How to use t

ntries (words, abbreviations, compounds, variant sp
ar in alphabetical order and are printed in bold type.

ish phrasal verbs come directly after the base verb and

ic superscripts indicate **homographs** (identically sp
nings).

IPA (International Phonetic Alphabet) is used for all **p**
uding American pronunciations.

e brackets are used to show **irregular plural forms**
s and adjectives.

nine forms of nouns and adjectives are shown unless they are identical to the
culine form. Spanish nouns are followed by their gender.

an numerals are used for the **grammatical divisions** of a word, and Arabic
erals for **sense divisions.**

swung dash represents the entry word in examples and idioms. The ► sign in-
ices **a block of set expressions, idioms and proverbs.** Key words are
erlined as a guide.

ous kinds of **meaning indicators** are used to guide users to the required trans-
n:

reas of specialization

efinitions or **synonyms,** typical **subjects** or **objects** of the entry

egional vocabulary and variants are shown both as headword and trans-
tions

anguage registers

en a word or expression has no direct translation, there is an **explanation** or a
ural equivalent (≈). Where a translation may be unclear, it is followed by an
anation in brackets.

and *v.t.* invites the reader to consult a **model entry** for further information.

DICCIONARIO

Cambridge Klett Compact

Español – Inglés
English – Spanish

CAMBRIDGE
UNIVERSITY PRESS

PUBLISHED BY THE PRESS SYNDICATE OF THE UNIVERSITY OF CAMBRIDGE
The Pitt Building, Trumpington Street, Cambridge, United Kingdom

CAMBRIDGE UNIVERSITY PRESS
The Edinburgh Building, Cambridge CB2 2RU, UK
40 West 20th Street, New York NY10011-4211, USA
477 Williamstown Road, Port Melbourne, VIC 3207, Australia
Ruiz de Alarcón 13, 28014 Madrid, Spain
Dock House, The Waterfront, Cape Town 8001, South Africa

http://www.cambridge.org

First published 2002

Printed in Germany at Clausen und Bosse, Leck

Typeface: Univers Black, Weidemann

A catalogue record for this book is available from the British Library

Library of Congress Cataloguing in Publication data applied for

ISBN 0521 802989 paperback

ISBN 0521 752981 paperback + CD-ROM

Editorial Management: María Teresa Gondar Oubiña

Contributors: Peter Bereza, Alexander Burden, Roser Calvet i Riera, Anne Choffrut, Majka Dischler, Maite Ferré Simó, Susan Frisbie Rabelo, Laura García Codony, Concepción Gil Bayo, Tim Gutteridge, Stephen John Hackett, Kay Hollingsworth, Melva Josefina Márquez Rojas, Matthew C. Maxwell, Ana María Peris Moreno, Josep Ràfols i Ventosa, Carlos Gerardo Rodríguez Penagos, James Robert Gurney Salter, Judith Santolaria Antolín, Anja Tauchmann, Stephen Alan Trott, Sandra Vilamitjana Parellada, Tessa Wigley

Typesetting: Dörr und Schiller GmbH, Stuttgart
Data processing: Andreas Lang, conTEXT AG für Information und Kommunikation, Zürich

Índice

Contents

Introducción

El *Diccionario Cambridge Klett Compact* es un diccionario bilingüe completamente nuevo destinado a estudiantes de inglés de habla española y a estudiantes de español de habla inglesa. En su confección y edición ha participado un gran número de hablantes nativos de ambas lenguas, lo que lo convierte en una herramienta lingüística amplia y actualizada.

En el diccionario se halla reflejado tanto el inglés británico como el inglés americano y proporciona, de esta manera, una guía fiable del inglés como lengua internacional. Al mismo tiempo ofrece una amplia cobertura tanto del español peninsular como del español de América Latina y constituye, por tanto, una herramienta útil de aprendizaje para cualquier estudiante de español en cualquier país de lengua española.

El diccionario incluye, además, una ayuda complementaria para el aprendizaje de aquellos aspectos que acostumbran a resultar más dificultosos a los estudiantes; por ejemplo, modelos de conjugaciones de los dos idiomas y una sección especial dedicada a los 'falsos amigos' que pueden confundir al estudiante.

Le deseamos que la consulta de este diccionario y el aprendizaje del nuevo idioma le reporten unos momentos agradables.

Este diccionario se puede adquirir con o sin CD-ROM. Si desea obtener más información, visítenos en nuestra dirección:

dictionary.cambridge.org

Introduction

The *Diccionario Cambridge Klett Compact* is a completely new bilingual dictionary for Spanish-speaking learners of English and English-speaking learners of Spanish. It has been written and edited by a large team of native speakers of both languages so that it provides an up-to-date and comprehensive language tool.

It covers British English and American English, so that it provides a reliable guide to English as an international language. It also has good coverage of the Spanish from Spain and Spanish from Latin America so that for learners of Spanish it can help them in all of the Spanish-speaking world.

The dictionary provides extra help with many areas that learners find difficult. For example, there is full information about the verb patterns of the the two languages and there is a special section on the 'false friends' that can be confusing for learners.

We hope that you enjoy using this book and that you enjoy learning your new language.

You can buy this book with or without a CD-ROM and you can find out more information on our website at:

dictionary.cambridge.org

La pronunciación del español
Spanish pronunciation

Remarkable differences can be observed in Spanish pronunciation, both within the various regions of the Iberian Peninsula and also in the individual countries where Spanish is spoken. Contrary to general opinion, these differences are stronger within Spain than between the various Spanish-speaking countries in America. In bilingual regions of the Iberian Peninsula like Catalonia, Valencia, the Balearic Islands, the Basque Provinces and Galicia, the pronunciation of Spanish is strongly influenced by the native languages of these areas. In other regions, on the other hand, the phonetic features of a range of dialects have been mixed into spoken Spanish. A particularly characteristic and autonomous note is evident in Andalusian pronunciation, for instance in the case of this dialect's own special **ceceo: s**, **z** and **c** are pronounced with an interdental fricative /th/(**káza**, as opposed to *casa* **kása**).
Generally, Castilian pronunciation is considered the standard pronunciation as it represents the closest approximation to the written form. This is also the pronunciation on which the following descriptions are based.

Vowels

Symbol	Graphic representation	Examples
[a]	a	san, acción
[e]	e	pez, saber
[i]	i	sí, mirar
[o]	o	con
[u]	u	tú, dibujo

Semi-vowels resp. semi-consonants

Symbol	Graphic representation	Examples	Notes
[i̯]	i, y	baile, hoy, despreciéis	*occurs in the diphthongs* ***ai, ei, oi*** *resp.* ***ay, ey, oy*** *and as the final element in triphthongs*
[j]	i	bieldo, apreciáis	*when* ***i*** *is pronounced as the first element in diphthongs and triphthongs*
[u̯]	u	auto, causa	*occurs in the diphthongs* ***au, eu, ou***
[w]	u	bueno, cuerda	*when* ***u*** *is pronounced as the first element in diphthongs or triphthongs*

Consonants

Symbol	Graphic representation	Examples	Notes
[p]	p	pato	
[b]	b, v	vacío, hombre	*plosive: pronounced in the absolute initial sound after a pause and in the medial after a preceding nasal*
[β]	b, v	objeto, pueblo	*fricative: pronounced when it does not occur in the absolute initial sound or after* ***m, n.***
[m]	m, n	mamá, convivir	*every non-word-final* ***m*** *and* ***n*** *before* [p] [b]
[ɱ]	n	enfermo, infusión	*every* ***n*** *which comes before* ***f***

[n]	n	**n**adie, e**n**tre	
[ṇ]	n	qui**n**ce, co**n**cie**n**cia	***n*** *together with a following* [θ]
[n̪]	n	co**n**denar, ca**n**tar	*dentalised* ***n:*** *together with a following* [t] *or* [d]
[ŋ]	n	ci**n**co, fi**n**gir	*syllable-final* ***n*** *together with a following velar consonant*
[ɲ]	ñ, n	vi**ñ**a, co**n**cha	***ñ*** *in the initial sound of the syllable and in syllable-final* ***n*** *before a palatal consonant*
[f]	f	café	
[k]	k, c, q	**k**ilo, **c**asa, **q**ue, a**c**tor	*occurs in the groupings* ***c + a,o,u*** *and* ***qu + e,i*** *and with syllable-final* ***c***
[g]	g, gu	**g**arra, **gu**erra,	*plosive: occurs in the absolute initial sound or in the medial sound with preceding nasal in the groupings* ***g + a,o,u*** *and* ***gu + e,i***
[x]	j, g	ro**j**o, **g**irar, **g**ente	*equivalent to* ***j*** *and to the groupings* ***g + e,i***
[ɣ]	g, gu	a**g**ua, ale**g**re, esti**g**ma	*fricative: occurs in the groupings* ***g + a,o,u*** *and* ***gu + e,i,*** *when it does not come in the absolute initial sound or follow* ***n***
[t]	t	le**t**ra, **t**ío	*plosive: equivalent to* ***d*** *in the absolute initial sound or after* ***n*** *or* ***l***
[d]	d	**d**edo, con**d**e, cal**d**o	*plosive: equivalent to* ***d*** *when it occurs in the absolute initial sound or follows* ***n*** *or* ***l***
[ð]	d,t	ca**d**a, escu**d**o, juventu**d**	*fricative: equivalent to* ***d*** *when it does not occur in the absolute initial sound or follow* ***n*** *or* ***l***
[θ]	c, z	**c**ero, **z**ar**z**a, cru**z**	*occurs in the groupings* ***c + e,i*** *and* ***z + a,o,u*** *and in the final sound*
[l]	l	**l**ibro, b**l**oque, sa**l**	
[l̟]	l	a**l**ce	*interdental* ***l:*** *occurs together with a following* [θ]
[l̪]	l	a**l**tura, ca**l**do	*dental* ***l:*** *occurs together with a following* [t] *or* [d]
[ʎ]	ll, l	**ll**ueve, co**l**cha	*equivalent to* ***ll*** *and syllable-final* ***l*** *before a palatal consonant*
[s]	s	así, coser	
[r]	r	ca**r**o, p**r**isa	*equivalent to the letter* ***r*** *when it occurs at the beginning of a word or follows* ***n, l, s***
[rr]	r, rr	**r**oca, hon**r**ado	*equivalent to* ***-rr-*** *and* ***r-, -r-*** *at the beginning of a word or at the beginning of a syllable after* ***n, l, s***
[tʃ]	ch	**ch**ino	
[ɟ]	y, hi	cón**y**uge, in**y**ección, **y**unque	*palatal affricate: fricative when* ***y, hi*** *occurs in the initial sound of a syllable*
[<ʃ>]	sh	**sh**ock	*like English* ***sh****ock,* ***sh****ow*

Hispano-American pronunciation bears the closest similarity to that of the Andalusian region. Among the phonetic peculiarities to be encountered in the Hispano-American linguistic areas, the following phenomena are the most prominent:

yeismo
The **ll** is pronounced like a **y** (**yovér**, as opposed to *llover* **llovér**). This phonetic phenomenon is usual not only in Spanish-speaking areas of America but also in various regions of Spain like Andalusia, the Canary Islands, Extremadura, Madrid and Castilian subregions. The assumption that the **yeísmo** is a phonetic feature of all Hispano-American countries is false. The standard pronunciation of **ll** is maintained in subregions of Chile, Peru, Columbia and Ecuador.

A further peculiarity is the pronunciation of **y** as a dʒ (**adʒér**, as opposed to *ayer* **aɟér**) in Argentina, Uruguay and subregions of Ecuador and Mexico.

seseo

z and **c** (θ) are pronounced like **s** (**sínko**, as opposed to *cinco* **θínko**). This dialectal peculiarity is widespread not only in Hispano-America but also in subregions of Andalusia and on the Canary Islands.
In the vernacular pronunciation of some areas of Spain and Hispano-America, one also encounters aspiration of the **s** in the final sound (**lah kása**, as opposed to *las casas* – **las kásas**), which may even disappear altogether (**mímo**, as opposed to *mismo* **mísmo**). Both phenomena are considered vulgar and should therefore be avoided.

Símbolos fonéticos del inglés
English phonetic symbols

[ɑː]	plant, farm, father	[l]	lamp, oil, ill
[aɪ]	life	[m]	man, am
[aʊ]	house	[n]	no, manner
[æ]	man, sad	[ɒ]	not, long
[b]	been, blind	[ɔː]	law, all
[d]	do, had	[ɔɪ]	boy, oil
[ð]	this, father	[p]	paper, happy
[e]	get, bed	[r]	red, dry
[eɪ]	name, lame	[s]	stand, sand, yes
[ə]	ago, better	[ʃ]	ship, station
[ɛː]	bird, her	[t]	tell, fat
[eə]	there, care	[tʃ]	church, catch
[ʌ]	but, son	[ʊ]	push, look
[f]	father, wolf	[uː]	you, do
[g]	go, beg	[ʊə]	poor, sure
[ŋ]	long, sing	[v]	voice, live
[h]	house	[w]	water, we, which
[ɪ]	it, wish	[z]	zeal, these, gaze
[iː]	bee, me, beat, belief	[ʒ]	pleasure
[ɪə]	here	[dʒ]	jam, object
[j]	youth	[θ]	thank, death
[k]	keep, milk		

A

A, a *f* A, a; ~ **de Antonio** A for Andrew *Brit,* A for Abel *Am*
a *prep* **1.** (*dirección*) to; **ir ~ Barcelona/Suiza** to go to Barcelona/Switzerland; **llegar ~ Madrid** to arrive in Madrid; **ir ~ casa de alguien** to go to sb's house; **ir ~ la escuela/~l cine** to go to school/to the cinema **2.** (*posición*) at; **estar sentado ~ la mesa** to be sitting at the table; **esperar ~ la puerta de la casa** to wait at the front door; **~ la derecha** on the right; **~l sur** (**de**) to the south (of); **~l sol** in the sun **3.** (*distancia*) **~ 10 kilómetros de aquí** 10 kilometres (away) from here **4.** (*tiempo*) at; (*hasta*) until; **~ las tres** at three o'clock; **~ mediodía** at noon; **~ los veinte años** at (the age of) twenty; **~l poco rato** shortly after; **¿~ cuántos estamos?** what's the date? **5.** (*modo*) **~ pie** on foot; **ir ~ pie** to walk; **~ mano** by hand; **~ oscuras** in the dark; **tortilla a la española** Spanish omelette **6.** (*precio*) **¿~ cómo está?** how much is it?; **~ 2 euros el kilo** (at) 2 euros a [*o* per] kilo **7.** (*relación*) **el partido terminó dos ~ dos** the game ended two all **8.** (*complemento indirecto*) to; **dio su fortuna ~ los pobres** he/she gave his/her fortune to the poor **9.** (*complemento directo*) **he visto ~ tu hermano** I've seen your brother **10.** (*con infinitivo*) to; **empezó ~ correr** he/she began to run **11.** (*complemento de verbo*) **oler ~ gas** to smell of gas; **jugar ~ los dados** to play dice ►**¡~ <u>que</u> llueve mañana!** I bet it'll rain tomorrow!; **~ Pedro le gusta mucho nadar, ¿~ <u>que</u> sí, Pedro?** Pedro likes swimming a lot; don't you, Pedro?
abacado *m AmL* BOT (*aguacate*) avocado, alligator pear *Am*
abacorar *vt AmL* (*acosar*) to hound
abad(esa) *m(f)* abbot *m,* abbess *f*
abadía *f* abbey
abajeño, -a *adj AmL* coastal
abajo **I.** *adv* **1.** (*movimiento*) down; **calle ~** down the street; **cuesta ~** downhill; **de arriba ~** from top to bottom **2.** (*estado*) down (below); (*en casa*) downstairs; **boca ~** face down; **hacia ~** down, downwards; **el ~ firmante** the undersigned; **de veinte para ~** twenty or under; **véase más ~** see below **II.** *interj* **¡~ el dictador!** down with the dictator!
abalanzarse <z→c> *vr* **~ a la ventana** to dash (over) to the window; **~ sobre** [*o* **contra**] **algo** to pounce on sth
abalear *vt Col* (*disparar*) to shoot
abanderado, -a *m, f* **1.** (*en actos públicos*) standard-bearer **2.** (*pionero*) champion
abandonado, -a *adj* **ser** (*descuidado*) neglected; (*desaseado*) slovenly
abandonar **I.** *vi* DEP to withdraw **II.** *vt* **1.** (*dejar*) to leave; (*desamparar*) to abandon; **niño abandonado** abandoned baby; **le ~on sus fuerzas** his/her strength deserted him/her; **estar abandonado a sí mismo** to be left to one's own devices **2.** (*renunciar*) to give up **3.** INFOR (*interrumpir*) to leave **III.** *vr:* **~se** **1.** (*entregarse*) to give oneself over **2.** (*ir desaliñado*) to let oneself go
abandono *m* **1.** (*abandonamiento*) abandonment; **~ de servicio** giving-up work; **~ de la víctima** denial of assistance **2.** (*renuncia*) renunciation; (*de una empresa, idea*) giving-up **3.** (*descuido*) neglect; **en un momento de ~** in a moment of weakness
abanicar <c→qu> **I.** *vt* to fan **II.** *vr:* **~se** to fan oneself
abanico *m* fan; **en** (**forma de**) **~** fan-shaped; **un ~ de posibilidades** a range of possibilities
abaratar **I.** *vt* (*bienes*) to make cheaper; (*precios*) to lower; **~ costes** to cut costs **II.** *vr:* **~se** to become cheaper
abarca *f* sandal
abarcar <c→qu> *vt* **1.** (*comprender*) to include; **~ con la vista** to take in; **~ muchas cosas a la vez** to have one's work cut out **2.** (*contener*) to contain ►**quien mucho abarca poco <u>aprieta</u>** *prov* don't bite off more than you can chew
abarquillarse *vr* (*papel*) to crinkle; (*madera*) to warp
abarrotado *adj* completely full; **~ de gente** crowded
abarrotar *vt* **~ algo de algo** to pack sth with sth
abarrote *m* **1.** NÁUT stop-gap **2.** *Cuba, Méx* (*tienda*) grocery store **3.** *pl, Cuba, Méx* (*comestibles*) groceries *pl*
abarrotería *f* **1.** *AmL* (*ferretería*) ironmonger's *Brit,* hardware store *Am* **2.** *Guat* (*abacería*) retail grocery
abastecedor(a) *m(f)* supplier
abastecer *irr como crecer* **I.** *vt* (*proveer*) **~ de** [*o* **con**] **algo** to provide with sth; COM to supply with sth **II.** *vr:* **~se ~se de** [*o* **con**] **algo** to provide oneself with sth
abastecimiento *m* **1.** (*provisión*) **~ de** [*o* **con**] **algo** provision of sth; **~ de aguas** water supply **2.** COM **~ de** [*o* **con**] **algo** supply of sth
abastero *m* **1.** *Chile* (*de carne*) wholesale livestock dealer **2.** *Méx* (*de artículos de consumo*) purveyor
abasto *m* **1.** (*abastecimiento*) supply **2.** (*provisiones*) provisions *pl* ►**no <u>dar</u> ~ con algo** to be unable to cope with sth
abatí *m sin pl* **1.** *Arg* (*maíz*) maize *Brit,* corn *Am* **2.** *Arg, Par* (*bebida*) maize liquor
abatible *adj* **asiento ~** folding seat
abatido, -a *adj* **1.** (*desanimado*) dejected **2.** (*mercancía*) depreciated
abatimiento *m* **1.** (*desánimo*) dejection **2.** (*derribo*) demolition **3.** (*desmontaje*) dismantling
abatir **I.** *vt* **1.** (*muro, casa*) to demolish; (*árbol*) to fell, to chop down *Am;* (*velas*) to

lower; (*avión*) to shoot down; ~ **el respaldo** to recline the back-rest **2.** (*desmontar*) to dismantle **3.** (*humillar*) to humiliate **4.** (*debilitar*) to lay low **II.** *vr:* ~**se** **1.** (*desanimarse*) to become dejected **2.** (*precipitarse*) ~**se sobre algo** to pounce on sth **3.** (*ceder*) to yield

abdicación *f* abdication; ~ **al trono** abdication from the throne

abdicar <c→qu> *vt* **1.** (*monarca*) to abdicate; **la reina abdicó la corona en su hija** the queen abdicated in favour of her daughter; ~ **la presidencia** to resign the presidency **2.** (*ideales*) to renounce

abdomen *m* abdomen

abdominal **I.** *adj* abdominal **II.** *m* DEP press-up *Brit,* sit-up *Am*

abecé *m* ABC, alphabet; **el** ~ **de la matemática** the fundamentals of mathematics ►**no saber el** ~ not to have a clue; **ser el** ~ **de algo** to be the basis of sth

abecedario *m* alphabet

abedul *m* (*madera, árbol*) birch

abeja *f* bee; ~ **reina** queen bee; ~ **obrera** worker (bee) ►**estar como** ~ **en flor** to be in top form; **ser como una** ~ to be a hard worker

abejón *m* drone

abejorro *m* **1.** (*insecto*) bumblebee **2.** (*escarabajo*) cockchafer ►**ser un** ~ to be a pain (in the neck)

aberración *f* **1.** (*desviación*) aberration; ~ **mental** mental aberration **2.** (*disparate*) absurdity **3.** *AmL* (*error*) mistake

aberrante *adj* **1.** (*anormal*) aberrant **2.** (*disparatado*) crazy

abertura *f* **1.** (*acción*) opening **2.** (*hueco*) hole **3.** (*franqueza*) openness

abeto *m* fir; ~ **rojo** spruce

abiertamente *adv* **1.** (*francamente*) openly **2.** (*patentemente*) clearly

abierto *m* DEP ~ **de tenis** tennis open championship

abierto, **-a** **I.** *pp de* **abrir** **II.** *adj* **1.** (*no cerrado*) open; ~ **a nuevas ideas** open to new ideas; **en campo** ~ in the open country; **un libro** ~ an open book **2.** (*persona*) open-minded; **la gente aquí es muy abierta** people here are very open-minded

abigarrado, **-a** *adj* many-coloured *Brit,* many-colored *Am*

abismado, **-a** *adj* **1.** (*absorto*) engrossed **2.** (*sorprendido*) amazed

abismal *adj* enormous; (*odio*) profound

abismar **I.** *vt* **1.** (*sumir*) to cast down; ~ **a alguien en la desesperación** to plunge sb into despair **2.** (*confundir*) to confuse **II.** *vr:* ~**se** **1.** (*hundirse*) to sink **2.** *AmL* (*asombrarse*) to be amazed

abismo *m* **1.** GEO abyss **2.** (*infierno*) hell **3.** (*diferencia*) chasm; **entre tus opiniones y las mías hay un** ~ there's a world of difference between our opinions

abjurar *vi, vt* ~ (**de**) **algo** to renounce sth

ablandar **I.** *vi* (*viento*) to drop; (*frío*) to become less severe **II.** *vt* **1.** (*poner blando*) to soften **2.** (*calmar*) to soothe **III.** *vr:* ~**se** **1.** (*ponerse blando*) to soften **2.** (*persona*) to relent

abnegación *f* self-denial; **con** ~ selflessly

abnegado, **-a** *adj* selfless

abobado, **-a** *adj* silly

abocado, **-a** *adj* (*vino*) smooth

abocar <c→qu> **I.** *vt* (*líquido*) to pour **II.** *vr:* ~**se** (*reunirse*) to meet up

abocetar *vt* to sketch

abochornar **I.** *vt* **1.** (*calor*) to oppress; **este calor me abochorna** I'm suffocated by this heat; **estoy abochornado** I'm stifled **2.** (*avergonzar*) to embarrass **II.** *vr:* ~**se** **1.** (*avergonzarse*) ~**se de** [*o* **por**] **algo** to be embarrassed by sth **2.** (*plantas*) to wilt

abofetear *vt* to slap

abogacía *f* legal profession; **ejercer la** ~ to practise *Brit* [*o* practice *Am*] law

abogado, **-a** *m, f* **1.** JUR lawyer; (*notario*) solicitor *Brit,* lawyer *Am;* (*en tribunal*) barrister, attorney *Am;* ~ **defensor** defending counsel, defense lawyer; ~ **divorcista** divorce lawyer; ~ **de oficio** court-appointed counsel, duty solicitor **2.** (*defensor*) advocate ►**ser un** ~ **de las causas perdidas** to be a champion of lost causes

abogar <g→gu> *vi* (*apoyar*) ~ **por** [*o* **en favor de**] **algo** to advocate sth

abolengo *m* ancestry; **de rancio** ~ of noble descent

abolición *f* abolition

abolir *irr vt* to abolish

abolladura *f* dent

abollar *vt* to dent

abolsarse *vr* **1.** (*tela*) to become baggy **2.** (*deformarse*) to become deformed; (*pared*) to bulge

abombado, **-a** *adj* **1.** (*combado*) bulging **2.** *AmS* (*atontado*) dopey

abombar **I.** *vt* to make convex **II.** *vr:* ~**se** **1.** (*abultarse*) to bulge **2.** *CSur, Ecua, Nic* (*alimentos*) to go bad

abominable *adj* abominable

abominación *f* abomination

abominar *vt, vi* **1.** (*aborrecer*) to loathe **2.** (*renegar*) ~ **de alguien** to condemn sb

abonable *adj* **1.** (*cantidad*) payable **2.** (*letra de cambio*) due

abonado, **-a** *m, f* (*a revistas, espectáculo, al teléfono*) subscriber; (*a electricidad, gas*) customer

abonar **I.** *vt* **1.** (*garantizar*) to guarantee **2.** (*pagar*) to pay; ~ **en cuenta** to credit to an account; **para** ~ **en cuenta** A/C payee only **3.** (*terreno*) to fertilize **4.** PREN to subscribe to; ~ **a alguien a una revista** (*convencer*) to persuade sb to take out a subscription to a magazine; (*como regalo*) to take out a subscription to a magazine for sb **II.** *vr:* ~**se** to subscribe; ~**se a la temporada de ópera** to buy a season ticket to the opera

abono *m* **1.** TEAT season ticket; **sacar un ~** to buy a season ticket **2.** PREN subscription **3.** (*para transporte público*) season ticket; **~ mensual** monthly ticket; **~ de 10 viajes** 10-journey ticket **4.** (*pago*) payment; **~ en cuenta** credit **5.** (*fertilizante*) fertilizer, manure; **~ químico** chemical fertilizer **6.** (*de la tierra*) fertilizing

abordable *adj* **1.** (*persona*) approachable **2.** (*tema*) that can be discussed; **no ~** taboo

abordaje *m* boarding; **tomar al ~** to board

abordar **I.** *vt* **1.** (*barco*) to board (*in attack*); (*chocar*) to ram **2.** (*persona*) to approach **3.** (*tema*) to discuss; (*problema*) to tackle **II.** *vi* NÁUT to dock

aborigen **I.** *adj* aboriginal **II.** *mf* aborigine

aborrecer *irr como crecer vt* **1.** (*sentir aversión*) to loathe; **~ a alguien de muerte** not to be able to abide sb **2.** (*exasperar*) to infuriate **3.** (*aburrir*) to bore

aborrecible *adj* detestable; (*persona*) loathsome

aborrecimiento *m* **1.** (*aversión*) loathing **2.** (*antipatía*) dislike

abortar **I.** *vi* **1.** (*provocado*) to have an abortion **2.** (*espontáneo*) to have a miscarriage **3.** (*fracasar*) to fail **II.** *vt* (*provocar un aborto*) to abort; (*hacer fracasar*) to cause to fail

aborto *m* **1.** (*provocado*) abortion **2.** (*espontáneo*) miscarriage

abota(r)gado, -a *adj* bloated

abota(r)garse <g→gu> *vr* to become bloated

abotonar *vt* to button up

abovedar *vt* **1.** (*formar*) to vault **2.** (*cubrir*) to cover (with a vault)

abra *f* **1.** (*bahía pequeña*) cove **2.** *AmL* (*desmonte*) clearing

abrasador(a) *adj* (*calor*) scorching

abrasar **I.** *vi* (*sol*) to scorch; (*comida*) to be burning hot **II.** *vt* **1.** (*quemar*) to burn; (*ácidos*) to corrode; **¡cuidado!, este café abrasa la lengua** take care not to burn your tongue on the coffee! **2.** (*plantas*) to dry up **3.** (*dolor*) to sear; (*estómago*) to irritate; **la sed me abrasa (la garganta)** I have a raging thirst **4.** (*odio*) to consume **III.** *vr:* **~se** **1.** (*quemarse*) to burn (up) **2.** (*morirse*) *t. fig* **~se en deseos de algo** to be desperate for sth; **~se de impaciencia por algo** to be desperately impatient to do sth

abrasión *f* **1.** GEO, TÉC abrasion **2.** MED graze

abrasivo *m* abrasive

abrasivo, -a *adj* abrasive; **líquido ~** abrasive liquid

abrazadera *f* **1.** TIPO bracket **2.** TÉC clamp

abrazar <z→c> **I.** *vt* **1.** (*persona*) to embrace **2.** (*contener*) to include; (*abarcar*) to take in **3.** (*doctrina*) to embrace; (*religión*) to adopt **II.** *vr:* **~se** to embrace (each other)

abrazo *m* embrace; **dar un ~ a alguien** to give sb a hug; **un (fuerte) ~** (*en cartas*) with best wishes

abreboca *m* **1.** *inf* (*aperitivo*) appetizer **2.** *Arg* (*persona distraída*) absent-minded person

abrebotellas *m inv* bottle opener

abrecartas *m inv* letter opener

abrelatas *m inv* tin opener, can opener *Am*

abrevadero *m* **1.** (*pila*) water trough **2.** (*lugar*) watering place

abrevar *vt* (*ganado*) to water

abreviación *f* **1.** (*abreviatura*) *t.* LING abbreviation **2.** (*de un texto*) abridgement

abreviado, -a *adj* abridged; (*corto*) short

abreviar **I.** *vt* **1.** (*acortar*) to shorten **2.** (*palabras*) to abbreviate **3.** (*texto*) to abridge **II.** *vi* to hurry

abreviatura *f* abbreviation

abridor *m* opener

abrigado, -a *adj* (*con ropa*) **estar** [*o* **ir**] **~** to be wrapped up warm

abrigar <g→gu> **I.** *vt* **1.** (*proteger: del viento, frío*) to protect **2.** (*cubrir*) to cover **3.** (*tener*) to hold; **~ esperanzas** to cherish hopes; **~ proyectos** to harbour *Brit* [*o* harbor *Am*] plans **II.** *vr:* **~se** to wrap up (warm)

abrigo *m* **1.** (*prenda*) coat; **~ de pieles** fur coat; **de ~** warm **2.** (*refugio*) shelter; **al ~ de** protected by ►**ser de ~** to be tough

abril *m* April; *v.t.* **marzo** ►**tener trece ~es** *inf* to be thirteen (years old)

abrillantado, -a *adj* **1.** *AmL* (*brillante*) shining **2.** *Arg* **fruta abrillantada** glazed fruit

abrillantar *vt* **1.** (*hacer brillar*) to polish **2.** (*piedras preciosas*) to cut and polish

abrir *irr* **I.** *vt* **1.** (*algo cerrado*) to open; (*paraguas*) to put up; (*grifo*) to turn on; (*con la llave*) to unlock; (*luz*) to turn on; (*silla plegable*) to open out; **~ la cabeza a alguien** to split sb's head open; **~ una calle al tráfico** to open a street to traffic; **~ a golpes** to knock open; **~ de par en par** to open wide; **a medio ~** (*puerta*) half-open **2.** (*canal, túnel*) to dig; (*agujero*) to bore **3.** (*perspectivas, mercado*) to open up **4.** (*comenzar, inaugurar*) to open; (*curso*) to begin **5.** (*ir en cabeza*) to lead **II.** *vi* (*tiempo*) to brighten up ►**en un ~ y cerrar de ojos** in the twinkling of an eye **III.** *vr:* **~se** **1.** (*puerta, herida*) to open; **la ventana se abre al jardín** the window opens (out) onto the garden **2.** (*confiar*) to confide **3.** (*perspectivas*) to open up **4.** *inf* (*irse*) to beat it

abrochar *vt* (*con broches*) to fasten; (*con hebillas*) to buckle; (*con botones*) to button (up); **abróchense los cinturones (de seguridad)** fasten your seat belts

abrogar <g→gu> *vt* to abrogate

abrojo *m* **1.** BIO thistle **2.** *Ven* (*urticaria*) rash

abroncar <c→qu> *vt inf* **1.** (*echar una bronca*) to tick off, to tell off *Am* **2.** (*abuchear*) to boo

abrumador(a) *adj* **1.** (*agobiador*) overwhelming **2.** (*apabullante*) crushing

abrumar *vt* **1.** (*agobiar*) to overwhelm **2.** (*con trabajo, elogios*) to wear out

abrupto, -a *adj* **1.** (*camino, abismo*) steep **2.** (*carácter*) abrupt

absceso *m* abscess

absentismo *m* absenteeism; ~ **laboral** absenteeism from work
ábside *m* ARQUIT apse
absolución *f* **1.** JUR acquittal; ~ **por falta de pruebas** acquittal owing to lack of evidence **2.** REL absolution; **dar la ~ a alguien** to give absolution to sb
absolutamente *adv* (*completamente*) absolutely, completely; **está ~ de acuerdo con nosotros** he/she completely agrees with us; ~ **nada** nothing at all; **es ~ posible** it's quite possible
absoluto, **-a** *adj* absolute ►**nada en ~** nothing at all; **en ~** not at all
absolver *irr como volver vt* **1.** JUR to acquit **2.** REL to absolve
absorbente *adj* **1.** (*esponja, trapo*) absorbent **2.** (*película, libro*) absorbing; (*trabajo, persona*) demanding
absorber *vt* **1.** (*tierra, esponja*) *t.* FÍS to absorb **2.** (*aspiradora*) to suck (up) **3.** (*cautivar*) to engross **4.** (*incorporar*) to incorporate; (*empresa*) to take over
absorción *f* **1.** (*de líquidos*) *t.* FÍS absorption **2.** ECON takeover
absorto, **-a** *adj* **1.** (*pasmado*) amazed **2.** (*entregado*) absorbed
abstemio, **-a I.** *adj* abstemious; (*completamente*) teetotal **II.** *m, f* teetotaller *Brit,* teetotaler *Am,* non-drinker *Am*
abstención *f t.* POL abstention
abstenerse *irr como tener vr* (*privarse de*) *t.* POL to abstain; ~ **de votar** to abstain; ~ **del tabaco** to refrain from smoking; **rogamos que se abstengan de realizar visitas** we request you to refrain from visiting
abstinencia *f* abstinence; (*de alcohol*) abstemiousness; (*completa*) teetotalism; ~ **de consumo** cutting down on consumption; **síndrome de ~** withdrawl symptoms
abstinente *adj* abstinent; (*de alcohol*) abstemious; (*completamente*) teetotal
abstracción *f* abstraction
abstracto, **-a** *adj* abstract; **en ~** in the abstract
abstraer *irr como traer* **I.** *vt* to abstract **II.** *vr* **~se en algo** to be absorbed in sth; **~se de algo** to detach oneself from sth; **consiguió ~se de los gritos en la calle** he/she managed not to be distracted by the shouting in the street
abstraído, **-a** *adj* lost in thought; **estar ~ en algo** to be preoccupied by sth
abstruso, **-a** *adj form* abstruse
absurdo *m* absurdity; **reducir algo al ~** to reduce sth to absurdity [*o* absurdum]
absurdo, **-a** *adj* absurd
abubilla *f* hoopoe
abuchear *vt* to boo; (*silbando*) to hiss
abucheo *m* booing; (*silbidos*) hissing
abuelo, **-a** *m, f* **1.** grandfather *m,* grandmother *f;* **los ~s** the grandparents **2.** *fig* elderly person ►**éramos pocos y parió la abuela** *inf* that was all we needed
abulense I. *adj* of/from Avila **II.** *mf* native/inhabitant of Avila
abulia *f* apathy
abúlico, **-a** *adj* weak-willed
abultado, **-a** *adj* bulky; (*labios*) thick
abultar I. *vi* to take up a lot of room **II.** *vt* **1.** (*aumentar*) to increase **2.** (*exagerar*) to exaggerate
abundancia *f* (*cantidad*) abundance; (*de bienes*) plenty; **en ~** in abundance; **nadar en la ~** to be rolling in money; **vivir en la ~** to be affluent
abundante *adj* abundant; ~ **en algo** abounding in sth; **~s lluvias** heavy rains; **una cosecha muy ~** a plentiful harvest
abundar *vi* to abound; ~ **en algo** to be rich in sth
aburrido, **-a** *adj* **1.** *estar* (*harto*) bored; **estar ~ de algo** to be bored of [*o* with *Am*] sth; **tus chistes me tienen ~** I'm tired of your jokes **2.** *ser* (*pesado*) boring
aburrimiento *m* **1.** (*tedio*) boredom **2.** (*fastidio*) bore
aburrir I. *vt* **1.** (*hastiar*) to bore **2.** (*fastidiar*) to weary **II.** *vr:* **~se** to be [*o* become] bored; **~se de algo** to become bored of sth, to tire of sth *Am*
abusar *vi* **1.** (*usar indebidamente*) ~ **de algo** to misuse sth; ~ **de su salud** to abuse one's health **2.** (*aprovecharse*) ~ **de alguien** to take advantage of sb **3.** (*sexualmente*) ~ **de alguien** to sexually abuse sb; (*violar*) to rape sb
abusivo, **-a** *adj* improper; (*precios*) outrageous
abuso *m* **1.** (*de poder*) misuse; ~ **de autoridad** abuse of authority; ~ **deshonesto** indecent assault **2.** (*cosa abusiva*) **este precio es un ~** this is an outrageous price
abyección *f* wretchedness
abyecto, **-a** *adj* wretched
a.C. *abr de* **antes de Cristo** AD
a/c 1. *abr de* **a cuenta** on account **2.** *abr de* **al cuidado de** c/o
acá *adv* here; ~ **y allá** here and there; **para ~** over here; **¡ven ~!** come here!
acabado *m* TÉC finish
acabado, **-a** *adj* **1.** (*completo*) finished **2.** (*salud*) ruined **3.** (*sin posibilidades*) finished off
acabar I. *vi* **1.** (*terminar*) to end; ~ **bien/mal** to turn out well/badly; ~ **en punta** to end in a point **2.** (*una acción*) ~ **de hacer algo** to have just done sth; **ella acaba de llegar** she's just arrived; **el libro acaba de publicarse** the book has just been published **3.** (*destruir, agotar*) ~ **con algo** to finish sth off; ~ **con alguien** to put paid to sb; **este niño ~á conmigo** this child will be the death of me **4.** (*finalmente*) **~ás por comprenderlo** you'll understand it in the end; **~ás por volverme loco** you'll end up driving me mad **II.** *vt* **1.** (*terminar*) to finish **2.** (*consumir*) to finish off; ~ **todas las ga-**

lletas to eat up all the biscuits **III.** *vr:* **~se** to come to an end; **la mantequilla se ha acabado** there's no butter left; **todo se acabó** it's all over; **¡se acabó!** and that's that!
acabóse *m inf* **¡esto es el ~!** that really is the limit!
acacia *f* acacia
academia *f* **1.** (*corporación*) academy **2.** (*colegio*) (private) school; **~ militar** military academy
académico, -a *adj* academic
acaecer *irr como crecer vi* to happen
acaecimiento *m* happening, occurrence
acahual *m Méx* (*girasol*) sunflower
acalambrarse *vr AmL* to get a cramp; **se le acalambró una pierna** he/she got a cramp in his/her leg
acallar *vt* **1.** (*hacer callar*) to silence **2.** (*apaciguar*) to pacify; (*conciencia*) to assuage; (*hambre*) to satisfy
acalorado, -a *adj* heated
acalorar **I.** *vt* **1.** (*dar calor*) to heat **2.** (*enfadar*) to inflame **II.** *vr:* **~se** **1.** (*sofocarse*) **se acaloró al correr** he/she got hot (while) running **2.** (*apasionarse*) **~se con algo** to get worked up over sth **3.** (*enfadarse*) **~se por algo** to get angry about sth; **se acalora por nada** he/she gets all het up about nothing *inf*
acampar *vi* to camp; (*tropa*) to encamp
acanalar *vt* **1.** (*hacer canales*) to furrow **2.** TÉC to groove
acantilado *m* cliff
acantilado, -a *adj* steep
acaparar *vt* **1.** (*objetos*) to hoard **2.** (*apoderarse*) **~se de algo** to lay claim to sth; **~ todas las miradas** to captivate everyone's attention
acapillar *vt Méx* (*atrapar*) to seize
acaramelar **I.** *vt* to coat with caramel **II.** *vr:* **~se** (*novios*) to be all over each other
acariciar *vt* **1.** (*persona, animal*) to caress **2.** (*idea, plan*) to toy with
acarrear *vt* **1.** (*transportar*) to transport **2.** (*ocasionar*) to cause
acarreo *m* **1.** (*transporte*) transport **2.** (*importe*) haulage
acartonado, -a *adj* **1.** (*persona*) wizened **2.** (*cutis*) shrivelled *Brit,* shriveled *Am*
acartonarse *vr* **1.** (*tela*) to become stiff **2.** (*persona*) to become wizened **3.** (*cutis*) to shrivel up
acaso **I.** *m* chance; **el ~ hizo que ...** *+subj* as chance would have it... **II.** *adv* maybe; **¿está ~ enfermo?** is he/she ill by any chance? ►**por si ~** (*en caso de*) in case; (*en todo caso*) just in case
acatamiento *m* **1.** (*respeto*) respect **2.** (*de las leyes*) **~ de algo** compliance with sth
acatar *vt* **1.** (*respetar*) to respect **2.** (*obedecer*) to obey **3.** *Col, Guat, PRico* (*caer en cuenta*) to realize
acatarrarse *vr* to catch a cold
acaudalado, -a *adj* well-off
acaudalar *vt* to acquire
acaudillar *vt* to lead
acceder *vi* **1.** (*consentir*) to agree; **~ a una petición** to agree to a request **2.** (*tener acceso*) to gain access **3.** (*ascender*) to accede; **~ a la presidencia** to assume the presidency; **~ a un cargo** to fill an office; **~ al trono** to succeed to the throne
accesible *adj* **1.** (*persona*) approachable **2.** (*lugar*) accessible **3.** (*precios*) affordable **4.** (*explicación*) comprehensible
accésit *m inv* consolation [*o* second *Am*] prize
acceso *m* **1.** (*a pie, en vehículo*) access; **de fácil ~** (easily) accessible; **libre ~** free access **2.** (*ataque*) attack **3.** INFOR access
accesorio *m* **1.** (*de vestidos*) accessory **2.** (*utensilio*) implement **3.** *pl* (*de máquinas*) spare parts *pl*
accesorio, -a *adj* accessory
accidentado, -a **I.** *adj* **1.** (*terreno*) rugged **2.** (*difícil*) difficult **II.** *m, f* injured person
accidental *adj* **1.** (*no esencial*) incidental **2.** (*casual*) casual
accidentarse *vr* to have an accident
accidente *m* **1.** (*suceso desgraciado*) accident; **~ en cadena** pile-up; **~ de circulación** traffic [*o* road] accident; **por ~** by accident; **sufrir un ~** to have an accident **2.** MED faint **3.** (*desnivel*) unevenness; **~s geográficos** geographical features
acción *f* **1.** (*acto*) act; **¡~!** CINE action!; **un hombre de ~** a man of action; **entrar en ~** to go into action; **poner en ~** to put into action **2.** (*influencia*) action; **~ recíproca** interaction; **de rápida ~** rapid-action; **de ~ retardada** (*bomba*) delayed-action **3.** MIL action **4.** FIN share; **~ común** ordinary share *Brit,* common share *Am;* **~ preferente** preference share *Brit,* preferred share *Am* **5.** JUR action; **~ por daños y perjuicios** action for damages; **~ popular** incidental action
accionamiento *m* TÉC operation, drive *Am*
accionar **I.** *vi* to gesticulate **II.** *vt* TÉC to operate; **~ un cohete** to fire a rocket
accionista *mf* shareholder, stockholder
acebo *m* holly
acechar *vt* **1.** (*espiar*) to spy on **2.** (*esperar*) to lie in wait for
acecho *m* spying; **estar al ~** to lie in wait
acecinar **I.** *vt* **1.** (*salar*) to salt **2.** (*ahumar*) to cure **II.** *vr:* **~se** to get thinner
aceitada *f* **1.** *AmL* oiling **2.** *AmL, inf* (*soborno*) kickback
aceitar *vt* **1.** (*motor, gozne*) to oil **2.** (*ensalada*) to dress; (*pan*) to coat with oil
aceite *m* oil; **~ bruto** crude oil; **~ comestible** cooking oil; **~ esencial** essential oil; **~ lubrificante** lubricating oil ►**echar ~ al fuego** to add fuel to the flames
aceitera *f* **1.** (*recipiente*) oil-can **2.** *pl* (*vinagreras*) cruet
aceitoso, -a *adj* oily
aceituna *f* olive ►**llegar a las ~s** to arrive late
aceitunado, -a *adj* olive(-green)

aceituno *m* olive tree
aceleración *f* acceleration
acelerador *m* **1.** AUTO accelerator *Brit,* gas pedal *Am;* **pisar el** ~ to step on the gas **2.** FÍS ~ **de partículas** particle accelerator
acelerar **I.** *vi* to accelerate; **¡no aceleres tanto!** don't accelerate so hard!, don't go so fast! *Am* **II.** *vt* to accelerate; ~ **el paso** to walk faster
acelga *f* chard
acémila *f* **1.** (*animal*) mule **2.** *pey* (*persona*) ass *Brit,* jackass *Am*
acento *m* **1.** (*prosódico*) stress; **el** ~ **cae en la primera sílaba** the stress falls on the first syllable **2.** (*pronunciación, signo*) accent; **hablar inglés sin** ~ to speak English without any accent; **esta palabra se escribe sin** ~ this word is written without an accent **3.** (*entonación*) tone **4.** (*énfasis*) emphasis; **poner especial** ~ **en algo** to put special emphasis on sth
acentuación *f* (*prosódica*) stress; (*ortográfica*) accentuation
acentuado, -a *adj* **1.** (*al pronunciar*) stressed; (*al escribir*) with an accent; **no** ~ unstressed; (*sin tilde*) unaccented **2.** (*marcado*) marked
acentuar <*1. pres:* acentúo> **I.** *vt* **1.** (*al pronunciar*) to stress; (*al escribir*) to write with an accent **2.** (*resaltar*) to highlight **3.** (*aumentar*) to increase **II.** *vr:* **~se** *AmL* (*una enfermedad*) to become worse
aceña *f* water mill
acepción *f* sense, meaning
aceptable *adj* acceptable
aceptación *f* **1.** (*aprobación*) approval; **tener** ~ to be popular [*o* successful] **2.** COM, JUR acceptance
aceptado *interj AmL* (*vale*) OK
aceptar *vt* **1.** (*recibir*) to accept **2.** (*aprobar, conformarse*) to approve; ~ **un compromiso** to accept an agreement; ~ **hacer algo** to agree to do sth
acequia *f* **1.** (*canal de riego*) irrigation ditch **2.** *Méx* (*albañal*) drain, gutter *Am*
acera *f* pavement *Brit,* sidewalk *Am* ►**ser de la** ~ **de enfrente** *inf* to be gay
acerado, -a *adj* **1.** (*de acero*) steel **2.** (*mordaz*) biting
acerbo, -a *adj* **1.** (*gusto*) sharp **2.** (*despiadado*) cruel; (*crítica, tono*) harsh
acerca *prep* ~ **de** (*sobre*) about; (*en relación a*) concerning
acercamiento *m* approach
acercar <c→qu> **I.** *vt* **1.** (*poner más cerca*) to bring nearer; **acerca la silla a la mesa** draw the chair up to the table **2.** (*traer*) to bring over **3.** *inf* (*llevar*) to take, to bring **II.** *vr:* **~se** **1.** (*aproximarse*) **~se a alguien/algo** to approach sb/sth **2.** (*ir*) to come [*o* go] round; **~se a la tienda a por patatas** to go round to the shop for potatoes
acerico *m* pincushion
acero *m* steel
acérrimo, -a **I.** *superl de* **acre** **II.** *adj* (*defensor, partidario*) staunch; (*enemigo*) bitter
acertado, -a *adj* **1.** (*correcto*) correct **2.** (*atinado*) accurate **3.** (*conveniente*) apt
acertar <e→ie> **I.** *vi* **1.** (*dar*) to hit; ~ **al blanco** to hit the mark **2.** (*hacer con acierto*) to be right; **acertaste en protestar** you were right to protest **3.** (*por casualidad*) ~ **a hacer algo** to happen to do sth **4.** (*conseguir*) **no acerté a encontrar la respuesta** I didn't manage to find the answer **5.** (*encontrar*) ~ **con algo** to come across sth **II.** *vt* **1.** (*dar en el blanco*) to hit **2.** (*encontrar*) to find **3.** (*adivinar*) to get right
acertijo *m* riddle
acervo *m* store; ~ **cultural** cultural heritage
acético, -a *adj* acetic
acetona *f* acetone
achacar <c→qu> *vt* to attribute
achachay *interj Col, Ecua* expressing cold, brrrrr
achacoso, -a *adj* sickly; **estar** ~ to be ailing
achalay *interj Arg, Perú* wow
achantar **I.** *vt inf* to intimidate **II.** *vr:* **~se** *inf* to hide away; (*no atreverse*) to back down
achaparrado, -a *adj* **1.** (*persona*) stocky **2.** (*objeto*) squat
achaque *m* **1.** (*dolencia*) ailment **2.** (*excusa*) pretext
achatado, -a *adj* flattened; **nariz achatada** snub nose; (*como un boxeador*) boxer's nose
achatar **I.** *vt* to flatten; ~ **la nariz a alguien** to break sb's nose **II.** *vr:* **~se** to become flat
achicar <c→qu> **I.** *vt* **1.** (*empequeñecer*) to make smaller **2.** (*intimidar*) to intimidate **3.** (*agua*) to bale out **II.** *vr:* **~se** **1.** (*empequeñecerse*) to become smaller; (*ropa*) to shrink **2.** (*acoquinarse*) to take fright; (*no atreverse*) not to dare **3.** *AmL* (*humillarse*) to demean oneself
achicharrar **I.** *vt* **1.** (*calor*) to scorch; **estoy achicharrado** I'm boiling (hot) **2.** (*comida*) to burn **3.** (*atosigar*) to harass **II.** *vr:* **~se** **1.** (*comida*) to get burnt **2.** (*persona*) to be sweltering; (*planta*) to be wilting (in the heat)
achichiguar *vt Méx* **1.** (*servir de niñera*) to babysit **2.** (*malcriar*) to cosset
achichinque *m Méx* (*adulador*) groupie
achicoria *f* chicory
achinado, -a *adj* **1.** (*rasgos*) oriental; **ojos ~s** slanting eyes **2.** *CSur* (*aplebeyado*) coarse
achiote *m AmC, Bol, Méx* **1.** BOT annatto tree **2.** (*pigmento*) annatto
achipolarse *vr Méx* **1.** (*personas*) to grow sad **2.** (*plantas*) to wither
achiquillado, -a *adj* **1.** *Méx* (*infantil*) childish **2.** *Chile* (*como un muchacho*) boyish
achira *f AmS* BOT canna
achís *interj* atishoo *Brit,* atchoo *Am*
achispar **I.** *vt* to cheer up **II.** *vr:* **~se** to become tipsy
acholado, -a *adj CSur, Perú, Bol* **1.** (*mestizo*)

mestizo (*of mixed Spanish American and American Indian descent*) **2.** (*acobardado*) intimidated

acholar I. *vt Chile, Perú, Bol* **1.** (*avergonzar*) to embarrass **2.** (*amilanar*) to scare **II.** *vr:* **~se** *CSur, Perú, Bol* (*acobardarse*) to become intimidated

achuchado, -a *adj inf* **1.** (*duro*) tough **2.** (*de dinero*) broke **3.** (*débil*) feverish

achuchar *vt* **1.** *inf* (*persona*) to stir up; **~ a un perro contra alguien** to set a dog on sb **2.** *inf* (*estrujar*) to crush **3.** (*atosigar*) to harass **4.** *inf* (*acariciar*) to caress; (*abrazar*) to embrace; (*manosear*) to fondle

achuchón *m inf* **1.** (*abrazo*) squeeze **2.** (*empujón*) shove **3.** (*achaque*) indisposition

achucutado, -a *adj* **1.** *AmL* (*abatido*) depressed **2.** *Ven, Hond, Guat* (*triste*) sad

achucutarse *vr Col, Ecua,* **achucuyarse** *vr AmC* **1.** (*humillarse*) to shame **2.** (*acobardarse*) to chicken out *inf*

achumado, -a *adj Ecua* drunk

achumarse *vr Ecua* to get drunk

achunchar *vt AmL* (*avergonzar, amedrentar*) to humiliate

achura *f AmS* (*despojos de res*) offal

achurar *vt CSur* **1.** (*res*) to gut **2.** (*persona*) to stab to death

achuras *fpl Arg* offal

aciago, -a *adj* ill-fated; **un día ~** a fateful day

acíbar *m* **1.** BOT aloe **2.** (*amargura*) bitterness

acicalarse *vr* to get dressed up

acicate *m* **1.** (*espuela*) spur **2.** (*estímulo*) stimulus

acidez *f* acidity; **~ de estómago** MED heartburn, acid indigestion *Am*

ácido *m* **1.** QUÍM acid; **~ cianhídrico** hydrocyanic acid; **~ clorhídrico** hydrochloric acid; **~s grasos insaturados** unsaturated fatty acids **2.** *inf* (*droga*) acid

ácido, -a *adj* **1.** (*agrio*) sour **2.** (*mordaz*) sharp **3.** QUÍM acidic

acídulo, -a *adj* sharp-tasting

acierto *m* **1.** (*en el tiro*) accuracy **2.** (*éxito*) success; (*en la lotería*) right number; **el casarte ha sido un ~** you did well to get married **3.** (*habilidad*) skill; **hacer algo con ~** to do sth skilfully

acitrón *m Méx* GASTR candied citron

aclamación *f* **1.** (*aplauso*) applause **2.** POL **por ~** by acclamation [*o* acclaim *Am*]

aclamar *vt* **1.** (*vitorear*) to cheer **2.** POL to acclaim

aclaración *f* **1.** (*clarificación*) clarification **2.** (*explicación*) explanation **3.** (*de un crimen*) solution; (*de un secreto*) revelation

aclarar I. *vt* **1.** (*hacer más claro*) to lighten; **~ el bosque** to clear [*o* thin out] the forest; **~ la voz** to clear one's throat **2.** (*un líquido*) to thin (down) **3.** (*la ropa*) to rinse **4.** (*explicar*) to explain **5.** (*crimen*) to solve; (*secreto*) to reveal **II.** *vr:* **~se 1.** (*problema, cuestión*) to be clarified **2.** *inf* (*entender*) to catch on; **no te aclaras contigo mismo** you don't know what you want **III.** *vimpers* **está aclarando** it's brightening up

aclaratorio, -a *adj* explanatory

aclimatación *f* acclimatization *Brit,* acclimation *Am*

aclimatar I. *vt* to acclimatize *Brit,* to acclimate *Am* **II.** *vr:* **~se** to get acclimatized *Brit* [*o* acclimated *Am*]

acné *m o f sin pl* acne

acobardar I. *vt* to frighten; (*con palabras*) to intimidate; **le acobarda el fuego** he/she is afraid of fire **II.** *vr:* **~se 1.** (*desanimarse*) **~se ante** [*o* **frente a**] **algo** to flinch from sth **2.** (*intimidarse*) to be frightened; **se acobarda de sí misma** he is afraid of his own shadow

acogedor(a) *adj* welcoming, inviting

acoger <g→j> **I.** *vt* to welcome; (*recibir*) to receive **II.** *vr:* **~se 1.** (*refugiarse*) to take refuge **2.** (*ampararse*) to shelter **3.** (*basarse*) to resort; **~se a algo** to avail oneself of sth

acogida *f* welcome; (*recibimiento*) reception; **encontrar una buena ~** to be well received; **el cantante tuvo una buena ~** the singer was received with applause; **el proyecto no tuvo una buena ~** the project didn't meet with approval

acogotar *vt* **1.** (*matar*) to kill (*with a blow to the head*) **2.** (*intimidar*) to pressurize *Brit,* to pressure *Am* **3.** (*derribar*) to knock down

acojonado, -a *adj vulg* **1.** (*asustado*) frightened, scared shitless *Am;* (*acobardado*) intimidated; **ahora está ~** he/she is frightened now **2.** (*impresionado*) impressed; (*asombrado*) amazed

acojonante *adj vulg* **1.** (*fantástico*) fantastic **2.** (*impresionante*) incredible

acojonar I. *vt vulg* **1.** (*asustar*) to frighten, to scare the shit out of *Am;* (*intimidar*) to intimidate **2.** (*impresionar*) to impress; (*asombrar*) to amaze **II.** *vr:* **~se** *vulg* **1.** (*asustarse*) to become frightened, to be scared shitless *Am;* (*acobardarse*) to back down; **no ~se** not to be frightened **2.** (*asombrarse*) to be amazed

acolchar *vt* to quilt

acólito *m* **1.** (*monaguillo*) altar boy **2.** *pey* (*seguidor*) follower

acometer I. *vi* to attack **II.** *vt* **1.** (*embestir*) to attack **2.** (*emprender*) to undertake **3.** (*ataque de tos, fiebre*) to attack; (*risa, sueño*) to overcome; **lo acometió la risa** he was overcome by laughter

acometida *f* **1.** (*embestida*) attack **2.** (*acceso*) fit **3.** TÉC connection

acomodado, -a *adj* **1.** (*cómodo*) comfortable **2.** (*rico*) well-off; **tener una vida acomodada** to live comfortably **3.** (*apropiado*) suitable **4.** (*precio*) reasonable

acomodador(a) *m(f)* TEAT, CINE usher

acomodar I. *vt* **1.** (*adaptar*) to adapt **2.** (*colocar*) to place **3.** (*albergar*) to accommodate **4.** (*proporcionar empleo*) **~ de algo (a alguien)** to take on (sb) as sth **5.** (*conciliar*) to reconcile II. *vi* **si te acomoda** if it suits you III. *vr:* ~**se** 1. (*adaptarse*) to adapt oneself; ~**se con todo** to put up with everything 2. (*ponerse cómodo*) to make oneself comfortable

acomodaticio, **-a** *adj* 1. (*adaptable*) adaptable 2. *pey* (*oportunista*) opportunistic

acomodo *m* 1. (*arreglo*) arrangement 2. (*acuerdo*) agreement 3. (*ocupación*) employment, job, post *Brit;* **buscar** ~ to look for a job 4. *AmL* (*soborno*) bribe

acompañado, **-a** *adj* accompanied; **bien/mal** ~ in good/bad company; **iba acompañada por su padre** she was accompanied by her father

acompañamiento *m* 1. *t.* MÚS accompaniment 2. (*cortejo*) retinue 3. TEAT extras *pl,* supporting cast *Am* 4. (*de comidas*) accompaniment, side dish *Am*

acompañante *mf* 1. (*de una dama*) escort 2. (*en el coche*) passenger

acompañar *vt* 1. (*ir con*) *t.* MÚS to accompany; ~ **a alguien a casa** to see sb home; ~ **a alguien en un viaje** to go with sb on a journey; ~ **a alguien de compras** to go shopping with sb; ~ **a alguien con la guitarra/al piano** to accompany sb on the guitar/on the piano; ~ **el pollo con arroz y verduras** to serve the chicken with rice and vegetables 2. (*hacer compañía*) ~ **a alguien** to keep sb company 3. (*adjuntar*) to enclose 4. (*ir incluido*) **el informe acompaña a la carta** the report is enclosed with the letter

acompasado, **-a** *adj* 1. MÚS rhythmic 2. (*pausado*) measured

acompasar *vt* 1. MÚS ~ **algo** to mark the rhythm of sth 2. (*adaptar*) ~ **algo a** [*o* **con**] **algo** to fit sth in with sth

acomplejado, **-a** *adj* full of complexes

acomplejar I. *vt* to give a complex II. *vr:* ~**se** to get a complex

aconchar I. *vt* 1. (*guarecer*) to shelter 2. *Méx* (*reprender*) to tell off II. *vr:* ~**se** 1. (*arrimarse*) to come alongside 2. NÁUT to run aground 3. *Chile, Perú* (*sedimentarse*) to settle; ~ **a alguien los meados** *inf* to chicken out 4. *Chile, Perú* (*serenarse*) to calm down

acondicionado, **-a** *adj* **bien/mal** ~ in good/bad condition

acondicionador *m* 1. (*de aire*) air-conditioner 2. (*para el pelo*) conditioner

acondicionar *vt* 1. (*preparar*) to prepare; (*arreglar*) to arrange 2. (*equipar*) to equip 3. (*climatizar*) to air-condition

acongojar *vt* to distress

aconsejable *adj* advisable

aconsejado, **-a** *adj* (*prudente*) sensible

aconsejar *vt* to advise; ~ **algo a alguien** to recommend sth to sb; **esto aconseja prudencia** this calls for caution

acontecer *irr como crecer vi* to happen

acontecimiento *m* event

acopiar *vt* to gather together

acopio *m* 1. (*de comida, bienes*) store; **hacer** ~ **de algo** to stock up with [*o* on *Am*] sth; **hacer** ~ **de paciencia** to draw on all one's reserves of patience; **hacer** ~ **de valor** to muster one's courage 2. (*compra*) stock

acoplado *m RíoPl* trailer

acoplamiento *m* 1. (*de máquinas, vagones*) coupling 2. ELEC connection

acoplar I. *vt* 1. (*ajustar*) to adjust; (*juntar*) to join 2. (*piezas, remolque*) to fit together 3. ELEC to connect 4. (*adaptar*) to adapt II. *vr:* ~**se** to adapt

acoquinar I. *vt* to intimidate II. *vr:* ~**se** to allow oneself to be intimidated, to chicken out *Am, inf*

acorazar <z→c> I. *vt* to armour-plate *Brit,* to armorplate *Am* II. *vr:* ~**se** to arm oneself

acorazonado, **-a** *adj* heart-shaped

acordar <o→ue> I. *vt* 1. (*convenir*) to agree 2. (*decidir*) to decide 3. MÚS to tune II. *vr* ~**se de algo/alguien** to remember sth/sb; **si mal no me acuerdo** if my memory serves me right; **¡acuérdate de decírselo!** remember to tell him/her!

acorde I. *adj* 1. (*conforme*) agreed; **estar** ~ **con alguien** to be in agreement with sb; ~ **con el medio ambiente** in keeping with the environment 2. MÚS harmonious II. *m* MÚS chord; ~ **mayor/menor** major/minor chord; **a los** ~**s de un vals** to the strains of a waltz

acordeón *m* accordion

acordonar *vt* 1. (*botas*) to lace up 2. (*un sitio*) to cordon off

acorralar *vt* 1. (*ganado*) to round up 2. (*cercar*) to fence in 3. (*intimidar*) to intimidate; (*con preguntas*) to corner

acortar I. *vt* to shorten; (*duración*) to cut down; (*distancia*) to reduce; ~ **camino** to take a short cut; ~ **un pantalón unos centímetros** to take up a pair of trousers by a few centimetres II. *vr:* ~**se** to become shorter

acosar *vt* 1. (*perseguir*) to hound 2. (*asediar*) to harass; ~ **a alguien a** [*o* **con**] **preguntas** to pester sb with questions

acosijar *vt Méx* (*acosar*) to hound

acoso *m* relentless pursuit; *fig* harassment; ~ **sexual** sexual harassment

acostar <o→ue> I. *vt* to put to bed II. *vr:* ~**se** 1. (*descansar*) to lie down; **estar acostado** to be lying down 2. (*ir a la cama*) to go to bed; ~**se con alguien** to go to bed with sb 3. *AmC, Méx, Col* (*dar a luz*) to give birth

acostumbrado, **-a** *adj* accustomed; **mal** ~ spoilt

acostumbrar I. *vi* ~ **a hacer algo** to be used to doing sth; **como se acostumbra a decir** as they say II. *vt* ~ **a alguien a hacer algo** to get sb used to doing sth III. *vr:* ~**se a algo** to get accustomed [*o* used] to sth

acotación *f* 1. (*nota*) margin note, annotation 2. TEAT stage direction 3. (*cota*) elevation mark

acotamiento *m* 1. (*acotación*) fencing

2. *Méx* (*arcén*) hard shoulder, shoulder *Am*

acotar *vt* 1. (*delimitar*) to delimit; **terreno acotado** private property 2. (*un plano*) ~ **algo** to mark elevations on sth 3. (*un texto*) to annotate

ácrata I. *adj* 1. (*anárquico*) anarchic 2. (*anarquista*) anarchistic II. *mf* anarchist

acre[1] *adj* <acérrimo> 1. (*áspero*) bitter 2. (*ácido*) sour 3. (*mordaz*) scathing; (*tono*) harsh

acre[2] *m* (*medida de tierra*) acre

acrecentar <e→ie> *vt*, **acrecer** *irr como crecer vt* to increase

acreditado, **-a** *adj* (*reputado*) reputable

acreditar I. *vt* 1. (*atestiguar*) to vouch for 2. (*autorizar*) to authorize 3. (*diplomático*) to accredit; ~ **como embajador** to accredit as ambassador 4. (*dar reputación*) to do credit 5. FIN to credit II. *vr:* ~**se** 1. (*adquirir reputación*) to get a reputation 2. (*dar crédito de uno mismo*) to prove one's worth

acreedor(**a**) I. *adj* **hacerse** ~ **a** [*o* **de**] **algo** to be worthy of sth II. *m(f)* FIN creditor

acribillar *vt* 1. (*abrir agujeros*) to riddle; **acribillado a balazos** riddled with bullets; **anoche me han acribillado los mosquitos** last night I was eaten alive by the mosquitoes 2. (*importunar*) to pester; ~ **a alguien a preguntas** to pester sb with questions

acrílico, **-a** *adj* acrylic; **fibra acrílica** acrylic fibre

acrimonia *f v.* **acritud**

acriollarse *vr AmL* to go native

acritud *f* 1. (*acrimonia*) acrimony; **contestar con** ~ to reply bitterly 2. (*de un dolor*) harshness

acrobacia *f* acrobatics *pl;* ~ **aérea** aerobatics *pl*, stunt flying *Am*

acróbata *mf* acrobat

acrobático, **-a** *adj* acrobatic

acrónimo *m* acronym

acta *f* 1. (*de una reunión*) minutes *pl;* **levantar** ~ **de algo** to draw up a document of sth; **hacer constar en** ~ to record in the minutes 2. (*certificado*) certificate 3. JUR act; ~ **de acusación** bill of indictment; **Acta Única Europea** Single European Act

actitud *f* 1. (*corporal*) posture; ~ **de ataque** threatening stance; ~ **de extrema cautela en cuanto a algo** policy of extreme caution with regard to sth 2. (*disposición*) attitude; **adoptar una** ~ **reservada** to adopt a reserved attitude 3. (*comportamiento*) behaviour *Brit,* behavior *Am;* **adoptar una** ~ **incomprensible** to behave incomprehensibly

activamente *adv* actively

activar *vt* 1. (*avivar*) to stimulate 2. (*acelerar*) to speed up; ~ **la digestión** to aid digestion 3. QUÍM, FÍS, INFOR to activate; ~ **una bomba** to detonate a bomb

actividad *f* 1. (*general*) activity; (*ocupación*) occupation; ~ **profesional** profession; **las** ~**es artísticas de una país** the cultural activities of a country [*o* city]; **en** ~ active; **volcán en** ~ active volcano; **entrar en** ~ to go into action 2. (*diligencia*) diligence

activo *m* FIN assets *pl;* ~ **circulante** current assets; ~ **fijo** fixed assets

activo, **-a** *adj* active; (*sustancia, medicamento*) effective

acto *m* 1. (*acción*) action; ~ **de cortesía** act of courtesy; ~ **jurídico** (*válido*) legal act; (*negocio*) legal transaction; ~ **penal** criminal act; ~ **sexual** sexual act; ~ **de violencia** act of violence; ~ **de voluntad** professed intention; **cometer** ~**s de gamberrismo** to commit acts of vandalism; **hacer** ~ **de presencia** to put in an appearance 2. (*ceremonia*) ceremony; ~ **conmemorativo** commemoration; ~ **estatal** state occasion; ~ **necrológico** funeral service 3. TEAT act ▸ ~ **seguido...** immediately after ...; **en el** ~ immediately, on the spot

actor, **actriz** *m, f* TEAT, CINE actor *m,* actress *f;* ~ **de cine** film actor; ~ **suplente** understudy; **primer** ~ principal actor, leading man

actor(**a**) *m(f)* plaintiff

actriz *f v.* **actor**

actuación *f* 1. (*conducta*) conduct; **la** ~ **de la policía** the police action 2. (*actividad*) activity; (*desempeño de un cargo*) performance 3. TEAT, MÚS performance; ~ **en directo** live performance 4. *pl* JUR legal proceedings *pl*

actual *adj* 1. (*de ahora*) present 2. (*corriente*) current

actualidad *f* 1. (*presente*) present; **en la** ~ at present 2. (*cualidad*) topicality, currentness; **de** ~ topical; **ser de gran** ~ to be topical

actualizar <z→c> *vt* to bring up to date

actualmente *adv* at the moment, currently

actuar <*1. pres:* actúo> *vi* 1. (*obrar, hacer*) to work 2. (*tener efecto*) ~ **sobre algo** to have an effect on sth 3. TEAT to act; ~ **en directo** to perform live; ~ **de Don Juan** to play Don Juan; **ella no actúa en esta función** she doesn't appear in this performance 4. JUR to appear; ~ **contra alguien** to take legal proceedings against sb

acuache *m Méx* (*compinche*) mate *Brit,* pal *Am*

acuarela *f* watercolour *Brit,* watercolor *Am*

acuario *m* aquarium

Acuario *m* Aquarius

acuartelar *vt* 1. MIL to billet 2. (*dividir*) to divide into quarters

acuático, **-a** *adj* aquatic; **parque** ~ waterpark

acuchamarse *vr Ven* (*entristecerse*) to get depressed

acuchillar *vt* 1. (*herir*) to knife; (*matar*) to stab to death 2. (*parqué*) to sand down; (*muebles*) to scrape

acuciante *adj* urgent

acuciar *vt* 1. (*dar prisa*) to hurry up 2. (*incitar*) to urge

acuclillarse *vr* to squat

acudiente *m Col* (*tutor*) tutor

acudir *vi* 1. (*ir*) to go; ~ **a una cita** to keep an appointment; ~ **al trabajo/a la puerta** to go to work/to the door; ~ **a las urnas** to go to the polls; ~ **a la memoria de alguien** to come to sb's mind **2.** (*corriendo*) ~ **a alguien** to go to help sb; ~ **en socorro de alguien** to come to sb's aid **3.** (*recurrir*) ~ **a** to turn to

acueducto *m* aqueduct

acuerdo *m* **1.** (*convenio*) *t.* POL agreement; **Acuerdo General sobre Aranceles y Comercio** General Agreement on Tariffs and Trade; **Acuerdo Monetario Europeo** European Monetary Agreement; **llegar a un** ~ to reach an agreement **2.** (*decisión*) decision; **tomar un** ~ to pass a resolution **3.** (*conformidad*) agreement; **estar de** ~ **con alguien** to agree with sb; **ponerse de** ~ to come to an agreement; **sin ponerse de** ~ without reaching (an) agreement; **de común** ~ by mutual consent ▶**¡de** ~**!** I agree!, OK!; **de** ~ **con** in accordance with

acuerpado, **-a** *adj Bol* (*corpulento*) hefty

acular *vt* AUTO to back

acullá *adv elev* **1.** (*lugar*) over there **2.** (*dirección*) yonder

acullicar *vi Arg, Bol, Chile, Perú* (*mascar coca*) to chew coca leaves

acullico *m Arg, Bol, Perú* (*bola de coca*) small ball of coca

acumuchar *vt Chile* (*acumular*) to pile up

acumulación *f* **1.** (*amontonamiento*) accumulation **2.** (*de cosas reunidas*) collection

acumulador *m* ELEC accumulator

acumular *vt* **1.** (*reunir*) to collect **2.** (*amontonar*) *t.* ELEC to accumulate

acunar *vt* to rock (to sleep)

acuñar *vt* **1.** (*monedas*) to mint **2.** (*palabras*) to coin **3.** TÉC to wedge

acuoso, **-a** *adj* watery; (*fruta*) juicy

acupuntura *f* acupuncture

acurí *m Col, Ven* ZOOL agouti, guinea pig

acurrucarse <c→qu> *vr* to curl up; (*agacharse*) to crouch; (*a causa del frío*) to huddle up; ~ **en un sillón** to curl up in an armchair

acusación *f* **1.** (*inculpación*) accusation; ~ **de corrupción** charge of corruption **2.** JUR (*en juicio*) charge; (*escrito*) indictment; ~ **constitucional** *charge concerning an infringement of the constitution;* ~ **particular** private prosecution

acusado, **-a** **I.** *adj* **1.** (*claro, evidente*) pronounced **2.** (*marcado*) marked **II.** *m, f* accused

acusador(a) *m(f)* accuser

acusar *vt* **1.** (*culpar*) to accuse; **lo acusan de asesinato** he is accused of murder **2.** (*en juicio*) to charge **3.** (*en la escuela*) to tell on **4.** (*traslucir*) to reveal; TÉC to register **5.** ECON to confirm; ~ **recibo de un pedido** to acknowledge receipt of an order

acusativo *m* LING accusative

acuse *m* ~ **de recibo** acknowledgement of receipt

acústica *f* **1.** (*ciencia*) acoustics *sing* **2.** (*de un sitio*) acoustics *pl*

acústico, **-a** *adj* acoustic

acutí *m Arg, Par, Urug* ZOOL agouti

adagio *m* **1.** (*proverbio*) adage **2.** MÚS adagio

adalid *m* **1.** (*caudillo*) leader **2.** (*defensor*) champion

adán *m* slovenly fellow; **vas hecho un** ~ you look a mess

Adán *m* Adam; ~ **y Eva** Adam and Eve

adaptable *adj* adaptable

adaptación *f* **1.** (*acomodación*) adaptation **2.** LIT, MÚS, TEAT adaptation; **la** ~ **de una obra de teatro al cine** the film version of a play

adaptador *m* TÉC adapter

adaptar **I.** *vt* **1.** (*acomodar*) to adapt; **bien adaptado al grupo** well adapted to the group **2.** (*edificio*) to convert; ~ **un piso para oficina** to convert a flat into an office **3.** (*ajustar*) to adjust; ~ **algo a algo** to adapt sth to sth **4.** LIT, MÚS, TEAT, CINE to adapt; ~ **una novela a la pantalla** to adapt a novel for the screen **II.** *vr:* ~**se** to adapt; **se han adaptado muy bien el uno al otro** they have fitted in very well with each other

adecentar **I.** *vt* to tidy up **II.** *vr:* ~**se** to tidy oneself up

adecuado, **-a** *adj* **1.** (*apto*) appropriate **2.** (*palabras*) fitting; (*conveniente*) suitable; **la decoración de tu casa es muy adecuada** your house is very well decorated

adecuar *vt, vr:* ~**se** to adapt

adefesio *m* **1.** (*prenda*) rag, ridiculous costume **2.** (*persona*) scarecrow; **estar hecho un** ~ to look a sight

a. de (J)C. *abr de* **antes de (Jesu)cristo** BC

adelantado, **-a** *adj* **1.** (*precoz*) precocious **2.** (*avanzado*) advanced; **estar muy** ~ to be very advanced ▶**por** ~ in advance

adelantamiento *m* **1.** (*avance*) advance; (*progreso*) progress **2.** (*del coche*) overtaking *Brit,* passing *Am;* **realizar un** ~ to overtake *Brit,* to pass *Am*

adelantar **I.** *vi* **1.** (*reloj*) to be fast **2.** (*progresar*) to progress; **no adelanto nada en francés** I'm not making any progress in French **3.** (*coche*) to overtake *Brit,* to pass *Am* **II.** *vt* **1.** (*reloj*) to put forward **2.** (*avanzar*) to move forward; ~ **unos pasos** to go forward a few steps **3.** (*coche, persona*) to overtake *Brit,* to pass *Am* **4.** (*viaje, partida*) to bring forward **5.** (*idea*) to put forward **6.** (*paga*) to advance **7.** (*obtener ventaja*) to gain; **¿qué adelantas con esto?** where does that get you? **III.** *vr:* ~**se** **1.** (*reloj*) to be fast **2.** (*avanzarse*) to go forward **3.** (*llegar antes*) to get ahead **4.** (*anticiparse*) to anticipate; **te has adelantado a mis deseos** you've anticipated my wishes

adelante *adv* forward, ahead *Am;* **llevar un plan** ~ to carry forward a plan, to go ahead with a plan *Am;* **sacar una familia** ~ to provide for a family; **¡**~**!** come in!; **seguir** ~ to go (straight) on; **véase más** ~ see below

adelanto *m* **1.** (*progreso*) progress; **~s técnicos** technical innovations **2.** (*anticipo*) advance

adelgazar <z→c> **I.** *vi, vr:* **~se** to lose weight **II.** *vt* **1.** (*cosas*) to make thin **2.** (*peso*) to reduce

ademán *m* **1.** (*gesto*) gesture; **hacer ~ de salir** to make as if to leave **2.** (*actitud*) attitude; **en ~ de** getting ready to

además *adv* besides, moreover

adenda *f* addendum

adentrarse *vr* **1.** (*entrar*) **~ en algo** to go into sth; (*penetrar*) to penetrate into sth **2.** (*estudiar a fondo*) to study thoroughly

adentro *adv* (*lugar y movimiento*) inside; **mar ~** out to sea; **tierra ~** inland; **el grito le salió de muy ~** his/her cry came from deep within

adentros *mpl* innermost being; **para sus ~** inwardly; **guardar algo para sus ~** to keep sth to oneself

adepto, **-a** *m, f* **1.** (*afiliado*) follower **2.** (*partidario*) supporter

aderezar <z→c> *vt* **1.** (*preparar*) to prepare **2.** (*guisar*) to stew **3.** (*condimentar*) to season; (*ensalada*) to dress

aderezo *m* **1.** (*de un guiso*) preparation **2.** (*condimentación*) seasoning; (*de, para una ensalada*) dressing **3.** (*joyas*) set of jewels

adeudar **I.** *vt* **1.** (*deber*) to owe **2.** (*cargar*) to charge; **~ una cantidad en cuenta** to debit an account for a sum **II.** *vr:* **~se** to run into debt; **~se mucho** to get deep into debt

adherencia *f* **1.** (*adhesión*) adherence; AUTO roadholding, road grip *Am* **2.** (*conexión*) connection

adherir *irr como sentir* **I.** *vt* (*sello*) to stick **II.** *vr:* **~se** **1.** (*pegarse*) to adhere **2.** (*a una opinión*) to adhere, to support **3.** (*a un partido*) **~se a un partido** to join a party

adhesión *f* **1.** (*adherencia*) adhesion **2.** (*a una opinión*) adherence, support **3.** (*apoyo*) **~ a alguien** support of sb **4.** (*a una asociación*) **~ a algo** membership of sth

adhesivo *m* **1.** (*sustancia*) adhesive; **~ multiuso** all-purpose adhesive **2.** (*pegatina*) sticker

adhesivo, **-a** *adj* adhesive

adicción *f* addiction; **~ a las drogas** drug addiction

adición *f* (*añadidura*) *t.* MAT addition

adicional *adj* additional

adicionar *vt* to add

adicto, **-a** **I.** *adj* **1.** (*leal*) devoted **2.** (*que tiene adicción*) addicted; **~ a las drogas** addicted to drugs; **~ a la televisión** *inf* addicted to television **II.** *m, f* **1.** (*dependiente*) addict **2.** *CSur* (*partidario*) **~ a alguien** supporter of sb

adiestrar *vt* (*personas, animales*) to train

adifés **I.** *adj Guat* (*difícil*) difficult **II.** *adv Ven* (*adrede*) on purpose

adinerado, **-a** *adj* wealthy

adiós **I.** *interj* **1.** (*despedida*) goodbye, bye **2.** (*al pasar*) hello, hi **II.** *m* farewell; **decir ~ a alguien** to say goodbye to sb

adiposo, **-a** *adj* adipose; **tejido ~** fatty tissue

aditamento *m* **1.** (*añadidura*) addition **2.** (*complemento*) complement

aditivo *m* additive

aditivo, **-a** *adj* additional

adivinanza *f* riddle

adivinar *vt* **1.** (*el futuro*) to foretell **2.** (*conjeturar*) to guess; (*acertar*) to guess correctly; **¡adivina cuántos años tengo!** guess how old I am! **3.** (*vislumbrar*) to glimpse

adjetivo *m* adjective; **~ numeral** numeral

adjudicación *f* **1.** (*de un premio, un pedido, una beca*) award(ing) **2.** (*en una subasta*) sale

adjudicar <c→qu> **I.** *vt* **1.** (*premio, encargo, beca*) to award **2.** (*en una subasta*) to knock down *Brit,* to sell at auction *Am* **II.** *vr:* **~se** **1.** (*apropiarse*) to appropriate **2.** (*victoria, premio*) to win

adjuntar *vt* to enclose

adjunto, **-a** *adj* **1.** (*junto*) enclosed **2.** (*auxiliar*) assistant; **profesora adjunta** UNIV senior lecturer *Brit,* associate professor *Am*

administración *f* **1.** (*dirección, organización, órgano*) administration; **la ~ española** the Spanish authorities; **la ~ de correos** the postal service; **~ de una cuenta** managing [*o* running *Brit*] of an account; **~ de fincas** property management; **~ municipal** town/city council **2.** (*de medicamentos, de sacramentos*) administering **3.** *Arg* (*gobierno*) government

administrador(a) *m(f)* administrator; (*gerente*) manager; **~ de la masa** receiver

administrar *vt* **1.** (*dirigir, cuidar*) administer; **~ justicia** to dispense justice **2.** (*racionar*) to ration **3.** (*suministrar*) to supply **4.** (*medicamentos, sacramentos*) to administer

administrativo, **-a** **I.** *adj* administrative **II.** *m, f* clerk

admirable *adj* admirable

admiración *f* **1.** (*respeto, adoración*) admiration **2.** (*asombro*) amazement **3.** (*signo*) exclamation mark [*o* point *Am*]; (*frase*) exclamation

admirado, **-a** *adj* amazed; **me quedé admirada de tus conocimientos** I was amazed at your knowledge

admirador(a) *m(f)* admirer

admirar *vt* **1.** (*adorar, apreciar*) to admire **2.** (*asombrar*) to amaze

admisible *adj* admissible

admisión *f* **1.** (*en una asociación, universidad*) **~ en algo** admission [*o* acceptance] to sth **2.** TÉC inlet

admitir *vt* **1.** (*en una asociación, universidad*) **~ en algo** to admit to sth **2.** (*aceptar*) to accept; **~ los métodos de alguien** to accept sb's methods **3.** (*reconocer*) to recognize **4.** (*permitir*) to permit; **~ una queja** JUR to accept a complaint; **el asunto no admite dilación** the matter allows no delay; **es cosa admitida que...** it is generally admitted that ... **5.** (*tener capacidad*) to hold

admonición *f* admonition; ADMIN warning
ADN *m abr de* **ácido desoxirribonucleico** DNA
adobar *vt* **1.** (*con salsa*) to marinade; (*carne*) to pickle **2.** (*piel*) to tan **3.** *inf* (*amañar*) to fiddle
adobe *m* adobe
adobo *m* **1.** (*salsa*) marinade **2.** (*con salsa*) marinating; (*para conservar*) pickling **3.** (*de pieles*) tanning
adocenado, **-a** *adj* mediocre
adoctrinar *vt* **1.** (*de ideas*) to indoctrinate **2.** (*enseñar*) to instruct; ~ **a alguien sobre algo** to instruct sb about sth
adolecer *irr como crecer vi* (*ponerse enfermo*) to fall ill; (*padecer*) to suffer; **este chico adolece de falta de imaginación** this boy suffers from a lack of imagination
adolescencia *f* adolescence
adolescente **I.** *adj* adolescent **II.** *mf* teenager
adonde *adv* (*relativo*) where; **el pueblo ~ iremos es muy bonito** the village we'll go to is very pretty
adónde *adv* (*interrogativo*) where
adondequiera *adv* ~ **que** +*subj* wherever
adopción *f* adoption
adoptar *vt* to adopt
adoptivo, **-a** *adj* **1.** (*personas*) adoptive, foster *Am* **2.** (*cosas*) adopted, foster *Am*
adoquín *m* **1.** (*piedra*) cobblestone **2.** *inf* (*persona*) blockhead
adoquinado *m* (*suelo*) cobbles *pl*
adoquinar *vt* to cobble
adorable *adj* adorable
adorar *vt* to adore; (*idolatrar*) to worship
adormecer *irr como crecer* **I.** *vt* **1.** (*personas*) to make sleepy **2.** (*dolor*) to numb **II.** *vr:* ~**se** to fall asleep
adormecido, **-a** *adj*, **adormilado**, **-a** *adj* (*cansado*) sleepy
adormilarse *vr* to doze
adornar **I.** *vt* to adorn; (*con ornamentos*) to decorate **II.** *vr:* ~**se** to adorn oneself
adorno *m* adornment; (*decoración*) decoration; (*ornamento*) ornament; **árbol de ~** ornamental tree; **la lámpara sólo está de ~** the lamp is just for decoration; **estar de ~** *fig* to be for show
adosado, **-a** *adj* **casa adosada** semi-detached house *Brit,* duplex *Am,* two-family house *Am*
adosar *vt* **1.** (*apoyar*) ~ **a algo** to lean against sth **2.** ARQUIT ~ **a algo** to build onto sth
adquirir *irr vt* **1.** (*conseguir*) to acquire; ~ **un hábito** to acquire a habit **2.** (*comprar*) to purchase
adquisición *f* acquisition; (*de una empresa*) takeover; ~ **de lenguas** acquisition of languages; **este coche es una buena ~** this car is a good buy
adquisitivo, **-a** *adj* acquisitive; **poder ~** purchasing power
adrede *adv* on purpose
adrenalina *f* adrenalin
adriático, **-a** *adj* Adriatic; **mar Adriático** Adriatic (Sea)
Adriático *m* Adriatic
adscribir *irr como escribir vt* **1.** (*atribuir*) to assign **2.** (*destinar*) to appoint
aduana *f* **1.** (*tasa*) customs duty; **declaración de ~s** customs declaration; **despacho de ~** customs clearance; **sin ~** duty-free **2.** (*oficina*) customs office; **pase por la ~, por favor** go through customs, please **3.** (*juego*) *dice game*
aduanero, **-a** **I.** *adj* customs; **exento de derechos ~s** duty-free; **sujeto a derechos ~s** dutiable **II.** *m, f* customs officer
aducir *irr como traducir vt* (*razón, motivo*) to put forward; (*prueba*) to provide
adueñarse *vr* to take possession; ~ **del poder** to take over power; **el pánico se adueñó de él** panic got the better of him
adulación *f* flattery
adulador(a) **I.** *adj* flattering **II.** *m(f)* flatterer
adular *vt* to flatter
adulterar *vt* to falsify; (*alimentos*) to adulterate
adulterio *m* adultery
adúltero, **-a** **I.** *adj* adulterous **II.** *m, f* adulterer
adulto, **-a** **I.** *adj* **1.** (*persona, animal*) adult **2.** (*desarrollado*) mature **II.** *m, f* adult
adusto, **-a** *adj* **1.** (*persona*) stern **2.** (*paisaje*) bleak **3.** (*región, casa*) austere **4.** (*clima*) harsh
advenedizo, **-a** **I.** *adj* **1.** (*forastero*) foreign **2.** *pey* (*arribista*) upstart **II.** *m, f* **1.** (*forastero*) newcomer **2.** *pey* (*arribista*) upstart
advenimiento *m* advent; (*de un monarca*) accession; **esperar algo como el santo ~** *inf* to wait impatiently for sth
adverbial *adj* adverbial
adverbio *m* adverb; ~ **de modo/de lugar/de tiempo** adverb of manner/of place/of time
adversario, **-a** *m, f* opponent
adversidad *f* **1.** (*contrariedad*) adversity **2.** (*desgracia*) setback
adverso, **-a** *adj* adverse; (*enemigo*) hostile; (*clima*) harsh
advertencia *f* **1.** (*amonestación*) warning **2.** (*indicación*) advice
advertido, **-a** *adj* experienced; **estar ~ del peligro** to be aware of the danger
advertir *irr como sentir vt* **1.** (*reparar*) to notice; **advirtió mis intenciones** he/she guessed my intentions **2.** (*indicar*) to point out **3.** (*llamar la atención*) ~ **algo** to draw attention to sth **4.** (*avisar*) to warn; (*aconsejar*) to advise
adviento *m* Advent
advocar <c→qu> *vt AmL* JUR to advocate
adyacencia *f RíoPl* (*proximidad*) proximity; **en las ~s** in the vicinity
adyacente *adj* adjacent
aéreo, **-a** *adj* **1.** (*del aire*) aerial; (*tráfico*) air; **base aérea** MIL airbase; **compañía aérea** airline (company); **por vía aérea** (by) airmail **2.** (*ligero*) light
aeróbic *m* aerobics

aerobús *m* airbus
aerodeslizador *m* hovercraft
aerodinámico, -a *adj* aerodynamic; (*vehículo*) streamlined
aeródromo *m* aerodrome
aeroespacial *adj* aerospace
aerofaro *m* beacon
aerolínea *f* airline
aeromodelismo *m* construction of model airplanes
aeromoza *f Méx, AmS* (*azafata*) air hostess, stewardess *Am*
aeronauta *mf* aeronaut
aeronáutica *f* aeronautics
aeronave *f* airship; ~ **espacial** spaceship
aeroplano *m* aeroplane *Brit,* airplane *Am*
aeropuerto *m* airport
aerosol *m* **1.** (*suspensión*) aerosol **2.** (*espray*) spray **3.** (*recipiente*) spray can
aerotrén *m* aerotrain
afabilidad *f* affability
afable *adj* affable
afamado, -a *adj* famous
afamar *vt* to make famous
afán *m* **1.** (*ahínco*) eagerness **2.** (*ambición*) ~ **de algo** urge for sth; ~ **de lucro** profit motive; **con** ~ eagerly; **poner mucho** ~ **en algo** to put a lot of effort into sth **3.** (*anhelo*) ~ **de algo** longing for sth; ~ **de notoriedad** hunger for publicity
afanador(a) *m(f)* **1.** *Arg* (*carterista*) pick-pocket; (*descuidero*) sneak thief **2.** *Méx* (*para la limpieza*) cleaner
afanar **I.** *vi* to work hard **II.** *vt CSur, inf* to steal, to pinch **III.** *vr:* **~se** (*esforzarse*) to toil (away)
afano *m Arg, inf* theft
afanoso, -a *adj* **1.** (*trabajoso*) laborious **2.** (*persona*) industrious
afarolarse *vr Chile, Perú, inf* to get worked up
afear *vt* **1.** (*desfigurar*) to disfigure **2.** (*censurar*) to censure
afección *f* **1.** MED condition **2.** (*inclinación*) inclination
afeccionarse *vr CSur* ~ **de algo/alguien** to take a liking to sth/sb
afectación *f* affectation; **comportarse con** ~ to behave affectedly
afectado, -a *adj* (*amanerado*) affected
afectar **I.** *vt* **1.** (*influir*) to concern **2.** (*dañar*) to harm; MED to attack **3.** (*impresionar*) to affect **4.** (*aparentar*) to feign **5.** *AmL* (*girar*) to transfer **6.** *AmL* (*destinar dinero*) ~ **a algo** to set aside for sth **II.** *vr:* **~se** *AmL* to fall ill
afectísimo, -a *adj* **suyo** ~ yours truly
afectivo, -a *adj* **1.** (*de afecto*) affective **2.** (*sensible*) emotional **3.** (*cariñoso*) affectionate
afecto *m* **1.** (*pasión*) emotion **2.** (*cariño*) ~ **a algo/alguien** affection for sth/sb
afecto, -a *adj* **1.** (*inclinado*) ~ **a algo/alguien** inclined towards sth/sb **2.** (*agregado*) attached **3.** (*sujeto*) **estar** ~ **al pago de impuestos** to be taxable **4.** (*afectado*) **estar** ~ **de algo** to be afflicted with sth
afectuoso, -a *adj* **1.** (*cariñoso*) affectionate **2.** (*cordial*) kind; **afectuosamente** yours affectionately
afeitada *f Arg,* **afeitado** *m* shave; **afeitado húmedo** wet shave
afeitar **I.** *vt* (*persona*) to shave; **máquina de** ~ (safety) razor **II.** *vr:* **~se** to shave
afeite *m* **1.** (*cosmético*) cosmetic(s), make-up **2.** (*adorno*) embellishment
afelpado, -a *adj* velvety; **sillón** ~ plush-covered armchair
afeminado *m* **1.** (*como una mujer*) effeminate man **2.** *pey* (*blando*) softy
afeminado, -a *adj* effeminate
afeminar *vt, vr:* **~se** **1.** (*hacer(se) afeminado*) to become effeminate **2.** (*ablandarse*) to become soft
aferrar **I.** *vt* to grasp **II.** *vr:* **~se** **1.** (*agarrarse*) ~ **a algo** to cling on [*o* to] sth **2.** (*obstinarse*) to stand by
Afganistán *m* Afghanistan
afgano, -a *adj, m, f* Afghan
afianzamiento *m* **1.** (*sujeción*) fastening **2.** (*aseguramiento*) securing **3.** (*firmeza*) strength **4.** JUR surety
afianzar <z→c> **I.** *vt* **1.** (*sujetar*) to fasten; (*con clavos*) to nail down; (*con puntales*) to prop up; (*con tornillos*) to screw on **2.** (*dar firmeza*) to strengthen; (*asegurar*) to secure **II.** *vr:* **~se** **1.** (*apoyarse*) to lean **2.** (*afirmarse*) to become established
afiche *m AmL* poster
afición *f* **1.** (*inclinación*) liking; **cobrar** [*o* **tomar**] **una** ~ **por** [*o* **a**] **algo** to develop [*o* take] a liking for [*o* to] sth; **tener** [*o* **sentir**] **una** ~ **hacia** [*o* **a**] **algo** to be fond of sth **2.** (*pasatiempo*) hobby; **de** ~ as a hobby; **hacer algo por** ~ to do sth as a hobby **3.** (*afecto*) affection **4.** (*hinchada*) fans *pl*
aficionado, -a **I.** *adj* **1.** (*que siente afición*) **ser** ~ **a la arquitectura** to be keen on architecture; **ser** ~ **a tocar la flauta** to be fond of playing the flute **2.** (*no profesional*) amateur **II.** *m, f* **1.** (*entusiasta*) lover; DEP fan; ~ **a la ópera** opera lover **2.** (*no profesional*) amateur
aficionar **I.** *vt* ~ **a alguien a algo** to get sb interested in sth **II.** *vr* **~se a algo** (*acostumbrarse*) to take a liking to sth; **~se a alguien** to become fond of sb
afilado, -a *adj* **1.** (*nariz*) pointed; (*dedos*) long; (*cara*) thin; **tener uñas afiladas** *inf* to be light-fingered **2.** (*mordaz*) biting; **lengua afilada** *fig* sharp tongue
afilalápices *m inv* pencil sharpener
afilar **I.** *vt* **1.** (*cuchillo, lápiz*) to sharpen **2.** (*sentidos*) to sharpen **II.** *vr:* **~se** **1.** (*sentido*) to get sharp **2.** (*cara*) to grow thin
afiliación *f* (*acto, pertenencia*) affiliation; ~ **política** political affiliation
afiliado, -a **I.** *adj* affiliated **II.** *m, f* member; ~

a un sindicato trade union member

afiliar I. *vt* (*incorporar*) ~ **a algo** to admit into sth II. *vr:* ~**se** ~**se a algo** to join sth

afín *adj* related

afinar I. *vi* (*cantando*) to sing in tune; (*tocando*) to play in tune II. *vt* 1. (*hacer más fino*) to refine; (*perfeccionar*) to perfect; ~ **la puntería** to sharpen one's aim 2. (*lápiz*) to sharpen 3. (*metales*) to purify 4. MÚS to tune

afincado, **-a** I. *adj* 1. (*que posee fincas*) landed 2. (*establecido*) established; **desde hace tiempo están ~s en Salamanca** they settled in Salamanca some time ago II. *m, f* landowner

afincarse <c→qu> *vr* to become established

afinidad *f* 1. (*semejanza*) similarity; ~ **de caracteres** relatedness of character 2. (*por parentesco*) relationship; **son parientes por** ~ they are related by marriage

afirmación *f* 1. (*confirmación*) confirmation; (*de preguntas*) affirmation; **contestar algo con afirmaciones** to answer in the affirmative 2. (*aseveración*) assertion

afirmar I. *vt* 1. (*decir sí*) to affirm; (*dar por cierto*) to confirm; ~ **con la cabeza** to nod in agreement 2. (*aseverar*) to state 3. (*asentar*) to secure II. *vr:* ~**se** 1. (*confirmarse*) to be confirmed 2. (*ratificarse*) ~**se en algo** to reaffirm sth

afirmativamente *adv* affirmatively; **responder** ~ to respond affirmatively; **responder** ~ **a algo** to reply in the affirmative to sth

afirmativo, **-a** *adj* affirmative; **en caso** ~ if so; **respuesta afirmativa** positive answer

aflicción *f* ~ **por algo/alguien** grief for sth/sb; **dar** ~ **a alguien** to cause sb worry

aflictivo, **-a** *adj*, **afligente** *adj AmL* upsetting

afligir <g→j> I. *vt* 1. (*apenar*) to upset 2. (*atormentar*) to afflict II. *vr:* ~**se** ~**se por** [*o* **de**] **algo** to get upset about [*o* over] sth

aflojar I. *vi* to slacken II. *vt* 1. (*nudo*) to loosen 2. (*cuerda*) to slacken (off) 3. *inf* (*dinero*) to fork out 4. (*velocidad*) to reduce; ~ **el paso** to slacken one's pace; **un tira y afloja** a tug-of-war III. *vr:* ~**se** to slacken

aflorar *vi* 1. (*salir a la superficie*) to come to the surface; (*agua subterránea*) to emerge 2. (*apuntar*) to appear

afluencia *f* 1. (*gente*) crowd; ~ **de votantes** turnout (at the polls) 2. (*abundancia*) abundance

afluente *m* tributary

afluir *irr como huir vi* 1. (*río*) ~ **a algo** to flow into sth; (*calle*) to lead into sth 2. (*gente*) to flock; ~ **a un concierto/a Madrid** to flock to a concert/to Madrid

afluxionarse *vr* 1. *AmC* (*hincharse*) to swell 2. *Col, Cuba* (*acatarrarse*) to catch cold

afonía *f* hoarseness; **tener** ~ to be hoarse

afónico, **-a** *adj* hoarse

aforar *vt* 1. (*cantidad*) to assess 2. (*mercancía*) to value 3. (*instrumentos de medida*) to gauge

aforismo *m* aphorism

aforo *m* 1. (*de una cantidad*) assessment 2. (*en un estadio, teatro*) capacity; **la sala tiene un** ~ **de 300 personas** the hall can seat 300 people 3. TÉC gauging

afortunado, **-a** *adj* fortunate; **¡qué afortunada eres!** how lucky you are!

afrenta *f* 1. (*vergüenza*) affront 2. (*ofensa*) insult; **hacer una** ~ **a alguien** to insult sb

afrentar I. *vt* to insult II. *vr:* ~**se** to take offence *Brit*, to take offense *Am*

afrentoso, **-a** *adj* 1. (*ofensivo*) insulting 2. (*vergonzoso*) outrageous

África *f* Africa

africano, **-a** *adj, m, f* African

afrodisiaco *m*, **afrodisíaco** *m* aphrodisiac

afrontar *vt* 1. (*hacer frente*) to face up to; ~ **un problema** to tackle a problem 2. (*enfrentar*) to confront

afrutado, **-a** *adj* fruity

afuera *adv* (*estado, movimiento*) outside; **la parte de** ~ the outside; **¡~!** *inf* get out of here!

afueras *fpl* outskirts *pl;* ~ **de la ciudad** outskirts of the city

agachar I. *vt* (*cabeza*) to lower II. *vr:* ~**se** 1. (*encogerse*) to crouch 2. *AmL* (*ceder*) to give in

agache *m* 1. *Col* (*mentira*) fib 2. *Cuba* **andar de** ~ to be on the run 3. *Ecua* (*de tapadillo*) **de** ~ on the sly

agalla *f* (*de un pez*) gill; **tener ~s** *fig* to have guts

agarrada *f inf* row; **tener una** ~ to have a row

agarradera *f AmL*, **agarradero** *m* 1. (*asidero*) handle 2. (*enchufe*) influence 3. (*excusa*) excuse

agarrado, **-a** *adj* stingy

agarrador *m* (*para cosas calientes*) oven glove *Brit*, pot holder *Am*

agarrar I. *vi* 1. (*echar raíces*) to take root 2. (*comida*) to stick 3. (*coche*) to grip the road; **agarró y salió** *inf* he/she upped and left II. *vt* 1. (*tomar*) to take 2. (*asir*) to grasp 3. (*delincuente, oportunidad*) to seize 4. (*enfermedad, rabieta*) to catch; ~ **una borrachera** to get drunk; ~ **una pulmonía** to catch pneumonia III. *vr:* ~**se** 1. (*asirse*) to hold on; **agárrate, que te voy a contar qué me pasó ayer** *inf* just hold on! Wait till you hear what happened to me yesterday 2. (*reñir*) to have a fight 3. (*comida*) to stick 4. *inf* (*tomar como pretexto*) to take as a pretext; ~**se al retraso del tren para justificarse** to use the train's late arrival as an excuse 5. *AmL* (*coger*) to catch; (*frutas*) to pluck

agarrotar I. *vt* 1. (*entumecer*) to stiffen up 2. (*atar*) to tie tight 3. (*oprimir*) to squeeze tight II. *vr:* ~**se** 1. (*entumecerse*) to go numb 2. (*por el miedo*) to go rigid with fear 3. TÉC to seize up

agasajar *vt* 1. (*recibir*) to receive in great style

2. (*con comida*) to wine and dine; **el embajador fue agasajado con un banquete** a banquet was given in the ambassador's honour **3.** (*con regalos*) to lavish

agasajo *m* **1.** (*recibimiento*) splendid reception **2.** (*con comida*) lavish hospitality **3.** (*regalo*) present

agatas *adv Par, RíoPl* **1.** (*con dificultad*) with great difficulty **2.** (*casi no*) hardly; ~ **sabe leer** he/she can barely read **3.** (*tan sólo, escasamente*) barely; ~ **hace una hora** barely an hour ago

agaucharse *vr AmS* to imitate or dress like a gaucho; **tras tantos años de vida en el campo se agauchó mucho** after so many years in the country he/she had become very gaucho-like

agazaparse *vr* **1.** *inf* (*agacharse*) to crouch **2.** (*esconderse*) to hide

agencia *f* **1.** (*empresa*) agency; ~ **de colocaciones** employment agency; ~ **inmobiliaria** estate agency; ~ **de noticias** news agency [*o* service]; ~ **de publicidad** advertising agency; ~ **de transportes** carriers; **Agencia Tributaria** tax office; ~ **de viajes** travel agency **2.** (*sucursal*) branch

agenciar **I.** *vt inf* to get **II.** *vr:* ~**se** to get hold of; **agenciárselas** to manage; **agénciatelas como puedas** try to get by as best you can

agenciero, **-a** *m, f* **1.** *Arg* (*de negocios*) representative; (*de lotería*) lottery vendor **2.** *Chile* (*prestamista*) pawnbroker

agenda *f* **1.** (*calendario*) diary, engagement book *Am;* ~ **de bolsillo** pocket diary; **tener una** ~ **apretada** to have a full agenda **2.** (*cuaderno*) notebook **3.** (*orden del día*) agenda

agente[1] *mf* **1.** (*representante*) representative; (*de un artista, escritor*) agent; (*corredor*) agent, broker; ~ **autorizado** authorized agent; ~ **de bolsa** stockbroker; ~ **exclusivo** exclusive agent; ~ **de la propiedad inmobiliaria** estate agent *Brit,* realtor *Am;* ~ **de transportes** carrier **2.** (*funcionario*) ~ **de aduanas** customs officer; ~ **judicial** bailiff; ~ **de policía** policeman **3.** (*espía*) secret agent

agente[2] *m t.* MED (*cosa*) agent

agigantado, **-a** *adj* gigantic; **a pasos** ~**s** by leaps and bounds

ágil *adj* **1.** (*de movimiento*) agile **2.** (*mental*) alert, quick-witted **3.** (*estilo*) lively

agilidad *f* **1.** (*física*) agility; ~ **de dedos** dexterity **2.** (*mental*) acumen

agilizar <z→c> *vt* to speed up

agitación *f* **1.** (*movimiento*) movement; (*de un líquido*) stirring **2.** *t.* POL (*intranquilidad*) agitation; (*excitación*) excitement

agitado, **-a** *adj* (*vida*) hectic

agitar **I.** *vt* **1.** (*mover*) to move; (*bandera, pañuelo*) to wave; (*botella*) to shake; **agítese antes de usarlo** shake well before use **2.** (*intranquilizar*) to worry; (*excitar*) to excite **3.** (*sublevar*) to rouse **II.** *vr:* ~**se** **1.** (*moverse*) to move about; (*con el cuerpo*) to wriggle; (*bandera*) to wave; (*mar*) to get rough **2.** (*excitarse*) to get excited; (*preocuparse*) to get upset

aglomeración *f* agglomeration; ~ **de gente** crowd of people; ~ **urbana** urban sprawl

aglomerar **I.** *vt* (*reunir*) to gather (together); (*amontonar*) to pile up **II.** *vr:* ~**se** to crowd (together)

aglutinar *vt* **1.** (*pegar*) to agglutinate **2.** (*unir*) to unite; *fig* to bring together

agnóstico, **-a** *adj, m, f* agnostic

agobiado, **-a** *adj* **1.** (*cansado*) exhausted; ~ **por los años** weighed down by the years **2.** *fig* **estar** ~ **de trabajo** to be overloaded with work; **estoy** ~ **de deudas** I'm burdened with debts

agobiante *adj* **1.** (*trabajo*) overwhelming **2.** (*persona*) tiresome **3.** (*silencio, calor*) oppressive

agobiar **I.** *vt* **1.** (*abrumar*) to overwhelm; ~ **a alguien con alabanzas** to overwhelm sb with praise; **¡no me agobies!** *inf* don't keep going on at me! **2.** (*calor*) to suffocate; (*tristeza*) to depress **II.** *vr:* ~**se** **1.** (*sentirse abatido*) to feel overwhelmed **2.** (*atarearse*) to work hard **3.** (*angustiarse*) ~**se por algo** to be weighed down with sth

agobio *m* **1.** (*carga*) burden **2.** (*cansancio*) exhaustion; (*de trabajo*) overwork **3.** (*opresión*) oppression; (*angustia*) anxiety

agolpamiento *m* crowd

agolparse *vr* **1.** (*personas*) to crowd (together) **2.** (*líquido*) to stream; **se agolparon las lágrimas en sus ojos** tears welled up in his/her eyes **3.** (*sucesos, pensamientos*) to come in quick succession

agonía *f* **1.** (*del moribundo*) death throes *pl* **2.** (*angustia*) anguish **3.** (*de una civilización*) decline

agónico, **-a** *adj* **período** ~ hour of death; **estar** ~ to be dying

agonizar <z→c> *vi* **1.** (*morir*) to be dying **2.** (*terminar*) to come to an end

agorero, **-a** **I.** *adj* ominous **II.** *m, f* soothsayer

agostar **I.** *vt* **1.** (*plantas*) to wither **2.** (*malograr*) to ruin **II.** *vr:* ~**se** to dry up

agosto *m* **1.** (*mes*) August **2.** (*período*) harvest (time); **hacer su** ~ to make a killing; *v.t.* **marzo**

agotado, **-a** *adj* **1.** (*producto*) out of stock **2.** (*persona*) exhausted

agotador(a) *adj* exhausting; **hace un calor** ~ the heat is unbearable

agotamiento *m* exhaustion

agotar **I.** *vt* **1.** (*existencias*) to use up **2.** (*mercancía*) to deplete **3.** (*paciencia, tema, posibilidad*) to exhaust **4.** (*cansar*) to tire (out) **II.** *vr:* ~**se** **1.** (*mercancía*) to run out; **esta edición se agotó enseguida** this edition sold out immediately **2.** (*pilas*) to run down [*o* out *Am*] **3.** (*fuerzas*) to give out; (*conversación*) to dry up **4.** (*cansarse*) to wear oneself out

agraciado, **-a** *adj* **1.** (*gracioso*) graceful

2.(*bien parecido*) attractive 3.(*afortunado*) lucky; **salir ~ en la lotería** to win in the lottery

agraciar *vt* 1.(*conceder*) to award; **fue agraciado con un premio** he/she was awarded a prize 2.(*vestido, adorno*) to enhance; **este traje le agracia la figura** this dress flatters her figure

agradable *adj* 1.(*ameno*) pleasant; **~ al paladar** tasty; **es ~ a la vista** it is pleasing to the eye 2.(*persona*) **~ con alguien** pleasant to sb

agradar *vi* to please; **me agrada oír música** I like listening to music; **me agrada esta gente** I like these people; **quieres ~ a todos** you want to please everyone

agradecer *irr como crecer vt* to thank; **te agradezco la invitación** thanks for the invitation; **les agradezco que me lo hayan dicho** I'm grateful to you for having told me; **le ~ía mucho si** *+subj* I'd be very grateful if; **no sabes ~ mi trabajo** you don't appreciate my work; **el campo ha agradecido la lluvia** the rain has done the fields good

agradecido, -a *adj* 1.(*que agradece*) **~ por algo** grateful for sth; **le estaría muy ~ que me contestara lo antes posible** I should be very grateful if you would reply as soon as possible; **le estoy sumamente ~** I am exceedingly grateful (to you); **le quedamos muy ~s** we are very grateful (to you) 2.(*que compensa*) worthwhile

agradecimiento *m* gratitude

agrado *m* 1.(*afabilidad*) affability; **tratar a alguien con ~** to treat sb kindly 2.(*complacencia*) willingness; **decidir según su ~** to decide as one likes; **he recibido con ~ su carta** I was very pleased to receive your letter; **esto no es de mi ~** this isn't to my liking

agrandar I. *vt* to make bigger; **~ la importancia de algo** to exaggerate the importance of sth II. *vr:* **~se** to get bigger

agrario, -a *adj* agrarian; **crédito ~** agrarian credit; **población agraria** rural population

agravamiento *m* 1. MED worsening 2.(*recrudecimiento*) aggravation

agravante I. *adj* aggravating II. *m o f* aggravating factor

agravar I. *vt* (*enfermedad, situación*) to make worse, to aggravate II. *vr:* **~se** (*enfermedad, situación*) to worsen

agraviar I. *vt* 1.(*ofender*) to offend 2. JUR to harm II. *vr:* **~se** to be offended

agravio *m* 1.(*ofensa*) offence *Brit,* offense *Am* 2. JUR grievance; **~ material** material damage; **sufrir ~s** to suffer injustice

agraz *m* 1.(*uva*) sour grape; **en ~** prematurely 2.(*zumo*) sour grape juice 3.(*amargura*) bitterness

agredir *vt* to attack; **~ a alguien de palabra** to attack sb verbally

agregación *f* adding; **~ de un municipio** incorporation

agregado *m* 1.(*conglomerado*) aggregate 2.(*aditamento*) addition

agregado, -a *m, f* 1.(*diplomático*) attaché; **~ comercial** commercial attaché; **~ militar** military attaché 2.(*adjunto*) assistant 3. UNIV assistant professor *Brit,* associate professor *Am*

agregar <g→gu> I. *vt* 1.(*añadir*) to add 2.(*persona*) to appoint II. *vr:* **~se** to join; **~se a alguien** to join sb

agremiar I. *vt* to unionize II. *vr:* **~se** to form a union

agresión *f* aggression

agresividad *f* aggressiveness

agresivo, -a *adj* aggressive

agresor(a) I. *adj* aggressor II. *m(f)* aggressor, assailant

agreste *adj* 1.(*campestre*) country 2.(*terreno*) rough 3.(*vegetación*) wild 4.(*persona*) uncouth

agriar I. *vt* 1.(*alimentos*) to sour 2.(*persona*) to make bitter II. *vr:* **~se** 1.(*alimentos*) to turn sour 2.(*persona*) to become embittered [*o* bitter]

agrícola *adj* agricultural; **cooperativa ~** agricultural cooperative

agricultor(a) *m(f)* farmer

agricultura *f* agriculture

agridulce *adj* bittersweet; GASTR sweet-and--sour

agrietar I. *vt* to crack II. *vr:* **~se** to crack; (*tela, pared*) to become cracked; (*piel, labios*) to become chapped

agrimensor(a) *m(f)* surveyor

agrimensura *f* surveying

agringarse <g→gu> *vr AmL: to imitate or adopt the customs of a foreigner*

agrio, -a *adj* 1.(*sabor*) sour 2.(*crítica*) sharp 3.(*carácter*) bitter

agripado, -a *adj Col, inf* (*griposo*) **estar ~** to have the flu

agro *m* farming

agronomía *f* agronomy

agrónomo, -a *m, f* agronomist

agropecuario, -a *adj* agricultural, farming

agroturismo *m* agrotourism

agrupación *f* 1.(*agrupamiento*) grouping 2.(*conjunto*) group; **~ de municipios** municipal association 3.(*asociación*) society 4. MIL unit

agrupar I. *vt* to group (together); **~ algo por temas** to group sth by subject II. *vr:* **~se** to form a group

agua *f* 1.(*líquido*) water; **~ de colonia** eau de cologne; **~s depuradas** purified water; **~ con gas** sparkling water; **~ del grifo** tap water; **~ de mar** seawater; **~ de nieve** meltwater; **~ potable** drinking water; **¡hombre al ~!** man overboard!; **claro como el ~** crystal clear 2.(*lluvia*) rain; **~ nieve** sleet; **esta noche ha caído mucha ~** it rained a lot last night 3. *pl* (*mar, río, manantial*) waters *pl;* **~s interiores** inland waters; **~s jurisdiccionales** territorial waters; **~s residuales** sewage; **~s termales** thermal waters; **~s abajo/arriba** downstream/upstream **4.** *pl* (*orina*) urine; **~s menores** urine; **hacer ~s** to urinate ▶**quedar en ~ de borrajas** to come to nothing; **volver las ~s a su cauce** to go back to normal; **estoy con el ~ hasta el cuello** I'm up to my neck in it; **como ~ de mayo** very welcome; **no hallar ~ en el mar** to act stupid; **llevar el ~ a su molino** to turn things to one's advantage; **~ pasada no mueve molino** *prov* it's no use crying over spilt milk; **sacar ~ a las piedras** to make something out of nothing; **no llegará el ~ al río** it won't go that far; **estar entre dos ~s** to be sitting on the fence; **es ~ pasada** that's water under the bridge; **hacer ~** (*buque*) to take in water; (*negocio*) to founder; **tomar las ~s** to take the waters

aguacate *m* avocado, alligator pear *Am*

aguacero *m* downpour; **cayó un ~** there was a cloudburst

aguachento, -a *adj AmL v.* **aguado**

aguachirle *f pey* dishwater

aguacil *m CSur* ZOOL dragonfly

aguada *f* **1.** (*lugar*) watering place **2.** (*provisión*) water supply

aguado, -a *adj* watered-down; (*fruta*) tasteless

aguafiestas *mf inv, inf* spoilsport, party pooper *Am*

aguafuerte *m* etching; **grabar al ~** to etch

aguaitar *vt* **1.** *Arg, Cuba* (*acechar*) to lie in wait for **2.** *Col* (*esperar*) to wait; **~ unos días** to wait a few days; **~ algo/a alguien** to wait for sth/sb

aguamarina *f* aquamarine

aguamiel *f* **1.** (*bebida*) mead **2.** *AmL* (*jugo del maguey*) maguey juice

aguanieve *f* sleet

aguanoso, -a *adj* (*fruta*) watery; (*suelo*) waterlogged

aguantable *adj* bearable

aguantadero *m Arg, Urug* hide-out

aguantar I. *vt* **1.** (*sostener*) to hold; (*sujetar*) to hold tight **2.** (*soportar*) to bear; (*tolerar*) to put up with; **no aguanto más** I can't bear it any more; **no poder ~ a alguien** not to be able to stand sb; **esta película no se aguanta** this film is unbearable; **~ la mirada de alguien** to hold sb's stare **3.** (*durar*) to last; **este abrigo ~á mucho** this coat will last for a long time **4.** (*contener*) to contain; **~ la risa** to hold back one's laughter **II.** *vr:* **~se 1.** (*contenerse*) to restrain oneself **2.** (*soportar*) to put up with it; (*tener paciencia*) to be patient **3.** (*conformarse*) to resign oneself **4.** (*sostenerse*) to support oneself; **~se de pie** to stay standing

aguante *m* **1.** (*paciencia*) patience; **tener mucho ~** to be very patient **2.** (*resistencia*) endurance; (*de persona*) stamina

aguar <gu→gü> **I.** *vt* **1.** (*mezclar con agua*) to water (down) **2.** (*frustrar*) to spoil **II.** *vr:* **~se 1.** (*llenarse de agua*) to fill with water; **no pude evitar que se me ~an los ojos** I couldn't stop my eyes from watering; **nuestras vacaciones se ~on** our holidays were spoilt [*o* spoiled] by rain **2.** (*estropearse*) to be spoilt [*o* spoiled]

aguardar I. *vt* to wait for; **~ unos días** to wait a few days; **~ algo/a alguien** to await sth/sb **II.** *vr:* **~se** to be awaited

aguardiente *m* brandy

aguarrás *m* turpentine

agudeza *f* **1.** (*del cuchillo, de la crítica*) sharpness; **~ visual** keenness of sight **2.** (*perspicacia*) perspicacity **3.** (*ingenio*) wittiness

agudizar <z→c> **I.** *vt* **1.** (*hacer agudo*) to sharpen **2.** (*agravar*) to make worse **II.** *vr:* **~se** (*situación, enfermedad*) to worsen

agudo, -a *adj* **1.** (*afilado*) sharp **2.** (*sagaz*) shrewd; **vista aguda** keen sight **3.** (*ingenioso*) witty; (*mordaz*) scathing **4.** (*intenso: dolor, enfermedad*) acute; (*olor*) pungent **5.** (*sonido*) piercing **6.** (*grave*) severe **7.** LING *stressed on the last syllable*

agüero *m* omen; **de mal ~** ill-omened; **ser de buen ~** to augur well

aguerrido, -a *adj* (*fuerte*) hardened

aguijar *vt* **1.** (*animales*) to goad **2.** (*estimular*) to urge on; **~ el paso** to make haste

aguijón *m* **1.** (*punta*) goad **2.** ZOOL, BOT sting, stinger *Am* **3.** (*estímulo*) stimulus

aguijonear *vt* **1.** (*animales*) to goad **2.** (*estimular*) to spur on **3.** (*inquietar*) to upset

águila *f* **1.** (*animal*) eagle; **~ real** golden eagle **2.** (*persona*) very clever; **ser un ~ para los negocios** to have a great deal of business acumen

aguileño, -a *adj* aquiline; **rostro ~** angular face

aguinaldo *m* tip (*given at Christmas*)

agüita *f Perú, inf* dough

agüitado, -a *adj Méx* gloomy

aguja *f* **1.** (*general*) needle; **~ de gancho** crochet hook; **~ de punto** knitting needle; **buscar una ~ en un pajar** to look for a needle in a haystack **2.** (*de una jeringa*) hypodermic needle **3.** (*del reloj*) hand; (*de otros instrumentos de medición*) pointer **4.** NÁUT **~ (de marear)** ship's compass **5.** FERRO point **6.** (*de una torre*) spire; **~ de la iglesia** church steeple; **las torres de esa catedral terminan en ~s** the towers of that cathedral are topped with spires **7.** BOT pine needle **8.** GASTR **carne de ~** fore rib *Brit*, rib roast *Am*

agujerear *vt* to make holes in; (*orejas*) to pierce

agujero *m* hole; **~ (en la capa) de ozono** hole in the ozone layer; **tapar un ~** to fill a hole

agujetas *fpl* stiffness

agusanarse *vr* to get maggoty

aguzado, -a *adj* (*puntiagudo, sagaz*) sharp

aguzar <z→c> *vt* **1.** (*afilar*) to sharpen **2.** (*avivar*) **~ la atención** to heighten one's attention; **~ los sentidos** to sharpen one's senses; **~ la vista** to look more carefully

aherrumbrarse *vr* to rust

ahí I. *adv* (*lugar*) there; **~ está** there he/she/it is; ~ **viene** there he/she/it comes; **llámame de** ~ call me from there; ~ **está el problema** that's the problem; **me voy por** ~ I'm going that way ►**¡~ es nada!** not bad!; ~ **me las den todas** *inf* I couldn't care less; **por ~, por ~** something like that **II.** *conj* **de ~ que...** that is why ...

ahijado, -a *m, f* **1.** (*del padrino*) godchild **2.** *fig* protégé *m,* protégée *f*

ahijar *irr como airar vt* to adopt

ahínco *m* **1.** (*afán*) zeal **2.** (*empeño*) effort **3.** (*insistencia*) insistence

ahíto, -a *adj* (*harto*) satiated

ahogado, -a *adj* **1.** (*persona*) drowned; (*sin ventilación*) stifling **2.** (*lleno*) **estar ~ de trabajo** to be snowed under with work

ahogar <g→gu> **I.** *vt* **1.** (*en el agua*) to drown **2.** (*estrangular*) to strangle **3.** (*asfixiar*) to suffocate **4.** (*angustiar*) to oppress **II.** *vr:* **~se 1.** (*en el agua*) to drown **2.** (*asfixiarse*) to suffocate; **~se de calor** to be sweltering (in the heat) **3.** (*motor*) to flood ►**~se en un vaso de agua** to make mountains out of molehills

ahogo *m* **1.** (*sofocación*) breathlessness **2.** (*asfixia*) asphyxiation **3.** (*angustia*) anguish **4.** (*apuro*) hardship; **~s económicos** financial difficulties

ahondar I. *vi* **1.** (*raíces*) to put down roots **2.** (*tema, cuestión*) **~ en algo** to go deeply into sth **II.** *vt* **1.** (*profundizar*) to deepen **2.** (*introducir*) to introduce **III.** *vr:* **~se** to go in more deeply

ahora *adv* now; (*dentro de un momento*) very soon; ~ **bien** now then; **de ~ en adelante** from now on; **hasta** ~ up to now; **por** ~ for the present; ~ **ríe,** ~ **llora** laughing one minute, crying the next; **¡~ (lo entiendo)!** now I've got it!; **¡~ sí que hemos tenido suerte!** we were really lucky there!; ~ **mismo vengo** I'm just coming; **acaba de salir ~ mismo** he/she has just gone out; **¡ven ~ mismo!** come right now!; **¿y ~ qué?** what now?

ahorcado, -a *m, f* hanged person

ahorcar <c→qu> **I.** *vt* to hang; ~ **los libros** to give up one's studies **II.** *vr:* **~se** to hang oneself

ahorita *adv AmL* (*ahora*) right away

ahorrador(a) I. *adj* thrifty **II.** *m(f)* saver

ahorrar I. *vt* to save; (*economizar*) to economize; ~ **fuerzas** to save [*o* conserve] one's energy; ~ **esfuerzos a alguien** to save sb the trouble; **ahórrame explicaciones** spare me your explanation **II.** *vr:* **~se** (*evitar*) to save oneself

ahorrativo, -a *adj* thrifty

ahorrista *mf AmL* saver

ahorro *m* (*acción, cantidad*) saving

ahuecar <c→qu> **I.** *vt* **1.** (*vaciar*) to hollow out **2.** (*tierra*) to break up; (*colchón*) to plump up **II.** *vr:* **~se 1.** (*ave*) to ruffle (up) its feathers **2.** (*envanecerse*) to give oneself airs **3.** (*papel pintado*) to blister

ahuevarse *vr Col, vulg* (*acobardarse*) to chicken out

ahulado *m* **1.** *AmC, Méx* (*mantel*) (oilcloth) table cover; **pon el ~ en la mesa** put the tablecloth on the table **2.** *pl, AmC* (*zapatos*) rubber shoes *pl*

ahumado, -a *adj* **1.** (*color*) smoky; (*cristal*) tinted **2.** (*salmón*) smoked

ahumar I. *vi* to smoke **II.** *vt* **1.** GASTR to smoke **2.** (*llenar de humo*) to fill with smoke; (*una colmena*) to smoke out **III.** *vr:* **~se 1.** (*ennegrecerse*) to become blackened **2.** (*un guiso*) to acquire a burnt taste

ahuyentar *vt* **1.** (*espantar*) to frighten off [*o* away] **2.** (*dudas*) to dispel

aindiado, -a *adj AmL* Indian-looking

airar *irr* **I.** *vt* to anger **II.** *vr:* **~se** to get angry

airbag *m* airbag

aire *m* **1.** (*atmósfera*) air; ~ **acondicionado** air conditioning; **Ejército del Aire** air force; **al ~ libre** in the open air; **echar una moneda al ~** to toss a coin (into the air); **tomar el ~** to go for a stroll; **dejar una pregunta en el ~** to leave a question open; **cambiar de ~s** to have a change of air; **¡~!** *inf* beat it! **2.** (*viento*) wind; **corriente de ~** draught *Brit,* draft *Am;* **corre ~** it's draughty; **hoy hace ~** it's windy today **3.** (*aspecto*) appearance; **no me gusta el ~ de este hombre** I don't like the look of this man; **tener ~ de despistado** to look absent-minded; **darse ~s de grandeza** to have pretensions of grandeur; **darse ~s de intelectual** to give oneself an intellectual air; **¡tiene unos ~s!** he/she is always putting on airs! **4.** (*garbo*) elegance **5.** MÚS tune, air **6.** *Arg, Par* (*cuello*) stiff neck

aireado, -a *adj* (*lugar*) ventilated

airear I. *vt* to air **II.** *vr:* **~se 1.** (*ventilarse*) to air **2.** (*coger aire*) to get some fresh air; (*resfriarse*) to catch a chill

airón *m* **1.** ZOOL heron **2.** (*penacho, adorno*) crest

airoso, -a *adj* graceful; **salir ~ de algo** to acquit oneself well in sth

aislado, -a *adj* (*individual*) isolated

aislamiento *m* **1.** (*retiro*) isolation **2.** *t.* TÉC (*apartamiento*) insulation; ~ **acústico** soundproofing

aislante I. *adj* insulating; **cinta ~** insulating [*o* electrical *Am*] tape **II.** *m* insulator

aislar I. *vt* **1.** (*general*) to isolate **2.** TÉC to insulate; **aislado contra el ruido** soundproof **II.** *vr:* **~se** to isolate oneself

ajá *interj* aha

ajado, -a *adj* (*persona*) worn out; (*cara*) wrinkled

ajamonarse *vr pey, inf* to acquire a middle age spread

ajar *vt* (*cosa, persona*) to wear out

ajardinado, -a *adj* landscaped

ajedrecista *mf* chessplayer

ajedrez *m sin pl* **1.** DEP chess **2.** (*tablero y figuras*) chess set

ajenjo *m* **1.** BOT wormwood **2.** (*bebida*)

absinthe
ajeno, **-a** *adj* **1.** (*de otro*) somebody else's; **la felicidad ajena** other people's happiness **2.** *ser* (*impropio*) inappropriate; **esto es ~ a su carácter** this is alien to his/her character **3.** *estar* (*ignorante*) ignorant; **estar ~ a** [*o* **de**] **algo** to be unaware of sth; **vivía ~ a todo lo que pasaba en el mundo** he/she lived unaware of what was happening in the world **4.** (*carente, exento*) **~ a** [*o* **de**] lacking; **~ de piedad** pitiless; **~ de preocupaciones** carefree; **él es ~ a todo eso** he is not involved in that
ajetrear **I.** *vt* to overwork **II.** *vr:* **~se** to tire oneself out; (*darse prisa*) to rush around
ajetreo *m* (*de personas*) drudgery; (*en un sitio*) bustle
ají *m AmS, Ant* **1.** (*arbusto*) pepper (plant) **2.** (*pimentón*) chilli *Brit,* chili *Am;* (*de las Indias*) cayenne (pepper)
ajilimoje *m,* **ajilimójili** *m* GASTR garlic and pepper sauce; **con todos sus ~s** with all the trimmings
ajillo *m* GASTR **al ~** with garlic
ajipa *f And* Jerusalem artichoke
ajo *m* **1.** BOT garlic; (*diente*) clove of garlic **2.** *inf* (*taco*) swearword ►**andar tieso como un ~** *inf* to be stuck-up; **andar** (**metido**) **en el ~** *inf,* **estar en el ~** *inf* to be mixed up in it
ajotar *vt* **1.** *AmC, Ant* (*azuzar*) to incite **2.** *Cuba* (*desdeñar*) to scorn
ajuar *m* **1.** (*de la novia*) trousseau **2.** (*de una casa*) furnishings *pl*
ajumarse *vr Col, Cuba, PRico, inf* to get drunk
ajuntarse *vr inf* to live together
ajustable *adj* adjustable; **sábanas ~s** fitted sheets
ajustado, **-a** *adj* **1.** (*ropa*) tight **2.** (*adecuado*) fitting
ajustar **I.** *vi* to fit **II.** *vt* **1.** (*adaptar*) *t.* TÉC to adjust; **~ un vestido** to take in a dress; **~ una correa** to adjust a strap **2.** (*una pieza dentro de otra*) to fit **3.** (*acordar*) to reconcile **III.** *vr:* **~se** **1.** (*ponerse de acuerdo*) to come to an agreement **2.** (*adaptarse*) to adapt; **no ~se al tema** not to keep to the subject; **~se a la verdad** to stick to the truth
ajuste *m* **1.** (*adaptación*) adjustment; **~ financiero** financial adjustment **2.** (*graduación*) graduation; **~ de brillo** brightness control **3.** (*encaje*) fitting **4.** (*acuerdo*) compromise; **~ de cuentas** settling of scores
ajusticiar *vt* to execute
al = **a** + **el** *v.* **a**
ala *f* wing; (*de hélice*) propeller blade; (*de mesa*) leaf; (*de sombrero*) brim; (*del tejado*) eaves *pl* ►**tener demasiadas ~s** to be overconfident; **estar tocado del ~** *inf* to be crazy; **ahuecar el ~** to get going; **cortar las ~s a alguien** to clip sb's wings; **dar ~s a alguien** to encourage sb; **le faltan ~s para...** he/she lacks the courage to ...
Alá *m* Allah
alabanza *f* praise; **deshacerse en ~s para con alguien** to shower praises on sb; **hacer una ~ de alguien** to sing sb's praises
alabar **I.** *vt* **~ a alguien por algo** to praise sb for sth; **alabado sea el Señor** praise be to God **II.** *vr:* **~se** to boast
alabastro *m* alabaster
alabear **I.** *vt* to warp **II.** *vr:* **~se** (*madera*) to warp
alacena *f* larder
alacrán *m* **1.** ZOOL scorpion **2.** (*persona*) **ser un ~** to be a gossip **3.** (*gancho*) hook
alado, **-a** *adj* **1.** (*con alas*) winged **2.** (*ligero*) swift
ALALC *abr de* **Asociación Latinoamericana de Libre Comercio** LAFTA
alambicado, **-a** *adj* **1.** (*sutil*) subtle **2.** (*rebuscado*) convoluted
alambicar <c→qu> *vt* **1.** (*destilar*) to distil *Brit,* to distill *Am* **2.** (*una expresión*) to refine; (*el lenguaje*) to polish; **diálogos alambicados** polished dialogues
alambique *m* still
alambrada *f* (*valla*) wire fence; (*con espinas*) barbed wire fence; (*red*) wire netting; **~ eléctrica** electric fence
alambrado *m* (*red*) wire netting; (*valla*) wire fence
alambrar *vt* to wire
alambre *m* wire; **~ de espinas** barbed wire
alambrera *f* **1.** (*de ventana*) wire screen **2.** (*de brasero, chimenea*) fireguard **3.** (*de alimentos*) wire cover
alambrista *mf* tightrope walker
alameda *f* **1.** (*lugar*) poplar grove **2.** (*paseo*) avenue; (*de álamos*) tree-lined avenue
álamo *m* (*madera*) *t.* BOT poplar; **~ temblón** aspen
alarde *m* show; **hacer ~ de algo** to make a show of sth
alardear *vi* **~ de algo** (*presumir*) to boast about sth
alardeo *m Méx* (*alarde*) showing off
alargado, **-a** *adj* elongated
alargar <g→gu> **I.** *vt* **1.** (*la extensión*) to lengthen; **~ la pierna** to stretch one's leg; **~ el cuello** to crane one's neck; **~ la mano** to hold out one's hand **2.** (*la duración*) to prolong **3.** (*retardar, diferir*) to delay **4.** (*el dinero*) to spin out **II.** *vr:* **~se** **1.** (*en la extensión*) to lengthen; **no te alargues** be brief; **~se en cumplidos** to be full of compliments **2.** (*retardarse*) to be delayed
alarido *m* shriek
alarife *m* **1.** (*arquitecto*) architect **2.** (*albañil*) bricklayer **3.** *Arg* (*persona lista*) smart customer *inf*
alarma *f* **1.** (*general*) alarm; **~ por ozono** ozone warning; **falsa ~** false alarm; **dar la ~** to raise the alarm; **ha saltado la ~ del banco** the alarm in the bank has gone off **2.** (*susto*) scare; (*inquietud*) worry; **~ social** social unrest

A

alarmar **I.** *vt* **1.** (*dar la alarma*) to alarm **2.** (*inquietar*) to worry; (*asustar*) to frighten; **noticia alarmante** terrible news **II.** *vr:* ~**se** (*inquietarse*) to get worried; (*asustarse*) to take fright

alarmista *mf* alarmist

alavés, -esa **I.** *adj* of/from Álava **II.** *m, f* native/inhabitant of Álava

alazán, -ana *adj* (*caballo*) sorrel

alba *f* dawn; **al rayar** [*o* **romper**] **el** ~ at daybreak

albacea *mf* executor

albaceteño, -a **I.** *adj* of/from Albacete **II.** *m, f* native/inhabitant of Albacete

albacora *f Chile, Perú, Méx* swordfish

albahaca *f* basil

albanés, -esa *adj, m, f* Albanian

Albania *f* Albania

albañal *m* **1.** (*conducto*) sewer **2.** (*lugar*) dung heap **3.** (*lugar sucio*) mess

albañil *mf* **1.** (*constructor*) builder **2.** (*artesano*) bricklayer

albañilería *f* **1.** (*profesión*) bricklaying **2.** (*materias*) brickwork; **obra de** ~ bricklaying [*o* mason *Am*] (work)

albarán *m* delivery note, invoice

albarda *f* packsaddle ►~ **sobre** ~ again and again

albaricoque *m* apricot

albaricoquero *m* apricot tree

albatros *m inv* albatross

albazo *m Perú* (*serenata*) morning serenade

albear *vi Arg* to get up very early

albedrío *m* whim; **libre** ~ free will; **a** [*o* **según**] **mi** ~ just as I like

alberca *f* cistern, reservoir

albergar <g→gu> **I.** *vt* to house **II.** *vr:* ~**se** to lodge

albergue *m* (*refugio*) refuge; (*alojamiento*) lodging; ~ **juvenil** youth hostel; ~ **de montaña** mountain hut

albino, -a *adj, m, f* albino

albóndiga *f* (*de carne*) meatball; (*de pescado*) fish rissole

albor *m* **1.** (*luz, comienzo*) dawn **2.** (*blancor*) whiteness

alborada *f* **1.** (*alba*) dawn **2.** (*canción*) dawn song **3.** MIL reveille

alborear *vi t. fig* to dawn; **al** ~ **el día** at break of day

albornoz *m* (*de baño*) bathrobe

alborotado, -a *adj* **1.** (*excitado*) excited **2.** (*irreflexivo*) rash

alborotar **I.** *vi* (*armar jaleo*) to make a racket; (*niños*) to romp about **II.** *vt* **1.** (*excitar*) to excite **2.** (*desordenar*) to agitate **3.** (*sublevar*) to stir up **III.** *vr:* ~**se** **1.** (*excitarse*) to get excited **2.** (*sublevarse*) to riot

alboroto *m* **1.** (*vocerío*) racket; (*ruido*) noise **2.** (*bulla*) uproar; (*disturbio*) disturbance **3.** (*inquietud, zozobra*) worry

alborozado, -a *adj* jubilant

alborozar <z→c> **I.** *vt* to delight **II.** *vr:* ~**se** to be overjoyed

alborozo *m* joy

albricias *fpl inf* **¡~!** good news!, congratulations

albufera *f* lagoon

álbum *m* <álbum(e)s> album; ~ **infantil** picture book

albumen *m* albumen

albur *m* ZOOL bleak ►**correr un** ~ to run a risk; **al** ~ at random

alburear **I.** *vt CRi* to disturb **II.** *vi* **1.** *Col* (*recibir dinero*) to get money **2.** *Cuba* (*engañar*) to deceive **3.** *Méx* (*hacer juegos de palabras*) to play on words

alcachofa *f* **1.** BOT artichoke **2.** (*de ducha*) shower head; (*de regadera*) sprinkler

alcahuete, -a *m, f* **1.** (*trotaconventos*) pimp, procurer *m,* procuress *f* **2.** (*encubridor*) go-between **3.** (*chismoso*) gossip

alcahuetear *vi* **1.** (*servir, hacer de alcahuete*) to pimp, to procure; **¿por qué consientes que él alcahuetee entre ti y ese muchacho?** why do you allow him to pair you off with that guy? **2.** (*chismorrear*) to gossip

alcalde(sa) *m(f)* mayor

alcaldía *f* **1.** (*oficio*) post of mayor **2.** (*oficina*) mayor's office

álcali *m* alkali

alcalino, -a *adj* alkaline

alcamonero, -a *adj Ven* (*entrometido*) meddlesome; (*de novedades*) newsy

alcance *m* **1.** (*distancia*) range; **misil de corto** ~ short-range missile; **de** ~ **limitado** short-range; **al** ~ **de la mano** within reach; **al** ~ **de todos los bolsillos** within everybody's means; **tener la victoria a su** ~ to have victory within one's grasp **2.** (*importancia*) importance; **de mucho/poco** ~ of great/little importance **3.** (*déficit*) deficit ►**la noticia de último** ~ the latest news; **ser persona de pocos** ~**s** to be a person of limited talents; **dar** ~ **a alguien** to catch up with sb

alcancía *f* money box *Brit,* piggy bank *Am*

alcanfor *m* camphor

alcanforar **I.** *vt* **1.** (*untar*) to anoint **2.** (*mezclar*) to camphorate; **alcohol alcanforado** camphorated alcohol **II.** *vr:* ~**se** **1.** *Col, Ven* (*evaporarse*) to vaporize **2.** *Hond* (*perderse*) to make oneself scarce *inf*

alcantarilla *f* **1.** (*cloaca*) sewer **2.** (*sumidero*) drain

alcantarillado *m* sewer system, drains *pl*

alcanzar <z→c> **I.** *vi* to reach; **este cañón alcanza 10 kilómetros** this gun has a range of 10 kilometres; **el dinero no alcanza para pagar la comida** the money's not enough to pay for the food; **no alcanzo a todo el trabajo** I can't manage to do all the work **II.** *vt* **1.** (*dar alcance*) to catch up (with); **el ladrón fue alcanzado** the thief was caught; **ve tirando, ya te ~é** keep going, I'll catch up with you **2.** (*llegar*) to reach; ~ **un acuerdo** to reach an agreement; **el disparo le alcanzó en la**

pierna the shot struck his leg; ~ **fama** to become famous **3.** (*entender*) to grasp **III.** *vr:* **~se no se me alcanza qué intentas con ello** I can't figure out what you mean by that

alcaparra *f* caper

alcatraz *m* **1.** ZOOL gannet **2.** BOT arum

alcaucil *m* **1.** (*alcachofa*) artichoke **2.** *Arg* (*trotaconventos*) pimp

alcázar *m* **1.** (*palacio*) palace **2.** MIL fortress

alce *m* elk, moose

alcista **I.** *adj* **mercado ~ de la bolsa** bull [*o* bullish] market; **movimiento ~ de los precios** upward trend in prices **II.** *mf* speculator, bull

alcoba *f* bedroom

alcohol *m* alcohol; ~ **de quemar** methylated spirit; **bebida sin ~** non-alcoholic drink; **no tomo ~** I don't drink alcohol; **estar bajo los efectos del ~** to be under the influence of alcohol

alcohólico, -a *adj, m, f* alcoholic

alcoholímetro *m* Breathalyzer® *Brit,* drunkometer *Am*

alcoholismo *m sin pl* alcoholism

alcoholista **I.** *adj Arg* drunk; **un hombre ~** a drunken man **II.** *mf Arg* drunkard

alcoholizado, -a *adj* alcoholic

alcoholizar <z→c> **I.** *vt* to alcoholize **II.** *vr:* **~se** to become an alcoholic

Alcorán *m* Koran

alcornoque *m* **1.** BOT cork oak **2.** (*persona*) (**pedazo de**) ~ idiot

alcotán *m* hobby

alcotana *f* pickaxe

alcurnia *f* ancestry; **de ~** of noble birth

alcuza *f* cruet

aldaba *f* **1.** (*picaporte*) doorknocker **2.** (*para ventanas, puertas*) bolt ▸**tener buenas ~s** *inf* to have influence

aldea *f* small village

aldeano, -a **I.** *adj* **1.** (*de la aldea*) village **2.** (*ignorante*) rustic **II.** *m, f* **1.** (*de la aldea*) villager **2.** (*inculto*) country bumpkin

aldehído *m* aldehyde

aleación *f* alloy; ~ **ligera** light alloy

alear *vt* to flutter ▸**ir aleando** to be getting better

aleatorio, -a *adj* random, fortuitous

alebrestarse *vr Col, inf* (*alborotarse*) to become agitated

aleccionador(a) *adj* instructive

aleccionar *vt* to instruct; **esto te ~á para no volver a hacer lo mismo** this will teach you not to do the same thing again

aledaño, -a *adj* adjoining

aledaños *mpl* outskirts *pl*

alegación *f* **1.** JUR (*declaración*) declaration; (*escrito*) statement; ~ **de culpabilidad** plea of guilty **2.** *pl* (*objeciones*) objections *pl*

alegar <g→gu> **I.** *vt* to cite; (*pruebas*) to produce; ~ **dolor de cabeza** to claim to have a headache **II.** *vi AmL* (*discutir*) to argue

alegato *m* **1.** (*escrito*) bill of indictment; (*oral*) plea **2.** *AmL* (*disputa*) argument

alegoría *f* allegory

alegrar **I.** *vt* **1.** (*a personas*) to make happy **2.** (*cosas*) to brighten up **II.** *vr:* **~se** **1.** (*sentir alegría*) **~se de** [*o* **con**] **algo** to be glad about sth; **me alegro de verle de nuevo** I'm pleased to see you again; **nos alegramos de que haya aceptado la invitación** we're glad that he/she has accepted the invitation; **me alegro (por ti)** I'm so happy for you **2.** (*beber*) to get tipsy

alegre *adj* **1.** (*contento*) happy; (*divertido*) merry; (*color*) bright; (*habitación*) pleasant; **un espíritu/una cara ~** a cheerful nature/face; **estoy ~ de que** *+subj* I'm pleased that; **estar más ~ que unas pascuas** to be pleased as Punch **2.** (*frívolo*) frivolous; **llevar una vida ~** to lead a free-and-easy life **3.** *inf* (*achispado*) merry; **estar ~** to be tipsy

alegría *f* **1.** (*gozo*) happiness; (*buen humor*) cheerfulness; (*alborozo*) merriment; **llevarse una gran ~** to be very happy **2.** BOT (*ajonjolí*) sesame

alegrón *m inf* thrill; **con esta noticia me has dado un ~** you've really delighted me with this news; **con esta noticia me he llevado un ~** I've been thrilled by this news

alegrón, -ona *adj Arg* tipsy

alejamiento *m* removal; *fig* aloofness

alejar **I.** *vt* **1.** (*distanciar*) to remove **2.** (*ahuyentar*) to drive away; **aleja estos pensamientos de tu cabeza** banish these thoughts from your mind **II.** *vr:* **~se** to move away; (*retirarse*) to withdraw; **todos se alejan de él** everyone avoids him

alelar **I.** *vt* to stupefy **II.** *vr:* **~se** to be stupefied

aleluya **I.** *interj* hallelujah **II.** *m o f* REL hallelujah; **estar de ~** to rejoice

alemán *m* (*lengua*) German; **alto ~** High German, standard German; **decir algo en ~** to say sth in German

alemán, -ana *adj, m, f* German

Alemania *f* Germany; **República Federal de ~** Federal Republic of Germany

alentado, -a *adj* (*valiente*) brave

alentar <e→ie> **I.** *vi* **1.** (*respirar*) to breathe **2.** (*estar vivo*) to be alive **II.** *vt* to encourage **III.** *vr:* **~se** **1.** (*animarse*) to take heart **2.** *Hond, Méx, Col, Ecua* (*restablecerse*) to get well

alerce *m* larch

alergia *f* allergy; ~ **a la primavera** hay fever; ~ **alimentaria** food allergy; ~ **al polen** pollen allergy; **esto me da ~** I'm allergic to this

alérgico, -a *adj* allergic; **es ~ a estos temas** *inf* he/she really isn't keen on these subjects

alergólogo, -a *m, f* allergist

alero *m* **1.** ARQUIT eaves *pl* **2.** AUTO wing, fender *Am* **3.** DEP winger

alerón *m* **1.** AVIAT aileron **2.** AUTO spoiler; ~ **delantero/trasero** front/back spoiler

alerta **I.** *adj* alert; **estar ~ de algo** to be alert to sth **II.** *f* alert; **dar la ~** to give the alarm; **poner**

en ~ a alguien to put sb on the alert **III.** *interj* watch out

aleta *f* **1.**(*general*) wing **2.**(*de un buzo*) flipper; (*de un pez*) fin

aletargar <g→gu> **I.** *vt* to become drowsy **II.** *vr:* **~se** to get drowsy

aletear *vi* **1.**(*ave*) to flutter **2.**(*pez*) to wriggle **3.** *inf* (*cobrar fuerza*) to regain one's strength

aleteo *m* **1.**(*de un ave*) fluttering (of the wings) **2.**(*de un pez*) wriggling

alevín *m* **1.**(*pez*) fry, young fish **2.**(*principiante*) beginner

alevosía *f* treachery; **con ~** treacherously

alevoso, -a *adj* treacherous

alfa *f* alpha; **~ y omega** *fig* the beginning and the end, Alpha and Omega

alfabético, -a *adj* alphabetic(al); **estar por orden ~** to be in alphabetical order

alfabetizar <z→c> *vt* to teach to read and write

alfabeto *m* alphabet

alfalfa *f* alfalfa, lucerne

alfaque *m* sandbank

alfar *m* **1.**(*taller*) pottery **2.**(*arcilla*) clay

alfarería *f* (*obrador, oficio*) pottery

alfarero, -a *m, f* potter

alféizar *m* windowsill

alfeñique *m* (*persona*) wimp *inf*

alférez *m* MIL second lieutenant

alfil *m* (*en ajedrez*) bishop

alfiler *m* **1.**(*aguja*) pin **2.**(*broche*) brooch; **~ de corbata** tiepin; **~ de gancho** *CSur, Ecua, Perú* safety pin **3.**(*pinza*) pincers *pl* ►**llevo la lección prendida con ~es** I'm badly prepared for the exam; **ir de veinticinco ~es** to be dressed up to the nines; **no caber un ~** to be bursting at the seams

alfiletero *m* needle case

alfombra *f* carpet; **~ persa** Persian carpet

alfombrado *m AmL* (*alfombra*) carpeting

alfombrar *vt* to carpet

alfombrilla *f* **1.**(*estera*) mat; **~ de baño** bath mat **2.** MED German measles **3.** INFOR mousemat *Brit,* mousepad *Am*

alforja *f* bag; (*de caballería*) saddlebag ►**sacar los pies de las ~s** to come out of one's shell

alga *f* alga

algarabía *f* **1.**(*griterío*) uproar **2.**(*lengua*) Arabic **3.** BOT broom

algarada *f* outcry

algarroba *f* **1.** BOT carob **2.**(*fruto del algarrobo*) carob bean

algarrobo *m* carob tree

algazara *f* clamour *Brit,* clamor *Am;* (*de alegría*) jubilation

álgebra *f* MAT algebra

álgido, -a *adj* **1.**(*culminante*) **el período ~ del Barroco** the high point of the Baroque period; **la crisis está en su momento más ~** the crisis has reached a climax **2.**(*muy frío*) freezing; **fiebre álgida** MED shivering fit

algo I. *pron indef* (*en frases afirmativas*) something; (*en negativas, interrogativas y condicionales*) anything; **~ es ~** it's better than nothing; **¿quieres ~?** do you want anything?; **¿apostamos ~?** do you want to bet?; **esta película es ~ aparte** this film is something special; **me suena de ~** it seems familiar to me; **se cree ~** he/she thinks he/she is something; **por ~ lo habrá dicho** he/she must have had a reason for saying it **II.** *adv* a little; **aún falta ~ hasta llegar** there's still a bit to go; **~ así como** something like

algodón *m* **1.**(*planta, tejido*) cotton; **una camisa de ~** a cotton shirt; **~ en rama** raw cotton **2.**(*cosmético*) cotton wool *Brit,* cotton *Am* **3.**(*dulce*) candy floss *Brit,* cotton candy *Am* ►**criado entre algodones** pampered

algodonero, -a I. *adj* cotton **II.** *m, f* **1.**(*comerciante*) cotton dealer **2.**(*cultivador*) cotton grower

alguacil *m* bailiff

alguien *pron indef* (*en frases afirmativas*) somebody, someone; (*en interrogativas y condicionales*) anybody, anyone; **¿hay ~ aquí?** is anybody [*o* anyone] there?; **~ me lo ha contado** somebody [*o* someone] told me; **se cree ~** he/she thinks he/she is somebody [*o* someone]

algún *adj v.* **alguno¹**

alguno, -a¹ *adj* <algún> **1.**(*antepuesto*) some; (*en frases negativas e interrogativas*) any; **¿alguna pregunta?** any questions?; **de alguna manera** somehow; **en algún sitio** somewhere; **alguna vez** sometimes; **algún día** some day **2.**(*postpuesto: ninguno*) no, not any; **en sitio ~** nowhere; **persona alguna** no one

alguno, -a² *pron indef* somebody, someone; **~s de los presentes** some of those present; **~s ya se han ido** some have already gone; **¿tienes caramelos? – sí, me quedan ~s** do you have any sweets? – yes, I still have some left; **los niños han vuelto a hacer alguna de las suyas** the children have been up to their tricks again

alhaja *f* **1.**(*de piedras preciosas*) piece of jewellery [*o* jewelry *Am*]; (*de bisutería*) costume jewellery [*o* jewelry *Am*] **2.**(*objeto de valor*) treasure **3.** *inf* (*persona*) **¡esta chica es una ~!** this girl's a real gem; **¡menuda ~, este niño!** this boy's a fine one!

alhajado, -a *adj Col* (*rico*) wealth

alhajera *f Arg, Chile* jewel box

alharaca *f* fuss

alhelí *m* <alhelíes> wallflower

alheña *f* **1.** BOT privet **2.**(*polvo*) henna

aliado, -a I. *adj* allied **II.** *m, f* ally; **los ~s** POL the Allies

alianza *f* **1.**(*pacto*) alliance; **Alianza Atlántica** Atlantic Alliance, NATO **2.**(*anillo*) wedding ring

aliar <*1. pres:* alío> **I.** *vt* to ally **II.** *vr:* **~se** to ally oneself

alias *adv, m inv* alias

alicaído, -a *adj* weak; (*deprimido*) dejected

alicantino, **-a** I. *adj* of/from Alicante II. *m, f* native/inhabitant of Alicante
alicates *mpl* pliers *pl;* ~ **universales** combination pliers
aliciente *m* incentive
alienación *f* alienation
aliento *m* 1.(*respiración, vaho*) breath; **mal** ~ bad breath; **sin** ~ out of breath; **cobrar** ~ to get one's breath back; **esto me quita el** ~ this takes my breath away; **tomar** ~ to take a breath 2.(*ánimo*) courage; **dar** ~ **a alguien** to encourage sb
aligátor *m* alligator
aligerar I. *vi* to hurry (up) II. *vt* 1.(*cargas*) to lighten 2.(*aliviar*) to alleviate 3.(*acelerar*) to quicken; ~ **el paso** to quicken one's pace
alimaña *f* 1.(*animal*) pest; ~**s** vermin 2.(*persona*) animal, brute
alimentación *f* 1.(*nutrición*) food; (*aprovisionamiento*) feeding; **industria de la** ~ food industry 2.(*de animales*) feeding 3.(*de un horno, una caldera*) stoking; (*de una máquina*) feeding; ~ **de energía** energy supply; ~ **de papel** INFOR sheetfeed
alimentador *m* TÉC feeder; ~ **de hojas sueltas** INFOR cut-sheet feed
alimentador(**a**) *adj* TÉC feeder
alimentar I. *vi* to be nourishing II. *vt* 1.(*nutrir*) to feed; ~ **el odio** to fuel hatred 2.(*horno, caldera*) to stoke; (*máquina*) to feed; ~ **la máquina con energía** to supply the machine with energy 3. INFOR ~ **un ordenador con datos** to feed data into a computer III. *vr* ~**se de algo** to live on sth
alimenticio, **-a** *adj* 1.(*nutritivo*) nourishing 2.(*alimentario*) food; **industria alimenticia** food industry; **pensión alimenticia** maintenance *Brit,* alimony *Am;* **productos** ~**s** foodstuffs *pl*
alimento *m* 1.(*sustancia*) food; **los** ~**s** foodstuffs *pl;* ~**s congelados** frozen food 2.(*alimentación*) nourishment; **de mucho/poco** ~ full of/lacking nutritional value 3. *pl* JUR (*asistencia financiera*) alimony
alimón *m* **al** ~ together
alineación *f,* **alineamiento** *m* 1.(*general*) alignment; **no** ~ POL non-alignment 2. DEP line-up
alinear I. *vt* 1.(*poner en línea*) to line up 2. DEP to select; (*para un partido*) to field 3. POL **país no alineado** non-aligned country II. *vr:* ~**se** 1.(*ponerse en fila*) to line up 2. POL to align oneself
aliñar *vt* 1.(*condimentar*) to season; (*ensalada*) to dress 2.(*preparar*) to prepare
aliño *m* 1.(*condimento*) seasoning; (*para ensalada*) dressing 2.(*acción*) preparation
alioli *m sauce of garlic and olive oil*
alisar *vt* 1.(*una superficie*) to smooth down; (*un terreno*) to level (off) 2.(*el pelo*) to smooth
alisio *adj* **vientos** ~**s** trade winds
aliso *m* (*madera*) *t.* BOT alder
alistado, **-a** *adj* 1.(*rayado*) striped 2.(*recluta*) enlisted
alistamiento *m* 1.(*inscripción*) enrolment 2.(*lista*) list 3. MIL enlistment
alistar I. *vt* 1.(*inscribir*) to enrol 2.(*enumerar*) to list 3. MIL to recruit; (*en la marina*) to enlist II. *vr:* ~**se** 1.(*inscribirse*) to enrol 2. MIL to enlist
aliteración *f* alliteration
aliviadero *m* overflow channel
aliviar I. *vi* to quicken one's pace II. *vt* 1.(*carga*) to lighten; **tienes que** ~ **la maleta** you'll have to reduce the weight of the suitcase 2.(*de una preocupación*) to relieve 3.(*dolor, pena*) to alleviate; ~ **un bloqueo económico** to relax an economic blockade III. *vr:* ~**se** 1.(*dolor, pena*) to ease off [*o* up] 2.(*de una enfermedad*) to recover
alivio *m* 1.(*aligeramiento*) relief 2.(*de una enfermedad*) recovery; (*mejoría*) improvement ▶**ser de** ~ *inf* to be horrible; **pescar un catarro de** ~ *inf* to get an awful cold; **vestir de** ~ to be in mourning
aljaba *f* quiver
aljibe *m* 1.(*cisterna*) cistern 2.(*tanque*) tank 3.(*barco*) tanker
allá *adv* 1.(*lugar, dirección*) there; **el más** ~ REL the hereafter; **¿cuánto se tarda de aquí** ~**?** how long does it take to go there?; **ponte más** ~ move further over 2.(*tiempo*) back; ~ **por el año 1964** round about 1964; ~ **en tiempos de Maricastaña** in the olden days ▶**¡**~ **tú!** *inf* that's your problem!
allanamiento *m* 1.(*de un terreno*) levelling *Brit,* leveling *Am* 2.(*de dificultades*) removal 3. JUR ~ **de morada** breaking and entering
allanar I. *vt* 1.(*terreno, camino*) to level (out) 2.(*construcción*) to demolish 3.(*dificultades*) to remove 4. JUR ~ **una casa** to break into a house II. *vr:* ~**se** to agree; **no se allana nunca** he/she never gives way
allegado, **-a** I. *adj* close II. *m, f* relative
allegar <g→gu> *vt* (*recursos*) to gather together; (*pruebas, datos*) to collect
allende *elev* I. *adv* on the other side; ~ **de ser guapa, es agradable** besides being pretty, she's pleasant as well II. *prep* beyond; ~ **las montañas** beyond the mountains
allí *adv* (*lugar, dirección*) there; ~ **cerca, por** ~ over there; **¡**~ **viene!** he's/she's just coming!; **hasta** ~ as far as that
alma *f* 1.(*espíritu, persona*) soul; **agradecer con el** ~ to thank with all one's heart; **me arranca el** ~ it's heartbreaking; **me llega al** ~ I'm deeply touched; **lo siento en el** ~ I'm terribly sorry; **no tener** ~ to be heartless; **fue el** ~ **de la fiesta** he/she was the life and soul of the party 2.(*ánimo*) spirit 3. TÉC core ▶~ **de cántaro** simpleton; **como** ~ **que lleva el diablo** *inf* like a bat out of hell; **un** ~ **de Dios** a good soul; **estar con el** ~ **en un hilo** *inf* to have one's heart in one's mouth; ~ **en pena** lost soul; **¡**~ **mía!** my darling!; **se le cayó el** ~ **a**

los pies *inf* his/her heart sank
almacén *m* **1.** (*depósito*) warehouse; ~ **al por mayor** wholesale warehouse; **franco en** ~ ex-works; **tener en** ~ to have in stock **2.** (*tienda*) **grandes almacenes** department store
almacenaje *m,* **almacenamiento** *m* **1.** (*de mercancías*) *t.* INFOR storage; ~ **definitivo** permanent storage **2.** (*tasa*) storage charge
almacenar *vt* (*mercancías*) *t.* INFOR to store; ~ **en disco duro** to store on the hard disk
almacenero, -a *m, f CSur* (*dueño*) grocer
almacenista *mf* wholesaler
almadreña *f* wooden shoe
almanaque *m* almanac
almeja *f* **1.** ZOOL clam **2.** *vulg* (*vagina*) cunt
almena *f* merlon
almendra *f* **1.** (*fruta*) almond; ~**s garapiñadas** sugar almonds **2.** (*semilla*) kernel **3.** *inf* (*guijarro*) pebble
almendro *m* almond tree
almeriense **I.** *adj* of/from Almería **II.** *mf* native/inhabitant of Almería
almiar *m* hayrick *Brit,* haystack *Am*
almíbar *m* syrup; **melocotón en** ~ peach in syrup
almibarado, -a *adj* sugary
almibarar *vt* to preserve in syrup; ~ **a alguien** to butter sb up
almidón *m* starch; (*cola*) paste
almidonado, -a *adj* (*acicalado*) spruced up
almidonar *vt* to starch
alminar *m* minaret
almirantazgo *m* admiralty
almirante *m* admiral
almirez *m* mortar
almizcle *m* musk
almizclero *m* musk deer
almohada *f* **1.** (*cojín*) cushion; (*de la cama*) pillow **2.** (*funda*) pillowcase ►**consultar algo con la** ~ *inf* to sleep on sth
almohadilla *f* (*cojín*) small cushion; (*acerico*) pin cushion; ~ **de tinta** inkpad
almohadón *m* cushion; (*del sofá*) sofa cushion
almoneda *f* **1.** (*subasta*) auction **2.** (*saldo*) clearance sale
almorranas *fpl* piles *pl*
almorzar *irr como forzar* **I.** *vi* **1.** (*a mediodía*) to have lunch **2.** *reg* (*desayunar*) to have breakfast **II.** *vt* **1.** (*a mediodía*) to have for lunch **2.** *reg* (*desayunar*) to have for breakfast
almuerzo *m* **1.** (*al mediodía*) lunch; ~ **de negocios** business lunch; **¿qué hay de ~?** what's for lunch? **2.** *reg* (*desayuno*) breakfast
almuerzo-coloquio *m* <almuerzos-coloquio> working lunch
aló *interj AmC, AmS* TEL hello; ~**, ¿quién es?** hello, who's speaking?
alocado, -a *adj* **1.** (*loco*) crazy **2.** (*imprudente*) reckless **3.** (*revoltoso*) rebellious
alocución *f* speech
alojamiento *m* **1.** (*lugar*) accommodation **2.** (*acción*) housing; MIL billeting
alojar **I.** *vt* **1.** (*albergar*) to accommodate **2.** (*procurar alojamiento*) to house; (*tropa*) to billet **3.** (*cosa*) to lodge **II.** *vr:* ~**se** **1.** (*hospedarse*) to stay; MIL to be billeted **2.** (*meterse*) ~**se en algo** to put up at sth
alondra *f* lark
alopatía *f* allopathy
alopecia *f sin pl* alopecia
alpaca *f* **1.** (*tela*) *t.* ZOOL alpaca **2.** (*aleación*) nickel silver, German silver
alpargata *f* espadrille ►**no tener ni para** ~**s** not to have a penny to one's name
Alpes *mpl* **los** ~ the Alps + *pl vb,* Alps
alpinismo *m sin pl* mountaineering, mountain climbing
alpinista *mf* mountaineer, mountain climber
alpino, -a *adj* Alpine; **refugio** ~ mountain refuge
alpiste *m* **1.** BOT canary grass **2.** (*para pájaros*) birdseed **3.** *inf* (*alcohol*) **le gusta mucho el** ~ he's/she's a boozer ►**no tener para** ~ *inf* to be on one's uppers
alquería *f* farm
alquilado, -a *m, f PRico* (*sirviente*) hireling
alquilar **I.** *vt* **1.** (*dejar*) to rent (out), to let **2.** (*tomar en alquiler*) to rent **II.** *vr:* ~**se** (*destinado a ser alquilado*) to be let; **se alquila** to let *Brit,* for rent *Am*
alquiler *m* **1.** (*acción*) renting, letting; ~ **de coches** car-hire *Brit,* car-rental *Am;* ~ **con opción de compra** leasing **2.** (*precio*) rent, rental
alquimia *f* alchemy
alquimista *mf* alchemist
alquitrán *m* tar
alquitranar *vt* to tar
alrededor *adv* **1.** (*local*) around; ~ **de la plaza** around the square; **un viaje** ~ **de la tierra** a round-the-world voyage **2.** (*aproximadamente*) ~ **de** around
alrededores *mpl* surroundings *pl;* (*de una ciudad*) outskirts *pl*
Alsacia *f* Alsace; ~**-Lorena** Alsace-Lorraine
alsaciano, -a *adj, m, f* Alsatian
alta *f* **1.** (*documento*) (certificate of) discharge; **dar el** ~ to discharge; **dar de** ~ **del hospital** to discharge from hospital **2.** (*inscripción*) registration; (*ingreso*) membership; **darse de** ~ **en** (**el registro de**) **una ciudad** to register as being resident in a city; **darse de** ~ **en una asociación** to become a member of an association; **dar de** ~ **a alguien en un partido** to admit sb as a member to a party
altamente *adv* highly; ~ **contaminado** highly contaminated; ~ **cualificado** highly qualified
altanería *f* arrogance, haughtiness
altanero, -a *adj* arrogant, haughty
altar *m* altar; ~ **mayor** high altar ►**quedarse para adornar** ~**es** to be left on the shelf; **poner a alguien en los** ~**es** to put sb on a pedestal; **tener a alguien en los** ~**es** to be full

of admiration for sb
altavoz *m* loudspeaker
alterable *adj* **1.** (*plan*) alterable **2.** (*alimento*) perishable **3.** (*persona*) changeable
alteración *f* **1.** (*de planes*) alteration, change; FIN fluctuation; ~ **del horario** change [*o* alteration] to the timetable **2.** (*perturbación*) disturbance **3.** (*turbación*) unrest **4.** (*irritación*) irritation **5.** (*altercado*) dispute **6.** (*adulteración*) adulteration
alterado, **-a** *adj* upset
alterar I. *vt* **1.** (*cambiar*) to alter **2.** (*perturbar*) to disturb **3.** (*turbar*) to upset; (*irritar*) to irritate **4.** (*adulterar*) to adulterate **II.** *vr:* **~se 1. ~se por algo** (*aturdirse*) to get upset over sth; (*irritarse*) to be irritated by sth **2.** (*cambiar*) to alter **3.** (*alimentos*) to go off [*o* bad]; (*leche*) to go sour
altercado *m* argument, altercation *form*
altercar <c→qu> *vi* to argue
alternar I. *vi* **1.** (*turnarse*) to alternate; **los veranos cálidos han alternado con los lluviosos** warm summers have alternated with rainy ones; ~ **en el volante** to take turns at the wheel **2.** (*tratar*) ~ **con alguien** to associate with sb; **es persona que alterna** he/she is a good mixer **3.** (*en un club nocturno*) to go clubbing **II.** *vt* to alternate; ~ **el trabajo con la diversión** to alternate between periods of work and leisure **III.** *vr* **~se en algo** to take turns at sth
alternativa *f* **1.** (*opción*) alternative; **no le queda otra** ~ **que...** he/she has no other alternative than ... **2.** TAUR *ceremony in which a novice becomes a fully-qualified bullfighter;* **dar la** ~ **a alguien para algo** *fig* to consider sb mature enough to do sth
alternativamente *adv* alternatively
alternativo, **-a** *adj* **1.** (*opcional*) alternative **2.** (*con alternación*) alternating
alterne *m* **chica de** ~ hostess; **bar de** ~ singles bar
alterno, **-a** *adj* alternate; **cultivo** ~ AGR crop rotation; **en días ~s** every other day
alteza *f* **1.** (*tratamiento*) nobleness; **Su Alteza Real** His/Her/Your Royal Highness **2.** (*calidad*) eminence
altibajos *mpl* **1.** (*de un terreno*) undulations *pl* **2.** (*cambios*) ups *pl* and downs; **es una persona con muchos** ~ **en su estado de ánimo** he's/she's very changeable
altillo *m* **1.** (*piso*) mezzanine (floor) **2.** (*desván*) attic
altiplanicie *f*, **altiplano** *m* high plateau
Altísimo *m* **el** ~ the Almighty
altisonante *adj* high-flown
altitud *f* height, altitude; **a una** ~ **de 1500 metros** at a height of 1,500 metres
altivez *f* arrogance, haughtiness
altivo, **-a** *adj* (*soberbio*) arrogant, haughty
alto I. *interj* halt; **¡~ el fuego!** cease fire! **II.** *m* **1.** (*descanso*) stop; ~ **el fuego** ceasefire; **dar el** ~ to order to halt **2.** (*altura*) height; **medir 8 metros de** ~ to be 8 metres high **3.** (*collado*) hill **4.** *pl* (*piso alto*) upstairs **III.** *adv* (*en un lugar elevado*) high (up); **ponlo en lo más** ~ put it as high up as possible; **de** ~ **abajo** from top to bottom ▶**pasar por** ~ to ignore; **pasar una pregunta por** ~ to overlook a question; **pasar un saludo por** ~ to ignore a greeting; **por todo lo** ~ splendidly
alto, **-a** *adj* **1.** (*en general*) high; **un** ~ **cargo** a high-ranking position; **la alta Edad Media** the high Middle Ages; **notas altas** MÚS high notes; **artículos de cuero de alta calidad** high-quality leather goods; **~s funcionarios** high officials; **tener un** ~ **concepto de alguien** to have a high opinion of sb **2.** (*persona, árbol*) tall; (*edificio*) high, tall **3.** (*en la parte superior*) upper; **clase alta** upper class **4.** GEO (*territorio, río*) upper; **la alta montaña** the high mountains; **el** ~ **Tajo** the Upper Tajo **5.** (*idioma, época*) high **6.** (*tiempo*) late; **a altas horas de la noche** late at night **7.** (*río*) in spate *Brit,* swollen *Am;* (*mar*) rough; **el río está** ~ the river is swollen **8.** (*sonido*) loud; **hablar en voz alta** to speak loudly
altoparlante *m AmL* loudspeaker
altozano *m* small hill
altramuz *m* lupin
altruismo *m sin pl* altruism
altruista I. *adj* altruistic **II.** *mf* altruist
altura *f* **1.** (*altitud*) height; **de gran** ~ high; **de poca** ~ low; **a gran** ~ at a great height; **una montaña de 2000 metros de** ~ a 2000-metre-high mountain; **el avión pierde** ~ the plane is losing altitude **2.** (*estatura*) height **3.** (*de un sonido*) pitch **4.** (*excelencia*) excellence **5.** *pl* (*cielo*) heaven ▶**estar a la** ~ **del betún** *inf* to look really stupid; **estar a la** ~ **de las circunstancias** to rise to the occasion; **estar a la** ~ **de Valencia** to be in the vicinity of Valencia; **a estas ~s** at this point
alubia *f* bean
alucinación *f* hallucination
alucinado, **-a** *adj inf* (*asombrado*) **miraba** ~ **a la chica** he looked at the girl in amazement; **me quedé** ~ **al leerlo en el periódico** I was stunned on reading it in the newpaper
alucinante *adj inf* **1.** (*estupendo*) fantastic **2.** (*increíble*) incredible
alucinar I. *vi inf* **1.** (*hablando*) to hallucinate; **¡tú alucinas!** *fig* you're crazy! **2.** (*quedar fascinado*) to be fascinated; **aluciné con sus conocimientos de chino** I was amazed by his/her knowledge of Chinese **II.** *vt inf* **1.** (*pasmar*) to amaze **2.** (*fascinar*) to fascinate
alud *m* **1.** (*de nieve*) avalanche **2.** (*de gente*) **un** ~ **de gente** a throng of people
aludir *vi* (*referirse*) to allude; (*mencionar*) to mention; **darse por aludido** (*ofenderse*) to take it personally; **no darse por aludido** not to take the hint
alumbrado *m* lighting; ~ **público** street lighting
alumbramiento *m* **1.** (*iluminación*) lighting

2.(*parto*) childbirth

alumbrar I. *vi* 1.(*iluminar*) to give off light; **la lámpara alumbra poco** the lamp doesn't give off much light 2.(*parir*) to give birth II. *vt* 1.(*iluminar*) to light (up); (*a alguien*) to shine a light on 2.(*parir*) to give birth to III. *vr:* **~se** *inf* to get tipsy

aluminio *m* aluminium *Brit,* aluminum *Am*

alumnado *m* (*de escuela*) pupils *pl;* (*de universidad*) students *pl*

alumno, -a *m, f* (*de escuela*) pupil; (*de universidad*) student

alunizaje *m* moon landing

alunizar <z→c> *vi* to land on the moon

alusión *f* 1.(*mención*) ~ **a algo** mention of sth 2.(*insinuación*) allusion; **hacer una ~ a algo** to allude to sth

alusivo, -a *adj* ~ **a algo** regarding sth; **dijo una frase alusiva a la situación** he/she said a few words about the situation

aluvión *m* 1.(*inundación*) *t. fig* flood 2.(*sedimento*) alluvium; **tierra de ~** alluvial soil

álveo *m* riverbed

alveolo *m,* **alvéolo** *m* 1. ANAT alveolus 2.(*del panal*) cell

alza *f* 1.(*elevación*) rise; **~ abusiva de los precios** extortionate price rise; **ir** [*o* **estar**] **en ~** (*precios*) to be rising; (*persona*) to be up-and-coming 2.(*de un zapato*) raised insole 3.(*de un arma*) sight

alzada *f* 1.(*de un caballo*) height 2. JUR appeal

alzado *m* AROUIT elevation

alzado, -a *adj* 1.(*fijado*) fixed 2.(*sublevado*) raised 3. *AmL* (*montaraz*) wild; (*en celo*) on heat

alzamiento *m* uprising

alzar <z→c> I. *vt* 1.(*levantar*) to lift (up); (*precio, voz*) to raise 2.(*poner vertical*) to put up 3.(*sostener*) to hold up 4.(*quitar*) to remove; (*colcha, mantel*) to take off; (*mesa*) to put away; (*campamento*) to break 5.(*construir*) to erect 6. AGR (*cosecha*) to gather in II. *vr:* **~se** 1.(*levantarse, destacar*) to rise (up); **allí se alza la universidad** the university buildings rise up over there 2. JUR to appeal 3. *AmL* (*animales*) to become wild 4. *AmL* (*sublevarse*) to revolt 5. *AmL* (*robar*) to steal; **~se con la pasta** *inf* to make off with the money [*o* dough]

ama *f* (*dueña*) mistress; (*propietaria*) owner; **~ de casa** housewife; **~ de cría** wet nurse; **~ de llaves** housekeeper

amabilidad *f* kindness; **tuvo la ~ de avisarme** he/she was kind enough to warn me; **le agradezco su ~** thank you for your kindness

amable *adj* kind; **ser ~** (**para**) **con alguien** to be kind to sb; **¿sería Ud. tan ~ de explicármelo?** would you be so kind as to explain it to me?

amadrinar *vt* ~ **algo** to act as sponsor to sth; **~ a alguien** to be godmother to sb

amaestrar *vt* 1.(*animales*) to train; (*caballos*) to break in 2. *pey* (*niños*) to train

3.(*instruir*) to coach

amagar <g→gu> I. *vi* 1.(*amenazar*) to threaten; **estaba amagando la guerra cuando...** war was threatening to break out when ... 2.(*enfermedad*) to show the first symptoms II. *vt* 1.(*indicar*) **amagó un golpe** he/she made as if to strike 2.(*amenazar*) to threaten; **~ a alguien con algo** to threaten sb with sth

amago *m* 1.(*amenaza*) threat 2.(*indicio*) hint 3. DEP feint

amainar I. *vi* to abate II. *vt* NÁUT to shorten

amalaya *interj AmL* I wish

amalgama *f* 1. QUÍM amalgam 2.(*mezcla*) mixture

amalgamar I. *vt* 1. TÉC to amalgamate 2.(*mezclar*) to mix 3.(*unir*) to unite II. *vr:* **~se** to amalgamate

amamantar *vt* (*bebé*) to breastfeed; (*cachorro*) to suckle

amancebamiento *m* cohabitation

amancebarse *vr* to cohabit

amanecer I. *vimpers* to dawn; **está amaneciendo** it's getting light II. *irr como crecer vi* to wake up III. *m* dawn; **al ~** at dawn

amanecida *f AmL* dawn

amanerado, -a *adj* 1.(*persona*) affected 2.(*estilo*) mannered

amanerarse *vr* (*persona*) to become affected

amanezquera *f Méx, PRico* (*alba*) dawn; **en la** [*o* **de**] **~** at daybreak

amansador *m Méx* (*domador*) horse breaker

amansar I. *vt* 1.(*animal*) to tame 2.(*persona*) to subdue; (*sosegar*) to calm down II. *vr:* **~se** to become tame

amante I. *adj* **soy poco ~ de hablar en público** I don't like speaking in public II. *mf* (*querido, aficionado*) lover; **un ~ de la naturaleza** a nature-lover

amanuense *mf* 1.(*secretario*) secretary 2.(*copista*) copyist

amañar I. *vt* 1.(*plan, asunto*) to fix; **~ una solución** to cook up a solution 2.(*resultado, documento*) to fake II. *vr* **~se con alguien** to get along well with sb; **amañárselas** (**para todo**) to manage to get by (in everything)

amaño *m* skill; **con ~** skilfully *Brit,* skillfully *Am*

amapola *f* poppy ▶**ponerse como una ~** to turn as red as a beetroot [*o* beet *Am*]

amar *vt* to love

amaraje *m* water landing; **efectuar el ~** to splash down

amarar *vi* to land on water

amargar <g→gu> I. *vt* to make bitter; **~ la vida a alguien** to make life difficult for sb II. *vi* to be bitter; **la verdad amarga** the bitter truth III. *vr:* **~se** to become bitter

amargo, -a *adj* bitter

amargor *m,* **amargura** *f* bitterness; **llorar con ~** to weep bitterly

amarillear *vi* to turn [*o* go] yellow

amarillento, -a *adj* yellowish; (*fotografía,*

papel) yellowed

amarillismo *m sin pl* sensationalism

amarillo, -a *adj* **1.** (*color*) yellow **2.** (*pálido*) pale

amarra *f* **1.** NÁUT hawser **2.** *pl* (*apoyo*) connections *pl*

amarradero *m* **1.** (*poste*) post, bollard **2.** (*argolla*) mooring ring **3.** NÁUT berth

amarrado, -a I. *pp de* **amarrar II.** *adj Arg, Par, PRico, Urug* (*tacaño*) mean *Brit,* stingy *Am;* (*innoble*) ignoble

amarrar I. *vt* **1.** (*atar*) to tie up **2.** NÁUT to moor **3.** *inf* (*empollar*) to swot *Brit,* to cram *Am;* **estar** [*o* **ir**] **amarrado** (*haber empollado*) to have crammed; (*tener enchufe*) to have good connections ►**tener a alguien muy amarrado** *inf* to keep sb under tight control **II.** *vr:* **~se** *AmL* to get married

amartelarse *vr* **1.** (*enamorarse*) **~se de alguien** to fall in love with sb **2.** (*ponerse cariñoso*) to smooch *inf*

amartillar *vt* **1.** (*arma*) to cock **2.** *inf* (*negocio*) to secure

amartizaje *m* landing on Mars

amasandería *f Chile* bakery

amasar *vt* **1.** (*masa*) to knead **2.** (*fortuna*) to amass **3.** *pey* (*tramar*) to concoct

amasiato *m Méx, CRi, Perú* (*concubinato*) concubinage

amasijar *vt AmL* (*dar paliza*) to give a beating; (*pegar brutalmente*) to beat to a pulp

amasijo *m* **1.** (*para hacer pan*) dough **2.** (*acción de amasar*) kneading **3.** (*argamasa*) mortar **4.** *inf* (*mezcla*) mixture **5.** *inf* (*intriga*) scheme

amateur I. *adj* amateur **II.** *mf* <amateurs> amateur

amatista *f* amethyst

amatorio, -a *adj* amatory

amauta *m Bol, Perú* **1.** (*mago y sabio de los incas*) Incan sage **2.** (*autoridad en pueblo indio*) village elder

amazacotado, -a *adj* **1.** (*colchón*) lumpy **2.** (*recargado*) overloaded; **un informe ~ de datos** a report crammed with facts; **estuvimos ~s en el tranvía** we were packed into the tram like sardines

amazona *f* **1.** (*mujer*) amazon **2.** DEP rider **3.** (*traje*) riding habit

ambages *mpl* **¡habla sin ~!** don't beat about the bush!

ámbar *adj, m inv* amber

Amberes *m* Antwerp

ambición *f* ambition; **~ de poder** hunger for power; **sin ambiciones** unambitious; **mi ~ en la vida es...** my ambition in life is ...

ambicionar *vt* to aspire to; **sólo ambiciono salud** I only want to be healthy

ambicioso, -a *adj* ambitious

ambientación *f* **1.** CINE, LIT setting **2.** (*ambiente*) atmosphere **3.** RADIO sound effects *pl*

ambientador *m* air freshener

ambientar I. *vt* **1.** (*novela*) to set; **~ la acción de una novela en el siglo pasado** to set a novel in the last century; **la novela está ambientada en Lima** the novel is set in Lima **2.** (*fiesta*) to enliven **II.** *vr:* **~se 1.** (*aclimatarse*) to adjust **2.** (*en una fiesta*) to get into the mood

ambiente *m* **1.** (*aire*) air **2.** (*medio*) surroundings *pl;* **medio ~** environment; **nocivo para el medio ~** harmful to the environment **3.** (*social*) milieu **4.** (*atmósfera*) atmosphere; **dar ~** to create a favourable atmosphere; **no había ~ en la calle** there wasn't much happening in the street; **el ~ en la reunión estaba caldeado** the atmosphere at the meeting was very tense **5.** *CSur, Perú* (*habitación*) room; **un departamento de cuatro ~s** a four-room flat

ambigüedad *f* ambiguity; **sin ~es** unambiguous

ambiguo, -a *adj* **1.** (*de doble significado*) ambiguous **2.** LING *having two genders*

ámbito *m* **1.** (*contorno*) surroundings *pl* **2.** (*espacio*) area; **en el ~ nacional** on a national level

ambivalente *adj* ambivalent

ambo *m Arg* two-piece suit

ambos, -as *adj* both

ambulancia *f* **1.** (*vehículo*) ambulance **2.** MIL field hospital **3.** FERRO **~ de correos** mail wagon

ambulante I. *adj* walking; **circo ~** travelling circus; **vendedor ~** pedlar *Brit,* peddler *Am;* **venta ~** peddling **II.** *mf* **~ de correos** railway post-office employee

ambulatorio *m* outpatient department

ambulatorio, -a *adj* outpatient

ameba *f* amoeba *Brit,* ameba *Am*

amedrentar I. *vt* **1.** (*asustar*) to scare **2.** (*intimidar*) to intimidate **II.** *vr:* **~se 1.** (*asustarse*) to get scared **2.** (*intimidarse*) to be intimidated

amelcochar I. *vt Arg, Méx, Par* (*almíbar*) to thicken **II.** *vi* **1.** *Cuba* (*enamorarse*) to fall in love **2.** *Méx* (*reblandecerse*) to soften

amén I. *m* amen; **decir ~ a todo** to agree to everything; **no decir ni ~** not to say a word; **en un decir ~** *inf* in a flash **II.** *prep* **~ de** except for

amenaza *f* **1.** (*intimidación*) threat; **bajo la ~ de violencia** under the threat of violence **2.** (*peligro*) menace

amenazador(a) *adj* **1.** (*tono*) threatening; **gesto ~** threatening gesture **2.** (*que anuncia peligro*) menacing

amenazar <z→c> **I.** *vt* (*intimidar*) to threaten; **el jefe lo ha amenazado con despedirle** the boss has threatened him with dismissal **II.** *vi, vt* (*presagiar*) to threaten; **amenaza tormenta** there's a storm in the offing; **está amenazando lluvia** it's threatening to rain

amenidad *f* **1.** (*carácter de lo agradable*)

pleasantness **2.** (*entretenimiento*) entertainment **3.** (*distracción*) enjoyment
amenizar <z→c> *vt* **1.** (*hacer agradable*) to make pleasant **2.** (*entretener*) to entertain **3.** (*conversación*) to liven up
ameno, **-a** *adj* **1.** (*agradable*) pleasant **2.** (*entretenido*) entertaining
América *f* America; ~ **Central** Central America; ~ **Latina** Latin America; ~ **del Norte/del Sur** North/South America ►**hacer las ~s** to make a fortune

> Many Spaniards emigrated to Latin America in the 19th and 20th centuries. The expression "**hacer las Américas**" refers directly to this fact and more or less means to make one's fortune in the Americas.

americana *f* jacket
americanismo *m* LING Americanism
americanista *mf* Americanist
americano, **-a** **I.** *adj* (*de América del Sur*) South American; (*estadounidense*) American; **el estilo de vida** ~ the American way of life **II.** *m, f* (*de América del Sur*) South American; (*estadounidense*) American
amerindio, **-a** **I.** *adj* American Indian, Amerindian **II.** *m, f* American Indian, Amerindian
amerizar <z→c> *vi* to land on water
ametralladora *f* machine gun
ametrallar *vt* to machine-gun
amianto *m* asbestos
amigable *adj* friendly
amígdala *f* tonsil
amigdalitis *f inv* tonsillitis *Brit,* tonsilitis *Am*
amigo, **-a** **I.** *adj* **1.** (*que tiene la amistad, amistoso*) friendly; **es muy amiga mía** she's a good friend of mine; **somos (muy) ~s desde la infancia** we've been close friends since our childhood **2.** (*aficionado, partidario*) **ser ~ de algo** to be fond of sth; **soy más ~ de veranear en el campo que en la costa** I prefer spending the summer in the country rather than at the seaside; **soy ~ de decir las cosas claras** I'm in favour of calling a spade a spade; **este tipo es muy ~ de lucir** this guy is a great one for showing off ►**¡y tan ~s!** and that's that! **II.** *m, f* **1.** (*general*) friend; ~ **de lo ajeno** thief; ~ **por correspondencia** penfriend *Brit,* penpal *Am;* **hacerse ~ de alguien** to make friends with sb; **poner a alguien cara de pocos ~s** to look grimly at sb **2.** (*amante*) lover **3.** (*adepto*) supporter
amiguete *m inf* pal, mate *Brit,* buddy *Am*
amilanar **I.** *vt* **1.** (*intimidar*) to intimidate **2.** (*desanimar*) to discourage **II.** *vr:* **~se** **1.** (*acobardarse*) to become frightened **2.** (*abatirse*) to become discouraged
aminoácido *m* amino acid
aminorar **I.** *vi* to diminish **II.** *vt* to reduce; ~ **el paso** to slacken one's pace
amistad *f* **1.** (*entre amigos*) friendship; **tener ~ con alguien** to be friendly with sb; **trabar ~ con alguien** to become friends with sb; **hacer las ~es con alguien** to make it up with sb **2.** *pl* (*amigos*) friends *pl*
amistar **I.** *vi Méx* to befriend **II.** *vr:* **~se** *CSur* to become friends
amistoso, **-a** *adj* (*persona, cosa*) friendly, amicable; **partido** ~ friendly match; **llegar a un acuerdo** ~ to come to an amicable agreement
amnesia *f sin pl* amnesia
amnistía *f* amnesty; **Amnistía Internacional** Amnesty International; **conceder ~ a alguien** to grant an amnesty to sb
amnistiar <*1. pres:* amnistío> *vt* to grant an amnisty
amo *m* **1.** (*de la casa*) head of the household **2.** (*propietario*) owner **3.** (*patrón*) boss; **ser el ~ en algo** to be the boss in sth ►**ser el ~ del cotarro** *inf* to be the top dog; **hacerse el ~ (de una asociación)** to become the leader (of an association)
amodorrarse *vr* to become drowsy [*o* sleepy]
amojonar *vt* to mark the boundary of
amoldar **I.** *vt* **1.** (*ajustar al molde*) to adjust **2.** (*moldear*) to mould *Brit,* to mold *Am* **3.** (*acomodar*) to adapt **II.** *vr:* **~se** to adapt oneself
amonarse *vr inf* to get tipsy
amonestación *f* **1.** (*advertencia*) warning; (*reprensión*) reprimand; **tarjeta de ~** DEP yellow card **2.** (*de los novios*) marriage banns *pl;* **correr las amonestaciones** to publish the banns
amonestar **I.** *vt* **1.** (*advertir*) to warn; (*reprender*) to reprimand **2.** (*los novios*) to publish the banns of **II.** *vr:* **~se** to have the banns published
amoníaco *m* ammonia
amontonar **I.** *vt* **1.** (*tierra, heno*) to pile up **2.** (*conocimientos, dinero*) to accumulate; **los refugiados estaban amontonados en el transbordador** the refugees were crowded together on the ferry **II.** *vr:* **~se** **1.** (*cosas*) to pile up **2.** (*personas*) to crowd together **3.** (*sucesos, noticias*) to accumulate
amor *m* love; ~ **al prójimo** love for one's neighbour; ~ **propio** self-esteem; ~ **a primera vista** love at first sight; **¡~ mío!** my love!; **mi gran ~ es el cine** my great passion is the cinema; **hacer el ~ con alguien** *inf* to make love with sb; **hacer algo con ~** to do sth lovingly ►**por ~ al arte** for nothing; **en ~ y compaña** in peace and harmony; **¡por ~ de Dios!** for God's sake!; **con [*o* de] mil ~es** with the greatest of pleasure; ~ **con ~ se paga** *prov* one good turn deserves another
amoratado, **-a** *adj* purple; **un ojo ~** a black eye; **tengo los labios ~s de frío** my lips are blue with cold; **tengo el brazo ~ de la caída** my arm is bruised from the fall
amordazar <z→c> *vt* **1.** (*poner mordaza*) to gag **2.** (*hacer callar*) to silence, to gag
amorfo, **-a** *adj* shapeless, amorphous

amorío(s) *m(pl) pey* love affair
amoroso, -a *adj* 1. (*de amor*) loving 2. (*cariñoso*) ~ **con/para con alguien** affectionate to/towards sb 3. (*tierra, tela*) soft 4. (*tiempo*) mild
amorrar I. *vi inf* 1. (*bajar la cabeza*) to hang one's head 2. (*mostrar enfado*) to sulk II. *vr:* ~**se** 1. *inf* (*enfadarse*) to get angry 2. *inf* (*al beber*) ~**se a la botella** to put the bottle to one's lips
amortiguador *m* AUTO shock absorber
amortiguar <gu→gü> *vt* (*sonido*) to muffle; (*golpe, caída*) to cushion; (*pena, dolor*) to soothe; (*sentimiento*) to deaden; ~ **los faros** AUTO to dim one's headlights
amortización *f* 1. (*de una deuda*) repayment 2. (*fiscal*) depreciation
amortizar <z→c> *vt* 1. (*deuda*) to pay off 2. (*fiscalmente*) to write off 3. (*inversión*) to recover 4. (*empleos*) to cut back on
amoscarse <c→qu> *vr*, **amostazarse** <z→c> *vr inf* to go into a huff
amotinado, -a I. *adj* rebel II. *m, f* rebel
amotinar I. *vt* to stir up II. *vr:* ~**se** to rebel
amparar I. *vt* to protect; ~ **a alguien** to shelter sb; **la constitución ampara la libertad de religión** the constitution guarantees religious freedom II. *vr:* ~**se** to seek protection; ~**se bajo algo** to shelter behind sth; **se ampara en una ley antigua** he/she has recourse to an old law; **el espía se amparó en la oscuridad para escapar** the spy escaped under cover of darkness
amparo *m* 1. (*protección*) protection; **estar al ~ de alguien** to be under sb's protection; **al ~ de la oscuridad** under cover of darkness 2. (*refugio*) shelter
amperio *m* amp
ampliación *f* 1. (*engrandecimiento*) enlargement; (*de un número, el capital*) increase; (*de un territorio*) expansion; (*de un edificio, una carretera*) extension; ~ **del surtido** stock enlargement 2. (*de conocimientos*) broadening 3. (*de un sonido*) amplification; ~ **de RAM** INFOR RAM expansion
ampliamente *adv* 1. (*cumplidamente*) amply 2. (*extensamente*) extensively; **las condiciones han mejorado** ~ conditions have considerably improved
ampliar <*1. pres:* amplío> *vt* 1. (*hacer más grande*) to enlarge; (*capital, número*) to increase; (*territorio*) to expand; (*edificio, carretera*) to extend; **edición ampliada** extended edition 2. (*conocimientos*) to broaden 3. (*sonido*) to amplify
amplificador *m* amplifier
amplificar <c→qu> *vt* to amplify
amplio, -a *adj* 1. (*casa*) spacious; (*jardín, parque*) extensive 2. (*vestido*) loose-fitting 3. (*informe*) detailed; (*experiencia, poderes*) wide-ranging; (*red de comunicaciones*) extensive; (*interés*) broad; **una derrota amplia** a serious defeat; **amplias partes de la población** large sections of the population; **en un sentido más** ~ in a wider sense
amplitud *f* 1. (*extensión*) extent; (*de conocimientos*) range; (*de un informe*) extensiveness; ~ **de miras** broad-minded; ~ **del surtido** ECON range of stock; **de gran** ~ wide-ranging 2. (*de una casa*) roominess; (*de un jardín, parque*) extensiveness 3. FÍS amplitude
ampolla *f* 1. (*en la piel, burbuja*) blister; **tener ~s en los pies** to have blisters on one's feet 2. (*garrafa*) flask 3. (*para inyecciones*) ampoule *Brit,* ampule *Am* ►**levantar** ~**s** to get people's backs up
ampolleta *f Arg* lightbulb
ampuloso, -a *adj* pompous
amputar *vt* to amputate
amuchar *vt Arg, Bol, Chile* to multiply
amueblar *vt* to furnish
amuermado, -a *adj inf* 1. *ser* boring 2. *estar* bored
amuermar I. *vt inf* 1. (*aburrir*) to bore 2. (*calor*) to make drowsy II. *vr:* ~**se** *inf* to get bored
amularse *vr Méx* 1. (*mercancía*) to become unsellable 2. (*persona*) to get stubborn
amuleto *m* amulet
amurallar *vt* to wall
anabolizante *m* anabolic steroid
anacarado, -a *adj* pearly
anacardo *m* 1. BOT cashew tree 2. (*fruto*) cashew (nut)
anaconda *f* anaconda
ánade *mf* duck
anagrama *m* anagram
anal *adj* anal
anales *mpl* 1. HIST annals *pl* 2. (*de una universidad, sociedad*) records *pl*
analfabetismo *m sin pl* illiteracy
analfabeto, -a *m, f* illiterate (person)
analgésico *m* painkiller
análisis *m inv* 1. (*general*) *t.* MAT analysis; ~ **de sistemas** INFOR systems analysis; ~ **de la situación económica** analysis of the economic situation; **¿qué ~ haces de la situación?** what's your analysis of the situation? 2. MED test; ~ **del grupo sanguíneo** blood test (*to determine blood group*)
analista *mf* 1. (*de anales*) chronicler 2. (*que analiza*) analyst; ~ **político** political analyst; ~ **de sistemas** INFOR systems analyst; **el médico mandó las pruebas al** ~ the doctor sent the samples to the laboratory
analítico, -a *adj* analytic(al)
analizar <z→c> *vt* 1. (*examinar*) *t.* MED to analyse *Brit,* to analyze *Am* 2. LING to parse
analogía *f* analogy; **por ~ con algo** on the analogy of sth
análogo, -a *adj* analogous
ananá(s) *m CSur* pineapple
anaquel *m* shelf
anaranjado, -a *adj* orange
anarquía *f* anarchy
anárquico, -a *adj* anarchic

anarquismo *m sin pl* anarchism
anarquista I. *adj* anarchist II. *mf* anarchist
anatema *m o f* 1. (*maldición*) curse; **lanzar ~s contra alguien** to hurl abuse at sb 2. (*condena*) condemnation 3. (*excomunión*) anathema
anatematizar <z→c> *vt* 1. (*maldecir*) to curse 2. (*condenar*) to condemn 3. (*excomulgar*) to anathematize
anatomía *f* anatomy
anatómico, -a *adj* 1. MED anatomical 2. (*adaptado al cuerpo*) anatomically designed
anca *f* 1. (*de animal*) haunch; **~s de rana** frogs' legs 2. (*cadera*) hip 3. *pl, inf* (*nalgas*) backside ▸**montar a las ~s** to sit behind
ancestral *adj* 1. (*relativo a los antepasados*) ancestral 2. (*antiguo*) ancient
ancho *m* width; **~ de vía** AUTO, FERRO gauge *Brit,* gage *Am;* **tener** [*o* **medir**] **cinco metros de ~** to be five metres wide
ancho, -a *adj* (*vasto*) wide; (*vestidos*) loose-fitting; **~ de espaldas** broad-shouldered; **a lo ~** widthways; **un árbol tumbado a lo ~ de la calle** a tree lying across the street ▸**estar a sus anchas** to feel at ease; **en este pueblo estoy a mis anchas** I feel at home in this village; **se queda tan ~ cuando dice tonterías** he doesn't turn a hair when he talks nonsense; **venir a alguien muy ~** to be too much for sb
anchoa *f* anchovy
anchura *f* width; (*de un vestido*) looseness
ancianidad *f* old age
anciano, -a I. *adj* old II. *m, f* old man
ancla *f* anchor; **echar ~s** to drop anchor; **levar ~s** to weigh anchor
ancladero *m* anchorage
anclar *vi, vt* to anchor; **estar anclado** to be anchored
áncora *f* anchor
ancuviña *f Chile* 1. (*sepelio*) burial 2. (*tumba*) grave; **cavar una ~** to dig a grave
andadas *fpl* **volver a las ~** to revert to [*o* to fall back into] old habits
ándale *interj Méx* (*adios*) bye; (*deprisa*) come on
Andalucía *f* Andalusia
andaluz(a) *adj, m(f)* Andalusian
andamiaje *m,* **andamio** *m* scaffolding
andanada *f* volley; **lanzar una ~ contra alguien** *fig* to give sb a dressing-down; **por ~s** *Arg* in excess
andante *adj* errant; **parecer un cadáver ~** to look like death (warmed up)
andanza *f* 1. (*aventura*) adventure 2. (*suerte*) **buena ~** good fortune; **mala ~** misfortune
andar *irr* I. *vi* 1. (*caminar*) to walk; **~ a caballo** to ride (a horse); **~ a gatas** to go on all fours; (*bebés*) to crawl; **~ con paso majestuoso** to strut; **~ de prisa** to go quickly; **~ detrás de algo** to be after sth; **desde la estación hay 10 minutos andando** it's 10 minutes walk from the station; **esta niña andaba ya a los ocho meses** this girl was already walking at the age of eight months 2. (*reloj, coche*) to go *Brit,* to run *Am;* (*máquina*) to work 3. (*tiempo*) to pass 4. (*estar*) **¿dónde está el periódico? – ~á por ahí** where's the newspaper? – it'll be around here somewhere; **~ atareado** to be busy; **~ metido en un asunto** to be involved in a matter; **~ haciendo algo** to be doing sth; **anda mucha gente buscando empleo** there are a lot of people looking for a job; **te ando llamando desde hace una hora** I've been trying to call you for an hour; **~ con gente de bien** to mix with respectable people; **los precios andan por las nubes** prices are sky-high; **~ mal de dinero** to be short of money; **andar mal de inglés** to be poor in English; **~emos por los 30 grados** it must be about 30 degrees; **~ por los 30** to be about 30; **no andes en mi escritorio** don't go rummaging in my desk ▸**dime con quien andas y te diré quien eres** *prov* your friends are a guide to your character; **~ a la que salta** to seize the opportunity; **¡anda!** good heavens! II. *vt* **he andado toda la casa para encontrarte** I've looked all over the house for you III. *m* walk, gait
andariego, -a I. *adj* fond of travelling II. *m, f* wanderer
andas *fpl* portable platform ▸**llevar a alguien en ~** to treat sb with great respect
andén *m* 1. FERRO platform 2. (*de muelle*) quayside 3. (*corredor*) corridor 4. (*de un puente*) footpath
Andes *mpl* **los ~** the Andes + *pl vb,* Andes
andinismo *m sin pl, AmL* mountaineering, mountain climbing
andinista *mf AmL* mountaineer, mountain climber
andino, -a *adj* Andean
Andorra *f* Andorra

> **Andorra** is a small democratic state (only 467 square kilometres in area) that has a parlamentary principality as its form of government. It borders France to the north and east and Spain to the west and south.

andorrano, -a *adj, m, f* Andorran
andrajo *m* rag
andrajoso, -a *adj* ragged
andurrial *m Arg, Ecua, Perú* (*paraje pantanoso*) muddy road
andurrial(es) *m(pl)* godforsaken place
anécdota *f* anecdote
anegar <g→gu> I. *vt* 1. (*inundar*) to flood 2. (*ahogar*) to drown; **~ una sublevación en sangre** to suppress a revolt with violence II. *vr:* **~se** 1. (*campo*) to flood 2. (*ahogarse*) to drown; **~se en lágrimas** to dissolve into tears
anejo *m* 1. (*edificio*) annexe *Brit,* annex *Am* 2. (*carta*) enclosure 3. (*libro, revista*) supplement 4. (*en un libro*) appendix 5. INFOR attachment 6. (*pueblo*) district
anejo, -a *adj* (*a edificios*) joined; (*a cartas*)

enclosed

anemia *f sin pl* anaemia *Brit,* anemia *Am*

anémona *f* anemone

anestesia *f* anaesthesia *Brit,* anesthesia *Am*

anestesiar *vt* to anaesthetize *Brit,* to anesthetize *Am*

anestésico *m* anaesthetic *Brit,* anesthetic *Am*

anestesista *mf* anaesthetist *Brit,* anesthetist *Am*

anexión *f* annexation

anexionar *vt* to annex

anexo *m v.* **anejo**

anexo, -a *adj v.* **anejo, -a**

anfibio *m* (*animal, vehículo*) amphibian; (*avión*) seaplane

anfibio, -a *adj* amphibious; **animal ~** amphibious animal; **vehículo ~** amphibious vehicle

anfiteatro *m* **1.**(*local*) amphitheatre *Brit,* amphitheater *Am* **2.**(*en la universidad*) lecture theatre *Brit,* lecture hall *Am*

anfitrión, -ona *m, f* host *m,* hostess *f*

ánfora *f* **1.**(*cántaro*) amphora **2.** *Méx* (*electoral*) ballot box

angarillas *fpl* **1.**(*andas*) litter **2.**(*vinagreras*) cruet

ángel *m* angel; **~ de la guarda** guardian angel; **tener mucho ~** to be very charming

angelical *adj* angelic(al); **rostro ~** angelic face

angina *f* **~ de pecho** angina (pectoris); **~s** sore throat

anglicismo *m* anglicism

angoleño, -a *adj, m, f* Angolan

angosto, -a *adj* narrow

angostura *f* **1.**(*estrechez*) narrowness **2.**(*paso estrecho*) narrows *pl*

anguila *f* **1.** ZOOL eel **2.** NÁUT slipway

angula *f* elver

angular **I.** *adj* angular **II.** *m* **1.** FOTO **gran ~** wide-angle lens **2.**(*herramienta*) angle iron **3. piedra ~** cornerstone

ángulo *m* **1.** MAT angle; **~ recto** right angle; **en ~** angled; **~ de tiro** DEP angle of fire **2.**(*rincón*) corner **3.**(*arista*) edge **4.**(*de vista*) angle of vision

anguloso, -a *adj* **1.**(*lugar*) full of twists and turns **2.**(*cara*) angular

angurria *f AmL: inf* **1.**(*ganas*) craving; (*hambre*) ravenous hunger; *pey* (*glotonería*) gluttony **2.**(*codicia*) greed

angurriento, -a *adj AmL* **1.** *pey* (*glotón*) gluttonous; (*hambriento*) greedy; *t. fig* (*devorador*) voracious **2.**(*codicioso*) avaricious

angustia *f* **1.**(*temor*) anguish; **~ vital** angst **2.**(*aflicción*) anxiety; **dar ~** to make anxious **3.**(*aprieto*) distress

angustiar **I.** *vt* **1.**(*acongojar*) to distress **2.**(*causar temor*) to frighten **3.**(*afligir*) to worry **II.** *vr:* **~se** **1.**(*afligirse*) to get worried **2.**(*atemorizarse*) to get scared

angustioso, -a *adj* **1.**(*lleno de angustia*) anguished **2.**(*inquietante*) worrying **3.**(*sofocante*) distressing

anhelante *adj* (*ansioso*) longing; **estar ~ por algo** to be longing for sth

anhelar **I.** *vi* to pant **II.** *vt* to long for

anhelo *m* **~ de algo** longing for sth

anidar **I.** *vi* **1.**(*hacer nido*) to nest **2.**(*morar*) to live **II.** *vt* to take in

anilla *f* **1.**(*aro t. para pájaros*) ring; (*de puro*) band **2.** *pl* DEP rings *pl*

anillo *m* ring; **~ de boda** wedding ring; **~ (de crecimiento)** BOT growth ring ►**venir como ~ al dedo** to be just right; **ese vestido te viene como ~ al dedo** this dress suits you perfectly; **no se me caen los ~s por...** it's not beneath me to ...

ánima *f* soul ►**a las ~s** in the evening

animación *f* **1.**(*acción de animarse*) *t.* CINE, INFOR animation; **dar ~** to animate **2.**(*viveza*) liveliness **3.**(*actividad*) activity; **había mucha ~ en la calle** the street was very busy

animado, -a *adj* **1.**(*persona*) in high spirits; **no estar muy ~** not to be very cheerful **2.**(*lugar*) busy **3.**(*actividad*) lively **4.**(*tener ganas*) **estar ~ a hacer algo** to be keen on doing sth **5.** INFOR **~ por ordenador** computer-animated

animador(a) **I.** *adj* encouraging **II.** *m(f)* **1.**(*artista*) entertainer **2.**(*de turistas*) host *m,* hostess *f* **3.**(*presentador*) presenter **4.** DEP cheerleader

animadversión *f* hostility; **sentir ~ por alguien** to feel hostile towards sb

animal **I.** *adj* **1.**(*relativo a los animales*) animal; **comportamiento ~** animal behaviour **2.**(*grosero*) rude; **el aspecto ~ del hombre** the animal side of man **II.** *m* **1.** ZOOL animal; **~es de caza** game; **~ de compañía** pet; **~ de presa** predator; **comer como un ~** *inf* to eat like a horse **2.** *pey* (*persona ignorante*) fool; (*bruta*) brute

animalada *f inf* **1.**(*disparate*) (piece of) nonsense **2.**(*barbaridad*) disgrace; **¡qué ~!** how outrageous! **3.**(*cantidad*) massive amount

animar **I.** *vt* **1.**(*infundir vida*) to liven up **2.**(*alentar*) to encourage **3.**(*persona triste*) to cheer up **4.**(*habitación*) to brighten up; (*economía*) to stimulate **II.** *vr:* **~se** **1.**(*cobrar vida*) to liven up **2.**(*atreverse*) to dare **3.**(*decidirse*) to decide; **¡por fin te has animado a escribir (una carta)!** so you've finally decided to write (a letter)!; **¿te animas?** will you have a go? **4.**(*alegrarse*) to cheer up

ánimo *m* **1.**(*espíritu*) spirit; **no estoy con ~s de...** I don't feel like ... **2.**(*energía*) energy; (*valor*) courage; **cobrar ~** to take heart; **dar ~** to encourage; **¡~!** cheer up! **3.**(*intención*) intention; **con ~ de...** with the intention of ...; **sin ~ de lucro** non-profit-making; **sin ~ de ofender a nadie** without wishing to offend anyone

animosidad *f* (*animadversión*) animosity

animoso, -a *adj* (*valeroso*) brave

aniñado, -a *adj* childlike; *pey* childish

aniquilar **I.** *vt* **1.**(*destruir*) to annihilate; ~

todas las esperanzas to destroy all hope **2.** (*salud*) to ruin **3.** (*desanimar*) to shatter **II.** *vr:* **~se 1.** (*desaparecer*) to be annihilated **2.** (*deteriorarse*) to deteriorate

anís <anises> *m* **1.** (*planta*) anise; (*semilla*) aniseed **2.** (*licor*) anisette

aniversario *m* anniversary; ~ **de bodas** wedding anniversary; ~ **de muerte de alguien** anniversary of sb's death

ano *m* ANAT anus; ~ **artificial** colostomy

anoche *adv* (*al atardecer*) last night; **antes de ~** the night before last; ~ **no pude dormir** I couldn't sleep last night

anochecer **I.** *irr como crecer vimpers* **anochece** it's getting dark **II.** *irr como crecer vi* **anochecimos en Burgos** we arrived in Burgos at nightfall **III.** *m* nightfall; **al ~** at nightfall

anodino, **-a** *adj* **1.** (*cosa*) insipid **2.** (*persona*) bland **3.** MED anodyne

ánodo *m* anode

anomalía *f* anomaly

anonadar **I.** *vt* **1.** (*pasmar*) to astound; (*maravillar*) to overwhelm; **la noticia me dejó anonadado** I was astonished by the news **2.** (*aniquilar*) to destroy **3.** (*descorazonar*) to discourage **II.** *vr:* **~se 1.** (*descorazonarse*) to be discouraged **2.** (*aniquilarse*) to be destroyed

anonimato *m* anonymity; **mantener el ~** to remain anonymous

anónimo *m* **1.** (*autor*) anonymous author; (*escrito*) anonymous work **2.** (*anonimato*) anonymity; **guardar el ~** to preserve one's anonymity

anónimo, **-a** *adj* anonymous; **sociedad anónima** ECON limited liability company *Brit,* public corporation *Am*

anorak <anoraks> *m* anorak

anorexia *f* anorexia

anormal *adj* (*no normal*) abnormal; ~ (**físico**) physically handicapped; ~ (**síquico**) mentally handicapped

anotación *f* **1.** (*acción de anotar*) annotation; (*en un registro*) record **2.** (*nota*) note **3.** FIN entry; ~ **de intereses** credit (entry)

anotar *vt* (*apuntar*) to note (down); (*en un registro*) to record

anquilosamiento *m* paralysis

anquilosar **I.** *vt* to paralyze **II.** *vr:* **~se 1.** (*las articulaciones*) to get stiff **2.** (*paralizarse*) to become paralyzed **3.** (*mentalmente*) to ossify

ánsar *m* goose

ansia *f* **1.** (*angustia*) anguish **2.** (*intranquilidad*) anxiety **3.** (*afán*) longing; ~ **de poder** craving for power **4.** *pl* (*náusea*) nausea

ansiar <*1. pres:* ansío> *vt* to long for; **el momento ansiado** the long-awaited moment; **lograr la tan ansiada copa** to win the much-longed-for cup; ~ **el regreso de alguien** to long for sb's return

ansiedad *f* anxiety

ansiosamente *adv* **esperamos ~ su visita** we eagerly await your visit; **la esperaba ~ en la estación** he waited for her anxiously in the station

ansioso, **-a** *adj* **1.** (*intranquilo*) anxious **2.** (*anheloso*) eager **3.** (*impaciente*) impatient **4.** (*codicioso*) greedy

antagónico, **-a** *adj* **1.** (*opuesto*) opposed **2.** (*rival*) antagonistic

antagonismo *m* (*oposición*) opposition; (*rivalidad*) antagonism

antagonista *mf* antagonist

antaño *adv* long ago

antártico, **-a** *adj* Antarctic; **el polo ~** the South Pole; **Océano Glacial Antártico** Antarctic Ocean

Antártida *f* Antarctica

ante **I.** *m* **1.** ZOOL elk **2.** (*piel*) suede **II.** *prep* **1.** (*posición, con movimiento*) before **2.** (*en vista de*) in view of **3.** (*adversario*) faced with

anteanoche *adv* the night before last

anteayer *adv* the day before yesterday

antebrazo *m* ANAT forearm

antecámara *f* anteroom

antecedente **I.** *adj* foregoing **II.** *m* **1.** LING antecedent **2.** *pl* (*circunstancias*) history; (*de una persona*) background; **~s penales** criminal record; **estar en ~s de algo** to be well informed about sth; **poner a alguien en ~s de algo** to fill sb in about sth

anteceder *vt* to precede

antecesor(**a**) *m(f)* **1.** (*en un cargo*) predecessor **2.** (*antepasado*) ancestor

antedicho, **-a** *adj* aforementioned, above-mentioned

antediluviano, **-a** *adj* antediluvian

antelación *f* **con ~** in advance; **con la debida ~** in good time

antemano *adv* **de ~** in advance; **calcular de ~** to calculate in advance

antena *f* **1.** ZOOL antenna **2.** (*de telecomunicaciones*) aerial *Brit,* antenna *Am;* ~ **colectiva** communal aerial; ~ **interior** indoor aerial; **estar en ~** to be on the air; **el programa lleva un año en ~** the programme [*o* program *Am*] has been running for a year **3.** NÁUT lateen yard ►**estar con las ~s puestas** *irón* to be all ears

anteojeras *fpl* blinkers *pl Brit,* blinders *pl Am*

anteojo *m* **1.** (*catalejo*) telescope **2.** *pl* (*gemelos*) opera glasses *pl;* (*prismáticos*) binoculars *pl;* (*lentes*) spectacles *pl*

antepasado, **-a** *m, f* ancestor

antepecho *m* **1.** (*barandilla*) handrail **2.** (*pretil*) parapet

antepenúltimo, **-a** *adj* last but two *Brit,* third from the last *Am*

anteponer *irr como poner* **I.** *vt* **1.** (*poner delante*) ~ **algo a algo** to place sth in front of sth **2.** (*dar preferencia*) to give priority to **II.** *vr:* **~se 1.** (*ponerse delante*) **~se a alguien** to stand in front of sb **2.** (*tener preferencia*) to be preferred

anteproyecto *m* draft

anterior I. *adj* previous; **la noche ~ había llovido** the night before it had rained; **en la página ~** on the preceding [*o* previous] page; **el presidente ~** the previous president II. *prep* **~ a** prior to

anterioridad I. *f* anteriority II. *prep* **con ~ a** prior to, before

anteriormente *adv* before, previously

antes I. *adv* 1. (*de tiempo*) before; (*hace un rato*) just now; (*antiguamente*) formerly; (*primero*) first; **poco ~** shortly before; **piénsate ~ lo que dices** think before you speak; **ahora como ~** still; **~ con ~, cuanto ~** as soon as possible; **~ de nada** first of all; **~ que nada** above all; **los cardenales van ~ que los obispos** cardinals come before bishops 2. (*comparativo*) rather II. *prep* **~ de** before III. *conj* 1. (*temporal*) before; **~ (de) que llegues** before you arrive 2. (*adversativo*) **no estoy satisfecho con el examen, ~ bien decepcionado** I'm not happy with the examination, on the contrary, I'm disappointed IV. *adj* **ya habíamos visto a esta chica el día ~** we had already seen this girl the previous day

antesala *f* anteroom; **hacer ~** to wait (to be received)

antiaéreo, -a *adj* MIL anti-aircraft **antialcohólico, -a** I. *adj* teetotal II. *m, f* teetotaller **antiatómico, -a** *adj* **refugio ~** fall-out shelter **antibalas** *adj inv* bullet-proof

antibiótico *m* antibiotic

antibloqueo *m* **sistema ~ de frenos** anti-lock braking system

anticiclón *m* anticyclone

anticipación *f* 1. (*de una fecha*) bringing forward *Brit,* moving up *Am* 2. (*de un suceso*) anticipation 3. COM advance; **con ~** (*pago*) in advance

anticipadamente *adv* in advance; **jubilar ~ a alguien** to retire sb early

anticipado, -a *adj* (*elecciones*) early; **pagar por ~** to pay in advance

anticipar I. *vt* 1. (*fecha*) to bring forward *Brit,* to move up *Am* 2. (*suceso*) to anticipate; **no anticipemos los acontecimientos** let's not anticipate events 3. (*dinero*) to advance; **~ una paga sobre el sueldo** to give an advance on a salary II. *vr* **~se a alguien** to beat sb to it; **el verano se ha anticipado este año** summer is early this year; **los invitados se han anticipado** the guests have arrived early

anticipo *m* 1. (*del sueldo*) advance; **~ sobre el sueldo** advance on a salary 2. (*de un pago*) advance payment

anticonceptivo *m* contraceptive, birth control method

anticonceptivo, -a *adj* contraceptive, birth-control; **píldora anticonceptiva** contraceptive pill

anticongelante *m* antifreeze **anticonstitucional** *adj* unconstitutional **anticorrosivo** *m* anticorrosive

anticuado, -a *adj* old-fashioned

anticuario, -a *m, f* (*vendedor*) antique dealer

anticuarse *vr* to become old-fashioned

anticucho *m Perú* kebob

anticuerpo *m* antibody **antideportivo, -a** *adj* unsporting **antideslizante** *adj* (*superficie*) non-slip; (*neumático*) non-skid **antidoping** *adj inv* **control ~** drugs test

antídoto *m* antidote

antieconómico, -a *adj* uneconomic(al)

antier *adv AmL, inf* the day before yesterday **antiestético, -a** *adj* unattractive

antifaz *m* mask

antifris *m inv, AmL* anti-freeze

antigás *adj inv* **máscara ~** gasmask

antigualla *f pey* 1. (*objeto*) piece of junk 2. (*costumbre, estilo*) relic

antiguamente *adv* once, long ago

antigubernamental *adj* anti-governmental

antigüedad *f* 1. (*edad antigua*) antiquity; **la ~ clásica** classical antiquity 2. (*objeto*) antique 3. (*edad*) age; **tener una ~ de 100 años** to be 100 years old 4. (*en una empresa*) seniority; **tengo 5 años de ~ (en el trabajo)** I've been working for 5 years (in the job)

antiguo, -a *adj* <antiquísimo> 1. (*de muchos años*) old; (*relación*) long-standing 2. (*anticuado*) antiquated; (*muy anticuado*) ancient; **a la antigua** in the old-fashioned way; **está chapado a la antigua** he is old-fashioned 3. (*de la antigüedad*) ancient 4. (*anterior*) former 5. (*en un cargo*) **es el más ~ en esta empresa** he's the most senior member of staff in this firm

antihigiénico, -a *adj* unhygienic **antiinflacionista** *adj* anti-inflationary; **lucha ~** fight against inflation **antiinflamatorio, -a** *adj* anti-inflammatory

antílope *m* antelope

antinatural *adj* unnatural

antinomia *f* antinomy

antiparras *fpl inf* specs *pl*

antipatía *f* antipathy; **~ a** [*o* **contra**] **alguien** antipathy for sb

antipático, -a *adj* unpleasant

antipirético *m* MED, **antipirina** *f AmL* MED antipyretic, antifebrile

antiquísimo, -a *adj superl de* **antiguo**

antirreglamentario, -a *adj* unlawful; **entrada antirreglamentaria** DEP foul **antirrobo** *m* anti-theft device **antisemita** I. *adj* anti-Semitic II. *mf* anti-Semite **antisemitismo** *m sin pl* anti-Semitism

antiséptico, -a *adj* antiseptic **antisísmico, -a** *adj* earthquake-proof **antisocial** *adj* antisocial **antiterrorista** *adj* antiterrrorist; **lucha ~** fight against terrorism

antítesis *f inv* antithesis

antojadizo, -a *adj* capricious

antojarse *vimpers* 1. (*encapricharse*) **se le antojó comprarse un coche nuevo** he/she took it into his/her head to buy a new car; **se me antojó un helado** I fancied an ice cream;

hace siempre lo que se le antoja he/she always does as he/she pleases **2.** (*tener la sensación*) **se me antoja que no vas a venir** I've a feeling that you're not going to come; **se me antoja que va a nevar** I think it's going to snow

antojitos *mpl Méx* GASTR appetizers *pl*

antojo *m* **1.** (*capricho*) whim; **a mi** ~ as I please **2.** (*de una embarazada*) craving; **tener ~s** (*ganas*) to have cravings; *CSur* (*estar embarazada*) to be pregnant **3.** (*mancha*) birthmark **4.** *Méx* (*apetito*) appetite

antología *f* anthology ►**de** ~ (*memorable*) excellent

antonomasia *f* **por** ~ par excellence

antorcha *f* torch

antro *m pey* (*local*) dive; **un ~ de corrupción** a den of iniquity

antropófago, -a *m, f* cannibal

antropología *f* anthropology

antropólogo, -a *m, f* anthropologist

anual *adj* **1.** (*que dura un año, que sucede cada año*) annual, yearly; **informe** ~ annual report **2.** (*planta*) annual

anualidad *f* annuity; ~ **vitalicia** life annuity

anualmente *adv* annually, yearly

anuario *m* yearbook

anubarrado, -a *adj* cloudy

anudar **I.** *vt* **1.** (*hacer un nudo*) to knot **2.** (*juntar*) to join **II.** *vr:* **~se** to become knotted; **~se la voz** to get a lump in one's throat

anulación *f* **1.** (*de una ley*) repeal **2.** (*de una sentencia*) overturning **3.** (*de un matrimonio*) annulment **4.** (*de un contrato, un pedido, una subscripción*) cancellation **5.** (*de una decisión, un permiso*) revocation

anular **I.** *vt* **1.** (*ley*) to repeal **2.** (*sentencia*) to overturn **3.** (*matrimonio*) to annul **4.** (*contrato, pedido, subscripción, cita*) to cancel **5.** (*decisión, permiso*) to revoke **6.** (*tren, autobús*) to cancel **7.** DEP (*gol*) to disallow **8.** (*persona*) to subjugate **II.** *vr:* **~se** (*persona*) to limit oneself **III.** *adj* **1.** (*relativo al anillo*) annular **2.** (*de forma de anillo*) ring-shaped

anunciación *f* announcement

anunciar **I.** *vt* **1.** (*dar noticia de algo*) to announce; **acaban de ~ la llegada del vuelo** they've just announced the arrival of the flight **2.** (*dar publicidad*) to advertise **3.** (*presagiar*) to herald **II.** *vr:* **~se** **1.** (*hacerse publicidad*) to be advertised **2.** (*el verano*) to be heralded

anuncio *m* **1.** (*de una noticia*) announcement **2.** (*publicidad: en la TV*) advertisement, commercial *Am;* (*publicidad: en un periódico*) advertisement, ad *inf;* ~ **en internet** banner; ~ **por palabras** classified advertisement

anverso *m* obverse

anzuelo *m* **1.** (*para pescar*) (fish-)hook **2.** *inf* (*aliciente*) bait, lure; **echar el** ~ to offer a bait; **echar el ~ a alguien** to lure sb; **morder** [*o* **picar en**] [*o* **tragar**] **el** ~ to take the bait

añadidura *f* addition; **por** ~ in addition

añadir *vt* **1.** (*agregar*) to add; **a esto hay que ~ que...** there's also the fact that ... **2.** (*alargar*) to lengthen; ~ **dos centímetros a las mangas** to lengthen the sleeves by two centimetres [*o* centimeters *Am*]

añagaza *f* **1.** (*para aves*) decoy **2.** (*ardid*) ruse

añares *mpl Arg* ages *pl*

añejo, -a *adj* old; (*vino*) mature

añicos *mpl* fragments *pl;* **hacer algo** ~ to smash sth up; **estoy hecho** ~ *inf* I'm shattered

añil *m* **1.** BOT indigo **2.** (*color*) indigo blue

año *m* year; ~ **bisiesto** leap year; ~ **civil** calendar year; ~ **luz** light year; ~ **natural** calendar year; ~ **nuevo** New Year; **la víspera de ~ nuevo** New Year's Eve; ~ **de servicio** year of service; **los ~s 60** the sixties; **por los ~s 60** in the sixties; **en el ~ 1960** in 1960; **el ~ de la pera** the year one; **cumplir ~s** to have a birthday; **cumplir 60 ~s** to turn sixty; **necesitar ~s** to take years; **¿cuántos ~s tienes?** how old are you?; **Juan le saca cinco ~s a Pepe** Juan is five years older than Pepe; **los ~s no pasan en balde** the years take their toll; **los ~s corren que vuelan** the years fly by ►**estar de buen** ~ (*saludable*) to look well; (*gordo*) to be plump; **un hombre entrado en ~s** an elderly man; **por él no pasan los ~s** he doesn't seem to get any older; **quitarse ~s** to be older than one admits; **a mis ~s** at my age

añoranza *f* yearning; (*morriña*) homesickness

añorar *vt* to yearn for; (*tener morriña*) to be homesick for; ~ **los viejos tiempos** to long for the old days

añoso, -a *adj* aged

aojada *f Col* (*tragaluz grande*) skylight; (*pequeña*) bull's eye

aojar *vt* (*hechizar*) to bewitch

aorta *f* aorta

aovado, -a *adj* oval

aovar *vi* to lay eggs

aovillarse *vr* to curl up

apabullante *adj* overwhelming

apabullar *vt* **1.** (*achicar*) to intimidate; (*confundir*) to confuse; (*abatir*) to crush; **me quedé apabullado cuando oí la noticia** I was devastated when I heard the news **2.** (*humillar*) to humiliate

apacentar <e→ie> *vt, vr:* **~se** to graze

apacible *adj* **1.** (*persona*) placid **2.** (*temperamento*) even **3.** (*tiempo*) mild **4.** (*viento*) gentle

apaciguar <gu→gü> **I.** *vt* **1.** (*persona*) to pacify **2.** (*calmar*) to calm down; (*dolor*) to ease **II.** *vr:* **~se** to calm down

apadrinar *vt* **1.** (*ser padrino*) ~ **a alguien** (*en un bautizo*) to be sb's godfather; (*en una boda*) to be sb's best man **2.** (*proteger*) to protect **3.** (*patrocinar*) to sponsor

apagado, -a *adj* **1.** (*volcán*) extinct **2.** (*sonido*) muffled **3.** (*persona*) lifeless **4.** (*color*) dull

apagar <g→gu> **I.** *vt* **1.** (*luz, cigarrillo, fuego*) to put out; ~ **el fuego con una manta**

to put out [*o* to extinguish] the fire with a blanket **2.** (*sed*) to quench **3.** (*hambre*) to satisfy **4.** (*protesta, disturbio*) to suppress **5.** (*televisor, radio*) to switch off **6.** (*vela*) to snuff **7.** (*color*) to tone down ►**estar apagado** (*person*) to not be in form; **¡apaga y vámonos!** that's enough! **II.** *vr:* **~se 1.** (*fuego, pipa, luz*) to go out **2.** (*sonido*) to die away **3.** (*color*) to fade

apagón *m* blackout; ELEC power cut

apaisado, -a *adj* landscape; **formato ~** landscape format

apalabrar *vt* to arrange

apalancar <c→qu> **I.** *vt* to lever up *Brit,* to jack up *Am* **II.** *vr:* **~se** *inf* to install oneself

apaleada *f Arg, Méx,* **apaleamiento** *m* **1.** (*zurra*) drubbing **2.** (*de una alfombra*) beating

apalear *vt* **1.** (*a alguien*) to thrash, to beat **2.** (*una alfombra*) to beat **3.** AGR to winnow; **~ un árbol** to shake the branches of a tree; **~ un manzano** to knock fruit from an apple tree

apalizar <z→c> *vt* to beat up; **el equipo fue apalizado** *fig* the team were thrashed

apancle *m Méx* irrigation ditch

apandorgarse *vr Perú* **1.** (*emperezarse*) to become lazy **2.** (*repantingarse*) to grow stout **3.** (*vaguear*) to be indolent

apantallado, -a *adj Méx* overwhelmed

apañado, -a *adj* **1.** (*hábil*) skilful *Brit,* skillful *Am* **2.** (*adecuado*) suitable **3.** *inf* **estás ~ si crees que te voy a ayudar** you're quite mistaken if you think I'm going to help you

apañar I. *vt* (*remendar*) to mend ►**¡ya te ~é yo!** I'll give you what for! **II.** *vr:* **~se 1.** (*darse maña*) to contrive to **2.** (*arreglárselas*) to manage; **no sé cómo te las apañas** I don't know how you manage; **¡apáñatelas como puedas!** get by as best you can!

apaño *m* **1.** (*acción de apañar*) mending **2.** (*remiendo*) patch **3.** (*chanchullo*) scam **4.** (*amorío*) affair ►**encontrar un ~** to find a solution

aparador *m* **1.** (*mueble*) sideboard **2.** (*escaparate*) shop window **3.** (*taller*) workshop

aparato *m* **1.** (*utensilio*) *t.* DEP apparatus; **~ indicador** meter; **~ de precisión** precision instrument; **~ de televisión** television set; **~ para la ventilación** ventilation system; **gimnasia de ~s** apparatus gymnastics **2.** TEL receiver; **ponerse al ~** to come to the phone; **el señor X está al ~** Mr X is on the phone **3.** (*avión*) plane **4.** (*vendaje*) bandage **5.** ANAT system; **~ digestivo** digestive system **6.** (*ostentación*) pomp **7.** POL (*de un partido*) machine

aparatoso, -a *adj* **1.** (*ostentoso*) ostentatious **2.** (*desmedido*) excessive; **un accidente ~** a spectacular accident

aparcamiento *m* **1.** (*acción*) parking **2.** (*lugar*) car park *Brit,* parking lot *Am*

aparcar <c→qu> *vt* **1.** (*coche*) to park **2.** (*decisión*) to put off

aparear I. *vt* **1.** (*animales*) to mate **2.** (*formar un par*) to pair; **~ personas** to pair people off **II.** *vr:* **~se 1.** (*animales*) to mate **2.** (*formar un par*) to form a pair

aparecer *irr como crecer* **I.** *vi* to appear; (*algo inesperado*) to turn up; **~ ante la opinión pública** to appear in public; **han aparecido casos de difteria** some cases of diphtheria have appeared **II.** *vr:* **~se** to appear

aparejado, -a *adj* (*adecuado*) suitable; **llevar** [*o* **traer**] **~** to entail

aparejador(a) *m(f)* foreman builder *m,* forewoman builder *f*

aparejo *m* **1.** (*arnés*) harness **2.** (*poleas*) block and tackle **3.** (*jarcia*) tackle **4.** (*imprimación*) sizing **5.** (*construcción*) bond **6.** *pl* (*utensilios*) equipment

aparentar *vt* to feign; **trata de ~ que es rico** he tries to make out that he's rich; **~ estar enfermo** to pretend to be ill; **no aparentas la edad que tienes** you don't look your age

aparente *adj* **1.** (*que parece y no es*) apparent **2.** (*perceptible a la vista*) visible **3.** (*de buen aspecto*) attractive

aparentemente *adv* apparently, seemingly

aparición *f* **1.** (*acción*) appearance **2.** (*visión*) apparition

apariencia *f* appearance; **en ~** apparently; **guardar las ~s** to keep up appearances ►**las ~s engañan** *prov* appearances can be deceptive

aparragarse *vr* **1.** *Chile, Hond, Méx, Par* (*achaparrarse*) to remain stunted **2.** *Chile* (*agazaparse*) to crouch

apartado *m* **1.** (*cuarto*) spare room **2.** (*párrafo*) paragraph **3.** ADMIN **~ de Correos** post office box

apartado, -a *adj* **1.** (*lugar*) isolated **2.** (*persona*) unsociable

apartamento *m* apartment, flat *Brit*

apartamiento *m* (*separación*) separation

apartar I. *vt* **1.** (*separar*) to separate **2.** (*poner a un lado*) to put aside; **~ a alguien para decirle algo** to take sb aside to tell him/her sth; **~ el plato** to push the plate aside; **¡aparta la mano del taladro!** take your hand off the drill! **3.** (*de un cargo*) to remove **4.** (*de un propósito*) to dissuade **5.** (*la vista*) to avert **6.** (*la atención*) to divert **II.** *vr:* **~se 1.** (*separarse*) to separate **2.** (*de un camino*) to turn off; **¡apártate!** get out of the way! **3.** (*del tema*) to deviate

aparte I. *adv* (*en otro sitio*) apart; **por correo ~** under separate cover; **he sumado los euros y, ~, los dólares** I've added up the euros and the dollars separately; **esta cuestión debe tratarse ~** this question must be dealt with on its own **II.** *prep* **1.** (*separado*) **él estaba ~ del grupo** he was separated from the group **2.** (*además de*) **~ de** apart from; **esta sopa ~ de mala está fría** besides tasting bad, this soup is cold as well; **~ de esto, perdí las llaves** apart from that, I lost the keys **III.** *m* (*de un escrito*) paragraph; **punto y ~** new para-

A

graph **IV.** *adj inv* **1.** (*singular*) special **2.** (*separado*) separate; **en un plato** ~ on a separate plate

apasionado, -a **I.** *adj* **1.** (*con pasión, temperamento*) passionate **2.** (*entusiasta*) enthusiastic **II.** *m, f* enthusiast

apasionante *adj* exciting

apasionar **I.** *vt* to fill with enthusiasm **II.** *vr:* **~se** **1.** (*entusiasmarse*) **~se por algo** to become enthusiastic about sth **2.** (*enamorarse*) **~se por alguien** to fall passionately in love with sb

apatía *f* apathy

apático, -a *adj* apathetic

apátrida *adj* stateless

apatusco *m Ven* **1.** (*intriga*) intrigue **2.** (*fingimiento*) pretence *Brit,* pretense *Am*

Apdo. *abr de* **Apartado de Correos** PO Box

apeadero *m* **1.** (*poyo*) mounting block **2.** FERRO halt **3.** (*en un camino*) stopping place

apear **I.** *vt inf* (*disuadir*) to dissuade **II.** *vr:* **~se** (*de un vehículo*) to get out; (*de un caballo*) to dismount

apechugar <g→gu> *vi* ~ **con** to put up with stoically; ~ **con las consecuencias** to suffer the consequences; ~ **con una tarea complicada** to take on a difficult task

apedrear **I.** *vimpers* to hail **II.** *vt* to throw stones at; (*lapidar*) to stone (to death) **III.** *vr:* **~se** (*cosecha*) to be damaged by hail

apegado, -a *adj* **estar ~ a alguien** to be attached to sb

apegarse <g→gu> *vr* to become attached

apego *m* attachment; **tener un gran ~ a algo** to be very attached to sth

apelación *f* **1.** JUR (*recurso*) appeal **2.** *fig* remedy; **esto no tiene** ~ there's nothing to be done

apelar *vi* **1.** (*invocar*) to appeal; (*referirse*) to refer **2.** (*recurrir: a alguien*) to turn; (*a algo*) to resort; ~ **a todos los medios** to try everything **3.** JUR (*recurrir*) to appeal; **la sentencia ha sido apelada** an appeal has been lodged against the judgement

apelativo *m* **1.** (*apellido*) name **2.** (*sobrenombre*) nickname; ~ **cariñoso** pet name **3.** LING common noun

apellidar **I.** *vt* to name **II.** *vr:* **~se** to be called; **se apellida Martínez** his/her surname is Martínez

apellido *m* surname; ~ **de soltera** maiden name; **primer** ~ father's surname; **por el ~ no caigo** the name doesn't mean anything to me

> Every Spaniard has two surnames (**apellidos**): the first one is the father's name and the second is the mother's. If, for example, Señora Iglesias Vieira and Señor González Blanco were to become parents, the child's surname would be González Iglesias.

apelmazar <z→c> **I.** *vt* to compress **II.** *vr:* **~se** **1.** (*colchón, cojín*) to become hard **2.** (*nieve*) to crust **3.** (*harina*) to become lumpy **4.** (*lana, pelo*) to become matted

apelotonar **I.** *vt* **1.** (*cosas*) to roll into a ball **2.** (*personas*) to crowd together **II.** *vr:* **~se** **1.** (*personas, cosas*) to mass, to crowd together; **~se en la entrada** to throng at the entrance; **en esta calle se apelotonan los coches** the traffic gets snarled up in this street **2.** (*formarse grumos*) to become lumpy

apenar **I.** *vt* to sadden **II.** *vr:* **~se** **1.** (*afligirse*) **~se por algo** to grieve over [*o* at] sth **2.** *AmC* (*sentir vergüenza*) **~se por algo** to feel embarrassed about sth

apenas **I.** *adv* **1.** (*casi no*) hardly; ~ **había nadie** there was hardly anybody [*o* anyone] there **2.** (*tan solo*) just; (*escasamente*) barely; ~ **hace un mes que estudio alemán** I've been learning German for just a month; ~ **hace una hora** barely an hour ago; **tengo ~ 10 libras en el bolsillo** I've just 10 pounds in my pocket **II.** *conj* (*tan pronto como*) as soon as; ~ **salí a la calle, se puso a llover** as soon as I went out into the street it began to rain

apéndice *m* **1.** (*de un libro*) appendix; (*tomo separado*) supplement **2.** (*complemento*) appendage **3.** ANAT appendix; ~ **vermiforme** veriform appendix

apendicitis *f inv* appendicitis

apensionarse *vr* **1.** *Arg, Chile, Méx* (*entristecerse*) to become sad **2.** *Col* (*inquietarse*) to become distressed

apercibimiento *m* **1.** (*acto*) preparation **2.** (*amonestación, advertencia*) warning

apercibir **I.** *vt* **1.** (*preparar*) to prepare **2.** (*avisar*) to warn **3.** (*amonestar*) ~ **a alguien por algo** to rebuke sb for sth **4.** JUR to warn; **lo han apercibido con el despido** they have threatened him with dismissal **II.** *vr:* **~se** **1.** (*prepararse*) **~se a** [*o* **para**] **algo** to prepare for sth **2.** (*percatarse*) **~se de algo** to notice sth; **me he apercibido de lo importante que es el examen** I've become aware of how important the examination is

aperitivo *m* **1.** (*bebida*) aperitif **2.** (*comida*) appetizer ► **¡y ésto es tan solo el ~!** and that's only the beginning!

aperos *mpl* (*utensilios*) farming equipment

apertura *f* **1.** (*reunión, teatro, cuenta, en ajedrez*) opening **2.** (*testamento*) reading; ~ **de un crédito** opening of a credit

apesadumbrar **I.** *vt* to sadden **II.** *vr* **~se por algo** to grieve over [*o* at] sth

apestar **I.** *vi* ~ **a algo** to stink of sth **II.** *vt* ~ **algo** to stink sth out **III.** *vr:* **~se** *AmL* (*contagiarse*) to become infected

apestoso, -a *adj* **1.** (*que apesta*) stinking, stinky *inf* **2.** (*fastidioso*) annoying

apetecer *irr como crecer vi* **1.** (*tener ganas de*) to feel like; **¿qué te apetece?** what would you like?; **¿un viaje? – sí, me apetece la idea** a trip? yes – the idea appeals to me; **me apetece un helado** I feel like an ice cream

2. (*gustar*) **una copa de vino siempre apetece** a glass of wine is always welcome; **este libro me apetece más** this book appeals to me more

apetecible *adj* attractive; (*objetivo*) desirable

apetencia *f* **1.** (*apetito*) appetite **2.** (*deseo*) ~ **de algo** desire for sth

apetito *m* **1.** (*de comida*) ~ **de algo** appetite for sth; **abrir el** ~ to whet one's appetite **2.** (*deseo*) ~ **de algo** desire for sth; ~ **sexual** sexual appetite

apetitoso, **-a** *adj* **1.** (*que despierta el apetito*) appetizing **2.** (*sabroso*) tasty **3.** (*deseable*) desirable

apiadar **I.** *vt* to move to pity; **su mala suerte apiada a sus vecinos** his/her misfortune moved his/her neighbours to pity **II.** *vr* **~se de** to take pity on; **¡Dios, apiádate de nosotros!** may God have mercy on us!

ápice *m* **1.** (*punta*) apex **2.** (*cúspide*) top **3.** (*nada*) iota; **no ceder un** ~ not to yield an inch; **no entender un** ~ not to understand the slightest thing

apicultor(a) *m(f)* beekeeper

apicultura *f* beekeeping, apiculture

apilar **I.** *vt* to pile up **II.** *vr:* **~se** to pile up

apiñar **I.** *vt* **1.** (*cosas*) to cram; **apiñó las cosas en el coche y partieron** he/she crammed the things into the car and they set off **2.** (*personas*) to crowd together; (*animales*) to herd together **II.** *vr:* **~se** to crowd together

apio *m* celery

apirularse *vr Chile* to dress up

apisonadora *f* steamroller

apisonar *vt* to roll flat

aplacar <c→qu> **I.** *vt* **1.** (*persona*) to calm down **2.** (*dolor*) to soothe **3.** (*hambre*) to satisfy **4.** (*sed*) to quench **II.** *vr:* **~se** to calm down

aplanamiento *m* **1.** (*allanamiento*) levelling *Brit,* leveling *Am* **2.** (*desánimo*) dejection

aplanar **I.** *vt* **1.** (*allanar*) to level **2.** (*aplastar*) to flatten **3.** (*desanimar*) to discourage **II.** *vr:* **~se** to get discouraged

aplastante *adj* overwhelming; (*derrota*) crushing; (*lógica, prueba*) devastating

aplastar *vt* **1.** (*chafar*) to flatten; **el desprendimiento de piedras aplastó a dos personas** the rockfall crushed two people **2.** (*con la mano*) to squash; ~ **un cigarrillo** to stub out a cigarette **3.** (*con el pie*) to crush **4.** (*derrotar*) to overwhelm **5.** (*persona*) to devastate

aplatanarse *vr* **1.** (*entregarse a la indolencia*) to become lethargic **2.** *Cuba, PRico* (*adoptar las costumbres*) to go native

aplaudir **I.** *vi* to applaud, to clap; **el publico rompió a** ~ the audience burst into applause **II.** *vt* **1.** (*palmear, alabar*) to applaud **2.** (*aprobar*) to approve

aplauso *m* applause; **salva de ~s** storm of applause; **digno de** ~ *fig* worthy of applause

aplazamiento *m* **1.** (*fecha, viaje, partido*) postponement; (*reunión*) postponement, adjournment **2.** (*decisión*) deferment

aplazar <z→c> *vt* **1.** (*fecha, viaje, partido*) to postpone; (*reunión*) to postpone, to adjourn (*after having begun*); ~ **el viaje una semana** to postpone the trip by one week; **la reunión se aplaza hasta nueva orden** the meeting is adjourned until further notice **2.** (*decisión*) to defer **3.** *AmL* (*suspender*) to fail

aplicación *f* **1.** (*de pintura, crema*) application **2.** (*utilización*) use; (*uso práctico*) application, use; **las múltiples aplicaciones del plástico** the various applications [*o* uses] of plastic

aplicado, **-a** *adj* (*trabajador*) hardworking

aplicar <c→qu> **I.** *vt* **1.** (*poner sobre: pintura, crema*) to apply; ~ **dando un ligero masaje** apply, massaging lightly; ~ **un lazo a un vestido** to sew a bow onto a dress; ~ **el oído a la puerta** to put one's ear to the door; **aplicado con regularidad...** applied regularly ... **2.** (*utilizar*) to use; ~ **una máquina para un trabajo** to use a machine for a job; ~ **el freno** to apply the break; ~ **un tipo de interés** to apply a rate of interest **3.** JUR ~ **una sanción** to impose; **la ley no se puede** ~ **en este caso** the law is not applicable in this case **II.** *vr:* **~se** **1.** (*esforzarse*) to apply oneself; **~se al estudio** to apply [*o* to devote] oneself to one's studies **2.** (*emplearse*) to be used

aplique *m* **1.** (*lámpara*) wall lamp, sconce **2.** TEAT prop

aplomo *m* (*seguridad*) self-confidence, composure; **perder el** ~ to lose one's composure

apocamiento *m* timidity

apocar <c→qu> **I.** *vt* to intimidate **II.** *vr:* **~se** to lose heart

apodar **I.** *vt* (*dar un sobrenombre*) to call; (*un apodo*) to nickname **II.** *vr* **~se...** (*tener el sobrenombre*) to be called ...; (*el apodo*) to be nicknamed ...

apoderado, **-a** *m, f* **1.** JUR proxy **2.** COM agent

apoderar **I.** *vt* **1.** (*en general*) to authorize **2.** JUR to grant power of attorney to **II.** *vr:* **~se** to take possession; **el espía se apoderó del maletín** the spy seized the briefcase; **~se de los clientes de la competencia** to woo customers away from competitors; **~se del liderato** to go into the lead

apodo *m* nickname

apogeo *m* **1.** ASTR apogee **2.** (*cumbre*) summit; **estar en el** ~ **de su carrera** to be at the peak of one's career; **el** ~ **del Barroco** the height of the baroque period

apolillado, **-a** *adj* **1.** (*de polilla*) moth-eaten **2.** (*anticuado*) antiquated

apolillar **I.** *vt* to eat away **II.** *vr:* **~se** to get moth-eaten

apolillo *m Arg* (*el dormir*) sleep

apolismado, **-a** *adj* **1.** *AmL* (*magullado*) damaged **2.** *Col, Méx, PRico* (*raquítico*) sickly **3.** *CRi* (*holgazán*) lazy **4.** *Méx, Ven* (*deprimido*) depressed **5.** *PRico* (*tonto*) stupid;

(*simple*) simple

apolítico, **-a** *adj* apolitical

apología *f* defence *Brit,* defense *Am*

apoltronarse *vr* **1.** (*emperezarse*) to get lazy **2.** (*repantigarse*) to lounge

apoplejía *f* stroke

apoquinar *vt inf* to fork out; **apoquina lo que me debes** pay up what you owe me

aporrear I. *vt* **1.** (*dar golpes*) to beat; ~ **el piano** to bang on the piano; ~ **la máquina de escribir** to hammer away on the typewriter; ~ **la puerta** to bang [*o* hammer] on the door **2.** (*molestar*) to bother; **esta música me aporrea los oídos** (*por estar muy alta*) this music is deafening; (*por ser mala*) this music is unbearable **II.** *vr:* ~**se** to toil

aportación *f* **1.** (*contribución*) contribution; **hacer una** ~ **a un trabajo** to make a contribution to a job **2.** (*donación*) donation **3.** ECON (*capital*) investment; ~ **dineraria** cash contribution; ~ **en especie** contribution in kind

aportar I. *vt* **1.** (*contribuir*) to contribute; **he aportado algo a la fiesta** I've made a contribution to the party; **no aporta nada ir a esa conferencia** it's not worth going to that conference **2.** (*información, evidencia, testigos, pruebas*) to provide **3.** (*traer*) to bring; ~ **al matrimonio** to bring to the marriage **II.** *vi* **1.** (*llegar a puerto*) to reach port **2.** (*recalar*) to show up; **hace tiempo que no aporta por aquí** he/she hasn't put in an appearance here for quite a while

aposentar I. *vt* to lodge, to put up **II.** *vr* ~**se en algo** to lodge [*o* put up] at sth; MIL to be billeted in sth

aposento *m* **1.** (*hospedaje*) lodging; **nos dieron** ~ they put us up **2.** (*cuarto*) room

aposición *f* apposition

apósito *m* (*vendaje*) dressing; (*adhesivo*) sticking plaster *Brit,* adhesive tape *Am*

aposta *adv* on purpose

apostar <o→ue> **I.** *vi* ~ **por algo/alguien** to back sth/sb; ~**las a** [*o* **con**] **alguien** to compete with sb **II.** *vt, vr:* ~**se 1.** (*hacer una apuesta*) to bet; **¿qué/cuánto apostamos?** what/how much shall we bet?; **¿qué te apuestas a que no lo hace?** I bet you he/she won't do it; ~ **doble contra sencillo que...** I bet you two to one that ...; **puedes** ~ **la cabeza que...** you can bet your life that ... **2.** (*poner*) to position (oneself)

apóstata *mf* apostate

apostatar *vi* to apostatize; ~ **de la fe cristiana** to break with the Christian faith

a posteriori *adv* with hindsight

apostilla *f* marginal note

apóstol *m* apostle; **Hechos de los Apóstoles** Acts of the Apostles; **ser un buen** ~ *fig* to be a good disciple

apostrofar *vt* to apostrophize

apóstrofo *m* LING apostrophe

apostura *f* good looks *pl*

apoteósico, **-a** *adj* tremendous; **éxito** ~ tremendous success

apoteosis *f inv* **1.** (*de un héroe*) apotheosis **2.** (*de un espectáculo*) climax

apoyabrazos *m inv* armrest

apoyacabezas *m inv* headrest

apoyar I. *vt* **1.** (*colocar sobre*) to rest; (*contra*) to lean **2.** (*fundar*) to base; ~ (**con pruebas**) to support **3.** (*confirmar*) to confirm **4.** (*patrocinar*) to back; (*ayudar*) to stand by; ~ **una moción/un ascenso** to support a motion/a promotion; ~ **una reforma** to back a reform **II.** *vi* ARQUIT to rest **III.** *vr:* ~**se 1.** (*descansar sobre*) to rest; ~**se en** [*o* **contra**] **algo** to lean on sth; ~**se con los brazos** to prop oneself up with one's arms; ~**se con la mano** to support oneself with one's hand **2.** (*fundarse*) to be based

apoyo *m* **1.** (*sostén, soporte*) support **2.** (*respaldo*) backing, support; (*ayuda*) help; **prestar** ~ **a un plan** to support [*o* back] a plan; **tener un** ~ **en alguien** to have sb's support [*o* backing]; **cuenta con mi** ~ you can rely on me; **en** ~ **de** in support of

apreciable *adj* **1.** (*observable*) noticeable; ~ **al oído** audible **2.** (*considerable*) considerable **3.** (*digno de estima*) worthy

apreciación *f* **1.** (*juicio*) assessment **2.** (*de una moneda*) appreciation **3.** (*de una casa*) valuation **4.** (*del tamaño*) estimation **5.** (*captación*) detection

apreciado, **-a** *adj* (*en cartas*) ~**s Sres** Dear Sirs

apreciar *vt* **1.** (*estimar*) to appreciate; **aprecio los perros** I like dogs; **si aprecias tu vida, ¡desaparece de aquí!** if you value your life, get out of here!; **aprecio la libertad** I value my liberty **2.** (*una moneda*) to appreciate **3.** (*una casa*) to value **4.** (*tamaño, distancia*) to estimate **5.** (*captar*) to detect; **de lejos no se aprecia ningún sonido** no sound can be heard from afar; **este cronómetro aprecia centésimas de un segundo** this chronometer indicates hundredths of a second; **el médico apreció una contusión en el pecho** the doctor detected bruising in the chest **6.** (*valorar*) to assess

aprecio *m* **1.** (*afecto*) affection; **te tengo un gran** ~ I'm very fond of you **2.** (*estima*) esteem; **gran** ~ high opinion; **tengo un gran** ~ **por este político** I hold this politician in high regard **3.** FIN valuation

aprehender *vt* **1.** (*coger*) to apprehend; (*botín, contrabando*) to seize **2.** (*percibir*) to perceive **3.** (*comprender*) to understand

aprehensión *f* **1.** (*acción de coger*) apprehension; (*del botín*) seizure **2.** (*percepción*) perception **3.** (*comprensión*) understanding

apremiante *adj* pressing

apremiar I. *vt* **1.** (*acuciar*) to urge (on) **2.** (*compeler*) to compel **II.** *vi* (*urgir*) to be urgent; **el tiempo apremia** time is pressing

apremio *m* **1.** (*situación apremiante*) urgent situation; **por** ~ **de tiempo** because time is short **2.** (*coacción*) compulsion **3.** JUR legal proceedings *pl*

aprender *vt* to learn; **fácil de** ~ easy to learn; ~ **a leer** to learn to read; ~ **de la historia** to learn from history; ~ **de memoria** to learn by heart; **¿dónde has aprendido estos malos modales?** where did you learn such bad manners?; **siempre se aprende algo nuevo** you live and learn

aprendiz(a) *m(f)* apprentice; **entrar de** ~ to become an apprentice; **trabajar de** ~ to work as an apprentice ►**ser** ~ **de mucho, maestro de nada** *prov* to be jack of all trades and master of none *prov*

aprendizaje *m* **1.** (*acción de aprender*) learning; ~ **en línea** internet-based learning **2.** (*formación profesional*) apprenticeship; **contrato de** ~ contract of apprenticeship; **puesto** [*o* **tiempo**] **de** ~ apprenticeship

aprensión *f* **1.** (*recelo*) apprehension; **me da** ~ **decírtelo** I daren't tell you **2.** (*asco*) disgust; **he cogido** ~ **a la leche** I've taken a strong dislike to milk; **me da** ~ **beber de este vaso** I find it disgusting to drink from this glass **3.** (*temor*) fear; (*impresión*) impression; **tener la** ~ **de que...** +*subj* (*temer*) to be afraid that ...; (*creer*) to have the impression that ... **4.** (*figuración*) imagining; **son aprensiones suyas** those are just his/her strange ideas

aprensivo, **-a** *adj* overanxious; (*hipocondríaco*) hypochondriacal

apresar *vt* **1.** (*hacer presa*) to seize **2.** (*delincuente, nave*) to capture

aprestar **I.** *vt* **1.** (*preparar*) to prepare **2.** (*telas*) to size **II.** *vr:* **~se** to prepare

apresurado, **-a** *adj* **1.** (*con prisa*) hurried; **andar con paso** ~ to walk quickly **2.** (*con excesiva prisa*) hasty

apresuramiento *m* hurry, haste

apresurar **I.** *vt* **1.** (*dar prisa*) to hurry **2.** (*acelerar*) to speed up; ~ **el paso** to quicken one's step; ~ **la salida del viaje** to depart hastily **II.** *vr:* **~se** to hurry; **¡no te apresures!** take your time!

apretado, **-a** *adj* **1.** (*oprimido*) oppressed **2.** (*tapón, tornillo*) tight; (*vestido*) close-fitting, tight; (*cinta, cuerda*) taut **3.** (*personas*) tight-fisted **4.** (*difícil*) **un caso** ~ an awkward case; **verse** [*o* **estar**] **muy** ~ to be in a very difficult situation **5.** (*apurado*) **estar** ~ **de dinero** to be short of money; **estar** ~ **de tiempo** to be short of time

apretar <e→ie> **I.** *vi* **1.** (*calor*) to become oppressive; (*dolor*) to become intense; (*lluvia*) to become heavier **2.** (*vestido*) to be too tight; **la americana me aprieta por detrás** the jacket is too tight around the back **3.** (*deudas, problemas*) ~ **a alguien** to weigh heavily on sb **4.** (*esforzarse*) **tenemos que** ~ **si queremos aprobar** we'll have to make more of an effort if we want to pass; **si aprietas un poco puedes ganar el partido** if you put more effort into it, you can win the game **5.** (*exigir*) **este profesor aprieta mucho en los exámenes** this professor demands a lot in the examinations **II.** *vt* **1.** (*hacer presión*) to press; ~ **un botón** to press a button; ~ **algo contra el pecho** to press sth against one's chest; ~ **el tubo de la pasta de dientes** to squeeze the toothpaste tube; ~ **el acelerador** to step on the accelerator; ~ **la ropa en la maleta** to pack clothes into the suitcase **2.** (*estrechar, sujetar fuertemente*) ~ **las cuerdas de la guitarra** to tighten the strings of the guitar; ~ **los dientes** to grit one's teeth; ~ **filas** to close ranks; ~ **las letras** to squeeze letters together; ~ **las manos** to clasp one's hands; ~ **el puño** to clench one's fist; ~ **un nudo/un tornillo** to tighten a knot/a screw **III.** *vr:* **~se** **1.** (*estrecharse*) to become narrower **2.** (*agolparse*) to crowd together **3.** (*ceñirse*) **~se el cinturón** to tighten one's belt

apretón *m* **1.** (*presión*) squeeze **2.** (*sprint*) sprint **3.** (*aprieto*) jam *inf* **4.** (*apretura*) crush

apretujar **I.** *vt* *inf* to squeeze **II.** *vr:* **~se** to squeeze together

apretura *f* **1.** (*de gente*) throng **2.** (*escasez*) shortage **3.** (*aprieto*) jam *inf*

aprieto *m* jam, fix; ~ **económico** financial difficulties; **estar en un** ~ to be in a jam; **poner a alguien en un** ~ **con una pregunta** to embarrass sb with a question; **sacar a alguien de un** ~ to get sb out of a fix

a priori *adv* a priori

aprisa *adv* quickly

aprisionar *vt* **1.** (*poner en prisión*) to imprison **2.** (*sujetar con cadenas*) to shackle **3.** (*atar*) to bind **4.** (*inmovilizar*) to immobilize; (*pillar*) to catch; **quedarse aprisionado en el barro** to be trapped in the mud

aprobación *f* (*de una decisión, un proyecto, una moción*) approval; (*de una ley*) passing; **murmullo de** ~ murmur of approval; **encontrar la** ~ **de alguien** to meet with sb's approval

aprobado *m* ENS pass; **he sacado un** ~ **en historia** I've passed history

aprobar <o→ue> **I.** *vt* **1.** (*decisión, propuesta, proyecto, moción*) to approve; (*ley*) to pass; ~ **las condiciones** to agree to the conditions; **la censura no aprobaba muchas películas** the board of censors didn't pass many films; **la solicitud fue aprobada** the application was approved **2.** (*examen, a un alumno*) to pass **II.** *vi* ENS to pass

aproches *mpl* *AmL* **1.** (*proximidad*) surrounding districts *pl* **2.** (*parentesco*) relation **3.** (*vía de acceso*) approaches *pl*

apronte *m* *AmL* preparation

apropiación *f* **1.** (*apoderamiento*) appropriation; ~ **indebida** misappropriation **2.** (*aplicación adecuada*) application **3.** (*adaptación*) adaptation

apropiado, **-a** *adj* **1.** (*adecuado*) ~ **a** [*o* **para**] **algo** suitable for sth **2.** (*oportuno*) appropriate; (*precio*) reasonable

apropiar I. *vt* 1. (*adaptar*) to adapt 2. *AmL* (*premio, beca*) to award; (*encargo*) to assign II. *vr* **~se de algo** to appropriate sth
aprovechable *adj* usable
aprovechado, **-a** *adj* 1. (*alumno, trabajador*) hardworking 2. (*calculador*) opportunistic
aprovechamiento *m* exploitation; **~ del tiempo libre** use of one's leisure time
aprovechar I. *vi* 1. (*valer*) to be of use 2. (*progresar*) **mi hijo no aprovecha en los estudios** my son isn't making progress in his studies ►**¡que aproveche!** enjoy your meal! II. *vt* to make good use of; (*abusar*) to exploit; **~ una idea** to exploit an idea; **~ un invento** to capitalize on an invention; **~ el máximo de algo** to get the most out of sth III. *vr:* **~se** 1. (*sacar provecho*) **~se de algo** to profit by [*o* from] sth; **ellos hacen el trabajo sucio y luego los otros se aprovechan** they do the dirty work and then others get the benefit 2. (*abusar*) to take advantage; **~se de una mujer** to take advantage of a woman 3. (*explotar*) **~se de alguien** to exploit sb
aprovisionar *vt* **~ de** [*o* **con**] **algo** to supply with sth
aproximación *f* 1. (*acercamiento*) approach 2. (*en una lotería*) consolation prize
aproximado, **-a** *adj* approximate
aproximar I. *vt* to bring nearer; **aproxima la silla a la mesa** draw your chair up to the table; **~ opiniones** to bring opinions closer together II. *vr:* **~se** to approach; **~se con la silla a la ventana** to move one's chair over to the window; **~se a los 50** to be getting on for 50; **se aproxima a la realidad** it comes close to the truth; **se aproxima agosto** August is approaching; **las tropas se aproximan** the troops are getting closer
aptitud *f* 1. (*talento*) aptitude; **~ para algo** aptitude for sth 2. (*conveniencia*) suitability; **~ para algo** fitness for sth; **~ para el servicio militar** fitness for military service; **tener ~es físicas para la natación** to have the physical requirements for swimming
apto, **-a** *adj* suitable; **~ para algo** fit for sth; **~ para el servicio militar** fit for military service; **la película no es apta para menores** the film is not suitable for minors
apuesta *f* 1. (*juego*) bet; **corredor de ~s** bookmaker 2. (*cantidad*) bid
apuesto, **-a** *adj* handsome
apuntador(a) *m(f)* TEAT prompter; **en esta película no se salva ni el ~** *fig* nobody is spared in this film
apuntalar *vt* to prop up
apuntar I. *vi* to appear; (*día*) to break; (*trigo*) to sprout; (*estación*) to come; **apunta la primavera** spring is coming; **la recuperación económica empieza a ~** economic recovery is starting II. *vt* 1. (*con un arma*) **~ a algo** to aim at sth; **¡apunten!** take aim! 2. (*con el dedo*) **~ a algo** to point at sth 3. (*anotar*) to note (down) 4. (*inscribir*) to enroll; (*en una lista*) to enter 5. (*naipes*) **~ a algo** to stake on sth 6. (*tela*) to darn 7. (*dictar*) to dictate; TEAT to prompt 8. (*insinuar*) to hint at; **~ algo y no dar** to make a promise and fail to keep it 9. (*indicar*) to point out; **~ que...** to point out that ...; **todo apunta en esta dirección** everything points in this direction III. *vr:* **~se** 1. (*inscribirse*) **~se a algo** to enrol in sth; (*en una lista*) to enter one's name in sth; **~se a un club** to join a club 2. (*el vino*) to go sour 3. (*éxito, tanto*) to score 4. (*victoria*) to achieve
apunte *m* 1. (*escrito*) note; **tomar ~s** to take notes; **¿me dejas los ~s de física?** can you lend me your physics notes? 2. (*bosquejo*) sketch 3. FIN entry
apuñalar *vt* to stab
apuradamente *adv* 1. (*exactamente*) precisely 2. (*con dificultad*) with difficulty
apurado, **-a** *adj* 1. (*falto*) **~ de dinero** hard up; **~ de tiempo** short of time 2. (*dificultoso*) difficult; **verse ~** to be in a fix 3. (*con esmero*) careful 4. *AmL* (*apresurado*) hurried; **estar ~** to be in a hurry; **hacer un trabajo a las apuradas** to do a job hurriedly
apurar I. *vt* 1. (*vaso*) to drain; (*plato*) to finish off 2. (*paciencia, reservas*) to exhaust; **~ todos los medios** to try everything 3. (*atosigar*) to harass; **¡no me apures, mi paciencia tiene un límite!** don't hassle me, my patience is limited!; **ya vendrás cuando te apure el hambre** you'll come when you're hungry 4. (*investigación*) to examine thoroughly 5. (*avergonzar*) to embarrass; **me apura decirle que no tengo dinero** I'm embarrassed to tell him/her that I don't have any money 6. *AmL* (*dar prisa*) to hurry II. *vr:* **~se** 1. (*preocuparse*) to worry; **¡no te apures por eso!** don't worry about that! 2. *AmL* (*darse prisa*) to hurry up; **¡no te apures!** there's no hurry
apuro *m* 1. (*aprieto*) fix; (*dificultad*) difficulty; **estar en un ~** to be in a fix; **sacar a alguien de un ~** to get sb out of a fix; **poner en ~** to put in an awkward position 2. (*estrechez*) financial need; **sufrir grandes ~s** to be in financial difficulties 3. (*vergüenza*) embarrassment; **me da ~ pedirle el dinero** it's embarrassing for me to ask him/her for money 4. *AmL* (*prisa*) hurry
aquejado, **-a** *adj* **~ de** afflicted by
aquejar *vt* 1. (*afligir*) to grieve 2. (*enfermedad*) to afflict; **lo aquejaba una enfermedad grave** he suffered from a serious disease
aquel *m* **tener un ~** to have a certain something
aquel, **-ella** I. *adj dem* <aquellos, -as> that, those *pl;* **aquella casa es nuestra** that house is ours; **¿qué fue del hombre ~?** what became of that man?; **¿estabais de acuerdo en ~ punto?** did you agree on that point?; **en aquellos tiempos** in those days II. *pron dem* *v.* **aquél, aquélla, aquello**

aquél, **aquélla**, **aquello** <aquéllos, -as> *pron dem* that (one), those (ones); ~ **me gusta, éste no** I like that one, not this one; **¿qué es aquello?** what's that?; **como decía** ~ as the former said; **sólo pueden participar** ~**s que sepan inglés** only those with a knowledge of English may participate; **esta teoría se diferencia de aquélla** this theory differs from that one; ~ **que colabore recibirá un premio** each person who contributes will receive a prize; **oye, ¿qué hay de aquello?** hey, how about it?

aquí *adv* **1.**(*lugar, dirección*) here; (**por**) ~ **cerca** around here; ~ **dentro** in here; **éste de** ~ this fellow here; **¡ah,** ~ **estás!** oh, there you are!; **andar de** ~ **para allá** to walk up and down; **mira** ~ **dentro** look in here; **de** ~ **hasta allí hay 10 minutos a pie** it's 10 minutes walk from here; **mejor ir por** ~ it's better to go this way **2.**(*de tiempo*) **de** ~ **en adelante** from now on; **de** ~ **a una semana** a week from now; **hasta** ~ up till now

aquietar **I.** *vt* **1.**(*apaciguar*) to calm (down) **2.**(*aliviar*) to allay **II.** *vr:* ~**se** to calm down; ~**se con una explicación** to be content with an explanation

ara¹ *f* altar ►**dar la vida en** ~**s de una idea** to sacrifice one's life for an idea; **en** ~**s de la paz** in the interests of peace; **acogerse a las** ~**s de alguien** to take refuge with sb

ara² *m AmL* parrot

árabe **I.** *adj* **1.**(*país*) Arab **2.**(*palabra*) Arabic **3.**(*península*) Arabian **4.**(*de los moros*) Moorish **II.** *mf* **1.**(*de un país árabe*) Arab **2.**(*lengua*) Arabic

Arabia *f* Arabia; ~ **Saudita** Saudi Arabia

arábigo, **-a** *adj* Arab; (*número*) Arabic

arado *m* plough *Brit*, plow *Am*

Aragón *m* Aragon

aragonés, **-esa** *adj, m, f* Aragonese

arancel *m* (*tarifa*) tariff; (*impuesto*) duty

arancelario, **-a** *adj* tariff, customs

arándano *m* bilberry, blueberry *Am*

arandela *f* TÉC washer

araña *f* **1.** ZOOL spider; **tela de** ~ spider's web, spiderweb *Am* **2.**(*candelabro*) chandelier

arañar **I.** *vt* **1.**(*rasguñar*) to scratch **2.** *inf*(*reunir*) to scrape together; **con un poco de suerte** ~**é un aprobado** with a little luck I'll scrape a pass **3.**(*tocar*) to play; ~ **la guitarra** to play the guitar **II.** *vi* to scratch **III.** *vr:* ~**se** to scratch oneself

arañazo *m* scratch; **dar un** ~ **a alguien** to scratch sb; **defenderse a** ~ **limpio** to defend oneself stubbornly

arar *vt* to plough *Brit*, to plow *Am*

arbitraje *m* **1.**(*juicio*) arbitration **2.** DEP (*en fútbol, etc*) refereeing; (*en tenis, etc*) umpiring

arbitral *adj* arbitral; **jurisdicción** ~ arbitral jurisdiction

arbitrar **I.** *vt* **1.**(*disputa*) ~ **algo** to arbitrate in sth **2.**(*medios, recursos*) to provide **3.** DEP (*en fútbol, etc*) to referee; (*en tenis, etc*) to umpire **II.** *vi* to adjudge

arbitrariedad *f* **1.**(*cualidad*) arbitrariness **2.**(*acción*) arbitrary act

arbitrario, **-a** *adj* arbitrary

arbitrio *m* **1.**(*decisión de un juez*) adjudication **2.**(*voluntad*) free will; **estar al** ~ **de alguien** to be at sb's discretion; **dejar algo al** ~ **de alguien** to leave sth to sb's discretion **3.**(*salida*) way out **4.** *pl* (*impuesto*) ~**s municipales** municipal taxes

árbitro, **-a** *m, f* **1.**(*mediador*) arbitrator **2.**(*fútbol, boxeo*) referee; (*tenis*) umpire

árbol *m* **1.** BOT tree; ~ **de Navidad** Christmas tree; ~ **de la ciencia** tree of knowledge; ~ **genealógico** family tree **2.** TÉC (*eje*) shaft **3.** NÁUT mast ►**los** ~**es no le dejan ver el bosque** he can't see the wood for the trees; **del** ~ **caído todos hacen leña** *prov* there are always those who will seek to benefit from another's misfortune

arbolado *m*, **arboleda** *f* woodland

arbóreo, **-a** *adj* **1.**(*relativo al árbol*) tree, arboreal *form;* **masa arbórea** tree population **2.**(*parecido*) tree-like

arboricultura *f* forestry

arbusto *m* shrub, bush

arca *f* chest; (*para dinero*) safe; **las** ~**s del estado** the treasury ►~ **de la alianza** REL Ark of the Covenant; ~ **de Noé** Noah's Ark; ~ **del pan** *inf* stomach, breadbasket *inf;* **ser un** ~ **cerrada** to be very reserved

arcada *f* **1.** ARQUIT arcade **2.** *pl* (*náusea*) retching

arcaico, **-a** *adj* (*anticuado*) archaic

arcángel *m* archangel

arcano *m* mystery

arcano, **-a** *adj* arcane

arce *m* maple

arcén *m* edge; (*de carretera*) hard shoulder *Brit*, shoulder *Am*

archiconocido, **-a** *adj inf* very well-known

archimillonario, **-a** *m, f* multimillionaire

archipiélago *m* archipelago; **el** ~ **canario** the Canary Islands

archisabido, **-a** *adj inf* very well-known; **esto está ya** ~ this is a well-known fact

archivador *m* **1.**(*mueble*) filing cabinet **2.**(*carpeta*) file

archivador(**a**) *m(f)* archivist

archivar *vt* (*documentos*) to file; INFOR to store; (*asunto: por un tiempo*) to put on file; (*para siempre*) to close the file on

archivero, **-a** *m, f* archivist

archivo *m* **1.**(*lugar*) archive(s); ~ **fotográfico** picture library; **constar en los** ~**s** to be on record **2.** *pl* (*documentos*) archives *pl* **3.** INFOR file

arcilla *f* clay; ~ **de alfarería** potter's clay

arcilloso, **-a** *adj* clayey

arco *m* **1.** ARQUIT arc; ~ **de medio punto** round arch **2.**(*arma*) *t.* MÚS bow **3.** *t.* MAT, ELEC arc; ~ **iris** rainbow; ~ **parlamentario** political spectrum; ~ **voltaico** arc lamp **4.** *AmL* DEP goal

arcón *m* large chest

arder *vi* **1.** (*quemar, llamear*) to burn; ~ **con fuerza** to blaze; ~ **sin llama** to smoulder; ~ **por los cuatro costados** to be ablaze; ~ **de fiebre** to have a very high temperature; ~ **de pasión** to be inflamed with passion; ~ **de rabia** to be mad with rage; **me arde la garganta** my throat is burning; **la reunión está que arde** things are getting heated at the meeting; **estoy que ardo** (*enfadado*) I'm furious **2.** + *en, fig* **ardo en deseos de conocerte** I'm dying to get to know you; **Valencia arde en fiestas** the festivities in Valencia are at their height; **el país arde en guerra** war is raging in the country

ardid *m* ruse

ardiente *adj* **1.** (*pasión, deseo, fiebre*) burning **2.** (*sed*) raging **3.** (*persona*) passionate **4.** (*color*) bright

ardilla *f* squirrel

ardor *m* **1.** (*calor*) heat; ~ **de estómago** heartburn **2.** (*fervor*) ardour *Brit*, ardor *Am*; **el ~ de su mirada** the ardour [*o* ardor *Am*] of his/her look; **en el ~ del combate** in the heat of battle

ardoroso, **-a** *adj* **1.** (*apasionado*) ardent **2.** (*caliente*) hot; (*calor*) burning

arduo, **-a** *adj* arduous

área *f t.* MAT area; **un ~ de 200 metros cuadrados** an area of 200 square metres [*o* meters *Am*]; ~ **de descanso** AUTO lay-by *Brit*, rest stop *Am*; ~ **de castigo** DEP penalty area; ~ **metropolitana** metropolitan area; ~ **de no fumar** no-smoking area

arena *f* **1.** (*materia*) sand; **~s movedizas** quicksand **2.** (*escenario*) arena ►**edificar sobre ~** to build upon sandy ground; **sembrar en ~** to labour *Brit* [*o* labor *Am*] in vain

arenal *m* sandy area

arenga *f* **1.** *inf* (*discurso*) harangue **2.** *Chile* (*disputa*) argument

arengar <g→gu> *vt* to harangue

arenoso, **-a** *adj* sandy

arenque *m* herring; **~s ahumados** kippers *pl*

arepa *f AmL: cornmeal griddlecake*

arequipa *f Col, Méx: type of milk pudding*

arete *m* earring

argamasa *f* mortar

Argel *m* Algiers

Argelia *f* Algeria

argelino, **-a** *adj, m, f* Algerian

Argentina *f* Argentina

> **Argentina** (official title: **República Argentina**) lies in the southern part of South America. It is the second largest country in South America after Brazil. The capital of Argentina is **Buenos Aires**. The official language of the country is Spanish and the monetary unit is the **peso argentino**.

argentino, **-a** *adj, m, f* Argentinian

argolla *f* **1.** (*anilla*) ring **2.** *Chile, Col, Hond, Méx* (*alianza*) wedding ring

argot <argots> *m* (*marginal*) slang; (*profesional*) jargon

argucia *f* **1.** (*argumento falso*) fallacy **2.** (*truco*) trick

argüende *m Méx* (*chisme*) gossip

argüir *irr como huir* **I.** *vt* **1.** (*alegar*) to argue **2.** (*deducir*) to deduce **3.** (*probar*) to prove **II.** *vi* to argue

argumentación *f* line of argument

argumentar *vi, vt* to argue

argumento *m* **1.** (*razón*) argument; (*razonamiento*) reasoning **2.** LIT, CINE, TEAT plot **3.** *AmL* (*discusión*) discussion; (*alegato*) argument

aria *f* aria

aridez *f* aridity

árido, **-a** *adj* (*terreno*) arid, dry; (*tema*) dry

Aries *m inv* Aries

ariete *m* MIL battering ram; DEP striker

ario, **-a** *adj, m, f* Aryan

arisco, **-a** *adj* (*persona*) surly, unfriendly; (*animal*) skittish

arista *f* edge

aristocracia *f* aristocracy

aristócrata *mf* aristocrat

aristocrático, **-a** *adj* aristocratic

aritmética *f* arithmetic

aritmético, **-a** *adj* arithmetical

arlequín *m* harlequin

arma *f* **1.** (*instrumento*) weapon, arm; **un ~ homicida** a murder weapon; ~ **blanca** knife; ~ **de fuego** firearm; ~ **reglamentaria** regulation weapon; **llegar a las ~s** to become violent; **pasar a alguien por las ~s** to shoot sb; **rendir las ~s** to surrender [*o* to lay down] one's arms; **tomar las ~s** to take up arms; **¡apunten ~s!** take aim!; **¡descansen ~s!** order arms! **2.** (*sección del ejército*) arm **3.** *pl* (*blasón*) arms *pl* ►**ser un ~ de doble filo** to be a double-edged sword; **ser de ~s tomar** to be bold

armada *f* **1.** (*fuerzas navales*) navy; **un oficial de la ~** a naval officer **2.** (*escuadra*) fleet; HIST armada

armadillo *m* armadillo

armado, **-a** *adj* armed; ~ **de algo** armed with sth

armador(a) *m(f)* shipowner

armadura *f* **1.** (*de caballero*) armour *Brit*, armor *Am*; **una ~** a suit of armour [*o* armor *Am*] **2.** (*de gafas*) frame; (*de cama*) bedstead; (*de edificio*) framework

armamento *m* (*de una persona*) arms *pl*; (*de un país*) armaments *pl*

armar **I.** *vt* **1.** (*persona, ejército*) to arm; ~ **a alguien de** [*o* **con**]**...** to arm sb with ... **2.** (*embarcación*) to fit out **3.** TÉC to assemble; (*tienda de campaña*) to pitch **4.** *inf* (*jaleo*) to stir up; (*ruido*) to raise; **~la** to start a row ►**~ a alguien caballero** to knight sb; ~ **un Cristo** *inf* to kick up a stink **II.** *vr* **~se de** [*o* **con**] **algo** to arm oneself with sth ►**~se de paciencia** to muster one's patience; **~se de valor** to pluck

up courage
armario *m* cupboard; ~ **empotrado** built-in cupboard; ~ (**ropero**) wardrobe
armatoste *m* monstrosity (*huge useless object*)
armazón *m o f* (*armadura*) frame; (*de edificio*) skeleton
Armenia *f* Armenia
armenio, **-a** *adj, m, f* Armenian
armería *f* **1.** (*tienda*) gunsmith's (shop) **2.** (*museo*) armoury *Brit,* armory *Am*
armero *m* gunsmith
armiño *m* **1.** (*animal*) stoat **2.** (*piel*) ermine
armisticio *m* armistice
armonía *f* harmony; **falta de** ~ (*entre personas*) discord; **su comportamiento no estuvo en** ~ **con la solemnidad del acto** his/her behaviour wasn't in keeping with the solemnity of the ceremony
armónica *f* harmonica, mouth organ
armónico, **-a** *adj* harmonic
armonio *m* harmonium
armonioso, **-a** *adj* harmonious
armonizar <z→c> **I.** *vi* to harmonize; ~ **con** (*colores*) to blend with; **estos dos objetos armonizan** these two objects go together **II.** *vt* to harmonize; ~ **colores** to harmonize colours; ~ **ideas** to reconcile ideas
arnés *m* **1.** (*armadura*) armour, armor *Am* **2.** *pl* (*caballería*) harness
árnica *f* arnica
aro *m* **1.** (*argolla*) ring; (*para jugar, hacer gimnasia*) hoop **2.** *Arg* (*arete*) earring **3.** *AmL* (*anillo de boda*) wedding ring ►**entrar** [*o* **pasar**] **por el** ~ to knuckle under
aroma *m* (*olor*) scent; (*de café*) aroma
aromático, **-a** *adj* aromatic
aromatizante *adj, m* aromatic
aromatizar <z→c> *vt* **1.** (*perfumar*) to scent **2.** GASTR to flavour *Brit,* to flavor *Am*
arpa *f* harp
arpía *f* harpy
arpón *m* harpoon
arquear **I.** *vt* **1.** (*doblar*) to bend; (*espalda*) to arch; **el gato arqueó su lomo** the cat arched its back **2.** (*cejas*) to raise **II.** *vr:* ~**se** (*doblarse*) to bend; (*espalda*) to arch
arqueo *m* **1.** (*de espalda*) *t.* ARQUIT arching **2.** COM cashing up **3.** NÁUT capacity
arqueología *f* archaeology, archeology *Am*
arqueológico, **-a** *adj* archaeological, archeological *Am*
arqueólogo, **-a** *m, f* archaeologist, archeologist *Am*
arquero, **-a** *m, f* **1.** archer **2.** *Arg* DEP goalkeeper
arquetípico, **-a** *adj* archetypal
arquetipo *m* archetype
arquitecto, **-a** *m, f* architect; ~ **interiorista** interior designer; ~ **técnico** quantity surveyor
arquitectónico, **-a** *adj* architectural
arquitectura *f* architecture
arrabal *m* (*periferia*) suburb; (*barrio bajo*) slum area; **vivir en los** ~**es** to live on the outskirts
arrabalero, **-a** **I.** *adj* **1.** (*de periferia*) suburban; (*de un barrio bajo*) from the slums **2.** (*grosero*) vulgar **II.** *m, f* **1.** (*de barrio bajo*) slumdweller **2.** (*grosero*) vulgar person
arracachada *f Col* silliness; **no dijeron más que** ~**s** they said nothing but nonsense
arracimarse *vr* to bunch together
arraigado, **-a** *adj* deep-rooted
arraigar <g→gu> *vi, vr:* ~**se** *t. fig* to take root
arraigo *m t. fig* rooting; **de mucho** ~ deep-rooted
arramblar *vi* ~ **con** to make off with
arrancada *f* **1.** (*salida*) (sudden) start **2.** DEP (*en halterofilia*) snatch
arrancar <c→qu> **I.** *vt* **1.** (*planta, flor*) to pull up; **el viento arrancó el árbol** the wind uprooted the tree **2.** (*pegatina, póster*) to tear off; (*página*) to tear out **3.** (*muela*) to extract, to pull (out); (*clavo*) to pull out **4.** (*quitar con violencia*) to snatch (away); **le** ~**on el arma** they wrenched the weapon from him/her; **el ladrón le arrancó el bolso de la mano** the thief snatched her handbag from her hand; **la granada le arrancó un brazo** the grenade blew off his/her arm; **la corriente arrancó el puente** the current swept away the bridge **5.** (*vehículo, motor*) to start **6.** (*conseguir: aplausos*) to draw; ~ **aplausos al público** to draw applause from the audience; ~ **una promesa a alguien** to force a promise out of sb; ~ **un secreto a alguien** to worm a secret out of sb; ~ **una victoria** to snatch (a) victory **II.** *vi* **1.** (*vehículo, motor*) to start **2.** (*iniciar: persona*) ~ **a hacer algo** to start doing sth; ~ **a correr** to start running; ~ **a cantar** to burst out singing **3.** (*provenir*) to stem; (*comenzar*) to begin; **esto arranca del siglo XV** this goes back to the 15th century
arranque *m* **1.** (*comienzo*) start; **en el** ~ **de la temporada** at the start of the season **2.** AUTO starting; ~ **automático** self-starter **3.** (*arrebato*) outburst; **un** ~ **de cólera/celos** a fit of anger/jealousy; **en un** ~ impulsively **4.** (*prontitud*) promptness; (*decisión*) initiative; **tener** ~ **para hacer algo** to have initiative to do sth **5.** ARQUIT base **6.** INFOR start-up
arras *fpl thirteen coins that the bridegroom gives the bride during the wedding*
arrasar **I.** *vt* (*destruir: edificios*) to demolish; (*región*) to devastate **II.** *vi* to triumph; POL to sweep the board **III.** *vr:* ~**se** (*ojos*) to fill with tears
arrastrado, **-a** *adj* poor, wretched; **traer una vida arrastrada** to have a wretched life
arrastrar **I.** *vt* **1.** (*tirar de*) to pull; (*algo pesado*) to drag; ~**on la caja montaña arriba** they dragged the box up the mountain; **el agua arrastra las piedras** the water sweeps the stones along; **el viento arrastra las hojas** the wind sweeps away the leaves; ~ **los pies**

(**al caminar**) to drag one's feet **2.** (*impulsar*) ~ **a alguien a hacer algo** to lead sb to do sth; **lo pude ~ al cine** I was able to drag him to the cinema; **no te dejes ~ por ese problema** don't get carried away by that problem **3.** (*producir*) to have as a consequence; **eso le arrastró dolores de cabeza** that caused him/her to have headaches **II.** *vi* (*vestido, cortinas*) to trail on the ground **III.** *vr:* **~se 1.** (*reptar*) to crawl; **~se por el suelo** to crawl along; **se arrastró hasta la habitación** he/she dragged himself/herself to the room **2.** (*humillarse*) to grovel

arrastre *m* (*de objetos, bultos*) dragging; (*en pesca*) trawling ►**estar para el ~** *inf* (*cosa*) to be ruined; (*persona*) to be a wreck

arre *interj* gee up *Brit,* giddap *Am*

arreada *f Arg, Chile, Méx* rustling

arrear I. *vt* **1.** (*ganado*) to drive **2.** *inf* (*golpe*) to give **II.** *vi inf* to hurry along; **¡arrea!** (*rápido*) get a move on!; (*atiza*) good heavens!

arrebañaduras *fpl* leftovers *pl*

arrebatado, -a *adj* **1.** (*alocado*) hasty, violent **2.** (*impetuoso*) rash **3.** (*rostro*) flushed

arrebatar I. *vt* **1.** (*arrancar*) to snatch (away); **el viento le arrebató el sombrero** the wind blew off his/her hat; **fue arrebatado por la corriente** he was swept away by the current; **~ la vida a alguien** to take sb's life; **~ la victoria a alguien** to snatch victory from sb **2.** (*extasiar*) to captivate **3.** (*conmover*) to move **II.** *vr:* **~se** (*exaltarse*) to get carried away

arrebato *m* **1.** (*arranque*) outburst; **un ~ de cólera** a fit of anger **2.** (*éxtasis*) ecstasy

arrebujar I. *vt* **1.** (*arrugar*) to crumple up **2.** (*envolver*) to wrap up **II.** *vr:* **~se** to wrap oneself up; **~se en una manta** to wrap oneself up in a blanket

arrecho, -a *adj Col, inf* **1.** (*vigoroso*) vigorous **2.** (*cachondo*) horny, randy **3.** (*enfadado*) angry

arrechucho *m inf* (*de salud*) indisposition; **le dio un ~** he/she had a bad turn

arreciar *vi* **1.** (*viento*) to get stronger; (*lluvia*) to get heavier **2.** (*críticas*) to intensify

arrecife *m* reef

arredrar I. *vt* **1.** (*hacer retroceder*) to drive back **2.** (*asustar*) to frighten **II.** *vr:* **~se 1.** (*echarse atrás*) **~se ante algo** to draw back from sth; **~se ante alguien** to shrink (away) from sb **2.** (*asustarse*) to get scared; **sin ~se** without flinching

arreglado, -a *adj* **1.** (*ordenado*) tidy; (*cuidado*) neat **2.** (*elegante*) smart **3.** (*moderado: precio*) reasonable ►**¡estamos ~s!** now we're in trouble!; **estás arreglado si crees que te ayudaré** you're very much mistaken if you think I'm going to help you; **¡vas ~ si piensas que...!** you're in for a big surprise if you think ...!

arreglar I. *vt* **1.** (*reparar*) to repair; (*ropa, zapatos*) to mend; **esta sopa te ~á el estómago** this soup will do your stomach good **2.** (*ordenar*) to tidy up; **~ la habitación** to tidy up the room; **~ la habitación para los invitados** to get the room ready for the guests; **~ una mesa con flores** to adorn a table with flowers **3.** (*preparar*) to get ready; **~ a los niños para salir** to get the children ready for going out **4.** (*pelo*) to do **5.** (*resolver: asunto*) to sort out **6.** (*acordar*) to arrange; **~ las cuentas con alguien** to get even with sb **7.** MÚS to arrange ►**¡ya te ~é yo!** *inf* I'll sort you out! **II.** *vr:* **~se 1.** (*vestirse, peinarse*) to get ready **2.** (*componérselas*) to manage; **no sé cómo te las arreglas** I don't know how you manage; **¿cómo te has arreglado para convencerlo?** how did you manage to convince him? **3.** (*ponerse de acuerdo*) to come to an agreement; (*solucionarse*) to work out; **al final todo se arregló** everything worked out all right in the end **4.** (*mejorar*) to get better; **el tiempo se está arreglando** the weather is getting better

arreglo *m* **1.** (*reparación*) repair **2.** (*solución*) solution; **no tienes ~** you're a hopeless case; **este trabajo ya no tiene ~** this job is completely botched **3.** (*acuerdo*) agreement; **llegar a un ~** to reach a settlement; **con ~ a lo convenido** as agreed; **obré con ~ a las normas** I worked in accordance with the regulations **4.** MÚS arrangement

arrellanarse *vr* to settle comfortably; **~ en algo** to settle oneself in sth

arremangar <g→gu> *vt, vr:* **~se** to roll up; **~se la camisa** to roll up one's sleeves; **arremángate** roll up your sleeves

arremeter *vi* **1.** (*criticar*) to attack; **~ contra alguien** to attack sb **2.** (*embestir*) to charge

arremetida *f* **1.** (*crítica*) attack **2.** (*embestida*) charge

arremolinarse *vr* **1.** (*hojas, polvo, agua*) to swirl around **2.** (*gente*) to mill around

arrendador(a) *m(f)* (*de casa*) landlord *m,* landlady *f;* (*de terreno, negocio*) *t.* JUR lessor

arrendamiento *m* **1.** (*alquiler*) rent; (*de terreno, negocio*) lease; **~ financiero** leasing **2.** (*contrato*) contract

arrendar <e→ie> *vt* (*propietario*) to rent, to let; (*inquilino*) to rent, to lease

arrendatario, -a *m, f* (*de una casa*) tenant; (*de un terreno, negocio*) *t.* JUR lessee, leaseholder

arreos *mpl* (*de caballerías*) harness

arrepentido, -a *adj* **1.** (*lamentándose*) sorry; REL repentant; **estar ~ de algo** to be sorry about sth, to regret sth **2.** (*delincuente*) reformed; **un terrorista ~** a reformed terrorist

arrepentimiento *m* (*lamento*) regret; REL repentance

arrepentirse *irr como sentir vr* (*lamentar*) to regret; REL to repent; **~ de algo** to regret sth; REL to repent of sth

arrestar *vt* to arrest; MIL to confine to barracks

arresto *m* **1.** (*detención*) arrest; **estar bajo ~** to be under arrest **2.** (*reclusión*) imprisonment; MIL detention; ~ **domiciliario** house arrest **3.** *pl* (*arrojo*) daring; **tener ~s** to be bold

arrevesado, **-a** *adj CSur, PRico* complicated; **un crucigrama bastante** ~ a rather difficult crossword puzzle

arria *f AmL* train of pack animals

arriar <*1. pres:* arrío> *vt* **1.** (*bandera*) to lower **2.** (*cabo, cadena*) to loosen **3.** (*inundar*) to flood

arriba *adv* **1.** (*posición*) above; (*en una casa*) upstairs; **más** ~ higher up; **te espero** ~ I'll wait for you upstairs; **lo** ~ **mencionado** the aforementioned; **la habitación de** ~ (*de encima*) the room above; **el piso de** ~ (*el último*) the top floor; **de** ~ **abajo** from top to bottom; (*persona*) from head to foot; **ensuciarse de** ~ **abajo** to get dirty from head to foot [*o* toe]; **leer un libro de** ~ **abajo** to read a book from cover to cover; **¡manos ~!** hands up! **2.** (*dirección*) up, upwards; **río** ~ upstream; **¡~!** get up! **3.** (*cantidad*) **tener de 60 años para** ~ to be over 60; **precios de 100 euros para** ~ prices from 100 euros upwards **4.** *CSur* **de** ~ (*gratis*) free (of charge); (*sin merecerlo*) for no reason

arribar *vi* **1.** NÁUT to reach port **2.** *AmL* (*llegar*) to arrive

arribista *mf* arriviste; (*en sociedad*) social climber

arriendo *m v.* **arrendamiento**

arriesgado, **-a** *adj* **1.** (*peligroso*) risky, dangerous **2.** (*atrevido*) daring

arriesgar <g→gu> **I.** *vt* **1.** (*vida, reputación*) to risk **2.** (*en el juego*) to stake **3.** (*hipótesis, afirmación*) to venture **II.** *vr:* **~se** to take a risk; **~se a hacer algo** to risk doing sth

arrimar **I.** *vt* **1.** (*acercar*) to bring closer **2.** (*apoyar*) ~ **algo a** to lean sth against **II.** *vr:* **~se** **1.** (*acercarse*) to come close(r); **~se a algo** to move closer to sth; **~se al poder** to seek the protection of the authorities **2.** (*apoyarse*) **~se a algo** to lean against sth; **el niño se arrimó a su madre** the child snuggled up to his mother

arrinconado, **-a** *adj* **1.** (*apartado*) remote **2.** (*desatendido*) neglected **3.** (*olvidado*) forgotten

arrinconar **I.** *vt* **1.** (*objeto*) to put in a corner **2.** (*enemigo*) to corner **3.** (*deshacerse de*) to get rid of **4.** (*rehuir*) to ignore **II.** *vr:* **~se** to withdraw from the world

arriscado, **-a** *adj* **1.** (*arriesgado*) risky **2.** (*escabroso*) craggy **3.** (*atrevido*) bold

arroba *f* **1.** INFOR at **2.** (*unidad de peso*) ≈ 11,502 kg

arrobar **I.** *vt* to entrance **II.** *vr:* **~se** to become entranced

arrobo *m* ecstasy; REL trance

arrocero, **-a** **I.** *adj* rice; **industria arrocera** rice industry **II.** *m, f* rice grower

arrodillarse *vr* to kneel (down)

arrogancia *f* arrogance

arrogante *adj* arrogant

arrogarse <g→gu> *vr* to assume; ~ **la facultad de juzgar a los demás** to presume to judge other people

arrojado, **-a** *adj* daring

arrojar **I.** *vt* **1.** (*lanzar*) to throw; **el caballo arrojó al jinete** the horse threw the rider **2.** (*emitir*) to emit, to give off [*o* out]; **la chimenea arroja humo** the chimney is giving off smoke; ~ **un mal olor** to give off a bad smell **3.** (*expulsar*) to throw out **4.** *AmL, inf* (*vomitar*) to throw up **5.** (*un resultado*) to produce; ~ **beneficios** to yield profits; ~ **fallos** to contain errors; **mi cuenta arroja un saldo de 800 euros** my account shows a balance of 800 euros **II.** *vr:* **~se** to throw oneself; **~se al agua** to jump into the water

arrojo *m* daring; **con** ~ boldly

arrollador(a) *adj* **1.** (*mayoría*) overwhelming; (*fuerza*) devastating **2.** (*carácter, vitalidad, optimismo*) irresistible

arrollar *vt* **1.** (*enrollar*) to roll up **2.** (*atropellar*) to run over **3.** DEP (*derrotar*) to crush **4.** (*riada, agua*) to sweep away

arropar **I.** *vt* **1.** (*abrigar*) to wrap up; (*en la cama*) to tuck in **2.** (*proteger*) to protect **II.** *vr:* **~se** (*abrigarse*) to wrap oneself up; (*en la cama*) to tuck oneself up; **¡arrópate bien!** wrap up warm!

arrorró *m AmS* lullaby

arrostrar *vt* (*consecuencias*) to face up to; (*peligro*) to face

arroyo *m* **1.** (*riachuelo*) stream **2.** (*cuneta*) gutter; **salir del** ~ to climb out of the gutter

arroz *m* rice; ~ **con leche** rice pudding

arrozal *m* ricefield

arruga *f* **1.** (*en la piel*) wrinkle **2.** (*en papel, tela*) crease; **este vestido hace ~s** this dress creases

arrugar <g→gu> **I.** *vt* **1.** (*piel*) to wrinkle **2.** (*papel, tela*) to crease **II.** *vr:* **~se** **1.** (*piel*) to wrinkle, to get wrinkled **2.** (*papel, tela*) to crease, to get creased **3.** (*achicarse*) to get scared

arruinar **I.** *vt* **1.** (*causar ruina*) to ruin **2.** (*destruir*) to destroy **3.** (*fiesta, vacaciones*) to spoil; (*plan*) to wreck **II.** *vr:* **~se** to be ruined

arrullar **I.** *vt* (*a un niño*) to lull to sleep **II.** *vi* (*paloma*) to coo **III.** *vr:* **~se** to bill and coo

arrullo *m* **1.** (*para niños*) lullaby **2.** (*de paloma*) cooing

arrumbar *vt* **1.** (*cosa*) to discard **2.** (*persona*) to ignore

arsenal *m* **1.** (*de armas, municiones*) arsenal **2.** NÁUT dockyard

arsénico *m* arsenic

arte *m o f* (*m en sing, f en pl*) **1.** (*disciplina artística*) art; ~ **culinario** culinary art; ~ **dramático** drama; ~ **narrativo** narrative art; **~s plásticas** visual arts; **~s y oficios** arts and crafts; **bellas ~s** fine arts; **el séptimo** ~ the cinema *Brit,* the movies *Am* **2.** (*habilidad*) skill; **tener mucho** ~ **para la pintura** to be a really skilled painter **3.** (*maña*) trick; **conseguir algo por malas ~s** to obtain sth by trickery; **desplegó todas sus ~s para convencerlo** she used all her wiles to convince him ►**como por ~ de** magia as if by magic; **no tener ~ ni** parte **en algo** to have nothing whatsoever to do with sth; **~s de** pesca fishing tackle

artefacto *m* (*aparato*) appliance; (*mecanismo*) device; ~ **explosivo** explosive device

artemisa *f* mugwort

arteria *f* **1.** ANAT artery **2.** (*de tráfico*) thoroughfare

arterio(e)sclerosis *f inv* arteriosclerosis

artesa *f* trough

artesanal *adj* craft; **industria ~** craft industry

artesanía *f* **1.** (*arte*) craftsmanship; **jarrón de ~** handmade vase **2.** (*obras*) handicrafts *pl*

artesano, -a *m, f* artisan, craftsman *m,* craftswoman *f*

artesonado *m* coffered ceiling

artesonado, -a *adj* coffered

ártico *m* **1.** (*océano*) Arctic Ocean **2.** (*región*) Arctic

ártico, -a *adj* Arctic

articulación *f* **1.** ANAT, TÉC joint **2.** LING articulation

articulado, -a *adj* articulated; **camión ~** articulated lorry

articular I. *vt* **1.** TÉC to join together **2.** LING to articulate **II.** *adj* articular

articulista *mf* feature writer

artículo *m* **1.** (*objeto*) article; COM commodity; **~s de consumo** consumer goods; **~s de lujo** luxury goods; **~s de primera necesidad** basic commodities; **~s de tocador** toiletries **2.** PREN, JUR, LING article **3.** (*en un diccionario*) entry

artífice *mf* **1.** (*artista*) artist **2.** *fig* architect

artificial *adj* artificial

artificio *m* **1.** (*mecanismo*) device; (*aparato*) appliance **2.** (*habilidad*) skill; (*truco*) trick; **un ~ técnico** a technical contrivance **3.** *pey* (*afectación*) affectation; **hablar con ~** to speak affectedly

artillería *f* artillery

artillero *m* gunner

artilugio *m* gadget

artimaña *f* (sly) trick

artista *mf* **1.** (*de bellas artes*) artist **2.** (*de circo, teatro*) artist(e) *m(f);* (*de cine*) actor *m,* actress *f* **3.** (*experto*) expert; **es un ~ en su especialidad** he's an expert in his field

artístico, -a *adj* artistic

artrítico, -a I. *adj* arthritic **II.** *m, f* person with arthritis

artritis *f inv* arthritis

artrosis *f inv* arthrosis

arzobispo *m* archbishop

as *m t. fig* ace; **un ~ del volante** an ace driver

asa *f* handle

asado *m* **1.** GASTR roast **2.** *Arg* (*comida*) barbecue

asador *m* **1.** (*pincho*) spit **2.** (*aparato*) spit roaster **3.** (*restaurante*) rotisserie

asadura *f* offal

asalariado, -a I. *adj* wage-earning **II.** *m, f* wage earner

asaltante *mf* attacker; (*de banco*) raider

asaltar *vt* **1.** (*fortaleza, ciudad*) to storm; (*banco*) to break into, to raid **2.** (*persona*) to attack, to assault; **~ a alguien con preguntas** to bombard sb with questions **3.** (*pensamiento*) to cross one's mind; (*duda*) to assail; **me asaltó una idea** I was struck by an idea; **me asaltó el pánico** I got into a panic

asalto *m* **1.** (*a una fortaleza, ciudad*) storming; **~ a algo** storming of sth; **tomar por** [*o* **al**] **~** to take by storm **2.** (*a un banco*) raid; **~ a un banco/a alguien** raid on a bank/of sb **3.** (*a una persona*) attack, assault **4.** DEP (*en boxeo*) round; (*en esgrima*) bout

asamblea *f* assembly; (*reunión*) meeting; **~ general** general assembly; **~ plenaria** plenary meeting; **~ de trabajadores** workers' meeting

asambleísta *mf* assemblyman *m,* assemblywoman *f*

asar I. *vt* **1.** GASTR to roast; **~ a la parrilla** to grill **2.** (*a preguntas*) to pester **II.** *vr:* **~se** to roast; **en esta casa se asa uno vivo** *inf* it's absolutely roasting in this house

asbesto *m* asbestos

ascendencia *f* **1.** (*linaje*) ancestry, descent; **de ~ escocesa** of Scottish descent **2.** (*antepasados*) ancestors *pl* **3.** (*origen*) origin

ascendente I. *adj* ascending; **en orden ~** in ascending order; **la carrera ~ de un pistón** the up-stroke of a piston **II.** *m* ascendant

ascender <e→ie> **I.** *vi* **1.** (*subir*) to rise; DEP to go up; **el equipo asciende a primera** (**división**) the team goes up to the first division **2.** (*escalar*) to climb **3.** (*de empleo*) to be promoted **4.** COM **~ a** (*cuenta*) to come to; (*cantidad*) to amount to **II.** *vt* to promote

ascendiente[1] *mf* (*antepasado*) ancestor

ascendiente[2] *m* (*influencia*) influence

ascensión *f* **1.** (*a una montaña, al trono*) ascent **2.** (*de Cristo*) Ascension

ascenso *m* **1.** (*de precio, temperatura*) rise **2.** (*a una montaña*) ascent **3.** (*de equipo, empleado*) promotion; **el ~ a primera** (**división**) the promotion to the first division

ascensor *m* lift *Brit,* elevator *Am;* **tomar el ~** to take the lift

ascético, -a *adj* ascetic

asco *m* **1.** (*sensación*) disgust, loathing; **tomar ~ a algo** to get sick of sth; **este olor me da ~** this smell makes me feel sick; **las espinacas me dan ~** I loathe spinach; **este hombre me da ~** I really detest this man; **hacer ~s a algo** to turn up one's nose at sth; **¡qué ~ de gente!** *inf* what dreadful people!; **¡qué ~!** how awful! **2.** (*situación*) **estar hecho un ~** (*lugar*) to be a mess; (*persona*) to feel low; **estar muerto de ~** to be bored stiff; **ser un ~** to be disgusting

ascua *f* ember ►**arrimar el ~ a su sardina** to feather one's nest; **estar en** [*o* **sobre**] **~s** to be on tenterhooks; **pasar algo sobre ~s** to deal with sth superficially; **tener a alguien en ~s** to keep sb on tenterhooks

aseado, -a *adj* (*limpio*) clean, tidy; (*arreglado*) smart

asear I. *vt* to clean up II. *vr:* **~se** to tidy oneself up

asechanza *f* 1. (*trampa*) trap 2. *pl* (*intrigas*) intrigues *pl*

asediar *vt* 1. MIL to besiege 2. (*importunar*) to bother

asedio *m* 1. MIL siege 2. (*fastidio*) nuisance

asegurado, -a *adj, m, f* insured

asegurador(a) *m(f)* (*persona*) insurance agent

aseguradora *f* (*empresa*) insurance company

asegurar I. *vt* 1. (*fijar*) to secure; **~ una puerta con una cadena** to secure a door with a chain 2. (*afirmar*) to affirm; **asegura no haber dicho nada** she maintains that she did not say anything 3. (*prometer*) to assure; (*garantizar*) to ensure; **se lo aseguro** I assure you; **aseguró que no lo sabía** he/she assured that he/she didn't know 4. (*mediante un seguro*) to insure II. *vr:* **~se** 1. (*comprobar*) to make sure; **~se de que funciona** to make sure that it works 2. (*hacerse un seguro*) to insure oneself

asemejarse *vr* to be alike; **~ a algo** to resemble sth, to be like sth

asentaderas *fpl inf* behind

asentado, -a *adj* 1. (*juicioso*) sensible 2. (*estable*) settled; (*empresa*) established

asentar <e→ie> I. *vt* 1. (*poner*) to place; (*campamento*) to pitch; **~ los cimientos** to lay the foundations; **la lluvia ha asentado el polvo** the rain has caused the dust to settle 2. (*sentar*) to seat; **~ en el trono** to seat on the throne 3. (*población*) to found 4. (*estómago*) to settle 5. (*golpe*) to fetch 6. (*principios*) to lay down II. *vr:* **~se** to settle

asentimiento *m* assent

asentir *irr como sentir vi* to agree; **~ a algo** to agree to sth; **~ con la cabeza** to nod in agreement

aseo *m* 1. (*acción*) cleaning; (**cuarto de**) **~** bathroom 2. (*estado*) cleanliness; **~ personal** personal hygiene 3. *pl* (*servicios públicos*) toilets *pl Brit,* restrooms *pl Am*

aséptico, -a *adj* 1. MED aseptic 2. (*desapasionado*) dispassionate; (*frío*) cold

asequible *adj* 1. (*precio*) reasonable; **esta casa no es ~ para nosotros** this house is beyond our means 2. (*objetivo*) attainable; (*plan*) feasible 3. (*persona*) approachable

aserradero *m* sawmill

aserrar <e→ie> *vt* to saw

aserto *m* assertion

asesinar *vt* to murder; (*personaje público*) to assassinate

asesinato *m* murder; (*de personaje público*) assassination; **robo con ~** robbery with murder

asesino, -a I. *adj t. fig* murderous; **ballena asesina** killer whale II. *m, f* murderer; (*de personaje público*) assassin; **~** (**a sueldo**) hit man

asesor(a) I. *adj* advisory II. *m(f)* 1. (*consejero*) adviser, consultant; **~ legal** legal adviser 2. JUR assessor

asesoramiento *f* advice

asesorar I. *vt* to advise II. *vr* **~se en algo** to take advice about sth; **~se con un médico/abogado** to take medical/legal advice

asesoría *f* 1. (*oficio*) consultancy 2. (*oficina*) consultant's office

asestar *vt* (*propinar*) to deal; **~ una puñalada a alguien** to stab sb; **~ un tiro a alguien** to fire a shot at sb

aseveración *f* assertion

aseverar *vt* (*afirmar*) to affirm; (*asegurar*) to assure; (*con energía*) to assert

asfaltado *m* 1. (*acción*) asphalting 2. (*capa*) asphalt

asfaltar *vt* to asphalt

asfalto *m* asphalt

asfixia *f* suffocation, asphyxia

asfixiante *adj* suffocating; **una atmósfera ~** a stifling atmosphere; **hace un calor ~** the heat is suffocating

asfixiar I. *vt* (*persona*) to suffocate; (*humo, gas*) to asphyxiate II. *vr:* **~se** to suffocate

así I. *adv* 1. (*de este modo*) in this way; **lo hizo ~** he/she did it like this; **~ es como lo hizo** that's how he/she did it; **yo soy ~** that's the way I am; **no puedes decir esto ~ como ~** you just can't say that; **no puedes tomar esta decisión ~ como ~** you can't take [*o* make] this decision just like that; **¡~ es!** that's right!; **¡~ es la vida!** that's life; **¿no es ~?** isn't it?; **por ~ decirlo** so to speak 2. (*ojalá*) **¡~ revientes!** I hope you die! 3. (*de extrañeza*) **¿~ que me dejas?** so you're leaving me? 4. (*de esta medida, cantidad*) **~ de grande** this big; **era ~ de feo** he was that ugly 5. *elev* (*temporal*) **~ que se fueron, lavamos los platos** as soon as they left, we washed the dishes ►**~ y todo** even so; **~ o asá** *inf* one way or another; **¿~ qué?** what now?; **~ ~** so-so II. *conj* 1. (*concesiva*) **~ se esté muriendo de frío...** even though he's/she's freezing ...; **~ lo ahorques no dará su brazo a torcer** no matter what you say to him, he won't back down 2. (*consecutiva*) **empezó a llover ~ que nos quedamos en casa** it began to rain, so we stayed indoors; **sólo hay una plaza libre, ~** (**es**) **que decídete pronto** there's only one free seat, so make up your mind; **te esperaré en la calle; ~ pues, no te retrases** I'll wait for you in the street, so don't be late 3. (*comparativa*) **~ el uno como el otro** both one and the other; **~ en la tierra como en el cielo** on earth as it is in heaven III. *adj inv* like

this, like that; **un sueldo** ~ a salary of that amount; **una cosa** ~ something like that
Asia *f* Asia; ~ **menor** Asia Minor
asiático, **-a** *adj, m, f* Asian, Asiatic
asidero *m* **1.** (*asa*) handle **2.** (*pretexto*) pretext
asiduidad *f* **1.** (*frecuencia*) frequency **2.** (*regularidad*) regularity
asiduo, **-a** *adj* **1.** (*frecuente*) frequent **2.** (*regular*) regular; **un** ~ **cliente de este local** a regular in this bar
asiento *m* **1.** (*silla*) seat; ~ **delantero** front seat; ~ **trasero** [*o* **de atrás**] rear seat; **tomar** ~ to take a seat **2.** (*sitio*) site **3.** (*de vasija, botella*) bottom **4.** (*poso*) sediment **5.** (*en una cuenta*) entry; ~ **de cierre** closing entry
asignación *f* **1.** *t.* INFOR assignment; (*de recursos*) allocation; ~ **de una tecla** assignment of a key **2.** FIN allowance
asignar *vt t.* INFOR to assign; (*recursos*) to allocate; (*subvención*) to award
asignatura *f* subject; ~ **pendiente** *subject which has to be retaken*
asilado, **-a** *m, f* POL political refugee
asilar **I.** *vt* POL to grant political asylum **II.** *vr:* **~se** to take refuge; POL to seek political asylum
asilo *m* **1.** POL asylum; **pedir/conceder** ~ to seek/to grant political asylum **2.** (*refugio*) refuge, shelter **3.** (*de ancianos*) (old people's) home **4.** (*de huérfanos*) orphanage
asimetría *f* asymmetry
asimétrico, **-a** *adj* asymmetric(al)
asimilación *f* assimilation
asimilar *vt t.* BIO to assimilate
asimismo *adv* likewise, also
asir *irr* **I.** *vt* (*sujetar*) to seize **II.** *vr* **~se a algo** to seize sth
asistencia *f* **1.** (*presencia*) attendance, presence; **sin la** ~ **del presidente** in the president's absence **2.** (*ayuda*) assistance, help; ~ **financiera** financial assistance; ~ **letrada** JUR legal aid; ~ **médica** medical care; ~ **social** social work
asistencial *adj* welfare; **servicios ~es** welfare services
asistenta *f* **1.** (*ayudante*) assistant **2.** (*para limpiar*) cleaning woman
asistente *mf* **1.** (*ayudante*) assistant **2.** (*persona presente*) **los ~s** those present ►~ social social worker
asistido, **-a** *adj* assisted; ~ **por ordenador** computer-assisted; **dirección asistida** power(-assisted) steering; **fecundación/respiración asistida** artificial insemination/respiration
asistir **I.** *vi* **1.** (*ir*) ~ **a algo** to attend sth; **no voy a** ~ I won't go **2.** (*estar presente*) to be present; **asistieron unas 50 personas** some 50 people were present **3.** (*presenciar*) ~ **a algo** to witness sth **II.** *vt* **1.** (*estar presente en*) to attend **2.** (*ayudar*) to help, assist; ~ **a un enfermo** to care for a patient
asma *m sin pl* asthma
asmático, **-a** *adj, m, f* asthmatic
asno *m* **1.** ZOOL donkey, ass **2.** *inf* (*persona*) ass
asociación *f* association; **siempre pienso en él en** ~ **con...** I always think of him in connection with ...; **Asociación Europea de Libre Cambio** European Free Trade Area; **Asociación de Padres de Alumnos** parent-teacher association; ~ **de vecinos** residents' association
asociado, **-a** **I.** *adj* associated; (*miembro*) associate **II.** *m, f* **1.** (*socio*) associate **2.** (*miembro*) member **3.** COM (*de una empresa*) partner
asociar **I.** *vt* **1.** *t.* POL to associate; **la asocio con alguien** I associate her with sb **2.** (*juntar*) to join **3.** COM to take into partnership **II.** *vr:* **~se** to associate; COM to become partners, to form a partnership; **~se con alguien** (*hacer compañía*) to join sb
asolar <o→ue> *vt* (*destruir*) to devastate
asoleada *f Col, Chile, Guat* (*insolación*) sunstroke
asomar **I.** *vt* **1.** (*mostrar*) to show **2.** (*parte del cuerpo*) to stick out; ~ **la cabeza por la ventana** to put one's head out of the window **II.** *vi* (*verse*) to show; (*aparecer*) to appear; **asoma el día** day is breaking **III.** *vr:* **~se** **1.** (*mostrarse*) to show up; **~se al balcón** to come out onto the balcony; **¡asómate!** put your head out! **2.** (*una parte del cuerpo*) to stick out **3.** (*acercarse*) to pop in; **¿por qué no te asomas un rato?** why don't you pop in for a bit?
asombrar **I.** *vt* (*pasmar*) to amaze **II.** *vr* **~se de algo** to be amazed at sth
asombro *m* amazement; **poner cara de** ~ to look amazed; **no salir de su** ~ not to get over one's amazement
asombroso, **-a** *adj* amazing
asomo *m* hint; **hay ~s de recuperación económica** there are signs of economic recovery; **no pienso en ello ni por** ~ I don't give it the slightest thought; **¿tienes miedo? – ni por** ~ are you afraid? – not in the slightest; **sin el menor** ~ **de...** without the slightest trace of ...
asonancia *f* assonance
asonante *adj* assonant
asorocharse *vr AmS* to get altitude sickness
aspa *f* **1.** (*figura*) cross; **marcar con un** ~ to mark with a cross; **en forma de** ~ cross-shaped **2.** (*de molino*) sail; (*de ventilador*) blade
aspamento *m Arg,* **aspaviento** *m* fuss; **hacer ~s** to make a fuss
aspecto *m* **1.** (*apariencia*) appearance; **tener buen/mal** ~ to look/not to look well **2.** (*punto de vista*) aspect; **bajo ese** ~ from that point of view
áspero, **-a** *adj* **1.** (*superficie*) rough **2.** (*terreno*) rugged **3.** (*sabor*) sour **4.** (*persona, voz, tono*) harsh; **tener un carácter** ~ to be bad-tempered **5.** (*clima*) tough
aspersión *f* sprinkling; **riego por** ~ watering by sprinkler

aspersor *m* sprinkler
aspiración *f* **1.** (*inspiración*) breathing in **2.** (*pretensión*) aspiration; **tener grandes aspiraciones** to have great aspirations **3.** LING aspiration
aspirador *m v.* **aspiradora**
aspiradora *f* vacuum cleaner, hoover *Brit;* **pasar la** ~ to vacuum
aspirante *mf* aspirant; (*a un empleo*) applicant; POL candidate
aspirar I. *vt* **1.** (*inspirar*) to breathe in, inhale; **salir a** ~ **aire fresco** to go out to get a breath of fresh air **2.** (*aspirador*) to suck in **3.** LING to aspirate **II.** *vi* **1.** (*inspirar*) to breathe in **2.** (*pretender*) to aspire; ~ **a mucho en la vida** to have high aims in life
aspirina® *f* aspirin®
asquear I. *vt* **1.** (*dar asco*) to disgust **2.** (*fastidiar*) to bother **II.** *vr:* ~**se** to feel disgusted
asquerosidad *f* disgusting mess; **esta casa está hecha una** ~ this house is filthy
asqueroso, -a *adj* disgusting; (*sucio*) filthy
asta *f* **1.** (*de martillo, pincel*) handle; (*de bandera*) flagpole; **a media** ~ at half mast **2.** (*cuerno*) horn
asterisco *m* asterisk
asteroide *m* asteroid
astil *m* **1.** (*mango*) handle **2.** (*de la balanza*) beam
astilla *f* **1.** (*esquirla*) splinter; **clavarse una** ~ to get a splinter **2.** *pl* (*para fuego*) firewood
astillar *vt, vr:* ~(**se**) to splinter
astillero *m* shipyard
astracán *m* astrakhan
astral *adj* astral
astringente *adj, m* astringent
astro *m t. fig* star; ~ **de la pantalla** film star
astrofísica *f* astrophysics
astrología *f* astrology
astrólogo, -a *m, f* astrologer
astronauta *mf* astronaut
astronáutica *f* astronautics
astronave *f* spaceship
astronomía *f* astronomy
astronómico, -a *adj t. fig* astronomical
astrónomo, -a *m, f* astronomer
astucia *f* **1.** (*sagacidad*) astuteness, shrewdness; **actuar con** ~ to be crafty **2.** (*ardid*) trick
asturiano, -a *adj, m, f* Asturian
Asturias *f* Asturias; **el Príncipe de** ~ the Prince of Asturias (*Spanish crown prince*)
astuto, -a *adj* astute, shrewd; (*con malicia*) crafty
asueto *m* (*descanso*) time off; (*vacaciones*) holiday; (**día de**) ~ day off; **un rato de** ~ a break
asumir *vt* **1.** (*responsabilidad*) to assume, to take on; (*cargo*) to take over; (*actitud*) to adopt; (*gastos*) to agree to pay **2.** (*suponer*) to assume; **la catástrofe está asumiendo proporciones espantosas** the catastrophe is assuming frightening proportions
asunción *f* assumption
Asunción *f* REL Assumption
asunto *m* **1.** (*cuestión*) matter; **ir al** ~ to get to the point; **el** ~ **es que...** the thing is (that) ...; **¡~ concluido!** that's the end of it!; **ocúpate de tus ~s** mind your own business **2.** (*negocio*) business; **tener ~s en el extranjero** to have business dealings abroad; **el ministro está envuelto en un** ~ **sucio** the minister is mixed up in a dubious affair **3.** LIT (*tema*) theme; (*argumento*) plot **4.** ARTE subject **5.** (*amorío*) affair **6.** POL **Ministerio de Asuntos Exteriores** Foreign Office *Brit,* State Department *Am;* **Ministro de Asuntos Exteriores** Foreign Secretary *Brit,* Secretary of State *Am*
asustadizo, -a *adj* (*persona*) jumpy; (*animal*) easily startled
asustar I. *vt* to scare, to frighten; **la responsabilidad no me asusta** I'm not afraid of the responsibility **II.** *vr:* ~**se** to be scared, to be frightened; ~**se de algo** to be frightened at sth; **no te asustes** don't be frightened
atacante *mf* **1.** (*agresor*) attacker, assailant **2.** DEP striker
atacar <c→qu> **I.** *vt* **1.** (*embestir, agredir, criticar*) to attack; ~ **por la espalda** to attack from behind **2.** (*sueño*) to overcome **3.** (*problema*) to tackle **II.** *vi t.* DEP to attack; ~ **por las bandas** to attack from the wings
attaché *m AmC, PRico* paper clip
atadijo *m,* **atado** *m* bundle
atadura *f* **1.** (*acción*) tying **2.** (*cuerda*) rope, string **3.** (*entre personas*) tie, bond **4.** (*obstáculo*) restriction
atajar I. *vi* to take a short cut; **por este camino atajamos mucho** this road cuts short our route considerably **II.** *vt* **1.** (*detener*) to stop; (*agua*) to stem **2.** (*cortar el paso*) to head off **3.** (*discurso*) to interrupt
atajo *m* short cut; **ir por un** ~ to take a short cut ►**echar por el** ~ *inf* to take the easy way out
atalaya *f* **1.** (*torre*) watchtower **2.** (*lugar elevado*) vantage point
atañer <*3. pret:* atañó> *vimpers* **eso no te atañe** that doesn't concern you; **por lo que atañe a tu empleo** as far as your job is concerned
ataque *m* **1.** (*embestida, agresión crítica*) attack; ~ **por sorpresa** surprise attack; **pasar al** ~ to go on the offensive **2.** *t.* MED attack, fit; ~ **al** [*o* **de**] **corazón** heart attack; ~ **de nervios** nervous breakdwon; ~ **de tos** fit of coughing
atar I. *vt* **1.** (*sujetar*) to tie; (*juntar*) to tie together; (*cerrar*) to tie up; (*cautivo*) to bind; ~ **a alguien las manos a la espalda** to tie sb's hands behind his/her back; ~ **al perro** to tie up the dog **2.** (*comprometer*) **esta profesión te ata mucho** this profession ties you down a lot ►**dejar algo atado y bien atado** to finish sth off completely; ~ **corto a alguien** to keep a tight rein on sb; **estar de** ~ to be raving mad

II. *vr:* ~**se** to do up; ~**se los zapatos** to lace up one's shoes

atarazana *f* dockyard

atardecer **I.** *irr como crecer vimpers* **atardece** it's getting dark **II.** *m* dusk; **al** ~ at dusk

atareado, -a *adj* busy; **andar muy** ~ to be very busy

atarear **I.** *vt* to give a job to **II.** *vr:* ~**se** to work hard

atascar <c→qu> **I.** *vt* to block **II.** *vr:* ~**se** **1.** (*cañería*) to get blocked (up); **el desagüe se ha atascado** the drain has got blocked (up) **2.** (*coche*) to get stuck **3.** (*mecanismo*) to jam **4.** (*en un discurso*) to get stuck, to dry up *inf* **5.** (*negociaciones*) to get bogged down

atasco *m* **1.** (*de una cañería*) blockage **2.** (*de un mecanismo*) blocking; ~ **de papel** INFOR paper jam **3.** (*de tráfico*) traffic jam

ataúd *m* coffin

ataviar <*1. pres:* me atavío> *vt, vr:* ~**se** to dress up

atavío *m* attire

ate *m Méx* GASTR *fruit paste*

ateísmo *m* atheism

atejonarse *vr Méx* **1.** (*agacharse*) to crouch; (*esconderse*) to hole up *inf* **2.** (*volverse astuto*) to become sharp

atemorizar <z→c> **I.** *vt* to scare, to frighten **II.** *vr* ~**se** (**de algo**) to get scared (at sth)

atemperar *vt* **1.** (*crítica*) to temper **2.** (*cólera*) to curb **3.** (*temperatura*) to moderate

Atenas *f* Athens

atenazar <z→c> *vt* **1.** (*miedo*) to grip **2.** (*duda*) to torment

atención *f* **1.** (*interés*) attention; **falta de** ~ inattentiveness; **digno de** ~ noteworthy; **¡~, por favor!** your attention please!; **estamos llamando la** ~ we're attracting attention; **los coches no me llaman la** ~ I'm not very interested in cars; **llamar la** ~ **de alguien sobre** [*o* **a**] **algo** to draw sb's attention to sth; **mantener la** ~ **de alguien** to hold sb's attention; **prestar** ~ **a algo** to pay attention to sth; (*escuchar*) to listen to sth; **absorber la** ~ **de alguien** to command sb's attention; **en** ~ **a este hecho** in view of this fact **2.** (*cuidado*) attention, care; ~ **médica** medical care **3.** (*en cartas*) **a la** ~ **de...** for the attention of ... **4.** (*cortesía*) kindness; **colmar a alguien de atenciones** to make a real fuss over [*o* of *Brit*] sb; **tener muchas atenciones con alguien** to be very nice to sb ▶<u>**llamar**</u> **la** ~ **a alguien** to rebuke sb

atender <e→ie> **I.** *vt* **1.** (*prestar atención a*) to pay attention to; (*escuchar*) to listen to **2.** (*seguir: consejo, recomendación*) to heed; (*deseo, petición*) to comply with; ~ **una solicitud** to grant a request **3.** (*cuidar*) ~ **a alguien** to care for sb **4.** (*tratar*) to treat **5.** (*despachar*) to serve; **¿lo atienden?** are you being served? **6.** (*llamada*) to answer; ~ **el teléfono** to mind the telephone **7.** (*tener en cuenta*) to take into account **II.** *vi* **1.** (*prestar atención*) to pay attention; (*escuchar*) to listen **2.** (*tener en cuenta*) ~ **a algo** to take sth into account; **atendiendo a las circunstancias actuales** bearing in mind present circumstances **3.** (*perro*) ~ **por...** to answer to the name of ...

atenerse *irr como tener vr* ~ **a** (*reglas*) to abide by; (*lo dicho*) to stand by, to keep to; ~ **a lo seguro** to play (it) safe; **me atengo a lo que dije antes** I'm sticking to what I said before; **saber a qué** ~ to know where one stands; (*en un futuro*) to know what to expect; **si no lo haces, atente a las consecuencias** if you don't do it, you'll bear the consequences

atentado *m* (*ataque*) attack, assault; (*crimen*) crime; ~ **contra alguien** assassination attempt on sb; ~ **terrorista** terrorist attack; **ser víctima de un** ~ to be the victim of an assassination attempt; **esta ley es un** ~ **contra la libertad de expresión** this law is a threat to freedom of speech

atentamente *adv* (*final de carta*) (**muy**) ~ (*si la carta empieza "Dear Sir"*) yours faithfully; (*si la carta empieza "Dear Mr X"*) yours sincerely *Brit,* sincerely yours *Am*

atentar *vi* **1.** (*cometer atentado*) ~ **contra alguien** to make an attempt on sb's life **2.** (*infringir*) ~ **contra la ley** to break the law

atento, -a *adj* **1.** (*observador*) attentive; **estar** ~ **a la conversación** to follow the conversation closely; **estar** ~ **al peligro** to be aware of the danger **2.** (*cortés*) kind; **es muy** ~ **de su parte** it's most kind of you; **estuvo muy** ~ **con nosotros** he was very considerate towards us; **es muy** ~ **con las mujeres** he's very gallant towards women

atenuación *f* **1.** attenuation; (*del dolor*) easing **2.** JUR extenuation

atenuante **I.** *adj* extenuating **II.** *f* **1.** *pl* JUR extenuating circumstances *pl* **2.** *AmL* (*perdón*) excuse

atenuar <*1. pres:* atenúo> **I.** *vt* **1.** to attenuate; (*dolor*) to ease **2.** JUR to extenuate **II.** *vr:* ~**se** **1.** to be attenuated; (*dolor*) to ease **2.** JUR to be extenuated

ateo, -a **I.** *adj* atheistic **II.** *m, f* atheist; **ser** ~ to be an atheist

aterciopelado, -a *adj* velvety

aterirse *irr como abolir vr* to become numb; **quedarse aterido** to be stiff with cold

aterrador(a) *adj* terrifying; **noticias** ~**as** terrible news

aterrar **I.** *vt* (*atemorizar*) to terrify; (*sobresaltar*) to startle **II.** *vr:* ~**se** (*sobresaltarse*) to be startled; (*tener miedo*) to be afraid

aterrizaje *f* landing; ~ **con daños** (**para el avión**) crash-landing; ~ **forzoso** forced landing; ~ **movido/suave** bumpy/soft landing

aterrizar <z→c> *vi* to land

aterrorizar <z→c> **I.** *vt* **1.** POL, MIL to terrorize **2.** (*causar terror*) to terrify; **me aterroriza volar** I'm terrified of flying **II.** *vr:* ~**se** (*tener miedo*) to be afraid; (*sobresaltarse*) to be startled

atesorar *vt* **1.**(*tesoros*) to store up; **este museo atesora pinturas de gran valor** this museum has a collection of very valuable paintings **2.** ECON to hoard **3.**(*virtudes*) to possess

atestado *m* ~ (**policial**) statement

atestar *vt* **1.** JUR to attest **2.**(*llenar*) ~ **de algo** to pack with sth; **la maleta está atestada** the suitcase is packed full; **el palacio de deportes estaba atestado de gente** the sports centre [*o* center *Am*] was crammed with people

atestiguar <gu→gü> *vt* to testify to

atiborrar **I.** *vt* to stuff **II.** *vr* ~**se de algo** to stuff oneself with sth

ático *m* attic; (*de lujo*) penthouse

atildado, **-a** *adj* elegant

atildar **I.** *vt* to tidy (up) **II.** *vr:* ~**se** to dress up

atinado, **-a** *adj* accurate

atinar **I.** *vi* **1.**(*acertar*) ~ **con algo** to hit on [*o* upon] sth; **no atiné con la respuesta** I didn't come up with the answer **2.**(*al disparar*) to hit the target **3.**(*encontrar*) ~ **con algo** to find sth **4.**(*lograr hacer*) ~ **a hacer algo** to manage to do sth **II.** *vt* to find

atípico, **-a** *adj* atypical

atisbar **I.** *vt* to spy on **II.** *vr:* ~**se** to be discerned

atisbo *m* spying; **un ~ de esperanza** a glimmer of hope; **en Marte hay ~s de vida** there are signs of life on Mars

atizar <z→c> **I.** *vt* **1.**(*fuego*) to poke **2.**(*pasión*) to rouse **3.**(*bofetada*) to give **II.** *vr* ~**se un trago** to take a drink **III.** *vi* **¡atiza!** good heavens!

atlántico, **-a** *adj* Atlantic

Atlántico *m* **el** ~ the Atlantic

atlas *m inv* atlas

atleta *mf* athlete

atlético, **-a** *adj* athletic

atletismo *m sin pl* athletics

atmósfera *f* atmosphere

atole *m AmC: drink prepared with cornmeal gruel*

atolladero *m* **1.**(*atascadero*) mire **2.**(*apuro*) jam; **estar en un** ~ to be in a fix; **sacar a alguien de un** ~ to get sb out of a jam

atollar *vi, vr:* ~**se** to get bogged down

atolón *m* atoll

atolondrado, **-a** *adj* (*insensato*) bewildered; (*tonto*) stupid

atolondramiento *m* **1.**(*de los sentidos*) bewilderment **2.**(*por una desgracia*) consternation **3.**(*irreflexión*) thoughtlessness

atolondrar **I.** *vt* to stun **II.** *vr:* ~**se** *t. fig* to be stunned

atomía *f AmL* evil act; **decir ~s** (*decir tonterías*) to talk nonsense; (*injuriar*) to mouth off *inf*

atómico, **-a** *adj* atomic; **refugio** ~ fallout shelter

atomizador *m* spray

átomo *m* atom

atónito, **-a** *adj* amazed

átono, **-a** *adj* unstressed

atontado, **-a** *adj* **1.**(*tonto*) stupid **2.**(*distraído*) inattentive

atontar **I.** *vt* **1.**(*aturdir*) to stun **2.**(*entontecer*) to bewilder **II.** *vr:* ~**se** **1.**(*aturdirse*) to be stunned **2.**(*entontecer*) to get bewildered

atorar **I.** *vt* to stop up **II.** *vr:* ~**se** **1.**(*atascarse*) to get clogged [*o* stopped] up **2.**(*al hablar*) to falter

atormentar **I.** *vt* **1.**(*torturar*) to torture **2.**(*molestar*) to harass; (*mortificar*) to torment **II.** *vr:* ~**se** to torment oneself

atornillador *m* screwdriver

atornillar *vt* (*sujetar*) to screw down; (*fijar*) to screw on; (*juntar*) to screw together; ~ **en la pared** to screw into the wall; ~ **fuertemente** to screw tight

atorozarse *vr AmC* **1.**(*atascarse*) to block up **2.**(*al hablar*) to choke up

atorrante *mf CSur, inf* tramp

atosigar <g→gu> **I.** *vt* **1.**(*apremiar*) to harass **2.**(*importunar*) to pester **II.** *vr:* ~**se** to be harassed; **no te atosigues** don't get worked up

atracadero *m* mooring

atracador(a) *m(f)* bank robber

atracar <c→qu> **I.** *vi* NÁUT to berth **II.** *vt* **1.** NÁUT to moor **2.**(*asaltar*) to hold up **3.** *inf* (*atiborrar*) ~ **de algo** to stuff with sth **III.** *vr inf* ~**se de algo** to stuff oneself with sth

atracción *f* **1.** *t.* FÍS attraction; ~ **universal** gravity **2.** *pl* (*diversiones*) entertainment; **parque de atracciones** amusement park

atraco *m* hold-up; ~ **a un banco** bank robbery; ~ **a mano armada** armed robbery

atracón *m inf* blowout; **darse un ~ de dulces** to stuff oneself with sweets; **darse un ~ de televisión** to watch too much television

atractivo *m* attraction; ~ **sexual** sex appeal

atractivo, **-a** *adj* attractive

atraer *irr como traer* **I.** *vt* (*cautivar*) to attract; (*ganarse*) to win over; ~ **a los inversores** to attract investors; ~ **a alguien a su bando** to get sb on one's side; **el cebo atrae a los peces** the bait lures the fish; **sentirse atraído hacia alguien** to feel drawn towards sb **II.** *vr* (*ganarse*) to win; ~**se las simpatías de alguien** to win sb's affections; ~**se las iras del público** to incur public anger

atragantarse *vr* **1.**(*al comer*) ~ **con algo** to choke on sth; **me he atragantado con una espina** a fish bone has got stuck in my throat; **este profesor se me ha atragantado** *fig* I can't bear this teacher **2.**(*al hablar: atascarse*) to become tongue-tied; (*trabucarse*) to get mixed up

atrancar <c→qu> **I.** *vt* (*puerta*) to bolt **II.** *vr:* ~**se** **1.**(*tubo*) to become blocked **2.**(*un coche, al hablar*) to get stuck

atrapar *vt* **1.**(*coger*) to trap; (*ladrón*) to catch; (*animal escapado*) to capture; **el portero atrapó la pelota** the goalkeeper caught the ball; ~**on al ladrón en plena faena** they caught the thief red-handed **2.** (*conseguir*) ~ **una novia** *inf* to get oneself a girlfriend; ~ **un empleo** to land a job

atrás *adv* **1.** (*hacia detrás*) back, backwards; **contar** ~ to count down; **dar un paso** ~ to take a step backwards [*o* back]; **ir marcha** ~ (**con el coche**) to reverse *Brit,* to back up *Am;* **quedar** ~ to fall behind; **volver** ~ to go back; ¡~! get back! **2.** (*detrás*) back, behind; **rueda de** ~ rear wheel; **dejar** ~ **a los perseguidores** to leave one's pursuers behind; **quedarse** ~ to remain behind; **sentarse** ~ to sit at the back **3.** (*de tiempo*) **años** ~ years ago; **la amistad venía de** ~ we/they had been friends for a long time ▸**echarse** ~ **de un acuerdo** to back out of an agreement; **volverse** ~ to back down

atrasado, -a *adj* **1.** (*en el estudio, desarrollo*) behind; (*país*) backward; **viven 20 años ~s** they're 20 years behind the times **2.** (*pago*) overdue **3.** (*tarde*) late; **llegué** ~ **a la reunión** I arrived late for the meeting; **el reloj va** ~ the watch is slow

atrasar **I.** *vt* **1.** (*aplazar*) to postpone; **la historia atrasa unos años esta batalla** history fixes the date of this battle some years earlier **2.** (*reloj*) to put back **3.** (*progreso*) to slow down **II.** *vr:* **~se** **1.** (*quedarse atrás*) to remain behind **2.** (*retrasarse*) to be late; **el tren se ha atrasado** the train is late; **~se en los plazos** to be behind in one's instalments

atraso *m* **1.** (*en una carrera*) slowness **2.** (*de un tren*) delay **3.** (*de un país*) backwardness **4.** FIN arrears *pl*

atravesar <e→ie> **I.** *vt* **1.** (*persona*) ~ **la calle/la frontera** to cross the street/the border; ~ **la sala/la ciudad** to cross the hall/the town; ~ **un río nadando** to swim across a river; **hemos atravesado Francia** (**con el coche**) we drove across France; ~ **un momento difícil** to go through a difficult time **2.** (*cuerpo*) ~ **algo con una aguja** to pierce sth with a needle; ~ **algo taladrando** to bore through sth; **la bala le atravesó el corazón** the bullet went through his/her heart; **el avión atraviesa las nubes** the plane breaks through the clouds; **la lluvia atravesó el abrigo** the rain penetrated the coat; **una cicatriz le atraviesa el pecho** a scar runs across his/her chest **3.** (*poner de través*) to lay across; ~ **un coche en medio de la calle** to park a car diagonally across the road **II.** *vr:* **~se** **1.** (*ponerse entremedio*) **no te atravieses en mi camino** don't get in my way; **se me ha atravesado una miga en la garganta** a crumb has got stuck in my throat; **cuando estoy nervioso se me atraviesan las palabras** when I'm worked up, I get tongue-tied **2.** (*en una conversación*) **~se en algo** to butt into sth **3.** (*no soportar*) **se me atraviesa ese tipo** I can't stand that fellow

atrayente *adj* attractive

atreverse *vr* (*osar, insolentarse*) to dare; ~ **a hacer algo** to dare to do sth; ~ **a afrontar un problema** to venture to tackle a problem; **¿cómo te atreves a hablarme así?** how dare you speak to me like that?; **¡no te atreverás!** you wouldn't dare!

atrevido, -a *adj* **1.** (*persona, vestido*) daring **2.** (*insolente*) insolent

atrevimiento *m* **1.** (*audacia*) boldness **2.** (*descaro*) cheek *Brit,* nerve *Am*

atribución *f* **1.** (*de un hecho*) attribution **2.** (*competencia*) authority; **atribuciones de un empleado** an employee's area of responsibility; **tiene atribuciones mías para llevar las negociaciones** I've authorized him/her to conduct the negotiations

atribuible *adj* attributable

atribuir *irr como huir* **I.** *vt* **1.** (*hechos, cualidades*) to attribute; ~ **la culpa de algo a alguien** to blame sth on sb; ~ **a alguien grandes facultades** to attribute great capabilities to sb; **atribuye el accidente a un defecto de los frenos** he/she puts the accident down to brake failure **2.** (*funciones*) to confer **II.** *vr:* **~se** **1.** (*hechos, cualidades*) to claim for oneself **2.** (*facultades*) **~se todo el poder** to assume absolute power

atribular **I.** *vt* **1.** (*apesadumbrar*) to trouble **2.** (*atormentar*) to torment **II.** *vr:* **~se** **1.** (*apenarse*) **~se con** [*o* **por**] **algo** to grieve about sth **2.** (*atormentarse*) **~se con** [*o* **por**] **algo** to be tormented by sth

atributo *m* **1.** *t.* LING attribute **2.** (*emblema*) emblem

atril *m* **1.** MÚS music stand **2.** (*de mesa*) lectern

atrincherar *vt, vr:* **~se** to entrench (oneself)

atrio *m* atrium

atrocidad *f* **1.** (*cosa atroz*) atrocity **2.** (*disparate*) foolish remark; **¡no digas ~es!** don't talk nonsense!; **este artículo está lleno de ~es** this article is full of outrageous comments **3.** (*gran cantidad*) **tener una** ~ **de dinero** to be rolling in money

atronador(a) *adj* deafening; (*aplauso*) thunderous

atropellar **I.** *vt* **1.** (*vehículo*) to run over; **por poco me atropellan** I was almost run over **2.** (*empujar*) to push past; (*derribar*) to knock down **3.** (*agraviar*) to insult **4.** (*leyes*) to violate; ~ **la lengua** to murder the language **5.** (*un trabajo*) to do hurriedly **II.** *vi* ~ **por todo** to disregard everything **III.** *vr:* **~se** to rush

atropello *m* **1.** (*colisión*) collision; (*accidente*) accident **2.** (*empujón*) push; (*derribo*) knocking down **3.** (*insulto*) insult **4.** (*injusticia*) outrage; **¡esto es un ~!** this is preposterous! **5.** (*prisa*) rushing; **tomar una decisión sin prisas ni ~s** not to rush a decision

atroz *adj* **1.** (*horroroso*) atrocious **2.** (*cruel*) cruel **3.** (*inhumano*) inhuman **4.** (*muy grande*) huge

atuendo *m* (*atavío*) outfit

atufar **I.** *vt* **1.** (*marear*) to make feel sick **2.** (*enfadar*) to annoy **II.** *vr:* **~se** **1.** (*marearse*)

to feel sick **2.** (*enfadarse*) to get annoyed
atún *m* tuna (fish)
aturdido, **-a** *adj* **1.** (*pasmado*) stunned **2.** (*irreflexivo*) thoughtless
aturdimiento *m* **1.** (*por un golpe, por una mala noticia*) daze **2.** (*irreflexión*) thoughtlessness
aturdir **I.** *vt* **1.** (*los sentidos*) to stupefy **2.** (*pasmar*) to stun **II.** *vr:* **~se** *t. fig* to be stunned
atur(r)ullar **I.** *vt* to confuse **II.** *vr:* **~se** to get flustered
atusar **I.** *vt* **1.** (*el peinado*) to smooth **2.** (*el pelo, la barba*) to trim **II.** *vr:* **~se** to do oneself up
audacia *f* boldness, audacity
audaz *adj* bold, audacious
audible *adj* audible
audición *f* **1.** (*acción, facultad*) hearing **2.** (*concierto*) concert **3.** TEAT audition; **pasar una ~** (*actor, instrumentista, cantante*) to audition
audiencia *f* **1.** TEL, RADIO, POL audience; **nivel de ~** viewing figures *pl* **2.** JUR (*sesión*) hearing; (*sala*) courtroom; (*tribunal*) court
audífono *m* **1.** (*para sordos*) hearing aid **2.** *AmL* (*auricular*) receiver
auditivo *m* TEL earpiece
auditivo, **-a** *adj* ANAT hearing
auditor(a) *m(f)* ECON, FIN auditor
auditorio *m* **1.** (*público*) audience **2.** (*sala*) auditorium
auge *m* **1.** (*cumbre*) peak; (*de una época*) heyday; **en el ~ de su belleza** at the height of her beauty **2.** (*mejora*) improvement
augurar *vt* to predict
augurio *m* prediction
aula *f* **1.** (*de escuela*) classroom **2.** (*de universidad*) lecture theatre *Brit,* lecture hall *Am;* **~ magna** main lecture theatre
aullar *irr vi* (*animal*) to howl
aullido *m* howl
aumentable *adj* **1.** (*de tamaño*) expandable **2.** (*de cantidad*) capable of being increased
aumentar **I.** *vi* **1.** (*en general*) to increase; (*temperatura, precios*) to rise, to increase; **~ de volumen** to increase in volume; **~ de velocidad** to speed up; **~ de altura** to become taller; **~ de peso** to get heavier; **los disturbios aumentan** the disturbances are spreading **2.** (*en extensión*) to extend; **~ mucho** to extend greatly **II.** *vt* **1.** to increase; (*multiplicar*) to multiply; (*precios*) to raise, to increase **2.** (*de extensión*) to extend; **~ el poder/el dominio** to extend the power/the authority **III.** *vr:* **~se** **1.** (*en cantidad*) to increase **2.** (*en extensión*) to extend
aumentativo *m* LING augmentative
aumento *m* **1.** increase; (*de la temperatura*) rise; (*de valor*) appreciation; **~ de precio** price rise **2.** (*en la extensión*) expansion
aun **I.** *adv* even; **~ así** even so; **ni ~** not even **II.** *conj* **~ cuando** even though; **~ no comprando nada, no me llega el dinero** even when I don't buy anything, I don't have enough money
aún *adv* still; **~ más** even more; **~ no** yet; **¿~ no ha llegado?** hasn't he arrived yet?
aunar *irr como aullar* **I.** *vt* **1.** (*unir*) to unite; **~ esfuerzos** to join forces **2.** (*unificar*) to unify **3.** (*armonizar*) to harmonize **II.** *vr:* **~se** to unite
aunque *conj* **1.** (*concesiva: a pesar de que, incluso si*) even though; **~ es viejo, aún puede trabajar** although he's old, he can still work; **la casa, ~ pequeña, está bien** the house is nice, even if it's small; **tengo que conseguirte ~ me cueste la vida** I must have you, even if it costs me my life; **~ parezca extraño** however strange it may seem; **tengo que regalarle ~ sea un boli** I must give him/her a present, even if it's only a biro **2.** (*adversativa*) but
aúpa *interj* up, up you get ►**de ~** *inf* tremendous
au pair *mf* au pair
aupar *irr como aullar vt* **1.** (*a un niño*) to lift up **2.** (*ayudar a subir*) to help up; **~ a alguien a la presidencia** to help sb become president
aura *f* (*atmósfera*) aura; **tiene una ~ misteriosa** he/she has a mysterious aura
áureo, **-a** *adj* golden
aureola *f* (*de alguien*) halo
auricular **I.** *adj* (*de la oreja*) aural; **testigo ~** ear-witness; **dedo ~** little finger **II.** *m* **1.** TEL receiver; **coger/colgar el ~** to pick up/put down the receiver **2.** *pl* (*de música*) headphones *pl*
aurora *f t. fig* dawn
auscultar *vt* **1.** MED **el médico lo auscultó** the doctor sounded his chest **2.** (*sondear*) to sound out
ausencia *f* **1.** (*estado de ausente*) absence **2.** (*falta*) lack; **~ de interés** lack of interest; **en ~ de algo mejor** for want of something better **3.** PSICO mental blackouts ►**en ~ del gato bailan los ratones** *prov* when the cat's away the mice will play *prov;* **hacer a alguien buenas ~s** to speak kindly of sb in his/her absence; **tener buenas ~s** to have a good reputation; **brillar por su ~** to be conspicuous by one's absence
ausentarse *vr* (*irse*) to go away; **~ de la ciudad** to leave town
ausente *adj* **1.** (*no presente*) absent; **estar ~** to be absent; **estar ~ del trabajo** to be off work **2.** (*distraído*) distracted
auspiciar *vt* **1.** (*presagiar*) to predict **2.** (*patrocinar*) to back
auspicios *mpl* **1.** (*protección*) protection **2.** (*presagio*) prediction **3.** (*patrocinio*) auspices *pl*
austeridad *f* austerity
austero, **-a** *adj* austere
austral *adj* southern
Australia *f* Australia
australiano, **-a** *adj, m, f* Australian

Austria *f* Austria

austriaco, -a, austríaco, -a *adj, m, f* Austrian

autenticar <c→qu> *vt* to authenticate

autenticidad *f* authenticity; **sobre la ~ de tus palabras tengo mis dudas** I have my doubts about the truth of your words; **no creo en la ~ de esta información** I don't believe that this information is reliable

auténtico, -a *adj* **1.** (*verdadero*) authentic; **un ~ fracaso** an absolute failure; **hacía un calor ~** it was really hot; **es un ~ maestro en su especialidad** he's an absolute expert in his field **2.** (*palabra*) credible **3.** (*información*) reliable

autista *adj* autistic

auto *m* **1.** (*resolución*) decision **2.** *pl* (*actas*) proceedings *pl* **3.** AUTO car ▶**constar en ~s** to be proven; **estar en ~s** to be in the picture; **poner en ~s** to put in the picture

autoabastecerse *vr* **~ de algo** to be self-sufficient in sth **autoadhesivo, -a** *adj* self-adhesive

autobiografía *f* autobiography **autobiográfico, -a** *adj* autobiographic(al)

autobús *m* bus

autocar <autocares> *m* coach *Brit,* bus *Am*

autocarril *m Bol, Chile, Nic* (*autovía*) dual carriageway *Brit,* divided highway *Am*

autocensura *f* self-censorship

autochoque *m* bumper car

autocine *m* drive-in cinema

autocracia *f* autocracy

autócrata *mf* autocrat

autocrático, -a *adj* autocratic

autocrítica *f* self-criticism

autóctono, -a *adj* indigenous

autodefensa *f* self-defence *Brit,* self-defense *Am* **autodeterminación** *f* self-determination **autodidacto, -a I.** *adj* self-taught **II.** *m, f* self-taught person **autodominio** *m* self-control

autoescuela *f* driving school

autoestop *m* **hacer ~** to hitch-hike

autoestopista *mf* hitch-hiker

autoevaluación *f* self-evaluation **autofinanciación** *f* self-financing **autogestión** *f* self-management **autogobierno** *m* self-government

autógrafo *m* (*firma*) autograph

autolavado *m* car wash

autómata *m* **1.** (*aparato*) automatic device **2.** (*robot*) robot **3.** *pey* (*persona*) automaton

automático *m* press stud *Brit,* snap fastener *Am*

automático, -a *adj* automatic; **dispositivo ~** automatic mechanism; **fusil ~** automatic rifle; **la puerta se cierra de modo ~** the door snaps shut; (*en un metro*) the door closes automatically; **su despido fue ~** he/she was dismissed without notice

automatización *f* automation

automatizar <z→c> *vt* to automate

automotivarse *vr* to motivate oneself

automóvil *m* car; **~ de carreras** racing car; **~ eléctrico** electrically powered car; **~ todo terreno** all-terrain vehicle; **Salón del Automóvil** motor show

automovilismo *m* DEP motoring

automovilista *mf* motorist, driver

automovilístico, -a *adj* car; **parque ~** fleet of vehicles

autonomía *f* **1.** (*de una personal*) autonomy; **~ colectiva** free collective bargaining; **~ municipal** municipal self-administration; **en esta empresa no tengo ~ para tomar decisiones** in this company I've no scope for making my own decisions **2.** (*territorio*) autonomous region

autonómico, -a *adj* autonomous; **proceso ~** process leading to autonomy; **política autonómica** regional policy; **elecciones autonómicas** regional elections

autónomo, -a *adj* **1.** POL autonomous; **la comunidad autónoma de Galicia** the autonomous region of Galicia **2.** (*trabajador*) self-employed; **trabajar de ~** to be self-employed; **¿cuánto pagas de ~s?** how much do you pay for your private health insurance?

autopista *f* motorway *Brit,* freeway *Am;* **~ de datos** INFOR data highway; **~ de la información** INFOR information highway; **~ de peaje** toll motorway *Brit,* turnpike *Am*

autopsia *f* MED autopsy

autor(a) *m(f)* **1.** LIT author; MÚS composer; **derechos de ~** royalties; **una novela de ~ desconocido** a novel by an anonymous author **2.** (*de un acto*) originator; (*de una conspiración*) conspirator; (*de un crimen*) perpetrator; (*de un atentado*) assassin **3.** (*de un invento*) inventor; (*de un descubrimiento*) discoverer

autoridad *f* **1.** (*en general*) authority; **~ del estado** state official; **~ judicial** jurisdiction; **~ de los padres** parental authority; **estar bajo la ~ de alguien** to be under sb's control; **¡aquí soy yo la ~!** I make the decisions here! **2.** *(pl)* (*policía*) authorities *pl;* **desacato a la ~** contempt (of court) **3.** (*experto*) authority

autoritario, -a *adj* authoritarian

autorización *f* authorization; (*para vender alcohol*) licence *Brit,* license *Am;* **~ de acceso** INFOR access privileges; **~ para hacer algo** authorization to do sth

autorizado, -a *adj* **1.** (*facultado*) authorized; **persona no autorizada** unauthorized person; **~ para firmar** authorized to sign; **de fuentes autorizadas** from approved sources **2.** (*oficial*) official

autorizar <z→c> *vt* **1.** (*consentir*) to approve; **mi jefe me ha autorizado para ausentarme** my boss has given me permission to be off **2.** (*facultar*) to authorize **3.** (*dar derecho*) to entitle; **que sea mi jefe no le autoriza para insultarme** even though you're my boss, it doesn't give you the right to insult me; **este hecho nos autoriza a pensar**

que... this fact gives us reason to believe that ...

autorretrato *m* self-portrait **autoservicio** *m* self-service

autostop *m* **hacer** ~ to hitch-hike

autostopista *mf* hitch-hiker

autosuficiencia *f* self-sufficiency; *pey* smugness **autosuficiente** *adj* self-sufficient; *pey* smug

autosugestión *f* autosuggestion

autovía *f* (*carretera*) dual carriageway *Brit,* divided highway *Am*

auxiliar[1] **I.** *adj* assistant; **profesor** ~ UNIV assistant professor; (*en la escuela*) supply teacher **II.** *mf* assistant; ~ **administrativo** administrative assistant; ~ **técnico sanitario** medical technician; ~ **de vuelo** flight attendant **III.** *vt* **1.** (*dar auxilio*) to help **2.** REL to give the last rites to

auxiliar[2] *m* LING auxiliary verb

auxilio *m* help; **~s espirituales** REL last rites; **primeros ~s** first aid; **pedir** ~ to ask for help; **pedir** ~ **a alguien** to ask for sb's help

avalancha *f* avalanche

avance *m* **1.** *t.* MIL advance; ~ **de los precios** price rise **2.** (*avanzo*) balance **3.** (*presupuesto*) estimate **4.** CINE, TV ~ **de algo** trailer for sth; ~ **informativo** news summary

avanzado, -a *adj* advanced

avanzar <z→c> **I.** *vi* **1.** (*seguir adelante*) *t.* MIL to advance; ~ **por una calle** to go along a street; ~ **hacia alguien** to go towards sb; **a medida que el tiempo avanzaba** as time went by **2.** (*progresar*) to progress; **no** ~ **nada** not to make any headway; **esta tendencia está avanzando** this trend is gaining ground **II.** *vt* to advance; ~ **un pie** to put a foot forward

avaricia *f* **1.** (*codicia*) greed **2.** (*tacañería*) avarice

avaricioso, -a *adj,* **avariento, -a** *adj* **1.** (*codicioso*) greedy **2.** (*tacaño*) avaricious

avaro, -a I. *adj* miserly; **ser muy** ~ **de algo** to be very mean with sth **II.** *m, f* miser

avasallar I. *vt* **1.** (*subyugar*) to subjugate **2.** (*atropellar*) to steamroller **II.** *vr:* **~se** to submit

avatares *mpl* **los ~es de la vida** life's ups and downs; **los ~es de la suerte** the vagaries of fortune

Avda. *abr de* **Avenida** Av(e).

ave *f* bird; **~s de corral** poultry; ~ **de paso** migratory bird; ~ **rapaz** [*o* **de rapiña**] bird of prey

AVE *m abr de* **Alta Velocidad Española** high-speed train

avecinarse *vr* to approach

avellana *f* hazelnut

avellano *m* hazel (tree)

avemaría *f* Hail Mary ▸**saberse algo como el** ~ to know sth inside out; **al** ~ at dusk; **en un** ~ in the twinkling of an eye

avena *f* oats *pl*

avenencia *f* **1.** (*acuerdo*) agreement **2.** (*armonía*) harmony; **en buena** ~ in harmony **3.** JUR settlement

avenida *f* **1.** (*de un río*) flood **2.** (*calle*) avenue

avenido, -a *adj* **dos personas bien avenidas** two good friends; **una pareja mal avenida** an ill-matched couple

avenir *irr como venir* **I.** *vt* to reconcile **II.** *vr:* **~se 1.** (*entenderse*) to get on **2.** (*ponerse de acuerdo*) **~se en algo** to agree on sth; **no ~se a...** not to agree to ...; **~se a dialogar** to agree to hold talks

aventajado, -a *adj* (*alumno*) outstanding; **de estatura aventajada** extremely tall

aventajar *vt* **1.** (*ser mejor*) to surpass **2.** (*en una carrera*) to overtake *Brit,* to pass *Am;* ~ **a todos** to get ahead of everyone **3.** (*anteponer*) to prefer

aventar <e→ie> **I.** *vt* **1.** (*echar aire a algo*) to fan **2.** (*dispersar el viento*) to blow away **3.** (*el grano*) to winnow **II.** *vr:* **~se 1.** *inf* (*pirárselas*) to beat it **2.** (*las velas*) to billow out

aventón *m Méx, inf* push; **dar un** ~ to give a lift; **ir de** ~ to ride free

aventura *f* **1.** (*extraordinaria*) adventure; **espíritu de** ~ spirit of adventure **2.** (*arriesgada*) venture **3.** (*amorosa*) affair

aventurado, -a *adj* risky

aventurar I. *vt* **1.** (*arriesgar*) to venture **2.** (*algo atrevido*) to dare **II.** *vr:* **~se** to dare; **perdieron dinero al ~se en el mundo editorial** they lost money when they went into publishing

aventurero, -a I. *adj* adventurous; **espíritu** ~ thirst for adventure **II.** *m, f* adventurer

avergonzado, -a *adj* (*sonrisa*) embarrassed; **sentirse** ~ to be ashamed

avergonzar *irr* **I.** *vt* to shame **II.** *vr* **~se de** [*o* **por**] **algo/alguien** to be ashamed of sth/sb

avería *f* **1.** AUTO breakdown **2.** (*de una mercadería*) damage **3.** TÉC fault **4.** NÁUT average; ~ **gruesa/simple** general/petty average

averiar <*1. pres:* averío> **I.** *vt* to damage **II.** *vr:* **~se 1.** AUTO to break down **2.** TÉC to fail **3.** NÁUT to be damaged

averiguación *f* **1.** (*haciendo pesquisas*) inquiry **2.** (*al dar con*) discovery

averiguar <gu→gü> *vt* **1.** (*inquiriendo*) to inquire into **2.** (*dar con*) to discover; **averigua a qué hora sale el tren** find out (at) what time the train leaves

averigüetas *m inv, Méx* busybody

aversión *f* aversion

avestruz *m* ostrich

avezado, -a *adj* accustomed; ~ **en los negocios** business-minded

avezar <z→c> **I.** *vt* to accustom **II.** *vr:* **~se** to get used to

aviación *f* **1.** AVIAT aviation; **compañía de** ~ airline (company) **2.** MIL air force

aviador(a) *m(f)* aviator

aviar <*1. pres:* avío> **I.** *vt* **1.** (*maleta*) to pack;

A

(*comida*) to prepare; (*mesa*) to set **2.** (*dar*) to provide; ~ **de algo** to provide with sth **3.** (*apresurar*) ~ **a alguien** to hurry sb up; **diles que vayan aviando** tell them to get a move on; **estar aviado** (*en un apuro*) to be in a tight spot **4.** *AmS* (*prestar*) to lend **II.** *vr:* ~**se** **1.** (*arreglarse*) to get ready **2.** (*espabilarse*) to get by

avícola *adj* poultry

avicultura *f* poultry farming

avidez *f* **1.** (*ansia*) eagerness; ~ **de algo** eagerness for sth **2.** (*codicia*) greed

ávido, **-a** *adj* **1.** (*ansioso*) eager; ~ **de algo** eager for sth **2.** (*codicioso*) greedy

avieso, **-a** *adj* **1.** (*objeto*) crooked **2.** (*persona*) wicked

avilés, **-esa** **I.** *adj* of/from Ávila **II.** *m, f* native/inhabitant of Ávila

avinagrarse *vr* **1.** (*vino*) to turn sour **2.** (*persona*) to become bitter

avío *m* **1.** (*apresto*) preparation **2.** (*provisión*) provision **3.** *AmS* (*de dinero, de utensilios*) loan **4.** *pl* (*utensilios*) ~**s de coser** sewing things; ~**s de escribir** stationery ►**¡al** ~**!** get on with it!

avión *m* **1.** AVIAT aeroplane *Brit,* airplane *Am;* ~ **a reación** jet (plane); **por** ~ (*correos*) by airmail; **ir en** ~ **a Mallorca** to fly to Majorca **2.** ZOOL martin

avioneta *f* light aircraft

avisado, **-a** *adj* **1.** (*prudente*) sensible **2.** (*sagaz*) informed; **mal** ~ ill-advised

avisador *m* ~ **de movimientos** movement sensor

avisar *vt* **1.** (*dar noticia*) to notify; **avísame cuando estés de vuelta** let me know when you're back; **nos avisó que venía a cenar** he/she told us that he/she was coming to dinner; **llegar sin** ~ to arrive unannounced **2.** (*poner sobre aviso*) to warn **3.** (*llamar*) to call

aviso *m* **1.** (*notificación*) notification; (*en una cartelera*) notice; (*por el altavoz*) announcement; ~ **de llegada** COM (acknowledgement of) receipt; ~ **de salida** FERRO departure announcement; ~ **de siniestro** accident report; **hasta nuevo** ~ until further notice; **sin previo** ~ without notice **2.** (*advertencia*) warning; ~ **de bomba** bomb warning; **estar sobre** ~ to be warned; **poner sobre** ~ to warn; **servir a alguien de** ~ to be a lesson to sb **3.** (*consejo*) advice **4.** (*prudencia*) prudence **5.** *AmL* (*en el periódico*) advertisement

avispa *f* wasp

avispado, **-a** *adj* sharp

avispero *m* **1.** (*nido*) wasps' nest **2.** (*avispas*) swarm of wasps ►**meterse en un** ~ to get oneself into a mess

avispón *m* hornet

avistar *vt* to sight

avituallar *vt* to supply with food

avivar *vt* (*dar viveza*) to enliven; (*fuego*) to stoke; (*pasión*) to arouse; (*color, luz*) to brighten; (*sentidos*) to sharpen; ~ **el paso** to increase one's pace

avizor *adj* **estar ojo** ~ to be alert

avizorar *vt* to spy on

axila *f* **1.** ANAT armpit **2.** BOT axillary bud

axioma *m* axiom

ay *interj* **1.** (*de dolor*) ouch **2.** (*de pena, de sorpresa*) oh **3.** (*de miedo*) oh, my God; **¡~, qué divertido!** oh, how funny! **4.** (*de amenaza*) **¡~ si vienes tarde!** you'll regret it if you come late!; ~ **del que...** +*subj* woe betide [*o* to] anyone who ...

ayer *adv* yesterday; ~ (**por la**) **noche** last night; ~ **hace una semana** a week ago yesterday; **de** ~ **acá** overnight; **¡parece que fue** ~**!** it seems like only yesterday!; **no he nacido** ~ I wasn't born yesterday

ayo, **-a** *m, f* tutor

ayuda[1] *f* **1.** (*auxilio*) help; **perro de** ~ watchdog; **eso no me sirve de ninguna** ~ that doesn't help me **2.** (*lavativa*) enema

ayuda[2] *m* helper

ayudado, **-a** *m, f Col* **1.** (*brujo*) witchdoctor; (*de tribu*) medicine man **2.** (*endemoniado*) possessed person

ayudante *mf* **1.** (*que ayuda*) helper **2.** (*cargo*) assistant; (*en una escuela*) supply teacher *Brit*

ayudar **I.** *vt* **1.** (*socorrer*) to help; ~ **a alguien en el trabajo** to help sb with his/her work; ~ **a alguien a levantarse** to help sb up; ~ **a alguien a salir del coche** to help sb to get out of the car; ~ **a pasar la calle** to help across the road; ~ **a misa** to serve at mass; **¡Dios me ayude!** God help me!; **¿le puedo** ~ **en algo?** can I help you with anything?; ~ **a conseguir un trabajo** to help to get a job **2.** (*temporalmente*) to help out **II.** *vr:* ~**se** **1.** (*mutuamente*) to help each other **2.** (*valerse de*) to help oneself

ayunar *vi* to fast

ayunas *adv* **estar en** ~ to not have eaten anything; (*ignorante*) never to understand anything

ayuno *m* fast

ayuno, **-a** *adj* **estar** ~ **de experiencia** to have no experience; **estoy** ~ **de lo que aquí se dice** I've no idea what it's all about

ayuntamiento *m* **1.** (*corporación*) district council; (*de una ciudad*) town/city council **2.** (*edificio*) town/city hall

azabache *m* jet; **ojos de** ~ jet-black eyes

azada *f* hoe

azafata *f* **1.** AVIAT air hostess; ~ **de congresos** conference hostess **2.** *Chile, Col* (*bandeja*) tray

azafrán *m* saffron

azahar *m* orange blossom

azalea *f* azalea

azar *m* **1.** (*casualidad*) chance; **juegos de** ~ games of chance; **al** ~ at random; **por** ~ by chance **2.** (*imprevisto*) misfortune; **los** ~**es de la vida** life's ups and downs

azarar **I.** *vt* to shame **II.** *vr:* ~**se** **1.** (*avergonzarse*) to be ashamed **2.** (*ruborizarse*) to blush

3. (*turbarse*) to get confused
azaroso, **-a** *adj* 1. (*proyecto*) hazardous; **una vida azarosa** an eventful life 2. (*persona*) unlucky
Azerbaiyán *m* Azerbaijan
azogue *m* mercury ▸**tener** ~ **en el cuerpo** to be fidgety; **ser uno como el** ~ to be restless; **temblar como** ~ to shake like a leaf
azor *m* goshawk
azoramiento *m* 1. (*nerviosismo*) excitement; (*ante un acto público*) stage fright 2. (*turbación*) confusion
azorar I. *vt* 1. (*poner nervioso*) to excite 2. (*turbar*) to confuse II. *vr:* **~se** 1. (*alterarse*) to get upset; (*ante un acto público*) to get stage fright 2. (*turbarse*) to get flustered
Azores *fpl* **las** ~ the Azores + *pl vb*
azoro *m* 1. *AmC* (*fantasma*) ghost 2. *AmC* (*aparición*) apparition 3. *Méx, Perú, PRico* (*azoramiento*) bewilderment
azotaina *f* spanking; **dar una** ~ to spank
azotar *vt* 1. (*con un látigo*) to whip; (*con nudos*) to scourge; (*con la mano*) to thrash, to spank; **el viento me azota (en) la cara** the wind is lashing my face 2. (*producir daños*) to devastate; **una epidemia azota la región** an epidemic is causing havoc in the region
azote *m* 1. (*látigo*) whip; (*con nudos*) scourge 2. (*golpe*) lash; (*golpe en las nalgas*) spank
azotea *f* terrace roof ▸**estar mal de la** ~ *inf* to be off one's rocker
azteca I. *adj* Aztec; **el equipo** ~ (*en fútbol*) Mexico II. *mf* Aztec

> The Indian tribe of the **aztecas** built up a vast and powerful empire between the 14th and 16th centuries in the southern and central part of Mexico, which was conquered by the Spanish in 1521. The language of the **aztecas** was **náhuatl**.

azúcar *m* sugar; ~ **de cortadillo** rock candy; ~ **en polvo** icing sugar; **tener el** ~ **muy alto** MED to have a very high blood-sugar level
azucarar I. *vt* to sugar II. *vr:* **~se** (*cristalizarse*) to crystallize
azucarero *m* (*recipiente*) sugar basin, sugar bowl *Am*
azucena *f* Madonna lily
azufrar *vt* to sulphurize, to sulfurize *Am*
azufre *m* sulphur, sulfur *Am*
azul *adj* blue; ~ **celeste** sky blue; ~ **marino** navy blue; ~ **verdoso** greenish-blue
azulado, **-a** *adj* bluish
azulejo *m* 1. (*para pared*) (glazed) tile 2. ZOOL blue wrasse 3. (*aciano*) cornflower
azulgrana *adj* blue and scarlet; **el equipo** ~ DEP Barcelona Football Club
azumbrado, **-a** *adj inf* tipsy
azuzar <z→c> *vt* to incite

B

B, **b** *f* B, b; ~ **de Barcelona** B for Benjamin *Brit*, B for Baker *Am*
baba *f* 1. (*de la boca*) spittle; **caérse a alguien la** ~ **por alguien** to dote on sb 2. (*del caracol*) slime
babasfrías *m inv, Col, inf* fool
babastibias *m inv, Ecua* fool
babear *vi* to dribble, to drool
babel *m o f* 1. (*desorden*) confusion 2. (*sitio*) bedlam
babero *m* bib
Babia *f* **estar en** ~ to be daydreaming
bable *m dialect of Asturias*
babor *m* NÁUT port; **a** ~ on the port side
babosa *f* 1. ZOOL slug 2. *AmL* (*tontería*) stupid thing
babosada *f AmC, Méx* (*bobería*) silliness
babosear *vi inf* to drool, to dribble
baboso, **-a** I. *adj* 1. (*lleno de baba*) slimy 2. (*zalamero*) fawning 3. *AmL* (*tonto*) silly II. *m, f* 1. (*joven*) brat 2. (*zalamero*) fawning individual
babucha *f* slipper
babuino *m* baboon
baca *f* (*portaequipajes*) roof rack, luggage rack
bacalao *m* 1. (*pez, pescado*) cod; (*salado*) salt cod 2. MÚS techno music ▸**cortar el** ~ to run the show
bacán I. *m AmL* (*rico*) rich guy, sugar daddy II. *adj Perú* (*estupendo*) great
bacanal *f* bacchanalia; (*orgía*) orgy
bachata *f RDom, PRico* party
bachatear *vi AmL* to go out on the town
bache *m* 1. (*en la calle*) pothole 2. AVIAT air pocket 3. (*en la producción*) slump 4. (*psíquico*) bad patch
bacheado, **-a** *adj* bumpy
bachicha *mf CSur, Perú, pey* (*italiano*) dago, wop
bachiller *mf* school-leaver; **título de** ~ ≈ secondary graduate, ≈ highschool graduate *Am*
bachillerato *m* (*título*) *certificate of secondary education;* (*estudios*) *high school education for 14–17-year-olds*
bacía *f* 1. (*recipiente*) basin 2. (*para animales*) feeding trough
bacilo *m* bacillus
backup *m* <backups> INFOR backup
bacteria *f* bacteria
bactericida I. *adj* bactericidal II. *m* bactericide
bacteriológico, **-a** *adj* bacteriological
bacteriólogo, **-a** *m, f* bacteriologist
báculo *m* 1. (*bastón*) staff 2. (*del obispo*) crosier 3. (*apoyo*) support
badajo *m* 1. (*de campana*) clapper 2. *inf* (*persona*) chatterbox
badajocense I. *adj* of/from Badajoz II. *mf* native/inhabitant of Badajoz
badana *f* sheepskin ▸**zurrar la** ~ **a alguien** to

B

tan sb's hide
badén *m* 1. (*desnivel*) dip 2. (*en carreteras*) drainage channel
badil *m* fire shovel
bádminton *m* DEP badminton
badulaquear *vi* 1. (*hacer tonterías*) to act like a fool 2. *Arg, Col, Chile, Perú* (*engañar*) to swindle
bafle *m* (loud)speaker
bagaje *m* 1. MIL baggage 2. (*saber*) ~ **cultural** cultural knowledge
bagatela *f* trifle
bagayo *m* 1. *Arg, inf* (*equipaje*) baggage 2. *Arg, inf* (*objetos robados*) stolen goods *pl* 3. *Arg, inf* (*prostituta*) whore
bagre I. *adj* 1. *Bol, Col* (*cursi*) coarse 2. *Guat, Hond, ElSal* (*inteligente*) clever II. *m* 1. *AmL* ZOOL catfish 2. *And* (*antipático*) unpleasant person 3. *And* (*mujer fea*) old bag 4. *CRi* (*prostituta*) slut
bah *interj* 1. (*incredulidad*) never 2. (*desprecio*) that's nothing 3. (*conformidad*) OK
Bahamas *fpl* **las** (**islas**) ~ the Bahamas
bahía *f* bay
bailable I. *adj* **música** ~ dance music II. *m* dance number
bailador(**a**) I. *adj* dancing II. *m(f)* dancer (of flamenco)
bailar I. *vi* 1. (*danzar*) to dance 2. (*caballo*) to prance 3. (*objetos*) to move; (*peonza*) to spin; TÉC to have play; **hacer** ~ **una peonza** to spin a top ▶ ~ **con la más fea** to get the short end of the stick; **¡que me quiten lo bailado!** *inf* nobody can take away the good times I've had!; **otro que tal** ~ he/she is just as bad II. *vt* to dance
bailarín, **-ina** I. *adj* dancing II. *m, f* dancer; (*de ballet*) ballet dancer
baile *m* 1. (*acto*) dancing 2. (*danza*) dance 3. (*fiesta*) dance party; (*de etiqueta*) ball 4. MED ~ **de San Vito** St Vitus' dance
bailongo *m inf* dance
bailotear *vi* 1. (*bailar*) to dance about 2. (*brincar*) to leap about
baja *f* 1. (*disminución*) decrease; (*de precio, de temperatura*) drop 2. (*cese de trabajo*) vacancy; ~ **por maternidad** maternity leave; **darse de** ~ (*temporalmente*) to take time off; (*por enfermedad*) to be on sick leave; (*definitivamente*) to give up one's job; **estar de** ~ (**por enfermedad**) to be off sick 3. (*en una asociación*) resignation; **dar de** ~ **a alguien** to expel sb 4. (*documento*) discharge certificate; (*del médico*) sick note 5. MIL casualty 6. FIN slump
bajada *f* 1. (*descenso*) descent; ~ **de tipos de interés** ECON fall in interest rates; ~ **de bandera** minimum fare 2. (*camino*) way down 3. (*pendiente*) slope
bajamar *f* low tide
bajar I. *vi* 1. (*ir hacia abajo*) to go down; (*venir hacia abajo*) to come down; ~ **en ascensor** to go/come down in the lift; ~ **las escaleras** to go/come down the stairs 2. (*apearse*) ~ **de** (*de un caballo*) to dismount, to get down from; (*de un coche*) to get out of 3. (*las aguas*) to fall 4. (*disminuir*) to decrease; (*temperatura*) to drop; (*hinchazón*) to go down 5. (*adelgazar*) to lose weight II. *vt* 1. (*transportar*) to bring down; (*coger*) to take down; ~ **las persianas** to lower the blinds 2. (*precios*) to lower 3. (*voz*) to lower; (*radio*) to turn down 4. (*ojos*) to drop 5. INFOR to download 6. *Cuba, inf* (*pagar*) pay III. *vr:* ~**se** 1. (*descender*) ~**se de** (*de un caballo*) to dismount; (*de un coche*) to get out of 2. (*inclinarse*) to bend down 3. (*humillarse*) to lower oneself
bajativo *m AmL* digestive
bajeza *f* 1. (*acción humillante*) mean act; (*acción vil*) vile act 2. (*carácter*) baseness 3. (*humildad*) lowliness
bajío *m* 1. (*banco de arena*) sandbank 2. *AmL* (*terreno bajo*) lowland
bajista I. *adj* FIN bearish; **tendencia** ~ bearish tendency II. *mf* 1. MÚS bass player 2. FIN bear
bajo I. *m* 1. (*instrumento*) bass 2. (*persona*) bass player 3. *pl* (*piso*) ground floor *Brit,* first floor *Am* 4. *pl* (*banco de arena*) sandbank 5. *pl* (*parte inferior*) underneath; (*de una prenda*) hemline II. *adv* 1. (*posición*) below 2. (*voz*) quietly III. *prep* 1. (*colocar debajo*) below 2. (*por debajo de*) underneath; ~ **llave** under lock and key; ~ **la lluvia** in the rain; ~ **fianza** on bail; ~ **la condición de que** +*subj* on condition that
bajo, **-a** <más bajo *o* inferior, bajísimo> *adj* 1. *estar* (*en lugar inferior*) low 2. *ser* (*de temperatura*) low; (*de estatura*) short; **baja tensión** ELEC low tension; **con la cabeza baja/los ojos** ~**s** with head/eyes lowered; **tener la moral baja** to be in poor spirits 3. (*voz*) low; (*sonido*) soft 4. (*color*) pale 5. (*metal*) base 6. (*comportamiento*) mean 7. (*clase social*) humble 8. (*calidad*) poor
bajón *m* 1. (*descenso*) decline; (*de precios*) drop; FIN slump 2. (*de la salud*) worsening 3. MÚS bassoon
bakalao *m* MÚS techno music
bala *f* 1. (*proyectil*) bullet; ~ **de fogueo** blank cartridge; **como una** ~ like a flash 2. (*fardo*) bale
balacear *vt AmL* (*herir o matar*) to shoot; (*disparar contra*) to shoot at
balada *f* ballad
baladí *adj* <baladíes> trivial, worthless
baladronada *f* boast
balalaica *f* MÚS balalaika
balance *m* 1. (*vaivén*) oscillation; (*en la danza*) rocking; NÁUT rolling 2. COM (*resultado*) balance; **hacer un** ~ to draw up a balance 3. (*comparación*) comparison; **hacer** (**el**) ~ to take stock of the situation 4. (*vacilación*) hesitation
balancear I. *vt* 1. (*mecer*) to sway; (*acunar*) to rock 2. (*equilibrar*) to balance II. *vr:* ~**se** 1. (*columpiarse*) to swing 2. NÁUT to roll
balanceo *m* 1. (*vaivén*) swaying; NÁUT rocking

2. (*vacilación*) hesitation

balancín *m* 1. (*de los equilibristas*) balancing pole 2. (*columpio*) seesaw, teeter-totter *Am* 3. (*silla*) rocking chair; (*en el jardín*) swing hammock 4. (*yugo*) yoke

balandra *f* sloop

balandrista *m* yachtsman *m,* yachtswoman *f*

balandro *m* yacht

balanza *f* 1. (*pesa*) scales *pl;* **inclinar el fiel de la ~** *fig* to tip the scales 2. COM balance; **~ de pagos** balance of payments

Balanza *f* ASTR Libra

balar *vi* to bleat

balaustrada *f* balustrade

balazo *m* 1. (*tiro*) shot 2. (*herida*) bullet wound

balbucear *vi, vt v.* **balbucir**

balbuceo *m* stammering; (*de niños*) babbling

balbucir *vi, vt* to stammer; (*niño*) to babble

Balcanes *mpl* **los ~** the Balkans

balcón *m* 1. (*de casa*) balcony 2. (*mirador*) observation point

balconada *f* row of balconies

balda *f* shelf

baldado, **-a** *adj* 1. (*tullido*) crippled 2. *inf* (*muy cansado*) knackered *Brit*

baldaquín *m* canopy

baldar *vt* 1. (*paralizar*) to paralyze; (*lisiar*) to disable 2. (*perjudicar*) to harm

balde *m* bucket ►**obtener algo de ~** to get sth for nothing; **en ~** in vain

baldío *m* AGR wasteland, uncultivated land

baldío, **-a** *adj* 1. (*terreno*) uncultivated 2. (*inútil*) useless; (*en balde*) vain

baldón *m* 1. (*acción*) insult 2. (*situación*) disgrace

baldosa *f* paving stone, floor tile

baldosado *m Col, Chile* (*suelo*) tiled floor

baldosín *m* tile

balear I. *vt AmL* **~ a alguien** (*disparar contra*) to shoot at sb; (*herir, matar*) to shoot sb II. *vr:* **~se** *AmL* 1. (*disparar*) to exchange shots 2. (*disputar*) to argue III. *adj* Balearic IV. *mf* native/inhabitant of the Balearic Islands

Baleares *fpl* **las (islas) ~** the Balearics

baleo *m AmL* (*disparo*) shot

balero *m AmL* (*juego*) cup and ball

balido *m* bleat

balín *m* 1. (*bala*) small bullet 2. (*bolita de plomo*) pellet

balística *f sin pl* ballistics

baliza *f* (*señal*) marker; NÁUT buoy; AVIAT beacon; FERRO signal; AUTO warning light

balizar <z→c> *vt* 1. (*con boyas*) to mark with buoys 2. (*iluminar*) to light

ball *f AmL* 1. (*balón*) ball 2. (*proyectil*) shell

ballena *f* whale

ballenero *m* 1. (*barco*) whaling ship 2. (*pescador*) whaler

ballesta *f* 1. TÉC spring 2. HIST crossbow

ballet <ballets> *m* ballet

balneario *m* 1. (*baños*) spa 2. (*estación*) health resort

balompié *m* football *Brit,* soccer *Am*

balón *m* 1. DEP ball 2. (*recipiente para gases*) bag 3. (*botella esférica*) canister 4. NÁUT spinnaker 5. (*en los tebeos*) speech balloon 6. METEO balloon ►**echar balones fuera** to evade the question

baloncesto *m* basketball

balonmano *m* handball

balonvolea *m* volleyball

balotaje *m Méx* voting

balsa *f* 1. (*charca*) pool; (*estanque*) pond 2. NÁUT (*barca*) ferry; (*plataforma*) raft; **~ neumática** rubber dinghy ►**ser una ~ de aceite** (*mar*) to be as calm as a millpond

balsámico, **-a** *adj* 1. (*vinagre*) balsamic 2. (*tranquilizador*) soothing

bálsamo *m* balm

báltico, **-a** I. *adj* Baltic; **el mar ~** the Baltic Sea; **los países ~s** the Baltic countries II. *m, f* native/inhabitant of the Baltic countries

baluarte *m* bastion; **un ~ de la libertad** a bulwark of freedom

balumba *f* 1. (*montón*) heap; **una ~ de ropa** a bundle of clothes 2. *AmS* (*barullo*) racket

bambalina *f* TEAT drop(-scene); **entre ~s** backstage

bambolear I. *vt* to swing, to sway II. *vr:* **~se** to swing, to sway

bamboleo *m* swaying

bambolla *f* ostentation

bambú *m* bamboo

banal *adj* banal

banalidad *f* banality

banalizar <z→c> *vt* to trivialize

banana *f AmL* banana

bananero, **-a** *adj* banana; **república bananera** *pey* banana republic

banano *m AmL* banana tree

banasta *f* large basket

banca *f* 1. (*en el mercado*) stall 2. *AmL* (*asiento*) bench 3. FIN banking; **~ electrónica** electronic banking 4. (*en juegos de azar*) bank 5. *AmS* (*influencia*) influence; **tener ~** to have pull

bancal *m* (*en un jardín*) patch; (*en una pendiente*) terrace

bancario, **-a** *adj* bank(ing); **cuenta bancaria** bank account

bancarrota *f* bankruptcy

banco *m* 1. (*asiento*) bench 2. FIN bank; **~ en casa** home banking; **Banco Interamericano de Desarrollo** Inter-American Development Bank; **Banco Central Europeo** Central European Bank; **Banco Europeo de Inversiones** European Investment Bank; **~ emisor** issuing bank; **Banco Mundial** World Bank 3. TÉC bench, work table; **~ de pruebas** test bed; *fig* testing ground 4. GEO stratum 5. (*de peces*) shoal ►**~ de datos** INFOR databank; **~ de sangre** bloodbank

banda *f* 1. (*cinta*) band; (*franja*) strip; **~ de frecuencia** RADIO frequency band; **~ sonora** CINE soundtrack; **estar fuera de ~** DEP to be out **2.** GEO (*de montaña*) side; (*de río*) bank **3.** (*pandilla*) gang; ~ **terrorista** terrorist group **4.** (*de música*) band; (*de música moderna*) group **5.** FIN ~ **de fluctuación** fluctuation range **6.** (*billar*) cushion **7.** (*como insignia*) sash

bandada *f* **1.** (*de pájaros*) flock; (*de peces*) shoal **2.** (*de personas*) gang

bandazo *m* **1.** NÁUT lurch; **dar ~s** to roll from side to side **2.** (*cambio*) marked shift

bandear I. *vt* **1.** *AmC* (*perseguir a alguien*) to chase; (*herir de gravedad*) to seriously wound **2.** *Arg, Par, Urug* (*taladrar*) to drill **3.** *Arg, Par, Urug* (*un río*) to cross **4.** *Guat* (*pretender*) to court **5.** *Urug* (*herir con palabras*) to hurt; (*inculpar*) to charge **II.** *vr:* **~se 1.** (*mecerse*) to rock **2.** (*en la vida*) to shift for oneself

bandeja *f* tray; ~ **de entrada** in-tray; ~ **de salida** out-tray; **pasar la** ~ to pass the hat around; **servir en** ~ to hand on a plate

bandera *f* flag ►**estar hasta la** ~ *inf* to be packed full

banderazo *m* DEP starting signal

banderilla *f* **1.** TAUR banderilla (*short decorated lance*) **2.** (*tapa*) *cocktail snack on a stick*

banderillero *m* TAUR banderillero (*bullfighter who uses the banderillas*)

banderín *m* **1.** (*bandera*) small flag; (*triangular*) pennant **2.** (*persona*) flag-bearer

banderola *f* **1.** (*como señal*) signalling [*o* signaling *Am*] flag **2.** MIL pennant **3.** *CSur* (*ventana*) fanlight *Brit,* transom *Am*

bandido, -a *m, f* **1.** (*criminal*) bandit **2.** (*persona pilla*) rogue

bando *m* **1.** (*edicto*) edict **2.** (*proclama*) proclamation **3.** (*partido*) faction **4.** (*de pájaros*) flock; (*de peces*) shoal

bandolera *f* (*correa*) bandoleer

bandolerismo *m sin pl* banditry

bandolero, -a *m, f* bandit

bandolina *f* MÚS mandolin

bangladesí *adj, mf* Bangladeshi

banjo *m* MÚS banjo

banking *m sin pl* banking; ~ **electrónico** e-banking

banquero, -a *m, f* banker

banqueta *f* **1.** (*taburete*) stool; (*para los pies*) footstool **2.** *AmC* (*acera*) pavement *Brit,* sidewalk *Am*

banquete *m* banquet

banquetear I. *vi* to feast **II.** *vt* to banquet

banquillo *m* **1.** (*banco pequeño*) bench; (*para los pies*) footstool; JUR dock **2.** DEP bench

bañada *f AmL* (*baño*) swim; (*de pintura*) coat

bañadera *f AmL* bath *Brit,* bathtub *Am*

bañado *m Arg, Bol, Par* marshland

bañador *m* (*de mujer*) swimming costume *Brit,* swimsuit *Am;* (*de hombre*) swimming trunks

bañar I. *vt* **1.** (*lavar*) to bath *Brit,* to bathe *Am* **2.** (*sumergir*) to immerse **3.** (*mar*) to bathe **4.** (*recubrir*) to coat; **bañado en sudor** bathed in sweat **5.** (*iluminar*) to flood with light **II.** *vr:* **~se 1.** (*lavarse*) to have a bath *Brit,* to bathe *Am* **2.** (*en el mar*) to bathe, to have a swim

bañera *f* bath, bathtub *Am*

bañero, -a *m, f* (swimming) pool attendant

bañista *mf* **1.** (*en una playa*) bather **2.** (*en un balneario*) patient at a spa

baño *m* **1.** (*acto*) bathing; ~ **de fijación** FOTO fixation; ~ (**de**) **María** GASTR bain-marie; ~ **de sangre** bloodbath **2.** (*cuarto*) bathroom; **ir al** ~ to go to the toilet **3.** (*capa de pintura*) coat; (*de chocolate*) coating **4.** *pl* (*balneario*) spa; **~s termales** hot springs; **ir a los ~s** to go to the spa

baptista *mf* REL Baptist

baptisterio *m* **1.** (*pila bautismal*) font **2.** (*lugar*) baptistery

baqueta *m* **1.** MIL ramrod **2.** MÚS drumstick

baquetazo *m* (*golpe*) heavy blow; (*caída*) heavy fall

baquetear *vt* to annoy

bar *m* **1.** (*café*) café; (*tasca*) bar **2.** FÍS bar

barahúnda *f* uproar

baraja *f* pack [*o* deck *Am*] of cards; **una** ~ **de posibilidades** *fig* a range of possibilities

barajar *vt* **1.** (*los naipes*) to shuffle **2.** (*mezclar*) to mix up **3.** (*varias posibilidades*) to consider; **se barajan varios nombres** several names are being bandied about **4.** (*caballo*) to rein in **5.** *CSur* (*detener*) to catch

baranda *f* **1.** (*de balcón*) handrail **2.** (*de billar*) cushion

barandilla *f* **1.** (*de balcón*) handrail **2.** (*pasamanos*) banister

baratijas *fpl* cheap goods *pl; pey* junk

baratillo *m* **1.** (*tienda*) junk shop **2.** (*puesto*) junk stall **3.** (*mercadillo*) flea market **4.** (*artículos*) junk

barato I. *m* (*venta*) bargain sale **II.** *adv* cheap(ly)

barato, -a *adj* cheap

barba *f* **1.** (*mentón*) chin **2.** (*pelos*) beard; **dejarse** ~ to grow a beard; **por** ~ per head **3.** *pl* (*de peces*) barbels *pl* **4.** *pl* (*de papel*) ragged edges *pl* ►**subirse a las ~s de alguien** to be disrespectful to sb

barbacoa *f* barbecue

barbado *m* **1.** (*plantón*) cutting **2.** (*hijuelo*) shoot

barbar *vi* **1.** (*hombre*) to grow a beard **2.** (*planta*) to take root

barbaridad *f* **1.** (*crueldad*) barbarity; **¡qué ~!** how terrible! **2.** (*temeridad*) rash act **3.** (*disparate*) nonsense **4.** *inf* (*cantidad*) loads *pl*

barbarie *f* savagery

bárbaro, -a I. *adj* **1.** (*cruel*) savage **2.** *inf* (*estupendo*) tremendous **3.** HIST barbarian **II.** *m, f* **1.** (*grosero*) brute **2.** HIST barbarian

barbear *vt* **1.** *AmC, Par* (*afeitar*) to shave **2.** *AmC, Méx* (*adular*) to fawn on

barbecho *m* fallow (land); **estar en** ~ to be fallow

barbería *f* barber's (shop)

barbero *m* barber

barbilampiño I. *adj* smooth-faced II. *m* novice

barbilla *f* **1.** (*mentón*) chin **2.** (*barba*) beard

barbitúrico *m* barbiturate

barbo *m* barbel

barbudo, -a *adj* bearded

barca *f* **1.** (*embarcación*) (small) boat; **dar un paseo en** ~ to take a boat ride **2.** *pl* (*columpio*) swing boat

barcaza *f* barge

Barcelona *f* Barcelona

barcelonés, -esa I. *adj* of/from Barcelona II. *m, f* native/inhabitant of Barcelona

barchilón, -ona *m, f AmL* (*curandero*) healer

barco *m* ship; ~ **cisterna** tanker; ~ **de pasajeros** passenger ship; ~ **de vapor** steamer; ~ **de vela** sailing ship

baremo *m* **1.** (*tabla de cuentas*) table **2.** (*de tarifas*) price list **3.** (*escala de valores*) range of values

bargueño *m* small cabinet

bario *m* barium

barítono *m* MÚS baritone

barman *m* <bármanes> barman, bartender

barniz *m* **1.** (*laca*) polish; (*para madera*) varnish **2.** (*para loza*) glaze **3.** (*cosa superficial*) gloss

barnizado *m* **1.** (*efecto*) varnish **2.** (*acción*) varnishing

barnizar <z→c> *vt* **1.** (*pintar*) to put a gloss on; (*madera*) to varnish **2.** (*loza*) to glaze

barómetro *m* barometer

barón, -onesa *m, f* baron *m,* baroness *f*

barquero, -a *m, f* (*en un bote*) boatman *m,* boatwoman *f;* (*en una barca de pasaje*) ferryman *m,* ferrywoman *f*

barquilla *f* **1.** (*barca*) small boat **2.** (*de un globo*) basket **3.** NÁUT log **4.** *AmC* (*galleta*) ice-cream cone

barquillo *m* wafer

barra *f* **1.** (*pieza larga*) bar; ~**s asimétricas** DEP asymmetric bars; ~ **de ejercicios** DEP exercise bar; ~ **de labios** lipstick; **desodorante en** ~ deodorant stick **2.** (*de pan*) loaf; (*de chocolate*) bar **3.** (*en un bar*) bar; ~ **americana** singles bar **4.** (*raya*) dash; (*signo gráfico*) slash; MÚS bar **5.** (*barrera*) barrier **6.** (*palanca*) lever **7.** (*bajío estrecho*) sandbank **8.** INFOR ~ **de comandos** taskbar; ~ **de desplazamiento** scroll bar; ~ **espaciadora** space bar; ~ **de inversa** backslash **9.** *AmL* (*pandilla*) gang **10.** *AmS* (*público*) public

barrabasada *f* dirty trick

barraca *f* **1.** (*vivienda provisional*) cabin **2.** (*choza*) hut **3.** *reg* (*vivienda rústica*) thatched farmhouse **4.** *AmL* MIL barracks **5.** *AmL* (*almacén*) storage shed **6.** (*barracón*) big hut

barracón *m* big hut

barracuda *f* barracuda

barranco *m* **1.** (*despeñadero*) cliff **2.** (*cauce*) ravine **3.** (*dificultad*) obstacle

barredera *f* street-cleaning vehicle

barredor(a) *m(f)* streetsweeper

barreminas *m inv* MIL minesweeper

barrena *f* **1.** (*taladrador*) drill **2.** AVIAT spin

barrenar *vt* **1.** (*perforar*) to drill **2.** (*planes*) to foil; (*leyes*) to violate

barrendero, -a *m, f* sweeper

barreno *m* **1.** (*barrena grande*) large drill **2.** (*perforación*) borehole; (*lleno de pólvora*) blasthole

barreño *m* washing-up basin

barrer *vt* **1.** (*habitación*) to sweep **2.** (*un obstáculo*) to sweep aside **3.** *inf* (*derrotar*) to defeat ►~ **para** [*o* **hacia**] **dentro** to look after number one

barrera *f* **1.** (*barra*) barrier; ~ **lingüística** language barrier; ~ **del sonido** sound barrier **2.** (*valla*) fence **3.** DEP wall **4.** TAUR barrier

barriada *f* **1.** (*barrio*) district **2.** *AmL* (*barrio pobre*) shanty town

barricada *f* barricade

barriga *f* **1.** (*vientre*) belly **2.** (*de una vasija*) rounded part **3.** (*de una pared*) bulge ►**rascarse la** ~ to laze about, to twiddle one's thumbs

barrigón *m* big belly

barrigón, -ona I. *adj* pottbellied II. *m, f* pot-bellied individual

barril *m* **1.** (*cuba*) barrel; **cerveza de** ~ draught beer **2.** *AmL* (*cometa*) hexagonal kite

barrilete *m* **1.** (*barril pequeño*) small keg **2.** (*que usan los carpinteros*) clamp **3.** (*en un revolver*) cylinder **4.** *AmL* (*cometa*) hexagonal kite

barrio *m* **1.** (*zona de una ciudad*) district, neighbourhood *Brit,* neighborhood *Am;* ~ **chino** red-light district; ~ **comercial** business quarter **2.** (*arrabal*) suburb ►**irse al otro** ~ *inf* to snuff it

barriobajero, -a *adj pey* **1.** (*de un barrio bajo*) slum **2.** (*vulgar*) coarse

barrizal *m* mire

barro *m* **1.** (*lodo*) mud **2.** (*arcilla*) clay; **de** ~ earthenware **3.** (*granito*) pimple

barroco I. *m sin pl* baroque II. *adj* **1.** (*del periodo barroco*) baroque **2.** (*elaborado*) overelaborate, gaudy *pej*

barrote *m* **1.** (*barra*) (heavy) bar; **entre** ~**s** *fig, inf* behind bars **2.** (*para reforzar*) crosspiece

barruntar(se) *vt, vr* to conjecture

barrunto *m* **1.** (*conjetura*) conjecture; (*sospecha*) suspicion **2.** (*indicio*) sign

bartola *f inf* **tumbarse a la** ~ to be idle

bártulos *mpl* belongings *pl*

barullo *m inf* **1.** (*ruido*) din **2.** (*desorden*) confusion

basa *f* **1.** (*de una columna*) base **2.** (*base*) basis

basalto *m* basalt

basar I. *vt* **1.** (*asentar*) to base **2.** (*fundar*) to ground II. *vr* ~**se en algo** (*teoría*) to be based on sth; (*persona*) to base oneself on sth

basca *f* **1.** MED (*espasmo*) nausea; **tener** ~**s** to feel sick **2.** *inf* (*arrebato*) fit of rage **3.** (*en animales*) rabies **4.** *inf* (*gentío*) gang

bascosidad *f* **1.** (*suciedad*) filth **2.** *Ecua* (*insulto*) obscenity

bascoso, **-a** *adj* **1.** MED queasy **2.** *Col, Ecua* (*nauseabundo*) nauseating **3.** *Col, Ecua* (*indigno*) contemptible, vile **4.** *Col, Ecua* (*obsceno*) obscene

báscula *f* scales *pl*

bascular *vi* **1.** (*inclinarse*) to tilt **2.** (*oscilar*) to seesaw

base *f* **1.** (*lo fundamental*) basis; ~ **de datos** INFOR database; **elaborado a ~ de algo** drawn up on the basis of sth; **partir de la ~ de que...** to start with the idea that ... **2.** ARQUIT, MIL, DEP base **3.** POL rank and file **4.** MAT base; (*superficie*) area; (*línea*) base line ▶**a ~ de** <u>**bien**</u> *inf* really well

básico, **-a** *adj* (*t. quím*) basic

Basilea *f* Basle, Basel

basílica *f* basilica

basilisco *m* **1.** (*mito*) basilisk **2.** *AmL* ZOOL iguana

basket *m sin pl* basketball

basta *f* **1.** (*hilván*) tacking *Brit,* basting *Am* **2.** *AmL* (*bastilla*) hem

bastante **I.** *adj* enough; **tengo ~ frío** I'm quite cold **II.** *adv* (*suficientemente*) sufficiently; (*considerablemente*) rather; **con esto tengo ~** this is enough for me

bastar **I.** *vi* to be enough; **¡basta!** that's enough! **II.** *vr* **~se (uno) solo** to be self-sufficient

bastardía *f* **1.** (*degeneración*) bastardy **2.** (*bajeza*) meanness

bastardilla *f* TIPO italics *pl*

bastardo, **-a** **I.** *adj* **1.** (*hijo*) bastard **2.** BOT hybrid **3.** (*vil*) wicked **II.** *m, f* bastard

bastedad *f* coarseness

bastidor *m* **1.** TÉC frame(work); (*de coche*) chassis *inv* **2.** (*de ventana*) frame **3.** TEAT wing; **entre ~es** behind the scenes

bastilla *f* hem

bastimento *m* **1.** (*provisión*) supply **2.** (*embarcación*) vessel

bastión *m* bastion

basto, **-a** *adj* **1.** (*grosero*) rude; (*vulgar*) coarse **2.** (*superficie*) rough **3.** (*mal hecho*) roughly made

bastón *m* **1.** (*para andar*) stick; (*para esquiar*) ski pole **2.** (*de mando*) baton; **empuñar el ~** to take command

bastoncillo *m diminutivo de* **bastón** small stick; ~ **de algodón** cotton bud *Brit,* cotton swab *Am,* Q-tip® *Am*

bastos *mpl* clubs *pl* (*in Spanish card pack*) ▶<u>**pintan**</u> ~ things are getting difficult

basura *f* **1.** (*desperdicios*) rubbish *Brit,* garbage *Am;* ~ **del hogar** domestic rubbish; **echar algo a la ~** to throw sth away **2.** (*lo despreciable*) trash

basural *m AmL* rubbish dump *Brit,* garbage dump *Am*

basurear *vt Arg, Urug* **1.** *vulg* (*tratar despectivamente*) to treat like shit **2.** (*vencer*) to defeat

basurero *m* **1.** (*vertedero*) rubbish dump *Brit,* garbage dump *Am* **2.** (*recipiente*) dustbin *Brit,* trashcan *Am*

basurero, **-a** *m, f* dustman *m Brit* dustwoman *f Brit,* garbage collector *Am*

bata *f* **1.** (*albornoz*) dressing gown **2.** (*guardapolvos*) overalls *pl Brit,* coverall *Am* **3.** (*de laboratorio*) lab coat; (*de hospital*) white coat

batacazo *m* **1.** (*golpe*) thump **2.** (*caída*) heavy fall; **se pegó un ~** *inf* he/she came a cropper **3.** *CSur, PRico* (*golpe de suerte*) stroke of luck

bataclán *m AmL* striptease show

bataclana *f AmL* chorus girl, stripper

batahola *f inf* rumpus

batalla *f* **1.** MIL (*episodio bélico*) battle; ~ **campal** pitched battle; *fig* bitter dispute **2.** (*lucha interior*) struggle **3.** AUTO wheelbase

batallar *vi* **1.** (*con armas*) to fight; ~ **por algo** to battle over sth **2.** (*disputar*) to quarrel

batallita *f* story

batallón *m* **1.** MIL battalion **2.** *inf* (*grupo*) group

batán *m* **1.** (*máquina*) fulling mill **2.** *AmL* (*piedra lisa*) millstone **3.** *Chile* (*tintorería*) dry cleaner's

batanear *vt* to beat

batata **I.** *adj CSur* (*tímido*) shy **II.** *f* **1.** (*planta*) sweet potato plant **2.** (*tubérculo*) sweet potato **3.** *CSur* (*susto*) shock **4.** *CSur* (*vergüenza*) embarrassment **5.** *AmL* ~ **de la pierna** calf

bate *m* DEP bat; ~ **de béisbol** baseball bat

bateador(a) *m(f)* DEP batter

batear *vt* DEP to bat

batería[1] *f* **1.** *t.* TÉC battery; ~ **de cocina** pots and pans; ~ **solar** solar panel; **aparcar en ~** to park adjacent to the kerb [*o* curb *Am*] **2.** TEAT footlights **3.** MÚS (*en orquesta*) percussion; (*en conjunto*) drums *pl*

batería[2] *mf,* **baterista** *mf* drummer

batida *f* **1.** (*de los cazadores*) beat **2.** (*de la policía*) raid **3.** *AmL* (*paliza*) beating, thrashing

batido *m* **1.** (*bebida*) milk shake; ~ **de fresa** strawberry milk shake **2.** (*masa*) dough **3.** (*de huevos*) batter

batidor *m* **1.** (*instrumento*) whisk **2.** (*en la caza*) beater **3.** (*explorador*) scout

batidora *f* (*de mano*) whisk; (*electrica*) mixer, blender

batiente **I.** *adj* flapping **II.** *m* **1.** (*marco de ventana*) frame; (*de puerta*) jamb **2.** (*hoja de ventana, puerta*) leaf **3.** MÚS damper **4.** (*roca*) reef

batifondo *m CSur, inf* (*alboroto*) uproar; (*disturbio*) commotion; (*zozobra*) uneasiness

batín *m* (man's) dressing gown

batir **I.** *vt* **1.** (*golpear*) to beat; (*el viento*) to beat against; (*las olas*) to crash against; (*la lluvia*) to beat down on; ~ **palmas** to clap **2.** (*metal*) to beat **3.** (*moneda*) to mint

4. (*casa*) to knock down 5. (*toldo*) to flap 6. (*privilegio*) to do away with 7. (*enemigo*) to defeat; ~ **un récord** to beat a record 8. MIL to beat 9. (*un terreno*) to comb 10. *CSur* (*denunciar*) to inform on II. *vr:* ~**se** 1. (*combatir*) to fight 2. (*en duelo*) to fight a duel

batista *f* cambric

batracio *m* batrachian

baturrillo *m* hotchpotch *Brit,* hodgepodge *Am*

baturro, **-a** I. *adj inf* (*rudo*) rough II. *m, f Aragonese peasant*

batuta *f* MÚS baton ►**llevar la** ~ to be in charge

baúl *m* 1. (*mueble*) trunk; ~ **de viaje** trunk 2. *AmL* (*portamaletas*) boot *Brit,* trunk *Am* 3. *inf* (*vientre*) belly

bausán, **-ana** I. *adj* 1. (*tonto*) stupid 2. *AmL* (*perezoso*) lazy II. *m, f* simpleton

bautismal *adj* baptismal; **pila** ~ font

bautismo *m* baptism; ~ **de sangre** first combat

bautista *mf* Baptist; **San Juan Bautista** St John the Baptist

bautizar <z→c> *vt* 1. REL to baptize; (*nombrar*) to christen 2. *inf* (*mojar*) to drench 3. *inf* (*leche*) to water; ~ **el vino** to water down the wine

bautizo *m* baptism; (*ceremonia*) christening; (*fiesta*) christening party

bauxita *f* bauxite

baya *f* berry

bayeta *f* 1. (*para fregar*) washing-up cloth, dish cloth 2. (*tela de lana*) baize

bayoneta *f* bayonet

bayoya *m PRico, RDom* uproar

baza *f* 1. (*naipes*) trick; **meter** ~ **en algo** *inf* to butt in on sth 2. (*provecho*) benefit; **sacar** ~ **de algo** to profit from sth

bazar *m* 1. (*mercado*) bazaar 2. (*gran almacén*) large shop

bazo *m* ANAT spleen

bazofia *f* 1. (*comida*) pigswill 2. (*restos de comida*) leftovers *pl* 3. (*cosa*) filthy thing

bazuca *f* bazooka

be *f letter B*

beata *f inf* (*moneda*) one peseta

beatería *f* 1. (*devoción exagerada*) sanctimoniousness 2. (*devoción falsa*) affected piety

beatificación *f* beatification

beatificar <c→qu> *vt* to beatify

beatitud *f* beatitude

beato, **-a** I. *adj* 1. (*piadoso*) devout 2. (*beatificado*) beatified 3. *elev* (*feliz*) blessed II. *m, f* 1. (*hermano*) lay brother *m,* lay sister *f* 2. (*persona beatificada*) beatified person 3. (*exageradamente devota*) devout person

bebe, **-a** *m, f AmL* baby

bebé *m* baby

bebedera *f Méx* drinking spree

bebedero *m* 1. (*para animales*) waterhole; (*para animales domésticos*) drinking trough 2. (*de jarro*) spout

bebedizo *m* 1. (*medicinal*) potion 2. (*enamoradizo*) love potion

bebedor(**a**) I. *adj* given to drinking II. *m(f)* drinker

bebendurria *f AmL, inf* drinking binge

bebé-probeta *m* <bebés-probeta> test-tube baby

beber I. *vi, vt* 1. (*líquido*) to drink; ~ **de la botella** to drink from the bottle; ~ **a sorbos** to sip; ~ **de un trago** to gulp 2. (*información*) to absorb II. *vr:* ~**se** to drink up; **bebérselo todo** to drink it all up

bebible *adj* drinkable

bebida *f* drink, beverage *form;* ~ **alcohólica** alcoholic drink; ~ **energética** energy drink; **darse a la** ~ to take to drink

bebido, **-a** *adj* (*borracho*) drunk

beca *f* (*de estudios*) grant; (*por méritos*) scholarship; **conceder una** ~ **a alguien** to award a grant to sb

becada *f* woodcock

becar <c→qu> *vt* to award a grant to

becario, **-a** *m, f* grant holder; (*por méritos*) scholarship holder

becerro *m* HIST register

becerro, **-a** *m, f* yearling calf; **el** ~ **de oro** the golden calf

bechamel *f* white sauce

bedel(**a**) *m(f)* beadle, proctor

beduino, **-a** I. *adj* Bedouin II. *m, f* Bedouin

befa *f* jeer

befarse *vr* ~ **de alguien/algo** to jeer at sb/sth

befo *m* lip (of horse)

befo, **-a** *adj* 1. (*belfo*) thick-lipped 2. (*zambo*) knock-needed

begonia *f* begonia

beicon *m sin pl* bacon

beige *adj* beige

béisbol *m sin pl* DEP baseball

bejuco *m* liana

Belcebú *m* Beelzebub

beldad *f elev* beauty

belduque *m AmL* pointed sword

belén *m* 1. (*nacimiento*) crib, Nativity scene 2. *inf* (*confusión*) confusion

Belén *m* Bethlehem

belfo *m* 1. (*de animales*) lip 2. (*de personas*) prominent lower lip

belga *adj, mf* Belgian

Bélgica *f* Belgium

Belgrado *m* Belgrade

Belice *m* Belize

beliceño, **-a** *adj, m, f* Belizean

belicista I. *adj* belligerent II. *mf* warmonger

bélico, **-a** *adj* warlike

belicosidad *f* aggressiveness

belicoso, **-a** *adj* (*población*) warlike; (*persona*) aggressive

beligerancia *f* belligerency

beligerante I. *adj* belligerent II. *mf* belligerent individual

bellaco, **-a** I. *adj* cunning II. *m, f* rascal

bellaquear *vi* 1. (*persona*) to cheat 2. *AmL*

(*caballo*) to shy
bellaquería *f* **1.**(*acción*) dirty trick **2.**(*cualidad*) cunning
belleza *f* beauty
bello, **-a** *adj* beautiful
bellota *f* **1.**(*fruto*) acorn **2.**(*capullo*) bud
bemba *f AmL, pey* lip
bembo, **-a** *adj AmL* thick-lipped
bembudo, **-a** *adj AmL* thick-lipped
bemol **I.** *adj* MÚS flat **II.** *m* MÚS flat ▸**tener** ~**es** to be difficult
benceno *m* benzene
bencina *f* benzine
bendecir *irr como decir vt* **1.**(*sacerdote*) to bless; ~ **la mesa** to say grace **2.**(*alabar*) to praise **3.**(*consagrar*) to consecrate **4.**(*una cosa*) to approve
bendición *f* **1.**(*acto*) blessing **2.**(*cosa magnífica*) marvel **3.** *pl* (*casamiento*) wedding ceremony
bendito, **-a** **I.** *adj* **1.** REL blessed; (*agua*) holy; (*santo*) saintly; **¡~ sea!** *inf* thank God! **2.**(*dichoso*) lucky **3.**(*simple*) simple-minded **II.** *m, f* kind soul
benedictino, **-a** *adj, m, f* REL Benedictine
benefactor(a) **I.** *adj* beneficient **II.** *m(f)* benefactor
beneficencia *f* **1.**(*organización*) charity **2.**(*virtud*) beneficience
beneficiado, **-a** *adj, m, f* beneficiary
beneficiar **I.** *vt* **1.**(*favorecer*) to benefit **2.**(*tierra*) to cultivate **3.**(*mina*) to work **4.**(*mineral*) to refine **5.** *AmL* (*animal*) to slaughter **II.** *vr:* ~**se** **1.**(*sacar provecho*) ~**se de algo** to benefit from sth **2.** *pey* (*enriquecerse*) ~**se de algo** to take advantage of sth
beneficiario, **-a** *m, f* beneficiary; (*de una letra de crédito*) assignee; ~ **de la pensión** receiver of the pension
beneficio *m* **1.**(*bien*) good **2.**(*provecho*) profit; **a ~ de** for the benefit of **3.** FIN profit **4.**(*cargo eclesiástico*) living **5.** *AmL* (*matanza*) slaughter
beneficioso, **-a** *adj* **1.**(*favorable*) beneficial **2.**(*útil*) useful **3.**(*productivo*) profitable
benéfico, **-a** *adj* **1.**(*que hace bien*) beneficial **2.**(*caritativo*) charitable
benemérito, **-a** *adj* worthy; **la Benemérita** the Civil Guard
beneplácito *m* **1.**(*permiso*) approval **2.**(*consentimiento*) consent
benévolo, **-a** *adj* **1.**(*favorable*) benevolent **2.**(*clemente*) indulgent
bengala *f* flare; (*pequeña*) sparkler
benignidad *f* **1.**(*de una persona*) kindness **2.**(*del clima*) mildness **3.** MED benignancy
benigno, **-a** *adj* **1.**(*persona*) kind; **ser ~ con alguien** to be kind to sb **2.**(*clima*) mild **3.** MED benign
benjamín, **-ina** *m, f* **1.**(*hijo menor*) youngest child **2.**(*de un grupo*) youngest member
beodo, **-a** **I.** *adj* drunk **II.** *m, f* drunkard
berbén *m Méx* (*escorbuto*) scurvy
berberecho *m* cockle
berbiquí *m* brace and bit
bereber, **beréber** *adj, mf* Berber
berenjena *f* aubergine *Brit,* eggplant *Am*
berenjenal *m* **1.** aubergine bed *Brit,* eggplant patch *Am* **2.** *fig* (*lío*) mess; **meterse en un ~** to get into a mess
bergante *m* scoundrel
berilio *m* beryllium
berilo *m* beryl
Berlín *m* Berlin
berlina *f* **1.**(*vehículo*) saloon (car) *Brit,* sedan *Am* **2.** *AmL* (*pastel*) jam doughnut *Brit,* jelly donut *Am*
berlinés, **-esa** **I.** *adj* Berlin **II.** *m, f* Berliner
bermejo, **-a** *adj* red; (*de animales*) reddish-brown
bermellón *m* vermilion
bermudas *mpl* Bermuda shorts *pl*
Berna *f* Berne
berrear *vi* **1.**(*animal*) to bellow; (*oveja*) to bleat **2.**(*llorar*) to howl **3.** *inf* (*cantar desentonadamente*) to howl **4.**(*chillar*) to screech
berrido *m* **1.**(*de animales*) bellow; (*de ovejas*) bleating **2.**(*lloro*) howl **3.** *inf* (*canto desentonado*) howling **4.**(*chillido*) screech
berrinche *m inf* **1.**(*llorera*) tantrum **2.**(*enfado*) rage
berrinchudo, **-a** *adj AmL* on heat
berro *m* watercress
berza *f* cabbage
berzal *m* cabbage patch
berzotas *mf inv, inf* chump
besar **I.** *vt* **1.**(*personas*) to kiss **2.** *inf* (*objetos*) to touch **II.** *vr:* ~**se** **1.**(*personas*) to kiss each other **2.**(*tocarse dos objetos*) to touch; (*chocar*) to bump into each other
beso *m* **1.**(*entre personas*) kiss; **comerse a alguien a ~s** to smother sb with kisses **2.**(*entre objetos*) bump
bestia[1] **I.** *adj* stupid **II.** *mf* **1.**(*persona bruta*) brute; (*grosera*) boor **2.**(*ignorante*) ignoramus
bestia[2] *f* **1.** ZOOL animal **2.**(*animal salvaje*) (wild) beast
bestial *adj* **1.**(*propio de una bestia*) bestial **2.**(*muy brutal*) brutal **3.** *inf* (*muy intensivo*) tremendous; (*muy grande*) huge; (*muy bueno*) marvellous *Brit,* marvelous *Am*
bestialidad *f* **1.**(*cualidad*) bestiality **2.**(*crueldad*) brutality **3.** *inf* (*gran cantidad*) huge amount
best seller *m inv,* **bestséller** *m inv* bestseller
besucón, **-ona** **I.** *adj* fond of kissing **II.** *m, f* **es una besucona** she's very fond of kissing
besugo *m* **1.** ZOOL bream; **ojos de ~** *inf* bulging eyes **2.** *inf* (*persona*) idiot; **¡no seas ~!** don't be an idiot!
besuquear *vt* to cover with kisses
betabel *f Méx* (*remolacha*) beetroot *Brit,* beet *Am;* ~ **forrajera** fodder beet
betarraga *f AmL* beetroot *Brit,* beet *Am*
betún *m* **1.** QUÍM bitumen **2.**(*para el calzado*)

shoe polish; **negro como el** ~ as black as pitch

bezo *m* thick lip

biaba *f Arg, Urug* (*cachetada*) slap; (*paliza*) beating; **dar la** ~ (*pegar*) to beat up; (*derrotar*) to defeat

bianual *adj* biannual; BOT biennial

biatlón *m* DEP biathlon

biberón *m* feeding bottle

Biblia *f* Bible

bíblico, -a *adj* biblical

bibliobús *m* mobile library

bibliófilo, -a *m, f* bibliophile, book lover

bibliografía *f* bibliography

bibliográfico, -a *adj* bibliographic(al)

biblioteca *f* **1.** (*local*) library; ~ **de consulta** reference library **2.** (*mueble*) bookcase **3.** (*estantería*) bookshelves *pl*

bibliotecario, -a *m, f* librarian

bicameral *adj* POL bicameral

bicarbonato *m* bicarbonate; ~ **sódico** bicarbonate of soda, baking soda, sodium bicarbonate

bicéfalo, -a *adj* two-headed

bicentenario *m* bicentenary, bicentennial *Am*

bíceps *m inv* ANAT biceps *inv*

bicha *f* **1.** *inf* (*serpiente*) snake **2.** (*figura*) mermaid

bicharraco *m* **1.** *pey* (*bicho*) ugly creature **2.** (*persona*) odd creature

bicho *m* **1.** (*animal*) (small) animal; (*insecto*) bug **2.** TAUR bull **3.** *inf* (*persona*) unpleasant person; ~ **raro** weirdo; **mal** ~ rogue **4.** *vulg* (*pene*) prick

bici *f inf abr de* **bicicleta** bike

bicicleta *f* bicycle; ~ **de carreras** racing bike; ~ **estática** exercise bike; ~ **de montaña** mountain bike

bicoca *f* **1.** *inf* (*ganga*) bargain **2.** *inf* (*pequeñez*) trifle **3.** *AmL* (*de eclesiásticos*) skull cap

bicolor *adj* two-colour *Brit,* two-color *Am*

bidé *m* <bidés>, **bidet** *m* <bidets> bidet

bidireccional *adj* two-way; INFOR bidirectional

bidón *m* steel drum

biela *f* **1.** TÉC connecting rod **2.** (*de la bicicleta*) crank

bieldo *m* winnowing fork

Bielorrusia *f* Belorussia

bielorruso, -a *adj, m, f* Belorussian

bien **I.** *m* **1.** (*bienestar*) well-being **2.** (*bondad moral*) good **3.** (*provecho*) benefit **4.** *pl* ECON goods *pl* **5.** *pl* (*posesiones*) property; (*riqueza*) wealth; ~**es inmuebles** real estate; ~**es de la tierra** agricultural produce **II.** *adv* **1.** (*de modo conveniente*) properly; (*correctamente*) well; ~ **mirado** well thought of; **estar** ~ **de salud** to be in good health; **estar (a)** ~ **con alguien** to get on well with sb; **hacer algo** ~ to do sth well; **hacer** ~ **en** +*infin* to do well to +*infin;* **¡pórtate** ~**!** behave yourself!; **tener a** ~ +*infin* to see fit to +*infin;* **te está** ~ that serves you right **2.** (*con gusto*) willingly **3.** (*seguramente*) surely **4.** (*muy*) very; (*bastante*) quite; **es** ~ **fácil** it's very simple **5.** (*asentimiento*) all right; **¡está** ~**!** OK! ▸**ahora** ~ however; ~ **que mal** one way or another **III.** *adj* well-off **IV.** *conj* **1.** (*aunque*) ~ **que** although; **si** ~ even though **2.** (*o...o*) ~**...**~**...** either ... or ... **3.** (*apenas*) **no** ~**...(cuando...)** no sooner ... (than ...) **V.** *interj* well done

bienal **I.** *adj* biennial **II.** *f* biennial show

bienaventurado *adj* **1.** REL blessed **2.** (*feliz*) fortunate

bienaventuranza *f* **1.** REL (*gloria*) bliss; **las** ~**s** the Beatitudes **2.** (*felicidad*) happiness

bienestar *m* **1.** (*estado, sentimiento*) well-being **2.** (*riqueza*) prosperity; **estado del** ~ welfare state

bienhablado, -a *adj* well-spoken

bienhechor(a) **I.** *adj* beneficent **II.** *m(f)* benefactor

bienintencionado, -a *adj* well-meaning

bienio *m* two-year period

bienpensante *adj, mf* orthodox

bienquistar **I.** *vt* to reconcile **II.** *vr:* ~**se** (*hacer amistad*) to become friendly; ~ **con alguien** (*congraciar*) to win sb over

bienquisto, -a *adj* ~ **de** [*o* **por**] **alguien** well-liked by sb

bienvenida *f* welcome; **dar la** ~ **a alguien** to welcome sb

bienvenido, -a **I.** *interj* welcome; **¡**~ **a casa!** welcome home!; **¡**~ **a España!** welcome to Spain! **II.** *adj* welcome

bies cortar al ~ to cut on the bias

bifásico, -a *adj* ELEC two-phase

bife *m CSur* **1.** (*carne*) steak **2.** *inf* (*sopapo*) slap

bifocal *adj* bifocal

bifurcación *f* **1.** (*de un camino*) fork **2.** INFOR branch

bifurcarse <c→qu> *vr* to fork

bigamia *f* bigamy

bígamo, -a **I.** *adj* bigamous **II.** *m, f* bigamist

bigote *m* **1.** (*de hombre*) moustache, mustache *Am;* **estar de** ~**(s)** *inf* to be terrific **2.** *pl* (*de animal*) whiskers *pl* **3.** *AmL* (*croqueta*) croquette

bigotudo, -a *adj* with a big moustache

bigudí *m* curler

bikini *m* bikini

bilateral *adj* bilateral

biliar *adj* biliary; **cálculo** ~ gallstone

bilingüe **I.** *adj* bilingual **II.** *mf* bilingual person

bilingüismo *m sin pl* bilingualism

bilis *f inv* **1.** ANAT bile **2.** (*cólera*) spleen; **no tuve más remedio que tragar** ~ I had no choice but to put up with it

billar *m* **1.** (*juego*) billiards; ~ **americano** pool **2.** (*mesa*) billiard table

billete *m* **1.** (*pasaje*) ticket; ~ **de ida y vuelta** return ticket *Brit,* roundtrip ticket *Am;* **sacar un** ~ to get a ticket **2.** FIN note *Brit,* bill *Am* **3.** (*de lotería*) ticket; ~ **premiado** winning

ticket **4.** (*mensaje breve*) note
billetera *f,* **billetero** *m* wallet *Brit,* billfold *Am*
billón *m* billion *Brit,* trillion *Am*
billonario, **-a** *m, f* billionaire
bimba *f AmL* (*embriaguez*) **pegarse una** ~ to get drunk
bimensual *adj* twice-monthly
bimestral *adj* (*cada dos meses*) bi-monthly; (*que dura dos meses*) two-month
bimotor I. *adj* twin-engined II. *m* twin-engined plane
binario, **-a** *adj* binary
bingo *m* (*juego*) bingo; (*sala*) bingo hall
binoculares *mpl* binoculars *pl*
binóculo *m* pince-nez
bioactivo, **-a** *adj* bioactive
biobasura *f* biorefuse
biodegradable *adj* biodegradable
biodiversidad *f* biodiversity
bioenergía *f* bioenergy
biofísica *f* biophysics
biogenética *f* biogenetics
biografía *f* biography
biografiar <*1. pres:* biografío> *vt* ~ **a alguien** to write the biography of sb
biógrafo *m CSur* (*cine*) cinema
biógrafo, **-a** *m, f* (*persona*) biographer
biología *f* biology
biólogo, **-a** *m, f* biologist
biomasa *f* biomass
biombo *m* (folding) screen
biomecánica *f* biomechanics
biónico, **-a** *adj* bionic
biopsia *f* biopsy
bioquímica *f* biochemistry
biorritmo *m* biorhythm
biosfera *f* biosphere
biosistema *m* biosystem
biotecnología *f* biotechnology
biotipo *m* biotype
biótopo *m* biotope
bipartidismo *m* POL two-party system
bípedo, **-a** *adj, m, f* biped
biplano *m* biplane
biplaza *adj, m* two-seater
bipolaridad *f* FÍS bipolarity
biquini *m* bikini
birlar *vt inf* (*hurtar*) to pinch *Brit,* to swipe *Am;* **Carlos me birló el lápiz** Carlos pinched my pencil
Birmania *f* Burma
birmano, **-a** *adj, m, f* Burmese
birome *m o f CSur* ballpoint ben, biro® *Brit*
birra *f inf* beer
birrete *m* **1.** (*de clérigos*) biretta **2.** (*de catedráticos, jueces*) cap
birria *f* **1.** (*persona*) drip; **el delantero centro es una** ~ the centre forward is useless; **va hecho una** ~ he looks really scruffy **2.** (*objeto*) rubbish, trash; **la película es una** ~ the film is rubbish
birriondo, **-a** *adj Méx* **1.** (*callejero*) street; (*animales*) jumpy; **disturbios** ~**s** street riots *pl;* **perro** ~ mutt **2.** (*enamoradizo*) easily infatuated **3.** (*cachondo*) randy *inf*
biruje *m AmL,* **biruji** *m* cold wind
bis I. *interj* encore II. *m* MÚS encore III. *adv* **1.** MÚS bis **2.** (*piso*) **7** ~ 7A
bisabuelo, **-a** *m, f* great-grandfather *m,* great--grandmother *f*
bisagra *f* hinge
bisar *vt* MÚS to give as an encore, to repeat
bisbis(e)ar *vt inf* **1.** (*musitar*) to mutter **2.** (*cuchichear*) to whisper
biscote *m* rusk
bisel *m* bevel
bisexual *adj* bisexual
bisexualidad *f sin pl* bisexuality
bisiesto *adj* **año** ~ leap year
bisílabo, **-a** *adj* two-syllable
bismuto *m* bismuth
bisnieto, **-a** *m, f* great-grandson *m,* great--granddaughter *f*
bisonte *m* (*americano*) buffalo; (*europeo*) bison
bisoñé *m* toupée
bisoño, **-a** I. *adj* inexperienced II. *m, f* (*novato*) novice
bisté *m* <bistés>, **bistec** *m* <bistecs> steak
bisturí *m* scalpel
bisutería *f* costume jewellery [*o* jewelry *Am*]
bit *m* <bits> INFOR bit; ~ **de parada** stop bit
bíter *m* bitters
bitoque *m* **1.** (*tapón*) bung **2.** *AmC* (*cloaca*) sewer **3.** *AmL* (*cánula de jeringa*) cannula **4.** *Méx, RíoPl* (*grifo*) faucet
bizantino, **-a** I. *adj* **1.** (*de Bizancio*) Byzantine **2.** *fig* hair-splitting II. *m, f* Byzantine
bizarría *f* **1.** (*valentía*) bravery **2.** (*gallardía*) dash **3.** (*generosidad*) generosity
bizarro, **-a** *adj* **1.** (*valiente*) brave **2.** (*apuesto*) dashing **3.** (*generoso*) generous **4.** (*extravagante*) odd
bizco, **-a** *adj* cross-eyed; **dejar a alguien** ~ *fig* to leave sb speechless
bizcocho I. *adj Méx* (*cobarde*) cowardly II. *m* **1.** GASTR sponge cake **2.** NÁUT hardtack
biznieto, **-a** *m, f v.* **bisnieto**
bizquear *vi* to squint
bizquera *f AmL* (*estrabismo*) squint; **tener** ~ to have a squint
bla-bla-bla *m* bla-bla-bla
blanca *f* **1.** MÚS minim *Brit,* half note *Am* **2.** (*pieza de dominó*) double-blank ►**estar sin** ~ to be broke
Blancanieves *f* Snow White
blanco *m* **1.** (*color*) white; **película en** ~ **y negro** black and white film **2.** (*de animal*) white patch **3.** (*espacio en un escrito*) blank space; **cheque en** ~ blank cheque [*o* check *Am*] **4.** (*diana*) target; **dar en el** ~ *fig* to hit the mark ►**se me quedó la mente en** ~ my mind went blank; **pasar la noche en** ~ to have a sleepless night; ~ **del ojo** white of the eye;

<u>quedarse</u> **en** ~ to go blank
blanco, -a I. *adj* 1. (*de tal color*) white 2. (*tez*) pale II. *m, f* white man *m,* white woman *f*
blancura *f* whiteness
blandear I. *vt* to persuade II. *vi* to begin to yield
blandengue *adj pey* soft, mushy
blandir I. *vt* to brandish II. *vi, vr:* ~**se** to wave about
blando, -a *adj* 1. (*objeto*) soft; **créditos** ~**s** ECON soft credits 2. (*carácter: suave*) mild; (*blandengue*) soft; (*cobarde*) cowardly; ~ **de corazón** soft-hearted 3. (*constitución*) weak 4. (*clima*) mild 5. (*lluvia, tono*) gentle 6. (*luz*) soft
blandura *f* 1. (*de una cosa*) softness 2. (*del carácter: suavidad*) mildness; (*blandenguería*) softness 3. (*lisonja*) flattery 4. (*del aire*) mildness 5. (*emplasto*) plaster
blanquear I. *vi* to whiten II. *vt* 1. (*poner blanco*) to whiten 2. (*pared*) to whitewash 3. (*dinero*) to launder 4. (*tejido*) to bleach 5. (*metal*) to blanch
blanquecino, -a *adj* whitish
blanqueo *m* 1. (*el poner blanco*) whitening 2. (*de una pared*) whitewashing 3. (*de tejido*) bleaching 4. (*de dinero*) laundering
blasfemar *vi* 1. REL to blaspheme 2. (*maldecir*) ~ **de algo** to swear about sth
blasfemia *f* 1. REL blasphemy 2. (*injuria*) insult 3. (*taco*) swearword
blasfemo, -a I. *adj* blasphemous II. *m, f* blasphemer
blasón *m* 1. (*escudo de armas*) coat of arms 2. (*honor*) honour *Brit,* honor *Am;* (*gloria*) glory 3. *pl* (*abolengo*) noble ancestry
blasonar I. *vt* to emblazen II. *vi* ~ **de algo** to boast about sth
blázer *m* blazer
bledo *m* goosefoot ►**(no) me** <u>**importa**</u> **un** ~ I couldn't care less
blindado *m* MIL armour-plated *Brit,* armor-plated *Am;* **puerta blindada** reinforced door
blindaje *m* armour (plating) *Brit,* armor (plating) *Am*
blindar *vt* to armour(-plate) *Brit,* to armor(-plate) *Am*
bloc *m* <blocs> 1. (*cuaderno*) notepad 2. (*calendario*) calendar pad
blofear *vi AmL* (*engañar*) to bluff
blofero, -a *m, f,* **blofista** *mf AmC, PRico* braggart, bluffer
blonda *f* 1. (*encaje*) blond lace 2. (*de papel*) (paper) doily
bloque *m* 1. block; ~ **de viviendas** block of flats 2. POL bloc ►<u>**en**</u> ~ en bloc
bloquear I. *vt* 1. (*cortar el paso*) to block 2. (*aislar*) to cut off 3. TÉC to jam 4. MIL (*asediar*) to blockade 5. FIN to freeze 6. DEP to block 7. (*obstaculizar*) to obstruct 8. (*interrumpir*) to cut off II. *vr:* ~**se** 1. (*una cosa*) to jam 2. (*una persona*) to have a mental block
bloqueo *m* 1. (*de un paso*) blocking; ~ **comercial** COM trade embargo 2. (*aislamiento*) cutting off 3. TÉC (*de un mecanismo*) jamming 4. MIL blockade 5. DEP block 6. (*de un proceso: estancamiento*) deadlock; (*interrupción*) cutting off 7. (*mental*) block
bluff *m* <bluffs> 1. (*finta*) feint 2. *AmL* (*fanfarronería*) bluff
blusa *f* 1. (*de mujer*) blouse 2. (*bata*) smock
blusón *m* smock
boa *f* boa
boato *m* ostentation
bobada *f* silly thing; **decir** ~**s** to talk nonsense
bobalicón, -ona I. *adj* 1. (*tonto*) silly 2. (*simple*) simple(-minded) II. *m, f* 1. (*tonto*) fool 2. (*simplón*) simpleton
bobear *vi* 1. (*hacer bobadas*) to fool about 2. (*decir bobadas*) to talk nonsense
bobina *f* 1. ELEC coil 2. (*de película, hilo*) reel
bobinar *vt* to wind
bobo, -a I. *adj* 1. (*tonto*) silly 2. (*simple*) simple II. *m, f* 1. (*tonto*) fool 2. (*simplón*) simpleton
boca *f* 1. ANAT mouth; ~ **abajo** face down(ward); ~ **arriba** face up(ward); **estaba tumbada** ~ **abajo/arriba** she was lying on her stomach/on her back; **andar de** ~ **en** ~ to be the subject of gossip 2. (*abertura*) opening; ~ **de metro** underground entrance *Brit,* subway entrance *Am;* ~ **de riego** hydrant 3. (*agujero*) hole 4. (*de cañón*) muzzle 5. (*de río, volcán*) mouth 6. (*de vino*) taste 7. TÉC (*de herramienta*) cutting edge 8. MÚS mouthpiece 9. INFOR slot ►**echar por la** ~ **sapos y** <u>**culebras**</u> to swear black and blue, to rant and rave; **quedarse con la** ~ <u>**abierta**</u> to be dumbfounded; **a** <u>**pedir**</u> **de** ~ perfectly
boca a boca *m sin pl* mouth-to-mouth resuscitation
bocacalle *f* 1. (*entrada de una calle*) street entrance 2. (*calle secundaria*) side street
bocadillo *m* 1. (*sandwich*) sandwich 2. (*refrigerio*) snack 3. (*tira cómica*) balloon, bubble
bocadito *m* 1. *Cuba* (*cigarrillo*) cigarette (*wrapped in tobacco leaf*) 2. *Cuba, RíoPl: coconut or sweet potato dessert*
bocado *m* 1. (*mordisco*) mouthful; ~ **de Adán** Adamns apple 2. (*freno*) bit
bocajarro *adv* **a** ~ (*tirar*) point-blank; **decir algo a** ~ to say sth straight out
bocamanga *f* 1. (*abertura*) hole for the head (in a cape) 2. (*puño*) cuff
bocana *f* estuario
bocanada *f* 1. (*de humo*) puff 2. (*de comida, bebida*) mouthful; **echar** ~**s** *fig* to boast
bocatero, -a *m, f Ven, Hond, Cuba,* **bocaza(s)** *mf* (*inv*) loudmouth; (*fanfarrón*) boaster
bocera *f* 1. (*restos de comida*) crumbs *pl* on the mouth; (*restos de bebida*) smears *pl* on the mouth 2. (*pupa*) cold sore
boceras *mf inv* (*tonto*) fool; (*que habla mucho*) bigmouth
boceto *m* sketch

B

bocha *f* **1.** (*bola*) bowl; (**juego de**) **las ~s** bowls, bowling *Am* **2.** *AmL, inf* (*cabeza*) nut

bochar *vt inf* **1.** *AmL* (*rechazar*) to reject **2.** *Arg* (*fracasar*) to fail

boche *m* **1.** (*hoyo*) hole in the ground **2.** *Arg* (*alemán*) German **3.** *CSur, inf* (*bronca*) telling-off **4.** *AmL, inf* (*repulsa*) snub

bochinche *m* **1.** (*tumulto*) uproar; (*alboroto*) riot **2.** *AmL* (*chisme*) piece of gossip

bochorno *m* **1.** METEO sultry weather **2.** (*sofocación*) stifling atmosphere **3.** (*vergüenza*) shame; **me da ~ que esté mirando** it embarrasses me that he/she is looking

bochornoso, **-a** *adj* **1.** METEO sultry **2.** (*vergonzoso*) shameful

bocina *f* **1.** (*de gramófono, auto*) horn; **tocar la ~** to blow the horn **2.** (*caracola*) large shell **3.** MÚS trumpet **4.** (*megáfono*) megaphone

bocinar *vi* **1.** (*por el cuerno*) to trumpet **2.** AUTO to blow the horn

bocinazo *m* **1.** AUTO blast **2.** *inf* (*grito*) bellow; **pegar un ~ a alguien** to yell at sb

bocio *m* goitre *Brit,* goiter *Am*

boda *f* **1.** (*ceremonia*) wedding **2.** (*fiesta*) wedding reception; **noche de ~s** wedding night

bodega *f* **1.** (*depósito de vino*) wine cellar **2.** (*tienda*) wine shop; (*taberna*) bar **3.** (*despensa*) pantry **4.** (*tienda*) grocery store **5.** NÁUT (*en un puerto*) storeroom; (*en un buque*) hold

bodegón *m* **1.** (*taberna*) bar **2.** (*casa de comidas*) cheap restaurant **3.** ARTE still life

bodeguero, **-a** *m, f* **1.** (*en una bodega*) owner of a wine cellar **2.** *Cuba* (*en una abacería*) grocer

bodoque *m* **1.** (*en un bordado*) raised tuft **2.** *Méx* (*chichón*) bump **3.** *Méx* (*pelota de papel, de lana*) lump; (*de lodo, de masa*) gob **4.** *Méx* (*cosa mal hecha*) badly made thing, sloppy job *inf* **5.** *inf* (*persona tonta*) blockhead

bodrio *m* **1.** *inf* (*cosa*) rubbish, trash; **esta película es un ~** this film is rubbish **2.** *inf* (*comida*) hotchpotch; **la comida fue un ~** the meal was terrible **3.** *AmL* (*confusión*) mess

body *m* <bodies> body

BOE *m abr de* **Boletín Oficial del Estado** ≈ Hansard *Brit,* ≈ The Congressional Record *Am*

bóer *adj, mf* <bóers> Boer

bofe *m* lung; **echar los ~s** (**por algo**) *inf* to slog one's guts out (for sth)

bofetada *f* cuff, smack *Am;* **dar una ~ a alguien** to slap sb

bofia *f inf* cops *pl*

boga *f* **1.** NÁUT rowing **2.** (*moda*) vogue; **estar en ~** to be in vogue

bogador(**a**) *m(f)* rower

bogar <g→gu> *vi* **1.** (*remar*) to row **2.** (*navegar*) to sail

bogavante *m* lobster

bogotano, **-a** **I.** *adj* of/from Bogotá **II.** *m, f* native/inhabitant of Bogotá

Bohemia *f* Bohemia

bohemio, **-a** *adj, m, f* bohemian

bohío *m AmL* rustic hut (*made of wood and branches, cane or straw*)

boicot <boicots> *m* boycott

boicotear *vt* to boycott

boicoteo *m* boycott

boina *f* beret

boj *m* (*arbusto*) box tree; (*madera*) boxwood

bol *m* **1.** (*tazón*) bowl **2.** (*red de pesca*) dragnet; (*lance de red*) casting **3.** (*bolo*) skittle

bola *f* **1.** (*cuerpo esférico*) ball; **~ del mundo** globe; **~ de nieve** snowball **2.** (*canica*) marble; **jugar a las ~s** to play marbles **3.** *inf* (*mentira*) fib; (*rumor*) rumour *Brit,* rumor *Am* **4.** *pl, vulg* (*testículos*) balls *pl,* nuts *pl Am;* **en ~s** *inf* naked, in starkers *Brit, inf,* in the buff *Am, inf* ►**no dar pie con ~** to be unable to do anything right; **ir a su ~** to go one's own way

bolada *f* **1.** (*en los bolos*) throw; (*en el billar*) stroke **2.** *AmL* (*suerte*) piece of luck

bolado *m AmL* (*asunto*) matter

bolazo *m CSur: inf* **1.** (*disparate*) twaddle *Brit,* bunk *inf* **2.** (*mentira*) lie, bull(shit) *vulg*

bolchevique *adj, mf* Bolshevik

boleadoras *fpl CSur* (*especie de lazo*) bolas *pl*

bolear **I.** *vi* **1.** (*en el billar*) to play for fun **2.** *inf* (*contar mentiras*) to tell fibs **II.** *vt* **1.** (*la pelota*) to play **2.** *CSur* (*cazar*) to hunt; (*atrapar*) to catch with a lasso **3.** *Méx* (*zapatos*) to polish **4.** (*alumno*) to fail

bolera *f* bowling alley

bolero *m* MÚS bolero

boleta *f* **1.** (*entrada*) ticket **2.** (*pase*) pass **3.** (*libranza*) bill of exchange, draft *Am* **4.** MIL billet **5.** *AmL* (*documento*) permit **6.** *AmL* (*para votar*) ballot (paper)

boletería *f AmL* (*taquilla*) ticket agency [*o* office]; TEAT box office

boletero, **-a** *m, f AmL* (*taquillero*) ticket clerk

boletín *m* **1.** (*publicación*) bulletin; **~ informativo** news bulletin **2.** (*informe*) report; **~ de noticias** news report **3.** (*cédula*) form

boleto *m* **1.** *AmL* (*entrada, billete*) ticket **2.** (*de quiniela*) coupon **3.** *Arg* (*mentira*) lie

boli *m inf abr de* **bolígrafo** (ballpoint) pen, biro®

boliche *m* **1.** (*bola*) jack **2.** (*juego de bochas*) bowls; (*de bolos*) skittles **3.** (*bolera*) bowling alley **4.** *AmL* (*establecimiento*) grocery shop **5.** *Arg, inf* (*bar*) bar

bólido *m* **1.** ASTR meteorite **2.** AUTO racing car

bolígrafo *m* (ballpoint) pen, biro®

bolillo *m* **1.** (*para hacer encajes*) bobbin; **trabajar al ~** to make lace by hand **2.** *Col* (*de tambor*) drumstick **3.** *Méx* (*panecillo*) bread roll

bolita *f* **1.** *CSur* (*canica*) marble **2.** *Chile* (*balota*) ballot

bolívar *m* bolivar

Bolivia *f* Bolivia

Bolivia is the fifth largest country in South America. Although **Sucre** is the capital, the seat of government is in **La Paz**, the largest city in the country. In addition to Spanish, the official languages of Bolivia are **quechua** and **aimara** (also known as **aimará**). The monetary unit is the **boliviano**.

boliviano *m* (*moneda*) boliviano
boliviano, -a *adj, m, f* Bolivian
bollería *f* (*establecimiento*) baker's; (*bollos*) buns *pl*, baked goods *pl*
bollo *m* **1.** (*panecillo*) bun; (*pastelillo*) cake **2.** (*abolladura*) dent; (*chichón*) lump **3.** (*cosmética*) puff **4.** (*confusión*) mix-up **5.** *CSur, inf* (*puñetazo*) punch
bolo *m* **1.** DEP skittle; **(juego de) ~s** skittles **2.** (*píldora*) large pill **3.** (*tonto*) nitwit **4.** TEAT (*compañía*) travelling company *Brit*, road company *Am*; (*papel*) guest star; **el grupo hizo muchos ~s en verano** the company put on a lot of shows in the summer
bolsa *f* **1.** (*saco*) bag; **~ de agua caliente** hot-water bottle **2.** (*bolso*) handbag, purse *Am*; **~ de plástico** plastic bag; **~ de la compra** shopping bag **3.** (*pliegue en la ropa*) crease **4.** (*caudal*) wealth; **~ de estudios** educational grant **5.** FIN stock exchange; **~ de trabajo** employment bureau; **~ negra** *AmL* black market; **~ de valores** stock exchange **6.** *AmL* (*bolsillo*) pocket **7.** *pl* ANAT **~s de los ojos** bags under the eyes
bolsear *vt AmC, Méx, inf* **~ a alguien** to pick sb's pocket; **~ algo a alguien** to sponge sth off sb
bolsillo *m* **1.** (*en una prenda de vestir*) pocket; **edición de ~** pocket edition **2.** (*monedero*) purse; **rascarse el ~** *inf* to fork out
bolsista *mf* **1.** FIN stockbroker **2.** *AmC* (*carterista*) pickpocket
bolso *m* **1.** bag; (*bolsa pequeña*) handbag, purse *Am* **2.** (*en una vela*) bulge; **hacer ~** to belly out
boludo, -a *inf* **I.** *adj Arg, Urug* (*imbécil*) stupid **II.** *m, f Arg, Urug* (*imbécil*) jerk
bomba **I.** *f* **1.** *t.* MIL bomb; **~ de mano** hand grenade; **~ de relojería** time bomb **2.** TÉC pump; **~ neumática** air pump; **dar a la ~** to pump **3.** (*de lámpara*) shade **4.** *AmL* (*bola*) ball **5.** *AmL* (*pompa*) bubble **6.** *AmL, inf* (*borrachera*) **pegarse una ~** to get drunk ►**a <u>prueba</u> de ~s** bomb-proof; **<u>estar</u> ~** *inf* (*mujer*) to be gorgeous; (*comida*) to be great **II.** *adj inf* astounding; **éxito ~** great success; **pasarlo ~** to have a great time
bombacha *f CSur* (*ropa interior*) knickers *pl Brit*, panties *pl*
bombacho *adj* **pantalón ~** baggy trousers *pl*
bombardear *vt* **1.** MIL to bomb **2.** (*abrumar*) to overwhelm **3.** FÍS to bombard
bombardeo *m* **1.** MIL bombing; **~ aéreo** air raid **2.** FÍS bombardment
bombardero *m* (*avión*) bomber
bombazo *m* **1.** (*explosión*) bomb explosion **2.** *inf* (*sensación*) bombshell
bombeador(a) *m(f) Arg* bomber
bombear **I.** *vt* **1.** MIL to shell **2.** (*un líquido*) to pump **3.** (*un balón*) to lob **4.** *CSur* (*explorar*) to reconnoitre, to reconnoiter *Am* **II.** *vr:* **~se** **1.** (*persona*) to put on airs **2.** (*objeto*) to bulge
bombeo *m* **1.** (*de líquidos*) pumping **2.** (*convexidad*) bulging
bombero *m* **1.** (*oficio*) fireman **2.** *pl* (*cuerpo*) fire brigade; **coche de ~s** fire engine
bombilla *f* **1.** ELEC (light) bulb **2.** *AmS* (*caña*) drinking straw
bombillo *m* **1.** (*de una cerradura*) thief tube **2.** *AmC* (*bombilla*) light bulb
bombín *m* **1.** (*sombrero*) bowler hat **2.** (*bomba de aire*) bicycle pump
bombita *f Arg* (*bombilla*) bulb
bombo *m* **1.** MÚS (*tambor grande*) bass drum **2.** (*en un sorteo*) drum **3.** (*elogio*) exaggerated praise ►**tener la <u>cabeza</u> hecha un ~** to have a splitting headache; **anunciar algo a ~ y <u>platillo</u>** to announce sth with a lot of hype
bombón *m* **1.** (*golosina*) chocolate **2.** *inf* (*mujer*) **es un ~** she's gorgeous
bombona *f* **1.** (*vasija*) carboy **2.** (*de gas*) cylinder
bombonera *f* **1.** (*caja de bombones*) chocolate box **2.** (*vivienda*) cosy little place
bómper *m AmC* (*parachoques*) bumper
bonachón, -ona *adj* **1.** (*buenazo*) kindly **2.** (*crédulo*) naive **3.** (*cándido*) simple
bonaerense **I.** *adj* of/from Buenos Aires province **II.** *mf* native/inhabitant of Buenos Aires province
bonanza *f* **1.** NÁUT calm conditions *pl* **2.** MIN rich vein of ore **3.** (*prosperidad*) prosperity
bondad *f* **1.** (*cualidad de bueno*) goodness **2.** (*amabilidad*) kindness; **tenga la ~ de seguirme** be so kind as to follow me
bondadoso, -a *adj* good-natured, kind
bondi *m Arg, inf* (*bus*) bus
bonete *m* **1.** (*gorro*) cap **2.** ZOOL reticulum
bonetería *f Méx* (*mercería*) draper's shop
bóngalo *m AmL* (*casa pequeña*) bungalow
bongo *m AmL* (*canoa*) small canoe; (*balsa*) small raft
bongó <bongoes> *m* bongo (drum)
boniato *m* sweet potato
bonificación *f* **1.** (*abono*) improvement **2.** (*gratificación*) bonus **3.** (*rebaja*) discount
bonificar <c→qu> *vt* **1.** (*abonar*) to improve **2.** (*gratificar*) to discount
bonito **I.** *m* ZOOL bonito **II.** *adv AmL* nicely
bonito, -a *adj* pretty
bonitura *f AmL* (*hermosura*) beauty
bono *m* **1.** (*vale*) voucher **2.** COM bond
bonoloto *f state-run lottery*
bonsái *m* <bonsais> bonsai
bonzo *m* REL Buddhist monk
boñiga *f*, **boñigo** *m* cow pat
boqueada *f* gasp; **dar las ~s** to be dying
boquear **I.** *vi* **1.** (*abrir la boca*) to gape

2. (*estar muriéndose*) to be at death's door 3. (*estar acabándose*) to be in its final stages **II.** *vt* (*palabras*) to utter
boquera *f* **1.** (*en un canal de riego*) sluice **2.** (*en un pajar*) hatch **3.** (*en los labios*) cold sore
boqueras *mf inv, inf* loudmouth
boquerón *m* **1.** (*abertura grande*) wide opening **2.** ZOOL (fresh) anchovy
boquete *m* (*abertura estrecha*) opening; (*en una pared*) hole
boquiabierto, -a *adj* **1.** (*con la boca abierta*) open-mouthed **2.** (*admirado*) astonished; **dejar a alguien ~** to astonish sb
boquilla *f* **1.** MÚS mouthpiece **2.** (*de cigarrillos*) cigarette holder; (*de pipa*) mouthpiece; **~ de filtro** filter tip **3.** (*de bolso*) clasp **4.** (*de lámpara*) lamp-holder **5.** TÉC nozzle ▸**decir algo de ~** to say sth without meaning it
borboll(e)ar *vi* to bubble
borbollón *m* borbotón
Borbón *m* HIST Bourbon
borbónico, -a *adj* Bourbon
borbotón *m* bubbling; **hablar a borbotones** to talk ten to the dozen; **salir a borbotones** (*agua*) to gush out
borda *f* **1.** NÁUT (*borde del costado*) gunwale; **motor fuera (de) ~** outboard motor; **echar algo por la ~** *t. fig* to throw sth overboard **2.** NÁUT (*vela mayor*) mainsail **3.** (*choza*) hut
bordada *f* NÁUT tack; **dar ~s** (*un barco*) to tack; (*una persona*) to move to and fro
bordado *m* embroidery
bordado, -a *adj* **1.** (*adornado*) embroidered **2.** (*perfecto*) superbly executed
bordador(a) *m(f)* embroiderer *m*, embroideress *f*
bordar *vt* **1.** (*adornar*) to embroider; (*un motivo*) to decorate **2.** (*ejecutar con primor*) to do superbly
borde **I.** *adj* **1.** (*planta*) wild **2.** (*hijo*) illegitimate **3.** *inf* (*persona*) difficult, stroppy **II.** *m* **1.** (*de camino*) verge; (*de mesa*) edge **2.** (*de río*) bank **3.** (*de vestido*) hem; (*como adorno*) border **4.** (*de sombrero*) brim
bordear **I.** *vt* **1.** (*ir por el borde*) to skirt; (*en coche*) to drive along **2.** (*hallarse en el borde*) to border on **3.** (*aproximarse*) to verge on; **su comportamiento bordea la locura** his/her behaviour borders on madness **II.** *vi* NÁUT to tack
bordillo *m* kerb *Brit*, curb *Am*
bordo *m* **1.** NÁUT board; **ir a ~** to go on board **2.** *Méx* (*presa*) dam
bordón *m* **1.** (*bastón*) staff **2.** (*estribillo*) refrain; (*muletilla*) pet phrase **3.** MÚS (*cuerda*) bass string; (*de tripa*) gut
boreal *adj* northern; **hemisferio ~** northern hemisphere
borgoña *m* burgundy
borla *f* **1.** (*adorno*) tassel **2.** (*para empolvarse*) powder puff
borne *m* ELEC terminal
bornear **I.** *vt* (*dar vuelta*) to bend; (*torcer*) to twist; (*ladear*) to incline **II.** *vi* NÁUT to swing at anchor **III.** *vr:* **~se** to bulge
boro *m* boron
borona *f AmL* maize bread *Brit*, corn bread *Am*
borra *f* **1.** (*relleno*) stuffing **2.** (*pelusa*) fluff **3.** (*sedimento*) sediment **4.** (*palabras sin sustancia*) padding
borrachera *f* **1.** (*ebriedad*) drunkenness; **agarrar una ~** to get drunk **2.** (*juerga*) drinking binge **3.** (*exaltación*) intoxication **4.** (*disparate*) absurdity
borracho, -a **I.** *adj* **1.** *ser* (*alcohólico*) hard drinking **2.** *estar* (*ebrio*) drunk; **estar ~ como una cuba** *inf* to be as drunk as a lord **3.** (*exaltado*) **~ de algo** elated with sth **4.** (*pastel*) soaked in liqueur **II.** *m, f* drunk
borrador *m* **1.** (*primer escrito*) rough draft **2.** (*cuaderno*) scribbling pad **3.** (*para la pizarra: trapo*) duster; (*esponja*) board rubber, board eraser
borradura *f* crossing-out, erasure
borrajear *vi, vt* to scribble
borrar **I.** *vt* **1.** (*con goma de borrar*) to rub out, to erase; (*con esponja*) to wipe off **2.** (*tachar*) to cross out **3.** INFOR to delete **4.** (*huellas*) to remove **5.** (*difuminar*) to efface **II.** *vr:* **~se** **1.** (*volverse no identificable*) to blur **2.** (*retirarse*) **~se de algo** to resign from sth
borrasca *f* **1.** (*temporal*) squall; (*tempestad*) storm **2.** (*peligro*) hazard; (*riesgo*) risk; (*contratiempo*) setback **3.** (*orgía*) spree
borrascoso, -a *adj* **1.** METEO stormy; **Cumbres Borrascosas** Wuthering Heights **2.** (*desenfrenado*) tempestuous
borrego, -a *m, f* **1.** (*cordero*) lamb **2.** (*persona*) meek person **3.** *AmL* (*noticia falsa*) hoax
borregos *mpl* **1.** (*nubes*) fleecy clouds *pl* **2.** (*olas*) white horses *pl*
borreguil *adj* meek
borrico *m* TÉC sawhorse
borrico, -a *m, f* donkey
borrón *m* **1.** (*mancha*) stain **2.** (*defecto*) blemish **3.** (*borrador*) rough draft; (*de un cuadro*) sketch ▸**hacer ~ y cuenta nueva** to wipe the slate clean
borronear *vt* **1.** (*borrajear*) to scribble **2.** (*dibujar*) to doodle
borroso, -a *adj* **1.** (*escrito, dibujo*) smudgy; (*escritura*) unclear **2.** (*foto*) blurred
boruquear *vt Méx* to be rowdy
boscaje *m* **1.** (*bosque denso*) thicket **2.** (*pintura*) woodland scene
boscoso, -a *adj* wooded
Bósforo *m* Bosphorus
Bosnia Herzegovina *f* Bosnia and Herzegovina
bosnio, -a *adj, m, f* Bosnian
bosorola *f CRi, Méx* (*borra*) sediment
bosque *m* **1.** (*lugar*) wood; **~ de coníferas** coniferous woodland; **~ frondoso** broad-

leaved woodland; ~ **pluvial** rainforest **2.** (*barba*) thick beard
bosquejar *vt* to sketch
bosquejo *m* sketch
bosta *f* dung, droppings *pl*
bostezar <z→c> *vi* to yawn
bostezo *m* yawn
bota **I.** *adj Méx* **1.** (*torpe*) dim **2.** (*borracho*) drunk **II.** *f* **1.** (*calzado*) boot; **estar con las ~s puestas** *fig* to be ready to go; **ponerse las ~s** *inf* to strike it rich **2.** (*botella de cuero*) wineskin **3.** (*cuba*) large barrel
botado, -a **I.** *adj* **1.** *AmC* (*malgastador*) spendthrift **2.** *Ecua* (*resignado*) resigned; (*resuelto*) resolute **3.** *Guat* (*tímido*) shy **4.** *Méx* (*barato*) dirt cheap **II.** *m, f Méx* foundling
botador(a) *adj AmL* (*derrochador*) spendthrift
botadura *f* launching
botánica *f sin pl* botany
botánico, -a **I.** *adj* botanical **II.** *m, f* botanist
botar **I.** *vi* **1.** (*pelota*) to bounce **2.** (*persona*) to jump **3.** (*caballo*) to rear (up) ▶**estar** (**uno**) **que bota** to be hopping mad **II.** *vt* **1.** (*lanzar*) to throw; (*la pelota contra el suelo*) to bounce **2.** NÁUT (*barco*) to launch; (*el timón*) to put over **3.** *AmL* (*tirar*) to throw away **4.** *AmL* (*expulsar*) to fire; **lo ~on del colegio** he was expelled from school **5.** *AmL* (*derrochar*) to squander **6.** *AmL* (*extraviar*) to lose **III.** *vr:* **~se** (*caballo*) to buck
botaratada *f inf* wild scheme
botarate *m* **1.** (*hombre alborotado*) madcap **2.** *AmL* (*derrochador*) spendthrift
bote *m* **1.** (*golpe*) blow **2.** (*salto*) jump; **pegar un ~** to jump **3.** (*de pelota*) bounce; **la pelota dio cuatro ~s** the ball bounced four times **4.** (*vasija*) jar; **~ de cuestación** collecting tin **5.** (*en la lotería*) jackpot **6.** (*en los bares*) kitty **7.** NÁUT boat; **~ salvavidas** lifeboat ▶**a ~ pronto** (*adj*) sudden; (*adv*) suddenly; **chupar del ~** *inf* to feather one's nest; **darse el ~** *inf* to beat it; **estar de ~ en ~** to be packed; **la tiene en el ~** *inf* he's got her in his pocket
botella *f* bottle; **~ de cerveza** bottle of beer; **cerveza de ~** bottled beer
botellero *m* **1.** (*fabricante*) bottler **2.** (*estantería*) wine-rack
botepronto *m* DEP half-volley
botica *f* **1.** (*farmacia*) pharmacy, chemist's *Brit,* drugstore *Am* **2.** (*tienda*) haberdashery
boticario, -a *m, f* chemist *Brit,* druggist *Am*
botija *f* **1.** (*vasija*) earthenware jug **2.** *inf* (*persona gorda*) fat person **3.** *AmL* (*tesoro*) buried treasure
botijo *m* **1.** (*vasija*) earthenware drinking jug **2.** (*tren*) excursion train
botín *m* **1.** (*calzado*) high shoe **2.** MIL booty
botina *f* ankle boot
botiquín *m* **1.** (*en casa*) medicine chest **2.** (*de emergencia*) first-aid kit
botón *m* **1.** (*en vestidos*) button **2.** ELEC knob; **~ de muestra** sample; *fig* illustration; **~ de opciones** INFOR option button **3.** (*en instrumentos de viento*) key **4.** BIO (*capullo*) bud; **~ de oro** buttercup **5.** *CSur, pey* (*policía*) cop
botonadura *f* (set of) buttons *pl*
botones *m inv* **1.** (*en un hotel*) bellboy **2.** *pey* (*recadero*) errand boy
boutique *f* boutique
bóveda *f* **1.** ARQUIT vault; **~ celeste** firmament **2.** (*cripta*) vault **3.** (*forma abombada*) dome
bovino, -a *adj* bovine
bovinos *mpl* bovines *pl*
box *m* **1.** (*para caballos*) stall **2.** *AmL* (*boxeo*) boxing **3.** *AmC* (*postal*) postbox *Brit,* mailbox *Am* **4.** *pl* AUTO pits *pl;* **entrar en ~es** to make a pit-stop
boxeador(a) *m(f)* boxer
boxear *vi* to box
boxeo *m* boxing
boya *f* buoy; (*en una red*) float
boyante *adj* **1.** (*flotante*) buoyant; (*barco*) high in the water **2.** (*próspero*) prosperous; **el negocio va ~** business is booming
boyar *vi* **1.** NÁUT to be afloat again **2.** *AmL* (*flotar*) to float
boyero *m* **1.** (*cuidador*) cowherd **2.** *Col* goad
boy scout <boy scouts> *mf* boy scout
bozal *m* **1.** (*de perro*) muzzle **2.** *AmL* (*cabestro*) halter; (*cuerda*) headstall
bozo *m* **1.** (*pelos*) down **2.** (*cabestro*) halter; (*cuerda*) headstall
bracear *vi* **1.** (*mover los brazos*) to swing one's arms **2.** (*nadar*) to swim **3.** (*esforzarse*) to make an effort **4.** (*forcejear*) to struggle **5.** NÁUT to measure in fathoms
bracero *m AmL* **1.** (*jornalero*) farmhand **2.** (*peón*) labourer *Brit,* laborer *Am*
braga *f* **1.** (*de bebé*) nappy *Brit,* diaper *Am* **2.** *pl* (*de mujer*) panties *pl* **3.** *pl* (*de hombre*) breeches *pl* ▶**dejar a alguien en ~s** *inf* to leave sb penniless; **estar en ~s** *inf* to be broke
bragado, -a *adj* **1.** (*malintencionado*) malicious **2.** (*decidido*) resolute
bragapañal *m* disposable nappy *Brit,* disposable diaper *Am*
bragazas *m inv* henpecked husband
bragueta *f* flies *pl Brit,* fly *Am*
braguetazo *m* marriage for money; **dar el ~** to marry for money
braille *m* Braille
brainstorming *m sin pl* tormenta de ideas, brainstorming
bramadero *m* **1.** (*del ciervo*) rutting ground **2.** *AmL* (*estaca para atar animales*) tethering post
bramante *m* twine
bramar *vi* **1.** (*animal*) to roar; (*ciervo*) to bellow **2.** (*persona*) to bluster; **está que brama** he/she is furious **3.** (*viento*) to howl **4.** (*oleaje*) to thunder
bramido *m* **1.** (*animales*) roar; (*ciervos*) bellow **2.** (*persona*) blustering **3.** (*viento*) howling **4.** (*oleaje*) thundering
brandy *m* brandy

branquia *f* gill

branquial *adj* branchial

brasa *f* ember; **a la** ~ grilled

brasero *m* **1.** (*como calefacción*) brazier **2.** *AmL* (*fuego*) fireplace; (*hogar*) hearth

Brasil *m* (**el**) ~ Brazil

brasileño, **-a** *adj, m, f* Brazilian

brava *f Cuba* (*golpe*) punch; **dar una** ~ to intimidate; **a la** ~, **por las** ~**s** *Arg, Cuba, Méx, PRico* by force

bravata *f* **1.** (*amenaza*) threat **2.** (*bravuconada*) piece of bravado

bravío *m* fierceness

bravío, **-a** *adj* **1.** (*animal: salvaje*) wild; (*sin domar*) untamed **2.** (*planta*) wild **3.** (*persona: indómita*) impetuous; (*rústica*) uncouth

bravo **I.** *interj* well done **II.** *m* thug

bravo, **-a** *adj* **1.** (*valiente*) brave **2.** (*bueno*) excellent **3.** (*salvaje: animal, persona*) wild; (*mar*) stormy; (*terreno*) rugged **4.** (*áspero*) rough **5.** (*fanfarrón*) boastful **6.** *AmL* (*picante*) hot

bravucón, **-ona** **I.** *adj* boastful **II.** *m, f* braggart

bravuconada *f* boasting

bravura *f* **1.** (*de los animales*) ferocity **2.** (*de las personas*) bravery **3.** *pey* (*bravata*) boasting

braza *f* **1.** NÁUT (*unidad de longitud*) fathom (*1,80 m*); (*cabo*) brace **2.** DEP breast stroke

brazada *f* **1.** (*movimiento de los brazos*) movement of the arms; (*al nadar*) stroke **2.** (*cantidad*) armful

brazalete *m* **1.** (*pulsera*) bracelet **2.** (*banda*) armband

brazo *m* **1.** ANAT arm; ~ **derecho** *fig* right-hand man; ~ **de gitano** GASTR Swiss roll, jelly roll *Am;* **cruzarse de** ~**s** to fold one's arms; *fig* to stand by and do nothing; **dar el** ~ **a torcer** to give way; **ir cogidos del** ~ to walk arm-in-arm; **recibir a alguien con los** ~**s abiertos** to welcome sb with open arms **2.** (*de una silla*) arm **3.** GEO (*del río*) branch; (*del mar*) sound **4.** ZOOL foreleg **5.** BIO limb **6.** (*poder*) power **7.** *pl* (*jornaleros*) workers *pl* **8.** *pl* (*protectores*) backers *pl*

brea *f* **1.** (*alquitrán*) tar **2.** (*pez*) pitch

breakdance *m sin pl* break dancing

brear *vt* **1.** (*maltratar*) to abuse; ~ **a alguien a golpes** to beat sb up **2.** (*burlarse*) ~ **a alguien** to make fun of sb

brebaje *m* **1.** (*bebida*) brew **2.** (*medicina*) potion

brecha *f* **1.** MIL breach **2.** (*abertura*) opening; (*en una pared*) gap **3.** (*impresión*) impression **4.** (*herida en la cabeza*) gash ►<u>**estar**</u> **en la** ~ to be in the thick of things

brécol(**es**) *m*(*pl*) broccoli

brega *f* **1.** (*riña*) quarrel **2.** (*lucha*) struggle **3.** (*trabajo duro*) slog

bregar <g→gu> *vi* **1.** (*reñir*) to quarrel **2.** (*luchar*) to struggle **3.** (*trabajar duro*) to slave away, to slog away *Brit*

bresca *f* honeycomb

Bretaña *f* Brittany; **Gran** ~ Great Britain

brete *m* fetters *pl;* **estar en un** ~ to be in a jam; **poner a alguien en un** ~ to put sb on the spot

bretón, **-ona** *adj, m, f* Breton

breva *f* **1.** (*higo*) early fig **2.** (*cigarro*) flat cigar **3.** *AmL* (*tabaco*) chewing tobacco **4.** (*ganga*) piece of luck; **¡no caerá esa** ~**!** no such luck!

breve **I.** *adj* **1.** (*de duración*) brief; **en** ~ shortly **2.** (*de extensión*) short **II.** *m* PREN short news item

brevedad *f* **1.** (*corta duración*) brevity; **a la mayor** ~ **posible** as soon as possible **2.** (*corta extensión*) shortness

brevete *m* **1.** (*membrete*) letterhead **2.** *Perú* (*permiso de conducir*) driving licence *Brit,* driver's license *Am*

breviario *m* **1.** (*libro de rezos*) prayer book **2.** (*compendio*) compendium

brezo *m* heather

briago, **-a** *adj Méx, inf* drunk

bribón, **-ona** **I.** *adj* **1.** (*pícaro*) rascally **2.** (*vago*) idle **II.** *m, f* **1.** (*bellaco*) rogue **2.** (*pícaro*) scoundrel **3.** (*niño*) rascal

bribonada *f* piece of mischief

bricolaje *m* do-it-yourself

brida *f* **1.** (*de la caballería*) bridle **2.** (*del sombrero*) chinstrap **3.** TÉC (*reborde*) flange; (*arandela*) clamp **4.** *pl* MED adhesion

bridge *m* bridge

brigada[1] *f* **1.** MIL brigade **2.** (*de obreros*) gang **3.** (*de policía*) squad

brigada[2] *m* MIL sergeant-major

brillante **I.** *m* diamond **II.** *adj* **1.** (*luz, color*) bright; (*joya, conversación*) sparkling **2.** (*compañía*) brilliant

brillantez *f t. fig* brilliance

brillantina *f* brilliantine, hair cream

brillar *vi* to shine; ~ **por su ausencia** *irón* to be conspicuous by one's absence

brillo *m* **1.** (*cualidad*) shine; (*reflejo de luz*) glow; **dar** ~ **a algo** to polish sth **2.** (*gloria*) splendour *Brit,* splendor *Am* **3.** (*excelencia*) brilliance

brincar <c→qu> *vi* **1.** (*saltar*) to hop; (*hacia arriba*) to jump **2.** (*pasar de un tema a otro*) to skip **3.** (*alterarse*) to fly into a rage; ~ **de alegría** to jump for joy; ~ **de rabia** to dance with rage

brinco *m* hop; **dar** ~**s** to hop; **de un** ~ in one bound

brindar **I.** *vi* (*levantar la copa*) to drink a toast; ~ **por alguien** to drink to sb **II.** *vt* **1.** (*ofrecer*) to offer **2.** TAUR to dedicate **III.** *vr* ~**se a hacer algo** to offer to do sth

brindis *m inv* **1.** (*el levantar los vasos*) toast; **echar un** ~ to drink a toast **2.** (*frase con que se brinda*) dedication

brío *m* **1.** (*energía*) spirit **2.** (*pujanza*) drive **3.** (*garbo*) elegance

brioso, **-a** *adj* **1.** (*con energía*) spirited **2.** (*con pujanza*) vigorous **3.** (*con garbo*) elegant

brisa *f* breeze

británico, **-a** I. *adj* British; **Inglés Británico** British English II. *m, f* Briton *Brit,* Britisher *Am*

brit-pop *m* MÚS Brit-pop

brizna *f* 1.(*hebra*) strand 2. BOT blade; (*de judías*) string 3.(*porción diminuta*) scrap; **no tiene ni una ~ de humor** he/she has no sense of humour whatsover 4. *AmL* (*llovizna*) drizzle

broca *f* TÉC (*taladro*) bit

brocado *m* brocade

brocal *m* rim; (*de pozo*) mouth

brocha *f* 1.(*pincel grueso*) brush; **de ~ gorda** crudely painted; *fig* slapdash; **pintor de ~ gorda** house painter 2.(*de afeitar*) shaving brush 3. *inf* (*mal pintor*) dauber

brochazo *m* brush stroke

broche *m* 1.(*en la ropa*) clasp; (*de adorno*) brooch; **~ de oro** *fig* finishing touch 2. *AmL* (*sujetapapeles*) paper clip 3. *pl, AmL* (*gemelos*) cufflinks *pl*

brocheta *f* skewer

broker *m* FIN broker

broma *f* 1.(*gracia*) fun, kidding *Am* 2.(*tontería*) joke; **~ pesada** practical joke; **decir algo en ~** to be kidding; **gastar ~s a alguien** to play jokes on sb; **~s aparte...** joking apart ...; **estoy de ~** I'm not serious; **no estoy para ~s** I'm in no mood for jokes; **no hay que andar con ~s con él** he doesn't put up with any nonsense; **¡ni en ~** no way!

bromear *vi* to joke, to kid *Am;* **¿bromeas?** are you kidding?

bromista I. *adj* fond of jokes II. *mf* joker

bromo *m* bromine

bromuro *m* bromide

bronca *f* 1.(*riña*) row; **se armó una ~ tremenda** there was a tremendous row 2.(*reprimenda*) ticking-off *Brit,* chewing-out 3.(*tumulto*) uproar 4. *AmL* (*enfado*) anger; **me da ~** it makes me mad

bronce *m* bronze

bronceado *m* 1.(*de un objeto*) bronze finish 2.(*de la piel: efecto*) tan; (*acción*) tanning

bronceado, **-a** *adj* 1.(*objeto*) bronze 2.(*piel*) tanned

bronceador *m* suntan lotion

broncear I. *vt* 1.(*un objeto*) to bronze 2.(*la piel*) to tan II. *vr:* **~se** to get a (sun)tan

bronco, **-a** *adj* 1.(*voz*) gruff 2.(*metal: tosco*) rough; (*quebradizo*) brittle 3.(*genio*) surly 4. *AmL* (*caballo*) untamed

bronquedad *f* 1.(*de la voz*) gruffness 2.(*tosquedad de metales*) roughness; (*delicadez*) brittleness 3.(*del genio*) surliness

bronquio *m* ANAT bronchial tube

bronquitis *f inv* MED bronchitis

broquel *m t. fig* (*escudo*) shield

broqueta *f* skewer

brotar I. *vi* 1. BOT to sprout; (*árbol*) to grow; (*semilla*) to germinate 2.(*agua*) to flow 3.(*enfermedad*) to break out II. *vt* (*terreno*) to bring forth; (*planta*) to sprout

brote *m* 1. BOT shoot; **~s de soja** bean sprouts 2.(*comienzo*) origin 3.(*erupción*) outbreak

broza *f* 1.(*hojas*) dead leaves *pl;* (*ramas*) brushwood 2.(*arbustos*) undergrowth 3.(*palabras inútiles*) padding

bruces *adv* **caer de ~** to fall headlong; **darse de ~ con alguien** (*chocar*) to crash into sb; (*hallar casualmente*) to run into sb

bruja *f* 1.(*hechicera*) witch 2.(*lechuza*) barn owl

Brujas *f* Bruges

brujería *f* witchcraft

brujo *m* 1.(*hechicero*) wizard 2. *AmL* (*curandero*) medicine man

brújula *f* 1.(*compás*) compass; (*aguja*) magnetic needle; **perder la ~** *fig* to lose one's bearings 2.(*mira*) guide

brulote *m AmS* (*taco*) swear word

bruma *f* mist

brumoso, **-a** *adj* misty

bruñido *m* 1.(*acto*) polishing 2.(*brillo*) polish

bruñir <*3. pret:* bruñó> *vt* 1.(*sacar brillo*) to polish 2. *inf* (*maquillar*) to make up 3. *AmL* (*molestar*) to pester

brusco, **-a** *adj* 1.(*repentino*) sudden; **un ~ aumento** a sharp increase 2.(*person*) abrupt

Bruselas *f* Brussels

brusquedad *f* 1.(*de un suceso*) suddenness 2.(*de un comportamiento*) abruptness; **con ~** sharply

brutal *adj* 1.(*violento*) brutal 2.(*desconsiderado*) tactless 3. *inf* (*enorme*) huge 4. *inf* (*estupendo*) tremendous

brutalidad *f* 1.(*calidad de bruto*) brutality 2.(*acción violenta*) brutal act; (*cruel*) cruel act 3.(*cantidad excesiva*) huge amount 4.(*estupidez*) stupidity

bruto *adj* 1.(*tosco*) uncut; **diamante en ~** rough diamond 2.(*peso*) gross

bruto, **-a** I. *adj* 1.(*brutal*) brutal 2.(*rudo*) uncouth 3.(*estúpido*) ignorant II. *m, f* 1.(*persona brutal*) brute 2.(*idiota*) idiot

bucal *adj* (of the) mouth; **higiene ~** oral hygiene

búcaro *m* (*jarra*) clay pitcher; (*arcilla*) fragrant clay; (*florero*) vase

buceador(**a**) *m(f)* diver

bucear *vi* 1.(*nadar*) to dive 2.(*investigar*) **~ en algo** to delve into sth

buceo *m* diving

buchada *f* mouthful

buche *m* 1.(*en las aves*) crop 2. *inf* (*estómago*) belly 3.(*bocanada*) mouthful 4.(*pliegue en la ropa*) crease 5.(*lo más íntimo*) inner thoughts *pl;* **guardar algo en el ~** to keep sth hidden

bucle *m* 1.(*rizo de cabello*) curl 2.(*onda*) *t.* INFOR loop

bucólico, **-a** *adj* pastoral; LIT bucolic

buda *m* Buddha

budín *m* pudding

budismo *m sin pl* Buddhism

budista *adj, mf* Buddhist

buen *adj v.* **bueno**

B

buenamente *adv* **1.**(*fácilmente*) easily **2.**(*voluntariamente*) voluntarily

buenaventura *f* **1.**(*suerte*) good luck **2.**(*adivinación*) fortune; **echar la ~ a alguien** to tell sb's fortune

buenazo, **-a** **I.** *adj* good-natured **II.** *m, f* good-natured person

bueno *interj* OK

bueno, **-a** *adj* <mejor *o* más bueno, el mejor *o* bonísimo *o* buenísimo> *delante de un substantivo masculino: buen* **1.**(*calidad*) good; (*tiempo*) fine; (*constitución*) sound; (*decisión*) right; **~s días** good morning; **buenas tardes/noches** good afternoon/evening; **buen viaje** have a good journey; **hace ~** it's nice weather; **dar algo por ~** to accept sth; **estar de buenas** to be in a good mood; **lo que tiene de ~ es que...** the good thing about it is that ...; **por las buenas o por las malas** by fair means or foul **2.**(*apropiado*) suitable **3.**(*fácil*) easy; **el libro es ~ de leer** the book is easy to read **4.**(*honesto*) honest; (*bondadoso*) kindly; (*niño*) well-behaved; **es buena gente** he/she is a nice person **5.**(*sano*) healthy **6.** *inf* (*atractivo*) attractive; **está buenísima** she's hot stuff **7.**(*bonito*) fine; **¡buena la has hecho!** *irón* you've done it now!; **¡estaría ~!** *fig* I should think not!

Buenos Aires *m* Buenos Aires

buey *m* **1.** ZOOL ox **2.** *AmC* (*cornudo*) cuckold

búfalo *m* buffalo

bufanda *f* scarf

bufar *vi* **1.**(*resoplar*) to snort; (*gato*) to spit; **está que bufa** he/she is really furious **2.** *AmL* (*oler mal*) to stink

bufé *m v.* **bufet**

bufeo *m Ant, Hond, Méx* (*delfín*) dolphin; (*tonina*) tuna

bufet *m AmL* **1.**(*aparador*) sideboard **2.**(*cena fría*) cold supper **3.**(*restaurante*) dining-room

bufete *m* **1.**(*escritorio*) desk **2.**(*de abogado*) lawyer's office; **abrir ~** to set up in practice **3.**(*clientela*) lawyer's clients *pl* **4.**(*aparador*) sideboard

bufido *m* **1.**(*resoplido*) snort **2.**(*exabrupto*) sharp remark **3.**(*gato*) hiss

bufón, **-ona** **I.** *adj* clownish **II.** *m, f* **1.**(*bromista*) joker **2.** TEAT buffoon

bufonada *f* **1.**(*burla*) joking **2.** TEAT comic piece

buganvilla *f* bougainvillea

buhardilla *f* **1.**(*ventana*) dormer window **2.**(*desván*) loft **3.**(*vivienda*) garret

búho *m* **1.** ZOOL owl **2.**(*persona*) unsociable person **3.**(*línea de autobús*) night bus

buhonería *f* pedlar's [*o* peddler's *Am*] wares *pl*

buhonero *m* pedlar *Brit,* peddler *Am*

buitre *m* **1.** ZOOL vulture, buzzard **2.** *inf* (*persona*) sponger

buitrear *vi* **1.** *AmL* (*cazar*) to kill **2.** *CSur* (*vomitar*) to throw up

bujía *f* **1.**(*vela*) candle **2.**(*candelero*) candlestick **3.** AUTO sparking plug *Brit,* spark plug *Am* **4.** FÍS candlepower

bula *f* (papal) bull

bulbo *m* bulb

bule *m Méx* BOT gourd

bulevar *m* boulevard

Bulgaria *f* Bulgaria

búlgaro, **-a** *adj, m, f* Bulgarian

bulimia *f sin pl* MED bulimia

bulla *f* **1.**(*ruido*) racket **2.**(*aglomeración*) mob **3.**(*confusión*) fuss **4.** *AmL* (*pelea*) brawl

bullabesa *f* GASTR fish soup, bouillabaisse

bullanguero, **-a** **I.** *adj* rowdy **II.** *m, f* troublemaker

bulldozer, **bulldózer** *m* bulldozer

bullicio *m* **1.**(*ruido*) uproar **2.**(*tumulto*) commotion

bullicioso, **-a** *adj* noisy

bullir <*3. pret:* bulló> **I.** *vi* **1.**(*hervir*) to boil; (*borbotar*) to bubble; **le bulle la sangre** (**en las venas**) *fig* he/she is a bundle of energy **2.**(*agitarse*) to move; (*moverse*) to stir **3.**(*pulular*) to swarm **II.** *vt* to move **III.** *vr:* **~se** to budge

bulo *m* false rumour *Brit,* false rumor *Am*

bulto *m* **1.**(*tamaño*) size; **a ~** roughly; **de ~** bulky; **escurrir el ~** *inf* to pass the buck **2.**(*importancia*) importance; (*esencia*) substance; **un error de ~** a major error **3.**(*cuerpo indistinguible*) mass **4.**(*fardo*) bundle **5.**(*paquete*) piece of luggage **6.** MED swelling

bumerán, **bumerang** *m* boomerang; **efecto ~** boomerang effect

bungaló *m*, **bungalow** *m* bungalow

búnker *m* MIL bunker

buñuelo *m* **1.**(*pastel*) doughnut *Brit,* donut *Am* **2.**(*chapuza*) botched job

BUP *m abr de* **Bachillerato Unificado Polivalente** *secondary studies for pupils aged 14–17, now supplanted by the ESO*

buque *m* **1.**(*barco*) ship; **~ de pasajeros** passenger ship; **~ de carga** freighter; **~ de guerra** warship; **~ insignia** flagship; **~ de vapor** steamer **2.**(*casco*) hull **3.**(*cabida*) tonnage

buqué *m* (*de vino*) bouquet

buque-cisterna *m* <buques-cisterna> tanker

buraco *m Arg, Par, Urug* hole

burata *f Ven, inf* cash, dough *Am, inf*

burbuja *f* bubble

burbujear *vi* to bubble

burdel *m* brothel

Burdeos *m* Bordeaux

burdo, **-a** *adj* (*tosco*) coarse; (*excusa*) clumsy

bureo *m* amusement; **ir de ~** to have a good time

burgalés, **-esa** **I.** *adj* of/from Burgos **II.** *m, f* native/inhabitant of Burgos

burgo *m* **1.**(*aldea*) hamlet **2.** HIST (*castillo*) castle

burgués, **-esa** **I.** *adj t. pey* bourgeois, middle-class **II.** *m, f t. pey* bourgeois *m,* bourgeoise *f*

burguesía *f* bourgeoisie

buril *m* engraver's chisel
Burkina Faso *f* Burkina-Faso
burla *f* **1.** (*mofa*) taunt; **hacer ~ de alguien** to make fun of sb **2.** (*broma*) joke; **~s aparte** joking apart **3.** (*engaño*) hoax
burlador(a) **I.** *adj* mocking **II.** *m(f)* **1.** (*mofador*) mocker **2.** (*bromista*) practical joker **3.** (*seductor*) seducer
burlar **I.** *vt* **1.** (*mofarse*) to mock **2.** (*engañar*) to cheat **3.** (*frustrar*) to frustrate **4.** (*eludir*) to evade; (*orden*) to disregard; (*bloqueo*) to run **5.** (*seducir*) to seduce **II.** *vr:* **~se** to joke
burlesco, -a *adj* **1.** (*jocoso*) comic **2.** LIT burlesque
burlete *m* (*de la puerta*) draught excluder *Brit,* weather stripp(ing) *Am*
burlón, -ona **I.** *adj* mocking **II.** *m, f* **1.** (*mofador*) mocker **2.** (*guasón*) joker, wag *Brit*
buró *m* **1.** (*escritorio*) bureau **2.** *AmL* (*mesa de noche*) bedside table
burocracia *f* bureaucracy
burócrata *mf* bureaucrat
burocrático, -a *adj* bureaucratic
burocratización *f* bureaucratization
burocratizar <z→c> *vt* to bureaucratize
burrada *f* **1.** *inf* (*disparate*) silly thing; **decir ~s** to talk nonsense **2.** *inf* (*cantidad grande*) load **3.** (*manada*) drove of donkeys
burro *m* **1.** TÉC sawhorse **2.** *AmC* (*escalera*) step ladder **3.** *AmC* (*columpio*) swing
burro, -a **I.** *adj* **1.** (*tonto*) stupid **2.** (*obstinado*) obstinate **II.** *m, f* **1.** ZOOL donkey; **~ de carga** *t. fig* beast of burden **2.** (*persona tonta*) idiot; **~ cargado de letras** pompous ass **3.** (*persona obstinada*) obstinate person **4.** (*persona trabajadora*) hard worker ▶**esto es un ~ con dos albardas** that's saying the same thing twice over; **apearse del ~** to recognize one's mistake; **no ver tres en un ~** to be as blind as a bat
bursátil *adj* stock exchange
bus *m t.* INFOR bus
busaca *f* **1.** *Col, Ven* (*bolsa*) bag **2.** *Ven* (*cartera*) satchel
busca[1] *f* search; **en ~ de alguien** in search of sb
busca[2] *m* bleeper *Brit,* beeper *Am*
buscabullas **I.** *adj* troublemaking **II.** *mf inv* troublemaker
buscador *m* INFOR searcher
buscapié *m* hint
buscapleitos *mf inv, AmL* troublemaker
buscar <c→qu> *vi, vt* to look for; **enviar a alguien a ~ algo** to send sb to fetch sth; **ir a ~ algo** to go and look for sth; **me viene a buscar a las 7** he/she is picking me up at 7; **él se lo ha buscado** he brought it on himself; **~ tres pies al gato** to complicate matters; **'se busca'** 'wanted'
buscatesoros *mf inv* treasure-seeker
buscavidas *mf inv* **1.** (*curioso*) busybody **2.** (*diligente*) hustler
buscona *f* whore
buseta *f Col, Ven* (*pequeño autobús*) minibus
busilis *m inv, inf* difficulty; **dar en el ~** to put one's finger on the spot
búsqueda *f t.* INFOR search
busto *m* bust
butaca *f* **1.** (*silla*) armchair **2.** (*de cine, de teatro*) stall *Brit,* seat *Am*
butacón *m* large armchair
butano **I.** *adj* orange **II.** *m* **1.** QUÍM butane (gas) **2.** (*color*) orange
butifarra *f* **1.** (*salchicha*) *Catalan sausage* **2.** *AmL* (*media*) (badly-fitting) stocking
butrón *m inf* break-in
buzo *m* **1.** (*buceador*) diver **2.** (*mono*) overalls *pl Brit,* coverall *Am*
buzón *m* (*de correos*) letterbox *Brit,* mailbox *Am;* **~ (electrónico)** INFOR mailbox
byte *m* INFOR byte; **~ de control** control byte

C

C, c *f* C, c; **~ de Carmen** C for Charlie
C/ *abr de* **calle** St
cabal **I.** *adj* **1.** (*completo*) complete **2.** (*persona*) honest **II.** *m* **no estar en sus ~es** not to be in one's right mind
cábala *f* **1.** REL cabbala **2.** (*intriga*) intrigue **3.** *pl* (*suposición*) supposition
cabalgadura *f* (*de montura*) mount; (*de carga*) beast of burden
cabalgar <g→gu> **I.** *vi* to ride **II.** *vt* **1.** (*a caballo*) to ride **2.** (*el macho a la hembra*) to mount
cabalgata *f* procession, cavalcade
caballa *f* mackerel
caballada *f* **1.** (*manada*) drove of horses **2.** *AmL* (*animalada*) asinine thing to say or do
caballerango *m Méx* groom
caballeresco, -a *adj* **1.** HIST knightly **2.** (*galante*) chivalrous
caballería *f* **1.** (*montura*) mount **2.** MIL cavalry
caballeriza *f* stable
caballerizo *m* groom
caballero *m* **1.** (*señor, galán*) gentleman **2.** HIST knight
caballerosidad *f* gentlemanliness
caballeroso, -a *adj* gentlemanly
caballete *m* **1.** (*de mesa*) trestle **2.** (*de cuadro*) easel
caballito *m* **1.** ZOOL **~ de mar** sea horse **2.** *pl* (*en una feria*) merry-go-round, carousel *Am*
caballo *m* **1.** (*animal*) horse; **a ~** on horseback; **ir a ~** to ride; **~ de batalla** *fig* hobby horse **2.** (*ajedrez*) knight **3.** DEP **~ (de saltos)** jumper **4.** AUTO horsepower **5.** (*naipes*) queen **6.** *inf* (*heroína*) smack
cabaña *f* **1.** (*choza*) cabin **2.** AGR livestock
cabaré *m,* **cabaret** *m* <cabarets> cabaret

cabecear I. *vi* 1. (*mover la cabeza*) to shake one's head 2. (*dormitar*) to nod off II. *vt* DEP to head

cabecera *f* 1. (*de una cama, de la mesa*) head; (*plaza de honor*) seat of honour [*o* honor *Am*]; **médico de** ~ general practioner, G.P. 2. (*del periódico*) masthead

cabecilla *mf* ringleader

cabellera *f* 1. (*de la cabeza*) hair; (*abundante*) mane 2. ASTR tail (of a comet)

cabello *m* hair; **se le pusieron los ~s de punta** his/her hair stood on end; **traído por los ~s** far-fetched

cabelludo, **-a** *adj* hairy; BOT fibrous

caber *irr vi* 1. (*tener espacio*) ~ **en algo** to fit in [*o* into] sth; **no ~ en sí de...** to be beside oneself with ...; **esta falda no me cabe** this skirt doesn't fit me 2. (*ser posible*) to be possible

cabestrillo *m* MED sling

cabeza[1] *f* 1. *t.* ANAT, TÉC head; ~ **de ajo** bulb of garlic; ~ **atómica** atomic warhead; ~ **de lectura** INFOR read head; ~ **de partido** administrative centre [*o* center *Am*]; ~ **abajo** upside down; ~ **arriba** upright; **de** ~ headfirst; **por** ~ a head; **abrirse la** ~ to split one's head open; **asentir con la** ~ to nod (one's head); **negar con la** ~ to shake one's head; **se me va la** ~ I feel dizzy; **de la ~ a los pies** from head to toe; **estar mal de la** ~ *inf* to be out of one's mind; **jugarse la** ~ to risk one's life; **levantar** ~ to pull through; **métetelo en la** ~ get it into your head; **algo se le pasa a alguien por la** ~ sth crosses sb's mind; **quitarse algo de la** ~ to put sth out of one's mind; **sentar** (**la**) ~ to settle down; **tener la ~ dura** to be stubborn; **traer a alguien de** ~ to drive sb crazy; **este chico tiene** ~ this boy is clever; **tener ~ para los negocios** to be business-minded 2. (*extremo*) top; **ir en** ~ DEP to be in the lead 3. AGR (*res*) head

cabeza[2] *m* head; ~ **de familia** head of the family; ~ **rapada** skinhead

cabezada *f* blow on the head; **dar** [*o* **echar**] **una** ~ *inf* to have a nap

cabezazo *m* 1. (*golpe*) blow on the head; **darse un** ~ to bang one's head 2. DEP header

cabezón, **-ona** I. *adj* 1. (*de cabeza grande*) with a big head 2. *inf* (*obstinado*) pigheaded II. *m, f* pigheaded person

cabezonería *f inf* pigheadedness

cabezota *mf inf* pigheaded person

cabida *f* space

cabina *f* cabin; (*en la playa*) cubicle; ~ **de control** TÉC control room; ~ **del piloto** cockpit; ~ **de proyección** projection room; ~ **de teléfonos** telephone box *Brit,* phone booth *Am*

cabinera *f Col* air hostess, stewardess

cabizbajo, **-a** *adj* with head bowed; (*triste*) dejected

cable *m t.* ELEC (*telegrama*) cable; **se le cruzaron los ~s** *inf* he/she lost control; **echar un ~ a alguien** *inf* to help sb out

cablegrafiar <*1. pres:* cablegrafío> *vt* to cable

cabo *m* 1. (*extremo*) end; **al fin y al** ~ in the end; **de ~ a rabo** from beginning to end; **llevar a** ~ to carry out; **no dejar ningún ~ suelto** to leave no loose ends 2. GEO cape; **Ciudad del Cabo** Cape Town 3. MIL corporal 4. NÁUT rope ▸**al** ~ **de** after

cabotaje *m* coastal shipping

cabra *f* goat; ~ **montés** wild goat; **estar como una** ~ *inf* to be off one's head

cabrear I. *vt inf* to infuriate; **estar cabreado** to be furious II. *vr:* **~se** *inf* to get angry

cabrero, **-a** *m, f* goatherd

cabrestante *m* 1. TÉC winch 2. NÁUT capstan

cabrío, **-a** *adj* goatish

cabriola *f* caper; **hacer ~s** to caper about

cabritillo, **-a** *m, f* kid

cabro *m AmS* billy goat

cabrón *m* billy goat

cabrón, **-ona** *m, f vulg* bastard, bugger

cabronada *f vulg* dirty trick

cábula *f* 1. *Arg, Par* (*amuleto*) amulet 2. *Arg* (*cábala*) cabal 3. *Chile, Méx, Perú, PRico* (*ardid*) ruse

caca *f inf* 1. (*excremento*) pooh *Brit,* poop *Am;* (*lenguaje infantil*) number two 2. (*chapuza*) rubbish

cacahuate *m Méx* (*cacahuete*) peanut

cacahuete *m* peanut

cacalote *m AmC* 1. GASTR popcorn 2. *inf* (*disparate*) silly thing

cacao *m* 1. (*planta*) cacao 2. *inf* (*jaleo*) to-do; **pedir** ~ *AmL* to give in

cacarear I. *vi* 1. (*gallinas*) to cackle 2. *inf* (*presumir*) to brag II. *vt inf* (*presumir*) to brag about

cacarizo, **-a** *adj Méx* pitted

cacastle *m AmC, Méx* 1. (*esqueleto*) skeleton 2. (*armazón*) pack frame (*fitted on shoulders to aid in carrying loads*)

cacatúa *f* 1. ZOOL cockatoo 2. *inf* (*mujer*) old bag

cacería *f* 1. (*partida*) hunting 2. (*piezas*) bag

cacerola *f* saucepan

cachafaz *adj AmS* roguish

cachalote *m* sperm whale

cachar *vt* 1. *AmC, Col, Chile* (*cornear*) to gore 2. *Arg, Nic, Urug* (*asir*) to seize 3. *AmC* (*hurtar*) to steal 4. *Arg, Chile* (*agarrar*) to grab 5. *AmL* (*al vuelo*) to catch in mid-air 6. *Chile* (*sospechar*) to suspect 7. *AmS, inf* (*burlarse*) to make fun of

cacharpas *fpl AmS* odds *mpl* and ends

cacharro *m* 1. (*recipiente*) pot 2. *pey, inf* (*aparato*) gadget 3. *pey, inf* (*trasto*) piece of junk; **¡quita ese ~ de ahí!** get rid of that junk!

cachas[1] I. *adj inv* 1. *inf* (*fuerte*) strong 2. *vulg* (*sexy*) sexy II. *fpl inf* bottom

cachas[2] *mf inv, inf* (*hombre*) hunk; (*mujer*) muscular woman

cachaza *f* 1. (*lentitud*) slowness 2. (*flema*)

phlegm
cachazudo, **-a** *adj* **1.** (*lento*) slow **2.** (*flemático*) phlegmatic
cachear *vt* to frisk
cachemir *m* cashmere
cacheo *m* searching, frisking
cachete *m* **1.** (*golpe*) slap **2.** (*carrillo*) (fat) cheek
cachetear *vt AmL* to slap
cachetón, **-ona** *adj AmL* (*mofletudo*) chubby-cheeked
cachimba *f AmL* **1.** (*pipa*) pipe **2.** (*cartucho*) cartridge
cachiporra *f* truncheon
cachivache *m* junk; **tienes la cocina llena de ~s** your kitchen is full of junk
cachondear *vr:* **~se** *vulg* **~ de uno** to take the mickey out of sb
cachondeo *m* **1.** *inf* (*broma*) joke; (*juerga*) good time; **tomar algo a ~** to take sth as a joke; **esto es un ~** this is a joke **2.** *vulg* (*burla*) farce
cachondo, **-a** **I.** *adj* **1.** *vulg* (*sexual*) sexy, horny; **poner a alguien ~** to turn sb on **2.** *inf* (*gracioso*) funny **3.** (*perra*) on heat **II.** *m, f* **1.** *vulg* (*juerguista*) reveller **2.** *inf* (*gracioso*) joker; **es un ~** he's a real laugh
cachorro, **-a** **I.** *adj AmL* despicable **II.** *m, f* (*de tigre*) cub; (*de perro, lobo*) pup(py)
cachudo, **-a** *adj* **1.** *AmL* (*animal*) horned **2.** *Méx* (*persona*) long-faced
cacique *m* **1.** (*jefe indio*) chief **2.** (*tirano*) tyrant
caciquismo *m pey: system of petty tyranny run by the local political boss*
caco *m inf* burglar
cacto *m* cactus
cada *adj* each; **~ uno/una** each one; **libros a 5 euros ~ uno** books at 5 euros each; **~ hora** hourly; **~ día** daily; **~ vez más/peor** more and more/worse and worse; **¿~ cuánto?** how often?
cadalso *m* **1.** (*tarima*) platform **2.** (*patíbulo*) scaffold
cadáver *m* (*de personas*) corpse; (*de animales*) carcass
cadavérico, **-a** *adj* **1.** (*muerto*) cadaverous **2.** (*pálido*) deathly pale
cadena *f* **1.** *t. fig* (*objeto, sucesión*) chain; **~ alimentaria** BIO food chain; **~ (antideslizante)** AUTO snow chain; **~ hotelera** hotel chain; **~ humana** human chain; **~ perpetua** JUR life imprisonment; **trabajo en ~** assembly-line work; **atar un perro con ~** to chain up a dog; **choque en ~** pile-up; **reacción en ~** chain reaction **2.** GEO mountain chain **3.** RADIO, TV network; **~ de sonido** sound system
cadencia *f* **1.** (*ritmo*) rhythm **2.** LING, MÚS cadence
cadera *f* hip
cadete *m* MIL cadet
cadmio *m* cadmium
caducar <c→qu> *vi* **1.** (*documento*) to expire; **este pasaporte está caducado** this passport has expired **2.** (*producto*) **la leche está caducada** the milk is past its sell-by date
caducidad *f* **1.** (*de un documento*) expiry; **fecha de ~** date of expiry **2.** (*de productos*) **fecha de ~** sell-by date
caduco, **-a** *adj* **1.** (*personas*) senile **2.** (*perecedero*) perishable **3.** (*árbol*) deciduous
caer *irr* **I.** *vi* **1.** (*objeto, persona*) to fall (down); (*fecha, precio*) to fall; **~ al suelo** to fall to the ground; **~ en manos de alguien** to fall into sb's hands; **dejarse ~** *inf* (*abandonarse*) to let oneself go; (*presentarse*) to show up; **tu amigo me cae bien/mal** *fig* I like/I don't like your friend; **estar al ~** *inf* to be about to happen **2.** (*presidente*) to fall from power **3.** (*comida*) **~ bien a** to agree with **4.** (*vestidos*) to suit **5.** *inf* (*encontrarse*) to be (located); **¿por dónde cae Jerez?** whereabouts is Jerez? **6.** (*atacar*) **~ sobre algo/alguien** to fall on sth/sb **II.** *vr:* **~se** (*desplomarse*) to collapse; (*un avión*) to crash; (*pelo, dientes*) to fall out; (*casa*) to fall down; **~se de culo** to fall on one's backside; **se me ha caído el pañuelo** I've dropped my handkerchief; **~se de sueño** to be ready to drop
café *m* **1.** (*bebida*) coffee; **~ con leche** white coffee; **~ solo** black coffee; **tomar un ~** to have a coffee **2.** (*local*) café **3.** (*planta*) coffee tree; (*semilla*) coffee bean
cafeína *f* caffeine
cafetal *m* coffee plantation
cafetera *f* **1.** (*jarra*) coffee pot; **~ eléctrica** coffeemaker **2.** *inf* (*vehículo*) old banger
cafetería *f* café
cafeto *m* coffee tree
cafre *mf pey, inf* moron
cagalera *f inf* **tener ~** to have the runs
cagar <g→gu> **I.** *vi vulg* to have a shit **II.** *vt vulg* to mess up; **¡ya la hemos cagado!** now we're really in the shit! **III.** *vr:* **~se** *vulg* (*de miedo*) to shit oneself; **¡me cago en diez!** shit!
caída *f* **1.** (*bajada brusca, de un imperio*) fall; (*de aviones*) crash; **~ del cabello** hair loss; **~ de gobierno** fall of the government; **~ del sistema** INFOR system crash; **la ~ del muro de Berlín** the fall of the Berlin wall; **esta calle tiene mucha ~** this street is very steep; **las cortinas tienen una bonita ~** the curtains hang well **2.** (*de agua*) waterfall **3.** FIN fall in prices **4.** (*puesta*) **a la ~ del sol** at sunset
caído, **-a** **I.** *adj* (*flojo*) drooping; (*abatido*) crestfallen **II.** *m, f* **1.** (*persona*) person who has fallen **2.** (*en la guerra*) soldier killed in action; **los ~s** the fallen
caigo *1. pres de* **caer**
caimán *m* caiman
Cairo *m* **El ~** Cairo
caja *f* **1.** (*recipiente*) box; **~ fuerte** safe; **~ de herramientas** *t.* INFOR tool box; **~ de música** musical box; **~ negra** AVIAT black box **2.** (*carcasa*) case; **~ de cambios** AUTO gearbox; ~

torácica ANAT thoracic cavity **3.** FIN fund; **Caja (Postal) de Ahorros** (Post Office) savings bank

cajero, **-a** *m, f* cashier; ~ **automático** cash dispenser

cajeta *f* **1.** *Arg* (*cepo*) trap **2.** *AmC* GASTR toffee-like sweet

cajetilla *f* (*caja pequeña*) small box; (*de cigarrillos*) packet of cigarettes *Brit,* pack of cigarettes *Am*

cajón *m* (*caja grande*) big box; (*de embalaje*) crate; (*deslizante*) drawer; ~ **de salida** DEP starting gate; **eso es de** ~ *inf* that goes without saying

cajuela *f Méx* AUTO boot, trunk *Am*

cake *m AmL* cake

cal *f* lime; **cerrar a** ~ **y canto** to shut firmly

cala *f* **1.** (*bahía*) cove **2.** NÁUT hold **3.** (*en el terreno*) probe

calabacín *m* courgette *Brit,* zucchini *Am*

calabaza *f* **1.** BOT pumpkin **2.** *pey* (*persona*) dummy ►**dar** ~**s a alguien** (*un suspenso*) to fail sb; (*una negativa*) to give sb the brush-off

calabozo *m* **1.** (*mazmorra*) dungeon **2.** (*celda*) (prison) cell

calada *f inf* puff; **¿me das una** ~**?** will you let me have a puff?

caladero *m* fishing ground

calado *m* **1.** (*bordado*) open work **2.** NÁUT draught

calaguasca *f Col* GASTR raw brandy

calamar *m* squid

calambrazo *m* attack of cramp

calambre *m* **1.** (*eléctrico*) electric shock **2.** (*muscular*) cramp; ~ **de estómago** stomach cramp

calamidad *f* **1.** (*catástrofe*) calamity; (*desastre*) disaster **2.** *inf* (*persona*) disaster

calamitoso, **-a** *adj* calamitous

calandria *f* **1.** ZOOL calandra lark **2.** (*máquina*) calender; (*para ropa*) mangle

calaña *f* **ser de mala** ~ to be bad

calar I. *vi* **1.** (*líquido*) to soak in **2.** (*material*) to be permeable **II.** *vt* **1.** (*líquido*) to soak; **el chaparrón me ha calado la chaqueta** the downpour has drenched my jacket **2.** (*con un objeto*) to pierce **3.** (*afectar*) ~ **a alguien** to make an impression on sb **4.** (*una prenda*) to do openwork on **5.** (*cortar*) to cut a piece out of **6.** *inf* (*desenmascarar*) to see through **7.** (*motor*) to stall **8.** NÁUT to draw **III.** *vr:* ~**se 1.** (*mojarse*) to get soaked **2.** (*motor*) to stall **3.** (*gorra*) to pull down

calato, **-a** *adj Perú* naked

calavera *f* skull

calcáneo *m* ANAT heel bone

calcañar *m* ANAT heel

calcar <c→qu> *vt* **1.** (*dibujar*) to trace **2.** (*imitar*) to copy; **es calcado a su padre** he's the spitting image of his father

calceta *f* knitting

calcetín *m* sock

calcificar <c→qu> **I.** *vt* to calcify **II.** *vr:* ~**se** to calcify

calcinar I. *vt* **1.** (*carbonizar*) to burn **2.** QUÍM to calcine **II.** *vr:* ~**se** to burn

calcio *m* calcium

calco *m* **1.** (*de dibujos*) tracing **2.** (*imitación*) imitation **3.** LING calque

calcomanía *f* transfer

calculador(a) *adj* calculating

calculadora *f* calculator; ~ **de bolsillo** pocket calculator

calcular *vt* **1.** (*computar*) to calculate **2.** (*aproximadamente*) to estimate; **calculo que llegaré sobre las diez** I reckon that I'll arrive around ten

cálculo *m* **1.** *t.* ECON (*matemático, cómputo*) calculation; ~ **diferencial** differential calculus; ~ **mental** mental arithmetic; ~ **de probabilidades** theory of probability; **hacer un** ~ **de algo** to calculate sth **2.** (*suposición*) conjecture **3.** MED stone

caldear I. *vt* **1.** (*calentar*) to heat (up) **2.** (*acalorar*) to inflame **II.** *vr:* ~**se 1.** (*calentarse*) to heat up **2.** (*acalorarse*) to get heated

caldera *f* **1.** (*caldero*) cauldron *Brit,* caldron *Am* **2.** TÉC boiler

calderilla *f* small change

caldero *m* cauldron *Brit,* caldron *Am*

caldo *m* **1.** GASTR broth **2.** (*vino*) wine **3.** BIO ~ **de cultivo** culture medium; *fig* breeding ground

caldoso, **-a** *adj* soggy

calefacción *f* heating

calefactor *m* **1.** (*aparato*) heater **2.** (*persona*) heating engineer

calefón *m Arg* gas water heater

caleidoscopio *m* kaleidoscope

calendario *m* calendar; ~ **de taco** tear-off calendar; ~ **de trabajo** schedule

calentador *m* heater; (*para la cama*) bedwarmer

calentamiento *m* **1.** (*caldeamiento*) warming **2.** DEP warm-up

calentar <e→ie> **I.** *vi* (*dar calor*) to be warm **II.** *vt* **1.** (*caldear*) to heat (up); (*con calefacción*) to warm (up); ~ **al rojo vivo** to make red-hot **2.** (*enfadar*) to anger **3.** *vulg* (*sexualmente*) to turn on **4.** *inf* (*pegar*) to give a good hiding **III.** *vr:* ~**se 1.** (*caldearse*) to heat up **2.** (*enfadarse*) to get angry **3.** DEP to warm up

calentura *f* **1.** (*fiebre*) fever **2.** (*en los labios*) cold sore

calenturiento, **-a** *adj* **1.** (*febril*) feverish **2.** (*exaltado*) rash **3.** (*indecente: pensamiento*) dirty

calesita *f Arg, Par* merry-go-round

caleta *f* **1.** (*cala*) cove **2.** *AmL* (*barco*) coaster

calibrar *vt* **1.** (*medir*) to gauge, to gage *Am;* TÉC to calibrate **2.** (*calcular*) to weigh up

calibre *m* **1.** (*diámetro*) calibre *Brit,* caliber *Am;* **eso es una mentira de** ~ *inf* that's a whopping lie **2.** (*instrumento*) gauge, gage *Am*

caliche *m* **1.** (*pared*) flake of lime **2.** (*piedrecilla*) pebbly particle **3.** (*maca en la fruta*)

bruise
calidad *f* 1.(*clase, característica*) quality; **de alta** ~ high-quality; **de primera** ~ top-quality; **en** ~ **de** as 2.(*prestigio*) importance
cálido, -a *adj* (*país*) hot; *fig* warm
caliente *adj* 1.(*cálido*) warm; (*ardiente*) hot 2.(*acalorado*) heated; **poner(se)** ~ *vulg* to get randy
califa *m* caliph
calificación *f* 1.(*denominación*) description; (*evaluación*) assessment 2.(*cualificación*) qualification; ~ **profesional** professional qualification 3.(*nota*) mark, grade
calificado, -a *adj* 1.*t.* JUR (*cualificado*) qualified 2.(*reconocido*) well-known
calificar <c→qu> *vt* 1.(*definir*) ~ **de algo** to describe as sth 2.(*evaluar*) to assess 3.ENS to mark, to grade
calificativo *m* description, qualifier
California *f* California
caligrafía *f* calligraphy
calina *f* 1.(*neblina*) mist 2.(*polución*) smog
cáliz *m* 1.REL chalice 2.BOT calyx
caliza *f* limestone
callado, -a *adj* 1.*estar* (*sin hablar*) silent; (*silencioso*) quiet 2.*ser* (*reservado*) quiet
callampa *f* 1.*Col, Chile, Perú* (*seta*) mushroom 2.*Chile* (*sombrero*) felt hat
callana *f* 1.*AmS* (*vasija*) earthenware pan 2.*Chile* (*reloj*) large pocket watch 3.*Perú* (*tiesto*) flowerpot
callar I.*vi, vr* **~se de** [*o* **por**] **algo** (*no hablar*) to keep quiet because of sth; (*enmudecer*) to fall silent due to sth; **¡cállate de una vez!** just shut up! II.*vt* (*un asunto*) to keep quiet about; (*un secreto*) to keep; **hacer** ~ **a uno** to make sb keep quiet
calle *f* street; (*en la autopista*) *t.* DEP lane; ~ **comercial** shopping street; ~ **de dirección única** one-way street; ~ **peatonal** pedestrian street; ~ **sin salida** cul-de-sac; ~ **arriba/abajo** up/down the street; **hacer la** ~ *inf* to streetwalk; **quedarse en la** ~ *inf* to be out of a job
callejear *vi* to stroll around
callejero *m* street directory
callejón *m* alley; ~ **sin salida** cul-de-sac
callista *mf* chiropodist
callo *m* 1.(*callosidad*) callus; (*ojo de gallo*) corn; **dar el** ~ *inf* to slave away 2.*pl* GASTR tripe
calma *f* 1.(*tranquilidad, silencio*) calm; ~ **chicha** NÁUT dead calm 2.(*serenidad*) calmness; **¡(con)** ~**!** calm down! 3.*inf* (*indolencia*) indolence
calmante I.*adj* (*que tranquiliza*) sedative; (*para dolores*) soothing II.*m* (*tranquilizante*) tranquillizer *Brit,* tranquilizer *Am;* (*analgésico*) painkiller
calmar I.*vi* (*viento*) to abate II.*vt* 1.(*tranquilizar*) to calm (down) 2.(*dolor*) to relieve; (*hambre*) to satisfy III.*vr:* **~se** 1.(*tranquilizarse*) to calm down 2.(*dolor*) to ease off
calmoso, -a *adj* 1.(*tranquilo*) calm 2.*inf* (*indolente*) sluggish
caló *m* gipsy [*o* gypsy *Am*] slang
calor *m* 1.(*de un cuerpo, afecto*) warmth 2.(*clima*) heat; ~ **sofocante** stifling heat; **hace mucho** ~ it's very hot 3.(*entusiasmo*) passion
caloría *f* calorie; **bajo en ~s** low-calorie
calorífero, -a *adj* heat-producing, heat-emitting
calote *m RíoPl* swindle
caluma *f Perú* (*desfiladero*) Andean gorge
calumnia *f* slander
calumniar *vt* to slander
caluroso, -a *adj* 1.(*clima*) hot 2.*fig* warm; **un recibimiento** ~ a warm reception
calva *f* 1.(*en la cabeza*) bald patch 2.(*en un tejido*) worn spot
calvario *m* REL Stations *pl* of the Cross; **pasar un** ~ to suffer agonies
calvero *m* clearing
calvicie *f* baldness
calvo, -a I.*adj* 1.(*en la cabeza*) bald; **estar** ~ to be bald 2.(*tejido*) threadbare 3.(*sin vegetación*) bare II.*m, f* bald person
calza *f* 1.(*media*) stocking 2.(*cuña*) wedge
calzada *f* 1.(*carretera*) (paved) road 2.(*carril*) carriageway *Brit,* lane
calzado *m* footwear
calzador *m* shoehorn
calzar <z→c> I.*vt* 1.(*poner zapatos*) to put on; (*esquís*) to clip on 2.(*llevar puesto*) to wear 3.(*poner una cuña*) to wedge II.*vr:* **~se** (*zapatos*) to put one's shoes on; (*esquís*) to clip one's skis on
calzón *m AmL* (*pantalón*) trousers *pl*
calzoncillo(s) *m(pl)* men's underpants *pl*
calzoneras *fpl Méx* (*pantalón de montar*) riding pants *pl*
cama *f* 1.(*mueble*) bed; ~ **elástica** trampoline; **caer en** ~ to fall ill 2.(*de animales*) lair
camada *f* 1.(*de animales*) litter 2.*pey* (*cuadrilla*) gang
camafeo *m* cameo
camaleón *m t. fig* chameleon
cámara[1] *f* 1.FOTO camera; ~ **de vídeo** video camera; **a** ~ **lenta** in slow motion 2.(*consejo*) house; **Cámara Alta** POL upper house; **Cámara Baja** POL lower house 3.(*receptáculo, en un arma*) chamber; ~ **frigorífica** cold-storage room
cámara[2] *mf* CINE cameraman *m,* camerawoman *f*
camarada *mf* 1.POL comrade 2.(*amigo*) companion
camaradería *f* comradeship
camarero, -a *m, f* 1.(*en restaurantes*) waiter *m,* waitress *f;* **¡~!** waiter! 2.(*en la barra*) barman *m,* barmaid *f* 3.(*de habitación*) room waiter *m,* room waitress *m* 4.(*en un barco*) steward *m,* stewardess *f*
camarilla *f t. pey* clique
camarín *m* dressing room
camarón *m* prawn, shrimp

C

camarote *m* NÁUT cabin, berth
camarotero *m AmL* (*camarero de barco*) steward
camastro *m* hard old bed
cambalache *m* swap
cambiable *adj* **1.** COM exchangeable **2.** (*variable*) changeable
cambiador *m Chile* switchman
cambiante *adj* **1.** (*irisado*) iridescent **2.** (*inestable*) changeable **3.** *pey* (*veleidoso*) moody
cambiar **I.** *vi* (*transformarse, alterar*) to change; ~ **de casa** to move (house); ~ **de coche** to buy a new car; ~ **de marcha** AUTO to change gear **II.** *vt* **1.** (*trocar, algo comprado*) to (ex)change; ~ **dinero** to change money; ~ **unas palabras con alguien** to exchange a few words with sb **2.** (*variar*) to change; ~ **algo de lugar** to move sth **III.** *vr* **1.** (*transformarse*) ~ **en algo** to change [*o* turn] into sth **2.** (*de ropa*) to change; (*de casa*) to move; ~**se a otra ciudad** to move to another town
cambiavía *m AmL* switchman
cambiazo *m* big change ▸**dar el ~ a alguien** *inf* to pull a fast one on sb
cambio *m* **1.** (*alteración, sustitución, transformación*) change; ~ **de aceite** AUTO oil change; ~ **climático** climatic change; ~ **de domicilio** change of address; ~ **de marchas** gear lever, gear *Am;* ~ **de tendencia** new trend; **hay un ~ en el horario** there's a change in the timetable; **a las primeras de ~** at the first opportunity; **en ~** however **2.** (*intercambio, en un comercio*) exchange; ~ **de impresiones** exchange of views; **libre ~** COM free trade; **a ~ de algo** in exchange for sth **3.** FIN exchange rate; ~ **de divisa** [*o* **de moneda**] foreign exchange; **al ~ del día** at the current exchange rate **4.** (*suelto*) change; **¿tiene ~ de 100 euros?** can you change 100 euros? **5.** TÉC gear change *Brit,* gearshift *Am;* ~ **de marchas** gearbox, transmission **6.** DEP substitution
cambista *mf* **1.** (*que cambia dinero*) moneychanger **2.** (*en la banca*) foreign exchange clerk
Camboya *f* Cambodia
cambuto, -a *adj Perú* (*menudo y rechoncho*) small and chubby
camelar *vt inf* **1.** (*engañar*) to cajole **2.** (*seducir*) to seduce
camelia *f* camellia
camello, -a *m, f* **1.** ZOOL camel **2.** *inf* (*persona*) drug dealer
camelo *m inf* **1.** (*timo*) con **2.** (*adulación*) flattery
camerino *m* TEAT dressing room
Camerún *m* Cameroon
camilla *f* **1.** (*angarillas*) stretcher **2.** (*cama de hospital*) hospital bed
camillero, -a *m, f* stretcher-bearer
camilucho, -a *m, f AmL* Indian day labourer
caminar **I.** *vi* **1.** (*ir*) to go; (*a pie*) to walk **2.** (*río*) to flow **3.** (*astro*) to move **4.** *AmL* (*funcionar*) to work **II.** *vt* (*distancia*) to cover
caminata *f* long walk
camino *m* **1.** (*senda*) path; (*más estrecho*) track; (*calle*) road; **a medio ~** halfway (there); **de ~ a Londres** on the road to London; **abrirse ~** to make one's way; **ponerse en ~** to set out [*o* off]; **ir por buen/mal ~** *fig* to be on the right/wrong track **2.** (*distancia*) way; **está a dos horas de ~** it's two hours' journey away **3.** (*manera*) way **4.** INFOR path ▸**todos los ~s llevan a Roma** *prov* all roads lead to Rome; ~ **de rosas** bed of roses; **su vida no ha sido ningún ~ de rosas** his/her life has been no bed of roses

> **Santiago de Compostela**, the capital of Galicia has been an important place of pilgrimage for the Roman Catholic Church since the 9th century. The **Camino de Santiago** which leads to **Santiago de Compostela** is a route that is travelled every year by thousands of pilgrims from all over the world.

camión *m* AUTO lorry *Brit,* truck *Am;* ~ **de la basura** dustcart *Brit,* garbage truck *Am;* ~ **volquete** dumper, dumptruck *Am*
camionero, -a *m, f* lorry driver *Brit,* truck driver *Am*
camioneta *f* **1.** (*furgoneta*) van; ~ **de reparto** delivery van **2.** *AmL* (*autobús*) bus
camisa *f* **1.** (*prenda*) shirt; ~ **de fuerza** straitjacket; **cambiar de ~** to change sides; **no me llegaba la ~ al cuerpo** *inf* I was scared stiff **2.** (*funda*) case; (*de disco*) sleeve **3.** (*de reptil*) slough ▸**meterse en ~ de once varas** to bite off more than one can chew
camisería *f* shirtmaker's (shop)
camiseta *f* **1.** (*exterior*) T-shirt **2.** (*interior*) vest *Brit,* undershirt *Am* **3.** DEP shirt
camisón *m* nightdress, nightgown *Am*
camomila *f* camomile
camorra *f* **1.** *pey, inf* (*escándalo*) row; **buscar ~** to go looking for trouble **2.** (*mafia*) Camorra
camorrear *vi RíoPl* to quarrel
camorrista **I.** *adj* troublemaking **II.** *mf* troublemaker
camote *m AmL* **1.** (*batata*) sweet potato **2.** (*molestia*) nuisance **3.** (*amante*) lover
camotear *vi Méx* (*vagabundear*) to roam
campamento *m* camp; ~ **de veraneo** summer camp
campana *f* bell; ~ **extractora de humos** extractor hood; **el coche dio tres vueltas de ~** the car turned over three times; **echar las ~s a vuelo** *inf* to let everybody know
campanada *f* chime; **dar la ~** *fig* to cause a stir
campanario *m* bell tower
campanilla *f* **1.** (*campana pequeña*) small bell; (*de la puerta*) bell **2.** ANAT uvula **3.** BOT bellflower
campante *adj inf* **1.** (*tranquilo*) calm; **que-**

darse tan ~ not to bat an eyelid **2.** (*satisfecho*) (self-)satisfied

campaña *f* **1.** (*campo*) countryside; **tienda de** ~ tent **2.** MIL, POL campaign; AGR season; ~ **de acoso y derribo** smear campaign; ~ **antitabaco** anti-smoking campaign; ~ **electoral** electoral [*o* election] campaign **3.** COM sales drive

campar *vi* to camp

campear *vi* **1.** *AmL* (*ir de acampada*) to camp **2.** *inf* (*arreglárselas*) **ir campeando** to get by **3.** (*sobresalir*) to abound

campechana *f* **1.** *Méx, Cuba* (*bebida*) cocktail **2.** NÁUT fantail grating

campechano, **-a** *adj* **1.** (*llano*) straightforward **2.** (*cordial*) cheerful

campeón, **-ona** *m, f* champion

campeonato *m* championship; **de** ~ *inf* terrific

campera *f CSur* windcheater

campesino, **-a** **I.** *adj* **1.** (*del campo*) rural; (*de la gente del campo*) country **2.** *t. pey* (*de un labrador*) peasant **II.** *m, f* **1.** (*que vive, trabaja*) countryman *m,* countrywoman *f;* **los ~s** country people **2.** *t. pey* (*labrador*) peasant

camping *m* **1.** (*campamento*) camping site **2.** (*actividad*) camping; **hacer** ~ to go camping

campiña *f* (*campo*) countryside; (*de cultivo*) farmland

campirano, **-a** *adj* **1.** *AmL* (*patán, rural*) rustic **2.** *Méx* (*campesino*) peasant **3.** *Méx* (*entendido en el campo*) good at farming **4.** *Méx* (*que maneja bien caballos*) skilled at handling horses

campista *mf* **1.** (*en las vacaciones*) camper **2.** *Méx* MIN mine leaseholder

campo *m* **1.** (*opuesto a ciudad*) countryside; (*de cultivo*) field; **gente del** ~ country people; **ir al** ~ to go into the country; **tener** ~ **libre para hacer algo** *fig* to be free to do sth **2.** *t.* DEP, MIL (*terreno*) field; ~ **de tiro** firing range **3.** *t.* POL, MIL (*campamento*) camp; ~ **de concentración** HIST concentration camp; ~ **de trabajo** work camp **4.** *t.* FÍS, INFOR (*área del saber*) field; ~ **de actuación** field of activity; ~ **para entradas** INFOR input field; ~ **de opción** INFOR option field; ~ **visual** field of vision

camposanto *m* cemetery

campus *m inv* campus

camuflaje *m* camouflage

camuflar *vt t. fig* to camouflage

cana *f* **1.** (*pelo blanco*) white hair; **echar una** ~ **al aire** *fig* to let one's hair down **2.** *Arg, inf* (*policía*) police **3.** *Arg, inf* (*prisión*) jail

Canadá *m* (**el**) ~ Canada

canal *m o f* **1.** *t.* ANAT (*cauce artificial*) canal **2.** GEO (*paso natural*) channel; **el Canal de la Mancha** the English Channel; **el Canal de Panamá** the Panama Canal **3.** (*canalón*) gutter **4.** TV channel; ~ **de televisión** television channel

canalización *f* **1.** (*de un río*) canalization **2.** (*alcantarillado*) sewerage system

canalizar <z→c> *vt* **1.** (*un río*) to canalize **2.** (*encauzar*) to channel

canalla *mf pey* swine

canallada *f* mean thing (to do)

canalón *m* gutter

canana *f* **1.** (*cinturón*) cartridge belt **2.** *AmL, inf* (*canallada*) dirty trick

Canarias *fpl* **las Islas** ~ the Canary Islands

canario *m* canary

canario, **-a** **I.** *adj* of/from the Canary Islands **II.** *m, f* (*de Canarias*) native/inhabitant of the Canary Islands

canasta *f* basket

canastero, **-a** *m, f* **1.** (*que fabrica canastas*) basket maker **2.** *Chile* (*panadería*) baker's helper

canastilla *f* **1.** (*cestita*) small basket; ~ **de costura** sewing basket **2.** (*del bebé*) layette **3.** *Arg, PRico* (*de la novia*) hope chest

cancanear *vi* **1.** *inf* (*vagar*) to wander about **2.** *AmL* (*tartamudear*) to stutter; (*hablar entrecortadamente*) to speak haltingly

cancel *m* **1.** (*en la puerta*) inner door **2.** (*mampara*) folding screen

cancelación *f* **1.** (*anulación, de una cita*) cancellation **2.** FIN (*de una cuenta*) closing; (*de una deuda*) payment; (*de un cheque*) stopping; ~ **de un pedido** cancellation of an order

cancelar *vt* **1.** (*anular*) to cancel; ~ **una cita** to cancel an appointment **2.** (*rescindir*) to rescind **3.** FIN (*una cuenta*) to close; (*una deuda*) to pay (off); (*un cheque*) to stop

cáncer *m* **1.** *t. fig* MED cancer **2.** ASTR Cancer

cancerígeno, **-a** *adj* carcinogenic

canceroso, **-a** *adj* cancerous; **tumor** ~ cancerous tumour

cancha *f* **1.** DEP (*de deporte*) sports field; (*de tenis, baloncesto*) court **2.** *AmL* (*hipódromo*) racecourse *Brit,* racetrack *Am* **3.** *AmL* (*de un río*) broad part of a river **4.** *AmL* (*espacio*) space

canchero, **-a** *m, f Arg* groundsman

canciller *mf* **1.** POL chancellor **2.** *AmL* (*de Asuntos Exteriores*) foreign minister

cancillería *f* **1.** POL chancellery **2.** *AmL* (*Asuntos Exteriores*) foreign ministry

canción *f* song; ~ **de moda** pop song; ~ **popular** folk song; (**es**) **siempre la misma** ~ (it's) always the same old story

cancionero *m* **1.** MÚS songbook **2.** LIT anthology (of verse)

canco *m* **1.** *Bol* (*nalga*) buttocks *pl* **2.** *Chile* (*olla*) earthenware casserole **3.** *Chile* (*tiesto*) flowerpot

cancona **I.** *adj Chile* broad-hipped **II.** *f Chile* broad-hipped woman

candado *m* padlock

candela *f* candle

candelabro *m* candelabra

candelejón, **-ona** *adj Chile, Col, Perú* (*inocente*) naïve

candelero *m* candlestick; **estar en el** ~ *fig* to be in the limelight

candelilla *f* 1. MED catheter 2. BOT (*inflorescencia*) inflorescence 3. BOT (*amento*) ament, catkin 4. *CRi, Chile, Hond* (*luciérnaga*) glow-worm 5. *Cuba* (*hilván*) overstitch

candente *adj* 1. (*al rojo*) red-hot 2. (*palpitante*) burning

candidato, -a *m, f* 1. (*aspirante*) applicant 2. POL candidate; ~ **al título** DEP contender for the title

candidatura *f* 1. (*presentación*) application; POL candidature 2. (*lista*) list of candidates 3. (*papeleta*) ballot paper

candidez *f v.* **candor**

cándido, -a *adj v.* **candoroso**

candil *m* 1. (*lámpara*) oil lamp 2. *AmL* (*candelabro*) candelabra

candilejas *fpl* TEAT footlights *pl*

candinga *f* 1. *Chile* (*necedad*) absurdity 2. *Hond* (*maraña*) mess

candonga *f* 1. *inf* (*mofa*) joking 2. *inf* (*mulo*) mule 3. NÁUT storm sail 4. *Col* (*pendiente*) earring

candor *m* 1. (*inocencia*) innocence 2. (*ingenuidad*) naivety *Brit,* naiveté *Am;* (*simplicidad*) simplicity

candoroso, -a *adj* 1. (*inocente*) innocent 2. (*ingenuo*) naive; (*simple*) simple

caneca *f* 1. (*licorera*) liquor bottle 2. *Col* (*basurero*) trash can 3. *Cuba* (*de agua caliente*) hot-water bottle 4. *AmL* (*barril*) drum; (*balde*) bucket

caneco, -a *adj Bol* (*embriagado*) tipsy

canela *f* cinnamon; **¡esto es ~ fina!** *fig* this is exquisite!

canelón *m* 1. (*desagüe*) (roof)gutter 2. *pl* GASTR cannelloni 3. (*carámbano*) icicle

canesú *m* 1. (*en una prenda*) bodice 2. *AmS* (*escote*) yoke

canfín *m AmC* (*petróleo*) petrol *Brit,* gasoline *Am*

cangrejo *m* (*crustáceo*) crab; ~ **de río** crayfish

cangrina *f Col* discomfort

cangro *m Col, Guat* MED (*cáncer*) cancer

canguro¹ *m* ZOOL kangaroo

canguro² *mf inf* (*persona*) baby-sitter

caníbal *adj, mf* cannibal

canica *f* marble

canícula *f* 1. (*período*) dog days *pl* 2. ASTR Sirius

canijo, -a *adj* 1. *pey* (*endeble*) feeble; (*pequeñajo*) puny 2. *AmL* (*malvado*) sly

canilla *f* 1. ANAT (*hueso alargado*) long bone; (*tibia*) shinbone 2. TÉC (*carrete*) bobbin 3. *Arg, Par, Urug* (*grifo*) tap

canillera *f AmL* 1. (*espinillera*) shin guard 2. (*temblor*) trembling

canillita *m AmS* newspaper vendor

canino *m* canine (tooth)

canje *m* 1. (*intercambio*) exchange 2. (*de un vale*) cashing (in)

canjear *vt* 1. (*intercambiar*) to exchange 2. (*cambiar*) to cash (in)

canoa *f* 1. *t.* DEP (*bote a remo*) canoe; (*tronco*) dugout (canoe); ~ **canadiense** Canadian canoe 2. (*a motor*) motor boat 3. *AmL* (*artesa*) feeding trough

canódromo *m* dog track

canon *m* 1. (*precepto*) rule 2. REL, ARTE, LIT canon 3. ECON levy

canónico, -a *adj* canonical

canónigo *m* REL canon

canonizar <z→c> *vt* REL to canonize

canoso, -a *adj* grizzled

cansado, -a *adj* 1. *estar* (*fatigado*) tired 2. *estar* (*harto*) tired 3. *ser* (*fatigoso*) tiring; **un viaje ~** a tiring journey 4. *ser* (*aburrido*) boring 5. *ser* (*molesto*) tiresome 6. *AmL* **a las cansadas** at long last

cansador(a) *adj Arg* 1. *ser* (*fatigoso*) tiring 2. *ser* (*aburrido*) boring 3. *ser* (*molesto*) tiresome

cansancio *m* 1. (*fatiga*) tiredness; (*agotamiento*) exhaustion; **estoy muerto de ~** I'm dead tired 2. (*hastío*) boredom

cansar I. *vi* 1. (*fatigar*) to tire 2. (*hastiar*) to be tiresome II. *vt* 1. (*fatigar*) to tire (out) 2. (*hastiar*) to bore III. *vr:* **~se** 1. (*fatigarse*) to tire oneself out 2. (*hartarse*) **~se de algo** to get tired of sth

cansera *f* 1. *inf* (*cansancio*) fatigue; (*enojo*) annoyance; **sus quejas me causan ~** his/her complaining annoys me 2. *Col* (*tiempo malgastado*) wasted effort

cansino, -a *adj* 1. (*cansado*) weary 2. (*lento*) slow

Cantabria *f* Cantabria

cantábrico, -a *adj* Cantabrian; **el Mar Cantábrico** the Bay of Biscay

cantaletear *vt AmL* to harp on

cantante I. *adj* singing; **llevar la voz ~** *fig* to call the tune II. *mf* singer

cantar I. *vi, vt* 1. (*personas, pájaros*) to sing; (*gallo*) to crow; (*grillo*) to chirp; (*ranas*) to croak; **en menos que canta un gallo** *inf* in no time at all 2. (*alabar*) to sing the praises of 3. *inf* (*confesar*) to talk 4. (*en el juego*) to declare 5. *inf* (*oler mal*) to stink II. *m* song; (*copla popular*) folksong

cántaro *m* pitcher; **estar lloviendo a ~s** to be raining cats and dogs

cantautor(a) *m(f)* singer-songwriter

cante *m* singing; ~ **jondo** Flamenco singing ►<u>**dar**</u> **el** ~ to stand out

cantera *f* 1. (*pedrera*) quarry 2. DEP young local club players

cantero *m* 1. (*picapedrero*) stonemason 2. *AmL* (*sembradío*) flowerbed

cántico *m* REL canticle

cantidad I. *f* 1. (*porción*) quantity; (*número*) number; **una gran ~ de** lots of; **¿qué ~ necesitas?** how much do you need? 2. (*suma de dinero*) sum II. *adv inf* a lot

cantilena *f* song ►**la** <u>**misma**</u> ~ *inf* the same old story

cantimplora *f* 1. (*botella de campaña*) water

bottle *Brit,* canteen *Am* **2.** (*sifón*) syphon
cantina *f* **1.** (*en estaciones*) buffet; (*en cuarteles*) canteen **2.** (*bodega*) wine cellar
cantinela *f v.* **cantilena**
canto *m* **1.** (*acción*) singing; (*canción*) song; ~ **gregoriano** Gregorian chant; ~ **de los pájaros** birdsong; **estudia** ~ he's/she's studying singing **2.** (*alabanza*) song of praise **3.** LIT hymn **4.** (*esquina*) corner; (*arista, borde*) edge; (*de un vestido*) hem **5.** (*en un cuchillo*) back; (*en un libro*) fore-edge; **poner de** ~ to put on end **6.** (*grosor*) thickness **7.** (*guijarro*) pebble
cantón *m* **1.** (*esquina*) corner **2.** ADMIN, POL canton **3.** MIL cantonment
cantonera *f* (*de un libro*) corner piece; (*de metal*) corner bracket; (*armario*) corner unit
cantor(a) **I.** *adj* singing; **los canarios son muy ~es** canaries sing a lot **II.** *m(f) elev* singer
canuto *m* **1.** (*tubo*) tube **2.** *inf* (*porro*) joint
caña *f* **1.** AGR, BOT, MÚS reed; (*tallo de cereal*) stalk; (*junco*) cane; ~ **de azúcar** sugar cane **2.** ANAT (*de la pierna*) shinbone; (*tuétano*) marrow **3.** (*de pescar*) (fishing) rod **4.** (*de un arma, una columna*) shaft **5.** (*en el calzado*) leg **6.** (*de cerveza*) glass
cañada *f* **1.** (*barranco*) gully, gulch *Am* **2.** AGR (*camino de ganado*) cattle track
cañamazo *m* **1.** (*arpillera*) sackcloth, burlap **2.** (*para bordar*) embroidery fabric
cáñamo *m* **1.** (*planta*) hemp **2.** (*tejido*) canvas; **de** ~ hempen
cañería *f* pipe; ~ **del agua** plumbing
cañizal *m,* **cañizar** *m* reedbed
caño *m* **1.** (*tubo*) tube; (*de la fuente*) spout; (*chorro*) jet **2.** (*desagüe*) drainpipe
cañón *m* **1.** (*tubo*) tube; ~ **de escopeta** barrel; **de dos cañones** double-barrelled *Brit,* double-barreled *Am* **2.** MIL cannon; (*artillería*) gun; ~ **de nieve** snow cannon; **carne de** ~ cannon fodder **3.** (*de una pluma*) quill **4.** GEO canyon; **el Cañón del Colorado** the Grand Canyon
cañonazo *m* **1.** (*disparo*) cannon shot **2.** *inf* (*en el fútbol*) powerful shot
cañonera *f* **1.** (*en una fortificación*) embrasure **2.** *AmL* (*pistolera*) holster
caoba **I.** *adj* (**color**) ~ mahogany **II.** *f* **1.** (*madera*) mahogany **2.** (*árbol*) mahogany tree
caos *m inv* chaos
caótico, -a *adj* chaotic
cap. *abr de* **capítulo** ch.
capa *f* **1.** *t.* TAUR (*prenda*) cape **2.** (*cobertura*) covering; (*recubrimiento*) layer; (*baño*) coating; ~ **aislante** insulating layer; ~ **de nieve** covering of snow **3.** (*estrato*) layer; ~ **de ozono** ozone layer **4.** GEO, MIN stratum ▸**defender a ~ y espada** to defend with all one's might; **hacer de su ~ un sayo** to do as one pleases; **andar** [*o* **estar**] **de ~ caída** *inf* to be down in the mouth
capacho *m* (large) basket, hamper
capacidad *f* **1.** *t.* FÍS (*cabida*) capacity **2.** (*aptitud*) aptitude; ~ **adquisitiva** purchasing power; ~ **negociadora** negotiating skills *pl;* ~ **de persuasión** persuasiveness **3.** JUR capacity **4.** *AmL* (*persona dotada*) talented person
capacitación *f* (*capacidad*) capacity; (*formación*) training; JUR (*habilitación*) capacitation
capacitado, -a *adj* ~ **para algo** to be qualified for [*o* to do] sth
capacitar **I.** *vt* **1.** (*formar*) to train; (*preparar*) to prepare **2.** *AmL* JUR (*habilitar*) to capacitate **II.** *vr:* **~se** to qualify
capar *vt* **1.** *inf* (*un pollo*) to caponize; (*animal o persona*) to castrate **2.** (*limitar*) to curtail
caparazón *m t. fig* shell
capataz *m* foreman
capaz *adj* **1.** (*con cabida*) capacious **2.** (*apto*) fit **3.** (*en condiciones*) capable **4.** *AmL* (*tal vez*) perhaps
capazo *m* **1.** (*espuerta*) (large)basket **2.** (*de bebé*) carrycot
capcioso, -a *adj* (*engañoso*) deceitful; (*insidioso*) cunning
capea *f bullfight with young bulls*
capear *vt* **1.** TAUR to make passes with the cape **2.** (*engañar*) to take in **3.** (*esquivar*) to dodge
capellán *m* **1.** (*con capellanía*) chaplain **2.** (*clérigo*) clergyman
capelo *m* **1.** (*sombrero cardenalicio*) cardinal's hat **2.** (*dignidad eclesiástica*) cardinalate **3.** *Cuba, PRico, Ven* (*de doctor*) academic cap, mortarboard *Am*
caperuza *f* (pointed) hood
capi *m* **1.** *AmS* (*maíz*) maize *Brit,* corn *Am* **2.** *Bol* (*harina*) white cornflour
capicúa *m* **1.** (*número*) symmetrical [*o* reversible] number **2.** (*palabra*) palindrome
capilla *f* REL chapel; ~ **ardiente** funeral chapel
capisayo *m* **1.** REL bishop's mantelletta **2.** *Col* (*camiseta*) vest *Brit,* undershirt *Am*
capital[1] **I.** *adj* essential; **letra** ~ *AmL* capital letter(s); **pena** ~ capital punishment; **de ~ importancia** of prime importance **II.** *m* ECON, FIN capital; ~ **fijo** fixed capital; ~ **a plazo** fixed-term deposit; **bienes de** ~ capital goods
capital[2] *f* (*de país*) capital (city); (*de provincia*) provincial capital
capitalismo *m* capitalism
capitalista **I.** *adj* capitalist(ic) **II.** *mf* capitalist
capitalizar <z→c> *vt* **1.** ECON, FIN to capitalize **2.** (*copar*) to seize
capitán *m* **1.** MIL, NÁUT, DEP captain; ~ **general** MIL commander-in-chief **2.** AVIAT flight lieutenant *Brit,* captain *Am* **3.** (*de una banda*) leader
capitanear *vt* **1.** MIL to command **2.** (*dirigir*) to lead **3.** (*equipo*) to captain
capitel *m* ARQUIT capital
capitolio *m* capitol; **el Capitolio** the Capitol
capitulación *f* **1.** MIL surrender **2.** (*acuerdo*) agreement
capitular **I.** *adj* REL chapter **II.** *vi* **1.** (*acordar*) to agree to [*o* on] **2.** (*rendirse*) to surrender
capítulo *m t.* REL chapter
capo *m* (*jefe mafioso*) mob boss

C

capó *m* bonnet *Brit,* hood *Am*

capón I. *adj* castrated II. *m* 1. (*pollo*) capon 2. (*coscorrón*) rap on the head

caporal *m* 1. MIL squadron leader, corporal *Am* 2. (*jefe*) leader 3. AGR foreman

capota *f* AUTO convertible roof *Brit,* convertible top *Am*

capote *m* 1. (*abrigo sin mangas*) cloak; ~ **de monte** *AmL* poncho 2. TAUR cape; **echar un ~ a alguien** *fig* to give sb a helping hand

capotera I. *adj* **aguja** ~ cloak needle II. *f Hond* (*percha*) clothes peg; (*perchero*) coat rack

capricho *m* 1. (*antojo*) whim; **a ~** as you/he/she like; **darse un ~** to allow oneself sth 2. MÚS capriccio

caprichoso, -a *adj* 1. (*antojadizo*) capricious 2. *pey* (*inconstante*) moody 3. *pey* (*arbitrario*) arbitrary

Capricornio *m* Capricorn

cápsula *f* 1. *t.* ANAT, BOT (*receptáculo*) capsule; ~ **espacial** AVIAT space capsule 2. (*tapón*) cap

captación *f* 1. (*obtención*) obtaining 2. (*registro*) registration; ~ **de datos** INFOR data capture 3. (*atracción*) attraction

captar I. *vt* 1. (*recoger*) to collect; (*capital*) to raise 2. (*percibir*) to make out 3. TEL to pick up 4. CINE, FOTO to take 5. INFOR to capture 6. (*comprender*) to grasp II. *vr:* **~se** to be obtained

captura *f* 1. (*apresamiento*) capture 2. (*detención*) arrest 3. NÁUT seizure 4. (*piezas cobradas*) catch

capturar *vt* 1. (*apresar*) to capture 2. (*detener*) to arrest 3. NÁUT to seize 4. (*cazar, pescar*) to catch

capucha *f* 1. *v.* **capuchón** 2. TIPO circumflex (accent)

capuchino *m* (*café*) capuccino

capuchino, -a *adj, m, f* Capuchin

capuchón *m* 1. (*para la cabeza*) hood 2. (*tapa*) top, cap

capujar *vt Arg* (*captar al vuelo*) to catch in mid-air

capullo *m* 1. BOT (*de flor*) bud 2. ZOOL cocoon; **salir del ~** to hatch out 3. *inf* (*prepucio*) foreskin 4. *vulg* (*canalla*) bastard

caqui I. *adj* khaki II. *m* 1. (*color, tela*) khaki 2. BOT persimmon

cara I. *f* 1. (*rostro*) face; ~ **a ~** face to face; **a ~ descubierta** openly; **(no) dar la ~ por alguien** (not) to come to sb's defense; **echar en ~** to reproach; **hacer** [*o* **plantar**] **~ a** to face up to; **partir** [*o* **romper**] **la ~ a alguien** *inf* to smash sb's face in 2. (*expresión*) expression; ~ **de póker** *inf* poker face; **una ~ larga** a long face; **una ~ de pocos amigos** *inf* a sour look; **salvar la ~** to save face 3. (*aspecto*) look; **tener buena/mala ~** to look good/bad 4. (*lado*) side; (*de una moneda*) face; ~ **o cruz** heads or tails 5. *inf* (*osadía*) nerve; **¡qué ~!** what cheek!; **tener mucha ~** to have some nerve II. *prep* (*en dirección a*) (**de**) **~ a** facing; **de ~ al futuro** with an eye to the future III. *conj* **de ~ a** +*infin* in order to +*infin*

carabela *f* NÁUT caravel

carabina *f* 1. (*fusil*) carbine 2. *inf* (*acompañanta*) chaperon

carabinero *m* police officer

caracol *m* 1. ZOOL snail 2. (*concha*) conch (shell) 3. ANAT cochlea 4. (*de pelo*) curl

caracola *f* conch

caracolillo *m* 1. (*caracol pequeño*) small snail 2. *AmL* (*café*) *high quality small-beaned coffee* 3. (*de pelo*) kiss-curl

carácter <caracteres> *m* 1. *t.* TIPO, INFOR, BIO (*en general*) character; **(no) tiene ~** he/she has (no) character; **sin ~** characterless; ~ **de separación** hyphen 2. (*índole*) nature; **con ~ de** as 3. *AmL* (*personaje*) character

característica *f* characteristic

característico, -a I. *adj* characteristic; **rasgo ~** characteristic II. *m, f* CINE, TEAT character actor *m,* character actress *f*

caracterizar <z→c> I. *vt* 1. (*marcar*) to characterize 2. (*describir*) to describe 3. TEAT to play II. *vr:* **~se** 1. (*destacar*) to be characterized 2. CINE, TEAT to play a role convincingly

caracú *m CSur* GASTR marrow

caradura *mf inf* shameless person

carajillo *m inf: coffee with a dash of brandy*

carajo *m vulg* prick ►**en el quinto ~** miles away; **irse al ~** to go to hell; (*estropearse*) to go to the dogs; **al ~ con...** to hell with ...; **¡~!** hell!

caramanchel *m* 1. *Perú* (*cobertizo*) shed 2. *Chile* (*taberna*) canteen

caramba *interj inf* **¡(qué) ~!** (*enfado*) damn!; (*extrañeza*) good heavens!

carámbano *m* icicle

carambola *f* 1. *inf* (*trampa*) trick 2. (*en el billar*) cannon; **de** [*o* **por**] **~** *inf* by pure chance 3. BOT carambola

caramelo *m* 1. (*azúcar quemado*) caramel; **(de) color ~** caramel-coloured *Brit,* caramel-colored *Am* 2. (*golosina*) sweet *Brit,* candy *Am*

carantoña *f* (*zalamería*) piece of flattery; **hacer ~s a uno** to butter sb up

caraota *f Ven* (*haba*) kidney bean

carapacho *m* 1. ZOOL (*caparazón*) carapace, shell 2. *Cuba* GASTR *shellfish cooked in the shell*

caraqueño, -a I. *adj* of/from Caracas II. *m, f* native/inhabitant of Caracas

carátula *f* 1. (*careta*) mask 2. *pey* (*farándula*) show-business people 3. (*portada*) title page; (*de un disco*) album [*o* CD] cover

caravana *f* 1. (*remolque*) caravan *Brit,* trailer *Am* 2. (*embotellamiento*) tailback 3. (*recua*) caravan

carbón *m* coal; ~ **de leña** [*o* **vegetal**] charcoal; **dibujo al ~** ARTE charcoal drawing; **papel ~** carbon paper

carbonato *m* carbonate

carbonera *f* 1. (*horno*) charcoal kiln 2. (*almacén*) coal cellar

carbonero, **-a** I. *adj* coal II. *m*, *f* 1. (*productor*) charcoal burner 2. (*vendedor*) coal merchant

carbonilla *f* 1. (*polvo de carbón*) coal dust 2. *AmL* (*carboncillo*) charcoal

carbonizar <z→c> I. *vt* 1. (*abrasar*) to char 2. QUÍM to carbonize II. *vr:* **~se** to carbonize

carbono *m* carbon; **dióxido de ~** carbon dioxide

carburador *m* TÉC carburettor *Brit*, carburetor *Am*

carburante *m* fuel

carburar I. *vt* to carburet II. *vi inf* (*funcionar*) to work

carburo *m* carbide

carcajada *f* guffaw; **reírse a ~s** to roar with laughter; **soltar una ~** to burst out laughing

carcajear *vi, vr:* **~se** 1. (*reírse a carcajadas*) to roar with laughter 2. *inf* (*no respetar*) **~se de algo/alguien** to have a good laugh at sth/sb

carcasa *f* TÉC casing

cárcel *f* prison; **~ de régimen abierto** open prison; **tres años de ~** three years imprisonment; **estar en la ~** to be in prison; **ir a parar a la ~** to end up in prison

carcelero, **-a** *m, f* prison officer, jailer

carcinoma *m* MED carcinoma

carcoma *f* 1. ZOOL woodworm 2. (*polvillo*) wood dust (*left by woodworm*) 3. (*destrucción lenta*) slow destruction

carcomer I. *vt* 1. (*corroer*) to eat away [*o* into] 2. (*minar*) to undermine II. *vr:* **~se** *fig* to decay

carcomido, **-a** *adj* 1. (*madera*) eaten away 2. *fig* decayed

cardar *vt* 1. (*proceso textil*) to card 2. (*el pelo*) to backcomb

cardenal *m* 1. REL, ZOOL cardinal 2. (*hematoma*) bruise

cárdeno, **-a** *adj* (*color*) purple; (*res*) black and white; (*agua*) opaline blue

cardiaco, **-a** *adj*, **cardíaco**, **-a** *adj* heart; MED cardiac; **ataque ~** heart attack; **paro ~** cardiac arrest

cardinal *adj* cardinal; **los cuatro puntos ~es** the four cardinal points; **número ~** LING cardinal number

cardiología *f* MED cardiology

cardiólogo, **-a** *m, f* MED cardiologist

cardiovascular *adj* MED cardiovascular

cardo *m* 1. BOT thistle 2. *pey, inf* (*desabrido*) prickly character

cardume(n) *m* 1. (*banco de peces*) shoal [*o* school] of fish 2. *CSur, inf* (*abundancia*) great quantity

carear I. *vt* 1. JUR (*confrontar*) to bring face to face 2. (*cotejar*) to compare II. *vr:* **~se** (*enfrentarse*) to confront; JUR to come face to face

carecer *irr como crecer vi* **~ de algo** to lack sth; **carece de importancia/de sentido** it's not important/it doesn't make sense; **tu afirmación carece de lógica** your assertion is illogical

carencia *f* 1. (*falta*) lack 2. ECON (*escasez*) shortage, scarcity 3. MED **~ de algo** deficiency in sth

carente *adj* **~ de algo** lacking in sth, devoid of sth; **~ de escrúpulos** unscrupulous; **~ de interés** uninteresting

careo *m t.* JUR confrontation

carestía *f sin pl* 1. (*escasez*) scarcity 2. ECON (*encarecimiento*) high cost; **la ~ de la vida** the high cost of living

careta *f* mask; **quitar la ~ a alguien** *t. fig* to unmask sb

carga *f* 1. (*acto*) loading; **permitida ~ y descarga** loading and unloading 2. (*cargamento*) load; (*flete*) freight; **animal de ~** pack animal; **buque de ~** freighter 3. (*obligación*) obligation; **ser una ~ para alguien** to be a burden on sb 4. MIL, FIN charge; **~ explosiva** exposive charge; **~ policial** baton charge; **¡a la ~!** MIL charge!; **~ fiscal** [*o* **impositiva**] tax burden

cargado, **-a** *adj* 1. (*con cargamento*) **~ con** [*o* **de**] **algo** loaded with sth; (*lleno*) full of sth; **~ de problemas** laden with problems 2. FÍS, TÉC **la batería está cargada** the battery is charged 3. (*pesado*) heavy; **un ambiente ~** *fig* a tense atmosphere 4. (*fuerte*) strong; **un café muy ~** very strong coffee 5. *inf* (*borracho*) drunk

cargador *m* 1. (*oficio*) loader 2. (*en un arma*) chamber

cargamento *m* (*acto*) loading; (*carga*) load, cargo

cargar <g→gu> I. *vi* 1. (*llevar*) **~ con algo** to carry sth 2. MIL (*atacar*) **~ contra** [*o* **sobre**] **alguien** to charge at sb 3. (*reposar*) to lie; ARQUIT to rest; **~ en cuenta a uno** FIN to charge to sb's account II. *vt* 1. *t.* MIL to load; **~ las tintas** *fig* to lay it on thick 2. (*achacar*) to attribute; **~ a alguien con las culpas** to put the blame on sb 3. FIN (*en una cuenta*) to charge 4. *inf* (*irritar*) to annoy; **este tipo me carga** this guy is getting on my nerves 5. *inf* (*suspender*) **a Paco le han cargado las mates** Paco has failed in maths 6. INFOR to load 7. *AmL* (*llevar*) to have; **¿cargas dinero?** do you have any money on you? III. *vr:* **~se** 1. (*llenarse*) **~se de algo** to fill up with sth 2. *inf* (*romper*) to smash up; **¡te la vas a ~!** *fig* you're in for it! 3. *inf* (*matar*) to do in

cargo *m* 1. FIN (*cantidad debida*) charge; **~ a cuenta** debit; **con ~ a nosotros** at our expense 2. (*puesto*) post; **desempeñar un ~** to hold a position 3. (*responsabilidad*) responsibility; (*deber*) duty; **estoy a ~ de las correcciones** I'm responsible for the corrections; **~ de conciencia** feeling of guilt

carguero *m* NÁUT freighter; (*de contenedores*) container ship

cariar <*1. pres:* carío> I. *vt* MED to cause to decay II. *vr:* **~se** MED to decay

caribe I. *adj* 1. *AmL* (*caribeño*) Caribbean 2. *AmL* (*antropófago*) cannibalistic 3. *AmL* (*cruel*) cruel 4. *Ant* (*furioso*) furious II. *m* 1. (*indígena*) Carib 2. *AmL* (*cruel*) savage

C

Caribe *m* **el** (**Mar**) ~ the Caribbean (Sea)
caribeño, **-a** **I.** *adj* Caribbean **II.** *m, f* native/inhabitant of the Caribbean area
caricatura *f* (*dibujo*) caricature, cartoon
caricaturista *mf* caricaturist, cartoonist
caricia *f* caress; **hacer ~s a alguien** to caress sb
caridad *f* (*amor al prójimo, generosidad*) charity; (*limosna*) alms *pl;* **hacer obras de ~** to do works of charity; **¡una limosna, por ~!** alms!
caries *f inv* MED tooth decay, caries
carillón *m t.* MÚS carillon
carimbo *m Bol* branding iron
Carintia *f* Carinthia
cariño *m* **1.** (*afecto*) affection; (*amor*) love; **hacer algo con ~** to do sth lovingly; **sentir ~ por alguien** to be fond of sb **2.** (*persona querida*) **¡~** (**mío**)! (my) dear! **3.** (*mimo*) caress; **hacer ~s** *inf* to caress
cariñoso, **-a** *adj* ~ **con alguien** affectionate [*o* tender] towards sb
carioca **I.** *adj* of/from Rio de Janeiro; (*brasileño*) Brazilian **II.** *mf* native/inhabitant of Rio de Janeiro
carisma *m* charisma
caritativo, **-a** *adj* charitable
cariz *m* **1.** (*aspecto*) look; **esto toma buen ~** this is looking good **2.** METEO outlook
carmelito, **-a** *adj AmL* (*marrón claro*) light brown
carmesí *adj* crimson
carmín **I.** *adj* carmine **II.** *m* **1.** (*color*) carmine **2.** BOT dog rose **3.** (*pintalabios*) (**barra de**) ~ lipstick
carnal *adj* **1.** REL carnal; **trato ~** sexual intercourse **2.** (*consanguíneo*) full; **somos primos ~es** we're first cousins
carnaval *m* carnival; REL shrovetide
carnaza *f* bait
carne *f* **1.** (*del cuerpo, pulpa*) flesh; **echar ~s** to put on weight; **ser uña y ~** to be inseparable; **los placeres de la ~** the pleasures of the flesh **2.** (*alimento, plato*) meat; **~ asada** roast meat; **~ de cerdo/vacuna** pork/beef; **~ picada** mince *Brit,* ground meat *Am* ►**poner toda la ~ en el asador** to risk all; **~ de gallina** gooseflesh; **ser de ~ y hueso** (*auténtico*) to be real; (*humano*) to be quite human
carné *m* <carnés> identity card; **~ de estudiante/de identidad** student/identity card; **~ de conducir** driving licence *Brit,* driver's license *Am*
carneada *f AmL* **1.** (*matanza*) slaughter **2.** (*matadero*) slaughterhouse
carnear *vt* **1.** *CSur* (*matar: un animal*) to slaughter; (*una persona*) to murder brutally **2.** *Chile* (*engañar*) to cheat **3.** *Méx* (*apuñalar*) to stab (to death)
carnero *m* **1.** ZOOL ram **2.** *CSur* (*débil*) weakling; (*desertor de huelga*) blackleg
carnet *m* <carnets> *v.* **carné**
carnicería *f* **1.** (*tienda*) butcher's (shop), meatshop **2.** (*masacre*) massacre
carnicero, **-a** **I.** *adj* **1.** (*carnívoro*) carnivorous **2.** (*sanguinario*) bloodthirsty **II.** *m, f* butcher
carnitas *fpl AmC* GASTR barbecued pork
carnívoro, **-a** *adj* carnivorous; **animal ~** carnivore
carnoso, **-a** *adj* fleshy
caro *adv* dear(ly) *Brit;* **esto nos costará ~** *fig* this'll cost us dear
caro, **-a** *adj* (*costoso, querido*) expensive, dear *Brit*
carótida *f* ANAT carotid (artery)
carozo *m CSur* stone (*of fruit*)
carpa *f* **1.** ZOOL carp **2.** (*entoldado gigante*) marquee; **~ del circo** big top **3.** *AmL* (*tienda de campaña*) tent **4.** *AmL* (*puesto de mercado*) market stall
Cárpatos *mpl* **los** (**Montes**) ~ the Carpathians
carpeta *f* **1.** (*portafolios*) folder; **~ de anillas** ring binder **2.** (*de un disco*) cover, sleeve **3.** (*cubierta*) cover
carpincho *m AmL* ZOOL capybara
carpintería *f* carpentry
carpintero, **-a** *m, f* carpenter; **pájaro ~** woodpecker
carpir *vt AmL* to hoe
carraca *f* **1.** *pey* (*objeto*) piece of junk; (*vehículo*) (old) jalopy **2.** (*carcamal*) wreck **3.** (*matraca*) ratchet **4.** ZOOL blue wrasse
carraspear *vi* to clear one's throat
carraspera *f* hoarseness
carrasposo, **-a** *adj* **1.** (*ronco*) hoarse **2.** *Col, Ecua, Ven* (*áspero*) rough
carrera *f* **1.** (*movimiento*) run **2.** (*recorrido*) journey; (*de un astro*) course **3.** DEP (*competición*) race; **~ de armamento** (**nuclear**) (nuclear) arms race; **~ de relevos** relay race; **coche de ~s** racing car **4.** (*profesión*) profession; **~ profesional** career **5.** (*estudios superiores*) degree course; **persona de ~** graduate; **hacer una ~** to study **6.** (*calle*) street; *AmL* (*avenida*) avenue; **hacer la ~** *inf* to be on the game **7.** (*en un tejido*) ladder
carreta *f* wagon
carrete *m t.* FOTO, TÉC (*bobina*) spool, reel; **~ de película** roll of film
carretera *f* (main) road; **~ de circunvalación** ring road *Brit,* bypass *Am,* beltway *Am*
carretilla *f* wheelbarrow
carriel *m Col, inf* (*bolso de bandolera*) shoulder-bag
carril *m* **1.** (*en la carretera*) lane; **~ de adelantamiento/lento** fast/slow lane **2.** *t.* TÉC (*raíl*) rail
carrilano, **-a** *m, f Chile* **1.** (*ferroviario*) railway worker **2.** (*bandolero*) bandit
carrillo *m inf* cheek
carrilludo, **-a** *adj* chubby-cheeked
carrito *m* (*de supermercado*) trolley *Brit,* shopping cart *Am*
carro *m* **1.** (*vehículo*) cart; **~ acorazado** [*o* **blindado**] armoured [*o* armored *Am*] car; **el**

Carro Mayor/Menor ASTR the Big/Little Dipper; **¡para el ~!** *inf* hold your horses! **2.** *AmL* (*coche*) car **3.** (*de una máquina de escribir*) carriage
carrocería *f* bodywork
carromato *m* (*entoldado*) covered wagon; (*roulotte*) caravan *Brit,* trailer *Am; pey* (*coche*) old banger
carroña *f* carrion
carroza *f* carriage
carruaje *m* carriage; (*de caballos*) coach
carrusel *m* **1.** (*tiovivo*) merry-go-round, carousel *Am* **2.** (*ecuestre*) cavalcade
carta *f* **1.** (*misiva, escrito*) letter; **~ certificada** registered letter; **~s al director** letters to the editor; **~ de porte** bill of lading; **~ de presentación** [*o* **de recomendación**] letter of introduction; **echar una ~** to post [*o* mail *Am*] a letter **2.** *t.* JUR (*documento*) document; **~ credencial** letter of credence; **Carta Magna** Magna Carta; **tomar ~s en un asunto** to intervene in a matter **3.** (*naipes*) card; **jugar a las ~s** to play (at) cards; **echar las ~s a alguien** to tell sb's fortune **4.** GEO (*mapa*) map; **~ astral** ASTR astral chart **5.** (*menú*) menu **6.** TV **~ de ajuste** test card *Brit,* test pattern *Am*
cartabón *m* set square
cartapacio *m* **1.** (*cuaderno*) notebook **2.** (*carpeta*) folder **3.** (*en una mesa*) desk pad
cartearse *vr* to correspond
cartel *m* poster; (*rótulo*) sign; TEAT bill; **prohibido fijar ~es** bill posters will be prosecuted; **tener buen ~** *fig* to be well-known
cártel *m* ECON cartel
cartelera *f* **1.** (*en el periódico*) entertainment guide; **estar en ~** to be on **2.** (*tablón*) notice board; TEAT, CINE publicity board
cárter *m* **1.** TÉC housing **2.** AUTO sump *Brit,* oil pan *Am*
cartera *f* (*de bolsillo*) wallet; (*de mano*) handbag, purse *Am;* (*de herramientas*) toolbag; (*portafolios*) portfolio; (*escolar*) (school) satchel; **ministro sin ~** POL minister without portfolio; **~ de valores** FIN securities portfolio; **~ de pedidos** ECON order book
carterista *mf* pickpocket
cartero, -a *m, f* postman *m Brit,* postwoman *f Brit,* mailman *m Am,* mailwoman *f Am*
cartílago *m* cartilage
cartilla *f* **1.** (*catón*) first reader **2.** (*cuaderno*) notebook; **~ de ahorros** savings book; **~ sanitaria** health attention card, NHS card *Brit* **3.** *AmL* (*carnet*) identity card
cartografía *f* cartography
cartón *m* **1.** (*material*) cardboard; **caja de ~** cardboard box **2.** (*envase*) carton; **~ de leche** carton of milk; **un ~ de tabaco** a carton of cigarettes **3.** ARTE cartoon **4.** *AmL* (*en periódicos*) cartoon
cartonaje *m* cardboard packaging
cartuchera *f* (*canana*) cartridge belt; (*bolsa*) cartridge clip
cartucho *m* **1.** *t.* MIL cartridge; **~ de tinta** ink cartridge; **~ de fogueo** blank cartridge **2.** (*envoltura: en forma de cucurucho*) cone; (*en forma de tubo*) roll
cartuja *f* Carthusian monastery
cartulina *f* thin cardboard; **~ amarilla** DEP yellow card
casa *f* **1.** (*edificio*) house; **~ adosada** semi-detached house; **~ de campo** country house; **~ de citas** brothel; **venta de ~ en ~** door-to-door selling **2.** (*vivienda*) flat **3.** (*hogar, en un juego*) home; **ir a ~** to go home; **¿vienes a mi ~?** will you come (over) to my place?; **vengo de ~** I'm coming from home; **en ~** at home; **estoy en ~ de Paco** I'm at Paco's (place); **llevar la ~** to run the house; **no parar en ~** to be always on the go; **todo queda en ~** it'll stay in the family **4.** ECON (*empresa*) firm; **~ discográfica** record company; **~ editorial** publishing house **5.** (*estirpe*) **~ real** royal family ►**echar** [*o* **tirar**] **la ~ por la ventana** *inf* to spare no expense
casabe *m AmL* GASTR cassava bread
casaca *f* (*de hombre*) frock coat; **~ de montar** hacking jacket
casadero, -a *adj* marriageable
casal *m* **1.** AGR (*de labranza*) farmhouse **2.** (*casa solariega*) country house **3.** *AmS* (*pareja*) couple; **un ~ de águilas** a pair of eagles
casamiento *m* **1.** (*matrimonio*) marriage **2.** (*boda*) wedding
casar I. *vi* **1.** *elev* (*casarse*) to marry **2.** (*combinar*) to match **II.** *vt* **1.** (*unir en matrimonio*) to marry; **estar** [*o* **ser**] **casado** to be married; **los recién casados** the newlyweds **2.** (*combinar*) to combine; (*piezas*) to join together **3.** JUR (*anular*) to annul **III.** *vr* **~se con alguien** to get married to sb; **~se en** [*o* **por**] **la Iglesia** to get married in church; **~se por lo civil** to get married in a registry office
cascabel *m* (little) bell; **serpiente de ~** rattlesnake ►**poner el ~ al gato** to bell the cat
cascada *f* waterfall; (*artificial*) cascade
cascado, -a *adj* **1.** (*roto*) broken (down) **2.** (*decrépito*) decrepit **3.** (*voz*) hoarse
cascajo *m* **1.** (*pedazo*) (broken) piece **2.** (*persona*) wreck; (*cosa*) piece of junk; **~s** rubbish **3.** (*gravilla*) piece of gravel
cascanueces *m inv* nutcracker
cascar <c→qu> **I.** *vi* **1.** *inf* (*charlar*) to chatter **2.** *vulg* (*morir*) to kick the bucket **II.** *vt* **1.** (*romper*) to crack; **~ un huevo/una nuez** to crack an egg/a nut **2.** *inf* (*pegar*) to clout **III.** *vr:* **~se 1.** (*romperse*) to crack; (*estropearse*) to break **2.** *inf* (*envejecer*) to get old
cáscara *f* shell; **~ de huevo** eggshell; **~ de limón** lemon peel; **¡~s!** *fig, inf* wow!
cascarón *m* **1.** (*de huevo*) shell **2.** NÁUT cockleshell
cascarrabias *mf inv, inf* cantankerous person, grouch
cascarudo *m Arg* beetle
casco *m* **1.** (*para la cabeza*) helmet; **los ~s**

C

azules the blue helmets (*members of the U.N. peacekeeping force*) **2.** *inf* (*cabeza*) head; **ligero de ~s** featherbrained; **calentarse los ~s** to agonize over **3.** (*pezuña*) hoof **4.** (*de un barco*) hull **5.** (*botella*) (empty) bottle **6.** (*centro ciudad*) city centre *Brit,* downtown *Am;* **el ~ antiguo** the old part of the city **7.** (*cascote*) piece of rubble **8.** TÉC (*cuerpo*) casing; **~ de presión** pressure casing **9.** *pl* (*auriculares*) headphones *pl*
cascote *m* piece of rubble; **~s** rubble
caseína *f* casein
caserío *m* **1.** (*granja*) farmhouse **2.** (*aldea*) hamlet
casero, **-a** **I.** *adj* **1.** (*hecho en casa*) homemade; **cocina casera** plain [*o* home-style] cooking; **remedio ~** household remedy **2.** (*hogareño*) home-loving **II.** *m, f* **1.** (*propietario*) landlord *m,* landlady *f* **2.** (*administrador*) caretaker
caseta *f* **1.** (*barraca*) hut; (*de feria*) booth; (*de muestras*) stand; **~ del perro** kennel, doghouse *Am;* **~ de tiro** shooting gallery **2.** (*cabina*) cabin
casete[1] *m o f* (*cinta*) cassette; **~ de vídeo** video cassette
casete[2] *m* **1.** (*aparato*) cassette recorder **2.** (*pletina*) cassette deck
casi *adv* almost; **~ ~** very nearly
casilla *f* **1.** (*caseta*) hut; **sacar a alguien de sus ~s** *fig* to drive sb mad **2.** (*en la cuadrícula*) box **3.** (*en un tablero*) square **4.** (*en un casillero*) pigeonhole
casillero *m* set of pigeonholes
casimba *f AmL* (*hoyo*) well; (*manantial*) spring; (*barril*) bucket
casino *m* **1.** (*casa de juego*) casino **2.** (*club*) club
caso *m* **1.** *t.* JUR,LING (*hecho*) case; (*circunstancia*) circumstance; **~ aislado** isolated case; **~ de fuerza mayor** case of force majeure; **¡eres un ~!** *inf* you're a right one!; **yo, en tu ~...** if I were you ...; **en ~ de** *+infin* in the event of; **dado** [*o* **llegado**] **el ~** if it comes to it; **dado el ~ de que** *+subj* supposing (that); **en ~ contrario** otherwise; **en cualquier ~** in any case; **en ningún ~** on no account; **en último ~** as a last resort; **en tal ~** in such a case; **en todo ~** in any case **2.** (*atención*) notice; **hacer ~ a alguien** (*considerar*) to pay attention to sb; (*obedecer*) to obey sb; (*creer*) to believe sb
caspa *f* dandruff
Caspio *m* **(el) Mar ~** (the) Caspian Sea
caspiroleta *f AmL* GASTR eggnog
casquete *m* **1.** (*casco*) helmet **2.** (*gorrilla*) cap; **~ polar** polar cap
casquillo *m* **1.** (*de bala*) cartridge case **2.** (*de bombilla*) light fitting
cassette[1] *m o f v.* **casete**[1]
cassette[2] *m v.* **casete**[2]
casta *f* **1.** (*raza*) race; **de ~ le viene al galgo** *fig* it runs in the family **2.** (*linaje*) lineage **3.** (*clase social*) caste
castaña *f* **1.** (*fruto*) chestnut; **~s asadas** roast chestnuts **2.** *inf* (*golpe*) blow; **darse una ~** to give oneself a knock **3.** *inf* (*bofetada*) slap; (*puñetazo*) thump **4.** *inf* (*borrachera*) drunkenness; **coger una ~** to get tight **5.** *inf* (*rápido*) **a toda ~** flat out
castañal *m,* **castañar** *m* chestnut grove
castañetear *vi* **1.** (*dedos*) to snap; **me castañeteaban los dientes de frío** my teeth were chattering with cold **2.** (*tocar las castañuelas*) to play the castanets
castaño *m* chestnut tree
castaño, **-a** *adj* brown
castañuela *f* castanet
castellano *m* LING (*español*) Spanish; (*variedad*) Castilian
castellano, **-a** **I.** *adj* Castilian; **la lengua castellana** the Spanish language **II.** *m, f* Castilian
castellanohablante *adj* Spanish-speaking
castidad *f* chastity; **cinturón de ~** chastity belt
castigar <g→gu> **I.** *vt* **1.** (*punir*) **~ por algo** to punish for sth; **¡castigado sin postre!** as a punishment you'll go without dessert! **2.** (*físicamente*) to beat; *fig* to castigate **3.** (*seducir*) to seduce **II.** *vr:* **~se** to castigate oneself
castigo *m* **1.** (*punición*) punishment **2.** (*aflicción*) affliction
Castilla *f* Castile
Castilla-La Mancha *f* Castile and La Mancha
Castilla-León *f* Castile and León
castillo *m t.* NÁUT (fore)castle; **~ de arena** sandcastle; **~ de naipes** house of cards; **hacer ~s en el aire** *fig* to build castles in the air
castizo, **-a** *adj* **1.** (*típico*) typical **2.** (*auténtico*) authentic
casto, **-a** *adj* chaste
castor *m* beaver
castración *f* **1.** AGR gelding **2.** *t.* MED castration
castrar *vt* **1.** AGR to geld **2.** *t.* MED to castrate
casual *adj* chance; **por un ~** *inf* by chance
casualidad *f* chance; **de** [*o* **por**] **~** by chance; **¡qué ~!** what a coincidence!; **da la ~ que conozco a tu mujer** it so happens that I know your wife
casualmente *adv* by chance
casulla *f* chasuble
cata *f* sampling; **~ de vinos** wine-tasting
cataclismo *m* cataclysm
catacumbas *fpl* catacombs *pl*
catador(a) *m(f)* **1.** (*catavinos*) taster **2.** (*entendido*) connoisseur
catadura *f* **1.** (*cata*) tasting **2.** (*aspecto*) look(s); **sujeto de mala ~** nasty-looking character
catalán *m* (*lengua*) Catalan
catalán, **-ana** *adj, m, f* Catalan, Catalonian
catalejo *m* telescope
catalizador *m* **1.** *t.* QUÍM, TÉC catalyst **2.** AUTO catalytic converter
catalogar <g→gu> *vt* **1.** (*registrar*) to cata-

logue *Brit,* to catalog *Am* **2.** (*clasificar*) to class; ~ **a alguien de algo** to classify sb as sth

catálogo *m* catalogue *Brit,* catalog *Am;* ~ **de materias/por autores** subject/author index; **casa de ventas por** ~ mail-order company; **en** ~ available

Cataluña *f* Catalonia

catamarán *m* DEP catamaran

cataplasma *f* **1.** MED poultice **2.** *inf* (*pesado*) bore

catapulta *f* catapult

catapultar *vt* to catapult

catar *vt* **1.** (*probar*) to taste **2.** (*experimentar*) to experience

catarata *f* **1.** (*salto de agua*) waterfall; **las ~s del Niágara** the Niagara Falls **2.** MED cataract

catarro *m* (*enfriamiento*) cold; MED catarrh; ~ **de nariz** headcold

catarsis *f inv* catharsis

catastro *m* cadastre *Brit,* cadaster *Am;* **oficina del** ~ land registry

catástrofe *f* catastrophe

catastrófico, -a *adj* catastrophic; **zona catastrófica** disaster area

catastrofismo *m* alarmism

catchup *m* <catchups> ketchup

cate *m inf* **1.** (*suspenso*) **me han dado dos ~s** I've failed two subjects **2.** (*bofetada*) whack

catear *vt inf* (*suspender*) to fail, to flunk *Am*

catecismo *m* REL catechism

cátedra *f* **1.** ENS (*púlpito*) lectern **2.** ENS (*docencia*) chair; **sentar** ~ to lay down the law; *irón* to pontificate

catedral *f* cathedral; **como una** ~ *fig* massive; (*alto*) huge

catedrático, -a *m, f* ENS professor; ~ **de instituto** ≈ secondary-school teacher

categoría *f* **1.** *t.* FILOS (*clase*) category; ~ **fiscal** tax bracket **2.** (*calidad*) quality; **de primera** ~ first-class **3.** (*rango*) rank; **dar** ~ to lend prestige; **tener mucha/poca** ~ to be important/unimportant

catequesis *f inv* **1.** REL catechesis **2.** (*clase*) religious instruction

caterva *f pey* load(s); (*de personas*) bunch

catete *m Chile* **1.** GASTR pork-broth porridge **2.** (*diablo*) devil

catéter *m* MED catheter

cateto, -a *m, f* yokel

catolicismo *m* REL (Roman) Catholicism

católico, -a *adj, m, f* (Roman) Catholic

catón *m* reader, primer *Am*

catorce *adj inv, m* fourteen; *v.t.* **ocho**

catorceavo, -a, catorzavo, -a *adj, m, f* fourteenth; *v.t.* **octavo**

catre *m t. pey* plank bed; (*de campaña*) camp bed; *inf* (*cama*) bed, sack *inf;* **llevar a alquien al** ~ to lay sb *vulg*

Cáucaso *m* **el** ~ the Caucasus

cauce *m* **1.** GEO (*lecho*) river bed **2.** (*acequia*) irrigation channel **3.** (*camino*) channel, course; ~ **jurídico** [*o* **legal**] JUR legal action; ~ **reglamentario** official channel

cauchal *m AmL* rubber plantation

caucho *m* **1.** (*sustancia*) rubber; **árbol del** ~ rubber tree **2.** *AmL* (*neumático*) tyre *Brit,* tire *Am*

caución *f* **1.** (*cautela*) caution **2.** JUR security

caudal **I.** *adj* tail **II.** *m* **1.** (*de agua*) volume **2.** (*dinero*) fortune; **caja de ~es** safe **3.** (*abundancia*) abundance; **un** ~ **de conocimientos** a wealth of knowledge

caudaloso, -a *adj* **1.** (*río*) large **2.** (*rico*) rich **3.** (*cantidad*) abundant

caudillaje *m* **1.** *t.* POL leadership **2.** *Arg, Chile, Perú, pey* (*caciquismo*) bossism

caudillo *m* MIL, POL leader; **el Caudillo** *Franco's nickname during his dictatorship*

caula *f AmL* (*estratagema*) trick

causa *f* **1.** *t.* POL (*origen, ideal*) cause; (*motivo*) reason; **a** [*o* **por**] ~ **de** on account of; **la** ~ **de su despido** the reason for his/her dismissal; **morir por la** ~ to die for the cause **2.** JUR lawsuit; (*proceso*) trial; **entender en una** ~ to handle a case; **instruir una** ~ to initiate legal proceedings *pl*

causante **I.** *adj* causing **II.** *mf* originator; (*culpable*) person responsible

causar *vt* to cause; ~ **alegría** to make happy; ~ **daño** to cause damage; ~ **efecto** to have an effect; ~ **problemas** to cause problems; ~ **risa a alguien** to make sb laugh; ~ **trabajo** to make work

causeo *m Chile* GASTR snack

cáustico, -a *adj* caustic

cautela *f* (*precaución*) caution

cauteloso, -a *adj* (*prudente*) cautious

cauterizar <z→c> *vt* MED to cauterize

cautivador(a) *adj* captivating

cautivar *vt* **1.** (*apresar*) to capture **2.** (*fascinar*) to captivate **3.** (*seducir*) to seduce

cautiverio *m,* **cautividad** *f* captivity

cautivo, -a *adj, m, f* captive

cauto, -a *adj* cautious

cava *m* cava

> **Cava** is referred to as the Spanish Champagne. This quality sparkling white wine is produced in champagne cellars in the northeast of Spain.

cavar *vi, vt* to dig

caverna *f* **1.** (*cueva*) cave; (*gruta*) cavern; **los hombres de las ~s** cavemen **2.** MED cavern

cavernícola *mf* **1.** (*troglodita*) cave dweller **2.** *inf* (*retrógrado*) reactionary

caviar *m sin pl* caviar

cavidad *f t.* MED cavity

cavilar *vt* ~ **algo** to ponder (on) sth

caviloso, -a *adj* suspicious

cayado *m* **1.** (*del pastor*) crook **2.** (*del prelado*) crozier

caza[1] *f* **1.** (*montería*) hunting; **ir de** [*o* **a la**] ~ to go hunting **2.** (*animales*) game; ~ **mayor** big game; **carne de** ~ game

caza[2] *m* MIL fighter plane

cazabombardero *m* MIL fighter-bomber
cazador(a) I. *adj* hunting II. *m(f)* (*persona*) hunter *m,* huntress *f;* ~ **furtivo** poacher
cazadora *f* bomber jacket; ~ **de piel** leather jacket
cazadotes *m inv* fortune hunter
cazar <z→c> *vt* 1. (*atrapar*) to hunt; (*perseguir*) to pursue; (*con una trampa*) to trap 2. (*coger*) to catch 3. (*conseguir*) to get 4. (*probar la culpabilidad*) to catch out; (*sorprender*) to surprise 5. *inf* (*engañar*) to take in
cazarrecompensas *mf inv* bounty hunter
cazatalentos *mf* 1. *inv* ECON headhunter 2. CINE, DEP talent spotter *Brit,* talent scout *Am*
cazavirus *adj inv* INFOR anti-virus; **programa** ~ anti-virus programme [*o* program *Am*]
cazo *m* 1. (*puchero*) saucepan 2. (*cucharón*) ladle 3. *inf* (*chulo*) pimp
cazuela *f* casserole
cazurro, -a I. *adj* 1. (*hosco*) sullen 2. (*obstinado*) stubborn 3. (*torpe*) slow-witted 4. (*grosero*) coarse II. *m, f* 1. (*hosco*) sullen person 2. (*obstinado*) stubborn person 3. (*patán*) boor
c.c., C.C., c/c *f* 1. COM *abr de* **cuenta corriente** C/A 2. ELEC *abr de* **corriente continua** D.C.
CC.OO. *fpl abr de* **Comisiones Obreras** *Spanish communist federation of trade unions*
CE¹ *f* HIST *abr de* **Comunidad Europea** EC
CE² *m abr de* **Consejo de Europa** Council of Europe
ceba *f* 1. (*engorde*) fattening 2. (*alimento*) feed 3. (*de un horno*) stoking
cebada *f* barley
cebar I. *vt* 1. (*engordar*) to fatten (up) 2. (*horno*) to stoke (up) 3. (*un arma*) to prime 4. (*el anzuelo, una trampa*) to bait 5. (*máquina*) to start; (*cohete*) to fire 6. (*esperanza*) to nourish; (*cólera*) to inflame II. *vr:* ~**se** 1. (*entregarse*) ~**se en algo** to devote oneself to sth 2. (*ira*) to vent one's anger; **se cebó en él** he/she vented his/her anger on him 3. (*alimentarse*) to feed
cebiche *m AmS* GASTR ceviche (*dish of raw fish marinated in lemon juice*)
cebo *m* 1. (*alimento*) feed 2. (*de un anzuelo*) bait; *t. fig* lure 3. (*en un arma*) primer 4. (*en un horno*) fuel
cebolla *f* 1. BOT (*comestible*) onion 2. BOT (*bulbo*) bulb 3. *inf* (*cabeza*) head
cebollar *m* field of onions
cebolleta *f* 1. BOT (*cebolla tierna*) spring onion *Brit,* scallion *Am* 2. BOT (*tallo fino, muy aromático*) chive 3. *vulg* (*pene*) prick
cebra *f* zebra; **paso de** ~ AUTO zebra crossing *Brit,* crosswalk *Am*
cebú *m* zebu
cecear *vi to pronounce the Spanish 's' as 'z'*
ceceo *m* 1. (*en algunas regiones*) *pronunciation of the Spanish 's' as 'z'* 2. (*defecto*) lisp

In certain regions, for example in certain areas of Andalusia, the Spanish 's' is pronounced as a 'z'. This linguistic phenomenon is referred to as **ceceo**, e.g. 'cocer' instead of 'coser'.

cedazo *m* 1. (*para cribar*) sieve 2. (*para pescar*) large net
ceder I. *vi* 1. (*renunciar*) to renounce; (*de una pretensión*) to give up 2. (*disminuir*) to diminish; **cedió la fiebre** the fever went down; **cedió la lluvia** the rain eased off 3. (*capitular*) ~ **a algo** to give in to sth 4. (*cuerda, rama, puente*) to give way; (*cuero*) to give II. *vt* 1. (*dar*) to hand over 2. (*transferir*) to transfer 3. DEP (*balón*) to pass 4. AUTO **"ceda el paso"** "give way" *Brit,* "yield" *Am*
cedro *m* cedar
cedrón *m AmS* BOT lemon verbena
cédula *f* certificate; ~ **de ahorro** savings certificate; ~ **de cambio** bill of exchange; ~ **de citación** summons; ~ **personal** identity card; ~ **real** royal charter
CEE *f* HIST *abr de* **Comunidad Económica Europea** EEC
céfiro *m* zephyr, west wind
cegar *irr como fregar* I. *vi* to go [*o* become] blind II. *vt* 1. (*quitar la vista*) to blind; **le ciega la ira** he/she is blinded by rage 2. (*ventana*) to wall up; (*con clavos*) to nail up; (*pozo*) to fill up III. *vr:* ~**se** 1. (*ofuscarse*) to be blinded; ~**se de ira** to be blinded by rage 2. (*tubo*) to get blocked up
cegatón, -ona *pey* I. *adj inf* (*corto de vista*) near-sighted II. *m, f inf* poor-sighted person
ceguera *f t. fig* blindness
Ceilán *m* Ceylon
ceja *f* 1. (*entrecejo*) eyebrow; **fruncir las** ~**s** to knit one's eyebrows; **tener a alguien entre** ~ **y** ~ *inf* to have it in for sb 2. (*borde*) rim 3. MÚS (*instrumento de cuerda*) nut; (*instrumento de teclado*) pressure bar 4. MÚS (*para elevar el tono*) capo
cejar *vi* 1. (*en discusiones*) to climb down 2. (*cesar*) to give up; **sin** ~ unceasingly
cejijunto, -a *adj* 1. (*fisonomía*) having eyebrows that meet (in the middle) 2. (*adusto*) severe
celada *f* 1. (*yelmo*) helmet 2. (*emboscada*) ambush 3. (*trampa*) trap
celador(a) *m(f)* watchman; (*de aparcamientos*) parking attendant; (*de cárcel*) prison warden *Brit,* prison guard *Am;* (*de escuela*) monitor
celaje *m* 1. METEO cloudy sky 2. *AmL* (*fantasma*) ghost
celar *vt* (*vigilar*) to keep a watchful eye on
celda *f* (*pequeño espacio, de colmena*) cell; (*en prisión*) prison cell; ~ **de castigo** solitary confinement; ~ **acolchada** padded cell
celdilla *f* 1. (*de colmena*) cell 2. ARQUIT niche 3. BOT seed capsule
celebérrimo, -a *adj superl de* **célebre**

celebración *f* 1. (*acto, festividad*) celebration; **la ~ de una misa** the celebration of a Mass 2. (*aplausos*) applause 3. (*organización*) holding

celebrar I. *vt* 1. (*mérito, acontecimiento*) to celebrate 2. (*reuniones*) to hold; **~ una subasta** to hold an auction 3. (*alegrarse*) to be delighted 4. (*aplaudir*) to applaud 5. (*llegada*) to welcome 6. (*ventajas*) to dwell on 7. (*un chiste*) to laugh at 8. (*tratado*) to conclude II. *vi* REL to celebrate [*o* to say] Mass III. *vr:* **~se** 1. (*fiesta*) to be celebrated 2. (*reunión, partido*) to be held

célebre <celebérrimo> *adj* 1. (*famoso*) **~ por algo** famous for sth 2. *inf* (*gracioso*) witty

celebridad *f* 1. (*alguien ilustre*) celebrity 2. (*renombre*) fame 3. (*festejo*) celebration

celeridad *f* swiftness

celeste *adj* 1. (*célico*) celestial; **cuerpos ~s** heavenly bodies 2. (*color*) sky blue

celestial *adj* 1. (*del cielo*) celestial, heavenly; (*delicioso*) heavenly 2. *irón, inf* (*tonto*) silly

celibato *m* 1. REL celibacy 2. (*soltería*) single state

célibe I. *adj* 1. REL celibate 2. (*soltero*) single II. *mf* unmarried person

celo *m* 1. (*afán*) zeal 2. *pl* (*por amor*) jealousy; **tener ~s** to be jealous 3. *pl* (*sospecha*) mistrust 4. *pl* (*envidia*) envy 5. (*ciertos animales de caza: macho*) rut; (*hembra*) heat; **estar en ~** (*macho*) to be in rut; (*hembra*) to be on heat 6. (*autoadhesivo*) adhesive tape *Brit,* Scotch® tape

celosía *f* 1. (*rejilla*) lattice 2. (*contraventanas*) slatted shutter; (*persianas*) (Venetian) blinds *pl*

celoso, -a *adj* 1. (*con fervor*) **~ en algo** zealous in sth 2. (*exigente*) **~ de algo** conscientious about sth 3. (*con celos*) jealous 4. (*con envidia*) envious 5. (*con dudas*) distrustful

celta I. *adj* Celtic II. *mf* Celt

célula *f* BIO, POL cell; **~ fotoeléctrica** photoelectric cell

celular *adj* 1. BIO cellular 2. (*cárcel*) **prisión ~** solitary confinement; **coche ~** police van

celulitis *f inv* MED cellulitis

cementar *vt* TÉC to cement

cementerio *m* 1. (*camposanto*) cemetery; **~ de coches** used-car scrapyard 2. (*depósito*) dump; **~ nuclear** nuclear waste dump

cemento *m* ARQUIT, ANAT cement; **~ armado** reinforced concrete

cena *f* supper; **la Última Cena** the Last Supper

cenáculo *m* 1. (*tertulia*) group; (*reunión*) meeting 2. (*de literatura*) literary group 3. (*camarilla*) clique 4. REL cenacle

cenador *m* 1. (*comedor*) dining room 2. (*en el jardín*) arbour *Brit,* arbor *Am*

cenaduría *f Méx* eating house (*serving only at night*)

cenagal *m* 1. (*con cieno*) bog 2. *inf* (*problema*) mess; **estar en un ~** to be in a fix

cenagoso, -a *adj* boggy

cenar I. *vi* to have supper [*o* dinner]; **hoy hemos cenado lentejas** we had lentils for supper [*o* dinner] today II. *vt* to have for supper [*o* dinner]

cencerrear *vi* 1. (*con cencerros*) to ring 2. (*tocar mal*) to play badly 3. (*bisagras*) to creak 4. (*traquetear*) to rattle; (*golpetear*) to knock; (*estruendo*) to make a noise

cencerro *m* (*de res*) cowbell; **estar como un ~** *inf* to be crazy

cenefa *f* 1. (*adorno*) border; (*encaje de bolillos*) pillow lace 2. (*de techos, muros*) frieze

cenicero *m* ashtray

cenicienta *f,* **Cenicienta** *f* Cinderella

ceniciento, -a *adj* ash-coloured [*o* colored *Am*]

cenit *m* zenith

ceniza *f* 1. (*residuo de algo quemado*) ash; **Miércoles de Ceniza** Ash Wednesday; **reducir algo a ~s** to reduce sth to ashes 2. *pl* (*restos mortales*) ashes *pl*

cenizo *m* 1. BOT goosefoot 2. (*que trae mala suerte*) jinx

cenobio *m* REL (*monjes*) monastery; (*monjas*) convent

censar I. *vi* to carry out a census II. *vt* to take a census of

censo *m* 1. (*de habitantes, estadística*) census; **~ electoral** POL electoral roll 2. FIN (*gravamen: sobre una finca*) ground rent

censor(a) *m(f)* censor

censura *f* 1. (*crítica*) censorship; **~ cinematográfica** film censorship; **someter a la ~** to censor 2. (*entidad*) censor's office 3. FIN **~ de cuentas** auditing 4. POL **moción de ~** motion of censure 5. (*vituperación*) condemnation

censurar *vt* 1. (*juzgar*) to censure; **~on todas las escenas violentas** all the violent scenes were taken out 2. (*vituperar*) to condemn

centauro *m* centaur

centavo *m* 1. (*centésima parte*) hundredth (part) 2. (*del dólar*) cent, penny *Am* 3. *AmC, CSur* FIN (*moneda*) centavo

centavo, -a *adj* hundredth; *v.t.* **octavo**

centella *f* 1. (*rayo*) flash of lightning 2. (*chispa*) spark 3. (*destello*) sparkle

centell(e)ar *vi* 1. (*relámpago*) to flash 2. (*fuego*) to spark 3. (*estrella*) to twinkle 4. (*ojos, gema*) to glitter

centelleo *m* 1. (*del relámpago*) flashing 2. (*de las llamas*) sparking 3. (*de las estrellas*) twinkling 4. (*de los ojos, de una gema*) glittering

centena *f* hundred

centenar *m* 1. (*cien*) hundred 2. AGR rye field

centenario *m* centenary *Brit,* centennial *Am*

centenario, -a *adj, m, f* centenarian

centeno *m* rye

centésimo *m Chile, Pan, Urug* FIN (*moneda*) centesimo

centésimo, -a I. *adj* (*parte, numeración*) hundredth; **la centésima parte de...** a hun-

C

dredth of ... II. *m, f* hundredth (part)

centígrado *m* centigrade; **grado** ~ degree centigrade

centigramo *m* centigram, centigramme *Brit*

centilitro *m* centilitre *Brit,* centiliter *Am*

centímetro *m* centimetre *Brit,* centimeter *Am*

céntimo I. *adj* hundredth II. *m* 1. (*centésima parte*) hundredth part 2. FIN (*moneda española*) hundredth part of a peseta; *CRi, Par, Ven* centimo; ~ **de euro** eurocent; **estar sin un** ~ to be broke

centinela *mf* 1. (*de museo, banco*) guard 2. MIL sentry

centollo *m* spider crab

centrado, -a *adj* 1. (*en el centro*) centred *Brit,* centered *Am* 2. (*forma de ser*) stable

central I. *adj* central; **Europa Central** Central Europe; **comité** ~ central committee; **estación** ~ main station II. *f* 1. (*oficina*) head office; ~ **de Correos** general [*o* main] post office; ~ **telefónica** TEL telephone exchange; (*de una empresa*) (telephone) switchboard 2. TÉC plant; ~ **depuradora** waterworks; ~ **eléctrica** electric power station; ~ **hidroeléctrica** hydroelectric power station; ~ **nuclear** nuclear power station; ~ **térmica** oil-fired power station

centralismo *m* POL centralism

centralista I. *adj* POL centralist II. *mf* 1. POL advocate of centralism 2. *AmC, Ant* (*del ingenio azucarero*) sugar-mill owner

centralita *f* TEL switchboard

centralización *f* centralization

centralizar <z→c> *vt* to centralize

centrar I. *vt* 1. TÉC (*colocar*) to centre *Brit,* to center *Am* 2. (*aunar esfuerzos*) to concentrate 3. (*interés, atención*) to focus II. *vi, vt* DEP (*fútbol*) to centre *Brit,* to center *Am* III. *vr:* ~**se** 1. (*basarse*) to centre *Brit,* to center *Am* 2. (*familiarizarse*) ~**se en algo** to get to know sth; (*en un trabajo*) to settle (down) to sth 3. (*interés, atención, miradas*) to focus

céntrico, -a *adj t.* TÉC central; **punto** ~ focal point; **piso** ~ an apartment in the centre of town

centrifugación *f* **programa de** ~ spin-drying programme, program *Am*

centrifugadora *f* spin-dryer; TÉC centrifuge

centrifugar <g→gu> *vt* to spin-dry; TÉC to centrifuge

centrífugo, -a *adj* centrifugal; **fuerza centrífuga** centrifugal force

centrismo *m* POL centrism

centrista I. *adj* POL centrist; **partido** ~ centrist party II. *mf* POL centrist

centro *m* 1. *t.* POL, DEP (*el medio*) centre *Brit,* center *Am;* (*de la ciudad*) town centre *Brit,* downtown *Am;* ~ **de gravedad** centre [*o* center *Am*] of gravity; ~ **industrial** industrial centre [*o* center *Am*] 2. (*institución*) centre *Brit,* center *Am;* ~ **de computación** computer centre [*o* center *Am*]; ~ **de enseñanza** teaching institution; ~ **comercial** shopping centre [*o* center *Am*], mall *Am* 3. ANAT ~ **nervioso** nerve centre [*o* center *Am*]

centroafricano, -a *adj, m, f* Central African

Centroamérica *f* Central America

centroamericano, -a *adj, m, f* Central American

centrocampista *mf* DEP midfielder

Centroeuropa *f* Central Europe

centuplicar <c→qu> *vt* to increase a hundredfold

céntuplo *m* hundredfold

centuria *f elev* century

centurión *m* HIST centurion

ceñido, -a *adj* 1. (*vestido*) tight-fitting, figure-hugging 2. (*forma de expresión*) sparing

ceñir *irr* I. *vt* 1. *t.* MIL (*rodear*) to surround 2. (*ponerse*) to put on; (*cinturón*) to buckle on 3. (*acortar*) to shorten 4. (*abreviar*) to shorten II. *vr:* ~**se** 1. (*ajustarse*) to limit oneself; (*al hablar*) to be brief; ~**se al presupuesto** to keep to the budget 2. (*vestido*) to be close-fitting 3. (*ponerse*) to put on; **se ciñó el cinturón** he/she buckled on his/her belt

ceño *m* frown; **fruncir** [*o* **arrugar**] **el** ~, **mirar con** ~ (*disgustado, enojado*) to frown

ceñudo, -a *adj* 1. (*mirada*) grim 2. (*persona: disgustada*) frowning

cepa *f* 1. *t.* BOT (*tronco*) stump; (*en la vid, origen*) stock; **de pura** ~ real 2. MED strain

cepillar I. *vt* 1. (*cabello, traje*) to brush 2. TÉC (*madera*) to plane 3. *inf* (*robar*) to rip off 4. *AmL, inf* (*adular*) to butter up 5. *inf* (*ganar*) to win 6. (*suspender*) to fail, to flunk *Am* II. *vr:* ~**se** 1. *inf* (*robar*) to rip off 2. *inf* (*devorar*) to polish off 3. *inf* (*gastarse dinero*) to squander 4. *inf* (*matar*) to bump off 5. *vulg* (*seducir*) to make it with; ~**se a una chica** to screw a girl

cepillo *m* 1. (*para el cabello*) brush; (*para un traje*) clothes brush; (*de limpiar*) scrubbing brush; ~ **de barrer** broom; ~ **de dientes** toothbrush; **pasar el** ~ to brush 2. TÉC (*para madera*) plane 3. (*en misa*) collection box

cepo *m* 1. (*caza*) trap; **caer en el** ~ to fall into the trap 2. (*grilletes*) stocks *pl* 3. *pl* AUTO wheel clamp

ceporro, -a I. *adj inf* (*ignorante*) dim-witted II. *m, f inf* dimwit; **dormir como un** ~ to sleep like a log

cera *f* wax; (*de vela*) candle-wax; ~ **de los oídos** earwax; ~ **para suelos** wax polish; **museo de** ~ wax museum; **blanco como la** ~ white as a sheet

cerámica *f* ceramics *pl*

ceramista *mf* potter

cerbatana *f* blowpipe *Brit,* blowgun *Am*

cerca I. *adv* 1. (*en el espacio*) near; **aquí** ~ near here; **mirar de** ~ to look closely at 2. (*en el tiempo*) close II. *prep* 1. (*lugar*) ~ **de** near 2. (*cantidad*) about III. *f* fence

cercado *m* 1. (*valla*) fence 2. (*recinto*) enclosure

cercanía *f* 1. (*proximidad*) closeness; (*vecin-*

dad) neighbourhood *Brit,* neighborhood *Am* **2.** *pl* (*alrededores*) outskirts *pl*
cercano, -a *adj* near
cercar <c→qu> *vt* **1.** (*vallar*) to fence in; (*rodear*) to enclose **2.** (*rodear*) to surround **3.** MIL (*sitiar*) to besiege; (*rodear*) to encircle
cercenar *vt* **1.** (*mutilar*) to cut off **2.** MED (*miembro*) to amputate **3.** (*sueldo*) to cut (back)
cerciorar **I.** *vt* to convince **II.** *vr:* **~se** to make sure
cerco *m* **1.** (*círculo*) circle; (*anillo*) ring; (*borde*) rim **2.** (*valla*) fence **3.** (*de barril*) hoop **4.** ASTR, METEO halo **5.** MIL siege
cerda *f* **1.** ZOOL sow **2.** (*pelo*) bristle; ~ **de cerdo** pigs bristle
cerdada *f pey* dirty trick
Cerdeña *f* Sardinia
cerdo, -a **I.** *adj* (*sucio*) dirty **II.** *m, f* **1.** ZOOL pig; **carne de** ~ pork **2.** (*insulto*) swine
cereales *mpl* cereals *pl,* grain
cerebelo *m* ANAT cerebellum
cerebro *m* **1.** ANAT (*en su totalidad*) brain; (*parte mayor*) cerebrum **2.** (*inteligencia*) brains *pl*
ceremonia *f* **1.** (*acto, celebración, misa*) ceremony **2.** (*cortesía*) formality; **sin ~s** without any fuss
ceremonial *adj, m* ceremonial
ceremonioso, -a *adj* **1.** (*solemne*) ceremonious; (*formal*) formal **2.** (*persona*) stiff
cereza *f* cherry
cerezo *m* **1.** (*árbol*) cherry tree **2.** (*madera*) cherry wood
cerilla *f* **1.** (*fósforo*) match **2.** (*vela*) wax taper **3.** (*cerumen*) earwax
cerillero *m AmL* (*cajita*) matchbox
cerillo *m* **1.** *Méx* (*fósforo*) match **2.** (*vela*) wax taper
cerner <e→ie> **I.** *vt* **1.** (*cribar*) to sieve, to sift **2.** (*observar*) to observe **II.** *vr* **~se sobre algo** to hover over sth
cernícalo *m* **1.** ZOOL kestrel **2.** (*persona*) boor
cernir *irr vt* **1.** (*cribar*) to sieve, to sift **2.** (*observar*) to observe; (*cielo, horizonte*) to scan
cero *m* **1.** *t.* MAT (*punto inicial, valor*) zero; **ocho** (**grados**) **bajo/sobre** ~ eight below/above zero; **partir de** ~ to start from scratch **2.** *inf* (*coche policía*) police car
cerote *m* **1.** *inf* (*miedo*) panic **2.** TÉC (*cera y pez*) shoemaker's wax **3.** *AmC, Méx, inf* (*excremento*) stool; **estar hecho un** ~ to look a mess
cerrado, -a *adj* **1.** *estar* (*no abierto*) closed; (*con llave*) locked; **la puerta está cerrada** the door is closed; **a puerta cerrada** behind closed doors; **aquí huele a** ~ it smells stuffy in here **2.** *estar* METEO (*cielo*) overcast **3.** *ser* (*actitud*) reserved **4.** *ser* (*espeso*) thick; (*denso*) dense; **noche cerrada** dark night **5.** *ser* (*característico*) typical; (*acento*) broad **6.** LING (*fonética*) closed **7.** *ser* (*curva*) sharp **8.** *ser* (*lerdo*) thick; ~ **de mollera** *inf* very dense
cerradura *f* **1.** (*dispositivo*) lock; ~ **antirrobo** steering(-wheel) lock **2.** (*acción*) closing; (*con llave*) locking
cerrajería *f* **1.** (*taller*) locksmith's (shop) **2.** (*oficio*) locksmith's craft
cerrajero, -a *m, f* locksmith
cerramiento *m* **1.** (*acción*) closing **2.** (*alrededor*) enclosure
cerrar <e→ie> **I.** *vt* **1.** (*paraguas, ojos*) to close; (*carta*) to seal; ~ **los oídos** to turn a deaf ear; ~ **el pico** *inf* to keep one's trap shut; ~ **archivo** INFOR to close a file **2.** (*con llave*) to lock **3.** (*carretera, puerto, establecimiento*) to close; ~ **el paso a alguien** to bar sb's way **4.** (*agujero, brecha*) to block (up); (*agua*) to turn off **5.** (*terreno*) to close off; (*con un cerco*) to enclose **6.** (*actividad, ciclo, negociación*) to conclude **II.** *vi* **1.** (*puerta, ventana*) to close **2.** (*acabar*) to end **3.** (*atacar*) ~ **contra alguien** to attack sb **III.** *vr:* **~se** **1.** (*puerta*) **la puerta se cerró sola** the door closed by itself **2.** (*herida*) to heal (up) **3.** (*obstinarse*) to persist **4.** (*el cielo*) to become overcast **5.** (*ser intransigente*) to close one's mind **6.** (*agruparse*) to crowd together
cerrazón *f* **1.** (*torpeza*) dimness **2.** (*obstinación*) stubbornness **3.** METEO (*nubes*) storm clouds
cerril *adj* **1.** (*terreno*) rough **2.** (*obstinado*) obstinate **3.** (*torpe*) dense **4.** (*tosco*) uncouth **5.** (*caballerías*) wild
cerrilismo *m* **1.** (*tosquedad*) uncouthness **2.** (*obstinación*) obstinacy
cerro *m* **1.** (*colina*) hill; (*peñasco*) crag; **irse por los ~s de Úbeda** *inf* to go off on a tangent; (*decir tonterías*) to talk (a lot of) rubbish **2.** ZOOL (*cuello*) neck; (*espinazo*) back
cerrojazo *m inf* **echar** ~ **a algo** to slam sth shut; *fig* to put an end to sth
cerrojo *m* bolt; **echar el** ~ **a la puerta** to bolt the door
certamen *m* competition
certero, -a *adj* **1.** (*acertado*) accurate **2.** (*diestro en tirar: tirador*) crack **3.** (*informado*) well-informed
certeza *f* certainty
certidumbre *f* certainty
certificación *f* **1.** (*acción, documento*) certification **2.** JUR (*atestación*) attestation
certificado *m* certificate; ~ **de aptitud** testimonial; ~ **de asistencia** certificate of attendance; ~ **escolar** school report; ~ **médico** medical certificate
certificado, -a *adj* **1.** JUR certified **2.** (*correos*) registered; **carta certificada** registered letter
certificar <c→qu> *vt* **1.** *t.* JUR (*afirmar*) to certify **2.** (*correos*) to register
certísimo, -a *adj superl de* **cierto**
cerumen *m* earwax
cervato *m* fawn
cervecería *f* **1.** (*bar*) pub *Brit,* bar **2.** (*fábrica*) brewery

cervecero *m* brewer
cervecero, -a *adj* beer; (*industria*) brewing
cerveza *f* beer; ~ **de barril** draught beer; ~ **negra** dark beer, stout; ~ **rubia** lager beer
cervical *adj* **1.** ANAT neck **2.** MED cervical
Cervino *m* **el Monte** ~ the Matterhorn
cerviz *f* ANAT nape of the neck
cesación *f*, **cesamiento** *m* cessation; ~ **del fuego** ceasefire
cesante **I.** *adj* **1.** (*suspendido*) suspended **2.** (*parado*) unemployed **II.** *mf* laid-off civil servants
cesantía *f* **1.** (*situación*) redundancy; (*paro*) unemployment **2.** (*suspensión*) suspension **3.** (*paga*) severance pay
cesar **I.** *vi* **1.** (*parar*) to stop; **sin** ~ ceaselessly **2.** (*en una profesión*) ~ **en algo** to leave sth **II.** *vt* **1.** (*pagos*) to stop **2.** (*despedir*) to dismiss; (*funcionario*) to dismiss
cesárea *f* caesarean
cese *m* **1.** (*que termina*) cessation; (*interrupción*) suspension; ~ **de pagos** suspension of payments, temporary receivership *Brit* **2.** (*de obrero*) sacking; (*de funcionario*) dismisaal; ~ **en el cargo** to retire from office **3.** JUR (*proceso*) abandonment
cesio *m* caesium *Brit*, cesium *Am*
cesión *f* **1.** (*entrega*) transfer **2.** JUR cession
césped *m* grass; **'prohibido pisar el ~'** 'keep off the grass'
cesta *f* basket
cestería *f* **1.** (*tienda*) basketwork shop **2.** (*artesanía*) basketwork **3.** (*artículos*) basketwork articles
cestero, -a *m, f* **1.** (*que fabrica*) basketmaker **2.** (*que vende*) basket seller
cesto *m t.* DEP basket; ~ **de los papeles** wastepaper basket, wastebasket *Am*
cesura *f* caesura
ceta *f* Z
cetáceo *m* cetacean
cetrería *f* falconry
cetrino, -a *adj* **1.** (*amarillento, verdoso*) greenish-yellow **2.** (*melancólico*) melancholy
cetro *m* **1.** (*vara*) sceptre *Brit*, scepter *Am*; **empuñar el** ~ *elev* to ascend the throne **2.** (*supremacía*) rule **3.** DEP championship; **ostentar el** ~ to reign supreme
ceutí **I.** *adj* of/from Ceuta **II.** *mf* native/inhabitant of Ceuta
cf. *abr de* **compárese** cf.
chabacanería *f* vulgarity
chabacano, -a *adj* vulgar
chabola *f* **1.** (*casucha*) shack **2.** *pl* (*barrio*) shanty town
chabolismo *m* shanty-town conditions *pl*, slums *pl*
chacal *m* jackal
chacalín *m AmC* ZOOL shrimp
chacanear *vt Chile* (*montura*) to spur on
chácara *f Par, Nic, Bol* **1.** (*granja*) small farm **2.** MED ulcer
chacarero, -a *m, f AmL* farmer; (*trabajador*) farm labourer
chacha *f inf* (*niñera*) nursemaid; (*criada*) maid; (*de limpieza*) cleaning lady
cháchara *f inf* (*charla*) chatter; **andar** [*o* **estar**] **de** ~ to have a chat
chacharear *vi inf* to chatter
chacho, -a *m, f inf* (*muchacho, muchacha*) boy *m*, girl *f*
chacolotear *vi* to clatter
chacota *f* **1.** (*jolgorio*) merriment **2.** (*broma*) joke; **echar** [*o* **tomar**] **algo a** ~ to take sth as a joke
chacotearse *vr* ~ **de algo/alguien** to make fun of sth/sb
chacra *f AmL* (*granja*) small farm; (*finca*) country estate
Chad *m* Chad
chafar **I.** *vt* **1.** (*aplastar*) to flatten *fig*, to squelch; (*arrugar*) to crease; (*deshacer*) to mess up **2.** (*confundir*) to confuse; **quedar(se) chafado** to be speechless **3.** (*estropear*) to spoil; **le ~on sus proyectos** they spoiled his/her plans **II.** *vr*: **~se** (*aplastarse*) to be flattened; (*deshacerse*) to be messed up; (*arrugarse*) to be creased
chafarrinón *m* **1.** (*mancha*) spot **2.** (*cuadro*) daub
chaflán *m* **1.** (*bisel*) bevel (edge) **2.** (*en una calle*) street corner; (*en un edificio*) house corner
chagra *mf Ecua* (*labriego*) peasant
cháguar *m AmS* BOT caraguata, Paraguayan sisal
chal *m* shawl
chalado, -a **I.** *adj inf* crazy; **estar ~ por alguien** to be crazy about sb **II.** *m, f inf* nutcase
chaladura *f inf* **1.** (*locura*) (piece of) madness **2.** (*enamoramiento*) infatuation
chalanear **I.** *vi* **1.** (*traficar*) to deal **2.** (*regatear*) to haggle (over) **II.** *vt AmL* (*un caballo*) to break in; (*adiestrar*) to train
chalar **I.** *vt inf* to drive crazy **II.** *vr*: **~se** *inf* to go crazy; **~se por alguien** to be crazy about sb
chalé *m* (*casa unifamiliar*) detached family home; (*de campo*) country house; (*villa*) chalet
chaleco *m* waistcoat *Brit*, vest *Am*; ~ **salvavidas** life jacket
chalina *f* **1.** (*pañuelo*) scarf **2.** *Arg, Col, CRi* (*chal*) narrow shawl
chalupa *f* NÁUT launch
chamaco, -a *m, f Cuba, Méx* **1.** (*muchacho*) boy; (*muchacha*) girl **2.** (*novio*) boyfriend; (*novia*) girlfriend
chamagoso, -a *adj Méx* (*mugriento*) filthy
chamaril(l)ero, -a *m, f* **1.** (*que vende objetos viejos*) secondhand dealer **2.** (*tahúr*) cardsharp
chambelán *m* chamberlain
chambón, -ona *adj inf* **1.** (*afortunado*) lucky **2.** (*descuidado*) slovenly
chamborote *adj Ecua* **1.** (*de nariz larga*) long-nosed **2.** (*loc*) **pimiento** ~ long white pepper

chamico *m AmL* BOT thorn apple
chamiza *f* **1.** (*planta*) thatch **2.** (*leña*) brushwood
chamizo *m* **1.** (*árbol*) charred tree; (*leño*) charred log **2.** (*choza*) thatched hut **3.** *pey* (*vivienda*) shack
champán *m,* **champaña** *m* champagne
Champaña *f* Champagne
champiñón *m* mushroom
champú *m* shampoo; ~ **anticaspa** anti-dandruff shampoo
chamuscado, **-a** *adj* **1.** (*quemado*) scorched **2.** *inf* (*receloso*) suspicious **3.** *inf* (*amoscado*) cross
chamuscar <c→qu> **I.** *vt* (*quemar*) to scorch; (*aves*) to singe **II.** *vr:* ~**se** **1.** (*quemarse*) to get scorched **2.** *inf* (*ponerse receloso*) to become suspicious **3.** *inf* (*amoscarse*) to go into a huff
chamusquina *f* (*quemadura*) scorching; (*de aves*) singeing; **esto huele a** ~ *inf* (*sospechoso*) this smells fishy; (*peligroso*) there's trouble in store
chance *m o f AmC* (*oportunidad*) chance
chancear **I.** *vi* to joke **II.** *vr:* ~**se** to make fun
chancero, **-a** *adj* joking
chanchería *f AmL* pork butcher's shop
chanchero, **-a** *m, f* pork butcher
chancho *m AmL* pig
chancho, **-a** *adj AmL* **1.** (*marrano*) dirty **2.** (*desaseado*) slovenly
chanchullo *m inf* swindle, fiddle
chancla *f* **1.** (*zapato viejo*) old shoe **2.** (*zapatilla*) slipper **3.** (*de playa*) flip flop
chancleta *f* **1.** (*chinela*) slipper **2.** *AmL* (*bebé*) baby girl **3.** *inf* (*persona inepta*) fool **4.** *AmL, pey* (*mujer*) slut
chanclo *m* **1.** (*zueco*) clog **2.** (*zapato de goma*) (rubber) overshoe, galosh
chándal *m* <chándals> tracksuit
changa *f* **1.** *inf* (*trato*) (unimportant) business deal **2.** *Arg* (*ocupación*) trade **3.** *AmS* (*transporte*) portering **4.** *AmS, Cuba* (*broma*) joke
changador *m* **1.** *AmS* (*cargador*) carrier **2.** *Arg* (*temporero*) casual worker
changar <g→gu> *vt* (*romper*) to break; (*descomponer*) to split up; (*destrozar*) to destroy
chanta *mf Arg, inf* (*impostor*) fraud
chantaje *m* blackmail
chantajear *vt* to blackmail
chantajista *mf* blackmailer
chantar *vt* **1.** (*poste*) to drive in **2.** *inf* (*vestir*) to put on; ~ **el abrigo a alguien** to help sb on with his/her coat **3.** (*verdad, impertinencia*) **se lo he chantado** I told it to him/her straight to his/her face **4.** *Chile* (*golpe*) to deal
chanza *f* joke; **estar de** ~ to be joking
chapa *f* **1.** (*metal*) sheet **2.** (*lámina*) plate; (*de madera*) panel **3.** (*contrachapado*) plywood **4.** (*tapón*) (bottle)cap **5.** (*colorete*) rouge, blusher *Am;* (*chapeta*) flush (in the cheeks) **6.** (*placa*) shield *Brit,* badge *Am* **7.** *AmL* (*cerradura*) lock **8.** *pl* (*juego*) *game played with bottlecaps*
chapar *vt* **1.** (*con un metal*) to plate; (*con oro*) to gold-plate; (*con madera*) to veneer; (*con baldosines*) to tile; **chapado a la antigua** old-fashioned **2.** (*comentario*) to come out with
chaparra *f* kermes oak
chaparreras *fpl Méx* (*pantalones para montar a caballo*) chaps *pl*
chaparro *m* dwarf oak
chaparro, **-a** **I.** *adj inf* squat **II.** *m, f inf* shorty
chaparrón *m* **1.** (*lluvia fuerte*) downpour; (*chubasco*) cloudburst **2.** *inf* (*cantidad grande*) barrage
chapeado *m* **1.** (*de metal*) metal plate; ~ **de oro** gold plate **2.** (*de madera*) veneer **3.** (*de baldosines*) tiling
chapeado, **-a** *adj* **1.** (*de metal*) metal-plated; (*de oro*) gold-plated **2.** (*de madera*) veneered **3.** (*de baldosines*) tiled
chapear **I.** *vt* **1.** (*con un metal*) to plate; (*con oro*) to gold-plate; (*con madera*) to veneer; (*con baldosines*) to tile **2.** *AmL* (*la tierra*) to weed **II.** *vi* (*chacolotear*) to clatter
chapero *m inf* **1.** (*prostituto*) male prostitute, rent boy *inf* **2.** (*homosexual*) queer
chapetón, **-ona** **I.** *adj AmL* newly arrived **II.** *m, f AmL* Spaniard in America
chapín, **-ina** *m, f* Guatemalan
chapisca *f AmC* AGR (*cosecha de maíz*) maize [*o* corn *Am*] harvest
chapista *mf* **1.** (*planchista*) tinsmith **2.** (*de carrocería*) panel beater
chapistería *f* **1.** (*planchistería*) tinsmith's forge **2.** (*de carrocería*) car-body works *pl*
chapitel *m* ARQUIT (*de una torre*) spire; (*de una columna*) capital
chapopote *m Ant, Méx* (*asfalto*) asphalt
chapotear **I.** *vi* (*persona*) to paddle; (*agua*) to splash (around) **II.** *vt* to moisten
chapucear *vt* (*hacer mal y rápido*) to botch
chapucero, **-a** **I.** *adj* **1.** (*mal y rápido*) shoddy **2.** (*embustero*) deceitful **II.** *m, f* **1.** (*chambón*) bungler **2.** (*embustero*) cheat
chapulín *m* **1.** *AmL* (*langosta*) large cicada **2.** *AmC* (*niño*) child
chapurr(e)ar *vt* **1.** (*idioma*) to speak badly **2.** *inf* (*bebidas*) to mix
chapuza *f* **1.** (*chapucería*) shoddy job **2.** (*trabajo*) odd job
chapuzar <z→c> **I.** *vt* to dive in **II.** *vi, vr:* ~**se** to dive in
chapuzón *m* dip; **darse un** ~ to go for a dip
chaqué *m* morning coat
chaqueta *f* (*cazadora*) jacket; **cambiar de** [*o* **la**] ~ *fig* to change sides
chaquetear *vi* **1.** (*cambiar de ideas*) to change sides **2.** (*acobardarse*) to go back on one's word
chaquetero, **-a** **I.** *adj* opportunistic **II.** *m, f* POL turncoat
chaquetilla *f* bolero
chaquetón *m* long jacket; (*cazadora*) wind-

cheater *Brit,* windbreaker *Am*
charada *f* charade
charanga *f* **1.** (*banda*) brass band **2.** *AmL* (*baile*) dance
charca *f* pond
charco *m* puddle, pool
charcón, -ona *adj Arg, Bol, Urug* (*flaco*) skinny
charcutería *f* **1.** (*productos*) cooked or cured pork products *pl* **2.** (*tienda*) ≈ delicatessen
charla *f* **1.** (*conversación*) chat; **estar de ~** to have a chat **2.** (*conferencia*) talk
charlar *vi* **1.** (*conversar*) to chat **2.** (*parlotear*) to chatter
charlatán, -ana **I.** *adj* talkative **II.** *m, f* **1.** (*hablador*) chatterbox **2.** (*chismoso*) gossip **3.** (*vendedor*) hawker **4.** (*curandero*) charlatan
charlatanería *f* **1.** (*locuacidad*) talkativeness **2.** (*palabrería*) sales talk **3.** (*curanderismo*) charlatanism
charnela *f* hinge
charol *m* **1.** (*barniz*) varnish **2.** (*cuero*) patent leather **3.** *AmL* (*bandeja*) tray
charqui *m AmS* (*charque*) beef jerky
charrán *m* rascal
charretera *f* **1.** (*insignia*) epaulette **2.** (*liga*) garter
charro, -a **I.** *adj* **1.** (*salmantino*) Salamancan **2.** *pey* (*rústico*) rustic; (*habla*) coarse **3.** (*de mal gusto*) in bad taste; (*chillón*) flashy **II.** *m, f* **1.** (*persona*) native/inhabitant of Salamanca **2.** *pey* (*tosco*) boor
chárter *adj inv* charter; **vuelo ~** charter flight
chasca *f* **1.** (*ramaje*) brushwood **2.** *CSur* (*pelo*) mop of hair
chascar <c→qu> **I.** *vi* **1.** (*con la lengua*) to click; (*con el látigo*) to crack; (*con los dedos*) to snap **2.** (*madera*) to creak; (*fuego*) to crackle **II.** *vt* (*comida*) to gulp down
chascarrillo *m* funny story
chasco *m* **1.** (*burla*) joke **2.** (*decepción*) disappointment; (*fracaso*) failure
chasco, -a *adj CSur* crinkly
chasis *m inv* **1.** AUTO chassis **2.** FOTO plateholder
chasque *m AmS* (*mensajero*) Indian messenger
chasquear **I.** *vt* **1.** (*burlar*) to play a trick on **2.** (*decepcionar*) to disappoint **3.** (*faltar*) to let down **II.** *vi* **1.** (*con la lengua*) to click; (*con el látigo*) to crack; (*con los dedos*) to snap **2.** (*madera*) to creak; (*fuego*) to crackle
chasqui *m AmS* (*chasque*) Indian courier
chasquido *m* **1.** (*de lengua*) click; (*de látigo*) crack **2.** (*de la madera*) creak
chatarra *f* **1.** (*metal viejo*) scrap (metal) **2.** (*trastos*) junk, lumber *Brit* **3.** *inf* (*dinero*) change
chatarrería *f* scrap yard
chatarrero, -a *m, f* scrap merchant
chato, -a **I.** *adj* **1.** (*nariz*) snub **2.** (*persona*) snub-nosed **3.** (*objeto*) blunt; (*aplastado*) flattened **II.** *m, f inf* (*tratamiento cariñoso*) kid
chatre *adj Chile, Ecua* (*elegante*) elegantly dressed
chaucha *f AmS* **1.** (*judía verde*) green bean **2.** (*patata*) new potato **3.** *pl* (*calderilla*) small change
chauchera *f Chile, Ecua* (*monedero*) purse
chauvinista **I.** *adj* chauvinist(ic) **II.** *mf* chauvinist
chaval(a) *m(f)* **1.** *inf* (*chico, chica*) kid; (*joven*) young man *m,* young woman *f* **2.** *inf* (*novio*) boyfriend *m,* girlfriend *f*
chaveta *f* **1.** (*remache*) rivet **2.** (*pasador*) pin; **estar mal de la ~** *inf* to have a screw loose
che **I.** *interj AmS* hey **II.** *f name of the former spanish letter 'ch'*
chécheres *mpl Col, CRi* things *pl*
checo, -a **I.** *adj* Czech; **República Checa** Czech Republic **II.** *m, f* Czech
checo(e)slovaco, -a **I.** *adj* Czechoslovak(ian) **II.** *m, f* Czechoslovakian
cheli *m Madrid slang*
chelín *m* (*moneda*) shilling
chelista *mf* cellist
chelo *m* cello
chepa *f inf* hump ►**subirse a la ~ de alguien** to be disrespectful to sb
cheposo, -a **I.** *adj* hunchbacked **II.** *m, f pey, inf* hunchback
cheque *m* cheque, check *Am* **~ bancario** bank cheque [*o* check *Am*]; **~ en blanco** blank cheque [*o* check *Am*]; **~ cruzado** crossed cheque [*o* check *Am*]; **~ sin fondo** bounced cheque [*o* check *Am*]; **~ de viaje** traveller's cheque [*o* check *Am*]; **cobrar un ~** to cash a cheque [*o* check *Am*]; **librar** [*o* **extender**] **un ~** to make out a cheque [*o* check *Am*]
chequear **I.** *vt AmL* (*comprobar*) to check **II.** *vr:* **~se** to have a checkup
chequeo *m* (*de la salud*) checkup; (*de un mecanismo*) service
chequera *f AmL* cheque book *Brit,* checkbook *Am*
Chequia *f* Czech Republic
chévere **I.** *adj Ven, inf* terrific, smashing *Brit* **II.** *mf Cuba, PRico, Ven* braggart
chic **I.** *adj inv* chic **II.** *m sin pl* elegance
chica **I.** *adj* **1.** (*pequeña*) small **2.** (*joven*) young **II.** *f* **1.** (*niña, tratamiento cariñoso*) girl **2.** (*joven*) young woman **3.** (*criada*) maid
chicano, -a *m, f* Chicano (*person of Mexican origin living in the USA*)
chicarrón, -ona **I.** *adj* sturdy **II.** *m, f* sturdy kid
chicha **I.** *f* **1.** *inf* (*carne*) meat; **tener pocas ~s** (*delgado*) to be slim **2.** *AmL* GASTR chicha (*alcoholic beverage made from corn, grape, pineapple, etc.*) ►**ni ~ ni limonada** neither chalk nor cheese *Brit,* neither fish nor fowl *Am* **II.** *adj* NÁUT **calma ~** dead calm
chicharra *f* **1.** ZOOL cicada **2.** (*juguete*) rattle **3.** ELEC buzzer
chicharrón *m* **1.** (*carne*) piece of burnt meat

2. *inf* (*persona*) sunburnt person 3. GASTR crackling (of pork)

chichi I. *adj AmC* (*fácil*) easy II. *m vulg* vagina, pussy *vulg*

chichón *m* bump

chicle *m* chewing gum

chico I. *adj* 1. (*pequeño*) small 2. (*joven*) young II. *m* 1. (*niño, tratamiento cariñoso*) boy 2. (*joven*) young man 3. (*para los recados*) errand boy

chicote *m AmL* (*látigo*) whip

chiflado, -a I. *adj inf* crazy; **estar ~ por alguien** to be crazy about sb II. *m, f inf* nutcase

chifladura *f* 1. (*locura*) craziness; (*empeño*) keenness 2. (*antojo*) whim

chiflar I. *vt inf* (*gustar*) to be crazy about; **me chiflan las aceitunas** I love olives II. *vr:* **~se** *inf* 1. (*pirrarse*) **~se por alguien** to be crazy [*o* mad] about sb *Brit* 2. (*volverse loco*) to go crazy

chiflón *m AmL* (*viento*) gale; (*corriente*) draught *Brit,* draft *Am;* **un ~ de aire** a blast of air

chigüín *m AmC* (*chavalín*) kid

chiíta *adj, mf* Shiite

chile *m* (*especia*) chilli, chili *Am*

Chile *m* Chile

> The capital of **Chile** (official title: **República de Chile**) is **Santiago (de Chile)**. Running from north to south, the country is over four thousand kilometres in length with an average width of just one hundred and eighty kilometres. The official language of the country is Spanish and the monetary unit is the **peso chileno**.

chileno, -a *adj, m, f* Chilean

chillar *vi* 1. (*persona*) to yell; **¡no me chilles!** don't shout at me! 2. (*animal salvaje*) to howl; (*ave, frenos*) to screech 3. (*puerta*) to creak 4. (*colores*) to clash 5. *AmL* (*sollozar*) to sob

chillido *m* 1. (*de persona*) yell 2. (*de animal salvaje*) howl; (*de ave, frenos*) screech 3. (*puerta*) creak 4. *AmL* (*sollozo*) sob

chillón, -ona I. *adj* 1. (*persona*) loud 2. (*voz*) shrill 3. (*color*) gaudy II. *m, f* loudmouth

chilote *m Méx: drink made of chilli and pulque*

chilpayate *m Méx, inf* (*muchacho*) kid; **los ~s** the kids

chimenea *f* 1. *t.* GEO (*de un edificio*) chimney 2. (*hogar*) fireplace

chimpancé *mf* chimpanzee

china *f* 1. (*piedra*) pebble 2. *AmL* (*india*) Indian woman; (*mestiza*) half-caste woman 3. *AmL* (*amante*) mistress

China *f* (**la**) ~ China

chinchar I. *vt* 1. *inf* to pester 2. *inf* (*matar*) to kill II. *vr:* **~se** *inf* to get upset; **¡chínchate!** so there!, tough luck!

chinche[1] *m o f* ZOOL bedbug

chinche[2] *mf inf* (*pelmazo*) pain

chincheta *f* drawing pin *Brit,* thumbtack *Am*

chinchilla *f* chinchilla

chinchudo, -a *adj Arg, inf* **estar ~** to be angry

chincol *f AmS* ZOOL crown sparrow

chinela *f* slipper

chingado, -a *adj inf* 1. (*frustrado*) annoyed 2. (*estropeado*) lousy

chingar <g→gu> I. *vt* 1. *vulg* (*joder*) to fuck 2. *inf* (*molestar*) to annoy 3. *inf* (*bebidas alcohólicas*) to drink II. *vr:* **~se** *inf* 1. (*emborracharse*) to get plastered 2. *AmL, inf* (*frustrarse*) to be a washout 3. *AmL* (*fallar*) to fail

chingo, -a *adj* 1. *AmC* (*animal sin rabo*) with a cropped tail 2. *AmC, Ven* (*chato*) flat-nosed 3. *AmC* (*corto*) short 4. *CRi* (*desnudo*) naked 5. *Ven* (*ansioso*) anxious 6. *Col, Cuba* (*pequeño*) tiny 7. *Nic* (*bajo*) short

chingue *m Chile* ZOOL skunk

chinita *f* 1. (*piedrecita*) small stone; **poner ~s a alguien** *fig* to make trouble for sb 2. *Chile* (*insecto*) ladybird *Brit,* ladybug *Am*

chino *m AmL* (*indio*) Indian; (*mestizo*) mestizo

chino, -a I. *adj* Chinese II. *m, f* Chinese man *m,* Chinese woman *f* ►**engañar a alguien como a un ~** *inf* to take sb for a ride

chip *m* INFOR chip

chipichipi *m Méx* (*llovizna*) drizzle

Chipre *f* Cyprus

chipriota *adj, mf* Cypriot

chiqueo *m* 1. *Cuba, Méx* (*mimo*) pampering 2. *AmC* (*contoneo*) swagger

chiquillada *f* 1. (*niñería*) childishness 2. (*travesura*) childish prank

chiquillería *f* kids *pl*

chiquillo, -a I. *adj* young II. *m, f* (*niño*) (small) child; (*chico*) (little) boy; (*chica*) (little) girl

chiquito, -a I. *adj inf* very small II. *m, f inf* kid; **no andarse con chiquitas** (*actuar sin miramiento*) not to beat about the bush

chirigota *f* joke

chirimbolo *m inf* 1. (*chisme*) thingummyjig 2. *pl* things *pl*

chirimoya *f* custard apple

chiringuito *m* kiosk (*selling snacks and drinks*)

chiripa *f* 1. *inf* (*suerte*) stroke of luck; (*casualidad favorable*) fluke 2. (*en el juego*) lucky break

chirle *adj* 1. (*soso*) tasteless 2. *inf* (*sin interés*) dull; (*sin substancia*) wishy-washy

chirlo *m* 1. (*herida*) gash 2. (*cicatriz*) scar

chirola *f* 1. *Arg* (*moneda*) *old coin made of nickel* 2. *Chile* (*moneda*) *silver 20 centavo coin* 3. *pl, Arg* (*calderilla*) small change

chirona *f inf* jail, clink *inf*

chirriar <*1. pres:* chirrío> *vi* 1. (*metal*) to squeak; (*madera*) to creak 2. (*pájaros*) to chirp

chirrido *m* 1. (*del metal*) squeaking; (*de la madera*) creaking 2. (*de los pájaros*) chirping

chis *interj* (*silencio*) sh; (*oye*) hey

chisme *m* **1.** (*habladuría*) piece of gossip; **andar** [*o* **ir**] **con ~s** to gossip **2.** (*objeto*) thingummyjig; **recoge esos ~s** put away those things

chismorrear *vi* to gossip

chismoso, **-a** **I.** *adj* gossiping **II.** *m, f* gossip

chispa *f* **1.** *t.* ELEC spark; **echar ~s** to give off sparks; *fig* to be hopping mad **2.** (*ingenio*) wit; **ser una ~** to be (very) lively **3.** (*gota*) drop (of rain) **4.** *inf* (*borrachera*) drunkenness **5.** (*una pizca*) **una ~ de...** a bit of ...

chispazo *m t.* ELEC spark; (*descarga*) spark discharge

chispear **I.** *vi* **1.** (*centellear*) to spark **2.** (*brillar*) to sparkle **II.** *vimpers* (*lloviznar*) to drizzle

chisporrotear *vi* (*despedir chispas*) to throw off sparks; (*el fuego*) to crackle

chistar *vi* to speak; **no ~** not to say a word

chiste *m* **1.** (*cuento*) funny story; (*broma*) joke; **~ verde** dirty joke; **no tiene ~ la cosa** that's not at all funny **2.** (*gracia*) point

chistera *f* **1.** (*sombrero*) top hat **2.** (*cesta*) (fish) basket

chistoso, **-a** **I.** *adj* funny **II.** *m, f* joker

chita *f* ANAT anklebone; **a la ~ callando** *fig* on the sly

chitón *interj* ssh

chiva *f Col, inf* (*noticia*) (piece of) news

chivar *vr:* **~se** *inf* **1.** (*hablar*) to grass **2.** *AmL* (*enojarse*) to get annoyed

chivatazo *m inf* tip-off; **dar el ~** to give a tip-off

chivatear *vi* **1.** *Arg, Chile* (*chillar*) to shout **2.** *AmS* (*alborotar los niños*) to make a ruckus **3.** *inf* (*delatar*) to squeal; **~ contra alguien** to squeal on sb

chivato, **-a** *m, f inf* (*informador*) grass *Brit,* stool pigeon *Am;* (*en la escuela*) tell-tale

chivo, **-a** *m, f* kid; **~ expiatorio** scapegoat

choapino *m Chile* potato-beetle larva

chocante *adj* **1.** (*raro*) strange; (*sorprendente*) startling **2.** (*escandaloso*) shocking **3.** *AmL* (*fastidioso*) annoying; (*repugnante*) disgusting

chocar <c→qu> **I.** *vi* **1.** (*vehículos*) **~ contra algo** to collide with sth; (*dar*) to crash into sth; (*coches*) to run into sth **2.** (*proyectil*) to smash **3.** (*encontrarse*) **~ con alguien** to come across sb; (*personas*) to run into sb; (*discutir*) to have words with sb; **chocó con su jefe** he/she clashed with his/her boss **II.** *vt* **1.** (*entrechocar*) **~ las copas** to clink glasses **2.** (*sorprender*) to surprise **3.** (*perturbar*) to startle; (*escandalizar*) to shock **4.** *AmL* (*repugnar*) to disgust; **me chocan sus opiniones** I can't stand his/her opinions

chocarrería *f* **1.** (*chiste*) coarse joke; (*dicho*) crude story **2.** (*acción*) crude act

chocarrero, **-a** *adj* coarse

chochear *vi* **1.** (*por vejez*) to dodder (around); *inf* (*atontar*) to become stupid **2.** (*sentir cariño*) to dote

chocho, **-a** **I.** *adj* **1.** (*senil*) doddering; *inf* (*lelo*) stupid **2.** (*chiflado*) doting **II.** *m, f* **1.** (*dulce*) sweet **2.** *inf* (*follón*) **montar un ~** to make a fuss **3.** *inf* (*montón*) load **4.** *vulg* (*coño*) cunt

choclo *m* **1.** (*zueco*) clog **2.** *AmS* (*maíz*) maize *Brit,* corn *Am;* (*mazorca tierna*) green ear of maize **3.** *AmS* GASTR sweet tamale

choclón *m Chile* POL rally

chocolate *m* **1.** (*para comer*) chocolate **2.** *inf* (*hachís*) dope, hash *inf*

chocolatera *f* **1.** (*vasija*) chocolate pot **2.** *inf* (*vehículo*) old crock

chocolatería *f* **1.** (*establecimiento*) *café specializing in hot chocolate drinks* **2.** (*fábrica*) chocolate factory

chocolatina *f* chocolate bar

chofer *m,* **chófer** *m* (*de un automóvil*) driver; (*personal*) chauffeur; (*de un camión*) lorry driver *Brit,* truck driver *Am*

chollo *m inf* **1.** (*suerte*) luck **2.** (*ganga*) bargain **3.** (*trabajo*) cushy job

cholo, **-a** *m, f AmL* **1.** (*indio*) *Indian integrated into Creole society* **2.** (*mestizo*) mestizo

chomba *f Arg* (*polo*) polo shirt

chongo *m* **1.** *Méx, inf* (*trenza*) braid; (*moño*) knot, bun **2.** *Chile* (*cuchillo*) blunt knife

chopera *f* poplar grove

chopo *m* black poplar

choque *m* **1.** (*impacto*) impact **2.** (*colisión*) crash; **~ de frente** head-on collision **3.** (*encuentro*) clash; (*disputa*) conflict **4.** *t.* MED (*susto*) shock

choricear *vt inf* to swipe

chorizo *m* chorizo (*hard pork sausage*)

chorizo, **-a** *m, f inf* petty thief; (*carterista*) pickpocket

chorlito *m* plover; **cabeza de ~** *fig* scatterbrain

choro *m* **1.** *Chile* (*mejillón*) large mussel **2.** *AmS, inf* (*ladrón*) thief

chorote *m Méx, Ven* (*chocolate*) chocolate drink

chorrada *f* **1.** *inf* (*tontería*) stupid remark **2.** *inf* (*cosa superflua*) trivial thing **3.** (*chorrillo*) extra drop

chorrear *vi* **1.** (*fluir*) to gush (out) **2.** (*gotear*) to drip **3.** (*concurrir lentamente*) to trickle in

chorrillo *m* (*de agua*) thin stream; (*de un ingrediente*) small drop

chorro *m* **1.** (*hilo*) trickle; (*porción*) squirt; (*de un ingrediente*) drop **2.** (*torrente*) stream; *t.* TÉC jet; **avión a ~** jet plane; **beber a ~s** *to drink without putting one's lips to the bottle;* **llover a ~s** to pour **3.** *Arg, inf* (*ladrón*) thief

chotear **I.** *vi* to romp **II.** *vr:* **~se** *inf* to make fun

choteo *m* **1.** (*burla*) joke **2.** (*diversión*) amusement

choto, **-a** *m, f* **1.** (*cría de la cabra*) kid **2.** (*de la vaca*) calf

choza *f,* **chozo** *m* **1.** (*cabaña*) hut **2.** (*vivienda*) hovel

chubasco *m* **1.**(*aguacero*) (heavy) shower **2.**(*contratiempo*) setback
chubasquero *m* raincoat, windbreaker *Am*
chúcaro, **-a** *adj Arg, inf* **1.**(*poco amable*) awkward **2.**(*huraño*) shy
chuchería *f* **1.**(*bocado*) titbit *Brit,* tidbit *Am;* (*dulce*) sweet **2.**(*menudencia*) trinket
chucho *m* **1.** *inf*(*perro*) mutt **2.** *AmL* (*escalofrío*) shivers *pl;* (*fiebre*) fever
chucrú *m,* **chucrut** *m,* **chucruta** *f sin pl* sauerkraut
chueco, **-a** *adj AmL* **1.**(*pies*) bow-legged **2.** *inf*(*torcido*) crooked
chufa *f* tiger nut
chufla *f* joke
chulada *f* **1.**(*insolencia*) impudence **2.** *inf* (*cosa estupenda*) marvellous thing
chulear **I.** *vi, vr:* **~se** (*jactarse*) to brag **II.** *vr:* **~se** to make fun
chulería *f* **1.**(*jactancia*) bragging **2.**(*frescura*) boldness
chuleta **I.** *f* **1.**(*costilla*) chop **2.** *inf* (*apunte*) crib (sheet) **3.** *inf* (*bofetada*) punch **II.** *adj inf* cheeky; **ponerse ~** to get fresh
chuletón *m* T-bone steak
chulo *m* **1.**(*gandul*) layabout; (*mal educado*) lout **2.** *inf* (*proxeneta*) pimp **3.**(*dandi*) dandy
chulo, **-a** **I.** *adj* **1.**(*jactancioso*) boastful; (*presumido*) conceited **2.**(*fresco*) cheeky; **ponerse ~** to get cocky **3.** *inf* (*elegante*) smart; (*lindo*) pretty **II.** *m, f* **1.**(*fanfarrón*) flashy type **2.**(*exagerador*) braggart
chumbera *f* prickly pear cactus
chumbo *m* (*fruto*) prickly pear
chunga *f inf* joke; **estar de ~** to be in high spirits
chungo, **-a** *adj inf* **1.**(*malo*) bad; (*comida*) spoiled, off *Brit* **2.**(*persona: rara*) odd; (*enfermiza*) poorly
chunguearse *vr* **1.** *inf* (*bromear*) to crack jokes **2.** *inf*(*embromar*) to make fun
chuño *m AmS* (*fécula de patata*) potato starch
chupa *f* **1.** HIST doublet; **poner a alguien como ~ de dómine** *inf* to wipe the floor with sb **2.**(*chaqueta*) leather jacket; (*chaleco*) waistcoat *Brit,* vest *Am* **3.** *AmC* (*borrachera*) drunkenness
chupa-chups® *m inv* lollipop
chupada *f* (*paja*) suck; (*cigarrillo*) puff
chupado, **-a** *adj* **1.**(*flaco*) skinny; (*consumido*) emaciated **2.**(*vestido*) tight **3.** *inf*(*fácil*) dead easy *Brit,* a cinch *Am* **4.** *AmL* (*borracho*) drunk
chupaflor *m AmC* ZOOL hummingbird
chupamirto *m Méx* ZOOL hummingbird
chupar **I.** *vt* **1.**(*extraer*) to suck out; (*aspirar*) to suck in; (*absorber*) to absorb **2.**(*caramelo*) to suck; (*helado*) to lick **3.**(*cigarrillo*) to smoke, to puff on **4.**(*salud*) to sap **II.** *vi* **1.** *inf* (*mamar*) to suckle **2.**(*aprovecharse*) to sponge; **~ del bote** to line one's pocket **3.** *AmL, inf*(*beber*) to booze; (*fumar*) to smoke **III.** *vr:* **~se** **1.**(*secarse*) to get very thin **2.** *inf* (*aguantar*) to sit out, to put up with
chupatintas *m inv, pey* **1.**(*oficinista*) clerk **2.**(*escritor*) penpusher
chupe *m* **1.** *inf*(*chupete*) dummy *Brit,* pacifier *Am;* (*chupador*) sucker **2.** *CSur, Ecua, Perú* GASTR spicy chowder
chupete *m* **1.**(*del bebé*) dummy, pacifier *Am;* (*del biberón*) teat **2.** *AmL* (*pirulí*) lollipop
chupetear *vi, vt* to lick
chupetón *m* **1.**(*chupada*) suck **2.** *inf*(*marca de un beso*) lovebite
chupo *m Col* (*del biberón*) teat
chupón, **-ona** **I.** *adj* **1.**(*chupador*) sucking **2.**(*parásito*) scrounging **II.** *m, f* scrounger
churrasco *m* **1.**(*carne*) steak **2.**(*barbacoa*) barbecue
churrete *m* spot
churro *m* **1.**(*fritura*) *slice of fried dough;* **¡vete a freír ~s!** get stuffed! **2.**(*chapuza*) (piece of) shoddy work **3.**(*suerte*) piece of luck **4.** *Col* (*persona atractiva*) good looker

> **Churro** is the term for fritters. The most typical of Spanish breakfasts comprises **chocolate** (hot chocolate) **con churros**. **Churros** can be obtained either in a **churrería**, in a **cafetería**, or they can be bought **en un puesto de churros** (at a kiosk in the street).

churro, **-a** *adj* **1.**(*lana*) coarse **2.**(*cordero*) one-year old
churumbel *m* (*voz gitana*) kid
chusco *m* crust (of bread)
chusco, **-a** **I.** *adj* droll **II.** *m, f* joker
chusma *f* rabble, riffraff
chutar **I.** *vt* to shoot; **esto va que chuta** *inf* it's going well **II.** *vr:* **~se** *inf* to shoot up
chute *m inf* shot; (*droga*) fix
chuza *f* **1.** *Arg, Urug* (*lanza*) pike **2.** *Arg* (*gallo*) cock's spur **3.** *Méx* (*juego: bolos*) strike **4.** *pl, Arg* (*pelo*) rats' tails
chuzar <z→c> *vt Col* (*punzar*) to prick
chuzo *m* HIST pike; **caen ~s** *fig* (*lluvia*) to pour; (*nieve*) to snow heavily
Cía *abr de* **compañía** Co.
cianuro *m* cyanide
ciática *f* sciatica
ciberbar *m,* **cibercafé** *m* cybercafé
ciberespacio *m* cyberspace
cibernauta *mf* cybernaut
cibernética *f* cybernetics *pl*
cibersexo *m* cybersex
cicatear *vi inf* to be stingy with
cicatería *f* stinginess
cicatero, **-a** **I.** *adj* stingy **II.** *m, f* skinflint
cicatriz *f* scar
cicatrizar <z→c> **I.** *vi, vr:* **~se** to heal (up) **II.** *vt* to heal
ciclamen *m* cyclamen
ciclismo *m* DEP cycling
ciclista **I.** *adj* cycle **II.** *mf t.* DEP cyclist
ciclo *m* (*en general*) cycle; **~ económico**

economic cycle; ~ **del rey Arturo** Arthurian cycle
ciclomotor *m* moped, motorbike
ciclón *m* cyclone
ciclope *m,* **cíclope** *m* Cyclops
ciclostil(o) *m* cyclostyle
cicloturismo *m* cycle touring
cicuta *f* hemlock
ciego, -a I. *adj* 1. (*privado de la vista*) blind; **quedarse** ~ to go blind 2. (*taponado*) blocked II. *m, f* blind man *m,* blind woman *f* III. *adv* **a ciegas** blindly; **obrar a ciegas** to act thoughtlessly
cielo I. *m* 1. (*atmósfera*) sky; **a** ~ **raso** in the open air; **el reino de los ~s** the Kingdom of Heaven; **como caído del** ~ out of the blue 2. (*apelativo cariñoso*) darling II. *interj* **¡~s!** good heavens!
ciempiés *m inv* centipede
cien *adj inv* a [*o* one] hundred; **al** ~ **por** ~ one hundred per cent; *v.t.* **ochocientos**
ciénaga *f* swamp
ciencia *f* 1. (*saber*) knowledge; **a** [*o* **de**] ~ **cierta** for sure 2. (*disciplina*) science; **~s físicas** physical science; **~s políticas** political science; **~s (naturales)** natural science(s)
ciencia-ficción *f sin pl* science fiction
cieno *m* mud
científico, -a I. *adj* scientific II. *m, f* scientist
ciento I. *adj* <cien> *inv* a [*o* one] hundred; *v.t.* **ochenta** II. *m* **~s de huevos** hundreds of eggs; **el cinco por** ~ five per cent
cierre *m* 1. *t.* ECON, FIN (*conclusión*) closing; (*clausura*) closure; PREN time of going to press; ~ **del ejercicio** close of the financial year; ~ **patronal** lockout; **hora de** ~ closing time 2. (*dispositivo*) closing device; ~ **centralizado** AUTO central locking 3. *Arg* (*cremallera*) zip fastener, zipper *Am*
cierro *m Chile* (*sobre*) envelope
ciertamente *adv* certainly
cierto *adv* certainly; **por** ~ by the way
cierto, -a *adj* <certísimo> 1. (*verdadero*) true; (*seguro*) sure; **una información cierta** a correct piece of information; **estar en lo** ~ to be right; **lo** ~ **es que...** the fact is that ... 2. (*alguno*) a certain; ~ **día** one day
ciervo, -a *m, f* deer
cierzo *m* north wind
cifra *f* 1. (*guarismo*) figure; ~ **de negocios** ECON turnover; ~ **de ventas** ECON sales figures 2. (*clave*) code; **en** ~ in code 3. (*monograma*) monogram 4. (*resumen*) summary
cifrar I. *vt* 1. (*codificar*) to code 2. (*calcular*) to reckon 3. (*esperanza*) to place II. *vr* **~se en algo** to amount to sth
cigala *f* crayfish
cigarra *f* cicada
cigarrera *f* 1. (*vendedora*) cigar seller 2. (*que elabora*) cigar maker 3. (*caja*) cigar box 4. (*petaca*) cigar case
cigarrillo *m* cigarette
cigarro *m* cigar
cigüeña *f* 1. (*ave*) stork 2. (*manivela*) crank
cigüeñal *m* AUTO crankshaft
cilindrada *f* AUTO cubic capacity
cilindro *m* cylinder; (*en un reloj*) drum
cima *f t. fig* summit; ~ **del árbol** tree top; ~ **del monte** mountain peak
cimarrón, -ona *adj AmL* wild
cimbo(r)rio *m* ARQUIT dome
cimbrar, cimbrear I. *vt* 1. (*agitar*) to shake 2. (*golpear*) to beat 3. (*doblar*) to bend II. *vr:* **~se** 1. (*agitarse*) to sway 2. (*doblarse*) to bend
cimbreo *m* 1. (*agitación*) swaying 2. (*golpe*) blow
cimbronazo *m* 1. (*golpe*) blow (with the flat of a sword) 2. *AmL* (*temblor nervioso*) jolt 3. *AmL* (*tirón del lazo*) yank 4. *AmL* (*temblor de tierra*) earthquake
cimentación *f* 1. (*fundamento*) foundations *pl* 2. (*edificación*) laying of foundations
cimentar <e→ie> *vt* 1. (*fundar*) to found 2. (*fundamentar*) to lay the foundations of 3. (*afinar oro*) to refine 4. (*consolidar*) to strengthen
cimiento *m* foundation
cimpa *f Perú* braid
cinc *m* zinc
cincel *m* chisel
cincelar *vt* to chisel
cincha *f* (*caballo*) girth, cinch
cinchar *vt* (*caballo*) to girth, to cinch
cinco I. *adj inv* five ►**estar sin** ~ to be broke II. *m* five; **¡choca esos ~!** give me five!; *v.t.* **ocho**
cincuenta *adj inv, m* fifty; *v.t.* **ochenta**
cincuentavo *m* fiftieth; *v.t.* **octavo**
cincuentavo, -a *adj* fiftieth; *v.t.* **octavo**
cincuentena *f unit consisting of fifty parts;* **una** ~ **de personas** about fifty people
cincuentenario *m* fiftieth anniversary
cine *m* 1. (*arte*) cinema, movies *pl Am;* ~ **mudo/sonoro** silent/talking films; ~ **negro** film noir; **me gusta el** ~ I like films 2. (*sala*) cinema, movie theater *Am;* ~ **de barrio** local cinema, local movie theater *Am;* **ir al** ~ to go to the cinema
cineasta *mf* film-maker; (*director*) director; (*aficionado*) film buff
cineclub *m* <cineclubs> film club
cinema *m* cinema, movies *pl Am*
cinemateca *f* film library
cinematografía *f* cinematography
cinematógrafo *m* 1. (*proyector*) projector 2. (*cine*) cinema
cingalés, -esa *adj, m, f* Singhalese
cíngaro, -a *adj, m, f* gipsy *Brit,* gypsy
cínico, -a I. *adj* (*descarado*) shameless; (*escéptico*) cynical II. *m, f t.* FILOS cynic
cinismo *m* (*descaro*) shamelessness; (*escepticismo*) cynicism
cinta *f* 1. (*tira*) band; ~ **adhesiva** adhesive tape; ~ **aislante** insulating tape; ~ **métrica** tape measure; ~ **del pelo** hair ribbon; ~ **de vídeo** videotape; ~ **virgen** blank tape; ~

transportadora conveyor belt **2.** (*hilera de baldosas*) tile skirting **3.** (*red de pesca*) tuna fish net
cinto *m* **1.** (*cinturón*) belt **2.** (*cintura*) waist
cintura *f* waist; ~ **de avispa** wasp waist
cinturón *m* **1.** (*ceñidor, correa*) belt; ~ **salvavidas** lifebelt; **ponerse el** ~ to fasten one's seatbelt; **apretarse el** ~ *fig* to tighten one' belt **2.** ASTR ring **3.** (*de una ciudad*) belt
cipe *adj AmC* (*enfermizo*) sickly, runty
ciprés *m* cypress
circense *adj* circus
circo *m* **1.** (*arena*) circus; ~ **ambulante** travelling [*o* traveling *Am*] circus **2.** GEO cirque
circuito *m* **1.** *t.* ELEC circuit; ~ **integrado** integrated circuit; **corto** ~ short circuit **2.** DEP circuit, track
circulación *f* **1.** *t.* ECON (*ciclo*) circulation; ~ **sanguínea** (blood) circulation; **retirar de la** ~ to withdraw from circulation **2.** (*tránsito*) traffic
circular **I.** *adj* circular **II.** *vi* **1.** (*recorrer*) to circulate **2.** (*personas*) to walk (around); **¡circulen!** move along! **3.** (*vehículos*) to drive (around) **III.** *f* circular
circulatorio, **-a** *adj* MED circulatory
círculo *m* circle; ~ **de amistades** circle of friends; ~ **vicioso** vicious circle
circuncidar *vt* to circumcise
circuncisión *f* circumcision
circundar *vt* to surround
circunferencia *f t.* MAT circumference
circunlocución *f* circumlocution
circunnavegar <g→gu> *vt* to circumnavigate
circunscribir *irr como escribir* **I.** *vt t.* MAT to circumscribe **II.** *vr:* ~**se** to limit oneself
circunscripción *f* **1.** (*distrito*) electoral district **2.** *t.* MAT (*concreción*) circumscription
circunscrito, **-a** *pp de* **circunscribir**
circunspecto, **-a** *adj* circumspect
circunstancia *f* circumstance; **en estas** ~**s** in these circumstances
circunstancial *adj* circumstantial
circunvalación *f* **carretera de** ~ bypass
cirílico, **-a** *adj* Cyrillic
cirineo, **-a** **I.** *adj* of Cyrene **II.** *m, f* helper
cirio *m* **1.** (*vela*) candle **2.** *inf* (*jaleo*) row
cirro *m* cirrus
cirrosis *f inv* MED cirrhosis
ciruela *f* plum; ~ **pasa** prune
ciruelo *m* **1.** (*pruno*) plum tree **2.** *inf* (*tonto*) idiot
cirugía *f* MED surgery; ~ **estética** cosmetic surgery
cirujano, **-a** *m, f* MED surgeon
ciscar <c→qu> **I.** *vt inf* to dirty, to soil **II.** *vr:* ~**se** *inf* to do one's business
cisco *m* **1.** (*carbón*) coaldust; **estar hecho un** ~ *inf* to be a wreck **2.** (*jaleo*) row
Cisjordania *f* (the) West Bank
cisma *m* **1.** REL schism **2.** (*desacuerdo*) disagreement
cisne *m* swan
cister *m*, **císter** *m* REL Cistercian Order
cisterna **I.** *adj* tank; **barco** ~ tanker **II.** *f* cistern, tank *Am*
cisura *f* **1.** (*fisura*) crack **2.** (*cicatriz*) scar **3.** (*incisión*) incision
cita *f* **1.** (*convocatoria*) appointment **2.** (*encuentro*) meeting; (*romántico*) date; ~ **anual** annual meeting; ~ **a ciegas** blind date; **tener una** ~ **con alguien** to be meeting sb; (*romántico*) to have a date with sb **3.** (*mención*) quotation
citación *f* **1.** JUR summons **2.** (*el mencionar*) quotation
citar **I.** *vt* **1.** (*convocar*) to arrange to meet **2.** (*mencionar*) to quote **3.** JUR to summon **II.** *vr:* ~**se** to arrange to meet
cítara *f* MÚS zither
citología *f* cytologie; **hacer una** ~ to have a smear test
cítrico, **-a** *adj* citric
cítricos *mpl* citrus fruits *pl*
ciudad *f* town; (*más grande*) city; ~ **hermanada** twin town; ~ **industrial** industrial town [*o* city]; ~ **de origen** home town; ~ **universitaria** university campus; ~ **dormitorio** dormitory town
ciudadanía *f* **1.** (*nacionalidad*) citizenship **2.** (*conjunto de ciudadanos*) citizenry, citizens *pl* **3.** (*civismo*) civic responsibility
ciudadano, **-a** **I.** *adj* **1.** (*de la ciudad*) city **2.** (*del ciudadano*) civic **II.** *m, f* **1.** (*residente*) resident **2.** (*súbdito*) citizen
ciudad-estado <ciudades-estado> *f* city-state
ciudadrealeño, **-a** **I.** *adj* of/from Ciudad Real **II.** *m, f* native/inhabitant of Ciudad Real
cívico, **-a** *adj* **1.** (*de la ciudad, del ciudadano*) civic **2.** (*del civismo*) public-spirited
civil **I.** *adj* civil; **derecho** ~ civil law; **guerra** ~ civil war **II.** *m* **1.** *inf* (*persona*) civil guard **2.** (*paisano*) civilian
civilización *f* civilization
civilizar <z→c> *vt* to civilize
civismo *m* community spirit, civic-mindedness
cizalla *f* **1.** (*recorte*) metal clippings **2.** *pl* (*tijeras*) wire-cutters *pl*
cizallar *vt* to cut with wire cutters
cizaña *f* **1.** BOT darnel **2.** (*enemistad*) discord **3.** (*adversidad*) trouble
cizañero, **-a** **I.** *adj* scheming **II.** *m, f* **1.** (*intrigante*) troublemaker **2.** (*pendenciero*) quarrelsome person
cl *abr de* **centilitro** centilitre *Brit,* centiliter *Am*
clamar **I.** *vi* to cry out **II.** *vt* to demand
clamor *m* **1.** (*lamento*) lament **2.** (*toque de campana*) tolling, knell
clamoroso, **-a** *adj* **1.** (*acompañado de clamor*) **acogida clamorosa** rousing reception **2.** (*éxito*) resounding
clan *m* clan
clandestinidad *f* **1.** (*secreto*) secrecy **2.** POL

underground

clandestino, **-a** *adj* **1.** (*secreto*) secret; **reunión clandestina** secret meeting **2.** (*ilegal*) **movimiento** ~ underground movement

claqué *f* tap dancing

claqueta *f* CINE clapperboard

clara *f* **1.** (*del huevo*) white **2.** (*bebida*) shandy *Brit, Aus*

claraboya *f* skylight

claramente *adv* clearly

clarear I. *vi* **1.** (*amanecer*) to grow light; **al ~ el día** at dawn **2.** (*despejarse*) to clear up **3.** (*concretarse*) to become clear II. *vt* to brighten III. *vr:* **~se** **1.** (*transparentarse*) to be transparent **2.** (*descubrirse*) to reveal oneself

clarete *m* rosé (wine)

claridad *f* **1.** (*luminosidad*) brightness **2.** (*lucidez*) clarity

clarificación *f* **1.** (*iluminación*) illumination **2.** (*aclaración*) clarification

clarificar <c→qu> *vt* **1.** (*iluminar*) to illuminate **2.** (*aclarar*) to clarify

clarín *m* **1.** (*instrumento*) bugle **2.** (*músico*) bugler

clarinete *m* **1.** (*instrumento*) clarinet **2.** (*músico*) clarinet(t)ist

clarividencia *f* **1.** (*perspicacia*) discernment **2.** (*instinto*) intuition **3.** (*percepción*) clairvoyance

clarividente I. *adj* **1.** (*perspicaz*) discerning **2.** (*que percibe*) clairvoyant II. *mf* clairvoyant

claro I. *interj* of course II. *m* **1.** (*hueco*) gap **2.** (*calvero*) clearing **3.** (*calva*) bald patch III. *adv* clearly

claro, **-a** *adj* **1.** (*iluminado*) bright; **azul ~** light blue **2.** (*ilustre*) famous **3.** (*evidente*) clear; **poner** [*o* **sacar**] **en ~** to clarify **4.** (*fino*) thin

claror *m* brightness

claroscuro *m* chiaroscuro

clase *f* **1.** (*tipo*) kind; **trabajos de toda ~** all kinds of jobs **2.** *t.* BIO (*categoría, grupo social*) class; ~ **turista** tourist class; ~ **media** middle class **3.** ENS class; (*aula*) classroom; **dar ~s** to teach

clasicismo *m* classicism

clásico, **-a** I. *adj* classical; *fig* classic II. *m, f* classic

clasificación *f* **1.** (*ordenación*) sorting; **~ en grupos** sorting into groups **2.** *t.* BIO classification

clasificador *m* **1.** (*archivador*) filing cabinet **2.** (*personal*) classifier **3.** (*carpeta*) ring binder

clasificar <c→qu> I. *vt* **1.** (*ordenar*) **~ por algo** to sort according to sth **2.** BIO **~ por algo** to classify under sth II. *vr:* **~se** to qualify

clasismo *m* class-consciousness

claudicación *f* **1.** (*de principios*) abandonment **2.** (*cesión*) giving way [*o* in]

claudicar <c→qu> *vi* **1.** (*principios*) **~ de algo** to abandon sth **2.** (*ceder*) to give way [*o* in]

claustro *m* **1.** (*galería, convento*) cloister **2.** (*conjunto de profesores*) senate **3.** (*reunión de profesores*) senate meeting

claustrofobia *f* PSICO claustrophobia

cláusula *f* JUR, LING clause; (*ley*) article

clausura *f* **1.** (*cierre*) closure; **sesión de ~** closing session **2.** (*en un convento*) cloister

clausurar *vt* to close

clavado, **-a** *adj* **1.** (*semejante*) very similar **2.** (*exacto*) **a las dos clavadas** (at) two sharp **3.** (*confuso*) astonished

clavar I. *vt* **1.** (*hincar*) to knock in **2.** (*enclavar*) to nail **3.** (*fijarse*) to fix; **tener la vista clavada en algo** to have one's eyes fixed on sth **4.** *inf* (*engañar*) to cheat **5.** (*engastar*) to set **6.** *inf* (*dar*) to give **7.** *inf* (*cobrar*) to rip off II. *vr* **~se una astilla en el dedo** to get a splinter in one's finger

clave I. *adj inv* key II. *f* **1.** (*secreto*) **~ de algo** key to sth **2.** (*código*) code; **~ de acceso** password; **en ~** coded **3.** ARQUIT keystone **4.** MÚS clef

clavel *m* carnation

clavetear *vt* **1.** (*clavar clavos*) to nail up **2.** (*terminar*) to conclude **3.** (*guarnecer*) to decorate with studs

clavicémbalo *m* harpsichord

clavicordio *m* clavichord

clavícula *f* collar bone

clavija *f* **1.** TÉC pin **2.** MÚS (*de guitarra*) peg **3.** (*enchufe*) plug ►<u>**apretar**</u> **las ~s a alguien** to put the screws on sb

clavo *m* **1.** (*punta*) nail; **dar en el ~** to hit the nail on the head **2.** (*especia*) clove **3.** (*callo*) corn

claxon *m* horn

clemencia *f* mercy

clemente *adj* merciful

clementina *f* tangerine

cleptómano, **-a** I. *adj* PSICO kleptomaniac II. *m, f* PSICO kleptomaniac

clerical *adj* clerical

clérigo *m* clergyman; (*sólo iglesia católica*) priest

clero *m* clergy

clic *m* click

cliché *m* **1.** (*tópico*) cliché **2.** FOTO negative

cliente, **-a** *m, f* customer; (*de un abogado*) client; ~ **fijo** regular customer

clientela *f* customers *pl;* (*de un abogado*) clients *pl*

clima *m* **1.** (*atmósfera*) atmosphere **2.** GEO climate

climatización *f* air conditioning

climatizador *m* air conditioner

climatizar <z→c> *vt* to air-condition

climatología *f* climatology

clímax *m inv* climax

clínica *f* clinic

clínico *m* clinical

clip *m* **1.** (*sujetapapeles*) paper clip **2.** (*pinza*) clip **3.** TV video (clip)

clítoris *m inv* clitoris

cloaca *f* sewer; ZOOL cloaca

clon *m* **1.** BIO clone **2.** (*payaso*) clown

clonar *vt* to clone
clónico, **-a** *adj* clonal
cloquear *vi* to cluck
clorato *m* chlorate
cloro *m* chlorine
clorofila *f* chlorophyl(l)
cloruro *m* chloride
club <clubs *o* clubes> *m* club; ~ **de alterne** hostess bar; ~ **deportivo** sports club
clueca *f* broody hen
cm *abr de* **centímetro** cm.
coacción *f* coercion
coaccionar *vt* to coerce
coagulación *f* coagulation, clotting
coagular I. *vt* to coagulate II. *vr:* ~**se** to coagulate, to clot
coágulo *m* clot
coalición *f* coalition
coaligarse <g→gu> *vr* to form an alliance
coartada *f* alibi
coartar *vt* **1.** (*libertad*) to restrict **2.** (*persona*) to inhibit
coautor(a) *m(f)* co-author
coba *f* lie; **dar ~ a alguien** to suck up to sb
cobalto *m* cobalt
cobarde I. *adj* cowardly II. *m* coward
cobardía *f* cowardice
cobaya *m o f* guinea pig
cobertizo *m* **1.** (*tejado*) canopy **2.** (*cabaña*) shed
cobertor *m* bedspread, counterpane *Brit*
cobertura *f* **1.** (*cobertor*) bedspread; (*que cubre*) cover **2.** COM (*acción*) coverage
cobija *f* **1.** (*cubierta*) cover **2.** ARQUIT (*teja*) ridge-tile **3.** *AmL* (*manta*) blanket **4.** *pl, AmL* (*ropa de cama*) bedclothes *pl;* **pegárse a alguien las ~s** to oversleep
cobijar I. *vt* **1.** (*cubrir*) to cover **2.** (*proteger*) to shelter **3.** (*acoger*) to give shelter to II. *vr:* ~**se** (*protegerse*) to take shelter
cobijo *m* shelter
cobo *m AmC, Ant* **1.** ZOOL giant sea snail **2.** (*persona*) unsociable person; **ser un ~** to be shy
cobra *f* cobra
cobrador(a) *m(f)* **1.** COM (*que cobra*) collector **2.** (*de tranvía*) conductor
cobrar I. *vt* **1.** (*recibir*) to receive; (*suma*) to collect; (*cheque*) to cash; (*sueldo*) to earn; **¿me cobra, por favor?** can I pay, please? **2.** (*exigir*) to levy; (*intereses*) to charge; (*deudas*) to recover **3.** (*conseguir*) ~ **ánimos** to pluck up courage; ~ **fama** to become famous **4.** (*cuerda*) to haul in II. *vi* **1.** (*sueldo*) to get one's wages **2.** *inf* **recibir una paliza** to get a beating; **¡que vas a ~!** you're going to get it! III. *vr:* ~**se** to cash up; *fig* to claim
cobre *m* **1.** QUÍM copper **2.** *pl* MÚS brass **3.** *AmL* (*moneda*) copper coin
cobrizo, **-a** *adj* coppery
cobro *m* **1.** (*como fuente financiera*) takings *pl* **2.** (*acto de cobrar*) recovery **3.** FIN (*impuestos*) collection; (*pago*) payment; ~ **por adelantado** advance payment; ~ **pendiente** outstanding payment; **llamar a ~ revertido** to reverse the charges **4.** *pl* COM arrears *pl*
coca *f* **1.** BOT coca **2.** (*droga*) cocaine **3.** (*de pelo*) coil, bun **4.** *inf* (*cabeza*) nut *Brit,* noodle *inf* **5.** *inf* (*refresco*) Coke®
cocaína *f* cocaine
cocainómano, **-a** *m, f* cocaine addict
cocción *f* **1.** (*acto*) cooking **2.** (*duración*) cooking time; (*en el horno*) baking time
cocear *vi* to kick
cocer *irr* I. *vt* **1.** (*cocinar*) to cook; (*hervir*) to boil; (*al horno*) to bake **2.** (*cerveza*) to brew; (*cerámica*) to fire II. *vi* **1.** (*cocinar*) to cook **2.** (*hervir*) to boil **3.** (*fermentar*) to ferment III. *vr:* ~**se** **1.** (*cocinarse*) to be cooked **2.** (*tramarse*) to be going on **3.** (*sufrir*) to suffer greatly **4.** *inf* (*pasar calor*) to be sweltering
cocha *f* **1.** MIN water tank **2.** *AmS* (*laguna*) lagoon; (*charco*) puddle
cochambroso, **-a** *adj inf* (*sucio*) filthy; (*asqueroso*) disgusting; (*maloliente*) stinking
cochayuyo *m AmS* BOT rockweed
coche *m* **1.** (*automóvil*) car; ~ **de bomberos** fire engine; ~ **de carreras** DEP racing car; ~ **de línea** coach *Brit,* bus *Am;* **ir en ~** to go by car **2.** (*de caballos*) coach, carriage; ~ **de equipajes** luggage van *Brit,* baggage car *Am*
coche-bomba <coches-bomba> *m* car bomb
coche-cama <coches-cama> *m* FERRO sleeping car
cochecito *m* pram *Brit,* baby carriage *Am*
coche-patrulla <coches-patrulla> *m* patrol car
cochera *f* garage; ~ **de tranvías** (*almacén*) tram depot
coche-restaurante <coches-restaurante> *m* FERRO dining car
coche-vivienda <coches-vivienda> *m* (large) caravan
cochinada *f,* **cochinería** *f inf* filthy thing
cochinilla *f* **1.** ZOOL (*insecto*) cochineal insect **2.** ZOOL (*crustáceo*) woodlouse
cochinillo *m* piglet; ~ **asado** roast suckling pig
cochino, **-a** I. *adj inf* filthy II. *m, f* **1.** ZOOL (*macho*) pig; (*hembra*) sow **2.** *inf* (*guarro*) swine
cocho *m Chile* **1.** (*bebida*) hot maize drink **2.** GASTR pudding made with toasted flour
cocido *m* stew (*made with chickpeas and meat*)
cociente *m* MAT quotient; ~ **intelectual** IQ
cocina *f* **1.** (*habitación*) kitchen **2.** (*aparato*) cooker, stove *Am* **3.** (*arte*) cookery, cooking; **la ~ francesa** French cooking [*o* cuisine]; **libro de ~** cookery book, cookbook *Am*
cocinar I. *vt* to cook II. *vi* **1.** (*guisar*) to cook **2.** *inf* (*inmiscuirse*) to meddle
cocinero, **-a** *m, f* cook
cocinilla *f* (*portátil*) camping stove; (*de gas*) gas stove

coco *m* 1. BOT (*fruto*) coconut 2. BOT (*árbol*) coconut palm 3. *inf* (*cabeza*) head; (*cerebro*) brain; **comerse el** ~ to worry 4. *inf* (*ogro*) bogeyman 5. ZOOL (*larva*) grub 6. BIO (*bacteria*) coccus

cocodrilo *m* crocodile

cocoliche *m Arg, Urug* LING *pidgin Spanish of Italian immigrants*

cocotero *m* coconut palm

coctel <coctels> *m,* **cóctel** <cócteles> *m* cocktail

coctelera *f* cocktail shaker

cocuy *m AmL* 1. BOT agave 2. (*bebida alcohólica*) maize [*o* corn *Am*] liquor 3. ZOOL firefly

cocuyo *m AmL* 1. ZOOL firefly 2. AUTO rear light

codazo *m* nudge (with one's elbow)

codear I. *vi* to nudge; (*más fuerte*) to elbow II. *vr:* ~**se** to rub shoulders [*o* elbows]

codera *f* elbow patch

códice *m* codex

codicia *f* 1. (*en general*) greed; ~ **de algo** greed for sth 2. (*de posesiones ajenas*) covetousness

codiciar *vt* to covet

codicioso, -a *adj* covetous

codificación *f* 1. (*con señales*) coding; *t.* INFOR encoding 2. JUR codification

codificar <c→qu> *vt* 1. JUR to codify 2. (*con señales*) to code; *t.* INFOR to encode

código *m* code; ~ **de circulación** highway code; **Código Civil** civil code; ~ **de barras** bar code; **mensaje en** ~ coded message; ~ **bancario** bank sorting code; ~ **postal** postcode *Brit,* zip code *Am*

codillo *m* 1. ZOOL elbow 2. GASTR knuckle of pork 3. (*de un árbol*) stump (of a branch) 4. TÉC (*doblez*) elbow joint

codo *m* 1. ANAT elbow; ~ **de tenis** tennis elbow; **empinar el** ~ *inf* to go on the booze; **trabajar** ~ **a** ~ to work side by side; **hablar por los** ~**s** *inf* to talk nonstop 2. TÉC (*doblez*) elbow joint 3. (*de camino*) bend (in the road)

codorniz *f* quail

coeficiente *m* MAT coefficient

coercer <c→z> *vt* 1. (*obligar*) ~ **a algo** to constrain to sth; *t.* JUR to coerce into sth 2. (*cohibir*) to restrain 3. (*coartar*) to restrict

coerción *f* constraint; *t.* JUR coercion

coetáneo, -a *adj, m, f* contemporary

coexistencia *f* coexistence

coexistir *vi* to coexist

cofia *f* cap

cofradía *f* 1. (*hermandad*) brotherhood 2. (*gremio*) guild 3. (*asociación*) association

cofre *m* 1. (*caja*) chest; (*baúl*) trunk 2. (*de joyas*) jewel case

cofundador(a) *m(f)* co-founder

cogedero *m* (*mango*) handle

cogedor *m* dustpan

coger <g→j> I. *vt* 1. (*agarrar*) to take hold, to seize; (*objeto caído*) to pick up; **le cogió del brazo** he/she took him by the arm; **le cogió en brazos** he/she picked him up in his arms 2. (*tocar*) to touch 3. (*quitar*) to take away; (*en la aduana*) to confiscate 4. (*atrapar*) to catch; (*apresar*) to capture 5. (*flores*) to pick; ~ **la cosecha** to harvest 6. AUTO (*atropellar*) to knock down 7. (*trabajo*) to take (up) 8. (*hábito*) to acquire; ~ **cariño a alguien** to get fond of sb; ~ **el hábito de fumar** to start smoking 9. (*enfermedad*) to catch; ~ **frío** to catch a cold; **ha cogido una gripe** he's/she's caught the flu 10. (*una noticia*) to receive 11. (*sorprender*) to find 12. (*obtener*) to get; **¿vas a** ~ **el piso?** are you going to take the flat? 13. RADIO to pick up 14. (*tomar*) to take; ~ **el tren/autobús** to take the train/bus 15. *AmL, vulg* (*copular*) to screw II. *vi* 1. (*planta*) to take 2. (*tener sitio*) to fit 3. *AmL, vulg* (*copular*) to screw III. *vr* 1. (*pillarse*) catch; ~**se los dedos en la puerta** to catch one's fingers in the door 2. *inf* (*robar*) to steal

cogestión *f* joint management

cogida *f* 1. TAUR goring 2. (*de frutas*) picking 3. *AmL, vulg* (*cópula*) screw

cognición *f* cognition

cognitivo, -a *adj* PSICO cognitive

cogollo *m* 1. (*de col, lechuga*) heart; (*de árbol*) top 2. (*brote*) bud 3. (*algo selecto*) best part 4. (*núcleo*) core

cogorza *f* pillar **una buena** ~ *inf* to get plastered

cogote *m* 1. (*de la cabeza*) back of the head 2. (*nuca*) scruff of the neck; **estar hasta el** ~ *inf* to have had enough

cogotudo *m AmL* self-made man

cohabitación *f t.* POL cohabitation

cohabitar *vi* 1. (*convivir*) to live together 2. *pey* (*amancebarse*) to cohabit

cohecho *m* bribery

coherencia *f* coherence

coherente *adj* coherent

cohesión *f* cohesion

cohesionar *vt* to unite

cohete *m* rocket

cohibición *f* 1. (*intimidación*) intimidation 2. (*inhibición*) inhibition 3. (*restricción*) restraint

cohibido, -a *adj* 1. (*intimidado*) intimidated 2. (*tímido*) shy 3. (*inhibido*) inhibited 4. (*refrenado*) restrained

cohibir *irr como prohibir* I. *vt* 1. (*intimidar*) to intimidate 2. (*incomodar*) to inhibit 3. (*refrenar*) to restrain II. *vr:* ~**se** to feel inhibited

coima *f* 1. HIST concubine 2. *pey* (*amante*) mistress 3. (*puta*) whore 4. *And, CSur* (*soborno*) bribe; (*dinero*) rake-off

coimear *vt AmS* (*sobornar*) to bribe

coincidencia *f* 1. (*simultaneidad*) coincidence; **¡qué** ~**!** what a coincidence! 2. (*acuerdo*) agreement 3. (*concordancia*) concordance 4. (*encuentro*) meeting

coincidente *adj* 1. (*simultáneo*) coincidental 2. (*concordante*) concordant 3. (*en el mismo lugar*) meeting

coincidir *vi* 1. (*sucesos*) to coincide 2. (*to-

parse) to meet; ~ **con alguien** to meet sb **3.** (*concordar*) to agree; ~ **con alguien** to agree with sb
coipo *m Arg, Chile* ZOOL coypu
coito *m* coitus, (sexual) intercourse
cojear *vi* (*persona, animal*) to limp; (*mueble*) to wobble; *fig* (*tener defecto*) to have a weak point; **saber de qué pie cojea alguien** to know sb's weaknesses
cojera *f* limp
cojín *m* cushion
cojinete *m* TÉC bearing
cojo, -a I. *adj* **1.** (*persona, animal*) lame; **a la pata coja** on one leg **2.** (*mueble*) wobbly II. *m, f* lame person
cojón *m vulg* **1.** *pl* (*testículos*) balls *pl* **2.** *pl* (*interjecciones*) **¡cojones!** God damn it!, bloody hell! *Brit;* **es una música de cojones** it's really cool music
cojonudo, -a *adj vulg* fantastic, fucking great *vulg*
cojudo, -a *adj AmL* (*tonto*) stupid
col *f* cabbage; ~**es de Bruselas** Brussels sprouts
cola *f* **1.** ANAT (*rabo*) tail; (*de conejo*) scut **2.** (*de vestido*) train; **llevar la** ~ to wear a train **3.** (*al esperar*) queue, line; **hacer** ~ to queue (up), to line up; **ponerse a la** ~ to join the queue [*o* line] **4.** (*de un cometa*) tail **5.** (*pegamento*) glue **6.** *vulg* (*pene*) prick **7.** *AmL, inf* **pedir** ~ to ask for a lift
colaboración *f* collaboration; (*periódico*) contribution
colaboracionismo *m* POL collaboration
colaborador(a) I. *adj* collaborating II. *m(f)* collaborator; LIT contributor
colaborar *vi* **1.** (*cooperar*) to collaborate **2.** LIT to contribute
colación *f* **1.** JUR (*mención*) official mention **2.** *inf* (*mencionar*) **sacar algo a** ~ to bring sth up **3.** (*comida*) light meal
colada *f* **1.** (*de ropa*) washing **2.** (*blanquear con lejía*) bleaching **3.** QUÍM lye **4.** (*montaña*) defile *liter*
coladera *f* **1.** (*pasador*) strainer **2.** *Méx* (*alcantarilla*) sewer
coladero *m* strainer, colander
colado, -a *adj inf* (*enamorado*) ~ **por alguien** crazy about sb
colador *m* sieve, strainer
colapsar I. *vt* (*tráfico*) to bring to a standstill II. *vi, vr:* ~**se 1.** (*tráfico*) to come to a standstill **2.** MED to collapse
colapso *m* **1.** MED collapse **2.** (*destrucción*) destruction; (*paralización*) standstill
colar <o→ue> I. *vt* **1.** (*filtrar*) to filter **2.** (*metal*) to cast **3.** (*ropa: blanquear*) to bleach; (*en remojo*) to soak **4.** *inf* (*en la aduana*) to slip through II. *vi* **1.** (*penetrar: líquido*) to seep (through); (*aire*) to get in **2.** *inf* (*información*) to be credible; **a ver si cuela** let|s see if it comes off III. *vr:* ~**se 1.** *inf* (*entrar*) to slip in **2.** (*en una cola*) to jump the queue [*o* line] **3.** *inf* (*equivocarse*) to be wrong; **¡te colaste!** you're way out!
colcha *f* bedspread, counterpane *Brit*
colchón *m* mattress; ~ **de agua** water bed
colchonería *f store which sells mattresses*
colchoneta *f* **1.** (*colchón neumático*) airbed; (*colchón isotermo*) foam mattress **2.** DEP (*gimnasia*) mat
colear *vi* **1.** (*la cola*) to wag **2.** (*durar*) to last
colección *f* collection
coleccionar *vt* to collect
coleccionista *mf* collector
colecta *f* **1.** REL (*en misa*) collect **2.** (*recaudación*) collection (for charity)
colectividad *f* group
colectivizar <z→c> *vt* to collectivize
colectivo *m* **1.** POL collective, group **2.** *Méx* (*microbús*) minibus
colectivo, -a *adj* **1.** (*todos juntos*) collective; **acción colectiva** joint action **2.** (*global*) comprehensive
colector *m* **1.** ELEC collector **2.** (*canalización*) (main) sewer
colega *mf* **1.** (*compañero*) colleague **2.** (*homólogo*) counterpart **3.** *inf* (*amigo*) pal, mate *Brit,* buddy
colegiado, -a I. *adj* collegiate II. *m, f* **1.** (*miembro*) member **2.** DEP (*árbitro*) referee
colegial(a) I. *adj* **1.** (*de un colegio*) school **2.** (*inexperto*) inexperienced II. *m(f)* **1.** (*alumno*) schoolboy *m,* schoolgirl *f* **2.** (*inexperto*) inexperienced person
colegiarse *vr* **1.** (*afiliarse*) to become a member of a professional association **2.** (*organizarse*) to form a professional association
colegio *m* **1.** ENS school; **ir al** ~ to go to school **2.** *AmL* (*universidad*) college; ~ **mayor** hall of residence **3.** (*corporación*) professional association; ~ **de abogados** bar association
colegir *irr como elegir vt* **1.** (*juntar*) to collect **2.** (*deducir*) to gather
cólera¹ *m* MED cholera
cólera² *f* (*ira*) anger; **acceso de** ~ fit of anger
colérico, -a I. *adj* **1.** (*de temperamento*) bad-tempered **2.** (*furioso*) furious II. *m, f* irascible person
colesterol *m* cholesterol
coletilla *f* **1.** (*peinado*) ponytail; TAUR bullfighter's pigtail **2.** (*de un escrito*) postscript **3.** (*palabra*) tag question
colgado, -a *adj* **1.** (*cuadro*) hung up; (*bandera*) hung out **2.** (*suspendido*) failed
colgador *m* (*en general*) hanger; (*gancho*) (coat)hook; (*percha*) coat-hanger
colgante I. *adj* hanging; **puente** ~ (*entre dos lados*) suspension bridge; (*de castillo*) drawbridge II. *m* **1.** ARQUIT festoon **2.** (*joya*) pendant
colgar *irr* I. *vt* **1.** (*pender, ahorcar*) ~ **algo** to hang sth; (*decorar*) to decorate with sth; ~ **el teléfono** to put down the phone **2.** (*dejar*) ~ **los libros** to abandon one's studies **3.** *inf* (*suspender*) to fail **4.** (*atribuir*) to attribute II. *vi* **1.** (*pender*) to hang; (*de arriba para abajo*) to

C

hang down; (*lengua del perro*) to droop **2.** TEL (*auricular*) to hang up **III.** *vr:* **~se** to hang oneself

colibrí *m* hummingbird

cólico *m* MED colic

coliflor *f* cauliflower

coligado, **-a** **I.** *adj* (*unido*) united; (*aliado*) allied **II.** *m, f* ally

coligarse <g→gu> *vr* to form an alliance

colilla *f* cigarette end, fag end, butt

colín *m* **1.** *AmC, Ant* ZOOL American bobwhite **2.** (*pan*) breadstick

colina *f* hill

colindar *vi* ~ **con algo** to adjoin sth

colirio *m* eye drops *pl*

colisión *f* collision

colisionar *vi* ~ **con** [*o* **contra**] **algo** to collide with sth; *fig* to conflict with sth

collado *m* **1.** (*colina*) hill **2.** (*puerto*) pass

collage *m* ARTE collage

collar *m* **1.** (*adorno*) necklace; ~ **de perlas** string of pearls; ~ **de perro** dog collar **2.** (*insignia*) chain (of office) **3.** TÉC (*aro*) collar

colmado *m* **1.** (*tienda*) grocer's shop, grocery **2.** (*restaurante*) snack bar

colmado, **-a** *adj* (*lleno*) full; (*repleto*) heaped; **un año** ~ **de felicidad** a very happy year

colmar **I.** *vt* **1.** (*vaso*) ~ **de algo** to fill to the brim with sth **2.** (*alabanzas*) ~ **de algo** to heap on sth **3.** (*esperanzas*) to fulfil *Brit,* to fulfill *Am* **II.** *vr:* **~se** to be fulfilled

colmena *f* beehive

colmenar *m* apiary

colmenero, **-a** *m, f* beekeeper

colmillo *m* eyetooth; (*de elefante*) tusk; (*de perro*) fang; **enseñar los ~s** *fig* to show one's teeth

colmo *m* (*lo máximo*) height; **el** ~ **de la elegancia** the height of elegance ►**¡esto es el ~!** this is the last straw!; **para** ~ on top of everything

colocación *f* **1.** (*empleo*) job **2.** (*disposición*) placing **3.** COM (*inversión*) investment **4.** DEP (*posición*) position

colocado, **-a** *adj inf* (*bebido*) plastered, pissed *Brit;* (*drogado*) high, stoned

colocar <c→qu> **I.** *vt* **1.** (*emplazar*) to place; (*según un orden*) to arrange; (*poner*) to put; (*cuadro*) to hang; (*cartel*) to put up **2.** DEP (*balón*) to kick; (*flecha*) to shoot **3.** COM (*invertir*) to invest; (*mercancías*) to sell **4.** (*empleo*) to find a job for **5.** (*casar*) to marry off **6.** *inf* (*encarcelar*) to lock up **II.** *vr:* **~se** **1.** (*empleo*) to get a job **2.** (*sombrero, gafas*) to put on **3.** (*posicionarse*) to place oneself; (*sentarse*) to sit (down) **4.** *inf* (*alcohol*) to get plastered; (*drogas*) to get high; (*heroína*) to shoot up

Colombia *f* Colombia

> **Colombia** (official title: **República de Colombia**) lies in the northwestern part of South America, between the Caribbean and the Pacific Ocean. The capital (**Santa Fe de**) **Bogotá** is also the largest city in the country. The official language of **Colombia** is Spanish and the monetary unit is the **peso**.

colombiano, **-a** *adj, m, f* Colombian

colombicultura *f* pigeon breeding

colombino, **-a** *adj* of Columbus

colon *m* ANAT colon

Colón *m* **1.** (*Cristóbal*) Columbus **2.** (*moneda*) colon

colonia *f* **1.** BIO, POL (*aglomeración*) colony **2.** *pl* (*para niños*) holiday camp **3.** (*barrio*) suburb **4.** (*perfume*) cologne

Colonia *f* Cologne; **agua de** ~ eau de cologne

coloniaje *m AmL* **1.** (*período*) colonial period **2.** (*sistema*) system of colonial government **3.** *pey* (*esclavitud*) slavery

colonialismo *m* colonialism

colonialista *adj, mf* colonialist

colonización *f* **1.** POL (*conquista*) colonization **2.** (*población*) settling

colonizador(a) **I.** *adj* colonizing **II.** *m(f)* **1.** (*conquistador*) colonizer **2.** (*poblador*) settler

colonizar <z→c> *vt* **1.** (*conquistar*) to colonize **2.** (*poblar*) to settle

colono *m* **1.** (*de una colonia*) settler **2.** (*labrador*) tenant farmer

coloquial *adj* LING colloquial

coloquio *m* **1.** (*conversación*) conversation; (*científico*) colloquium **2.** (*congreso*) conference

color *m* **1.** (*en general*) colour *Brit,* color *Am;* **película en** ~ colour [*o* color *Am*] film; **un hombre de** ~ a coloured [*o* colored *Am*] man; **huevos de** ~ *AmL* brown eggs; **nuestros ~es** DEP our team; **mudar de** ~ (*palidecer*) to turn pale; (*ruborizarse*) to blush; **subido de** ~ risqué; **sacar los ~es a alguien** to embarrass sb **2.** (*sustancia*) dye **3.** POL (*ideología*) hue ►**verlo todo de** ~ **de rosa** to see everything through rose-tinted spectacles

coloración *f* **1.** (*acto*) colouring *Brit,* coloring *Am* **2.** (*resultado, carácter*) coloration

colorado, **-a** *adj* **1.** (*rojo*) red; **ponerse** ~ to blush **2.** (*coloreado*) coloured *Brit,* colored *Am*

colorante **I.** *adj* colouring *Brit,* coloring *Am* **II.** *m* colouring *Brit,* coloring *Am*

colorar *vt* to colour *Brit,* to color *Am*

colorear **I.** *vt* **1.** (*dar color*) to colour *Brit,* to color *Am;* (*pintar*) to paint; (*teñir*) to dye, to tint **2.** (*al relatar*) to portray in a favourable [*o* favorable *Am*] light **II.** *vi* **1.** (*frutos*) to redden **2.** (*tirar a rojo*) to be reddish

colorido *m* colour(ing) *Brit,* color(ing) *Am*

colosal *adj* colossal

coloso *m* **1.** (*estatua*) colossus **2.** (*persona*) giant; (*en un campo*) colossus

columbrar *vt* **1.** (*divisar*) to make out **2.** (*solución*) to begin to see

columna *f* **1.** *t.* MIL (*pilar, periódico*) column

2. ANAT ~ **vertebral** spinal column 3. *fig* (*apoyo*) pillar
columnista *mf* columnist
columpiar I. *vt* 1. (*balancear*) to swing (to and fro) 2. (*mecer*) to push on a swing II. *vr:* **~se** to swing
columpio *m* 1. (*para niños*) swing 2. *AmL* (*mecedora*) rocking chair
colza *f* rape
coma[1] *m* MED coma
coma[2] *f* LING comma
comadre *f* 1. *inf* (*comadrona*) midwife 2. (*madrina*) godmother 3. *inf* (*vecina*) neighbour *Brit,* neighbor *Am* 4. *inf* (*amiga íntima*) bosom friend 5. *inf* (*chismosa*) gossip 6. *inf* (*celestina*) go-between
comadrear *vi inf* to gossip
comadreja *f* weasel
comadrona *f* midwife
comandancia *f* 1. (*mando*) command 2. (*cuartel*) command headquarters 3. MIL, NÁUT (*zona*) command
comandante *m* 1. MIL commander; (*grado*) commanding officer 2. NÁUT captain 3. AVIAT squadron leader
comandar *vi, vt* to command
comando *m* 1. MIL command 2. INFOR ~ **de arranque** start command
comarca *f* (*zona*) area; (*región*) region
comba *f* 1. (*curvatura*) bend; (*de madera*) warp; (*de una cuerda*) sag 2. (*cuerda*) skipping rope; (*juego*) skipping; **saltar a la** ~ to skip
combar I. *vt* to bend; (*madera*) to warp II. *vr:* **~se** to bend; (*madera*) to warp; (*cuerda*) to sag
combate *m* 1. (*lucha*) combat; (*batalla*) battle 2. DEP (*competición*) competition; (*partido*) match; ~ **de boxeo** boxing match; **fuera de** ~ out of action
combatiente *adj, mf* combatant
combatir I. *vi* to fight II. *vt* 1. (*luchar*) to fight 2. (*rebatir*) to combat
combativo, **-a** *adj* combative
combi *m* fridge-freezer, refrigerator-freezer *Am*
combinación *f* 1. (*composición*) combination; *t.* MAT permutation; ~ **ganadora** winning combination 2. QUÍM compound 3. (*de transportes*) connection 4. (*lencería*) slip
combinado *m* cocktail
combinar I. *vi* to go II. *vt* 1. (*componer*) to combine 2. (*unir*) to unite; ~ **ideas** to link ideas 3. (*coordinar*) to coordinate 4. MAT to permutate III. *vr:* **~se** to combine; *pey* (*compincharse*) to band together
combustible I. *adj* combustible II. *m* fuel
combustión *f* combustion
comecocos *m inv* 1. *inf* (*obsesión*) obsession 2. (*juego*) Pacman
comedia *f* 1. TEAT (*obra*) play; (*divertida*) comedy 2. CINE comedy 3. *inf* (*farsa*) farce; **hacer** ~ to pretend
comediante, **-a** *m, f* 1. CINE, TEAT actor 2. (*farsante*) fraud
comedido, **-a** *adj* 1. (*moderado*) moderate; (*contenido*) restrained 2. *AmL* (*servicial*) obliging
comedimiento *m* 1. (*moderación*) moderation; (*contenimiento*) restraint 2. (*modestia*) modesty 3. (*cortesía*) courtesy 4. *AmL* (*disposición*) willingness
comediógrafo, **-a** *m, f* playwright
comedirse *irr como pedir vr* 1. (*moderarse*) to behave moderately; (*contenerse*) to show restraint 2. *AmL* (*ofrecerse*) to offer
comedor *m* 1. (*sala*) dining room; (*en una empresa*) canteen; ~ **universitario** refectory 2. (*mobiliario*) dining-room furniture
comején *m AmL* 1. (*termita*) termite 2. (*zozobra*) nagging uneasiness
comensal *mf* fellow diner
comentador(a) *m(f)* commmentator
comentar *vt* 1. (*hablar sobre algo*) to talk about; (*hacer comentarios*) to comment on; (*explicar*) to explain 2. (*una obra: criticar*) to discuss, to review; (*interpretar*) to interpret 3. *pey* (*cotillear*) ~ **algo** to gossip about sth 4. *inf* (*contar*) to mention
comentario *m* 1. (*general*) comment; (*análisis*) commentary 2. *pl* (*murmuraciones*) gossip
comentarista *mf* commentator
comenzar *irr como empezar* I. *vi* to begin, to commence; ~ **por hacer algo** to begin by doing sth; ~ **a trabajar** to begin to work; **para** ~ to begin with II. *vt* to begin, to commence *form*
comer I. *vi* 1. (*alimentarse*) to eat; **dar de** ~ **a un animal** to feed an animal; ~ **caliente** to have a warm meal 2. (*almorzar*) to have lunch; **antes/después de** ~ before/after lunch ►~ **por siete** to eat like a horse II. *vt* 1. (*ingerir*) to eat 2. *fig* (*consumir*) to consume 3. (*corroer*) to eat away 4. (*colores*) to fade 5. (*dilapidar*) to squander 6. (*en juegos*) to take ►**sin ~lo ni beberlo** without asking for it; **me echaron la culpa a mí sin ~lo ni beberlo** I got blamed although I had nothing to do with it III. *vr:* **~se** 1. (*ingerir*) to eat up; **~se a alguien a besos** to smother sb with kisses; **está para comérsela** she looks a treat 2. (*corroer*) to eat away 3. (*colores*) to fade 4. (*palabras*) to skip; (*al pronunciar*) to slur
comercial[1] I. *adj* commercial II. *mf* (*profesión*) sales representative
comercial[2] *m AmL* (*anuncio*) commercial
comercialización *f* 1. (*de un producto*) marketing 2. (*de un acontecimiento*) commercialization
comercializar <z→c> *vt* 1. (*producto*) to market 2. (*acontecimiento*) to commercialize
comerciante, **-a** *m, f* shopkeeper; (*negociante*) dealer
comerciar *vi* 1. (*tener trato con*) ~ **con un país** to trade with a country 2. (*traficar en*) ~ **en algo** to deal in sth
comercio *m* 1. (*actividad*) trade; ~ **exterior**

foreign trade; ~ **al por mayor** wholesale trade **2.** (*tienda*) shop **3.** (*relaciones*) dealings *pl*
comestibles *mpl* foods; **tienda de** ~ grocer's (shop), grocery
cometa¹ *m* ASTR comet
cometa² *f* (*de papel*) kite
cometer *vt* **1.** *t.* JUR to commit; (*error*) to make **2.** COM to give commission
cometido *m* (*encargo*) assignment; (*tarea*) task; (*obligación*) commitment
comezón *f* **1.** (*picor*) itch **2.** (*malestar*) uneasiness
cómic *m* <cómics> comic
comicios *mpl* **1.** (*elecciones*) elections *pl* **2.** HIST comitia
cómico, -a **I.** *adj* (*relativo a la comedia*) comedy; (*divertido*) comical **II.** *m, f* comedian
comida *f* **1.** (*alimento*) food; (*plato*) meal; (*cocina*) cooking; ~ **de** [*o* **para**] **animales** pet food; ~ **basura** junk food; ~ **casera** plain [*o* homestyle] cooking; ~ **francesa** French cuisine; ~ **rápida** fast food; **cama y** ~ bed and board **2.** (*horario*) ~ **principal** main meal (of the day) **3.** (*almuerzo*) lunch; ~ **de negocios** business lunch **4.** *Col, Perú, Chile* (*cena*) supper
comidilla *f inf* special interest; **ser la** ~ **del pueblo** to be the talk of the town
comienzo *m* (*principio*) beginning; **al** ~ at first; **a ~s de mes** at the beginning of the month
comillas *fpl* inverted commas; **entre** ~ in inverted commas
comilona *f inf* feast, blowout *inf*
comino *m* cumin; **no valer un** ~ not to be worth anything
comisaría *f* **1.** (*edificio*) ~ **de policía** police station, precinct *Am* **2.** (*cargo*) commissionership
comisariato *m AmL* company store; (*almacén*) warehouse
comisario, -a *m, f* **1.** (*delegado*) commissioner **2.** (*de policía*) superintendant, chief police inspector
comisión *f* **1.** (*cometido*) assignment **2.** (*delegación*) commission; (*comité*) committee; **Comisión Europea** European Commission; ~ **permanente** standing committee **3.** COM commission; **a** ~ on a commission basis **4.** ADMIN ~ **de servicios** secondment
comisionado, -a *m, f* commissioner
comisionar *vt* to commission
comisura *f* ANAT (*del cráneo*) commissure; ~ **de los labios** corner of the mouth
comité *m* committee; ~ **de empresa** works committee
comitiva *f* procession; ~ **fúnebre** cortège
como **I.** *adv* **1.** (*del modo que*) as, like; **hazlo** ~ **quieras** do it any way you like; ~ **quien** [*o* **aquel que**] **dice** so to speak; **blanco** ~ **la nieve** white as snow; **vivía** ~ **un hermitaño** he lived like a hermit **2.** (*comparativo*) as; **es tan alto** ~ **su hermano** he's as tall as his brother **3.** (*aproximadamente*) about; **hace** ~ **un año** about a year ago **4.** (*y también*) as well as **5.** (*en calidad de*) as; **trabaja** ~ **camarero** he works as a waiter **II.** *conj* **1.** (*causal*) as, since; ~ **no tengo tiempo, no voy** I'm not going because I haven't time; **lo sé,** ~ **que lo vi** I know because I saw it **2.** (*condicional*) if **3.** (*con "si" +subj o con "que"*) as if **4.** (*final*) ~ **para** in order to **5.** (*temporal*) as soon as
cómo **I.** *adv* **1.** (*modal, exclamativo*) how; **¿~ estás?** how are you?; **¿~ (dice)?** sorry?, pardon?; **según y** ~ it all depends **2.** (*por qué*) why; **¿~ (no)?** why not?; **¡~ no!** certainly! **II.** *m* **el** ~ the how
cómoda *f* chest (of drawers), dresser *Am*
comodidad *f* **1.** (*confort*) comfort **2.** (*conveniencia*) convenience
comodín *m* **1.** (*en juegos*) joker **2.** (*palabra*) all-purpose word **3.** INFOR wild card **4.** (*pretexto*) pretext
cómodo, -a *adj* **1.** *ser* (*cosa*) comfortable; (*conveniente*) convenient **2.** *ser* (*perezoso*) lazy **3.** *estar* (*a gusto*) comfortable; **¡ponte ~!** make yourself comfortable!
comoquiera **I.** *adv* somehow **II.** *conj* **1.** (*causal*) ~ **que** *+subj* since **2.** (*concesiva*) ~ **que** *+subj* in whatever way; ~ **que sea eso** however that may be
compact (disc) *m* compact disc
compacto *m* **1.** (*disco*) compact disc **2.** (*reproductor*) compact disc player **3.** (*equipo*) compact hi-fi system
compacto, -a *adj* **1.** (*textura, tamaño*) compact; (*denso*) dense; (*firme*) firm; **disco** ~ compact disc **2.** (*escritura*) close
compadecer *irr como crecer* **I.** *vt* to feel sorry for **II.** *vr* **~se de alguien/algo** to (take) pity (on) sth/sb
compadre *m* **1.** (*padrino*) godfather **2.** (*amigo*) friend, mate *Brit,* buddy
compadrear *vi* **1.** (*de compadraje*) to be pals **2.** *CSur* (*presumir*) to show off
compadreo *m pey* chumminess
compadrito *m AmS* (*chulo, bravucón*) braggart
compaginación *f* **1.** (*compatibilización*) combining **2.** (*paginación*) page makeup
compaginar **I.** *vt* **1.** (*combinar*) to combine **2.** (*paginar*) to page up **II.** *vr:* **~se** **1.** (*combinar*) to combine **2.** (*armonizar*) to go together
compañerismo *m* companionship; (*camaradería*) comradeship; DEP team spirit
compañero, -a *m, f* **1.** (*persona*) companion; (*amigo*) friend; (*pareja*) partner; *t.* POL comrade; ~ **de clase** schoolmate; UNIV fellow student; ~ **de piso** flatmate, roommate; ~ **de trabajo** workmate **2.** (*cosa*) other one (of a pair)
compañía *f* company; **animal de** ~ pet; **hacer** ~ **a alguien** to keep sb company
comparación *f* comparison; **no hay ni punto de** ~ there's no comparison
comparar **I.** *vt* to compare **II.** *vr:* **~se** to be

compared
comparativo *m* comparative
comparecencia *f t.* JUR appearance (in court); **no** ~ failure to appear
comparecer *irr como crecer vi t.* JUR to appear (in court)
comparsa *mf* **1.** TEAT extra **2.** (*desfile de carnaval*) *group of people with float*
compartimentar *vt* to compartmentalize
compartim(i)ento *m* compartment
compartir *vt* **1.** (*tener en común*) to share **2.** (*repartirse*) to share (out)
compás *m* **1.** (*en dibujo*) compass **2.** (*ritmo*) beat; MÚS time **3.** AVIAT, NÁUT (*brújula*) compass
compasión *f* ~ **de alguien** pity on sb, compassion [*o* sympathy] with sb; **sin** ~ pitiless(ly)
compasivo, **-a** *adj* compassionate, sympathetic
compatibilidad *f* compatibility
compatibilizar <z→c> *vt* to reconcile
compatible *adj* compatible
compatriota *mf* compatriot, fellow citizen
compeler *vt* to compel
compendiar *vt* to summarize
compendio *m* **1.** (*resumen*) summary; (*manual*) textbook **2.** (*epítome*) epitome
compenetración *f* (mutual) understanding; (*fusión*) interpenetration
compenetrarse *vr* **1.** QUÍM (*fusionarse*) to interpenetrate **2.** (*identificarse*) to reach an understanding
compensación *f* compensation
compensar *vt* ~ **de algo** to compensate for sth
competencia *f* **1.** *t.* COM, DEP (*competición*) competition; (*rivalidad*) rivalry; ~ **desleal** unfair competition **2.** *t.* LING competence **3.** (*responsabilidad*) responsibility; **esto (no) es de mi** ~ I'm not responsible for this
competente *adj* competent
competer *vi* (*corresponder*) ~ **a alguien** to be the responsibility of sb
competición *f* competition
competidor(a) **I.** *adj* competing **II.** *m(f) t.* ECON competitor
competir *irr como pedir vi* **1.** (*enfrentarse*) ~ **por algo** to compete for sth **2.** (*igualarse*) to rival each other
competitividad *f* competitiveness
competitivo, **-a** *adj* competitive
compilador *m* INFOR compiler
compilar *vt t.* INFOR to compile
compincharse *vr pey, inf* to team up
compinche *mf pey, inf* mate *Brit,* buddy
complacencia *f* **1.** (*agrado*) willingness; (*satisfacción*) satisfaction; (*placer*) pleasure **2.** (*indulgencia*) indulgence
complacer *irr como crecer* **I.** *vt* (*gustar*) to please; ~ **una petición** to grant a request **II.** *vr:* ~**se** (*gustar*) ~**se en algo** to be pleased to sth
complaciente *adj* **1.** (*servicial*) obliging **2.** (*indulgente*) ~ **para** [*o* **con**] **alguien** indulgent towards sb
complejidad *f* complexity
complejo *m* complex
complejo, **-a** *adj* complex
complementar **I.** *vt* to complement; (*completar*) to complete **II.** *vr:* ~**se** to complement each other
complemento *m* **1.** *t.* LING complement **2.** (*culminación*) culmination **3.** (*paga*) supplementary payment, bonus; (*recargo*) surcharge **4.** *pl* (*accesorio*) accessory
completamente *adv* completely
completar **I.** *vt* to complete **II.** *vr:* ~**se** to complete each other
completo, **-a** *adj* (*íntegro*) complete; (*perfecto*) perfect; (*total*) total; (*lleno*) full; (*cine, espectáculo*) sold out; **pensión completa** full board; **la obra completa de Lorca** the complete works of Lorca
complexión *f* **1.** (*constitución*) constitution, build **2.** *AmL* (*tez*) complexion
complicación *f* **1.** *t.* MED (*problema*) complication **2.** (*complejidad*) complexity
complicar <c→qu> **I.** *vt* **1.** (*dificultar*) to complicate **2.** (*implicar*) to involve **II.** *vr:* ~**se** **1.** (*dificultarse*) to get complicated **2.** (*embrollarse*) to get involved
cómplice *mf t.* JUR accomplice; **hacerse** ~ **de alguien/algo** to become sb's accomplice
complicidad *f* complicity
compló *m* <complós>, **complot** *m* <complots> conspiracy
componente *m* **1.** *t.* TÉC component; MAT, QUÍM constituent; ~**s lógicos** INFOR software **2.** (*miembro*) member
componer *irr como poner* **I.** *vt* **1.** (*formar*) to put together; (*organizar*) to organize **2.** (*constituir*) to make up **3.** *t.* MÚS to compose **4.** TIPO to set (up) **5.** (*recomponer*) to repair **6.** (*asear*) to arrange **7.** *AmL* (*castrar*) to castrate **8.** *AmL* (*hueso*) to set **II.** *vr:* ~**se** **1.** (*constituirse*) to consist **2.** (*arreglarse*) to tidy oneself up **3.** *AmL* (*mejorarse*) to get better
comportamiento *m* conduct, behaviour *Brit,* behavior *Am; t.* TÉC performance
comportar **I.** *vt* to involve; **esto (no) comporta que** +*subj* this (doesn't) mean(s) that **II.** *vr:* ~**se** to behave
composición *f* **1.** *t.* LIT, MÚS composition **2.** TIPO typesetting; **taller de** ~ composing room
compositor(a) *m(f)* composer
compost *m sin pl* compost
compostación *f*, **compostaje** *m* composting
compostura *f* **1.** (*realización*) composition **2.** (*corrección*) repair **3.** (*aspecto*) tidiness **4.** (*comedimiento*) composure
compota *f* compote
compra *f* purchase; ~**s** shopping; **ir de** ~**s** to go shopping
comprador(a) *m(f)* buyer; (*cliente*) customer
comprar **I.** *vt* **1.** (*adquirir*) to buy; ~ **al con-**

tado to pay cash; ~ **a plazos** to buy on hire-purchase, to buy on an installment plan **2.** (*corromper*) to buy off **II.** *vr:* **~se** to buy

comprender *vt* **1.** (*entender*) to understand; **hacerse** ~ to make oneself understood; ~ **mal** to misunderstand **2.** (*contener*) to comprise; (*abarcar*) to take in; (*incluir*) to include

comprensible *adj* understandable, comprehensible

comprensión *f* **1.** (*capacidad*) understanding; (*entendimiento*) comprehension **2.** (*inclusión*) inclusion

comprensivo, -a *adj* **1.** (*benévolo*) understanding **2.** (*tolerante*) tolerant **3.** (*inclusivo*) comprehensive

compresa *f* **1.** *t.* MED (*apósito*) compress **2.** (*higiénica*) sanitary towel *Brit,* sanitary napkin *Am*

compresión *f* compression

compresor *m* compressor

comprimido *m* pill

comprimir **I.** *vt* **1.** *t.* FÍS, TÉC to compress **2.** (*reprimir*) to restrain **II.** *vr:* **~se** to control oneself

comprobación *f* **1.** (*control*) checking **2.** (*verificación*) verification; (*confirmación*) confirmation; (*prueba*) proof

comprobante **I.** *adj* (*justificante*) justifying; (*de control*) supporting **II.** *m* voucher, proof

comprobar <o→ue> *vt* **1.** (*controlar*) to check **2.** (*verificar*) to verify; (*confirmar*) to confirm; (*justificar*) to justify; (*probar*) to prove

comprometedor(a) *adj* compromising

comprometer **I.** *vt* **1.** (*implicar*) to involve **2.** (*exponer*) to endanger **3.** (*arriesgar*) to put at risk **4.** (*obligar*) to commit **II.** *vr:* **~se** **1.** (*implicarse*) to compromise oneself **2.** (*obligarse*) to commit oneself; **~se** (**en matrimonio**) to get engaged

compromiso *m* **1.** (*vinculación*) commitment; (*obligación*) obligation; **visita de** ~ formal visit; **sin** ~ without obligation; (**soltero y**) **sin** ~ free and single **2.** (*promesa*) promise; ~ **matrimonial** engagement **3.** (*acuerdo*) agreement **4.** (*aprieto*) awkward situation **5.** (*cita*) engagement

compuerta *f* (*de una presa*) sluice gate

compuesto *m t.* QUÍM compound

compulsa *f* certified copy

compulsar *vt* **1.** JUR to certify **2.** (*cotejar*) to compare

compulsivo, -a *adj* compulsive

compungido, -a *adj* **1.** (*contrito*) remorseful **2.** (*triste*) sad

compungir <g→j> **I.** *vt* to make remorseful **II.** *vr:* **~se** (*sentir arrepentimiento*) to feel remorseful

computación *f* **1.** (*cálculo*) calculation **2.** INFOR computing

computador *m AmL* computer

computador(a) *adj* computer

computadora *f AmL* computer

computar *vt* **1.** (*calcular*) to calculate **2.** (*considerar*) to count

computerizar <z→c> *vt* to computerize

cómputo *m* calculation; ~ **de votos** count of votes

comulgar <g→gu> *vi* **1.** REL to take communion **2.** (*estar de acuerdo*) to agree

común **I.** *adj* common; **de ~ acuerdo** by common consent; **sentido** ~ common sense; **fuera de lo** ~ out of the ordinary; **poco** ~ unusual; **por lo** ~ usually **II.** *m* POL **los Comunes** the Commons *Brit*

comuna *f* **1.** *t.* HIST commune **2.** *AmL* (*municipio*) municipality

comunal *adj* ADMIN, POL communal; **elecciones ~es** municipal elections

comunicación *f* **1.** (*en general*) communication; **ponerse en ~ con alguien** to get in touch with sb **2.** (*comunicado*) message; (*ponencia*) paper **3.** (*conexión*) connection; ~ **telefónica** telephone call **4.** (*transmisión*) transmission **5.** (*de transporte*) link **6.** *pl t.* TEL communications *pl*

comunicado *m* communiqué; ~ **de prensa** press release

comunicar <c→qu> **I.** *vi* **1.** (*estar unido*) to be joined; (*estar en contacto*) to be connected **2.** (*conectar*) to connect **3.** (*teléfono*) to be engaged [*o* busy *Am*] **II.** *vt* **1.** (*informar*) to inform **2.** (*transmitir*) to communicate **3.** (*unir*) to connect; (*contactar*) to contact **4.** (*al teléfono*) to put through **III.** *vr:* **~se** **1.** (*entenderse*) to communicate **2.** (*relacionarse*) to be connected

comunicativo, -a *adj* communicative

comunidad *f* community; ~ **de vecinos** residents' association; ~ **autónoma** autonomous region

comunión *f* communion

comunismo *m* POL communism

comunista **I.** *adj* POL communist(ic) **II.** *mf* POL communist

comunitario, -a *adj* **1.** (*colectivo*) communal **2.** (*municipal*) community **3.** POL (*Comunidad Europea*) Community

con **I.** *prep* **1.** (*compañía,instrumento, modo*) with; **estar ~ la gripe** to have the flu; ~ **el tiempo...** with time ... **2.** MAT **3 ~ 5** 3 point 5 **3.** (*actitud*) (**para**) ~ to, towards **4.** (*circunstancia*) ~ **este tiempo...** in this weather ... **5.** (*a pesar de*) in spite of **II.** *conj* + *infin* if; ~ **que** +*subj* as long as; ~ **sólo que** +*subj* if only

conato *m* **1.** (*intento*) attempt **2.** (*empeño*) effort

concatenación *f* (*acción*) linking

concatenar *vt* to link together

concavidad *f* concavity

cóncavo, -a *adj* concave

concebir *irr como pedir* **I.** *vi* to conceive **II.** *vt* to conceive; ~ **esperanzas** to have hopes

conceder *vt* **1.** (*otorgar*) to grant; (*asignar*) to give; ~ **la palabra a alguien** to give sb the floor; ~ **un premio** to award a prize **2.** (*admi-*

tir) to concede

concejal(a) *m(f)* town [*o* city] councillor *Brit,* councilman *m Am,* councilwoman *f Am*

concejo *m* council

concelebrar *vt* REL to concelebrate

concentración *f* concentration; ~ **pacífica** peaceful demonstration

concentrado *m* (*extracto*) concentrate

concentrar **I.** *vt* to concentrate **II.** *vr:* ~**se** **1.** (*reunirse*) to assemble; (*agruparse*) to gather together **2.** (*centrarse*) to concentrate

concepción *f* conception

concepto *m* **1.** (*noción*) notion; (*plan*) concept **2.** (*opinión*) opinion **3.** (*motivo*) **bajo** [*o* **por**] **ningún** ~ on no account **4.** (*calidad*) **en** ~ **de** by way of

conceptual *adj* conceptual

conceptualizar <z→c> *vt* to conceptualize

concernir *irr como cernir vi* to concern; **en** [*o* **por**] **lo que concierne a alguien...** as far as sb is concerned ...

concertación *f* coordination; ~ **social** social harmony

concertar <e→ie> **I.** *vi t.* LING to agree **II.** *vt* **1.** (*arreglar*) to arrange **2.** MÚS (*afinar*) to tune **3.** (*armonizar*) to harmonize **III.** *vr:* ~**se** **1.** (*ponerse de acuerdo*) to come to an agreement **2.** *pey* (*compincharse*) to band together

concertista *mf* MÚS soloist

concesión *f* **1.** *t.* COM concession **2.** (*de una beca, de un premio*) awarding

concesionario, -a *m, f* dealer

concha *f* **1.** (*del molusco*) shell; (*de tortuga*) tortoiseshell **2.** TEAT prompt box **3.** *AmL* (*descaro*) nerve **4.** *AmL, vulg* (*vulva*) cunt ►**tener más ~s que un galápago** *inf* to be a slippery customer

conchabar **I.** *vt* **1.** (*mezclar*) to mix **2.** *AmL* (*contratar*) to hire **II.** *vr:* ~**se** *inf* to plot; **estar conchabado con alguien** to be in league with sb

conchudo, -a *adj* **1.** (*con conchas*) conchiferous **2.** *AmL, inf* (*sinvergüenza*) shameless **3.** *Méx, Col, inf* (*indolente*) sluggish

conciencia *f* **1.** (*conocimiento*) awareness; **tomar ~ de algo** to become aware of sth **2.** (*moral*) conscience; **a** ~ conscientiously; **libertad de** ~ freedom of worship; (**sin**) **cargo de** ~ (without) remorse; **me remuerde la** ~ my conscience is pricking me

concienciar **I.** *vt* **1.** (*persuadir*) to persuade **2.** (*sensibilizar*) to make aware **II.** *vr:* ~**se** **1.** (*convencerse*) to convince oneself **2.** (*sensibilizarse*) to become aware

concienzudo, -a *adj* conscientious

concierto *m* **1.** MÚS (*función*) concert; (*obra*) concerto **2.** (*disposición*) order **3.** (*armonía*) harmony **4.** *t.* ECON (*acuerdo*) agreement

conciliación *f* conciliation; (*reconciliación*) reconciliation; ~ **laboral** arbitration

conciliador(a) *adj* conciliatory

conciliar **I.** *vt* **1.** (*reconciliar*) to reconcile; (*armonizar*) to harmonize **2.** *fig* ~ **el sueño** to get to sleep **II.** *vr:* ~**se** (*reconciliarse*) to be reconciled

concilio *m t.* REL council

concisión *f* concision

conciso, -a *adj* concise

concitar *vt* to arouse

conciudadano, -a *m, f* fellow citizen

conclave *m,* **cónclave** *m* **1.** REL conclave **2.** (*reunión*) meeting

concluir *irr como huir* **I.** *vi* to end; **¡asunto concluido!** that's settled! **II.** *vt* **1.** (*terminar*) to complete; (*negocio*) to conclude **2.** (*deducir*) ~ **de algo** to conclude from sth **III.** *vr:* ~**se** to end

conclusión *f* conclusion; **en** ~ (*en suma*) in short; (*por último*) in conclusion; **llegar a la ~ de que...** to come to the conclusion that ...

concluyente *adj* conclusive; (*determinante*) decisive, unequivocal

concomitante *adj* concomitant

concordancia *f* **1.** (*correspondencia*) concordance **2.** LING agreement

concordar <o→ue> **I.** *vi* **1.** (*coincidir*) to coincide **2.** LING to agree **II.** *vt* **1.** (*armonizar*) to reconcile **2.** LING to make agree

concordia *f* harmony

concreción *f* **1.** (*precisión*) sticking **2.** (*acumulación*) agglomeration **3.** MED stone

concretar **I.** *vt* **1.** (*precisar*) to put in concrete form **2.** (*limitar*) to limit **II.** *vr:* ~**se** to limit oneself

concretizar <z→c> *vt v.* **concretar**

concreto, -a *adj* concrete; **en** ~ specifically

concubina *f* concubine

conculcar <c→qu> *vt* to violate

concurrencia *f* **1.** (*coincidencia*) coincidence **2.** (*asistencia*) attendance **3.** (*público*) audience **4.** (*competencia*) competition

concurrido, -a *adj* crowded

concurrir *vi* **1.** (*coincidir en el lugar*) to come together; (*en el tiempo*) to coincide **2.** (*concursar*) ~ **por algo** to compete for sth **3.** (*participar*) to take part **4.** (*presenciar*) ~ **en algo** to attend sth

concursante *mf* **1.** (*aspirante*) candidate **2.** (*participante*) competitor, contestant

concursar **I.** *vi* to compete **II.** *vt* JUR ~ **a alguien** to declare sb bankrupt [*o* insolvent]

concurso *m* **1.** *t.* DEP competition **2.** (*oposición*) (public) competition **3.** (*coincidencia*) coincidence **4.** (*ayuda*) help

condado *m* **1.** (*título*) countship **2.** (*territorio*) county, shire *Brit;* HIST earldom

conde(sa) *m(f)* count *m,* countess *f*

condecoración *f* MIL decoration

condecorar *vt* MIL to decorate

condena *f* sentence, conviction; **cumplir una** ~ to serve a sentence

condenado, -a **I.** *adj inf* condemned **II.** *m, f* **1.** (*reo*) convicted person, convict **2.** REL **los ~s** the damned **3.** *inf* (*endemoniado*) wretch **4.** *inf* (*niño*) rascal

condenar **I.** *vt* **1.** (*sentenciar, reprobar*) to

condemn **2.** REL to damn **3.** (*tapiar*) to wall up **II.** *vr:* ~**se** **1.** REL to be damned **2.** (*acusarse*) to confess

condensador *m* ELEC condenser

condensar **I.** *vt* to condense **II.** *vr:* ~**se** to condense

condesa *f v.* **conde**

condescendencia *f* **1.** (*dignación*) condescension **2.** (*transigencia*) ~ **con algo/alguien** acquiescence to [*o* in] sth/sb

condescender <e→ie> *vi* **1.** (*avenirse*) ~ **con algo/alguien** to agree to st/with sb **2.** (*rebajarse*) to condescend

condescendiente *adj* **1.** (*benévolo*) kind **2.** (*complaciente*) obliging **3.** (*arrogante*) condescending

condición *f* **1.** (*índole de una cosa*) nature **2.** (*estado, requisito*) condition; **a ~ de que** +*subj* on condition that, providing **3.** (*situación*) position **4.** (*clase*) social class

condicional **I.** *adj t.* LING conditional **II.** *m* LING conditional

condicionar *vt* **1.** (*supeditar*) ~ **a algo** to make conditional on sth **2.** (*acondicionar*) to condition

condimentar *vt* to season, to flavour *Brit,* to flavor *Am*

condimento *m* seasoning, flavouring *Brit,* flavoring *Am*

condolencia *f* condolence, sympathy

condolerse <o→ue> *vr* ~**se de algo** to sympathize with sth

condón *m* condom

condonación *f* (*de una deuda*) writing off

condonar *vt* (*deuda*) to write off

cóndor *m* condor

conducción *f* **1.** (*transporte*) transport(ation) **2.** (*coche*) driving; ~ **temeraria** reckless driving **3.** (*conducto, administración*) management

conducir *irr como traducir* **I.** *vt* **1.** (*llevar*) to take; (*transportar*) to transport **2.** (*guiar*) to guide **3.** (*arrastrar*) to lead **4.** (*pilotar*) to drive **5.** (*mandar*) to direct **II.** *vi* **1.** (*dirigir*) to lead **2.** (*pilotar*) to drive **III.** *vr:* ~**se** to behave

conducta *f* **1.** (*comportamiento*) conduct, behaviour *Brit,* behavior *Am* **2.** (*mando*) management

conductismo *m* PSICO behaviourism *Brit,* behaviorism *Am*

conducto *m* **1.** (*tubo*) pipe **2.** MED canal; ~ **auditivo** ear canal **3.** (*mediación*) channels *pl*

conductor *m* FÍS conductor

conductor(a) **I.** *adj* conductive; **hilo ~** conductor wire **II.** *m(f)* **1.** (*chófer*) driver **2.** (*jefe*) leader

conectar **I.** *vt* **1.** (*enlazar*) to connect **2.** (*enchufar*) to plug in **II.** *vi* to communicate

conejera *f* **1.** (*madriguera*) burrow, warren *fig,* overcrowded room **2.** *t. fig* den

conejillo *m* ~ **de Indias** *t. fig* guinea pig

conejo, **-a** *m, f* rabbit

conexión *f* **1.** *t.* TEL connection **2.** *pl* (*amistades*) connections *pl*

confabularse *vr* to plot

confección *f* making; (*de vestidos*) dressmaking

confeccionar *vt* to make; (*plan*) to draw up

confederación *f* confederation

confederar **I.** *vt* to confederate **II.** *vr:* ~**se** to form a confederation

conferencia *f* **1.** (*charla*) lecture **2.** (*encuentro*) conference **3.** (*plática*) talk **4.** (*llamada telefónica*) call

conferenciante *mf,* **conferentista** *mf AmL* lecturer

conferir *irr como sentir vt* to confer

confesar <e→ie> **I.** *vt* **1.** (*admitir*) to confess **2.** REL (*declarar*) to confess; ~ **a alguien** to confess, to hear sb's confession **II.** *vr:* ~**se** to confess; ~**se culpable** to admit one's guilt

confesión *f* confession

confes(i)onario *m* confessional (box)

confesor *m* confessor

confeti *m* confetti

confiado, **-a** *adj* **1.** *ser* (*crédulo*) trusting **2.** *estar* (*presumido*) vain; (*de sí mismo*) self-confident

confianza *f* **1.** (*crédito*) trust; **amiga de ~** close friend **2.** (*esperanza*) confidence **3.** (*en uno mismo*) self-confidence **4.** (*familiaridad*) familiarity **5.** *pl* (*familiaridad excesiva*) familiarities *pl*

confiar <*1. pres:* confío> **I.** *vi* ~ **en algo/alguien** to trust in sth/sb **II.** *vt* to entrust **III.** *vr* ~**se a alguien** to confide in sb

confidencia *f* secret

confidencial *adj* confidential

confidente *mf* **1.** (*cómplice*) confidant *m,* confidante *f* **2.** (*espía*) informer

configuración *f* **1.** (*formación*) shaping **2.** (*forma*) shape **3.** INFOR configuration

configurar **I.** *vt* **1.** (*formar*) to shape **2.** INFOR to configure **II.** *vr:* ~**se** to take shape

confín **I.** *adj* bordering **II.** *m* **1.** (*frontera*) border **2.** (*final*) limit

confinar **I.** *vi* ~ **con algo** to border on sth **II.** *vt* to confine

confirmación *f t.* REL confirmation

confirmar **I.** *vt t.* REL to confirm **II.** *vr:* ~**se** to be confirmed

confiscación *f* confiscation

confiscar <c→qu> *vt* to confiscate

confitar *vt* (*en almíbar*) to preserve in syrup; (*con azúcar*) to candy

confitería *f* cake [*o* pastry] shop, sweet shop *Brit,* candy shop *Am*

confitura *f* jam

conflagración *f* war

conflictividad *f* disputes *pl*

conflicto *m* conflict

confluencia *f* confluence

confluir *irr como huir vi* (*ríos, calles*) to meet

conformación *f* shape

conformar **I.** *vt* **1.** (*contentar*) to satisfy **2.** (*formar*) to shape **3.** (*ajustar*) to adjust **II.** *vi*

to agree **III.** *vr:* **~se 1.** (*contentarse*) to be satisfied **2.** (*ajustarse*) to adjust
conforme I. *adj* (*adecuado*) **estar ~ con algo** to be satisfied with sth **II.** *prep* according to **III.** *conj* (*como*) as
conformidad *f* **1.** (*afinidad*) similarity **2.** (*aprobación*) approval
confort *m sin pl* comfort
confortable *adj* comfortable
confortar I. *vt* **1.** (*vivificar*) to strengthen **2.** (*alentar*) to encourage; (*consolar*) to comfort **II.** *vr:* **~se 1.** (*reanimarse*) to regain one's strength **2.** (*consolarse*) to take comfort
confraternizar <z→c> *vi* to fraternize
confrontación *f* **1.** (*comparación*) comparison **2.** (*enfrentamiento*) confrontation
confrontar I. *vt* **1.** (*comparar*) to compare **2.** (*enfrentar*) to confront **II.** *vr* **~se con alguien** to face up to sb
Confucionismo *m* FILOS Confucianism
confundir I. *vt* **1.** (*trastocar*) to mistake **2.** (*mezclar*) to mix up **3.** (*embrollar*) to confuse **II.** *vr:* **~se 1.** (*mezclarse*) to mix **2.** (*embrollarse*) to get confused
confusión *f* confusion
confuso, -a *adj* confused
congelación *f* **1.** (*solidificación*) freezing; **~ salarial** pay freeze **2.** frostbite; MED
congelador *m* **1.** (*electrodoméstico*) freezer **2.** (*compartimento en la nevera*) ice [*o* freezer] compartment
congelar I. *vt t. fig* to freeze **II.** *vr:* **~se 1.** (*solidificarse*) to freeze **2.** (*helarse*) to get frostbitten
congénere *mf* **el ladrón y sus ~s** the thief and others like him, the likes of the thief
congeniar *vi* **congeniar con** to get on [*o* along] with
congénito, -a *adj* congenital
congestión *f t.* MED congestion
congestionar I. *vt t.* MED to congest **II.** *vr:* **~se** *t.* MED to become congested
conglomerar I. *vt* to conglomerate **II.** *vr:* **~se** to conglomerate
Congo *m* **el ~** the Congo
congoja *f* **1.** (*pena*) sorrow **2.** (*desconsuelo*) anguish
congola *f Col* (*pipa de fumar*) pipe
congoleño, -a, congolés, -esa *adj, m, f* Congolese
congraciar I. *vt* to win over **II.** *vr:* **~se** to ingratiate oneself
congratular I. *vt* to congratulate **II.** *vr* **~se de** [*o* **por**] **algo** to congratulate oneself on sth
congregación *f* **1.** (*reunión*) meeting **2.** REL congregation
congregar <g→gu> **I.** *vt* to bring together **II.** *vr:* **~se** to gather
congresal *mf AmL* member of a congress
congresista *mf* **1.** POL delegate, congressman *m,* congresswoman *f* **2.** (*asisitente a un congreso*) congress member
congreso *m* **1.** POL congress **2.** (*reunión*) congress, convention
congrio *m* conger eel
congruencia *f* **1.** (*coherencia*) coherence **2.** MAT congruence
cónico, -a *adj* conical
conífera *f* conifer
conjetura *f* conjecture
conjeturar *vt* to speculate
conjugación *f* conjugation
conjugar <g→gu> *vt* **1.** (*combinar*) to combine **2.** LING to conjugate
conjunción *f* conjunction
conjuntamente *adv* jointly; **~ con** together with
conjuntar I. *vi* to match; **~ con** to go with **II.** *vt* to harmonize **III.** *vr:* **~se** to come together
conjuntivitis *f inv* conjunctivitis
conjunto *m* **1.** (*unido*) unit **2.** (*totalidad*) whole; **en ~** as a whole **3.** (*en representaciones artísticas*) ensemble **4.** (*ropa*) outfit **5.** MAT set
conjura *f,* **conjuración** *f* conspiracy
conjurar I. *vi* to conspire **II.** *vt* **1.** (*invocar*) to beseech **2.** (*alejar*) to ward off **III.** *vr:* **~se** to conspire
conllevar *vt* **1.** (*implicar*) to involve **2.** (*soportar*) to bear
conmemoración *f* commemoration
conmemorar *vt* to commemorate
conmemorativo, -a *adj* commemorative
conmigo *pron pers* with me
conminar *vt* **1.** (*amenazar*) to threaten **2.** JUR to warn
conmiseración *f* commiseration
conmoción *f* **1.** MED concussion **2.** *fig* shock
conmocionar *vt* **1.** MED to concuss **2.** *fig* to shake
conmovedor(a) *adj* **1.** (*conmocionando*) stirring **2.** (*sentimental*) moving
conmover <o→ue> **I.** *vt* **1.** (*emocionar*) to move **2.** (*sacudir*) to shake **II.** *vr:* **~se 1.** (*emocionarse*) to be moved **2.** (*sacudirse*) to be shaken
conmutación *f t.* LING commutation
conmutador *m* ELEC switch
conmutar *vt* **1.** (*cambiar*) to exchange **2.** (*una pena*) **~ por algo** to commute to sth **3.** ELEC to switch
connaturalizar <z→c> **I.** *vt* to accustom **II.** *vr* **~se con algo** to get accustomed to sth
connivencia *f* collusion
cono *m* cone; **Cono Sur** GEO *Argentina, Chile, Paraguay and Uruguay*

> The economic union between the four countries in the most southerly part of Latin America, **Argentina**, **Chile**, **Paraguay** and **Uruguay** is referred to as **Cono Sur**.

conocedor(a) I. *adj* **~ de algo** knowledgeable about sth **II.** *m(f)* expert
conocer *irr como crecer* **I.** *vt* **1.** (*saber, tener*

trato) to know; ~ **de vista** to know by sight; **dar a** ~ to make known **2.** (*reconocer*) to recognize **3.** (*descubrir*) to get to know **4.** (*por primera vez*) to meet; **les conocí en una fiesta** I met them at a party **II.** *vi* ~ **de algo** to know about sth **III.** *vr:* ~**se 1.** (*tener trato*) to know each other **2.** (*persona*) to know oneself

conocido, -a I. *adj* (well-)known **II.** *m, f* acquaintance

conocimiento *m* **1.** (*saber*) knowledge **2.** (*entendimiento*) understanding **3.** (*consciencia*) consciousness **4.** *pl* (*nociones*) knowledge

conque *conj inf* so

conquense I. *adj* of/from Cuenca **II.** *mf* native/inhabitant of Cuenca

conquista *f* conquest

conquistador(a) I. *adj* conquering **II.** *m(f)* **1.** conqueror **2.** *pl* (*de América*) conquistadores

conquistar *vt* to conquer

consagración *f* **1.** REL consecration **2.** (*dedicación*) dedication

consagrar I. *vt* **1.** REL to consecrate **2.** (*dedicar*) to dedicate **II.** *vr:* ~**se 1.** (*dedicarse*) to devote oneself **2.** (*acreditarse*) to distinguish oneself

consanguíneo, -a I. *adj* related by blood **II.** *m, f* blood relation

consciencia *f* consciousness

consciente *adj* conscious; **estar** ~ MED to be conscious; **ser** ~ **de algo** to be aware of sth

conscripción *f Arg* (*servicio militar*) conscription

conscripto *m AmS* (*quinto*) recruit, conscript

consecución *f* attainment

consecuencia *f* **1.** (*efecto*) consequence; **a** ~ **de** as a result of **2.** (*coherencia*) consistency

consecuente *adj* consistent

consecuentemente *adv* **1.** (*por consiguiente*) consequently **2.** (*con consistencia*) consistently

consecutivo, -a *adj* consecutive

conseguido, -a *adj* successful

conseguir *irr como seguir vt* **1.** (*obtener*) to get **2.** (*tener éxito*) ~ **obtener una beca** to succeed in obtaining a grant

consejero, -a *m, f* **1.** (*guía*) adviser, counselor, consultant **2.** (*miembro de un consejo*) member; ~ **delegado** managing director **3.** (*de una autonomía*) minister

consejo *m* **1.** (*recomendación*) piece of advice **2.** (*organismo*) council; **Consejo Europeo** Council of Europe **3.** (*reunión*) meeting

consenso *m* consensus

consensuar <*1. pres:* consensúo> *vt* to reach a consensus on

consentido, -a *adj* **1.** (*mimado*) spoiled **2.** (*tolerante*) complaisant

consentimiento *m* ~ **para algo** consent to sth

consentir *irr como sentir* **I.** *vi* (*admitir*) ~ **en algo** to agree to sth **II.** *vt* **1.** (*autorizar*) to allow; (*tolerar*) to tolerate **2.** (*mimar*) to spoil **3.** (*aguantar*) to put up with

conserje *mf* **1.** (*encargado*) caretaker *Brit,* janitor *Am* **2.** (*hotel*) concierge, receptionist **3.** (*portero*) (hall) porter

conserjería *f* **1.** (*cargo*) job of caretaker **2.** (*oficina*) caretaker's office **3.** (*hotel*) reception (desk)

conserva *f* **1.** (*enlatado*) tinned food *Brit,* canned food *Am* **2.** (*conservación*) preserving

conservación *f* **1.** (*mantenimiento*) maintenance **2.** (*guarda*) conservation **3.** (*conserva*) preserving

conservador(a) I. *adj* conservative **II.** *m(f)* **1.** (*guardador*) curator **2.** POL conservative, Tory *Brit*

conservante *m* preservative

conservar I. *vt* **1.** (*mantener*) to maintain **2.** (*guardar*) to conserve **3.** (*hacer conservas*) to can **4.** (*continuar la práctica*) to preserve **II.** *vr:* ~**se** to survive; (*mantenerse*) to keep

conservatorio *m* conservatory

considerable *adj* considerable

consideración *f* **1.** (*reflexión*) consideration; **en** ~ **a** in consideration of **2.** (*respeto*) respect

considerado, -a *adj* **1.** (*tener en cuenta*) considered **2.** (*apreciado*) respected **3.** (*atento*) considerate

considerar I. *vt* to consider **II.** *vr:* ~**se** to consider oneself

consigna *f* **1.** MIL motto **2.** POL instruction **3.** (*depósito de equipajes*) left-luggage (office) *Brit,* checkroom *Am*

consignar *vt* **1.** (*asignar*) to assign **2.** (*protocolar*) to record **3.** (*poner en depósito*) to deposit in left-luggage [*o* baggage-check *Am*] **4.** COM to dispatch

consignatario, -a *m, f* **1.** (*destinatario*) addressee **2.** COM consignee

consigo *pron pers* **tiene el libro** ~ he/she has the book with him/her; **lléveselo** ~ take it with you

consiguiente *adj* resulting; **por** ~ consequently

consistencia *f* consistency

consistente *adj* consistent; (*argument*) sound; GASTR thick; ~ **en** consisting of

consistir *vi* **1.** (*componerse*) ~ **en algo** to consist of sth **2.** (*radicar*) ~ **en algo** to lie in sth

consistorio *m* **1.** REL consistory **2.** ADMIN town council

consola *f* **1.** (*mesa*) console table **2.** ELEC console; (*de videojuegos*) video console

consolación *f* consolation

consolador *m* (*vibrador*) vibrator, dildo *vulg*

consolar <o→ue> **I.** *vt* to console **II.** *vr:* ~**se** to console oneself

consolidación *f* consolidation

consolidar I. *vt* to consolidate **II.** *vr:* ~**se** to be consolidated

consomé *m* consommé

consonancia *f* **1.** (*rima*) rhyme **2.** (*armonía*)

harmony; **en ~ con** in keeping with
consonante I. *adj* 1. (*que rima*) rhyming 2. (*armonioso*) harmonious II. *f* LING consonant
consorcio *m* consortium
consorte *mf* 1. (*partícipe*) partner 2. (*cónyuge*) spouse 3. *pl* JUR accomplices *pl*, co-litigants *pl* 4. *pey, inf* (*compinche*) mate *Brit*, buddy
conspicuo, **-a** *adj* eminent
conspiración *f* conspiracy
conspirar *vi* to conspire
constancia *f* 1. (*firmeza*) constancy 2. (*perseverancia*) perseverance 3. (*certeza*) certainty 4. (*prueba*) proof; **dejar ~ de algo** to show evidence of sth
constante *adj* constant
Constanza *f* Constance; **Lago de ~** Lake Constance
constar *vi* 1. (*ser cierto*) to be clear 2. (*figurar*) to be on record; **hacer ~ algo** to put sth on record 3. (*componerse*) to consist
constatar *vt* to confirm
constelación *f* constellation
consternación *f* consternation
consternar I. *vt* to dismay II. *vr:* **~se** to be dismayed
constipado *m* cold
constipado, **-a** *adj* **estar ~** to have a cold
constipar *vr:* **~se** to catch a cold
constitución *f* 1. *t.* POL constitution 2. (*establecimiento*) setting-up 3. (*composición*) make-up
constitucional *adj* constitutional
constituir *irr como huir* I. *vt* 1. (*formar*) to constitute 2. (*ser*) to be 3. (*establecer*) to establish 4. (*designar*) **~ en algo** to designate as sth II. *vr:* **~se** (*convertirse*) **~se en algo** to become sth
constitutivo, **-a** *adj* constituent
constreñimiento *m* constraint
constreñir *irr como ceñir vt* 1. (*obligar*) to constrain 2. MED to constrict 3. (*cohibir*) to restrict
constricción *f* constriction
construcción *f* 1. (*acción*) construction 2. (*sector, edificio*) building; **~ aneja** annexe
constructivo, **-a** *adj* constructive
constructor(a) *m(f)* builder
construir *irr como huir vt* 1. (*casa*) to build; (*erigir*) to erect 2. LING to construe
consubstancial *adj v.* **consustancial**
consuelo *m* consolation
cónsul *mf* consul
consulado *m* 1. (*lugar*) consulate 2. (*cargo*) consulship
consulta *f* 1. (*acción*) consultation 2. (*de un médico*) surgery; **horas de ~** surgery hours 3. (*asesoramiento*) **~ popular** POL referendum
consultar *vt* to consult
consultor(a) I. *adj* consulting; **empresa ~a** consultancy firm II. *m(f)* consultant
consultoría *f* consultancy; (*empresa*) consultancy (firm)
consultorio *m* 1. (*establecimiento*) consultancy; (*de un médico*) surgery 2. (*en la radio*) phone-in
consumación *f sin pl* consummation
consumar *vt* to carry out; **~ el matrimonio** JUR to consummate the marriage
consumición *f* 1. (*bar*) drink; **~ mínima** minimum charge 2. (*agotamiento*) consumption
consumidor(a) *m(f)* consumer
consumir I. *vt* 1. (*gastar, destruir*) to consume 2. (*acabar*) to use 3. (*comer*) to eat 4. (*afligir*) to wear out II. *vr:* **~se** 1. (*persona*) to waste away 2. (*gastarse*) to be consumed
consumismo *m* consumerism
consumo *m* consumption; **bienes de ~** consumer goods; **sociedad de ~** consumer society
consustancial *adj* consubstantial
contabilidad *f* 1. (*sistema*) accounting 2. (*profesión*) accountancy
contabilizar <z→c> *vt* to enter
contable I. *adj* countable II. *mf* accountant
contactar *vi, vt* **~ con alguien** to contact sb
contacto *m* 1. (*tacto, persona*) contact 2. AUTO ignition 3. FOTO contact print
contado *m* **pagar al ~** to pay (in) cash
contador *m* (*del agua, de la luz*) meter
contados, **-as** *adj* (*raro*) scarce; **tiene los días ~** his/her days are numbered
contagiar I. *vt* to transmit, to infect II. *vr* **~se de algo** to become infected with sth
contagio *m* contagion
contagioso, **-a** *adj* contagious; **tener una risa contagiosa** to have a contagious laugh
contaminación *f* pollution; **~ acústica** noise pollution; **~ ambiental** environmental pollution
contaminante I. *adj* polluting II. *m* pollutant
contaminar I. *vt* 1. (*infestar*) to pollute 2. (*contagiar*) to infect 3. (*corromper*) to corrupt II. *vr:* **~se** 1. (*infectarse*) to become contaminated 2. (*contagiarse*) to become infected 3. (*corromperse*) to be corrupted
contante *adj* **~ y** <u>**sonante**</u> in hard cash
contar <o→ue> I. *vi* 1. (*hacer cuentas, valer*) to count 2. (+ *con: confiar*) **~ con alguien/algo** to rely on sth/sb 3. (+ *con: tener en cuenta*) **~ con algo** to expect sth II. *vt* 1. (*numerar, incluir*) to count; **sin ~ con** without taking into account 2. (*narrar*) to tell; **¿qué cuentas?** (*saludo*) how's it going? III. *vr:* **~se** to be counted
contemplación *f* 1. (*observación*) contemplation 2. REL meditation 3. *pl* (*miramientos*) indulgence
contemplar *vt* 1. (*mirar*) to look at 2. (*considerar*) to consider 3. (*complacer*) to spoil 4. REL to meditate
contemplativo, **-a** *adj* contemplative
contemporáneo, **-a** *adj, m, f* contemporary
contemporizar <z→c> *vi* **~ con algo/alguien** to be accommodating towards sth/sb

C

contención *f* (*de agua, etc*) containment
contender <e→ie> *vi* ~ **por algo** to contend for sth
contendiente *mf* contender
contenedor *m* **1.** (*general*) container **2.** (*basura*) bin container *Brit,* (trash) dumpster *Am* **3.** (*escombros*) skip *Brit,* dumpster *Am*
contener *irr como tener* **I.** *vt* **1.** (*encerrar*) to contain **2.** (*refrenar*) to hold back; (*respiración*) to hold **II.** *vr:* **~se** to contain oneself
contenido *m* **1.** (*incluido, significado*) contents *pl* **2.** (*concentración*) content
contentar I. *vt* to satisfy **II.** *vr:* **~se** to be contented
contento, -a *adj* **1.** (*alegre*) happy **2.** (*satisfecho*) content
contestación *f* **1.** (*respuesta*) answer **2.** (*protesta*) protest
contestador *m* answerphone, answering machine
contestar I. *vt* (*responder*) to answer **II.** *vi* **1.** (*responder*) to answer **2.** (*replicar*) to answer back
contestatario, -a *m, f* rebel
contexto *m* context
contienda *f* **1.** (*disputa*) dispute **2.** (*batalla*) conflict
contigo *pron pers* with you; **me siento** ~ I'll sit beside you
contiguo, -a *adj* adjoining
continencia *f* continence
continental *adj* continental
continente *m* **1.** GEO continent **2.** (*aspecto*) air; (*compostura*) bearing **3.** (*cosa*) container
contingencia *f* **1.** (*eventualidad*) eventuality **2.** *t.* FILOS contingency **3.** (*riesgo*) risk
contingentar *vt* to establish quotas for
contingente I. *adj* possible **II.** *m* **1.** ECON quota **2.** MIL contingent
continuación *f* continuation; **a** ~ (*después*) next; (*en un escrito*) as follows
continuar <*1. pres:* continúo> **I.** *vi* to continue; **~á** to be continued **II.** *vt* to continue
continuidad *f* continuity
continuo, -a *adj* continuous; **movimiento** ~ perpetual motion
contonearse *vr* to swing one's hips, to wiggle
contorno *m* **1.** (*de una figura*) outline **2.** (*de la cintura*) waist measurement **3.** *(pl)* (*territorio*) surrounding area
contra[1] **I.** *prep* against; **tener algo en** ~ to object **II.** *m* **los pros y los ~s** the pros and the cons
contra[2] *f* **1.** (*dificultad*) snag **2.** (*oposición*) **llevar la** ~ **a alguien** to contradict sb **3.** (*guerrilla*) contra
contraataque *m* MIL counterattack
contrabajo *m* **1.** (*instrumento*) double bass **2.** (*músico*) double-bass player
contrabandista *mf* smuggler; ~ **de armas** gunrunner
contrabando *m sin pl* **1.** (*comercio*) smuggling; **pasar algo de** ~ to smuggle sth in **2.** (*mercancía*) contraband
contracción *f* **1.** *(pl)* MED contractions *pl* **2.** *t.* LING contraction
contrachapado *m* plywood
contrachapado, -a *adj* plywood; **mesa contrachapada** plywood table; **madera contrachapada** plywood
contracorriente *f sin pl* crosscurrent
contractual *adj* contractual
contracultura *f sin pl* alternative society
contradecir *irr como decir* **I.** *vt* to contradict **II.** *vr:* **~se** (*persona*) to contradict oneself
contradicción *f* contradiction
contradictorio, -a *adj* contradictory
contraer *irr como traer* **I.** *vt* **1.** (*encoger*) to contract **2.** (*adquirir: deudas*) to contract; (*enfermedad*) to catch, to contract *form* **3.** (*limitar*) to limit **II.** *vr:* **~se 1.** (*encogerse*) to contract **2.** (*limitarse*) to limit oneself
contraespionaje *m* counterespionage
contrafuerte *m* **1.** ARQUIT buttress **2.** (*zapato*) heel stiffener **3.** GEO spur
contrahecho, -a *adj* **1.** (*deforme*) deformed; (*persona*) hunchbacked **2.** (*falsificado*) counterfeit
contraindicación *f* MED contraindication
contralor *m AmL* FIN treasury inspector
contraloría *f AmL* treasury inspector's office
contraluz *m o f* back light(ing)
contramanifestación *f* counter-demonstration
contramedida *f* countermeasure
contraofensiva *f* counteroffensive
contraoferta *f* counteroffer
contraorden *f* countermand *form*
contrapartida *f* **1.** (*compensación*) compensation **2.** (*contabilidad*) balancing entry
contrapelo *adj* **a** ~ *t. fig* the wrong way
contrapesar *vt* to counterbalance, to offset
contrapeso *m* counterweight
contraponer *irr como poner* **I.** *vt* **1.** (*comparar*) to compare **2.** (*oponer*) to contrast **II.** *vr:* **~se** to be contrasted
contraportada *f* back cover [*o* page]
contraposición *f* comparison
contraprestación *f* consideration
contraproducente *adj* counterproductive
contrapunto *m* MÚS counterpoint
contrariar <*1. pres:* contrarío> *vt* **1.** (*oponerse*) to oppose; (*plan*) to thwart **2.** (*disgustar*) to upset
contrariedad *f* **1.** (*inconveniente*) obstacle **2.** (*disgusto*) annoyance
contrario, -a I. *adj* (*opuesto*) contrary; (*perjudicial*) harmful; **al** ~ on the contrary; **en caso** ~ otherwise; **de lo** ~ or else; **llevar la contraria a alguien** to oppose [*o* contradict] sb **II.** *m, f* opponent
contrarreembolso *m* C.O.D., cash on delivery
contrarreforma *f sin pl* HIST Counter-Reformation
contrarrestar *vt* **1.** (*neutralizar*) to counter-

act **2.** DEP to return
contrasentido *m* **1.** (*contradicción*) contradiction **2.** (*disparate*) piece of nonsense
contraseña *f* **1.** (*santo y seña*) password **2.** (*marca*) countermark
contrastar **I.** *vi* to contrast **II.** *vt* **1.** (*oro*) to hallmark **2.** (*peso*) to verify
contraste *m* **1.** *t.* FOTO contrast **2.** MED contrast medium **3.** (*persona*) inspector of weights and measures; (*oficina*) weights and measures office **4.** (*señal*) hallmark
contratación *f* contracting; ~ **bursátil** FIN trading (*on the stock exchange*)
contratar *vt* **1.** (*trabajador*) to hire; (*artista*) to sign up **2.** (*encargar*) to contract
contratiempo *m* setback
contratista *mf* contractor
contrato *m* contract; ~ **de alquiler** lease; ~ **colectivo** wage agreement
contravención *f* JUR contravention; ~ **de contrato** breach of contract
contravenir *irr como venir vt* to contravene
contraventana *f* shutter
contravidriera *f* double window
contrayente **I.** *adj* contracting **II.** *mf* contracting party; (*de un matrimonio*) bridegroom *m*, bride *f*
contribución *f* **1.** (*aportación*) contribution; **aportar una ~ a algo** to make a contribution to sth **2.** (*impuesto*) tax; ~ **municipal** council tax, local tax
contribuir *irr como huir* **I.** *vi* **1.** (*ayudar*) to contribute **2.** (*tributar*) to pay taxes **II.** *vt* (*aportar*) to contribute; (*pagar*) to pay
contribuyente *mf* taxpayer
contrición *f sin pl* contrition
contrincante *mf* opponent
contrito, **-a** *adj* contrite
control *m* control; (*inspección*) inspection; ~ **al azar** spot check; ~ **a distancia** TÉC remote control
controlador *m* INFOR driver; ~ **de la impresora** printer driver
controlador(a) *m(f)* controller; ~ **de vuelo** [*o* **de tráfico aéreo**] air traffic controller
controlar **I.** *vt* (*confirmar*) to check; (*regir*) to control **II.** *vr:* **~se** to control oneself
controversia *f* controversy
controvertido, **-a** *adj* controversial
controvertir *irr como sentir* **I.** *vi* to argue **II.** *vt* to discuss
contumacia *f sin pl* **1.** (*porfía*) obstinacy **2.** JUR contempt (of court)
contumaz *adj* (*obstinado*) obstinate
contundencia *f sin pl* force
contundente *adj* **1.** (*objeto*) contusive **2.** *fig* convincing; **prueba ~** conclusive proof
conturbación *f sin pl* perturbation
conturbar **I.** *vt* (*intranquilizar*) to trouble; (*turbar*) to perturb **II.** *vr:* **~se** (*intranquilizarse*) to be troubled; (*turbarse*) to become perturbed
contusión *f* MED bruise
contusionar *vt* to bruise
convalecencia *f* convalescence
convalecer *irr como crecer vi* ~ **de algo** to convalesce after sth
convaleciente *mf* convalescent
convalidación *f* **1.** (*de un título*) (re)validation **2.** (*confirmación*) confirmation, recognition
convalidar *vt* **1.** (*título*) to (re)validate **2.** (*confirmar*) to confirm, to recognize
convencedor(a) *adj* convincing
convencer <c→z> **I.** *vt* **1.** (*persuadir*) to persuade **2.** (*satisfacer*) **no me convence ese piso** I'm not at all sure about that flat **II.** *vr:* **~se** to be convinced
convencido, **-a** *adj* sure
convencimiento *m sin pl* (*convicción*) conviction; **tengo el ~ de que...** I'm convinced that ...
convención *f* convention
convencional *adj* conventional
conveniencia *f* **1.** (*provecho*) usefulness; **matrimonio de ~** marriage of convenience **2.** (*acuerdo*) agreement **3.** (*oportunidad*) opportunity
conveniente *adj* **1.** (*adecuado*) suitable **2.** (*provechoso*) advisable; (*útil*) useful **3.** (*decente*) fitting
convenio *m* agreement
convenir *irr como venir* **I.** *vi* **1.** (*acordar*) to agree **2.** (*ser oportuno*) to be advisable **3.** (*corresponder*) to suit **II.** *vr* **~se en algo** to agree on sth
convento *m* **1.** (*de monjes*) monastery **2.** (*de monjas*) convent
convergencia *f* convergence
convergente *adj* convergent
converger <g→j> *vi*, **convergir** <g→j> *vi* **1.** (*líneas*) to converge **2.** (*coincidir*) to coincide
conversación *f* conversation
conversador(a) *m(f)* conversationalist
conversar *vi* to talk
conversión *f* conversion
converso, **-a** *m, f* convert; HIST converted Jew or Moor
convertible *adj, m* convertible
convertir *irr como sentir* **I.** *vt* **1.** (*transformar*) ~ **en algo** to turn into sth **2.** *t.* REL to convert **3.** COM, TÉC to convert **II.** *vr:* **~se** **1.** (*transformarse*) **~se en algo** to turn into sth **2.** REL to convert
convexidad *f sin pl* convexity
convexo, **-a** *adj* convex
convicción *f* conviction
convicto, **-a** *adj* convicted
convidado, **-a** *m, f* guest
convidar **I.** *vt* to invite **II.** *vr:* **~se** **1.** (*invitarse*) to invite oneself **2.** (*ofrecerse*) to offer one's services
convincente *adj* convincing
convite *m* **1.** (*invitación*) invitation **2.** (*banquete*) banquet

C

convivencia *f* living together; *fig* co-existence

convivir *vi* to live together; *fig* to coexist

convocar <c→qu> *vt* **1.** (*citar para algo*) to summon; (*reunir*) to call (together); MIL to call up; **me ~on al examen** I was called for the examination **2.** (*concurso*) to announce **3.** (*reunión*) to call

convocatoria *f* **1.** (*citación*) summons **2.** MIL call-up papers *Brit,* draft papers *Am* **3.** (*de un concurso*) official announcement **4.** (*de una conferencia*) notification

convoy *m* **1.** MIL convoy **2.** *inf* (*vinagreras*) cruet

convulsión *f* **1.** MED convulsion **2.** POL upheaval **3.** GEO tremor

convulsionar *vt* **1.** MED to produce convulsions in **2.** *t.* GEO, POL to convulse

conyugal *adj* marital

cónyuge *mf form* spouse; **los ~s** the married couple

coña *f vulg* **1.** (*broma*) joking, piss-taking *Brit;* **tomar algo a ~** to take sth as a joke; **¡ni de ~!** no way! **2.** (*lata*) annoyance; **eres la ~** you're a pain in the neck [*o* ass *Am*] **3.** (*estupidez*) rubbish

coñá *m,* **coñac** *m* <coñacs> cognac

coñazo *m vulg* pain in the arse [*o* ass *Am*]; **¡esto es un ~!** this is a drag!

coñete *adj Chile, Perú, inf* (*tacaño*) stingy, tight *inf*

coño **I.** *interj vulg* damn, bloody hell *Brit* **II.** *m vulg* cunt, fanny *Brit,* pussy *Am;* **vive en el quinto ~** he/she lives in the back of beyond; **¿qué ~ te importa?** why the hell does it matter to you? **III.** *adj Chile, vulg: pejorative term for a Spaniard*

cooperación *f* cooperation

cooperador(a) *m(f)* collaborator

cooperante *mf* (overseas) voluntary worker

cooperar *vi* **1.** (*juntamente*) to cooperate **2.** (*participar*) to collaborate

cooperativa *f* cooperative, co-op

cooperativista *mf* member of a cooperative

cooperativo, -a *adj* cooperative

coordenada *f* MAT coordinate

coordinación *f* coordination

coordinador(a) **I.** *adj* coordinating **II.** *m(f)* coordinator

coordinar *vt* to coordinate

copa *f* **1.** (*vaso*) glass; **una ~ de vino** a glass of wine; **una ~ para el vino** a wine glass; **ir de ~s** to go out for a drink; **tener una ~ de más** to have had one too many **2.** (*de árbol*) top **3.** (*de sujetador*) cup **4.** (*de sombrero*) crown; **sombrero de ~** top hat **5.** DEP cup

copar *vt* **1.** MIL (*rodear*) to surround; (*cortar la retirada*) to cut off **2.** (*acorralar*) to corner; **estar copado** to be stuck; (*negociaciones*) to be bogged down **3.** (*premios*) to win; **~ la banca** (*en un juego*) to sweep the board

copartícipe *mf* (*codueño*) joint owner; (*socio*) partner

copatrocinar *vt* to co-sponsor

cópec *m* <copecks>, **copeca** *f* kopeck

Copenhague *m* Copenhagen

copete *m* **1.** (*de persona*) tuft (of hair) **2.** (*de ave*) crest; (*de caballo*) forelock **3.** (*altanería*) haughtiness **4.** (*linaje*) **ser de alto ~** to be aristocratic

copetín *m* **1.** *Méx* (*copa de licor*) glass of liquor; (*aperitivo*) aperitif **2.** *Arg* (*cóctel*) cocktail

copetón, -ona *adj Col* tipsy; **estar ~** to be slightly drunk

copia *f* **1.** (*de un escrito*) copy; (*al carbón*) carbon copy; **~ en limpio** fair copy; **~ de seguridad** INFOR back-up copy **2.** ARTE (*imagen*) copy; (*réplica*) replica **3.** FOTO print **4.** CINE, TIPO copy

copiadora *f* photocopier, xerox® *machine Am*

copiar *vt* **1.** (*general*) to copy **2.** (*fotocopiar*) to photocopy, to xerox® *Am*

copiloto, -a *m, f* AVIAT copilot; AUTO co-driver

copioso, -a *adj* (*exuberante*) copious; (*abundante*) abundant

copista *mf* copyist

copla *f* **1.** LIT verse **2.** MÚS popular song

copo *m* flake; **~ de nieve** snowflake; **~s de maíz** cornflakes

copón *m* REL ciborium; **del ~** *inf* tremendous

copresidente, -a *m, f* joint president

coprocesador *m* INFOR co-processor

coproducir *vt* CINE to co-produce

coproductor(a) *m(f)* CINE co-producer

copropietario, -a *m, f* co-owner

copucha *f Chile* **1.** (*mentira*) lie **2.** (*vejiga de animal*) bladder

cópula *f* **1.** BIO copulation **2.** LING copula

copulación *f* copulation

copular *vi, vr:* **~se** to copulate

coque *m* MIN coke

coqueta *f* **1.** (*chica, mujer*) flirt **2.** (*mueble*) dressing table

coquetear *vi* to flirt

coquetería *f* coquetry

coqueto, -a *adj* **1.** (*que coquetea*) flirtatious **2.** (*encantador*) charming **3.** (*vanidoso*) vain **4.** (*objeto*) pretty

coracha *f AmL* leather bag

coraje *m* **1.** (*valor*) courage; **tener ~** to be courageous **2.** (*ira*) anger; **dar ~** to make angry

coral **I.** *adj* **1.** (*color*) coral **2.** MÚS choral **II.** *m* **1.** *t.* ZOOL coral **2.** (*composición*) chorale **III.** *f* (*coro*) choir

Corán *m* REL Koran

coraza *f* **1.** MIL cuirass **2.** NÁUT armour-plating *Brit,* armor-plating *Am* **3.** ZOOL shell **4.** *fig* shield

corazón *m* **1.** *t. fig* ANAT heart; **blando de ~** soft-hearted; **duro de ~** hard-hearted; **de todo ~** with all one's heart; **con el ~ en la mano** with one's heart on one's sleeve; **hacer algo de ~** to do sth willingly; **tener un ~ de oro** to have a heart of gold; **no tener ~** to be heartless **2.** BOT core **3.** (*coraje*) **hacer de tripas ~** to

pluck up courage **4.** (*apelativo cariñoso*) ~ (**mío**) darling
corazonada *f* **1.** (*presentimiento*) hunch **2.** (*impulso*) sudden impulse **3.** (*acto*) impulsive act
corbata *f* tie
corbatín *m* bow tie
corbeta *f* NÁUT corvette
Córcega *f* Corsica
corcel *m* LIT steed
corchea *f* quaver
corchete *m* **1.** (*broche*) hook and eye; (*pieza*) hook **2.** TIPO square bracket
corcho **I.** *m* **1.** (*material, tapón*) cork **2.** (*en la pesca*) float **II.** *interj* for heaven's sake
corcovado, **-a** **I.** *adj* hunchbacked **II.** *m, f* hunchback
corcovar *vt* to bend
corcovear *vi* **1.** (*caballo*) to buck **2.** (*gato*) to arch its back
cordaje *m* **1.** (*de un instrumento, de una raqueta*) strings *pl* **2.** (*de una embarcación*) rigging
cordel *m* **1.** (*cuerda delgada*) cord **2.** (*cañada*) cattle track
corderillo *m* (*piel*) lambskin
cordero *m* **1.** (*carne*) mutton, lamb **2.** (*piel*) lambskin
cordero, **-a** *m, f* lamb
cordial **I.** *adj* **1.** (*persona*) cordial **2.** MED tonic **II.** *m* cordial
cordialidad *f* cordiality
cordillera *f* mountain range
cordillerano, **-a** *adj AmL* GEO Andean
córdoba *m Nic* (*moneda*) cordoba
Córdoba *f* Cordova [*o* Cordoba]
cordobés, **-esa** *adj, m, f* Cordovan
cordón *m* **1.** (*cordel*) cord; (*del uniforme*) braid; (*de zapatos*) shoelace; ~ **umbilical** ANAT umbilical cord **2.** ELEC flex *Brit,* cord *Am* **3.** NÁUT strand **4.** MIL cordon **5.** *CSur* (*de la acera*) kerb *Brit,* curb *Am*
cordura *f* **1.** (*razón*) good sense **2.** (*juicio*) wisdom **3.** (*prudencia*) prudence
Corea *f* Korea
coreano, **-a** *adj, m, f* Korean
corear *vt* **1.** (*cantando*) to chant **2.** (*asentir*) to echo **3.** *fig* (*aclamar*) to applaud
coreografía *f* choreography
coreógrafo, **-a** *m, f* choreographer
coriáceo, **-a** *adj* leathery
corintio, **-a** *adj, m, f* Corinthian
corinto **I.** *adj inv* maroon **II.** *m* Corinth
corista[1] *mf* MÚS chorister
corista[2] *f* TEAT chorus girl
cornada *f* **1.** (*golpe*) butt **2.** (*herida*) goring
cornamenta *f* **1.** (*de animales*) horns *pl;* (*de ciervos*) antlers *pl* **2.** (*del marido*) cuckold's horns *pl*
córnea *f* cornea
cornear *vt* **1.** (*golpear*) to butt **2.** (*herir*) to gore
corneja *f* crow
córner *m* DEP corner
corneta *f* **1.** (*instrumento*) cornet; (*en el ejército*) bugle; **hacer algo a toque de** ~ *fig* to do sth on command **2.** (*música*) cornet player **3.** (*de los sordos*) ear trumpet
corneta *m* **1.** (*músico*) cornet player **2.** MIL bugler
cornisa *f* cornice; **la** ~ **cantábrica** the Cantabrian Coast
cornucopia *f* **1.** (*cuerno*) cornucopia **2.** (*espejo*) ornamental mirror
cornudo **I.** *adj* (*marido*) cuckolded **II.** *m* cuckold
cornudo, **-a** *adj* (*animal*) horned
coro *m* ARQUIT, MÚS choir; **a** ~ in unison; **hacer** ~ **a alguien** to back sb up
corola *f* corolla
corolario *m* corollary
corona *f* **1.** *t.* POL (*adorno*) crown **2.** (*de flores*) garland, wreath **3.** (*de eclesiásticos*) tonsure **4.** (*de santos*) halo **5.** (*de los dientes*) crown **6.** ASTR corona
coronación *f* **1.** (*de un rey*) coronation **2.** (*de una acción*) culmination **3.** ARQUIT crown
coronar *vt* to crown; **para ~lo...** *fig* to crown it all ...
coronario, **-a** *adj* coronary
coronel(a) *m(f)* colonel
coronilla *f* crown (of the head); **estar hasta la** ~ **de algo** *inf* to be fed up to the back teeth with sth
corotos *mpl AmL* (*bártulos*) things *pl*
corpiño *m* bodice; *CSur* (*sujetador*) bra
corporación *f* **1.** *t.* COM corporation; ~ **de estudiantes** students' society **2.** HIST guild
corporal *adj* physical
corporativo, **-a** *adj* corporate
corpóreo, **-a** *adj* bodily
corpulencia *f* **1.** (*de alguien*) heftiness **2.** (*de algo*) massiveness
corpulento, **-a** *adj* **1.** (*persona*) hefty **2.** (*cosa*) massive
corpus *m sin pl* LING corpus
Corpus *m sin pl* REL Corpus Christi
corpúsculo *m* corpuscle
corral *m* **1.** (*cercado*) yard; (*redil*) stockyard; (*para la pesca*) fish weir; (*para gallinas*) chicken run **2.** HIST, TEAT open-air theatre **3.** (*lugar sucio*) pigsty **4.** (*para niños*) playpen
corralón *m* **1.** (*patio*) large yard **2.** (*casa de vecindad*) tenement **3.** *CSur* (*maderería*) lumberyard
correa *f* **1.** (*tira*) strap **2.** (*cinturón*) belt **3.** TÉC ~ **de transmisión** driving belt, drive **4.** (*afilador*) strop **5.** (*perro*) lead, leash **6.** (*elasticidad*) elasticity **7.** *inf* (*aguante*) **tener** ~ to be long-suffering
correaje *m t.* TÉC belts *pl*
corrección *f* **1.** TIPO proofreading; (*de ruta*) course correction **2.** (*represión*) rebuke **3.** (*cualidad*) correctness; (*comportamiento*) courtesy, (good) manners *pl*
correccional *m* reformatory

C

correctivo *m* corrective
correcto, **-a** *adj* correct
corrector(**a**) I. *adj* correcting II. *m(f)* TIPO proofreader
corredera *f* 1. TÉC slide; **puerta de** ~ sliding door 2. (*pista*) racetrack 3. (*cucaracha*) cockroach 4. *inf* (*alcahueta*) procuress *form*
corredizo, **-a** *adj* **nudo** ~ slipknot; **puerta corrediza** sliding door
corredor *m* corridor
corredor(**a**) *m(f)* 1. DEP (*a pie*) runner; ~ **de coches** racing driver; ~ **de fondo** long-distance runner 2. COM agent; ~ **de fincas** estate agent *Brit*, real estate broker *Am*
correduría *f* 1. (*oficio*) brokerage 2. (*comisión*) commission
corregible *adj* correctable
corregir *irr como elegir* I. *vt* 1. *t.* TIPO to correct 2. (*reprender*) to rebuke II. *vr:* ~**se** 1. (*en la conducta*) to change one's ways 2. (*al expresarse*) to correct oneself
correlación *f* correlation
correlacionar *vi, vt* to correlate
correlativo, **-a** *adj form* correlative
correligionario, **-a** *m, f* 1. REL coreligionist 2. POL fellow supporter
correntada *f AmL* (*rápido*) rapids *pl*
correo *m* 1. (*persona*) courier 2. (*correspondencia*) post *Brit*, mail *Am;* ~ **aéreo** airmail; ~ **certificado** registered [*o* certified] mail; ~ **electrónico** e-mail; ~ **urgente** special delivery; **a vuelta de** ~ by return post [*o* mail *Am*]; **echar al** ~ to post *Brit*, to mail *Am* 3. (*barco*) mail boat; (*tren*) mail train
Correos *mpl* post office; **ir a** ~ to go to the post office
correoso, **-a** *adj* tough
correr I. *vi* 1. (*caminar*) to run; **echarse a** ~ (*partir*) to start to run; (*escaparse*) to run off; **salir corriendo** to run out 2. (*apresurarse*) to rush; **a todo** ~ at top speed 3. (*conducir*) to go fast 4. (*tiempo*) to pass (quickly); **el mes que corre** this month; **en los tiempos que corremos...** at the present time ... 5. (*líquido*) to flow 6. (*viento*) to blow 7. (*camino*) to run 8. (*moneda*) to be valid 9. (*rumor*) to circulate 10. (*estar a cargo de*) **eso corre de** [*o* **por**] **mi cuenta** (*gastos*) I'm paying for that; (*un asunto*) I'm responsible for that ►**el que no corre, vuela** ≈ opportunity knocks but once *prov* II. *vt* 1. (*un mueble*) to move; (*una cortina*) to draw; (*un cerrojo*) to slide 2. (*un nudo*) to undo 3. (*un lugar*) to travel over; ~ **mundo** to travel widely 4. MIL to overrun 5. (*un caballo*) to race 6. (*la caza*) to chase 7. (*avergonzar*) to embarrass 8. (*tener*) ~ **la misma suerte** to suffer the same fate; **corre prisa** it's urgent ►**dejar** ~ **algo** not to worry about sth; ~**la** to make a night of it III. *vr:* ~**se** 1. (*moverse*) to move 2. (*avergonzarse*) to get embarrassed 3. *vulg* (*eyacular*) to come 4. (*colores*) to run 5. (*excederse*) to go too far
correría *f* 1. MIL raid 2. *pl* (*recorridos*) travels *pl*
correspondencia *f* 1. (*correo*) post *Brit*, mail *Am;* (*de cartas*) correspondence; **curso por** ~ correspondence course; **llevar la** ~ to attend to the correspondence 2. (*equivalente*) correspondence 3. (*conformidad*) agreement 4. (*entre medios de transporte*) connection
corresponder I. *vi* 1. (*equivaler*) to correspond 2. (*armonizar*) to match 3. (*convenir*) to tally 4. (*contestar*) to respond 5. (*pertenecer*) to belong 6. (*incumbir*) to concern; **no me corresponde criticarlo** it's not for me to criticize him 7. (*comunicar*) to communicate; (*medios de transporte*) to connect II. *vr:* ~**se** 1. (*ser equivalente, escribirse*) to correspond; (*armonizar*) to match; (*convenir*) to agree 2. (*comunicarse*) to communicate with each other
correspondiente *adj* 1. (*oportuno*) corresponding 2. (*apropiado*) appropriate 3. (*respectivo*) respective
corresponsabilizar <z→c> *vt* to make jointly responsible
corresponsable *adj* jointly responsible
corresponsal *mf* correspondent
corretaje *m* 1. (*negocio*) brokerage 2. (*comisión*) commission
corretear *vi* 1. (*vagar*) to stroll around 2. (*niños*) to run about
corrida *f* 1. TAUR bullfight 2. (*carrera*) run; **decir algo de** ~ to reel off sth from memory 3. *vulg* (*orgasmo*) orgasm
corrido, **-a** *adj* 1. *t.* ARQUIT (*sin interrupción*) continuous 2. (*cantidad: larga*) large; **un quilo** ~ a good kilo 3. *estar* (*avergonzado*) embarrassed; (*confuso*) confused 4. *ser* (*astuto*) astute
corriente I. *adj* 1. (*fluente*) running 2. (*actual*) current; (*moneda*) valid; **estar al** ~ **de algo** to be aware of sth; **ponerse al** ~ **de algo** to get to know about sth 3. (*ordinario*) ordinary 4. (*normal*) normal II. *f* 1. (*de agua, electricidad*) current; ~ **de aire** draught *Brit*, draft *Am;* ~ **alterna** alternating current; **hace** ~ there's a draught [*o* draft *Am*]; **ir contra la** ~ to swim against the tide; **seguir** [*o* **llevar**] **la** ~ **a alguien** to play along with sb 2. ARTE, LIT (*tendencia*) tendency
corrimiento *m* 1. (*movimiento*) movement 2. GEO slipping; ~ **de tierras** landslide 3. (*vergüenza*) embarrassment; (*timidez*) shyness
corro *m* 1. (*círculo*) circle; **hacer** ~ (*hacer un círculo*) to form a circle; (*hacer sitio*) to make room 2. AGR plot 3. (*juego*) ring-a-ring-a-roses
corroboración *f* corroboration
corroborar *vt* to corroborate
corroer *irr como roer* I. *vt* 1. (*un material*) to corrode 2. (*una persona*) consume; **el remordimiento lo corroe** he's consumed by remorse II. *vr:* ~**se** to corrode
corromper I. *vt* 1. (*descomponer*) to rot; (*un texto*) to corrupt 2. (*sobornar*) to bribe 3. (*enviciar*) to debauch; (*pervertir*) to corrupt

4. *inf* (*enojar*) to annoy **II.** *vi* to smell bad **III.** *vr:* ~**se** **1.** (*descomponerse*) to rot; (*alimentos*) to go bad **2.** (*degenerar*) to become corrupted
corronchoso, -a *adj AmL* (*basto*) coarse
corrosca *f Col* broad-brimmed straw hat
corrosión *f* corrosion
corrosivo, -a *adj* **1.** (*sustancia*) corrosive **2.** (*estilo*) caustic
corrupción *f* **1.** (*descomposición*) decay **2.** (*de la moral, de un texto*) corruption **3.** (*soborno*) bribery, graft **4.** (*seducción*) seduction
corrupto, -a *adj* corrupt
corruptor(a) **I.** *adj* corrupting **II.** *m(f)* corrupter
corsario *m* HIST corsair
corsé *m* corset
corso, -a *adj, m, f* Corsican
cortacésped *m* lawnmower
cortada *f* **1.** (*rebanada*) slice **2.** *AmL* (*herida*) cut
cortado *m* GASTR *coffee with only a little milk*
cortado, -a *adj* **1.** (*leche: mala*) sour; (*cuajada*) curdled **2.** (*persona: tímida*) shy; (*avergonzada*) self-conscious, embarrassed **3.** (*estilo*) abrupt
cortafuegos *m inv* **1.** AGR firebreak, firebreak *Brit,* fire lane *Am* **2.** ARQUIT firewall
cortapisa *f* **1.** (*restricción*) restriction **2.** (*obstáculo*) obstacle; **hablar sin ~s** to talk freely; **poner ~s a alguien** to put obstacles in sb's path **3.** (*gracia*) wit
cortaplumas *m inv* penknife
cortar **I.** *vt* **1.** (*tajar*) to cut; (*por el medio*) to cut through; (*en pedazos*) to cut up; (*quitar*) to cut off; (*un traje*) to cut out; (*un árbol*) to cut down; (*la carne*) to carve; (*leña*) to chop; (*el césped*) to mow; (*pelo*) to trim; INFOR to cut; ~ **al rape** to cut close; **¡corta el rollo!** that's enough! **2.** DEP (*la pelota*) to slice **3.** (*una bebida, una película, cartas*) to cut **4.** (*el agua*) to cut off; (*la corriente*) to switch off **5.** (*una carretera*) to cut **6.** (*la comunicación*) to cut off **II.** *vi* **1.** (*tajar*) cut **2.** (*romper*) **ha cortado con su novio** she has split up with her boyfriend **III.** *vr:* ~**se** **1.** (*persona*) to cut oneself **2.** (*turbarse*) to become embarrassed; **no se cortó ni un pelo** he/she wasn't embarrassed in the least **3.** (*leche*) to turn; (*cuajarse*) to curdle **4.** (*piel*) to get chapped **5.** TEL to get cut off
cortaúñas *m inv* nailclippers *pl*
corte[1] *m* **1.** (*herida, tajo, de un traje*) cut **2.** (*de pelo*) haircut **3.** TÉC section; ~ **transversal** cross section **4.** (*de un libro*) edge **5.** ELEC ~ **de corriente** power cut ▸**hacer a alguien un ~ de mangas** ≈ to give sb the V-sign; **dar** ~ to embarrass; **¡qué ~!** how embarrassing!
corte[2] *f* court
cortedad *f* **1.** (*pequeñez*) smallness; (*escasez*) shortness **2.** (*timidez*) bashfulness **3.** (*de poco entendimiento*) stupidity
cortejar *vt* to court
cortejo *m* **1.** (*halago*) courtship **2.** (*séquito*) retinue **3.** (*desfile*) procession
Cortes *fpl* POL Spanish parliament
cortés *adj* polite
cortesana *f* courtesan
cortesano, -a *adj* **1.** (*palaciego*) court **2.** (*cortés*) courteous
cortesano *m* courtier
cortesía *f* **1.** (*cortesanía*) courtesy; (*gentileza*) politeness; **fórmula de** ~ polite expression **2.** (*en una carta*) concluding formula
corteza *f* **1.** (*de un tronco*) bark; (*del queso*) rind; (*de una fruta*) peel; (*del pan*) crust; **la ~ terrestre** GEO the earth's crust **2.** (*exterioridad*) outward appearance; (*rusticidad*) roughness
cortijo *m* **1.** (*finca*) country estate **2.** (*casa*) country house
cortina *f* curtain; ~ **de humo** MIL smokescreen; **correr/descorrer la** ~ to draw/to draw back the curtain
corto, -a *adj* **1.** (*pequeño*) short; ~ **de oído** hard of hearing; ~ **de vista** short-sighted; **se ha casado de** ~ she got married in a short dress; **a la corta o a la larga...** sooner or later ... **2.** (*breve*) brief **3.** (*de poco entendimiento*) slow **4.** (*tímido*) shy
cortocircuito *m* ELEC short circuit
cortometraje *m* CINE short
coruñés, -esa **I.** *adj* of/from Corunna **II.** *m, f* native/inhabitant of Corunna
corva *f* ANAT back of the knee
corzo, -a *m, f* roe deer
cosa *f* **1.** (*en general*) thing; **la trata como una** ~ he treats her like an object; **eso es ~ tuya/mía** that's your/my affair; **¿sabes una ~?** do you know what?; **no me queda otra ~ que...** I have no alternative but ...; **ser una ~ nunca vista** to be unique; **no valer gran** ~ not to be worth much; **tal como están las ~s...** as things stand ...; **como si tal** ~ as if nothing had happened; **esas son ~s de Inés** that's typical of Inés **2.** *pl* (*pertenencias*) things *pl*
cosaco *m* Cossack ▸**beber como un** ~ to drink like a fish
coscacho *m AmS, inf* (*capón*) rap on the head
coscorrón *m* **1.** (*golpe*) bump on the head **2.** (*contratiempo*) setback
cosecha *f* **1.** AGR harvest **2.** (*conjunto de frutos*) crop; **de ~ propia** home-grown
cosechadora *f* combine harvester
cosechar *vi, vt* to harvest
cosechero, -a *m, f* harvester
coser **I.** *vt* **1.** (*un vestido*) to sew; (*un botón*) to sew on; (*un roto*) to sew up; ~ **a alguien a balazos** to riddle sb with bullets **2.** MED to stitch (up) **II.** *vi* to sew; **esto es ~ y cantar** this is child's play **III.** *vr* ~**se con** [*o* **contra**] **alguien** to snuggle up to sb

cosido *m* sewing
cosmética *f* cosmetics *pl*
cosmético, **-a** *adj* cosmetic
cósmico, **-a** *adj* cosmic
cosmografía *f* ASTR cosmography
cosmología *f* ASTR cosmology
cosmonauta *mf* cosmonaut
cosmonave *f* spaceship
cosmopolita *adj, mf* cosmopolitan
cosmos *m sin pl* cosmos
coso *m* **1.** (*plaza*) festival ground **2.** *reg* (*calle principal*) main street **3.** TAUR ~ **taurino** bullring
cosquillas *fpl* **hacer** ~ to tickle; **tener** ~ to be ticklish; **buscar las** ~ **a alguien** *fig* to try to stir sb up
cosquillear *vt* to tickle
cosquilleo *m* tickling
costa *f* **1.** GEO coast; **Costa Azul** Côte d'Azur; **Costa de Marfil** Ivory Coast **2.** FIN cost; **a toda** ~ at any price **3.** *pl* JUR costs *pl*

> **Costa del Sol** is the name of a coast in southern Spain, running from **Tarifa** (in the west) to **Almería** (in the east). It incorporates the following four **provincias**: **Cádiz**, **Málaga**, **Granada** and **Almería**. The coast of **Málaga** is probably the most well known (especially **Marbella** and **Fuengirola**) and is where Spanish celebrities particularly like taking their holidays.

costado *m* **1.** (*lado*) side; **por los cuatro ~s** through and through **2.** MIL flank; **entrar de** ~ to come in sideways
costal *m* sack; **eso es harina de otro** ~ *fig* that's something quite different
costalearse *vr Chile* **1.** (*recibir un costalazo*) to fall heavily **2.** *fig* (*sufrir una decepción*) to be disappointed
costanera *f* **1.** (*repecho*) steep slope **2.** *pl* (*maderos*) rafters *pl* **3.** *Arg* (*paseo marítimo*) jetty
costar <o→ue> *vi, vt* **1.** (*valer*) to cost; ~ **caro** to be expensive; **esto te va a** ~ **caro** this is going to cost you dear; **cueste lo que cueste** cost what it may **2.** (*resultar difícil*) **me cuesta convencerlo** I find it difficult to persuade him
Costa Rica *f* Costa Rica

> **Costa Rica** lies in Central America and borders the countries Nicaragua and Panama as well as the Pacific and the Caribbean. The capital of **Costa Rica** is **San José**. Spanish is the official language of the country and the monetary unit is the **colón**.

costarriqueño, **-a** *adj, m, f* Costa Rican
coste *m* **1.** (*costo*) cost; ~ **de la vida** cost of living **2.** (*precio*) price
costear **I.** *vt* **1.** (*pagar*) to pay for **2.** NÁUT to sail along the coast of **II.** *vr:* **~se** to cover the expenses
costeño, **-a** **I.** *adj* coastal **II.** *m, f* coastal dweller
costero, **-a** *adj* coastal
costilla *f* **1.** *t.* ANAT, ARQUIT rib **2.** GASTR chop **3.** *irón* (*mujer*) better half
costillar *m* **1.** (*costillas*) ribs *pl* **2.** *inf* (*tórax*) ribcage
costo *m* **1.** (*coste*) cost **2.** *AmL* (*esfuerzo*) effort
costoso, **-a** *adj* **1.** (*en dinero*) expensive **2.** (*en esfuerzo*) difficult
costra *f* **1.** MED scab **2.** (*corteza*) crust
costumbre *f* **1.** (*hábito*) habit; **de** ~ **se levanta bastante tarde** he/she usually gets up rather late; **como de** ~ as usual **2.** (*tradición*) custom **3.** *pl* (*conjunto de tradiciones*) customs *pl*
costura *f* **1.** *t.* MED seam **2.** (*coser*) sewing, needlework **3.** (*confección*) dressmaking; **alta** ~ haute couture
costurera *f* (*modista*) dressmaker; (*zurcidora*) seamstress
costurero *m* sewing box
cota *f* **1.** (*armadura*) doublet **2.** GEO height above sea level
cotejar *vt* to compare
cotejo *m* comparison
cotidiano, **-a** *adj* daily
cotilla *mf inf* gossip
cotillear *vi inf* to gossip
cotilleo *m inf* gossip
cotillo, **-a** *adj inf* gossipy
cotización *f* **1.** (*de acciones*) price **2.** (*pago de una cuota*) contribution
cotizar <z→c> **I.** *vt* **1.** FIN ~ **a algo** to stand at sth **2.** (*estimar*) to value **II.** *vi* (*pagar*) to pay contributions **III.** *vr:* **~se** **1.** FIN ~ **a algo** to sell at sth **2.** (*ser popular*) to be valued
coto *m* **1.** (*vedado*) ~ **de caza** game [*o* hunting] preserve **2.** (*mojón*) boundary stone **3.** (*límite*) limit
cotorra *f* **1.** (*papagayo*) parrot **2.** (*urraca*) magpie **3.** *inf* (*persona habladora*) chatterbox **4.** *pey, inf* (*chivato*) telltale *Brit,* tattletale *Am*
cotorrear *vi inf* to chatter
cototo *m AmL, inf* (*chichón*) bump
COU *m abr de* **Curso de Orientación Universitaria** *one-year pre-university course*
covacha *f* **1.** (*cueva*) small cave **2.** *pey* (*vivienda*) dump
coxis *m inv* ANAT coccyx
coyote *m* coyote
coyuntura *f* **1.** ANAT joint **2.** (*oportunidad*) opportunity **3.** (*situación*) situation, circumstances *pl* **4.** ECON current economic situation
coyuntural *adj* ECON current
coz *f* **1.** (*patada*) kick; **dar coces** to kick **2.** (*culatada*) recoil **3.** (*retroceso del agua*) backward flow **4.** (*grosería*) rude remark
crack *m* **1.** ECON crash **2.** (*droga*) crack
cráneo *m* ANAT skull
crápula[1] *m* rake

crápula² *f* **1.** (*embriaguez*) drunkenness **2.** (*libertinaje*) licentiousness
craso, -a *adj* **1.** (*gordo*) fat **2.** (*burdo*) coarse
cráter *m* crater
creación *f* creation; *fig* the world
creador(a) **I.** *adj* creative **II.** *m(f)* creator; Dios ~ God, the Creator
crear **I.** *vt* **1.** (*hacer*) to create **2.** (*fundar*) to establish **3.** INFOR ~ **archivo** to make a new file **II.** *vr:* ~**se** to be created
creatividad *f* creativity
creativo, -a *adj* creative
crecer *irr* **I.** *vi* **1.** (*aumentar*) to grow, to increase **2.** (*relativo a la luna*) to wax **3.** (*relativo al agua*) to rise **II.** *vr:* ~**se** (*persona*) to grow more confident
creces *fpl* **1.** (*aumento*) increase **2.** (*exceso*) **con** ~ fully
crecida *f* **1.** (*riada*) flood **2.** (*crecimiento*) (sudden) growth
creciente *adj* growing, increasing
crecimiento *m* **1.** *t.* ECON growth **2.** (*moneda*) appreciation
credencial **I.** *adj* accrediting **II.** *fpl* credentials
credibilidad *f* credibility
crédito *m* **1.** FIN (*préstamo*) credit; ~ **puente** bridging loan; **dar a** ~ to loan; **pedir un** ~ to ask for a loan **2.** (*fama*) reputation **3.** (*confianza*) **dar** ~ **a algo/alguien** to believe in sth/sb
credo *m* **1.** (*creencias*) beliefs *pl* **2.** (*oración, dogma*) creed
credulidad *f* credulity
crédulo, -a *adj* credulous
creencia *f* belief; REL faith
creer *irr como leer* **I.** *vi* ~ **en Dios/alguien** to believe in God/sb **II.** *vt* **1.** (*dar por cierto*) to believe; **¡quién iba a ~lo!** who would have believed it!; **no te creo** I don't believe you; **hacer ~ algo a alguien** to make sb believe sth **2.** (*pensar*) **¡ya lo creo!** I should think so! **III.** *vr:* ~**se** **1.** (*tener por probable*) to believe **2.** (*considerarse*) to believe oneself to be; **¡qué te has creído!** what do you take me for?
creíble *adj* credible, believable
creído, -a *adj* **1.** *ser inf* (*vanidoso*) conceited **2.** *estar* (*seguro*) sure
crema **I.** *adj* cream **II.** *f* **1.** cream; ~ **antiarrugas** anti-wrinkle cream **2.** (*natillas, pasta*) custard; **la ~ y la nata** *fig* the crème de la crème **3.** LING diaeresis *Brit,* dieresis *Am*
cremación *f* **1.** (*incineración*) cremation **2.** (*combustión de desechos*) incineration
cremallera *f* **1.** (*cierre*) zip fastener *Brit,* zipper *Am* **2.** TÉC rack; **tren de** ~ rack [*o* cog] railway
crematístico, -a *adj* financial
crematorio *m* crematorium
crematorio, -a *adj* **horno** ~ crematorium
cremosidad *f* creaminess
cremoso, -a *adj* creamy
crencha *f* parting *Brit*
crep¹ *m* (*tela*) crepe
crep² *f* GASTR crêpe
crepé *m* **1.** (*suela, tejido*) crepe **2.** (*postizo*) hairpiece
crepería *f* creperie
crepitación *f* crackling
crepitar *vi* to crackle
crepuscular *adj* twilight
crepúsculo *m* twilight, dusk; ~ **matutino** dawn
cresa *f* **1.** (*huevos*) eggs *pl* (*of queen bee*) **2.** (*gusano*) maggot
creso *m* Croesus
crespo, -a *adj* **1.** (*rizado*) curly **2.** (*irritado*) irritated **3.** (*estilo*) involved
crespón *m* (*tela*) crepe
cresta *f* **1.** (*del gallo*) (cocks)comb **2.** (*de una ola, de una montaña*) crest **3.** (*plumas*) crest **4.** (*cabello*) tuft
creta *f* chalk
Creta *f* Crete
cretense *adj, mf* Cretan
cretino, -a *m, f t. fig* cretin
cretona *f* cretonne
creyente *mf* believer
cría *f* **1.** (*el criar*) rearing, raising **2.** (*cachorro*) baby animal **3.** (*camada*) litter **4.** (*pájaro*) brood
criadero *m* **1.** (*plantel*) nursery **2.** (*vivero*) breeding ground **3.** MIN vein
criadero, -a *adj* fertile
criado, -a *m, f* servant
criador *m* (*Dios*) **el Criador** the Creator
criador(a) *m(f)* **1.** (*de animales*) breeder **2.** (*de vinos*) wine grower
criandera *f AmL* wet nurse
crianza *f* **1.** (*lactancia*) lactation **2.** (*educación*) upbringing **3.** (*vinos*) maturing
criar <*1. pres:* crío> **I.** *vt* **1.** (*alimentar*) to feed; (*mamíferos*) to suckle **2.** (*reproducir y cuidar*) to breed **3.** (*ser propicio*) to produce **4.** (*educar*) to bring up **5.** (*referente al vino*) to mature **II.** *vi* (*animal*) to have young **III.** *vr:* ~**se** to grow up
criatura *f* **1.** *t. fig* creature **2.** (*niño*) child **3.** (*feto*) foetus
criba *f* **1.** (*tamiz*) sieve **2.** *fig* (*proceso*) selection process
cribar *vt* to sieve
cric *m* jack
Crimea *f* Crimea
crimen *m* crime
criminal *adj, mf* criminal
criminalidad *f* criminality
criminalista *mf* criminal lawyer
criminología *f* criminology
crin *f* **1.** (*cerda*) mane **2.** (*filamento*) esparto grass
crío, -a *m, f inf* kid
criollo, -a *adj, m, f* Creole
cripta *f* crypt
críptico, -a *adj* cryptic
criptografía *f* cryptography

criptograma *m* cryptogram
criptón *m* krypton
crisálida *f* chrysalis
crisantemo *m* chrysanthemum, chrysanth
crisis *f inv* crisis; ~ **nerviosa** nervous breakdown
crisma[1] *m* REL chrism
crisma[2] *f inf* (*cabeza*) head
crisol *m* **1.** (*recipiente*) crucible; *fig* melting pot **2.** (*prueba*) test
crispación *f* **1.** (*contracción*) contraction **2.** (*irritación*) tension
crispar **I.** *vt* **1.** (*contraer*) to contract **2.** (*exasperar*) to exasperate **II.** *vr:* ~**se** **1.** (*contraerse*) to contract **2.** (*exasperarse*) to become exasperated
cristal *m* **1.** (*cuerpo*) crystal **2.** (*vidrio*) glass **3.** *elev* (*agua*) water **4.** (*ventana*) window
cristalera *f* **1.** (*aparador*) glass cabinet **2.** (*puertas*) French windows *pl*
cristalería *f* **1.** (*empresa*) glassworks *pl* **2.** (*objetos*) glassware
cristalero, **-a** *m, f* **1.** (*colocador*) glazier **2.** (*limpiador*) window cleaner
cristalino *m* MED crystalline lens
cristalino, **-a** *adj* **1.** (*de cristal*) crystalline **2.** (*transparente*) crystal-clear
cristalizar <z→c> **I.** *vi, vr:* ~**se** to crystallize **II.** *vt* to crystallize
cristiandad *f* Christendom
cristianismo *m* Christianity
cristianizar <z→c> *vt* to Christianize
cristiano *m inf* **1.** (*persona*) person **2.** (*castellano*) Spanish; **hablar en** ~ *fig* to speak plainly
cristiano, **-a** *adj, m, f* Christian
cristo *m* **1.** (*crucifijo*) crucifix **2.** *inf* (*persona*) **todo** ~ everyone
Cristo *m* Christ ►**donde** ~ **perdió el gorro** *inf* in the middle of nowhere; **donde** ~ **dio las tres voces** *inf* in the back of beyond
criterio *m* **1.** (*norma*) criterion **2.** (*discernimiento*) judgement **3.** (*opinión*) opinion
crítica *f* **1.** (*juicio*) criticism **2.** (*prensa*) review, write-up; **tener buenas** ~**s** to get good reviews; (*análisis*) critique
criticable *adj* reprehensible *form*
criticar <c→qu> **I.** *vt* to criticize **II.** *vi* to gossip
crítico, **-a** **I.** *adj* critical **II.** *m, f* critic
criticón, **-ona** *m, f* faultfinder
Croacia *f* Croatia
croar *vi* (*rana*) to croak
croata *adj, mf* Croat(ian)
croché *m* **1.** (*ganchillo*) crochet; **hacer** ~ to crochet **2.** DEP hook
crol *m* crawl
cromar *vt* to chromium-plate
cromo *m* **1.** QUÍM chromium **2.** (*estampa*) (picture) card; ~**s de béisbol** baseball cards; **estar** [*o* **ir**] **hecho un** ~ to look wonderful *iron*
cromosfera *f* chromosphere
cromosoma *m* chromosome
crónica *f* **1.** HIST chronicle **2.** (*prensa*) (feature) article; (*reportaje*) report
crónico, **-a** *adj t.* MED chronic
cronista *mf* **1.** HIST chronicler **2.** (*periodista*) journalist
crono *m* DEP **1.** (*tiempo*) time; ~ **personal** personal best time **2.** (*cronómetro*) stopwatch
cronología *f* chronology, sequence of events
cronológico, **-a** *adj* chronological
cronometrador(a) *m(f)* DEP timekeeper
cronometraje *m* DEP timekeeping
cronometrar *vt* to time
cronómetro *m* chronometer; DEP stopwatch
croquet *m* croquet
croqueta *f* ≈ croquette
croquis *m inv* sketch, outline
cross *m inv* DEP cross-country running
crótalo *m* **1.** ZOOL rattlesnake **2.** (*instrumento*) castanet
cruasán *m* croissant
cruce *m* **1.** (*acción*) crossing **2.** (*intersección*) crossing, intersection **3.** (*mezcla*) crossing, cross; ~ **de peatones** pedestrian crossing **4.** (*interferencia*) interference **5.** BIO cross
cruceiro *m* FIN cruzeiro
crucero *m* **1.** ARQUIT transept **2.** (*cruciferario*) crossbearer **3.** NÁUT (*buque*) cruiser **4.** (*viaje*) cruise
cruceta *f* **1.** NÁUT crosstree **2.** (*en la labor*) cross-stitch
crucial *adj* **1.** (*en forma de cruz*) cross-shaped **2.** (*decisivo*) crucial
crucificado *m* **el Crucificado** Christ
crucificar <c→qu> *vt* to crucify
crucifijo *m* crucifix
crucifixión *f* crucifixion
cruciforme *adj* cross-shaped
crucigrama *m* crossword (puzzle)
crudelísimo, **-a** *adj superl irr de* **cruel**
crudeza *f* **1.** (*rigor*) harshness **2.** (*rudeza*) coarseness **3.** (*crueldad*) cruelty
crudo *m* crude oil
crudo, **-a** *adj* **1.** (*sin cocer, natural*) raw **2.** (*aplicado al tiempo*) harsh **3.** (*blanco-amarillento*) yellowish-white **4.** (*despiadado*) cruel **5.** (*de difícil digestión*) difficult to digest
cruel *adj* <crudelísimo> ~ **con alguien** cruel to sb
crueldad *f* ~ **con alguien** cruelty to sb
cruento, **-a** *adj* bloody
crujía *f* ARQUIT bay; (*iglesia*) *passage between choir and altar*
crujido *m* **1.** (*de papel*) rustling **2.** (*de dientes*) grinding **3.** (*de madera*) creaking
crujiente *adj* **1.** (*dientes*) grinding **2.** (*pan tostado*) crunchy
crujir *vi* **1.** (*papel, hojas*) to rustle **2.** (*dientes*) to grind **3.** (*madera*) creak **4.** (*huesos*) crack
crup *m* MED croup
crupier *m* croupier
crustáceo *m* crustacean
cruz *f* **1.** (*aspa, crucifijo*) cross; ~ **gamada** swastika; **Cruz Roja** Red Cross **2.** (*de una*

moneda) reverse; **¿cara o ~?** heads or tails? **3.** (*de un árbol*) *top of trunk where branches begin* **4.** (*de un animal*) withers *pl* **5.** ASTR (Southern) Cross **6.** (*suplicio*) burden; **llevar una ~** to have a cross to bear
cruzada *f* crusade
cruzado *m* crusader
cruzado, -a *adj* **1.** BIO **animal ~** crossbred animal **2.** (*ropa*) **chaqueta cruzada** double-breasted jacket
cruzamiento *m* BIO crossing
cruzar <z→c> **I.** *vt* **1.** (*atravesar*) to cross; **~ los brazos/las piernas** to cross one's arms/legs; **~ algo con una raya** to cross out sth **2.** BIO to cross **3.** (*condecorar*) to decorate **II.** *vi* to cross **III.** *vr:* **~se 1.** (*caminos*) to cross **2.** (*encontrarse*) to meet; **~se con alguien** to pass sb **3.** *t.* MAT to intersect
CTNE *f abr de* **Compañía Telefónica Nacional de España** *former name of the Spanish national telephone company*
cu *f* (name of the letter) q
cuácara *f* **1.** *Col, Ven* (*levita*) frock coat **2.** *Chile* (*camisa ordinaria*) workman's blouse; (*chaqueta*) jacket
cuaderna *f* NÁUT frame (rib)
cuaderno *m* notebook; **~ de bitácora** NÁUT logbook
cuadra *f* **1.** (*de caballos*) stable **2.** (*conjunto de caballos*) stables *pl* **3.** (*lugar sucio*) pigsty **4.** (*sala*) hall; (*para dormir*) large room **5.** *AmL* (*manzana de casas*) block (of houses)
cuadrada *f* MÚS breve
cuadradillo *m* **1.** (*regla*) square ruler **2.** (*pieza de tela*) gusset
cuadrado *m* **1.** *t.* ASTR square; **elevar al ~** to square **2.** (*regla*) ruler **3.** (*trozo de tela*) gusset **4.** (*barra*) die
cuadrado, -a *adj* **1.** (*forma*) square; **tener la cabeza cuadrada** to be pigheaded **2.** (*macizo*) solid; **tenerlos ~s** *inf* to have balls *vulg* **3.** (*corpulento*) hefty
cuadragenario, -a I. *adj* forty-year-old **II.** *m, f* forty-year-old (person)
cuadragésimo, -a *adj, m, f* fortieth; *v.t.* **octavo**
cuadrangular *adj* quadrangular
cuadrángulo *m* quadrangle
cuadrante *m* **1.** ASTR, MAT quadrant **2.** (*reloj de sol*) sundial **3.** RADIO dial
cuadrar I. *vi* **1.** (*ajustarse, convenir*) to fit in **2.** (*coincidir*) to tally **II.** *vt t.* MAT to square **III.** *vr:* **~se 1.** MIL to stand to attention **2.** (*pararse un caballo*) to stand stock-still **3.** *inf* (*plantarse*) to dig one's heels in
cuadratura *f* ASTR, MAT quadrature
cuadrícula *f* grid squares *pl;* **papel de ~** squared [*o* gridded] paper
cuadricular I. *adj* squared **II.** *vt* to divide into squares
cuadriga *f* four-in-hand; (*en la antigua Roma*) quadriga
cuadrilátero *m* **1.** (*polígono*) quadrilateral **2.** DEP ring
cuadrilla *f* **1.** (*brigada*) squad **2.** (*de amigos*) group **3.** (*de trabajo*) work team **4.** *pey* (*de maleantes*) gang
cuadro *m* **1.** (*cuadrado*) square; **a ~s** plaid, chequered *Brit,* check(er)ed *Am* **2.** (*pintura*) painting **3.** (*marco*) frame **4.** (*bancal*) flowerbed **5.** (*escena*) scene **6.** (*descripción*) description **7.** (*gráfico*) **~ sinóptico** synoptic chart **8.** MIL officers *pl* **9.** TÉC panel
cuadrúpedo *m* quadruped
cuádruple I. *adj* quadruple, four-fold **II.** *m* quadruple
cuadruplicar <c→qu> *vt, vr:* **~se** to quadruple
cuádruplo *m* quadruple
cuádruplo, -a *adj* quadruple
cuajada *f* curd
cuajar I. *vi* **1.** (*espesarse*) to thicken; (*la nieve*) to lie **2.** *inf* (*realizarse*) to come off **II.** *vt* **1.** (*leche*) to curdle **2.** (*cubrir*) to cover **III.** *vr:* **~se 1.** (*coagularse*) to coagulate **2.** (*llenarse*) **~se de algo** to fill (up) with sth **3.** (*leche*) to curdle **IV.** *m* fourth stomach
cuajo *m* **1.** (*sustancia*) rennet **2.** *fig* phlegm ▶ **de ~** completely
cual *pron rel* **1.** (*relativo explicativo*) **el/la ~** (*persona*) who, whom; (*cosa*) which; **lo ~** which; **los/las ~es** (*personas*) who, whom; (*cosas*) which; **cada ~** everyone **2.** (*relativo correlativo*) **hazlo tal ~ te lo digo** do it just as I tell you (to); **sea ~ sea su intención** whatever his/her intention may be
cuál I. *pron interrog* which (one); **¿~ es el tuyo?** which is yours? **II.** *pron indef* **1.** (*distributivo*) **~ más ~ menos** some more, some less **2.** (*ponderativo*) **tengo tres hermanas a ~ más bella** I've three sisters, each more beautiful than the other
cualesquier(a) *pron indef pl de* **cualquiera**
cualidad *f* quality
cualificación *f* **1.** (*calificación*) qualification **2.** (*clasificación*) rating
cualificar <c→qu> *vt* to qualify
cualitativo, -a *adj* qualitative
cualquiera I. *pron indef* (*delante de un substantivo: cualquier*) any; **en un lugar ~** anywhere; **a cualquier hora** at any time; **cualquier cosa** anything; **de cualquier modo** whichever way; (*de todas maneras*) anyway; **¡~ lo puede hacer!** anybody can do it! **II.** *mf* **ser una ~** *pey* to be a whore
cuan *adv* how; **cayó ~ largo era** he/she fell his/her whole length
cuando *conj* **1.** (*presente, pasado*) when; **de ~ en ~** from time to time **2.** (*futuro; +subj*) when; **~ quieras** when(ever) you want **3.** (*relativo*) **el lunes es ~ no trabajo** I don't work on Mondays **4.** (*condicional*) if; **~ más** [*o* **mucho**] at (the) most; **~ menos** at least **5.** (*aunque*) **aun ~** even if
cuándo *adv* when
cuantía *f* **1.** (*suma*) amount **2.** (*importancia*)

C

importance
cuántica *f* FÍS quantum theory
cuantificación *f* quantification
cuantificar <c→qu> *vt* **1.** (*expresar numéricamente*) to quantify **2.** FÍS to quantize
cuantioso, **-a** *adj* substantial
cuantitativo, **-a** *adj* quantitative
cuanto **I.** *adv* ~ **antes** as soon as possible; ~ **antes mejor** the sooner the better; ~ **más que...** all the more that ...; ~ **más lo pienso, menos me gusta** the more I think about it, the less I like it **II.** *prep* (*por lo que se refiere a*) **en** ~ **a** as regards **III.** *conj* **1.** (*temporal*) **en** ~ (**que**) as soon as **2.** (*puesto que*) **por** ~ **que** inasmuch as **IV.** *m* FÍS quantum
cuanto, **-a** **I.** *pron rel* **1.** (*neutro*) all that (which); **tanto...~** as much ... as; **dije** (**todo**) ~ **sé** I said all that I know **2.** *pl* all those that; **la más hermosa de cuantas conozco** the most beautiful of those I know **II.** *pron indef* **unos ~s/unas cuantas** some, several
cuánto *adv* **1.** (*interrogativo*) how much **2.** (*exclamativo*) how; **¡~ llueve!** how hard it's raining!
cuánto, **-a** **I.** *adj* **¿~ vino?** how much wine?; **¿~s libros?** how many books?; **¿~ tiempo?** how long?; **¿cuántas veces?** how often? **II.** *pron interrog* how much [*o* many]; **¿~ hay de aquí a Veracruz?** how far is it from here to Veracruz?
cuarenta **I.** *adj inv* forty **II.** *m* forty; *v.t.* **ochenta** ▸cantar **las ~ a alguien** to give sb a piece of one's mind
cuarentavo *m* fortieth; *v.t.* **octavo**
cuarentavo, **-a** *adj* fortieth; *v.t.* **octavo**
cuarentena *f* **1.** (*aislamiento*) quarantine **2.** (*cuarenta unidades*) **una ~ de veces** about forty times
cuarentón, **-ona** **I.** *adj* fortyish **II.** *m, f* forty-year-old
cuaresma *f* REL Lent
cuarta *f* **1.** (*cuarta parte*) quarter **2.** (*medida*) span **3.** MÚS fourth
cuartear **I.** *vt* **1.** (*dividir en cuartos*) to quarter **2.** (*zigzaguear*) to zigzag up [*o* down] **II.** *vr:* **~se** to crack
cuartel *m* **1.** (*cuarta parte*) quarter **2.** MIL (*acuartelamiento*) encampment; ~ **general** headquarters *pl* **3.** MIL (*edificio*) barracks *pl* **4.** (*perdón*) mercy
cuartelero, **-a** *adj* barracks
cuartelillo *m* (*de policía*) police station
cuarteo *m* **1.** (*división*) division **2.** (*grieta*) crack
cuarteto *m* MÚS quartet
cuartilla *f* (*hoja*) sheet of paper
cuarto *m* **1.** (*habitación*) room; ~ **de aseo** lavatory; ~ **de baño** bathroom; ~ **de estar** living room; ~ **trastero** lumber room **2.** *(pl), inf* (*dinero*) money, dough *inf;* **tener cuatro ~s** to have to watch every penny **3.** (*de un caballo*) **~s delanteros/traseros** forequarters *pl* hindquarters *pl*
cuarto, **-a** **I.** *adj* fourth **II.** *m, f* quarter; ~ **creciente/menguante** first/last quarter; ~ **de final** DEP quarterfinal; **un ~ de hora** a quarter of an hour; **es la una y/menos ~** it's a quarter past/to one; *v.t.* **octavo**
cuartucho *m pey* poky room
cuarzo *m* quartz
cuate, **-a** *m, f* **1.** *Méx* (*gemelo*) twin **2.** *Guat, Méx* (*amigo*) mate *Brit,* buddy
cuaternario *m* GEO **el ~** the Quaternary (period)
cuaternario, **-a** *adj* quaternary
cuatrero, **-a** *m, f* rustler
cuatrienal *adj* **1.** (*repetición*) four-yearly **2.** (*duración*) four-year
cuatrienio *m* four-year period
cuatrillizo, **-a** *m, f* quadruplet
cuatrimestre *m* four-month period
cuatrimotor *adj* four-engined
cuatro *adj inv, m* four; *v.t.* **ocho**
cuatrocientos, **-as** *adj* four hundred; *v.t.* **ochocientos**
cuatrojos *mf inv, inf* four-eyes
cuba *f* (*tonel*) barrel; **estar como una ~** *inf* (*borracho*) to be plastered
Cuba *f* Cuba

> **Cuba** (official title: **República de Cuba**) is the largest of the West Indian Islands. The capital and also the largest city in Cuba is **La Habana**. The official language of the country is Spanish and the monetary unit is the **peso cubano**.

cubano, **-a** *adj, m, f* Cuban
cubata *f* GASTR rum and coke
cubertería *f* cutlery, silverware
cubeta *f* **1.** (*cubo*) pail **2.** FOTO tray **3.** (*de un termómetro*) bulb
cubicar <c→qu> *vt* MAT **1.** (*multiplicar*) to cube **2.** (*medir el volumen*) to measure the volume of
cúbico, **-a** *adj t.* MAT cubic
cubículo *m* cubicle
cubierta *f* **1.** (*cobertura*) cover; (*de un libro*) jacket; (*de una rueda*) tyre *Brit,* tire *Am;* ~ **de cama** bedspread **2.** NÁUT deck **3.** ARQUIT roof **4.** (*pretexto*) pretext
cubierto *m* **1.** *t.* GASTR (*servicio de mesa*) place setting; **poner un ~** to set a place **2.** (*cubertería*) set of cutlery; **los ~s** the cutlery, the silverware *Am* **3.** (*techumbre*) **ponerse a ~** to take cover
cubierto, **-a** **I.** *pp de* **cubrir** **II.** *adj* **1.** (*cielo*) overcast **2.** FIN **cheque no ~** bounced cheque
cubil *m* lair
cubilete *m* **1.** (*en juegos*) cup **2.** (*molde*) mould *Brit,* mold *Am* **3.** GASTR pie
cubismo *m* ARTE cubism
cubitera *f* ice tray
cubito *m* ~ **de hielo** ice cube
cúbito *m* ANAT ulna
cubo *m* **1.** (*recipiente*) bucket; ~ **de basura**

dustbin *Brit,* trashcan *Am* **2.** (*de una rueda*) hub **3.** *t.* MAT cube

cubrecama *m* bedspread

cubrimiento *m* (*de un acontecimiento*) coverage

cubrir *irr como abrir* **I.** *vt* **1.** (*tapar*) to cover **2.** *t. fig* DEP, MIL, ZOOL, PREN to cover **3.** (*vacante*) to fill **4.** (*deuda*) to repay **II.** *vr:* **~se 1.** (*taparse*) to cover oneself **2.** (*ponerse el sombrero*) to put on one's hat **3.** (*el cielo*) to become overcast **4.** MIL to take cover **5.** (*protegerse*) to cover oneself

cuca *f* **1.** (*chufa*) tiger nut **2.** (*oruga*) caterpillar **3.** *inf* (*jugadora*) compulsive gambler **4.** *vulg* (*pene*) prick **5.** *pl, inf* (*dinero*) dough

cucar <c→qu> *vt* (*guiñar*) to wink

cucaracha *f* cockroach

cuchara *f* spoon; ~ **de palo** wooden spoon; ~ **sopera** soup spoon; **meter** (**su**) ~ (*entrometerse*) to meddle

cucharada *f* (*porción*) spoonful; **una ~ grande/pequeña** a tablespoonful/teaspoonful; **a ~s** in spoonfuls; **meter su ~** *fig* to meddle

cucharadita *f* (*cuchara*) teaspoon; (*medida*) teaspoonful

cucharilla *f* teaspoon

cucharón *m* ladle

cuchichear *vi* to whisper

cuchicheo *m* whispering

cuchilla *f* **1.** (*de afeitar*) razor blade **2.** (*de cocina*) kitchen knife; (*de carnicero*) cleaver **3.** (*hoja*) blade

cuchillada *f* **1.** (*navajazo*) slash; (*corte*) cut **2.** (*herida*) stab wound; **andar a ~s con alguien** *fig* to be bitterly hostile to sb

cuchillería *f* knife shop, cutler's *Brit*

cuchillero *m* **1.** (*persona*) cutler **2.** (*abrazadera*) bracket

cuchillo *m* **1.** (*para cortar*) knife; ~ **de bolsillo** pocket knife; ~ **de cocina** kitchen knife; ~ **de monte** hunting knife; **pasar a ~** to put to the sword **2.** (*de la ropa*) gore **3.** ARQUIT support

cuchitril *m* **1.** (*pocilga*) pigsty **2.** *fig* (*habitación*) hole

cuchuco *m Col* GASTR pork and barley soup

cuchufleta *f* joke

cuclillas *fpl* **estar en ~** to be squatting

cuclillo *m* cuckoo

cuco *m* cuckoo

cuco, -a *adj* **1.** (*astuto*) crafty **2.** (*bonito*) pretty

cucufato, -a **I.** *adj Bol, Perú* sanctimonious **II.** *m, f Bol, Perú* hypocrite

cucurucho *m* **1.** (*de papel*) cone **2.** (*de helado*) ice-cream cone **3.** (*gorro cónico*) pointed hat

cuello *m* **1.** ANAT neck; ~ **uterino** cervix; **alargar el ~** to crane one's neck; **estar con el agua al ~** to be in a tight spot **2.** (*de una prenda*) collar; ~ **alto** polo neck *Brit,* turtleneck *Am;* ~ **de pico** V-neck; ~ **redondo** crew neck **3.** (*de un recipiente*) neck; ~ **de botella** *fig* bottleneck

cuenca *f* **1.** GEO basin; ~ **del río** river basin **2.** (*región*) valley **3.** (*recipiente*) wooden bowl **4.** (*de los ojos*) socket

cuenco *m* **1.** (*vasija*) bowl **2.** (*concavidad*) hollow

cuenta *f* **1.** (*cálculo*) counting; (*calculación final*) calculation; ~ **atrás** countdown; **~s atrasadas** outstanding debts *pl;* **rendición de ~s** balance; **Tribunal de Cuentas** National Audit Office; **por ~ del Estado** at the public expense; **pagar la ~** to pay the bill; **trabajar por ~ propia** to be self-employed; **establecerse por su ~** to set up one's own business; **a ~ de alguien** on sb's account; **echar ~s** to reflect; **dar ~ de algo** to report on sth; **ajustar las ~s a alguien** to get even with sb; **ajuste de ~s** act of revenge; **caer en la ~** to catch on; **hablar más de la ~** to talk too much; **a fin de ~s** after all; **en resumidas ~s** in short; **perder la ~** to lose count **2.** (*en el banco*) account; ~ **corriente** [*o* **de giros**] current account; ~ **de crédito** loan account; **abonar en ~** to credit; **abrir una ~** to open an account; **girar a una ~** to transfer to an account **3.** (*consideración*) **tener en ~** to bear in mind; **tomar en ~** to take into consideration; **darse ~ de algo** to realize sth **4.** (*de un collar*) bead ▶**hacer la ~ de la <u>vieja</u>** to count on one's fingers

cuentagotas *m inv* dropper; **con** [*o* **a**] ~ *fig* bit by bit

cuentakilómetros *m inv* (*de velocidad*) speedometer, odometer *Am*

cuentarrevoluciones *m inv* tachometer

cuentista *mf* **1.** (*chismoso*) gossip **2.** (*fanfarrón*) braggart **3.** (*narrador*) storyteller; LIT short-story writer

cuento *m* **1.** LIT (*historieta*) story; ~ **chino** *inf* tall story; ~ **de hadas** fairy tale [*o* story]; ~ **de nunca acabar** never-ending story; **tener mucho ~** *inf* (*presumir*) to boast a lot; (*exagerar*) to exaggerate everything; **dejarse de ~s** to stop beating about the bush **2.** ARQUIT, TÉC brace ▶**eso es como el ~ de la <u>lechera</u>** don't count your chickens before they're hatched; **<u>venir</u> a ~** to matter; **no <u>venir</u> a ~** to be beside the point

cuerda *f* **1.** (*gruesa*) rope; (*delgada*) string; ~ **floja** tightrope; ~ **métrica** tape measure; **andar en la ~ floja** *fig* to be in an unstable position; **ser de la misma ~** *fig* to be cast in the same mould [*o* mold *Am*]; **bajo ~** secretly **2.** (*del reloj*) spring; **dar ~ al reloj** to wind up one's watch; **dar ~ a alguien** to encourage sb **3.** ANAT **~s vocales** vocal chords **4.** (*de instrumentos*) string; ~ **metálica** steel string; ~ **de tripa** gut string; **juego de ~s** set of strings; **apretar las ~s** *fig* to tighten up

cuerdo, -a *adj* **1.** (*de juicio sano*) **estar ~** to be sane **2.** (*razonable*) sensible

cueriza *f AmL* (*zurra*) beating

cuerno *m* **1.** MÚS, ZOOL horn; ~ **de la abun-**

C

dancia horn of plenty, cornucopia; **poner a alguien los ~s** *inf* to be unfaithful to sb **2.** *inf* (*exclamativo*) **¡y un ~!** my foot!; **irse al ~** to be ruined; (*plan*) to fall through; **¡que se vaya al ~!** he/she can go to hell!

cuero *m* **1.** (*piel*) leather; **~ cabelludo** scalp; **~ curtido** tanned hide; **estar en ~s** *inf* to be stark naked; **dejar a alguien en ~s** *inf* to fleece sb **2.** (*recipiente*) wineskin

cuerpear *vi Arg, Urug, inf* (*esquivar*) to dodge

cuerpo *m* **1.** (*del hombre o del animal*) body; (*sólo el tronco*) trunk; (*de una mujer*) figure; (*cadáver*) corpse, cadaver; **a ~ descubierto** unarmed; **una foto de ~ entero** a full-length photo(graph); **luchar ~ a ~** to fight hand-to-hand; **dar con el ~ en tierra** to fall down; **tomar ~** to take shape; **estar de ~ presente** to lie in state; **hacer de(l) ~** to relieve oneself; **haz lo que te pida el ~** do what you feel like doing **2.** *t.* FÍS (*objeto*) body **3.** (*corporación, colección*) body; **~ de bomberos** fire brigade *Brit*, fire department *Am*; **~ diplomático** diplomatic corps; **~ docente** teaching staff **4.** (*grosor*) thickness; **~ de letra** TIPO point size; **tener poco ~** to be thin **5.** (*parte principal*) main body; (*de iglesia*) nave ▶**vivir a ~ de rey** to live like a king

cuervo *m* raven, crow; **cría ~s y te sacarán los ojos** *prov* a dog bites the hand that feeds it *prov*

cuesta *f* slope; **~ abajo/arriba** downhill/uphill; **un camino en ~** an uphill road; **llevar a alguien/algo a ~s** to carry sb/sth on one's back; **la ~ de enero** January (*when, following Christmas spending, people are often short of money*)

cuestación *f* charity collection

cuestión *f* question, matter; **~ de confianza** POL vote of confidence; **~ de gustos** question of taste; **~ secundaria** minor matter; **eso es otra ~** that's another matter; **la ~ es pasarlo bien** the main thing is to enjoy oneself

cuestionable *adj* questionable

cuestionar *vt* to question

cuestionario *m* questionnaire

cuete *m Méx* **1.** (*loncha de carne*) slice of meat **2.** (*borrachera*) drunken spree; **traer un ~** to be plastered

cueva *f* cave; (*sótano*) cellar; **~ de ladrones** *fig* den of thieves

cuidado *m* care; **¡~!** careful!; **¡~ con el escalón!** mind the step!; **¡anda con ~!** watch your step!; **de ~** serious; **eso me tiene sin ~** I couldn't care less about that; **salir de ~** (*mejorar*) to be out of danger; (*dar a luz*) to give birth

cuidador(a) *m(f)* caregiver; *Arg* nurse

cuidadora *f Méx* nanny

cuidadoso, -a *adj* careful

cuidar **I.** *vi* to take care **II.** *vt* to look after **III.** *vr:* **~se** to look after oneself; **~se mucho de (no) hacer algo** to take good care not to do sth; **¡cuídate!** take care!

cuita *f* worry

cuitado, -a *adj* worried

culata *f* **1.** (*del fusil*) butt; **salir el tiro por la ~** to backfire **2.** (*del caballo*) croup, hindquarters *pl*

culebra *f* snake

culebrón *m* **1.** *aumentativo de* **culebra** big snake **2.** TV soap opera **3.** (*hombre cazurro*) wily character **4.** (*mujer intrigante*) scheming woman

culera *f* seat (of trousers)

culinario, -a *adj* culinary

culminación *f* **1.** (*lo máximo*) culmination **2.** ASTR zenith

culminante *adj* **punto ~** high point

culminar *vi* to culminate

culo *m* **1.** (*trasero*) bottom, backside *Brit;* **caer de ~** to fall on one's backside; *fig* to be amazed; **lamer el ~ a alguien** *vulg* to lick sb's arse; **ser ~ de mal asiento** *inf* to be restless; **tonto del ~** berk *Brit;* **¡vete a tomar por el ~!** *vulg* piss off! **2.** (*de vaso o botella*) bottom

culpa *f* fault; JUR guilt; **echar la ~ a alguien** to blame sb; **y ¿qué ~ tengo yo?** and how am I to blame (for that)?

culpabilidad *f* guilt

culpabilizar <z→c> *vt* to blame

culpable **I.** *adj* guilty; **declarar ~** to find guilty **II.** *mf* culprit

culpar **I.** *vt* **~ de** [*o* **por**] **algo** to blame for sth **II.** *vr* **~se de** [*o* **por**] **algo** to be to blame for sth

cultismo *m* (*palabra culta*) learned word

cultivable *adj* arable, cultivable

cultivador(a) *m(f)* **1.** (*persona*) grower; **~ de vino** wine grower **2.** (*instrumento*) cultivator

cultivar *vt* **1.** *t. fig* AGR to cultivate; **~ la tierra** to farm the land **2.** (*bacterias*) to culture

cultivo *m* **1.** AGR (*acto*) cultivation; (*resultado*) crop; **~ de regadío** irrigated crop **2.** (*de bacterias*) culture

culto *m* **1.** (*veneración*) worship; **~ de la personalidad** personality cult **2.** REL **~ divino** divine service

culto, -a *adj* (*persona*) educated, cultured

cultura *f* culture; **~ ambiental** environmental conservation; **~ general** general knowledge

cultural *adj* cultural

culturismo *m* body-building

culturista *mf* body-builder

culturización *f* education

culturizar <z→c> *vt* to educate

cuma *f* **1.** *AmC* (*machete*) long knife **2.** *Perú* (*comadre*) godmother

cumbre *f* **1.** (*cima*) summit **2.** (*reunión*) summit meeting **3.** (*culminación*) height

cumiche *m AmC* baby of the family

cumpleaños *m inv* birthday

cumplido *m* compliment; **visita de ~** formal [*o* courtesy] visit; **hacer algo por ~** to do sth out of courtesy

cumplido, -a *adj* **1.** (*acabado*) completed; **¡misión cumplida!** mission accomplished!

2. (*abundante*) plentiful 3. (*cortés*) courteous 4. (*con el servicio militar finalizado*) **un soldado** ~ an ex-serviceman

cumplidor(a) I. *adj* reliable II. *m(f)* reliable person

cumplimentar *vt* 1. (*felicitar*) to congratulate 2. (*visita de cumplido*) to pay one's respects to 3. (*una orden*) to carry out 4. (*un impreso*) to complete

cumplimiento *m* 1. (*observación*) fulfilment; ~ **de un deber** performance of a duty; **no** ~ non-fulfilment 2. (*cumplido*) compliment

cumplir I. *vi* 1. (*hacer su deber*) ~ **con su deber/su promesa** to do one's duty/to keep one's promise; **hacer algo sólo por** ~ to do sth as a matter of form; ~**é por ti** I'll act on your behalf 2. (*soldado*) to finish one's military service 3. (*plazo*) to end II. *vt* 1. (*una orden*) to carry out 2. (*una promesa*) to keep 3. (*un plazo*) to keep to 4. (*el servicio militar*) to do 5. (*una prestación*) to make 6. (*una pena*) to serve 7. (*las leyes*) to observe 8. (*años*) **en mayo cumplo treinta años** I'm thirty years old in May III. *vr:* ~**se** to be fulfilled

cúmulo *m* 1. (*amontonamiento*) heap 2. METEO cumulus

cuna *f* cradle; **canción de** ~ lullaby

cundir *vi* 1. (*dar mucho de sí*) to be productive; (*el arroz*) to swell; **esta comida cunde mucho** this food is very nourishing 2. (*un trabajo*) to go well 3. (*mancha, epidemia, un rumor, una noticia*) to spread

cuneco, -a *m, f Ven* baby of the family

cuneta *f* ditch

cuña *f* 1. (*traba*) wedge 2. *fig* (*enchufe*) influence 3. MED bedpan

cuñado, -a *m, f* brother-in-law *m,* sister-in-law *f*

cuño *m* 1. (*troquel*) die stamp 2. *t. fig* stamp; **de nuevo** ~ (*palabra*) newly-coined

cuota *f* 1. (*porción*) quota; (*de una deuda*) instalment; ~ **de crecimiento** rate of increase; ~ **de mercado** market share 2. (*contribución*) fee; ~ **de socio** membership fee

cupé *m* AUTO coupé

cupido *m* 1. (*de la mitología romana*) Cupid 2. *fig* (*mujeriego*) womanizer

cupo I. *3. pret de* **caber** II. *m* 1. ECON quota 2. MIL draught *Brit,* draft *Am*

cupón *m* coupon; (*de lotería*) lottery ticket; ~ **de descuento** discount coupon

cupón-respuesta *m* <cupones-respuesta> reply coupon

cuprífero, -a *adj* copper

cúpula *f* 1. (*media esfera*) dome 2. (*máximos dirigentes*) leading members *pl;* ~ **dirigente** top management 3. BOT cup 4. NÁUT turret

cura[1] *m* priest

cura[2] *f* 1. (*curación*) cure 2. (*tratamiento*) treatment; ~ **para adelgazar** diet; ~ **de almas** REL cure of souls; ~ **de deshabituación** cure for drug addiction [*o* alcoholism]; **primera** ~ first aid

curable *adj* curable

curación *f* (*tratamiento*) treatment

curado, -a *adj* 1. (*sanado*) cured 2. (*endurecido*) hardened 3. (*salado, ahumado*) cured 4. *AmL* (*borracho*) drunk

curanderismo *m* folk healing; *pey* quack medicine

curandero, -a *m, f* 1. (*mago*) witch doctor 2. (*charlatán*) quack (doctor)

curar I. *vi* to recover II. *vt* 1. (*a un enfermo: tratar*) to treat; (*sanar*) to cure 2. (*ahumar, salar*) to cure 3. (*pieles*) to tan 4. (*madera*) to season 5. (*hilos y lienzos*) to bleach III. *vr:* ~**se** to recover; ~**se en salud** to take precautions

curare *m* curare

curativo, -a *adj* curative

curcuncho, -a *adj AmL* (*corcovado*) hunchbacked

curda *f inf* drunkenness; **agarrar una** ~ to get tight

curdo, -a I. *adj* Kurdish II. *m, f* Kurd

curia *f* 1. REL Curia 2. (*tribunal*) bar

curiosear *vi* to look round; (*fisgar*) to snoop

curiosidad *f* 1. (*indiscreción, objeto*) curiosity; **despertar la** ~ **de alguien** to arouse sb's curiosity 2. (*pulcritud*) neatness

curioso, -a I. *adj* 1. (*indiscreto, interesante*) curious; **estar** ~ **por saber algo** to be curious to know sth; **¡qué** ~**!** how curious! 2. (*aseado*) neat II. *m, f* 1. (*indiscreto*) busybody, snoop 2. (*mirón*) onlooker, bystander 3. *AmL* (*curandero*) quack doctor

currante *mf inf* worker

currar *vi inf,* **currelar** *vi inf* to work

currículo *m* curriculum

curriculum (vitae) *m,* **currículum (vitae)** *m* curriculum vitae

curro *m inf* (*trabajo*) job

currutaco, -a *adj inf* flashy

curry *m* curry

cursar *vt* 1. (*cursos*) to take; (*asignatura*) to study 2. (*tramitar*) to file; (*una orden*) to issue; (*un telegrama, un mensaje*) to send; (*una solicitud*) to pass on 3. (*frecuentar*) to frequent

cursi I. *adj inf* 1. (*una persona*) affected, twee *Brit* 2. (*una cosa*) kitschy, tasteless II. *mf inf* affected person

cursilada *f inf,* **cursilería** *f inf* 1. (*acción cursi*) pretentious act 2. (*calidad de cursi*) affectation

cursillista *mf* member (*of a short course*)

cursillo *m* short course; ~ **de socorrismo** life-saving classes

cursiva *f* italics *pl*

cursivo, -a *adj* cursive

curso *m* 1. (*transcurso*) course; ~ **de agua** watercourse; **estar en** ~ to be going on; **en el** ~ **del año** in the course of the year; **tomar un** ~ **favorable** to go favourably; **dar** ~ **a una solicitud** to deal with an application 2. (*de enseñanza*) course; ~ **acelerado** crash course; **asistir a un** ~ to take part in a course; **perder el** ~ to fail a subject 3. FIN (*circulación*)

estar en ~ to be in circulation
cursor *m* **1.** INFOR cursor **2.** TÉC slide
curtido *m* **1.** (*cuero*) tanned hide **2.** (*acción*) tanning **3.** *fig* experienced
curtido, **-a** *adj* **1.** *fig* hardened **2.** (*cuero*) tanned
curtidor(**a**) *m(f)* tanner
curtiduría *f* tannery
curtiembre *f AmL* **1.** (*taller*) tannery **2.** (*acción*) tanning
curtir I. *vt* **1.** (*tratar pieles, broncearse*) to tan **2.** (*acostumbrar a la vida dura*) to harden **II.** *vr:* **~se 1.** (*ponerse moreno*) to become tanned **2.** (*acostumbrarse a la vida dura*) to become inured
curva *f* curve
curvar *vt, vr:* **~se** to bend
curvatura *f* curvature
curvilíneo, **-a** *adj* MAT curvilinear
curvo, **-a** *adj* curved
cusca *f* **1.** *Méx* (*prostituta*) whore **2.** *Col* (*embriaguez*) drunkenness **3.** *Col* (*colilla de cigarro*) butt ►**hacer la ~ a alguien** *inf* to play a dirty trick on sb
cuscurro *m* (*de pan*) crust
cuscús *m inv* couscous
cusma *f AmS* coarse woollen Indian shirt
cúspide *f* **1.** MAT apex **2.** *fig* pinnacle
custodia *f* **1.** (*guarda*) custody; **bajo ~** in custody; **estar bajo la ~ de alguien** to be in sb's care **2.** (*ostensorio*) monstrance
custodiar *vt* to guard
custodio, **-a** *m, f* guardian
cususa *f AmC* uncured rum
cutáneo, **-a** *adj* skin
cutícula *f* cuticle
cutis *m inv* skin, complexion
cutre I. *adj* **1.** (*tacaño*) stingy, mean *Brit* **2.** (*sórdido*) seedy, grotty, crummy *inf;* **ropa ~** cheap clothes *pl* **II.** *mf* miser
cutrería *f*, **cutrez** *f* **1.** (*tacañería*) stinginess, meanness *Brit* **2.** (*sordidez*) seediness, shabbiness
cuyo, **-a** *pron rel* whose; **por cuya causa** for which reason
C.V. 1. *abr de* **curriculum vitae** CV **2.** *abr de* **caballos de vapor** HP, h.p.

D

D, **d** *f* D, d; **~ de Dolores** D for David *Brit,* D for dog *Am*
D. *abr de* **Don** Mr
Dª *abr de* **Doña** Mrs
dactilar *adj* **huellas ~es** fingerprints *pl*
dádiva *f* (*regalo*) gift
dadivoso, **-a** *adj* generous
dado[1] *m* **1.** (*cubo*) die; **~s** dice *pl;* **tirar el ~** to throw a die **2.** *pl* (*juego*) dice; **jugar a los ~s** to play dice; **jugarse una cerveza a los ~s** to play dice for a glass of beer
dado[2] *conj* **1.** (*ya que*) **~ que llueve...** given that it's raining ... **2.** (*supuesto que*) **~ que sea demasiado difícil...** supposing it's too difficult ...
dado, **-a** *adj* (*supuesto, determinado*) given; **dada la coyuntura actual...** given the current situation ...; **en el caso ~** in this particular case ►**no ser ~** *Méx* to be brave; **ser ~ a algo** to be given to sth
daga *f* dagger; *PRico* (*machete*) machete
daiquiri *m Cuba* daiquiri
dalia *f* dahlia
dálmata *m* dalmatian
daltónico, **-a** *adj* colour-blind *Brit,* color-blind *Am*
dama *f* **1.** (*señora*) lady; **~ de honor** (*de la reina*) lady-in-waiting; (*de la novia*) bridesmaid; **primera ~** POL first lady **2.** *pl* (*juego*) (**juego de**) **~s** draughts *Brit,* checkers *pl Am*
damajuana *f* demijohn
damasco *m* **1.** (*tejido*) damask **2.** *AmL* (*fruta*) damson
damnificar <c→qu> *vt* (*persona*) to injure; (*cosa*) to damage
danés *m* **gran ~** Great Dane
danés, **-esa I.** *adj* Danish **II.** *m, f* Dane
danta *f Ven, Col* ZOOL tapir
Danubio *m* Danube
danza *f* dance ►**en ~** *inf* on the go
danzar <z→c> **I.** *vi* **1.** (*bailar, girar*) to dance **2.** (*moverse*) to run about **II.** *vt* to dance
danzarín, **-ina** *m, f* dancer
dañar I. *vi* to harm **II.** *vt* (*cosa*) to damage; (*persona*) to injure; **~ la imagen** to ruin the image **III.** *vr:* **~se** to get damaged; (*fruta, cosecha*) to go bad
dañero, **-a** *adj Ven* (*embaucador*) misleading
dañino, **-a** *adj* harmful
daño *m* **1.** (*perjuicio*) damage; **~ material** physical damage; **~s ecológicos** environmental harm; **~s y perjuicios** JUR damages **2.** (*dolor*) hurt; **hacer ~ a alguien** to hurt sb; **hacerse ~** to hurt oneself; **no hace ~** it doesn't hurt
dar *irr* **I.** *vt* **1.** (*entregar*) to give; **~ una patada a alguien** to kick sb; **~ un abrazo a alguien** to hug sb; **¿a quién le toca ~** (**las cartas**)? whose turn is it to deal?; **~ forma a algo** to shape sth; **~ permiso** to give permission; **~ importancia a algo** to consider sth important **2.** (*producir*) **la vaca da leche** the cow yields milk; **este árbol da naranjas** this tree bears oranges **3.** (*celebrar*) to give; **~ clases** to teach; **~ una conferencia** to give a talk; **~ una fiesta** to give a party **4.** (*causar*) **~ gusto** to please; **~ miedo** to be frightening; **me das pena** I feel sorry for you **5.** (*presentar*) **~ una película** to show a film; **¿dónde dan la película?** where's the film showing?; **¿qué dan en la ópera?** what's showing at the opera house? **6.** (*expresar*) **~ las buenas noches** to

say goodnight; ~ **la enhorabuena a alguien** to congratulate sb; ~ **el pésame a alguien** to give one's condolences to sb; ~ **recuerdos** to send one's regards **7.** (*comunicar: una noticia, un mensaje*) to give **8.** (*hacer*) ~ **un paseo** to go for a walk; **no da golpe** *inf* he/she is bone-idle *Brit* **9.** (*encender*) to turn on; ~ **el agua** to turn the water on; ~ **la luz** to turn the light on **10.** (*sonar*) **el reloj ha dado las dos** the clock has chimed two o'clock **11.** (*aplicar: crema*) to apply **12.** (+ *'de'*) ~ **a alguien de alta** MED to discharge sb; MIL to pass sb as fit; ~ **a alguien de baja** MED to put sb on sick leave; MIL to discharge sb; (*miembro*) to expel sb **13.** (+ *'a'*) ~ **a conocer algo** to let sth be known; ~ **a entender algo a alguien** to let sb know sth ▶**dale que te pego** *inf* on and on; **estar dale que dale con un mismo tema** *inf* to keep going on about the same topic **II.** *vi* **1.** (+ *'a'*) **el balcón da a la calle/al norte** the balcony faces the street/north; **la ventana da al patio** the window opens onto the courtyard **2.** (+ *'con'*) ~ **con alguien en la calle** to run into sb in the street; ~ **con la solución** to find the solution **3.** (+ *'contra'*) ~ **contra algo** to hit sth; **la piedra ha dado contra el cristal** the stone hit the glass **4.** (*caer*) ~ **de espaldas/de narices en el suelo** to land on one's back/on one's face on the ground; ~ **en la trampa** to fall into the trap **5.** (*acertar*) ~ **en el blanco** *fig* to hit the target; ~ **en el clavo** *fig* to hit the nail on the head **6.** (+ *'para'*) **esta tela da para dos vestidos** this cloth will be enough for two dresses; **da para vivir** it's enough to live on **7.** (+ *'por'* + *adjetivo*) ~ **a alguien por inocente** to assume sb is innocent; ~ **a alguien por muerto** to take sb for dead; ~ **por concluido algo** to treat sth as concluded; ~ **el libro por leído** to assume that the book has been read **8.** (+ *'por'* + *verbo*) **le ha dado por dejarse el pelo largo** he/she has decided to grow his/her hair long **9.** (+ *'que'* + *verbo*) ~ **que decir** to give cause for comment; ~ **que hablar** to be the topic of conversation; ~ **que hacer** to be a lot of work; ~ **que pensar** to give cause for thought ▶**¡qué más da!** *inf* what does it matter?; ~ **de sí** (*jersey*) to stretch **III.** *vr:* **~se 1.** (*suceder*) to happen **2.** (*frutos*) to grow **3.** (+ *'a': consagrarse*) to devote oneself; (*entregarse*) to surrender; **~se a la bebida** to give oneself over to drink **4.** (+ *'contra'*) **~se contra algo** to hit sth **5.** (+ *'por'* + *adjetivo: creerse*) **~se por algo** to believe oneself to be sth; **~se por aludido** to take the hint; **~se por vencido** to give up; **~se por enterado** to show that one has understood **6.** (+ *'a'* + *verbo*) **~se a conocer** (*persona*) to make oneself known; (*noticia*) to become known; **~se a entender** to hint **7.** (+ *'de'*) **~se de baja** to sign off; **~se de alta** to sign up; **~se de alta en Hacienda** to register with the Inland Revenue; **dárselas de valiente** *inf* to pretend to be brave **8.** (+ *sustantivo*) **~se un baño** to have a bath; **~se cuenta de algo** to realize sth; **~se prisa** to hurry up; **~se un susto** to get a fright

dardo *m* **1.** (*arma*) spear **2.** (*del juego*) dart; **jugar a los ~s** to play darts **3.** (*pulla*) cutting remark

dársena *f* dock

datar *vi, vt* to date

dátil *m* date

dativo *m* dative

dato *m* **1.** (*circunstancia*) fact; **~s personales** personal details **2.** (*cantidad*) figure **3.** (*fecha*) date **4.** *pl* INFOR data *pl;* **~s de entrada/de salida** input/output data; **~s fijos** fixed data; **elaborar ~s** to compile data

dcha. *abr de* **derecha** rt.

d. de J.C. *abr de* **después de Jesucristo** AD

de *prep* **1.** (*posesión*) **el reloj ~ mi padre** my father's watch; **los hijos ~ Ana** Ana's children **2.** (*origen*) from; **ser ~ Italia/~ Lisboa** to come from Italy/from Lisbon; ~ **Málaga a Valencia** from Malaga to Valencia; **el avión procedente ~ Lima** the plane from Lima; **un libro ~ Goytisolo** a book by Goytisolo; ~ **ti a mí** from you to me **3.** (*material, cualidad*) of; ~ **oro** of gold, gold; ~ **madera** of wood, wooden; **un hombre ~ buen corazón** a good-hearted man **4.** (*temporal*) from; ~ **niño** as a child **5.** (*finalidad*) **máquina ~ escribir** typewriter; **hora ~ comer** mealtime **6.** (*causa*) of, from **7.** (*condición*) ~ **haberlo sabido no habríamos ido** if we had known we wouldn't have gone **8.** (*partitivo*) **dos platos ~ sopa** two bowls of soup; **un vaso ~ agua** a glass of water **9.** (+ *nombre propio*) **la ciudad ~ Cuzco** the city of Cuzco; **el tonto ~ Luis lo ha roto** that idiot Luis broke it; **pobre ~ mí** poor me

deambular *vi* to wander around

debajo I. *adv* underneath **II.** *prep* ~ **de** (*local*) below, under; (*con movimiento*) under; **pasar por ~ del puente** to go under the bridge

debate *m* **1.** POL debate **2.** (*charla*) discussion

debatir I. *vt* **1.** POL to debate **2.** (*considerar*) to discuss **II.** *vr:* **~se** to struggle; **~se entre la vida y la muerte** to hover between life and death

debe *m* debit

deber I. *vi* (*suposición*) **debe de estar al llegar** he/she should arrive soon; **deben de ser las nueve** it must be nine o'clock **II.** *vt* **1.** (*estar obligado*) to have to; **no ~ías haberlo dicho** you shouldn't have said it **2.** (*tener que dar*) to owe **III.** *vr:* **~se 1.** (*tener por causa*) **~se a algo** to be due to sth; (*agradeciendo algo*) to be thanks to sth **2.** (*estar obligado*) to have a duty; **se debe a su profesión** his/her job is his/her vocation **IV.** *m* **1.** (*obligación*) duty; ~ **de conciencia** moral duty **2.** *pl* (*tareas*) homework*;* **tener muchos ~es** to have a lot of homework; **dar muchos ~es** to set a lot of homework

D

debido *prep* ~ **a** due to
debido, **-a** *adj* (*conveniente, necesario*) proper; **como es** ~ as is proper
débil *adj* weak; (*sonido*) faint; (*luz*) dim
debilidad *f* ~ **por algo** weakness for sth
debilitar *vt* to weaken
debitar *vt AmL* to debit
débito *m* debt; (*debe*) debit; ~ **conyugal** marital duty
debocar <c→qu> *vi Arg, Bol* to vomit
debut <debuts> *m* debut; **hacer su** ~ to make one's debut; (*teatro*) opening, first performance
debutar *vi* to make one's debut
década *f* decade; **la** ~ **de los 40** the 40s
decadencia *f* **1.** (*decaimiento*) decay; ~ **moral** decadence **2.** (*de un imperio*) decline
decadente *adj* (*en declive*) declining; (*moralmente*) decadent
decaer *irr como caer vi* to decline; ~ **en fuerza** to lose strength; ~ **el ánimo** to get [*o* become] discouraged; **decae de ánimo** he/she is losing heart
decaído, **-a** *adj* **1.** (*abatido*) downhearted **2.** (*débil*) weak
decaimiento *m* **1.** (*afligimiento*) dejection **2.** (*debilidad*) weakness
decálogo *m* REL Decalogue
decano, **-a** *m, f* UNIV dean
decapitar *vt* to decapitate
decatlón *m* decathlon
decena *f* ten; ~**s** MAT tens; ~**s de miles** tens of thousands; **una** ~ **de huevos** ten eggs
decencia *f* decency
decenio *m* decade
decente *adj* **1.** (*decoroso*) decent **2.** (*honesto*) upright **3.** (*respetable*) respectable
decepción *f* disappointment; **llevarse una** ~ to be disappointed
decepcionar *vt* to disappoint
deceso *m* death, decease *form*
decibel(**io**) *m* decibel
decididamente *adv* **1.** (*resueltamente*) resolutely **2.** (*definitivamente*) decidedly
decidido, **-a** *adj* determined
decidir **I.** *vi* to decide **II.** *vt* **1.** (*determinar, acordar*) to decide **2.** (*mover a*) to persuade **III.** *vr* ~**se por/en contra de algo** to decide in favour [*o* favor *Am*] of/against sth
décima *f* tenth ►**tener** ~**s** to have a slight temperature
decimal *adj* decimal; **número** ~ decimal number
décimo *m* (*de lotería*) *tenth share of a lottery ticket*
décimo, **-a** **I.** *adj* tenth **II.** *m, f* tenth; (*de lotería*) *tenth share of a lottery ticket; v.t.* **octavo**
decimoctavo, **-a** *adj* eighteenth; *v.t.* **octavo**
decimocuarto, **-a** *adj* fourteenth; *v.t.* **octavo**
decimonono, **-a** *adj*, **decimonoveno**, **-a** *adj* nineteenth; *v.t.* **octavo**
decimoquinto, **-a** *adj* fifteenth; *v.t.* **octavo**
decimoséptimo, **-a** *adj* seventeenth; *v.t.* **octavo**
decimosexto, **-a** *adj* sixteenth; *v.t.* **octavo**
decimotercero, **-a** *adj*, **decimotercio**, **-a** *adj* thirteenth; *v.t.* **octavo**
decir *irr* **I.** *vi* **1.** (*expresar*) ~ **algo de alguien** to say sth about sb; ~ **que sí** to say yes; **diga** [*o* **dígame**] TEL hello; **es** [*o* **quiere**] ~ in other words; **¡no me digas!** *inf* really!; ~ **por** ~ to talk for talking's sake; **por** ~**lo así** to put it like that; **el qué dirán** what people will say; **¡quién lo diría!** who would have thought it!; **y que lo digas** you can say that again; **y no digamos** not to mention; **dicen de él que es un buen profesor** they say he is a good teacher **2.** (*contener*) to say; **la regla dice lo siguiente:...** the rule says the following: ... **3.** (*armonizar*) to suit; ~ **con algo** to go with sth **II.** *vt* **1.** (*expresar*) to say; (*comunicar*) to tell; ~ **algo para sí** to say sth to oneself; **¡no digas tonterías!** *inf* don't talk rubbish!; **dicho y hecho** no sooner said than done; **como se ha dicho** as has been said **2.** (*mostrar*) to show; **su cara dice alegría** he/she has a happy face ►**no es muy guapa, que digamos** she's not exactly pretty **III.** *vr* **¿cómo se dice en inglés?** how do you say it in English?; **¿cómo se dice 'ropa' en inglés?** how do you say 'ropa' in English? **IV.** *m* saying ►**ser un** ~ to be a manner of speaking
decisión *f* **1.** (*resolución*) resolution; (*acuerdo*) decision; **tomar una** ~ to take [*o* make] a decision **2.** (*firmeza*) determination; **tener** ~ to be determined
decisivo, **-a** *adj* decisive
declamar *vt* to declaim; (*versos*) to recite
declaración *f* **1.** (*a la prensa*) declaration; **hacer declaraciones** to make a statement **2.** JUR statement; ~ **final** closing statement; **prestar** ~ to give evidence; **tomar** ~ **a alguien** to take sb's statement **3.** (*de bienes, impuestos*) ~ **de la renta** income-tax return; **hacer una** ~ **de valor de algo** to declare the value of sth
declarar **I.** *vi* **1.** (*testigo*) to testify, to give evidence **2.** (*a la prensa*) to make a statement **II.** *vt* **1.** (*manifestar*) to declare; ~ **abierta la reunión** to declare the meeting open; ~ **a alguien culpable/inocente** to convict/acquit sb **2.** (*ingresos, a aduanas*) to declare **III.** *vr:* ~**se** **1.** (*aparecer*) to break out **2.** (*manifestarse*) to declare oneself; ~**se en huelga** to go on strike; ~**se inocente** to plead innocent; ~**se en quiebra** to declare oneself bankrupt
declinación *f* **1.** (*disminución*) decline **2.** LING declension
declinar **I.** *vi* **1.** (*disminuir*) to decline **2.** (*extinguirse*) to come to an end **II.** *vt* (*rechazar*) *t. fig* to decline
declive *m* **1.** (*del terreno*) slope; **en** ~ sloping; **en fuerte** ~ steeply sloping **2.** (*decadencia*) decline; **en** ~ in decline
decodificar *vt* to decode
decolaje *m AmL* take-off

decolar *vi AmL* to take off
decolorar I. *vt* 1. QUÍM to discolour *Brit,* to discolor *Am* 2. (*el sol*) to bleach II. *vr:* ~**se** to fade
decomisar *vt* to confiscate
decoración *f* 1. (*adorno*) decoration 2. (*con muebles*) furnishing 3. TEAT scenery
decorado *m* TEAT set
decorador(**a**) *m(f)* decorator; TEAT set designer; ~ **de interiores** interior designer [*o* decorator]; ~ **de escaparates** window-dresser
decorar *vt* 1. (*adornar*) to decorate 2. (*con muebles*) to furnish; ~ **con moqueta** to carpet
decorativo, **-a** *adj* decorative
decoro *m* 1. (*dignidad*) dignity; **con** ~ with dignity; **vivir con** ~ to live with dignity 2. (*respeto*) respect; **guardar el** ~ to show respect 3. (*pudor*) decency; **con** ~ decently
decoroso, **-a** *adj* 1. (*decente*) decent 2. (*digno*) dignified
decrecer *irr como crecer vi* to decrease; (*nivel, fiebre*) to fall; ~ **en intensidad** to diminish in intensity
decrépito, **-a** *adj* 1. (*persona*) decrepit 2. (*cosa*) battered 3. (*sociedad*) declining
decretar *vt* to decree
decreto *m* decree; ~ **gubernamental** government decree
decúbito *m* position; ~ **prono/supino** prone/supine position
dedal *m* thimble
dédalo *m* 1. (*laberinto*) labyrinth 2. (*lío*) mess
dedear *vt Méx* to finger
dedicación *f* 1. (*consagración*) consecration 2. (*entrega*) dedication, commitment; ~ **plena** (*en el trabajo*) full-time 3. (*dedicatoria*) dedication
dedicar <c→qu> I. *vt* 1. (*destinar*) to dedicate 2. (*consagrar*) to consecrate II. *vr:* ~**se** to devote oneself; ~**se a algo** (*profesionalmente*) to work as sth; ~**se a la enseñanza** to be a teacher; **¿a qué se dedica Ud.?** what do you do?
dedicatoria *f* dedication
dedillo *m inf* **saberse algo al** ~ to know sth inside out
dedo *m* (*de mano*) finger; (*de pie*) toe; ~ **anular** ring finger; ~ **corazón** middle finger; ~ **gordo** big toe; ~ **índice** index finger, forefinger; ~ **meñique** little finger *Brit,* pinkie *Am;* ~ **pulgar** thumb; **chuparse el** ~ *inf* to suck one's thumb; **señalar a alguien con el** ~ to point sb out ►**no tener dos ~s de frente** *inf* to be as thick as two short planks; **estar a dos ~s de algo** to be within in an inch of sth; **estar para chuparse los ~s** *inf* to be absolutely delicious; **¿crees que me chupo el dedo?** do you think I was born yesterday?; **hacer** [*o* **ir a**] ~ to hitch-hike; **no mover un** ~ to not lift a finger; **pillarse los ~s** to get one's fingers burnt; **nombrar a** ~ to hand-pick; **poner el** ~ **en la llaga** to touch a nerve
deducción *f* 1. (*derivación*) deduction 2. ECON deduction; (*fiscal*) allowance, deduction; ~ **estándar** basic allowance; ~ **por hijo** child tax allowance
deducir *irr como traducir vt* 1. (*derivar*) to deduce 2. (*descontar*) to deduct
defecación *f* defecation
defecar <c→qu> *vi* to defecate
defecto *m* 1. (*carencia*) lack; **en** ~ **de** in the absence of; **en su** ~ (*cosa*) if it is unavailable; (*persona*) in his/her absence 2. (*falta*) defect; ~ **físico** physical defect; ~ **genético** genetic defect
defectuoso, **-a** *adj* faulty, defective
defender <e→ie> I. *vt* 1. (*ideas, contra ataques*) *t.* JUR to defend 2. (*proteger*) to protect II. *vr:* ~**se** 1. (*contra ataques*) to defend oneself 2. (*arreglárselo*) to get by; **¿hablas francés? – me defiendo** do you speak French? – I can get by
defendible *adj* defensible
defensa[1] *f* 1. (*contra ataques*) *t.* JUR, DEP defence *Brit,* defense *Am;* **en legítima** ~ JUR in self-defence; **acudir en** ~ **de alguien** to come to sb's defence 2. *pl t.* BIO defences *pl Brit,* defenses *pl Am;* **tener** ~**s** to have resistance 3. *Méx* (*paragolpes*) bumper *Brit,* fender *Am*
defensa[2] *mf* DEP defender
defensiva *f* defensive; **a la** ~ on the defensive
defensivo, **-a** *adj* defensive
defensor(**a**) I. *adj* defending II. *m(f)* defender; ~ **de la naturaleza** environmental campaigner
deferencia *f* (*consideración*) deference; (*cortesía*) courtesy; **por** ~ **a algo** in deference to sth; **tener la** ~ **de...** +*infin* to be so kind as to ...
deferente *adj* deferential
deferir *irr como sentir vi* to defer
deficiencia *f* 1. (*insuficiencia*) lack 2. (*defecto*) deficiency
deficiente I. *adj* 1. (*insuficiente*) lacking 2. (*defectuoso*) deficient II. *mf* ~ **mental** mentally handicapped person
déficit *m inv* 1. FIN deficit; ~ **presupuestario** budget deficit 2. (*escasez*) shortage
deficitario, **-a** *adj* (*empresa*) loss-making; (*cuenta*) in deficit
definición *f* (*aclaración*) *t.* TV definition; **por** ~ by definition
definido, **-a** *adj* (*claro*) *t.* LING definite
definir I. *vt* to define II. *vr:* ~**se** to take a stand
definitivo, **-a** *adj* 1. (*irrevocable*) final 2. (*decisivo*) decisive ►**en definitiva** in short
deforestation *f* deforestation
deformación *f* 1. (*alteración*) distortion 2. (*desfiguración*) deformation; ~ **física** physical deformity
deformar I. *vt* 1. (*alterar*) to distort 2. (*desfigurar*) to deform II. *vr:* ~**se** to become deformed; (*jersey*) to lose its shape
deforme *adj* 1. (*imagen*) distorted 2. (*cuerpo*) deformed
deformidad *f* MED deformity
defraudar *vt* 1. (*estafar*) to cheat; ~ **a Ha-**

D

cienda to evade one's taxes **2.** (*decepcionar*) to disappoint
defunción *f* death; **certificado de** ~ death certificate
degeneración *f* **1.** (*proceso*) degeneration **2.** (*estado*) degeneracy
degenerar *vi* to degenerate
deglutir *vt* to swallow
degolladero *m* **1.** (*cuello*) throat **2.** (*matadero*) slaughterhouse **3.** (*cadalso*) scaffold
degollar <o→ue> *vt* **1.** (*matar*) ~ **un animal** to slit an animal's throat; ~ **a alguien** (*decapitar*) to behead sb; (*cortar la garganta*) to slit sb's throat **2.** *inf* (*malograr*) to make a hash of
degradación *f* **1.** (*humillación*) humiliation **2.** (*en el cargo*) demotion **3.** (*deterioro*) deterioration; ~ **del medio ambiente** environmental damage **4.** (*en pintura*) ~ **de color** colour gradation
degradante *adj* demeaning
degradar **I.** *vt* **1.** (*en el cargo*) to demote **2.** (*calidad*) to worsen; ~ **el medio ambiente** to damage the environment **3.** (*humillar*) to humiliate **4.** (*color*) to tone down **II.** *vr* to degrade [*o* demean] oneself
degüello *m* **1.** (*degolladura*) slaughter **2.** (*decapitación*) beheading ►**tirar a alguien a** ~ *inf* to have it in for sb
degustación *f* tasting; ~ **de vinos** wine tasting
degustar *vt* to taste
dehesa *f* pasture
deidad *f* (*dios*) deity
deificar <c→qu> *vt* **1.** (*divinizar*) to deify **2.** (*ensalzar*) to idolize
dejadez *f* **1.** (*falta de aseo*) slovenliness **2.** (*pereza*) laziness **3.** (*negligencia*) neglect
dejado, **-a** *adj* **1.** *ser* (*descuidado*) slovenly **2.** *estar* (*abatido*) dejected
dejar **I.** *vi* ~ **de hacer algo** to stop doing sth; **no dejes de escribirles** don't fail to write them; **¡no deje de venir!** make sure you come! **II.** *vt* **1.** (*en general*) to leave; ~ **el libro sobre la mesa** to leave the book on the table; ~ **acabado** to finish; ~ **caer** to drop; ~ **claro** to make clear; ~ **constancia de algo** to put sth on record; ~ **a deber** to owe; ~ **en libertad** to set free; ~ **algo para mañana** to leave sth for tomorrow; ~ **a alguien en paz** to leave sb in peace; **¡déjanos en paz!** leave us alone!; ~ **mucho que desear** to leave a lot to be desired; ~ **algo sin lavar** to not wash sth; ~ **triste** to sadden **2.** (*abandonar*) to leave; ~ **la carrera** to drop out of university **3.** (*ganancia*) to give **4.** (*permitir: algo*) to allow, to let; **no me dejan salir** they won't let me go out **5.** (*entregar*) to give; (*prestar*) to lend; (*en herencia*) to leave; ~ **un recado** to leave a message; ~ **algo en manos de alguien** to leave sth in sb's hands ►**¡déjalo ya!** forget about it! **III.** *vr:* ~**se** **1.** (*descuidarse*) to neglect oneself **2.** (*olvidar*) to forget ►~**se caer** to hint; ~**se llevar** to let oneself get carried away; ~**se querer** to let oneself be loved
deje *m* hint; **se te nota un** ~ **catalán** you have a slight Catalan accent
dejo *m* **1.** (*entonación*) inflection; (*acento*) accent **2.** (*regusto*) *t. fig* aftertaste
del *v.* = **de** + **el** *v.* **de**
delación *f* delation, accusation
delantal *m* apron, pinafore *Brit*
delante **I.** *adv* **1.** (*ante, en la parte delantera*) in front; **de** ~ from the front; **abierto por** ~ open at the front **2.** (*enfrente*) opposite **II.** *prep* ~ **de** in front of; ~ **mío** [*o* **de mí**] in front of me
delantera *f* **1.** (*parte anterior*) front (part) **2.** (*primera fila*) front row **3.** (*distancia*) lead; **coger la** ~ **a alguien** to gain a lead on sb; **llevar la** ~ **a alguien** to have a lead over sb **4.** DEP forward line
delantero *m* **1.** (*parte anterior*) front (part) **2.** DEP forward; ~ **centro** centre [*o* center *Am*] forward
delantero, **-a** *adj* front
delatar **I.** *vt* **1.** (*denunciar*) to inform on **2.** (*manifestar*) to reveal **II.** *vr:* ~**se** to give oneself away
delegación *f* **1.** (*atribución, comisión*) delegation; ~ **de poderes** delegation; **actuar por** ~ **de alguien** to act on behalf of sb **2.** (*oficina*) local office; (*filial*) branch; **Delegación de Hacienda** (local) tax office **3.** *Méx* (*comisaría*) police station; (*ayuntamiento*) council
delegado, **-a** *m, f* delegate; ~ **gubernamental** government representative
delegar <g→gu> *vt* **1.** (*encargar*) ~ **algo en alguien** to delegate sth to sb **2.** (*transferir*) to transfer
deleitar **I.** *vt* to delight **II.** *vr* ~**se con** [*o* **en**] **algo** to delight in sth
deleite *m* delight; **con** ~ with pleasure
deletrear *vt* to spell
deleznable *adj* **1.** (*frágil*) fragile **2.** (*inconsistente*) weak; (*despreciable*) contemptible
delfín *m* dolphin
delgado, **-a** *adj* thin; (*esbelto*) slender
deliberado, **-a** *adj* **1.** (*tratado*) considered **2.** (*intencionado*) deliberate
deliberar *vi, vt* **1.** (*reflexionar*) to deliberate **2.** (*discutir*) ~ **sobre** [*o* **acerca de**] **algo** to discuss sth
delicadeza *f* **1.** (*finura*) delicacy; **con** ~ delicately **2.** (*debilidad*) weakness **3.** (*miramiento*) attentiveness; **tener la** ~ **de...** to be thoughtful enough to ...
delicado, **-a** *adj* **1.** (*fino, frágil*) delicate **2.** (*exquisito*) fine **3.** (*atento*) thoughtful **4.** (*enfermizo*) frail; **ser** ~ **de salud** to suffer from poor health **5.** (*asunto*) delicate **6.** (*exigente*) demanding
delicia *f* delight
delicioso, **-a** *adj* (*persona, cosa*) delightful; (*comida*) delicious

delictivo, -a *adj* criminal; **acto** ~ criminal act

delimitar *vt* **1.** (*terreno*) to mark out **2.** (*definir*) to define

delincuencia *f* crime, delinquency; ~ **juvenil** juvenile delinquency

delincuente **I.** *adj* criminal **II.** *mf* criminal; ~ **reincidente** persistent offender

delineante *mf* draughtsman *m Brit,* draughtswoman *f Brit,* draftsman *m Am,* draftswoman *f Am*

delinear *vt* to draw

delinquir <qu→c> *vi* to commit an offence [*o* offense *Am*]

delirante *adj* **1.** *t.* MED delirious **2.** (*idea*) crazy

delirar *vi* **1.** (*desvariar*) to be delirious **2.** (*disparatar*) to talk nonsense

delirio *m* **1.** (*enfermedad*) delirium **2.** (*ilusión*) delusion; ~ **de grandezas** delusions of grandeur

delito *m* crime; ~ **contra los derechos humanos** human rights violation; ~ **de guerra** war crime; **cuerpo del** ~ corpus delicti; ~ **común** common offence

delta *m* **1.** GEO delta **2.** DEP **ala** ~ (*aparato*) hang-glider; (*actividad*) hang-gliding

demacrarse *vr* to become haggard

demagogia *f* demagogy, demagogism *pej*

demanda *f* **1.** (*petición*) request; ~ **de empleo** job application; ~ **de extradición** JUR extradition request; **en** ~ **de algo** in search of sth **2.** COM ~ **de algo** demand for sth; ~ **adicional** surplus demand; ~ **agregada** total demand; ~ **energética** energy demands *pl;* **tener mucha** ~ to be in great demand **3.** JUR action, lawsuit; **presentar una** ~ **contra alguien** to bring an action against sb

demandado, -a **I.** *adj* (*solicitado*) requested **II.** *m, f* JUR defendant

demandante **I.** *adj* JUR **parte** ~ plaintiff **II.** *mf* claimant; JUR plaintiff

demandar *vt* **1.** (*pedir*) to ask for; (*solicitar*) to request **2.** JUR ~ **por algo** to sue [*o* file a suit] for sth

demarcación *f* **1.** (*delimitación*) demarcation; **línea de** ~ line of demarcation **2.** (*terreno*) area

demás **I.** *adj* other; **...y ~...** (*y otros*) ... and other ...; **y** ~ (*etcétera*) and so on; **por lo** ~ otherwise **II.** *adv* besides, moreover; **por** ~ more; **está por** ~ **que** *+subj* there is no point (in)

demasía *f* **1.** (*exceso*) excess; **en** ~ in excess **2.** (*insolencia*) insolence

demasiado *adv* (+ *adj*) too; (+ *verbo*) too much; **comió** ~ he/she ate too much

demasiado, -a *adj* (*singular*) too much; (*plural*) too many; **hace** ~ **calor** it's too hot; **demasiado vino** too much wine; **demasiados libros** too many books

demencia *f* **1.** MED dementia; ~ **senil** senile dementia **2.** (*locura*) madness, insanity

demencial *adj,* **demente** *adj* insane, mad

demérito *m* **1.** (*falta de mérito*) fault **2.** (*perjuicio*) disadvantage; **obrar en** ~ **de alguien** to count against sb

democracia *f* democracy

demócrata **I.** *adj* democratic **II.** *mf* democrat

democratacristiano, -a **I.** *adj* Christian Democrat(ic) **II.** *m, f* Christian Democrat

democrático, -a *adj* democratic

democratizar <z→c> **I.** *vt* to democratize **II.** *vr:* ~**se** to become democratic

demográfico, -a *adj* demographic; **explosión demográfica** population explosion; **estadísticas demográficas** vital statistics

demoledor(a) *adj* (*ataque*) devastating; (*argumento*) overwhelming; (*crítica*) merciless

demoler <o→ue> *vt* **1.** (*edificio*) to demolish **2.** *fig* (*destruir*) to destroy

demonio *m* **1.** (*espíritu*) demon **2.** (*diablo*) devil; **ser el mismísimo** ~ to be a real devil ►**tener el** ~ **en el cuerpo** to never stop; **de mil** ~**s** dreadful; **saber a** ~**s** to taste awful; **tentar al** ~ to tempt fate; **¡vete al ~!** go to hell!; **cómo/dónde/qué ~s...** how/where/what the hell ...; **como un** ~ like a madman; **ponerse como un** ~ to go mad; **ese** ~ **de mujer/de niño...** that devil of a woman/of a child ...; **¡~(s)!** damn!

demora *f* delay

demorar **I.** *vt* to delay **II.** *vr:* ~**se** **1.** (*retrasarse*) ~**se en hacer algo** to delay in doing sth **2.** (*detenerse*) to be held up

demostración *f* **1.** (*prueba*) test **2.** (*argumentación*) proof **3.** (*explicación*) explanation **4.** (*exteriorización*) display **5.** (*exhibición*) exhibition, demonstration

demostrar <o→ue> *vt* **1.** (*probar*) to demonstrate **2.** (*mostrar, exhibir*) to show **3.** (*explicar*) to explain **4.** (*expresar*) to express

demostrativo, -a *adj* **1.** (*probatorio*) evidential; **documento** ~ **del pago** document showing proof of payment **2.** LING demonstrative; **pronombre** ~ demonstrative pronoun

demudado, -a *adj* (*pálido*) pale

demudar **I.** *vt* **1.** (*variar*) to alter; **la mala noticia le demudó el rostro** he/she was visibly distressed by the bad news **2.** (*desfigurar*) to distort **II.** *vr:* ~**se** **1.** (*de color*) to go pale **2.** (*desfigurarse*) to change

denegar *irr como fregar vt* **1.** (*negar*) to deny; ~ **un derecho a alguien** to deny sb a right **2.** (*rechazar*) to refuse; ~ **una solicitud** to reject a request

denigrar *vt* **1.** (*humillar*) to denigrate **2.** (*calumniar*) to vilify **3.** (*injuriar*) to insult

denominación *f* **1.** (*nombre*) name **2.** (*acción*) naming; **Denominación de Origen** *guarantee of region of origin of wine or food* **3.** FIN denomination

denominador *m* MAT denominator; **reducir a un común** ~ *t. fig* to reduce to a common denominator

denominar **I.** *vt* (*llamar*) to name **II.** *vr:* ~**se**

to be called
denotar *vt* (*significar*) to denote
densidad *f* density
denso, -a *adj* **1.** (*compacto*) dense **2.** (*espeso*) thick **3.** (*pesado*) heavy
dentado, -a *adj* toothed; (*filo*) serrated; BOT dentate; **rueda dentada** TÉC cog(wheel)
dentadura *f* teeth *pl;* ~ **postiza** false teeth
dental *adj* dental
dentellada *f* **1.** (*mordisco*) bite; **comer algo a ~s** to wolf sth down; **matar a alguien a ~s** (*fiera*) to tear sb to bits; **pelearse a ~s** to fight tooth and nail **2.** (*herida*) toothmark
dentera *f* **dar ~ a alguien** (*dar grima*) to set sb's teeth on edge; *inf* (*dar envidia*) to make sb jealous
dentición *f* **1.** (*aparición*) teething **2.** (*dientes*) teeth
dentífrico *m* toothpaste
dentífrico, -a *adj* **pasta dentífrica** toothpaste
dentista **I.** *adj* dental **II.** *mf* dentist
dentro **I.** *adv* inside; **a ~** inside; **desde ~** from within; **por ~** inside **II.** *prep* **1.** (*local*) **~ de** inside **2.** (*con movimiento*) **~ de** into; **mirar ~ de la habitación** to look into the room **3.** (*temporal*) **~ de** within; **~ de poco** soon ► **~ de lo que cabe** all things considered; **~ de lo posible** as far as possible
denuncia *f* **1.** (*acusación*) accusation; **hacer una ~ ante alguien por algo** to make [*o* file] a complaint to sb about sth; **hacer una ~ por falta de pago** to make an official complaint due to non-payment **2.** (*de una injusticia*) denunciation; **ser una ~ de algo** to expose sth **3.** (*tratado*) cancellation
denunciar *vt* **1.** (*acusar*) **~ a alguien por algo** to accuse sb of sth **2.** (*delatar*) to betray **3.** (*hacer público*) to expose; **oficial, quiero ~ un robo** officer, I want to report a robbery **4.** (*tratado*) to cancel
denuncio *m And* (*denuncia*) report
Dep. *abr de* **departamento** department
D.E.P. *abr de* **descanse en paz** R.I.P.
deparar *vt* to bring; **nunca se sabe lo que a uno le ~á el destino** you never know what fate has in store for you
departamento *m* **1.** (*de un establecimiento*) *t.* UNIV department; **~ de contabilidad** accounts department **2.** (*de un objeto*) compartment **3.** (*ministerio*) ministry **4.** (*distrito*) district **5.** FERRO compartment **6.** *AmL* (*apartamento*) flat *Brit,* apartment *Am*
departir *vi* to converse
dependencia *f* **1.** (*sujeción*) dependency; **vivir en ~ de alguien** to be dependent on sb **2.** (*sucursal*) branch **3.** (*empleados*) personnel **4.** (*sección*) section **5.** *pl* (*habitaciones*) rooms *pl*
depender *vi* **depender de algo/alguien** to depend on sth/sb; **¡depende!** it depends!; **depende de ti** it's up to you
dependiente *adj* **~ de algo/alguien** dependent on sth/sb
dependiente, -a *m, f* dependant *Brit,* dependent *Am;* (*de una tienda*) shop assistant
depilación *f* hair removal; **~ a la cera** waxing
depilar **I.** *vt* to remove hair from **II.** *vr* **~se las cejas** to pluck one's eyebrows; **~se las piernas** (*con cera*) to wax one's legs; (*con maquinilla*) to shave one's legs
depilatorio *m* hair remover
depilatorio, -a *adj* depilatory
deplorable *adj* deplorable; **espectáculo ~** dreadful scene
deplorar *vt* **1.** (*lamentar*) to regret deeply **2.** (*condenar*) to deplore
deponer *irr como poner* **I.** *vt* **1.** (*destituir*) to remove; (*monarca*) to depose; **~ de un cargo** to remove from a position **2.** (*deshacerse de*) to set aside; **~ las armas** to lay down one's weapons **II.** *vi* to give evidence, to testify
deportación *f* deportation
deportar *vt* to deport
deporte *m* sport; **~ de (alta) competición** competitive sport; **~ hípico** equestrian sport; **~s de invierno** winter sports; **hacer ~** to practise [*o* practice *Am*] sports
deportista **I.** *adj* sporty **II.** *mf* sportsman *m,* sportswoman *f;* **~ aficionado** amateur sportsman *m,* amateur sportswoman *f;* **~ profesional** professional sportsman *m,* professional sportswoman *f*
deportividad *f* DEP sportsmanship
deportivo *m* **1.** (*club*) sports club **2.** (*automóvil*) sports car
deportivo, -a *adj* sporting; **noticias deportivas** sports news; **(zapatillas) deportivas** sports shoes, trainers *pl Brit*
depositar **I.** *vt* to put; FIN to deposit; (*cadáver*) to lay out; **~ su confianza en alguien** to place one's trust in sb **II.** *vr:* **~se** to settle
depósito *m* **1.** (*acción de guardar*) keeping; **en ~** bonded **2.** (*acción de poner al cuidado*) depositing **3.** (*depósito*) warehouse; **~ de armas** weapons store; **~ de cadáveres** morgue, mortuary; **~ de equipajes** FERRO left-luggage office *Brit,* checkroom *Am;* **~ judicial** police morgue; **~ de objetos perdidos** lost property office *Brit,* lost-and-found *Am* **4.** (*del wáter*) cistern, tank *Am* **5.** AUTO petrol tank *Brit,* gas tank *Am* **6.** *t.* FIN deposit; **hacer un ~** to make a deposit
depravar **I.** *vt* to corrupt **II.** *vr:* **~se** to become depraved
depre *f inf* **estar con la ~** to be feeling down
depreciación *f* (*desvalorización*) depreciation; **~ monetaria** devaluation
depreciar **I.** *vt* (*desvalorizar*) to depreciate; (*moneda*) to devalue **II.** *vr:* **~se** to depreciate
depredación *f* (*saqueo*) pillage
depredador(a) **I.** *adj* **1.** ZOOL predatory **2.** (*saqueador*) pillaging **II.** *m(f)* predator
depredar *vt* (*saquear*) to pillage
depresión *f* **1.** (*tristeza*) depression **2.** GEO

hollow **3.** ECON, METEO depression; ~ **cíclica** cyclical depression; ~ **económica** recession, slump

depresivo, **-a** *adj* **1.** (*que deprime*) depressing **2.** (*propenso a*) depressive

deprimir **I.** *vt* (*abatir*) to depress **II.** *vr:* **~se** (*abatirse*) to become depressed

deprisa *adv* fast, quickly; ~ **y corriendo** in a rush

depuración *f* purification; POL purge

depurado, **-a** *adj* (*estilo*) polished

depuradora *f* (*de agua*) water-treatment plant; ~ **de aguas residuales** sewage plant

depurar *vt* **1.** (*purificar*) to purify; ~ **el estilo** to polish one's style **2.** POL to purge

derecha *f* **1.** (*diestra*) right **2.** (*lado*) right-hand side; **a la** ~ (*estar*) on the right; (*ir*) to the right; **doblar a la** ~ to turn right; **tengo a mi madre a la** ~ my mother is on my right; **rebasar por la** ~ to go down to the right **3.** POL right (wing); **de** ~(**s**) right-wing

derechamente *adv* **1.** (*directamente*) directly **2.** (*correctamente*) rightly

derechista **I.** *adj* POL right-wing **II.** *mf* POL right-winger

derecho **I.** *adv* straight **II.** *m* **1.** (*legitimidad*) right; ~ **de asociación** freedom of association; ~ **de libertad de conciencia y culto** right to freedom of conscience and worship; **~s de pago de indemnización** right to receive compensation; **~s de propiedad intelectual** intellectual property rights; ~ **de sufragio** right to vote; **con** ~ **a** with the right to; **miembro de pleno** ~ full member; **estar en su** (**perfecto**) ~ to be within one's rights; **hacer uso de un** ~ to exercise one's right; **por** ~ **propio** in one's own right; **tener** ~ **a** to have the right to; **el** ~ **al pataleo** *inf* the right to complain **2.** (*jurisprudencia, ciencia*) law; ~ **criminal** criminal law; ~ **político** political law; **estudiar** ~ to study law; **conforme a** ~ lawful; **de** ~ by right **3.** (*de un papel, una tela*) right side **4.** *pl* (*impuestos*) duties *pl;* **~s de exportación** export duties; **libre de ~s** duty-free; **sujeto a ~s** subject to duty **5.** *pl* (*honorarios*) fee(s); **~s de mediación** intermediary fee; **~s de autory** royalties, copyright ►**¡no hay ~!** *inf* it's not fair!

derecho, **-a** *adj* **1.** (*diestro*) right; **lado** ~ right-hand side **2.** (*recto*) straight **3.** (*erguido*) upright; **ponerse** ~ to stand up straight **4.** (*justo*) honest; **a derechas** fairly **5.** (*directo*) direct

derivación *f* **1.** *t.* LING derivation; MAT derivative; ~ **a tierra** ELEC earth connection **2.** FERRO branch **3.** (*de agua*) channel

derivado *m* derivative

derivar **I.** *vi* **1.** (*proceder*) to derive **2.** (*tornar*) ~ **hacia algo** to turn towards sth **3.** NÁUT to drift **II.** *vt* **1.** *t.* MAT, LING (*deducir*) to derive **2.** (*desviar*) to divert; ~ **una conversación hacia otro tema** to move on to another topic **3.** ELEC to shunt **III.** *vr* **~se de algo** to come from sth

dermatólogo, **-a** *m, f* dermatologist

dérmico, **-a** *adj* skin, dermal

dermoprotector(**a**) *adj* kind to the skin, skin-friendly

derogación *f* **1.** (*de una ley*) repeal **2.** (*disminución*) decrease

derogar <g→gu> *vt* (*una ley*) to repeal

derramamiento *m* spilling; (*de sangre, lágrimas*) shedding

derramar **I.** *vt* **1.** (*verter*) to pour; (*sin querer*) to spill; (*lágrimas, sangre*) to shed **2.** (*repartir*) ~ **un gasto** to share out an expense **II.** *vr:* **~se** **1.** (*esparcirse: líquidos*) to spill; (*otros*) to scatter **2.** (*desaguar*) ~ **en algo** to leak onto sth **3.** (*diseminarse*) to spread

derrame *m* **1.** *v.* **derramamiento** **2.** (*desbordamiento*) overflow **3.** MED haemorrhage *Brit,* hemorrhage *Am;* ~ **cerebral** brain haemorrhage *Brit,* brain hemorrhage *Am*

derrapar *vi* to skid

derredor *m* surroundings; **en** ~ around

derrengado, **-a** *adj* **1.** (*deslomado*) broken **2.** (*torcido*) twisted **3.** (*exhausto*) exhausted

derretir *irr como pedir* **I.** *vt* **1.** (*deshacer*) to melt **2.** (*derrochar*) to squander **II.** *vr:* **~se** **1.** (*deshacerse*) to melt **2.** *inf* (*consumirse*) **~se de calor** to be boiling hot; **estar derretido** (**de amor**) **por alguien** to be crazy about sb

derribar *vt* **1.** (*edificio*) to demolish, to knock down, to tear down; (*puerta*) to batter down; (*árbol*) to fell; (*avión*) to shoot down **2.** (*jinete*) to knock off; (*boxeador*) to knock down **3.** (*del cargo, poder*) to remove; (*gobierno*) to overthrow **4.** (*humillar*) to humiliate

derribo *m* **1.** (*caída provocada*) knocking down; (*de un avión*) downing; (*de un futbolista*) trip **2.** (*demolición*) demolition **3.** (*escombros*) rubble

derrocar <c→qu> *vt* **1.** (*despeñar: persona*) to knock over; (*edificio*) to knock down, to tear down **2.** (*destituir*) to remove

derrochador(**a**) *adj, m(f)* spendthrift

derrochar *vt* **1.** (*despilfarrar*) to squander **2.** *inf* (*tener en abundancia*) to be brimming with

derroche *m* **1.** (*despilfarro*) waste **2.** (*exceso*) profusion

derrota *f* **1.** (*fracaso*) defeat **2.** NÁUT course **3.** (*senda*) path

derrotado, **-a** *adj* **1.** (*vencido*) defeated **2.** (*harapiento*) ragged **3.** (*deprimido*) despondent

derrotar **I.** *vt* **1.** (*vencer*) to defeat **2.** (*desmoralizar*) to demoralize **II.** *vr:* **~se** NÁUT to drift off course

derrotero *m* (*rumbo*) course; **ir por nuevos ~s** *fig* to follow a new course

derrotista *mf* defeatist

derruir *irr como huir vt* **1.** (*derribar*) to knock [*o* tear] down **2.** (*destruir*) to destroy

derrumbamiento *m* 1.(*de un edificio*) demolition 2.(*de una persona*) collapse 3.(*de tierras*) landslide
derrumbar I. *vt* 1.(*despeñar, derruir*) to knock [*o* tear] down 2.(*moralmente*) to devastate II. *vr:* ~**se** 1.(*edificio*) to fall down 2.(*esperanzas*) to collapse
desabastecido, **-a** *adj* without supplies
desaborido, **-a** I. *adj* insipid II. *m, f* bore
desabotonar *vt, vr:* ~**se** to unbutton
desabrido, **-a** *adj* 1.(*comida*) insipid 2.(*tiempo*) bad 3.(*persona*) disagreeable
desabrigado, **-a** *adj* unprotected; **estar** ~ (*persona*) to be too lightly dressed
desabrochar *vt, vr:* ~**se** (*botones, hebillas, ganchos*) to undo, to unfasten; (*cordones*) to untie
desacatar *vt* to disobey
desacato *m* ~ **a algo** disrespect for sth; JUR contempt (of court)
desacertado, **-a** *adj* 1.(*equivocado*) mistaken 2.(*inapropiado*) unfortunate
desacierto *m* mistake
desaconsejado, **-a** *adj* not advised
desaconsejar *vt* to advise against; ~ **algo a alguien** to advise sb against sth
desacorde *adj* 1. MÚS discordant 2.(*opinión*) conflicting; **estar** ~ **con algo/alguien** to not agree with sb/sth
desacostumbrado, **-a** *adj* (*fuera de la rutina*) unaccustomed; (*no común*) unusual
desacostumbrar I. *vt* ~ **a alguien de algo** to break sb of the habit of sth II. *vr* ~**se a** [*o* **de**] **hacer algo** (*perder el hábito*) to get out of the habit of doing sth; (*perder la rutina*) to become unused to sth
desacreditar I. *vt* to discredit II. *vr:* ~**se** to become discredited
desactivar *vt* (*explosivos*) to defuse
desacuerdo *m* (*discrepancia*) disagreement; **estar en** ~ to disagree
desafiador(**a**) I. *adj* defiant II. *m(f)* challenger
desafiar <*1. pres:* desafío> I. *vt* 1.(*retar*) to challenge 2.(*hacer frente a*) to defy II. *vr:* ~**se** to challenge each other
desafilado, **-a** *adj* blunt
desafinado, **-a** *adj* (*tono*) out of tune
desafinar *vi* MÚS (*al cantar*) to sing out of tune; (*al tocar*) to play out of tune; (*instrumento*) to be out of tune
desafío *m* 1.(*reto, prueba*) challenge 2.(*duelo*) duel
desaforado, **-a** *adj* 1.(*fuera de la ley*) lawless 2.(*desmedido*) excessive
desafortunado, **-a** *adj* unlucky
desafuero *m* outrage
desagradable *adj* unpleasant; **ser** ~ **al tacto/gusto** to feel/taste unpleasant
desagradar *vi* to displease; **me desagrada...** I don't like ...
desagradecido, **-a** *adj* ungrateful
desagrado *m* displeasure
desagraviar I. *vt* 1.(*excusarse*) to apologize 2.(*compensar*) to compensate II. *vr* ~**se de algo** to make amends for sth
desagravio *m* amends *pl;* (*compensación*) compensation; **en** ~ **de** as amends for
desaguar <gu→gü> I. *vi* 1.(*desembocar*) to flow 2.(*verterse*) to spill II. *vt* (*desecar*) to drain; ~ **el sótano** to pump water out of the cellar III. *vr:* ~**se** (*verterse*) to spill
desagüe *m* plughole, drain *Am*
desaguisado *m* 1.(*agravio*) offence *Brit,* offense *Am* 2. *inf* (*lío*) mess
desaguisado, **-a** *adj* 1.(*ilegal*) illegal 2.(*escandaloso*) outrageous
desahogado, **-a** *adj* 1.(*lugar*) spacious; (*prenda*) loose 2.(*adinerado*) well-off 3.(*descarado*) shameless
desahogar <g→gu> I. *vt* 1.(*aliviar*) to relieve 2.(*consolar*) to console II. *vr:* ~**se** 1.(*desfogarse*) to let off steam 2.(*confiarse*) ~**se con alguien** to tell one's troubles to sb; ~**se de un disgusto con alguien** to get sth off one's chest by talking to sb 3.(*recuperarse*) to recover
desahogo *m* 1.(*alivio*) relief 2.(*reposo*) rest 3.(*holgura económica*) comfort 4.(*descaro*) brazenness
desahuciado, **-a** *adj* 1.(*enfermo*) hopeless 2.(*inquilino*) dispossessed
desahuciar I. *vt* 1.(*enfermo*) to declare past saving 2.(*inquilino*) to evict 3.(*quitar la esperanza*) to deprive of hope II. *vr:* ~**se** to lose all hope
desahucio *m* eviction
desairado, **-a** *adj* 1.(*humillado*) insulted 2.(*desgarbado*) clumsy 3.(*ropa*) shabby
desairar *irr como airar vt* 1.(*humillar*) to insult 2.(*desestimar*) to slight 3.(*rechazar*) to snub
desaire *m* 1.(*humillación*) insult 2.(*desprecio*) disdain 3.(*desatención*) discourtesy
desajustar I. *vt* 1.(*desordenar*) to put out of balance; (*aparato*) to put out of order 2.(*aflojar*) to loosen II. *vr:* ~**se** 1.(*desavenir*) to break down 2.(*aflojarse*) to come loose
desajuste *m* 1.(*desorden*) imbalance 2.(*desconcierto*) confusion 3.(*de aparatos*) breakdown
desalentador(**a**) *adj* discouraging
desalentar <e→ie> I. *vt* (*desesperanzar*) to discourage II. *vr:* ~**se** to lose heart
desaliento *m* 1.(*falta de valor*) dismay 2.(*de fuerzas*) weakness
desaliñado, **-a** *adj* shabby
desaliño *m* shabbiness
desalmado, **-a** I. *adj* heartless II. *m, f* swine
desalojar I. *vi* to move out II. *vt* (*abandonar: casa*) to vacate; (*puesto*) to leave; (*persona*) to eject; (*cosa*) to dislodge
desalquilar I. *vt* (*dejar libre*) to stop renting II. *vr:* ~**se** to remain vacant
desamor *m* 1.(*falta de amor*) indifference 2.(*aborrecimiento*) dislike
desamparado, **-a** I. *adj* 1.(*persona*) defence-

less *Brit,* defenseless *Am* **2.** (*vagabundo*) homeless **3.** (*lugar*) exposed **4.** (*casa*) abandoned **II.** *m, f* **los ~s** the poor and homeless
desamparar *vt* **1.** (*dejar*) to abandon **2.** (*desasistir*) to fail to help
desamparo *m* **1.** (*falta de protección*) defencelessness *Brit,* defenselessness *Am* **2.** (*abandono*) abandonment
desamueblado, -a *adj* unfurnished
desamueblar *vt* **~ algo** to remove the furniture from sth
desandar *irr como andar vt* **~ lo andado** to retrace one's steps; *fig* to go back to square one; **no se puede ~ lo andado** *prov* it's no use crying over spilt milk *prov*
desangrar I. *vt* **1.** (*animales*) to bleed **2.** (*pantanos*) to drain **3.** (*arruinar*) to bleed dry **II.** *vr:* **~se 1.** (*perder mucha sangre*) to bleed heavily **2.** (*morirse*) to bleed to death
desanimado, -a *adj* **1.** (*persona*) downhearted **2.** (*lugar*) lifeless
desanimar I. *vt* to discourage **II.** *vr:* **~se** to lose heart
desánimo *m* dejection
desanudar *vt* (*nudo*) to untie
desapacible *adj* unpleasant
desaparecer *irr como crecer vi* to disappear; **~ del mapa** to vanish off the face of the earth; (*en guerra*) to go missing, to be missing in action
desaparecido, -a I. *adj* missing **II.** *m, f* missing person
desaparición *f* (*el perderse*) disappearance
desapego *m* indifference
desapercibido, -a *adj* **1.** (*inadvertido*) unnoticed; **pasar ~** to go unnoticed **2.** (*desprevenido*) unprepared; **coger ~** to catch unawares [*o* off guard]
desaplicado, -a *adj* lazy
desaprensivo, -a *adj* unscrupulous
desaprobar <o→ue> *vt* **1.** (*conducta*) **~ algo** to disapprove of sth **2.** (*solicitud*) to reject
desaprovechado, -a *adj* **1.** (*infructuoso*) fruitless **2.** (*malogrado*) wasted
desaprovechar *vt* to waste
desarmador *m* **1.** (*gatillo*) trigger **2.** *Méx* (*destornillador*) screwdriver
desarmar I. *vi* POL to disarm **II.** *vt* **1.** (*dejar sin armas*) to disarm; (*argumentos*) to confound **2.** (*desmontar*) to take apart
desarme *m* POL disarmament
desarraigar <g→gu> *vt* **1.** (*árbol, persona*) to uproot **2.** (*costumbre, creencia*) to eradicate
desarraigo *m* **1.** (*de árbol, persona*) uprooting **2.** (*de costumbre, creencia*) eradication
desarreglado, -a *adj* (*cuarto, persona*) untidy; (*vida*) disorganized
desarreglar *vt* **1.** (*desordenar*) to mess up **2.** (*perturbar*) to disturb
desarreglo *m* **1.** (*desorden: cuarto, persona*) untidiness; (*vida*) confusion **2.** (*desperfecto, molestia*) problem; (*en el coche*) trouble
desarrollar I. *vt* **1.** (*aumentar*) to develop; **~ relaciones comerciales** to develop trade relations **2.** (*tratar en detalle*) to expound **3.** (*desenrollar*) to unroll **II.** *vr:* **~se 1.** (*progresar*) to develop **2.** (*tener lugar*) to take place
desarrollo *m* **1.** *t.* FOTO development; **ayuda al ~** development aid; **país en vías de ~** developing country **2.** (*crecimiento*) growth; **~ profesional** professional development
desarrugar <g→gu> *vt* to smooth out
desarticular I. *vt* **1.** (*mecanismo*) to dismantle **2.** (*articulación*) to dislocate **3.** (*grupo*) to break up **II.** *vr:* **~se 1.** (*mecanismo*) to come apart; (*piezas*) to come loose **2.** (*articulación*) to become dislocated **3.** (*grupo*) to break up
desaseado, -a *adj* (*sucio*) dirty; (*desordenado*) untidy
desasir *irr como asir* **I.** *vt* **~ algo** to let go of sth **II.** *vr:* **~se 1.** (*desprenderse*) to come off **2.** (*desacostumbrarse*) to let go
desasosegar *irr como fregar* **I.** *vt* to worry **II.** *vr:* **~se** to become uneasy
desasosiego *m* unease
desastrado, -a *adj* **1.** (*desaliñado*) untidy; (*harapiento*) shabby **2.** (*infortunado*) unlucky, wretched
desastre *m* disaster; **ser un ~** *inf* (*alguien*) to be hopeless; (*algo*) to be a flop
desastroso, -a *adj* disastrous
desatado, -a *adj* **1.** (*desligado*) untied **2.** (*desenfrenado*) wild; **estar ~** to be out of control
desatar I. *vt* **1.** (*soltar*) to untie; (*nudo, paquete, zapatos*) to undo **2.** (*causar*) to unleash **II.** *vr:* **~se 1.** (*soltarse*) to untie oneself; (*nudo*) to come undone **2.** (*desligarse*) to free oneself **3.** (*desencadenarse: tormenta*) to break; (*crisis*) to erupt **4.** (*perder la contención*) **~se en improperios** to let loose a stream of abuse
desatascar <c→qu> *vt* **1.** (*desobstruir*) to unblock **2.** (*sacar del atascadero*) to pull out **3.** (*activar*) to get going
desatención *f* **1.** (*distracción*) inattention **2.** (*descortesía*) discourtesy
desatender <e→ie> *vt* **1.** (*desoír*) to ignore **2.** (*abandonar*) to neglect
desatento, -a *adj* **1.** (*distraído*) inattentive; (*negligente*) careless **2.** (*descortés*) **~ con alguien** impolite to sb
desatinado, -a *adj* **1.** (*desacertado*) foolish **2.** (*irreflexivo*) rash
desatinar *vi* (*conducta*) to act foolishly; (*palabras*) to say stupid things
desatino *m* **1.** (*error*) mistake; (*torpeza*) blunder **2.** (*tontería*) rubbish
desatornillador *m AmL* screwdriver
desatornillar *vt* to unscrew; **~ un tornillo** to remove a screw
desatracar <c→qu> *vi* NÁUT to cast off
desatrancar <c→qu> *vt* **1.** (*puerta*) to unbolt **2.** (*desatascar*) to unblock
desautorizado, -a *adj* unauthorized
desautorizar <z→c> *vt* (*inhabilitar*) to

deprive of authority; (*prohibir*) to ban; (*desmentir*) to deny
desavenencia *f* **1.** (*desacuerdo*) disagreement **2.** (*discordia*) friction
desavenir *irr como venir* **I.** *vt* to cause to fall out **II.** *vr:* **~se** to fall out
desaventajado, -a *adj* **1.** (*poco ventajoso*) unfavourable *Brit,* unfavorable *Am* **2.** (*inferior*) inferior
desayunar **I.** *vi* to have [*o* eat] breakfast; **~ fuerte** to eat a large breakfast **II.** *vt* **~ algo** to have sth for breakfast
desayuno *m* breakfast
desazón *f* **1.** (*desasosiego*) unease **2.** (*malestar*) discomfort **3.** (*picor*) itch
desazonar **I.** *vt* **1.** (*enfadar*) to annoy **2.** (*inquietar*) to worry **II.** *vr:* **~se** **1.** (*enfadarse*) to get annoyed **2.** (*inquietarse*) to worry
desbancar <c→qu> *vt* to oust
desbandarse *vr* **1.** MIL to disband **2.** *fig* to scatter
desbarajuste *m* chaos; **¡esto es un ~ total!** this is a total mess!
desbaratar **I.** *vt* **1.** (*desunir, dispersar*) to break up **2.** (*desmontar*) to take apart **3.** (*arruinar*) to ruin **II.** *vr:* **~se** **1.** (*separarse*) to break up **2.** (*estropearse*) to break down **3.** (*fracasar*) to fail
desbloquear *vt* **1.** (*desatascar*) *t.* POL to unblock **2.** FIN to unfreeze
desbocado, -a *adj* **1.** (*herramienta*) worn **2.** (*escote*) wide **3.** (*persona: deslenguado*) foulmouthed; (*enloquecida*) mad **4.** (*caballo*) runaway
desbocar <c→qu> **I.** *vt* **1.** (*cacharro*) to chip **2.** (*enloquecer*) to drive mad [*o* crazy] **II.** *vr:* **~se** **1.** (*enloquecer*) to go mad [*o* crazy] **2.** (*caballo*) to bolt
desbordamiento *m* overflowing; INFOR overflow; *fig* outbreak
desbordante *adj* (*alegría, entusiasmo*) boundless; **~ de alegría** brimming with happiness
desbordar **I.** *vr:* **~se** **1.** (*líquido*) to overflow; (*río*) to overflow, to burst its banks *Brit* **2.** (*vicio*) to get out of control **II.** *vi* to overflow; **~ de alegría** to be brimming with happiness; **~ de emoción** to be full of emotion **III.** *vt* (*exceder*) to exceed; **esto desborda mi paciencia** this is the final straw
desbravar *vt* **1.** (*domar*) to tame; (*caballo*) to break (in) **2.** (*dominar*) to bring under control
descabalgar <g→gu> *vi* to dismount
descabellado, -a *adj* preposterous
descabellar *vt* **1.** TAUR to give the coup de grâce to (*to kill the bull by sticking a sword in its neck*) **2.** (*desgreñar*) to ruffle
descabezado, -a *adj* headless
descabezar <z→c> *vt* **1.** (*decapitar*) to behead **2.** (*podar*) to top, to cut the tops off **3.** **~ un sueñecito** to have a nap
descafeinado, -a *adj* **1.** (*café*) decaffeinated **2.** *fig* (*falto de fuerzas*) watered-down
descalabrar **I.** *vt* **~ a alguien** to injure sb on the head ►**salir descalabrado** to come off badly **II.** *vr:* **~se** (*en la cabeza*) to injure one's head
descalabro *m* **1.** (*herida*) serious injury **2.** (*revés*) setback; **sufrir un ~** (*derrota*) to suffer a defeat
descalcificar <c→qu> *vt* decalcify
descalificación *f* disqualification
descalificar <c→qu> *vt* to disqualify
descalzar <z→c> **I.** *vt* **~ a alguien** to take sb's shoes off **II.** *vr:* **~se** (*alguien*) to take one's shoes off
descalzo, -a *adj* **1.** (*sin zapatos*) barefoot **2.** *fig* (*indigente*) destitute
descambiar *vt inf* to swap, to change back, to exchange
descaminar **I.** *vt* to misdirect ►**ir descaminado** to be on the wrong track **II.** *vr:* **~se** **1.** (*perderse*) to get lost **2.** (*descarriarse*) to go astray
descampado *m* piece of open ground; **en ~** in the open
descansado, -a *adj* **1.** *estar* (*bien dormido*) rested **2.** *ser* (*cómodo*) restful
descansar **I.** *vi* **1.** (*reposar*) to rest; **descanse en paz** (*difunto*) rest in peace **2.** (*recuperarse*) to recover **3.** (*dormir*) to sleep; **¡que descanses!** sleep well! **4.** (*apoyar*) to rest **5.** (*confiar*) to trust **II.** *vt* **1.** (*apoyar*) to rest **2.** (*aliviar*) to relieve **III.** *vr:* **~se** (*confiarse*) to trust (*en* in)
descansillo *m* landing
descanso *m* **1.** (*reposo*) rest; **día de ~** day of rest, day off **2.** (*recuperación*) recovery **3.** (*tranquilidad*) peace **4.** (*pausa*) *t.* DEP break; (*alto*) pause; **sin ~** without a break **5.** (*alivio*) relief **6.** (*apoyo*) support **7.** (*descansillo*) landing
descapotable **I.** *adj* **coche ~** convertible **II.** *m* convertible
descarado, -a *adj* **1.** (*desvergonzado*) shameless **2.** (*evidente*) blatant
descararse *vr* (*insolentarse*) **~ con alguien** to be impudent [*o* cheeky *Brit*] to sb
descarga *f* **1.** (*de mercancías*) unloading **2.** (*disparo*) discharge; (*disparos*) volley; **una ~ de golpes** a hail of blows **3.** ELEC, FÍS, FIN discharge; **~ eléctrica** (*calambre*) electric shock
descargar <g→gu> **I.** *vi* **1.** (*desembocar*) to flow **2.** (*tormenta*) to break **II.** *vt* **1.** (*carga*) to unload; **~ el vientre** to move one's bowels **2.** ELEC, FÍS to discharge; (*corriente*) to use up **3.** (*disparar*) to fire; **~ un golpe sobre...** to land a blow on ... **4.** (*desahogar*) to vent; **~ su mal humor en** [*o* **sobre**] **alguien** to vent one's bad temper on sb **5.** (*aliviar*) to relieve; FIN to discharge **6.** JUR (*absolver*) to acquit (*de* of); (*librar*) to release **7.** INFOR to download **III.** *vr:* **~se** **1.** (*vaciarse*) to empty; ELEC, FÍS to discharge; (*pila*) to go flat, to run out **2.** (*librarse*) to unburden oneself **3.** (*desahogarse*) to let off steam

descargo *m* **1.** (*descarga*) unloading **2.** FIN discharge **3.** (*liberación*) release **4.** (*justificación*) excuse; **en mi ~** in my defence [*o* defense *Am*] **5.** (*absolución*) acquittal; **testigo de ~** witness for the defence [*o* defense *Am*]
descarnado, -a *adj* **1.** (*sin carne*) scrawny; (*huesudo*) bony; (*flaco*) thin **2.** (*acre*) brutal **3.** *fig* bare
descaro *m* cheek
descarriar <*1. pres:* descarrío> **I.** *vt* **1.** (*animal*) to separate from the herd **2.** (*descaminar*) to misdirect **II.** *vr:* **~se 1.** (*perderse*) to get lost **2.** (*descaminarse*) to go astray
descarrilamiento *m* derailment
descarrilar *vi* to be derailed
descartar I. *vt* (*propuesta*) to reject; (*posibilidad*) to rule out **II.** *vr:* **~se** (*naipes*) to discard
descascarar I. *vt* (*pelar*) to peel; (*nuez*) to shell **II.** *vr:* **~se** to chip
descascarillarse *vr* (*loza*) to chip; (*pintura*) to peel
descendencia *f* descendents *pl;* **tener ~** to have offspring
descendente *adj* **1.** (*en caída*) descending **2.** (*en disminución*) diminishing
descender <e→ie> **I.** *vi* **1.** (*ir abajo*) to descend; (*a un valle, una mina*) to go down **2.** (*disminuir*) to diminish **3.** (*proceder*) to be descended **II.** *vt* **1.** (*llevar*) to take down **2.** (*una escalera*) to go down
descendiente *mf* descendant
descenso *m* **1.** (*bajada*) descent; **carrera de ~** DEP downhill race **2.** (*cuesta, pendiente*) slope **3.** (*disminución, caída*) decline; ECON downturn
descentralizar <z→c> *vt* to decentralize
descerrajar *vt* **1.** (*puerta*) to force **2.** (*tiro*) **~ a alguien** to fire at sb
descifrar *vt* (*mensaje, código*) to decipher; (*problema*) to figure out
descocado, -a *adj* **1.** (*descarado*) impudent **2.** (*indecente*) brazen
descoco *m* **1.** (*descaro*) impudence **2.** (*indecencia*) brazenness
descodificador *m* decoder
descodificar <c→qu> *vt* to decode
descojonante *adj inf* hilarious
descojonarse *vr inf* (*reír*) **~se de alguien/algo** to piss oneself laughing
descolgar *irr como colgar* **I.** *vt* **1.** (*quitar*) to take off **2.** (*teléfono*) to pick up **3.** (*bajar*) to take down ►**andar descolgado** *inf* to be left out **II.** *vr:* **~se 1.** (*bajar*) to come down **2.** (*aparecer*) to turn up **3.** (*dejar caer*) to drop
descollar <o→ue> *vi* to stand out; **Goya descolló en la pintura de su tiempo** Goya stands out among the artists of his time
descolorar *vt, vr,* **descolorir** *vt, vr:* **~se** *v.* **decolorar**
descomedido, -a *adj* **1.** (*excesivo*) excessive **2.** (*insolente*) rude
descomedirse *irr como pedir vr* to go too far
descompaginar *vi* to upset
descompasado, -a *adj* **1.** (*sin proporción*) out of all proportion **2.** MÚS out of time
descompensar I. *vt* to unbalance; **estar descompensado** to be unbalanced **II.** *vr:* **~se** to unbalance
descomponer *irr como poner* **I.** *vt* **1.** (*desordenar*) to mess up **2.** (*separar*) to take apart **3.** (*corromper*) *t.* QUÍM to decompose **4.** (*enfurecer*) to anger **II.** *vr:* **~se 1.** (*desmembrarse*) to come apart **2.** (*corromperse*) to decay **3.** (*enfermar*) to become ill **4.** (*encolerizarse*) to lose one's temper
descomposición *f* **1.** (*separación*) separation; QUÍM decomposition **2.** (*corrupción*) decay **3.** (*diarrea*) **~** (**de vientre**) diarrhoea *Brit,* diarrhea *Am*
descompostura *f* **1.** (*desarreglo*) disorder **2.** (*descomedimiento*) rudeness
descompuesto, -a I. *pp de* **descomponer II.** *adj* **1.** (*desordenado*) untidy **2.** (*podrido*) rotten **3.** (*alterado*) upset; **ponerse ~ de rabia** to lose one's temper **4.** (*enfermo*) ill
descomunal *adj* enormous
desconcertar <e→ie> *vt* **1.** (*desbaratar*) to ruin; (*planes*) to upset **2.** (*pasmar*) to confuse; **estar desconcertado** to be disconcerted
desconchado *m* (*de loza*) chip; (*en la pared*) *place where paint has come off*
desconcierto *m* **1.** (*desarreglo*) disorder **2.** (*desorientación*) confusion
desconectar I. *vi, vt* to disconnect; (*radio, tele*) to switch off; (*desenchufar*) to unplug **II.** *vi inf* to switch off
desconfiado, -a *adj* distrustful
desconfianza *f* distrust
desconfiar <*1. pres:* desconfío> *vi* **~ de alguien/algo** to mistrust sb/sth
descongelar I. *vt* **1.** (*comida*) to thaw out; (*el frigorífico*) to defrost **2.** FIN to unfreeze; **~ los salarios** to lift a wage freeze **II.** *vr:* **~se** (*comida*) to thaw out; (*el frigorífico*) to defrost
descongestionar *vt* to unblock; MED to clear
desconocer *irr como crecer vt* **1.** (*ignorar*) **~ algo** to be unaware of sth **2.** (*subestimar*) to underestimate **3.** (*no conocer*) to not know; (*no reconocer*) to not recognize **4.** (*no aceptar*) to deny; **~ la paternidad** to disown one's paternity
desconocido, -a I. *adj* unknown; (*correos*) address unknown; **estar ~** (*cambiado*) to be unrecognizable **II.** *m, f* stranger; **un completo ~** a total stranger
desconocimiento *m* **1.** (*ignorancia*) ignorance; **por ~ de los hechos** without full knowledge of the facts **2.** (*ingratitud*) ingratitude
desconsiderado, -a *adj* inconsiderate
desconsolado, -a *adj* (*triste*) grief-stricken; (*inconsolable*) unconsolable
desconsolar <o→ue> **I.** *vt* to distress **II.** *vr:* **~se** to lose hope
desconsuelo *m* distress; **daba ~ verlo** it was sad to see him like that

D

descontado, **-a** *adj* (*descartado*) discounted ►**dar algo por** ~ to take sth for granted; **por** ~ of course

descontar <o→ue> *vt* 1. (*restar*) to take away 2. (*letras*) to discount 3. (*descartar*) to disregard; **descontando que fuera...** +*subj* assuming that it was not ...

descontento *m* dissatisfaction

descontento, **-a** *adj* dissatisfied

descontrol *m* loss of control

descontrolarse *vr* (*máquina*) to go out of control; (*persona*) to go wild

descorazonar I. *vt* to discourage II. *vr*: ~**se** to lose heart

descorchador *m* corkscrew

descorchar *vt* (*botella*) to uncork

descorrer I. *vt* to draw; (*cortinas, cerrojo*) to draw back; ~ **el cerrojo** to unbolt the door II. *vr*: ~**se** to open

descortés *adj* impolite

descortesía *f* discourtesy

descoser I. *vt* (*costura*) to unpick *Brit*, to unstitch; **tengo la manga descosida** my sleeve is coming apart at the seam II. *vr*: ~**se** 1. (*costura*) to come apart at the seam; **se me ha descosido un botón** one of my buttons has come off 2. *inf* to fart

descosido, **-a** *adj* **como un** ~ (*loco*) like mad; **hablar como un** ~ to talk one's head off

descoyuntar *vt* 1. (*dislocar*) to dislocate 2. (*falsear*) to distort ►**estar descoyuntado** *inf* to be dead beat

descrédito *m* discredit; **caer en** ~ to fall into disrepute

descreído, **-a** *adj* sceptical *Brit*, skeptical *Am*

descremar *vt* (*milk*) to skim

describir *irr como escribir vt* 1. (*explicar*) to describe 2. (*trazar*) to trace

descripción *f* description; JUR statement, particulars *pl*

descuajaringar <g→gu> I. *vt* to break into pieces II. *vr*: ~**se** *inf* (*cansarse*) to be knackered; ~ **de risa** to laugh one's head off

descuartizar <z→c> *vt* to cut up; (*en cuatro*) to quarter

descubierto *m* 1. (*lugar*) **al** ~ in the open; MIN opencast 2. (*bancario*) overdraft; **al** [*o* **en**] ~ (*cuenta, cheque*) overdrawn; **quedarse en** ~ to be overdrawn 3. (*en evidencia*) **poner algo al** ~ to bring sth into the open; **quedar al** ~ to be revealed

descubierto, **-a** I. *pp de* **descubrir** II. *adj* open; (*sin techo*) open-air; (*cielo*) clear; (*cabeza*) uncovered; (*paisaje*) bare

descubridor(a) *m(f)* discoverer

descubrimiento *m* 1. (*tierras, invento*) discovery 2. (*revelación*) disclosure; JUR detection

descubrir *irr como abrir* I. *vt* 1. (*destapar*) to uncover 2. (*encontrar*) to discover 3. (*averiguar*) to find out 4. (*inventar*) to invent 5. (*revelar*) to reveal 6. (*desenmascarar*) to unmask II. *vr*: ~**se** 1. (*salir a la luz*) to come out 2. (*traicionarse*) to give oneself away 3. (*desenmascararse*) to reveal oneself 4. (*saludo*) to raise one's hat

descuento *m* 1. (*deducción*) discount 2. (*rebaja*) reduction; COM discount; ~ **por pago al contado** cash discount; ~ **por cantidad** quantity discount; ~ **al por mayor** discount on bulk purchase; ~ **por not tener siniestros** no claims bonus 3. (*de letras de cambio: acción*) discounting; (*cantidad*) discount 4. DEP injury time

descuidado, **-a** *adj* 1. *ser* (*falto de atención*) inattentive; (*de cuidado*) careless; (*imprudente*) negligent; (*desaseado*) slovenly; (*desaliñado*) untidy 2. *estar* (*abandonado*) neglected; (*desprevenido*) unprepared; **aspecto** ~ untidiness; **coger** ~ **a alguien** to catch sb off his/her guard

descuidar I. *vi* ¡**descuida!** don't worry! II. *vt* 1. (*desatender*) to neglect 2. (*ignorar*) to overlook III. *vr*: ~**se** 1. (*abandonarse*) to neglect oneself, to let oneself go 2. (*distraerse*) to be distracted

descuidero, **-a** *m, f* pickpocket

descuido *m* 1. (*falta de atención*) inattentiveness; (*de cuidado*) carelessness; (*imprudencia*) negligence 2. (*error*) oversight; **por** ~ inadvertently

desde I. *prep* 1. (*temporal: pasado*) since; (*a partir de*) from; ~**...hasta...** from ... until ...; ~ **ahora** (**en adelante**) from now on; ¿~ **cuándo?** since when?; ¿~ **cuándo vives aquí?** how long have you lived here (for)?; ~ **entonces** since then; ~ **hace un mes** for a month; ~ **hace poco/mucho** for a short/long time; ~ **hoy/mañana** from today/tomorrow; ~ **el principio** from the beginning; ~ **ya** from now on 2. (*local*) from; **te llamo** ~ **el aeropuerto** I'm calling from the airport II. *adv* ~ **luego** (*por supuesto*) of course; **¿vienes con nosostros? – ¡~ luego!** are you coming with us? – of course I am!; **hace un tiempo horroroso – ¡~ luego!** the weather is dreadful – absolutely! III. *conj* ~ **que** since

desdecir *irr como decir* I. *vi* to be unworthy; ~ **de los suyos** to let one's family down II. *vr*: ~**se de algo** to withdraw sth, to take sth back; ~**se de una promesa** to go back on a promise

desdén *m* disdain

desdentado, **-a** *adj* toothless

desdeñable *adj* 1. (*insignificante*) insignificant; **nada** ~ far from negligible 2. (*despreciable*) despicable

desdeñar *vt* 1. (*despreciar*) to scorn 2. (*rechazar*) to spurn

desdeñoso, **-a** *adj* disdainful; (*soberbio*) contemptuous

desdibujar I. *vt* to blur II. *vr*: ~**se** to become blurred

desdicha *f* 1. (*desgracia*) misfortune; (*suceso*) calamity 2. (*miseria*) misery

desdichado, **-a** *adj* unfortunate; **es un** ~ he is an unfortunate wretch

desdoblar I. *vt* 1. (*desplegar*) to unfold;

(*extender*) to open out, to spread out **2.** (*dividir*) to divide **3.** (*duplicar*) to double **II.** *vr:* **~se 1.** (*abrirse*) to open out **2.** (*dividirse*) to divide **3.** (*duplicarse*) to double

desdoro *m* dishonour *Brit,* dishonor *Am*

deseable *adj* desirable

desear *vt* to want; (*sexualmente*) to desire; **~ suerte a alguien** to wish sb luck; **hacerse ~** to play hard to get; **¿desea algo más?** would you like anything else?; **dejar mucho que ~** to leave a lot to be desired

desecar <c→qu> **I.** *vt* (*pantano*) to dry out; (*alimentos, aire*) to dry **II.** *vr:* **~se** to dry up

desechable *adj* **1.** (*de un solo uso*) disposable; **guantes ~s** disposable gloves; **botellas ~s** non-returnable bottles **2.** (*despreciable*) despicable; **nada ~** far from negligible

desechar *vt* **1.** (*tirar*) to throw away **2.** (*descartar*) to rule out; (*desestimar*) to reject **3.** (*desdeñar*) to scorn

desecho(s) *m(pl)* (*restos*) remains *pl;* (*residuos*) residue; (*basura*) waste; **~s tóxicos** toxic waste; **de ~** waste; **el ~ de la sociedad** the dregs of society

desembalar *vt* to unpack

desembarazado, -a *adj* **1.** (*expedito*) free **2.** (*desenvuelto*) free and easy

desembarazar <z→c> **I.** *vt* **1.** (*desocupar*) to empty **2.** (*despejar*) to clear; (*librar*) to free **II.** *vr:* **~se** to free oneself **III.** *vi Chile* (*dar a luz*) to give birth

desembarazo *m* **1.** (*despejo*) clearing **2.** (*desenvoltura*) ease

desembarcadero *m* landing stage; (*puente*) jetty, wharf

desembarcar <c→qu> **I.** *vi* **1.** (*descargar*) to disembark **2.** (*una escalera*) to lead to **II.** *vt* **1.** (*descargar*) to unload **2.** (*transportar*) to transport

desembarco *m* (*arribada*) landing

desembargar <g→gu> *vt* **~ algo** to lift the embargo on sth

desembarque *m* **1.** (*arribada*) landing **2.** (*descarga*) unloading

desembarrancar <c→qu> *vt* to refloat

desembocadura *f* **1.** (*de un río*) mouth **2.** (*desagüe*) outlet

desembocar <c→qu> *vi* **1.** (*río*) **~ en** to flow into **2.** (*situación*) **~ en** to result in

desembolsar *vt* **1.** (*sacar*) **~ algo** to take sth out of one's pocket **2.** (*pagar*) to pay, to pay out *Brit;* (*gastar*) to spend

desembolso *m* **1.** (*pago*) payment **2.** (*gasto*) expense

desembozar <z→c> **I.** *vt* **1.** (*descubrir*) to uncover **2.** (*desatrancar*) to unblock **II.** *vr:* **~se 1.** (*descubrirse*) to uncover oneself **2.** (*desatrancarse*) to become unblocked

desembragar <g→gu> AUTO **I.** *vi* to release the clutch **II.** *vt* to release

desembrollar *vt inf* **1.** (*madeja*) to disentangle **2.** (*asunto*) to sort out

desembuchar **I.** *vi inf* (*confesar*) to come clean; **¡desembucha de una vez!** out with it! **II.** *vt* **~ algo** to come clean about sth

desempacar <c→qu> *vt* to unpack

desempapelar *vt* (*paquete*) to unwrap; **~ una habitación** to strip the wallpaper of a room

desempaquetar *vt* to unwrap

desempatar *vi* to break the tie

desempate *m* breakthrough

desempeñar *vt* **1.** (*préstamo*) to pay off **2.** (*cargo*) to hold; (*trabajo*) to carry out; **~ un papel** to play a role

desempeño *m* **1.** (*de un préstamo*) repayment **2.** (*ejercicio*) fulfilment *Brit,* fulfillment *Am;* (*realización*) performance

desempleado, -a **I.** *adj* unemployed **II.** *m, f* unemployed person

desempleo *m* unemployment

desempolvar *vt* **1.** (*limpiar*) to dust **2.** (*lo olvidado*) to revive, to brush up

desencadenar **I.** *vt* **1.** (*soltar*) to unleash **2.** (*provocar*) to trigger **II.** *vr:* **~se** to break loose

desencajar **I.** *vt* (*sacar*) to dismantle; MED to dislocate; (*cara*) to distort **II.** *vr:* **~se** (*salirse*) to come apart; MED to dislocate

desencantar **I.** *vt* **1.** (*desilusionar*) to disillusion; (*decepcionar*) to disappoint **2.** (*desembrujar*) **~ algo** to break the spell on sth **II.** *vr:* **~se** to become disillusioned

desencanto *m* **1.** (*decepción*) disappointment **2.** (*desilusión*) disillusion

desenchufar *vt* to unplug

desencoger <g→j> **I.** *vt* **1.** (*extender*) to spread out **2.** (*estirar*) to stretch **II.** *vr:* **~se 1.** (*extenderse*) to spread out **2.** (*estirarse*) to stretch **3.** (*desempacharse*) to come out of one's shell

desencolarse *vr* to come unstuck

desencuadernar **I.** *vt* (*libro*) to remove the binding from **II.** *vr:* **~se** *t. fig* to fall apart

desenfadado, -a *adj* **1.** (*desenvuelto*) self-assured **2.** (*carácter*) easy-going **3.** (*ropa*) casual

desenfado *m* openness; (*sin inhibiciones*) naturalness

desenfocado, -a *adj* FOTO out of focus

desenfrenado, -a *adj* frantic

desenfreno *m* lack of restraint

desenganchar **I.** *vt* **1.** (*gancho*) to unhook **2.** (*soltar*) to take off; (*caballos*) to unhitch **3.** FERRO to uncouple **II.** *vr:* **~se** *inf* (*de la droga*) to get off drugs

desengañar **I.** *vt* (*desilusionar*) to disillusion; **~ a alguien** (*abrir los ojos*) to shatter sb's illusions **II.** *vr:* **~se** (*decepcionarse*) to be disappointed; **pronto te ~ás** (*verás claro*) you'll soon see the truth

desengaño *m* disillusion; **sufrir un ~ amoroso** to have an unhappy love affair

desengrasar *vt* to remove the grease from

desenlace *m* outcome; **la película tiene un ~ feliz** the film has a happy ending

desenlazar <z→c> **I.** *vt* **1.** (*desatar*) to untie

D

2. (*resolver*) to clear up **II.** *vr:* **~se** (*resolverse*) to be resolved; TEAT to end

desenmarañar *vt* **1.** (*desenredar*) to untangle **2.** (*desentrañar*) to figure out

desenmascarar **I.** *vt* to unmask; *fig* to expose **II.** *vr:* **~se** to remove one's mask; *fig* to reveal oneself

desenredar **I.** *vt t. fig* to unravel; (*pelo*) to untangle **II.** *vr:* **~se** *inf* (*librarse*) to extricate oneself

desenroscar <c→qu> *vt* **1.** (*abrir, sacar de la rosca*) to unscrew **2.** (*desenrollar*) to unwind

desentenderse <e→ie> *vr* **1.** (*despreocuparse*) **~ de algo** to want nothing to do with sth; **~ de un problema** to wash one's hands of a problem **2.** (*fingir ignorancia*) **~ de algo** to pretend to not know about sth; **hacerse el desentendido** to turn a deaf ear

desenterrar <e→ie> *vt* **1.** to dig up, to disinter *form;* (*cadáver*) to exhume **2.** (*encontrar*) to find; **~ viejos recuerdos** to rake up old memories

desentonar *vi* **1.** (*cantar*) to sing out of tune; (*tocar*) to play out of tune **2.** (*no combinar*) to not go [*o* match]; **con esa ropa desentonas en la fiesta** with those clothes you'll be out of place at the party

desentorpecer *irr como crecer vt* **1.** (*desembarazar*) to clear **2.** (*desentumecer*) to loosen up **3.** (*afinar*) to polish up

desentrañar *vt* (*descubrir*) to unravel

desentumecer *irr como crecer vt* to loosen up; DEP to warm up

desenvoltura *f* self-confidence; (*descaro*) cheek, gall

desenvolver *irr como volver* **I.** *vt* **1.** (*desempaquetar*) to unwrap **2.** (*desenrollar*) to unwind; (*desdoblar*) to unfold **3.** (*descubrir*) to discover **4.** (*desarrollar*) to develop **II.** *vr:* **~se** **1.** (*llevarse*) to get on with **2.** (*manejarse*) to handle oneself

desenvuelto, **-a** **I.** *pp de* **desenvolver** **II.** *adj* (*resuelto*) self-assured; (*descarado*) impudent

deseo *m* **1.** (*anhelo*) wish; **~ imperioso** burning desire; **tener ~s de venganza** to want to get one's revenge; **tengo grandes ~s de que vengan** I really hope they come; **formular un ~** to make a wish **2.** (*necesidad*) need **3.** (*ansia*) longing **4.** (*sexual*) desire **5.** (*impulso*) whim

deseoso, **-a** *adj* **estar ~ de hacer algo** (*ansioso*) to be eager to do sth; **estoy ~ de conocerlo** I'm dying to meet him

desequilibrado, **-a** *adj* unbalanced; (*trastornado*) (mentally) disturbed

desequilibrar **I.** *vt* **1.** (*descompensar*) to unbalance **2.** (*trastornar*) to disturb **II.** *vr:* **~se** **1.** (*descompensarse*) to unbalance **2.** (*psíquicamente*) to become disturbed

desequilibrio *m* **1.** (*falta de equilibrio*) lack of balance; (*descompensación, desproporción*) imbalance **2.** (*trastorno*) disturbance; **~ mental** mental instability

desertar *vi* **1.** MIL to desert; **~ de** to desert from; **~ a** to go over to **2.** *fig* (*abandonar*) to abandon

desértico, **-a** *adj* desert

desertor(a) *m(f)* deserter

desesperación *f* **1.** (*desmoralización*) desperation, despair; **con ~** desperately; **caer en la ~** to become desperate **2.** (*enojo*) exasperation **3.** (*que desespera*) **ser una ~** to be a cause of despair; **tu manera de trabajar es mi ~** the way you work exasperates me

desesperado, **-a** *adj* **1.** (*desmoralizado*) desperate; (*situación*) hopeless; **correr/gritar como un ~** to run/shout like mad; **hacer algo a la desesperada** to do sth as a last resort **2.** (*enojado*) exasperated

desesperante *adj* **1.** (*sin esperanza*) hopeless; **resulta ~...** there is no point ...; **¡eres ~!** you're a disaster! **2.** (*exasperante*) exasperating; **tu comportamiento es ~** your behaviour drives me to despair

desesperar **I.** *vt* **1.** (*quitar la esperanza*) **~ a alguien** to cause sb to lose hope **2.** (*exasperar*) to exasperate **II.** *vi* to despair; **no desesperes de que sigan vivos** don't lose hope, they're still alive **III.** *vr:* **~se** **1.** (*perder la esperanza*) to give up hope; **¡no te desesperes!** don't give up! **2.** (*lamentarse*) **~ por algo** to despair of sth **3.** (*despecharse*) to despair

desestimar *vt* **1.** (*despreciar*) **~ algo** to have a low opinion of sth **2.** (*rechazar*) to reject; **~ una demanda/una reclamación** to reject a demand/a claim

desfachatez *f* cheek

desfalcar <c→qu> *vt* (*dinero*) to embezzle

desfalco *m* embezzlement

desfallecer *irr como crecer* **I.** *vi* **1.** (*debilitarse*) to weaken **2.** (*colapsar*) to collapse; (*desmayarse*) to faint **3.** (*perder el ánimo*) to lose heart; **después de una hora empezó a ~** after an hour he/she began to flag **II.** *vt* **1.** (*debilitar*) to weaken **2.** (*desanimar*) to discourage

desfallecimiento *m* **1.** (*debilidad*) weakening **2.** (*desmayo*) faint; (*colapso*) collapse; **~ de ánimo** loss of heart; **~ (de las fuerzas)** loss of strength; **poco antes de llegar a la meta le sobrevino el ~** just before reaching the end, he/she collapsed

desfasado, **-a** *adj* **1.** (*anticuado: persona*) old-fashioned; (*cosa*) antiquated; **estar ~** to be behind the times **2.** TÉC out of phase

desfase *m* (*diferencia*) gap; **~ con la realidad** lack of realism; **¡que ~!** *inf* wild!

desfavorable *adj* unfavourable *Brit,* unfavorable *Am*

desfavorecer *irr como crecer vt* **1.** (*perjudicar*) to discriminate against **2.** (*sentar mal*) **este clima me desfavorece** this climate doesn't suit me **3.** (*oponerse*) to be against

desfigurar *vt* **1.** (*afear: las facciones*) to disfigure; (*el cuerpo, el tipo*) to deform

2. (*deformar*) to deface; (*una imagen, la realidad*) to distort; (*un texto*) to mutilate **3.** (*disfrazar*) to disguise **4.** (*ocultar*) to hide

desfiguro *m Méx* (*cosa ridícula*) silly stunt; **hacer un** ~ to make a fool of oneself

desfiladero *m* GEO gorge

desfilar *vi* **1.** (*marchar en fila*) *t.* MIL to walk in file; **desfilaron ante la reina** they paraded before the queen **2.** (*salir*) to file out

desfile *m* **1.** (*acción*) marching; (*de tropas*) march-past; (*parada*) parade; POL march; (*en una fiesta*) procession; ~ **de modelos** fashion show **2.** (*personas*) procession; **participar en el** ~ to join the procession

desflorar *vt* **1.** (*a una mujer*) to deflower **2.** (*estropear*) to spoil; (*gastar*) to use up

desfogar <g→gu> **I.** *vt* **1.** (*un sentimiento*) to vent; ~ **su ira** to vent one's anger; ~ **su mal humor en** [*o* **con**] **alguien** to take it out on sb **2.** (*un fuego*) to fan **II.** *vi* (*tormenta*) to break **III.** *vr:* ~**se** to let off steam; ~**se en** [*o* **con**] **alguien** (*ira*) to take one's anger out on sb; (*frustración*) to take one's frustration out on sb

desgajar **I.** *vt* **1.** (*arrancar*) to tear off; (*romper*) to break; (*ramas*) to snap off; ~ **una página de un libro** to tear a page out of a book **2.** (*separar*) to tear apart **3.** (*despedazar*) to tear to pieces **II.** *vr:* ~**se** (*desprenderse*) to come off; (*romperse*) to break off; (*rama*) to snap off

desgana *f* **1.** (*inapetencia*) lack of appetite; **comer con** ~ to eat without appetite **2.** (*falta de interés*) lack of enthusiasm; **con** ~ without enthusiasm

desganado, -a *adj* **estar** ~ (*sin apetito*) to have no appetite; (*sin entusiasmo*) to have lost one's enthusiasm

desgañitarse *vr* (*gritar*) to shout one's head off; (*enronquecerse*) to shout oneself hoarse

desgarbado, -a *adj* **1.** (*sin garbo*) ungainly **2.** (*larguirucho*) gangling

desgarrador(a) *adj* heartrending

desgarrar **I.** *vt* **1.** (*partir*) to tear; (*en muchos pedazos*) to tear to pieces; ~ **un paquete** to tear open a parcel **2.** (*causar pena*) **esto me desgarra el corazón** this breaks my heart; **estas imágenes desgarran el corazón** these pictures are heartbreaking **II.** *vr:* ~**se** **1.** (*romperse*) to tear **2.** (*anímicamente*) **se me desgarra el corazón al pensar que no voy a verte nunca más** it breaks my heart to think I'll never see you again

desgarro *m* **1.** (*rotura*) tear **2.** (*descaro*) cheek; **contestar con** ~ to answer insolently, to talk back **3.** *AmL* (*esputo*) spittle

desgastar **I.** *vt* **1.** (*estropear*) to wear out; **este pantalón está desgastado por las rodillas** these trousers are worn at the knees **2.** (*consumir*) to use up **3.** (*cansar*) to wear out **II.** *vr:* ~**se** **1.** (*consumirse*) to wear out; (*color*) to fade **2.** (*acabarse*) to run out **3.** (*debilitarse*) to wear oneself out

desgaste *m* **1.** (*fricción*) wear; ~ **natural** wear and tear **2.** (*consumo*) consumption

desglosar *vt* **1.** (*una hoja*) to detach **2.** (*una cuestión*) to treat separately; ~ **los gastos** to itemize expenses

desgobernar <e→ie> *vt* **1.** (*un país*) to misgovern; (*de una institución*) to mismanage; ~ **un asunto** to mishandle an affair **2.** (*los huesos*) to dislocate **3.** (*perturbar*) to disturb

desgobierno *m* **1.** (*de un país*) misgovernment; (*una institución*) mismanagement **2.** (*desorden*) disorder

desgracia *f* **1.** (*suerte adversa*) bad luck; **por** ~ unfortunately; **este año estoy de** ~ this year I've had nothing but bad luck; **tuve la** ~ **de perder todo mi dinero en el bingo** I was unlucky enough to lose all my money at bingo; **tiene la** ~ **de ser sordo** he has the misfortune of being deaf; **he tenido la** ~ **de...** I've been unlucky enough to ...; **para mayor** ~ to top it off **2.** (*acontecimiento*) misfortune; **llevar una temporada de** ~**s** to have one disaster after another; **en el accidente no hubo** ~**s personales** in the accident nobody was hurt; **es una** ~ **que...** +*subj* it's a terrible shame that ...; **eres una verdadera** ~ you're an absolute disgrace **3.** (*pérdida de gracia*) disgrace; **caer en** ~ to fall from grace, to fall into disgrace ▶ ~ **compartida, menos sentida** *prov* misery loves company *prov;* **las** ~**s nunca vienen solas** *prov* it never rains but it pours *prov*

desgraciadamente *adv* unfortunately

desgraciado, -a **I.** *adj* **1.** (*sin suerte*) unlucky; **ser** ~ (*tener mala suerte*) to be unlucky; (*no llegar a nada*) to be a disaster **2.** (*infeliz*) miserable **3.** (*que implica desgracia*) unfortunate; **fue una intervención desgraciada** it was an unfortunate intervention **4.** (*pobre*) poor **II.** *m, f* **1.** (*sin suerte*) unlucky person **2.** (*infeliz*) **es un** ~ he's a poor wretch **3.** (*pobre*) poor person **4.** (*persona sin valor*) **ser un** ~ to be worthless **5.** *pey* (*miserable*) scoundrel, rotter

desgraciar **I.** *vt* **1.** (*estropear*) to ruin **2.** (*disgustar*) to displease **II.** *vr:* ~**se** (*malograrse*) to be ruined

desgranar *vt* **1.** (*maíz, trigo*) to thresh; (*habas*) to shell; ~ (**las cuentas de**) **un rosario** to tell one's beads **2.** (*repetir*) ~ **insultos/palabrotas** to reel off a stream of abuse/obscenities; ~ **mentiras** to tell a string of lies

desgravable *adj* tax-deductible

desgravación *f* **1.** (*reducción de un impuesto*) tax allowance, tax deduction **2.** (*de un gasto*) tax relief; ~ **sobre bienes de capital** capital allowance; ~ **por cargas familiares** tax allowance [*o* deduction] for dependants

desgravar *vt* **1.** (*suprimir: un impuesto, un derecho*) to exempt from **2.** (*reducir*) ~ **el tabaco** (*bajar el impuesto*) to reduce the tax on tobacco; (*el arancel*) to reduce the duties on tobacco **3.** (*deducir*) to deduct

desgreñado, -a *adj* dishevelled

desguace *m* **1.** (*lugar*) scrapyard *Brit,* breaker's yard **2.** (*acción*) scrapping *Brit,* wrecking **3.** (*materiales*) scrap ►**estar para el** ~ *inf* to have had it

desguazar <z→c> *vt* **1.** (*desmontar*) to take to pieces **2.** (*reducir a chatarra*) to scrap *Brit,* to break up, to wreck; ~ **algo** (*quitar las partes útiles*) to use sth for scrap

deshabitado, **-a** *adj* (*edificio*) empty; **ciudad deshabitada** ghost town; **una región muy deshabitada** a very sparsely populated region

deshabitar *vt* **1.** (*un edificio*) to abandon; ~ **una casa** to vacate a house **2.** (*despoblar*) to empty

deshacer *irr como hacer* **I.** *vt* **1.** (*un paquete*) to unwrap; (*una costura*) to unpick; (*un nudo*) to undo; (*la cama*) to mess up; (*un aparato*) to dismantle; (*una maleta*) to unpack; ~ **los puntos** to unpick [*o* undo] the stitches; ~ **un error** to rectify a mistake **2.** (*romper*) to break; (*en pedazos*) to tear apart; (*cortar*) to cut up; (*una res*) to butcher; (*una tela*) to tear to pieces; (*a golpes*) to knock to pieces **3.** (*arruinar*) to ruin; (*plan*) to spoil, to thwart *form* **4.** (*disolver*) to dissolve; (*hielo*) to melt; (*contrato, negocio*) to dissolve; ~ **una casa** *fig* to move home **5.** MIL to rout ►**no intentes** ~ **lo hecho** what's done can't be undone; **ser el que hace y deshace** to be the boss **II.** *vr:* ~**se 1.** (*descomponerse*) to come apart; (*hielo*) to melt; (*desaparecer*) to disappear; **se me ha deshecho el helado** my ice cream has melted; ~**se en cumplidos** to be full of praise; ~**se de impaciencia** to be dying of impatience; ~**se en lágrimas** to burst into tears; ~**se en llanto** to cry one's heart out; ~**se de nervios** to be a nervous wreck; ~**se por algo** to try one's hardest to do sth; **se deshace por complacernos** he/she does everything possible to please us; ~**se a trabajar** to work oneself into the ground; ~**se empollando** to tire oneself out studying **2.** (*romperse*) to break; (*costura, nudo*) to come undone; (*pastel*) to fall apart; (*silla*) to fall to pieces **3.** (*desprenderse*) to come away; ~**se de algo** (*venderlo*) to offload sth; ~**se de alguien** (*librarse de, asesinar*) to get rid of sb; (*despedir*) to say goodbye to sb

desharrapado, **-a** *adj* ragged

deshecho, **-a** **I.** *pp de* **deshacer** **II.** *adj* **1.** (*deprimido*) devastated; **dejar a alguien** ~ to leave sb shattered **2.** (*cansado*) tired; **estar** ~ to be exhausted **3.** (*tormenta*) violent; (*lluvia*) heavy

deshelar <e→ie> **I.** *vt* (*hielo, nieve*) to melt; (*una nevera*) to defrost **II.** *vr:* ~**se** (*hielo*) to melt; (*nieve*) to thaw; (*nevera*) to defrost

desheredar *vt* to disinherit

deshidratar **I.** *vt* to dry; (*cuerpo*) to dehydrate **II.** *vr:* ~**se** to dry out; (*cuerpo*) to dehydrate

deshielo *m* **1.** (*el deshelar*) thawing; (*de la nevera*) defrosting **2.** (*clima*) *t.* POL thaw

deshilachar *vt, vr:* ~**se** to fray

deshilvanado, **-a** *adj* (*discurso*) disjointed

deshinchar **I.** *vt* **1.** (*sacar el aire*) to deflate **2.** (*una inflamación*) to reduce **3.** (*cólera*) to vent **II.** *vr:* ~**se 1.** (*perder aire*) to deflate; **se me ha deshinchado la rueda de la bici** my bicycle tyre [*o* tire *Am*] is flat **2.** (*una inflamación*) to go down **3.** *inf* (*deponer la vanidad*) to get down off one's high horse

deshojado, **-a** *adj* **1.** (*árbol*) leafless **2.** (*libro*) **un libro** ~ a book with pages missing

deshojar **I.** *vt* **1.** BOT to strip the leaves from; ~ **una flor** to pull the petals off a flower **2.** (*un libro*) to tear the pages out of **II.** *vr:* ~**se 1.** BOT (*un árbol*) to lose its leaves; (*una flor*) to lose its petals **2.** (*un libro*) to lose its pages

deshollinar *vt* **1.** (*la chimenea*) to sweep **2.** (*limpiar*) to clean off soot **3.** (*curiosear*) to take a close look at

deshonesto, **-a** *adj* **1.** (*inmoral*) indecent **2.** (*tramposo*) dishonest

deshonor *m* (*afrenta*) dishonour *Brit,* dishonor *Am*

deshonra *f* (*afrenta*) disgrace; **ser una** ~ **para la empresa** (*desacreditar*) to be a disgrace to the company; **tener algo a** ~ (*como insulto*) to take offence [*o* offense *Am*] at sth; (*como humillante*) to think sth is beneath one

deshonrar *vt* to disgrace; (*ofender*) to offend; (*humillar*) to humiliate; ~ **a alguien** (*desacreditar*) to bring disgrace on sb

deshonroso, **-a** *adj* **1.** (*que causa deshonra*) disgraceful **2.** (*poco honroso*) dishonest

deshora *f* inconvenient time; **hablar a** ~(**s**) to interrupt; **venir a** ~(**s**) (*en un momento inconveniente*) to come at a bad moment; (*demasiado tarde*) to arrive too late; **dormir a** ~**s** to sleep at odd hours

deshuesado, **-a** *adj* **1.** (*fruta*) stoned **2.** (*carne*) boned

desidia *f* **1.** (*descuido*) carelessness; **me molesta tu** ~ **en el trabajo** I don't like your lack of attention to your work **2.** (*pereza*) laziness

desierto *m* **1.** GEO desert **2.** (*lugar despoblado*) wasteland; **predicar en el** ~ *fig* to preach to the winds

desierto, **-a** *adj* **1.** (*sin gente*) deserted **2.** (*como un desierto*) desert **3.** (*sin participantes*) **una subasta desierta** an auction without bidders; **el premio fue declarado** ~ the prize was not awarded; **dar por** ~ **un concurso** to declare a competition void

designación *f* **1.** (*nombramiento*) appointment; ~ **de candidatos** selection of candidates **2.** (*nombre*) name; ~ **del contenido** contents

designar *vt* **1.** (*dar un nombre*) to designate; ~ **a alguien con un apodo** to give sb a nickname **2.** (*destinar*) to assign; (*elegir*) to choose; (*fecha*) to set; (*nombrar*) to appoint (*para* to); ~ **un abogado** to appoint a lawyer; ~ **un candidato** to select a candidate; ~ **un representante** to nominate a representative

designio *m* **1.** (*plan*) plan **2.** (*propósito*) intention **3.** (*deseo*) wish; **su** ~ **es conver-**

tirse en multimilionario his/her ambition is to be a multimillionaire

desigual *adj* **1.** (*distinto*) unequal; **ser muy ~** to be very different **2.** (*injusto*) unfair **3.** (*irregular*) uneven **4.** (*inconstante*) inconsistent

desigualdad *f* **1.** (*diferencia*) inequality **2.** (*injusticia*) unfairness **3.** (*irregularidad*) unevenness **4.** (*del carácter*) inconsistency; (*del tiempo*) changeability

desilusión *f* **1.** (*desengaño*) disappointment; **sufrir una ~** to be disappointed **2.** (*desencanto*) disillusion

desilusionante *adj* (*que desencanta*) disillusioning

desilusionar **I.** *vt* **1.** (*quitar la ilusión*) to disillusion **2.** (*decepcionar*) to disappoint **II.** *vr:* **~se** **1.** (*perder la ilusión*) to become disillusioned; (*ver claro*) to see things for what they are **2.** (*decepcionarse*) to be disappointed

desinencia *f* ending; **~ nominal** noun ending

desinfectante *m* disinfectant

desinfectar *vt* to disinfect

desinflado, -a *adj* (*rueda*) flat

desinflar **I.** *vt* (*sacar el aire*) to deflate **II.** *vr:* **~se** (*perder aire*) to go down; **se me ha desinflado la rueda de atrás** my back tyre [*o* tire *Am*] is flat

desintegración *f* **1.** (*de una cosa*) disintegration; (*debido al clima*) erosion; FÍS fission; QUÍM decomposition **2.** (*de un territorio, un grupo*) breakup

desintegrar **I.** *vt* **1.** (*disgregarse*) to disentegrate; (*una piedra*) to erode; FÍS to split; QUÍM to decompose **2.** (*un grupo, un país*) to break up **II.** *vr:* **~se** **1.** (*disgregarse*) to disentegrate; (*edificio, muro*) to fall down; FÍS to split; QUÍM to decompose **2.** (*grupo*) to break up; (*partido*) to fall apart

desinterés *m* **1.** (*indiferencia*) indifference; **sentir ~ por algo** to not be interested in sth **2.** (*altruismo*) altruism; (*generosidad*) generosity; **hacer algo con ~** to do sth without thinking about personal gain

desinteresado, -a *adj* **1.** (*indiferente*) indifferent; (*en un conflicto*) impartial **2.** (*altruista*) altruistic; (*generoso*) generous

desintoxicación *f* detoxification

desintoxicar <c→qu> **I.** *vt* to detoxify **II.** *vr:* **~se** **1.** to undergo detoxification; (*de alcohol*) to dry out **2.** *fig* to get away from it all

desistir *vi* **1.** (*de un proyecto*) **~ de algo** to give up sth; **no ~é de convencerte** I'll do my best to persuade you; **no hay manera de hacerles ~ de su propósito** there is no way of getting them to back down **2.** (*renunciar a*) **~ de un derecho** to waive a right; **~ de un cargo** to resign from a post; **~ de una petición** to withdraw a request; **~ de un contrato** to withdraw from a contract

deslavazado, -a *adj* **1.** (*lacio*) limp; **este traje te queda ~** this dress doesn't really suit you **2.** (*incoherente*) disjointed **3.** (*insulso*) insipid

desleal *adj* (*infiel*) disloyal; (*traidor*) treacherous; **competencia ~** unfair competition; **publicidad ~** misleading advertising; **ser ~ a su patria** to betray one's country; **ser ~ con su partido** to betray one's party; **has sido ~ a tu familia** you have been disloyal to your family; **ten cuidado con lo que le cuentes, es una persona muy ~** be careful what you tell him/her, he/she isn't very trustworthy; **ser ~ con** [*o* **a**] **alguien** (*injusto*) to treat sb unfairly

deslealtad *f* **1.** (*infidelidad*) disloyalty **2.** (*injusticia*) unfairness

desleír *irr como reír* **I.** *vt* (*disolver*) to dissolve **II.** *vr:* **~se** to dissolve

deslenguado, -a *adj* **1.** (*desvergonzado*) foul-mouthed; **ser ~** to be foul-mouthed **2.** (*chismoso*) gossipy; **ser ~** to be a gossip; **¡no seas ~!** don't be such a gossip!

desliar <*1. pres:* deslío> **I.** *vt* to undo **II.** *vr:* **~se** to come undone

desligar <g→gu> **I.** *vt* **1.** (*un nudo*) to undo; (*un enredo*) to untangle; (*una persona*) to untie **2.** (*un asunto*) to clear up **3.** (*separar*) to separate; **~ intereses particulares de los de la empresa** to separate private interests from those of the company **4.** (*de un compromiso*) to release **II.** *vr:* **~se** **1.** (*un nudo*) to come undone; (*persona*) to get out of; (*un enredo*) to unravel **2.** (*un asunto*) to be resolved **3.** (*de un compromiso*) to be released; **no poder ~se de algo** to be unable to get out of sth

deslindar *vt* **1.** (*un lugar*) to demarcate; **~ una finca** to mark the boundary of a farm; **~ dos provincias** to mark the boundary between two provinces **2.** (*determinar*) to outline; **~ dos temas** to distinguish between two topics

desliz *m* **1.** (*error*) slip; (*indiscreción*) indiscretion **2.** (*adulterio*) affair

deslizante *adj* **1.** (*que desliza, que hace deslizar*) slippery, slippy **2.** (*corredizo*) sliding

deslizar <z→c> **I.** *vt* **1.** (*pasar*) **~ la mano sobre algo** to run one's hand over sth; **~ un sobre por debajo de una puerta** to slip an envelope under the door **2.** (*incluir con disimulo*) to slip; **~ algo en una conversación** to slip sth into a conversation **II.** *vi* to slip **III.** *vr:* **~se** **1.** (*resbalar*) **~ sobre algo** to slide over sth; **~se por un tobogán** to go down a slide; **las lágrimas se deslizaban por sus mejillas** the tears slid down his/her cheeks; **con la tormenta se han deslizado algunas tejas** the storm has blown a few tiles off **2.** (*escaparse*) to slip away; **el ladrón se deslizó entre los clientes** the thief slipped away through the customers **3.** (*el tiempo*) to slip away **4.** (*cometer un errror*) to slip up; (*una indiscreción*) to slip out

deslomar **I.** *vt* **1.** (*dañar*) **~ a alguien** to break sb's back **2.** (*agotar*) to exhaust **II.** *vr:*

D

~**se** **1.** (*dañarse*) to do one's back in **2.** (*trabajar*) to work oneself to death

deslucido, **-a** *adj* **1.** (*ropa*) shabby **2.** (*actuación*) lacklustre *Brit*, lackluster *Am* **3.** (*sin gracia*) dull

deslucir *irr como lucir* **I.** *vt* **1.** (*estropear*) to ruin; **la lluvia deslució la procesión** the rain ruined the parade **2.** (*quitar el lustre: metal*) to tarnish; (*una prenda, un tejido, colores*) to fade **3.** (*desacreditar*) to discredit **II.** *vr:* ~**se** **1.** (*fracasar*) to fail **2.** (*perder el lustre*) to lose one's shine; (*colores*) to fade; (*metal*) to become dull **3.** (*desacreditarse*) to be discredited

deslumbrador(**a**) *adj*, **deslumbrante** *adj* (*impresionante*) dazzling; (*mujer*) stunning

deslumbrar *vt* to dazzle

deslustrar *vt* **1.** (*quitar el brillo*) to tarnish **2.** (*gastar*) to wear out; (*una prenda, un tejido, colores*) to fade **3.** (*estropear*) to ruin **4.** (*un vidrio*) to frost **5.** (*desacreditar*) to discredit

desmadrado, **-a** *adj* (*desenfrenado*) wild

desmadrarse *vr inf* (*desenfrenarse*) to go wild; (*alocarse*) to go mad; **¡no te desmadres!** don't go over the top!

desmadre *m* **1.** (*comportamiento*) outrageous behaviour [*o* behavior *Am*]; **la policía acabó con el ~ entre los hinchas** the police put an end to the mayhem between the fans **2.** (*caos*) chaos; **tus fiestas acaban siendo un ~** your parties are always completely wild

desmalezar <z→c> *vt AmL* to weed, to clear brush

desmán *m* **1.** (*salvajada*) outrage; **cometer desmanes contra alguien** to commit outrages against sb **2.** (*exceso*) excess; **debido a sus desmanes con la bebida** due to his/her excessive drinking **3.** (*desgracia*) misfortune; **he sufrido muchos desmanes** a lot of bad things have happened to me

desmandado, **-a** *adj* **1.** (*rebelde*) rebellious; (*caballo*) runaway **2.** (*violento*) violent **3.** (*desmadrado*) wild

desmandarse *vr* **1.** (*rebelarse*) to rebel; (*descontrolarse*) to get out of control; (*un caballo*) to bolt **2.** (*insolentarse*) to be insolent; (*insultar*) to be rude; (*cometer actos violentos*) to become violent **3.** (*apartarse*) to go off on one's own; ~ **del rebaño** to stray from the flock

desmano *m* **a ~** out of the way

desmantelar *vt* **1.** (*derribar*) to knock down; (*un edificio*) to demolish **2.** (*desmontar*) to take apart; (*bomba*) to dismantle; (*escenario*) to take down **3.** (*abandonar*) to abandon; (*liquidar*) to liquidate **4.** NÁUT (*desarbolar*) to unmast

desmañado, **-a** **I.** *adj* clumsy; **es muy ~ para trabajos manuales** he's very clumsy with his hands **II.** *m, f* **ser un ~** (*torpe*) to be clumsy; (*chapucero*) to be shoddy

desmaquillador *m* make-up remover

desmaquillador(**a**) *adj* **leche ~a** make-up remover

desmaquillarse *vr* to take one's make-up off

desmayado, **-a** *adj* **1.** (*sin conocimiento*) unconscious **2.** (*sin fuerza*) exhausted; (*color*) faded

desmayar **I.** *vi* (*desanimarse*) to lose heart **II.** *vr:* ~**se** (*desvanecerse*) to faint; **se desmayó en mis brazos** he/she fainted in my arms

desmayo *m* **1.** (*desvanecimiento*) faint; **hablar con ~** to speak in a small voice **2.** (*desánimo*) dismay **3.** (*debilidad*) weakness

desmedido, **-a** *adj* excessive; **tener un apetito ~** to have an enormous appetite; **afición desmedida por la bebida** excessive drinking

desmedirse *irr como pedir vr* **1.** (*excederse*) to go too far; ~ **en la bebida** to drink to excess **2.** (*insolentarse*) to be insolent; (*insultar*) to be rude

desmedrado, **-a** *adj* (*flaco, débil*) puny

desmejorar **I.** *vt* (*estropear*) to ruin; (*gastar*) to wear out **II.** *vi* to deteriorate; **con la gripe has desmejorado mucho** the flu has really weakened you **III.** *vr:* ~**se** **1.** (*estropearse*) to be ruined; (*gastarse*) to wear out, to go downhill *inf* **2.** (*perder la salud*) to deteriorate

desmelenado, **-a** *adj* (*despeinado*) tousled

desmembrar <e→ie> **I.** *vt* **1.** (*desunir*) to break up; (*una institución*) to dismantle; (*un cuerpo*) to dismember; **la bomba le desmembró la mano** the bomb took his/her hand off **2.** (*escindir*) to separate **II.** *vr:* ~**se** **1.** (*desunirse*) to break up **2.** (*escindirse*) to separate (*de* from)

desmentir *irr como sentir* **I.** *vt* **1.** (*negar*) to deny; ~ **a alguien** (*contradecir*) to contradict sb; (*decir que miente*) to accuse sb of lying; **el artículo desmiente la historia** the article disproves the story **2.** (*demostrar que es falso*) to refute; ~ **una sospecha** to refute an accusation; **las pruebas desmienten tus palabras** the evidence contradicts what you have said **3.** (*desdecir*) ~ **algo/a alguien** to be unworthy of sth/sb; **con su comportamiento desmiente a su familia** with this behaviour [*o* behavior *Am*] he/she is letting down his/her family; **este vino desmiente su marca** this wine doesn't do justice to its label **II.** *vi* to be out of line **III.** *vr* ~**se** to contradict oneself

desmenuzable *adj* crumbly

desmenuzar <z→c> **I.** *vt* **1.** (*deshacer*) to break into small pieces; (*fish*) to flake; (*con un cuchillo*) to chop up; (*con los dedos*) to crumble; (*raspar*) to grate; (*moler*) to grind; (*papel*) to tear up **2.** (*analizar*) to scrutinize **II.** *vr:* ~**se** to crumble

desmerecer *irr como crecer* **I.** *vt* (*no merecer*) to not deserve; **desmereces mi amor** you don't deserve my love **II.** *vi* **1.** (*decaer*) to decline; (*belleza*) to lose one's looks **2.** (*ser inferior*) ~ **de alguien/algo** to be worse than sb/sth; ~ **en talento de alguien** to be less talented than sb; **tu último libro no**

desmerece de los anteriores your latest book maintains the standard of the previous ones; **desmereces de tu familia** your family are too good for you

desmesurado, **-a** *adj* **1.** (*enorme*) enormous **2.** (*excesivo*) excessive; (*ambición*) boundless; (*pretensiones*) exaggerated; **beber de una forma desmesurada** to drink to excess **3.** (*desvergonzado*) shameless; (*descortés*) rude; (*ofensivo*) offensive

desmesurarse *vr* **1.** (*excederse*) to go too far **2.** (*atreverse*) to be daring **3.** (*insultar*) to be rude

desmigajar **I.** *vt* to crumble **II.** *vr:* **~se** to crumble

desmilitarizar <z→c> *vt* to demilitarize

desmirriado, **-a** *adj* (*flaco*) skinny; (*raquítico*) puny

desmochar *vt* **1.** (*despuntar*) to cut the top off; (*plantas*) to pollard **2.** (*mutilar*) to mutilate

desmontable *adj* (*que se puede quitar*) detachable; (*sacar*) removable; (*deshacer*) that can be taken apart; (*doblar*) foldable

desmontar **I.** *vt* **1.** (*un mecanismo*) to disassemble **2.** (*una pieza: quitar*) to detach; (*sacar*) to remove **3.** (*una estructura, un edificio*) to take down **4.** (*un bosque*) to cut down **5.** (*un terreno*) to clear **6.** (*un montón de tierra*) to level **7.** (*una pistola*) to uncock **8.** (*de un caballo, de una moto*) to throw **II.** *vi* (*de un caballo*) to dismount; (*de una moto*) to help get down from **III.** *vr:* **~se** (*bajarse*) to dismount

desmonte *m* **1.** (*de un terreno*) levelling *Brit,* leveling *Am* **2.** (*de un bosque*) clearance, cut *Brit* **3.** (*escombros*) heap of soil **4.** *pl* AGR clearing

desmoralizador(a) *adj* **1.** (*que desanima*) demoralizing **2.** (*que corrompe*) corrupting

desmoralizar <z→c> **I.** *vt* **1.** (*desanimar*) to demoralize; **la crítica la ha desmoralizado mucho** the criticism has really got [*o* gotten *Am*] to her **2.** (*corromper*) to corrupt **II.** *vr:* **~se** **1.** (*desanimarse*) to lose heart; (*perder la confianza*) to lose one's confidence; **las tropas se iban desmoralizando** the soldiers were gradually becoming demoralized **2.** (*corromperse*) to be corrupted

desmoronamiento *m* **1.** (*arruinamiento*) ruin; (*de un edificio*) collapse **2.** (*disminución: de un imperio, una ideología*) decline; (*de una persona*) breakdown; (*de un sentimiento*) weakening; **la crisis económica produjo el ~ de mi fortuna** the economic crisis used up all my wealth

desmoronar **I.** *vt* (*deshacer*) to wear away; (*edificio*) to ruin; GEO to erode **II.** *vr:* **~se** **1.** (*deshacerse*) to fall to pieces; (*un edificio, un muro*) to fall down; QUÍM to decay **2.** (*disminuir*) to decline; (*sentimiento*) to weaken **3.** (*persona*) to fall apart

desnatar *vt* (*la leche*) to skim; **leche sin ~** whole milk

desnaturalizado, **-a** *adj* **1.** (*alimentos*) adulterated **2.** (*hijo*) ungrateful; **madre desnaturalizada** uncaring mother **3.** QUÍM denatured

desnaturalizar <z→c> **I.** *vt* **1.** (*expatriar*) to denaturalize **2.** (*desvirtuar*) to denature; (*aspecto*) to spoil; (*carácter*) to ruin; **~ la competencia** to distort the marketplace **3.** QUÍM to denature **II.** *vr:* **~se** (*expatriarse*) to abandon one's country

desnivel *m* **1.** (*diferencia de altura*) drop; (*pendiente*) slope **2.** (*desequilibrio*) imbalance; (*disparidad*) inequality; **~ cultural** cultural difference [*o* gap] **3.** (*altibajo*) unevenness

desnivelar **I.** *vt* **1.** (*un terreno*) to make uneven **2.** (*desequilibrar*) to unbalance; (*balanza*) to tip **II.** *vr:* **~se** **1.** (*torcerse*) to twist; (*calle*) to become uneven **2.** (*perder el equilibrio*) to become unbalanced

desnucar <c→qu> **I.** *vt* **1.** (*herir*) **~ a alguien** to break sb's neck **2.** (*matar*) to kill; **~ una gallina** to wring a chicken's neck; **~ el conejo de un golpe en el cogote** to kill the rabbit with a blow to its neck **II.** *vr:* **~se** to break one's neck

desnuclearizado(a) *adj* nuclear-free

desnudar **I.** *vt* **1.** (*desvestir*) to undress **2.** (*descubrir*) to strip **II.** *vr:* **~se** (*desvestirse*) to undress

desnudez *f* **1.** (*persona*) nudity **2.** *fig* bareness

desnudo *m* ARTE nude

desnudo, **-a** *adj* **1.** (*desvestido*) naked, nude; **~ de (la) cintura para arriba/abajo** naked from the waist up/down **2.** (*con poca ropa*) half-naked **3.** (*despojado*) bare **4.** (*pobre*) penniless; **este mes me he quedado ~** *inf* this month I haven't got a penny **5.** (*claro*) clear; **al ~** clearly; **decir a alguien la verdad desnuda** to tell sb the plain truth **6.** (*desprovisto*) **~ de algo** devoid of sth

desnutrición *f* malnutrition, undernourishment

desnutrido, **-a** *adj* undernourished

desobedecer *irr como crecer vi, vt* to disobey

desobediencia *f* disobedience; MIL insubordination

desobediente *adj* disobedient; MIL insubordinate

desocupación *f* **1.** (*desembarazo*) ease; (*evacuación*) vacation **2.** (*paro*) unemployment **3.** (*ociosidad*) leisure

desocupado, **-a** **I.** *adj* **1.** (*parado*) unemployed **2.** (*vacío*) empty; (*vivienda*) vacant; (*paso, plaza*) clear; (*ocioso*) idle; **estoy ~** I'm not busy **II.** *m, f* unemployed person

desocupar **I.** *vt* **1.** (*desembarazar*) to clear; (*evacuar*) to evacuate; **~ una vivienda** to vacate a property **2.** (*vaciar*) to empty **II.** *vr:* **~se** **1.** (*de una ocupación*) to get away; **cuando pueda ~me** when I'm free **2.** (*quedarse vacante*) to be vacant **III.** *vi AmL* (*parir*) to give birth

desodorante **I.** *adj* (*para el hogar*) deoderizing; (*para el cuerpo*) deoderant; **espray** ~ (*para el cuerpo*) deodorant spray; (*para el hogar*) air freshener spray **II.** *m* (*para el cuerpo*) deodorant; ~ **en barra** stick deodorant; ~ **antitranspirante** antiperspirant

desoír *irr como oír vt* ~ **algo** to not listen to sth

desolación *f* **1.** (*devastación*) desolation **2.** (*desconsuelo*) distress

desolado, **-a** *adj* **1.** (*desierto*) desolate **2.** (*desconsolado*) devastated

desolar <o→ue> **I.** *vt* (*destruir, afligir*) to devastate **II.** *vr:* ~**se** to be devastated

desolladero *m* slaughterhouse

desollar <o→ue> *vt* **1.** (*quitar la piel*) to flay, to skin; ~ **a alguien vivo** *fig* to fleece sb, to skin sb alive **2.** (*causar daño económico*) to fleece; (*engañar*) to deceive **3.** (*maltratar*) to mistreat **4.** (*criticar*) to lambast

desorbitado, **-a** *adj* **1.** (*ojos*) bulging, bug-eyed *inf* **2.** (*exagerado*) exaggerated; (*desmedido*) exhorbitant

desorbitar I. *vt* (*exagerar*) to exaggerate; (*dar demasiada importancia*) to blow out of proportion **II.** *vr:* ~**se** (*asunto*) to get out of control; **se le ~on los ojos** *fig* he/she was flabbergasted

desorden *m* **1.** (*desarreglo*) mess; (*confusión*) chaos; ~ **público** public disturbance; **la casa está en** ~ the house is in a mess **2.** (*exceso*) excess **3.** *pl* (*alboroto*) disorders *pl* **4.** MED disorder

desordenado, **-a** *adj* **1.** (*desorganizado*) jumbled; (*persona, cosa*) messy; (*vida*) chaotic **2.** (*excesivo*) excessive

desordenar *vt* (*turbar*) to mess up; (*mezclar*) to mix up; (*pelo*) to ruffle

desorganización *f* lack of organization; **en esta empresa llevan una ~ increíble** this company is completely disorganized

desorganizar <z→c> **I.** *vt* to disrupt; (*planes*) to disturb **II.** *vr:* ~**se** (*persona, empresa*) to be disorganized

desorientación *f* **1.** (*extravío*) disorientation **2.** (*confusión*) confusion **3.** (*falta de orientación*) loss of direction

desorientar I. *vt* **1.** (*extraviar*) to lose one's bearings, to disorientate *Brit,* to disorient *Am* **2.** (*confundir*) to confuse **II.** *vr:* ~**se 1.** (*extraviarse*) to become disorientated *Brit,* to become disoriented *Am* **2.** (*confundirse*) to become confused

desovar *vi* (*pez, anfibio*) to spawn; (*insecto*) to lay eggs

despabilado, **-a** *adj* **1.** (*listo*) smart **2.** (*despierto*) alert

despabilar I. *vt* **1.** (*despertar*) to wake up **2.** (*avivar*) to sharpen up; **en la mili ya lo ~án** in the army they'll soon show him what's what; **es muy perezosa, pero en el colegio ya la ~án** she's very lazy, but at school they'll soon make her sharpen up **3.** (*acabar deprisa*) to finish off; (*fortuna*) to squander; (*comida*) to eat up **4.** (*robar*) to steal **5.** (*matar*) to kill **II.** *vi* **1.** (*darse prisa*) to hurry up **2.** (*avivarse*) **si quieres empezar a trabajar por tu cuenta, tienes que** ~ if you want to work for yourself, you'll have to get your act together **III.** *vr:* ~**se 1.** (*sacudir el sueño*) to waken up **2.** (*darse prisa*) to hurry up **3.** (*avivarse*) to get one's act together; **se ha despabilado desde que va al colegio** he/she has really come to life since starting school **4.** *AmL* (*marcharse*) to leave

despachante *mf RíoPl* COM customs officer

despachar I. *vt* **1.** (*enviar*) to send, to ship; (*mercancías*) to dispatch **2.** (*concluir*) to finish off; (*buque*) to clear out **3.** (*resolver*) to decide; (*discutir*) to discuss **4.** (*atender*) to serve, to wait on **5.** (*vender*) to sell **6.** (*matar*) to kill **7.** (*comer, beber*) to polish off **8.** *inf* (*despedir*) to dismiss, to sack *Brit,* to fire *Am* **II.** *vi* **1.** (*acabar*) to finish **2.** (*atender*) to do business; **por las tardes no despachan en esta tienda** this shop doesn't open in the evenings **3.** (*conversar*) ~ **con alguien** to consult with sb **III.** *vr:* ~**se 1.** (*darse prisa*) to hurry up **2.** (*desahogarse*) to let off steam; ~**se a (su) gusto con alguien** to speak frankly to sb **3.** (*desembarazarse*) ~**se de alguien** to rid oneself of sb

despacho *m* **1.** (*oficina*) office; (*en casa*) study; ~ **de abogado** lawyer's office; ~ **de aduana** customs office; ~ **de patentes** patent office; **mesa de** ~ desk **2.** (*envío*) sending **3.** (*de un asunto*) resolution; (*entrevista*) consultation **4.** (*de clientes*) service; **sólo tenemos ~ por las mañanas** we only see clients in the morning **5.** (*venta*) sale; **géneros sin** ~ unsaleable [*o* unsellable *Am*] goods; **no tener buen** ~ to sell slowly; **tener buen** ~ to sell well **6.** (*despido*) dismissal **7.** (*de un pedido*) dispatch, shipping; (*de la correspondencia, el equipaje*) sending; (*de un buque*) clearance **8.** (*muebles*) office furniture; **comprarse un ~ nuevo** to refurnish one's office **9.** (*taquilla*) ticket office; (*tienda*) shop; ~ **de billetes** [*o* **boletos**] *AmL* FERRO ticket office; ~ **de localidades** TEAT, CINE box [*o* ticket] office **10.** (*parte*) message; (*telegrama*) telegram; (*entre gobiernos*) dispatch; ~ **judicial** legal dispatch

despachurrar I. *vt* **1.** (*aplastar*) to squash; (*reventar*) to burst **2.** (*embrollar*) to mix up; **despachurras todos los chistes** you're dreadful at telling jokes **3.** (*apabullar*) to silence; **me dejó despachurrado** I was left speechless; **lo despachurró con sus argumentos** he/she silenced him with his/her arguments **II.** *vr:* ~**se** to flatten; (*fruta*) to squash

despacio I. *adv* **1.** (*lentamente*) slowly; **por allí viene caminando** ~ here he/she comes, walking slowly; **en esta oficina las cosas van** ~ in this office things move slowly **2.** (*calladamente*) quietly **II.** *interj* take it easy

despampanante *adj* (*mujer*) stunning

despancar <c→qu> *vt AmS* (*maíz*) to husk

desparejado, **-a** *adj* odd; **este calcetín está**

~ this is an odd sock; **estos calcetines están ~s** these socks don't match

desparpajo *m* **1.** (*desenvoltura*) self-confidence; (*en el hablar*) ease; **con ~** confidently **2.** (*habilidad*) skill; **con ~** skilfully **3.** (*frescura*) cheek; **con ~** cheekily

desparramar **I.** *vt* **1.** (*dispersar*) to scatter; **~ los juguetes sobre el suelo** to scatter the toys across the floor; **~ su atención** to allow one's attention to wander **2.** (*un líquido*) to spill **3.** (*malgastar*) to waste **4.** (*una noticia*) to spread **5.** *Arg, Méx, PRico* (*diluir*) to dilute **II.** *vr:* **~se** **1.** (*dispersarse*) to scatter; **el rebaño se desparramó por el campo** the flock spread out across the field; **al pasar el coche los pájaros se ~on** when the car went past the birds scattered **2.** (*un líquido*) to spill **3.** (*divertirse*) to enjoy oneself **4.** (*dispersar su atención*) to allow one's attention to wander

desparramo *m* **1.** *Chile, Cuba* (*desparramiento*) scattering **2.** *Chile, Urug* (*desbarajuste*) disorder

despatarrado, **-a** *adj* **1.** (*espatarrado*) **estar ~** to have one's legs wide apart; (*en un sofá*) to sprawl **2.** (*pasmado*) astonished **3.** (*asustado*) frightened

despatarrar **I.** *vt* **1.** (*asombrar*) to astonish **2.** (*asustar*) to frighten **II.** *vr:* **~se** **1.** (*espatarrarse*) to open one's legs wide; **se despatarró sobre la cama** he/she sprawled on the bed **2.** (*pasmarse*) to be astonished **3.** (*caerse*) to go sprawling; **~se de risa** to split one's sides laughing **4.** *inf* (*una mujer*) to spread one's legs

despavorido, **-a** *adj* terrified

despechar **I.** *vt* (*indignar*) to anger **II.** *vr* **~se contra alguien** to get angry with sb

despecho *m* **1.** (*animosidad*) spite, rancour *Brit,* rancor *Am* **2.** (*desesperación*) despair **3.** **a ~ de algo** in spite of sth

despectivo, **-a** *adj* **1.** (*despreciativo*) contemptuous; (*desdeñoso*) disdainful; (*tono*) derogatory; **tratar de manera despectiva** to treat with a lack of respect **2.** LING pejorative

despedazar <z→c> **I.** *vt* (*romper*) to smash; (*en mil pedazos*) to tear to pieces; (*con un cuchillo, una tijera*) to cut up; (*con las manos*) to tear up; (*el corazón*) to break; **la bomba le despedazó la mano** the bomb blew his/her hand off **II.** *vr:* **~se** **1.** (*romperse*) to smash; (*en mil pedazos*) to fall to pieces; (*muro*) to fall down; (*cristal*) to shatter; (*globo*) to burst **2.** (*apenar*) **se me despedazó el alma cuando vi tanta miseria** *fig* seeing such misery broke my heart

despedida *f* **1.** (*separación*) goodbye, farewell **2.** (*acto oficial*) send-off; (*fiesta*) leaving party; **~ de soltero** stag night [*o* party]; **~ de soltera** hen night [*o* party]; **cena de ~** farewell dinner; **mañana le dan la ~ en el palacio** tomorrow they are giving her a send-off in the palace **3.** (*en una carta*) close

despedir *irr como pedir* **I.** *vt* **1.** (*decir adiós*) to say goodbye; **~ a alguien con una fiesta** to give sb a leaving party; **salió a ~me a mi coche** he/she came out to the car to say goodbye to me; **vinieron a ~me al aeropuerto** they came to the airport to see me off **2.** (*echar*) to throw out; (*de un empleo*) to dismiss, to sack *Brit,* to fire *Am* **3.** (*difundir*) to give off; (*emitir*) to emit; **el volcán despide fuego** the volcano gives off flames **4.** (*lanzar*) to launch; (*flecha*) to fire **5.** (*apartar de sí*) to get rid of **II.** *vr:* **~se** **1.** (*decir adiós*) to say goodbye **2.** (*dejar un empleo*) to leave; **~se de un trabajo** to leave a job **3.** (*de obtener, conseguir algo*) **despídete de ese dinero** say goodbye to that money; **despídete este mes de salir por las noches** this month you can forget about going out in the evening

despegado, **-a** *adj* **1.** (*poco cariñoso*) distant **2.** (*áspero*) unfriendly **3.** (*suelto*) unstuck

despegar <g→gu> **I.** *vt* to unstick; **~ dos hojas** to separate two pages; **sin ~ los labios** without a word **II.** *vi* to take off; **la economía no despega** the economy is stagnant **III.** *vr:* **~se** **1.** (*desprenderse*) to come off; (*deshacerse*) to come apart **2.** (*perder el afecto*) **~se de alguien** to lose one's feelings for sb

despego *m* **1.** (*falta de cariño*) coldness **2.** (*falta de afecto*) lack of feeling; **sentir ~ por alguien** to feel nothing for sb **3.** (*falta de interés*) indifference

despegue *m* AVIAT, ECON take-off; (*cohete*) blast-off, lift-off

despeinado, **-a** *adj* unkempt

despeinar **I.** *vt* to ruffle **II.** *vr* **me despeiné** I ruffled my hair

despejado, **-a** *adj* **1.** (*sin nubes, obstáculos*) clear **2.** (*ancho*) wide; (*habitación*) spacious **3.** (*listo*) smart **4.** (*despierto*) alert; (*cabeza*) clear

despejar **I.** *vt* **1.** (*un lugar, una mesa*) to clear; (*sala*) to tidy up; **~ la calle de nieve** to clear the street of snow **2.** (*una situación*) to clarify; (*un misterio*) to clear up **3.** (*una persona*) **el aire fresco despejó mi mente** the fresh air cleared my mind **4.** DEP to clear; **~ el tiro a córner** to concede a corner **II.** *vr:* **~se** **1.** (*cielo, misterio*) to clear up **2.** (*despabilarse*) to wake up; (*mentalmente*) to sharpen one's wits **3.** (*adquirir desenvoltura*) to gain self-confidence **4.** (*un enfermo*) to improve; **se ha despejado un poco** he/she is feeling a bit better

despeje *m* (*en fútbol, hockey*) clearance

despejo *m* **1.** (*de un lugar*) clearing **2.** (*en el trato*) self-confidence **3.** (*entendimiento*) understanding

despellejar **I.** *vt* **1.** (*desollar*) to flay, to skin **2.** *inf* (*criticar*) to lambast *form,* to cut to bits, to skin alive **3.** *inf* (*desvalijar*) to fleece **II.** *vr:* **~se** to peel

despelotarse *vr inf* **1.** (*desnudarse*) to strip off, to strip down **2.** (*de risa*) to split one's sides

despeluzar <z→c> *vt, vr v.* **despeluznar**

despeluznante *adj* terrifying

despeluznar I. *vt* 1. (*causar miedo*) to terrify 2. (*pelo*) to ruffle 3. *Cuba* (*desplumar*) to pluck II. *vr* to be terrified; **se despeluz(n)ó (del miedo que tenía)** it made his/her hair stand on end

despensa *f* 1. (*fresquera*) larder, pantry 2. (*provisiones*) provisions *pl* 3. (*comestibles*) groceries 4. *Arg* (*almacén*) shop

despeñadero *m* 1. GEO precipice 2. (*riesgo*) danger; **meterse en un** ~ to get into danger

despeñadero, **-a** *adj* sheer

despeñar I. *vt* to throw down; ~ **a alguien por un precipicio** to throw sb over a cliff II. *vr:* ~**se** to throw oneself down; **el motorista se despeñó por el talud** the driver went headlong down the slope

desperdiciar *vt* to waste; (*ocasión*) to miss

desperdicio *m* 1. (*residuo*) rubbish *Brit,* garbage *Am;* ~**s biológicos** biological waste 2. (*malbaratamiento*) waste; **no tener** ~ *irón* to be good from start to finish *iron*

desperdigar <g→gu> *vt, vr:* ~**se** to scatter

desperezarse <z→c> *vr* to stretch

desperfecto *m* 1. (*deterioro*) damage 2. (*defecto*) fault, defect; **esta máquina tiene un pequeño** ~ this machine has a slight defect

despertador *m* (*reloj*) alarm clock

despertar <e→ie> I. *vt* to wake up II. *vr:* ~**se** to wake up III. *m* awakening

despiadado, **-a** *adj* (*inhumano*) ruthless; (*cruel*) cruel

despichar *vi inf* to peg out, to bite the dust

despido *m* (*descontratación*) dismissal, sack; ~ **colectivo** wholescale redundancies

despierto, **-a** *adj* 1. (*insomne*) awake 2. (*listo*) smart; **mente despierta** sharp mind

despilfarrador(a) I. *adj* wasteful; (*con dinero*) spendthrift II. *m(f)* wasteful person; (*con dinero*) spendthrift

despilfarrar *vt* to waste; (*dinero*) to squander

despilfarro *m* (*derroche*) waste; (*de dinero*) squandering

despintar I. *vt* 1. (*colores*) to wash out 2. (*la realidad*) to misrepresent 3. *Chile, PRico* ~ **a alguien** (*apartar la mirada*) to look away from sb; (*perder de vista*) to lose sight of sb II. *vr:* ~**se** 1. (*borrarse*) to fade; ~**se con el sol** to fade with the sunlight 2. *inf* (*de la memoria*) **este asunto no se me despinta** I can't forget what happened

despiojar *vt* to delouse

despistado, **-a** I. *adj* absent-minded II. *m, f* **eres un** ~ you're absent-minded

despistar I. *vt* (*confundir*) to confuse; (*desorientar*) to mislead II. *vr:* ~**se** 1. (*perderse*) to get lost 2. (*desconcertarse*) to become confused

despiste *m* 1. (*distracción*) confusion 2. (*error*) slip; **un** ~ **lo tiene cualquiera** anyone can make a mistake

desplante *m* rude remark

desplazado, **-a** *adj* (*no integrado*) out of place; (*trasladado*) displaced

desplazamiento *m* 1. (*traslado*) displacement 2. (*remoción*) removal

desplazar <z→c> *vt* 1. (*mover*) to move 2. (*suplantar*) to displace

desplegable *adj* folding; **silla** ~ folding chair

desplegar *irr como fregar vt* 1. (*abrir*) to open out; (*desdoblar*) to unfold; (*bandera*) to unfurl 2. MIL to deploy 3. (*desarrollar*) to develop; ~ **toda su fantasía** to give free rein to one's imagination

despliegue *m* 1. (*desdoblamiento*) unfolding 2. MIL deployment

desplomarse *vr* 1. (*casa, persona*) to collapse 2. (*desviarse*) to go off course

desplumar *vt* 1. (*plumas*) to pluck 2. (*robar*) to fleece; ~ **a alguien jugando a las cartas** to clean sb out at cards

despoblación *f* depopulation

despoblado *m* (*yermo*) deserted place

despoblado, **-a** *adj* depopulated

despoblar <o→ue> *vt* 1. (*de habitantes*) to depopulate 2. (*un bosque*) to clear; **el huracán despobló la zona de árboles** the hurricane blew down all the trees in the area

despojar I. *vt* to strip; **la** ~**on de todo** they took everything she had; ~ **de un derecho a alguien** to deprive sb of a right II. *vr:* ~**se** 1. (*desistir*) ~**se de algo** to give up sth 2. (*quitar*) ~ **de algo** to remove sth; (*ropa*) to take off

despojo *m* 1. (*presa*) spoils *pl;* ~ **del mar** flotsam and jetsam 2. *pl* (*restos*) leftovers *pl;* (*del matadero*) offal; (*escombros*) rubble; (*mortales*) mortal remains

desposado, **-a** *adj* (*recién casado*) newly wed

desposar I. *vt* to marry II. *vr:* ~**se con** to get married to

desposeer *irr como leer* I. *vt* 1. (*expropiar*) to dispossess 2. (*no reconocer*) to not recognize; **la desposeyeron de sus derechos** they deprived her of her rights 3. (*destituir*) to oust; ~ **a alguien de su cargo** to remove sb from his/her position 4. (*desplumar*) ~ **a alguien de algo** to fleece sb of sth II. *vr:* ~**se** 1. (*renunciar*) ~**se de algo** to give up sth 2. (*desapropiarse*) ~**se de algo** to relinquish sth

desposorio(s) *m(pl)* 1. (*esponsales*) engagement, betrothal *form* 2. (*matrimonio*) marriage

despostar *vt AmS* to joint meat

déspota *mf* despot

despótico, **-a** *adj* despotic

despotismo *m* despotism

despotricar <c→qu> *vi inf* 1. (*chochear*) to be senile 2. (*maldecir*) ~ **de algo/alguien** to rant and rave about sth/sb

despreciable *adj* contemptible; **nada** ~ to not be sneered at

despreciar I. *vt* 1. (*menospreciar*) to despise 2. (*rechazar*) to spurn; (*oferta*) to turn down II. *vr:* ~**se** to run oneself down

despreciativo, **-a** *adj* disdainful

desprecio *m* contempt

desprender I. *vt* 1. (*soltar*) to release 2. (*olor, gas*) to give off 3. (*deducir*) to deduce; **de su aviso desprendemos que...** from his/her warning we can deduce that ... II. *vr:* **~se** 1. (*soltarse*) to untie oneself 2. (*deshacerse*) to come undone; (*desembarazarse*) to rid oneself of; **~se de cualquier duda** to get rid of any doubts; (*renunciar*) to part with 3. (*deducirse*) **de tu comportamiento se desprende que...** from your behaviour [*o* behavior *Am*] one can see that ...

desprendido, -a *adj* (*generoso*) generous; (*altruista*) disinterested

desprendimiento *m* 1. (*separación*) separation; **~ de tierras** landslide; **~ de retina** detached retina 2. (*generosidad*) generosity

despreocupación *f* 1. (*indiferencia*) indifference 2. (*insensatez*) carelessness

despreocupado, -a *adj* 1. (*negligente*) careless 2. (*tranquilo*) unconcerned

despreocuparse *vr* 1. (*tranquilizarse*) to stop worrying 2. (*desatender*) **~se de algo** to neglect sth

despresar *vt AmS* to carve

desprestigiar I. *vt* to discredit II. *vr:* **~se** 1. (*rebajarse*) to fall into discredit 2. (*perder reputación*) to see one's reputation suffer

desprevenido, -a *adj* unprepared; **coger a alguien ~** to catch sb unawares [*o* off guard]

desproporción *f* disproportion

desproporcionado, -a *adj* disproportionate

despropósito *m* stupid remark; **decir ~s** to make stupid remarks

desproveer *irr como proveer vt* to deprive

desprovisto, -a *adj* **~ de** lacking; **el estadio está ~ de las normas de seguridad necesarias** the stadium lacks the necessary safety provisions

después I. *adv* 1. (*tiempo*) after; **~ de la cena** after supper; **una hora ~** an hour later 2. (*espacio*) **~ de la torre** behind the tower 3. (*concesivo*) **~ de todo** after all II. *conj* **~ (de) que** after

despuntar I. *vt* (*gastar la punta*) to blunt; (*quitarla*) to remove the tip of II. *vi* 1. (*flor*) to bud; (*planta*) to sprout 2. (*amanecer*) to dawn; **al ~ la aurora** at the break of dawn 3. (*distinguirse*) to stand out; **despunta en inglés** he/she excels at English III. *vr:* **~se** (*gastarse*) to become blunt

desquiciado, -a *adj inf* disturbed

desquiciar I. *vt* 1. (*desencajar*) to unhinge 2. (*alterar*) to disturb II. *vr:* **~se** to become unstable

desquitar *vt, vr:* **~se** 1. (*resarcir*) to win back; **~se de una pérdida** to make good a loss 2. (*desagraviar*) **~ de algo** to make up for sth 3. (*vengar*) to get even with

desquite *m* 1. (*satisfacción*) satisfaction 2. (*venganza*) revenge; **tomar(se) el ~** to avenge oneself

desrielar *vi AmL* to derail

destacable *adj* outstanding

destacado, -a *adj* outstanding

destacamento *m* MIL detachment, detail

destacar <c→qu> I. *vi* to stand out; **~ en el deporte** to excel at sports II. *vt* (*realzar*) to emphasize III. *vr:* **~se** (*descollar*) to stand out

destajo *m* piecework; **trabajar a ~** to do piecework; *fig* to work hard; **hablar a ~** *inf* to talk nineteen to the dozen; **a ~** *Arg, Chile* (*a ojo*) by guesswork

destapar I. *vt* 1. (*abrir*) to open; **~ la olla** to take the lid off the pot 2. (*desabrigar*) to uncover 3. (*secretos*) to reveal II. *vr:* **~se** 1. (*perder la tapa*) to lose its lid 2. (*desabrigarse*) to be uncovered 3. *inf* (*desnudarse*) to strip off, to strip down 4. (*descubrirse*) to be revealed 5. (*desahogarse*) **~se con** [*o* **haciendo**] **algo** to let off steam by doing sth

destaponar *vt* 1. (*una botella*) to uncork 2. (*obstrucción*) to unplug 3. *Perú* (*abrir*) to open

destartalado, -a *adj* ramshackle

destellar *vi* to sparkle

destello *m* 1. (*rayo*) ray 2. (*reflejo*) glint 3. (*resplandor*) sparkle 4. (*indicio*) glimmer

destemplado, -a *adj* 1. (*sonido*) out of tune 2. (*voz*) harsh 3. (*tiempo*) unpleasant 4. (*persona*) bad-tempered

destemplanza *f* 1. (*inmoderación*) excess; **con ~** excessively 2. (*tiempo*) unsettledness 3. (*malestar*) indisposition

destemplar I. *vt* 1. (*sonido*) to be out of tune 2. (*perturbar*) to disturb II. *vr:* **~se** 1. (*alterarse*) to get upset 2. (*indisponerse*) to become ill

desteñido, -a *adj* (*descolorido*) faded; (*manchado*) discoloured *Brit,* discolored *Am*

desteñir *irr como ceñir* I. *vi* (*descolorarse*) to fade; (*despintar*) to run II. *vt* 1. (*descolorar*) to fade; QUÍM to bleach 2. (*manchar*) to stain III. *vr:* **~se** (*descolorarse*) to fade; (*despintar*) to run, to bleed

desternillarse *vr* **~ de risa** to laugh one's head off

desterrar <e→ie> *vt* 1. (*exiliar*) to exile; **~ a alguien del país** to exile sb from the country 2. (*alejar*) to banish

destetar *vt* to wean

destiempo *m* **a ~** at the wrong moment

destierro *m* 1. (*pena*) exile 2. (*lugar*) (place of) exile 3. (*lugar muy alejado*) remote place

destilación *f* (*alcohol*) distillation; (*petróleo*) refining

destilar I. *vi* to distil *Brit,* to distill *Am* II. *vt* 1. (*alambicar*) to distil *Brit,* to distill *Am* 2. (*filtrar*) to filtrate 3. (*soltar*) to give off 4. (*sentimiento*) to exude; **la crítica destila mala leche** the criticism is full of spite

destilería *f* distillery; **~ de petróleo** oil refinery

destinar *vt* 1. (*dedicar*) to dedicate; (*asignar*) to assign 2. (*enviar*) to send 3. (*designar*) to appoint; **~ a alguien para Ministro de**

Defensa to appoint sb as Minister of Defence [*o* Defense *Am*] **4.** MIL to post

destinatario, **-a** *m, f* (*correo*) addressee; (*mercancía*) consignee

destino *m* **1.** (*hado*) fate; **tuvo un ~ muy triste** he/she met an unhappy end **2.** (*empleo*) job, post *Brit;* **pedir un importante ~ en el gobierno** to apply for an important position in the government **3.** (*destinación*) destination; **estación de ~** destination station; **puerto de ~** destination port; **el barco sale con ~ a México** the boat is bound for Mexico **4.** (*finalidad*) purpose

destitución *f* dismissal; **~ del cargo** removal from one's post [*o* office *Am*]

destituir *irr como huir vt* **1.** (*despedir*) to dismiss; **~ al jefe de gobierno** to remove the head of the government **2.** *elev* (*privar*) **~ a alguien de algo** to deprive sb of sth

destornillador *m* **1.** (*herramienta*) screwdriver, turnscrew *Brit;* **~ de estrella** cross-point screwdriver *Brit,* Philips screwdriver *Am* **2.** GASTR screwdriver

destornillar *vt* to unscrew

destrabar **I.** *vt* to untie **II.** *vr:* **~se** to come undone

destral *m* hatchet

destreza *f* skill; **~ manual** dexterity; **con ~** skilfully *Brit,* skillfully *Am*

destripador(a) *m(f) fig* murderer; **Jack el ~** Jack the Ripper

destripar *vt* **1.** (*despanzurrar: persona, animal*) to disembowel; (*pez*) to gut **2.** (*despachurrar*) *t. fig* to crush **3.** (*estropear*) to ruin

destrísimo, **-a** *adj superl de* **diestro**

destrozar <z→c> *vt* **1.** (*despedazar*) to smash; (*libro*) to rip up; (*ropa*) to tear up; **~ un vehículo** (*conduciendo*) to smash up a vehicle **2.** (*moralmente*) to shatter; **estar destrozado** to be an emotional wreck **3.** *inf* (*físicamente*) to shatter; **el viaje me ha destrozado** I'm absolutely exhausted from the journey; **he trabajado todo el día y estoy destrozado** I've been working all day and now I'm knackered **4.** (*planes*) to ruin **5.** (*enemigo, cosecha*) to destroy

destrozo *m* **1.** (*daño*) damage **2.** (*acción*) destruction

destrozón, **-ona** *adj, m, f inf* destructive; **este niño es un ~** this child leaves a trail of destruction in his wake

destrucción *f* destruction

destructivo, **-a** *adj* destructive

destruir *irr como huir vt* **1.** (*destrozar*) to destroy **2.** (*física o moralmente*) to shatter **3.** (*aniquilar*) to annihilate

desubicado, **-a** *adj AmL* out of place; *fig* disorientated *Brit,* disoriented *Am*

desuncir <c→z> *vt* to unyoke

desunión *f* **1.** (*separación*) separation **2.** (*discordia*) disunity

desunir **I.** *vt* **1.** (*separar*) to separate **2.** (*enemistar*) **~ a dos personas** to cause discord between two people **II.** *vr:* **~se** **1.** (*separar*) to separate **2.** (*enemistar*) to fall out

desusado, **-a** *adj* **1.** (*anticuado*) old-fashioned **2.** (*insólito*) unusual

desuso *m* **caer en ~** to fall into disuse; (*máquina*) to become obsolete

desvaído, **-a** *adj* **1.** (*colores*) faded **2.** (*persona*) dull; **es una mujer desvaída** she's a bit insipid

desvalido, **-a** *adj* needy

desvalijar *vt* to clean out *inf*

desvalimiento *m* destitution

desvalorización *f* depreciation; **~ monetaria** monetary devaluation

desvalorizar <z→c> *vt* to devalue

desván *m* loft, attic

desvanecer *irr como crecer* **I.** *vt* **1.** (*color*) to tone down **2.** (*dudas*) to dispel; **~ las sospechas de alguien** to allay sb's suspicions **II.** *vr:* **~se** **1.** (*desaparecer*) to disappear; (*alcohol*) to evaporate; (*colores, esperanzas*) to fade; (*enojo*) to abate; **el entusiasmo se desvaneció rápidamente** the enthusiasm soon abated **2.** (*desmayarse*) to faint

desvanecimiento *m* **1.** (*desaparición*) disappearance **2.** (*mareo*) faint; **tener un ~** to faint

desvariar <*1. pres:* desvarío> *vi* (*delirar*) to be delirious; (*decir incoherencias*) to talk nonsense

desvarío *m* **1.** (*locura*) madness; **los ~s de una imaginación enfermiza** the crazed imaginings of a sick mind **2.** (*delirio*) delirium **3.** (*monstruosidad*) monstrosity

desvelar **I.** *vt* **1.** (*sueño*) **~ a alguien** to keep sb awake **2.** (*revelar*) to reveal **II.** *vr:* **~se** **1.** (*no dormir*) to stay awake **2.** (*esmerarse*) **~se por algo/alguien** to devote oneself to sth/sb

desvelo *m* **1.** (*insomnio*) insomnia **2.** (*despabilamiento*) alertness **3.** *(pl)* (*celo*) jealousy **4.** *(pl)* (*atención*) efforts *pl*

desvencijado, **-a** *adj* dilapidated

desvencijar **I.** *vt* to break **II.** *vr:* **~se** to fall to pieces

desventaja *f* disadvantage, drawback

desventajoso, **-a** *adj* disadvantageous; (*condiciones*) unfavourable *Brit,* unfavorable *Am;* **apariencia desventajosa** unprepossessing appearance

desventura *f* misfortune

desventurado, **-a** *adj* unfortunate; **una familia desventurada** an ill-fated family

desvergonzado, **-a** *adj* **1.** (*sinvergüenza*) shameless **2.** (*descarado*) brazen

desvergonzarse *irr como avergonzar vr* to lose all sense of shame; **~ con alguien** to be rude to sb

desvergüenza *f* shamelessness

desvestir *irr como pedir vt, vr:* **~se** to undress

desviación *f* **1.** (*torcedura*) deviation; **~ de la columna vertebral** curvature of the spine; **~ jurídica** miscarriage of justice **2.** (*del tráfico*) diversion, detour; (*bocacalle*) turning

3. (*aberración*) deviance

desviado, -a *adj* (*diferente*) deviant

desviar <*1. pres:* desvío> I. *vt* (*del camino, dinero*) to divert; (*de un propósito*) to distract; ~ **una cuestión** to avoid a problem II. *vr:* **~se** 1. (*del camino*) to be diverted; (*del tema*) to be distracted; (*de una idea, intención*) to be put off; **la brigada se desvió hacia la izquierda** the brigade turned towards the left 2. (*extraviarse*) to get lost

desvincular I. *vt* to dissociate II. *vr:* **~se** to dissociate oneself

desvío *m* 1. (*desviación*) deviation 2. (*carretera*) detour; (*temporal*) diversion, detour 3. (*despego*) indifference

desvirgar <g→gu> *vt* to deflower

desvirtuar <*1. pres:* desvirtúo> *vt* (*argumento, prueba*) to undermine; (*rumor*) to scotch; ~ **la competencia** to distort the marketplace

desvivirse *vr* 1. (*chiflarse*) ~ **por alguien** to be crazy about sb; **se desvive por ella** he's head over heels in love with her 2. (*afanarse*) ~ **con** [*o* **por**] **alguien** to be utterly devoted to sb; **se desvivió por conseguir este documento** he/she went to every length imaginable to get this document

detallado, -a *adj* detailed; **una lista detallada** an itemized list

detallar *vt* 1. (*pormenorizar*) to detail, to itemize 2. COM to retail

detalle *m* 1. (*pormenor*) detail; **en** [*o* **al**] ~ in detail; **venta al** ~ retail sales; **entrar en ~s** to go into details 2. (*finura*) nice gesture; **has tenido un ~ regalándome las flores** it was very kind of you to give me the flowers

detallista I. *adj* precise; *pey* pedantic II. *mf* 1. (*minucioso*) perfectionist 2. COM retailer 3. (*considerado*) thoughtful person

detectable *adj* detectable

detectar *vt* to detect

detective *mf* detective

detector *m* detector; ~ **de humo** smoke detector

detención *f* 1. (*parada*) stopping; (*de la correspondencia*) withholding; ~ **del crecimiento** inhibition of growth 2. JUR arrest; ~ **ilegal** false imprisonment; ~ **preventiva** preventive detention, remand in custody; ~ **domiciliaria** house arrest 3. (*dilación*) delay; **sin** ~ without delay 4. (*prolijidad*) detail; **describir con** ~ to describe in detail; **ha corregido el examen con** ~ he/she took great care in marking the exam

detener *irr como tener* I. *vt* 1. (*parar*) to stop; (*correspondencia*) to withhold; ~ **los progresos de una enfermedad** to halt the evolution of a disease 2. JUR to arrest 3. (*retener*) ~ (**en su poder**) to keep (in one's power) II. *vr:* **~se** 1. (*pararse*) to stop 2. (*entretenerse*) **~se en algo** to pass one's time doing sth

detenidamente *adv* thoroughly, carefully

detenido, -a I. *adj* 1. (*minucioso*) thorough 2. (*arrestado*) arrested 3. (*apocado*) timid 4. (*escaso*) insufficient II. *m, f* person under arrest

detenimiento *m* 1. (*minuciosidad*) care; **con** ~ thoroughly 2. (*tardanza*) delay; **con** ~ late 3. JUR arrest

detentar *vt* to hold unlawfully

detergente I. *adj* detergent II. *m* detergent; ~ **para lavar la ropa** washing powder *Brit,* laundry detergent *Am;* ~ **lavavajillas** washing-up liquid *Brit,* dish liquid *Am*

deteriorar I. *vt* 1. (*empeorar*) to worsen 2. (*romper*) to break 3. (*gastar*) to wear out II. *vr:* **~se** 1. (*empeorarse*) to worsen 2. (*estropearse*) to spoil; **mercancía deteriorada** spoiled goods

deterioro *m* 1. (*desmejora*) deterioration; ~ **de calidad** decline in quality 2. (*daño*) damage; **sin** ~ undamaged; ~ **debido al almacenamiento** damaged in storage 3. (*desgaste*) wear and tear 4. (*echarse a perder*) spoiling; **sujeto a** ~ perishable; **de fácil** ~ easily spoilt

determinación *f* 1. (*fijación*) establishment; ~ **de los daños** ascertainment of damages; ~ **de objetivos** setting of objectives 2. (*decisión*) decision; **tomar una** ~ to take [*o* make] a decision; **con** ~ determinedly 3. (*audacia*) determination

determinado, -a *adj* 1. (*cierto*) *t.* LING definite 2. (*atrevido*) determined 3. (*preciso*) specific

determinante I. *adj* decisive; **palabra** ~ LING determiner II. *m* decisive factor; MAT determinant

determinar I. *vt* 1. (*fijar*) to establish; (*plazo*) to fix 2. (*decidir*) to decide; JUR to settle; ~ **un pleito** to adjudicate a (court) case 3. (*causar*) to determine 4. (*motivar*) ~ **a alguien a hacer algo** to determine sb to do sth II. *vr:* **~se por algo** to decide in favour [*o* favor *Am*] of sth; **~se a hacer algo** to decide to do sth

detestable *adj* loathsome

detestar *vt* to detest, to loathe

detonación *f* 1. (*acción*) detonation 2. (*ruido*) explosion

detonador *m* detonator

detonante I. *adj* 1. (*explosivo*) explosive 2. *AmL* (*que molesta*) discordant II. *m* (*causa*) cause

detonar I. *vi* to detonate, to set off II. *vt* to detonate

detractor(a) I. *adj* denigrating II. *m(f)* detractor

detrás I. *adv* 1. (*local*) behind; **allí** ~ over there, behind that; **entrar por** ~ to come in through the back; **me asaltaron por** ~ they attacked me from behind 2. (*en el orden*) **el que está** ~ the next one; **primero estás tu y ~ van mis amigos** *fig* you're more important to me than my friends II. *prep* 1. (*local: tras*) ~ **de** behind; ~ **de la carta** on the back of the letter; **quedar ~ de los otros** to be behind the others; **ir ~ de alguien** to be looking for sb;

hablar mal (**por**) ~ **de alguien** to criticize sb behind his/her back **2.** (*en el orden*) **uno** ~ **de otro** one after another

detrimento *m* **1.** (*daño*) harm; **causa** ~ **de la salud** it damages your health **2.** (*perjuicio*) detriment; **en** ~ **de alguien** to sb's detriment; **en** ~ **de su salud** at cost to his/her health

deuda *f* **1.** (*débito*) debt; ~ **activa** productive debt; ~ **contraída** debt; ~ **del Estado** Treasury notes/bonds; ~ **externa** foreign debt; ~ **interna** internal debt; ~ **pública** national debt; ~ **a pagar** debt due; ~ **pendiente** outstanding debt; ~ **vencida** mature debt; **cargado de ~s** burdened with debt; **contraer ~s** to get into debt; **sin ~s** free of debt **2.** (*moral*) debt; **estar en** ~ **con alguien** to be indebted to sb; **lo prometido es** ~ a promise is a promise **3.** (*pecado*) **y perdónanos nuestras ~s...** and forgive us our trespasses ...

deudor(a) **I.** *adj* indebted; **saldo** ~ debit balance **II.** *m(f)* debtor; ~ **solidario** joint debtor

devaluación *f* devaluation

devaluar <*1. pres:* devalúo> *vt* to devalue

devanar **I.** *vt* to wind **II.** *vr:* **~se** *Cuba* (*reírse mucho*) to split one's sides laughing **2. ~se los sesos** to rack one's brains

devaneo *m* **1.** (*amorío*) flirtation **2.** (*distracción*) distraction **3.** (*locura*) delusion

devastación *f* devastation

devastar *vt* to devastate

devengar <g→gu> *vt* **1.** (*salario*) to earn **2.** (*intereses*) to yield; **interTs devengado** accrued interest

devenir *irr como venir vi* **1.** (*acaecer*) to occur **2.** (*convertirse*) ~ **en algo** to become sth

devoción *f* **1.** (*religión*) religious belief; **fingir** ~ to feign belief **2.** (*oración*) devotion **3.** (*respeto*) devotion; **rezar con** ~ to pray devoutly **4.** (*obediencia*) obedience; **estar a la** ~ **de alguien** to be at sb's disposal **5.** (*fervor*) fervour *Brit,* fervor *Am;* **amar con** ~ to love devotedly; **hacer con** ~ to do with great devotion; **tener** ~ **a un santo** to venerate a saint **6.** (*afición*) attachment

devocionario *m* prayer book

devolución *f* return; ~ **a origen** return to sender; FIN refund; ~ **de impuestos** tax refund, tax return; **'no se admiten devoluciones'** 'no refunds'

devolver *irr como volver* **I.** *vt* **1.** to return; *fig* to restore; ~ **bien por mal** to repay evil with good; ~ **un favor** to return a favour [*o* favor *Am*]; ~ **la visita** to return a visit; **devuélvase al remitente** (*en cartas*) return to sender; **esta máquina no devuelve cambio** this machine does not give change; ~ **la pelota al defensa** to pass the ball back to the defender **2.** (*vomitar*) to throw up **II.** *vr:* **~se** *AmL* (*volver*) to return; **~se a casa** to go back home

devorador(a) *adj* **hambre ~a** ravenous hunger

devorar *vt* to devour; ~ **la comida** to wolf down one's food; **la enfermedad devoró sus fuerzas** the illness consumed his/her strength; **me devora la impaciencia** I am consumed with impatience

devoto, -a **I.** *adj* **1.** (*religioso*) devout **2.** (*adicto*) devoted; ~ **admirador de los Beatles** loyal [*o* keen *Brit*] fan of the Beatles **II.** *m, f* **1.** (*creyente*) devotee **2.** (*admirador*) enthusiast

deyección *f* **1.** (*volcán*) ejecta **2.** (*defecación*) defecation **3.** *pl* (*heces*) faeces *pl Brit,* feces *pl Am*

DGT *f* **1.** (*turismo*) *abr de* **Dirección General de Turismo** *Spanish department for tourism* **2.** (*tráfico*) *abr de* **Dirección General de Tráfico** *Spanish department for traffic*

día *m* day; ~ **de año nuevo** New Year's day; ~ **de cumpleaños** birthday; **el** ~ **D** D-day; ~ **de descanso** rest day; ~ **de los difuntos** All Souls' Day; ~ **festivo** holiday; ~ **hábil** [*o* **laborable**] working day; **el** ~ **del juicio final** Judgement Day; ~ **lectivo** school day; ~ **libre/de baja** day off; ~ **de Reyes** Epiphany; ~ **del santo** saint's day; **cambio del** ~ today's exchange rate; **al abrir el** ~ at the break of day; **al caer el** ~ at the close of day; **al otro** ~ by the next day; **antes del** ~ before the break of day; **de hoy en ocho ~s** eight days from now; **de un** ~ **a otro** from one day to the next; **cualquier** ~ any day; **durante ~s enteros** for days at a time; **una diferencia como del** ~ **a la noche** as different as you can get; **un** ~ **sí y otro no,** ~ **por medio** *AmL* every other day; ~ **y noche** day and night; **el** ~ **de hoy** nowadays; **el** ~ **de mañana** in the future; **el** ~ **menos pensado** one fine day; **el** ~ **que...** the day that ...; **el otro** ~ the other day; **en su** ~ in his/her day; **hoy** (**en**) ~ nowadays; **un buen** ~ one fine day; **un** ~ **de estos** one of these days; **un** ~ **u otro** some day; **hace buen** ~ it's nice weather; **a ~s** at times; **de** ~ by [*o* during the] day; **del** ~ today's; ~ **a** ~ day by day; ~ **tras** [*o* **por**] ~ day after day; **de** ~ **en** ~ from day to day; **¡buenos ~s!** hello; (*por la mañana*) good morning; **¡hasta otro ~!** until another day! ▸**hay más ~s que <u>longanizas</u>** *inf* there will be other days; **<u>mañana</u> será otro** ~ tomorrow is another day; **tiene los ~s <u>contados</u>** his/her days are numbered; **<u>entrado</u> en ~s** getting on; **¡no en <u>mis</u> ~s!** over my dead body!; **un** ~ **y <u>otro</u>** ~ again and again; **todo el <u>santo</u>** ~ the whole day long; **<u>alcanzar</u> a alguien en ~s** to outlive sb; **<u>dar</u> a alguien el** ~ to ruin sb's day; **<u>estar</u> al** ~ to be up to date; **no <u>pasar</u> los ~s por alguien** to not look a day older; **un** ~ **<u>es</u> un** ~ it's just one day; **<u>tener</u> ~s** (*viejo*) to be old; (*de mal humor*) to be bad-tempered; **<u>vivir</u> al** ~ to live from day to day

diabetes *f inv* diabetes

diabético, -a *adj, m, f* diabetic

diablo *m* devil; **ser un** ~ **de hombre** to be an absolute devil; **tener el** ~ **en el cuerpo** to be a little devil; **abogado del** ~ devil's advocate; **duele como el** ~ it hurts like hell ▸**¡con <u>mil</u>**

~s! hell!; **de mil ~s** hellish; **aquí hay mucho ~** *inf* there is something fishy going on here; **más sabe el ~ por viejo que por sabio** *prov* the older, the wiser *prov;* **anda el ~ suelto** *inf* there's trouble brewing; **aquí anda el ~** everything is going wrong; **dar de comer al ~** *inf* to curse; **dar al ~** *inf* to send to hell; **darse al ~** *inf* to blow one's top; **¡vete al ~!** go to hell!; **¿cómo ~s...?** how on earth ...?; **¡qué ~s!** hell!; **¿qué ~s pasa aquí?** what the hell is going on here?; **¡~s!** damn!

diablura *f* prank

diabólico, -a *adj* **1.** (*maligno*) diabolic(al) **2.** (*complicado*) fiendish

diadema *f* (*corona*) diadem; (*joya*) tiara; (*del pelo*) hairband

diáfano, -a *adj* **1.** (*transparente*) transparent **2.** (*translúcido*) translucent **3.** (*claro*) clear; **un argumento ~** a clear argument

diafragma *m* **1.** FOTO, ANAT diaphragm **2.** (*anticonceptivo*) (Dutch) cap *Brit,* diaphragm *Am*

diagnosis *f inv* diagnosis

diagnosticar <c→qu> *vt* to diagnose

diagnóstico *m* **1.** (*diagnosis*) diagnosis; **~ precoz** early diagnosis **2.** (*análisis*) analysis

diagonal **I.** *adj* diagonal; **en ~** diagonally **II.** *f* diagonal

diagrama *m* diagram; **~ de bloques** block diagram; **~ esquemático** schematic diagram; **~ de puntos** scatter diagram; **~ de flujo** flowchart

dial *m* dial; **~ de velocidad** AUTO speedometer

dialectal *adj* dialect

dialéctica *f* dialectics *pl*

dialecto *m* dialect

diálisis *f inv* dialysis

dialogar <g→gu> *vi* (*hablar*) to talk; **~ con alguien** to have a conversation with sb; **escrito en forma dialogada** written in the form of a dialogue [*o* dialog *Am*]

diálogo *m* **1.** (*conversación*) conversation **2.** LIT dialogue *Brit,* dialog *Am*

diamante *m* diamond; **bodas de ~** diamond wedding; **~ brillante** brilliant; **~ (en) bruto** rough [*o* uncut] diamond

diametralmente *adv* diametrically; **~ opuesto** diametrically opposed

diámetro *m* diameter

diana *f* **1.** MIL reveille; **a toque de ~** *fig* highly disciplined **2.** (*objeto*) target **3.** (*del blanco*) bull's-eye; **hacer ~** to hit the bull's-eye

diantre *interj inf* damn

diapasón *m* MÚS range; **~ normal** standard pitch; (*objeto*) tuning fork; (*de voz*) pitch-pipe; (*guitarra*) fingerboard; **bajar/subir el ~** *inf* to turn the volume up/down

diapositiva *f* slide

diariero, -a *m, f AmS* paperboy, newspaper vendor

diario *m* **1.** (*periódico*) (daily) newspaper; **~ de avisos** classified advertising newspaper **2.** (*dietario*) journal; **~ de navegación** NÁUT log **3.** (*memorias*) diary **4.** (*gastos*) daily expenses

diario, -a *adj* daily; **a ~** daily; **de ~** everyday; **uniforme de ~** service uniform

diarismo *m AmL* (*periodismo*) journalism

diarrea *f* diarrhoea *Brit,* diarrhea *Am*

dibujante *mf* (*lineal*) draughtsman *m,* draughtswoman *f;* **~ proyectista** architectural draughtsman *m,* architectural draughtswoman *f;* (*de bocetos*) sketcher; (*de caricaturas, dibujos animados*) cartoonist

dibujar **I.** *vt* **1.** (*trazar*) to draw; **~ copiando** to draw from a copy; **~ según modelo** to draw from a model; **~ a pulso** to draw freehand; **~ a lápiz** to draw in pencil **2.** (*describir*) to describe **II.** *vr:* **~se** to be outlined

dibujo *m* **1.** (*acción*) drawing **2.** (*resultado*) drawing; **~ acotado** contour drawing; **~s animados** cartoons **3.** (*muestra*) illustration; **con ~s** illustrated **4.** (*estampado*) pattern

dicción *f* **1.** (*declamación*) declamation **2.** (*pronunciación*) diction; (*estilo*) eloquence

diccionario *m* dictionary; **~ de artes y ciencias** dictionary of art and science; **~ enciclopédico** encyclopaedic [*o* encyclopedic *Am*] dictionary; **~ de inglés-español** English-Spanish dictionary

dicha *f* (*suerte*) luck; **~ conyugal** marital bliss; **por ~** fortunately; **nunca es tarde si la ~ es buena** *prov* better late than never *prov*

dicharachero, -a **I.** *adj* funny **II.** *m, f* joker

dicho *m* **1.** (*ocurrencia*) observation **2.** (*refrán*) saying **3.** *pl* (*al casarse*) vows *pl;* **tomarse los ~s** to take one's vows ►**del ~ al hecho hay mucho trecho** *prov* it's easier said than done *prov*

dicho, -a **I.** *pp de* **decir** **II.** *adj* **dicha gente** the said people; **~ y hecho** no sooner said than done

dichoso, -a *adj* **1.** (*feliz*) **~ de algo** happy to sth **2.** *irón* (*maldito*) blessed

diciembre *m* December; *v.t.* **marzo**

dictado *m* **1.** (*escuela*) dictation **2.** *fig* (*inspiración*) dictate; **seguir los ~s de la conciencia** to follow one's conscience

dictador(a) *m(f)* dictator

dictadura *f* dictatorship

dictáfono *m* Dictaphone®

dictamen *m* **1.** (*peritaje*) opinion; **~ en juicio** legal opinion; **dar ~** to give advice **2.** (*informe*) report; **~ facultativo** medical report **3.** (*opinión*) opinion; **tomar ~ de alguien** to consult with sb **4.** JUR **~ judicial** legal judgment

dictaminar *vi* to pronounce judgement

dictar *vt* **1.** (*un dictado*) to dictate **2.** (*una sentencia*) to pass **3.** (*una ley*) to enact **4.** (*un discurso*) to give **5.** *AmS* (*clases*) to teach **6.** *fig* (*sugerir*) to suggest

didáctico, -a *adj* didactic; **material ~** teaching material

diecinueve *adj inv, m* nineteen; *v.t.* **ocho**

dieciocho *adj inv, m* eighteen; *v.t.* **ocho**

dieciséis *adj inv, m* sixteen; *v.t.* **ocho**

D

dieciseisavo, **-a** *adj, m, f* sixteenth; *v.t.* **octavo**

diecisiete *adj inv* seventeen; *v.t.* **ocho**

diecisieteavo, **-a** *adj, m, f* seventeenth; *v.t.* **octavo**

diente *m* **1.**(*de la boca*) tooth; ~ **canino** canine (tooth); ~ **incisivo** incisor; ~ **de leche** milk tooth; ~ **molar** molar; ~**s postizos** false teeth; ~ **picado** tooth with caries; **armado hasta los ~s** armed to the teeth; **daba ~ con ~** his/her teeth were chattering **2.** TÉC tooth; (*de horquilla*) prong; **de dos ~s** two-pronged **3.** BOT ~ **de ajo** clove of garlic; ~ **de león** dandelion ▸**decir algo entre ~s** to mumble sth; **poner los ~s largos a alguien** to make sb green with envy; **pelar el ~** *AmL, inf* to smile flirtatiously; **tener buen ~** to have a healthy appetite; **volar ~** *AmL* (*comer*) to stuff one's face

diesel *m* diesel

diestro *m* (*torero*) matador

diestro, **-a** <destrísimo *o* diestrísimo> *adj* **1.**(*a la derecha*) right; **a ~ y siniestro** *fig* left, right and centre [*o* center *Am*] **2.**(*hábil*) skilful *Brit,* skillful *Am* **3.**(*astuto*) cunning **4.**(*que usa la mano derecha*) right-handed

dieta *f* **1.**(*para adelgazar*) diet; ~ **absoluta** starvation diet; **estar a ~** to be on a diet; **poner alguien a ~** to put sb on a diet **2.**(*alimentación*) ~ **alimenticia** diet; ~ **básica** staple diet **3.**(*asamblea*) diet **4.** *pl* (*retribución*) allowance, expenses *pl;* (*de diputados*) salary

dietético, **-a** *adj* dietary; **régimen ~** diet; **médico ~** dietician

diez *adj inv, m* ten; *v.t.* **ocho**

diezmar *vt* (*aniquilar*) to decimate

difamación *f* defamation; (*escrita*) libel; (*oral*) slander

difamar *vt* to defame; (*por escrito*) to libel; (*hablando*) to slander

difamatorio, **-a** *adj* defamatory; (*escrito*) libellous *Brit,* libelous *Am;* (*hablando*) slanderous

diferencia *f* **1.**(*desigualdad*) difference; ~ **de los tipos de interés** interest differential/margin; **a ~ de algo** unlike [*o* in contrast with] sth **2.**(*desacuerdo*) disagreement; **arreglar (las) ~s** to settle one's differences **3.** MAT difference; ~ **de caja** cash deficit

diferencial[1] **I.** *adj* **1.**(*variable*) variable **2.** MAT differential **II.** *f* MAT differential

diferencial[2] *m* AUTO differential (gear)

diferenciar **I.** *vi* to differentiate **II.** *vt* **1.**(*distinguir*) to distinguish **2.** MAT to differentiate **III.** *vr:* ~**se** to differ

diferendo *m AmS* (*disputa*) dispute

diferente **I.** *adj* different; **~s veces** several times; **España es ~** Spain is different **II.** *adv* differently; **piensa muy ~** he/she has a very different way of thinking

diferir *irr como sentir* **I.** *vi* to differ; ~ **de algo** to be different from sth **II.** *vt* to postpone; ~ **el pago** to delay payment; **transmisión en diferido** pre-recorded broadcast

difícil *adj* difficult; ~ **de explicar** difficult to explain; **de ~ acceso** hard to get to

difícilmente *adv* with difficulty; **un material ~ soluble** a substance which is hard to dissolve; (*apenas*) hardly

dificultad *f* difficulty; **estar en ~es** to be in difficulty; **expresarse con ~** to express oneself with difficulty; **poner ~es a alguien** to put sb in a difficult position; **ahí está la ~** that's where the problem lies

dificultar *vt* to hinder; ~ **la circulación** to obstruct the traffic

dificultoso, **-a** *adj* difficult; (*laborioso*) heavy-going

difteria *f* diphtheria

difuminar *vt* (*dibujo*) to stump, to blur; (*luz*) to diffuse

difundir **I.** *vt* to spread; (*gas*) to give off; ~ **por la radio** to broadcast on the radio **II.** *vr:* ~**se** to spread; **la niebla se difundió por todo el valle** the fog spread right across the valley; **la novedad se ha difundido por toda la ciudad** the news has spread throughout the city

difunto, **-a** **I.** *adj* deceased; **el ~ presidente** the late president **II.** *m, f* deceased person; **día de ~s** All Souls' Day; **misa de ~s** Requiem (mass)

difusión *f* **1.**(*expansión, divulgación*) dissemination; TV, RADIO broadcast; ~ **de productos** distribution of products **2.**(*prolijidad*) lengthiness

difuso, **-a** *adj* **1.**(*extendido*) widespread **2.**(*vago, prolijo*) diffuse

digerir *irr como sentir vt* **1.**(*la comida*) to digest **2.**(*a una persona*) to stomach; (*noticia, libro*) to absorb

digestión *f* (*de alimentos*) digestion; **tener mala ~** to have stomach problems; **corte de ~** stomach cramp

digestivo, **-a** *adj* digestive; **aparato ~** ANAT digestive system

digital **I.** *adj* **1.**(*dactilar*) finger; **huellas ~es** fingerprints **2.** INFOR, TÉC digital; **ingreso ~** digital input; **ordenador ~** digital computer **II.** *m* foxglove

digitalizar <z→c> *vt* to digitize *Brit,* to digitalize *Am*

dígito **I.** *adj* digital **II.** *m* MAT, INFOR digit; ~ **de verificación** verification number; ~ **de control** check bit

dignarse *vr* ~ **hacer algo** to condescend to do sth; **se dignaron invitarnos a su fiesta** *irón* they deigned to invite us to their party

dignatario, **-a** *m, f* dignitary

dignidad *f* **1.**(*respeto*) dignity; **con ~** with dignity **2.**(*decencia*) decency **3.**(*cargo*) office

digno, **-a** *adj* **1.**(*merecedor*) deserving; ~ **de compasión** worthy of sympathy; ~ **de confianza** trustworthy; ~ **de fe** worth believing in; ~ **de mención** worth mentioning; ~ **de ver** worth seeing **2.**(*adecuado*) fitting

3. (*noble*) noble 4. (*con gravedad*) dignified
digresión *f* (*del tema*) digression
dije *m* (*colgante*) charm; **ser un ~** *inf* (*persona*) to be a treasure [*o* jewel]
dilación *f* (*aplazamiento*) postponement; (*retraso*) delay; **sin ~** without delay
dilapidar *vt* to squander; **~ una fortuna** to squander a fortune
dilatación *f* 1. (*ampliación*) expansion; MED dilation; **~ del mercado** COM expansion of the market 2. (*desahogo*) calm
dilatado, -a *adj* 1. (*pupila*) dilated 2. (*extenso*) extensive
dilatar I. *vt* 1. (*extender*) to expand; MED to dilate 2. (*aplazar*) to postpone; **~ la reunión** to postpone the meeting 3. (*retrasar*) to delay 4. (*prolongar*) to prolong II. *vr:* **~se** 1. (*extenderse*) to expand 2. *AmL* (*demorar*) to delay
dilatorio, -a *adj* dilatory
dilema *m* dilemma; **encontrarse en un ~** to be in a dilemma
diligencia *f* 1. (*esmero*) diligence 2. (*agilidad*) skill 3. (*trámite*) paperwork; **~s policiales** police proceedings; **evacuar una ~** to resolve a matter; **hacer ~s** to do business 4. (*asunto administrativo*) procedure; **~ judicial/policial** legal/police procedures; **~s preparatorias** initial proceedings; **~s de prueba** taking of evidence 5. (*nota oficial*) communication; **~ de notificación** official notification 6. (*carreta*) stagecoach
diligente *adj* 1. (*cuidadoso, aplicado*) diligent 2. (*ágil*) able
dilucidar *vt* to elucidate
dilución *f* 1. (*de líquidos, colores*) dillution 2. (*de sólidos*) dissolving
diluir *irr como huir* I. *vt* 1. (*líquidos, colores*) to dilute; **sin ~** undiluted 2. (*sólidos*) to dissolve; **dejar ~ en la boca** to allow to dissolve in one's mouth II. *vr:* **~se** to dissolve
diluviar *vimpers* to pour with rain
diluvio *m* 1. (*lluvia*) downpour 2. *inf* (*abundancia*) shower; **~ de balas** hail of bullets
dimanar *vi* to emanate; **tu éxito dimana de tu constancia** your success stems from your perseverance
dimensión *f* (*extensión, tamaño, medida*) dimension; *fig* magnitude; **de dos dimensiones** in two dimensions; **la ~ cultural** the cultural aspect; **una edificio de grandes dimensiones** a large building; **un escándalo de grandes dimensiones** a major scandal; **este asunto está alcanzando dimensiones inesperadas** this affair is turning out to be bigger than people expected
dimes *mpl* **~ y diretes** *inf* tittle-tattle; **andar en ~ y diretes** to quibble
diminutivo *m* LING diminutive
diminutivo, -a *adj* diminutive; **lente diminutiva** diminishing lens
diminuto, -a *adj* tiny
dimisión *f* resignation; **presentar la ~** to resign
dimitir *vt, vi* to resign; **~ de un cargo** to resign (from) a position; **dimitió de presidente del club** he/she resigned as club president
Dinamarca *f* Denmark
dinamarqués, -esa I. *adj* Danish II. *m, f* Dane
dinámica *f* dynamics *pl*
dinámico, -a *adj* dynamic
dinamismo *m* (*energía*) dynamism
dinamita *f* dynamite
dinamitar *vt* to dynamite
dinamizar *vt* to vitalize
dinamo *f*, **dínamo** *f* dynamo
dinastía *f* dynasty
dineral *m* fortune; **costar un ~** *inf* to cost a fortune
dinero *m* money; **~ blanco** silver coins; **~ en caja** cash in hand; **~ electrónico** e-cash; **~ metálico** [*o* **contante y sonante**] hard [*o* ready] cash; **~ de rescate** ransom money; **~ de curso legal** legal tender; **~ negro** undeclared money; **~ en reserva** cash reserve; **~ suelto** loose change; **hacer ~** to make money; **pagar en ~** to pay in cash; **estar mal de ~** to be short of money; **ser alguien de ~** to be rich ►**~ en manos de necio como agua se va** *prov* a fool and his money are soon parted *prov;* **los ~s del sacristán cantando se vienen y cantando se van** *prov* easy come, easy go; **~ ahorrado, ~ ganado** *prov* a penny saved is a penny earned *prov*
dinosaurio *m* dinosaur
dintel *m* ARQUIT lintel
diñar *vt inf* to give; **~la** *inf* to kick the bucket
dio *3. pret de* **dar**
diócesis *f inv* diocese
diodo *m* diode
dioptría *f* dioptre *Brit,* diopter *Am*
dios(a) *m(f)* god *m,* goddess *f*
Dios *m* God; **~ Hombre** Jesus Christ; **~ mediante** God willing; **~ te bendiga** God bless you; **¡~ nos libre!** Heaven help us!; **¡~ sabe!** God knows!; **~ sabe que estuve ahí** I swear I was there; **~ tenga en su gloria** God rest his/her soul; **¡alabado sea ~!** praise the Lord!; **así ~ me asista** JUR so help me God; **~ lo llamó** he/she went to meet his/her maker; **¡~ mío!** my God!; **¡ay ~!** oh dear!; **¡santo ~!** my God! ►**costar ~ y ayuda** to take a lot of work; **a la buena de ~** at random; **armar la de ~ es Cristo** *inf* to raise a hell of a row; **a ~ rogando y con el mazo dando** *prov* trust in God but keep your powder dry *prov;* **como ~ le trajo al mundo** stark naked; **¡~ nos coja confesados!** Lord help us!; **todo ~** everyone; **~ aprieta pero no ahoga** *prov* God strikes not with both hands *prov;* **~ los cría y ellos se juntan** *prov* birds of a feather flock together *prov;* **~ dirá** time will tell; **hacer algo como ~ manda** to do sth properly; **si ~ quiere** God willing; **¡sabe ~!** God only knows!; **que sea lo que ~ quiera** if it is meant to be; **¡válgame ~!** good God!; **¡vaya por ~!** for Heaven's sake!;

D

venga ~ **y lo vea** I'll eat my hat; **¡vive ~!** I swear to God!; **vivir como** ~ to live like a lord; **¡a ~!** goodbye!; **¡por ~!** for God's sake!

dióxido *m* dioxide

dioxina *f* dioxin

diploma *m* diploma; ~ **de asistencia** attendance certificate; ~ **de bachiller(ato)** *school-leaving certificate equivalent to A-levels in the UK and high school graduation in the USA;* ~ **de capitán** captain's commission; ~ **de maestría** teaching certificate; ~ **de reconocimiento** official diploma; ~ **universitario** university title

diplomacia *f* **1.** (*política, tacto*) diplomacy **2.** (*cuerpo*) diplomatic corps **3.** (*carrera*) diplomatic career

diplomado, -a *adj* qualified; **traductora diplomada** qualified translator

diplomático, -a I. *adj* diplomatic **II.** *m, f* diplomat

diptongo *m* diphthong

diputación *f* **1.** (*delegación*) deputation; ~ **permanente de Cortes** *standing committee of the Spanish parliament;* ~ **provincial** provincial delegation of government **2.** (*personas*) delegation **3.** (*cargo*) post of member of parliament **4.** *Méx* (*edificio*) town hall

diputado, -a *m, f* member of parliament; ~ **en** [*o* **a**] **Cortes** member of the Spanish parliament; ~ **independiente** independent (member)

dique *m* **1.** (*rompeolas*) dike; ~ **de abrigo** breakwater **2.** NÁUT dry dock; ~ **flotante** floating dock **3.** (*freno*) brake; **poner un ~ a algo** to restrain sth

dirección *f* **1.** (*rumbo*) direction; ~ **de la circulación** direction of traffic; ~ **única** one-way; ~ **prohibida** no entry; ~ **de marcha** gear control; ~ **visual** viewing direction; **en ~ longitudinal** lengthwise; **en ~ opuesta** in the opposition direction; **el viento soplaba en ~ oeste** the wind was blowing from the east; **salir con ~ a España** to leave for Spain **2.** (*administración, mando*) direction; ~ **central** central control; ~ **general** head office; ~ **comercial** business management; ~ **del Estado** state control; ~ **política** political control; ~ **regional** regional government; **alta ~** senior management **3.** (*guía*) direction; ~ (**artística**) TEAT artistic direction; ~ **de personal** personnel management; **bajo la ~ de** directed by **4.** (*señas*) address; ~ **comercial** business address; ~ **de correo electrónico** e-mail address **5.** AUTO steering; ~ **asistida** power steering

directa *f* AUTO top gear; (*coche automático*) drive ►**poner la ~** *inf* to go all out

directiva *f* **1.** (*dirección*) board (of directors) **2.** (*instrucción*) directive

directivo, -a I. *adj* managing; **junta directiva** managing committee **II.** *m, f* **1.** (*ejecutivo*) director; (*manager*) manager **2.** (*de la junta directiva*) member of the board of directors

directo *m* **1.** FERRO through train **2.** DEP straight (punch)

directo, -a *adj* **1.** (*recto*) straight **2.** (*inmediato, franco*) direct; **transmisión en ~** live broadcast; **un tren ~** a through train; **seguir el camino más ~** to take the shortest route

director(a) I. *adj* managing **II.** *m(f)* director; (*jefe*) manager; ~ **accidental** [*o* **en funciones**] acting director; ~ **administrativo** administrative director; ~ **de departamento** department manager; ~ (**de escena**) CINE, TEAT director; ~ (**de escuela**) headmaster *m Brit,* headmistress *f Brit,* principal *mf Am;* ~ **de fábrica** factory manager; ~ **general** managing director; ~ **de la obra** project manager; ~ **de orquesta** conductor; ~ **invitado** guest conductor; ~ **de sucursal** branch manager; ~ **técnico** technical director; ~ **de la tesis** doctoral advisor

directorio *m* **1.** (*junta*) governing body **2.** (*manual*) directory **3.** (*agenda*) address book **4.** INFOR directory; ~ **raíz** root [*o* parent] directory **5.** (*guía de teléfonos*) telephone directory *Brit,* phonebook *Am*

directriz *f* **1.** (*orientación*) guideline **2.** MAT directrix

dirigente *mf* leader; **los ~s** the leadership; **preparar a los ~s** to train the leadership

dirigible I. *adj* steerable **II.** *m* (*globo*) airship

dirigido, -a *adj* (*sistemas*) remote-controlled

dirigir <g→j> **I.** *vt* **1.** (*un coche, un buque*) to steer **2.** (*el tráfico*) to direct **3.** (*un envío, palabras*) to address **4.** (*la vista*) to turn; ~ **todas sus atenciones a algo** *fig* to focus all one's effort on sth **5.** (*una nación*) to lead; (*empresa*) to manage; (*finca*) to run; (*orquesta, debate*) to conduct; ~ **una casa** to run a household **6.** (*por un camino*) to lead **7.** CINE, TEAT, TV to direct; **una película dirigida por...** a film directed by ... **II.** *vr:* **~se 1.** (*a un lugar*) **~se a** to head for/towards **2.** (*a una persona*) **~se a alguien** to address sb

dirimir *vt* **1.** (*contrato, matrimonio*) to annul **2.** (*asunto, disputa*) to settle; ~ **los empates** to break a tie

discapacitado, -a *adj* disabled, handicapped

discernimiento *m* **1.** (*acción de distinguir*) differentiation; (*capacidad de distinguir*) discernment **2.** (*juicio*) discrimination; **obrar sin ~** to behave indiscriminately

discernir *irr como cernir vt* (*diferenciar*) to differentiate; ~ **entre lo bueno y lo malo** to distinguish between good and bad

disciplina *f* discipline

disciplinado, -a *adj* disciplined

disciplinar *vt* **1.** (*someter*) to discipline **2.** (*enseñar*) to instruct

disciplinario, -a *adj* disciplinary; **sanción disciplinaria** disciplinary measure

discípulo, -a *m, f* **1.** (*alumno*) pupil **2.** (*seguidor*) disciple

disc-jockey <dis yoqueis> *mf* DJ, disc jockey

disco *m* **1.** (*lámina circular*) disc *Brit,* disk *Am;* (*en el teléfono*) dial; ~ **de freno** brake disc [*o* disk *Am*]; ~ **de horario** parking permit; ~ **de señales** FERRO signal (disc) **2.** MÚS record; ~ **de larga duración** LP; **siempre pones el mismo** ~ *inf* you always go on about the same thing; **¡cambia el ~ ya!** *inf* give it a break! **3.** DEP discus **4.** (*semáforo*) traffic light **5.** INFOR disk; ~ **de arranque** boot disk; ~ **duro** hard disk; ~ **flexible** floppy (disk)

discográfico, -a *adj* record

díscolo, -a *adj* disobedient

disconforme *adj* **1.** (*persona*) in disagreement **2.** (*cosa*) incompatible

disconformidad *f* **1.** (*con algo, entre personas*) disagreement; **se te nota tu ~ con la decisión** you obviously disagree with the decision **2.** (*de cosas*) incompatibility

discontinuidad *f* **1.** (*inconstancia*) discontinuity **2.** (*interrupción*) interruption

discontinuo, -a *adj* **1.** (*inconstante*) discontinuous **2.** (*interrumpido*) interrupted

discordancia *f* **1.** (*disconformidad*) disagreement; **hubo ~s a la hora de elegir un representante** there was a clash over the choice of representative **2.** MÚS discordance, dissonance

discordante *adj* **1.** (*opinión*) conflicting **2.** MÚS discordant, dissonant

discordar <o→ue> *vi* **1.** (*cosas*) to clash **2.** (*personas*) to disagree **3.** (*instrumento*) to be out of tune

discorde *adj* **1.** (*persona*) in disagreement **2.** MÚS discordant

discordia *f* discord

discoteca *f* **1.** (*local*) disco(thèque) **2.** (*discos*) record collection

discreción *f* discretion; ~ **absoluta** strict privacy; **a** ~ at one's discretion; **bajo** ~ confidentially; **con** ~ tactfully; **entregarse a** ~ MIL to surrender unconditionally

discrecional *adj* discretional; **cuestión** ~ optional matter; **parada** ~ request stop

discrepancia *f* **1.** (*entre cosas*) discrepancy **2.** (*entre personas*) disagreement

discrepante *adj* divergent

discrepar *vi* **1.** (*diferenciarse*) to differ **2.** (*disentir*) to dissent; **discrepo de lo que Ud. piensa sobre eso** I disagree with what you think about that

discreto, -a *adj* (*reservado*) discreet; (*cantidad*) modest

discriminación *f* **1.** (*perjuicio*) discrimination **2.** (*diferenciación*) differentiation; **de difícil** ~ difficult to distinguish between

discriminar *vt* **1.** (*diferenciar*) to differentiate (between) **2.** (*perjudicar*) to discriminate against

discriminatorio, -a *adj* discriminatory

disculpa *f* **1.** (*perdón*) apology; **admitir una** ~ to accept an apology; **pedir ~s** to apologize; **eso no tiene** ~ there is no excuse **2.** (*pretexto*) excuse; **¡qué ~ más tonta!** what a stupid excuse!; **¡no valen ~s!** no excuses!

disculpable *adj* pardonable

disculpar **I.** *vt* **1.** (*perdonar*) to forgive; **discúlpame por no haberte escrito** forgive me for not writing to you **2.** (*justificar*) to justify; **tu inexperiencia no disculpa ese comportamiento** your inexperience does not excuse such behaviour [*o* behavior *Am*] **II.** *vr:* **~se** to apologize; **~se con alguien por algo** to apologize to sb for sth

discurrir **I.** *vi* **1.** (*pensar*) ~ **sobre algo** to ponder on sth **2.** (*andar*) to roam; **los niños discurrían por la feria** the children wandered around the fair **3.** (*río*) to flow **4.** (*transcurrir*) to pass **II.** *vt* to come up with

discurso *m* **1.** (*arenga*) speech; ~ **de clausura** closing speech; ~ **de recepción** opening speech; ~ **solemne** formal speech; **pronunciar un** ~ to make a speech **2.** (*plática*) talk **3.** (*disertación escrita*) dissertation; (*oral*) presentation **4.** (*raciocinio*) reasoning **5.** (*transcurso*) passing

discusión *f* **1.** (*debate*) discussion; ~ **del presupuesto** POL budget debate; ~ **pública** public debate **2.** (*riña*) argument; **entablar una** ~ to start an argument; **sin** ~ without argument [*o* question]

discutible *adj* **1.** (*disputable*) debatable **2.** (*dudoso*) doubtful

discutido, -a *adj* controversial

discutir **I.** *vi, vt* **1.** (*hablar*) to discuss; ~ **un asunto** to discuss sth; ~ **un plan a fondo** to discuss a plan in detail; ~ **el recorte del presupuesto** to debate the budget cut; ~ **sobre el precio** to argue about the price **2.** (*opinar diferentemente*) ~ **de** [*o* **sobre**] **algo** to argue about [*o* over] sth **II.** *vt* (*contradecir*) **siempre me discutes lo que digo** you always contradict what I say

disecar <c→qu> *vt* **1.** ANAT to dissect **2.** (*preparar un animal muerto*) to stuff **3.** (*secar una flor*) to press

disección *f* ANAT dissection

diseminar **I.** *vt* **1.** (*semillas*) to disperse **2.** (*noticias*) to spread **II.** *vr:* **~se** to spread

disensión *f* **1.** (*desavenencia*) disagreement **2.** (*riña*) quarrel

disentería *f* MED dysentery

disentimiento *m* disagreement

disentir *irr como sentir vi* to dissent; **disiento de tu opinión** I disagree with you; **en religión disentimos profundamente** we have deep differences regarding religion

diseñador(a) *m(f)* **1.** (*dibujante*) artist **2.** (*decorador*) designer

diseñar *vt* **1.** (*crear*) to design **2.** (*dibujar*) to draw; (*delinear*) to draught *Brit,* to draft *Am* **3.** (*proyectar*) to plan

diseño *m* **1.** (*dibujo*) drawing; (*boceto*) sketch; (*esbozo*) outline; ~ **de construcción** construction plan; ~ **de página** *t.* INFOR page design **2.** (*forma*) design; ~ **ergonómico** ergonomic design **3.** (*en tejidos*) pattern **4.** (*descripción*) description

D

disertación *f* (*escrita*) dissertation; (*oral*) presentation

disertar *vi* (*por escrito*) to write a dissertation; (*oralmente*) to give a presentation, to expound

disfraz *m* **1.** (*para engañar*) disguise; (*para la cara*) mask; (*traje*) fancy dress, costume; MIL camouflage **2.** (*disimulación*) pretence *Brit,* pretense *Am;* **presentarse sin ~** to be frank

disfrazar <z→c> **I.** *vt* **1.** (*enmascarar*) to disguise; (*la cara*) to cover with a mask; MIL to camouflage **2.** (*escándalo*) to cover up; (*voz*) to disguise; (*sentimiento*) to hide; **~ su embarazo** to conceal one's pregnancy; **~ su tristeza con una sonrisa** to hide one's sadness behind a smile **II.** *vr:* **~se de** (*enmascararse*) to disguise oneself as

disfrutar *vi, vt* **1.** (*gozar*) **~ de algo** to enjoy sth; **~ de excelente salud** to enjoy excellent health; **~ de licencia** to be on leave **2.** (*poseer*) **~ de algo** to have sth (*de*); **este coche disfruta de muchas comodidades** this car has a number of features for your added comfort **3.** (*utilizar*) to have the use; (*sacar provecho*) to have the benefit

disfrute *m* **1.** (*goce*) enjoyment **2.** (*aprovechamiento*) benefit

disgregación *f* disintegration; FÍS splitting; GEO, METEO erosion

disgregar <g→gu> **I.** *vt* **1.** (*materia*) to disintegrate; FÍS to split **2.** (*gente*) to disperse **II.** *vr:* **~se 1.** (*gente*) to disperse; **el público se disgregó al terminar el espectáculo** the audience dispersed when the show ended **2.** (*materia*) to disintegrate; FÍS to split

disgustar **I.** *vt* **1.** (*desagradar*) to displease; **me disgusta** I don't like it **2.** (*enfadar*) to anger; (*ofender*) to offend **II.** *vr:* **~se 1.** (*enfadarse*) **~se por** [*o* **de**] **algo** to get angry about sth **2.** (*ofenderse*) **~se por algo** to be offended about sth; **se ha disgustado por tus comentarios** he/she took offence [*o* offense *Am*] at your comments **3.** (*reñir*) **~se con alguien** to quarrel with sb

disgusto *m* **1.** (*desagrado*) displeasure; (*repugnancia*) repulsion; **estar a ~** to be ill at ease **2.** (*aflicción*) suffering; (*molestia*) annoyance; (*enfado*) anger; **dar un ~ a alguien** (*afligir*) to cause sb suffering; (*causar molestias*) to annoy sb **3.** (*pelea*) quarrel

disidencia *f* **1.** (*desavenencia*) disagreement **2.** POL dissent

disidente *adj, mf* dissident

disimulación *f* **1.** (*fingimiento*) pretence *Brit,* pretense *Am* **2.** (*ocultación*) concealment **3.** (*tolerancia*) tolerance

disimulado, -a **I.** *adj* **1.** (*fingido*) feigned **2.** (*encubierto*) concealed **3.** (*engañoso*) misleading; (*hipócrita*) hypocritical **II.** *m, f* **1.** (*hipócrita*) hypocrite **2. hacerse el ~** to feign ignorance

disimular **I.** *vi* to pretend **II.** *vt* **1.** (*ocultar*) to conceal; **~ el miedo** to hide one's fear; **no ~ algo** to not hide sth; **la falda disimulaba su barriga** the skirt made her stomach look smaller **2.** (*paliar*) to make better **3.** (*tolerar*) to tolerate; **~ algo a alguien** to tolerate sth from sb

disimulo *m* **1.** (*fingimiento*) pretence *Brit,* pretense *Am;* (*engaño*) deceit; **con ~** furtively **2.** (*tolerancia*) tolerance

disipación *f* **1.** (*desvanecimiento*) dispelling; (*volatilización*) dispersal; *fig* scattering **2.** (*libertinaje*) dissipation **3.** (*derroche*) waste

disipado, -a *adj* **1.** (*libertino*) dissipated **2.** (*que derrocha*) wasteful

disipador(a) **I.** *adj* wasteful **II.** *m(f)* spendthrift

disipar **I.** *vt* **1.** (*nubes, niebla*) to disperse; (*dudas*) to dispel; **el sol disipa las nieblas** the sun disperses the clouds; **~ el cansancio** to dispel one's tiredness **2.** (*derrochar*) to squander **II.** *vr:* **~se** to disperse; (*dudas*) to vanish; **~se en humo** (*desaparecer*) to vanish into thin air; (*fracasar*) to go up in smoke

dislate *m* **1.** (*absurdo*) absurdity **2.** (*disparate*) nonsense

dislexia *f* dyslexia

disléxico, -a *adj, m, f* dyslexic

dislocación *f* **1.** MED dislocation **2.** (*desplazamiento*) displacement; GEO fault **3.** (*desfiguración*) dismemberment

dislocar <c→qu> **I.** *vt* **1.** MED to dislocate **2.** (*desplazar*) to displace **3.** (*desfigurar*) to dismember **II.** *vr:* **~se 1.** (*deshacerse*) to come apart **2.** (*desarticularse*) to be dislocated

disminución *f* decrease; **~ de los gastos** fall in spending; **~ de la natalidad** decline in the birth rate; **~ de la pena** JUR remission of sentence; **~ de peso** weight loss; **~ de los precios** fall in prices; **~ de la presión** TÉC loss of pressure; **~ de la producción** fall in production; **~ de riesgo** risk reduction; **~ de tamaño** reduction in size; **~ de la tensión** reduction of tension; **~ del valor** depreciation; **~ de las ventas** fall in sales; **ir en ~** to diminish

disminuir *irr como huir* **I.** *vi* (*en intensidad*) to diminish; (*número*) to decrease; (*existencias*) to decline; **~ de tamaño** to shrink **II.** *vt* to diminish; (*precio, sueldo*) to lower; (*velocidad*) to reduce; **~ de tamaño** to make smaller; **~ en duración** to make shorter; **~ la ganancia** to reduce profits

disnea *f* MED laboured [*o* labored *Am*] breathing

disociación *f* separation

disociar *vt, vr:* **~se** to separate

disoluble *adj* **1.** (*contrato*) rescindible **2.** QUÍM soluble

disolución *f* **1.** (*dilución*) dissolution; (*de la familia*) break-up; (*de las costumbres*) dissoluteness; **~ de contrato** rescission of a contract **2.** QUÍM solution

disoluto, -a **I.** *adj* dissolute **II.** *m, f* debauchee

disolvente *m* QUÍM solvent; (*para pintura*) thinner

disolver *irr como volver vt, vr:* ~**se** (*manifestación*) to dissolve; (*reunión*) to break up

disonancia *f* **1.** MÚS dissonance **2.** (*desproporción*) difference **3.** (*discordancia*) discord

dispar *adj* dissimilar

disparado, -a *adj* **salir** ~ to rush off

disparador *m* **1.** (*de un arma*) trigger; **poner en el** ~ *inf* to drive to distraction **2.** FOTO shutter release; ~ **automático** automatic shutter release

disparar **I.** *vt* (*un proyectil, el arma*) to fire; ~ **un tiro/flechas a** [*o* **contra**] **alguien** to fire a shot/arrows at sb; ~ **una piedra contra alguien** to throw a stone at sb **II.** *vi* **1.** (*tirar*) to fire; ~ **contra alguien** to fire at sb; **esta pistola no dispara bien** this pistol doesn't fire well **2.** *AmL* (*caballo*) to bolt **III.** *vr:* ~**se** **1.** (*arma*) to go off **2.** (*precios*) to shoot up **3.** (*salir corriendo*) to rush off; (*caballo*) to bolt **4.** (*desbocarse*) to blow one's top

disparatado, -a *adj* **1.** (*absurdo*) nonsensical **2.** *inf* (*desmesurado*) outrageous

disparatar *vi* (*hablar*) to talk nonsense; (*obrar*) to act foolishly

disparate *m* **1.** (*insensatez: acción*) foolish act; (*comentario*) foolish remark; (*idea*) foolish idea **2.** *inf* (*mucho*) **me gusta un** ~ I really love him/her/it; **costar un** ~ to cost a fortune

disparidad *f* disparity; ~ **de precios** ECON difference in prices

disparo *m* **1.** (*el disparar*) firing **2.** (*tiro*) shot; ~ **al aire** shot into the air; ~ **de partida** firing of starting pistol

dispendio *m* (*derroche*) waste; (*de dinero*) squandering

dispensa *f* (*excepción*) exemption; REL dispensation; ~ **de edad** JUR exemption on grounds of age

dispensable *adj* (*impedimento*) dispensable; (*error*) forgivable

dispensador *m*, **dispensadora** *f* (*aparato*) dispenser

dispensar *vt* **1.** (*otorgar*) to give out; ~ **cuidados a alguien** to care for sb; ~ **favores/atención a alguien** to lavish favours/attention on sb; ~ **ovaciones/elogios a alguien** to shower sb with acclaim/praise; **le** ~**on un tratamiento privilegiado** they gave him/her special treatment **2.** (*librar*) to release; (*de molestias*) to relieve; ~ **a alguien de su cargo** to relieve sb of his/her position; ~ **a alguien del servicio militar** to exempt sb from military service; **me** ~**on del castigo** they let me off being punished **3.** (*excusar*) to forgive; **dispénseme que le interrumpa** forgive me for interrupting

dispensario *m* dispensary; ~ **sanitario** (health) clinic

dispepsia *f* dyspepsia

dispersar **I.** *vt* to spread; (*personas, animales*) to disperse; MIL to put to flight; (*una manifestación*) to break up; (*light*) to diffuse; FÍS to scatter; ~ **sus energías** to divide one's energy **II.** *vr:* ~**se** (*semillas*) to be dispersed; (*personas, animales*) to disperse; MIL to spread out

dispersión *f* dispersion; FÍS diffusion; ~ **de la luz** diffusion of light; ~ **de la nubosidad** dispersion of the clouds; **pintura de** ~ emulsion paint; **la** ~ **de las tropas** the dispersal of the troops; **la** ~ **de los manifestantes** the breaking up of the demonstration

disperso, -a *adj* scattered; MIL in disarray

displicencia *f* **1.** (*desagrado*) displeasure; **tratar con** ~ to treat with contempt **2.** (*desaliento*) indifference

displicente *adj* contemptuous

disponer *irr como poner* **I.** *vi* to have the use; **puede** ~ **de mí cuando Ud. quiera** I am at your disposal; ~ **de tiempo** to have time **II.** *vt* **1.** (*colocar*) to place; ~ **las sillas en círculo** to set out the chairs in a circle **2.** (*preparar*) to prepare; (*la mesa*) to lay; ~ **las camas para los huéspedes** to make the beds for the guests **3.** (*determinar*) to stipulate; ~ **en testamento** to dispose of in a will **III.** *vr:* ~**se** **1.** (*colocarse*) to position oneself **2.** (*prepararse*) to get ready; **me disponía a escribir la carta cuando…** I was getting ready to write the letter when …

disponibilidad *f* **1.** (*disposición*) availability **2.** *pl* (*dinero*) resources *pl;* **nuestras** ~**es no nos permitirán nunca comprar una casa** it will never be within our means to buy a house

disponible *adj* available

disposición *f* **1.** (*colocación*) arrangement; ~ **del espacio** organization of space **2.** (*de ánimo, salud*) disposition **3.** (*para algún fin*) preparation; ~ **de servicio** service provision; **estar en** ~ **de hacer algo** to be ready to do sth **4.** (*disponibilidad*) availability; **de libre** ~ freely available; **estoy a su** ~ I am at your disposal; **poner a** ~ to make available **5.** (*talento*) aptitude; **tener** ~ **para la música** to have an aptitude for music **6.** (*resolución*) agreement; ~ **legal** legal provision; **última** ~ last will and testament; **tomar las disposiciones precisas** to take the appropriate measures

dispositivo *m* device; ~ **de alarma** burglar alarm; ~ **antirrobo** anti-theft device; ~ **de cambio de velocidades** AUTO gears *pl;* ~ **sensitivo** TÉC sensor; ~ **de televisión** video security system; ~ **de visualización** INFOR monitor; ~ **táctico** MIL plan of action; ~ **intrauterino** MED intrauterine device

dispuesto, -a **I.** *pp de* **disponer** **II.** *adj* **1.** (*preparado*) ready; ~ **para el uso** ready to use; **estar** ~ **para salir** to be ready to go out; **estar** ~ **a trabajar/a negociar** to be prepared to work/to negotiate **2.** (*habilidoso*) capable **3.** (*de buen cuerpo*) well-built **4.** (*de ánimo, salud*) **estar bien** ~ (*ánimo*) to be in a good frame of mind; (*de salud*) to be well; **estar mal** ~ (*ánimo*) to be in a poor frame of mind; (*de salud*) to be indisposed

disputa *f* (*pelea*) fight; (*conversación*) argu-

D

ment; ~ **legal** legal dispute; **sin** ~ without argument [*o* question]; **en** ~ at issue
disputable *adj* disputable
disputado, -a *adj* hard-fought
disputar I. *vi* to argue II. *vt* 1. (*controvertir*) to dispute 2. (*competir*) to compete for; ~ **una carrera** to contest a race III. *vr:* **~se** to compete with one another (for); **todos se disputan la foto** they all want the photograph
disquete *m* INFOR floppy disk; ~ **de arranque** start-up disk; ~ **de destino** destination drive; ~ **para instalación** setup disk
disquetera *f* disk drive
disquisición *f* treatise
distancia *f t. fig* distance; ~ **focal** FÍS focal length; ~ **entre ruedas** AUTO inter-wheel spacing; ~ **de seguridad** safe distance; ~ **visual** visibility; **a** ~ (*lejos*) far away; (*desde lejos*) from a distance; **¿a qué ~?** how far?; **acortar ~s** to close the gap; **cubrir ~s** to cover a lot of ground; **guardar las ~s** *fig* to keep one's distance; **tener a alguien a** ~ to keep sb at arm's length
distanciado, -a *adj t. fig* distant; **están ~s** *fig* they have drifted apart
distanciamiento *m fig* distance
distanciar I. *vt* to distance II. *vr:* **~se** 1. (*de una persona*) to drift apart 2. (*de un lugar*) to move away
distante *adj t. fig* distant
distar *vi* to be distant; **disto mucho de creerlo** that's very hard for me to believe
distender <e→ie> *vt* 1. (*estirar*) to stretch 2. (*aflojar*) to loosen; *fig* to relax
distensión *f* 1. (*relajación*) easing of tension; POL détente; TÉC slackening 2. MED strain
distinción *f* 1. (*diferenciación*) distinction; **a ~ de algo** in contrast to sth; **no hacer** ~ to make no distinction; **sin ~ de** irrespective of 2. (*claridad*) clarity 3. (*honor*) distinction 4. (*elegancia*) refinement; (*educación*) good manners *pl*
distinguible *adj* 1. (*diferenciable*) distinguishable 2. (*visible*) visible
distinguido, -a *adj* 1. (*ilustre*) distinguished 2. (*elegante*) refined 3. (*en cartas*) Dear; ~ **amigo:...** Dear Sir, ...
distinguir <gu→g> I. *vt* 1. (*diferenciar*) to distinguish; **no ~ lo blanco de lo negro** *inf* to not be able to tell left from right 2. (*señalar*) to single out 3. (*divisar*) to make out 4. (*condecorar*) to honour *Brit,* to honor *Am;* (*tratar mejor*) to favour *Brit,* to favor *Am;* ~ **a alguien con su confianza** to honour [*o* honor *Am*] sb with one's trust II. *vr:* **~se** 1. (*poder ser visto*) to be noticeable 2. (*ser diferente*) to be different
distintivo *m* emblem
distintivo, -a *adj* **característica distintiva** distinguishing characteristic
distinto, -a *adj* 1. (*diferente*) different; **es ~ a** [*o* **de**] **los demás** he is different from the others; **operaciones distintas a la actividad de la empresa** activities which are different from the company's usual business 2. (*nítido*) distinct 3. *pl* (*varios*) various
distorsión *f* 1. MED sprain 2. FÍS distortion 3. (*falseamento*) distortion; **distorsiones de competencia** distortion of the market
distorsionar I. *vt* to distort II. *vr:* **~se** MED to sprain
distracción *f* 1. (*entretenimiento*) pastime 2. (*falta de atención*) distraction 3. JUR ~ **de fondos** embezzlement
distraer I. *vt* 1. (*entretener*) to entertain 2. (*dinero*) to embezzle 3. (*desviar*) to divert II. *vr:* **~se** 1. (*entretenerse*) to amuse oneself; **el niño se distrae sólo** the child amuses himself 2. (*no atender*) to be distracted
distraído, -a I. *adj* 1. (*desatento*) distracted 2. (*entretenido*) entertaining 3. *Chile, Méx* (*mal vestido*) badly dressed II. *m, f* **hacerse el ~** to pretend to not notice
distribución *f* 1. (*repartición, disposición*) distribution; (*de correo*) delivery; ~ **de agua** water distribution; ~ **de equipajes** baggage reclaim; ~ **del espacio** spatial distribution; ~ **de funciones** division of functions; ~ **de información** distribution of information 2. COM distribution; ~ **exclusiva** exclusive distribution; ~ **mayorista** wholesale distribution 3. FIN sharing out; ~ **de beneficios** profit breakdown 4. CINE, TÉC distribution; **armario de ~** ELEC connection cabinet
distribuidor *m* 1. TÉC distributor; ~ **automático** automatic dispenser; ~ **automático de billetes** ticket dispenser 2. COM dealer
distribuidor(a) *m(f)* distributor; ~ **exclusivo** exclusive distributor; ~ **industrial** industrial retailer; ~ **oficial** official dealer
distribuir *irr como huir* I. *vt* 1. (*repartir*) to distribute; (*disponer*) to arrange; (*una tarea*) to allocate; (*el correo*) to deliver 2. COM to distribute 3. FIN to share out II. *vr:* **~se** to divide up
distributivo, -a *adj* distributive; **justicia distributiva** retributive justice (*branch of law dealing with redistribution of incomes through taxation*)
distrito *m* district; ~ **electoral** constituency; ~ **industrial** industrial area; ~ **judicial** jurisdiction; ~ **de policía** police district
disturbio *m* disturbance, riot
disuadir *vt* to dissuade; ~ **a alguien de algo** to dissuade sb from sth
disuasión *f* dissuasion; POL, MIL deterrence
disuasivo, -a *adj* dissuasive; POL, MIL deterrent; **poder ~** deterrent
disuelto, -a *pp de* **disolver**
disyuntiva *f* choice
disyuntivo, -a *adj* disjunctive; **conjunción disyuntiva** LING disjunctive (conjunction)
dita *f* 1. *AmC, Chile* debt 2. ECON (*cosa*) bond; (*persona*) bondsman
DIU *m* MED *abr de* **dispositivo intrauterino** IUD

diurético, **-a** *adj* diuretic
diurno, **-a** *adj* daily; **trabajo** ~ day work; **luz diurna artificial** artificial daylight
diva *f* diva
divagación *f* 1. (*desviación*) digression 2. *pl* (*sin concierto*) ramblings *pl*
divagar <g→gu> *vi* 1. (*desviarse*) to digress 2. (*hablar sin concierto*) to ramble
diván *m* divan
divergencia *f* divergence
divergente *adj* divergent; **opiniones** ~**s** differing opinions
divergir <g→j> *vi t.* MAT to diverge; (*opiniones*) to differ; (*personas*) to disagree
diversidad *f* diversity
diversificación *f* 1. (*variedad*) diversity 2. ECON diversification
diversificar <c→qu> I. *vt* to diversify; ~ **los horizontes** to broaden one's horizons II. *vr:* ~**se** to diversify
diversión *f* 1. (*entretenimiento*) entertainment 2. (*pasatiempo*) pastime 3. MIL diversion
diverso, **-a** *adj* 1. (*distinto*) distinct; (*desemejante*) dissimilar 2. (*variado*) diverse 3. ~**s** (*varios*) various; (*muchos*) many
divertido, **-a** *adj* 1. (*alegre*) amusing 2. (*que hace reír*) funny 3. *AmL* (*achispado*) tipsy
divertir *irr como sentir* I. *vt* 1. (*entretener*) to amuse; **sus bromas me divierten** his/her jokes are funny 2. (*apartar*) to divert II. *vr:* ~**se** 1. (*alegrarse*) to amuse oneself (*en* with); **¡que te diviertas!** enjoy yourself! 2. (*distraerse*) to be distracted
dividendo *m* dividend; **arrojar** ~**s** to pay dividends
dividir I. *vt* 1. (*partir*) to divide; ~ **por la mitad** to divide in two 2. (*distribuir*) to distribute 3. (*separar*) to separate; **divide y vencerás** *prov* divide and conquer *prov;* (*sembrando discordia*) to disunite 4. (*agrupar*) to divide up 5. MAT ~ **algo entre** [*o* **por**] **dos** to divide sth by two II. *vr:* ~**se** 1. (*partirse*) to divide 2. (*agruparse*) to divide up into 3. (*enemistarse*) to fall out
divieso *m* MED boil
divinidad *f* 1. (*ser divino*) divinity 2. (*deidad*) deity 3. *inf* (*preciosidad*) **esta mujer es una** ~ that woman is absolutely divine
divinizar <z→c> *vt* 1. (*deificar*) to deify 2. (*santificar*) to sanctify 3. (*glorificar*) to exalt
divino, **-a** *adj* divine, heavenly
divisa *f* 1. (*insignia*) emblem 2. (*mote*) motto 3. (*en el escudo*) device 4. *pl* (*moneda*) (foreign) currency
divisar *vt* (*percibir*) to make out; **divisé a lo lejos un vehículo** in the distance I made out a vehicle
divisible *adj* divisible; **ser** ~ **por dos** to be divisible by two
división *f* 1. (*partición*) *t.* MAT division 2. (*separación*) separation 3. (*parte*) portion 4. MIL division 5. (*desavenencia*) disagreement 6. (*de un discurso*) part 7. LING hyphen
divisor *m* MAT divisor; **máximo común** ~ highest common factor
divisoria *f* 1. dividing lines 2. GEO watershed
divisorio, **-a** *adj* dividing; **línea divisoria de las aguas** watershed
divorciado, **-a** I. *adj* divorced II. *m, f* divorcee
divorciar I. *vt* to divorce II. *vr:* ~**se** to get divorced; **ella se divorció de él** she divorced him
divorcio *m* 1. (*separación*) divorce 2. (*discrepancia*) disagreement; ~ **de opiniones** difference of opinions
divulgación *f* disclosure; (*publicación*) publication; **libro de** ~ popularizing book
divulgar <g→gu> I. *vt* (*propagar*) to spread; (*dar a conocer*) to make known; (*popularizar*) to popularize II. *vr:* ~**se** (*propagarse*) to spread; (*conocerse*) to become known
Dn. *abr de* **don** ≈ Mr *Brit,* ≈ Mr. *Am* (*used with the forename*)
DNI *m abr de* **Documento Nacional de Identidad** ID
Dña. *abr de* **doña** ≈ Mrs *Brit,* ≈ Mrs. *Am*
do <does> *m* (*de la escala diatónica*) C; (*de la solfa*) doh; ~ **bemol** C flat; ~ **de pecho** high C; **dar el** ~ **de pecho** *fig* to make a great effort; ~ **sostenido** C sharp
dobladillo *m* (*pliegue*) hem; (*del pantalón*) turn-up, cuff
doblador(**a**) *m(f)* CINE dubbing actor *m,* dubbing actress *f*
doblaje *m* CINE dubbing
doblar I. *vt* 1. (*arquear*) to bend 2. (*plegar*) to fold; **no** ~ do not bend 3. (*duplicar*) to be twice as much as; **mi madre me dobla en edad** my mother is twice my age 4. (*una película*) to dub 5. (*rodear*) to go round; ~ **la esquina** to turn the corner 6. (*convencer*) to convince II. *vi* 1. (*redoblar*) to double 2. (*torcer*) to turn (*a* towards) 3. (*hacer dos papeles*) to play two roles 4. (*campanas*) to toll III. *vr:* ~**se** 1. (*inclinarse*) to bend down 2. (*ceder*) to give in
doble[1] I. *adj inv* 1. (*duplo*) double; ~ **clic** double click; **contabilidad por partida** ~ double-entry bookkeeping; **tener** ~ **nacionalidad** to have dual nationality; ~ **personalidad** split personality 2. (*hipócrita*) two-faced; **Pedro es muy** ~ Pedro is very two-faced II. *mf t.* CINE double
doble[2] *m* 1. (*duplo*) double 2. (*pliegue*) fold 3. (*toque de campanas*) knell 4. (*tenis*) (**partido de**) ~**s** doubles (match)
doble[3] *f* doubles *pl*
doblegar <g→gu> I. *vt* 1. (*torcer*) to 2. (*persuadir*) to persuade II. *vr:* ~**se** 1. (*torcerse*) to twist 2. (*someterse*) to give in; **se doblegó a mis súplicas** he/she gave in to my pleas
doblez[1] *m* (*pliegue*) fold
doblez[2] *m o f* (*hipocresía*) duplicity
doce *adj inv, m* twelve; *v.t.* **ocho**

doceavo, **-a** *adj* twelfth; *v.t.* **octavo**
docena *f* dozen; **una ~ de huevos** a dozen eggs; **la ~ del fraile** baker's dozen
docencia *f* teaching; **dedicarse a la ~** to be a teacher
doceno, **-a** *adj* twelfth; *v.t.* **octavo**
docente I. *adj* teaching II. *mf* teacher; UNIV lecturer *Brit,* professor *Am*
dócil *adj* 1. (*sumiso*) obedient 2. (*manso*) docile 3. (*metal*) ductile
docilidad *f* 1. (*sumisión*) obedience 2. (*mansedumbre*) docility 3. (*del metal*) ductability
docto, **-a** *adj* learned; **~ en leyes** well-versed in the law
doctor(**a**) *m(f)* doctor
doctorado *m* 1. (*grado*) doctorate 2. (*estudios*) **curso de ~** doctoral course
doctoral *adj* UNIV doctoral; **tesis ~** doctoral thesis
doctorando, **-a** *m, f* PhD student
doctorar *vt, vr:* **~se** to gain one's doctorate [*o* PhD]; **~se en historia** to do a doctorate [*o* PhD] in history
doctrina *f* 1. (*teoría*) doctrine 2. (*sabiduría*) learning 3. (*catecismo*) catechism
documentación *f* 1. (*estudio*) information 2. (*documentos*) documentation; (*del coche*) vehicle documents *pl,* car papers *pl*
documentado, **-a** *adj* 1. (*identificado*) documented; (*personas*) with papers 2. (*informado*) informed
documental *adj, m* documentary
documentar I. *vt* 1. (*probar*) to document 2. (*instruir*) to inform II. *vr:* **~se** to inform oneself
documento *m* document; **~s de envío** dispatch documents; **Documento Nacional de Identidad** ID, identity card
dodotis® *m inv* nappy *Brit,* diaper *Am,* pampers® *Am*
dogal *m* (*de animal*) halter; (*de verdugo*) noose
dogma *m* dogma
dogmático, **-a** *adj* dogmatic
dogo *m* bulldog
dólar *m* dollar
dolencia *f* ailment; **~ respiratoria** respiratory complaint
doler <o→ue> I. *vi* to hurt; **me duele la cabeza** I have a headache II. *vr:* **~se** 1. (*quejarse*) **~se de algo** to complain about sth 2. (*arrepentirse*) to regret (*de*)
dolido, **-a** *adj* hurt; **estoy ~ por tus palabras** I feel hurt by your remarks
doliente *adj* 1. (*enfermo*) ill 2. (*afligido*) sorrowful
dolo *m* 1. (*engaño*) fraud 2. JUR **con ~** under false pretences [*o* pretenses *Am*]
dolor *m* pain; **~ de cabeza** headache; **estar con ~es** to have labour [*o* labor *Am*] pains; **retorcerse de ~** to writhe in pain; **tengo ~ de barriga** I have (a) stomach ache
dolorido, **-a** *adj* 1. (*dañado*) painful; **tener la rodilla dolorida** to have hurt one's knee 2. (*apenado*) sad
doloroso, **-a** *adj* 1. (*lastimador*) painful 2. (*lamentable*) regrettable
doloso, **-a** *adj* fraudulent
doma *f* taming; (*de caballos*) breaking-in
domable *adj* (*animal*) tamable; (*caballo*) breakable
domador(**a**) *m(f)* (*de circo*) tamer
domar *vt,* **domeñar** *vt* to tame
domesticado, **-a** *adj* **animal ~** domestic animal
domesticar <c→qu> *vt* 1. (*animales*) to domesticate 2. (*personas*) to bring under control
doméstico, **-a** I. *adj* domestic; **vuelo ~** national flight; **animal ~** pet; **gastos ~s** household expenses II. *m, f* (domestic) servant
domiciliación *f* (*orden permanente*) standing order; (*de recibos*) direct debit; (*de una letra de cambio*) bank transfer
domiciliar I. *vt* 1. (*un recibo*) to pay by direct debit; **~ el alquiler** to pay the rent by standing order; **~ la nómina** to pay the salary direct into sb's account 2. (*dar domicilio*) to house II. *vr:* **~se** to reside
domiciliario, **-a** *adj* home; **arresto ~** JUR house arrest
domicilio *m* (*de alguien*) residence; (*una empresa*) address; **reparto a ~** home delivery; **~ social** registered office
dominación *f* 1. (*el dominar*) domination 2. (*poder*) power
dominante *adj* dominant; **~ en el mercado** dominant in the marketplace
dominar I. *vi* 1. (*imperar*) to rule 2. (*sobresalir*) to stand out 3. (*predominar*) to predominate II. *vt* 1. (*conocer*) to have a good knowledge of; (*idioma*) to have a good command of 2. (*reprimir*) to control; **~ el odio** to overcome one's hatred 3. (*sobresalir*) to dominate 4. (*divisar*) to look out over III. *vr:* **~se** to control oneself
domingas *fpl inf* boobs *pl*
domingo *m* Sunday; **~ de Resurrección** Easter Sunday; **~ de Ramos** Palm Sunday; *v.t.* **lunes**
dominguero, **-a** I. *adj* Sunday II. *m, f pey* Sunday driver
dominical I. *adj* Sunday; **descanso ~** Sunday off; **oración ~** Lord's Prayer II. *m* PREN Sunday supplement
dominicano, **-a** *adj, m, f* GEO, REL Dominican
dominio *m* 1. (*dominación*) control; **~ de sí mismo** self-control 2. (*poder*) authority 3. (*territorio*) domain 4. (*campo*) subject 5. (*posesión*) ownership; **ser del ~ público** *fig* to be common knowledge
dominó <dominós> *m* (*juego*) dominoes *pl*
don *m* gift; **tener ~ de gentes** to have a way with people; **tener el ~ de palabra** to have a way with words
don, **doña** *m, f* ≈ Mr *m,* Mrs *f Brit,* ≈ Mr. *m,*

≈ Mrs. *f Am* (*used in combination with the forename*)

donación *f* donation; JUR gift

donador(a) *m(f)* donor

donaire *m* **1.** (*gracia*) grace **2.** (*chiste*) witticism

donante *mf* donor

donar *vt* to donate

donativo *m* donation

doncella *f* **1.** (*criada*) maid **2.** *elev* (*muchacha*) maiden

donde *adv* where; **a** [*o* **hacia**] **~...** where ... to; **de ~...** where ... from; **en ~** where; **la calle ~ vivo** the street where I live; **estuve ~ Luisa** I was at Luisa's

dónde *pron interrog, rel* where; **¿a** [*o* **hacia**] **~?** where to?; **¿de ~?** where from?; **¿en ~?** where?; **¿~ se habrá enterado?** where can he/she have found out?

dondequiera *adv* **1.** (*en cualquier parte*) anywhere **2.** (*donde*) wherever; **~ que estés** wherever you are

donjuán *m* womanizer

donoso, -a *adj* graceful

donostiarra **I.** *adj* of/from San Sebastian **II.** *mf* native/inhabitant of San Sebastian

donosura *f* **1.** (*garbo*) grace **2.** (*gracia*) wit

donut *m* <donuts> doughnut *Brit*, donut *Am*

doña *f v.* **don**

dopar *vt, vr:* **~se** DEP to take drugs

doping *m sin pl* drug-taking

dorada *f* (*pez*) gilthead bream

dorado, -a *adj* golden

dorar **I.** *vt* **1.** (*sobredorar*) to gild **2.** (*tostar*) to brown **3.** (*suavizar*) to sweeten; **~ la píldora** to sugar the pill **II.** *vr:* **~se** to go brown

dormilón, -ona *m, f inf* sleepyhead

dormir *irr* **I.** *vi* **1.** (*descansar*) to sleep; **~ a pierna suelta** to be fast [*o* sound] asleep; **~ de un tirón** to sleep right through the night; **~ sobre algo** *fig* to sleep on sth; **quedarse dormido** to fall asleep **2.** (*pernoctar*) to spend the night; **~ en casa de alguien** to sleep at sb's house **3.** (*reposar*) to rest **4.** (*descuidarse*) to let things slide **II.** *vt* (*a un niño*) to get to sleep; (*a un paciente*) to put to sleep; **~ la borrachera/mona** *inf* to sleep off one's hangover; **~ la siesta** to have a siesta [*o* nap]; **¡no hay quien duerma a este niño!** it's impossible to get this child to sleep!; **esta monotonía me duerme** this monotony is sending me to sleep **III.** *vr:* **~se** **1.** (*adormecerse*) to fall asleep; **se me ha dormido el brazo** I've got pins and needles in my arm; **~se en los laureles** to rest on one's laurels **2.** (*descuidarse*) to not pay attention

dormitar *vi* to doze

dormitorio *m* **1.** (*en una casa*) bedroom; (*muebles*) bedroom furniture [*o* set] **2.** (*en un colegio*) dormitory

dorsal **I.** *adj* ANAT dorsal; **espina ~** backbone **II.** *m* DEP number

dorso *m* (*reverso*) *t.* ANAT back; **~ de la mano** back of the hand; **véase al ~** please turn over

dos **I.** *adj inv* two; **~ puntos** colon; **de ~ en ~** two by two; **están a ~** DEP it's two-all ►**cada ~ por tres** all the time; **en un ~ por tres** in a flash **II.** *m* two; **los/las ~** both ►**como ~ y ~ son cuatro** as sure as night follows day; *v.t.* **ocho**

doscientos, -as *adj* two hundred; *v.t.* **ochocientos**

dosel *m* (*baldaquín*) canopy; **cama con ~** four-poster (bed)

dosificar <c→qu> *vt* to measure out

dosis *f inv* dose; **una buena ~ de paciencia** a lot of patience; (*drugs*) fix *inf*

dotación *f* **1.** (*equipamiento*) equipping **2.** (*personal: de un buque*) crew; (*de una fábrica*) workforce; (*de una oficina*) staff **3.** (*financiación*) endowment **4.** (*donación*) donation **5.** (*ajuar*) dowry

dotado, -a *adj* **1.** (*con talento*) gifted **2.** (*hombre:genitales*) endowed

dotar *vt* **1.** (*constituir dote*) to give as a dowry **2.** (*equipar*) **~ de** [*o* **con**] **algo** to equip with sth **3.** (*señalar bienes*) to endow **4.** (*financiar*) to provide funds for **5.** (*con sueldo*) to provide

dote¹ *m o f* (*ajuar*) dowry

dote² *f* (*aptitud*) gift; **~ de mando** leadership ability

doy *1. pres de* **dar**

Dpto. **1.** *abr de* **departamento** (*sección*) department **2.** *AmL abr de* **departamento** (*distrito*) administrative district

Dr(a). *abr de* **doctor(a)** Dr *Brit*, Dr. *Am*

draga *f* dredge

dragaminas *m inv* minesweeper

dragar <g→gu> *vt* to dredge

dragón *m* **1.** (*monstruo*) dragon **2.** (*reptil*) flying dragon; **~ marino** (*pez*) weever fish

drama *m* drama; TEAT play

dramático, -a *adj* dramatic; **autor ~** playwright

dramatismo *m* dramatism

dramatizar <z→c> *vt* dramatize

dramaturgo, -a *m, f* playwright

dramón *m inf* melodrama, tear-jerker *Am*

drapear *vt* to drape

drástico, -a *adj* drastic

drenaje *m* drainage

drenar *vt* to drain

driblar *vi, vt* DEP to dribble; **~ a un contrario** to dribble round an opponent

dril *m* (*tela*) drill, duck

droga *f* drug, dope *inf;* **~ sintética** synthetic drug

drogadicto, -a **I.** *adj* addicted to drugs **II.** *m, f* drug addict

drogado, -a *adj* **estar ~** to be drugged

drogar <g→gu> **I.** *vt* to drug **II.** *vr:* **~se** to take drugs

drogata *mf pey, inf* junkie

drogodelincuencia *f* drug-related crime

drogodependencia *f* drug addiction

droguería *f shop selling soap, shampoo,*

cleaning materials etc.

dromedario *m* dromedary

drupa *f* drupe

dublinés, -esa I. *adj* of/from Dublin II. *m, f* Dubliner

ducado *m* (*territorio*) duchy

ducal *adj* ducal

ducha *f* 1. (*para ducharse*) shower 2. MED douche ►**recibir una ~ de agua fría** to receive a shock

duchar I. *vt* to shower II. *vr:* **~se** to have [*o* take] a shower

ducho, -a *adj* skilled

dúctil *adj* 1. (*condescendiente*) easy going 2. (*dilatable*) stretchable; (*flexible*) pliable

duda *f* (*indecisión, incredulidad*) doubt; **salir de ~s** to dispel one's doubts; **sin ~ (alguna)** without a doubt; **no cabe la menor ~** there is not the slightest doubt; **poner algo en ~** to question sth

dudable *adj* doubtful

dudar I. *vi* 1. (*desconfiar*) **~ de algo** to doubt sth 2. (*vacilar*) to hesitate II. *vt* to doubt

dudosamente *adv* doubtfully

dudoso, -a *adj* 1. (*inseguro*) doubtful 2. (*indeciso*) undecided 3. (*sospechoso*) dubious

duelo *m* 1. (*desafío*) duel; **retar a ~** to challenge to a duel 2. (*pesar*) grief 3. (*funerales*) mourning 4. (*cortejo*) funeral procession

duende *m* 1. (*espíritu*) elf; (*fantasma*) ghost 2. **tener ~** to have charm

dueño, -a *m, f* 1. (*propietario*) owner; (*amo*) boss; **~ y señor** lord and master; **hacerse ~ de algo** (*apropiarse*) to take possession of sth; (*dominar*) to take command of sth; **ser ~ de sí mismo** (*empresario*) to be one's own boss; **no ser ~ de sí mismo** (*dominarse*) to not be in control of oneself; **poner a alguien como no digan dueñas** *inf* to call sb every name under the sun 2. (*de familia*) head

duermevela *m o f* (*sueño ligero*) light sleep; (*sueño agitado*) restless sleep

dulce I. *adj* 1. (*referente al sabor*) sweet 2. (*suave*) soft 3. (*agradable*) pleasant 4. (*metal*) soft 5. (*agua*) fresh II. *m* 1. (*postre*) dessert 2. (*almíbar*) syrup 3. (*golosina*) sweet *Brit,* candy *Am;* **a nadie le amarga un ~** *inf* gifts are always welcome

dulcificar <c→qu> *vt* 1. (*azucarar*) to sweeten 2. (*suavizar*) to soften; (*hacer más grato*) to sugar

dulzor *m,* **dulzura** *f* 1. (*sabor*) sweetness 2. (*suavidad*) softness 3. (*bondad*) goodness

duna *f* dune

dundera *f AmL* (*bobada*) stupidity

dundo, -a *adj AmL* (*bobo*) silly

dúo *m* duet; **cantar a ~** to sing a duet

duodécimo, -a *adj* twelfth; *v.t.* **octavo**

duodenal *adj* MED **úlcera ~** duodenal ulcer

duodeno *m* ANAT duodenum

dúplex *m* ARQUIT duplex

duplicado *m* duplicate; **por ~** in duplicate

duplicar <c→qu> *vt, vr:* **~se** to duplicate

duplicidad *f* (*falsedad*) duplicity

duplo *m* double

duplo, -a *adj* double

duque(sa) *m(f)* duke, duchess *m, f*

durabilidad *f* durability

durable *adj* durable; (*producto*) long-lasting

duración *f* duration, length; (*de un préstamo*) term; **de larga ~** long-term

duradero, -a *adj* long-lasting

durante *prep* during; **hablar ~ una hora** to talk for an hour

durar *vi* 1. (*extenderse*) to last; **~ todo el día** to last the whole day 2. (*permanecer*) to stay 3. (*resistir*) to last

durazno *m AmL* (*fruta*) peach; (*árbol*) peach tree

dureza *f* 1. (*rigidez*) hardness; **~ de vientre** constipation 2. (*callosidad*) hard skin

durmiente I. *adj* sleeping; **la Bella Durmiente** Sleeping Beauty II. *mf* sleeper

duro I. *m* five-peseta coin II. *adv* hard ►**¡dale ~!** *inf* go at it!; (*a personas*) hit him/her as hard as you can!; **quedarse ~** *Arg, inf* to be amazed

duro, -a *adj* hard; **~ de corazón** hard-hearted; **~ de oído** hard of hearing; **a duras penas** barely; **estoy contigo a las duras y las maduras** I'll stick with you through thick and thin

DVD *abr de* **videodisco digital** DVD

E

E, e *f* E, e; **~ de España** E for Edward *Brit,* E for easy *Am*

e *conj* (*before 'hi' or 'i'*) **madres ~ hijas** mothers and daughters

E *abr de* **Este** E

ea *interj* (*animando*) come on

ebanista *mf* cabinetmaker, woodworker

ébano *m* ebony

ebrio, -a *adj elev* 1. (*borracho*) inebriated 2. (*extasiado*) **~ de** beside oneself with; (*ciego*) blind with

ebullición *f* 1. (*de líquidos*) boiling 2. (*agitación*) turmoil

eccema *m* MED eczema

echado, -a *adj* 1. (*postrado*) lying down; **estar ~** to be lying down; **~ para adelante** *inf* pushy 2. *Nic, CRi* (*indolente*) idle

echar I. *vt* 1. (*tirar*) to throw; (*carta*) to post *Brit,* to mail *Am;* (*a la basura, al suelo*) to throw out; **la suerte está echada** the die is cast 2. (*verter*) to pour; **~ en algo** to pour into sth 3. (*expulsar*) to throw out; (*despedir*) to sack *Brit,* to fire *Am* 4. *inf* (*crecer: pelo*) to grow; (*hojas, flores*) to sprout 5. (*emitir*) to give off; **~ humo** to let out smoke 6. (*tumbar*) to lie down 7. (*proyectar*) to show; TEAT to stage; **en el cine echan 'Titanic'** 'Titanic' is on at the cinema [*o* movie theater *Am*] **8.** (*calcular*) **te echo 30 años** I reckon you're 30 **9.** (*tiempo, esfuerzo*) **eché dos horas en acabar** it took me two hours to finish **10.** *Perú* (*emborracharse*) **~le** to get drunk **11.** *Chile* (*echar a correr*) **~las** to beat it **II.** *vi* **1.** (*lanzar*) to throw **2.** (*verter*) to pour **3.** (*empezar*) to begin; **~ a correr** to break into a run **III.** *vr:* **~se 1.** (*postrarse*) to lie down; **me eché en la cama** I lay down in bed **2.** (*lanzarse*) to jump; **~se sobre algo/alguien** to fall upon sth/sb; **~se a los pies de alguien** to throw oneself down before sb; **~se atrás** *fig* to have second thoughts **3.** (*empezar*) to begin; **~se a llorar** to burst into tears; **~se a la bebida** to take to drink **4.** *inf* (*iniciar una relación*) **~se un novio** to get a boyfriend

echarpe *m* stole; *AmL* (*chal*) shawl

echón, -ona *Ven* **I.** *adj* conceited **II.** *m, f* braggart

eclesiástico *m* clergyman

eclesiástico, -a *adj* ecclesiastical

eclipsar I. *vt* **1.** ASTR to eclipse **2.** (*oscurecer*) to darken **3.** *fig* to outshine **II.** *vr:* **~se 1.** (*sufrir un eclipse*) to be eclipsed **2.** (*decaer*) to decline

eclipse *m* eclipse; **~ solar** solar eclipse

eco *m* **1.** *t. fig* echo; **hacer ~** *fig* to have an impact; **tener ~** *fig* to arouse interest; **~s de sociedad** PREN gossip column **2.** (*repercusión*) consequence

ecografía *f* ultrasound scan

ecología *f* ecology

ecológico, -a *adj* ecological; **daños ~s** environmental damage; **producción ecológica** AGR organic farming

ecologismo *m sin pl* green movement, environmentalism

ecologista I. *adj* ecological **II.** *mf* ecologist, environmentalist

economato *m* cooperative store

economía *f* **1.** (*situación, sistema*) economy; **~ de desechos** recycling industry; **~ forestal** forestry sector; **~ sumergida** black economy; **~ de escala** economy of scale; **~ de oferta** supplyside economy **2.** (*ciencia*) economics; **~ de la empresa** business economics; **~ política** political economics **3.** (*ahorro*) saving **4.** (*moderación*) thrift(iness) **5.** (*cosa ahorrada*) savings *pl;* **hacer ~s** to economize

económico, -a *adj* **1.** ECON economic; **año ~** financial year; **estudiar Ciencias Económicas** to study economics **2.** (*barato*) cheap; (*ahorrador*) economical; (*persona*) thrifty

economista *mf* economist

economizar <z→c> *vi, vt* to economize; **no ~ esfuerzos** to spare no effort; **~ esfuerzos** to save one's efforts

ecosistema *m* ecosystem

ecotest *m* ecotest

ecu, ECU *m abr de* **European Currency Unit** ecu, ECU

ecuación *f* equation

ecuador *m* equator; **paso del ~** half-way point

Ecuador *m* Ecuador

> **Ecuador** lies in the northwestern part of South America. It borders Colombia to the north, Peru to the east and south and the Pacific Ocean to the west. The capital is **Quito**. The official language of the country is Spanish and the monetary unit of **Ecuador** is the **sucre**.

ecuánime *adj* **1.** (*justo*) fair; (*imparcial*) impartial **2.** (*sereno*) level-headed

ecuanimidad *f* **1.** (*imparcialidad*) impartiality **2.** (*calma*) composure

ecuatorial *adj* equatorial

ecuatoriano, -a I. *adj* of/from Ecuador **II.** *m, f* native/inhabitant of Ecuador

ecuestre *adj* equestrian

ecuménico, -a *adj* universal

eczema *m* MED eczema

edad *f* **1.** (*años*) age; **~ para jubilarse** retirement age; **~ del pavo** adolescence; **mayor de ~** adult; **menor de ~** minor; **ser mayor/menor de ~** to be of/under age; **a la ~ de...** at the age of ...; **¿qué ~ tiene?** how old is he/she?; **de mi ~** of my age; **de cierta ~** getting on in years; **llegar a la mayoría de ~** to come of age; **de mediana ~** middle-aged; **la tercera ~** old [*o* retirement] age **2.** (*época*) age, era; **la ~ media** the Middle Ages; **la ~ de piedra** the Stone Age

edema *m* oedema

edén *m* Eden; *fig* (*paraíso*) paradise

edición *f* **1.** (*impresión, conjunto de ejemplares*) edition; **~ de bolsillo** paperback edition **2.** (*de un acontecimiento*) **la presente ~ del Festival de Cine** this year's Film Festival

edicto *m* **1.** (*aviso*) announcement **2.** JUR edict

edificable *adj* with planning permission

edificación *f* (*construcción*) construction

edificante *adj* edifying

edificar <c→qu> *vt* **1.** (*construcción*) to build **2.** (*moral*) to edify

edificio *m* building

edil(a) *m(f)* town councillor *Brit,* councilman *m Am,* councilwoman *f Am*

Edimburgo *m* Edinburgh

editar *vt* **1.** (*publicar*) to publish **2.** (*preparar*) to edit

editor *m* INFOR editor

editor(a) *m(f)* **1.** (*que publica*) publisher **2.** (*que prepara textos*) editor

editorial[1] I. *adj* **1.** (*publicar*) publishing **2.** (*preparar*) editing; **casa ~** publishing house; **éxito ~** best-seller **II.** *f* publisher

editorial[2] *m* editorial

editorialista *mf* leader writer

Edo. *Méx, Ven abr de* **Estado** State

edredón *m* eiderdown; **~ nórdico** duvet,

quilt *Brit,* comforter *Am*

educación *f* **1.**(*instrucción*) education, teaching; ~ **de adultos** adult education; ~ **ambiental** environmental education; ~ **física** ENS physical education; ~ **a distancia** distance learning; ~ **permanente** permanent education; **Educación General Básica** HIST education for children aged 6 to 14; **Educación preescolar** nursery school education; ~ **vial** road education; **Ministerio de Educación y Ciencia** Ministry of Education and Science **2.**(*comportamiento*) manners *pl;* **este niño no tiene** ~ this child has no manners **3.**(*crianza*) upbringing

educado, -a *adj* **1.**(*culto*) cultured, cultivated **2.**(*cortés*) (**bien**) ~ polite; **mal** ~ rude

educar <c→qu> *vt* **1.**(*dar instrucción*) to educate **2.**(*criar*) to bring up; **los padres educan a los hijos** children are brought up by their parents **3.**(*facultades*) to improve; **debes** ~ **tu oído** you should train your ear

educativo, -a *adj* (*instructivo*) educational

edulcorante *m* sweetener

edulcorar *vt* to sweeten

edutenimiento *m sin pl* edutainment

EEB *f abr de* **encefalopatía espongiforme bovina** MED BSE

EE.UU. *mpl abr de* **Estados Unidos** USA

efe *f* (*letra*) f; **la letra** ~ the letter f

efectista *adj* for effect

efectivamente *adv* in fact

efectividad *f* effectiveness

efectivo *m* (*dinero*) cash; ~ **electrónico** electronic cash; **en** ~ (in) cash

efectivo, -a *adj* **1.**(*que hace efecto*) effective **2.**(*auténtico*) real; **un éxito** ~ a real success; **hacer** ~ to put into action; (*cheque*) to cash **3.**(*no interino*) fixed

efecto *m* **1.** effect; ~ **boomerang** boomerang effect; ~ **invernadero** greenhouse effect; ~ **retardado** delayed reaction; ~**s secundarios** side effects; **hacer** ~ to have an effect; **hacer buen** ~ (*impresión*) to make a good impression; **tener** ~ to take effect; **llevar a** ~ to carry out; **en** ~ indeed; **para los** ~**s** effectively; **con** ~**s retroactivos** retroactively **2.** COM asset

efectuar <*1. pres:* efectúo> **I.** *vt* to carry out; (*viaje*) to go on; ~ **una compra** to make a purchase; ~ **una llamada** to make a phone call **II.** *vr:* ~**se** (*tener lugar*) to take place; (*realizarse*) to be carried out

efemérides *fpl* PREN list of the day's anniversaries

efervescente *adj* (*líquido*) fizzy; **pastilla** ~ soluble pill

eficacia *f* **1.**(*de persona*) efficiency; (*de medida*) effectiveness; ~ **económica** economic efficiency; **con** ~ effectively; **sin** ~ useless **2.** TÉC efficiency

eficaz *adj* (*persona*) efficient; (*medida*) effective

eficiencia *f* (*persona*) efficiency; (*medida*) effectiveness

eficiente *adj* (*persona*) efficient; (*medida*) effective

efusión *f* **1.**(*cordialidad*) effusion; **con gran** ~ very effusively **2.**(*derramamiento*) spillage

efusivo, -a *adj* effusive

EGB *f* HIST *abr de* **Educación General Básica** *education for children aged 6 to 14*

Egeo *m* Aegean; **el mar** ~ the Aegean Sea

egipcio, -a *adj, m, f* Egyptian

Egipto *m* Egypt

eglefino *m* haddock

ego *m* PSICO ego

egocéntrico, -a *adj* egocentric, self-centred *Brit,* self-centered *Am*

egoísmo *m sin pl* selfishness, egoism

egoísta I. *adj* selfish, egoistical; **ser un** ~ to be very selfish **II.** *mf* selfish person, egoist

egregio, -a *adj* eminent, illustrious

egresado, -a I. *adj* graduate **II.** *m, f Arg, Chile* (*universidad, escuela*) graduate

egresar *vi Arg, Chile* (*escuela*) to finish school; (*universidad*) to graduate

eh *interj* **1.**(*advertencia*) OK; **no vuelvas a hacerlo, ¿~?** don't do it again, OK? **2.**(*susto, incomprensión*) **¿~?** eh?

ej. *abr de* **ejemplo** example

eje *m* **1.** TÉC, MAT axle; ~ **anterior** front axle **2.**(*centro*) ~ **de la conversación** core of the conversation; **ser el** ~ **de atención** to be the centre [*o* center *Am*] of attention; **el Eje** HIST the Axis

ejecución *f* execution; (*de proyectos*) implementation; ~ **de un pedido** carrying out of an order; ~ **de la sentencia** JUR execution of sentence; **poner en** ~ to carry out

ejecutar *vt* to execute; (*ley*) to enforce

ejecutiva *f* executive (body)

ejecutivo, -a I. *adj* **1.**(*que decide*) *t.* JUR executive; **comité** ~ executive [*o* administrative] committee; **poder** ~ executive power **2.**(*urgente*) urgent **II.** *m, f* (*en cargo directivo*) executive; (*empleado*) manager; ~ **de marketing** marketing executive, executive [*o* administrative] committee

ejemplar I. *adj* exemplary; **un alumno** ~ a model student **II.** *m* (*ejemplo*) example; (*de libro*) copy; (*de revista*) issue; ~ **de muestra** sample

ejemplarizar <z→c> *vi AmL* to serve as an example

ejemplificar <c→qu> *vt* to exemplify

ejemplo *m* example; **dar buen** ~ to set a good example; **poner por** ~ to give as an example; **por** ~ for example; **sin** ~ unprecedented; **predicar con el** ~ to practise what one preaches; **tomar por** ~ to take as an example

ejercer <c→z> **I.** *vt* (*profesión*) to practise *Brit,* to practice *Am;* (*derechos*) to exercise **II.** *vi* (*como abogado, médico*) to practise *Brit,* to practice *Am;* (*de profesor*) to work

ejercicio *m* **1.**(*de una profesión*) practice; **en** ~ practising *Brit,* practicing *Am* **2.** DEP exercise; (*entrenamiento*) training; **el médico me**

recomendó hacer ~ my doctor advised me to take [*o* do] exercise; **tener falta de** ~ to be out of practice **3.** ENS (*para practicar*) exercise; (*prueba*) test **4.** MIL ~ **de las armas** weapons training; ~ **de combate** combat exercise **5.** ECON ~ **contable** tax year; ~ (**económico**) financial year

ejercitar **I.** *vt* **1.** (*profesión*) to practise *Brit,* to practice *Am;* (*actividad*) to carry out; ~ **la cirurgía** to work as a surgeon **2.** (*desarrollar*) to develop **3.** (*adiestrar*) to train **II.** *vr:* **~se** to train; **~se en natación** to do swimming training

ejército *m* MIL (*tropas*) army; (*fuerzas armadas*) armed forces; ~ **del aire** air force

ejote *m AmC, Méx* string bean

el, **la**, **lo** <los, las> *art def* **1.** the; **el perro** the dog; **la mesa** the table; **los amigos/las amigas** the friends; **prefiero ~ azul al amarillo** I prefer the blue one to the yellow one **2.** *lo + adj* **lo bueno/malo** the good/bad thing; **lo antes** [*o* **más pronto**] **posible** as soon as possible; **hazlo lo mejor que puedas** do it the best you can **3.** + *nombres geográficos* **el Canadá** Canada; **la China/India** China/India **4.** + *días de semana* **llegaré el domingo** I'll arrive on Sunday; **los sábados no trabajo** I don't work on Saturdays **5.** + *nombre propio, inf* **he visto a la Carmen** I saw Carmen **6.** + *que* **lo que digo es...** what I'm saying is ...; **lo que pasa es que...** the thing is that ... **7.** *como interj* **¡la de gente que vino!** so many people came!

él *pron pers, 3. sing m* **1.** (*sujeto*) he **2.** (*tras preposición*) him; **el libro es de** ~ (*suyo*) the book is his

elaboración *f* **1.** (*fabricación*) manufacture; (*tratamiento*) treatment **2.** (*de comidas*) preparation; **de ~ casera** home-made **3.** (*de una idea*) development; (*de una obra*) construction

elaborar *vt* **1.** (*fabricar*) to manufacture; (*preparar*) to prepare **2.** (*una idea*) to develop; (*una obra*) to construct

elación *f AmL* elation, exaltation

elasticidad *f* elasticity

elástico *m* elastic

elástico, **-a** *adj* elastic; (*concepto*) ambiguous; (*horario, persona*) flexible; (*tela*) stretch

Elba *m* **1.** (*río*) **el** ~ the (river) Elbe **2.** (*isla*) Elba

ele *f* L, l; **la letra** ~ the letter l

elección *f* (*selección*) choice; *t.* POL election; **elecciones legislativas** general election; ~ **parcial** by-election; ~ **de la profesión** career choice; **lo dejo a su** ~ the choice is yours

electo, **-a** *adj* elect

elector(a) **I.** *adj* electing **II.** *m(f)* voter; **los ~es** the electorate

electorado *m* electorate

electoral *adj* electoral; **colegio** ~ electoral college

electricidad *f* to electricity

electricista **I.** *adj* electrical **II.** *mf* electrician

eléctrico, **-a** *adj* (*que usa electricidad*) electric; (*relacionado*) electrical; **máquina eléctrica** electrical appliance

electrificar <c→qu> *vt* to electrify

electrizar <z→c> *vt t. fig* to electrify

electrocardiograma *m* electrocardiogram

electrocución *f* electrocution

electrocutar *vt* to electrocute

electrodo *m* electrode; ~ **positivo/negativo** positive/negative electrode

electrodoméstico *m* household [*o* electrical] appliance

electroimán *m* electromagnet

electromagnético, **-a** *adj* electromagnetic

electrón *m* electron

electrónica *f* electronics

electrónico, **-a** *adj* electronic; **microscopio** ~ electron microscope; **correo** ~ e-mail

electrotecnia *f* electrical engineering

electrotécnico, **-a** *adj* related to electrical engineering

elefante, **-a** *m, f* elephant *m;* ~ **marino** elephant seal ►**ver ~s volando** to believe anything

elegancia *f* elegance; (*buen gusto*) tastefulness

elegante *adj* elegant; (*con buen gusto*) tasteful

elegantoso, **-a** *adj inf* posh *Brit*

elegir *irr* **I.** *vi, vt* (*escoger*) to choose; **a ~ entre** to be chosen from **II.** *vt* POL to elect

elementado, **-a** *adj Chile, Col* (*alelado*) bewildered

elemental *adj* basic; **conocimientos ~es** basic knowledge

elemento *m* **1.** (*componente, persona*) element; ~ **base** basic element; **tener ~s de juicio** to be able to judge; ~ **decisivo** crucial factor **2.** *pl* (*fuerzas naturales*) elements *pl* **3.** *pl* (*nociones fundamentales*) **~s de matemáticas** basic mathematics *pl* **4.** *pl* (*medios*) resources *pl*

elenco *m* **1.** (*catálogo*) list, catalogue *Brit,* catalog *Am* **2.** TEAT cast **3.** *AmL* (*personal*) staff **4.** *Chile, Perú* (*equipo*) team

elepé *m* LP, album

elevación *f* **1.** (*subida*) rise **2.** GEO elevation

elevado, **-a** *adj* (*alto*) elevated; (*nivel, estilo*) refined; MAT raised to the power of

elevador *m* **1.** *AmC* (*ascensor*) lift *Brit,* elevator *Am* **2.** *Arg* (*para cargas*) goods [*o* freight] elevator

elevalunas *m inv* AUTO electric window-winder, automatic windows

elevar **I.** *vt* **1.** (*subir*) to raise; ~ **al trono** to put on the throne **2.** MAT ~ **a** to raise to the power of; **tres elevado a cuatro** three to the power of four **3.** (*enviar*) to present; ~ **una protesta** to lodge a complaint **II.** *vr:* **~se** **1.** (*tener altura*) to rise **2.** (*tener precio*) **~se a** to amount to; (*cotización*) to stand at **3.** (*hallarse*) to stand

eliminación *f* **1.** (*supresión, de errores*) elimination; (*de aranceles*) abolition; (*de basura, residuos*) disposal **2.** MED discharge **3.** DEP elimination

eliminar *vt* **1.** (*suprimir, matar*) to eliminate; ~ **la competencia** to eliminate the competition **2.** DEP to knock out; **fueron eliminados en la cuarta prueba** they went out in the fourth round

eliminatoria *f* **1.** (*competición*) knockout competition *Brit,* playoff **2.** (*vuelta*) qualifying round; (*atletismo*) heat

elipse *f* ellipse

elipsis *f inv* ellipsis

elite *f,* **élite** *f* elite; **de** ~ top-class

elitista *adj* elitist

elixir *m* elixir

ella *pron pers, 3. sing f* **1.** (*sujeto*) she **2.** (*tras preposición*) her; **el abrigo es de** ~ (*suyo*) the coat is hers

ellas *pron pers, 3. pl f* **1.** (*sujeto*) they **2.** (*tras preposición*) them; **el coche es de** ~ (*suyo*) the car is theirs

ello *pron pers, 3. sing neutro* **1.** (*sujeto*) it **2.** (*tras preposición*) it; **para** ~ for it; **por** ~ that is why; **estar en** ~ to be doing it; **¡a ~!** let's do it!

ellos *pron pers, 3. pl m* **1.** (*sujeto*) they **2.** (*tras preposición*) them; **estos niños son de** ~ (*suyos*) these children are theirs

elocuencia *f* eloquence; **con** ~ eloquently

elocuente *adj* eloquent; **las pruebas son ~s** *fig* the evidence speaks for itself

elogiar *vt* to eulogize *form,* to praise

elogio *m* eulogy, praise; **hacer ~s** to eulogize; **recibir ~s** to be praised; **digno de** ~ praiseworthy

elote *m AmC* maize [*o* corn *Am*] cob

eludir *vt* (*evitar*) to elude; (*preguntas*) to evade; ~ **su responsabilidad** to shirk one's responsibility

emanar **I.** *vi* **1.** (*escaparse*) ~ **de** to emanate from *form;* (*líquido*) to ooze from **2.** (*tener su origen*) ~ **de** to stem from **II.** *vt* to give off

emancipación *f* emancipation

emancipar **I.** *vt* (*liberar*) to free; (*feminismo*) to emancipate **II.** *vr:* **~se** to become emancipated

embadurnar **I.** *vt* **1.** (*manchar*) ~ **algo de** [*o* **con**] **algo** to smear sth with sth **2.** (*pintar*) to daub **II.** *vr* **~se de** [*o* **con**] **algo** to be smeared with sth

embajada *f* embassy

embajador(a) *m(f)* ambassador

embalaje *m* (*envoltorio*) packaging; (*acción*) packing

embalar **I.** *vt* to pack **II.** *vr:* **~se** **1.** (*correr*) to dash off **2.** *inf* (*hablar mucho*) to talk nineteen to the dozen

embalsamar *vt* **1.** (*cadáveres*) to embalm **2.** (*perfumar*) to perfume

embalsar *vt* to dam

embalse *m* **1.** (*pantano*) reservoir **2.** (*acción*) damming **3.** *Arg* (*presa*) dam

embarazada **I.** *adj* (*encinta*) pregnant; **estar ~ de seis meses** to be six months pregnant; **quedarse** ~ to become [*o* get] pregnant **II.** *f* pregnant woman

embarazado, -a *adj* (*cohibido*) awkward

embarazar <z→c> *vt* **1.** (*estorbar*) to get in the way **2.** (*cohibir*) ~ **a alguien** to make sb feel awkward **3.** (*dejar encinta*) ~ **a alguien** to get sb pregnant

embarazo *m* **1.** (*gravidez*) pregnancy; **interrupción del** ~ abortion **2.** (*cohibición*) awkwardness; **causar ~ a alguien** to make sb feel awkward **3.** (*impedimento*) obstacle

embarazoso, -a *adj* awkward

embarcación *f* (*barco*) vessel; ~ **de recreo** pleasure craft

embarcadero *m* pier, wharf

embarcar <c→qu> **I.** *vi* to go on board; (*avión*) to board **II.** *vt* **1.** (*en barco*) to stow **2.** (*avión*) to put on board **3.** (*en un asunto*) to involve **III.** *vr:* **~se** **1.** (*en barco*) to embark **2.** (*avión*) to board **3.** (*en un asunto*) to become involved

embargar <g→gu> *vt* **1.** (*retener*) to confiscate **2.** (*absorber*) to overcome **3.** (*molestar*) to bother

embargo **I.** *m* **1.** COM embargo **2.** (*retención*) confiscation **II.** *conj* **sin** ~ however

embarque *m* **1.** (*de material*) loading **2.** (*de personas*) boarding; **tarjeta de** ~ boarding card

embarrada *f Cuba, PRico, And* **1.** (*desliz*) blunder **2.** (*tontería*) foolishness, stupid act

embarrancar <c→qu> **I.** *vi* (*barco*) to run aground; *fig* to get stuck **II.** *vr:* **~se** to run aground

embarullar **I.** *vt inf* to mix up **II.** *vr:* **~se** *inf* to get mixed up

embate *m* **1.** (*del mar*) pounding **2.** (*acometida*) onslaught

embaucador(a) **I.** *adj* deceitful **II.** *m(f)* cheat

embaucar <c→qu> *vt* to cheat

embeber **I.** *vi* to shrink **II.** *vt* **1.** (*absorber*) to absorb **2.** (*empapar*) to soak up **3.** (*contener*) to contain **III.** *vr:* **~se** **1.** (*empaparse*) **~se de algo** to be soaked in sth **2.** (*enfrascarse*) to become absorbed

embejucarse *vr Col, inf* (*disgustarse*) to get upset; (*encolerizarse*) to get angry

embelesar **I.** *vi, vt* to captivate **II.** *vr* **~se de** [*o* **con**] **algo** to be captivated by sth

embellecer *irr como crecer vt* **1.** (*hacer más bonito*) to beautify **2.** (*idealizar*) to idealize

embestida *f* onslaught

embestir *irr como pedir* **I.** *vi* to charge **II.** *vt* **1.** (*atacar*) to attack; (*coche*) to crash into **2.** *inf* (*pidiendo*) to ask for money

emblema *m* emblem; (*de marca*) logo

embobar **I.** *vt* (*asombrar*) to amaze; (*fascinar*) to fascinate **II.** *vr* **~se en** [*o* **con**] **algo** to be amazed by sth; (*de fascinación*) to be fascinated by sth

embocadura *f* **1.** (*entrada*) entrance; (*de un río*) mouth **2.** (*vino*) taste **3.** MÚS mouthpiece
embocar <c→qu> *vt* (*enfilar*) ~ **algo** to slip into sth; **embocó la bola** he/she putted the ball
embolador *m Col, inf* shoeshine
embolar **I.** *vt Col, inf* (*zapatos*) to shine **II.** *vr:* **~se** *AmC* to get drunk
embolia *f* embolism; ~ **cerebral** brain clot
émbolo *m* TÉC piston
embolsar *vt* to pocket
emboquillado *m* filter
emborrachar **I.** *vt* **1.** (*a alguien*) to make drunk **2.** GASTR ~ **con algo** to soak in sth **II.** *vr:* **~se** **1.** (*beber*) to get drunk **2.** (*los colores*) to run
emborrascarse <c→qu> *vr* **1.** METEO to cloud over **2.** (*negocio*) to falter
emborronar *vt* **1.** (*de tachaduras*) to cover with blots and smudges **2.** (*escribir*) to scribble
emboscada *f* ambush; **tender una ~ a alguien** to lay an ambush for sb
emboscarse <c→qu> *vr* (*para atacar*) to lie in ambush
embotellado, **-a** *adj* (*bebida*) bottled; **vino ~** bottled wine
embotellamiento *m* **1.** (*de vino*) bottling **2.** (*de tráfico*) jam
embotellar **I.** *vt* **1.** (*líquido*) to bottle **2.** (*tráfico*) to block **3.** *inf* (*lección*) to swot up *inf* **II.** *vr:* **~se** **1.** (*tráfico*) to get congested **2.** *inf* (*lección*) to swot
embozar <z→c> **I.** *vt* **1.** (*rostro*) to cover **2.** (*hecho*) to hide **II.** *vr:* **~se** (*rostro*) to cover one's face
embragar <g→gu> AUTO **I.** *vi* to engage the clutch **II.** *vt* to engage
embrague *m* AUTO clutch
embriagar <g→gu> **I.** *vi, vt* **1.** (*emborrachar*) to inebriate **2.** (*enajenar*) to hypnotize; **este perfume embriaga** this perfume is intoxicating **II.** *vr:* **~se** (*emborracharse*) to get drunk
embriaguez *f* **1.** (*borrachera*) inebriation; **en estado de ~** inebriated **2.** (*enajenación*) delight
embrión *m* BIO embryo; (*idea*) beginnings *pl*
embrionario, **-a** *adj* embryonic
embrollar **I.** *vt* **1.** (*liar*) to mess up; **embrollas todo lo que tocas** you mess everything up; **lo embrollas más de lo necesario** you're overcomplicating things **2.** *CSur* (*engañar*) to deceive **II.** *vr:* **~se** to get tangled up; **~se en algo** to get involved in sth
embrollo *m* **1.** (*lío*) mess; (*de hilos*) tangle; **meterse en un ~** to get into a mess **2.** (*embuste*) swindle; **no me vengas con ~s** don't try and fool me **3.** (*chanchullo*) dodgy business; **este negocio seguro que es un ~** I'm sure that's a dodgy business
embromado, **-a** *adj AmL: inf* **1.** (*difícil*) hard **2.** (*molesto*) annoyed
embromar *vt* **1.** (*gastar una broma*) to play a joke on **2.** (*engatusar*) to wheedle **3.** *AmL* (*fastidiar*) to annoy
embroncarse <c→qu> *vr Arg, inf* to get angry
embrujado, **-a** *adj* bewitched; **casa embrujada** haunted house
embrujar *vt* **1.** (*haciendo brujería*) to captivate **2.** (*embelesar*) to hypnotize
embuchado *m* **1.** GASTR sausage **2.** (*para ocultar*) decoy **3.** POL electoral fraud
embudo *m* **1.** (*aparato*) funnel; **en forma de ~** funnel-shaped; **aplicar la ley del ~** to apply one-sided rule **2.** (*trampa*) deceit **3.** (*de tráfico*) bottleneck
embuste *m* **1.** (*mentira*) lie **2.** (*estafa*) swindle
embustero, **-a** **I.** *adj* lying; **¡qué tío más ~!** what a swindler! **II.** *m, f* **1.** (*mentiroso*) liar **2.** (*estafador*) swindler
embute *m Méx, inf* (*soborno*) bribe
embutido *m* sausage
embutir **I.** *vt* **1.** to pack; ~ **lana en un cojín** to pack wool into a cushion; **íbamos embutidos en el tranvía** in the tram we were packed in like sardines **2.** (*el embutido*) to stuff **II.** *vr* **~se de algo** to stuff oneself with sth
eme *f* M, m; **la letra ~** the letter m; **mandar a alguien a la ~** *inf* (*mierda*) to tell sb to eff off
emergencia *f* **1.** (*acción*) appearance **2.** (*suceso*) emergency; **estado de ~** state of emergency; **plan de ~** emergency plan; **declarar el estado de ~ en una zona** to declare a state of emergency in an area
emergente *adj* **país ~** emergent country
emerger <g→j> *vi* **1.** (*del agua*) to emerge; **mi jefe emergió de la nada** my boss is a self-made man **2.** (*de la superficie*) to surface
emeritense **I.** *adj* of/from Mérida **II.** *mf* native/inhabitant of Mérida
emigración *f* emigration; (*animales*) migration
emigrado, **-a** *m, f,* **emigrante** *mf* emigrant; POL emigré
emigrar *vi* to emigrate; (*animales*) to migrate
eminencia *f* **1.** (*talento*) expert; **ser una ~ en su campo** to be an expert in one's field; **ser una ~ en literatura contemporánea** to be a specialist in contemporary literature **2.** GEO height **3.** (*título*) Eminence
eminente *adj* **1.** (*sobresaliente*) outstanding **2.** (*elevado*) high
emisión *f* **1.** TV, RADIO (*difusión*) broadcast; (*en directo*) live broadcast; (*programa*) programme *Brit,* program *Am* **2.** (*de radiación, calor, luz*) emission; **emisiones contaminantes** pollution **3.** FIN issue
emisor(a) *adj* **1.** TV, RADIO broadcasting **2.** FIN **banco ~** issuing bank
emisora *f* broadcasting station; ~ **clandestina** pirate station; ~ **de radio** radio station; ~ **de televisión** television station
emitir *vt* **1.** TV, RADIO to broadcast; (*en directo*) to broadcast live **2.** (*luz, calor, olor, radiación*)

to emit, to give off; (*humo*) to let off **3.** (*grito*) to let out **4.** (*dictamen*) to give **5.** FIN to issue

emoción *f* **1.** (*sentimiento*) emotion; (*conmoción*) excitement; **lleno de emociones** full of thrills; **palabras llenas de** ~ words full of emotion; **llorar de** ~ to cry with emotion; **sin** ~ without emotion; **sentir una honda** ~ to feel a deep emotion; **dar rienda suelta a sus emociones** to give free rein to one's emotions **2.** (*turbación*) excitement

emocional *adj* emotional

emocionante *adj* **1.** (*excitante*) exciting, thrilling **2.** (*conmovedor*) moving

emocionar **I.** *vt* **1.** (*apasionar*) to excite; **este libro no me emociona** this book doesn't do anything for me; **sólo la idea ya lo emocionaba** the idea alone was enough to excite him **2.** (*conmover*) to move; **los espectadores estaban emocionados** the spectators were moved; **tus palabras me ~on** I found your words very moving **II.** *vr:* **~se** **1.** (*conmoverse*) to be moved **2.** (*turbarse*) to get flustered; (*alegrarse*) to get excited

emolumentos *mpl* salary; (*de un libro*) royalties *pl;* (*honorarios*) fees *pl*

emoticón *m* emoticon, smiley

emotivo, **-a** *adj* **1.** (*persona*) emotional **2.** (*palabras*) moving

empacar <c→qu> **I.** *vi AmL* to pack **II.** *vt* to pack

empachado, **-a** *adj* **estoy** ~ (*indigestado*) I've got indigestion; (*harto*) I'm so full I feel sick

empachar **I.** *vt* **1.** (*indigestar*) to give indigestion **2.** (*turbar*) to bother; **para decirlo no me empacha que estés delante** I don't mind saying it in front of you **II.** *vr:* **~se** **1.** (*indigestarse*) to get indigestion; (*comer demasiado*) to eat too much **2.** (*turbarse*) to get flustered; **no ~se de expresar sus sentimientos** not to be afraid of showing one's feelings

empacho *m* **1.** (*indigestión*) indigestion; **tengo un** ~ **de dulces** I've eaten too many sweets; **tengo un** ~ **de televisión** I'm sick of watching television **2.** (*turbación*) fluster; **no tengo** ~ **en...** I don't mind ...

empadronamiento *m* registration in local census bureau; **oficina de** ~ register office

empadronar **I.** *vt* to register (for a census) **II.** *vr:* **~se** to register (for a census)

empalagar <g→gu> **I.** *vt* **1.** (*alimento*) to be oversweet **2.** (*persona*) to cloy upon; **tanta cortesía me empalaga** I find all this politeness cloying; **esta película empalaga** this film is too treacly **II.** *vr* **~se de** [*o* **con**] **algo** (*hastiarse*) to get sick of sth

empalagoso, **-a** *adj* **1.** (*alimento*) oversweet **2.** (*persona*) cloying **3.** (*película*) treacly

empalmar **I.** *vi* **1.** (*dos trenes*) to link up **2.** (*dos caminos, ríos*) ~ **con algo** to meet sth; **esta carretera empalma con la nacional** this road joins up with the national highway **II.** *vt* (*maderos, tubos*) to fit together; (*cables,película*) to splice; (*teléfono*) to connect; ~ **a puerta** DEP to shoot on goal **III.** *vr:* **~se** (*sexualmente*) to get a hard-on

empalme *m* **1.** (*acción: de maderos, tubos*) fitting together; (*de cable, película*) splice; (*del teléfono*) connection **2.** (*punto: de maderos, tubos*) join; (*del teléfono*) connection; (*estación*) FERRO transfer station **3.** (*erección*) hard-on

empanada *f* **1.** GASTR pie (*usually containing meat or tuna*)*;* ~ **mental** *inf* complete mix-up **2.** (*timo*) swindle

empanadilla *f* small pasty

empanar *vt* **1.** (*rebozar*) to coat in breadcrumbs **2.** (*rellenar*) to fill

empantanarse *vr* (*terreno*) to flood; *fig* to get bogged down

empañarse *vr* (*ventana*) to mist up; (*ojos*) to fill with tears; (*reputación*) to become tainted

empañetar *vt AmL* (*encalar*) to plaster

empapar **I.** *vt* **1.** (*mojar*) to soak; **la lluvia ha empapado el suelo** the rain has soaked the floor; **el vendaje está empapado de sangre** the bandage is soaked with blood **2.** (*absorber*) to soak up **II.** *vr:* **~se** **1.** (*mojarse*) to get soaked **2.** (*un tema*) **~se de algo** to become versed in sth

empapelar **I.** *vi, vt* (*las paredes*) to (wall)paper **II.** *vt* **1.** (*objeto*) to wrap up **2.** *inf* (*encausar*) to prosecute

empaque *m* **1.** (*gravedad*) portentousness; **andaba con gran** ~ he/she walked with great pomp **2.** (*semblante*) air; (*del rostro*) expression; **su** ~ **era grave** he/she had a severe expression **3.** (*el empaquetar*) packing **4.** *AmL* (*desfachatez*) cheek

empaquetador(a) *m(f)* packer

empaquetar *vt* **1.** (*objetos*) to pack **2.** (*personas*) ~ **en algo** to fit into sth **3.** MIL to punish

emparedado *m* sandwich

emparejar **I.** *vi* **1.** (*ponerse al lado*) ~ **con alguien** to catch up with sb **2.** (*ponerse al nivel*) to draw level **II.** *vt* **1.** (*juntar*) to pair up; **ya estoy emparejado** I've already got a partner; **me quieren** ~ **con ella** they want to pair me up with her **2.** (*nivelar*) to level **3.** (*ventana*) to leave slightly open **III.** *vr:* **~se** (*formar pareja*) to make a pair; (*parejas*) to pair up; **en el siguiente partido quedé emparejado con Juan** in the next game I was Juan's partner

emparentado, **-a** *adj* ~ **con algo** related to sth; **está bien** ~ he married into an important family

emparentar <e→ie> *vi* ~ **con una familia** to marry into a family

empastador(a) *m(f) AmL* (book)binder

empastar *vt* **1.** (*rellenar*) to fill; (*cubrir*) to cover; ~ **un diente** to have a tooth filled; ~ **la cara con crema** to cover one's face with cream **2.** (*libro*) to bind

empaste *m* **1.** MED filling; **tengo dos muelas con** ~ I've got fillings in two of my back teeth **2.** (*relleno*) filling; (*cubrir*) covering

empatar I. *vi* 1. DEP to draw; ~ **a uno** to draw one-all; **estar empatados a puntos en la clasificación** to have the same points in the league table 2. POL to tie II. *vt* 1. *AmL* (*cuerdas*) to tie together; ~ **mentiras** to tell one lie after another 2. *CRi, PRico* (*amarrar*) to moor 3. *Ven, Col* (*importunar*) to annoy

empate *m* 1. DEP draw; **gol del** ~ the equalizer 2. POL tie

empatía *f* empathy

empavonar I. *vt AmL* (*pringar*) to grease II. *vr:* ~**se** *AmC* to get dressed up

empecinarse *vr* ~ **en algo** to be stubborn about sth

empedernido, **-a** *adj* 1. (*incorregible*) incorrigible; **bebedor** ~ hardened drinker; **fumador** ~ chain smoker; **solterón** ~ confirmed bachelor 2. (*insensible*) unfeeling

empeine *m* instep

empelotado, **-a** *adj* 1. (*confuso*) confused 2. *AmL, inf* (*desnudo*) starkers 3. *Méx* (*colado por alguien*) infatuated

empelotarse *vr* 1. *inf* (*enredarse*) to get into a wrangle 2. *AmL, inf* (*desnudarse*) to strip

empeñado, **-a** *adj* 1. (*obstinado*) **estar** ~ (**en hacer algo**) to be determined (to do sth); **lo vi** ~ **en invitarme** I realized that he was set on inviting me 2. (*discusión*) heated

empeñar I. *vt* (*objetos*) to pawn; ~ **la palabra** to give one's word II. *vr:* ~**se** 1. (*insistir*) to insist; **se empeña en hablar contigo** he/she insists on speaking to you; **no te empeñes** don't go on about it; **si te empeñas en beber este vino asqueroso...** if you insist on drinking this disgusting wine ... 2. (*endeudarse*) to get into debt 3. (*mediar*) to mediate

empeño *m* 1. (*afán*) determination; **con** ~ determinedly; **tengo** ~ **por** [*o* **en**] **sacar la mejor nota** I'm determined to get the highest mark; **pondré** ~ **en...** I will try my best to ... 2. (*compromiso*) commitment 3. (*de objetos*) pawning; **casa de** ~**s** pawnbroker's

empeorar I. *vt* to make worse; **con tus palabras lo has acabado de** ~ what you've said has just made it worse II. *vi, vr:* ~**se** to worsen

empequeñecer *irr como crecer vt* 1. (*disminuir*) to make smaller 2. (*quitar importancia*) to trivialize

emperador *m* 1. POL emperor 2. ZOOL swordfish

emperatriz *f* empress

emperrarse *vr inf* (*obstinarse*) to be bent [*o* dead set] on

empezar *irr vi, vt* to begin, to start; **empezó de la nada** he/she started with nothing; **¡no empieces!** don't start!; ~ **con buen pie** to get off to a good start; **para** ~ **me leeré el periódico** to begin with, I'll read the newspaper; **para** ~ **no tengo dinero y, además, no tengo ganas** first of all, I have no money, and what's more, I don't feel like it

empiezo *m Col, Ecua, Guat* (*comienzo*) beginning

empinado, **-a** *adj* 1. (*pendiente*) steep 2. (*edificio*) high

empinar I. *vt* 1. (*poner vertical*) to stand up 2. (*alzar*) to raise; ~ **una botella** to raise a bottle (*in order to drink*); ~ **la cabeza** to raise one's head; ~ **el codo** *inf* to have a drink, to booze *inf* II. *vr:* ~**se** 1. (*persona*) to stand on tiptoes; (*animal*) to stand on its hind legs 2. (*un edificio*) to tower

empipada *f AmL* binge; **darse una** ~ **de chocolate** to have a chocolate binge

empiparse *vr AmL* to have a binge

empírico, **-a** *adj* empirical

emplaste *m* plaster

emplasto *m* poultice

emplazamiento *m* 1. (*lugar, situación*) location 2. JUR summons *pl* 3. MIL emplacement

emplazar <z→c> *vt* 1. (*citar*) to call; JUR to summon; **le emplazo para darme una respuesta mañana** you have until tomorrow to give me an answer 2. (*situar*) to locate; MIL to emplace; **este monumento no está bien emplazado aquí** this isn't the best place for this monument

empleado, **-a** *m, f* employee; ~ **de oficina** office worker; ~ **de ventanilla** clerk; **los** ~**s de una empresa** company personnel [*o* staff]

empleador(a) *m(f) AmL* employer

emplear I. *vt* 1. (*usar: medio, técnica, método*) to use; (*tiempo*) to spend; **¡podrías** ~ **mejor el tiempo!** you could use your time better!; **¡ya te está bien empleado!** it serves you right!; **dar algo por bien empleado** to be satisfied at the results of sth 2. (*dinero*) to invest; **he empleado todo el dinero en la casa** I've put all my money into the house 3. (*colocar*) to employ; (*ocupar*) to engage; **en estos momentos no estoy empleado** I'm unemployed at the moment II. *vr:* ~**se** 1. (*colocarse*) ~**se de** [*o* **como**] **algo** to be employed as sth 2. (*usarse*) to be used 3. (*esforzarse*) ~**se a fondo** to put everything into sth

empleo *m* 1. (*trabajo*) job, post *Brit;* (*ocupación*) employment; **pleno** ~ full employment; **no tener** ~ to be out of work; **crear** ~ to create employment; **solicitud de** ~ job application 2. (*uso, técnica, método*) use; (*tiempo*) spending; **modo de** ~ instructions for use; **el** ~ **de materias primas y energía** the use of raw materials and energy

emplomadura *f* 1. (*cubrimiento*) lead covering 2. (*precinto*) leading 3. (*plomo*) leadwork 4. *AmL* (*empaste*) filling

emplomar *vt* 1. (*cubrir*) to cover with lead 2. (*precintar*) to seal with lead 3. *AmL* (*empastar*) to fill 4. *Col, Guat* (*enredar*) to entangle

emplumar *vt inf* to stick sb with sth

empobrecer *irr como crecer* I. *vt* to impoverish; **la edad empobrece los reflejos** age slows one's reflexes II. *vi, vr:* ~**se** to become poorer; **este terreno se ha empobrecido** this soil has become less fertile

empobrecimiento *m* 1. (*depauperación*) impoverishment 2. (*empeoramiento*) worsening

empollar I. *vi* 1. *inf* (*estudiante*) to swot 2. *AmL* (*ampollar*) to blister II. *vt* 1. (*ave*) to brood 2. *inf* (*lección*) to swot up; **estar empollado de algo** to have swotted up on sth

empollón, **-ona** *m, f inf* swot

empolvar I. *vt* to cover with dust II. *vr*: **~se** (*el rostro*) to powder

emponchado, **-a** *adj* 1. *AmL* (*astuto*) sharp, crafty 2. *Arg, Ecua, Perú, Urug* (*con poncho*) wearing a poncho 3. *Arg, Bol, Perú* (*sospechoso*) suspicious

emponzoñar *vt* to poison

emporio *m* 1. (*ciudad*) trading place; (*centro comercial*) shopping centre [*o* center *Am*], (shopping) mall *Am* 2. (*centro cultural*) cultural centre [*o* center *Am*] 3. *AmC* (*almacén*) store

empotrado, **-a** *adj* fitted, built-in

empotrar *vt* 1. (*en una pared*) to fit *Brit*, to build in 2. (*chocar*) to crash

empotrerar *vt AmL* to put out to pasture

emprendedor(a) *adj* resourceful, enterprising

emprender *vt* 1. (*trabajo*) to begin; (*negocio*) to set up; **~ la marcha** to set out; **~ la vuelta** to go back; **~ el vuelo** to take off; **al anochecer la emprendimos hacia la casa** at nightfall we set off back to the house 2. *inf* (*principiar una acción*) **~la con alguien** to take it out on sb; **~la a insultos con alguien** to begin insulting sb

empresa *f* 1. ECON enterprise; (*compañía*) company; **~ de mensajería** courier company; **mediana ~** medium-sized company; **pequeña ~** small company; **~ matriz** parent company; **~ privada** private enterprise; **~ pública** state-owned company 2. (*iniciativa*) resourcefulness 3. (*operación*) task

empresarial *adj* 1. (*del empresario*) entrepreneurial 2. (*de la empresa*) business; (*compañía*) company

empresario, **-a** *m, f* 1. ECON businessman *m*, businesswoman *f*; **pequeño ~** small businessman 2. TEAT impresario

empréstito *m* loan; **~ público** government loan

empujar *vi, vt* 1. (*dar empujón*) to push; (*con violencia*) to shove; (*multitud*) to elbow, to shoulder; **me empujó hacia atrás** he/she pushed me back; **me empujó contra la pared** he/she pushed me against the wall 2. (*empleado*) to dismiss 3. (*instar*) to urge; **su familia le empuja a que se case** his family is urging him to get married 4. (*intrigar*) to intrigue

empuje *m* 1. (*acción*) pushing 2. FÍS force; **~ ascensional** upward force 3. (*energía*) energy; (*resolución*) drive; **persona de ~** pushy person; **no tienes el ~ suficiente para llevar la empresa** you don't have enough drive to run the company

empujón *m* push; (*violento*) shove, shove; **dar un ~ a alguien** to give sb a shove; **entrar en un local a empujones** to push one's way into a place; **si no le damos un ~ al trabajo no lo acabaremos** if we don't push ahead with it we won't finish it

empuntar I. *vi* 1. (*irse*) to go away 2. *Col, inf* **~las** to beat it *inf* II. *vt* 1. TAUR (*empitonar*) to gore 2. *Col, Ecua* (*encarrilar*) to direct towards III. *vr*: **~se** *Ven* (*obstinarse*) to dig one's heels in

empuñadura *f* (*puño*) handle; (*de un bastón*) grip; **de una espada** hilt

empuñar *vt* 1. (*tomar*) to take; (*asir*) to grip; **~ las armas** to take up arms 2. (*un puesto*) to land 3. *Chile* (*la mano*) to clench

empurrarse *vr AmC* to get irritated

emú *m* emu

emulación *f* 1. (*imitación*) emulation 2. (*competencia*) competition

emular *vt* 1. (*imitar*) to emulate 2. (*competir*) **~ algo** to compete with sth

émulo, **-a** *m, f* 1. (*imitador*) imitator 2. (*oponente*) competitor

emulsión *f* emulsion

en *prep* 1. (*lugar: dentro*) in; (*encima de*) on; (*con movimiento*) in, into; **el libro está ~ el cajón** the book is in the drawer; **pon el libro ~ el cajón** put the book in the drawer; **he dejado las llaves ~ la mesa** I've left the keys on the table; **coloca el florero ~ la mesa** put the vase on the table; **~ la pared hay un cuadro** there is a painting on the wall; **pon el póster ~ la pared** put the poster on the wall; **estar ~ el campo/~ la ciudad/~ una isla** to be in the countryside/in the city/on an island; **~ Escocia** in Scotland; **vacaciones ~ el mar** holidays at the seaside; **jugar ~ la calle** to play in the street; **vivo ~ la calle George** I live in George Street; **estoy ~ casa** I'm at home; **estoy ~ casa de mis padres** I'm at my parents' house; **trabajo ~ una empresa japonesa** I work in a Japanese company 2. (*tiempo*) in; **~ el año 2005** in 2005; **~ mayo/invierno/el siglo XIX** in may/winter/the 19th century; **~ otra ocasión** on another occasion; **~ aquellos tiempos** in those times [*o* days]; **~ un mes/dos años** in a month/two years; **lo terminaré ~ un momento** I'll finish it in a moment; **~ todo el día** all [*o* the whole] day 3. (*modo, estado*) **~ absoluto** not at all; **~ construcción** under construction; **~ flor** in flower; **~ venta** for sale; **~ vida** while living; **~ voz alta** aloud; **de dos ~ dos** two at a time; **decir algo ~ español** to say something in Spanish; **pagar ~ libras** to pay in pounds 4. (*medio*) **papá viene ~ tren/~ coche** dad is coming by train/by car; **he venido ~ avión** I came by air [*o* plane]; **lo reconocí ~ la voz** I recognised him by his voice 5. (*ocupación*) **doctor ~ filosofía** Ph.D in Philosophy; **trabajo ~ ingenie-**

ría genética I work in genetic engineering; **estar ~ la policía** to be in the police force; **estar ~ la mili** to be doing military service; **trabajar ~ Correos/~ una fábrica** to work in the postal service/in a factory **6.** (*con verbo*) **pienso ~ ti** I am thinking of you; **no confío ~ él** I don't trust him; **ingresar ~ un partido** to join a party; **ganar ~ importancia** to gain in importance **7.** (*cantidades*) **aumentar la producción ~ un 5%** to increase production by 5%; **me he equivocado sólo ~ 3 euros** I was only wrong by 3 euros **8.** ECON **~ fábrica** ex-works; **franco ~ almacén** ex-store

enagua(s) *f(pl)* underskirt

enajenación *f* **1.** (*de una propiedad*) transfer **2.** (*de la mente*) derangement; **~ mental** insanity **3.** (*embeleso*) delight **4.** (*distracción*) distraction **5.** (*entre personas*) estrangement

enajenar **I.** *vt* **1.** (*una posesión*) to transfer **2.** (*enloquecer*) to drive mad **3.** (*turbar*) to disturb; (*fascinar*) to fascinate **II.** *vr:* **~se 1.** (*de una posesión*) **~se de algo** to transfer sth **2.** (*enloquecer*) to go mad **3.** (*de alguien*) to become estranged

enaltecer *irr como crecer vt* **1.** (*ensalzar*) to praise **2.** (*dignificar*) to ennoble

enamoradizo, -a *adj* romantic; **es un joven ~** he is a young romantic

enamorado, -a **I.** *adj* **~ (de alguien/algo)** in love (with sb/sth); **estuvimos un tiempo ~s** we were in love for a time **II.** *m, f* lover *m, f;* **día de los ~s** St Valentine's Day

enamorar **I.** *vt* (*conquistar*) to win the heart of; **mi profesora me ha enamorado** I've fallen in love with my teacher **II.** *vr* **~se (de alguien/algo)** to fall in love (with sb/sth)

enanito, -a *m, f* **Blancanieves y los siete ~s** Snow White and the Seven Dwarfs

enano, -a **I.** *adj* tiny **II.** *m, f* **1.** (*persona*) dwarf **2.** *inf* (*criatura*) kid; **disfrutar como un ~** *inf* to have a whale of a time; **te vengaste como un ~** *inf* you really got your own back

enarbolar *vt* (*bandera*) to hoist; (*cartel*) to stick up; (*espada*) to wield

enarcar <c→qu> **I.** *vt* **1.** (*arquear*) to bend; (*las cejas*) to arch **2.** (*tonel*) to hoop **II.** *vr:* **~se 1.** (*arquearse*) to arch **2.** (*encogerse*) to shrink **3.** *Méx* (*caballo*) to rear

enardecer *irr como crecer* **I.** *vt* **1.** (*personas*) to fire with enthusiasm; (*pasiones*) to kindle; **~ los ánimos** to raise spirits **2.** (*enfervorizar*) to inflame **3.** (*sexualmente*) to arouse **II.** *vr:* **~se 1.** (*pasiones*) to be kindled **2.** (*entusiasmarse*) **~se por algo** to become enthusiastic about sth **3.** MED (*inflamarse*) to become inflamed **4.** (*sexualmente*) to be aroused

encabezado *m Guat, Méx* (*titular*) heading

encabezamiento *m* **1.** (*de un escrito, libro, artículo*) heading **2.** (*de una carta: parte superior*) letterhead; (*tratamiento*) form of address; (*primeras líneas*) opening

encabezar <z→c> *vt* **1.** (*lista, grupo*) to head; (*institución*) to be the head of **2.** (*un escrito*) to be at the top of; (*un artículo*) to be the title of; **~ un libro con una cita** to open a book with a quotation **3.** (*una carta: la parte superior*) to head; (*el tratamiento*) to title; (*las primeras líneas*) to open

encabritarse *vr* **1.** (*animal, vehículo*) to rear up **2.** (*persona*) to lose one's temper

encadenar *vt* **1.** (*poner cadenas*) to chain (up) **2.** *fig* (*unir*) to connect, to link up; (*atar*) to tie down

encajar **I.** *vi* **1.** *t.* TÉC to fit; (*cerradura*) to bolt; **la puerta encaja mal** the door doesn't fit properly; **esta puerta no encaja con este marco** this door doesn't fit into this frame **2.** (*datos, hechos*) to fit in; **las dos declaraciones encajan** the two statements fit together; **¡ves como todo encaja!** see how everything fits!; **este chiste no encaja aquí** this joke is out of place here **II.** *vt* **1.** *t.* TÉC to fit; **~ en algo** to clamp into sth; **~ dos piezas** to fit two pieces together; **~ la ventana en el marco** to fit the window into the frame; **~ el sombrero en la cabeza** to stick a hat on one's head; **~ la funda en la máquina** to put the covering over the machine **2.** *inf* **~ un tiro a alguien** to shoot sb; **~ un golpe a alguien** to hit sb **3.** *inf* (*aceptar*) to take; **no ~ la muerte de alguien** not to take sb's death well; **no sabes ~ una broma** you don't know how to take a joke **4.** (*gol*) to let in **5.** *inf* (*soltar*) to come out with; **~ una reprimenda a alguien** to give sb a talking-to; **nos encajó todas sus vacaciones** we had to listen to him/her telling us all about his/her holidays **6.** *inf* (*endilgar*) to palm off on sb; **~ una tarea a alguien** to palm a task off on sb **7.** (*insertar*) to fit; **tenemos que ~ esta historia en la edición de mañana** we have to fit this story into tomorrow's edition **III.** *vr:* **~se 1.** (*empotrarse*) **~se en algo** to crash into sth **2.** *AmL, inf* (*aprovecharse*) to go too far **3.** (*atascarse*) to jam

encaje *m* **1.** (*acción*) fitting **2.** (*tejido*) lace

encajonar **I.** *vt* **1.** (*en cajones*) to put in a drawer; (*en cajas*) to box (up) **2.** (*a la fuerza*) to cram; **estábamos encajonados en el coche** we were crammed into the car **3.** *fig* (*cortar la salida*) to box in **II.** *vr:* **~se 1.** (*apretarse*) **~se en algo** to squeeze into sth **2.** (*un río*) to narrow down

encalambrarse *vr AmL* **1.** (*calambre*) to cramp up **2.** (*de frío*) to become numb

encalar *vt* to whitewash

encallar *vi* **1.** (*barco*) to run aground **2.** (*asunto*) to founder; (*negociaciones*) to break down

encallecer *irr como crecer* **I.** *vi, vr:* **~se** (*piel*) to harden **II.** *vr:* **~se** (*persona*) to become inured

encalmarse *vr* to calm down

encaminar **I.** *vt* **1.** (*orientar*) to guide; **¿me puede ~ al pueblo más próximo, por favor?** can you tell me how to get to the nearest village, please?; **estar bien encaminado**

to be on the right track **2.** (*dirigir*) to direct; ~ **sus pasos hacia el pueblo** to head towards the village; ~ **la mirada/la conversación hacia un punto** to direct one's gaze/the conversation towards a point; ~ **los esfuerzos hacia una meta** to focus one's efforts on a goal; **medidas encaminadas a reducir el paro** measures intended to reduce unemployment; ~ **los negocios hacia algo** to steer one's business towards sth **II.** *vr* ~**se a/hacia algo** to head for/towards sth; ~**se a la meta** to focus on the goal

encamotarse *vr AmL, inf* ~ **de alguien** to fall in love with sb

encandilar I. *vt* to dazzle; **tu belleza lo encandiló** your beauty captivated him; **escuchar encandilado** to listen in raptures **II.** *vr:* ~**se 1.** *fig* (*luz, emociones*) to light up **2.** *AmL* (*asustarse*) to be scared **3.** *PRico* (*enfadarse*) to get angry

encanecer *irr como crecer vi, vr:* ~**se 1.** (*pelo*) to go grey *Brit,* to go gray *Am;* **pelo encanecido** grey hair *Brit,* gray hair *Am* **2.** (*persona*) to get old

encantado, -a *adj* **1.** (*satisfecho*) delighted; **estar** ~ **de** [*o* **con**] **algo/alguien** to be delighted with sth/sb; **¡**~ **(de conocerle)!** pleased to meet you!; **estoy** ~ **con mi nuevo trabajo** I love my new job; **estoy** ~ **de la vida** I am thrilled **2.** (*distraído*) **estar** ~ to have one's head in the clouds **3.** (*embrujado*) haunted

encantador(a) I. *adj* **1.** (*persona*) charming; (*bebé*) lovely, adorable **2.** (*fiesta, lugar*) lovely **3.** (*música*) beautiful **II.** *m(f)* charmer; ~ **de serpientes** snake charmer

encantamiento *m* spell

encantar *vt* **1.** (*hechizar*) to bewitch; (*serpientes*) to charm **2.** (*gustar*) **me encanta viajar** I love to travel; **me encantan los dulces** I love sweet things; **me encanta que te preocupes por mí** I love the fact that you care about me **3.** (*cautivar*) to captivate; (*fascinar*) to fascinate

encanto *m* **1.** (*hechizo*) spell; **romper el** ~ to break the spell **2.** (*atractivo*) charm; **¡es un** ~ **de niño!** what an adorable child!

encañado *m* **1.** (*tubos*) drain **2.** (*cañas*) pipes *pl;* (*plantas*) trellis

encapotarse *vr* (*cielo*) to become overcast [*o* cloudy]

encapricharse *vr* **1.** (*con una cosa*) ~**se con algo** to be taken by sth **2.** (*con una persona*) to become infatuated, to have a crush on; **te has encaprichado con ella** you're infatuated with her

encapuchado, -a *adj* hooded

encaramar I. *vt* **1.** (*alzar*) to raise; ~ **a alguien a la fama mundial** to make sb world-famous **2.** (*alabar*) to praise **II.** *vr:* ~**se 1.** (*subir*) ~**se a un árbol** to climb a tree; ~**se a una escalera** to climb a staircase **2.** (*de categoría*) to rise; ~**se a lo más alto de la empresa** to rise to the top of the company

encarar I. *vt* **1.** (*persona, cosa*) to bring face to face **2.** (*riesgo*) to face up to **3.** (*fusil*) ~ **a algo/alguien** to aim at sth/sb **II.** *vr:* ~**se 1.** (*dos personas*) to be face to face **2.** (*a una dificultad*) ~**se a algo** to face up to sth **3.** *inf* (*a un superior*) ~**se a alguien** to stand up to sb

encarcelación *f,* **encarcelamiento** *m* imprisonment

encarcelar *vt* to imprison; **estar encarcelado** to be in prison

encarecer *irr como crecer vt* **1.** COM to raise the price of **2.** (*alabar*) to praise **3.** (*subrayar*) to emphasize; **encareció la necesidad de aprender idiomas** he/she stressed the need to learn languages **4.** (*insistir*) to urge; **me encareció que no dejara de visitarla** she urged me not to stop visiting her

encarecidamente *adv* strongly; **le ruego** ~**...** I have to insist ...

encarecimiento *m* **1.** COM price increase; **el** ~ **de la vida** the increase of the cost of living **2.** (*acentuación*) emphasis **3.** (*insistencia*) **con** ~ insistently

encargado, -a I. *adj* in charge **II.** *m, f* person in charge; ~ **de negocios** chargé d'affaires; ~ **de campo** groundsman; ~ **de curso** course director; ~ **de obras** site manager; ~ **de prensa** press officer

encargar <g→gu> **I.** *vt* **1.** (*encomendar*) to put in charge; **lo** ~**on del departamento de ventas** they put him in charge of the sales department; **encargó a su hija a una vecina** he asked a neighbour [*o* neighbor *Am*] to look after his daughter **2.** (*comprar*) to order **3.** (*mandar*) to ask; **me han encargado que ocupe la presidencia** I have been asked to take over the presidency **4.** JUR to commission **II.** *vr* ~**se de algo** to take responsibility for sth; **tengo que** ~**me aún de un par de cosas** I still have to get a couple of things done

encargo *m* **1.** (*pedido*) order; ~ **por anticipado** advance order; **hacer un nuevo** ~ to make another order **2.** (*trabajo*) job; **traje de** ~ tailor-made suit; **de** ~ to order; **por** ~ **de** at the request of; **hacer** ~**s** to run errands; **tener** ~ **de hacer algo** to be commissioned to do sth; **este vestido te viene como hecho de** ~ this dress really suits you

encariñado, -a *adj* **estar** ~ **con algo** to be very attached to sth; **estar** ~ **con alguien** to be fond of sb

encariñarse *vr* ~ **con algo** to get attached to sth; ~ **con alguien** to grow fond of sb; **el niño se ha encariñado con su tía** the child has become attached to his aunt

encarnación *f* incarnation; **la** ~ **del horror** the embodiment of horror

encarnado, -a *adj* **1.** (*color carne*) flesh coloured [*o* colored *Am*]; (*rosado*) pink; (*rojo*) red **2.** (*persona*) incarnate; **era el diablo** ~ it was the devil incarnate

encarnar I. *vi* REL to incarnate **II.** *vt* (*represen-*

tar) to represent; ~ **a** CINE, TEAT to play the role [*o* part] of

encarnizado, **-a** *adj* **1.**(*lucha*) bloody **2.**(*herida*) sore; (*ojo*) bloodshot **3.**(*persona*) cruel

encarnizamiento *m* cruelty; (*de la lucha*) fury; (*ensañamiento*) bloodthirstiness

encarpetar *vt* to file away; (*encuadernar*) to bind; *AmL* (*dar carpetazo*) to shelve

encarrilar *vt* **1.** FERRO to put on rails; **ir encarrilado** to be on the right track **2.**(*dirigir*) to guide

encartar *vt* JUR to summon

encasillado *m* (*de un crucigrama*) grid

encasillar **I.** *vt* **1.**(*meter en casillas*) to pigeonhole **2.**(*clasificar*) to classify **3.**(*considerar*) to consider; **me ~on como un comunista** they considered me a communist **4.** CINE, TEAT to typecast **II.** *vr* **~se en algo** to limit oneself to sth, to be classified as sth

encasquetar **I.** *vt* **1.**(*sombrero*) to put on firmly **2.**(*dar*) ~ **un golpe a alguien** to hit sb **3.**(*una idea*) to get into one's head **4.**(*endilgar*) to lumber with; **nos ~on la parte peor** we were lumbered [*o* stuck] with the worst part; **me encasquetó un rollo tremendo** I had to listen to him going on and on **II.** *vr:* **~se** **1.**(*sombrero*) to put on one's head **2.**(*idea*) **se te ha encasquetado esa idea** you've got this idea into your head

encausar *vt* JUR to prosecute; (*acusar*) to accuse

encauzar <z→c> *vt* (*corriente*) to channel; (*debate*) to lead; ~ **su vida** to sort out one's life

encéfalo *m* MED brain

encefalopatía *f* encephalopathy; ~ **espongiforme bovina** bovine spongiform encephalopathy, mad cow disease *inf*

encenagarse <g→gu> *vr* **1.**(*con barro*) to get covered in mud **2.**(*pervertirse*) to become corrupt

encendedor *m* lighter

encender <e→ie> **I.** *vi* (*fuego*) to catch fire; (*motor*) to fire **II.** *vt* **1.**(*cigarrillo*) to light; ~ **un conflicto** to stir up a conflict **2.**(*conectar*) to switch on **3.**(*pasiones*) to arouse **4.** AUTO, TÉC to ignite **III.** *vr:* **~se** **1.**(*desencadenarse*) to break out **2.**(*inflamarse*) to ignite **3.**(*luz*) go come on; (*ruborizarse*) to blush

encendido *m* AUTO, TÉC ignition; ~ **automático** automatic ignition; ~ **defectuoso** faulty ignition

encendido, **-a** *adj* **1.**(*conectado*) **estar** ~ to be on; **la luz está encendida** the light is on **2.**(*ardiente*) burning; (*cigarrillo*) lighted; (*apasionado*) passionate; **estar** ~ to be lit **3.**(*rojo*) red

encerado *m* blackboard

encerar *vt* to wax; (*lustrar*) to polish

encerrar <e→ie> **I.** *vt* **1.**(*depositar, recluir*) to lock in [*o* up]; ~ **entre paréntesis** to put in brackets **2.**(*contener*) to contain; **la oferta encerraba una trampa** the offer held a trap **II.** *vr:* **~se** to lock oneself in; *fig* to cut oneself off

encerrona *f* trap; **preparar una ~ a alguien** to frame [*o* lay a trap for] sb

encestar *vi* DEP to score a basket

enchastrar *vt CSur* to dirty

enchilada *f AmC* enchilada

enchilado, **-a** *adj Méx* **1.**(*bermejo*) ruddy **2.**(*colérico*) angry; (*rabioso*) furious

enchilar **I.** *vt AmC* **1.** GASTR to season with chilli **2.**(*molestar*) to annoy **3.**(*decepcionar*) to disappoint **II.** *vr:* **~se** *AmC* (*enfurecerse*) to blow one's top

enchinar **I.** *vt Méx* (*enrizar*) to curl **II.** *vr:* **~se** *Méx* **1.**(*ponerse carne de gallina*) to get gooseflesh **2.**(*acobardarse*) to be frightened

enchinchar **I.** *vt* **1.** *Guat, RDom* (*incomodar*) to annoy **2.** *Méx* ~ **a alguien** (*hacer perder el tiempo*) to waste sb's time **II.** *vr:* **~se** **1.** *Arg* (*malhumorarse*) to be in a bad mood; **¿estás enchinchado?** are you in a bad mood? **2.** *Guat, Méx, Perú, PRico* (*llenarse de chinches*) to be infested with bugs

enchironar *vt inf* to throw in jail

enchivarse *vr Col, Ecua* to get furious

enchufar *vt* **1.** ELEC to plug in **2.** TÉC (*conectar*) to connect **3.**(*acoplar*) to couple **4.** *inf* (*persona*) ~ **a alguien** to get a job for sb (by pulling strings)

enchufe *m* **1.**(*clavija*) plug **2.**(*toma*) socket **3.** *inf* (*contactos*) **tener** ~ *inf* to have connections **4.**(*trabajo*) good job (*which has been obtained by pulling strings*) **5.** INFOR plug-in

enchutar *vt AmC* **1.**(*embutir*) ~ **de algo** to fill with sth **2.**(*introducir*) to introduce

encía *f* ANAT gum

enciclopedia *f* encyclopaedia *Brit,* encyclopedia *Am;* ~ **en ocho volúmenes** an eight-volume encyclopedia; **ser una ~ viviente** to be a walking encyclopedia

enciclopédico, **-a** *adj* encyclopaedic *Brit,* encyclopedic *Am;* **diccionario** ~ encyclopedic dictionary

encierro *m* **1.**(*reclusión*) confinement; (*prisión*) imprisonment; (*aislamiento*) isolation; (*como protesta*) sit-in **2.**(*lugar*) quiet spot; (*cercado*) enclosure **3.** TAUR *running of bulls in the San Fermin festival in Pamplona*

> Strictly speaking, **encierro** a term from the **tauromaquia** (art of bullfighting), refers to the following two processes: the bulls are first driven into the arena pens and then locked up in the **toril** (bull cage). For many people this represents the actual **fiesta** (public festival).

encima **I.** *adv* **1.**(*arriba: con contacto*) on top; (*sin tocar*) above **2.** *fig* **echarse ~ de alguien** to attack sb; **se nos echa el tiempo ~** time is running out; **quitarse algo de ~** (*librarse*) to get sth off one's back; **quitar a alguien un peso de ~** to take a weight off sb's mind; **se me ha quitado un peso de ~** that's a weight off my mind; **tener algo** ~ to be saddled with sth; **ya tenemos bastante** ~ we've got enough on our plate; **llevaba mucho dinero** ~ he/she had a lot of money on him/her **3.** (*además*) besides; **te di el dinero y** ~ **una botella de vino** I gave you the money and a bottle of wine as well **4.** (*superficialmente*) **por** ~ superficial(ly) **II.** *prep* **1.** (*local: con contacto*) ~ **de** on top of; **con queso** ~ with cheese on top; **el libro está** ~ **de la mesa** the book is on the table; **estar** ~ **de alguien** *fig* to be on sb's case [*o* back] **2.** (*local: sin contacto*) (**por**) ~ **de** above; **viven** ~ **de nosotros** they live above us; **por** ~ **de todo** above all; **por** ~ **de la media** above average **3.** (*con movimiento*) (**por**) ~ **de** over; **pon esto** ~ **de la cama** put this over the bed; **cuelga la lámpara** ~ **de la mesa** hang the light above the table; **¡por** ~ **de mí!** *fig* over my dead body!; **ése pasa por** ~ **de todo** *fig* he only cares about himself **4.** (*más alto*) **el rascacielos está por** ~ **de la catedral** the skyscraper is higher than the cathedral **5.** (*en contra de*) **por** ~ **de alguien** against one's will

encimera *f* worktop, counter *Am*

encina *f* holm oak

encinta *adj* pregnant; **dejar** ~ **a alguien** to get sb pregnant

enclave *m* enclave

enclenque *adj* (*enfermizo*) sickly; (*débil*) weak; (*flaco*) puny

encocorar I. *vt inf* to irritate **II.** *vr:* ~**se** *inf* to get annoyed

encoger <g→j> **I.** *vi* (*tejido*) to shrink **II.** *vt* **1.** (*contraer*) to contract **2.** (*reducir*) to shrink **3.** (*desalentar*) to depress; **verlo así me encoge el ánimo** it depresses me to see him like this **III.** *vr:* ~**se 1.** (*contraerse*) to contract; (*persona*) to cringe; ~**se de hombros** *fig, inf* to shrug one's shoulders **2.** (*reducirse*) to shrink **3.** (*acobardarse*) to get scared

encolar *vt* to glue

encolerizar <z→c> **I.** *vt* to incense **II.** *vr:* ~**se** to be incensed

encomendar <e→ie> **I.** *vt* **1.** (*recomendar*) to recommend **2.** (*confiar*) ~ **algo a alguien** to entrust sth to sb **II.** *vr:* ~**se** to commend; ~**se a Dios** to commend one's soul to God

encomendería *f Perú* COM grocery store

encomiar *vt* to praise

encomienda *f* **1.** (*encargo*) assignment **2.** (*encomio*) praise **3.** (*recomendación*) recommendation **4.** (*beneficio*) payment **5.** (*recado*) errand **6.** *AmL* (*postal*) parcel

encomio *m* praise; **digno de** ~ praiseworthy

enconar I. *vt* **1.** (*agravar*) to worsen; (*agudizar*) to intensify; (*espolear*) to spur on **2.** (*exasperar*) to exasperate **3.** (*inflamar*) to inflame **II.** *vr:* ~**se 1.** (*inflamarse*) to become inflamed **2.** (*agravarse*) to worsen; (*agudizarse*) to intensify **3.** (*ensañarse*) ~**se con alguien** to vent one's rage on sb

encono *m* (*rencor*) spite

encontradizo, -a *adj* **hacerse el** ~ to contrive a meeting

encontrado, -a *adj* (*opuesto*) opposite; **opiniones encontradas** conflicting opinions

encontrar <o→ue> **I.** *vt* **1.** (*hallar*) to find **2.** (*coincidir con*) to come across **3.** (*considerar*) to find; (*notar*) to be conscious of **II.** *vr:* ~**se 1.** (*estar*) to be **2.** (*sentirse*) to feel **3.** (*citarse*) ~**se con alguien** to meet sb **4.** (*coincidir*) ~**se con alguien** to run [*o* bump] into sb **5.** (*hallar*) to find; ~**se con algo** to come across sth; **me encontré con que el coche se había estropeado** I found that the car had broken down; ~**se con un problema** to come up against a problem; ~**se con una sorpresa desagradable** to have a nasty surprise; **no sé lo que me** ~**é cuando llegue** I don't know what I'll find when I arrive; ~**se todo hecho** *inf* to be born with a silver spoon in one's mouth

encontronazo *m inf* crash; **darse un** ~ to have a collision; **tener un** ~ **con alguien** to quarrel with sb; (*enfrentamiento*) to clash with sb

encorvado, -a *adj* hunched; **un viejecito** ~ a stooped old man

encorvar I. *vt* (*cosa*) to bend; (*cuerpo*) to stoop **II.** *vr:* ~**se** (*cosa*) to become bent; (*madera*) to warp; (*persona*) to become hunched

encrespar I. *vt* **1.** (*rizar*) to frizz; **el viento encrespó las aguas** the wind churned up the waters **2.** (*erizar*) to stand on end **3.** (*irritar*) to annoy; (*excitar*) to excite **II.** *vr:* ~**se 1.** (*rizarse*) to curl **2.** (*erizarse*) to stand on end **3.** (*irritarse*) to get annoyed

encrucijada *f* (*cruce*) crossroads *inv,* intersection; **estar en una** ~ *fig* to be at a crossroads [*o* turning point]

encuadernación *f* **1.** (*encuadernado*) binding **2.** (*cubierta*) cover; ~ **en pasta** hardback; ~ **en rústica** paperback **3.** (*taller*) bookbinder's

encuadernador(a) *m(f)* bookbinder

encuadernar *vt* to bind; **encuadernado en rústica** paperback; **encuadernado en pasta** hardback; **sin** ~ unbound

encuadrar *vt* **1.** *t.* CINE, FOTO, TV (*enmarcar*) to frame **2.** (*encajar*) to insert **3.** (*incluir*) to include

encubierto, -a I. *pp de* **encubrir II.** *adj* **tus palabras son una acusación encubierta** what you've said is a veiled accusation

encubridor(a) *m(f)* JUR accessory after the fact

encubrir *irr como abrir vt* **1.** (*cubrir*) to cover **2.** (*ocultar*) to hide; (*silenciar*) to hush up; (*escándalo, crimen*) to cover up; (*un delincuente*) to harbour *Brit,* to harbor *Am*

encuentro *m* **1.** (*acción*) encounter; **ir al** ~ **de alguien** to go to meet sb **2.** (*cita, reunión*) meeting **3.** (*encontronazo*) confrontation; MIL encounter **4.** DEP match, game; ~ **amistoso** DEP

friendly match [*o* game]
encuerado, **-a** *adj Cuba, Méx* **1.** (*desharrapado*) shabby **2.** (*desnudo*) naked
encuerar *vt, vr:* **~se** *AmL* to undress, to strip
encuerista *mf AmL* stripper
encuesta *f* **1.** (*sondeo*) opinion poll; **~ estadística** statistical survey; **~ no oficial** straw poll; **hacer una ~** to carry out an opinion poll **2.** (*investigación*) inquiry; **~ judicial** judicial inquiry
encularse *vr Arg: inf* **1.** (*ofenderse*) **~se por algo** to get pissed off about sth **2.** (*enojarse*) to get angry
enculebrado, **-a** *adj Col, inf* (*endeudado*) indebted
encumbrar **I.** *vt* **1.** (*levantar*) to raise **2.** (*socialmente*) to elevate; **~ a alguien a la fama** to make sb famous **3.** (*exaltar*) to praise **II.** *vr:* **~se** **1.** (*elevarse*) to rise **2.** (*engrandecerse*) to be ennobled **3.** (*envanecerse*) to be vain
ende *adv* **por ~** therefore
endeble *adj* **1.** (*débil*) weak; (*enfermizo*) sickly **2.** (*inconsistente*) flimsy
endémico, **-a** *adj* **1.** MED endemic **2.** (*continuo*) constant
endemoniado, **-a** *adj* **1.** (*poseso*) possessed **2.** (*malo*) bad **3.** *inf* (*difícil, tremendo*) awful; **tienes un genio ~** you've got a terrible temper; **tengo un hambre endemoniada** I'm dying of hunger **4.** *inf* (*travieso*) naughty; **¡~s chiquillos!** damn kids! *inf*
endenantes *adv AmL, inf* a bit before
enderezar <z→c> *vt* **1.** (*poner derecho*) to straighten **2.** (*corregir*) to straighten out
endeudarse *vr* to get into debt; (*favor*) to be indebted, to owe a favour [*o* favor *Am*]
endiablado, **-a** *adj v.* **endemoniado**
endibia *f* chicory *Brit,* endive *Am*
endilgar <g→gu> *vt inf* **1.** (*cargar*) **~ algo a alguien** to offload sth onto sb; **me ~on sus opiniones moralistas** they inflicted their moralistic opinions on me **2.** (*una tarea*) **me ~on el trabajo sucio** I got stuck with the dirty work **3.** (*encaminar*) to guide
endomingarse <g→gu> *vr* to put on one's Sunday best; **ir endomingado** to wear one's Sunday best
endosar *vt* FIN to endorse; (*traspasar*) to pass on; **~ una letra** to endorse a document
endoso *m* endorsement; **~ de una letra** endorsement of a document; **sin ~** unendorsed
endovenoso, **-a** *adj* intravenous; **por vía endovenosa** intravenously
endrina *f* sloe
endrino *m* blackthorn
endrino, **-a** *adj* bluish-black
endrogarse <g→gu> *vr* **1.** *AmL* (*drogarse*) to take drugs **2.** *Méx, Perú* (*endeudarse*) to get into debt
endulzar <z→c> *vt* **1.** (*poner dulce*) to sweeten **2.** (*suavizar*) to soften
endurecer *irr como crecer* **I.** *vt* **1.** (*poner duro*) to harden; TÉC to chill; ANAT to stiffen **2.** (*mente*) to toughen; (*persona*) to inure **3.** (*hacer resistente*) to strengthen **II.** *vr:* **~se** **1.** (*ponerse duro*) to get tough; (*sentimientos*) to become hardened **2.** (*hacerse resistente*) to be strengthened **3.** (*agudizarse*) to become more intense
endurecimiento *m* **1.** (*dureza*) hardness **2.** (*proceso*) hardening; **~ de las arterias** hardening of the arteries **3.** (*resistencia*) harshness **4.** (*terquedad*) stubbornness
ene **I.** *adj inv* MAT x; **~ veces** x times **II.** *f* (*letra*) N, n; **la letra ~** the letter n
enebrina *f* juniper berry
enebro *m* juniper
eneldo *m* dill
enema *m* (*lavado*) enema; **poner un ~ a alguien** to give sb an enema
enemigo, **-a** <enemicísimo> **I.** *adj* enemy; (*hostil*) hostile; **país ~** hostile country **II.** *m, f* enemy; (*contrario*) opponent; **~ acérrimo** sworn enemy; **~s mortales** mortal enemies *pl;* **ser ~ de algo** to be opposed to sth
enemistad *f* enmity; (*hostilidad*) animosity
enemistar **I.** *vt* to make enemies of **II.** *vr:* **~se** to become enemies
energético, **-a** *adj* energy; **fuentes energéticas** sources of energy; **valor ~** (*de alimentos*) calories *pl*
energía *f t.* FÍS energy; (*fuerza*) force; **~ nuclear** nuclear energy; **~ eólica** wind power; **con ~** *fig* forcefully; **con toda su ~** with all one's force; **sin ~** *fig* feebly; **la glucosa da ~** glucose gives you energy; **emplear todas las ~s en algo** to put all one's energies into sth
enérgico, **-a** *adj* **1.** (*fuerte*) energetic **2.** (*decidido*) firm **3.** (*estricto*) tough; **ponerse ~ con alguien** to get tough with sb **4.** (*efectivo*) effective
energúmeno, **-a** *m, f inf* lout, boor; **se puso a gritar como un ~** he started shouting like a maniac
enero *m* January; **la cuesta de ~** the post-Christmas slump; *v.t.* **marzo**
enervante *adj* (*irritante*) annoying
enervar **I.** *vt* **1.** (*debilitar*) to enervate **2.** *inf* (*poner nervioso*) to irritate **II.** *vr:* **~se** **1.** (*debilitarse*) to be enervated **2.** *inf* (*ponerse nervioso*) to get flustered
enésimo, **-a** *adj* MAT nth; **por enésima vez** *inf* for the thousandth [*o* umpteenth] time
enfadar **I.** *vt* **1.** (*irritar*) to anger; **estar enfadado con alguien** to be angry [*o* mad] with sb **2.** *AmL* (*aburrir*) to bore **II.** *vr:* **~se** to get angry; **~se con alguien** to get angry [*o* mad] with sb
enfado *m* (*enojo*) anger; (*molestia*) annoyance
énfasis *m o f inv* emphasis; (*insistencia*) insistence; **poner ~ en algo** to emphasize sth
enfático, **-a** *adj* emphatic; (*insistente*) insistent
enfatizar <z→c> **I.** *vt* to emphasize **II.** *vt* to

emphasize
enfermar I. *vi, vr* ~(**se**) **de algo** to get ill [*o* sick] with sth II. *vt* to make ill [*o* sick]
enfermedad *f* illness; (*específica*) disease; ~ **del hígado** liver disease; **ausencia por** ~ sickness [*o* sick] leave; **costar una** ~ *fig* to take its toll
enfermera *f* nurse
enfermería *f* infirmary
enfermero *m* male nurse; (*camillero*) stretcher-bearer
enfermizo, -a *adj* 1. (*de mala salud*) sickly 2. (*morboso*) sick
enfermo, -a I. *adj* ill, sick; ~ **del corazón** suffering heart disease; ~ **de gravedad** seriously ill; **caer** ~ **de algo** to come down with sth; **ponerse** ~ to get ill; **esta situación me pone** ~ this situation is really getting me down II. *m, f* ill person; (*paciente*) patient
enfervorizar <z→c> I. *vt* to enthuse II. *vr:* ~**se** to become enthused
enfilar I. *vi* to head II. *vt* 1. (*poner en fila*) to put in a row 2. (*enhebrar*) to string 3. (*poner en línea*) to line up 4. (*ruta*) to take; **enfilamos la carretera** we went down the road
enfisema *m* MED emphysema
enflaquecer *irr como crecer* I. *vi, vr:* ~**se** to become thin II. *vt* to make thin
enfocar <c→qu> *vt* 1. (*ajustar*) to focus; **mal enfocado** out of focus 2. (*iluminar*) ~ **algo** to shine light upon sth 3. (*una cuestión*) to approach; (*considerar*) to consider; **no enfocas bien el problema** you're not addressing the issue properly
enfoque *m* 1. (*punto de vista*) opinion, stance 2. (*planteamiento*) approach; (*concepción*) conception
enfrascar <c→qu> I. *vt* to bottle II. *vr* to get wrapped up in; ~**se en la lectura** to immerse oneself in reading
enfrentamiento *m* confrontation; (*encontronazo*) collision; (*pelea*) fight; ~**s callejeros** street-fighting
enfrentar I. *vt* 1. (*encarar*) to bring face to face; (*confrontar*) to confront 2. (*hacer frente*) to face up to; ~ **los hechos** to face the facts II. *vr:* ~**se** 1. (*encararse*) to come face to face 2. (*afrontarse*) ~**se con alguien** to face up to sb 3. (*pelearse*) to fight; **los manifestantes se ~on con la policía** the demonstrators clashed with the police 4. (*confrontar*) to confront 5. (*oponerse*) to oppose; **estar enfrentado a alguien** to be up against sb
enfrente I. *adv* 1. (*en el lado opuesto*) opposite; **allí** ~ over there; **la casa de** ~ the house opposite 2. (*en contra*) **tendrás a tu familia** ~ your family will be against you II. *prep* (*local: frente a*) ~ **de** opposite; ~ **mío** [*o* **de mí**] opposite me; ~ **del teatro** opposite the theatre; **vivo** ~ **del parque** I live opposite the park; **ponerse** ~ **de alguien** *fig* to be opposed to sb
enfriamiento *m* 1. (*pérdida de temperatura*) cooling; ~ **económico** economic slowdown 2. (*resfriado*) cold; **pillar un** ~ *inf* to catch a cold [*o* chill]
enfriar <*1. pres:* enfrío> I. *vi* to cool (down) II. *vt* to cool; *fig* to cool down; ~ **el vino** to chill the wine III. *vr:* ~**se** 1. (*perder calor*) to cool (down) 2. (*refrescar, apaciguarse*) to cool off 3. (*acatarrarse*) to catch a cold
enfundar I. *vt* (*espada, cuchillo*) to sheathe; **pistola** to put back in the holster II. *vr:* ~**se** (*ropa*) to put on
enfurecer *irr como crecer* I. *vt* to enrage II. *vr:* ~**se** 1. (*encolerizarse*) to be furious 2. (*mar*) to become rough
enfurruñar *vr:* ~**se** to get in a huff
engajado, -a *adj Col, CRi* curly
engalanar I. *vt* (*decorar*) to decorate; (*adornar*) to embellish II. *vr:* ~**se** to do oneself up, to get dressed up
enganchar I. *vt* 1. (*sujetar*) to hook; (*remolque*) to hitch up; (*caballerías*) to harness 2. (*prender*) to catch on; TAUR to impale 3. *inf* (*atrapar*) to catch; (*convencer*) to persuade 4. MIL to recruit 5. FERRO, TÉC to couple II. *vr:* ~**se** 1. (*sujetarse*) ~**se de algo** to get hooked on sth 2. (*prenderse*) ~**se de** [*o* **con**] **algo** to get caught on sth 3. (*enredarse*) to get caught up; ~**se en una pelea** to get caught up in a fight 4. MIL to sign up for the army 5. *inf* (*drogarse*) ~**se a** to get hooked on; **estar enganchado** to be hooked
enganche *m* 1. (*gancho*) hook 2. (*acto*) hooking 3. MIL recruitment, enlistment *Am*
engañabobos *mf inv, inf* (*timador*) con artist, conman *m,* conwoman *f*
engañar I. *vi* to deceive; **las apariencias engañan** *prov* looks [*o* appearances] are deceiving *prov* II. *vt* 1. (*desorientar*) to confuse 2. (*mentir*) to deceive; (*estafar*) to cheat; ~ **a alguien** (*ser infiel*) to cheat on sb; (*burlarse*) to laugh at sb; ~ **el hambre** to stave off one's hunger; **dejarse** ~ to fall for it *inf* III. *vr:* ~**se** 1. (*equivocarse*) to be wrong 2. (*hacerse ilusiones*) to get excited; **¡no te engañes con esta oferta!** don't get all excited about this offer!
engañifa *f inf,* **engañifla** *f Chile* trap
engaño *m* 1. (*mentira*) deceit 2. (*truco*) trick 3. (*error*) mistake 4. (*ilusión*) illusion
engañoso, -a *adj* 1. (*persona*) deceitful 2. (*algo: falaz*) false; (*equívoco*) incorrect; **publicidad engañosa** false advertising
engaratusar *vt AmC, Col* (*engatusar*) to coax
engarce *m* 1. (*engarzado*) setting 2. (*montura*) mount(ing) 3. (*unión*) coupling
engarzar <z→c> I. *vt* 1. (*trabar*) to join together 2. (*montar*) to set II. *vr:* ~**se** *AmL* to get caught up
engastar *vt* to set
engaste *m* 1. (*engastado*) setting 2. (*montura*) set
engatusar *vt* to sweet-talk; ~ **a alguien para que haga algo** to coax sb into doing sth

engavetar *vt Guat* to pigeon-hole; ~ **a alguien** to shelve sb

engendrar *vt* **1.** (*concebir*) to beget *liter* **2.** (*causar*) to give rise to; **la pobreza engendra violencia** poverty gives rise to violence

engendro *m* **1.** (*persona fea*) freak **2.** (*idea*) piece of claptrap

englobar *vt* **1.** (*incluir*) to include, to comprise **2.** (*reunir*) to bring together **3.** (*resumir*) to summarize

engolillarse *vr* **1.** *Cuba* (*contraer deudas*) to get into debt **2.** *Perú* (*encolerizarse*) to lose one's temper

engolosinar **I.** *vt* ~ **a alguien** (*atraer*) to entice sb; (*engatusar*) to beguile sb **II.** *vr* ~**se con algo/alguien** to be attracted to sth/sb; (*encariñarse*) to be taken by sth/sb

engomar *vt* **1.** (*con cola*) to put glue on **2.** (*cabello*) to put gel on

engordar **I.** *vi* **1.** (*ponerse gordo*) to get fat **2.** (*aumentar de peso*) to gain weight; **he engordado tres kilos** I've gained three kilos **3.** (*poner gordo*) to be fattening **4.** *inf* (*enriquecerse*) to get rich **II.** *vt* AGR to fatten

engorro *m* **1.** (*impedimento*) snag **2.** (*molestia*) nuisance

engorroso, **-a** *adj* awkward; (*molesto*) bothersome

engranaje *m* **1.** TÉC gear; (*mecanismo*) cogs *pl* **2.** (*sistema*) gearing

engranar **I.** *vi* to interlock **II.** *vt* **1.** (*endentar*) to fit **2.** (*enlazar*) to connect

engrandecer *irr como crecer vt* **1.** (*aumentar*) to increase; (*acrecentar*) to enlarge; (*elevar*) to ennoble **2.** (*exagerar*) to exaggerate **3.** (*enaltecer*) to praise

engrasar *vt* **1.** (*con grasa*) to grease; (*enaceitar*) to oil **2.** AUTO, TÉC (*lubricar*) to lubricate **3.** (*manchar*) to stain

engrase *m* **1.** (*engrasado*) greasing; AUTO, TÉC lubrication **2.** (*grasa*) grease; (*lubricante*) lubrication

engreído, **-a** *adj* **1.** (*envanecido*) conceited **2.** *AmL* (*mimado*) spoilt

engreír *irr como reír* **I.** *vt* **1.** (*envanecer*) to make arrogant **2.** *AmL* (*mimar*) to pamper **II.** *vr:* ~**se** **1.** (*envanecerse*) to become vain; (*presumir*) to boast **2.** *AmL* (*hacerse mimado*) to become spoilt

engrifarse *vr* **1.** *Col* (*volverse altivo*) to become arrogant **2.** *Méx* (*irritarse*) ~**se** to get annoyed; (*malhumorarse*) to lose one's temper

engrosar <o→ue> **I.** *vi, vr:* ~**se** **1.** (*engordar*) to become fatter **2.** (*aumentar*) to increase **II.** *vt* **1.** (*engordar*) to fatten **2.** (*aumentar*) to increase; (*multiplicar*) to multiply

engrudo *m* paste

engualichar *vt Arg* **1.** (*endemoniar*) ~ **a alguien** to put a spell on sb **2.** (*al amante*) ~ **a alguien** to have power over sb

enguandocar *vt Col* (*adornar*) to adorn; (*recargar*) to overload

enguaraparse *vr AmC* (*fermentar*) to ferment

enguatar *vt* to fill (with padding), to quilt

engubiar *vt Urug* to defeat

engullir <*3. pret:* engulló> *vt* **1.** (*tragar*) to swallow **2.** (*atropelladamente*) to devour **3.** *pey* (*comer*) to gobble down

enharinar *vt* (*rebozar*) to coat with flour; (*espolvorear*) to sprinkle with flour

enhebrar *vt* **1.** (*pasar hebra*) to thread **2.** (*ensartar*) to string together

enhiesto, **-a** *adj* **1.** (*derecho*) straight; (*erguido*) upright **2.** (*alto*) high

enhorabuena *f* congratulations *pl;* **dar la ~ a alguien** to congratulate sb; **estar de ~** to be on top of the world; **¡~!** congratulations!

enigma *m* enigma; **descifrar/plantear un ~** to unravel/to pose an enigma

enigmático, **-a** *adj* enigmatic; (*misterioso*) mysterious

enjabonar *vt* **1.** (*al lavar*) to soap **2.** *inf* (*dar coba*) to butter up, to sweet talk **3.** *inf* (*regañar*) to tick off

enjalbegar <g→gu> *vt* to whitewash

enjambre *m* **1.** (*de abejas*) swarm **2.** (*muchedumbre*) throng

enjaular *vt* (*encerrar*) to lock up; (*en una jaula*) to cage

enjetarse *vr Arg, Méx* **1.** (*enojarse*) to get angry **2.** (*ofenderse*) to take offence [*o* offense *Am*]

enjuagar <g→gu> *vt* to rinse

enjuague *m* **1.** *t.* TÉC rinse **2.** (*manejo*) rinsing **3.** (*líquido*) ~ **bucal** mouthwash

enjugamanos *m inv, AmL* hand-towel

enjugar <g→gu> **I.** *vt* **1.** (*secar*) to dry; (*limpiar*) to wipe (off) **2.** (*una deuda*) to write off **II.** *vr:* ~**se** **1.** (*secarse*) to dry **2.** (*adelgazar*) to lose weight

enjuiciar *vt* **1.** (*juzgar*) to analyze; (*censurar*) to criticize **2.** (*procesar*) to prosecute; (*sentenciar*) to sentence

enjutarse *vr Guat, Ven* **1.** (*enflaquecerse*) to become thin **2.** (*achicarse*) to get smaller; (*encogerse*) to shrink

enjuto, **-a** *adj* scrawny; ~ **de carnes** thin

enlace *m* **1.** (*conexión*) connection **2.** *t.* ELEC, FERRO (*empalme*) link; (*unión*) join; ~ **ferroviario** railroad link **3.** (*entrelazado*) joining **4.** (*boda*) wedding **5.** (*contacto*) link; ~ **policial** police informer **6.** QUÍM bond; (*sistema*) bonding **7.** INFOR link

enlatados *mpl Col* (*comestibles en latas*) tinned *Brit* [*o* canned *Am*] food

enlatar *vt* to tin *Brit,* to can *Am;* **programa enlatado** TV prerecorded programme [*o* program *Am*]

enlazar <z→c> **I.** *vi* (*transporte*) to link up **II.** *vt* **1.** (*atar*) to tie; (*unir*) to join; (*entrelazar*) to interlink **2.** *t.* ELEC, TÉC (*empalmar*) to connect **III.** *vr:* ~**se** (*casarse*) to marry

enloquecedor(a) *adj* maddening

enloquecer *irr como crecer* **I.** *vi, vr:* ~**se** to go out of one's mind, to go mad; ~ **de dolor** to be in terrible pain; ~ **de rabia** to be raging mad; ~ **por alguien** to be mad [*o* crazy] about sb **II.** *vt* to madden, to drive crazy; **me enloquecen los pasteles** I'm mad [*o* crazy] about cakes

enlozado *m AmL* enamel finish, glaze

enlozar <z→c> *vt AmL* to enamel, to glaze

enlucido *m* plaster

enlucir *irr como lucir vt* **1.** (*con yeso*) to plaster **2.** (*lustrar*) to polish

enlutar I. *vt* **1.** (*en el vestir*) to dress in mourning; **mujeres enlutadas** women dressed in mourning **2.** (*ensombrecer*) to darken; (*entristecer*) to sadden **II.** *vr:* **~se** to wear black

enmadrar *vr:* **~se** to be tied to one's mother's apron strings

enmarañar I. *vt* **1.** (*enredar*) to mix up **2.** (*confundir*) to confuse; (*complicar*) to complicate **II.** *vr:* **~se 1.** (*enredarse*) to get mixed up **2.** (*confundirse*) to get confused; (*complicarse*) to get complicated

enmarcar <c→qu> *vt* to frame; (*encajar*) to place

enmascarar I. *vt* **1.** (*poner máscara*) to mask; (*disfrazar*) to disguise **2.** (*ocultar*) to hide; (*encubrir*) to cover up **II.** *vr:* **~se 1.** (*con una máscara*) to wear a mask; (*disfrazarse*) to disguise oneself **2.** (*encubrirse*) to cover one's tracks

enmendar <e→ie> **I.** *vt* **1.** (*corregir*) to correct; ~ **la plana a alguien** to find fault with sb **2.** (*modificar*) to modify; (*una ley*) to amend **II.** *vr:* **~se** to mend one's ways

enmicar <c→qu> *vt Méx* (*cubrir con plástico*) to cover in plastic

enmienda *f* **1.** (*corrección*) correction; **no tener** ~ *fig* to be beyond repair **2.** (*modificación*) modification; (*de una ley*) amendment **3.** (*indemnización*) compensation

enmohecer *irr como crecer vi, vr:* **~se 1.** (*cubrirse de moho*) to go mouldy *Brit,* to go moldy *Am;* (*pudrirse*) to rot **2.** (*caer en desuso*) to become rusty

enmudecer *irr como crecer* **I.** *vi* **1.** (*perder el habla*) to be struck dumb; ~ **de miedo** to be struck speechless with fear **2.** (*callar*) to go silent **II.** *vt* to silence

ennegrecer *irr como crecer* **I.** *vt* **1.** (*poner negro*) to blacken **2.** (*oscurecer*) to darken; (*ensombrecer*) to sadden **II.** *vr:* **~se 1.** (*ponerse negro*) to blacken **2.** (*oscurecerse*) to darken; (*ensombrecer*) to sadden

ennoblecer *irr como crecer vt* **1.** (*conceder el título*) to ennoble **2.** (*mejorar*) to enhance; (*refinar*) to refine **3.** (*enaltecer*) to exalt; **nos ennoblece su presencia** we are honoured [*o* honored *Am*] by your presence

enojar I. *vt* **1.** (*enfadar*) to anger **2.** (*molestar*) to annoy **II.** *vr:* **~se 1.** (*enfadarse*) to get angry **2.** (*molestarse*) to get cross

enojo *m* **1.** (*enfado*) anger; **con** ~ angrily **2.** (*molestia*) annoyance

enojón, **-ona I.** *adj Chile, Ecua, Méx* (*enojadizo*) touchy **II.** *m, f Chile, Ecua, Méx* (*enojadizo*) a quick-tempered person

enojoso, **-a** *adj* **1.** (*enfadoso*) vexing **2.** (*molesto*) annoying **3.** (*complicado*) complicated; (*trabajoso*) strenuous

enorgullecer *irr como crecer* **I.** *vt* to fill with pride **II.** *vr:* **~se** to be proud

enorme *adj* enormous; (*gigantesco*) huge; (*desmedido, extraordinario*) remarkable, monstrous *pej*

enormidad *f* **1.** (*tamaño*) enormity; *fig* lot; **trabajó una** ~ he/she worked a lot **2.** (*cantidad*) great number; **una** ~ **de dinero** a lot of money

enrabiar I. *vt* to enrage **II.** *vr:* **~se** to get angry

enraizado, **-a** *adj* rooted; **una costumbre muy enraizada** a deep-seated tradition

enraizar *irr vi* to set [*o* put] down roots

enrastrojarse *vr AmL* to get dirty

enredadera *f* climbing [*o* trailing] plant

enredar I. *vi* (*niño*) to get into mischief; **¡no andes enredando con las cerillas!** don't play with the matches! **II.** *vt* **1.** (*liar*) to mix up; (*confundir*) to confuse **2.** (*enemistar*) to make enemies of **III.** *vr:* **~se 1.** (*cuerda, asunto*) to get mixed up **2.** (*planta*) to climb **3.** *inf* (*amancebarse*) to have an affair

enredo *m* **1.** (*de alambres*) tangle **2.** (*mentira*) troublemaking **3.** (*asunto*) muddle **4.** (*intriga*) intrigue **5.** (*engaño*) deceit **6.** (*amorío*) affair **7.** *pl, inf* (*trastos*) stuff

enrejado *m* (*de hierro*) grating; (*de caña*) fence

enrejar *vt* (*ventana*) to put a grating over; (*huerta*) to fence in

enrevesado, **-a** *adj* (*intrincado*) complicated; (*camino, carretera*) winding; (*difícil*) difficult

enriquecer *irr como crecer* **I.** *vt* **1.** (*hacer rico, engrandecer, metal, tierra*) to enrich **2.** (*adornar*) to embellish **II.** *vr:* **~se** to get rich; **~se** (**a costa ajena**) to get rich (at other people's expense)

enriquecimiento *m* enrichment; ~ **injusto** JUR embezzlement

enrocar *vi* (*ajedrez*) to castle

enrojecer *irr como crecer* **I.** *vi* to blush; ~ **de ira** to go red with anger; (*con fiebre*) to flush **II.** *vt* (*cielo*) to redden **III.** *vr:* **~se** (*persona*) to blush; (*cielo*) to redden

enrolar *vt* **1.** NÁUT to enrol *Brit,* to enroll *Am* **2.** MIL to enlist

enrollar I. *vt* (*cartel*) to roll up; (*cuerda*) to coil **II.** *vr:* **~se** *inf* **1.** (*extenderse demasiado*) to go on and on; **~se como una persiana** to talk the hind leg off a donkey **2.** (*ligar*) **~se con alguien** to take up with sb **3.** (*saber estar*) to get on well

enronquecer *irr como crecer* **I.** *vt* to make hoarse **II.** *vi, vr:* **~se** to go hoarse

enroscar <c→qu> **I.** *vt* **1.** (*enrollar*) to wind; ~ **el hilo en el palo** to wind the thread around the stick **2.** (*tornillo*) to screw in **3.** (*tapa*) to twist on **II.** *vr:* **~se** to curl up; **la**

serpiente se enroscó en la rama the snake coiled itself round the branch
enrostrar *vt AmL* to throw in one's face
enrular *vt CSur* to curl

Anyone who visits **Mallorca** brings **ensaimadas** with them, at least every Spanish tourist does. An **ensaimada** is a light spiral-shaped pastry that can be filled with sweet **cabello de ángel**, a type of mashed pumpkin filling.

ensalada *f* **1.** salad; ~ **de frutas** fruit salad **2.** (*confusión*) mix-up
ensaladera *f* salad bowl

Ensaladilla rusa: Take jacket potatoes, cooked vegetables (carrots, green beans, peas), olives, and hard-boiled eggs. Finely chop all these ingredients (similar to potato salad), then add tuna and dress the dish with mayonnaise and a little vinegar.

ensalmo *m* (*conjuro*) charm; (**como**) **por** ~ as if by magic
ensalzar <z→c> **I.** *vt* (*dignificar*) to dignify; (*alabar*) to praise **II.** *vr:* ~**se** to boast
ensamblar *vt* to assemble
ensanchar **I.** *vt* to widen **II.** *vr:* ~**se** to widen
ensanche *m* **1.** (*ampliación*) enlargement; (*de anchura*) widening **2.** (*ciudad*) suburb; **zona de** ~ area for urban development
ensangrentar <e→ie> *vt* to cover in blood
ensartar *vt* **1.** (*perlas*) to string **2.** (*pinchar*) to skewer **3.** (*hablar*) to reel off
ensayar **I.** *vt* **1.** TEAT to rehearse **2.** (*probar*) to test; (*examinar*) to examine **II.** *vr* ~**se en algo** to rehearse sth
ensayo *m* **1.** TEAT rehearsal; ~ **general** dress rehearsal **2.** LIT essay **3.** (*prueba*) test; (*experimento*) experiment; **tubo de** ~ test tube
enseguida *adv* at once, straight [*o* right] away
ensenada *f* **1.** (*mar*) inlet **2.** *Arg* (*corral*) meadow
enseña *f* insignia; (*estandarte*) standard
enseñante *mf* teacher
enseñanza *f* **1.** (*sistema*) education; ~ **primaria** primary education; ~ **privada** private education; ~ **pública** public education; ~ **secundaria** secondary education; ~ **superior** higher education **2.** (*docencia*) teaching; ~ **a distancia** distance learning; ~ **universitaria** university education; **método de** ~ teaching method; **dedicarse a la** ~ to be a teacher **3.** (*lección*) lesson; **de lo ocurrido en el pasado no has sacado ninguna** ~ you haven't learned anything from past events
enseñar *vt* **1.** (*instruir, dar clases*) to teach; (*explicar*) to explain; **él me enseñó la poca química que sé** he taught me the little I know about chemistry; **ella me enseñó a tocar la flauta** she taught me how to play the flute; **hay que** ~ **con el ejemplo** you have to lead by example; **¡la vida te** ~**á!** life is the best teacher!; **¡ya te** ~**é yo a obedecer!** I'll teach you a bit of obedience! **2.** (*mostrar*) to show; **te enseñé a hacer las camas** I showed you how to make beds; ~ **el camino a alguien** to show sb the way **3.** (*dejar ver*) to show; (*presentar*) to present; (*exhibir*) to exhibit
enseñorearse *vr* ~ **de algo** to take over sth
enseres *mpl* belongings *pl;* (*útiles*) tools *pl;* (*mobiliario*) goods *pl*
ensillar *vt* to saddle
ensimismarse *vr* **1.** (*absorberse*) to become absorbed; ~ **en recuerdos/una lectura** to become engrossed in one's memories/reading **2.** *Col, Chile* (*engreírse*) to become vain
ensoberbecerse *irr como crecer vr* (*persona*) ~ **de algo** to boast about sth
ensombrecer *irr como crecer* **I.** *vt* (*oscurecer*) to darken; (*ofuscar*) to cast a shadow over **II.** *vr:* ~**se** **1.** (*entristecerse*) to become sad **2.** (*oscurecerse*) to darken
ensoñación *f* daydream
ensopar **I.** *vt AmS* (*empapar*) to soak **II.** *vr:* ~**se** *AmS* to get soaked
ensordecedor(**a**) *adj* deafening
ensordecer *irr como crecer* **I.** *vi* (*quedarse sordo*) to go deaf **II.** *vt* (*ruido*) to deafen
ensortijado, **-a** *adj* curly
ensortijar *vt* (*pelo*) to curl
ensuciar **I.** *vt* to dirty **II.** *vr:* ~**se** **1.** (*mancharse*) to get dirty; ~**se de algo** to be stained with sth **2.** (*reputación*) to tarnish **3.** *inf* (*excremento*) to soil oneself
ensueño *m* dream; **de** ~ fantastic
entablar *vt* **1.** (*conversación*) to strike up; (*negociaciones*) to begin; (*amistad*) to establish; (*juicio*) to file; ~ **relaciones comerciales** to establish trade links **2.** (*suelo*) to put floorboards on **3.** (*ajedrez*) to set up
entablillar *vt* to splint
entallado, **-a** *adj* taken in at the waist
entallar **I.** *vt* (*vestido*) to take in at the waist **II.** *vi, vr:* ~**se** to fit; **la chaqueta entalla bien** the jacket fits well
entarimado *m* floorboards *pl*
ente *m* **1.** FILOS being **2.** (*autoridad*) body; **el Ente Público** the public sector **3.** (*persona*) geek
entecarse <c→qu> *vr Chile* (*emperrarse*) to be stubborn
enteco, **-a** *adj* sickly
entendederas *fpl inf* brains *pl;* **es muy corto de** ~ he's pretty dim [*o* dumb]
entendedor(**a**) *m(f)* expert ►**a buen** ~, **con pocas palabras bastan** *prov* a word to the wise is sufficient *prov*
entender <e→ie> **I.** *vi* **1.** (*comprender*) to understand **2.** (*saber*) ~ **mucho de algo** to know a lot about sth; **no** ~ **nada de algo** to know nothing about sth **II.** *vt* **1.** (*comprender*) to understand; **dar a** ~ **que...** to imply that

E

…; **dar a ~ a alguien que…** to give sb to understand that …; **lo entendieron mal** they misunderstood it; **si entiendo bien Ud. quiere decir que…** am I right in saying that what you mean is that …; **¿qué entiende Ud. por 'acuerdo'?** what do you understand by 'agreement'?; **ellos ya se harán ~** they'll soon make themselves understood; **no ~ ni jota/papa** *inf* not to understand a thing; **no entiende una broma** he/she can't take a joke **2.** (*creer*) to think; **yo entiendo que sería mejor si** +*subj* I think it would be better if; **yo no lo entiendo así** that's not the way I see it; **tengo entendido que…** (*según creo*) I believe that …; (*según he oído*) I've heard that … **III.** *vr:* **~se** **1.** (*llevarse*) to get on **2.** (*ponerse de acuerdo*) to agree; **para el precio entiéndete con mi socio** as regards the price, reach an agreement with my partner **3.** *inf* (*liarse*) to have an affair **4.** *inf* (*desenvolverse*) to manage; **no me entiendo con este lío de cables** I can't manage with this tangle of leads; **¡que se las entienda!** let him/her get on with it! **5.** (*expresiones*) **¡yo me entiendo!** I know what I'm doing!; **pero ¿cómo se entiende?** *inf* but what does it mean?; **eso se entiende por sí mismo** this is self-explanatory **IV.** *m* opinion; **a mi ~** the way I see it

entendido, **-a** **I.** *adj* **1.** (*listo*) clever, smart **2.** (*experto*) **~ en algo** expert on sth; **no se dio por ~** he pretended he hadn't heard **3.** (*claro*) **queda ~ que…** it is clear that …; **queda ~ que te acompaño a casa** of course I'll take you home; **bien ~ que…** on the understanding that … **II.** *m, f* expert; (*vinos*) connoisseur; **es un gran ~ en informática** he'a real expert on computers; **hacerse el ~** to act smart

entendimiento *m sin pl* **1.** (*razón*) reason; (*facilidad de comprensión*) understanding; **obrar con ~** to go about things reasonably; **un hombre de mucho ~** a very reasonable man **2.** (*acuerdo*) agreement

enterado, **-a** *adj* **~ de algo** (*iniciado*) aware of sth; (*conocedor*) knowledgeable about sth; **yo ya estaba ~ del incidente** I already knew about the incident; **no se dio por ~** he pretended not to have understood

enteramente *adv* wholly

enterar **I.** *vt* **1.** (*informar*) **~ de algo** to tell about sth **2.** *Méx, CRi, Hond* COM to pay **II.** *vr* **~ de algo** (*descubrir*) to find out about sth; (*saber*) to hear about sth; **me enteré de la explosión por la radio** I heard about the explosion on the radio; **no me enteré de nada hasta que me lo dijeron** I wasn't aware of anything until they told me; **pasa las hojas sin ~se de lo que lee** he/she spends hours reading without taking anything in; **¡para que se entere!** *inf* that'll teach him/her/you!; **para que te enteres…** for your information …

entereza *f sin pl* **1.** (*determinación*) strength of mind **2.** (*aplomo*) aplomb **3.** (*integridad*) integrity; **a la muerte de su madre demostraron mucha ~** they showed great fortitude when their mother died

enterizo, **-a** *adj* in one piece

enternecer *irr como crecer* **I.** *vt* **1.** (*ablandar*) to soften **2.** (*conmover*) to move; (*hacer ceder*) to make relent **II.** *vr:* **~se** (*conmoverse*) to be touched; (*ceder*) to relent

entero, **-a** *adj* **1.** (*completo*) *t.* MAT whole, entire; **por ~** completely; **se pasa días ~s sin decir ni una palabra** he/she goes for days at a time without speaking; **el espejo salió ~ de aquí** when the mirror left here it was in one piece; **la comisión entera se declaró a favor** the whole committee declared themselves to be in favour [*o* favor *Am*]; **el juego de café no está ~** some of the coffee service is missing **2.** (*persona integra*) honest

enterrador(a) *m(f)* (*sepulturero*) gravedigger

enterramiento *m* (*funeral*) burial; (*tumba*) grave

enterrar <e→ie> **I.** *vt* **1.** (*a un muerto*) to bury; **¡ésa nos ~á a todos!** *inf* she will outlive the lot of us! **2.** (*un objeto*) to bury; (*no muy profundo*) to cover up **3.** (*ilusiones, esperanzas*) to abandon **II.** *vr:* **~se** (*recluirse*) to hide oneself away

enterratorio *m AmS* (*cementerio*) Indian burial ground

entibiar **I.** *vt* (*líquido*) to cool; *fig* to soften **II.** *vr:* **~se** (*líquido*) to become lukewarm; *fig* to soften

entidad *f* **1.** (*asociación*) organization; **~ aseguradora** insurance firm; **~ crediticia** credit company; **~ jurídica** legal entity; **~ bancaria** bank **2.** (*importancia*) importance

entierro *m* **1.** (*inhumación*) burial; **¡no pongas esa cara de ~!** don't look so glum! **2.** (*funeral*) funeral **3.** (*comitiva*) funeral procession

entintar *vt* (*manchar*) to stain; (*teñir*) to dye; TIPO to ink

entonación *f* LING, MÚS intonation

entonar **I.** *vi* **1.** (*canción*) to sing in tune **2.** (*armonizar*) to go well; **los colores de las cortinas no entonan con los de la pared** the colours [*o* colors *Am*] of the curtains don't go well with the walls **II.** *vt* **1.** (*canción*) to sing **2.** (*fortalecer*) to liven up

entonces *adv* **1.** (*temporal*) then; **desde ~** from then on; **hasta ~** until then; **en** [*o* **por**] **aquel ~** at that time **2.** (*modal*) then; **¿y ~ qué pasó?** and what happened next?; **¿pues ~ por qué te extraña si no vienen?** then why are you surprised that they don't come?; **¡~!** I should think so!; **si lo amas ¿~ por qué no se lo dices?** if you love him, then why don't you tell him?

entontecer *irr como crecer* **I.** *vi, vr:* **~se** to become a moron **II.** *vt* to stupefy

entornar *vt* (*puerta*) to leave slightly open

entorno *m* surroundings *pl;* (*medio ambiente*) environment; (*mundillo*) world, sphere

entorpecer *irr como crecer vt* **1.** (*movimiento*) to make slow [*o* clumsy]; (*frío*) to numb; **el frío me entorpecía los dedos** the cold numbed my fingers **2.** (*dificultar*) to hamper; (*retrasar*) to slow down **3.** (*sentidos*) to dull

entrabar *vt AmS* to interfere

entrada *f* **1.** (*puerta*) entrance; (*para coche*) door; ~ **a la autopista** motorway slip road *Brit,* (entry) ramp *Am;* ~ **trasera** back door **2.** (*acción*) entrance; **hacer una** ~ to make an entrance; **se prohibe la** ~ no entry [*o* admittance] **3.** (*comienzo*) entry; (*en un cargo*) start; ~ **en funciones** starting date; ~ **en vigor** coming into force; **de** ~ right from the start; **así de** ~ **tu idea no me pareció mal** at first your idea didn't strike me as bad **4.** (*cine, teatro*) ticket; ~ **gratuita** free entry [*o* admission] **5.** (*público*) audience; **en el estreno hubo una gran** ~ a great number of people were at the première **6.** GASTR first course, entrée **7.** *pl* (*pelo*) **tiene ~s** his/her hair is receding **8.** MÚS entry; **dar la** ~ to enter **9.** (*en diccionario*) entry **10.** (*depósito*) deposit; **ya hemos dado la** ~ **para el coche** we've already paid the deposit [*o* down payment] for the car **11.** COM income; ~ **de pedidos** orders *pl* **12.** FIN **~s y salidas** income and costs **13.** INFOR input **14.** DEP tackle

entrado, -a *adj* **un señor** ~ **en años** an elderly gentleman; **llegamos entrada la noche** we arrived when it was already dark; **hasta muy** ~ **el siglo XVII** until well into the seventeeth century

entrador(a) *adj* **1.** *AmS* (*animoso*) spirited; (*atrevido*) daring **2.** *Arg* (*simpático*) friendly **3.** *AmL* (*enamoradizo*) romantic **4.** *Chile* (*entremetido*) interfering **5.** *Guat, Nic* (*compañero*) companionable

entrampar **I.** *vt* **1.** (*animal*) to trap **2.** (*engañar*) to deceive **3.** *inf* (*embrollar*) to mess up **4.** *inf* (*deudas*) to indebt *form* **II.** *vr:* **~se** to get into debt

entrante[1] *adj* (*próximo*) next; **a primeros del mes** ~ at the start of next month

entrante[2] *m* GASTR first course, starter

entraña *f* **1.** *pl* (*órganos*) entrails *pl;* **echar las ~s** *inf* to throw up; **¡hijo de mis ~s!** *inf* my darling child!; **por mis hijos doy las ~s** *inf* I'd give anything for my children **2.** (*lo esencial*) core **3.** *pl* (*carácter*) nature; **de buenas ~s** good-natured **4.** *pl* (*interior*) core; **las ~s de la tierra** the bowels of the earth

entrañable *adj* (*amistad*) intimate; (*película, persona*) endearing; (*recuerdo*) fond

entrañar *vt* to involve; ~ **graves peligros** to entail serious dangers

entrar **I.** *vi* **1.** (*pasar*) to enter; ~ **por la ventana** to come in through the window; ~ **por la fuerza** to break in; **el tren entra en la estación** the train enters the station; **me entró por un oído y me salió por otro** it went in one ear and out the other; ~ **con buen pie** to start off on the right foot; **¡entre!** come in! **2.** (*caber*) to fit; ~ **en el armario** to fit into the wardrobe [*o* closet *Am*]; **no me entra el anillo** I can't get the ring on; **el corcho no entra en la botella** the cork won't fit into the bottle; **por fin he hecho** ~ **el tapón** I've finally got the lid on **3.** (*penetrar*) to go in; **el clavo entró en la pared** the nail went into the wall; **¡no me entra en la cabeza cómo pudiste hacer eso!** I can't understand how you could do this! **4.** (*empezar*) to begin; ~ **en relaciones** to start a relationship; **el verano entra el 21 de junio** summer begins on the 21st of June; **después entré a trabajar en una casa más rica** afterwards I started working in a wealthier household; **cuando entró de alcalde** when he/she was elected mayor; **no** ~ **en detalles** not to go into details; ~ **en calor** to warm up; ~ **en vigor** to come into force; **me entró la tentación** I was tempted; **me entró un mareo** I became dizzy; **me entró el sueño** I became sleepy; **me entró el hambre** I became hungry **5.** (*como miembro*) ~ **en algo** to become a member of sth; ~ **en la Academia de Ciencias** to be admitted to the Royal Academy of Science **6.** (*formar parte*) **en un kilo entran tres panochas** you can get three corncobs to the kilo; **eso no entraba en mis cálculos** I hadn't reckoned on this; **en esta receta no entran huevos** there are no eggs in this recipe **7.** MÚS to come in **8.** DEP to tackle **9.** INFOR to access **10.** (*dar*) **esperemos que no te entre la gripe** we hope you don't get the flu; **le ha entrado la costumbre de...** he/she's got into the habit of ... **11.** *inf* (*entender*) **las matemáticas no me entran** I can't get the hang of mathematics **12.** *inf* (*soportar*) **su hermano no me entra** I can't stand his/her brother **13.** *inf* (*relacionarse, tratar*) **no sabe** ~ **a las chicas** he doesn't know how to chat up [*o* pick up] girls; **a él no sabes como ~le** you don't know how to deal with him **14.** (*opinar*) **yo en eso no entro** [*o* **ni entro ni salgo**] *inf* I've got nothing to do with this **II.** *vt* to put; ~ **el coche en el garaje** to put the car into the garage

entre *prep* **1.** (*dos cosas*) between; (*más de dos cosas*) among(st); **salir de** ~ **las ramas** to emerge from among(st) the branches; **pasar por** ~ **las mesas** to go between the tables; ~ **semana** during the week; **ven** ~ **las cinco y las seis** come between five and six; ~ **tanto** meanwhile; **lo cuento** ~ **mis amigos** I consider him as one of my friends; **un ejemplo** ~ **muchos** one of many examples; **el peor** ~ **todos** the worst of the lot; **llegaron veinte** ~ **hombres y mujeres** twenty men and women arrived; **se la llevaron** ~ **cuatro hombres** she was carried off by four men; **lo hablaremos** ~ **nosotros** we'll speak about it

E

among(st) ourselves; ~ **el taxi y la entrada me quedé sin dinero** what with the taxi and the ticket I had no money left; **lo dije ~ mí** I was speaking to myself; **¡guárdalo ~ los libros!** keep it amongst your books; **me senté ~ los dos** I sat down between the two of them **2.** MAT **ocho ~ dos son cuatro** eight divided by two is four

entreabierto, **-a** *adj* ajar

entreabrir *irr como abrir vt* to open slightly

entreacto *m* (*intermedio*) interval

entrecano, **-a** *adj* greying *Brit,* graying *Am*

entrecejo *m* (*ceño*) brow; **fruncir el ~** to frown

entrecomillar *vt* to put in inverted commas *Brit,* to put in quotes [*o* quotation marks]

entrecortado, **-a** *adj* (*respiración*) uneven, laboured *Brit,* labored *Am;* (*voz*) halting; **con la voz entrecortada por los sollozos** with a voice broken with sobs

entrecruzar <z→c> *vt, vr:* **~se** to interweave; (*miradas*) to cross; (*cintas*) to interlace

entredicho *m* **1.** (*prohibición*) ban **2.** (*duda*) **poner algo en ~** to put sth in question; **poner en ~ la veracidad** to question the truth

entrega *f* **1.** (*dedicación*) dedication **2.** (*fascículo*) instalment *Brit,* installment *Am;* **novela por ~s** serialized novel **3.** (*de documentos*) delivery; (*ceremonia*) giving; **~ de premios** prizegiving; **~ de títulos** UNIV graduation ceremony; **hacer ~ de algo** to hand sth over **4.** COM delivery; **~ a domicilio** home delivery; **talón de ~** delivery sheet; **pagadero a la ~** payable on delivery; **~ contra reembolso** collect on delivery **5.** MIL surrender; (*de prisioneros*) release

entregar <g→gu> **I.** *vt* **1.** (*dar*) to give, to hand over [*o* in]; **~la** *inf* to kick the bucket **2.** (*carta*) to deliver **3.** MIL to surrender; (*prisioneros*) to hand over **II.** *vr:* **~se 1.** (*desvivirse*) to take to; **~se a la bebida** to take to drink **2.** (*delincuente*) to give oneself up **3.** MIL to surrender **4.** (*sexo*) to yield

entrelazar <z→c> *vt, vr:* **~se** to join, to (inter)weave

entremedias *adv* **1.** (*local*) between; (*más de dos cosas*) amongst; **~ de...** somewhere between ... **2.** (*temporal*) meanwhile

entremeses *mpl* hors d'oeuvres *pl,* appetizers *pl Am*

entremeterse *vr* to interfere, to butt in *inf*

entremetido, **-a** **I.** *adj* interfering **II.** *m, f* busybody

entremezclar *vt* to intermingle

entrenador(**a**) *m(f)* DEP coach

entrenamiento *m* **1.** DEP training session **2.** (*práctica*) training

entrenar *vt, vr:* **~se** to train

entrepierna *f* **1.** (*muslo, pantalón*) crotch; **esto se me pasa por la ~** *vulg* I don't give a shit about this **2.** *Chile* (*de baño*) swimsuit

entreplanta *f* mezzanine

entresacar <c→qu> *vt* **1.** (*escoger*) to pick out; (*elegir*) to choose **2.** (*pelo*) to thin out

entresijo *m fig* secret; **los ~s** the ins and outs

entresuelo *m* mezzanine, first floor

entretanto *adv* meanwhile

entretecho *m CSur* (*desván*) attic

entretejer *vt* **1.** (*meter*) to weave in **2.** (*entrelazar*) to interweave

entretela *f* inner lining

entretener *irr como tener* **I.** *vt* **1.** (*divertir*) to entertain; **sabe cómo ~ a los niños** he/she knows how to entertain the children **2.** (*apartar la atención*) to distract **3.** (*asunto*) to delay; **~ a alguien con excusas** to keep giving sb excuses **4.** (*detener*) to hold up **II.** *vr:* **~se 1.** (*pasar el rato*) to amuse oneself; **~se con revistas** to amuse oneself by reading magazines **2.** (*tardar*) to delay; **¡no te entretengas!** don't dilly dally! **3.** (*apartar la atención*) to be distracted

entretenido, **-a** *adj* entertaining

entretenimiento *m* **1.** (*diversión*) entertainment; (*pasatiempo*) activity; **en el bosque hay mucho ~ para los niños** children can have a great time in the forest **2.** (*conservación*) upkeep

entretiempo *m sin pl* between season; (*primavera*) spring; (*otoño*) autumn

entrever *irr como ver vt* **1.** (*objeto*) to glimpse **2.** (*sospechar*) to surmise; (*intenciones*) to guess

entreverar **I.** *vt* to intermingle **II.** *vr:* **~se** *Arg, Perú* to jumble together

entrevero *m CSur* **1.** (*confusión*) jumble **2.** (*riña*) brawl **3.** (*escaramuza*) skirmish

entrevista *f* **1.** (*inteviú*) interview; **hacer una ~ a alguien** to interview sb; **~ de trabajo** job interview **2.** (*reunión*) meeting

entrevistar **I.** *vt* to interview **II.** *vr:* **~se** (*entrevista*) to be interviewed; (*reunión*) to have a meeting

entristecer *irr como crecer* **I.** *vt* to sadden **II.** *vr:* **~se** to be saddened

entrometerse *vr* to interfere

entrometido, **-a** *adj, m, f v.* **entremetido**

entroncar <c→qu> *vi* **1.** (*tener parentesco*) **~ con alguien** to be related to sb **2.** *AmL* (*tren*) to connect

entronque *m* **1.** (*parentesco*) relations *pl* **2.** *AmL* (*tren*) connection

entrucharse *vr Méx* **1.** (*entremeterse*) **~ en algo** to interfere with sth **2.** (*enamorarse*) **~ de alguien** to fall in love with sb

entuerto *m* (*agravios*) wrongdoing, offence *Brit,* offense *Am*

entumecerse *irr como crecer vr* (*frío*) to go numb; (*músculo*) to stiffen; (*hinchazón*) to swell

entumecido, **-a** *adj* (*frío*) numb; (*pierna, rígido*) stiff; (*hinchado*) swollen

enturbiar *vt* to darken

entusiasmar **I.** *vt* to enthuse **II.** *vr:* **~se** to get enthusiastic

entusiasmo *m sin pl* enthusiasm

entusiasta I. *adj* enthusiastic II. *mf* enthusiast
entusiástico, **-a** *adj* enthusiastic
enumeración *f* enumeration
enumerar *vt* to enumerate; (*escrito*) to set down
enunciado *m* 1. (*de problema*) setting out 2. (*texto*) summary 3. LING statement
enunciar *vt* (*explicar*) to set out; (*expresar*) to state
enunciativo, **-a** *adj* **oración enunciativa** declarative sentence
envalentonar I. *vt* to spur II. *vr:* **~se** to become brave
envanecer *irr como crecer* I. *vt* to make vain II. *vr:* **~se** 1. (*enorgullecerse*) to become proud 2. (*engreírse*) to become vain
envasar *vt* to package; (*en latas*) to tin *Brit,* to can *Am;* (*en botellas*) to bottle
envase *m* 1. (*paquete*) package; (*recipiente*) container; (*botella*) bottle 2. (*casco*) bottle; **~ sin retorno** non-returnable bottle 3. (*acción*) packing; **~ al vacío** vacuum packing
envejecer *irr como crecer vt, vr:* **~se** to age
envenenar *vt* to poison
envergadura *f* (*importancia*) magnitude; (*alcance*) scope; **de gran ~** far-reaching
envés *m* back
enviado, **-a** *m, f* envoy; **~ especial** PREN, TV, RADIO special correspondent
enviar <*1. pres:* envío> *vt* to send; **~ por correo** to post *Brit,* to mail *Am*
envidia *f* envy; **tener ~ a alguien** to envy sb; **tener ~ de algo** to be jealous of sth; **daba ~ verlo de lo guapo que iba** it made me envious to see how handsome he looked; **lo corroe la ~** he is eaten up by jealousy
envidiable *adj* enviable
envidiar *vt* to envy; **¡mucho tienes tú que ~le a ella!** *irón* you've got no reason to be jealous of her!
envidioso, **-a** *adj* envious
envío *m* sending; (*expedición*) issue; **~ a domicilio** home delivery; **~ contra reembolso** cash on delivery; **~ urgente** urgent delivery; **~ con valor declarado** declared value delivery; **gastos de ~** postage and packing *Brit,* shipping and handling *Am*
enviudar *vi* to be widowed; (*una mujer*) to become a widow; (*un hombre*) to become a widower
envoltorio *m* 1. (*lío*) bundle 2. (*embalaje*) wrapping 3. (*caramelo*) wrapper
envoltura *f* (*capa exterior*) covering; (*embalaje*) wrapping
envolver *irr como volver* I. *vt* 1. (*en papel*) to wrap; **~ con** [*o* **en**] **algo** to wrap up in sth 2. (*empaquetar, ropa*) to pack; **~ con** [*o* **en**] **algo** to pack in sth; (*para regalo*) to gift-wrap 3. (*implicar*) to involve 4. (*rodear*) to envelop II. *vr* **~se** to get involved; **el policía se envolvió en un asunto sospechoso** the policeman got mixed up in a shady business
envuelto, **-a** *pp de* **envolver**
enyesar *vt* to plaster
enzarzar *vr:* **~se en** to get involved [*o* entangled] in
enzima *m o f* enzyme
eñe *f* Ñ, ñ; **la letra ~** the letter ñ
eólico, **-a** *adj* wind; **central eólica** wind power plant
EP *f abr de* **Educación Primaria** primary education
epa *interj AmL* (*saludo*) hi!; (*llamar la atención*) hey!; (*accidente*) (wh)oops!
épica *f* epic
epicentro *m* epicentre *Brit,* epicenter *Am*
épico, **-a** *adj* epic; **poema ~** epic poem
epidemia *f* epidemic
epidermis *f inv* epidermis
epifanía *f* Epiphany, Twelfth Night
epígrafe *m* 1. (*título*) title 2. (*inscripción*) epigraph
epilepsia *f* epilepsy
epiléptico, **-a** *adj, m, f* epileptic
epílogo *m* (*de libro*) epilogue *Brit,* epilog *Am*
episcopal *adj* episcopal; **sede ~** bishop's palace
episodio *m* 1. *t.* MÚS, LIT, TV episode 2. (*etapa*) stage 3. (*suceso*) incident
epitafio *m* epitaph
época *f* 1. HIST epoch, age; **coches de ~** classic cars *pl;* **muebles de ~** antique furniture; **trajes de ~** historical [*o* period] costumes *pl;* **un invento que hizo ~** an epoch-making invention 2. (*tiempo*) time; **~ de las lluvias** rainy season; **es la ~ más calurosa del año** it is the hottest time of the year; **en aquella ~** at that time
epopeya *f* LIT epic
equidad *f sin pl* 1. (*justicia*) fairness 2. (*de precios*) equity
equilátero, **-a** *adj* MAT equilateral
equilibrado, **-a** *adj* balanced; (*sensato*) sensible
equilibrar *vt, vr:* **~se** to balance
equilibrio *m* 1. (*en general*) balance; **mantener el ~** to keep one's balance; **perder el ~** to lose one's balance; **para llegar a fin de mes tengo que hacer muchos ~s** *fig* I have to do a juggling act to make my money last until the end of the month 2. (*contrapeso*) counterweight 3. (*armonía, mesura*) balance
equilibrista *mf* tightrope artist
equino, **-a** *adj* equine
equinoccio *m* equinox
equipaje *m* (*maletas*) baggage, luggage *Am;* **entrega de ~s** baggage check-in; **exceso de ~** excess baggage; **registro de ~** baggage inspection; **hacer el ~** to pack; **~ de mano** hand baggage [*o* luggage *Am*]
equipal *m Méx* 1. (*silla de mimbre*) rustic wicker chair 2. (*silla de cuero*) leather chair
equipamiento *m* **~ de serie** AUTO standard equipment
equipar *vt* to equip; (*de ropa*) to fit out
equiparable *adj* comparable

equiparar *vt* **1.** (*igualar*) to put on the same level **2.** (*comparar*) to compare, to liken

equipo *m* **1.** (*grupo*) team; (*turno*) shift; ~ **gestor** management team; ~ **de investigadores** research team; **trabajo en** ~ teamwork **2.** DEP team; **carrera por ~s** team race; **caerse con todo el** ~ *inf* to completely fluff [*o* blow] it; **el** ~ **de casa/de fuera** the home/visiting team **3.** (*utensilios*) equipment; ~ **de alta fidelidad** hi-fi system; ~ **productivo** productive equipment; **bienes de** ~ capital goods *pl*

equis I. *adj inv* X; ~ **euros** X number of euros; **el señor** ~ Mr X **II.** *f inv* **1.** (*letra*) X, x; **la letra** ~ the letter x **2.** *Col* (*serpiente*) snake

equitación *f sin pl* horseriding; **escuela de** ~ horseriding [*o* riding] school

equitativamente *adv* equitably

equitativo, **-a** *adj* equitable; **hicieron un reparto** ~ **de las ganancias** they shared out the profits equally

equivalencia *f* equivalence

equivalente I. *adj* equivalent; **una cantidad** ~ **a diez dólares** an amount equivalent to ten dollars **II.** *m* equivalent; **el** ~ **a diez días de trabajo** the equivalent of ten days' work

equivaler *irr como valer vi* to be equivalent; **la negativa equivaldría a la ruptura de las negociaciones** saying no would mean the breakdown of negotiations; **lo que equivale a decir que...** which is the same as saying that ...

equivocación *f* mistake; (*error*) error; (*malentendido*) misunderstanding; (*confusión*) mix-up; **por** ~ by mistake

equivocadamente *adv* by mistake

equivocado, **-a** *adj* mistaken; **número** ~ wrong number

equivocar <c→qu> **I.** *vt* **1.** (*confundir*) to get wrong; **equivoqué los sobres de las cartas** I mixed up the envelopes for the letters **2.** (*desconcertar*) to throw **II.** *vr:* **~se** to be wrong; **~se en** [*o* **de**] **algo** to be wrong about sth; **~se de camino** to take the wrong way; **~se al escribir/al hablar** to make a mistake (when) writing/when speaking; **~se al hacer una cuenta** to make a mistake in one's calculations; **~se al leer** to misread; **~se de número** (**de teléfono**) to dial the wrong number; **~se de tranvía** to take the wrong tram; **~se de puerta** to take the wrong door

equívoco *m* (*doble sentido*) ambiguity; (*malentendido*) misunderstanding

equívoco, **-a** *adj* **1.** (*con dos sentidos*) ambiguous **2.** (*dudoso*) doubtful

era[1] *f* **1.** (*período*) era; ~ **postcomunista** the post-communist era; ~ **terciaria** tertiary era **2.** (*para trigo*) threshing floor

era[2] *3. imp de* **ser**

erario *m* revenue; **el** ~ **público** the public treasury

ere *f* R, r; **la letra** ~ the letter r

erección *f* **1.** (*del pene*) erection **2.** (*de monumentos*) building

erecto, **-a** *adj* (*tieso*) erect; (*cuerpo*) upright

eremita *mf* hermit

eres *2. pres de* **ser**

erguido, **-a** *adj* (*derecho*) upright

erguir *irr* **I.** *vt* to raise; ~ **el cuello** to straighten one's neck; **con la cabeza erguida** with one's head held high **II.** *vr:* **~se** **1.** (*ponerse de pie*) to stand up straight; (*en una silla*) to sit up (straight); **el perro se irguió sobre las patas traseras** the dog rose up on its hind legs **2.** (*engreírse*) to boast

erial I. *adj* fallow **II.** *m* fallow field

erigir <g→j> **I.** *vt* **1.** (*construir*) to build; ~ **un andamio** to put up scaffolding **2.** (*fundar*) to establish **3.** (*nombrar*) to appoint; **la erigieron presidente** she was named president **II.** *vr:* **~se** **1.** (*declararse*) **~se en algo** to declare oneself to be sth **2.** (*hacer de*) **~se en algo** to act as sth

erizado, **-a** *adj* **1.** BOT prickly **2.** (*pelo*) on end

erizar <z→c> **I.** *vt* **1.** (*el pelo*) to make stand on end; **el frío me erizó el vello** the cold gave me goose pimples; **el miedo me erizó los cabellos** I was so frightened my hair stood on end **2.** (*un asunto*) to complicate; **estar erizado de dificultades** to be full of problems; **la vida está erizada de espinas** life is full of difficulties; **el camino está erizado de obstáculos** the way is littered with obstacles **II.** *vr:* **~se** **1.** (*pelo*) to stand on end; **mis cabellos se ~on del susto** I was so shocked my hair stood on end; **se me erizó el vello de tanto frío** it was so cold I had goose pimples **2.** (*persona*) to stiffen

erizo *m* **1.** (*mamífero*) hedgehog **2.** (*pez*) globefish **3.** (*del castaño*) burr, shell **4.** (*de mar*) sea urchin **5.** *inf* (*persona*) grouch **6.** (*defensa*) spike

ermita *f* hermitage

ermitaño *m* hermit crab

ermitaño, **-a** *m, f* hermit

erogación *f* **1.** *Arg, Méx, Par* (*pago*) costs *pl* **2.** *Ven, Col* (*donativo*) contribution

erogar <g→gu> *vt Arg, Col* (*pagar*) to pay; (*bienes*) to distribute

erógeno, **-a** *adj* erogenous

erosión *f* **1.** (*desgaste*) wearing away, wear and tear; (*desaparición*) disappearance; ~ **monetaria** gradual devaluation **2.** GEO erosion **3.** (*de la piel*) graze **4.** (*de alguien*) decline; **sufrir** ~ to go into decline; (*perder influencia*) to lose influence; (*perder prestigio*) to lose prestige

erosionar I. *vt* **1.** (*desgastar*) to wear away **2.** GEO to erode; **el agua erosiona las rocas** water erodes rocks **3.** (*la piel*) to abrade **4.** (*a alguien*) to harm; **el artículo erosionó al partido** the article damaged the party **II.** *vr:* **~se** to decline; (*perder prestigio*) to lose prestige; (*perder influencia*) to lose influence

erótico, **-a** *adj* erotic

erotismo *m* eroticism, erotism

errabundo, **-a** *adj* (*sin orientación*) wandering; (*vagabundo*) vagrant

erradicar <c→qu> *vt* to eradicate; (*una planta*) to uproot; (*una institución*) to abolish; (*una enfermedad*) to stamp out

errar *irr* **I.** *vi* **1.** (*equivocarse*) to err; ~ **en algo** to make a mistake in sth; ~ **en la respuesta** to give the wrong answer; ~ **en el camino** to take the wrong road; *fig* to make the wrong choice **2.** (*andar vagando*) to wander; (*vagabundear*) to live on the streets; ~ **por algo** to roam around sth; **ir errando por las calles** to wander the streets **II.** *vt* (*no acertar*) to miss; ~ **la vocación** to choose the wrong career **III.** *vr* ~**se en algo** to make a mistake in sth

errata *f* errata

erre *f* RR, rr; **la letra** ~ the letter rr; ~ **que** ~ *inf* stubbornly; **él está,** ~ **que** ~**, empeñado en subir a la montaña** he absolutely insists on going up the mountain

erróneo, **-a** *adj* erroneous; **decisión errónea** wrong decision

error *m* **1.** (*falta*) fault; ~ **de cálculo** miscalculation; ~ **de operación** INFOR operative error; ~ **ortográfico** spelling mistake; ~ **freudiano** Freudian slip; **cometer un** ~ to make a mistake; **has cometido un** ~ **muy grave** you have made a very serious mistake **2.** (*equivocación*) mistake; (*descuido*) oversight; **estar en el** ~ to be wrong; **por** ~ by mistake **3.** FÍS, MAT (*diferencia*) error **4.** (*conducta reprochable*) misconduct **5.** JUR ~ **judicial** miscarriage of justice **6.** TIPO ~ **de imprenta** misprint

eructar *vi* to belch, to burp

eructo *m* belch, burp

erudición *f* erudition; (*sabiduría*) wisdom

erudito, **-a** **I.** *adj* **1.** (*persona*) erudite; ~ **a la violeta** *pey* pseudo-intellectual; (*sabio*) wise **2.** (*obra*) scholarly; **conocimientos** ~**s** extensive knowledge **II.** *m, f* scholar; (*sabio*) man of learning; (*experto*) expert; **es un** ~ **en filosofía** he is a philosophy scholar

erupción *f* **1.** GEO eruption; ~ **volcánica** volcanic eruption **2.** MED rash

es *3. pres de* **ser**

esa(**s**) *adj, pron dem v.* **ese**, **-a**

ésa(**s**) *pron dem v.* **ése**

esbeltez *f* **1.** (*delgadez*) slenderness **2.** (*altura*) height **3.** (*gracia*) grace **4.** (*elegancia*) elegance

esbelto, **-a** *adj* **1.** (*delgado*) slender **2.** (*alto*) tall **3.** (*grácil*) graceful **4.** (*elegante*) elegant; **un hombre** ~ a well-proportioned man

esbirro *m* **1.** *pey* (*que comete actos violentos*) henchman, goon *inf;* (*sicario*) assasin **2.** (*alguacil*) constable **3.** (*de las autoridades*) representative

esbozar <z→c> *vt* **1.** (*dibujo*) to sketch **2.** (*un tema*) to outline; ~ **un discurso** to summarize a speech **3.** (*una sonrisa*) **esbozó una sonrisa** a smile formed upon his/her lips

esbozo *m* **1.** (*dibujo*) sketch **2.** (*de un proyecto*) outline

escabechar *vt* **1.** GASTR to marinate **2.** *inf* (*suspender*) to fail **3.** *inf* (*matar*) to do in

escabeche *m* **1.** (*adobo*) marinade; **atún en** ~ pickled tuna; **poner en** ~ to marinade **2.** (*alimento: pescado*) pickled fish; ~ **de pollo** marinated chicken

escabechina *f* **1.** *inf* (*en un examen*) **en el examen hubo gran** ~ lots of people failed the exam **2.** (*destrozo*) damage; (*carnicería*) bloodbath; **hacer una** ~ to wreak havoc

escabel *m* (*taburete*) stool; (*para los pies*) footstool

escabroso, **-a** *adj* **1.** (*áspero*) rough; (*terreno*) uneven **2.** (*asunto*) thorny **3.** (*indecente*) obscene

escabullirse <*3. pret:* se escabulló> *vr* **1.** (*desaparecer*) to slip away; ~ (**por**) **entre la multitud** to slip away [*o* sneak off] through the crowd **2.** (*escurrirse*) to slip through; **la trucha se me escabulló** (**de entre las manos**) the trout slipped through my fingers

escacharrar **I.** *vt* **1.** (*objeto*) to break **2.** (*plan, proyecto*) to spoil; **la lluvia nos escacharró la fiesta** the rain spoilt the party; **escacharró nuestros planes** it wrecked our plans **II.** *vr:* ~**se** **1.** (*objeto*) to break; **se me ha escacharrado la escultura** my sculpture has broken **2.** (*plan, proyecto*) to be spoilt; **nuestros planes se** ~**on por culpa de la lluvia** our plans were spoilt by the rain

escafandra *f* diving [*o* wet] suit; ~ **autónoma** scuba diving outfit; ~ **espacial** space suit

escala *f* **1.** *t.* MÚS (*serie, proporción, de mapa*) scale; ~ **de colores** range of colours [*o* colors *Am*], colour [*o* color *Am*] scale; ~ **de cuotas** payment scale; ~ **de descuentos** range of discounts; ~ **de grados** degree scale; ~ **impositiva** tax bracketing; ~ **de reproducción** scale of reproduction; ~ **de Richter** Richter scale; ~ **de salarios**, ~ **de valores** set of values, salary scale; **a** ~ to scale; **hacer** ~**s** to do scales; **un mapa a** ~ **1:100.000** a map with a 1:100,000 scale; ~ **milimétrica** millimetre scale **2.** (*medida*) level; **a** ~ **mundial** on a world scale; **a** ~ **nacional** on a national scale; **en gran** ~ on a large scale; **comprar en gran** ~ to buy in bulk; **fabricación en gran** ~ large-scale production; **ser de mayor** ~ to be on a large scale **3.** (*parada, puerto*) stop; AVIAT stopover; ~ **forzada** forced landing; **el avión tuvo que hacer** ~ **en París** the plane had to land in Paris; **hacer** ~ **en un puerto** to make a stop at a port **4.** (*escalera*) ladder; ~ **de cuerda** rope ladder

escalada *f* **1.** (*subida*) climb, ascent; ~ **libre** free climbing; ~ **en roca** rock climbing **2.** (*a una posición, cargo*) promotion **3.** (*aumento*) increase; (*de un conflicto, la violencia*) escalation

escalafón *m* (*de cargos*) ranking; (*de sueldos*) salary scale; **subir en el** ~ to move up in the ranking

escalar **I.** *vi* **1.** (*en las montañas, socialmente*) to climb **2.** (*profesionalmente*) to rise

II. *vt* 1. (*subir*) to go up; (*una montaña*) to climb; **has escalado las cimas del poder** you have reached the summit of power 2. (*ladrón*) to break into; **~on la habitación por la ventana** they got into the room through the window 3. (*una posición*) to rise to; **escaló el cargo más alto de la empresa** he/she rose to the highest position in the company 4. MIL to escalate

escaldado, -a *adj* 1. (*quemado*) scalded 2. (*escarmentado*) cautious; **salir ~** to learn one's lesson

escaldadura *f Arg* (*lastimadura*) chafing

escaldar I. *vt* 1. (*metal*) to make red hot 2. MED to scald; (*inflamar*) to inflame II. *vr:* **~se** 1. (*persona*) to be scalded 2. (*piel*) to become chafed

escalera *f* 1. (*escalones*) staircase, stairs; AVIAT stairway; **~ abajo** downstairs; **~ arriba** upstairs; **~ de caracol** spiral staircase; **~ mecánica** [*o* **automática**] escalator; **~ de servicio** service stairs 2. (*escala*) ladder; **~ de bomberos** firemen's ladder; **~ de cuerda** rope ladder; **~ doble** stepladder; **~ de incendios** fire escape; **~ de mano** ladder; **~ de tijera** stepladder; **subir la ~** to go up the ladder 3. (*naipes*) run; **~ de color real** royal flush

escalfar *vt* to poach

escalinata *f* main staircase; (*fuera*) outside steps *pl*

escalofriante *adj* 1. (*pavoroso*) chilling; **película ~** scary film *Brit,* scary movie *Am* 2. (*asombroso*) hair-raising

escalofrío *m* 1. (*sensación*) chill; **al abrir la ventana sentí ~s** I felt a chill when I opened the window; **el libro me produjo ~s** the book sent shivers down my spine; **cierra la puerta, tengo ~s** close the door, I feel chilly 2. MED shiver

escalón *m* 1. (*de una escala*) rung; **~ lateral** side step 2. (*nivel*) step; **subir un ~** (*profesionalmente*) to move up the ladder; **este libro es un ~ hacia el éxito** this book is a stepping stone on the way to success; **descender un ~ en la opinión pública** to go down in the eyes of the public 3. MIL echelon

escalonado, -a *adj* 1. (*terreno*) terraced 2. (*precio*) graded; **tarifa escalonada** graded fare 3. (*horario, vacaciones*) staggered 4. (*pelo*) layered

escalonar *vt* 1. (*situar*) to spread out; **~ puestos de vigilancia** to set look-out posts at regular intervals 2. (*terreno*) to terrace 3. (*precio*) to grade 4. (*horarios, vacaciones*) to stagger 5. (*pelo*) to layer

escalope *m* escalope; **~ a la vienesa** Wiener schnitzel

escalpelo *m* scalpel

escama *f* 1. (*placa*) *t.* ZOOL, BOT scale; **~s de jabón** soap flakes; **tener más ~s que un besugo** *fig* to be impossible to resolve 2. *inf* (*recelo*) suspicion; **le salieron ~s** he/she began to have doubts

escamado, -a *adj* 1. (*piel, superficie*) scaly 2. *inf* (*receloso*) cautious

escamar I. *vt* 1. (*el pescado*) to scale 2. *inf* (*inquietar*) to make suspicious II. *vr:* **~se** *inf* to smell a rat; **me escamé al oír la noticia** I was worried when I heard the news; **me escamé de tu respuesta** I was suspicious of your response

escamocha *f Méx* (*sobras*) leftovers *pl*

escamoso, -a *adj* scaly; (*piel*) flaky

escamotear *vt* 1. (*ilusionista*) to whisk out of sight 2. (*quitar*) to remove; (*robar*) to palm 3. (*ocultar*) to hide; (*información*) to withhold; **~ la verdad/un asunto** to cover up the truth/a matter

escampar *vimpers* **espera hasta que escampe** wait until it clears

escanciar *vt* to pour

escandalizar <z→c> I. *vi* to cause an upset II. *vt* 1. (*indignar*) to scandalize 2. (*horrorizar*) to horrify 3. (*impactar*) to shock 4. (*alborotar*) **ayer por la noche escandalizaste la casa con tus gritos** last night you woke up the whole house with your shouting III. *vr:* **~se** 1. (*indignarse*) **~se de** [*o* **por**] **algo** to be scandalized by sth 2. (*estar horrorizado*) **~se de** [*o* **por**] **algo** to be horrified at sth

escándalo *m* 1. (*ruido*) uproar; **armar un** [*o* **dar el**] **~** to make a scene; **se armó un ~** there was a terrible uproar 2. (*hecho inmoral*) scandal; **~ público** public scandal; **causar ~** to cause a scandal; **la piedra del ~** the root of the scandal; **estos precios son un ~** these prices are outrageous; **tu comportamiento es un ~** your behaviour [*o* behavior *Am*] is a disgrace; **de ~** scandalous 3. (*pasmo*) **¡qué ~!** can you believe it?

escandaloso, -a *adj* 1. (*ruidoso*) noisy; (*alborotado*) uproarious 2. (*inmoral, irritante*) scandalous; **precios ~s** outrageous prices 3. (*revoltoso*) unruly; **esta clase es escandalosa** this class is rowdy [*o* out of control]

Escandinavia *f* Scandinavia

escandinavo, -a *adj, m, f* Scandinavian

escanear *vt* to scan

escáner *m* scanner

escaño *m* 1. (*banco*) bench 2. POL (*acta de diputado*) seat

escapada *f* (*huida*) escape; (*viaje*) short trip

escapar I. *vi* 1. (*de la cárcel, de un peligro*) to escape; (*de un encierro*) to evade; **logré ~** I managed to escape; **es imposible ~ a esta ley** it is impossible to dodge this law 2. (*deprisa, ocultamente*) to get away; **~ de casa** to run away from home; **el ladrón escapó por la ventana** the thief got away through the window II. *vr:* **~se** 1. (*de la cárcel, de un peligro*) to escape; (*de un encierro*) to evade 2. (*deprisa, ocultamente*) to get away; **~se de casa** to run away from home; **el ladrón se escapó por la ventana** the thief got away through the window; **algunas cosas se escapan al poder de la voluntad** some things are beyond one's power **3.** (*agua, gas*) to leak **4.** (*decir*) to come out; **se me ha escapado que te vas a casar** I let it slip that you were getting married **5.** (*soltarse*) to get away; **se escapó un tiro** a shot was let loose; **se me ha escapado su nombre** I've forgotten your name; **se me ha escapado el autobús** I've missed the bus; **se me ha escapado la mano** my hand slipped; **se me ha escapado la risa** I couldn't help laughing; **se me escapó un suspiro** I let out a sigh **6.** (*pasar inadvertido*) to go unnoticed; **no se te escapa ni una** you don't miss a thing

escaparate *m* **1.** (*de una tienda*) shop window; **estar en el ~** *fig* to be in the limelight **2.** (*estantería*) bookcase **3.** *AmL* (*armario*) dresser **4.** *inf* (*pecho*) cleavage; **tener mucho ~** to have a big cleavage

escaparatista *mf* window dresser [*o* decorator]

escapatoria *f* **1.** (*lugar*) escape; **no hay ~** *fig* there's no way out **2.** (*excusa*) excuse **3.** (*solución*) way out; **es la única ~ que tienes** it's your only way out; **no tener ~** to have no way out; (*cláusula*) loophole

escape *m* **1.** (*de un gas, líquido*) leak **2.** (*solución*) way out; **no tenía ~** (*de una amenaza*) there was no way out; **no había ningún ~ a la situación** there was no way out of the situation **3.** (*rápidamente*) **a ~** like a shot; **dame a ~ las tijeras** quickly, pass me the scisssors

escápula *f* shoulder blade

escaquearse *vr inf* to skive off

escarabajo *m* beetle

escaramujo *m* wild [*o* dog] rose

escaramuza *f* **1.** (*lucha*) skirmish **2.** (*discusión*) row

escarapelar I. *vt* **1.** *Col, CRi, Méx* (*descascarar*) to peel **2.** *Col* (*manosear*) to handle; (*ajar*) to wear out **II.** *vr:* **~se** *Méx, Perú* **1.** (*atemorizarse*) to be scared **2.** (*temblar*) to shudder

escarbar I. *vi* **1.** (*en la tierra*) **~ en algo** to dig sth **2.** (*escudriñar*) **~ en algo** to investigate sth; (*entremeterse*) to pry into sth **II.** *vt* **1.** (*la tierra*) to dig up; **~ la arena** to dig up sand **2.** (*la lumbre*) to poke **3.** (*tocar*) **~ algo** to pick at sth **4.** (*limpiar*) to clean; **~ los dientes** to pick one's teeth **5.** (*investigar*) to investigate; (*entremeterse*) to pry into **III.** *vr:* **~se** to pick; **no te escarbes la herida** don't pick at the sore; **~se las orejas** to scratch [*o* pick] one's ears

escarceo *m* **1.** *pl* (*divagaciones*) distractions *pl;* **~s políticos** political comings and goings; **sin ~s** without hesitation; **~ amoroso** fling **2.** *pl* (*vueltas*) prancing; **el caballo dio ~s** the horse pranced about **3.** (*oleaje*) ripple

escarcha *f* frost

escarchar I. *vt* (*frutas*) to crystallize **II.** *vimpers* **ha escarchado** it's frosty

escarlata *adj* scarlet

escarlatina *f* MED scarlet fever

escarmentar <e→ie> **I.** *vi* **1.** (*desengañarse*) to realize the truth; **~ en cabeza ajena** to learn from sb else's mistakes **2.** (*enmendarse*) to learn one's lesson **II.** *vt* **1.** (*castigar*) to punish **2.** (*reprender*) to reprimand **3.** (*desengañar*) to teach a lesson; **quedar** [*o* **estar**] **escarmentado de algo** to learn one's lesson from sth

escarmiento *m* **1.** (*lección*) lesson; **me sirvió de ~** it taught me a lesson **2.** (*penalización*) punishment; (*pena*) sentence

escarnecer *irr como crecer vt* (*burlarse*) to mock; (*ridiculizar*) to deride

escarnio *m* scorn; **con ~** scornfully

escarola *f* curly endive

escarpado, -a *adj* (*terreno*) rugged; (*montaña*) steep and craggy

escarpia *m* hook

escasamente *adv* scarcely; **hace ~ dos horas que se han ido** they left only two hours ago

escasear I. *vi* **1.** (*faltar*) to be scarce; **escasea la leche** milk is scarce **2.** (*ir a menos*) to diminish **II.** *vt* (*dar con escasez*) to skimp on

escasez *f* **1.** (*insuficiencia*) shortage; **comprar con ~** to spend sparingly **2.** (*falta*) shortage; **~ de lluvias** lack of rain; **~ de viviendas** housing shortage; **una región con ~ de agua** a region with scarce rainfall **3.** (*pobreza*) neediness; **vivir con ~** to live in need

escaso, -a *adj* **1.** (*insuficiente*) insufficient, scant(y); (*tiempo*) little; **~ de palabras** of few words; **viento ~** light wind; **andar ~ de dinero** to be short of money; **estar ~ de tiempo** to be short of time; **tener escasas posibilidades de ganar** to have little chance of winning; **en dos horas escasas** in only two hours **2.** (*mezquino*) mean

escatimar *vt* to skimp; **no ~ gastos/medios** not to skimp on costs/means; **~ el aplauso a alguien/algo** to be sparing in the applause for sb/sth; **me escatimó parte del dinero** he/she didn't give me some of the money

escayola *f* **1.** (*yeso*) plaster **2.** MED plaster; **¿cuándo te quitan la escayola?** when are they taking the plaster off? **3.** (*estuco*) stucco

escayolar *vt* MED to put a plaster-cast on; **llevar el brazo escayolado** to have an arm in plaster

escena *f* **1.** (*parte del teatro*) stage; **aparecer en ~** to appear on stage; **poner en ~** to stage; **puesta en ~** staging; **salir a la ~** to go on stage; **salir de la ~** to go off stage **2.** (*lugar, parte de una obra*) scene; **~ final** final scene; **cambio de ~** change of scene; **~ del crimen** scene of the crime; **desaparecer de ~** (*marcharse*) to leave the scene; (*morirse*) to pass on; **poner en ~** to put on stage; **salir a ~** (*aparecer*) to make an appearance **3.** (*arte*) theatre *Brit,* theater *Am;* **dedicarse a la ~** to devote oneself to the stage **4.** LIT scene **5.** (*suceso, reproche*) scene; **~ de celos** display of jealousy; **hacer una ~ ridícula** to make a ridiculous scene

escenario *m* 1. (*parte del teatro*) stage 2. (*lugar, situación*) scene; ~ **del crimen** scene of the crime; **un cambio de** ~ a change of scene

escénico, **-a** *adj* scenic; **efectos** ~**s** stage effects *pl;* **escuela de arte** ~ drama school; **palco** ~ stage

escenografía *f* 1. (*decoración*) set design 2. (*decorados*) set

escenógrafo, **-a** *m, f* set designer

escepticismo *m sin pl* (*desconfianza*) scepticism *Brit,* skepticism *Am*

escéptico, **-a** I. *adj* (*desconfiado*) sceptical *Brit,* skeptical *Am;* **ser** ~ **respecto a algo** to be sceptical [*o* skeptical *Am*] about sth II. *m, f* sceptic *Brit,* skeptic *Am;* **es un** ~ **de la homeopatía** he doesn't take homoepathy seriously

escindir I. *vt* 1. (*dividir*) to divide; (*partido*) *t.* FÍS to split 2. (*separar*) to separate 3. (*cortar*) to split II. *vr:* ~**se** 1. (*dividirse*) ~**se en algo** to divide into sth; (*partido*) to split into sth 2. (*separarse*) to separate

escisión *f* 1. (*división*) division; (*de un partido*) split; *t.* FÍS splitting 2. (*separación*) separation; MED excision

esclarecer *irr como crecer vt* 1. (*explicar*) to clear up; (*un crimen, misterio*) to shed light upon; ~ **un asunto** to clear up a matter 2. (*iluminar*) to illuminate 3. (*afamar*) ~ **a alguien** to make sb famous

esclarecido, **-a** *adj* 1. (*ilustre*) great; (*famoso*) famous 2. (*lugar*) clear

esclarecimiento *m* 1. (*explicación*) explanation 2. (*fama*) fame 3. (*iluminación*) illumination

esclavitud *f* 1. (*sistema*) slavery, servitude; **someter a la** ~ to submit to slavery 2. (*dependencia*) dependence

esclavizar <z→c> I. *vt* 1. (*cautivar*) to enslave 2. (*dominar*) to control; ~ **a alguien** (*hacer depender*) to make sb dependent; **la empresa te ha esclavizado** you're a slave to the company II. *vr:* ~**se** to become a slave

esclavo, **-a** I. *adj* 1. (*cautivo*) slave 2. (*dominado*) dependent; (*obediente*) obedient; **eres esclava de tu familia** you do everything your family wants; **ser** ~ **del alcohol** to be a slave to alcohol II. *m, f* slave; **ser el** ~ **de alguien** (*obedecer*) to be sb's slave; (*estar enamorado*) to be at sb's command; **ser un** ~ **de algo** *fig* to be dependent on sth; **eres un** ~ **del alcohol** you can't live without alcohol

esclerosis *f inv* sclerosis; ~ **múltiple** multiple sclerosis

esclusa *f* 1. (*recinto*) lock; TÉC sluice 2. (*puerta*) lock gate

escoba *f* 1. (*para barrer*) broom, brush *Brit;* **no vender ni una** ~ *inf* to be completely useless; (*de bruja*) broomstick 2. BOT broom 3. *inf* (*mujer*) frump

escobazo *m* 1. (*golpe*) knock [*o* smack] with a brush; **echar a alguien a** ~**s** *inf* to throw sb out 2. *Arg, Chile* (*barredura*) **dar un** ~ **al suelo** to give the floor a quick sweep

escobilla *f* 1. (*cepillo*) *t.* ELEC brush; (*de baño*) toilet brush 2. (*escoba*) broom 3. (*brezo*) heather 4. (*cardencha*) teasel 5. (*del limpiaparabrisas*) windscreen wiper pad *Brit,* windshield wiper blade *Am* 6. (*plumero*) feather duster

escobillar I. *vi AmL* (*zapatear*) to tap or shuffle the feet II. *vt* to brush

escocedura *f* 1. (*picor*) smarting, stinging 2. (*irritación*) inflammation; (*ampolla*) blister

escocer *irr como cocer* I. *vi* 1. (*picar*) to sting 2. (*ofender*) to be offended; (*irritar*) to be annoyed; **no me escuece que no me hayan invitado** I'm not annoyed at not being invited II. *vr:* ~**se** 1. (*inflamarse*) to redden 2. (*dolerse*) to be sore; (*enfadarse*) to get angry

escocés *m* 1. (*lengua*) (Scottish) Gaelic 2. (*tela*) tartan 3. (*bebida*) Scotch

escocés, **-esa** I. *adj* Scottish; **cuadros escoceses** tartan; **falda escocesa** kilt; (*para mujeres*) tartan skirt II. *m, f* Scot, Scotsman *m,* Scotswoman *f*

Escocia *f* Scotland

escoger <g→j> I. *vi* to choose; **no has sabido** ~ you've made the wrong choice II. *vt* 1. (*elegir, seleccionar*) to choose 2. (*decidirse*) to decide

escogido, **-a** *adj* 1. *ser* (*selecto*) finest; (*persona*) upper class; **mercancías escogidas** top quality goods 2. *estar* (*elegido*) taken; **estos plátanos están ya muy** ~**s** all the good bananas have gone

escolar I. *adj* academic; **curso** ~ academic year; **edad** ~ school-going age II. *mf* schoolboy *m,* schoolgirl *f*

escolaridad *f* (*en una escuela*) schooling, education; **libro de** ~ reports *pl;* **la** ~ **es obligatoria** education is compulsory; **perder la** ~ not to be eligible to take an exam

escolarización *f* education; ~ **obligatoria** compulsory education; **esta región tiene una tasa de** ~ **muy baja** this area has a very low enrolment [*o* enrollment *Am*]

escolarizar <z→c> *vt* to educate; ~ **una región** to educate a region

escolero, **-a** *m, f Perú* (*escolar*) schoolboy *m,* schoolgirl *f*

escollar *vi* 1. (*barco*) to hit a reef 2. *Arg, Chile* (*proyecto*) to fail

escollo *m* 1. (*peñasco*) rock; (*dificultad*) difficulty 2. (*riesgo*) pitfall; **sortear un** ~ to overcome an obstacle

escolta *f* 1. MIL (*acompañante*) escort; **buque de** ~ escort ship; **dar** ~ **a alguien** to escort sb 2. (*acompañamiento*) escort 3. (*guardaespaldas*) bodyguard; (*guardia*) guard

escoltar *vt* to escort

escombrera *f* tip *Brit,* dump *Am*

escombro(s) *m(pl)* rubble; **hacer** ~ *Arg* to exaggerate

esconder I. *vt* (*ocultar*) to hide; (*tapar*) cover

up; **su comportamiento esconde alguna intención** his/her behaviour [*o* behavior *Am*] is trying to hide something; **el fondo del mar esconde muchas riquezas** the ocean bed has many secret treasures **II.** *vr:* **~se** (*persona, cosas*) to hide

escondidas *adv* **a ~** secretly; **a ~ del profesor** behind the teacher's back

escondido, -a *adj* **1.**(*secreto*) hidden; **en ~** hidden away **2.**(*retirado*) remote

escondido(s) *m(pl) AmL* hide and seek

escondite *m* **1.**(*juego*) hide and seek; **jugar al ~** to play hide and seek **2.**(*lugar*) hiding place

escondrijo *m* hideout

escopeta *f* (*arma*) shotgun; **~ de aire comprimido** air rifle [*o* gun *Am*]; **~ de cañones recortados** sawn-off shotgun

escopetear *vt* **1.** *Méx* (*con indirectas*) to be snide about **2.** *Ven* (*contestar mal*) to give an unpleasant reply to

escorbuto *m* scurvy

escorchar *vt Arg* (*molestar*) to annoy; (*enfadar*) to anger; **¡no me escorches la paciencia!** don't try my patience!

escoria *f* **1.**(*residuo mineral*) slag **2.**(*hez*) dregs *pl* **3.**(*despreciable*) scum; **la ~ de la sociedad** the scum of society

Escorpio *m* Scorpio

escorpión *m* (*alacrán*) scorpion

Escorpión *m* Scorpio

escotado *m* neckline

escotado, -a *adj* with a low neckline; **lleva un vestido muy ~** she's wearing a dress with a plunging neckline

escotadura *f* (*cortadura*) cut; (*en el cuello*) neckline

escotar **I.** *vt* **1.**(*cortar un escote*) to cut **2.**(*ajustar*) to cut to fit **3.**(*pagar*) to pay one's share **II.** *vi* **~ entre todos** to club together (to buy sth)

escote *m* **1.**(*en el cuello*) neckline; **~ en pico** V-neck **2.**(*busto*) bust **3.**(*dinero*) share; **pagar a ~** to split the price; **pagaron la cena a ~** they went Dutch on the dinner bill

escotilla *f* hatchway

escozor *m* **1.**(*picor*) burning **2.**(*resentimiento*) resentment **3.**(*pena*) pain

escrachar *vt* **1.** *AmL* (*tachar*) to strike out, to eliminate **2.** *PRico* (*estropear*) to ruin **3.** *Arg, inf* (*arruinar*) to wreck

escracho *m RíoPl* **1.**(*cara fea*) mug *inf* **2.**(*esperpento*) fright

escribanía *f* **1.**(*juego*) writing set **2.**(*mueble*) desk **3.** *AmL* (*notaría*) notary

escribano *m* **1.**(*notario*) notary **2.**(*secretario judicial*) court clerk **3.**(*amanuense*) scribe **4.** ZOOL bunting

escribiente *mf* scribe

escribir *irr* **I.** *vi, vt* write; **~ algo a mano** to write sth by hand; **~ algo a máquina** to typewrite sth; **escrito a mano** handwritten; **escrito a máquina** typewritten; **¿cómo se escribe tu nombre?** how do you spell your name? **II.** *vr:* **~se** to write (to each other); **se escriben mucho** they write to each other a lot; **estaba escrito que acabarían casándose** it was in their stars to get married

escrito *m* **1.**(*carta*) letter; (*nota*) note; **por ~** in writing **2.**(*literario, científico*) text; JUR brief, writ **3.** *pl* (*obras*) writings *pl;* **los ~s de Oscar Wilde** Oscar Wilde's works

escrito, -a **I.** *pp de* **escribir** **II.** *adj* written; **con la emoción escrita en su cara** with excitement written all over his/her face

escritor(a) *m(f)* writer

escritorio *m* **1.**(*mesa*) desk **2.**(*oficina*) office **3.** INFOR desktop

escritura *f* **1.**(*acto*) writing **2.**(*signos*) script; **~ fonética** phonetic script **3.**(*documento*) deed; **~ de propiedad** title deeds; **~ de hipoteca** mortgage deeds; **~ de seguro** insurance certificate; **~ social** company registration; **mediante ~** in writing; **las Sagradas Escrituras** REL the Holy Scriptures

escriturar *vt* to put down in deed

escroto *m* scrotum

escrúpulo *m* **1.**(*duda*) scruple; **~s de conciencia** pangs of conscience; **ser una persona sin ~s** to be completely unscrupulous; **no tener ~s en hacer algo** to have no qualms about doing sth **2.**(*escrupulosidad*) scrupulousness **3.**(*asco*) disgust; **me da ~ beber de latas** I think it's disgusting to drink out of cans

escrupulosidad *f* scrupulousness

escrupuloso, -a *adj* **1.**(*meticuloso*) scrupulous **2.**(*honrado*) principled **3.**(*quisquilloso*) fussy

escrutar *vt* **1.**(*mirar*) to scrutinize **2.**(*recontar*) to count

escrutinio *m* **1.**(*examen*) scrutiny **2.**(*recuento*) count **3.**(*votación*) vote

escuadra *f* **1.**(*para dibujar*) set square; **~ de delineante** draughtsman's [*o* draftsman's *Am*] square; **a ~** at right angles **2.**(*de apoyo, fijación*) bracket **3.** MIL (*de infantería*) squad; (*de naves, aviones*) squadron **4.** MIL (*cargo*) (squad) corporal **5.**(*cuadrilla*) team **6.** DEP corner (of the net)

escuadrilla *f* AVIAT squadron

escuadrón *m* MIL squadron

escuálido, -a *adj* (*flaco*) scrawny; (*macilento*) emaciated

escualo *m* shark

escucha¹ *m* MIL scout

escucha² *f* (*de conversaciones*) listening; **~ telefónica** telephone tapping; **servicio de ~** monitoring service; **estar a la ~** to be listening; **~ electrónica** electronic surveillance

escuchar **I.** *vi* **1.**(*atender*) to listen **2.**(*en secreto*) to eavesdrop **3.**(*obedecer*) to pay attention **II.** *vt* **1.**(*oír*) to listen to; (*seguir*) to follow; (*en secreto*) to eavesdrop; **~ un concierto** to listen to a concert; **~ una conversación telefónica** to tap into a telephone conversation; **~ (la) radio** to listen to the radio

2. (*prestar atención*) to pay attention; **¡escúchame bien!** pay attention to what I'm saying! **III.** *vr:* **~se** to like the sound of one's own voice

escuchimizado *adj inf* puny

escudar **I.** *vt* (*proteger*) to shield **II.** *vr* **1.** (*excusarse*) **~se en algo** to use sth as an excuse **2.** (*ampararse*) **~se con algo** to take refuge in sth

escudería *f* DEP racing car team

escudilla *f* bowl

escudo *m* **1.** (*arma*) shield **2.** (*amparo*) defence *Brit,* defense *Am;* (*persona*) protector **3.** (*emblema*) **~** (**de armas**) coat of arms **4.** (*moneda*) escudo (*monetary unit of Chile and Portugal*)

escudriñar **I.** *vt* **1.** (*examinar*) to scrutinize; (*una habitación*) to search **2.** (*mirar*) to scour; **~ el cielo en busca de aviones** to scour the skies in search of planes **II.** *vi* **~ en la intimidad de alguien** to invade sb's privacy

escuela *f* **1.** (*institución, edificio*) school; (*de enseñanza primaria*) primary school, elementary school; **Escuela de Bellas Artes** School of Fine Arts; **~ de conducir** driving school; **~ de idiomas** language school; **~ normal** teacher training college; **~ de párvulos** nursery school; **~ superior técnica** polytechnic; **~ taller** workshop **2.** (*método de enseñanza*) method **3.** (*conocimientos*) teaching; **ha tenido buena ~** he/she has been well taught; **la vida es la mejor ~** life is the best teacher **4.** (*estilo, seguidores*) school; **la ~ holandesa/de Durero** the Dutch school/the Dürer school; **su ejemplo ha hecho ~** his/her work has set an example **5.** (*doctrina*) belief

escueto, **-a** *adj* **1.** (*sin adornos*) bare **2.** (*lenguaje*) concise; *pey* curt; **explicar algo de forma escueta** to explain sth briefly **3.** (*desembarazado*) frank

escuincle *m Méx, inf* (*chiquillo*) baby, kid

esculcar <c→qu> *vt AmC, Col, Méx* (*registrar*) to go through

esculpir *vt* **1.** (*modelar*) to sculpt; **~ a cincel** to sculpt using a chisel; **~ en madera** to carve in wood; **~ una figura en mármol** to sculpt a figure in marble **2.** (*grabar*) to engrave

escultor(**a**) *m(f)* sculptor *m,* sculptress *f;* **~ de madera** wood carver

escultura *f* sculpture; **~ de madera** wood carving

escultural *adj* **1.** (*escultórico*) sculptural; **arte ~** sculpture **2.** (*bello*) statuesque; **esta chica tiene medidas ~es** this girl has got beautiful curves

escupidera *f* **1.** (*para escupir*) spittoon **2.** *AmL* (*orinal*) chamberpot

escupir **I.** *vi* **1.** (*por la boca*) to spit **2.** *inf* (*contar*) to spit it out **II.** *vt* **1.** (*por la boca*) to spit out; **~ sangre** to spit blood **2.** (*pagar*) to cough up **3.** (*arrojar*) to give out; **~ fuego** to belch smoke; **el volcán escupe lava** the volcano spits lava **4.** (*tratar mal*) to abuse; **~ a alguien** to insult sb **5.** *inf* (*decir*) to spit out; **escupe lo que sabes** spill the beans

escupitajo *m* gob of spit

escurreplatos *m inv* plate rack

escurridizo, **-a** *adj* slippery; (*idea*) elusive; **lazo ~** slipknot

escurrido, **-a** *adj* **1.** (*flaco*) thin; **~ de caderas** slim-hipped; **~ de pecho** flat-chested **2.** (*ropa*) tight **3.** *Méx, PRico* (*avergonzado*) embarrassed

escurridor *m* **1.** (*colador*) drainer, colander **2.** (*escurreplatos*) dish drainer, plate rack *Brit* **3.** (*de una lavadora*) wringer

escurrir **I.** *vi* (*gotear, ropa*) to drip; (*verdura*) to drain **II.** *vt* **1.** (*ropa*) to wring out; (*platos, verdura*) to drain **2.** (*deslizar*) to slip; **~ la mano por encima de algo** to run one's hand over sb; **escurrió el dinero en mi bolsillo** he/she slipped the money into my pocket **3.** (*una vasija*) to empty; **~ la** (**botella de**) **cerveza** to empty the bottle of beer **III.** *vr:* **~se** **1.** (*resbalar*) to slip **2.** (*escaparse*) to slip out; **el pez se me escurrió de** (**entre**) **las manos** the fish slipped out of my hands; **~se por un agujero** to slip through a hole; **~ el bulto** *inf* to dodge the issue **3.** (*desaparecer*) to slip away; **~se** (**por**) **entre la gente** to slip away in the crowd **4.** (*gotear*) to drip; (*lágrima*) to trickle **5.** *inf* (*dar*) to overdo

esdrújulo, **-a** *adj with the accent falling on the third-last syllable: e.g., 'esdrújulo', 'número'*

ese *f* S, s; **la letra ~** the letter s; **ir haciendo ~s** *inf* to stagger [*o* reel] from side to side

ese, **-a** **I.** *adj* <esos, -as> that; **¿~ coche es tuyo?** is that car yours?; **esas sillas están en el medio** those chairs are in the way; **el chico ~ no me cae bien** I don't like that boy **II.** *pron dem v.* **ése, ésa, eso**

ése, **ésa**, **eso** <ésos, -as> *pron dem* that, that one; **me lo ha dicho ésa** that girl told me; **¿por qué no vamos a otro bar? – ~ no me gusta** why don't we go to another bar? – I don't like that one; **llegaré a eso de las doce** I'll arrive at about twelve o'clock; **estaba trabajando, en eso** (**que**) **tocaron al timbre** I was working when I heard the bell; **¡a ~!** get him!; **¡no me vengas con ésas!** come off it!; **me ofrecieron mucho dinero pero, ¡ni por ésas!** they offered to pay me a lot, but not on your life!; **eso mismo te acabo de decir** that's what I've just said; **aun con eso prefiero quedarme en casa** even so, I'd rather stay at home; **lejos de eso** just the opposite; **no es eso** it's not that; **por eso** (**mismo**) that's why; **¿y eso?** what do you mean?; **¿y eso qué?** so what?; **¡eso sí que no!** defintely not!; *v.t.* **ese, -a**

esencia *f* **1.** (*naturaleza*) essence; **se dice que el irlandés es por ~ hablador** it is said that the Irish are talkative by nature **2.** (*fondo*) base; **ser de ~** to be very pure; **en ~** in essence

3. QUÍM essence; ~ **de café** coffee essence; ~ **de rosas** essence of roses 4. (*colmo*) height; **ser la ~ de la arrogancia** to be the height of arrogance
esencial *adj* 1. (*sustancial*) fundamental; **elemento ~** essential element; **lo ~** the main thing 2. (*indispensable*) essential; **alimento/aceite ~** essential food/oil
esencialmente *adv* essentially
esfera *f* 1. MAT sphere 2. (*del reloj*) face, dial 3. (*ámbito*) *t.* ASTR field; ~ **de actividad** area of activity; ~ **de influencia** sphere of influence 4. (*clase*) class; **las altas ~s de la sociedad** the upper classes
esférico *m* DEP ball
esférico, -a *adj* spherical
esferográfico *m AmS* (*bolígrafo*) ball-point pen
esfinge *f* 1. (*animal fabuloso*) sphinx; **ser una ~** *fig* to be inscrutable 2. ZOOL hawk moth
esfínter *m* ANAT sphincter
esforzado, -a *adj* courageous
esforzar *irr como forzar* I. *vt* 1. (*forzar*) to force; (*vista, voz*) to strain; ~ **demasiado la vista** to strain one's eyes 2. (*dar ánimo*) to encourage II. *vr:* **~se** (*moralmente*) to strive; (*físicamente*) to make an effort
esfuerzo *m* 1. (*acción de esforzarse*) effort; **sin ~** effortlessly; **hacer un ~** to make an effort; **me ha costado muchos ~s conseguirlo** it took me a lot of effort to manage it 2. (*económico*) strain; **hacer un ~** to tighten one's belt 3. (*valor*) courage 4. (*vigor*) energy 5. TÉC stress
esfumar I. *vt* (*contornos*) to blur; (*colores*) to tone down II. *vr:* **~se** 1. (*desaparecer*) to fade away; (*contornos*) to blur 2. *inf* (*marcharse*) to beat it; **¡esfúmate!** beat it!
esgrima *f* fencing; **practicar la ~** to do fencing
esgrimir *vt* 1. (*blandir*) to wield 2. (*argumento*) to use
esgrimista *mf AmL* fencer
esguince *m* 1. MED sprain; **hacerse un ~ en el tobillo** to sprain one's ankle 2. (*movimiento*) sidestep 3. (*gesto*) frown
eslabón *m* 1. (*de una cadena*) link 2. (*entre acontecimientos*) step; **el ~ perdido** the missing link
eslalon *m* slalom
eslavo, -a *adj, m, f* Slav
eslogan *m* slogan
eslora *f* NÁUT length of a ship
eslovaco, -a I. *adj* Slovakian II. *m, f* Slovak
Eslovaquia *f* Slovakia
Eslovenia *f* Slovenia
esloveno, -a *adj, m, f* Slovenian
esmaltar *vt* 1. (*metal, cerámica*) to enamel 2. (*adornar de colores*) to paint 3. (*embellecer*) to beautify
esmalte *m* 1. (*barniz*) varnish; (*sobre metal, porcelana*) enamel; ~ **de laca** lacquer enamel; **sin ~** unenamelled *Brit,* unenameled *Am* 2. (*de uñas*) nail polish [*o* varnish *Brit*] 3. (*labor*) enamelling *Brit,* enameling *Am* 4. (*color*) smalt 5. (*de los dientes*) enamel 6. (*lustre*) shine 7. (*adorno*) embellishment
esmerado, -a *adj* 1. (*persona*) painstaking 2. (*obra*) professional
esmeralda I. *adj* emerald II. *f* emerald; ~ **oriental** corundum
esmerarse *vr* 1. (*obrar con esmero*) to take pains; ~ **en la limpieza** to clean conscientiously 2. (*esforzarse*) ~ **en algo** to make an effort with sth 3. (*lucirse*) to make a good impression; **hoy te has esmerado en la comida** today's lunch was wonderful
esmeril *m* (*roca*) emery; **papel de ~** emery paper
esmerilar *vt* to polish using emery
esmero *m* care; **con ~** with great care
esmirriado, -a *adj* (*flaco*) scrawny; (*raquítico*) puny
esmoquin *m* dinner jacket *Brit,* tuxedo *Am*
esnifar *vt inf* (*cocaína*) to snort; (*pegamento, pintura*) to sniff
esnob I. *adj* snobbish II. *mf* snob
esnobismo *m* snobbery
eso *pron dem v.* **ése**
ESO *f abr de* **Educación Secundaria Obligatoria** (compulsory) secondary education up to age sixteen
esófago *m* oesophagus *Brit,* esophagus *Am*
esos *adj v.* **ese**
ésos *pron dem v.* **ése**
esotérico, -a *adj* esoteric
esoterismo *m sin pl* esoteric nature
espabilada *f Col* (*parpadeo*) blink; **en una ~** in a second
espabilado, -a *adj* 1. (*listo*) smart 2. (*despierto*) awake
espabilar I. *vi* 1. (*darse prisa*) to hurry up 2. (*avivarse*) to liven up; **si quieres empezar a trabajar por tu cuenta, tienes que ~** if you want to be self-employed, you'll have to shake up II. *vt* 1. (*despertar*) to wake up 2. (*avivar*) to get one's act together *inf,* to shake up; **en la mili ya lo ~án** he's having to shake up in the army; **es muy perezosa, pero en el colegio ya la ~án** she's very lazy, but when she gets to school she'll have to change her act 3. (*acabar deprisa*) to hurry; (*fortuna*) to squander; (*comida*) to wolf down 4. (*robar*) to swipe 5. (*matar*) to bump off III. *vr:* **~se** 1. (*sacudir el sueño*) to wake oneself up; (*la pereza*) to get busy; **tómate un café para ~te** have a coffee to wake yourself up 2. (*darse prisa*) to hurry up 3. (*avivarse*) **se han espabilado desde que van al colegio** they've livened up since they started school 4. *AmL* (*marcharse*) to head off
espachurrar I. *vt inf* to squash II. *vr:* **~se** to get squashed
espaciador *m* space bar
espacial *adj* space; **estación ~** space station
espaciar I. *vt* (*sillas*) to separate; (*alumnos*) to

E

distribute; (*letras*) to space out; ~ **las visitas** to spread out [*o* to stagger] the visits; ~ **los árboles** to space out the trees **II.** *vr:* ~**se** (*en un discurso*) to go on at length, to expatiate *form*

espacio *m* **1.** (*área*) *t.* ASTR space; (*superficie*) area; (*trayecto*) distance; ~ **sideral** outer space; ~ **vacío** empty space; ~ **verde** green belt; ~ **virtual** cyberspace; ~ **vital** living space; ~ **web** web site; **a doble** ~ double-spaced **2.** (*que ocupa un cuerpo*) room, space; **este armario ocupa demasiado** ~ this wardrobe takes up too much space **3.** (*de tiempo*) period; **en el** ~ **de dos meses** in a period of two months; **por** ~ **de tres horas** for a three hour period **4.** (*programa*) programme *Brit,* program *Am;* ~ **informativo** news bulletin; ~ **publicitario** advertising spot

espacioso, -a *adj* (*lugar*) spacious, roomy

espada[1] *m* **1.** TAUR bullfighter **2.** ZOOL swordfish

espada[2] *f* **1.** (*arma*) sword; ~ **negra** foil; **desnudar la** ~ to unsheathe one's sword; **el despido era mi** ~ **de Damocles** the possibility of losing my job hung over me like a sword of Damocles; **tu respuesta es una** ~ **de dos filos** [*o* **de doble filo**] your answer is a double-edged sword; **de capa y** ~ cloak-and-dagger **2.** (*naipes*) spade; **pintan** ~**s** spades are trumps ►**estar entre la** ~ **y la pared** to be between the devil and the deep blue sea

espadachín *m* **1.** (*esgrimidor*) swordsman **2.** (*fanfarrón*) loudmouth; (*pendenciero*) troublemaker

espadaña *f* **1.** (*campanario*) bell tower [*o* gable] **2.** BOT bullrush

espagueti(s) *m(pl)* spaghetti; ~**s a la boloñesa** spaghetti bolognese

espalda *f* **1.** ANAT back; **ancho de** ~**s** broad-shouldered; **ser cargado de** ~**s** to be hunched; **andar de** ~**s** to walk backwards; **con las manos en la** ~ with one's hands clasped behind one's back; **estar a** ~**s de alguien** to be behind sb; **estar de** ~**s a la pared** to have one's back to the wall; **atacar por la** ~ to attack from the rear; **coger a alguien por la** ~ *fig* to take sb by surprise; **doblar la** ~ *fig* to put one's back into a task; **volver la** ~ **a alguien** *fig* to turn one's back on sb; **hablar a** ~**s de alguien** to talk behind sb's back; **me caí de** ~**s al oír eso** *inf* I was astonished to hear that; **tener las** ~**s muy anchas** *fig* to put up with a lot; **tener las** ~**s bien guardadas** *inf* to have friends in high places; **la responsabilidad recae sobre mis** ~**s** the responsibility is on my shoulders; **vivir de** ~**s a la realidad** to live in the clouds **2.** DEP backstroke; **100 metros** ~ 100 metres [*o* meters *Am*] backstroke; **¿sabes nadar** ~**?** do you know how to swim backstroke?; **nadar de** ~**s va bien para la columna** swimming backstroke is good for your spine **3.** (*de un edificio*) back **4.** (*de un animal*) back; (*para el consumo*) shoulder

espaldero *m Ven* **1.** (*guardaespaldas*) bodyguard **2.** (*asistente de un militar*) henchman

espaldilla *f* **1.** (*de una res*) shoulder **2.** ANAT shoulder blade

espanglis *m* Spanglish

espantadizo, -a *adj* **1.** (*persona*) jittery **2.** (*caballo*) skittish

espantajo *m* **1.** (*espantapájaros*) scarecrow; **tal como vas vestido pareces un** ~ dressed like that, you look a fright [*o* like a scarecrow] **2.** (*fantoche*) bogeyman

espantamoscas *m inv* fly-swatter

espantapájaros *m inv* scarecrow

espantar **I.** *vt* **1.** (*dar susto*) to shock; (*dar miedo*) to frighten **2.** (*ahuyentar a un animal*) to shoo away; (*asustándolo*) to frighten off **3.** (*asombrar*) to awe **II.** *vr:* ~**se** **1.** (*personas*) ~**se de** [*o* **por**] **algo** to be scared of sth **2.** (*animales*) to be shooed away; (*asustándolos*) to be frightened off

espanto *m* **1.** (*miedo*) fright; **¡qué** ~**!** how awful!; **hace un calor de** ~ it's terribly hot; **los precios son de** ~ prices are outrageous; **estar curado de** ~**s** *inf* to have been around a few years **2.** (*terror*) horror **3.** (*enfermedad*) shock **4.** *AmL* (*fantasma*) ghost

espantosidad *f AmC, Col, PRico* (*horror*) horror

espantoso, -a *adj* **1.** (*horroroso*) horrible **2.** (*feo*) hideous **3.** (*asombroso*) awesome

España *f* Spain

> **España** (official title: **Reino de España**) is a constitutional monarchy with a two-chamber system. The king, **Juan Carlos I**, was appointed Head of State on 22.11.1975. The successor to the throne is Crown Prince **Felipe de Asturias**. The official language of the country is Spanish. Since 1978, **el gallego** (Galician), **el catalán** (Catalan) and **el euskera/el vasco** (Basque) have also been recognised as national languages.

español *m* Spanish; **clases de** ~ Spanish classes; **aprender** ~ to learn Spanish; **traducir al** ~ to translate into Spanish

español(a) **I.** *adj* Spanish; **a la** ~**a** Spanish-style **II.** *m(f)* Spaniard

esparadrapo *m* adhesive [*o* medical] tape

esparcimiento *m* **1.** (*acción*) spreading **2.** (*diversión*) fun

esparcir <c→z> **I.** *vt* **1.** (*cosas*) to spread out; (*líquido*) to spill; **el viento ha esparcido los papeles de la mesa** the wind has blown the papers off the table **2.** (*mancha*) to spread over **3.** (*noticia*) to spread **4.** (*distraer*) ~ **el ánimo** to amuse oneself **II.** *vr:* ~**se** **1.** (*cosas*) to spread out **2.** (*noticias*) to spread **3.** (*distraerse*) to relax; **¿qué haces para** ~**te?** what do you do for fun?

espárrago *m* asparagus; ~ **triguero** wild asparagus; **¡vete a freír** ~**s!** *inf* get lost!; **estar hecho un** ~ *fig* to be as thin as a rake; **ser un**

~ to be a wet blanket
esparraguera *f* asparagus plant
espartano, **-a** *adj* spartan
espartillo *m AmL,* **esparto** *m* esparto
espasmo *m* spasm
espasmódico, **-a** *adj* spasmodic
espatarrarse *vr* to sprawl out
espátula *f* **1.** TÉC trowel **2.** (*manualidades*) palette [*o* putty] knife **3.** MED spatula
especia *f* spice
especial *adj* **1.** (*no habitual*) special; (*adecuado*) perfect; **edición/comisión/escuela** ~ special edition/committee/school; **en** ~ in particular; **¿qué has hecho hoy? – nada en** ~ what did you do today? – nothing special; **no pensaba en nada en** ~ I wasn't thinking of anything in particular; **él es para mí alguien muy** ~ he means a lot to me **2.** (*raro*) peculiar
especialidad *f* **1.** (*de un restaurante, una empresa*) speciality *Brit,* specialty *Am* **2.** (*rama*) field; DEP speciality *Brit,* specialty *Am*
especialista *mf* **1.** (*experto*) specialist **2.** (*médico*) specialist **3.** CINE stuntman *m,* stuntwoman *f*
especialización *f* specialization; **mi ~ es la física cuántica** my field is quantum physics
especializar <z→c> *vi, vr:* **~se** to specialize; **personal especializado** skilled staff
especialmente *adv* (*específicamente*) specially; **lo he hecho ~ para ti** I made it specially for you; (*particularmente, sobre todo*) especially
especie *f* **1.** *t.* BOT, ZOOL (*clase*) species *inv;* **~ amenazada de extinción** endangered species; **la ~ animal** animals *pl;* **ese es una ~ de cantante** he's a kind of singer; **gente de todas las ~s** all kinds of people; **un hombre de mala ~** an unpleasant man **2.** COM **pagar en ~s** to pay in kind **3.** (*rumor*) rumour *Brit,* rumor *Am;* **corre la ~ que...** people are saying that ...
especificación *f* **1.** (*precisión*) specification; **especificaciones técnicas** technical specifications **2.** (*explicación*) explanation
especificar <c→qu> *vt* **1.** (*explicar*) to explain; **el ministro especificó los problemas actuales de la economía** the minister spelled out the present economic problems; **no ~ los pormenores de las negociaciones** not to give details of the negotiations **2.** (*citar*) to specify; (*enumerar*) to enumerate
específico, **-a** *adj* specific; **el significado ~ de una palabra** the specific meaning of a word
espécimen *m* <especímenes> **1.** (*ejemplar*) specimen; **~ de lujo** prime example **2.** (*muestra*) sample
espectacular *adj* spectacular
espectáculo *m* **1.** TEAT show; (*de variedades*) variety show; **~ de circo** circus; **~ deportivo** sporting event **2.** (*visión*) sight **3.** *inf* (*escándalo*) **dar el ~** to make a spectacle [*o* scene]
espectador(**a**) *m(f)* spectator
espectro *m* **1.** (*fantasma*) phantom, spectre *Brit,* specter *Am* **2.** FÍS spectrum
especulación *f* speculation
especulador(**a**) *m(f)* speculator
especular *vi* **1.** *t.* FIN (*conjeturar*) to speculate; **~ en la Bolsa** to speculate on the stock market **2.** (*meditar*) to speculate
especulativo, **-a** *adj* **1.** (*que especula*) speculative **2.** (*teórico*) theoretical
espejado *m AmL* mirror-like
espejismo *m* **1.** (*óptico*) mirage **2.** (*de la imaginación*) illusion
espejo *m* mirror; **~ retrovisor** car mirror, rear-view mirror; **mirarse al ~** to look at oneself in the mirror; **el cine es el ~ de la vida** the cinema reflects real life
espeluznante *adj* horrific
espera *f* **1.** (*acción, duración*) wait; **tuvimos dos horas de ~** we had a two-hour wait; **estoy a la ~ de recibir la beca** I'm waiting to hear about the grant; **esta ~ me saca de quicio** this waiting around is really getting to me **2.** (*estado*) waiting; **lista de ~** waiting list; **en ~ de su respuesta** (*final de carta*) looking forward to hearing from you; **en ~ de tu carta, te mando el paquete** I'm sending you the parcel and look forward to hearing from you **3.** (*paciencia*) patience **4.** (*plazo*) period; **no tener ~** to be urgent; **sin ~** immediate; **quien espera, desespera** *prov* a watched pot never boils *prov*
esperanza *f* hope; **~ de vida** life expectancy; **no tener ~s** to have no hope; **abrigar ~s** to foster hopes; **estar en estado de buena ~** to be pregnant [*o* expecting]; **poner las ~s en algo** to put one's hopes into sth; **tener ~s de conseguir un puesto de trabajo** to have hopes of getting a job; **veo el futuro con ~** I'm hopeful about the future; **con ~ no se come** *prov* who lives by hope will die by hunger
esperanzador(**a**) *adj* hopeful
esperanzar <z→c> **I.** *vt* to give hope to **II.** *vr* **~se en algo** to become hopeful about sth
esperar **I.** *vi* **1.** (*aguardar*) to wait; **~ al aparato** (*teléfono*) to stay on the line; **hacerse ~** to keep people waiting; **es de ~ que** *+subj* it is to be expected that; **esperemos y veamos cómo evolucionan las cosas** let's wait and see how things develop; **¡que se espere!** let him wait!; **¿a qué esperas?** what are you waiting for?; **espera, que no lo encuentro** hold on, I can't find it; **ganaron la copa tan esperada** they won the long-awaited cup; **uno sólo tiene que ~ a que las cosas lleguen** all things come to those who wait **2.** (*confiar*) to hope; **~ en alguien** to place one's hope in sb **II.** *vt* **1.** (*aguardar*) to wait for; **hace una hora que lo espero** I've been waiting for you for an hour; **hacer ~ a alguien** to keep sb waiting; **la respuesta no se hizo ~** the answer was not long in coming; **te espero mañana a las nueve** I'll be waiting for you tomorrow at nine

o'clock; **me van a ~ al aeropuerto** they're meeting me at the airport; **nos esperan malos tiempos** there are bad times in store for us; **espero su decisión con impaciencia** (*final de carta*) I'm looking forward to hearing from you; **te espera una prueba dura** a hard test awaits you **2.** (*un bebé, recibir, pensar*) to expect; **ya me lo esperaba** I expected it **3.** (*confiar*) to hope; **espero que nos veamos pronto** I hope to see you soon; **esperando recibir noticias tuyas...** looking forward to hearing from you ...; **espero sacar grandes ganancias de este negocio** I hope to make a lot of profit out of this business; **espero que sí** I hope so

esperma *m* sperm

espermatozoide *m* spermatozoid

esperpéntico, -a *adj* grotesque

esperpento *m* **1.** (*persona*) fright **2.** (*desatino*) piece of nonsense **3.** (*estilo literario*) *literary style coined by Valle Inclán*

espesar **I.** *vt* (*líquido*) to thicken **II.** *vr:* **~se** (*bosque*) to become denser

espeso, -a *adj* **1.** (*cabello, niebla, bosque, líquido*) thick **2.** (*persona*) untidy **3.** *Arg, Perú, Ven* (*molesto*) bothersome

espesor *m* **1.** (*grosor*) thickness; (*nieve*) depth **2.** (*densidad*) density

espesura *f* **1.** (*del cabello, bosque*) thickness; (*de un líquido*) density **2.** (*bosque*) thicket

espetar *vt* **1.** (*ave, objeto*) to skewer **2.** *inf* (*de repente*) to come out with; **~ una bronca a alguien** to give sb a telling-off; **~ un sermón a alguien** to give sb a talking-to; **~ cuatro verdades a alguien** *fig* to give sb a piece of one's mind

espía *mf* spy; (*de la policía*) informer; (*infiltrado*) infiltrator; **~ doble** double agent

espiantar **I.** *vi, vr:* **~se** *CSur, inf* (*alejarse*) to head off; (*huir*) to escape **II.** *vt CSur* (*hurtar*) to steal

espiar <*1. pres:* espío> **I.** *vi* (*hacer espionaje*) to spy **II.** *vt* to spy on; (*para la policía*) to inform on

espichar *vt Col, inf* (*aplastar*) to squash

espiga *f* **1.** BOT ear; **dibujo de ~** herringbone **2.** (*madera*) dowel

espigado, -a *adj* **1.** (*forma*) tall **2.** (*maduro*) ripe **3.** (*árbol*) tall; (*persona*) lanky

espigarse <g→gu> *vr* to shoot up

espigón *m* **1.** (*dique*) mole; (*rompeolas*) breakwater **2.** (*espiga*) ear **3.** (*de un clavo*) point **4.** (*aguijón*) sting

espina *f* **1.** (*de pescado*) bone **2.** BOT thorn **3.** (*astilla*) splinter **4.** ANAT **~** (**dorsal**) spine **5.** (*inconveniente*) problem; **esto me da mala ~** *inf* I don't like the look of this **6.** (*pesar*) frustration; **sacarse una ~** *inf* (*desquitarse*) to get even; (*desahogarse*) to let it all out; **tener una ~ clavada** to have sth hanging over one

espinaca *f* spinach

espinal *adj* spinal; **médula ~** spinal chord

espinazo *m* ANAT spinal column; **doblar el ~** *fig* to work hard

espinilla *f* **1.** ANAT shin; **dar a alguien una patada en la ~** to kick sb in the shin **2.** (*grano*) blackhead; **sacarse una ~** to get rid of a blackhead

espino *m* **1.** BOT **~ albar** hawthorn **2.** TÉC **alambre de ~** barbed wire

espinoso, -a *adj,* **espinudo, -a** *adj AmC, CSur* **1.** (*planta*) thorny; (*pescado*) bony **2.** (*problema*) tricky

espionaje *m* espionage; **~ industrial** industrial espionage; **servicio de ~ británico** British secret service

espira *f* spiral

espiración *f* MED exhalation

espiral **I.** *adj* spiral; **escalera ~** spiral staircase **II.** *f* spiral

espirar **I.** *vi* (*aire*) to exhale **II.** *vt* (*olor*) to give off

espiritismo *m sin pl* spiritualism; **sesión de ~** seance

espiritista *adj* spiritualist

espíritu *m* spirit; (*alma*) soul; (*inteligencia*) mind; (*idea principal*) essence, nature; **~ de compañerismo** brotherly spirit; **~ de contradicción** contrariness; **~ emprendedor** hard-working nature; **~ deportivo** sportsmanship; **~ de la época** spirit of the age; **~ de observación** (*don*) gift of observation; **el Espíritu Santo** REL the Holy Spirit; **~ de solidaridad** spirit of solidarity; **pobre de ~** mean-spirited; **exhalar el ~** to breathe one's last; **cobrar ~** to take shape; **levantar el ~ a alguien** to lift sb's spirits; **tener un ~ de rebelión** to have a spirit of rebellion; **hacer algo con ~ alegre** to go about sth cheerfully; **evocar los ~s** to call upon the spirits

espiritual *adj* spiritual; **vida ~** spiritual life; **mantenemos una relación puramente ~** we have a purely Platonic relationship

espita *f* **1.** (*de una cuba*) tap *Brit,* faucet *Am;* (*del gas*) gas-tap *Brit,* gas spigot *Am;* () **2.** (*palmo*) span **3.** *inf* (*borracho*) drunk

esplendidez *f* **1.** (*generosidad*) generosity **2.** (*magnificencia*) splendour *Brit,* splendor *Am*

espléndido, -a *adj* **1.** (*generoso*) generous **2.** (*aspecto*) splendid; (*día*) beautiful; (*comida*) lovely; (*ocasión, idea, resultado*) excellent

esplendor *m* splendour *Brit,* splendor *Am*

esplendoroso, -a *adj* splendid

espliego *m* lavender

esplín *m* (*melancolía*) spleen

espolear *vt* **1.** (*al caballo*) to spur **2.** (*a alguien*) to spur on

espoleta *f* (*de bomba*) fuse

espolvorear *vt* to sprinkle

esponja *f* **1.** (*para lavar*) *t.* ZOOL sponge; **~ de baño** bath sponge; **beber como una ~** *inf* to drink like a fish; **¡pasemos la ~!** *inf* let's forget about it! **2.** (*persona*) sponger *Brit,* sponge *Am,* leech *Am*

esponjoso, **-a** *adj* (*masa*) fluffy; (*pan*) light
espontáneamente *adv* spontaneously
espontaneidad *f* spontaneity
espontáneo *m* TAUR *bullfight spectator who enters the ring to participate*
espontáneo, **-a** *adj* spontaneous; (*saludo*) natural; **curación espontánea** spontaneous healing
espora *f* spore
esporádico, **-a** *adj* sporadic
esportivo, **-a** *adj AmL* **1.** (*deportivo*) sporting **2.** (*afectando descuido*) casual
esposar *vt* to handcuff
esposas *fpl* (*manillas*) handcuffs *pl;* **colocar las ~ a alguien** to handcuff sb
esposo, **-a** *m, f* spouse; (*marido*) husband; (*mujer*) wife; **le presento a mi esposa** this is my wife; **salude a su ~ de mi parte** give my regards to your husband; **los ~s** the bride and groom
espray *m* **1.** (*líquido*) spray **2.** (*envase*) aerosol
esprint *m* sprint
esprintar *vt* to sprint
esprínter *mf* sprinter
espuela *f* **1.** (*de caballo*) spur; **poner las ~s a alguien** to spur sb on **2.** *inf* (*la última copa*) one for the road; **tomar la ~** to have one for the road
espuerta *f* carrier; **a ~s** in sackloads
espuma *f* (*burbujas*) foam; (*de las olas*) spray; (*de jabón*) lather; (*de cerveza*) head; **~ de afeitar** shaving foam; **crecer como la ~** *inf* (*persona*) to shoot up; (*cosa*) to grow very quickly
espumadera *f* skimmer
espumarajo *m* **1.** *pey* (*espuma*) froth **2.** (*de la boca*) foam; **echar ~s por la boca** *fig* to be foaming at the mouth
espumilla *f* **1.** (*tejido*) gauzy fabric **2.** *AmL* GASTR (*merengue*) meringue
espumillón *m* tinsel
espumoso, **-a** *adj* (*masa*) foamy; (*líquido*) sparkling; **vino ~** sparkling wine
espurio, **-a** *adj* **1.** (*falso*) spurious **2.** (*persona*) illegitimate
esputo *m* spit(tle); MED sputum
esqueje *m* cutting
esquela *f* **1.** (*nota*) notice of death **2.** (*necrológica*) ~ (**mortuoria**) obituary notice; **publicar una ~** to publish an obituary
esquelético, **-a** *adj* **1.** ANAT skeletal **2.** (*persona*) scrawny
esqueleto *m* **1.** ANAT skeleton; **después de la operación quedé hecho un ~** after the operation I was so thin I looked like a skeleton; **esta noche vamos a mover el ~** *inf* tonight we're going to dance **2.** (*de un avión, barco*) shell; (*de un edificio*) framework
esquema *m* **1.** (*gráfico*) sketch; **en ~** in rough **2.** (*de una clase*) summary; **tengo que hacer el ~ del discurso** I have to make an outline for the speech **3.** (*idea*) idea; **romper los ~s** to shake up sb's ideas
esquemático, **-a** *adj* schematic
esquematizar *vt* to outline
esquí *m* **1.** (*patín*) ski; **~ de fondo** cross-country ski **2.** (*deporte*) skiing; **~ acuático** water-skiing
esquiador(**a**) *m(f)* skier; **~ de fondo** cross-country skier
esquiar <*1. pres:* esquío> *vi* to ski
esquila *f* **1.** (*cencerro*) cowbell; (*campanilla*) small bell **2.** (*esquileo*) shearing
esquilar *vt* **1.** (*ovejas*) to shear; (*perros*) to clip; **esta tarde iré a que me esquilen** *inf* this afternoon I'm going to get my hair cut **2.** (*timar*) to rip off
esquileo *m* (*acción*) shearing
esquilmar *vt* **1.** (*frutos*) to harvest **2.** (*la tierra*) to exhaust **3.** (*explotar*) to exploit
esquimal **I.** *adj* Eskimo; **perro ~** husky **II.** *mf* Eskimo
esquina *f* corner; **casa que hace ~** house on the corner; **hacer un saque de ~** DEP to take a corner; **a la vuelta de la ~** around the corner; **doblar la ~** to turn the corner
esquinar **I.** *vi* to be on the corner **II.** *vt* **1.** (*objetos*) to turn round **2.** (*maderos*) to square **III.** *vr:* **~se** to have a quarrel
esquinazo *m inf* corner; **dar ~ a alguien** (*dejar plantado*) to stand sb up; (*rehuir*) to avoid sb
esquirla *f* splinter, chip
esquirol *mf* scab, blackleg
esquivar **I.** *vt* **1.** (*golpe*) to dodge **2.** (*problema*) to shirk **3.** (*encuentro*) ~ **algo** to get out of sth **4.** (*a alguien*) to avoid **II.** *vr:* **~se** to back out
esquivo, **-a** *adj* **1.** (*huidizo*) evasive **2.** (*arisco*) aloof
esquizofrenia *f* schizophrenia
esquizofrénico, **-a** *adj, m, f* schizophrenic
esta *adj v.* **este**, **-a**
ésta *pron dem v.* **éste**
estabilidad *f* stability; (*de una amistad*) firmness; (*del carácter*) steadiness, stability; **~ de los precios** price stability
estabilización *f* stability
estabilizar <z→c> **I.** *vt* to stabilize; (*amistad*) to establish **II.** *vr:* **~se** to stabilize
estable *adj* stable; (*trabajo*) steady; (*carácter*) steadfast, stable
establecer *irr como crecer* **I.** *vi* to **II.** *vt* **1.** (*fundar*) to establish; (*grupo de trabajo*) to set up; (*sucursal, tienda*) to open; (*principio, récord*) to set; (*orden, escuela*) to found **2.** (*colocar*) to place; (*campamento*) to set up; (*colonos*) to settle; (*conexión*) to establish **III.** *vr* **~se de algo** (*instalarse*) to set oneself up as sth
establecimiento *m* **1.** (*fundación, relaciones*) establishment; (*de un grupo de trabajo*) setting-up; (*de una sucursal*) opening; (*de un principio, récord*) setting; (*del orden, de una escuela*) founding **2.** (*de colonia*)

E

settlement

establo *m* **1.** (*cuadra*) stable, barn; **esta casa es un ~** *fig* this house is a pigsty **2.** *Cuba* (*cochera*) depot; (*para alquilar*) garage

estaca *f* (*palo*) post; (*para tienda*) peg; (*garrote*) stick

estacada *f* fence; **dejar a alguien en la ~** to leave sb in the lurch; **quedarse en la ~** to be left in the lurch

estación *f* **1.** (*año, temporada*) season; **~ de las lluvias** rainy season **2.** *t.* RADIO, TV, FERRO station; (*parada*) stop; **~ de autobuses** bus station; **~ central** central station; **~ de destino** destination; **~ de metro** underground station *Brit,* subway station *Am* **3.** (*centro*) *t.* REL station, centre *Brit,* center *Am;* **~ meteorológica** weather station; **~ orbital** orbiting space station; **~ de servicio** service [*o* gas *Am*] station

estacionamiento *m* **1.** AUTO (*acción*) parking; (*espacio*) parking place [*o* space]; (*lugar*) car park **2.** (*colocación*) placing **3.** MIL (*posición*) positioning **4.** (*estabilización*) stabilization

estacionar **I.** *vt* **1.** AUTO to park **2.** (*colocar*) to place **3.** MIL to position **II.** *vr:* **~se** **1.** AUTO to park **2.** (*alguien*) to stabilize **3.** (*parar*) to stabilize; **la producción se ha estacionado** production has stabilized

estacionario, **-a** *adj* stable

estada *f AmL,* **estadía** *f* **1.** (*estancia*) stay **2.** (*de un modelo*) session **3.** COM (*tiempo*) demurrage; (*tarifa*) cost of such a delay

estadía *f AmL* (*estancia*) stay

estadio *m* **1.** DEP stadium **2.** MED stage

estadística *f* statistics *pl*

estadístico, **-a** **I.** *adj* statistical **II.** *m, f* statistician

estado *m* **1.** (*condición*) condition; (*situación*) state; **~ de alarma** state of alert; **~ civil** marital status; **~ de las cosas** (*general*) state of affairs; **~ de gracia** state of grace; **~ de la economía** state of the economy; **~ de derecho** constitutional state; **~ de emergencia** state of emergency; **~ financiero** financial situation; **~ gaseoso** gaseous state; **~ de guerra** state of war; **el cuarto ~** (*periodismo*) the press; **~ de necesidad** JUR state of necessity; **en buen ~ de conservación** in a good state of upkeep; **en ~ de embriaguez** in a state of inebriation; **estar en ~ interesante** [*o* **de buena esperanza**] to be pregnant; **en ~ de merecer** marriageable **2.** POL state; **~ comunitario** community state; **~ miembro** member state; **presupuestos del ~** state budget; **~ totalitario** police state **3.** MIL **~ mayor** (general) staff; **~ de sitio** martial law **4.** FIN **~ de cuentas** balance statement; **~ de los gastos** statement of expenses

Estados Unidos *mpl* United States *pl* of America

estadounidense **I.** *adj* of/from the United States, American **II.** *mf* native/inhabitant of the United States, American

estafa *f* swindle

estafador(**a**) *m(f)* swindler

estafar *vt* to swindle; **la cajera me ha estafado el cambio** the checkout assistant has shortchanged me

estafeta *f* (*correos*) sub-post office *Brit,* branch post office *Am*

estafilococo *m* MED staphylococcus

estagnación *f AmC* stagnation

estaje *m AmL* piecework

estajear *vi AmL* to do as piecework

estajero, **-a** *m, f AmL* pieceworker, freelancer

estalactita *f* stalactite

estalagmita *f* stalagmite

estallar *vi* **1.** (*globo, neumático*) to burst; (*bomba*) to explode, to go off; (*cristales*) to shatter; (*látigo*) to crack; **estalló una ovación** applause broke out; **me estalla la cabeza** I have a splitting headache **2.** (*revolución, incendio*) to break out; (*tormenta*) to break; **al ~ la guerra** when the war broke out **3.** (*risa*) to burst out; **~ en llanto** to burst into tears; **estaba enfadado y al final estalló** he was angry and he finally snapped

estallido *m* **1.** (*ruido*) explosion; (*de un globo*) bursting **2.** (*de una revolución*) outbreak; **~ de cólera** outbreak of cholera

Estambul *m* Istanbul

estampa *f* **1.** (*dibujo*) illustration; **~ de la Virgen** image of the Virgin Mary **2.** (*huella*) imprint **3.** (*impresión*) impression; (*aspecto*) appearance; **un caballo de magnífica ~** a splendid-looking horse; **tienes mala ~** you look terrible; **¡maldita sea tu ~!** damn you!; **ser la viva ~ de la pobreza** to be the incarnation of poverty; **ser la viva ~ de su padre** *inf* to be the spitting image of one's father

estampado *m* **1.** (*tejido*) print; **no me gusta este ~** I don't like this design **2.** (*metal*) engraving

estampado, **-a** *adj* printed

estampar **I.** *vt* **1.** (*en papel, tela*) to print; (*con relieve*) to stamp; **~ un dibujo en una camiseta** to print a design on a T-shirt **2.** TÉC (*una chapa*) to press; (*un motivo en una chapa*) to stamp; **se me quedó estampado en la cabeza** *fig* it imprinted itself on my memory **3.** (*huella*) to imprint; **~ una firma** to sign one's name; **~ la firma al pie del documento** to sign at the foot of the document **4.** *inf* (*arrojar*) to hurl **5.** *inf* (*dar*) to give; **~ una bofetada a alguien** to give sb a slap; **~le un beso a alguien en la cara** to plant a kiss on sb's face **II.** *vr* **~se con algo** *inf* to crash into sth

estampida *f* stampede

estampido *m* bang; **~ del trueno** peal of thunder; **dar un ~** to bang

estampilla *f* **1.** (*sello*) rubber stamp **2.** *AmL* (*de correos*) stamp

estancamiento *m* **1.** (*del agua*) stagnation **2.** (*de una mercancía*) monopolization **3.** (*de* *los negocios*) breakdown; (*de un proceso*) deadlock; ~ **coyuntural** matrimonial deadlock **4.** ECON recession

estancar <c→qu> **I.** *vt* **1.** (*un río*) to stagnate; **aguas estancadas** stagnant water **2.** (*mercancía*) to monopolize **3.** (*proceso*) to hold up **II.** *vr:* ~**se** **1.** (*río*) to be held back **2.** (*negocio*) to falter; **quedarse estancado** to get stuck; **me he estancado en los estudios** I've got bogged down in my studies

estancia *f* **1.** (*permanencia*) stay; ~ **en un hospital** stay in hospital **2.** (*habitación*) room **3.** *AmL* (*hacienda*) estate **4.** *Cuba, Ven* (*quinta*) smallholding **5.** (*poesía*) stanza

estanciera *f Arg* (*furgoneta*) station wagon

estanciero, -a *m, f CSur, Col, Ven* **1.** (*de ganado*) cattle farmer **2.** (*de latifundios*) landowner

estanco *m* **1.** (*establecimiento*) tobacconist's (*also selling stamps*) **2.** (*monopolio*) monopoly

estanco, -a *adj* **1.** NÁUT watertight **2.** (*separado*) independent

estándar **I.** *adj* standard; **tipo** ~ standard version **II.** *m* standard

estandarizar <z→c> *vt* to standardize

estandarte *m* banner

estanque *m* **1.** (*en un parque*) pool, pond **2.** (*para el riego*) tank

estanquero, -a *m, f* tobacconist

estanquillo *m* **1.** *Ecua* (*taberna*) tavern **2.** *Méx* (*tienda*) small shop or stall

estante *m* **1.** (*tabla*) shelf; (*para libros*) bookshelf **2.** (*estantería para libros*) bookcase

estantería *f* shelves *pl;* (*para libros*) bookcase

estañar *vt Ven* **1.** (*herir*) to wound **2.** TEC to tin; (*soldar*) to solder

estaño *m* tin; ~ **para soldar** solder

estar *irr* **I.** *vi* **1.** (*hallarse*) to be; (*un objeto: derecho*) to stand; (*tumbado*) to lie; (*colgando*) to hang; **Valencia está en la costa** Valencia is on the coast; **¿está Pepe?** is Pepe there?; **¿dónde estábamos?** where were we?; **como estamos aquí tú y yo** as you and I are here; **ya lo hago yo, para eso estoy** I'll do it, that's why I'm here; **¿está la comida?** is lunch ready? **2.** (*sentirse*) to be; **¿cómo estás?** how are you?; **ya estoy mejor** I'm better; **hoy no estoy bien** today I'm not well **3.** (+ *adjetivo, participio*) to be; ~ **asomado al balcón** to be looking out over the balcony; ~ **cansado** to be tired; ~ **sentado** to be sitting; ~ **ubicado** *AmL* to be located; ~ **viejo** to be old; **el asado está rico** the roast is delicious; **está visto que...** it is obvious that ... **4.** (+ *bien, mal*) ~ **mal de azúcar** to be running out of sugar; ~ **mal de la cabeza** to be off one's head; ~ **mal de dinero** to be short of money; **eso te está bien empleado** *inf* it serves you right; **esa blusa te está bien** that blouse suits you; **este peinado no te está bien** this hairstyle doesn't suit you **5.** (+ *a*) ~ **al caer** (*persona*) to be about to arrive; (*suceso*) to be about to happen; **están al caer las diez** it's almost ten o'clock; ~ **al día** to be up to date; **estamos a uno de enero** it's the first of January; **¿a qué estamos?** what day is it?; **las peras están a 2 euros el kilo** pears cost 2 euros a kilo; **el cuadro está ahora a 8.000 libras** the painting now costs 8,000 pounds; **las acciones están a 12 euros** the shares are at 12 euros; **Sevilla está a 40 grados** it is 40 degrees in Seville; **el termómetro está a diez grados** the thermometer shows ten degrees; **están uno a uno** they're drawing one-all; ~ **a examen** to be under examination; **estoy a lo que decida la asamblea** I will follow whatever the assembly decides; **estoy a oscuras en este tema** I'm in the dark about this matter **6.** (+ *con*) to be; **estoy con mi novio** I'm with my boyfriend; **en la casa estoy con dos más** I share the house with two others; **estoy contigo en este punto** I agree with you on that point **7.** (+ *de*) to be; ~ **de broma** to be joking; ~ **de charla** to be chatting; ~ **de mal humor** to be in a bad mood; ~ **de parto** to be in labour [*o* labor *Am*]; ~ **de pie** to be standing; ~ **de suerte** to be lucky; ~ **de secretario** to be working as a secretary; ~ **de viaje** to be travelling [*o* traveling *Am*]; **en esta reunión estoy de más** I'm not needed in this meeting; **esto que has dicho estaba de más** there's no call for what you've just said **8.** (+ *en*) **el problema está en el dinero** the problem is the money; **yo estoy en que él no dice la verdad** I believe he's not telling the truth; **no estaba en sí cuando lo hizo** he/she wasn't in control of himself/herself when he/she did it; **siempre estás en todo** you don't miss a thing; **estoy en lo que tú dices** I agree with you **9.** (+ *para*) ~ **para morir** to feel like dying; **hoy no estoy para bromas** today I'm in no mood for jokes; **el tren está para salir** the train is about to leave **10.** (+ *por*) **estoy por llamarle** I think we should call him/her; **eso está por ver** we don't know that yet; **la historia de esta ciudad está por escribir** the history of this city has not been written yet; **este partido está por la democracia** this party believes in democracy **11.** (+ *gerundio*) to be; **¿qué estás haciendo?** what are you doing; **estoy haciendo la comida** I'm making lunch; **siempre estás viendo la tele** you're always watching television; **he estado una hora esperando el autobús** I've been waiting for the bus for an hour; **estoy escribiendo una carta** I'm writing a letter; **¡lo estaba viendo venir!** I saw it coming!; **este pastel está diciendo cómeme** this cake is crying out to be eaten **12.** (+ *que*) **estoy que no me tengo** I can hardly stand up I'm so tired; **está que trina** he/she's furious **13.** (+ *sobre*) **estáte sobre este asunto** look after this matter; **siempre tengo que** ~ **sobre mi hijo para que coma** I always have to force my son to eat; **ser una persona que siempre está**

sobre sí (*serena*) to always be in control of oneself **14.** (*entendido*) **a las 10 en casa, ¿estamos?** 10 o'clock at home, OK? **II.** *vr:* **~se 1.** (*hallarse*) to be **2.** (*permanecer*) to stay; **~se de charla** to be chatting; **te puedes ~ con nosotros** you can stay with us; **me estuve con ellos toda la tarde** I spent the whole afternoon with them; **¡estáte quieto!** keep still; **¡estáte callado!** shut up!

estarcir *vt* to stencil

estárter *m* choke

estatal *adj* state

estática *f sin pl* statics

estático, **-a** *adj* static; (*pasmado*) rooted to the spot

estatua *f* statue

estatuaria *f* statues *pl*

estatuilla *f* statuette; CINE Oscar

estatura *f* stature; (*altura*) height; **¿qué ~ tienes?** how tall are you?; **es un hombre de ~ pequeña** he's a short man; **su ~ política** his/her political stature

estatus *m inv* status

estatutario, **-a** *adj* statutory

estatuto *m* **1.** (*de una sociedad*) rule **2.** JUR, POL statute; (*de autonomía*) statute of autonomy; **~ de los trabajadores** employment legislation

este *m* **1.** (*punto*) east; **Alemania del Este** East Germany **2.** (*viento*) easterly

este, **-a** **I.** *adj* <estos, -as> this; **~ perro es mío** this dog is mine; **esta casa es nuestra** this house is ours; **estos guantes son míos** these gloves are mine **II.** *pron dem v.* **éste, ésta, esto**

éste, **ésta**, **esto** <éstos, -as> *pron dem* him, her, this; (**a**) **éstos no los he visto nunca** I've never seen them; **~ se cree muy importante** this guy thinks he's very important; **antes yo también tenía una camisa como ésta** I used to have a shirt like this before, too; (**estando**) **en esto** [*o* **en éstas**], **llamaron a la puerta** and then, someone called at the door; **¡ésta sí que es buena!** *irón* that's a good one!, that's brilliant!; **te lo juro, por ésta**(**s**) I swear to God!; *v.t.* **este, -a**

estela *f* **1.** NÁUT wake **2.** (*de avión*) slipstream, vapour [*o* vapor *Am*] trail **3.** (*rastro*) trail; **dejar una ~ de recuerdos** to leave a lot of memories in one's wake **4.** ARQUIT stele

estelar *adj* **1.** ASTR stellar; **sistema ~** stellar system **2.** (*extraordinario*) **invitado ~** star guest; **programa ~** TV star programme *Brit,* star program *Am*

estelaridad *f Chile* (*popularidad*) stardom; **tener una gran ~** to be a star

estenografía *f* shorthand

estenografiar <*1. pres:* estenografío> *vt* to take down in shorthand

estentóreo, **-a** *adj* (*voz, risa*) booming

estepa *f* **1.** GEO steppe **2.** BOT rockrose

estera *f* matting

estercolero *m* **1.** (*montón*) dunghill **2.** (*lugar*) rubbish tip *Brit,* garbage heap *Am*

estéreo **I.** *adj inf* stereo **II.** *m* **1.** (*estereofonía*) stereophonics **2.** (*equipo*) stereo

estereofónico, **-a** *adj* stereophonic

estereotipado, **-a** *adj* stereotyped; **frase estereotipada** hackneyed expression

estereotipo *m* stereotype

estéril *adj* **1.** (*persona*) sterile; (*mujer*) infertile **2.** (*tierra*) barren **3.** (*trabajo*) mundane; (*esfuerzo*) useless; (*discusión*) pointless

esterilidad *f* **1.** (*de una persona*) sterility **2.** (*tierra*) barrenness

esterilizar <z→c> *vt* to sterilize

esterilla *f* **1.** (*estera*) mat; **~ eléctrica** electric blanket; **~ del camping** camping mat **2.** *Ecua* (*rejilla*) **silla de ~** wicker chair

esterlina *adj* **libra ~** pound sterling

esternón *m* MED sternum, breastbone

estero *m* **1.** *AmL* (*pantano*) bog **2.** *Cuba* (*ría*) estuary **3.** *Chile, Ecua* (*arroyo*) stream **4.** *Ven* (*aguazal*) pool; **estar en el ~** to be up the creek without a paddle

esteroide *m* steroid

estertor *m* (*respiración*) rasp; (*de la muerte*) death rattle

esteta *mf* aesthete

estética *f* aesthetics *Brit,* esthetics *Am*

esteticien *mf* beautician, aesthetician *Brit,* esthetician *Am*

estético, **-a** *adj* aesthetic *Brit,* esthetic *Am;* **cirugía estética** plastic [*o* cosmetic] surgery; **no ~** unaesthetic *Brit,* unesthetic *Am*

estetoscopio *m* stethoscope

estiaje *m* (*nivel*) low water

estibador *m* stevedore, docker *Brit,* longshoreman

estibar *vt* **1.** (*cargar*) to load **2.** (*distribuir*) to trim

estiércol *m* manure; **sacar el ~** *fig* to do the dirty work

estigma *m* stigma; (*en el cuerpo*) mark; REL stigmata *pl*

estigmatizar <z→c> *vt* to stigmatize; REL to mark with stigma

estilar **I.** *vt* to usually do; **estila levantarse pronto** he/she usually gets up early **II.** *vr:* **~se** to be in fashion; **ya no se estila llevar pantalones acampanados** it's no longer in fashion to wear bell bottoms

estilista *mf* **1.** LIT stylist **2.** (*diseño*) designer, stylist

estilístico, **-a** *adj* stylistic

estilizar <z→c> *vt* to stylize; (*adelgazar*) to make slim

estilo *m* **1.** *t.* ARTE, LIT (*modo*) style; **~ de la fuente** INFOR font style; **al ~ de** in the style of; **~ de vida** lifestyle; **por el ~** like that; **¿estás mal?, pues yo estoy por el ~** are you not feeling well? neither am I; **algo por el ~** something similar; **ya me habían dicho algo por el ~** I'd already been told something like that **2.** DEP style; **~ libre** freestyle; **~ (de) pecho** breaststroke **3.** LING **~ directo/indirecto**

direct/indirect speech **4.** BOT style
estilográfica *f* fountain pen
estima *f* esteem; **tener a alguien en mucha ~** to hold sb in high esteem
estimación *f* **1.** (*aprecio*) esteem; **~ propia** self-esteem **2.** (*evaluación*) estimate; **~ de ventas** sales forecast
estimado, -a *adj* **1.** (*apreciado*) respected **2.** (*en cartas*) **~ Señor** Dear Sir
estimar **I.** *vt* **1.** (*apreciar*) to apppreciate, to value; **~ a alguien mucho** to appreciate sb a lot; **~ a alguien poco** not to think much of sb; **~ en demasía** to overrate **2.** (*tasar*) to estimate **3.** (*valorar*) **~ en algo** to value at sth **4.** (*juzgar*) to judge; **lo estimó oportuno** he/she considered it appropriate; **~ que...** to consider that ... **5.** JUR (*una demanda*) to admit **II.** *vr:* **~se** **1.** (*apreciarse*) to value each other **2.** (*calcularse*) **~se en algo** to be valued at sth
estimulante *m* stimulant
estimular *vt* **1.** (*excitar*) to stimulate; (*en la sexualidad*) to excite, to turn on *inf* **2.** (*animar*) to encourage; ECON to stimulate
estímulo *m* **1.** (*incentivo*) incentive; ECON boost; **~ de la exportación** an export incentive **2.** MED stimulus
estío *m elev* summer
estipendio *m* stipend
esti(p)tiquez *f AmL* (*estreñimiento*) constipation
estipulación *f* **1.** (*convenio*) agreement **2.** JUR stipulation
estipular *vt* **1.** (*acordar*) to stipulate **2.** (*fijar*) to fix
estirado, -a *adj* (*adusto*) severe; (*engreído*) haughty, snooty *inf*
estirar **I.** *vi* to stretch; **no estires más que se rompe la cuerda** if you stretch it any more the rope will break **II.** *vt* **1.** (*alargar*) to stretch out; (*suma*) to spin out; (*un discurso*) to draw out; **~ el bolsillo** to spin out one's resources **2.** (*alisar*) to smoothe; **~ la masa** to roll out the dough; **aún tengo que ~ la cama** I still have to make the bed **3.** (*extender*) to stretch **4.** (*tensar*) to tighten; **~ la piel** to have a face-lift **5.** (*piernas, brazos*) to stretch out; **voy a salir a ~ un poco las piernas** I'm going to stretch my legs a little; **~ demasiado un músculo** to overstretch a muscle; **~ el cuello** to crane (one's neck); **~ la pata** *inf* to kick the bucket *inf* **6.** (*alambre*) to draw **III.** *vr:* **~se** to stretch; (*crecer*) to shoot up
estirón *m* **1.** (*tirón*) pull **2.** (*crecimiento*) **dar un ~** *inf* to shoot up
estirpe *f* stock; JUR heirs *pl*
estival *adj* summer
esto *pron dem v.* **éste**
estocada *f* **1.** *t.* TAUR swordthrust **2.** (*herida*) stab wound
Estocolmo *m* Stockholm
estofa *f pey* (*calidad*) class; **gente de baja ~** lower class people
estofado *m* (meat) stew
estofar *vt* **1.** (*guisar*) to stew **2.** (*enguatar*) to quilt
estoico, -a *adj* stoical
estola *f* stole
estólido, -a **I.** *adj* dim-witted **II.** *m, f* dullard
estomacal *adj* stomach; **trastorno ~** stomach upset
estómago *m* stomach; **dolor de ~** stomachache; **tener buen ~** *fig* to be tough; **tener a alguien sentado en el ~** *fig* not to like sb; **se me revolvió el ~** it turned my stomach
Estonia *f* Estonia
estonio, -a *adj, m, f* Estonian
estoque *m* **1.** (*espadín*) rapier; **estar hecho un ~** *fig* to be as thin as a rake **2.** BOT gladiolus
estorbar **I.** *vi* **1.** (*obstaculizar*) to get in the way **2.** (*molestar*) to be annoying **II.** *vt* **1.** (*impedir*) to stop **2.** (*obstaculizar*) to hinder **3.** (*molestar*) to bother
estorbo *m* **1.** (*molestia*) nuisance; **sal de casa, que sólo eres un ~** leave the house, you're only getting in the way **2.** (*obstáculo*) obstacle
estornino *m* starling
estornudar *vi* to sneeze
estornudo *m* sneeze
estos *adj v.* **este, -a**
estrabismo *m sin pl* squint
estrado *m* dais; **~ del testigo** JUR witness box; **citar a alguien para ~s** to subpoena [*o* call as a witness]
estrafalario, -a *adj inf* **1.** (*ropa*) shabby **2.** (*extravagante*) outlandish; (*ridículo*) preposterous
estragar <g→gu> *vt* **1.** (*dañar*) to damage **2.** (*embotar*) to numb; (*gusto*) to pervert
estrago *m* damage; **hacer grandes ~s en la población civil** to wreak havoc upon the civil population
estragón *m* tarragon
estrambótico, -a *adj* eccentric
estramonio *m* thorn apple
estrangulación *f t.* MED strangulation; **~ de intestinos** strangulation of the intestines
estrangulador *m* AUTO **~ de aire** choke; TEC throttle
estrangulador(a) *m(f)* (*asesino*) strangler
estrangulamiento *m* **1.** (*de persona*) strangulation **2.** (*estorbo*) blockage **3.** (*estrechamiento*) bottleneck
estrangular **I.** *vt* **1.** (*asesinar*) to strangle **2.** MED to strangulate **3.** TÉC to throttle **II.** *vr:* **~se** to be strangled
estraperlista *mf* black marketeer
estraperlo *m* **1.** (*tráfico*) black market; **adquirir algo de ~** to buy sth on the black market **2.** (*mercancía*) black market goods *pl*
Estrasburgo *m* Strasbourg
estratagema *m* **1.** (*artimaña*) ploy **2.** MIL strategy
estratega *mf* strategist
estrategia *f* strategy
estratégico, -a *adj* strategic

estrato *m t.* GEO stratum; ~ **social** social stratum

estrechamente *adv* **1.** (*pobremente*) in austerity; **vivimos** ~ we barely make ends meet **2.** (*íntimamente*) closely **3.** (*rigurosamente*) strictly

estrechar **I.** *vt* **1.** (*angostar*) to narrow; (*ropa*) to take in **2.** (*abrazar*) to hug; (*la mano*) to shake **3.** (*amistad*) to deepen; **hemos estrechado nuestra relación** our relationship has become closer **4.** (*obligar*) to oblige **II.** *vr:* **~se** **1.** (*camino*) to become narrower **2.** *inf* (*en un asiento*) to squeeze in **3.** (*dos personas*) to become close; **~se las manos** to shake hands **4.** (*amistad*) to deepen **5.** (*económicamente*) to live on a minimum; **~se el cinturón** *inf* to tighten one's belt

estrechez *f* **1.** (*espacial*) narrrowness; ~ **de espíritu** mean-spiritedness **2.** (*rigidez*) strictness **3.** (*de amistad*) deepening **4.** (*escasez*) shortage; (*apuro*) jam; ~ **de dinero** lack of money **5.** *pl* (*económicamente*) neediness

estrecho *m* GEO strait; ~ **de Gibraltar** strait of Gibraltar

estrecho, **-a** *adj* **1.** (*angosto*) narrow; **él es muy** ~ **de caderas** he's got very narrow hips; **hacérselas pasar estrechas a alguien** *inf* to give sb a hard time **2.** (*amistad*) close **3.** (*ropa, lugar*) tight **4.** (*rígido*) strict **5.** *inf* (*sexualmente*) prudish

estregar *irr como fregar* **I.** *vt* **1.** (*frotar*) to rub; (*cepillar, para limpiar*) to scrub **2.** (*sacar brillo*) to shine **II.** *vr:* **~se** to rub

estrella *f* **1.** ASTR, CINE star; ~ **fija** fixed star; ~ **fugaz** shooting star; ~ **de Venus** the planet of Venus; **una nueva** ~ **del teatro** a new star of the stage; **querer contar las ~s** *fig* to aim for the moon; **poner a alguien por las ~s** to praise sb to the skies; **ver las ~s** (**de dolor**) *fig* to see stars **2.** (*destino*) fate; **haber nacido con buena** ~ to have been born under a lucky star; **tener buena/mala** ~ to be lucky/unlucky **3.** TIPO asterisk **4.** ZOOL ~ **de mar** starfish

estrellado, **-a** *adj* **1.** (*esteliforme*) star-shaped **2.** (*noche, cielo*) starry; **cielo** ~ starry sky **3.** (*avión*) crashed

estrellar **I.** *adj* star **II.** *vt* (*romper*) to smash; (*arrojar*) to hurl; ~ **huevos en una sartén** to break eggs in a frying pan **III.** *vr:* **~se** **1.** (*chocar*) **~se contra** [*o* **en**] **algo** to crash into sth; **~se con alguien** *fig* to bump into sb **2.** (*avión*) to crash; (*barco*) to break up; (*globo*) to burst; **~se contra** [*o* **en**] **algo** to collide with sth **3.** (*fracasar*) to fail

estrellato *m* stardom

estremecedor(**a**) *adj* **1.** (*emoción*) moving **2.** (*horrible*) harrowing

estremecer *irr como crecer* **I.** *vt* **1.** (*conmover*) to move **2.** (*hacer tiritar*) to make tremble **II.** *vr:* **~se** **1.** (*por un suceso, de un susto*) to be shocked; **se estremecieron sus creencias** their beliefs were rocked **2.** (*temblar*) to shiver

estremecimiento *m* **1.** (*emoción*) shock **2.** (*de cañonazo, terremoto*) rumble **3.** (*de frío, miedo*) shivering **4.** (*de susto*) shock

estrenar **I.** *vt* **1.** (*usar*) to use for the first time; (*ropa*) to wear for the first time; (*edificio*) to inaugurate; ~ **un piso** to move into a new flat; **sin** ~ brand new; **estos guantes están sin** ~ these gloves are brand new **2.** CINE, TEAT to première **3.** (*trabajo*) to start; ~ **un cargo** to have one's first day in a job [*o* post *Brit*] **II.** *vr:* **~se** **1.** (*carrera artística*) to make one's debut **2.** CINE, TEAT to be premièred **3.** (*trabajo*) to open, to start work

estreno *m* **1.** (*uso*) first use; (*edificio*) opening; ~ **de piso** showing of new flat *Brit,* house-warming *Am;* **ser de** ~ to be brand new **2.** (*de un actor, un músico*) debut; (*de una obra*) première

estreñido, **-a** *adj* constipated

estreñimiento *m* constipation

estreñir *irr como ceñir vt* (*comida*) to constipate; **las judías me estriñen** green beans give me constipation

estrépito *m* **1.** (*ruido*) din; **reírse con** ~ to laugh loudly **2.** (*ostentación*) fanfare; **con gran** ~ ostentatiously

estrepitoso, **-a** *adj* (*risa, aplausos*) loud; (*fracaso*) spectacular

estreptococo *m* MED streptococcus

estrés *m* stress; **producir** ~ to be stressful

estresante *adj* stressful

estresar *vt* to stress

estría *f* **1.** ARQUIT flute **2.** *pl* (*rayas*) grooves *pl;* **~s del embarazo** stretchmarks *pl* from pregnancy

estriado, **-a** *adj* **1.** ARQUIT fluted **2.** (*con rayas*) ribbed

estribación *f* GEO foothills *pl*

estribar *vi* to lie; **nuestro éxito estriba en nuestra larga experiencia** our success is due to our lengthy experience; **la dificultad estriba en la falta de práctica** the problem lies in the lack of practice

estribillo *m* **1.** MÚS chorus **2.** LIT refrain **3.** (*frase*) catchphrase; **siempre** (**con**) **el mismo** ~ *fig* always the same old story

estribo *m* **1.** (*de jinete*) stirrup; **estar sobre los ~s** *fig* to be careful; **perder los ~s** *fig* to fly off the handle **2.** (*del coche*) running board; (*de moto*) footrest **3.** (*entibo*) buttress **4.** (*respaldo*) grip

estribor *m* NÁUT starboard

estricnina *f* strychnine

estricto, **-a** *adj* **1.** (*severo*) strict **2.** (*exacto*) exact

estridente *adj* shrill; (*vestir*) loud

estripazón *m AmC* **1.** (*apertura*) opening **2.** (*destrozo*) mutilation

estrofa *f* (*de poema*) stanza; (*de canción*) verse

estrógeno *m* oestrogen *Brit,* estrogen *Am*

estroncio *m sin pl* strontium

estropajo *m* 1. (*de fregar*) scourer; **poner a alguien como un** ~ to lay into sb; **servir de** ~ *fig* to work like a slave 2. BOT loofah
estropajoso, **-a** *adj* 1. (*seco*) dry; (*carne*) tough 2. (*pelo*) straw-like 3. (*tartajoso*) slurring 4. (*andrajoso*) ragged
estropear I. *vt* 1. (*deteriorar: planes, comida*) to spoil; (*televisor*) to break; (*cosecha*) to ruin; **con lo que dijiste, lo has estropeado todo** by saying that, you have ruined everything 2. (*aspecto*) to spoil; **desde la muerte de su mujer está muy estropeado** since his wife died he looks terrible; **está muy estropeado por la enfermedad** the disease has had a very bad effect on him II. *vr:* **~se** 1. (*deteriorarse*) to spoil 2. (*averiarse*) to break down; (*comida*) to go off; (*planes*) to be spoilt
estropicio *m* 1. (*destrozo*) mess 2. (*alboroto*) uproar
estructura *f* structure; (*edificio*) framework
estructural *adj* structural; **problemas ~es** structural [*o* organizational] problems *pl*
estructurar I. *vt* to structure; (*clasificar*) to classify II. *vr:* **~se** to be structured
estruendo *m* 1. (*ruido*) din 2. (*alboroto*) uproar 3. (*ostentación*) ostentation
estruendoso, **-a** *adj* deafening; (*aplauso*) thunderous
estrujar I. *vt* 1. (*apretar, naranja*) to squeeze 2. (*machacar*) to crush; (*papel*) to crumple up 3. (*al saludar*) to hug II. *vr:* **~se** 1. (*entre mucha gente*) to push 2. (*apretujarse*) to squeeze together; **~se los sesos** *inf* to rack one's brains
estucar <c→qu> *vt* to plaster, to stucco
estuche *m* case; (*cajita*) little box; ~ **de gafas** spectacle [*o* glasses] case; ~ **de joyas** jewel box; ~ **de violín** violin case
estuco *m* plaster, stucco
estudiado, **-a** *adj* (*amanerado*) affected
estudiante *mf* 1. (*de universidad*) student; ~ **de ciencias** science student 2. (*de escuela*) pupil
estudiantil *adj* student; **movimiento** ~ student movement
estudiar I. *vi, vt* 1. (*aprender, observar*) to study; ~ **para médico** to study to be a doctor; **dejar de** ~ to drop out 2. (*analizar*) to analyze, to study II. *vt* 1. (*reflexionar*) to think about; **lo ~é** I'll think about it 2. (*obra de teatro*) to learn
estudio *m* 1. (*trabajo intelectual*) studying; **dedicarse tres horas todos los días al** ~ to devote three hours every day to studying 2. (*ensayo, obra*) study; (*informe*) report; (*investigación*) research; ~ **de impacto ambiental** environmental impact study; **estar en** ~ to be under study 3. MÚS étude 4. ARTE, TV studio; ~ **cinematográfico** cinema studio; ~ **radiofónico** radio studio; ~ **de registro de sonido** sound studio 5. MED (*prueba*) test 6. (*taller*) studio 7. (*piso*) bedsit 8. *pl* (*carrera*) studies *pl;* **cursar ~s** to study; **no se me dan bien los ~s** I'm not good at studying; **tener ~s** to have studied
estudioso, **-a** I. *adj* studious II. *m, f* scholar
estufa *f* heater; ~ **eléctrica** electric fire [*o* heater]
estulticia *f elev* inanity
estupefacción *f* 1. (*asombro*) amazement; (*sorpresa*) surprise 2. (*espanto*) fright 3. MED stupefaction
estupefaciente *m* MED narcotic; (*droga*) drug
estupefacto, **-a** *adj* 1. (*atónito*) amazed 2. (*espantado*) shocked
estupendo, **-a** *adj* fantastic; **¡~!** great!
estupidez *f* stupidity
estúpido, **-a** I. *adj* stupid II. *m, f* idiot
estupor *m* 1. (*asombro*) amazement 2. (*espanto*) shock 3. MED stupor
estupro *m* rape (*of a minor*)
esturión *m* sturgeon
esvástica *f* swastika
ETA *abr de* **Euzkadi Ta Askatasuna** ETA (*radical Basque separatist movement*)
etapa *f* (*fase*) stage; (*época*) phase; **por ~s** in stages; **quemar ~s** *fig* to come along quickly; **quemar ~s con el coche** *fig* to speed along
etarra I. *adj* **un comando** ~ an ETA cell II. *mf* ETA member
etc. *abr de* **etcétera** etc.
etcétera etcetera
éter *m* ether
etéreo, **-a** *adj* ethereal
eternidad *f* eternity; **tardar una** ~ to take a lifetime
eternizar <z→c> I. *vt* to make last forever; *pey* (*alargar*) to spin out II. *vr:* **~se** to take ages; **~se en algo** to take ages doing sth
eterno, **-a** *adj* eternal; (*discurso*) long-winded
ética *f* 1. *t.* FILOS (*moral*) ethics; ~ **profesional** professional code of conduct 2. (*decencia*) decency; **no tener** ~ to have no sense of decency
ético, **-a** *adj* ethical
etílico, **-a** *adj* 1. QUÍM ethyl 2. (*alcohólico*) alcoholic; **borrachera etílica** drunkenness; **en estado** ~ drunk
etimología *f sin pl* etymology
etimológico, **-a** *adj* etymological
etíope *adj, mf* Ethiopian
Etiopía *f* Ethiopia
etiqueta *f* 1. (*rótulo*) label; ~ **del precio** price tag 2. (*convenciones*) etiquette; ~ **de la red** netiquette; ~ **de palacio** court etiquette; **de** ~ (*solemne*) formal; (*ceremonioso*) ceremonial; **función de** ~ formal function; **traje de** ~ formal [*o* evening] dress; **ir de** ~ *inf* to be dressed up
etiquetar *vt* to label; (*encasillar*) to stereotype
etnia *f* (*pueblo*) ethnic group
étnico, **-a** *adj* ethnic
etnología *f sin pl* ethnology
etnólogo, **-a** *m, f* ethnologist
eucalipto *m* eucalyptus

eucaristía *f* Eucharist
eufemismo *m* euphemism
euforia *f* euphoria
eufórico, **-a** *adj* euphoric
eunuco *m* eunuch
Eurasia *f* Eurasia
euro *m* euro
eurocheque *m* eurocheque *Brit,* eurocheck *Am*
eurocomisario, **-a** *m, f* POL Eurocommissioner
eurocracia *f* POL eurocracy
eurodiputado, **-a** *m, f* member of the European Parliament, MEP
euroescéptico, **-a** *m, f* eurosceptic
Europa *f* Europe
europarlamentario, **-a** *m, f* member of the European Parliament, MEP
europeidad *f* Europeanness
europeísmo *m sin pl* Europeanism
europeísta *adj, mf* pro-European
europeizar *irr como enraizar vt* to Europeanize
europeo, **-a** I. *adj* European; **Consejo Europeo** Council of Europe II. *m, f* European
eurotúnel *m* Channel tunnel
euscaldún, **-una** *adj* Basque-speaking
Euskadi *m* Basque Country
euskera *adj,* **eusquera** *adj* Basque
eutanasia *f* euthanasia, mercy killing
evacuación *f* 1. (*personas, edificios*) evacuation 2. MED excretion
evacuar *vt* 1. (*ciudad, población*) to evacuate 2. (*diligencias, trámites*) to carry out; (*deber*) to fulfil *Brit,* to fulfill *Am;* (*consulta*) to perform; (*negocio, trato*) to conclude 3. MED ~ (**el vientre**) to have a bowel movement
evadir I. *vt* (*evitar: problema, persona*) to avoid; (*peligro, riesgo*) to avert; ~ **la mirada de alguien** to avoid sb's gaze II. *vr:* **~se** to get away
evaluación *f* 1. (*valoración*) valuation 2. ENS assessment; (*examen*) exam(ination)
evaluar <*1. pres:* evalúo> *vt* 1. (*valorar*) to value 2. (*apreciar*) ~ **en algo** to price at sth 3. (*analizar*) *t.* ENS to assess
evangélico, **-a** I. *adj* evangelical II. *m, f* evangelist
evangelio *m* Gospel; **el Evangelio según San Mateo** the Gospel according to St Matthew; **decir el** ~ *fig* to speak the truth
evaporación *f* evaporation
evaporar I. *vt* (*convertir en vapor*) to evaporate II. *vr:* **~se** 1. (*convertirse en vapor*) to evaporate 2. (*desaparecer*) to vanish; (*persona*) to disappear into thin air
evasión *f* evasion; ~ **de impuestos** ECON tax evasion; (*fuga*) escape; **lectura de** ~ escapist literature; ~ **de la realidad** escape from reality
evasiva *f* 1. (*rodeo*) evasions *pl;* **dar ~s** to hedge 2. (*pretexto*) excuse 3. (*escapatoria*) way out
evasivo, **-a** *adj* evasive; (*ambiguo*) ambiguous, non-committal
evento *m* 1. (*incidente*) incident, event; **a todo** ~ in any event; ~ **social** social event 2. DEP meeting
eventual *adj* 1. (*posible*) possible; (*accidental*) fortuitous; (*provisional*) temporary; **trabajo** ~ casual job 2. (*adicional*) extra; **ingresos ~es** extra income
eventualidad *f* 1. (*cualidad*) contingency 2. (*inseguridad*) insecurity 3. (*hecho*) eventuality
eventualmente *adv* fortuitously; (*tal vez*) possibly
evidencia *f* (*certidumbre*) evidence; **poner algo en** ~ (*probar*) to prove sth; (*hacer claro*) to make sth clear; **poner a alguien en** ~ to make sb look bad
evidenciar *vt* (*demostrar*) to show; (*patentizar*) to indicate
evidente *adj* evident; (*pruebas*) manifest
evidentemente *adv* evidently; **¡~!** of course!
evitar I. *vt* 1. (*prevenir*) to prevent; (*molestias, disgustos*) to avoid; **no pude ~ que declarasen** I couldn't keep [*o* prevent] them from testifying; **pude ~ mayores estragos** I was able to prevent further damage 2. (*rehuir*) to avoid; **antes de los examenes evito salir por la noche** I try not to go out at night before the exams II. *vr:* **~se** 1. (*cosas*) to avoid 2. (*personas*) to avoid each other
evocación *f* 1. (*de espíritus*) invocation 2. (*recuerdo*) evocation
evocar <c→qu> *vt* 1. (*espíritus*) to invoke 2. (*recordar*) to evoke; (*revivir*) to relive; **estuvimos toda la tarde evocando nuestra niñez** we spent the whole afternoon remembering our childhood; **tu presencia evocó en mí el recuerdo de tu madre** your being there made me remember your mother
evolución *f* 1. *t.* MED (*desarrollo*) progress 2. (*cambio*) transformation; **experimentar una** ~ to undergo a transformation 3. BIO evolution 4. MIL manoeuvre *Brit,* maneuver *Am* 5. *pl* (*vueltas*) turns *pl*
evolucionar *vi* 1. (*desarrollarse*) to progress 2. (*cambiar*) to transform 3. MED to evolve 4. (*dar vueltas*) to turn 5. MIL to manoeuvre *Brit,* to maneuver *Am*
ex I. *adj* ~ **novia** ex-girlfriend II. *mf inf* ex
exacción *f* (*cobro*) collection; (*impuesto*) tax(ation)
exacerbar I. *vt* 1. (*dolor*) to intensify; (*crisis*) to deepen, to exacerbate 2. (*irritar*) to aggravate II. *vr:* **~se** 1. (*dolor*) to intensify; (*crisis*) to deepen 2. (*irritarse*) to become irritated
exactitud *f* 1. (*precisión*) accuracy 2. (*veracidad*) exactitude 3. (*puntualidad*) punctuality
exacto, **-a** *adj* 1. (*con precisión*) accurate; (*al copiar algo*) faithful 2. (*correcto*) correct; **eso no es del todo** ~ that's not exactly true 3. (*puntual*) punctual
exageración *f* exaggeration
exagerado, **-a** I. *adj* exaggerated; (*publici-

dad) distorted; (*precio*) steep; (*en los gestos*) theatrical **II.** *m, f* **¡eres un ~!** don't exaggerate!

exagerar *vi, vt* **1.** (*sobrepasarse*) to exaggerate; **~ los precios** to charge excessive prices; **~ los gestos** to behave theatrically; **pienso que ese paso sería ~** I think such a step would be going too far **2.** (*al relatar*) to exaggerate; **¡anda, anda, no exageres tanto!** *inf* come on, stop exaggerating!

exaltación *f* **1.** (*gloria*) exaltation **2.** (*entusiasmo*) enthusiasm; (*pasión*) fervour *Brit,* fervor *Am;* (*excitación*) excitement

exaltado, -a I. *adj* **1.** (*sobreexcitado*) over-excited; (*apasionado*) passionate; (*entusiasmado*) enthusiastic **2.** (*violento*) extreme **3.** (*radical*) radical **II.** *m, f* **1.** (*nervioso*) excitable person **2.** POL extremist **3.** (*loco*) lunatic

exaltar I. *vt* **1.** (*elevar*) to exalt **2.** (*realzar*) **~ a alguien** to praise sb **II.** *vr* **~se con algo** (*apasionarse*) to become excited about sth; (*obsesionarse*) to become obsessed with sth

examen *m* **1.** (*prueba, reflexión*) examination; **~ de conciencia** soul-searching; **~ de conductor** driving test; **~ de ingreso** entrance exam; **~ de selectividad** *Spanish university entrance exam;* **presentarse a un ~** to sit for an exam; **tribunal de exámenes** examination board; **aprobar/suspender un ~** to pass/fail an exam **2.** (*médico*) examination; **someterse a un ~** to have a check-up **3.** TÉC test; AUTO check **4.** (*estudio*) examination; (*indagación*) research

examinador(a) *m(f)* examiner

examinar I. *vt* **1.** *t.* MED (*poner un examen, reflexionar*) to examine **2.** TÉC, AUTO to inspect **3.** (*estudiar*) to study, to examine; (*observar*) to observe **4.** ADMIN, JUR to examine; **para ~lo** for examination; **al ~lo** upon examination **II.** *vr:* **~se** (*en una prueba*) to sit [*o* take] an exam; **mañana me examino de francés** tomorrow I've got my French exam; **volver a ~se** to resit [*o* retake] an exam

exangüe *adj* **1.** (*desangrado*) bloodless **2.** (*agotado*) exhausted **3.** (*muerto*) lifeless

exánime *adj* **1.** (*inánime*) lifeless **2.** (*debilitado*) weak

exasperación *f* (*ira*) exasperation

exasperante *adj* exasperating

exasperar I. *vt* to exasperate **II.** *vr:* **~se** to get exasperated

excarcelar *vt* to release from prison

excavación *f* excavation; (*arqueológica*) dig

excavadora *f* excavator

excavar *vt* to excavate; (*en arquelogía*) to dig

excedencia *f* (*laboral*) leave

excedente I. *adj* **1.** (*sobrante*) surplus **2.** (*funcionario*) redundant; (*temporalmente*) on (extended) leave **II.** *m* surplus; **~ en la balanza comercial** trade surplus

exceder I. *vi* to be greater; **~ de algo** to exceed sth **II.** *vt* (*aventajar: persona*) to outdo; (*cosa*) to be better than **III.** *vr:* **~se 1.** (*sobrepasar*) **~se en algo** to excel at sth; **~se a sí mismo** to outdo oneself **2.** (*pasarse*) to go too far; **has vuelto a ~te** you've overstepped the mark again; **te excedes en el uso de tacos** you swear too much

excelencia *f* **1.** (*exquisitez*) excellence; **por ~** par excellence **2.** (*cargo*) Excellency

excelente *adj* excellent

excelentísimo, -a *adj* honourable *Brit,* honorable *Am;* **el ~ Ayuntamiento de Cádiz** the Cadiz city council; **el ~ señor Presidente** his excellency, the President

excelso, -a *adj* **1.** *elev* (*muy eminente*) illustrious **2.** (*excelente*) excellent

excentricidad *f* eccentricity; **estoy harta de tus ~es** I've had it up to here with your eccentric behaviour [*o* behavior *Am*]

excéntrico, -a *adj, m, f* eccentric

excepción *f* exception; **~ de la regla** exception to the rule; **con ~ de algunos casos** with a few exceptions; **sin ~ (ninguna)** without exception; **de ~** unique; **un vino de ~** an exceptionally good wine; **a** [*o* **con**] **~ de** with the exception of; **todo el mundo a** [*o* **con**] **~ de mí** everybody except me ►**la ~ confirma la regla** (*prov*) it is the exception which proves the rule

excepcional *adj* (*extraordinario*) exceptional; (*raro*) unusual

excepto *adv* except; **todo el mundo ~ yo** everybody except me; **~ algunos casos** with the exception of some cases

exceptuar <*1. pres:* exceptúo> *vt* to except; **~ de un deber** to release sb from a duty

excesivo, -a *adj* excessive; **exposición excesiva** FOTO over-exposure

exceso *m* **1.** (*abuso, demasía*) excess; **~ de alcohol** excessive drinking; **~ de capacidad** overcapacity; **~ de demanda** excess demand; **~ de deudas** too many debts; **~ de equipaje** excess baggage; **~ de peso** excess weight; **~ de velocidad** speeding; **en ~** in excess; **comer con** [*o* **en**] **~** to overeat; **solía beber hasta el ~** he/she used to drink to excess **2.** FIN surplus **3.** *pl* (*libertinaje*) indulgence; **en su juventud cometió muchos ~s** in his youth he indulged in a lot of excess **4.** *pl* (*desorden*) chaos

excitable *adj* excitable; (*irritable*) temperamental; **muy ~** very highly-strung

excitación *f* **1.** (*exaltación*) excitement; (*sexual*) arousal **2.** (*irritación*) nervousness **3.** (*incitación*) stimulation

excitar I. *vt* **1.** (*incitar*) to incite; (*apetito*) to stimulate **2.** (*poner nervioso*) to put on edge **3.** (*sexualmente*) to arouse **II.** *vr:* **~se 1.** (*enojarse*) to become agitated, to get all worked up *inf* **2.** (*sexualmente*) to become aroused

exclamación *f* **1.** (*frase*) exclamation; **signo de ~** exclamation mark **2.** (*grito*) cry; **lanzar una ~ de sorpresa** to cry out in surprise

exclamar *vi, vt* **1.** (*declamar*) to exclaim

E

2. (*gritar*) to cry
excluir *irr como huir vt* **1.** (*expulsar, eliminar*) to exclude; (*descartar*) to rule out **2.** (*rechazar*) to reject
exclusión *f* **1.** (*eliminación*) exclusion; **a/con ~ de** excluding; **con ~ de la prensa** press-free **2.** (*expulsión*) expulsion **3.** (*rechazo*) rejection
exclusiva *f* **1.** (*privilegio*) sole rights *pl* **2.** (*monopolio*) monopoly **3.** PREN exclusive; (*primicia*) scoop
exclusivamente *adv* exclusively
exclusive *adv* exclusively; **cerrado hasta el 27 de agosto ~** closed up to and including the 26th of August
exclusivo, -a *adj* exclusive; **contrato/modelo ~** exclusive contract/model
excma. *adj abr de* **excelentísima** honourable *Brit,* honorable *Am*
excmo. *adj abr de* **excelentísimo** honourable *Brit,* honorable *Am*
excombatiente *mf* ex-serviceman *m Brit,* ex-servicewoman *f Brit,* veteran *Am*
excomulgar <g→gu> *vt* REL to excommunicate
excomunión *f* excommunication
excoriación *f* graze
excoriar *vt* to graze
excrecencia *f* outgrowth
excremento *m* excretion
exculpar I. *vt* JUR to acquit **II.** *vr:* **~se** to be acquitted
excursión *f* **1.** (*paseo*) excursion, trip; **~ a pie** hike; **ir de ~** to go on an excursion [*o* outing] **2.** (*de estudios*) field trip
excursionista *mf* daytripper, excursionist; (*a pie*) hiker; (*turista*) sightseer
excusa *f* **1.** (*pretexto*) excuse **2.** (*disculpa*) apology; **presentar sus ~s** to apologize **3.** (*justificación*) justification
excusable *adj* justifiable
excusado *m* toilet
excusar I. *vt* **1.** (*justificar*) to justify **2.** (*disculpar*) to excuse **3.** (*eximir*) to let off **4.** (*evitar*) to avoid **5.** (+ *inf*) **excusas venir** you don't have to come **II.** *vr* **~se de algo** to apologize for sth
execrable *adj* loathsome
exención *f* exemption; **~ de derechos de aduana** exemption from import/export duty; **~ de impuestos** tax exemption; **~ del servicio militar** exemption from military service
exento, -a *adj* exempt, free; **~ de aranceles** duty-free; **~ de averías** free of breakdowns; **~ de impuestos** tax free; **~ de mantenimiento** free of maintenance; **rentas exentas del impuesto** tax-free income; **estar ~ de la jurisdicción local** to be beyond local jurisdiction
exequias *fpl* funeral rites *pl*
exfoliante *m* exfoliating cream/lotion
exfoliar I. *vt* to exfoliate; **la falta de humedad exfolia la piel** lack of moisture dries out the skin **II.** *vr:* **~se** (*pintura*) to peel; (*corteza*) to flake
exhalación *f* **1.** (*aire*) exhalation **2.** (*suspiro*) sigh **3.** (*rayo*) flash of lightning; **pasar corriendo como una ~** to go past like a streak of lightning **4.** (*estrella*) shooting star
exhalar I. *vt* **1.** (*aire*) to exhale, to breathe out **2.** (*emanar*) to give off **3.** (*suspiros, quejas*) to let out **II.** *vr* **~se** to hurry
exhaustivo, -a *adj* exhaustive; **de forma exhaustiva** thoroughly
exhausto, -a *adj* exhausted, knackered *inf*
exhibición *f* **1.** (*ostentación*) display **2.** (*exposición*) exhibition **3.** (*presentación*) show; **~ cinematográfica** film festival; **~ deportiva** sports festival
exhibicionismo *m sin pl* **1.** (*sexual*) indecent exposure, flashing *inf* **2.** (*deseo de exhibirse*) showing-off
exhibicionista *mf* **1.** (*sexual*) flasher **2.** (*presuntuoso*) show-off
exhibir I. *vt* **1.** (*mostrar*) to exhibit **2.** (*ostentar*) to show off **3.** JUR to show **II.** *vr:* **~se** to put on a show; **~se en público** to expose oneself
exhortación *f* **1.** (*ruego*) exhortation **2.** (*amonestación*) warning
exhortar *vt* **1.** (*rogar*) to exhort **2.** (*amonestar*) to warn
exhumar *vt* **1.** (*cadáver*) to exhume **2.** (*recordar*) to relive
exigencia *f* **1.** (*demanda*) demand; **tener ~s** *inf* to be very demanding **2.** (*requisito*) requirement
exigente *adj* demanding
exigible *adj* (*obligación*) enforceable; JUR payable on demand
exigir <g→j> *vt* **1.** (*solicitar*) to ask for, to demand; **el docente exige demasiado** the teacher is asking for too much **2.** (*reclamar, pedir*) to demand; **la carta exige contestación** the letter needs to be answered
exiguo, -a *adj* meagre *Brit,* meager *Am*
exil(i)ado, -a I. *adj* exiled **II.** *m, f* exile
exil(i)ar I. *vt* to exile **II.** *vr:* **~se** to go into exile; **muchos chilenos se ~on en España** many Chilean people sought exile in Spain
exilio *m* exile
eximio, -a *adj elev* illustrious; **un ejemplo ~** a paramount example
eximir I. *vt* to exempt; **~ de obligaciones** to free from obligations; **~ de responsabilidades** to release from responsibilities **II.** *vr:* **~se** to be exempted
existencia *f* **1.** (*vida*) existence **2.** *pl* COM stock; **en ~** in stock; **liquidacion de ~s** stock liquidation; **renovar las ~s** to renew stocks; **en tanto haya ~s** as soon as stocks are in
existencial *adj* existential
existente *adj* **1.** (*que existe*) existing **2.** COM in stock
existir *vi* to exist, to be; **existen numerosas actividades** there are many activities; **cree que existen ovnis** he believes that UFOs exist

exitazo *m inf* howling success, smash hit

éxito *m* success; ~ **de taquilla** box office hit; ~ **de ventas** sales success; **con** ~ successfully; **sin** ~ without success; **tener** ~ to be successful

exitoso, **-a** *adj* successful

éxodo *m* exodus; ~ **rural** rural depopulation; ~ **urbano** urban depopulation; (*de tecnicos, científicos, etc.*) brain drain

exonerar *vt* **1.** (*eximir*) to exempt **2.** (*culpa*) to exonerate **3.** (*relevar*) to relieve; ~ **a alguien de su cargo** to remove sb from his/her position

exorbitante *adj* **1.** (*excesivo*) excessive; (*precio*) exorbitant **2.** (*exagerado*) exaggerated

exorcismo *m* exorcism

exornar *vt* to enhance; LIT to embellish

exótico, **-a** *adj* exotic

exotismo *m* exoticism

expandir **I.** *vt* **1.** (*dilatar*) to expand **2.** (*divulgar*) to spread **II.** *vr:* ~**se** **1.** (*dilatarse*) to expand **2.** (*extenderse, divulgarse*) to spread

expansión *f* **1.** (*dilatación*) expansion; POL enlargement **2.** (*extensión*) extension **3.** (*crecimiento*) growth **4.** (*difusión*) spread **5.** (*diversión*) recreation

expansionarse *vr* **1.** (*dilatarse*) to expand **2.** *inf* (*sincerarse*) to talk openly **3.** *inf* (*divertirse*) to relax

expansivo, **-a** *adj* **1.** (*dilatable*) expansive **2.** (*comunicativo*) open

expatriar <*1. pres:* expatrío> **I.** *vt* **1.** (*exiliar*) to exile **2.** (*quitar la ciudadanía*) to deprive of citizenship **II.** *vr:* ~**se** **1.** (*exiliarse*) to go into exile **2.** (*renunciar a la ciudadanía*) to renounce one's citizenship

expectación *f* **1.** (*expectativa*) expectation; **con** ~ expectantly **2.** (*emoción*) excitement

expectante *adj* (*atento*) expectant

expectativa *f* **1.** (*expectación*) expectation; **estar a la** ~ **de algo** to be on the lookout for sth **2.** (*perspectiva*) prospect; ~ **de vida** life expectancy

expectorante *adj* MED expectorant

expectorar *vt* to expectorate

expedición *f* **1.** (*viaje*) expedition; ~ **científica** scientific expedition; ~ **militar** military expedition **2.** (*grupo*) expedition **3.** (*remesa*) shipment; (*acción*) shipping; (**empresa de**) ~ shipping agent; **oficina de** ~ issuing [*o* shipping] office **4.** (*documento*) issue

expedicionario, **-a** **I.** *adj* expeditionary **II.** *m, f* member (of an expedition)

expediente *m* **1.** (*asunto judicial*) proceedings *pl;* **instruir un** ~ to open proceedings **2.** (*legajo*) file; (*sumario*) record; ~ **académico** academic [*o* student] record **3.** (*administrativo*) file **4.** (*trámite*) requirement; **cubrir el** ~ *inf* to keep up appearances

expedir *irr como pedir vt* **1.** (*carta*) to send; (*pedido*) to ship; ~ **por avión** to send by air mail; ~ **por correo** to send by post [*o* mail *Am*]; ~ **por vía marítima** to send by sea **2.** (*documento*) to issue

expeditar *vt* **1.** *AmL* (*acelerar*) to speed up **2.** *AmC, Méx* (*despachar*) to send

expedito, **-a** *adj* **1.** (*desembarazado*) free **2.** (*rápido*) swift

expeler *vt* (*sangre, excreto*) to expel; (*aire, humo*) to give out

expendedor *m* ~ **automático** vending machine; ~ **de bebidas/cigarrillos** soft drink/cigarette vending machine

expendedor(**a**) **I.** *adj* **máquina** ~**a de billetes/tabaco** ticket/cigarette vending machine **II.** *m(f)* vendor

expendio *m And, Méx, Ven* (*estanco*) shop

expensas *fpl* costs *pl;* **a** ~ **de** at the expense of; **vivir a** ~ **de alguien** to live off sb

experiencia *f* **1.** (*práctica, vivencia*) experience; ~ **docente** teaching experience; **falta de** ~ **laboral** lack of work experience; **tener mucha/poca** ~ to have a lot of/little experience; **saber algo por** ~ **propia** to know sth from experience **2.** (*experimento*) experiment

experimentado, **-a** *adj* **1.** (*con experiencia*) experienced **2.** (*comprobado*) tested; **no** ~ **en animales** (*en etiquetas*) not tested on animals

experimental *adj* experimental

experimentar **I.** *vi* to experiment **II.** *vt* **1.** (*sentir*) to experience **2.** (*hacer experimentos*) to experiment with; (*probar*) to test **3.** (*sufrir*) to register; ~ **un alza** to register a rise; ~ **un aumento** to register an increase; ~ **una caída** to register a fall; ~ **una pérdida** to register a loss

experimento *m* experiment

experto, **-a** **I.** *adj* expert **II.** *m, f* **1.** (*conocedor*) expert **2.** (*perito*) specialist

expiación *f* **1.** (*purgación*) expiation **2.** (*castigo*) serving

expiar <*1. pres:* expío> *vt* **1.** (*purgar*) to expiate **2.** (*pena*) to serve

expirar *vi* **1.** (*morir*) to expire; (*cultura*) to die out **2.** (*plazo*) to expire; **antes de** ~ **el mes** before the end of the month

explanada *f* (*espacio*) flat area

explanar *vt* **1.** (*allanar*) to level, to grade **2.** (*explicar*) to explain

explayar **I.** *vt* to extend; ~ **la mirada** to look around **II.** *vr:* ~**se** **1.** (*extenderse*) to spread **2.** (*expresarse*) to speak at length; ~**se con alguien** (*confiarse*) to talk openly to sb **3.** (*divertirse*) to enjoy oneself

explicable *adj* **1.** (*que se puede explicar*) explicable, explainable **2.** (*comprensible*) understandable

explicación *f* **1.** (*aclaración*) explanation; **pedir explicaciones** to ask for explanations **2.** (*motivo*) reason; **sin dar explicaciones** without giving reasons **3.** (*interpretación*) interpretation **4.** *pl* (*excusas*) reason; **dar explicaciones** to justify

explicar <c→qu> **I.** *vt* **1.** (*manifestar*) to tell **2.** (*aclarar, exponer*) to explain **3.** (*interpretar*) to interpret **4.** (*justificar*) to justify **II.** *vr:* ~**se**

1. (*comprender*) to understand; **no me lo explico** I don't understand it 2. (*disculparse*) to apologize 3. (*articularse*) to express oneself; **¿me explico?** do I make myself clear?; **ella se explica muy bien** she expresses herself very clearly

explicativo, **-a** *adj* explanatory

explícito, **-a** *adj* explicit

exploración *f* 1. MIL reconnaissance (mission) 2. MED examination 3. (*investigación*) exploration

explorador(a) I. *adj* 1. MIL reconnaissance 2. (*investigador*) explorative II. *m(f)* 1. MIL scout 2. (*scout*) Boy Scout *m*, Girl Guide *f Brit*, Girl Scout *f Am* 3. (*investigador*) explorer

explorar *vt* 1. MIL to reconnoitre *Brit*, to reconnoiter *Am* 2. MED to analyze 3. (*investigar*) to explore

explosión *f* 1. (*estallido*) explosion, boom; ~ **demográfica** population boom; **gran** ~ FÍS big bang; **motor de** ~ internal combustion engine; **hacer** ~ to explode 2. (*detonación*) detonation; (*voladura*) blasting; ~ **fallida** undetonated explosive 3. (*arrebato*) outburst; ~ **de carcajadas** guffaws

explosionar *vi, vt* to explode

explosivo *m* explosive

explosivo, **-a** *adj* explosive; **artefacto** ~ explosive device

explotación *f* 1. (*aprovechamiento*) exploitation; AGR plantation; MIN working; ~ **abusiva** exploitation; ~ **a cielo abierto** opencast mining; ~ **de la energía** harnessing of energy; ~ **minera** mine 2. (*empresa*) management 3. (*abuso*) exploitation

explotar I. *vi* 1. (*estallar*) to explode; ~ **en carcajadas** to burst out laughing 2. (*tener un arrebato*) to blow up *inf* II. *vt* 1. (*recursos, terreno*) to exploit; AGR to cultivate; MIN to exploit; ~ **pozos petrolíferos** to exploit oil wells 2. (*empresa*) to manage 3. (*abusar*) to exploit

expoliar *vt* to ransack

expolio *m* 1. (*acción*) ransacking 2. (*botín*) loot 3. *inf* (*alboroto*) din

exponente *m* 1. (*ejemplo*) example; (*índice*) index 2. MAT exponent

exponer *irr como poner* I. *vt* 1. (*mostrar*) to show, to display 2. (*hablar*) to set out 3. (*exhibir*) to exhibit 4. (*proponer*) to put forward 5. (*explicar*) to explain 6. (*arriesgar*) to endanger 7. (*abandonar*) to abandon 8. FOTO to expose II. *vr:* **~se** 1. (*descubrirse*) to expose oneself 2. (*arriesgarse*) to endanger oneself

exportación *f* export

exportador(a) I. *adj* exporting II. *m(f)* exporter

exportar *vt* to export

exposición *f* 1. (*explicación*) explanation 2. (*informe*) report 3. (*exhibición*) exhibition; ~ **universal** world('s) fair 4. FOTO exposure

expósito, **-a** I. *adj* abandoned II. *m, f* abandoned child, foundling *liter*

expositor(a) *m(f)* 1. (*que exhibe*) exhibitor 2. (*que aclara*) exponent 3. (*mueble*) display case

exprés I. *adj inv* express; **café** ~ espresso; **olla** ~ pressure cooker II. *m* (*tren*) express

expresamente *adv* 1. (*literalmente*) clearly 2. (*deliberadamente*) expressly

expresar I. *vt* to express II. *vr:* **~se** to express oneself

expresión *f* 1. expression; **reducir a la mínima** ~ to reduce to the bare minimum 2. *pl* (*saludos*) greetings *pl*

expresionismo *m sin pl* ARTE expressionism

expresionista *adj, mf* expressionist

expresivo, **-a** *adj* 1. (*vivo*) expressive 2. (*revelador*) revealing 3. (*significativo*) meaningful 4. (*afectuoso*) affectionate

expreso I. *m* 1. (*tren*) express 2. (*correo*) special delivery II. *adv* express

expreso, **-a** *adj* 1. (*explícito*) express 2. (*claro*) clear 3. (*rápido*) express; **tren** ~ express train; **enviar una carta por (correo)** ~ to send a letter by special delivery

exprimidor *m* squeezer

exprimir *vt* 1. (*frutas*) to squeeze; ~ **a alguien para que hable** *fig* to put pressure on sb to talk 2. (*ropa*) to wring 3. (*persona*) to exploit, to bleed (dry) *inf*

expropiación *f* expropriation; ~ **forzosa** compulsory purchase

expropiar *vt* to expropriate

expuesto, **-a** I. *pp de* **exponer** II. *adj* 1. (*peligroso*) risky 2. (*sin protección*) exposed 3. (*sensible*) vulnerable; ~ **a perturbaciones** vulnerable to disturbances; (~ *a la vista*) on display

expugnar *vt* to conquer

expulsar *vt* 1. (*a alguien*) to expel, to kick out *inf*; (*del país*) to deport; (*excluir*) to bar; ~ **a alguien de la escuela** to expel sb from school; ~ **a alguien del campo de juego** DEP to send sb off the pitch [*o* field]; ~ **de la sala** to eject from the room 2. (*emitir*) to give off, to expel

expulsión *f* 1. (*de alguien*) expulsion; (*del país*) deportation; DEP sending off *Brit*, expulsion; ~ **de la escuela** expulsion from school 2. (*emisión*) expulsion

expurgar <g→gu> *vt* 1. (*purificar*) to clean out 2. (*censurar*) to expurgate

exquisitez *f* exquisiteness; (*manjar*) delicacy

exquisito, **-a** *adj* exquisite; (*comida*) delicious

éxtasis *m inv* ecstacy

extemporáneo, **-a** *adj* 1. (*a destiempo*) unseasonable; **son unas temperaturas extemporáneas para esta altura del año** these are unusual temperatures for this time of year 2. (*inoportuno*) inopportune; (*inadecuado*) inappropriate

extender <e→ie> I. *vt* 1. (*papeles, mantequilla, pintura*) to spread 2. (*desplegar*) to unfold; ~ **la mano** to reach out one's hand

3. (*ensanchar*) to widen; (*agrandar*) to enlarge; ~ **la vista** to look around **4.** (*propagar*) to spread **5.** (*escribir*) to write out; (*documento*) to draw up **II.** *vr:* ~**se 1.** (*terreno*) to extend; (*en la cama*) to stretch out **2.** (*prolongarse*) to last **3.** (*difundirse, expresarse*) ~**se por algo** to extend over sth; ~**se en discusiones interminables** to get bogged down in endless discussions

extendido, -a *adj* **1.** (*amplio*) widespread; **un parentesco muy** ~ a far-reaching set of family relations **2.** (*prolongado*) long **3.** (*conocido*) well-known; **estar muy** ~ to be very well-known **4.** (*detallado*) extensive **5.** (*mano, brazos*) outstretched

extensible *adj* **1.** (*ampliable*) extensible; **cable** ~ extension lead *Brit,* extension cord *Am* **2.** (*desplegable*) folding; **mesa** ~ folding table **3.** (*elástico*) elastic **4.** (*plazo*) extendible

extensión *f* **1.** (*dimensión*) extent; (*longitud*) length; **en toda la** ~ **de la palabra** in all senses of the word; **por** ~ by extension **2.** (*difusión*) spreading **3.** (*duración*) length **4.** (*ampliación*) enlargement; ~ **hacia el este** POL enlargement towards the east; ~ **eléctrica** extension lead *Brit* [*o* cord *Am*] **5.** TEL extension

extensivo, -a *adj* extensive; **hacer extensiva una invitación a alguien** to extend an invitation to sb; **hacer ~s sus saludos a alguien** to offer one's greetings to sb

extenso, -a *adj* **1.** (*amplio*) extensive **2.** (*dilatado*) lengthy, drawn-out

extenuar <*1. pres:* extenúo> *vt* **1.** (*agotar*) to exhaust **2.** (*debilitar*) to weaken

exterior **I.** *adj* **1.** (*de fuera*) external, exterior; **aspecto** ~ external appearance; **espacio** ~ outer space **2.** (*extranjero*) foreign; **Ministerio de Asuntos Exteriores** Foreign Office *Brit,* State Department *Am;* **relaciones ~es** external relations *pl* **II.** *m* **1.** (*parte de afuera, apariencia*) exterior **2.** *pl* CINE location shots *pl*

exteriorizar <z→c> *vt* (*manifestar*) to show; (*revelar*) to reveal

exteriormente *adv* externally, outwardly

exterminar *vt* **1.** (*aniquilar*) to exterminate **2.** (*devastar*) to destroy

exterminio *m* **1.** (*aniquilación*) extermination **2.** (*devastación*) destruction

externo, -a *adj* external; **consultorios ~s** outpatients' department; **de uso** ~ MED external use only

extinción *f* **1.** (*apagado*) extinguishing; ~ **de incendios** fire extinguishing **2.** ECOL extinction; **en vías de** ~ threatened by extinction **3.** (*de obligación, derecho*) end; (*de contrato*) termination

extinguir <gu→g> **I.** *vt* **1.** (*apagar*) to extinguish **2.** (*finalizar*) to terminate **II.** *vr:* ~**se 1.** (*apagarse*) to be extinguished **2.** (*finalizar*) to be terminated; ECOL to become extinct

extinto, -a **I.** *adj* **1.** (*especie, volcán*) extinct **2.** (*fuego*) extinguished **3.** *AmS, Méx* (*muerto*) deceased **II.** *m, f AmS, Méx* deceased

extintor *m* ~ **de incendios** fire extinguisher

extirpación *f* **1.** MED extraction; (*de un miembro*) amputation **2.** (*erradicación*) eradication **3.** (*desarraigo*) extirpation

extirpar *vt* **1.** MED to extract; (*miembro*) to amputate **2.** (*erradicar*) to eradicate **3.** (*arrancar*) to extirpate

extorsión *f* **1.** (*chantaje*) extorsion **2.** (*molestia*) nuisance; **ser una** ~ to be a pain *inf*

extorsionar *vt* **1.** (*chantajear*) to extort **2.** (*molestar*) to bother

extra[1] **I.** *adj* **1.** (*adicional*) extra; **horas ~s** overtime; **paga** ~ bonus **2.** (*excelente*) extra special; **de calidad** ~ top quality **II.** *prep* ~ **de** in addition to **III.** *m* **1.** (*complemento*) extra; (*en periódico, revista*) special supplement **2.** (*paga*) bonus

extra[2] *mf* **1.** CINE, TV extra **2.** (*ayudante*) helper

extracción *f* **1.** (*sacar*) removal; (*de un diente*) extraction; ~ **de sangre** extraction [*o* drawing] of blood **2.** (*lotería*) draw **3.** *t.* MIN (*origen*) extraction

extraconyugal *adj* extramarital

extractar *vt* to extract; (*resumir*) to summarize

extracto *m* **1.** (*resumen*) summary **2.** (*pasaje*) extract; ~ **impreso** INFOR printed extract **3.** QUÍM extract

extractor *m* ~ **de humo** extractor fan

extradición *f* extradition

extraditar *vt* to extradite

extraer *irr como traer vt* **1.** (*sacar*) to remove; (*dientes*) to extract; ~ **de un libro** to extract from a book **2.** QUÍM, MIN to extract **3.** MAT to extract

extraescolar *adj* extracurricular

extrafino, -a *adj* top quality **extrajudicial** *adj* extrajudicial

extralimitarse *vr* to go too far; ~ **en sus funciones** to overstep one's bounds; ~ **en sus esfuerzos** to make a superhuman effort

extranjería *f* status of aliens; **ley de** ~ immigration law

extranjero *m* abroad

extranjero, -a **I.** *adj* foreign; **lengua extranjera** foreign language **II.** *m, f* foreigner

extrañamente *adv* strangely

extrañar **I.** *vt* **1.** (*desterrar*) to deport **2.** (*sorprender*) to surprise; **¡no me extraña!** I'm not surprised! **3.** (*echar de menos*) to miss **II.** *vr* ~**se de algo** to find sth strange

extrañeza *f* **1.** (*rareza*) strangeness; **causar** ~ to cause surprise **2.** (*perplejidad*) surprise

extraño, -a **I.** *adj* **1.** (*raro, forastero*) strange, odd; (*extranjero*) foreign **2.** (*peculiar*) peculiar; (*extraordinario*) remarkable **II.** *m, f* (*forastero*) outsider, stranger; (*extranjero*) foreigner

extraoficial *adj* unofficial; **una declaración** ~ an off-the-record statement

extraordinario *m* PREN special supplement

extraordinario, -a *adj* **1.** (*fuera de lo nor-*

mal) extraordinary; (*muy bueno*) fantastic **2.** (*por añadidura*) special **3.** (*raro*) strange **4.** (*sorprendente*) surprising

extraparlamentario, -a *adj* extraparliamentary

extrarradio *m* outskirts *pl*

extrasensorial *adj* extrasensory

extraterrestre **I.** *adj* extraterrestrial **II.** *mf* extraterrestrial, alien

extravagancia *f* **1.** (*rareza*) strangeness **2.** (*excentricidad*) eccentricity

extravagante **I.** *adj* **1.** (*raro*) odd **2.** (*excéntrico*) eccentric **II.** *mf* eccentric

extraviado, -a *adj* **1.** (*cosa*) lost **2.** (*animal*) stray

extraviar <*1. pres:* extravío> **I.** *vt* **1.** (*despistar*) to confuse **2.** (*perder*) to lose; (*dejar*) to leave **II.** *vr:* **~se** **1.** (*errar el camino*) to get lost **2.** (*perderse*) to get lost; (*carta*) to go missing *Brit*, to get lost in the mail *Am* **3.** (*descarriarse*) to stray; *fig* to go astray

extremado, -a *adj* **1.** (*excesivo*) excessive **2.** (*exagerado*) extreme

Extremadura *f* Extremadura

extremar **I.** *vt* to carry to extremes; **~ la prudencia** to be extremely cautious; **la policía extremó las medidas de seguridad** the police tightened security measures **II.** *vr* **~se en algo** to put a lot of work into sth

extremaunción *f* REL extreme unction

extremeño, -a **I.** *adj* of/from Extremadura **II.** *m, f* native/inhabitant of Extremadura

extremidad *f* **1.** (*cabo*) end; (*punta*) tip **2.** *pl* ANAT limb

extremismo *m* extremism; (*religioso*) fundamentalism; **~ derechista** right-wing extremism

extremista *adj, mf* extremist

extremo *m* **1.** (*cabo*) end; **a tal ~** to such an extreme; **con** [*o* **en**] **~** a lot; **en último ~** in the last resort; **pasar de un ~ a otro** to go from one extreme to another; **los ~s se tocan** opposite ends of the spectrum meet up **2.** (*asunto*) matter; **en este ~** on this point **3.** (*punto límite*) extreme; **esto llega hasta el ~ de...** this goes so far as ... **4.** *pl* (*aspavientos*) **hacer ~s** to go wild

extremo, -a **I.** *adj* **1.** (*intenso*) extreme **2.** (*distante*) furthest; **los barrios más ~s** the outermost areas **3.** (*límite*) extreme **II.** *m, f* DEP winger, outside forward; **~ derecha** right winger, right outside forward

extrínseco, -a *adj* (*externo*) extrinsic(al); **circunstancias extrínsecas** extrinsic circumstances

extrovertido, -a *adj* PSICO outgoing

exuberancia *f* exuberance

exuberante *adj* exuberant; (*vegetación*) lush

exultar *vi* to exult

eyaculación *f* ejaculation

eyacular *vi* to ejaculate

F

F, f *f* F, f; **~ de Francia** F for Frederick *Brit*, F for Fox *Am*

fa *m inv* MÚS F; **~ sostenido** F sharp

fabada *f* bean stew (*typical dish of Asturias prepared with pork products*)

fábrica *f* **1.** (*lugar de producción*) factory; **~ de cerveza** brewery; **en** [*o* **ex**] **~** ex-works *Brit* **2.** (*de ladrillo, piedra*) masonry; **obra de ~** stonework **3.** (*invención*) fabrication; **~ de mentiras** pack [*o* tissue] of lies **4.** (*edificio*) building

fabricación *f* manufacturing; **~ en masa** mass production

fabricante *mf* **1.** (*que fabrica*) manufacturer **2.** (*dueño*) factory owner

fabricar <c→qu> *vt* **1.** (*producir*) to manufacture; **~ cerveza** to brew beer **2.** (*construir*) to build **3.** (*inventar*) to fabricate

fabril *adj* industrial; (*de la fabricación*) manufacturing

fábula *f* **1.** LIT fable **2.** *inf* (*invención*) tale **3.** (*relato mitológico*) myth **4.** **¡de ~!** terrific!, smashing!

fabulador(a) *m(f)* **1.** (*fabulista*) writer of fables **2.** (*que inventa cosas fabulosas*) storyteller

fabuloso, -a *adj* **1.** (*inventado*) fabulous; **personaje ~** ficticious character **2.** (*extraordinario*) fabulous

facción *f* **1.** (*banda*) guerrilla band **2.** (*de un partido*) faction **3.** *pl* (*rasgos*) (facial) features *pl*

faccioso, -a **I.** *adj* rebellious **II.** *m, f* **1.** (*rebelde*) rebel **2.** (*de un partido*) member of a faction

faceta *f* facet; (*aspecto*) aspect, side

faceto, -a *adj Méx* **1.** (*chistoso*) facetious **2.** (*presuntuoso*) cocksure

facha[1] **I.** *adj pey, inf* fascist **II.** *mf pey, inf* fascist

facha[2] *f inf* appearance, look; **tener una ~ sospechosa** to look suspicious; **estar hecho una ~** *inf* to look a sight

fachada *f* **1.** (*de un edificio*) façade **2.** (*apariencia*) façade, front; **su buen humor es pura ~** his/her good humour is pure pretence [*o* pretense *Am*]

fachendear *vi inf* to swank *inf*

fachendoso, -a **I.** *adj inf* swanky *inf* **II.** *m, f inf* swank *inf*

fachero *m Arg, inf* nice-looking man

fachinal *m Arg* marshland

facial *adj* facial

fácil *adj* **1.** (*sin dificultades*) easy, simple; **la ventana es ~ de abrir** the window is easy to open; **es más ~ de decir que de hacer** *prov* easier said than done *prov* **2.** (*cómodo*) undemanding **3.** (*probable*) probable; **es ~ que** +*subj* it is likely that; **es ~ que nieve** it may well snow **4.** (*carácter*) easy-going **5.** (*mujer*) loose *pej*

facilidad *f* 1.(*sin dificultad*) ease 2.(*dotes*) facility; **tener ~ para algo** to have an ability for sth; **tener ~ para los idiomas** to have a flair for languages 3. *pl* facilities *pl*; **ofrecer** [*o* **dar**] **~es a alguien para algo** to offer [*o* give] sb facilities for sth

facilitar *vt* 1.(*favorecer*) to facilitate; (*posibilitar*) to make possible 2.(*suministrar*) to furnish, to supply

fácilmente *adv* 1.(*sin dificultad*) easily 2.(*con probabilidad*) probably

facineroso, **-a** *m, f* 1.(*delincuente*) criminal 2.(*malvado*) wicked person

facistol *m* lectern

facón *m RíoPl: gaucho's knife*

facsímil(e) *m* 1.(*reproducción*) facsimile 2. TEL fax

factibilidad *f* feasibility

factible *adj* feasible, viable

fáctico, **-a** *adj* factual; **los poderes ~s** the institutions holding effective control

factor *m t.* MAT (*causa*) factor; **~ de riesgo** risk factor

factoría *f* factory

factótum *m inf* factotum

factura *f* 1.(*cuenta*) bill; (*recibo*) receipt; **pasar ~** to render an account; **su holgazanería le pasa ahora ~** *inf* he/she is now having to pay the price for his/her idleness 2.(*hechura*) **esta chaqueta es de buena ~** this jacket is well made

facturación *f* 1.(*elaboración de una factura*) invoicing 2. FERRO registration 3. COM turnover 4.(*equipaje*) check-in

facturar *vt* 1.(*cobrar*) to bill; **~ los gastos de transporte** to bill for transport costs 2. COM (*ganar*) to earn; **nuestra compañía factura tres millones de euros al mes** our company is bringing in three million euros a month 3. FERRO to register 4. AVIAT **~ (el equipaje)** to check in

facultad *f* 1.(*atribuciones*) authority; **tener ~ para hacer algo** to have the authority to do sth; **conceder ~es a alguien (para hacer algo)** to authorize sb (to do sth) 2.(*aptitud*) faculty; **recobró sus ~es** he/she recovered his faculties 3. UNIV faculty 4. *pl* (*dotes*) faculties *pl*

facultar *vt* to authorize; **este título me faculta para ejercer la abogacía** this qualification entitles me to practise [*o* practice] law *Am*

facultativo, **-a** I. *adj* 1.(*potestativo*) optional 2. UNIV faculty 3.(*del médico*) medical II. *m, f* doctor

facundia *f* 1.(*verbosidad*) verbosity *form* 2.(*locuacidad*) talkativeness

facundo, **-a** *adj* 1.(*verboso*) verbose *form* 2.(*locuaz*) talkative

fado *m* MÚS fado

faena *f* 1.(*tarea*) task; **~s domésticas** chores *pl* 2. *inf* (*mala pasada*) dirty trick; **hacer una ~ a alguien** to play a dirty trick on sb 3. TAUR *bullfighter's performance, especially with the cape*

faenar I. *vi* 1.(*pescar*) to fish 2.(*laborar*) to work II. *vt* (*matar reses*) to slaughter animals

faenero, **-a** *m, f Chile* field worker

fagot[1] *mf* MÚS bassoonist

fagot[2] *m* MÚS bassoon

fagotista *mf* MÚS bassoonist

failear *vt AmC, RíoPl* COM (*documentos*) to file; (*en una carpeta*) to put in a folder

faíno, **-a** *adj Cuba* simple

fair play *m sin pl* DEP fair play

faisán *m* pheasant

faja *f* 1.(*para ceñir*) corset, girdle; (*para abrigar*) sash 2.(*distintivo honorífico*) sash 3.(*franja*) strip 4.(*de libros*) promotional band

fajada *f* 1. *Ant* (*ataque*) attack, assault 2. *Arg, inf* (*paliza*) beating; **le han dado una buena ~** they gave him a hell of a beating 3. *Ven* (*chasco*) disappointment

fajar I. *vt* 1.(*envolver*) to wrap; (*periódicos*) to put a wrapper on 2. *AmL* (*golpear*) to strike II. *vr:* **~se** 1.(*ponerse una faja*) to put on a girdle [*o* sash] 2. *AmL* (*pelearse*) to fight III. *vi* **~ con alguien** to fight with sb

fajilla *f AmL* wrapper

fajín *m* 1. *diminutivo de* **faja** 2.(*de generales, funcionarios*) sash

fajina *f* 1.(*en la era*) rick 2.(*de leña*) faggots *pl Brit,* fagots *pl Am*

fajita *f* GASTR *appetizer of grilled meat wrapped in a corn tortilla*

fajo *m* 1.(*papeles*) bundle; **~ de billetes** *inf* wad of dough *inf* 2. *pl* (*de bebé*) baby's swaddling clothes

falacia *f* deceit

falange *f* 1. MIL, HIST, ANAT phalanx 2. POL **la Falange (Española)** the (Spanish) Falange

falangista *adj, mf* Falangist

falaz *adj* false; **apariencia ~** deceptive appearance

falca *f* wedge

falcado, **-a** *adj* sickle-shaped

falcar <c→qu> *vt reg* to secure with wedges

falda *f* 1.(*vestido*) skirt; **~ pantalón** culottes; **~ plisada** pleated skirt; **~ tubo/recta** straight skirt; **estar pegado a las ~s de una mujer** to be under a woman's thumb; **se ha criado bajo las ~s de mamá** he/she has been brought up tied to his/her mother's apron strings 2.(*regazo*) lap 3.(*de una mesa camilla*) table cover 4.(*de una montaña*) lower slope 5. GASTR brisket 6.(*de sombrero*) brim 7. *inf* (*mujer*) **es asunto de ~s** it is to do with women; **le tiran mucho las ~s** he is a real ladies' man

faldellín *m Ant, Ven* christening robe

faldeo *m Arg, Chile* (*ladera*) mountainside

faldero *m* 1.(*hombre*) womanizer 2.(*animal*) **perro ~** lapdog

faldón *m* 1.(*de una camisa*) (shirt-)tail 2.(*de una funda*) flap 3. ARQUIT gable 4.(*de la chi-*

menea) fireplace

falencia *f Col* bankruptcy, insolvency

falibilidad *f* fallibility

falible *adj* (*erróneo*) fallible; (*engañoso*) deceitful

fálico, **-a** *adj* phallic

falla *f* **1.** (*defecto*) defect; (*en un sistema*) fault **2.** GEO fault **3.** *Col* ENS day's absence (*from school*)

fallar **I.** *vi* **1.** JUR to pronounce sentence **2.** (*malograrse: proyecto*) to fail; (*plan, intento*) to miscarry **3.** (*no funcionar*) to go wrong; **le ~on los nervios** his/her nerves let him/her down; **algo le falla** there is sth wrong with him/her; **no falla nunca** (*cosa*) it never fails; (*persona*) you can always count on her/him **4.** (*romperse*) to break **5.** (*no cumplir con su palabra*) ~ **a alguien** to let sb down; (*en una cita*) to stand sb up **II.** *vt* **1.** JUR to pronounce sentence on; ~ **la absolución** to acquit; ~ **un pleito** to rule on a case **2.** (*premio*) to award **3.** DEP to miss **4.** (*en el juego de naipes*) to trump

> The **Fallas** is the name of the largest public festival in Valencia on March 19th, which is **día del padre** (Father's Day) in Spain. **Fallas** are figures made from papier-mâché that are humorous caricatures, mainly of well-known public figures. They are burned during the "**noche del fuego**" on March 19th.

fallecer *irr como crecer vi* to pass away, to die

fallecido, **-a** **I.** *adj* deceased, late **II.** *m, f* deceased

fallecimiento *m* death

fallero, **-a** *m, f person who participates in las Fallas*

fallido, **-a** **I.** *adj* **1.** (*proyecto*) unsuccessful; (*intento*) abortive **2.** COM (*deuda*) bad **3.** (*en quiebra*) bankrupt **II.** *m, f* irrecoverable loan

fallo *m* **1.** JUR sentence **2.** (*error*) error; (*omisión*) omission; ~ **humano** human error; **este asunto solo tiene un pequeño** ~ this matter only has one small shortcoming [*o* hitch] **3.** (*certamen*) decision **4.** TÉC breakdown **5.** (*en el juego de naipes*) void **6.** (*fracaso*) failure **7.** MED ~ **cardíaco/renal** heart/kidney failure

falluto, **-a** *adj RíoPl, inf* (*en el comportamiento*) unreliable; (*en el modo de ser*) two-faced, hypocritical

falo *m elev* phallus

falocracia *f* male chauvinism

falopa *f Arg, inf* (*droga*) drugs *pl*

falopero, **-a** *m, f Arg, inf* (*adicto*) addict

falsario, **-a** **I.** *adj* counterfeit **II.** *m, f* (*mentiroso*) liar

falseable *adj* falsifiable, forgeable

falseador(a) *m(f)* forger

falseamiento *m* forgery

falsear **I.** *vi* **1.** (*flaquear*) to weaken **2.** MÚS to be out of tune **II.** *vt* **1.** (*adulterar al referir*) to misrepresent; (*verdad*) to distort **2.** (*falsificar materialmente*) to counterfeit

falsedad *f* (*en el carácter*) falseness; (*hipocresía*) hypocrisy

falsete *m* MÚS falsetto; **cantar en** ~ to sing falsetto

falsificación *f* (*acto, objeto*) forgery; ~ **de billetes** counterfeiting of banknotes

falsificador(a) *m(f)* (*de documentos*) forger; (*de moneda*) counterfeiter

falsificar <c→qu> *vt* to forge, to falsify; ~ **la verdad** to distort the truth

falso *adv* **en** ~ (*falsamente*) falsely; **jurar en** ~ to commit perjury; **coger a alguien en** ~ to catch sb out [*o* in a lie]; **dar un golpe en** ~ (*movimiento*) to miss the mark; **dar un paso en** ~ (*tropezar*) to stumble; (*equivocarse*) to make a mistake; **sonar** ~ to ring false

falso, **-a** **I.** *adj* **1.** (*no cierto, no auténtico*) false; **¡~!** not true! **2.** (*no natural*) artificial; (*pseudo*) pseudo; **llave falsa** fake key; **puerta falsa** false door **3.** (*caballería*) vicious **II.** *m, f* (*mentiroso*) liar; (*hipócrita*) hypocrite

falta *f* **1.** (*carencia*) lack; (*ausencia*) absence; ~ **de dinero** shortage of money; ~ **de educación** lack of education; ~ **de liquidez** liquidity problem; **echar en** ~ **algo/a alguien** to miss sth/sb; **me hace** ~ **dinero** I need money; **¡ni** ~ **que hace!** there is absolutely no need! **2.** (*equivocación*) error; ~ **ortográfica** spelling error; **sin ~s** with no mistakes; **sin** ~ without fail **3.** DEP foul **4.** JUR default; (*omisión censurable*) misdemeanour *Brit,* misdemeanor *Am* ►**a** ~ **de pan, buenas son tortas** *prov* half a loaf is better than none *prov*

faltar *vi* **1.** (*no estar*) to be missing; (*persona*) to be absent; ~ **a clase** to miss class; ~ **a una cita** not to turn up to an appointment; **me faltan mis llaves** my keys are missing **2.** (*necesitarse*) ~ (**por**) **hacer** to be still to be done; **nos falta dinero para...** we do not have enough money to ...; **me falta tiempo para hacerlo** I need time to do it; **no falta quien...** there is always sb who ...; **falta** (**por**) **saber si...** we need to know if ...; **¡no ~ía** [*o* **faltaba**] **más!** it is the limit!; (*respuesta a agradecimiento*) you are welcome!; (*asentir amablemente*) of course!; **por si algo faltaba...** as if it were not enough already ...; **¡lo que faltaba!** that is the last straw! **3.** (*temporal: quedar*) to be left; **faltan cuatro días para tu cumpleaños** your birthday is in four days; **falta mucho para que vengan** they won't be here for a long time yet; **falta poco para las doce** it is nearly twelve o'clock; **faltan diez para las nueve** *AmL* it is ten to nine; **poco le faltó para llorar** he/she was on the verge of tears **4.** (*no cumplir*) ~ **a una promesa** to break a promise; **nunca falta a su palabra** he/she never goes back on his/her word **5.** (*ofender*) to be rude; ~ **a alguien** to be disrespectful [*o* rude] to sb **6.** (*cometer una falta*) ~ **en algo** to make a mistake **7.** *elev* (*morir*) to expire

falto, **-a** *adj* (*escaso*) ~ **de algo** short of sth; (*desprovisto*) lacking in sth; ~ **de recursos** lacking in resources; **estar ~ de cariño** to be in need of love [*o* lacking affection]

faltón, **-ona** *adj inf* **1.** (*que falta a su palabra*) unreliable, fly-by-night *inf* **2.** (*negligente*) negligent, remiss **3.** *AmL* (*vago*) idle, do-nothing **4.** (*grosero*) rude

faltriquera *f* pocket; (*a la cintura*) *a pouch tied around the waist and under the apron or skirt*

fama *f* **1.** (*gloria*) glory; (*celebridad*) fame; **tener ~** to be famous; **dar ~ a algo/alguien** to make sth/sb famous; **unos tienen la ~ y otros cardan la lana** *prov* some do all the work while others get all the glory *prov* **2.** (*reputación*) reputation; **tener ~ de fanfarrón** to have a reputation of being boastful; **ser de mala ~** to have a bad reputation **3.** (*rumor*) rumour *Brit,* rumor *Am;* **corre la ~ de que** there is a rumour [*o* rumor *Am*] going round that

famélico, **-a** *adj* starving

familia *f* **1.** (*pareja e hijos*) family; (*que comparten una casa*) household; ~ **numerosa** large family (*for administrative purposes, a family with three or more children*)*;* **cabeza de ~** head of the household **2.** (*parentela*) relatives *pl;* ~ **política** in-laws *pl;* **libro de ~** *book recording the details of a family, including births, deaths, marriages, etc.;* **de buena ~** from a good family; **eso viene de ~** that runs in the family; **en ~** with the family; **ser de la ~** to be one of the family; **acordarse de la ~ de alguien** *inf* to insult sb **3.** (*hijos*) family

familiar **I.** *adj* **1.** (*íntimo*) intimate; **asunto ~** personal matter; **economía ~** domestic economy **2.** (*conocido*) familiar **3.** LING colloquial **II.** *mf* (*pariente*) relative

familiaridad *f* (*confianza*) intimacy; (*trato familiar*) familiarity

familiarizar <z→c> **I.** *vt* (*acostumbrar*) to familiarize **II.** *vr:* **~se** to familiarize oneself, to get to know; **~se con un sistema nuevo** to familiarize oneself with a new system

famoso, **-a** *adj* **1.** (*conocido*) ~ **por algo** famous for sth **2.** *inf* (*sonado*) talked-of

fan *mf* <fans> (*admirador*) fan; (*de fútbol*) supporter

fanático, **-a** **I.** *adj* fanatical **II.** *m, f* **1.** *inf* (*hincha*) fan; **es una fanática del rock** she is crazy about rock **2.** *pey* (*extremista*) fanatic

fanatismo *m sin pl* fanaticism

fané *adj AmL, inf* (*arrugado*) crumpled, rumpled; (*marchito*) withered

fanfarria *f* **1.** *inf* (*jactancia*) bragging **2.** MÚS (*banda*) (military [*o* brass]) band; (*música*) fanfare

fanfarrón, **-ona** **I.** *adj inf* (*chulo*) swanky **II.** *m, f inf* (*bravucón*) braggart, swank

fanfarronada *f inf* brag, baloney

fanfarronear *vi inf* to brag

fangal *m* quagmire

fango *m* **1.** (*lodo*) mud; **baños de ~** MED mudbath **2.** (*deshonra*) dishonour *Brit,* dishonor *Am*

fangoso, **-a** *adj* muddy

fantasear **I.** *vi* **1.** (*soñar*) to fantasize **2.** (*presumir*) to boast, to pose **3.** (*soñar despierto*) to daydream **II.** *vt* to invent

fantaseo *m* fantasizing

fantasía *f* **1.** (*imaginación*) imagination; (*cosa imaginada*) fantasy; **joyas de ~** imitation jewellery; **¡déjate de ~s!** come down to earth! *inf* **2.** LIT fantastic tale **3.** MÚS fantasia

fantasioso, **-a** **I.** *adj* **1.** (*inventado*) fanciful; **idea fantasiosa** fanciful idea **2.** (*fachendoso*) swanky *inf* **II.** *m, f* poseur *form,* show-off

fantasma **I.** *m* **1.** (*aparición*) ghost; **andar como un ~** to be lifeless; **aparecer como un ~** to appear from [*o* out of] nowhere **2.** (*visión*) phantom **3.** *inf* (*fanfarrón*) boaster, poseur *form* **II.** *adj* ghost; **empresa ~** dummy company

fantasmada *f inf* pose

fantasmagoría *f* phantasmagoria; TEAT optical illusion

fantasmagórico, **-a** *adj* phantasmagorical; TEAT with optical illusion

fantasmal *adj* phantom, illusory

fantasmón, **-ona** **I.** *adj inf* posey **II.** *m, f* poseur *form,* show-off

fantástico, **-a** *adj* **1.** (*irreal*) fantastic, imaginary **2.** *inf* (*fabuloso*) fantastic, fabulous

fantochada *f* **1.** (*fantasmada*) pose **2.** (*tontería*) silly act [*o* remark]

fantoche *m* **1.** (*títere*) puppet **2.** (*mamarracho*) sight **3.** (*fantasmón*) poseur; *form* phony *inf*

fañoso, **-a** *adj Ven* twanging

FAO *f* **1.** *abr de* **Organización de las Naciones Unidas para la Agricultura y la Alimentación** FAO **2.** *abr de* **fabricación asistida por ordenador** CAM

FAQ *abr de* **frequently asked questions** FAQ

faquir *m* fakir

faralá *f* <faralaes> **1.** (*volante*) flounce **2.** *inf* (*oropel*) frills *pl,* frippery

farallón *m* (*mar, lago*) out-jutting rock

faramallear *vi Chile, Méx* to brag

farándula *f* **1.** (*farsa*) farce **2.** TEAT the stage, theatre [*o* theater *Am*] world **3.** *inf* (*palabrería*) blarney, bamboozling *inf*

faraón *m* Pharaoh

faraónico, **-a** *adj* pharaonic

fardada *f inf* showing off

fardar *vi inf* (*presumir*) to boast; (*impresionar*) to make an impression

fardo *m* **1.** (*bulto*) package; (*de ropa*) bundle **2.** *inf* (*beso*) podge *Brit,* tub *Am*

fardón, **-ona** *adj inf* **1.** (*chulo*) swanky *inf,* boastful **2.** (*vistoso*) showy; (*coche*) swish, flashy *inf*

farero, **-a** *m, f* lighthouse keeper

F

farfullar I. *vi inf* (*balbucear*) to splutter II. *vt inf* (*chapucear*) to botch
farfullero, **-a** *m, f inf* 1. (*tartamudo*) splutterer 2. (*chapucero*) botcher
farináceo, **-a** *adj* floury, farinaceous
faringe *f* ANAT pharynx, throat
faringitis *f inv* MED pharyngitis
fariña *f AmS* coarse cassava flour
farisaico, **-a** *adj* 1. (*fariseo*) Pharisaic(al) 2. (*falso*) hypocritical
fariseo, **-a** *m, f* 1. (*de la secta judía*) Pharisee 2. (*hipócrita*) hypocrite
farmacéutico, **-a** I. *adj* pharmaceutical; **industria farmacéutica** pharmaceutical industry; **productos ~s** pharmaceutical products II. *m, f* chemist *Brit,* druggist *Am*
farmacia *f* 1. (*tienda*) chemist's *Brit,* drugstore *Am;* ~ **de guardia** all-night chemist's [*o* drugstore *Am*] 2. (*ciencia*) pharmacy
fármaco *m* medicine, drug
farmacodependencia *f* drug dependence
farmacólogo, **-a** *m, f* pharmacologist
faro *m* 1. AUTO headlight; ~ **antiniebla** fog light [*o* lamp] 2. NÁUT lighthouse
farol *m* 1. (*lámpara*) lamp; (*de papel*) Chinese lantern; ~ (**de calle**) streetlight 2. DEP bluff 3. *inf* (*fanfarronada*) idle boast, swank *inf;* (*patraña*) tall story; **tirarse un** ~ to show off 4. *pl AmL* (*ojos*) eyes; **¡adelante con los ~es!** *inf* go for it!
farola *f* street light [*o* lamp]; (*poste*) lamppost
farolazo *m AmC, Méx* swig of liquor
farolear *vi inf* to brag, to swank *inf*
farolero, **-a** I. *adj inf* bragging II. *m, f* 1. (*oficio*) lamplighter 2. (*fanfarrón*) show-off
farolillo *m* Chinese lantern; ~ **rojo** *inf* team [*o* competitor] in last place
farra *f* **estar** [*o* **ir**] **de** ~ *inf* to party
fárrago *m* jumble, hotch-potch *Brit,* hodge-podge *Am*
farragoso, **-a** *adj* jumbled-up
farrear I. *vi CSur, inf* to paint the town red II. *vr:* **~se** *RíoPl* (*dinero*) to squander, to blow *inf*
farrista I. *adj CSur* fun-loving; **mi hija es muy** ~ my daughter is always out living it up II. *mf CSur* (*que le gusta ir a fiestas*) party-loving
farruco, **-a** I. *adj* defiant; **ponerse** ~ **con alguien** to get cocky with sb II. *m, f RíoPl: Galician or Asturian immigrant*
farruto, **-a** *adj Bol, Chile* puny
farsa *f* 1. TEAT (*farándula*) theatre *Brit,* theater *Am;* (*sainete*) farce 2. (*engaño*) sham
farsante I. *adj inf* sham II. *mf inf* charlatan
FAS *fpl* MIL *abr de* **Fuerzas Armadas** the (armed) forces
fascículo *m* 1. ANAT fascicle 2. (*de libro*) instalment *Brit,* installment *Am*
fascinación *f* fascination; **sentir** ~ **por algo** to be fascinated by [*o* drawn to] sth
fascinador(**a**) *adj,* **fascinante** *adj* fascinating; (*persona*) captivating; (*libro*) enthralling
fascinar I. *vi, vt* (*encantar*) to fascinate; (*libro*) to enthral *Brit,* enthrall *Am* II. *vr:* **~se** to be fascinated
fascismo *m sin pl* fascism
fascista I. *adj* fascist(ic) II. *mf* fascist
fascistoide *adj* fascist-like
fase *f* 1. (*período, estado*) phase 2. ELEC, FÍS, QUÍM phase; **de tres ~s** three-phase; (*nave espacial*) stage
fast food *m o f sin pl* fast food
fastidiado, **-a** *adj inf* 1. (*enfermo*) unwell 2. (*molesto*) annoyed 3. (*estropeado*) broken; **andar** ~ **de...** to have a bad ...; **ando** ~ **de dinero/tiempo estos dias** I don't have enough money/time these days; **anda** ~ **de la rodilla** he has a bad knee
fastidiar I. *vt* 1. (*molestar*) to annoy; **¡no te fastidia!** *inf* you must be joking! 2. *inf* (*estropear*) ruin 3. (*causar hastío*) to sicken 4. (*aburrir*) to bore II. *vr:* **~se** *inf* 1. (*enojarse*) to get cross; **¡fastídiate!** stuff it! *inf;* **¡hay que ~se!** it's unbelievable! 2. (*aguantarse*) to put up with it 3. *AmL* (*perjudicarse*) to harm
fastidio *m* 1. (*disgusto*) bother; **¡vaya ~!** what a nuisance; (*mala suerte*) misfortune 2. (*aburrimiento*) bore 3. (*hastío*) repugnance
fastidioso, **-a** *adj* 1. (*molesto*) annoying 2. (*aburrido*) boring 3. (*pesado*) dull; **persona fastidiosa** a bore
fasto *m* 1. (*pompa*) pomp 2. *pl* (*anales*) annals *pl*
fastuosidad *f* lavishness
fastuoso, **-a** *adj* (*casa, boda*) sumptuous; (*persona*) flashy
fatal I. *adj* 1. (*inevitable*) unavoidable; **el momento** ~ the inevitable [*o* fateful moment] 2. (*desagradable*) disagreeable 3. (*funesto*) fatal; (*mortal*) mortal; **mujer** ~ femme fatale 4. JUR not extendable 5. *inf* (*muy mal*) awful II. *adv inf* awfully; **el examen me fue** ~ my exam was a disaster
fatalidad *f* 1. (*desgracia*) misfortune 2. (*destino*) fate
fatalismo *m sin pl* fatalism
fatalista I. *adj* fatalistic II. *mf* 1. (*que sigue el fatalismo*) fatalist 2. *inf* (*pesimista*) pessimist
fatídico, **-a** *adj* 1. (*que predice el futuro*) prophetic 2. *inf* (*algo*) fateful 3. (*terrible*) horrible
fatiga *f* 1. (*cansancio*) weariness, fatigue *form;* ~ **visual** eye strain 2. (*sofocos*) shortness of breath 3. TÉC fatigue 4. *pl* (*sacrificios*) hardship
fatigado, **-a** *adj* 1. (*agotado*) worn-out 2. (*sofocado*) short of breath 3. TÉC with fatigue
fatigador(**a**) *adj* (*que cansa*) tiring; (*que molesta*) annoying
fatigar <g→gu> I. *vt* 1. (*cansar*) to tire, to fatigue *form* 2. (*molestar*) to annoy; (*importunar*) to pester II. *vr:* **~se** 1. (*agotarse*) to wear oneself out; (*ojos*) to strain 2. (*esforzararse*) to exert oneself 3. (*sofocarse*) to get short of

breath

fatigoso, **-a** *adj* **1.** (*trabajo*) tiring **2.** (*persona*) tiresome; (*jadeante*) panting

fatuidad *f* (*vanidad*) conceit; (*inmodestia*) immodesty

fatuo, **-a** *adj* **1.** (*presumido*) conceited; (*jactancioso*) boastful **2.** (*necio*) fatuous

fauces *fpl* **1.** ZOOL fauces *pl* **2.** *AmL* (*dientes*) teeth

fauna *f* fauna

fauno *m* faun

fausto *m* (*lujo*) sumptousness; (*ostentación*) ostentation

fausto, **-a** *adj* fortunate

favela *f AmL* **1.** (*casucha*) shanty **2.** *pl* (*barrio*) shanty town

favor *m* **1.** (*servicio*) favour *Brit,* favor *Am;* (*ayuda*) good turn; **por** ~ please; **hacer un** ~ **a alguien** to do sb a favour; **¡hágame el** ~ **de dejarme en paz!** would you please leave me alone!; **te lo pido por** ~ I am begging you; **hagan el** ~ **de venir puntualmente** please be punctual; ~ **con** ~ **se paga** *prov* one good turn deserves another *prov* **2.** (*gracia*) favour *Brit,* favor *Am;* **a** [*o* **en**] ~ **de alguien** in sb's favour; **tener a alguien a su** ~ to have sb on your side; **a** ~ **del viento/de la corriente** with the wind/the current **3.** (*beneficio*) **voto a** ~ vote for; **estar a** ~ **de algo** to be in favour of sth; **votar a** ~ **de alguien** to vote for sb

favorable *adj* **1.** (*propicio*) favourable *Brit,* favorable *Am* **2.** (*optimista*) promising **3.** (*benévolo*) kind

favorecedor(**a**) *adj* becoming; **es un vestido muy** ~ **para ti** the dress is very becoming on you

favorecer *irr como crecer* **I.** *vt* **1.** (*beneficiar*) to benefit **2.** (*ayudar*) to help **3.** (*dar preferencia*) to favour *Brit,* to favor *Am* **4.** (*prendas de vestir*) to become **II.** *vr:* **~se** to benefit

favorecido, **-a** *adj* **1.** (*propiciado*) favoured *Brit,* favored *Am* **2.** (*fotografía*) **has salido** ~ **en la foto** you have come out well in the photo

favoritismo *m* (*nepotismo*) nepotism; (*parcialidad*) favouritism *Brit,* favoritism *Am*

favorito, **-a** **I.** *adj* favourite *Brit,* favorite *Am;* **plato** ~ favourite dish **II.** *m, f* **1.** (*del rey*) favourite *Brit,* favorite *Am;* ~ **del público** the public's darling; **la favorita del rey** the king's mistress **2.** DEP (the) favourite *Brit,* (the) favorite *Am*

fax *m inv* fax; **mandar un** ~ **a una empresa/a Suecia** to send a fax to a company/to Sweden

faxear *vt* to fax

fayuca *f Méx, inf* black market; **tabaco de** ~ contraband tobacco

fayuquero, **-a** *m, f Méx, inf* smuggler

faz *f* **1.** *elev* (*rostro*) face **2.** (*anverso*) obverse

FCC *abr de* **fluorclorocarbonados** CFC

fe *f* **1.** (*religión*) faith; ~ **en Dios** faith in God; **doy profesión de** ~ I profess my faith **2.** (*confianza*) faith; **digno de** ~ worthy of trust; **dar** ~ **a algo/alguien** to vouch for sth/sb; **dar** ~ **de algo** to certify sth; **tener** ~ **en alguien** to believe in sb; **de buena/mala** ~ in good/bad faith **3.** (*lealtad*) fidelity **4.** (*certificado*) certificate; ~ **de bautismo/de matrimonio** certificate of baptism/marriage certificate; ~ **de erratas** errata

fealdad *f* **1.** (*monstruosidad*) ugliness **2.** (*indignidad*) indignity

febrero *m* February; *v.t.* **marzo**

febril *adj* (*fiebre*) feverish; **acceso** ~ sudden temperature; (*actividad*) hectic

fecal *adj* faecal *Brit,* fecal *Am;* **sustancias ~es** faecal matter

fecha *f* **1.** (*data*) date; (*señalada*) day; ~ **de caducidad** expiry [*o* expiration] date; (*de comida*) sell-by date; ~ **de cierre** closing date; ~ **clave** decisive day; ~ **de las elecciones** Polling day *Brit,* Election day *Am;* ~ **de entrega** date of delivery; ~ **límite/tope** deadline; **sin** ~ undated; **en la** ~ **fijada** on the agreed day; **hasta la** ~ until now, so far; **adelantar/atrasar la** ~ **de algo** to bring forward/put back the date of sth; **¿cuál es la** ~ **de hoy?** what is the date today? **2.** ECON date; **a 30 días** ~ at 30 days' sight **3.** *pl* (*época*) days *pl;* **en estas ~s** around this time

fechable *adj* datable

fechado, **-a** *adj* (*en cartas*) ~ **el...** dated ...

fechador *m* date-stamp

fechar *vt* to date

fechoría *f* **1.** (*delito*) misdemeanour *Brit,* misdemeanor *Am* **2.** (*travesura*) prank

fécula *f* starch

fecundación *f* fertilization

fecundar *vt t.* BIO to fertilize

fecundidad *f* **1.** (*fertilidad*) fertility **2.** (*abundancia*) abundance **3.** (*productividad*) productiveness

fecundizar <z→c> *vt* to fertilize

fecundo, **-a** *adj* **1.** (*prolífico*) prolific **2.** (*tierra*) fertile; (*campo*) productive **3.** (*creador*) fertile

FED *m* POL *abr de* **Fondo Europeo de Desarrollo** EDF

fedatario *m* (public) notary

federación *f* federation

federado, **-a** *adj* federate; **estado** ~ federate state

federal **I.** *adj* federal; (*partidario del federalismo*) federalist; **estado** ~ federal state; **república** ~ federal republic **II.** *mf* federalist

federalismo *m sin pl* federalism

federalista *adj, mf* federalist

federalizar <z→c> **I.** *vt* to federalize **II.** *vr:* **~se** to form a federation

federar **I.** *vt* (*aliarse*) to unite; (*federalizar*) to federate **II.** *vr:* **~se** (*unirse*) to become a member; (*federalizarse*) to form a federation

federativo, **-a** *adj* federative

fehaciente *adj* indisputable; JUR irrefutable; **copia** ~ certified true copy

felación *f* fellatio
felicidad *f* 1. (*alegría*) happiness 2. (*dicha*) good fortune; **¡~es!** (*boda, nacimiento, etc*) congratulations!; (*Navidad*) Merry Christmas; (*cumpleaños*) happy birthday; **te deseamos muchas ~es** we wish you all the best
felicitación *f* 1. (*enhorabuena*) congratulation 2. (*tarjeta*) greetings card
felicitar I. *vt* **~ a alguien por algo** to congratulate sb on sth II. *vr* **~se por algo** to be glad about sth; **~se de que** +*subj* to be glad that
feligrés, -esa *m, f* parishioner, church member
felino, -a *adj* feline
feliz *adj* 1. (*dichoso*) happy; **¡~ Navidad!** merry Christmas!; **¡~ viaje!** have a good journey [*o* trip]! 2. (*exitoso*) fortunate, successful
felón, -ona I. *adj* 1. (*traidor*) treacherous 2. (*infame*) wicked II. *m, f* 1. (*traidor*) traitor 2. (*infame*) villain
felonía *f* 1. (*deslealtad*) disloyalty 2. (*infamia*) infamy *form* 3. *AmL* JUR serious offence *Brit*, felony *Am*
felpa *f* 1. (*peluche*) plush 2. *inf* (*paliza*) beating, licking 3. *inf* (*reprimenda*) telling-off
felpeada *f Arg, Urug, CSur, inf* dressing-down
felpudo *m* doormat
felpudo, -a *adj* (*tela*) plushy; (*moqueta*) shaggy
femenino *m* LING feminine
femenino, -a *adj* 1. (*de sexo femenino*) female; **equipo ~** women's team 2. (*afeminado*) effeminate 3. LING feminine
feminidad *f* femininity
feminismo *m sin pl* (*doctrina*) feminism; (*movimiento*) feminist movement
feminista *adj, mf* feminist
fémur *m* ANAT femur, thigh-bone *inf*
fenecer *irr como crecer vi* 1. (*morirse*) to die 2. *elev* (*acabarse*) to end
fenicio, -a *adj, m, f* Phoenician
fénix *m* phoenix
fenomenal I. *adj* 1. (*extraordinario*) incredible; (*estupendo*) terrific 2. *inf* (*tremendo*) tremendous 3. (*fenoménico*) phenomenal II. *adv inf* terrifically
fenómeno I. *adj inv, inf* marvellous *Brit*, marvelous *Am*; **¡~!** terrific! II. *m* 1. *t.* FILOS, MED (*suceso*) phenomenon; (*maravilla*) marvel 2. (*genio*) genius 3. (*monstruo*) freak III. *adv* marvellously *Brit*, marvelously *Am*
feo I. *m inf* 1. (*grosería*) insult; **hacer un ~ a alguien** to snub [*o* slight] sb 2. (*aspecto*) ugly person II. *adv inf* bad, badly
feo, -a *adj* 1. (*espantoso*) ugly; **dejar ~ a alguien** *fig* to show sb up [*o* in a bad light]; **tener las cartas muy feas** *fig* to have very bad cards; **la cosa se está poniendo fea** things aren't looking too good 2. (*reprobable*) bad; **está muy ~ lo que hiciste** what you did was really nasty [*o* rotten] ►**ser más ~ que Picio** to be (as) ugly as sin; **le tocó bailar con la más fea** he/she drew the short straw
feracidad *f* fertility
feraz *adj* fertile
féretro *m* coffin
feria *f* 1. (*exposición*) fair, show; **~ de muestras** trade fair 2. (*fiesta*) festival 3. (*verbena*) fair; **puesto de ~** stand
feriado, -a *adj AmL* holiday; **día ~** bank [*o* legal] holiday
ferial I. *adj* (*de exposición*) fair, show; **recinto ~** trade fair pavilion II. *m* fair; (*lugar*) fair-ground
feriante *mf* 1. (*que exhibe*) exhibitor; (*en la verbena*) stall holder 2. (*que compra*) fairgoer
feriar I. *vi* to take time off II. *vt* 1. (*mercar*) to buy 2. (*vender*) to sell 3. (*permutar*) to exchange, to barter
fermentación *f* fermentation
fermentar I. *vi* 1. (*vino*) to ferment 2. (*agitarse*) to get in a state, to work oneself up II. *vt* to ferment
fermento *m* 1. (*sustancia*) fermenting agent 2. (*origen*) cause
ferocidad *f* 1. (*salvajismo*) ferocity 2. (*crueldad*) savagery
feroz *adj* 1. (*salvaje*) fierce 2. (*cruel, violento*) savage 3. *inf* (*muy grande*) huge
férreo, -a *adj* 1. (*de hierro, tenaz*) iron 2. (*del ferrocarril*) railway *Brit*, railroad *Am*
ferrería *f* foundry
ferretería *f* 1. (*tienda*) ironmonger's, hardware store 2. (*ferrería*) ironworks *pl*
ferretero, -a *m, f* ironmonger, hardware dealer
férrico, -a *adj* ferrous
ferrocarril *m* 1. (*vía*) railway line *Brit*, railroad *Am* 2. (*tren*) railway; **~ de cremallera** rack railway *Brit*, rack railroad *Am*; **~ de vía ancha** wide-gauge railway *Brit*, wide-gauge railroad *Am*; **por ~** by rail
ferrocarrilero, -a *adj AmL, inf* (*ferroviario*) railway *Brit*, railroad *Am*; **el transporte ~** rail transport
ferroviario, -a I. *adj* railway *Brit*, railroad *Am* II. *m, f* railway worker *Brit*, railroad worker *Am*
ferruginoso, -a *adj* 1. (*agua, mineral*) ferrous 2. (*color*) rust-coloured *Brit*, rust-colored *Am*
ferry *m* ferry
fértil *adj* 1. (*tierra*) fertile; **estar en edad ~** to be of reproductive age 2. (*rico*) rich
fertilidad *f* fertility; (*t. de tierra*) productiveness
fertilización *f* (*de tierra*) fertilization; **~ in vitro** in vitro fertilization
fertilizante *m* fertilizer
fertilizar <z→c> *vt* to fertilize
férula *f* 1. (*palmeta*) cane 2. (*cirugía*) splint 3. (*poder abusivo*) tyranny
férvido, -a *adj elev* 1. (*hirviente*) fervid 2. (*sentimiento*) ardent
ferviente *adj* fervent
fervor *m* 1. *t.* REL fervour *Brit*, fervor *Am*

2.(*calor*) intense heat **3.**(*entusiasmo*) enthusiasm; **con** ~ ardently
fervoroso, **-a** *adj* fervent
festejar I. *vt* **1.**(*celebrar*) to celebrate **2.**(*galantear*) to court, to woo **3.** *AmL* (*azotar*) to beat II. *vr:* ~**se** to enjoy oneself
festejo *m* **1.**(*conmemoración*) celebration **2.**(*galanteo*) courtship **3.** *pl* (*actos públicos*) festival, public festivities *pl*
festín *m* **1.**(*celebración*) celebration **2.**(*banquete*) feast
festinar *vt AmC* **1.**(*agasajar*) to wine and dine **2.**(*arruinar*) to ruin **3.**(*apremiar*) to hasten
festival *m* festival; ~ **de cine** film festival
festividad *f* **1.**(*conmemoración*) festivity **2.**(*día*) feast
festivo, **-a** *adj* **1.**(*de fiesta*) festive, celebratory; **día** ~ bank holiday **2.**(*humorístico*) humorous, entertaining; (*persona*) witty
festón *m* **1.**(*guirnalda*) garland **2.**(*remate cosido*) scallop
festonear *vt* **1.**(*bordar*) to scallop **2.**(*adornar*) to festoon
feta *f Arg* slice
fetal *adj* foetal *Brit,* fetal *Am*
fetén I. *adj inv, inf* **1.**(*auténtico*) authentic **2.**(*excelente*) smashing II. *f inf* (*verdad*) truth
fetiche *m* fetish
fetichismo *m sin pl* fetishism
fetichista I. *adj* fetishistic II. *mf* fetishist
fetidez *f* fetidness *form*
fétido, **-a** *adj* fetid *form;* **bomba fétida** stink bomb
feto *m* **1.** MED foetus *Brit,* fetus *Am* **2.** *inf* (*feo*) ugly sod *inf*
feúcho, **-a** *adj inf* unattractive, plain
feudal *adj* feudal, manorial; **señor** ~ feudal lord
feudalismo *m sin pl* **1.**(*sistema*) feudalism **2.**(*época*) feudal era
feudo *m* fief; **este pueblo es un** ~ **de los socialistas** this town is a socialist stronghold
fiabilidad *f* **1.**(*de una persona*) trustworthiness **2.**(*de una empresa, de datos*) reliability
fiable *adj* **1.**(*persona*) trustworthy **2.**(*empresa*) reliable
fiaca *f Arg, inf* (*pereza*) laziness
fiado, **-a** *adj* trusting; **comprar al** ~ to buy on credit
fiador *m* (*de puerta*) catch; (*de pistola*) safety catch
fiador(**a**) *m(f)* backer, bondsman; **salir** ~ **por alguien** to stand surety [*o* bail] for sb
fiambre I. *adj* **1.** GASTR cold **2.** *inf* (*noticia*) stale; (*discurso*) old hat II. *m* **1.** GASTR cold meat **2.** *inf* (*cadáver*) stiff; **ese está** ~ that one is stone-dead
fiambrera *f* (*cesta*) picnic basket; (*para el almuerzo*) lunch pail [*o* box]; (*caja*) Tupperware® container
fianza *f* **1.**(*depósito*) deposit **2.**(*garantía*) security **3.**(*fiador*) surety, bail; **en libertad bajo** ~ free [*o* out] on bail
fiar <*1. pres:* fío> I. *vi* **1.**(*al vender*) to give credit; **en esa tienda no fían** that shop does not give credit **2.**(*confiar*) to trust; **es de** ~ he/she is trustworthy II. *vt* **1.**(*garantizar*) to stand surety [*o* bail] for **2.**(*dar crédito*) to sell on credit **3.**(*confiar*) to entrust III. *vr* ~**se de algo/alguien** to trust sth/sb; **no te fíes de lo que dice** don't trust what he/she says
fiasco *m* fiasco
fibra *f* **1.** *t.* BIO, MED (*filamento*) fibre *Brit,* fiber *Am;* ~ **muscular** muscle fibre [*o* fiber *Am*]; ~ **de vidrio** fibreglass *Brit,* fiberglass *Am* **2.**(*vigor*) energy; **no tiene** ~ **suficiente para llevar la empresa** he/she has not got enough drive run the business
fibroso, **-a** *adj t.* MED fibrous
ficción *f* **1.**(*simulación*) simulation **2.**(*invención*) invention; ~ **novelesca** fiction
ficha *f* **1.**(*de ruleta*) chip; (*de dominó*) domino; (*de ajedrez*) piece, man **2.**(*para una máquina*) token; (*de teléfono*) telephone token; (*de guardarropa*) cloakroom [*o* checkroom *Am*] token **3.**(*tarjeta informativa*) (index) card; (*en el trabajo*) card; ~ **perforada** INFOR punched card; ~ **policial** police record; ~ **técnica** technical specifications **4.** DEP signing **5.**(*bribón*) rascal
fichaje *m* DEP signing (up)
fichar I. *vi* **1.** DEP to sign **2.**(*en el trabajo*) to clock in II. *vt* **1.**(*registrar*) to enter; ~ **a alguien** (*la policía*) to open a file on sb; **estar fichado** to have a police record **2.** *inf* (*desconfiar*) to mistrust **3.** DEP to sign up **4.**(*anotar informaciones*) to record
fichero *m* **1.**(*archivador*) filing-cabinet; (*caja*) box file **2.** INFOR file
ficticio, **-a** *adj* ficticious
ficus *m* rubber plant
fidedigno, **-a** *adj* reliable
fideicomiso *m* trust
fidelidad *f* **1.**(*lealtad*) fidelity, faithfulness **2.**(*precisión*) precision; **alta** ~ high fidelity
fideo *m* **1.** GASTR fine noodle **2.** *inf* (*persona*) beanpole
fiduciario, **-a** I. *adj* fiduciary II. *m, f* trustee
fiebre *f* fever; ~ **del heno** hay fever; ~ **del juego** compulsive gambling; ~ **del oro** gold rush; ~ **palúdica** malaria; **tener poca** ~ to have a slight temperature
fiel I. *adj* **1.**(*persona*) faithful; **ser** ~ **a una promesa** to keep a promise; **siempre me han sido** ~**es** they have always been loyal to me **2.**(*retrato*) faithful **3.**(*memoria*) accurate II. *m* **1.**(*seguidor*) faithful **2.**(*de una balanza*) needle, pointer; **él podría inclinar el** ~ **de la balanza** he could tip the scales [*o* balance] **3.** *pl* REL the faithful
fieltro *m* felt
fiera *f* **1.** ZOOL wild animal **2.** TAUR bull **3.**(*persona*) animal; **llegó hecho una** ~ *inf* he arrived in a furious state; (*persona astuta*) wizard, whizz *Brit,* whiz *Am*

F

fiereza *f* **1.** (*de un animal*) ferocity, ferociousness **2.** (*de una persona*) cruelty

fiero, **-a** *adj* **1.** (*feroz*) fierce **2.** (*cruel*) cruel **3.** (*feo*) ugly **4.** (*fuerte*) terrible

fierro *m AmL* **1.** (*hierro*) iron **2.** (*del ganado*) branding iron

fiesta *f* **1.** (*día*) holiday; **¡Felices Fiestas!** Merry Christmas and a Happy New Year!; **hoy hago ~** I have taken the day off today **2.** (*celebración*) celebration; **~** (**mayor**) festival; **aguar la ~** *inf* to be a wet blanket **3.** *pl* (*caricias*) **hacer ~s a alguien** to caress sb **4.** *inf* (*humor*) **estar de ~** to be in a very cheerful mood **5.** *inf* (*asunto*) **tengamos la ~ en paz** let's agree to differ

fifí *m AmL* (*señorito*) playboy, man-about-town

fifiriche *adj AmL* (*enclenque*) weak

fig. *abr de* **figurativo** fig

figura *f* **1.** *t.* ARTE, MAT (*de un cuerpo*) figure; **~ decorativa** (*persona*) formal figure; **un vestido que realza la ~** (*que adelgaza*) a dress which enhances the figure; (*que modela*) a dress which moulds [*o* molds *Am*] the figure **2.** (*cara, mueca*) face; (*aspecto*) countenance **3.** (*imagen*) image; **se distinguía la ~ de un barco** you could make out the shape of a boat **4.** TEAT character **5.** (*personaje*) figure; **las grandes ~s del deporte** great sporting [*o* sports *Am*] figures **6.** (*ilustración*) illustration **7.** (*de la baraja*) *court card* **8.** MÚS note

figuración *f* **1.** ARTE representational art **2.** (*imaginación*) imagination **3.** CINE extras *pl*

figurado, **-a** *adj* **1.** (*lenguaje*) metaphorical **2.** (*uso*) figurative; **en sentido ~** in a figurative sense

figurante *mf* CINE, TEAT extra

figurar **I.** *vi* **1.** (*encontrarse*) to figure; **no figura en la lista** it is not on the list; **figura en el puesto número tres** he appears in third place **2.** (*destacar*) to stand out **3.** (*aparentar*) to pose; **le gusta un montón ~** he loves putting on airs **II.** *vt* **1.** (*representar*) to represent **2.** TEAT to appear **3.** (*simular*) to pretend; **figuró no haber oído el comentario** he pretended not to have heard the comment **III.** *vr:* **~se** to imagine; **¡figúrate!** just think!; **no vayas a ~te que...** don't go thinking that ...

figurativo, **-a** *adj* figurative; **no ~** non-figurative

figurín *m* **1.** (*dibujo*) fashion design [*o* drawing]; (*modelo*) model **2.** (*persona*) flashy person **3.** (*revista*) fashion magazine

figurita *f Arg* picture card

figurón *m inf* pompous person, stuffed shirt *inf*

figuroso, **-a** *adj Chile, Méx* (*extravagante en el vestir*) loud-dressing

fija *f* **1.** *CSur* (*en una apuesta*) sure bet **2.** *Arg* (*arpón*) harpoon

fijación *f* **1.** (*sujeción*) fixation; (*con chinchetas*) sticking up; (*con cuerdas*) tying up; (*con cola*) gluing on; (*con clavos*) nailing; (*con cadenas*) chaining; (*con tornillos*) screwing on **2.** (*de precio, regla*) fixing **3.** (*de la mirada*) fixedness **4.** (*de esquíes*) ski binding **5.** (*obsesión*) **tener una ~ por alguien** to have a fixation with [*o* on] sb

fijado *m* FOTO fixing

fijador *m* **1.** (*para el pelo*) hair gel **2.** (*de pintura*) fixative **3.** FOTO fixer

fijar **I.** *vt* **1.** (*sujetar*) to fix; (*con cuerdas*) to tie up; (*con cola*) to glue on; (*con clavos*) to nail; (*con cadenas*) to chain; (*con tornillos*) to screw on; **~ con chinchetas** to stick up with drawing pins; **~ una placa en la pared** to fix a plaque on the wall; **prohibido ~ carteles** bill posters prohibited **2.** (*la mirada*) to fix; **~ la atención en algo** to concentrate on sth **3.** (*residencia, precio*) to establish **4.** *t.* QUÍM to fix **II.** *vr:* **~se** **1.** (*en un lugar*) to establish oneself **2.** (*atender*) to pay attention; **no se ha fijado en mi nuevo peinado** he/she has not noticed my new hairdo; **ese se fija en todo** nothing escapes him; **fíjate bien en lo que te digo** listen carefully to what I have to say **3.** (*mirar*) to notice; **no se fijó en mí** he/she did not notice me

fijeza *f* **1.** (*seguridad*) certainty **2.** (*persistencia*) persistence; **mirar con ~ a alguien** to stare fixedly at sb

fijo, **-a** **I.** *adj* **1.** (*estable*) stable; **cliente ~** regular client; **precio ~** fixed price **2.** (*idea*) fixed **3.** (*mirada*) steady **4.** (*trabajador*) permanent **II.** *adv* with certainty; **saber algo de ~** to know sth for sure

fila *f* **1.** (*hilera*) row; **~ de coches** line of cars; **en ~ india** in single file; **aparcar en doble ~** to double-park; **en ~** in line; **salir de la ~** to step out of line **2.** MIL rank; **¡en ~s!** fall in!; **¡rompan ~s!** fall out!; **llamar a ~s** to call up *Brit,* to draft *Am* **3.** *inf* (*tirria*) dislike **4.** MAT row **5.** *pl* (*de un partido*) ranks *pl*

filamento *m* **1.** (*de un tejido*) thread **2.** ELEC filament **3.** BOT fibre *Brit,* fiber *Am*

filantropía *f sin pl* philanthropy

filántropo *mf* philanthropist

filarmónico, **-a** *adj* Philharmonic; **orquesta filarmónica** Philharmonic Orchestra

filatelia *f* philately, stamp collecting

filatelista *mf* philatelist, stamp collector

filete *m* **1.** GASTR (*solomillo*) steak; (*lonja*) fillet *Brit,* filet *Am* **2.** (*ribete*) edging **3.** ARQUIT, TIPO fillet **4.** (*tornillo*) thread **5.** TÉC border

filetear *vt* **1.** (*un vestido*) to hem **2.** GASTR to fillet *Brit,* to filet *Am* **3.** (*tornillo*) to thread **4.** TÉC to edge

filfa *f inf* **1.** (*mentira*) lie **2.** (*engañifa*) fraud

filiación *f* **1.** (*origen*) filiation; (*de ideas*) relation **2.** (*datos personales*) particulars *pl* **3.** (*en un partido*) affiliation

filial **I.** *adj* filial; **equipo ~** DEP sister club **II.** *f* **1.** COM subsidiary **2.** REL dependency

filibustero *m* HIST buccaneer; POL filibuster

filigrana *f* **1.** (*de orfebrería*) filigree **2.** (*en un papel*) watermark

Filipinas *fpl* **las ~** the Philippines

filipino, **-a** *adj, m, f* Philippine

filisteo, **-a** *adj, m, f* HIST Philistine
film *m* CINE, FOTO film *Brit,* movie *Am;* ~ **transparente** Cling wrap® *Brit,* Saran wrap® *Am*
filmación *f* 1.(*de reportaje*) footage 2.(*rodaje*) filming, shooting
filmadora *f* camera
filmar *vt* to film, to shoot
filme *m* film *Brit,* movie *Am*
fílmico, **-a** *adj* film *Brit,* movie *Am*
filmina *f* slide
filmografía *f* films, movies *Am*
filmoteca *f* film archive
filo *m* 1.(*de cuchillo*) blade; **un arma de dos ~s** *fig* a double-edged sword 2.(*entre dos partes*) dividing line 3. *AmC* (*hambre*) hunger ►**al ~ del amanecer** dot on dawn; **al ~ de la medianoche** at the stroke of midnight
filología *f* philology; ~ **germánica** Germanic language and literature; ~ **hispánica** Hispanic language and literature
filólogo, **-a** *m, f* philologist
filón *m* 1. MIN seam 2.(*negocio*) gold mine
filoso, **-a** *adj AmL* (*afilado*) sharp
filosofar *vi* to philosophize
filosofía *f* 1.(*disciplina*) philosophy 2.(*serenidad*) calm; **tomar las cosas con ~** to be philosophical about things
filosófico, **-a** *adj* philosophical
filósofo, **-a** *m, f* philosopher
filoxera *f* (*insecto*) phylloxera
filtración *f* 1.(*de un líquido*) leak, seepage; (*de la luz*) filtration 2.(*de información*) leak
filtrador *m* filter
filtrar I. *vi* 1.(*líquido*) to leak (out), to seep; (*luz*) to filter 2.(*tubería*) to leak II. *vt* 1.(*por un filtro*) to filter; (*llamadas*) to screen 2.(*datos*) to leak 3.(*noticia*) to percolate III. *vr:* **~se** 1.(*líquido*) to seep; (*luz*) to filter 2.(*noticia*) to percolate 3.(*dinero*) to dwindle
filtro *m* 1.(*tamiz*) filter; **cigarrillo con ~** filter tip cigarette; ~ **solar** sunscreen 2.(*poción*) philtre *Brit,* philter *Am*
filudo, **-a** *adj AmL* sharp
fin *m* 1.(*término*) end; ~ **de semana** weekend; **a ~(es) de mes** at the end of the month; **algo toca a su ~** sth is coming to an end; **poner ~ a algo** to put an end to sth; **sin ~** neverending; **al ~ y al cabo**, **a ~ de cuentas** after all 2.(*propósito*) aim; **~es deshonestos** immoral purposes; **a ~ de que** *+subj* so that ►**el ~ justifica los medios** *prov* the end justifies the means *prov*
finado, **-a** *m, f* deceased
final[1] I. *adj* (*producto, resultado*) end; (*fase, examen*) final; (*solución*) ultimate; **el juicio ~** REL the Final [*o* last] Judgement; **palabras ~es** last words II. *m* end; (*de un libro*) ending; MÚS finale; **película con ~ feliz** film with a happy ending; **al ~ no nos lo dijo** in the end he did not tell us
final[2] *f* DEP (*partido*) final; (*ronda*) finals *pl*
finalidad *f* purpose; FILOS finality
finalista *mf t.* FILOS finalist
finalización *f* finalization; ~ **de contrato** completion of a contract
finalizar <z→c> I. *vi* to finish; (*plazo*) to end II. *vt* to end; (*discurso*) to conclude
finalmente *adv* finally, at last
financiación *f* financing, funding; ~ **de los partidos** political party financial backing
financiador(a) *m(f)* financial backer
financiar *vt* to finance
financiera *f* finance company
financiero, **-a** I. *adj* financial II. *m, f* financier
financista *mf AmL* 1.(*experto en finanzas*) financial expert 2.(*el que financia*) financier
finanzas *fpl* finances *pl*
finar *vi* to die
finca *f* (*urbana*) (town) property, urban real estate *Am;* (*rústica*) (country) property [*o* real estate *Am*]
finés, **-esa** I. *adj* Finnish II. *m, f* Finn
fineza *f* 1.(*delgadez*) fineness 2.(*suavidad*) softness 3.(*de calidad*) excellence 4.(*cumplido*) compliment 5.(*regalo*) gift 6.(*primor*) exquisiteness
fingido, **-a** *adj* fake, make-believe; (*persona*) false
fingidor(a) *m(f)* (*de una enfermedad*) *person who pretends to be ill;* (*de sentimientos*) *person who feigns a feeling*
fingimiento *m* 1.(*de una enfermedad*) pretence *Brit,* pretense *Am;* (*de un sentimiento*) feigning 2.(*engaño*) trick; (*hipocresía*) hypocrisy
fingir <g→j> I. *vi* to pretend II. *vt* to pretend; (*sentimiento*) to feign
finiquitar *vt* 1.(*cuenta*) to settle 2. *inf* (*asunto*) to wind up
finiquito *m* settlement, acquittance; (*documento*) final discharge
finisecular *adj* turn-of-the-century, fin-de-siècle *liter*
finito, **-a** *adj* finite; **número ~** MAT finite number
finlandés, **-esa** I. *adj* Finnish II. *m, f* Finn
Finlandia *f* Finland
fino *m* dry sherry
fino, **-a** *adj* 1.(*delgado*) fine; **lluvia fina** fine rain 2.(*liso*) smooth, even 3.(*de calidad*) excellent; **oro ~** refined gold; **tener un paladar ~** to have a discriminating palate 4.(*sentido*) acute 5.(*cortés*) polite; **modales ~s** refined manners 6.(*astuto*) shrewd 7.(*metal*) precious
finolis I. *adj inv, inf* la-di-da, hoity-toity II. *mf inv, inf* affected person
finta *f t.* DEP feint; **hacer una ~** to feint
finura *f* 1.(*delgadez*) fineness 2.(*suavidad*) smoothness 3.(*calidad*) excellence 4.(*cortesía*) refinement 5.(*astucia*) shrewdness
fiordo *m* fjord, fiord
fique *m Col* BOT sisal
firma *f* 1.(*en documentos*) signature 2.(*de un acuerdo*) signing 3.(*empresa*) firm
firmamento *m* firmament

F

firmante *mf* signatory, signer; **el/la abajo** ~ the undersigned

firmar *vi, vt* to sign; ~ **autógrafos** to sign autographs; ~ **un cheque** (*para pagar*) to sign a cheque [*o* check *Am*]; (*para cobrar*) to endorse a cheque [*o* check *Am*]; ~ **un tratado / acuerdo** to sign [*o* subscribe to] a treaty/an agreement

firme I. *adj* (*fijo*) firm; (*estable*) steady; (*seguro*) secure; (*carácter*) resolute; (*postura corporal*) straight; (*amistad*) strong; **con mano** ~ with a firm hand; **esta mesa no está** ~ this table is unsteady; **es** ~ **en sus propósitos** he/she is resolute in his/her intentions; **¡~s!** MIL attention! II. *m* 1. (*de la carretera*) road surface 2. (*de guijo*) roadbed III. *adv* **de** ~ (*fuertemente*) strongly; (*sin parar*) steadily; **estudiar de firme** to study hard; **el calor aprieta de** ~ the heat is intense

firmeza *f* 1. (*solidez*) solidity; (*de un mueble*) sturdiness 2. (*de una creencia*) firmness; ~ **de carácter** resolution 3. (*perseverancia*) perseverance

firulete *m* 1. *CSur* (*adorno*) cheap adornment 2. *RíoPl* (*paso de tango*) tango step

fiscal I. *adj* 1. (*del fisco*) fiscal 2. (*de los impuestos*) tax II. *mf* 1. JUR public prosecutor *Brit,* district attorney *Am;* **Fiscal General del Estado** Attorney General 2. (*interventor*) auditor, inspector

fiscalía *f* office of the public prosecutor *Brit,* district attorney's office *Am*

fiscalidad *f* taxation

fiscalización *f* audit; (*de impuestos*) tax inspection

fiscalizador(a) *m(f)* auditor; (*de impuestos*) tax inspector

fiscalizar <z→c> *vt* to audit; (*lo fiscal*) to inspect

fisco *m* exchequer, treasury

fisgar <g→gu> I. *vi* (*indagar*) ~ **en algo** to snoop into [*o* about] sth; **le encanta** ~ **en mis asuntos** she loves prying into my affairs II. *vt* 1. (*pescar*) to harpoon 2. (*con el olfato*) to sniff out

fisgón, -ona *m, f pey* 1. (*que indaga*) nosy Parker 2. (*que se burla*) mocker

fisgonear *vi pey* ~ **en algo** to pry into sth

física *f* physics *pl*

físicamente *adv* physically

físico *m* physique; **tener un buen** ~ (*cuerpo*) to have a good physique; (*aspecto general*) to be good-looking

físico, -a I. *adj t.* FÍS physical; **educación física** ENS physical education II. *m, f* physicist

fisiología *f* physiology

fisiólogo, -a *m, f* physiologist

fisión *f* FÍS, BIO fission

fisionar *vt* to undergo fission

fisionomía *f v.* **fisonomía**

fisioterapeuta *mf* physiotherapist

fisioterapia *f* physiotherapy

fisonomía *f* 1. (*general*) physiognomy 2. (*del rostro*) face 3. (*aspecto*) appearance 4. (*rasgos*) features *pl*

fisonomista *mf* physiognomist; **¿eres un buen ~?** do you have a good memory for faces?

fístula *f* 1. MED fistula 2. (*tubo*) tube

fisura *f* 1. (*grieta*) fissure, crack 2. MED (*en un hueso*) hairline fracture 3. MED (*en el ano*) fissure

flac(c)idez *f* 1. (*de las carnes*) flabbiness 2. (*de la piel*) flaccidity

flác(c)ido, -a *adj* 1. (*carnes*) flabby 2. (*piel*) flaccid 3. (*vestiduras*) loose

flaco *m* weak point [*o* spot]

flaco, -a *adj* 1. (*delgado*) thin; **los años de las vacas flacas** the lean years 2. (*escaso*) poor; **rendimientos ~s** poor performance 3. (*débil*) weak; **punto** ~ weak spot

flacucho, -a *adj pey, inf* skinny

flagelar I. *vt* 1. (*azotar*) to flog; REL to flagellate 2. (*verbalmente*) to censure II. *vr:* **~se** to flagellate oneself

flagelo *m* whip; (*azote*) scourge

flagrante I. *adj* (*evidente*) flagrant II. *adv* **en** ~ red-handed

flamante *adj inf* 1. (*vistoso*) flamboyant 2. (*nuevo*) brand-new

flamear I. *vi* 1. (*llamear*) to flame 2. (*bandera*) to flap II. *vt* 1. GASTR to flambé 2. MED to disinfect (*using a flame*)

flamenco *m* 1. ZOOL flamingo 2. (*cante*) flamenco 3. (*lengua*) Flemish

> The **flamenco**, a very traditional form of song and dance from **Andalucía**, is known the world over. The origins of the **flamenco** can be found in the rich traditions of three national groups: the Andalusians, the Moors and the Gypsies. The song and dance movements (solo or duet) are always accompanied by a rhythmic clapping of hands and clicking of fingers together with various cries.

flamenco, -a I. *adj* 1. (*andaluz*) flamenco; **cante** ~ flamenco 2. (*de Flandes*) Flemish 3. (*chulo*) cocky II. *m, f* Fleming

flan *m* crème caramel; **estar hecho un** ~ to be shaking like a leaf

flanco *m* flank, side

Flandes *m* Flanders

flanquear *vt* 1. (*estar al lado*) to flank 2. MIL to outflank

flaquear *vi* 1. (*fuerzas*) to flag; (*salud*) to decline 2. (*en un examen*) to be poor 3. (*demanda*) to slacken 4. (*edificio*) to be on the point of giving way 5. (*ánimo*) to lose heart

flaqueza *f* 1. (*de flaco*) thinness 2. (*debilidad*) weakness

flas *m,* **flash** *m inv* 1. FOTO flash 2. (*noticia*) newsflash

flato *m* 1. MED flatulence 2. *AmC* (*melancolía*) melancholy

flatoso, -a *adj AmL* (*miedoso*) apprehensive

flatulencia *f* MED flatulence
flauta[1] *f* ~ (**dulce**) recorder; ~ (**travesera**) flute
flauta[2] *mf,* **flautista** *mf* flautist *Brit,* flutist *Am*
flebitis *f inv* MED phlebitis
flecha *f* **1.** (*arma*) arrow; **ser rápido como una** ~ *fig* to be as quick as lightning **2.** (*de torre*) spire **3.** (*de viga*) rise
flechar **I.** *vi* to have the bow drawn **II.** *vt* **1.** (*un arco*) to draw **2.** *inf* (*enamorar*) to sweep sb off his/her feet
flechazo *m* **1.** (*de flecha*) arrow shot **2.** *inf* (*de amor*) **lo nuestro fue un** ~ ours was love at first sight
fleco *m* **1.** (*adorno*) fringe **2.** (*del pelo*) fringe **3.** *pl* (*de vestido*) frayed edges *pl* **4.** *pl fig* (*asunto*) final [*o* small] details *pl*
fleje *m* iron hoop
flema *f* **1.** (*calma*) imperturbability **2.** (*mucosidad*) phlegm
flemático, -a **I.** *adj* phlegmatic **II.** *m, f* phlegmatic person
flemón *m* **1.** MED conjunctivitis **2.** (*dental*) gumboil
flequillo *m* fringe; ()
fleta *f AmC* **1.** (*friega*) rubbing **2.** (*zurra*) thrashing; (*castigo*) spanking
fletador(**a**) *m(f)* **1.** (*de avión*) charterer **2.** COM freighter **3.** (*pasajeros*) carrier
fletamento *m* **1.** (*de avión*) charter **2.** COM (*apelocción*) fringe, freightage **3.** (*contrato*) freight **4.** (*pasajeros*) carrier
fletán *m* halibut
fletar **I.** *vt* **1.** (*avión*) to charter **2.** COM to freight **3.** *AmL* (*vehículo*) to hire, to rent **4.** *CSur* (*despedir*) to fire **II.** *vr:* ~**se** *AmC* (*fastidiarse*) to get annoyed
flete *m* **1.** (*carga*) cargo, freight **2.** COM (*tasa*) freight **3.** *AmL* (*tarifa*) hire charge
flexibilidad *f* **1.** (*de palo*) flexibility; (*de músculo*) suppleness **2.** (*de una persona*) flexibility; ~ **de precios** price flexibility
flexibilizar <z→c> *vt* to make (more) flexible
flexible *adj* **1.** (*palo*) flexible; (*músculo*) supple **2.** (*persona*) flexible; **horario** ~ flexitime
flexión *f* **1.** (*del cuerpo*) flexion, bending; (*plancha*) press-up; ~ **de brazos en la espaldera** pull-up **2.** LING inflection **3.** GEO monoclinal fold
flexionar *vt* to flex, to bend
flexo *m* flexible table lamp
flipado, -a *adj inf* freaked *inf;* (*drogado*) stoned, high
flipante *adj inf* amazing, far-out *inf,* awesome *inf;* (*drogas*) mind-bending
flipar **I.** *vt inf* **este actor me flipa** I love this actor **II.** *vi, vr:* ~**se** *inf* (*drogas*) to be spaced-out [*o* on a high], to get high [*o* stoned]
flipper *m* pinball machine
flirt *m* <flirts> flirt
flirtear *vi* to flirt
flirteo *m* flirtation
flojear *vi* **1.** (*disminuir*) to diminish; (*calor*) to ease up **2.** (*en una materia*) ~ **en algo** to be poor at sth
flojedad *f* **1.** (*debilidad*) weakness **2.** (*pereza*) slackness
flojera *f inf* **1.** (*debilidad*) weakness; **cogió** ~ **de piernas** his legs went weak **2.** (*pereza*) slackness
flojo, -a *adj* **1.** (*cuerda*) slack; (*nudo*) loose **2.** (*vino, café, argumento*) weak; (*viento*) light; (*luz*) feeble; ~ **de carácter** spineless; **estoy** ~ **en inglés** I am weak in English; **la política me la trae floja** *vulg* I don't give a damn about politics **3.** (*cosecha*) poor **4.** (*obrero*) slack **5.** *AmL* (*cobarde*) cowardly
floppy *m* INFOR floppy disk
flor *f* **1.** BOT (*planta*) flowering plant; (*parte de la planta*) flower, bloom; **estar en** ~ to be in flower [*o* bloom]; **camisa de** ~**es** flowery shirt **2.** (*lo más selecto*) flower; **la** ~ **y la nata de la sociedad** the cream of society; **la** ~ **de la canela** *fig* the best; **la** ~ **de la vida** the prime of life **3.** (*piropo*) compliment **4.** (*de los metales*) iridescence **5.** (*de las pieles*) grain **6.** (*virginidad*) virginity **7.** (*del vino*) lees *pl* **8.** (*nivel*) **pasó volando a** ~ **de tierra** the plane skimmed over the ground; **tengo los nervios a** ~ **de piel** my nerves are frayed
flora *f* flora
floración *f* **1.** (*acción*) flowering **2.** (*tiempo*) flowering season
florear **I.** *vi* **1.** (*la espada*) to flourish **2.** MÚS to play a trill [*o* appogiatura] **3.** *AmL* (*florecer*) to flower **II.** *vt* **1.** (*adornar*) to adorn with flowers **2.** (*harina*) to sift **3.** (*naipes*) to stack **4.** (*piropear*) to compliment
florecer *irr como crecer* **I.** *vi* **1.** (*planta*) to flower, to bloom **2.** (*industria*) to flourish **II.** *vr:* ~**se** to grow mould *Brit,* to grow mold *Am*
floreciente *adj* **1.** (*planta*) flowering **2.** (*industria*) flourishing
florecimiento *m* **1.** (*de una planta*) flowering **2.** (*de una industria*) flourishing
Florencia *f* Florence
florentino, -a *adj, m, f* Florentine
floreo *m* **1.** (*conversación*) empty talk **2.** MÚS ornament
florería *f CSur, Bol, Perú* (*floristería*) florist's, flower shop
florero *m* **1.** (*jarrón*) vase; **estar de** ~ *fig* to be just for decoration **2.** (*maceta*) flowerpot
floresta *f* **1.** (*bosque*) wood, forest **2.** (*de poemas*) anthology
florete *m* DEP foil
floricultor(**a**) *m(f)* floriculturist
floricultura *f* floriculture
florido, -a *adj* **1.** (*con flores*) flowery; (*floreciente*) flowering; **árbol** ~ tree in flower [*o* bloom] **2.** (*selecto*) select **3.** (*lenguaje*) florid
florín *m* florin
floripondio *m pey* **1.** (*flor*) large flower

2. (*adorno*) gaudy adornment, frippery *Brit*
florista *mf* florist
floristería *f* florist's, flower shop
floritura *f* heavy ornamentation
flota *f* fleet
flotación *f* **1.** floating, flotation, floatation; **línea de** ~ NÁUT waterline **2.** TÉC buoyancy **3.** FIN flotation, floatation
flotador *m* **1.** TÉC (*de pesca*) float **2.** (*en barcos*) float; (*para niños*) rubber ring **3.** (*cisterna*) ballcock **4.** *inf* (*michelines*) roll of fat
flotar *vi* **1.** (*en agua: activamente*) to stay afloat; (*pasivamente*) to be suspended; (*en aire*) to float **2.** (*bandera*) to wave **3.** FIN to float
flote *m* **estar a** ~ to be afloat; **mantenerse a** ~ *t. fig* to manage to keep one's head above water; **sacar a** ~ **una empresa** to get a business going
fluctuación *f* **1.** (*oscilación*) fluctuation **2.** (*irresolución*) uncertainty
fluctuante *adj* fluctuating
fluctuar <*1. pres:* fluctúo> *vi* to fluctuate; **estoy fluctuando entre comprarme un coche o no** I can't decide whether to buy a car or not
fluidez *f* **1.** (*de líquido*) fluidity **2.** (*de expresión*) **hablar con** ~ **un idioma extranjero** to speak a foreign language fluently
fluido *m* **1.** (*líquido*) fluid **2.** ELEC current **3.** (*expresión*) fluent
fluido, **-a** *adj* **1.** (*alimento*) liquid; **es** ~ **de palabra** he speaks with ease **2.** (*tráfico*) free-flowing
fluir *irr como huir vi* **1.** (*correr*) to run; (*brotar*) to flow **2.** (*palabras*) to flow
flujo *m* **1.** (*de un líquido*) flow; ~ **de datos** *t.* INFOR data flow; ~ **de palabras** stream [*o* flood] of words **2.** (*de la marea*) rising tide **3.** MED discharge; ~ **de vientre** diarrhoea *Brit,* diarrhea *Am;* ~ **menstrual** menstrual flow
fluminense **I.** *adj* of/from Rio de Janeiro **II.** *mf* native/inhabitant of Rio de Janeiro
flúor *m* fluorine
fluorescencia *f* fluorescence
fluorescente **I.** *adj* fluorescent; **tubo** ~ fluorescent tube **II.** *m* fluorescent light
flus *m* **1.** *Ant, Col, Ven* (*terno*) suit of clothes **2.** *ElSal* (*racha de buena suerte*) lucky streak
fluvial *adj* fluvial; **puerto** ~ river port
FM *f abr de* **Frecuencia Modulada** FM
FMI *m abr de* **Fondo Monetario Internacional** IMF
fobia *f* **1.** MED phobia **2.** (*aversión*) aversion
foca *f* **1.** ZOOL seal **2.** (*piel*) sealskin **3.** *pey* (*gordo*) whale
focal *adj* focal; **distancia** ~ focal length
focalizar <z→c> *vt* to focus on
foche **I.** *adj Chile* (*maloliente*) smelly **II.** *mf Chile* (*persona corrompida*) corrupt person, rotten apple *inf*
foco *m* **1.** FÍS, MAT focus **2.** (*centro*) focal point; ~ **de infección** source of infection **3.** (*lámpara*) light; (*estadio*) floodlight; (*teatro*) spotlight **4.** *AmL* (*bombilla*) light bulb
fofo, **-a** *adj* flabby; **estoy** ~ I am flabby
fogaje *m Arg, Col, PRico, Ven* (*bochorno*) stifling heat
fogata *f* (*en el campo*) bonfire; (*de alegría*) blaze; (*como baliza*) flare
fogón *m* **1.** (*de la cocina*) stove **2.** (*de máquinas de vapor*) furnace; FERRO firebox **3.** (*de un cañón*) vent **4.** *AmL* (*fogata*) fire
fogonazo *m* **1.** (*de arma*) flash **2.** (*de pólvora*) flare
fogonero *m* stoker
fogosidad *f* **1.** (*de pasión*) passion **2.** (*de persona*) ardour *Brit,* ardor *Am* **3.** (*de debate*) animation
fogoso, **-a** *adj* **1.** (*pasión*) passionate **2.** (*persona*) ardent **3.** (*debate*) animated **4.** (*caballo*) spirited
fogueado, **-a** *adj AmL* expert
foguear **I.** *vt* **1.** (*un arma*) to fire a blank (cartridge) **2.** MIL to get used to gunfire **3.** (*a penalidades*) to harden **II.** *vr:* ~**se** to become hardened
fogueo *m* **bala de** ~ blank (cartridge)
foguerear **I.** *vt Chile, Cuba* (*quemar*) to burn off **II.** *vi* (*hacer una hoguera*) to make a fire
foja *f AmL* sheet; ~ **de servicios** record
folclor(**e**) *m* folklore
folclórico, **-a** **I.** *adj* traditional **II.** *m, f* singer of flamenco
folclorista *mf* folklore specialist
fólder *f AmL* (*carpeta*) folder
foliación *f* foliation
foliar **I.** *adj* foliar **II.** *vt* TIPO to foliate
folio *m* **1.** (*hoja de papel*) sheet (of paper) **2.** (*de un libro*) leaf
folk *m sin pl* MÚS folk music
follador *m* **1.** (*que afuella*) bellows operator **2.** *vulg* (*fornicador*) shagger *Brit*
follaje *m* **1.** (*de árbol, bosque*) foliage **2.** (*adorno*) decoration of branches and leaves **3.** (*en un texto, al hablar*) waffle, wordiness
follar[1] **I.** *vi vulg* to fuck **II.** *vt* **1.** *vulg* (*coitar*) to fuck **2.** *vulg* (*fastidiar*) to bug *inf* **3.** (*deshacer*) to destroy
follar[2] <o→ue> **I.** *vt* **1.** (*soplar*) to blow with bellows **2.** *inf* (*suspender*) to screw up **II.** *vr:* ~**se** *vulg* to silently fart, the butler's revenge *inf*
folletín *m* newspaper serial; **novela de** ~ pulp novel
folletinesco, **-a** *adj* pulp
folleto *m* pamphlet; ~ **publicitario** advertising leaflet, flier
follón *m inf* **1.** (*alboroto*) row; **armar un** ~ to cause a commotion **2.** (*asunto enojoso*) trouble
follón, **-ona** *adj* **1.** (*chulo*) swaggering **2.** (*holgazán*) lazy
follonero, **-a** *m, f* troublemaker
fome *adj Chile* (*aburrido*) boring; **más** ~ **que jugar solo a la escondida** duller than playing hide-and-seek by yourself

fomentar *vt* 1.(*empleo*) to promote; (*economía*) to boost 2.(*discordias*) to foment

fomento *m* 1.(*del empleo*) promotion; (*de la economía*) boosting; **Banco Internacional de Reconstrucción y Fomento** International Bank for Reconstruction and Development 2.(*de discordias*) fuelling *Brit,* fueling *Am*

fonda *f* inn

fondeadero *m* anchorage

fondeado, -a *adj AmL* well-off, well-heeled *Am*

fondear I. *vi* NÁUT to anchor II. *vt* 1.(*anclar*) to anchor 2.(*sondear*) to sound 3.(*registrar*) to search; (*una cuestión*) to examine thoroughly; ~ **un asunto** to examine a matter thoroughly

fondeo *m* 1. NÁUT anchoring; (*sondeo*) sounding 2.(*registro*) search

fondillos *mpl* (*pantalones*) seat; (*trasero*) behind

fondista *mf* 1.(*de una fonda*) innkeeper 2. DEP long-distance runner

fondo *m* 1.(*de un cajón*) back; (*del río*) bed; (*de un valle*) bottom; **los bajos ~s** the underworld [*o* low life]; **en el ~ de su corazón** in his/her heart of hearts; **en este asunto hay mar de ~** there are underlying issues in this matter; **tocar ~** ECON to hit bottom 2.(*de un edificio*) depth; **al ~ del pasillo** at the end of the corridor; **mi habitación está al ~ de la casa** my bedroom is at the back of the house 3.(*lo esencial*) essence; **artículo de ~** editorial; **en el ~** at bottom; **ir al ~ de un asunto** to go to the heart of the matter; **tratar un tema a ~** to seriously discuss a subject; **hay un ~ de verdad en lo que dices** there is sth of truth in what you say; **su carta tiene un ~ amargo** his/her letter had a bitter undertone to it 4.(*índole*) nature, disposition; **persona de buen ~** a good person at heart; **tiene un buen ~** he/she has a happy disposition 5.(*de un cuadro*) background; (*de una tela*) background colour [*o* color *Am*]; **ruido/música de ~** background noise/music 6.(*conjunto de cosas, biblioteca*) collection 7. DEP long-distance; **corredor de ~** long-distance runner; **esquiador de ~** cross-country skier 8. FIN, POL fund; **~ común** kitty; **Fondo Monetario Internacional** International Monetary Fund; **Fondo Social Europeo** European Social Fund; **a ~ perdido** non-recoverable 9. *pl* (*medios*) funds *pl;* **~s públicos** public funds; **cheque sin ~s** bad cheque *Brit,* bad check *Am* 10. NÁUT sea bed; **tocar ~** to touch bottom; **irse a ~** to sink

fondón, -ona *adj pey, inf* big-bottomed

fonema *m* LING phoneme

fonética *f* phonetics *pl*

fono *m Chile* (*auricular del teléfono*) receiver

fonógrafo *m* FÍS phonograph

fonología *f* LING phonology

fonoteca *f* sound archive, sound [*o* music] library

fontanería *f* 1.(*acción, conducto*) plumbing 2.(*establecimiento*) plumber's

fontanero, -a I. *adj* (*natural*) spring; (*artificial*) fountain II. *m, f* plumber

footing *m sin pl* jogging; **hacer ~** to jog

forajido, -a I. *adj* outlawed II. *m, f* outlaw, bandit

foral *adj* 1.(*de los privilegios*) *referring to the privileges obtained by the granting of charters in the Middle Ages to certain towns* 2.(*de la jurisdicción*) jurisdictional 3.(*de las leyes*) statutory

foráneo, -a *adj* 1.(*de otro lugar*) outside 2.(*extraño*) alien

forastero, -a I. *adj* 1.(*de otro lugar*) outside; (*extranjero*) foreign 2.(*extraño*) alien II. *m, f* stranger; (*extranjero*) foreigner

forcejear *vi* 1.(*esforzarse*) to struggle 2.(*resistir*) to resist

forcejeo *m* 1.(*esfuerzo*) struggle 2.(*resistencia*) resistance

fórceps *m inv* forceps *pl*

forense I. *adj* forensic; **médico ~** forensic surgeon II. *mf* pathologist

forestal *adj* forest, woodland; **camino ~** forest track; **repoblación ~** afforestation; **guarda ~** forester *Brit,* forest ranger *Am*

forestar *vt* to afforest

forfait *m* 1. COM fixed price 2.(*esquiar*) ski pass

forfaiting <forfaitings> *m* COM price fixing

forja *f* 1.(*fragua*) forge 2.(*ferrería*) ironworks *pl* 3.(*creación*) forging 4.(*argamasa*) mortar

forjar I. *vt* 1.(*metal*) to forge 2.(*muro*) to build; (*revocar*) to render 3.(*inventar*) to invent 4.(*crear*) to forge; (*imperio*) to build II. *vr:* **~se** 1.(*imaginarse*) to imagine; **~ ilusiones** to build castles in the air 2.(*crear*) to make

forma *f* 1.(*figura*) form, shape; **las ~s de una mujer** a woman's curves; **en ~ de gota** in the shape of a drop; **dar ~ a algo** (*formar*) to shape sth; (*precisar*) to spell out 2.(*manera*) way; **~ de comportamiento** way of behaviour [*o* behavior *Am*]; **~ de pago** method of payment; **defecto de ~** JUR defect of form; **tiene una extraña ~ de andar** he/she has a strange way of walking; **de ~ libre** freely; **en ~ escrita** written; **en (buena y) debida ~** duly; **de ~ que** so that; **de todas ~s,...** anyway, ...; **lo haré de una ~ u otra** I will do it one way or another; **no hay ~ de abrir la puerta** this door is impossible to open 3.(*comportamiento*) manners *pl* 4.(*molde*) mould *Brit,* mold *Am* 5.(*condición*) **estar en ~** to be fit [*o* in good shape] 6. DEP form

formación *f* 1.(*creación*) creation; (*de una sociedad*) formation; **~ del balance** establishment of the balance sheet; **~ de humo** forming of smoke 2. *t.* MIL (*de personas*) formation; **~ política** political group; **~ de tropas** military force; **desfilar en ~ cerrada** to march past in close formation 3.(*educación*) education; ~ **de adultos** adult education; ~ **escolar** school education; ~ **profesional** vocational training **4.** GEO formation **5.** (*forma*) form

formal *adj* **1.** (*relativo a la forma*) formal; **requisito** ~ formal requirement **2.** (*serio*) serious; (*polite*) educated; (*cumplidor*) reliable **3.** (*oficial*) official; **una invitación** ~ a formal invitation; **tiene novio** ~ she has a steady boyfriend

formalidad *f* **1.** (*seriedad*) seriousness; (*exactitud*) correctness **2.** *pl* ADMIN, JUR formalities *pl* **3.** (*norma de comportamiento*) formality

formalismo *m* formalism

formalizar <z→c> **I.** *vt* **1.** (*dar forma*) to formalize **2.** (*solemnizar*) to solemnize; ~ **un noviazgo** (*comprometerse*) to become engaged; (*casarse*) to marry **3.** JUR to formalize; ~ **un contrato** to formalize a contract; ~ **una solicitud** to formalize a motion **II.** *vr:* ~**se** **1.** (*formarse*) to be formalized **2.** (*volverse formal*) to grow up

formar I. *vi* **1.** MIL to fall in **2.** (*figurar*) to figure **II.** *vt* **1.** (*dar forma*) to form, to shape **2.** (*constituir*) to form; MIL to form up; ~ **parte de** to form part of **3.** (*educar*) to train; (*enseñar*) to teach **III.** *vr:* ~**se** **1.** (*crearse*) to form; MIL to fall in **2.** (*ser educado*) to be educated; **se ha formado a sí mismo** he is self-taught **3.** (*desarrollarse*) to develop **4.** (*hacerse*) to form; ~**se una idea de algo** to form an impression of sth

formatear *vt* INFOR to format

formateo *m* INFOR formatting

formativo, **-a** *adj* **1.** *t.* LING (*que da forma*) formative **2.** (*educativo*) educational; (*instructivo*) instructive

formato *m* format; (*tamaño*) size; ~ **de datos** INFOR data format; ~ **de texto** INFOR text format; ~ **vertical** vertical format

formica® *f sin pl* Formica®

formidable *adj* **1.** *inf* (*estupendo*) fantastic **2.** (*enorme*) enormous **3.** (*temible*) awesome

formón *m* **1.** (*escoplo*) chisel **2.** (*sacabocados*) punch

fórmula *f* **1.** *t.* MAT, QUÍM formula; ~ **de despedida** (*carta*) closing formula, close; **coche de** ~ **1** DEP Formula One car **2.** *AmL* MED prescription

formulación *f* **1.** (*de una idea*) formulation; ~ **de balances** drawing up of the balance; ~ **de la propuesta** drawing up of a proposal **2.** FÍS formula

formular I. *adj* formulaic **II.** *vt* **1.** (*expresar con una fórmula*) to express with a formula **2.** (*manifestar*) to formulate; ~ **demanda** to file a claim [*o* suit]; ~ **denuncia** to lodge a complaint **3.** (*recetar*) to prescribe

formulario *m* **1.** (*impreso*) form; ~ **para giro postal** postal order form **2.** (*colección de fórmulas*) formulary; (*de recetas*) recipe book

formulario, **-a** *adj* **1.** (*cortés*) formal **2.** (*formular*) formulaic

formulismo *m* formalism; (*burocrático*) red tape

fornicar <c→qu> *vi* **1.** (*realizar el acto sexual*) to fornicate **2.** (*cometer adulterio*) to commit adultery

fornido, **-a** *adj* well-built, husky

foro *m* **1.** (*plaza*) forum; ~ **romano** Roman forum **2.** JUR (*lugar*) court of law **3.** JUR (*curia*) the Bar **4.** TEAT upstage area; **irse por el** ~ *inf* to slip away unnoticed

forofo, **-a** *m, f* fan, buff

forrado, **-a** *adj* **1.** (*con forro*) lined **2.** *inf* (*rico*) stinking rich *inf*

forraje *m* **1.** (*pasto*) hay; (*verde*) grass; *AmL* (*seco*) feed **2.** *inf* (*fárrago*) hotchpotch *Brit*, hodgepodge *Am*

forrar I. *vt* (*el exterior, una pared*) to face; (*el interior, una prenda*) to line; (*una butaca*) to upholster; (*un libro*) to cover; ~ **con algodón** to cover with cotton **II.** *vr:* ~**se** *inf* **1.** (*enriquecerse*) to make a packet **2.** (*hartarse*) ~**se de algo** to stuff oneself with sth

forro *m* **1.** (*exterior, de una pared*) facing; (*interior, de una prenda*) lining; (*de una butaca*) upholstery; (*de un libro*) cover **2.** NÁUT sheathing **3.** AUTO ~ **de freno** brake lining **4.** *inf* (*en absoluto*) **ni por el** ~ at all **5.** *AmL, vulg* (*preservativo*) condom, rubber *Am;* (*gilipollas*) asshole *vulg*

fortachón, **-ona** *adj inf* beefy

fortalecedor(a) *adj* **1.** (*vigorizador*) invigorating **2.** (*que da ánimo*) encouraging **3.** (*reforzante*) fortifying, revitalizing

fortalecer *irr como crecer* **I.** *vt* **1.** (*vigorizar*) to invigorate **2.** (*animar*) to encourage **3.** (*reforzar*) to fortify **II.** *vr:* ~**se** **1.** (*vigorizarse*) to fortify oneself **2.** (*volverse más fuerte*) to become stronger

fortalecimiento *m* **1.** (*de una cosa*) fortifying **2.** (*del cuerpo*) toughening **3.** (*del ánimo*) encouragement

fortaleza *f* **1.** (*fuerza*) strength; **de poca** ~ not very tough **2.** (*virtud*) fortitude **3.** (*robustez*) robustness **4.** MIL fortress, stronghold

fortificación *f* **1.** (*fortalecimiento*) strengthening **2.** MIL (*acción*) fortifying **3.** MIL (*obra*) fortification

fortificar <c→qu> **I.** *vt* **1.** (*fortalecer*) to strengthen **2.** MIL to fortify **II.** *vr:* ~**se** **1.** (*fortalecerse*) to fortify oneself **2.** MIL to build fortifications

fortín *m* **1.** (*fuerte*) fort **2.** (*defensa*) bunker

fortísimo, **-a** *adj superl de* **fuerte**

fortuito, **-a** *adj* fortuitous, chance

fortuna *f* **1.** (*suerte*) fortune; **por** ~ (*afortunadamente*) fortunately; (*por casualidad*) luckily; **probar** ~ to try one's luck **2.** (*destino*) fate **3.** (*capital*) fortune; **su voz era su** ~ her voice was her asset

fórum *m* forum

forúnculo *m* MED boil, furuncle

forzado *m* **1.** (*presidiario*) convict **2.** (*galeote*) galley slave

forzado, **-a** *adj* 1. (*artificial*) forced; **trabajos ~s** hard labour [*o* labor *Am*] 2. (*ocupado*) occupied

forzar *irr* I. *vt* 1. (*obligar*) to force 2. (*un acontecimiento*) to bring about 3. (*violar*) to rape 4. (*esforzar*) to force; (*voz*) to strain 5. (*obligar a entrar*) to push in; (*a abrirse*) to force open II. *vr:* **~se** 1. (*obligarse*) to force oneself 2. (*esforzarse*) to push oneself

forzosamente *adv* (*inevitablemente*) unavoidablly; (*obligatoriamente*) necessarily

forzoso, **-a** *adj* forced, necessary; **aterrizaje ~** forced landing; **venta forzosa** compulsary sale

forzudo, **-a** *adj* strong

fosa *f* 1. (*hoyo*) pit; (*alargado*) MIL, GEO trench; **~ séptica** septic tank 2. (*sepultura*) grave; **~ común** common grave 3. ANAT fossa; **~ nasal** nostril

fosfato *m* phosphate

fosforecer *irr como crecer vi* to phosphoresce

fosforescencia *f* phosphoresence

fosforescente *adj* phosphorescent; **pintura ~** luminous paint

fósforo *m* 1. QUÍM phosphorus 2. (*cerilla*) match

fósil I. *adj* 1. GEO fossil 2. *inf* (*anticuado*) antiquated II. *m* fossil

fosilizado, **-a** *adj* GEO fossilized

fosilizarse <z→c> *vr* 1. GEO to fossilize 2. *inf* (*persona*) to turn into an old fossil

foso *m* 1. (*hoyo*) hole; (*alargado*) ditch; MIL trench; (*fortaleza*) moat 2. MÚS, TEAT orchestra pit 3. DEP pit 4. (*en un garaje*) inspection pit

foto *f* photo; **~ (tamaño) carnet** passport photo

fotocopia *f* photocopy

fotocopiadora *f* photocopier

fotocopiar *vt* to photocopy

fotoeléctrico, **-a** *adj* photoelectric

fotogénico, **-a** *adj* photogenic

fotografía *f* 1. (*imagen*) photograph; **~ aérea** aerial photograph; **~ en color** colour [*o* color *Am*] photograph; **~ (tamaño) carnet** passport photograph; **albúm de ~s** photo(graph) album 2. (*arte*) photography

fotografiar <*1. pres:* fotografío> I. *vi* to photograph II. *vt* 1. (*hacer fotos*) to photograph 2. (*describir*) to describe in detail III. *vr:* **~se** to have one's photo taken

fotográfico, **-a** *adj* photographic; **máquina fotográfica** camera; **papel ~** photographic paper

fotógrafo, **-a** *m, f* photographer

fotograma *m* 1. CINE still 2. FOTO photogram

fotomatón *m* 1. (*mecanismo*) photo automaton 2. (*cabina*) photo booth 3. (*foto*) passport-size photo

fotomodelo *mf* photographic model

fotomontaje *m* photomontage

fotonovela *f* photostory

fotoquímica *f* photochemistry

fotorreportaje *m* report with photographs, illustrated feature

fotosíntesis *f sin pl* photosynthesis

fotovoltaico, **-a** *adj* photovoltaic

FP *f abr de* **Formación Profesional** vocational training, technical education

frac *m* <fracs *o* fraques> tails *pl*

fracasar *vi* 1. (*no tener éxito*) to fail; **la película fracasó** the film was a flop; **~ en un examen** to fail an exam 2. NÁUT to break up

fracaso *m* 1. (*acción*) failure 2. (*fiasco*) fiasco 3. (*desastre*) disaster

fracción *f* 1. (*división*) division; (*ruptura*) rupture; (*de una cantidad*) splitting up 2. (*parte*) fraction; (*de un objeto*) fragment; (*de una organización*) splinter group; **~ parlamentaria** parliamentary faction 3. MAT, QUÍM fraction

fraccionamiento *m* 1. (*división*) division; (*ruptura*) rupturing; (*de una cantidad*) splitting up; (*de una organización*) splintering 2. QUÍM fractionation

fraccionar I. *vt* 1. (*dividir*) to divide; (*romper*) to break up; (*una cantidad*) to split up; **~ el pago** to pay in instalments [*o* installments *Am*]; (*una organización*) to break away 2. QUÍM to fractionate II. *vr:* **~se** to fractionalize; (*grupo*) to split up

fraccionario, **-a** *adj* 1. MAT fractional; **número ~** fraction 2. POL factional 3. (*incompleto*) incomplete

fractura *f* 1. (*rotura*) break; MED fracture; **~ simple/complicada** closed/compound fracture 2. GEO (*falla*) fault

fracturar I. *vt* to break; (*una caja fuerte*) to force II. *vr:* **~se** to fracture

fragancia *f* fragrance; (*perfume*) perfume; (*vino*) bouquet

fragata *f* 1. NÁUT frigate 2. ZOOL frigate bird

frágil *adj* 1. (*objeto*) fragile 2. (*constitución, salud*) delicate; (*anciano*) frail 3. (*carácter*) weak; **tener una memoria ~** to have a bad memory

fragilidad *f* 1. (*de un objeto*) fragility 2. (*de la constitución, salud*) delicacy; (*de un anciano*) frailty 3. (*del carácter*) weakness

fragilizar <z→c> *vt* to weaken

fragmentación *f* fragmentation; (*en muchos pedazos*) breaking up; (*de un cristal*) shattering

fragmentar I. *vt* (*dividir*) to fragment, to divide; (*en muchos pedazos*) to break up; (*romper*) to break; (*una roca*) to split II. *vr:* **~se** (*cristal*) to shatter; (*roca*) to split

fragmentario, **-a** *adj* 1. (*compuesto*) compound 2. (*incompleto*) fragmentary

fragmento *m* 1. (*parte*) fragment; (*de un cristal*) splinter; (*de una roca*) chip; (*de un tejido*) remnant; (*de un papel*) scrap 2. LIT, MÚS (*parte*) fragment, excerpt

fragor *m* din

fragoroso, **-a** *adj* deafening

fragosidad *f* 1. (*de un monte*) ruggedness

2.(*de un camino*) unevenness 3.(*lugar*) roughness; (*lleno de arbustos*) denseness
fragoso, -a *adj* 1.(*áspero*) rough 2.(*ruidoso*) noisy
fragua *f* forge
fraguar <gu→gü> I. *vi* 1.(*cemento*) to set 2.(*idea*) to devise II. *vt* (*metal*) to forge; **¿qué estás fraguando?** *fig* what are you scheming?
fraile *m* 1. REL friar 2.(*en un vestido*) accidental turn-up 3. TIPO *part of a page which fails to be printed*
frambuesa *f* raspberry
frame *m* INFOR frame
francés, -esa I. *adj* French; **tortilla francesa** plain omelette II. *m, f* Frenchman *m,* Frenchwoman *f*
Francfort *m* Frankfurt
franchute *mf pey* Frog, Frenchy
Francia *f* France
franciscano, -a I. *adj* 1. REL Franciscan 2. *AmL* (*pardo*) dun II. *m, f* Franciscan
francmasonería *f* freemasonry
franco *m* 1.(*moneda francesa, belga, suiza*) franc 2.(*lengua*) Frankish
franco, -a I. *adj* 1.(*sincero*) frank 2.(*generoso*) generous 3.(*libre*) free; **puerto** ~ free port; ~ **a bordo** free on board; ~ **de derechos** duty-free; ~ **en fábrica** ex-factory 4.(*claro*) patent 5. HIST Frankish 6.(*francés*) French II. *m, f* Frank
francófilo, -a *adj* Francophile
francófono, -a I. *adj* francophone, French-speaking II. *m, f* French-speaking person
francotirador *m* 1.(*guerrillero*) guerrilla; (*tirador emboscado*) sniper 2.(*persona aislada*) loner; **ser un** ~ to be a loner
franela *f* 1.(*tejido*) flannel 2. *AmL* (*camiseta*) T-shirt
franelear *vi Arg, inf* to pet
franja *f* 1.(*guarnición*) border 2.(*tira*) strip; **en la misma** ~ **horaria** in the same time zone
frankfurt *m* GASTR frankfurter, hot dog *inf*
franquear I. *vt* 1.(*carta*) to pay postage on; **a** ~ **en destino** postage paid at destination 2.(*desobstruir*) to clear 3. *inf* (*río*) to cross; ~ **el paso** to open the way; (*obstáculo*) to get round 4.(*conceder*) to grant 5.(*dar libertad*) to free II. *vr:* ~**se** to have a heart-to-heart talk
franqueo *m* 1.(*sellos*) postage; **sin** ~ without stamps 2.(*acción: de una carta*) franking 3.(*de una salida*) opening
franqueza *f* 1.(*sinceridad*) frankness; **admitir algo con** ~ to openly admit sth 2.(*generosidad*) generosity 3.(*familiaridad*) intimacy 4.(*exención*) exemption
franquicia *f* 1.(*de franqueo*) exemption; ~ **postal** free postage 2. ECON franchise
franquiciador(a) I. *adj* COM franchise II. *m(f)* COM franchiser
franquismo *m sin pl* 1.(*régimen*) Franco's regime 2.(*movimiento*) Francoism
franquista I. *adj* Francoist II. *mf* Francoist
fraques *pl de* **frac**
frasco *m* 1.(*botella*) flask; (*de perfume*) perfume bottle; ~ **pulverizador** sprayer 2. *AmL: measurement of liquids, 2.37 litres*
frase *f* 1.(*oración*) sentence 2.(*locución*) expression; (*refrán*) saying; (*expresión famosa*) well-known phrase; ~ **hecha** idiom; ~ **proverbial** proverb 3.(*sin valor*) cliché 4.(*estilo*) style 5. MÚS phrase
fraseología *f* 1. LING phraseology 2.(*verbosidad*) verbiage
fraternal *adj* fraternal, brotherly
fraternidad *f* fraternity
fraternizar <z→c> *vi* 1.(*unirse*) to mingle with; POL to sympathize with 2.(*alternar*) to fraternize
fratricidio *m* fratricide
fraude *m* fraud; ~ **fiscal** tax fraud [*o* evasion]; **cometer** ~ to commit a fraudulent act
fraudulento, -a *adj* fraudulent; **publicidad fraudulenta** misleading advertising
fray *m* REL Brother
frazada *f AmL* blanket; (*de lana*) woollen blanket
frecuencia *f t.* FÍS frequency; **con** ~ frequently
frecuentar *vt* 1.(*lugar*) to frequent 2.(*a alguien*) to be in touch with 3.(*acción*) to do sth frequently
frecuente *adj* 1.(*repetido*) frequent 2.(*usual*) common
fregadero *m* (kitchen) sink
fregado *m* 1.(*limpieza*) cleaning; (*de los platos*) washing-up *Brit,* dishes *Am* 2. *inf* (*enredo*) mess 3. *pey* (*pelea*) brawl
fregado, -a *adj* 1. *AmL* (*descarado*) cheeky; (*fastidioso*) tiresome 2. *AmL* (*astuto*) sly 3. *AmC* (*severo*) strict
fregador *m* 1.(*fregadero*) sink 2.(*estropajo*) scourer
fregar *irr vt* 1.(*frotar*) to rub 2.(*limpiar: el suelo*) to scrub; (*con fregona*) to mop; (*los platos*) to wash up 3. *AmL, inf* (*molestar*) to annoy
fregona *f* 1.(*utensilio*) mop 2. *pey* (*sirvienta*) drudge, skivvy *Brit* 3. *pey* (*mujer ordinaria*) common woman
freidora *f* fryer
freír *irr* I. *vt* 1.(*guisar*) to fry; (*en mucho aceite*) to deep-fry; **mandar a alguien a** ~ **espárragos** *inf* to tell sb to get lost 2. *inf* (*molestar*) to annoy 3. *inf* (*matar*) to bump off *inf;* ~ **a balazos** to shoot dead II. *vr:* ~**se** 1.(*alimento*) to fry 2. *inf* (*persona*) to find it hot; **aquí te fríes** it's boiling here
fréjol *m Perú* BOT, GASTR (*frijol*) bean
frenada *f Arg, Chile* (*frenazo*) sudden braking
frenar I. *vt* 1.(*hacer parar*) to stop 2.(*un impulso, persona*) to restrain; (*un desarollo*) to check, to curb II. *vi* to brake; ~ **en seco** to slam on the brakes III. *vr* ~**se en algo** to restrain oneself from (doing) sth
frenazo *m* 1. AUTO sudden braking; **pegar un** ~ to step on the brakes 2.(*del desarrollo*) curb; **sufrir un** ~ *fig* to suffer a setback

frenesí *m* **1.** (*exaltación*) frenzy **2.** (*locura*) wildness; (*delirio furioso*) passion
frenético, -a *adj* **1.** (*exaltado*) frenzied; **aplauso** ~ frenzied applause **2.** (*loco*) wild **3.** (*furioso*) furious
freno *m* **1.** TÉC brake; ~ **de mano** handbrake *Brit,* emergency brake *Am* **2.** (*para un caballo*) bit **3.** (*contención*) curb; **tirar del** ~ **a alguien** to hold sb back; **no tener** ~ not to hold back
frente[1] *f* **1.** (*parte de la cara*) forehead; **fruncir la** ~ to frown; **hacer** ~ **a alguien** to stand up to sb; **hacer** ~ **a algo** to face up to sth; **no tener dos dedos de** ~ *inf* to be as thick as two short planks **2.** (*cara*) face; ~ **a** ~ face to face; **bajó la** ~ he/she bowed his/her head
frente[2] **I.** *m* **1.** (*delantera*) front; (*de un edificio*) façade, face; **al** ~ (*dirección*) ahead; (*lugar*) in front; **de** ~ head-on; **¡de ~!** MIL forward march!; **estar al** ~ **de algo** to be in charge of sth; **ponerse al** ~ to take charge **2.** POL, METEO, MIL front; **un** ~ **frío** a cold front **3.** (*de un escrito*) top margin **II.** *prep* **1.** ~ **a** (*enfrente de*) opposite; (*delante de*) in front of; (*contra*) as opposed to; (*ante*) in the face of **2. en** ~ **de** opposite
fresa I. *adj* strawberry-coloured [*o* colored *Am*] **II.** *f* **1.** BOT strawberry **2.** TÉC milling cutter, drill
fresadora *f* milling machine, rotary tool
fresal *m* strawberry bed
fresar *vt* to mill
fresco *m* **1.** (*frescor*) freshness, cool air; (*frío moderado*) coolness; (*viento*) cool; **salir a tomar el** ~ to go out to get some fresh air; **hoy hace** ~ it is cool today **2.** ARTE fresco **3.** *AmL* (*refresco*) soft drink
fresco, -a I. *adj* **1.** (*frío*) cool; (*prenda*) lightweight, cool; (*cutis*) fresh, rosy **2.** (*reciente*) fresh; **noticia fresca** up-to-date news; **queso** ~ cottage cheese **3.** (*descansado*) fresh **4.** *inf* (*desvergonzado*) fresh, cheeky **5.** (*impasible*) cool **6.** (*equivocado*) **estar** ~ *inf* to be wrong **II.** *m, f inf* cheeky person
frescor *m* **1.** (*frío moderado*) coolness; (*frescura*) freshness **2.** ARTE colour of flesh *Brit,* color of flesh *Am*
frescura *f* **1.** (*frescor*) freshness, cool air; (*frío moderado*) coolness **2.** (*desvergüenza*) cheek **3.** (*desembarazo*) naturalness; **con** ~ freely
fresno *m* ash
fresquera *f* food safe *Brit*
fresquería *f AmL: establishment where drinks are made and sold*
frialdad *f* **1.** (*frío*) coldness **2.** (*despego*) coolness; **me trató con** ~ he/she was cool towards me **3.** (*impasibilidad*) coolness **4.** (*falta de sentimientos*) indifference; (*frigidez*) frigidity **5.** (*estilo*) impersonality; (*del ambiente*) lack of warmth
fricandó *m* GASTR fricandeau
fricasé *m* GASTR fricassee
fricción *f* **1.** (*resistencia*) friction **2.** (*del cuerpo*) rub; (*con linimento*) massage **3.** (*desavenencia*) friction; (*disputa*) fight
friccionar *vt* (*en seco*) to rub; (*con linimento*) to massage
friega *f* **1.** (*fricción*) rub **2.** *AmL* (*molestia*) bother **3.** *inf* (*zurra*) beating
friegaplatos *m inv* dishwasher
frigidez *f* frigidity
frígido, -a *adj* frigid
frigorífico *m* **1.** (*nevera*) fridge, refrigerator **2.** (*local*) cold store
frigorífico, -a *adj* refrigeratory; **camión** ~ refrigerator lorry *Brit,* refrigerator truck *Am*
frijol *m,* **fríjol** *m AmL* bean
frío *m* cold; **hace** ~ it is cold; **hace un** ~ **que pela** it is bitterly cold; **coger** ~ to catch cold; **tener** ~ to be cold; **no dar a alguien ni** ~ **ni calor** to leave sb indifferent
frío, -a *adj* **1.** (*no caliente*) cold **2.** (*relación*) cool **3.** (*falto de sentimientos*) indifferent; (*frígida*) frigid **4.** (*impasible*) impassive **5.** (*inexpresivo*) inexpressive; (*ambiente*) impersonal
friolento, -a *adj AmL* (*friolero*) sensitive to the cold
friolera *f* **1.** *irón* (*insignificante*) trifle; **ganaron la** ~ **de 50 millones en la loto** they won a mere fifty million in the lottery **2.** *inf* (*montón*) pile
friolero, -a *adj* sensitive to the cold
frisa *f* **1.** (*tela*) woolen fabric **2.** *Arg, Chile* (*pelo*) nap **3.** *PRico, RDom* (*manta*) blanket **4.** MIL palisade **5.** NÁUT weatherstripping
frisar I. *vi* to border **II.** *vt* (*tejido*) to frizz
friso *m* **1.** ARQUIT frieze **2.** (*de la pared*) wainscot
frisón, -ona *adj, m, f* Frisian
fritanga *f pey* (*comida frita*) (greasy) fried food; **hueles a** ~ you reek of fried food
frito *m* fry
frito, -a I. *pp de* **freír II.** *adj* **1.** (*comida*) fried **2.** *inf* (*dormido*) **quedarse** ~ to fall fast asleep **3.** *inf* (*muerto*) dead; **quedarse** ~ to kick the bucket; **dejar a alguien** ~ to snuff sb **4.** *inf* (*harto*) **estar** ~ **con algo** to be fed up with sth; **me tienen** [*o* **traen**] **frito con sus preguntas** I am fed up with their questions
frivolidad *f* **1.** (*ligereza*) frivolity **2.** (*coquetería*) coquetry **3.** (*trivialidad*) triviality **4.** (*sensualidad*) sensuality
frívolo, -a *adj* **1.** (*ligero*) light **2.** (*coqueto*) coquettish **3.** (*superficial*) frivolous, superficial **4.** (*sensual*) sensual
fronda *f* **1.** (*hoja*) frond **2.** *pl* (*follaje*) foliage
frondosidad *f* **1.** (*de una planta*) leafiness; (*de un bosque*) luxuriance **2.** (*follaje*) foliage
frondoso, -a *adj* (*planta, árbol*) leafy; (*bosque*) lush
frontal I. *adj* **1.** ANAT frontal **2.** (*relativo al frente*) front **3.** (*de frente*) head-on **II.** *m* **1.** ANAT frontal bone **2.** REL frontal
frontera *f* **1.** (*límite*) border; **atravesar la** ~ to cross the frontier **2.** (*frontispicio*) frontispiece; (*de un edificio*) façade
fronterizo, -a *adj* (*en la frontera*) frontier;

(*país*) border(ing); **paso ~** border post
frontero *adj* opposite, facing
frontis *m inv* (*frontispicio*) frontispiece; (*de un edificio*) façade
frontispicio *m* **1.**(*delantera*) front; (*de un edificio*) façade **2.**(*de un libro*) frontispiece **3.** ARQUIT pediment **4.**(*cara*) face
frontón *m* **1.**(*juego*) pelota **2.**(*pared*) wall (*used to play pelota*) **3.**(*pista*) pelota court; (*edificio*) *building in which pelota is played* **4.** ARQUIT frontispiece, pediment
frotación *f,* **frotadura** *f* **1.**(*acción*) rubbing; (*con cepillo*) brushing **2.**(*efecto*) friction
frotamiento *m* (*acción de frotar*) rubbing; (*con cepillo*) brushing
frotar I. *vt* to rub; (*con cepillo*) to brush; (*con un estropajo*) to scrub **II.** *vr:* **~se** to rub oneself; **~se con una toalla** to rub oneself with a towel
frotis *m* MED smear
fructífero, -a *adj* fruitful
fructificación *f* **1.**(*de una planta*) fruitfulness **2.**(*de un esfuerzo*) fruition
fructificar <c→qu> *vi* **1.**(*planta*) to bear fruit **2.**(*esfuerzo*) to come to fruition
frugal *adj* frugal
frugalidad *f* frugality
fruición *f* delight
frunce *m* gather, shirr
fruncimiento *m* **1.**(*pliegue*) pleat, shirring **2.**(*arrugamiento*) puckering *pl* **3.**(*de los labios*) pursing; (*de la frente*) wrinkling; (*del entrecejo*) frowning
fruncir <c→z> **I.** *vt* **1.**(*tela*) to gather, to shirr; (*arrugar*) to pucker **2.**(*labios*) to purse; (*frente*) to wrinkle; **~ el entrecejo** to frown **II.** *vr:* **~se** to affect modesty
fruslería *f* **1.**(*baratija*) trifle **2.** *inf* (*bagatela*) nothing **3.** *inf* (*tontería*) silly thing
frustración *f* **1.**(*de planes*) thwarting; (*fracaso*) failure; (*de una esperanza*) frustration **2.**(*desilusión*) disappointment
frustrado, -a *adj* (*persona*) frustrated; (*intento*) failed
frustrar I. *vt* **1.**(*estropear*) to thwart; **~ las esperanzas de alguien** to frustrate sb's hopes **2.**(*decepcionar*) to discourage **II.** *vr:* **~se 1.**(*plan*) to fail **2.**(*esperanzas*) to be disappointed
fruta *f* fruit; **~ de Aragón** passion fruit; **~ del tiempo** seasonal fruit; **~s tropicales** tropical fruits; **de postre comimos ~** we had fruit for dessert
frutal I. *adj* fruit **II.** *m* fruit tree
frutería *f* greengrocer's
frutero *m* **1.**(*recipiente*) fruit bowl **2.** ARTE still life
frutero, -a I. *adj* fruit; **es muy ~** he eats a lot of fruit **II.** *m, f* fruit seller, fruiterer *Brit*
fruticultura *f* fruit growing
frutilla *f* **1.**(*cuenta*) rosary bead **2.** *AmL* (*fresón*) strawberry
fruto *m* **1.** BOT fruit **2.**(*hijo*) offspring **3.**(*rendimiento*) fruit; (*resultado*) result **4.**(*ganancia*) profit; *t.* JUR (*provecho*) benefit
fucsia[1] **I.** *adj* (*color*) fuschia-coloured [*o* colored *Am*] **II.** *m* fuschia
fucsia[2] *f* BOT fuschia
fue 1. *3. pret de* **ir 2.** *3. pret de* **ser**
fuego *m* **1.** fire; **¿me das ~?** can you give me a light?; **~s artificiales** fireworks *pl;* **a ~ lento** GASTR over a low heat; *fig* little by little; **prender** [*o* **pegar**] **~ a algo** to set sth alight [*o* on fire]; **echar ~ por los ojos** to look daggers at sb **2.** MIL firing; **estar entre dos ~s** to be caught in the crossfire [*o* middle]; **arma de ~** firearm **3.**(*ardor*) ardour *Brit,* ardor *Am;* **en el ~ de la discusión** in the heat of the discussion
fuel *m* refined oil
fuelle *m* **1.**(*instrumento, de una cámara*) bellows *pl* **2.**(*de un vestido*) fold **3.**(*de un carruaje*) folding top **4.** *inf* (*pulmones*) lungs *pl;* (*aguante*) stamina **5.** *inf* (*soplón*) telltale *Brit,* tattletale *Am*
fuente *f* **1.**(*manantial*) spring **2.**(*construcción*) fountain **3.**(*plato llano*) platter; (*plato hondo*) (serving) dish **4.**(*origen*) source; **~s bien informadas** reliable sources
fuera I. *adv* **1.**(*lugar*) outside; **por ~** on the outside; **de ~** from the outside; **el nuevo maestro es de ~** the new teacher is not from here; **estar ~ de lugar** to be irrelevant [*o* out of place] **2.**(*dirección*) out; **¡~!** out!; **¡~ con esto!** no way!; **¡~ de mi vista!** out of my sight!; **echar a alguien ~** to throw sb out; **hacia ~** outwards; **salir ~** to go out **3.**(*tiempo*) out; **~ de plazo** past the deadline **4.** *inf* (*de viaje*) away; **me voy ~ una semana** I am going away for a week **II.** *prep* **1.** *t. fig* (*local*) out of; **estar ~ de casa** to be away from home; **~ de juego** DEP offside; **~ de serie** exceptional **2.**(*excepto*) **~ de** outside of **III.** *conj* **~ de que** *+subj* apart from the fact that **IV.** *m* boo
fueraborda *m* **1.**(*motor*) outboard motor **2.**(*embarcación*) outboard motor boat
fuereño, -a I. *adj AmL, inf* (*forastero*) outside, foreign **II.** *m, f AmL, inf* (*forastero*) outsider
fuero *m* **1.**(*privilegio*) privilege **2.**(*jurisdicción*) jurisdiction; **en mi ~ interno** inwardly **3.**(*código*) code
fuerte I. *adj* <fortísimo> **1.**(*resistente*) strong; (*robusto*) tough; **caja ~** safe; **hacerse ~** to entrench oneself; **ser ~ de carácter** to be strong-willed **2.**(*musculoso*) strong; (*gordo*) fat **3.**(*intenso*) intense; (*sonido*) loud; (*comida, golpe*) heavy; (*abrazo, beso*) big; **un vino ~** a full-bodied wine **4.**(*valiente*) brave **5.**(*sólido*) solid; (*duro*) hard; (*tela*) thick **6.**(*genio*) **tener un carácter** [*o* **genio**] **muy ~** to be quick-tempered **7.**(*poderoso*) powerful **8.**(*versado*) **estar ~ en matemáticas** to be good at mathematics **9.**(*considerable*) considerable **10.**(*violento*) disturbing; (*expresión*) nasty; **palabra ~** rude word **11.**(*terreno*) rough **12.** LING (*vocal*) *the Spanish*

vowels a, e, o; (*forma*) *when the word stress falls on the word stem* **13.** MIL fortified **II.** *m* **1.** (*de una persona*) strong point **2.** MIL fort **3.** MÚS forte **4.** (*auge*) zenith **III.** *adv* **1.** (*con fuerza*) strongly; (*con intensidad*) intensely **2.** (*en voz alta*) aloud **3.** (*en abundancia*) copiously; **desayunar** ~ to have a large breakfast

fuerza *f* **1.** *t.* FÍS (*capacidad física*) strength; *t.* FÍS (*potencia*) force; ~ **de ánimo** strength of mind; ~ **de voluntad** willpower; **tiene más ~ que yo** he/she is stronger than I am; **sin ~s** weak, drained; **se le va la ~ por la boca** he/she is all talk [*o* hot air] **2.** (*capacidad de soportar*) toughness; (*eficacia*) effectiveness **3.** (*poder*) power; ~ **de disuasión** powers of dissuasion; ~ **mayor** act of God, force majeure **4.** (*violencia*) force; **a** [*o* **por**] **la** ~ willy-nilly; **por** ~ (*por necesidad*) out of necessity; (*con violencia*) by force; **recurrir a la** ~ to resort to violence **5.** (*intensidad*) intensity **6.** (*expresividad*) expressiveness **7.** *pl* POL political groups *pl;* MIL forces *pl;* **~s del orden público** forces of law and order **8.** ELEC power **9.** (*usando*) **a ~ de** by means of; **lo ha conseguido todo a ~ de trabajo** he/she has achieved everything through hard work

fuete *m AmL* (*látigo*) whip

fuga *f* **1.** (*huida*) flight; (*de la cárcel*) escape; **darse a la** ~ to escape, to run away; ~ **de capital** flight of capital; ~ **de cerebros** brain drain **2.** (*en tubos*) leak; (*de líquido*) leakage; (*de gas*) escape; **la cañería tiene una** ~ the pipe has a leak; **hubo una ~ de gas/petróleo** there was a gas/oil leak **3.** MÚS fugue **4.** (*auge*) peak

fugacidad *f* brevity; (*caducidad*) transitoriness

fugarse <g→gu> *vr* to flee; (*de casa*) to run away; (*para casarse*) to elope; ~ **de la cárcel** to escape from prison

fugaz *adj* fleeting; (*caduco*) short-lived; **estrella** ~ shooting star

fugitivo, -a I. *adj* fugitive; (*belleza*) transitory **II.** *m, f* fugitive; (*de la cárcel*) escapee

fulana *f pey* whore

fulano, -a *m, f* **1.** (*evitando el nombre*) so-and-so **2.** (*persona indeterminada*) guy, Joe Bloggs *Brit,* John Doe *Am;* **no me importa lo que digan ~ y mengano** I do not care what Tom, Dick or Harry say **3.** (*amante*) lover

fular *m* **1.** (*tela*) fine silk **2.** (*pañuelo*) foulard, silky scarf

fulcro *m* fulcrum

fulero, -a *adj inf* **1.** (*embustero*) lying **2.** (*chapucero*) **eres muy** ~ you are a bungler

fulgor *m* (*resplandor*) radiance; (*centelleo*) sparkle; (*de una superficie*) gleam

fulgurante *adj* **1.** (*rápido*) rapid; **su carrera fue** ~ he/she rose rapidly in his/her career **2.** (*dolor*) intense

fulgurar *vi* (*resplandecer*) to shine; (*centellear*) to sparkle; (*espejear*) to gleam

fullería *f* **1.** (*trampa*) trick; (*en el juego*) cheating; **hacer ~s** to cheat **2.** (*treta*) ruse

fullero, -a I. *adj* **1.** (*tramposo*) tricky **2.** *inf* (*astuto*) crafty **II.** *m, f* **1.** (*tramposo*) trickster; (*en el juego*) cheat, cardsharper **2.** *inf* (*astuto*) crafty individual

fulminación *f* **1.** (*aniquilación*) destruction **2.** (*de un explosivo*) fulmination **3.** (*emisión*) emission; (*de amenazas*) threatening **4.** (*de una sentencia*) sentencing

fulminante I. *adj* **1.** *t.* MED (*inesperado*) sudden **2.** (*explosivo*) explosive **3.** (*mirada*) withering **II.** *m* gunpowder

fulminar I. *vi* to explode **II.** *vt* **1.** (*dañar*) to strike down; (*aniquilar*) to destroy; (*matar*) to electrocute; **un rayo/el cáncer lo fulminó** he was struck down by lightning/cancer **2.** (*arrojar*) to hurl **3.** (*imponer*) to impose; ~ **una censura** to impose censorship **4.** (*amenazar*) to threaten angrily

fumadero *m* smoking room; ~ **de opio** opium den

fumador(a) I. *adj* **zona de no ~es** no-smoking area **II.** *m(f)* smoker; **no** ~ non-smoker

fumar I. *vi, vt* to smoke **II.** *vr:* **~se 1.** (*fumar*) to smoke **2.** *inf* (*gastar*) to squander **3.** *inf* (*faltar*) to cut; **~se la clase** to skive off school

fumigar <g→gu> *vt* to fumigate

fumista *mf* stove installer [*o* maker]

funambulesco, -a *adj* **1.** (*extravagante*) extravagant **2.** (*relativo al funámbulo*) acrobatic; (*como un funámbulo*) like a tightrope walker

funámbulo, -a *m, f* tightrope walker

función *f* **1.** *t.* BIO, MAT (*papel*) function; **el precio está en ~ de la calidad** the price depends on the quality **2.** (*cargo*) office; (*tarea*) duty; **entrará en ~ mañana** he/she will take up her duties tomorrow; (*cargo*) he/she will enter into office tomorrow; **el ministro en funciones** acting minister **3.** (*acto formal*) function; CINE showing; TEAT performance; ~ **doble** double feature; ~ **de noche** late show

funcional *adj* functional

funcionalidad *f* functionality

funcionamiento *m* **1.** (*marcha*) running; ~ **administrativo** running of the administration; ~ **del mercado** market organization; **poner en** ~ to bring into operation **2.** (*rendimiento*) performance; (*manera de funcionar*) operation; **en estado de** ~ in working order; (*máquina*) working

funcionar *vi* to function; (*estar trabajando*) to be working; **el coche no funciona bien** the car is not going properly; **la televisión no funciona** the television does not work; **No Funciona** (*cartel*) out of order

funcionario, -a *m, f* (*de una organización*) employee; (*del Estado*) civil servant

funda *f* (*cubierta*) cover; (*para gafas*) glasses case; (*de libro*) (dust) jacket; (*de almohada*) pillowcase; (*de butaca*) loose cover; (*de revólver*) holster; ~ **nórdica** duvet

fundación *f* **1.** (*creación*) foundation, found-

F

ing **2.** (*institución*) foundation **3.** (*justificación*) foundation, fundament **4.** (*de una estructura*) foundations *pl*

fundado, -a *adj* well-founded

fundador(a) **I.** *adj* founder, founding **II.** *m(f)* founder

fundamental *adj* **1.** fundamental; (*esencial*) essential; (*básico*) basic; **argumento ~** key argument; **conocimientos ~es** rudimentary knowledge **2.** MAT cardinal

fundamentalismo *m sin pl* fundamentalism

fundamentalista *adj, mf* fundamentalist

fundamentar *vt* **1.** ARQUIT to lay the foundations of **2.** (*basar*) to base **3.** (*establecer*) to establish

fundamento *m* **1.** ARQUIT foundations *pl* **2.** (*base*) basis **3.** (*motivo*) grounds; **sin ~** groundless **4.** (*formalidad*) sensibleness; (*seriedad*) seriousness; **hablar sin ~** not to talk seriously **5.** *pl* (*conocimientos*) fundamentals *pl*

fundar **I.** *vt* **1.** (*crear*) to found **2.** TÉC to found **3.** (*basar*) to base; (*justificar*) to found **II.** *vr:* **~se** **1.** (*basarse*) to base oneself; (*tener su justificación*) to be founded **2.** (*asentarse*) to be established

fundición *f* **1.** (*de un metal*) smelting **2.** (*en una forma*) casting **3.** (*de ideas*) fusion **4.** (*taller*) foundry **5.** (*hierro*) cast iron **6.** TIPO font

fundidor *m* founder

fundillo *m* **1.** *AmL* (*fondillos*) seat of trousers **2.** *Méx* (*trasero*) bottom

fundir **I.** *vt* **1.** (*deshacer*) to melt **2.** (*dar forma*) to found, to cast **3.** (*bombilla*) to fuse; (*plomo*) to blow **4.** (*unir*) to unite; (*empresas*) to merge **5.** *inf* (*gastar*) to squander **II.** *vr:* **~se** **1.** (*deshacerse*) to melt **2.** (*bombilla*) to fuse; (*plomo*) to blow **3.** (*unirse*) to unite; (*empresas*) to merge **4.** *inf* (*arruinarse*) to become ruined; (*negocio*) to go bankrupt

fundo *m Chile, Perú* (*finca*) country property

fúnebre *adj* **1.** (*triste*) mournful **2.** (*sombrío*) gloomy **3.** (*de los difuntos*) funerary; **coche ~** hearse; **pompas ~s** (*ceremonia*) funeral; (*empresa*) undertaker's

funeral **I.** *adj* funerary, funereal **II.** *m* **1.** (*entierro*) burial **2.** *pl* (*misa*) funeral, obsequies *pl*

funeraria *f* funeral parlour

funerario, -a *adj* funeral

funesto, -a *adj* **1.** (*aciago*) ill-fated **2.** (*desgraciado*) terrible **3.** *inf* (*sin talento*) inept

fungible *adj* ECON consumable

fungicida **I.** *adj* fungicidal **II.** *m* fungicide

fungir <g→j> *vi* **1.** *AmL* (*un cargo*) to hold the post **2.** *AmC* (*presumir*) to give oneself airs

funicular **I.** *adj* funicular; (*de cable aéreo*) cable; **tren ~** cable [*o* funicular] railway **II.** *m* funicular; **~ aéreo** cable car

furcia *f pey* whore, tart *inf*

furgón *m* **1.** (*carro*) wagon; (*camioneta*) van **2.** FERRO (*para el equipaje*) luggage van *Brit,* baggage car *Am;* (*para mercancías*) wagon *Brit,* freight car *Am;* **~ de cola** train rear wagon *Brit,* caboose *Am*

furgoneta *f* van

furia *f* **1.** (*ira, ímpetu*) fury **2.** (*persona*) **estaba hecha una ~** she was furious **3.** *inf* (*energía*) energy **4.** (*auge*) zenith

furibundo, -a *adj* **1.** (*furioso*) furious **2.** *inf* (*entusiasta*) enthusiastic; (*extremado*) extreme

furioso, -a *adj* **1.** (*furibundo*) furious **2.** (*loco*) beside oneself **3.** (*violento*) violent; (*tempestad*) raging **4.** (*tremendo*) tremendous; (*sentimiento*) intense

furor *m* **1.** (*ira*) fury **2.** (*ímpetu*) impulse **3.** (*energía*) drive **4.** (*auge*) craze; **hacer ~** to be the (latest) thing **5.** (*afición*) passion **6.** (*locura*) frenzy **7.** MED **~ uterino** nymphomania

furtivo, -a *adj* furtive; **cazador ~** poacher

furúnculo *m* MED boil

fusa *f* MÚS demisemiquaver *Brit,* thirty-second note *Am*

fuselaje *m* AVIAT fuselage

fusible **I.** *adj* fusible **II.** *m* fuse

fusil *m* rifle

fusilamiento *m* **1.** (*ejecución*) execution (by firing squad) **2.** *inf* (*de textos*) cribbing

fusilar *vt* **1.** (*ejecutar*) to execute, to shoot **2.** *inf* (*copiar*) to crib

fusilería *f* **1.** (*fusiles*) rifles **2.** (*soldados*) fusiliers **3.** (*fuego*) gunfire

fusilero *m* fusilier, rifleman

fusión *f* **1.** (*fundición*) fusion **2.** (*unión*) union; ECON merger

fusionar **I.** *vi* to fuse **II.** *vt* **1.** (*deshacer*) to fuse **2.** (*unir*) to fuse; (*empresas*) to merge **III.** *vr:* **~se** to fuse; (*empresas*) to merge

fusta *f* **1.** (*látigo*) riding whip **2.** (*leña*) brushwood **3.** (*tejido*) woollen cloth

fustán *m AmL* (*combinación*) lady's slip

fuste *m* **1.** (*madera*) wood **2.** (*vara*) pole; (*de una lanza*) shaft **3.** ARQUIT shaft **4.** (*importancia*) importance; (*sustancia*) solidity; (*de una persona*) consequence **5.** (*arzón*) pommel

fustigar <g→gu> *vt* **1.** (*azotar*) to whip **2.** (*reprender*) to reprimand

fútbol *m* football *Brit,* soccer *Am;* **~ americano** American football, football *Am*

futbolín *m* table football

futbolista *mf* DEP football player *Brit,* soccer player *Am*

futbolístico, -a *adj* footballing, football *Brit,* soccer *Am*

fútbol-sala *m sin pl* DEP indoor football, five-a-side football *Brit*

fútil *adj* trivial

futileza *f Chile* (*pequeñez*) trifle

futilidad *f* triviality

futre *m AmL, pey* stuck-up person, toff

futurible **I.** *adj* possible; (*acontecimiento*) likely; (*persona*) potential **II.** *mf* potential candidate

futurismo *m sin pl* Futurism

futuro *m* **1.** *t.* LING (*tiempo*) future **2.** FIN **compra de ~s** purchase of futures
futuro, **-a** **I.** *adj* future **II.** *m, f inf* intended
futurólogo, **-a** *m, f* futurologist

G

G, **g** *f* G, g; **~ de Granada** G for George
gabacho, **-a** *m, f pey* (*francés*) Froggy
gabán *m* overcoat
gabardina *f* **1.** (*tela*) gabardine **2.** (*prenda*) raincoat
gabarra *f* NÁUT (*para carga y descarga*) barge; (*más pequeña*) lighter; (*remolcada*) tug
gabela *f* tax
gabinete *m* **1.** (*estudio*) study; (*salita*) private sitting room; **~ de prensa** press office **2.** POL cabinet **3.** (*tocador*) dressing room **4.** (*museo*) museum **5.** (*de médico*) office
Gabón *m* Gabon
gabonés, **-esa** *adj, m, f* Gabonese
gacela *f* gazelle ►**correr como una ~** to run like the wind
gaceta *f* **1.** (*publicación*) gazette **2.** *inf* (*persona*) gossip, grapevine
gacetilla *f* **1.** (*de un periódico*) news-in-brief section; (*notas de sociedad*) gossip column **2.** (*noticia*) news item
gacetillero, **-a** *m, f* journalist; (*de chismorreo*) gossip columnist
gacha *f* **1.** *pl* (*comida*) ≈ porridge **2.** *inf* (*barro*) mud
gachí <gachís> *f inf* bird, chick
gacho, **-a** *adj* drooping; **orejas gachas** floppy ears; **sombrero ~** slouch hat; **con las orejas gachas** with one's tail between one's legs
gachó *m inf* guy, bloke
gachumbo *m Col, Ecua* hollowed-out fruit shell
gaditano, **-a** **I.** *adj* of/from Cadiz **II.** *m, f* native/inhabitant of Cadiz
gaélico, **-a** *adj* Gaelic
gafa *f* **1.** *pl* (*anteojos*) glasses *pl;* **~s de bucear** diving mask; **llevar ~s** to wear glasses; **ponerse las ~s** to put one's glasses on **2.** (*varilla*) earpiece **3.** TÉC (*grapa*) staple **4.** TÉC (*abrazadera*) clamp
gafar *vt* **1.** *inf* (*mala suerte*) to jinx **2.** (*con las uñas*) to claw **3.** (*con grapas*) to staple
gafe *m* **1.** (*cenizo*) jinx **2.** (*aguafiestas*) party-pooper, wet-blanket
gag *m* <gags> gag
gago, **-a** **I.** *adj AmL* stuttering **II.** *m, f* stutterer
gaita *f* **1.** MÚS (*gallega*) bagpipes *pl;* (*zamorana*) hurdy-gurdy **2.** *inf* (*cuello*) neck **3.** *inf* (*lata*) **vaya ~ tener que hacer eso** having to do that is a real pain ►**estar hecho una ~** to be in a bad way
gaitero, **-a** *m, f* (*de gaita gallega*) (bag)piper; (*de gaita zamorana*) hurdy-gurdy player
gajes *mpl* fees *pl* ►**~ del oficio** *irón* occupational hazards; **son ~ del oficio** it's all in a day's work
gajo *m* **1.** (*de naranja*) segment **2.** (*racimo*) bunch **3.** (*rama*) branch
gala *f* **1.** (*fiesta*) gala **2.** (*garbo*) elegance **3.** (*selecto*) best **4.** *pl* (*vestido*) finery, (fine) clothes *pl* ►**hacer ~ de algo** to take pride in sth
galáctico, **-a** *adj* galactic
galaico, **-a** *adj* Galician
galaicoportugués, **-esa** *adj* Galician-Portuguese
galán *m* **1.** (*hombre*) handsome man **2.** (*novio*) beau **3.** TEAT (*papel*) leading man **4.** (*mueble*) (clothes) valet
galante *adj* **1.** (*atento*) gallant **2.** (*mujer*) flirtatious **3.** (*historia*) risqué
galanteador(a) *adj* flirtatious
galantear *vt* to woo
galantería *f* **1.** (*hacia una mujer*) gallantry **2.** (*amabilidad*) politeness **3.** (*generosidad*) generosity **4.** (*cumplido*) compliment
galápago *m* turtle
galardón *m* prize
galardonar *vt* to award a prize to; **~ a alguien con un título** to confer a title on sb
galaxia *f* (*universo*) galaxy
galbana *f inf* laziness
galena *f* MIN galena, lead sulphide *Brit,* lead sulfide *Am*
galeno *m inf* doctor, physician *Am*
galeón *m* NÁUT galleon
galeote *m* galley slave
galera *f* **1.** NÁUT galley **2.** ZOOL mantis shrimp **3.** TIPO galley **4.** MAT dividing line **5.** *AmL* (*cobertizo*) shed **6.** *AmL* (*sombrero: de copa*) top hat; (*de hongo*) bowler hat
galerada *f* galley proof
galería *f* **1.** (*corredor, de arte*) gallery **2.** *pl* (*grandes almacenes*) department store; (*centro comercial*) shopping centre *Brit,* shopping center *Am,* mall *Am* **3.** *pl* (*bulevar*) arcade **4.** MIN, TEAT gallery; **hablar para la ~** to play to the gallery
galerista *mf* art gallery owner
galerón *m* **1.** *AmS* (*romance*) ballad **2.** *Col, Ven* MÚS folkdance and song **3.** *CRi, ElSal* (*cobertizo*) shed
galés, **-esa** **I.** *adj* Welsh **II.** *m, f* Welshman *m,* Welshwoman *f*
Gales *m* (**el País de**) ~ Wales
galgo, **-a** *m, f* greyhound; **~ inglés** whippet
galguerías *fpl Col* (*golosinas*) sweets *pl Brit,* candies *pl Am*
Galia *f* Gaul
Galicia *f* Galicia
galicismo *m* French loan word(s), Gallicism
galimatías *m inv* **1.** (*lenguaje*) gibberish **2.** (*enredo*) jumble
gallardear *vi* **1.** (*ostentar gallardía*) to act with self-assurance **2.** (*presumir*) to show off,

to strut

gallardía *f* **1.** (*apostura*) poise **2.** (*garbo*) style, elegance **3.** (*valentía*) bravery

gallardo, **-a** *adj* **1.** (*de aspecto*) elegant **2.** (*garboso*) dashing **3.** (*valiente*) brave **4.** (*generoso*) noble

gallear **I.** *vi* **1.** (*fanfarronear*) to brag **2.** (*alzar la voz*) to shout **3.** (*creerse importante*) to strut around **II.** *vt* (*el gallo a la gallina*) to tread

gallego, **-a** **I.** *adj* Galician **II.** *m, f* **1.** (*habitante*) Galician **2.** *AmS, pey* (*español*) Spaniard

galleguismo *m word or phrase of Galician origin*

galleta *f* **1.** (*dulce*) biscuit *Brit,* cookie *Am;* (*salada*) cracker **2.** *inf* (*bofetada*) slap, smack **3.** MIN anthracite briquet [*o* briquette], nuts *pl*

galletero *m* biscuit tin *Brit,* cookie tin *Am*

gallina *f* **1.** (*hembra del gallo*) hen; ~ **clueca** brooding hen **2.** *inf* (*cobarde*) chicken **3.** (*juego*) **jugar a la ~ ciega** to play blind man's buff ▶~ **en corral ajeno** fish out of water; **acostarse con las ~s** to go to bed very early

gallinazo *m* turkey buzzard

gallinero *m* **1.** (*corral*) chicken coop, henhouse **2.** TEAT *inf* gallery, gods *pl Brit*

gallito *m inf* **ser un ~** to be a tough guy; **ponerse ~** to act tough

gallo *m* **1.** (*ave*) cock, rooster *Am;* ~ **de pelea** fighting cock; ~ **silvestre** capercaillie **2.** (*pez*) (John) dory **3.** (*engreído*) show-off **4.** MÚS false note; **soltar un ~** to let out a squeak **5.** (*esputo*) phlegm **6.** *AmL* (*hombre fuerte*) tough guy ▶**alzar el ~** to put on airs; **en menos que canta un ~** in an instant [*o* flash]; **si el dinero fuera mío, otro ~ nos cantara** *inf* if it was my money, it would be another story

galo, **-a** **I.** *adj* **1.** (*de la Galia*) Gaulish **2.** (*francés*) French **II.** *m, f* **1.** (*de la Galia*) Gaul **2.** (*francés*) Frenchman *m,* Frenchwoman *f*

galón *m* **1.** (*cinta*) braid **2.** MIL (*distintivo*) stripe, decoration **3.** (*medida inglesa*) gallon

galopada *f* gallop

galopante *adj* galloping

galopar *vi* to gallop

galope *m* gallop

galopín *m* **1.** (*golfillo*) urchin **2.** (*granuja*) rascal **3.** (*granujilla*) ragamuffin, whippersnapper

galpón *m AmL* shed

galuchar *vi Col, Cuba, PRico, Ven* to gallop

galvanismo *m sin pl* FÍS galvanism

galvanización *f* **1.** MED galvanization **2.** TÉC electroplating

galvanizar <z→c> *vt* **1.** TÉC to electroplate **2.** (*una institución*) to galvanize

gama *f* **1.** MÚS gamut; (*escala*) scale **2.** (*escala*) range; **una ~ amplia/reducida de productos** a wide/narrow range of products

gamada *adj* **cruz ~** swastika

gamba *f* prawn, shrimp

gamberrada *f* act of hooliganism; **hacer ~s** to horse around *inf*

gamberro, **-a** *m, f* hooligan, yobbo *inf*

gambeta *f AmL* **1.** (*distensión*) swerve **2.** (*evasiva*) dodge **3.** (*fútbol*) dummy; **hacer ~s** to dribble

gamín, **-ina** *m, f Col* (*pilluelo*) urchin

gamma *f* gamma

gamo *m* fallow deer

gamonal *m AmL: local political boss*

gamonalismo *m AmL* caciquism

gamuza *f* **1.** (*animal*) chamois **2.** (*piel*) chamois (leather) **3.** (*paño*) duster

gana *f* desire; **tener ~s de hacer algo** to feel like doing sth; **tengo ~s de irme de vacaciones** I feel like going on holiday; **son ~s de fastidiar** *inf* they're just trying to be difficult; **de buena/mala ~** willingly/unwillingly; **me quedé con las ~s de verlo** I wish I'd been able to see him; **no me da la (real) ~** *inf* I can't be bothered; **venir en ~** to feel like; **no me viene en ~** I don't feel like it; **este es feo con ~s** *inf* he's bloody ugly

ganadería *f* **1.** (*ganado*) livestock **2.** (*crianza*) livestock farming **3.** (*comercio*) livestock trade

ganadero, **-a** **I.** *adj* livestock **II.** *m, f* **1.** (*criador: de vacas*) cattle farmer; (*de cerdos*) pig farmer; (*de ovejas*) sheep farmer **2.** (*tratante: de vacas*) cattle merchant; (*de cerdos*) pig merchant; (*de ovejas*) sheep merchant

ganado *m* **1.** (*reses*) livestock *pl;* ~ **bovino** [*o* **vacuno**] cattle *pl;* ~ **cabrío** goats *pl;* ~ **ovino** sheep *inv;* ~ **porcino** pigs *pl* **2.** *AmL* (~ *vacuno*) cattle *pl* **3.** *inf* (*de personas*) crowd

ganador(a) **I.** *adj* winning **II.** *m(f)* winner

ganancia *f* **1.** (*beneficio*) profit **2.** (*sueldo*) earnings *pl*

ganancial *adj* pertaining to earnings or profit; **bienes ~es** property acquired during marriage

ganancioso, **-a** *adj* **1.** (*que da ganancia*) profitable **2.** (*beneficiado*) **salir ~ de algo** to make a profit from sth

ganapán *m* **1.** *pey* (*trabajador*) odd-job man **2.** (*rudo*) lout

ganar **I.** *vi* **1.** (*vencer*) to win **2.** (*mejorar*) ~ **en algo** to improve at sth; ~ **en condición social** to better oneself socially **con esto sólo puedes salir ganando** you can't lose with this; **no gana para sustos** with her it is one thing after another **II.** *vt* **1.** (*trabajando*) to earn; **con ese negocio consiguió ~ mucho dinero** he/she made a lot of money out of that business **2.** (*jugando*) win; (*a alguien*) to beat; **le he ganado 30 euros** I won 30 euros from him/her **3.** (*adquirir*) to gain; (*libertad*) to win; ~ **conocimientos de algo** to acquire knowledge of sth; ~ **experiencia** to gain experience; ~ **peso** to put on weight; **¿qué esperas ~ con esto?** what do you hope to gain by that?; **4.** (*llegar a*) to reach; ~ **la orilla** to reach the shore **5.** (*aventajar*) ~ **a alguien en algo** to be better than sb at sth **6.** MIL (*ciudad*) to take **7.** (*convencer*) to win over **III.** *vr:*

~**se** **1.**(*dinero*) to earn; **si no me sale, me la gano** *inf* if I don't get it right, I'm in trouble; **¡te la vas a ~!** *inf* you're for it **2.**(*a alguien*) to win over
ganchillo *m* **1.**(*gancho*) hook **2.**(*labor*) crochet; **hacer** ~ to crochet
gancho *m* **1.**(*instrumento*) hook **2.** DEP (*boxeo*) hook; (*baloncesto*) hook shot **3.**(*de árbol*) stump **4.**(*algo que atrae*) bait **5.** *AmL* (*horquilla*) hairpin **6.**(*garabato*) scrawl **7.**(*atractivo*) **tener** ~ to be attractive **8.**(*persona*) decoy
ganchudo, **-a** *adj* hooked
gandido, **-a** *adj Col, pey* (*glotón*) gluttonous
gandinga *f* **1.**(*mineral*) fine washed ore **2.** *Cuba, PRico* GASTR offal [*o* liver] stew
gandul(**a**) **I.** *adj* lazy **II.** *m(f)* layabout
gandulear *vi* to loaf about
gandulería *f* loafing
ganga *f* **1.**(*oferta*) bargain; **a precio de** ~ at a bargain price; **¡menuda ~ este nuevo jefe!** *irón* we've got our work cut out with the new boss **2.** ZOOL sandgrouse **3.** MIN slag
ganglio *m* ANAT ganglion; ~ **linfático** lymph gland
gangosear *vi* to speak through one's nose
gangoso, **-a** **I.** *adj* nasal **II.** *adv* **hablar** ~ to speak through one's nose
gangrena *f* MED gangrene
gangrenarse *vr* to become gangrenous
gángster *mf* gangster
ganguear *vi* to speak through one's nose
gangueo *m* twang
gansada *f inf* silly thing; **hacer ~s** to clown about; **decir ~s** to talk nonsense
gansear *vi inf* **1.**(*hacer gansadas*) to clown about, to goof around *Am* **2.**(*decir gansadas*) to talk nonsense
ganso, **-a** *m, f* **1.**(*ave: hembra*) goose; (*macho*) gander **2.** *inf* (*perezoso*) lazybones *inv* **3.** *inf* (*estúpido*) ninny, gubbins; **hacer el** ~ to clown about
Gante *m* Ghent
ganzúa[1] *f* (*llave*) picklock
ganzúa[2] *m* (*ladrón*) burglar
gañán *m* **1.**(*mozo*) farmhand **2.**(*tosco*) brute
gañido *m* (*de animal, persona*) howl; (*de perro*) yelp; (*de ave*) squawk
gañir <*3. pret:* gañó> *vi* (*animal, persona*) to howl; (*perro*) to yelp; (*ave*) to squawk
gañote *m* throat
garabatear **I.** *vt* (*al escribir*) to scribble; (*dibujando*) to doodle **II.** *vi* **1.** TÉC to use a hook **2.**(*al escribir*) to scribble **3.**(*andar con rodeos*) to beat around the bush
garabato *m* **1.**(*gancho*) hook **2.**(*al escribir*) scribble **3.**(*atractivo*) appeal **4.**(*al dibujar*) doodle
garaje *m* garage
garambaina *f* **1.**(*adorno*) frippery **2.** *pl* (*tonterías*) nonsense **3.** *pl* (*ademanes*) mannerisms **4.** *pl* (*garabatos*) scrawl
garandumba *f AmS* flat river boat
garante **I.** *adj* responsible **II.** *mf* guarantor
garantía *f* **1.**(*seguridad*) guarantee; **sin** ~ (*en la lotería*) no liability assumed **2.** FIN (*aval*) guarantee, collateral; (*caución*) surety **3.** COM guarantee; **~s constitucionales** POL constitutional rights
garantir *irr como abolir vt v.* **garantizar**
garantizador(**a**) *m(f)* guarantor
garantizar <z→c> *vt* **1.**(*asegurar*) to guarantee; **no está garantizado que él sea el orador** it's not certain that he'll be the speaker **2.** JUR to act as guarantor for
garañón *m* **1.**(*asno*) stud jackass [*o* donkey]; (*camello*) stud camel **2.** *AmL* (*caballo semental*) stud
garapiña *f* **1.**(*galón*) braid **2.** GASTR sugar icing [*o* coating]

> In Latin America **garapiña** (or **garrapiña**) is a refreshing drink, which is prepared from pineapple rinds, water and milk.

garapiñar *vt* to coat with sugar
garbancero, **-a** **I.** *adj* chickpea **II.** *m, f* chick-pea seller
garbanzo *m* chickpea ▶**por un ~ no se descompone la olla** *prov* nobody is irreplaceable *prov;* **ser el ~ negro** (**de la olla**) to be the black sheep of the family; **ganarse los ~s** *inf* to earn one's living
garbear **I.** *vi* **1.**(*afectar garbo*) to put on airs **2.**(*trampear*) to cheat (for a living) **II.** *vt* **1.**(*garbas*) to bind into sheaves **2.**(*robar*) to steal **III.** *vr:* ~**se** to go for a stroll
garbeo *m* stroll
garbillar *vt* to sieve, to sift
garbillo *m* **1.**(*criba*) sieve **2.** MIN screen
garbo *m* **1.**(*elegancia*) elegance; (*de movimiento*) grace(fulness) **2.**(*brío*) dash **3.**(*generosidad*) generosity **4.**(*de un escrito*) style
garboso, **-a** *adj* **1.**(*elegante*) elegant **2.**(*brioso*) dashing **3.**(*generoso*) generous
garceta *f* **1.**(*ave*) egret **2.**(*pelo*) sidelock
gardenia *f* gardenia
garduña *f* marten
garete *inf* **ir**(**se**) **al** ~ (*proyecto*) to go down the tubes; NÁUT to go adrift
garfa *f* claw
garfio *m* hook
gargajear *vi* to spit phlegm
gargajo *m* phlegm, gob *inf*
garganta *f* **1.**(*gaznate*) throat; (*cuello*) neck; (*empeine*) instep; **tener buena** ~ to have a good voice; **se me hizo un nudo en la ~ de lo nervioso que estaba** I was so nervous I had a lump in my throat **2.**(*de un objeto*) neck **3.** GEO (*quebrada*) gorge, ravine; (*angostura*) narrow pass **4.** TÉC, ARQUIT neck
gargantilla *f* **1.**(*collar*) (short) necklace; (*de perlas*) string of pearls **2.**(*cinta*) choker
gárgaras *fpl* gargles *pl;* **hacer** ~ to gargle; **¡vete a hacer ~!** *inf* get lost!
gargarear *vi Chile, Guat, Perú* (*barbotear*) to

G

gargle

gargarizar <z→c> *vi* to gargle

gárgola *f* ARQUIT gargoyle

garita *f* **1.** (*de centinelas*) sentry box **2.** (*de portero*) lodge **3.** FERRO signal box **4.** (*de fortificación*) lookout post, watch tower

garito *m* **1.** (*local*) nightclub; (*de juego*) gambling den; (*antro*) dive, joint **2.** (*ganancia*) winnings *pl*

garlar *vi inf* to chatter

garlito *m* trap; **caer en el ~** *fig* to fall into the trap

garlopa *f* jack [*o* long] plane

garnacha *f* **1.** (*uva*) garnacha (*purplish grape*) **2.** (*vino*) garnacha (*sweet wine made from garnacha grapes*)

garra *f* **1.** (*de animal*) claw; **caer en las ~s de alguien** to fall into sb's clutches; **la policía le echó la ~** the police got hold of him **2.** *pey* (*mano*) paw **3.** NÁUT hook **4.** *pl, AmL* (*harapos*) rags, tatters *pl* **5.** *inf* (*brío*) **tener ~** to be compelling [*o* appealing]; **este equipo tiene ~** this team has real class

garrafa *f* (*pequeña*) carafe; (*más grande*) demijohn; **vino de ~** cheap wine

garrafal *adj* (*muy grande*) enormous; (*muy malo*) terrible

garrapata *f* tick

garrapatear *vi, vt* to scribble, to scrawl

garrapiña *f v.* **garapiña**

garrapiñar *vt v.* **garapiñar**

garrido, **-a** *adj* **1.** (*gallardo*) smart **2.** (*atractivo: hombre*) handsome; (*mujer*) pretty

garrocha *f* TAUR goad

garronear *vi Arg* to goad

garrotazo *m* blow with a stick [*o* club]

garrote *m* **1.** (*palo*) stick **2.** (*ligadura*) tourniquet **3.** (*de ejecución*) garotte

garrotillo *m sin pl* MED croup

garrucha *f* pulley

garrulería *f* chatter

gárrulo, **-a** *adj* **1.** (*pájaro*) twittering **2.** (*persona*) talkative **3.** (*arroyo*) babbling; (*viento*) howling

garúa *f AmL* (*llovizna*) drizzle

garuar *vimpers AmL* (*lloviznar*) to drizzle

garza *f* heron

garzón, **-ona** *m, f AmL* (*camarero*) waiter *m*, waitress *f*

gas *m* **1.** (*fluido*) gas; **~ natural** natural gas; **bombona de ~** gas cylinder; **cartucho de ~** gas cartridge; **cocina de ~** gas cooker *Brit,* gas stove *Am;* **agua con ~** carbonated water; **agua sin ~** still water **2.** *inf* AUTO **dar ~** to accelerate; **ir a todo ~** to go at full speed; **quedarse sin ~** *fig* to run out of steam **3.** *pl* (*en el estómago*) **~es** wind

gasa *f* **1.** (*tela*) gauze; **~ hidrófila** surgical gauze **2.** MED lint **3.** (*pañal*) nappy liner *Brit,* diaper liner *Am* **4.** (*de luto*) crêpe

gascón, **-ona** **I.** *adj* of/from Gascony **II.** *m, f* Gascon

gasear *vt* **1.** (*agua*) to carbonate **2.** QUÍM to gasify **3.** (*matar*) to gas

gaseiforme *adj* gaseous

gaseosa *f* lemonade, soda

gaseoso, **-a** *adj* **1.** (*bebida*) fizzy **2.** (*gaseiforme*) gaseous

gasfitería *f AmL* plumbing

gasificación *f* **1.** (*de bebida*) carbonation **2.** QUÍM gasification

gasificar <c→qu> *vt* **1.** (*bebida*) to carbonate **2.** QUÍM (*transformar en gas*) to gasify

gasista *m* gasman

gasoducto *m* gas pipeline

gasógeno *m* gasogene

gasoil *m,* **gas-oil** *m* diesel

gasóleo *m* diesel

gasolina *f* petrol *Brit,* gas(oline) *Am;* **~ sin plomo** unleaded petrol *Brit* [*o* gasoline *Am*]; **~ súper** three-star petrol *Brit* [*o* gasoline *Am*]; **echar ~** to fill up with petrol *Brit* [*o* gasoline *Am*]

gasolinera *f* **1.** (*establecimiento*) petrol station *Brit,* gas station *Am* **2.** (*lancha*) motorboat

gastado, **-a** *adj* **1.** (*vestido, zapato*) worn out; (*cuello*) frayed; (*talón*) worn down; (*suelo*) worn; (*neumático*) bare; (*pilas*) used up **2.** (*expresión*) hackneyed **3.** (*persona*) worn out

gastador *m* **1.** MIL (*zapador*) sapper **2.** (*condenado*) convict

gastador(a) **I.** *adj* extravagant, lavish **II.** *m(f)* spendthrift

gastar **I.** *vt* **1.** (*dinero*) to spend **2.** (*vestido, zapato, neumático*) to wear out; (*talón, suelo*) to wear down **3.** (*tiempo*) to spend **4.** (*electricidad*) to use **5.** (*consumir, usar*) use; **¿qué talla/número gastas?** what size are you? **6.** (*tener*) **~ mal/buen humor** to be bad/good-humoured *Brit,* to be bad/good-humored *Am* **7.** (*poseer*) to have **II.** *vr:* **~se** **1.** (*dinero*) to spend **2.** (*vestido*) to wear out **3.** (*consumirse*) to run out

Gasteiz *m* Vitoria

gasto *m* **1.** *pl* (*de dinero*) spending; (*en un negocio*) costs *pl;* ECON, COM (*desembolso*) expenditure; (*costos adicionales*) expenses *pl;* **~s adicionales** extra charges; **~s pagados** all expenses paid; **~s corrientes** running costs; **~s de inscripción** inscription charges *pl;* **~s de personal** staff costs *pl;* **~s generales** overhead (expenses); **el ~ público** public expenditure; **~s de representación** expenses *pl* **2.** (*de fuerza*) expenditure; **no merece el ~ de tanto tiempo** it's not worth spending so much time on it **3.** (*consumo*) consumption **4.** (*de una fuente*) flow

gástrico, **-a** *adj* gastric

gastritis *f inv* MED gastritis

gastroenteritis *f inv* MED gastroenteritis

gastronomía *f sin pl* (*arte culinaria*) gastronomy

gastronómico, **-a** *adj* gastronomic

gastrónomo, **-a** *m, f* **1.** (*que trabaja en gas-

tronomía) gastronome **2.**(*gourmet*) gourmet
gata *f* **1.**(*hembra del gato*) (she-)cat **2.**(*nubecilla*) hill cloud **3.**(*madrileña*) woman from Madrid
gatas andar a ~ to crawl
gateado, **-a** *adj* feline; **marmol** ~ veined marble
gatear **I.** *vi* **1.**(*trepar*) to climb, to clamber **2.**(*ir a gatas*) to crawl **3.** *AmL* (*enamorar*) to seduce **II.** *vt* **1.**(*arañar*) to scratch **2.** *inf* (*robar*) to swipe
gatera *f* **1.**(*de gatos*) catflap **2.** NÁUT cat hole **3.** *AmL* (*verdulera*) vegetable seller
gatillo *m* **1.**(*percusor*) trigger; **apretar el** ~ to pull the trigger **2.**(*de dentista*) forceps *pl* **3.**(*de cuadrúpedo*) nape (of neck) **4.**(*ratero*) petty thief
gato *m* **1.**(*félido*) cat; (*macho*) tomcat **2.**(*astuto*) fox **3.**(*madrileño*) man from Madrid **4.** TÉC (*de coche*) jack; (*de carpintero*) vice **5.**(*para dinero*) moneybag ▶**llevarse el ~ al agua** *inf* to bring [*o* pull] it off; **el Gato con Botas** Puss in Boots; **dar ~ por liebre a alguien** *inf* to rip sb off; **cuando el ~ no está los ratones bailan** when the cat's away, the mice will play; **éramos cuatro ~s** *inf* there was hardly anyone else there; **aquí hay ~ encerrado** *inf* there's something fishy going on here; **~ escaldado del agua fría huye** *prov* once bitten twice shy; **de noche todos los ~s son pardos** all cats are grey [*o* gray *Am*] in the night; **ser ~ viejo** to be an old hand
GATT *m abr de* **Acuerdo General sobre Aranceles y Comercio** GATT
gatuno, **-a** *adj* feline, catlike
gatuperio *m* **1.**(*mezcla*) hotchpotch *Brit*, hodgepodge *Am* **2.**(*embrollo*) dirty business
gauchaje *m CSur* gauchos *pl*
gauchear *vi* **1.** *Arg, Urug* (*vivir como un gaucho*) to live as a gaucho **2.** *Arg* (*errar*) to rove
gaucho *m AmL* **1.**(*campesino*) gaucho **2.**(*jinete*) skilled horseman

> **Gauchos** were the cattle drovers or "cowboys" of the South American **Pampa**.

gaucho, **-a** *adj* **1.**(*de gaucho*) gaucho **2.** *AmL* (*grosero*) coarse **3.** *AmL* (*astuto*) cunning
gaveta *f* drawer
gavia *f* **1.**(*zanja*) ditch **2.** NÁUT (*vela*) topsail
gavilán *m* **1.**(*ave*) sparrow hawk **2.**(*de pluma*) nib **3.**(*de espada*) quillon **4.**(*del cardo*) thistle flower
gavilla *f* **1.**(*fajo*) bundle, sheaf **2.**(*cuadrilla*) band
gaviota *f* (sea)gull
gay *m* gay
gazapera *f* **1.**(*madriguera*) warren **2.**(*de mala gente*) den **3.**(*riña*) brawl
gazapo *m* **1.**(*conejo*) young rabbit **2.**(*en un periódico*) misprint **3.** *inf* (*al hablar*) slip
gazmoñería *f* **1.**(*mojigatería*) prudishness **2.**(*hipocresía*) hypocrisy
gazmoño, **-a** *adj* **1.**(*mojigato*) prudish **2.**(*hipócrita*) hypocritical
gaznápiro, **-a** *m, f* simpleton
gaznatada *f AmL* blow to the throat
gaznate *m* gullet
gazpacho *m* GASTR gazpacho

> **Gazpacho**, a cold vegetable soup made from **tomates** (tomatoes), **pepinos** (cucumbers), **pimientos** (peppers), **aceite de oliva** (olive oil) and a little **pan** (bread), is prepared in summer, especially in the south of Spain, in **Andalucía** and **Extremadura**.

GB *m* **1.** *abr de* **gigabyte** GB **2.** *abr de* **Gran Bretaña** GB
Gbit *m abr de* **gigabit** Gbit
Gbyte *m abr de* **gigabyte** GB
géiser *m* geyser
geisha *f* geisha
gel *m* gel
gelatina *f* **1.**(*sustancia*) gelatine, gelatin *Am* **2.** GASTR jelly
gelatinoso, **-a** *adj* **1.**(*como la gelatina*) gelatinous **2.**(*de gelatina*) jelly
gélido, **-a** *adj* icy
gema *f* **1.**(*piedra preciosa*) gem, jewel **2.** BOT bud, gemma
gemebundo, **-a** *adj* groaning, moaning
gemelo, **-a** **I.** *adj* twin; **hermanos ~s** twin brothers **II.** *m, f* (*mellizo*) twin
gemelos *mpl* **1.**(*anteojos*) binoculars *pl*; **~ de teatro** opera glasses **2.**(*de la camisa*) cufflinks *pl* **3.** ASTR **Gemelos** Gemini **4.** ANAT calves *pl*
gemido *m* **1.**(*de dolor*) groan; (*de pena*) moan; (*al llorar*) wail **2.**(*de animal*) whimper
geminación *f* **1.**(*duplicación*) duplication **2.** LING gemination
Géminis *m* Gemini
gemir *irr como pedir vi* **1.**(*de dolor*) to groan; (*de pena*) to moan **2.**(*animal*) to whine
gen *m* BIO gene
genciana *f* gentian
gendarme *m* policeman
genealogía *f* genealogy
genealógico, **-a** *adj* genealogical; **árbol ~** family tree
generación *f* **1.**(*producción*) generation; **instrucción de ~** INFOR generative instruction **2.**(*descendientes*) generation
generacional *adj* generational
generador *m* ELEC generator
generador(a) *adj* **1.**(*productivo*) productive; **medidas ~as de empleo** employment creation measures **2.** ELEC generating
general **I.** *adj* **1.**(*universal*) general; **cuartel ~** headquarters; **cultura ~** general knowledge; **junta ~ (extraordinaria)** (extraordinary) general meeting; **regla ~** general rule; **de uso ~** (*para todo uso*) multi-purpose, all-purpose; (*para todo el mundo*) for general use; **por lo**

~, **en** ~ in general, generally; **por regla** ~ as a (general) rule; **en** ~ **me siento satisfecho** overall, I'm satisfied; **en** ~ **hace mejor tiempo aquí** generally speaking, the weather is better here **2.** (*vago*) general; **tengo una idea** ~ **del tema** I have a general idea about the subject **II.** *m* general; ~ **en jefe** supreme commander

generalato *m* **1.** MIL (*grado*) generalship; (*oficiales*) generals *pl* **2.** REL generalship

generalidad *f* **1.** (*calidad general, validez general*) generality; **en la** ~ **de los casos** in most cases **2.** (*vaguedad*) **respondió con una** ~ he/she gave a vague reply; **hablar de** ~**es** to talk about nothing in particular **3.** *pl* (*conocimientos generales*) basic knowledge

Generalitat *f regional government of Catalonia*

generalización *f* **1.** (*universalización*) generalization **2.** (*difusión*) spread

generalizador(**a**) *adj* generalizing

generalizar <z→c> *vt* **1.** (*hacer general*) to generalize **2.** (*difundir*) to spread

generalmente *adv* **1.** (*en general*) generally **2.** (*ampliamente*) widely **3.** (*habitualmente*) generally

generar *vt* **1.** (*producir*) to generate; ~ **beneficios** to generate profits **2.** (*provocar*) to create; ~ **un clima de confianza** to create a climate of trust

generativo, **-a** *adj* generative

generatriz *f* **1.** FÍS generator **2.** MAT generatrix

genérico, **-a** *adj* **1.** (*de la especie*) generic; **medicamentos** ~**s** generic drugs **2.** LING **nombre** ~ common noun

género *m* **1.** BIO genus; ~ **humano** mankind, human race **2.** (*clase*) type, sort; **¿qué** ~ **de hombre es?** what sort of man is he?; **sin ningún** ~ **de dudas** without a shadow of a doubt; **tomar todo** ~ **de precauciones** to take every possible precaution **3.** LING gender **4.** LIT, ARTE genre; **el** ~ **novelístico** fiction; **el** ~ **lírico** lyric poetry **5.** COM (*artículo*) article; (*mercancía*) merchandise, goods *pl;* (*tela*) cloth; ~**s de punto** knitwear **6.** MÚS **el** ~ **lírico** opera; **el** ~ **chico** light opera, zarzuela **7.** (*manera*) manner

generosidad *f* **1.** (*dadivosidad*) generosity **2.** (*magnanimidad*) magnanimity

generoso, **-a** *adj* **1.** (*dadivoso*) generous; **ser** ~ **con** [*o* **para con**] **alguien** to be generous to sb **2.** (*magnánimo*) magnanimous **3.** (*abundante*) generous

génesis *f inv* genesis

Génesis *m* Genesis

genética *f sin pl* BIO genetics

genético, **-a** *adj* genetic

genial *adj* **1.** (*idea*) brilliant **2.** (*gracioso*) funny **3.** (*estupendo*) great

genialidad *f* **1.** (*cualidad*) genius **2.** (*acción*) stroke of genius

genio *m* **1.** (*carácter*) character; **tener mal** ~ to be bad-tempered; **tener mucho** ~ to be very temperamental **2.** (*persona*) genius; **el** ~ **de Cervantes** Cervantes the genius **3.** (*empuje*) drive **4.** (*de una época*) spirit **5.** (*ser fabuloso*) genie **6.** ARTE genius

genista *f* broom

genital *adj* genital

genitales *mpl* genitals *pl*

genitivo *m* LING genitive

genocidio *m* genocide

Génova *f* Genoa

gente *f* **1.** (*personas*) people *pl;* ~ **de armas** men at arms; **la** ~ **joven/mayor** young/old people; ~ **menuda** (*niños*) children; **a este partido le preocupa la** ~ this party cares about people; **tienes que tratar más con la** ~ you should spend more time with other people; **¿qué dirá la** ~**?** what will people say?; **tener don de** ~**s** to have a way with people **2.** (*personal*) staff **3.** MIL (*tropa*) troop; NÁUT crew **4.** *inf* (*parentela*) family; **¿qué tal tu** ~**?** how are your folks? **5.** *AmL* (*honrado*) honest people

gentil **I.** *adj* **1.** (*pagano*) pagan **2.** (*apuesto*) dashing; (*elegante*) elegant **3.** (*amable*) considerate **II.** *mf* pagan, heathen

gentileza *f* **1.** (*garbo*) elegance **2.** (*cortesía*) kindness; **¿tendría Ud. la** ~ **de ayudarme?** would you be so kind as to help me?

gentilicio, **-a** *adj* **nombre** ~ *noun describing people from a particular place*

gentío *m sin pl* crowd

gentuza *f pey* rabble; **¡qué** ~**!** what a rabble!

genuflexión *f* genuflection

genuino, **-a** *adj* (*persona*) genuine; (*manuscrito*) authentic; (*amor*) true; **es un caso** ~ **de histeria** it is a genuine case of hysteria

geodesia *f* geodesy

geografía *f sin pl* geography

geográfico, **-a** *adj* geographical

geógrafo, **-a** *m, f* geographer

geología *f sin pl* geology

geológico, **-a** *adj* geological

geólogo, **-a** *m, f* geologist

geometría *f sin pl* geometry

geométrico, **-a** *adj* geometri(cal)

geopolítico, **-a** *adj* geopolitical

Georgia *f* Georgia

georgiano, **-a** *adj, m, f* Georgian

geranio *m* geranium

gerencia *f* (*de una empresa, un teatro*) management; (*de un banco*) directors *pl*

gerente *mf* (*de una gran empresa*) director, general manager; (*de una pequeña empresa*) manager; (*de un departamento*) head

geriatra *mf* geriatrician

geriatría *f sin pl* geriatrics *pl*

geriátrico, **-a** *adj* geriatric; **clínica geriátrica** geriatric hospital

gerifalte *m* **1.** (*persona*) bigwig **2.** (*halcón*) gerfalcon [*o* gyrfalcon]

germánico, **-a** **I.** *adj* **1.** (*de Germania*) Germanic **2.** (*de Alemania*) German **II.** *m, f* German

germanio *m* germanium
germanismo *m word or phrase of German origin*
germanista *mf* Germanist, German scholar
germanización *f* Germanization
germanizar <z→c> *vt* to Germanize, to make German
germano, **-a** *adj, m, f v.* **germánico**
germanófilo, **-a** *adj* Germanophilic
germanófobo, **-a** *adj* Germanophobic
germanooccidental *adj, mf* West German
germanooriental *adj, mf* East German
germen *m* **1.** BIO germ; ~ **de trigo** wheatgerm **2.** (*origen*) origin
germicida *m* germicide
germinación *f* germination
germinar *vi* **1.** BOT to germinate **2.** (*sospechas*) to arouse; ~ **en** to give rise to
gerontocracia *f* POL gerontocracy
gerontología *f sin pl* gerontology
gerundense **I.** *adj* of/from Gerona **II.** *mf* native/inhabitant of Gerona
gerundio *m* LING gerund
gesta *f* heroic deed, exploit; LIT epic poem or narrative
gestación *f* **1.** (*de una persona, un animal*) gestation **2.** (*de un plan, proyecto*) preparation; (*de un complot*) hatching; **el proyecto está en** ~ the project is at the planning stage
gestar **I.** *vt* to gestate **II.** *vr:* ~**se** (*proceso*) to develop; (*plan, proyecto*) to be prepared; (*complot*) to be hatched
gesticulación *f* **1.** (*con las manos*) gesticulation **2.** (*con la cara*) face-pulling; (*de dolor*) grimace
gesticular *vi* **1.** (*con las manos*) to gesticulate **2.** (*con la cara*) to pull faces; (*de dolor*) to grimace
gestión *f* **1.** (*diligencia*) measure; **hacer gestiones** to take measures [*o* steps] **2.** (*de una empresa*) management; **la** ~ **del gobierno** the government's management of the country; **la** ~ **al frente de la escuela** school management **3.** INFOR ~ **de ficheros** file management
gestionar *vt* **1.** (*asunto*) to conduct **2.** (*negocio*) to manage
gesto *m* **1.** (*con el cuerpo*) movement; (*con la mano*) gesture; (*con el rostro*) expression; **torcer el** ~ to scowl **2.** (*semblante*) face **3.** (*acto*) gesture; **un** ~ **de apoyo** a gesture of support
gestor(a) **I.** *adj* managing **II.** *m(f) person who handles official matters on the behalf of his/her client*
gestoría *f agency handling official matters*
gestual *adj* gestural; **lenguaje** ~ body language
gestualidad *f* (*del rostro*) expressiveness; (*del cuerpo*) body language
ghanés, **-esa** *adj, m, f* Ghanese
GHz *abr de* **gigahertz** GHz
giba *f* **1.** (*chepa*) hump, hunch **2.** (*bulto*) lump **3.** (*molestia*) nuisance
gibar *vt* **1.** (*concorvar*) to bend **2.** *inf* (*jorobar*) to bother, to hassle
gibón *m* gibbon
gibosidad *f* hump
Gibraltar *m* Gibraltar
gibraltareño, **-a** *adj, m, f* Gibraltarian
Giga *m* Giga
gigabyte *m* gigabyte; ~**s por segundo** gigabytes per second
gigante **I.** *adj* giant, gigantic **II.** *m* **1.** (*ser*) giant **2.** (*en fiesta popular*) *papier maché giant* ►**un** ~ **con pies de barro** an idol with feet of clay
gigantesco, **-a** *adj* gigantic
gigantismo *m sin pl* MED giantism [*o* gigantism]
gigoló *m* gigolo
gilipollas *mf inv, vulg* jerk, wanker
gilipollez *f vulg* bullshit; **decir gilipolleces** to talk rubbish
gimnasia *f* **1.** DEP gymnastics *pl;* ~ **rítmica** rhythm gymnastics; **hacer** ~ to do gymnastics **2.** ENS gym **3.** (*ejercicio*) **hacer** ~ to do exercises
gimnasio *m* gymnasium; ~ (**de musculación**) gym
gimnasta *mf* gymnast
gimnástico, **-a** *adj* gymnastic
gimotear *vi* **1.** *pey* (*gemir*) to groan **2.** (*lloriquear*) to whimper, to whine
gimoteo *m* **1.** (*gemidos*) groan **2.** (*lloriqueo*) whimper, whining
ginebra *f* gin
Ginebra *f* Geneva
ginebrino, **-a** **I.** *adj* of/from Geneva **II.** *m, f* native/inhabitant of Geneva
ginecología *f sin pl* gynaecology *Brit,* gynecology *Am*
ginecológico, **-a** *adj* gynaecological *Brit,* gynecological *Am*
ginecólogo, **-a** *m, f* gynaecologist *Brit,* gynecologist *Am*
ginesta *f* broom
gingivitis *f inv* MED gingivitis
gira *f* **1.** (*de un día*) (day)trip, excursion; (*más larga*) tour **2.** (*de un artista*) tour; **estar de** ~ to be on tour
girado, **-a** *m, f* FIN drawee
giralda *f* weathervane; (*en forma de gallo*) weathercock
girar **I.** *vi* **1.** (*dar vueltas*) to revolve; (*con rapidez*) to spin **2.** (*conversación*) ~ **en torno a algo** to revolve around sth **3.** (*beneficios*) **este negocio gira mucho** this business has a big turnover **4.** (*torcer*) to turn **II.** *vt* **1.** (*dar la vuelta*) to turn; ~ **la vista** to look round **2.** COM (*dinero*) to send; ~ **a cargo de alguien** (*letra*) to draw on sb
girasol *m* sunflower
giratorio, **-a** *adj* revolving
giro *m* **1.** (*vuelta, cariz*) turn; **un** ~ **de volante** a turn of the steering wheel; **tomar un** ~

G

favorable/negativo to take a turn for the better/worse; **me preocupa el ~ que toma este asunto** I don't like the way this issue is developing **2.** LING (*locución*) expression **3.** COM (*letra*) draft; ~ **postal** money order **4.** COM (*de una empresa*) business turnover

gitanada *f* **1.** (*engaño*) contemptible trick **2.** (*zalamería*) wheedling

gitanear *vi inf* to wheedle

gitanería *f* **1.** *inf* (*halago*) wheedling praise **2.** (*grupo*) band of gipsies [*o* gypsies *Am*] **3.** (*vida*) gipsy [*o* gypsy *Am*] way of life **4.** (*acción*) gipsy [*o* gypsy *Am*] saying

gitano, **-a** **I.** *adj* **1.** (*de los gitanos*) gipsy *Brit,* gypsy *Am* **2.** *inf* (*zalamero*) wheedling **II.** *m, f* **1.** (*calé*) gipsy *Brit,* gypsy *Am;* **ir hecho un ~** *inf* to look like a tramp **2.** *inf* (*estafador*) swindler **3.** GASTR **brazo de ~** Swiss roll *Brit,* jelly roll *Am*

glaciación *f* glaciation

glacial *adj* **1.** (*helado*) icy cold; **zona ~** polar region **2.** (*persona*) cold

glaciar *m* GEO glacier

gladiador *m* gladiator

gladiolo *m,* **gladíolo** *m* gladiolus

glande *m* ANAT glans penis

glándula *f* ANAT gland

glandular *adj* glandular

glasé *m* glacé silk

glasear *vt* (*alimentos, papel*) to glaze; (*tarta*) to ice

glaucoma *m* MED glaucoma

glicerina *f* glycerine *Brit,* glycerin *Am*

global *adj* **1.** (*total*) overall; **valoración ~** total value **2.** (*cantidad*) total **3.** (*informe*) comprehensive **4.** (*mundial*) global

globalidad *f* totality

globalización *f* **1.** (*de un problema*) overall treatment **2.** (*generalización*) generalization **3.** (*mundialización*) globalization

globalizante *adj* generalizing

globalizar <z→c> *vt* **1.** (*problema*) to give an overall view of **2.** (*generalizar*) to generalize **3.** (*mundializar*) to globalize

globo *m* **1.** (*esfera*) sphere; ~ **de una lámpara** (round) lampshade; ~ **ocular** eyeball **2.** (*tierra, mapa*) globe **3.** (*para niños*) balloon; ~ (**aerostático**) hot-air balloon **4.** *inf* (*borrachera*) **tener un ~** to be plastered **5.** *inf* (*enfado*) anger **6.** *inf* (*preservativo*) condom, johnny *Brit,* rubber *Am* **7.** DEP (*tenis*) lob **8.** (*comics, tebeos*) speech balloon [*o* bubble] ►**en ~** as a whole

globular *adj* **1.** (*de globo*) spherical **2.** (*de glóbulo*) globular

globulina *f* BIO globulin

glóbulo *m* ANAT corpuscle ~ **blanco/rojo** white/red corpuscle

gloria[1] *f* **1.** (*fama*) glory; **Goya es una ~ nacional** Goya is a national treasure **2.** (*paraíso*) heaven; **conseguir la ~** to go to heaven; **estar en la ~** *inf* to be in seventh heaven **3.** (*esplendor*) glory ►**sin pena ni ~** whitout any ado; **oler/saber a ~** to smell/taste delicious

gloria[2] *m* REL gloria, doxology

gloriarse <*1. pres:* me glorío> *vr* **1.** (*presumir*) **~se de algo** to boast about sth **2.** (*complacerse*) **~se de** [*o* **en**] **algo** to glory in sth

glorieta *f* **1.** (*cenador*) arbour *Brit,* arbor *Am* **2.** (*plazoleta*) (small) square **3.** (*rotonda*) roundabout

glorificación *f* glorification

glorificar <c→qu> **I.** *vt* to glorify **II.** *vr* **~se de algo** to boast about sth

glorioso, **-a** *adj* **1.** *t.* REL glorious **2.** (*jactancioso*) boastful

glosa *f* **1.** ~ **a algo** (*aclaración*) explanation on sth; (*anotación*) note on sth; (*comentario*) comment on sth **2.** LIT gloss **3.** MÚS variation

glosar *vt* **1.** (*anotar*) to annotate **2.** (*comentar*) to comment on; LIT to gloss **3.** (*tergiversar*) to deliberately misinterpret

glosario *m* glossary

glotis *f sin pl* ANAT glottis

glotón *m* glutton

glotón, **-ona** **I.** *adj* gluttonous, greedy **II.** *m, f* glutton, gannet *inf*

glotonear *vi* to be gluttonous

glotonería *f* gluttony

glucemia *f* MED glycaemia *Brit,* glycemia *Am*

glucosa *f* glucose

gluten *m* **1.** (*cola*) glue **2.** BOT gluten

glúteo *m* ANAT gluteous *pl,* buttocks *pl*

glutinoso, **-a** *adj* glutinous

gnomo *m* gnome

gnosis *f inv* REL gnosis

gnosticismo *m sin pl* REL gnosticism

gobernabilidad *f sin pl* governability

gobernable *adj* **1.** (*país*) governable **2.** (*nave*) steerable

gobernación *f* government

gobernador(**a**) **I.** *adj* governing **II.** *m(f)* governor

gobernanta *f AmL* **1.** (*niñera*) nanny **2.** (*institutriz*) governess **3.** (*ama de llaves*) housekeeper

gobernante *mf* ruler

gobernar <e→ie> *vt* **1.** POL (*mandar*) to govern **2.** (*dirigir*) to manage; (*nave*) to steer; ~ **una casa** to run a household **3.** (*máquina*) to handle, to run **4.** (*a una persona*) to rule

gobierno *m* **1.** POL government; ~ **autonómico** regional government; ~ **central** central government; **en círculos afines al ~** in the corridors of power **2.** (*ministros*) cabinet; ~ **en la sombra** shadow cabinet **3.** (*del gobernador*) governorship; (*residencia*) governor's residence **4.** (*dirección*) management **5.** (*de una nave*) steering **6.** (*de una máquina*) handling

goce *m* pleasure, enjoyment

godo, **-a** **I.** *adj* Gothic **II.** *m, f* **1.** HIST Goth **2.** *AmC, pey* (*español*) Spaniard

gofre *m* waffle

gol *m* DEP goal; ~ **del empate** equalizer;

meter un ~ to score (a goal) ▸**meter un** ~ **a alguien** *inf* to put one over [*o* pull a fast one] on sb

gola *f* **1.**(*gorguera*) ruff **2.**(*garganta*) throat

golazo *m* DEP great goal

goleador(a) *m(f)* DEP goalscorer

golear *vt* DEP to score a lot of goals against, to hammer

goleta *f* NÁUT schooner

golf *m sin pl* DEP golf

golfa *f* **1.** *inf*(*puta*) slut, hussy **2.** *v.* **golfo, -a**

golfear *vi* to loaf about

golfista *mf* DEP golfer

golfo *m* GEO gulf

golfo, -a **I.** *adj* (*niño*) naughty **II.** *m, f* **1.**(*pilluelo*) urchin **2.**(*vagabundo*) tramp **3.**(*sinvergüenza*) scoundrel

gollería *f* delicacy

gollete *m* **1.** ANAT (*garganta*) throat **2.**(*de vasija*) neck

golondrina *f* **1.**(*pájaro*) swallow **2.** *reg* (*barca*) motorboat

golondrino *m* **1.**(*pájaro*) young swallow **2.**(*vagabundo*) drifter, rolling stone

golosina *f* **1.**(*manjar*) delicacy **2.**(*dulce*) sweet *Brit,* candy *Am* **3.**(*deseo*) fancy *Brit,* desire **4.**(*cosa apetitosa*) titbit *Brit,* tidbit *Am*

golosinear *vi* to nibble at sweets [*o* candy *Am*]

goloso, -a **I.** *adj* **1.**(*de dulces*) sweet-toothed **2.**(*apetitoso*) appetizing; **es una oferta muy golosa** it's a very tempting offer **II.** *m, f* **ser un** ~ to have a sweet tooth

golpe *m* **1.**(*impacto*) blow; (*choque*) bump; ~ **de Estado** coup (d'état); ~ **de pincel** brushstroke; **un** ~ **de tos** a fit of coughing; **andar a** ~**s** to be always fighting; **abrirse de** ~ (*door, window*) to fly open; **cerrar la puerta de** ~ to slam the door shut; **dar un** ~ to strike; **me he dado un** ~ **en la cabeza** I've banged my head; **parar un** ~ to stop a blow; **me lo tragué de un** ~ I downed it in one go [*o* all at once] **2.**(*ruido*) bang **3.**(*ocurrencia*) witty remark **4.**(*atraco*) hold-up **5.**(*gran cantidad*) crowd; ~ **de gente** lots of people **6.** TÉC (*pestillo*) spring bolt **7.**(*sorpresa*) shock **8.**(*de vestido*) flap **9.**(*en el boxeo*) punch; ~ **bajo** punch below the belt; ~ **franco** free kick ▸**de** ~ (**y porrazo**) (*al mismo tiempo*) at the same time; (*de repente*) suddenly; **a** ~ **de vista** at a glance; **no pegó ni** ~ *inf* he didn't lift a finger

golpear **I.** *vi* **1.**(*dar un golpe*) to hit **2.**(*latir*) to throb, to beat **3.** TÉC (*motor*) to knock **II.** *vt* to hit; (*puerta*) to knock on **III.** *vr* ~**se la cabeza** to bang one's head

golpetear **I.** *vi* **1.**(*dar golpes*) to hammer **2.**(*traquetear*) to rattle **II.** *vt* to hammer

golpista *mf* participant in a coup (d'état)

goma *f* **1.**(*sustancia*) rubber; ~ **de borrar** rubber *Brit,* eraser *Am;* ~ **elástica** (*sustancia*) rubber; (*objeto*) elastic band; ~ **de pegar** glue **2.** *inf* (*preservativo*) condom, johnny *Brit,* rubber *Am* **3.** *AmL* (*resaca*) hangover

goma-dos *f sin pl* plastic explosive

gomaespuma *f* foam rubber

gomería *f Arg* COM tyre [*o* tire *Am*] dealer, tyre [*o* tire *Am*] workshop

gomero *m AmL* (*árbol*) rubber tree

gomina® *f* hair [*o* styling] gel

gominola *f* winegum *Brit,* gumdrop *Am*

gomosidad *f* **1.**(*elasticidad*) elasticity **2.**(*adherencia*) stickiness

gomoso *m* sticky

gónada *f* ANAT gonad

góndola *f* **1.**(*de Venecia*) gondola **2.** *AmL* bus

gondolero *m* gondolier

gong *m* <gongs>, **gongo** *m* gong

gonorrea *f* MED gonorrhoea *Brit,* gonorrhea *Am*

gordo *m* **1.**(*grasa*) fat **2.**(*lotería*) **el** ~ first prize (in the lottery), the jackpot; **sacar el** ~ *fig* to bring home the bacon

gordo, -a **I.** *adj* **1.**(*persona*) fat; (*comida*) fatty; (*tejido*) thick **2.**(*suceso*) important; (*salario*) big; **una mentira gorda** a big lie; **ha pasado algo muy** ~ sth serious has happened ▸**se armó la gorda** *inf* all hell broke loose; **me cae** ~ I don't like him **II.** *m, f inf* fat man, fat woman *m, f*

gordura *f* (*obesidad*) fatness; (*corpulencia*) corpulence; (*tejido adiposo*) fat

gorgojo *m* **1.**(*insecto*) weevil **2.** *inf* (*persona*) midget

gorgoritear *vi inf* to warble

gorgotear *vi* **1.**(*hacer ruido*) to gurgle; (*arroyo*) to babble **2.**(*burbujear*) to bubble

gorgoteo *m* **1.**(*ruido*) gurgle; (*de un arroyo*) babbling **2.**(*borboteo*) bubbling

gorguera *f* **1.**(*gola*) ruff **2.**(*de la armadura*) gorget

gorila *m* **1.**(*animal*) gorilla **2.** *inf* (*portero*) bouncer **3.** *inf* (*guardaespaldas*) bodyguard **4.** *inf*(*matón*) thug

gorjear **I.** *vi* **1.**(*personas*) to twitter **2.**(*pájaros*) to chirp **II.** *vr:* ~**se** **1.**(*niño*) to gurgle **2.** *AmL* (*burlarse*) to make fun of

gorjeo *m* **1.**(*de personas*) twittering; (*de bebés*) gurgling **2.**(*de pájaros*) chirping

gorra *f* **1.**(*prenda*) cap; ~ **de visera** peaked cap *Brit,* baseball cap *Am* **2.**(*para niños*) bonnet ▸**de** ~ *inf* (*gratis*) free; **andar** [*o* **vivir**] **de** ~ *inf* to sponge

gorrear *vi, vt inf* to scrounge; **¿te puedo** ~ **un cigarrillo?** can I cadge a cigarette off you?

gorrero *m inf* scrounger

gorrinada *f* (*acción injusta*) dirty trick

gorrinera *f* pigsty

gorrino, -a *m, f* **1.**(*cochinillo*) suckling pig; (*cerdo*) pig; (*cerda*) sow **2.** *pey* (*persona*) pig

gorrión *m* **1.**(*pardal*) sparrow **2.** *AmC* (*colibrí*) hummingbird

gorro *m* hat; (*de uniforme*) cap; ~ **para bebés** baby's bonnet; ~ **de natación** bathing cap; ~ **de papel** paper hat ▸**estar hasta el** ~ **de algo**

to be fed up with sth
gorrón *m* **1.**(*piedra*) pebble, cobblestone **2.**TÉC pivot
gorrón, -ona *m, f* **1.** *inf* (*aprovechado*) scrounger **2.** *AmC* (*egoísta*) selfish person
gorronear *vi v.* **gorrear**
gorronería *f inf* scrounging
gota *f* **1.**(*de líquido*) drop; **café con unas ~s de ron** coffee with a dash of rum; **el agua salía ~ a ~ del grifo** the water dripped out of the tap; **apurar el vaso hasta la última ~** to drain the glass to the last drop; **parecerse como dos ~s de agua** to be like two peas in a pod **2.**(*pizca*) drop; **no queda ni ~ de agua** there's not a drop of water left; **no tiene ni una ~ de paciencia** he/she doesn't have an ounce of patience **3.**METEO **~ fría** cold front **4.**MED (*enfermedad*) gout **5.**(*gotero*) **el ~ a ~** the drip ▸**la ~ que colma el vaso** the last straw; **sudar la ~ gorda** *inf* to sweat blood
gotear **I.** *vi* **1.**(*líquido*) to drip; (*escurrir*) trickle **2.**(*salirse*) to leak **II.** *vimpers* **está goteando** it's drizzling, it's spitting (with rain) *Brit*
goteo *m* **1.**(*gotear*) drip(ping) **2.**MED drip *Brit*
gotera *f* **1.**(*filtración, grieta*) leak; **hay una ~ en el baño** there's a leak in the bath(room) **2.**(*mancha*) stain **3.**(*achaque*) complaint **4.** *pl, AmL* (*afueras*) outskirts *pl*
gotero *m* **1.**MED drip **2.** *AmL* (*cuentagotas*) dropper
gótico, -a *adj* Gothic
gotoso, -a **I.** *adj* MED gouty **II.** *m, f* MED gout-sufferer
gozada *f inf* delight
gozar <z→c> **I.** *vi* **1.**(*complacerse*) to enjoy oneself **2.**(*disfrutar*) **~ de algo** to enjoy sth; **~ de una increíble fortuna** to be incredibly wealthy **II.** *vt* **1.**(*disfrutar*) to enjoy **2.**(*poseer carnalmente*) to possess **III.** *vr:* **~se** to enjoy oneself; **~se en** to take pleasure in
gozne *m* hinge
gozo *m* **1.**(*delicia*) delight; (*placer*) pleasure **2.**(*alegría*) joy **3.**(*del fuego*) flame ▸**mi ~ en un pozo** all for nothing
gr. *abr de* **gramo** g.
grabación *f* **1.**(*de disco*) recording **2.**TV (*de una serie*) shooting **3.**INFOR copying
grabado *m* **1.**ARTE (*acción*) engraving **2.**ARTE (*copia*) print; **~ al agua fuerte** etching; **~ en madera** woodcut **3.**(*ilustración*) illustration
grabador(a) *m(f)* engraver
grabadora *f* TÉC tape recorder
grabadura *f* (*acción, efecto*) recording; (*en piedra*) engraving; (*en madera*) cutting
grabar **I.** *vt* **1.**ARTE to engrave; (*en madera*) to cut **2.**(*disco*) to record **3.**INFOR to copy **4.**(*fijar*) to engrave **II.** *vr:* **~se** to become engraved
gracejo *m* wit, humour *Brit,* humor *Am*
gracia *f* **1.** *pl* (*agradecimiento*) **¡~s!** thanks!; **¡muchas ~s!** thanks a lot!; **¡~s a Dios!** thank God!; **te debo las ~s** I owe you my thanks; **no me ha dado ni las ~s** he/she didn't even say "thank you"; **~s a tus esfuerzos lo conseguí** thanks to your efforts, I managed it **2.**REL grace **3.**(*perdón*) mercy **4.**(*favor*) favour *Brit,* favor *Am* **5.**(*agrado*) **me cae en ~** I like him/her **6.**(*garbo*) elegance; **está escrito con ~** it's elegantly written **7.**(*chiste*) joke; **no tiene (ni) pizca de ~** it's not in the least bit funny; **no me hace nada de ~** I don't find it funny in the least; **si lo haces se va la ~** if you do it it loses its charm; **este cómico tiene poca ~** this comedian isn't very funny; **la ~ es que...** the funny thing is that ...; **no estoy hoy para ~s** I'm not in a mood for jokes today **8.** *irón* (*ocurrencia*) **hoy ha hecho otra de sus ~s** he/she has been up to his/her tricks again
grácil *adj* graceful
gracilidad *f* gracefulness
gracioso, -a **I.** *adj* **1.**(*atractivo*) attractive **2.**(*chistoso*) funny; **para mí no fue nada ~** I didn't find it at all funny **3.**(*gratis*) free **II.** *m, f* TEAT comic character; **algún ~ me ha escondido las llaves** some joker has hidden my keys; **no te hagas el ~ conmigo** don't try to play the clown with me
grada *f* **1.**(*de un estadio*) tier; **las ~s** the terraces **2.**(*peldaño*) step **3.**AGR harrow **4.**NÁUT slipway **5.** *pl* (*escalinata*) steps *pl* **6.** *pl, AmL* (*atrio*) courtyard
gradación *f* **1.**(*escalonamiento*) gradation **2.**MÚS gradation **3.**(*retórica*) climax
gradería *f,* **graderío** *m* **1.**(*de un estadio*) terraces *pl* **2.** *fig* crowd
grado *m* **1.**(*nivel*) degree; **~ de confianza** degree of trust; **quemaduras de primer ~** MED first-degree burns; **en ~ sumo** greatly, highly **2.**(*parentesco*) degree **3.**ENS year; **~ elemental** basic level **4.**UNIV degree; **~ de doctor** doctorate **5.**MAT degree; **~ centígrado** degree centigrade **6.**LING **~ comparativo** degree of comparison **7.**MIL (*rango*) rank **8.**(*de alcohol*) degree
graduable *adj* adjustable
graduación *f* **1.**(*regulación*) adjustment **2.**(*en grados*) graduation; (*en niveles, de personas*) grading; (*de precios*) regulation **3.**(*de un vino*) strength; **~ alcohólica** alcohol content **4.**MIL rank **5.**UNIV graduation
graduado, -a **I.** *adj* graduate(d) **II.** *m, f* **1.**UNIV graduate; **~ en ingeniería** engineering graduate **2.**ENS **~ escolar** *school-leaving certificate*
gradual *adj* gradual
gradualmente *adv* **1.**(*en grados*) by degrees **2.**(*progresivamente*) gradually
graduar <*1. pres:* **gradúo**> **I.** *vt* **1.**(*regular*) to regulate **2.**TÉC to graduate; **~ la vista a alguien** to test sb's eyesight **3.**(*en niveles*) to classify; (*precios*) to regulate **4.**UNIV to confer a degree on **5.**MIL to confer a rank on; **~ a alguien de coronel** to confer the rank of colonel on sb **II.** *vr:* **~se** to graduate; **se graduó en económicas** he/she graduated in economics

grafía *f* (*escritura*) writing; (*ortografía*) spelling

gráfica *f* graph

gráfico *m* graph; ~ **de tarta** pie chart; **tarjeta de ~s** INFOR graphics card

gráfico, **-a** *adj* **1.** (*de la escritura*) written **2.** (*del dibujo*) illustrated; **diccionario** ~ visual dictionary **3.** (*claro*) graphic **4.** *fig* expressive

grafismo *m* **1.** (*grafía*) handwriting **2.** (*aspecto estético*) vivid writing style **3.** INFOR computer graphics

grafista *mf* graphic artist [*o* designer]

grafito *m* MIN graphite

grafología *f sin pl* graphology

grafólogo, **-a** *m, f* graphologist

gragea *f* MED (sugar-coated) pill

grajear *vi* **1.** (*el grajo*) to caw **2.** (*un bebé*) to gurgle

grajilla *f* jackdaw

grajo *m* **1.** (*ave*) rook **2.** (*charlatán*) chatter-box **3.** *AmL* (*sobaquina*) body odour *Brit,* body odor *Am*

gral. *adj abr de* **general** gen.

gramática *f* LING grammar; ~ **generativa** transformational grammar ►**tener mucha ~ parda** *inf* to be worldy-wise

gramatical *adj* grammatical; **regla** ~ grammatical rule

gramático, **-a** *m, f* grammarian

gramilla *f AmL* (*hierba*) lawn, grass

gramo *m* gramme *Brit,* gram *Am*

gramófono *m* gramophone *Brit,* phonograph *Am*

gramola *f* **1.** (*gramófono*) gramophone *Brit,* phonograph *Am* **2.** (*en un bar*) jukebox

gran *adj v.* **grande**

grana **I.** *adj* (*color*) scarlet **II.** *f* **1.** (*acción*) seeding **2.** (*semilla*) seed **3.** (*cochinilla*) cochineal

granada *f* **1.** (*fruto*) pomegranate **2.** (*proyectil: de mano*) grenade; (*de artillería*) shell

granadilla *f* **1.** (*fruto*) passion fruit **2.** *AmC* (*planta*) passionflower

granadino, **-a** **I.** *adj* of/from Granada **II.** *m, f* native/inhabitant of Granada

granado *m* pomegranate tree

granado, **-a** *adj* **1.** (*ilustre*) distinguished **2.** (*maduro*) mature **3.** (*alto*) tall

granar *vi* to seed

granate **I.** *adj* burgundy **II.** *m* MIN garnet

Gran Bretaña *f* Great Britain

grancanario, **-a** **I.** *adj* of/from Grand Canary **II.** *m, f* native/inhabitant Grand Canary

grande **I.** *adj* <más grande *o* mayor, grandísimo> (*precediendo un substantivo singular: gran*) **1.** (*de tamaño*) big; (*número, cantidad*) large; **gran ciudad** big city; **una habitación** ~ a large room; **una gran suma de dinero** a large sum of money; **una gran mentira** a big lie; **gran velocidad** high speed; **vino gran cantidad de gente** a lot of people came; **tengo un gran interés por...** I'm very interested in ...; **no me preocupa gran cosa** I'm not very worried about it **2.** *inf* (*de edad*) grown-up **3.** (*moralmente*) great; **un gran hombre** a great man; **una gran idea** a great idea ►**ir ~ a alguien** to be too much for sb; **pasarlo en ~** to have a great time; **vivir a lo ~** to live in style **II.** *m* **1.** (*prócer*) great; **los ~s de la industria** the major industrial players **2.** (*título*) **Grande de España** Spanish Grandee

grandemente *adv* (*mucho*) greatly; (*extremadamente*) extremely

grandeza *f* **1.** (*tamaño*) size; **delirio de ~** delusions of grandeur **2.** (*excelencia de cosas, de personas*) greatness **3.** (*de un Grande*) status of grandee

grandilocuencia *f* grandiloquence

grandilocuente *adj* grandiloquent

grandiosidad *f* impressiveness, grandeur

grandioso, **-a** *adj* impressive; (*rimbombante*) grandiose

grandullón, **-ona** *adj* oversized

granear *vt* **1.** (*semilla*) to sow **2.** (*pólvora*) to sieve **3.** ARTE to grain

granel **carga a ~** bulk order; **a ~** (*sin envase*) loose; (*líquido*) by volume; (*en abundancia*) in abundance

granero *m* granary; (*de granja*) barn; **Castilla es el ~ de España** Castile is the granary of Spain

granítico, **-a** *adj* **1.** (*de granito*) granite **2.** (*parecido al granito*) granitic

granito *m* MIN granite

granizada *f* **1.** (*pedrisco*) hailstorm **2.** (*de balas*) hail

granizado *m* iced drink; ~ **de café** ≈ iced coffee

granizar <z→c> *vimpers* to hail

granizo *m* hail

granja *f* **1.** (*finca*) farm **2.** (*establecimiento*) dairy store

granjear **I.** *vt* **1.** (*ganado*) to farm **2.** (*adquirir*) to earn **II.** *vr:* **~se** to earn

granjero, **-a** *m, f* farmer

grano *m* **1.** (*de cereales, sal, arena*) grain; (*de café*) bean; (*de mostaza*) seed; **~s** grain; ~ **de uva** grape **2.** (*de piel*) spot, pimple **3.** TÉC grain; **de ~ duro** coarse-grained; **de ~ fino** fine-grained ►**aportó su ~ de arena** he/she did his/her bit; **de un ~ (de arena) hace una montaña** he/she always makes a mountain out of a molehill; **apartar el ~ de la paja** to separate the wheat from the chaff; **ir al ~** to get to the point

granoso, **-a** *adj* grainy

granuja[1] *m* **1.** (*pilluelo*) rascal **2.** (*bribón*) scoundrel; **el muy ~ me ha engañado** that scoundrel has cheated me

granuja[2] *f* **1.** (*uva*) grapes *pl* **2.** (*de las frutas*) seeds *pl*

granujada *f* **1.** (*travesura*) prank **2.** (*bribonada*) dirty trick

granujería *f* **1.** (*travesura*) prank **2.** (*bribonada*) dirty trick **3.** (*de pillos*) bunch of raga-

G

muffins **4.**(*de bribones*) bunch of scoundrels
granujiento, -a *adj* **1.**(*cara*) spotty, pimply **2.**(*superficie*) grainy
granulación *f* granulation
granulado *m* granules *pl*
granular I. *adj* grainy **II.** *vt* to granulate
granuloso, -a *adj* grainy
grapa *f* **1.**(*para papeles, madera*) staple **2.**(*licor*) grappa
grapadora *f* stapler
grapar *vt* to staple
grasa[1] *f* **1.** ANAT fat; ~ **de cerdo** pork fat; **cocinar sin** ~ to cook without fat [*o* grease]; **tener mucha** ~ **en los muslos** to have fat thighs **2.** TÉC (*lubricante*) oil, grease **3.**(*mugre*) grime **4.** MIN **las ~s** slag
grasa[2] *Arg* **I.** *adj inf, pey* common **II.** *m inf, pey* **ser un** ~ to be common
grasiento, -a *adj* fatty; (*de aceite*) greasy
graso, -a *adj* **1.**(*grasiento*) fatty; **piel grasa** oily skin; **pelo graso** greasy hair **2.**(*gordo*) fat
gratén *m* GASTR **al** ~ au gratin
gratificación *f* **1.**(*recompensa*) reward; (*sobre objetos perdidos*) compensation **2.**(*del sueldo*) bonus; ~ **de Navidad** Christmas bonus **3.**(*propina*) tip **4.**(*satisfación*) gratification
gratificante *adj* gratifying
gratificar <c→qu> *vt* **1.**(*recompensar*) ~ **a alguien por algo** to reward sb for sth; **se ~á a quien lo encuentre** there is a reward for the finder **2.**(*en el trabajo*) ~ **a alguien** to give sb a bonus **3.**(*complacer*) to gratify
gratinador *m* grill
gratinar *vt* GASTR to cook au gratin, to brown on top
gratis *adv* free
gratitud *f* gratitude
grato, -a *adj* **1.**(*agradable*) pleasant; ~ **al paladar** tasty; **tu novio me ha dado una grata impresión** your boyfriend seems very nice; **tu visita me es muy grata** I'm very glad you could come **2.**(*en una carta*) **me es** ~ **comunicarle que...** I am pleased to inform you that ...
gratuidad *f* **1.**(*de gratis*) **reclamar la** ~ **de la enseñanza/la sanidad** to demand free education/health services **2.**(*arbitrariedad*) arbitrariness **3.**(*algo infundado*) unjustified remark
gratuito, -a *adj* **1.**(*gratis*) free **2.**(*arbitrario*) arbitrary **3.**(*infundado*) groundless; **es una acusación gratuita** the accusation is groundless; **este rumor es** ~ this rumour [*o* rumor *Am*] is without foundation; **lo que has hecho ha sido bastante** ~ what you did was quite unnecessary
grava *f* gravel
gravable *adj* taxable
gravamen *m* **1.**(*carga*) burden **2.**(*de los ingresos*) tax
gravar *vt* **1.**(*cargar*) to burden **2.** FIN to tax; ~ **algo con un impuesto** to impose a tax on sth
grave *adj* **1.**(*objeto*) heavy **2.**(*enfermedad*) serious; **está** ~ he/she is very ill **3.**(*persona, situación*) serious; **este es un momento** ~ **para la industria** this is a difficult time for the industry **4.**(*estilo*) solemn **5.**(*sonido*) deep **6.** LING **acento** ~ grave accent; **palabra** ~ word whose stress falls on the penultimate syllable
gravedad *f* **1.** FÍS gravity; **centro de** ~ centre of gravity **2.** MED seriousness; **estar herido de** ~ to be seriously injured **3.** MÚS (*de los sonidos*) depth **4.**(*de un estilo*) solemnity **5.**(*de una situación, de un asunto*) seriousness
gravidez *f elev* pregnancy
grávido, -a *adj* **1.**(*mujer*) pregnant **2.** *elev* (*cargado*) ~ **de algo** laden with sth
gravilla *f* gravel
gravitación *f* FÍS gravitation
gravitar *vi* **1.** FÍS to gravitate **2.**(*un cuerpo*) ~ **sobre algo** to rest on sth **3.**(*recaer*) ~ **sobre** to loom over
gravitatorio, -a *adj* gravitational
gravoso, -a *adj* **1.**(*pesado*) burdensome **2.**(*costoso*) expensive
graznar *vi* (*cuervo*) to caw; (*ganso*) to honk; (*pato*) to quack
graznido *m* (*de cuervo*) caw; (*de ganso*) honk; (*de pato*) quack
greca *f* **1.**(*adorno*) frieze **2.** *AmL* (*cafetera eléctrica*) coffee machine
Grecia *f* Greece
grecolatino, -a *adj* Greco-Latin
grecorromano, -a *adj* Greco-Roman
greda *f* **1.**(*arcilla*) clay **2.**(*para desengrasar*) fuller's earth
gredal *m* claypit
gregal *adj* gregarious
gregario, -a *adj* **1.**(*persona*) gregarious **2.**(*soldado*) common
gregarismo *m sin pl* gregariousness
gregoriano, -a *adj* Gregorian
greguería *f* uproar, hullabaloo
gremial I. *adj* **1.**(*de una asociación*) relating to an association **2.**(*de un sindicato*) relating to a trade union **3.** HIST guild **II.** *mf* **1.**(*de una asociación*) association member **2.**(*de un sindicato*) union member
gremialismo *m sin pl* **1.**(*mundo de*) system of associations **2.**(*doctrina*) collectivism **3.**(*tendencia*) tendency to form associations
gremio *m* **1.**(*asociación*) association **2.**(*sindicato*) trade union **3.** HIST guild
greña *f* mop [*o* mat] of hair, rats' tails *pl* ►**andar a la** ~ **con alguien** to squabble [*o* bicker] with sb
greñudo, -a *adj* (*pelo*) tangled, matted
gres *m* **1.**(*arcilla*) potter's clay **2.**(*producto*) earthenware
gresca *f* **1.**(*bulla*) uproar, racket **2.**(*riña*) quarrel
grial *m* grail
griego, -a *adj, m, f* Greek
grieta *f* **1.**(*en la pared, una taza*) crack; (*en la piel*) chap **2.**(*desacuerdo*) rift

grifa *f* hash, dope, pot

grifo *m* 1. TÉC tap *Brit,* faucet *Am;* **agua del** ~ tap water; **abrir/cerrar el** ~ to turn the tap on/off; **he dejado el** ~ **abierto** I've left the tap running 2. (*mitología*) griffon 3. *Perú, Ecua, Bol* (*gasolinera*) petrol station *Brit,* gas station *Am*

grifo, -a *adj inf* stoned, high (on dope)

grillarse *vr* 1. *inf* (*persona*) to go nuts 2. (*tubérculo*) to sprout

grillera *f* 1. (*agujero*) cricket hole 2. (*jaula*) cricket cage 3. *inf* (*lugar*) **esto es una** ~ this place is a madhouse 4. (*de la policía*) police van

grillete *m* 1. (*cepo*) shackle, fetter 2. NÁUT shackle

grillo *m* 1. (*insecto*) cricket 2. (*de tubérculo*) shoot 3. *pl* (*grilletes*) shackles *pl*

grima *f* **me da** ~ (*asco*) it's disgusting; (*dentera*) it sets my teeth on edge

grimillón *m Chile* multitude

gringada *f AmL: inf* 1. (*truco sucio*) dirty trick 2. (*grupo de gringos*) group of gringos

gringo *m inf* gibberish; **hablar en** ~ to talk double Dutch

gringo, -a *m, f AmL: inf* 1. (*persona*) gringo (*North American or North European*) 2. (*de EE.UU.*) Yank(ee)

gripa *f AmL* flu, influenza

gripal *adj* MED flu, influenza

griparse *vr* TÉC to seize up

gripe *f* MED flu, influenza

griposo, -a I. *adj* MED **estar** ~ to have the flu II. *m, f* flu patient

gris I. *adj* 1. (*color*) grey *Brit,* gray *Am;* ~ **marengo** charcoal grey *Brit,* charcoal gray *Am;* **de ojos** ~**es** grey-eyed *Brit,* gray-eyed *Am* 2. (*persona*) boring II. *m* 1. (*color*) grey *Brit,* gray *Am* 2. (*viento*) cold wind 3. HIST (*policía*) *member of Spanish National Police*

grisáceo, -a, *adj* greyish *Brit,* grayish *Am*

grisma *f Chile, Guat, Hond* (*pizca*) pinch

grisú *m* <grisúes *o* grisús> MIN firedamp

gritadera *f Col, Ven* (*griterío*) loud shouting

gritar I. *vt* 1. (*dar gritos*) to shout at; **¡a mí no me grites!** don't you shout at me! 2. (*reprender*) to tell off 3. (*en un concierto*) to boo II. *vi* to shout, to yell

griterío *m* uproar

grito *m* shout; ~ **de protesta** cry of protest; **pegar un** ~ to shout, to yell; **me lo dijo a** ~**s** he/she told me in a very loud voice; **a** ~ **limpio** [*o* **pelado**] at the top of one's voice; **la región está pidiendo a** ~**s ayuda internacional** the region is crying out for international support ▸**poner el** ~ **en el** cielo **por algo** to raise hell about sth; **ser el** último ~ to be the (latest) rage

groenlandés, -esa I. *adj* Greenland II. *m, f* Greenlander

Groenlandia *f* Greenland

grogui *adj* groggy, half-asleep

grosella *f* (red)currant

grosería *f* 1. (*descortesía*) rudeness 2. (*ordinariez*) vulgarity 3. (*tosquedad*) crudeness 4. (*estupidez*) stupidity 5. (*observación*) rude comment; (*palabrota*) swearword

grosero, -a *adj* 1. (*descortés*) rude 2. (*ordinario*) vulgar 3. (*tosco*) crude

grosor *m* thickness

grotesco, -a *adj* grotesque

grúa *f* 1. (*máquina*) crane 2. (*vehículo*) tow truck, breakdown van *Brit,* wrecker *Am*

gruesa *f* (*cantidad*) gross

grueso *m* 1. (*espesor*) thickness 2. (*parte principal*) main part 3. MED (*intestino*) large intestine 4. COM **vender en** ~ to sell in bulk 5. TIPO downstroke

grueso, -a *adj* 1. (*persona*) stout 2. (*objeto, tela*) thick 3. (*mar*) **mar gruesa** heavy seas 4. (*broma*) crude

grulla *f* crane

grumete *m* NÁUT cabin boy

grumo *m* 1. (*coágulo*) lump; ~ **de sangre** blood clot 2. (*de lechuga*) heart 3. (*de planta*) shoot

grumoso, -a *adj* lumpy

gruñido *m* 1. (*de cerdo, persona*) grunt 2. (*del perro*) growl 3. *fig* (*queja*) grumble 4. (*de puerta*) creak

gruñir <*3. pret:* gruñó> *vi* 1. (*cerdo, person*) to grunt 2. (*perro*) to growl 3. *fig* (*quejarse*) to grumble 4. (*puerta*) to creak

gruñón, -ona I. *adj inf* grumbling, whingeing II. *m, f inf* grumbler; **es un viejo** ~ he's a grumpy old man

grupa *f* hindquarters *pl;* **volver** ~**s** MIL to turn around

grupal *adj* group

grupo *m* 1. (*conjunto*) group; ~ (**industrial**) COM corporation; ~ **parlamentario** POL parliamentary group; ~ **de presión** POL pressure group; ~ **principal** INFOR main group; **trabajo en** ~ groupwork 2. TÉC unit

grupúsculo *m* POL small group

gruta *f* (*artificial*) grotto; (*natural*) cave

guaca *f AmL* 1. (*tumba*) tomb 2. (*tesoro*) buried treasure 3. (*hucha*) money box; **hacer** ~ to make money

guacal *m AmC, Col, Ven* (*calabaza, jícara*) gourd

guacamayo *m* macaw

guacamol(e) *m AmL* GASTR guacamole

guacamote *m Méx* manioc

guachada *f AmL, inf* (*canallada*) dirty trick

guachimán *m AmL* (*vigilante*) watchman

guacho, -a *m, f AmS* (*huérfano*) orphan; (*expósito*) abandoned child

guadal *m Arg* sandy bog

guadalajareño, -a I. *adj* of/from Guadalajara II. *m, f* native/inhabitant of Guadalajara

guadaña *f* 1. (*herramienta*) scythe 2. (*muerte*) **la Guadaña** the Grim Reaper

guadañar *vt* to scythe

guagua *f* 1. *AmC* (*autobús*) bus 2. *CSur* (*bebé*) baby 3. (*trivialidad*) trifle

guajiro, **-a** I. *adj* peasant II. *m, f Cuba* white peasant
gualdo, **-a** *adj* yellow; **la bandera roja y gualda** the Spanish flag
guamazo *m Méx* punch
guamúchil *m Méx* (*planta*) camachile
guanábano *m AmL* (*árbol*) soursop tree; (*fruta*) custard apple
guanaco *m* (*mamífero*) guanaco
guanaco, **-a** I. *adj AmL* (*tonto*) simple; (*lento*) slow II. *m, f* 1. *AmL* (*tonto*) simpleton 2. *AmC, pey* native of El Salvador
guanajo, **-a** *m, f Cuba, PRico* 1. (*pavo*) turkey 2. (*bobo*) fool, idiot
guanche *m* 1. (*persona*) original inhabitant of the Canary Islands 2. HIST (*lengua*) language of the original inhabitants of the Canary Islands
guandoca *f Col* (*cárcel*) prison
guango, **-a** *adj Méx* baggy
guano *m* 1. (*excrementos*) guano 2. *CSur* (*estiércol*) dung
guantada *f* slap; **dar una ~ a alguien** to slap sb
guantazo *m v.* **guantada**
guante *m* glove; **~ cibernético** INFOR data glove ▸**colgar los ~s** (*boxeador*) to hang up one's gloves; (*futbolista*) to hang up one's boots; **le echaron el ~ al ladrón** they caught the thief; **ir** [*o* **sentar**] **como un ~** to fit like a glove; **recoger el ~** to take up the challenge
guantear *vt AmL* (*abofetear*) to slap (around)
guantelete *m* gauntlet
guantera *f* AUTO glove box [*o* compartment]
guantero, **-a** *m, f* glovemaker
guapear *vi inf* 1. (*ostentar*) to dress showily 2. (*fanfarronear*) to boast about, to swank *Brit*
guaperas I. *adj inf* good-looking II. *m inv, inf* heart-throb; **va de ~** he thinks he's a real heart-throb
guaperío *m* **el ~** the jet set
guapeza *f* 1. (*aspecto: en general*) good looks *pl;* (*de mujer*) prettiness; (*de hombre*) handsomeness 2. (*en los vestidos*) elegance 3. (*valentonería*) bravery; *pey* bravado 4. *pey* flashiness
guapo *m* 1. (*galán*) handsome man 2. *AmL, pey* (*pendenciero*) bully
guapo, **-a** *adj* 1. (*atractivo: en general*) good-looking; (*de mujer*) pretty; (*de hombre*) handsome 2. (*en el vestir*) **estar** [*o* **ir**] **~** to look smart 3. *AmL* (*valiente*) brave
guaquero, **-a** *m, f AmL* graverobber; (*ilegal*) plunderer (*person who digs for ancient Indian archaeological valuables*)
guaraca *f AmL* (*honda*) catapult; (*látigo*) whip
guaraná *f PRico* BOT guaraná, paullinia
guarangada *f AmL* (*grosería*) rude comment
guaraní *adj, m* Guaraní
guarapo *m AmL* (*jugo*) sugar-cane juice; (*bebida*) sugar-cane liquor
guarapón *m AmS* broad-brimmed hat
guarda[1] *mf* guard; **~ forestal** forester *Brit,* forest ranger *Am;* (*cuidador*) custodian, keeper; **~ jurado** security guard
guarda[2] *f* 1. (*acto*) guarding, safekeeping 2. (*protección*) protection 3. (*de un libro*) flyleaf 4. (*de la ley*) observance 5. *pl* (*de llave*) guard; (*de cerradura*) ward 6. *pl* (*de abanico*) outer ribs *pl*
guardabarrera *mf* crossing [*o* gate] keeper
guardabarros *m inv* mudguard *Brit,* fender *Am*
guardabosque(**s**) *mf* (*inv*) 1. (*de caza*) gamekeeper 2. (*guarda forestal*) forester *Brit,* forest ranger *Am*
guardacostas *m inv* coastguard
guardaespaldas *mf inv* bodyguard
guardagujas *mf inv* FERRO pointsman *m,* pointswoman *f Brit,* switchman *m,* switchwoman *m Am*
guardameta *mf* DEP goaltender, goalkeeper
guardapolvo *m* (*mono*) overalls *pl*
guardar I. *vt* 1. (*vigilar*) to guard 2. (*proteger*) to protect 3. (*ley*) to observe 4. (*conservar*) to keep; **~ un sitio** to keep a place; **~ un trozo de pastel a alguien** to save a piece of cake for sb; **guárdame esto, que ahora vengo** keep this for me, I'll be back soon [*o* right back] 5. (*poner*) **¿dónde has guardado las servilletas?** where did you put the serviettes?; **~ el dinero en el banco** to keep money in the bank; **~ algo en el bolsillo** to put sth in one's pocket 6. (*quedarse con*) to keep 7. (*ahorrar*) to save; **~ las fuerzas** to save one's strength 8. INFOR to save II. *vr:* **~se** 1. (*evitar*) **~se de hacer algo** to be careful not to do sth 2. (*protegerse*) **~se de algo/alguien** to be on one's guard against sth/sb
guardarropa[1] *m* 1. (*cuarto*) cloakroom *Brit,* checkroom *Am* 2. (*armario*) wardrobe
guardarropa[2] *mf* 1. (*de vestuario*) cloakroom attendant *Brit,* checkroom attendant *Am* 2. TEAT (*guardarropía*) wardrobe
guardarropía *m* 1. TEAT (*accesorios*) props *pl* 2. TEAT (*cuarto*) wardrobe ▸**de ~** make-believe
guardería *f* (*centro educativo*) nursery; (*en hipermercado*) crèche
guardia[1] *f* 1. (*vigilancia*) duty; **¿cuál es la farmacia de ~?** which chemist is on the emergency rota? *Brit,* which pharmacy is open 24 hours? *Am;* **estar de ~** to be on duty; MIL to be on guard duty 2. (*protección*) **estar en ~** to be on one's guard; **poner a alguien en ~** to put sb on his/her guard 3. DEP guard; **bajar la ~** to lower one's guard; **en ~** (*esgrima*) en garde 4. (*instituciones*) **la Guardia Civil** the Civil Guard; **~ municipal** [*o* **urbana**] local police
guardia[2] *mf* **~ civil** civil guard; **~ municipal** [*o* **urbano**] local policeman; **~ de tráfico** traffic policeman *m,* traffic policewoman *f*
guardián, **-ana** *m, f* 1. (*protector*) guardian; **perro ~** watchdog 2. (*en el zoo*) (zoo)keeper
guardilla *f* 1. (*habitación*) attic room 2. (*ven-*

tana) attic window **3.** (*buhardilla*) attic, garret

guarecer *irr como crecer* **I.** *vt* **1.** (*proteger*) to protect **2.** (*albergar*) to shelter; **lo guarecí en mi casa** I took him in **3.** (*curar*) to cure **II.** *vr:* **~se** (*cobijarse*) to take refuge; ~ **de la lluvia** to take shelter from the rain

guarida *f* **1.** (*de animales*) den, lair **2.** (*refugio*) hideout

guarismo *m* MAT numeral; (*cifra*) cipher

guarnecer *irr como crecer vt* **1.** (*adornar*) ~ **algo con** [*o* **de**] **algo** to adorn sth with sth; GASTR to garnish sth with sth; (*vestido*) to trim sth with sth **2.** MIL (*ciudad*) to garrison **3.** (*equipar*) ~ **con** [*o* **de**] **algo** to equip with sth; (*proveer*) to provide with sth

guarnición *f* **1.** GASTR *accompaniment to a main dish;* (*adorno*) garnish; **chuletas de cordero con ~** (**de patatas y ensalada**) lamb chops served with salad and potatoes **2.** (*adorno*) adornment; (*en vestido*) trimming; (*en joya*) setting **3.** MIL garrison **4.** *pl* (*arreos*) harness

guarrada *f inf* **1.** (*mala pasada*) dirty trick **2.** (*palabras*) swear [*o* dirty] word(s) **3.** (*asquerosidad*) **ser una ~** (*sucio*) to be filthy; (*asqueroso*) to be disgusting; **¡qué ~ de baño!** what a filthy bathroom!; **¡qué ~ de fotografía!** what a disgusting photograph!

guarrería *f v.* **guarrada**

guarro, **-a** **I.** *adj* **1.** (*cosa*) disgusting; **chiste ~** dirty joke **2.** (*persona*) dirty; (*moralmente*) smutty **II.** *m, f* pig

guasa *f* **1.** (*burla*) joke; **estar de ~** to be joking; **tiene ~ que...** *+subj* it's ironic that ... **2.** (*sosería*) dullness

guasanga *f AmL* (*bullanga*) hubbub

guasca *f AmL* (*látigo*) whip

guasearse *vr* to joke; ~ **de alguien/algo** to make fun of sb/sth

guasería *f Arg, Chile* (*grosería*) rudeness, obscenity

guaso, **-a** *adj CSur* **1.** (*rústico*) peasant **2.** (*tosco*) coarse

guasón, **-ona** *m, f* joker

guata *f* **1.** (*algodón*) cotton padding **2.** *AmL* (*barriga*) belly

guate *m AmC, Méx: maize stalks used for fodder*

Guatemala *f* Guatemala

> **Guatemala** (official title: **República de Guatemala**) lies in Central America. The capital is also called **Guatemala**. The official language of the country is Spanish and the monetary unit of **Guatemala** is the **quezal**.

guatemalteco, **-a** *adj, m, f* Guatemalan

guateque *m inf* party

guatero *m Chile* hot-water bottle

guau *interj* (*perro*) woof, bow-wow; (*persona*) wow

guay *adj inf* great, cool

guayaba *f* **1.** (*fruto*) guava **2.** (*jalea*) guava jelly **3.** *AmL* (*mentira*) lie

guayabo *m* guava tree

guayacán *m AmL* BOT lignum-vitae tree

Guayana *f* Guyana

guayanés, **-esa** *adj, m, f* Guyanese

guayar **I.** *vt Ant* to grate **II.** *vr:* **~se** *PRico* to get drunk

gubernamental *adj* **1.** (*relativo a*) governmental **2.** (*partidario*) loyalist

gubernativo, **-a** *adj* governmental; **policía gubernativa** national police

gubia *f* TÉC gouge

guepardo *m* cheetah

güero, **-a** **I.** *adj AmL* (*rubio: pelo, persona*) blond(e); (*tez*) fair **II.** *m, f AmL* (*rubio*) blond *m,* blonde *f*

guerra *f* war; **la ~ civil española** the Spanish Civil War; **la ~ de las galaxias** star wars; ~ **de precios/tarifas** price/tariff war; ~ **santa** holy war; **la Primera/Segunda Guerra Mundial** the First/Second World War; **guerra química/psicológica/biológica** chemical/psychological/biological warfare; **ir a la ~** to go to war; **estar en pie de ~** to be on a war footing; **tener la ~ declarada a alguien** *inf* to have it in for sb; **dar mucha ~** *inf* to be a real handful; **en ~** at war

guerrear *vi* **1.** (*hacer guerra*) to wage war **2.** (*resistir*) to resist

guerrera *f* trench coat

guerrero, **-a** **I.** *adj* **1.** (*de guerra*) warlike **2.** (*travieso*) naughty **3.** (*revoltoso*) rebellious **II.** *m, f* warrior

guerrilla *f* **1.** (*guerra*) guerrilla warfare **2.** (*partida*) guerrilla band

guerrillear *vi* to wage guerrilla warfare

guerrillero, **-a** *m, f* guerrilla (fighter)

gueto *m* ghetto

guía[1] *mf* (*de un grupo*) guide; ~ **turístico** tourist guide

guía[2] *m* **1.** MIL scout **2.** (*manillar*) handlebar

guía[3] *f* **1.** (*pauta*) guidance, guideline **2.** (*persona*) guide **3.** (*manual*) handbook; ~ **comercial** trade directory; ~ **de ferrocarriles** railway [*o* railroad *Am*] timetable; ~ **telefónica** telephone directory, phone book *Am;* ~ **turística** travel guide(book) **4.** (*de planta*) main stem **5.** TÉC guide **6.** (*del bigote*) end **7.** *PRico* (*volante*) steering wheel **8.** *pl* (*riendas*) reins *pl*

guiar <*1. pres:* guío> **I.** *vt* **1.** (*a alguien*) to guide **2.** (*conversación*) to direct **3.** (*planta*) to train **II.** *vr* **~se por algo** to be guided by sth; **me guío por mi instinto** I follow my instincts

guija *f* pebble

guijarro *m* **1.** (*canto*) pebble **2.** *pl* (*en playa*) pebbles *pl*

guijo *m* gravel

guillarse *vr inf* **1.** (*chiflarse*) to go nuts **2.** (*irse*) **guillárselas** to beat it

guillotina *f* **1.** (*de ejecución, para papel*) guillotine **2.** TÉC **ventana de ~** sash window

guillotinar *vt* to guillotine
guinda *f* **1.** (*fruta*) morello cherry **2.** NÁUT (*de arboladura*) height **3.** *inf* (*remate*) **poner la ~ a algo** to top sth off; **y la ~ fue que...** and the best bit was that ...
guindilla *f* GASTR chilli pepper *Brit,* chili pepper *Am*
guindo *m* (*árbol*) (morello) cherry tree ►**caerse del ~** *inf* to catch [*o* cotton] on; **subirse al ~** *inf* to have one's head in the clouds
guineo *m AmL* (*banana*) banana
guiñapo *m* **1.** (*trapo*) rag **2.** (*andrajoso*) bedraggled person; **estar hecho un ~** to be a wreck **3.** (*degradado*) down-and-out **4.** (*debilucho*) weakling
guiñar **I.** *vt* **~ el ojo a alguien** to wink at sb **II.** *vi* **1.** (*con el ojo*) to wink **2.** NÁUT to yaw
guiño *m* wink; **hacer un ~ a alguien** to wink at sb
guiñol *m* **1.** (*teatro*) puppet show **2.** (*títere*) puppet
guión *m* **1.** CINE, TV script **2.** (*de una conferencia*) outline **3.** LING (*de compuesto, al fin de renglón*) hyphen; (*en diálogo*) dash **4.** (*persona*) scriptwriter **5.** (*real*) standard **6.** (*de procesión*) banner
guionista *mf* CINE screenwriter; TV scriptwriter
guipar *vt inf* **1.** (*ver*) to see, to spot **2.** (*entender*) to catch on to, to see through
guipuzcoano, -a **I.** *adj* of/from Guipuzcoa **II.** *m, f* native/inhabitant of Guipuzcoa
guiri *mf pey* **1.** (*extranjero*) foreigner **2.** (*guardia*) civil guard
guirigay *m* <guirigayes *o* gurigáis> *inf* **1.** (*lenguaje*) gibberish **2.** (*griterío*) uproar **3.** (*barullo*) hubbub
guirlache *m* (hard) nougat
guirnalda *f* garland
guisa *f* **a ~ de** like; **de tal ~** in such a way; **no puedes hacerlo de esta ~** you can't do it like that
guisado *m* stew
guisante *m* pea
guisar **I.** *vt* **1.** (*cocinar*) to cook; (*con salsa*) to stew, to braise **2.** (*tramar*) to prepare **II.** *vr:* **~se** to cook; **se está guisando** it's cooking; **tú te lo guisas, tú te lo comes** *prov* as you make your bed so must you like in it *prov*
guiso *m* **1.** (*plato*) dish **2.** (*en salsa*) stew
guisote *m pey* poor quality stew, concoction
güisqui *m* whisky *Brit,* whiskey *Am*
guita *f* **1.** (*cuerda*) twine, packthread **2.** *inf* (*dinero*) dough, curd
guitarra *f* (*instrumento*) guitar ►**venir como una ~ en un entierro** to be completely out of place; **chafar la ~ a alguien** to mess it up for sb
guitarrero, -a *m, f* **1.** (*fabricante*) guitar maker **2.** (*guitarrista*) guitarist
guitarrista *mf* guitarist
güito *m* **1.** *inf* (*sombrero*) hat **2.** (*de albaricoque*) stone
gula *f* gluttony
gulasch *m* goulash
guripa *m inf* **1.** (*soldado*) soldier **2.** (*guardia*) policeman, cop *Am* **3.** (*golfo*) rogue
gurrumino *m* henpecked husband
gurrumino, -a *adj* **1.** (*tacaño*) stingy, mean *Brit* **2.** (*pequeño*) puny
gurú *m* guru
gusanillo *m* worm ►**entrarle a uno el ~ de algo** *inf* to get the bug [*o* an irresistible urge] for sth; **matar el ~** *inf* (*comiendo*) to kill one's hunger; (*bebiendo*) to quench one's thirst
gusano *m* **1.** (*lombriz*) worm; **~ de tierra** earthworm; **~ de luz** glow-worm **2.** (*oruga*) caterpillar **3.** (*larva de mosca*) maggot **4.** *fig* (*persona despreciable*) worm
gustar **I.** *vi* **1.** (*agradar*) **me gusta nadar/el helado** I like swimming/ice cream; **me gustan estos zapatos** I like this shoes; **¿te gusta estar aquí?** do you like it here?; **¡así me gusta!** well done!; **como Ud. guste** as you wish; **cuando guste** whenever you like [*o* want] **2.** (*apasionarse*) **~ de** *+infin* to enjoy **3.** (*atraer*) **me gusta tu hermano** I fancy your brother **4.** (*querer*) **me gustas** I like you **5.** (*condicional*) **me ~ía saber...** I would like to know ... **II.** *vt* (*probar*) to taste
gustativo, -a *adj* taste
gustazo *m* **1.** (*placer*) great pleasure; **tuve el ~ de darle la mano** I had the great pleasure of shaking his/her hand; **darse el ~ de algo** to treat oneself to sth **2.** (*ante una desgracia*) satisfaction
gustillo *m* **1.** (*sabor*) aftertaste, tang **2.** (*sensación*) kick; **da ~ ver que le regañan a ella también** I get a kick out of seeing her criticised for a change
gusto *m* **1.** (*sentido*) taste; **una broma de mal ~** a joke in bad taste; **no hago nada a su ~** nothing I do pleases him/her; **lo ha hecho a mi ~** he/she did it to my satisfaction; **sobre ~s no hay nada escrito** there's no accounting for tastes **2.** (*sabor*) taste, flavour *Brit,* flavor *Am;* **~ a algo** taste of sth; **huevos al ~** eggs cooked to order **3.** (*placer*) pleasure; **con ~** with pleasure; **~s caros** expensive tastes *pl;* **coger ~ a algo** to take [*o* develop] a liking to sth; **encontrar ~ en algo** to find enjoyment in sth; **derretirse de ~** to swoon with pleasure; **estar a ~** to feel comfortable; **tanto ~ en conocerla – el ~ es mío** pleased to meet you – the pleasure is all mine; **hago lo que me viene en ~** I do what I please; **cantan que da ~** they sing wonderfully
gustoso, -a *adj* **1.** (*sabroso*) tasty, savoury *Brit,* savory *Am* **2.** (*con gusto*) **te acompañaré ~** I'd be glad to accompany you **3.** (*agradable*) pleasant
gutapercha *f* gutta-percha
gutural *adj* guttural, throaty
gym-jazz *m* DEP jazz gymnastics *pl*
gymkhana *f* gymkhana

H

H, h *f* H, h; ~ **de Huelva** H for Harry *Brit,* H for How *Am*

ha *interj* ah, ha; **¡~, ~!** Ha, ha!

haba *f* broad bean ►**son ~s contadas** there's no doubt about it; **en todas partes cuecen ~s** *prov* it's the same the world over

Habana *f* **la** ~ Havana

habanero, -a *adj, m, f* Havanan

habano *m* (*cigar*) Havana cigar

haber *irr* **I.** *aux* **1.** (*en tiempos compuestos*) to have; **ha ido al cine** he/she has gone to the cinema; **he comprado el periódico** I've bought the newspaper **2.** (*de obligación*) ~ **de hacer algo** to have to do sth; **has de hacerlo** (*sin falta*) you must do it; **han de esforzarse más** they must make more of an effort **3.** (*futuro*) **han de llegar pronto** they will [*o* should] be here soon **4.** (*imperativo*) **no tengo sitio – ¡~ venido antes!** there's no room – you should have come earlier! **II.** *vimpers* **1.** (*ocurrir*) **ha habido un terremoto en Japón** there has been an earthquake in Japan; **¿qué hay?** what's the news?; **¿qué hay, Pepe?** how's it going, Pepe? **2.** (*efectuarse*) to take place; **hoy no hay cine** the cinema is closed today; **ayer hubo reunión** there was a meeting yesterday; **después habrá baile** there'll be a dance afterwards **3.** (*existir*) **aquí no hay agua** there is no water here; **eso es todo... ¡y ya no hay más!** that's all ... and nothing more!; **¿hay algo entre tú y ella?** is there something going on between you two?; **hay poca gente que...** there are few people who ...; **hay quien cree que...** some people think that ...; **¡muchas gracias! – no hay de qué** thanks a lot! – not at all; **no hay quien me gane al ping-pong** nobody can beat me at table tennis **4.** (*hallarse, estar*) **hay un cuadro en la pared** there is a painting on the wall; **había un papel en el suelo** there was a piece of paper on the floor; **no hay leche/platos en la mesa** there is no milk/there are no plates on the table; **¿había mucha gente?** where there many people? **5.** (*tiempo*) **había una vez...** once there was ... **6.** (*obligatoriedad*) **¡hay que ver cómo están los precios!** my God! look at those prices!; **hay que trabajar más** we have to work harder; **no hay que olvidar que...** we must not forget that ... **III.** *vt* **compra cuantos sellos pueda** ~ buy as many stamps as you can **IV.** *vr* **habérselas con alguien** to be up against sb **V.** *m* **1.** (*capital*) assets *pl;* **tener algo en su** ~ *fig* to have sth to one's credit **2.** (*en cuenta corriente*) balance, account; **pasaré la cantidad a tu** ~ I'll pay the amount into your account **3.** *pl* (*emolumentos*) assets *pl*

habichuela *f* (kidney) bean; (*judía blanca*) haricot bean

hábil *adj* **1.** (*diestro*) skilled; **ser** ~ **para algo** to be skilled at sth **2.** (*en el oficio*) **ser** ~ **en algo** to be good at sth **3.** (*astuto*) shrewd; **una respuesta** ~ a clever response **4.** JUR working; **días ~es** working days

habilidad *f* **1.** (*destreza*) skill; **no tengo gran** ~ **con las manos** I'm not very skilful with my hands **2.** (*facultad*) ability **3.** (*astucia*) shrewdness **4.** (*gracia*) grace; **se mueve con** ~ she moves gracefully

habilidoso, -a *adj* **1.** (*diestro*) skilful, able **2.** (*astuto*) shrewd **3.** (*gracioso*) graceful

habilitación *f* **1.** JUR (*de personas*) ~ **para algo** entitlement to sth **2.** (*de empleo*) paymaster's duties **3.** (*oficina*) paymaster's office **4.** (*de un espacio*) fitting out

habilitar *vt* **1.** (*a personas*) to train, to teach; JUR to entitle, to empower; (*documentos*) to authorize **2.** COM (*dar capital*) to fund, to finance **3.** (*proveer*) ~ **de algo** to provide with sth; ~ **horas de visita** to provide with visiting hours **4.** (*espacio*) to fit out

habiloso, -a *adj AmL* **1.** (*hábil*) skilled, skilful *Brit,* skillful *Am* **2.** (*astuto*) shrewd

habitabilidad *f sin pl* habitability

habitable *adj* liveable

habitación *f* **1.** (*cuarto*) room; (*dormitorio*) bedroom; ~ **individual** single room **2.** (*vivienda*) dwelling **3.** (*acción*) living

habitáculo *m* **1.** (*vivienda*) dwelling **2.** ECOL (*espacio*) habitat **3.** AUTO interior

habitante *mf* inhabitant; **¿cuántos habitantes tiene Madrid?** what is the population of Madrid?

habitar **I.** *vi* to live **II.** *vt* to live in; **hace tiempo que habita en Escocia** he/she has been living in Scotland for some time now

hábitat *m* <hábitats> habitat

hábito *m* **1.** (*costumbre*) habit; **he dejado el** ~ **de fumar** I gave up smoking **2.** REL (*sotana*) habit; (*orden*) insignia ►**el** ~ **no hace al monje** *prov* clothes don't make the man

habitual *adj* regular; **cliente** ~ regular client; **bebedor** ~ habitual drinker; **lo dijo con su ironía** ~ he said it with his customary irony

habituar <*1. pres:* habitúo> *vt, vr* ~(**se**) **a algo** to get used to sth

habla *f* **1.** (*facultad*) speech, diction; **quedarse sin** ~ to be left speechless **2.** (*acto*) speech; **un país de** ~ **inglesa** an English-speaking country; **¡Juan al ~!** TEL Juan speaking! **3.** (*manera, dialecto*) way of speaking

hablado, -a *adj* spoken; **bien** ~ well-spoken; **el francés** ~ spoken French; **ser mal** ~ to be foul-mouthed

hablador(a) **I.** *adj* talkative **II.** *m(f)* **1.** (*cotorra*) chatterbox **2.** (*chismoso*) gossip

habladuría *f* rumour *Brit,* rumor *Am;* **~s** gossip

hablante *mf* speaker

hablantina *f Col, Ven* talkative

hablar **I.** *vi* **1.** (*decir*) to speak, to talk; ~ **a gritos** to shout; ~ **alto/bajo** to speak loudly/softly; ~ **entre dientes** to mutter; **déjeme**

H

terminar de ~ let me finish; ~ **claro** to speak frankly; **el autor no habla de este tema** the author does not address this topic; **la policía le ha hecho** ~ the police have made him talk; **los números hablan por sí solos** the figures speak for themselves; **¡no ~ás en serio!** you must be joking!; **por no ~ de...** not to mention ...; **¡y no se hable más!** and that's an end to it; **¡ni ~!** no way! **2.** (*conversar*) ~ **con alguien** to talk to sb; ~ **con franqueza** to talk sincerely; ~ **por teléfono** to talk on the telephone; **no he podido ~ con él** I haven't managed to speak to him; ~ **por los codos** *inf* to talk nineteen to the dozen **II.** *vt* **1.** (*idioma*) to speak **2.** (*decir*) to say; ~ **a alguien (de algo/alguien)** to talk to sb (about sth/sb); **no me habló en toda la noche** he/she didn't say a word all night **3.** (*asunto*) **lo hablaré con tu padre** I'll talk about it with your father **III.** *vr:* **~se** to talk to each other; **no se hablan** they are not on speaking terms; **no se habla con su madre** he/she doesn't talk to his/her mother; **nos hablamos de tú** we are on familiar terms

hablilla *f* rumour *Brit,* rumor *Am*

hablista *mf* elegant speaker

hacedero, -a *adj* practicable, feasible

hacedor(a) *m(f)* **1.** (*creador*) maker, creator; **el Hacedor** REL the Maker **2.** (*de una hacienda*) administrator

hacendado, -a **I.** *adj* landowning **II.** *m, f* **1.** (*de una hacienda*) landowner **2.** *AmS* (*de ganado*) livestock farmer, rancher *Am*

hacendoso, -a *adj* hard-working

hacer *irr* **I.** *vt* **1.** (*producir*) to make; (*coche t.*) to manufacture; **la casa está hecha de madera** the house is made of wood; **Dios hizo al hombre** God created man **2.** (*realizar*) to do; (*libro*) to write; **¿qué hacemos hoy?** what shall we do today?; ~ **una llamada** to make a phone call; **demuestra lo que sabes** ~ show us what you can do; **hazlo por mí** do it for me; **a medio** ~ half-finished; **hicimos la trayectoria en tres horas** we did the journey in three hours; **¡Dios mío, qué has hecho!** my God! what have you done?; **lo hecho, hecho está** there's no use crying over spilt milk; **puedes ~ lo que quieras** you can do whatever you want; **¿qué haces por aquí?** what are you doing round here?; **¡me la has hecho!** you've let me in for it; **la ha hecho buena** he's/she's really messed things up **3.** (*pregunta*) to ask; (*observación*) to make; (*discurso*) to make, to give **4.** (*ocasionar: ruido*) to make; (*daño*) to cause; ~ **destrozos** to wreak havoc; ~ **sombra** to cast a shadow; **no puedes ~me esto** you can't do this to me **5.** (*construir*) to build **6.** (*procurar*) to make; **¿puedes ~me sitio?** can you fit me in? **7.** (*transformar*) ~ **pedazos algo** to smash sth up; **estás hecho un hombre** you're a man now; **¿quién te hace el pelo?** who does your hair? **8.** (*conseguir: dinero, amigos*) to make **9.** (*llegar*) ~ **puerto** to enter harbour *Brit* [*o* harbor *Am*]; ~ **noche en...** to spend the night in ... **10.** (*más sustantivo*) ~ **el amor** to make love; ~ **caso a alguien** to pay heed to sb; ~ **cumplidos** to pay compliments; ~ **deporte** to do sport; ~ **frente a algo/alguien** to face up to sth/sb; ~ **la maleta** to pack; ~ **uso de algo** to make use of sth **11.** (*más verbo*) ~ **creer algo a alguien** to make [*o* have] sb believe sth; ~ **venir a alguien** to make sb come; **hazle pasar** let him in; **no me hagas contarlo** don't make me say it **12.** (*limpiar*) **hacer las escaleras** *inf* to do the steps **13.** TEAT ~ **una obra** to do [*o* put on] a play; ~ **el papel de Antígona** to play the role of Antigone **14.** ENS (*carrera*) to study, to do; **¿haces francés o inglés?** are you doing French or English? **15.** GASTR (*comida, pastel*) to make; (*patatas*) to do; **quiero la carne bien hecha** I want the meat well done **II.** *vi* **1.** (*convenir*) **eso no hace al caso** that's not relevant **2.** (*oficio*) ~ **de algo** to work as sth **3.** (*con preposición*) **por lo que hace a Juan...** as regards Juan ...; **hizo como que no me vio** he pretended he hadn't seen me **III.** *vr:* **~se** **1.** (*volverse*) to become; **~se del Madrid** to become a Madrid supporter **2.** (*crecer*) to grow **3.** (*simular*) to pretend; **se hace a todo** he's always pretending; **hacerse el sueco** to pretend not to hear; **~se la víctima** to act like a victim **4.** (*habituarse*) **~se a algo** to get used to sth **5.** (*dejarse hacer*) **~se una foto** to have one's picture taken **6.** (*conseguir*) **~se respetar** to instill respect; **~se con el poder** to seize power **7.** (*resultar*) to be; **se me hace muy difícil creer eso** it's very difficult for me to believe that **IV.** *vimpers* **1.** (*tiempo*) **hace frío/calor** it is cold/hot; **hoy hace un buen día** it's a nice day today **2.** (*temporal*) **hace tres días** three days ago; **no hace mucho** not long ago; **desde hace un día** since yesterday

hacha *f* **1.** (*herramienta*) axe, hatchet **2.** (*antorcha*) torch **3.** (*vela*) large candle ►**ser un ~ en algo** to be brilliant [*o* an ace] at sth

hachazo *m* stroke of the axe

hache *f* H, h; **la** ~ the letter h ►**por ~ o por be** for one reason [*o* thing] or another

hachear *vt* to cut (with an axe), to chop

hachero *m* **1.** (*candelero*) torch stand, candleholder **2.** (*persona*) woodcutter, lumberjack

hachís *m* hashish

hacia *prep* **1.** (*dirección*) towards, to; **el pueblo está más ~ el sur** the village lies further to the south; **el pueblo está yendo ~ Valencia** the village is on the way to Valencia; **fuimos ~ allí** we went that way; **vino ~ mí** he/she came towards me **2.** (*cerca de*) near **3.** (*respecto a*) regarding

hacienda *f* **1.** (*finca*) country estate **2.** (*bienes*) ~ **pública** public finance

Hacienda *f* (*ministerio*) the Treasury, the Exchequer *Brit;* (*administración*) the Inland Revenue; **el Ministro de Economía y** ~ the

Chancellor of the Exchequer; **¿pagas mucho a ~?** do you pay a lot of tax?

hacinamiento *m* **1.**(*de haces*) piling **2.**(*de objetos*) stacking; (*de personas*) (over)crowding

hacinar **I.** *vt* to pile **II.** *vr:* **~se** (*personas*) to (over)crowd; (*objetos*) to stack

hacker *mf* (*pirata informático*) hacker

hada *f* fairy; **cuento de ~s** fairy tale; **~ madrina** fairy godmother

hado *m* fate

Haití *m* Haiti

haitiano, **-a** *adj, m, f* Haitian

hala *interj* **1.**(*sorpresa*) well, well **2.**(*prisa*) come on

halagador(a) *adj* flattering

halagar <g→gu> *vt* to flatter

halago *m* **1.**(*acción*) flattery **2.**(*palabras*) flattering words *pl*, compliment

halagüeño, **-a** *adj* **1.**(*halagador*) flattering **2.**(*prometedor*) encouraging

halcón *m* **1.** ZOOL falcon **2.** POL hawk

halconero, **-a** *m, f* falconer

hálito *m* **1.**(*aliento*) breath **2.**(*vapor*) steam **3.** *elev* (*viento*) breeze

hall *m* hall

hallar **I.** *vt* **1.**(*encontrar*) to find; (*sin buscar*) to come across **2.**(*inventar*) to invent **3.**(*averiguar*) to check **4.**(*darse cuenta*) to realize **5.**(*tierra*) to discover **II.** *vr:* **~se** **1.**(*sitio*) to be **2.**(*estado*) to feel; **no me hallo a gusto aquí** I don't feel comfortable here; **se halló con la resistencia de su partido** he met opposition from his party

hallazgo *m* **1.** discovery **2.** *pl* findings *pl*

halo *m* halo

halógeno *m* halogen

haltera *f* DEP weight, dumbbell

halterofilia *f* DEP weightlifting

halterófilo, **-a** *m, f* DEP weightlifter

hamaca *f* **1.**(*cama*) hammock **2.**(*tumbona*) deckchair **3.** *AmL* (*mecedora*) rocking chair

hamacar <c→qu> *vt, vr:* **~(se)** *AmS, Guat* to rock

hambre *f* **1.**(*apetito*) hunger; **huelga de ~** hunger strike; **matar el ~** to kill one's hunger; **me ha entrado (el) ~** I'm getting hungry; **morirse de ~** to die of hunger; **tener ~** to be hungry **2.**(*de la población*) starvation **3.**(*deseo*) **~ de algo** longing for sth; **~ de poder** hunger for power ▶**a buen ~ no hay pan duro** *prov* hunger is the best sauce; **ser más listo que el ~** to be no fool

hambrear *vi AmL* **1.**(*hacer pasar hambre*) to starve **2.**(*mendigar*) to be hungry

hambriento, **-a** *adj* **1.**(*con hambre*) hungry **2.**(*muerto de hambre*) starving **3.**(*deseoso*) **estar ~ de poder** to be hungry for power

hambrón, **-ona** *m, f pey* glutton

hambruna *f AmL* famine

hamburguesa *f* GASTR hamburger; **~ con queso** cheeseburger

hamburguesería *f* hamburger bar

hampa *f* **1.**(*gente*) underworld **2.**(*modo de vida*) criminal class

hampón *m* **1.**(*maleante*) crook **2.**(*valentón*) thug

hamster *m* hamster

handicap *m* handicap

hangar *m* AVIAT hangar

haragán, **-ana** *m, f* loafer

haraganear *vi* to loaf around

haraganería *f* loafing around

harakiri *m* hara-kiri

harapiento, **-a** *adj* ragged, in tatters

harapo *m* rag

hardware *m* hardware

harem *m*, **harén** *m* harem

harina *f* **1.** GASTR flour; **~ integral** wholemeal [*o* wholewheat *Am*] flour; **~ de trigo** wheat flour **2.**(*polvo*) powder ▶**esto es ~ de otro costal** this is a horse of a different colour *Brit* [*o* color *Am*]

harinear *vimpers Ven* to drizzle

harinoso, **-a** *adj* **1.**(*parecido a la harina*) floury **2.**(*con harina*) with flour

harmonía *f* harmony

harnero *m* sieve

hartar *irr* **I.** *vt* **1.**(*saciar*) **~ a alguien** to give sb their fill **2.**(*fastidiar*) **me harta con sus chistes** I'm getting sick of his/her jokes **II.** *vr:* **~se** **1.**(*saciarse*) to eat one's fill; (*en exceso*) to eat too much **2.**(*cansarse*) to get fed up; **~se de reír** to laugh oneself silly; **me he hartado del tiempo que hace en Escocia** I'm sick of [*o* fed up with] this weather in Scotland

hartazgo *m* glut; **darse un ~ (de dulces)** to have a binge (on the sweets); **tengo un ~ de televisión** I've been watching too much television

harto, **-a** **I.** *adj* **1.**(*repleto*) full; (*en exceso*) too full **2.**(*sobrado*) **tengo hartas razones** I have plenty of reasons **3.**(*cansado*) **estar ~ de alguien/algo** to be sick of [*o* fed up with] sb/sth **II.** *adv* (*sobrado*) (more than) enough; (*muy*) a lot of

hartura *f* (over)abundance

hasta **I.** *prep* **1.**(*de lugar*) to; **te llevo ~ la estación** I'll give you a lift to the station; **volamos ~ Madrid** we're flying to Madrid; **~ cierto punto** to a certain degree, up to a point **2.**(*de tiempo*) until, up to until; **~ ahora** up to now; **~ el próximo año** up until next year **3.**(*en despedidas*) **¡~ luego!** see you later!; **¡~ la vista!** see you again!; **¡~ la próxima!** until next time! **II.** *adv* even **III.** *conj* **~ cuando come lee el periódico** he/she even reads the newspaper while he's/she's eating; **no consiguió un trabajo fijo ~ que cumplió 40 años** he/she didn't get a steady job until he/she was forty

hastiar <*1. pres:* hastío> **I.** *vt* **1.**(*aburrir*) to bore **2.**(*hartar, repugnar*) to sicken **II.** *vr* **~se de alguien/algo** to get fed up with sb/sth

hastío *m* **1.**(*tedio*) boredom; **¡qué ~!** what a bore! **2.**(*repugnancia*) disgust

H

hatajo *m* **1.** (*de ganado*) small herd **2.** (*de personas*) bunch, cluster
hatillo *m* belongings *pl;* (*de ropa*) bundle
hato *m* **1.** (*de ropa*) belongings **2.** (*de ganado*) *small group of livestock animals* **3.** (*montón*) a whole lot
Hawai *m* Hawaii
hawaiano, **-a** *adj, m, f* Hawaiian
haya *f* **1.** (*arbol*) beech **2.** (*madera*) beechwood
Haya *f* **La** ~ the Hague
hayal *m* beech grove
hayuco *m* beech nut
haz *m* **1.** (*hato*) bunch; (*de papeles*) sheaf **2.** FÍS face; **sobre el** ~ **de la tierra** on the face of the earth
haza *f* plot of cultivable land
hazaña *f* feat, exploit
hazmerreír *m inv* laughing stock; **es el** ~ **de la gente** he's the butt of everyone's jokes
HB *m abr de* **Herri Batasuna** *Basque nationalist political coalition*
he *1. pres de* **haber**
hebilla *f* buckle
hebra *f* **1.** (*hilo*) thread **2.** (*fibra*) fibre; **tabaco de** ~ loose tobacco
hebreo *m* **1.** (*lengua*) Hebrew **2.** *inf* (*mercader*) merchant **3.** *inf* (*usurero*) usurer
hebreo, **-a** *adj, m, f* Hebrew
hebroso, **-a** *adj* fibrous
hecatombe *f* hecatomb
hechicería *f* **1.** (*arte*) witchcraft **2.** (*hechizo*) spell
hechicero, **-a** *m, f* **1.** (*brujo*) sorcerer **2.** (*de tribu*) witch doctor
hechizar <z→c> *vt* **1.** (*encantar*) to cast a spell on **2.** (*captivar*) captivate, to enchant
hechizo *m* spell; **romper el** ~ to break the spell
hecho *m* **1.** (*circunstancia*) fact **2.** (*acto*) action, deed; ~ **delictivo** criminal act; **los Hechos de los Apóstoles** the Acts of the Apostles **3.** (*suceso*) event; JUR deed; **exposición de los ~s** statement of events; **lugar de los ~s** scene of the crime; **los ~s que causaron el incendio** the events that gave rise to the fire ►**de** ~ in fact
hecho, **-a** *adj* **1.** (*maduro*) mature; **vino** ~ mature wine **2.** (*cocido*) cooked; **me gusta la carne hecha** I like meat well done; **el pollo está demasiado** ~ the chicken is overcooked **3.** (*acabado*) finished; **frase hecha** set phrase; **traje** ~ ready-made suit **4.** (*adulto*) **un hombre** ~ **y derecho** a real man
hechura *f* **1.** (*factura*) making; **de buena** ~ well-made **2.** (*de un vestido*) tailoring **3.** (*obra*) work; (*de Dios*) creation **4.** (*del cuerpo*) shape
hectárea *f* hectare
hectogramo *m* hectogramme *Brit,* hectogram *Am*
hectolitro *m* hectolitre *Brit,* hectoliter *Am*
hectómetro *m* hectometre *Brit,* hectometer *Am*
heder <e→ie> *vi* ~ **a algo** to stink of sth
hediondez *f* stench
hediondo, **-a** *adj* **1.** (*fétido*) fetid **2.** (*repugnante*) repulsive **3.** (*obsceno*) obscene
hedonismo *m sin pl* hedonism
hedonista **I.** *adj* hedonistic **II.** *mf* hedonist
hedor *m* stench; ~ **a huevos podridos** stench of rotten eggs
hegemonía *f* hegemony
hegemónico, **-a** *adj* hegemonic
helada *f* frost; **las primeras ~s del año** the first frosts of the year; **anoche cayó una** ~ there was a frost last night
heladera *f* (*nevera*) refrigerator, fridge; **este sitio es una** ~ it's absolutely freezing here
heladería *f* ice cream parlour *Brit* [*o* parlor *Am*]
heladero, **-a** *m, f* ice cream seller
helado *m* **1.** (*postre*) ice cream **2.** (*sorbete*) sorbet
helado, **-a** *adj* **1.** (*frío*) freezing; (*congelado*) frozen; **estoy** ~ I'm freezing; **el lago está** ~ the lake is frozen; **las cañerías están heladas** the pipes are frozen **2.** (*pasmado*) **me quedé** ~ I was left speechless; (*de miedo*) I was petrified **3.** (*altivo*) aloof
helador, **-a** *adj* (*viento*) freezing
heladora *f* **1.** (*nevera*) ice-box, refrigerator **2.** (*para helados*) ice cream maker [*o* machine]
helaje *m Col* intense cold, frost
helar <e→ie> **I.** *vt* **1.** (*congelar*) to freeze **2.** (*pasmar*) to astonish **II.** *vimpers* to freeze **III.** *vr:* **~se** **1.** (*congelarse*) to freeze; **el lago se ha helado** the lake has frozen over **2.** (*morir*) to freeze to death **3.** (*pasar frío*) to be frozen [*o* ice cold]; **~se de frío** to get chilled to the bone
helecho *m* fern, bracken
helénico, **-a** *adj* **1.** (*antiguo*) Hellenic **2.** (*actual*) Greek
helenista *mf* Hellenist
hélice *f* **1.** TÉC propeller **2.** ANAT, MAT helix; **la doble** ~ the double helix
helicoidal *adj* helicoidal
helicóptero *m* helicopter
helio *m* helium
heliocéntrico, **-a** *adj* heliocentric
helipuerto *m* heliport
helvético, **-a** *adj, m, f* Swiss
hematíe *m* MED red blood cell [*o* corpuscle]
hematoma *m* bruise; MED haematoma *Brit,* hematoma *Am*
hembra *f* **1.** *t.* ZOOL, ELEC female **2.** TÉC female; (*tornillo*) nut
hembraje *m AmS* **1.** (*de ganado*) herd of female animals **2.** *pey* (*de mujeres*) gaggle
hemeroteca *f* newspaper archive
hemiciclo *m* **1.** (*semicírculo*) semicircle **2.** (*sala*) semicircular hall; (*parlamento*) floor **3.** POL (*en España, Congreso de Diputados*) Parliament chamber
hemiplejia *f,* **hemiplejía** *f* MED hemiplegia,

semi-paralysis

hemipléjico, -a I. *adj* hemiplegic, semi-paralysed *Brit,* semi-paralyzed *Am* II. *m, f* hemiplegic, person suffering partial paralysis

hemisférico, -a *adj* hemispherical

hemisferio *m* hemisphere

hemofilia *f* MED haemophilia *Brit,* hemophilia *Am*

hemoglobina *f* BIO haemoglobin *Brit,* hemoglobin *Am*

hemograma *m* MED blood count

hemorragia *f* MED haemorrhage *Brit,* hemorrhage *Am*

hemorroides *fpl* haemorrhoids *pl Brit,* hemorrhoids *pl Am*

hemostático *m* MED haemostatic *Brit,* hemostatic *Am*

henar *m* (*terreno*) hay field; (*pajar*) hayloft

henchir *irr como pedir* I. *vt* to fill; ~ **los pulmones de aire** to fill one's lungs with air II. *vr:* ~**se** (*hartarse de comida*) to stuff oneself

hender <e→ie> I. *vt* 1. (*algo de madera*) to split; (*algo de plástico*) to cut 2. (*abrirse paso*) to make one's way through 3. (*mar*) to plough; **el barco hendía las aguas** the ship ploughed the waves II. *vr:* ~**se** to split

hendidura *f* 1. (*raja*) split; (*en la pared, en un jarrón*) crack 2. (*de una guía*) groove

hendija *f AmL* (*rendija*) crack

hendimiento *m* splitting

hendir *irr como cernir vt v.* **hender**

henequén *m AmL* henequen (*plant and fabric derived from it*)

henil *m* hayloft

heno *m* hay; **fiebre del** ~ hay fever

hepático, -a *adj* hepatic; **cirrosis hepática** cirrhosis of the liver

hepatitis *f inv* MED hepatitis

heptágono I. *adj* heptagonal II. *m* heptagon

heptatlón *m* DEP heptathlon

heráldica *f sin pl* heraldry

heráldico, -a *adj* heraldic

herbáceo, -a *adj* 1. (*de hierba*) herbaceous 2. (*de hierbas medicinales*) homeopathic

herbajar I. *vi* to graze II. *vt* to put out to pasture

herbaje *m* 1. (*lugar*) pasture 2. (*comida*) grass

herbario I. *adj* herbal II. *m* herbalist

herbicida *m* herbicide

herbívoro *m* herbivore

herbolario *m* health food shop

herbolario, -a *m, f* herbalist

herboristería *f v.* **herbolario**

herborizar <z→c> *vi* to collect herbs

hercio *m* FÍS hertz

hercúleo, -a *adj* Herculean; **una empresa hercúlea** a Herculean task

heredable *adj* able to be inherited

heredad *f* 1. (*finca*) estate 2. (*terreno*) piece of land

heredar *vt* to inherit; **propiedad heredada** inherited property; **problemas heredados del franquismo** problems handed down from Franco's time

heredero, -a *m, f* heir; **el** ~ **del trono** the heir to the throne; **el príncipe** ~ the crown prince

hereditario, -a *adj* hereditary; **enfermedad hereditaria** hereditary disease

hereje *mf* REL heretic

herejía *f* 1. REL heresy 2. (*calumnia*) insult 3. (*fechoría*) evil deed 4. (*rebeldía*) rebellion

herencia *f* 1. JUR inheritance 2. (*legado*) legacy; **una** ~ **de la antigüedad** a legacy of the past

herético, -a *adj* heretical

herida *f* 1. (*lesión*) wound; **tocar a alguien en la** ~ *fig* to find somebody's weak [*o* sore] spot 2. (*ofensa*) affront

herido, -a I. *adj* 1. (*lesionado*) injured; MIL wounded; ~ **de gravedad** seriously injured; MIL mortally wounded 2. (*ofendido*) hurt, offended II. *m, f* injured person; MIL wounded soldier; **los** ~**s** the wounded; **en el atentado no hubo** ~**s** nobody was wounded in the attack

herir *irr como sentir* I. *vt* 1. (*lesionar*) to injure; MIL to wound 2. (*golpear*) to hit 3. (*flecha*) to sink into 4. MÚS (*instrumento de cuerda*) to pluck; (*instrumento de tecla*) to strike 5. (*sol*) to beat down 6. (*ofender*) to hurt, to offend; **no quisiera** ~ **susceptibilidades** I wouldn't want to hurt anybody's feelings 7. (*acertar*) to hit II. *vr:* ~**se** to be injured

hermafrodita *adj, m* hermaphrodite

hermana *f* sister; *v.t.* **hermano**

hermanado, -a *adj* twinned; **ciudad hermanada** twinned city

hermanamiento *m* 1. (*de ciudades*) twinning 2. (*acción*) joining

hermanar I. *vt* (*unir*) to join; (*de ciudades*) to twin; **Santiago está hermanada con...** Santiago is twinned with ... II. *vr:* ~**se** to be twinned

hermanastro, -a *m, f* stepbrother *m,* stepsister *f*

hermandad *f* (*de hombres*) brotherhood; (*de mujeres*) sisterhood; REL religious association

hermano, -a *m, f* (*pariente*) brother *m,* sister *f;* ~ **de padre** half-brother (*on the father's side*)*;* ~ **político** brother-in-law; **hermano de leche** foster brother; ~**s siameses** Siamese twins; **mi** ~ **mayor/pequeño** my elder/younger brother; **tengo tres** ~**s** (*sólo chicos*) I have three brothers; (*chicos y chicas*) I have three brothers and sisters; **medio** ~ half-brother; **lenguas hermanas** sister tongues

hermético, -a *adj* hermetic(al); (*al aire*) airtight; (*al agua*) watertight

hermetismo *m* secrecy; **el** ~ **entre las personas de su confianza es absurdo** it's absurd for people he/she trusts to behave so secretively

hermetizar <z→c> *vt* to seal (hermetically)

hermosear *vt* 1. (*a una persona*) to beautify 2. (*a una cosa*) to embellish, to adorn

H

hermoso, **-a** *adj* **1.** (*paisaje, mujer*) beautiful; (*hombre*) handsome **2.** (*día*) lovely **3.** (*niño*) pretty; (*sanote*) robust **4.** (*persona*) good **5.** (*gesto*) nice
hermosura *f* beauty
hernia *f* MED hernia
herniarse *vr* to rupture oneself; *irón* to work very hard; **¡no te herniarás, no!** *irón* don't burst a blood vessel!
héroe *m* hero; (*protagonista*) main character
heroicidad *f* **1.** (*hazaña*) feat (of heroism) **2.** (*cualidad*) heroic qualities
heroico, **-a** *adj* heroic
heroína *f* **1.** (*de héroe*) heroine; (*protagonista*) main character **2.** (*droga*) heroin
heroinómano, **-a** *m, f* heroin addict
heroísmo *m sin pl* heroism
herpes *m o f inv* MED herpes
herrador *m* (black)smith, farrier
herradura *f* **1.** (*de caballo*) horseshoe; **camino de** ~ bridle path **2.** ZOOL horseshoe bat
herraje(**s**) *m(pl)* ironwork
herramienta *f* tool; ~ **agrícola** agricultural machinery; **caja de** (**las**) ~**s** tool box
herrar <e→ie> *vt* **1.** (*caballo*) to shoe **2.** (*a un animal*) to brand
herrería *f* blacksmith's, smithy
herrerillo *m* tit
herrero *m* blacksmith; **en casa del** ~, **cuchillo de palo** *prov* the shoemaker's wife is always worst shod
herrete *m* (metal) tip
herrumbre *f* rust
herrumbroso, **-a** *adj* rusty
hertz *m* FÍS hertz
hervidero *m* **1.** (*manantial*) hot spring; **un** ~ **de intrigas** a hotbed of intrigue **2.** (*multitud*) throng
hervido *m* **1.** (*de los alimentos, líquidos*) boiling; (*a fuego lento*) simmering **2.** (*burbujeo*) bubbling **3.** *AmS* (*cocido*) stew
hervidor *m* **1.** (*de cocina, para el agua*) kettle; (*de cocina, para la leche*) milk pan **2.** TÉC boiler
hervir *irr como sentir* **I.** *vi* **1.** (*alimentos*) to boil; (*a fuego lento*) to simmer **2.** (*burbujear*) to bubble **3.** (*el mar*) to be choppy **4.** (*persona*) to get angry; ~ **en cólera** to lose one's temper; **le hierve la sangre** his/her blood is boiling **5.** (*abundar*) **esta calle hierve en rumores** the street is a hotbed of rumours [*o* rumors *Am*] **II.** *vt* **1.** (*bullir*) to boil **2.** (*desinfectar*) to sterilize
hervor *m* **1.** (*acción*) boil; **dar un** ~ **a algo** to bring sth to the boil; **levantar el** ~ to come to the boil; **le falta un** ~ *fig* he's got a screw loose **2.** (*burbujeo*) bubbling **3.** (*de la juventud*) fervour *Brit*, fervor *Am*
heterodoxo, **-a** *adj* heterodox
heterogeneidad *f* heterogeneity
heterogéneo, **-a** *adj* heterogeneous
heterosexual *adj, mf* heterosexual
heterosexualidad *f sin pl* heterosexuality
hexadecimal *adj* hexadecimal
hexaedro *m* MAT hexahedron
hexagonal *adj* hexagonal
hexágono *m* hexagon
hez *f* **1.** (*poso*) sediment **2.** *pl* (*escoria*) dregs *pl* **3.** *pl* (*excrementos*) faeces *pl Brit*, feces *pl Am*
hibernación *f* **1.** ZOOL hibernation **2.** MED deep sleep
hibernal *adj* **1.** (*temporada*) winter **2.** ZOOL hibernating
hibernar *vi* to hibernate
hibisco *m* hibiscus
hibridación *f* hybridization
híbrido *m* BIO hybrid
híbrido, **-a** *adj* hybrid; **computador** ~ hybrid computer
hidalgo *m* HIST nobleman
hidalgo, **-a** *adj* **1.** (*de los nobles, noble*) noble **2.** (*generoso*) gentlemanly
hidra *f* **1.** (*pólipo*) hydra **2.** (*en la mitología*) Hydra
hidratante *adj* moisturizing; **crema** ~ moisturizer
hidratar *vt* **1.** QUÍM to hydrate **2.** (*piel*) to moisturize
hidrato *m* hydrate
hidráulica *f* hydraulics *pl*
hidráulico, **-a** *adj* hidraulic
hídrico, **-a** *adj* **1.** (*relativo al agua*) water **2.** (*que contiene agua*) hydric
hidroavión *m* seaplane
hidrocarburo *m* hydrocarbon
hidrodinámico, **-a** *adj* hydrodynamic
hidroeléctrico, **-a** *adj* hydroelectric; **central hidroeléctrica** hydroelectric power station
hidrófilo, **-a** *adj* QUÍM hydrophilic
hidrofobia *f* **1.** MED (*fobia al agua*) hydrophobia **2.** (*rabia*) rabies
hidrófobo, **-a** *adj* **1.** QUÍM hydrophobic **2.** (*rabioso*) rabid
hidrófugo, **-a** *adj* water-resistant
hidrogenar *vt* to hydrogenize
hidrógeno *m* hydrogen
hidrografía *f sin pl* hydrography
hidrográfico, **-a** *adj* hydrographic
hidrológico, **-a** *adj* hydrological
hidropesía *f* MED dropsy
hidrópico, **-a** *adj* dropsical
hidroplano *m* **1.** AVIAT seaplane **2.** NÁUT hydroplane
hidrosfera *f* GEO hydrosphere
hidrosoluble *adj* water-soluble
hidrostático, **-a** *adj* hydrostatic
hidroterapia *f* MED hydrotherapy
hidróxido *m* hydroxide
hiedra *f* ivy
hiel *f* **1.** (*bilis*) bile **2.** (*amargura*) bitterness; **echar la** ~ to sweat blood **3.** *pl* (*adversidades*) troubles *pl*
hielera *f* **1.** *Chile, Méx* (*nevera portátil*) ice chest **2.** *Arg* (*cubitera*) icecube tray
hielo *m* **1.** (*del agua*) ice; ~ **en la carretera**

black ice; ~ **picado** crushed ice; **el barco ha quedado aprisionado en el** ~ the ship is trapped in the ice; **capa** [*o* **manta**] **de** ~ icecap **2.** *pl* (*helada*) frost, cold spell **3.** (*frialdad*) coldness; **romper el** ~ to break the ice ▸**quedarse de** ~ to be stunned

hiena *f* hyena

hierático, -a *adj* hieratic

hierba *f* **1.** (*planta*) grass; *t.* MED herb; ~ **medicinal** medicinal herb; **infusión de ~s** herbal tea; **mala** ~ weed; **tenis sobre** ~ lawn tennis; **está jugando mejor sobre** ~ **esta temporada** his grass court game has improved this season **2.** *inf* (*droga*) grass ▸**y otras ~s** *irón* and such like; **mala** ~ **nunca muere** *prov* the Devil looks after his own; **como la mala** ~ like wildfire; **segar la** ~ **en verde** to cut the grass while it's green

hierbabuena *f* mint

hierbajo *m* weed

hierra *f AmL* branding

hierro *m* **1.** (*metal*) *t.* DEP iron; **edad del** ~ Iron Age; **salud de** ~ iron constitution; **voluntad de** ~ iron will **2.** (*del ganado*) branding iron **3.** (*para marcar*) brand **4.** (*de lanza*) tip of spear **5.** (*arma*) weapon **6.** (*herramienta, golf*) iron **7.** *pl* (*grilletes*) shackles *pl* **8.** *pl* (*cadenas*) chains *pl* ▸**quitar** ~ **a un asunto** to play sth down

hifi *adj* hi-fi

hígado *m* **1.** ANAT liver **2.** *pl* (*valor*) guts *pl* ▸**me pone del** ~ it really gets on my nerves

higiene *f* hygiene; ~ **personal** personal cleanliness [*o* hygiene]

higiénico, -a *adj* hygienic; **compresa higiénica** sanitary towel *Brit,* sanitary napkin *Am;* **papel** ~ toilet paper

higienización *f* cleaning

higienizar <z→c> *vt* to clean

higo *m* **1.** (*fruto*) fig; ~ **chumbo** prickly pear **2.** *inf* (*cosa sin valor*) **esto me importa un** ~ I don't give a toss; **esto no vale un** ~ this is a load of rubbish **3.** (*algo arrugado*) **estar hecho un** ~ (*persona*) to be wizened; (*ropa*) to be crumpled

higrómetro *m* hygrometer

higuera *f* fig tree ▸**estar en la** ~ to have one's head in the clouds

hijastro, -a *m, f* stepson *m,* stepdaughter *f*

hijo, -a *m, f* **1.** (*parentesco*) son *m,* daughter *f;* ~ **adoptivo** adopted son; **un** ~ **de papá** Daddy's boy; ~ **político** son-in-law; ~ **predilecto** (**de una ciudad**) favourite [*o* favorite *Am*] son; ~ **de puta** *vulg* bastard; ~ **único** only child; **pareja sin ~s** childless couple; **como cualquier** ~ **de vecino** just like everybody else; **es** ~ **de Madrid** he's from Madrid **2.** *pl* (*descendencia*) children *pl,* offspring

híjole *interj Méx, inf* (*caramba*) Jesus

hijuela *f* **1.** (*de camino*) track **2.** (*de herencia*) part of an inheritance **3.** (*de una institución*) branch

hijuelar *vt Chile* to parcel

hila *f* **1.** (*acción*) spinning **2.** *pl* (*hebras*) fibre *Brit,* fiber *Am*

hilacha *f,* **hilacho** *m* ravelled [*o* raveled *Am*] thread

hilada *f* **1.** (*hilera*) line **2.** ARQUIT course

hilado *m* **1.** (*acción*) spinning **2.** (*hilo*) thread; (*en la industria*) yarn; **fábrica de ~s** yarn factory

hilador(a) *m(f)* spinning machine

hiladora *f* spinner

hilandería *f* **1.** (*actividad, arte*) spinning **2.** (*fábrica*) textile mill

hilandero *m* (*lugar*) spinner's

hilandero, -a *m, f* spinner

hilar *vt* **1.** (*hilo, araña*) to spin **2.** (*inferir*) to work out **3.** (*cavilar*) to ponder; ~ **fino** *fig* to split hairs

hilarante *adj* hilarious; **gas** ~ laughing gas

hilaridad *f* hilarity; **esta comedia provoca la** ~ **del público** this comedy has the audience in stitches

hilatura *f* **1.** (*fábrica*) textile [*o* spinning] mill **2.** (*fabricación*) spinning

hilaza *f* **1.** (*hilo*) thread **2.** (*en la industria*) yarn

hilera *f* **1.** (*fila, de cosas iguales*) row, line; MIL file; **colocarse en la** ~ to get into line **2.** TÉC drawplate **3.** ARQUIT ridgepiece

hilo *m* **1.** (*para coser*) thread; (*más resistente*) yarn; (*para bordar*) floss; ~ **bramante** twine; ~ **dental** dental floss; ~ **de perlas** string of pearls; **cortar el** ~ **de la vida a alguien** *fig* to cut short sb's life; **mover los ~s** *fig* to pull the strings; **pender de un** ~ *fig* to hang by a thread **2.** (*tela*) linen **3.** TÉC wire; ~ **conductor** thread; **telegrafía sin ~s** wireless telegraphy **4.** (*de un discurso*) gist; **no sigo el** ~ **de la película** I'm not following this film; **perder el** ~ (**de la conversación**) to lose the thread (of the conversation); **recoger el** ~ **de la historia** to pick up the thread of the story **5.** (*de un líquido*) trickle **6.** MÚS ~ **musical** piped music

hilván *m* **1.** (*costura*) tacking, basting *Am* **2.** (*hilo*) tacking [*o* basting *Am*] thread

hilvanado *m* tacking, basting *Am*

hilvanar *vt* **1.** (*vestido*) to tack, to baste *Am* **2.** (*frases*) to weave together; **un discurso mal hilvanado** an incoherent speech

himen *m* ANAT hymen

himeneo *m* nuptials *pl*

himno *m* hymn; ~ **nacional** national anthem

hincapié *m* hold; **hacer** ~ **en algo** to emphasize sth

hincar <c→qu> **I.** *vt* **1.** (*clavar*) to stick; ~ **el diente en algo** *fig, inf* to get one's teeth into sth **2.** (*pie*) to get a strong foothold, to stand firmly **II.** *vr* **~se de rodillas** to kneel down

hincha[1] *mf* (*seguidor*) fan

hincha[2] *f inf* (*tirria*) grudge

hinchable *adj* inflatable; **colchón** ~ inflatable mattress; **muñeca** ~ blow-up doll

hinchada *f* supporters *pl*

hinchado, -a *adj* **1.** (*pie, madera*) swollen

H

2. (*estilo*) wordy, verbose **3.** (*persona*) pompous

hinchamiento *m* swelling

hinchar **I.** *vt* **1.** (*globo*) to blow up; (*neumático*) to inflate; (*estómago*) to swell; ~ **la bici** to inflate the bike tyres [*o* tires *Am*] **2.** (*exagerar*) to exaggerate; **¡no lo hinches!** come off it! **3.** (*río*) to swell **4.** *AmL* (*molestar*) to bother **II.** *vr:* ~**se** **1.** (*pierna*) to swell; **se me ha hinchado mucho el pie** my foot's really swollen **2.** (*engreírse*) to become conceited **3.** *inf* (*de comer*) ~**se** (**de algo**) to stuff oneself (with sth) **4.** (*hacer mucho*) ~**se a mirar/a escuchar algo** to look at/to listen to sth non-stop; ~**se a insultar a alguien** to go overboard insulting sb

hinchazón *f* **1.** (*del pie, madera*) swelling; (*del río*) flooding **2.** (*soberbia*) conceit **3.** (*de un estilo*) pomposity

hindi *m* hindi

hindú *mf* **1.** (*indio*) Indian **2.** (*del hinduismo*) Hindu

hinduismo *m sin pl* REL Hinduism

hinojo *m* **1.** (*planta*) fennel **2.** HIST (*rodilla*) knee; **de** ~**s** on one's knees; **ponerse de** ~**s** to get down on one's knees

hipar *vi* **1.** (*tener hipo*) to have hiccups **2.** (*perros*) to pant **3.** (*fatigarse*) to get tired **4.** (*sollozar*) to whine **5.** (*desear*) ~ **por algo/alguien** to long for sth/sb

hiper *m inf* superstore, hypermarket *Brit*

hiperacidez *f* hyperacidity

hiperactividad *f* hyperactivity

hiperactivo, **-a** *adj* hyperactive

hipérbola *f* MAT hyperbola

hipérbole *f* LIT hyperbole

hiperbólico, **-a** *adj* MAT hyperbolic

hipercrítico, **-a** *adj* hypercritical, overcritical

hiperenlace *m* hyperlink

hiperinflación *f* COM hyperinflation

hipermercado *m* superstore, hypermarket *Brit*

hipermétrope *adj* MED long-sighted

hipermetropía *f* MED long-sightedness

hiperrealismo *m sin pl* hyperrealism

hipersensibilidad *f sin pl* hypersensitivity

hipersensible *adj* hypersensitive, oversensitive

hipertensión *f* MED high blood pressure

hipertenso, **-a** **I.** *adj* suffering from high blood pressure **II.** *m, f* person with high blood pressure; **mi padre es** ~ my father has high blood pressure

hipertexto *m* hypertext

hipertrofia *f* MED hypertrophy

hipertrofiarse *vr* to grow out of all proportion

hípica *f sin pl* (*general*) horsemanship; (*montar*) riding; (*carreras*) horse racing

hípico, **-a** *adj* equestrian, horse

hipido *m* whimper, sob

hipnosis *f inv* hypnosis

hipnótico *m* MED sedative

hipnótico, **-a** *adj* hypnotic

hipnotismo *m* hypnotism

hipnotización *f* hypnotizing

hipnotizador(a) *m(f)* hypnotizer

hipnotizar <z→c> *vt* to hypnotize

hipo *m* **1.** (*fisiológico*) hiccup; **tener** ~ to have (the) hiccups **2.** (*deseo*) ~ **de algo** longing for sth; **...que quita el** ~ *fig* ... that takes your breath away **3.** (*tirria*) grudge

hipocondría *f* MED hypochondria

hipocondríaco, **-a** *adj, m, f* hypochondriac

hipocrático, **-a** *adj* Hippocratic; **el juramento** ~ the Hippocratic oath

hipocresía *f* hypocrisy

hipócrita **I.** *adj* hypocritical **II.** *mf* hypocrite

hipodérmico, **-a** *adj* MED hypodermic

hipódromo *m* DEP racecourse, racetrack *Am*

hipófisis *f inv* ANAT pituitary gland

hipogastrio *m* ANAT hypogastric

hipopótamo *m* hippopotamus

hipoteca *f* mortgage

hipotecable *adj* mortgageable

hipotecar <c→qu> *vt* to mortgage; **si haces eso** ~**ás tu libertad** if you do that you're signing away your freedom

hipotecario, **-a** *adj* mortgage; **crédito** ~ mortgage loan

hipotensión *f* MED low blood pressure

hipotenso, **-a** **I.** *adj* suffering from low blood pressure **II.** *m, f* **ser** ~ to have low blood pressure

hipotenusa *f* MAT hypotenuse

hipotermia *f* MED hypothermia; **muerte por** ~ death from hypothermia

hipótesis *f inv* hypothesis

hipotético, **-a** *adj* hypothetical; **es totalmente** ~ **que...** we cannot be at all sure that ...

hipotónico, **-a** *adj, m, f* hypotonic

hippie, **hippy** **I.** *adj* hippy; **moda** ~ hippy style **II.** *mf* hippy

hiriente *adj* hurtful

hirsuto, **-a** *adj* **1.** (*pelo*) hairy, shaggy **2.** (*planta*) bristly **3.** (*carácter*) surly, brusque

hirviente *adj* boiling

hisopear *vt* to sprinkle (with holy water)

hisopo *m* **1.** (*planta*) hyssop **2.** (*de iglesia*) aspergillum

hispalense **I.** *adj* of/from Seville **II.** *mf* native/inhabitant of Seville

hispánico, **-a** *adj* **1.** (*de España*) Spanish **2.** (*de Hispania*) Hispanic; **Filología Hispánica** Spanish Language and Literature

hispanidad *f sin pl* **1.** (*calidad*) Spanishness **2.** (*conjunto*) Spanish-speaking world

hispanismo *m* UNIV Hispanism

hispanista *mf foreign expert on Spanish history and culture*

hispanizar <z→c> *vt, vr:* ~**se** to take on Spanish customs

hispano, **-a** **I.** *adj* **1.** (*español*) Spanish **2.** (*en EE.UU.*) Hispanic **II.** *m, f* **1.** (*español*) Spaniard **2.** (*en EE.UU.*) Hispanic

Hispanoamérica *f* Spanish America

> **Hispanoamérica** is a generic term that includes all countries of Central and South America, where Spanish is (officially) spoken. There are nineteen states in total:**Argentina**, **Bolivia**, **Chile**, **Colombia**, **Costa Rica**, **Cuba**, **Ecuador**, **El Salvador**, **Guatemala**, **Honduras**, **México**, **Nicaragua**, **Panamá**, **Paraguay**, **Perú**, **Puerto Rico**, **República Dominicana**, **Uruguay** and **Venezuela**. In contrast, the collective term **Latinoamérica** (or **América Latina**) applies to all those countries of Central and South America that were colonised by the Spaniards, Portugese and French.

hispanoamericano, **-a** *adj, m, f* Spanish American

hispanohablante I. *adj* Spanish-speaking; **los países ~s** Spanish-speaking countries II. *mf* Spanish speaker

histeria *f* hysteria

histérico, **-a** I. *adj* hysterical II. *m, f* hysterical person

histerismo *m* hysteria

histología *f* MED histology

historia *f* 1. (*antigüedad*) history; ~ **natural** natural history; ~ **universal** universal [*o* world] history; **pasar a la** ~ (*ser importante*) to go down in history; (*no ser actual*) to be out of date 2. *t. inf* story; **cuenta la ~ completa** tell the whole story; **ésa es la misma ~ de siempre** it's the same old story; **eso sólo son ~s** that doesn't prove anything; **ya sabes la ~** you know what I'm talking about; **¡déjate de ~s!** stop fooling around; **¡no me vengas con ~s!** come off it

historiador(**a**) *m(f)* historian

historial I. *adj* historical II. *m* 1. (*antecedentes*) file, record; ~ **delictivo** police record 2. (*currículo*) curriculum vitae; ~ **profesional** professional background; **este hecho no empañará el ~ de esta institución** this will not tarnish the reputation of this institution; **él tiene un ~ intachable** he has an impeccable record

historiar *vt* 1. (*contar*) to tell the story of 2. ARTE to paint 3. *AmL* (*enmarañar*) to complicate

historicismo *m* historicism

histórico, **-a** *adj* (*que tiene que ver con la historia*) historical; (*acontecimiento*) historic; **un miembro ~ del partido** a longstanding party member

historieta *f* 1. (*anécdota*) anecdote 2. (*con viñetas*) comic strip

historiografía *f sin pl* historiography

historiógrafo, **-a** *m, f* historiographer

histrión *m* 1. HIST histrion 2. (*actor*) actor 3. (*payaso*) clown 4. (*efectista*) playactor

histriónico, **-a** *adj* histrionic

histrionismo *m* 1. (*teatralidad*) acting 2. (*efectismo*) histrionics *pl*

hitleriano, **-a** *adj* Hitlerian

hito *m* (*mojón*) milestone ▸**mirar a alguien de ~ en ~** to stare at sb

hit-parade *m* (*los cuarenta*) top forty

hobby *m* <hobbies> hobby

hocicar <c→qu> I. *vt* (*hozar*) ~ **algo** to root about [*o* around] in sth II. *vi* 1. (*caerse*) to fall flat on one's face 2. *inf* (*dificultad*) to run into trouble 3. NÁUT (*amorrar*) to pitch 4. (*dar de bruces*) to run [*o* bump] into III. *vt, vi* (*tocar*(*se*)) to nuzzle

hocico *m* 1. (*morro*) muzzle; (*de cerdo*) snout 2. *inf* (*cara*) mug; **caer de ~s** to fall on one's face; **estar de ~s** to be in a bad mood; **meter el ~ en todo** *fig* to stick one's nose in everything 3. *vulg* (*boca*) rubber lips *pl*

hocicudo, **-a** *adj AmL* 1. (*persona*) thick-lipped 2. (*animal*) long-snouted

hockey *m sin pl* hockey; ~ **sobre hielo/hierba** ice/field hockey

hogar *m* 1. (*casa*) home; ~ **del pensionista** old people's home; ~ **de adopción** foster home; **artículos para el ~** household items; **persona sin ~** homeless person 2. (*familia*) family; **la vida del ~** family life; **crear un ~** to start a family 3. (*de cocina, de tren*) boiler; (*de chimenea*) hearth; (*de fundición*) furnace

hogareño, **-a** *adj* 1. (*ambiente*) family 2. (*persona*) homeloving

hogaza *f large loaf of bread*

hoguera *f* 1. (*en un campamento*) bonfire; (*de alegría*) blaze 2. HIST (*ejecución*) stake; **morir en la ~** to be burnt at the stake

hoja *f* 1. (*de una planta*) leaf; (*pétalo*) petal; **~s del bosque** forest leaves; **árbol sin ~s** leafless tree; **los árboles vuelven a echar ~s** the leaves on the trees are sprouting again 2. (*de papel*) sheet; ~ **de lata** tinplate; ~ **volante** leaflet, flyer *Am;* ~ **de una mesa** (**extensible**) table flap; **pasar la ~** to turn the page; ~ **de movilización** MIL call-up paper; **no hay** [*o* **tiene**] **vuelta de ~** *fig* there's no doubr about it 3. (*formulario*) form; ~ **de estudios** educational record; ~ **de pedido** order form; ~ **de servicios** service record; **tener una buena ~ de servicios** to have a good record 4. (*de arma*) blade; ~ **de afeitar** razor blade 5. (*de ventana*) pane

hojalata *f* tinplate

hojalatería *f* (*local*) tinsmith's; (*mercancía*) tinware

hojalatero *m* tinsmith, tin worker

hojaldre *m* puff pastry; **pastel de ~** puff

hojarasca *f* 1. (*hojas*) fallen [*o* dead] leaves 2. (*estilo*) waffle; **tus promesas son ~** your promises don't mean a thing

hojear *vt* to browse through

hojoso, **-a** *adj* leafy

hojuela *f* 1. (*hoja*) small leaf 2. GASTR pancake; (*aceitunas*) crushed olives 3. *AmC* (*hojaldre*) puff pastry

hola *interj* hello

holán *m AmC* (*lienzo*) canvas

holanda *f* cheese; (*tela*) fine linen

Holanda *f* the Netherlands

holandés, -esa I. *adj* Dutch; **la escuela holandesa** ARTE the Dutch school II. *m, f* Dutchman *m,* Dutchwoman *f*

holding *m* <holdings> COM holding company; **el ~ de empresas fiduciarias** the holding of fiduciary companies

holgado, -a *adj* 1. (*vestido*) loose 2. (*espacioso*) spacious; **en este coche se va ~** there's lots of space in this car; **ir ~ de tiempo** to have plenty of time

holganza *f* 1. (*ociosidad*) leisure; (*agradable*) rest 2. (*diversión*) enjoyment; (*regocijo*) merriment

holgar *irr como colgar* I. *vi* 1. (*sobrar*) to be unnecessary; **huelgan las palabras** what can you say?; **huelga decir que...** needless to say that ... 2. (*descansar*) to relax II. *vr:* **~se** 1. (*alegrarse*) **~se de** [*o* **con**] **algo** to be pleased with sth 2. (*divertirse*) **~se de algo** to have a good time with sth

holgazán, -ana *m, f* layabout

holgazanear *vi* to laze [*o* loaf] arodun

holgazanería *f* laziness

holgorio *m v.* **jolgorio**

holgura *f* 1. (*de vestido*) looseness 2. TÉC play 3. (*bienestar*) **vivir con ~** to live comfortably

holladura *f* 1. (*acción*) treading 2. (*huella*) footprint

hollar <o→ue> *vt* 1. (*pisar*) to step on; (*dejar huellas*) to leave footprints 2. (*despreciar*) to trample on

hollejo *m* skin (*of grape or olive*)

hollín *m* soot

holocausto *m* 1. (*genocidio*) holocaust 2. REL sacrifice

holografía *f* holography

holÓgrafo, -a *adj* holograph

holograma *m* hologram

hombracho *m,* **hombrachón** *m* strong man; *pey* brute

hombrada *f* feat of prowess, manly act

hombradía *f v.* **hombría**

hombre I. *m* 1. (*varón*) man; **el ~ de la calle** *fig* the man in the street; **~ de las cavernas** caveman; **~ de confianza** right-hand man; **~ de estado** statesman; **~ del montón** nobody special; **~ de negocios** businessman; **~ de paja** front man; **el ~ medio** the average man; **el ~ del saco** the bogeyman *Brit,* the boogeyman *Am;* **ser ~ de dos caras** to be two-faced; **el ~ del tiempo** the weatherman; **el defensa fue al ~** DEP the defender went for the man; **¡está hecho un ~!** he's become a man!; **hacer un ~ de alguien** to make a man out of sb; **se comportó como un ~** he behaved like a man; **¡~ al agua!** man overboard! 2. (*especie humana*) **el ~** mankind 3. *inf* (*marido*) man II. *interj* (*sorpresa*) well, well; (*duda*) well...; **¡~!, ¿qué tal?** hey! how's it going?; **¡cállate, ~!** give it a rest, eh!; **¡pero, ~!** but, come on!; **¡sí, ~!** yes, of course!

hombre-anuncio *m* <hombres-anuncio> sandwich man

hombrear I. *vi* to play the man II. *vr* **quiere ~se con su padre** he wants to play at being a man with his father

hombrecillo *m* little man; (*sin importancia*) insignificant man

hombre-lobo *m* <hombres-lobo> werewolf

hombre-mono *m* <hombres-mono> apeman

hombrera *f* 1. (*almohadilla*) shoulder pad 2. (*de uniforme*) epaulet(te) 3. (*de armadura*) shoulder plate

hombre-rana *m* <hombres-rana> frogman

hombría *f* 1. (*conducta*) uprightness 2. (*comportamiento*) manliness; **un acto de ~** a worthy action

hombro *m* 1. ANAT shoulder; **ancho de ~s** broad-shouldered; **cargado de ~s** round-shouldered; **encogerse de ~s** to shrug one's shoulders; **llevar algo a ~s** carry sth on one's shoulders 2. TIPO *part of typographical letter that does not leave a mark* ►**arrimar el ~** to lend a hand; **echarse al ~** to put one's shoulder to the wheel; **mirar a alguien por encima del ~** to look down one's nose at sb

hombruno, -a *adj* mannish; **mujer hombruna** mannish woman

homenaje *m* 1. (*el honrar*) tribute; **hacer una fiesta en ~ de alguien** to celebrate in honour [*o* honor *Am*] of sb; **rendir ~ a alguien** to pay homage to sb 2. HIST obedience, allegiance

homenajear *vt* to pay tribute to

homeópata *mf* homeopath

homeopatía *f sin pl* homeopathic medicine

homeopático, -a *adj* homeopathic

homicida I. *adj* homicidal; **el arma ~** the murder weapon II. *mf* (*planeado*) murderer *m,* murderess *f;* (*no planeado*) person guilty of manslaughter

homicidio *m* homicide; (*planeado*) murder; (*no planeado*) manslaughter; **~ frustrado** attempted murder; **brigada de ~s** murder squad

homínido *m* BIO hominid

homo *adj inf* gay

homogeneidad *f sin pl* homogeneity

homogeneización *f* homogenization

homogeneizar <z→c> *vt* 1. *t.* QUÍM to homogenize 2. (*uniformar*) to standardize

homogéneo, -a *adj* homogeneous, uniform

homógrafo *m* homograph

homógrafo, -a *adj* homographic

homologable *adj* equivalent; **el récord no es ~** the record cannot be accepted

homologación *f* 1. (*de una escuela*) validation, accreditation 2. DEP (*de un récord*) official recognition 3. TÉC (*de un casco*) authorization 4. JUR (*de un arreglo*) confirmation; (*de* *un convenio*) ratification

homologar <g→gu> I. *vt* 1. (*escuela*) to validate 2. DEP (*récord*) to recognize officially 3. TÉC to authorize; **homologar un casco** to authorize a helmet 4. JUR (*arreglo*) to confirm; (*convenio*) to ratify II. *vr:* **~se** to be officially recognized

homólogo, -a I. *adj* equivalent II. *m, f* counterpart; **el presidente mejicano y su ~ francés** the Mexican president and his French counterpart

homónimo *m* namesake

homónimo, -a I. *adj* homonymous II. *m, f* homonym

homosexual *adj, mf* homosexual

homosexualidad *f sin pl* homosexuality

honda *f* sling

hondo *m* depth

hondo, -a *adj* deep; **en lo ~ del valle** in the depths of the valley; **respirar ~** to breathe deeply; **cante ~** *purist Flamenco musical style*

hondonada *f* GEO depression, hollow

hondura *f* depth; **meterse en ~s** *fig* to get into deep water

Honduras *f* Honduras

> **Honduras** lies in Central America and borders **Nicaragua**, **El Salvador** and **Guatemala** as well as the Caribbean and the Pacific Ocean. The capital is **Tegucigalpa**. Spanish is the official language of the country and the monetary unit of **Honduras** is the **lempira**.

hondureño, -a *adj, m, f* Honduran

honestidad *f sin pl* honesty

honesto, -a *adj* honest

hongo *m* 1. BOT fungus; (*comestible*) mushroom 2. (*sombrero*) bowler (hat) ►**estar solo como un ~** to be as lonely as a cloud

honor *m* honour *Brit,* honor *Am;* **cuestión de ~** matter of honour; **¡palabra de ~!** word of honour!; **¡por mi ~!** on my honour!; **hacer ~ a su fama** to honour his/her name; **es para mí un gran ~** it is a great honour for me; **hacer los ~es** to do the honours

honorabilidad *f* honour *Brit,* honor *Am*

honorable *adj* honourable *Brit,* honorable *Am*

honorario, -a *adj* honorary; **cónsul ~** honorary consul

honorarios *mpl* fees *pl*

honorífico, -a *adj* honorary

honra *f* 1. (*honor, reputación*) honour *Brit,* honor *Am;* **¡a mucha ~!** I'm proud of it! 2. REL **~s fúnebres** funeral proceedings

honradez *f* (*honestidad*) honesty; (*integridad*) integrity; **falta de ~** lack of integrity

honrado, -a *adj* (*íntegro, moral*) honourable *Brit,* honorable *Am;* (*decente*) upright; **llevar una vida honrada** to lead an honourable [*o* honorable *Am*] life

honrar I. *vt* to honour *Brit,* to honor *Am;* **nos honra con su presencia** he honours [*o* honors *Am*] us with his presence II. *vr* **~se con** [*o* **de**] **algo** to be an honour [*o* honor *Am*] for sb

honrilla *f* self-esteem

honroso, -a *adj* honourable *Brit,* honorable *Am*

hontanar *m* spring

hopo *m* 1. (*rabo*) bushy tail 2. (*mechón*) tuft

hora *f* 1. (*de un día*) hour; **~s de consulta** surgery hours; **~s extraordinarias** overtime; **~ feliz** happy hour; **~(s) punta** rush hour; **un cuarto de ~** a quarter of an hour; **media ~** half an hour; **una ~ y media** an hour and a half; **a última ~** at the last minute; **a primera/última ~ de la tarde** in the early/late afternoon; **noticias de última ~** last-minute news; **el pueblo está a dos ~s de camino** the village is two hours' walk away; **estuve esperando ~s y ~s** I was waiting for hours and hours; **a la ~** on time 2. (*del reloj*) time; **¿qué ~ es?** what time is it?, what's the time?; **¿a qué ~ vendrás?** what time are you coming?; **adelantar la ~** to put [*o* set] the clock forward; **poner el reloj en ~** to set one's watch; **retrasar la ~** to put [*o* set] the clock back; **me ha dado** [*o* **tengo**] **~ para el martes** I've got an appointment for Tuesday 3. (*tiempo*) time; **a la ~ de la verdad...** when it comes down to it ...; **comer entre ~s** to eat between meals; **estar en ~s bajas** to be feeling down; **no lo dejes para última ~** don't leave it till the last minute; **tener** (**muchas**) **~s de vuelo** *fig* to be (very) experienced; **ven a cualquier ~** come at any time; **ya va siendo ~ que tomes tus propias decisiones** it is about time that you made your own decisions 4. REL prayer 5. *pl* (*mitología*) **las ~s** the seasons

horadar *vt* to perforate

hora-hombre <horas-hombre> *f* ECON man-hour; **con las huelgas se pierden al año miles y miles de horas-hombre** thousands and thousands of man-hours are lost every year as a result of strikes

horario *m* 1. (*escolar, de medio de transporte*) timetable, schedule *Am;* (*de consulta*) surgery hours; **~ de atención al público** opening hours; **~ flexible** flexitime; **~ de oficina** office hours; **¿qué ~ hacen?** what hours do they work?; **tenemos ~ de tarde** we work evenings 2. (*manecilla del reloj*) hour hand

horario, -a *adj* hourly

horca *f* 1. (*para colgar*) gallows *pl* 2. (*bieldo*) winnowing fork 3. (*horquilla*) pitchfork

horcajadas a ~ astride

> **Horchata** is a refreshing drink from Valencia made from **chufas** (a specific type of almond), **azúcar** (sugar) and **agua** (water).

horda *f* 1. (*de salvajes*) horde 2. (*banda*) violent group

horizontal I. *adj* horizontal II. *f* horizontal

position
horizontalidad *f sin pl* horizontality
horizonte *m* horizon
horma *f* **1.** TÉC (*molde*) mould *Brit,* mold *Am* **2.** (*muelle*) ~ **de zapatos** shoetree ►**encontrar la** ~ **de su** **zapato** *inf* to meet one's match
hormiga *f* ant; ~ **blanca** white ant; **ser una** ~ *fig* to be always working
hormigón *m* concrete; ~ **armado** reinforced concrete
hormigonera *f* concrete mixer
hormiguear *vi* **1.** (*picar*) to tingle, to itch **2.** (*gente, insectos*) to swarm; ~ **de algo** to seethe [*o* teem] with sth
hormigueo *m* **1.** (*picor*) pins and needles; **tengo un** ~ **en la espalda** my back is itching **2.** (*multitud*) swarming
hormiguero *m* **1.** (*de hormigas*) anthill **2.** (*de gente*) swarm; **la plaza era un** ~ **de gente** the square was seething with people
hormiguero, -a *adj* related to ants; **oso** ~ anteater
hormona *f* hormone
hormonal *adj* hormone, hormonal
hormonar *vt* to treat with hormones
hornacina *f* ARQUIT (vaulted) niche
hornada *f* **1.** (*de horno*) batch, ovenload **2.** (*conjunto*) **una** ~ **de médicos** a whole lot of doctors
hornalla *f AmL* **1.** (*parrilla*) barbecue **2.** (*del fogón*) hotplate **3.** (*horno*) oven
hornear *vt* to bake
hornero, -a *m, f* baker
hornillo *m* (*cocina*) stove; (*de una cocina*) ring; ~ **de gas** gas ring; ~ **portátil** portable cooker
horno *m* **1.** (*cocina*) oven; ~ **microondas** microwave oven; **recién salido del** ~ straight from [*o* out of] the oven; **asar al** ~ to oven roast **2.** TÉC furnace; ~ **crematorio** cremation furnace; **alto** ~ blast furnace; (*para cerámica*) kiln ►**no está el** ~ **para** **bollos** this is not the right time
horóscopo *m* horoscope
horqueta *f* **1.** (*horca*) winnowing fork **2.** (*horquilla*) pitchfork **3.** (*de un árbol*) fork
horquilla *f* **1.** (*del pelo*) hairclip *Brit,* bobby pin *Am;* (*de moño*) hairpin **2.** (*de bicicleta, árbol*) fork **3.** TÉC yoke
horrendo, -a *adj v.* **horroroso**
hórreo *m* raised granary
horrible *adj* **1.** (*horroroso*) horrible; **un crimen** ~ a ghastly crime; **una historia** ~ a horrible story **2.** (*muy feo*) grotesque
horripilante *adj* horrifying
horripilar **I.** *vt* **1.** (*erizar*) ~ **a alguien** to make one's hair stand on end; **estas historias me horripilan** I'm horrified by these stories **2.** (*horrorizar*) to horrify **II.** *vr:* ~**se** to be horrified
horrísono, -a *adj* dreadful; **un griterío** ~ a frightful clamour [*o* clamor *Am*]
horror *m* **1.** (*miedo, aversión*) horror; **tener** ~ **a algo** to have a horror of sth; **siento** ~ **a la oscuridad** I'm terrified of the dark; **me da** ~ **verte con esta corbata** you look terrible with that tie on; **el diseño moderno me parece un** ~ I don't like modern design at all; **¡qué** ~**!** *inf* how horrible! **2.** *pl* (*actos*) **los** ~**es de la guerra** the atrocities of war **3.** *inf* (*mucho*) **ganar un** ~ **de dinero** to earn a lot of money; **hoy hace un** ~ **de frío** it's hellishly cold today; **me cuesta** ~**es** it's very hard for me; (*me gusta* ~*es el regalo*) I absolutely love the gift
horrorizar <z→c> **I.** *vt* to horrify; **me horrorizó ver el accidente** I was horrified by the accident **II.** *vr* ~**se de algo** to be horrified [*o* terrified] by sth
horroroso, -a *adj* horrifying; **una escena horrorosa** a terrible scene; **su última novela es horrorosa** his last novel is awful
hortaliza *f* vegetable
hortelano, -a *m, f* market gardener *Brit,* truck gardener *Am;* ~ **aficionado** amateur gardener
hortensia *f* hydrangea
hortera[1] **I.** *adj* vulgar, tasteless, tacky **II.** *m inf* vulgar person
hortera[2] *f* wooden bowl
horterada *f inf* tasteless thing; **este vestido es una** ~ this dress is completely tasteless; **esta película es una** ~ this film is so tacky
hortícola *adj* horticultural; **productos** ~**s** horticultural produce
horticultor(a) *m(f)* gardener
horticultura *f sin pl* horticulture
hortofrutícula *adj* fruit and vegetable gardening
hortofruticultura *f sin pl* fruit and vegetable growing
hosco, -a *adj* **1.** (*persona*) gruff **2.** (*ambiente*) unpleasant, hostile
hospedaje *m* **1.** (*acción, situación*) residence; **dar** ~ **a alguien** to put sb up **2.** (*coste*) rent
hospedar **I.** *vt* to accommodate **II.** *vr:* ~**se** to stay
hospedería *f* **1.** (*fonda*) inn **2.** (*en convento*) hospice
hospedero, -a *m, f* innkeeper
hospiciano, -a *m, f* **1.** (*niño*) orphan **2.** (*pobre*) poor person
hospicio *m* **1.** (*para niños*) children's home **2.** (*para pobres, en un monasterio*) hospice
hospital *m* hospital; ~ **militar** military hospital
hospitalario, -a *adj* **1.** (*acogedor*) welcoming, hospitable **2.** (*de hospital*) hospital
hospitalidad *f sin pl* hospitality
hospitalización *f* **1.** (*envío*) hospitalization **2.** (*estancia*) stay in hospital
hospitalizar <z→c> *vt* to hospitalize; **ayer** ~**on a mi madre** yesterday my mother went into hospital; **estoy hospitalizado desde**

el domingo I've been in hospital since Sunday

hosquedad *f* **1.** (*de una persona*) gruffness **2.** (*de un lugar*) dismalness

hostal *m* cheap hotel

hostelería *f* **1.** ECON hotel business **2.** ENS hotel management; **escuela superior de ~** school of hotel management

hostelero, **-a** **I.** *adj* hotel **II.** *m, f* hotelier

hostería *f* inn

hostia **I.** *f* **1.** REL host; (*sin consagrar*) wafer **2.** *vulg* (*bofetada*) clout, smack; (*golpe*) bash; **darse una ~** (*chocar*) to smash **3.** *vulg* (*uso hiperbólico*) **¡me cago en la ~!** for fuck's sake; **¡este examen es la ~!** fucking hell! what an exam!; **hace un tiempo de la ~** (*malo*) the weather's really shitty; (*bueno*) the weather's fantastic; **iba a toda ~** he was going full speed **II.** *interj vulg* Jesus

hostiar *vt vulg* (*bofetada, golpe*) to belt

hostigador(a) *adj* annoying

hostigamiento *m* **1.** (*fustigación*) whipping **2.** (*molestia*) annoyance **3.** (*apremio*) harrassment

hostigante *adj Col* (*sabor*) sickly; (*persona*) annoying

hostigar <g→gu> *vt* **1.** (*fustigar*) to whip **2.** (*molestar*) to bother; (*con observaciones*) to harrass **3.** (*incitar*) to incite **4.** MIL to make small attacks

hostigoso, **-a** *adj Chile, Guat, Perú* cloying

hostil *adj* hostile; **le hicieron un recibimiento ~** he was given a hostile reception

hostilidad *f* hostility

hostilizar <z→c> *vt* **1.** (*hostigar*) to annoy **2.** MIL to attack

hostión *m vulg* heavy clout

hotel *m* **1.** (*establecimiento*) hotel; **~ residencia** boarding house, guesthouse **2.** (*casa*) country house, villa; (*mansión*) mansion

hotelero, **-a** **I.** *adj* hotel; **industria hotelera** hotel business **II.** *m, f* hotelier, hotelkeeper

hotelito *m* (*casa*) house; (*de vacaciones*) holiday home

hovercraft *m* <hovercrafts> hovercraft

hoy *adv* today; **~ (en) día** nowadays; **llegará de ~ a mañana** it will arrive any time now; **de ~ en adelante** from now on; **los niños de ~ (en día)** children nowadays; **llegará de ~ a mañana** it will arrive today or tomorrow

hoya *f* **1.** (*hoyo*) hollow **2.** (*sepultura*) grave **3.** GEO (*hondonada*) plain

hoyo *m* **1.** (*concavidad*) hollow **2.** (*agujero*) hole **3.** (*sepultura*) grave

hoyuelo *m* dimple

hoz *f* **1.** AGR sickle **2.** GEO (*desfiladero*) defile; (*garganta*) gorge

hozar <z→c> **I.** *vi* to root around **II.** *vt* to root around in

huacal *m And, Méx: wooden box*

huachafoso, **-a** *adj Perú* affected, pretentious

huaico *m Perú* landslide

huarache *m Méx* **1.** (*sandalia*) sandal **2.** GASTR *corn dough filled with fried beans*

huarmi *f AmS* **1.** (*mujer muy trabajadora*) hardworking woman **2.** (*ama de casa*) housewife

huasca *f AmL* (*látigo*) whip

huaso, **-a** **I.** *adj AmS* (*campesino*) peasant **II.** *m, f AmS* (*campesino*) peasant

hubo *3. pret de* **haber**

hucha *f* **1.** (*alcancía*) moneybox, piggy bank **2.** (*ahorros*) savings

hueco *m* **1.** (*agujero*) hole; **~ del ascensor** lift well *Brit,* elevator shaft *Am;* **~ de la mano** hollow of the hand; **~ de la ventana** window space **2.** (*lugar*) space; **hazme un ~** move over **3.** (*tiempo*) time; **hazme un ~ para mañana** make time for me tomorrow

hueco, **-a** *adj* **1.** (*ahuecado*) hollow; (*vacío*) empty **2.** (*sonido*) resonant **3.** (*tierra*) soft **4.** (*palabras*) empty **5.** (*persona*) vain; **ponerse ~** to become vain; **tener la cabeza hueca** *pey* to be thick **6.** (*estilo*) trite

huecograbado *m* TIPO photogravure

huelga *f* strike; **~ de advertencia** warning strike; **~ de brazos caídos** sit-down strike; **~ general** general strike; **~ de hambre** hunger strike; **~ salvaje** wildcat strike; **convocar una ~** to call a strike; **declararse en** [*o* **hacer**] **~** to go on strike; **en esta fábrica estamos en ~** we're on strike in this factory

huelguista *mf* striker

huelguístico, **-a** *adj* strike

huella *f* **1.** (*señal*) mark; **~ de un animal** animal track; **~ dactilar** fingerprint **2.** (*vestigio*) trace; (*pasos*) footsteps; **seguir las ~s de alguien** to follow sb's footsteps

huelveño, **-a** **I.** *adj* of/from Huelva **II.** *m, f* native/inhabitant of Huelva

huérfano, **-a** **I.** *adj* orphan; **ser ~ de padre** to have no father; **quedarse ~** to become an orphan; **la ciudad se queda huérfana en invierno** the city empties in winter **II.** *m, f* orphan

huero, **-a** *adj* (*discurso*) trite; (*huevo*) rotten; **la cosa ha salido huera** it was a bit of a disaster

huerta *f* (*frutales*) orchard; (*hortalizas*) market garden *Brit,* truck garden *Am*

huertero, **-a** *m, f Arg, Nic, Perú* market gardener *Brit,* truck gardener *Am*

huerto *m* (*hortalizas*) vegetable patch; (*frutales*) orchard; **~ familiar** allotment ►**llevar a alguien al ~** *inf* (*engaño*) to lead sb up the garden path; (*sexo*) to seduce sb [*o* have sex with]

huesa *f* shallow grave

huesera *f Chile* ossuary

hueso *m* **1.** ANAT bone; **carne sin ~** boneless meat; **te voy a romper los ~s** *inf* I'm going to kick your face in; **estar en los ~s** to be a rack of bones **2.** (*de fruto*) stone, pit *Am* **3.** (*faena*) task; **un ~ duro de roer** a hard nut to crack; **este profesor es un ~** this teacher's really strict **4.** *AmL* (*trabajo*) hard work ►**dar con**

sus ~s en la cárcel to end up in jail; calado hasta los ~s soaked to the skin; dar en ~ *inf* to come a cropper
huésped *m t.* BIO host
huésped(a) *m(f)* guest
hueste *f* **1.** HIST (*ejército*) host **2.** (*de un partido*) supporters
huesudo, -a *adj* **1.** (*persona*) big-boned **2.** (*carne*) bony
hueva *f* roe
huevada *f AmL, inf* (*estupidez*) stupid thing
huevear *vi AmS, inf* (*hacer tonterías*) to fool around
huevera *f* egg cup; (*cartón*) egg crate
huevería *f shop that sells eggs*
huevero *m* (*que fabrica*) egg producer
huevero, -a *m, f* (*que vende*) egg seller
huevo *m* **1.** BIO egg; ~ **duro** hard-boiled egg; ~**s fritos** fried eggs; ~ **pasado por agua** soft-boiled egg; ~**s revueltos** scrambled eggs; **clara de** ~ egg white; **ir pisando ~s** to go very slowly and/or carefully; **poner un** ~ to lay an egg; *vulg* to have [*o* take] a shit **2.** *AmL* (*valor*) guts *pl* **3.** *vulg* (*testículo*) ball; **¡estoy hasta los ~s!** I've had it up to here!; **me importa un** ~ I don't give a shit; **¡tiene ~s la cosa!** that's quite something!; **poner algo a alguien a** ~ to make sth very easy for sb; **me costó un** ~ (*de dinero*) it cost loads; (*de dificultades*) it was damn difficult; **¡y un ~!** like hell!
huevonear *vi Méx, vulg* to piss around
huida *f* flight; ~ **del lugar del accidente** flight from the scene of the accident; **no hay ~ posible** there's no way out
huidizo, -a *adj* **1.** (*persona*) elusive **2.** (*momento*) fleeting
huido, -a *m, f* escaped prisoner
huir *irr* **I.** *vi* (*escapar*) to flee; ~ **de casa** to run away from home; **el tiempo huye** time flies; **pudieron ~ de sus perseguidores** they managed to give their pursuers the slip **II.** *vt, vi* (*evitar*) ~ **(de) algo** to keep away from sth; ~ **(de) alguien** to avoid sb
huiro *m AmS* (*alga*) seaweed
hule *m* **1.** (*para la mesa*) tablecloth **2.** (*tela*) oilcloth **3.** *AmL* (*caucho*) rubber
hulero, -a *m, f AmL* rubber tapper
hulla *f* fossil coal; ~ **blanca** hydroenergy
hullero, -a *adj* coal; **período** ~ GEO Carboniferous period
humanamente *adv* humanly; **hacer todo lo ~ posible** to do everything humanly possible
humanidad *f* **1.** (*género humano*) **la** ~ mankind; **un crimen contra la** ~ a crime against humanity **2.** (*naturaleza, caridad humana*) humanity **3.** *inf* (*corpulencia*) fatness **4.** *pl* (*letras*) arts
humanismo *m sin pl* humanism
humanista *mf* humanist
humanístico, -a *adj* humanistic
humanitario, -a *adj* humanitarian; **organización humanitaria** humanitarian organization
humanitarismo *m sin pl* humanitarianism
humanización *f sin pl* **1.** (*dignificación*) humanization **2.** ARTE humanizing
humanizador(a) *adj* humanizing
humanizar <z→c> **I.** *vt* (*dignificar, arte*) to humanize **II.** *vr:* ~**se** to become human
humano, -a *adj* **1.** (*del hombre*) human **2.** (*manera de ser*) humane
humanoide *m* humanoid
humareda *f* cloud of smoke
humazo *m* thick smoke
humear I. *vi* **1.** (*humo*) to smoke **2.** (*vapor*) to steam **3.** (*enemistad*) to linger on, to smolder **4.** (*engreírse*) to act vain **II.** *vr:* ~**se** to give oneself airs
humectador *m* humidifier
humectante *adj* moisturizing
humedad *f* humidity; (*agradable*) moisture; (*desagradable*) dampness
humedal *m* wetland
humedecer *irr como crecer vt* to moisten
húmedo, -a *adj* (*mojado*) wet; (*agradable*) moist; (*desagradable*) damp; (*con vapor*) humid; (*aire*) muggy
húmero *m* ANAT humerus
humidificar <c→qu> *vt* to humidify
humildad *f* **1.** (*modestia*) humility, humbleness **2.** (*religiosa*) meekness **3.** (*social*) lowliness
humilde *adj* **1.** (*modesto*) humble; **un ~ trabajador** a humble worker **2.** (*en sentido religioso*) meek **3.** (*condición social*) poor; **ser de orígenes ~s** to be of humble origin
humillación *f* **1.** (*degradación*) humiliation **2.** (*vergüenza*) shame
humillante *adj* humiliating
humillar I. *vt* **1.** (*degradar*) to humiliate **2.** (*avergonzar*) to shame **II.** *vr:* ~**se** to lower oneself
humo *m* **1.** (*de combustión*) smoke; **señal de** ~ smoke signal; **en ese bar siempre hay** ~ it's always smoky in that bar; **la chimenea echa** ~ the chimney pours out smoke; **tragar el ~ al fumar** to inhale cigarette smoke **2.** (*vapor*) steam **3.** (*al cocinar*) smoke, steam **4.** *pl* (*vanidad*) conceit; **bajar los ~s a alguien** to take sb down a peg; **subírse los ~s a la cabeza** to put on airs; **tener muchos ~s** to be very conceited
humor *m* **1.** (*cualidad, humorismo*) humour *Brit,* humor *Am;* ~ **negro** gallows humour *Brit* [*o* humor *Am*]; **¡pero no tienes sentido del ~ o qué!** have you got no sense of humour *Brit* [*o* humor *Am*]? **2.** (*ánimo*) mood; **estar de buen/mal** ~ to be in a good/bad mood; **no estoy de ~ para bailar** I'm not in the mood for dancing **3.** MED (*líquido*) humour *Brit,* humor *Am*
humorada *f* (*dicho, broma*) witticism; **dejémonos de ~s** let's stop beating around the bush
humorado, -a *adj* **bien/mal** ~ (*por un momento*) in a good/bad mood; (*carácter*)

even-tempered/bad-tempered
humorismo *m sin pl* comedy
humorista *mf* comic, humorist; (*dibujante*) cartoonist
humorístico, **-a** *adj* comic
humus *m sin pl* humus
hundido, **-a** *adj* **1.**(*ojos*) deep-set; (*techo*) collapsed **2.**(*persona*) downcast, demoralized
hundimiento *m* **1.**(*de un barco*) sinking **2.**(*de un edificio*) *t.* ECON collapse **3.**GEO (*depresión*) hollow
hundir **I.** *vt* **1.**(*barco*) to sink **2.**(*sumergir*) ~ **la mano en el agua** to put one's hand in the water; ~ **los pies en el barro** to sink one's feet into the mud **3.**(*suelo*) to cave in **4.**(*arruinar*) to ruin; (*proyecto*) to cause to fail; (*empresa*) to bankrupt; (*esperanzas*) to destroy; **la crisis económica ha hundido a muchos empresarios** the economic crisis has ruined many businessmen **II.** *vr:* **~se** **1.**(*barco*) to sink **2.**(*edificio*) to collapse; (*suelo*) to cave in; **el rublo se hunde** the rouble is plummeting **3.**(*fracasar*) to fail, to lose it; **me he hundido en el tercer set** I lost it in the third set
húngaro, **-a** *adj, m, f* Hungarian
Hungría *f* Hungary
huno, **-a** **I.** *adj* HIST Hun **II.** *m, f* HIST Hun
huracán *m* hurricane; **las tropas pasaron como un ~ por la ciudad** the troops stampeded through the city; (*persona*) whirlwind of energy
huracanado, **-a** *adj* tempestuous; **vientos ~s** hurricane winds
huraño, **-a** *adj* **1.**(*insociable*) unsociable **2.**(*hosco*) surly
hurgar <g→gu> **I.** *vt, vi* **1.**(*remover*) ~ **en algo** to poke about in sth; ~ **el fuego** to poke the fire **2.**(*fisgonear*) ~ **en algo** to look [*o* rummage] through sth **II.** *vr* **~se la nariz** to pick one's nose
hurgón *m* (*de fuego*) poker
hurgonear *vt* to jab, to poke
hurguetear *vt AmL* ~ **algo** rummage about in sth
hurí *f* houri
hurón, **-ona** *m, f* **1.**(*animal*) ferret **2.** *inf* (*husmeador*) nosy parker **3.** *inf* (*huraño*) unsociable
huronear *vi* **1.**(*cazar*) to hunt with ferrets **2.**(*fisgonear*) to nose around, to snoop
huronera *f* **1.**(*madriguera*) ferret hole **2.**(*escondrijo*) hiding place; (*de ladrones*) den; (*escondite*) hideout
hurra *interj* hooray
hurtadillas **a ~** secretly; **lo hizo a ~ de su novia** he did it behind his girlfriend's back
hurtar **I.** *vt* **1.**(*robar*) to steal; (*en tiendas*) to shoplift **2.**(*con el peso*) to give sb short measure **3.**(*mar*) to eat away **4.**(*cuerpo*) to avoid **5.**(*ocultar*) to hide **II.** *vr* **~se a algo** to keep away from sth
hurto *m* **1.**(*acción*) stealing; (*en tiendas*) shoplifting **2.**(*cosa*) stolen property
húsar *m* MIL hussar
husmear **I.** *vt* (*perro*) to sniff **II.** *vi* (*perro*) to sniff around; (*fisgonear*) to nose around
husmeo *m* **1.**(*de un perro*) sniffing **2.**(*fisgoneo*) nosing around, snooping
huso *m* **1.**(*textil*) spindle **2.**GEO ~ **horario** time zone
huy *interj* **1.**(*de dolor*) ow **2.**(*de asombro*) wow

I

I, **i** *f* I, i; ~ **de Italia** I for Isaac *Brit,* I for Item *Am;* ~ **griega** y
ibérico, **-a** *adj* Iberian; **Península Ibérica** Iberian Peninsula
Iberoamérica *f* Latin America
iberoamericano, **-a** *adj, m, f* Latin American
ibicenco, **-a** **I.** *adj* of/from Ibiza **II.** *m, f* native/inhabitant of Ibiza
Ibiza *f* Ibiza
iceberg *m* <icebergs> iceberg; **la punta del ~** the tip of the iceberg
icono *m,* **ícono** *m* REL, INFOR icon
iconoclasta **I.** *adj* iconoclastic **II.** *mf* iconoclast
iconografía *f* iconography
ictericia *f sin pl* MED jaundice
ictiología *f sin pl* ichthyology
I+D *abr de* **Investigación y Desarrollo** R & D
ida *f* departure; **billete de ~** single (ticket); **billete de ~ y vuelta** return (ticket)
idea *f* **1.** *t.* FILOS idea; ~ **fundamental** basic idea; **ni ~** no idea; **dar a alguien (una) ~ de algo** to give sb an idea of [*o* about] sth; **tener la ~ de hacer algo** to have the idea of doing sth **2.**(*propósito*) intention; **tener ~ de hacer algo** to have the intention of doing sth; **llevar ~ de hacer algo** to intend to do sth **3.** *pl* (*convicciones*) ideas *pl*
ideal *adj, m* ideal
idealismo *m* idealism
idealista **I.** *adj* idealistic **II.** *mf* idealist
idealización *f* idealization
idealizar <z→c> *vt* to idealize
idear *vt* **1.**(*concebir*) to conceive **2.**(*inventar*) to think up **3.**(*trazar un proyecto*) to design; (*un plan*) to devise
ideario *m* **1.**(*conjunto de ideas*) doctrine **2.**(*ideología*) ideology
ídem *pron* ditto
idéntico, **-a** *adj* **1.**(*igual*) identical; **es ~ a su madre** he/she is just like his/her mother **2.**(*semejante*) same
identidad *f* **1.**(*personalidad*) identity; **carné de ~** identity card; **no pude probar mi ~** I was unable to prove my identity **2.**(*coinciden-*

I

cia) sameness

identificable *adj* identifiable

identificación *f* **1.** (*de alguien*) identification **2.** INFOR password

identificar <c→qu> **I.** *vt* **1.** (*reconocer*) to recognize; (*establecer la identidad*) to identify **2.** (*equiparar*) to categorize **II.** *vr:* **~se 1.** (*demostrar la identidad*) to identify **2.** (*solidarizarse*) to sympathize **3.** (*compenetrarse*) **~se con alguien/algo** to identify oneself with sb/sth

ideología *f* ideology

ideólogo, **-a** *m, f* ideologist, idealogue

idílico, **-a** *adj* idyllic

idilio *m* **1.** LIT idyll **2.** (*relación amorosa*) love affair

idioma *m* language; **hablar el mismo ~** *fig* to be on the same wavelength

idiomático, **-a** *adj* idiomatic

idiosincrasia *f* idiosyncrasy, quirk

idiota **I.** *adj* idiotic, stupid **II.** *mf* **1.** MED subnormal person **2.** (*estúpido*) idiot

idiotez *f* **1.** *t.* MED imbecility **2.** (*estupidez*) idiocy

ido, **-a** *adj* **1.** *inf* (*mal de la cabeza*) crazy **2.** (*despistado*) absent-minded **3.** *AmC* (*borracho*) drunk

idólatra **I.** *adj* **1.** (*que rinde culto*) idolatrous **2.** (*que ama excesivamente*) adoring **II.** *mf* **1.** (*quien rinde culto*) idolater *m,* idolatress *f* **2.** (*quien ama una persona o cosa*) adorer

idolatrar *vt* **1.** (*rendir culto*) to worship **2.** (*adorar*) to adore; (*amar*) to idolize

idolatría *f* **1.** (*culto*) idolatry **2.** (*adoración*) adoration

ídolo *m* **1.** (*persona*) idol **2.** *pey* (*divinidad*) idol, deity; (*efigie*) graven image

idoneidad *f* **1.** (*aptitud*) suitability **2.** (*capacidad*) aptitude

idóneo, **-a** *adj* apt

iglesia *f* church; **casarse por la ~** to have a church wedding

iglú *m* igloo

ígneo, **-a** *adj* igneous

ignición *f* **1.** (*combustión*) combustion; (*incandescencia*) incandescence **2.** (*inicio de una combustión*) ignition

ignífugo, **-a** *adj* (*que protege contra el fuego*) fireproof; (*que no se quema*) noninflammable *Brit,* nonflammable *Am*

ignominia *f* ignominy, disgrace

ignominioso, **-a** *adj* ignoble, ignominious

ignorancia *f* **1.** (*desconocimiento*) ignorance **2.** (*incultura*) lack of culture [*o* education]; **la ~ es atrevida** *prov* a little learning [*o* knowledge] is a dangerous thing

ignorante **I.** *adj* **1.** (*desconocedor*) **~ de algo** ignorant about [*o* of] sth **2.** (*inculto*) uncultured, uneducated **II.** *mf pey* dunce, ignoramus

ignorar *vt* **1.** (*desconocer, no saber*) **~ algo** to be ignorant of sth **2.** (*no hacer caso*) to ignore

igual[1] **I.** *adj* **1.** (*idéntico*) identical; (*semejante*) same; **nunca he visto cosa ~** I've never seen anything like it **2.** (*llano*) flat **3.** (*constante: temperaturas, clima*) stable; (*ritmo*) steady **4.** MAT equal **5.** (*lo mismo*) **a mí me pasó ~** the same (thing) happened to me; **habla ~ que su padre** he/she speaks just like his/her father; **¡es ~!** it doesn't matter ►**al ~ que...** as well as ... **II.** *mf* equal; **no tiene ~** he/she has no equal **III.** *adv inf* (*quizá*) **~ no viene** he/she might not come

igual[2] *m* MAT equal(s) sign

igualación *f* **1.** (*igualamiento*) equalization; (*equiparación*) matching **2.** (*allanamiento*) flattening **3.** (*nivelación*) levelling *Brit,* leveling *Am* **4.** (*ajuste*) adjustment **5.** (*convenio*) agreement; (*pago*) retainer

igualada *f* equalizer

igualado, **-a** *adj* **1.** (*parecido*) similar **2.** (*empatado*) level

igualar **I.** *vt* **1.** (*hacer igual*) to equalize; (*equiparar*) to match **2.** (*allanar*) to flatten (out) **3.** (*nivelar*) to level **4.** (*ajustar*) to even out **II.** *vi* **1.** (*equivaler*) to be equal **2.** (*combinar*) to match **III.** *vr:* **~se 1.** (*parecerse*) **~se a** [*o* **con**] **alguien** to be similar to sb **2.** (*compararse*) to equate **3.** (*ponerse al igual*) to make equal, to equate

igualdad *f* **1.** equality; (*uniformidad*) sameness, uniformity; **~ de derechos** equal rights; **en ~ de condiciones** all things (being) equal; **estar en ~ de condiciones** to be on an equal footing **2.** (*semejanza*) similarity **3.** (*regularidad*) steadiness; (*de superficie*) smoothness

igualitario, **-a** *adj* egalitarian

igualitarismo *m sin pl* egalitarianism

igualmente **I.** *interj* and the same to you **II.** *adv* equally

iguana *f* iguana

ijada *f* **1.** ANAT abdominal cavity **2.** (*dolor*) pain in the side, stitch

ikurriña *f flag of the Basque Country*

ilegal *adj* illegal, unlawful

ilegalidad *f* illegality

ilegible *adj* **1.** (*la letra*) illegible **2.** (*el contenido*) unreadable

ilegitimar *vt* **1.** (*asunto*) to invalidate **2.** (*hijo*) to disinherit

ilegitimidad *f* **1.** (*asunto*) illegality **2.** (*hijo*) illegitimacy

ilegítimo, **-a** *adj* **1.** (*asunto*) illegal **2.** (*hijo*) illegitimate; (*relación*) adulterous **3.** (*exigencia*) illegitimate

ileso, **-a** *adj* unharmed, unhurt; **salir** [*o* **resultar**] **~** to be unscathed

iletrado, **-a** *adj* **1.** (*inculto*) uncultured **2.** (*analfabeto*) uneducated

ilícito, **-a** *adj* illegal, illicit

ilimitado, **-a** *adj* unlimited

ilocalizable *adj* **el médico está ~** the doctor cannot be found

ilógico, **-a** *adj* illogical

iluminación *f* **1.** (*el alumbrar*) *t.* ARTE illumination **2.** (*alumbrado*) lighting; (*como adorno*) illuminations *pl* **3.** REL enlightenment

iluminado, -a *adj* **1.** (*un lugar*) *t.* ARTE illuminated; (*un monumento*) lit up **2.** REL enlightened

iluminar *vt* **1.** (*alumbrar*) *t.* ARTE to illuminate; (*un monumento*) to light up **2.** *fig* to enlighten, to illuminate

ilusión *f* **1.** (*alegría*) excitement; **ese viaje me hace mucha ~** I'm excited about the journey **2.** (*esperanza*) hope; **no te hagas ilusiones** do not get your hopes up **3.** (*sueño*) illusion **4.** (*espejismo*) (optical) illusion

ilusionante *adj* exciting

ilusionar **I.** *vt* **1.** (*entusiasmar*) to excite; **estar ilusionado con algo** to be excited about sth; **me ilusiona mucho hacer ese viaje** I'm very excited about that journey **2.** (*hacer ilusiones*) to raise false hopes **3.** (*engañar*) to delude **II.** *vr:* **~se** **1.** (*alegrarse*) to be excited **2.** (*esperanzarse*) **el proyecto le ilusiona mucho** the project has got his hopes up

ilusionismo *m* illusionism, conjuring

ilusionista *mf* illusionist

iluso, -a **I.** *adj* gullible **II.** *m, f* dreamer

ilusorio, -a *adj* **1.** (*engañoso*) illusory **2.** (*de ningún efecto*) ineffective

ilustración *f* **1.** (*imagen, instrucción*) illustration; **~ gráfica** graphic illustration; (*explicación*) explanation **2.** HIST **la Ilustración** the Enlightenment

ilustrado, -a **I.** *adj* **1.** (*con imágenes*) illustrated **2.** (*instruido*) enlightened **3.** (*de la Ilustración*) pertaining to the Enlightenment **II.** *m, f* learned [*o* erudite] person

ilustrador(a) **I.** *adj* **1.** (*ilustrativo, aclarativo*) illustrative **2.** (*instructivo*) enlightening **II.** *m(f)* illustrator

ilustrar **I.** *vt* **1.** (*con imágenes, aclarar*) to illustrate **2.** (*instruir*) to enlighten **II.** *vr:* **~se** to enlighten oneself

ilustrativo, -a *adj* **1.** (*aclarador*) illustrative **2.** (*sintomático*) representative

ilustre *adj* (*famoso*) illustrious; (*egregio*) distinguished

imagen *f* **1.** (*representación mental, fama*) image; **ser la viva ~ de alguien** to be the spitting [*o* living] image of sb **2.** TV picture **3.** (*escultura sagrada*) idol, graven image; (*pintura*) icon

imaginable *adj* imaginable

imaginación *f* (*imaginativa, fantasía*) imagination; **ni por ~** on no account

imaginar **I.** *vt* to imagine; **~ fantasmas** to imagine things **II.** *vr:* **~se** **1.** (*representarse*) to imagine oneself; **me lo imagino** I can imagine [*o* picture] it **2.** (*figurarse*) to imagine, to suppose

imaginario, -a *adj t.* MAT imaginary, unreal

imaginativo, -a *adj* imaginative

imán *m* **1.** *t. fig* (*hierro*) magnet **2.** REL imam

iman(t)ar *vt* to magnetize

imbatibilidad *f sin pl* invincibility

imbatible *adj* unbeatable

imbebible *adj* undrinkable

imbécil *adj, mf t.* MED imbecile

imbecilidad *f t.* MED imbecility, subnormality

imberbe *adj* **1.** (*sin barba*) clean-shaven **2.** *pey* (*inmaduro*) beardless

imborrable *adj* **1.** (*lápiz, tinta*) indelible **2.** (*acontecimiento*) unforgettable

imbricación *f* **1.** ARQUIT imbrication **2.** (*superposición*) overlapping; (*entrecruzamiento*) criss-crossing

imbricar <c→qu> **I.** *vt* to imbricate **II.** *vr:* **~se** **1.** (*superponerse*) to overlap **2.** (*entrecruzarse*) to criss-cross **3.** (*entrelazarse*) to interlace

imbuido, -a *adj* imbued; **~ de algo** imbued with sth

imbuir *irr como huir* **I.** *vt* **1.** (*inculcar*) to imbue **2.** (*transmitir*) to infuse **II.** *vr* **~se de algo** to imbibe sth

IME *m abr de* **Instituto Monetario Europeo** EMI

imitable *adj* imitable

imitación *f* **1.** (*copia, reproducción*) imitation; **a ~ de...** as an imitation of ... **2.** (*como falsificación*) imitation; **perlas de ~** imitation pearls **3.** (*parodia*) impression

imitado, -a *adj* **1.** (*copiado*) imitated **2.** (*falso*) imitation

imitador(a) *m(f)* (*copista*) imitator; (*parodista*) impersonator

imitar *vt* to imitate, to copy; (*parodiar*) to impersonate; **~ una firma** to forge a signature; (*asemejarse*) to imitate

impaciencia *f* impatience

impacientar **I.** *vt* to make impatient **II.** *vr:* **~se** to become impatient

impaciente *adj* impatient; **estamos ~s por empezar** we are eager to start

impactar *vt* **1.** (*un acontecimiento*) to make an impact **2.** (*un proyectil*) to strike

impacto *m* **1.** (*choque de un proyectil*) impact; (*huella*) damage; *fig* repercussions *pl* **2.** *AmL* (*en el boxeo*) punch **3.** (*golpe emocional*) shock, impact; **~ (medio)ambiental** environmental impact **4.** INFOR hit

impagable *adj* **1.** (*no pagable*) unpayable **2.** (*inapreciable*) priceless

impago *m* non-payment; **~ de impuestos** non-payment of taxes

impalpable *adj* **1.** (*intocable, intangible*) impalpable **2.** (*sutil*) tenuous

impar **I.** *adj* **1.** (*número, sin par*) odd **2.** ANAT single **3.** (*sin igual*) unique, peerless **II.** *m* odd number

imparable *adj* unstoppable

imparcial *adj* **1.** (*sin tomar partido, justo*) impartial **2.** (*sin prejuicios*) unbiased

imparcialidad *f* (*falta de parcialidad, de prevención*) impartiality, fairness

impartir *vt* **1.** (*dar, comunicar*) to give **2.** (*conferir*) to impart *form*

impasibilidad *f* impassiveness

impasible *adj* impassive

impavidez *f* sangfroid, intrepidness

impávido, -a *adj* self-possessed, intrepid

impecable *adj* **1.** *ser* (*correcto*) impeccable **2.** *estar* (*nuevo*) **el motor del coche está ~** the car's engine is in perfect condition

impedido, -a **I.** *adj* disabled; **estar ~ para algo** to be incapacitated for sth **II.** *m, f* disabled person

impedimento *m* **1.** (*que imposibilita algo*) restraint **2.** (*obstáculo*) impediment, hindrance; (*acerca del matrimonio*) impediment **3.** MED handicap

impedir *irr como pedir vt* **1.** (*imposibilitar*) to prevent, to keep from **2.** (*obstaculizar*) to impede, to hinder **3.** (*estorbar*) to impede

impeler *vt* **1.** (*empujar, impulsar*) to impel, to drive **2.** (*incitar*) to urge; **fue impelido a robar por sus amigos** he was pushed into stealing by his friends

impenetrabilidad *f* **1.** (*inaccesibilidad, incomprensibilidad*) impenetrability **2.** (*impermeabilidad*) imperviousness

impenetrable *adj* **1.** (*inaccesible, incomprensible*) impenetrable **2.** (*impermeable*) impervious

impenitencia *f* impenitence

impenitente *adj* (*empedernido*) impenitent; (*incorregible*) incorrigible

impensable *adj* unthinkable

impensado, -a *adj* **1.** (*repentino*) sudden **2.** (*imprevisto*) unforeseen; (*inesperado*) unexpected

impepinable *adj inf* unquestionable

imperar *vi* to reign; *fig* to prevail

imperativo *m* **1.** LING imperative **2.** *pl* (*necesidad*) imperative

imperativo, -a *adj* **1.** (*autoritario*) imperative; (*imperioso*) imperious **2.** (*exigente*) demanding; (*obligatorio*) imperative

imperceptible *adj* **1.** (*inapreciable*) imperceptible **2.** (*minúsculo*) minute

imperdible **I.** *adj* unlosable **II.** *m* safety pin

imperdonable *adj* unpardonable, inexcusable

imperecedero, -a *adj* imperishable; *fig* everlasting

imperfección *f* imperfection, flaw

imperfecto *m* LING imperfect

imperfecto, -a *adj* imperfect, flawed

imperial *adj* imperial

imperialismo *m* POL imperialism

impericia *f* **1.** (*ineptitud*) inaptitude **2.** (*inexperiencia*) inexperience **3.** (*torpeza*) ineptitude

imperio *m* **1.** (*territorio*) empire; *t. fig* realm **2.** (*mandato*) reign **3.** (*autoridad*) sovereignty **4.** (*altanería*) imperiousness

imperioso, -a *adj* **1.** (*autoritario*) imperious **2.** (*urgente, forzoso*) imperative

impermeabilidad *f* impermeability

impermeabilizar <z→c> *vt* **1.** (*un tejido*) to waterproof **2.** (*una abertura*) to make watertight

impermeable **I.** *adj* impermeable **II.** *m* raincoat

impersonal *adj t.* LING impersonal

impertérrito, -a *adj* (*impávido*) imperturbable; (*sin miedo*) fearless

impertinencia *f* **1.** (*insolencia, descaro*) impertinence, impudence **2.** (*inoportunidad*) inappropriateness

impertinente **I.** *adj* **1.** (*insolente, descarado*) impertinent, impudent **2.** (*inoportuno*) inopportune **3.** (*pesado*) exacting **II.** *mf* impertinent person

imperturbabilidad *f* imperturbability

imperturbable *adj* imperturbable

ímpetu *m* **1.** (*vehemencia*) vehemence **2.** (*brío*) impetus, energy **3.** (*violencia*) impetus, force

impetuosidad *f* impetuousity

impetuoso, -a *adj* **1.** (*temperamento*) impetuous **2.** (*movimiento*) hasty; (*fuerza*) vehement **3.** (*acto*) impetuous, rash

impiedad *f* **1.** (*falta de fe*) impiety **2.** (*de piedad*) pitilessness

impío, -a **I.** *adj* **1.** (*irreligioso, irrespetuoso*) impious **2.** (*inclemente*) pitiless **II.** *m, f* non-believer, infidel

implacable *adj* **1.** (*imposible de ablandar*) implacable **2.** (*riguroso*) relentless

implantación *f* **1.** MED implant **2.** (*introducción*) implantation **3.** (*asentamiento*) settlement **4.** (*generalización*) establishment

implantar **I.** *vt* **1.** *t.* MED to implant **2.** (*asentar*) to establish **3.** (*instituir*) to found, to institute **4.** (*introducir*) to introduce **II.** *vr:* **~se** to become established

implementar *vt AmL* **1.** (*un método*) to introduce **2.** (*un plan*) to implement; (*una orden, un deber*) to carry out

implemento *m AmL* (*utensilio*) tool; (*accesorio*) implement; **~s agrícolas** farming equipment

implicación *f* **1.** (*inclusión*) inclusion **2.** (*en un delito*) implication **3.** (*consecuencia*) implications *pl* **4.** (*significado*) significance

implicar <c→qu> **I.** *vt* **1.** (*incluir*) to involve **2.** (*significar*) to imply; **eso implica que...** this means that ... **II.** *vr:* **~se** to be [*o* become] involved

implícito, -a *adj* **1.** (*incluido*) implicit **2.** (*sobreentendido*) understood **3.** (*tácito*) tacit

implorar *vt* (*a alguien*) to implore; (*algo*) to beg; **~ (el) perdón** to beg forgiveness

impoluto, -a *adj* immaculate

imponderable *adj* imponderable

imponderables *mpl* imponderables *pl*

imponente **I.** *adj* **1.** (*impresionante*) imposing **2.** (*que infunde respeto*) awesome **3.** (*inmenso*) enormous; (*grandioso*) grand **4.** *inf* (*atractivo*) gorgeous **II.** *mf* FIN depositor

imponer *irr como poner* **I.** *vt* **1.** (*idea, sanciones*) to impose; **~ a** [*o* **sobre**] **alguien** (*carga, impuestos*) to impose on [*o* upon] sb

2. (*nombre*) to give **3.** (*respeto*) to command **4.** FIN to levy, to tax; (*invertir*) to deposit **II.** *vi* to impress **III.** *vr:* **~se** **1.** (*hacerse necesario*) to become necessary; (*hacerse ineludible*) to become unavoidable **2.** (*hacerse obedecer*) **se impuso a los demás** he/she made his/her authority felt **3.** (*prevalecer*) **~se a algo** to prevail over sth **4.** (*tomar como obligación*) **me impuse una hora de ejercicio diario** I imposed an hour's daily exercise on myself

imponible *adj* **1.** FIN taxable; **no ~** tax free, tax exempt *Am* **2.** (*importación*) dutiable **3.** *inf* (*ropa*) unwearable

impopular *adj* unpopular

impopularidad *f* unpopularity

importación *f* **1.** (*acción*) importation **2.** (*producto*) import

importador(a) **I.** *adj* importing **II.** *m(f)* importer

importancia *f* **1.** (*interés*) importance; **sin ~** unimportant; **restar** [*o* **quitar**] **~ a algo** to play sth down **2.** (*extensión*) scope, magnitude **3.** (*trascendencia*) significance **4.** (*prestigio, influencia*) importance; **se daba ~ ante los demás** he gave himself airs in front of everyone else

importante *adj* **1.** (*de gran interés*) important; **lo ~ es** *+infin* the important thing is *+infin* **2.** (*dimensión*) considerable **3.** (*cantidad*) significant **4.** (*calidad*) high **5.** (*situación*) good **6.** (*persona influyente*) important

importar **I.** *vt* **1.** (*mercancía*) to import **2.** (*precio*) to cost, to amount to; (*valer*) to be worth **3.** (*traer consigo*) to imply, to involve **II.** *vi* to matter, to mind; **no importa la hora que sea** it doesn't matter what time it is; **¿a ti qué te importa?** what has it got to do with you?; **¿te importa esperar?** do you mind waiting?; **me importa un pepino** *inf* I couldn't care less

importe *m* (*cuantía*) value; (*total*) amount

importunar *vt* (*incomodar, molestar*) to pester, to importune *form*

importunidad *f* **1.** (*incomodidad, molestia*) importunity **2.** (*indiscreción*) tactlessness

importuno, -a *adj* **1.** (*incómodo, molesto*) importunate **2.** (*indiscreto*) tactless **3.** (*inoportuno*) inopportune

imposibilidad *f* impossibility

imposibilitado, -a *adj* **1.** (*impedido*) disabled; (*paralítico*) paralytic **2.** (*de acudir*) **el despegue se vio ~ por la niebla** the take-off was impeded by the fog

imposibilitar *vt* (*impedir*) to impede, to make impossible; (*evitar*) to prevent

imposible **I.** *adj* **1.** (*irrealizable*) impossible **2.** *inf* (*insoportable*) impossible, unbearable **3.** *AmL* (*repugnante*) horrid **II.** *m* **lo ~** the impossible

imposición *f* **1.** (*de una carga, condena, condiciones*) imposition **2.** (*de impuestos*) taxation **3.** (*de un nombre*) giving **4.** REL **~ de manos** laying-on of hands **5.** FIN deposit

impositiva *f AmL* tax office

impositivo, -a *adj* **1.** FIN tax **2.** *CSur* (*imperativo*) imperative

impostergable *adj* that cannot be postponed

impostor(a) **I.** *adj* **1.** (*difamador*) slanderous **2.** (*tramposo*) fraudulent **II.** *m(f)* **1.** (*difamador*) slanderer **2.** (*tramposo*) impostor, imposter

impostura *f* **1.** (*calumnia*) slander **2.** (*trampa*) imposture, fraud

impotencia *f* **1.** (*falta de poder*) *t.* MED impotence **2.** (*incapacidad*) incapacity **3.** (*indefensión*) helplessness

impotente *adj* **1.** (*sin poder*) impotent, powerless **2.** (*incapaz*) incapable **3.** (*desvalido*) helpless **4.** MED impotent

impracticable *adj* **1.** (*irrealizable*) unfeasible **2.** (*intransitable*) impassable

imprecación *f* curse, imprecation *form*

imprecar <c→qu> *vt* to curse, to imprecate *form*

imprecisión *f* **1.** (*falta de precisión*) inexactness **2.** (*falta de determinación*) vagueness

impreciso, -a *adj* **1.** (*no preciso*) imprecise **2.** (*indefinido*) vague

impredecible *adj* unpredictable; (*suceso*) unforeseeable

impregnar **I.** *vt* **1.** (*empapar, un tejido*) to impregnate, to saturate **2.** (*penetrar*) to penetrate **3.** (*influir*) **el derecho romano impregna nuestras leyes** Roman law influences our laws **II.** *vr:* **~se** to become impregnated

impremeditado, -a *adj* **1.** (*impensado*) unpremeditated **2.** (*irreflexivo*) unintentional **3.** (*involuntario*) inadvertent

imprenta *f* **1.** (*técnica, arte*) printing **2.** (*taller*) printer's **3.** (*impresión*) print **4.** BIO **~ genética** genetic imprint **5.** (*máquina*) press

imprescindible *adj* (*ineludible*) essential; (*obligatorio*) necessary; (*insustituible*) indispensable

impresentable **I.** *adj* unpresentable **II.** *mf* embarrassment

impresión *f* **1.** (*huella*) imprint **2.** TIPO printing, impression **3.** INFOR print-out **4.** FOTO print **5.** (*grabación*) recording **6.** (*sensación, opinión*) impression; **cambiar impresiones** to compare notes

impresionable *adj* **1.** (*fácil de impresionar*) impressionable **2.** (*sensible*) susceptible **3.** TIPO, INFOR printable

impresionante *adj* **1.** (*emocionante, de gran efecto*) impressive, striking **2.** (*magnífico*) magnificent

impresionar **I.** *vt* **1.** (*emocionar, inculcar*) to impress; (*conmover*) to move **2.** FOTO to print **3.** (*grabar*) to cut **II.** *vr:* **~se** (*emocionarse*) to be impressed; (*conmoverse*) to be moved

impresionismo *m* ARTE impressionism

impreso *m* **1.** (*hoja*) sheet **2.** (*formulario*) form **3.** (*envío*) printed matter; **~ publicitario** leaflet, flyer *Am*

I

impreso, **-a** *pp de* **imprimir**
impresor, **-a** I. *adj* printing II. *m, f* printer
impresora *f* INFOR printer; ~ **de inyección de tinta** ink-jet printer; ~ **láser** laser printer
imprevisible *adj* unforeseeable; (*persona*) unpredictable
imprevisión *f* 1. (*despreocupación*) thoughtlessness; (*descuido*) carelessness 2. (*ligereza*) imprudence
imprevisto *m* 1. (*algo inesperado*) contingency, sth unexpected 2. *pl* (*gastos*) unexpected expenses
imprevisto, **-a** *adj* (*no previsto*) unforeseen; (*inesperado*) unexpected
imprimir *irr vt* 1. TIPO, INFOR to print 2. (*editar*) to publish 3. (*reproducir*) to reproduce 4. *t. fig* (*un sello*) to stamp 5. (*inculcar*) to instil
improbabilidad *f* improbability, unlikelihood
improbable *adj* improbable, unlikely
ímprobo, **-a** *adj* 1. *elev* (*inmoral*) immoral 2. (*esfuerzo*) huge, tremendous; (*trabajo*) mammoth
improcedente *adj* 1. (*inoportuno*) inopportune; (*extemporáneo*) ill-timed 2. (*inadecuado*) inappropriate 3. (*antirreglamentario*) irregular; JUR inadmissable
improductividad *f* 1. (*falta de productividad, rendimiento*) unproductiveness 2. (*falta de rentabilidad*) unprofitability
improductivo, **-a** *adj* 1. (*no productivo, sin rendimiento*) unproductive 2. (*antieconómico*) unprofitable
impronta *f* 1. (*impresión*) impression 2. (*molde*) mould *Brit,* mold *Am* 3. *fig* mark
impronunciable *adj* unpronounceable
improperio *m* (*ofensa*) offense; (*insulto*) insult
impropiedad *f* 1. (*inexactitud en el lenguaje*) impropriety; (*incorrección*) incorrectness 2. (*inoportunidad*) inappropriateness 3. (*ineptitud*) ineptitude
impropio, **-a** *adj* 1. (*inoportuno*) improper, unfitting; **ese comportamiento es ~ en él** that behaviour is not usual in [*o* not worthy of] him 2. (*inadecuado*) inappropriate
improrrogable *adj* 1. (*no prolongable*) non-extendable, non-extendible 2. (*no aplazable*) that cannot be postponed
improvisación *f* improvisation
improvisado, **-a** *adj* impromptu, improvised
improvisar *vt* to improvise; *inf* TEAT to ad-lib
improviso, **-a** *adj* unexpected; **de ~** unexpectedly; **coger a alguien de ~** to surprise sb
imprudencia *f* 1. (*irreflexión, descuido*) imprudence, carelessness 2. JUR negligence; **~ temeraria** criminal negligence; (*conducir*) reckless driving
imprudente *adj* 1. (*irreflexivo*) imprudent; (*insensato*) unwise 2. (*incauto*) incautious 3. (*indiscreto*) indiscreet 4. JUR negligent
impudicia *f* (*desvergüenza*) shamelessness
impúdico, **-a** *adj* indecent, immodest; (*obsceno*) lewd
impudor *m* (*desvergüenza*) shamelessness
impuesto *m* FIN tax; ~ **sobre la renta** income tax; ~ **sobre la propiedad** property tax; ~ **sobre el Valor Añadido** Value Added Tax; **libre de ~s** tax-free, duty-free; **sujeto a ~s** taxable, dutiable
impugnación *f* 1. *t.* JUR contest(ation); ~ **de un testamento** probate action 2. (*negación*) refutation 3. (*objeción*) counterargument
impugnar *vt* 1. *t.* JUR to contest 2. (*combatir*) to dispute; (*una teoría*) to challenge
impulsar *vt* 1. (*empujar*) to impel 2. (*incitar*) to incite 3. (*estimular*) to motivate; (*promover*) to instigate
impulsión *f* 1. TÉC drive 2. *elev* (*empuje*) impetus
impulsivo, **-a** I. *adj* impulsive II. *m, f* impulsive person
impulso *m* 1. (*empujón*) push 2. (*estímulo*) impulse, stimulus; ~ **sexual** sex drive 3. (*empuje*) drive 4. FÍS momentum
impulsor(a) I. *adj* **fuerza ~a** driving force II. *m(f)* catalyst
impune *adj* unpunished
impunidad *f* impunity
impureza *f* 1. *t.* REL impurity 2. (*obscenidad*) foulness
impuro, **-a** *adj* 1. *t.* REL impure 2. (*obsceno*) lewd
imputabilidad *f* imputability
imputable *adj* imputable, attributable
imputación *f* 1. (*insinuación*) insinuation 2. (*acusación*) imputation
imputar *vt* 1. (*atribuir*) to impute 2. (*cargar*) to charge 3. COM to impute
inabarcable *adj* impossible to encompass; (*inmenso*) vast
inacabable *adj* never-ending, interminable
inaccesibilidad *f* inaccessibility
inaccesible *adj* 1. (*objeto, razonamiento*) ~ **para alguien** inaccessible to sb 2. (*persona*) inaccessible, unapproachable 3. (*inalcanzable*) beyond one's reach
inacción *f* 1. (*inactividad*) inaction 2. (*ociosidad*) idleness
inaceptable *adj* unacceptable
inactividad *f* 1. (*inacción, de una sustancia*) inactivity; (*desocupación*) unemployment 2. MED inactivity
inactivo, **-a** *adj* 1. (*persona*) inactive; (*desocupado*) jobless 2. (*funcionamiento, sustancia*) *t.* MED inactive 3. (*volcán*) dormant
inadaptable *adj* unadaptable
inadaptación *f* inability to adapt
inadecuación *f* inadequacy
inadecuado, **-a** *adj* inadequate
inadmisible *adj* inadmissible
inadvertencia *f* inadvertence, oversight
inadvertido, **-a** *adj* 1. (*descuidado*) inadvertent; **me cogió ~** it caught me unprepared 2. (*desapercibido*) unnoticed
inagotable *adj* inexhaustible; (*persona*) tire-

less
inaguantable *adj* unbearable, intolerable
inalámbrico, **-a** *adj* TEL cordless, wireless
inalcanzable *adj* unattainable, beyond one's reach
inalienable *adj* inalienable
inalterable *adj* **1.** (*invariable, permanente*) unalterable **2.** (*imperturbable*) impassive
inalterado, **-a** *adj* unchanged
inamovible *adj* fixed, immovable
inanición *f* starvation
inanidad *f* inanity
inanimado, **-a** *adj,* **inánime** *adj* inanimate
inapelable *adj* **1.** JUR unappealable, not open to appeal **2.** (*inevitable*) definitive
inapetencia *f* loss [*o* lack] of appetite
inaplazable *adj* **1.** (*impostergable*) that can't be postponed, undeferable **2.** (*urgente*) urgent, pressing
inaplicable *adj* inapplicable
inapreciable *adj* **1.** (*imperceptible*) inappreciable **2.** (*de gran valor*) priceless
inaprensible *adj* **1.** (*inasible*) elusive **2.** (*incomprensible*) incomprehensible
inasequible *adj* out of reach; **esa casa es ~ para nuestro bolsillo** that house is beyond our means
inaudible *adj* inaudible
inaudito, **-a** *adj* **1.** (*sin precedente*) unprecedented **2.** (*vituperable*) outrageous
inauguración *f* **1.** (*puente, exposición*) opening **2.** (*estatua*) unveiling **3.** (*comienzo*) inauguration
inaugural *adj* inaugural
inaugurar *vt* **1.** (*puente*) to open **2.** (*estatua*) to unveil **3.** (*comenzar*) to inaugurate
inca *adj, m* Inca

> The **incas** were a small Indian tribe, who lived in **Perú**. In the 15th century, however, they expanded their empire, which ultimately covered present-day Colombia, Ecuador, Peru and Bolivia, and extended south into the northern part of Argentina and Chile.

incaico, **-a** *m, f* Inca
incalculable *adj* **1.** (*invalorable, no cuantificable*) incalculable **2.** (*comportamiento*) invaluable
incalificable *adj* **1.** (*indecible*) inexpressible, indescribable **2.** (*reprobable*) reproachable
incanato *m Chile, Perú* HIST Incan period
incandescente *adj* **1.** FÍS (*metal*) incandescent **2.** (*temperamento, pasión*) fiery
incansable *adj* tireless
incapacidad *f* **1.** (*ineptitud*) incompetence **2.** (*psíquica*) incapacity; (*física*) disability **3.** (*falta de abilidad*) inability, incapability
incapacitación *f* (*minusvalía*) *t.* JUR incapacitation
incapacitado, **-a** **I.** *adj* **1.** (*incapaz*) incapacitated **2.** (*incompetente*) incompetent **3.** (*para negocios*) unemployable **II.** *m, f* **1.** (*minusválido*) disabled person **2.** JUR (*para negocios*) incapacitated person
incapacitar *vt* **1.** JUR to disqualify; (*para negocios*) to incapacitate **2.** (*impedir*) to impede
incapaz *adj* **1.** (*inepto*) incapable **2.** JUR (*sin capacidad legal*) incapacitated, incompetent **3.** (*sin talento*) inept
incasable *adj* **1.** (*imposible de casar*) unmarriageable **2.** JUR *unable to marry without legal autorization*
incautación *f* seizure, confiscation
incautarse *vr* **1.** (*confiscar*) **~se de algo** to confiscate sth **2.** (*adueñarse*) **~se de algo** to appropriate sth
incauto, **-a** *adj* **1.** (*sin cautela*) incautious; (*confiado*) credulous **2.** (*ingenuo*) naive
incendiar **I.** *vt* **~ algo** (*sin intención*) to unintentionally set sth on fire; (*intencionalmente*) to set fire to sth, to commit arson **II.** *vr:* **~se** to catch fire
incendiario, **-a** *adj, m, f* incendiary
incendio *m* fire; **~ intencionado** arson
incentivar *vt* to motivate, to offer incentives to
incentivo *m* incentive
incertidumbre *f* **1.** (*inseguridad*) incertitude **2.** (*duda*) incertitude, uncertainty
incesante *adj* incessant
incesto *m* incest
incestuoso, **-a** *adj* incestuous
incidencia *f* **1.** *t.* MAT incidence **2.** (*consecuencia*) repercussion **3.** (*efecto*) impact
incidente **I.** *adj* incidental **II.** *m* incident
incidir *vi* **1.** (*consecuencias*) **~ en algo** to impinge on [*o* affect] sth **2.** *elev* (*falta*) **~ en un error** to fall into error **3.** FÍS to incise; **~ en algo** to incise in sth **4.** (*tema*) **~ en algo** to touch on sth **5.** MED **~ en algo** to make an incision in sth
incienso *m* incense
incierto, **-a** *adj* (*dudoso*) doubtful, uncertain; (*falso*) untrue
incineración *f* incineration; (*de personas*) cremation
incinerador *m* **1.** TÉC incinerator **2.** (*para cadáveres*) crematorium
incinerador(a) *adj* **1.** TÉC incinerating **2.** (*para cadáveres*) crematory
incineradora *f* **1.** *v.* **incinerador(a)** **2.** (*para basuras*) incinerator
incinerar *vt* **1.** TÉC to incinerate **2.** (*cadáveres*) to cremate
incipiente *adj* incipient
incisión *f t.* MED incision
inciso *m* **1.** TIPO subsection **2.** LING (*paréntesis*) parenthesis; (*coma*) comma **3.** (*al relatar*) aside **4.** (*en documentos*) interpolation
incitación *f* **1.** (*instigación*) incitement **2.** (*ánimo*) animation
incitante *adj* **1.** (*instigador*) inciting **2.** (*que anima*) animating
incitar *vt* **1.** (*instigar*) to incite **2.** (*animar*) to

animate
incívico, **-a** *adj* antisocial
incivil *adj*, **incivilizado**, **-a** *adj* 1. (*inculto*) uncivilised 2. (*rudo*) uncivil
inclemencia *f* 1. (*falta de clemencia*) inclemency, unmercifulness 2. (*clima*) inclemency; (*invierno*) harshness; (*paisaje*) bleakness; **las ~s del tiempo** the inclemency of the weather
inclinación *f* 1. (*declive*) slope 2. (*reverencia, con la cabeza*) bow 3. (*afecto*) ~ **por alguien/algo** inclination for [*o* to] sb/sth 4. (*tendencias*) propensity, tendency
inclinado, **-a** *adj* 1. (*ángulo, de cuerpo*) inclined 2. (*dispuesto*) ~ **a algo** inclined to [*o* towards] sth
inclinar I. *vt* to incline II. *vr:* **~se** 1. (*reverencia*) to bow; (*árboles*) to bend 2. (*propender*) to incline 3. (*preferir*) **~se por algo** to have a penchant for sth
incluir *irr como huir vt* 1. (*comprender, contener*) to include, to enclose, to contain; **todo incluido** all-inclusive 2. (*formar parte*) to include
inclusa *f* ≈ orphanage (*home for abandoned children*)
inclusión *f* inclusion; **con ~ de...** with the inclusion of
inclusive *adv* inclusively
incluso I. *adv* inclusively II. *prep* including; **habéis aprobado todos, ~ tú** you have all passed, even you
incluso, **-a** *adj* included
incoar *vt* 1. (*comenzar*) to initiate 2. JUR (*proceso*) to institute proceedings
incógnita *f* 1. MAT (*magnitud*) variable 2. (*enigma*) enigma; (*secreto*) secret; **despejar la ~** (*enigma*) to solve the enigma; (*secreto*) to disclose the secret
incógnito, **-a** *adj* incognito
incoherencia *f* incoherence
incoherente *adj* incoherent
incoloro, **-a** *adj* colourless *Brit*, colorless *Am*
incólume *adj* intact, unscathed
incombustible *adj* incombustible
incomible *adj* inedible, uneatable
incomodar I. *vt* to inconvenience, to incommode *form* II. *vr:* **~se** 1. (*molestarse*) **no te incomodes, que abro yo** don't trouble yourself, I'll open the door 2. *CSur* (*enfadarse*) to become angry
incomodidad *f*, **incomodo** *m* 1. (*inconfortable*) uncomfortableness, discomfort 2. (*molestia*) inconvenience, uneasiness
incómodo, **-a** *adj* 1. (*inconfortable*) uncomfortable; **estar ~** to be uncomfortable 2. (*molesto*) tiresome
incomparable *adj* incomparable
incompatibilidad *f* incompatibility; **~ de oficios** job incompatibility
incompatible *adj* incompatible
incompetencia *f* incompetence
incompetente *adj* incompetent
incompleto, **-a** *adj* incomplete
incomprensible *adj* 1. (*no inteligible*) incomprehensible 2. (*inexplicable*) inexplicable
incomprensión *f* 1. (*no querer comprender*) unwillingness to understand 2. (*no poder comprender*) incomprehension
incomunicación *f* 1. (*aislamiento*) isolation 2. (*en prisión*) solitary confinement 3. (*falta de comunicación*) lack of communication
incomunicado, **-a** *adj* 1. (*aislado*) incommunicado 2. (*en prisión*) **el preso estuvo 6 días ~** the prisoner spent 6 days in solitary confinement
incomunicar <c→qu> *vt* 1. (*aislar*) to isolate 2. (*bloquear*) to cut off
inconcebible *adj* 1. (*inimaginable*) inconceivable 2. (*inadmisible*) unacceptable
inconciliable *adj* irreconcilable
inconcluso, **-a** *adj* unfinished
inconcreción *f* imprecision
inconcreto, **-a** *adj* imprecise
incondicional I. *adj* unconditional II. *mf* 1. (*amigo*) faithful [*o* steadfast] friend 2. (*servil*) devoted person, yes man *pej*
inconexo, **-a** *adj* unconnected
inconformista *mf* nonconformist
inconfundible *adj* unmistakable
incongruencia *f* (*incoherencia*) incongruity
incongruente *adj* (*contradictorio*) incongruous
inconmensurable *adj* 1. (*que no puede medirse*) incommensurate 2. (*enorme*) immense
inconmovible *adj* 1. (*cosas*) immutable 2. (*personas*) steadfast
inconsciencia *f* 1. (*desmayo*) unconsciousness 2. (*insensatez*) senselessness; (*irresponsabilidad*) thoughtlessness; (*ignorancia*) unawareness
inconsciente *adj* 1. *estar* (*desmayado*) unconscious 2. *ser* (*insensato*) senseless; (*irresponsable*) thoughtless; (*ignorante*) unaware 3. *ser* (*gesto*) involuntary
inconsistencia *f* flimsiness
inconsistente *adj* 1. (*irregular*) uneven 2. (*poco sólido*) flimsy; (*argumento*) weak
inconsolable *adj* inconsolable, broken-hearted
inconstancia *f* inconstancy
inconstante *adj* 1. (*irregular*) inconstant 2. (*caprichoso*) changeable
inconstitucionalidad *f* unconstitutionality
incontable *adj* 1. (*innumerable*) countless 2. (*inenarrable*) unmentionable; LING uncountable
incontenible *adj* 1. (*irrefrenable*) unrestrainable 2. (*fuera de control*) uncontrollable 3. (*risa, júbilo, impulso*) irrepressible
incontestable *adj* 1. (*innegable*) incontestable 2. (*pregunta*) unanswerable
incontinencia *f t.* MED incontinence
incontrolado, **-a** I. *adj* 1. (*que no puede controlarse*) uncontrolled 2. (*que no puede verifi-*

carse) unverified **3.** (*violento*) violent **II.** *m, f* unruly [*o* uncontrolled] person

incontrovertible *adj* incontrovertible

inconveniencia *f* **1.** (*descortesía*) discourtesy **2.** (*disparate*) absurd remark **3.** (*no adecuado*) inappropriateness

inconveniente **I.** *adj* **1.** (*descortés*) discourteous; (*disparate*) absurd **2.** (*no adecuado*) inappropriate **3.** (*no aconsejable*) unadvisable **II.** *m* **1.** (*desventaja*) disadvantage **2.** (*obstáculo*) inconvenience

incordiar *vt* to bother; **¡deja de ~!** stop being so irritating!

incordio *m inf* (*molestia*) bother, pest

incorporación *f* **1.** (*al enderezarse*) straightening up; (*al sentarse*) sitting up **2.** (*integración, en un equipo*) incorporation; **~ a filas** MIL induction

incorporar **I.** *vt* **1.** (*a un grupo*) **~ a** [*o* **en**] **algo** to incorporate in [*o* into] sth **2.** (*a una persona*) to include **II.** *vr:* **~se** **1.** (*enderezarse*) to sit up **2.** (*en el trabajo*) **mañana me incorporo al nuevo trabajo** tomorrow I start my new job **3.** (*agregarse*) **~se a** [*o* **en**] **algo** to join sth **4.** MIL (*a filas*) to join up

incorrección *f* **1.** (*no correcto*) inaccuracy **2.** (*falta*) error, mistake **3.** (*descortesía*) discourtesy

incorrecto, -a *adj* **1.** (*erróneo*) erroneous **2.** (*descortés*) impolite

incorregible *adj* incorrigible

incorruptible *adj* incorruptible

incorrupto, -a *adj* **1.** (*personas*) undefiled **2.** (*cosas*) uncorrupted

incredibilidad *f* unbelievability

incredulidad *f* **1.** (*desconfianza*) incredulity **2.** REL (*sin fe*) lack of faith

incrédulo, -a **I.** *adj* **1.** (*desconfiado*) incredulous **2.** REL (*sin fe*) unbelieving **II.** *m, f* **1.** (*desconfiado*) incredulous person **2.** REL (*sin fe*) unbeliever; (*escéptico*) sceptic *Brit,* skeptic *Am*

increíble *adj* incredible

incrementar **I.** *vt* to increase; (*intensificar*) to intensify **II.** *vr:* **~se** to increase

incremento *m* **1.** (*aumento*) increment **2.** (*crecimiento*) increase

increpar *vt* to rebuke

incriminar *vt* JUR to incriminate

incruento, -a *adj* bloodless

incrustación *f* **1.** (*proceso*) embedding **2.** ARTE inlaying **3.** MED incrustation **4.** (*costra*) incrustation

incrustar **I.** *vt* ARTE (*con madera*) to inlay **II.** *vr:* **~se** **1.** (*introducirse*) to embed itself **2.** MED to encrust

incubación *f* incubation (period)

incubadora *f* incubator

incubar *vt, vr:* **~se** to incubate

incuestionable *adj* unquestionable

inculcar <c→qu> **I.** *vt* **1.** (*enseñar*) to instil, to instill *Am;* **~ a sus hijos la fe religiosa** to instill [*o* to inculcate] the religious beliefs in [*o* into] his children **2.** (*infundir*) to inculcate; **el nuevo entrenador ha inculcado un espíritu nuevo en el equipo** the new coach has inculcated the team with a new spirit **II.** *vr:* **~se** to be obstinate; **~ en algo** to be obstinate about sth

inculpación *f* accusation

inculpar *vt* **~ a alguien de algo** to accuse sb of sth; JUR to charge sb with sth

inculto, -a *adj* **1.** (*sin instrucción*) uneducated **2.** (*comportamiento*) unrefined, uncouth **3.** AGR (*sin cultivar*) uncultivated

incultura *f* lack of education [*o* culture]

incumbencia *f* responsibility, incumbency *form;* **no es de tu ~** it's none of your business

incumbir *vi* **1.** (*atañer*) to concern **2.** ADMIN (*ser de la competencia*) **~ a alguien** to be incumbent on [*o* upon] sb

incumplimiento *m* non-compliance; **~ de contrato** breach of contract

incumplir *vt* to break, to fail to fulfil [*o* fulfill *Am*]

incurable **I.** *adj* **1.** (*enfermedad*) incurable **2.** (*sin esperanza*) hopeless **II.** *mf* incurable person

incurrir *vi* **1.** (*situación mala*) **incurrió en el desprecio de su jefe** he brought on his boss's scorn; **~ en una falta** to commit an error; **~ en viejas costumbres** to go back to old habits **2.** (*odio*) to incur

incursión *f* incursion, strike

indagación *f* investigation, enquiry *Brit,* inquiry *Am*

indagar <g→gu> *vt* **~ algo** to investigate, to look into sth

indebido, -a *adj* **1.** (*cantidades*) wrong **2.** (*injusto*) wrongful; (*ilícito*) illicit; **respuesta indebida** inappropriate reply

indecencia *f* **1.** (*persona*) indecency; (*obscenidad*) obscenity **2.** (*acción*) indecency, outrage; (*dicho*) unseemliness

indecente *adj* **1.** (*inadecuado*) improper **2.** (*obsceno*) indecent; (*sin vergüenza*) shameless **3.** (*guarro*) filthy, indecent

indecisión *f* **1.** (*irresolución*) iresolution **2.** (*vacilación*) hesitation, indecision

indeciso, -a *adj* **1.** (*irresoluto*) irresolute **2.** (*que vacila*) indecisive **3.** (*resultado*) inconclusive

indecoroso, -a *adj* **1.** (*indecente*) indecent **2.** (*incorrecto*) indecorous

indefendible *adj* indefensible

indefensión *f* defencelessness *Brit,* defenselessness *Am*

indefenso, -a *adj* defenceless *Brit,* defenseless *Am*

indefinible *adj* indefinable, undefinable

indefinidamente *adv* indefinitely

indefinido, -a *adj t.* LING indefinite

indeformable *adj* that keeps its shape

indelicadeza *f* **1.** (*vulgaridad*) vulgarity **2.** (*desconsideración*) indelicacy

indelicado, -a *adj* indelicate

indemne *adj* **1.** (*persona*) unharmed **2.** (*cosa*) undamaged
indemnización *f* indemnity, indemnification; ~ **de despido** unemployment compensation, severance pay
indemnizar <z→c> *vt* **1.** (*daños y perjuicios*) to indemnify; ~ **de** [*o* **por**] **algo** to indemnify for sth **2.** (*gastos*) to reimburse
independencia *f* independence; **con ~ de algo** independently of sth
independentismo *m* POL independence movement
independiente *adj* **1.** (*libre*) independent; **un piso ~** an individual flat **2.** (*profesión, sin partido*) independent **3.** (*soltero*) single
independización *f* (*liberación*) liberation; (*adolescente*) emancipation
independizar <z→c> **I.** *vt* to make independent **II.** *vr:* **~se 1.** (*liberarse*) to become independent **2.** (*adolescente*) to become independent [*o* emancipated]
indescifrable *adj* indecipherable
indescriptible *adj* indescribable
indeseable I. *adj* undesirable **II.** *mf* undesirable [*o* despised] person
indestructible *adj* indestructible
indeterminación *f* **1.** (*inconcreción*) indeterminacy **2.** (*indecisión*) indecision
indeterminado, **-a** *adj* **1.** (*inconcreto*) indeterminate **2.** (*indeciso*) indecisive
indexación *f* **1.** indexation **2.** INFOR indexing
indexar *vt* INFOR to index
India *f* **la ~** India; **las ~s** the Indies
indiada *f AmL: a group of Indians*
indicación *f* **1.** (*señal*) indication; (*por escrito*) observation; **~ de las fuentes** source reference **2.** MED (*síntoma*) symptom; (*en recetas*) directions *pl* **3.** (*consejo*) advice; **por ~ de...** on the advice of ... **4.** *pl* (*instrucciones*) instructions *pl*
indicado, **-a** *adj* **1.** (*aconsejable*) advisable; (*adecuado*) indicated; **eso es lo más ~** that is the most suitable **2.** MED (*tratamiento*) recommended
indicador *m* indicator; TÉC gauge, gage *Am;* ECON index; **~ de carretera** roadsign; **~ de gasolina** fuel gauge [*o* gage *Am*]
indicar <c→qu> *vt* **1.** TÉC (*aparato*) to register **2.** (*señalar, sugerir*) to indicate; (*mostrar*) to show **3.** MED to prescribe
indicativo, **-a** *adj t.* LING indicative
índice *m* **1.** (*biblioteca, catálogo*) index, catalogue, catalog *Am;* (*libro*) table of contents **2.** (*dedo*) index finger, forefinger **3.** (*estadísticas*) rate; **~ de audiencia** audience ratings; **~ de paro** unemployment rate; **~ de Precios al Consumidor** Retail Price Index **4.** TÉC pointer; (*de reloj*) hand
indicio *m* **1.** (*señal*) sign **2.** JUR indication **3.** (*vestigio*) trace
indiferencia *f* indifference
indiferente *adj* indifferent; **me es ~** it doesn't make any difference to me
indígena I. *adj* indigenous, native; (*en Latinoamérica*) Latin American **II.** *mf* native; (*en Latinoamérica*) Latin American
indigencia *f* poverty
indigente I. *adj* destitute **II.** *mf* destitute person
indigestar I. *vt* to cause indigestion to **II.** *vr:* **~se 1.** (*empacharse*) **~se de** [*o* **por**] **algo** to get indigestion from sth **2.** *inf* (*hacerse antipático*) to be detestable **3.** *AmL* (*inquietarse*) to worry
indigestión *f* MED indigestion; **contraer una ~** to get indigestion
indigesto, **-a** *adj ser* indigestible, hard to digest
indignación *f* indignation
indignado, **-a** *adj* **~ por algo** indignant about [*o* at] sth
indignante *adj* infuriating, outrageous
indignar I. *vt* to infuriate, to outrage **II.** *vr* **~se por algo** to become indignant [*o* infuriated] about sth
indignidad *f* indignity
indigno, **-a** *adj* **1.** (*desmerecedor*) unworthy; **~ de confianza** unworthy of trust **2.** (*vil*) contemptible
índigo *m* indigo
indio, **-a I.** *adj* **1.** (*de la India*) Indian **2.** (*de América*) American Indian **II.** *m, f* **1.** (*de la India*) Indian **2.** (*de América*) American Indian ▶**hacer el ~** (*tonterías*) to fool around [*o* about]; (*el ridículo*) to act the fool
indirecta *f inf* hint, insinuation; **lanzar** [*o* **soltar**] **una ~** to drop a hint
indirecto, **-a** *adj* indirect; **complemento ~** LING indirect object
indisciplina *f* indiscipline, lack of discipline
indisciplinado, **-a I.** *adj* (*falto de disciplina*) undisciplined; (*desobediente*) disobedient; (*insumiso*) insubordinate **II.** *m, f* (*desobediente*) disobedient person; (*insumiso*) insubordinate person
indiscreción *f* **1.** (*no guardar un secreto*) indiscretion **2.** (*observación*) faux pas, gaffe **3.** (*curiosidad*) nosiness
indiscreto, **-a** *adj* **1.** (*imprudente*) imprudent **2.** (*que no guarda secretos*) indiscreet
indiscriminado, **-a** *adj* indiscriminate
indiscutible *adj* indisputable
indisociable *adj* inseparable; QUÍM indissoluble
indispensable *adj* indispensable; **lo** (**más**) **~** the most essential; **el requisito ~ es...** the key requisite is ...
indisponer *irr como poner* **I.** *vt* **1.** (*enemistar*) **~ a uno contra otro** to set one person against another **2.** (*de salud*) to indispose **II.** *vr:* **~se 1.** (*enemistarse*) to quarrel **2.** (*ponerse mal*) to become indisposed
indisposición *f* (*de salud, desgana*) indisposition
indispuesto, **-a** *adj* **1.** (*enfermizo, con desgana*) indisposed **2.** (*enemistado*) at odds

3. (*reacio*) unwilling
indistintamente *adv* **1.** (*indiscriminadamente*) indiscriminately; **se aplica a todos los niños** ~ it applies to all the children without distinction **2.** (*irreconocible*) indistinctly
indistinto, -a *adj* **1.** *elev* (*indiferenciado*) undifferentiated **2.** (*igual*) indistinguishable **3.** (*difuso*) vague; (*poco claro*) indistinct
individual *adj* **1.** (*personal*) personal; (*peculiar*) individual **2.** (*simple*) single **3.** *CSur* (*idéntico*) identical
individualista **I.** *adj* individualistic **II.** *mf* individualist
individualizar <z→c> *vt* to individualize; (*diferenciar*) to single out
individuo *m* **1.** (*espécimen*) individual **2.** (*miembro*) member **3.** *pey* (*sujeto*) individual, character
indivisible *adj* indivisible
indócil *adj* **1.** (*desobediente*) unruly **2.** (*cabezota*) wilful *Brit*, willful *Am*
indoctrinar *vt AmL* to indoctrinate; *fig* to brainwash
indocumentado, -a *adj* **1.** *ser* (*no registrado*) unregistered **2.** *estar* (*sin documentos*) without papers [*o* means of identification]
índole *f* nature, kind
indolencia *f* **1.** (*apatía*) apathy **2.** (*indiferencia*) indifference **3.** (*desgana*) indolence
indolente *adj* **1.** (*apático*) apathetic **2.** (*indiferente*) indifferent **3.** (*con desgana*) indolent
indomable *adj* **1.** (*que no se somete*) indomitable **2.** (*indomesticable*) untameable **3.** (*fuera de control*) unmanageable
indómito, -a *adj* **1.** (*indomable*) indomitable **2.** (*rebelde*) rebellious
Indonesia *f* Indonesia
indonesio, -a *adj, m, f* Indonesian
inducción *f* **1.** ELEC, FILOS induction **2.** (*instigación*) inducement
inducir *irr como traducir vt* **1.** ELEC (*corriente*) to induce **2.** (*instigar*) to induce; ~ **a error** to lead astray, to mislead **3.** FILOS (*razonar*) to induce; **de todo esto induzco que...** from all this I induce that ...
inductor(a) *adj* **1.** ELEC (*corriente*) inductor **2.** (*instigador*) inducer
indudable *adj* undeniable; **es** ~ **que...** it is certain that ...
indulgencia *f* **1.** REL (*pecados*) indulgence, remission **2.** *elev* (*cualidad*) indulgence; **proceder sin** ~ **contra...** to proceed without leniency against ...
indultar *vt* **1.** JUR (*perdonar*) to pardon; (*después del proceso*) to reprieve; ~ **a alguien de la pena de muerte** to grant sb a reprieve from the death penalty **2.** (*eximir*) to exempt
indulto *m* **1.** (*perdón total*) pardon **2.** (*perdón parcial*) remission **3.** (*exención*) exemption
indumentaria *f* **1.** (*ropa*) clothing, clothes *pl;* (*vestir*) dress **2.** HIST (history of) costume [*o* apparel]
industria *f* **1.** COM industry; ~ **del automóvil** car [*o* automobile *Am*] industry **2.** (*empresa*) business; (*fábrica*) factory **3.** (*dedicación*) industry **4.** (*maña*) adeptness; (*pericia*) expertise
industrial **I.** *adj* industrial; **nave** ~ industrial warehouse; **planta** ~ industrial plant; **polígono** ~ industrial estate, industrial park **II.** *mf* industrialist; (*fabricante*) manufacturer
industrialización *f* industrialization
industrializar <z→c> *vt, vr:* ~**se** to industrialize
industrioso, -a *adj* **1.** (*trabajador*) industrious **2.** (*mañoso*) dexterous, dextrous
inédito, -a *adj* **1.** (*no publicado*) unpublished **2.** (*desconocido*) unknown **3.** (*nuevo*) original, new
inefable *adj* ineffable, inexpressible
inefectivo, -a *adj* **1.** (*sin resultado*) ineffective, ineffectual **2.** COM (*no rentable*) unprofitable
ineficacia *f* **1.** (*sin resultado*) ineffectiveness **2.** COM (*sin rentabilidad*) lack of profitability **3.** (*de una persona*) inefficiency
ineficaz *adj* **1.** (*cosa*) ineffective **2.** (*persona*) ineffectual
ineficiente *adj* inefficient
INEM *m abr de* **Instituto Nacional de Empleo** *national employment agency*
inenarrable *adj* indescribable
inepcia *f AmL* **1.** (*ineptitud*) ineptitude **2.** (*necedad*) imbecility
ineptitud *f* **1.** (*incapacidad*) ineptitude; ~ **para algo** ineptitude in sth **2.** (*incompetencia*) incompetence; ~ **para algo** incompetence in sth
inepto, -a *adj* **1.** (*incapaz*) inept; ~ **para algo** inept at sth **2.** (*incompetente*) incompetent; ~ **para algo** incompetent at sth
inequívoco, -a *adj* unequivocal; (*inconfundible*) unmistakable
inercia *f t.* FÍS inertia; **por** ~ mechanically
inerme *adj* **1.** (*desarmado*) unarmed **2.** BIO (*sin aguijón*) without a sting; (*sin púas*) without spines **3.** (*indefenso*) defenceless
inerte *adj* **1.** (*sin vida*) inanimate **2.** (*inmóvil*) inert
inescrutable *adj elev* inscrutable
inesperado, -a *adj* unexpected
inestabilidad *f* **1.** (*fragilidad*) *t.* TÉC fragility **2.** (*variabilidad*) instability
inestable *adj* **1.** (*frágil*) *t.* TÉC fragile **2.** (*variable*) unstable
inestimable *adj* inestimable
inevitable *adj* inevitable, unavoidable
inexactitud *f* **1.** (*no exacto*) inexactitude, inaccuracy **2.** (*error*) incorrection
inexacto, -a *adj* **1.** (*no exacto*) inexact **2.** (*erróneo*) inaccurate
inexcusable *adj* **1.** (*ineludible*) unavoidable **2.** (*sin disculpa*) inexcusable
inexistencia *f* non-existence
inexistente *adj* non-existent
inexorable *adj elev* inexorable

I

inexperiencia *f* inexperience
inexperto, **-a** *adj* inexpert; (*sin experiencia*) inexperienced
inexplicable *adj* inexplicable
inexpresivo, **-a** *adj* **1.** (*cara, mirada*) impassive, inexpressive **2.** (*cosa*) inexpressive
inexpugnable *adj* **1.** (*inconquistable*) impregnable **2.** (*irreductible*) unyielding
inextricable *adj* **1.** (*enmarañado*) inextricable **2.** (*complicado*) intricate
infalible *adj* infallible
infamante *adj* shameful
infamar *vt* to defame
infame *adj* **1.** (*vil*) wicked **2.** (*muy malo*) vile
infamia *f* **1.** (*canallada*) infamy **2.** (*deshonra*) dishonour *Brit,* dishonor *Am*
infancia *f* **1.** (*niñez, niños*) childhood; **enfermedades de la ~** childhood illnesses **2.** (*etapa inicial*) infancy
infante, **-a** *m, f* **1.** *elev* (*niño, niña*) infant; **jardín de ~s** *AmL* nursery school *Brit,* preschool *Am* **2.** (*príncipe, princesa*) infante *m,* infanta *f* **3.** (*soldado*) infantryman, foot soldier
infantería *f* MIL infantry
infanticida **I.** *adj* **madre ~** infanticidal mother **II.** *mf person who commits infanticide*
infantil *adj* **1.** (*referente a la infancia*) infant; **trabajo ~** child labour *Brit,* child labor *Am;* **sonrisa ~** child's smile **2.** *pey* (*ingenuo*) infantile
infarto *m* heart attack
infatigable *adj* tireless
infausto, **-a** *adj* unfortunate
infección *f* MED **1.** (*contaminación*) contagion **2.** (*afección*) infection
infeccioso, **-a** *adj* MED infectious; **enfermedad infecciosa** contagious illness
infectar **I.** *vt* **1.** MED (*contagiar*) to transmit **2.** *inf* (*contaminar*) to infect **3.** (*corromper*) to corrupt **II.** *vr:* **~se** **1.** (*contagiarse*) **~se de SIDA** to catch AIDS **2.** (*inflamarse*) to become infected
infecto, **-a** *adj* **1.** (*contagiado*) **~ de algo** infected with sth **2.** (*nauseabundo*) nauseating **3.** (*corrupto*) corrupt, tainted
infecundidad *f* infertility
infelicidad *f* **1.** (*falta de felicidad*) unhappiness **2.** (*suerte adversa*) misfortune
infeliz **I.** *adj* **1.** (*no feliz*) unhappy **2.** *inf* (*ingenuo*) ingenuous **II.** *mf inf* **1.** (*desgraciado*) wretch **2.** (*buenazo*) kind-hearted person
inferior **I.** *adj* **1.** (*debajo*) lower; **labio ~** lower lip **2.** (*de menos calidad*) inferior **3.** (*menos*) **~ a algo** lesser than sth **4.** (*subordinado*) subordinate **II.** *mf* inferior
inferioridad *f* inferiority; **estar en ~ de condiciones** to be at a disadvantage
inferir *irr como sentir* **I.** *vt* **1.** (*deducir*) to infer; **~ de** [*o* **por**] **algo** to infer from sth **2.** (*ocasionar*) to occasion **3.** (*causar*) to cause **II.** *vr:* **~se** to be deducible
infernal *adj* infernal; **ruido ~** infernal din
infértil *adj* infertile
infertilidad *f sin pl* infertility
infestar *vt* **1.** (*inundar*) **~ de algo** to overrun with sth **2.** (*infectar*) **~ de algo** to infect with sth **3.** (*causar*) to ravage **4.** (*corromper*) **~ de algo** to corrupt with sth
inficionar *vt* **1.** (*contaminar*) to infect **2.** (*envenenar*) to poison **3.** *form* (*corromper*) to corrupt
infidelidad *f* **1.** (*deslealtad*) infidelity, unfaithfulness **2.** (*incredulidad*) unbelief
infiel **I.** *adj* <infidelísimo> **1.** (*desleal*) unfaithful **2.** (*pagano*) heathen **3.** (*inexacto*) imprecise **II.** *mf* pagan
infiernillo *m* camp(ing) [*o* portable] stove
infierno *m* **1.** *t.* REL hell; **me mandó al ~** he/she told me to go to hell **2.** (*en la mitología*) underworld
infiltración *f t.* POL infiltration
infiltrar **I.** *vt* **1.** (*penetrar*) to infiltrate, to penetrate **2.** (*inculcar*) to imbue **II.** *vr:* **~se en algo** **1.** (*penetrar*) to penetrate sth **2.** (*introducirse*) to infiltrate sth
ínfimo, **-a** *adj* **1.** (*muy bajo*) very low **2.** (*mínimo*) minimal **3.** (*vil*) vile
infinidad *f* **1.** (*cualidad de infinito*) infinity **2.** (*gran número*) enormous quantity
infinitivo *m* infinitive
infinito *m t.* MAT infinity
infinito, **-a** *adj* **1.** (*ilimitado*) limitless; (*cosas no materiales*) boundless **2.** (*incontable*) infinite
infinitud *f sin pl* infinitude
inflable *adj* inflatable
inflación *f* **1.** *t.* ECON inflation **2.** (*exceso*) excess
inflacionista *adj* ECON inflationist
inflamable *adj* (in)flammable
inflamación *f* **1.** *t.* MED inflammation **2.** TÉC ignition; **punto de ~** ignition point
inflamar **I.** *vt* **1.** (*encender*) to ignite **2.** (*excitar*) *t.* MED to inflame **II.** *vr:* **~se** *t.* MED to become inflamed
inflamatorio, **-a** *adj* MED inflammatory
inflar **I.** *vt* **1.** (*llenar de aire*) to inflate **2.** (*exagerar*) to exaggerate **II.** *vr* **1.** (*hincharse*) **~se de algo** to swell with sth **2.** *inf* (*de comida*) to stuff oneself
inflexibilidad *f* **1.** (*rigidez*) inflexibility **2.** (*firmeza*) firmness
inflexible *adj* **1.** (*rígido*) inflexible **2.** (*firme*) firm
inflexión *f* **1.** (*de la voz*) *t.* MAT, LING inflection, inflexion **2.** (*torcimiento*) bend
infligir <g→j> *vt* (*dolor*) to inflict; **~ un castigo** to inflict a punishment; **~ daño** to cause injury
influencia *f* influence; **tener ~** to be influential
influenciar **I.** *vt* to influence **II.** *vr:* **~se** to be influenced
influir *irr como huir* **I.** *vi* **1.** (*contribuir*) **~ en** [*o* **sobre**] **algo** to have a hand in sth **2.** (*actuar*)

~ **en algo** to have an influence on sth **II.** *vt* to influence
influjo *m* influence
influyente *adj* influential
información *f* **1.** information **2.** (*noticias*) news + *sing vb* **3.** MIL intelligence **4.** TEL directory enquiries *pl Brit*
informador(a) *m(f)* **1.** (*informante*) informant; (*de policía*) informer **2.** (*periodista*) reporter
informal *adj* **1.** (*desenfadado*) informal, casual; **lenguaje** ~ informal language **2.** (*no cumplidor*) unreliable
informalidad *f* informality
informante *mf* informant
informar I. *vt* **1.** (*comunicar*) to inform; (*periodista*) to report **2.** *elev* (*fundamentar*) to found **II.** *vi* JUR to plead **III.** *vr* ~**se de algo** to find out about sth
informática *f* computer [*o* computing] science
informático, -a I. *adj* **fallo** ~ computer error **II.** *m, f* computer expert
informativo *m* news broadcast, news programme *Brit,* news program *Am;* **el** ~ **de las nueve** the nine o'clock news
informativo, -a *adj* informative; **boletín** ~ (*por escrito, radial*) (news) bulletin
informatización *f* computerization
informatizar <z→c> *vt* to computerize
informe I. *adj* **1.** (*sin forma*) shapeless **2.** (*indefinido*) undefined **II.** *m* report
infortunado, -a *adj* unfortunate
infortunio *m* misfortune, adversity
infotainment *m* infotainment
infracción *f* infraction; (*administrativa*) breach; ~ **de tráfico** traffic offence [*o* offense *Am*]
infractor(a) I. *adj* offending **II.** *m(f)* infractor, offender
infraestructura *f* **1.** (*construcción*) foundations *pl* **2.** (*medios*) infrastructure
infrahumano, -a *adj* subhuman
infranqueable *adj* impassable, insurmountable *fig*
infrarrojo, -a *adj* infrared
infrautilización *f* underuse
infrautilizar <z→c> *vt* to underuse
infravalorar *vt* to undervalue, to underestimate
infrecuencia *f* infrequency
infrecuente *adj* infrequent
infringir <g→j> *vt* to infringe; ~ **la ley** to break the law
infructuoso, -a *adj* fruitless; (*fracasado*) unsuccessful
ínfula *f pl* (*soberbia*) pretensions *pl;* **darse** ~**s** to put on airs (and graces)
infundado, -a *adj* unfounded
infundio *m* lie
infundir *vt* (*deseo*) to infuse; (*respeto*) to command; (*temor*) to intimidate; (*sospechas*) to instil
infusión *f* infusion; (*de hierbas*) herb(al) tea
ingeniar I. *vt* to devise **II.** *vr:* ~**se** to contrive, to manage
ingeniería *f* engineering; **escuela de** ~ school of engineering
ingeniero, -a *m, f* engineer
ingenio *m* **1.** (*inventiva*) ingenuity, ingeniousness **2.** (*talento para contar*) wit **3.** (*persona*) gifted person, genius **4.** (*maña*) aptitude **5.** (*máquina*) device
ingenioso, -a *adj* **1.** (*hábil*) skilful *Brit,* skillful *Am* **2.** (*listo*) ingenious
ingente *adj* enormous; ~ **cantidad** huge quantity
ingenuidad *f* **1.** (*inocencia*) ingenuousness, candour *Brit,* candor *Am* **2.** (*torpeza*) naivety
ingenuo, -a *adj* ingenuous, candid
ingerir *irr como sentir vt* **1.** (*referente a medicamentos*) to take **2.** (*beber, comer*) to ingest
ingestión *f* **1.** (*referente a medicamentos*) taking, intake **2.** (*el beber, comer*) ingestion, consumption
Inglaterra *f* England
ingle *f* ANAT groin
inglés, -esa I. *adj* English **II.** *m, f* Englishman *m,* Englishwoman *f*
inglete *m* **1.** MAT forty-five degree angle **2.** (*ensambladura*) mitre joint *Brit,* miter joint *Am*
ingobernable *adj* **1.** (*no gobernable*) ungovernable **2.** (*no dirigible*) unmanageable
ingratitud *f* ingratitude
ingrato, -a *adj* ungrateful; ~ (**para**) **con alguien** ungrateful to sb; (*tarea*) thankless
ingravidez *f* weightlessness, lack of gravity
ingrávido, -a *adj* **1.** (*falta de gravedad*) lacking in gravity, weightless **2.** (*ligero*) light
ingrediente *m* **1.** (*sustancia*) ingredient **2.** (*elemento*) element
ingresar I. *vi* **1.** (*inscribirse*) ~ **en algo** to become a member of sth **2.** (*hospitalizarse*) to be admitted to hospital **II.** *vt* **1.** FIN (*cheque*) to pay in, to deposit **2.** (*hospitalizar*) to hospitalize **3.** (*percibir*) to earn
ingreso *m* **1.** (*inscripción*) entry; **examen de** ~ entrance exam **2.** (*ceremonia*) initiation **3.** (*alta*) incorporation **4.** (*en una cuenta*) deposit **5.** *pl* (*retribuciones*) income
íngrimo, -a *adj AmL* (*solitario*) solitary
inhábil *adj* **1.** (*persona: torpe*) clumsy; (*incompetente*) inept **2.** JUR **día** ~ non-working day
inhabilidad *f* ineptitude
inhabilitar *vt* JUR **1.** (*incapacitar*) ~ **para algo** to incapacitate for sth **2.** (*prohibir*) ~ **a** (**hacer**) **algo** to disqualify from (doing) sth
inhabitable *adj* uninhabitable
inhabitado, -a *adj* uninhabited
inhabitual *adj* unusual
inhalador *m* MED inhaler
inhalar *vt t.* MED to inhale, to breathe in
inherente *adj* inherent; ~ **a algo** inherent in

sth

inhibición *f* **1.** (*represión*) repression **2.** (*abstención*) abstention **3.** MED, JUR inhibition

inhibir **I.** *vt* **1.** (*reprimir*) to repress **2.** BIO, JUR to inhibit **II.** *vr* **~se de algo** to abstain from sth; **~se de hacer algo** to refrain from doing sth

inhibitorio, **-a** *adj* JUR inhibitive

inhospitalario, **-a** *adj* inhospitable, unfriendly

inhóspito, **-a** *adj* inhospitable

inhumación *f* inhumation, burial

inhumano, **-a** *adj* (*no humano*) inhuman; (*sin compasión*) inhumane

inhumar *vt elev* to inhume, to bury

INI *m abr de* **Instituto Nacional de Industria** *national industry institute*

iniciación *f* **1.** (*comienzo*) beginning, commencement **2.** (*introducción*) **~ a** [*o* **en**] **algo** initiation to sth **3.** (*de un novato*) initiation

iniciado, **-a** **I.** *adj* initiated **II.** *m, f* initiate

iniciador(a) *m(f)* initiator, pioneer

inicial **I.** *adj* inital; **fase ~** initial phase **II.** *f* (*letra*) initial

iniciar **I.** *vt* **1.** (*comenzar*) to begin **2.** (*introducir*) to initiate **3.** INFOR to log in [*o* on]; **~ el funcionamiento del ordenador** to log in [*o* on] to a computer **II.** *vr:* **~se** **1.** (*comenzar*) to begin **2.** (*introducirse en*) **ella sola se inició en la lectura** she taught herself to read

iniciativa *f* initiative; **~ privada** ECON private enterprise

inicio *m* beginning

inigualable *adj* incomparable, unrivalled *Brit,* unrivaled *Am*

inimaginable *adj* unimaginable

ininteligible *adj* unintelligible; (*escritura*) illegible

ininterrumpido, **-a** *adj* uninterrupted

iniquidad *f* **1.** (*injusticia*) iniquity **2.** (*infamia*) wickedness

injerencia *f* interference

injerir *irr como sentir* **I.** *vt* **1.** (*introducir*) to introduce; **~ en algo** to introduce into sth **2.** (*injertar*) to graft **II.** *vr:* **~se** to interfere

injertar *vt* (*plantas*) *t.* MED to graft

injerto *m* **1.** (*acción de injertar*) grafting **2.** (*brote*) *t.* MED graft

injuria *f* (*con palabras*) insult, affront; (*con acciones*) harm; JUR slander

injuriar *vt* (*con palabras*) to insult; (*con acciones*) to injure

injurioso, **-a** *adj* injurious

injusticia *f* injustice, unfairness

injustificado, **-a** *adj* unjustified

injusto, **-a** *adj* **1.** (*no justo*) unjust, unfair **2.** (*injustificado*) *t.* JUR inequitable

inmaculado, **-a** *adj* **1.** (*limpísimo*) immaculate **2.** (*impecable*) impeccable

inmadurez *f sin pl* immaturity

inmaduro, **-a** *adj* immature

inmediaciones *fpl* surroundings *pl,* vicinity

inmediatamente *adv* **1.** (*sin demora*) immediately **2.** (*directamente*) directly

inmediato, **-a** *adj* **1.** (*sin demora*) immediate; **de ~** immediately, right away **2.** (*directo*) direct **3.** (*próximo*) adjacent

inmejorable *adj* unbeatable, excellent

inmemorable *adj,* **inmemorial** *adj* immemorial; **desde tiempos ~es** since [*o* from] time immemorial

inmensidad *f* **1.** (*extensión*) immensity **2.** (*cantidad*) vastness

inmenso, **-a** *adj* immense

inmerecido, **-a** *adj* undeserved

inmersión *f* (*sumersión*) *t.* ASTR immersion

inmerso, **-a** *adj* immersed; *fig* involved

inmigración *f* immigration

inmigrante *mf* immigrant

inmigrar *vi* to immigrate

inmigratorio, **-a** *adj* immigratory

inminente *adj* imminent

inmiscuir *irr como huir* **I.** *vt* to put in **II.** *vr:* **~se** to interfere, to meddle

inmisericorde *adj* hard-hearted

inmobiliaria *f* **1.** (*construcción*) construction company **2.** (*venta, alquiler*) estate agency *Brit,* real estate office [*o* agency] *Am*

inmobiliario, **-a** *adj* property

inmoderado, **-a** *adj* immoderate

inmodestia *f* immodesty

inmodesto, **-a** *adj* immodest

inmolación *f* immolation, sacrifice

inmolar *vt, vr:* **~(se)** **Jesús se inmoló por los hombres** Jesus sacrificed himself for mankind

inmoral *adj* immoral; (*en cuestiones sexuales*) indecent

inmoralidad *f* **1.** (*indignidad*) immorality **2.** (*indecencia*) indecency

inmortal *adj* immortal

inmortalidad *f* immortality

inmortalizar <z→c> **I.** *vt* to immortalize **II.** *vr:* **~se** to be immortalized

inmóvil *adj* immobile; (*inamovible*) unmovable; (*quieto*) still, motionless

inmovilidad *f* immobility

inmovilización *f* **1.** (*incapaz de moverse*) paralysis; MED, MIL immobilization **2.** COM lock-up

inmovilizar <z→c> **I.** *vt* **1.** (*paralizar*) to paralyse; **~ a alguien** to put sb out of action **2.** MED to immobilize **3.** COM to lock up **II.** *vr:* **~se** to become immobilized

inmueble *adj, m* property

inmundicia *f* **1.** (*suciedad*) filth **2.** (*indecencia*) immorality **3.** (*basura*) rubbish *Brit,* garbage *Am*

inmundo, **-a** *adj* filthy; (*asqueroso*) disgusting

inmune *adj* **1.** MED immune **2.** (*exento*) **~ de algo** exempt from sth

inmunidad *f* immunity

inmunizar <z→c> **I.** *vt* to immunize; (*vacunar*) to vaccinate **II.** *vr:* **~se** to safeguard oneself

inmunodeficiencia *f* MED immunodeficiency; **síndrome de ~ adquirida** Acquired

Immune Deficiency Syndrome
inmunología *f* MED immunology
inmutabilidad *f* **1.** (*inmodificable*) immutability **2.** (*imperturbable*) impassivity
inmutable *adj* **1.** (*inmodificable*) immutable **2.** (*imperturbable*) imperturbable
inmutar I. *vt* **1.** (*afectar*) to affect **2.** (*variar*) to alter **II.** *vr:* **~se** to be affected; **sin ~se** without turning a hair [*o* batting an eye], impassively
innato, **-a** *adj* innate, inborn; **tiene un talento ~** he has an natural talent
innavegable *adj* **1.** (*aguas*) unnavigable **2.** (*embarcación*) unseaworthy
innecesario, **-a** *adj* unnecessary
innegable *adj* undeniable
innoble *adj* ignoble
innovación *f* innovation
innovador(a) I. *adj* innovative, novel **II.** *m(f)* innovator
innovar *vt* to innovate
innumerable *adj* innumerable; **un gentío ~** countless people
inobservancia *f* non-observance
inocencia *f* **1.** (*falta de culpabilidad, ingenuidad*) innocence **2.** (*falta de malicia*) harmlessness, candour *Brit,* candor *Am*
inocentada *f* **1.** (*tontada: comentario*) naive remark; (*acción*) naive action **2.** (*broma*) ≈ *April fool joke, in Spain played on 28th December;* **gastar una ~ a alguien** to play a practical joke on sb
inocente *adj* **1.** (*sin culpa*) innocent **2.** (*sin malicia*) harmless **3.** (*ingenuo*) innocent, ingenuous
inocuidad *f sin pl* innocuousness, harmlessness
inocular *vt* **1.** MED to inoculate **2.** (*serpientes*) to administer an antitoxin
inocuo, **-a** *adj* innocuous, harmless
inodoro *m* toilet
inodoro, **-a** *adj* odourless *Brit,* odorless *Am*
inofensivo, **-a** *adj* inoffensive
inoficioso, **-a** *adj AmL* useless, idle
inolvidable *adj* unforgettable
inoperante *adj* ineffective
inopinado, **-a** *adj* unexpected
inoportunidad *f* **1.** (*fuera de lugar*) inappropriateness **2.** (*fuera de tiempo*) inopportuneness, untimeliness
inoportuno, **-a** *adj* **1.** (*fuera de lugar*) inappropriate **2.** (*fuera de tiempo*) inopportune, untimely
inorgánico, **-a** *adj* **1.** (*no viviente*) inorganic **2.** (*no organizado*) disorganized
inoxidable *adj* rustproof; (*acero*) stainless
input *m* <inputs> INFOR input
inquebrantable *adj* (*decisión*) unwavering; (*cosa*) unbreakable
inquietante *adj* (*preocupante*) worrying; (*perturbador*) disturbing
inquietar I. *vt* to worry **II.** *vr* **~se con** [*o* **por**] **algo** to worry about sth
inquieto, **-a** *adj* **1.** *estar* (*intranquilo*) anxious **2.** *ser* (*desasosegado*) restless
inquietud *f* **1.** (*intranquilidad*) anxiety **2.** (*desasosiego*) restlessness **3.** (*preocupación*) worry **4.** *pl* (*anhelos*) aspirations *pl*
inquilino, **-a** *m, f* tenant, lessee
inquina *f* aversion
inquirir *irr como adquirir vt* to enquire *Brit,* to inquire *Am*
inquisición *f* investigation
Inquisición *f* Inquisition, The Holy Office
inquisidor *m* inquisitor
inquisidor(a) *adj* inquisitive
inri *m* REL INRI; **para más ~** *fig* to make matters worse
insaciable *adj* insatiable; (*sed*) unquenchable
insalubre *adj* unhealthy, insalubrious *form*
insalubridad *f* unhealthiness
insalvable *adj* unsalvageable; (*obstáculo*) insuperable
insanable *adj* incurable
insano, **-a** *adj* **1.** (*insalubre*) unhealthy **2.** (*loco*) insane
insatisfacción *f sin pl* dissatisfaction
insatisfactorio, **-a** *adj* unsatisfactory
insatisfecho, **-a** *adj* dissatisfied
inscribir *irr como escribir* **I.** *vt* **1.** (*registrar*) to register; **a los dos días de nacer la inscribieron en el registro civil** two days after she was born they registered her birth **2.** (*grabar*) to inscribe; **~ en algo** to inscribe on sth **3.** (*alistar*) to enrol *Brit,* to enroll *Am;* **~ en algo** to enrol for [*o* on] sth **4.** MAT to inscribe **II.** *vr:* **~se 1.** (*registrarse*) to register; **se inscribió en la oficina de empleo** he registered at the Job Centre **2.** *t.* UNIV (*alistarse*) to enrol *Brit,* to enroll *Am;* **~se en algo** to enrol for [*o* on] sth
inscripción *f* **1.** (*registro*) registration **2.** (*alistamiento*) *t.* UNIV enrolment *Brit,* enrollment *Am;* **~ en la universidad** enrolment at university; **~ en un curso** enrolment on a course **3.** (*escrito grabado*) inscription
inscrito, **-a** *pp de* **inscribir**
insecticida *m* insecticide
insecto *m* insect
inseguridad *f* insecurity
inseguro, **-a** *adj* insecure
inseminación *f* insemination
inseminar *vt* to inseminate
insensatez *f* **1.** (*falta de sensatez*) foolishness **2.** (*disparate*) stupidity
insensato, **-a** *adj* foolish
insensibilidad *f* **1.** (*física o afectiva*) insensitivity **2.** (*resistencia*) immunity
insensibilizar <z→c> **I.** *vt* to render insensitive; MED to desensitize **II.** *vr:* **~se 1.** (*no sentir*) to become insensitive **2.** (*resistir*) to become immune
insensible *adj* **1.** (*física o afectivamente*) insensitive **2.** (*resistente*) immune **3.** (*imperceptible*) imperceptible
inseparable *adj* inseparable
inserción *f* **1.** (*inclusión*) inclusion; **~ social**

social insertion **2.** MED implant

insertar **I.** *vt* **1.** (*llave, moneda, texto*) to insert **2.** (*anuncio*) to place **II.** *vr:* ~**se** **1.** (*músculo*) to be attached **2.** (*tumor*) ~**se en algo** to invade sth

inservible *adj* useless

insidia *f* **1.** (*asechanzas, trampa*) trap **2.** (*engaño*) deception, trick **3.** (*mala pasada*) treacherous act

insidioso, **-a** **I.** *adj* **1.** (*intrigante*) scheming **2.** (*capcioso*) treacherous **3.** (*enfermedad*) insidious **II.** *m, f* **1.** (*intrigante*) schemer **2.** (*capcioso*) treacherous person

insigne *adj* (*personaje público*) distinguished; (*científico*) eminent

insignia *f* **1.** (*de asociación*) badge; (*honorífica*) decoration; (*militar*) insignia **2.** (*bandera*) flag, ensign

insignificancia *f* **1.** (*pequeñez, no importancia*) insignificance **2.** (*no significancia*) triviality

insignificante *adj* **1.** (*pequeño, no importante*) insignificant **2.** (*no significante*) trivial

insinceridad *f* insincerity

insincero, **-a** *adj* (*no sincero*) insincere

insinuación *f* **1.** (*alusión*) allusion **2.** (*engatusamiento*) insinuation

insinuante *adj* **1.** (*palabras*) insinuating **2.** (*comportamiento*) ingratiating **3.** (*seductor*) suggestive

insinuar <*1. pres:* insinúo> **I.** *vt* **1.** (*dar a entender*) to insinuate; **¿qué estás insinuando?** what are you insinuating? **2.** (*hacer creer*) **¿quién te ha insinuado eso?** who has put that into your head? **II.** *vr:* ~**se** **1.** (*engatusar*) ~**se a alguien** to get in with sb **2.** *inf* (*amorosamente*) ~**se a alguien** to flirt with sb **3.** (*cosa*) to be discernible

insipidez *f* **1.** (*de comida*) insipidness **2.** (*de persona: aburrida*) dullness; (*sin espíritu*) listlessness

insípido, **-a** *adj* **1.** (*comida*) insipid **2.** (*persona: aburrida*) dull; (*sin espíritu*) listless

insistencia *f* **1.** (*perseverancia*) persistence **2.** (*énfasis*) insistence; **pedir algo con** ~ to press for sth

insistente *adj* **1.** (*perseverante*) persistent; (*machacón*) insistent **2.** (*con énfasis*) pressing

insistir *vi* **1.** (*perseverar*) to persist; ~ **en algo** to persist in sth **2.** (*exigir, recalcar*) to insist; ~ **en algo** to insist on sth

insobornable *adj* incorruptible

insociable *adj,* **insocial** *adj* unsociable

insolación *f* **1.** METEO *period of unbroken sunshine* **2.** MED sunstroke

insolencia *f* **1.** (*impertinencia*) impertinence, disrepect **2.** (*arrogancia*) arrogance

insolentarse *vr* to become insolent; ~ **con alguien** to be insolent to sb

insolente *adj* **1.** (*impertinente*) impertinent **2.** (*arrogante*) insolent

insolidario, **-a** *adj* unsupportive; (*egoísta*) selfish

insólito, **-a** *adj* **1.** (*inhabitual*) unusual, uncommon **2.** (*extraordinario*) unwonted *form*

insoluble *adj* **1.** (*no soluble*) insoluble **2.** (*insolucionable*) insoluble

insolvencia *f* bankruptcy; ECON insolvency

insolvente **I.** *adj* bankrupt; ECON insolvent **II.** *mf* insolvent

insomnio *m* MED insomnia, sleeplessness

insondable *adj* bottomless, unfathomable *fig*

insonorización *f* soundproofing

insonorizar <z→c> *vt* to soundproof

insoportable *adj* unbearable

insoslayable *adj* unavoidable, inevitable

insospechable *adj* **1.** (*imprevisible*) unforeseeable **2.** (*sorprendente*) surprising

insospechado, **-a** *adj* **1.** (*no esperado*) unexpected **2.** (*no sospechado*) unsuspected, unforeseen

insostenible *adj* unsustainable

inspección *f* **1.** (*reconocimiento*) inspection; **Inspección de Trabajo** Inspectorate **2.** (*de equipaje*) check **3.** (*de trabajo*) supervision **4.** (*de una máquina*) *t.* TÉC inspection; **Inspección Técnica de Vehículos** ≈ MOT test

inspeccionar *vt* **1.** (*reconocer*) *t.* TÉC to inspect **2.** (*equipaje*) to check **3.** (*trabajo*) to supervise

inspector(**a**) *m(f)* **1.** (*controlador*) inspector **2.** ENS school inspector

inspiración *f* **1.** (*de aire*) inhalation **2.** (*ideas*) inspiration

inspirar **I.** *vt* **1.** (*aire*) to inhale **2.** (*ideas, confianza*) to inspire **II.** *vr:* ~**se** ~**se en algo/alguien** to be inspired by sth/sb

instalación *f* **1.** (*acción*) installation; (*de baño*) plumbing **2.** (*lo instalado*) TÉC fitting; (*objeto fijo*) fixture; (*objetos movibles*) fittings *pl Brit,* furnishings *pl Am* **3.** *pl* (*edificio*) installation; **instalaciones deportivas** sports facilities *pl*

instalador(**a**) *m(f)* installer, fitter

instalar **I.** *vt* **1.** (*calefacción, teléfono*) to install, to instal *Am;* (*baño*) to plumb, to fit **2.** (*alojar*) to accommodate **3.** (*en un cargo*) to install, to instal *Am* **II.** *vr:* ~**se** **1.** (*en una ciudad*) to settle; **me instalé en un sillón** I installed myself in an armchair **2.** (*negocio*) to set up

instancia *f* **1.** (*acción de instar*) urging **2.** (*solicitud*) application; (*petición formal*) petition **3.** JUR instance; **en última** ~ *fig* as a last resort

instantánea *f* FOTO snapshot

instantáneo, **-a** *adj* instantaneous; (*efecto, café*) instant; **la muerte fue instantánea** death was instantaneous

instante *m* instant; **al cabo de un** ~ the next instant; **en un** ~ in an instant; **pienso en ti a cada** ~ I think of you constantly; **¡un** ~**!** one moment!

instar *vi, vt* (*pedir*) to urge; ~ **a algo** to press for sth; **le** ~**on a que aceptara el puesto** they urged him to accept the post

instauración *f* **1.** (*de imperio*) foundation **2.** (*de democracia*) establishment **3.** (*de plan*) implementation

instaurar *vt* **1.** (*imperio*) to found **2.** (*democracia*) to establish **3.** (*plan*) to implement

instigación *f* **1.** instigation; (*a algo malo*) incitement **2.** (*de las masas*) rousing

instigador(a) **I.** *adj* **1.** instigating; (*a algo malo*) inciting **2.** (*de las masas*) rousing **II.** *m(f)* instigator; (*a algo malo*) inciter

instigar <g→gu> *vt* **1.** to instigate; (*a algo malo*) to incite **2.** (*a las masas*) to rouse

instintivo, -a *adj* instinctive

instinto *m* instinct; ~ **de supervivencia** survival instinct

institución *f* **1.** (*social*) institution; ~ **penitenciaria** prison **2.** (*fundación*) foundation **3.** (*establecimiento: de comité*) setting-up; (*de derecho*) institution; (*de beca*) creation; (*de norma, de horario*) introduction

institucional *adj* institutional

institucionalizar <z→c> *vt* to institutionalize

instituir *irr como huir vt* **1.** (*fundar*) to found **2.** (*establecer: comisión*) to set up; (*derecho*) to institute; (*beca*) to create; (*norma*) to introduce

instituto *m* **1.** ENS (*de bachillerato*) secondary school, high school *Am* **2.** (*científico*) institute; **Instituto Monetario Europeo** European Monetary Institute; **Instituto Nacional de Empleo** Employment Service **3.** REL order **4.** (*establecimiento*) ~ **de belleza** beauty salon

institutriz *f* governess

instrucción *f* **1.** (*enseñanza*) teaching; (*en una máquina*) instruction **2.** (*conocimientos*) knowledge; (*formación*) training **3.** *pl* (*órdenes*) instructions *pl*, directions *pl*; (*directrices*) guidelines *pl* **4.** JUR (*proceso*) proceedings *pl*

instructivo, -a *adj* instructive, educational

instructor(a) **I.** *adj* **juez** ~ JUR examining magistrate *Brit* **II.** *m(f)* (*en escuela*) teacher; (*en empresa*) *t.* MIL instructor

instruido, -a *adj* educated

instruir *irr como huir vt* **1.** (*enseñar*) to teach; (*en una máquina*) to instruct; (*en tarea específica*) to train **2.** (*informar*) to inform **3.** JUR (*proceso*) to prepare

instrumentación *f* instrumentation

instrumental **I.** *adj t.* MÚS instrumental **II.** *m* **1.** LING instrumental case **2.** (*de médico*) *t.* MÚS instruments *pl*

instrumentalizar <z→c> *vt* to use as an instrument

instrumentar *vt t.* MÚS to orchestrate, to arrange, to score

instrumentista *mf* **1.** (*músico*) instrumentalist **2.** (*fabricante*) maker of musical instruments **3.** (*de quirófano*) *member of the surgical staff in charge of the instruments*

instrumento *m* instrument

insubordinación *f* insubordination

insubordinar **I.** *vt* to rouse to rebellion, to stir up **II.** *vr:* ~**se** to rebel

insubsanable *adj* **1.** (*daño*) irreparable **2.** (*deficiencia*) unrectifiable **3.** (*dificultad*) insurmountable

insuficiencia *f* **1.** (*cualidad*) insufficiency **2.** (*escasez*) deficiency; (*falta*) lack **3.** (*incompetencia*) incompetence **4.** MED failure

insuficiente **I.** *adj* insufficient; (*conocimientos*) inadequate **II.** *m* ENS fail; **he sacado un ~ en inglés** I got a fail in English

insuflar *vt* **1.** MED to pump into **2.** (*ánimo*) to raise

insufrible *adj* insufferable

insular *adj* insular

insulina *f* MED insulin

insulso, -a *adj* **1.** (*comida*) insipid, tasteless **2.** (*persona, película*) dull

insultante *adj* insulting; (*de modo grosero*) rude

insultar *vt* **1.** (*con insultos*) to insult **2.** (*con injurias*) to abuse

insulto *m* **1.** (*palabra gruesa*) insult **2.** (*injuria*) abuse

insumisión *f* **1.** (*de un pueblo*) rebelliousness **2.** MIL *refusal to do military service* **3.** (*intransigencia*) intransigence

insumiso *m one who refuses to do military service or its alternative*

insuperable *adj* **1.** (*dificultad*) insuperable, insurmountable; (*persona*) unrivalled *Brit*, unrivaled *Am* **2.** (*resultado*) unbeatable

insurgente **I.** *adj* insurgent **II.** *mf* insurgent

insurrección *f* insurrection; ~ **militar** mutiny

insustancial *adj* **1.** (*sin sustancia*) insubstantial **2.** (*sin interés*) uninteresting **3.** (*no importante*) unimportant, insignificant **4.** (*superficial*) superficial

insustituible *adj* irreplaceable

intachable *adj* irreproachable; (*comportamiento*) faultless

intacto, -a *adj* **1.** (*no tocado*) untouched **2.** (*no dañado*) intact **3.** (*puro*) pure **4.** (*no tratado*) untreated

intangible *adj* **1.** (*inviolable*) inviolable **2.** (*intocable, inmaterial*) intangible

integración *f* integration

integrador *m* integrator

integral **I.** *adj* **1.** (*completo*) integral, full **2.** (*pan*) wholemeal, wholegrain; (*arroz*) brown rice **3.** (*elemento*) integral, intrinsic **4.** MAT integral; **cálculo** ~ integral calculus **II.** *f* MAT integral

integrar **I.** *vt* **1.** (*constituir*) to constitute, to comprise **2.** (*en conjunto*) *t.* MAT to integrate **II.** *vr:* ~**se** to integrate

integridad *f* **1.** (*totalidad*) entirety **2.** (*honradez*) integrity **3.** (*física*) physical well-being

integrismo *m* **1.** (*ideológico*) fundamentalism **2.** (*católico*) orthodoxy

. (*ideológico*) fundamentalist
...thodox catholic
... *adj* **1.** (*completo*) whole **2.** (*per-*
...onest, upright
...ecto *m* intellect
...telectual **I.** *adj* intellectual; (*interés*) studious; (*facultad*) intelligent, scholarly **II.** *mf* intellectual
inteligencia *f* **1.** (*capacidad*) intelligence **2.** (*comprensión*) comprehension **3.** (*acuerdo*) understanding **4.** POL intelligence; **servicio de ~** MI5 *Brit,* CIA *Am*
inteligente *adj* intelligent
inteligibilidad *f sin pl* intelligibility
inteligible *adj* **1.** (*comprensible*) comprehensible **2.** (*sonido*) *t.* FILOS intelligible
intemperancia *f* **1.** (*intolerancia*) intolerance **2.** (*intransigencia*) intransigence **3.** (*falta de moderación*) intemperance, excess
intemperante *adj* **1.** (*intolerante*) intolerant **2.** (*intransigente*) intransigent **3.** (*no moderado*) intemperate
intemperie *f* **1.** (*el aire libre*) **a la ~** out in the open; **dormir a la ~** to sleep outdoors **2.** (*del clima*) harsh climate; (*mal tiempo*) inclement weather
intempestivo, **-a** *adj* **1.** (*observación*) inopportune **2.** (*visita*) ill-timed
intención *f* **1.** (*propósito*) intention; (*propósito firme*) resolution; **sin ~** unintentionally; **con ~** deliberately; **tener segundas intenciones** to have an ulterior motive; **tener buenas intenciones** to mean well **2.** (*idea*) idea **3.** (*objetivo*) intent
intencionado, **-a** *adj* intentional; JUR premeditated; **bien ~** (*acción*) well-meant; (*persona*) well-meaning; **mal ~** unkind; (*persona*) malicious
intencionalidad *f* intention; JUR premeditation
intendencia *f* **1.** MIL service corps, quartermaster corps *Am* **2.** (*dirección*) management **3.** *CSur* (*distrito*) district
intendente *m* **1.** MIL quartermaster-general **2.** (*de empresa*) manager **3.** *CSur* (*de un distrito*) mayor
intensidad *f* **1.** (*fuerza*) *t.* FÍS intensity; (*de tormenta*) severity **2.** (*de palabras*) vehemence **3.** (*de viento*) force **4.** (*de luz*) brightness
intensificación *f sin pl* intensification
intensificar <c→qu> **I.** *vt* to intensify **II.** *vr:* **~se** (*tensión*) to heighten; (*tráfico, calor*) to increase; (*conflicto*) to intensify
intensivo, **-a** *adj* intensive
intenso, **-a** *adj* **1.** (*fuerza, olor*) strong **2.** (*palabras*) vehement **3.** (*tormenta*) severe **4.** (*frío, calor*) intense
intentar *vt* **1.** (*probar*) to attempt, to try **2.** (*proponerse*) to intend, to mean
intento *m* **1.** (*lo intentado*) attempt, try **2.** (*propósito*) aim
intentona *f inf* reckless attempt
interacción *f* interaction
interactivo, **-a** *adj* interactive
intercalación *f* insertion; **~ de líneas** insert
intercalar **I.** *adj elev* interpolated; (*día*) intercalary **II.** *vt* (*en un periódico*) to insert
intercambiar **I.** *vt* to interchange; (*opiniones*) to exchange; (*cosas*) to swap; **~ correspondencia con alguien** to correspond with sb **II.** *vr:* **~se** (*lugares*) to exchange places
intercambio *m* exchange
interceder *vi* to intercede; **~ en favor de alguien** to intercede on behalf of sb
interceptar *vt* **1.** (*comunicaciones*) to cut off; (*el paso de algo, pelota*) to intercept; (*tráfico*) to hold up, to stop **2.** (*mensaje, conversación telefónica*) to intercept **3.** (*calle*) to block off
intercesión *f* **1.** (*en favor de alguien*) intercession **2.** (*en secuestro*) intervention
intercomunicador *m* intercom
intercomunicar <c→qu> *vt* to intercommunicate
intercontinental *adj* intercontinental
intercultural *adj* intercultural
interdisciplinar *adj,* **interdisciplinario**, **-a** *adj* interdisciplinary
interés *m* **1.** (*importancia*) concern **2.** (*deseo, atención*) interest; **tengo mucho ~ en que...** it is of interest to me that ...; **tengo ~ por saber...** I'm interested in knowing ...; **no poner ~ en algo** to show [*o* to take] no interest in sth **3.** (*provecho*) interest; **el ~ público** the public's interest; **esto redunda en ~ tuyo** this redounds to your credit **4.** FIN interest; (*rendimiento*) yield; **un 10 % de ~** 10 % interest; **dar mucho ~** to give a lot of interest
interesadamente *adv* selfishly; **actuar ~** (*por propio interés*) to act selfishly; (*por interés material*) to act in one's own interest
interesado, **-a** **I.** *adj* **1.** (*con interés*) interested **2.** (*parcial*) biased, prejudiced **3.** (*egoísta*) selfish, self-seeking **II.** *m, f* **1.** the interested party, the person concerned **2.** (*egoísta*) selfish person
interesante *adj* interesting; **hacerse el ~** to show off [*o* play to the gallery]
interesar **I.** *vi* to be of interest; **este tema no me interesa** this subject is of no interest to me **II.** *vt* **1.** (*inspirar interés*) to interest **2.** (*atraer*) to attract, to appeal **III.** *vr:* **~se** **1.** (*mostrar interés*) **~se por algo** to become interested in sth **2.** (*preguntar por*) **~se por algo** to ask about sth; **~se por la salud de alguien** to ask after sb's health
interface *m* INFOR interface
interfecto, **-a** **I.** *adj* murdered **II.** *m, f* **1.** JUR murder victim **2.** *inf* (*susodicho*) the person mentioned [*o* in question]
interferencia *f t.* FÍS, LING interference
interferir *irr como sentir vi t.* FÍS to interfere; **~ en algo** to interfere with [*o* in] sth; **eso no interfiere en mi decisión** that does not influence my decision

interfono *m* intercom

intergubernamental *adj* intergovernmental

interinidad *f* 1. (*cualidad*) temporariness; **estar en situación de** ~ to be in a temporary job 2. (*de un cargo*) duration

interino, -a I. *adj* 1. (*funcionario, plaza*) temporary 2. POL interim II. *m, f* 1. (*suplente*) stand-in 2. (*funcionario*) temporary [*o* acting] incumbent; (*maestro*) supply teacher

interior I. *adj* interior; **decoración** ~ interior decoration; (*sin costa*) inland; **mercado** ~ COM (*de la UE*) internal market; (*de Inglaterra*) home [*o* domestic] market; **ropa** ~ underwear; **la vida** ~ **de una persona** a person's inner life II. *m* 1. (*lo de dentro*) interior; **el** ~ **de un país** the interior of a country; **Ministerio del Interior** POL Home Office *Brit,* Department of the Interior *Am;* **en el** ~ **de...** inside ... 2. DEP inside-forward

interiores *mpl* 1. (*entrañas*) insides *pl* 2. *inf* (*de una cosa*) innards *pl* 3. ARQUIT house interiors *pl* 4. CINE (*secuencias*) interior shots *pl;* (*decorados*) film sets *pl* 5. *Col* (*calzoncillos*) men's underpants *pl*

interioridad *f* 1. (*cualidad*) inwardness 2. *pl* (*de alguien*) intimacies *pl;* (*de una familia*) family secrets *pl*

interiorista *mf* 1. (*arquitecto*) interior designer 2. (*diseñador*) interior decorator [*o* designer]

interiorizar <z→c> *vt* to internalize; (*emociones*) to repress

interiormente *adv* 1. (*en su interior*) inside 2. (*internamente*) internally

interjección *f* LING interjection, exclamation

interlocutor(a) *m(f)* speaker, interlocutor *form;* ~**es sociales** ECON management and workers' representatives

intermediario, -a I. *adj* intermediary II. *m, f* 1. (*mediador*) mediator, intermediary; (*enlace*) go-between 2. (*comerciante*) middleman

intermedio *m* interval

intermedio, -a *adj* 1. (*capa*) intermediate 2. (*período de tiempo*) intervening 3. (*calidad*) **mandos** ~**s** middle management; (*tamaño*) medium

interminable *adj* interminable, endless

intermitencia *f* 1. (*calidad*) intermittency 2. MED intermittence 3. AUTO indicator

intermitente *m* intermittence; AUTO indicator *Brit,* turn signal *Am*

internación *f v.* **internamiento**

internacional *adj* international; **derecho** ~ JUR international law; **partido** ~ DEP international game

internacionalidad *f* international nature

internacionalización *f* internationalization

internacionalizar <z→c> *vt* to internationalize

internado *m* boarding school

internado, -a I. *adj* boarding II. *m, f* 1. (*alumno*) boarder 2. (*demente*) inmate

internamiento *m* 1. (*en hospital*) admission, confinement; ~ **en algo** admission to sth 2. MIL internment; ~ **en algo** internment in sth

internar I. *vt* 1. (*penetrar*) to lead inland 2. (*ingresar*) ~ **en** (*hospital*) to admit to; (*asilo*) to commit to 3. MIL to intern II. *vr:* ~**se** 1. (*penetrar*) *t.* DEP to enter 2. (*en tema*) ~**se en algo** to delve into sth

internauta *mf* INFOR Internet user

internet *f sin pl* INFOR Internet

interno, -a I. *adj* internal; **régimen** ~ (*de una empresa*) internal management; (*de un partido*) internal affairs II. *m, f* (*en colegio*) boarder; (*en cárcel*) inmate; MED resident doctor, houseman

interpelación *f* POL interpellation; JUR appeal, plea

interpolación *f* MAT interpolation

interponer *irr como poner* I. *vt* 1. (*entre varias cosas*) to interpose; (*entre dos cosas: silla*) to place; (*papel*) to insert; (*alguien*) to come 2. (*en un asunto*) to intervene 3. JUR to bring, to lodge II. *vr:* ~**se** to intervene

interposición *f* 1. (*entre varias cosas*) interposition; (*de una silla*) placing between; (*de un papel*) insertion; (*de alguien*) coming between 2. (*en un asunto*) intervention 3. JUR bringing, lodging

interpretable *adj* (*texto*) interpretable; MÚS, TEAT performable

interpretación *f* 1. (*de texto*) interpretation; (*traducción oral*) interpreting 2. TEAT performance; MÚS rendering; **escuela de** ~ TEAT stage [*o* acting] school

interpretar *vt* 1. (*texto, traducir oralmente*) to interpret 2. TEAT to perform; MÚS to render

interpretativo, -a *adj* interpretative, interpretive; **fuerza interpretativa** interpretative ability

intérprete[1] *mf* 1. (*de texto*) scholar 2. (*actor*) performer 3. (*traductor*) interpreter, translator

intérprete[2] *m* INFOR interpreter

interprofesional *adj* **Salario Mínimo Interprofesional** minimum wage

interpuesto, -a *pp de* **interponer**

interregional *adj* interregional

interrelacionado, -a *adj* interrelated

interrelacionar *vt* to interrelate

interrogación *f* 1. (*de policía*) interrogation, questioning 2. (*signo*) question mark

interrogador(a) I. *adj* questioning II. *m(f)* 1. (*que pregunta*) questioner 2. (*policía*) interrogator, cross-examiner

interrogante[1] I. *adj* questioning II. *m* question

interrogante[2] *m o f* questioner

interrogar <g→gu> *vt* 1. (*hacer preguntas*) to question 2. (*policía*) to interrogate

interrogativo, -a *adj* 1. (*mirada*) questioning 2. LING (*pronombre, oración*) interrogative

interrogatorio *m* interrogation, (cross-)examination

interrumpir *vt* 1. (*cortar*) to interrupt; (*brus-*

camente al hablar) to break; (*tráfico*) to hold up **2.** (*estudios*) to terminate; ~ **las vacaciones** (*por unos días*) to temporarily interrupt one's holidays; (*definitivamente*) to cut short one's holidays

interrupción *f* **1.** (*corte*) break; (*del tráfico*) stoppage, hold-up; **sin** ~ uninterruptedly **2.** (*de los estudios*) termination

interruptor *m* ELEC switch, socket *Am*

intersección *f* intersection, crossing, junction

intersticio *m* (*espacio*) *t.* BIO interstice; (*en pared*) crack; (*entre placas*) fissure

interurbano, **-a** *adj* intercity; **conferencia interurbana** TEL intercity call

intervalo *m*, **intérvalo** *m* (*lapso de tiempo*) *t.* MÚS interval; **a ~s** at intervals

intervención *f* **1.** (*participación*) participation **2.** (*en conflicto*) intervention; (*en temas familiares*) involvement **3.** (*mediación*) mediation **4.** POL intervention **5.** MED operation **6.** (*del teléfono*) tapping; (*del correo*) interception

intervencionismo *m* POL interventionism

intervenir *irr como venir* **I.** *vi* **1.** (*tomar parte*) to participate **2.** (*en conflicto*) to intervene **3.** (*mediar*) to mediate **4.** (*suceder*) to occur **II.** *vt* **1.** MED to operate on **2.** (*incautar*) to seize **3.** (*teléfono*) to tap; (*correo*) to intercept **4.** COM to audit

interventor(**a**) *m(f)* **1.** COM auditor **2.** POL supervisor

interviú *m o f* interview

intestinal *adj* intestinal

intestino *m* **1.** ANAT intestine; **el** ~ **grueso** the large intestine; **el** ~ **delgado** the small intestine **2.** *pl* (*tripas*) intestines *pl*, bowels *pl*

intestino, **-a** *adj* internal; **luchas intestinas** (*en un país*) domestic disputes *pl;* (*en un partido*) internal wrangling

íntimamente *adv* **1.** (*estrechamente*) closely **2.** (*en lo íntimo*) intimately

intimar **I.** *vi* to become intimate [*o* friendly] **II.** *vt* to require

intimidación *f* intimidation

intimidad *f* **1.** (*personal*) heart of hearts **2.** *pl* (*sexuales*) private parts *pl;* (*asuntos*) personal matters *pl;* (*privacidad*) privacy **3.** (*vida privada*) private life

intimidar **I.** *vt* to intimidate **II.** *vr:* **~se** to be intimidated

intimidatorio, **-a** *adj* intimidating

íntimo, **-a** *adj* **1.** (*interior, interno*) inner, innermost **2.** (*amigo*) intimate, close **3.** (*velada*) intimate **4.** (*conversación*) private

intocable **I.** *adj* untouchable **II.** *mf* untouchable

intolerable *adj* intolerable

intolerancia *f* intolerance

intolerante *adj* intolerant

intoxicación *f* (*alimentos*) food poisoning; (*alcohol*) intoxication

intoxicar <c→qu> *vt, vr:* ~(**se**) to poison

intracomunitario, **-a** *adj* intra-EU

intraducible *adj* untranslatable

intragable *adj* unpalatable, unbearable *fig*

intranet *f sin pl* INFOR Intranet

intranquilidad *f sin pl* uneasiness

intranquilizador(**a**) *adj* worrying

intranquilizar <z→c> *vt, vr:* ~(**se**) to worry

intranquilo, **-a** *adj* **1.** (*nervioso*) edgy **2.** (*preocupado*) worried, uneasy **3.** (*excitado*) agitated, restless

intransferible *adj* untransferable

intransigencia *f* **1.** (*falto de condescendencia*) intransigence **2.** (*intolerancia*) intolerance

intransigente *adj* **1.** (*no condescendiente*) intransigent **2.** (*intolerante*) intolerant

intransitable *adj* impassable

intransitivo, **-a** *adj* LING intransitive

intrascendencia *f sin pl* triviality

intrascendente *adj* trivial

intratable *adj* **1.** (*persona*) impossible **2.** (*material*) unusable **3.** (*asunto*) intractable **4.** (*enfermedad*) untreatable

intrepidez *f* intrepidity, fearlessness

intrépido, **-a** *adj* intrepid

intriga *f* **1.** (*maquinación*) intrigue **2.** (*de una película*) suspense

intrigante **I.** *adj* **1.** (*persona*) scheming **2.** (*película*) gripping **II.** *mf* schemer

intrigar <g→gu> **I.** *vi* to scheme **II.** *vt* to intrigue

intrincado, **-a** *adj* (*bosque*) thick; (*camino*) twisting; (*nudo*) intricate; (*situación*) complicated

intrincar <c→qu> *vt* (*hilos*) to tangle; (*asunto*) to complicate

intrínseco, **-a** *adj* **1.** (*interior*) intrinsic; **valor** ~ intrinsic value **2.** (*propio*) inherent **3.** (*esencial*) intrinsic

introducción *f* **1.** (*de una llave, de un disquete*) insertion, introduction; (*de clavo*) hammering in; (*de medidas*) introduction; INFOR (*de datos*) input **2.** (*de moda*) introduction; (*de mercancías*) launching **3.** (*de libro*) preface **4.** MÚS overture, prelude

introducir *irr como traducir* **I.** *vt* **1.** (*llave, disquete*) to insert, to put in; (*clavo*) to hammer in; (*medidas*) to introduce; INFOR (*datos*) to enter, to input **2.** (*moda*) to introduce **3.** (*discordia*) to sow **II.** *vr:* **~se** **1.** (*meterse*) to get in(to) **2.** (*en un ambiente*) ~ **en algo** to enter into sth **3.** (*moda*) to be introduced **4.** (*entrometerse*) to interfere

introductorio, **-a** *adj* introductory; **capítulo** ~ introduction

intromisión *f* interference

introspección *f* introspection

introversión *f* introversion

introvertido, **-a** *adj* introverted

intrusión *f* trespass; (*en la vida privada*) intrusion

intruso, **-a** **I.** *adj* intrusive **II.** *m, f* **1.** intruder; (*en reunión*) interloper **2.** (*en fiesta*) gatecrasher

intuición *f* intuition; **saber algo por ~** to know sth intuitively

intuir *irr como huir vt* **1.** (*reconocer*) to intuit *form* **2.** (*presentir*) to sense; **intuyo que...** I have a hunch that ...

intuitivo, **-a** *adj* intuitive

inundación *f* flood(ing)

inundar *vt* to flood

inusitado, **-a** *adj* **1.** (*inhabitual*) unusual, uncommon **2.** (*extraordinario*) unwonted **3.** (*raro*) uncommon

inusual *adj* **1.** (*inhabitual*) unusual **2.** (*extraordinario*) unwonted

inútil **I.** *adj* **1.** (*que no sirve*) useless; MIL unfit **2.** (*esfuerzo*) vain **3.** (*sin sentido*) futile **II.** *mf* (*torpe*) incompetent person

inutilidad *f* uselessness; (*laboral*) incapacity; MIL unfitness

inutilizar <z→c> *vt* **1.** (*objeto*) to render useless; (*sello*) to cancel; (*instalaciones*) to render unusable **2.** (*al enemigo*) to defeat

invadir *vt* **1.** MIL (*país*) to invade **2.** (*entrar en gran número*) to overrun; **los hinchas invadieron el campo** the fans invaded the pitch [*o* field] **3.** (*plaga*) to infest **4.** (*tristeza, dudas*) to assail **5.** (*jurisdicción*) to encroach on; (*privacidad*) to intrude on

invalidar *vt* (*anular*) to invalidate; (*declarar nulo*) to declare null and void; JUR (*matrimonio, contrato*) to annul; (*acuerdo, ley*) to rescind

invalidez *f* **1.** invalidity; (*nulidad*) nullity; JUR (*de matrimonio*) annulment; (*de acuerdo, ley*) rescindment **2.** MED disability; **pensión de ~** disability allowance

inválido, **-a** **I.** *adj* **1.** MED disabled **2.** (*acuerdo*) invalid; JUR null and void **II.** *m, f* disabled person, invalid

invariable *adj t.* MAT invariable

invasión *f* **1.** *t.* MIL, MED invasion **2.** (*de plaga*) plague **3.** (*en jurisdicción*) encroachment; (*en privacidad*) intrusion **4.** MED spreading, infestation

invasor(**a**) **I.** *adj* invasive **II.** *m(f)* invader

invectiva *f* invective

invencible *adj* **1.** (*inderrotable*) invincible **2.** (*insuperable*) unbeatable **3.** (*obstáculo*) unsurmountable

invención *f* invention; (*mentira*) lie

invendible *adj* unsaleable; COM unmarketable

inventar *vt* to invent

inventariar <*1. pres:* inventarío> *vt* to make an inventory of

inventario *m* **1.** (*recuento*) stocktaking, inventory **2.** (*lista*) inventory, list

inventiva *f* inventiveness

invento *m* invention

inventor(**a**) *m(f)* inventor

inverificable *adj* unverifiable

invernada *f* **1.** *elev* (*estación*) winter season **2.** (*hibernación*) hibernation **3.** *CSur* (*invernadero*) winter pasture **4.** *Méx* (*cosecha*) winter crop **5.** *Ven* (*aguacero*) heavy rainstorm

invernadero *m* greenhouse, hothouse; **el efecto ~** the greenhouse effect

invernal *adj* winter; (*tiempo*) wintry; **sueño ~** ZOOL winter sleep, hibernation

invernar <e→ie> *vi* ZOOL to winter; (*los que duermen*) to hibernate

inverosímil *adj* **1.** (*increíble*) implausible **2.** (*que no parece verdad*) improbable, hard to believe

inverosimilitud *f* **1.** (*falta de credibilidad*) implausibility **2.** (*falta de probabilidad*) improbability

inversión *f* **1.** COM, FIN (*dinero*) investment **2.** (*efecto de invertir*) inversion

inversionista *mf* investor

inverso, **-a** *adj* inverse, opposite; **a la inversa** inversely; **y a la inversa** vice versa; **en orden ~** in reverse order

inversor(**a**) *m(f)* investor

invertebrado, **-a** *adj* **1.** ZOOL (*sin columna vertebral*) invertebrate **2.** (*débil*) spineless

invertido, **-a** **I.** *adj* **1.** (*al revés*) inverted; (*volcado*) upside-down **2.** (*sexualmente*) homosexual **II.** *m, f* homosexual

invertir *irr como sentir vt* **1.** (*orden*) to invert **2.** (*volcar*) to turn upside down **3.** (*dinero*) to invest

investidura *f* (*en un cargo*) investiture; REL ordination

investigación *f* **1.** (*indagación*) investigation; (*averiguación*) enquiry *Brit,* inquiry *Am;* **~ de mercado** market research **2.** (*ciencia*) research **3.** (*estudio*) study

investigador(**a**) **I.** *adj* investigative; **comisión ~a** investigatory commission **II.** *m(f)* investigator, researcher; **~ privado** private detective

investigar <g→gu> *vt* **1.** (*indagar*) to investigate; (*averiguar*) to enquire *Brit,* to inquire *Am* **2.** (*en la ciencia*) to research

investir *irr como pedir vt* (*en un cargo*) to confer; **la invistieron doctor honoris causa por la Universidad de Salamanca** she was given an honorary PhD from the University of Salamanca

inveterado, **-a** *adj* (*costumbre*) inveterate, long-standing

inviabilidad *f sin pl* non-viability

inviable *adj* non-viable, unfeasible

invicto, **-a** *adj* unbeaten

invidencia *f* blindness

invidente **I.** *adj* blind **II.** *mf* blind person

invierno *m* **1.** (*estación*) winter **2.** *AmL* (*lluvias*) rainy season **3.** *AmC* (*aguacero*) shower

inviolabilidad *f* POL (*de derechos*) inviolability

inviolable *adj* POL (*derechos*) inviolable

invisibilidad *f* invisibility

invisible *adj* invisible

invitación *f* **1.** (*a una fiesta, una acción*) invitation **2.** (*tarjeta*) invitation card

invitado, **-a** **I.** *adj* invited **II.** *m, f* guest; **~ de honor** guest of honour [*o* honor *Am*]

invitar *vt* **1.** (*convidar*) to invite; **esta vez invito yo** this time it's on me **2.** (*instar*) to press; (*rogar*) to beg; (*tentar*) to be inviting [*o* tempting]
invocación *f* invocation
invocar <c→qu> *vt* **1.** (*dirigirse*) to invoke; (*suplicar*) to implore, to appeal **2.** (*alegar*) to allege **3.** JUR (*apoyarse en una ley*) to invoke
involución *f* **1.** POL reaction **2.** BIO involution, regression
involucionista *adj, mf* POL reactionary
involucrar **I.** *vt* to involve **II.** *vr:* **~se 1.** (*inmiscuirse*) to interfere **2.** (*intervenir*) to become [*o* get] involved
involuntariedad *f* **1.** (*por obligación*) involuntariness **2.** (*falta de voluntad*) unwillingness **3.** (*sin querer*) unintentionality
involuntario, -a *adj* **1.** (*sin querer*) unintentional **2.** (*por obligación*) involuntary
involutivo, -a *adj* regressive
invulnerabilidad *f* **1.** (*que no puede ser herido*) invulnerability **2.** (*insensibilidad*) insensitiveness
invulnerable *adj* **1.** (*que no puede ser herido*) invulnerable **2.** (*insensible*) insensitive; **es ~ a las críticas** he/she is insensitive to the criticism
inyección *f* **1.** MED injection **2.** TÉC fuel injection; **motor de ~** fuel-injected engine
inyectable **I.** *adj* MED injectable **II.** *m* MED injection
inyectar *vt* to inject
inyector *m t.* TÉC injector
ion *m* ion
ionosfera *f* ionosphere
IPC *m* ECON *abr de* **Índice de Precios al Consumo** RPI
ir *irr* **I.** *vi* **1.** (*general*) to go; **¡voy!** I'm coming!; **¡vamos!** let's go!, come on!; **~ a pie** to go on foot; **~ en bicicleta** to go by bicycle; **~ a caballo** to go on horseback; **tengo que ~ a París** I have to go to Paris; **~ detrás de una chica** to chase after a girl **2.** (*ir a buscar*) **iré por el pan** I'll go and get the bread **3.** (*progresar*) to go; **¿cómo va la tesina?** how is the dissertation going?; **¿cómo te va?** how are things?; **va para médica** she is a budding doctor [*o* studying to be a doctor]; **en lo que va de año** so far this year; **~ de culo** *vulg* to be headed straight for disaster **4.** (*diferencia*) **de dos a cinco van tres** two from five leaves three **5.** (*referirse*) **eso no va por ti** I'm not referring to you; **¿tú sabes de lo que va?** do you know what it is about? **6.** (*interj: sorpresa*) **¡vaya coche!** what a car!; **¡qué va!** of course not! **7.** (*con verbo*) **iban charlando** they were chatting; **voy a hacerlo** I'm going to do it **8.** (*edad*) **~ para viejo** to be getting on **II.** *vr:* **~se 1.** (*marcharse*) to leave **2.** (*dirección*) to go; **~se para el sur** to go southwards; **~se por las ramas** to beat about the bush **3.** (*resbalar*) to slip **4.** (*perder*) to leak
ira *f* anger, wrath *form*
iracundo, -a *adj* irate
Irán *m* Iran
iraní *adj, mf* Iranian
Iraq *m* Iraq
iraquí *adj, mf* Iraqi
irascible *adj* irascible
irgo *1. pres de* **erguir**
irguió *3. pret de* **erguir**
iridio *m* iridium
iridiscente *adj* iridescent
iris *m* ANAT iris; **arco ~** rainbow
irisar **I.** *vi* to be iridescent **II.** *vt* to make iridescent
Irlanda *f* Ireland
irlandés, -esa **I.** *adj* Irish **II.** *m, f* Irishman *m*, Irishwoman *f*
ironía *f* irony; **~ del destino** quirks of fate
irónico, -a **I.** *adj* ironic **II.** *m, f* ironic person
ironizar <z→c> *vt* to be ironic
IRPF *m abr de* **Impuesto sobre la Renta de las Personas Físicas** personal income tax
irracional *adj* (*contra la razón*) irrational; (*contra la lógica*) illogical; **número ~** MAT irrational number; **ser ~** to be unreasonable
irracionalidad *f sin pl* irrationality
irradiación *f* **1.** (*de material nuclear*) radiation **2.** MED (*tratamiento*) radiotherapy; (*dolor*) diffusion
irradiar **I.** *vt* **1.** (*emitir*) to radiate **2.** (*difundir*) to diffuse **3.** (*tratamiento*) to irradiate **II.** *vi* to radiate **III.** *vr:* **~se** to be diffused, to be disseminated *form*
irrazonable *adj* irrational
irreal *adj* unreal
irrealidad *f* unreality
irrealizable *adj* unrealizable, unfeasible
irrebatible *adj*, **irrechazable** *adj* irrefutable
irreconciliable *adj* irreconcilable
irreconocible *adj* unrecognizable
irrecuperable *adj* irretrievable
irreductible *adj* uncompromising
irreflexión *f* recklessness, thoughtlessness
irreflexivo, -a *adj* **1.** (*acción*) reckless **2.** (*persona*) rash **3.** (*precipitado*) hasty
irrefrenable *adj* **1.** (*desarrollo*) uncontrollable **2.** (*persona*) irrepressible
irrefutable *adj* irrefutable
irregular *adj* **1.** (*desigual*) irregular, uneven **2.** (*contra las reglas*) irregular; (*sin reglas*) without rules; (*anómalo*) anomalous *form*
irregularidad *f* **1.** (*desigualdad, del terreno*) irregularity, unevenness **2.** (*contra las reglas*) irregularity; (*sin reglas*) absence of rules
irrelevante *adj* irrelevant
irremediable *adj* **1.** (*inevitable*) inevitable **2.** (*irreparable*) irremediable **3.** (*daño físico*) irreversible
irremisible *adj* **1.** (*falta*) unpardonable **2.** (*pérdida*) irretrievable
irrenunciable *adj* **1.** (*imprescindible*) indispensable **2.** (*destino*) inescapable
irreparable *adj* **1.** (*que no se puede reparar*)

irreparable; (*incompensable*) which cannot be compensated **2.** (*daño físico*) irreversible
irrepetible *adj* unique
irreprimible *adj* irrepressible
irreprochable *adj* irreproachable
irreproducible *adj* **1.** (*irrepetible*) unrepeatable **2.** (*que ya no se puede fabricar*) irreplaceable
irresistible *adj* **1.** (*atractivo*) irresistible **2.** (*inaguantable*) unbearable
irresoluble *adj* unsolvable
irresolución *f* **1.** (*indecisión*) indecisiveness **2.** (*vacilación*) irresolution
irresoluto, **-a** *adj* **1.** (*indeciso*) indecisive **2.** (*vacilante*) irresolute **3.** (*problema*) unsolved
irrespetuoso, **-a** *adj* disrespectful
irrespirable *adj* **1.** (*por tóxico*) unbreathable **2.** (*aire*) stale, suffocating
irresponsabilidad *f* **1.** (*falta de responsabilidad*) absence of responsibility; (*por minoría de edad*) absence of legal responsibility (*as a minor*) **2.** (*desconsideración*) irresponsibility **3.** COM (*sociedades*) absence of liability
irresponsable **I.** *adj* **1.** (*no responsable*) irresponsible; ~ **de algo** not responsible for sth **2.** COM (*sociedades*) ~ **de algo** not liable for sth **II.** *mf* irresponsible person
irreverencia *f* irreverence
irreverente *adj* irreverent
irreversible *adj* irreversible
irrevocable *adj* **1.** (*no revocable*) irrevocable; (*firme*) firm **2.** (*inamovible*) unalterable
irrigación *f* **1.** AGR (*regadío*) irrigation **2.** MED (*del recto*) administration of an enema; (*vagina*) douching
irrigar <g→gu> *vt* **1.** AGR (*regar*) to irrigate **2.** MED (*la sangre*) to oxygenate
irrisorio, **-a** *adj* derisory; **a precios ~s** at ridiculous [*o* ridiculously low] prices
irritabilidad *f sin pl* irritability
irritable *adj* irritable
irritación *f* **1.** MED (*órgano*) inflammation; (*de piel*) irritation **2.** (*enfado*) irritation
irritante *adj* **1.** (*enojar, molesto*) irritating **2.** MED (*órgano*) inflamed
irritar **I.** *vt* **1.** (*enojar, molestar*) to irritate **2.** MED (*órgano*) to inflame **II.** *vr:* **~se** **1.** (*enojarse*) to become irritated **2.** MED (*órgano*) to become inflamed
irrompible *adj* **1.** (*material*) unbreakable **2.** (*amistad*) solid
irrumpir *vi* ~ **en algo** to burst into sth
irrupción *f* **1.** (*entrada*) irruption **2.** MIL (*invasión*) invasion; (*ataque*) raid
IRTP *m abr de* **impuesto sobre el rendimiento del trabajo personal** PAYE
isla *f* island
Islam *m* REL Islam
islámico, **-a** *adj* Islamic
islamización *f* Islamization
islandés, **-esa** **I.** *adj* Icelandic **II.** *m, f* Icelander
Islandia *f* Iceland
isleño, **-a** **I.** *adj* island **II.** *m, f* islander
islote *m* islet
isobara *f*, **isóbara** *f* METEO isobar
isotónico, **-a** *adj* isotonic
Israel *m* Israel
israelí *adj, mf* Israeli
israelita *adj, mf* Israelite
istmo *m* GEO isthmus
itacate *m Méx* (*provisión*) travel(ling) provisions
Italia *f* Italy
italiano, **-a** *adj, m, f* Italian
itálico, **-a** HIST **I.** *adj* Italic **II.** *m, f* Italic; (*letra*) italics *pl*
itinerante *adj* itinerant, traveling *Brit,* travelling *Am*
itinerario *m* **1.** (*ruta*) itinerary **2.** FERRO (*horario*) timetable *Brit,* schedule *Am* **3.** AVIAT (*vuelo*) route
ITV *f abr de* **Inspección Técnica de Vehículos** MOT test
IVA *m abr de* **impuesto sobre el valor añadido** VAT
izada *f AmL* raising
izar <z→c> *vt* NÁUT to hoist
izcuinche *m Méx* **1.** (*perro callejero*) mangy stray dog **2.** (*niño callejero*) street urchin
izda. *adj,* **izdo.** *adj abr de* **izquierda, izquierdo** left
izquierda *f* **1.** (*mano*) left hand **2.** POL left **3.** (*lado*) left side; **a la ~** to the left
izquierdista **I.** *adj* POL left-wing, leftist **II.** *mf* POL left-winger, leftist
izquierdo, **-a** *adj* left; *fig* crooked; (*zurdo*) left-handed; **levantarse con el pie ~** to get up on the wrong side of the bed

J

J

J, **j** *f* J, j; ~ **de Juan** J for Jack *Brit,* J for Jig *Am*
ja *interj* ha
jabalí *m* <jabalíes> wild boar
jabalina *f* **1.** ZOOL female wild boar **2.** DEP javelin
jabato *m* **1.** ZOOL young wild boar **2.** (*hombre*) daredevil; **luchar como un ~** to fight like a lion
jabato, **-a** *adj* brave
jabón *m* **1.** (*para lavar*) soap; **pastilla de ~** bar of soap **2.** *PRico, Arg* (*susto*) fright ►**dar ~ a alguien** to soft-soap sb; **dar un ~ a alguien** to give sb a hard time
jabonar *vt* **1.** (*con jabón*) to soap **2.** *inf* (*reprender*) to tell off
jaboncillo *m* **1.** (*de tocador*) (bar of) toilet soap **2.** (*de sastre*) French chalk
jabonera *f* **1.** (*para depositar jabón*) soapdish **2.** BOT soapwort

jabonoso, **-a** *adj* soapy
jabugo *m type of Spanish ham* (*from Jabugo*)
jaca *f* **1.** (*yegua*) mare **2.** *pey* (*caballo*) nag **3.** *AmL* (*gallo*) (fighting) cock
jacal *m Méx, Ven* hut
jacalear *vi Méx* to spread rumours [*o* rumors *Am*]
jacarandá *m AmL* BOT jacaranda
jacarandoso, **-a** *adj* merry
jacarero, **-a** *m, f inf* joker
jacinto *m* hyacinth
jaco *m* **1.** (*caballo pequeño*) small horse **2.** *pey* (*caballo*) nag
jactancia *f* boasting, boastfulness
jactancioso, **-a** **I.** *adj* boastful **II.** *m, f* boaster
jactarse *vr* **jactarse de algo** to boast of [*o* about] sth
jaculatoria *f* short prayer
jacuz(**z**)**i**® *m* Jacuzzi®
jade *m* jade
jadear *vi* to pant
Jaén *m* Jaen
jaenero, **-a**, **jaenés**, **-esa** **I.** *adj* of/from Jaen **II.** *m, f* native/inhabitant of Jaen
jaez *m* **1.** (*de caballo*) harness **2.** (*clase, condición*) kind, ilk; **persona de mal** ~ bad type; **no te fíes de gente de ese** ~ don't trust that sort of people
jaguar *m* jaguar
jagüel *m*, **jagüey** *m AmL* (*balsa*) pool; (*cisterna*) cistern
jaiba **I.** *adj* **1.** *Ant, Méx* (*astuto*) cunning **2.** *Cuba* (*perezoso*) lazy **II.** *f AmL* (*cangrejo*) crab
jáibol *m Méx* whisky and soda, highball *Am*
jalada *f Méx, Ven: inf* **1.** (*exageración*) exaggeration **2.** (*reprimenda*) ticking-off
jalado, **-a** *adj* **1.** *Méx, Ven* (*exagerado*) exaggerated **2.** *AmL* (*demacrado*) emaciated **3.** *AmL* (*obsequioso*) obliging **4.** *AmL* (*borracho*) drunk
jalar **I.** *vt AmL* **1.** (*una cuerda*) to pull **2.** (*una persona*) to attract **3.** *inf* (*comer*) to guzzle, to wolf down **II.** *vi Bol, PRico, Urug, Ven* (*largarse*) to clear off **III.** *vr:* **~se** *AmL* (*emborracharse*) to get drunk
jalea *f* jelly
jalear *vt* (*animar*) to encourage
jaleo *m* **1.** (*barullo*) commotion; **armar** ~ to kick up a row [*o* fuss] **2.** (*desorden*) confusion; **me he armado un** ~ **con los nombres** *inf* I've got the names all mixed up **3.** (*riña*) quarrel
jalón *m* **1.** (*vara*) pole **2.** (*hito*) landmark, milestone
jalonar *vt* **1.** (*un terreno*) to stake out **2.** (*marcar*) to mark
jamar **I.** *vt inf* (*comer*) to hoover *Brit*, to scarf (down) *Am* **II.** *vr:* **~se** *inf* (*atracarse*) to stuff oneself
jamás *adv* never; ~ **de los jamases** never in your life; ~ **había tenido la oportunidad** I'd/he'd/she'd never had the chance; **¿habías leído** ~ **algo parecido?** had you ever read anything like it?; **nunca digas nunca** ~ never (ever) say never; **nunca** ~ never again
jamba *f* (*de la ventana*) reveal, window post; (*de la puerta*) door post
jamelgo *m inf* (*caballo*) nag
jamón *m* ham; ~ **dulce** [*o* **de York**] boiled ham; ~ **serrano** cured ham ►**¡y un ~!** *inf* get away!
Japón *m* Japan
japonés, **-esa** *adj, m, f* Japanese
jaque *m* **1.** DEP check; ~ **mate** checkmate; **dar** ~ to check **2.** *inf* (*perdonavidas*) big talker ►**tener a alguien en** ~ *fig* to keep sb in check
jaquear *vt* DEP to check
jaqueca *f* (severe) headache, migraine; **este tipo me da** ~ *inf* this guy's getting to me
jara *f* **1.** BOT rockrose **2.** *Guat, Méx* (*flecha*) arrow
jarabe *m* syrup; (*para la tos*) cough mixture [*o* syrup] ►**dar** ~ **de palo a alguien** *inf* to give sb a thrashing; ~ **de pico** *inf* empty talk
jarana *f* **1.** *inf* (*juerga*) spree; **ir de** ~ *inf* to go on a spree **2.** *Méx* MÚS *small guitar* **3.** *AmL* (*burla*) joke **4.** *AmC* (*deuda*) debt **5.** *Col* (*embuste*) trick
jaranear **I.** *vi inf* (*ir de copas*) to go out on the town; (*divertirse*) to live it up **II.** *vt Col* (*importunar*) to pester
jaranero, **-a** *m, f* **ser un** ~ to be a reveller [*o* reveler *Am*]
jarcia *f* NÁUT rigging
jardín *m* (*césped*) garden; (*flores, plantas*) garden; ~ **de infancia** (*hasta los tres años*) creche *Brit*, nursery school; (*a partir de tres años*) kindergarten; **los jardines de una ciudad** the municipal parks; **trabajar en el** ~ to garden
jardinear *vt AmL* to garden
jardinera *f* **1.** (*profesión*) (woman) gardener **2.** (*maceta*) window box ►**a la** ~ à la jardiniere
jardinería *f* gardening
jardinero, **-a** *m, f* gardener
jareta *f* **1.** (*para ceñir*) casing; **cinturón de** ~ drawstring waist **2.** (*dobladillo*) hem; (*pliegue*) tuck **3.** *CRi, Par* (*bragueta*) trouser fly, zip *Brit*, zipper *Am*
jarocho, **-a** *adj* **1.** (*rudo, insolente*) boorish, uncouth **2.** *AmL* (*natural de Veracruz*) native of Veracruz
jarra *f* jar; (*de agua*) jug, pitcher *Am;* (*de café*) mug ►**ponerse de** [*o* **en**] **~s** to stand with arms akimbo
jarro *m* jug, pitcher; (*de agua*) pitcher; **echar un** ~ **de agua fría** *fig* to pour cold water on
jarrón *m* vase
jartón, **-ona** *m, f AmC, Méx* (*comilón*) greedy-guts *inf*
jaspeado, **-a** *adj* speckled; (*tela, lana*) variegated
jauja *f* earthly paradise; **¡pero te crees que esto es Jauja!** where do you think you are?;

para ti la vida es **Jauja** you're living in clover
jaula *f* (*para animales*) cage
jauría *f* pack of hounds
jazmín *m* jasmine
jazz *m sin pl* MÚS jazz; **tocar** ~ to jazz
J.C. *abr de* **Jesucristo** J.C.
jebe *m* **1.** (*alumbre*) alum **2.** *AmL* (*caucho*) rubber
jeep *m* <jeeps> jeep
jefatura *f* **1.** (*cargo*) leadership **2.** (*sede*) ~ **del gobierno** seat of government; ~ **de policía** police headquarters
jefazo *m inf* big boss
jefe, -a *m, f* (*de una organización, empresa*) head, boss; (*de un departamento*) head; (*de una banda*) leader; ~ **de filas** DEP team captain; ~ **de gobierno** head of the government; ~ **de(l) Estado** head of state; ~ **de partido** party leader; **redactor** ~ editor-in-chief; **en mi casa no soy yo el ~, sino mi mujer** it's my wife who wears the trousers [*o* pants], not me
jengibre *m* ginger
jeque *m* sheik(h)
jerarca *mf* high official
jerarquía *f* hierarchy
jerárquico, -a *adj* hierarchical
jerez *m* sherry
jerga *f* (*lenguaje*) jargon
jergón *m* **1.** (*colchón*) rough mattress, pallet **2.** *inf* (*persona*) oaf
jeribeque *m* **hacer ~s** to make faces
jerigonza *f* **1.** (*galimatías*) gibberish **2.** (*jerga*) jargon
jeringa *f* (*instrumento*) syringe
jeringar <g→gu> *vt* **1.** (*con la jeringa*) to syringe **2.** *inf* (*molestar*) to pester
jeringuilla *f* syringe
jeroglífico *m* **1.** (*signo*) hieroglyph(ic) **2.** (*pasatiempo*) rebus, puzzle
jeroglífico, -a *adj* hieroglyphic
jersey *m* pullover, jumper *Brit;* ~ **de cuello alto** roll-neck *Brit* [*o* turtleneck *Am*] sweater
Jerusalén *m* Jerusalem
Jesucristo *m* Jesus Christ
jesuita *adj, m* Jesuit
Jesús *m* Jesus ►**en un** (**decir**) ~ in a flash; **¡~!** (*al estornudar*) bless you!; (*interjección*) good heavens!
jet[1] *m* <jets> (*avión*) jet
jet[2] *f sin pl* (*alta sociedad*) jet set
jeta *f* **1.** *inf* (*cara*) mug, dial; **ése tiene una ~ increíble** *fig* what incredible cheek that guy has **2.** (*labios*) lips **3.** (*del cerdo*) snout
ji *interj* ha
jíbaro, -a *adj* **1.** *AmL* (*campesino*) country, peasant; (*costumbres, vida*) rural **2.** *AmL* (*planta, animal*) wild **3.** *Ant, Méx* (*huraño*) shy
jibia *f* cuttlefish
jícama *f Méx* BOT edible tuber
jícaro *m AmC* (*árbol*) calabash tree
jicotera *f AmC, Méx* wasps' nest
jienense, -a **I.** *adj* of/from Jaen **II.** *m, f* native/inhabitant of Jaen
jijona *m* soft nougat (*made in Jijona*)
jilguero *m* goldfinch
jincho, -a *adj Col, inf* (*borracho*) drunk
jineta *f* genet
jinete *m* (*persona*) horseman; (*profesional*) rider
jinetear *vt AmL* (*domar*) to break in (horses)
jinetera *f Cuba, inf* prostitute
jiote *m Méx* MED impetigo
jipa *f Col* Panama hat
jira *f* **1.** (*jirón*) strip of cloth **2.** (*picnic*) picnic **3.** (*excursión*) outing
jirafa *f* **1.** ZOOL giraffe **2.** (*para el micro*) boom
jirón *m* shred; **hacer algo jirones** to tear sth to shreds
jitazo *m Méx* hit
jitomate *m Méx* (*tomate*) tomato
JJ.OO. *abr de* **Juegos Olímpicos** Olympic Games
jo *interj* **1.** (*so*) whoa **2.** (*sorpresa*) **¡~!** well, well!
jobillo *m PRico, inf* **irse de ~s** to play truant
jockey *m* jockey
jocosidad *f* **1.** (*cualidad*) humour *Brit,* humor *Am* **2.** (*chiste*) joke
jocoso, -a *adj* humourous, jocular
jocundo, -a *adj* jovial
joda *f Arg, vulg* (*broma*) joke; **lo dije en** ~ I was only joking
joder **I.** *vt vulg* **1.** (*copular*) to fuck, to screw **2.** (*fastidiar*) to piss off; **¡no me jodas!** piss off! **3.** (*echar a perder*) to fuck up **4.** (*robar*) to pinch **II.** *vi vulg* to fuck **III.** *vr:* **~se** *vulg* **1.** (*fastidiarse*) to get pissed off; **¡jódete!** piss [*o* fuck] off!; **¡hay que ~se!** to hell with it!; **¡no te jode!** you must be off your head! **2.** (*echar a perder*) **nuestra amistad se ha jodido** our friendship's gone down the drain [*o* tubes *Brit*]; **la tele se ha jodido** the telly's buggered **IV.** *interj vulg* shit
jodido, -a **I.** *pp de* **joder** **II.** *adj vulg* **1.** (*cansado*) buggered; **estoy** ~ I'm buggered **2.** (*difícil*) fucking difficult; **es ~ tener que trabajar tanto** it's damned hard [*o* bloody tough *Brit*] having to work so much
jodón, -ona **I.** *adj Méx, inf* fucking [*o* bloody *Brit*] annoying **II.** *m, f Méx, inf* pain in the neck
joint-venture, joint venture *f* ECON joint venture
jojoba *f AmL* BOT jojoba
jolgorio *m* merriment
jolín *interj,* **jolines** *interj* sugar
jopé *interj* sugar
Jordania *f* Jordan
jordano, -a *adj, m, f* Jordanian
jornada *f* **1.** (*de trabajo*) working day; (*tiempo trabajado*) hours of work; ~ **continua** *continuous timetable without lunch break, finishing early;* ~ **partida** split shift; **trabajo media** ~ I work half a day [*o* part-time] **2.** (*viaje*) day's journey; (*andando*) day's march

J

[*o* walk]; **este pueblo está a dos ~s de viaje** this village is two days' journey away **3.** *pl* (*congreso, simposio*) conference

jornal *m* (*paga*) day's wage [*o* pay]; **trabajar a ~** to be paid by the day

jornalero, -a *m, f* day labourer *Brit,* day laborer *Am*

joroba *f* **1.** (*de persona*) hunched back **2.** (*de camello*) hump **3.** *inf* (*molestia*) nuisance

jorobado, -a **I.** *adj* hunchbacked **II.** *m, f* hunchback

jorobar **I.** *vt inf* to annoy **II.** *vr:* **~se** *inf* **1.** (*enojarse*) to get annoyed **2.** (*aguantar*) to put up with it; **si no le gusta, ¡que se jorobe!** if he doesn't like it, he can lump it!

jorongo *m Méx* poncho

joropo *m Col: popular dance of the Colombian lowlanders*

jota *f* **1.** (*letra*) j **2.** (*baile*) *Aragonese dance* ▸**no entender** [*o* **saber**] **ni ~** *inf* not to have a clue; **no ver ni ~** *inf* not to see a thing

joto *m* **1.** *Col* (*paquete*) bundle **2.** *Méx, pey* (*homosexual*) queer

joven **I.** *adj* young; **de muy ~** in early youth **II.** *mf* young man *m,* young woman *f;* **los jóvenes** young people

jovial *adj* cheerful, jovial

joya *f* **1.** (*alhaja*) jewel; (*piedra*) gem; **las ~s** jewellery, jewelry *Am* **2.** (*persona, cosa*) gem; **esta mujer de la limpieza es una ~** this cleaning lady is a real treasure; **este niño es una ~** this child is a little gem

joyería *f* **1.** (*joyas*) jewellery *Brit,* jewelry *Am* **2.** (*tienda*) jeweller's shop *Brit,* jeweler's shop *Am*

joyero *m* jewel case

joyero, -a *m, f* jeweller *Brit,* jeweler *Am*

juanete *m* (*del pie*) bunion

jubilación *f* **1.** (*acción*) retirement; **~ anticipada** early retirement **2.** (*pensión*) pension

jubilado, -a *m, f* pensioner, retiree; **aquí viven muchos ~s** lots of retired people live round here

jubilar **I.** *vt* **1.** (*a alguien*) to pension off **2.** *inf* (*un objeto*) to take out of circulation; **~ algo** to get rid of sth **II.** *vr:* **~se** **1.** (*retirarse*) to retire **2.** *AmC* (*hacer novillos*) to play truant

júbilo *m* joy, jubilation

jubiloso, -a *adj* jubilant; **estar ~** to be joyful

judaico, -a *adj* Jewish, Judaic

judas *m* traitor

judía *f* **1.** (*mujer*) Jewess **2.** bean; **~ verde** green bean

judicatura *f* **1.** (*cargo*) office of judge, judgeship **2.** (*de un país*) judicature, judiciary **3.** **~ del trabajo** ≈industrial law

judicial *adj* judicial

judío, -a **I.** *adj* Jewish **II.** *m, f* Jew

judo *m* DEP judo

juego *m* **1.** (*diversión*) game; **~ de mesa** board game; **~ de los roles** role-playing; **hacer ~s malabares** to juggle; **tengo mal ~** I've a bad hand; **perder dinero en el ~** to gamble money away **2.** DEP play; **~ en blanco** nil draw; **~ limpio** fair play; **~ sucio** foul play; **fuera de ~** (*persona*) offside; (*balón*) out of play; **entrar/poner en ~** to come/to bring into play **3.** (*conjunto*) set; **~ de café** coffee set; **~ de mesa** dinner service; **hacer ~** to match **4.** TÉC play; **esta llave no hace ~ con la cerradura** this key doesn't turn in the lock ▸**desgraciado en el ~, afortunado en amores** *prov* lucky at cards, unlucky in love *prov;* **hacer el ~ a alguien haciendo algo** to play into one's rival's hands by doing sth; **tomarse algo a ~** to take sth as a joke; **vérsele a alguien el ~** to know what sb is up to

juerga *f* spree; **ayer estuve de ~** *inf* I was (out) partying [*o* on a spree] yesterday; **anoche se armó una ~ increíble en ese bar** *inf* there was a real party going on in that bar last night; **correrse unas cuantas ~s** *inf* to go out at night quite a bit

jueves *m inv* Thursday; **Jueves Santo** Maundy Thursday ▸**no es nada del otro ~** it's nothing to write home about; *v.t.* **lunes**

juez *mf t.* JUR judge; **~ de instrucción** JUR examining magistrate; **~ de paz** justice of the peace; **ser ~ y parte** to be biased; **~ de línea** [*o* **de banda**] DEP linesman

jugada *f* **1.** DEP play; **~ de ajedrez** chess move; **~ antirreglamentaria** foul play; **las ~s de Michael Jordan encandilaban al público** the audience loved Michael Jordan's plays; **Ronaldo hizo una ~ genial** Ronaldo made a great move **2.** (*jugarreta*) bad turn; **hacer** [*o* **gastar**] **una ~ a alguien** to play a dirty trick on sb

jugador(a) **I.** *adj* **mi marido es muy ~** my husband like to gamble a lot **II.** *m(f) t.* DEP player

jugar *irr* **I.** *vi* **1.** (*a un juego, deporte*) to play; **~ limpio/sucio** to play fair/unfairly; **¿quién juega?** (*juego de mesa*) whose move it?; (*partido en la TV, radio*) who's playing?; **¿puedo ~?** can I join in?; **¿a qué juegas?** *fig* what are you playing at? **2.** (*bromear*) to play about; **hacer algo por ~** to do sth for fun **3.** (*en un negocio*) to speculate; **~ a la bolsa** to speculate on the stock exchange **4.** (*hacer juego*) to match **II.** *vt* **1.** (*un juego, una partida*) to play **2.** (*apostar*) to gamble; **~ fuerte** to play for high stakes **3.** (*una carta*) to play; (*una torre*) to move; **¿quién juega?** whose turn is it?; (*al ajedrez*) whose move is it? **III.** *vr:* **~se** **1.** (*la lotería*) to be drawn **2.** (*apostar*) **~se algo** to gamble [*o* to bet] on sth; **¿qué te juegas que...?** (do you) want to bet that ...? **3.** (*arriesgar*) to risk; **~se el todo por el todo** to stake one's all ▸**jugársela a alguien** to take sb for a ride

jugarreta *f inf* **1.** (*jugada*) bad move **2.** (*trampa*) dirty trick; **hacer una ~ a alguien** to pull a fast one on sb

juglar *m* HIST, LIT, MÚS minstrel

jugo *m* **1.** (*de fruta, carne*) juice; **~s gástricos**

gastric juices **2.** (*esencia*) essence; **declaraciones con mucho** ~ *fig* important declarations ►sacar el ~ a alguien to squeeze sb dry
jugoso, **-a** *adj* (*fruta, carne*) juicy
juguete *m* **1.** (*objeto*) toy; **el barco era un ~ de las olas** *fig* the boat was at the mercy of the waves **2.** *pl* COM toys *pl*
juguetear *vi* **1.** (*con las llaves, una pelota*) to play **2.** (*los niños*) to romp
juguetería *f* toyshop
juguetón, **-ona** *adj* playful
juicio *m* **1.** (*facultad para juzgar*) reason **2.** (*razón*) sense; **falta de** ~ lack of common sense; **recobrar el** ~ to come to one's senses; **tú no estás en tu sano** ~ you're not in your right mind **3.** (*opinión*) opinion; **a mi** ~ to my mind; **emitir un ~ sobre algo** to pass judgement on sth **4.** JUR trial; ~ **criminal** criminal proceedings; **llevar a alguien a** ~ to take sb to court; **el** (**día del**) **Juicio final** REL the Last Judgement
juicioso, **-a** *adj* (*sensato*) sensible; (*acertado*) fitting
juil *m Méx* ZOOL *Mexican lake trout;* **si el ~ no abriera la boca, no lo pescarían** *prov* silence is golden *prov*
julepe *m* **1.** (*castigo*) punishment; (*reprimenda*) telling-off; **dar ~ a alguien** (*castigar*) to punish sb; (*dar una reprimenda*) to give sb a dressing-down **2.** *AmL* (*miedo*) scare **3.** *AmL* (*ajetreo*) drudgery; **dar un ~ a alguien** *inf* to make sb sweat
julia *f* **1.** ZOOL snakefish **2.** *Méx, inf* (*coche celular*) police van, paddy wagon *Am*
julio *m* **1.** (*mes*) July; *v.t.* **marzo** **2.** FÍS joule
juma *f AmL, inf* drunkenness
jumado, **-a** *adj AmL, inf* drunk
jumarse *vr Col, Cuba* to get drunk
jumento *m* donkey
jumo *m PRico* drunkenness
jumo, **-a** *adj AmL* (*borracho*) drunk
juncal *adj* (*gallardo*) slim
junco *m* **1.** BOT reed **2.** (*bastón*) (walking) stick, cane **3.** (*embarcación*) junk
jungla *f* jungle
junio *m* June; *v.t.* **marzo**
júnior *m* <juniors> junior
junta *f* **1.** (*comité*) committee; (*consejo*) council; ~ **calificadora** ENS examining board; ~ **directiva** COM board of directors; ~ **militar** MIL military junta; ~ **municipal** POL district council **2.** (*reunión*) meeting; ~ **general** general meeting; **celebrar** ~ to hold a board meeting; ~ **de accionistas** shareholders' meeting **3.** TÉC (*de dos ladrillos, tablas*) joint; (*de dos tubos*) junction; (*sellado*) seal
juntar **I.** *vt* **1.** (*aproximar*) ~ **la mesa a la pared** to move the table over to the wall; ~ **las sillas** to put the chairs together **2.** (*unir*) to join **3.** (*reunir: personas*) to assemble; (*objetos*) to put together; (*dinero*) to collect **4.** (*puerta, ventana*) to pull to **II.** *vr:* **~se** **1.** (*reunirse*) to meet **2.** (*unirse*) to come together **3.** (*aproximarse*) to come closer **4.** (*vivir juntos*) to move in (together); **se han juntado** they've started living together
junto **I.** *adv* **hablaba por teléfono y trabajaba en el ordenador, todo** ~ he/she was on the phone and at his/her computer at the same time **II.** *prep* **1.** (*local*) ~ **a** near to; **¿quién es el que está ~ a ella?** who's the man at her side?; **estábamos ~ a la entrada** we were at the entrance; **pasaron ~ a nosotros** they walked past us **2.** (*con movimiento*) ~ **a** beside; **he puesto la botella ~ a las otras** I've put the bottle beside the others; **pon la silla ~ a la mesa** put the chair next to the table **3.** (*con, en compañía de*) ~ **con** together with
junto, **-a** *adj* joined; **nos sentamos todos ~s** we all sat together; **me las pagarás todas juntas** you'll pay for that
juntura *f* TÉC (*de dos ladrillos, tablas*) joint; (*de dos tubos*) junction; (*sellado*) seal
jupiarse *vr AmC* to get drunk
jura *f* oath; (*acto*) swearing in
juraco *m AmL* hole
jurado *m* **1.** JUR (*miembro*) juror; (*tribunal*) jury **2.** (*de un examen*) qualified examiner **3.** (*de un concurso*) panel member
jurado, **-a** *adj* qualified; **intérprete** ~ sworn interpreter
juramentar **I.** *vt* to swear in **II.** *vr:* **~se** to be sworn in
juramento *m* **1.** *t.* JUR (*jura*) oath; **falso** ~ perjury; **estar bajo** ~ to be on oath; **tomar ~ a alguien** to swear sb in **2.** (*blasfemia*) swearword
jurar *vt, vi* to swear; ~ **por alguien** to swear by sb; ~ **en falso** to commit perjury; ~ **por todos los santos** to swear blind; **jurársela(s) a alguien** *inf* to swear vengeance on sb
jurel *m* horse mackerel
jurero, **-a** *m, f Chile, Ecua* (*testigo falso contratado*) false witness
jurídico, **-a** *adj* legal, lawful
jurisdicción *f* **1.** JUR (*potestad*) jurisdiction; ~ **militar** military law; **ese caso no está dentro de la ~ de este tribunal** that case does not come within the jurisdiction of this court **2.** (*territorio*) administrative district
jurisdiccional *adj* jurisdictional, judicial; **no** ~ extrajudicial; **aguas ~es** territorial waters
jurisperito, **-a** *m, f* legal expert
jurisprudencia *f* **1.** (*legislación*) jurisprudence **2.** (*ciencia*) science of law
jurista *mf* jurist
jurungar <g→gu> *Ven* **I.** *vt* to bore **II.** *vr:* **~se** to get bored
justamente *adv* **1.** (*con justicia*) justly **2.** (*precisamente*) precisely **3.** (*ajustadamente*) **este vestido viene ~ al cuerpo** this dress is close-fitting
justicia *f* **1.** (*cualidad, poder judicial*) justice; **en ~, él merece ganar el premio** in all fairness, he deserves to win the prize; **hacer ~ a**

J

alguien to do sb justice **2.**(*derecho*) law; **administrar** ~ to administer justice
justiciero, -a *adj* (*justo*) just; (*severo*) strict
justificable *adj* justifiable
justificación *f* **1.**(*disculpa*) justification; **no hay ~ para lo que has hecho** there's no excuse for what you've done **2.**(*prueba*) proof, evidence; (*documento*) document
justificante *m* supporting evidence; (*de ausencia*) note of absence
justificar <c→qu> **I.** *vt* **1.**(*disculpar*) to justify; **mi desconfianza es justificada** my distrust is vindicated **2.**(*probar*) to prove; (*con documentos*) to substantiate **II.** *vr:* **~se** to justify oneself
justipreciar *vt* (*apreciar*) to assess; (*tasar*) to evaluate
justiprecio *m* (*aprecio*) assessment; (*tasación*) valuation, appraisal
justo I. *adv* **1.**(*exactamente*) right; **llegué ~ a tiempo** I arrived just in time **2.**(*escasamente*) scarcely; **tengo ~ para vivir** I've just enough to live on **II.** *mpl* the just
justo, -a *adj* **1.**(*persona, decisión*) just **2.**(*exacto*) exact; (*acertado*) correct; **el peso ~** the correct weight; **¿tiene el dinero ~? es que no tengo cambio** do you have the exact amount (of money)? I don't seem to have any change **3.**(*escaso*) **ha venido muy justo el dinero** money's been very tight **4.**(*ajustado*) close-fitting; **este abrigo me viene ~** this coat is rather tight for me
juvenil I. *adj* youthful, young **II.** *mf* DEP **juego con los ~es** I'm in the junior team
juventud *f* **1.**(*edad*) youth **2.**(*estado*) early life **3.**(*jóvenes*) young people
juzgado *m* **1.**(*jueces, local*) court; **~ de guardia** police court; **~ de lo penal** criminal court **2.**(*territorio*) juridical district
juzgar <g→gu> **I.** *vt* **1.**(*juez: decidir*) to judge; (*condenar*) to sentence **2.**(*opinar sobre*) to judge; (*considerar*) to consider, to deem; **~ mal a alguien** to misjudge sb; **juzgo necesario avisarle** I consider it necessary to inform him/her/you; **le ~on de maleducado** they considered him ill-mannered; **no te juzgo capaz de hacerlo** I don't think you're capable of doing it **II.** *vi* **1.**(*juez*) to judge **2.**(*opinar*) **~ sobre apariencias** to judge by appearances; **a ~ por como me mira, debe conocerme** judging by how he/she is looking at me, he/she must know me

K

K, k *f* K, k; **~ de Kenia** K for King
kaki *adj* khaki
karaoke *m* karaoke
karate *m*, **kárate** *m* DEP karate
kart *m* <karts> go-cart
kartin(g) *m* <kartin(g)s> DEP go-carting
katiuska *f* gumboot, Wellintons *pl*
kayac *m* <kayacs> DEP kayak
Kazajstán *m* Kazakhstan
KB *m* INFOR *abr de* **kilobyte** KB
kéfir *m* kefir (*type of yoghurt*)
keniano, -a *adj, m, f* Kenyan
keniata *adj, mf* Kenyan
kerosén *m AmS* kerosene
keroseno *m* kerosene, paraffin
ketchup *m* <ketchups> ketchup
kg *abr de* **kilogramo** kg
kibutz *m* <kibutzs> kibbutz
kikirikí *m* cock-a-doodle-doo
kilo *m* kilo
kilocaloría *f* kilocalorie
kilociclo *m* kilocycle
kilogramo *m* kilogramme *Brit,* kilogram *Am*
kilohercio *m* kilohertz
kilolitro *m* kilolitre *Brit,* kiloliter *Am*
kilometraje *m* **1.** AUTO mileage *Brit,* milage *Am* **2.**(*distancia*) distance in kilometres *Brit* [*o* kilometers *Am*]; **hay que recorrer un buen ~** we've got a fair bit of distance to cover
kilometrar *vt* to measure in kilometres *Brit* [*o* kilometers *Am*]
kilométrico, -a *adj* **1.**(*en kilómetros*) kilometric **2.**(*muy largo*) very long; (*escrito*) lengthy
kilómetro *m* kilometre *Brit,* kilometer *Am*
kilotón *m* kiloton
kilovatio *m* kilowatt
kilovatio-hora *m* <kilovatios-hora> kilowatt hour
kínder *m inv,* **kindergarten** *m inv, AmL* kindergarten, nursery school
kit *m* <kits> kit
kl *abr de* **kilolitro** kl
kleenex® *m inv,* **klínex**® *m inv* Kleenex®, tissue
km *abr de* **kilómetro** km.
km/h *abr de* **kilómetro por hora** km/h
K.O. *adj abr de* **knock-out** knock-out; **dejar ~ a alguien** to knock sb out
Kremlin *m* Kremlin
Kurdistán *m* Kurdistan
kurdo, -a I. *adj* Kurdish **II.** *m, f* Kurd
kuwaití *adj, mf* Kuwaiti
kv *abr de* **kilovatio** kw
kv/h *abr de* **kilovatio-hora** kw/h

L

L, l *f* L,l; **~ de Lisboa** L for Lucy *Brit,* L for Love *Am*
l *abr de* **litro(s)** l
l. 1. *abr de* **libro** bk **2.** *abr de* **ley** l
L. 1. *abr de* **Ley** l **2.** *abr de* **lira(s)** L, l

la I. *art def v.* **el, la, lo** II. *pron pers, f sing* 1. *objeto directo: f sing* her; (*cosa*) it; **¡tráeme~!** bring her/it to me!; **mi bicicleta y ~ tuya** my bicycle and yours 2. (*con relativo*) **~ que...** the one that ...; **~ cual** which III. *m* MÚS A; **en ~ bemol menor** in A flat minor

laberíntico, -a *adj* labyrinthine; *fig* rambling

laberinto *m* 1. (*lugar*) labyrinth, maze 2. (*maraña*) tangle

labia *f inf* glibness; **tener mucha ~** to be a smooth talker

labial *adj* labial

lábil *adj* 1. *t.* QUÍM (*carácter*) labile 2. (*frágil*) frail

labio *m* 1. (*boca*) lip; **~ leporino** harelip; **cerrar los ~s** to close one's mouth; **morderse los ~s** *fig* to keep back what one thinks; **estar sin despegar los ~s** to not say a word 2. (*borde*) rim 3. *pl* (*vulva*) labia *pl*

labioso, -a *adj Ecua* (*adulador*) honey-tongued

labor *f* work; (*de coser*) needlework; (*labranza*) ploughing *Brit,* plowing *Am;* **no estoy por la ~** I don't feel like it; **~ de ganchillo** crochet work; **ocupación: sus ~es** occupation: housewife; **hacer ~es** to do needlework

laborable *adj* 1. AGR arable 2. (*de trabajo*) **día ~** working day

laboral *adj* labour *Brit,* labor *Am*

laborar I. *vi* 1. (*gestionar*) **~ por** [*o* **en favor de**] **algo** to strive for sth 2. (*intrigar*) to scheme II. *vt v.* **labrar**

laboratorio *m* laboratory, lab

laborear *vt* 1. *v.* **labrar** 2. MIN to work

laboreo *m* 1. AGR farm work 2. MIN working

laboriosidad *f* diligence, industriousness

laborioso, -a *adj* 1. (*trabajador*) hard-working, industrious 2. (*difícil*) arduous

laborismo *m* POL Labour Movement

laborista I. *adj* **partido ~** Labour Party II. *mf* *member of the Labour Party*

labrado *m* 1. (*acción*) working; AGR tillage 2. (*resultado*) result; (*dibujo*) fine detail; (*de un cristal*) etching 3. (*campo*) cultivated land 4. *pl* (*tierra*) ploughed fields *pl Brit,* plowed fields *pl Am*

labrado, -a *adj* 1. (*telas*) embroidered; (*objetos*) wrought; (*madera*) carved; (*cristal*) etched 2. AGR tilled; **campo ~** ploughed field

labrador(a) *m(f)* farmhand

labrantío *m* land for cultivation

labrantío, -a *adj* 1. (*cultivado*) sown 2. (*cultivable*) arable

labranza *f* 1. (*cultivo*) tillage 2. (*trabajo*) work 3. (*hacienda*) farm

labrar *vt* 1. (*trabajar un material*) to work; (*un dibujo*) to draw; (*cristal*) to etch; **sin ~** plain 2. (*cultivar, en jardín*) to work; (*arar*) to plough *Brit,* to plow *Am* 3. MIN to work 4. (*coser*) to sew; (*bordar*) to embroider 5. (*acuñar*) to coin 6. (*causar gradualmente*) to bring about; **~ la felicidad de alguien** to make sb happy; **~ la perdición de alguien** to bring sb to ruin

labriego, -a *m, f* farmworker

laburante *mf Arg, Urug, inf* worker

laburar *vi Arg, Urug, inf* to work

laburo *m Arg, Urug, inf* work

laca *f* 1. (*pintura*) lacquer, shellac 2. (*para el pelo*) hairspray; (*para las uñas*) nail varnish, nail polish

lacayo *m* 1. (*criado*) footman 2. *pey* (*adulador*) lackey

lacerante *adj* cutting; (*dolor*) searing; (*grito*) piercing

lacerar *vt* 1. (*herir*) to injure; **~ el alma** to wound the soul 2. (*magullar*) to bruise 3. (*la honra*) to damage

lachear *vt Chile* to chat up

lacho I. *adj Chile, Perú* (*hombre enamoradizo*) easily enamored; (*acostumbrado a galantear*) womanizing II. *m Chile, Perú* (*enamorado*) lover; (*pisaverde*) dandy

lacio, -a *adj* 1. (*marchito*) withered 2. (*flojo*) limp; (*cabello*) straight, lank

lacón *m* ham

lacónico, -a *adj* brief; (*persona*) laconic

lacra *f* 1. (*de una enfermedad*) mark; (*cicatriz*) scar 2. (*vicio*) blight

lacrar *vt* 1. (*cerrar*) to seal 2. (*contagiar*) to impair the health of 3. (*perjudicar*) to blight

lacre *m* sealing wax

lacrimógeno, -a *adj* (*de lágrimas*) tear; **gas ~** tear gas; (*sentimental*) soupy; **película lacrimógena** *pey* tearjerker

lacrimoso, -a *adj* 1. (*lloroso*) tearful 2. (*lastimoso*) sorrowful 3. (*quejumbroso*) whining

lactancia *f* 1. (*acción*) nursing, breastfeeding 2. (*período*) pre-weaning period

lactante I. *adj* still on milk II. *mf* unweaned infant

lactar I. *vt* to nurse, to breastfeed II. *vi* to nurse

lacteado, -a *adj* milk; **papilla lacteada** milk-based baby formula

lácteo, -a *adj* milk, dairy; *fig* milky; **vía láctea** ASTR Milky Way

láctico, -a *adj* lactic

lactosa *f* lactose

lacustre *adj* lacustrine; **construcciones ~s** lake dwellings

ladeado, -a *adj* tilted; **el cuadro está ~** the picture is lopsided

ladear I. *vt* 1. (*inclinar*) to slant; (*un sombrero*) to tip 2. (*desviar*) to skirt; **~ un problema** to get around a problem II. *vi* (*caminar*) to walk lopsided; (*desviarse*) to turn off III. *vr:* **~se** 1. (*inclinarse*) to lean 2. *Chile* (*enamorarse*) **~se de alguien** to fall in love with sb

ladera *f* slope, hillside

ladilla *f* crab louse

ladino, -a *adj* (*taimado*) cunning

lado *m* 1. *t.* MAT side; **a ambos ~s** on both sides; **por el ~ materno** on the mother's side;

ir de un ~ a otro to go back and forth; **dormir del ~ izquierdo** to sleep on ones left side; **por todos ~s** everywhere; **al ~** nearby; **la casa de al ~** the house next-door; **al ~ de** (*junto a*) beside, next to; **al ~ mío, a mi ~** next to me, by my side; **por un ~..., y por el otro ~...** on the one hand..., and on the other hand... **2.** (*borde*) edge; (*extremo*) end; (*parte*) side **3.** (*lugar*) **por el ~ del río** by the river; **ir a algún otro ~** to go somewhere else; **~ a ~** side by side **4.** (*punto de vista*) side; **por el ~ ecológico** on the ecological side; **el ~ bueno de la vida** the good side of life; **su ~ débil** his weak spot **5.** (*camino*) direction; **tomar por otro ~** to go another way **6.** (*partido*) **me puse de tu ~** I sided with you ►**dejar de ~ a alguien** to ignore sb; **mirar de ~ a alguien** to look out of the corner of one's eye at sb
ladrar *vi* (*perro*) to bark; (*amenazar*) to growl ►**perro que ladra no muerde** *prov* his bark is worse than his bite
ladrido *m* **1.** (*perro*) bark **2.** *pey* (*calumnia*) slander
ladrillo *m* **1.** (*de construcción*) brick **2.** *inf* **ser un ~** (*película, libro*) to be deadly dull
ladrón *m* (*enchufe*) multiple socket
ladrón, -ona I. *adj* thieving **II.** *m, f* (*bandido*) thief, robber; **~ cuatrero** treacherous thief ►**piensa el ~ que todos son de su condición** *prov* we all judge others by our own standards; **la ocasión hace al ~** *prov* opportunity makes the thief *prov*
ladronzuelo, -a *m, f* (*ratero*) petty thief
lagar *m* **1.** (*aceite*) oil press; (*vino*) winepress **2.** (*edificio*) press house
lagartear I. *vt* **1.** *Chile* to pinion **2.** *Col* (*hacer chanchullos*) to finagle **II.** *vi Guat, Méx* (*cazar lagartos*) to catch lizards
lagartija *f* small lizard
lagarto I. *m* **1.** (*reptil*) lizard **2.** *AmL* (*caimán*) alligator **II.** *interj* touch wood! *Brit,* knock on wood! *Am*
lagarto, -a I. *adj* sly **II.** *m, f* (*persona*) crafty fellow
lagartón, -ona I. *adj* shrewd; *pey* sly **II.** *m, f* sharp fellow; *pey* sly devil *m,* sly bitch *f*
lago *m* lake
lágrima *f* **1.** (*del ojo*) tear **2.** (*de vino*) drop ►**llorar ~s de sangre por algo** to shed bitter tears for sth; **llorar a ~ viva** to weep bitterly; **deshacerse en ~s** to burst into tears
lagrimal I. *adj* lachrymal **II.** *m* corner of the eye
lagrimear *vi* **1.** (*llorar*) to cry easily **2.** (*ojos*) to water
lagrimoso, -a *adj* **1.** (*triste*) tearful **2.** (*ojos*) watery
laguna *f* **1.** (*agua salada*) lagoon; (*dulce*) small lake **2.** (*omisión*) gap; **~ en la memoria** memory lapse
laicado *m* laity
laicalización *f Chile* secularization
laicalizar <z→c> *vt Chile* to secularize
laico, -a I. *adj* lay **II.** *m, f* layman *m,* laywoman *f*

> The term **laísmo** refers to the incorrect or perhaps non-standard usage of **la(s)** as the indirect object instead of **le(s)**, e.g. "**La regalé una novela de Borges**" instead of "**Le regalé una novela de Borges**". Such use is commonly accepted in certain regions but not accepted by most Spanish speakers.

laja *f* flat stone; **~ de pizarra** slate slab
lama *f* **1.** (*cieno*) silt **2.** (*de metal*) slat
lambiche *adj Méx, vulg* (*adulador*) arse-licking *Brit,* ass-kissing *Am*
lameculos *mf inv, vulg* arselicker *Brit*
lamedura *f* licking
lamentable *adj* regrettable
lamentación *f* **1.** (*acción*) lamentation **2.** (*expresión*) lament
lamentar I. *vt* to regret; **lo lamento** I'm sorry **II.** *vr* **~se de algo** to complain about sth
lamento *m* lament
lameplatos *mf inv* **1.** *inf* (*goloso*) glutton **2.** (*pobre*) scrounger
lamer I. *vt* **1.** (*pasar la lengua*) to lick **2.** (*tocar*) to lap; **las olas lamen las arenas** the waves lap against the shore ►**mejor lamiendo que mordiendo** it's easier to catch a bear with honey than with vinegar **II.** *vr:* **~se** to lick oneself; **~se de gusto** to lick one's lips
lamido *m* licking
lamido, -a *adj* **1.** (*flaco*) scrawny **2.** (*pálido*) pale **3.** (*relamido*) affected **4.** (*gastado*) worn out
lámina *f* **1.** (*hojalata*) tin plate; (*hoja de metal*) sheet; (*segmento*) lamina; **~ para proyector** projector plate **2.** TIPO plate **3.** (*ilustración*) print; **con ~s** illustrated
laminador *m* (*empresa*) rolling mill
laminar I. *adj* **1.** (*en forma de lámina*) laminar **2.** (*formado de láminas*) laminated **II.** *vt* **1.** (*cortar*) to split **2.** (*guarnecer*) to laminate
lampa *f And* (*pala*) shovel; (*azada*) pick
lámpara *f* **1.** (*luz*) lamp, light; **~ de alarma** warning light; **~ fluorescente** fluorescent lamp; **~ de pie** standard lamp **2.** TV, RADIO valve *Brit,* tube *Am* **3.** (*mancha*) grease stain
lamparazo *m Col* drink
lamparilla *f* (*luz*) small lamp
lamparón *m* **1.** (*mancha*) grease stain **2.** MED scrofula
lampiño, -a *adj* (*sin barba*) beardless; (*sin pelo*) hairless
lana *f* **1.** (*material, tela*) wool; **~ esquilada** fleece; **perro de ~s** poodle **2.** *vulg* (*dinero*) dough; **tienen mucha ~** they're loaded ►**unos cardan la ~ y otros cobran la fama** some do all the work and others get all the credit; **cardar la ~ a alguien** to give sb a good telling off
lanar *adj* wool-bearing; **ganado ~** sheep
lance *m* **1.** (*acción*) throw; (*red*) cast

2. (*trance*) critical moment 3. (*pelea*) quarrel; ~ **de honor** duel 4. (*juego*) move 5. *inf* (*compra*) secondhand; **comprar de** ~ to buy secondhand; **de** ~ at a bargain price 6. (*episodio*) ~ **de amor** love afair; ~ **de fortuna** stroke of luck

lancha *f* 1. (*piedra*) flat stone; ~ **de pizarra** slate slab 2. (*bote*) motorboat; ~ **a remolque** barge; ~ **de salvamento** lifeboat

lanchar *vi Ecua* 1. (*nublarse*) to become overcast 2. (*helar*) to freeze

lancinante *adj* (*dolor*) stabbing

landa *f* moorland

lanero, **-a** *adj* wool

langosta *f* 1. (*insecto*) locust; **por esta nevera ha pasado la** ~ *inf* sb has polished off everything in the fridge 2. (*crustáceo*) lobster

langostino *m* prawn

langucia *f AmL* hunger

languidecer *irr como crecer vi* (*debilitarse*) to languish; (*persona*) to languish (away); (*flores*) to droop; (*fuego*) to die down; ~ **de amor** to pine; **la conversación languideció** the conversation flagged

languidez *f* 1. (*debilidad*) weakness 2. (*espíritu*) listlessness

lánguido, **-a** *adj* 1. (*débil*) weak 2. (*espíritu*) languid

lanilla *f* (*pelillo*) nap

lanolina *f* lanolin

lanoso, **-a** *adj*, **lanudo**, **-a** *adj* woolly, wooly *Am*; (*oveja*) wool-bearing

lanza *f* 1. (*arma*) lance 2. (*carro*) pole ►quebrar ~s to cross swords, to argue; romper **una** ~ **en favor de alguien** to stick up for sb

lanzabengalas *m inv* flare gun

lanzacohetes *m inv* rocket launcher

lanzada *f* (*golpe*) spear thrust; (*herida*) lance wound

lanzadera *f* shuttle; (*plataforma*) platform, launch(ing) pad

lanzado, **-a** *adj* 1. (*decidido*) determined; (*emprendedor*) enterprising 2. (*impetuoso*) impetuous; (*fogoso*) forward

lanzador(a) *m(f)* thrower; (*beisbol*) bowler, pitcher

lanzallamas *m inv* flamethrower

lanzamiento *m* throw; ~ **de bombas** dropping of bombs; ~ **comercial** commercial promotion, product launch; ~ **espacial** space launch; ~ **de peso** DEP shot put

lanzamisiles *m inv* missile-launcher

lanzar <z→c> I. *vt* 1. (*arrojar*) ~ **a algo/alguien** to throw at [*o* to] sth/sb; ~ **peso** to put the shot 2. (*al mercado*) to launch II. *vr* **~se a/sobre algo/alguien** to throw oneself at/against sth/sb; **~se a correr** to break into a run; **~se al agua** to dive into the water; **~se en paracaídas** to parachute; **~se en picado** to nosedive; **~se a algo** to undertake sth

lanzaroteño, **-a** I. *adj* of/from Lanzarote II. *m, f* native/inhabitant of Lanzarote

laña *f* (*grapa*) clamp

lapa *f* 1. ZOOL limpet 2. *inf* (*persona*) nuisance; **pegarse como una** ~ to stick like a leech

La Paz *f* La Paz

lapicera *f Arg, Urug* (*pluma*) ballpoint pen

lapicero *m* 1. (*lápiz*) pencil 2. (*recipiente*) penholder

lápida *f* stone tablet; ~ **conmemorativa** memorial tablet; ~ **mortuoria** gravestone

lapidar *vt* to stone

lapidario, **-a** *adj* 1. (*piedras preciosas*) lapidary 2. (*categórico*) categorical, scathing; **frase lapidaria** *memorable phrase*

lápiz *m* pencil; ~ **de labios** lipstick; ~ **de ojos** eye pencil; ~ **de color** crayon, wax crayon *Brit*; ~ **de pizarra** chalk

lapón, **-ona** I. *adj* Lapp II. *m, f* (*habitante*) Lapp, Laplander

Laponia *f* Lapland

lapso *m* 1. (*período*) ~ (**de tiempo**) lapse 2. *v.* **lapsus**

lapsus *m inv* blunder; ~ **linguae** slip of the tongue

laquear *vt* to lacquer

lar *m* 1. (*fuego*) hearth 2. (*hogar*) home

lardo *m* 1. (*tocino*) lard 2. (*grasa*) animal fat

largar <g→gu> I. *vt* 1. (*soltar*) to release 2. *inf* (*golpe*) to land; (*bofetada*) to let fly 3. *inf* (*discurso*) to give 4. *inf* (*deshacerse de*) ~ **algo a alguien** to unload sth on sb; **siempre larga el trabajo a los demás** he/she is always unloading work on others 5. (*revelar*) to tell; **si te lo digo, lo ~ás a todos** if I tell you, you'll go and tell everyone II. *vr:* **~se** 1. (*irse*) to leave; (*de casa*) to leave home 2. *AmL* (*comenzar*) to begin; **~se a hacer algo** to start to do sth III. *vi inf* to talk a lot, to yack

largo I. *adv* (*en abundancia*) plenty; **tenemos comida para** ~ we've got plenty of food; ~ **y tendido** at length ►a lo ~ **de la playa** along the beach; a **lo** ~ **del día** throughout the day; ¡~ (**de** aquí)! clear off! II. *m* (*longitud*) length; **nadar tres ~s** to swim three lengths of the pool; **diez metros de** ~ ten metres long

largo, **-a** *adj* 1. (*tamaño, duración*) long; **a** ~ **plazo, a la larga** in the long term [*o* run]; **a la larga o a la corta** sooner or later; **a lo** ~ **de los años** throughout the years; **dar largas a algo** to put off doing sth; **el pantalón te está** ~ your trousers are too long for you; **ir de** ~ to be in a long dress; (*de gala*) to be in formal dress; **pasar de** ~ to pass by; *fig* to ignore; **tener cincuenta años ~s** to be well past 50; **tener las manos largas** (*pegar*) to be free with one's hands; (*robar*) to be light-fingered 2. (*extensivo*) lengthy; (*mucho*) abundant; **por** ~ for a long time 3. *inf* (*astuto*) shrewd

largometraje *m* full-length [*o* feature] film

larguero *m* 1. (*carpintería*) long beam 2. DEP crossbar

largueza *f* 1. (*largura*) length 2. (*generosidad*) largesse 3. (*liberalidad*) liberality

larguirucho, **-a** *adj inf* lanky

largura *f* length
laringe *f* larynx
laringitis *f inv* laryngitis
larva *f* larva
larvado, **-a** *adj* latent
las I. *art def v.* **el, la, lo** II. *pron pers f pl* 1. (*objeto directo*) them; **¡míra~!** look at them! 2. (*con relativo*) ~ **que...** the ones that ...; ~ **cuales** those which 3. (*laísmo*) *improper use of 'la' and 'las' as indirect objects instead of 'le' and 'les'*
lascar <c→qu> *vt* 1. NÁUT to pay out 2. *Méx* (*lastimar*) to bruise
lascivia *f* 1. (*lujuria*) lasciviousness 2. (*indecencia*) lewdness 3. (*sensualidad*) lust
lascivo, **-a** *adj* 1. (*sensual*) lustful 2. (*lujurioso*) lascivious 3. (*indecente*) lewd
láser *m* laser
lasitud *f* lassitude
laso, **-a** *adj* 1. (*cansado*) weary 2. (*pelo*) lank 3. (*cuerda*) slack
lástima *f* 1. (*compasión*) pity; **dar** [*o* **causar**] ~ to inspire pity; **me da mucha** ~ I feel very sorry for him/her; **su último libro da** ~ his/her latest book is pathetic; **de** [*o* **por**] ~ out of pity; **estar hecho una** ~ to be a sorry sight; **¡qué ~!** what a pity! 2. (*lamentación*) complaint
lastimadura *f* injury
lastimar I. *vt* 1. (*herir*) to hurt; **las botas me han lastimado los pies** my feet hurt from my boots 2. (*agraviar*) to offend II. *vr:* **~se** 1. (*herirse*) to hurt oneself 2. (*quejarse*) **~se de algo** to complain about sth
lastimero, **-a** *adj*, **lastimoso**, **-a** *adj* 1. (*daño*) harmful 2. (*lástima*) pitiful
lastra *f* flagstone
lastrar *vt* 1. (*poner peso*) to ballast 2. (*subrayar*) to emphasize
lastre *m* 1. (*cantera*) gravel 2. NÁUT ballast 3. (*estorbo*) dead weight; **ser un** ~ to be a burden
lata *f* 1. (*metal*) tin 2. (*envase*) tin *Brit*, can *Am* 3. (*conversación*) long boring conversation 4. *inf* (*pesadez, aburrido*) bore; **dar la** ~ to be a nuisance; **¡vaya ~!** (*fastidio*) what a pain!
latazo *m inf* 1. (*tontería*) foolishness 2. (*pesadez*) pain; **ser un** ~ (*pesado*) to be a drag; (*fastidioso*) bother; (*aburrido*) bore; **dar el** ~ to be a nuisance
latear *vi AmL* 1. (*aburrir a alguien*) to bore 2. (*parlotear*) **se pasa el día lateando** he/she spends all day blabbing away
latente *adj* latent
lateral *adj* 1. (*lado*) lateral 2. (*secundario*) secondary
latería *f* 1. (*conjunto de latas*) cans *pl* of preserves; **la ~ de su despensa** the canned goods in her pantry 2. *AmL* (*hojalatería*) tinsmith's shop
latido *m* 1. (*corazón*) heartbeat; (*herida, arteria*) throbbing 2. (*perro*) yelp
latifundio *m large landed estate*
latifundista *mf owner of a large estate*
latigazo *m* 1. (*golpe*) whiplash 2. (*chasquido*) crack of a whip 3. (*destino*) stroke of fate 4. (*reprimenda*) tongue lashing 5. *inf* (*trago*) swig
látigo *m* whip
latiguear I. *vi* to crack a whip II. *vt AmL* to flog
latiguillo *m* 1. (*efectismo*) hamming 2. (*muletilla*) catchphrase; (*expresión*) platitude
latín *m* Latin; **saber (mucho)** ~ *inf* to know what's what, to know a thing or two
latino, **-a** I. *adj* Latin; **América Latina** Latin America II. *m, f* Latin; *AmL* (*latinoamericano*) Latin American
Latinoamérica *f* Latin America
latinoamericano, **-a** *adj, m, f* Latin American
latir *vi* 1. (*corazón*) to beat; (*arteria, herida*) to throb 2. (*perros*) to yelp
latitud *f* 1. GEO, ASTR latitude 2. (*extensión*) breadth
lato, **-a** *adj* (*amplio*) broad; (*extendido*) extensive; **en sentido** ~ in the broad sense
latón *m* brass
latoso, **-a** *adj* bothersome
latrocinio *m* larceny
laúd *m* MÚS lute
laudable *adj* praiseworthy
laudatorio, **-a** *adj* laudatory; **discurso** ~ eulogistic speech
laudo *m* decision
laureado, **-a** *adj* 1. (*coronado*) crowned with laurel 2. (*premiado*) laureate, prize-winning
laurear *vt* 1. (*coronar*) to crown with laurel 2. (*premiar*) to award
laurel *m* 1. (*árbol*) laurel 2. (*condimento*) bay leaf 3. *pl* (*honor*) honour *Brit*, honor *Am;* **dormirse en los ~es** to rest on one's laurels
lauro *m* 1. (*laurel*) laurel 2. (*gloria*) glory
lava *f* (*volcán*) lava
lavable *adj* washable; (*color*) colourfast *Brit*, colorfast *Am*
lavabo *m* 1. (*pila*) washbasin *Brit*, sink *Am* 2. (*cuarto*) toilet *Brit*, bathroom *Am*
lavacoches *m inv* (*instalación*) car wash
lavacristales *mf inv* window cleaner
lavadero *m* (*de ropa*) laundry; (*en el río*) washing place
lavado *m* wash; ~ **en seco** dry-cleaning; MED lavage; ~ **de cerebro** *fig* brainwashing; ~ **de cara** *fig* facelift
lavadora *f* washing machine
lavafaros *m inv* AUTO headlamp washer
lavanda *f* lavender
lavandería *f* laundry, launderette *Brit*, laundromat *Am*
lavaplatos *m inv* 1. (*electrodoméstico*) dishwasher 2. *Col, inf* (*fregadero*) (kitchen) sink
lavar I. *vt* (*limpiar*) to wash; ~ **la cabeza** to wash one's hair; ~ **los platos** to wash up II. *vr:*

~**se** to wash; ~**se los dientes** to brush [*o* clean *Brit*] one's teeth
lavarropas *f inv, Arg* (*lavadora*) washing machine
lavativa *f* **1.**(*enema*) enema **2.**(*instrumento*) enema bag
lavatorio *m* **1.**MED lotion, wash **2.**REL maundy; ~ **del Jueves Santo** feet-washing on Maundy Thursday **3.***AmL* (*lavabo*) lavatory *Brit*, washroom *Am*
lavavajillas *m inv* **1.**(*electrodoméstico*) dishwasher **2.**(*detergente*) washing-up liquid
lavotear I. *vt* to wash quickly and badly **II.** *vr:* ~**se** *inf* to wash quickly
laxante *m* laxative
laxar *vt* **1.**(*relajar*) to relax **2.**(*vientre*) to loosen up
laxitud *f* laxity
laxo, -a *adj* **1.**(*flojo*) slack **2.**(*moral*) lax
lazada *f* (*de zapato*) bow
lazareto *m* (*de contagiosos*) quarantine station
lazo *m* **1.**(*nudo*) bow **2.**(*para caballos*) lasso; (*para conejos*) snare **3.**(*cinta*) ribbon **4.**(*vínculo*) tie; ~**s afectivos** emotional bonds
lda., ldo. *abr de* **licenciado, -a** graduate
le *pron pers* **1.** *objeto indirecto: m sing* him; *f sing* her; *forma cortés* you; **¡da~ un beso!** give him/her a kiss!; **si Ud. quiere, ~ puedo llamar el lunes** if you like, I can phone you on Monday **2.** *reg, objeto directo: m sing* him **3.** *forma cortés* you
leal *adj* loyal
lealtad *f* loyalty
lebrel *m* greyhound
lección *f* **1.**(*lectura*) reading **2.** *(pl)* (*enseñanza escolar*) lessons *pl;* **tomar lecciones de matemáticas** to take mathematics classes **3.**UNIV lecture **4.**(*tema a estudiar*) lesson; **¿te tomo la ~?** *inf* should I test you? **5.**(*advertencia*) warning; **dar una ~ a alguien** to teach sb a lesson; **¡que te sirva de ~!** let that be a lesson to you!
lechada *f* **1.**(*para blanquear*) whitewash **2.**(*argamasa*) grout
lechal I. *adj* (*cachorro*) suckling; **cordero ~** suckling lamb **II.** *m* (*cordero*) baby lamb
lechar *adj* **1.**(*cachorro*) suckling; **corzo ~** unweaned fawn, *of roe deer* **2.**(*productor*) **vaca ~** milk [*o* milch *Brit*] cow
leche *f* **1.**(*líquido*) milk; ~ **en polvo** powdered milk; ~ **entera** whole milk; ~ **desnatada** skimmed milk; ~ **semidesnatada** low fat milk; ~ **desmaquillante** cleansing milk **2.** *vulg* (*esperma*) spunk **3.** *inf* (*golpe*) blow; **¡te doy una ~!** I'm going to belt you one! **4.** *inf* (*hostia*) **¡~s!** damn it!; **ser la ~** to be too much; **estar de mala ~** to be in a foul mood; **tener mala ~** to be vindictive; **a toda ~** at full speed
lechera *adj, f v.* **lechero**
lechería *f* dairy
lechero, -a I. *adj* milk **II.** *m, f* milkman *m,* milkwoman *f*
lechigada *f* litter
lecho *m* bed; (*río*) riverbed
lechón, -ona *m, f* **1.**(*animal*) suckling pig **2.** *pey* (*persona*) fat slob
lechosa *f AmL* BOT papaya
lechoso, -a *adj* milky
lechuga *f* lettuce ►**como una ~** as fresh as a daisy; **ser más fresco que una ~** *inf* to have a lot of nerve
lechuguino, -a *m, f pey* (*presumido*) dandy
lechuza *f* barn owl
lectivo, -a *adj* **ciclo ~** ENS school cycle; UNIV academic cycle; **día ~** school day
lector *m* INFOR reader
lector(a) *m(f)* **1.**(*que lee*) reader; (*en voz alta*) lector **2.**(*profesor*) conversation assistant **3.**(*aparato*) player; ~ **de CD** CD player
lectorado *m* assistantship
lectura *f* **1.** *t.* INFOR (*acción de leer, instrumento*) reading; (*disertación*) dissertation; ~ (**en voz alta**) reading aloud; **el portavoz dio ~ al comunicado** the spokesman read the communiqué **2.**(*obra*) reading material **3.**(*conocimientos*) knowledge; **ser de mucha ~** to be well-read **4.**(*perspectiva*) interpretation
leer *irr vt* **1.**(*percibir, instrumento*) to read; ~ **en voz alta** to read aloud **2.**(*interpretar*) to interpret; ~ **en la cara de alguien** to see from sb's expression
legación *f* legation
legado *m* **1.**POL legacy; REL legate **2.**(*herencia*) legacy
legajo *m* dossier
legal *adj* **1.**(*determinado por la ley*) legal; **medicina ~** forensic medicine **2.**(*conforme a la ley*) lawful **3.**(*fiel*) trustworthy
legalidad *f* legality; **al filo de la ~** semi-legal; **fuera de la ~** unlawful
legalista *adj* legalistic
legalización *f* **1.**(*autorización*) legalization, legalisation *Brit* **2.**(*atestamiento*) authentication
legalizar <z→c> *vt* **1.**(*autorizar*) to legalize **2.**(*atestar*) to authenticate
légamo *m* (*cieno*) mud
legaña *f* sleep, rheum; **tienes ~s** you have sleep in your eyes
legar <g→gu> *vt* **1.**(*legado*) to bequeath **2.**(*enviar*) to delegate
legendario, -a *adj* legendary; (*famoso*) renowned
legible *adj* legible
legión *f* **1.**MIL legion **2.**(*multitud*) crowd; **hay comida para una ~** there's enough food to feed an army
legionario, -a I. *adj* legionary **II.** *m, f* legionnaire
legionella *f* MED Legionnaire's disease
legislación *f* **1.**(*acción*) lawmaking **2.**(*leyes*) legislation
legislador(a) I. *adj* legislative **II.** *m(f)* **1.**(*que*

L

legisla) legislator **2.** *AmL* (*parlamentario*) member of parliament

legislar *vi* to legislate

legislativo, **-a** *adj* legislative; **poder** ~ legislative power

legislatura *f* **1.** (*período*) term of office **2.** *AmL* (*parlamento*) legislative body

legitimación *f* **1.** (*legalización*) authentication **2.** (*habilitación*) recognition **3.** (*hijo*) legitimization, legitimisation *Brit*

legitimar **I.** *vt* **1.** (*dar legitimidad*) to authenticate **2.** (*habilitar*) to recognize **3.** (*hijo*) to make legitimate **II.** *vr:* **~se** to establish one's title

legítimo, **-a** *adj* **1.** (*legal*) legitimate; **defensa legítima** self-defense **2.** (*verdadero*) genuine **3.** (*hijo*) legitimate

lego, **-a** **I.** *adj* **1.** (*no eclesiástico*) lay **2.** (*ignorante*) uninformed **II.** *m, f* lay brother *m,* lay sister *f;* **ser un ~ en el tema** to know nothing about the subject

legua *f* league; **a la ~** miles away; **se ve a la ~ que no dicen la verdad** it's obvious that they're lying

leguleyo, **-a** *m, f pey* pettifogging lawyer, shyster

legumbre *f* **1.** (*planta*) legume **2.** (*fruta seca*) pulse; (*fruta fresca*) vegetable; **frutas y ~s** fruit and vegetables

leíble *adj* readable

leído, **-a** *adj* **1.** (*persona*) well-read **2.** (*revista*) widely-read

> The term **leísmo** refers to the incorrect or perhaps non-standard usage of **le(s)** as the indirect object instead of **lo(s)** or **la(s)**, e.g. "**Les visité ayer, a mis hermanas**" instead of "**Las visité ayer, a mis hermanas**". Such use is commonly accepted in certain regions but not accepted by most Spanish speakers.

lejanía *f* distance

lejano, **-a** *adj* faraway; (*parentesco*) distant; **en un futuro no muy ~** in the not-so-distant future

lejía *f* **1.** QUÍM lye **2.** (*para lavar, decolorar*) bleach

lejos **I.** *adv* far; **~ de algo** far from sth; **a lo ~** in the distance; **de ~** from afar; **ir demasiado ~** *t. fig* to go too far; **es de ~ la mejor soprano** she is by far the best soprano; **llegar ~** *fig* to go far; **sin ir más ~** *fig* to take an obvious example **II.** *prep* **~ de** far from; **está muy ~ de mí hacer algo** *fig* I have no intention of intervening in sth

lelo, **-a** **I.** *adj inf* **1.** *ser* (*tonto*) silly, goofy *Am* **2.** *estar* (*pasmado*) stunned; (*mareado*) dizzy **II.** *m, f* (*persona*) dolt, gubbins, dork *Am*

lema *m* **1.** (*tema*) theme; (*mote*) motto **2.** (*contraseña*) watchword

lencería *f* **1.** (*telas*) linen; (*ropa de cama*) bed linen **2.** (*tienda de telas*) draper's shop; (*de ropa interior*) lingerie shop; **~ de un almacén** linen room **3.** (*ropa interior*) underwear

lengón, **-ona** *adj Col* (*deslenguado*) outspoken

lengua *f* **1.** ANAT tongue; **lo tengo en la punta de la ~** I have it on the tip of my tongue; **morderse la ~** *t. fig* to bite one's tongue; **¿te ha comido alguien la ~?** has the cat got your tongue?; **sacar la ~ a alguien** to stick ones tongue out at sb; **se me trabó la ~** I got tongue-tied; **tener la ~ demasiado larga** *fig* to talk too much **2.** LING tongue; **~ materna** mother tongue; **~ oficial** official language **3.** (*forma*) tongue; **~ de agua** tongue of water ►**tener la ~ de trapo** *inf* to stutter and stammer; **estar con la ~ fuera** to be out of breath; **tener una ~ viperina** to be a backbiter; **atar la ~ a alguien** to silence sb; **dar a la ~** to gab; **desasir la ~ a alguien** to loosen sb's tongue; **aquí alguien se ha ido de la ~** sb here has spilled the beans; **tirar a alguien de la ~** to pump sb for information; **volar ~** *AmC* (*hablar*) to gossip

lenguado *m* sole

lenguaje *m* language; **~ técnico** technical language

lenguaraz *adj* talkative

lenguaz *adj* garrulous

lengüeta *f* **1.** (*zapato*) tongue; (*balanza*) pointer **2.** MÚS reed

lengüetear *vi AmL, inf* to stick one's tongue out

lengüilargo, **-a** *adj inf* impudent

lenguón, **-ona** **I.** *adj AmL* (*calumniador*) backbiting; (*chismoso*) gossipy **II.** *m, f AmL* (*calumniador*) backbiter; (*chismoso*) gossip

lenidad *f sin pl* lenience

lenificar <c→qu> *vt* to soothe

lenitivo, **-a** *adj* alleviating

lente *m o f* **1.** (*gafas*) eyeglasses *pl;* **llevar ~s** to wear glasses **2.** *t.* FOTO (*cristal*) lens; **~ convergente** converging lens; **~ de aumento** magnifying glass

lenteja *f* lentil; **dar algo por un plato de ~s** *fig* to sell sth of value for sth worthless; **ganarse las ~s** *fig* to earn one's daily bread

lentejuela *f* sequin, spangle

lenticular *adj* lenticular

lentilla *f* contact lens

lentitud *f* slowness; *fig* slow-wittedness; **con ~** slowly

lento, **-a** *adj* slow; *fig* slow-witted; (*enfermedad*) lingering; **a cámara lenta** in slow motion; **a paso ~** slowly; **cocinar a fuego ~** to cook over low heat [*o* a low flame]; **quemar a fuego ~** *fig* to burn slowly

leña *f sin pl* **1.** (*madera*) firewood; **echar ~ al fuego** to add more firewood; *fig* to add fuel to the flames **2.** (*castigo*) beating; **¡~ con él!** let him have it!; **dar ~** to give a beating; **repartir ~** to dish out blows; **recibir ~** to get beaten up ►**hacer ~ del árbol caído** to kick somebody

when he is down; **llevar** ~ **al** <u>**monte**</u> to carry coals to Newcastle
leñador(a) *m(f)* woodcutter, lumberjack
leñazo *m inf* bash; **¡qué** ~ **se pegó con su coche!** he/she really crashed his car!; **darse un** ~ **en la cabeza** to bash one's head
leñe *interj* damn it!
leño *m* **1.** (*de árbol*) log **2.** (*tonto*) blockhead
leñoso, -a *adj* woody
Leo *m* Leo
león *m* lion; *AmL* (*puma*) puma, cougar *Am;* ~ (**marino**) sea lion ►**no es tan** <u>**fiero**</u> **el** ~ **como lo pintan** *inf* it's not as bad as it looks
leonado, -a *adj* tawny
leonera *f* **1.** (*jaula*) lion's cage **2.** (*habitación*) messy room
leonés, -esa **I.** *adj* of/from León **II.** *m, f* native/inhabitant of León
leonino, -a *adj* **1.** (*animal*) leonine **2.** (*contrato*) unfair
leontina *f* watch chain
leopardo *m* leopard
leotardo(s) *m(pl)* leotards *pl,* tights *pl*
Lepe saber más que ~ to be very sharp
lépero, -a **I.** *adj* **1.** *AmC* (*grosero*) coarse; (*vil*) rotten **2.** *Cuba* (*perspicaz*) shrewd **3.** *Ecua, inf* (*arruinado*) broke **II.** *m, f AmC* pauper
leporino, -a *adj* harelike; **labio** ~ harelip
lepra *f* MED *sin pl* leprosy
leprosario *m Méx* leper colony
leproso, -a **I.** *adj* leprous **II.** *m, f* leper
lerdear *vi AmC, Arg* **1.** (*hacer algo con pesadez*) to be sluggish **2.** (*demorarse*) to take a long time; (*llegar tarde*) to be late
lerdo, -a *adj* slow, sluggish
leridano, -a **I.** *adj* of/from Lérida **II.** *m, f* native/inhabitant of Lérida
les *pron pers* **1.** *m pl, reg* (*objeto directo*) them; (*forma cortés*) you **2.** *mf pl* (*objeto indirecto*) them; (*forma cortés*) you
lesbiana *f* lesbian
lésbico, -a *adj* lesbian
lesear *vi Chile* to fool around
lesera *f AmL* stupidity
lesión *f* injury; ~ **cardiaca** heart damage
lesionar **I.** *vt* **1.** (*herir*) to injure **2.** (*dañar*) to damage **II.** *vr:* ~**se** to get hurt
lesivo, -a *adj* harmful
leso, -a *adj* injured
letal *adj elev* lethal
letanía *f* litany; **¡ya está éste con su ~!** there he/she goes again with his usual story
letárgico, -a *adj* lethargic
letargo *m* lethargy
letón, -ona **I.** *adj* Latvian, Lettish **II.** *m, f* Latvian, Lett
Letonia *f* Latvia
letra *f* **1.** (*signo*) letter; ~**s de molde** block letters; ~ **mayúscula/minúscula** capital/small letter; **con** ~ **mayúscula/minúscula** in capitals/small letters; **al pie de la** ~ to the letter; ~ **por** ~ word for word; **poner cuatro** ~**s a alguien** to drop sb a line; **tener las** ~**s gordas** *fig* to be perfectly clear **2.** (*escritura*) handwriting; **de su puño y** ~ in his own handwriting **3.** *pl* (*saber*) learning, letters; UNIV arts *pl;* **aprender las primeras** ~**s** *fig* to learn one's ABC; **hombre de** ~**s** man of letters **4.** MÚS lyrics *pl* **5.** COM ~ (**de cambio**) bill of exchange; ~ **al portador** draft payable to the bearer; ~ **a la vista** sight draft; **girar una** ~ **a cargo de alguien** to draw a bill on sb
letrado, -a **I.** *adj* learned **II.** *m, f* lawyer
letrero *m* notice, sign
leucemia *f sin pl* MED leukaemia *Brit,* leukemia *Am*
leucocito *m* leucocyte *Brit,* leukocyte *Am*
leva *f* **1.** MIL levy **2.** (*barco*) weighing anchor
levadizo, -a *adj* **puente** ~ drawbridge
levadura *f* **1.** (*masa*) leavening yeast; ~ **en polvo** baking powder **2.** (*hongo*) yeast
levantamiento *m* **1.** (*amotinamiento*) uprising **2.** (*alzar*) lifting; ~ **del cadáver** removal of the corpse
levantar **I.** *vt* **1.** (*alzar*) to lift, to raise; (*del suelo*) to pick up; (*algo tumbado, inclinado*) to straighten; (*polvo, telón*) to raise; (*cartel*) to take down; (*un campamento*) to strike; (*las anclas*) to weigh; ~ **el vuelo** to take off; **después del fracaso ya no levantó cabeza** he never recovered from the fiasco **2.** (*despertar, provocar*) to awaken; **no queremos** ~ **sospechas** we don't want to arouse suspicion; ~ **polémica** to give rise to controversy **3.** (*construir*) to build; (*monumento*) to erect; (*muro*) to put up **4.** (*suprimir*) to remove; (*embargo, castigo*) to lift **5.** (*mapa*) to draw up; ~ **acta de algo** to draw up a report on sth **6.** (*voz*) to raise; ~ **la voz a alguien** to raise one's voice to sb **7.** (*mirada, mano*) to raise **8.** (*caza*) to flush out **II.** *vr:* ~**se** **1.** (*de la cama*) to get up; ~**se con el pie izquierdo** *fig* to get out of bed on the wrong side **2.** (*sobresalir*) to stand out **3.** (*sublevarse*) to rebel; **se ~on pocas voces críticas** very few protested **4.** (*viento*) to rise **5.** *inf* (*robar*) to swipe, to pinch **6.** (*telón*) to rise **7.** (*sesión*) to adjourn; **se levanta la sesión** the meeting is closed, court is adjourned
levante *m sin pl* **1.** (*Este*) east **2.** (*viento*) east wind
levantisco, -a *adj* rebellious
levar *vt* ~ (**las**) **anclas** to weigh anchor
leve *adj* (*enfermedad*) mild; (*peso, sanción*) light; (*error*) slight; (*pecado*) venial
levedad *f sin pl* lightness
levitar *vi* to levitate
lexicalizar <z→c> *vt* to lexicalize
léxico *m* **1.** (*diccionario*) lexicon **2.** (*vocabulario*) vocabulary
lexicón *m* lexicon
ley *f* **1.** JUR, REL, FÍS law; ~ **del embudo** *inf* one-sided law; **Ley Fundamental** Fundamental Law; **Ley General Tributaria** Tax Law; ~ **marcial** martial law; ~ **orgánica** constitu-

L

tional law; **la ~ de la oferta y demanda** the law of supply and demand; **~ de prescripción** statute of limitations; **la ~ seca** the Prohibition; **la ~ de la selva, la ~ del más fuerte** the law of the jungle; **fuerza de ~** force of law; **proyecto de ~** bill; **hacer algo con todas las de la ~** to do sth properly; **hecha la ~, hecha la trampa** every law has its loophole; **respetar las ~es del juego** to follow the rules of the game; **regirse por la ~ del embudo** to have one law for oneself, and one for everyone else; **según la ~ vigente** in accordance with the law currently in force; **se le aplicó la ~ de la fuga al reo** the prisoner was shot while trying to escape; **ser de ~** *inf* to be reliable **2.** *pl* (*estudio*) Law **3.** (*oro*) legal standard of fineness; (*monedas*) genuine; **oro de ~** standard gold; **ser de buena ~** *fig* to be genuine

leyenda *f* **1.** LIT, REL legend **2.** (*plano*) caption **3.** (*moneda*) inscription

lezna *f* awl

liana *f* liana

liar *<1. pres:* lío*>* **I.** *vt* **1.** (*fardo*) to tie up; (*paquete*) to wrap up; **~ el petate** *inf* to pack up and go **2.** (*cigarrillo*) to roll **3.** *inf* (*engañar*) to take in; (*enredar*) to mix up; **¡ahora sí que la hemos liado!** we've really done it now! **II.** *vr:* **~se 1.** *inf* (*juntarse*) to become lovers **2.** (*embarullarse*) to get complicated; **~se la manta a la cabeza** *inf* to throw caution to the winds [*o* take the plunge] **3.** (*ponerse a*) **~se a golpes con alguien** to start fighting with sb

libanés, -esa *adj, m, f* Lebanese

Líbano *m* **El ~** Lebanon

libar *vi* (*abeja*) to suck

libelo *m* libel

libélula *f* dragonfly

liberación *f* liberation, release

liberal I. *adj t.* POL liberal; (*generoso*) generous **II.** *mf* Liberal

liberalidad *f* (*generosidad*) generosity

liberalización *f* liberalization

liberalizar <z→c> *vt* to liberalize

liberar *vt* to liberate, to set free; (*eximir*) to exempt

liberiano, -a *adj, m, f* Liberian

líbero *m* DEP sweeper

libérrimo, -a *adj superl de* **libre**

libertad *f* **1.** (*libre arbitrio*) liberty; **~ de culto** freedom of worship; **~ de expresión** freedom of speech; **~ de prensa** freedom of the press; **en ~ bajo fianza** on bail; **en ~ condicional** on parole; **poner en ~** to set free; **tomarse demasiadas ~es** to take too many liberties **2.** (*naturalidad*) familiarity

libertar *vt* to liberate

libertario, -a *adj, m, f* libertarian

libertinaje *m* libertinage

libertino, -a I. *adj* dissolute **II.** *m, f* libertine

Libia *f* Libya

libidinoso, -a *adj* lustful

libido *f sin pl* libido

libio, -a *adj, m, f* Libyan

libra *f* pound; **~ esterlina** pound sterling; **una ~ de judías** a pound of beans

Libra *f* Libra

librado, -a *adj* **salir bien ~ de algo** to come out of sth unscathed, to be successful in sth; **salir mal ~** to come out the worse for wear, to fail

libramiento *m,* **libranza** *f* order of payment; (*de un cheque*) payment

librar I. *vt* **1. ~ de algo/alguien** (*dejar libre*) to free from sth/sb; (*salvar*) to save from sth/sb; **¡líbreme Dios!** God [*o* Heaven] forbid!; **y líbranos del mal** and deliver us from evil **2.** COM to draw; **~ una letra a cargo de alguien** to draw a draft on sb **II.** *vi inf* (*tener libre*) **hoy libro** I have today off **III.** *vr* **~ de algo/alguien** (*deshacerse*) to get rid of sth/sb; (*salvarse*) to escape from sth/sb; **~se de una buena** to have a narrow escape

libre <libérrimo> *adj* **1.** (*en general*) free; (*independiente*) independent; **zona de ~ cambio** free trade area; **~ de franqueo** no postage necessary; **dar vía ~** to give the green light; **estar ~ de preocupaciones** to be free from worries; **la imaginación es ~** imagination is free to wander; **eres bien ~ de hacerlo** you are quite free to do so **2.** (*soltero*) single **3.** (*descarado*) forward

librea *f* (*traje*) livery

librecambio *m sin pl* free trade

librería *f* **1.** (*tienda*) bookshop; **~ de depósito** book warehouse; **~ de ocasión** secondhand bookshop **2.** (*papelería*) stationer's **3.** (*biblioteca*) library **4.** (*estantería*) bookcase

librero, -a *m, f* bookseller

libreta *f* **1.** (*cuaderno*) notebook; (*para notas*) notepad **2.** (*de ahorros*) bank book

libro *m* (*escrito*) book; (*volumen*) volume; **~ de bolsillo** paperback; **~ blanco** white paper; **~ científico** science book; **~ de cocina** cookery book *Brit,* cookbook *Am;* **~ de consulta** reference book; **~s de contabilidad** account book; **~ de escolaridad** school record; **~ de familia** *official booklet in which details of one's marriage and children's birthdates, etc. are registered;* **~ ilustrado** picture book; **~ de reclamaciones** complaints book; **los Libros Sagrados** the Holy Scriptures; **~ de texto** textbook ▸**hablar como un ~ abierto** to express oneself clearly; **hablar como un ~ cerrado** not to express oneself clearly; **colgar los ~s** to abandon one's studies

licencia *f* **1.** (*permiso*) licence *Brit,* license *Am;* (*para un libro*) authorization; **~ de conducir** *Méx, Cuba* driving licence *Brit,* driver's licence *Am;* **~ de obras** building permit; **~ de pesca/de armas** fishing/gun licence **2.** (*soldado*) **estar tres días de ~** to be on leave for three days **3.** (*libertad*) liberty

licenciado, -a *m, f* **1.** (*estudiante*) graduate; **~ en economía** Economics graduate **2.** (*soldado*) discharged soldier

licenciar I. *vt* (*despedir*) to dismiss; (*soldado*)

to discharge II. *vr:* ~**se** to graduate; **se licenció en psicología** he got a degree in psychology
licenciatura *f* 1.(*título*) degree 2.(*carrera*) university studies *pl*
licencioso, -a *adj* (*persona*) licentious; (*conducta*) dissolute
liceo *m* 1.(*sociedad*) literary society 2. *AmL* (*colegio*) secondary school
licitación *f* 1.(*concurso*) tender; **sacaron el proyecto a** ~ the project was put out to tender 2.(*subasta*) bidding
licitador(a) *m(f)* bidder
licitar *vt* to bid
lícito, -a *adj* 1.(*permitido*) allowed 2.(*justo*) fair 3.(*legal*) lawful
licitud *f sin pl* legality
licor *m* liquor; (*de frutas*) liqueur
licra® *f* Lycra®
licuadora *f* (*batidora*) blender; (*para fruta*) liquidizer
licuar <*1. pres:* licúo> *vt* 1. FÍS to liquate 2.(*fruta*) to liquefy 3. MIN to eliquate
líder *mf* leader; **la empresa** ~ the leading company
liderar *vt* 1.(*ser el primero*) to lead; **el equipo que lidera la clasificación** the team at the top of the table 2.(*dirigir*) to head
liderato *m,* **liderazgo** *m sin pl* leadership; **capacidad de** ~ leadership capability
lidia *f* fight; TAUR bullfight
lidiar *vt, vi* to fight; ~ **con los niños** *fig* to contend with the kids
liebre *f* hare; ~ **marina** sea hare ▸**levantar la** ~ to let the cat out of the bag; **donde menos se piensa salta la** ~ things always happen when you least expect them to
lienzo *m* 1.(*tela*) cloth; (*para cuadros*) canvas 2.(*óleo*) painting
liga *f* 1.(*alianza*) league 2.(*prenda*) suspender, garter 3. DEP league
ligadura *f* 1.(*lazo*) bond 2. *fig* (*traba*) tie 3. MÚS ligature
ligamento *m* ANAT ligament
ligar <g→gu> I. *vi inf* (*tontear*) to flirt; ~ **con alguien** (*conocer*) to get off with sb, to pick sb up II. *vt* 1.(*atar*) to tie 2.(*metal*) to alloy 3.(*unir*) to join 4. MÚS (*notas*) to slur III. *vr:* ~**se** 1.(*unirse*) to join 2. *inf* (*tontear*) to flirt
ligazón *f* (*unión*) link
ligerear *vi Chile* (*apresurarse*) to walk quickly
ligereza *f* 1.(*rapidez*) swiftness 2.(*levedad*) lightness 3.(*error*) thoughtless act; (*indiscreción*) indiscretion
ligero, -a *adj* 1.(*leve, ingrávido*) light; (*ruido*) soft; **ir muy** ~ **de ropa** to be lightly clad 2.(*ágil*) nimble ▸**hacer algo a la ligera** to do sth without thinking; **tomarse algo a la ligera** to not take sth seriously
lignito *m* MIN lignite
ligón *m* womanizer; **ser un** ~ to be a Don Juan
ligona *f* flirt
ligue *m inf* 1.(*acción*) pick-up; **dicen que tiene un** ~ **con el director** they say she's having an affair with the director 2.(*persona*) chat-up, pick-up
liguero *m* suspender belt, garter belt *Am*
liguero, -a *adj* DEP league; **competición liguera** league competition
lija *f* 1.(*papel*) sandpaper; ~ **esmeril** emery paper; (*piel*) shagreen 2. ZOOL dogfish
lijadora *f* sander
lijar *vt* to sand
lijoso, -a *adj Cuba* stuck-up
lila[1] I. *adj* lilac coloured *Brit,* lilac colored *Am* II. *f* BOT lilac
lila[2] *m* (*color*) lilac
lile *adj Chile* weak
liliputiense *adj, mf* Lilliputian
lima *f* 1.(*instrumento*) file; **rebajar con la** ~ to file down 2. BOT (*fruta*) lime; (*árbol*) lime tree ▸**comer como una** ~ *inf* to eat like a horse
limadura *f* 1.(*pulido*) polishing 2. *pl* (*partículas*) filings
limar *vt* 1.(*pulir*) to file; *fig* to perfect 2.(*consumir*) to wear down
limaza *f* slug
limbo *m* 1. REL limbo; **estar en el** ~ (*distraído*) to be distracted; (*atontado*) to be bewildered; (*no enterarse*) to be oblivious 2.(*de vestido*) hem
limeño, -a I. *adj* of/from Lima II. *m, f* native/inhabitant of Lima
limitación *f* limitation; (*de una norma*) restriction; **sin limitaciones** unlimited; **el plan tiene sus limitaciones pero ha sido eficaz** despite its shortcomings, the plan has been effective
limitado, -a *adj* 1.(*poco*) scant; (*medios*) limited; **un número** ~ a limited number 2.(*tonto*) slow-witted
limitar I. *vi* ~ **con algo** to border on sth II. *vt* to limit; (*libertad*) to restrict; (*definir*) to fix the boundaries of III. *vr:* ~**se** to confine oneself
límite *m* limit; ~ **de crédito** credit limit; **situación** ~ extreme situation; **sin** ~**s** limitless; **la fecha** ~ **para entregarlo es el...** the deadline for turning it in is ...
limítrofe *adj* bordering; **países** ~**s** neighbouring *Brit* [*o* neighboring *Am*] countries
limo *m* mud
limón *adj, m* lemon
limonada *f* lemonade; ~ **de vino** sangria (*type of sangria made of wine and lemonade*)
limonar *m* 1. AGR lemon grove 2. *Guat* (*limonero*) lemon tree
limonero *m* lemon tree
limosna *f* alms *pl;* **pedir** ~ to beg
limosnear *vi* to beg
limosnero, -a I. *adj* charitable II. *m, f AmL* (*pedigüeño*) beggar
limoso, -a *adj* muddy
limpiabarros *m inv* footscraper
limpiabotas *mf inv* bootblack

L

limpiachimeneas *mf inv* chimney sweep
limpiacristales[1] *mf inv* (*persona, producto*) window cleaner
limpiacristales[2] *m inv* (*producto*) window cleaning fluid
limpiador *m* cleaner
limpiador, **-a** **I.** *adj* cleaning; **leche ~a** cleansing milk **II.** *m, f* cleaner
limpiamuebles *m inv* furniture polish
limpiaparabrisas *m inv* windsreen wiper, windshield wiper *Am*
limpiar **I.** *vt* **1.** (*suciedad*) to clean; (*dientes*) to brush; (*chimenea*) to sweep; **~ el polvo** to dust; **~ en seco** to dry-clean **2.** (*librar*) to clear; **~ de culpas** to exonerate **3.** *inf* (*robar*) to nick **II.** *vi* (*quitar la suciedad*) to clean **III.** *vr:* **~se** to clean; (*nariz*) to wipe; (*dientes*) to brush
límpido, **-a** *adj elev* (*limpio*) limpid
limpieza *f* **1.** (*lavar*) washing; (*casa, zapatos*) cleaning; **~ de cutis** facial; **~ a fondo** thorough cleaning; **hacer la ~** to do the cleaning; **señora de la ~** cleaning lady **2.** (*estado*) cleanness, cleanliness **3.** (*eliminación*) cleansing; POL purge **4.** (*habilidad*) skill, precision
limpio *adv* (*sin trampas*) fairly; **jugar ~** to play fair ►**escribir en ~** to make a clean copy; **¿qué has sacado en ~ de todo este asunto?** what do you make of all this?; **en ~** (*dinero*) net
limpio, **-a** *adj* **1.** (*cocina, persona, agua*) clean; (*aire*) pure; (*almendra*) shelled **2.** *fig* honorable ►**lo dejaron ~** *inf* (*sin dinero*) they cleaned him out; **no sacar nada en ~ de algo** to make neither head nor tail of sth
limpión *m* **1.** (*lavado*) wash; **dar un ~ a alguien** to give sth a wipe **2.** *AmL* (*trapo*) dishcloth
limusina *f* AUTO limousine
linaje *m* lineage; **de rancio ~** of ancient descent
linaza *f* flax seed; **aceite de ~** linseed oil
lince *m* lynx; **tener ojos de ~** to be sharp-eyed; **ser un ~** *fig* to be very sharp
linchamiento *m* lynching
linchar *vt* to lynch
lindar *vi* **~ con algo** to border on sth
linde *m o f,* **lindero** *m* boundary; (*camino*) edge
lindeza *f* **1.** (*bonito*) prettiness **2.** (*gracioso*) witty remark **3.** *pl, irón* (*insulto*) insult; **me llamó "idiota" y otras ~s parecidas** he called me an "idiot" and other such compliments
lindo, **-a** *adj* pretty; (*niño*) lovely, cute; **divertirse a lo ~** to have a great time
línea *f* **1.** *t.* MAT, MIL, ECON (*raya*) line; **~ de intersección** intersecting line; **~ de meta** DEP (*fútbol*) goal line; (*atletismo*) finishing line; **~ recta** straight line; **fracasar en toda la ~** to fail completely **2.** (*renglón*) line; **~ en blanco** blank line; **leer entre ~s** to read between the lines; **te pongo cuatro ~s para...** I'm writing you just a few lines to ... **3.** (*de transporte*) line; (*trayecto*) route; **~ aérea** airline; **~ férrea** railway [*o* railroad *Am*] line; **coche de ~** coach *Brit,* long-distance bus *Am* **4.** TEL telephone line; **~ para el fax** fax line; **~ roja** hotline; **no hay ~** the line is dead [*o* down] **5.** (*pariente*) line; **por ~ materna** on his mother's side **6.** (*tipo*) figure; **guardar la ~** to watch one's figure **7.** (*directriz*) policy **8.** (*fábrica*) **~ de montaje** assembly line
lineal *adj t.* MAT, ARTE linear
linfa *f* BIO lymph
linfático, **-a** *adj* lymphatic; **gánglio ~** lymph node
lingotazo *m inf* swig; **pegarse un ~** to take a swig
lingote *m* ingot; (*de acero*) pig
lingüista *mf* linguist
lingüística *f* linguistics
lingüístico, **-a** *adj* linguistic
linier *m* <liniers> DEP linesman
linimento *m* liniment
lino *m* **1.** BOT flax **2.** (*tela*) linen
linóleo *m* linoleum
linterna *f* **1.** (*de mano*) torch, flashlight **2.** (*farol*) lantern; **~ mágica** magic lantern **3.** (*faro*) lighthouse
lío *m* **1.** (*embrollo*) mess; **¡déjame de ~s!** don't come to me with your problems!; **me hago un ~ con tus explicaciones** I'm getting all confused by your explanation; **¡me meto en cada ~!** I always get myself in such scrapes!; **no entiendo ese ~** I can't make anything of that mess **2.** (*de ropa*) bundle **3.** *inf* (*relación*) affair; **sé que tienes un ~ por ahí** I know you're having an affair
liofilizar <z→c> *vt* to freeze-dry, to lyophilize
lioso, **-a** *adj* (*difícil*) complicated; **persona liosa** troublemaker
lipidia *f* **1.** *AmC* (*pobreza*) poverty; (*miseria*) misery **2.** *Cuba, Méx* (*impertinencia*) impertinence
lipidiar *vt Cuba, Méx, PRico* to annoy
lipotimia *f* blackout
liquelique *m Col, Ven* white linen jacket
liquen *m* lichen
liquidación *f* **1.** (*de una mercancía*) sale; **~ por fin de temporada** (*invierno*) end of season sale; (*verano*) summer sale; **~ total** clearance sale **2.** (*de una empresa*) liquidation **3.** (*de una factura*) payment; (*cuenta*) settlement
liquidar *vt* **1.** (*licuar*) to liquefy **2.** *inf* (*acabar*) to liquidate; (*matar*) to kill; **lo ~on** *inf* they bumped him off **3.** (*mercancía*) to sell; **~ las existencias** to sell off all merchandise **4.** (*cerrar*) to close **5.** (*factura*) to settle
liquidez *f* **1.** (*agua*) fluidity **2.** COM liquidity
líquido *m* **1.** (*agua*) liquid; **~ amniótico** amniotic fluid; **~ de frenos** brake fluid **2.** (*saldo*) cash; **~ imponible** taxable income
líquido, **-a** *adj* **1.** (*material, consonante*)

liquid **2.** (*dinero*) cash; **renta líquida** disposable income

lira *f* **1.** (*moneda*) lira **2.** (*instrumento*) lyre

lírica *f* poetry

lírico, **-a** **I.** *adj* **1.** LIT lyric(al) **2.** MÚS lyrical **II.** *m, f* utopian; *AmL* lyric poet

lirio *m* lily; ~ **de los valles** lily of the valley

lirismo *m sin pl* **1.** LIT lyricism **2.** (*sentimentalismo*) emotionalism

lirón *m* dormouse; **dormir como un** ~ to sleep like a log

Lisboa *f* Lisbon

lisboeta **I.** *adj* of/from Lisbon **II.** *mf* native/inhabitant of Lisbon

lisiado, **-a** **I.** *adj* crippled **II.** *m, f* cripple

lisiar **I.** *vt* (*lesionar*) to injure; (*mutilar*) to maim **II.** *vr:* ~**se** to become disabled

liso, **-a** *adj* **1.** (*superficie*) smooth; (*pelo*) straight; **los 100 metros** ~**s** the 100 metre flat race **2.** (*tela, vestido*) plain

lisonja *f* flattery

lisonjear *vt* to flatter

lisonjero, **-a** **I.** *adj* flattering **II.** *m, f* flatterer

lista *f* **1.** (*enumeración*) list; ~ **de la compra** shopping list; ~ **del censo electoral** electoral roll; ~ **única** slate (*list of party candidates on a single ticket*); **estar en la** ~ **de espera** to be on the waiting list; **pasar** ~ (*leer*) to take roll call; (*controlar siempre*) to check on **2.** (*tira, de madera*) strip; (*estampado*) stripe; **a** ~**s** striped

listado *m* list

listado, **-a** *adj* striped

listar *vt* to list

listillo, **-a** *m, f* smart aleck, clever cloggs

listín *m* (*de teléfonos*) directory

listo, **-a** *adj* **1.** *ser* (*inteligente*) clever; (*sagaz*) shrewd; (*hábil*) skilful; **pasarse de** ~ to be too clever by half **2.** *estar* (*preparado*) ready; ~ **para enviar** *t.* INFOR ready to send; ~ **para el envío/para el tiraje** ready to ship/print; ~ **para despegar** ready for takeoff; **estás** ~ **si crees que...** *inf* you've got another think coming if you think that ...

listón *m* (*madero*) lath; **poner el** ~ **muy alto** *fig* to set very high standards

lisura *f* **1.** (*llano*) evenness **2.** *AmL* (*frescura*) impudent remark **3.** *fig* (*ingenuidad*) naivety; (*franqueza*) frankness

litera *f* (*cama*) bunk; FERRO couchette; NÁUT berth

literal *adj* literal

literario, **-a** *adj* literary; **lenguaje** ~ literary language

literato, **-a** *m, f* man *m* of letters, woman *f* of letters

literatura *f* literature; ~ **barata** pulp fiction; **¡eso es sólo hacer** ~**!** that's only words, but no action!

litigante *adj, mf* litigant

litigar <g→gu> *vt* **1.** *t.* JUR (*disputar*) to dispute **2.** (*llevar a juicio*) to be in dispute

litigio *m* **1.** (*disputa*) dispute; **en caso de** ~ in the case of dispute; **en** ~ in dispute **2.** (*juicio*) lawsuit

litografía *f* **1.** ARTE (*proceso*) lithography **2.** (*grabado*) lithograph

litoral **I.** *adj* coastal **II.** *m* (*costa*) coast; (*playa*) shore

litri *adj inf* pretentious, hoity-toity

litro *m* litre *Brit,* liter *Am;* **un** ~ **de leche** a litre *Brit* [*o* liter *Am*] of milk

litrona *f inf* litre bottle of beer *Brit,* liter bottle of beer *Am*

Lituania *f* Lithuania

lituano, **-a** *adj, m, f* Lithuanian

liturgia *f* liturgy

liviandad *f* (*frivolidad*) triviality

liviano, **-a** *adj* **1.** (*trivial*) light **2.** (*ligero*) light; (*error*) trivial

lividez *f* lividness

lívido, **-a** *adj* **1.** (*amoratado*) livid; ~ **de frío** livid with cold **2.** (*pálido*) ashen

llaga *f* **1.** (*herida*) wound; (*úlcera*) ulcer; (*ampolla*) sore **2.** (*pena*) sorrow

llagar <g→gu> **I.** *vt* (*herir*) to wound; (*rozar*) to cause a sore **II.** *vr:* ~**se** **1.** (*ulcerarse*) to get a sore **2.** (*herirse*) to get hurt; ~**se** (**los pies**) to get sores (on your feet)

llama *f* **1.** (*fuego*) flame; *fig* burning passion **2.** ZOOL llama

llamada *f* **1.** (*voz*) call; ~ **al orden** call to order; ~ **del programa** INFOR program call **2.** (*de teléfono*) phonecall; ~ **urbana** local call; ~ **a cobro revertido** reverse charge call **3.** (*gesto*) gesture **4.** (*a la puerta golpeando*) knock; (*con el timbre*) ring **5.** (*en un libro*) reference mark **6.** MIL call-up, conscription *Brit,* draft *Am*

llamado, **-a** *adj* (*conocido como*) called; (*supuesto*) so-called

llamado *m AmS v.* **llamamiento**

llamador *m* **1.** (*picaporte*) doorknocker **2.** (*timbre*) doorbell

llamamiento *m* **1.** (*exhortación*) appeal; (*soldado*) call-up; **hacer un** ~ **a todos** to issue an appeal to all **2.** MIL ~ **a filas** call to arms **3.** JUR (*citación*) summons, subpoena

llamar **I.** *vt* **1.** (*voz*) to call; (*por teléfono*) to telephone, to ring up *Brit;* ~ **a declarar a alguien** to call on sb to testify; ~ **a filas** MIL to call up *Brit,* to draft *Am;* **te llaman al teléfono** you're wanted on the phone; ~ **a capítulo a alguien** to tell sb off; ~ **al perro con un silbido** to whistle to the dog **2.** (*denominar*) to call; **lo llamé idiota a la cara** I called him an idiot to his face **3.** (*despertar*) to wake up; ~ **la atención** (*reprender*) to reprimand; (*ser llamativo*) to attract attention; ~ **la atención sobre algo** to draw attention to sth **II.** *vi* **1.** (*a la puerta golpeando*) to knock; (*con el timbre*) to ring; **¿quién llama?** who is it? **2.** *inf* (*gustar*) to appeal; **el chocolate no me llama nada** chocolate just doesn't appeal to me **III.** *vr:* ~**se** to be called; **¿cómo te llamas?** what's your name?; **¡como me llamo David,**

que lo harás! *inf* you will do it, as sure as my name is David!

llamarada *f* **1.** (*llama*) blaze **2.** (*rubor*) sudden flush

llamarón *m Chile, Col, Ecua* sudden blaze

llamativo, -a *adj* (*traje*) flashy; (*color*) loud

llamear *vi* to blaze

llana *f* (*herramienta*) trowel

llanca *f Chile* MIN *bluish-green copper ore*

llaneza *f sin pl* simplicity

llanito, -a *m, f inf* Gibraltarian

llano *m* plain

llano, -a *adj* **1.** (*liso*) flat; (*terreno*) level **2.** (*campechano*) straightforward **3.** LING paroxytone **4.** (*sencillo*) **el pueblo** ~ the common people

llanta *f* **1.** *AmL* (*rueda*) tyre *Brit,* tire *Am* **2.** (*cerco*) (metal) rim; ~ **de aleación** alloy wheel

llantería *f sin pl, AmL* weeping and wailing

llantina *f inf* uninterrupted weeping

llanto *m* crying

llanura *f* plain

llapa *f AmS* extra

llave *f* **1.** *t. fig* (*instrumento*) key; ~ **de contacto** AUTO ignition key; ~ **maestra** master key; **ama de ~s** housekeeper; ~ **en mano** (*coche*) on the road; **~s en mano** (*casa*) available for immediate occupancy; **echar la** ~ to lock; **estar bajo** ~ to be under lock and key; **la ~ no entra** the key doesn't fit; **la ~ para descubrir el secreto** the key to the secret; **meter/sacar la** ~ to put in/pull out the key **2.** MÚS (*trompeta*) valve; (*órgano*) stop; (*instrumentos de viento*) key **3.** (*grifo*) tap *Brit,* faucet *Am* **4.** (*tuerca*) spanner; ~ **inglesa** adjustable spanner, monkey wrench **5.** (*interruptor*) switch **6.** TIPO bracket **7.** DEP hold, armlock

llavero *m* (*utensilio*) key ring

llegada *f* **1.** (*al destino*) arrival **2.** (*meta*) finishing line

llegar <g→gu> **I.** *vi* **1.** (*al destino, el correo*) to arrive; (*avión*) to land; (*barco*) to dock; ~ **a la meta** DEP to reach the finishing line; **estar al ~** to be about to arrive; ~ **a Madrid/al hotel** to arrive in Madrid/at the hotel; ~ **tarde** to be late; **¡todo llegará!** all in good time!; **¡hasta ahí podíamos ~!** that's the limit! **2.** (*recibir*) **no me ha llegado el dinero** I haven't received the money **3.** (*durar*) to live; ~ **a viejo** to live to old age; ~ **a los ochenta** to reach the age of eighty; **el enfermo no ~á a la primavera** the patient won't make it to spring; **este gobierno no ~á a 2 años** this government won't last two years **4.** (*ascender*) to amount to; **la cinta no llega a tres metros** the ribbon is less than 3 m long; **no llega a 20 euros** it's less than 20 euros **5.** (*lograr*) **ese ~á lejos** that fellow will go far; ~ **a ser muy rico** to become very rich; **llegamos a recoger 8.000 firmas** we managed to get 8,000 signatures; ~ **a ministro** to succeeding in becoming a minister; **nunca ~é a entenderte** I'll never understand you **6.** (*ser suficiente*) to be enough **7.** (*tocar*) ~ **a** [*o* hasta] **algo** to reach sth; **el niño no llega a los productos de limpieza** the child can't get at the cleaning products; **no me llegas ni a la suela de los zapatos** you can't hold a candle to me **II.** *vr:* **~se** (*ir*) to go; **~se por casa de alguien** to stop by [*o* to go round *Brit*] sb's house

llenador(a) *adj Chile* filling; **esta fruta es muy ~a** this fruit is very filling

llenar I. *vt* **1.** (*atestar*) to fill; ~ **de algo** to fill with sth; **es necesario ~ esa laguna** *fig* this gap must be filled; **los niños ~on el suelo de papeles** the children littered the floor with papers; **~se los bolsillos de caramelos** to fill one's pockets with sweets *Brit* [*o* candy *Am*] **2.** (*comida*) to be filling; **la pasta llena mucho** pasta is very filling **3.** (*cumplimentar*) to fill in [*o* out] **4.** (*colmar*) ~ **de algo** to overwhelm with sth; **nos llenó de regalos** we were showered with gifts **5.** (*satisfacer*) to satisfy **6.** (*agradecer*) to be grateful for **II.** *vr:* **~se de algo** *inf* **1.** (*comida*) to stuff oneself with sth **2.** (*irritarse*) to be fed up with sth

lleno *m* (*teatro, auditorio*) full house

lleno, -a *adj* (*recipiente*) full; **luna llena** full moon; ~ **de** full of, filled with; **a la planta le da el sol de ~** the plant is directly in the sun; **el autobús iba ~** the bus was full; **estoy ~** *inf* I'm full; **el escritorio estaba ~ de papeles** the desk was covered with papers

llevadero, -a *adj* bearable

llevar I. *vt* **1.** (*a un destino, acompañar*) to take; (*transportar*) to transport; (*en brazos*) to carry; (*viento*) to blow; (*comida*) to take out; ~ **a alguien en el coche** to give sb a lift; ~ **algo a alguien** to take sth to sb; **dos pizzas para ~, por favor** two pizzas to take away, please **2.** (*exigir, cobrar*) to charge; (*costar*) to cost; **me llevó un dineral reparar el tejado** it cost me a fortune to fix the roof; **este trabajo lleva mucho tiempo** this work takes a lot of time **3.** (*tener*) ~ **consigo** to be carrying, to have **4.** (*conducir*) to lead; ~ **de la mano** to lead by the hand; ~ **consigo** [*o* **aparejado**] to include; **esto no lleva a ninguna parte** this isn't getting us anywhere **5.** (*ropa*) to wear **6.** (*coche*) to drive **7.** (*finca*) to run **8.** (*estar*) to have been; ~ **estudiando tres años** to have been studying for three years; **llevo cuatro días aquí** I've been here for four days **9.** (*gestionar*) to manage; ~ **las cuentas** to manage the accounts; **el abogado que lleva el caso** the lawyer handling the case **10.** (*inducir*) ~ **a algo** to lead to sth, to induce sth; **me llevó a pensar que...** it led me to think that ... **11.** (*exceder*) to exceed; **te llevo dos años** I'm two years older than you; **me llevas dos centímetros** you are two cm taller than me **12.** (*tener como ingrediente*) **esta receta lleva 12 huevos** this recipe calls for 12 eggs; **¿lleva picante?** does it have hot pepper? ►**dejarse** ~ **por algo** to be carried away with sth;

dejarse ~ **por alguien** to let sb influence you; ~ **las de perder** to look like losing; **¿qué tal lo llevas?** how are you holding up? **II.** *vr:* ~**se 1.** (*coger*) to take; **la riada se llevó** (**por delante**) **el puente** the flood washed away the bridge; ~**se dos años** to be two years older **2.** (*ganar*) to win; ~**se la mayor/peor parte** to get the best/worst of it **3.** (*estar de moda*) to be in fashion; **ya no se llevan los zapatos de plataforma** platform shoes are no longer in fashion **4.** (*soportarse*) to get along; **mi jefe y yo nos llevamos bien** my boss and I get along well; ~**se a matar** to hate each other ▸**...y me llevo cuatro** MAT ... and carry four

llicIla *f Bol, Ecua, Perú* blanket (*carried on the back by Indian women*)

llicta *f Bol* GASTR potato meal cake (*type of hard cake eaten while chewing coca to give flavour to the coca ball*)

llorar I. *vi* **1.** (*lágrimas*) to cry, to weep; **desahogarse llorando** to relieve one's feelings by crying; **la película te hacía** ~ the film made you cry; **me lloran los ojos** my eyes are watering; ~ **de alegría** to cry for joy; **de** ~ enough to make one cry; **lloramos de risa** we laughed till we cried **2.** (*vid, árbol*) to bleed ▸**quien no llora no mama** *inf* if you don't ask, you don't get **II.** *vt* **1.** (*lágrimas*) ~ **por algo/alguien** to cry over sth/sb; *fig* to mourn sth/sb; ~ **la muerte de alguien** to mourn sb's death **2.** (*quejarse*) to whine **3.** (*lamentar*) to bemoan

llorera *f inf* fit of crying, blubbering

llorica *mf inf* crybaby, whiner

lloriquear *vi* to whimper, to snivel

lloriqueo *m* whimpering

lloro(s) *m(pl)* crying; **con estos ~s no conseguirás nada** this crying won't get you anywhere

llorón, -ona I. *adj* always crying; **sauce** ~ weeping willow **II.** *m, f* crybaby, whiner

lloroso, -a *adj* tearful

llovedizo, -a *adj* (*techo*) leaky; **agua llovediza** rainwater

llover <o→ue> *vi, vt, vimpers* to rain; **está lloviendo** it's raining; **llueve a mares** [*o* **a cántaros**] it's pouring; **siempre llueve sobre mojado** it never rains but it pours; **como llovido del cielo** heaven sent; **llueven las malas noticias** it's one piece of bad news after another; **me escucha como quien oye** ~ *inf* it's water off a duck's back to him/her, in one ear and out the other; **ya ha llovido mucho desde entonces** *fig* a lot has happened since then

llovida *f AmL* rain; **¡qué ~!** what a downpour!

llovizna *f* drizzle

lloviznar *vimpers* **está lloviznando** it's drizzling

lluqui *adj Ecua* (*zurdo*) left-handed

lluvia *f* **1.** (*chubasco*) rain; ~ **de estrellas** meteor shower; **época de las ~s** rainy season; ~ **ácida** acid rain; ~ **radiactiva** fallout **2.** (*cantidad*) shower; **hubo una** ~ **de protestas** there was a shower of protests **3.** *AmL* (*ducha*) shower

lluvioso, -a *adj* rainy; **tiempo** ~ rainy weather

lo I. *art def v.* **el, la, lo II.** *pron pers m y neutro sing* **1.** (*objeto: masculino*) him; (*neutro*) it; **¡lláma~!** call him!; **¡haz~!** do it! **2.** (*con relativo*) ~ **que...** what; ~ **cual** which; ~ **que quiero decir es que...** what I mean is that ...

loa *f* (*alabanza*) praise

loable *adj* commendable

loar *vt* to praise

lobato *m* **1.** (*lobo*) wolf cub **2.** (*cachorro*) cub

lobezno *m* wolf cub

lobisón *m Arg, Par, Urug* werewolf

lobo, -a *m, f* wolf; ~ **cerval** lynx; ~ **de mar** old salt; ~ **marino** seal; **en esa ocasión le vimos las orejas al** ~ that time we saw his/her true colours *Brit* [*o* colors *Am*]; **meterse en la boca del** ~ to go into the lion's den; **ser un** ~ **con piel de oveja** to be a wolf in sheep's clothing; **tener un hambre de ~s** to be as hungry as a wolf

lóbrego, -a *adj* gloomy

lóbulo *m* ANAT lobe; ~ **de la oreja** earlobe

local I. *adj* local; **periódico** ~ local newspaper **II.** *m* locale; COM premises *pl;* ~ **público** public building

localidad *f* **1.** (*municipio*) town **2.** (*entrada*) ticket; (*asiento*) seat

localismo *m* regionalism; *pey* (*chovinismo*) provincialism, parochialism

localista *adj pey* parochial, of local interest; **escritor** ~ parochial writer

localización *f* **1.** (*búsqueda*) finding; AVIAT tracking **2.** (*posición*) location

localizar <z→c> *vt* **1.** (*encontrar*) to find; ~ **por teléfono** to get in touch by phone **2.** (*limitar*) to localize; AVIAT to track; (*fuego, epidemia*) to confine

locería *f AmL* crockery

loche *m Col* ZOOL loach

loción *f* **1.** (*líquido*) lotion; ~ **capilar** hair lotion; ~ **tónica** after-shave **2.** (*crema*) lotion; ~ **bronceadora** suntan lotion; ~ **hidratante** moisturizing cream **3.** (*fricción*) massage

loco, -a I. *adj* **1.** (*chalado*) mad, crazy; **a lo ~, a tontas y a locas** any old way; **estar** ~ **de atar** to be raving [*o* stark staring] mad; **estar** ~ **por la música** to be crazy about music; **estar** ~ **con la bicicleta** to be wild about one's bike; **estar** ~ **de contento** to be elated; **estar medio** ~ to be not all there **2.** (*maravilloso*) tremendous; **tener una suerte loca** to be incredibly lucky **II.** *m, f* madman; **casa de ~s** *t. fig* madhouse; **cada** ~ **con su tema** to each his own; **hacerse el** ~ to act dumb; **hacer el** ~ to act the fool; **tener una vena de** ~ to have a streak of madness

locomoción *f* locomotion

locomotor, -a *adj* locomotive

locomotora *f* locomotive

L

locomotriz *adj* locomotive
locro *m AmS: meat and vegetable stew*
locuacidad *f* talkativeness
locuaz *adj* loquacious; (*charlatán*) talkative
locución *f* (*expresión*) phrase; ~ **prepositiva** prepositional phrase
locura *f* **1.** (*enajenación mental*) madness; ~ **bovina** mad cow disease; **querer con** ~ to be madly in love with; **una casa de** ~ a dream house **2.** (*disparate*) crazy thing; **andar haciendo** ~**s** to be doing foolish things
locutor(**a**) *m(f)* speaker
locutorio *m* **1.** (*claustro*) locutory **2.** TEL telephone box *Brit,* telephone booth *Am*
lodazal *m* mudhole
lodo *m* mud
logia *f* **1.** ARQUIT loggia **2.** (*reunión*) lodge
lógica *f* logic
lógico, **-a** *adj* logical; (*normal*) natural
logística *f* logistics *pl*
logístico, **-a** *adj* logistic
logopeda *mf* speech therapist
logopedia *f* speech therapy
logotipo *m* (*distintivo*) logotype; (*de una empresa, un producto*) logo
logrado, **-a** *adj* successful, well done; **te ha quedado muy** ~ **el cuadro** you've done a wonderful job on that painting
lograr I. *vt* to achieve; (*premio*) to win; **logré convencerla** I managed to convince her **II.** *vr:* ~**se** to be successful
logrero, **-a** *m, f* moneylender
logro *m* achievement
logroñés, **-esa I.** *adj* of/from Logroño **II.** *m, f* native/inhabitant of Logroño
loma *f* hill
lomada *f AmS* hill
lombriz *f* worm; ~ **intestinal** tapeworm; ~ **de tierra** earthworm
lomo *m* **1.** (*espalda*) back; **agachar el** ~ *inf* to work very hard; **sobar el** ~ **a alguien** *inf* to butter sb up; **ser un mentiroso de tomo y** ~ to be an out-and-out liar **2.** (*solomillo*) loin **3.** (*de libro*) spine **4.** (*de cuchillo*) back
lona *f* canvas
loncha *f* slice; (*beicon*) rasher
lonchería *f AmC, Méx* lunch counter
londinense I. *adj* London **II.** *mf* Londoner
Londres *m* London
longanimidad *f sin pl, elev* forbearance
longánimo, **-a** *adj elev* forbearing
longaniza *f spicy pork sausage;* **hay mas días que** ~**s** there's all the time in the world
longevidad *f sin pl* longevity
longevo, **-a** *adj* (*que dura*) long-lived; (*viejo*) very old
longitud *f* length; **salto de** ~ DEP long jump; **cuatro metros de** ~ four metres [*o* meters *Am*] long; **cincuenta grados** ~ **este/oeste** fifty degrees longitude east/west; **estar en la misma** ~ **de onda** *fig* to be on the same wavelength
longitudinal *adj* **corte** ~ longitudinal section
longitudinalmente *adv* longitudinally, lengthwise
longui(**s**) *mf inv* **hacerse el** ~ *inf* to play dumb
lonja *f* **1.** COM public exchange **2.** (*loncha*) slice
lonjear *vt* **1.** *Arg* (*cortar*) to slice **2.** *Arg, inf* (*azotar*) to give a good thrashing to
loor *m elev* praise; **en** ~ **de la Virgen María** in praise of the Virgin Mary
loquear *vi inf* to clown around
loquera *f* **1.** (*manicomio*) madhouse **2.** *AmL* (*locura*) madness
lora *f Col* (*loro*) parrot
Lorena *f* Lorraine
loro *m* **1.** ZOOL parrot; **repetir como un** ~ to repeat parrot fashion; **hablar como un** ~ to talk non-stop **2.** *pey, inf* (*mujer*) old hag
los I. *art def v.* **el, la, lo II.** *pron pers m y neutro pl* **1.** (*objeto directo*) them; **¡lláma~!** call them! **2.** (*con relativo*) ~ **que...** the ones that ...; ~ **cuales** which
losa *f* **1.** (*piedra*) slab; (*lápida*) gravestone **2.** (*baldosa*) tile
lote *m* **1.** (*parte*) share; COM lot **2.** (*toqueteo*) **darse** [*o* **pegarse**] **el** ~ to get off with
lotería *f* lottery; ~ **primitiva** weekly lottery; **administración de** ~ office selling lottery tickets; **a Juan le tocó la** ~ John won the lottery; **un décimo de la** ~ a tenth share of a lottery number; **¡con ese hijo te tocó la** ~**!** you really struck gold with that son of yours!; **jugar a la** ~ to play the lottery
loto[1] *m* **1.** (*planta*) lotus **2.** (*flor*) lotus flower
loto[2] *f inf* lottery
Lovaina *f* Louvain
loza *f* earthenware; (*vajilla*) crockery; ~ **fina** china
lozanía *f sin pl* **1.** (*vegetación*) lushness **2.** (*persona: robustez*) vigour *Brit,* vigor *Am;* (*salud*) healthiness
lozano, **-a** *adj* **1.** (*planta*) lush **2.** (*persona: robusta*) vigorous; (*saludable*) healthy
lubina *f* sea bass
lubricante *m* lubricant
lubricar <c→qu> *vt* to lubricate
lúbrico, **-a** *adj* (*obsceno*) lewd
lubrificante *m* lubricant
lubrificar <c→qu> *vt* to lubricate
Lucayas *fpl* **islas** ~ the Bahamas
lucense I. *adj* of/from Lugo **II.** *mf* native/inhabitant of Lugo
Lucerna *f* Lucerne
lucernario *m* skylight
lucero *m* **1.** (*estrella*) bright star **2.** (*en la frente de cuadrúpedos*) star
lucha *f* fight; DEP wrestling; ~ **cuerpo a cuerpo** hand-to-hand fighting [*o* combat]; ~ **contra la droga** the fight against drugs
luchador(**a**) *m(f)* fighter; DEP wrestler
luchar *vi* ~ **por algo** to fight for sth, to struggle for sth
luche *m Chile* **1.** (*juego*) hopscotch **2.** BOT,

GASTR sea lettuce

lucidez *f sin pl* **1.** (*estado*) lucidity; **antes de morir tuvo todavía un momento de ~** before dying he had one last moment of lucidness **2.** (*clarividencia*) clarity; (*sagacidad*) clear-headedness

lucido, -a *adj* **1.** (*brillante*) outstanding **2.** (*selecto*) select

lúcido, -a *adj* **1.** (*clarividente*) clear-sighted; (*sagaz*) astute **2.** (*sobrio*) clear-headed

luciérnaga *f* firefly

lucio *m* pike

lucir *irr* **I.** *vi* **1.** (*brillar*) to shine; **esa lámpara luce muy poco** this lamp gives off very little light **2.** (*compensar*) to compensate; (*verse*) to look good; **el vestido no le luce** the dress doesn't look good on her; **es un trabajo pesado y que no luce** it's hard work, though it doesn't look it; **ese collar luce mucho con el vestido rojo** that necklace goes really well with the red dress; **este jersey hecho a mano no luce** this handmade sweater doesn't look much; **me he pasado la mañana recogiendo, pero no me luce** I've spent the whole morning tidying though you'd never know it; **no te luce el dinero que tienes** no one would ever know you are wealthy **II.** *vt* (*exhibir*) to display; **lucía un bronceado impecable** he/she was showing off her perfect tan **III.** *vr:* **~se 1.** (*exhibirse*) to display **2.** (*destacarse*) to stand out; **¡ahora sí que nos hemos lucido!** *irón* now we've really made a mess of it!

lucrarse *vr* to profit

lucrativo, -a *adj* lucrative; **no ~** not profitable; **sin fines ~s** non-profit making

lucro *m* profit; **con ánimo de ~** for profit; **organización sin ánimo de ~** non-profit organisation

luctuoso, -a *adj* sorrowful

lúdico, -a *adj* ludic; **el aspecto ~ de la vida** the fun side of life

luego **I.** *adv* **1.** (*después*) later; **¡hasta ~!** see you later! **2.** (*entonces*) then **3.** (*por supuesto*) **desde ~** of course **II.** *conj* **1.** (*así que*) and so **2.** (*después de*) **~ que** as soon as

lugar *m* **1.** (*sitio, localidad, situación*) place; **el ~ de autos** the scene of the incident; **en primer/segundo ~** first/second; **tener ~** to take place; **en algún ~ de la casa** somewhere in the house; **hacerse una composición de ~** to consider the pros and cons; **la observación está fuera de ~** that comment is out of place; **en ~ de** instead of; **yo en ~ de usted...** if I were you ... **2.** (*motivo*) **no des ~ a que te reprendan** don't give them any cause for reproach; **dar ~ a un escándalo** to give rise to a scandal

lugareño, -a *adj, m, f* local

lugarteniente *m* deputy

lúgubre *adj* (*sombrío*) gloomy

lugués, -esa **I.** *adj* of/from Lugo **II.** *m, f* native/inhabitant of Lugo

lujo *m* luxury; **permitirse el ~ de...** to treat oneself to the luxury of ...; **un ~ asiático** the ultimate in luxury; **con gran ~ de detalles** with a wealth of detail; **darse el ~ de** to give oneself the pleasure of

lujoso, -a *adj* luxurious

lujuria *f* lechery, lust

lujurioso, -a **I.** *adj* lecherous **II.** *m, f* lecher

lulo *m Chile* (*bulto cilíndrico*) small cylindrical bundle

lumbago *m* MED lumbago

lumbar *adj* lumbar

lumbre *f sin pl* (*llamas*) fire; (*brasa*) glow; **¿me das ~?** can you give me a light?; **sentados al amor de la ~** sitting by the fireside; **poner a la ~** to put on the stove

lumbrera *f* **1.** (*claraboya*) skylight **2.** (*talento*) leading light

luminarias *fpl* (*para fiestas*) decorative lights

luminosidad *f* luminosity; (*astro, día*) brightness

luminoso, -a *adj* **1.** (*brillante*) bright, luminous; (*día*) light; **anuncio ~** illuminated [*o* neon] sign; **potencia luminosa** illuminating power **2.** (*excelente*) brilliant

luna *f* **1.** ASTR moon; (*luz*) moonlight; **~ creciente/menguante** waxing/waning moon; **~ llena/nueva** full/new moon; **~ de miel** honeymoon; **media ~** half moon; **a la luz de la ~** in the moonlight; **estar en la ~** to be daydreaming; **pedir la ~** to ask for the moon; **tener ~s** *fig* to have whims **2.** (*cristal*) plate glass; (*espejo*) mirror; **~s del coche** car windows ▶**quedarse a la ~ de Valencia** to be disappointed

lunar **I.** *adj* lunar **II.** *m* **1.** (*en la piel*) mole **2.** (*en una tela*) polka-dot **3.** (*mancha*) stain

lunarejo, -a **I.** *adj AmL* **1.** (*persona con lunares*) with moles on the face **2.** (*animal con lunares*) spotted **II.** *m, f AmL* (*persona con lunares*) person with moles

lunático, -a *adj* lunatic

lunes *m inv* Monday; **~ de carnaval** the last Monday before Lent; **~ de Pascua** Easter Monday; **el ~** on Monday; **el ~ pasado** last Monday; **el ~ que viene** next Monday; **el ~ por la noche/al mediodía/por la mañana/por la tarde** Monday night/at midday/morning/afternoon; (**todos**) **los ~** every Monday, on Mondays; **en la noche del ~ al martes** in the small hours of Monday; **el ~ entero** all day Monday; **cada dos ~** (**del mes**) every other Monday; **hoy es ~, once de marzo** today is Monday, March 11th; **pasar de ir al trabajo el ~** not to go to work on Monday

luneta *f* **1.** (*adorno*) crescent-shaped ornament **2.** (*anteojo*) lens

lunfardismo *m Arg* slang word

lupa *f* magnifying glass; **mirar con ~** to examine meticulously

lupanar *m* brothel

lúpulo *m* **1.** BOT hop plant **2.** (*cerveza*) hops

lustrabotas *mf inv, AmL* shoeshine

L

lustrador *m Arg, Nic* shoeshine boy
lustrar *vt* to polish; (*zapatos*) to shine
lustre *m* **1.**(*brillo*) lustre *Brit,* luster *Am;* **sacar ~ a los zapatos/a los muebles** to polish shoes/furniture; **tener ~** *fig* to be famous or noble **2.** *AmL* (*betún*) shoe polish
lustrín *m Chile* shoeshine stall
lustrina *f Chile* (*betún*) shoe polish
lustro *m* lustrum; **en el último ~** *elev* in the last five years
lustroso, **-a** *adj* shiny; **estar ~** *fig* to be radiant
luto *m* mourning; (*vestido*) mourning clothes; **ir de ~** to wear mourning; **estar de ~ por alguien** to be in mourning for sb; **declarar día de ~ nacional** to declare a day of national mourning
luxación *f* MED dislocation
Luxemburgo *m* Luxembourg
luxemburgués, **-esa** **I.** *adj* of/from Luxembourg **II.** *m, f* native/inhabitant of Luxembourg
luz *f* **1.**(*resplandor*) light; **~ corta** dipped headlights; **~ larga** full beam; **~ natural** natural light; **~ trasera** rear light, tail light *Am;* **traje de luces** bullfighter's suit; **a la ~ del día** in daylight; **a media ~** in subdued light; **claro como la ~ del día** crystal clear; **dar a ~** to give birth; **¡~ de mis ojos!** the apple of my eye!; **sacar a la ~** *fig* to bring to light; **salir a la ~** *fig* to come to light; **arrojar ~ sobre un asesinato** to shed light on the murder; **a la ~ de los nuevos datos...** in the light of the new data ... **2.**(*energía*) electricity; **¡da la ~!** turn on the light!; **se fue la ~** the power went off **3.**(*fuente de luz*) light source; (*lámpara*) light; **apagar/encender la ~** to turn off/on the light **4.** ARQUIT aperture **5.** *pl* (*inteligencia*) intelligence; **el Siglo de las Luces** the Age of Enlightenment; **ser de pocas luces** to be dim-witted; **tener pocas luces** to be stupid; **a todas luces** evidently

M

M, **m** *f* M, m; **~ de María** M for Mary *Brit,* M for Mike *Am*
Mª *abr de* **María** *abbreviation for the name Mary*
maca *f* (*daño*) damage; (*en un mueble*) defect; (*fruta*) bruise; (*del carácter*) blemish
macabí *m Cuba* cunning person, shark *fig*
macabro, **-a** *adj* macabre
macaco, **-a** **I.** *adj Cuba, Chile* (*feo*) ugly **II.** *m, f* **1.** ZOOL macaque **2.** *AmL, pey* Chink
macagua *f* **1.** *AmS* (*ave*) laughing falcon **2.** *Ven* (*serpiente*) large poisonous snake **3.** *Cuba* BOT macaw-tree
macana *f* **1.**(*tontería*) piece of nonsense **2.**(*mentira*) lie **3.** ECON unsaleable goods *pl* **4.** *AmL* (*porra*) baton, truncheon *Brit*
macaneador(a) *m(f) Arg, inf* fibber
macanear **I.** *vi CSur* **1.**(*disparatar*) to act rashly **2.**(*hacer tonterías*) to act foolishly; (*decir tonterías*) to talk nonsense **3.**(*mentir*) to lie **II.** *vt inf* (*chapucear*) to botch
macanudo, **-a** *adj AmL, inf* fantastic, super
macarra *m inf* **1.**(*chorizo*) lout, roughneck *Am* **2.**(*chulo*) pimp
macarrón *m* **1.** *pl* (*pasta*) macaroni **2.**(*bollo*) macaroon
macedonia *f* **~ (de frutas)** fruit salad
macerar **I.** *vt* **1.**(*con golpes*) to macerate **2.** GASTR to marinate **3.**(*mortificar*) to mortify **II.** *vr:* **~se** to mortify oneself
maceta *f* **1.**(*tiesto*) flowerpot **2.** *Chile* (*ramo*) bunch of flowers **3.**(*martillo*) mallet
macetero *m* flowerpot stand; *AmL* flowerpot
machacar <c→qu> **I.** *vt* **1.**(*triturar*) to pound **2.**(*insistir*) to insist on, to harp on **3.** *inf* (*estudiar*) to swot up **4.** *inf* (*destruir*) to crush **II.** *vr:* **~se** *inf* to wear oneself out; **machacársela** *vulg* to have a wank *Brit,* to jerk off
machacón, **-ona** *adj pey* insistent; **¡no seas ~!** (*no insistas*) stop going on and on!
machamartillo **a ~** very firmly; **creer algo a ~** to firmly believe sth; **repetir algo a ~** to repeat sth ad nauseam
machete *m* **1.** machete **2.** *Arg, Urug, Col, inf* (*chuleta*) crib (sheet)
machetear **I.** *vt, vi Arg, Col, inf* (*copiar*) to copy **II.** *vr:* **~se** *Méx* (*trabajar*) to work; *inf* (*empollar*) to swot
machetero, **-a** *m, f* **1.** cutter **2.**(*que corta la caña de azúcar*) cane-cutter **3.** *Arg, inf* (*copión*) copycat **4.** *Méx* (*empollón*) plodder
machismo *m* male chauvinism; (*virilidad*) manliness, masculinity
machista *adj* (male) chauvinistic
macho **I.** *m* **1.** ZOOL (*masculino*) male; **~ cabrío** billy goat **2.** *inf* (*machote*) tough guy **3.**(*pieza*) male part **4.** ARQUIT buttress **II.** *adj* **1.**(*masculino*) male **2.**(*fuerte*) macho
machona *f AmL, inf* butch
machote **I.** *m* **1.** *inf* (*hombre*) (tough) guy **2.** *AmL* (*borrador*) (rough) draft; (*modelo*) model **II.** *adj inf* **1.**(*viril*) manly **2.**(*valiente*) brave
machucar <c→qu> *vt* **1.**(*golpear*) to pound **2.**(*destruir*) to destroy; (*aplastar*) to crush
machucho, **-a** *adj* **1.** *estar pey* (*viejo*) old; **¡qué ~!** how old he is! **2.** *ser* (*tranquilo*) serene
macilento, **-a** *adj* **1.**(*pálido*) wan; (*cansado*) haggard **2.**(*flaco*) gaunt **3.**(*triste*) sombre *Brit,* somber *Am*
macizo *m* **1.**(*masa*) solid mass; (*trozo*) chunk **2.** GEO massif **3.**(*plantas*) flowerbed **4.** ARQUIT section **5.** *pl* GASTR soused sardines *pl*
macizo, **-a** *adj* **1.**(*oro, puerta*) solid; **de plata maciza** of solid silver **2.**(*persona*) robust; **estar ~** to be robust; **un tío ~** a well-built guy

3. (*sólido*) solid 4. (*mujer*) stacked *inf;* (*hombre*) well-built
macramé *m* macramé
macroinstrucción *f* INFOR macro
mácula *f* 1. (*mancha*) spot; *fig* stain; **sin** ~ *fig* pure 2. *inf* (*engaño*) trick
macuto *m* 1. (*mochila*) rucksack *Brit,* backpack *Am;* MIL kit bag 2. *inf* (*joroba*) hump 3. *Ven* (*de los mendigos*) begging basket
madama *f RíoPl* (*patrona de burdel*) madame
madeja *f* 1. (*de hilo*) skein, hank; **enredar la** ~ *fig* to complicate matters 2. (*cabello*) mat 3. *pey* (*hombre dejado*) slob; (*perezoso*) layabout
madera *f* 1. (*de los árboles*) wood; ~ **prensada** particle board, chipboard; (*cortada*) timber, lumber *Am;* **de** ~ wooden; **tocar** ~ to touch [*o* knock on *Am*] wood; **¡toca ~!** touch [*o* knock on *Am*] wood!; **ser de la misma** ~ to be just the same; **tener** ~ **de** to have the makings of; **tener** [*o* **ser de**] **buena/mala** ~ (not) to have what it takes 2. *inf* (*policía*) **la** ~ the law 3. MÚS (*instrumentos*) woodwinds *pl*
maderaje *m,* **maderamen** *m* timbers *pl;* ~ **de techo** roof timbers
maderería *f* timber yard, lumber yard *Am*
madero *m* 1. (*viga*) beam; (*tablón*) board 2. (*persona*) oaf
madona *f* Madonna
madrastra *f* 1. (*pariente*) stepmother 2. *pey* (*mala madre*) bad mother
madraza *f inf* mother hen *fig;* **es una verdadera** ~ she is a really devoted mother
madre *f* 1. (*de familia*) mother; ~ **de alquiler** surrogate mother; ~ **de leche** wet nurse; ~ **política** mother-in-law; **futura** ~ mother-to-be; **¡~ (mía)!** goodness me!; **¡~ de Dios!** Holy Mary!; **como su ~ lo/la parió** *inf* in his/her birthday suit; **¡la ~ que lo parió!** *vulg* the bastard!; **¡la ~ que te parió!** *vulg* you bastard!; **¡viva la ~ que te parió!** *inf* well done!; **¡tu ~!** *inf* up yours! *vulg;* **de puta** ~ *vulg* (fucking) great! *vulg;* **el ciento y la** ~ *inf* (all) the world and his wife *Brit,* everyone and his brother *Am;* **sacar a alguien de** ~ *inf* to drive sb mad [*o* nuts]; **los alquileres se están saliendo de** ~ *inf* rents are becoming ridicuously high 2. REL **la ~ Teresa** Mother Theresa; ~ **superiora** Mother Superior 3. (*origen*) cradle; ~ **patria** mother country; **ahí está la ~ del cordero** *inf* that is the crux of the matter 4. GEO river bed 5. TÉC wooden support 6. GASTR dregs *pl*
madrear *vt* 1. *Méx* (*romper a golpes*) to bash up 2. *Méx, vulg* (*pegar fuerte*) to beat up
madrejón *m Arg* watercourse
madreperla *f* mother of pearl
madreselva *f* honeysuckle
Madrid *m* Madrid
madriguera *f* 1. (*guarida*) den; (*de conejo*) burrow; (*de ratón*) hole; (*de zorro*) earth; (*de tejón*) set 2. (*escondrijo*) lair
madrileño, -a I. *adj* of/from Madrid; **las noches madrileñas** the Madrid nights II. *m, f* native/inhabitant of Madrid
madrina *f* 1. (*de bautismo*) godmother 2. (*de boda*) ~ (**de boda**) maid of honour *Brit* [*o* honor *Am*] 3. (*de un artista, una asociación*) patroness
madrugada *f* 1. (*alba*) dawn; **en la** [*o* **de**] ~ in the early morning; **salimos de viaje de** ~ we set off in the early hours; **a las cinco de la** ~ at five in the morning 2. (*madrugón*) **pegarse una** ~ to get up very early
madrugador(a) I. *adj* 1. (*que se levanta pronto*) **ser muy** ~ to be an early riser [*o* earlybird] 2. *inf* (*astuto*) smart II. *m(f)* early riser
madrugar <g→gu> *vi* to get up early; **tienes que ~ más para ganarme** *fig* you will have to be quicker off the mark to beat me ►**a quien madruga, Dios le ayuda** *prov* the early bird catches the worm *prov;* **no por mucho ~ amanece más temprano** *prov* ≈ everything will happen at its appointed time
madrugón *m* **darse un** ~ to get up very early
maduración *f* (*de fruta*) ripening; (*de persona*) maturing
madurar I. *vt* 1. (*hacer maduro: fruta*) to ripen; (*persona*) to mature 2. (*reflexionar sobre*) to think over II. *vi, vr:* **~se** (*volverse maduro: fruta*) to ripen; (*persona*) to mature
madurez *f* (*de fruta*) ripeness; (*de persona*) maturity; (*de un plan*) readiness; **estar en la** ~ to be middle-aged
maduro, -a *adj* (*fruta*) ripe; (*persona: prudente*) mature; (*mayor*) adult; (*plan*) ready; **una manzana demasiado madura** an overripe apple; **en la edad madura** middle-aged; **estar a las duras y a las maduras** to take the bad with the good
maestría *f* 1. (*habilidad*) mastery; **con** ~ skilfully *Brit,* skillfully *Am* 2. (*título*) Master's degree
maestro, -a I. *adj* 1. (*principal*) master 2. (*con gran conocimiento*) master; **obra maestra** masterpiece 3. (*animal*) trained II. *m, f* 1. (*profesor*) teacher 2. (*persona de gran conocimiento*) master 3. (*capataz*) overseer; ~ **de cocina** master chef; ~ **de obras** foreman 4. (*lo que enseña*) school; **la vida es la mejor maestra** life is the best school 5. MÚS master
mafia *f* **la Mafia** the Mafia
mafioso, -a I. *adj* of the Mafia II. *m, f* mafioso
maganzón, -ona I. *adj Col, CRi* lazy II. *m, f Col, CRi* lazybones *inv inf*
magdalena *f* (*pastel*) sweet muffin ►**estar como una Magdalena** to be inconsolable; **llorar como una Magdalena** to cry like a child
magia *f* magic; **como por arte de** ~ as if by magic
mágico, -a I. *adj* 1. (*misterioso*) magic; **varita mágica** magic wand 2. (*maravilloso*) marvellous *Brit,* marvelous *Am* II. *m, f* magic
magín *m inf* creativity
magisterio *m* 1. (*labor*) teaching; **dedicarse al** ~ to be a teacher 2. (*profesión*) teaching; **estudiar** ~ to study to become a teacher

3. (*maestros*) teachers *pl*
magistrado, **-a** *m, f* 1. (*funcionario superior*) senior civil servant 2. JUR (*juez*) magistrate; (*miembro del Tribunal Supremo*) Supreme Court judge
magistral *adj* 1. ENS teaching 2. (*con maestría*) masterly 3. (*tono*) affected
magistratura *f* 1. (*oficio*) magistracy, judgeship 2. (*jueces*) magistracy, judges 3. (*funcionarios*) senior civil servants *pl*
magma *m* magma
magnanimidad *f* magnanimity
magnánimo, **-a** *adj* magnanimous
magnate *m* tycoon; ~ **de las finanzas** finance magnate; ~ **de la prensa** press baron
magnesio *m* magnesium
magnético, **-a** *adj* magnetic; *fig* (*que atrae*) attractive
magnetismo *m* magnetism; **ejercer un intenso ~ sobre alguien** to have a lot of influence over sb
magnetizar <z→c> *vt* 1. (*un cuerpo*) to magnetize 2. (*hipnotizar*) to hypnotize 3. (*entusiasmar*) to enthuse; (*retener la atención*) to captivate
magnetofón *m* tape recorder
magnetofónico, **-a** *adj* recording; **cinta magnetofónica** (recording) tape
magnetófono *m* tape recorder
magnificencia *f* 1. (*esplendor*) magnificence 2. (*liberalidad*) lavishness
magnífico, **-a** *adj* 1. (*lujoso*) sumptuous; (*valioso*) valuable 2. (*excelente*) magnificent 3. (*liberal*) lavish 4. (*título*) **Magnífico Señor Rector** Chancellor *Brit*, Rector *Am*
magnitud *f* magnitude; **la ~ de este problema es alarmante** the magnitude of this problem is alarming
magno, **-a** *adj* (*importante*) great; **Alejandro Magno** Alexander the Great; **aula magna** main hall
magnolia *f* magnolia
magnolio *m* magnolia
mago, **-a** *m, f* magician; **los Reyes Magos** the Magi, the Three Kings [*o* Wisemen]
magra *f* slice of ham
magrear *vt vulg* to feel up
magro *m* (*como el lomo*) tenderloin; *inf* (*carne magra*) lean meat
magro, **-a** *adj* lean
magua *f Cuba, PRico, Ven* (*contrariedad*) setback
magüey *m AmL* BOT maguey
magulladura *f*, **magullamiento** *m* bruising
magullar *vt* to bruise
mahometano, **-a** *adj, m, f* Muslim, Mohammedan
mahonesa *f* mayonnaise
maicena® *f* cornflour *Brit*, cornstarch *Am*
maicillo *m* AGR maize *Brit*, corn *Am*
maíz *m* sweetcorn *Brit*, corn *Am*
maizal *m* maize field *Brit*, cornfield *Am*
majada *f* 1. (*aprisco*) fold 2. (*estiércol*) dung, cowpat
majaderear *vt AmL* to annoy
majadería *f* 1. (*tontería*) idiocy; **¡no hagas caso a sus ~s!** don't pay any attention to his idiocies! 2. (*imprudencia*) foolishness
majadero, **-a** I. *adj* 1. (*insensato*) silly 2. (*porfiado*) pestering 3. (*imprudente*) foolish; (*loco*) crazy II. *m, f* 1. (*imbécil*) idiot 2. (*porfiador*) pest
majagua *f Cuba* 1. (*árbol*) *type of linden tree* 2. (*chaqueta*) suit jacket
majamama *f Chile* jumble
majar *vt* 1. (*en un mortero*) to crush 2. (*en la era*) to thresh 3. (*molestar*) to pester 4. *inf* (*azotar*) to smack
majara, **majareta** I. *adj inf* crazy, nuts II. *mf inf* crackpot
majarete *m* 1. *Cuba* (*galanteador*) Don Juan 2. *PRico* (*confusión*) commotion 3. *Ant, Ven* (*postre*) blancmange (*made with corn, milk and sugar*)
maje I. *adj Méx, inf* gullible II. *mf Méx, inf* sucker
majestad *f* 1. (*título*) Majesty; **Su Majestad** Your Majesty 2. (*majestuosidad*) majesty
majestuosidad *f* majesty
majestuoso, **-a** *adj* majestic
majo, **-a** *adj* 1. (*bonito*) lovely; (*guapo*) attractive 2. (*agradable*) pleasant 3. (*ataviado*) stylish, smart *Brit*; **ponte maja para la fiesta** dress up for the party
mal I. *adj v.* **malo** II. *m* 1. (*daño*) harm; (*injusticia*) wrong; (*sufrimiento*) suffering; **la caída del dólar le ha hecho mucho ~** the fall of the dollar has done him a lot of harm 2. (*lo malo*) bad thing; **el ~ menor** the lesser evil; **decir ~ de alguien** to talk badly of sb; **menos ~** thank goodness 3. (*inconveniente*) problem; **el ~ está en que...** the problem is that ... 4. (*enfermedad*) illness; ~ **de montaña** mountain sickness; ~ **de vientre** stomach complaint 5. (*desgracia*) misfortune ►**el ~ de ojo** the evil eye; **bien vengas, ~, si vienes solo** *prov* it never rains but it pours; **no hay ~ que por bien no venga** *prov* every cloud has a silver lining; **no te preocupes, no hay ~ que por bien no venga** don't worry, it's an ill wind that blows nobody any good; **el que escucha su ~ oye** *prov* those who listen at doors never hear good of themselves III. *adv* 1. (*de mala manera, insuficientemente*) badly; **dejar ~ a alguien** to show sb in a bad light; **estar ~ de dinero** to be badly off; **esto acabará ~** this will end badly; **vas a acabar ~** you are going to come to a bad end; **este chico va de ~ en peor** this boy is going from bad to worse; **me sentó ~ que te fueras sin despedirte** I was hurt that you went without saying goodbye; **mi nueva compañera de trabajo me cae ~** I don't like my new workmate 2. (*equivocadamente*) wrongly 3. (*difícilmente*) ~ **podrás ganar con esta moto** you'll be hard-pressed

to win with this motorbike **4.** (+ *a mal*) **tomarse algo a ~** to take sth badly; **tomarse a ~ un consejo** to take a piece of advice badly; **¡no te lo tomes tan a ~!** don't take it so badly!; **estoy a ~ con mi vecino** I'm on bad terms with my neighbour **5.** (*mal que bien*) **~ que bien, el negocio sigue funcionando** better or worse, the business is still working; **~ que bien, tendré que ir al dentista este mes** whether I like it or not, I will have to go to the dentist this month; **aprobar los exámenes más ~ que bien** to scrape through the exams

malabarismo *m* (*juegos malabares*) juggling; **hacer ~s para mantener su puesto de trabajo** *fig* to do a balancing act to keep one's job

malabarista *mf* (*artista*) juggler

malaconsejar *vt* to badly advise; **actuar malaconsejado** to act on bad advice

malacostumbrado, -a *adj* **estar ~** (*mimado*) to be spoilt; (*sin modales*) to be badly brought-up; (*vicioso*) to have bad habits

malacostumbrar **I.** *vt* **1.** (*mimar*) to spoil **2.** (*educar mal*) to bring up badly **3.** (*viciar*) **~ a algo** to get into the bad habit of sth **II.** *vr:* **~se** to get into a bad habit

Málaga *f* Malaga ►**salir de ~ para entrar en Malagón** to jump out of the frying pan into the fire, to go from bad to worse

malagradecido, -a *adj* ungrateful

malagueño, -a **I.** *adj* of/from Malaga **II.** *m, f* native/inhabitant of Malaga

malandante *adj* unfortunate; **persona ~** unfortunate person

malandanza *f* (*desgracia*) misfortune; (*golpe*) blow

malandrín, -ina **I.** *adj* roguish **II.** *m, f* rogue

malanga **I.** *adj Cuba* cowardly **II.** *f* **1.** (*sombrero de paja*) straw hat **2.** *RDom* (*pelo*) **pelar a alguien la ~** to cut sb's hair **3.** *AmC, Méx* (*planta*) taro

malapata *mf* (*patoso*) clumsy oaf; **tener ~** (*poca destreza*) to be maladroit; (*malas intenciones*) to have wicked intentions; (*mala suerte*) to be unlucky; **la cosa tiene ~** *fig* it is ill-starred [*o* fated]

malaria *f* malaria

Malasia *f* Malaysia

malasombra **I.** *adj* **1.** (*desastrado*) scruffy **2.** (*malvado*) wicked **II.** *mf* **1.** (*desastre*) disaster **2.** (*mala persona*) wicked person

malaventura *f* **1.** (*desgracia*) unhappiness; (*golpe*) blow **2.** (*mala suerte*) misfortune

malayo, -a *adj, m, f* Malay, Malayan

malbaratar *vt* **1.** (*vender barato*) to sell at too low a price **2.** (*malgastar*) to squander; **malbarató toda la herencia en sólo un año** he/she squandered the entire inheritance in just one year

malcarado, -a *adj* **1.** (*repulsivo*) repulsive **2.** (*enfadado*) cross; (*furioso*) furious; (*malhumorado*) grumpy

malcomer *vi* **1.** (*poco, cosas de mala calidad*) to eat badly; **el dinero sólo da para ~** the money isn't sufficient to eat properly **2.** (*sin ganas*) to eat without appetite

malcriadez *f AmC, AmS* ill-breeding; (*descortesía*) rudeness

malcriado, -a *adj* (*mal educado*) spoilt; (*descortés*) rude

malcriar <*1. pres:* malcrío> *vt* to bring up badly; (*mimar*) to spoil

maldad *f* evil, wickedness

maldecir *irr* **I.** *vt* to curse, to damn; **¡te maldigo!** I curse you! **II.** *vi* **1.** (*jurar*) to swear **2.** (*hablar mal*) to speak ill; (*difamar*) to speak evil **3.** (*quejarse*) **~ de algo/alguien** to complain about sth/sb

maldición *f* **1.** (*imprecación*) curse; **parece que le ha caído una ~** he/she seems to be cursed; **en el mismo año le cayó la ~ del mago** that same year the curse the magician had put on him/her was fulfilled **2.** (*juramento*) swear word; **soltar una ~ contra alguien** to swear at sb

maldito, -a **I.** *pp de* **maldecir** **II.** *adj* **1.** (*endemoniado*) damned; **¡maldita sea!** *inf* damn (it)!; **¡~ seas!** *vulg* damn you!; **maldita la idea que tengo del tema** *inf* I don't have a clue about the subject; **~ el caso que me hacen** *inf* they aren't taking a blind bit of notice of me; **no vale la maldita pena** *inf* there's absolutely no bloody point; **¡maldita la gracia (que me hace)!** I don't find it in the least bit funny!; **¡malditas las ganas (que tengo)!** I haven't the slightest wish to! **2.** (*maligno*) wicked; **¡vete, ~!** go away, you blasted nuisance!; **soltar la maldita** to talk nineteen to the dozen

maldoso, -a *adj Méx* wicked

maleable *adj* **1.** (*forjable*) malleable **2.** (*flexible*) pliable **3.** (*dócil*) pliant

maleante **I.** *adj* **1.** (*delincuente*) delinquent; **gente ~** delinquents **2.** (*maligno*) miscreant **II.** *mf* **1.** (*delincuente*) delinquent **2.** (*persona maligna*) miscreant

malear **I.** *vt* **1.** (*pervertir*) to pervert **2.** (*dañar: a alguien*) to harm; (*algo*) to spoil; (*perjudicar*) to harm **II.** *vr:* **~se** to go to the dogs

malecón *m* **1.** (*dique*) dyke **2.** (*rompeolas*) breakwater **3.** FERRO embankment **4.** (*embarcadero*) jetty

maledicencia *f* (evil) talk

maleducado, -a *adj* **1.** (*sin modales*) ill-mannered; (*niño*) ill-bred; **tu amigo es muy ~** your friend is very ill-mannered **2.** (*descortés*) rude **3.** (*mimado*) spoilt

maleducar *vt* to spoil

maleficio *m* **1.** (*hechizo*) curse **2.** (*daño*) harm

maléfico, -a **I.** *adj* **1.** (*perjudicial*) harmful **2.** (*que hechiza*) who casts spells; **poder ~** evil power **II.** *m, f* sorcerer

malentendido *m* misunderstanding

malestar *m* **1.** (*físico*) malaise **2.** (*espiritual*) uneasiness

M

maleta[1] *f* suitcase; **hacer la ~** to pack one's suitcase

maleta[2] *m* (*diletante*) dilettante; DEP amateur; **este fontanero es un ~** this plumber is an amateur

maletera *f Col, Méx,* **maletero** *m* AUTO boot *Brit,* trunk *Am*

maletero, -a *m, f* **1.** (*en las estaciones*) porter **2.** *Chile* (*ladrón*) thief

maletín *m* (*de aseo*) toilet bag; (*para herramientas*) tool box; (*en una bici*) pannier; **~ (de viaje)** overnight bag

malevaje *m Arg* ruffians *pl*

malevolencia *f* **1.** (*malignidad*) malevolence **2.** (*animosidad*) animosity; **no me trates con ~** do not treat me with animosity

malévolo, -a *adj* malevolent

maleza *f* **1.** (*hierbas malas*) weeds *pl;* **el jardín se está llenando de ~** the garden is becoming overrun with weeds **2.** (*matorral*) thicket

malgastador(a) **I.** *adj* wasteful **II.** *m(f)* spendthrift

malgastar *vt* to waste; **~ todo el dinero en tabaco** to squander all the money on cigarettes; **~ dinero en el bingo** to waste money on bingo; **con él no haces más que ~ tu paciencia** with him you are only wasting your patience; **~ el tiempo charlando** to waste time chatting; **~ una oportunidad** to waste an opportunity

malhadado, -a **I.** *adj* (*desventurado*) ill-fated **II.** *m, f* ill-fated person; **ha sido toda su vida un ~** he has been unlucky all his life

malhechor(a) **I.** *adj* delinquent **II.** *m(f)* delinquent, wrongdoer

malherir *irr como sentir vt* to seriously injure

malhumorado, -a *adj* **1.** *ser* bad-tempered **2.** *estar* **estar ~** to be in a bad mood

malicia *f* **1.** (*intención malévola*) malice; **hacer todo con ~** to do everything with malice **2.** (*maldad*) wickedness **3.** (*picardía*) mischievousness; **tener mucha ~** to be full of mischief **4.** (*interpretación maliciosa*) distrust **5.** *inf* (*sospecha*) suspicion; **tengo mis ~s** I have my suspicions; **no tener ~** to be very trusting

maliciar *vt, vr:* **~se** **1.** (*sospechar*) to suspect; **no malicies de cualquiera** do not distrust just anyone; **~ de todo** to be suspicious of everything **2.** (*pervertir*) to pervert

malicioso, -a *adj* **1.** (*con intención malévola*) malicious **2.** (*maligno*) malign **3.** (*que sospecha malicia*) suspicious

malignidad *f* **1.** (*de persona*) evilness **2.** MED malignance

maligno, -a *adj* (*pernicioso*) malign; (*persona*) spiteful; (*sonrisa*) malicious; MED malignant

malinchista **I.** *adj Méx* preferring foreign things **II.** *mf Méx* person who prefers foreign things

malintencionado, -a *adj* unkind

malinterpretar *vt* to misinterpret

malla *f* **1.** (*de un tejido*) mesh, weave; **de ~(s) ancha(s)/estrecha(s)/fina(s)** open/close/fine weave; **caer en las ~s de alguien** *fig* to fall prey to sb **2.** (*tejido*) cloth **3.** (*vestido*) leotard **4.** *pl* (*pantalones*) leggings *pl* **5.** *AmL* (*de baño*) swimming costume *Brit,* swimsuit *Am*

mallo *m* **1.** (*mazo*) mallet **2.** (*juego*) croquet; (*terreno para este juego*) croquet field **3.** *Chile* (*guiso de patatas*) potato stew

Mallorca *f* Majorca

mallorquín, -ina **I.** *adj* of/from Majorca **II.** *m, f* native/inhabitant of Majorca

malnutrido, -a *adj* malnourished

malo, -a **I.** *adj* <peor, pésimo> (*precediendo un sustantivo masculino: mal*) **1.** (*en general*) bad; **mala gestión** mismanagement; **malas palabras** bad words; **tengo mala cabeza para los números** I am no good with numbers; **eres ~ de entender** you are difficult to understand; **fumar es ~ para la salud** smoking is bad for your health; **de mala gana** unwillingly; **me gusta la casa, lo ~ es que es demasiado cara** I like the house, the problem is that it is too expensive; **tener mala mano para algo** to have no talent for sth; **siempre anda con malas mujeres** he is always with flighty women; **se casó sin decirnos ni una mala palabra** he/she got married without saying a single word to us; **es ~ para madrugar** he is bad at getting up early; **~ sería si no llegáramos a una solución** it would be really bad if we did not find a solution; **tener mala suerte** to be unlucky; **hace un tiempo malísimo** the weather is really bad; **el trabajo en las minas es muy ~** the work in the mines is very hard; **me vino de malas** it happened at a very inconvenient time for me; **la chapa de este coche es mala** the bodywork of this car is poor; **hacer un trabajo de mala manera** to do a job badly **2.** *ser* (*falso*) false **3.** *ser* (*malévolo*) nasty; **tener mal genio** to have a bad temper; **una mala persona** a nasty person; **venir de malas** to have a hostile attitude **4.** *estar* (*enfermo*) ill; **caer ~** to become ill **5.** *ser* (*travieso*) naughty **6.** *estar* (*estropeado*) spoilt; (*leche*) off *Brit,* gone bad [*o* sour]; (*ropa*) worn-out ►**más vale ~ conocido que bueno por conocer** *prov* better the devil you know **II.** *adv* **si no pagas voluntariamente tendré que intentarlo por las malas** if you don't pay voluntarily I will have to take steps to force you to; **hoy te llevo al dentista aunque sea por las malas** today I am taking you to the dentist even if I have to drag you there; **podemos llegar a un acuerdo por las buenas o por las malas** we can reach an agreement by fair means or foul; **estoy a malas con mi jefe** I am at daggers drawn with my boss; **se pusieron a malas por una tontería** they fell out with each other over an insignificance; **andar a malas** to be on bad terms; **han vuelto a fallar un penalti, hoy están de ~s** they have failed to score a penalty again, today they are out of luck **III.** *m, f* (*persona*) bad man *m,* bad woman *f;* CINE baddie; **los ~s de la peli** the bad guys

malograr I. *vt* **1.** (*desaprovechar*) to waste; **has malogrado la ocasión** you have wasted the occasion **2.** (*frustrar*) to frustate **3.** (*estropear*) to ruin **II.** *vr:* **~se 1.** (*fallar*) to fail; **se han malogrado mis esperanzas** my hopes have come to nothing **2.** (*estropearse*) to be ruined **3.** (*desarrollarse mal*) to turn out badly **4.** (*morir demasiado pronto*) to die an untimely death; (*morir en un accidente*) to die in an accident **5.** (*interrumpirse*) to be interrupted

maloliente *adj* foul-smelling; **me molestan tus cigarros ~s** your smelly cigarettes annoy me

malparar *vt* (*persona*) to come off badly; **salió malparado de la pelea** he came off worse in the fight; **salir malparado de un asunto** to come off badly in a matter

malparir *vi* to have a miscarriage

malpensado, -a *adj* evil-minded; **no seas tan ~** don't be so cynical

malquerencia *f* **1.** (*antipatía*) antipathy; **sentir mucha ~ hacia alguien** to feel great antipathy towards sb **2.** (*mala voluntad*) ill will; **sentir ~ hacia alguien** to bear sb ill will

malquistar I. *vt* to set against; **me has malquistado con tu familia** you have set your family against me **II.** *vr:* **~se** to fall out

malsano, -a *adj* **1.** (*insano, enfermizo*) unhealthy **2.** (*moralmente*) unwholesome

malsonante *adj* (*sonido*) jarring; (*palabra*) nasty; (*doctrina*) dangerous; **ruidos ~s** jarring noises

malta *f* **1.** *t.* AGR malt **2.** *Arg* (*cerveza*) beer

maltés, -esa *adj, m, f* Maltese

maltón, -ona I. *adj AmS* overgrown **II.** *m, f AmS* overgrown youth

maltraído, -a *adj Bol, Chile, Perú* disheveled

maltratar *vt* **1.** (*tratar mal, causar daño físico, psíquico*) to maltreat **2.** (*insultar*) ~ (**de palabra**) to abuse (verbally) **3.** (*estropear*) to damage

maltrato *m* **1.** (*físico, psíquico*) maltreatment, abuse **2.** (*insulto*) (verbal) abuse **3.** (*de una cosa*) misuse

maltrecho, -a *adj* **1.** (*golpeado*) battered **2.** (*deprimido*) low

malura *f Chile* pain or discomfort

malva I. *adj* mauve **II.** *f* mallow; **estar criando ~s** *inf* to be pushing up daisies; **ser (como) una ~** *inf* to be meek and mild

malvado, -a I. *adj* wicked; **una persona malvada** a wicked person **II.** *m, f* wicked person

malvavisco *m* marsh mallow

malvender *vt* to sell at a loss

malversar *vt* to misappropriate, to embezzle

malversión *f* embezzlement, misappropriation

Malvinas *fpl* Falkland Islands *pl*

malvís *m inv* song thrush

malvón *m Arg, Méx, Par, Urug* BOT geranium

mama *f* **1.** (*pecho*) breast; (*ubre*) udder **2.** *inf* (*mamá*) mummy *Brit,* mommy *Am*

mamá *f inf* mummy *Brit,* mommy *Am*

mamada *f* **1.** (*acción*) breastfeeding; **el bebé se queda dormido después de cada ~** the baby always falls asleep after breastfeeding **2.** (*cantidad mamada*) breastfeed **3.** *AmL* (*ganga*) bargain; **¡vaya ~!** what a bargain! **4.** *vulg* (*felación*) blow job; **dar una ~ a alguien** to give sb a blow [*o* French] job, to go down on sb

mamadera *f AmL* (*biberón*) baby bottle

mamar I. *vt, vi* **1.** (*en el pecho*) to breastfeed; **no le des de ~ tanto al niño** don't breastfeed the baby so much **2.** (*adquirir*) **has mamado la pereza** (**con la leche**) you acquired your laziness at your mother's breast **3.** *inf* (*comer*) to wolf (down) **4.** *vulg* **mamársela a alguien** to give sb a blow job **II.** *vr:* **~se** *vulg* (*emborracharse*) to get sloshed

mamario, -a *adj* mammary

mamarracho *m* **1.** (*persona que viste mal*) sight; (*ridícula*) ridiculous person **2.** (*cosa mal hecha*) botch; (*fea*) hideous thing; (*sin valor*) piece of junk **3.** (*persona despreciable*) despicable person

mameluco *m* **1.** (*bobo*) idiot **2.** *AmL* (*de bebé*) romper suit

mamífero I. *adj* mammalian **II.** *m* mammal

mamila *f* **1.** ANAT (*mujer*) mammilla **2.** ANAT (*hombre*) nipple **3.** *Méx* (*biberón*) baby bottle

mamografía *f* MED mammogram, mammograph

mamón, -ona *m, f* **1.** *vulg* jerk; (*hombre*) prick; (*mujer*) bitch **2.** *AmL, inf* (*borracho*) drunk

mamonear *vt Guat, Hond* **1.** (*golpear*) to beat **2.** (*retardar*) to postpone **3.** (*pasar el tiempo con futilezas*) to waste time

mamotreto *m pey* **1.** (*libro*) hefty tome **2.** (*armatoste*) cumbersome object; **esta butaca es un ~** this armchair is a cumbersome piece of furniture

mampara *f* screen (door), (room) divider

mamporro *m inf* clout; **darse un ~ contra algo** to bash oneself against sth; **con el hielo me pegué un ~ en medio de la calle** I went sprawling on the ice in the middle of the street

mampostería *f* **1.** (*obra*) rubblework; **~ de ladrillos en bruto** brickwork **2.** (*oficio*) drystone walling

mamúa *f Arg, Urug, vulg* (*borrachera*) **agarrarse una ~** to get smashed

mamut <mamuts> *m* mammoth

manada *f* (*rebaño de vacas, ciervos*) herd; (*de ovejas, aves*) flock; (*de peces*) shoal; (*de lobos*) pack; **~ de gallinas** brood of hens; **~ de gente** crowd of people; **una ~ de curiosos** a crowd of onlookers; **llegaron en** [*o* **a**] **~s al concierto** people arrived at the concert in droves; **pasamos la frontera en ~** we crossed

M

over the border en masse

Managua *m* Managua

manantial I. *adj* running II. *m* 1. (*fuente natural*) spring; ~ **caliente** hot spring; ~ **medicinal** health spa 2. (*fuente artificial*) fountain 3. (*origen*) source

manar I. *vt* to flow with; **la fuente mana agua fría** the fountain flows with cold water; **la herida no paraba de ~ sangre** the wound wouldn't stop flowing with blood II. *vi* 1. (*surgir*) to well; **el agua manaba sucia de la fuente** dirty water welled from the fountain 2. (*fluir fácilmente*) to flow; **las palabras manaban de su boca** the words flowed from his/her mouth

manatí *m* manatee

manazas *mf inv, inf* clumsy person, klutz *Am*; **ser un ~** to be clumsy

mancha *f* 1. (*en la ropa, piel*) dirty mark; (*de tinta*) stain; (*salpicadura*) spot; (*de maquillaje*) smudge 2. (*toque de color*) fleck; **este perro es blanco con ~s negras** this dog is white with black patches; **la corbata tiene ~s azules y blancas** the tie has splashes of blue and white 3. (*boceto*) sketch 4. (*deshonra*) stain; **sin ~** stainless

Mancha *f* **canal de la ~** the (English) Channel

manchado, **-a** *adj* 1. (*ropa, mantel*) stained 2. (*cara, fruta*) dirty 3. (*caballos, vacas*) dappled; (*salpicado*) spotted

manchar I. *vt* 1. (*ensuciar*) to dirty 2. (*desprestigiar*) to sully II. *vr:* **~se** (*ensuciarse*) to get dirty

manchego, **-a** I. *adj* of/from la Mancha II. *m, f* native/inhabitant of la Mancha

mancilla *f* stain; **sin ~** pure

mancillar *vt* to sully

manco, **-a** I. *adj* 1. (*de un brazo*) one-armed; (*de una mano*) one-handed; **es ~ de la mano izquierda/derecha** (*le falta*) he/she lacks a left/right hand; (*la tiene inutilizada*) his/her left/right hand is useless; **no ser** (**cojo ni**) **~** (*ser hábil*) to be dexterous; (*ser largo de manos*) to be light-fingered 2. (*defectuoso*) faulty; (*incompleto*) incomplete II. *m, f* (*con un brazo*) one-armed man; (*con una mano*) person who is missing a hand

mancomunar I. *vt* to join together II. *vr:* **~se** to unite

mancomunidad *f* 1. (*comunidad*) community 2. JUR joint ownership [*o* responsibility]

mancornas *fpl Col, Chile* cuff links *pl*

mancuernillas *fpl Méx* cuff links *pl*

manda *f* legacy, bequest

mandadero, **-a** *m, f* messenger; (*de recados*) errand boy *m*, errand girl *f*; (*de oficina*) office boy *m*, office girl *f*

mandado *m* (*encargo*) errand; (*orden*) order; (*compra*) purchase; **hacer un ~** to run an erand

mandamás *mf pey, inf* big shot

mandamiento *m* 1. (*orden*) order; **~ de detención** arrest warrant; **~ judicial** court order 2. (*precepto*) precept 3. REL commandment

mandar I. *vt* 1. (*ordenar*) to order; **~ a alguien que** +*subj* to order sb to; **lo que Ud. mande** whatever you say 2. (*prescribir*) to prescribe 3. (*dirigir*) to lead; (*gobernar*) to govern 4. (*encargar*) **~ buscar/hacer/venir** to ask to fetch/do/come 5. (*enviar*) to send; **~ al cuerno** *inf* to send to hell 6. TÉC to control; **mandado a distancia** remote controlled II. *vr:* **~se** to manage alone

mandarín *m* 1. (*idioma*) Mandarin 2. *pey, inf* (*funcionario*) mandarin

mandarina *f* mandarin, tangerine

mandatario, **-a** *m, f* agent; **primer ~** POL head of state; JUR attorney

mandato *m* 1. (*orden*) order; (*prescripción*) prescription; (*delegación*) delegation; **~ judicial** injunction; **~ de pago** warrant for payment; **por ~ de las leyes** by law 2. POL mandate; **~ internacional** international mandate; **~ parlamentario** parliamentary mandate

mandíbula *f* 1. ANAT jaw; **reír**(**se**) **a ~ batiente** to laugh one's head off 2. TÉC clamp; **~ prensora** vice; **~ de sujeción** clamp

mandil *m* 1. (*delantal*) apron; (*de cuero*) leather apron 2. *AmL* (*de caballería*) cloth (*used to rub down a horse*)

mandilón *m pey, inf* wimp

mandinga *m* 1. *AmL, inf* (*diablo*) devil 2. *Arg, inf* (*muchacho*) scamp

mando *m* 1. (*poder*) control; MIL command; (*del presidente*) term of office; **don de ~** leadership qualities; **estar al ~ de** to be in command of; **estar bajo el ~ de alguien** to be under sb's command; **tener el ~ y el palo** *inf* to rule the roost 2. (*quien lo tiene*) **~s intermedios de una empresa** middle management of a business; **alto ~** MIL high command 3. TÉC control; **~ a distancia** remote control; **~ manual** manual control; **botón de ~** control button

mandolina *f* MÚS mandolin

mandón, **-ona** I. *adj* bossy II. *m, f* bossy person

manducar <c→qu> *vi, vt inf* to gobble, to scarf *Am*

manecilla *f* 1. (*del reloj*) hand 2. (*broche*) clasp 3. TÉC pointer 4. (*signo*) sign (*clenched fist with extended index finger to draw attention to sth*)

manejable *adj* 1. (*objeto*) user-friendly 2. (*persona*) tractable 3. AUTO manoeuvrable *Brit*, maneuverable *Am*

manejar I. *vt* 1. (*usar*) to use; (*máquina*) to operate; *fig* to handle; **~ un cuchillo** to use a knife; **manejas bien las cifras** you are good with numbers; **saber ~ el dinero** to know how to handle money; **'¡manéjese con cuidado!'** 'handle with care!' 2. INFOR to use 3. (*dirigir*) to handle; **~ intereses** to manage interests 4. (*a alguien*) to manage; **maneja al**

marido a su antojo she can twist her husband round her little finger **5.** *AmL* (*un coche*) to drive **II.** *vr:* **~se** to manage; **saber ~se en la vida** to know how to get on in life; **manejárselas** *inf* to get by

manejo *m* **1.** (*uso*) use; (*de una máquina*) operation; *fig* handling; **~ de animales** handling of animals; **~ a distancia** remote control **2.** INFOR management; **~ de errores** error management; **~ de la memoria** memory management; **~ de información** information management **3.** (*trato*) handling **4.** (*de un negocio*) running **5.** *AmL* (*de un coche*) driving **6.** *pl* (*intrigas*) machinations *pl*

manera *f* **1.** (*forma, modo*) manner, way; **~ de decir** way of saying; **~ de obrar** way of doing things; **~ de pensar** way of thinking; **~ de proceder** way of acting; **es su ~ de ser** that's the way he/she is; **~ de ver las cosas** way of seeing things; **a la ~ de sus abuelos** in the way their grandparents did; **a la ~ de la casa** in the habitual way; **a ~ de** a sort of; **a mi ~** my way; **a mi ~ de ver** to my way of looking at things; **de la ~ que sea** somehow or other; **de cualquier ~**, **de todas ~s** anyway; **de esta ~** that way; **de ~ que** (*finalidad*) so that; **mañana tienes que madrugar, de ~ que es mejor que te acuestes pronto** tomorrow you have to get up early, so you had better get to bed early; **¿de ~ que sacaste mala nota?** so you got a bad mark, did you?; **de ninguna ~** no way; **se echó a gritar de tal ~ que...** *inf* he/she started to shout in such a way that ...; **de una ~ o de otra** one way or another; **en cierta ~** in a way; **en gran ~** largely; **no hay ~ de...** there is no way that ...; **¡qué ~ de llover!** just look at the rain!; **sobre ~** a lot; **primero se lo dije de buena ~** first I said it to him nicely; **contestar de mala ~** to answer rudely; **hacer las cosas de mala ~** to do things badly **2.** *pl* (*modales*) manners *pl;* **¡estas no son ~s!** this is no way to behave!

maneto, **-a** *adj* **1.** *Hond* (*manos*) one-handed **2.** *Guat, Ven* (*piernas*) knock-kneed

manga *f* **1.** (*del vestido*) sleeve; **de ~s cortas/largas** short-/long-sleeved; **estar en ~s de camisa** to be in shirt-sleeves; **¡a buenas horas ~s verdes!** *inf* a bit late in the day!; **andar ~ por hombro** *inf* to be a mess; **poner algo ~ por hombro** *inf* to turn sth inside out; **sacarse algo de la ~** *fig* to come up with sth; **hacer un corte de ~s a alguien** to give sb the finger; **ser más corto que las ~s de un chaleco** *fig* to be as thick as two short planks; **tener (la)** [*o* **ser de**] **~ ancha** *fig* to be lenient; **tienen algo en la manga** they are keeping sth up their sleeve **2.** (*tubo*) hose **3.** AVIAT **~ de aire** windsock **4.** METEO **~ de viento** tornado; **~ de agua** waterspout **5.** GASTR (*filtro*) muslin strainer; (*pastelera*) pastry bag, icing bag *Brit* **6.** *inf* (*borrachera*) drunkenness **7.** *Arg, pey* (*grupo de personas*) mob ▸**hacer ~s y capirotes** to completely ignore; **tirar la ~** to ask for a loan

manganeta *f Hond* trick

mangante *mf inf* **1.** (*ladrón*) thief **2.** (*holgazán*) loafer **3.** (*mendigo*) beggar

manganzón, **-ona** *m, f AmL* loafer

mangar <g→gu> *vt inf* to swipe, to nick; (*en tiendas*) to shoplift

mangle *m AmL* BOT mangrove tree

mango *m* **1.** (*puño*) knob; (*alargado*) handle; **tener la sartén por el ~** *fig* to hold the reins **2.** BOT mango tree **3.** (*fruta*) mango

mangoneador(a) *adj* **1.** (*entrometido*) meddlesome **2.** (*dominador*) dominating **3.** (*vago*) idle

mangonear **I.** *vi inf* **1.** (*entrometerse*) to meddle **2.** (*vaguear*) to loaf **II.** *vt inf* to wangle; **está mangoneando todo** he/she has got a finger in every pie

mangoneo *m inf* **1.** (*entremetimiento*) meddling **2.** (*vagancia*) idleness

manguear *vt Arg, inf* (*dinero*) to scrounge

manguera *f* (*tubo*) hose

mangueta *f* **1.** (*listón*) batten **2.** (*palanca*) lever **3.** (*retrete*) U-bend

manguito *m* **1.** (*mitón*) muff **2.** (*protección*) oversleeve **3.** (*cilindro hueco*) sleeve **4.** (*anillo*) hoop

maní *m* peanut

manía *f* **1.** (*locura*) mania **2.** (*extravagancia*) eccentricity, quirk **3.** (*obsesión*) obsession; **tener ~ por la moda** to be obsessed with fashion **4.** *inf* (*aversión*) aversion; **tener ~ a alguien** not to be able to stand sb; **coger ~ a alguien** to take a dislike to sb

maniaco, **-a**, **maníaco**, **-a** **I.** *adj* maniacal **II.** *m, f* maniac; **~ sexual** sex maniac

maniatar *vt* **~ a alguien** to tie sb's hands up; **lo ~on a la silla** they tied his hands to the chair

maniático, **-a** **I.** *adj* **1.** (*extravagante*) fussy **2.** (*loco*) manic **3.** (*obsesivo*) neurotic **II.** *m, f* **1.** (*extravagante*) fusspot **2.** (*loco*) maniac; **un ~ del fútbol** a football fanatic; **ser un ~ del cine** to be crazy about films; **un ~ de la limpieza** a cleaning maniac

manicomio *m* psychiatric hospital; *fig* (*casa de locos*) madhouse

manicura *f* manicure

manicuro, **-a** *m, f* manicurist

manido, **-a** *adj* **1.** (*alimentos*) off; (*fruta*) overripe **2.** (*objetos*) worn; (*libro*) tatty; (*ropa*) shabby **3.** (*trillado*) hackneyed **4.** (*oculto*) hidden

manifestación *f* **1.** (*expresión*) expression; **como ~ de cariño** as an expression of love **2.** (*reunión*) demonstration

manifestante *mf* demonstrator

manifestar <e→ie> **I.** *vt* **1.** (*declarar*) to declare **2.** (*mostrar*) to show **II.** *vr:* **~se** **1.** (*declararse*) to declare oneself; **~se a favor/en contra de algo** to declare oneself in favour *Brit* [*o* favor *Am*] of/against sth **2.** (*revelarse*) to show oneself **3.** (*política*) to demonstrate

manifiesto *m* manifesto

manifiesto, -a *adj* (*evidente*) manifest; **poner de ~** (*revelar*) to show [*o* make clear]; (*expresar*) to declare

manigua *f Cuba* jungle

manija *f* handle

manilargo, -a I. *adj* **1.** (*hurtador*) light-fingered **2.** (*dadivoso*) generous II. *m, f* petty thief

manilla *f* **1.** *v.* **manija** **2.** (*del reloj*) hand **3.** *pl* (*para prisioneros*) handcuffs *pl* **4.** (*pulsera*) bracelet

manillar *m* handlebars *pl*

maniobra *f* **1.** (*operación manual*) handling **2.** (*uso*) use **3.** (*ardid*) ploy; **~s fraudulentas** fraudulent tactics **4.** MIL manoeuvre *Brit,* maneuver *Am;* **estar de ~s** to be on manoeuvres *Brit* [*o* maneuvers *Am*] **5.** (*vehículo*) manoeuvre *Brit,* maneuver *Am;* FERRO shunting; (*movimiento*) movement

maniobrable *adj* manoeuvrable *Brit,* maneuverable *Am;* **un vehículo fácilmente ~** a highly manoeuvrable *Brit* [*o* maneuverable *Am*] car

maniobrar I. *vi* **1.** MIL to carry out manoeuvres *Brit* [*o* maneuvers *Am*] **2.** (*intrigar*) to scheme II. *vt* **1.** (*manejar*) to handle **2.** (*manipular*) to manipulate

manipulación *f* **1.** (*empleo*) use, handling **2.** (*elaboración*) making **3.** (*alteración*) manipulation

manipular *vt* **1.** (*maniobrar*) to manoeuvre *Brit,* to maneuver *Am;* (*máquina*) to operate **2.** (*elaborar*) to make **3.** (*alterar*) to manipulate **4.** (*interferir*) **~ algo** to interfere with sth **5.** (*manosear*) **~ algo** to fiddle with sth

maniquí <maniquíes> *m* **1.** (*modelo*) model **2.** (*muñeco*) puppet, dummy **3.** (*para ropa*) mannequin

manir *irr como abolir vt* (*carne*) to hang

manirroto, -a *adj* spendthrift

manita *f* **hacer ~s** *inf* to canoodle, to snog *Brit;* **ser un ~s** to be dexterous, to be good with one's hands

manito *m Méx* mate *Brit,* pal

manivela *f* handle

manjar *m* **1.** (*comestible*) food **2.** (*exquisitez*) delicacy

mano *f* **1.** ANAT hand; **a ~ alzada** (*votación*) by a show of hands; **a ~ armada** armed; **a ~s llenas** in abundance; **nunca alcé la ~ contra mis hijos** I never raised my hand to my children; **apretón de ~s** handshake; **bajo ~** underhand; **cargar las ~s** to overdo it; **coger a alguien con las ~s en la masa** to catch sb red-handed; **cogidos de las ~s** hand in hand; **comer de la ~ de alguien** *fig* to eat out of sb's hand; **me lo prometió con la ~ en el corazón** he promised me with his hand on his heart; **dar de ~** (*al trabajo*) to leave work; **echar una ~ a alguien** to give sb a hand; **dejar algo en ~s de alguien** to leave sth in sb's hands; **echar ~ de alguien** to make use of sb; **ser de ~ abierta/cerrada** *fig* to be generous/tight-fisted; **estar al alcance de la ~** to be within (arm's) reach; **estar ~ sobre ~** *fig* to be idle; **hecho a ~** hand-made; **irse a las ~s** to come to blows; **su vida se le había ido de las ~s** his/her life has got out of hand; **se le ha ido la ~** (*desmesura*) he/she has overdone it; (*violencia*) he/she has lost control; **se lavó las ~s (como Pilatos) en el asunto** he washed his hands of the matter; **llevar a alguien de la ~** to lead sb by the hand; *fig* to guide sb; **~ a ~** *fig* hand in hand; **¡~s a la obra!** to work!; **meter ~** to take action; **meter ~ a alguien** *inf* to touch sb up; **pedir la ~ de alguien** to ask for sb's hand in marriage; **no voy a poner las ~s en el fuego por nadie** I am not going to risk my neck for anyone; **si a ~ viene...** if it drops into my lap ...; **echar ~ de algo** to draw on sth; **traer algo entre ~s** to be up to sth; **tomarle la ~ a algo** *inf* to take sth up; **untar la ~ a alguien** to grease sb's palm; **¡venga esa ~!** let's shake on it! **2.** ZOOL (*de un mono*) hand; (*de un perro*) paw; **~ de ave** bird's claw; **~ de cerdo** pig's trotter **3.** (*reloj*) hand **4.** (*lado*) **~ derecha/izquierda** right-/left--hand side; **a [*o* de] la ~ derecha** on the right(-hand side) **5.** (*capa*) coat; **una ~ de pintura** a coat of paint; **la pared necesita una ~ de pintura** the wall needs a coat of paint **6.** (*trabajador*) hand; **~ de obra** labour *Brit,* labor *Am;* **~ de obra especializada** skilled labour *Brit* [*o* labor *Am*] **7.** (*habilidad*) skill; **tener buena ~ para coser** to be good at sewing; **tener ~ izquierda** to be tactful; **tener ~ con** to have a way with; **~ de santo** sure remedy **8.** (*de naipes*) hand; **ser ~** to lead **9.** (*de ajedrez*) game ▶**muchas ~s en un plato hacen mucho garabato** *prov* too many cooks spoil the broth

manojo *m* bunch; **~ de llaves** bunch of keys; **ser un ~ de nervios** to be a bundle of nerves

manopla *f* **1.** (*guante*) mitten **2.** (*para lavarse*) flannel *Brit,* washcloth *Am*

manoseado, -a *adj* **1.** (*sobado*) worn **2.** (*trillado*) hackneyed

manosear *vt* to handle; *pey* to paw

manotazo *m* smack; **dar ~s** to smack

manoteador(a) I. *adj CSur* (*caballo piafador*) pawing II. *m(f)* **1.** *Arg, Méx* (*ratero*) thief **2.** (*que mueve mucho las manos*) gesticulator

manotear *vi* to gesticulate

manotón *m* slap

mansalva *adv* **a ~** (*sobre seguro*) without risk; (*traidoramente*) point-blank; (*en gran cantidad*) in abundance

mansarda *f AmC, AmS* attic

mansedumbre *f* **1.** (*suavidad*) gentleness **2.** (*sumisión*) meekness

mansión *f* **1.** (*casa suntuosa*) mansion **2.** (*morada*) dwelling

manso, -a *adj* **1.** (*dócil*) docile **2.** (*animales*) tame **3.** (*aguas*) quiet **4.** (*aire*) still **5.** (*clima*) mild

manta[1] *f* **1.** (*de cama*) blanket; **a ~** in abundance; **liarse la ~ a la cabeza** (*actuar con decisión*) to take it on oneself to do sth; (*de modo irreflexivo*) to recklessly decide to do sth; **tirar de la ~** to let the cat out of the bag **2.** (*zurra*) beating **3.** ZOOL manta

manta[2] *mf* (*persona torpe*) oaf

manteca *f* **1.** (*grasa*) fat; **~ de cerdo** lard **2.** (*mantequilla*) butter; **como ~** as soft as butter; **eso no se le ocurre ni al que asó la ~** *inf* nobody in their right mind would do that

mantecado *m* **1.** (*bollo*) pastry cake (*type of shortbread*) **2.** (*helado*) icecream (*made from a custard base*)

mantecoso, -a *adj* **1.** (*de manteca*) greasy; (*sabor*) buttery **2.** (*consistencia*) soft; (*carne*) fatty

mantel *m* tablecloth; **comer a ~es** to dine formally; **estar a mesa y ~** to have free board; **poner/levantar los ~es** *fig* to lay/clear the table

mantelería *f* table linen

mantener *irr como tener* **I.** *vt* **1.** (*conservar, relaciones*) to maintain; (*orden*) to keep; **~ a punto** to keep in working order; **mantiene la línea** she keeps her figure; **~ la calma** to keep calm **2.** (*perseverar*) **~ algo** to keep sth up **3.** (*sustentar*) to maintain; **~ correspondencia con alguien** to keep up a correspondence with sb **4.** (*sostener*) to support **5.** (*proseguir*) to continue; **~ una conversación con alguien** to hold a conversation with sb **II.** *vr:* **~se 1.** (*sostenerse*) to support oneself **2.** (*continuar*) to continue **3.** (*perseverar*) to keep; **se mantiene en sus trece** *inf* he/she is sticking to his/her guns **4.** (*sustentarse*) to support oneself

mantenido, -a *adj* kept

mantenimiento *m* **1.** (*alimentos*) sustenance **2.** TÉC maintenance; **~ de datos** INFOR database update; **sin ~** maintenance-free **3.** (*de una propiedad*) upkeep

mantequilla *f* butter

mantequillera *f AmL: butter dish*

mantilla *f* **1.** (*de mujer*) mantilla **2.** (*de niño*) swaddling clothes *pl;* **el negocio está en ~s** *inf* the business is in its infancy; **estar en ~s sobre algo** *inf* to be in the dark about sth **3.** (*de caballo*) horse blanket

manto *m* **1.** (*prenda*) cloak; (*talar*) gown **2.** (*capa*) layer; **el ~ ácido de la piel** the acid layer of the skin **3.** (*velo*) veil **4.** MIN seam **5.** GEO **~ terrestre** earth's crust **6.** BOT **~ vegetal** humus

mantón *m* shawl

mantudo, -a I. *adj* (*ave*) with droopy wings **II.** *m, f AmC* masked [*o* disguised] person

manual I. *adj* **1.** (*con las manos*) manual, hand; **trabajos ~es** handicrafts *pl* **2.** (*manejable*) user-friendly **II.** *m* manual, handbook; **~ de referencia** reference book; **~ de instrucciones** instruction manual

manubrio *m* **1.** (*puño*) stock **2.** (*manivela*) handle; **piano de ~** barrel organ

manufactura *f* **1.** (*acción, producto*) manufacture **2.** (*taller*) factory

manufacturar *vt* to manufacture

manuscrito *m* manuscript

manuscrito, -a *adj* handwritten

manutención *f* **1.** (*alimentos*) keep **2.** TÉC maintenance

manzana *f* **1.** (*fruta*) apple; **la ~ de la discordia** the bone of contention; **sano como una ~** as fit as a fiddle **2.** (*conjunto de casas*) block; **dar la vuelta a la ~** to go round the block **3.** *AmL* ANAT (*nuez*) Adam's apple

manzanilla *f* **1.** (*planta*) camomile **2.** (*flor*) camomile flower **3.** (*infusión*) camomile tea **4.** (*vino*) manzanilla (*type of dry sherry*)

manzano *m* apple tree

maña *f* **1.** (*habilidad*) skill, dexterity; **tener ~ para algo** to have a knack for sth **2.** (*astucia*) craftiness **3.** *pl* (*caprichos*) whims *pl;* **tiene ~s** he/she has his/her little whims ►**más vale ~ que fuerza** *prov* better brains than brawn

mañana[1] **I.** *f* (*temprano*) early morning; (*hasta el mediodía*) morning; **a las 5 de la ~** at 5 a.m.; **de la noche a la ~** overnight; **de ~** in the early morning; **por la ~** in the morning; **todas las ~s** every morning; **~ por la ~** tomorrow morning **II.** *adv* **1.** (*día*) tomorrow; **¡hasta ~!** see you tomorrow!; **~ será otro día** tomorrow is another day **2.** (*futuro*) tomorrow ►**no dejes para ~ lo que puedas hacer hoy** *prov* do not leave for tomorrow what you can do today

mañana[2] *m* tomorrow; **pasado ~** the day after tomorrow; **el día de ~** in the future

mañanero, -a I. *adj* **1.** (*madrugador*) early-rising **2.** (*de la mañana*) morning **II.** *m, f* early riser

mañanita *f* **1.** (*prenda*) bed jacket **2.** *Méx* (*canción*) serenade

mañero, -a *adj Arg, inf* fussy

maño, -a I. *adj* of/from Aragón **II.** *m, f* native/inhabitant of Aragón

mañosear *vi* **1.** *Chile, Perú* to act craftily **2.** *CSur, Méx* to be finicky

mañoso, -a *adj* **1.** (*hábil*) dexterous, handy **2.** (*sagaz*) guileful

mapa *m* map; **~ astronómico** map of the stars; **~ del tiempo** weather map; **borrar del ~** (*matar*) to wipe off the map [*o* the face of the earth]; **desaparecer del ~** to vanish into thin air; **no estar en el ~** *fig* to be out of this world

mapache *m,* **mapachín** *m AmL* raccoon

maqueta *f* **1.** ARQUIT (scale) model **2.** (*formato*) format; (*de libro*) dummy

maquetación *f* layout

maquetar *vt* to lay out

maquiavélico, -a *adj* (*retorcido*) Machiavellian

maquillador(a) *m(f) t.* TEAT make-up artist

maquillaje *m* **1.** (*acción*) application of make-up **2.** (*producto*) make-up

M

maquillar I. *vt* 1. (*poner base de fondo*) to apply foundation to; (*con pinturas*) to apply make-up to 2. (*disimular*) to disguise II. *vr:* **~se** (*con base de fondo*) to put on foundation; (*con pinturas*) to put on make-up

máquina *f* 1. (*artefacto*) machine; ~ **de afeitar** electric shaver [*o* razor]; ~ **de coser/lavar** sewing/washing machine; ~ **fotográfica** camera; ~ **de escribir automática** electric typewriter; ~ **destructora de documentos** paper-shredder; **a toda** ~ (at) full speed; **escrito a** ~ typed; **hecho a** ~ machine-made 2. (*aparato de monedas*) vending machine; ~ **de tabaco** cigarette dispenser; ~ **tragaperras** *inf* slot-machine 3. (*tren*) engine

maquinación *f* plot

maquinal *adj* mechanical, automatic

maquinar *vt* 1. (*urdir*) to scheme 2. (*trabajar*) to work

maquinaria *f* 1. (*máquinas*) machinery 2. (*mecanismo*) mechanism

maquinilla *f* (safety) razor

maquinista *mf* 1. (*conductor*) machinist; ~ **de trenes** train driver *Brit,* engineer *Am* 2. (*constructor*) engineer

maquinizar <z→c> *vt* to mechanize

mar *m o f* 1. GEO sea; **Mar Antártico** Antarctic Ocean; **Mar de las Antillas** Caribbean Sea; **Mar Artico** Artic Ocean; **Mar Báltico** Baltic Sea; **Mar de Irlanda** Irish Sea; **Mar Mediterráneo** Mediterranean Sea; **Mar del Norte** North Sea; **en alta** ~ offshore; ~ **adentro** high seas; ~ **de fondo** swell; ~ **gruesa/picada/rizada** heavy/rough/choppy sea; *fig* unrest; **por** ~ by sea; **hacerse a la** ~ to put out to sea; **al otro lado del** ~ overseas; **arar en el** ~ *fig* to labour *Brit* [*o* labor *Am*] in vain; **arrojarse a la** ~ *fig* to venture forth 2. *inf* **la** ~ **de...** there is an abundance of ...; **llueve a ~es** it is pouring with rain; **lloró a ~es** he/she cried his/her eyes out; **sudar a ~es** to pour with sweat; **ser la** ~ **de aburrido** to be excruciatingly boring; **ser la** ~ **de bonita** to be incredibly pretty ▶**quien no se aventura no pasa la** ~ *prov* nothing ventured, nothing gained; **echar pelillos al** ~ to let bygones be bygones, to bury the hatchet *Am*

maraca *f* maraca

maraña *f* 1. (*maleza*) thicket 2. (*lío*) mess; ~ **de cabello** tangle of hair; ~ **de hilo** tangle of threads 3. (*embuste*) fabrication

marasmo *m* 1. (*debilitamiento*) weakening 2. (*inmovilidad*) paralysis

maratón *m o f* marathon; **la reunión fue verdaderamente un** ~ the meeting was a real marathon

maravilla *f* 1. (*portento*) marvel; **a las mil ~s, de** ~ marvellously *Brit,* marvelously *Am;* **hablar ~s de alguien** to speak extremely well of sb; **hacer ~s** *fig* to work wonders 2. (*admiración*) wonder 3. BOT (*caléndula*) marigold

maravillar I. *vt* to amaze II. *vr* **~se de algo** to marvel at sth

maravilloso, -a *adj* marvellous *Brit,* marvelous *Am*

marbellí I. *adj* of/from Marbella II. *mf* native/inhabitant of Marbella

marca *f* 1. (*distintivo*) mark; ~ **de agua** watermark; ~ **de ganado** brand 2. (*de productos*) brand; ~ **registrada** registered trademark; **ropa de** ~ designer label; **un idiota de** ~ **mayor** a complete idiot 3. (*huella*) impression 4. DEP record 5. (*medida*) measurement 6. INFOR bookmark

marcadamente *adv* 1. (*claramente*) clearly 2. (*singularmente*) markedly 3. (*con énfasis*) emphatically

marcado, -a *adj* 1. (*señalado*) marked 2. (*evidente*) clear 3. (*singular*) singular 4. (*enfático*) emphatic

marcador *m* 1. (*tablero*) scoreboard; **abrir el** ~ to open the scoring; **cerraron el** ~ **con tres tantos** they finished the game with three goals 2. *Arg* (*rotulador*) marker pen

marcaje *m* DEP marking, cover(age)

marcapaso(s) *m* (*inv*) pacemaker

marcar <c→qu> I. *vt* 1. (*señalar*) to mark; (*ganado*) to brand; (*mercancías*) to label; ~ **una época** to denote an era; ~ **el compás** to beat time 2. (*resaltar*) to emphasize 3. (*teléfono*) to dial 4. (*cabello*) to style 5. DEP ~ **un gol** to score a goal; ~ **un punto** to score a point 6. DEP (*a un jugador*) to mark, to cover II. *vr:* **~se** to show

marcha *f* 1. (*movimiento*) progress; **poner en** ~ to start 2. (*caminata*) hike 3. (*curso*) course; ~ **de los negocios** business trend; **la** ~ **de los acontecimientos** the course of events; **sobre la** ~ along the way 4. (*velocidad*) gear; ~ **atrás** reverse; **a toda** ~ at full speed 5. *t.* MIL, MÚS march; ~ **silenciosa** silent march 6. (*salida*) departure; **¡en ~!** lets go! 7. *inf* (*acción*) action; **¡aquí hay mucha ~!** this is where the action is!; **ir de** ~ to go out on the town; **tener** ~ to be full of go

marchamo *m* 1. (*aduanas*) customs stamp 2. (*embutidos*) tag

marchante I. *adj* commercial II. *mf* dealer; ~ **de obras de arte** art dealer

marchantía *f AmC, PRico, Ven* clientele

marchar I. *vi* 1. (*ir*) to go; **¡marchando!** let's go! 2. (*funcionar*) to work; ~ **sobre ruedas** *fig* to go like clockwork II. *vr:* **~se** 1. (*irse*) to leave; **¿os marcháis?** are you leaving? 2. (*huir*) to flee; **~se del país** to flee the country

marchitar I. *vi* 1. (*plantas*) to wither 2. (*personas*) to be on the wane II. *vr:* **~se** to wither

marchito, -a *adj* withered

marchoso, -a *adj* 1. (*salidor*) fun-loving 2. (*elegante*) elegant

marcial *adj* martial; **artes ~es** martial arts; **ley** ~ martial law

marcianitos *mpl inf* little green men *pl*

marciano, -a *adj, m, f* Martian

marco *m* 1. (*recuadro*) frame; (*armazón*)

framework; **el ~ legal** the legal framework **2.** (*ambiente*) background **3.** (*moneda*) mark

marea *f* **1.** (*mar*) tide; **~ alta** high tide; **~ baja** low tide; **~ creciente** rising tide; **~ menguante** ebb tide; **~ negra** oil slick [*o* spill]; **~ viva** spring tide **2.** (*multitud*) flood; **una ~ humana** a flood of people

mareado, **-a** *adj* **1.** (*indispuesto*) sick; (*en el mar*) seasick; (*en el coche*) carsick; (*al viajar*) travel-sick; **estoy ~** I feel sick **2.** (*aturdido*) dizzy; *fig* confused **3.** (*bebido*) tipsy

marear **I.** *vt* **1.** *inf* (*molestar*) to pester **2.** MED to nauseate **3.** (*aturdir*) to make dizzy; *fig* to confuse **II.** *vr:* **~se** **1.** (*enfermarse*) to feel sick; (*en el mar*) to get seasick; (*al viajar*) to get travel-sick **2.** (*quedar aturdido*) to become dizzy; *fig* to become confused **3.** (*emborracharse*) to get tipsy

marejada *f* swell; *fig* unrest

maremagno *m*, **maremágnum** *m inv* **1.** (*multitud*) multitude **2.** (*confusión*) commotion

maremoto *m* tidal wave; (*seísmo*) seaquake

mareo *m* **1.** (*malestar*) nausea; (*en el mar*) seasickness; (*al viajar*) travel-sickness, motion sickness **2.** (*vértigo*) dizziness; **¡qué ~ de hombre!** *inf* what a nuisance that man is!

marfil *m* **1.** (*elefante*) ivory **2.** (*dentadura*) dentine

marfileño, **-a** **I.** *adj* **1.** (*nacionalidad*) of/from the Ivory Coast **2.** (*material*) ivory-like **II.** *m, f* native/inhabitant of the Ivory Coast

margarina *f* margarine

margarita *f* **1.** BOT daisy; **deshojar la ~** to play 'she loves me, she loves me not' **2.** (*bebida*) margarita **3.** ZOOL periwinkle **4.** (*perla*) pearl; **echar ~s a puercos** to cast pearls before swine **5.** TIPO daisywheel

margen *m o f* **1.** (*borde*) edge; **el ~ del río** the riverside [*o* riverbank]; **al ~** apart; **dejar al ~** to leave out; **mantenerse al ~ de algo** *fig* to keep out of sth **2.** (*página*) margin **3.** (*libertad*) leeway; **dar ~** to give leeway **4.** (*ganancia*) profit margin; **~ de costos** margin of costs; **~ de seguridad** safety margin

marginado, **-a** **I.** *adj* **1.** (*excluido*) excluded, marginalized **2.** (*aislado*) isolated **II.** *m, f* outcast

marginal *adj* **1.** (*al margen*) apart **2.** (*secundario*) secondary

marginar *vt* **1.** (*ignorar algo*) to disregard; (*a alguien*) to marginalize **2.** (*acotar*) to annotate in the margin

maría *f* **1.** *inf* (*ama de casa*) housewife **2.** *inf* (*marihuana*) grass, pot **3.** *inf* ENS easy subject

mariachi *m Méx* mariachi musician

marica *m vulg* **1.** (*homosexual*) queer, poof *Brit*, fag *Am* **2.** (*cobarde*) sissy **3.** (*insulto grosero*) berk *Brit*, asshole *Am*

Maricastaña *f* **tiempos de ~** *inf* years ago; **desde los tiempos de ~** from the year dot; **este chiste es de los tiempos de ~** that joke is as old as the hills

maricón *m vulg v.* **marica**

mariconada *f vulg* **1.** (*acción malintencionada*) dirty trick; **hacer una ~ a alguien** to play a dirty trick on sb **2.** (*tontería*) silly [*o* poncy *Brit*] thing to do

marido *m* husband; **mi ~** my husband

mariguana, **marihuana** *f sin pl* marijuana, marihuana

marimacho *m inf* butch (woman); (*niña*) tomboy; *pey* (*lesbiana*) dyke

marimandón, **-ona** *m, f inf* bossy boots

marimba *f* **1.** MÚS (*de maderas*) marimba **2.** MÚS (*tambor*) African drum **3.** *Arg* (*paliza*) beating

marimorena *f inf* rumpus; **armar la ~** to kick up a fuss; **se armó la ~** all Hell broke loose

marina *f* **1.** (*flota*) navy; **la ~ mercante** the merchant marine **2.** ARTE seascape **3.** GEO coastal region

marinera *f* **1.** (*blusa*) middy blouse **2.** *And* (*baile*) popular folk dance

marinero *m* sailor; **~ de agua dulce** *irón* landlubber

marinero, **-a** *adj* **1.** (*relativo al mar*) marine; **buque ~** seagoing boat; **pueblo ~** coastal town; **pescado a la marinera** *fish in a sauce with tomatoes, mussels and wine* **2.** (*relativo a la marina*) marine; **nudo ~** sailor's knot

marino *m* (*navegante*) sailor, seaman

marino, **-a** *adj* marine

marioneta *f* **1.** (*títere*) puppet, marionette **2.** *pl* (*teatro*) puppet show

mariposa *f* **1.** ZOOL butterfly; **~ nocturna** moth **2.** (*lámpara*) lamp (*wick floating in oil*) **3.** DEP butterfly stroke **4.** *pey* (*afeminado*) pansy ►**¡a otra cosa ~!** let's talk about something else!

mariposear *vi* **1.** (*ser inconstante*) to be fickle **2.** (*flirtear*) to flirt **3.** (*rondar*) **~ a alguien** to dance attendance on sb

mariquita[1] *f* ZOOL **1.** (*insecto*) ladybird **2.** (*perico*) parakeet

mariquita[2] *m inf* poof *Brit*, fag *Am*

marisabidilla *f inf* know-all

mariscal *m* marshal

marisco *m* seafood

marisma *f* marsh

marisquería *f* **1.** (*tienda*) seefood shop **2.** (*restaurante*) seafood restaurant

marital *adj* marital; **vida ~** married life

maritatas *fpl Guat, Hond* junk

marítimo, **-a** *adj* maritime, marine; **ciudad marítima** seaside town; **seguro ~** marine insurance

marjal *m* fen

marmita *f* pot

mármol *m* marble; **frío como el ~** as cold as stone; **de ~** of marble

marmóreo, **-a** *adj* marble(-like)

marmota *f* **1.** ZOOL marmot; **~ de América** groundhog **2.** *inf* (*dormilón*) sleepyhead **3.** *pey* (*criada*) maid

maroma *f* **1.** (*cuerda*) rope **2.** *AmL* (*pirueta*)

M

somersault **3.** *AmL* (*cambio de partido político*) change of political allegiance; (*de opinión*) change of opinion
maromo *m inf* guy, bloke *Brit*
marqués, -esa *m, f* marquis *m,* marquise *f*
marquesina *f* (glass) canopy, marquee
marquetería *f* marquetry; (*ebanistería*) cabinet-making
marrajo *m* shark
marrajo, -a *adj* (*toro*) vicious; (*persona*) crafty
marrana *f* **1.** (*cerda*) sow **2.** *pey, inf* (*mujer sucia*) slut; (*vil*) despicable woman
marranada *f inf* filthiness; (*acción*) a dirty trick
marrano *m* **1.** (*cerdo*) pig **2.** *pey, inf* (*hombre sucio*) dirty man; (*grosero*) rude man; (*vil*) despicable man
marrano, -a *adj* filthy
marrar *vi* **1.** (*errar*) to miss; ~ **el golpe** *fig* to miss the mark **2.** (*desviarse*) to stray
marras *adv* **tema de** ~ the same old subject; **la persona de** ~ the person in question; **lo de** ~ the same old thing
marrón **I.** *adj* brown **II.** *m* **1.** (*color*) brown **2.** *AmC* (*martillo*) hammer
marroquí *adj, mf* Moroccan
Marruecos *m* Morocco
marrullería *f* flattery; **déjate de ~s** cut the flattery; (*labia*) glibness
marrullero, -a **I.** *adj* flattering; (*con labia*) glib **II.** *m, f* flatterer
Marsella *f* Marseilles
marsellés, -esa *adj, m, f* Marseillaise
marsopa *f* porpoise
marsupial **I.** *adj* **animal** ~ marsupial **II.** *m* marsupial
marta *f* **1.** ZOOL marten; ~ **cebellina** sable **2.** (*piel*) sable
Marte *m* Mars
martes *m inv* Tuesday; **¡~ y trece!** Friday the thirteenth!; *v.t.* **lunes**
martill(e)ar *vt* **1.** (*golpear*) to hammer **2.** (*atormentar*) to torment **3.** (*repetir*) to repeat
martilleo *m* hammering
martillero *m Arg, Chile* auctioneer
martillo *m* **1.** (*herramienta*) hammer; ANAT malleus; **creer algo a macha** ~ to firmly believe sth; **repetir algo a macha** ~ to repeat sth ad nauseam **2. pez** ~ hammerhead **3.** (*subasta*) gavel
martín *m* ~ **pescador** kingfisher; ~ **del río** heron
martinete *m* **1.** ZOOL heron **2.** MÚS (*macillo*) hammer **3.** (*mazo*) hammer; (*para clavar estacas*) sledgehammer
martingala *f inf* sly trick, dodge
mártir *mf* martyr
martirio *m* REL martyrdom; *fig* torture
martirizar <z→c> *vt* to torture
maruja *f pey, inf* housewife (*used to refer to women whose sole interests are their homes, family, personal appearance and gossip*)
marxismo *m* Marxism
marxista *adj, mf* Marxist
marzo *m* March; **en** ~ in March; **a principios/a mediados/a fin(al)es de** ~ at the beginning/in the middle/at the end of March; **el 21 de** ~ the 21st of March; **el mes de** ~ **tiene 31 días** the month of March has 31 days; **el pasado** ~ **fue muy frío** last March was very cold
mas **I.** *m* manor **II.** *conj* LIT but, yet
más **I.** *adv* **1.** (*cantidad*) more; ~ **dinero/zapatos** more money/shoes **2.** (*comparativo*) more; ~ **intelligente/complicado** more intelligent/complicated; ~ **grande/pequeño** bigger/smaller; ~ **temprano/tarde** earlier/later; **correr** ~ to run more; **esto me gusta** ~ I like this better; ~ **acá** closer; ~ **adelante** (*local*) further forward [*o* on]; (*temporal*) later; **es** ~ **guapo que tú** he is more handsome than you; **cada día** [*o* **vez**] ~ more and more; **cuanto** ~ **mejor** the more the merrier; ~ **allá de esto** beyond this; ~ **de la cuenta** too much **3.** (*superlativo*) **el/la** ~ the most; **la** ~ **bella** the most beautiful; **el** ~ **listo de la clase** the cleverest in the class; **el modelo que** ~ **se lleva** the model that is most in fashion; **lo que** ~ **me gusta** what I most like [*o* like most]; **lo que** ~ **quieras** what you most want; **lo** ~ **probable es que llueva** it is likely to rain; **lo** ~ **pronto posible** as early as possible; ~ **que nunca** more than ever; **a lo** ~ at (the) most; **a** ~ **no poder** to the utmost; **a** ~ **tardar** at the latest; **todo lo** ~ at most **4.** (*con numerales, cantidad*) ~ **de treinta** more than thirty; **son** ~ **de las diez** it is after ten **5.** (*preferencia*) ~ **quiero la muerte que la esclavitud** I prefer death to slavery **6.** (*tan*) **¡está** ~ **guapa!** you look so beautiful; **¡qué tarde** ~ **apacible!** what a peaceful afternoon! **7.** (*con pronombre interrogativo, indefinido*) **¿algo ~?** anything else?; **no, nada** ~ no, nothing else **8.** (*en frases negativas*) **no puedo** ~ I have had it; **nunca** ~ never again **9.** MAT plus; **tengo tres libros,** ~ **los que he prestado** I have three books, plus those I have lent **10.** (*a más*) **a** ~ **y mejor** really; **llueve a** ~ **y mejor** it is raining with a vengeance; **divertirse a** ~ **y mejor** to have a really good time **11.** (*de más*) **de** ~ spare, more than enough; **hay comida de** ~ there is food to spare; **estar de** ~ not to be needed; **de lo** ~ very **12.** (*más bien*) ~ **bien** rather; **no es muy delgado; es** ~ **bien gordo** he is not very thin; rather he is fat **13.** (*más o menos*) **¿cómo te ha ido? –** ~ **o menos** how did it go? – so-so; ~ **o menos** (*aproximadamente*) more or less; **le va** ~ **o menos** he is doing so-so; **ni** ~ **ni menos** exactly **14.** (*por más que*) **por** ~ **que lo intento, no consigo dormirme** however hard I try, I cannot sleep ►**tener sus** ~ **y sus menos** to have one's good and one's bad points; **sin** ~ **acá ni** ~ **allá** without more ado; **el** ~ **allá** the beyond; **el que** ~ **y el que**

menos every single one; **quien ~ y quien menos** everyone; **es ~, ~ aún** what is more; **el no va ~** the last word; **el no va ~ (de la moda)** the latest fashion; **como el que ~** as well as the next man; **sin ~ ni ~** without more ado; **¿qué ~ da?** what difference does it make? **II.** *m* MAT plus sign
masa *f* **1.** (*pasta*) mixture; (*para hornear*) dough; **coger a alguien con las manos en la ~** to catch sb red-handed **2.** (*volumen, muchedumbre*) mass; **~ monetaria** money supply; **medios de comunicación de ~s** mass media; **en ~** en masse **3.** ELEC earth *Brit,* ground *Am*
masacrar *vt* to massacre
masacre *f* massacre
masaje *m* massage; **dar ~s** to massage; **darse ~s** to be massaged
masajista *mf* masseur *m,* masseuse *f*
masato *m AmS* GASTR **1.** (*mazamorra*) coconut sweet **2.** (*bebida*) *fermented maize or rice drink*
mascada *f* **1.** *AmL* (*tabaco*) *quid of chewing tobacco* **2.** (*boxeo*) uppercut **3.** *Col, Cuba, Chile* (*bocado*) bite **4.** *Méx* (*pañuelo*) silk kerchief
mascar <c→qu> *vt* **1.** (*masticar*) to chew **2.** (*mascullar*) to mumble **3.** (*presentir*) to have a premonition
máscara *f* **1.** (*careta*) mask; **traje de ~** fancy dress; **quitar la ~ a alguien** *fig* to unmask sb; **quitarse la ~** *fig* to reveal oneself **2.** *pl* (*fiesta*) fancy dress party **3.** (*enmascarado*) masquerade; (*de Carnaval*) carnival
mascarada *f* **1.** (*baile*) masquerade **2.** (*farsa*) farce
mascarilla *f* **1.** (*máscara*) mask **2.** (*protección*) face mask **3.** (*cosmética*) **~ exfoliante** face scrub; **~ facial** face pack **4.** (*molde*) cast
mascota *f* mascot; (*animal de compañía*) pet
masculinidad *f* masculinity
masculino *m* LING masculine
masculino, -a *adj* **1.** (*aspecto, rasgos*) masculine; **moda masculina** men's fashion **2.** LING **género ~** masculine form
mascullar *vt* to mumble
masía *f* manor house
masificación *f* overcrowding
masilla *f* putty
masita *f AmS* GASTR small cake
masivo, -a *adj* **1.** (*grande*) massive **2.** (*fuerte*) strong **3.** (*de masas*) mass
masón, -ona *m, f* Mason, Freemason
masoquista **I.** *adj* masochistic **II.** *mf* masochist
mastectomía *f* mastectomy
máster <másters> *m* master's degree
masticar <c→qu> *vt* **1.** (*mascar*) to chew **2.** (*meditar*) to ponder
mástil *m* **1.** NÁUT mast, spar **2.** (*poste*) post, pole **3.** MÚS (*guitarra, violín*) neck
mastín *m* mastiff
mastuerzo *m* **1.** BOT cress **2.** (*hombre*) idiot
masturbación *f* masturbation
masturbarse *vr* to masturbate
mata *f* **1.** (*matorral*) clump **2.** (*planta*) plant; (*arbusto*) bush **3.** *pl, inf* (*cabellera*) mop of hair
matadero *m* **1.** (*desolladero*) slaughterhouse; **ir al ~** *fig* to put one's life in danger; **llevar al ~** *fig* to send sb to his/her death **2.** (*fatiga*) strain
matador(a) **I.** *adj* **1.** (*que mata*) killer **2.** (*cansador*) killing **3.** *inf* (*ridículo*) ludicrous **II.** *m(f)* **1.** TAUR matador **2.** (*asesino*) killer
matamoscas *m inv* **1.** (*insecticida*) fly-spray **2.** (*objeto*) fly-swat **3.** (*trampa*) flypaper
matanza *f* **1.** (*el matar*) killing **2.** (*en batallas*) slaughter; **hacer una ~** to massacre **3.** (*carneada*) slaughter; **hacer la ~** to slaughter an animal **4.** GASTR cured pork products *pl*
matar **I.** *vt* **1.** (*quitar la vida*) to kill; **~ a golpes** to beat to death; **~ a palos** to club to death; **~ a puñaladas** to knife [*o* stab] to death; **~ a tiros** to shoot dead; **que me maten si yo esperaba una cosa así** *inf* I swear on my mother's grave that I didn't expect this **2.** (*carnear*) to slaughter **3.** (*saciar*) to assuage; (*hambre*) to satisfy; (*sed*) to quench **4.** (*luz, fuego*) to put out **5.** (*sellos*) to postmark **6.** (*redondear*) to round off **7.** (*naipes*) to top **8.** (*color, brillo*) to tone down **9.** (*acabar con alguien*) **~ a disgustos** to be the death of **10.** (*aniquilar*) to be the end of; (*el tiempo*) to kill; (*el aburrimiento, nerviosismo*) to alleviate **11.** (*molestar*) to annoy; **~ a preguntas a alguien** to drive sb mad with questions **II.** *vr:* **~se** **1.** (*suicidarse*) to kill oneself **2.** (*aniquilarse*) **te estás matando trabajando así** you are wearing yourself out working like that **3.** (*trabajar sin descanso*) **~se a trabajar** to work oneself to death; **~se por algo** to go out of one's way to do sth
matarife *mf* butcher
matarratas *m inv* **1.** (*raticida*) rat poison **2.** *pey, inf* (*aguardiente*) firewater; (*alcohol de mala calidad*) rotgut, hooch
matasanos *mf inv, irón, inf* quack
matasellos *m inv* postmark
matasuegras *m inv, inf* party blower
matazón *m AmL* (*matanza*) massacre
match *m* match
mate **I.** *adj* dull **II.** *m* **1.** (*ajedrez*) mate; **jaque ~** checkmate **2.** (*acabado*) matte **3.** *pl inf* (*matemáticas*) maths *Brit,* math *Am* **4.** *AmS* (*bebida*) maté tea (*herbal infusion drunk from a gourd*)

In South America **mate** means: 1. The maté plant, 2. The leaves of the maté plant, from which tea is made, 3. The tea itself, and 4. A container in which the tea is kept.

matemáticas *fpl* mathematics
matemático, -a **I.** *adj* mathematical **II.** *m, f*

M

mathematician

materia *f* 1. *t.* FÍS (*substancia*) matter; ~ **gris** ANAT grey matter; ~ **prima** raw material 2. (*tema*) subject, matter; **en** ~ **de** in the matter of 3. *t.* ENS (*disciplina*) subject; ~ **penal** JUR penal matter

material I. *adj* (*real*) tangible; **daño** ~ physical damage; **el autor** ~ **del hecho** the actual perpetrator of the deed II. *m* material; ~**es de construcción** building materials; ~ **de enseñanza** teaching material; ~ **de oficina** office equipment

materialismo *m* materialism

materialista I. *adj* materialistic II. *mf* materialist

materializar <z→c> I. *vt* 1. (*hacer material*) to bring into being 2. (*realizar*) to carry out 3. (*hacer aparecer*) to produce II. *vr:* ~**se** to materialize

materialmente *adv* materially; **ser** ~ **posible** to be physically possible

maternal *adj* maternal, motherly

maternidad *f* 1. (*el ser madre*) maternity 2. (*hospital*) maternity hospital; (*sala*) maternity ward

materno, **-a** *adj* maternal; **abuelo** ~ maternal grandfather; **lengua materna** mother tongue

matero, **-a** I. *adj AmS* mate-drinking II. *m, f* mate-drinker

matinal *adj* morning; **sesión** ~ (*congreso, conferencia*) morning session; CINE, TEAT matinee

matiné *f* matinée

matiz *m* 1. (*gradación*) shade 2. (*toque*) touch 3. (*sentido*) nuance

matizar <z→c> *vt* 1. (*combinar colores o tonos*) to blend; ~ **de rojo** to tinge with red 2. (*graduar*) to tint 3. (*de un sentido*) to tinge; ~ **una frase de significado irónico** to give a sentence an ironical slant; (*concretar*) to specify

matón, **-ona** *m, f* 1. (*chulo*) bully 2. (*guardaespaldas*) bodyguard 3. (*asesino*) murderer

matorral *m* thicket

matraca *f* 1. (*carraca*) rattle, noisemaker 2. *inf* (*fastidio*) **dar la** ~ to pester; **ser** ~ to be a bore

matraz *m* flask

matrero, **-a** *adj* 1. (*astuto*) cunning 2. (*receloso*) suspicious 3. (*engañoso*) deceitful 4. *AmS* (*fugitivo*) fugitive

matrícula *f* 1. (*documento*) registration document 2. (*inscripción*) enrolment *Brit,* enrollment *Am;* UNIV matriculation 3. AUTO (*placa*) number plate *Brit,* license plate *Am;* **número de la** ~ registration number *Brit,* license number *Am* 4. (*lista*) register 5. (*conjunto de alumnos*) student enrolment *Brit,* enrollment *Am* 6. ENS **aprobar con** ~ **de honor** to pass with distinction [*o* with highest honors *Am*] (*allowing student free enrolment in a subject for the following course*)

matricular I. *vt* to register; UNIV to enrol *Brit,* to enroll *Am* II. *vr* ~**se en la universidad** to enrol in the university

matrimonial *adj* matrimonial, marriage; **agencia** ~ dating agency; **vida** ~ married life

matrimonio *m* 1. marriage; ~ **canónico** church wedding; ~ **civil** civil wedding; **consumar el** ~ to consummate the marriage; **contraer** ~ to marry 2. (*marido y mujer*) married couple; **cama de** ~ double bed

matriz I. *f* 1. (*útero*) womb 2. (*molde*) cast 3. TIPO, MAT matrix 4. (*de un talonario*) stub II. *adj* **la casa** ~ **está en Sevilla** the parent company is in Seville; **lengua** ~ primal language

matrona *f* 1. (*comadrona*) midwife 2. (*de familia*) matron

maturrango, **-a** I. *adj* 1. *AmS* (*mal jinete*) **ser** ~ to be a poor rider 2. *Chile* (*tosco*) clumsy II. *m, f AmS* (*mal jinete*) poor horserider

matute *m* 1. (*contrabando*) smuggling; **de** ~ *fig* clandestinely; **pasar de** ~ to pass clandestinely; **viajar de** ~ to travel clandestinely 2. (*género*) contraband

matutino, **-a** *adj* morning; **periódico** ~ morning paper; **sesión matutina** morning session

maula[1] *mf inf* 1. (*tramposo*) cheat 2. (*inútil*) good-for-nothing

maula[2] *f* 1. (*baratija*) a piece of junk; **este coche es una** ~ this car is a piece of junk 2. (*engaño*) trick

maullar *irr como aullar vi* to miaow *Brit,* to meow *Am*

maullido *m* miaow *Brit,* meow *Am*

mauritano, **-a** *adj, m, f* Mauritanian

mausoleo *m* mausoleum

maxilar I. *adj* ANAT maxillary II. *m* jaw

máxima *f* maxim

máxime *adv* particularly

máximo, **-a** I. *adj* maximum; **rendimiento** ~ maximum output; **triunfo** ~ greatest triumph; **pon la radio al** ~ turn the radio as high as it goes II. *m, f* maximum; **como** ~ at most; (*temporal*) at the latest

maya[1] *f* BOT daisy

maya[2] *adj, m* Mayan

> The **mayas** were an Indian race of people native to Central America (present-day Mexico, Guatemala and Honduras) with a civilisation that was highly advanced in many fields. The great number of ruins bear witness to this fact, such as the pyramids constructed from blocks of stone, numerous inscriptions and drawings, and not least the very accurate calendar that these people possessed.

mayestático, **-a** *adj* majestic; **plural** ~ the royal we

mayo *m* 1. (*mes*) May; *v.t.* **marzo** 2. (*árbol*) maypole

mayonesa *f* mayonnaise

mayor I. *adj* 1. (*tamaño*) bigger; **la** ~ **parte**

the majority, most; **el ~ barco** the largest boat; **mal ~** greater evil; **~ que** bigger than; **comercio al por ~** wholesale trade; **se repartieron palos al por ~** *fig* many blows were dealt **2.** (*edad*) older; **~ que** older than; **mi hermano ~** my older [*o* big] brother; **el ~ de mis hermanos** the eldest of my brothers and sisters; **ser ~** to be grown-up; **ser ~ de edad** to be an adult, to be of legal age; **persona ~** elderly person; **los ~es** the adults, the grown-ups; **ya es ~ para esos juguetes** he/she is too old for [*o* has outgrown] those toys **3.** MÚS major; **tono ~** major key; **tercera ~** major third; **escala en do ~** scale of C major **II.** *m* **1.** MIL major **2.** (*superior*) superior **3.** *pl* (*ascendientes*) ancestors *pl*

mayoral *m* (*capataz*) foreman

mayorcito, -a *adj inf* **¡si ya eres ~!** what a big boy/girl you are now!; **¿no crees que ya eres mayor para eso?** don't you think you are a little too old for that?

mayordomo, -a *m, f* administrator; (*de una mansión*) butler

mayoría *f* majority; **~ de edad** (age of) majority; **llegar a la ~ de edad** to come of age; **~ relativa** relative majority; **la ~ tiene un coche** most [*o* the majority] have a car

mayorista **I.** *adj* wholesale; **comercio ~** wholesale business **II.** *mf* wholesaler

mayoritariamente *adv* mainly, preponderantly *form*

mayoritario, -a *adj* majority; **tener el apoyo ~** to have majority support

mayormente *adv* especially, particularly

mayúscula *f* capital (letter); **escribirse con ~** to be written with a capital (letter)

mayúsculo, -a *adj* (*grande*) big; **letra mayúscula** capital letter

maza *f* **1.** (*porra*) club **2.** (*para machacar*) pestle **3.** (*percusor*) hammer

mazacote *m* **1.** (*hormigón*) concrete; **esta esponja está hecha un ~** this sponge is rock hard **2.** *inf* (*comida*) stodge

mazacotudo, -a *adj AmL* dense

mazapán *m* marzipan

mazazo *m* blow; **dar ~s a alguien** *fig* to hurt sb; **la muerte de su hijo fue un ~ para él** the death of his son was a terrible blow for him

mazmorra *f* dungeon

mazo *m* **1.** (*martillo*) mallet **2.** (*del mortero*) pestle; (*grande*) sledgehammer **3.** (*manojo*) bundle

mazorca *f* (*del maíz*) cob; (*del cacao*) pod; **~ de maíz** corncob, ear of corn

me **I.** *pron pers* **1.** (*objeto directo*) me; **¡míra~!** look at me! **2.** (*objeto indirecto*) me; **da~ el libro** give me the book **II.** *pron reflexivo* **~ lavo** I wash myself; **~ voy** I am going; **~ he comprado un piso** I have bought myself a flat; **~ lavo el pelo** I wash my hair

meada *f* **1.** *inf* (*pis*) wee, pee; **echar una ~** to take a piss **2.** (*mancha de orina*) piss; **aquí hay una ~ de gato** a cat has pissed here

meadero *m vulg* bog *Brit*

meandro *m* (*curva*) meander

mear *vi, vr:* **~se** *inf* to piss; **el niño se ha meado en el pantalón** the boy has peed (in) his pants; **~se de risa** to die laughing

meato *m* ANAT meatus; **~ auditivo** auditory meatus; **~ urinario** urinary meatus

mecánica *f* mechanics

mecánico, -a **I.** *adj* mechanical **II.** *m, f* mechanic

mecanismo *m* mechanism; (*dispositivo*) device

mecanizar <z→c> *vt* **1.** (*automatizar*) to mechanize **2.** (*elaborar*) to shape

mecano® *m* (*juguete*) Meccano®

mecanografía *f* typewriting

mecanógrafo, -a *m, f* typist

mecate *m AmC, Col, Méx, Ven* (*cuerda*) rope

mecedora *f* rocking chair

mecenas *mf inv* patron

mecer <c→z> **I.** *vt* **1.** (*balancear*) to rock; (*columpiar*) to swing **2.** (*menear*) to move **II.** *vr:* **~se** **1.** (*balancearse*) to rock; (*columpiarse*) to swing **2.** (*menearse*) to move

mecha *f* **1.** (*pabilo*) wick; (*de explosivos*) fuse **2.** (*gasa*) swab **3.** (*mechón*) tuft **4.** *pl* (*mechones teñidos*) highlights *pl*, streaks *pl*; **hacerse ~s** to have highlights [*o* streaks] put in **5.** (*tocino*) streak **6.** *inf* (*prisa*) **a toda ~** very fast **7.** *inf* (*fastidio*) **aguantar ~** to grin and bear it

mechero *m* **1.** (*encendedor*) lighter **2.** (*quemador*) burner

mechificar <c→qu> *vi AmS* to trick

mechón *m* tuft

mechudo, -a *adj AmL* (*desgreñado*) unkempt

meco, -a *adj* **1.** *Méx* (*grosero*) rude **2.** *Méx* (*bermejo con negro*) blackish red; **toro ~** blackish red bull

medalla *f* medal; **~ militar** military decoration

medallista *mf* (*ganador*) medal winner, medallist *Brit*, medalist *Am*

medallón *m* medallion

médano *m*, **medaño** *m* **1.** (*duna*) dune **2.** (*bajío*) sandbank

media *f* **1.** (*promedio*) average **2.** (*calceta*) stocking; *AmL* (*calcetín*) sock

mediacaña *f* bead

mediación *f* mediation

mediado, -a *adj* (*medio lleno*) half full; (*work*) half-completed; **para ~s de semana** by the middle of the week [*o* by midweek]

mediador(a) *m(f)* mediator

mediana *f* **1.** AUTO central reservation *Brit*, median strip *Am* **2.** MAT median

medianero, -a **I.** *adj* (*en medio*) **pared medianera** party [*o* dividing] wall **II.** *m, f* (*intermediario*) mediator

medianía *f* **1.** (*término medio*) average **2.** (*mediocridad*) mediocrity **3.** (*persona*) **ser una ~** (*inteligencia*) to not be very bright

M

mediano, **-a** *adj* **1.**(*calidad*) average **2.**(*tamaño*) medium; **talla mediana** medium **3.** ECON medium-sized

medianoche *f* **1.**(*hora*) midnight; **a ~** at midnight **2.**(*panecillo*) small soft roll

mediante **I.** *adj* **Dios ~** God willing **II.** *prep* by means of; (*a través de*) through

mediar *vi* **1.**(*intermediar*) to mediate **2.**(*interceder*) **~ por alguien** to intercede on behalf of sb **3.**(*realizar hasta la mitad*) to half do **4.**(*interponerse*) to intervene **5.**(*transcurrir*) to happen **6.**(*existir*) to exist; **entre tú y yo media un abismo** there is a world of difference between you and me

mediato, **-a** *adj* next but one

medicación *f* medication

medicamento *m* medicine

medicar <c→qu> **I.** *vt* to medicate; (*recetar*) to prescribe **II.** *vr:* **~se** to take medicine

medicina *f* medicine; **la ~ naturista** natural remedies

medicinal *adj* medicinal; **balón ~** medicine ball; **hierba ~** medicinal plant

medición *f* measurement

médico, **-a** **I.** *adj* medical; **cuerpo ~** medical corps **II.** *m, f* doctor; **Colegio de Médicos** Medical Association; **~ de cabecera** family doctor; **~ forense** forensic surgeon; **~ naturista** homeopath

medida *f* **1.**(*medición*) measurement **2.**(*dimensión*) measurement; **a la ~** (*ropa*) made-to-measure; **tomar la(s) ~(s)** to take the measurement(s); **hasta cierta ~** up to a point; **en la ~ de lo posible** as far as possible; **a ~ que** as **3.** LIT metre *Brit,* meter *Am* **4.**(*prudencia*) prudence; **con ~** with care **5.**(*moderación*) moderation; **sin ~** without moderation **6.**(*acción*) measure; **tomar ~s** to take measures ►**¡vaya ~ de pata!** *AmL, inf* what a clanger *Brit* [*o* blooper *Am*]!

medidor *m* **1.**(*instrumento*) gauge **2.** *AmL* (*contador*) meter

medidor(a) **I.** *adj* measuring; **reloj ~** stopwatch **II.** *m(f)* gauge *Brit,* gage *Am*

medieval *adj* medieval

medio *m* **1.**(*mitad*) middle; **en ~ de** in the middle of; **en ~ de todo** in the middle of it all; **meterse por ~** to intervene; **quitar de en ~** to get rid of; **quitarse de en ~** to get out of the way; **de ~ a ~** smack on **2.**(*instrumento*) means; **~ de transporte** means of transport; **por ~ de** by means of **3.** PREN, RADIO, TV medium; **~s de comunicación** the media **4.**(*entorno*) surroundings *pl;* **~ ambiente** environment **5.** DEP halfback **6.** *Cuba* (*moneda*) five cent coin **7.** *pl* (*fuentes*) sources *pl* **8.** *pl* (*capital*) means *pl;* **estar corto de ~s** to be hard-up

medio, **-a** **I.** *adj* **1.**(*mitad*) half; **a las cuatro y media** at half past four; **litro y ~** one and a half litres *Brit* [*o* liters *Am*]; **mi media naranja** *fig* my other half **2.**(*promedio*) **ciudadano ~** average person **II.** *adv* half; **~ vestido** half dressed; **a ~ asar** half done; **~ dormido, dormido a medias** half asleep; **tomar a medias** to share; **ir a medias** to go halves

medioambiental *adj* environmental

mediocre *adj* mediocre

mediocridad *f* mediocrity

mediodía *m* **1.**(*hora*) midday; **al ~** at noon **2.**(*sur*) south

medir *irr como pedir* **I.** *vt* **1.**(*calcular*) to measure; **¿cuánto mides?** how tall are you? **2.**(*sopesar*) to weigh; **~ los riesgos** to weigh up the risks **3.**(*moderar*) to moderate **II.** *vi* to measure **III.** *vr:* **~se** to be moderate; **~se con alguien** to measure oneself against sb

meditabundo, **-a** *adj* meditative

meditación *f* meditation

meditar *vt, vi* to meditate

mediterráneo, **-a** *adj* Mediterranean; **isla mediterránea** Mediterranean island

Mediterráneo *m* Mediterranean

medrar *vi* **1.**(*crecer*) to grow **2.**(*avanzar*) to thrive

medroso, **-a** **I.** *adj* **1.** *estar* frightened **2.** *ser* apprehensive **II.** *m, f* coward

médula *f* **1.** ANAT marrow; **~ espinal** spinal cord **2.** BOT pith **3.**(*meollo*) core; **hasta la ~** to the core; **hay que llegar a la ~ de las cosas** you have to get to the core of the matter; **estar hasta la ~** *inf* to be fed up

medular *adj* **1.**(*tuétano*) marrow; (*médula espinal*) spinal **2.**(*esencial*) essential; **parte ~** fundamental part

medusa *f* jellyfish

mefítico, **-a** *adj* **1.**(*dañino*) contaminated, noxious **2.**(*fétido*) fetid

megaciclo *m* megacycle

megáfono *m* megaphone

megalomanía *f* megalomania

megalómano, **-a** *adj* megalomaniac

megavatio *m* megawatt

mejicano, **-a** *adj, m, f* Mexican

Méjico *m* Mexico

mejilla *f* cheek; **poner la otra ~** to turn the other cheek

mejillón *m* mussel

mejor **I.** *adj* **1.**(*compar*) better; **~ que** better than; **es ~ que no vayas** +*subj* it is better that you don't go; **cambiar a ~** to change for the better; **pasar a ~ vida** to pass away **2.**(*superl*) **el/la/lo ~** the best; **el ~ alumno** the best student; **la ~ nota** the best mark; **~ postor** highest bidder; **el ~ día** the best day **II.** *adv* better; **a lo ~** maybe; **~ que ~** better still [*o* yet]; **en el ~ de los casos** at best; **~ quiero un coche viejo que una moto** I prefer to have an old car than a motorbike

mejora *f* **1.**(*mejoramiento*) improvement; **~ salarial** (pay) rise *Brit,* (pay) raise *Am* **2.**(*puja*) higher bid

mejorable *adj* improvable

mejoramiento *m* improvement

mejorana *f* marjoram

mejorar **I.** *vt* **1.**(*perfeccionar*) to improve

2. (*superar*) to surpass; (*subasta*) to outbid **II.** *vi, vr:* **~se 1.** (*enfermo*) to get better; **¡que se mejore!** I hope you get better soon! **2.** (*tiempo*) to improve

mejoría *f* improvement

mejunje *m* **1.** (*cosmético, medicamento*) mixture **2.** *pey* concoction

melancolía *f* melancholy

melancólico, -a I. *adj* melancholic **II.** *m, f* melancholic person

melanina *f* melanin

melanoma *m* MED melanoma

melena *f* **1.** (*crin*) mane **2.** (*pelo*) long hair (*shoulder-length or longer, worn loose*)*;* **soltarse la ~** *t. fig* to let one's hair down

melenudo, -a I. *adj* long-haired **II.** *m, f* long-haired person; *pey* (*haragán*) layabout

melifluo, -a *adj* mellifluous

melillense I. *adj* of/from Melilla **II.** *mf* native/inhabitant of Melilla

melindre *m* **1.** (*con miel y harina*) fried honeyed pastry; (*con mazapán*) marzipan sweet **2.** *pl* (*delicadeza exagerada*) mincing ways *pl;* (*afectada*) affectation; **hacer ~s** to affect

melindroso, -a I. *adj* (*delicado*) dainty; (*afectado*) affected **II.** *m, f* (*persona delicada*) dainty person; (*afectada*) affected person

melisa *f* lemon balm

mella *f* **1.** (*hendidura*) nick **2.** (*hueco*) gap **3.** (*merma*) decrease; **hacer ~** to make an impression

mellar *vt* **1.** (*hacer mellas*) to nick **2.** (*disminuir*) to shrink

mellizo, -a I. *adj* **1.** (*gemelo*) twin **2.** (*igual*) identical **II.** *m, f* twin

melocotón *m* **1.** (*fruto*) peach **2.** *inf* (*borrachera*) **anoche cogí un melocotón** I got plastered last night

melocotonero *m* peach tree

melodía *f* melody

melódico, -a *adj* melodic

melodrama *m* melodrama

melodramático, -a *adj* melodramatic

melómano, -a *m, f* music lover

melón *m* **1.** (*fruto*) melon **2.** *inf* (*cabeza*) nut, noggin *Am* **3.** *pl vulg* (*pechos*) tits *pl,* boobs *pl*

melón, -ona *m, f inf* nutter

melopea *f inf* (*borrachera*) drunkenness

meloso, -a *adj* sweet

membrana *f* membrane; **~ mucosa** mucous membrane

membrete *m* letterhead

membrillo *m* (*árbol*) quince tree; (*fruto*) quince; **carne** [*o* **dulce**] **de ~** quince jelly

membrudo, -a *adj* brawny

memela *f Méx* GASTR *thin maize tortilla*

memo, -a I. *adj* idiotic **II.** *m, f* idiot

memorable *adj* memorable

memorándum *m* <memorandos> memorandum

memoria *f* **1.** (*facultad, recuerdo*) memory; **a la** [*o* **en**] **~ de** in memory of; **de ~** by heart; **flaco de ~** forgetful; **hacer ~** to try and remember; **traer a la ~** to bring to mind; **venir a la ~** to come to mind **2.** (*informe*) report **3.** INFOR memory **4.** *pl* (*autobiografía*) autobiography

memorial *m* **1.** (*petición*) petition **2.** (*agenda*) notebook **3.** (*boletín*) newsletter

memorizar <z→c> *vt* **1.** (*aprender*) to memorize **2.** INFOR to store

mena *f* MIN ore

menaje *m* household furnishings *pl;* **~ de cocina** kitchen utensils

mención *f* mention; **digno de ~** worth mentioning; **hacer ~ de** to mention

mencionar *vt* to mention

menda I. *pron pers, inf* yours truly; **aquí el** [*o* **este**] **~ no dijo nada** yours truly didn't say anything **II.** *pron indef, inf* **un ~** a guy

mendicante I. *adj* mendicant **II.** *mf* beggar

mendicidad *f* begging; **vivir de la ~** to live by begging

mendigar <g→gu> *vi, vt* **~ algo** to beg for sth

mendigo, -a *m, f* beggar

mendrugo *m* **1.** (*trozo de pan*) crust **2.** *inf* (*torpe*) clodhopper

menear I. *vt* to move; (*cabeza*) to shake; **~ la cola** to wag one's tail **II.** *vr:* **~se 1.** (*moverse*) to move **2.** *inf* (*apresurarse*) to get a move on **3. meneársela** *vulg* to wank *Brit,* to jerk off *Am*

meneo *m* **1.** (*brusco*) jolt **2.** *inf* (*vapuleo*) beating; **dar un ~ a alguien** to give sb a beating

menester *m* **1.** (*necesidad*) need; **ser ~** to be necessary; **haber ~ de algo** to need sth **2.** *pl* (*tareas*) jobs *pl*

menesteroso, -a I. *adj* needy **II.** *m, f* needy person

menestra *f* vegetable stew

menestral(a) *m(f)* artisan

mengano, -a *m, f* **fulano y ~** so-and-so

mengua *f* **1.** (*disminución*) decrease; **sin ~ de** without a diminishing of; JUR without detriment to **2.** (*carencia*) lack; **sin ~** sufficient **3.** (*descrédito*) discredit

menguante *f* **1.** (*marea*) ebb; (*estiaje*) low water level **2.** (*mengua*) decrease

menguar <gu→gü> **I.** *vi* to diminish **II.** *vt* to decrease; (*punto*) to reduce

meninge *f* ANAT meninx, meninges *pl;* **me estrujé las ~s** *inf* I racked my brains

meningitis *f inv* MED meningitis

menisco *m* ANAT meniscus

menopausia *f* MED menopause, change of life

menor I. *adj* **1.** (*tamaño*) smaller; **~ que** smaller than; (*número*) smaller; **al por ~** COM retail; **no dar la ~ importancia a algo** not to give sth the least importance; **Asia Menor** Asia Minor **2.** (*edad*) younger; **~ que** younger than; **~ de edad** underage; **el ~ de mis hermanos** the youngest of my brothers **3.** MÚS minor; **tono ~** minor key; **tercera ~** minor third **II.** *mf* (*persona*) minor; **esta película no**

M

es apta para ~es this film is not suitable for under-eighteens
Menorca *f* Minorca
menorista I. *adj Chile, Méx* retail II. *mf Chile, Méx* (*minorista*) retailer
menorquín, -ina *adj, m, f* Minorcan
menos I. *adv* 1. (*contrario de más*) less; **a ~ que** unless; **el/la ~** the least; **el coche (el) ~ caro** the least expensive car; **eso es lo de ~** that is the least important thing; **lo ~** the least; **al** [*o* **por lo**] **~** at least; **aún ~** even less; **cuanto ~... (tanto) más** the less ... the more; **de ~** short; **echar de ~** to miss; **en ~ de nada** in no time; **ir a ~** to decrease; **~ de 20 personas** fewer than 20 people; **~ de una hora** less than an hour; **~ mal** thank goodness; **¡ni mucho ~!** not at all!; **son las ocho ~ diez** it's ten minutes to eight; **cada vez ~ tiempo/casos** less and less time/fewer and fewer cases 2. MAT minus 3. (*excepto*) except; **todo ~ eso** anything but that II. *m* MAT minus
menoscabar *vt* 1. (*disminuir*) to diminish 2. (*dañar*) to impair; *fig* to damage 3. (*desacreditar*) to discredit
menoscabo *m* 1. (*disminución*) decrease 2. (*daño*) impairment; *fig* damage; **sufrir ~** to suffer damage
menospreciable *adj* despicable
menospreciar *vt* 1. (*despreciar*) to underrate 2. (*desdeñar*) to despise 3. (*subestimar*) to underestimate
menosprecio *m* 1. (*desprecio*) underrating 2. (*desdén*) scorn 3. (*subestimación*) underestimate
mensaje *m* message; **~ de error** INFOR error message; **~ (de) radio** radio communication; **~ de socorro** SOS message
mensajería *f* messenger [*o* courier] service
mensajero, -a I. *adj* messenger; **paloma mensajera** messenger [*o* carrier] pigeon II. *m, f* messenger
menso, -a *adj Méx* (*necio*) stupid
menstruación *f* menstruation
menstruar <*1. pres:* menstrúo> *vi* to menstruate
mensual *adj* monthly; **revista ~** monthly (magazine)
mensualidad *f* 1. (*sueldo*) monthly salary 2. (*paga*) monthly payment; (*compra aplazada*) monthly instalment *Brit* [*o* installment *Am*]; **~ del alquiler** month's rent
mensurar *vt* to measure
menta *f* 1. (*planta*) mint 2. (*infusión*) mint tea 3. (*extracto*) menthol; **caramelo de ~** mint
mentado, -a *adj* well-known; (*mencionado*) above-mentioned
mental *adj* mental; **cálculo ~** mental arithmetic
mentalidad *f* mentality
mentalizar <z→c> I. *vt* (*preparar*) to prepare (mentally); (*concienciar*) to make aware; **~ a alguien de algo** to make sb aware of sth II. *vr:* **~se** (*prepararse*) to prepare oneself (mentally); (*concienciarse*) to make oneself aware
mentar <e→ie> *vt* to mention
mente *f* 1. (*pensamiento*) mind; **tener en (la) ~** to have in mimd; **no puedo quitarme esa idea de la ~** I cannot get that idea out of my head; **el nombre se me ha ido de la ~** the name has gone right out of my head; **tengo la ~ en blanco** my mind is a complete blank; **traer a la ~** to bring to mind 2. (*intelecto*) intellect
mentecato, -a I. *adj* silly II. *m, f* fool
mentir *irr como sentir vi* 1. (*engañar*) to lie; **miente más que habla** he/she is a compulsive liar; **¡miento!** I tell a lie!, I am wrong! 2. (*inducir a error*) to be misleading
mentira *f* (*embuste*) lie; **~ piadosa** white lie; **¡parece ~!** I can hardly believe it!
mentiroso, -a I. *adj* (*persona*) lying II. *m, f* liar
mentís *m inv* denial; **dar un ~ a algo** to deny sth
mentol *m* menthol
mentón *m* chin
mentor *m* mentor
menú *m* <menús> *t.* INFOR menu
menudear I. *vi* to be frequent II. *vt* to do frequently; **~ sus visitas** to make frequent visits
menudencia *f* 1. (*pequeñez*) trifle 2. (*meticulosidad*) meticulousness 3. *pl* (*del cerdo*) pork products *pl*
menudillos *mpl* (*despojos*) giblets *pl*
menudo, -a *adj* 1. (*minúsculo*) minuscule 2. (*pequeño y delgado*) slight 3. (*fútil*) futile 4. (*exclamación*) **¡menuda película!** what a film!; **¡~ lío has armado!** what a fuss you have created! 5. COM **por** [*o* **a**] **la menuda** retail ▸**a ~** often
meñique I. *m* little finger, pinkie, pinky *Am* II. *adj inf* tiny
meollo *m* 1. (*sesos*) brains *pl* 2. (*médula*) marrow 3. (*fundamento*) essence, crux
mequetrefe *m inf* good-for-nothing
meramente *adv* merely
mercachifle *m pey* 1. (*comerciante*) hawker 2. (*avaro*) moneygrubber
mercader *m* merchant; **~ de grueso** wholesaler
mercadería *f* merchandise
mercadillo *m* street market, flea market
mercado *m* market; **~ de capitales** investment market; **~ de divisas** foreign exchange market; **~ exterior/interior** overseas/domestic market; **el ~ de Madrid** the Madrid market; **~ alcista/bajista** bull/bear market; **~ de trabajo** labour market; **~ único europeo** European Single Market; **~ de valores** securities market; **hay ~ los sábados** there is a market on Saturdays
mercancía *f* goods *pl;* **tren de ~s** goods [*o* freight] train
mercante I. *adj* mercantile II. *mf* (*barco*) merchantman

mercantil *adj* mercantile

merced *f* mercy; ~ **a** thanks to; **estar a ~ de alguien** to be at sb's mercy

mercenario, **-a** *adj, m, f* mercenary

mercería *f* **1.**(*tienda*) haberdasher's shop *Brit,* notions store *Am* **2.**(*artículos*) haberdashery *Brit,* notions *pl Am*

mercurio *m* mercury

Mercurio *m* Mercury

merecedor(a) *adj* deserving; **hacerse ~ de algo** to earn sth

merecer *irr como crecer* **I.** *vt* **1.**(*ser digno de*) to deserve; **merece que lo ahorquen** he deserves to be hung; **merece respeto de nuestra parte** he/she deserves our respect; **este libro merece mención** this book deserves a mention **2.**(*valer*) to be worthy of; **no merece la pena** it is not worth it **II.** *vi* ~ **bien de algo** to be deserving of sth **III.** *vr:* **~se** to deserve

merecido *m* deserts *pl;* **se llevó su ~** he got his just deserts

merendar <e→ie> **I.** *vt* to have for tea, to have for an afternoon snack **II.** *vi* to have tea, to have an afternoon snack; (*en el campo*) to picnic **III.** *vr:* **~se** *inf* to wangle; **~se a alguien** to get the better of sb

merendero *m* picnic area

merengue *m* **1.**(*dulce*) meringue **2.**(*persona débil*) weakling **3.** *CSur, inf*(*lío*) mess

meridiano *m* meridian

meridiano, **-a** *adj* **1.**(*del mediodía*) midday **2.**(*evidente*) clear

meridional **I.** *adj* south; **Andalucía está en la España ~** Andalucía is in southern Spain **II.** *mf* southerner

merienda *f* **1.**(*comida por la tarde*) tea, afternoon snack **2.**(*picnic*) picnic; **ir de ~** to go for a picnic; ~ **de negros** *fig* free-for-all

mérito *m* **1.**(*merecimiento*) merit; **hacer ~s** to prove oneself worthy; **callarse sus ~s** to hide one's light under a bushel **2.**(*valor*) worth; **de ~** (*obra*) excellent; (*persona*) worthy

meritorio, **-a** **I.** *adj* meritorious **II.** *m, f* (*aprendiz*) apprentice; (*empleado sin sueldo*) unpaid employee [*o* trainee]

merlo *m AmL* ZOOL wrasse

merluza *f* **1.** ZOOL hake **2.** *vulg* (*borrachera*) **coger una buena ~** to get sloshed; **estar (con la) ~** to be sloshed

merluzo, **-a** *adj inf* silly

merma *f* decrease; ~ **de peso** loss of weight

mermar **I.** *vt* to lessen; (*sueldo*) to cut; ~ **peso** to reduce weight **II.** *vi, vr:* **~se** to decrease

mermelada *f* jam; ~ **de naranja** marmalade

mero **I.** *adv* **1.** *AmC, Méx* (*pronto*) soon **2.** *Méx* (*muy*) very **3.** *Méx* (*precisamente*) precisely **II.** *m* **1.** ZOOL grouper **2.** *Méx* (*jefe*) boss

mero, **-a** *adj* **1.**(*sencillo*) simple **2.**(*sin nada más*) mere; **la mera verdad** the plain truth **3.** *Méx* (*preciso*) precise **4.** *Méx* (*propio*) own

merodear *vi* to prowl; ~ **por un sitio** to hang about a place

merolico, **-a** *m, f Méx* **1.**(*vendedor charlatán*) quack **2.**(*persona charlatana*) chatterer

mes *m* **1.**(*período*) month; **a principios/a mediados/a fin(al)es de ~** at the beginning/in the middle/at the end of the month; **5.000 pesetas al ~** 5000 pesetas a month; **todos los ~es** every month; **el ~ corriente** this month; **el ~ que viene** next month; **el ~ pasado** last month; **hace un ~** a month ago; **con un ~ de anticipo** a month's salary in advance **2.**(*sueldo*) ~ (**de trabajo**) monthly salary **3.** *inf* (*menstruación*) period; **tengo el ~** I have my period

mesa *f* **1.**(*mueble*) table; ~ **de despacho** office desk; ~ **de tertulia** coffee table; **vino de ~** table wine; **bendecir la ~** to say grace; **poner la ~** to lay [*o* set] the table; **quitar la ~** to clear the table; **en la ~** (*comiendo*) at the table; **¡a la ~!** food's ready!; **servir una ~** to serve a table; **tener a alguien a ~ y a mantel** to give sb free board; **vivir** [*o* **estar**] **a ~ puesta** to live a life of leisure **2.**(*junta directiva*) board **3.** POL ~ **electoral** *officials in charge of a polling station* **4.** GEO plateau **5.** INFOR ~ **digitalizadora** digitizer **6.**(*pensión*) board; ~ **y cama** board and lodging

mesar *vt, vr* **~se los pelos,** ~ **sus pelos** to tear one's hair out

mesero, **-a** *m, f Méx* (*camarero*) waiter *m,* waitress *f*

meseta *f* GEO plateau

mesías *m* Messiah

mesilla *f* small table; ~ **de noche** bedside table, nightstand *Am*

mesón *m* inn, tavern

mesonero, **-a** *m, f* innkeeper

mestizo, **-a** **I.** *adj* **1.**(*entre blancos e indios*) mestizo **2.**(*entre dos razas*) mixed-race **II.** *m, f* **1.**(*entre blancos e indios*) mestizo **2.**(*entre dos razas*) person of mixed race

> A **mestizo** in Latin America means a person of mixed race whose parents were of white (i.e. European) and Indian origin. (In Brazil, **mestizos** are known as **mamelucos**.)

mesura *f* **1.**(*moderación*) moderation **2.**(*cortesía*) courtesy, civility **3.**(*calma*) calm

meta[1] *f t. fig* winning post; (*portería*) goal; **la ~ de su vida** his/her aim in life; **fijarse una ~** to set oneself a goal

meta[2] *mf* (*portero*) goalkeeper *Brit,* goaltender *Am*

metabolismo *m* metabolism

metadona *f* methadon(e)

metafísica *f* FILOS metaphysics

metafísico, **-a** **I.** *adj* **1.** FILOS metaphysical **2.**(*difícil*) subtle **II.** *m, f* metaphysician

metáfora *f* metaphor

metafórico, **-a** *adj* metaphorical

metal *m* **1.**(*material*) metal; ~ **noble** precious metal; ~ **pesado** heavy metal **2.** (*de voz*) timbre **3.** (*instrumento*) brass instrument **4.** (*dinero*) **el vil** ~ filthy lucre

metálico *m* (*monedas*) coins *pl;* **en** ~ in cash; **premio en** ~ cash prize

metálico, **-a** *adj* metallic; **tela metálica** (metal) screening

metalurgia *f* metallurgy

metalúrgico, **-a** **I.** *adj* metallurgical; **industria metalúrgica** metallurgical industry **II.** *m, f* metallurgist

metamorfosear **I.** *vt* to transform **II.** *vr:* ~**se** to metamorphose

metamorfosis *f inv* **1.** ZOOL, GEO metamorphosis **2.** (*en una persona*) transformation

metano *m* methane

metástasis *f inv* MED metastasis

metedura *f* **¡vaya** ~ **de pata!** *inf* what a clanger *Brit* [*o* blooper *Am*]!

metelón, **-ona** *adj Méx* meddling

meteórico, **-a** *adj* **1.** METEO meteorological **2.** (*rápido*) meteoric

meteorismo *m* flatulence

meteorito *m* meteorite

meteoro *m* **1.** METEO meteorological phenomenon **2.** ASTR meteor

meteorología *f sin pl* meteorology

meteorológico, **-a** *adj* meteorological; **informe** ~ weather forcast; **estación meteorológica** weather station

meteorólogo, **-a** *m, f* meteorologist; TV, RADIO weather forecaster, weatherman

meter **I.** *vt* **1.** (*introducir*) to insert; (*poner*) to put; ~ **en una caja** to put in a box; **¡mete el enchufe!** put the plug in!; ~ **un clavo en la pared** to hammer a nail into the wall; ~ **el coche en el garaje** to put the car in the garage; ~ **a alguien en la cárcel** to put sb in jail **2.** (*invertir*) to invest; ~ **en el banco** to put in the bank **3.** (*en costura*) to take in **4.** DEP ~ **un gol** to score a goal **5.** (*de contrabando*) to smuggle **6.** *inf* (*encasquetar*) to palm off; (*vender*) to sell; (*enjaretar*) to foist; **nos metió una película aburridísima** he foisted a really boring film on us; **le metieron tres meses de cárcel** they gave him/her three months in jail **7.** *inf* (*pegar*) ~ **un puñetazo a alguien** to punch sb **8.** (*provocar*) ~ **miedo/un susto a alguien** to frighten/startle sb; ~ **prisa a alguien** to hurry sb (up); ~ **ruido** to be noisy **9.** (*hacer participar*) to involve; ~ **a toda la familia en el asunto** to involve the whole family in the matter **10.** (*emplear*) to employ; ~ **a alguien a fregar platos** to set sb to work washing dishes; ~ **a una chica de peluquera** to put a girl to work as a hairdresser ►**a** <u>**todo**</u> ~ *inf* as fast as possible **II.** *vr:* ~**se** **1.** (*introducirse*) to put; ~**se el dedo en la nariz** to stick one's finger in one's nose; **se lo ha metido en la cabeza que...** he/she has got it into his/her head that ...; **¡métetelo donde te quepa!** *vulg* go and stick it up your arse *Brit* [*o* ass *Am*]! **2.** (*entrar en un lugar*) to enter; **lo vi** ~**se en un cine** I saw him go into the cinema; ~**se entre la gente** to mingle with the people; **se metió en el armario** he/she got into the wardrobe; **¿dónde se habrá metido?** where has he/she got to?; ~**se para adentro** to go inside **3.** (*entrar indebidamente*) to enter unlawfully **4.** *inf* (*aceptar algo*) **¿cuándo se te** ~**á esto en la cabeza?** when will you get it into your head? **5.** (*inmiscuirse*) to meddle; **¡no te metas donde no te llaman!** mind your own business! **6.** (*provocar*) ~**se con alguien** to provoke sb **7.** (*comenzar un oficio*) ~**se monja** to become a nun; ~**se a actor** to become an actor

metiche *adj Méx* (*entrometido*) meddlesome

meticuloso, **-a** **I.** *adj* meticulous **II.** *m, f* meticulous person

metida *f inf* (*avance*) **dar una** ~ **a algo** to give sth a boost; **tengo que darle una buena** ~ **a los estudios** I have to give my studies a real boost

metido *m inf* (*reprimenda*) ticking off; **pegar un** ~ **a alguien** to give sb a ticking off

metido, **-a** *adj* **1.** (*introvertido*) ~ **en sí mismo** withdrawn **2.** (*envuelto*) involved; **sigue estando muy** ~ **en el negocio a pesar de su edad** he is still very involved in the business in spite of his age **3.** (*con abundantes*) ~ **en carnes** chubby; ~ **en años** elderly **4.** *inf* (*relación*) **está muy** ~ **con esa chica** he is very involved with that girl; **está muy** ~ **con la dirección de la empresa** he is in with the management of the company **5.** (*puesto*) **la llave está metida** the key is in

metl *m Méx* (*agave*) agave

metódico, **-a** **I.** *adj* methodical **II.** *m, f* methodical person

metodismo *m* Methodism

metodista *adj, mf* Methodist

método *m* **1.** (*sistema*) method; **proceder con** ~ to proceed methodically **2.** (*libro*) manual; **un** ~ **de guitarra** a guitar manual

metodología *f* methodology

metomentodo **I.** *adj inv* nosy **II.** *mf inv, inf* nosy parker; **ser un** ~ to be a real busybody

metraje *m* length; **película de largo** ~ feature-length film; **película de corto** ~ short (film)

metralla *f* **1.** (*munición*) shell; **fuego de** ~ shellfire **2.** (*trozos*) shrapnel

metralleta *f* sub-machine gun, tommy gun

métrica *f* LIT metrics

métrico, **-a** *adj* metric

metro *m* **1.** (*unidad*) metre *Brit,* meter *Am;* ~ **cuadrado** square metre *Brit* [*o* meter *Am*]; ~ **cúbico** cubic metre *Brit* [*o* meter *Am*] **2.** (*para medir*) ruler; ~ **de cinta** tape measure; ~ **plegable** folding ruler **3.** FERRO underground *Brit,* subway *Am* **4.** *t.* MÚS (*poesía*) metre *Brit,* meter *Am*

metrópoli *f* (*urbe*) metropolis; (*capital*) capital

metropolitano *m* FERRO underground *Brit,* subway *Am*
metropolitano, -a *adj* **1.**(*de la capital*) metropolitan **2.**(*de la urbe*) city
mexicano, -a *adj, m, f v.* **mejicano**
México *m* Mexico

México or **Méjico** (official title: **Estados Unidos Mexicanos**) lies in Central America and borders the USA in the north. The capital, **Ciudad de México** (Mexico City), has almost twenty million inhabitants. Spanish is the official language of the country and the monetary unit is the **peso**. The original inhabitants of Mexico, the **aztecas** (Aztecs), referred to themselves as **mexica**.

mezcal *m Méx* BOT mescal
mezcla *f* **1.**(*sustancia*) mixture; ~ **de carburantes** blend of fuel; ~ **explosiva** *t. fig* explosive mixture **2.**(*acto*) mixing **3.**(*tela*) mixed fibres *Brit,* mixed fibers *Am;* **sin** ~ pure **4.**(*argamasa*) mortar
mezclar I. *vt* **1.**(*unir*) to blend; GASTR (*añadir*) to mix **2.**(*revolver*) to muddle; (*confundir*) to mix up **3.**(*involucrar*) to involve **II.** *vr:* ~**se 1.**(*inmiscuirse*) to meddle **2.**(*en un grupo de personas*) ~**se entre los espectadores** to mingle with the spectators; ~**se con gente de mucho dinero** to mix with wealthy people **3.**(*revolverse*) to mix
mezcolanza *f pey* hotchpotch *Brit,* hodgepodge *Am*
mezquindad *f* **1.**(*tacañería*) stinginess, meanness *Brit* **2.**(*acto vil*) mean action
mezquino, -a I. *adj* **1.**(*tacaño*) stingy, mean *Brit* **2.**(*innoble*) ignoble **3.**(*insuficiente*) inadequate **4.**(*despreciable*) despicable **5.**(*miserable*) small-minded **II.** *m, f* miser
mezquita *f* mosque
mg. *abr de* **miligramo** mg
mi I. *adj* (*antepuesto*) my; ~ **amigo/casa** my friend/house; ~**s amigos** my friends **II.** *m inv* MÚS E; ~ **mayor** E major; ~ **menor** E minor
mí *pron pers* me; **a** ~ (*objeto directo*) me; (*objeto indirecto*) to me; **para** ~ for me; **¿y a ~ qué?** so what?; **para** ~ (**que**)… I think (that) …; **por** ~ as far as I'm concerned; **por** ~ **que se quede** as far as I'm concerned he/she can stay; **por** ~ **mismo** by myself; **¡a** ~ **con esas!** don't give me that!; **¡a** ~**!** (*¡socorro!*) help!
miaja *f* crumb
miau miaow *Brit,* meow *Am*
mica *f* **1.** MIN mica **2.** *And* (*orinal*) chamber pot **3.** *AmC, inf* (*borrachera*) drunkenness
micción *f* urination
miche *m* **1.** *CRi* (*pendencia*) brawl **2.** *Chile* (*juego*) game of marbles
michelín *m* roll of fat, spare tyre *Brit* [*o* tire *Am*]
mico *m* **1.** ZOOL long-tailed monkey **2.** *inf* (*persona fea*) hideous person **3.** *inf* (*niño*) little monkey, tyke *Am* ►**dar** ~ **a alguien** *inf* (*dejar plantado*) to stand sb up; **dar el** ~ **a alguien** *inf* (*engañar*) to take sb in; **quedarse hecho un** ~ *inf* (*avergonzado*) to be ashamed; **volverse** ~ **para hacer algo** *inf* to go mad [*o* crazy] trying to do sth
micro *m* (*micrófono*) mike
microbio *m* microbe
microbús *m* minibus **microchip** *m* microchip **microficha** *f* microfiche **microfilm** *m* <microfilm(e)s> microfilm
microfilmar *vt* to microfilm
micrófono *m* microphone
microonda *f t.* FÍS (*cocina*) microwave; **horno (de)** ~**s** microwave (oven) **microorganismo** *m* micro-organism
microscópico, -a *adj* microscopic; **de tamaño** ~ *inf* of microscopic size
microscopio *m* microscope; ~ **de 60 aumentos** microscope with x60 magnification; ~ **electrónico** electron microscope
microtenis *m inv, AmL* table tennis
miedo *m* **1.**(*angustia*) fear; **por** ~ **a** [*o* **de**] for fear of; **por** ~ **de que** +*subj* for fear that; **meter** ~ **a alguien** to frighten sb; **dar** ~ to be frightening; **me entró** [*o* **dio**] ~ I became frightened; **morirse de** ~ to be petrified; **cagarse de** ~ *vulg* to shit oneself (with fear) **2.** *inf* (*maravilloso*) **de** ~ terrific; **el concierto estuvo de** ~ the concert was terrific **3.** *inf* (*terrible*) **de** ~ dreadful; **hace un frío de** ~ it is dreadfully cold ►**al que mal vive, el** ~ **le sigue** *prov* ≈ those who act badly always live in fear; **a quien** ~ **han, lo suyo le dan** *prov* ≈ fear is the tool of a tyrant
miedoso, -a I. *adj ser* fearful **II.** *m, f* apprehensive person, scaredy-cat *inf*
miel *f* (*de abeja*) honey; ~ **blanca** bees' honey; **luna de** ~ honeymoon; **quedarse con la** ~ **en los labios** to be left wanting more; **si encima me pagan el viaje ¡~ sobre hojuelas!** if they also pay for the trip it would be the icing on the cake!; **hacerse de** ~ to go all sugary ►**no hay** ~ **sin hiel** *prov* there is no rose without a thorn; ~ **sobre hojuelas** even better; **hazte de** ~ **y te comerán las moscas** *prov* ≈ if you are too good people will take advantage of you
mielga *f* **1.** BOT alfalfa **2.** ZOOL dogfish
miembro I. *m* **1.** *pl* (*extremidades*) limbs *pl* **2.**(*pene*) ~ (**viril**) male member **3.** *t.* LING, MAT (*socio*) member; **no** ~ non-member; ~ **de pleno derecho** full member; **hacerse** ~ **de** to join **4.**(*parte*) component **II.** *adj* **los Estados** ~**s** the member states
mientes *fpl* thoughts *pl;* **caer en** (**las**) ~ to come to mind; **parar** [*o* **poner**] ~ **en algo** to give sth great thought; **traer a las** ~ to recall; **todo se le vino a las** ~ everything came back to him/her; **¡ni por** ~**!** never!
mientras I. *adv* meanwhile; ~ (**tanto**) in the meantime **II.** *conj* ~ (**que**) while; ~ (**que**) +*subj* as long as; ~ **se ríe no se llora** you cannot laugh and cry at the same time; ~ **más le**

M

dan más pide el niño the more the child gets, the more he/she wants
miércoles *m inv* Wednesday; ~ **de ceniza** Ash Wednesday; ~ **santo** Easter Wednesday; *v.t.* **lunes**
mierda *f vulg* **1.** (*heces*) shit **2.** (*porquería*) muck **3.** (*persona, cosa despreciable*) **el maestro nuevo es una** ~ the new teacher is lousy; **esta película es una** ~ this film is a piece of shit; **¡2.000 pesetas, una ~!** 2000 pesetas, that's peanuts!; **es una** ~ **de coche** the car is a piece of junk; **no valer una** ~ to be a load of crap; **cubrirse de** ~ to discredit oneself **4.** (*borrachera*) **¡vaya** ~ **que cogí ayer!** God, I got sloshed yesterday! **5.** (*expresiones*) **¡~!** shit!; **¡una ~!** like hell!; **¡a la ~!** to hell with it!; **¡(vete) a la ~!** get lost!; **¡eso te importa una ~!** you don't give a damn about that!; **mandar a alguien a la** ~ to tell sb to go to hell; **¿qué** ~ **ocurre?** what the hell is going on?; **irse a la** ~ to go to the dogs; **no comerse ni (una)** ~ to get absolutely nowhere
mies *f* **1.** (*cereal maduro*) (ripe) corn **2.** (*temporada*) harvest (time) **3.** *pl* (*campos*) cornfields *pl*
miga *f* **1.** (*pan*) bread (*not the crust*); (*trocito*) crumb; **hacer buenas/malas ~s con alguien** to get on well/badly with sb; **hacer ~s a alguien** to leave sb in a sorry state; **estar hecho** ~ (*cansado*) to be shattered; **hacer ~s** to destroy **2.** (*esencia*) essence; **esto tiene su** ~ there is something behind this
migaja *f* **1.** (*trocito*) crumb; **una** ~ **de algo** a scrap of sth **2.** *pl* (*sobras*) leftovers *pl*
migración *f* **1.** (*emigración*) emigration **2.** ZOOL migration
migraña *f* migraine
mijo *m* millet
mil I. *adj inv* thousand; **dos** ~ **millones** two billion; **ya se lo he dicho** ~ **veces** I have already told him/her hundreds of times **II.** *m* **1.** (*número*) thousand **2.** (*cantidad indefinida*) **~es** thousands; **a ~es** by the thousand; **~es y ~es** thousands and thousands; **varios ~es de dólares** several thousand dollars; **a las** ~ **(y quinientas)** very late; **pasar las** ~ **y una** to be a huge amount
milagro *m* miracle; **hacer ~s** to work wonders; **contar la vida y ~s de alguien** to tell all the gory details about sb's life; **esta vez se escapó de** ~ this time he/she had a lucky escape; **si sales de ésta, solo saldrás de** ~ if you get out of this, it will be a miracle; ~ **(sería) que** +*subj* it would be a miracle if
milagroso, -a *adj* **1.** miraculous **2.** (*maravilloso*) marvellous *Brit,* marvelous *Am*
Milán *m* Milan
milanés, -esa I. *adj* Milanese **II.** *m, f* Milanese
milanesa *f* breaded escalope
milano *m* red kite
milenario *m* millennium
milenario, -a *adj* millennial
milenio *m* millennium
milenrama *f* yarrow
mili *f inf* military service; **ir a** [*o* **hacer**] **la** ~ to do military service; **¿ya hiciste la ~?** have you done your military service?; **tener mucha** ~ *inf* to be an old hand
milibar *m* FÍS millibar
milicia *f* **1.** (*tropa*) military; ~ **nacional** (*ciudadanos*) militia **2.** (*actividades militares*) military operation
miligramo *m* milligram **mililitro** *m* millilitre *Brit,* milliliter *Am* **milímetro** *m* millimetre *Brit,* millimeter *Am*
militante I. *adj* militant **II.** *mf* (*de un partido*) militant, active member
militar I. *vi* **1.** (*cumplir el servicio*) to serve **2.** (*en un partido*) to be an active member of; ~ **en favor de/contra algo** to campaign for/against sth **II.** *adj* military; **los altos mandos ~es** the military high command **III.** *m* soldier
milla *f* mile; ~ **marina** nautical mile
millar *m* thousand; **protestaron a ~es** they protested by the thousand
millo *m AmC, Méx* type of millet
millón *m* million; **mil millones** a billion; **cuatro millones de habitantes** four million inhabitants; **un** ~ **de gracias** a million thanks
millonada *f inf* (*muchísimo dinero*) fortune
millonario, -a *m, f* millionaire, millionairess *f*
milonga *f* **1.** MÚS popular dance **2.** *And, CSur* (*fiesta*) party **3.** *And, CSur, inf* (*trola, mentira*) tall story
milpa *f AmL* **1.** (*campo*) cornfield **2.** (*planta*) maize *Brit,* corn *Am*
milpiés *m inv* millipede
mimar *vt* **1.** (*consentir*) to indulge; (*excesivamente*) to spoil **2.** (*favorecer*) to favour *Brit,* to favor *Am*
mimbre *m* **1.** (*material*) wicker; **de** ~ wicker; **muebles de** ~ wicker furniture; **silla de** ~ wicker chair **2.** (*ramita*) piece of wicker
mimbrera *f* osier; (*sauce*) willow
mimeografiar <*1. pres:* mimeografío> *vt AmL* to mimeograph
mimeógrafo *m AmL* mimeograph
mimetismo *m* mimicry
mímica *f* **1.** (*facial*) mime **2.** (*señas*) sign language **3.** (*ademanes*) gesticulation
mímico, -a *adj* imitative; TEAT mimetic
mimo *m* **1.** (*actor*) mimic; **hacer** ~ **de alguien** to mimic sb **2.** (*caricia*) caress; **necesitar mucho** ~ to need a lot of affection **3.** (*condescencia*) spoiling; **le dan demasiado** ~ they spoil him **4.** (*con cariño*) **realizo mi trabajo con** ~ I carry out my work with love
mimosa *f* mimosa
mimoso, -a *adj* **1.** (*mimado*) spoilt **2.** *ser* (*cariñoso*) affectionate **3.** *estar* (*apegado*) clinging
mina *f* **1.** MIN mine; ~ **de carbón** coal mine; **este negocio es una** ~ this business is a gold mine **2.** (*pasillo subterráneo*) underground passage **3.** (*explosivo*) mine; ~ **de mar** under-

water mine; ~ **de tierra** landmine **4.** (*de lápiz, bolígrafo*) lead

minar **I.** *vt* **1.** (*excavar, colocar minas*) to mine **2.** (*debilitar*) to undermine **II.** *vr:* **~se** *inf* (*hartarse*) to become fed up

minarete *m* minaret

mineral **I.** *adj* mineral; **agua** ~ mineral water **II.** *m* **1.** GEO mineral **2.** MIN ore

mineralogía *f sin pl* mineralogy

minería *f* mining

minero, **-a** **I.** *adj* mining **II.** *m, f* (*trabajador*) miner

minga **I.** *interj RíoPl, inf* no way!, like hell! **II.** *f And* communal work

mingaco *m Chile: communal work done by neighbours*

miniatura *f* miniature

minibús *m* minibus **minifalda** *f* miniskirt

minifundio *m* smallholding

minifundista *mf* smallholder

minigolf *m* minigolf

minimizar <z→c> *vt* **1.** (*simplificar*) to minimize **2.** (*subestimar*) to underestimate

mínimo *m* minimum; ~ **de presión** METEO trough of low pressure; **un** ~ **de respeto** a minimum of respect; **como** ~ (*cantidad*) as a minimum; **como** ~ **podrías llamar por teléfono** you could at least phone; **reducir al** ~ to reduce to the bare minimum

mínimo, **-a** *adj superl de* **pequeño** minimum; **las temperaturas mínimas** the minimum temperatures; **cifra mínima** minimum figure; **la mínima obligación posible** the slightest obligation possible; **sin el más** ~ **ruido** without the least noise; **no ayudar en lo más** ~ to be no help at all

minino, **-a** *m, f inf* pussy [*o* kitty] (cat)

miniprímer *m o f* hand blender

miniserie *f* miniseries

ministerial *adj* (*de minister*) ministerial; (*de gobierno*) governmental

ministerio *m* **1.** (*cartera, edificio*) ministry **2.** (*cargo*) ministerial office

ministro, **-a** *m, f* **1.** (*de un gobierno*) minister; **primera ministra** prime minister; ~ **sin cartera** minister without portfolio; **Ministro de Economía y Hacienda** Chancellor of the Exchequer *Brit,* Treasury Secretary *Am;* **Ministro de Educación y Ciencia** Education Minister *Brit,* Education Secretary *Am;* **Ministro del Interior** Home Secretary *Brit,* Secretary of the Interior *Am* **2.** JUR court official **3.** (*en la embajada*) diplomat

minivacaciones *fpl* short break **minivestido** *m* minidress

minoría *f* minority; ~ **de bloqueo** blocking minority; ~ **de edad** minority

minoridad *f* minority

minorista **I.** *adj* retail **II.** *mf* retailer

minoritario, **-a** *adj* minority

minucia *f* (*de poca importancia*) trifle

minuciosidad *f* meticulousness

minucioso, **-a** *adj* meticulous

minúscula *f* LING lower case; **en ~s** in lower case [*o* small] letters; **escribirse con** ~ to be written in lower case

minúsculo, **-a** *adj* **1.** (*muy pequeño*) minuscule, minute **2.** LING **letra minúscula** lower-case [*o* small] letter

minusvalía *f* **1.** (*física*) handicap, disability **2.** COM capital loss

minusválido, **-a** **I.** *adj* handicapped **II.** *m, f* handicapped person

minusvalorar *vt* to undervalue

minuta *f* **1.** (*cuenta*) lawyer's bill **2.** (*borrador*) rough draft; (*copia*) carbon copy **3.** (*apunte*) note **4.** (*menú*) menu

minutero *m* minute hand

minuto *m* minute; **sin perder un** ~ at once; **vuelvo en un** ~ I will be [*o* back in a minute] right back

mío, **-a** *pron pos* **1.** (*de mi propiedad*) mine; **el libro** ~ the book is mine; **la botella es mía** the bottle is mine; **¡ya es ~!** I have it! **2.** (*tras artículo*) **el ~/la mía** mine; **los ~s** (*cosas*) mine; (*parientes*) my family; **ésta es la mía** *inf* this is just what I want; **he vuelto a hacer una de las mías** I have been up to it again; **eso es lo** ~ that is my strong point **3.** (*tras substantivo*) of mine; **una amiga mía** a friend of mine; **¡amor ~!** my darling!; (**no**) **es culpa mía** it is (not) my fault

miocardio *m* ANAT myocardium

mioma *m* MED myoma, myogenic tumour *Brit* [*o* tumor *Am*]

miope **I.** *adj* myopic, short-sighted **II.** *mf* short-sighted person

miopía *f* myopia, short-sightedness

mira *f* **1.** (*para apuntar*) sight **2.** MIL watchtower; **estar en la** ~ **de alguien** to be in sb's sights **3.** (*mirada*) gaze; **pusieron la** ~ **en el cuadro/la chica** (*atención*) their gaze fixed on the picture/the girl; **he puesto la** ~ **en esa casa** (*aspirar*) I have set my sights on that house; **con amplias ~s** broad-minded; **de ~s estrechas** narrow-minded; **con ~s a** with a view to **4.** *(pl)* (*intención*) intention; **con ~s desinteresadas** disinterestedly

mirada *f* look; ~ **perdida** faraway look; **devorar con la** ~ to gaze hungrily at; **echar una** ~ **a algo** to glance at sth; **levantar la** ~ to look up; **apartar la** ~ to look away; **ser el blanco de las ~s** to be stared at; **volver la** ~ **atrás** to look back

mirado, **-a** *adj* **1.** (*respetuoso*) respectful **2.** *inf* (*delicado*) considerate **3.** (*cuidadoso*) discreet **4.** (*respetado*) **estar bien/mal** ~ (*persona*) to be well/badly thought of; **está mal** ~ **ir sin regalo** it is not the done thing to go without a present **5.** (*si bien se mira*) **bien ~, ...** all things considering [*o* considered], ...

mirador *m* **1.** (*balcón*) glassed-in balcony; (*ventana*) bay window **2.** (*atalaya*) viewpoint

miramiento *m* **1.** (*consideración*) consideration; **tener** ~ **con alguien** to have[*o* show] consideration for sb; **sin** ~ inconsiderately;

M

andar con ~**s** to tread carefully; **sin** ~**s de** without considering **2.** (*cuidado*) discretion; **sin** ~ indiscreetly **3.** (*timidez*) hesitation **4.** *pl* (*cortesías*) civilities *pl*, courtesies *pl*

mirar I. *vt* **1.** (*observar*) to observe; (*ver*) to look at; ~ **fijamente a alguien** to stare at sb; ~ **algo por encima** to give sth a quick look (over) **2.** (*buscar*) to look for **3.** (*prestar atención*) to watch; **mira bien el dinero que te devuelven** check the change they give you; **¡mira el bolso!** keep an eye on the bag!; **¡pero mira lo que estás haciendo!** but look what you are doing! **4.** (*meditar*) to think about; **mirándolo bien, bien mirado** taking everything into consideration **5.** (*tener en cuenta*) to take into account; **siempre estás mirando tu porvenir** you always have your future in mind; ~ **el dinero** to be careful of the money **6.** (*estimar*) ~ **bien/mal** to have a good/poor opinion of; ~ **con buena/mala cara** to approve/disapprove of **II.** *vi* **1.** (*dirigir la vista*) to look; ~ **por la ventana** to look out of the window; ~ **por un agujero** to look through a hole; ~ **atrás** to look back; ~ **alrededor** to look around **2.** (*buscar*) to look for; **siempre miramos por nuestros hijos** we always look out for our children **3.** (*dar*) **la casa mira al este** the house faces east; **la ventana mira al mar** the window overlooks [*o* gives on to] the sea **4.** (*de aviso, exclamativo*) **¡mira! ya llega** look! here he/she comes; **mira, mira, con que tú también apareces por aquí** well, well, so you're here too; **mira, mira, déjate de tonterías** that is enough, stop being silly; **¡pues, mira por donde...!** surprise, surprise ...!; **mire, ya se lo he explicado tres veces** look, I have already explained it to him/her three times **5.** (*tener en cuenta*) **mira, que no nos queda mucho tiempo** look, we do not have much time left; **mira que si se cae este jarrón** just imagine if the vase fell **6.** (*ir a ver, considerar, afectar*) **mira (a ver) si han llegado ya** go and see if they have arrived yet; **quedarse mirando** (*sorprendido*) to stop and stare; **por lo que mira a...** as regards .... **7.** (*mira que*) **mira que es tonta, ¿eh?** she really is silly, isn't she? ►**ser de mírame y no me toques** to be very delicate **III.** *vr:* ~**se** (*verse*) to look at oneself; ~**se a los ojos** to look into another's eyes; ~**se en el espejo** to look at oneself in the mirror; **se mire como se mire** however [*o* no matter how] you look at it; **si bien se mira** taking everything into consideration

mirasol *m* sunflower

miriápodo *m* myriapod

mirilla *f* (*en la puerta, pared*) peephole *Brit*, eyehole *Am;* FOTO viewer

miriñaque *m* **1.** HIST (*crinolina*) hoop skirt **2.** *CSur* FERRO cowcatcher

mirlo *m* **1.** ZOOL blackbird **2.** *inf* (*lengua*) **debes aprender a achantar el** ~ you have to learn to hold your tongue

mirón, -ona I. *adj* inquisitive **II.** *m, f* **1.** (*espectador curioso*) onlooker; *pey* (*de intimidades*) snoop; (*voyeur*) peeping Tom **2.** INFOR lurker

mirra *f* myrrh

misa *f* REL (*ceremonia*) mass; ~ **de difuntos** requiem mass; ~ **del gallo** midnight mass; **ir a** ~ to go to mass; **ayudar a** ~ to assist at mass; **cantar** ~ to sing mass; **decir** ~ to say mass ►**no saber de la** ~ **la media** [*o* **la mitad**] *inf* not to know the half [*o* the first thing] of it; **no se puede estar en** ~ **y repicar** you can't be in two places at once; **eso va a** ~ *inf* and that's a fact

misántropo, -a I. *adj* misanthropic **II.** *m, f* misanthrope

miscelánea *f* (*revoltijo*) miscellany

miserable I. *adj* **1.** (*pobre*) poor **2.** (*lamentable*) pitiful **3.** (*tacaño*) stingy **4.** (*poco, mísero*) miserable; **un sueldo** ~ a miserable wage **II.** *mf* **1.** (*desdichado*) wretch; (*que da pena*) poor thing **2.** (*canalla*) swine

miseria *f* **1.** (*pobreza*) poverty; **caer en la** ~ to become impoverished; **vivir en la** ~ to live in poverty **2.** (*poco dinero*) pittance **3.** (*tacañería*) stinginess **4.** *pl* (*infortunios*) misfortunes *pl*

misericordia *f* **1.** (*compasión*) compassion **2.** (*perdón*) forgiveness

misericordioso, -a *adj* **1.** (*que siente*) compassionate **2.** (*que perdona*) forgiving

mísero, -a *adj v.* **miserable**

misil *m* missile; ~ **antiaéreo** anti-aircraft missile

misión *f* mission; (*embajada*) embassy, legation; POL assignment

misionero, -a *m, f* missionary

mismamente *adv* **1.** (*sólo*) only **2.** (*literalmente*) literally **3.** (*hasta*) even; **da** ~ **escalofríos** it sends shivers down your spine **4.** (*en realidad*) actually **5.** *inf* (*precisamente*) just; **ayer** ~ **estuvimos hablando de ello** only yesterday we were talking about it

mismo *adv* **1.** (*incluso*) even; **me duele sentado** ~ it hurts me even when I am sitting down **2.** (*manera*) **así** ~ in that way **3.** (*justamente*) **ahí** ~ just there; **aquí** ~ right here; **ayer** ~ only yesterday **4.** (*ejemplo*) **nos podemos ver el miércoles** ~ we could meet on Wednesday, say

mismo, -a *adj* **1.** (*idéntico*) **el/lo** ~**/la misma** the same; **al** ~ **tiempo** at the same time; **da lo** ~ it does not matter; **por lo** ~ for that reason; **lo** ~ **José como** [*o* **que**] **María** both José and María; **lo** ~ **que coma o no coma, sigo engordando** (it makes no difference) whether I eat or not, I keep putting on weight; **lo** ~ **no vienen** they might not come; **quedamos** [*o* **seguimos**] **en las mismas** we are where we were **2.** (*semejante*) **el**~**/la misma/lo** ~ the same; **llevar la misma falda** to wear an identical skirt **3.** (*reflexivo*) myself; **te perjudicas a ti** ~ you harm yourself; **yo**

misma lo vi I myself saw him/it; **lo hizo por sí misma** she did it (all) by herself; **lo podemos hacer nosotros ~s** we can do it ourselves **4.** (*precisamente*) **este ~ perro fue el que me mordió** that very dog was the one which bit me; **¡eso ~!** exactly! **5.** (*hasta*) actual; **el ~ embajador asistió a la fiesta** the ambassador himself attended the party; **mi misma familia me abandonó** my own family abandonded me

miss *f* Miss; ~ **España** Miss Spain

misterio *m* (*enigma, secreto*) mystery; **obrar con ~** to act mysteriously

misterioso, -a *adj* mysterious

mística *f sin pl* mysticism

místico, -a I. *adj* mystical II. *m, f* mystic

mistificar <c→qu> *vt* **1.** (*burlarse*) to hoax **2.** (*falsear*) to misrepresent

mistol *m Arg, Par* BOT jujube tree

mitad *f* **1.** (*parte igual*) half; ~ **hombre ~ bestia** half man, half beast; **a ~ de precio** at half price; **cara ~** (*cónyuge*) other half; **mezcla harina y agua, ~ y ~** mix flour and water, half and half [*o* in equal amounts]; **reducir a la ~** to halve; **¿estás contenta? – ~ y ~** are you happy?– so-so **2.** (*medio*) middle; **en ~ del bosque** in the middle of the forest; **cortar por la ~** to cut in half **3.** DEP half

mítico, -a *adj* mythical, mythological

mitigar <g→gu> I. *vt* **1.** (*dolores*) to alleviate; (*sed*) to quench; (*hambre*) to take the edge off; (*temperamento*) to pacify; ~ **la inquietud de alguien** to set sb's mind at rest **2.** (*colores, luz*) to subdue; (*calor*) to mitigate II. *vr:* **~se 1.** (*dolores*) to lessen **2.** (*color, luz*) to become subdued

mitin *m* political meeting, rally

mito *m* myth

mitología *f* mythology

mitológico, -a *adj* mythological

mitón *m* mitten

mitote *m Méx* **1.** (*jaleo*) uproar; (*caos*) riot **2.** (*danza*) *ritual Aztec dance*

mitra *f* mitre *Brit,* miter *Am*

mixto *m* (*fósforo*) match

mixto, -a *adj* mixed

mixtura *f* mixture

ml. *abr de* **mililitro** ml

mm. *abr de* **milímetro** mm

mobiliario *m* furniture

moca *m* **1.** (*café*) mocha **2.** *Ecua* (*ciénaga*) quagmire

mocasín *m* moccasin

mocedad *f* youth

mocetón, -ona *m, f* (*chico*) strapping lad; (*chica*) big girl

mochales *adj inv, inf* **estar ~** to be crazy

mochila *f* rucksack *Brit,* backpack *Am;* (*de un soldado*) pack; (*de un estudiante*) satchel; (*para bebés*) baby carrier

mochilero, -a *m, f* backpacker; **ir de mochilera** to go backpacking

mocho, -a *adj* **1.** (*vaca*) hornless; (*árbol*) pollarded **2.** (*cabeza*) cropped **3.** *AmL* (*mutilado*) mutilated

mochuelo *m* **1.** ZOOL small owl **2.** *inf* (*carga*) burden; **cargar a alguien con el ~** to stick sb with the dirty work; **siempre me toca cargar con el ~** I am always stuck [*o* lumbered *Brit*] with the job; **cada ~ a su olivo** *fig* to each his own

moción *f t.* POL motion; **presentar una ~ de censura** to put forward a censure motion

moco *m* **1.** (*materia*) mucus; (*de la nariz*) snot; **limpiarse los ~s** to wipe one's nose **2.** (*del pavo*) wattle; **no es ~ de pavo** *fig* it's nothing to sneeze [*o* sniff] at **3.** (*de una mecha*) snuff; **a ~ de candil** by candlelight ►**llorar a ~ tendido** *inf* to cry one's eyes out

moco, -a *adj inf* (*borracho*) plastered; (*drogado*) high

mocoso, -a I. *adj* runny-nosed II. *m, f pey* brat

moda *f* fashion; **vestido/peinado de ~** fashionable dress/hairstyle; **estar de ~** to be fashionable; **ponerse/pasar de ~** to come into/go out of fashion; **ir a la (última) ~** to follow the (latest) fashion

modal I. *adj* modal II. *mpl* manners *pl;* **~es de la mesa** table manners; **¡qué ~es son estos!** what manners are these!; **¿has olvidado tus ~es?** have you forgotten your manners?

modalidad *f* form; **~es de un contrato** types of contract

modelar *vt* to model; *fig* to fashion

modelo *mf* **1.** (*de modas*) model **2.** ARTE, FOTO model; **~ vivo** live model

modelo *m* **1.** (*ejemplo*) model; **un político ~** a model politician; **hacer algo según el ~** to do sth according to the model; **~ fuera de mercado** *t.* COM discontinued model **2.** (*esquema*) design

módem *m* INFOR modem

moderación *f* **1.** (*comedimiento*) moderation; **comer con ~** to eat in moderation **2.** TV, RADIO presentation **3.** (*de un debate*) chairing

moderado, -a I. *adj* (*propuesta, persona, velocidad*) moderate; (*precio, petición*) reasonable; (*castigo*) light II. *m, f* POL moderate

moderador(a) I. *adj* moderating II. *m(f)* **1.** TV, RADIO presenter, moderator *Am* **2.** (*de un debate*) chairperson, moderator *Am*

moderar I. *vt* **1.** (*disminuir*) to moderate **2.** TV, RADIO to present **3.** (*debate*) to chair II. *vr:* **~se** to calm down

modernismo *m* modernism

modernización *f* modernization

modernizar <z→c> I. *vt* to modernize II. *vr:* **~se** to modernize oneself, to come up to date

moderno, -a *adj* modern; **edad moderna** present day; **historia moderna** modern history

modestia *f* **1.** (*humildad, sencillez*) modesty; **~ aparte** modesty apart [*o* aside]; **vestir con ~** to dress discreetly **2.** (*conformidad*) conformity **3.** (*de una mujer*) demureness

modesto, -a *adj* **1.** (*humilde, sencillo*) modest **2.** (*poco complicado*) simple **3.** (*mujer*) demure

módico, -a *adj* modest

modificación *f* (*de plan*) modification; (*de tema*) alteration; LING qualification; ~ **de estatutos** modification of statutes

modificar <c→qu> **I.** *vt* (*plan*) to modify; (*texto*) to revise; (*tema*) to alter; LING to qualify **II.** *vr:* ~**se** to adapt

modismo *m* idiom

modista *mf* dressmaker

modisto *m* fashion designer

modo *m* **1.** (*manera*) way; ~ **de andar/hablar/pensar** way of walking/talking/thinking; **hazlo a tu** ~ do it your way; **de este** ~ in this way; **de ningún** ~ no way; **hacer algo de cualquier** ~ to do sth any old how; **encontrar un** ~ **de resolver el problema** to find a way to solve the problem; **he encontrado el** ~ **de hacerlo** I have found the way to do it; **no es** ~ **de hablar a un superior** that is no way to speak to a superior; **de cualquier** ~ **no hubieran ido** anyway they would not have gone; **de** ~ **que lo has conseguido** so you have managed it; **utilizar el paraguas a** ~ **de espada** to use the umbrella as a sword; **en cierto** ~ in a way; **de un** ~ **u otro** one way or another; **de todos** ~**s no hubo heridos** at any rate no one was injured; **de todos** ~**s, lo volvería a intentar** anyway, I would try again; **de todos** ~**s es mejor que te vayas** in spite of everything it would be better for you to go **2.** LING mood **3.** INFOR mode; ~ **de operación** operational mode **4.** *pl* (*comportamiento*) manners *pl;* **tener buenos/malos** ~**s** to have good/bad manners; **decir algo con buenos/malos** ~**s** to say sth politely/rudely; **¿qué** ~**s son esos?** what manners are these?

modorra *f* drowsiness

modorro, -a *adj* **1.** (*somnoliento*) drowsy **2.** (*torpe*) lumbering **3.** (*atontado*) dazed **4.** (*fruta*) shrivelled *Brit,* shriveled *Am*

modoso, -a *adj* **ser** [*o* **estar**] ~ to be well-mannered

modular *vt, vi* to modulate

módulo *m* **1.** *t.* ARQUIT, ELEC (*de un mueble*) unit **2.** (*de una prisión*) wing **3.** ENS, INFOR module **4.** MÚS modulation **5.** AVIAT ~ **de mando** command module

mofa *f* mockery; **hacer** ~ **de algo** to scoff at sth

mofar *vi, vr* ~**se de algo/alguien** to scoff at sth/sb

mofeta *f* **1.** ZOOL skunk **2.** MIN noxious gas

moflete *m* chubby cheek

mofletudo, -a *adj* chubby-cheeked

mogolla *m Col* GASTR dark wholegrain bread

mogollón *m* **1.** *inf* (*cantidad*) load(s); **había** ~ **de gente en la fiesta** there were loads of people at the party; **había** ~ **de público en el pabellón** there were masses of spectators in the pavilion **2.** *inf* (*lío*) mess

mohín *m* face; **hacer un** ~ **gracioso** to pull a funny face

mohíno, -a *adj* **1.** (*enfadado*) sulky; (*de mal humor*) grumpy **2.** (*triste*) glum

moho *m* **1.** BOT mould *Brit,* mold *Am;* **no (dejar) criar** ~ (*alimentos*) to be eaten immediately; (*un objeto*) to be in constant use **2.** (*óxido*) rust **3.** (*desidia*) laziness

mohoso, -a *adj* **1.** (*de moho*) mouldy *Brit,* moldy *Am* **2.** (*oxidado*) rusty

mojama *f* salted dried tuna

mojar **I.** *vt* **1.** (*con un líquido*) to wet; (*ligeramente*) to moisten; (*para planchar*) to dampen **2.** (*el pan*) to dunk **3.** *inf* (*celebrar*) to celebrate **4.** *inf* (*apuñalar*) to stab **II.** *vi inf* (*en un asunto*) to get involved **III.** *vr:* ~**se** **1.** (*con un líquido*) to get wet; **no te mojes los pies en el charco** do not get your feet wet in the puddle **2.** *inf* (*comprometerse*) to get involved

mojarra *f Arg* short broad knife

mojicón *m* **1.** GASTR sponge cake **2.** *inf* (*puñetazo*) punch in the face

mojigato, -a *adj* **1.** (*gazmoño*) prudish **2.** (*hipócrita*) hypocritical

mojón *m* **1.** (*hito*) boundary stone; ~ **kilométrico** milestone **2.** (*poste*) post

mol *m* mole

molar **I.** *adj* **1.** (*de muela*) **diente** ~ molar **2.** (*de moler*) grinding **II.** *m* molar **III.** *vi inf* **1.** (*gustar*) **este libro mola** this book is really cool; **me molan las rubias** I am into [*o* I go for] blonds; **me mola ese tío** I really like that guy **2.** (*llevarse*) to be in; **ahora mola llevar pelo corto** nowadays short hair is in

Moldavia *f* Moldavia

moldavo, -a *adj, m, f* Moldavian

molde *m* **1.** TÉC, GASTR mould *Brit,* mold *Am;* TIPO form; **pan de** ~ sliced bread; **letras de** ~ block letters; **romper** ~**s** to break the mould *Brit* [*o* mold *Am*] **2.** (*modelo*) model

moldeador *m* (*para el cabello*) perm

moldear *vt* **1.** (*formar*) to mould *Brit,* to mold *Am;* **diversas circunstancias han moldeado su vida** diverse circumstances have shaped his/her life **2.** (*vaciar*) to cast

moldura *f* **1.** (*listón*) trim **2.** ARQUIT moulding *Brit,* molding *Am*

mole[1] *f* (*masa*) mass

mole[2] *m Méx* GASTR **1.** (*salsa*) sauce; ~ **verde** green sauce **2.** (*guiso*) stew

> **Mole** is the name given to a Mexican chilli sauce. Cayenne pepper from the chilli plant gives this sauce its characteristic sharp taste.

molécula *f* molecule

molecular *adj* molecular; **biología** ~ molecular biology

moler <o→ue> *vt* **1.** (*café, trigo*) to grind; (*aceitunas*) to press **2.** (*fatigar*) to exhaust; **estoy molido de la excursión** the trip has exhausted me **3.** (*molestar*) to bother **4.** (*estropear*) to ruin

molestar I. *vt* (*estorbar*) to inconvenience; (*fastidiar*) to bother; (*dolores*) to hurt; (*enfadar*) to annoy; **esta camisa me molesta** this shirt annoys me; **este dolor en la espalda me molesta** this pain in my shoulder bothers me II. *vr:* **~se** 1. (*tomarse la molestia*) to bother; **ni siquiera te has molestado en comprobarlo** you haven't even taken the trouble to check it; **no te molestes en ir allí** don't bother to go there; **no te molestes por mí** don't put yourself out for me; **no tendrías que haberte molestado** you shouldn't have bothered 2. (*ofenderse*) to take offence *Brit,* to take offense *Am;* **se ha molestado por tu comentario** he/she has taken offence *Brit* [*o* offense *Am*] at what you said

molestia *f* 1. (*fastidio*) bother; (*por dolores*) discomfort; **ser una ~** to be a nuisance; **no es ninguna ~** it doesn't bother me 2. (*inconveniente*) trouble; **no es ninguna ~ (para mí)** it is no trouble (for me); **tomarse la ~** to take the trouble; **perdonen las ~s** we apologize for the inconvenience caused 3. (*enfado*) annoyance 4. (*dolor*) discomfort

molesto, -a *adj* 1. *ser* (*desagradable*) unpleasant; (*fastidioso*) troublesome 2. *estar* (*enfadado*) **~ por algo** annoyed about sth; (*ofendido*) hurt by sth 3. *estar* (*incómodo*) uncomfortable; **estoy ~ por el vendaje** the bandage is uncomfortable

molicie *f* 1. *elev* (*blandura*) softness 2. (*comodidad*) **vivir en la ~** to live a life of luxury

molido, -a *adj inf* (*cansado*) **estoy ~** I am worn out; **el trabajo me ha dejado ~** the work has left me worn out

molinero, -a I. *adj* milling II. *m, f* miller

molinete *m* 1. (*en una ventana*) ventilator 2. (*juguete*) windmill *Brit,* pinwheel *Am*

molinillo *m* 1. (*aparato*) **~ de café** coffee grinder 2. (*juguete*) windmill *Brit,* pinwheel *Am* 3. (*para batir*) wooden stirrer

molino *m* 1. (*máquina*) mill; **~ de papel** paper mill 2. (*inquieto*) restless person 3. (*pesado*) irksome person

mollar *adj* 1. (*fruta*) soft; (*carne*) tender 2. (*persona*) gullible 3. (*trabajo*) cushy

mollejas *fpl* sweetbreads *pl*

mollera *f* 1. (*de la cabeza*) crown 2. (*fontanela*) fontanelle *Brit,* fontanel *Am;* **la ~ se cierra** the fontanelle is closing; **tener la ~ cerrada** *fig* to be old enough to reason 3. (*seso*) brain; **eso no me entra en la ~** I just do not understand that; **ser duro de ~** to be stubborn

mollete *m* 1. (*pan*) muffin 2. (*moflete*) plump cheek 3. *Bol* GASTR *bread made quickly and poorly*

molo *m Chile* (*rompeolas*) breakwater; (*dique*) seawall

molón, -ona *adj* 1. *inf* (*bonito*) pretty 2. (*presumido*) vain 3. *Guat, Ecua, Méx* (*fastidioso*) tiresome

molusco *m* mollusc

momentáneo, -a *adj* 1. (*instantáneo*) momentary 2. (*provisional*) provisional; **hacer un arreglo ~** to find a provisional solution 3. (*temporal*) temporary

momento *m* 1. (*instante*) instant, moment; **¡espera un ~!** wait a moment!; **de un ~ a otro** at any time now; **al ~** immediately; **en cualquier** [*o* **en todo**] **~** at any time; **el ~ decisivo** the moment of truth; **en el ~ adecuado** at the appropriate time; **en el ~ de la salida** when they were about to start; **en este ~ hay demasiado paro** at the moment there is too much unemployment; **en este ~ estaba pensando en ti** I was just thinking about you; **de ~, no te puedo decir nada** for the moment, I can't tell you anything; **de ~ leeré el periódico y luego...** for the time being I'll read the newspaper and then ...; **de** [*o* **por el**] **~ no sé nada de él** for the moment I haven't heard from him; **en un ~ de flaqueza** in a moment of weakness; **la tensión aumentaba por ~s** the tension was growing ever stronger [*o* stronger and stronger]; **aparecer en el último ~** to arrive at the last moment; **en todo ~ mantuvo la calma** at all times he/she remained calm; **no tengo un ~ libre** I do not have one free moment; **hace un ~ que ha salido** he/she left a moment ago; **este estudiante me pregunta a cada ~** this student is always asking me questions 2. (*período*) period; **atravieso un mal ~** I am going through a bad patch 3. (*actualidad*) present; **la música del ~** present-day music 4. (*situación*) moment 5. FÍS momentum

momia *f* 1. (*egipcia*) mummy 2. (*persona*) painfully thin person

momificar <c→qu> *vt* to mummify

momio *m inf* cushy job; **este trabajo es un ~** this is a cushy job; **este traje es un ~** this suit is a bargain; **de ~** free

momio, -a *adj* lean

mona *f* 1. ZOOL female monkey; (*especie*) Barbary ape 2. *inf* (*borrachera*) drunken state; **coger una ~** to get drunk; **estar como una ~** to be drunk; **dormir la ~** to sleep off a hangover 3. GASTR **~ de Pascua** Easter cake ▸**aunque la ~ se vista de seda, ~ se queda** *prov* you can't make a silk purse from a sow's ear; **vete a freír ~s** *inf* go jump in the lake; **estar hecho una ~** to feel mortified

Mónaco *m* Monaco

monada *f* 1. (*zalamería*) flattery 2. (*gracia*) antics *pl* 3. *pl* (*amaneramiento*) affectation 4. (*algo bonito*) **es una ~ de chica** that girl is a beauty; **¡qué ~ de vestido!** what a gorgeous dress!; **este bebé es una ~** this baby is a cute little thing

monaguillo, -a *m, f* altar boy

monarca *mf* monarch

monarquía *f* monarchy

monárquico, -a I. *adj* 1. (*de la monarquía*) monarchic 2. (*partidario*) monarchist II. *m, f* monarchist

M

monasterio *m* monastery
monda *f* **1.** (*acción*) peeling **2.** (*peladura*) peel **3.** (*poda*) pruning ►**ser la ~** *inf* to be terrific; **este pueblo es la ~, nadie sabe dónde está el cine** this village is the pits, nobody knows where the cinema is
mondadientes *m inv* toothpick
mondadura *f* **1.** (*acción*) peeling **2.** *pl* (*peladuras*) peelings *pl*
mondar **I.** *vt* **1.** (*plátano, patata, palo*) to peel; (*guisantes*) to shell; (*rama*) to pare **2.** (*árbol*) to prune **II.** *vr:* **~se** **1.** (*pelarse*) to peel **2.** (*limpiar*) **~se los dientes** to clean one's teeth with a toothpick **3.** *inf* (*reírse*) **~se** (**de risa**) *inf* to die laughing
mondo, -a *adj* **1.** (*cabeza*) shaven **2.** *inf* (*de dinero*) **quedarse ~** (**y lirondo**) to be broke ►**~ y lirondo** *inf* plain, pure and simple
mondongo *m* **1.** entrails *pl,* innards *pl* **2.** (*carne*) sausage meat
moneda *f* **1.** (*pieza*) coin; **~ de cinco peniques** five pence coin; **~ de 5/10/25 centavos** nickel/dime/quarter; **~ suelta** change; **teléfono de ~s** pay phone; **pagar a alguien con la misma ~** *fig* to pay sb back tit for tat; **la otra cara de la ~** the other side of the coin; **esto es ~ corriente** *fig* that is the norm; **si él me ofrece calidad, yo le pago en buena ~** *fig* if he offers me quality, I'll see him right **2.** (*de un país*) currency; **~ base** base currency; **~ de curso legal** legal tender; **~ extranjera** foreign currency; **~ fuerte/débil** strong/weak currency; **~ nacional** local currency; **~ única europea** European single currency
monedero *m* **1.** (*bolsa*) purse **2.** (*persona*) **~ falso** counterfeiter
monegasco, -a **I.** *adj* of/from Monaco **II.** *m, f* native/inhabitant of Monaco
monería *f* (*gracia*) antics *pl*
monetario, -a *adj* monetary; **institución monetaria** monetary institution; **tormentas monetarias** monetary turmoil
mongólico, -a **I.** *adj* MED of Down's syndrome **II.** *m, f* MED person with Down's syndrome; **ser un ~** to have Down's syndrome
mongolismo *m sin pl* MED Down's syndrome
monigote *m* **1.** (*dibujo mal hecho*) childlike drawing; (*figura*) stick figure; **hacer ~s** (*figuras humanas*) to draw stick figures; (*borrones*) to doodle **2.** (*muñeco*) rag doll, paper doll **3.** (*persona*) spineless individual, wimp
monitor *m* TÉC, TV, INFOR monitor; (*pantalla*) screen
monitor(a) *m(f)* (*de un deporte*) coach, trainer; (*de un campamento*) camp leader; **~ de natación** swimmimg instructor
monitorio, -a *adj* admonitory; **carta monitoria** admonitory letter
monja *f* nun, sister
monje *m* monk, brother
monjil **I.** *adj* nun-like; **llevar una vida ~** *fig* to lead the life of a hermit; (*muy recatado*) prudish **II.** *m* nun's habit
mono *m* **1.** ZOOL monkey; **¿tengo ~s en la cara?** *inf* what are you staring at?; **hacer ~s a alguien** to make a sign to sb **2.** (*fantoche*) nobody; **en esta casa soy el último ~** in this house I am a nobody **3.** (*traje*) overalls *pl;* (*de mecánico*) boiler suit *Brit,* coveralls *pl Am;* (*de calle*) jumpsuit *Am* **4.** *inf* (*de drogas*) withdrawal symptoms *pl;* **tener el ~** to be suffering from withdrawal symptoms; **le entra el ~** he gets withdrawal symptoms **5.** (*persona fea*) ugly devil **6.** (*joven tonto*) silly youth **7.** (*dibujo*) cartoon
mono, -a *adj* **1.** (*niño*) cute; (*chica*) pretty; (*vestido*) lovely **2.** *Col, inf* (*rubio*) blonde
monóculo *m* monocle
monocultivo *m* monoculture, singlecrop farming
monogamia *f sin pl* monogamy
monógamo, -a *adj* monogamous
monografía *f* monograph
monograma *m* monogram
monolingüe *adj* monolingual
monólogo *m* monologue; TEAT soliloquy
monopatín *m* skateboard
monopolio *m* monopoly
monopolizar <z→c> *vt* COM to monopolize, to corner (a market); **~ la atención de alguien** to monopolize sb's attention
monosílabo *m* monosyllable; **responder con ~s** to answer in monosyllables
monosílabo, -a *adj* monosyllabic
monotonía *f* monotony
monótono, -a *adj* monotonous
monóxido *m* monoxide
monseñor *m* monsignor
monserga *f inf* **1.** (*lengua*) drivel; **¡no me vengas con ~s!** don't spout drivel at me! **2.** (*lata*) bore; **este trabajo es una ~** this job is a bore
monstruo **I.** *m* **1.** (*ser fantástico*) monster **2.** (*persona fea*) hideous person **3.** (*persona perversa*) fiend **4.** (*artista*) superstar **II.** *adj inv* **una actuación ~** a magnificent performance
monstruosidad *f* monstrosity; **eso que dices es una ~** what you are saying is a monstrosity
monstruoso, -a *adj* **1.** (*desfigurado*) disfigured **2.** (*terrible*) monstrous; **es ~ tener que estudiar durante el verano** it is monstrous to have to study during the summer **3.** (*enorme*) huge
monta *f* **1.** (*de maquinaria*) assembly; (*de joyas*) setting **2.** (*de caballo*) mating season; (*acto*) mounting **3.** (*importe*) total **4.** (*importancia*) importance; **de poca ~** unimportant
montacargas *m inv* (service) lift *Brit,* (freight) elevator *Am*
montador(a) *m(f)* **1.** TÉC (*de máquinas*) fitter, assembler **2.** CINE editor
montaje *m* **1.** TÉC assembly **2.** CINE editing; FOTO montage **3.** TEAT decor **4.** (*engaño*) set-up
montante *m* **1.** (*importe*) total **2.** (*de puerta*)

jamb; (*de ventana*) mullion

montaña *f* 1. GEO (*monte*) mountain; (*zona*) mountains *pl;* ~ **rusa** big dipper; **prefiero la ~ al mar** I prefer the mountains to the seaside; **la fe mueve ~s** faith will move mountains 2. (*de cosas*) difficulty ▸**hacer una ~ de un grano de arena** to make a mountain out of a molehill; **grande como una** ~ as big as a house

montañero, -a *m, f* mountaineer

montañés, -esa I. *adj* 1. (*de la montaña*) highlander 2. (*de Santander*) of/from Santander II. *m, f* native/inhabitant of Santander

montañismo *m* mountaineering

montañoso, -a *adj* mountainous

montar I. *vi* 1. (*subir a una bici, un caballo*) to get on; (*en un coche*) to get in; ~ **en** (*una bici, un caballo*) to get onto; (*en un coche*) to get into; **tanto monta que vaya como que no** *fig* it doesn't matter whether I go or not 2. (*ir a caballo*) to ride; ~ **en bici** to ride a bycicle 3. (*una cuenta*) ~ **a** to come to II. *vt* 1. (*subir en un caballo*) to mount; **no montes al niño en el alféizar** don't sit the lad on the window-sill 2. (*ir a caballo*) to ride 3. (*acaballar, cubrir*) to cover 4. (*máquina*) to assemble; (*tienda*) to open 5. (*clara de huevo*) to beat; (*nata*) to whip 6. (*casa*) to furnish 7. (*negocio*) to set up 8. TEAT to stage 9. (*diamante*) to set 10. (*arma*) to cock 11. CINE to edit 12. *inf* (*excursión*) to organize 13. (*guardia, ejército*) to mount 14. *inf* (*lío*) ~**la** to kick up a fuss; ~ **un número** to make a scene III. *vr:* ~**se** 1. (*subir*) to climb; **no te montes ahí** do not climb up there 2. *inf* (*arreglárselas*) **¿cómo te lo montas con el trabajo?** how do you manage with the work?; **no nos lo montamos muy bien entre nosotros** we are not coping very well on our own; **me lo monto solo** I manage on my own

montaraz *adj* 1. (*salvaje*) wild 2. (*resistente*) tough 3. (*tosco*) coarse 4. (*arisco*) unsociable

monte *m* 1. (*montaña*) mountain; **el ~ de los Olivos** the Mount of Olives 2. (*bosque*) ~ **alto** woodland; ~ **bajo** scrub; **batir el** ~ (*cazar*) to go hunting; (*buscar*) to beat the undergrowth; **echarse al** ~ to take to the hills 3. *pl* (*cordillera*) mountain range 4. (*establecimiento*) ~ **de piedad** state-owned pawnshop ▸**no todo el ~ es orégano** *prov* all that glitters is not gold

montepío *m* 1. (*caja para viudas*) fund for widows; (*para huérfanos*) fund for orphans 2. (*pensión de viuda*) widow's pension; (*de huérfano*) orphan's pension

montera *f* 1. (*gorra*) cap; **ponerse el mundo por** ~ *fig* not to be affected by the opinion of others 2. (*de una galería*) glass roof

montería *f* hunting

montés, -esa *adj* wild; **cabra montesa** mountain goat; **gato** ~ wildcat

montículo *m* mound

monto *m* total

montón *m* heap; **un ~ de ropa** a heap of clothes; **había un ~ de gente** there were a lot of people; **tengo problemas a montones** *inf* I have loads of problems; **tomar montones de pastillas** *inf* to take loads of pills; **ser del** ~ to be ordinary; **tener una cara del** ~ to have a run-of-the-mill face; **la bomba atómica redujo Hiroshima a un ~ de escombros** the atomic bomb reduced Hiroshima to a pile of rubble

montura *f* 1. (*arnés*) harness; (*silla*) saddle 2. (*animal*) mount 3. (*de gafas*) frame; (*de una joya*) setting

monumental *adj* 1. (*grande, de importancia*) monumental; (*error*) tremendous 2. (*de monumento*) **el Madrid** ~ the sights of Madrid

monumento *m* memorial; (*grande*) monument; ~ **funerario** gravestone; ~ **de la literatura** literary work of art; **los ~s de una ciudad** the sights of a city; **esta casa es un ~ nacional** this house is a listed building; **esta chica es un** ~ this girl is beautiful

monzón *m o f* monsoon

moña *f* 1. (*lazo*) bow 2. *inf* (*borrachera*) drunken state; **estar** ~ to be drunk

moño *m* 1. (*pelo*) bun 2. (*lazo*) bow 3. (*plumas*) crest 4. *Col* (*capricho*) whim 5. *Chile* (*pelo*) hair; (*copete*) forelock 6. *pl* (*adornos*) frippery 7. *inf* (*expresiones*) **quitar ~s a alguien** to bring sb down a peg (or two); **ponerse ~s** to put on airs (and graces); **estar hasta el ~ de algo** to be fed up to the back teeth with sth; **se me ha puesto en el ~ de...** I have taken it into my head to ...

MOPU *m abr de* **Ministerio de Obras Públicas y Urbanismo** *Spanish ministerial department in charge of public transport infrastructure and planning, now called Fomento*

moquear *vi* to have a runny nose

moqueta *f* fitted carpet, carpet *Am*

mora *f* 1. BOT (*del moral*) mulberry; (*de la zarzamora*) blackberry 2. JUR delay

morada *f* 1. (*casa*) abode 2. (*residencia*) residence 3. (*estancia*) stay; **la eterna** ~ heaven

morado, -a *adj* purple; **poner un ojo ~ a alguien** to give sb a black eye; **pasarlas moradas** to have a bad time; **ponerse ~ (comiendo)** *inf* to gorge [*o* stuff] oneself

moral I. *adj* 1. (*ético*) moral; **código** ~ code of ethics; **tengo la certidumbre** ~ I have the moral conviction 2. (*espiritual*) spiritual II. *f* morals *pl;* ~ **relajada** relaxed morals; **tú y yo no tenemos la misma** ~ you and I do not have the same principles; **levantar la ~ a alguien** to boost sb's morale; **hay que tener ~ para hacer eso** you have to be sure of yourself to do that; **tener más ~ que el Alcoyano** to keep one's morale high in the face of overwhelming difficulties

moraleja *f* moral

moralidad *f* (*cualidad*) morality

moralista *mf* moralist

moralizar <z→c> I. *vi* to moralize II. *vt* to

improve the morals of
morapio *m inf* red (wine), red plonk
moratón *m* bruise
moratoria *f t.* FIN moratorium; ~ **nuclear** moratorium on nuclear weapons testing
mórbido, **-a** *adj* **1.** (*enfermo*) ill **2.** (*suave*) soft
morbo *m* **1.** (*enfermedad*) illness **2.** (*interés malsano*) morbid fascination; **este partido de fútbol tiene mucho** ~ this football game has created a lot of unhealthy interest; **el color negro me da** ~ I find black a morbid colour
morbosidad *f* morbidity
morboso, **-a** *adj* **1.** (*clima*) unhealthy **2.** (*placer, imaginación*) morbid
morcilla *f* **1.** GASTR black pudding, blood sausage **2.** TEAT improvisation **3.** *Cuba* (*mentira*) lie **4.** *inf* (*fastidiar*) **¡que te den ~!** *vulg* get stuffed!
morcillo *m* shin; (*carne*) shoulder
mordaz *adj* **1.** (*comentario*) caustic; (*crítica*) scathing **2.** (*sabor*) bitter **3.** (*corrosivo*) corrosive
mordaza *f* **1.** (*en la boca*) gag; **quieren ponerme una** ~ *fig* they want to shut me up **2.** TÉC clamp
mordedor(a) *adj* liable to bite; **perro ladrador, poco** ~ *prov* his bark is worse than his bite
mordedura *f* bite
morder <o→ue> **I.** *vt* **1.** (*con los dientes*) to bite; **te voy a hacer ~ el polvo** I am going to crush you; **está que muerde** *inf* he/she is furious **2.** (*corroer*) to corrode **3.** *AmL* (*estafar*) to cheat **II.** *vr:* **~se** to bite; **¡no te muerdas las uñas!** don't bite your nails; **tuve que ~me la lengua** I had to bite my tongue; **no ~se la lengua** to say what one thinks
mordida *f* **1.** *Méx, inf* (*acción*) bite; (*dinero*) bribe **2.** *Arg v.* **mordisco**
mordisco *m* bite, nibble
mordisquear *vt* ~ **algo** to nibble at sth
morena *f* **1.** ZOOL moray eel **2.** (*pan*) wholemeal [*o* wholegrain] bread **3.** GEO moraine
moreno *m* mixture of ground coal and vinagre (*used by shearers to cure cuts*)
moreno, **-a** **I.** *adj* brown; (*de piel*) swarthy; (*de cabello*) dark-haired; (*de ojos*) brown-eyed **II.** *m, f* **1.** (*negro*) coloured person *Brit,* colored person *Am* **2.** *Cuba* (*mulato*) mulatto
morera *f* mulberry tree
morete *m AmC,* **moretón** *m inf* bruise
morfema *m* LING morpheme
morfina *f* morphine
morfinómano, **-a** **I.** *adj* addicted to morphine **II.** *m, f* morphine addict
morgue *f AmL* morgue
moribundo, **-a** **I.** *adj* dying **II.** *m, f* dying person
morigeración *f elev* moderation
morigerado, **-a** *adj elev* **1.** (*moderado*) moderate **2.** (*bien criado*) well brought-up **3.** (*de buenas costumbres*) well-behaved
morigerar *vt elev* to moderate
morir *irr* **I.** *vi* **1.** (*perecer*) to die; (*en catástrofe, guerra, accidente*) to be killed; ~ **de hambre/sed** to die of starvation/thirst; ~ **ahogado** (*en agua*) to drown; (*en humo*) to asphyxiate, to suffocate; ~ **de viejo** to die of old age; ~ **en un incendio** to die in a fire; ~ **a causa de las graves heridas** to die from serious wounds; **murió al pie del cañón** he died with his boots on **2.** (*tarde*) to draw to a close; (*luz*) to fade away; (*tradición*) to die out; (*camino*) to peter out; (*río*) to finish; (*sonido*) to die away **II.** *vr:* **~se** **1.** (*perecer*) to die; (*planta*) to wither; **se le ha muerto su padre** his/her father has died; **¡así te mueras!** *inf* good riddance to you! **2.** (*con 'de'*) **~se de hambre/de sed** to die of starvation/thirst; **~se de frío** to freeze to death; **~se de vergüenza** to die of shame; **~se de risa** to die laughing; **~se de pena** to pine away **3.** (*con 'por'*) **me muero por conocer a tu nueva novia** I am dying to meet your new girlfriend; **me muero (de ganas) por saber lo que te dijo** I am dying to know what she/he said to you; **me muero por ella** I am crazy about her **4.** (*miembro del cuerpo*) to become numb
mormón, **-ona** *adj, m, f* Mormon
moro, **-a** **I.** *adj* (*musulmán*) Muslim **II.** *m, f* Muslim; **ser un** ~ *inf* to be chauvinistic; **¡hay ~s en la costa!** *fig* watch out!; **¡no hay ~s en la costa!** *fig* the coast is clear!
morochos *mpl Ven* twins *pl*
morondo, **-a** *adj* bare
moroso, **-a** **I.** *adj* **1.** (*deudor*) slow to pay up **2.** *elev* (*lento*) slow; (*estilo*) drawn-out; **el río avanza de manera morosa** the river advances at a slow pace **II.** *m, f* debtor in arrears, defaulter
morral *m* **1.** (*de las caballerías*) nosebag **2.** (*zurrón*) knapsack
morralla *f* **1.** (*cosas*) trifles *pl* **2.** (*gente*) rabble **3.** (*pescados*) small fry
morrear *vt, vr:* **~se** *vulg* to neck, to snog
morriña *f sin pl, inf* (*nostalgia*) homesickness
morro *m* **1.** ZOOL (*hocico*) snout **2.** (*de persona*) **~s** (*labios*) lips; (*boca*) mouth; **beber a ~** to drink straight from the bottle; **me caí de ~s** I fell flat on my face; **te voy a partir los ~s** *inf* I'm going to smash your face in; **estar de ~(s)** *fig* to be angry; **torcer el ~** *fig* to pout; **tiene un ~ que se lo pisa** *inf* he/she has a real nerve; **lo hizo así, por el ~** *inf* he/she did it like that, quite brazenly; **se quedó el dinero por (todo) el ~** *inf* he brazenly kept all the money **3.** (*de pistola*) muzzle; (*de barco, avión, coche*) nose **4.** (*montículo*) hillock
morrocotudo, **-a** *adj inf* **1.** (*formidable*) terrific **2.** (*susto, disgusto*) dreadful
morrón **I.** *adj* **pimiento ~** sweet red pepper **II.** *m inf* (*golpe*) blow
morsa *f* walrus
morse *m* Morse code; **señal ~** Morse code signal

mortadela *f* mortadella, ≈ bologna

mortaja *f* **1.** (*sábana*) shroud; (*vestidura*) burial clothes *pl* **2.** *AmL* (*de cigarrillo*) cigarette paper

mortal I. *adj* **1.** (*sujeto a la muerte*) mortal; **los restos ~es** the mortal remains; **los ~es** mankind **2.** (*que la causa*) mortal, lethal; **pecado ~** mortal sin; **peligro ~** mortal danger; **tener un odio ~ a alguien** to have a deadly hatred of sb **3.** (*pesado*) deadly; (*aburrido*) dreary **II.** *mf* mortal

mortalidad *f* **1.** (*cualidad*) mortality **2.** (*número*) mortality rate

mortandad *f* loss of life; **el virus ébola causó una gran ~ en Zaire** Ebola fever caused a carnage in Zaire; **la ~ de la guerra en Ruanda** the bloodbath during the war in Rwanda

mortecino, -a *adj* (*luz*) dim; (*color*) muted; (*fuego*) dull

mortero *m* **1.** *t.* MIL (*cuenco*) mortar **2.** (*cemento*) cement, mortar

mortífero, -a *adj* deadly

mortificación *f* **1.** (*tormento*) torment **2.** *t.* REL (*humillación*) mortification

mortificar <c→qu> **I.** *vt* **1.** (*atormentar*) to torment **2.** *t.* REL (*humillar*) to mortify **II.** *vr:* **~se 1.** (*atormentarse*) to be tormented **2.** REL to mortify oneself **3.** *Méx* (*avergonzarse*) to be ashamed

mortuorio, -a *adj* death

moruno, -a *adj* Moorish; **pincho ~** spicy meat kebab

mosaico *m* mosaic

mosca *f* **1.** ZOOL fly; **por si las ~s** *inf* just in case; **tener la ~ detrás de la oreja** *inf* to be suspicious; **estar ~** *inf* (*receloso*) to be suspicious; (*enfadado*) to be cross; **no se oía el vuelo de una ~** you could have heard a pin drop; **papar ~s** *inf* to be spellbound; **¿qué ~ te ha picado?** what's bugging you?; **andar cazando ~s** to spend time on futile things **2.** (*barba*) goatee **3.** (*persona*) nuisance, bore; **~ cojonera** *vulg* fucking [*o* bloody *Brit*] pest; **~ muerta** hypocrite **4.** *inf* (*dinero*) dough, dosh; **aflojar la ~** to shell out

moscada *adj* **nuez ~** nutmeg

moscarda *f* blowfly, bluebottle

moscardón *m* **1.** ZOOL (*moscarda*) blowfly, bluebottle; (*tábano*) horsefly; (*avispón*) hornet **2.** (*persona*) pest

moscatel *m* Muscatel

moscón *m v.* **moscardón**

moscón, -ona *m, f* blowfly

moscovita *adj, mf* Muscovite

Moscú *m* Moscow

mosqueado, -a *adj* **1.** *inf* (*enfadado*) cross; **estar ~ con alguien** to be cross with sb **2.** (*moteado*) spotted; (*vaca*) mottled

mosquearse *vr inf* (*ofenderse*) to take offence *Brit,* to take offense *Am;* (*enfadarse*) to get angry

mosqueo *m* anger; **coger un ~ de aúpa** to fly into a rage

mosquetero *m* **1.** (*soldado*) musketeer **2.** *Arg, Bol* (*en una fiesta*) party-crasher

mosquetón *m* **1.** (*arma*) carbine **2.** (*anilla*) snap ring

mosquita *f* **~ muerta** hypocrite; **se hace la ~ muerta** he/she looks as if butter wouldn't melt in his/her mouth

mosquitero *m* mosquito net(ting)

mosquito *m* mosquito; (*pequeño*) gnat

mostaza *f* mustard; (*semilla*) mustard seed; **(de) color ~** mustard(-yellow)

mosto *m* grape juice

mostrador *m* **1.** (*tienda*) counter; (*escaparate*) shop window **2.** (*bar*) bar **3.** (*ventanilla*) window

mostrar <o→ue> **I.** *vt* (*enseñar*) to show; (*presentar*) to display; **¡no muestres tu miedo!** do not reveal your fear! **II.** *vr:* **~se** to appear; **~se amigo** to be friendly

mota *f* **1.** (*partícula*) speck; **~ (de polvo)** speak of dust **2.** (*mancha*) spot; (*lunar*) mole

mote *m* **1.** (*apodo*) nickname; **~ cariñoso** pet name **2.** *AmL* (*maíz*) boiled maize *Brit* [*o* corn *Am*]

moteado, -a *adj* (*ojos*) flecked; (*tela*) dotted; (*huevos*) speckled

motear *vt* to fleck, to speckle

motejar *vt* (*tildar*) to brand

motel *m* motel

motero, -a *m, f* biker

motete *m* **1.** MÚS motet **2.** *AmS* bundle

motín *m* uprising; (*militar*) mutiny; **un ~ en la cárcel** a prison riot

motivación *f* motivation

motivar *vt* **1.** (*incitar*) to motivate **2.** (*explicar*) to explain **3.** (*provocar*) to cause; **los puntos que motivan el presente contrato son...** the points which give rise to the present contract are ...

motivo *m* **1.** (*causa*) reason behind; (*crimen*) motive; **con ~ de...** on the occasion of ...; **por este ~** for this reason; **carecer de ~ alguno** to have no point whatsoever **2.** (*tela*) motif

moto *f inf* motorbike; **~ acuática** jet ski; **~ para la nieve** snowmobile; **ir en ~** to ride a motorbike; **iba como una ~** *inf* he/she was going like a bat out of hell; **estar como una ~** to be wound up; **ponerse como una ~** (*sexual*) to get horny; (*enfadado*) to get furious

motocicleta *f* motorcycle; **ir en ~** to go by motorcycle

motociclismo *m sin pl* motorcycling

motociclista *mf* motorcyclist

motoneta *f AmL* motor scooter

motor *m* **1.** *t. fig* motor; **~ de búsqueda** INFOR search engine; **~ de explosión** internal combustion engine; **~ de reacción** jet engine; **vehículo de ~** motor vehicle **2.** (*causa*) cause

motor(a) *adj* motor; **nervio ~** motor nerve

motora *f* motorboat

motorismo *m sin pl* motorcycling

motorista *mf* **1.** DEP motorcyclist **2.** (*chófer*)

motorist, driver **3.** (*policía*) motorized policeman
motorizar <z→c> *vt* to motorize; **estar motorizado** *inf* to have wheels [*o* a car]
motosierra *f* chain saw
motriz *adj* driving; **fuerza** ~ driving force
movedizo, **-a** *adj* **1.** (*móvil*) moving; **arenas movedizas** quicksand; *fig* dangerous ground **2.** (*inconstante*) changeable
mover <o→ue> **I.** *vt* **1.** (*desplazar*) to move; ~ **la cola** to wag one's tail; ~ **la cabeza** (*asentir*) to nod (one's head); (*negar*) to shake one's head **2.** (*ajedrez*) to move **3.** (*incitar*) to rouse; ~ **a alguien a compasión** to move sb; ~ **a alguien a lágrimas** to move sb to tears **4.** INFOR to move; ~ **archivo** move file **II.** *vr:* **~se** to move; **¿nos movemos o qué?** shall we make a move?; **¡venga, muévete!** come on! get a move on!
movible *adj* **1.** (*pieza*) movable **2.** (*carácter*) changeable
movida *f* **1.** *inf* fuss; **¡qué ~!** (*lío*) what a business! **2.** (*ambiente*) scene
movido, **-a** *adj* **1.** (*foto*) blurred **2.** (*activo*) active; (*vivo*) lively; **he tenido un día muy** ~ I have had a very busy day **3.** MÚS rhythmic
móvil **I.** *adj* mobile **II.** *m* **1.** (*para colgar*) mobile **2.** (*crimen*) motive **3.** TEL mobile (phone), cellphone *Am*
movilidad *f sin pl* mobility
movilización *f* **1.** (*recursos, tropas*) mobilization **2.** (*huelga*) industrial action **3.** (*dinero*) release
movilizar <z→c> *vt* **1.** (*ejército, recursos, fuerzas*) to mobilize **2.** (*dinero*) to release
movimiento *m* **1.** *t.* FÍS movement; ~ **vibratorio** vibratory movement; **hacer ~s** ARQUIT to subside; **poner en** ~ to put [*o* set] in motion; **había mucho ~ en las tiendas** the shops were busy **2.** (*ajedrez*) move **3.** MÚS (*velocidad*) tempo; (*tiempo*) movement **4.** HIST, LIT, POL movement; **el Movimiento (Nacional)** *ruling political organization in Francoist Spain* **5.** COM movement; **~s bursátiles** stock-market movements
moza *f* (*chica*) girl; **¡está ya hecha una ~!** she is a big girl now!
mozambiqueño, **-a** *adj, m, f* Mozambican
mozo *m* **1.** (*criado*) servant; ~ **(de café)** waiter; ~ **(de estación)** porter; ~ **de hotel** bellboy **2.** (*soldado*) recruit
mozo, **-a** **I.** *adj* **1.** (*joven*) young; **la gente moza** the youth **2.** (*soltero*) single **II.** *m, f* (*chico*) lad; (*chica*) girl; (*joven*) youth, young man; **¡pero si estás hecho un ~!** (*a un chico*) what a strapping lad you are!; (*a un adulto*) you are nothing but a lad!
mu **I.** *interj* (*vaca*) moo **II.** *m* **no decir ni** ~ *inf* not to say a word
mucamo, **-a** *m, f AmL* (*criado*) servant; (*criada*) maid
muceta *f* (*del doctor, juez*) cape
muchacha *f* **1.** *v.* **muchacho** **2.** (*criada*) maid
muchachada *f AmL* group of youths
muchacho, **-a** *m, f* (*chico*) boy; (*chica*) girl
muchedumbre *f* **1.** (*de cosas*) collection; **salió volando una ~ de pájaros** a flock of birds flew off **2.** (*de personas*) crowd
mucho, **-a** **I.** *adj* a lot of; ~ **vino** a lot of wine, much wine; **~s libros** a lot of books, many books; **esto es ~ para ella** this is too much for her; **hace ya ~ tiempo que...** it has been a long time since ...; **muchas veces** lots of times; **eso me parece ~ decir** I think that is going a bit far ►**mal de ~s, consuelo de tontos** *prov* ≈ only a fool finds comfort in the fact that a misfortune is shared by others **II.** *adv* (*intensidad*) very; **trabajar/esforzarse** ~ to work/to try hard; (*cantidad*) a lot; (*mucho tiempo*) for a long time; (*muchas veces*) many times; (*a menudo*) often; **lo sentimos** ~ we are very sorry; **no hace ~ estuvo aquí** he was here not long ago; **es con ~ el más simpático** he is by far the most pleasant; **¡pero que muy ~!** extremely!; **lo tenemos en** ~ we think highly of him; **por ~ que se esfuercen, no lo conseguirán** however hard they try, they will not manage it; **ni ~ menos** far from it; **como** ~ at (the) most
mucosa *f* mucus
mucosidad *f* (*moco*) mucosity
mucoso, **-a** *adj* mucous; **membrana mucosa** mucous membrane
muda *f* **1.** (*ropa interior*) change of underwear; (*cama*) change of sheets **2.** (*serpiente*) slough, shedding of skin **3.** (*pájaro, pelo*) moult *Brit,* molt *Am* **4.** (*voz*) **está de** ~ his voice is breaking
mudable *adj* changeable
mudanza *f* (*de casa*) move; **camión de ~s** removal van, moving van; **estar de** ~ to be moving house
mudar **I.** *vi, vt* **1.** (*cambiar*) to change; ~ **(de) pluma** to moult *Brit,* to molt *Am;* ~ **(de) piel** to slough, to shed; **los años le han mudado el** [*o* **de**] **carácter** the years have altered his/her character **2.** (*de ropa*) to change **II.** *vr:* **~se** **1.** (*casa*) to move (house); **nos mudamos (de aquí)** we are moving (from here); **~se a Granada** to move to Granada; **~se a una casa nueva** to move to a new house **2.** (*ropa*) **~se (de ropa)** to change clothes
mudez *f sin pl* muteness, dumbness; (*silencio*) silence
mudo, **-a** **I.** *adj* dumb; **cine** ~ silent films *Brit,* silent movies *Am;* **quedarse ~ de asombro** to be speechless with amazement **II.** *m, f* mute [*o* dumb] person
mueble **I.** *m* **1.** (*pieza*) piece of furniture; ~ **bar** drinks cabinet; ~ **biblioteca** bookcase; **cama** ~ foldaway bed; ~ **zapatero** shoe cupboard; ~ **de cocina** kitchen unit **2.** *pl* furniture; **con/sin ~s** furnished/unfurnished; **~s de cocina** kitchen units [*o* cabinets]; **~s de época** period furniture; **~s tapizados** uphol-

stered furniture **II.** *adj* JUR **bienes ~s** movable goods, personal property

mueca *f* face; **hacer ~s** to pull faces; (*de dolor, disgusto*) grimace

muela *f* **1.** (*diente*) molar; **~s del juicio** wisdom teeth; **~ picada** molar with tooth decay; **dolor de ~s** toothache **2.** (*molino*) millstone **3.** (*para afilar*) grindstone

muelle **I.** *m* **1.** (*resorte*) spring; (*reloj*) mainspring **2.** (*puerto*) wharf; **~ flotante** floating quay **3.** (*andén*) loading dock **II.** *adj* (*blando*) soft; (*cómodo*) comfortable

muérdago *m* mistletoe

muerte *f* **1.** (*acción de morir*) death; **~ forestal** forest destruction; **~ subita** MED crib death; **~ a traición** death by treachery; **pena de ~** death penalty; **condenar a ~** to condemn [*o* sentence] to death; **morir de ~ natural** to die of natural causes; **está luchando contra la ~** he/she is fighting for his/her life; **estar enfermo de ~** to be at death's door; **está en su lecho de ~** he/she is on his/her deathbed; **hasta que la ~ os separe** (*matrimonio*) till death do you part **2.** (*asesinato*) murder **3.** (*destrucción*) destruction ►**cada ~ de un obispo** once in a blue moon; **de mala ~** lousy, crummy; **un hotel de mala ~** a grotty hotel; **a ~** to death; **a ese tipo lo odio a ~** I detest that man; **llevarse un susto de ~** to have a dreadful fright

muerto, -a **I.** *pp de* **morir** **II.** *adj* dead; **cal muerta** slaked [*o* hydrated] lime; **horas muertas** period of inactivity; **naturaleza muerta** still life; **estar ~ (de cansancio)** to be exhausted; **estar ~ de hambre/sed** to be ravenous/dying of thirst; **para mí esa está muerta** I disown her; **caerse ~** to drop dead; **no tener dónde caerse ~** *inf* to be penniless; **punto ~** AUTO neutral **III.** *m, f* dead person; (*difunto*) deceased; (*cadáver*) corpse; (*víctima*) victim; **están tocando a ~s** the bells are tolling for a death; **ahora me cargan el ~ a mí** *inf* now they are laying the blame on me; **hacerse el ~** (*callado*) to keep as quiet as a mouse; (*quieto, t. fig*) to play dead; (*nadando*) to float; **ser un ~ de hambre** to be a nobody

muesca *f* nick; (*ranura*) groove

muesli *m* muesli

muestra *f* **1.** (*mercancía*) sample; **~ gratuita** free sample; **feria de ~s** trade fair **2.** (*prueba*) proof; **~ de amistad** token of friendship **3.** (*demostración*) demonstration; **dar ~(s) de valor** to give a demonstration of courage; **de ~, un botón** one example will suffice **4.** (*de labores*) example; **~ de bordado/punto** example of embroidery/knitting **5.** MED **~ de sangre/orina** blood/urine sample [*o* specimen] **6.** (*rótulo*) sign ►**por la ~ se conoce el paño** *prov* a friend in need is a friend indeed

muestrario *m* collection of samples

muestreo *m* sampling

mugido *m* **1.** (*vaca*) moo **2.** (*viento, mar*) roar

mugir <g→j> *vi* **1.** (*vaca*) to moo **2.** (*viento, agua*) to roar

mugre *f sin pl* grime

mugriento, -a *adj* grubby

mujer *f* woman; **~ de edad** elderly lady; **~ fácil** loose woman; **~ fatal** femme fatale; **~ de la limpieza** cleaning lady; **~ de la calle** prostitute; **una ~ de rompe y rasga** a woman who knows what she wants (and how to get it); **ser una ~ de su casa** to be a good housewife; **tomar ~** to take a wife; **está hecha toda una ~** she really is grown-up; **esto es cosa de ~es** this is women's stuff

mujerero, -a *adj AmC, AmS* (*mujeriego*) woman-chasing, skirt-chasing

mujeriego *m* womanizer

muladar *m* (*basurero*) rubbish dump *Brit,* trash dump *Am;* (*estiércol*) dunghill

mulato, -a **I.** *adj* (*mestizo*) mulatto; (*color*) brown-skinned **II.** *m, f* mulatto

mulero, -a *m, f RíoPl* **1.** *inf* (*mentiroso*) liar **2.** *inf* (*tramposo*) cheat

muleta *f* **1.** (*apoyo*) crutch; **andar con ~s** to walk with crutches **2.** TAUR *red cloth attatched to a stick used by a matador*

muletilla *f* (*coletilla*) tag; (*palabra*) pet word; (*frase*) catch phrase

mullido, -a *adj* soft

mullir <*3. pret:* mulló> *vt* **1.** (*almohada*) to fluff up **2.** (*tierra*) to dig over; (*cepas*) to hoe

mullo *m* **1.** ZOOL (*salmonete*) red mullet **2.** *Ecua* (*abalorio*) coloured *Brit* [*o* colored *Am*] bead

mulo, -a *m, f* (*caballo y asna*) hinny; (*asno y yegua*) mule

multa *f* fine; **poner una ~ a alguien** to fine sb

multar *vt* to fine; **me han multado con 3.000 pesetas** I've been fined 3000 pesetas

multicines *mpl* multiplex

multicolor *adj* multicoloured *Brit,* multicolored *Am;* TIPO polychromatic

multicopista *f* duplicator

multiforme *adj* multifarious

multilingüe *adj* multilingual

multimedia *adj inv* multimedia; **programa ~ de computadora** multimedia computer program

multimillonario, -a *m, f* multimillionaire

multinacional *adj, f* multinational

múltiple *adj* multiple; (*variado*) multifarious; **~s veces** numerous times

multiplicación *f t.* MAT multiplication

multiplicar <c→qu> **I.** *vi, vt* **1.** MAT **~ por algo** to multiply by sth; **tabla de ~** multiplication table **2.** (*reproducir, aumentar*) to multiply **II.** *vr:* **~se** **1.** (*reproducirse*) to multiply; **¡creced y multiplicaos!** REL go forth and multiply! **2.** (*desvivirse*) to be everywhere at the same time

multiplicidad *f* multiplicity

múltiplo, -a *adj, m, f* multiple

multitud *f* **1.** (*cantidad*) multitude; **una ~ de flores** a great number of flowers **2.** (*gente*) multitude, crowd; (*vulgo*) masses *pl*

M

multitudinario, **-a** *adj* multitudinous
multiuso *adj inv* multi-purpose
mundanal *adj,* **mundano**, **-a** *adj* **1.**(*del mundo*) of the world; (*terrenal*) worldly **2.**(*extravagante*) society
mundial *adj* world; **campeonato ~ de fútbol** World Cup; **guerra ~** world war; **a nivel ~** worldwide
mundillo *m* **1.** *inf* (*ambiente*) world; **el ~ de la música** the world of music; **ella se maneja bien en ese ~** she gets on well in that circle **2.**(*encaje*) lace pillow
mundo *m* **1.**(*tierra*) earth; (*planeta*) planet; (*globo*) world; **~ profesional** professional world; **el ~ antiguo** the ancient world; **el otro ~** the next world; **no sabemos si en los otros ~s hay vida** we do not know if there is life on the other planets; **dar la vuelta al ~** to go round the world; **echar al ~** to give birth to; **venir al ~** to be born; **irse de este ~** to die; **se bañaban como Dios los/las trajo al ~** they swam in the nude; **ver ~** to travel a lot; **andar por esos ~s de Dios** *inf* (*estar de viaje*) to be travelling all over the place; (*estar perdido*) to be lost; **recorrer medio ~** to visit many countries; **con la mayor tranquilidad del ~** with the utmost calm; **rápidamente se le cae el ~ encima** he/she quickly gets discouraged; **vive en otro ~** *fig* he/she lives in a world of his/her own; **este ~ es un pañuelo** it is a small world; **desde que el ~ es ~** since the world began; **ponerse el ~ por montera, reírse del ~** not to care what others think/say; **hacer un ~ de algo** to make a mountain out of a molehill; **así va** [*o* **anda**] **el ~** that is the way things are; **no es nada del otro ~** it is nothing out of this world; **por nada del ~** not for the world; **dejó el ~ y se metió monja** she left this world and became a nun **2.**(*humanidad*) **todo el ~** everyone, everybody; **a la vista de todo el ~** for the whole world to see; **todo el ~ sabe que...** everyone knows that ...; **lo sabe medio ~** nearly everyone knows that **3.**(*experiencia*) worldliness; **Lola tiene mucho ~** Lola is worldly-wise
mundología *f sin pl, inf* worldly wisdom
Múnich *m* Munich
munición *f* (*de armas*) ammunition
municipal *adj* municipal; **parque ~** municipal park; **término ~** municipality
municipio *m* **1.**(*población*) municipality, borough **2.**(*ayuntamiento*) town hall **3.**(*concejo*) town council
munificencia *f sin pl* munificence
munir **I.** *vt CSur* **~ de algo** to provide with sth; **ir munido de los documentos necesarios** to have the necessary documents **II.** *vr CSur* **~se de algo** to provide oneself with sth; **~se del equipo necesario** to provide oneself with the necessary equipment; **~se de suficientes provisiones** to equip oneself with sufficient provisions
muñeca *f* **1.**(*brazo*) wrist **2.**(*juguete*) doll **3.**(*maniquí*) dummy; **~ hinchable** inflatable doll **4.** *fig* (*niña*) doll, cutie *Am*
muñeco *m* **1.**(*juguete*) doll; **~ articulado** jointed doll; **~ de nieve** snowman **2.** *pey* (*monigote*) puppet
muñequera *f* wristband
muñón *m* stump
mural **I.** *adj* wall **II.** *m* mural
muralla *f* wall
murciélago *m* bat
murga *f inf* (*banda*) street band; **dar la ~ a alguien** to bother sb; **¡deja de darme la ~!** stop bothering [*o* bugging] me!
murmullo *m* **1.**(*voz*) whisper; (*cuchicheo*) murmur **2.**(*hojas*) rustling; (*agua*) murmur
murmuración *f* (*calumnia*) slander; (*cotilleo*) gossip
murmurar **I.** *vi, vt* (*entre dientes*) to mutter; (*susurrar*) to murmur; **~ al oído de alguien** to whisper in sb's ear **II.** *vi* **1.**(*gruñir*) to grumble **2.**(*criticar*) to criticize; (*chismorrear*) to gossip **3.**(*agua*) to murmur; (*hojas*) to rustle
muro *m* wall; **~ de contención** retaining wall; **Muro de las Lamentaciones** the Wailing Wall; **~ medianero** party [*o* dividing] wall
murria *f sin pl, inf* (*tristeza*) gloominess, blues
murrio, **-a** *adj* gloomy, blue
mus *m card game*
musa *f* muse; **se le sopló la ~** he/she was inspired; (*en un juego*) he/she was on a lucky streak
musaraña *f* **1.** ZOOL shrew **2.** *fig* (*bicho*) small animal; (*insecto*) bug; **pensar en las ~s** *fig* to have one's head in the clouds **3.**(*nubecilla*) film
muscular *adj* muscular
musculatura *f* musculature
músculo *m* muscle; **~ deltoide** deltoid muscle; **ser ~ puro** to be all muscle
musculoso, **-a** *adj* muscular
muselina *f* muslin
museo *m* museum; **~ etnográfico** museum of ethnography
musgo *m* moss
música *f* **1.**(*sonido*) music; (*partituras*) score; **~ folclórica** traditional music; **~ ratonera** *inf* cabaret [*o* pub] music; **~ sacra** sacred music; **~ de cámara** chamber music; **~ ambiental** muzak, canned [*o* piped] music; **~ ligera** easy listening; **banda de ~** band; **caja de ~** music box; **¡véte con la ~ a otra parte!** *inf* get out of here!; **tus palabras nos sonaron a ~ celestial** you were spouting nonsense; **tener talento para la ~** to be musical **2.**(*orquesta*) orchestra
musical **I.** *adj* musical; **composición ~** musical composition **II.** *m* musical
músico, **-a** **I.** *adj* musical **II.** *m, f* musician; (*compositor*) composer; **~ ambulante** itinerant musician
musicología *f sin pl* musicology
musicólogo, **-a** *m, f* musicologist
musitar *vi* **1.**(*balbucear*) to mumble; (*susu-

rrear) to whisper; ~ **al oído de alguien** to whisper in sb's ear **2.** (*hojas*) to rustle
muslo *m* (*persona*) thigh; (*animal*) leg
mustela *f* weasel
mustio, -a *adj* **1.** (*flores*) wilting **2.** (*triste*) low
musulmán, -ana *adj, m, f* Muslim
mutable *adj* mutable
mutación *f* **1.** (*transformación, genes*) mutation **2.** TEAT scene change **3.** METEO appreciable change
mutilado, -a *m, f* cripple; ~ **de guerra** disabled war veteran
mutilar *vt* **1.** (*cuerpo*) to mutilate **2.** (*recortar*) to cut
mutis *m inv* **1.** TEAT exit; ~ **por el foro** quick exit; **hacer** ~ to exit **2.** (*silencio*) **¡~!** shh!
mutismo *m* silence; **no hay manera de sacarlo de su** ~ there is no way of making him break his silence
mutual **I.** *adj* mutual **II.** *f CSur* mutual benefit society
mutualidad *f* **1.** (*cooperativa*) mutual benefit society; ~ **de accidentes de trabajo** mutual insurance company; ~ **obrera** workers' mutual society **2.** (*reciprocidad*) mutuality
mutuo, -a *adj* mutual
muy *adv* very; **es** ~ **improbable que...** +*subj* it is very unlikelythat ...; ~ **a pesar mío** much to my dismay; ~ **de tarde en tarde** once in a blue moon; ~ **de mañana** in the very early morning; **¿y qué ha hecho el ~ tunante?** and what has the little devil done?; **le saluda ~ atentamente,** (*en cartas*) yours faithfully [*o* sincerely]; **¡dejarnos plantados: eso es ~ de María!** to leave us in the lurch: that is typical of María!; **es Ud. ~ libre de hacer lo que quiera** you are absolutely free to do what you like; **¡guárdate ~ mucho de irlo contando por ahí!** *inf* be very careful not to go around talking about it!

N

N, n *f* N, n; ~ **de Navarra** N for Nelly *Brit,* N for Nan *Am*
naba *f* turnip
nabo *m* **1.** BOT turnip **2.** *vulg* (*pene*) cock **3.** ARQUIT main pillar
nácar *m* mother-of-pearl, nacre; **de** ~ nacreous, pearly
nacarado, -a *adj,* **nacarino, -a** *adj* nacreous, pearly
nacatamal *m AmC, Méx* GASTR pork tamale
nacer *irr como crecer vi* **1.** (*venir al mundo*) to be born; **nací el 29 de febrero** I was born on the 29th of February; **no nací ayer** I wasn't born yesterday; **haber nacido para la música** to be a natural for music; **volver a** ~ to have a very narrow escape **2.** (*del huevo*) to hatch **3.** (*germinar*) to germinate **4.** (*astr*) to be created; **nace una estrella** a star is born **5.** (*día*) to rise; **al ~ el día** at the break of day **6.** (*originarse*) to stem; (*arroyo*) to begin; (*surgir*) to arise; **nació una duda en su mente** *elev* a doubt was sown in his/her mind ▸**nadie nace enseñado** *prov* we all have to learn; **no con quien naces, sino con quien paces** *prov* it's your environment that counts, not your birth
nacido, -a **I.** *pp de* **nacer** **II.** *adj* **bien** ~ (*origen*) born into a good family; (*comportamiento*) noble; ~ **de padres ricos** born into a well-off family **III.** *m, f* **recién** ~ newborn; **los ~s el 2 de abril** those born on the 2nd of April; **un mal** ~ a born villain
naciente[1] **I.** *adj fig* incipient, budding **II.** *m* (*oriente*) orient; (*este*) east
naciente[2] *f Arg, Par* spring
nacimiento *m* **1.** (*venida al mundo*) birth; **de** ~ by birth; **ciego de** ~ born blind; **lugar de** ~ birthplace; **partida de** ~ birth certificate; (*belén*) Nativity scene **2.** (*linaje*) family; **ser de humilde** ~ to be of humble birth **3.** (*comienzo*) beginning; ~ **del pelo** root (of hair)
nación *f* nation; (**la Organización de**) **las Naciones Unidas** the United Nations (Organization)
nacional *adj* national; **carretera** ~ (*en el Reino Unido*) A [*o* arterial] road; (*en los Estados Unidos*) highway; **moneda** ~ national currency; **producto** ~ national product; **renta** ~ national income; **vuelos ~es** domestic flights
nacionalidad *f* (*ciudadanía*) nationality, citizenship; **ser de ~ española** to have Spanish nationality, to be a Spanish national
nacionalismo *m sin pl* nationalism
nacionalista *adj, mf* nationalist
nacionalización *f* (*persona*) naturalization, nationalization; (*expropiación*) expropriation
nacionalizar <z→c> **I.** *vt* (*persona*) to naturalize, to nationalize **II.** *vr* **~se español** to obtain Spanish nationality
naco *m* **1.** *AmC* (*cobarde*) coward **2.** *AmC* (*marica*) queer **3.** *Arg* (*miedo*) fear
nada **I.** *pron indef* nothing; **¡gracias! – ¡de ~!** thank you! – not at all!; **¡pues ~!** well all right then; **por ~ se queja** he/she complains about the slightest thing; **como si** ~ as if nothing had happened; **le costó ~ más y ~ menos que...** it cost him/her the fine sum of ...; ~ **menos que el director** the director himself; **no servir para** ~ to be useless **II.** *adv* not at all; ~ **más** (*solamente*) only; (*no más*) no more; **¡~ más!** enough!; ~ **de** ~ absolutely nothing; **no ser ~ difícil** not to be difficult at all; **¡~ de eso!** none of that!; **¡y ~ de llegar tarde!** no arriving late!; **¡casi ~!** hardly anything!; **antes de** ~ (*sobre todo*) above all; (*primero*) first of all; **para** ~ not in the slightest **III.** *f* nothing, nothingness; **salir de la** ~ to appear out of

nowhere; **la ~ de nuestras vidas** *elev* the emptiness of our lives

nadador(a) *m(f)* swimmer

nadar *vi* to swim; **~ en deudas** to be swimming in debt

nadería *f* nothing important

nadie *pron indef* nobody, anybody, no one; **no ví a ~** I didn't see anybody, I saw nobody; **no vino ~** nobody came; **tú no eres ~ para decir...** who are you to say ...?; **un don ~** a nobody; **tierra de ~** no man's land

nadita I. *f Ecua, Méx* **en ~ estuvo que lo mataran** they almost killed him II. *adv Méx* in no time

nado *adv* **a ~** afloat, swimming; **cruzar algo a ~** to swim across sth

nafta *f* 1. QUÍM naphtha 2. *CSur* (*gasolina*) petrol *Brit*, gasoline *Am*

nagual *f Méx, Hond* witch doctor

nagualear *vi* 1. *Méx* (*mentir*) to lie 2. *Méx* (*robar*) to swipe

naif *adj* naive; ARTE naive, primitive

nailon *m* nylon

naipe *m* 1. (*carta*) card 2. *pl* (*baraja*) pack of cards

najarse *vr inf* to beat it, to scram

nalga *f* buttock; **~s** bottom

namibio, -a *adj, m, f* Namibian

nana *f* 1. (*canción*) lullaby 2. (*niñera*) nanny

nanay *interj inf* no way!

napia(s) *f(pl) inf* conk

Nápoles *m* Naples

napolitano, -a *adj, m, f* Neapolitan

naranja I. *f* 1. BOT orange 2. ARQUIT **media ~** dome ►**¡~s (de la China)!** no way!; **tu media ~** your better half II. *adj* **(de color) ~** orange

naranjada *f* orangeade

naranjado, -a *adj* orangey

naranjal *m* orange grove

naranjo *m* orange tree

narcisismo *m sin pl* narcissism, egoism

narcisista *adj* narcissistic

narciso *m* 1. BOT daffodil, narcissus *inv* 2. (*persona*) narcissist

narco *m inf* drug dealer [*o* trafficker]

narcosis *f inv* MED narcosis

narcoterrorismo *m sin pl* drugs terrorism

narcótico *m* narcotic

narcótico, -a *adj* narcotic

narcotizar <z→c> *vt* to narcotize

narcotraficante *mf* drug dealer [*o* trafficker]

narcotráfico *m* drug dealing [*o* trafficking]

narigada *f Ecua* pinch of snuff

narigón *m inf* big nose

narigón, -ona *adj* big-nosed

narigudo, -a *adj* (*narigón*) big-nosed

nariz *f* 1. ANAT nose; **~ chata** flat nose; **~ ganchuda** hooked nose; **~ respingona** turned-up nose; **~ aguileña** aquiline nose; **dar a alguien con la puerta en las narices** to slam the door in sb's face; **darse de narices con alguien** *inf* to bump straight into sb; **sonarse/limpiarse la ~** to blow/wipe one's nose; **romper las narices a alguien** to smash sb's face in; **no ver más allá de sus narices** *inf* to be short-sighted; **quedarse con un palmo de narices** *inf* to be let down 2. *inf* (*eufemismo por 'cojones'*) **estar hasta las narices** to have had it up to here; **hasta que se me hinchen las narices** until I lose my rag; **lo hizo por narices** he/she did it because he/she felt like it; **¡(qué) narices!** no way; **tener narices** to be too much; **¡tócate las narices!** would you believe it? 3. (*intuición*) suspicions *pl;* **me da en la ~ que...** I've got a funny feeling that...

narizudo, -a *adj Méx* (*narigudo*) large-nosed

narración *f* narration

narrador(a) *m(f)* narrator; (*que cuenta la historia*) storyteller

narrar *vt* 1. (*contar*) to narrate 2. (*informar*) to tell

narrativa I. *adj* narrative II. *f* literature

nasal *adj* nasal

nata *f* 1. (*producto*) cream; **~ montada** whipped cream 2. (*sobre un líquido*) film 3. (*lo más selecto*) the best; **la crema y ~ de la sociedad** the crème de la crème of society

natación *f* DEP swimming

natal *adj* native, home; **ciudad ~** home town; **país ~** native country [*o* land]

natalicio, -a *adj* birthday

natalidad *f* birth; **índice de ~** birth rate; **de fuerte/baja ~** with a high/low birth rate

natatorio, -a *adj* swimming; **vejiga natatoria** ZOOL swimming bladder

natillas *fpl* custard

natividad *f* nativity

nativo, -a I. *adj* 1. (*natal*) native, home; **lengua nativa** native [*o* mother] tongue; **profesor ~** native teacher 2. (*metal*) native II. *m, f AmL* native

nato, -a *adj* born; **un triunfador ~** a born winner

natural I. *adj* 1. (*no artificial, sencillo*) natural; **de tamaño ~** life-sized; **esto es lo más ~ del mundo** (*normal*) it is the most natural thing in the world; (*lógico*) it makes perfect sense 2. (*nacido*) **ser ~ del Reino Unido** to be a British natural; **hijo ~** illegitimate child II. *m* native

naturaleza *f* 1. (*campo*) nature; **~ muerta** still life; **en plena ~** in the heart of the countryside 2. (*manera*) nature 3. (*índole*) type; **de ~ pública** of the public domain

naturalidad *f sin pl* naturalness; **lo dijo con mucha ~** he said it very naturally

naturalizar <z→c> I. *vt* to naturalize; **~ costumbres** to take on customs; **~ un animal** to acclimatize an animal II. *vr* **~se a algo** (*habituarse*) to get used to sth

naufragar <g→gu> *vi* 1. (*hundirse*) to sink 2. (*no hundir del todo*) to be wrecked; (*personas*) to be shipwrecked 3. (*fracasar*) to fall through

naufragio *m* 1. (*accidente*) shipwreck 2. (*fracaso*) failure; (*de negociaciones*) breakdown

náufrago, -a I. *adj* shipwrecked II. *m, f* shipwrecked sailor, castaway
nauseabundo, -a *adj* nauseating
náuseas *fpl* sick feeling; **tengo** ~ I feel sick; **dar** ~ **a alguien** to make sb feel sick
náutica *f sin pl* navigation
náutico, -a *adj* nautical; **club** ~ yacht club
nava *f* plain
navaja *f* 1. (*cuchillo*) (pocket) knife; ~ **de afeitar** razor; ~ **automática** flick knife *Brit,* switchblade *Am* 2. ZOOL (*molusco*) razor clam 3. (*colmillo*) tusk; (*aguijón*) sting
navajada *f,* **navajazo** *m* 1. (*golpe*) stabbing 2. (*herida*) stab [*o* knife] wound, gash
navajero, -a *m, f* (*delincuente*) thug who carries a knife
naval *adj* naval
navarro, -a I. *adj* of/from Navarra II. *m, f* native/inhabitant of Navarra
nave *f* 1. NÁUT ship, vessel 2. AVIAT ~ (**espacial**) spaceship, spacecraft 3. (*en una iglesia*) nave; ~ **central** main nave 4. (*almacén*) warehouse 5. (*fábrica*) factory unit ►**quemar las ~s** to burn one's bridges
navegable *adj* navigable; **rutas ~s** navigable routes
navegación *f* navigation
navegador *m* INFOR browser
navegante *mf* navigator; ~ **de internet** Net surfer
navegar <g→gu> I. *vi, vt* to navigate; ~ **veinte nudos por hora** to sail at 20 knots an hour; ~ **contra la corriente** to go against the flow; ~ **por la web** to surf the net II. *vi* (*vagar*) to roam
Navidad *f* Christmas; **¡feliz ~!** merry Christmas!
navideño, -a *adj* Christmas; (*ambiente*) festive
naviero, -a I. *m, f* shipowner II. *adj* shipping
navío *m* ship
nazi *adj, mf* HIST Nazi
nazismo *m sin pl* Nazism
N. de la R. *abr de* **Nota de la Redacción** Ed.
N. del T. *abr de* **Nota del Traductor** T.N.
NE *abr de* **Nordeste** NE
neblina *f* mist; *fig* haze
neblinoso, -a *adj* 1. (*nebuloso*) foggy 2. (*brumoso*) misty
nebuloso, -a *adj* 1. (*brumoso*) misty 2. (*nuboso*) cloudy 3. (*vago*) hazy 4. (*oscuro*) obscure
necedad *f* stupidity; **no decir más que ~es** to talk a lot of nonsense
necesariamente *adv* necessarily
necesario, -a *adj* necessary; **es ~ que haya más acuerdo** there is a need for more agreement; **la lluvia hizo ~ quedarse en casa** the rain meant we had to stay at home
neceser *m* (*de aseo*) toilet bag; (*de costura*) sewing box; (*de afeitar*) shaving kit; (*de herramientas*) tool box; (*de maquillaje*) cosmetic bag
necesidad *f* 1. (*ser preciso*) need, necessity; **de primera ~** essential; **no tiene ~ de trabajar** there is no need for him/her to work 2. (*requerimiento*) need; **tener ~ de algo** to be in need of sth 3. (*apuro*) difficulty; (*penurias*) suffering 4. *pl* (*evacuación corporal*) **hacer sus ~es** to relieve oneself
necesitado, -a I. *adj* (*pobre*) needy; **estar ~ de amor** to be in need of love II. *m, f* poor person; **los ~s** the poor
necesitar I. *vt* 1. (*precisar*) to need; **se necesita piso** flat wanted *Brit,* apartment wanted *Am* 2. (*tener que*) to need to; **necesitas comer algo** you've got to eat something II. *vi* (*precisar*) ~ **de algo** to need sth
necio, -a I. *adj* idiotic II. *m, f* idiot
nécora *f* fiddler crab
necrófago, -a I. *adj* necrophagous, carrion-eating II. *m, f* carrion-eater
necrología *f* 1. (*biografía*) obituary 2. (*nota*) list of deaths
necrológico, -a *adj* necrological
necrosis *f* MED necrosis; (*gangrena*) gangrene
néctar *m* nectar
nectarina *f* nectarine
neerlandés, -esa I. *adj* Dutch II. *m, f* Dutchman *m,* Dutchwoman *f*
nefando, -a *adj* abominable
nefario, -a *adj* terrible
nefasto, -a *adj* awful; (*día*) horrible
nefrítico, -a *adj* MED suffering from nephritis
nefritis *f* MED nephritis
negación *f* 1. (*desmentir*) denial 2. (*denegar*) refusal 3. LING negative; **es la ~ del arte** it is anything but art
negado, -a I. *adj* ~ **para algo** useless at sth II. *m, f* **ser un ~ para las matemáticas** to be no good at maths *Brit* [*o* math *Am*]; **ser un ~ para las labores de la casa** to be useless at housework
negar *irr como fregar* I. *vt* 1. (*desmentir*) to deny 2. (*rehusar*) to refuse; (*rechazar*) to reject; ~ **con la cabeza** to shake one's head II. *vr:* **~se** to refuse
negativa *f* (*negación*) denial; (*rehusamiento*) refusal; (*rechazo*) rejection
negativo *m* FOTO negative
negativo, -a *adj* negative; **tu respuesta fue negativa** your answer was negative
negligencia *f* 1. (*descuido*) carelessness 2. (*abandono*) neglect 3. JUR negligence
negligente I. *adj* 1. (*descuidado*) careless; **ser ~ en** [*o* **para**] **su trabajo** to be a careless worker 2. JUR negligent II. *mf* JUR negligent party
negociable *adj* negotiable; **el precio es ~** the price is open to negotiation
negociación *f* (*convenio*) negotiation; ~ **colectiva** collective bargaining; **entrar en negociaciones con alguien** to enter into negotiations with sb
negociado *m* 1. (*dependencia*) section; **jefe de ~** head of department 2. *AmS* (*negocio*)

suspicious deal
negociador(a) I. *adj* negotiating II. *m(f)* 1. (*comerciante*) merchant 2. (*mediador*) negotiator
negociante *mf* 1. (*comerciante*) dealer 2. *pey* moneygrubber
negociar I. *vi* (*comerciar*) to deal II. *vi, vt* (*dialogar, concertar*) to negotiate
negocio *m* 1. (*comercio*) business; ~ **al detalle** retail business; **hombre/mujer de ~s** businessman/businesswoman 2. (*asunto*) matter; **eso no es ~ mio** it's none of my business ▶**hacer un ~ redondo** *inf* to do a good bit of business
negra *f* MÚS crotchet *Brit,* quarter note *Am*
negrada *f Cuba* HIST slaves (*body of slaves belonging to a plantation*)
negrero, -a *m, f* 1. (*que trata con esclavos*) slave dealer 2. (*tirano*) slave driver 3. *CSur* (*aprovechado*) parasite
negrilla *f,* **negrita** *f* TIPO bold face
negro, -a I. *adj* black; ~ **del sol** suntanned; ~ **como la boca del lobo** pitch-black; ~ **como el carbón** as black as coal ▶**estar/ponerse** ~ *inf* to be/get furious; **pasarlas negras** *inf* to have a terrible time; **tener la negra** *inf* to be jinxed; **verse ~ para hacer algo** *inf* to have a hard time doing sth; **verse** ~ [*o* **pasarlas negras**] **para encontrar algo** *inf* to have a hard time finding sth; **verlo todo** ~ to be very pessimistic II. *m, f* 1. (*persona*) black; **trabajar como un** ~ *inf* to work like a slave 2. (*escritor*) ghost writer 3. *Arg, inf* (*cariño*) darling
negrura *f* blackness
negruzco, -a *adj* blackish
neme *m Col* asphalt
nene, -a *m, f inf* (*niño*) baby; (*expresión de cariño*) dear
nenúfar *m* water lily
neocapitalismo *m sin pl* ECON neocapitalism
neoclasicismo *m sin pl* neoclassicism
neoclásico, -a *adj* neoclassical
neófito, -a *m, f* 1. (*bautizado*) *recently baptized person* 2. (*iniciado*) novice
neolatino, -a *adj* LING Neo-Latin; **lenguas neolatinas** Romance languages
neolítico *m* neolithic
neologismo *m* neologism
neón *m* neon
neoyorquino, -a I. *adj* of/from New York II. *m, f* New Yorker
neozelandés, -esa I. *adj* of/from New Zealand II. *m, f* New Zealander
nepalés, -esa I. *adj* Nepalese II. *m, f* Nepalese person
nepotismo *m sin pl* nepotism
Neptuno *m* Neptune
nervadura *f* 1. ARQUIT ribs *pl* 2. BOT venation 3. BIO veins *pl*
nervio *m* 1. (*conductor*) nerve; **ataque de ~s** nervous breakdown; **crispar los ~s a alguien, poner a alguien los ~s de punta** *inf* (*enfadar*) to drive sb mad [*o* crazy]; (*poner nervioso*) to get on sb's nerves; **ponerse de los ~s** to get nervous [*o* flustered]; **estar atacado de los ~s** to be a nervous wreck; **ser un puro ~** *inf* to be a bundle of nerves; **tener ~s de acero** to have nerves of steel 2. (*tendón*) sinew 3. BOT vein 4. (*libro*) band 5. (*ímpetu*) impetus; **esta empresa tiene ~** this company is dynamic
nerviosidad *f* 1. (*tensión*) tension 2. (*nerviosismo*) nervousness
nerviosismo *m* nervousness
nervioso, -a *adj* 1. ANAT nervous; **el sistema ~** the nervous system 2. (*intranquilo*) excitable
nervudo, -a *adj* tough; (*apariencia*) sinewy, wiry
neto, -a *adj* 1. (*claro*) clear 2. (*no bruto*) net
neumático I. *adj* pneumatic; **martillo ~** pneumatic drill II. *m* tyre *Brit,* tire *Am*
neumonía *f* MED pneumonia
neura *f inf* obsession
neural *adj* neural
neurología *f sin pl* MED neurology
neurólogo, -a *m, f* MED neurologist
neurona *f* ANAT neuron, neurone *Brit*
neurosis *f inv* neurosis
neurótico, -a *adj, m, f* neurotic
neurotizar <z→c> *vt inf* ~ **a alguien** to make sb neurotic
neutral *adj, mf* neutral
neutralidad *f* neutrality
neutralización *f* neutralization
neutralizar <z→c> I. *vt* to neutralize II. *vr:* **~se** to be neutralized
neutro, -a *adj* 1. *t.* QUÍM neutral 2. ZOOL sexless 3. LING neuter; **género ~** neuter gender
neutrón *m* FÍS neutron
nevada *f* snowfall; (*tormenta*) snowstorm
nevado, -a *adj* 1. (*cubierto*) snow-covered; (*montaña*) snow-capped 2. (*blanco*) snow-white
nevar <e→ie> *vimpers* to snow
nevazón *f Arg, Chile, Ecua* METEO blizzard, snowstorm
nevera *f* (*frigorífico*) fridge; (*portátil*) cool box; **este cuarto es una ~** this room is freezing
nevisca *f* light snowfall
neviscar <c→qu> *vimpers* to snow lightly
nexo *m* 1. nexus 2. LING connective
ni *conj* ~... ~... neither ... nor ...; **no fumo ~ bebo** I don't smoke or drink, I neither smoke nor drink; ~ (**siquiera**) not even; **¡~ lo pienses!** don't even let it cross your mind!; **sin más ~ más** without any further ado; **¡~ que fueras tonto!** anyone would think you were stupid!; ~ **bien...** *Arg* as soon as ...
nica *adj Nic, inf* Nicaraguan
Nicaragua *f* Nicaragua

Nicaragua lies in Central America, bordering Honduras to the north, Costa Rica to the south, the Caribbean to the east and the Pacific Ocean to the west. The capital of Nicaragua is **Managua**. The official language of the country is Spanish and the monetary unit is the **córdoba**.

nicaragüense *adj, mf* Nicaraguan
nicho *m* niche
nicotina *f* nicotine
nidada *f* **1.** (*huevos*) clutch (of eggs) **2.** (*polluelos*) brood
nidal *m* **1.** (*lugar*) nest **2.** (*huevo*) brooding egg **3.** (*escondite*) hiding place
nidificar <c→qu> *vi* ZOOL to nest
nido *m* **1.** (*lecho*) den; ~ **de ladrones** den of thieves; ~ **de discordias** hotbed of dissent; **caerse del** ~ *fig* to come down to earth with a bump **2.** (*nidal*) nest
niebla *f* fog; **hay** ~ it is foggy
nieto, **-a** *m, f* grandchild, grandson *m*, granddaughter *f*; **los nietos** the grandchildren
nieve *f* **1.** (*precipitación*) snow; ~ **carbónica** dry ice; **a punto de** ~ GASTR stiff; **copo de** ~ snowflake **2.** *inf* (*cocaína*) coke, snow **3.** *AmC* (*helado*) ice cream
NIF *m abr de* **Número de Identificación Fiscal** Fiscal Identity Number
nigeriano, **-a** *adj, m, f* Nigerian
nigua *f AmC* ZOOL jigger flea
Nilo *m* Nile
nilón *m* nylon
nimbo *m* METEO nimbus
nimiedad *f* (*insignificancia*) trifle
nimio, **-a** *adj* insignificant
ninfa *f* **1.** (*mitología*) nymph **2.** (*joven*) girl **3.** ZOOL nymph
ninfómana *f* nymphomaniac
ningún *adj indef v.* **ninguno**
ninguno, **-a I.** *adj indef* (*precediendo un substantivo masculino singular: ningún*) any; **por ningún lado** anywhere; **de ninguna manera** in no way; **ninguna vez** never; **en ningún sitio** nowhere; **no hay ningún peligro** there is no danger **II.** *pron indef* anything, nothing; (*personas*) anybody, nobody; **no quiso venir** ~ nobody wanted to come
niña *f* **1.** (*chica, persona no adulta*) girl **2.** ANAT pupil; **eres como las ~s de mis ojos** *fig* you are the apple of my eye
niñera *f* nanny; (*canguro*) babysitter
niñería *f* **1.** (*de niños*) childish act **2.** *inf* (*pequeñez*) triviality
niñez *f* childhood; *fig* infancy
niño *m* **1.** (*persona no adulta*) boy; ~ **bien** *inf* rich kid; ~ **de la bola** the baby Jesus; ~ **mimado** (*favorito*) spoilt child; ~ **de pecho** babe-in-arms; ~ **probeta** test tube baby; **¡no seas ~!** don't act like a child! **2.** *reg* (*joven*) young
nipón, **-ona I.** *adj* Japanese **II.** *m, f* native/inhabitant of Japan
níquel *m* nickel
niqui *m* (*camiseta*) T-shirt
nitidez *f* brightness; FOTO clarity
nítido, **-a** *adj* bright; FOTO clear
nitrato *m* nitrate; ~ **de plata** silver nitrate
nítrico, **-a** *adj* nitric; **ácido** ~ nitric acid
nitrito *m* nitrite
nitro *m* nitre, saltpetre
nitrógeno *m* nitrogen
nitroglicerina *f* nitroglycerine
nitroso, **-a** *adj* nitrous
nivel *m* **1.** (*estándar*) standard; ~ **de vida** standard of living; **estar al** ~ to come up to scratch; **estar al** ~ **de lo exigido** to rise to the occasion **2.** (*horizontalidad, grado, cota*) level; ~ **de burbuja** TÉC spirit level; ~ **estilístico** stylistic level; **paso a** ~ level crossing *Brit*, grade crossing *Am;* ~ **de la riada** flood level; **sobre el** ~ **del mar** above sea level
nivelación *f* levelling *Brit*, leveling *Am;* ~ **del presupuesto** balancing the budget
nivelado, **-a** *adj* level; (*horizontal*) horizontal
nivelar I. *vt* to level; (*parcela*) to level out **II.** *vr:* **~se** to level out; **~se con alguien** to catch up with sb
níveo, **-a** *adj elev* snowy, snow-white
nixtamal *m Méx* corn (*specially processed for tortilla-making*)
NO *abr de* **Noroeste** NW
no *adv* **1.** (*respuesta*) no; **¡que ~!** I tell you it isn't! **2.** + *adjetivo* non-; ~ **protegido** non-protected **3.** + *verbo* not; **~... nada** not ... anything; **~... nadie** not ... anyone; **~... nunca** not ... ever, never; ~ **lo compró** he/she did not buy it; ~ **tal** not at all; ~ **ya** not only; **ya** ~ not any more, no longer; **hoy** ~ **tengo clase** I don't have class today; ~ **tiene más que un abrigo** he/she only has one coat; ~ **quedan más que dos botellas** there are only two bottles left; ~ **querer más hijos** not to want any more children; ~ **quiero hablar más de esto** I don't want to talk about this any more **4.** (*retórica*) **¿~?** isn't he/she?, don't we/they? ▸ ~ **bien** +*subj* as soon as; **el** ~ **va más** the best, the state-of-the-art; **tener un** ~ **sé qué** to have something special; **a** ~ **ser que** +*subj* unless; **¡a que ~!** do you want to bet?; **¿cómo ~?** of course; **o, si** ~ otherwise
nº *abr de* **número** No.
nobiliario, **-a** *adj* noble
nobilísimo, **-a** *adj superl de* **noble**
noble I. *adj* <nobilísimo> **1.** *t.* QUÍM (*aristócrata*) noble **2.** (*bueno*) upright **3.** (*honesto*) honest **II.** *mf* nobleman *m*, noblewoman *f*
nobleza *f* **1.** (*linaje, hidalguía*) nobility **2.** (*bondad*) uprightness **3.** (*honestidad*) honesty
noche *f* **1.** (*contrario de día*) night; ~ **cerrada** complete darkness; **Noche Vieja** New Year's Eve, Hogmanay *Scot;* **buenas ~s** (*saludo*) good evening; (*despedida*) good night; **turno de** ~ night shift; **media** ~ midnight; **a media** ~ at midnight; **por la** ~ at night; **toda la** ~ all night long; **ayer (por la)** ~ last night; **hacerse**

de ~ to get dark; **hacer** ~ **en** to spend the night in **2.** (*tarde*) evening **3.** (*oscuridad*) darkness; **es de** ~ it's dark; **no veo más que** ~ **a mi alrededor** *elev* I am surrounded by darkness ►**ser como la** ~ **y el día** to be as different as night and day, to be like chalk and cheese *Brit;* **de la** ~ **a la mañana** overnight; **pasar una** ~ **en blanco** not to sleep a wink all night

Nochebuena *f* Christmas Eve; **en** ~ on Christmas Eve

nochecita *f AmL* dusk, nightfall

nocherniego, **-a** *adj, m, f v.* **noctámbulo**

nochero *m* **1.** *CSur* (*vigilante*) nightwatchman **2.** *Col* (*mesilla*) bedside table

Nochevieja *f* New Year's Eve, Hogmanay *Scot*

noción *f* **1.** (*idea*) idea; **perder la** ~ **del tiempo** to completely forget about the time **2.** *pl* (*fundamentos*) base; **tengo nociones de francés** I know a bit of French

nocividad *f* harmfulness

nocivo, **-a** *adj* harmful; ~ **para la salud** damaging to health

noctámbulo, **-a** **I.** *adj* (*trasnochador*) **ser** ~ to be a night-bird; (*salir*) to go out at night **II.** *m, f* (*trasnochador*) night worker; (*que sale*) night owl

nocturno *m* MÚS nocturne

nocturno, **-a** *adj* **1.** (*de noche*) night; **la vida nocturna** nightlife **2.** BOT, ZOOL nocturnal

nodo *m* node

nodriza *f* **1.** (*ama*) wet-nurse **2.** (*transporte*) **avión** ~ mother aeroplane *Brit,* mother airplane *Am;* **buque** ~ supply ship

nódulo *m* nodule

Noé *m* REL Noah; **el arca de** ~ Noah's ark

nogal *m,* **noguera** *f* walnut tree

nómada **I.** *adj* nomadic; **pueblo** ~ nomadic people **II.** *mf* nomad

nomás *adv AmL* **1.** (*solamente*) only; ~ **que** +*subj* unless; **¡pase** ~**!** come straight in! **2.** (*nada más*) and that was all **3.** (*apenas*) hardly

nombradía *f* (*reputación*) reputation; (*fama*) fame; **de gran** ~ of great repute

nombrado, **-a** *adj* **1.** (*que se nombra*) named **2.** (*fama*) famous

nombramiento *m* **1.** (*designación*) appointment; (*military*) commission **2.** (*documento*) title

nombrar *vt* **1.** (*citar*) to quote; (*mencionar*) to mention **2.** (*llamar*) to call **3.** (*designar*) to appoint; (*militar*) to commission

nombre *m* **1.** (*designación*) name; ~ **y apellido** name and surname, full name; ~ **de familia** surname *Brit,* last name *Am;* ~ **ficticio** false name; ~ **de pila**, **primer** ~ Christian [*o* first] name; ~ **del producto** product name; ~ **de soltera** maiden name; **de** ~, ~ **artístico** stage name, by name; **sin** ~ nameless; **en** ~ **de** on behalf of; **a su propio** ~ in his/her own name; **conocer a alguien de** ~ to know sb by name; **dar su** ~ to give one's name; **poner un** ~ **a alguien** to give sb a name; **llamar a las cosas por su** ~ *fig* to call a spade a spade; **tu conducta no tiene** ~ your behaviour *Brit* [*o* behavior *Am*] is a disgrace; **reservar a** ~ **de X** to book in X's name **2.** (*reputación*) reputation; **de** ~ famous **3.** LING noun; ~ **común** common noun; ~ **propio** proper noun

nomenclátor *m* catalogue of names

nomenclatura *f* nomenclature

nomeolvides *f inv* forget-me-not

nómina *f* **1.** (*lista*) list; (*de sueldos*) payroll **2.** (*haberes*) salary

nominación *f* appointment, nomination

nominal *adj* **1.** (*relativo al nombre*) nominal; **citación** ~ personal summons; **valor** ~ nominal value **2.** LING noun

nominalmente *adv* nominally

nominar *vt* to nominate

nominativo *m* LING nominative

nominativo, **-a** *adj* nominative

non **I.** *adj* odd **II.** *m* odd number; **de** ~ odd; **estar** [*o* **quedar**] **de** ~ *inf* to be the odd one out; **decir** (**que**) ~**es** *fig* to say no

nonada *f* trifle

nonagésimo, **-a** *adj* ninetieth; *v.t.* **octavo**

nonato, **-a** *adj* **1.** (*nacimiento*) born by caesarean [*o* cesarean *Am*] section **2.** (*no existente*) unborn

nono, **-a** *adj* ninth; *v.t.* **octavo**

noquear *vt* to knock out

nordeste *m* **1.** (*dirección*) North East **2.** (*viento*) northeasterly

nórdico, **-a** *adj* **1.** (*del norte*) northern, northerly; **la ciudad más nórdica de España** the most northerly city in Spain **2.** HIST Nordic **3.** (*escandinavo*) Scandinavian

noreste *m v.* **nordeste**

noria *f* **1.** (*para agua*) water wheel **2.** *inf* (*trabajo*) treadmill *fig;* **este trabajo es una** ~ this job is a pain in the neck **3.** (*columpio*) big wheel *Brit,* Ferris wheel *Am*

norirlandés, **-esa** **I.** *adj* Northern Irish **II.** *m, f* native/inhabitant of Northern Ireland

norma *f* **1.** (*regla*) rule; (*general*) norm, standard; ~**s de circulación** highway code; ~ **técnica** technical norm; **observar la** ~ to follow the rules; **como** ~ (**general**) as a rule **2.** (*escuadra*) set square

normal *adj* **1.** (*habitual*) normal; **gasolina** ~ two-star petrol *Brit,* regular gas *Am* **2.** (*según la norma*) regulation

normalizar <z→c> *vt* **1.** (*volver normal*) to normalize **2.** (*reglar*) to regulate

normalmente *adv* normally; (*habitualmente*) usually

normando, **-a** *adj, m, f* Norman

normativa *f* rules *pl;* ~ **comunitaria** POL Community regulations *pl;* **según la** ~ **vigente** according to current rules

normativo, **-a** *adj* normative

noroeste *m* **1.** (*dirección*) North West **2.** (*viento*) northwesterly

norte *m* **1.** (*punto cardinal*) north; **el** ~ **de**

España Northern Spain; **al** ~ **de** north of **2.** (*viento*) northerly **3.** (*polo ártico*) North Pole **4.** (*guía*) aim; **ha perdido el** ~ *fig* he/she has lost his/her way; **sin** ~ aimless **5.** (*objetivo*) objective

norteamericano, **-a** *adj, m, f* North American; (*de los EE.UU.*) American

nortear **I.** *vt* NÁUT to steer to the north **II.** *vi* **1.** NÁUT to veer northwards **2.** (*viento*) **nortea** the north wind is blowing **III.** *vr:* **~se** *Méx* to get lost; **al dar la vuelta nos norteamos** we lost out way when we turned around

norteño, **-a** **I.** *adj* Northern **II.** *m, f* Northerner

nortino, **-a** *adj, m, f Chile, Perú* (*norteño*) northern

Noruega *f* Norway

noruego, **-a** *adj, m, f* Norwegian

nos **I.** *pron pers* us; **tu primo nos pegó** your cousin hit us; **nos escribieron una carta** they wrote a letter to us **II.** *pron reflexivo* ourselves, each other

nosocomio *m AmL* (*hospital*) hospital

nosotros, **-as** *pron pers, 1. pl* **1.** (*sujeto*) we **2.** (*tras preposición*) us

nostalgia *f* (*de lugar*) homesickness; (*del pasado*) nostalgia; ~ **de alguien** longing for sb; **tengo** ~ **de María** I'm longing to see María again

nostálgico, **-a** *adj* (*de un lugar*) homesick; (*del pasado*) nostalgic; ~ **de alguien** longing (for) sb; **sentimiento** ~ sentimental longing; **estar** ~ to be nostalgic

nota *f* **1.** (*anotación*) note; ~ **al pie de la página** footnote; ~ **preliminar** preliminary notes **2.** (*apunte*) note; **tomar** ~ to take notes; **tomar** (**buena**) ~ **de algo** to take (good) note of sth **3.** (*aviso*) letter; ~ **circular** circular **4.** (*calificación*) mark *Brit,* grade *Am;* **sacar malas ~s** to get bad marks *Brit* [*o* grades *Am*] **5.** (*factura*) receipt; ~ **de caja** receipt **6.** (*cuenta*) bill **7.** (*detalle*) touch; **una** ~ **individual** a personal touch **8.** MÚS note ►<u>**dar**</u> **la** ~ to stand out (in a negative way); <u>**dejar**</u> **mala** ~ to leave a bad impression; <u>**forzar**</u> **la** ~ to go too far

notabilidad *f* **1.** (*importancia*) noteworthiness **2.** (*personalidad*) **es una** ~ he/she's quite a character; **es una** ~ **en su género** he/she's an expert in his/her field

notable **I.** *adj* remarkable; (*suma*) considerable **II.** *m* **1.** ENS *in the Spanish education system the qualification equivalent to 7 or 8 on a scale of ten* **2.** *pl* (*personas importantes*) notables *pl*

notación *f* **1.** (*sistema*) notation; ~ **musical** musical notation; ~ **fonética** phonetic script **2.** MAT, QUÍM annotation

notar *vt* **1.** (*percibir*) to notice; (*calor*) to feel; **hacer** ~ to point out; **hacerse** ~ to stand out; **no se te nota nada** you wouldn't notice **2.** (*apuntar*) to write (a note)

notaría *f* **1.** (*profesión*) profession of notary **2.** (*despacho*) notary's office

notariado, **-a** *adj* profession of notary

notarial *adj* JUR legal; (*hecho por el notario*) notarial

notario, **-a** *m, f* notary

noticia *f* (piece of) news; **las ~s** the news; ~ **falsa** a false news item; ~ **de prensa** press report; ~ **bomba** bombshell; **ser** ~ to be in the news; **~s de última hora** latest news; **no tener** ~ **de alguien** to not have heard from sb; **tener** ~ **de algo** to have heard about sth; **andar atrasado de ~s** not to be up to date (with the news)

noticiario *m* RADIO, TV news report, newscast *Am;* ~ **deportivo** sports news

notificación *f* notification; ~ **de accidentes** accident report; ~ **por escrito** written notification; ~ **pública** public notification; ~ **de la sentencia** delivery of verdict

notificar <c→qu> *vt* to notify; **hacer** ~ to let it be known

notoriedad *f* **1.** (*nombradía*) fame; **adquirir** ~ to become well-known **2.** (*evidencia*) clarity

notorio, **-a** *adj* **1.** (*conocido*) well-known **2.** (*evidente*) obvious

novatada *f* **1.** (*broma*) prank, hazing *Am;* **gastar la** ~ **a alguien** to play a trick on sb; **pagar la** ~ to learn the hard way **2.** *inf* (*complicación*) beginner's mistake

novato, **-a** *m, f* (*en un lugar*) new boy *m,* new girl *f;* (*en una actividad*) beginner

novecientos, **-as** *adj* nine hundred; *v.t.* **ochocientos**

novedad *f* **1.** (*acontecimiento*) new development; **¿hay alguna ~?** anything new?; **las últimas ~es** the latest; **el enfermo sigue sin ~es** the patient's condition is unchanged; **¡sin ~ en el frente!** all quiet on the front! **2.** (*cosa*) novelty; (*libro*) new publication

novedoso, **-a** *adj AmL* novel

novel **I.** *adj* new; (*sin experiencia*) inexperienced **II.** *mf* beginner

novela *f* novel; ~ **corta** novella; ~ **por entregas** serialized novel; ~ **policíaca** detective story; ~ **rosa** romance; **¡déjate de ~s!** stop dreaming!

novelar **I.** *vi* to write novels **II.** *vt* to make into a novel

novelesco, **-a** *adj* novel; *fig* amazing

novelista *mf* novelist

novelística *f sin pl* fiction

noveno, **-a** *adj, m, f* ninth; *v.t.* **octavo**

noventa *adj inv, m* ninety; *v.t.* **ochenta**

novia *f v.* **novio**

noviar *vi CSur* to go steady; ~ **con alguien** to be going out with sb

noviazgo *m* **1.** (*para casarse*) engagement **2.** *inf* (*relación*) relationship

novicio, **-a** *m, f* **1.** REL novice **2.** (*principiante*) beginner **3.** (*persona recatada*) shy person

noviembre *m* November; *v.t.* **marzo**

novillada *f* TAUR *bullfight with young bulls and less experienced bullfighters*

novillero, **-a** *m, f* **1.** (*torero*) apprentice bullfighter **2.** (*escuela*) truant
novillo, **-a** *m, f* young bull ►**hacer** ~**s** to play truant
novio, **-a** *m, f* **1.** (*para casarse*) bridegroom *m,* bride *f;* **los** ~**s** (*en la boda*) the bride and groom; (*después de la boda*) the newly-weds; **viaje de** ~**s** honeymoon **2.** (*en relación amorosa*) boyfriend *m,* girlfriend *f;* **echarse novia** to get a girlfriend; **tontear con el** ~ to flirt with one's boyfriend ►**compuesta y sin** ~ all dressed up and nowhere to go
novísimo, **-a** *adj* brand new; (*noticia*) latest
nubarrón *m* storm cloud
nube *f* cloud; ~ **de humo y gases** cloud of smoke and chemicals; ~ **de mosquitos** cloud of mosquitos; ~ **de verano** *t. fig* passing cloud; (*pequeñez*) trifle; **descargar una** ~ to rain ►**bajar de las** ~**s** to come back down to earth; **estar por las** ~**s** (*precios*) to be sky-high; **poner a alguien por las** ~**s** to praise sb to the skies; **ponerse por las** ~**s** *inf* (*persona*) to go up the wall; **vivir en las** ~**s** to have one's head in the clouds
núbil *adj* nubile
nublado **I.** *adj* cloudy **II.** *m* METEO cloud cover
nublar **I.** *vt* **1.** (*nubes*) to cloud **2.** (*mente*) to get confused; (*ojos*) to mist over **II.** *vr:* ~**se** **1.** (*nubes*) to cloud over **2.** (*mente*) to get confused; (*ojos*) to mist over; **se me nubló la vista** my eyes clouded over
nubosidad *f* cloudiness
nuboso, **-a** *adj* cloudy
nuca *f* ANAT nape, back of the neck
nuclear *adj* nuclear; **energía** ~ nuclear energy [*o* power]
núcleo *m* **1.** QUÍM nucleus **2.** (*centro*) hub; ~ **de una idea** core of an idea; ~ **urbano** town
nudillo *m* ANAT knuckle
nudo *m* **1.** *t.* NÁUT (*atadura*) knot; ~ **corredizo** slipknot; **deshacer el** ~ to untie the knot; **hacer un** ~ **en la garganta** to get a lump in one's throat **2.** (*madera*) knot; ~ **de rama** fork in a branch; **sin** ~**s** smooth **3.** (*punto de reunión*) centre *Brit,* center *Am;* ~ **de comunicaciones** communications centre *Brit* [*o* center *Am*]; ~ **ferroviario** junction **4.** (*cosa que une*) **el** ~ **de la amistad** the ties of friendship **5.** (*dificultad*) **el** ~ **del problema es...** the crux of the problem is ... **6.** NÁUT (*velocidad*) knot
nudoso, **-a** *adj* knotty; (*madera*) gnarled
nuera *f* daughter-in-law
nuestro, **-a** **I.** *adj pos antepuesto* our; ~ **hijo/nuestra hija** our son/daughter; ~**s nietos** our grandchildren; **por nuestra parte** on our side **II.** *pron pos* **1.** (*propiedad*) **la casa es nuestra** the house is ours; **¡ya es** ~**!** *fig* we've got it! **2.** *tras artículo* **el** ~**/la nuestra/lo** ~ ours; **los** ~**s** our people; (*parientes*) our family; **¡eso es lo** ~**!** that's what we're good at!; **ésta es la nuestra** *fig, inf* this is our chance **3.** *tras substantivo* of ours, our; **una amiga nuestra** a friend of ours; **es culpa nuestra** it is our fault
nueva *f* piece of news; **esto me coge de** ~**s** this is news to me; **no te hagas de** ~**s** don't pretend you didn't know; **la buena** ~ good tidings *pl*
nuevamente *adv* **1.** (*otra vez*) again **2.** (*últimamente*) recently
Nueva York *f* New York
Nueva Zelandia *f* New Zealand
nueve *adj inv, m* nine; *v.t.* **ocho**
nuevo, **-a** **I.** *adj* new; **de** ~ again; **sentirse como** ~ to feel like a new man; **¿qué hay de** ~**?** what's new?; **hasta** ~ **aviso** until our next communication **II.** *m, f* new person
nuez *f* **1.** BOT walnut; ~ **de anacardo** cashew nut; ~ **de coco** coconut; ~ **moscada** nutmeg; **cascar nueces** to crack nuts **2.** ANAT Adam's apple; **apretar la** ~ **a alguien** *inf* to wring sb's neck
nulidad *f* **1.** (*no válido*) nullity; **declarar la** ~ **de algo** to declare sth invalid **2.** *inf* (*persona*) nonentity; **ser una** ~ to be useless
nulo, **-a** *adj* **1.** (*inválido*) null; **declarar** ~ to declare invalid; **voto** ~ invalid vote **2.** (*incapaz*) useless; **soy** ~ **para el deporte** I'm no good at sports
núm. *abr de* **número** No.
numen *m elev* (*del artista*) inspiration
numeración *f* **1.** (*sistema*) numbering system; ~ **arábiga** Arabic numerals; ~ **correlativa** correlated sequence; ~ **decimal** decimal system **2.** (*acción*) numbering
numerador *m* **1.** MAT numerator **2.** (*aparato*) meter; (*sello*) stamp
numeral **I.** *adj* numeral **II.** *m* LING number
numerar *vt* **1.** (*poner números*) to number; ~ **correlativamente** to make a correlated sequence; (*páginar*) to paginate; **sin** ~ unnumbered **2.** (*contar*) to number off
numerario *m* cash
numerario, **-a** *adj* **1.** (*de números*) full **2.** (*fijo*) permanent; (*profesor*) tenured
numéricamente *adv* numerically
numérico, **-a** *adj* numerical
número *m* **1.** MAT number; ~ **cardinal** cardinal number; ~ **primo** prime number; ~ **quebrado** fraction; **en** ~**s redondos** in round numbers; **aprender de** ~**s** *inf* to learn one's sums; **hacer** ~**s** to do one's sums; **hacer** ~**s para ver si...** to calculate if ... **2.** (*cantidad*) number; ~ **de habitantes** number of inhabitants; **sin** ~ innumerable **3.** *t.* LING (*cifra, edición*) number; ~ **de matrícula** registration number *Brit,* license number *Am;* ~ **de identificación personal** PIN (personal identification number); ~ **de zapatos** shoe size; **es el** ~ **uno de la clase** he's the top of the class; ~ **suelto** odd number; **el** ~ **1000** number 1,000 **4.** (*ejemplar*) copy; ~ **atrasado** back issue **5.** (*actución*) ~ **de baile** dance number; **montar un** ~ to make a scene
numeroso, **-a** *adj* numerous; **familia numerosa** large family

nunca *adv* never; ~ **jamás** never ever; **más que** ~ more than ever
nuncio *m* **1.** REL nuncio **2.** (*que anuncia*) messenger; *fig* harbinger
nupcial *adj* nuptial; **corona** ~ bridal wreath
nupcias *fpl* nuptials *pl;* **segundas** ~ remarriage; **posteriores** ~ later wedding
nurse *f AmL* **1.** (*niñera*) nanny; (*extranjera*) au-pair **2.** (*enfermera*) nurse
nutria *f* otter
nutricio, **-a** *adj* (*nutritivo*) nutritious
nutrición *f* nutrition
nutrido, **-a** *adj* **1.** (*alimentado*) fed; **bien** ~ well-fed; **mal** ~ undernourished **2.** (*numeroso*) ample; (*biblioteca*) well-stocked
nutrir **I.** *vt* **1.** (*alimentar*) to feed; (*piel*) to nourish **2.** (*fortalecer*) to strengthen **II.** *vr* **~se de** [*o* **con**] **algo** to feed off sth
nutritivo, **-a** *adj* nutritious; **valor** ~ nutritional value

Ñ

Ñ, **ñ** *f* Ñ, ñ

> The **eñe** is the trade mark of the Spanish **alfabeto**. Up until a few years ago the 'ch', - **la che** - (directly after the 'c') and the 'll' - **la elle** - (after the 'l') were also part of the alphabet, as they are both independent sounds in their own right. This had to be changed, however, in order to internationalise the Spanish alphabet, i.e. bring it into line with other languages.

ña *f AmC, AmS, inf* (*señora*) lady, Missis
ñácara *f Chile* sore, ulcer
ñandutí *m CSur* Paraguayan lace
ñangotarse *vr* **1.** *PRico, RDom* (*ponerse en cuclillas*) to squat **2.** *PRico* (*someterse*) to yield **3.** *PRico* (*perder el ánimo*) to lose heart
ñaña *f Chile, Perú* elder sister
ñapango, **-a** *adj Col* mestizo, half-breed
ñaque *m* junk
ñata *f AmL, inf* conk *Brit,* beak *Am*
ñato, **-a** **I.** *adj* **1.** *CSur* (*chato*) snub-nosed **2.** *Col* (*gangoso*) nasal **II.** *m, f AmL* guy
ñeque **I.** *adj AmC* strong **II.** *m* **1.** *Chile, Ecua, Perú* (*fuerza*) strength; (*energía*) vim **2.** *Perú* (*valor, coraje*) courage
ñire *m Chile* BOT antarctic beech
ño *m AmC, AmS, inf* (*señor*) *abbreviated form of 'señor' used only before the first name*
ñoco, **-a** *adj AmS* (*sin dedo*) missing a finger; (*sin mano*) missing a hand
ñoñería *f* **1.** (*simpleza*) inanity **2.** (*dengues*) silliness
ñoño, **-a** **I.** *adj inf* **1.** (*soso*) insipid; (*aburrido*) boring **2.** (*tonto*) inane **3.** (*remilgado*) prudish **II.** *m, f inf* **1.** (*tonto*) idiot **2.** (*aburrido*) bore
ñoqui *m* gnocchi
ñorbo *m Ecua, Perú* BOT passionflower
ñu *m* gnu
ñudo *m* knot; **al** ~ *AmL, inf* in vain
ñuto, **-a** *adj AmS, Arg, Perú* (*ablandado*) tenderized

O

O, **o** *f* O, o; ~ **de Oviedo** O for Oliver *Brit,* O for Oboe *Am* ▸**no saber hacer la 'o' con un canuto** not to know a thing
o, **ó** *conj* or; ~**...**, ~**...** either ..., or ...; ~ **sea** in other words; ~ **bien** or else; ~ **mejor dicho** or rather
O *abr de* **oeste** W
oasis *m inv* oasis
obcecación *f* stubborn insistence
obcecar <c→qu> **I.** *vt* to blind **II.** *vr:* **~se** to be blinded, to stubbornly insist
obedecer *irr como crecer* **I.** *vt* (*orden, a alguien*) to obey; (*instrucciones*) to follow; **hacerse** ~ to make people obey **II.** *vi* (*provenir*) to be due; (*responder*) to respond
obediencia *f* obedience
obediente *adj* obedient
obelisco *m* obelisk
obertura *f t.* MÚS overture
obesidad *f* obesity
obeso, **-a** *adj* obese
óbice *m elev* **no ser** ~ **para que alguien** +*subj* not to prevent sb from
obispado *m* REL **1.** (*cargo*) bishopric **2.** (*diócesis*) diocese
obispo *m* REL bishop ▸**trabajar para el** ~ to work for nothing
óbito *m* demise *form*
obituario *m* **1.** (*libro*) register of deaths **2.** *AmL* (*defunción*) demise **3.** *AmL* (*del periódico*) obituary
objeción *f* objection; ~ **de conciencia** conscientious objection; **poner** ~ **a algo** to object to sth
objetar *vt* to object; **tengo algo que** ~ I have an objection
objetividad *f* objectivity
objetivo *m* **1.** (*finalidad*) goal; **tener como** ~ to have as one's goal **2.** FOTO lens **3.** (*blanco*) target
objetivo, **-a** *adj* objective
objeto *m* **1.** (*cosa*) object; ~ **de enseñanza** teaching aid; ~ **de lujo** luxury item; ~ **de valor** valuables *pl;* **la mujer** ~ woman as an object; **~s perdidos** lost property **2.** (*motivo*) purpose; **el** ~ **de la presente es...** the purpose of this letter is ...; **con** (**el**) [*o* **al**] ~ **de...** in order to ...; **no tener** ~ to be pointless;

Ñ O

tener por ~ to have as one's aim **3.** LING object

objetor(**a**) *m(f)* dissenter; ~ **de conciencia** conscientious objector

oblea *f* **1.** (*hostia*) wafer; **estar hecho una** ~ *inf* to be as thin as a rake **2.** (*sello*) stamp

oblicuidad *f* obliquity

oblicuo, **-a** *adj* oblique, slanted

obligación *f* **1.** (*deber*) obligation; ~ **alimenticia** duty to provide maintenance; ~ **de comunicación** need to reply; ~ **de secreto** obligation to maintain confidentiality; **contraer una** ~ to undertake an obligation; **cumplir con una** ~ to fulfil *Brit* [*o* to fulfill *Am*] an obligation; **dedicarse a sus obligaciones** to devote oneself to one's duties; **faltar a sus obligaciones** to neglect one's duties; **tener la** ~ **de hacer algo** to be obliged to do sth **2.** (*deuda*) liability; (*documento*) bond

obligado, **-a** *adj* **1.** *estar* obliged **2.** *ser* (*imprescindible*) obligatory; **tema** ~ compulsory topic; **es** ~**...** one must ... **3.** *estar* (*agradecido*) grateful

obligar <g→gu> **I.** *vt* **1.** (*forzar*) to force; (*comprometer*) to oblige **2.** *Chile, Arg* (*invitar*) to invite to drink **II.** *vr:* ~**se** to commit oneself

obligatoriedad *f* obligation; **de** ~ **general** universally compulsory; ~ **de visado** visa requirement; ~ **del voto** requirement to vote

obligatorio, **-a** *adj* obligatory; **asignatura obligatoria** compulsory subject; **compromiso** ~ binding commitment; **no** ~ not compulsory; (*oferta*) not binding; **es** ~ **llevar puesto el casco** helmets must be worn

oblongo, **-a** *adj* oblong

obnubilación *f* **1.** (*trastorno*) confusion **2.** (*ofuscación*) fascination **3.** (*vista*) blurring

obnubilar *vt* **1.** (*trastornar*) to confuse **2.** (*ofuscar*) to fascinate

oboe *m* MÚS **1.** (*instrumento*) oboe **2.** (*músico*) oboist

obra *f* **1.** (*creación, labor*) work; ~ **de arte** work of art; ~ **benéfica** charitable act; ~**s completas** collected [*o* complete] works; ~ **de consulta** reference work; ~ **maestra** masterpiece; ~ **meritoria** commendable act; ~ **de teatro** play; **por** ~ (**y gracia**) **de** thanks to; **¡manos a la** ~**!** let's get to work! **2.** (*construcción*) building work; (*lugar en construcción*) construction site; (*edificio*) building; ~ **de caminos, canales y puertos** civil engineering; ~**s públicas** public works; ~ **de reforma** renovation; ~ **de romanos** *fig* Herculean task; ~ **vieja** old building; **mano de** ~ labour *Brit,* labor *Am;* **estar en** ~**s** to be under construction ►~**s son amores y no buenas razones** *prov* actions speak louder than words; ~ **empezada, medio acabada** *prov* the hardest part is getting started *prov*

obradera *f Col, Guat, Pan* (*diarrea*) diarrhoea *Brit,* diarrhea *Am*

obrador *m* **1.** (*taller*) workshop **2.** (*de confitería*) bakery

obrador(**a**) **I.** *adj* working **II.** *m(f)* worker

obraje *m* **1.** *CSur* sawmill **2.** *Méx* butcher's shop

obrajero, **-a** *m, f* **1.** *AmL* (*propietario de un obraje*) sawmill owner **2.** *Arg, Par* (*peón de un obraje*) sawmill worker **3.** *AmL* (*artesano*) craftsman **4.** *Méx* (*carnicero*) pork butcher

obrar I. *vi* **1.** (*actuar*) to act; ~ **contra las buenas costumbres** to behave badly; ~ **a tontas y a locas** *inf* to act rashly **2.** *vulg* (*defecar*) to move one's bowels **3.** (*encontrarse*) to find oneself **II.** *vi, vt* **1.** (*hacer efecto*) to have an effect on; ~ **buen efecto** to be effective; ~ **sobre alguien/algo** to act on sb/sth **2.** (*construir*) to build **3.** (*hacer*) to do; (*trabajar*) to work; **sin** ~ unworked

obrerismo *m* **1.** POL labour movement *Brit,* labor movement *Am* **2.** (*conjunto*) working class movement

obrerista I. *adj* working-class **II.** *mf* labour *Brit* [*o* labor *Am*] movement activist

obrero, **-a I.** *adj* (*relativo al trabajo*) working; (*relativo al obrero*) working-class **II.** *m, f* worker; ~ **agrícola** agricultural labourer *Brit* [*o* laborer *Am*]; ~ **asalariado** labourer *Brit,* laborer *Am,* paid worker; ~ **eventual** temporary [*o* seasonal] worker; ~ **desocupado** unemployed worker; ~ **especializado** [*o* **cualificado**] skilled worker; ~ **fijo** permanent employee; **ser alguien** ~ **de su propia ruina** to be the author of one's own downfall

obscenidad *f* obscenity

obsceno, **-a** *adj* obscene

obscurecer *irr como crecer vt v.* **oscurecer**

obscuridad *f v.* **oscuridad**

obscuro, **-a** *adj v.* **oscuro**

obsequiar *vt* **1.** (*con atenciones*) to honour *Brit,* to honor *Am;* (*con bebidas*) to toast; (*con regalos*) to bestow **2.** (*agasajar*) to lavish attention on; (*festejar*) to celebrate; ~ **con su presencia** to honour *Brit* [*o* to honor *Am*] with one's presence; ~ **a alguien con un banquete** to hold a banquet in sb's honour **3.** *AmL* (*regalar*) to give

obsequio *m* **1.** (*regalo*) gift **2.** (*agasajo*) attention; **¡hágame Ud. este** ~**!** please do this favour *Brit* [*o* favor *Am*] for me!; **en** ~ **de alguien** in honour *Brit* [*o* honor *Am*] of sb

obsequioso, **-a** *adj* (*cortés*) attentive

observación *f* **1.** (*contemplación, vigilancia*) observation **2.** (*comentario*) remark; ~ **marginal** note **3.** (*observancia*) observance

observador(**a**) **I.** *adj* observant **II.** *m(f)* observer

observancia *f* observance

observante *adj* (*orden*) observant

observar *vt* **1.** (*contemplar, cumplir*) to observe **2.** (*orden*) to follow; (*normas, plazos*) to adhere to **3.** (*notar*) to notice; **hacer** ~ **algo a alguien** to bring sth to sb's attention

observatorio *m* observatory; ~ **astronómico** observatory; ~ **meteorológico** weather station

obsesión *f* obsession

obsesionado, **-a** *adj* obsessed; **está ~ con ella** he is obsessed with [*o* by] her

obsesionar I. *vt* to obsess; **el fútbol lo obsesiona** he is obsessed with [*o* by] football II. *vr:* **~se** to be obsessed; **~se con algo/alguien** to be obsessed by [*o* with] sth/sb

obsesivo, **-a** *adj* obsessive

obseso, **-a** I. *adj* obsessed II. *m, f* obsessive person; **~ del sexo** sex maniac

obsoleto, **-a** *adj* obsolete

obstaculizar <z→c> *vt* to hinder; **~ la carretera** to obstruct [*o* block] the road; **~ el progreso** to hinder progress

obstáculo *m* **1.** obstacle; **salvar un ~** to overcome an obstacle; **triunfar ante todos los ~s** to triumph in the face of great odds; **poner ~s a alguien** to hinder sb **2.** COM barrier; **~s comerciales** trade barriers **3.** DEP hurdle

obstante *adv* **no ~** nevertheless

obstar I. *vi* to stand in the way II. *vimpers* to be a hindrance; **eso no obsta para que...** +*subj* that does not prevent ...

obstetra *mf* MED obstetrician

obstetricia *f* MED obstetrics *pl*

obstinación *f* **1.** (*terquedad*) obstinacy **2.** (*tenacidad*) persistence

obstinado, **-a** *adj* **1.** (*terco*) obstinate **2.** (*tenaz*) persistent **3.** (*intransigente*) unyielding

obstinarse *vr* to persist; **~ en su silencio** to remain silent; **~ contra algo/alguien** to hold firm against sth/sb

obstrucción *f* obstruction; MED blockage; **~ de la autoridad** JUR ≈ obstruction of duty

obstruir *irr como huir* I. *vt* **1.** (*el paso, acción*) to obstruct **2.** (*una tubería*) to block II. *vr:* **~se** to get blocked

obtención *f* obtaining; QUÍM extraction; **~ de alimentos** food production; **~ de datos** data collection; **~ de la velocidad máxima** attainment of maximum speed

obtener *irr como tener vt* to obtain; QUÍM to extract; (*resultado, ventaja*) to gain; **~ un pedido** to receive an order; **difícil de ~** not easily obtainable

obtenible *adj* obtainable

obturación *f* **1.** (*cierre*) closure; (*bloqueo*) blockage **2.** (*de dientes*) filling

obturador *m* FOTO shutter

obturar *vt* **1.** (*cerrar*) to close; (*bloquear*) to block **2.** (*los dientes*) to fill

obtuso, **-a** *adj* **1.** (*cosa*) blunt **2.** (*persona*) obtuse

obús *m* **1.** (*artillería*) howitzer **2.** (*proyectil*) shell **3.** AUTO valve core

obviar I. *vi* (*ser un obstáculo*) to stand in the way II. *vt* **1.** (*evitar*) to avoid **2.** (*eliminar*) to remove; **~ un problema** to get round a problem

obvio, **-a** *adj* obvious; **es ~** it's obvious; **lo ~ del mensaje** the clarity of the message

oc *abr de* **ondas cortas** SW

oca *f* **1.** ZOOL goose; **¡es la ~!** *inf* it's the best! **2.** (*juego*) snakes *pl* and ladders **3.** BOT oxalis

ocasión *f* occasion; **coche de ~** second hand car; **libros de ~** bargain [*o* cut-price] books; **aprovechar la ~** to make the most of the opportunity; **desperdiciar la ~** to waste the opportunity; **en esta ~** on this occasion; **llegada la ~** when the occasion arises; **en ocasiones** sometimes; **en la primera ~** at the first opportunity; **con ~ de** on the occasion of; **dar a alguien ~ para quejarse** to give sb cause to complain ▸**la ~ hace al ladrón** *prov* opportunity makes the thief *prov;* **la ~ la pintan calva** *prov* strike while the irón is hot *prov,* make hay while the sun shines *prov*

ocasional *adj* **1.** (*no habitual*) occasional; **trabajo ~** temporary work **2.** (*casual*) chance **3.** (*para una ocasión*) occasional **4.** (*causante*) causative; **enfermedad ~** underlying illness

ocasionar *vt* **~ algo** to cause sth, to bring sth about; **~ dolores de cabeza a alguien** to give sb a headache

ocaso *m* **1.** ASTR setting; (*del sol*) sunset; (*oeste*) west **2.** (*final*) end **3.** (*decadencia*) decline

occidental *adj* western; **potencias ~es** Western powers

occidente *m* GEO west; **el ~** the West

occipucio *m* MED occiput

occiso, **-a** *adj form* murdered

OCDE *f abr de* **Organización para la Cooperación y el Desarrollo Económicos** OECD

Oceanía *f* Oceania

océano *m* **1.** (*mar*) ocean; **Océano Austral** Southern Ocean; **Océano Boreal** Arctic Ocean **2.** *fig* (*cantidad*) sea; **un ~ de gente** a sea of people; **un ~ de sangre** a sea of blood; **un ~ de gente salía del concierto** a huge throng of people left the concert

oceanografía *f* oceanography

ocelote *m* ocelot

ochava *f AmL* (*chaflán*) corner house; (*de un edificio*) cant

ochenta I. *adj inv* **1.** eighty; **los años ~** the eighties; **un hombre de alrededor de ~ años** a man of about eighty years of age; **una mujer en sus ~** a woman in her eighties **2.** (*octogésimo*) eightieth II. *m* eighty

ocho I. *adj inv* eight; **jornada de ~ horas** eight-hour day; **~ veces mayor/menor que...** eight times bigger/smaller than ...; **a las ~** at eight (o'clock); **son las ~ y media de la mañana/tarde** it is half past eight in the morning/evening; **las ~ y cuarto/menos cuarto** a quarter past/to eight; **a las ~ en punto** at eight o'clock precisely [*o* on the dot]; **el ~ de agosto** the eighth of August; **dentro de ~ días** in a week's time; **de aquí a ~ días** a week from now ▸**echar a alguien con los ~s y los nueves** to be blunt with sb; **ser más chulo que un ~** *inf* to be a right show off; **dar igual ~ que ~** not to care less II. *m* eight

ochocientos, **-as** *adj* eight hundred; **esta basílica fue construida hace ~ años** this basilica was built eight hundred years ago; **vinieron más de ochocientas personas** more than eight hundred people came

ocio *m* leisure; ~ **anual** annual holidays *pl;* **horas de** ~ spare time; **entregarse al** ~ to lead a life of leisure

ociosear *vi AmS* to be at leisure, to loaf around *inf*

ociosidad *f* idleness ►**la** ~ **es la** madre **de todos los vicios** *prov* the devil makes work for idle hands *prov,* idleness is the root of all evil *prov*

ocioso, **-a** *adj* **1.** *estar* (*inactivo*) idle **2.** *ser* (*inútil*) useless; **palabras ociosas** talking for talking's sake

oclusión *f* LING, METEO occlusion

ocote *m Méx* BOT ocote pine

ocre *adj* ochre *Brit,* ocher *Am*

octagonal *adj* octagonal

octágono *m* octagon

octava *f* LIT, MÚS octave

octavilla *f* (*volante*) leaflet; ~ **difamatoria** defamatory leaflet

octavo, **-a I.** *adj* eighth; **en** ~ **lugar** in eighth place; (*enumeración*) eighth; **estoy en** ~ **curso** I am in eighth year; **la octava parte** an eighth **II.** *m, f* eighth

octeto *m* **1.** MÚS octet **2.** INFOR byte

octogésimo, **-a** *adj* eightieth; *v.t.* **octavo**

octubre *m* October; *v.t.* **marzo**

óctuplo, **-a** *adj* eightfold

ocular I. *adj* ocular; **examen** ~ eye test; **testigo** ~ eyewitness **II.** *m* eyepiece

oculista *mf* MED ophthalmologist

ocultación *f,* **ocultamiento** *m* concealment; ~ **fiscal** tax evasion

ocultar I. *vt* (*cosa*) to hide; (*información, delito*) to conceal; ~ **la cara entre** [*o* **con**] **las manos** to cover one's face with one's hands **II.** *vr:* ~**se** to hide

ocultismo *m* **el** ~ the occult

oculto, **-a** *adj* (*escondido*) hidden; (*secreto*) secret; **de** ~ incognito; **en** ~ in secret; **traerse algo** ~ to keep sth hidden

ocupación *f* **1.** (*trabajo*) occupation; ~ **lucrativa** well-paid job; ~ **del ocio** occupation of leisure time; ~ **temporal** temporary job; **sin** ~ unemployed **2.** (*apoderamiento*) *t.* MIL occupation; ~ **hotelera** hotel occupancy; **primera** ~ **de un apartamento** first occupation of a flat *Brit* [*o* apartment *Am*]; **zona de** ~ occupied zone

ocupacional *adj* occupational

ocupado, **-a** *adj* **1.** (*sitio*) occupied **2.** (*persona*) busy **3.** (*línea de teléfono*) engaged *Brit,* busy *Am*

ocupante I. *adj* MIL occupying **II.** *mf* **1.** (*de vehículo*) occupant; (*de tren, avión*) passenger **2.** (*de un edificio*) resident

ocupar I. *vt* **1.** (*lugar, teléfono*) *t.* MIL to occupy **2.** (*un cargo*) to hold; (*vacante*) to fill **3.** (*tiempo, espacio, asiento*) to take up **4.** (*vacante*) to fill **5.** (*a una persona*) to keep busy **6.** (*tiempo, espacio*) to take up **II.** *vr* ~**se de** [*o* **con**] **algo** to busy oneself with sth; ~**se de alguien** (*cuidar*) to look after sb; **ella se ocupó de todo** she took care of everything

ocurrencia *f* **1.** (*idea*) idea; **¡qué** ~ **pensar que es mi culpa!** imagine saying that it was my fault!; **dijo que podía comerse 20 panecillos, ¡qué** ~**!** he/she said that he/she could eat 20 rolls, what nonsense!; **se bañó en el mar en pleno invierno, ¡qué** ~**!** he/she swam in the sea in the middle of winter, what a thing to do!; **tener la** ~ **de...** to have the bright idea of ... **2.** (*suceso*) occurrence

ocurrente *adj* witty

ocurrir I. *vi* to happen; **¿qué ocurre?** what's wrong?; **¿qué te ocurre?** what's the matter?; **lo que ocurre es que...** the thing is that ...; **cuida de que no vuelva a** ~ **algo semejante** make sure the same thing doesn't happen again **II.** *vr:* ~**se** to occur; **no se me ocurre nada** I can't think of anything; **no se le ocurre más que decir tonterías** he/she does nothing but talk nonsense; **¿cómo se te ocurrió esa tontería?** what on earth made you think of a stupid thing like that?; **nunca se me hubiese ocurrido pensar que...** I never would have imagined that ...

oda *f* LIT ode

odiar *vt* to hate; ~ **a alguien a muerte** to have an undying hatred for sb, to hate sb's guts *inf*

odio *m* hate, hatred; **hacer algo por** ~ **a alguien** to do sth out of hatred for sb

odiosidad *f* **1.** (*carácter*) hatefulness **2.** (*aversión*) odiousness **3.** *AmL* (*molestia*) irksomeness

odioso, **-a** *adj* **1.** (*hostil*) nasty **2.** (*repugnante*) horrible **3.** *AmL* (*fastidioso*) annoying

odisea *f* odyssey

odontología *f* MED dentistry

odontólogo, **-a** *m, f* MED dentist

odre *m* (*cuero*) wineskin

OEA *f abr de* **Organización de los Estados Americanos** OAS

oeste *m* **1.** (*punto*) west; **el lejano** ~ the wild [*o* far] west; **película del** ~ western; **hacia el** ~ westward(s); **al** ~ **de...** west of ... **2.** (*viento*) westerly

ofender I. *vt* **1.** (*humillar*) to offend; ~ **la vista** to be an eyesore; ~ **a Dios** to offend God; **hacerse el ofendido** to take offence *Brit* [*o* offense *Am*] **2.** (*herir*) to insult **II.** *vr:* ~**se** to take offence [*o* offense *Am*]; **¡no te ofendas conmigo!** don't get angry with me!

ofensa *f* offence, offense *Am;* **dicho sea sin** ~ **de nadie** I say this without wishing to offend anyone

ofensiva *f* offensive; **tomar la** ~ to go on the offensive

ofensivo, **-a** *adj* **1.** (*hiriente*) offensive **2.** (*dañino*) damaging; ~ **para el medio ambiente** environmentally damaging **3.** (*que ataca*) attacking

ofensor(**a**) *adj* (*de ofensa*) offending; (*de

ataque) attacking

oferta *f* **1.** (*propuesta*) offer; ~ **de empleo** job offer; ~ **especial** special offer; **estar de** ~ to be on special offer; **este supermercado tiene muchas ~s** this supermarket has lots of special offers; **hacer mayor** ~ to outbid **2.** COM tender, bid **3.** ECON supply; ~ **y demanda** supply and demand; ~ **excesiva** oversupply

ofertar *vt* to offer; **invitar a alguien a** ~ to invite sb to bid

office *m small room adjoining the kitchen used as a dining area or utility room*

offset *m* offset

oficial *adj* official; **boletín** ~ official gazette

oficial(**a**) *m(f)* **1.** (*oficio manual*) (skilled) worker; (*administrativo*) clerk; ~ **de albañil** builder's mate; ~ **cervecero** brewery worker; ~ **de obra** building worker; ~**a de peluquería** hairdresser; ~**a** (**de secretaría**) secretary **2.** MIL officer; ~ **de complemento** reserve officer; ~ **marinero** ship's officer **3.** (*funcionario*) civil servant; ~ **del juzgado** court clerk; ~ **de la justicia** sheriff; ~ **del registro civil** registry clerk

oficialidad *f* **1.** (*carácter*) official nature **2.** MIL officers *pl*

oficialismo *m* **1.** *Arg* (*burocracia*) bureaucracy **2.** *AmL* (*del gobierno*) the government and its party members

oficialista **I.** *adj* **1.** *AmL* (*burocrático*) bureaucratic **2.** *AmL* (*del gobierno*) governmental **II.** *mf AmL: fervent follower of the government's policy*

oficializar <z→c> *vt* to make official

oficiar **I.** *vt* **1.** REL to celebrate **2.** (*comunicar*) to inform **II.** *vi inf* (*obrar*) to act; ~ **de intérprete** to act as interpreter

oficina *f* office; ~ **de asistencia social** social security office; ~ **de correos** post office; ~ **de cuenta** accounts *pl* office; ~ **de empleo** job centre *Brit,* job office *Am;* ~ **de información matrimonial** *marriage advice office;* ~ **de maquinaria** machine room; ~ **de matrícula** registration office; ~ **de objetos perdidos** lost property (office); ~ **de pasaportes** passport office

oficinista *mf* office worker

oficio *m* **1.** (*trabajo manual*) trade; ~ **de ebanista** cabinet-making; ~ **especializado** skilled trade; **ejercer un** ~ to have a trade; **sin** ~ **ni beneficio** out of work; **tomar algo por** ~ *fig* to do sth out of habit; **ser del** ~ *inf* to be on the game **2.** (*profesión*) profession; **de** ~ by trade; **gajes del** ~ occupational hazards; **son gajes del** ~ it's all in a day's work **3.** (*función*) function; **defensor de** ~ JUR defence counsel *Brit,* defense counsel *Am* (*paid for by the state*)*;* **de** ~ ex officio; **ofrecer sus buenos ~s** to offer one's services **4.** (*escrito*) official document **5.** REL service; ~ **de difuntos** funeral service; **Santo Oficio** Holy Office

oficioso, **-a** *adj* **1.** (*extraoficial*) unofficial; **mentira oficiosa** white lie **2.** (*activo*) diligent **3.** (*servicial*) obliging

ofidios *mpl* snakes *pl*

ofimática *f* INFOR office automation

ofrecer *irr como crecer* **I.** *vt* to offer; ~ **un banquete** to give a meal; ~ **grandes dificultades** to present a lot of difficulties; ~ **un sacrificio** to offer up a sacrifice; **vamos a** ~ *inf* we're going for a drink **II.** *vr:* ~**se** (*brindarse*) to offer oneself; **¿se le ofrece algo?** do you need anything?; **¿qué se le ofrece?** may I help you?

ofrecimiento *m* **1.** (*oferta*) offer **2.** REL offering

ofrenda *f* offering; (*sacrificio*) sacrifice

ofrendar *vt* to offer; (*sacrificar*) to sacrifice

oftalmía *f* MED ophthalmia

oftálmico, **-a** *adj* ophthalmic

oftalmología *f* MED ophthalmology

oftalmólogo, **-a** *m, f* MED ophthalmologist

ofuscación *f,* **ofuscamiento** *m* **1.** (*vista*) blindness **2.** (*de la mente*) confusion **3.** (*de alguien*) blinding

ofuscar <c→qu> **I.** *vt* **1.** (*cegar*) to blind **2.** (*la mente*) to confuse; ~ (**la mente**) **a alguien** to confuse sb **II.** *vr* ~**se en algo** to insist on sth; ~**se con una idea** to be obsessed by an idea

ogro *m t. fig* ogre

ohmio *m* FÍS ohm

oída *f* **conocer a alguien de ~s** to have heard about sb; **saber algo de ~s** to have heard about sth

oído *m* **1.** (*sentido*) hearing; **aprender de** ~ to learn by ear; **aplicar el** ~ to listen carefully; **aguzar el** ~ to prick up one's ears; **tener buen** ~ to have a good ear; **duro de** ~ hard of hearing **2.** ANAT ear; **cera de ~s** ear wax; ~ **interno/medio/externo** inner/middle/outer ear; **zumbido de ~s** buzzing in the ears; **me zumban los ~s** my ears are buzzing [*o* ringing]; **cerrar los ~s a algo** to turn a deaf ear to sth; **dar ~s a alguien** (*escuchar*) to listen to sb; (*creer*) to believe sb; **hacer ~s de mercader** to pretend not to hear; **ladrar a alguien al** ~ to yell into sb's ear; **llegar a ~s de alguien** to come to sb's notice [*o* attention]; **pegarse al** ~ to be catchy; **ser todo ~s** to be all ears ►**¡~ al parche!** look out!; **regalar los ~s** to flatter

oír *irr vt* (*sentir*) to hear; (*escuchar*) to listen; **¡oye!** hey!; **¡oye, ven aquí!** come here!; **¿oyes?** do you understand?; **¡oiga!** excuse me!; **¡Dios te oiga!** may your prayers be answered!; **como lo oyes** believe it or not; **lo que hay que** ~ what next?; ~ **decir que...** to hear that ...; **parece que no has oído bien** you don't seem to have heard properly; **ya me oirá** he/she hasn't heard the last of me; **no se oye el vuelo de una mosca** you could hear a pin drop ►~**, ver y callar** *prov* hear no evil, see no evil, speak no evil; ~ **como quien oye llover** not to be listening

ojal *m* **1.** (*para botones*) buttonhole **2.** (*ojete*)

O

eyelet

ojalá *interj* I hope so, I wish; **¡~ tuvieras razón!** if only you were right!

ojeada *f* glance; **echar una ~ a algo** to glance at sth; **¿puedes echar una ~ a mi maleta?** (*vigilar*) could you keep an eye on my suitcase?

ojear *vt* **1.** (*mirar con atención*) to stare at **2.** (*pasar la vista*) to glance at **3.** (*la caza*) to beat

ojeras *fpl* bags *pl* (under the eyes); **tener ~** to have dark circles under one's eyes

ojeriza *f* grudge; **tener ~ a alguien** to bear a grudge against sb

ojeroso, -a *adj* haggard, tired

ojete *m* **1.** (*ojal*) eyelet **2.** *vulg* (*ano*) arsehole *Brit,* asshole *Am* **3.** *Arg, Méx* (*vagina*) vagina

ojímetro *m inf* **a ~** at a rough guess

ojiva *f* ARQUIT (*arco*) pointed arch

ojival *adj* pointed

ojo **I.** *m* **1.** ANAT eye; **~ de buey** NÁUT porthole; **~ de gallo** *fig* corn; **~ morado** black eye; **~s rasgados** almond [*o* slanting] eyes; **~s saltones** [*o* **de rana**] bulging eyes; **a ~** by eye; **aguzar los ~s** to narrow one's eyes; **con ~s de cordero degollado** with a sad look; **los niños llenan antes los ~s que la barriga** children's eyes are always bigger than their stomachs; **mirar con buenos/malos ~s** to approve/disapprove of; **pasar los ~s por algo** to run one's eyes over sth; **¡qué ~ tienes!** you don't miss a thing!; **tener ~ clínico** to be a good diagnostician; *fig* to be very observant **2.** (*agujero*) hole; **~ de aguja** eye of a needle; **~ de cerradura** keyhole; **~ del huracán** eye of the storm; **~ de patio** opening; **~ de un puente** span of a bridge; **meterse por el ~ de una aguja** to be very sharp ►**donde pone el ~, pone la bala** he/she is a good shot; **no parecerse ni en el blanco de los ~s** to be as different as chalk and cheese *Brit;* **poner los ~s en blanco** to roll one's eyes; **costar un ~ de la cara** to cost an arm and a leg; **no tener ~s en la cara** to be blind; **~s que no ven, corazón que no siente** *prov* out of sight, out of mind *prov;* **a ~ de buen cubero** roughly; **mirar con unos ~s redondos como platos** to look wide-eyed; **a ~s cerrados** without thinking; **con los ~s cerrados** with complete confidence; **andar con cien ~s** to be on one's guard; **cuatro ~s** *pey* four-eyes; **cuatro ~s ven más que dos** *prov* two heads are better than one *prov;* **poner delante de los ~s de alguien** to make clear to sb; **ser el ~ derecho de alguien** to be the apple of sb's eye; **¡dichosos los ~s que te ven!** *irón* it's great to see you after so long!; **estar entrampado hasta los ~s** to be up to one's neck in debt; **a ~s vistas** visibly; **en un abrir y cerrar de ~s** in a flash; **andar con ~** to be careful; **cerrar los ~s a algo** to shut one's eyes to sth; **clavar los ~s en algo** to lay eyes on sth; **comerse con los ~s** to devour with one's eyes; **echar el ~ a algo/alguien** to have one's eye on sth/sb; **echar un ~ a algo/alguien** to take a look at sth/sb; (*vigilar*) to keep an eye on sth/sb; **meter algo a alguien por los ~s** to shove sth down sb's throat; **no pegar ~** to not sleep a wink; **no saber dónde poner los ~s** not to know which way to turn; **sacarle los ~s a alguien** to kill sb; **ser todo ~s** to give one's full attention; **tener ~** (*cuidado*) to be careful; **tiene mucho ~ con los turistas** he/she is good at dealing with tourists; **tener a alguien entre ~s** (*estar enfadado*) to be angry with sb; (*tener manía*) to have it in for sb; **¡mis ~s!** my darling!; **~ por ~ (y diente por diente)** *prov* an eye for an eye (a tooth for a tooth) **II.** *interj* (be) careful, look out; **¡~ con ese tipo!** watch out for that guy! ►**¡~ al dinero que es el amor verdadero!** you can't live on thin air!

ojota *f AmL* (*sandalia*) sandal

okey **I.** *adj* okay **II.** *m AmL* okay; **dar el ~** to give the go ahead **III.** *adv* okay

okupa *mf inf* squatter

ola *f* wave; **~ de calor** heatwave; **~ de frío** cold spell

olé *interj* ≈ bravo

> **Olé** (or **ole**) is not only a cry of encouragement during a bullfight or a Flamenco dance, but also a general cry of enthusiasm and joy. **¡Olé!** is associated worldwide with Spain and its folklore.

oleada *f t. fig* wave; **~ de gente** throng of people

oleaginoso, -a *adj* oily

oleaje *m* swell, surf

óleo *m* **1.** (*aceite*) oil **2.** ARTE oil paint; **cuadro al ~** oil painting; **pintar al ~** to paint in oil **3.** REL **administrar los ~s** to anoint sb with holy oil

oleoducto *m* pipeline

oleoso, -a *adj* oily

oler *irr* **I.** *vi* to smell; **~ a algo** to smell of sth; **~ bien** to smell good **II.** *vt* to smell; **~ una flor** to smell a flower; **~ el peligro** to smell danger

olfa *mf RíoPl* **1.** *inf* (*chupamedias*) bootlicker **2.** *inf* (*persona servil*) toady

olfatear **I.** *vt* **1.** (*oliscar*) to sniff **2.** (*husmear*) to smell out **II.** *vi* **1.** (*oliscar*) to sniff **2.** (*curiosear*) to nose about

olfativo, -a *adj* olfactory

olfato *m* sense of smell; **tener (buen) ~** *fig* to have a good nose [*o* instinct]

oliente *adj* smelling; **mal ~** bad-smelling, smelly

oligarquía *f* oligarchy

oligofrenia *f* mental deficiency

oligofrénico, -a **I.** *adj* mentally deficient **II.** *m, f* mental retard

olimpiada *f,* **olimpíada** *f* Olympics + *pl vb*

olímpico, -a *adj* Olympic

oliscar <c→qu> *vi* **1.** (*oler*) to smell **2.** *v.* **olfatear**

olisquear *vt, vi v.* **olfatear**
oliva I. *adj* (**verde**) ~ olive (green) II. *f* 1. BOT (*árbol*) olive tree; (*fruta*) olive 2. (*color*) olive (green)
oliváceo, **-a** *adj* olive-green
olivarero, **-a** *adj* olive; **región olivarera** olive-growing region
olivo *m* olive tree; **el Monte de los Olivos** REL the Mount of Olives
olla *f* 1. (*para cocinar*) pot; ~ **exprés** pressure cooker; ~ **de grillos** *inf* madhouse; **tengo la cabeza como una ~ de grillos** *inf* my head is buzzing 2. GASTR stew
olmo *m* elm
olor *m* smell; **buen** ~ good smell; (*fragancia*) scent; ~ **corporal** body odour *Brit* [*o* odor *Am*]; **viene al ~ de tu dinero** he is after your money; **vivir en ~ de santidad** to lead the life of a saint; **tener ~ a** to smell of
olores *mpl Chile* (*especias*) spices *pl*
oloroso, **-a** *adj* fragrant
oloroso *m* GASTR full-bodied sherry
olote *m Méx* corncob
OLP *f abr de* **Organización para la Liberación de Palestina** PLO
olvidadizo, **-a** *adj* forgetful
olvidar *vt, vr:* **~se** to forget; **no ~ que...** (*considerar*) to remember that ...; **dejar olvidado** to leave be; **se me ha olvidado tu nombre** I've forgotten your name
olvido *m* 1. (*falta de memoria*) forgetfulness 2. (*omisión*) oversight, forgetting; ~ **de sí mismo** self-neglect; **caer en** (**el**) ~ to sink into oblivion; **enterrar en el** ~ to forget forever
ombligo *m* 1. ANAT navel, belly button *inf;* **se me encoge el** ~ *fig* I'm getting cold feet 2. (*centro*) centre *Brit,* center *Am;* **el ~ del mundo** the centre *Brit* [*o* center *Am*] of the world; **contemplarse el** ~ to self-gratify
ombú *m Arg* BOT umbra tree, ombu
ominoso, **-a** *adj* despicable
omisión *f* 1. (*supresión*) omission 2. (*negligencia*) negligence; ~ **de auxilio** JUR failure to render assistance 3. (*lapsus*) oversight
omiso, **-a** *adj* (*negligente*) negligent; **hacer caso ~ de algo** to take no notice of sth
omitir *vt* 1. (*no hacer*) to fail to do; **no ~ esfuerzos** to spare no effort 2. (*pasar por alto*) to omit
ómnibus *m* AUTO bus
omnímodo, **-a** *adj* all-embracing
omnipotencia *f* omnipotence
omnipotente *adj* almighty, omnipotent
omnipresencia *f* omnipresence
omnipresente *adj* ubiquitous
omnisciencia *f* omniscience
omnisciente *adj* omniscient, all-knowing
omnívoro, **-a** I. *adj* omnivorous II. *m, f* omnivore
omoplato *m,* **omóplato** *m* ANAT scapula, shoulder blade
OMS *f abr de* **Organización Mundial de la Salud** WHO
onagra *f* evening primrose; **aceite de ~** evening primrose oil
once I. *adj inv* eleven ►**estar a las ~ y cuarto** to have a screw loose; **estar a las ~** (*ropa*) to be askew II. *m* eleven; *v.t.* **ocho**
ONCE *f abr de* **Organización Nacional de Ciegos Españoles** *Spanish national organization for the blind*
onceno, **-a** *adj* eleventh; *v.t.* **octavo** ►**el ~, no estorbar** *inf* don't get in the way
oncología *f* MED oncology
onda *f t.* FÍS, RADIO wave; ~ **explosiva** [*o* **expansiva**] shockwave; **~s del pelo** waves *pl* of hair ►**¡qué buena ~!** *inf* that's really cool!; **estar en la misma ~** to be on the same wavelength; **estar en la ~ de algo** *inf* (*comprender*) to be on top of sth; (*seguir*) to keep up with sth
ondear *vi* (*formar*) to undulate; (*moverse*) to ripple; (*bandera*) to flutter
ondulación *f* 1. (*movimiento*) undulation; (*de agua*) ripple 2. (*formación*) wave; ~ **permanente** perm, permanent wave
ondulado, **-a** *adj* wavy; **cartón ~** corrugated cardboard
ondular I. *vi* (*formar ondas*) to ripple; (*moverse*) to undulate; (*bandera*) to flutter; (*culebra*) to slither II. *vt* to wave
ondulatorio, **-a** *adj* undulatory; **movimiento ~** wave motion
oneroso, **-a** *adj* 1. (*molesto*) onerous; (*gravoso*) burdensome 2. (*costoso*) costly 3. (*remunerable*) remunerative
ONG *f abr de* **Organización No Gubernamental** NGO
onírico, **-a** *adj* oniric
onomástica *f* 1. (*materia*) onomastics *pl* 2. (*día*) name-day, saint's day
onomástico, **-a** *adj* onomastic; **fiesta onomástica** *party to celebrate a name-day*
ONU *f abr de* **Organización de las Naciones Unidas** UNO
onubense I. *adj* of/from Huelva II. *mf* native/inhabitant of Huelva
onza *f* ounce
opa *mf CSur* 1. (*retrasado mental*) mental retard 2. (*simple*) fool
opacar <c→qu> *vt* 1. *AmL* (*hacer opaco*) to darken 2. *Méx* (*superar*) to outshine; **su belleza opaca a las de las demás** her beauty eclipses that of all others
opacidad *f* opacity
opaco, **-a** *adj* 1. (*no transparente*) opaque; **proyector de cuerpos ~s** overhead projector 2. (*sin brillo*) dull; (*oscuro*) gloomy 3. (*persona, voz*) gloomy
opalescente *adj* opalescent
ópalo *m* MIN opal
opción *f* 1. (*elección*) choice; (*posibilidad*) option; ~ **del menú** INFOR menu option 2. (*derecho*) right; ~ **al cambio** right to exchange 3. ECON, JUR option; ~ **de compra** option to purchase

opcional *adj* optional

OPEP *f abr de* **Organización de Países Exportadores de Petróleo** OPEC

ópera *f* **1.** MÚS opera; **teatro de la ~** opera house **2.** CINE, LIT **~ prima** author's first work

operación *f* **1.** MAT, MED operation; **~ quirúrgica** surgical operation **2.** (*actividad*) activity; (*negocio*) transaction; **~ por acciones** share trading; **~ de saneamiento** clean-up operation

operado, **-a** *adj* TÉC operated; **~ a mano** hand-operated; **~ por teclado** keyboard-controlled

operador(a) *m(f)* **1.** CINE projectionist; **~ de cámara** cameraman **2.** INFOR, TEL operator **3.** MED surgeon

operar **I.** *vi* **1.** (*actuar*) *t.* MIL to operate **2.** COM to do business; **~ con bancos** to do business with banks **3.** (*tener efecto*) to take effect **II.** *vt* **1.** MED to operate on **2.** (*producir un efecto*) to bring about; **~ milagros** to work miracles **III.** *vr:* **~se** to have an operation

operario, **-a** *m, f* worker; **~ sin cualificar** unskilled worker

operativo, **-a** *adj* **1.** (*efectivo*) operative **2.** INFOR **sistema ~** operating system

operatorio, **-a** *adj* MED operative

opereta *f* MÚS operetta

opinable *adj* (*discutible*) debatable; (*controvertido*) controversial

opinar **I.** *vi, vt* to think; **~ bien/mal de algo/alguien** to have a good/bad opinion of sth/sb; **¿tú qué opinas de** [*o* **sobre**] **esto?** what do you think about this?; **¿qué opinas del nuevo jefe?** what's your opinion of the new boss? **II.** *vi* to give an opinion; **¿puedo ~?** can I say what I think?

opinión *f* opinion; (*postura*) stance; (*punto de vista*) viewpoint; **en mi ~** in my opinion; **cambiar de ~** to change one's opinion [*o* mind]; **dar su ~** (**sobre algo**) to express an opinion (about sth); **ser de otra/la misma ~** to be of a different/the same opinion; **ser de la ~ que...** to be of the opinion that ...; **tener buena/mala ~ de algo/alguien** to have a good/bad opinion of sth/sb

opio *m* opium

opíparo, **-a** *adj* sumptuous

oponente **I.** *adj* opposing **II.** *mf* opponent

oponer *irr como poner* **I.** *vt* **1.** (*enfrentar*) to oppose; (*confrontar*) to confront **2.** (*objetar*) to object; **~ reparos** to raise objections; **~ resistencia** to offer resistance **II.** *vr:* **~se** **1.** (*rechazar*) to object; **~se a algo** to oppose sth **2.** (*enfrentarse*) to oppose each other **3.** (*obstaculizar*) to hinder **4.** (*ser contrario*) to be opposed **5.** (*estar enfrente*) to be opposite

oporto *m* GASTR port (wine)

oportunidad *f* **1.** (*posibilidad*) chance; (*ocasión*) opportunity; **a la primera ~** at the first opportunity; **una segunda ~** a second chance; **aprovechar la ~** to make the most of the opportunity; (**no**) **tener ~ de...** (not) to have the opportunity of ... **2.** (*cualidad*) opportuneness; (*temporal*) timeliness; (*adecuación*) appropriateness **3.** *pl* (*ofertas*) bargain buys *pl*

oportunismo *m* opportunism

oportunista *mf* opportunist

oportuno, **-a** *adj* **1.** (*adecuado, apropiado*) appropriate; **es muy ~** it is just what was needed; **en el momento ~** at the right moment **2.** (*propicio*) opportune **3.** (*al caso*) relevant **4.** (*permisible*) permissible

oposición *f* **1.** (*resistencia*) *t.* POL opposition; **encontrar ~** to meet opposition; **presentar ~** to oppose **2.** (*objeción*) objection **3.** (*contraposición*) comparison **4.** *(pl)* UNIV (competetive) examination (*for a public-sector job*); **por ~** by examination; **presentarse a unas oposiciones** to sit an examination (*for a public-sector job*)

opositar *vi* **~ a algo** to sit an examination for sth

opositor(a) **I.** *adj* opposing; **partido ~** opposing party **II.** *m(f)* **1.** (*oponente*) *t.* POL opponent **2.** (*candidato*) candidate (*in examination for a public-sector job*)

opresión *f* **1.** (*angustia*) anxiety **2.** (*represión*) oppression **3.** (*presión*) pressure; (*compresión*) compression

opresivo, **-a** *adj* **1.** (*agobiante, represivo*) oppressive; (*constringente*) restrictive; (*aire*) suffocating **2.** (*presionante*) pressing; (*comprimente*) compressive

opresor(a) **I.** *adj* oppressive **II.** *m(f)* oppressor

oprimir *vt* **1.** (*presionar*) to press; (*comprimir*) to compress **2.** (*agobiar*) to weigh down **3.** (*reprimir*) to oppress; (*constreñir*) to restrict

oprobio *m* disgrace

oprobioso, **-a** *adj* disgraceful

optar *vi* **1.** (*escoger*) **~ por algo/alguien** to opt for sth/sb **2.** (*aspirar*) to aspire **3.** (*solicitar*) **~ a algo** to apply for sth; **~ a un cargo** to apply for a position **4.** (*tener acceso*) to have access

optativo, **-a** *adj* optional; (**asignatura**) **optativa** optional subject

óptica *f* **1.** FÍS optics *pl* **2.** (*establecimiento*) optician's **3.** (*punto de vista*) viewpoint; **bajo esta ~** according to this point of view

óptico, **-a** **I.** *adj* **1.** ANAT optic; **nervio ~** optic nerve **2.** FÍS optical **II.** *m, f* optician

optimar *vt* to optimize, to optimise *Brit*

optimismo *m* optimism

optimista **I.** *adj* optimistic **II.** *mf* optimist

optimizar *vt* to optimize

óptimo *m* optimum

óptimo, **-a** **I.** *superl de* **bueno** **II.** *adj* (very) best; (*excelente*) excellent

opuesto, **-a** **I.** *pp de* **oponer** **II.** *adj* **1.** (*enfrente*) opposite; **al lado ~** on the other side; **en dirección opuesta** in the opposite direction **2.** (*diverso*) different; (*contrario, enfrentado*) opposing; **polo ~** *t. fig* opposite pole; **el sexo ~** the opposite sex **3.** (*enemigo*) enemy

opulencia *f* **1.** (*abundancia, exuberancia*)

opulence **2.** (*riqueza*) affluence

opulento, -a *adj* **1.** (*abundante, lujoso*) opulent **2.** (*rico*) affluent

oquedad *f* (*concavidad, vacío*) hollow

ora *conj elev* **~..., ~...** now ..., now ..., either ..., or ...

oración *f* **1.** REL prayer; **decir una ~** to say a prayer **2.** (*frase*) sentence; LING clause; (*discurso*) speech; **~ coordinada** coordinate clause; **~ subordinada** subordinate clause; **partes de la ~** parts of speech; **~ simple/compuesta** simple/compound sentence

oráculo *m* oracle

orador(a) *m(f)* orator; (*portavoz*) spokesperson

oral *adj* oral; **sexo ~** oral sex; **vista ~** JUR hearing; **por vía ~** MED orally

órale *interj Méx* (*animar*) come on; (*oiga*) hey; (*acuerdo*) OK, right

orangután *m* orang-utan

orar *vi elev* **~ por algo** to pray for sth; (*rogar*) to plead for sth

oratoria *f* **1.** (*retórica*) oratory **2.** (*elocuencia*) eloquence

oratorio *m* REL chapel

oratorio, -a *adj* oratorical

orbe *m* **1.** (*círculo*) circle; (*esfera*) sphere; (*terráqueo*) globe **2.** (*mundo*) world

órbita *f* **1.** ASTR, FÍS orbit; **~ planetaria** planetary orbit; **~ terrestre** terrestrial orbit; **poner en ~** to put into orbit; **estar en ~** *fig* to be up to date; **estar fuera de ~** *fig* to be out of touch **2.** (*ámbito*) sphere **3.** ANAT eye socket; **se me salían los ojos de las ~s** *fig* I couldn't believe my eyes

orca *f* killer whale

órdago *m* **de ~** *inf* terriffic

orden[1] <órdenes> *m* **1.** (*colocación, organización*) *t.* REL, ARQUIT order; **en ~** in order; **alterar el ~** to change the order; **llamar al ~** to call to order; **poner en ~** to put in order; **ser persona de ~** to be orderly; *fig* to be upright; **sin ~ ni concierto** without rhyme or reason, any old way **2.** (*sucesión*) order; **en** [*o* **por**] **su** (**debido**) **~** in the right order; **por ~** by order; **por ~ de antigüedad** in order of seniority **3.** (*categoría*) rank; **de primer/segundo ~** first-rate/second-rate; **del ~ de** in the order of **4.** JUR **~ constitucional** constitution; **~ jurídico** judicial order

orden[2] <órdenes> *f* **1.** (*mandato*) order; **~ de arresto** arrest warrant; **~ ministerial** ministerial decree; **~ de registro** search warrant; **órdenes son órdenes** orders are orders; **¡a la ~!** yes, sir!; **contrario a las órdenes** against orders; **dar una ~** to give an order; **cumplir una ~** to obey an order; **estar a las órdenes de alguien** to be at sb's command; **hasta nueva ~** until further notice; **tus deseos son órdenes para mí** *irón* your wish is my command; **estar a la ~ del día** *fig* to be the order of the day **2.** COM, REL order; **~ de entrega** delivery order; **~ de pago** payment order; **~ permanente** standing order; **por ~** by order; **por ~ de** to the order of; **entrar en una ~ (religiosa)** to join a religious order; **~ de caballería** HIST order of knighthood **3.** *pl* REL (*sacramento*) orders *pl;* **las órdenes mayores/menores** the major/minor orders

ordenación *f* **1.** (*disposición*) arrangement **2.** (*ordenanza*) order; (*regulación*) regulation; **~ jurídica** legal system; **~ territorial** regional development **3.** REL ordination

ordenado, -a **I.** *adj* **1.** *estar* (*en orden*) tidy, neat **2.** *estar* (*encaminado*) directed **3.** *ser* (*persona*) organized **II.** *m, f* REL ordained person

ordenador *m* computer; **~ de a bordo** car computer; **~ personal** personal computer; **~ portátil** laptop computer; **asistido por ~** computer-aided

ordenamiento *m* **1.** (*ordenación*) organization **2.** (*regulación*) legislation; **~ constitucional** constitution; **~ jurídico** judicial legislation

ordenancista *adj* strict

ordenanza[1] *f* **1.** (*ordenación*) organization **2.** (*medida*) order **3.** *pl* ADMIN, MIL regulations *pl*

ordenanza[2] *m* **1.** MIL orderly **2.** (*botones*) office assistant

ordenar **I.** *vt* **1.** (*arreglar*) to organize; (*habitación, armario*) to tidy; (*colocar*) to arrange; (*clasificar*) to order **2.** (*mandar*) to order **3.** REL to ordain **II.** *vr:* **~se** REL to be ordained

ordeña *f AmC, CSur, Méx* milking

ordeñadora *f* milkmaid

ordeñar *vt* to milk

ordeñe *m Arg, Cuba* milking

ordinal *adj, m* ordinal

ordinariez *f* (*vulgaridad*) vulgarity

ordinario, -a *adj* **1.** (*habitual*) usual; **de ~** usually **2.** (*grosero*) rude **3.** *t.* JUR (*regular*) ordinary

orear **I.** *vt* **1.** (*airear*) to air **2.** (*secar*) to dry **II.** *vr:* **~se** *inf* to get a breath of fresh air

orégano *m* oregano

oreja *f* **1.** ANAT ear; **aguzar las ~s** to prick up one's ears; **calentar las ~s a alguien** to box sb's ears; *fig* to give sb a dressing-down; **ser todo ~s** to be all ears **2.** (*sentido*) hearing **3.** (*lateral*) flap; (*lengüeta*) tongue; (*del zapato*) eyelet tab; **sillón de ~s** wing chair ►**ver las ~s al lobo** to have a close shave; **con las ~s gachas** with one's tail between one's legs; **agachar las ~s** to lose heart; **¡no agaches las ~s!** don't give up!; **enseñar la ~** to show one's true colours *Brit* [*o* colors *Am*]

orejera *f* **1.** (*en una gorra*) earflap **2.** *pl* (*en una cinta*) earmuffs *pl*

orejero, -a *m, f Chile, pey* telltale

orejón *m* GASTR dried apricot

orensano, -a **I.** *adj* of/from Orense **II.** *m, f* native/inhabitant of Orense

oreo *m* **1.** (*ventilación*) airing **2.** (*desecación*) drying

orfanato *m* orphanage
orfanatorio *m Méx* orphanage
orfandad *f* **1.** (*estado*) orphanhood **2.** (*pensión*) orphan's allowance
orfebre *mf* (*orífice*) goldsmith; (*platero*) silversmith
orfebrería *f* **1.** (*obra*) articles *pl* worked in precious metal; (*en oro*) articles *pl* worked in gold **2.** (*arte*) working of precious metals; (*en oro*) goldsmithing
orfelinato *m* orphanage
orfeón *m* MÚS choral society
orgánico, **-a** *adj* organic; **Ley Orgánica del Estado** basic law
organigrama *m* organization chart; ~ **del programa** INFOR flowchart
organillo *m* MÚS barrel organ
organismo *m* **1.** ANAT, BIO organism **2.** (*institución*) body; ~ **oficial** official body
organista *mf* MÚS organist
organización *f* organization; ~ **central** central organization; **Organización del Tratado del Atlántico Norte** North Atlantic Treaty Organization; **Organización No Gubernamental** Non-Governmental Organization
organizado, **-a** *adj* organized
organizador(a) **I.** *adj* organizing; **comité** ~ organizing committee **II.** *m(f)* (*de un evento*) organizer; ~ **de despacho** office organizer
organizar <z→c> **I.** *vt* to organize; (*una fiesta*) to hold **II.** *vr:* **~se** **1.** (*asociarse*) to organize oneself **2.** (*surgir*) to break out; **¡menuda se organizó!** all hell broke loose!; **se organizó una pelea** a fight broke out **3.** (*ordenar*) to arrange; **~se el tiempo** to organize one's time
organizativo, **-a** *adj* organizing
órgano *m* **1.** (*organismo*) *t.* ANAT organ; ~ **judicial** judicial body; **~s rectores** governing board; **~s sexuales** sexual organs **2.** MÚS organ; ~ **automático** automatic organ; ~ **electrónico** electric organ
orgasmo *m* orgasm
orgía *f* **1.** (*bacanal*) orgy **2.** (*desenfreno*) disinhibition
orgiástico, **-a** *adj* **1.** (*de bacanal*) orgiastic **2.** (*desenfrenado*) unrestrained
orgullo *m* **1.** (*satisfacción*) pride; ~ **por** [*o* **de**] **algo** pride in sth; ~ **profesional** professional pride; **sentir ~ por alguien/algo** to be proud of sb/sth; **tener el ~ de...** to be proud to ...; ~ **propio** self-respect **2.** (*soberbia*) arrogance
orgulloso, **-a** *adj* **1.** *estar* (*satisfecho*) proud; **sentirse ~ de algo/alguien** to feel proud of sth/sb **2.** *ser* proud; (*soberbio*) arrogant
orientación *f* **1.** (*situación*) situation **2.** (*posición*) position **3.** (*ajuste*) adjustment **4.** (*asesoramiento*) advice; (*dirección*) management; ~ **profesional** career [*o* vocational] guidance **5.** (*tendencia*) tendency; **tu ~ política** your political leanings
oriental **I.** *adj* **1.** (*del Este*) eastern; **Alemania Oriental** East Germany; **alfombra** ~ Persian rug **2.** (*del Extremo Oriente*) oriental **II.** *mf* Oriental
orientar **I.** *vt* **1.** (*dirigir*) to direct; **orientado a la práctica** with a practical focus **2.** (*ajustar*) to adjust **3.** (*asesorar*) to advise **4.** (*dirigir*) to manage **II.** *vr:* **~se** **1.** (*dirigirse*) to orientate oneself, to orient oneself *Am; fig* to find one's bearings; **~se bien** to have a good sense of direction; **se orientó muy bien en el trabajo** he settled in well in the job **2.** (*tender*) to tend
oriente *m* **1.** GEO east; **el Oriente Próximo, el Cercano Oriente** the Near East; **el Extremo Oriente, el Lejano Oriente** the Far East **2.** (*viento*) easterly
orífice *m* goldsmith
orificio *m* **1.** (*agujero*) orifice **2.** (*abertura*) opening; ~ **de salida** outlet
origen *m* **1.** (*principio*) origin; **texto/idioma de ~** source text/language **2.** (*causa*) cause; **dar ~ a algo, ser ~ de algo** to give rise to sth; **tener su ~ en algo** to have its origins in sth **3.** (*ascendencia*) descent **4.** (*procedencia*) origin; **de ~ español** of Spanish origin
original **I.** *adj* **1.** (*auténtico, creativo*) original; **versión ~** original version; **el pecado ~** original sin **2.** (*originario*) originating **3.** (*singular*) peculiar **II.** *m* original; **fiel al ~** faithful to the original
originalidad *f* **1.** (*autenticidad, creatividad*) originality **2.** (*singularidad*) peculiarity
originar **I.** *vt* **1.** (*causar*) to cause **2.** (*provocar*) to provoke **II.** *vr:* **~se** **1.** (*tener el origen*) to originate **2.** (*surgir*) to arise **3.** (*proceder*) **~se en algo** to spring from sth
originario, **-a** *adj* **1.** (*oriundo*) native; **es ~ de Chile** he comes from Chile **2.** (*de origen*) **país ~** country of origin **3.** (*original*) original; (*innato*) innate
orilla *f* **1.** (*borde*) edge **2.** (*ribera*) bank; **a ~s del Ebro** on the banks of the Ebro; ~ **de** *inf* on the edge of **3.** *pl, AmL* (*arrabales*) outskirts *pl*
orillar *vt* **1.** (*tela*) to hem; (*adornar*) to trim **2.** (*resolver*) to surmount **3.** (*sortear*) to skirt (around)
orillero, **-a** **I.** *adj AmL: pey* **1.** (*arrabalero*) low class **2.** (*grosero*) coarse **II.** *m, f AmL: pey* **1.** (*arrabalero*) common person **2.** (*grosero*) ill-bred person
orillo *m* selvage
orín *m* **1.** (*óxido*) rust; **cubierto de ~** rusty **2.** *(pl)* (*orina*) urine
orina *f* <orines> urine
orinal *m* chamber pot; (*de niño*) potty
orinar **I.** *vi, vt* to urinate; ~ **sangre** to urinate blood; **ir a ~** to go to the lavatory **II.** *vr:* **~se** to wet oneself; **~se en la cama** to wet the bed; **estoy orinándome** I need to urinate
oriundo, **-a** *adj* ~ **de** native to; **es ~ de Méjico** he comes from Mexico
orla *f* **1.** (*de tela*) edge; ~ **de luto** black border **2.** (*foto*) graduating-class photo [*o* picture]
orlar *vt* (*adornar*) to trim
ornamentación *f* adornment

ornamentar *vt* to adorn
ornamento *m* **1.** (*adorno*) ornament **2.** *pl* REL (*vestiduras*) vestments *pl*
ornar *vt* to adorn
ornato *m* adornment
ornitorrinco *m* duck-billed platypus
oro *m* **1.** (*metal*) gold; ~ **de ley** fine gold; **bañado en** ~ gold-plated; **de** ~ gold; **color** ~ golden; **valer su peso en** ~ to be worth one's weight in gold **2.** (*dinero*) money; **hacerse de** ~ to make one's fortune; **nadar en** ~ to be swimming in money ►**prometer a alguien el** ~ **y el moro** to promise sb the earth; **mi palabra es** ~ my word is my honour *Brit* [*o* honor *Am*]; **guardar como** ~ **en paño** to treasure; **no es** ~ **todo lo que reluce** *prov* all that glitters is not gold *prov*
orondo, **-a** *adj* **1.** (*gordo*) fat **2.** (*engreído*) smug
oropel *m* **1.** (*latón*) imitation gold leaf **2.** *t. pey* (*adorno*) tinsel
orquesta *f* MÚS orchestra
orquestar *vt t. fig* to orchestrate
orquestina *f* MÚS (*de baile*) (dance) band
orquídea *f* orchid
ortiga *f* nettle
orto *m* sunrise
ortodoncia *f* MED orthodontics *pl*
ortodoxo, **-a** **I.** *adj* orthodox; **ser católico** ~ to be a devout Catholic **II.** *m, f* orthodox
ortogonal *adj* right-angled
ortografía *f* spelling; **falta de** ~ spelling mistake
ortográfico, **-a** *adj* spelling; **reglas ortográficas** spelling rules; **reforma ortográfica** spelling reform
ortopeda *mf* MED orthopaedist *Brit*, orthopedist *Am*
ortopedia *f* MED orthopaedics *Brit*, orthopedics *Am*
ortopédico, **-a** MED **I.** *adj* orthopaedic *Brit*, orthopedic *Am;* **pierna ortopédica** artificial leg **II.** *m, f* orthopaedist *Brit*, orthopedist *Am*
ortopedista *mf* orthopaedist *Brit*, orthopedist *Am*
oruga *f* **1.** ZOOL caterpillar **2.** TÉC caterpillar track
orujo *m* **1.** (*residuo*) marc **2.** (*aguardiente*) *strong Spanish liqueur made from residue of grape skins after pressing*
orzuelo *m* MED stye
os **I.** *pron pers* (*objeto directo e indirecto*) you **II.** *pron reflexivo* yourselves; **¿~ marcháis?** are you leaving?
osa *f* **1.** ZOOL she-bear **2.** ASTR **la Osa Mayor/Menor** the Great/Little Bear ►**¡anda la ~!** *inf* good heavens!
osadía *f* daring; (*desfachatez*) boldness
osado, **-a** *adj* daring
osamenta *f* **1.** (*esqueleto*) skeleton **2.** (*restos mortales*) bones *pl*
osar *vi* to dare; **¿cómo osas decir esto?** how dare you say that!
oscense **I.** *adj* of/from Huesca **II.** *mf* native/inhabitant of Huesca
oscilación *f* **1.** (*vaivén*) oscillation **2.** (*variación*) fluctuation **3.** (*indecisión*) indecision
oscilante *adj* **1.** (*indeciso*) indecisive **2.** (*que varía*) fluctuating
oscilar *vi* **1.** (*en vaivén*) to oscillate **2.** (*péndulo*) to swing **3.** (*variar*) to fluctuate
oscilatorio, **-a** *adj* oscillatory
oscurecer *irr como crecer* **I.** *vimpers* to get dark **II.** *vt* **1.** *t. fig* (*privar de luz*) to darken **2.** (*confundir*) to confuse **III.** *vr:* **~se** **1.** *t. fig* (*volverse oscuro*) to darken **2.** *t. fig* (*debilitarse*) to wane **IV.** *m* dusk; **al** ~ at dusk
oscurecimiento *m* (*t. fig*) darkening; (*anochecer*) nightfall
oscuridad *f* **1.** (*falta de luz*) darkness; **en la** ~ in the dark **2.** (*falta de claridad*) obscurity; **en la** ~ in obscurity
oscuro, **-a** *adj* dark; *fig* obscure; **azul** ~ dark blue; **a oscuras** in the dark; **de** ~ **origen** of obscure origin
óseo, **-a** *adj* bony; **restos ~s** skeletal remains
osezno, **-a** *m, f* bear cub
osificar <c→qu> *vt, vr:* **~se** to ossify
osmosis *f sin pl*, **ósmosis** *f sin pl* osmosis
oso *m* bear; ~ **blanco** polar bear; ~ **de peluche** teddy bear; **fuerte como un** ~ as strong as an ox
ostensible *adj* obvious; **hacer** ~ to make evident
ostensivo, **-a** *adj* **1.** (*manifiesto*) evident **2.** (*ostentoso*) ostentatious
ostentación *f* display; (*jactancia*) ostentation; **hacer** ~ **de algo** to show sth; (*jactarse*) to flaunt sth
ostentar *vt* **1.** (*mostrar*) to show; (*jactarse*) to flaunt **2.** (*poseer*) to have; (*puesto, poder*) to hold
ostentoso, **-a** *adj* **1.** (*jactancioso*) ostentatious **2.** (*llamativo*) showy; (*provocativo*) provocative
ostra *f* oyster ►**aburrirse como una** ~ *inf* to be bored to death; **¡~s!** *inf* Jesus!
ostracismo *m* (*de la vida pública*) ostracism; (*exilio*) exile; **condenar al** ~ (*fig*) to ostracize
ostrogodo, **-a** **I.** *adj* Ostrogothic **II.** *m, f* Ostrogoth
otalgia *f* MED earache
OTAN *f abr de* **Organización del Tratado del Atlántico Norte** NATO
otario, **-a** *CSur* **I.** *adj* foolish **II.** *m, f* fool
otate *m Méx* BOT reed, rush
otear **I.** *vt* **1.** (*ver*) to scan **2.** (*escudriñar*) to scrutinize **3.** (*observar*) to watch **II.** *vi* to look; (*desde un alto*) to look down on
otero *m* hillock
otitis *f sin pl* MED inflammation of the ear; ~ **media** inflammation of the middle ear
otomana *f* ottoman
otomano, **-a** *adj, m, f* Ottoman
otomía *f Arg, Col* atrocity
otoñal *adj* (*lugar, tiempo*) autumnal; **un amor**

~ *fig* late love

otoño *m* (*estación*) autumn, fall *Am;* **a fin(al)es de** ~ at the end of autumn [*o* fall *Am*]; **el** ~ (**de la vida**) the autumn (of one's life)

otorgamiento *m* **1.** (*concesión*) concession; JUR execution; (*de documento*) drawing up; (*de contrato*) award; (*de licencia*) grant; ~ **de poder** bestowal of power **2.** (*consentimiento*) consent

otorgar <g→gu> *vt* **1.** (*conferir*) to confer; ~ **poderes** to confer powers **2.** (*conceder*) to concede; (*ayudas*) to offer; ~ **un plazo** to set a time limit **3.** (*expedir*) to issue; ~ **licencia** to grant a license **4.** (*acceder*) ~ **algo** to agree to sth; ~ **su consentimiento** to give one's consent

otorrinolaringólogo, **-a** *m, f* MED ear, nose and throat specialist

otro, **-a** **I.** *adj* another, other; **al** ~ **día** the next day; **el** ~ **día** the other day; **en otra ocasión** another time; **la otra semana** the other week; **en** ~ **sitio** in another place, somewhere else; **otra cosa** another thing; ~ **tanto** as much again; **otra vez** again; **¡otra vez será!** maybe another time!; **es** ~ **Mozart** he is another Mozart; **eso ya es otra cosa** that is much better; **¡hasta otra (vez)!** until the next time! **II.** *pron indef* **1.** (*distinto: cosa*) another (one); (*persona*) someone else; **~s** others; **el ~/la otra/lo** ~ the other (one); **ninguna otra persona, ningún** ~ nobody else; **de un sitio a** ~ from one place to another; **no** ~ **que...** none other than ...; **ésa es otra** (*cosa distinta*) that is different; *irón* (*aún peor*) that is even worse **2.** (*uno más*) another; **otras tres personas** three more people; **¡otra, otra!** more!

otrora *adv* formerly

otrosí *adv* furthermore

ovación *f* ovation; **dar/recibir una** ~ to give/receive an ovation

ovacionar *vt* to give an ovation

oval *adj,* **ovalado**, **-a** *adj* oval

óvalo *m* (*forma*) oval

ovario *m* ANAT ovary

oveja *f* sheep *inv;* (*hembra*) ewe; **la** ~ **negra de la familia** the black sheep of the family ►**cada** ~ **con su pareja** *prov* birds of a feather flock together *prov*

ovejero, **-a** **I.** *adj* sheep; **perro** ~ sheep dog **II.** *m, f* **1.** (*ganadero*) sheep breeder; (*pastor*) shepherd **2.** *AmL* (*perro*) sheep dog

overol *m AmL* overall

ovetense **I.** *adj* of/from Oviedo **II.** *mf* native/inhabitant of Oviedo

oviducto *m* oviduct

ovillar **I.** *vt* to wind into a ball; (*enrollar*) to wind up **II.** *vr:* **~se** to roll up into a ball

ovillo *m* ball; *fig* tangle; **hacerse un** ~ (*enredarse*) to get tangled up; (*encogerse*) to curl up into a ball; (*al hablar*) to get all tangled up

ovino, **-a** **I.** *adj* sheep; **ganado** ~ sheep *pl* **II.** *m, f* sheep *inv*

ovíparo, **-a** *adj* oviparous

ovni *m* UFO

ovoide **I.** *adj* ovoid, egg-shaped **II.** *m* **1.** MAT ovoid **2.** *AmL* (*pelota*) rugby ball

ovulación *f* ovulation

ovular *vi* to ovulate

óvulo *m* ANAT ovule

oxidable *adj* (*metal*) which rusts

oxidación *f* **1.** QUÍM oxidation **2.** (*metal*) rusting

oxidar **I.** *vt* **1.** QUÍM to oxidize **2.** (*metal*) to rust; **un hierro oxidado** a piece of rusty iron **II.** *vr:* **~se** **1.** (*metal*) to rust; (*mente*) to go rusty; **~se de no moverse** to rust through lack of use **2.** QUÍM to oxidize

óxido *m* **1.** QUÍM oxide **2.** (*orín*) rust

oxigenar **I.** *vt* **1.** (*cabello*) to bleach; (**rubio**) **oxigenado** platinum [*o* peroxide] blond(e) **2.** QUÍM to oxigenate; **agua oxigenada** (hydrogen) peroxide **II.** *vr:* **~se** *inf* to get some fresh air

oxígeno *m* QUÍM oxygen

oyente *mf* listener; (**libre**) ~ UNIV unmatriculated student

ozono *m* QUÍM ozone; **el agujero en la capa de** ~ the hole in the ozone layer

P

P, **p** *f* P, p; ~ **de París** P for Peter

pabellón *m* **1.** (*tienda*) bell tent **2.** (*bandera*) flag **3.** ARQUIT pavillion **4.** ANAT ~ **de la oreja** auricle, outer ear

pabilo *m,* **pábilo** *m* wick

pábulo *m* food; *fig* fuel; **dar** ~ **a rumores** to encourage rumours *Brit* [*o* rumors *Am*]

paca *f* (*fardo*) bale

pacato, **-a** *adj* **1.** (*mojigato*) prudish **2.** (*apacible*) gentle **3.** (*tímido*) shy

pacer *irr como crecer vi, vt* to graze

pacha *f* **1.** *Nic, Méx* (*botella aplanada*) flask **2.** *Nic* (*biberón*) baby's bottle

pachá *m* pasha; **vivir como un** ~ *fig* to live like a lord

pachacho, **-a** *adj Chile* short-legged

pachaco, **-a** *adj* **1.** *AmC* (*aplastado*) flattened **2.** *CRi* (*inútil, enclenque*) feeble

pachamama *f And* (*Madre Tierra*) Mother Earth

pachamanca *f And* **1.** (*plato*) barbecued meat **2.** (*horno*) barbecue pit

pachanga *f* **1.** *Cuba* (*danza*) *Cuban dance* **2.** *Col, inf* (*fiesta*) party

pacho, **-a** *adj* **1.** (*indolente*) lazy **2.** *Nic* (*flaco*) skinny

pachón, **-ona** **I.** *adj* **1.** (*perro*) shaggy; **perro** ~ shaggy dog **2.** *AmL* (*peludo*) hairy **II.** *m, f* **1.** ZOOL beagle **2.** *inf* (*persona*) calm quiet fellow

pachorra *f inf* slowness; **tener** ~ to be lackadaisical [*o* laid-back]
pachorriento, **-a** *adj AmS* phlegmatic, lackadaisical
pachucho, **-a** *adj* **1.** *inf* (*persona*) off-colour *Brit*, off-color *Am* **2.** (*fruta*) overripe
pachulí *m* patchouli
paciencia *f* patience; **se me ha acabado la** ~ I've run out of patience; **ése hace perder la** ~ **a un santo** he'd try the patience of a saint
paciente **I.** *adj* patient; **ser** ~ **con alguien** to be patient with sb **II.** *mf* patient
pacificación *f* pacification
pacificar <c→qu> **I.** *vi* to become peaceful **II.** *vt* (*apaciguar*) to pacify; (*reconciliar*) to reconcile **III.** *vr:* ~**se** to calm down; (*viento*) to abate
pacífico, **-a** *adj* peaceful; **carácter** ~ (*nación*) peacefulness
Pacífico *m* Pacific (Ocean)
pacifismo *m* pacifism
pacifista *adj, mf* pacifist
paco, **-a** *adj AmL* reddish
pacota *f Méx* (*pacotilla*) rabble
pacotilla *f* **1.** (*calidad inferior*) trashiness; **tienda de** ~**s** junk shop; **de** ~ (*mercancía*) shoddy; (*restaurante*) second-rate; **ser de** ~ to be shoddy **2.** *AmL* (*chusma*) rabble
pacotillero, **-a** **I.** *adj* second-rate; **tienda pacotillera** shop selling shoddy goods **II.** *m, f* **1.** (*vendedor*) street vendor **2.** *AmL* (*negociante que viaja*) street hawker
pactar **I.** *vi* to come to an agreement; **¡hay que** ~ **para sobrevivir!** you have to compromise if you want to get on! **II.** *vt* to agree on
pacto *m* agreement; (*contrato*) contract
padecer *irr como crecer* **I.** *vi* to suffer **II.** *vt* **1.** (*sufrir*) to suffer; ~ **algo** to suffer from sth; ~ **un error** to labour [*o* labor *Am*] under a misapprehension **2.** (*soportar*) to endure
padecimiento *m* **1.** (*sufrimiento*) suffering **2.** (*enfermedad*) ailment
padrastro *m* **1.** (*marido de madre*) stepfather **2.** (*mal padre*) cruel father **3.** (*pellejo*) hangnail
padrazo *m* **es un** ~ *inf* he's a great dad
padre **I.** *m* **1.** *t.* REL father; ~ **espiritual** confessor; **¡tu** ~**!** *inf* up yours! **2.** *pl* (*padre y madre*) parents *pl* **3.** *pl* (*antepasados*) forefathers *pl;* **dormir con sus** ~**s** to have passed away ►**tal** ~**, tal hijo** *prov* like father, like son **II.** *adj inf* tremendous; **un escándalo** ~ a huge scandal; **recibir una paliza de** ~ **y muy señor mío** to take one hell of a beating
padrenuestro *m* Lord's Prayer
padrillo *m CSur* stallion
padrinazgo *m* **1.** (*título*) godfathership **2.** (*protección*) patronage
padrino *m* (*de bautizo*) godfather; (*de boda*) best man; **tener buenos** ~**s** *fig* to know the right people
padrón *m* **1.** ADMIN (*registro*) (census) register **2.** *AmL* (*caballo*) stallion
padrote *m AmC, Méx* **1.** (*equino*) stallion; (*bovino*) breeding bull **2.** *inf* (*alcahuete*) pimp
paella *f* paella

> **Paella** is a Spanish rice dish containing various types of meat and fish, **marisco** (seafood) and **azafrán** (saffron), which gives the rice its characteristic dark-yellow colour. Originally from **Valencia**, paella is known today throughout the world.

paellera *f* paella dish
pág. *abr de* **página** p.
paga *f* **1.** (*sueldo*) pay **2.** (*acto*) payment
pagadero, **-a** *adj* **1.** (*a pagar*) due **2.** (*pagable*) payable
pagado, **-a** *adj* paid; (*en aduana*) duty paid; ~ **de sí mismo** full of oneself
pagador(**a**) *m(f)* payer
pagaduría *f* payment office
paganismo *m sin pl* paganism
pagano, **-a** **I.** *adj* pagan **II.** *m, f* **1.** (*infiel*) pagan **2.** *inf* (*pagador*) payer; **hacer de** ~ to always end up footing the bill
pagar <g→gu> **I.** *vt* **1.** (*gastos*) to pay; (*una deuda*) to repay; ~ **un anticipo** to make an advance payment; **una cuenta sin** ~ an unpaid bill; ~ **una deuda a plazos** to pay off a debt in instalments [*o* installments *Am*] **2.** (*expiar*) to atone for; ~ **una condena** to serve a sentence; **¡me las** ~**ás!** you'll pay for this! **3.** (*recompensar*) to repay; (*una visita*) to return; **¡Dios se lo pague!** God will reward you! **II.** *vr* **1.** (*aficionarse*) ~**se de algo** to take a liking to sth **2.** (*presumir*) to boast; ~**se de algo** to boast about sth **3.** (*contentarse*) to be content
pagaré *m* promissory note, IOU
página *f* **1.** (*hoja*) page; **pasar la** ~ (**adelante**) to turn the page **2.** (*episodio*) chapter **3.** TEL ~**s blancas** telephone directory; ~**s amarillas** yellow pages **4.** INFOR ~ **web** web site
paginación *f* pagination
paginar *vt* to paginate
pago *m* **1.** (*reintegro*) payment; ~ **adicional** supplement; ~ **extraordinario** one-off payment, bonus; ~ **inicial** down payment; ~ **a plazos** payment by instalments [*o* installments *Am*]; **día de** ~ pay day; **anticipar el** ~ to pay in advance; **sujeto a** ~ subject to payment; ~ **contra entrega** payment on delivery **2.** (*salario*) pay; ~ **anticipado** advance payment; ~ **por hora** hourly pay; ~ **por incapacidad** sick pay **3.** *fig* (*recompensa*) reward; **¿éste es el** ~ **que me das?** is this how you repay me? **4.** (*heredad*) estate **5.** *Arg, Perú* (*de nacimiento*) home region
pai *m AmL* GASTR pie
paila *f AmL* (*sartén*) frying pan
país *m* GEO, POL country; ~ **comunitario** member state (*of the European Union*); ~ **industrializado** industrialized country; ~

P

limítrofe neighbouring [*o* neighboring *Am*] country; ~ **en vías de desarrollo** developing country; ~ **en vías de industrialización** industrializing country

paisa *m AmL v.* **paisano**

paisaje *m* landscape; (*campo*) countryside

paisajista *mf* ARTE landscape artist

paisanada *f CSur* peasants *pl*

paisano, **-a** *m, f* **1.** (*no militar*) civilian; **ir de** ~ to be in plain clothes **2.** (*compatriota*) compatriot **3.** (*campesino*) peasant

Países Bajos *mpl* Netherlands

paja *f* **1.** (*hierba, caña*) straw; **cama de** ~ straw bed; **no pesar una** ~ to be as light as a feather; **no dormirse en las ~s** *inf* to be alert **2.** *vulg* (*masturbación*) **hacerse una** ~ *vulg* to wank *Brit,* to jerk off *Am*

pajar *m* haystack; (*lugar*) hayloft; **buscar una aguja en un** ~ *fig* to search for a needle in a haystack

pájara *f* **1.** (*ave*) hen **2.** (*cometa*) kite **3.** *pey* (*mujer*) slyboots *inf* **4.** *inf* (*desfallecimiento*) **me entró la** ~ I fainted

pajarera *f* aviary

pajarero, **-a I.** *adj* **1.** (*de pájaros*) bird; **redes pajareras** bird nets **2.** (*persona*) perky, cheerful **3.** (*telas*) bright-coloured *Brit,* bright-colored *Am* **4.** *AmL* (*caballos*) skittish **II.** *m, f* (*cazador de pájaros*) bird catcher; (*criador de pájaros*) bird breeder; (*vendedor de pájaros*) bird dealer

pajarita *f* (*corbata*) bow tie

pájaro *m* bird; ~ **bobo** penguin; ~ **carpintero** woodpecker; ~ **mosca** hummingbird; ~ **de cuenta** *inf* wily bird; ~ **gordo** *fig* big shot; **tener la cabeza llena de ~s** to be scatterbrained; **voló el** ~ *inf* the chance has gone ▶**más vale ~ en <u>mano</u> que ciento volando** *prov* a bird in the hand is worth two in the bush

pajarón, **-ona** *adj Arg, Chile, inf* scatterbrained

pajarraco *m inf* (*pillo*) rogue

paje *m* (*criado*) page

pajero *m CSur, vulg* wanker *Brit,* jerk-off *Am*

pajita *f* (drinking) straw

pajizo, **-a** *adj* **1.** (*con, de paja*) straw **2.** (*color, cabello*) straw-coloured *Brit,* straw-colored *Am*

pajolero, **-a** *adj inf* damned

pajonal *m CSur* scrubland

pajuela *f* **1.** (*para encender*) straw taper **2.** *Bol* (*cerilla*) match **3.** *Bol, Col* (*mondadientes*) toothpick

pajuerano, **-a** *m, f Arg, Bol, Urug, pey* (*paleto*) country bumpkin, hick *Am*

Pakistán *m* Pakistan

pakistaní *adj, mf* Pakistani

pala *f* **1.** (*para cavar*) spade; (*cuadrada*) shovel; ~ **mecánica** mechanical shovel; *AmL* bulldozer **2.** (*del timón*) rudder **3.** (*raqueta*) racket; (*bate*) bat **4.** (*hélice*) blade **5.** (*del calzado*) upper

palabra *f* word; ~ **clave** *t.* INFOR keyword, password; **~s cruzadas** crossword; ~ **extranjera** foreign word; **~s insultantes** rude words; ~ **de matrimonio** promise of marriage; **~s mayores** strong words; ~ **técnica** technical term; **juego de ~s** pun, play on words; **libertad de** ~ freedom of speech; **bajo** ~ on one's word of honour *Brit* [*o* honor *Am*]; **buenas ~s** empty words; **de pocas ~s** quiet; **ahorrar ~s** not to waste one's words; **aprender las ~s** to learn one's lines; **beber las ~s a alguien** to hang on sb's every word; **coger a alguien la** ~ to take sb at his word; **cumplir la** ~ to be as good as one's word; **dirigir la ~ a alguien** to speak to sb; **faltar a la** ~ to go back on one's word; **llevar la** ~ to speak; **medir las ~s** to choose one's words carefully; **no entender** ~ not to understand a single word; **quitar a alguien la ~ de la boca** to take the words right out of sb's mouth ▶**dejar a alguien con la ~ en la <u>boca</u>** to interrupt sb; **a ~s necias <u>oídos</u> sordos** *prov* sticks and stones will break my bones, but names will never hurt me *prov;* **poner <u>dos</u> ~s a alguien** to write sb a short note; **hablar a <u>medias</u> ~s** to drop hints; **decir la <u>última</u>** ~ to have the last word; **<u>de</u>** ~ (*oral*) by word of mouth; (*que cumple sus promesas*) honourable *Brit,* honorable *Am*

palabrería *f* (empty) words, hot air

palabrero, **-a I.** *adj* wordy **II.** *m, f* gasbag *Brit, inf*

palabrota *f* swearword

palaciego, **-a I.** *adj* palace **II.** *m, f* courtier

palacio *m* palace; (*casa grande*) mansion; **Palacio de las Cortes** Spanish parliament building; **Palacio de Justicia** law courts; ~ **municipal** town hall

palada *f* **1.** (*de la pala*) shovelful **2.** (*de remo*) stroke

paladar *m* palate; ~ **blando** soft palate; **tener buen** ~ (*vino*) to be smooth on the palate; (*persona*) to have a discerning palate

paladear *vt* **1.** (*degustar*) to taste **2.** (*saborear*) to savour *Brit,* to savor *Am;* ~ **un dulce** to allow a sweet to dissolve in one's mouth

palanca *f* **1.** (*pértiga*) lever; (*palanqueta*) crowbar; ~ **de mando** AVIAT, INFOR joystick **2.** (*influencia*) influence; **tener mucha** ~ to have a lot of influence **3.** (*en las piscinas*) rigid diving board **4.** AUTO ~ **de cambio** gear lever *Brit,* gearshift *Am*

palangana *f* washbasin

palanganear *vi AmL, inf* to brag

palanquear *vt AmL* **1.** (*apalancar*) to lever **2.** (*influenciar*) to influence

palanqueta *f* crowbar

palapa *f Méx* sunshade

palatal *adj* palatal

palatino, **-a** *adj* **1.** ANAT palatal; **hueso** ~ hard palate **2.** (*del palacio*) palace; **vida palatina** palace life

palco *m* TEAT box

palenque *m* **1.** (*palestra*) arena **2.** (*estacada*) fence

palenquear *vt Arg, Urug* to tether
paleontología *f sin pl* paleontology
Palestina *m* Palestine
palestino, **-a** *adj, m, f* Palestinian
paleta *f* **1.** (*pala*) (small) shovel; (*del albañil*) trowel **2.** (*del pintor*) palette **3.** (*de turbinas*) blade **4.** (*omóplato*) shoulder blade **5.** *Col, inf* (*helado*) ice lolly
paletada *f* shovelful; **una ~ de yeso** a shovelful of plaster
paletilla *f* (*omóplato*) shoulder blade
paleto *m* fallow deer
paleto, **-a** **I.** *adj* uncouth **II.** *m, f* yokel, hick *Am*
paliacate *m Méx* large brightly coloured [*o* colored *Am*] scarf
paliar <*1. pres:* palío, palio> *vt* **1.** (*delito*) to mitigate **2.** (*enfermedad*) to alleviate **3.** (*restar importancia*) to excuse
paliativo *m* palliative
paliativo, **-a** *adj* MED palliative; **remedio ~** palliative remedy
palidecer *irr como crecer vi* **1.** (*persona*) to turn pale **2.** (*cosa*) to fade
palidez *f* paleness
pálido, **-a** *adj* pale; (*estilo*) flat
palillo *m* **1.** (*palo*) (small) stick; **tener las piernas como ~s** *fig* to have legs like matchsticks; **tocar todos los ~s** *inf* to pull out all the stops **2.** (*para los dientes*) toothpick **3.** (*para el tambor*) drumstick
palio *m* (*baldaquín*) canopy; **recibir a alguien bajo ~** *fig* to roll out the red carpet for sb
palique *m inf* chat; **estar de ~ con alguien** to chat to sb
palisandro *m* rosewood
paliza[1] *f* **1.** (*zurra*) beating; **dar una buena ~** (*pegar*) to beat up; (*derrotar*) to thrash; **¡no me des la ~!** *fig* give me a break! **2.** *inf* (*esfuerzo*) slog; **¡qué ~ me he pegado subiendo la montaña!** climbing that mountain has exhausted me!
paliza[2] *mf inv, inf* (*pesado*) pain; **tu amigo es un ~(s)** your friend is a real bore
palma *f* **1.** (*palmera*) palm (tree); (*hoja de palmera*) palm leaf **2.** (*triunfo*) **llevarse la ~** to be the best **3.** ANAT palm; **conozco el barrio como la ~ de mi mano** *inf* I know the area like the back of my hand; **llevar a alguien en ~s** to treat sb with kid gloves **4.** *pl* (*ruido*) clapping; (*aplauso*) applause; **tocar las ~s** to clap; (*aplaudir*) to applaud
palmada *f* **1.** (*golpe*) pat **2.** *pl* (*ruido*) clapping; **~s de aplauso** applause; **dar ~s** to clap
palmar **I.** *m* palm grove; **ser más viejo que un ~** to be as old as the hills **II.** *vi inf* **~la** to kick the bucket
palmario, **-a** *adj* (*evidente*) clear
palmatoria *f* (*candelero*) candlestick
palmeado, **-a** *adj* **1.** (*figura*) palm-shaped **2.** ZOOL webbed
palmear *vi* (*aplaudir*) to clap
palmense **I.** *adj* of/from Las Palmas **II.** *mf* native/inhabitant of Las Palmas
palmera *f* palm (tree)
palmeral *m* palm grove
palmero, **-a** **I.** *adj* of/from the island of Palma **II.** *m, f* native/inhabitant of the island of Palma
palmípedas *fpl* web-footed birds *pl*
palmo *m* (hand)span; **con un ~ de la lengua fuera** *inf* with one's tongue hanging out ►**dejar a alguien con un ~ de narices** to disappoint sb badly; **~ a ~** inch by inch; **conocer algo ~ a ~** to know every inch of sth
palmotear *vi* to clap
palmoteo *m* (*aplauso*) clapping
palo *m* **1.** (*bastón*) stick; (*vara*) pole; (*garrote*) club; (*estaca*) post; **~ de la escoba** broomstick; **~ de hockey** hockey stick; **~ de la portería** goalpost **2.** NÁUT mast **3.** (*madera*) wood **4.** (*paliza*) beating; **andar a ~s** to be at each another's throats; **dar ~s de ciego** to thrash about wildly; *fig* to grope in the dark; **dar un ~ a alguien** *fig* to tear a strip off sb; (*cobrar mucho*) to rip sb off; **echar a alguien a ~s** to throw sb out; **liarse a ~s con alguien** to come to blows with sb; **moler a alguien a ~s** to beat sb black and blue ►**~ de agua** *AmL* downpour; **no dar un ~ al agua** not to do a stick of work; **de tal ~, tal astilla** *prov* like father, like son; **cada ~ que aguante su vela** *prov* everyone must face up to their responsibilities; **ser un ~** to be a setback
paloma *f* (*ave*) pigeon; (*blanca, como símbolo*) dove; **~ mensajera** carrier pigeon; **ser una ~ sin hiel** *fig* to be as gentle as a lamb
palomar *m* dovecote, pigeon loft
palomilla *f* **1.** ZOOL (*mariposa nocturna*) moth **2.** (*tornillo*) wing [*o* butterfly] nut
palomitas *fpl* GASTR popcorn
palomo *m* (cock) pigeon
palote *m* **1.** (*palillo*) drumstick **2.** (*ejercicio*) downstroke
palpable *adj* **1.** (*tangible*) palpable **2.** (*evidente*) clear
palpar *vt* **1.** (*tocar*) to touch **2.** *inf* (*magrear*) to touch up *Brit*, to feel up *Am* **3.** (*percibir*) to feel; **se palpaba el entusiasmo** you could feel the enthusiasm
palpitación *f* **1.** (*del pulso*) throb; (*del corazón*) beating; (*por estar excitado*) palpitation **2.** (*estremecimiento*) shudder
palpitante *adj* **1.** (*corazón*) throbbing **2.** *fig* (*emocionante*) exciting; (*interés*) burning; **un problema de ~ actualidad** a problem of the utmost relevance
palpitar *vi* **1.** (*contraerse*) to shudder; (*corazón, pulso*) to throb **2.** (*manifestarse*) **en sus palabras palpita la dulzura** his words are full of sweetness
pálpito *m* (*corazonada*) hunch
palta *f AmS* BOT avocado (pear)
palto *m CSur* BOT avocado pear tree

palúdico, **-a** *adj* MED malarial; **fiebre palúdica** malaria
paludismo *m* MED malaria
palurdo, **-a** I. *adj* uncouth II. *m, f* yokel, hick *Am*
palustre I. *adj* marsh; **planta** ~ marsh plant II. *m* trowel
pamela *f* broad-brimmed ladies' hat
pamema *f inf* 1. (*tontería*) silly thing 2. (*melindre*) flattery
pampa *f* GEO pampas + *sing/pl vb*

> The **pampa** is a flat, treeless, grassy steppe in Argentina. It is a very fertile agricultural area, because the moist soil, which consists mainly of fine sand, clay and earth, is ideally suited to the cultivation of cereals.

pámpano *m* 1. (*vástago*) vine shoot; **echar ~s** to put out shoots 2. (*hoja*) vine leaf
pampear *vi CSur* to travel over the pampas
pampero, **-a** I. *adj* of/from the Pampas II. *m, f* native/inhabitant of the Pampas
pampino, **-a** I. *adj Chile* of/from the Chilean pampas II. *m, f Chile* native/inhabitant of the Chilean pampas
pamplina *f inf* (*pamema*) silly thing
pamplonés, **-esa** I. *adj* of/from Pamplona II. *m, f* native/inhabitant of Pamplona
pamplonica *adj, mf inf v.* **pamplonés**
pan *m* 1. (*alimento*) bread; ~ **de azúcar** sugar loaf; ~ **candeal** white bread; ~ **integral** wholemeal bread; ~ **con mantequilla** bread and butter; ~ **de molde** sliced bread; ~ **de munición** (army) ration bread; ~ **rallado** breadcrumbs *pl;* **estar a ~ y agua** to be on (a strict diet of) bread and water; **ganarse el** ~ to earn one's living; **este año hay mucho** ~ it's been a good harvest this year 2. (*pieza*) **un ~ de jabón** a bar of soap 3. (*laminilla*) gold leaf ▶**comer ~ con corteza** (*ser independiente*) to fend for oneself; (*recuperar la salud*) to be on the mend; **¡el ~ de cada día!** the same old thing!; **no sólo de ~ vive el hombre** man cannot live by bread alone; **ser un pedazo de ~, quien da ~ a perro ajeno, pierde ~ y pierde perro** *prov:* ≈ *don't expect gratitude from strangers;* **a falta de ~, buenas son tortas** *prov* half a loaf is better than none, beggars can't be choosers; (**llamar**) **al ~, ~ y al vino, vino** *inf* to call a spade a spade; **ser más bueno que el** ~ to be very good-natured; **ser ~ comido** *inf* to be dead easy; **con su ~ se lo coma** *inf* that's his lookout [*o* problem]; **comer el ~ de alguien** to live off sb; **no se le cuece el** ~ he's/she's very impatient
pana *f* (*tejido*) corduroy
panacea *f* panacea, cure-all
panadería *f* bakery
panadero, **-a** *m, f* baker
panal *m* honeycomb
Panamá *m* Panama

> **Panamá** is divided in two by the Panama Canal and links Central America to North America. The capital, which is also called **Panamá**, is the largest city in the country. Spanish is the official language of the country, although English is widely used. The monetary unit of Panama is the **balboa**.

panameño, **-a** *adj, m, f* Panamanian
pancarta *f* placard
pancho *m Arg* GASTR (*perrito caliente*) hot-dog
pancho, **-a** *adj* (*tranquilo*) calm
pancista *mf* opportunist
pancita *f Méx* GASTR tripe
páncreas *m inv* pancreas
panda[1] *m* ZOOL panda
panda[2] *f v.* **pandilla**
pandear *vi, vr:* **~se** (*pared*) to bulge; (*viga*) to warp
pandereta *f*, **pandero** *m* MÚS tambourine
pandilla *f* band; (*de amigos*) group; ~ **de ladrones** gang of thieves
pandorga *f* 1. (*cometa*) kite 2. *inf* (*mujer gorda*) fat woman 3. (*barriga*) paunch 4. *Col* (*chanza, diablura*) prank
panecillo *m* roll
panegírico *m* panegyric
panegírico, **-a** *adj* eulogizing
panel *m* 1. (*carpintería, téc*) panel; ~ **de control** control panel 2. (*encuesta*) panel 3. (*que discute en público*) discussion panel
panela *f* 1. (*bizcocho*) maize cake, corn cake *Am* 2. *Col, CRi, Hond* (*azúcar*) brown sugar loaf
panera *f* 1. (*para trigo*) grain store 2. (*cesto*) bread bin, breadbox *Am*
pánfilo, **-a** *adj* 1. (*fácil de engañar*) gullible 2. (*lento*) slow
panfleto *m* pamphlet; *fig* propaganda
pánico *m* panic; **entrar en** ~ to panic; **tener ~ a algo** to be terrified of sth
pánico, **-a** *adj* panic
panificar <c→qu> *vt* ~ **algo** to make bread from sth
panizo *m* millet
panocha *f*, **panoja** *f* 1. (*de maíz*) corncob 2. (*espiga*) ear of corn; (*racimo*) cornstalk
panoli *inf* I. *adj* idiotic II. *mf* idiot
panorama *m* panorama; *fig* outlook; **el ~ de cráteres en la luna** the landscape of craters on the moon
panqué *m Cuba, Méx,* **panqueque** *m AmS* GASTR pancake
pantagruélico, **-a** *adj* (*comidas*) enormous; **banquete** ~ lavish feast
pantaleta(**s**) *f(pl) Méx, Ven* (*bragas*) knickers *pl Brit,* panties *pl*
pantalla *f* 1. (*de la lámpara*) shade 2. (*protección*) screen; **servirse de alguien como** ~ to hide behind sb; **servir de** ~ (*testaferro*) to be a figurehead 3. INFOR, TV, CINE screen; ~ **com-**

pleta full-size screen; ~ **cromática** colour [*o* color *Am*] screen; ~ **panorámica** wide screen; **estrella de la** ~ screen star; **pequeña** ~ *inf* TV

pantalón *m* trousers *pl,* pair of trousers; ~ **bombacho** (*amplio*) baggy trousers; (*hasta la pantorrilla*) knickers *pl Brit;* ~ **de pinzas** pleated trousers; ~ **tejano** [*o* **vaquero**] jeans *pl;* **llevar los pantalones** *fig* to wear the trousers [*o* pants]

pantanal *m* marshland

pantano *m* **1.** (*ciénaga*) marsh; (*laguna*) swamp **2.** *fig* (*atolladero*) fix **3.** (*embalse*) reservoir

pantanoso, **-a** *adj* marshy

panteón *m* **1.** HIST pantheon **2.** (*sepultura*) tomb; ~ **de familia** family vault **3.** *AmL* (*cementerio*) cemetery

panteonero, **-a** *m, f AmL* gravedigger

pantera *f* panther

pantimedia(**s**) *f(pl) Méx* tights *pl Brit,* pantyhose

pantis *mpl inf* tights *pl Brit,* pantyhose

pantomima *f* pantomime

pantorrilla *f* calf

pantufla *f,* **pantuflo** *m* slipper

panucho *m Méx* meat and bean stuffed tortilla

panul *m CSur* BOT (*apio*) celery

panza *f* **1.** (*barriga*) belly; (*de un recipiente*) bulge; **llenarse la** ~ to fill one's belly **2.** ZOOL stomach; (*rumiantes*) rumen

pañal *m* nappy *Brit,* diaper *Am;* **dejar en** ~**es a alguien** *fig* to leave sb way behind; **estar aún en** ~**es** *fig* to be still in its infancy; **en física estoy en** ~**es** I haven't got a clue about physics

pañería *f* **1.** (*comercio*) drapery *Brit,* dry goods *pl Am* **2.** (*tienda*) draper's (shop) *Brit,* dry goods store *Am*

pañetar *vt Col* (*una pared*) to skim with plaster

paño *m* **1.** (*tejido, trapo*) cloth; ~ **asargado** serge; ~ **de cocina** (*para fregar*) dishcloth; (*para secar*) tea towel *Brit,* dish towel *Am* **2.** (*ancho de una tela*) width **3.** (*mancha*) stain ►**ser el** ~ **de lágrimas de alguien** to be sb's shoulder to cry on; **andarse con** ~**s calientes** to do things by halves; **aplicar** ~**s calientes** to apply half measures; ~**s menores** underwear; **¡conozco el** ~**!** *inf* I know what's what!; **hay** ~ **que cortar** there's plenty to be getting on with

pañoleta *f* fichu

pañuelo *m* **1.** (*moquero*) handkerchief; **el mundo es un** ~ it's a small world **2.** (*pañoleta*) fichu; (*de cabeza*) headscarf, scarf

papa¹ *m* pope

papa² *f* **1.** *reg, AmL* (*patata*) potato; **no entender ni** ~ not to understand a thing **2.** *inf v.* **paparrucha 3.** *pl* (*comida*) purée

papá *m inf* **1.** (*padre*) dad; **Papá Noel** Father Christmas **2.** *pl* **los** ~**s** mum and dad

papachar *vt Méx* (*mimar*) to spoil

papada *f* (*de la persona*) double chin, jowl; (*del animal*) dewlap

papagayo *m* **1.** (*loro*) parrot **2.** (*hablador*) chatterbox; **hablar como un** ~ to be a real chatterbox **3.** (*pez*) parrot fish

papal I. *adj* papal **II.** *m AmL* potato field

papalote *m Ant, Méx* paper kite

papamoscas *m inv* **1.** ZOOL flycatcher **2.** *inf* (*papanatas*) halfwit

papamóvil *m* popemobile

papanatas *m inv, inf* halfwit

paparrucha *f inf,* **paparruchada** *f inf* **1.** (*noticia falsa*) piece of nonsense; (*patraña*) lie **2.** (*obra sin valor*) piece of trash; **ese libro es una** ~ this book is trash

papaya *f* pawpaw, papaya

papayo *m* pawpaw (tree)

papel *m* **1.** (*para escribir, material*) paper; (*hoja*) piece of paper; (*escritura*) piece of writing; ~ **de barba** untrimmed paper; ~ **de calcar** tracing paper; ~ **cebolla** onionskin (paper); ~ **continuo** continuous listing paper; ~ **de envolver** wrapping paper; ~ **de regalo** giftwrap; ~ **de estraza** brown paper; ~ **de aluminio** aluminium [*o* tin] foil; ~ **de seda** tissue paper; ~ **de fumar** cigarette paper; ~ **higiénico** toilet paper; ~ **de hilo** parchment paper; ~ **de lija** sandpaper; ~ **maché** papier mâché; ~ **moneda** banknotes *pl,* bills *pl Am;* ~ **de música** music paper; ~ **pautado** ruled paper; ~ **pintado** wallpaper; ~ **de plata** silver paper; ~ **reciclado** recycled paper; ~ **secante** blotting paper; ~ **de tornasol** litmus paper; ~ **mojado** *fig* worthless scrap of paper; **tus palabras fueron** ~ **mojado** your words were no more than empty promises; **ponerse más blanco que el** ~ to go as white as a sheet **2.** (*rol*) role; ~ **protagonista** leading role; ~ **secundario** supporting role; **hacer su** ~ to play one's part; **hacer un** ~ **ridículo** to make a fool of oneself; **hacer buen/mal** ~ to make a good/bad impression; **hacer el** ~ **de malo en la película** to play the role of the baddy in the film; **repartir los** ~**es** to assign the parts **3.** *pl* (*documentos*) documentation; (*de identidad*) identity papers *pl*

papela *f inf* ID papers *pl*

papeleo *m* (*trámites*) paperwork; ~ **burocrático** red tape

papelera *f* **1.** (*cesto*) wastepaper basket; (*en la calle*) litter bin **2.** (*fábrica*) paper mill **3.** (*mueble*) desk

papelería *f* stationer's

papelerío *m AmL* mass of papers

papelero, **-a I.** *adj* paper **II.** *m, f* (*vendedor*) stationer

papeleta *f* (*cédula*) slip of paper; (*en el examen*) result slip; ~ **del monte de piedad** pawn ticket; ~ **de propaganda** flier *Brit,* flyer *Am;* **menuda** ~ **le ha tocado** that's a nasty problem he's got

papelón *m* **1.** *pey* (*papel inútil*) scrap of paper **2.** *inf* (*actuación*) embarrassing behaviour *Brit,*

P

embarrassing behavior *Am;* **¡qué ~!** how embarrassing!; **hacer un ~** to make a spectacle of oneself

papelote *m,* **papelucho** *m* **1.** *pey* (*inútil*) scrap of paper **2.** (*reciclable*) pulped paper

papera *f* MED **1.** *pl* (*enfermedad*) mumps *pl* **2.** (*bocio*) goitre *Brit,* goiter *Am*

papi *m inf* dad(dy)

papilla *f* baby food; **dar ~ a alguien** *fig* to con sb; **echar la (primera) ~** *inf* to be as sick as a dog; **hacer ~ a alguien** *fig* to beat hell out of sb; **estar hecho ~** *fig* to be smashed to a pulp

papiro *m* papyrus

papo *m* **1.** (*buche: de animal*) dewlap; (*de ave*) crop; *inf* (*bocio*) goitre *Brit,* goiter *Am* **2.** (*papada*) double chin, jowl

paquebote *m* packet boat

paquete *m* **1.** *t. fig* (*atado*) packet; **~ postal** parcel **2.** *inf* (*castigo*) **meter un ~ a alguien** (*reprender*) to give sb a real telling-off; (*castigar*) to punish sb heavily **3.** *inf* (*genitales*) bulge; **marcar ~** to wear tight-fitting trousers

paquete, -a *adj Arg* smart

paquetear *vi Arg, Urug, inf: to show off how smartly dressed one is*

paquete-bomba *m* <paquetes-bomba> parcel bomb

paquetería *f* **1.** (*paquete*) parcels *pl* **2.** *Arg* (*vanidad*) vanity

paquidermo *m* pachyderm

paquistaní *adj, mf v.* **pakistaní**

par **I.** *adj* **1.** (*número*) even; **~es o nones** odds or evens **2.** (*igual*) equal; **a la ~** at the same time; **esta película entretiene a la ~ que instruye** this film is both entertaining and educational; **sin ~** without equal ▶**de ~ en ~** wide open; **abrir una ventana de ~ en ~** to open a window wide **II.** *m* **1.** (*dos cosas*) pair; **un ~ de zapatos/pantalones** a pair of shoes/trousers **2.** (*algunos*) **un ~ de minutos** a couple of minutes **3.** (*título*) peer

para **I.** *prep* **1.** (*destino*) for; **asilo ~ ancianos** old people's home; **un regalo ~ el niño** a present for the child **2.** (*finalidad*) for; **gafas ~ bucear** diving goggles; **servir ~ algo** to be useful for sth; **las frutas son buenas ~ guardar la línea** fruit is good for keeping in shape; **¿~ qué es esto?** what is this for? **3.** (*dirección*) to; **voy ~ Madrid** I'm going to Madrid; **mira ~ acá** look over here **4.** (*duración*) for; **~ siempre** forever; **con esto tenemos ~ rato** with this we've got enough for quite a while; **vendrá ~ Navidad/finales de marzo** he/she will come for Christmas/towards the end of March; **estará listo ~ el viernes** it will be ready for [*o* by] Friday; **diez minutos ~ las once** *AmL* ten to eleven **5.** (*contraposición*) for; **es muy activo ~ la edad que tiene** he is very active for his age **6.** (*trato*) **~ (con)** with; **es muy amable ~ con nosotros** he/she is very kind to us **7.** (+ *estar*) **estar ~...** (*disposición*) to be ready to ...; (*a punto de*) about to ...; **no estoy ~ bromas** I'm in no mood for jokes; **está ~ llover** it's about to rain; **está ~ llegar** he/she is about to arrive; **quiere estar ~ sí** he/she wants to be alone **8.** (*a juicio de*) **~ mí, esto no es lo mismo** in my opinion, this is not the same; **~ mí que va a llover** I think it's going to rain **II.** *conj* **1.** + *infin* to; **he venido ~ darte las gracias** I've come to thank you **2.** **~ que** +*subj* so that; **te mando al colegio ~ que aprendas algo** I send you to school so that you learn sth

parabién *m* congratulations *pl;* **dar el ~ a alguien** to congratulate sb

parábola *f* **1.** (*alegoría*) parable **2.** MAT curve, parabola

parabólica *f* satellite dish

parabólico, -a *adj* **1.** (*alegórico*) allegorical; **expresarse en sentido ~** to speak allegorically **2.** MAT parabolic **3.** TÉC satellite

parabrisas *m inv* AUTO windscreen *Brit,* windshield *Am*

paraca *f AmL* strong breeze from the Pacific

paracaídas *m inv* parachute

paracaidismo *m sin pl* parachuting

paracaidista *mf* DEP parachutist; MIL paratrooper

parachoques *m inv* AUTO bumper, fender *Am*

parada *f* **1.** (*de un autobús, tranvía*) stop; **~ de taxis** taxi rank **2.** (*acción de parar*) stopping; **~ de una fábrica** factory stoppage; **estoy cansada, tenemos que hacer una ~** I'm tired, we need to have a rest **3.** DEP, MIL parade; **paso de ~** marching step

paradero *m* (*de una persona*) whereabouts; (*de una cosa*) destination; **está en ~ desconocido** his whereabouts are unknown; **no logramos descubrir el ~ del paquete** we didn't manage to find out where the packet ended up

paradigma *m* (*ejemplo*) paradigm

paradisíaco, -a *adj* heavenly; **un placer ~** a heavenly delight

parado, -a **I.** *adj* **1.** (*que no se mueve*) stationary; **estar ~** to be motionless; (*fábrica*) to be at a standstill; **quedarse ~** to remain motionless; *fig* to be surprised; **me quedé tan ~ que no pude decir nada** I was so surprised I was left totally dumbstruck; **me has dejado ~** you have really surprised me **2.** (*sin empleo*) unemployed **3.** (*remiso*) slow **4.** (*tímido*) shy **5.** *AmL* standing (up) ▶**salir bien/mal ~ de algo** to come out of sth well/badly; **ser el peor ~ en algo** to be the one who comes off worst in sth **II.** *m, f* unemployed person; **los ~s** the unemployed; **~ de larga duración** long-term unemployed person

paradoja *f* paradox; **esto es una ~** this is absurd

parador *m* **1.** inn **2.** (*en España*) state-run luxury hotel

paraestatal *adj* semi-official

parafina *f* paraffin

parafrasear *vt* to paraphrase

paráfrasis *f inv* paraphrase
paragolpes *m inv, AmL* bumper, fender *Am*
parágrafo *m* paragraph; **...,** ~ **aparte** ..., new paragraph; *fig* ..., to change the subject
paraguas *m inv* umbrella
Paraguay *m* Paraguay

> **Paraguay** lies in South America and borders Bolivia, Brazil and Argentina. It is a landlocked country. The capital of Paraguay is **Asunción**. The official languages of the country are Spanish and **guaraní**. The monetary unit of the country is also called the **guaraní**.

paraguayo, -a *adj, m, f* Paraguayan
paragüero *m* (*mueble*) umbrella stand
paraíso *m* 1.(*en el cielo*) heaven; ~ **terrenal** earthly paradise; **entrar en el** ~ to go to heaven 2. TEAT gods *pl* 3. *Méx* (*gallinero*) henhouse
paraje *m* 1.(*lugar*) place; (*punto*) spot 2.(*estado*) state
paralela *f* 1. MAT parallel 2. *pl* DEP parallel bars *pl*; ~**s asimétricas** asymmetric bars
paralelo *m* 1.(*comparación*) comparison; **establecer un** ~ **entre dos cosas** to compare two things; **estos libros no admiten** ~ these books cannot be compared 2. GEO parallel 3. ELEC **conexión en** ~ parallel connection; **conectado en** ~ connected in parallel
paralelo, -a *adj* parallel; **líneas paralelas** parallel lines; **las calles son paralelas** the streets are parallel; **seguir caminos** ~**s** to develop along similar lines
paralelogramo *m* parallelogram
parálisis *f inv* paralysis; ~ **infantil** infantile paralysis; **sufre** ~ **de las piernas** his/her legs are paralysed [*o* paralyzed *Am*]
paralítico, -a I. *adj* (*persona*) paralysed *Brit*, paralyzed *Am* II. *m, f* paralytic
paralización *f* 1.(*del cuerpo*) paralysis 2.(*de un proyecto, un proceso*) halting; ~ **de una obra** halting of a building job
paralizar <z→c> I. *vt* 1.(*persona*) to paralyse *Brit*, to paralyze *Am*; **el miedo/el frío la paralizó** she was paralysed [*o* paralyzed *Am*] by fear/the cold 2.(*cosa*) to stop; ~ **un transporte** to paralyse [*o* to paraalyze *Am*] a means of transport II. *vr* 1.(*persona*) to be paralysed [*o* paralyzed *Am*] 2.(*cosa*) to stop
paramento *m* 1.(*adorno*) ornament; (*vestidura*) vestment 2.(*para un caballo*) trappings *pl*
parámetro *m* parameter
paramilitar *adj* paramilitary; **fuerzas** ~**es** paramilitary forces
páramo *m* 1.(*terreno desierto*) wilderness; (*infértil*) wasteland; (*altiplano*) barren plateau 2.(*lugar desamparado*) exposed place
parangón *m* 1.(*comparación*) comparison; **sin** ~ incomparable 2.(*semejanza*) similarity
parangonar *vt* 1.(*comparar*) to compare 2. TIPO to justify
paraninfo *m* UNIV (*salón*) auditorium, assembly hall
paranoia *f* paranoia
paranoico, -a I. *adj* paranoid II. *m, f* paranoic
parapente *m* paragliding
parapetarse *vr* to protect oneself; ~ **tras una excusa** to hide behind an excuse; **se parapetó en el hecho de que no tenía dinero** he used the excuse that he didn't have any money
parapeto *m* 1. MIL parapet; (*barricada*) barricade 2.(*baranda*) railing
paraplejía *f* paraplegia
parapléjico, -a *adj, m, f* paraplegic
parapsicología *f* parapsychology
parar I. *vi* 1.(*detenerse, cesar*) to stop; **hablar sin** ~ to talk without stopping; **¿para el tren en este pueblo?** does the train stop in this town?; **a la vuelta paramos en casa de mi tía** on the way back we'll stop at my aunt's house; **la máquina funciona sin** ~ the machine works non-stop; **mis hijos no me dejan** ~ my kids never give me a break; **mis remordimientos de conciencia no me dejan** ~ my guilty conscience doesn't give me any peace; **ha parado de llover** it has stopped raining; **no para de quejarse** he/she never stops complaining; **no para** (**de trabajar**) he never stops (working) 2.(*acabar*) to finish; **si sigues así irás a** ~ **a la cárcel** if you carry on like this you'll end up in jail; **la maleta fue a** ~ **a Bilbao** the suitcase ended up in Bilbao; **por fin, el paquete fue a** ~ **a tus manos** the packet finally reached you; **¿dónde iremos a** ~**?** what's the world coming to?; **¿en qué irá a** ~ **esto?** where will it all end?; **salimos bien/mal parados del asunto** we came out of the affair well/badly; **¿dónde quieres ir a** ~**?** what are you getting at?; **siempre venimos a** ~ **al mismo tema** we always end up talking about the same thing 3.(*alojarse, estar*) to live; **no sé dónde para** I don't know where he/she lives; **nunca para en casa** he/she is never at home; **siempre para en el mismo hotel** he/she always stays at the same hotel; **¿paras mucho en este bar?** *inf* do you come to this bar often? 4.(*convertirse*) **la tienda paró en un restaurante** the shop was converted into a restaurant II. *vt* 1.(*detener*) to stop; (*un golpe*) to block; (*un gol*) to save; (*el motor*) to turn off; **cuando se enfada no hay quien lo pare** when he gets angry there's no stopping him 2.(*en el juego*) to bet III. *vr* 1.(*detenerse*) to stop; **el reloj se ha parado** the clock has stopped; ~**se a pensar** to stop and think; ~**se a descansar** to stop to rest 2. *AmL* (*levantarse*) to get up
pararrayos *m inv* lightning conductor
parásito, -a I. *adj t. fig* parasitic II. *m, f t. fig* parasite
parásitos *mpl* RADIO statics *pl*, interference
parasol *m* 1.(*quitasol*) sunshade 2.(*en el*

P

coche) sun visor **3.** (*umbela*) canopy

parcela *f* **1.** (*terreno*) plot; ~ **de cultivo** cultivated plot; ~ **edificable** building plot **2.** (*parte*) portion

parcelar *vt* **1.** (*dividir*) to parcel out **2.** (*medir*) to measure out

parche *m* **1.** (*pegote*) patch; (*para una herida*) (sticking) plaster, Bandaid®; **bolsillo de ~** patch pocket; ~ **para el ojo** eye patch; **pegar un ~ a alguien** *inf* to put one over on sb; **poner un ~** to patch up **2.** (*retoque*) makeshift remedy; (*de pintura*) dab; **poner ~s** to patch up; *fig* to paper over the cracks **3.** (*piel del tambor*) drumskin **4.** (*tambor*) drum

parchear *vt* **1.** (*poner parches*) to patch (up) **2.** (*manosear*) to touch up *Brit,* to feel up *Am*

parchís *m* (*juego*) ludo *Brit,* parcheesi *Am*

parcial **I.** *adj* **1.** (*incompleto*) partial; **la venta ~ del terreno** the partial sale of the land **2.** (*arbitrario*) biased **II.** *mf* supporter

parcialidad *f* **1.** (*preferencia*) bias, favoritism **2.** (*grupo*) faction

parco, -a *adj* **1.** (*moderado*) moderate; (*sobrio*) frugal **2.** (*escaso*) meagre *Brit,* meager *Am;* ~ **en palabras** of few words; **ser ~ en conceder favores** to be sparing with one's favours [*o* favors *Am*]

pardiez *interj* HIST good gracious

pardillo *m* linnet

pardillo, -a **I.** *adj inf* **1.** (*palurdo*) uncouth **2.** (*ingenuo*) simple **II.** *m, f* **1.** (*palurdo*) yokel **2.** (*ingenuo*) simpleton

pardo, -a **I.** *adj* **1.** (*color*) greyish-brown; **oso ~** brown bear; **de ojos ~s** brown-eyed **2.** (*oscuro*) dark **3.** (*voz*) dull **II.** *m, f AmL* mulatto

pardusco, -a *adj* brownish

parear *vt* **1.** (*formar parejas*) to pair; (*atar*) to tie together; (*ropa*) to match up **2.** BIO to mate **3.** (*igualar*) to match

parecer **I.** *irr como crecer vi* (*tener cierto aspecto*) to seem; (*aparentar*) to appear; **a lo que parece** as far as one can tell; **tu idea me parece bien** I think your idea is a good one; **parece mayor de lo que es** he seems older than he is; **parece mentira que** +*subj* it seems incredible that; **aunque parezca mentira** though it may seem incredible; **me parece que no tienes ganas** I don't think you want to; **parece que va a llover** it looks like rain; **¿qué te parece?** what do you think?; **¿qué te parece el piso?** what do you think of the flat?; **si te parece bien,...** if you agree, ...; **me ha parecido oír un grito** I thought I heard a scream, if it's OK with you; **parecen hermanos** they look like brothers ►**quien no parece, perece** *prov* if you don't look after your own interests, nobody else will **II.** *irr como crecer vr* to look alike; **se parece a una estrella de cine** she looks like a film star; **te pareces mucho a tu madre** you look very much like your mother; **¡esto se te parece!** this looks like you! **III.** *m* **1.** (*opinión*) opinion; (*juicio*) judgement; **a mi ~** in my opinion; **arrimarse al ~ de la mayoría** to follow the opinion of the majority; **esto es cuestión de ~es** this is a matter of opinion **2.** (*aspecto, apariencia*) appearance; **ser de buen ~** to be good-looking; **al ~** apparently; **por el bien ~** for the sake of appearances

parecido *m* similarity, likeness; **tienes un gran ~ con tu hermana** you and your sister look very alike

parecido, -a *adj* **1.** (*semejante*) similar **2.** (*de aspecto*) **ser bien/mal ~** (*persona*) to be good/bad-looking; (*cosa*) to be appropriate/inappropriate

pared *f* **1.** (*tabique, muro*) wall; (*de una montaña*) face; (*separación*) partition; ~ **abdominal** stomach wall; ~ **maestra** (load-)bearing wall **2.** (*personas*) wall; (*cosas*) mountain ►**vivimos ~ por medio** we live next door; **estar blanco como la ~** to be as white as a sheet [*o* ghost]; **entre cuatro ~es** cooped up; **dejar a alguien pegado a la ~** to put sb on the spot; **quedarse pegado a la ~** to be put on the spot; **hablar a la ~** to talk to a brick wall; **¡cuidado, que estas ~es oyen!** careful, walls have ears!; **subirse por las ~es** to go up the wall; (*enfadarse*) to blow one's top; (*estar nervioso*) to be [*o* go] stir crazy

paredón *m* thick wall; **llevar a alguien al ~** to take sb before a firing squad

pareja *f* **1.** (*par*) couple; (*de la guardia civil*) pair of Civil Guards; ~ **de hecho** common law couple; **~s mixtas** DEP mixed doubles; **hacen buena ~** they make a good partnership [*o* couple]; **¿dónde está la ~ de este guante?** where is the other glove?; **su bondad y su modestia corrían ~s** his goodness was matched by his modesty; **no correr ~s** to be dissimilar **2.** (*compañero*) partner **3.** (*en los dados, los naipes*) pair

parejo, -a *adj* **1.** (*igual*) equal; (*semejante*) similar; **los caballos iban ~s** the horses were neck and neck **2.** (*llano*) smooth

parentela *f* relations *pl*

parentesco *m* relationship, kinship; ~ **por consanguinidad** blood relationship

paréntesis *m inv* **1.** (*signo*) bracket; **poner algo entre ~** to put sth in brackets; **entre ~** *fig* by the way; **abrir/cerrar el ~** to open/close brackets; *fig* to introduce/finish a digression **2.** (*oración*) digression **3.** (*interrupción*) interruption; **hicimos un ~ para almorzar** we had a break for lunch

paridad *f* **1.** (*comparación*) comparison **2.** FIN, ECON parity; ~ **adquisitiva** parity of purchasing power; ~ (**de cambio**) exchange parity **3.** (*igualdad*) equality; (*semejanza*) similarity; ~ **de fuerzas** parity of strength; **competir a ~ de medios** to compete on an equal basis

pariente, -a **I.** *adj* **1.** (*de la misma familia*) related **2.** (*parecido*) similar **II.** *m, f* **1.** (*familiar*) relative; **los ~s** the relations, the relatives; ~ **mayor** direct ancestor; ~**lejano/**

cercano distant/close relative **2.** *inf* (*marido, mujer*) other half; **mi** ~ my missus, my old man
parihuela(s) *f(pl)* stretcher
paripé *m* show; **hacer el** ~ to put on a show; (*presumir*) to show off; (*fingir*) to pretend; (*fingir cariño*) to put on a show of affection
parir I. *vt* **1.** (*dar a luz*) to give birth to **2.** (*producir*) to produce; (*causar*) to cause **II.** *vi* **1.** (*dar a luz*) to give birth **2.** (*descubrirse*) to come to light **3.** (*expresarse*) to express oneself; ~ **sin dificultad** to express oneself well ▶**poner a alguien a** ~ *inf* to run sb down
París *m* Paris
parisiense *adj, mf* Parisian
paritario, -a *adj* equal; **comité** ~ joint committee
paritorio *m* **1.** (*sala*) delivery room **2.** *AmC* (*parto*) birth
parking *m* <parkings> car park, parking lot *Am*
parlamentar *vi* **1.** (*hablar*) to talk **2.** (*negociar*) to negotiate
parlamentario, -a I. *adj* parliamentary; **debate** ~ parliamentary debate **II.** *m, f* **1.** (*diputado*) member of parliament **2.** (*negociador*) negotiator
parlamento *m* **1.** (*cámara*) parliament; **Parlamento Europeo** European Parliament **2.** *t.* TEAT (*discurso*) speech **3.** (*negociaciones*) negotiations *pl*
parlanchín, -ina I. *adj inf* talkative **II.** *m, f inf* (*persona*) chatterbox; (*indiscreta*) gossip
parlotear *vi* to chatter
parloteo *m* chat
parné *m inf* (*dinero*) dough
paro *m* **1.** (*parar: una fábrica*) shutdown; (*de trabajar*) stopping **2.** (*huelga*) ~ **laboral** strike; (*por parte de los empresarios*) lockout **3.** (*desempleo*) unemployment; ~ **forzoso** unemployment; **estar en** ~ to be unemployed; **cobrar el** ~ to be on the dole **4.** ZOOL tit; ~ **carbonero** coal tit
parodia *f* parody; **hacer una** ~ **de algo** to parody sth
parodiar *vt* to parody
parpadear *vi* **1.** (*ojos*) to blink; **sin** ~ *fig* without a second thought **2.** (*luz, llama*) to flicker
parpadeo *m* **1.** (*de los ojos*) blinking **2.** (*de una luz, una llama*) flicker
párpado *m* eyelid
parque *m* **1.** (*jardín*) park; ~ **de atracciones** funfair *Brit,* amusement park *Am;* ~ **natural** National Park; ~ **zoológico** zoo **2.** (*depósito*) depot; ~ **de bomberos** fire station, fire department *Am;* ~ **militar** military depot; ~ **temático** theme park **3.** (*conjunto*) collection; ~ **industrial** industrial park; ~ **de maquinaria** pool of machinery; ~ **móvil** fleet of (official) vehicles; ~ **de vehículos** fleet of vehicles, car pool **4.** (*para niños*) playpen
parqué *m* parquet
parqueadero *m AmL* car park, parking lot *Am*
parquear *vt AmL* to park
parquedad *f* frugality; **hablar con** ~ to be sparing with one's words
parquet *m* parquet
parquímetro *m* parking meter
parra *f* (*vid*) (grape)vine; **subirse a la** ~ (*enfadarse*) to hit the roof; (*darse importancia*) to get above oneself
párrafo *m v.* **parágrafo**
parral *m* **1.** (*parras*) vine; (*techo*) vine arbour *Brit,* vine arbor *Am* **2.** (*viña*) vineyard
parranda *f* spree; **ir de** ~ to go out on the town
parrilla *f* **1.** (*para la brasa*) grill; (*de un horno*) oven rack **2.** (*establecimiento*) grill(room) **3.** DEP ~ **(de salida)** (starting) grid **4.** *AmL* AUTO roof-rack
parrillada *f* grill; ~ **de pescado** grilled fish; ~ **de carne** mixed grill
párroco I. *adj* parish **II.** *m* parish priest
parroquia *f* **1.** (*territorio, fieles*) parish **2.** (*iglesia*) parish church **3.** (*clientela*) customers *pl*
parroquial *adj* parish; **iglesia** ~ parish church
parroquiano, -a I. *adj* parish **II.** *m, f* **1.** (*feligrés*) parishioner **2.** (*cliente*) customer
parsimonia *f* **1.** (*calma*) calm; (*lentitud*) deliberation; **con** ~ calmly **2.** (*en los gastos*) economy **3.** (*prudencia*) care; (*moderación*) moderation
parsimonioso, -a *adj* **1.** (*tranquilo*) calm; (*flemático*) phlegmatic **2.** (*ahorrador*) economical **3.** (*prudente*) careful; (*moderado*) moderate
parte[1] *f* **1.** (*porción, elemento*) part; (*de repuesto*) spare (part); ~ **alícuota** proportion; ~ **constitutiva** component part; ~ **esencial** vital part; ~ **del león** lion's share; ~ **del mundo** part of the world; **una cuarta** ~ a quarter; **de varias ~s** of several parts; **en** ~ in part; **en gran** ~ largely; **en mayor** ~ for the most part; ~ **por** ~ bit by bit; **tomar** ~ **en algo** to be involved in sth **2.** (*repartición*) division; ~ **hereditaria** share of the inheritance; **tener** ~ **en algo** to have a share in sth; **dar** ~ **a alguien en algo** to give sb a part of sth; **llevarse la peor/mejor** ~ to come off (the) worst/best **3.** (*lugar*) part; **¿a qué** ~ **vas?** where are you going?; **a ninguna** ~ nowhere; **en ninguna** ~ nowhere; **en cualquier** ~ anywhere; **por todas (las) ~s** everywhere; **en otra** ~ somewhere else; **¿de qué** ~ **de España es tu familia?** which part of Spain is your family from?; **no llevar a ninguna** ~ *fig* to lead nowhere **4.** *t.* JUR (*bando*) party; (*en una discusión*) participant; ~ **contratante** contracting party; ~ **laboral** employee **5.** (*lado*) side; ~ **de delante/de atrás** front/back; **dale recuerdos de mi** ~ give him/her my regards; **somos primos por** ~ **de mi padre/de mi madre** we are cousins on my father's/mother's side; **por mi** ~ **puedes hacer lo que quieras** as far

as I'm concerned you can do what you like; **estar de ~ de alguien** to be on sb's side; **ponerse de ~ de alguien** to take sb's side; **saber de buena ~** to know from a reliable source; **me tienes de tu ~** I'm on your side; **de ~ a ~** (*de un lado a otro*) from side to side; (*de arriba a abajo*) from top to bottom; **por otra ~** on the other hand; (*además*) what's more **6.** (*sección*) section; (*tomo*) volume; (*capítulo*) chapter **7.** TEAT, MÚS (*papel*) part **8.** *pl* (*genitales*) (private) parts *pl;* **me dio una patada en salva sea la ~** *inf* he gave me a kick in the you-know-whats **9.** (*temporal*) **de primeros de mes a esta ~** from the beginning of this month; **de unos cuantos días a esta ~** a few days from now ▸**tomar** [*o* **echar**] **algo a mala ~** to take sth as an insult

parte² *m* **1.** (*comunicado*) message; **dar ~** to report; **tienes que dar ~ del robo a la policía** you have to report the theft to the police **2.** RADIO, TV report; **~ meteorológico** weather report

partero, -a *m, f* midwife *f,* male midwife *m;* (*médico*) obstetrician

parterre *m* flower bed

partición *f* **1.** (*acción de partir*) partition **2.** MAT division

participación *f* **1.** (*intervención*) participation; **~ en los beneficios** profit-sharing **2.** (*parte*) share **3.** (*billete*) lottery ticket (*which is shared between several people*); (*parte que se juega*) stake **4.** (*anuncio*) notice; (*aviso*) warning

participante *mf* participant

participar I. *vi* **1.** (*tomar parte*) to participate; **los países participantes** the participating countries; **~ en un juego** to take part in a game; **participo en tu alegría** I share your happiness **2.** (*tener parte*) to have a part; **~ en una herencia** to share in an inheritance **3.** (*tener en común*) **~ de algo** to share sth; **participamos de la misma opinión** we are of the same opinion II. *vt* (*comunicar*) to inform

partícipe I. *adj* involved II. *mf* participant; **~ de algo** person involved in sth; **hacer a alguien ~ de algo** (*compartir*) to share sth with sb; (*informar*) to inform sb of sth

participio *m* LING participle; **~ activo** [*o* **de presente**] present participle; **~ pasivo** [*o* **de pretérito**] past participle

partícula *f* **1.** *t.* FÍS, QUÍM particle; **~ elemental** fundamental particle; **~s de polvo** dust particles **2.** LING particle; **~ prepositiva** prefix

particular¹ I. *adj* **1.** (*propio*) peculiar; (*individual*) individual; (*típico*) typical; (*personal*) personal; **el sabor ~ del azafrán** the special flavour [*o* flavor *Am*] of saffron **2.** (*raro*) peculiar **3.** (*extraordinario*) unusual; **caso ~** unusual case; **en ~** in particular; **posee un talento ~ para dibujar** he has a special talent for drawing **4.** (*privado*) private; **envíamelo a mi domicilio ~** send it to my home address **5.** (*determinado*) particular; **tenemos que concentrarnos en este problema ~** we must concentrate on this particular problem II. *mf* private individual; (*civil*) civilian

particular² *m* matter

particularidad *f* **1.** (*especialidad*) speciality *Brit,* specialty *Am;* (*singularidad*) distinctive feature; (*peculiaridad*) peculiarity; **la ~ de este método estriba en que...** the distinctive feature of this method is that ... **2.** (*rareza*) peculiarity **3.** (*detalle*) detail; (*circunstancia*) circumstance; **las ~es del crimen** the circumstances of the crime **4.** (*en el trato*) intimacy

particularizar <z→c> I. *vt* **1.** (*explicar*) to go into details about **2.** (*mostrar preferencia*) to favour *Brit,* to favor *Am* **3.** (*personalizar*) **~ en alguien** to make references to sb **4.** (*distinguir*) to distinguish; **sus saques particularizan su estilo de jugar** the distinctive feature of his/her style of play is his/her serve II. *vi* (*explicar*) to go into details

particularmente *adv* particularly

partida *f* **1.** (*salida*) departure **2.** (*envío*) consignment **3.** FIN item; **~ doble** double entry **4.** (*anotación*) entry; (*certificado*) certificate; **~ de defunción** death certificate **5.** (*juego*) game; **jugar una ~ de ajedrez** to play a game of chess **6.** (*grupo*) party; MIL faction; (*en un juego*) team; (*excursión*) trip; **~ de campo** excursion (to the country) **7.** (*muerte*) death **8.** (*lugar*) place

partidario, -a I. *adj* **1.** (*parcial*) biased **2.** (*seguidor*) **ser ~ de algo** to be in favour [*o* favor *Am*] of sth II. *m, f* **1.** (*seguidor*) follower; (*afiliado*) member; (*de un proyecto, una idea*) supporter **2.** (*guerrillero*) partisan

partidismo *m* **1.** (*parcialdad*) bias; (*a favor de un partido*) political bias, partisanism **2.** POL party loyalty

partido *m* **1.** POL party; **~ de clase media** middle-class party; **~ de derecha(s)/de izquierda(s)** left-wing/right-wing party; **~ obrero** worker's party; **~ pequeño** minority party; **~ popular** people's party; **sistema de ~ único** one-party system **2.** (*grupo*) group; **formar ~** to band together; **esta idea tiene mucho ~** this idea has a lot of supporters; **el candidato tenía cada vez menos ~** the candidate had less and less support; **la película tuvo mucho ~ en el extranjero** the film was very successful abroad **3.** DEP (*juego*) match; **~ amistoso** friendly **4.** (*equipo*) team **5.** (*para casarse*) match; **encontrar un buen ~** to make quite a catch **6.** ADMIN district; **~ judicial** administrative area; **cabeza de ~** administrative centre [*o* center *Am*] **7.** (*determinación*) determination; **tomar ~ a favor de algo/alguien** (*inclinarse*) to lean towards sth/sb; (*opinar*) to express an opinion on sth/sb; (*decidirse*) to choose sth/sb; **tomar ~** MIL to enlist **8.** (*provecho*) advantage; **de esto aún se puede sacar ~** sth can still be made of this;

no sacarás ~ de él you'll get nothing out of him/her; **saqué ~ del asunto** I profited from the affair **9.** *AmL* (*del pelo*) parting

partido, **-a** *adj* (*liberal*) generous

partidor *m* divider

partir I. *vt* **1.** *t.* MAT (*dividir*) to divide; **~ por la mitad** to divide into two halves; **estar a ~ un piñon** to be thick as thieves **2.** (*romper*) to break; (*madera*) to chop; (*una nuez*) to crack; **~ el pan** REL to break bread; **~ la cabeza a alguien** to crack sb's head open **3.** (*repartir*) to share out; (*clasificar*) to classify **4.** (*compartir*) to share **5.** (*una baraja*) to cut **II.** *vi* **1.** (*tomar como base*) to start; **a ~ de ahora** from now on; **a ~ de mañana** from tomorrow; **a ~ de las seis** from six o'clock onwards; **a ~ de entonces** since then **2.** (*salir de viaje*) to leave; (*ponerse en marcha*) to start; **partimos de Cádiz a las cinco** we left Cadiz at five o'clock **III.** *vr* **1.** (*rajarse*) to split; (*cristal*) to crack **2.** *inf* (*de risa*) **~se** (**de risa**) to split one's sides laughing

partisano, **-a** *m, f* partisan

partitivo, **-a** *adj* **1.** LING partitive **2.** (*que se puede partir*) divisible; (*que se puede romper*) breakable

partitura *f* MÚS score; (*hojas*) sheet music

parto *m* (*alumbramiento*) birth; **~ prematuro** premature birth; **dolores de ~** labour [*o* labor *Am*] pains *pl;* **estar de ~** to be in labour [*o* labor *Am*]; **esto es el ~ de los montes** *fig* this is an anticlimax

parturienta *f* **1.** (*que está de parto*) woman in labour [*o* labor *Am*] **2.** (*que acaba de parir*) woman who has just given birth

parva *f* **1.** AGR unthreshed grain **2.** (*montón*) heap

parvedad *f* **1.** (*escasez*) scarcity; (*pequeñez*) smallness; (*poquedad*) fewness **2.** (*para comer*) morsel

parvo, **-a** *adj* (*pequeño*) small; (*escaso*) scarce

parvulario *m* kindergarten; (*educación preescolar*) nursery school, preschool *Am*

párvulo, **-a** *m, f* infant; **escuela de ~s** nursery school, preschool *Am;* **clase de ~s** nursery class

pasa *f* (*uva seca*) raisin; **~ de Corinto** currant; **helado de ron y ~s** rum and raisin ice cream; **estar hecho una ~** *inf* to be as shrivelled [*o* shriveled *Am*] as a prune

pasable *adj* passable

pasabocas *m inv, Col* (*tapas*) appetizer

pasacalle *m* MÚS passacaglia; (*marcha*) lively march

pasada *f* **1.** (*paso*) passing; **hacer varias ~s** to make several passes; **de ~** when passing; *fig* in passing **2.** (*mano*) going-over; (*pintura*) coat; **dar una ~ a algo** to give sth another going-over; **dar otra ~ con agua limpia** to give another wipe with clean water **3.** *inf* (*comportamiento*) excess; **¡vaya (mala) ~!** what a thing to do!; **hacer una mala ~ a alguien** to play a dirty trick on sb **4.** *inf* (*exageración*) **¡es una ~!** it's way over the top! **5.** (*puntada*) tacking [*o* basting *Am*] stitch; (*costura*) row of stitches; **dar unas ~s a algo** to tack sth, baste sth *Am* **6.** (*con la plancha*) **sólo le voy a dar una ~** I'm just going to give it a quick iron **7.** (*en un juego*) pass

pasadero, **-a** *adj* passable

pasadizo *m* (*pasillo*) corridor; (*entre dos calles*) alley; **~ secreto** secret passageway

pasado *m* (*tiempo, vida*) past; LING past (tense); **en el ~** in the past; **son cosas del ~** it's all in the past

pasado, **-a** *adj* **1.** (*de atrás*) past; **el año ~** last year; **la conferencia del año ~** last year's conference; **~ mañana** the day after tomorrow; **~s dos meses** after two months; **~ de moda** out of fashion; (*vestido*) unfashionable **2.** (*estropeado: alimentos*) bad; (*fruta*) overripe; (*leche*) off, sour; (*mantequilla*) rancid; (*ropa*) worn-out; (*flores*) wilted; **el yogur está ~ de fecha** the yogurt is past its sell-by date **3.** (*muy cocido*) overcooked; **¿quieres el filete muy ~?** do you want the steak very well done?; **un huevo ~ por agua** a soft-boiled egg

pasador *m* **1.** (*alfiler*) pin; (*imperdible*) safety pin; (*broche*) clip; (*de corbata*) tiepin **2.** (*para el cabello*) hairclip, slide *Brit,* barrette *Am* **3.** (*cerrojo*) bolt **4.** (*colador*) colander **5.** *pl* (*gemelos*) cufflinks *pl*

pasadores *mpl* **1.** (*botón*) cufflinks *pl* **2.** *Perú* (*cordones*) shoelaces *pl*

pasaje *m* **1.** (*acción de pasar*) passing; (*de una calle, un territorio*) crossing **2.** (*derecho*) toll **3.** (*en barco*) voyage **4.** (*billete de avión*) (plane) ticket; (*de barco*) (boat) ticket; (*precio*) fare **5.** (*pasajeros*) passengers *pl* **6.** (*pasillo*) passage; **~ subterráneo** underground passage **7.** (*estrecho*) strait

pasajero, **-a I.** *adj* **1.** (*transitorio, breve*) passing; (*fugaz*) fleeting **2.** (*calle, plaza*) busy **II.** *m, f* (*viajero*) passenger; **tren de ~s** passenger train

pasamano(**s**) *m(pl)* handrail

pasamontañas *m inv* balaclava, ski mask *Am*

pasante I. *adj* (*viajante*) travelling *Brit,* traveling *Am* **II.** *mf* **1.** (*auxiliar*) assistant; (*de un abogado*) articled clerk; **~ de pluma** clerk **2.** (*profesor*) tutor

pasapalos *m inv, Méx, Ven* (*tapas*) appetizer

pasaporte *m* (*para viajar*) passport; **dar** (**el**) **~ a alguien** *inf* (*despedirlo*) to give sb their marching orders; (*matarlo*) to bump sb off

pasapuré(**s**) *m* (*inv*) vegetable mill; (*patatas*) potato masher

pasar I. *vi* **1.** (*por delante*) to pass; **~ corriendo** to run past; **~ desapercibido** to go unnoticed; **~ de largo** to go past; **pásate un momento por mi casa** drop round to my house; **dejar ~** (*por delante*) to allow to go past; **~ por encima de** (*un obstáculo*) to overcome; (*una persona*) to overlook; **el avión pasó por encima de los Pirineos** the plane flew over the Pyrenees; **~ por alto** *fig* to leave

P

out; **no dejes ~ la oportunidad** don't miss the opportunity **2.** (*por un hueco*) to go through; **el sofá no pasa por la puerta** the sofa won't go through the door; **el Ebro pasa por Zaragoza** the Ebro flows through Zaragoza; ~ **por una crisis** to go through a crisis **3.** (*trasladarse*) to move; **pasemos al comedor** let's go to the dining room **4.** (*acaecer*) to happen; **¿qué pasa?** what's up?; **¿qué te pasa?** what's wrong?; **pase lo que pase** whatever happens; **dejar ~ algo** to allow sth to happen; **lo que pasa es que...** the thing is that ... **5.** (*acabar*) to pass; **ya ha pasado la tormenta** the storm has passed; **cuando pasen las vacaciones...** when the holidays are over ... **6.** (*el tiempo*) to pass; **han pasado dos semanas sin llover** we have had two weeks without rain; **lo pasado, pasado** what's done is done **7.** (*ser transferido*) to be transferred **8.** (*poder existir*) to get by; **vamos pasando** we manage **9.** (*aparentar*) to pass for; **pasa por nuevo** it looks new; **podrías ~ por inglesa** you could be taken for an Englishwoman; **hacerse ~ por médico** to pass oneself off as a doctor **10.** (*cambiar*) to go; **paso a explicar porqué** and now I will (go on to) explain why; ~ **a mayores** to go from bad to worse **11.** (*ser admisible*) to pass; **arreglándolo aún puede ~** if we fix it it should still be okay; ~ **por un control** to pass a checkpoint **12.** (*no jugar*) to pass **13.** *inf* (*no necesitar*) **yo paso de salir** I don't want to go out; **paso de esta película** I can't be bothered with this film; **pasa de todo** he/she couldn't care less about anything **II.** *vt* **1.** (*atravesar*) to cross; ~ **el puente** to cross the bridge; ~ **el semáforo en rojo** to go through a red light **2.** (*por un hueco*) to go through; ~ **la tarjeta por la ranura** to swipe the card through the slot; ~ **algo por debajo de la puerta** to slide sth under the door **3.** (*trasladar*) to transfer; ~ **a limpio** to make a fair copy **4.** (*dar*) to pass; ~ **la pelota** to pass the ball **5.** (*una temporada*) to spend; ~ **el invierno en Mallorca** to spend the winter in Majorca; **~lo bien/mal** to have a good/bad time; **~lo en grande** to have a whale of a time; **¡que lo paséis bien!** enjoy yourselves! **6.** (*sufrir*) to experience; ~ **hambre** to go hungry; ~ **frío** to feel the cold; **has pasado mucho** you have been through a lot; **pasé un mal rato** I went through a difficult time **7.** (*transmitir*) to send; (*una película*) to show; (*una noticia*) to broadcast; (*dinero*) to give; ~ **un recado** to pass on a message; **me has pasado el resfriado** you've given me your cold; **le paso a la Sra. Ortega** I'll put you through to Señora Ortega **8.** (*sobrepasar*) to exceed; (*cierta edad*) to be older than; **he pasado los treinta** I am over thirty; **te paso en altura** I am taller than you **9.** (*hacer deslizar*) ~ **la mano por la mesa** to run one's hand over the table; ~ **la aspiradora** to vacuum **10.** (*tolerar*) to allow to pass **11.** (*aprobar*) to pass **12.** (*omitir*) to overlook **13.** (*leer sin atención*) to skim **14.** (*repasar*) to check; (*estudiar*) to study **15.** (*tragar*) to swallow; **no puedo ~me la pastilla** I can't swallow the pill **16.** (*colar*) to strain **17.** (*las hojas de un libro*) to turn **18.** (*géneros prohibidos*) to smuggle **III.** *vr* **1.** (*acabarse*) to pass; **se me han pasado las ganas** I don't feel like it any more; **ya se le ~á el enfado** his anger will soon subside; **~se de fecha** to miss a deadline **2.** (*exagerar*) to go too far; **~se de la raya** to go over the line; **~se de listo** to be too clever by half; **te has pasado de listo** you've been too clever for your own good; **te has pasado un poco con la sal** you've overdone the salt a bit **3.** (*por un sitio*) to visit; **me pasé un rato por casa de mi tía** I popped round to my aunt's house for a while; **se me pasó por la cabeza que...** it occurred to me that ...; **no se te pasará ni por la imaginación** you'll never be able to guess; **~se la mano por el pelo** to run one's hand through one's hair **4.** *t.* MIL (*cambiar*) to go over; **se ha pasado de trabajadora a perezosa** she has gone from being hard-working to being lazy **5.** (*olvidarse*) to be forgotten; **se me pasó tu cumpleaños** I forgot your birthday **6.** (*estropearse: alimentos, leche*) to spoil, to go off; (*fruta*) to overripen; (*mantequilla*) to go rancid; (*flores*) to wilt; **se ha pasado el arroz** the rice is overcooked; **~se de moda** to go out of fashion **7.** (*escaparse*) to be missed; **se me pasó la oportunidad** I missed my chance; **se me pasó el turno** I missed my turn

pasarela *f* **1.** (*para desfiles*) catwalk **2.** (*de un barco*) gangway **3.** (*puente provisional*) temporary bridge; (*para peatones*) walkway

pasarratos *m inv,* **pasatiempo** *m* **1.** (*diversión*) pastime; **los pasatiempos del periódico** the games and puzzles section of the newspaper **2.** (*hobby*) hobby

pascana *f* **1.** *AmS* (*etapa de un viaje*) stage **2.** *Arg, Bol, Perú* (*posada*) wayside inn

Pascua *f* **1.** (*de resurrección*) Easter; ~ **Florida** Easter Sunday; **mona de ~** Easter cake; **de ~s a Ramos** once in a blue moon; **hacer la ~ a alguien** *inf* to do the dirty on sb **2.** (*fiesta judía*) Passover **3.** *pl* (*navidad*) Christmas time; **dar las ~s a alguin** to wish sb a merry Christmas **4.** *pl* (*pentecostés*) Whitsun ►**tener** cara **de ~(s)** *inf* to be glowing with happiness; **¡y** santas **~s!** and that's that!; **estar** como **una(s) ~(s)** to be over the moon

pascual *adj* **1.** (*relativo a la pascua cristiana*) Easter **2.** (*relativo a la pascua judía*) Passover **3.** (*navideño*) Christmas **4.** (*de pentecostés*) Whitsun

pase *m* **1.** (*desfile*) parade; (*de moda*) fashion show **2.** DEP pass **3.** CINE showing **4.** (*en los naipes*) pass **5.** *t.* MIL (*permiso*) pass; (*licencia*) licence *Brit,* license *Am;* (*para entrar gratis*) free pass; (*para viajar en tren*) rail pass; ~ (**de transporte**) travel pass **6.** *AmL* (*pasaporte*) passport

paseandero, **-a** *adj CSur* fond of walking; **mi madre es a pesar de sus años muy paseandera** despite her age, my mother walks a lot

paseante *mf* walker; ~ (**en corte**) *inf* loafer

pasear I. *vt* **1.** (*en coche*) to take for a ride; (*a pie*) to take for a walk; ~ **al perro** to walk the dog; ~ **a un caballo** to exercise a horse **2.** (*llevar a todas las partes*) to take sb around **II.** *vi, vr* **1.** (*a pie*) to go for a walk; (*en coche*) to go for a drive; (*a caballo*) to ride **2.** (*caballo*) to trot **III.** *vr* (*estar ocioso*) to hang about

paseo *m* **1.** (*a pie*) walk; (*en coche, a caballo*) ride; (*en barco*) trip; **dar un** ~ to go for a walk; **¡vete a ~!** get lost!; **mandar a alguien a** ~ to tell sb to get lost **2.** (*para pasear*) avenue; ~ **marítimo** promenade, esplanade **3.** (*distancia*) short walk; **de aquí al colegio sólo hay un** ~ it's only a short walk from here to the school

pasillo *m* (*corredor*) passage; (*entre habitaciones, pisos*) corridor, hallway

pasión *f* **1.** (*ardor*) passion; ~ **de ánimo** melancholy; **con** ~ passionately; **sin** ~ without enthusiasm **2.** (*afecto*) passion; (*preferencia*) preference; **sentir** ~ **por el fútbol** to be passionate about football **3.** (*de Jesucristo*) Passion

pasional *adj* **1.** (*ardiente*) passionate; **crimen** ~ crime of passion **2.** REL Passion

pasionaria *f* **1.** (*flor*) passionflower **2.** (*fruto*) passion fruit

pasividad *f* passivity, passiveness

pasivo *m* **1.** (*deuda*) liabilities *pl* **2.** (*en el balance*) debit side **3.** LING passive **4.** (*pensión*) pension

pasivo, **-a I.** *adj* **1.** *t.* LING passive; **verbo** ~ passive verb; **voz pasiva** passive **2.** ECON **haber** ~ pension; **las clases ~s** pensioners **II.** *m, f* pensioner

pasmado, **-a I.** *adj* (*asombrado*) amazed; (*torpe*) slow **II.** *m, f* idiot

pasmar I. *vt* **1.** (*asombrar*) to astonish; **me has dejado pasmado** you have left me completely stunned; **no te quedes pasmado** don't just stand there **2.** (*enajenar*) to enthuse **3.** (*aturdir*) to bewilder **4.** (*enfriar*) to chill; **la helada ha pasmado las lechugas** the frost has spoilt the lettuces **II.** *vr* **1.** (*asombrarse*) to be astonished **2.** (*quedar fascinado*) **~se ante algo** to be fascinated by sth **3.** (*helarse*) to freeze; (*planta*) to be affected by frost

pasmo *m* **1.** (*asombro*) astonishment; (*admiración*) wonder **2.** (*objeto*) marvel; **ser el** ~ **de alguien** *inf* (*asombrar*) to astonish sb

pasmoso, **-a** *adj* amazing

paso I. *m* **1.** (*acción de pasar*) passing; (*en coche*) overtaking; **al** ~ on the way; **me salió al** ~ **en el pasillo** he waylaid me in the corridor; **ceder el** ~ (*a una persona*) to make way; (*en el tráfico*) to give way, to yield *Am;* **estar de** ~ to be passing through; **al** ~ **que come ve la tele** when eating, he watches TV; **de** ~ (*indirectamente*) by the way; **de** ~ **que vas al centro, puedes llevarme a la estación** on your way to the centre [*o* center *Am*], you could take me to the station; **nadie salió al** ~ **de sus mentiras** nobody put a stop to his lies **2.** (*movimiento*) step; (*progreso*) progress; **bailar a** ~ **de vals** to dance a waltz; **ir al** ~ to keep in step; **llevar el** ~ **al ritmo de una melodía** to march in time to a tune; **marcar el** ~ to mark the rhythm [*o* time]; **a cada** ~ at every step; **a** ~ **llano** smoothly; ~ **a** ~ step by step; **contar los ~s a alguien** to watch sb's every move; **dar un** ~ **adelante/atrás** to take a step forwards/backwards; **dar un** ~ **en falso** to trip; *fig* to make a false move; **he dado un enorme** ~ **en mis investigaciones** I have made enormous progress in my research **3.** (*velocidad*) pace; **a ~s agigantados** with giant steps; *fig* by leaps and bounds; **a buen** ~ quickly; **a** ~ **de tortuga** at snail's pace; **a este** ~ **no llegarás** at this speed you'll never get there; **a este** ~ **no conseguirás nada** *fig* at this rate you won't achieve anything **4.** (*sonido*) footstep; (*de un caballo*) sound of horse's hooves **5.** (*manera de andar*) walk; **salir de su** ~ to change one's ways **6.** (*pisada*) footprint; (*de un animal*) track; **seguir los ~s de alguien** to follow sb; *fig* to follow in sb's footsteps; **volver sobre sus ~s** to retrace one's steps **7.** (*distancia*) pace; **vive a dos ~s de mi casa** he lives very near to my house **8.** (*pasillo*) passage; (*en el mar*) strait; (*entre montañas*) pass; ~ **subterráneo** underground passage; **abrirse** ~ to open up a path for oneself; *fig* to make one's way; **esta puerta da** ~ **al jardín** this door leads to the garden; **¡prohibido el ~!** (*pasar*) no throughfare! *Brit,* no thruway; (*entrar*) no entry!; **andar en malos ~s** to fall into bad ways; **con este dinero puedo salir del** ~ with this money I can solve my problems; **sólo lo has dicho para salir del** ~ you only did it to get out of a jam **9.** (*para atravesar algo*) crossing; ~ **de cebra** zebra crossing; ~ **a nivel** level crossing; **¡~!** make way!; ~ **de ecuador** halfway point **10.** (*medida*) step; **dar todos los ~s necesarios** to take all the necessary steps; **no dar** ~ not to do anything **11.** (*de un contador*) unit; **marcar los ~s** to count the units **12.** (*de un escrito*) passage **II.** *adv* gently

pasota I. *adj inf* apathetic **II.** *mf inf* drop-out; **es un** ~ **total** he/she doesn't give a damn about anything

paspadura *f AmS* chapped skin

pasquín *m* wall poster

pasta *f* **1.** (*masa*) paste; (*para un pastel*) pastry; (*para paredes*) filler; (*para madera, ventanas*) putty; ~ **de dientes** toothpaste **2.** (*comida italiana*) pasta **3.** (*pastelería*) pastries *pl* **4.** (*encuadernación*) cover; **de** ~ **dura/blanda** hardback/softback **5.** *inf* (*dinero*) dough **6.** (*madera*) pulp; **tener** ~ **para algo** to be cut out for sth; **tiene** ~ **para**

P

ser ministro he's got what it takes to be a minister; **tener buena** ~ to be good-natured

pastar *vt, vi* to graze

pastel *m* 1.(*tarta*) cake; (*bollo*) pastry; (*de carne, pescado*) pie 2.(*lápiz*) pastel crayon 3.(*pintura*) pastel 4.(*chapucería*) botch 5.(*asunto*) **descubrir el** ~ to catch on; **vámonos antes de que se descubra el** ~ let's go before we get found out

pastelear *vi* 1.(*contemporizar*) to stall 2.(*chanchullear*) to wangle

pastelería *f* 1.(*comercio*) pastry shop; (*arte*) pastrymaking 2.(*pasteles*) pastries *pl*

pastelero, -a *m, f* 1.(*repostero*) pastrycook 2.(*contemporizador*) staller; **ser un** ~ to go with the flow, to be spineless

pastelillo *m* (*dulce*) pastry; (*de carne, pescado*) pie

pastelón *m* 1.GASTR large meat pie 2.*AmL* (*loseta para pavimentar*) large paving stone

pasteurizar <z→c> *vt* to pasteurize

pastiche *m* pastiche

pastilla *f* 1.(*medicinal*) tablet; ~ **contra el dolor** painkiller; ~ **para la garganta** throat lozenge; ~ **para la tos** cough drop 2.(*dulce*) sweet, candy *Am;* ~ **de café con leche** coffee-flavoured sweet *Brit,* coffee-flavored candy *Am* 3.(*trozo*) piece; ~ **de caldo** stock cube; ~ **de chocolate** bar of chocolate; ~ **de jabón** bar of soap; **ir a toda** ~ *inf* to go at full pelt

pastizal *m* pasture

pasto *m* 1.(*pastura*) grazing 2.(*pastizal*) pasture 3.(*hierba*) grass; ~ **seco** fodder 4.(*alimento*) feed 5.(*materia, rumores*) food; **ser** ~ **de las llamas** to go up in flames; **ser** ~ **de la murmuración** to be the subject of gossip 6.(*en abundancia*) **a todo** ~ at full pelt; **pudimos beber y comer a** ~ we ate and drank our fill 7.(*vino*) **de** ~ ordinary; **vino de** ~ table wine

pastor *m* 1.REL minister; (*obispo*) bishop 2.ZOOL ~ **alemán** Alsatian *Brit,* German shepherd *Am;* **perro** ~ sheepdog

pastor(a) *m(f)* (*de ganado*) herdsman *m;* (*de ovejas*) shepherd

pastorear *vt* 1.(*cuidar el ganado*) to look after; (*llevarlo a los pastos*) to graze 2.REL to guide 3.*AmC* (*mimar*) to spoil 4.*AmL* (*atisbar*) to spy on

pastoreo *m* grazing

pastoso, -a *adj* 1.(*blando*) soft 2.(*pegajoso*) sticky; (*espeso*) thick; **lengua pastosa** furred tongue 3.(*voz*) mellow 4.*AmL* (*región*) grassy

pata *f* 1.*inf* ANAT leg; (*de un perro, un gato*) paw; (*de una silla, una mesa*) leg; ~ **de gallo** BOT goosefoot; (*dibujo*) check; **~s de gallo** (*en el rostro*) crow's feet; ~ **de palo** wooden leg; **mala** ~ *inf* bad luck; **estirar la** ~ *inf* to kick the bucket; **ir a** ~ *inf* to go on foot; **~s arriba** upside down; **la habitación está ~s arriba** the room has been turned upside down; **poner todo ~s arriba** to turn everything upside down; **a la** ~ **coja** hopping; **a (la)** ~ **llana** simply; **a cuatro ~s** on all fours; **meter la** ~ *inf* (*cometer una indiscreción*) to put one's foot in it; **poner a alguien de ~s en la calle** *inf* to throw sb out 2.ZOOL (female) duck

patada *f* 1.(*contra algo*) kick; (*en el suelo*) stamp; **dar una** ~ **contra la pared** to kick the wall; **dar ~s en el suelo** to stamp one's feet; **romper una puerta a ~s** to kick a door down; **dar la** ~ **a alguien** to give sb the boot; **me da cien ~s** he/she really gets on my nerves; **echar a alguien a ~s** to kick sb out; **tratar a alguien a ~s** to treat sb like dirt; **a ~s** *fig* by the bucketload 2.*inf* (*paso*) step; (*de un caballo*) pace; **esto me ha costado muchas ~s** *fig* I've really had to work hard for this 3.(*huella de un pie*) footmark; (*de una pata*) pawprint

Patagonia *f* Patagonia; **ir a la** ~ to go to Patagonia

> **Patagonia** lies in the southern most part of Chile and Argentina, to the south of the Pampa. Unlike the Pampa, this vast, scantily cultivated, barren steppe is unsuited to the growth of cereals and is used mainly for rearing sheep.

patalear *vi* to kick; (*en el suelo*) to stamp one's feet; **está que patalea** he is furious; (*niño*) to throw a tantrum

pataleo *m* 1.(*acción de patalear*) kicking; (*en el suelo, ruido*) stamping 2.(*queja*) complaint; **derecho al** ~ *inf* right to complain

patán I.*adj* rustic; **ser** ~ *fig* to be uncouth II.*m* yokel, hick *Am*

patata *f* 1.potato; **~s fritas** chips *pl Brit,* French fries *pl Am;* **una bolsa de ~s fritas** a bag of crisps *Brit,* a bag of potato chips *Am;* **tortilla de** ~ Spanish omelette [*o* omelet *Am*]; **puré de ~(s)** mashed potatoes 2.*inf* (*basura*) dud; **este ordenador es una** ~ this computer is a piece of junk ►**no entender ni** ~ *inf* (*palabra*) not to understand a single word; (*ser tonto*) to be completely stupid; **¡~!** (*al hacer una foto*) cheese!

patatús *m inv, inf* (*desmayo*) faint; **le dio un** ~ he/she fainted; (*ataque*) fit

patear I.*vt* 1.(*dar golpes*) to kick; ~ **el estómago a alguien** to kick sb in the stomach 2.(*pisotear*) to trample 3.(*tratar rudamente*) to trample on II.*vi* 1.(*en el suelo*) to stamp; (*estar enfadado*) to be furious 2.(*andar mucho*) to tramp about; **estar pateando todo el día** to spend the whole day walking; **tuve que** ~ **para tener este éxito** I had to work really hard for this success

patentar *vt* to patent

patente I.*adj* 1.(*visible*) clear 2.(*evidente*)

patent; **hacer** ~ to establish; (*comprobar*) to prove; (*revelar*) to reveal **II.** *f* **1.** (*documento*) licence *Brit,* license *Am;* (*permiso*) permit; ~ **de comercio** trading permit [*o* license *Am*]; ~ **de sanidad** bill of health **2.** (*título*) title; ~ **de piloto** pilot's licence **3.** JUR patent; ~ **industrial** industrial patent; ~ **pendiente** patent pending; ~ **de privilegio** letters patent; **solicitar la** ~ to apply for a patent

patentizar <z→c> *vt* to make evident; (*comprobar*) to prove; (*revelar*) to reveal

patera *f* small boat

paternal *adj* paternal; **amor** ~ paternal [*o* fatherly] love

paternalismo *m* paternalism

paternidad *f* **1.** (*relación*) fatherhood; JUR paternity **2.** (*calidad*) fatherliness **3.** REL **Vuestra Paternidad** Father

paterno, -a *adj* paternal; **casa paterna** parental home; **mi abuelo** ~ my paternal grandfather

patero, -a I. *adj Chile* bootlicking **II.** *m, f Chile* bootlicker

patético, -a *adj* **1.** (*conmovedor*) moving; (*tierno*) tender; (*manifestando dolor*) painful **2.** *pey* (*exagerado*) pathetic

patibulario, -a *adj* **1.** (*relativo al patíbulo*) gallows; **horca patibularia** gallows *pl* **2.** (*terrible*) horrifying; **novela patibularia** horrifying novel

patíbulo *m* scaffold; (*horca*) gallows *pl*

patidifuso, -a *adj* stunned; (*de horror*) aghast; **me quedé** ~ I was aghast

patilla *f* **1.** (*de unas gafas*) sidepiece; (*de un madero*) peg **2.** *pl* (*pelo*) sideburns *pl*

patín *m* **1.** (*de hielo*) ice skate; (*de ruedas*) roller skate; **patines en línea** rollerblades **2.** (*patinete*) scooter **3.** (*de vela*) catamaran; (*de pedales*) pedal boat **4.** (*tabla*) skateboard **5.** TÉC shoe

patinador(a) I. *adj* skating **II.** *m(f)* (*de hielo*) (ice) skater; (*sobre ruedas*) (roller) skater; (*artístico sobre hielo*) ice dancer; (*sobre ruedas*) roller skate dancer; (*de velocidad*) speed skater

patinaje *m* **1.** (*sobre hielo*) (ice) skating; (*sobre ruedas*) (roller) skating; ~ **artístico** (*sobre hielo*) figure skating; (*sobre ruedas*) roller dancing *Brit;* ~ **de velocidad** speed skating **2.** (*deslizamiento*) slip; (*de un vehículo*) skid

patinar *vi* **1.** (*sobre patines de hielo*) to (ice) skate; (*sobre patines de ruedas*) to (roller) skate **2.** (*deslizarse*) to slip; (*un vehículo*) to skid **3.** (*equivocarse*) to slip up

patinazo *m* **1.** (*deslizamiento*) slip; (*de un vehículo*) skid **2.** *inf* (*equivocación*) blunder

patinete *m* scooter

patio *m* **1.** ARQUIT (*interior*) courtyard; (*entre dos casas*) back yard; ~ **de recreo** playground **2.** TEAT pit

patiperrear *vi Chile* to traipse around

patitieso, -a *adj* **1.** (*paralizado*) paralysed *Brit, Aus,* paralyzed *Am;* (*de frío*) frozen stiff; **quedarse** ~ **de frío** to be frozen stiff **2.** (*sorprendido*) stunned; **quedarse** ~ to be struck dumb **3.** (*presumido*) stuck-up

patito, -a *adj AmL* primrose yellow

patizambo, -a *adj* knock-kneed and/or bow-legged

pato, -a *m, f* **1.** ZOOL duck; (*macho*) drake **2.** *inf* (*torpe*) clumsy person ►**estar hecho un** ~ **(de agua)** *inf* to be extremely dull; **pagar el** ~ *inf* to carry the can

patochada *f* (*tontería*) piece of nonsense; **decir ~s** to talk rubbish

patógeno, -a *adj* MED pathogen; **germen** ~ harmful germ

patojo, -a I. *adj* crooked-legged; (*como un pato*) waddling **II.** *m, f Col, Guat* kid *inf*

patología *f* MED pathology

patológico, -a *adj t. fig* pathological

patólogo, -a *m, f* MED pathologist

patoso, -a *adj* **1.** (*soso*) boring **2.** (*torpe*) clumsy

patraña *f* lie, pack of lies

patria *f* native land; ~ **adoptiva** adoptive homeland; ~ **celestial** heaven; **madre** ~ mother country; *AmL* Spain

patriada *f CSur* rising

patriarca *m t.* REL patriarch

patrimonial *adj* hereditary; **bien** ~ inheritance

patrimonio *m* **1.** (*herencia*) inheritance; ~ **cultural** cultural heritage **2.** (*riqueza*) wealth

patrio, -a *adj* **1.** (*relativo a la patria*) native **2.** (*relativo al padre*) paternal

patriota I. *adj* patriotic **II.** *mf* **1.** (*que ama a su patria*) patriot **2.** (*compatriota*) compatriot

patriotero, -a I. *adj* jingoistic **II.** *m, f* jingoist

patriótico, -a *adj* patriotic

patriotismo *m* **1.** (*del patriota*) patriotism **2.** (*del patriotero*) jingoism

patrocinador(a) *m(f) t.* DEP sponsor

patrocinar *vt t.* DEP to sponsor

patrocinio *m* **1.** (*protección*) patronage **2.** DEP sponsorship

patrón *m* **1.** (*modelo*) model; (*de costura*) pattern **2.** FIN ~ **monetario** monetary standard

patrón, -ona *m, f* **1.** (*que protege*) patron *m,* patroness *f* **2.** (*jefe*) boss **3.** (*de una casa*) head; (*de una pensión*) landlord *m,* landlady *f* **4.** (*santo*) patron saint

patronal I. *adj* (*empresario*) employers'; **cierre** ~ lockout **II.** *f* **1.** (*asociación*) employers' organization **2.** (*fiesta*) **fiesta** ~ patron saint's day

patronato *m* **1.** (*protección*) patronage **2.** ECON employers' organization **3.** (*fundación*) foundation **4.** (*junta directiva*) board

patrono, -a *m, f* **1.** (*jefe*) boss **2.** (*de un feudo*) landowner **3.** (*miembro del patronato*) board member **4.** REL patron saint

patrulla *f t.* MIL (*de policía*) patrol; **estar de** ~ to be on patrol

patrullar *vi, vt* to patrol

P

patucos *mpl* (*para bebés*) bootees *pl;* (*para mayores*) bedsocks *pl*

patuleco, **-a** *adj AmC, AmS* (*de pies*) lame; (*de piernas*) bow-legged

paturro, **-a** *adj Col* short and stocky

paular *m* (*pantano*) marsh

paulatinamente *adv* gradually

paulatino, **-a** *adj* gradual

paupérrimo, **-a** *adj superl de* **pobre**

pausa *f* pause; **con** ~ unhurriedly

pausado, **-a** *adj* deliberate

pauta *f* **1.** (*modelo*) guide **2.** (*normas*) standard; **marcar la** ~ to set the example [*o* standard] **3.** (*falsilla*) lines *pl* (*on writing paper*) **4.** (*regla*) rule

pautado, **-a** *adj* lined

pava *f* **1.** ZOOL *v.* **pavo**, **-a** **2.** *AmL* (*olla*) pot; (*tetera*) tea kettle **3.** *AmL* (*sombrero*) straw hat **4.** *And, AmC* (*flecos*) fringe ►**pelar la** ~ *inf* (*los enamorados*) to court

pavada *f* **1.** *CSur* (*disparate*) piece of foolishness **2.** *CSur* (*poquísimo*) pittance **3.** *AmC* (*mala suerte*) piece of bad luck

pavear **I.** *vi* **1.** *CSur* (*hacer el tonto*) to fool about **2.** *CSur* (*pelar la pava*) to court **II.** *vt* **1.** *And, CSur* (*bromear*) to play a joke on **2.** *And* (*asesinar*) to bump off

pavimentar *vt* (*con adoquín, con losas*) to pave; (*con asfalto*) to surface

pavimento *m* **1.** (*recubrimiento: en una casa*) flooring; (*en la carretera*) surfacing **2.** (*material: en una casa*) floor; (*en una carretera*) surface

pavo *m inf* (*un duro*) five pesetas; **¡dame diez ~s!** give me fifty pesetas!; (*dólar*) buck *Am;* **me debes diez ~s** you owe me ten bucks; **soltar el** ~ to pay up

pavo, **-a** **I.** *m, f* **1.** ZOOL turkey; ~ **real** peacock **2.** (*persona*) idiot; **estar en la edad del** ~ *inf* to be at an awkward stage (*of one's adolescence*)*;* **comer** ~ *inf* to be a wallflower; **no es moco de** ~ *inf* it's not to be scoffed at [*o* sneezed]; **se me subió el** ~ *inf* I went as red as a beetroot [*o* beet *Am*]; **ir de** ~ *AmL* to travel for free **II.** *adj* idiotic

pavonearse *vr* to strut (about); **~se de algo** to show off about sth

pavor *m* terror

pavoroso, **-a** *adj* terrifying

payada *f CSur* MÚS *improvised gaucho minstrel song*

payador *m CSur* gaucho minstrel

payasada *f* clowning; *pey* idiotic behaviour *Brit* [*o* behavior *Am*]; **hacer ~s** to clown about

payasear *vi* to clown about

payaso, **-a** *m, f* **1.** (*del circo*) clown **2.** (*bromista*) joker; **¡deja de hacer el ~!** stop fooling about!

payés, **-esa** *m, f reg* peasant farmer (*from Catalonia or the Balearic Isles*)

payo, **-a** *m, f* non-gipsy *Brit,* non-gypsy *Am* (*gypsy term to refer to people who are not gypsies*)

paz *f* peace; (*tratado*) peace treaty; **hacer las paces** to make up; **no dar ~ a la lengua** not to stop talking; **estar en ~ con alguien** to be quits with sb; **¡a la ~ de Dios!** God be with you!; **¡déjame en ~!** leave me alone!; **¡...y en ~!** ... and that's that!; **que en ~ descanse** may he/she rest in peace

pazguato, **-a** **I.** *adj* simple **II.** *m, f* simpleton

pazo *m* manor house (*in Galicia*)

PCE *m abr de* **Partido Comunista Español** *Spanish Communist Party*

P.D. *abr de* **posdata** P.S.

pe *f* p; **de ~ a pa** *inf* from A to Z

peaje *m* **1.** (*de tránsito, de carretera*) toll **2.** (*taquilla*) tollbooth

peana *f* (*pedestal*) pedestal

peatón, **-ona** *m, f* pedestrian

peca *f* freckle

pecado *m* sin; ~ **capital** deadly sin; ~ **original** original sin; **sin** ~ without sin; *fig* unblemished; **pagar sus ~s** to pay for one's sins; **sería un ~ rechazarlos** it would be a crying shame to reject them; **¡estos niños de mis ~s!** *irón, inf* these children of mine!; **¡ay, José de mis ~s!** *irón, inf* oh, my beloved José!

pecador(**a**) **I.** *adj* sinning **II.** *m(f)* sinner

pecar <c→qu> *vi* **1.** REL to sin **2.** (*errar*) to go astray **3.** ~ **por exceso** to go too far; **peca por exceso de confianza** he/she is too confident by half; **éste no peca de hablador** he/she's not exactly talkative

pecarí *m AmL* ZOOL peccary

pecera *f* fish tank; (*en forma de globo*) fishbowl

pechada *f* **1.** *AmS* (*empujón*) shove **2.** *Arg, inf* (*sablazo*) touch for a loan

pechador(**a**) *m(f) Arg, inf* sponge(r), moocher *Am*

pechar *vt* **1.** (*pagar*) to pay **2.** (*empujar*) to push **3.** *Arg, inf* (*pedir*) to sponge, to mooch *Am;* ~ **a alguien** to sponge off sb

pechazo *m AmS, inf* sponging, mooching *Am*

pecho *m* **1.** ANAT breast, chest *Am;* **dar el ~ al bebé** to breastfeed the baby; **el bebé toma el** ~ the baby breastfeeds; **a ~ descubierto** (*sin armas*) unarmed; *fig* openly; **dar el ~ a alguien** *fig* to face up to sb; **gritar a todo** ~ to shout at the top of one's voice; **partirse el ~ por alguien** to slog one's guts out for sb **2.** (*pulmones*) lungs *pl* **3.** (*en la costura*) bust **4.** (*conciencia*) heart; **abrir su ~ a alguien** to open one's heart to sb; **tomarse algo muy a** ~ to take sth to heart **5.** (*coraje*) courage; **¡~ al agua!** courage!

pechuga *f* **1.** (*pecho de ave*) breast; ~ **de pollo** chicken breast **2.** *inf* (*de mujer*) bosom

pechugón, **-ona** *adj* **1.** *inf* (*de mucho pecho*) busty **2.** *AmL* (*descarado*) shameless **3.** *AmL* (*franco*) outspoken

pecíolo *m* leaf stalk

pecoso, **-a** *adj* freckly

pectoral **I.** *adj* **1.** ANAT pectoral **2.** (*contra la tos*) cough **II.** *m* MED pectoral

pecuario, **-a** *adj* livestock
pecueca *f Col, Ecua, Ven* **1.** (*pezuña*) hoof **2.** (*olor*) smell of feet
peculiar *adj* **1.** (*especial*) distinctive **2.** (*raro*) peculiar
peculiaridad *f* **1.** (*singularidad*) peculiarity **2.** (*distintivo*) distinguishing feature
peculio *m* private money; **pagar de su ~** to pay out of one's own money
pedagogía *f sin pl* pedagogy
pedagógico, **-a** *adj* pedagogical
pedagogo, **-a** *m, f* educator, teacher
pedal *m* pedal; MÚS (*sordina*) soft pedal; (*bajo*) pedal note; **pisar el ~** AUTO to accelerate
pedalear *vi* to pedal
pedante **I.** *adj* pretentious, pedantic **II.** *mf* pedant
pedantería *f* pedantry
pedazo *m* **1.** (*parte*) (big) piece; **~ de papel** piece of paper; **caerse a ~s** to fall apart, to fall to pieces; **estoy que me caigo a ~s** *inf* I'm absolutely exhausted; **hacerse ~s** to fall to pieces; **hacer ~s** to break; (*madera*) to smash up; (*un pastel*) to cut up; (*papel*) to tear up; (*con tijeras*) to cut to pieces **2.** (*persona*) **~ de mi alma** my darling; **ser un ~ de pan** to be very good-natured; **¡~ de alcornoque/animal!** *inf* you idiot!; **¡~ de bruto!** *inf* you brute!
pederasta *m* pederast
pedernal *m* flint
pedestal *m* **1.** (*cimiento*) pedestal; **poner a alguien en un ~** to put sb on a pedestal **2.** (*apoyo*) base
pedestre *adj* **1.** (*a pie*) pedestrian; **carrera ~** foot race **2.** (*chabacano*) vulgar
pediatra *mf* paediatrician *Brit,* pediatrician *Am*
pediatría *f sin pl* paediatrics *Brit,* pediatrics *Am*
pedicura *f* pedicure; **hacerse la ~** to have a pedicure
pedicuro, **-a** *m, f* chiropodist
pedida *f* **~ de mano** *asking for sb's hand in marriage*
pedido *m* COM (*de un servicio*) reservation; (*de un producto*) order; **~ suplementario** additional order; **enviar sobre ~** to supply on request; **a ~** to order; **a ~ de** at the request of
pedido, **-a** *adj* **1.** (*solicitado*) requested; **este anillo ya lo tiene ~ mi nieta** this ring has already been reserved for my granddaughter **2.** (*encargado*) ordered; **el armario ya está ~** the wardrobe has already been ordered
pedigrí *m* pedigree
pedigüeño, **-a** **I.** *adj* persistent **II.** *m, f* nuisance
pedilón, **-ona** *adj AmL* persistent
pedimento *m* (*petición*) request
pedinche *mf Méx* (*pedigüeño*) scrounger
pedir *irr vt* **1.** (*rogar*) to ask for; **~ algo a alguien** to ask sb for sth; **os pido que hagáis menos ruido** I'm asking you to make less noise; **~ prestado** to borrow; **a ~ de boca** just right **2.** (*exigir, cobrar*) to demand; (*necesitar*) to need; (*solicitar, demandar*) to request; **~ a gritos algo** *fig* to be crying out for sth; **una paella que no hay más que ~** a sublime paella **3.** (*encargar*) to order **4.** (*para casarse*) **~ la mano de alguien** to ask for sb's hand in marriage; **~ en matrimonio a alguien** to propose to sb **5.** (*mendigar*) to beg; **~ limosna** to beg; **están pidiendo para la Cruz Roja** they are collecting for the Red Cross
pedo *m vulg* **1.** (*ventosidad*) fart; **tirarse un ~** to fart **2.** *inf* (*borrachera*) drunkenness; **estar en ~** to be blind drunk; **ponerse en ~** to get blind drunk
pedofilia *f sin pl* paedophilia *Brit,* pedophilia *Am*
pedorrear *vi inf* to fart repeatedly
pedorreta *f inf* raspberry, Bronx cheer *Am;* **hacer una ~ a alguien** to blow a raspberry at sb
pedorro, **-a** **I.** *adj* (*de pedos*) farting; (*tonto*) stupid; (*pelma*) annoying **II.** *m, f* (*que tira pedos*) farter; (*tonto*) stupid fart; (*pelmazo*) bore, drag
pedrada *f* **1.** (*lanzar*) throw of a stone; **matar a alguien a ~s** to stone sb to death; **pegar una ~ a alguien** to throw a stone at sb **2.** (*ofensa*) wounding remark ►<u>**sentar**</u> **algo como una ~** to take sth very badly; <u>**venir**</u> **como ~ en ojo de boticario** to be just what the doctor ordered
pedrea *f* **1.** (*lanzar pedradas*) stoning; (*pelea*) stone-throwing fight **2.** METEO hailstorm **3.** (*lotería*) small prizes *pl* (*in lottery*)
pedregal *m* stony [*o* rocky] ground
pedregoso, **-a** *adj* stony
pedregullo *m CSur* gravel
pedrera *f* stone quarry
pedrería *f* (*piedras*) precious stones *pl;* (*joyas*) jewellery *Brit,* jewelry *Am*
pedrisco *m* METEO hail
pedrusco *m* **1.** (*piedra*) lump of stone **2.** *AmL* *v.* **pedregal**
pedúnculo *m* stalk
pega *f* **1.** *inf* (*dificultades*) difficulty; **poner ~s a** to find fault with; (*desventaja*) drawback, snag **2.** (*pregunta*) trick question **3.** (*falso*) **de ~** fake **4.** *CSur, Méx, inf* (*trabajo*) job
pegada *f CSur* **1.** (*mentira*) lie **2.** (*suerte*) piece of luck
pegadizo, **-a** **I.** *adj* **1.** (*pegajoso*) sticky; (*enfermedad*) contagious; **melodía pegadiza** catchy tune **2.** (*postizo*) false **3.** (*gorrón*) sponging, freeloading *Am* **II.** *m, f* sponge(r), freeloader *Am*
pegajoso, **-a** *adj* **1.** (*adhesivo*) sticky, adhesive **2.** (*persona*) tiresome; (*niño*) clinging **3.** MED contagious
pegamento *m* glue; **~ en barra** stick glue; **~ de contacto** bonding cement
pegar <g→gu> **I.** *vt* **1.** (*aglutinar*) to stick; **~ un sello** to attach [*o* stick on] a stamp; **no ~ ojo** not to sleep a wink **2.** (*con hilo, grapa*) to

P

attach **3.** (*muebles*) ~ **la mesilla a la cama** to put the side table right next to the bed **4.** (*contagiar*) to give **5.** (*fuego*) ~ **fuego a algo** to set fire to sth **6.** (*golpear*) to hit; ~ **una paliza a alguien** to beat sb up **7.** (*un grito*) to let out; (*un tiro*) to fire; ~ **una patada** to kick; ~ **una bofetada** to slap; ~ **un salto** to jump; ~ **un susto a alguien** to frighten sb **8.** INFOR to paste **9.** *AmL, inf* (*tener suerte*) to be lucky; ~**la** to get what one wants **10.** *Méx* (*atar*) to tie **II.** *vi* **1.** (*hacer juego*) to go together; **te pegan bien los zapatos con el bolso** those shoes go really well with the bag; **esto no pega ni con cola** this really doesn't go **2.** (*rozar*) ~ **en algo** to brush against sth; (*tocar*) to touch sth **3.** (*golpear*) to beat; **¡cómo pega el sol hoy!** *inf* the sun is really hot today! **4.** *inf* (*currar*) to work hard; **no** ~ **golpe** [*o* **palo al agua**] not to do a thing **III.** *vr* **1.** (*impactar*) ~**se con algo** to bump into sth; ~**se con alguien** to fight with sb; ~**se un tortazo en el coche** *inf* to crash one's car **2.** (*quemarse*) to stick to the pot **3.** (*entrometerse*) ~**se a algo** to interfere in sth **4.** (*aficionarse*) ~**se a algo** to acquire a liking for sth **5.** (*acompañar siempre*) ~**se a alguien** to stick to sb (like glue); (*perseguir*) to follow sb; **siempre anda pegado a mí** he/she is always following me about **6.** (*contagiarse*) **finalmente se me pegó el sarampión** I finally caught the measles **7.** *inf* (*engañar*) **pegársela a alguien** *inf* to trick sb; **pegársela al marido/a la mujer** to cheat on one's husband/one's wife **8.** *inf* (*darse*) ~**se la gran vida** to live it up; ~**se un tiro** to shoot oneself; ~**se un tiro en la cabeza** to shoot oneself in the head

pegatina *f* sticker

pegote *m* **1.** (*emplasto*) plaster, Band-Aid® **2.** *pey, inf* (*guisote*) stodgy mess **3.** *inf* (*persona*) hanger-on **4.** *inf* (*chapuza*) botch **5.** *inf* (*añadido feo*) **esa corbata es un** ~ that tie just doesn't go **6.** *inf* (*farol*) **tirarse** ~**s** to show off

peinado *m* hairstyle, hairdo; **hacerse un** ~ to have one's hair done

peinado, -a *adj* combed

peinador *m* **1.** (*para peinar, afeitar*) robe **2.** (*tocador*) dressing table

peinar I. *vt* **1.** (*desenredar*) to comb **2.** (*acicalar*) to style **II.** *vr* to comb one's hair; (*arreglar el pelo*) to style [*o* to do] one's hair

peine *m* (*para peinarse*) comb; **¡te vas a enterar de lo que vale un** ~**!** *fig* you'll soon find out what's what!; **¡ya apareció el** ~**!** *fig* so that's it!

peineta *f* Spanish ornamental comb

peinilla *f* **1.** *Col, Ecua* (*peine*) dressing comb **2.** *Col, Ecua, Pan, Ven* (*especie de machete*) large machete

p.ej. *abr de* **por ejemplo** e.g.

pejiguera *f inf* nuisance

pela *f* **1.** *inf* (*dinero*) **no me queda ni una sola** ~ I'm completely broke; **no me quedan más** ~**s** I've got no money left; ~ **larga** lots of dough **2.** (*estar pelando*) peeling

pelada *f* **1.** (*rapada*) haircut **2.** *CSur* (*calva*) bald head **3.** *AmL* (*error*) blunder

peladez *f* **1.** *And* (*pobreza*) poverty **2.** *Méx* (*palabrota*) obscenity

pelado *m inf* (*pobretón*) poor wretch

pelado, -a *adj* **1.** (*rapado*) shorn **2.** (*escueto, despojado*) bare **3.** *inf* (*números*) round; **esto vale las 5.000 peladas** this costs exactly 5000 **4.** *AmL, inf* (*sin dinero*) broke

peladuras *fpl* (*cáscaras*) peelings *pl*

pelagatos *m inv, inf* poor wretch

pelaje *m* **1.** (*piel*) coat, fur **2.** *pey* (*pinta*) appearance, looks *pl*

pelambre *m o f* **1.** (*pelo*) thick hair; (*de animales*) fur; (*pelambrera*) mop **2.** (*zona calva*) bald patch **3.** *AmL* (*habladurías*) rumours *pl*

pelambrera *f* **1.** (*pelo*) mop **2.** (*calvicie*) bald patch

pelandusca *f inf* floozie; (*puta*) whore

pelapatatas *m inv* potato peeler

pelar I. *vt* **1.** (*pelo*) to cut; (*rapar*) to shear; (*plumas*) to pluck; (*frutas, verduras*) to peel; (*animales*) to skin **2.** (*murmurar*) to criticize **3.** (*robar*) to fleece **4.** (*en el juego*) to clean out **5.** (*difícil*) **ser duro de** ~ to be a hard nut to crack **6.** *AmL, inf* (*dar una paliza*) to beat up **7.** *And, inf* (*morir*) ~**la** to kick the bucket **II.** *vi inf* **hace un frío que pela** it's freezing cold **III.** *vr* **1.** (*el pelo*) to have one's hair cut; **ir a** ~**se** to go for a haircut **2.** (*la piel*) to peel **3.** *vulg* (*masturbarse*) **pelársela** to have a wank *Brit*, to jerk off *Am* **4.** *inf* (*intensificador*) **corre que se las pela** she is a really fast runner; **pelárselas por algo** to be crazy about sth; **pelárselas por hacer algo** to do everything possible to do sth

pelaverduras *m inv* vegetable peeler

peldaño *m* step; (*escalera portátil*) rung

pelea *f* **1.** (*lucha*) fight **2.** (*verbal*) quarrel, argument; **buscar** ~ to be looking for trouble

pelear I. *vi* **1.** (*luchar*) to fight **2.** (*discutir*) to argue **3.** (*sufrir*) to suffer **4.** (*trabajar*) ~ **por algo** to struggle for sth **II.** *vr* **1.** (*con violencia*) ~**se por algo** to fight over sth **2.** (*verbal*) ~**se por algo** to argue about sth **3.** (*enemistarse*) to fall out

pelele *m* **1.** (*muñeco*) rag doll **2.** (*de bebés*) rompers *pl*; (*para dormir*) sleepsuit **3.** *inf* (*persona*) puppet

peleón *m inf* troublemaker

peleón, -ona *adj* quarrelsome; **vino** ~ cheap wine

peletería *f* **1.** (*costura*) furrier's; (*venta*) fur shop **2.** *AmC* (*zapatería*) shoe store

peliagudo, -a *adj* (*complicado*) tricky

pelícano *m*, **pelicano** *m* pelican

película *f* film, movie *Am*; ~ **en blanco y negro** black and white film; ~ **hablada** talkie; ~ **muda** silent film [*o* movie *Am*]; ~ **de suspense** thriller; ~ **de terror** horror film [*o* movie *Am*]; ~ **del oeste** western; **de** ~ *inf* sensational; **como de** ~ like sth out of the movies; **un matrimonio como de** ~ a wedding like you see in the movies; **poner en** ~ to film; **echar una** ~ to show a film; **¡allí ~s!** it's nothing to do with me!; **no saber de qué va la** ~ not to have a clue

peligrar *vi* to be in danger; **hacer** ~ to endanger

peligro *m* danger; ~ **de incendio** fire risk; **puesta en** ~ endangering; **correr (un gran)** ~ to be at (great) risk; **correr** ~ **de hacer algo** to run the risk of doing sth; **estar en** ~ **de muerte** to be in mortal danger; **fuera de** ~ out of danger; **poner en** ~ to endanger; **poniendo en** ~ **su propia vida** risking his/her own life

peligroso, **-a** *adj* dangerous

pelillo *m inf* (*pequeñez*) trifle; **echar ~s a la mar** to make up; **¡~s a la mar!** let bygones be bygones!

pelirrojo, **-a** I. *adj* red-haired II. *m, f* redhead, carrot-top *inf*

pella *f* 1. (*masa*) lump; ~ **de algodón** ball of cotton wool 2. *inf* (*dinero*) dough

pelleja *f* 1. (*de animal*) hide 2. *inf* (*persona muy delgada*) skinny person; **ser una** ~ to be all skin and bones 3. *vulg* (*prostituta*) whore 4. *pey* (*vieja antipática*) old bag

pellejerías *fpl Chile* hard times *pl*

pellejo *m* 1. (*de animal*) hide 2. (*de persona*) skin; **no tener más que el** ~ to be all skin and bones; **no caber en su** ~ *fig* to be bursting with pride; **quitar el** ~ **a alguien** *fig* to criticize sb; **si yo estuviera en tu ~...** *inf* if I were in your shoes ... 3. *inf* (*vida*) **salvar(se) el** ~ to save one's skin; **arriesgar el** ~ to risk one's neck; **para esto yo no daría mi** ~ I wouldn't risk my neck for that; **pagar con el** ~ to pay with one's life; **perder el** ~ to lose one's life 4. (*odre*) wineskin 5. (*fruta*) peel; (*salchicha*) skin 6. (*de las uñas*) hangnail 7. *inf* (*ebrio*) drunkard

pellizcar <c→qu> I. *vt* 1. (*repizcar*) to pinch 2. *inf* (*pizcar algo*) to take a pinch of; (*comida*) to nibble II. *vr* to pinch oneself

pellizco *m* 1. (*pizco*) pinch; **dar un** ~ **a alguien** to pinch sb 2. (*poquito: de sal*) pinch; (*de bocadillo*) nibble

pelma *m inf*, **pelmazo** *m inf* (*pesado*) bore, drag

pelo *m* 1. (*cabello*) hair; (*de animal*) fur; (*de ave*) plumage; (*de barba*) whisker; **tener el** ~ **rubio** to have fair hair; **tirar el** ~ (*perro*) to moult *Brit*, to molt *Am*; **cortarse el** ~ to have one's hair cut; **soltarse el** ~ to take one's hair down; *fig* to let one's hair down 2. (*vello*) down; (*pelusa*) fluff; (*de alfombra*) pile 3. *inf* (*categoría*) **de** ~ wealthy; **la gente de medio** ~ the hoi polloi; **luce buen** ~ he/she is doing well 4. (+ *al*) **al** ~ perfectly; **todo irá al** ~ everything will be fine; **el traje ha quedado al** ~ the suit looks great; **venir al** ~ to be just right, to happen [*o* come] at just the right time; **sin venir al** ~ inconveniently 5. *inf* (*poco*) **por un** ~ **te caes** you very nearly fell; **escaparse por un** ~ to escape by the skin of one's teeth; **no se mueve ni un** ~ **de aire** the air is completely still ▸**cortar un** ~ **en el aire** (*cuchillo*) to be as sharp as a razor; (*listo*) to be very clever; **no tener ~s en la lengua** *inf* not to mince words; **un hombre de** ~ **en pecho** a real man; **ponerse a uno los ~s de punta** to make one's hair stand on end; **no tocar un** ~ **(de la ropa) a alguien** *inf* not to lay a finger on sb; **contar algo con ~s y señales** *inf* to describe sth in great detail; **colgado de un** ~ hanging from a thread; **no tener (un)** ~ **de tonto** *inf* to be nobody's fool; **agarrarse a un** ~ to clutch at straws; **estar hasta los ~s** *inf* to be fed up; **tomar el** ~ **a alguien** *inf* to pull sb's leg; **no se te ve el ~, ¿por dónde andas?** *inf* I/we haven't seen you for ages, where have you been hiding?; **a** ~ (*la cabeza descubierta*) bare-headed; (*sin prepararse*) unprepared

pelón, **-ona** I. *adj* 1. (*calvo*) bald 2. (*rapado*) shaven-headed II. *m, f inf* (*pobre*) poor wretch

pelota[1] *f* 1. (*balón*) ball; **echar la** ~ **a alguien** *fig* to leave sb holding the baby; **devolver la** ~ **a alguien** (*argumentar*) to turn the tables on sb; (*vengarse*) to give sb a taste of their own medicine; **la** ~ **sigue en el tejado** *fig* things are still up in the air 2. (*juego*) pelota 3. *pl, vulg* (*testículos*) balls *pl*, ballocks *pl*; **tocar las ~s a alguien** to irritate sb; **y esto lo hago así porque me sale de las ~s, tocarse las ~s** to do absolutely nothing, I do it like this because I bloody well feel like it!; **¡fíjate, que tiene ~s!** I'll tell you one thing, he's got balls!; **¡y esto es así, por ~s!** that's how it is, and no arguing!; **de ~s** cool 4. *vulg* (*desnudo*) **en ~s** starkers; **dejar a alguien en ~s** (*juego*) to clean sb out; (*ropa*) to strip sb naked; **pillar a alguien en ~s** *fig* to catch sb with their trousers down ▸**hacer la** ~ **a alguien** to suck up to sb

pelota[2] *m inf* crawler

pelotazo *m* 1. (*con el pie*) shot; (*tirando*) throw; (*con la raqueta*) stroke 2. *inf* (*bebida*) slug; **meterse un** ~ to have a drink

pelotear I. *vi* 1. (*tenis*) to knock up; (*fútbol*) to have a kick about 2. (*de un sitio al otro*) to throw back and forth II. *vt* (*cuentas*) to check

pelotera *f inf* fight

pelotón *m* 1. (*de gente*) crowd; (*en carreras*) pack; MIL squad; ~ **de ejecución** firing squad 2. (*enredo*) tangle

pelotudo, **-a** I. *adj CSur, vulg* idiotic II. *m, f CSur, vulg* jerk

peluca *f* wig; **usar** ~ to wear a wig

peluche *m* 1. (*tejido*) plush 2. (*juguete*) soft toy; **oso** ~ teddy bear

pelucón *m And, inf* bigwig

pelucón, **-ona** *adj And, inf* long-haired

peludo, **-a** *adj* 1. hairy; (*con una barba*) bearded 2. *AmC, inf* (*difícil*) tricky

peluquería *f* hairdresser's; ~ **de señoras/señores** ladies'/gents'[*o* men's] hairdressers; **ir a la** ~ to go to the hairdresser's

P

peluquero, -a *m, f* hairdresser
peluquín *m* toupée; **¡ni hablar del ~!** it's out of the question!
pelusa *f* **1.** (*vello*) down; (*tejido*) fluff **2.** (*de polvo*) fluff **3.** *inf* (*celos*) jealousy; **sentir ~** to be jealous **4.** (*envidia*) envy; **sentir ~** to be envious
pelvis *f inv* pelvis
pena *f* **1.** (*tristeza*) sorrow; **ahogar las ~s** to drown one's sorrows **2.** (*lástima*) **ser una ~** to be a pity; **¡qué ~!** what a shame!; **me da mucha ~ el gato** I feel really sorry for the cat; **me da mucha ~ el tener que verlo así** it really upsets me to see him like this **3.** (*sanción*) punishment; **~ de cadena perpetua** life sentence; **~ capital** capital punishment; **~ pecuniaria** fine **4.** (*dificultad*) trouble; **pasar las ~s del purgatorio** to go through hell; **a duras ~s** with great difficulty; (*apenas*) scarcely; **sin ~ ni gloria** undistinguished; **valer la ~** to be worth the effort [*o* the trouble]; **¡allá ~s!** it's not my problem! **5.** *AmL* (*vergüenza*) shame; **tener ~** to be ashamed ►**so ~ que** +*subj* under pain of
penable *adj* punishable
penacho *m* **1.** (*de aves, adorno*) crest **2.** *inf* (*vanidad*) pride
penado, -a I. *adj* **1.** (*triste*) sad **2.** (*difícil*) difficult **3.** *AmL* (*tímido*) shy **II.** *m, f* convict
penal I. *adj* JUR penal; **antecedentes ~es** criminal record **II.** *m* **1.** (*prisión*) prison **2.** *AmL* (*falta*) foul (*inside the penalty area*) **3.** (*penalti*) penalty; (*en baloncesto*) free throw
penalidad *f* **1.** (*molestia*) hardship **2.** (*sanción*) punishment
penalización *f* penalization
penalizar <z→c> *vt* to penalize
penalti *m* **1.** (*falta*) foul (*inside the penalty area*); **área de ~s** penalty area **2.** (*sanción*) penalty; (*en baloncesto*) free throw; **casarse de ~** *inf* to have a shotgun wedding
penar I. *vt* (*delincuente, delito*) to punish **II.** *vi* **1.** (*padecer*) to suffer; **~ de amores** to be unhappy in love **2.** (*ansiar*) **~ por algo** to long for sth
penca *f* **1.** (*hoja*) fleshy leaf **2.** *AmL* (*borrachera*) **agarrarse una ~** to get drunk **3.** *And* (*atractivo*) **una ~ de hombre/de mujer** a really good-looking man/woman; **una ~ de casa** a gorgeous house
penco *m* **1.** (*jamelgo*) nag **2.** *And, inf* (*atractivo*) **un ~ de hombre/de mujer** a really good-looking man/woman **3.** *inf* (*holgazán*) layabout; (*inútil*) waster; (*torpe*) clod
pendejada *f AmL, inf* **1.** (*disparate*) foolishness; **¿cómo se te pudo ocurrir tal ~?** what ever made you think of such a stupid thing? **2.** (*acto cobarde*) cowardly act **3.** (*cualidad de cobarde*) cowardliness
pendejear *vi Col, inf* to mess around *inf*
pendejo, -a *m, f Arg, inf* (*necio*) fool
pendencia *f* fight; **armar ~** to start a fight
pendenciero, -a I. *adj* quarrelsome **II.** *m, f* troublemaker
pender *vi* **1.** (*colgar*) to hang **2.** JUR to be pending
pendiente[1] I. *adj* **1.** (*colgado*) hanging **2.** (*problema, asunto*) unresolved; (*cuenta, trabajo, pedido*) outstanding; **una cuenta ~ de pago** an outstanding account; **quedar ~ una asignatura** to have one subject left to pass (*as a resit or carried over to next year*) **3.** *inf* (*ocuparse*) **estate ~ del arroz** keep an eye on the rice; **¡tú estate ~ de lo tuyo!** mind your own business!; **estar ~ de los labios de alguien** (*estar atento*) to be hanging on sb's every word; **estoy ~ de si me conceden la beca o no** I'm waiting to see whether or not they'll give me the grant **4.** (*depender*) **estamos ~s de lo que digan nuestros padres** it all depends on what our parents say **II.** *m* (*de oreja*) earring; (*de nariz*) nose ring
pendiente[2] *f* (*cuesta, del tejado*) slope; **de mucha ~** steep
péndola *f* **1.** (*de reloj*) pendulum **2.** (*reloj*) pendulum clock
pendón *m* **1.** (*estandarte*) banner **2.** *inf* (*buscona*) floozie
péndulo *m* pendulum
pene *m* penis
penetración *f* **1.** (*acción*) penetration **2.** (*comprensión*) insight; (*inteligencia*) intelligence
penetrante *adj* **1.** (*profundo*) deep; (*dolor*) fierce **2.** (*frío*) biting; (*hedor*) strong; (*olor*) pervasive **3.** (*sonido*) penetrating; (*grito*) piercing
penetrar I. *vi* to penetrate **II.** *vt* **1.** (*atrevesar*) to penetrate **2.** (*entender*) to understand; **~ un misterio** to unravel a mystery; **~ una intención** to fathom an intention; **~ los pensamientos de alguien** to penetrate sb's thoughts **III.** *vr* **~se de algo** to become imbued with sth
penicilina *f* MED penicillin
península *f* GEO peninsula; **la Península Ibérica** the Iberian Peninsula

> The **Península Ibérica** (Iberian Peninsula) includes Spain and Portugal. The Spanish language makes use of this term (and the corresponding adjective **peninsular**), in order to differentiate between the Spanish mainland and the two Spanish island groups (**Baleares y Canarias**) as well as the country's territories in Africa (**Ceuta y Melilla**).

peninsular *adj* peninsular; **las temperaturas ~es** temperatures in the Iberian peninsula
penique *m* penny
penitencia *f* **1.** (*pena*) punishment; **imponer una ~ a alguien** to impose a punishment on sb **2.** REL penance; **hacer ~** to do penance **3.** (*arrepentimiento*) penitence
penitenciaría *f* prison, penitentiary *Am*

penitenciario, **-a** *adj* **1.** (*relativo a la penitenciaría*) prison **2.** (*relativo a la penitencia*) penitentiary
penitente *adj, mf* penitent
penoso, **-a** *adj* **1.** (*arduo*) laborious **2.** (*dificultoso*) difficult **3.** (*con pena*) upset **4.** *AmL* (*vergonzoso*) shameful
pensado, **-a** *adj* **1.** (*reflexionado*) considered; **esto está poco** ~ this hasn't been properly thought out; **lo tengo bien** ~ I have thought it through thoroughly; **tener** ~ **hacer algo** to have it in mind to do sth; **el día menos** ~ **volverá** just when it's least expected he/she will return **2.** (*persona*) **ser un mal** ~ to always be ready to think the worst
pensador(a) **I.** *adj* thinking **II.** *m(f)* thinker
pensamiento *m* **1.** (*acción, idea, objeto*) thought; **ya el** ~ **solo me da risa** the very thought of it makes me laugh **2.** (*intención*) intention **3.** (*mente*) mind; **tengo un problema en el** ~ there's sth on my mind; **¿cuándo te vino esa idea al** ~**?** when did that idea occur to you? **4.** (*apotegma*) maxim **5.** (*contenido*) thoughts *pl* **6.** BOT pansy
pensar <e→ie> **I.** *vi, vt* **1.** (*formar un juicio, reflexionar*) ~ (**en**) **algo** to think (about) sth; **todo pasa cuando menos se piensa** (**en ello**) everything happens when you least expect it; **¡ni ~lo!** don't even think about it!; **¡no quiero ni ~lo!** I don't even want to think about it!; **nos dio mucho que** ~ **que no hubiera regresado aún** the fact that he/she hadn't returned yet gave us a lot to think about; **esto es algo para ~lo bien** we need to think carefully about this; **lo hicimos sin ~lo** we did it without thinking; **sin ~lo me dio una bofetada** he suddenly slapped me; **pensándolo bien** on reflection **2.** (*considerar*) to consider **II.** *vi* (*opinar, suponer*) to think; **pienso que deberíamos irnos** I think we should go; ~ **muy mal de alguien** to think very badly of sb **III.** *vt* **1.** (*intención*) to think of; **pensábamos venir este fin de semana** we were thinking of coming this weekend; **lo pensó mejor y no lo hizo** he/she thought better of it and didn't do it **2.** (*inventar, tramar*) to think up
pensativo, **-a** *adj* thoughtful, pensive
pensión *f* **1.** (*paga*) pension; ~ **recibida de la empresa** occupational pension; ~ **de viudez** widow's pension; ~ **alimenticia** maintenance; **aún no cobra la** ~ (*no recibe la paga*) he/she doesn't get a pension yet; (*no tiene la edad*) he/she isn't a pensioner yet **2.** (*para huéspedes*) guesthouse **3.** (*precio por alojamiento*) (charge for) board and lodging; ~ **completa** full board
pensionado *m* ENS boarding school
pensionado, **-a** *m, f* (*jubilado*) pensioner
pensionar *vt* to give a pension to
pensionista *mf* **1.** (*jubilado*) pensioner **2.** (*huésped*) guest (*at boarding house*) **3.** (*alumno*) boarder
pentagonal *adj* pentagonal
pentágono *m* pentagon
pentagrama *m* MÚS stave, staff
pentatlón *m* pentathlon
Pentecostés *m* REL **1.** (*cristiano*) Whitsun; **Pascua de** ~ Whit Sunday **2.** (*judío*) Pentecost
penúltimo, **-a** *adj* penultimate, next-to-last
penumbra *f* semi-darkness; ASTR penumbra
penuria *f* **1.** (*escasez*) scarcity; **pasar muchas ~s** to suffer great hardship **2.** (*pobreza*) poverty
peña *f* **1.** (*roca*) crag **2.** (*grupo*) group; (*de aficionados*) club; (*tertulia*) circle; *inf* (*de jóvenes*) gang
peñasco *m* (*peña*) boulder
peñascoso, **-a** *adj* rocky
peñón *m* **1.** (*peñasco*) crag; **el Peñón** the Rock (of Gibraltar) **2.** (*monte*) mountain
peón *m* **1.** (*obrero*) unskilled labourer *Brit* [*o* laborer *Am*]; (*jornalero*) farmhand; *Méx* (*aprendiz*) apprentice **2.** (*en juegos*) piece; (*en ajedrez*) pawn
peonza *f* (*juguete*) spinning top
peor *adv, adj comp de* **mal**(**o**) worse; **en matemáticas soy** ~ **que tú** I am worse at maths than you are; **el** ~ **de la clase** the worst in the class; **el pequeño es el** ~ **de los dos** the little one is the worse of the two; **y verás, será** ~ **aún** you'll see, it will get even worse; **el** ~ **día, verás como te hablará** just when you least expect it, he/she will speak to you; **en el** ~ **de los casos** at worst; **si pasa lo** ~ if worst comes to worst; **pero lo** ~ **de todo fue...** but the worst thing of all was ...; **vas de mal en** ~ you're going from bad to worse; ~ **es nada** it's better than nothing
pepa *f* **1.** *AmL* (*pepita*) seed **2.** *And* (*mentira*) fib
Pepa *f inf* **¡viva la ~!** (*indiferencia*) who cares!; (*regocijo*) hurrah!, hurray! *Am*
Pepe *m* **ponerse como un** ~ *inf* to have a great time; **ver menos que** ~ **Leches** *inf* to be as blind as a bat
pepena *f* **1.** *Col* (*abanico*) fan **2.** *Méx* (*lo recogido*) collection; (*vísceras*) viscera
pepinillo *m* gherkin
pepino *m* **1.** (*para ensaladas*) cucumber; **eso me importa un** ~ *inf* I don't give two hoots about that **2.** (*melón*) unripe melon
pepita *f* BOT seed
pepsina *f* pepsin
pequeñajo, **-a** **I.** *adj inf* small **II.** *m, f inf* kid
pequeñez *f* **1.** (*tamaño*) smallness **2.** (*minucia*) trifle
pequeño, **-a** **I.** *adj* small, little; **ya desde** ~ **solía venir a este sitio** I've been coming here since I was little; **esta camisa me queda** ~ this shirt is too small for me **II.** *m, f* little one
pequeñoburgués, **-esa** *adj, m, f* petit bourgeois
pequinés *m* ZOOL Pekinese
pequinés, **-esa** *adj, m, f* Pekinese

P

pera I. *adj* posh; **niño** ~ posh brat *Brit,* little rich kid II. *f* 1. BOT pear 2. (*barba*) goatee 3. TÉC ~ **de goma** rubber bulb 4. *vulg* (*masturbación*) **hacerse una** ~ to wank *Brit,* to jerk off *Am* ►**pedir ~s al olmo** *inf* to ask for the impossible; **poner a alguien las ~s a cuarto** *inf* to tell sb a few home truths; **eso es la** ~ *inf* that's the limit; **tocarse la** ~ *vulg* to sit on one's backside

peral *m* pear tree

perca *f* perch

percance *m* (*contratiempo*) setback; (*por culpa propia*) blunder; (*de plan, proyecto*) hitch

per cápita *adv* per capita; **consumo** ~ per capita consumption

percatarse *vr* **~se de algo** (*darse cuenta*) to notice sth; (*comprender*) to realize sth

percebe *m* goose barnacle

percepción *f* 1. (*acción*) perception 2. (*idea*) notion; (*impresión*) impression 3. FIN receipt

perceptible *adj* 1. (*que puede comprenderse*) perceptible 2. FIN payable

perceptivo, -a *adj* perceptive

perceptor(a) *m(f)* recipient

percha *f* 1. (*en el armario*) hanger 2. (*perchero*) coat stand; (*en la tienda*) clothes rail; **vestido de** ~ ready-made dress 3. *AmC* (*chaqueta*) jacket 4. *inf* (*tipo*) build; **tener buena** ~ to have a good figure

perchero *m* ~ (**de pared**) coat rack; ~ (**de pie**) coat stand

percibir *vt* 1. (*notar*) to perceive 2. (*darse cuenta*) to notice 3. (*comprender*) to realize 4. (*cobrar*) to receive

percusión *f* 1. (*golpeo*) striking 2. TÉC percussion; **barra de** ~ percussion bar 3. MÚS percussion; **instrumento de** ~ percussion instrument

percusionista *mf* (*de bongos, congas*) percussionist; (*de batería*) drummer

perdedor(a) I. *adj* losing II. *m(f)* loser

perder <e→ie> I. *vt* 1. (*en general*) to lose; ~ **la cuenta** to lose count; **he perdido mis gafas** I've lost my glasses; ~ **terreno** *fig* to lose ground 2. (*malgastar*) to waste 3. (*no aprovechar*) **si llego tarde al espectáculo pierdo la entrada** if I arrive late for the show my ticket will be wasted 4. (*peso, costumbre*) to lose 5. (*oportunidad, tren*) to miss 6. (*ocasionar daños*) to destroy; **el fuego perdió todo el edificio** the fire destroyed the whole building; **esa equivocación nos perdió** that mistake was our undoing; **el juego lo ~á** gambling will be his undoing; **el régimen lo llevo muy bien, lo que me pierde es ver comer a los demás** I don't have a problem with the diet, it's seeing other people eat which leads me astray 7. ENS (*suspender*) ~ **el curso** to fail the year II. *vi* 1. (*en general*) to lose; **Portugal perdió por 1 a 2 frente a Italia** Portugal lost 2–1 against Italy; **vas a salir perdiendo** you're going to come off worst; **llevar todas las de** ~ to be fighting a losing battle; **lo echó todo a** ~ he/she lost everything; **la comida se quemó y todo se echó a** ~ the food was burnt and everything was completely ruined; **cómete esos plátanos que si no se echan a** ~ eat these bananas, otherwise they'll just go to waste 2. (*decaer*) to decline; **por mi profesión he perdido mucho en salud** my job has been very bad for my health 3. (*desteñir*) to fade III. *vr* 1. (*extraviarse*) to get lost; **¡qué se le habrá perdido por allí?** *fig* what is he/she doing there? 2. (*bailando, leyendo*) to lose oneself; **~se en palabrerías complicadas** (*hablando*) to get bogged down in complicated wordplay 3. (*desaparecer*) to disappear 4. (*arruinarse*) **~se por algo/alguien** to be ruined by sth/sb 5. (*desperdiciarse*) to be wasted; **se pierde mucha agua por falta de conciencia ecológica** a lot of water is wasted through lack of environmental awareness 6. (*ocasión*) to miss out; **si no te vienes, tú te lo pierdes** if you don't come, you'll be the one who misses out 7. (*extinguirse*) to die out; **poco a poco la minifalda se va perdiendo** miniskirts are slowly going out of fashion 8. (*anhelar*) **~se por algo/alguien** to be mad about sth/sb

perdición *f* 1. (*acción*) loss; (*daño*) ruin 2. (*moral*) perdition

pérdida *f* loss; ~ **de cabellos** hair loss; ~ **de conciencia** loss of consciousness; ~ **por fricción** wear; **esto es una** ~ **de tiempo** this is a waste of time; **es fácil de encontrar, no tiene** ~ it's easy to find, you can't miss it; **el edificio ha sufrido ~s enormes después del incendio** the building has been very badly damaged in the fire; **el coche tiene una leve** ~ **de aceite** the car has a slight oil leak; **~s humanas** victims; **no hubo que lamentar ~s humanas** fortunately there were no lives lost

perdidamente *adv* 1. (*con exceso*) **estar** ~ **enamorado** to be madly in love 2. (*inútilmente*) pointlessly

perdido, -a I. *adj* 1. (*que no se encuentra*) lost; **dar a alguien por** ~ to give sb up for lost; **dar algo por** ~ to give sth up for lost; *fig* to give up on sth; **estar** ~ to be lost 2. (*vicioso, sin salida*) lost; **estar loco** ~ *inf* to be completely insane [*o* mad *Brit*] 3. (*sucio*) **poner algo** ~ *inf* to make sth completely dirty; **ponerse** ~ **de pintura** *inf* to get covered in paint II. *m, f* 1. *inf* (*vago*) layabout; (*pobre*) poor wretch; **hacerse el** ~ *inf* to make oneself scarce 2. (*libertino*) waster

perdiz *f* partridge; **...y fueron felices y comieron perdices** ... and they lived happily ever after

perdón *m* 1. (*absolución, indulto*) pardon 2. (*disculpa*) **¡~!** sorry!; **¿~?** pardon?; **¡con ~!** if you'll excuse me!; **no cabe** ~ it's inexcusable; **pedir** ~ **a alguien** to ask for sb's forgiveness; (*disculparse*) to apologize to sb; **con** ~ **de la mesa, esto es una porquería** I hope you will excuse the expression at table, but this is a load of crap

perdonable *adj* forgivable

perdonar *vt* **1.** (*ofensa, deuda*) to forgive; (*pecado, pena*) to pardon; **no te perdono** I don't forgive you; **perdona que te interrumpa** forgive me for interrupting; **perdona, ¿puedo pasar?** excuse me, can I come through? **2.** (*obligación*) to let off; **te perdono los 20 euros** I'll forget about the 20 euros you owe me; **les he perdonado la tarde a mis empleados** I have given my employees the afternoon off **3.** (*dejar pasar*) **no ~ ningún esfuerzo** to spare no effort; **no ~ ningún medio** to use all possible means; **la guerra no perdona a nadie** war spares no-one

perdurable *adj* **1.** (*duradero*) long-lasting **2.** (*eterno*) everlasting

perdurar *vi* **1.** (*todavía*) to persist **2.** (*indefinidamente*) to last for ever; **su recuerdo ~á para siempre entre nosotros** his memory will always be with us

perecedero, **-a** *adj* **1.** (*pasajero*) transitory **2.** (*alimento*) perishable

perecer *irr como crecer vi* **1.** (*morir*) to perish; **~ de sed** to die of thirst **2.** (*daño, sufrimiento*) to suffer

peregrinación *f* REL pilgrimage; **ir en ~** to make a pilgrimage

peregrinar *vi* **1.** REL to make a pilgrimage **2.** (*viajar: a pie*) to wander; (*con vehículo*) to drive around; **para matricularme tuve que ~ por cientos de oficinas** to register I had to trek round hundreds of offices

peregrino, **-a** **I.** *adj* **1.** (*persona*) wandering **2.** (*extraño*) strange **3.** (*raro*) unusual **4.** (*extraordinario*) extraordinary **II.** *m, f* pilgrim

perejil *m* **1.** BOT parsley **2.** *pl* (*adornos*) trimmings *pl*

perenne *adj* **1.** (*perpetuo*) everlasting; BOT perennial **2.** (*constante*) constant

perentorio, **-a** *adj* **1.** (*urgente*) pressing, peremptory *liter* **2.** (*pago*) due **3.** (*decisión*) definite; **plazo ~** fixed time limit

pereza *f* **1.** (*gandulería*) laziness **2.** (*de movimientos*) slowness; **me dio ~ ir y me quedé en casa** I couldn't be bothered going so I stayed at home

perezosa *f Arg, Perú, Urug* deckchair

perezoso, **-a** *adj* **1.** (*gandul*) lazy **2.** (*movimiento*) unhurried **3.** *fig* **y ni corto ni ~ me soltó un sopapo** *inf* without stopping to think he/she slapped me

perfección *f* perfection; **estilo de gran ~** highly polished style; **hacer algo a la ~** to do sth to perfection

perfeccionamiento *m* perfection; (*de técnica, sistema*) improvement; (*profesional*) further training

perfeccionar *vt* to perfect; (*de técnica, sistema*) to improve

perfeccionista *adj, mf* perfectionist

perfectamente *adv* perfectly; **sabes ~ que...** you know perfectly well that ...; **te entiendo ~** I understand you perfectly; **es ~ comprensible** it is perfectly understandable; **¡~!** exactly!

perfecto *m* LING perfect tense

perfecto, **-a** *adj* **1.** perfect; **nadie es ~** nobody is perfect; **habla un inglés ~** he/she speaks perfect English; **un ~ caballero** a perfect gentleman; **eres un ~ idiota** you are a complete idiot **2.** LING **pretérito ~** past perfect

perfidia *f* **1.** (*deslealtad*) disloyalty **2.** (*traición*) betrayal

pérfido, **-a** *adj* **1.** (*desleal*) disloyal **2.** (*traidor*) treacherous

perfil *m* **1.** *t.* TÉC (*de cara*) profile; **de ~** in profile; **~ genético** genetic profile **2.** (*contorno*) outline **3.** (*de personalidad, doctrina*) characteristics *pl*; **el ~ del candidato** the description of the candidate

perfilar **I.** *vt* **1.** (*retocar*) to touch up **2.** (*sacar perfil*) to outline; TÉC to streamline **II.** *vr* **1.** (*distinguirse*) to stand out **2.** (*tomar forma*) to take shape

perforación *f* **1.** (*con máquina*) drilling; (*de oreja*) piercing; (*de papel*) punching; (*con muchos agujeros*) perforation **2.** (*agujeros, línea*) perforation

perforar *vt* (*con máquina*) to drill; (*oreja*) to pierce; (*papel*) to punch; (*para decorar, arrancar*) to perforate

perfumador *m* (*utensilio*) perfume spray

perfumar **I.** *vt* to perfume; **las flores perfuman la habitación** the smell of flowers fills the room **II.** *vi* to be fragrant

perfume *m* **1.** (*sustancia*) perfume **2.** (*olor*) fragrance

perfumería *f* **1.** (*tienda*) perfume shop **2.** (*productos*) perfume

pergamino *m* parchment; **libro (con encuadernación) en ~** parchment-bound book; **familia de ~s** ancient family

pericia *f* **1.** (*habilidad*) expertise **2.** (*práctica*) skill

pericial *adj* expert; **informe ~** expert report

perico *m* **1.** ZOOL parakeet **2.** *inf* (*puta*) whore **3.** *inf* (*cocaína*) snow

periferia *f* periphery; (*de ciudad*) outskirts *pl*

perifollo *m* **1.** BOT chervil **2.** *inf* (*adornos*) trimmings *pl*

perífrasis *f inv* circumlocution, wordiness

perifrástico, **-a** *adj* circumlocutory, long-winded

perilla *f* (*barba*) goatee ►venir **de ~s** to be just what was needed

perillán, **-ana** *m, f* **1.** (*niño*) rascal **2.** (*adulto*) rogue

perímetro *m* MAT perimeter

perineo *m* perineum

perinola *f* (*peonza*) (small) spinning top

periodicidad *f* frequency

periódico *m* (*diario*) newspaper

periódico, **-a** *adj* periodic; (*publicación*) periodical; **sistema ~** QUÍM periodic table

P

periodicucho *m pey* scandal sheet, rag
periodismo *m* (*profesión, estudios*) journalism
periodista *mf* journalist
periodístico, **-a** *adj* **1.** (*de los periodistas*) journalistic **2.** (*de los periódicos*) newspaper; **reportaje** ~ newspaper report
periodo *m*, **período** *m t.* MAT, FÍS, GEO (*tiempo, época, menstruación*) period; ~ **álgido** critical period; ~ **glacial** ice age; ~ **productivo** productive period; ~ **de prueba** trial period
peripecia *f* (*incidente*) vicissitude; **ha pasado por muchas ~s en esta vida** he/she has had many ups and downs in his/her life
peripuesto, **-a** *adj inf* dressed up to the nines; (*hombre*) all spruced up; (*mujer*) dolled up *Am*
periquete *m* **esto lo hago yo en un** ~ I can do that in no time; **estoy lista en un** ~ I'll be ready in a jiffy
periquito *m* parakeet
periscopio *m* periscope
perito, **-a** **I.** *adj* expert **II.** *m, f* **1.** (*experto*) expert **2.** UNIV graduate; ~ **agrónomo** agronomist; ~ **mercantil** accountant; **Escuela de Peritos** *professional training college*
peritoneo *m* peritoneum
perjudicar <c→qu> **I.** *vt* **1.** (*causar daño*) to damage; (*naturaleza, intereses*) to harm; (*proceso, desarrollo*) to hinder; **fumar perjudica la salud** smoking is bad for your health **2.** (*causar desventaja*) to disadvantage **II.** *vr* to harm oneself
perjudicial *adj* **1.** (*que causa daño*) harmful; ~ **para la salud** harmful to health **2.** (*desventajoso*) disadvantageous
perjuicio *m* **1.** (*daño: de imagen, naturaleza*) harm; (*de objeto*) damage; (*de libertad*) infringement; **causar ~s** to cause harm; **sin ~ de que** +*subj* despite the fact that **2.** (*detrimento*) detriment; **ir en ~ de alguien** to be to sb's detriment
perjurar *vi* **1.** (*en falso*) to commit perjury **2.** (*faltar al juramento*) to break one's oath
perjurio *m* **1.** (*en falso*) perjury **2.** (*faltar al juramento*) breaking one's word
perla *f* pearl; ~ **cultivada** cultured pearl; **eso viene de ~s** that is just what was needed
permanecer *irr como crecer vi* (*estar, seguir*) to remain; ~ **quieto** to keep still; ~ **invariable** to remain unchanged; ~ **dormido** to carry on sleeping; ~ **sentado** to remain seated
permanencia *f* **1.** (*estancia*) stay; (*duración*) duration; **luchar para lograr la ~ en primera** DEP to fight to stay in the first division **2.** (*persistencia*) persistence **3.** (*continuación*) continuation
permanente **I.** *adj* permanent; **estado** ~ permanent state **II.** *f* perm
permeabilidad *f* permeability
permeable *adj* permeable; ~ **al agua** permeable to water
permisible *adj* permissible
permisión *f* permission
permisionario, **-a** *m, f AmL* official agent
permisividad *f* permissiveness
permisivo, **-a** *adj* permissive
permiso *m* **1.** (*aprobación, autorización*) permission; **me dio ~ para hacerlo** he/she gave me permission to do it; **pedir ~ a alguien** to ask sb for permission **2.** (*licencia*) permit; ~ **de conducir** driving licence *Brit,* driver's license *Am;* ~ **de residencia/de trabajo** residence/work permit **3.** (*vacaciones*) leave; **pedir** ~ to request leave; **estar de** ~ MIL to be on leave
permitir **I.** *vt* **1.** (*consentir*) to permit; **¿me permite pasar/entrar/salir?** may I get past/enter/leave?; **no está permitido fumar** smoking is not allowed; **si me permite la expresión** if you will excuse the phrase **2.** (*autorizar*) to authorize **3.** (*hacer posible, tolerar*) to allow; **esta máquina permite trabajar el doble** this machine allows you to do twice as much work; **no permito que me levantes la voz** I won't allow you to raise your voice to me **II.** *vr* to allow oneself
permuta *f* exchange
permutar *vt* to exchange
pernera *f* (trouser) leg
pernicioso, **-a** *adj* damaging; (*tumor*) malignant; ~ **para algo/alguien** damaging to sth/sb
pernil *m* **1.** (*del cerdo*) leg of ham **2.** (*del pantalón*) (trouser) leg
pernio *m* hinge
perno *m* bolt
pernoctar *vi* to spend the night
pero **I.** *conj* but; (*sin embargo*) however; **¡~ si todavía es una niña!** but she is still only a child!; **¡~ si ya la conoces!** but you already know her!; **¿~ qué es lo que quieres?** what do you want? **II.** *m* (*objeción*) objection; **el proyecto tiene sus ~s** there are lots of problems with the project; **sin un** ~ no buts; **poner ~s a algo** to object to sth; **¡no hay ~ que valga!** there are no buts about it!; **poner ~s a todo** to object to everything
perogrullada *f* obvious truth
perol *m* (metal) cooking pot
peroné *m* fibula
peronista *adj, mf* Peronist
peroración *f* (*discurso*) speech
perorar *vi* **1.** (*dar discurso*) to make a speech; *pey* to hold forth **2.** *inf* (*hablar*) to ramble on **3.** (*pedir*) to ask persistently
peróxido *m* peroxide
perpendicular *adj, f* perpendicular
perpetrar *vt* to perpetrate
perpetuar <*1. pres:* perpetúo> **I.** *vt* **1.** (*recuerdo, memoria, nombre*) to preserve **2.** (*situación, error, mentira*) to perpetuate **II.** *vr* to be perpetuated
perpetuidad *f* **1.** (*continuidad*) continuity **2.** (*eternidad*) perpetuity; **a** ~ in perpetuity; **condenar a** ~ to condemn to life imprison-

ment
perpetuo, **-a** *adj* **1.** (*incesante*) perpetual; **nieves perpetuas** permanent snow **2.** (*vitalicio*) life; **cadena perpetua** life sentence
perplejo, **-a** *adj* perplexed
perra *f* **1.** ZOOL bitch; *v.t.* **perro I. 2.** (*obstinación*) obsession **3.** *inf* (*rabieta*) tantrum; **coger una ~** to throw a tantrum **4.** *inf* (*modorra*) sleepiness; (*pereza*) laziness **5.** (*mujer malvada*) bitch **6.** *inf* (*dinero*) penny; **no tener una ~** to be broke **7.** *inf* (*borrachera*) drunkenness; **cogerse una ~** to get pissed
perramus *m inv, Arg, Bol, Urug* (*impermeable*) raincoat
perrera *f* (*casita*) kennel; (*de perros callejeros*) dog pound
perrería *f* (*vileza*) dirty trick
perrilla *f Méx* (*orzuelo*) snare
perrito *m* **~ caliente** hot dog
perro, **-a I.** *m, f* (*macho*) dog; (*hembra*) bitch; **~ callejero** stray dog; **~ faldero** lapdog; **~ lazarillo** guide-dog; **echar los ~s a alguien** *inf* to tear sb to shreds; **morir como un ~** *inf* to die a lonely death ►**se llevan como el ~ y el gato** *inf* they fight like cat and dog; **ser como el ~ del hortelano** to be a dog in the manger; **¡venga ya, a otro ~ con ese hueso!** *inf* pull the other one!; **humor de ~s** *inf* filthy mood; **a ~ flaco todo son pulgas** *prov* misfortunes never come singly; **tiempo de ~s** *inf* filthy weather; **~ ladrador, poco mordedor** *prov* his bark is worse than his bite; **muerto el ~ se acabó la rabia** *prov* dead dogs don't bite; **ser ~ viejo** *inf* to be an old hand **II.** *adj* lousy; **llevar una vida perra** to lead a wretched life
persa I. *adj* Persian; **alfombra ~** Persian rug **II.** *mf* Persian
persecución *f* **1.** (*seguimento*) pursuit; **~ en coche** car chase **2.** (*acoso*) persecution
perseguir *irr como seguir vt* to chase; (*contrato, chica*) to pursue; **la policía persigue al fugitivo** the police are pursuing the fugitive; **me persigue la mala suerte** I am dogged by bad luck; **me persiguen los remordimientos** I am tormented by remorse; **el jefe me persigue todo el día** the boss is always on my back; **¡qué persigues con esto?** what do you hope to achieve by this?
perseverancia *f* **1.** (*insistencia*) **~ en algo** insistence on sth **2.** (*en trabajo, actividad*) **~ en algo** perseverance in sth **3.** (*firmeza*) resolve
perseverante *adj* **1.** (*insistente*) insistent **2.** (*constante*) persevering **3.** (*firme*) determined
perseverar *vi* **1.** (*insistir*) to insist **2.** (*mantener*) **~ en algo** to persevere in sth
Persia *f* Persia
persiana *f* blind
pérsico, **-a** *adj* Persian
persignarse *vr* to cross oneself
persistencia *f* **1.** (*insistencia*) insistence **2.** (*perduración*) persistence
persistente *adj* **1.** (*persona*) persistent **2.** (*acción, recuerdo*) lasting
persistir *vi* **1.** (*insistir*) to insist **2.** (*perdurar*) to persist
persona *f* person; **~ de contacto** contact; **~ (non) grata** persona (non) grata; **en ~** in person; **~ jurídica** legal entity; **~ mayor** adult, grown-up; **~ física** individual; **ser buena/mala ~** to be good/bad; **había muchas ~s** there were a lot of people; **no había ninguna ~ allí** there was nobody there; **se apareció en la ~ de...** he/she appeared in the form of ...; **ese es una ~ de cuidado** you need to be careful with him
personaje *m* **1.** (*personalidad*) personality; **~ de culto** cult figure; **es todo un ~** he/she is a real character **2.** TEAT, LIT character
personal[1] **I.** *adj* personal; **datos ~es** personal details; **pronombre ~** personal pronoun **II.** *m* **1.** (*plantilla*) personnel; (*en empresa*) staff; **~ de a bordo** AVIAT aircrew; **~ docente** teaching staff; **~ de tierra** AVIAT ground crew **2.** *inf* (*gente*) people *pl*
personal[2] *f* DEP foul
personalidad *f* personality
personalizar <z→c> *vt* **1.** (*hacer personal*) to personalize **2.** (*aludir*) to get personal
personarse *vr* to appear; **~ en juicio** to appear before the court; **persónese ante el director** report to the director; **el lunes tengo que personarme en el INEM** on Monday I have to go to the job centre *Brit* [*o* center *Am*]
personero, **-a** *m, f AmL* government representative
personificar <c→qu> *vt* to personify; **personifica la maldad** he is evil personified
perspectiva *f* **1.** (*general*) perspective **2.** (*vista*) view **3.** *pl* (*posibilidad*) prospects *pl* **4.** (*distancia*) **aún no disponemos de la ~ adecuada para valorar este periodo** we are still too close to the period to be able to judge it
perspicacia *f* insight
perspicaz *adj* **1.** (*vista*) keen **2.** (*persona*) perceptive
persuadir I. *vt* **1.** (*inducir*) to encourage; **le ~é para que no haga el viaje** I will try to persuade him not to make the journey **2.** (*convencer*) to persuade **II.** *vr* to be persuaded
persuasión *f* **1.** (*acto*) persuasion; **emplear todo su poder de ~** to use all one's powers of persuasion **2.** (*convencimiento*) belief
persuasivo, **-a** *adj* persuasive
pertenecer *irr como crecer vi* **1.** (*ser de*) to belong; **esta casa me pertenece** this house belongs to me; **esta cita pertenece a Hamlet** this is a quotation from Hamlet **2.** (*tener obligación*) **te pertenece a ti hacerlo** it is your duty to do it; **esto pertenece al Ministerio de Asuntos Exteriores** that's the Foreign Office's *Brit* [*o* State Department's *Am*] responsibility
perteneciente *adj* **~ a** belonging to; **los países ~s a la ONU** the countries which are

P

members of the UN; **todo lo ~ al caso** everything which is relevant to the case; **un cuadro ~ a la colección de Thyssen** a picture which belongs to the Thyssen collection
pertenencia *f* **1.** (*acción*) belonging; (*afiliación*) membership **2.** *pl* (*bienes*) belongings *pl* **3.** *pl* (*accesorios*) accessories *pl*
pértiga *f t.* DEP (*vara*) pole; **salto de ~** pole vault; **saltar con ~** to pole vault; **~ del trole** current-collecting pole, trolley pole
pertinacia *f* (*de lluvia, persona*) persistence
pertinaz *adj* (*lluvia, tos, persona*) persistent
pertinente *adj* **1.** (*oportuno*) appropriate **2.** (*datos, pregunta, comentario*) relevant, pertinent **3.** (*relativo*) **en lo ~ a...** with regard to ...
pertrechar **I.** *vt* to supply **II.** *vr* **~se de algo** (*de alimentos*) to supply oneself with sth; (*de equipamiento*) to equip oneself with sth
pertrechos *mpl* MIL supplies *pl*
perturbación *f* disturbance
perturbado, **-a** **I.** *adj* PSICO disturbed **II.** *m, f* **~** (**mental**) mentally disturbed person
perturbador(**a**) **I.** *adj* disturbing **II.** *m(f)* **1.** (*por hacer ruido*) disturber of the peace **2.** (*por alborotar*) troublemaker
perturbar *vt* to disturb; (*confundir*) to confuse
Perú *m* Peru

> **Perú** lies in the western part of South America. It is the third largest country after Brazil and Argentina. The capital and also the largest city in Peru is **Lima**. Both Spanish and **quechua** are the official languages of the country and the monetary unit is the **sol**. The original inhabitants of Peru were the **incas**.

peruano, **-a** *adj, m, f* Peruvian
perversidad *f* **1.** (*maldad*) wickedness **2.** (*sexual*) perversity
perversión *f* **1.** (*acción*) perversion; **~ de menores** corruption of minors **2.** (*cualidad*) perversity
perverso, **-a** *adj* **1.** (*malo*) wicked **2.** (*moral*) twisted **3.** (*sexual*) perverse
pervertido, **-a** **I.** *adj* perverted **II.** *m, f* pervert
pervertir *irr como sentir* **I.** *vt* to corrupt **II.** *vr* **1.** (*en costumbres, ideología*) to become corrupt **2.** (*depravarse*) to become perverted
pesa *f t.* DEP weight; **~ del reloj** clock weight; **hacer** (**entrenamiento de**) **~s** to do weight training; **levantamiento de ~s** weightlifting
pesadez *f* **1.** (*de objeto*) heaviness **2.** (*de movimiento*) slowness, sluggishness **3.** (*de sueño*) drowsiness **4.** (*de tarea*) boring nature **5.** (*de persona*) tiresome nature **6.** (*de viaje*) tediousness **7.** (*de lectura*) density; (*aburrido*) dullness **8.** (*de dibujo*) over-elaboration **9.** (*de estómago*) (acid) indigestion
pesadilla *f* nightmare
pesado, **-a** *adj* **1.** (*que pesa*) heavy; **tengo la cabeza pesada** my head feels rather stuffy; **tengo el estómago ~** my stomach is uncomfortably full **2.** (*lento*) slow **3.** (*molesto*) tiresome **4.** (*duro*) hard; **hacer un diccionario es ~** writing a dictionary is hard work **5.** (*aburrido*) boring **6.** (*sueño*) deep; (*tiempo*) oppressive; (*viaje*) tedious; (*lectura*) heavy going; (*dibujo*) over-elaborate
pesadumbre *f* **1.** affliction **2.** *elev* heaviness
pésame *m* condolences *pl;* **dar el ~** to offer one's condolences; **reciba mi más sincero ~ por la muerte de su hermana** please accept my condolences for the loss of your sister
pesantez *f* gravity
pesar **I.** *vi* **1.** (*tener peso*) to weigh; **esta caja pesa mucho** this box is very heavy; **pon encima lo que no pese** put the lightest things on top **2.** (*cargo, responsabilidad*) **~ sobre alguien** to weigh heavily on sb; (*problemas*) to weigh sb down **3.** (*hipoteca*) to affect **II.** *vt* **1.** (*objeto, persona*) to weigh; (*cantidad concreta*) to weigh out; **¿me puede ~ la fruta?** could you weigh this fruit for me? **2.** (*ventajas*) to weigh up **3.** (*disgustar*) **me pesa haberte mentido** I regret having lied to you; **mal que te pese...** much as you may dislike it ...; **pese a quien pese** come what may; **pese a que...** although ... **III.** *m* **1.** (*pena*) sorrow; **muy a ~ mío** to my great sadness **2.** (*remordimiento*) regret ►**a ~ de** in spite of; **a ~ de todo lo quiere intentar** in spite of everything, he/she wants to try it
pesaroso, **-a** *adj* **1.** (*afligido*) sad; **está ~ por haberlo dicho** he really regrets having said it **2.** (*disgustado*) upset **3.** (*preocupado*) worried
pesca *f* **1.** (*acción, oficio, industria*) fishing; **ir de ~** to go fishing; **~ de altura** deep-sea fishing; **~ de arrastre** trawling; **~ de bajura** inshore fishing; **y toda la ~** *fig, inf* and all the rest of the crew **2.** (*captura*) capture
pescadería *f* (*tienda*) fishmonger's *Brit,* fishmarket
pescadilla *f* whiting; **ser la ~ que se muerde la cola** *inf* to be a vicious circle
pescado *m* fish
pescador(**a**) *m(f)* (*de caña*) angler; (*de mar*) fisherman
pescar <c→qu> *vt* **1.** (*con caña, en barco*) to fish for; **ir a ~ sardinas** to fish for sardines **2.** (*resfriado*) to catch **3.** *inf* (*novio*) to land **4.** *inf* (*entender*) to understand **5.** (*sorprender*) to catch out
pescuezo *m* (scruff of the) neck; **retorcer el ~ a alguien** *inf* to wring sb's neck; **sacar el ~** *inf* to be snooty; **salvar el ~** *fig* to save one's skin
pese *adv* **~ a** in spite of, despite
pesebre *m* manger; (*de Navidad*) Nativity scene
pesero *m Méx* minibus
peseta *f* peseta; **cambiar la ~** *inf* to throw up
pesetero, **-a** *m, f* money-grubbing; **este comerciante es un ~** all this businessman

thinks about is money
pesimismo *m sin pl* pessimism
pesimista I. *adj* pessimistic II. *mf* pessimist
pésimo, **-a** *adj* dreadful
peso *m* 1. (*de objeto*) weight; **coger/perder** ~ to gain/lose weight; **¿qué ~ tiene?** how much does it weigh?; **vender a ~** to sell by weight; **eso cae por su propio ~** that goes without saying 2. (*pesadez*) heaviness; **tener ~ en las piernas** to have heavy legs 3. (*importancia*) weight; **es un gran ~ dentro de la empresa** he/she has a lot of influence within the business; **tener una razón de ~** to have a good reason 4. (*carga*) burden; **llevar el ~ de algo** to bear the burden of sth; **me saco un ~ de encima** that's taken a load off my mind 5. DEP (*bola*) shot 6. DEP (*boxeo*) ~ **gallo** bantamweight 7. (*moneda*) peso ►**comprar a ~ de oro** to pay way over the odds; **pagar a ~ de oro** to pay the earth
pespuntar *vt* to backstitch
pespunte *m* 1. (*acción, costura*) backstitching 2. (*puntada*) backstitch
pespuntear *vt* to backstitch
pesquero *m* fishing boat
pesquero, **-a** *adj* fishing
pesquisa[1] *f* inquiry; **hacer ~s** to make inquiries
pesquisa[2] *m Arg, Ecua, Par* detective
pestaña *f* eyelash; **quemarse las ~s** *fig* to burn the midnight oil
pestañ(e)ar *vi* to blink; **sin ~** without batting an eyelid
pestañeo *m* blinking
peste *f* 1. *t.* MED (*plaga*) plague; ~ **bubónica** bubonic plague 2. (*olor*) stench; **aquí hay una ~ increíble** it really stinks here 3. (*crítica*) **echar ~s de alguien** to heap abuse on sb
pesticida *m* pesticide
pestífero, **-a** *adj* 1. (*fétido*) foul-smelling 2. (*pernicioso*) pernicious
pestilencia *f* 1. (*olor*) stench 2. MED pestilence
pestilente *adj v.* **pestífero**
pestillo *m* (*de puerta, cerradura*) bolt; **echar el ~** to shoot the bolt; ~ **de golpe** spring bolt
petaca *f* 1. (*para cigarros*) cigarette case; (*para tabaco*) tobacco pouch 2. (*para bebidas*) hip flask 3. *AmL* (*caja*) box; (*baúl*) chest; (*cesto*) basket 4. *AmC* (*joroba*) hump
petacón, **-ona** *adj AmL* tubby
pétalo *m* petal
petanca *f* DEP bowls, petanque
petardo *m* 1. (*de fiesta*) firecracker; **tirar ~s** to let off firecrackers 2. (*estafa*) swindle; **pegar un ~ a alguien** to take sb for a ride 3. *inf* (*persona o cosa mala*) **ser un ~** to be a pain
petate *m* (*de soldado, marinero*) kit bag; **liar el ~** *fig* to pack up and go
petatearse *vr Méx* (*morirse*) to peg out *inf*
petenera *f* MÚS *Andalusian song;* **salirse por ~s** to go off on a tangent
petición *f* 1. (*ruego, solicitud*) request; **a ~ de...** at the request of ...; **¿has hecho ya la ~ de mano?** have you asked her to marry you yet? 2. (*escrito*) petition
peticionar *vt AmL* to petition
petirrojo *m* robin (redbreast)
petiso, **-a** I. *adj Arg, Urug* 1. (*pequeño*) small; (*muy pequeño*) tiny 2. (*enano*) short II. *m, f* short person
petisú *m* eclair
petitorio, **-a** *adj* petitionary
peto *m* 1. (*de armadura*) breastplate 2. (*de bebé, delantal*) bib 3. (*pantalón*) overalls, dungarees *pl Am*
pétreo, **-a** *adj* 1. (*como piedra, pedregoso*) stony 2. (*duro*) rock-hard
petrificación *f* petrification
petrificar <c→qu> I. *vt t. fig* to petrify II. *vr:* **~se** to turn to stone
petrodólar *m* ECON petrodollar
petróleo *m* 1. (*carburante*) petroleum, (crude) oil 2. (*de lámpara*) paraffin
petrolero *m* (*barco*) oil tanker
petrolero, **-a** I. *adj* 1. (*del carburante*) petrol, oil 2. (*de la lámpara*) paraffin II. *m, f* (*persona*) arsonist
petrolífero, **-a** *adj* oil-bearing; **campo ~** oilfield; **industria petrolífera** oil industry
petroquímica *f sin pl* petrochemistry
petulancia *f* 1. (*arrogancia*) arrogance 2. (*insolencia*) insolence 3. (*vanidad*) vanity
petulante *adj* 1. (*arrogante*) arrogant; (*creído*) conceited 2. (*insolente*) insolent
petunia *f* petunia
peyorativo, **-a** *adj* pejorative; **un comentario ~** a derrogatory remark
peyote *m AmL* BOT peyote cactus
pez[1] *m* ZOOL fish; **estar como (el) ~ en el agua** to be in one's element; **estar ~ en español** *inf* to have no idea of Spanish; **ese es un buen ~** he's a wily bird; **un ~ gordo** a big shot
pez[2] *f* 1. (*betún*) pitch 2. (*excremento*) meconium
pezón *m* 1. (*de mujer*) nipple 2. (*de animal*) teat 3. BOT stalk
pezuña *f* 1. (*de vaca, oveja*) hoof 2. *pl, inf* (*de persona*) feet *pl*
PHN *abr de* **Plan Hidrológico Nacional** *national water plan*
pi *f* MAT pi
piadoso, **-a** *adj* 1. (*misericordioso*) merciful; (*bondadoso*) compassionate 2. (*devoto*) pious
pialar *vt AmL* to lasso
pianista *mf* pianist
piano I. *m* piano; ~ **de cola** grand piano II. *adv* MÚS piano
piar <1. pres: pío> *vi* 1. (*pájaro*) to chirp 2. (*clamar*) ~ **por algo** to cry out for sth
piara *f* herd (of pigs)
PIB *m abr de* **Producto Interior Bruto** GDP
pibe, **-a** *m, f Arg* (*chico*) boy; (*chica*) girl
pibil *m Méx* GASTR chili sauce
pica *f* 1. (*lanza*) pike 2. *pl* (*de cartas*) spades

pl
picacho *m* peak
picada *f* **1.**(*de avispa*) sting; (*de serpiente*) bite **2.**(*de pez*) bite **3.** *CSur* (*tapas*) snack
picadero *m* **1.**(*para adiestrar*) ring; (*escuela*) riding school **2.** *inf* bachelor pad, diggings *pl*
picadillo *m* (*carne picada*) mince *Brit*, ground meat *Am;* (*para embutido, salchichas*) filling; **hacer ~ a alguien** *inf* to make mincemeat of sb
picado *m* (*de avión*) dive; **las acciones cayeron en ~** shares slumped; **su fama ha caído en ~** his reputation has plummeted
picado, -a *adj* **1.**(*con picaduras: abrigo*) moth-eaten; (*fruta*) rotten; (*muela*) decayed; (*cara*) pockmarked **2.**(*con agujeros*) perforated **3.**(*mar*) choppy **4.** *inf* (*enfadado*) annoyed
picador *m* **1.**(*adiestrador*) horse-breaker **2.** TAUR picador (*mounted bullfighter who goads the bull with a lance*) **3.** MIN faceworker
picadura *f* **1.**(*de insecto*) sting; (*de serpiente*) bite **2.**(*en ropa, metal*) hole **3.**(*tabaco*) cut tobacco **4.**(*caries*) cavity
picaflor *m* **1.** ZOOL hummingbird **2.** *AmL* (*tenorio*) Don Juan
picante **I.** *adj* **1.**(*comida*) spicy, hot **2.** *fig* risqué **II.** *m* **1.** GASTR spicy food **2.**(*de comida*) spiciness **3.**(*de expresión*) sauciness
picantería *f And* (*restaurante modesto*) small restaurant
picapica *f* (**polvos**) ~ (*de picores*) itching powder; (*de estornudos*) sneezing powder
picapleitos *m inv, pey* pettifogger, shyster
picaporte *m* **1.**(*aldaba*) doorknocker **2.**(*tirador*) door handle **3.**(*pestillo*) latch
picar <c→qu> **I.** *vi* **1.**(*sol, ojos*) to sting **2.**(*chile, pimienta*) to be hot **3.**(*pez, clientes*) to take the bait **4.**(*de la comida*) to snack **5.**(*tener picazón*) to itch; **me pica la espalda** my back is itchy **6.**(*avión*) to dive **7.**(*golpear*) **~ a la puerta** to knock on the door **8.**(*aspirar*) **~ muy alto** to aim too high **9.**(*ser*) **su actitud pica en valiente** his attitude is a brave one **II.** *vt* **1.**(*con punzón*) to prick, to pierce **2.**(*sacar*) **~ una aceituna de la lata** to fish an olive from the tin **3.**(*insecto*) to sting; (*serpiente*) to bite **4.**(*ave*) to peck **5.**(*desmenuzar*) to chop up; (*carne*) to mince; (*tabaco*) to shred **6.**(*caballo*) to spur on **7.**(*papel, tela*) to perforate; (*billete*) to punch **8.**(*ofender*) to irritate; **estar picado con alguien** to be annoyed with sb; **¿qué mosca te ha picado?** what's eating you? **9.**(*incitar*) to goad **10.** TIPO to insert **11.** INFOR to click on **III.** *vr* **1.**(*metal*) to rust; (*muela*) to decay; (*ropa*) to get moth-eaten; (*vino*) to turn sour; (*semillas*) to go off **2.**(*mar*) to become choppy **3.**(*ofenderse*) to become irritated; (*mosquearse*) to become angry; **~se por nada** to get irritated about the slightest thing; **siempre se pica cuando juega** he/she always becomes angry when playing **4.** *AmL* (*embriagarse*) to get tipsy
picardear **I.** *vi* to get into mischief **II.** *vr* to fall into bad ways
picardía *f* **1.**(*malicia*) roguishness; **lo dije con ~** I said it out of a sense of mischief **2.**(*travesura*) naughty trick **3.**(*broma*) joke
picaresco, -a *adj* **1.**(*astuto*) cunning **2.**(*comentario*) mischievous
pícaro, -a **I.** *adj* **1.**(*granuja*) roguish **2.**(*astuto*) cunning **3.**(*comentario*) naughty **II.** *m, f* (*granuja*) rogue ►**~ de siete suelas** *inf* out-and-out rogue
picarón *m AmL* (*buñuelo*) fritter
picatoste *m* crouton
picazón *f* **1.**(*comezón*) itch **2.**(*disgusto*) annoyance
picha *f vulg* (*pene*) dick, prick
pichanga *f* **1.** *Arg* (*vino*) wine (*not fully fermented*) **2.** *Bol* (*fácil*) **ser ~** to be a cinch *inf*
pichi *m* **1.**(*falda*) pinafore **2.** *CSur, inf* (*pipí*) pee, wee wee *childspeak*
pichicata *f Arg, inf* (*droga*) drugs *pl*
pichicatearse *vr Arg, inf* (*drogarse*) to take drugs
pichicatero, -a *m, f Arg, inf* (*adicto*) drug addict
pichicato, -a **I.** *adj AmC* stingy **II.** *m, f AmC* skinflint
pichichi *m* DEP top goal-scorer
pichín *m CSur, inf* (*pipí*) pee
pichincha *f* **1.** *Arg* (*ganga*) bargain **2.** *Chile* (*cantidad pequeña*) tiny bit; **con sólo una ~ de leche** with just a drop of milk
pichirre **I.** *adj Ven* (*tacaño*) stingy **II.** *mf Ven, inf* (*tacaño*) skinflint
pichón *m* young pigeon
pichón, -ona *m, f* (*querido*) darling
pichoso, -a *adj* **1.** *Col* (*de ojos llorosos*) watery-eyed **2.** *Ven* (*sucio*) dirty
pichula *f Chile, vulg* (*pene*) dick
pichulear *vt* **1.** *Chile* (*engañar*) to cheat **2.** *CSur* (*negociar*) to buy and sell (*on a small scale*)
picnic *m* picnic
pico *m* **1.**(*pájaro*) woodpecker **2.**(*del pájaro*) beak **3.** *inf* (*boca*) mouth, gob *Brit;* **¡cierra el ~!** shut your trap!; **~ de oro** the gift of the gab; **tener un buen ~** to be a smooth talker; **¡él de ~ todo lo que quieras!** he's always promising the earth!; **alguien se fue del ~** sb let the cat out of the bag; **¡ese se perderá por el ~!** his big mouth will be the end of him! **4.**(*herramienta*) pickaxe *Brit*, pickax *Am* **5.**(*montaña*) peak; **cortado a ~** sheer **6.**(*de jarra*) lip **7.**(*cantidad*) **llegar a las cuatro y ~** to arrive just after four o'clock; **tiene cuarenta y ~ de años** he/she is forty-something; **salir por un ~** to cost a lot
picor *m* (*en la piel*) itching; (*en la boca*) stinging, burning
picota *f* **1.**(*tortura*) pillory; **poner en la ~ a alguien** *fig* to pillory sb **2.** BOT cherry
picotada *f*, **picotazo** *m* (*de ave*) peck; (*de insecto*) sting; (*de serpiente*) bite; **pegar una**

~ (*ave*) to peck; (*insecto*) to sting; (*serpiente*) to bite; **arrancar a ~s** to peck off

picotear I. *vi* 1. (*comer*) to nibble 2. (*hablar*) to chatter II. *vt* to peck III. *vr* 1. (*personas*) to squabble 2. (*pájaros*) to peck

pictórico, -a *adj* pictorial; **técnica pictórica** painting technique

picudo, -a *adj* 1. (*puntiagudo*) pointed; (*anguloso*) angular 2. (*charlatán*) gossipy

pie *m* 1. (*extremidad, medida*) foot; **~s planos** flat feet; **~ de atleta** MED athlete's foot; **~ equino** clubfoot; **¿qué ~ calza Ud.?** what shoe size do you take?; **al ~ del árbol** at the foot of the tree; **al ~ de la carta** at the bottom of the letter; **a(l) ~ de (la) obra** on the spot; **a ~** on foot; **a ~ firme** steadfastly; **quedarse de ~** to remain standing; **estar de ~** to be standing; **ponerse de ~** to stand up; **caer de ~s** to land on one's feet; **ya sabemos de qué ~ cojea** *fig* now we know his weak spot; **tener los ~s en el suelo** *fig* to be realistic; **echar ~ a tierra** (*salir de coche*) to get out; (*salir de tren, autobús*) to get off; **se marchó del hospital por su propio ~** he left hospital under his own steam; **no hacer ~** (*en una piscina*) to be out of one's depth; **perder ~** (*en una piscina*) to get out of one's depth; **estoy cansada: no me tengo en ~** I am so tired I can barely stand; **con buen ~** *fig* on the right footing; **estar en ~ de guerra** to be on a war footing; **en ~ de igualdad** on an equal footing; **este informe está hecho con los ~s** *inf* this report is a dreadful piece of work; **ya tiene un ~ en el hoyo** *inf* he/she already has one foot in the grave; **este nació de ~** *inf* this one was born lucky; **no le des ~ para que se queje de ti** don't give him/her a chance to complain about you 2. TIPO **~ de imprenta** imprint; **~ de página** foot of the page 3. (*planta*) stem; (*tronco*) trunk; **~ de vid** vine stock 4. (*métrica*) foot 5. TEAT cue 6. (*trípode*) leg ► **~ de banco** *inf* stupid idea; **hoy no doy ~ con bola** I can't seem to do anything right today; **no tener ni ~s ni cabeza** to make no sense; **estar al ~ del cañón** to be ready for action; **~ de fuerza** *AmL* armed forces; **buscar tres ~s al gato** (*daño*) to ask for trouble; (*complicaciones*) to complicate matters; **seguir algo al ~ de la letra** to follow sth to the letter; **andarse con ~s de plomo** to tread very carefully; **poner ~s en polvorosa** to cut and run; **creer a ~(s) juntillas** to believe unquestioningly; **parar los ~s a alguien** *inf* to put sb in his/her place; **~s, ¿para qué os quiero?** time to leave!; **salir por ~s** *inf* to beat it; **de a ~** ordinary

piedad *f sin pl* 1. REL piety; (*compasión*) pity; **¡ten ~ de nosotros!** have pity on us! 2. ECON **monte de ~** pawnshop

piedra *f* 1. GEO, MED stone; **~ pómez** pumice stone; **~ preciosa** precious stone; **cartón ~** papier-mâché; **Edad de Piedra** Stone Age; **poner la primera ~** to lay the foundation stone; **lo saben hasta las ~s** the whole world knows; **lavado a la ~** stonewashed; **~ angular** *fig* cornerstone; **~ filosofal** *fig* philosopher's stone; **~ de toque** *fig* touchstone; **no te quejes que menos da una ~** *fig* don't complain, it's better than nothing; **no dejar ~ por mover** *fig* to leave no stone unturned; **no dejar ~ sobre ~** to raze to the ground; **cuando lo supimos nos quedamos de ~** we were absolutely stunned when we found out about it; **tirar la ~ y esconder la mano** to play the innocent; **tirarse ~s a su propio tejado** to foul one's own nest; **pasar a alguien por la ~** *inf* to lay sb 2. (*granizo*) hail 3. (*mechero*) flint

piel *f* 1. (*de persona*) skin; **estos niños son de la ~ del diablo** these children are little devils; **en esa empresa se dejó la ~** *inf* he/she worked himself/herself into the ground for that company 2. (*de animal*) skin, hide; (*con pelo*) fur; (*cuero*) leather; **un abrigo de ~es** a fur coat 3. (*de fruta*) skin ► **~ de gallina** goose-pimples *pl*; **se me puso la ~ de gallina oyendo su historia** hearing his story made my flesh crawl

pienso *m* (*ganado*) fodder; **~ completo** compound feed

pierna *f* (*extremidad*) leg; (*entre la rodilla y el pie*) lower leg; **~ ortopédica** artificial leg; **estirar las ~s** to stretch one's legs; **con las ~s cruzadas** with one's legs crossed; **dormir a ~ suelta** to be fast asleep; **en ~s** bare-legged

pieza *f* 1. (*pedazo*) piece; (*parte*) part; (*reproducción*) copy; **~ de artillería** artillery piece; **~ de recambio** spare part; **~ suelta** individual part; **un traje de dos ~s** a two-piece suit; **~ por ~** piece by piece; **vender a ~s** to sell by the piece 2. (*caza*) specimen; (*pesca*) catch 3. MÚS, TEAT piece 4. (*damas, ajedrez*) piece 5. *AmL* (*habitación*) room 6. (*moneda*) coin, piece 7. *inf* (*malicioso*) **¡menuda ~ está hecho ese!** what a little rascal he is! ► **quedarse de una ~** to be absolutely dumbfounded

pifia *f* 1. (*error*) blunder 2. *And* (*escarnio*) mockery

pigmentación *f* pigmentation

pigmento *m* pigment

pignorar *vt* to pawn

pija *f AmL, vulg* (*pene*) dick

pijada *f inf* (*tontería*) piece of nonsense; **¡esos son ~s!** what a load of nonsense!

pijama *m* pyjamas *pl*, pajamas *pl Am*

pije *m Chile, inf* (*fanfarrón*) toff *inf*

pijo *m vulg* (*pene*) dick; **¡y un ~!** like hell!

pijo, -a I. *adj inf* posh II. *m, f inf* posh youth; **niño ~** *pey* upper -class twit

pijotero, -a *adj* 1. *pey* (*fastidioso*) annoying 2. *AmL* (*tacaño*) stingy

pila *f* 1. (*recipiente*) basin; (*lavadero*) sink; (*fuente*) fountain; (*bautismal*) font; **nombre de ~** first name, Christian name 2. FÍS battery; **~ reversible** reversible battery; **ponerse las ~s** *inf* to get one's act together 3. (*montón*)

P

pile; **una ~ de libros** a pile of books **4.** ARQUIT pile **5.** INFOR **~ de discos** disk drive
pila-botón *f* <pilas-botón> (*batería*) watch battery
pilar *m* **1.** (*columna*) pillar **2.** (*apoyo*) prop **3.** (*en camino*) milestone
pilcha *f CSur, inf* (*prendas*) fine clothes *pl*
pilche *m And* wooden bowl
píldora *f* pill; **la ~** (**anticonceptiva**) the pill; **dorar la ~ a alguien** *inf* to sweeten the pill; **me tragué la ~** *fig* I fell for it
pileta *f* **1.** *Arg* (*de cocina*) kitchen sink **2.** *Arg* (*piscina*) swimming pool **3.** *RíoPl* (*abrevadero*) water trough **4.** *Arg* **tirarse a la ~** to go headlong into sth
pililа *f inf* (*pene de niño*) willy *Brit*
pililo, **-a** *m, f CSur, pey* tramp
pillaje *m* pillage
pillapilla *m inf* **jugar al ~** to play tag
pillar *vt* **1.** (*atropellar*) to knock down, to run over **2.** (*encontrar*) to find; (*en flagrante*) to catch; **me pillas de buen humor** you've caught me in a good mood; **la noche nos pilló en el monte** when night came we were still on the mountain; **eso no me pilla de sorpresa** that doesn't surprise me; **tu casa nos pilla de camino** your house is on our way; **Correos no nos pilla cerca** the Post Office isn't very near; **aquí te pillo, aquí te mato** *fig* to strike while the iron is hot **3.** (*entender*) to grasp **4.** (*robar*) to steal **5.** *Arg* (*orinar*) to piss
pillastre *m inf* rascal
pillín, **-ina** **I.** *adj inf* crafty **II.** *m, f inf* little rascal
pillo, **-a** **I.** *adj inf* crafty **II.** *m, f inf* rascal
pilmama *f Méx* nanny
pilme *m Chile* ZOOL blister beetle
pilón *m* **1.** (*lavadero*) basin; (*abrevadero*) drinking trough **2.** (*mortero*) mortar **3.** (*pesa*) weight **4.** ARQUIT pillar
piloncillo *m Méx* brown sugar
piloso, **-a** *adj* hairy
pilotar *vt* (*barco*) to steer; (*coche*) to drive; (*avión*) to fly
pilote *m* ARQUIT pile
pilotear *vt AmL* **1.** (*ayudar*) to guide **2.** (*negocio*) to run **3.** *Chile* (*explotar*) to exploit
piloto[1] **I.** *mf* **1.** NÁUT navigator; (*oficial*) first mate; (*práctico*) (harbour) pilot **2.** AVIAT pilot; **poner el ~ automático** to set the automatic pilot **3.** AUTO driver; **~ de carreras** racing driver **II.** *adj* (*de prueba*) test; (*de modelo*) show, model; **piso ~** show flat *Brit,* model apartment *Am;* **experiencia ~** test
piloto[2] *m* **1.** (*lámpara*) pilot light **2.** *Arg* (*impermeable*) raincoat
piltrafa *f* **1.** (*comida*) scrap **2.** (*persona*) wreck
pilucho, **-a** *adj Chile* naked
pimentero *m* **1.** BOT pepper plant **2.** (*vasija*) pepper pot
pimentón *m* paprika
pimienta *f* pepper; **~ en grano** peppercorns *pl*
pimiento *m* pepper; **~ encarnado** red pepper; **me importa un ~ lo que él diga** I couldn't care less what he says
pimpante *adj inf* **1.** (*elegante*) swish **2.** (*despreocupado*) unconcerned; **tan ~** as if nothing had happened
pimpón *m sin pl* DEP ping-pong
pinacate *m Méx* ZOOL black stinkbug
pinacoteca *f* art gallery
pináculo *m* pinnacle
pinar *m* pine grove
pincel *m* (paint)brush; (*de maquillaje*) make-up brush; **estar hecho un ~** to be stylishly dressed
pincelada *f* brushstroke; **dar las últimas ~s** *fig* to apply the finishing touches
pinchar **I.** *vi* **1.** (*rueda*) to puncture *Brit,* to have a flat (tire) *Am* **2.** (*fracasar*) to fail ►**ni ~ ni cortar** *inf* to not count for anything **II.** *vt* **1.** (*alfiler*) to prick **2.** (*estimular*) to prod; (*mortificar*) to wound **3.** (*inyección*) to give an injection; **tengo que ir al médico para que me pinche** I have to go the doctor's for an injection **4.** (*teléfono*) to tap **III.** *vr* **1.** (*alfiler*) to prick oneself **2.** (*rueda*) **se nos ha pinchado una rueda** one of our wheels has a puncture **3.** (*insulina*) to give oneself an injection **4.** *inf* (*drogarse*) to shoot up
pinchazo *m* **1.** (*espina*) prick; **me dieron unos ~s insoportables en el estómago** I had some really horrible shooting pains in the stomach **2.** (*neumático*) puncture, flat (tyre) *Brit,* flat (tire) *Am;* **tuvimos un ~ tras la curva** we had a puncture after the bend
pinche *mf* kitchen boy, cook's helper *Am*
pinchito *m* (*tapa*) snack; (*en un palillo*) *aperitif on a cocktail stick*
pincho *m* **1.** (*avispa*) sting; (*rosa*) thorn **2.** *v.* **pinchito**
pinciano, **-a** **I.** *adj* of/from Valladolid **II.** *m, f* native/inhabitant of Valladolid
pinedo *m AmC* pine grove
pinga *f Col, Méx, Perú, vulg* (*pene*) prick *vulg;* **¡de ~!** unreal!
pingajo *m inf* rag
pingo *m* **1.** *inf* (*harapo*) rag **2.** *pey* (*mujer*) slut **3.** *CSur* (*caballo*) horse ►**ir de ~** to go out on the town; **poner a alguien hecho un ~** to run sb down
pingonear *vi inf* to loaf about
ping-pong *m sin pl* ping-pong
pingüe *adj* (*negocio*) lucrative; **~s beneficios** fat profits
pingüino *m* penguin
pino *m* **1.** (*árbol, madera*) pine; **~ piñonero** stone pine **2.** DEP handstand ►**en el quinto ~** in the back of beyond
pinol(**e**) *m AmC* pinole, (*aromatic powder to mix in chocolate*)
pinta[1] *f* **1.** *t.* ZOOL (*mancha*) spot; (*gota*) drop; **a ~s** spotted **2.** *inf* (*aspecto*) appearance; **tener ~ de caro** to look expensive; **tener**

buena ~ (*dish*) to look tasty; (*persona*) to be attractive; **sacar por la** ~ to recognize

pinta² *f* (*medida*) pint

pintada *f* **1.** ZOOL guinea fowl **2.** (*pared*) (piece of) graffiti

pintado, **-a** *adj* (*animal*) spotted; **papel** ~ wallpaper; **eso viene como** ~ that is just what was needed; **el traje te sienta que ni** ~ *inf* the suit really suits you; **no lo puedo ver ni** ~ *inf* I can't stand even the sight of him

pintalabios *m inv* lipstick

pintar **I.** *vi* **1.** ARTE to paint **2.** (*bolígrafo*) to write **II.** *vt* **1.** (*pared*) to paint; (*con dibujos*) to decorate; ~ **de azul** to paint blue; **¡recién pintado!** wet paint! **2.** (*cuadro*) to paint; **¿qué pinta eso aquí?** *fig* what's that doing here?; **no** ~ **nada** *fig* (*persona*) to have no influence; (*asunto*) to be completely irrelevant **3.** (*describir*) to describe **III.** *vr* to do one's make-up

pinto, **-a** *adj* spotted

pintor(a) *m(f)* painter

pintoresco, **-a** *adj* picturesque, colourful *Brit,* colorful *Am*

pintura *f* **1.** (*arte*) painting; ~ **a la aguada** watercolour *Brit,* watercolor *Am;* ~ **al óleo** oil painting; ~ **rupestre** cave painting; **voy a clases de** ~ I go to painting classes **2.** (*cuadro*) painting; **no lo puedo ver ni en** ~ *inf* I can't stand him **3.** (*color*) paint; **caja de ~s** paintbox; **dar una capa de** ~ **a algo** to give sth a coat of paint

pinturero, **-a** **I.** *adj* fashion-conscious **II.** *m, f* dandy

pinza(s) *f(pl)* **1.** (*tenacilla*) tongs *pl;* TÉC pincers *pl* **2.** (*para la ropa*) (clothes) peg, (clothes) pin *Am* **3.** (*para depilar*) tweezers *pl* **4.** (*costura*) pleat **5.** (*de cangrejo*) claw

pinzón *m* finch

piña *f* **1.** (*pino*) pine cone **2.** (*fruta*) pineapple

piñón *m* **1.** (*pino*) pine nut; **estar a partir un** ~ **con alguien** *inf* to be thick as thieves **2.** TÉC pinion

pío *m* cheep; **no decir ni** ~ not to say a word; **¡~, ~, ~!** tweet, tweet!

pío, **-a** *adj* (*piadoso*) pious; (*bondadoso*) compassionate; **monte** ~ benefit fund; **obra pía** charitable deed

piocha *adj Méx, inf* (*magnífico*) great

piojo *m* louse; **estar como ~s en costura** *inf* to be packed in like sardines

piojoso, **-a** **I.** *adj* **1.** (*con piojos*) louse-infested; (*miserable*) lousy, crummy; (*sucio*) grotty **2.** *pey* (*mezquino*) mean **II.** *m, f pey* scoundrel

piola **I.** *adj Arg, inf* (*astuto*) clever **II.** *f AmS* (*cuerda*) cord

piolet *m* ice axe

piolín *m AmS* twine

pionero, **-a** *m, f* pioneer

pipa *f* **1.** (*fumador*) pipe; **preparar la** ~ to fill one's pipe; **fumar en** ~ to smoke a pipe **2.** (*tonel*) barrel **3.** (*de fruta*) pip, seed **4.** *CRi, inf* (*cabeza*) head **5.** *inf* (*pistola*) rod **6.** *pl* (*de girasol*) sunflower seed **7.** *inf* (*muy bien*) **lo pasamos** ~ we had a great time

pipe *m AmC* (*camarada*) buddy

pipeta *f* pipette

pipí *m inf* pee, wee wee *childspeak*

pipil *adj AmC* Mexican

pipiolo, **-a** *m, f* **1.** *irón* (*novato*) novice, greenhorn **2.** *Méx* (*niño*) kid

pipón, **-ona** **I.** *adj Ant, Arg, Ecua, inf* (*barrigón*) pot-bellied; (*harto*) stuffed **II.** *m, f PRico, inf* (*niño*) boy; (*niña*) girl

pique *m* **1.** (*rivalidad*) rivalry; **menudo** ~ **se traían entre ellos** they really hate each other **2.** *Arg, Par, Nic* (*camino*) trail **3.** (*hundirse*) **irse a** ~ (*barco*) to sink; (*plan*) to fail

piqueta *f* pickaxe *Brit,* pickax *Am*

piquete *m* **1.** (*huelga*) (strike) picket **2.** MIL squad

pira *f* (*hoguera*) pyre; ~ **funeraria** funeral pyre

pirado, **-a** **I.** *adj inf* crazy **II.** *m, f inf* nutcase

piragua *f* canoe

piragüismo *m* canoeing

piramidal *adj* pyramidal

pirámide *f* pyramid

piraña *f* piranha

pirarse *vr inf* to clear off; ~ **de la clase** to skip class

pirata **I.** *mf* pirate; ~ **aereo** hijacker; INFOR hacker **II.** *adj* pirate; **emisora** ~ pirate radio station

pirca *f AmC* stone wall

pirco *m Chile* GASTR succotash

pirenaico, **-a** *adj* Pyrenean; **el Aneto es el pico** ~ **más elevado** Aneto is the highest mountain in the Pyrenees

Pirineos *mpl* Pyrenees

piripi *adj inf* tipsy

pirómano, **-a** *m, f* pyromaniac

piropear *vt inf* to make flirtatious comments to

piropo *m* **1.** *inf* (*lisonja*) flirtatious comment; **echar ~s** to make flirtatious comments **2.** (*granate*) garnet

pirotecnia *f sin pl* pyrotechnics

pirrarse *vr inf* **~se por alguien** to be crazy about sb

pirueta *f* pirouette

piruja *f Méx, inf* hooker

piruleta *f,* **pirulí** *m* <pirulís> lollipop

pis *m inf* piss

pisa *f* **1.** (*acción de pisar*) treading **2.** *inf* (*paliza*) beating

pisada *f* **1.** (*acción*) footstep **2.** (*huella*) footprint; **seguir las ~s de alguien** *fig* to follow in sb's footsteps **3.** (*patada*) stamp of the foot

pisapapeles *m inv* paperweight

pisar *vt* **1.** (*poner el pie*) to tread; **¡no pises las flores!** don't tread on the flowers!; **me han pisado en el bus** sb trod on my foot on the bus; **ir pisando huevos** *fig* to tread carefully; ~ **los talones a alguien** *fig* to follow on sb's heels; ~ **fuerte** *fig* to make a big impact **2.** (*entrar*) to enter **3.** (*uvas, aceitunas*) to tread; (*tierra*) to tread down **4.** (*humillar*) to walk all over **5.** *inf* (*planes*) to pre-empt; **con su proyecto me pisan el terreno** their plan has beaten me to it; **me han pisado el tema** they have stolen my topic

piscicultura *f* fish farming

piscina *f* swimming pool; ~ **cubierta** indoor swimming pool

Piscis *m inv* Pisces

pisco *m* **1.** (*aguardiente*) *strong Peruvian liquor;* ~ **sour** *cocktail made with pisco, lemon and sugar* **2.** *Col, Ven* (*pavo*) turkey **3.** *Col, pey* (*hombre*) bloke *Brit,* guy

piscolabis *m inv, inf* snack

piso *m* **1.** (*pavimento*) floor; (*calle*) surface **2.** (*planta*) floor, storey *Brit,* story *Am;* **de dos ~s** with two floors **3.** (*vivienda*) flat *Brit,* apartment *Am* **4.** (*zapato*) sole **5.** MIN layer (*of workings*)

pisotear *vt* to trample; *fig* to walk all over

pisotón *m* stamp; **dar un ~ a alguien** to tread on sb's foot

pispear *vt Arg* (*birlar*) to nick *Brit,* to swipe

pista *f* **1.** (*huella*) trail; (*indicio*) clue; **estar sobre la buena** ~ to be on the right lines; **seguir la ~ a alguien** to follow sb's trail **2.** (*de circo*) ring; (*para atletismo, coches*) track; (*de tenis*) court; (*de baile*) floor; ~ **de aterrizaje** runway; ~ **de esquí** ski slope; ~ **de hielo** ice rink **3.** (*camino*) trail **4.** INFOR track

pistache *m* **1.** GASTR (*helado*) pistachio ice cream; (*dulce*) pistachio sweet **2.** *Méx* (*pistacho*) pistachio

pistacho *m* pistachio

pistero *m* (*taza*) cup with spout

pistilo *m* pistil

pisto *m* **1.** (*caldo*) chicken broth **2.** (*fritada*) vegetable stew (*made with tomato, onion, pepper and courgette*) **3.** (*mezcla*) hotchpotch *Brit,* hodgepodge *Am* **4.** *AmC* (*dinero*) dough ►darse ~ to show off

pistola *f* **1.** (*arma*) pistol **2.** (*del pintor*) spray gun

pistolera *f* **1.** (*funda*) holster **2.** *pl inf* ANAT *fat accumulated on hips*

pistolero *m* gunman

pistoletazo *m* pistol shot; ~ **de salida** *fig: starting signal*

pistón *m* **1.** (*émbolo*) piston **2.** (*de arma*) percussion cap **3.** MÚS key

pistonudo, -a *adj inf* great

pita *f* **1.** BOT agave, century plant **2.** *inf* (*gallina*) hen; **¡~, ~, ~!** tweet, tweet!, cluck! cluck!

pitada *f Arg, inf* (*calada*) puff; **¿me das una ~?** will you let me have a puff?

pitanza *f* **1.** (*ración*) daily ration; *inf* (*alimentos*) grub **2.** (*precio*) price

pitar **I.** *vt, vi* **1.** (*claxon*) to blow; **me pitan los oídos** my ears are buzzing **2.** (*pagar*) to pay **3.** *AmS* (*fumar*) to smoke **4.** *Chile* (*engañar*) to cheat **II.** *vi* **1.** *inf* (*funcionar*) to work **2.** *inf* (*deprisa*) **salir pitando** to rush off **3.** *inf* (*ser suficiente*) **¡con la mitad vas que pitas!** half of it should be more than enough!

pitido *m* whistle

pitillera *f* (*estuche*) cigarette case

pitillo *m* cigarette

pitiminí *m* BOT miniature rose; (*persona*) finicky person

pitiyanqui *m PRico* Yankee-lover

pito *m* **1.** (*silbato*) whistle; (*claxon*) horn; **tocar ~s** to click one's fingers; **entre ~s y flautas** *inf* what with one thing and another; **por ~s o por flautas** *inf* for one reason or another; **tomar a alguien por el ~ del sereno** *inf* to take no notice of sb; **no me importa un** ~ *inf* I don't give a damn about it; **no valer un** ~ *inf* to be completely worthless **2.** (*canica*) marble; **jugar a los ~s** to play marbles **3.** (*cigarro*) cigarette **4.** (*de vasija*) spout **5.** (*abucheo*) booing **6.** *inf* (*pene*) dick

pito, -a *adj inf* smart; **iba todo** ~ he looked really smart

pitón *m* **1.** ZOOL python **2.** (*cuerno*) budding horn; (*de toro*) horn **3.** (*pitorro*) spout

pitonisa *f* fortune teller

pitopausia *f inf* midlife crisis in males

pitorrearse *vr inf* to make fun

pitorreo *m inf* joking; **¡esto es un ~!** this is a joke!

pitorro *m* spout

pituco, -a **I.** *adj CSur* **1.** (*cursi*) affected, snooty **2.** (*muy acicalado*) overdressed **3.** (*nuevo rico*) nouveau riche **II.** *m, f CSur* **1.** (*cursi*) snob, toff *Brit* **2.** (*nuevo rico*) nouveau riche

pitufo *m inf* titch *Brit,* shrimp *Am*

pituita *f* mucus

pituitario, -a *adj* pituitary; **glándula pituitaria** pituitary gland

pivote *m* TÉC pivot

píxel *m* INFOR pixel

piyama *m AmL* pyjamas *pl,* pajamas *pl Am*

pizarra *f* **1.** (*roca*) slate **2.** (*encerado*) blackboard

pizarrín *m* slate pencil

pizarrón *m AmL* (*encerado*) blackboard

pizca *f* **1.** *inf* (*poco*) pinch, little bit; **una ~ de sal** a pinch of salt; **no tienes ni ~ de vergüenza** you have no shame whatsoever **2.** *Méx* (*cosecha*) harvest

pizcar <c→qu> *vt Méx* to pick

pizco *m* **1.** (*poco*) little bit **2.** *inf* (*pellizco*) pinch

pizpireta *adj* (*mujer*) vivacious

pizza *f* pizza

placa *f* **1.** (*lámina, plancha*) sheet; FOTO plate; INFOR board; ~ **base** INFOR motherboard; ~ **giratoria** FERRO turntable **2.** (*cartel*) plaque; ~ **conmemorativa** commemorative plaque **3.** AUTO number plate *Brit,* license plate *Am* **4.** MED ~ **dental** (dental) plaque

placar *m,* **placard** *m Arg, Urug* (*armario empotrado*) built-in cupboard, built-in closet *Am*

placebo *m* MED placebo
pláceme *m* congratulations *pl;* **dar el ~ a alguien** to congratulate sb
placenta *f* placenta
placentero, -a *adj* pleasant
placentino, -a I. *adj* of/from Plasencia II. *m, f* native/inhabitant of Plasencia
placer I. *m* 1.(*goce*) pleasure; **con sumo ~** with great pleasure; **casa de ~** brothel 2.(*arena*) sandbank II. *irr como crecer vi* to please; **¡haré lo que me plazca!** I will do as I please!
placero, -a *m, f AmL* (*vendedor*) street trader
plácet *m form* approval; **dar el ~ a un embajador** to accept an ambassador's credentials
placidez *f* calmness
plácido, -a *adj* calm
plaga *f* 1.AGR plague 2.(*calamidades*) disaster; (*lacra*) blight 3.(*abundancia*) glut; **este año hemos tenido una ~ de cerezas** this year we've had a glut of cherries
plagado, -a *adj* infested; **el texto estaba ~ de faltas** the text was full of mistakes; **la casa está plagada de cucarachas** the house is infested with cockroaches
plagar <g→gu> I. *vt* to infest; **~ de algo** to fill with sth; **~on la ciudad de carteles** they covered the city with posters II. *vr:* **~se** to become infested; **el pueblo se plagó de ratas** the village became infested with rats
plagiar *vt* 1.(*copiar*) to plagiarize 2.*AmL* (*secuestrar*) to kidnap
plagio *m* 1.(*copia*) plagiarism 2.*AmL* (*secuestro*) kidnapping
plan *m* 1.(*proyecto*) plan; **~ de emergencia** emergency plan; **si no tienes ~ para esta noche paso a buscarte** if you don't have anything planned for tonight I'll come round and fetch you 2.*inf* (*ligue*) date 3.*inf* (*actitud*) **esto no es ~** it's just not on; **en ~ de...** as ...; **está en un ~ que no lo soporto** I can't stand him when he behaves like this
plana *f* 1.(*folio*) page; **a toda ~** full-page; **un artículo en primera ~** a front-page article 2.(*caligrafía*) writing exercise 3.(*planicie*) plain 4.(*en una organización*) **la ~ mayor del partido** the party leadership
plancha *f* 1.(*lámina*) sheet; TIPO plate 2.(*para ropa*) iron 3.NÁUT gangway 4.*inf* (*desacierto*) blunder; **hacer** [*o* **tirarse**] **una ~** to put one's foot in it 5.GASTR grill; **a la ~** grilled 6.DEP (*gimnasia*) press-up
planchado *m* (*acción, ropa*) ironing
planchado, -a *adj* 1.*AmC* (*acicalado*) neat, smart *Brit* 2.(*anonadado*) flattened; **lo dejé ~** *inf* I left him speechless
planchar *vt* to iron
plancton *m sin pl* BIO plankton
planeador *m* AVIAT glider
planear I. *vi* (*ave*) to hover; AVIAT to glide II. *vt* to plan
planeta *m* planet
planetario *m* planetarium
planetario, -a *adj* planetary
planicie *f* plain
planificación *f* planning; **~ regional** local planning
planificar <c→qu> *vt* to plan
planilla *f* 1.ECON (*personal*) payroll 2.(*impreso*) form; **~ de cálculo** INFOR spreadsheet 3.*AmL* (*nómina*) payroll
planisferio *m* planisphere
plano *m* 1.MAT plane; **~ inclinado** inclined plane 2.(*mapa*) map; **levantar un ~** to draw a map 3.CINE **primer ~** close-up; **en primer ~** (*delante*) in the foreground 4.(*totalmente*) **de ~** directly; (*negar*) flatly; **aceptó de ~ nuestra propuesta** she accepted our suggestion straight away
plano, -a *adj* flat; **superficie plana** flat surface
planta *f* 1.BOT plant; **~ anual** annual; **~ de interior** houseplant; **~ medicinal** medicinal plant; **~ trepadora** climbing plant 2.(*pie*) sole 3.(*fábrica*) plant; **~ de abastecimientos de agua** waterworks; **~ de energía atómica/hidráulica** atomic/hydraulic power station; **~ incineradora** incineration plant; **~ de reciclaje de basuras** recycling plant; **~ siderúrgica** steel plant 4.(*piso*) floor, storey *Brit,* story *Am;* **~ alta** top floor; **~ baja** ground floor *Brit,* first floor *Am* 5.ARQUIT ground plan; (*proyecto*) building plan 6.(*aspecto*) **tener buena ~** to be good-looking
plantación *f* 1.(*acción*) planting 2.(*finca, terreno*) plantation
plantado, -a *adj inf* **bien ~** (*atractivo*) good-looking
plantar I. *vt* 1.(*bulbo*) to plant; **han plantado el monte** they have planted trees on the hillside 2.(*clavar*) to stick in; **~ una tienda de campaña** to pitch a tent 3.*inf* (*golpe*) to land; **~ un tortazo a alguien** to slap sb 4.*inf* (*cita*) to stand up; **desapareció y me dejó plantado** he/she disappeared and left me standing; **dejó plantada a su novia** he stood his girlfriend up; **lo ~on en la calle** they chucked him out 5.(*abandonar*) to abandon II. *vr:* **~se** 1.(*resistirse*) **~se ante algo** to stand firm in the face of sth 2.(*asno, perro*) to refuse to move 3.(*aparecer*) to get to; **se ~on en mi casa en un periquete** they arrived at my house in no time 4.(*negarse*) to refuse 5.(*en los naipes*) to stick; **aquí me planto** I'm sticking
planteamiento *m* 1.(*enfoque*) approach; **tu ~ de la cuestión no me parece el adecuado** your approach to the question strikes me as incorrect 2.MAT solution
plantear I. *vt* 1.(*asunto, problema*) to approach; **este problema está mal planteado** this problem has been incorrectly formulated 2.(*causar*) to cause; (*discusión*) to provoke 3.(*proponer*) to put forward, to pose II. *vr* 1.(*reflexionar*) to think about 2.(*cuestión*) to ask oneself; **ahora me planteo la pregunta si...** now I ask myself whether ...

P

plantel *m* **1.** (*conjunto*) group **2.** (*vivero*) nursery **3.** *Arg* (*plantilla*) staff
planteo *m Arg* demand
plantificar <c→qu> **I.** *vt* (*golpe*) to land; (*beso*) to plant **II.** *vr* to get there; **se plantificó allí al poco tiempo** he got there almost straight away
plantilla *f* **1.** (*empleados*) staff; ~ **de profesores** teaching staff **2.** (*de zapato*) insole **3.** (*zapatero*) sole **4.** (*patrón*) pattern **5.** (*equipo*) squad
plantío *m* **1.** (*acción de plantar*) planting **2.** (*terreno*) plot, patch **3.** (*lo plantado*) field of crops
plantón *m* **1.** (*planta*) seedling; (*rama*) cutting **2.** *inf* (*espera*) long wait; **dar un ~ a alguien** to stand sb up; **y ahora estoy de ~** I've been left waiting around
plañir <*3. pret:* plañó> *vi* to wail
plaqué *m* (*de oro*) gold-plating; (*de plata*) silver-plating
plaqueta *f* MED platelet
plasma *m* plasma
plasmar *vt* **1.** (*moldear*) to mould *Brit,* to mold *Am* **2.** (*representar*) to represent
plasta[1] *mf pey* bore, drag
plasta[2] *f* **1.** (*mal hecha*) botch **2.** (*blanda*) soft mass
plástica *f* plastic arts *pl;* (*escultura*) sculpture
plasticidad *f* plasticity; *fig* expressiveness
plástico *m* plastic; (*para envolver*) cling film *Brit,* plastic wrap *Am*
plástico, **-a** *adj* **1.** (*materia*) plastic **2.** (*expresivo*) expressive; **las artes plásticas** the plastic arts
plastificar <c→qu> *vt* to laminate
plastilina® *f* plasticene *Brit,* modelling clay *Brit,* modeling clay *Am*
plata *f* **1.** (*metal*) silver; ~ **labrada** silverwork; ~ **de ley** sterling silver; **bodas de ~** silver anniversary; (*de matrimonio*) silver wedding anniversary **2.** (*moneda*) silver coins *pl* **3.** *AmL* (*dinero*) money; **¡adiós mi ~!** *CSur, inf* what a disaster! ►**hablar en ~** to talk bluntly
plataforma *f* **1.** (*estrado*) platform **2.** (*tranvía*) platform; (*vagón*) flatbed truck; ~ **giratoria** turntable; ~ **petrolífera** oil rig; ~ **de lanzamiento** launch pad *Am* **3.** POL platform **4.** GEO ~ **continental** continental shelf
platal *m AmL* (*dineral*) fortune
plátano *m* **1.** (*árbol frondoso*) plane tree **2.** (*árbol frutal tropical*) banana tree; (*fruta*) banana; ~ **guineo** plantain
platea *f* stalls *pl Brit,* orchestra *Am*
plateado, **-a** *adj* (*con plata*) silver-plated; (*color*) silver
platear *vt* to silver-plate
platense *adj* **1.** (*de La Plata*) of/from La Plata **2.** (*de Río de La Plata*) native/inhabitant of the River Plate region
platería *f* **1.** (*tienda*) jeweller's *Brit,* jeweler's *Am* **2.** (*taller*) silversmith's **3.** (*vajilla*) silverware
platero, **-a** *m, f* silversmith; (*joyero*) jeweller *Brit,* jeweler *Am*
plática *f* **1.** (*conversación*) chat; **estar de ~** to be chatting **2.** (*sermón*) sermon
platicar <c→qu> *vi inf* to chat
platija *f* flounder
platillo *m* **1.** (*de una taza*) saucer **2.** (*de una balanza*) pan **3.** MÚS cymbal
platina *f* **1.** (*de microscopio*) slide **2.** TYPO platen **3.** (*de tocadiscos, casete*) deck
platino *m* **1.** QUÍM platinum **2.** *pl* AUTO contact points *pl*
plato *m* **1.** (*vajilla*) plate; (*para taza*) saucer; **tiro al ~** DEP clay pigeon shooting; **ahora tengo que pagar los ~s rotos** *fig* now I've got to pay the consequences; **tener cara de no haber roto un ~ en la vida** *inf* to look as if butter wouldn't melt in one's mouth; **comer en un mismo ~** *fig* to be bosom pals **2.** (*comida*) dish; ~ **combinado** *dish usually consisting of meat or fish and vegetables;* ~ **fuerte** main dish; *fig* main part; **hoy hay ~ único** today there is only one dish; **nos sirvieron tres ~s y postre** we were served three courses and dessert **3.** (*de balanza*) pan
plató *m* CINE (film) set
platón *m AmL* serving dish
platónico, **-a** *adj* platonic
platudo, **-a** *adj AmL* well-heeled
plausible *adj* **1.** (*loable*) laudable **2.** (*admisible*) acceptable
playa *f* **1.** (*mar*) beach; ~ **naturista** nudists' beach **2.** *AmL* (*espacio*) open space; ~ **de estacionamiento** car park, parking lot *Am*
play-back *m* <play-backs> playback; **cantar en ~** to mime a song
play-boy *m* <play-boys> playboy
playera *f Guat, Méx* (*camiseta*) T-shirt
playeras *fpl* (*zapatillas*) gym shoes *pl*
playo, **-a** *adj CSur* shallow; **plato ~** dinner plate
plaza *f* **1.** (*espacio*) square; (*de mercado*) marketplace; (*de toros*) bullring; ~ **de abastos** (central) food market; **fuimos a la ~ a comprar** we went to the market to do the shopping **2.** (*asiento*) seat; (*de garage, parking*) space **3.** (*empleo*) post **4.** (*en instituciones, viajes*) place
plazo *m* **1.** (*vencimiento*) period; ~ **de entrega** delivery date; ~ **de preaviso** notice period; **a corto/largo ~** in the short/long term; **fuera del ~** after the closing date; **en el ~ de un mes** within a month; **en el banco tengo dos millones a ~ fijo** I have two million in the bank in a fixed-term deposit; **¿cúando vence el ~ para la presentación de solicitudes?** when is the deadline for submitting applications? **2.** (*cantidad*) instalment *Brit,* installment *Am;* **a ~s** by instalments
plazoleta *f diminutivo de* **plaza**
pleamar *f* high tide
plebe *f sin pl* **1.** HIST masses *pl* **2.** *pey* (*chusma*)

rabble
plebeyo, **-a** I. *adj* 1. *t.* HIST plebeian 2. (*sin linaje*) common 3. (*inculto*) uneducated; (*grosero*) uncouth II. *m, f* 1. *t.* HIST plebeian 2. (*sin linaje*) commoner 3. (*grosero*) lout
plebiscito *m* plebiscite
plegable *adj* (*papel*) foldable; (*mueble*) folding; **silla** ~ folding chair
plegar *irr como fregar* I. *vt* (*doblar*) to fold; (*muebles*) to fold away II. *vr:* ~**se** to yield
plegaria *f* prayer
pleitear *vi* JUR to bring a lawsuit, to sue
pleito *m* 1. JUR lawsuit 2. (*disputa*) dispute
plenario, **-a** *adj* plenary; **sesión plenaria** plenary session
plenipotenciario, **-a** *adj, m, f* plenipotentiary
plenitud *f* 1. (*totalidad*) fullness; **sensación de** ~ sensation of fullness 2. (*apogeo*) height; **en la** ~ **de sus facultades físicas** at the height of his/her physical powers
pleno *m* plenary session; **el ayuntamiento en** ~ **aprobó la propuesta** the local council approved the proposal
pleno, **-a** *adj* full; ~ **empleo** full employment; **en el** ~ **uso de sus facultades mentales** in full command of his/her faculties; **le robaron a plena luz del día** they robbed him in broad daylight; **en** ~ **verano** at the height of summer
pletórico, **-a** *adj* full; ~ **de salud** bursting with health
pleura *f* pleura
pleuresía *f* MED pleurisy
plexiglás® *m sin pl* Perspex® *Brit,* Plexiglass® *Am*
plica *f* 1. sealed envelope 2. MÚS note stem
pliego *m* 1. (*hoja*) sheet 2. (*documento*) document; ~ **de cargos** list of charges; ~ **de condiciones** specifications *pl* 3. (*libro*) section
pliegue *m t.* GEO (*doblez*) fold
plinto *m* 1. ARQUIT plinth 2. DEP vaulting horse
plisar *vt* to pleat
plomada *f* (*albañilería*) plumb line; **echar la** ~ to drop the plumb line
plomazo *m* 1. *inf* (*pesado*) drag 2. (*perdigón*) shot
plomería *f Arg* (*fontanería*) plumber's
plomero *m Arg* (*técnico fontanero*) plumber
plomizo, **-a** *adj* 1. (*color*) lead-coloured *Brit,* lead-colored *Am* 2. (*material*) lead(en)
plomo *m* 1. (*metal*) lead; **gasolina sin** ~ unleaded petrol *Brit,* unleaded gas *Am;* **caer a** ~ to fall heavily 2. *inf* (*pesado*) **ser un** ~ to be a real drag 3. (*plomada*) plumb line 4. (*bala*) bullet 5. *pl* ELEC fuse
pluma *f* 1. (*ave*) feather; **cambiar la** ~ to moult *Brit,* to molt *Am* 2. (*escribir*) pen; ~ **estilográfica** fountain pen 3. (*escritor*) writer 4. (*estilo*) (writing) style ►**vestirse de** ~**s ajenas** to dress in borrowed finery; **quedarse cacareando y sin** ~**s** to remain defiant in defeat
plumada *f* stroke of the pen
plumaje *m* 1. (*ave*) plumage 2. (*adorno*) plume
plumario, **-a** *m, f AmC, Méx, pey* (*periodista*) hack
plumazo *m* (*trazo*) stroke of the pen; **suprimieron de un** ~ **las subvenciones** they abolished the subsidies at a stroke
plúmbeo, **-a** *adj* heavy; *fig* tedious
plumear *vt AmC* (*escribir*) to write
plumero *m* 1. (*para limpiar*) feather duster 2. (*plumier: estuche*) pencil case; (*caja*) pencil box 3. (*adorno*) plume ►**vérsele el** ~ **a alguien** to be obvious what sb is up to
plumier *m* (*estuche*) pencil case; (*caja*) pencil box
plumilla *f* nib
plumón *m* 1. (*ave*) down 2. (*cama*) feather bed
plural I. *adj* plural; **número** ~ plural II. *m* plural; ~ **mayestático** royal 'we'
pluralidad *f* plurality; **a** ~ **de votos** by majority vote
pluralizar <z→c> *vt* 1. (*generalizar*) to generalize; **tú cuenta lo que te pasó a ti y no pluralices** say what happened to you, but don't assume you're speaking for the rest of us 2. LING to form the plural
pluriempleo *m situation where various positions are filled by the same person*
plurifamiliar *adj* for several families
pluripartidismo *m* multi-party system
plus *m* 1. (*gratificación*) bonus; **de** ~ extra; ~ **de peligrosidad** danger money; ~ **por trabajar en días festivos** bonus for working on public holidays 2. (*ventaja*) advantage
pluscuamperfecto *m* LING pluperfect
plusmarquista *mf* record holder; **ser el** ~ **mundial de lanzamiento de jabalina** to hold the world record for javelin-throwing
plusvalía *f sin pl* ECON appreciation
plutonio *m* plutonium
pluvial *adj* rain
pluviosidad *f* rainfall
p.m. *abr de* **post meridiem** pm
P.M. *f abr de* **policía militar** MP
PN *m abr de* **peso neto** net weight
PNB *m abr de* **producto nacional bruto** GNP
PNN *m abr de* **producto nacional neto** NNP
PNV *m abr de* **Partido Nacionalista Vasco** *Basque Nationalist Party*
p.o. *abr de* **por orden** by order
población *f* 1. *t.* BIO (*habitantes*) population; ~ **activa** ECON working population 2. (*localidad: ciudad*) city; (*ciudad pequeña*) town; (*pueblo*) village
poblado *m* (*pueblo*) village; (*colonia*) settlement
poblado, **-a** *adj* 1. (*habitado*) inhabitated; (*con árboles*) wooded 2. (*cejas*) bushy; (*barba*) thick
poblador(**a**) *m(f)* (*habitante*) inhabitant; (*colono*) settler

P

poblar <o→ue> **I.** *vi, vt* **1.** (*colonizar*) to colonize **2.** (*de plantas*) to plant; (*de peces*) to stock; **han poblado el monte de pinos** they have planted the hillside with pines **3.** (*habitar*) to inhabit; **distintas especies pueblan el fondo del mar** various species inhabit the sea bed **II.** *vr:* **~se** to fill; **la costa se pobló rápidamente** the coast quickly filled with people

pobre **I.** *adj* **1.** (*no rico*) poor; **~ de algo** poor in sth; **es una lengua ~ de expresiones** it is a language with few expressions **2.** (*desgraciado*) unfortunate **3.** (*humilde*) humble **4.** (*exclamaciones*) **¡~ de ti si dices mentiras!** you'll be sorry if you lie! **II.** *mf* poor person; (*mendigo*) beggar; **los pobres** the poor *pl*

pobremente *adv* poorly

pobreza *f* **1.** (*necesidad*) poverty **2.** (*pusilanimidad*) cowardliness

pochismo *m Méx* **1.** *inf* (*angloamericanismo*) *anglicism introduced into Spanish* **2.** *inf* (*característica de los pochos*) *characteristic of Americanized Mexicans*

pocho, **-a** **I.** *m, f Méx, pey* Americanized Mexican **II.** *adj* **1.** (*fruta*) overripe **2.** (*persona*) off-colour *Brit,* off-color *Am*

pochoclo *m Arg* popcorn

pocilga *f t. fig* pigsty

pócima *f,* **poción** *f* potion; *pey* (*brebaje*) brew; **la ~ mágica** the magic potion

poco **I.** *m* **1.** (*cantidad*) **un ~ de azúcar** a little sugar; **acepta el ~ de dinero que te puedo dar** accept what little money I can give you; **espera un ~** wait a little **2.** *pl* few; **~s de los presentes lo sabían** few of those present knew it; **los ~s que vinieron...** the few who came ...; **es un envidioso como hay ~s** there are few people who are as jealous as him **II.** *adv* little; **escribir ~** to write little; **es ~ simpático** he is not very friendly; **nos da ~ más o menos lo mismo** it really doesn't make much difference to us; **~ a ~** bit by bit, little by little; **~ a ~ dejamos de creerle** we gradually stopped believing him; **a ~ de llegar...** shortly after arriving ...; **~ después** shortly afterwards; **dentro de ~** soon; **desde hace ~** since recently; **hace ~** recently, not long ago; **a/con/por ~ que se esfuerce lo conseguirá** with a little bit of effort he/she will get it; **por ~ me estrello** I very nearly crashed; **tener en ~ a alguien** to have a low opinion of sb; **y por si fuera ~...** and as if that wasn't enough ...

poco, **-a** <poquísimo> *adj* little; **~s** few; **aquí hay poca comida para dos personas** there's not much food here for two people; **hay pocas colecciones mejores que ésta** there are few collections better than this one; **tiene pocas probabilidades de aprobar** he has little chance of passing

podadera *f* secateurs *pl,* pruning shears *pl*

podar *vt* to prune

podenco *m breed of Spanish hunting dog*

poder **I.** *irr vi* to be able to; **puedo** I can; **puedes** you can; **no ~ más de hambre** to be starving; **yo a ti te puedo** *inf* I'm stronger than you; **no ~ con el alma** to be completely exhausted; **no puedes cogerlo sin permiso** you can't take it without permission; **no podemos abandonarlo** we can't abandon him; **¡bien pod(r)ías habérmelo dicho!** you could have told me!; **bien puede haber aquí un millón de abejas** there could easily be a million bees here; **no puedo verlo todo el día sin hacer nada** I can't stand seeing him do nothing all day long; **no puedo con mi madre** I can't cope with my mother; **la sala se llenó a más no ~** the room filled to bursting point; **de ~ ser, no dudes que lo hará** if it is at all possible, have no doubt that he/she will do it; **no pude menos que preguntarle qué hacía por allí** I couldn't help asking him/her what he/she was doing there; **lo menos que puedes hacer es llamar si vas a llegar tarde** the least you can do is phone if you're going to be late; **no puede ser** it is impossible; **a ~ ser** if possible **II.** *irr vimpers* **puede (ser) que después vuelva** maybe he/she will come back afterwards, he/she may come back afterwards; **¡puede!** maybe!; **¿se puede?** may I (come in)? **III.** *m* **1.** *t.* POL (*autoridad*) power; **~ absoluto** absolute power; **~ ejecutivo** executive power; **~ judicial** judicial power; **~ legislativo** legislative power; **los ~es fácticos** the powers that be; **los ~es públicos** the public authorities; **la división de ~es** the separation of powers; **el partido en el ~** the party in power; **subir al ~** to achieve power; **los documentos están en ~ del juez** the documents are in the hands of the judge; **haré todo lo que está en mi ~** I will do everything in my power **2.** (*autorización*) authority; **~ notarial** power of attorney; **por ~es** by proxy; **~ de decisión** decision-making power **3.** (*fuerza*) strength; **~ adquisitivo** ECON buying [*o* purchasing] power

poderío *m* **1.** (*autoridad*) power **2.** (*riqueza*) wealth **3.** (*fuerza*) strength

poderoso, **-a** *adj* **1.** (*influyente*) powerful **2.** (*rico*) wealthy **3.** (*eficaz*) effective

podio *m* podium

podólogo, **-a** *m, f* podiatrist, chiropodist

podredumbre *f* **1.** (*putrefacción*) decay **2.** (*depravación*) corruption

podrido, **-a** *adj* **1.** (*descompuesto*) *t. fig* rotten; **estar ~ de dinero** *inf,* **estar ~ en plata** *Arg, inf* to be filthy rich **2.** *Arg, inf* (*aburrido*) fed up

podrir *irr vt, vr v.* **pudrir**

poema *m* poem; **~ épico** epic poem; **~ en prosa** prose poem; **¡fue todo un ~!** (*gracioso*) it was really funny!; **estar hecho un ~** to be a real sight

poesía *f* **1.** (*género*) poetry **2.** (*poema*) poem; **libro de ~(s)** poetry book

poeta, **-isa** *m, f* poet *m(f),* poetess *f*

poética *f* poetics

poético, **-a** *adj t. fig* poetic; **arte poética** poetics; **licencia poética** poetic licence *Brit* [*o* license *Am*]
poetisa *f v.* **poeta**
póker *m sin pl* poker; **poner cara de** ~ to look poker-faced
polaco, **-a I.** *adj* Polish **II.** *m, f* (*persona*) Pole; (*idioma*) Polish
polaina *f* gaiter; (*pantalón*) leggings *pl*
polar *adj* polar; **Círculo Polar Ártico/Antártico** Arctic/Antarctic Circle; **la estrella** ~ Polaris, Pole Star
polaridad *f* polarity
polarización *f* polarization
polarizar <z→c> *vt* **1.** FÍS to polarize **2.** *fig* (*opinión*) to polarize; (*atención*) to focus; **el espectáculo polarizó la atención de los visitantes** the spectators were completely absorbed by the show
polca *f* MÚS polka
polea *f* pulley; (*roldana*) pulley wheel; **sistema de ~s** pulley system
polémica *f* controversy, polemic
polémico, **-a** *adj* polemical
polemizar <z→c> *vi* to argue; ~ **con alguien** to have an argument with sb
polen *m* pollen; **tengo alergia al** ~ I have hay fever
polera *f* **1.** *Chile* (*camiseta*) t-shirt **2.** *Arg* (*de cuello alto*) polo neck *Brit*, turtleneck *Am*
poli *f inf abr de* **policía** cops *pl*
poliamida *f* polyamide; (*textil*) nylon
policía[1] *f* police; **agente de** ~ police officer; **coche de** ~ police car; **comisaría de** ~ police station; **jefatura de** ~ police headquarters
policía[2] *mf* policeman *m*, policewoman *f*; **perro** ~ police dog
policiaco, **-a** *adj*, **policíaco**, **-a** *adj* police; **estado** ~ police state; **película/novela policíaca** detective film/novel
policial *adj v.* **policíaco**
policlínica *f*, **policlínico** *m* hospital
polideportivo *m* sports centre *Brit* [*o* center *Am*]
poliéster *m* polyester
polietileno *m* polythene *Brit*, polyethylene *Am*
polifacético, **-a** *adj* multi-faceted; (*persona*) many-sided
poligamia *f sin pl* polygamy
polígamo, **-a** *adj* polygamous
políglota I. *adj* polyglot **II.** *mf* polyglot
poligonal *adj* polygonal
polígono *m* **1.** MAT polygon **2.** (*terreno*) site; ~ **industrial** industrial estate [*o* park]
polilla *f* moth; **no tener** ~ **en la lengua** *inf* not to mince one's words
polimorfo, **-a** *adj* polymorphous
polinesio, **-a** *adj, m, f* Polynesian
polinización *f* pollination
polio *f inv* MED polio, poliomyelitis
pólipo *m* MED polyp
polisemia *f sin pl* LING polysemy
polisílabo, **-a** *adj* LING polysyllabic
politécnica *f* polytechnic, technical school
politécnico, **-a** *adj* polytechnic
política *f* politics; **Política Agraria Común** Common Agricultural Policy; ~ **interior/exterior** domestic/foreign policy; ~ **monetaria** monetary policy; ~ **pesquera** fishing policy
político, **-a I.** *adj* **1.** POL political; **ciencias políticas** political science; **economía política** political economy **2.** (*parentesco*) in-law; **hermano** ~ brother-in-law; **hermana política** sister-in-law **II.** *m, f* politician
politizar <z→c> *vt, vr* to become politicized
politólogo, **-a** *m, f* political scientist
póliza *f* **1.** JUR policy; **me he hecho una** ~ **de seguros** I have taken out an insurance policy **2.** (*sello*) stamp
polizón *mf* stowaway
polizonte *m pey* cop
polla *f* **1.** (*gallina*) hen; ~ **de agua** ZOOL moorhen **2.** *inf* (*chica*) chick **3.** *vulg* (*pene*) dick; **ni ~s en vinagre** don't come to me with bullshit; **¡y una** ~ **como una olla!** like hell! **4.** *AmL* (*carrera*) horse race
pollera *f* **1.** (*gallinero*) chicken coop **2.** *Arg* (*falda*) skirt
pollería *f* poultry shop
pollerudo I. *adj CSur* **1.** (*chismoso*) gossipy **2.** (*blando*) weak; **niño** ~ sissy; **hombre** ~ wimp **II.** *m CSur, pey* (*clérigo*) priest
pollina *f PRico, Ven* (*del pelo*) fringe *Brit*, bangs *pl Am*
pollino, **-a** *m, f* **1.** (*borrico*) (young) donkey **2.** *fig* (*tonto*) fool
pollito, **-a** *m, f* **1.** (*ave*) chick **2.** *fig* (*niño*) kid
pollo *m* **1.** GASTR chicken; ~ **asado** roast chicken **2.** (*cría*) young; (*de gallina*) chick; **sacar ~s** to breed chickens; **voló el** ~ *fig* the chance has gone **3.** (*joven*) kid; *inf* (*tío*) bloke *Brit*; **¿quién es ese ~?** who's that guy?
polluelo *m* chick
polo *m* **1.** GEO, FÍS, ASTR pole; ~ **norte/ártico/boreal** North Pole; ~ **sur/antártico/austral** South Pole; ~ **industrial** development region **2.** DEP polo **3.** (*camiseta*) polo neck **4.** (*helado*) ice lolly
pololear *vi AmS* (*coquetear*) to flirt
pololo, **-a** *m, f* **1.** *And* (*novio*) boyfriend *m*; (*novia*) girlfriend *f* **2.** *CSur* (*coqueto*) flirt
polonesa *f* MÚS polonaise
Polonia *f* Poland
poltrón, **-ona** *adj* lazy
poltrona *f* easy chair, recliner
polución *f* **1.** (*contaminación*) pollution; ~ **ambiental** environmental pollution **2.** (*semen*) emission
polvareda *f* dust cloud; **levantar una** ~ *fig* to cause an uproar
polvera *f* powder compact
polvo *m* **1.** (*suciedad*) dust; **quitar el** ~ to dust; **hacer** ~ (*algo*) to smash; (*a alguien*) to annihilate; **estoy hecho** ~ *inf* I'm exhausted;

hacer morder el ~ a alguien to humiliate sb; **sacudir a alguien el ~** *fig* to give sb a beating **2.** (*sustancia*) powder; **levadura en ~** powdered yeast **3.** *vulg* (*coito*) screw; **echar un ~** to screw **4.** *pl* (*cosmética*) powder

pólvora *f* gunpowder; **no haber inventado la ~** *inf* to be a bit dim

polvoriento, -a *adj* dusty

polvorín *m* powder magazine; **estamos sentados sobre un ~** *fig* we're sitting on a powder keg

polvorón *m crumbly shortbread, eaten at Christmas*

polvoso, -a *adj AmL* dusty

pomada *f* ointment; **~ contra mosquitos** mosquito repellent

pomelo *m* grapefruit

pómez *f* pumice

pompa *f* **1.** (*burbuja*) bubble **2.** (*esplendor*) pomp; (*ostentación*) display; **~s fúnebres** (*ceremonia*) funeral ceremony; (*funeraria*) funeral parlour *Brit* [*o* parlor *Am*]

pompis *m inv, inf* bottom, backside *Brit,* tush *Am*

pompo, -a *adj Col, Ecua* (*sin filo*) blunt

pomposidad *f* pomposity

pomposo, -a *adj* magnificent; (*grandilocuente*) high-flown; (*estilo*) pompous

pómulo *m* cheekbone

ponchada *f CSur, inf* (*cantidad*) stack; **una ~ de** a load of

ponche *m* punch

poncho *m* poncho

poncho, -a *adj AmL* lazy

ponderación *f* **1.** (*elogio*) eulogy **2.** (*el sopesar*) deliberation; **con ~** carefully **3.** (*en estadística*) weighting **4.** (*exageración*) exaggeration

ponderar *vt* **1.** (*sopesar*) to weigh up **2.** (*encomiar*) to praise

ponencia *f* (*conferencia*) paper; (*informe*) report

ponente *mf* (*en conferencia*) speaker; (*informador*) reporter

poner *irr* **I.** *vt* **1.** (*colocar*) to put; (*horizontalmente*) to lie; (*inyección*) to give; (*sellos, etiqueta*) to stick on; (*tirita*) to put on; (*huevos*) to lay; **pon el espejo mirando hacia mí** put the mirror facing towards me; **pon la ropa en el tendedero** hang the clothes on the line; **¿dónde habré puesto...?** where can I have put ...?; **lo pongo en tus manos** *fig* I leave it in your hands **2.** (*disponer*) to place; (*la mesa*) to lay, to set; **~ algo a disposición de alguien** to make sth available to sb **3.** (*encender*) to switch on; **pon el despertador para las cuatro** set the alarm for four o'clock; **~ en marcha** to start **4.** (*convertir*) to make; **~ de mal humor a alguien** to put sb in a bad mood; **la noticia me puso de buen humor** the news put me in a good mood; **~ colorado a alguien** to make sb blush; **el sol te pondrá moreno** the sun will give you a tan **5.** (*suponer*) to assume; **pon que no viene** let's assume he doesn't come; **pongamos que resolvemos el problema en dos días...** let's assume we solve the problem in two days ...; **pongamos el/por caso que no llegue a tiempo** let's consider what happens if she doesn't arrive on time **6.** (*exponer*) **~ la ropa a secar al sol** to put the clothes out to dry in the sun; **~ la leche al fuego** to put the milk on the stove; **~ en peligro** to endanger **7.** (*contribuir*) to put in; (*juego*) to bet; **¿cúanto has puesto tú en el fondo común?** how much have you put into the kitty?; **pusimos todo de nuestra parte** we did all that we could **8.** (*una expresión*) to take on; **~ mala cara** to look angry **9.** (*tratar*) to treat; **~ de idiota** *pey* to treat sb like a fool **10.** (*denominar*) to give; **le pusieron por** [*o* **de**] **nombre Manolo** they called him Manolo; **¿qué nombre le van a ~?** what are they going to call him/her? **11.** (*espectáculo*) to put on; **~ en escena** to stage; **¿qué ponen hoy en el cine?** what's on at the cinema today? **12.** (*imponer*) to impose; **nos han puesto muchos deberes** they have given us a lot of homework; **~ una multa** to impose a fine; **~ condiciones** to impose conditions **13.** (*instalar*) to install *Brit,* to instal *Am* **14.** (*a trabajar*) **tendrá que ~ a mis hijos a trabajar** I will have to send my children out to work; **puse a mi hijo de aprendiz de panadero** I found my son a position as an apprentice baker **15.** (*añadir*) to add **16.** (*escribir*) to write; (*un telegrama*) to send; **~ entre comillas** to put in inverted commas; **~ la firma** to sign; **~ un anuncio** to place an advertisement; **~ por escrito la propuesta** to put the proposal in writing; **te pongo cuatro letras para decirte que...** this is just a short note to tell you that ... **17.** (*estar escrito*) to say **18.** (*vestido, zapato*) to put on; **le pusieron el collar al cuello** they put his collar on **19.** (*teléfono*) to put through; **me puse al habla con mi amigo** I got through to my friend **II.** *vr:* **~se 1.** (*vestido, zapato*) to put on; **ponte guapo** make yourself look nice; **~se de invierno** to dress warmly; **~se de luto** to wear mourning clothes; **~se de largo** to dress up **2.** ASTR to set; **el sol se pone por el oeste** the sun sets in the west **3.** (*mancharse*) **se pusieron perdidos de barro** they got mud all over themselves **4.** (*comenzar*) to begin; **por la tarde se puso a llover** in the evening it started to rain **5.** (*con adjetivo o adverbio*) to become; **se puso chulo y no nos dejó entrar** he became rude and wouldn't let us in; **ponte cómodo** make yourself comfortable

póney *m* pony

pongo *1. pres de* **poner**

poni *m* pony

poniente *m* **1.** (*oeste*) west **2.** (*viento*) west wind

pontevedrés, -esa I. *adj* of/from Pontevedra **II.** *m, f* native/inhabitant of Pontevedra

ponzoña *f* poison
ponzoñoso, **-a** *adj* poisonous; *fig* harmful
pop I. *adj inv* pop II. *m inv* pop (music)
popa *f* 1. (*barco*) stern; **viento en** ~ following wind; **a** ~ astern 2. *inf* (*trasero*) bum *Brit,* butt *Am*
popero, **-a** *m, f inf* pop music fan
popó *m infantil* pooh *Brit,* poop *Am*
popocho, **-a** *adj Col* 1. (*repleto*) stuffed 2. (*rico*) loaded *inf* 3. (*gordo*) podgy *Brit,* pudgy *Am, inf*
popoff *adj inv, Méx, inf* posh
popote *m Méx* (*paja*) straw
populacho *m* masses *pl*
popular *adj* 1. (*del pueblo*) folk; **aire** ~ folk song 2. (*conocido*) well-known; (*admirado*) popular
popularidad *f* popularity
popularizar <z→c> I. *vt* to popularize; (*extender*) to spread II. *vr:* ~**se** to become popular
populoso, **-a** *adj* populous
popurrí *m* potpourri
poquedad *f* 1. (*escasez*) scarcity 2. (*pusilanimidad*) timidity 3. (*insignificancia*) insignificance
póquer *m* poker
poquito *adv* a little; **bébelo** ~ **a poco** drink it a little bit at a time
por *prep* 1. (*lugar: a través de*) through; (*vía*) via; (*en*) in; ~ **aquí** near here; **limpia la botella** ~ **dentro/fuera** clean the inside/outside of the bottle; **pasé** ~ **Madrid hace poco** I passed through Madrid recently; **adelantar** ~ **la izquierda** to overtake on the left; **volar** ~ **encima de los Alpes** to fly over the Alps; **ese pueblo está** ~ **Castilla** that town is in Castile; **la cogió** ~ **la cintura** he grasped her waist 2. (*tiempo*) in; ~ **la(s) mañana(s)** in the morning; **mañana** ~ **la mañana** tomorrow morning; ~ **la tarde** in the evening; **ayer** ~ **la noche** last night; ~ **noviembre** in November; ~ **fin** finally 3. (*a cambio de*) for; (*en lugar de*) instead of; (*sustituyendo a alguien*) in place of; **cambié el libro** ~ **el álbum** I exchanged the book for the album 4. (*agente*) by; **una novela** ~ **Dickens** a novel by Dickens 5. MAT (*multiplicación*) by 6. (*reparto*) per; **toca a cuatro** ~ **cabeza** it comes out at four each; **el ocho** ~ **ciento** eight per cent 7. (*finalidad*) for 8. (*causa*) because of; (*en cuanto a*) regarding; **lo merece** ~ **los esfuerzos que ha hecho** he/she deserves it for all his/her effort; **lo hago** ~ **ti** I'm doing it for you; ~ **desesperación** out of desperation; ~ **consiguiente** consequently; ~ **eso**, ~ **(lo) tanto** therefore, because of that; ~ **lo que a eso se refiere** as far as that is concerned; ~ **mí que se vayan** as far as I'm concerned, they can go; **no te preocupes** ~ **hacer muchas fotocopias** don't bother making lots of photocopies 9. (*preferencia*) in favour *Brit,* in favor *Am;* **estoy** ~ **comprarlo** I think we should buy it; **estar loco** ~ **alguien** to be crazy about sb 10. (*dirección*) **voy (a)** ~ **tabaco** I'm going to get some cigarettes 11. (*pendiente*) **este pantalón está** ~ **lavar** these trousers need to be washed 12. (*aunque*) however; ~ **muy cansado que esté no lo dejará a medias** however tired he is, he won't leave it unfinished 13. (*medio*) by means of; (*alguien*) through; **poner** ~ **escrito** to put in writing; **al** ~ **mayor** wholesale 14. (*interrogativo*) ¿~ **(qué)**? why? 15. ~ **si acaso** just in case 16. (*casi*) ~ **poco** almost; **por** ~ **me ahogo** I nearly drowned
porcelana *f* porcelain; (*vajilla*) china
porcentaje *m* percentage; ~ **de derechos del autor** author's royalties
porcentual *adj* percentage
porche *m* 1. (*pórtico*) porch, verandah *Am* 2. (*cobertizo*) arcade
porcino, **-a** *adj* pig; **ganado** ~ pigs *pl*
porción *f* portion; GASTR serving
pordiosear *vi* to beg
pordiosero, **-a** *m, f* beggar
porfía *f* persistence; **a** ~ in competition
porfiador(a) I. *adj* obstinate II. *m(f)* obstinate person
porfiar <*1. pres:* porfío> *vi* 1. (*insistir*) ~ **en algo** to insist on sth 2. (*disputar*) to quarrel
pormenor *m* detail
pormenorizado, **-a** *adj* detailed
pormenorizar <z→c> *vt* to describe in detail
porno *adj inv, m inf* porn
pornografía *f* pornography
pornográfico, **-a** *adj* pornographic
poro *m* pore
porongo *m* 1. *CSur* (*calabaza para el mate*) calabash 2. *Perú* (*lechera*) milk can
pororó *m CSur* (*palomitas*) popcorn
poroso, **-a** *adj* porous
poroto *m Chile* bean; (*guiso*) bean stew
porque *conj* 1. (*causal*) because; **lo hizo** ~ **sí** he/she did it because he/she wanted to 2. +*subj* (*final*) so that; **recemos** ~ **llueva** let us pray that it rains
porqué *m* reason
porquería *f inf* 1. (*suciedad*) filth 2. (*acto*) disgusting act 3. (*comida*) pigswill 4. (*cacharro*) piece of junk 5. (*pequeñez*) trifle
porqueriza *f* pigsty
porra *f* 1. (*bastón*) truncheon 2. GASTR *a large stick of fried batter* 3. *inf* (*expresión*) **¡vete a la** ~**!** *inf* go to hell!; **¡**~**(s)!** *inf* damn!
porrazo *m* blow; **de golpe y** ~ all of a sudden; **de un** ~ in one go
porreta *f* **en** ~**(s)** *inf* stark naked
porrista *mf Méx* fan
porro *m* 1. *inf* (*canuto*) joint, spliff *Brit* 2. (*puerro*) leek 3. *inf* (*torpe*) fool
porrón *m bottle with a long spout*
porrudo, **-a** *adj Arg* big-headed
portaaviones *m inv* aircraft carrier
portada *f* 1. (*fachada*) front 2. TIPO title page; PREN cover
portador(a) *m(f)* 1. (*de gérmenes*) carrier

2. COM bearer
portaequipaje(s) *m (inv)* 1. *(maletero)* boot *Brit,* trunk *Am* 2. *(baca, en tren)* luggage rack; *(en bicicleta)* carrier
portafolios *m inv* briefcase
portal *m* 1. *(zaguán)* hall 2. *pl (soportales)* arcade 3. REL ~ **de Belén** Nativity scene 4. INFOR portal
portalámpara(s) *m (inv) (de bombilla)* socket; *(de lámpara)* lamp-holder
portaligas *m inv, AmL (liguero)* suspender belt, garter belt *Am*
portalón *m* 1. ARQUIT large doorway 2. NÁUT gangway
portamaletas *m inv* AUTO boot *Brit,* trunk *Am*
portaminas *m inv* propelling pencil
portamonedas *m inv* purse
portante *m* **tomar el ~** *inf* to clear off; **dar el ~ a alguien** *inf* to sack sb, to fire sb
portar I. *vt (perro)* to fetch II. *vr:* **~se** to behave; **~se bien con alguien** to treat sb well; **el niño se porta bien/mal** the child is well-/badly behaved; **~se como un hombre** to act like a man; **nuestro equipo se ha portado** our team performed well
portátil *adj* portable; **máquina de escribir ~** portable typewriter; **ordenador ~** laptop
portavoz[1] *mf (persona)* spokesperson, spokesman *m,* spokeswoman *f*
portavoz[2] *m* 1. *(periódico)* organ 2. *(bocina)* megaphone
portazo *m* slam *(of the door)*; **dar un ~** to slam the door; **despedirse con un ~** to slam one's door on the way out; **dar a alguien un ~ en las narices** *inf* to slam the door in sb's face
porte *m* 1. *(transporte)* transport; **~ aéreo** air freight; **gastos de ~** transport costs; **a ~ debido** carriage forward 2. *(gastos de transporte)* transport costs *pl,* shipping 3. *(correo)* postage; **~ por expreso** express postage; **~ de un paquete** parcel post; **~ suplementario** additional postage charge 4. *(de buque)* capacity; **buque de gran ~** large vessel 5. *(aspecto)* appearance; **es un hombre de ~ distinguido** he has a distinguished air; **mostrar un ~ severo** to look strict
portear I. *vi* to slam the door II. *vt* to transport, to ship
portento *m* marvel; **niño ~** child prodigy; **ser un ~ de energía** to be full of energy
portentoso, -a *adj* marvellous *Brit,* marvelous *Am*
porteño, -a I. *adj* of/from Buenos Aires II. *m, f* native/inhabitant of Buenos Aires
portería *f* 1. *(en un edificio de viviendas)* porter's lodge 2. DEP goal
portero, -a *m, f* 1. *(conserje)* caretaker; *(en un edificio de viviendas)* porter; **~ automático** entryphone 2. *Arg (administrador)* building manager 3. DEP *(fútbol)* goalkeeper, goaltender
portezuelo *m Arg, Chile (paso de montaña)* pass
pórtico *m (porche)* porch; *(galería)* arcade
portilla *f* NÁUT porthole
portillo *m* 1. *(abertura)* gap 2. *(postigo)* wicket 3. *(entre montañas)* narrow pass 4. *(punto débil)* weak point
portorriqueño, -a *adj, m, f* Puerto Rican
portuario, -a I. *adj* port II. *m, f* docker
portugués, -esa *adj, m, f* Portuguese
porvenir *m* future; **lleno de ~** full of promise; **tener el ~ asegurado** to have a secure future; **un joven de ~** a young man with great prospects
pos I. *adv* **ir en ~ de algo/alguien** to pursue sth/sb; **van en ~ del éxito** they are striving for success II. *conj Méx, inf v.* **pues**
posada *f* 1. *(parador, fonda)* inn; *(pensión)* guest house 2. *(hospedaje)* lodging; **dar ~ a alguien** to give sb lodging; **hacer ~** to stop for the night; **pedir ~** to ask for shelter 3. *(casa)* residence
posaderas *fpl inf* bottom, backside
posadero, -a *m, f* landlord *m,* landlady *f*
posar I. *vi* 1. *(reposar)* to rest 2. *(modelo)* to pose II. *vt* 1. *(poner suavemente)* to place 2. *(carga)* to set down 3. *(mirada)* to rest III. *vr:* **~se** to settle; **el sol se posaba en el mar** the sun set over the sea; **el gorrión se posó en la rama** the sparrow alighted on the branch
posdata *f* postscript
pose *f (postura)* pose
poseedor(a) *m(f)* owner; *(póliza, acciones)* holder
poseer *irr como leer vt* to possess, to have; **~ una importante posición social** to occupy an important position in society; **~ a alguien a la fuerza** to rape sb
poseído, -a I. *adj* possessed; **~ de odio** full of hatred; **una chica poseída de su belleza** a girl obsessed by her own beauty II. *m, f* madman *m,* madwoman *f;* **gritar como un ~** to shout like one possessed
posesión *f (propiedad)* possession; **estoy en ~ de su atenta carta...** I have received your kind letter ...
posesionar I. *vt* **~ a alguien de algo** to hand sth over to sb II. *vr:* **~se** to take possession; **~se de un nuevo cargo** to take up a new position
posesivo, -a *adj t.* LING possessive
poseso, -a I. *adj* possessed II. *m, f* madman *m,* madwoman *f*
posguerra *f* postwar period *(in Spain, usually used to refer to the period after the Spanish Civil War)*
posibilidad *f* 1. *(lo posible)* possibility; **tener grandes ~es de éxito** to have a good chance of success 2. *(aptitud, facultad)* capability; **tienes ~es de llegar a ser un buen actor** you have the ability to become a good actor; **esto está por encima de mis ~es** this is beyond my capabilities 3. *pl (medios económicos)* means *pl;* **estás viviendo por encima de tus ~es** you are living beyond your means
posibilitar *vt* to make possible

posible I. *adj* possible; **hacer ~** to make possible; **hacer lo ~ para que** +*subj* to do everything possible so that; **hacer todo lo ~** to do everything one can; **hacer todo lo humanamente ~** to do everything humanly possible; **es muy ~ que lleguen tarde** they may very well arrive late; **es ~ que** +*subj* it is possible that; **es muy ~ que** +*subj* it is very likely that; **¡no es ~!** I can't believe it!; **¿será ~?** surely not?; **si es ~** if possible; **en lo ~** as far as possible; **lo antes ~** as soon as possible; **no lo veo ~** I don't think it's possible II. *m pl* (*recursos*) means *pl*

posiblemente *adv* possibly

posición *f t.* MIL (*colocación, postura*) position; **~ clave** vital position; **~ del cuerpo** posture; **~ del cursor** INFOR cursor position; **la ~ económica** the economic situation; **~ de empleado** position of employment; **la ~ geográfica** the geographic location; **en buena ~** in a good position; **de ~** of high social standing; **mi ~ ante este asunto...** my opinion on this affair ...; **tomar ~** to adopt a stance

positivo *m* FOTO print

positivo, **-a** *adj* **1.** *t.* MAT, FÍS (*afirmativo, favorable*) positive **2.** (*práctico*) practical; **un hombre ~** a practical man

poso *m* **1.** (*sedimento*) sediment; (*de café*) grounds *pl;* (*de vino*) lees *pl;* **hasta los ~s** *fig* to the very last drop **2.** (*descanso*) rest

posponer *irr como poner vt* **1.** (*postergar*) to relegate **2.** (*aplazar*) to postpone

postal I. *adj* postal, mail *Am;* **una fotografía tamaño ~** a postcard-sized photograph II. *f* postcard

poste *m t.* TEL (*pilar*) post; ELEC pylon; **~ indicador** signpost; **~ kilométrico** ≈ milestone ►**más serio que un ~** *inf* deadly serious

postema *f Méx* (*pus*) pus

póster *m* poster

postergar <g→gu> *vt* **1.** (*aplazar*) to postpone; **~ la fecha** to put back the date **2.** (*posponer injustamente*) to delay; **~ el ascenso de alguien** to pass sb over for promotion

posteridad *f* **1.** (*descendencia*) descendants *pl* **2.** (*generaciones venideras*) future generations *pl* **3.** (*futuro, fama póstuma*) posterity; **pasar a la ~** to be remembered by posterity

posterior *adj* **1.** (*de tiempo*) later; **~ a** after **2.** (*de lugar*) back; **~ a alguien** behind sb; **la parte ~ de la cabeza** the back of the head; **en la parte ~ del coche está el maletero** the boot is at the back of the car

posterioridad *f* posteriority; **con ~ de fecha** at a later date; **con ~** subsequently

posteriormente *adv* subsequently, later

postigo *m* **1.** (*puerta falsa*) blind door **2.** (*portillo*) wicket gate **3.** (*contraventana*) shutter

postín *m* **1.** (*lujo*) luxury; **de ~** luxurious **2.** (*presunción*) ostentation; **darse mucho ~** to show off

postinear *vi* to show off

postinero, **-a** *adj inf* vain

postizo *m* hairpiece

postizo, **-a** *adj* artificial; **cuello ~** detachable collar; **dentadura postiza** false teeth; **nombre ~** false name; **ojo ~** artificial eye; **pelo ~** wig

postor(a) *m(f)* bidder; **mejor ~** highest bidder

postración *f* **1.** (*humillación*) humiliation **2.** (*por enfermedad, aflicción*) prostration; **~ nerviosa** nervous breakdown

postrado, **-a** *adj* **1.** (*arrodillado*) prostrate **2.** (*humillado*) humiliated **3.** (*abatido*) prostrate; **~ de dolor** (*dolor físico*) in great pain; (*pena*) beside oneself with grief; **~ en cama** laid up in bed; **quedar ~ por una enfermedad** to be struck down by an illness **4.** (*desanimado*) depressed

postrar I. *vt* **1.** (*derribar*) to prostrate **2.** (*humillar*) to humiliate **3.** (*debilitar*) to weaken II. *vr:* **~se 1.** (*arrodillarse*) to prostrate oneself **2.** (*perder las fuerzas*) to become weak

postre *m* dessert; **a (la) ~** *fig* in the end, when all is said and done; **llegar a los ~s** *fig* to arrive too late

postrero, **-a** *adj* last

postrimerías *fpl* **1.** (*de persona*) final years *pl;* **estar en sus ~** to be at the end of one's life **2.** (*tiempo*) final stages *pl;* **en las ~ del siglo pasado** at the end of the last century

postulado *m* proposition

postulante, **-a** *m, f* **1.** (*solicitante*) petitioner **2.** REL postulant **3.** (*colecta*) collector

postular *vt* **1.** (*pedir*) to request; (*donativos*) to collect **2.** (*solicitar*) **~ algo** to petition for sth

póstumo, **-a** I. *adj* posthumous; **fama póstuma** posthumous fame II. *m, f* posthumous son *m,* posthumous daughter *f*

postura *f* **1.** (*colocación*) position; (*del cuerpo*) posture **2.** (*actitud*) attitude **3.** (*subasta*) bid; **~ mayor** highest bad; **hacer ~** to bid **4.** (*apuesta*) amount bet **5.** (*convenio*) agreed price **6.** (*conjunto de huevos*) clutch; (*poner huevos*) egg-laying **7.** BOT sapling **8.** (*puesta*) **~ del sol** sunset

post-venta I. *adj* after-sales; **servicio ~** after-sales service II. *f* warranty period

potable *adj* **1.** (*bebible*) drinkable; **agua ~** drinking water **2.** *inf* (*aceptable*) acceptable; **Juan es una persona ~** Juan is a nice guy

potaje *m* **1.** GASTR (*sopa*) soup; (*guiso*) stew (*containing pulses and vegetables*) **2.** (*legumbres secas*) pulses *pl Brit,* dried legumes *pl* (*beans, peas, lentils and chickpeas*) **3.** (*brebaje*) brew **4.** *inf* (*mezcla*) mixture

potar *vi, vt inf* (*vomitar*) to puke

potasio *m* potassium

pote *m* **1.** (*de barro, metal, para cocinar*) pot; (*para plantas*) flowerpot **2.** GASTR stew ►**darse ~** to show off

potencia *f* **1.** (*fuerza*) strength; (*capacidad*) capacity; **~ de carga** capacity; **~ explosiva** explosive power; **~ generativa** generative power; **~ imaginativa** imaginative power; ~

intelectual intellectual power; ~ **mágica** magic power; ~ **del motor** engine capacity; ~ **motriz** motive power; ~ **visual** visual acuity **2.** (*poder*) power; **gran** ~ great power **3.** INFOR ~ **de entrada/de salida** input/output capacity **4.** FILOS possibility; **en** ~ potential **5.** MAT power; **elevar a la cuarta** ~ to raise to the power of four

potencial **I.** *adj* **1.** (*que tiene potencia*) powerful **2.** (*posible*) potential **3.** LING **el modo** ~ the conditional tense **II.** *m* **1.** (*poder, capacidad*) power; ~ **financiero** financial muscle **2.** FÍS potential energy; ELEC potential difference **3.** LING conditional

potente *adj* **1.** (*poderoso*) powerful **2.** (*eficiente*) efficient **3.** (*sexualidad*) potent

potestad *f* authority; ~ **electoral** electoral authority; ~ **legislativa** legislative jurisdiction; ~ **reglamentaria** regulatory authority; **patria** ~ paternal authority

potingue *m pey* **1.** *inf* (*cosmético*) lotion; **darse** ~**s** to put on one's war paint **2.** (*bebida*) concoction

poto *m* **1.** *Perú* (*vaso*) clay bowl **2.** *And, inf* (*trasero*) bum *Brit,* butt *Am*

potranca *f* filly

potranco *m* colt

potrear **I.** *vt* **1.** *inf* (*incomodar*) to vex **2.** *AmL* (*domar*) to break **3.** *Guat, Perú* (*pegar*) to beat **II.** *vi* (*actuar como joven y no serlo*) to frisk about like a young colt

potro *m* **1.** ZOOL colt **2.** DEP vaulting horse **3.** (*de tortura*) rack; **tener a alguien en el** ~ *fig* to have sb on the rack **4.** (*de herrar*) shoeing frame **5.** (*lo que atormenta*) torment

poza *f* (*charca*) puddle

pozal *m* (*cubo*) well-bucket

pozo *m* **1.** (*manantial*) well; ~ **de garrucha** well (*from which water is drawn by a bucket*) **2.** (*hoyo profundo*) shaft; ~ **airón** ventilation shaft; ~ **de extracción** extraction shaft; ~ **de lobos** trap; ~ **negro** cesspool; ~ **petrolífero** oil well; ~ **de retrete** latrine; ~ **séptico** septic tank; **caer en un** ~ *fig* to fall into oblivion; **ser un** ~ **sin fondo** *fig* to be a bottomless pit; **ser un** ~ **de ciencia** *fig* to be a fount of knowledge **3.** *CSur* (*bache*) pothole

pozole *m Méx* GASTR (*guiso*) pozole (*stew of young maize, meat and chili*)

PP *m abr de* **Partido Popular** Popular Party (*Spanish conservative party*)

p.p. *abr de* **por poder** pp

práctica *f* **1.** (*experiencia*) experience; ~ **en la conducción** driving experience; **una** ~ **de muchos años** many years' experience; **adquirir** ~ to gain experience; **perder la** ~ to get out of practice; **tener** ~ **en algo** to have experience of sth **2.** (*ejercitación*) practice; ~ **profesional** professional practice **3.** (*cursillo*) practical course; ~ **preprofesional** vocational training **4.** (*realización*) practice; **en la** ~ in practice; **llevar a la** ~ to carry out; **poner en** ~ to put into practice; **poner en** ~ **una posibilidad** to put an idea into practice **5.** (*costumbre*) practice; ~ **judicial** normal legal practice; **la** ~ **de los negocios** business norms **6.** (*modo*) manner; (*método*) method; **la** ~ **comercial** business methods ►**la** ~ **hace al maestro** *prov* practice makes perfect

practicable *adj* **1.** (*realizable*) feasible **2.** (*camino, calle*) passable **3.** (*puerta, ventana*) that opens

practicar <c→qu> *vi, vt* to practise *Brit,* to practice *Am;* ~ **deporte** to play sport, to do sports; **estudió medicina, pero no practica** he/she studied medicine, but he/she doesn't work as a doctor; ~ **el español** to practise Spanish; ~ **una operación** to perform an operation

práctico *m* NÁUT pilot; ~ **de puerto** harbour [*o* harbor *Am*] pilot

práctico, -a **I.** *adj* practical; (*experimentado*) experienced **II.** *m, f* practitioner

pradera *f* grassland, prairie; (*prado*) meadow

pradería *f* meadowlands *pl*

prado *m* grassy field; (*para ganado*) meadow; (*para pasear*) park

Praga *f* Prague

pragmático, -a **I.** *adj* pragmatic **II.** *m, f* pragmatist

prángana *f Méx, PRico* extreme poverty

preámbulo *m* introduction, preamble; **sin** ~**s** *fig* without further ado; **no andarse con** ~**s** not to beat about the bush; **¡déjese de** ~**s!** get to the point!

preaviso *m* forewarning

prebenda *f* **1.** REL prebend **2.** *inf* (*trabajo*) soft job

precalentar <e→ie> **I.** *vt* to preheat **II.** *vr:* ~**se** DEP to warm up

precario, -a *adj* **1.** (*de poca estabilidad*) precarious **2.** unsafe

precaución *f* precaution; **tomar precauciones** to take precautions

precaver **I.** *vt* (*prevenir*) to prevent; (*evitar*) to avoid **II.** *vr* ~**se de algo/alguien** to take precautions against sth/sb; **hay que** ~**se de todas las eventualidades** you have to be prepared for all eventualities

precavido, -a *adj* cautious

precedencia *f* **1.** (*prioridad*) precedence; **dar** ~ **a alguien** to give precedence to sb **2.** (*superioridad*) superiority

precedente **I.** *adj* preceding **II.** *m* precedent; **sentar un** ~ to establish a precedent; **sin** ~**s** unprecedented

preceder *vt* **1.** (*anteceder*) to precede; **un banquete precedido de varios discursos** a banquet preceded by several speeches **2.** (*tener primacía*) ~ **a algo/alguien** to have priority over sth/sb; ~ **en categoría** to have a higher position

preceptista **I.** *adj* preceptive **II.** *mf* LIT theorist

preceptiva *f* precepts *pl*

preceptivo, -a *adj* compulsory

precepto *m* **1.** (*mandamiento*) order

2. (*norma*) precept; ~ **básico** basic principle; ~ **de conducta** rule of behaviour *Brit* [*o* behavior *Am*]; ~ **jurídico** law; ~ **de ley** legal precept

preceptor(a) *m(f)* tutor

preceptuar <*1. pres:* preceptúo> *vt* to establish

preces *fpl* **1.** (*oraciones*) prayers *pl* **2.** (*súplicas*) pleas *pl*

preciado, **-a** *adj* **1.** (*estimado*) prized **2.** (*jactancioso*) boastful; ~ **de sí mismo** boastful

preciarse *vr* ~ **de algo** to boast about sth

precintar *vt* to seal

precinto *m* (*sello*) seal; ~ **de aduana** customs seal

precio *m* price; ~ **abordable** reasonable price; ~ **alzado** fixed price; ~ **al consumidor** retail price; ~ **al contado** cash price; ~ **de conversión** conversion rate; ~ **de coste** cost price; ~ **al detalle** retail price; ~ **de fábrica** price ex-works, factory price; ~ **irrisorio** bargain price; ~ **al por mayor** wholesale price; ~ **preferente** preferential price; ~ **de presentación** introductory price; ~ **recomendado** recommended price; ~ **de rescate** ransom; ~ **de tarifa** list price; ~ **de temporada** seasonal price; ~ **unitario** single price; ~ **de venta al público** retail price; **a buen** ~ for a good price; **a** ~ **controlado** at a controlled price; **a mitad de** ~ at half price; **a poco** ~ cheaply; **a** ~ **de oro** for a very high price; **poner el** ~ to set the price; **¡qué** ~ **tiene el libro?** how much does this book cost?; **de todos los** ~**s** at all prices; **no tener** ~ *fig* to be priceless; **al** ~ **de la salud** at the cost of one's health; **querer conseguir algo a cualquier** ~ to want sth at any price; **poner** ~ **a la cabeza de alguien** to put a price on sb's head

preciosidad *f* value; **este cuadro es una** ~ this picture is very valuable; *fig* this picture is delightful; **esta chica es una** ~ this girl is lovely

precioso, **-a** *adj* **1.** (*valioso*) valuable **2.** (*hermoso*) lovely

precipicio *m* precipice; **estar al borde del** ~ *fig* to be on the brink of disaster

precipitación *f* **1.** (*prisa*) haste; **con** ~ hastily **2.** METEO rainfall

precipitadamente *adv* hastily

precipitado, **-a** *adj* (*apresurado*) hasty; **ser** ~ **en el hablar** to talk too soon

precipitar **I.** *vt* **1.** (*arrojar*) to throw down; **lo** ~**on por la ventana** they threw him out of the window **2.** (*apresurar*) to hasten; (*acelerar*) to hurry **II.** *vr:* ~**se** **1.** (*arrojarse*) to throw oneself down **2.** (*atacar*) ~**se sobre algo/alguien** to hurl oneself at sth/sb **3.** (*acontecimientos*) to happen very quickly; (*personas*) to act hastily; **¡no se precipite!** don't be hasty!

precisamente *adv* exactly; **¿tiene que ser** ~ **hoy?** does it have to be today, of all days?; ~ **por eso** for that very reason

precisar **I.** *vi* to be necessary **II.** *vt* **1.** (*determinar*) to specify; **hay algo que no consigo** ~ there's sth I can't put my finger on **2.** (*necesitar*) to need; **preciso tu ayuda** I need your help

precisión *f* **1.** (*exactitud*) precision; ~ **de funcionamiento** reliability; ~ **de tiro** accuracy; **instrumento de** ~ precision instrument; **hablar con** ~ to speak clearly **2.** (*determinación*) clarification; **hacer precisiones** to clarify matters **3.** (*necesidad*) need; **tener** ~ **de hacer algo** to need to do sth

preciso, **-a** *adj* **1.** (*necesario*) necessary; **es** ~ **que** +*subj* it is necessary to; **es** ~ **que nos veamos** we need to see each other; **si es** ~**...** if necessary ... **2.** (*exacto*) precise; **a la hora precisa** punctually

preclaro, **-a** *adj* illustrious; (*destacado*) outstanding

precocidad *f* **1.** (*del niño*) precociousness **2.** (*de tiempo*) earliness

precocinado, **-a** *adj* pre-cooked; **plato** ~ ready-cooked dish, convenience food

preconcebido, **-a** *adj* preconceived; **tener ideas preconcebidas** to have preconceived ideas

preconizable *adj* foreseeable

preconizar <z→c> *vt* to recommend

precordillera *f Arg* Andean foothills *pl*

precoz *adj* precocious; (*diagnóstico, cosecha*) early; **eyaculación** ~ premature ejaculation

precursor(a) **I.** *adj* preceding **II.** *m(f)* precursor

predecesor(a) *m(f)* **1.** (*en el cargo*) predecessor **2.** (*antepasados*) ancestor

predecir *irr como decir vt* to predict; (*tiempo*) to forecast

predestinado, **-a** *adj* predestined; **estar** ~ **al crimen** to be destined for a life of crime

predestinar *vt* to predestine

predeterminar *vt* to predetermine

prédica *f* (*sermon*) sermon; (*discurso*) speech

predicación *f* **1.** (*sermonear*) preaching **2.** (*sermón*) sermon

predicado *m* LING predicate

predicador(a) **I.** *adj* preaching **II.** *m(f)* preacher

predicar <c→qu> *vt* **1.** (*sermonear*) to preach; ~ **en desierto** to preach in the wilderness; ~ **con el ejemplo** to practise [*o* practice *Am*] what one preaches **2.** (*publicar*) to publish **3.** (*elogiar*) to praise **4.** (*amonestar*) to admonish ►**no se puede** ~ **y andar en la procesión** *prov* you can't be in two places at once; **una cosa es** ~ **y otra dar trigo** *prov* actions speak louder than words

predicativo, **-a** *adj* LING predicative

predicción *f* prediction; ~ **económica** economic forecast

predilección *f* predilection

predilecto, **-a** *adj* favourite *Brit,* favorite *Am;* **hijo** ~ favourite [*o* favorite *Am*] son; **plato** ~ favourite [*o* favorite *Am*] dish

predio *m* **1.** JUR estate; ~ **familiar** family estate; ~ **grande** large estate **2.** (*finca*) piece of land; ~ **familiar** family holding; ~ **pequeño** smallholding

predisponer *irr como poner* **I.** *vt* **1.** (*fijar por anticipado*) to agree beforehand; **predispongamos ya la fecha de nuestra próxima reunión** let's set the date of our next meeting now; **venía predispuesto a pelearse** he arrived in a mood for a quarrel **2.** (*influir*) to predispose; ~ **a alguien a favor/en contra de alguien** to bias sb in favour [*o* favor *Am*] of/against sb **3.** (*inclinar*) to make receptive; MED to predispose **II.** *vr* **1.** (*prepararse*) **~se a algo** to prepare oneself for sth **2.** (*tomar partido*) to have a bias; **~se a favor/en contra de alguien** to be biased in favour [*o* favor *Am*] of/against sb

predisposición *f t.* MED predisposition; (*tendencia*) tendency; ~ **al crimen** criminal predisposition; **tener ~ a engordar** to have a tendency to put on weight

predispuesto, -a **I.** *pp de* **predisponer** **II.** *adj* **1.** *ser* (*sensible*) predisposed; **ser ~ a coger los virus** to have a tendency to catch viruses **2.** *estar* (*prevenido*) prejudiced; **estar (mal) ~ contra alguien** to be prejudiced against sb

predominar *vi, vt* **1.** (*prevalecer*) to predominate; **aquí predomina la corrupción** corruption is very common here; **en este parque las palomas predominan en número sobre los gorriones** in this park there are more pigeons than sparrows **2.** (*sobresalir*) to stand out; ~ **en algo/sobre alguien** to stand out at sth/over sb

predominio *m* **1.** (*poder*) predominance **2.** (*preponderancia*) preponderance **3.** (*superioridad*) ~ **sobre alguien** superiority over sb

preeminencia *f* pre-eminence

preeminente *adj* pre-eminent

preescolar *adj* pre-school; **edad ~** pre-school age

preestreno *m* preview

preexistir *vi* to pre-exist

prefabricado, -a *adj* prefabricated; **casa prefabricada** prefabricated house

prefacio *m* (*libro*) preface; (*discurso*) introduction

preferencia *f* **1.** (*elección, trato*) preference; **mostrar ~ por alguien** to show a preference for sb **2.** (*predilección*) predilection; **sentir ~ por alguien** to be biased in favour of sb **3.** (*prioridad*) priority; ~ **de paso** right of way; **precio de ~** preferential price; **tener ~ ante alguien** to have priority over sb; **dar ~** to give preference; **de ~** preferably

preferentemente *adv* preferably

preferible *adj* preferable; **sería ~ que lo hicieras** it would be best if you did it

preferiblemente *adv* preferably

preferido, -a *adj* favourite *Brit,* favorite *Am*

preferir *irr como sentir vt* to prefer; **prefiero ir a pie** I prefer to walk; **prefiero que no venga** I would rather he/she didn't come

prefijar *vt* **1.** (*determinar*) to decide (in advance), to prearrange **2.** LING to prefix

prefijo *m* **1.** LING prefix **2.** TEL (dialling) code *Brit,* area code *Am*

pregón *m* proclamation; **con ~** *fig* with much ado; **sin ~** *fig* without a lot of fuss

pregonar *vt* **1.** (*en público*) to proclaim; ~ **mercancías** to publicize goods **2.** (*lo que estaba oculto*) to make public; ~ **a los cuatro vientos** *inf* to proclaim for all to hear; ~ **a tambor batiente** to proclaim loudly **3.** (*alabar*) to praise publicly

pregonero, -a *m, f* **1.** (*público*) town crier **2.** *inf* (*chismoso*) gossip

pregunta *f* **1.** (*demanda*) question; ~ **capciosa** trick question; **hacer ~s capciosas a alguien** to try to catch sb out; **estrechar a ~s a alguien** to bombard sb with questions; **a tal ~ tal respuesta** ask a silly question, get a silly answer; **estar a la cuarta ~** *inf* to be broke **2.** (*de datos*) inquiry

preguntar **I.** *vt* to ask; ~ **a alguien la lección** to test sb; ~ **a un sospechoso** to question a suspect; ~ **por alguien** to ask after sb ►**quien pregunta no <u>yerra</u>** *prov* he who asks questions won't go far wrong **II.** *vr* **~se si/cuándo/qué...** to wonder if/when/what ...

preguntón, -ona *adj* inquisitive, nosy *pej*

prehistórico, -a *adj* prehistoric

prejubilación *f* early retirement

prejuicio *m* prejudice

prejuzgar <g→gu> *vt* to prejudge

preliminar *adj* preliminary

preludio *m t.* MÚS prelude

premamá *adj inv* **vestido ~** maternity dress

prematuro, -a *adj* **1.** (*persona*) precocious **2.** (*antes de tiempo, apresurado*) premature; **detección prematura del cáncer** early detection of cancer; **nacimiento ~** premature birth

premeditación *f* premeditation; **con ~** premeditated

premeditadamente *adv* with premeditation

premeditado, -a *adj* premeditated

premeditar *vt* **1.** (*pensar*) to think about **2.** (*planear*) to plan; JUR to premeditate

premiación *f And* awarding (of prizes)

premiado, -a **I.** *adj* prizewinning **II.** *m, f* prizewinner; (*literatura, ciencias*) laureate

premiar *vt* **1.** (*recompensar*) to reward **2.** (*dar un premio*) to give [*o* award] a prize to

premier *mf* premier

premio *m* **1.** (*galardón*) prize; ~ **Nobel (de literatura)** Nobel prize (for/in literature); **conceder un ~** to award a prize **2.** (*recompensa*) reward; ~ **por hallazgo** finder's reward **3.** (*remuneración*) bonus; ~ **al ahorro** savings bonus; ~ **de antigüedad** long-service bonus **4.** (*lotería*) prize; **el ~ gordo** the jackpot **5.** (*ganador*) prizewinner; **García Márquez es ~ Nobel de literatura** García Márquez is a Nobel laureate in literature

premioso, **-a** *adj* 1. (*ajustado*) tight 2. (*molesto*) annoying 3. (*estrecho*) narrow 4. (*torpe*) slow 5. (*estricto*) strict

premisa *f* 1. (*condición*) premise 2. (*indicio*) indication

premonición *f* (*presentimiento*) premonition

premunir I. *vt AmL* ~ **de algo** to provide with sth II. *vr AmL* ~**se de algo** to provide oneself with sth

premura *f* 1. (*apuro*) pressure 2. (*prisa*) haste 3. (*falta*) lack

prenatal *adj* prenatal

prenda *f* 1. (*fianza*) guarantee; **en** ~ as security; **en** ~**s** as evidence; **hacer** ~ to hold as security; **soltar** ~ to commit oneself; **no soltar** ~ *inf* not to say a word; **a mí no me duelen** ~**s** I don't mind admitting it 2. (*pieza de ropa*) garment; ~**s interiores** underwear; ~ **protectora** protective clothing 3. (*cariño*) darling; **la** ~ **de mi corazón** my darling 4. (*cualidades*) talent; ~**s del espíritu** spiritual qualities; **un hombre de** ~**s** a talented man

prendar I. *vt* 1. (*tomar como prenda*) to take as security 2. (*ganar el afecto*) to captivate II. *vr* ~**se de alguien** *elev* to fall in love with sb

prendedor *m* (*broche*) brooch, pin; (*de corbata*) tiepin

prender I. *vi* (*planta, ideas*) to take root; (*medicamentos*) to take effect; **sus ideas prendieron fácilmente en la juventud** his ideas quickly took root among the young II. *vt* 1. (*sujetar*) to hold down; (*con alfileres*) to pin; (*con cola*) to stick; (*en un gancho*) to hang; (*el pelo*) to tie back; ~ **un alfiler de corbata** to put a tiepin on 2. (*detener*) to catch 3. (*fuego*) **el coche prendió fuego** the car caught fire 4. *AmL* (*encender*) to light; (*luz*) to turn on; ~ **un cigarillo** to light a cigarette III. *vr* 1. (*mujeres*) to dress up; ~**se una flor en el ojal** to put a flower in one's buttonhole 2. *PRico* (*emborracharse*) to get drunk

prendimiento *m* 1. (*captura*) capture 2. *Col, Ven* (*irritación*) irritation 3. *CSur* (*estreñimiento*) constipation

prensa *f* 1. (*máquina*) press; ~ **de uvas** wine press 2. (*imprenta*) printer's, press; **dar a la** ~ to send to the printer's; **estar en** ~ to be at the printer's 3. PREN press; ~ **amarilla** tabloids *pl;* ~ **especializada** specialist publications; **rueda de** ~ press conference; **libertad de** ~ freedom of the press; **secretario de** ~ press secretary; **Prensa y Relaciones Públicas** Public Relations; **tener buena/mala** ~ *fig* to get a good/bad press

prensar *vt* to press

prensil *adj* prehensile

preñada *adj* (*mujer*) pregnant

preñado, **-a** *adj* 1. (*animal*) pregnant 2. (*lleno*) full; **una nube preñada de agua** a cloud full of water; **una palabra preñada** a word loaded with meaning; ~ **de dificultades** full of difficulties; ~ **de emoción** full of emotion

preñar *vt* 1. (*mujer*) to make pregnant 2. (*animal*) to impregnate 3. (*llenar*) to fill

preñez *f* (*de la mujer, del animal*) pregnancy

preocupación *f* 1. (*desvelo*) worry; ~ **por algo/alguien** worry about sth/sb; **¡déjate de preocupaciones!** stop worrying!; **sin preocupaciones** unworried 2. (*pesadumbre*) worry; **causar preocupaciones a alguien** to be a cause of concern for sb 3. (*obsesión*) concern; **tu única** ~ **es el dinero** the only thing you care about is money 4. (*prejuicio*) prejudice

preocupado, **-a** *adj* worried; ~ **por algo/alguien** worried about sth/sb; **mi padre anda bastante** ~ my father is quite worried; **tener el espíritu** ~ **por algo** to be worried about sth

preocupante *adj* worrying

preocupar I. *vt* 1. (*inquietar*) to worry; **¿por qué preocupas tanto a tus padres?** why do you make your parents worry so much? 2. (*prevenir*) to prejudice II. *vr* 1. (*inquietarse*) ~**se por algo/alguien** to worry about sth/sb; **¡no se preocupe!** don't worry!; **¡no te preocupes tanto!** don't worry so much! 2. (*encargarse*) to take care; **no se preocupa de arreglar el asunto** he/she doesn't do anything to solve the problem 3. (*tener prejuicios*) to be biased

prepa *f Méx* (*preparatoria*) secondary school

preparación *f* 1. (*de un asunto, de la comida, de materias primas*) preparation; ~ **de datos** INFOR data processing 2. (*formación*) training; ~ **académica** education; ~ **especializada** specialist training; ~ **profesional** professional training; **sin** ~ untrained 3. (*farmacéutica*) preparation

preparado *m* preparation; ~ **listo** ready-made medicine; **¡**~**s, listos, ya!** ready, steady, go!

preparado, **-a** *adj* (*listo*) ready; ~ (**para funcionar**) ready for use; **tener** ~ to have ready

preparar I. *vt* 1. (*disponer: la comida, materias primas*) to prepare; **en esta escuela profesional te preparan bien** in this professional training school they give you a good training; **en inglés me prepara una profesora nativa** I am taught English by a teacher who is a native speaker; ~ **un buque para zarpar** to get a boat ready for a journey; ~ **el camino** to prepare the way; ~ **una casa para vivir en ella** to make a house ready for living in; ~ **un discurso** to write a speech; ~ **las maletas** to pack one's bags; **ya puedes** ~ **la maleta** *inf* it's time you were leaving; ~ **la tierra** to prepare the ground 2. QUÍM, ANAT to prepare 3. INFOR (*datos*) to process; (*programa*) to compile II. *vr* to get ready; **me preparaba a salir, cuando empezó a llover** I was getting ready to leave when it started raining; **se prepara una tormenta** there's a storm brewing; ~**se para cualquier eventualidad** to prepare oneself for any eventuality

preparativo *m* preparation

preparativo, **-a** *adj* preparatory
preparatoria *f Méx* college prep (*3-year pre-university course and the school where it is given*)
preparatorio, **-a** *adj* preparatory; **curso** ~ introductory course; **trabajos ~s** preliminary work
prepo *Arg* **de** ~ by force
preponderancia *f* preponderance
preponderante *adj* preponderant
preponderar *vi* to prevail
preposición *f* preposition
prepotente *adj* arrogant
prerrogativa *f* (*privilegio*) prerogative
presa *f* **1.** (*acción*) capture; **las llamas hicieron ~ en la casa** the house went up in flames; **ser ~ del terror** to be seized by terror **2.** (*objeto, de caza*) prey; **animal de ~** prey; **ave de ~** bird of prey; **hacer una ~** to make a kill **3.** (*dique*) dam **4.** (*colmillo*) fang **5.** (*uña*) talon **6.** (*acequia*) channel **7.** (*de comida*) piece of food **8.** DEP hold; ~ **de brazo** (*judo*) arm hold
presagiar *vt* to betoken *form;* **estas nubes presagian tormenta** these clouds mean there will be a storm
presagio *m* **1.** (*señal*) warning sign **2.** (*presentimiento*) premonition
presbicia *f* MED long-sightedness
presbiterio *m* presbytery
presbítero *m* priest
prescindible *adj* dispensable
prescindir *vi* **1.** (*renunciar a*) ~ **de algo/alguien** to do without sth/sb; **tenemos que ~ del coche** we will have to get rid of the car; **no podemos ~ de él** we can't do without him **2.** (*pasar por alto*) ~ **de algo/alguien** to overlook sth/sb; **han prescindido de mi opinión** they have ignored my opinion **3.** (*no contar*) ~ **de algo/alguien** to disregard sth/sb
prescribir *irr como escribir* **I.** *vi* (*plazo*) to expire **II.** *vt* (*indicar*) *t.* MED to prescribe; **prescrito por la ley** prescribed by law
prescripción *f* **1.** (*indicación*) indication **2.** MED prescription **3.** (*plazo*) expiry
presencia *f* **1.** (*asistencia*) presence; **sin la ~ del ministro** without the minister being present; **hacer acto de ~** to put in an appearance **2.** (*aspecto*) appearance; **buena ~** stylish appearance **3.** (*existencia*) **estamos en ~ del aeropuerto más grande de Europa** this is the largest airport in Europe; **la gente está asustada por la ~ de ladrones** people are scared by the presence of thieves; **la constante ~ de ese recuerdo no le dejaba dormir** the persistence of the memory did not allow him to sleep
presencial *adj* **testigo** ~ eyewitness
presenciar *vt* **1.** (*ver*) to witness **2.** (*asistir*) to attend; **10.000 personas ~on el concierto** 10,000 people attended the concert
presentable *adj* presentable; **ponerse** ~ to make oneself presentable
presentación *f* **1.** (*de una novela, una película*) launch(ing) **2.** (*de un número artístico*) presentation; TEAT show **3.** (*de instancia, dimisión*) submission; **el plazo de ~ de solicitudes finaliza hoy** the period for presenting requests ends today **4.** (*de argumentos, documento, propuesta*) presentation **5.** (*de personas*) introduction **6.** (*aspecto*) appearance **7.** *AmL* (*súplica*) petition
presentador(**a**) *m(f)* (*de programa*) presenter; (*de telediario*) newsreader
presentar **I.** *vt* **1.** (*mostrar*) to show **2.** (*ofrecer*) to offer; **el viaje presenta dificultades** the journey poses difficulties; **la ciudad presenta un aspecto de gala** the city is in festive mood; **este informe presenta los sucesos de una manera clara** this report sets out the events clearly **3.** TV, RADIO to present; TEAT to put on; (*presentador*) to introduce **4.** (*instancia, dimisión, trabajo*) to submit **5.** (*argumentos*) to put forward; (*pruebas, propuesta*) to submit **6.** (*pasaporte, documento*) to show **7.** (*persona*) to introduce; **te presento a mi marido** may I introduce you to my husband? **8.** (*candidato*) to propose **II.** *vr:* **~se** **1.** (*comparecer*) to present oneself; (*aparecer*) to turn up **2.** (*para elecciones*) **~se a** to stand at *Brit,* to run for *Am* **3.** (*concurso*) to enter
presente[1] **I.** *adj* **1.** (*que está*) present; **¡~!** present!; **estar** ~ to be present **2.** (*actual*) current **3.** (*este*) **la ~ edición** this edition; **la ~ tesina** this thesis **4.** (*a considerar*) **hay que tener ~ las circunstancias** one must consider the circumstances; **ten ~ lo que te he dicho** bear in mind what I have told you **5.** (*escrito*) **por la ~ deseo comunicarle que...** (*en una carta*) I write in order to tell you that ... **II.** *mf* (*asistente*) **los/las ~s** those present
presente[2] *m* **1.** (*actualidad*) present; **hasta el ~** until now; **por el ~** for the moment **2.** LING present (tense) **3.** (*regalo*) present, gift
presentimiento *m* premonition; **tengo el ~ de que...** I have a feeling that ...
presentir *irr como sentir vt* to have a premonition of; **presiento que mañana lloverá** I have a feeling it's going to rain tomorrow
preservación *f* preservation
preservar **I.** *vt* to protect **II.** *vr* to protect oneself
preservativo *m* condom
presidencia *f* **1.** (*mandato*) presidency; **asumir la ~** to take over the presidency; **esta orden viene de la ~** this order comes from the president **2.** (*edificio*) presidental palace **3.** (*de organización, asamblea: conjunto*) board; (*individuo*) chairperson, president; **asumir la ~** to take the chair
presidencial *adj* **1.** POL presidential **2.** (*de asamblea*) presiding
presidente *mf* **1.** POL president; ~ **del gobierno Aznar** Spanish Prime Minister, Aznar **2.** (*de asociación*) chairperson

presidiario, **-a** *m, f* convict
presidio *m* prison; **condenar a 20 años de** ~ to sentence to 20 years in prison
presidir *vt* **1.** (*ocupar presidencia*) to be president of **2.** (*mandar*) to rule **3.** (*dominar*) to dominate
presilla *f* fastener
presión *f* pressure; ~ **arterial** blood pressure; ~ **competitiva** competition; ~ **fiscal** tax burden; ~ **social** social pressure; **grupo de** ~ pressure group; **zona de altas presiones** METEO high pressure area; **cerrado a** ~ pressurized; **¿a qué ~ llevas las ruedas?** what is your tyre [*o* tire *Am*] pressure?; **estar bajo** ~ to be under pressure; **hacer ~ sobre alguien** to put pressure on sb; **no acepto presiones de nadie** I don't allow anyone to pressurize [*o* pressure *Am*] me
presionar *vt* **1.** (*apretar*) to press **2.** (*coaccionar*) to put pressure on
preso, **-a** *m, f* prisoner, (prison) inmate
prestación *f* **1.** (*de ayuda, servicio*) provision; ~ **por desempleo** unemployment benefit; **prestaciones en especie** payment in kind; ~ **de servicios** provision of services; **Prestación Social Sustitutoria** social service (*as an alternative to military service*) **2.** *pl* (*de coche*) features *pl;* **un coche con todas las últimas prestaciones** a car with all the latest features
prestado, **-a** *adj* borrowed; **voy de ~, el traje me lo han dejado** I'm wearing borrowed finery, sb lent me the suit; **vivir de ~ en casa de alguien** to live off sb else
prestamista *mf* moneylender; (*contra prenda*) pawnbroker; (*banco*) lending bank
préstamo *m* **1.** (*acción*) lending **2.** *t.* FIN (*lo prestado: para exposición*) loan; ~ **hipotecario** mortgage; ~ **a interés fijo** fixed-interest loan; **la duración de un** ~ the period of a loan **3.** LING loan word
prestancia *f* **1.** (*distinción*) distinction **2.** (*excelencia*) excellence
prestar **I.** *vt* **1.** (*dejar*) to lend; **¿me prestas la bici, por favor?** can I borrow your bike?; **el banco me ha prestado el dinero** I have borrowed money from the bank **2.** (*dedicar*) ~ **ayuda** to help; ~ **servicios** to provide services; ~ **colaboración** to cooperate; ~ **apoyo** to support **3.** (*declaración*) to make; (*juramento*) to swear **4.** (*atención*) to pay; ~ **silencio** to remain silent; ~ **paciencia** to be patient; ~ **oídos** to lend an ear **II.** *vi* (*dar de sí*) **los zapatos son pequeños pero ya ~án** the shoes are small but they will stretch; **este pantalón presta mucho** these trousers have stretched a lot; **esta cuerda no presta** this rope doesn't have any give **III.** *vr:* **~se 1.** (*ofrecerse*) to offer oneself; **se prestó a ayudarme en la mudanza** he/she offered to help me move house **2.** (*avenirse*) to accept **3.** (*dar motivo*) to give rise to; **tus palabras se prestan a confusión** your words lend themselves to misinterpretation
prestatario, **-a** *m, f* borrower
presteza *f* speed
prestidigitación *f* conjuring; **un número de** ~ a conjuring trick
prestidigitador(a) *m(f)* conjurer
prestigio *m* prestige; **una cuestión de** ~ a matter of honour *Brit* [*o* honor *Am*]; **hoy viene un conferenciante de** ~ today's speaker is very famous
prestigioso, **-a** *adj* prestigious
presto *adv* **1.** (*rápidamente*) quickly **2.** (*al instante*) at once
presto, **-a** *adj* **1.** (*listo*) ready **2.** (*rápido*) quick
presumido, **-a** *adj* **1.** (*arrogante*) arrogant **2.** (*vanidoso*) vain
presumir **I.** *vi* **1.** (*vanagloriarse*) ~ **de algo** to boast about sth **2.** ~ **más que una mona** *inf* to be as vain as a peacock **II.** *vt* to presume
presunción *f* **1.** (*sospecha*) assumption **2.** (*petulancia*) arrogance **3.** (*vanidad*) vanity
presunto, **-a** *adj* **1.** (*supuesto*) presumed; **el ~ asesino** the alleged murderer **2.** (*equivocadamente*) so-called
presuntuoso, **-a** *adj* conceited
presuponer *irr como poner vt* **1.** (*suponer*) to presuppose **2.** (*calcular*) to suppose
presupuestar *vt* **1.** POL, ECON to budget (for) **2.** (*gastos*) to calculate; ~ **los gastos en tres millones** to calculate the costs to be three million
presupuestario, **-a** *adj* budget(ary)
presupuesto *m* **1.** POL, ECON budget; ~ **anual** annual budget; **Presupuesto General del Estado** National Budget; **la confección del** ~ the drawing up of the budget **2.** (*cálculo*) estimate **3.** (*suposición*) assumption
presuroso, **-a** *adj* hurried; **iba ~ por la calle** he hurried down the street
pretender *vt* **1.** (*aspirar a*) to aspire to; ~ **subir de categoría** to be seeking promotion **2.** (*pedir*) to expect; **¿qué pretendes que haga?** what do you want me to do?; **no puedes ~ que te traten con corrección si...** you can't expect them to treat you with respect if ... **3.** (*tener intención*) to mean; **no pretendía molestar** I didn't mean to disturb you **4.** (*intentar*) to try to **5.** (*afirmar*) to affirm **6.** (*puesto*) to aspire to **7.** (*cortejar*) to woo
pretendiente *m* (*de trabajo*) applicant; (*de mujer*) suitor; (*a la corona*) pretender
pretensión *f* **1.** (*derecho*) claim; ~ **económica** financial demand **2.** (*ambición*) ambition; (*aspiración*) aim; **es una persona con muchas pretensiones** he is very ambitious; **es una persona con pocas pretensiones** he is easily pleased; **tener muchas pretensiones laborales** to be ambitious at work; **tiene la ~ de que vaya con él** he wants me to go with him **3.** *pl* (*vanidad*) **tiene pretensiones de actor** he fancies himself as an actor **4.** (*solicitud*) application
pretérito *m* LING past
pretérito, **-a** *adj* past

P

pretextar *vt* to use as an excuse; **pretextó que estaba enfermo** he pretended that he was ill; **siempre pretexta algo** he always has some excuse

pretexto *m* pretext; **a ~ de...** on the pretext of ...

pretil *m* **1.** (*de puente*) parapet **2.** *AmL* (*atrio*) forecourt

pretina *f* **1.** (*cinta*) band **2.** (*de calzoncillos*) waistband **3.** (*de prenda*) elastic **4.** (*cintura*) waist

prevalecer *irr como crecer vi* **1.** (*imponerse*) to prevail; **la verdad prevaleció sobre la mentira** truth prevailed over lies **2.** (*predominar*) to predominate; **en esta ciudad prevalecen los de derechas sobre los de izquierdas** in this city there are more right-wingers than left-wingers **3.** (*triunfar*) to win **4.** BOT to take root **5.** (*prosperar*) to thrive

prevaleciente *adj* (*moda*) current; (*costumbre*) prevailing

prevaricación *f* **1.** JUR perversion of the course of justice **2.** (*del deber*) dereliction of duty

prevaricar <c→qu> *vi* **1.** JUR to pervert the course of justice **2.** (*faltar al deber*) to fail to do one's duty **3.** *inf* (*desvariar*) to talk nonsense

prevención *f* **1.** (*precaución*) precaution **2.** *t.* MED (*acción*) prevention; **~ del cáncer** cancer prevention; **~ de accidentes** accident prevention; **~ de siniestros** crash prevention **3.** (*prejuicio*) prejudice; **tener ~ contra alguien** to be prejudiced against sb

prevenido, -a *adj* **1.** *estar* (*alerta*) **estar ~** to be prepared **2.** *ser* (*previsor*) prudent ►**hombre ~ vale por dos** *prov* forewarned is forearmed *prov*

prevenir *irr como venir* **I.** *vt* **1.** (*protegerse de, evitar*) to prevent **2.** (*advertir*) to warn **3.** (*predisponer*) to prejudice; **~ a alguien a favor de alguien/en contra de alguien** to prejudice sb in sb's favour [*o* favor *Am*]/against sb **4.** (*preparar*) to prepare; **~ las armas** to get ready for battle **5.** (*proveer*) **~ de algo** to provide with sth ►**más vale ~ que curar** *prov* prevention is better than cure, a stitch in time saves nine *prov* **II.** *vr:* **~se 1.** (*tomar precauciones*) to take precautions **2.** (*contra alguien*) to protect oneself **3.** (*proveerse*) **~se de algo** to provide oneself with sth **4.** (*prepararse*) to get ready

preventivo, -a *adj* preventive, preventative; **medida preventiva** preventive measure; **prisión preventiva** remand

prever *irr como ver vt* to foresee; (*esperar*) to expect

previo *m* TV, CINE playback

previo, -a *adj* previous; (**sin**) **~ aviso** (without) prior warning; **previa presentación del D.N.I.** on presentation of identity documents; **~ pago de la matrícula** on payment of the matriculation fee; **tuve una entrevista previa con él** I had a preliminary interview with him

previsible *adj* **1.** (*probable*) predictable **2.** (*que se puede prever*) foreseeable; **dentro de un futuro ~** in the foreseeable future; **era ~** it was to be expected

previsión *f* **1.** (*de prever*) prediction; **esto supera todas las previsiones** this surpasses all the predictions **2.** (*precaución*) precaution; **hay que tener ~ de futuro** one must plan for the future; **en ~ de...** as a precaution against ... **3.** (*cálculo*) forecast; **las previsiones económicas** the economic forecasts

previsor(a) *adj* **1.** (*con visión*) far-sighted **2.** (*precavido*) prudent

previsto, -a *adj* predicted; **el éxito estaba ~** the success had been expected; **todo lo necesario está ~** everything necessary has been prepared

prez *m o f* **1.** (*honor*) honour *Brit,* honor *Am* **2.** (*gloria*) glory

PRI *m abr de* **Partido Revolucionario Institucional** *Mexican ruling party from 1929 onwards*

prieto, -a *adj* **1.** (*apretado*) tight **2.** (*negro*) black; (*negruzco*) blackish **3.** (*tacaño*) stingy, mean *Brit* **4.** (*compacto*) compact

prima *f* **1.** (*pariente*) (girl) cousin; **~ hermana/segunda** first/second cousin **2.** FIN bonus; (*seguro*) insurance premium

primacía *f* **1.** *t.* MIL, POL (*supremacía*) supremacy **2.** (*prioridad*) priority

primada *f inf* piece of foolishness; **no hagas la ~ de comprarte este traje** don't be so stupid as to buy this suit; **me han hecho una ~** they've ripped me off

primar I. *vi* to be of great importance; **en esta escuela prima el orden** in this school the most important thing is good behaviour *Brit* [*o* behavior *Am*]; **aquí priman los enchufes sobre la capacidad personal** here contacts are more important than ability **II.** *vt* to reward

primario, -a *adj* **1.** (*principal, primero*) primary; **corriente primaria** ELEC primary current; **enseñanza primaria** primary education; **necesidades primarias** basic necessities **2.** (*persona*) primitive

primate *m* primate

primavera I. *adj* spring **II.** *f* **1.** (*estación*) spring; **estar en la ~ de la vida** *fig* to be in the prime of life **2.** BOT primrose **3.** *pl* (*años*) years

primaveral *adj* spring(like)

primer *adj v.* **primero, -a**

primera *f* **1.** AUTO first (gear); **ir en ~** to be in first (gear) **2.** FERRO, AVIAT first class; **viajar en ~** to travel first class

primeriza *f* first-time mother

primerizo, -a *m, f* (*novato*) novice

primero *adv* **1.** (*en primer lugar*) first; **~..., segundo...** first ..., second ...; **~ dice una cosa, luego otra** first he says one thing, then another **2.** (*antes*) rather

primero, -a I. *adj* (*ante sustantivo masculino: primer*) first; **primera calidad** top quality; **primera edición** first edition; **el Primer Mi-**

nistro the Prime Minister; **primera representación** première (performance); **estado ~** initial state; **a primera hora (de la mañana)** first thing (in the morning); **a ~s de mes** at the beginning of the month; **lo hice a la ~** I did it at the first attempt; **de primera** first-rate; **de primera calidad** top quality; **ser/estar de primera** to be really good; **desde un primer momento** from the outset; **en primer lugar** in the first place; **ocupar una de las primeras posiciones** to occupy one of the top positions; **lo ~ es lo ~** first things first; **para mí tú eres lo ~** for me you are more important than anything else; **lo ~ es ahora la familia** the most important thing now is the family **II.** *m, f* first; **el ~ de la carrera** the winner of the race; **el ~ de la clase** the top of the class; **estar entre los ~s** to be among the leaders; **eres el ~ en llegar** you are the first to arrive

primicia *f* **1.** (*lo primero*) first one **2.** PREN, TV, RADIO scoop **3.** *pl* (*frutos*) **las ~s** the first fruits

primitivo, -a *adj* primitive; **los habitantes ~s** the original inhabitants; **lotería primitiva** *Spanish state lottery;* **palabra primitiva** LING non-derived word

primo *m* **1.** (*pariente*) (boy) cousin; **~ hermano/segundo** first/second cousin **2.** *inf* (*ingenuo*) mug; **he hecho el ~: he pagado 50 euros por esto** I've been taken for a ride: I paid 50 euros for this; **¡no seas ~!** don't be such a fool!

primo, -a *adj* **1.** *elev* (*primero*) first; **materia prima** raw material **2.** (*primoroso*) exquisite **3.** (*excelente*) excellent **4.** MAT **número ~** prime number

primogénito, -a *adj, m, f* first-born

primor *m* **1.** (*habilidad*) skill **2.** (*esmero*) care; **hacer algo con ~** to take great care in doing sth

primordial *adj* **1.** (*más importante*) supreme; **este asunto es de interés ~** this affair is of fundamental concern **2.** (*fundamental*) essential, fundamental; **para vivir en Gran Bretaña es ~ hablar inglés** if you are going to live in Great Britain it is essential that you speak English

primoroso, -a *adj* **1.** (*hábil*) skilful *Brit,* skillful *Am* **2.** (*con esmero*) careful; **es un bordado ~** it is a delicate piece of embroidery **3.** (*excelente*) excellent; **labios ~s** beautiful lips

prímula *f* primrose

princesa *f v.* **príncipe, princesa**

principado *m* principality; **el Principado** Asturias; **el Principado de Andorra** the Principality of Andorra

principal[1] **I.** *adj* **1.** (*más importante*) principal; **el problema ~** the main problem; **su carrera profesional era lo ~ para él** his career was his main priority **2.** (*esencial*) essential **II.** *mf* (*de negocio: propietario*) owner; (*jefe*) boss

principal[2] *m* **1.** (*piso*) first floor *Brit,* second floor *Am* **2.** (*edición*) first edition

principalmente *adv* mainly, principally; **él ha sido ~ el que ha hecho el trabajo** he is the one who did most of the work

príncipe *adj* **edición ~** first edition

príncipe, princesa *m, f* prince *m,* princess *f;* **~ heredero** crown prince; **el Príncipe de Asturias** the Prince of Asturias (*title held by the heir to the Spanish throne*)*;* **~ azul** Prince Charming

principesco, -a *adj* princely

principiante *mf* beginner, novice

principio *m* **1.** (*comienzo*) beginning; **al ~** at the beginning; **ya desde el ~** right from the beginning; **desde un ~** from the first; **a ~s de diciembre** at the beginning of December; **dar ~ a algo** to start sth **2.** (*causa*) cause; (*origen*) origin; **el ~ de la discusión** the cause of the argument **3.** (*de ética*) principle; **sin ~s** unprincipled; **hombre de ~s** a man of principle(s); **por ~** on principle **4.** *t.* FÍS (*fundamento*) principle; **en ~** in principle **5.** QUÍM element **6.** *pl* (*de ciencia*) fundamentals *pl*

pringado, -a *m, f inf* (*primo*) chump, mug *Brit*

pringar <g→gu> **I.** *vt* **1.** (*manchar*) **~ de/con algo** to smear with sth **2.** (*mojar*) to dip **3.** *inf* (*herir*) to wound **4.** *inf* (*desacreditar*) to run down **II.** *vi* **1.** *pey, inf* (*en negocio*) to make a bit on the side **2.** *inf* (*trabajar*) to slog one's guts out **3.** *AmL* (*lloviznar*) to drizzle **4.** *inf* (*morir*) to snuff it **III.** *vr:* **~se 1.** (*mancharse*) **~se de/con algo** to cover oneself with sth **2.** (*en negocio*) to make a bit on the side; **se ha pringado en 200 marcos** *pey* he has raked off 200 marks

pringoso, -a *adj* **1.** (*grasiento*) greasy **2.** (*pegajoso*) sticky

pringue *m* **1.** (*grasa*) grease **2.** (*suciedad*) grime **3.** *inf* (*jugada*) **¿que tienes que repetir el trabajo? ¡vaya ~ tío!** *inf* you've got to do the work again? what a drag!

prioridad *f* **1.** (*anterioridad, urgencia*) priority; **de máxima ~** top priority; **dar ~ a un asunto** to give an affair priority **2.** AUTO right of way

prioritario, -a *adj* priority; **este plan es ~** this plan has priority

prisa *f* hurry; **a toda ~** at full speed; **de ~** quickly; **de ~ y corriendo** (*con demasiada prisa*) in a rush; (*rápidamente*) quickly; **no corre ~** there's no hurry; **¡date ~!** hurry up!; **meter ~ a alguien** to hurry sb; **tengo ~** I'm in a hurry; **no tengas ~** take your time

prisión *f* **1.** (*reclusión*) imprisonment; **~ celular** confinement in cells; **~ preventiva** remand **2.** (*edificio*) prison; **~ de alta seguridad** high-security prison; **estar en ~** to be in prison

prisionero, -a *m, f* prisoner; **hacer ~ a alguien** to take sb prisoner

prisma *m* **1.** (*figura*) prism **2.** (*perspectiva*)

P

angle

prismáticos *mpl* binoculars *pl*

privación *f* 1. (*desposesión*) deprivation; ~ **de libertad** JUR loss of liberty 2. (*carencia*) privation

privado *m* (*de rey*) royal favourite *Brit* [*o* favorite *Am*]; (*de ministro*) protégé

privado, -a *adj* 1. (*reunión, fiesta*) private; (*sesión*) closed 2. (*personal, confidencial*) private; **vida privada** private life; **en el trabajo es insoportable, pero en ~...** at work he is unbearable, but outside ...; **quisiera hablar en ~ contigo** I would like to speak to you in private 3. (*falto*) ~ **de...** without ...; ~ **de flexibilidad** (*cosa*) inelastic; (*persona*) inflexible; ~ **de inteligencia** slow-witted; ~ **de la libertad** deprived of one's freedom; ~ **de medios** without means

privanza *f* (*de príncipe*) favour *Brit,* favor *Am;* (*de ministro*) protection

privar I. *vt* 1. (*desposeer*) to deprive; ~ **a alguien del permiso de conducir** to take away sb's driving licence *Brit* [*o* driver's license *Am*]; ~ **a alguien de libertad** to deprive sb of his freedom; ~ **a alguien de un derecho** to deprive sb of a right; ~ **a alguien de un cargo** to remove sb from a position 2. (*prohibir*) to forbid; **no me prives de visitarte** don't stop me from visiting you 3. (*gustar*) to delight; **está privado por esa chica** he's crazy about that girl II. *vi* 1. (*estar de moda*) to be fashionable 2. (*influir*) to have influence III. *vr* to deny oneself; **no se privan de nada** they don't want for anything

privativo, -a *adj* (*propio*) exclusive; ~ **de alguien** exclusive to sb; **esta facultad es privativa del presidente** that power belongs exclusively to the president

privatización *f* privatization

privatizar <z→c> *vt* to privatize

privilegiado, -a I. *adj* privileged; (*memoria*) exceptional II. *m, f* privileged person

privilegiar *vt* to grant a privilege to

privilegio *m* privilege; ~ **fiscal** tax concession

pro I. *m o f* 1. (*provecho*) advantage; **valorar los ~s y los contras** to weigh up the pros and cons; **en ~ de** in favour [*o* favor *Am*] of; **campaña en ~ de la erradicación de las pruebas nucleares** campaign for the banning of nuclear tests 2. (*de bien*) **un hombre de ~** an honest man II. *prep* for

proa *f* NÁUT bow; AVIAT nose; **poner la ~ en un asunto** to tackle an affair; **poner la ~ a alguien** to take a stand against sb

probabilidad *f* 1. (*verosimilitud*) probability; **con toda ~** in all likelihood 2. (*posibilidad*) prospect; **hay ~es de rescatar los rehenes** there is a good chance of rescuing the hostages

probable *adj* 1. (*verosímil*) probable; **un resultado ~** a likely result; **lo más ~ es que...** chances are that ...; **el ~ campeón** the likely winner 2. (*que se puede probar*) provable

probablemente *adv* probably

probado, -a *adj* (*cosa, cualidad, método*) proven; (*trabajador*) experienced

probador *m* fitting room

probar <o→ue> I. *vt* 1. (*demostrar*) to prove; **todavía no está probado que sea culpable** it still hasn't been proved that he is guilty 2. (*experimentar*) to try; (*aparato*) to test 3. (*a alguien*) to test 4. (*vestido*) to try on 5. GASTR to taste; **no he probado nunca una paella** I have never tried paella II. *vi* (*intentar*) to try

probatorio, -a *adj* evidential

probatura *f inf* go; TEAT, CINE rehearsal

probeta *f* (*tubo*) test tube; ~ **graduada** graduated flask

probidad *f* probity

problema *m* (*cuestión, dificultad, ejercicio*) problem; ~**s de adaptación** teething problems; ~ **de liquidez** cash flow problem; **el planteamiento del ~** the way in which the problem is presented

problemática *f* problems *pl,* questions *pl*

problemático, -a *adj* problematic

probo, -a *adj* 1. (*honrado*) honest 2. (*íntegro*) upright

probóscide *f* proboscis

procacidad *f* 1. (*insolencia*) shamelessness 2. (*grosería*) obscenity

procaz *adj* 1. (*insolente*) shameless 2. (*grosero*) obscene

procedencia *f* 1. (*origen*) origin; **anunciar la ~ del tren** to announce where the train has come from 2. JUR legitimacy

procedente *adj* 1. (*oportuno*) appropriate 2. (*que viene de*) ~ **de** from; **el tren ~ de Nueva York con destino a Chicago** the train from New York to Chicago 3. JUR fitting

proceder I. *m* 1. (*comportamiento*) behaviour *Brit,* behavior *Am* 2. (*actuación*) (course of) action II. *vi* 1. (*familia*) to descend; (*de un lugar*) to come; (*pasión*) to spring 2. (*actuar*) to act 3. (*ser oportuno*) to be appropriate; **no ~** to be inappropriate; **ahora procede guardar silencio** now we (etc.) should remain silent; **táchese lo que no proceda** delete as applicable 4. (*pasar a*) to proceed 5. JUR (*iniciar un proceso*) to begin proceedings; (*procesar*) to process; **no procede** it is not appropriate

procedimiento *m* 1. (*actuación*) procedure; **¿qué ~ se puede seguir aquí?** what procedure should be followed here? 2. (*método*) method 3. JUR proceedings *pl*

prócer I. *adj* illustrious II. *m* national hero

procesado, -a *m, f* JUR defendant; **el ~** the accused

procesador *m* processor, computer *Am;* ~ **de textos** word processor

procesal *adj* (*costos, actuación*) legal; (*regla, derecho*) procedural

procesamiento *m* 1. JUR prosecution 2. INFOR processing; ~ **en línea** on-line processing

procesar *vt* **1.** JUR to prosecute; **le procesan por violación** he is being prosecuted for rape **2.** TÉC to process

procesión *f* **1.** *t.* REL (*marcha*) procession **2.** (*hilera*) line; (*de personas*) procession **3.** *inf* (*preocupación*) **permaneció tranquilo aunque la ~ iba por dentro** he remained outwardly calm, but he was actually rather worried

proceso *m* **1.** (*método*) process; **~ de una enfermedad** development of an illness **2.** (*procedimiento*) procedure **3.** JUR (*causa*) trial **4.** (*intervalo*) course

proclama *f* **1.** (*matrimonial*) banns *pl* **2.** (*política*) proclamation

proclamación *f* proclamation

proclamar **I.** *vt* **1.** (*hacer público*) to announce; **~ la República** to proclaim a Republic **2.** (*aclamar*) to acclaim **3.** (*sentimiento*) to declare **4.** (*ganador*) to declare; **fue proclamado Premio Nobel** he was awarded the Nobel Prize **II.** *vr* **~se presidente** to proclaim oneself president; **~se ganador** to declare oneself the winner

proclive *adj* prone

procrear *vt* **1.** (*engendrar*) to procreate **2.** (*reproducirse*) to reproduce

proctólogo, **-a** *m, f* MED proctologist *m, f*

procura *f* **1.** JUR power of attorney **2.** *Méx* **en ~ de** in an attempt to

procurador(**a**) *m(f)* attorney; (*en negocios*) agent

procurar **I.** *vt* **1.** (*intentar*) to try; **procura hacerlo lo mejor que puedas** do it to the best of your abilities; **procura que no te vean más por aquí** make sure you're not seen around here any more; **procura que no te oigan** make sure they don't hear you **2.** (*proporcionar*) to obtain **II.** *vr* to secure (for oneself)

prodigalidad *f* **1.** (*despilfarro*) wastefulness **2.** (*abundancia*) profusion

prodigar <g→gu> **I.** *vt* **1.** (*malgastar*) to waste **2.** (*dar*) to lavish **II.** *vr* **se prodigó en toda clase de atenciones con nosotros** he attended to our every need; **se prodigó en elogios hacia él** he/she showered him with praise; **se prodiga tanto en las explicaciones que nadie la entiende** her explanations are so detailed that nobody understands her

prodigio *m* prodigy; **niño ~** child prodigy

prodigioso, **-a** *adj* **1.** (*sobrenatural*) miraculous **2.** (*extraordinario*) marvellous *Brit,* marvelous *Am*

pródigo, **-a** *adj* **1.** (*malgastador*) wasteful; **el hijo ~** the prodigal son **2.** (*generoso*) generous; **la pródiga naturaleza** bountiful nature

producción *f* **1.** *t.* TÉC, CINE production; **~ en cadena** assembly line production; **~ por encargo** manufacture to order; **~ en masa** mass production; **~ a medida** made-to-measure fabrication **2.** (*productos*) output **3.** JUR (*de pruebas, documentos*) presentation

producir *irr como traducir* **I.** *vt* **1.** *t.* TÉC, CINE to produce; (*energía*) to generate **2.** (*beneficios*) to generate; (*intereses*) to yield **3.** (*alegría, impresión*) to create; (*aburrimiento, miedo*) to produce; (*daño, tristeza*) to cause **4.** JUR (*pruebas, documentos*) to present **II.** *vr:* **~se** **1.** (*fabricarse*) to be produced **2.** (*tener lugar*) to take place; **se produjo una crisis** a crisis occurred; **se ha producido una mejora** there has been an improvement **3.** (*ocurrir*) to occur; **cuando se produzca el caso...** as the case arises ...

productividad *f* (*de máquina, mina*) productivity; (*de negocio*) profitability; (*de tierra*) fertility

productivo, **-a** *adj* (*máquina, mina*) productive; (*negocio*) profitable; (*tierra*) fertile

producto *m* **1.** *t.* QUÍM, MAT (*objeto*) product; **~s básicos** commodities; **~s agrícolas** agricultural produce; **~ alimenticio** food item; **~s alimenticios** foodstuffs *pl;* **~ de belleza** beauty product; **~ estancado** product sold by state monopoly; **~s a granel** goods sold by bulk; **~ de línea blanca** no-name product; **~ de marca** brand-name product; **~s químicos** chemicals *pl;* **~s** (**semi**)**manufacturado** manufactured good; **~ terminado** finished product; **~ derivado** [*o* **secundario**] by-product **2.** (*de un negocio*) profit; (*de una venta*) proceeds *pl;* **Producto Interior Bruto** Gross Domestic Product; **Producto Nacional Bruto** Gross National Product

productor(**a**) **I.** *adj* producing **II.** *m(f)* producer

proemio *m* preface

proeza *f* exploit

profanar *vt* **1.** (*templo, cementerio*) to desecrate **2.** (*memoria, nombre*) to profane

profano, **-a** *adj* **1.** (*secular*) secular **2.** (*irreverente*) irreverent **3.** (*ignorante*) ignorant; **soy ~ en esta materia** I am not an expert in this subject

profecía *f* prophecy

proferir *irr como sentir vt* (*palabra, grito*) to utter; (*insulto*) to hurl; (*queja*) to express

profesar **I.** *vt* **1.** (*oficio*) to practise *Brit,* to practice *Am* **2.** (*admiración*) to declare **3.** (*religión, doctrina*) to profess **4.** ENS to teach **II.** *vi, vr:* **~se** to take one's vows

profesión *f* **1.** (*empleo*) profession; **la ~ más antigua del mundo** the world's oldest profession; **las profesiones liberales** the professions; **de ~** by profession **2.** (*de admiración*) declaration **3.** (*de religión, doctrina*) profession; **~ de fe** profession of one's faith ►hacer **~ de algo** to boast about sth

profesional **I.** *adj* **1.** (*de la profesión, no aficionado*) professional; **deportista ~** professional sportsman, sportswoman; **ética ~** professional ethics; **secreto ~** trade secret **2.** (*académico*) academic **II.** *mf* **1.** (*experto, no aficionado*) professional **2.** (*académico*) aca-

demic
profesionista *mf Méx* professional
profesor(a) *m(f)* (*no universitario*) teacher; (*universitario*) lecturer *Brit,* professor *Am;* (*catedrático*) senior teacher; ~ **agregado** senior lecturer *Brit,* assistant professor *Am;* ~ **numerario** [*o* **titular**] full professor
profesorado *m* **1.** (*cargo no universitario*) teaching post; (*cargo universitario*) lectureship *Brit,* professorship *Am* **2.** (*conjunto*) teaching staff *Brit,* faculty *Am*
profeta, -isa *m, f* prophet *m(f),* prophetess *f;* **nadie es ~ en su tierra** no one is a prophet in his own land
profetizar <z→c> *vt* to prophesy; *fig* (*adivinar*) to conjecture
profiláctico *m* condom
profiláctico, -a *adj* preventive, preventative
profilaxis *f inv* prophylaxis
prófugo *m* MIL deserter
prófugo, -a *m, f* JUR fugitive
profundamente *adv* profoundly; ~ **ofendido** deeply offended; ~ **sentido** heartfelt; **una persona ~ moral** a profoundly moral person
profundidad *f* depth; **analizar en ~** to analyse in depth; **tener mucha/poca ~** to be very deep/not very deep; **una cueva de cinco metros de ~** a cave five metres deep
profundizar <z→c> **I.** *vt* (*hoyo, zanja*) to make deeper; *fig* to study in depth **II.** *vi* ~ **en algo** to study [*o* to go into] sth in depth
profundo, -a *adj* (*hoyo, lago, voz*) deep; (*capa, estrato*) deep-lying; (*observación*) incisive; (*pena*) heartfelt; (*dificultad*) extreme; (*pensamiento, misterio*) profound; (*conocimiento*) thorough; **psicología profunda** deep psychology; **en lo más ~ de mi corazón** from the very bottom of my heart
profusión *f* profusion; ~ **de ideas** profusion of ideas; ~ **de trabajo** surplus of work; **con ~ de detalles** with a wealth of details; **hay gran ~ de noticias** there is a lot of news
profuso, -a *adj* profuse
progenie *f* **1.** (*casta*) lineage **2.** (*descendencia*) offspring, progeny
progenitor(a) *m(f)* **1.** (*antepasado*) for(e)bear **2.** (*mayor*) father *m,* mother *f;* **los ~es** the parents
programa *m* programme *Brit,* program *Am;* ~ **de las clases (de la Universidad)** (university) timetable; ~ **de estudios** study plan; ~ **de trabajo** work schedule; ~ **antivirus** INFOR antivirus program; ~ **aplicativo** INFOR application; ~ **contaminado** INFOR infected program; ~ **de demostración** INFOR trial software; ~ **de gráficas** INFOR graphics programme; ~ **de tratamiento de textos** INFOR word-processing package; **~s utilitarios** INFOR utilities *pl*
programación *f* **1.** (*acción*) programming **2.** TV, RADIO programme *Brit,* program *Am*
programador(a) *m(f)* programmer
programar *vt* to plan; **la conferencia está programada para el domingo** the talk is scheduled for Sunday; **¿qué tienes programado para esta tarde?** what have you got planned for this evening?
progre I. *adj inf* trendy; POL left-wing; **sus ideas son ~s** he/she is a lefty **II.** *mf* trendy liberal; POL lefty
progresar *vi* to make progress; (*enfermedad, ciencia*) to develop; ~ **profesionalmente** to progress [*o* get ahead] in one's career
progresión *f* **1.** (*avance*) progress **2.** MAT, MÚS progression
progresista I. *adj* progressive **II.** *mf* progressive person
progresivamente *adv* progressively; **recuperarse ~** to recover gradually
progresivo, -a *adj t.* FIN (*que progresa*) progressive; (*que aumenta*) increasing; **aspecto ~** LING continuous tense
progreso *m* progress
prohibición *f* prohibition
prohibido, -a *adj* ~ **fumar** no smoking; **fruto ~** forbidden fruit; **prohibida la entrada** no entry
prohibir *irr vt* to prohibit, to ban; **en los hospitales prohiben fumar** in hospitals smoking is not allowed
prohibitivo, -a *adj* prohibitive; **a precio ~** prohibitively expensive
prohijar *irr como airar vt t. fig* to adopt
prójimo *m* **1.** (*semejante*) fellow man; **amor al ~** love of one's neighbour *Brit* [*o* neighbor *Am*] **2.** *pey* (*sujeto*) specimen; **¡menudo ~ tenemos de vecino!** what a neighbour *Brit* [*o* neighbor *Am*] we've got!
prole *f* offspring *pl;* **padre con numerosa ~** father with several children
prolegómeno *m* (*a un escrito*) preface; (*al hablar*) introduction; **déjate de ~s y ve al grano** *inf* stop beating around the bush and get to the point
proletariado *m* proletariat
proletario, -a I. *adj* proletarian; **barrio ~** working-class area **II.** *m, f* proletarian
proliferación *f* **1.** (*en cantidad*) proliferation; **tratado de no ~ de armas nucleares** nuclear non-proliferation treaty **2.** *t.* MED (*incontrolada*) spread
proliferar *vi* **1.** (*en cantidad*) to proliferate **2.** (*epidemia, rumor*) to spread
prolífico, -a *adj* prolific
prolijo, -a *adj* **1.** (*extenso*) protracted **2.** (*esmerado*) detailed **3.** (*cargante*) long-winded
prólogo *m* (*de libro*) foreword; TEAT, DEP prelude
prolongación *f* extension; (*de decisión*) postponement
prolongado, -a *adj* prolonged; **un sobre ~** a long envelope
prolongar <g→gu> **I.** *vt* to extend; (*decisión*) to postpone; (*un estado*) to prolong **II.** *vr:* **~se** to continue; (*un estado*) to be pro-

longed; (*reunión*) to overrun; **la fiesta se prolongó hasta bien entrada la noche** the party carried on well into the night; **las negociaciones se están prolongando demasiado** the negotiations are dragging on for too long

promediar I. *vt* 1. (*repartir*) to divide in two 2. (*sacar promedio*) to average out II. *vi* 1. (*mediar*) to mediate 2. (*temporal*) **antes de ~ el año** before the year was halfway through; **promediaba el mes cuando...** the month was halfway through when ...

promedio *m* average; **veo la tele un ~ de dos horas al día** I watch an average of two hours' TV a day

promesa *f* promise; REL vow; **~ de matrimonio** promise of marriage; **el jefe me ha dado su ~ de que...** the boss has promised me that ...

prometedor(a) *adj* promising

prometer I. *vt* to promise; REL to vow; **te prometo que lo haré** I promise you I'll do it; **te prometo por mis muertos que...** I promise on my mother's grave that ...; **~ el oro y el moro** to promise the earth ►**lo prometido es deuda** *prov* a promise is a promise II. *vi* **este negocio promete** this business is promising III. *vr:* **~se** 1. (*novios*) to get engaged 2. (*esperar*) to hope; **prometérselas muy felices** to have high hopes

prometido, -a *m, f* fiancé *m,* fiancée *f*

prominencia *f* 1. (*abultamiento*) bulge 2. (*del terreno*) rise 3. MED swelling

prominente *adj* prominent

promiscuidad *f* 1. (*mezcla*) mixture 2. (*sexual*) promiscuity

promiscuo, -a *adj* 1. *pey* (*mezclado*) mixed 2. (*ambiguo*) ambiguous 3. (*sexualmente*) promiscuous

promoción *f* 1. (*de empresa, categoría, producto*) promotion 2. (*de licenciados*) year, graduating class; **ser de la misma ~** to have graduated in the same year

promocionar I. *vt* (*a empresa, de categoría, a producto*) to promote; **está promocionando su nueva película** she is promoting her new film II. *vi* DEP to be promoted

promontorio *m* 1. (*terreno*) promontory; (*colina*) hill 2. (*de papeles*) pile

promotor(a) *m(f)* 1. (*de altercado*) instigator 2. (*patrocinador*) sponsor; (*deportivo, artístico, de espectáculo*) promoter

promover <o→ue> *vt* 1. (*querella, escándalo*) to cause; (*proceso*) to advance 2. (*en el cargo*) to promote 3. (*aplausos*) to bring forth; (*altercado*) to instigate

promulgación *f* enactment; (*divulgación*) announcement

promulgar <g→gu> *vt* to enact; (*divulgar*) to announce

pronombre *m* LING pronoun

pronominal *adj* LING pronominal; **verbo ~** reflexive verb

pronosticar <c→qu> *vt* to forecast

pronóstico *m t.* ECON forecast; MED prognosis; DEP prediction; **lesiones de ~ reservado** injuries of unknown seriousness

prontitud *f* 1. (*celeridad*) speed; (*de ejecución*) promptness 2. (*de ingenio*) sharpness

pronto I. *adv* 1. (*rápido*) quickly 2. (*enseguida*) at once 3. (*temprano*) early ►**al ~** at first; **de ~** suddenly; **¡hasta ~!** see you!; **por de** [*o* **por lo**] **~** for the time being II. *conj* **tan ~ como** as soon as; **tan ~ como llegaron/lleguen** as soon as they arrived/arrive

pronto, -a *adj* 1. (*rápido*) quick; (*despierto*) sharp; **inteligencia pronta** lively intelligence 2. (*dispuesto*) ready; **estar ~** *CSur* to be ready

prontuario *m* 1. (*resumen*) summary 2. (*manual*) handbook

pronunciación *f* LING pronunciation

pronunciado, -a *adj* pronounced; (*pendiente, cuesta*) steep; **arrugas pronunciadas** deep lines; **acento ~** strong [*o* marked] accent; **una curva pronunciada** a sharp bend; **rasgos ~s** strong features

pronunciamiento *m* 1. (*alzamiento*) (pronouncement of a) military coup 2. JUR pronouncement; **~ judicial** legal judgement; **~ de sentencia** sentencing

pronunciar I. *vt* 1. (*articular*) to pronounce; **~ un brindis por alguien** to propose a toast in sb's honour *Brit* [*o* honor *Am*]; **~ un discurso** to make a speech; **~ unas palabras** to say a few words; **~ sentencia** to pass sentence 2. (*resaltar*) to emphasize II. *vr:* **~se** 1. (*levantarse*) to launch a military coup 2. (*apoyar*) to declare oneself 3. (*opinar*) **~se sobre algo** to state one's opinion on sth 4. (*acentuarse*) to become more pronounced

propagación *f* 1. (*multiplicación, reproducción*) propagation 2. (*extensión, transmisión*) spreading

propaganda *f* 1. (*publicidad, promoción*) publicity; **hacer ~** to advertise, to publicize 2. MIL, POL propaganda

propagar <g→gu> I. *vt* 1. (*multiplicar, reproducir*) to propagate 2. (*extender, divulgar*) to spread; **~ un rumor** to spread a rumour II. *vr:* **~se** 1. (*multiplicarse, reproducirse*) to propagate 2. (*extenderse, divulgarse, transmitirse*) to spread

propalar *vt, vr:* **~se** to spread

propano *m* propane

propasar I. *vt* to overstep II. *vr:* **~se** (*extralimitarse*) to go too far; (*excederse*) to overstep the mark; **~se con alguien** to take liberties with sb

propender *vi* **~ a algo** to tend towards sth; MED to be prone to sth

propensión *f* **~ a algo** tendency towards sth; MED predisposition to sth; **tener gran ~ a resfriarse** to catch colds very easily

propenso, -a *adj* (*a enfermedades*) susceptible; (*dispuesto*) inclined; **ser ~ a algo** to be prone to sth

propiamente *adv* (*realmente*) really; (*exacta-*

mente) exactly; ~ **dicho** strictly speaking

propiciar I. *vt* 1. (*aplacar*) to placate 2. (*favorecer*) to favour *Brit*, to favour *Am*; (*posibilitar*) to make possible; **el viento propició la extensión de las llamas** the wind helped the flames to spread II. *vr:* ~**se** (*conseguir*) to gain; **con sus palabras se propició el respeto de todos** with his/her words he/she won everyone's respect

propicio, **-a** *adj* 1. (*favorable*) favourable *Brit*, favorable *Am*; **en el momento** ~ at the right moment 2. (*dispuesto*) inclined; **mostrarse (poco)** ~ **para...** (not) to be prepared to ...

propiedad *f* 1. (*pertenencia*) property; (*inmuebles*) property, estate; (*derechos*) right; ~ **exclusiva** exclusive ownership; ~ **horizontal** joint ownership (*in a block of flats*); ~ **industrial** patent rights; ~ **intelectual** intellectual property; ~ **inmobiliaria** real assets *Brit*, real estate *Am*; ~ **mobiliaria** movable property; ~ **rústica** farm property; **un piso de mi** ~ a flat *Brit* [*o* an apartment *Am*] which I own; **tener algo en** ~ to own sth; **ser** ~ **de alguien** to be sb's property 2. *t.* FÍS (*cualidad*) property 3. (*corrección*) correctness; (*exactitud*) precision; **expresarse con** ~ to speak correctly

propietario, **-a** I. *adj* proprietary II. *m, f* owner; (*terrateniente*) landowner; (*casero*) landlord

propina *f* tipo; **dejar** ~ to leave a tip; **me dió dos libras de** ~ he/she gave me a two pound tip; **de** ~ *fig* for good measure

propinar *vt* (*golpes*) to give

propio, **-a** *adj* 1. (*de uno mismo*) own; **con la propia mano** with one's own hand; **entregar en propia mano** to deliver personally; **en defensa propia** in self-defence *Brit*, in self-defense *Am*; **es tu propia culpa** it's your own fault; **lo he visto con mis** ~**s ojos** I have seen it with my own eyes; **tengo piso** ~ I own my flat *Brit* [*o* apartment *Am*] 2. (*mismo*) same; **lo** ~ the same; **el** ~ **jefe** the boss himself; **al** ~ **tiempo** at the same time; **nombre** ~ LING proper noun 3. (*característico*) characteristic; **los productos** ~**s del país** the products of the country; **eso (no) es** ~ **de ti** that is (not) like you 4. (*apropiado*) proper

proponer *irr como poner* I. *vt* 1. (*sugerir, presentar*) to propose; ~ **un brindis por alguien** to propose a toast in sb's honour *Brit* [*o* honor *Am*] 2. (*plantear*) to put forward; ~ **un acertijo** to ask a riddle; ~ **una cuestión** to set out a matter II. *vr* to propose; (*tener intención*) to intend; **¿qué te propones?** what are you trying to do?

proporción *f* 1. (*relación, porcentaje*) proportion; **no guardar** ~ **con algo** to be out of proportion with sth; **en una** ~ **de 8 a 1** in a ratio of 8 to 1 2. *pl* (*dimensión*) proportions *pl*; **un accidente de enormes proporciones** a major accident

proporcional *adj* proportional; **reparto** ~ proportional distribution; **sistema** ~ POL proportional representation

proporcionar *vt* 1. (*facilitar*) to provide; (*conseguir, procurar*) to obtain; ~ **víveres a alguien** to provide sb with supplies 2. (*ocasionar*) to cause; ~ **disgustos a alguien** to upset sb 3. (*dar proporción*) to proportion; (*adecuar*) to fit 4. (*repartir*) to distribute 5. (*crear*) to create 6. (*producir*) to produce

proposición *f* 1. (*propuesta*) proposal; ~ **de ley** bill; ~ **de matrimonio** marriage proposal 2. (*solicitud*) request 3. (*oferta*) offer 4. LING (*oración*) sentence; (*parte*) clause

propósito I. *m* 1. (*intención*) intention; (*plan*) plan; **buenos** ~**s** good intentions; **tener el** ~ **de...** to intend to ... 2. (*objetivo*) objective ▸**fuera de** ~ irrelevant; **a** ~ (*adrede*) on purpose; (*adecuado*) suitable; (*por cierto*) by the way; **¡a** ~**! tu hermana viene mañana** talking of that, your sister is coming tomorrow II. *prep* **a** ~ **de** with regard to

propuesta *f* 1. (*proposición*) proposal 2. (*solicitud*) request 3. (*oferta*) offer 4. (*recomendación*) suggestion; **a** ~ **de alguien** on sb's suggestion; **formular una** ~ to draw up a proposal

propugnar *vt* 1. (*defender*) to defend 2. (*apoyar, promover*) to advocate

propulsar *vt* 1. TÉC to propel 2. (*fomentar*) to promote

propulsión *f* TÉC propulsion; ~ **delantera/trasera** AUTO rear-/front-wheel drive; ~ **a hélice** propeller power; ~ **por reacción** jet propulsion; ~ **total** AUTO four-wheel drive

prorrata *f* (*parte*) portion; (*cuota*) quota

prórroga *f* 1. (*prolongación*) prolongation; ECON extension; ~ **de pago** extension of payment deadline 2. (*dilatoria, retraso*) delay; (*aplazamiento*) deferral; (*cambio de fecha*) postponement 3. DEP extra time, overtime

prorrogación *f* extension

prorrogar <g→gu> *vt* 1. (*prolongar*) to prolong; ECON to extend 2. (*dilatar, retrasar*) to delay 3. *t.* JUR (*aplazar*) to defer; (*cambiar de fecha*) to postpone

prorrumpir *vi* 1. (*salir*) to burst forth 2. (*estallar*) to break out; ~ **en algo** to break out into sth

prosa *f* prose; **texto en** ~ piece of prose

prosaico, **-a** *adj* prosaic

prosapia *f* ancestry; **de mucha** ~ from an illustrious family

proscribir *irr como escribir vt* to ban

proscrito, **-a** I. *pp de* **proscribir** II. *m, f* exile

prosecución *f* 1. (*continuación*) continuation 2. *t.* JUR prosecution; (*de un fin*) pursuit; ~ **criminal** pursuit of a criminal

proseguir *irr como seguir* I. *vi* (*alguien*) to continue; (*mal tiempo*) to persist; ~ **con/en algo** to persist with sth II. *vt* 1. (*continuar*) *t.* JUR to continue; ~ **diligencias** to continue proceedings 2. (*un fin*) to pursue

prosista *mf* prose writer

prospección *f* MIN prospecting; ~ **petro-**

lífera oil prospecting; ~ **de mercado** ECON market research

prospecto *m* (*folleto*) prospectus; (*de instrucciones*) instruction leaflet; (*informativo*) (information) leaflet; (*de un medicamento*) directions *pl* for use

prosperar *vi* **1.** (*crecer*) to grow; (*florecer*) to thrive; (*tener éxito*) to prosper **2.** (*imponerse*) to become established

prosperidad *f* (*bienestar*) prosperity; ~ **económica** economic prosperity

próspero, **-a** *adj* **1.** (*feliz*) happy; **¡Próspero Año Nuevo!** Happy New Year! **2.** (*floreciente*) thriving **3.** (*rico, con éxito*) prosperous

próstata *f* prostate

prosternarse *vr* to prostrate oneself

prostíbulo *m* brothel

prostitución *f* prostitution; **ejercer la** ~ to be a prostitute

prostituir *irr como huir* **I.** *vt* to prostitute **II.** *vr:* ~**se** *t. fig* to prostitute oneself

prostituto, **-a** *m, f* male prostitute *m,* prostitute *f*

prosudo, **-a** *Chile, Ecua, Perú* **I.** *adj* affectedly formal **II.** *m, f* pompous person

protagonista **I.** *adj* **la actriz** ~ the leading actress; **el papel** ~ the leading role **II.** *mf* key participant; CINE, TEAT leading actor *m,* leading actress *f;* LIT main character

protagonizar <z→c> *vt* (*un papel*) to play; **un gran actor protagoniza esta película** a famous actor stars in this film

protección *f* **1.** (*salvaguarda*) protection; ~ **acústica** sound-proofing; ~ **antiaérea** anti-aircraft defences *Brit* [*o* defenses *Am*]; ~ **contra incendios** fire protection; ~ **sanitaria** health cover; **crema de alta** ~ high-protection sun cream; **poner a alguien bajo** ~ to place sb under protection; **tomar a alguien bajo su** ~ to take sb into one's protection **2.** *t.* POL (*mecenazgo, patrocinio*) patronage **3.** MIL defence *Brit,* defense *Am*

protector *m* (*cosa que protege*) protector; (*en boxeo*) mouthguard; ~ **labial** lip salve; ~ **solar** sunscreen

protector(**a**) **I.** *adj* protective; **casco** ~ protective helmet; **sociedad** ~**a de animales** society for the prevention of cruelty to animals **II.** *m(f)* **1.** (*persona*) protector **2.** *t.* POL (*mecenas*) patron **3.** (*patrocinador*) sponsor

protectorado *m* protectorate

proteger <g→j> **I.** *vt* **1.** *t.* ECOL (*resguardar, asegurar*) to protect **2.** *t.* POL (*como mecenas*) to act as a patron to **II.** *vr:* ~**se** to protect oneself; ~**se los ojos** to protect one's eyes

protegido, **-a** **I.** *adj* protected; ~ **contra escritura** INFOR write-protected; ~ **contra el uso indebido** protected against unauthorized use; ~ **por patente** protected by patent **II.** *m, f* protégé *m,* protégée *f*

proteína *f* protein

prótesis *f inv* prosthesis; ~ **auditiva** hearing aid

protesta *f* **1.** (*queja*) protest **2.** JUR objection **3.** (*aseveración*) protestation

protestante *adj, mf* REL Protestant

protestar **I.** *vi* to protest **II.** *vt* **1.** (*confesar*) to avow **2.** JUR to raise an objection

protestón, **-ona** **I.** *adj inf* grumbling **II.** *m, f inf* grouch

protocolo *m* protocol; **de** ~ formal

protón *m* proton

prototipo *m* prototype

protuberancia *f* protuberance; (*bulto*) bulge

protuberante *adj* protuberant

provecho *m* **1.** (*aprovechamiento*) use; (*ventaja*) advantage; (*producto*) yield; (*beneficio*) benefit; **para su propio** ~ for one's own use; **de** ~ useful; **nada de** ~ nothing of use; **en** ~ **de alguien** to sb's advantage; **sacar** ~ **de algo/alguien** to do benefit from sth/sb, to profit from sth/sb **2.** (*progreso*) progress; (*mejora*) improvement **3.** (*en comidas*) **¡buen ~!** enjoy your meal!, bon appétit!; **hacer** (**buen**) ~ to be beneficial

provechoso, **-a** *adj* beneficial; (*productivo*) productive; (*útil*) useful; (*ventajoso*) advantageous; (*saludable*) healthy

proveedor(**a**) **I.** *adj* supplying **II.** *m(f)* **1.** (*suministrador*) supplier **2.** INFOR provider

proveer *irr* **I.** *vi* to provide; ~ **a algo** to provide for sth; ~ **a las necesidades de alguien** to attend to sb's needs; **¡Dios ~á!** the Lord will provide! **II.** *vt* **1.** (*abastecer, suministrar*) to supply; ~ **de algo** to furnish with sth; (*dotar*) to provide with sth **2.** (*un puesto*) to fill; (*conceder*) to award **3.** JUR ~ **sobre algo** to give an interim ruling on sth **III.** *vr:* ~**se** to supply oneself; ~**se de algo** to provide oneself with sth

proveniente *adj* **el tren** ~ **de Madrid** the train from Madrid

provenir *irr como venir vi* ~ **de** to come from, to stem from

proverbial *adj* proverbial

proverbio *m* proverb

providencia *f* **1.** (*prevención, medida*) precaution **2.** JUR ruling; (*disposición*) measure; ~ **ejecutoria** writ of execution **3.** REL Providence

provincia *f* province; *AmS* (*estado*) state; **ciudad de** ~**s** provincial town

> The 17 **Comunidades Autónomas** in Spain are subdivided into 52 **provincias**. Consequently, the **Comunidad de Castilla-León**, for example, consists of the following nine **provincias**: **Ávila**, **Burgos**, **León**, **Palencia**, **Salamanca**, **Segovia**, **Soria**, **Valladolid** and **Zamora**.

provincial **I.** *adj* provincial; **capital** ~ provincial capital; **delegación** ~ provincial authority **II.** *m* REL provincial

provincialismo *m* provincialism; *pey* parochialism

provinciano, **-a** **I.** *adj t. pey* provincial **II.** *m, f* *t. pey* provincial

provisión *f* **1.**(*reserva*) supply; **provisiones** provisions *pl* **2.**(*suministro*) supply **3.**(*cobertura*) cover; (*reserva*) reserve **4.**(*comisión*) commission **5.**(*medida*) provision **6.**(*de un cargo*) filling **7.** JUR provision

provisional *adj* provisional; **gobierno** ~ provisional government; **medida** ~ temporary measure

provisto, **-a** **I.** *pp de* **proveer** **II.** *adj* provided; ~ **al efecto** provided for the purpose

provocación *f* **1.**(*ataque*) provocation; (*instigación*) instigation **2.**(*causa*) cause; MED (*del parto*) induction, induced labour *Brit* [*o* labor *Am*]

provocador *m* stirrer

provocador(a) **I.** *adj* provocative **II.** *m(f)* POL agitator

provocar <c→qu> **I.** *vt* **1.**(*incitar, irritar*) to provoke; (*excitar*) to arouse; (*instigar*) to instigate; POL to agitate; **¡no me provoques!** don't provoke me! **2.**(*causar*) *t.* MED to cause; (*artificialmente*) to induce; ~ **risa a alguien** to make sb laugh; ~ **lástima a alguien** to make sb feel sorry for one; ~ **un cambio** to bring about a change; ~ **una guerra** to start a war; ~ **una escena** to create a scene; ~ **un incendio** to start a fire **II.** *vi AmL* (*apetecer*) (**no**) **me provoca** I (don't) feel like it

provocativo, **-a** *adj* provocative

proxeneta *mf* (*de prostitutas*) pimp *m;* (*alcahuete*) procurer *m,* procuress *f*

próximamente *adv* soon

proximidad *f* **1.**(*cercanía*) proximity; **en las ~es** in the vicinity **2.**(*parentesco*) closeness

próximo, **-a** *adj* **1.**(*cercano*) near, neighbouring *Brit,* neighboring *Am;* (*temporal*) close; **en fecha próxima** shortly, soon; **estar ~ a...** to be close to ... **2.**(*siguiente*) next; **el ~ año** next year; **el ~ viernes** next Friday; **el ~ 3 de octubre** on the 3rd of October this year; **la próxima vez** the next time; **¡hasta la próxima!** see you soon!

proyección *f* **1.** FÍS, ARQUIT, CINE, PSICO projection; (*sesión*) screening **2.**(*lanzamiento*) throwing (forwards); (*impulso*) stimulation; ~ **de sombras** casting of shadows **3.**(*influencia*) influence; (*orientación*) orientation; **una empresa de ~ internacional** a business with a global presence **4.**(*proyecto*) planning

proyectable *adj* **asiento** ~ AVIAT ejector seat

proyectar **I.** *vt* **1.** FÍS, FOTO, CINE to project **2.**(*lanzar*) to throw **3.**(*luz*) to shine; (*sombra*) to cast **4.**(*planear, proponerse*) to plan **5.** *t.* TÉC (*diseñar*) to design **II.** *vr:* **~se** **1.**(*luz*) to be shone; (*sombra*) to be cast **2.** PSICO **~se en algo** to project onto sth **3.**(*orientarse*) to get one's bearings

proyectil *m* projectile; MIL missile; ~ **anticarro** anti-tank missile

proyecto *m* plan; (*proyección*) projection; (*borrador*) draft; (*propuesta*) proposal; ~ **de fin de carrera** UNIV final year project; (*en Letras*) final year dissertation; ~ **de ley** bill; **en ~** planned; **tener ~s** to have plans; **tener algo en ~** to be planning sth

proyector *m* FOTO, CINE projector; ~ **de cine** film projector; **de diapositivas** slide projector; ~ **de cuerpos opacos** overhead projector; ~ **de luz** floodlight

prudencia *f* **1.**(*precaución, previsión*) prudence; (*cautela*) caution **2.**(*cordura*) wisdom; (*astucia*) good sense **3.**(*moderación*) moderation

prudencial *adj* (*razonable*) reasonable; (*adecuado*) sufficient; (*previsor*) prudent; **una cantidad** ~ an adequate amount

prudenciarse *vr AmL* **1.**(*ser prudente*) to be cautious **2.**(*moderarse*) to be moderate **3.**(*conservar la calma*) to remain calm

prudente *adj* **1.**(*precavido, previsor*) prudent; (*cauteloso*) cautious **2.**(*razonable*) reasonable **3.**(*adecuado*) sufficient

prueba *f* **1.** *t.* TÉC (*test*) test; (*experimento*) experiment; ~ **de alcoholemia** breathalyser® test; ~ **de aptitud** aptitude test; ~ **al azar** random trial; ~ **de azúcar en la sangre** blood sugar test; **~s nucleares** nuclear tests; ~ **de paternidad** paternity test; **período de ~** trial period; **poner a ~** to try out; **someter a ~** to test; **sufrir una dura ~** to be put through a stern test; **a ~ de agua** waterproof; **a ~ de balas** bullet-proof; **a ~ de robo** theftproof; **a título de ~** as a test; **a toda ~** fully tested; *fig* cast-iron; ~ **de fuego** *fig* acid test **2.**(*comprobación*) proof; (*de ropa*) trying on; ~ **de degustación** tasting; (*cata*) (wine)-tasting **3.**(*examen*) exam; ~ **de acceso** entry exam **4.** DEP (*competición*) event; ~ **clasificatoria/eliminatoria** qualifier/eliminator **5.** TIPO proof; ~ **de imprenta** proof **6.**(*testimonio*) piece of evidence; ~ **circunstancial** circumstantial evidence; ~ **documental** documentary evidence; **dar ~s de afecto** to show one's affection; **en ~ de nuestro reconocimiento** as a token of our gratitude; **presentar la ~** to present the evidence; **ser ~ de algo** to be proof of sth; **tener ~s de que...** to have evidence that ...

prurito *m* MED **1.**(*picor*) itch **2.**(*afán*) urge

Prusia *f* Prussia

prusiano, **-a** *adj, m, f* Prussian

P.S. *abr de* **post scriptum** PS

(**p**)**seudonónimo** *m* pseudonym

(**p**)**sicoanálisis** *m sin pl* psychoanalysis

(**p**)**sicoanalista** *mf* psychoanalyst

(**p**)**sicodélico**, **-a** *adj* psychedelic

(**p**)**sicofármaco** *m* psychotropic drug

(**p**)**sicología** *f sin pl* (*ciencia, vida anímica*) psychology; ~ **infantil** child psychology; ~ **evolutiva** developmental psychology

(**p**)**sicológico**, **-a** *adj* psychological; **terror ~** psychological terror

(**p**)**sicólogo**, **-a** *m, f* psychologist; **es muy/poco ~** *inf* he is very/not very perceptive

(**p**)**sicópata** *mf* psychopath; ~ **sexual** sexual

psychopath

(**p**)**sicosis** *f inv* psychosis; ~ **colectiva** collective psychosis

(**p**)**sicosomático, -a** *adj* psychosomatic

(**p**)**sicoterapeuta** *mf* psychotherapist

(**p**)**sicoterapia** *f* psychotherapy

(**p**)**sique** *f* psyche

(**p**)**siquiatra** *mf* psychiatrist

(**p**)**siquiatría** *f* psychiatry

(**p**)**siquiátrico** *m* (*hospital*) mental [*o* psychiatric] hospital

(**p**)**siquiátrico, -a** *adj* psychiatric

(**p**)**síquico, -a** *adj* psychic, mental; **problemas ~s** mental problemas

PSOE *m abr de* **Partido Socialista Obrero Español** *Spanish Socialist Party*

pta. *f* <pt(a)s.> *abr de* **peseta** peseta

púa *f* **1.** (*espina*) spike; (*de planta*) thorn; (*de animal, pez*) spine, quill **2.** (*del peine*) tooth; (*de tenedor*) prong **3.** MÚS plectrum

pub <pubs> *m* bar, cocktail lounge

púber *adj* adolescent

pubertad *f* puberty

púbico, -a *adj* pubic; **zona púbica** pubic area

pubis *m inv* (*zona*) pubic area; (*hueso*) pubis

publicable *adj* publishable

publicación *f* **1.** (*acción, edición*) publication; ~ **electrónica** e-publication; ~ **reciente** recent publication **2.** *t.* JUR (*proclamación*) issue

publicar <c→qu> **I.** *vt* to publish; (*proclamar*) to make known; JUR to issue **II.** *vr:* **~se** to be published

publicidad *f* **1.** (*carácter público*) publicity; **dar** ~ to publicize; **este programa le ha dado mucha** ~ this programme [*o* program *Am*] has given him/her a lot of publicity **2.** (*propaganda*) advertising; ~ **disimulada** subliminal advertising; ~ **sobreimpresa** press advertising; ~ **en TV** TV advertisements *pl;* **hacer ~ de algo** to advertise sth

publicista *mf* publicist

publicitario, -a *adj* advertising

público *m* **1.** (*colectividad*) public; **en** ~ in public; **aparecer en** ~ to appear in public; **el gran** ~ the general public **2.** (*asistente*) audience; **para todos los ~s** for all audiences; CINE U-certificate *Brit,* rated G *Am;* **abierto/cerrado al** ~ open/closed to the public; **hoy hay poco** ~ there aren't many people today

público, -a *adj* **1.** (*no privado, estatal*) public; **deuda pública** national debt; **relaciones públicas** public relations; **el sector** ~ the public sector; **transporte** ~ public transport **2.** (*común*) public; **de utilidad pública** of general use **3.** (*conocido*) public; **escándalo** ~ public scandal; **hacer** ~ to make public; **hacerse** ~ to become known; **ser del dominio** ~ to be public domain

pucha *interj CSur* (*caramba*) **¡la ~!** damn!

pucherazo *m* ~ **electoral** electoral fraud

puchero *m* **1.** (*olla*) pot **2.** GASTR stew **3.** *inf* (*alimento*) grub; **ganarse el** ~ to earn a crust **4.** *inf* (*gestos*) **hacer ~s** to pout

pucho *m AmL* (*resto*) leftover; (*colilla*) cigarette butt

pudibundo, -a *adj pey* prudish

púdico, -a *adj v.* **pudoroso**

pudiente *adj* (*poderoso*) powerful; (*rico*) well-off

pudin *m* pudding

pudor *m* **1.** (*recato*) shyness; (*decencia*) decency; (*vergüenza*) shame **2.** (*modestia*) modesty

pudoroso, -a *adj* **1.** (*recatado*) shy; (*vergonzoso*) bashful; (*decente*) decent **2.** (*modesto*) modest

pudridero *m* (*estercolero*) compost heap; (*muladar*) midden; (*de cadáveres*) temporary vault

pudrir *irr* **I.** *vt* **1.** (*descomponer*) *t. fig* to rot **2.** *inf* (*molestar*) to annoy **II.** *vr:* **~se 1.** (*descomponerse*) *t. fig* to rot; **~se en la cárcel** *inf* to rot in prison; **¡ahí te pudras!** *vulg* go to hell! **2.** *Arg, inf* (*aburrirse*) to get bored

pueblerino, -a I. *adj t. pey* small-town **II.** *m, f* villager; *pey* yokel

pueblo *m* **1.** (*nación*) people; **el ~ bajo** the common people; **un hombre del** ~ a man of the people **2.** (*aldea*) village; (*población*) (small) town; ~ **costero** seaside town; ~ **de mala muerte** *inf* dead-end town; ~ **joven** *AmL* shanty town; **de** ~ from a small town; *pey* small-town

puente *m* **1.** NÁUT (*construcción, de las gafas*) bridge; ~ **levadizo** drawbridge; ~ **colgante** suspension bridge; ~ **aéreo** (*servicio*) shuttle; MIL airlift; ~ **dental** bridge; ~ **de mando** (compass) bridge; ~ **de maniobras** working deck; ~ **de paseo** promenade deck **2.** ELEC bridge (circuit); **hacer un ~ a un coche** to hot-wire a car **3.** (*fiesta*) long weekend (*a public holiday plus an additional day off*)*;* **hacer/tener** ~ to take/have a long weekend

puenting *m sin pl* bungee jumping

puerco, -a I. *adj* **1.** *estar inf* (*sucio*) filthy **2.** *ser* (*indecente*) gross **II.** *m, f* **1.** (*cerdo*) pig; (*macho*) hog; (*hembra*) sow; ~ **espín** porcupine **2.** *inf* (*persona sucia u obscena*) pig **3.** *inf* (*canalla*) swine

puericultor(**a**) *m(f)* MED paediatrician *Brit,* pediatrician *Am;* (*en la guardería*) nursery nurse

puericultura *f sin pl* (*general*) childcare, paediatrics *Brit,* pediatrics *Am*

pueril *adj* **1.** (*infantil*) infant; **edad** ~ childhood **2.** (*inmaduro*) childish

puerro *m* leek

puerta *f* **1.** (*abertura*) door; (*portal*) doorway; (*portalón*) portal; (*acceso*) entry; ~ **de la calle** front door; ~ **corredera** sliding door; ~ **cortafuego** fire door; ~ **de servicio** service door; ~ **de socorro** emergency exit; ~ **giratoria** revolving door; **día de ~s abiertas** open day; **quinta** ~ AUTO rear door; **entrar por la ~ grande** to make a grand entrance; **escuchar**

P

detrás de la ~ to eavesdrop; **a la** ~ **de casa** at the front door; **a** ~ **abierta** *t.* JUR in public; **a** ~ **cerrada** *t.* JUR in private; **a las** ~**s de la muerte** at death's door; **enseñar la** ~ **a alguien** to show sb the door; **estar a las** ~**s** *fig* to be on the brink; **dar a alguien con la** ~ **en las narices** to slam the door in sb's face; **de** ~**s adentro** *fig* in private; **ir de** ~ **en** ~ to go from door to door; **cerrar las** ~**s a alguien** *fig* to block sb's path; **poner a alguien en la** ~ (**de la calle**) to throw sb out; **eso es querer poner** ~**s al campo** *fig* that is like trying to turn back the waves; **por la** ~ **grande** *t. fig* in triumph; **tiene todas las** ~**s abiertas** *fig* he has a wealth of opportunities **2.** DEP goal; **disparo a** ~ shot at goal **3.** INFOR gate

puerto *m* **1.** NÁUT harbour *Brit,* harbor *Am;* (*ciudad*) port; ~ **deportivo** marina; ~ **franco** free port; ~ **interior** river port; ~ **marítimo** seaport; ~ **de matrícula** home port; **tomar** ~ to come into port **2.** (*de montaña*) pass **3.** INFOR port; ~ **para módem** modem port; ~ **de transmisión en paralelo/en serie** parallel/serial port **4.** (*refugio*) haven

Puerto Rico *m* Puerto Rico

> **Puerto Rico**, a state associated with the USA since 1952, consists of a main island and several small islands situated in the Greater Antilles. The capital of Puerto Rico is **San Juan**. The official languages of the country are both Spanish and English.

puertorriqueño, -a *adj, m, f* Puerto Rican

pues **I.** *adv* **1.** (*entonces*) then; (*así que*) so; **Ana quiere conocerte –** ~ **que venga** Ana wants to meet you – well, she should come then; **he vuelto a suspender –** ~ **estudia más** I've failed again – well, you should study more; ~ **entonces, nada** well that's it, then **2.** (*ilativo*) so; ~ **bien** okay; **la consecuencia es,** ~**, ...** so the result is ...; **dejémoslo,** ~ let's leave it, then **3.** (*causal*) **estudio inglés – ¡ah,** ~ **yo también!** I study English – ah, me too!; **yo soy de Salamanca –** ~ **yo, de Soria** I'm from Salamanca – I'm from Soria; **¿quién es? –** ~ **no sé** who is it? – I don't know **4.** (*expletivo*) well; **¿estuvisteis por fin en Toledo? –** ~ **no/sí** did you go to Toledo in the end? – no, I didn't/yes, I did; **¡**~ **esto no es nada!** this is nothing compared with what's to come!; **estoy muy cansado –** ~ **aún queda mucho camino** I'm very tired – well, there's still a long way to go; **¡qué caro! – ¿sí?** ~ **a mí me parece barato** how expensive! – do you think so? it seems cheap to me **5.** (*exclamativo*) **¡**~ **vaya lata!** what a pain!; **¡**~ **no faltaría más!** (*naturalmente*) but of course!; (*el colmo*) that's all we (etc.) need! **6.** (*interrogativo*) **no voy a salir – ¿**~ **cómo es eso?** I'm not going out – why not?; **¿**~ **qué quieres?** what do you want, then?; **¿y** ~**?** and?; **¿**~ **qué ha pasado?** so what happened? **7.** (*atenuación*) well; **¿por qué no viniste a la fiesta? –** ~ **es que tenía mucho que hacer** why didn't you come to the party? – well, I was really busy; **¿nos vemos mañana? –** ~ **no sé todavía** shall we meet tomorrow? – well, I'm not sure yet **8.** (*insistencia*) ~ **así es** well that's how it is; ~ **claro** but of course; **¡vamos** ~**!** come on then!; **¡**~ **entonces!** for that very reason! **II.** *conj* ~ **no me queda otro remedio, venderé el coche** so I don't have any choice, I'll sell the car; **no voy de viaje,** ~ **no tengo dinero** I'm not going on holiday because I don't have any money; ~ **que** *elev* since

puesta *f* **1.** (*general*) putting; ~ **a cero** resetting; ~ **al día** updating; ~ **en escena** TEAT staging; ~ **en funcionamiento** activation; ~ **en hora** setting (*of time*); ~ **en libertad** release; ~ **en marcha** start button; AUTO starter; ~ **en práctica** putting into effect; ~ **a punto** final check; AUTO service **2.** (*de aves*) laying **3.** (*de sol*) setting; ~ **de sol** sunset **4.** (*en el juego*) bet

puestero, -a *m, f* stallholder; (*en el mercado*) market trader

puesto *m* **1.** (*lugar*) place; (*posición*) position; ~ **de información** information point; ~ **de observación** ASTR observation station; MED observation post; **ceder/mantener el** ~ DEP to lose/keep one's place **2.** (*empleo*) job; (*cargo*) post; (*posición*) position **3.** (*tenderete*) stall; (*feria de muestras*) stand; (*chiringuito*) open-air bar; ~ **de periódicos** newspaper stand **4.** MIL post **5.** (*guardia*) post; ~ **de policía** police post; ~ **de socorro** first-aid station **6.** (*caza*) stand

puesto, -a **I.** *pp de* **poner** **II.** *adj* **1.** COM (*ex*) from; ~ **en fábrica** ex works **2.** *inf* (*arreglado*) **ir muy bien** ~ to be very smartly dressed; **tienen la casa muy bien puesta** they've done the house up very nicely; **tenerlos muy bien** ~**s** *vulg* to be a real man **3.** *inf* (*entendido*) **estar** ~ **en un tema** to be well-informed about a subject; ~ **al día** up to date **III.** *conj* ~ **que** given that

pufo *m inf* dirty trick; **meter un** ~ **a alguien** to pull a fast one on sb

pugna *f* (*lucha*) struggle; (*conflicto*) conflict

pugnar *vi* **1.** *t. fig* to fight **2.** (*esforzarse*) to strive; ~ **por algo/alguien** to struggle for sth/sb **3.** (*intentar*) ~ **por algo** to strive for sth

puja *f* **1.** (*esfuerzo*) effort **2.** (*en una subasta*) bid; ~ **mínima** minimum bid

pujante *adj* strong; *fig* vigorous

pujanza *f* (*fuerza*) strength; (*impulso*) drive; (*brío*) vigour *Brit,* vigor *Am*

pujar *vi* **1.** (*esforzarse*) to struggle; ~ **por** to strive for **2.** (*en una subasta*) to bid

pulcritud *f* **1.** (*aseo*) tidiness **2.** (*cuidado*) neatness; (*finura*) delicacy

pulcro, -a <pulquérrimo> *adj* **1.** (*aseado*) tidy **2.** (*cuidadoso*) neat; (*fino*) delicate

pulga *f* flea; INFOR bug; **tener ~s** to be restless; **tener malas ~s** *inf* to be bad-tempered; **buscar las ~s a alguien** *inf* to tease sb
pulgada *f* (*medida*) inch
pulgar I. *adj* **dedo** ~ thumb II. *m* thumb
Pulgarcito *m* LIT Tom Thumb
pulgón *m* aphid
pulguiento, **-a** *adj AmL* (*pulgoso*) flea-ridden
pulido *m* polishing; (*con cera*) waxing
pulido, **-a** *adj* 1. (*brillante*) polished 2. (*fino*) refined; (*estilo*) polished
pulidor *m* TÉC polisher
pulidor(**a**) *adj* TÉC polishing
pulimentar *vt* to polish; (*alisar*) to smooth; (*esmerilar*) to smooth with emery
pulimento *m* 1. *v.* **pulido** 2. (*sustancia*) polish
pulir I. *vt* 1. (*abrillantar*) to polish; (*suavizar*) to smooth; (*esmerilar*) to smooth with emery; (*con cera*) to wax 2. (*perfeccionar, refinar*) to polish up II. *vr:* **~se** 1. (*refinarse*) to become more refined 2. *inf* (*derrochar*) to squander
pulla *f* jibe *Brit,* gibe *Am*
pullman *m AmL* (*coche cama*) sleeping car
pullover *m AmL* (*jersey*) pullover
pulmón *m* lung; ~ **de acero** iron lung; ~ **acuático** aqualung; **gritar a pleno** ~ to shout at the top of one's voice [*o* lungs]; **enfermo de** ~ lung patient; **padecer de los pulmones** to have bad lungs
pulmonar *adj* MED pulmonary
pulmonía *f* MED pneumonia
pulóver *m AmL v.* **pullover**
pulpa *f* 1. ANAT soft matter; ~ **dental** dental pulp 2. (*de la fruta*) flesh; ~ **de madera** wood pulp
pulpería *f AmL* local shop, general store

> In Latin America a **pulpería** is a general store selling alcoholic drinks, where all kinds of items can be bought. **Pulperías** are very similar to the small **tiendas de pueblo** that are still frequently encountered in small villages in Spain.

pulpero, **-a** *m, f AmL* grocer
púlpito *m* pulpit
pulpo *m* 1. ZOOL octopus; **como un** ~ **en un garaje** *inf* completely out of place 2. (*sujeción*) bunjee strap
pulquería *f AmC, Méx* (*pulpería*) general store
pulquero, **-a** *m, f AmS, Méx* (*pulpero*) storekeeper
pulquérrimo, **-a** *adj superl de* **pulcro**
pulsación *f* 1. ANAT (*latido*) beat, throbbing 2. (*de una tecla*) striking; (*mecanografía*) key-stroke; ~ **doble** INFOR strikeover
pulsador *m* 1. (*tecla*) key 2. (*botón*) button 3. (*conmutador*) switch
pulsar *vt* 1. (*oprimir*) to press; (*teclado*) to strike; ~ **el timbre** to ring the bell 2. (*tomar el pulso*) to take the pulse of; ~ **la opinión pública** to gauge [*o* gage *Am*] public opinion
pulsera *f* bracelet; **reloj de** ~ wristwatch
pulso *m* 1. (*muñeca*) wrist; *fig* steadiness of hand; **a** ~ (*sin apoyarse*) freehand; (*por su propio esfuerzo*) on one's own; **con** ~ carefully; **tener buen** ~ to have a steady hand; **tomar el** ~ **a alguien** to take sb's pulse 2. (*desafío*) **echar un** ~ **a alguien** to arm wrestle sb
pulular *vi* 1. (*bullir*) **los turistas pululaban por la plaza** the square was swarming with tourists 2. (*multiplicarse*) to abound 3. (*brotar*) to swarm
pulverizador *m* (*aparato*) sprayer; (*botella*) spray bottle; (*atomizador*) atomizing spray; (*spray*) spray can
pulverizar <z→c> I. *vt* 1. (*reducir a polvo*) to pulverize; (*rallar*) to grate; (*moler*) to grind 2. (*atomizar*) to atomize 3. *fig* (*aniquilar*) to pulverize; (*argumento*) to destroy II. *vr:* **~se** to be pulverized
pum *interj* bang; **ni** ~ *inf* not a thing
puma *m* puma
pumita *f* MIN pumice stone
puna *f AmS* 1. (*altiplano*) Andean plateau 2. (*malestar*) altitude sickness
punción *f* MED puncture
pundonor *m* 1. (*honorabilidad*) dignity, sense of honour *Brit* [*o* honor *Am*] 2. (*honor*) honour *Brit,* honor *Am*
pundonoroso, **-a** *adj* (*honorable*) honourable *Brit,* honorable *Am*
punga *f Arg, inf,* **punguista** *m Arg, inf* (*carterista*) pickpocket
punible *adj* punishable
punición *f* punishment
punitivo, **-a** *adj* punitive
punki *adj, mf* punk
punta *f* 1. (*extremo*) end; (*de lengua, iceberg*) tip; (*de tierra*) headland; **hora**(**s**) ~ rush hour; **de** ~ **a** ~ from end to end; **lo tenía en la** ~ **de la lengua** it was on the tip of my tongue 2. (*pico*) point; **a** ~ **de navaja** at knifepoint; **a** ~ **de pistola** at gunpoint; **acabar en** ~ to come to a point; **sacar** ~ (*afilar*) to sharpen 3. (*un poco*) touch ▸**de** ~ **en** blanco all dressed up; estar **de** ~ **con alguien** to be annoyed with sb; ponerse **de** ~ **con alguien** to fall out with sb
puntada *f* (*costura*) stitch; (*pinchazo*) prick; *fig* hint
puntaje *m AmL v.* **puntuación**
puntal *m* 1. (*madero*) prop; *fig* (*apoyo*) mainstay 2. *AmL* (*refrigerio*) snack
puntapié *m* kick; **pegar un** ~ **a alguien** to kick sb; **tratar a alguien a ~s** *fig* to walk all over sb
puntear *vt* 1. (*marcar con puntos, motear*) to dot 2. (*dar puntadas*) to stitch 3. MÚS to pluck
puntería *f* 1. (*apuntar*) aim 2. (*destreza*) marksmanship; **tener buena/mala** ~ to be a good/bad shot
puntero *m* (*vara*) pointer

P

puntero, -a I. *adj* 1. (*con puntería*) accurate 2. (*sobresaliente*) leading; **tecnología puntera** cutting-edge technology; **el equipo ~** DEP the top team II. *m, f* leader

puntiagudo, -a *adj* (sharp-)pointed

puntilla *f* 1. (*encaje*) lace (edging) 2. (*marcador*) marker 3. (*puñal*) dagger (*used in bullfighting*); **dar la ~ a alguien** *fig* to finish sb off 4. (*del pie*) **de ~s** on tiptoe; **andar de ~s** to walk on tiptoe; **ponerse de ~s** to stand on tiptoe

punto *m* 1. (*general*) point; **~ álgido** crucial moment; **~ de arranque** starting point; **~ cardinal** point of the compass; **~ cero** starting point; **~ clave** key point; **no hay ~ de comparación** there's no comparison; **~ de destino** destination; **~ de ebullición** boiling point; **~ de encuentro** meeting place; **~ esencial** main point; **~ fuerte** strong point; **~ de intersección** intersection; **~ máximo** high point; **~ muerto** AUTO neutral; **~ de referencia** reference point; **~ a tratar** item (on the agenda); **~ de venta** point of sale; **~ de vista** point of view; **dar el ~ a algo** to get sth just right; **ganar por ~s** to win on points; **al ~** (*en seguida*) at once; **hasta tal ~ que...** to such a degree that ...; **de todo ~** absolutely; **la una en ~** exactly one o'clock; **en ~ a** with reference to; **hasta cierto ~** up to a point; **¿hasta qué ~?** how far?; **¡vamos por ~s!** let's take it step by step!; **a ~ de** on the point of; **está a ~ de llover** it's about to rain; **a ~ fijo** exactly; **¡~ en boca!** *inf* mum's the word!; **¡y ~!** *inf* and that's that!; **en su ~** *fig* just right 2. TIPO full stop; **~ y aparte** full stop, new paragraph; **~ y coma** semicolon; **~ final** full stop (*end of paragraph*); **poner ~ final a algo** *fig* to bring sth to an end; **~ y seguido** full stop (*no new paragraph*); **~s suspensivos** suspension points, dot, dot, dot *inf*; **dos ~s** colon; **poner los ~s sobre las íes** *fig* to dot the i's and cross the t's; **con ~s y comas** very precise 3. (*calceta, labor*) knitting; **~ de media** plain stitch; **chaqueta de ~** knitted jacket; **hacer ~** to knit 4. (*puntada*) stitch; **~ de sutura** MED stitch; **la herida necesitó diez ~s** the wound needed ten stitches 5. *pey* (*tipo*) bloke; **es un ~ filipino** he's a rogue 6. GASTR **a/en su ~** done; **batir a ~ de nieve** to beat until stiff 7. (*preparado*) **a ~** ready; **poner a ~** TÉC to fine-tune; (*ajustar*) to adjust; **tener a ~** to have ready 8. INFOR dot; **~ .com** dot.com

puntuación *f* 1. LING punctuation; **signo de ~** punctuation mark 2. (*calificación*) mark *Brit,* grade *Am;* DEP score; **sistema de ~** scoring system

puntual *adj* 1. (*concreto*) specific 2. (*exacto*) precise 3. (*sin retraso*) punctual

puntualidad *f* punctuality

puntualizar <z→c> *vt* (*especificar, precisar*) to specify; (*aclarar*) to clarify

puntuar <*1. pres:* puntúo> *vt* 1. (*un escrito*) to punctuate 2. (*conseguir puntos*) to score 3. (*calificar*) to mark *Brit,* to grade *Am;* DEP to score

punzada *f* (*dolor*) sharp pain; (*en los costados*) stitch

punzante *adj* 1. (*puntiagudo*) sharp 2. (*mordaz*) scathing

punzar <z→c> I. *vt* 1. (*pinchar*) to prick; (*agujererar*) to puncture 2. (*conciencia*) to prick II. *vi* (*doler*) to stab

punzó *adj CSur, Col* **rojo ~** bright red

punzón *m* punch; **para cuero** awl; (*sello*) stamp; (*cincel*) graver; (*taladro*) drilling bit; (*buril*) burin

puñado *m* handful; **a ~s** (*mucho*) by the handful; **un ~** *inf* (*mucho*) a lot

puñal *m* dagger; **poner a alguien el ~ al pecho** *fig* to hold a gun to sb's head

puñalada *f* stab; (*herida*) stab wound; *fig* blow; **coser a ~s** to stab repeatedly; **dar una ~ trapera a alguien** *fig* to stab sb in the back

puñeta *f vulg* 1. (*molestia*) **¡(qué) ~(s)!** hell!; **hacer la ~ a alguien** to screw things up for sb 2. (*bobada*) stupid thing; **¡déjate de ~s!** stop messing about!; **¿qué ~s estás diciendo?** what the hell are you on about?; **en la quinta ~** in the back of beyond 3. *AmL* (*masturbación*) wank *Brit,* jerk-off *Am* 4. *vulg* (*expresión de enfado*) **mandar a alguien a hacer ~s** to tell sb to go to hell; **¡vete a hacer ~s!** go to hell!

puñetazo *m* punch

puñetero, -a *adj inf* damn(ed); **el muy ~ no me ayudó** the bastard didn't help me

puño *m* 1. (*mano*) fist; **~ cerrado** clenched fist; **con el ~ en alto** with one's fist raised; **apretar los ~s** *fig* to struggle hard; **comerse los ~s** *fig* to be starving; **como un ~** (*huevo, mentira*) enormous; (*casa, habitación*) tiny; **verdades como ~s** fundamental truths; **de su ~ y letra** in his/her own hand; **meter a alguien en un ~** *fig* to intimidate sb; **tener a alguien en un ~** *fig* to have sb under one's thumb 2. (*puñado*) handful 3. (*mango*) handle; (*pomo*) hilt 4. (*de la ropa*) cuff; **~ vuelto** turned-up cuff

pupa *f* 1. (*ampolla*) blister; (*heridilla*) small wound; (*úlcera*) ulcer 2. *inf* (*dolor*) pain; **¡~!** ouch! 3. ZOOL pupa

pupila *f* pupil; **tener ~** *inf* to be sharp

pupilaje *m* (*tutela*) pupillage

pupilar *adj* pupillary

pupilo, -a *m, f* ward

pupitre *m* 1. (*escritorio*) desk 2. TÉC console; **~ de control** control panel

pupo *m Arg, Bol, Chile* navel

purasangre *adj, m* thoroughbred

puré *m* purée; **~ de patatas** mashed potatoes; **hacer ~** to purée; *fig* to beat to a pulp; **estar hecho ~** *fig* to be knackered

pureza *f* purity

purga *f* 1. (*medicamento*) purgative 2. (*eliminación*) purge

purgación *f* 1. MED purging 2. TÉC draining 3. *pl, inf* (*blenorragia*) gonorrhoea *Brit,* gonorrhea *Am*

purgante *adj, m* purgative

purgar <g→gu> **I.** *vt* **1.** *t. fig* to clean **2.** MED to purge **3.** (*evacuar*) to empty; (*aguas*) to drain **4.** (*expiar*) to expiate **5.** JUR to clear **II.** *vr:* **~se 1.** *t. fig* to clean oneself **2.** MED to take a purge

purgativo, -a *adj* purgative

purgatorio *m* purgatory

purificador *m* purifier; **~ de humos** smoke filter

purificador(a) *adj* **planta ~a** water treatment plant

purificar <c→qu> **I.** *vt t. fig* to purify **II.** *vr:* **~se** to be purified; *fig* to purify oneself

Purísima *f* **la ~** the Virgin (Mary)

purista *adj, mf* purist

puritano, -a I. *adj* puritanical **II.** *m, f* puritan

puro *m* cigar

puro, -a *adj* **1.** (*sin imperfecciones*) pure; (*auténtico*) authentic; **por pura cortesía** as a matter of courtesy; **pura lana** pure wool; **la pura verdad** the honest truth; **pura casualidad** sheer chance; **de ~ miedo** from sheer terror; **se cae de ~ bueno/tonto** he is unbelievably kind/stupid **2.** (*sin mezcla*) unadulterated **3.** (*íntegro*) whole

púrpura *adj, f* purple

purpúreo, -a *adj* purple

purrete, -a *m, f RíoPl, inf* (*chiquillo*) kid *inf*

purulento, -a *adj* purulent

pus *m sin pl* MED pus

pusilánime *adj* cowardly

pústula *f* MED pustule

puta *f vulg* whore; **casa de ~s** brothel; *fig* everyone for himself, to each his own; **ir de ~s** to go whoring; **hijo de ~** son of a bitch; **pasarlas ~s** to go through hell

putada *f vulg* **¡qué ~!** what a bloody nuisance!; **hacer una ~ a alguien** to play a dirty trick on sb

putañear *vi inf* to go whoring

putativo, -a *adj* putative

puteada *f AmS, vulg* swearword; **dar ~s** to swear

putear I. *vi vulg* (*ir de putas*) to go whoring **II.** *vt vulg* (*fastidiar*) to annoy; **me putea tanta gilipollez** all this stupidity really pisses me off; **estoy puteado** I'm really pissed off; **¡te han puteado bien!** they've really messed you about!

puticlub *m inf* singles bar

puto, -a *adj vulg* bloody; **¡de puta madre!** bloody brilliant!; **¡qué puta suerte!** what bloody awful luck!; **el ~ coche no arranca** the damn car won't start; **ni puta idea** not a bloody clue; **las estoy pasando putas** I'm having a really shitty time

putrefacción *f* decay

putrefacto, -a *adj* rotten

pútrido, -a *adj* putrid

puya *f* **1.** (*punta*) point **2.** (*injuria*) jibe *Brit,* gibe *Am;* **echar una ~ a alguien** to make a gibe at sb

puzzle *m* (*rompecabezas*) jigsaw (puzzle); *fig* puzzle

PVP *m abr de* **Precio de Venta al Público** RRP

Q

Q, q *f* Q, q; **~ de Quebec** Q for Queenie *Brit,* Q for Queen *Am*

qm *abr de* **quintal métrico** 100 kg

que I. *pron rel* **1.** (*con antecedente: personas, cosas*) that, which (*often omitted when referring to object*)*;* **la pelota ~ está pinchada** the ball that is punctured; **la pelota ~ compraste** the ball you bought; **la historia de ~ te hablé** the story I told you about; **reacciones a las ~ estamos acostumbrados** reactions which we are accustomed to; **el proyecto en el ~ trabajo** the project that I am working on; **la empresa para la ~ trabajo** the company that I work for **2.** (*con antecedente: personas*) who, whom (*often omitted when referring to the object*)*;* **la mujer que trabaja conmigo** the woman who works with me; **el rey al ~ sirvo** the king (whom) I serve **3.** (*sin antecedente*) **el/la/lo ~...** the one (that/who/which) ...; **los ~ hayan terminado** those who have finished; **el ~ quiera, ~ se marche** whoever wants to, can leave; **es de los ~...** he/she/it is the type that ...; **el ~ más y el ~ menos** every single one; **es todo lo ~ sé** that's all I know; **lo ~ haces** what you do; **no sabes lo difícil ~ es** you don't know how difficult it is **4.** (*con preposición*) **de lo ~ habláis** what you are talking about **II.** *conj* **1.** (*completivo*) that; **me pidió ~ le ayudara** he/she asked me to help him/her **2.** (*estilo indirecto*) that; **ha dicho ~...** he/she said that ... **3.** (*comparativo*) **más alto ~** taller than; **lo mismo ~** the same as **4.** (*porque*) because; **le ayudaré, seguro, ~ se lo he prometido** I'll help him/her, of course, because I promised **5.** (*para que*) **dio órdenes a los trabajadores ~ trabajaran más rápido** he/she ordered the workers to work faster **6.** (*sin que*) **no voy de vacaciones, ~ no me roben** I can't go on holiday without getting robbed **7.** (*de manera que*) **corre ~ vuela** he/she runs like the wind **8.** (*o, ya*) **~ paguen, ~ no paguen, eso ya se verá** we'll see whether they pay or not **9.** (*y*) **lo hizo él, ~ no yo** he did it, not me **10.** (*frecuentativo*) **y él dale ~ dale con la guitarra** and he kept on playing and playing the guitar **11.** (*explicativo*) **hoy no vendré, es ~ estoy cansado** I'm not coming in today because I'm tired; **no es ~ no pueda, es ~ no quiero** it's not that I can't, it's that I don't want to; **¿es ~ no puedes venir?** can't you come then?

12. (*enfático*) **¡~ sí/no!** I said "yes"/"no"!; **sí ~ lo hice** I did do it! **13.** (*de duda*) **¿~ no está en casa?** are you saying he/she isn't at home? **14.** (*exclamativo*) **¡~ me canso!** I'm getting tired!; **¡~ sea yo el que tenga que hacerlo!** I would be the one who has to do it! **15.** (*con verbo*) **hay ~ trabajar más** you/we/they have to work harder; **tener ~ hacer algo** to have to do something; **dar ~ hablar** to set tongues wagging ►**a la ~ llegue** as soon as he/she arrives; **a menos ~** *+subj* unless; **antes ~** before; **con tal (de) ~** *+subj* as long as; **por mucho ~ tú digas...** no matter what you say ...; **yo ~ tú...** if I were you ...

qué *adj, pron interrog* **1.** (*general*) what; (*cuál*) which; (*qué clase de*) what kind of; **¿por ~?** why?; **¿en ~ piensas?** what are you thinking about?; **¿para ~?** what for?; **¿de ~ hablas?** what are you talking about?; **¿a ~ esperas?** what are you waiting for?; **¿~ día llega?** what day is he/she arriving?; **¿~ cerveza tomas?** what kind of beer do you drink?; **¿a ~ vienes?** what are you here for?; **¿~ edad tienes?** how old are you?; **según ~ gente no la soporto** some people I just can't stand **2.** (*exclamativo*) **¡~ alegría!** how nice!; **¡~ gracia!** how funny!; **¡~ suerte!** what luck! **3.** (*cuán*) **¡~ magnífica vista!** what a magnificent view!; **¡mira ~ contento está!** look how happy he is! **4.** (*cuánto*) **¡~ de gente!** what a lot of people! ►**¿~ tal?** how are you [*o* things]?; **¿~ tal si salimos a cenar?** how about going out to dinner?; **¿y ~?** so what?; **¿y a mí ~?** and what about me?; **¿~?** well?; **~, ¿vienes o no?** well, are you coming, or not?

quebrada *f* **1.** (*paso*) ravine **2.** (*hendidura*) gap **3.** *AmL* (*arroyo*) stream

quebradizo, -a *adj* **1.** (*objeto*) brittle **2.** (*de salud*) sickly; (*persona mayor*) frail **3.** (*voz*) faltering

quebrado *m* MAT fraction

quebrado, -a *adj* **1.** (*empresa*) bankrupt **2.** (*herniado*) ruptured **3.** (*terreno*) rough **4.** (*rostro*) pale

quebrantado, -a *adj* **1.** (*salud*) **tengo las espaldas quebrantadas** my back is killing me; **la operación me dejó muy ~** the operation left me very weak **2.** (*pared*) cracked

quebrantar **I.** *vt* **1.** (*romper*) to break; (*cascar*) to crack; (*machacar*) to crush; **~ la prisión** to break out of prison **2.** (*ley, secreto*) to break; (*obligación*) to violate **3.** (*furia*) to diminish; (*autoridad*) to breach; (*salud*) to debilitate **II.** *vr:* **~se** (*estado de salud*) to be ruined; (*fuerza*) to be weakened

quebranto *m* **1.** (*de romper*) breaking; (*de cascar*) cracking; (*de machacar*) crushing **2.** (*económico*) heavy loss **3.** (*moral*) breakdown; (*físico*) weakening **4.** (*pena*) suffering

quebrar <e→ie> **I.** *vt* **1.** (*romper*) to break **2.** (*interrumpir*) to interrupt **3.** (*el cuerpo*) to bend **4.** (*rostro*) to distort **5.** (*ley*) to break **6.** (*suavizar*) to moderate **II.** *vi* **1.** (*con alguien*) to break up **2.** (*ceder*) to break down **3.** COM to go bankrupt **4.** (*intento*) to fail **5.** *Méx* (*darse por vencido*) to give in **III.** *vr:* **~se 1.** MED to rupture oneself **2.** (*la voz*) to go hoarse **3.** (*rostro*) to turn pale **4.** (*cuerpo*) to bend; **~se de dolor** to double over [*o* up] with pain

quebrazón *m AmL* **1.** (*resultado*) breakage **2.** (*acción*) shattering

quechua **I.** *adj* Quechua **II.** *mf* Quechuan

> **Quechua** is the name given both to the original inhabitants of **Perú** as well as their language. **Quechua** is the second official language of **Perú**.

quedada *f* **1.** *inf* (*burla*) joke; **lo de largarse en medio de la reunión fue sólo una ~** I was only fooling when I got up and left in the middle of the meeting **2.** *Méx, pey* (*solterona*) old maid

quedado, -a *adj Arg, Chile* slow

quedar **I.** *vi* **1.** (*permanecer*) to remain; **los problemas quedan atrás** the problems are a thing of the past; **¿cuánta gente queda?** how many people are left?; **~ a deber algo** to owe sth **2.** (*sobrar*) to be left; **no nos queda otro remedio que...** there's nothing left for us to do but ...; **no queda pan** there's no bread left; **no queda ningún ejemplar de este libro** there are no copies of this book left **3.** (*resultar*) **todo quedó en una simple discusión** it ended up in a mere argument; **~ acordado** to be arranged; **~ cojo** to go lame; **~ eliminado** to be eliminated; **~ en ridículo** to make a fool of oneself **4.** (*acordar*) **~ en algo** to agree to sth; **¡en qué habéis quedado?** what have you decided?; **quedamos a las 10** we agreed to meet at 10; **¿quedamos a las 10?** shall we meet at 10?; **primero dices una cosa y luego otra, ¿en qué quedamos?** first you say one thing and then another, make up your mind! **5.** (*estar situado*) to lie; **queda por/hacia el norte** it lies to the north; **quedar lejos de aquí** to be a long way from here **6.** (*faltar*) **quedan aún 100 km para llegar a casa** there are still 100 km left before we get home; **aún queda mucho por hacer** there's still a lot to do; **por mí que no quede** I'll do all that I can **7.** (*terminar*) to end; **... y ahí quedó el concierto** ... the concert ended there **8.** (*en una subasta*) **el cuadro queda por un millón de libras** the painting goes for one million pounds **9.** (*+ por*) **~ por cobarde** to come across as a coward; **algo queda por ver** sth remains to be seen **10.** (*+ bien/mal*) **~ bien/mal** to come off well/badly **11.** (*+ como*) **~ como un señor** to behave like a real gentleman; **~ como un idiota** to look a fool **II.** *vr:* **~se 1.** (*permanecer*) to stay; **~se atrás** to stay behind; **~se colgado** (*ordenador*) to block; **durante la tormenta nos quedamos**

a oscuras during the storm the lights went out; **cuando me lo dijo me quedé mudo** when he told me I was speechless **2.** (*resultar*) **~se ciego** to go blind; **~se viuda/viudo** to become a widow/widower; **al freír la carne se ha quedado en nada** when the meat was fried it shrunk to almost nothing **3.** (*conservar, adquirir*) **me quedo con el coche pequeño** I'll take the small car; **quédate con el libro** keep the book; **~se sin nada** to be left with nothing; **entre el mar y la montaña me quedo con el mar** if I have to choose between the sea and the mountains, I'll take the sea **4.** (*burlarse*) **~se con alguien** to make fun of sb

quehacer *m* chores *pl;* **los ~es de la casa** housework; **dar ~ a alguien** to assign work to sb

queja *f* complaint; **no tengo ~ de él** I have nothing against him

quejarse *vr* **1.** (*formular queja*) **~ de algo** to complain about sth; **se queja del frío** he complains about the cold; **¿qué tal te va el negocio? – bien, gracias, no puedo quejarme** how's business? – fine, thanks, I can't complain **2.** (*gemir*) **~ de algo** to moan about sth

quejica **I.** *adj* (*por dolor*) moaning; (*por manera de ser*) complaining; **¡no seas ~, hombre!** stop whining! **II.** *mf* complainer, bellyacher *inf;* (*criticón*) faultfinder

quejido *m* moan; (*constante*) lament; **~ de dolor** cry of pain; **dar ~s** to groan

quejoso, -a *adj* complaining; **estar ~ de alguien** to be annoyed at sb

quejumbroso, -a *adj* (*voz*) whining; (*por dolor*) moaning

quelite *m Méx* greens *pl*

quelonio *m* chelonian

queltehue *m Chile* ZOOL teruteru

quema *f* **1.** (*acción*) burning; (*completa*) incineration **2.** (*incendio, fuego*) fire; **huir de la ~** *fig* to flee from danger

quemada *f* **1.** *Arg, Méx* (*acción que pone en ridículo*) embarrassment **2.** *Méx* (*quemadura*) burn

quemado, -a *adj* burnt; **este político está ~** *inf* this politician is finished; **estar ~ con alguien** *inf* to have had it with sb

quemadura *f* burn; **~ de primer grado** first degree burn

quemar **I.** *vi* to burn; **cuidado, esta sopa quema** be careful, the soup is boiling hot **II.** *vt* **1.** (*comida, sol*) to burn; (*casa: completamente*) to burn down; **~ un bosque** to set fire to a forest; **este chili quema la garganta/la lengua** this chilli burns my throat/tongue **2.** (*planta: calor*) to scorch; (*frío*) to damage by frost **3.** (*fortuna*) to squander **4.** (*fastidiar*) to mess up **5.** *AmC* (*denunciar*) **~ a alguien** to inform against sb **III.** *vr:* **~se** **1.** (*arder*) to burn; **el bosque se quema** the forest is on fire; **me he quemado los cabellos** I've singed my hair **2.** (*herir*) to be hurt **3.** (*comida*) to burn; (*ligeramente*) to singe **4.** (*tener calor*) **me estoy quemando** I'm boiling **5.** (*por una pasión*) **~se de amor** to burn with love **6.** (*acertar*) **¡que te quemas!** you're getting warm!

quemarropa **disparar a ~** to shoot at very close range; **hacer preguntas a ~** to ask point-blank

quemazón *f* **1.** (*quema*) burning **2.** (*calor*) intense heat **3.** (*ardor*) **siento una ~ en el estómago** I have a burning sensation in my stomach

quemo *m Arg* **¡que ~!** how embarrassing!

quemón *m Méx* dope smoker

quena *f* MÚS *reed flute used in Andean music*

quepi(s) *m* (*inv*) (*gorro militar*) kepi

quepo *1. pres de* **caber**

queque *m Chile, Perú, AmC* (*bollo*) cake

querella *f* **1.** JUR lawsuit; **~ criminal** criminal action; **poner una ~ contra alguien** to sue sb **2.** (*discordia*) dispute

querellarse *vr* **1.** (*quejarse*) to complain; **~ por algo** to complain about sth **2.** JUR to bring an action

querencia *f* (*aprecio*) attachment; (*cariño*) affection; (*afición*) liking; **tomar ~ a algo/alguien** to take a liking to sth/sb

querendón, -ona *adj AmL* loving, affectionate

querer *irr* **I.** *vt* **1.** (*desear*) to desire; (*más suave*) to want; **como tú quieras** as you like; **has ganado, ¿qué más quieres?** you win, what more do you want?; **hacer algo queriendo/sin ~** to do something on purpose/unintentionally; **quisiera tener 20 años menos** I wish I were 20 years younger; **eso es lo que quería decir** that's what I meant to say; **quiero que sepáis que...** I want you to know that ...; **y yo, ¡qué quieres que le haga!** what do you expect me to do?; **donde quiera que esté** wherever he/she/it may be; **¡por lo que más quieras, deja ese tema!** for God's sake, change the subject! **2.** (*amar*) to like; (*más fuerte*) to love; **te quiero con locura** I love you madly **3.** (*pedir*) to require **4.** (*requerir*) **estas plantas quieren mucha agua** these plants need a lot of water ►**~ es <u>poder</u>** *prov* where there's a will, there's a way; **como quiera que <u>sea</u>** anyhow **II.** *vimpers* **parece que quiere llover** it looks like rain **III.** *m* love

querido, -a **I.** *adj* dear **II.** *m, f* (*amante*) lover; (*como vocativo*) darling

queroseno *m* kerosene *Am,* paraffin *Brit*

quesadilla *f* GASTR **1.** (*pastel*) cheesecake **2.** (*pastelillo*) pastry **3.** *AmL* (*tortilla*) quesadilla (*folded tortilla filled with a spicy mixture and topped with cheese*)

quesera *f* (*plato*) cheese dish

queso *m* **1.** GASTR cheese; **~ de bola** Edam cheese; **~ rallado** grated cheese **2.** *inf* (*pie*) foot; **te huelen los ~s** your feet smell

quicio *m* (*de puerta, ventana*) hinge post ►**sacar las <u>cosas</u> de ~** to make a mountain out of

Q

a molehill; **estar fuera de** ~ to be in disorder; **sacar a alguien de** ~ to drive sb up the wall *inf;* **me saca de** ~ **verla llorar** it gets on my nerves to see her crying

quico *m inf* toasted corn snack

quid *m* crux; **ese es el** ~ **de la cuestión** that is the crux of the matter; **dar en el** ~ to hit the nail on the head

quiebra *f* **1.** COM bankruptcy; **dar en** ~ to go bankrupt **2.** (*hendidura*) fissure; (*rotura*) break **3.** (*fracaso*) failure; (*pérdida*) loss, breakdown; **la** ~ **de los valores** the breakdown of values; **este asunto no tiene** ~ this can't go wrong

quiebro *m* **1.** (*movimiento*) dodge; **Maradona le hizo un** ~ **al defensa** Maradona dribbled around the defender **2.** (*gorgorito*) trill

quien *pron rel* **1.** (*con antecedente*) who, that, whom (*often omitted when referring to object*)*;* **el chico de** ~ **te hablé** that boy I told you about; **las chicas con** ~**es...** the girls with whom ... **2.** (*sin antecedente*) that; **hay** ~ **dice que...** some people say that ...; **no hay** ~ **lo aguante** nobody can stand him; ~ **opine eso...** whoever thinks so ...; ~ **más,** ~ **menos, todos tenemos problemas** everybody has problems

quién *pron interrog* who; **¿**~ **es?** (*llama*) who is it?; **¿**~**es son tus padres?** who are your parents?; **¿a** ~ **has visto?** who did you see?; **¿a** ~ **se lo has dado?** who did you give it to?; **¿**~ **eres tú para decirme esto?** who do you think you are telling me this?; **¿por** ~ **me tomas?** what do you take me for?; **¡**~ **tuviera 20 años!** If only I were 20!

quienquiera <quienesquiera> *pron indef* whoever; ~ **que sea que pase** whoever it is, come in

quieto, **-a** *adj* **1.** (*tranquilo*) calm; **no puede estar nunca** ~ (*niño*) he/she can never keep still **2.** (*parado*) motionless; **quedarse** ~ to stand still

quietud *f* **1.** (*calma*) calm **2.** (*inmovilidad*) stillness

quijada *f* jaw(bone)

quilate *m* carat *Brit,* karat *Am;* **de muchos** ~**s** *t. fig* of great value

quilco *m Chile* (large) basket

quilla *f* NÁUT keel

quillango *m CSur* (*manta de pieles*) fur blanket

quillay *m Arg, Chile* BOT soapbark tree

quilo *m* **1.** (*peso*) kilo(gramme) *Brit,* kilo(gram) *Am;* **sudar el** ~ *inf* to sweat blood **2.** *inf* (*dinero*) million

quilombo *m* **1.** *Chile* (*burdel*) whorehouse **2.** *Ven* (*choza*) hut **3.** *Arg* (*lío*) mess

quiltro *m Chile, pey* (*perro*) yapper, mutt *Am*

quimba *f* **1.** *AmL* (*garbo*) grace **2.** *AmL* (*sandalia*) sandal **3.** *pl Col* (*conflicto*) difficulties *pl*

quimbo *m Cuba* knife, machete

quimera *f* (*ilusión*) chimera *form*

química *f* chemistry

químico, **-a** **I.** *adj* chemical; **productos** ~**s** chemicals *pl* **II.** *m, f* chemist

quimioterapia *f* chemotherapy

quimono *m* kimono

quina *f* cinchona bark; **ser más malo que la** ~ *inf* to taste terrible; **tragar** ~ *fig* to put up with a lot

quincalla *f* **1.** (*objetos*) ironmongery *Brit,* hardware *Am* **2.** (*adornos*) trinkets *pl*

quincallería *f* **1.** (*tienda*) ironmonger's *Brit,* hardware store *Am* **2.** (*objetos*) ironmongery *Brit,* hardware *Am* **3.** (*adornos*) trinkets *pl*

quince **I.** *adj inv* fifteen; **dentro de** ~ **días** in a fortnight *Brit,* in fifteen days **II.** *m* fifteen; *v.t.* **ocho**

quincena *f* (*días*) fortnight *Brit,* fifteen days

quincenal *adj* fortnightly *Brit,* twice-monthly, bi-weekly; **revista** ~ fortnightly journal *Brit,* twice-monthly journal

quincuagésimo, **-a** *adj* fiftieth; *v.t.* **octavo**

quingos *m inv, AmL* zigzag

quiniela *f* **1.** (*juego*) sports pools *pl;* **jugar a las** ~**s** to do the pools **2.** (*boleto*) pools coupon **3.** *CSur* (*lotería*) lottery

quinientos, **-as** *adj* five hundred; *v.t.* **ochocientos**

quinina *f* quinine

quino *m AmL* BOT cinchona tree

quinqué *m* oil lamp

quinqui *mf inf* delinquent

quinta *f* **1.** (*casa*) country house **2.** MIL call-up, draft *Am;* **entrar en** ~**s** to be called up, to be drafted *Am;* **ese es de mi** ~ he is my age

quintaesencia *f* quintessence *elev*

quintal *m* quintal; ~ **métrico** 100 kgs

quintar *vt* MIL to call up, to draft *Am*

quinteto *m* MÚS quintet

quintillizo, **-a** *m, f* quintuplet

Quintín *m* **se armó la de San** ~ *inf* all hell broke loose

quinto *m* conscript, draftee *Am*

quinto, **-a** *adj, m, f* fifth; *v.t.* **octavo**

quintuplicar <c→qu> *vt* to quintuple

quíntuplo, **-a** *adj* quintuple

quiosco *m* **1.** (*de jardín*) gazebo **2.** (*de periódicos*) news-stand

quipo(s) *m(pl),* **quipu(s)** *m(pl) AmL* HIST quipu (*ancient Peruvian system of coloured threads and knots for recording facts and events*)

quiquiriquí *m* (*onomatopeya*) cock-a-doodle--doo

quirófano *m* operating theatre *Brit,* operating room *Am;* **pasar por el** ~ to be operated on

quirquincho *m CSur* **1.** ZOOL (*armadillo*) small armadillo **2.** (*guitarra*) charango

quirúrgico, **-a** *adj* surgical

quisicosa *f inf* riddle, puzzle

quiso *3. pret de* **querer**

quisque *pron indef, inf,* **quisqui** *pron indef, vulg* **cada** ~ every man-Jack; **todo** ~ anyone and everyone; **se lo dijo a todo** ~ he told every Tom, Dick and Harry

quisquilla *f* 1.(*pequeñez*) trifle 2.ZOOL shrimp

quisquilloso, **-a** *adj* 1.(*susceptible*) touchy 2.(*meticuloso*) fussy

quiste *m* MED cyst

quitaesmalte *m* nail varnish remover

quitagusto *m Ecua, Perú* (*intruso*) intruder

quitaipón *m* **de ~** detachable

quitamanchas *m inv* stain remover

quitamiedos *m inv* (*en carretera*) guardrail

quitanieves *f inv* snowplough *Brit,* snowplow *Am*

quitar I. *vt* 1.(*piel, funda*) to remove; (*sombrero, tapa, ropa*) to take off; (*botón*) to pull off; **~ la mesa** to clear the table; **una capucha de quita y pon** a detachable hood 2.(*desposeer*) to take; (*robar*) to steal; **me lo has quitado de la boca** *fig* you took the words right out of my mouth; **el café me quita el sueño** coffee keeps me awake; **ese asunto me quita el sueño** that matter is keeping me awake at night 3.(*mancha*) to get out; (*obstáculo*) to remove; (*dolor*) to relieve; (*vida*) to take 4.(*de plan, horario, texto*) to leave out 5.(*regla*) to do away with 6.(*apartar*) to get out of the way; (*mueble*) to remove; **¡quita!** (*no me molestes*) don't bother me!; (*deja eso*) leave that alone!; (*déjate de tonterías*) stop it!; **el médico me ha quitado de fumar** the doctor has told me to quit smoking 7.MAT to subtract; **quitando dos** taking away two ►**ni ~ ni <u>poner</u> en algo** not to have any say in sth II. *vr:* **~se** (*sombrero, gafas, ropa*) to take off; (*barba*) to shave off; **~se la vida** to commit suicide; **~se de la bebida** to give up drinking; **~se de encima algo/a alguien** to get rid of sth/sb; **quítate de mi vista** get out of my sight; **~se años** (**de encima**) to look years younger

quitasol *m* sunshade

Quito *m* Quito

quizá(**s**) *adv* perhaps, maybe; **~ y sin ~** without a doubt

R

R, **r** *f* R, r; **~ de Ramón** R for Roger

rabadilla *f* ANAT coccyx

rabanito *m* radish

rábano *m* radish; **~ picante** [*o* **blanco**] horseradish ►**tomar el ~ por las <u>hojas</u>** *inf* (*interpretación*) to get the wrong end of the stick; (*ejecución*) to get it back to front; **me <u>importa</u> un ~** *inf* I couldn't care less; **¡<u>y</u> un ~!** no way!; **déjame tu coche – ¡y un ~!** *inf* can I borrow your car? – no way!; **tu hermano es más listo que tú – ¡y un ~!** *inf* your brother is brighter than you – you must be joking!

rabí <rabíes> *m* REL rabbi

rabia *f* 1.MED (*hidrofobia*) rabies *pl* 2.(*furia*) rage; **¡qué ~!** how infuriating! 3.(*enfado, manía*) **tener ~ a alguien** (*enfado*) to be furious with sb; (*manía*) not to be able to stand sb; **tomar ~ a alguien** (*enfado*) to become furious with sb; (*manía*) to take a dislike to sb; **me da ~ sólo pensarlo** just thinking about it makes me mad; **con ~** angrily

rabiar *vi* 1.(*padecer rabia: animal*) to be rabid, to have rabies; (*persona*) to have rabies 2.(*enfadarse*) to be furious; **hacer ~ a alguien** to infuriate sb 3.(*sufrir*) to be in great pain; **~ de...** to be dying of ... 4.(*ansiar, desear*) **~ por...** to be dying to ... ►**<u>está</u> que rabia** *inf* (*picante*) it's incredibly hot; **<u>a</u> ~** (*mucho*) incredibly

rabieta *f* tantrum; **coger una ~** to throw a tantrum [*o* fit]

rabillo *m* **el ~ del ojo** the corner of the eye

rabimocho, **-a** *adj AmL* (*rabón*) short

rabino *m* rabbi

rabioso, **-a** *adj* 1.(*hidrofóbico*) rabid 2.(*furioso*) furious; (*desconsiderado*) inconsiderate 3. *inf* (*picante*) really hot 4. *fig* (*vehemente*) fervent; **un tema de rabiosa actualidad** a highly topical issue

rabo *m* 1.(*cola*) tail; **salir con el ~ entre las piernas** *inf* to go away with one's tail between one's legs; **aún queda el ~ por desollar** *inf* the worst is yet to come 2.(*extremo*) end 3.(*tallo*) stem 4. *vulg* (*pene*) cock

rabona *f CSur, inf* (*falta a la escuela*) truant; **hacer**(**se**) **la ~** to play truant

racanear I. *vi inf* to be stingy II. *vt inf* **~ algo a alguien** to be stingy with sth to sb; **~ dinero a alguien** not to give sb enough money

rácano, **-a** *adj* 1. *inf* (*tacaño*) mean 2. *inf* (*gandul*) lazy

racha *f* 1.(*de aire*) gust of wind 2.(*fase*) series; **tener buena/mala ~** to have a good/bad run; **a** [*o* **por**] **~s** in fits and starts; **arrancar un coche a ~s, dar una ~ a un coche** to jump-start a car

racial *adj* (*étnico*) racial; **disturbios ~es** race riots

racimo *m* bunch; **~ de uvas** bunch of grapes

raciocinio *m* 1.(*facultad, razón*) reason 2.(*proceso mental*) reasoning

ración *f* 1.(*tapa*) portion (*portion of food served as a large snack in a bar or restaurant*); **una ~ de patatas fritas** a portion of chips *Brit* [*o* French fries *Am*]; **una ~ de queso** a plate of cheese 2. en casa, helping, serving; (*en restaurante*) plate, portion 3.MIL ration ►**poner a alguien a <u>media</u> ~** to put sb on half rations

racional *adj* rational; (*razonable*) reasonable

racionalización *f* ECON, PSICO rationalization

racionalizar <z→c> *vt* to rationalize

racionamiento *m* rationing

racionar *vt* 1.(*repartir*) to ration out 2.(*limitar*) to ration

racismo *m sin pl* racism

racista *adj, mf* racist

radar *m* ELEC radar; **por ~** by radar

radiación *f* **1.** FÍS radiation; **~ solar** solar radiation **2.** RADIO, TV broadcasting

radiactividad *f* FÍS radioactivity

radiactivo, -a *adj* radioactive

radiado, -a *adj* **1.** (*forma*) radiate **2.** RADIO broadcast

radiador *m* (*de casa, coche*) radiator

radial *adj* **1.** (*forma*) radial; **músculo ~** ANAT radial muscle **2.** *AmL* RADIO radio

radiante *adj* (*brillante*) radiant; **~ de alegría/felicidad** radiant with joy/happiness; **estás ~ con ese vestido** you look wonderful in that dress; **está ~ con su nuevo trabajo** he/she is delighted with his/her new job

radiar I. *vi* **1.** (*irradiar*) to radiate **2.** RADIO to broadcast **II.** *vt* **1.** (*irradiar*) to radiate **2.** RADIO to broadcast; **un debate radiado** a radio debate **3.** MED to treat with X-rays **4.** *AmL* (*eliminar*) to delete

radical I. *adj* **1.** BOT, MAT (*t. extremado*) radical **2.** (*fundamental*) drastic **II.** *m* **1.** LING root **2.** MAT, QUÍM, PSICO radical **3.** MAT (*signo*) radical (sign) **III.** *mf* POL radical; **~ de derecha** extreme right-winger

radicalizar <z→c> **I.** *vt* to radicalize **II.** *vr:* **~se 1.** (*extremar*) to become radical **2.** (*agudizarse*) to intensify

radicar <c→qu> **I.** *vi* **1.** *fig* (*arraigar*) to take root; **el problema radica en su comportamiento** the problem lies in his/her behaviour *Brit* [*o* behavior *Am*] **2.** (*estar asentado*) to reside **3.** (*basarse*) **~ en algo** to be based on sth **4.** (*consistir*) **~ en algo** to consist of sth **II.** *vr:* **~se** (*establecerse*) to settle

radicheta *f Arg, Urug* (*achicoria*) chicory

radio[1] *f* RADIO, TEL **1.** (*radiodifusión*) radio; **hablar por la ~** to talk by radio; **retransmitir por ~** to send by radio **2.** (*receptor*) radio; (*radiotelefonía*) radiophone; **~ del coche** car radio; **dirigido por ~** radio-controlled **3.** (*emisora*) radio station; **~ pirata** pirate radio ►**~ macuto** *inf* the grapevine

radio[2] *m* **1.** MAT, ANAT radius; **en un ~ de varios kilómetros** within a radius of several kilometres **2.** (*en la rueda*) spoke **3.** QUÍM radium **4.** (*ámbito*) range; (*esfera*) field; **~ de acción** operational range; *fig* sphere of influence; **~ de alcance** reach; **~ de atracción** field of attraction; **~ visual** field of vision

radioactivo, -a *adj* radioactive

radioaficionado, -a *m, f* radio ham

radiocasete *m o f* radio cassette player

radiocomunicación *f* radio communication

radiodespertador *m* radio alarm (clock)

radiodifusión *f* broadcasting

radiodifusora *f AmL* radio transmitter

radioescucha *mf v.* **radioyente**

radiofonía *f* **1.** (*radiodifusión*) broadcasting **2.** (*radiotelefonía*) radio-telephony

radiofónico, -a *adj* RADIO, TEL radio; **guión ~** radio guide; **programa ~** (*programación*) radio schedule; (*emisión*) radio programme *Brit* [*o* program *Am*]

radiografía *f* **1.** (*técnica*) radiography **2.** (*placa*) radiograph, X-ray photograph

radiografiar <*1. pres:* radiografío> *vt* **1.** RADIO, TEL to radiograph **2.** MED to X-ray

radiólogo, -a *m, f* MED radiologist

radiopatrulla *f* patrol car

radiotaxi *m* radiocab

radiotelegrafiar <*1. pres:* radiotelegrafío> *vt* to radiotelegraph

radioterapia *f* MED radiotherapy

radioyente *mf* RADIO listener; **~ clandestino** illegal listener

RAE *f abr de* **Real Academia Española** Spanish Royal Academy (*organization which is responsible for setting linguistic standards for Spanish*)

Since its inception in 1714, the **Real Academia Española (RAE)** has made the standardisation and purity of the Spanish language one of its objectives.

raedera *f* scraper

raedura *f* **1.** (*rascado*) scrape **2.** (*brizna*) scraping **3.** MED graze

raer *irr vt* **1.** (*raspar*) to scrape **2.** MED to graze **3.** (*desgastar*) to wear out; (*deslucir*) to spoil

ráfaga *f* **1.** (*de aire*) gust **2.** (*de lluvia*) squall **3.** (*de luz, inspiración*) flash **4.** (*de disparos*) burst

ragú <ragús> *m* ragout

raído, -a *adj* (*deslucido*) spoilt; (*gastado*) worn-out; (*rozado*) scratched

raigambre *f* **1.** BOT (*raíces*) roots *pl* **2.** *fig* (*tradición*) tradition; **sin ~** rootless; **tener ~** to have strong roots; **mi familia es de ~ conservadora** my family has always been conservative

raíl *m* FERRO rail

raíz *f* **1.** ANAT, BOT *t. fig* root; **echar raíces** (*persona*) to put down roots; (*costumbre*) to take root; **como si hubiera echado raíces** *fig* well-established; **tener sus raíces en un lugar** *fig* to have one's roots in a place **2.** (*causa*) cause; (*origen*) origin; **a ~ de** because of; **tener su ~ en algo** to be due to sth **3.** MAT, LING root; **~ cuadrada/cúbica** square/cube root; **extraer la ~** to calculate the root ►**de ~** completely; **atajar de ~** to nip in the bud; **arrancar de ~** to destroy

raja *f* **1.** (*grieta*) crack; (*hendedura*) split **2.** (*abertura*) opening; (*separación*) gap **3.** *vulg* (*vulva*) cunt **4.** (*rodaja*) slice

rajada *f inf* **1.** *Arg* (*fuga*) flight **2.** *Méx* (*cobardía*) chickening out **3.** *Col* (*examen*) fail

rajadiablo(s) *m* (*inv*), *Chile* young rogue

rajante *adj Arg* (*definitivo*) definitive

rajar I. *vi* **1.** *inf* (*charlar*) to chatter **2.** *AmL, pey* (*hablar mal*) **~ de alguien** to slag sb off **II.** *vt* **1.** (*cortar*) to cut; (*abrir*) to cut open; (*hender*) to split; (*quitar*) to cut off; (*partir*) to cut up;

(*en rajas*) to slice **2.** *inf* (*apuñalar*) to knife **III.** *vr:* ~**se 1.** (*abrirse*) to split open; (*agrietarse*) to crack **2.** *inf* (*echarse atrás*) to back out **3.** *inf* (*disculparse*) to apologize **4.** (*cortarse*) to cut oneself

rajatabla a ~ (*estrictamente*) strictly; (*exactamente*) to the letter; (*a toda costa*) at all costs

raje *m Arg* **1.** *inf* (*huída*) flight; **al** ~ in a rush **2.** *inf* (*el despedir*) sacking, firing; **dar el** ~ **a alguien** to get rid of sb

rajo *m AmC* (*desgarrón*) tear; (*rotura*) rip

rajón, -ona *adj* **1.** *AmC, Méx* (*fanfarrón*) bragging **2.** *AmC* (*ostentoso*) lavish **3.** *Cuba, Méx* (*cobarde*) chicken *inf* **4.** *Méx* (*poco fiable*) unreliable

ralea *f pey* sort; **son todos de la misma** ~ they're all as bad as each other

ralentí *m sin pl* **1.** AUTO timing; **al** ~ ticking over **2.** CINE slow motion; **al** ~ in slow motion

rallador *m* grater

ralladura *f* gratings *pl;* ~ **de queso** grated cheese

rallar *vt* (*fino*) to grate; (*menos fino*) to shred

rally(**e**) <rallys> *m* rally

ralo, -a *adj* **1.** (*escaso*) scarce; (*árboles*) sparse; (*cabello*) thin; (*tejido*) threadbare **2.** *CSur* (*insustancial*) flimsy

rama *f* **1.** BOT, MAT (*t. de árbol*) branch; ~ **florida** flowering branch; ~**s secas** brushwood **2.** (*ámbito*) branch; ECON (*t. sector*) sector **3.** (*derivación*) branch **4.** (*parentesco*) branch; **por la** ~ **materna/paterna** on the mother's/father's side ►**andarse por las** ~**s** (*rodeos*) to beat about the bush; **irse por las** ~**s** (*desviarse*) to go off at *Brit* [*o* on *Am*] a tangent

ramada *f Chile* (*puesto de feria*) festival stand

ramaje *m* **1.** (*ramas*) branches **2.** (*follaje*) foliage

ramal *m* **1.** (*cabo*) strand **2.** (*ramificación*) branch; FERRO branch line

ramalazo *m* **1.** (*trallazo*) lash; (*marca*) weal; *fig* (*de dolor*) sharp pain **2.** *inf* (*parecido*) likeness; **tener un** ~ **a su padre** to look like one's father; **tener un** ~ **de loco** to be slightly mad

rambla *f* (*paseo*) boulevard

ramera *f pey* whore

ramificación *f* ramification; **ramificaciones** consequences *pl*

ramificarse <c→qu> *vr* to branch out

ramillete *m* bouquet

ramo *m* **1.** (*de flores*) bunch **2.** (*de árbol*) (small) branch **3.** (*ámbito*) area; ECON (*t. sector*) sector; ~ **de la construcción** construction sector; **del** ~ appropriate **4.** REL **Domingo de Ramos** Palm Sunday

rampa *f* (*inclinación*) ramp; (*en carretera*) access road *Brit,* ramp *Am;* **en** ~ sloping

rampla *f Chile* (*carrito de mano*) handtruck

ramplón, -ona *adj* **1.** (*basto*) coarse; (*chapucero*) shoddy **2.** (*vulgar*) vulgar; (*chabacano*) tasteless **3.** (*simplón*) dim

rana *f* frog; ~ **de San Antonio** jumping frog; **hombre** ~ frogman; **el príncipe** ~ the frog prince ►**cuando las** ~**s críen pelo** when pigs fly; **salir** ~ **a alguien** *inf* to be a disappointment to sb

ranchera *f AmL* **1.** (*canción*) *typical popular Mexican song* **2.** (*furgoneta*) estate car *Brit,* station wagon *Am*

ranchería *f* **1.** *Col* (*chabolas*) shantytown **2.** (*barraca*) bunkhouse

ranchero, -a *m, f* **1.** (*granjero*) rancher **2.** (*colono*) settler **3.** MIL cook

rancho *m* **1.** (*comida*) food; MIL mess; *pey* (*de mala calidad*) swill; **hacer el** ~ to cook **2.** (*granja*) ranch ►**hacer** ~ **aparte** to go one's own way

ranciarse *vr* to go rancid

rancio, -a *adj* **1.** (*grasas*) rancid **2.** (*antiguo*) ancient; *pey* (*anticuado*) old-fashioned

rancotán *adv AmL* (*al contado*) in cash

rango *m* **1.** (*categoría, puesto*) rank; **de primer/segundo** ~ first/second-level; **según el** ~ according to rank; **de** (**alto**) ~ high-ranking; **de** ~ **abolengo** of ancient lineage **2.** (*ordenación*) order

rangoso, -a *adj AmC* **1.** (*generoso*) generous **2.** (*ostentoso*) ostentatious

ranúnculo *m* buttercup

ranura *f* groove; (*muesca*) notch; (*junta*) joint; (*fisura*) slot

rapacidad *f* rapacity

rapapolvo *m inf* dressing down; **echar un** ~ **a alguien** to give sb a dressing down

rapar *vt* **1.** ~**se el pelo** (*afeitar*) to shave one's head; (*cortar*) to have one's hair cut very short **2.** *inf* (*mangar*) to snatch

rapaz I. *adj* **1.** (*ávido*) greedy **2.** (*expoliador*) rapacious **II.** *f* bird of prey

rapaz(**a**) *m(f)* kid; (*muchacho*) boy, lad *Brit;* (*niña*) girl, lass *Brit*

rape *m* **1.** ZOOL (*pescado*) monkfish **2.** *inf* (*afeitado*) quick shave; **al** ~ (*pelo*) closely cropped

rapé *m* snuff; **polvos de** ~ snuff powder

rapear *vi* MÚS to rap

rapidez *f* speed; ~ **de reflejos** quick reflexes; **con** (**gran**) ~ (very) quickly

rápido *m* **1.** (*tren*) express **2.** *pl* (*de un río*) rapids *pl*

rápido, -a *adj* **1.** (*veloz*) fast **2.** (*breve*) quick **3.** (*corriente*) running

rapiña *f* robbery; (*saqueo*) pillage

rapiñar *vt* to steal; (*saquear*) to pillage

raposo, -a *m, f* **1.** (*zorro*) fox **2.** (*astuto*) sly fox

raptar *vt* to kidnap

rapto *m* **1.** (*secuestro*) kidnapping; ~ **de un niño** child abduction **2.** (*arrebato*) fit; **en un** ~ **de celos/generosidad** in a fit of jealousy/generosity

raptor(**a**) *m(f)* kidnapper

raque *adj Ven* scrawny

raqueta *f* **1.** DEP (*pala*) bat **2.** DEP (*tenista*) racket **3.** (*para nieve*) snowshoe **4.** (*del croupier*) rake

raquítico, **-a** *adj* **1.** MED suffering from rickets **2.** *inf* (*enclenque*) sickly **3.** (*débil*) weak

raquitismo *m sin pl* MED rickets *pl*

raramente *adv* **1.** (*casi nunca*) rarely, seldom **2.** (*extrañamente*) strangely

rareza *f* **1.** (*cualidad*) rarity **2.** (*curiosidad*) strangeness **3.** (*peculiaridad*) peculiarity; (*manía*) eccentricity; **tener sus ~s** (*ser caprichoso*) to be a bit odd

rarífico, **-a** *adj Chile* implausible

raro, **-a** *adj* **1.** (*extraño, inesperado*) strange; **¡(qué) cosa más rara!** how strange! **2.** (*inusual*) unusual; (*poco común*) rare; **rara vez** rarely; **raras personas** few people; **no es ~ que...** +*subj* it's not surprising that ... **3.** FÍS, QUÍM rarefied; **gases ~s** rarefied gases

ras *m* level; **a(l) ~ de** on a level with; **a ~ de agua** at water level; **a ~ de tierra** at ground level; **volar a ~ de suelo** to hedgehop; **al ~** level

rasante **I.** *adj* close **II.** *f* slope; **cambio de ~** brow of a hill

rasar **I.** *vt* **1.** (*igualar*) to level **2.** (*rozar*) to skim **3.** (*arrasar*) to raze **II.** *vr:* **~se** (*cielo*) to clear

rasca *f* **1.** *inf* (*frío*) cold; **¡vaya ~ que hace!** it's freezing! **2.** *AmL* (*mona*) drunkenness; **pegarse una ~** to get plastered

rascacielos *m inv* skyscraper

rascar <c→qu> **I.** *vt* **1.** (*con las uñas*) to scratch **2.** (*raspar*) to scrape **3.** *irón, inf* (*instrumento*) **~ la guitarra** to bash away at the guitar; **~ el violín** to scrape away on the violin **II.** *vr:* **~se** **1.** (*con las uñas*) to scratch **2.** *AmS* (*achisparse*) to get tipsy

rascón, **-ona** *adj Méx* (*pendenciero*) troublemaker

rascuache *adj Méx: fam* **1.** (*miserable, pobre*) wretched **2.** (*de baja calidad*) cheap

rasgadura *f* tear, rip

rasgar <g→gu> **I.** *vt* **1.** (*romper por un lado*) to tear; (*en dos*) to tear in two; (*en pedazos*) to tear to pieces; (*abrir*) to tear open; **ojos rasgados** almond [*o* slanting] eyes **2.** (*cortar*) to cut **II.** *vr:* **~se** **1.** (*desgarrarse*) to tear **2.** *AmL, vulg* (*diñarla*) to kick the bucket

rasgo *m* **1.** (*del rostro*) feature; (*del carácter*) trait **2.** (*acción*) deed; **un ~ de generosidad** a fit of generosity **3.** (*trazo*) stroke; **a grandes ~s** in outline, in general

rasgón *m* tear

rasguear **I.** *vi* (*en la escritura*) to write with a flourish **II.** *vt* MÚS to strum

rasguñar **I.** *vt* **1.** (*arañar*) to scratch; (*herir*) to wound; (*cortar*) to cut **2.** ARTE to sketch **II.** *vr:* **~se** (*arañarse*) to scratch oneself; (*herirse*) to wound oneself; (*cortarse*) to cut oneself; **~se con algo** (*excoriarse*) to graze oneself against sth

rasguño *m* (*arañazo*) scratch; (*rasponazo*) scrape; (*excoriación*) chafing; **sin un ~** *fig* unscathed

raso *m* satin

raso, **-a** *adj* **1.** (*liso*) smooth; (*llano*) flat **2.** (*cielo*) clear; **al ~** in the open air **3.** (*al borde*) level; **una cucharada rasa** a level spoonful

raspa *f* **1.** (*del pescado*) backbone **2.** (*del cereal*) beard; (*de uva*) stalk **3.** *AmL* (*ratero*) pickpocket; (*ramera*) prostitute **4.** *fig, inf* (*delgado*) beanstalk

raspada *f Méx, PRico* (*reprimenda*) scolding

raspado *m* **1.** TÉC scraping; (*limado*) filing **2.** MED dilatation and curettage, D and C

raspador *m* **1.** (*instrumento*) scraper; (*lima*) file; MED curette **2.** (*de fósforos*) friction strip

raspadura *f* **1.** (*raspado*) scratching; (*con espátula*) scraping **2.** (*brizna*) scraping

raspaje *m Arg* MED curettage

raspar **I.** *vi* (*ser rasposo*) to be rough; (*en sorteos*) to scratch **II.** *vt* **1.** (*rascar*) to scratch **2.** MED to scrape **3.** (*rozar*) to brush **4.** *AmL, inf* (*mangar*) to swipe **5.** *AmS, inf* (*abroncar*) to yell at **III.** *vr:* **~se** to scratch oneself

raspón *m* **1.** (*arañazo*) scratch; (*excoriación*) chafing; (*rasguño*) scrape; (*de bala*) graze **2.** *Col* (*sombrero*) (large) straw hat

rasponazo *m* scratch

rasposo, **-a** *adj* rough

rasquetear *vt* **1.** *AmL* (*almohazar*) to groom **2.** *Arg* (*raer*) to scrape **3.** *AmS* (*caballo*) to curry

rasquiña *f AmL* (*comezón*) itch

rastra *f* (*rastrillo*) rake ►**a ~s** unwillingly; **ir a ~s** *inf* to drag along behind; **llevar a alguien a ~s** to drag sb along

rastrear **I.** *vt* **1.** (*seguir*) to track **2.** (*investigar*) **~ algo** to make inquiries about sth **3.** (*llevar arrastrando*) to drag **4.** (*registrar*) to go through **5.** (*minas*) to sweep **II.** *vi* **1.** (*investigar*) to make inquiries **2.** (*rastrillar*) to rake

rastrero, **-a** *adj* **1.** (*por el suelo*) creeping; **planta rastrera** creeper **2.** *pey* (*servil*) cringing **3.** *pey* (*despreciable*) despicable; (*canallesco*) base

rastrillar *vt* to rake

rastrillo *m* **1.** (*herramienta*) rake **2.** (*mercadillo*) flea market

rastro *m* **1.** (*indicio, pista*) trace; **ni ~** not a trace; **sin dejar (ni) ~** without trace; **seguir el ~ a** [*o* **de**] **alguien** to follow sb's trail **2.** (*mercadillo*) flea market **3.** (*herramienta*) rake

rastrojo *m* (*de paja*) stubble

rasurar **I.** *vt* to shave **II.** *vr:* **~se** to shave

rata[1] *f* ZOOL rat; **~ de alcantarilla** sewer rat; **escabullirse como una ~** to run and hide ►**~ de biblioteca** bookworm; **más pobre que las ~s** as poor as a church mouse; **hacerse la ~** *AmL* to play truant

rata[2] *mf* **1.** *inf* (*rácano*) miser **2.** (*descuidero*) pickpocket

ratear **I.** *vi* (*gatear*) to crawl **II.** *vt* **1.** *inf* (*mangar*) to nick **2.** *inf* (*racanear*) **~ algo** to be stingy with sth **3.** (*prorratear*) to share out

ratería *f* **1.** (*hurto*) theft **2.** (*racanería*) stinginess

ratero, **-a** *m, f* petty thief
raticida *m* rat poison
ratificación *f* **1.** JUR, POL ratification **2.** (*confirmación*) confirmation
ratificar <c→qu> **I.** *vt* **1.** JUR, POL to ratify **2.** (*confirmar*) to confirm **II.** *vr:* **~se 1.** JUR, POL to be ratified **2.** (*reafirmarse*) **~se en algo** to reaffirm sth
rato *m* while; (*momento*) moment; **a ~s** from time to time; **a cada ~** all the time; **al (poco) ~** shortly after; **de ~ en ~** from time to time; **en un ~ perdido** in a quiet moment; **todo el ~** the whole time; **un buen ~** for quite a time; **pasar un buen/mal ~** to have a good/bad time; **hacer pasar un mal ~ a alguien** to give sb a rough [*o* hard] time; **pasar el ~** to pass the time ►**¡hasta otro ~!** see you later!; **ser un ~ tonto** *inf* to be a bit stupid; **me gusta un ~** *inf* I really like it; **aún hay para ~** there's still plenty left to do; **tener para ~** to have lots to do; **un ~ (largo)** *inf* a lot
ratón *m* mouse; **~ de campo** fieldmouse; **~ (electrónico)** INFOR mouse ►**~ de biblioteca** bookworm
ratonera *f* **1.** (*trampa*) mousetrap; *fig* trap; **estar en una ~** *fig* to be caught in a trap; **caer en la ~** *fig* to fall into the trap **2.** (*agujero*) mousehole
ratonero *m* buzzard
raudal *m* torrent; **~ de palabras** flood of words ►**a ~es** in floods; **por la ventana entra la luz a ~es** the light came flooding through the window
raudo, **-a** *adj* rapid
raya *f* **1.** (*línea*) line; (*guión*) dash; **a ~s** (*paper*) lined; (*shirt*) striped; **tres en ~** (*juego*) noughts and crosses *Brit,* tic(k)-tac(k)-toe *Am* **2.** (*franja*) edge; (*cortafuegos*) firebreak **3.** (*del pelo*) parting *Brit,* part *Am;* **~ al lado/en medio** side/centre parting *Brit,* side/center part *Am;* **hacer la ~** to comb one's hair into a parting *Brit,* to part one's hair *Am* **4.** ZOOL ray, skate **5.** (*doblez*) fold **6.** (*cocaína*) line ►**pasar(se) de la ~** to go too far; **tener a alguien a ~** to keep sb in place [*o* under control]
rayado *m* **1.** (*líneas*) lines **2.** (*plumeado*) hatching **3.** (*rayajo*) scrawl
rayano, **-a** *adj* **~ en algo** bordering on sth
rayar I. *vi* **1.** (*lindar*) **~ con algo** to border on sth **2.** (*asemejarse*) **~ en algo** to come close to sth **3.** (*amanecer*) to break; **está rayando el alba** dawn is breaking; **al ~ el día** at the break of day **II.** *vt* **1.** (*marcar con rayas*) to line; (*plumear*) to hatch **2.** (*tachar*) to cross out **3.** (*arañar*) to scratch **4.** (*grabar*) to engrave **III.** *vr:* **~se** to get scratched
rayo *m* **1.** (*de luz*) ray; **~ de luna** shaft of moonlight **2.** (*radiación*) **~s infrarrojos** infrared rays; **~s X** X-rays; **~ láser** laser beam; **emitir ~s** to give out radiation **3.** (*relámpago*) (bolt of)lightning; **ha caído un ~ en la torre** the tower was hit by lightning **4.** (*infortunio*) (stroke of) bad luck **5.** (*radio*) spoke ►**¡~s (y centellas)!** good heavens!; **echar ~s y centellas** to be furious; **¡mal ~ te parta!** *inf* go to hell!; **como tocado por el ~** as if struck by lightning; **que me parta un ~ si no es verdad** *inf* I swear it on my mother's grave; **saber a ~s** to taste awful; **como un ~** in a flash
raza *f* **1.** (*casta*) race; (*estirpe*) strain; **de ~** (*perro*) pedigree; (*caballo*) thoroughbred; **de ~ blanca/negra** white/black **2.** (*temperamento*) character; **de (pura) ~** true
razón I. *f* **1.** (*discernimiento*) reason; (*entendimiento*) understanding; **puesto en ~** reasonable; **(no) atender a razones** (not) to listen to reason; **privar de la ~ a alguien** to drive sb out of his/her mind **2.** (*argumento*) argument; (*razonamiento*) reasoning; **ponerse a razones con alguien** to argue with sb; **venirse a razones con alguien** to reach an agreement with sb **3.** (*motivo*) reason; (*justificación*) justification; **~ de Estado** reasons *pl* of State; **~ de ser** raison d'être; **~ de más para** +*infin,* **~ de más para que** +*subj* more than enough reason to +*infin;* **la ~ por la que...** the reason why ...; **fuera de ~** unreasonable; **por ~ de algo** due to sth; **por razones de seguridad** for security reasons; **por una u otra ~** for one reason or another; **tener razones para...** +*infin* to have cause to ... **4.** (*acierto*) right; **la ~ de la fuerza** the doctrine that might is right; **¡con (mucha) ~!** quite rightly!; **sin ~** without justification; **cargarse de ~** to be convinced that one is right; **dar la ~ a alguien** to agree with sb; **llevar la ~** to be right; **tener (mucha) ~** to be (absolutely) right; **en eso (no) tienes ~** you are (not) right about that; **me asiste la ~** most people would agree with me **5.** (*información*) information; (*recado*) message; **~ aquí** inquire here; **dar ~ de alguien** to give information about sb; **dar ~ de sí** to report; *fig* to give a good account of oneself; **mandar ~ a alguien de algo** to send sb a message about sb; **pedir ~ de alguien** to ask sb for information **6.** MAT (*proporción*) ratio; **a ~ de tres por persona** at a rate of three per person; **a ~ del 10%** at 10%; **a ~ de 2 euros el kilo** at 2 euros per kilo **7.** JUR **~ social** trade name ►**entrar en ~** to come to one's senses; **hacer perder la ~ a alguien** to make sb lose control; **meter a alguien en ~** to make sb see sense; **perder la ~** to take leave of one's senses **II.** *prep* **en ~ de** (*en cuanto a*) as far as; (*a causa de*) because of
razonable *adj* **1.** (*sensato*) reasonable **2.** (*justo*) fair; (*adecuado*) sufficient
razonamiento *m* **1.** (*pensamientos, argumentación*) reasoning; (*reflexión*) reflection; **tus ~s no son convincentes** your argument is not convincing **2.** (*conversación*) discussion
razonar I. *vi* **1.** (*pensar, deducir, argumentar*) to reason **2.** (*juzgar*) to judge **3.** (*reflexionar*) to reflect **4.** (*conversar*) to discuss; **es inútil tratar de ~ con él** there's no point trying to reason with him **II.** *vt* **1.** (*exponer*) to show

2. (*fundamentar*) to establish

RDSI *f abr de* **Red Digital de Servicios Integrados** ISDN

re *m* MÚS (*de la escala diatónica*) D; (*de la solfa*) re; ~ **bemol** D flat; ~ **sostenido** D sharp

reabrir *irr como abrir vt t.* JUR to reopen

reacción *f* reaction; ~ **en cadena** chain reaction; ~ **excesiva** overreaction

reaccionar *vi* **1.** (*ante un estímulo*) ~ **a** [*o* **ante**] **algo** to react to sth **2.** (*responder*) ~ **a algo** to respond to sth **3.** (*repercutir*) ~ **en** [*o* **sobre**] **algo** to have repercussions on sth **4.** (*sobreponerse*) ~ **a algo** to overcome sth **5.** (*entrar en calor*) to get warm

reaccionario, **-a** *adj, m, f* reactionary

reacio, **-a** *adj* reluctant; **el pintor era ~ a mostrarse en público** the painter was reluctant to show his work; **es ~ a las fiestas** he/she is not very fond of parties

reactivar *vt* to reactivate; ECON to revive, to boost

reactivo *m* QUÍM reagent; (*indicador*) indicator; *fig* stimulant

reactor *m* **1.** (*motor*) jet engine **2.** (*avión*) jet **3.** FÍS reactor

readaptación *f* **1.** (*adaptación*) readaptation **2.** (*reintegración*) ~ **a algo** reintegration into sth; ~ **profesional** professional retraining

readaptar **I.** *vt* **1.** (*volver a adaptar*) to readapt **2.** (*reintegrar*) ~ **a algo** to reintegrate into sth **3.** (*profesión*) to retrain **II.** *vr:* **~se** **1.** (*adaptarse*) to readapt **2.** (*reintegrarse*) **~se a algo** to reintegrate into sth

readmisión *f* readmission; (*de despedidos*) re-employment

readmitir *vt* to readmit; (*despedidos*) to re-employ

reafirmar **I.** *vt* **1.** (*apoyar*) to reaffirm **2.** (*poner firme*) to make firm; (*la piel*) to tone up **3.** (*insistir*) ~ **algo** to insist on sth **II.** *vr:* **~se** **1.** (*confirmarse*) to reaffirm **2.** (*insistir*) **~se en algo** to insist on sth

reagrupar **I.** *vt* to regroup; (*redistribuir*) to redistribute **II.** *vr:* **~se** to regroup

reajustar *vt* **1.** (*adaptar*) to readjust **2.** (*reestructurar*) to restructure **3.** (*reorganizar*) to reorganize **4.** TÉC, ECON to adjust

reajuste *m* **1.** (*adaptación*) readjustment **2.** (*reestructuración*) restructuring **3.** (*reorganización*) reorganization; , ~ **de gobierno** cabinet reshuffle **4.** TÉC, ECON adjustment; ~ **salarial** wage settlement

real **I.** *adj* **1.** (*verdadero*) real; **basado en hechos ~es** based on a true story; **no me da la ~ gana** *inf* I don't feel like it **2.** (*del rey*) royal; **Alteza ~** Royal Highness; **palacio ~** royal palace **3.** (*espléndido*) splendid **II.** *m* **1.** (*dinero*) real (*old coin worth quarter of a peseta*); **estar sin un ~** *inf* to be pennniless **2.** (*de la feria*) fairground

realce *m* **1.** (*relieve*) relief **2.** (*esplendor*) splendour *Brit,* splendor *Am;* (*acento*) accent; **dar ~** to highlight

realengo, **-a** *adj* **1.** HIST Crown **2.** *AmL* (*sin amo*) ownerless; (*vagabundo*) stray

realeza *f* **1.** (*dignidad*) royalty **2.** (*grandeza*) magnificence; (*boato*) pomp

realidad *f* reality; (*verdad*) truth; ~ **virtual** virtual reality; **ajeno a la ~** far removed from reality; **hacer ~** to make come true; **hacerse ~** to happen; (*cumplirse*) to come true; **en ~** in fact

realismo *m sin pl* **1.** ARTE, LIT, CINE realism **2.** POL royalism

realista **I.** *adj* **1.** ARTE, LIT, CINE realistic **2.** POL royalist **II.** *mf* **1.** ARTE, LIT, FILOS, CINE realist **2.** POL royalist

realizable *adj* **1.** (*practicable*) practical; (*factible*) feasible **2.** ECON saleable; **bienes ~s** saleable goods

realización *f* **1.** (*ejecución*) execution **2.** (*materialización*) realization; (*cumplimiento*) fulfilment *Brit,* fulfillment *Am* **3.** (*organización*) organization **4.** ECON realization; ~ **de un pedido** fulfilment *Brit* [*o* fulfillment *Am*] of an order; ~ **de plusvalías** realization of capital gains **5.** CINE production

realizador(a) *m(f)* CINE, TV producer

realizar <z→c> **I.** *vt* **1.** (*efectuar*) to carry out; (*hacer*) to make **2.** (*hacer realidad*) to make real; (*sueños*) to fulfil *Brit,* to fulfill *Am* **3.** ECON to realize; (*ganancia, aportaciones*) to take **4.** CINE, TV to produce **5.** *AmL* (*notar*) to notice **II.** *vr:* **~se** **1.** (*desarrollarse*) to be carried out **2.** (*materializarse*) to happen; (*hacerse realidad*) to come true; (*cumplirse*) to be fulfilled

realmente *adv* (*en efecto, verdaderamente*) really; (*de hecho*) in fact

realquilar *vt* to sublet; **vivir en una vivienda realquilada** to live in a sublet property

realzar <z→c> *vt* **1.** (*labrar*) to emboss **2.** (*acentuar*) to bring out **3.** (*subrayar*) to highlight

reamargo, **-a** *adj AmL* very bitter

reamigo, **-a** *m, f AmL* very close friend; **son ~s del director** they are very close friends of the director

reanimación *f* **1.** revival **2.** MED resuscitation; (*posoperatorio*) reanimation; **unidad de ~** intensive care unit

reanimar **I.** *vt* **1.** (*reavivar*) to revive **2.** (*reactivar*) to reactivate **3.** (*animar*) to liven up **4.** MED to resuscitate **II.** *vr:* **~se** **1.** (*recuperar el conocimiento*) to regain consciousness **2.** (*restablecerse*) to become re-established **3.** (*animarse*) to liven up

reanudar *vt* to resume

reaparición *f* reappearance; TEAT, CINE comeback

reapertura *f* reopening

reata *f* **1.** (*correa*) rope (*used to keep animals in file*); (*animales*) packtrain; **una ~ de mulos** a pack of mules **2.** *AmL* (*de flores*) border ▸**de ~** (*sucesivamente*) one after the other; (*en hilera*) in single file

reavivar *vt, vr:* **~se** to revive

rebaba *f* (rough) edge; (*metales*) burr

rebaja *f* **1.**(*oferta*) sale; **~s de verano** summer sales; **estar de ~s** to have a sale on **2.**(*descuento*) discount; (*reducción*) reduction

rebajar **I.** *vt* **1.**(*abaratar*) to reduce **2.**(*humillar*) to put down **3.** *t.* FOTO (*mitigar*) to soften; (*debilitar*) to weaken; (*disminuir*) to lessen **4.**(*una bebida*) to dilute **5.**(*dispensar*) to let off **6.**(*gastar*) to wear down **II.** *vr:* **~se** **1.**(*humillarse*) to be humiliated **2.**(*condescender*) to lower oneself **3.**(*dispensarse*) to be let off

rebanada *f* slice

rebanar *vt* **1.**(*hacer rebanadas*) to slice **2.**(*partir*) to cut up

rebañar *vt* **1.**(*apurar*) to finish off; **~ el plato** to wipe the plate clean **2.** *pey* (*recoger*) to mop up

rebaño *m t. fig* herd

rebasar *vt* **1.**(*sobrepasar*) to exceed; MIL to overrun; **~ el límite** *fig* to overstep the mark; **esto rebasa los límites de mi paciencia** this is trying my patience **2.**(*exceder*) **~ en algo** to excel at sth

rebatir *vt* **1.**(*discutir*) to contest; (*refutar*) to refute; (*rechazar*) to reject **2.**(*repeler*) to repel **3.**(*batir*) to beat **4.**(*abatir*) to knock down

rebato *m* alarm; **tocar a ~** to sound the alarm

rebeca *f* cardigan

rebeco *m* chamois

rebelarse *vr* to rebel; (*oponerse*) to be opposed

rebelde **I.** *adj* **1.**(*indócil*) unruly; (*levantisco*) restless **2.**(*insurrecto*) rebellious **3.**(*persistente*) persistent **4.**(*difícil*) troublesome **5.** JUR defaulting **II.** *mf* **1.** rebel **2.** JUR defaulter

rebeldía *f* **1.**(*cualidad*) rebelliousness **2.**(*oposición*) opposition **3.** *t.* MIL (*insubordinación*) insubordination **4.** JUR default; **declarar a alguien en ~** to declare sb to be in default; **juzgar en ~** to judge by default

rebelión *f* rebellion

rebenque *m CSur* riding crop

reblandecer *irr como crecer vt, vr:* **~se** to soften

rebobinar *vt* (*retroceder*) to rewind

rebosante *adj* overflowing; **~ de agua/alegría** brimming with water/hapiness; **~ de salud** glowing with health

rebosar *vi* **1.**(*desbordar*) to overflow **2.**(*tener mucho*) **~ de** to be brimming with; **le rebosa el dinero** he/she is rolling in money; **le rebosa la soberbia** he/she is very arrogant; **la gota que hizo ~ el vaso** the final straw, the straw which broke the camel's back **3.**(*estar lleno*) to be full to the brim; (**lleno**) **a ~** full to the brim **4.**(*abundar*) to abound

rebotar **I.** *vi* **1.**(*botar*) to bounce; (*bala*) to ricochet **2.**(*chocar*) **~ en** [*o* **contra**] **algo** to bump into sth; **salir rebotado** to bounce back; *fig* to shoot off **II.** *vt* **1.**(*botar*) to bounce **2.** *inf* (*enfadar*) to anger **III.** *vr:* **~se** **1.**(*vino*) to turn **2.** *inf* (*enfadarse*) to get angry

rebote *m* (*bote*) bounce; DEP rebound; (*golpe*) blow; (*de bala*) ricochet; **de ~** on the rebound **2.** *inf* (*enfado*) **coger un ~** to have a fit

rebozar <z→c> **I.** *vt* **1.** GASTR (*con pan rallado*) to coat with breadcrumbs; (*con masa*) to coat with batter **2.**(*envolver*) to cover **II.** *vr:* **~se** to cover one's face

rebozo *m* **1.**(*velo*) ≈ cloak **2.**(*pretexto*) pretext; **sin ~** openly

rebujo *m* ball; (*trapos*) bundle; **hacer un ~ con la ropa** to gather clothes into a bundle

rebullir <*3. pret:* rebulló> *vi, vr:* **~se** to stir; **sin ~se** very quietly

rebumbio *m Méx* (*alboroto*) commotion

rebuscado, -a *adj* pedantic; (*palabras*) obscure; (*estilo*) contrived

rebuscar <c→qu> **I.** *vi* to search thoroughly **II.** *vt* (*buscar*) to search for **III.** *vr* **rebuscárselas** *CSur* (*defenderse*) to get by

rebuznar *vi* (*burro*) to bray

rebuzno *m* bray

recabar *vt* **1.**(*obtener*) to manage to obtain **2.**(*pedir*) to ask for

recadero, -a *m, f* messenger

recado *m* **1.**(*mensaje*) message; **dar un ~ a alguien** to give a message to sb; **¿puedes darle el siguiente ~?** could you give him/her this message? **2.**(*encargo*) errand; **hacer ~s** to do errands

recaer *irr como caer vi* **1.**(*enfermedad*) to relapse **2.**(*delito*) to reoffend; **~ en el mismo error una y otra vez** to repeat the same mistake again and again; **~ en la bebida** to start drinking again **3.**(*culpa*) to fall; **~ en alguien** (*herencia*) to fall to sb

recaída *f* relapse

recalar **I.** *vi* **1.** NÁUT to put in **2.**(*persona*) to appear **II.** *vt* to soak **III.** *vr:* **~se** to get soaked

recalcar <c→qu> *vt* **1.**(*palabras*) to stress **2.**(*apretar*) to squeeze **3.**(*llenar*) to fill; **~ la cuba con vino** to fill the barrel with wine

recalcificar *vt* MED to calcify

recalcitrante *adj* recalcitrant

recalentado *m Méx, inf* leftovers *pl*

recalentar <e→ie> **I.** *vt* **1.**(*comida*) to reheat **2.**(*aparato*) to overheat **II.** *vr:* **~se** (*motor*) to overheat

recámara *f* **1.**(*para ropa*) dressing room **2.**(*arma*) chamber

recamarera *f Méx* chambermaid

recambiar *vt* **1.**(*sustituir*) to substitute **2.**(*intercambiar*) to exchange

recambio *m* (*repuesto*) spare (part); (*envase*) refill

recapacitar **I.** *vt* to consider **II.** *vi* to think

R

things over
recapitulación *f* summary, summing up
recapitular *vt* to summarize, to sum up
recargado, **-a** *adj* (*exagerado*) overelaborate; (*lenguaje*) overblown
recargar <g→gu> *vt* **1.** (*pila*) to recharge **2.** (*decorar*) to overdecorate; **el vestido recargado de lazos y botones no se vendió** nobody bought the dress which was dripping with laces and buttons **3.** (*impuesto*) to increase **4.** (*carga*) to overload; ~ **de trabajo** to overload with work
recargo *m* (*tasas*) increase; (*sobreprecio*) surcharge; **llamada sin** ~ freephone call *Brit,* toll-free call *Am*
recatado, **-a** *adj* **1.** (*decoroso*) decent; (*modesto*) modest **2.** (*cauto*) cautious
recato *m* **1.** (*decoro*) decency **2.** (*cautela*) caution; (*pudor*) modesty
recauchutar *vt* AUTO (*llanta*) to retread
recaudación *f* **1.** (*cobro*) collection; (*cantidad*) takings *pl;* ~ **diaria** daily takings **2.** (*de impuestos*) collection; (*cantidad*) receipts *pl*
recaudar *vt* (*impuestos, dinero*) to collect
recaudería *f Méx* (*especiería*) grocery store
recaudo *m* **1.** (*ganancia*) collection **2.** JUR (*seguridad*) surety **3.** (*cuidado*) care; (*precaución*) precaution ►**estar a buen** ~ to be safe and sound; **poner algo a buen** ~ to put sth in safe keeping
recelar **I.** *vt* (*temer*) to fear **II.** *vi* to be suspicious; **recelo de mi secretaria** I don't trust my secretary
recelo *m* mistrust; **mirar algo con** ~ to be suspicious of sth
receloso, **-a** *adj* distrustful; **estar** ~ **de alguien** to be suspicious of sb; **ponerse** ~ to become suspicious; **poner** ~ **a alguien** to cause sb to be suspicious
recensión *f* PREN review
recepción *f* reception
recepcionista *mf* receptionist
receptáculo *m* (*cavidad*) receptacle
receptividad *f* receptiveness; MED susceptibility
receptivo, **-a** *adj* **1.** (*sensible*) receptive **2.** MED susceptible
receptor *m* (*radio, teléfono*) receiver; ~ **de televisión** TV set
receptor(a) *m(f)* recipient
recesión *f* ECON recession
receso *m AmL* (*vacaciones*) recess
receta *f* **1.** GASTR recipe; **¿cuál es tu** ~ **para ser feliz?** *fig* what's your formula for happiness? **2.** MED prescription; **con** ~ **médica** on prescription; **venta con** ~ available on prescription
recetar *vt* MED to prescribe
recetario *m* **1.** GASTR cookery book *Brit,* cookbook **2.** MED (*libro*) pharmacopoeia; (*talonario*) prescription pad; (*de un enfermo*) prescription record
rechazar <z→c> *vt* **1.** (*no aceptar*) to reject **2.** (*denegar, no tolerar*) to refuse; ~ **de plano las acusaciones** to flatly deny the accusations **3.** (*ataque*) to repel, to push back
rechazo *m* rejection; (*denegación*) refusal
rechiflar **I.** *vt* to whistle at **II.** *vr:* ~**se de** to make fun of
rechinamiento *m* squeaking; ~ **de dientes** grinding of teeth
rechinar **I.** *vi* to squeak; (*puerta*) to creak **II.** *vt* ~ **los dientes** to grind one's teeth
rechistar **I.** *vi* to grumble; **sin** ~ without complaining
rechoncho, **-a** *adj inf* tubby
rechupete **de** ~ delicious
recibidor *m* **1.** (*hotel, oficinas*) lobby **2.** (*casa*) entry (hall) **3.** (*persona*) recipient
recibimiento *m* **1.** (*acogida*) welcome; **le dispensaron un** ~ **multitudinario** they gave him/her a tumultuous welcome **2.** (*recibidor*) lobby
recibir **I.** *vt* **1.** (*tomar*) to receive **2.** (*personas*) to welcome **3.** (*aceptar*) to accept **II.** *vi* (*médico*) to see patients; (*ministro*) to see people **III.** *vr* ~**se de algo** *AmL* to graduate as sth; (*médico, abogado*) to qualify as sth
recibo *m* **1.** (*en tienda*) receipt; (*de la luz, del agua*) bill; ~ **de entrega** delivery note **2.** (*de una carta*) receipt; **acusar** ~ to acknowledge receipt **3.** (*recibidor*) lobby ►**si llaman, abre tú porque yo no estoy de** ~ if they call, can you go to the door? I don't want to see anybody; **ser de** ~ (*estar de moda*) to be in; (*ser apropiado*) to be acceptable
reciclaje *m* **1.** (*de materiales*) recycling **2.** ENS ~ **profesional** *fig* professional retraining; **curso de** ~ refresher course
reciclar *vt* **1.** TÉC to recycle **2.** (*formación*) to retrain
recién *adv* **1.** (*acabado de*) recently; ~ **cocido/pintado** freshly cooked/painted; **los** ~ **casados** the newly weds; **el** ~ **nacido** the newborn baby **2.** *AmL* (*en cuanto*) as soon as
reciente *adj* **1.** (*nuevo*) new; (*fresco*) fresh **2.** (*que acaba de suceder*) recent; **un libro de** ~ **publicación** a book which has recently been published
recientemente *adv* recently
recinto *m* enclosure; ~ **fortificado** fortified enclosure; ~ **universitario** university campus; ~ **ferial** fairgrounds *pl*
recio, **-a** **I.** *adj* **1.** (*fuerte*) strong **2.** (*rígido*) stiff; **en lo más** ~ **del invierno** in the depths of winter **II.** *adv* (*hablar*) loudly; (*llover*) heavily
recipiente *m* container; (*de vidrio, barro*) vessel
reciprocidad *f* reciprocity
recíproco, **-a** *adj* reciprocal; **...y a la recíproca** ... and vice versa
recital *m* MÚS concert, recital; LIT reading; *fig* exhibition

recitar *vt* to recite; ~ **maquinalmente el menú** to recite the menu from memory

reclamación *f* **1.**(*recurso*) protest; (*queja*) complaint **2.**(*exigencia*) claim; (*de deuda*) demand

reclamar I. *vi* **1.**(*protestar*) to protest **2.**(*quejarse*) ~ **por algo** to complain about sth **II.** *vt* (*pedir*) to claim; (*una deuda*) to demand; ~ **daños** to sue for damages; **nos reclaman el dinero que nos prestaron** they want us to repay the money which they lent us; **el terrorista es reclamado por la justicia sueca a Italia** the Swedish courts have asked Italy to hand over the terrorist; **España reclama Gibraltar** Spain claims sovereignty over Gibraltar

reclame *m Arg, Urug* advertisement

reclamo *m* **1.**(*caza, utensilio*) decoy; (*grito*) decoy call; **acudir al** ~ to answer the call **2.** COM advert(isement)

reclinable *adj* reclining; **asiento** ~ reclining chair

reclinar I. *vt* to lean; (*hacia atrás*) to lean back; **reclinó su cabeza contra** [*o* **sobre**] **mis hombros** he/she rested his/her head on my shoulders **II.** *vr:* ~**se** (*inclinarse*) to lean; (*apoyarse*) to rest

recluir *irr como huir* **I.** *vt* (*cárcel*) to imprison; (*hospital*) to confine **II.** *vr:* ~**se** to shut oneself away

reclusión *f* **1.** JUR imprisonment **2.**(*aislamiento*) seclusion

recluso, -a I. *adj* (*preso*) imprisoned; **la población reclusa vive en condiciones inhumanas** the prisoners live in inhuman conditions **II.** *m, f* prisoner

recluta *mf* (*voluntario*) recruit; (*obligado*) conscript, draftee *Am*

reclutamiento *m* recruiting

reclutar *vt* MIL to recruit; (*obligar*) to conscript, to draft *Am*

recobrar I. *vt* to recover; ~ **las fuerzas** to regain one's strength; ~ **las pérdidas** to make good one's losses; ~ **el sentido** to regain consciousness; ~ **la vista** to regain one's sight; ~ **las ganas de vivir** to recover one's enthusiasm for life **II.** *vr:* ~**se** to recover

recodo *m* (*río*) bend

recogedor *m* dustpan

recogepelotas *mf inv* DEP (*chico*) ballboy; (*chica*) ballgirl

recoger <g→j> **I.** *vt* **1.**(*buscar*) to collect; **te voy a** ~ **a la estación** I'll meet you at the station; **recogen las cartas a las ocho** they collect the post at eight o'clock *Brit,* they pick up the mail at eight *Am* **2.**(*coger*) to collect; (*ordenar*) to organize; (*guardar*) to keep; ~ **del suelo** to pick up from the floor; **¡es hora de ~!** let's call it a day! **3.**(*juntar*) to gather together **4.**(*cosecha*) to gather; ~ **el fruto de su trabajo** to reap the fruits of one's labour *Brit* [*o* labor *Am*] **5.**(*acoger*) to take in **6.**(*arremangar: vestido*) to lift up; (*pantalón*) to roll up **7.**(*cabello*) to gather up **8.**(*enrollar: velas*) to take in; (*cortinas*) to roll up **II.** *vr:* ~**se 1.**(*a casa*) to go home; (*a la cama*) to go to bed **2.** REL to withdraw

recogida *f* collection; ~ **de basuras** rubbish collection *Brit,* garbage collection *Am;* ~ **de beneficios** FIN profit taking; ~ **del correo** mail collection; ~ **de equipajes** AVIAT baggage reclaim *Brit,* baggage claim *Am*

recogido, -a *adj* **1.**(*acogedor*) welcoming **2.**(*retirado*) secluded

recolección *f* AGR harvest; (*periodo*) harvest time

recolectar *vt* **1.**(*cosas*) to gather **2.**(*frutos*) to harvest

recomendable *adj* recommendable

recomendación *f* recommendation; **con la ayuda de tu** ~ with the help of your recommendation; **por** ~ **de mi médico** on my doctor's advice; **al ser hijo del alcalde tiene muchas recomendaciones** being the mayor's son he has lots of contacts

recomendado, -a I. *adj* (*precio*) recommended; **precio de venta al público** ~ recommended retail price **II.** *m, f person who has obtained a job by means of contacts*

recomendar <e→ie> *vt* to advise; **nos recomendó no salir de casa** he/she advised us not to leave the house

recomenzar *irr como empezar vt* ~ **a** to begin again +*infin*

recompensa *f* reward; **ofrecer una** ~ **de 100 dólares por algo** to offer a reward of 100 dollars for sth; **¿es ésta la** ~ **a todos mis esfuerzos?** is this what I get for all my efforts?; **en** ~ as a reward

recompensar *vt* **1.**(*a alguien, un servicio*) ~ **por** [*o* **de**] **algo** to reward for sth **2.**(*de un daño*) to compensate; **fue recompensado por sus gastos** his/her expenses were paid

recomponer *irr como poner vt* (*reparar*) to repair, to put back together *inf;* (*reconstruir*) to rebuild

reconcentrar I. *vt* ~ **algo en algo** to concentrate sth on sth **II.** *vr* ~**se en algo** to concentrate on sth

reconciliación *f* reconciliation; **darse la mano en señal de** ~ to shake hands as a sign of reconciliation

reconciliar I. *vt* to reconcile **II.** *vr:* ~**se** to be reconciled

recóndito, -a *adj* hidden; **la casa está en lo más** ~ **del bosque** the house is hidden away in the depths of the forest; **en lo más** ~ **de mi corazón** in my heart of hearts

reconducir *vt* **1.**(*dirigir*) to reroute **2.** JUR to renew

reconfortar *vt* to comfort; (*consolar*) to console

reconocer *irr como crecer* **I.** *vt* **1.**(*identificar*) to recognize; ~ **a alguien por la voz** to recognize sb by his/her voice **2.**(*admitir*) to accept; (*un error*) to acknowledge; ~ **como hijo** to recognize as one's son **3.** (*examinar*) to check; MED to examine **4.** POL to recognize **5.** MIL to reconnoitre *Brit,* to reconnoiter *Am* **6.** (*advertir*) to warn; **reconociendo que...** in the knowledge that ... **II.** *vr:* ~**se 1.** (*declararse*) to admit; ~**se culpable** to admit one's guilt **2.** (*identificarse*) **no se reconoció a sí misma** she no longer knew who she was; **no me reconocí en la novela** I didn't recognize myself in the novel

reconocido, **-a** *adj* **1.** (*agradecido*) grateful **2.** (*aceptado*) recognized

reconocimiento *m* **1.** POL, JUR recognition; **el no ~ de Bosnia-Herzegovina** the non-recognition of Bosnia-Herzegovina; ~ **de firma** authorization of signature **2.** (*exploración*) inspection; ~ **médico** medical examination; ~ **precoz** MED early diagnosis; **vuelo de** ~ reconnaissance flight **3.** (*gratitud*) gratefulness; **en ~ de mi labor** in recognition of my work **4.** INFOR ~ **de errores** error recognition

reconquista *f* reconquest

> The **Reconquista** was ended after eight centuries of Moorish occupation by the reconquest of the Kingdom of **Granada**. For eight centuries, the sole objective of the Christian rulers had been to drive the arabs out of the **Península Ibérica**. Those Moors and Jews who wished to remain in Spain had to convert to the Christian faith.

reconquistar *vt* to reconquer; *fig* to win back

reconstituir *irr como huir vt* **1.** (*restablecer*) to re-establish **2.** (*rehacer*) to reconstruct; ~ **una escena histórica** to reconstruct a historical scene

reconstituyente *m* MED reconstituent

reconstrucción *f* **1.** (*país*) rebuilding **2.** JUR reconstruction

reconstruir *irr como huir vt* **1.** (*reedificar*) to rebuild **2.** (*componer*) to reconstruct; (*completar*) to complete

recontar <o→ue> *vt* **1.** (*contar*) to count; (*contar otra vez*) to recount **2.** (*cuento*) to retell

recontra *AmL, inf* **¡idiota! – ¡que te ~!** idiot! – the same to you!

recontrabueno, **-a** *adj AmL, inf* really good

recontracaro, **-a** *adj AmL, inf* really expensive

reconvenir *irr como venir vt* (*reprender*) ~ **por algo** to reproach for sth

Recopa *f* DEP Cup Winners' Cup

recopilación *f* compilation

recopilar *vt* to compile

récord <récords> *m* record

recordar <o→ue> **I.** *vi, vt* **1.** (*acordarse*) to remember **2.** (*traer a la memoria, semejar*) to remind; **recuérdale a mamá que me traiga el libro** remind mum *Brit* [*o* mom *Am*] to bring me the book; **este paisaje me recuerda (a) la Toscana** this landscape reminds me of Tuscany; **si mal no recuerdo** if I remember correctly **II.** *vi, vr:* ~**se** *Arg, Méx* (*despertarse*) to wake up **III.** *vr:* ~**se** (*acordarse*) to remember

recordatorio *m* **1.** (*comunión*) communion card; (*fallecimiento*) in memoriam card **2.** (*advertencia*) reminder

recorrer *vt* **1.** (*atravesar*) to cross; (*viajar por*) to travel around; ~ **Europa en bicicleta** to travel around Europe by bicycle **2.** (*trayecto*) to travel; **recorrimos tres kilómetros a pie** we walked three kilometres *Brit* [*o* kilometers *Am*] **3.** (*registrar*) to check; (*terreno*) to search **4.** (*texto*) to skim; ~ **con la vista** to look over

recortable *adj* cutout; **muñeca** ~ cutout doll

recortado, **-a** *adj* (*hoja*) uneven; (*costa*) rugged; (*cortado*) cut out

recortar **I.** *vt* **1.** (*figuras*) to cut out; (*barba, uñas*) to trim; (*quitar*) to cut off **2.** (*disminuir*) to cut (down) **II.** *vr:* ~**se** to stand out; **el perfil de las montañas se recorta sobre el horizonte** the outline of the mountains stands out against the horizon

recorte *m* **1.** (*periódico*) cutting **2.** (*rebajamiento*) cut(back) **3.** *pl* (*cortaduras*) cuttings *pl;* ~**s de papel/tela** scraps of paper/cloth

recostar <o→ue> **I.** *vt* **1.** (*apoyar*) to rest **2.** (*inclinar*) ~ **contra/en algo** to lean against/on sth; ~ **la espalda contra una columna** to lean one's back against a column **II.** *vr:* ~**se 1.** (*inclinarse*) ~**se contra/en algo** to lean against/on sth **2.** (*apoyarse*) to rest

recova *f* **1.** *CSur* (*arcadas*) arcade **2.** *And, Urug* (*mercado*) market

recoveco *m* **1.** (*escondrijo*) nook **2.** (*falta de claridad*) obscurity; **sin ~s** frankly; **persona con** ~ complicated person **3.** (*vuelta*) bend

recreación *f* **1.** (*reproducción*) reproduction **2.** (*diversión*) recreation

recrear **I.** *vt* **1.** (*reproducir*) to reproduce **2.** (*divertir*) to entertain **II.** *vr:* ~**se** to entertain oneself; **se recrea contemplando cuadros** he/she enjoys looking at pictures

recreativo, **-a** *adj* recreational; (**salón de juegos**) ~**s** amusement arcade

recreo *m* **1.** recreation; **de** ~ recreational; **casa de** ~ holiday home; **puerto de** ~ marina **2.** (*en el colegio*) break, recess *Am*

recriminación *f* **1.** (*reproche*) reproach **2.** (*acusación*) recrimination

recriminar *vt* **1.** (*reprochar*) to reproach **2.** (*acusar*) to accuse

recrudecer *irr como crecer vi, vr:* ~**se** to worsen; (*conflicto*) to intensify

recrudecimiento *m* worsening; (*combate*) intensification

recta *f* straight; **entrar en la ~ final** *t.* DEP to enter the final straight

rectamente *adv* (*honradamente*) justly

rectangular *adj* rectangular

rectángulo *m* rectangle

rectángulo, **-a** *adj* rectangular

rectificación *f* (*corrección*) correction
rectificar <c→qu> *vt* **1.**(*corregir*) to correct **2.**(*carretera*) to straighten
rectilíneo, -a *adj* **1.**(*forma*) rectilinear **2.**(*persona*) rigid
rectitud *f* (*honradez*) uprightness
recto[1] *adv* straight; **siga todo ~** go straight ahead [*o* on]
recto[2] *m* ANAT rectum
recto, -a *adj* **1.** *t.* MAT (*forma*) straight; **ángulo ~** right angle; **línea recta** straight line **2.**(*honrado*) upright
rector(a) **I.** *adj* principal; (*responsable*) governing **II.** *m(f)* ENS, REL rector; (*universidad*) vice-chancellor *Brit,* president *Am*
rectorado *m* rectorship; (*lugar*) rectorate; (*cargo*) UNIV vice-chancellorship *Brit,* presidency *Am*
recua *f* train (*of pack animals*)*;* **con él llegó toda su ~ de amigos** *inf* his band [*o* drove] of friends came along with him
recuadro *m* (*casilla*) box
recubierto *pp de* **recubrir**
recubrimiento *m* covering
recubrir *irr como abrir vt* to cover
recuento *m* count; **hacer el ~ de votos** to count the votes
recuerdo *m* **1.**(*evocación*) memory; **en** [*o* **como**] **~ de nuestro encuentro** in memory of our meeting; **traer al ~** to remind; **tener un buen ~ de algo** to have good memories of sth **2.**(*de un viaje*) souvenir **3.** *pl* (*saludos*) regards *pl;* **dales muchos ~s de mi parte** send them my regards; **María te manda muchos ~s** María sends you her regards
recular *vi* **1.**(*retroceder*) to go back; (*automóvil*) to reverse *Brit,* to back up *Am* **2.** *inf* (*ceder*) to give way
recuperación *f* **1.**(*recobrar*) recovery; MIL recapture; **~ de datos** INFOR data retrieval **2.** ECON recovery; **~ de las cotizaciones** share price recovery; **la ~ de los precios** rally of prices **3.**(*enfermo*) recovery **4.**(*papel, hierro*) recycling **5.**(*asignatura*) pass (*in a re-take exam*)*;* **examen de ~** re-sit (exam) **6.**(*rescate*) rescue
recuperar **I.** *vt* **1.**(*recobrar*) to recover; MIL to recapture **2.**(*tiempo*) to make up **3.**(*papel, hierro*) to recycle **4.**(*rescatar*) to rescue **5.**(*asignatura*) to pass (*a re-sit examination*)*;* **mi hijo no recuperó la física en el examen de septiembre** my son failed his physics re-sit **II.** *vr:* **~se** to recover
recurrir *vi* **1.** JUR to appeal **2.**(*acudir*) **~ a** (*una persona*) to turn to; (*una institución*) to resort to; **~ a la justicia** to turn to the law; **~ a todos los medios** to resort to every measure available; **no tener a quien ~** to have nobody to turn to; **si no me pagas ~é a un abogado** if you don't pay me I'm going to see a lawyer
recursivo, -a *adj Col* (*ocurrente*) resourceful
recurso *m* **1.** JUR appeal; **~ de apelación** appeal; **~ contencioso administrativo** action against the administration; **interponer un ~ contra la sentencia** to lodge an appeal against the sentence **2.**(*remedio*) solution; (*expediente*) expedient; **no me queda otro ~ que...** I have no alternative but ...; **como último ~** as a last resort **3.** *pl* (*bienes*) means *pl;* **familias sin ~s** families without means **4.** *pl* (*reservas*) resources *pl;* **~s naturales** natural resources; **ser una persona de ~s** to be resourceful; **el país cuenta con abundantes ~s minerales** the country has rich mineral resources
recusar *vt* to reject; JUR to challenge
red *f* **1.**(*malla*) net; **~ de arrastre** trawl net; **echar las ~es** to cast the nets **2.**(*sistema*) network; **~ comercial** business [*o* sales] network; **~ vial** road network; **han desarticulado una ~ de carteristas** they have broken up a gang of pickpockets **3.** ELEC mains *pl Brit,* power lines *pl;* **avería en la ~** mains failure *Brit,* power failure ►caer **en la ~** to fall into the trap
redacción *f* **1.** ENS writing; **hacer una ~ sobre el mar** to write a composition on the sea **2.** PREN editing
redactar *vt* to write; (*documento*) to edit; (*testamento*) to draw up
redactor(a) *m(f)* writer; PREN editor
redada *f* **1.**(*de la policía*) roundup, raid **2.**(*pescado*) catch; *fig* haul
redecilla *f* (*pelo*) hairnet; (*equipaje*) luggage rack
rededor *m* **al** [*o* **en**] **~** around; **al ~ de la casa** around the house
redención *f* **1.** REL redemption **2.**(*cautivo*) freeing **3.**(*finca*) redemption (*by repaying a loan*)
redentor(a) *m(f)* redeemer
redicho, -a *adj inf* pretentious
redil *m* fold; **volver al ~** *fig* to return to the fold
redimir *vt* **1.** REL to redeem **2.**(*esclavo*) to purchase the freedom of **3.**(*finca*) to redeem (*by repaying a loan*)
redistribución *f* redistribution
rédito *m* yield, revenue
redituar <*3. pres:* reditúa> *vt* to yield
redoblar **I.** *vt* **1.**(*aumentar*) to intensify **2.**(*clavo*) to clinch, to bend back **II.** *vi* (*tambor*) to play a roll on the drums; (*tormenta*) to intensify
redoble *m* drum roll
redomado, -a *adj* **1.**(*astuto*) sly **2.**(*total*) utter; **un tonto ~** an utter fool
redomón *adj AmS* half-trained
redonda *f* **1.**(*dehesa*) pasture; **en tres kilómetros a la ~** for three kilometres *Brit* [*o* kilometers *Am*] in all directions **2.** MÚS semibreve *Brit,* whole note *Am*
redondear *vt* to round off; **~ por defecto/por exceso** to round up/down
redondel *m* circle
redondela *f* **1.** *Arg, Chile* (*objeto circular*)

R

round object **2.** *Chile, inf* (*círculo*) circle
redondez *f* roundness ►**en toda la ~ de la Tierra** in the whole wide world
redondo, -a *adj* *t.* MAT (*circular*) round; (*redondeado*) rounded ►**un negocio ~** a great deal; **caer(se) ~** (*derrumbarse*) to fall flat; (*quedarse mudo*) to be struck dumb; **negarse en ~** to flatly deny
reducción *f* **1.** *t.* QUÍM, ECON (*disminución*) reduction; (*rebaja*) discount; (*de personal*) cut; **~ de la jornada laboral** reduction of the working day **2.** JUR remission **3.** FÍS, MAT reduction; **~ de quebrados** reduction of fractions **4.** MED setting
reducido, -a *adj* (*pequeño*) small; (*estrecho*) narrow; **tarifas reducidas** reduced rates
reducidor(a) *m(f)* *AmS* (*perista*) fence
reducir *irr como traducir* **I.** *vt* **1.** *t.* QUÍM (*disminuir*) to reduce; (*personal, gastos*) to cut; (*precios*) to lower **2.** (*foto, dibujo*) to reduce; **~ de escala** to scale down **3.** (*someter*) to subdue; **la policía redujo al agresor** the police overpowered the assailant **4.** (*convertir*) to reduce; **el fuego redujo la casa a cenizas** the fire reduced the house to ashes; **~/quedar reducido a escombros** to reduce/be reduced to rubble; **~ al absurdo algo** to make nonsense of sth **5.** (*limitar*) to reduce **6.** (*resumir*) to summarize; (*acortar*) to abbreviate **7.** MED to set **8.** MAT to reduce; **~ al común denominador** *t. fig* to reduce to the lowest common denominator **II.** *vi* AUTO to change down *Brit,* to shift into a lower gear *Am* **III.** *vr:* **~se** to come down
redundancia *f* redundancy
redundante *adj* redundant
redundar *vi* **eso redunda en beneficio nuestro** this works in our interest; **eso ~á en perjuicio vuestro** this will work against you
reedición *f* reissue; (*impresión*) reprint
reedificación *f* rebuilding
reedificar <c→qu> *vt* to rebuild
reeditar *vt* to republish; (*imprimir*) to reprint
reeducación *f* MED physiotherapy
reelección *f* re-election
reelegir *irr como elegir vt* to re-elect
reembolsar *vt* to repay, to reimburse
reembolso *m* (*devolución*) repayment; **enviar algo contra ~** to send sth cash on delivery
reemplazante *mf* *Méx* replacement
reemplazar <z→c> *vt* to replace; (*representar*) to substitute
reemplazo *m* **1.** (*sustitución*) replacement; DEP substitution **2.** (*tropas*) reserve; **ser del mismo ~** to have been called up together
reencarnación *f* reincarnation
reencauchar *vt* *Col, Perú* AUTO to retread
reencontrar <o→ue> **I.** *vt* to find again **II.** *vr:* **~se** to meet again
reencuentro *m* **1.** (*encuentro*) reunion **2.** (*choque*) collision **3.** MIL skirmish
reenganchar *vt* to re-enlist
reenviar <*1. pres:* reenvío> *vt* (*al remitente*) to return; (*a un nuevo destinatario*) to forward
reestreno *m* TEAT revival; TV rerun; CINE rehowing
reestructurar *vt* to restructure
refacción *f* snack
refaccionar *vt* *AmL* (*edificios*) to refurbish
refectorio *m* refectory
referencia *f* **1.** reference; **punto de ~** point of reference; **con ~ a** with reference to; **hacer una pequeña ~ a alguien** to make a slight reference to sb; **hacer una ~ a algo** to refer to sth **2.** *pl* (*informes*) report **3.** (*nota*) reference; **nuestra/su ~** (*en un escrito*) our/your ref. **4.** (*relato*) account
referéndum <referéndums> *m* POL (*popular*) referendum; (*sindical*) ballot
referente *adj* regarding; **(en lo) ~ a su queja** with regard to your complaint
referí *m* *AmL* DEP referee
referir *irr como sentir* **I.** *vt* **1.** (*relatar*) to recount **2.** (*remitir*) to refer **II.** *vr:* **~se** to refer; **en** [*o* **por**] **lo que se refiere a nuestras relaciones** with regard to our relationship; **no me estaba refiriendo a Ud.** I was not referring to you
refilón mirar de ~ a alguien to look sideways at sb; **el sol da en mi ventana de ~** the sun comes slanting through my window
refinado, -a *adj* refined
refinamiento *m* refinement
refinanciar *vt* ECON to refinance
refinar **I.** *vt* to refine **II.** *vr:* **~se** to become refined
refinería *f* refinery
refino, -a *adj* extra fine
reflector *m* (*foco*) spotlight; DEP floodlight; MIL searchlight
reflector(a) *adj* reflective
reflejar **I.** *vi, vt* to reflect; **tus palabras reflejan miedo** your words show fear **II.** *vr:* **~se** to be reflected
reflejo *m* **1.** (*luz, imagen*) reflection; **las esmeraldas despiden unos preciosos ~s verdes** emeralds give off lovely green sparkles; **su comportamiento es un fiel ~ de su estado de ánimo** his/her behaviour *Brit* [*o* behavior *Am*] is an accurate reflection of how he/she is feeling **2.** MED, PSICO reflex; **para ello hay que ser rápido de ~s** you need fast reflexes for that
reflejo, -a *adj* reflective; **movimiento ~** reflex
reflexión *f* **1.** (*consideraciones*) reflection; **con ~** on reflection; **sin ~** without thinking **2.** (*rayos*) reflection
reflexionar *vi, vt* to reflect; **reflexiona bien antes de dar ese paso** think carefully before doing that
reflexivo, -a *adj* **1.** (*sensato*) thoughtful **2.** (*reflectante*) reflecting **3.** LING reflexive
refluir *irr como huir vi* to flow back; (*la marea*) to ebb

reflujo *m* **1.** (*marea*) ebb **2.** MED reflux; ~ **gástrico** gastric reflux

refocilarse *vr pey* ~ **con** [*o* **en**] **algo** to enjoy sth

reforma *f* **1.** (*mejora, modificación*) reform; ~ **educativa** educational reform; ~ **monetaria** monetary reform; ~ **del sistema tributario** reform of the tax system **2.** ARQUIT (*reestructuración*) rebuilding; (*renovación*) renovation; **hacer una ~ en el cuarto de baño** to have one's bathroom refurbished **3.** REL **Reforma Protestante** Reformation **4.** (*reparación*) repair

reformar I. *vt* **1.** REL (*t. mejorar, modificar*) to reform; ~ **su conducta** to change one's ways **2.** (*a alguien*) to reform **3.** ARQUIT (*reestructurar*) to rebuild; (*renovar*) to renovate, to reform **4.** (*rehacer*) to redo **5.** (*deshacer*) to alter **II.** *vr:* **~se** to mend one's ways; **~se en el vestir** to dress better

reformatorio *m* reformatory; ~ **para delincuentes juveniles** borstal *Brit*

reformatorio, -a *adj* reforming

reformista I. *adj* reformist; **tendencias ~s** reformist tendencies; **ser** ~ to be a reformist **II.** *mf* reformist

reforzamiento *m* **1.** (*de algo*) reinforcement; (*con vigas*) strengthening **2.** (*de alguien*) encouragement

reforzar *irr como forzar* **I.** *vt* **1.** (*fortalecer*) to reinforce; (*con vigas*) to strengthen **2.** (*animar*) to encourage **II.** *vr:* **~se** to be reinforced

refractar I. *vt* to refract **II.** *vr:* **~se** to be refracted

refractario, -a *adj* **1.** QUÍM, FÍS heat-resistant **2.** (*rebelde*) recalcitrant; **ser ~ a algo** to be opposed to sth **3.** (*inmune*) immune

refrán *m* saying, proverb; **como dice el** ~ as the saying goes

refranero *m* LING collection of proverbs/sayings

refregar *irr como fregar* **I.** *vt* **1.** (*frotar*) to rub; ~ **con un cepillo** to scrub with a brush; ~ **la cacerola con un estropajo** to scrub the saucepan with a scouring pad **2.** *inf* (*reprochar*) ~ **algo a alguien** (**por las narices**) to rub sb's nose in sth **II.** *vr:* **~se** to rub; **~se los ojos** to rub one's eyes; **~se la manga contra la puerta recién pintada** to brush one's sleeve against the freshly painted door

refrenar I. *vt* to check **II.** *vr:* **~se** to restrain oneself

refrendar *vt* **1.** (*autorizar*) to approve **2.** (*un pasaporte*) to stamp **3.** (*aceptar*) to accept

refrescante *adj* refreshing

refrescar I. *vt* **1.** (*algo, a alguien*) to refresh; **el baño me ha refrescado** the bath has revived me **2.** (*cosas olvidadas*) to brush up; (*sentimiento*) to revive; ~ **la memoria** to refresh one's memory **II.** *vi* **1.** (*aire, viento*) to cool down **2.** (*dar fresco*) to refresh; **esta bebida refresca mucho** this drink is very refreshing **3.** (*beber*) to have a refreshing drink **4.** (*reponerse*) to refresh oneself **III.** *vr:* **~se 1.** (*aire, viento, cosa*) to cool down; **el día se ha refrescado** the weather has become cooler **2.** (*persona*) to cool down; (*beber*) to have a refreshing drink; **voy a ducharme para ~me** I'm going to have a shower to cool down; **~se con una cerveza** to have a nice cool drink of beer **3.** (*reponerse*) to freshen up **4.** (*tomar el fresco*) to get some fresh air **IV.** *vimpers* **por la tarde refresca** in the evening it gets cooler

refresco *m* **1.** (*bebida*) soft drink; (*gaseosa, naranjada*) fizzy drink **2.** (*comidas y bebidas*) refreshment; (*refrigerio*) snack

refriega *f* **1.** MIL skirmish **2.** *inf* (*pelea*) scuffle; (*violenta*) brawl

refrigeración *f* **1.** refrigeration; (*de una habitación*) air conditioning; ~ **por aire/agua** air/water-cooling **2.** (*refrigerio*) refreshment, snack

refrigerador *m* **1.** (*nevera*) refrigerator; (*cámara*) cool room; (*instalación*) cooling unit; (*líquido*) coolant, refrigerant **2.** (*de un automóvil*) cooling system

refrigerador(a) *adj* cooling; **aparato** ~ (*para comestibles*) refrigerator; (*para habitaciones*) air-cooling unit

refrigeradora *f Perú* (*nevera*) refrigerator

refrigerar I. *vt* (*enfriar*) to refrigerate; (*una habitación*) to air-condition **II.** *vr:* **~se 1.** (*enfriarse*) to cool down **2.** (*reponer fuerzas*) to freshen up

refrigerio *m* snack

refuerzo *m* **1.** (*reforzamiento*) reinforcement; (*viga*) strengthening; (*parche*) patch **2.** (*ayuda*) support **3.** *pl* MIL reinforcements *pl*

refugiado, -a *m, f* refugee; **el Alto Comisionado de las Naciones Unidas para los Refugiados** (**ACNUR**) United Nations High Commission for Refugees (UNHCR)

refugiarse *vr* (*en un lugar*) to take refuge; ~ **de algo** to flee from sth; ~ **en una mentira** to hide behind a lie; **se refugió en mis brazos** he/she sought shelter in my arms; **se refugió en la bebida** he/she turned to drink

refugio *m* **1.** (*protección, consuelo, lugar*) ~ **de algo** refuge from sth **2.** *t.* MIL (*construcción*) shelter; ~ (**montañero**) mountain shelter; ~ **nuclear** [*o* **atómico**] fallout shelter **3.** (*persona*) protector **4.** (*tráfico*) traffic island

refulgencia *f* brightness

refulgir <g→j> *vi* to shine

refundir I. *vt* **1.** (*metal: fundir*) to recast **2.** (*revisar*) to revise; (*obra*) to adapt **3.** (*reunir*) to join **4.** (*perder*) to lose **II.** *vr:* **~se 1.** (*reunirse*) to be joined **2.** *AmC* (*perderse*) to be lost

refunfuñar *vi* to grumble

refunfuñón, -ona I. *adj* grumpy **II.** *m, f* grouch

refutación *f* refutation

refutar *vt* to refute

regadera *f* **1.** (*recipiente*) watering can **2.** (*reguera*) irrigation channel ►**estar como**

R

una ~ *inf* to be as mad as a hatter
regaderazo *m Méx* shower
regadío *m* irrigation; **estos campos son de** ~ these fields are irrigated
regadío, **-a** *adj* **1.** (*de riego*) irrigation **2.** (*que se puede regar*) irrigable
regalado, **-a** *adj* **1.** (*cómodo*) easy; **llevar una vida regalada** to lead a life of luxury **2.** (*barato*) very cheap; **vender algo a precio** ~ to sell sth for a knock-down price; **a este precio el vestido es** ~ at this price they are practically giving the dress away **3.** (*delicado*) delicate **4.** (*deleitoso*) delightful; (*sabroso*) delicious
regalar **I.** *vt* **1.** (*obsequiar*) to give; **en esta tienda regalan la fruta** *fig* in this shop the fruit is dirt-cheap; ~ **los oídos a alguien** to flatter sb **2.** (*mimar*) to pamper **3.** (*deleitar*) to delight **4.** (*acariciar*) to stroke **II.** *vr:* ~**se** **1.** (*llevar buena vida*) to live very well **2.** (*proporcionarse*) to indulge oneself **3.** (*deleitarse*) ~ **con algo** to delight in sth
regalía *f* **1.** (*privilegio*) privilege; (*del Estado, la Corona*) prerogative **2.** (*pago*) bonus **3.** (*tasa*) royalties *pl*
regaliz *m* **1.** (*golosina*) liquorice *Brit,* licorice *Am* **2.** BOT liquorice plant
regalo *m* **1.** (*obsequio*) present, gift; **a este precio el coche es un** ~ at this price the car is a steal; **una cesta de fruta de** ~ **en cada habitación** a complimentary basket of fruit in each room **2.** (*gusto*) pleasure; **un** ~ **para la vista** a sight for sore eyes **3.** (*comodidad*) luxury
regalón, **-ona** *adj inf* (*niño*) pampered
regañadientes **a** ~ reluctantly, grudgingly
regañar **I.** *vt inf* to scold **II.** *vi* **1.** (*reñir*) to argue; (*dejar de tener trato*) to fall out; **ha regañado con su novio** (*reñir*) she has had a fight with her boyfriend; (*separarse*) she has split up with her boyfriend; **estoy regañado con mis vecinos** I have fallen out with my neighbours *Brit* [*o* neighbors *Am*] **2.** (*refunfuñar*) to grumble
regañina *f* **1.** (*reprensión*) telling off; **echar una** ~ **a alguien** to tell sb off, to give sb a telling off **2.** (*riña*) quarrel; **tener una** ~ **por algo** to quarrel about sth
regañón, **-ona** **I.** *adj* grumpy **II.** *m, f* grouch
regar *irr como fregar vt* **1.** (*con agua: una planta, el jardín*) to water; (*las calles*) to hose down; AGR to irrigate **2.** (*con un líquido*) to wet; (*mojar*) to soak; (*con algo menudo*) to sprinkle; ~ **el suelo con arena** to sprinkle sand on the ground; ~ **la alfombra con pintura** to spatter the carpet with paint; ~ **algo con lágrimas** to bathe sth with tears **3.** (*atravesar*) to cross
regata *f* DEP regatta
regate *m* dodge; (*con el balón*) dribble
regatear **I.** *vi* **1.** (*mercadear*) to haggle **2.** (*hacer regates*) to dodge; (*con el balón*) to dribble **II.** *vt* to haggle over
regateo *m sin pl* **1.** (*negociar*) haggling **2.** DEP dribbling
regazo *m* lap; *fig* warmth
regencia *f* **1.** (*gobierno*) regency **2.** (*dirección*) direction; (*de un negocio*) management
regeneración *f* regeneration
regenerar **I.** *vt* **1.** *t.* ELEC (*algo*) to regenerate **2.** (*a alguien*) to reform **II.** *vr:* ~**se** **1.** (*renovarse*) to regenerate; (*cabello*) to grow back **2.** (*reformarse*) to reform
regentar *vt* **1.** (*dirigir*) to manage **2.** (*ejercer*) to hold **3.** POL to govern
regente *mf* **1.** (*que gobierna*) regent **2.** (*que dirige*) director; (*un negocio*) manager
régimen *m* <regímenes> **1.** (*sistema*) system; (*reglamentos*) regulations *pl;* ~ **abierto** (*en una prisión*) open regime; ~ **legal de la seguridad social para jubilación e invalidez** social security system for retirement and invalidity; ~ **de patentes** patent regulation; ~ **penitenciario** prison system **2.** POL government **3.** (*dieta*) diet; ~ **de adelgazamiento** (slimming) diet; **estar a** ~ to be on a diet; **poner a alguien a** ~ to put sb on a diet **4.** (*manera de vivir*) lifestyle; **llevar un** ~ **de austeridad** to have an austere lifestyle **5.** LING government
regimiento *m* MIL regiment
regio, **-a** *adj* **1.** (*real*) royal **2.** (*magnífico*) magnificent
región *f* **1.** (*territorio*) region **2.** (*espacio*) area; (*del cuerpo*) region; ~ **abdominal** abdominal region
regional *adj* regional
regir *irr como elegir* **I.** *vt* **1.** (*gobernar*) to govern; (*dirigir*) to direct **2.** (*guiar*) to lead; (*ley*) to govern **3.** LING to take **II.** *vi* **1.** (*tener validez*) to apply **2.** (*funcionar*) to work **3.** *inf* (*estar cuerdo*) to be sane; **¡tú no riges!** you're out of your mind! **III.** *vr:* ~**se** to be guided
registrador(**a**) **I.** *adj* registering; **caja** ~**a** cash register **II.** *m(f)* **1.** (*funcionario*) registrar; ~ **de la propiedad** property [*o* land] registrar **2.** TÉC recorder; ~ **de sonidos** sound recorder
registrar **I.** *vt* **1.** (*examinar*) to search **2.** (*inscribir*) to record; (*una empresa, un patente*) to register **3.** (*incluir*) to include **4.** (*señalar*) to note; (*grabar*) to record ►**¡a mí que me registren!** I certainly didn't do it!, don't look at me! **II.** *vr:* ~**se** **1.** (*inscribirse*) to register **2.** (*observarse*) to be reported
registro *m* **1.** (*inspección*) search; ~ **de la casa** house search **2.** (*con un instrumento*) measurement; (*grabación*) recording **3.** (*inscripción*) recording; (*inclusión*) inclusion; (*de una empresa, una patente*) registration **4.** (*nota*) note; (*protocolo*) record; ~ **de entrada/de salida** note of arrival/departure; ~ **de inventario** inventory **5.** (*libro*) register; ~ **de autores** list of authors; ~ **electoral** electoral register; ~ **de entradas/salidas** visitors' book; ~ **de la propiedad** land register **6.** (*oficina, archivo*) registry; ~ **civil** registry

office; ~ **de la propiedad** land registry; ~ **de la propiedad industrial** industrial property registry **7.** (*abertura*) inspection hatch **8.** (*de un mecanismo*) regulator **9.** (*de un libro*) entry **10.** MÚS register; (*órgano*) stop; **tiene un ~ muy amplio** he/she has a very wide range ►**tocar todos los ~s** to pull out all the stops

regla *f* **1.** (*instrumento*) ruler; ~ **de cálculo** slide rule **2.** (*norma*) rule; **~s de exportación** COM export regulations; **la ~ de oro** the golden rule; **por ~ general** as a rule; **ser la ~** to be the rule; **la ~ es que** +*subj* the rule is that **3.** MAT ~ **de tres** rule of three; **las cuatro ~s** addition, subtraction, multiplication and division **4.** (*moderación*) moderation; **beber con ~** to drink in moderation **5.** (*menstruación*) period; **está con la ~** she has her period ►**la excepción confirma la ~** *prov* the exception confirms the rule *prov;* **por qué ~ de tres...** why on earth ...; **estar en ~** to be in order; **poner en ~** to put in order; **salir de la ~** to go too far

reglamentación *f* **1.** (*acción*) regulation; *pey* regimentation **2.** (*reglas*) rules *pl*

reglamentar *vt* to regulate; *pey* to regiment

reglamentario, -a *adj* **1.** (*relativo al reglamento*) regulatory **2.** (*conforme al reglamento*) regulation

reglamento *m* rules *pl;* (*de una organización*) regulations *pl;* ~ (**de funcionarios**) civil service regulations; ~ (**interno**) rules *pl;* ~ **de tráfico** traffic regulations

reglar **I.** *vt* **1.** (*reglamentar*) to regulate **2.** (*con líneas*) to line **II.** *vr:* **~se** **1.** (*sujetarse*) to be regulated **2.** (*moderarse*) to limit oneself

regocijado, -a *adj* joyful

regocijar **I.** *vr:* **~se** **1.** (*alegrarse*) **~se con algo** to delight in sth **2.** (*divertirse*) to amuse oneself **II.** *vt* to delight

regocijo *m* **1.** (*alegría*) delight; (*diversión*) pleasure; **esperar algo con ~** to be really looking forward to sth **2.** (*júbilo*) rejoicing

regodearse *vr* **1.** ~ **con** [*o* **en**] **algo** (*gozar*) to enjoy sth; (*alegrarse*) to delight in sth; **se regodea viéndome sufrir** he/she takes pleasure in seeing me suffer **2.** *inf* (*chacotear*) to joke around

regodeo *m* **1.** (*placer*) pleasure **2.** *inf* (*chacoteo*) joking; (*burla*) mockery **3.** *inf* (*fiesta*) party

regodeón, -ona *adj Chile, Col, inf* hard to please, fussy

regoldar *vi inf* to burp

regordete, -a *adj* chubby, plump

regresar **I.** *vi* (*volver*) to return, to go back **II.** *vt Méx* (*devolver*) to give back **III.** *vr:* **~se** *AmL* (*volver*) to return, to go back

regresión *f* **1.** (*retroceso*) regression **2.** (*declive*) decline

regresivo, -a *adj* regressive

regreso *m* (*vuelta*) return; (**viaje de**) ~ return journey; **estar de ~** to have returned

reguero *m* **1.** (*chorro*) irrigation channel **2.** (*señal*) trail ►**expandirse como un ~ de pólvora** to spread like wildfire

regulación *f* **1.** (*reglamentación*) regulation; ~ **administrativa** administrative regulations **2.** *t.* TÉC (*organización, ajustación*) adjustment; (*de un río*) channelling *Brit,* channeling *Am;* **de ~ automática** self-regulating; ~ **de la demanda** ECON management of demand

regulado, -a *adj* (*reglamentario*) regulatory

regulador *m* regulator; (*mecanismo*) control knob

regular **I.** *vt* **1.** *t.* TÉC (*organizar, ajustar*) to adjust **2.** (*reglamentar*) to regulate **3.** (*poner en orden*) to put in order **II.** *adj* **1.** (*conforme a una regla*) regular; **verbos ~es** regular verbs **2.** (*reglamentado, ordenado*) ordered **3.** (*estable*) stable **4.** (*uniforme*) regular **5.** (*mediano*) average; (*mediocre*) mediocre; (*nota*) satisfactory; **de tamaño ~** normal size ►**tu comportamiento no me parece ni medio ~** *inf* your behaviour *Brit* [*o* behavior *Am*] strikes me as most irregular; **por lo ~** as a rule **III.** *adv* so-so

regularidad *f* **1.** (*conformidad, uniformidad*) regularity; **con ~** regularly **2.** (*medianía*) averageness; (*mediocridad*) mediocrity **3.** (*puntualidad*) punctuality

regularizar <z→c> **I.** *vt* (*poner en orden*) to regularize; (*normalizar*) to standardize **II.** *vr:* **~se** (*regularse*) to be regulated; (*normalizarse*) to become standardized

regularmente *adv* (*normalmente*) usually

regurgitar *vi, vt* to regurgitate

regusto *m* aftertaste; **el cuadro tiene un cierto ~ surrealista** the picture has a slightly surrealist feeling

rehabilitación *f* **1.** *t.* JUR, MED (*de alguien*) rehabilitation; (*restitución*) restitution **2.** (*de una cosa*) repair; (*de un edificio*) refurbishment

rehabilitar **I.** *vt* **1.** *t.* JUR, MED (*a alguien*) to rehabilitate; (*restituir*) to return **2.** (*una cosa*) to repair; (*un edificio*) to refurbish; ~ **la memoria** [*o* **la buena fama**] **de alguien** to restore sb's reputation **II.** *vr:* **~se** to be rehabilitated

rehacer *irr como hacer* **I.** *vt* **1.** (*volver a hacer*) to redo; ~ **una carta** to rewrite a letter **2.** (*reconstruir*) to rebuild; (*reparar*) to repair; (*un edificio*) to refurbish; ~ **su vida con alguien** to rebuild one's life with sb **II.** *vr:* **~se** (*recuperar las fuerzas*) to recover one's strength; (*la salud*) to regain one's health; (*la tranquilidad*) to regain one's peace of mind; **~se de una desgracia** to recover from a misfortune

rehecho, -a **I.** *pp de* **rehacer** **II.** *adj* (*robusto*) thickset

rehén *m* **1.** (*persona*) hostage **2.** (*cosa*) pledge

rehogar <g→gu> *vt* to sauté

rehuir *irr como huir vt* **1.** (*eludir*) to avoid; ~ **a alguien** to avoid sb; ~ **una obligación** to shirk an obligation; **rehúye decir la verdad** he/she avoids telling the truth **2.** (*rechazar*) to reject

rehusar *vt* to refuse; (*una reclamación*) to reject; **¡rehusado!** rejected!; **rehúsa verme** he/she refuses to see me; ~ **una invitación** to decline an invitation

reimpresión *f* reprint; ~ **pirata** pirate copy

reimprimir *irr como imprimir vt* to reprint

reina *f* **1.** *t.* ZOOL (*soberana, la mejor*) queen; ~ **madre** queen mother; **abeja** ~ queen bee **2.** *inf* (*cariño*) darling

reinado *m t. fig* (*tiempo*) reign

reinar *vi* **1.** *t. fig* (*gobernar*) to reign **2.** (*dominar*) to prevail

reincidencia *f* relapse; JUR reoffending

reincidente **I.** *adj* reoffending **II.** *mf* (*delincuente*) reoffender

reincidir *vi* **1.** (*error*) ~ **en algo** to relapse into sth; ~ **en un delito** to reoffend; ~ **siempre en el mismo error** to keep making the same mistake **2.** MED to relapse

reincorporar **I.** *vt* ~ **a algo** to reincorporate into sth; ~ **a alguien a un puesto** to restore sb to a position; ~ **al servicio** to return to service **II.** *vr:* ~**se** (*a un sitio*) to return; (*a una organización*) to rejoin; ~**se al trabajo** to return to work

reineta *f* (*manzana*) pippin

reino *m* realm; (*de un monarca*) kingdom; **Reino Unido** United Kingdom

reintegración *f* **1.** (*reincorporación*) reintegration; (*en un cargo*) reinstatement **2.** (*de gastos*) reimbursement; ~ **de los daños** reimbursement for damages

reintegrar **I.** *vt* **1.** (*reincorporar*) to reintegrate; (*en un cargo*) to reinstate; ~ **a alguien a su puesto de trabajo** to reinstate sb in his/her job **2.** (*devolver*) to return; (*dinero*) to repay; (*desembolsos*) to reimburse **II.** *vr:* ~**se** **1.** (*reincorporarse*) to return; (*a una organización*) to rejoin; ~**se al trabajo** to return to work **2.** (*recobrar*) to recover

reintegro *m* **1.** (*reintegración*) reintegration; (*en un cargo*) reinstatement **2.** (*premio*) **me tocó un** ~ I won back my stake **3.** (*pago*) reimbursement; (*de la cuenta*) withdrawal; (*devolución*) repayment

reír *irr* **I.** *vi* **1.** (*desternillarse*) to laugh; **echarse a** ~ to burst out laughing; **no me hagas** ~ *fig* don't make me laugh **2.** (*sonreír*) to smile ►**el que ríe último ríe mejor** *prov* he who laughs last laughs longest [*o* best] *prov* **II.** *vr:* ~**se** **1.** (*desternillarse*) ~**se de algo** to laugh at sth; ~**se a carcajadas** to laugh loudly; ~**se en las barbas de alguien** to laugh in sb's face; ~**se hasta de su sombra** to laugh at the slightest provocation; **me río de tu dinero** *fig* I don't give a damn about your money; ~**se para sus adentros** to chuckle; ~**se tontamente** to giggle **2.** (*sonreír*) to smile **3.** (*burlarse*) ~**se de algo** to laugh at sth **4.** *inf* (*romperse*) to come apart **III.** *vt* ~ **algo** to laugh at sth

reiteración *f* repetition; JUR reoffending

reiteradamente *adv* repeatedly

reiterar **I.** *vt* to repeat; **te reitero las gracias** I thank you once again; **reiteró su intención de ayudarme** he/she repeated his/her intention of helping me **II.** *vr:* ~**se** to repeat; **se reiteró en su decisión de dejar de fumar** he/she reaffirmed his/her decision to stop smoking

reivindicación *f* ~ **de algo** claim to sth

reivindicar <c→qu> *vt* **1.** (*pedir*) to claim; (*exigir*) to demand **2.** (*recobrar*) to recover **3.** (*una acción*) to claim; ~ **un atentado** to claim responsibility for an attack

reja *f* **1.** (*barras*) grill; **estar entre** ~**s** *fig, inf* to be behind bars **2.** (*del arado*) ploughshare *Brit,* plowshare *Am* **3.** (*labor*) ploughing *Brit,* plowing *Am*

rejego *adj AmC, Méx* **1.** (*indomable*) wild; (*alzado*) untamed **2.** (*intratable*) unmanageable; (*enojadizo*) cranky

rejilla *f* **1.** (*enrejado*) grating **2.** (*parrilla*) grill **3.** (*brasero*) brazier **4.** (*tejido*) wickerwork **5.** (*para equipaje*) luggage rack

rejo *m* **1.** (*punta*) spike **2.** *AmL* (*látigo*) whip

rejón *m* (*barra*) spike; TAUR lance

rejoneador(a) *m(f)* TAUR bullfighter on horseback

rejoneo *m* TAUR bullfighting on horseback

rejuntar **I.** *vt* to join **II.** *vr inf* **han decidido** ~**se** they've decided to live together

rejuvenecer *irr como crecer* **I.** *vt* **1.** (*hacer más joven*) to rejuvenate; **este peinado te rejuvenece** this haircut makes you look much younger **2.** (*modernizar*) to modernize **II.** *vr:* ~**se** to be rejuvenated

relación *f* **1.** (*entre cosas, hechos*) relationship, relation; ~ **entre la causa y el efecto** relationship between cause and effect; **hacer** ~ **a algo** to refer to sth; **con** ~ **a su petición** with regard to your/his/her request **2.** (*entre dos magnitudes*) relationship; ~ **calidad-precio** value for money; **los gastos no guardan** ~ **con el presupuesto** the expenses bear no relation to the budget **3.** (*entre personas*) relationship; **relaciones públicas** public relations; **tener relaciones con alguien** to be in contact with sb; **tener muchas relaciones** (*amigos*) to have lots of friends; (*influyentes*) to have lots of contacts; **tienen buenas/malas relaciones** they have a good/bad relationship **4.** *pl* (*noviazgo, amorío*) relationship; **han roto sus relaciones** they have broken up; **mantienen relaciones** they are going out with each other; **mantener relaciones sexuales con alguien** to have a sexual relationship with sb **5.** (*relato*) account; (*informe*) report; **hacer una** ~ **de algo** to report on sth; **hacer una** ~ **detallada de algo** to make a detailed report about sth **6.** (*lista*) list

relacional *adj* relational; **base de datos** ~ INFOR relational database

relacionar **I.** *vt* **1.** (*poner en relación*) to

relate **2.** (*relatar*) to report **II.** *vr:* **~se 1.** (*estar relacionado*) to be related **2.** (*iniciar relaciones*) to strike up a relationship; (*mantener relaciones*) to mix; **~se mucho** (*tener amigos*) to have lots of friends; (*influyentes*) to have lots of contacts

relajación *f* **1.** (*distensión, distracción*) relaxation **2.** (*malas costumbres*) slackness **3.** (*debilitación*) weakening **4.** (*atenuación*) easing; **~ de la pena** reduction of the sentence **5.** MED sprain; (*de la hernia*) hernia

relajado, -a *adj* **1.** (*sosegado*) relaxed **2.** (*débil*) loose **3.** (*vicioso*) dissolute

relajadura *f Méx* (*hernia*) rupture

relajar I. *vt* **1.** (*distender, distraer*) to relax **2.** (*suavizar*) to ease; (*la pena*) to reduce **II.** *vr:* **~se 1.** (*distenderse, descansar*) to relax **2.** (*debilitarse*) to weaken **3.** (*suavizarse*) to ease **4.** (*viciarse*) to become dissolute

relamer I. *vt* to lick **II.** *vr:* **~se 1.** (*los labios*) to lick one's lips **2.** (*gozar*) **~se con algo** to relish sth; **~se con un manjar** to eat a delicacy with great relish **3.** (*gloriarse*) **~se de algo** to gloat over sth **4.** (*arreglarse*) to clean oneself up **5.** (*animal*) to lick its chops

relamido, -a *adj* **1.** (*arreglado*) prim and proper **2.** (*afectado*) affected

relámpago *m* flash of lightning; **ser (veloz como) un ~** to be as fast as lightning

relampaguear I. *vi* to sparkle **II.** *vimpers* **relampagueaba** there was lightning

relance *m* **1.** *Chile* (*piropo*) flirtatious compliment **2.** *Col* **de ~** (*al contado*) in cash

relatar *vt* (*información*) to report; (*una historia*) to tell

relatividad *f sin pl* FÍS relativity

relativizar <z→c> *vt* to play down

relativo *m* LING (*pronombre*) relative pronoun; **oración de ~** relative clause

relativo, -a *adj* **1.** (*referente*) relative; **un artículo ~ a...** an article about ... **2.** (*dependiente*) relative; **pronombre ~** relative pronoun; **ser ~ a algo** to be relative to sth **3.** (*poco*) limited

relato *m* report; LIT story; **~ corto** short story

relé *m* ELEC relay

relegar <g→gu> *vt* **1.** (*apartar*) to relegate; **ser relegado al olvido** to be consigned to oblivion; **~ algo a un plano secundario** to push sth into the background **2.** (*desterrar*) to banish

relente *f* night dew; **dormir al ~** to sleep out in the open

relevancia *f* importance, relevance

relevante *adj* **1.** (*importante*) important **2.** (*sobresaliente*) outstanding

relevar I. *vt* **1.** (*liberar*) to exempt; **~ a alguien de un juramento** to release sb from an oath; **~ a alguien de sus deudas** to release sb from his/her debts; **~ a alguien de sus culpas** to exonerate sb from blame for his/her actions **2.** JUR (*destituir*) to remove; **~ a alguien de un cargo** to relieve sb of his/her post **3.** (*reemplazar*) to place; MIL to relieve; DEP to substitute **4.** (*acentuar*) to highlight **II.** *vr:* **~se** to take turns

relevo *m* **1.** (*reemplazo*) change; **tomar el ~ de alguien** to take over from sb **2.** *(pl)* DEP (*competición*) relay; **carrera de ~s** relay race **3.** MIL change of the guard

relicario *m* **1.** (*para reliquias*) reliquary **2.** *AmL* (*medallón*) locket

relieve *m* **1.** ARTE, GEO relief; **en bajo ~** in bas-relief **2.** (*renombre*) prominence ►**poner de ~** to emphasize; **de ~** important

religión *f* **1.** (*creencia, doctrina*) religion; **~ reformada** Protestantism; **sin ~** godless **2.** (*virtud*) virtue **3.** (*orden*) **entrar en ~** to take vows

religiosidad *f* **1.** (*observancia*) religiosity, religiousness **2.** (*piedad*) piety **3.** (*puntualidad*) punctuality; (*exactitud*) thoroughness

religioso, -a I. *adj* **1.** (*relativo a la religión*) religious **2.** (*pío*) pious **3.** (*puntual*) punctual; (*exacto*) thorough **II.** *m, f* member of a religious order, monk *m,* nun *f*

relinchar *vi* to neigh, to whinny

relincho *m* **1.** (*de un caballo*) neigh, whinny **2.** (*de alguien*) whoop

reliquia *f* **1.** *t.* REL relic; **una ~ de familia** a family heirloom **2.** (*antigüedad*) collector's item **3.** MED after-effect

rellano *m* (*de escalera*) landing

rellena *f Col, Méx* (*morcilla*) blood sausage

rellenar *vt* **1.** (*llenar*) **~ de** [*o* **con**] **algo** to fill with sth; GASTR to stuff with sth; **~ los agujeros de yeso** to fill in the holes with plaster **2.** (*por completo*) to fill up; (*demasiado*) to overfill **3.** (*volver a llenar*) to refill **4.** (*completar*) to fill out **5.** *inf* (*dar de comer*) to feed up *Brit,* to put on the feedbag *Am*

relleno *m* **1.** (*material*) filling; GASTR stuffing **2.** (*superfluidad*) padding; **palabra de ~** filler

relleno, -a *adj* **1.** (*lleno*) full; (*demasiado*) stuffed full; GASTR stuffed **2.** *inf* (*gordo*) chubby

reloj *m* clock; (*de pulsera*) watch; **~ despertador** alarm clock; **~ para fichar** time clock; **~ de arena** hourglass; **~ de sol** sundial, **~ de caja** [*o* **de péndulo**] grandfather clock; **carrera contra ~** race against the clock; **trabajar contra ~** to work against the clock; **ser (como) un ~** (*mecanismo*) to go like clockwork; (*persona*) to be very punctual

relojear *vt Arg* **1.** (*tomar el tiempo*) to time **2.** *inf* (*controlar, espiar*) to keep tabs on; **~ a alguien de arriba abajo** to look sb up and down

relojería *f* clockmaker's; (*de relojes de pulsera*) watchmaker's

relojero, -a *m, f* clockmaker; (*de relojes de pulsera*) watchmaker

reluciente *adj* shining; **~ de limpio** shiny clean

relucir *irr como lucir vi* **1.** (*despedir, reflejar luz*) to shine **2.** (*sobresalir*) to stand out ►**sacar algo a ~** to bring sth up; **salir a ~** to come

R

up

reluctante *adj* reluctant

relumbrar *vi* **1.**(*emitir, reflejar luz*) to shine **2.**(*sobresalir*) to stand out

relumbrón *m* **1.**(*destello*) flash **2.**(*oropel*) flashiness ►**de** ~ flashy

remachado, **-a** *adj* **1.**(*nariz*) flat **2.** *Col* (*callado*) quiet

remachar **I.** *vt* **1.**(*golpear*) to hammer **2.**(*doblar*) to bend; (*aplastar*) to flatten **3.**(*sujetar*) to rivet **4.**(*subrayar*) to stress; ~ **algo a alguien** to stress sth to sb **II.** *vr:* ~**se** *Col* to remain silent

remanente **I.** *adj* remaining **II.** *m* remainder; COM surplus; (*contabilidad*) carry-over

remangar <g→gu> **I.** *vt* to roll up **II.** *vr:* ~**se** *t. fig* (*las mangas*) to roll up one's sleeves

remansarse *vr* (*corriente*) to be still

remanso *m* (*represa*) pool; (*agua muerta*) stagnant water ►~ **de paz** haven of peace

remar *vi* (*bogar*) to row

rematado, **-a** *adj* absolute; **un tonto** ~ an absolute idiot

rematar **I.** *vt* **1.**(*concluir*) to finish (off); (*terminar de hacer*) to put the finishing touches to; **nunca rematas lo que has empezado** you never finish what you start **2.**(*matar: animal*) to put out of its misery; (*persona*) to finish off **3.**(*una costura*) to finish off **4.**(*gastar*) to use up **5.** DEP to shoot **6.**(*en subasta*) to knock down **7.**(*vender*) to sell off (cheap) **II.** *vi* **1.** DEP to shoot **2.**(*terminar*) to end; **la torre remata en punta** the tower ends in a point

remate *m* **1.**(*conclusión*) conclusion; (*de un producto*) finishing touch; **dar ~ a un edificio** to put the finishing touches to a building **2.**(*final, extremo*) end; **poner ~ a un mueble** to ornament a piece of furniture **3.**(*matanza*) killing off, coup de grâce **4.**(*adjudicación*) sale by auction **5.**(*oferta*) highest bid **6.** DEP shot **7.**(*consumo*) consumption; **dar** ~ to use up **8.**(*venta*) sale (*at a low price*) ►**estar loco de** ~ to be as mad as a hatter; **ser tonto de** ~ to be completely stupid; **para** ~ to cap it all *Brit,* to top it all off *Am;* **por** ~ finally

remecer *irr como crecer vt, vr:* ~**se** *AmL* (*sacudir*) to shake

remedar *vt* (*imitar*) to imitate; (*parodiar*) to mimic

remediar *vt* **1.**(*evitar*) to prevent; **no me cae bien, no puedo ~lo** I don't like him/her, I can't help it **2.**(*acabar con*) to finish off; (*reparar*) to repair; (*compensar*) to make up for; **llorando no remedias nada** crying won't solve anything **3.**(*corregir*) to correct **4.**(*ayudar*) to help

remedio *m* **1.**(*arreglo*) remedy; (*compensación*) compensation; (*corrección*) correction; **no tener** ~ to be a hopeless case; **mi hermano no tiene** ~ my brother is beyond help; **tu problema/la crisis no tiene** ~ there is no solution to your problem/to the crisis; **no llores, ya no tiene** ~ don't cry, there's nothing that can be done now; **eso tiene fácil** ~ that is easy to fix; **no hay** ~ there's nothing we can do; **no tenemos** [*o* **no hay**] **más ~ que...** the only solution is ..., there is no choice but to ...; **poner ~ a un mal** to right a wrong; **sin** ~ (*inútil*) hopeless; (*sin falta*) inevitable; **un idealista sin** ~ an incurable idealist **2.**(*ayuda*) help; **buscar ~ en sus amigos** to turn to one's friends for help; **buscar ~ en la bebida** to turn to drink **3.** MED (*medio*) remedy; ~ **naturalista** natural remedy; ~ **casero** household [*o* home] remedy ►**es peor el ~ que la enfermedad** *prov* the remedy is worse than the disease; **¿qué ~?** what choice is there?

remedo *m* **1.**(*imitación*) imitation; (*mal hecha*) travesty **2.**(*parodia*) parody

rememorar *vt* to remember

remendar <e→ie> *vt* (*reparar*) to mend; (*con parches*) to patch; (*zurcir*) to darn

remera *f* **1.** ZOOL flight feather **2.** *Arg* (*camiseta*) T-shirt

remero, **-a** *m, f* rower, oarsman

remesa *f* consignment, shipment; FIN remittance

remezón *m AmL* (*sacudida*) shake

remiendo *m* **1.**(*reparación*) mending; (*con parches*) patching; (*zurcidura*) darning **2.**(*corrección*) correction **3.**(*extra*) addition **4.**(*parche*) patch **5.**(*mancha*) stain

remilgado, **-a** *adj* prim; (*quisquilloso*) fussy

remilgo *m* primness; (*quisquilloso*) fussiness; **sin ~s** without making a fuss; **hacer ~s** to make a fuss

reminiscencia *f* **1.**(*en una obra*) influence; **la ópera tiene ~s wagnerianas** the opera shows Wagnerian influences **2.**(*lo que sobrevive*) remainder **3.**(*recuerdo*) reminiscence

remirar **I.** *vt* (*volver a mirar*) to look at again; (*mirar intensamente*) to scrutinize; **por más que miro y remiro no encuentro tu libro** however much I search I cannot find your book **II.** *vr:* ~**se** **1.**(*poner cuidado*) ~**se en algo** to take great pains over sth **2.**(*mirar*) to observe carefully

remisible *adj* (*deuda, pena*) which can be cancelled *Brit* [*o* canceled *Am*]; (*pecado*) remissible

remisión *f* **1.**(*envío*) consignment **2.**(*referencia*) reference **3.**(*atenuación*) slackening **4.**(*de una obligación*) excusal; (*de los pecados*) forgiveness; (*de una deuda*) cancellation *Brit,* cancelation *Am;* (*de una pena*) release; **sin** ~ without fail **5.** MED remission

remiso, **-a** *adj* (*reacio*) reluctant; (*irresoluto*) hesitant; (*lento*) slow; **mostrarse ~ a hacer algo** to be reluctant to do sth

remite *m* sender's name and address

remitente *mf* sender

remitir **I.** *vt* **1.**(*enviar*) to send; FIN to remit; ~ **algo a alguien** to send sth to sb **2.**(*referirse*) to refer **3.** (*de una obligación*) to forgive; ~ **a alguien de una pena** to release sb from a punishment; ~ **a alguien de una deuda** to cancel sb's debt; ~ **a alguien de sus pecados** to forgive sb his/her sins **4.** (*aplazar*) to postpone; (*un juicio*) to adjourn **5.** (*confiar*) to entrust **6.** (*ceder*) to hand over **II.** *vi* (*calmarse*) to let up **III.** *vr:* ~**se 1.** (*referirse*) to refer **2.** (*calmarse*) to let up **3.** (*confiarse*) to trust; ~**se al juez** to abide by the ruling of the judge

remo *m* **1.** (*pala: con soporte*) oar; (*sin soporte*) paddle; **a(l)** ~ by rowing boat *Brit,* by rowboat *Am; fig* with difficulty **2.** DEP rowing ►**a** ~ **y vela** *inf* speedily; **andar al** ~ *inf* to work like a slave; **tomar el** ~ *inf* to take the helm

remodelación *f* redesign, remodelling *Brit,* remodeling *Am;* ~ **del gabinete** cabinet reshuffle

remodelar *vt* to redesign, to remodel; (*gobierno*) to reshuffle

remojar **I.** *vt* **1.** (*mojar, sumergir*) to soak; (*empapar*) to drench; (*ablandar*) to soften; (*galleta*) to dip **2.** (*celebrar*) to drink to **II.** *vr:* ~**se** (*mojarse*) to get wet; (*bañarse*) to have a dip

remojo *m* **1.** (*empapamiento, sumersión*) soaking; (*baño*) dip; **poner en** ~ to leave to soak **2.** (*celebración*) toast

remojón *m* **1.** (*empapamiento, sumersión*) soaking; **darse un** ~ **en la piscina** to have a dip in the pool **2.** (*baño*) dip

remolacha *f* beet; (*roja*) beetroot; (*de azúcar*) (sugar) beet

remolcador *m* **1.** (*camión*) breakdown truck *Brit,* tow truck *Am* **2.** (*barco*) tug

remolcador(a) *adj* **grúa** ~**a** breakdown truck *Brit,* tow truck *Am*

remolcar <c→qu> *vt* **1.** (*un barco*) to tug; (*un vehículo averiado*) to tow **2.** (*convencer*) to rope in

remolienda *f Arg, Urug, inf* (*juerga*) binge

remolino *m* **1.** (*movimiento*) whirl; (*de agua*) whirlpool; ~ **de viento** whirlwind **2.** (*pelo*) cowlick **3.** (*gente*) throng **4.** (*confusión*) commotion **5.** *inf* (*persona*) whirlwind

remolón, -ona **I.** *adj* lazy **II.** *m, f* (*vago*) slacker; (*que evita algo*) shirker; **hacerse el** ~ (*vaguear*) to be lazy; **siempre se hace el** ~ **a la hora de fregar** he/she always tries to get out of doing the washing-up

remolonear *vi, vr:* ~**se 1.** (*vaguear*) to be lazy **2.** (*evitar*) to shirk

remolque *m* **1.** (*arrastre*) tow **2.** (*vehículo*) trailer **3.** (*cuerda*) towrope; **llevar a** ~ to tow ►**hacer algo a** ~ to do sth reluctantly

remontar **I.** *vt* **1.** (*superar*) to overcome **2.** (*subir*) to go up; ~ **un río** (*navegar*) to go up a river; (*nadar*) to swim up a river **3.** (*elevar*) to fly; ~ **el vuelo** to soar **4.** (*la caza*) to beat **II.** *vr:* ~**se 1.** (*volar*) to climb; (*ave*) to soar **2.** (*gastos*) to amount **3.** (*pertenecer, retroceder*) to go back to; **la construcción de la iglesia se remonta al siglo pasado** the construction of the church dates from the past century; **el discurso se remonta a los orígenes del automóvil** the speech goes back to the origins of the automobile

remorder <o→ue> **I.** *vt* **1.** (*atormentar*) to torment **2.** (*morder*) to bite again **II.** *vr:* ~**se** to suffer remorse

remordimiento *m* remorse; **tener** ~**s (de conciencia) por algo** to feel remorseful about sth; **el** ~ **no lo deja dormir** he can't sleep for remorse

remotamente *adv* **1.** (*vagamente*) vaguely **2.** (*lejos*) distantly; (*hace tiempo*) long ago ►**ni** ~ not in the slightest, far from it

remoto, -a *adj* **1.** (*lejano*) remote; **en tiempos** ~**s** long ago **2.** (*improbable*) remote; **no existe ni la más remota posiblidad** there is not the slightest possibility; **no tener ni la más remota idea** to not have the slightest idea; **¡ni por lo más** ~**!** not on your life!

remover <o→ue> **I.** *vt* **1.** (*mover*) to remove **2.** (*agitar*) to shake; (*dar vueltas*) to stir; (*la ensalada*) to toss **3.** (*activar*) to stir up **II.** *vi* to investigate **III.** *vr:* ~**se 1.** (*moverse*) to roll about **2.** (*aguas*) to move about

remozar <z→c> *vt* to renovate

remunerable *adj* remunerable

remuneración *f* **1.** (*pago*) remuneration **2.** (*recompensa*) compensation **3.** (*rendimiento*) profit

remunerar *vt* **1.** (*pagar*) to remunerate; ~ **a alguien por un servicio** to pay sb for a service **2.** (*recompensar*) to compensate **3.** (*rendir*) to be profitable for

remunerativo, -a *adj* remunerative

renacer *irr como crecer vi* **1.** (*volver a nacer*) to be reborn **2.** (*regenerarse*) to revive; **sentirse** ~ to feel completely revived

renacimiento *m* **1.** ARTE, LIT renaissance **2.** *t.* FILOS, REL (*regeneración*) revival

renacuajo *m* tadpole

renacuajo, -a *m, f pey* shrimp

renal *adj* renal

Renania *f* Rhineland

rencilla *f* quarrel

rencor *m* ill feeling; **guardar** ~ **a alguien** to bear a grudge against sb

rencoroso, -a *adj* **1.** (*vengativo*) spiteful **2.** (*resentido*) resentful

rendición *f* **1.** (*capitulación, sumisión*) surrender **2.** (*entrega*) yield; ~ **de cuentas** balance **3.** (*utilidad*) usefulness **4.** (*fatiga*) exhaustion **5.** (*conquista*) conquest

rendidamente *adv* devotedly; **estar** ~ **enamorado de** to be besotted with

rendido, -a *adj* **1.** (*cansado*) exhausted **2.** (*sumiso*) submissive; **cayó** ~ **ante su belleza** he was enchanted by her beauty

rendija *f* crack

rendimiento *m* **1.** (*productividad*) yield; ECON (*máximo*) capacity; **a pleno** ~ at full capacity **2.** (*beneficio*) profit; **de gran** ~ very profitable **3.** (*cansancio*) exhaustion **4.** *pl* (*ingresos*) income **5.** (*humildad*) humility **6.** (*obsequiosidad*) servility

rendir *irr como pedir* **I.** *vt* **1.** (*rentar*) to yield; ~ **utilidad** to be useful; ~ **fruto** to bear fruit; **la inversión ha rendido mucho** the investment has been very profitable **2.** (*trabajar*) to produce; **estas máquinas rinden mucho** these machines are very productive **3.** (*tributar*) to attribute; ~ **las gracias a alguien** to thank sb; ~ **importancia a algo** to attribute importance to sth **4.** (*entregar*) to hand over; (*pruebas*) to bring; (*una confesión*) to make; ~ **cuentas** to settle the accounts; *fig* to account for one's actions; ~ **obsequios a alguien** to praise sb; ~ **las armas** to surrender one's arms **5.** (*vencer*) to defeat **6.** (*cansar*) to exhaust; **me rindió el sueño** I was overcome by tiredness **7.** (*substituir*) to replace **II.** *vr:* ~**se 1.** (*entregarse*) to surrender; ~**se al enemigo** to surrender to the enemy; ~**se a la evidencia de algo** to bow to the evidence of sth; ~**se a las razones de alguien** to yield to sb's arguments **2.** (*cansarse*) ~**se de cansancio** to give in to one's exhaustion

renegado, -a I. *adj* **1.** (*religión*) apostate **2.** *inf* (*carácter*) bad-tempered **II.** *m, f* **1.** (*religión*) apostate **2.** *inf* (*carácter*) grouch

renegar *irr como fregar* **I.** *vi* **1.** (*protestar*) ~ **de algo** to protest against sth **2.** (*renunciar*) to renounce; ~ **de la fe** to renounce one's faith; ~ **del partido** to renounce the party **II.** *vt* **1.** (*negar*) to deny **2.** (*detestar*) to detest

RENFE *f abr de* **Red Nacional de Ferrocarriles Españoles** *Spanish state railway company*

renglón *m* **1.** (*línea*) line; **poner cuatro renglones a alguien** to drop sb a line; **a ~ seguido** on the next line; *fig* straight away **2.** (*partida*) share

rengo, -a *adj CSur* (*cojo*) lame

renguear *vi CSur* (*cojear*) to limp

renguera *f CSur* limp

reno *m* reindeer

renombrado, -a *adj* (*célebre*) renowned

renombrar *vt* to name

renombre *m* renown; **una empresa de gran** ~ a very well-known company; **una persona de** ~ a famous person; **adquirir** ~ to become renowned; **gozar de** ~ to be renowned

renovación *f* renewal; (*de un edificio*) renovation

renovar <o→ue> *vt* to renew; (*una casa*) to renovate; (*un país*) to modernize; ~ **un pedido** to repeat a request; ~ **la pintura** to touch up the paintwork; ~ **la memoria** to refresh one's memory; ~ **un aviso** to repeat a warning

renquear *vi* to limp

renta *f* **1.** (*beneficio*) profit; (*ingresos*) income; ~ **per cápita** per capita income; ~**s públicas** national revenue **2.** (*pensión*) pension; ~ **por incapacidad laboral** invalidity benefit; ~ **vitalicia** life annuity; ~ **de viudez** widow's pension **3.** (*alquiler*) rent; **en** ~ for rent; **tomar a ~ un negocio** to lease out a business

rentabilidad *f* profitability; ~ **competitiva** cost-effectiveness; **dar una ~ de...** to yield profits of ...

rentable *adj* profitable

rentar I. *vt* **1.** (*beneficio*) to yield **2.** *AmL* (*alquilar*) to rent **II.** *vi* to be profitable; ~ **bien** to yield a good profit

rentero, -a *m, f* **1.** (*arrendatario*) tenant farmer **2.** *Arg* (*contribuyente*) tax payer

rentista *mf* **1.** (*pensionista*) pensioner **2.** (*hacendista*) tax expert

renuencia *f* reluctance

renuente *adj* reluctant

renuevo *m* **1.** (*tallo*) shoot **2.** (*renovación*) renewal

renuncia *f* **1.** (*abandono*) ~ **a** [*o* **de**] **algo** resignation from sth; ~ **del cargo** resignation from the post; ~ **al contrato** withdrawal from the contract; **presentar su** ~ to resign **2.** (*escrito*) waiver

renunciar *vi* **1.** (*desistir*) ~ **a** [*o* **de**] **algo** to renounce sth; ~ **al trono** to abdicate the throne; ~ **a un cargo** to resign from a post; ~ **a una herencia** to renounce an inheritance **2.** (*rechazar*) ~ **a algo** to reject sth

reñido, -a *adj* **1.** (*enojado*) angry; **estoy ~ con él** I have fallen out with him **2.** (*en oposición*) **estar** ~ *fig* to be incompatible **3.** (*encarnizado*) bitter

reñir *irr como ceñir* **I.** *vi* to quarrel; **¿has reñido con tu novio?** have you had a row with your boyfriend? ▶**dos no riñen si uno no quiere** it takes two to make a quarrel **II.** *vt* to scold

reo, -a I. *adj* accused **II.** *m, f* (*culpado*) defendant; (*autor*) culprit; ~ **de asesinato** murderer; ~ **habitual** persistent offender; ~ **preventivo** remand prisoner

reojo *m* **mirar de** ~ (*con hostilidad*) to look askance at; (*con disimulo*) to look out of the corner of one's eye at

reorganización *f* reorganization; ~ **del gobierno** government reshuffle

reorganizar <z→c> *vt* to reorganize; (*gobierno*) to reshuffle

reorientación *f* reorientation; ~ **política** political realignment

repanchigarse <g→gu> *vr,* **repantigarse** <g→gu> *vr* to sprawl out

reparable *adj* (*arreglable*) repairable

reparación *f* **1.** (*arreglo*) repair **2.** (*indemnización, enmienda*) compensation; ~ **de perjuicios** damages *pl*

reparar I. *vt* **1.** (*arreglar*) to repair; ~ **el daño** to repair the damage **2.** (*indemnizar, enmendar*) to compensate **3.** (*recuperar*) ~ **fuerzas** to recover one's strength; **con la siesta reparo fuerzas** a nap refreshes me **II.** *vi* ~ **en** (*advertir*) to notice; (*considerar*) to consider;

sin ~ **en gastos** regardless of the cost; **no ~ en sacrificios/gastos** to spare no effort/ expense **III.** *vr:* **~se** to restrain oneself

reparo *m* **1.** (*arreglo*) repair **2.** (*inconveniente*) problem; **sin ~ alguno** without any difficulty; **me da ~ decírselo** I don't like to say it; **tener ~s para** to be reluctant [*o* hesitant] to **3.** (*objeción*) objection; **sin ~** without reservation; **no andar con ~s** to have no reservations; **poner ~s a algo** to raise objections to sth

repartición *f* **1.** *v.* **repartimiento 2.** *AmL* (*oficina*) office

repartidor(a) *m(f)* (*recadero*) delivery man, delivery woman *m, f;* **~ de periódicos** newspaper boy *m,* newspaper girl *f*

repartimiento *m* (*distribución*) distribution; (*división*) division

repartir I. *vt* to distribute; (*correos*) to deliver **II.** *vr:* **~se 1.** (*colocarse*) to place oneself **2.** (*dividir*) to divide up; **~se el mercado** to divide up the market

reparto *m* **1.** (*distribución*) distribution; (*división*) division; **~ de contribuciones** allotment of taxes; **~ domiciliario** home delivery; **~ de equipajes** baggage reclaim; **~ postal** mail delivery; **camión de ~** (*furgoneta*) delivery van; (*grande*) delivery lorry *Brit,* delivery truck *Am* **2.** (*relación*) division; **~ de poderes** ECON division of power

repasador *m Arg, Urug* (*paño de cocina*) dish cloth

repasar *vt* **1.** (*la ropa*) to mend **2.** (*un texto, la lección*) to revise; **segunda edición repasada y corregida** second edition, revised and amended **3.** (*la cuenta*) to check **4.** (*una carta*) to reread

repaso *m* **1.** (*revisión*) review **2.** (*inspección*) check

repatear *vt inf* **1.** (*molestar*) to annoy; **me repatean cosas así** things like that really get to me **2.** (*disgustar*) to dislike; **su mujer me repatea** I can't stand his wife

repatriar *vt* to repatriate

repe *m Ecua* GASTR *mashed cooked bananas with milk and cheese*

repecho *m* (steep) slope; **a ~** uphill

repeinar I. *vt* to comb carefully; *pey* to doll up **II.** *vr:* **~se** to comb one's hair carefully; *pey* to doll oneself up

repelente I. *adj* **1.** (*rechazador*) repellent; **~ al agua** water-repellent **2.** (*repugnante*) repulsive **3.** (*redicho*) affected **II.** *mf* (*sabelotodo*) know-all *Brit,* know-it-all *Am*

repeler *vt* **1.** (*rechazar*) to repel; **los imanes se repelen mutuamente** magnets repel one another **2.** (*repugnar*) to disgust

repelo *m* **1.** (*pelo*) *hair which sticks up;* **a ~** against the grain **2.** (*repugnancia*) repugnance

repelón *m* **dar repelones** to tug one's hair ▸**ser más viejo que el ~** to be as old as the hills; **a repelones** (*con dificultad*) with difficulty; (*con resistencia*) unwillingly; **de ~** without stopping

repelús *m inf* sudden shiver; **las arañas me dan ~** spiders give me the creeps

repeluzno *m* (*escalofrío*) wave (of disgust)

repensar <e→ie> *vt* to reconsider

repente *m inf* (*movimiento*) start; (*ataque*) fit ▸**de ~** suddenly, all of a sudden; **de ~ se echó a llorar** suddenly he/she started to cry

repentino, -a *adj* sudden

repera *f* **¡eres la ~!** *inf* you really take the biscuit *Brit* [*o* cake *Am*]!

repercusión *f* **1.** (*efecto*) repercussion; **tener gran ~** (*éxito*) to meet with great success **2.** (*del choque*) reverberation

repercutir *vi* **1.** (*efecto*) **~ en algo** to have an effect on sth; **~ en la salud** to affect one's health **2.** (*del choque*) to rebound **3.** (*eco*) to reverberate

repertorio *m* **1.** (*lista*) list; **~ legislativo** legislative program **2.** *t.* TEAT repertoire, repertory

repesca *f inf* second chance; DEP play-off

repescar <c→qu> *vt inf* to give a second chance to

repetición *f* repetition; **~ de orden** repeat order; **fusil de ~** repeating rifle; **en caso de ~** in case of repetition

repetido, -a *adj* repeated; **repetidas veces** again and again; **tengo muchos sellos ~s** I have doubles of lots of my stamps

repetidor *m* TÉC repeater, booster

repetidor(a) I. *adj* repeating **II.** *m(f)* **1.** (*estudiante*) resit student *Brit,* repeating student **2.** (*profesor*) tutor (*who prepares students for resit examinations*)

repetir *irr como pedir* **I.** *vi* **1.** (*sabor*) to repeat; **los ajos repiten mucho** garlic comes back on you **2.** (*plato*) **~ de un plato de comida** to have second helpings of a dish **II.** *vt* (*reiterar, recitar*) to repeat; **~ curso** to stay down; **~ un pedido de mercancía** to reorder goods **III.** *vr:* **~se** to repeat oneself

repicar <c→qu> **I.** *vi* (*campanas*) to ring, to peal; (*castañuelas*) to click **II.** *vt* **1.** (*campanas*) to ring; (*instrumento*) to play **2.** (*despedazar*) to mince **III.** *vr:* **~se** to boast

repipi *adj* la-di-da; **niño ~** little know-all

repique *m* **1.** (*de las campanas*) peal **2.** *inf* (*riña*) squabble

repiquetear *vi, vt* to ring; (*castañuelas*) to click

repiqueteo *m* peal; (*castañuelas*) click

repisa *f* shelf; **~ de chimenea** mantelpiece; **~ de ventana** window ledge

replantear *vt* **1.** (*asunto*) to raise again; (*plan*) to revise; (*reconsiderar*) to rethink **2.** ARQUIT to lay out a ground plan of

replegar *irr como fregar* **I.** *vt* **1.** (*doblar*) to fold **2.** (*para atrás*) to fold back **II.** *vr:* **~se** MIL to fall back

repleto, -a *adj* **~ de algo** full of sth; (*demasiado*) crammed with sth; **tener una cartera repleta de billetes** to have a wallet full of notes *Brit* [*o* bills *Am*]; **el tren está ~** the train is packed; **estoy** ~ I'm full up; **está repleta de energía** she is full of energy

réplica *f* **1.** (*respuesta*) reply; (*objeción*) rebuttal **2.** ARTE replica

replicar <c→qu> **I.** *vt* to answer **II.** *vi* **1.** (*replicar*) to reply **2.** (*contradecir*) to contradict; **obedecer sin** ~ to obey without argument

repliegue *m* **1.** (*dobladura*) fold **2.** MIL withdrawal

repoblación *f* (*de personas*) repopulation; (*de plantas*) replanting; ~ **forestal** reafforestation *Brit,* reforestation *Am*

repoblar <o→ue> *vt* (*personas*) to repopulate; (*plantas*) to replant; (*árboles*) to reafforest *Brit,* to reforest *Am*

repollo *m* cabbage

repolludo, **-a** *adj fig* cabbage-headed; (*regordete*) chubby

reponer *irr como poner* **I.** *vt* **1.** (*volver a poner*) to put back; (*teléfono*) to hang up; (*máquina*) to put back into service; (*en su cargo*) to reinstate **2.** (*reemplazar*) to replace **3.** (*completar*) to replenish **4.** (*replicar*) to reply **5.** CINE to rerelease; TEAT to revive; TV to rerun **II.** *vr:* ~**se** to recover

reportaje *m* report; PREN article; ~ **gráfico** illustrated report; (*documental*) documentary

reportar **I.** *vt* **1.** (*refrenar*) to check **2.** (*proporcionar*) to bring **3.** *AmL* (*informar*) to report **II.** *vr:* ~**se** to restrain oneself

reporte *m* **1.** (*noticia*) news item **2.** TIPO transfer

reportear *vt AmL* (*entrevistar*) to interview

reportero, **-a** *m, f* reporter; ~ **gráfico** press photographer

reposabrazos *m inv* armrest

reposacabezas *m inv* headrest

reposado, **-a** *adj* peaceful; (*agua*) calm

reposapiés *m inv* footrest

reposar **I.** *vi* to rest; **aquí reposan los restos mortales de...** here lie the mortal remains of ... **II.** *vt* to settle; ~ **la comida** to let one's food settle **III.** *vr:* ~**se** (*líquidos*) to settle; (*vino*) to lie

reposera *f AmL* (*tumbona*) deckchair

reposición *f* **1.** (*de un objeto*) replacement; ~ **de existencias** replenishment of stocks; ~ **de maquinaria** replacement of machinery **2.** (*del mercado, de una persona*) recovery **3.** (*de una situación*) stabilization **4.** TEAT revival; TV rerun; CINE rerelease

reposo *m* (*tranquilidad*) peace; (*descanso*) rest; ~ **en cama** rest in bed, bed rest; **una máquina en** ~ a machine at rest

repostada *f AmC* (*contestación*) rude reply

repostar *vt* **1.** (*provisiones*) to stock up with **2.** (*vehículo*) to refuel; (*combustible*) to fill up with

repostería *f* **1.** (*pastelería*) cake [*o* pastry] shop **2.** (*oficio*) pastrymaking **3.** (*productos*) pastries *pl*

repostero, **-a** *m, f* pastrycook

reprender *vt* to reprimand; ~ **algo a alguien** to scold [*o* to reprimand] sb for sth

reprensión *f t.* JUR reprimand

represa *f* **1.** (*estancamiento*) pool **2.** (*construcción*) dam

represalia *f* reprisal; **en** ~ **por...** in retaliation for ...

represar **I.** *vt* (*agua*) to hold back; (*río*) to dam; *fig* to contain **II.** *vr:* ~**se** (*agua*) to be held back; (*río*) to be dammed

representación *f* **1.** (*substitución, delegación*) representation; ~ **colectiva** collective representation; ~ **exclusiva** exclusive representation; ~ **mayoritaria** majority representation; ~ **proporcional** POL proportional representation; **por** [*o* **en**] ~ **de** representing **2.** TEAT performance **3.** (*reproducción*) reproduction; (*ilustración*) illustration; ~ **digital** digital display **4.** (*idea*) idea **5.** (*autoridad*) standing; **ser hombre de** ~ to be a man of some standing

representante *mf* **1.** (*delegado, suplente*) representative; ~ **especial** special representative **2.** TEAT, CINE agent, manager; (*actor*) actor, actress *m, f* **3.** COM dealer, salesman *m,* saleswoman *f*

representar **I.** *vt* **1.** (*sustituir*) to represent **2.** (*actuar*) to act; (*una obra*) to perform; ~ **el papel de amante** to play the role of lover **3.** (*significar*) to mean **4.** (*encarnar, personificar*) to embody; (*reproducir*) to reproduce; (*ilustrar*) to illustrate; ~ **visualmente** INFOR to display visually **5.** (*aparentar*) to seem; **representa ser más joven** he/she seems younger **6.** (*evocar*) to evoke **II.** *vr:* ~**se** to imagine

representativo, **-a** *adj* representative; **gobierno** ~ representative government

represión *f* (*contención*) suppression; (*limitación*) repression; ~ **de crímenes** anti-crime measures

reprimenda *f* reprimand

reprimir **I.** *vt* to suppress **II.** *vr:* ~**se** **1.** (*contenerse*) to control oneself; ~**se de hablar** to refrain from speaking **2.** (*cohibirse*) to be repressed

reprobable *adj* reprehensible

reprobación *f* **1.** (*condenación*) condemnation **2.** (*rechazamiento*) rejection

reprobar <o→ue> *vt* to condemn

réprobo, **-a** *adj, m, f* reprobate

reprochable *adj* reprehensible

reprochar *vt* to reproach

reproche *m* reproach; **en son de** ~ in a reproachful tone; **hacer** ~**s a alguien por algo** to reproach sb for sth

reproducción *f* **1.** (*procreación*) reproduction; ~ **bovina** cattle breeding **2.** (*repetición*) repetition; (*copia*) reproduction; ~ (**de un libro**) copy (of a book); ~ **de un discurso** repeat of a speech; (*documentos*) duplication **3.** (*representación*) reproduction; ~ **magnetofónica** tape recording; ~ **radiofónica** radio reproduction

reproducir *irr como traducir* **I.** *vt* **1.** (*pro-*

crear) to reproduce **2.** (*repetir*) to repeat; (*copiar*) to reproduce; (*un libro*) to print; (*documento*) to duplicate **3.** (*representar*) to represent; (*imitar*) to imitate; (*contar*) to recount **II.** *vr:* **~se** to reproduce

reproductor *m* (*aparato*) playback machine; **~ de discos compactos** compact disc player; **~ de video** video recorder

reproductor(a) **I.** *adj* reproductive **II.** *m(f)* (*animal*) breeder

reptar *vi* to crawl

reptil *m* reptile

república *f* republic; **~ miembro** member republic; **~ bananera** *pey* banana republic

republicano, -a *adj, m, f* republican

repudiar *vt* **1.** (*rechazar*) to reject **2.** (*parientes*) to disown

repudio *m* **1.** (*rechazo*) rejection **2.** (*de parientes*) repudiation

repuesto *m* **1.** (*pieza*) spare part; **rueda de ~** spare tyre *Brit,* spare tire *Am* **2.** (*de alimentos*) supply

repuesto, -a *pp de* **reponer**

repugnancia *f* **1.** (*repulsión*) **~ a algo** repugnance for sth **2.** (*asco*) **~ a algo** disgust for sth; **tener ~ al pescado** to loathe fish **3.** (*resistencia*) reluctance; **hacer algo con ~** to do sth reluctantly

repugnante *adj* disgusting

repugnar **I.** *vi* **1.** (*producir aversión*) to repel; (*asquear*) to disgust; **me repugna la carne grasosa** fatty meat makes me sick **2.** (*disgustar*) to disgust **II.** *vt* (*rehusar*) to refuse

repujar *vt* (*metal*) to work in relief; (*cuero*) to emboss

repulsa *f* (*rechazo*) rejection

repulsar *vt* (*persona*) to rebuff; (*deseo*) to reject

repulsión *f* (*aversión*) aversion; (*asco*) disgust

repulsivo, -a *adj* repulsive

repunte *m RíoPl* (*alza*) rise; **el ~ del dólar causó sensación hoy en la bolsa** the dollar's upturn caused a sensation in the stock market today

reputación *f* reputation; **mujer de mala ~** woman of ill repute; **tener muy buena/mala ~** to have a very good/bad reputation; **un local con mala ~** a place with a bad reputation

reputar *vt* **1.** (*considerar*) **~ a alguien de** [*o* **por**] **algo** to consider sb to be sth **2.** (*apreciar*) to respect

requebrar <e→ie> *vt* (*a una mujer*) to flatter

requemado, -a *adj* **1.** (*color*) brown; (*piel*) tanned **2.** (*persona*) angry

requemar **I.** *vt* **1.** (*asar bien*) to roast; (*demasiado*) to burn **2.** (*plantas*) to scorch **3.** (*doler*) **~ la garganta/la lengua** to burn one's throat/tongue **II.** *vr:* **~se** **1.** (*quemarse*) to scorch **2.** (*enfadarse*) to become angry **3.** (*de un sentimiento*) **~se de algo** to be consumed with sth **4.** (*plantas*) to scorch

requenete *adj Ven* (*rechoncho*) tubby

requerimiento *m* **1.** (*requisitoria*) **~ de algo** demand for sth; (*escrito*) writ for sth; **~ de información** request for information; **a ~ de...** on the request of ...; **hacer el ~ para la publicación de las proclamas** to publish the (matrimonial) banns **2.** (*exigencia*) demand **3.** (*aviso*) warning

requerir *irr como sentir vt* **1.** (*necesitar*) to require; **esto requiere toda la atención** this calls for our fullest attention; **este asunto requiere mucho tiempo** this affair demands a lot of time **2.** (*amorosamente*) to woo; **~ de amores** to woo **3.** (*intimar*) to urge; **~ a alguien que...** *+subj* to urge sb to ...

requesón *m* cottage [*o* curd] cheese

requetebién *adv inf* really well

requetebueno, -a *adj AmL, inf* really good

requetecaro, -a *adj AmL, inf* really expensive

requiebro *m* (amorous) compliment

réquiem *m* MÚS requiem

requisa *f* **1.** (*inspección*) inspection **2.** (*confiscación*) confiscation; MIL requisition

requisar *vt* to confiscate; MIL to requisition

requisito *m* (*requerimiento*) requirement; (*condición*) condition; **ser ~ indispensable** to be absolutely essential; **~ previo** prerequisite; **exigir ciertos ~s** to demand certain requirements; **cumplir con los ~s** to fulfil *Brit* [*o* fulfill *Am*] the requirements; **con todos los ~s** *fig, inf* with everything just as it should be

res *f* **1.** (*animal*) beast; **~es de matadero** animals for slaughter; **carne de ~** beef **2.** *AmL* (*vaca*) head of cattle

resabio *m* **1.** (*sabor*) unpleasant aftertaste **2.** (*costumbre*) bad habit

resaca *f* **1.** (*olas*) undertow, undercurrent **2.** *inf* (*malestar*) hangover

resalado, -a *adj* lively

resaltar *vi* **1.** (*sobresalir, distinguirse*) to stand out; **hacer ~** to highlight **2.** (*rebotar*) to bounce

resalte *m,* **resalto** *m* (*saliente*) projection, ledge

resanar *vt* to restore; (*con oro*) to repair the gilding of

resarcir <c→z> **I.** *vt* **1.** (*compensar*) **~ de algo** to compensate for sth **2.** (*reparar*) to repay **II.** *vr* **~se de algo** to make up for sth

resbalada *f AmL, inf* slip

resbaladilla *f Méx* slide

resbaladizo, -a *adj* slippery

resbalar *vi* to slide; (*sin querer*) to slip; (*coche*) to skid; **¡cuidado con no ~!** be careful not to slip!

resbalín *m Chile* slide

resbalón *m* slip; **dar un ~** to slip

rescatar *vt* **1.** (*a un prisionero*) to rescue; (*con dinero*) to pay the ransom for **2.** (*a un náufrago*) to pick up **3.** (*un cadáver*) to recover **4.** (*algo perdido*) to recover **5.** (*una deuda*) to pay off **6.** (*tiempo*) to win back; **quisiera ~ mi juventud** I wish I could relive my youth **7.** ECON (*bonos*) to redeem **8.** *AmL* (*mercancías*) to peddle

rescate *m* **1.** (*de un prisionero*) rescue; (*con dinero*) ransoming **2.** (*de una prenda*) revival **3.** (*recuperación*) recovery; **con facultad de ~** redeemable **4.** (*dinero para rescatar*) ransom

rescindir *vt* (*la ley*) to repeal; (*un contrato*) to annul

rescisión *f* (*la ley*) repeal; (*un contrato*) annulment; **~ de una deuda** cancellation of a debt *Brit,* debt cancelation *Am*

rescoldo *m* **1.** (*borrajo*) embers *pl* **2.** (*sospecha*) lingering suspicion

resecar <c→qu> *vt* (*secar mucho*) to dry out; (*plantas*) to parch

reseco, -a *adj* **1.** (*muy seco*) very dry **2.** (*flaco*) skinny

resentido, -a *adj* **1.** *estar* (*ofendido*) resentful **2.** *estar* (*débil*) worn out **3.** *ser* (*rencoroso*) bitter

resentimiento *m* resentment

resentirse *irr como sentir vr* **1.** (*ofenderse*) **~ por** [*o* **de**] **algo** to feel resentful about sth **2.** (*sentir dolor*) **~ de** [*o* **con**] **algo** to suffer from sth; **~ del costado** to have a sore side; **todavía se resiente de las heridas del accidente** he/she is still suffering from the injuries he/she received in the accident **3.** (*debilitarse*) to be weakened; **los edificios se resintieron cuando abrieron el túnel** the buildings were weakened when they dug the tunnel

reseña *f* **1.** (*de un libro*) review **2.** (*de una persona*) description **3.** (*narración*) report **4.** MIL review

reseñar *vt* **1.** (*un libro*) to review **2.** (*una persona*) to describe **3.** (*resumir*) to summarize **4.** MIL to review

resero, -a *m, f CSur* (*arreador*) cowhand

reserva *f* **1.** (*previsión*) reservation; **~ de equipajes** *AmL* left luggage; **tener algo en ~** to hold sth in reserve **2.** FIN reserve; (*fondos*) reserves *pl* **3.** (*de plazas*) reservation; **hacer una ~** to reserve, to book **4.** (*biológica*) reserve **5.** MIL reserves *pl;* **pasar a la ~** to join the reserves **6.** (*discreción*) secrecy; **guardar la ~** to be discrete **7.** (*circunspección*) reserve; **~ mental** mental reservation; **sin la menor ~** unreservedly **8.** (*vino*) vintage **9.** (*lugar protegido*) reserve; (*para personas*) reservation; (*para animales*) wildlife reserve ►**a ~ de que** *+subj* unless

reservadamente *adv* in confidence

reservado *m* **1.** FERRO reserved compartment **2.** (*habitación*) reserved room

reservado, -a *adj* **1.** (*derecho*) reserved; **quedan ~s todos los derechos** all rights reserved **2.** (*callado*) reserved **3.** (*confidencial*) confidential; **fondos ~s** reptilian funds **4.** (*cauteloso*) cautious

reservar **I.** *vt* **1.** (*retener plaza*) to reserve; **~ un asiento** (*ocupar*) to occupy a seat; (*para un viaje*) to save a seat **2.** (*guardar*) to put by **3.** (*ocultar*) to conceal **II.** *vr:* **~se** (*conservarse*) to save oneself

resfriado *m* MED cold

resfriar <*3. pres:* resfría> **I.** *vi* to cool **II.** *vt* to cool off **III.** *vr:* **~se** **1.** (*enfriarse*) to get cold **2.** MED to catch a cold

resfrío *m AmL* cold

resguardar **I.** *vt* **1.** (*proteger*) **~ de algo** to protect from sth **2.** (*poner en seguridad*) to safeguard; **~ los derechos** to reserve the rights **II.** *vr* **~se de algo** to protect oneself from sth; **~se con un muro** to shelter behind a wall

resguardo *m* **1.** (*protección*) protection **2.** (*recibo*) receipt; (*vale*) voucher; **~ de almacén** warrant; **~ de entrega/de transferencia** proof of delivery/transfer

residencia *f* **1.** (*domicilio, estancia*) residence; **~ habitual** usual place of residence; **cambiar de ~** to change one's address **2.** (*casa lujosa*) residence; **~ real** royal residence; **~ señorial** palatial residence **3.** (*internado*) residence; (*colegio*) boarding school; **~ de ancianos** old people's home; **~ de huérfanos** children's home; **~ universitaria** hall of residence *Brit,* dormitory *Am* **4.** (*hostal*) small hotel

residencial **I.** *adj* residential **II.** *m* (*urbanización*) housing development

residente **I.** *adj* resident; **no ~** non-resident; **~ en el lugar** resident locally **II.** *mf* resident

residir *vi* **1.** (*habitar*) to reside **2.** (*radicar*) **~ en** to lie in

residual *adj* residual; **aguas ~es** sewage

residuo *m* **1.** (*resto*) residue; QUÍM residuum **2.** *pl* (*basura*) waste; (*géneros defectuosos*) leftovers *pl;* **~s de las fábricas** industrial waste; **~s radiactivos** radioactive waste; **~s tóxicos** toxic waste

resignación *f* resignation

resignar **I.** *vt* to resign from **II.** *vr:* **~se** to resign oneself; **~se con** [*o* **a**] **algo** to resign oneself to sth

resina *f* resin

resistencia *f* **1.** resistance; **~ a la autoridad** opposition to the authorities; **oponer ~** to offer resistance; **formar parte de la ~** to be part of the resistance; **la ~ francesa** the French Resistance **2.** (*aguante*) **~ física** stamina; **~ al choque** shock resistance; **~ al frío** resistance to the cold; **~ al pago** non-payment; **~ a la publicidad** publicity fatigue **3.** DEP **carrera de ~** endurance race **4.** ELEC resistor, resistance

resistente **I.** *adj* resistant; **~ al calor** heat-resistant; **~ a la intemperie** weatherproof; **~ a la lavadora** machine-washable; **~ a la luz** light-resistant; **~ a la rotura** shatterproof **II.** *mf* resistance fighter

resistir **I.** *vi, vt* **1.** (*oponer resistencia*) to resist; **~ a una tentación** to resist a temptation; **~ al enemigo** to resist the enemy; **resistió la enfermedad** he/she overcame the illness; **¡no resisto más!** I can't take any more! **2.** (*aguantar*) **no resisto la comida pesada** I can't cope handle heavy food; **no puedo ~ a esta persona** I can't stand this person **II.** *vr:* **~se** to resist

resolana *f AmL* **1.** (*calor reflejado*) reflected sunlight **2.** (*lugar a pleno sol*) sunny windless spot **3.** (*resplandor*) sun glare

resollar *vi* **1.** (*aspirar*) to breathe heavily; **~ comiendo** to slurp **2.** *inf* (*dar noticia de sí*) to show signs of life; **sin ~** without a word; **beber algo sin ~** to drink sth in one gulp; **trabajar horas y horas sin ~** to work for hours without a break

resolución *f* **1.** (*firmeza*) resolve **2.** (*decisión*) decision; POL resolution; **~ administrativa** administrative decision; **~ arbitral** refereeing decision; **~ judicial** adjudication; **tomar una ~** to take [*o* reach] a decision **3.** (*solución*) solution

resoluto, -a *adj* resolute

resolver *irr como volver* **I.** *vt* **1.** (*acordar*) to agree **2.** (*solucionar*) to solve; (*dudas*) to resolve **3.** (*decidir*) to decide **4.** (*disolver*) to dissolve **II.** *vr:* **~se** **1.** (*solucionarse*) to be solved **2.** (*decidirse*) to decide **3.** (*disolverse*) to dissolve

resonancia *f* resonance; **caja de ~** soundbox; **de ~ universal** of great importance; **tener ~** (*suceso*) to have an impact

resonante *adj* (*importante*) important; **con éxito ~** with tremendous success; **una victoria ~** a resounding victory

resonar <o→ue> *vi* to resound; **los gritos de angustia resuenan todavía en mis oídos** I can still hear the cries of anguish; **~ fuera de las fronteras** *fig* to be heard beyond the borders

resoplar *vi* to huff and puff; **~ de rabia** to snort angrily

resorte *m* **1.** (*muelle*) spring **2.** *fig* (*medio*) means *pl* ►**tocar todos los ~s** to pull out all the stops

resortera *f Méx* catapult *Brit,* slingshot *Am*

respaldar **I.** *vt* **1.** (*apoyar*) to support **2.** (*proteger*) to protect **3.** (*anotar*) to endorse **II.** *vr:* **~se** **1.** (*apoyarse*) to lean; (*hacia atrás*) to lean back; **~se en el sillón** to sit back in one's chair **2.** (*ampararse*) to seek shelter **III.** *m* support

respaldo *m* **1.** (*respaldar*) support **2.** (*reverso*) back; **en el ~** on the back **3.** (*apoyo*) support; (*protección*) protection

respectar *vi* (*verbo defectivo*) to regard; **por** [*o* **en**] **lo que respecta a él...** with regard to him ...

respectivamente *adv* respectively

respectivo, -a *adj* respective

respecto *m* (**con**) **~ a** with regard to; **al ~, con ~ a eso** in that regard; **a este ~** in this regard; **al ~ de** with regard to

respetabilidad *f* respectability

respetable *adj* **1.** (*digno de respeto*) respectable **2.** (*notable*) considerable

respetar *vt* **1.** (*honrar*) to respect; **hacerse ~** to command respect **2.** (*considerar*) to consider **3.** (*cumplir*) to observe

respeto *m* (*veneración*) respect; **~ a las leyes** respect for the law; **~ de un plazo** compliance with a time limit; **falta de ~** lack of respect; **tener mucho ~ a las tormentas** to be well aware of the dangers of storms; **¡mis ~s a su señora!** give your wife my regards! ►**campar por sus ~s** to do as one pleases; **faltar al ~ a alguien** to be disrespectful to(wards) sb; **ofrecer los ~s a alguien** to pay one's respects to sb; **de ~** respectable; **una persona de ~** a respectable person

respetuoso, -a *adj* respectful; **ser ~ con las leyes** to respect the law

respingar <g→gu> *vi* **1.** (*animal*) to buck, to balk **2.** (*falda*) to ride up **3.** (*refunfuñar*) to grumble

respingo *m* **1.** (*movimiento*) start; (*animal*) buck; **dar un ~** to start, to jump **2.** (*refunfuño*) grumbling

respingón, -ona *adj* **1.** (*levantado*) turned-up; **nariz respingona** snub nose **2.** (*animal*) nervous

respiración *f* (*inhalación*) breathing; (*aliento*) breath; **~ artificial** artificial respiration; **~ boca a boca** mouth to mouth resuscitation; **dificultad de ~** breathing difficulties; **cortar la ~** to hold one's breath; **faltar a uno la ~** to be breathless, to be short of breath

respirar *vi* to breathe; **~ aliviado** to breathe easily; **~ trabajosamente** to gasp for breath; **no me atrevo a ~ delante de él** I don't dare to open my mouth when he's around ►**¡déjame que respire!** leave me in peace! *Brit,* give me a break! *Am;* **ahora sé por dónde respira** now I know what makes him/her tick; **sin ~** without stopping; **escuchar sin ~** to listen with bated breath

respiratorio, -a *adj* respiratory; **vías respiratorias** air passages

respiro *m* **1.** (*respiración*) breathing **2.** (*pausa*) rest **3.** (*de alivio*) sign

resplandecer *irr como crecer vi* (*lucir, reflejar*) to shine; **~ de alegría** to glow with happiness; **~ por su inteligencia** to stand out for one's intelligence

resplandeciente *adj* shining; **~ de limpio** shiny clean

resplandor *m* brightness

responder *vi* **1.** (*contestar*) to reply; **el perro responde al nombre de...** the dog answers to the name of ... **2.** (*contradecir*) to contradict **3.** (*corresponder*) to correspond; (*cumplir con*) to obey **4.** (*ser responsable*) **~ por algo** to answer for sth **5.** (*garantizar*) **~ de** [*o* **por**] **algo** to guarantee [*o* vouch for] sth; **~ de una deuda** to guarantee a debt

respondón, -ona **I.** *adj* argumentative; (*niño*) cheeky *Brit,* sassy *Am* **II.** *m, f* argumentative person; (*niño*) cheeky child

responsabilidad *f* **1.** (*por un niño*) **~ de** [*o* **por**] **alguien** responsibility for sb; **~ propia**

R

personal responsibility; **exigir** ~ to demand that sb accept responsibility **2.** (*por un daño*) liability; ~ **civil** civility; ~ **del daño** liability for damages; **incurrir en** ~ to become liable; **no acepto la** ~ it has nothing to do with me
responsabilizar <z→c> **I.** *vt* ~ **de algo** to make responsible for sth **II.** *vr:* ~**se** **1.** (*asumir la responsabilidad*) ~**se de algo** to accept the responsibility for sth **2.** (*garantizar*) ~**se de algo** to guarantee sth; JUR to accept liability for sth
responsable **I.** *adj* ~ **de algo** responsible for sth; **ser civilmente** ~ to be liable **II.** *mf* (*encargado*) person in charge; (*culpable*) culprit
respuesta *f* answer; ~ **negativa** negative reply; **en** ~ **a su carta del...** in reply to your letter of ...; **dar la callada por** ~ to answer with silence; **por toda** ~ **se encogió de hombros** his/her only answer was a shrug of the shoulders
resquebrajadura *f* crack, chink
resquebrajar *vt, vr:* ~**se** to crack
resquemor *m* **1.** (*escozor*) sting **2.** (*resentimiento*) resentment, ill-feeling
resquicio *m* **1.** (*abertura*) crack **2.** (*ocasión*) opening; ~ **de esperanza** glimmer of hope
resta *f* MAT subtraction
restablecer *irr como crecer* **I.** *vt* to re-establish; (*democracia, paz*) to restore **II.** *vr:* ~**se** to recover
restablecimiento *m* **1.** (*recuperación*) re-establishment; (*de democracia, paz*) restoration **2.** (*cura*) recovery
restallar *vi* to crack; **hacer** ~ **el látigo** to crack the whip
restante **I.** *adj* remaining; **cantidad** ~ remainder **II.** *m* remainder
restañar *vt* (*la sangre*) to staunch *Brit,* to stanch *Am;* ~ **las heridas** *fig* to heal the wounds
restar **I.** *vi* to remain; **aún restan algunos días para finalizar el año** there are still a few days left until the end of the year **II.** *vt* to take away; ~ **energías a alguien** to drain sb's strength; **no** ~ **un ápice del mérito** not to detract in the slightest from the achievement; ~**se años** to seem much younger; ~ **importancia a algo** to play sth down; MAT to subtract
restauración *f* **1.** *t.* ARTE restoration; ~ **de la monarquía** restoration of the monarchy **2.** COM the restaurant business
restaurante *m* restaurant
restaurar *vt t.* ARTE to restore
restitución *f* **1.** (*devolución*) *t.* FIN return **2.** (*reposición*) replacement
restituir *irr como huir* **I.** *vt* **1.** (*devolver*) *t.* FIN to return **2.** (*restablecer*) to restore **II.** *vr:* ~**se** to go back
resto *m* (*lo que sobra*) rest; MAT remainder; ~**s de un buque** wreckage; **los** ~**s mortales** the mortal remains; **los** ~**s de la torre** the tower ruins; **lo recordaré el** ~ **de mis días** I will remember him for the rest of my life
restregar *irr como fregar* **I.** *vt* to rub; ~ **a alguien algo por las narices** *fig* to rub sb's nose in sth **II.** *vr:* ~**se** to rub; ~**se los ojos** to rub one's eyes
restregón *m* rub
restricción *f* (*limitación*) restriction; (*recorte*) cutback; ~ **de la natalidad** reduction of the birth rate; ~ **mental** evasiveness; **sin restricciones** freely
restrictivo, -a *adj* restrictive
restringir <g→j> *vt* to restrict
resucitar **I.** *vi* to resuscitate **II.** *vt* **1.** (*de la muerte*) to resuscitate **2.** (*un estilo, una moda*) to revive
resuello *m* breathing; **sin** ~ out of breath ►**meter a alguien el** ~ **en el cuerpo** to intimidate sb
resuelto, -a **I.** *pp de* **resolver** **II.** *adj* determined
resulta *f* result; **de** ~**s de algo** as a result of sth
resultado *m* result, outcome; ~ **del reconocimiento** (**médico**) results of the medical examination; **dar buen** ~ (*funcionar*) to work; (*no desgastarse*) to last; **dar mal** ~ (*no funcionar*) to fail; (*desgastarse*) to wear out fast; **tener por** ~ to lead to
resultar *vi* **1.** (*deducirse*) ~ **de algo** to result from sth **2.** (*surtir*) to be; ~ **muerto en un accidente** to be killed in an accident; ~ **en beneficio de alguien** to be to sb's benefit **3.** (*tener éxito*) to succeed, to work well **4.** (*comprobarse*) to turn out
resumen *m* **1.** (*sumario*) summary; **en** ~ in short **2.** (*extracto*) extract
resumidero *m AmL* **1.** (*alcantarilla*) drain **2.** (*pozo ciego*) cess pool
resumir **I.** *vt* to summarize **II.** *vr* ~**se en algo** to amount to sth
resurgimiento *m* resurgence; (*reaparición*)
resurgir <g→j> *vi* **1.** (*reaparecer*) to reappear **2.** (*renacer*) to be resurrected **3.** (*revivir*) to revive
resurrección *f* **1.** REL resurrection; **Pascua de Resurrección** Easter; **Domingo de Resurrección** Easter Sunday **2.** (*restablecimiento*) re-establishment
retablo *m* ARTE reredos, altarpiece
retacón, -ona *adj CSur* stubby
retaguardia *f* MIL rearguard ►**estar a la** ~ **de algo** to lag behind sth; **ir a la** ~ to bring up the rear; **quedarse en la** ~ to stay in the background; **a** [*o* **en**] ~ (*tarde*) late; **a** ~ **de** (*detrás de*) behind
retahíla *f* string; **soltar la** ~ to come out with a string of insults
retal *m* remnant
retama *f* broom
retar *vt* to challenge
retardar **I.** *vt* to delay **II.** *vr:* ~**se** to be late; **me he retardado** I was delayed
retardo *m* delay; **sufrir un** ~ to be delayed; **tener** ~ **con algo** to be late doing sth

retazo *m* **1.** (*retal*) remnant **2.** (*fragmento*) fragment; (*de conversación*) snippet

rete *adj Méx* (*muy*) very; **su hija es ~ alta** their daughter is very tall

retemblar <e→ie> *vi* to shake; **hacer ~** to shake

retén *m* **1.** MIL reserves *pl;* (*refuerzos*) reinforcements *pl* **2.** (*reserva*) stock

retención *f* **1.** (*custodia*) retention; (*deducción*) deduction; **~ fiscal** tax retention; **certificado de retenciones** certificate of tax retention **2.** (*memorizar*) retention **3.** (*moderación*) moderation **4.** (*tráfico*) hold-up

retener *irr como tener* **I.** *vt* **1.** (*conservar*) to retain; (*el pasaporte*) to withold; (*la respiración*) to hold **2.** (*recordar*) to retain; (*detener*) to detain **II.** *vr:* **~se** to restrain oneself

retentiva *f* memory

reticencia *f* **1.** (*indirecta*) insinuation; **andar con ~s** to drop hints **2.** (*renuencia*) reluctance **3.** (*reserva*) **~ ante** reticence towards

reticente *adj* **1.** (*discurso*) insinuating **2.** (*reacio*) reluctant

retículo *m* net

retina *f* ANAT retina; **desprendimiento de ~** detached retina

retintín *m* **1.** (*tonillo*) sarcastic tone **2.** (*son*) ringing

retirada *f* **1.** (*abandono*) abandonment; MIL retreat **2.** (*eliminación*) withdrawal **3.** (*jubilación*) retirement

retirado, **-a** **I.** *adj* **1.** (*lejos*) remote **2.** (*jubilado*) retired **II.** *m, f* retired person

retirar **I.** *vt* **1.** (*apartar*) to remove; (*tropas, dinero*) to withdraw **2.** (*echar*) to remove; **~on de la sala a los manifestantes** they removed the demonstrators from the hall **3.** (*recoger, quitar*) to take away **4.** (*desdecirse*) to withdraw **5.** (*negar*) to deny **6.** (*jubilar*) to retire **II.** *vr:* **~se** **1.** (*abandonar*) **~se de algo** to withdraw from sth **2.** *t.* MIL (*retroceder*) to retreat **3.** (*jubilarse*) to retire

retiro *m* **1.** (*pensión*) pension **2.** (*refugio*) retreat **3.** (*retraimiento*) withdrawal

reto *m* challenge

retobado, **-a** *adj* **1.** *AmC, Méx, Ecua* (*respondón*) insolent **2.** *AmC, Cuba, Ecua* (*indómito*) wild **3.** *Arg, Méx, Urug* (*enconado*) cheesed off *Brit, inf,* ticked off *inf*

retobar **I.** *vt CSur* (*forrar*) to cover with leather **II.** *vi Méx* (*rezogar*) to talk back

retocar <c→qu> *vt* **1.** (*corregir*) FOTO to retouch, to touch up **2.** (*perfeccionar*) to perfect

retoñar *vi* to sprout; *fig* to reappear

retoño *m* **1.** (*vástago*) shoot **2.** (*niño*) kid

retoque *m* **1.** (*corrección*) alteration; FOTO retouch **2.** FIN adjustment

retorcer *irr como cocer* **I.** *vt* **1.** (*torcer*) to twist **2.** (*enroscar*) to twine **II.** *vr:* **~se** **1.** (*enroscarse*) to twist **2.** (*de dolor*) to writhe

retorcido, **-a** *adj* **1.** (*complicado*) **pensar de manera retorcida** to think in a very confused way; **¡qué ~!** how complicated! **2.** (*maligno*) twisted; **una mente retorcida** a warped mind **3.** (*conceptuoso*) convoluted

retorcijón *m* stomach cramp

retorcimiento *m* **1.** (*torcedura*) twist **2.** (*vuelta*) turn **3.** (*encorvadura*) curve

retórica *f* rhetoric

retórico, **-a** **I.** *adj* rhetorical **II.** *m, f* rhetorician

retornable *adj* **botella (no) ~** (non-)returnable bottle

retornar **I.** *vi* to return **II.** *vt* to give back

retorno *m* return

retorta *f* retort

retortijón *m* **1.** (*ensortijamiento*) twist **2.** (*dolor*) cramp; **tengo un ~ de estómago** I have a cramp in my stomach

retozar <z→c> *vi* **1.** (*brincar*) to frolic **2.** (*coquetear*) to flirt

retozón, **-ona** *adj* playful

retracción *f* **1.** JUR retraction **2.** (*retroceso, retiro*) withdrawal **3.** (*impedimento*) obstacle **4.** MED retraction

retractación *f* retraction

retractar **I.** *vt* (*desdecirse*) to take back; JUR to retract **II.** *vr* **~se de algo** to withdraw from sth

retráctil *adj* retractable; BIO retractile

retraer *irr como traer* **I.** *vt* **1.** (*encoger*) to withdraw **2.** (*traer*) to bring back **3.** (*impedir*) to hinder **4.** JUR to retract **II.** *vr:* **~se** **1.** (*aislarse*) **~se a** [*o* **en**] **algo** to withdraw into sth **2.** (*retirarse*) **~se de algo** to withdraw from sth **3.** (*retroceder*) to retreat

retraído, **-a** *adj* (*reservado*) reserved; (*poco sociable*) withdrawn

retraimiento *m* reserve

retransmisión *f* broadcast; **~ deportiva** sports programme, sport(s) program; **~ por televisión** television broadcast; **~ en directo/diferido** live/pre-recorded broadcast

retransmitir *vt* to broadcast

retrasado, **-a** *adj* **1.** (*atrasado*) backward; **~ en tecnología** technologically backward **2.** (*anticuado*) old-fashioned **3.** (*no actual*) out of date **4.** (*subdesarrollado*) underdeveloped; **~ mental** mentally retarded

retrasar **I.** *vt* **1.** (*demorar*) to delay **2.** (*el reloj*) to put [*o* set] back **II.** *vi* **1.** (*el reloj*) to be slow **2.** (*no estar al día*) to be out of touch **III.** *vr:* **~se** to be late

retraso *m* **1.** (*demora*) delay **2.** (*del desarrollo*) underdevelopment **3.** (*de la deuda*) arrears *pl;* **tener ~ en los pagos** to be in arrears

retratar *vt* **1.** (*describir*) to depict, to portray **2.** (*fotografiar*) to photograph **3.** (*pintar*) to paint a portrait of

retratista *mf* (*dibujante*) portrait artist; (*fotógrafo*) portrait photographer

retrato *m* **1.** (*representación*) *t.* FOTO portrait **2.** (*descripción*) description ► **ser el vivo ~ de alguien** to be the spitting image of sb

retrato-robot <retratos-robot> *m* photo-

fit® picture
retreta *f* retreat
retrete *m* lavatory, toilet
retribución *f* reward; (*sueldo*) remuneration; **retribuciones dinerarias** money payment; **retribuciones en especie** payment in kind
retribuir *irr como huir vt* **1.** (*remunerar*) to remunerate **2.** *AmL* (*compensar*) to compensate
retro *adj inf* retro, old-fashioned looking
retroactividad *f* retroactivity
retroactivo, **-a** *adj* retroactive
retroalimentación *f* feedback
retroceder *vi* **1.** (*regresar*) to go back **2.** (*desistir*) to give up; (*echarse atrás*) to back down
retroceso *m* **1.** (*regresión*) reversal; ~ **en las negociaciones** setback in the negotiations **2.** MED relapse **3.** (*arma de fuego*) recoil, kick *inf*
retrógrado, **-a** *adj, m, f* reactionary
retropropulsión *f* AVIAT jet propulsion
retroproyector *m* overhead projector
retrospectivo, **-a** *adj* retrospective
retrovisor *m* AUTO rearview mirror; ~ **exterior** wing mirror, side mirror *Am;* **mirar por el espejo** ~ to look in the rearview mirror
retumbar *vi* to boom; (*resonar*) to resound
reuma *m o f,* **reúma** *m o f* MED rheumatism
reumático, **-a** *adj* rheumatic
reumatismo *m sin pl* MED rheumatism
reunificación *f* reunification
reunificar <c→qu> *vt* to reunify
reunión *f* **1.** (*encuentro, asamblea*) meeting; ~ **de los trabajadores** employees' meeting; ~ **de antiguos alumnos** class reunion; ~ **en la cumbre** summit meeting **2.** (*conferencia*) meeting; **estar en** ~ to be in a meeting; **celebrar una** ~ to hold a meeting **3.** (*el juntar*) collection **4.** (*grupo, invitados*) gathering
reunir *irr* **I.** *vt* **1.** (*congregar*) to assemble **2.** (*unir*) to gather **3.** (*juntar*) to reunite **4.** (*poseer*) to have; ~ **las cualidades necesarias** to have the necessary qualities **II.** *vr:* ~**se** **1.** (*congregarse*) to meet; (*informal*) to get together **2.** (*unir*) to gather **3.** (*juntarse*) to reunite
reválida *f* **1.** (*confirmación*) confirmation **2.** (*examen*) final examination
revalidar **I.** *vt* to confirm **II.** *vr:* ~**se** to be recognized
revaloración *f* re-evaluation; FIN revaluation
revalorización *f* FIN appreciation
revalorizar <z→c> *vt* **1.** to re-evaluate **2.** FIN to appreciate; (*subir el valor*) to increase the value of
revaluación *f* **1.** re-evaluation **2.** FIN revaluation; (*elevamiento*) appreciation
revaluar <*1. pres:* revalúo> *vt* **1.** to re-evaluate **2.** FIN to revalue; (*subir el valor*) to increase the value of
revancha *f* **1.** revenge; **tomarse la** ~ **por algo** to get one's own back for sth; **tomarse la** ~ to take one's revenge **2.** DEP return match
revelación *f t.* REL revelation
revelado *m* FOTO developing
revelar *vt* **1.** (*dar a conocer*) to reveal, to disclose **2.** FOTO to develop
revellín *m Cuba* (*dificultad*) difficulty ►**echar** ~ to provoke anger
revender *vt* to resell
revenir *irr como venir vi, vr:* ~**se** **1.** (*encoger*) to shrink **2.** (*agriarse*) to sour **3.** (*secarse*) to dry out
reventa *f* resale; (*entradas*) touting *Brit,* scalping *Am*
reventadero *m* **1.** *Col, Méx* (*hervidero*) bubbling spring **2.** *Chile* (*rompiente*) shoal
reventado, **-a** *adj* **1.** *inf* (*hecho polvo*) wiped out **2.** *Arg* (*sinuoso*) devious
reventar <e→ie> **I.** *vi* **1.** (*romperse*) to break; (*globo, neumático*) to burst; **lleno hasta** ~ full to bursting **2.** *vulg* (*morir*) to snuff it *Brit;* **¡que reviente!** I hope he/she drops dead! **II.** *vt* **1.** (*romper*) to break; (*globo, neumático*) to burst **2.** *inf* (*molestar*) to annoy **III.** *vr:* ~**se** **1.** (*romperse*) to break; (*globo, neumático*) to burst **2.** *vulg* (*morirse*) to snuff it *Brit*
reventón *m* AUTO **tener un** ~ to have a flat tyre
reverberación *f* (*de la luz*) reflection; (*del sonido*) reverberation
reverberar *vi* (*luz*) to reflect; (*sonido*) to reverberate
reverbero *m* **1.** *v.* **reverberación** **2.** (*farol*) reflecting light; AUTO reflector **3.** *AmL* (*hornillo*) spirit stove
reverdecer *irr como crecer vi* **1.** (*verdear*) to become green **2.** (*vigorizar*) to revive
reverencia *f* **1.** (*veneración*) reverence; **Su Reverencia** Your Reverence **2.** (*inclinación*) bow
reverenciar *vt* to revere
reverendísimo, **-a** *adj* Most Reverend; **Su Reverendísimo** Your Most Reverend
reverendo, **-a** **I.** *adj* revered; REL Reverend **II.** *m, f* Reverend
reverente *adj* respectful
reversa *f Chile, Col, Méx* AUTO reverse
reversibilidad *f* reversibility
reversible *adj* reversible
reversión *f* reversion
reverso *m* other side ►**el** ~ **de la medalla** the other side of the coin
revertir *irr como sentir vi* to revert; **revirtió en su beneficio** it worked to his/her advantage
revés *m* **1.** (*reverso*) other side; **al** [*o* **del**] ~ back to front; (*con lo de arriba abajo*) upside down; **te has puesto el jersey del** ~ you have put your jumper on back to front; (*dentro para fuera*) inside out; **poner a alguien del** ~ (*confundir*) to confuse sb; (*poner a caldo*) to be blunt with sb **2.** (*golpe*) blow with the back of the hand **3.** DEP backhand **4.** (*infortunio*) set-

back; ~ **de fortuna** stroke of bad luck

revestimiento *m t.* ARQUIT ~ **de/con algo** covering with sth

revestir *irr como pedir* **I.** *vt* **1.** (*recubrir*) ~ **con** [*o* **de**] **algo** to cover with sth; ~ **de cinc** to coat with zinc **2.** (*tener*) ~ **importancia** to assume importance **II.** *vr:* ~**se** (*aparentar*) ~**se con** [*o* **de**] **algo** to arm oneself with sth

reviejo, **-a** *adj* very old

revirado, **-a** *adj* **1.** *Arg, Urug, inf* (*loco*) dotty *Brit, inf,* nutty *inf* **2.** BOT twisted

revire *m Arg, Urug, inf* crazy idea; **le dió uno de sus ~s** he/she had one of his/her crazy ideas

revisada *f AmL* (*revisión*) check, review

revisar *vt* to check; TÉC to inspect; (*textos, edición*) to revise

revisión *f* check; TÉC inspection; JUR, TIPO revision; MED checkup

revisor(a) *m(f)* **1.** (*controlador*) inspector; ~ **de cuentas** auditor **2.** FERRO ticket inspector

revista *f* **1.** PREN magazine; **las ~s del corazón** the gossip magazines; ~ **electrónica** e-zine; ~ **especializada** special interest magazine; ~ **ilustrada** illustrated magazine **2.** *t.* MIL (*inspección*) inspection; **pasar ~ a las tropas** to inspect the troops **3.** (*espectáculo*) revue, variety show

revistero *m* magazine rack

revival *m* revival

revivificar <c→qu> *vt* to revive

revivir **I.** *vi* to revive **II.** *vt* to revive; (*evocar*) to relive

revocación *f* (*anulación*) annulment

revocar <c→qu> **I.** *vt* **1.** (*anular*) to annul **2.** (*apartar*) to dismiss **3.** (*hacer retroceder*) to recall **4.** (*enlucir*) to plaster **II.** *vi* (*humo*) to blow back

revolcar *irr como volcar* **I.** *vt* **1.** (*derribar*) to knock over **2.** *inf* (*vencer*) to defeat **3.** *inf* (*suspender*) to fail **II.** *vr:* ~**se** **1.** (*restregarse*) ~**se por algo** to roll around in sth **2.** (*obstinarse*) ~**se en algo** to insist on sth

revolcón *m* **dar un ~ a alguien** *fig* to wipe the floor with sb; **darse un ~** *inf* to have a roll in the hay *fig*

revolear *vt Méx, CSur* to whirl round

revolotear *vi* to flutter about

revoloteo *m* fluttering

revoltijo *m* **1.** (*embrollo*) jumble **2.** (*tripas*) tripe **3.** (*huevos*) scrambled eggs

revoltoso, **-a** **I.** *adj* **1.** (*travieso*) mischievous **2.** (*rebelde*) rebellious **3.** (*intrincado*) tangled **II.** *m, f* troublemaker

revoltura *f Méx* mixture

revolución *f* **1.** *t.* POL, ASTR (*cambio, rotación*) revolution; **número de revoluciones** number of revolutions **2.** (*inquietud*) disturbance

revolucionar *vt* **1.** (*amotinar*) to stir up **2.** (*transformar*) to revolutionize **3.** (*excitar*) to arouse interest in **4.** TÉC to increase the number of revolutions of

revolucionario, **-a** *adj, m, f* revolutionary

revoluta *f AmC v.* **revolución**

revolvedora *f Arg, Méx* (*de cemento*) cement mixer

revolver *irr como volver* **I.** *vt* **1.** (*mezclar*) to mix **2.** (*desordenar*) to mess up **3.** (*soliviantar*) to stir up **4.** (*investigar*) to investigate **5.** (*registrar*) to rummage through **II.** *vr:* ~**se** **1.** (*moverse*) to toss and turn; **se me revuelve el estómago** it makes my stomach turn **2.** (*enfrentarse*) to turn **3.** (*el tiempo*) to break

revólver *m* revolver

revoque *m* **1.** (*acción*) plastering **2.** (*material*) plaster

revuelco *m* (*golpe*) blow

revuelo *m* **1.** (*turbación*) disturbance; **causar ~** to disturb **2.** (*segundo vuelo*) second flight ▸**de ~** in passing

revuelta *f* **1.** (*tumulto*) disturbance **2.** (*rebelión*) revolt **3.** (*encorvadura*) bend; **carretera con muchas ~s** windy road **4.** (*cambio*) change

revuelto, **-a** **I.** *pp de* **revolver** **II.** *adj* **1.** (*agitado*) shaken **2.** (*desordenado*) chaotic **3.** (*tiempo*) unsettled **4.** (*irritado*) annoyed **5.** (*intrincado*) tangled **6.** (*huevos*) scrambled

revulsar *vt, vi Méx* (*vomitar*) to throw up

rey *m* king; **los Reyes** The King and Queen; **los Reyes Católicos** the Catholic Monarchs, Ferdinand and Isabella; **los Reyes Magos** the Magi, the Three Wise Men; **el día de Reyes** Epiphany, Twelfth Night ▸**lo mismo me da ~ que roque** it's all the same to me; **no temer ~ ni roque** to fear nothing and nobody; **a ~ muerto ~ puesto** off with the old, on with the new

reyerta *f* quarrel, fight

reyezuelo *m* goldcrest

rezagado, **-a** *m, f* straggler

rezagar <g→gu> **I.** *vt* **1.** (*dejar atrás*) to leave behind **2.** (*suspender*) to postpone **II.** *vr:* ~**se** to fall behind

rezar <z→c> **I.** *vt* ~ **por alguien** to pray for sb; ~ **una oración** to say a prayer **II.** *vi* **1.** (*decir*) to pray **2.** (*corresponder*) ~ **con algo** to apply to sth

rezo *m* **1.** (*el rezar*) praying **2.** (*oración*) prayer

rezongar <g→gu> *vi* to grumble

rezongón, **-ona** **I.** *adj inf* grumpy **II.** *m, f inf* grouch

rezumar *vi* **1.** (*filtrarse*) ~ **por algo** to ooze from sth; **el sudor le rezumaba por la frente** sweat beaded his/her forehead **2.** (*rebosar*) ~ **algo** to ooze with sth

RFA *f v.* **República Federal de Alemania** FRG

ría *f* **1.** GEO ≈ estuary, sea loch *Scot* **2.** DEP water break

riachuelo *m* stream

riada *f* flood

ribazo *m* steep bank

ribera *f* **1.** (*orilla*) bank **2.** (*tierra*) riverside **3.** (*vega*) fertile plain

ribete *m* **1.**(*galón*) trimming **2.**(*adorno*) adornment; (*de una narración*) embellishment **3.** *pl* (*indicios*) traces *pl*
ribetear *vt* to trim
ricamente *adv* **1.**(*con abundancia*) richly **2.**(*con placer*) splendidly
ricino *m* castor oil plant
rico, -a **I.** *adj* **1.**(*acaudalado*) rich; **es muy** ~ he/she is very rich **2.**(*sabroso*) delicious; **la comida está muy rica** the food is delicious **3.**(*abundante*) rich **4.**(*fructífero*) fertile **5.**(*excelente*) excellent **6.**(*simpático*) lovely, cute **II.** *m, f* **1.**(*rico*) rich person; **los ricos** the rich; **nuevo** ~ nouveau riche **2.** *inf*(*apelativo*) mate *Brit*
ricota *f Arg* GASTR ricotta cheese
ricura *f inf* **ser una** ~ to be adorable; **¡anda, ~!** come on, darling!
ridiculez *f* **1.**(*lo ridículo, nimiedad*) ridiculousness; **me pagan la ~ de tres dólares** I'm being paid the laughable sum of three dollars **2.**(*tontería*) stupidity
ridiculizar <z→c> *vt* to ridicule
ridículo, -a *adj* **1.**(*risorio*) ridiculous; **poner(se) en** ~ to make a fool of (oneself) **2.**(*tacaño*) stingy
riego *m* irrigation; ~ **sanguíneo** blood flow
riel *m* **1.** FERRO rail **2.**(*para cortinas*) bar; **los ~es de la cortina** the curtain rod
rienda *f* **1.**(*correa*) rein; **tener las ~s del poder** *fig* to hold the reins of power **2.** *pl* (*gobierno*) reins *pl* ►**a** ~ **suelta** *fig* wildly; **aflojar las ~s** to ease up; **dar** ~ **suelta a** to give free rein to; **llevar las ~s** to be in control; **tirar de la** ~ to pressurize *Brit,* to pressure *Am*
riesgo *m* risk; ~ **monetario** monetary risk; **a ~ de que...** +*subj* at the risk of ...; **a ~ y ventura de...** at the risk of ...; **por cuenta y ~ propios** at one's own risk and expense; **asumir un** ~ to assume a risk; **correr el ~ de...** to run the risk of ...; **estar asegurado a todo** ~ AUTO to have comprehensive insurance *Brit,* to have full coverage insurance; **exponer a un** ~ to expose to a risk; **exponerse a un** ~ to run a risk; ~ **profesional** occupational hazard
riesgoso, -a *adj AmL* **1.**(*arriesgado*) risky **2.**(*peligroso*) dangerous
rifa *f* **1.**(*sorteo*) raffle **2.**(*riña*) quarrel
rifar **I.** *vt* to raffle **II.** *vi* to quarrel
rifle *m* rifle
rigidez *f* **1.**(*inflexibilidad*) rigidity **2.**(*severidad*) strictness
rígido, -a *adj* **1.**(*inflexible*) rigid **2.**(*severo*) strict
rigor *m* **1.**(*severidad*) strictness **2.**(*exactitud*) rigorousness; **en** ~ strictly speaking **3.** METEO ~ **del invierno** depths of winter; ~ **del verano** height of summer ►**de** ~ de rigueur
riguroso, -a *adj* **1.**(*severo*) strict **2.**(*exacto*) rigorous **3.** METEO harsh
rija *f* (*riña*) quarrel
rijoso, -a *adj* **1.**(*lujurioso*) lustful; (*animal: macho*) in rut; (*hembra*) on heat **2.**(*pendenciero*) quarrelsome
rima *f* LIT rhyme; **tener** ~ to rhyme
rimar **I.** *vi* **1.**(*versificar*) to write poetry **2.**(*tener rima*) to rhyme **II.** *vt* to rhyme
rimbombante *adj* grandiloquent
rímel® *m* mascara
rin *m* **1.** *Ven* (*llanta*) rim **2.** *Perú* (*ficha telefónica*) telephone token
Rin *m* Rhine
rincón *m* **1.**(*esquina*) corner **2.**(*escondrijo, lugar tranquilo*) nook; **por todos los rincones** *fig* in every nook and cranny **3.** *inf* (*habitación*) room
rinconera *f* corner cupboard
ringlera *f* row
rinitis *f* MED rhinitis; ~ **alérgica** hay fever
rinoceronte *m* rhinoceros
riña *f* quarrel; ~ **de gallos** cockfight
riñón *m* **1.** ANAT kidney; **tener piedras en el** ~ to have kidney stones **2.** *pl* (*parte de la espalda*) lower back **3.** *fig* (*centro*) heart ►**tener el ~ bien cubierto** to be well off; **costar un** ~ to cost an arm and a leg; **tener riñones** to have guts
riñonera *f* **1.**(*faja*) cummerbund **2.**(*cinturón con bolsa*) bum bag *Brit, inf,* fanny pack *Am, inf*
río *m* river; ~ **abajo** downstream; ~ **arriba** upstream ►**tener un ~ de oro** to have a goldmine; **de perdidos al** ~ in for a penny, in for a pound, as well be hanged for a sheep as for a lamb; **pescar en ~ revuelto** to fish in troubled waters; **cuando el ~ suena, algo lleva** *prov* where there's smoke, there's fire
riojano, -a **I.** *adj* of/from La Rioja **II.** *m, f* native/inhabitant of La Rioja
rioplatense **I.** *adj* of/from the River Plate region **II.** *mf* native/inabitant of the River Plate region
ripio *m* **1.**(*cascajo*) rubble; **no valer un** ~ (*sin valor*) to be completely worthless; (*feo*) to be really ugly **2.**(*palabra inútil*) padding; **meter** ~ to waffle; **no perder** ~ not to miss a trick
riqueza *f* riches *pl*
risa *f* laughter; **digno de** ~ laughable; **estar muerto de** ~ to be laughing one's head off; **mondarse de** ~ to split one's sides laughing; **llorar de** ~ to laugh until one cries; **tener un ataque de** ~ to have a fit of the giggles; **tomar algo a** ~ to treat sth as a joke; **no quiero oír ~s a mis espaldas** I don't want any more laughing behind my back; **¡qué ~!** what a joke!; **no estoy para ~s** I'm in no mood for jokes
risco *m* crag
risotada *f* guffaw; **soltar una gran** ~ to guffaw
ríspido, -a *adj AmL* (*rudo*) coarse
ristra *f* **1.**(*trenza*) string; **una ~ de ajos/cebollas** a string of garlic/onions **2.** *inf* (*sarta*) string; **una ~ de mentiras** a string of lies
risueño, -a *adj* **1.**(*alegre*) smiling **2.**(*placentero*) pleasant **3.**(*próspero*) favourable *Brit,*

favorable *Am*

rítmico, -a *adj* rhythmic

ritmo *m* rhythm

rito *m* (*costumbre*) ritual; REL rite

ritual *adj, m* ritual

rival *adj, mf* rival

rivalidad *f* rivalry

rivalizar <z→c> *vi* ~ **por algo** to compete for sth

rizado, -a *adj* (*cabello*) curly

rizar <z→c> **I.** *vt* **1.** (*encrespar*) to curl **2.** (*plegar*) to crease **II.** *vr:* **~se** to curl

rizo *m* **1.** (*mechón*) curl; **rizar el ~** (*imponerse*) to win through; (*complicar*) to overcomplicate things **2.** (*tela*) velvet; **tela de ~** (*felpa*) terry towelling, terrycloth **3.** AVIAT loop; **rizar el ~** to loop the loop; *fig* to split hairs

rizo, -a *adj* curly

rizoma *m* rhizome

RNE *f abr de* **Radio Nacional de España** Spanish national radio network

robar *vt* **1.** (*hurtar: algo*) to steal; (*a alguien*) to rob; (*a alguien con violencia*) to mug; **me ~on en París** I was robbed in Paris; **me robó la novia** *inf* he stole my girlfriend; **esto roba mucho tiempo** this takes up a lot of time **2.** (*un río*) to carry away **3.** (*estafar*) to cheat **4.** (*en juegos*) to draw

robellón *m* yellow boletus

roble *m* oak; **estar como un ~** to be as fit as a fiddle

robo *m* **1.** (*hurto*) robbery; **~ con homicidio** theft and murder; **~ a mano armada** armed robbery; **~ con allanamiento** breaking and entering **2.** (*presa*) loot **3.** (*estafa*) swindle; **ser un ~** *fig* (*muy caro*) to be a rip-off; **¿20 libras? ¡qué ~!** twenty pounds? that's highway robbery!

robot <robots> *m* robot; **~ de cocina** food processor

robustecer *irr como crecer* **I.** *vt* to strengthen **II.** *vr:* **~se** to become strong

robusto, -a *adj* robust

roca *f* (*materia, peña*) rock; **ese hombre es una ~** that man is as solid as a rock

rocalla *f* stone chippings *pl*

roce *m* **1.** (*fricción*) brush **2.** (*huella*) scrape **3.** (*contacto*) contact; **tener mucho ~ con alguien** to have a lot of contact with sb **4.** (*pelea*) scrape

rochar *vt* **1.** AGR to clear ground **2.** *Chile* (*sorprender*) to catch red-handed

rochela *f Col, PRico, Ven* hullabaloo

rociar <*3. pres:* rocía> **I.** *vimpers* **ha rociado** dew has fallen **II.** *vt* **1.** (*regar*) to wash down **2.** (*esparcir*) to sprinkle

rocín *m* **1.** (*jamelgo*) nag; **ir de ~ a ruin** to go from bad to worse **2.** *inf* (*tosco*) lout

rocío *m* **1.** (*relente*) dew; **cae ~** dew is forming **2.** (*lluvia*) drizzle **3.** (*rociada*) sprinkling

rock **I.** *adj* rock; **grupo de música ~** rock group **II.** *m* MÚS rock

rockero, -a **I.** *adj* rock **II.** *m, f* (*fan*) rock fan; (*músico*) rock musician

rocoso, -a *adj* rocky; **Montañas Rocosas** Rocky Mountains, Rockies

rocote *m,* **rocoto** *m Bol, Ecua, Perú* (*pimiento*) (large) green pepper

rodaballo *m* turbot

rodada *f* wheel track

rodado, -a *adj* **1.** (*fluido*) smooth; **venir ~** (*sin dificultades*) to go smoothly; (*de perlas*) to come in very handy **2.** AUTO **tráfico ~** vehicular traffic **3.** (*caballo*) dappled

rodaja *f* **1.** (*rueda*) small wheel **2.** (*trozo*) slice

rodaje *m* **1.** CINE shooting **2.** (*rodar*) rolling; **cuando tengamos más ~** when we've got going **3.** (*impuesto*) road tax *Brit,* vehicle tax **4.** (*ruedas*) wheels *pl*

Ródano *m* Rhone

rodar <o→ue> **I.** *vi* **1.** (*dar vueltas, moverse sobre ruedas*) to roll; **~ por el suelo** to roll across the floor **2.** (*girar sobre el eje*) to turn **3.** (*deslizarse*) to slide **4.** (*abundar*) to abound **5.** (*ir*) to wander; **he rodado de tienda en tienda** I've wandered from shop to shop ▸**echarlo todo a ~** to spoil everything **II.** *vt* **1.** (*hacer dar vueltas*) to roll **2.** (*película*) to shoot **3.** (*coche*) to run in

rodear **I.** *vi* **1.** (*circunvalar*) to go round **2.** (*divagar*) to ramble **II.** *vt* **1.** (*cercar*) **~ de algo** to surround with sth **2.** (*hacer dar vueltas*) to turn **3.** (*un tema*) to avoid **III.** *vr* **~se de algo/alguien** to surround oneself with sth/sb

rodeo *m* **1.** (*desvío*) detour; **dar un ~** to take a detour; **conseguir algo con ~s** to achieve sth in a roundabout manner **2.** (*evasiva*) evasion **3.** DEP rodeo ▸**andar(se) con ~s** to beat about the bush; **dejarse de ~s** stop beating about the bush; **sin ~s** without beating about the bush

rodilla *f* **1.** ANAT knee; **de ~s** on one's knees; **ponerse de ~s** to kneel **2.** (*paño*) cloth

rodillera *f* **1.** (*protección*) kneepad **2.** (*del pantalón*) knee patch; **para que no salgan ~s al pantalón** so that the trousers don't go baggy at the knees

rodillo *m* **1.** TÉC roller **2.** (*de cocina*) rolling pin

roedor *m* rodent

roer *irr vt* **1.** (*ratonar*) **~ algo** to gnaw at sth; **los ratones royeron mi libro** the mice gnawed my book; **~se las uñas** to bite one's nails **2.** (*concomer*) **las preocupaciones me roen el alma** I'm worrying my life away

rogar <o→ue> *vt* to request; (*con humildad*) to beg; JUR to plead; **rogamos nos contesten inmediatamente nuestra carta** we would be grateful if you could give us an immediate reply; **¡te ruego que me escuches!** I beg you to listen to me!; **le gusta hacerse de ~** he/she likes playing hard to get

rojez *f* redness

rojizo, -a *adj* reddish

rojo, -a *adj* red; (*persona*) red-headed; **~ chi-**

llón/subido bright/deep red; ~ **burdeos** maroon ▶**al** ~ (vivo) red-hot; *fig* at fever pitch; **poner** ~ **a alguien** to make sb blush; **ponerse** ~ to go red
rol *m* **1.** (*papel*) role; **desempeñar un** ~ to play a role **2.** (*lista*) list; ~ **de pago** payroll
rollito *m* ~ **de primavera** GASTR spring roll, egg roll *Am*
rollizo, **-a** *adj* **1.** (*robusto*) plump **2.** (*cilíndrico*) round
rollo *m* **1.** *t.* FOTO (*de papel, alambre*) roll; **hacer un** ~ **de algo** to roll sth up **2.** *inf* (*cosa aburrida*) bore; **¡qué** ~ **de película!** what a boring film!; **soltar siempre el mismo** ~ to always come out with the same old stuff **3.** *inf* (*tipo de vida*) lifestyle; (*asunto*) affair; **montarse el** ~ to organize one's life; **ir a su** ~ to do as one likes; **tener mucho** ~ to be full of crap *inf;* **traerse un mal** ~ to be in a mess; **acaba con el** ~**, muchacho** get on with it, son; **corta el** ~ (*palabrería, mentiras*) cut the crap *inf;* **¿de qué va el** ~**?** what's it all about? **4.** (*del cuerpo*) roll (of fat) **5.** GASTR roll; **este niño está hecho un** ~ **de manteca** this child is a picture of health
Roma *f* Rome ▶**revolver** ~ **con Santiago para conseguir algo** to move heaven and earth to achieve sth
romana *f* scales *pl*
romance **I.** *adj* LING Romance **II.** *m* **1.** *t.* LIT (*aventura*) romance; ~ **de ciego** popular ballad; **tiene un** ~ **con la vecina** he's having an affair with his neighbour *Brit* [*o* neighbor *Am*] **2.** HIST (*castellano*) Castilian; **hablar en** ~ *fig* to speak plainly
románico, **-a** *adj* Romanesque
romanista *mf* Romanist
romano, **-a** **I.** *adj* **1.** (*de Roma*) Roman **2.** REL Roman Catholic **3.** (*latín*) Latin **II.** *m, f* (*de Roma*) Roman
romanticismo *m sin pl* romanticism; (*movimiento*) Romanticism
romántico, **-a** *adj, m, f* romantic
romaza *f* sorrel
rombal *adj* rhombic
rombo *m* rhombus; **en forma de** ~ diamond-shaped
romería *f* **1.** (*peregrinaje*) pilgrimage **2.** (*fiesta*) festival **3.** (*muchedumbre*) throng
romerito *m Méx* vegetables *pl*
romero *m* rosemary
romero, **-a** *adj, m, f* pilgrim
romo, **-a** *adj* **1.** (*sin punta*) blunt **2.** (*de nariz pequeña*) snub-nosed **3.** (*tosco*) coarse
rompecabezas *m inv* (*juego*) brainteaser; (*acertijo*) riddle
rompehielos *m inv* NÁUT icebreaker
rompehuelgas *mf inv* strikebreaker
rompeolas *m inv* breakwater
romper **I.** *vi* **1.** (*las olas*) to break **2.** (*empezar bruscamente*) to burst; ~ **a llorar** to burst into tears **3.** (*el día*) to break; **al** ~ **el día** at the break of day **4.** (*separarse*) to break up **II.** *vt* **1.** (*destrozar, quebrar*) to break; (*un cristal*) to shatter; (*un plato*) to smash; (*papel, tela*) to tear; (*los zapatos*) to wear out; (*un terreno*) to plough; ~ **algo a martillazos** to smash sth with a hammer; ~ **algo a golpes** to bash sth to pieces; ~ **algo doblando** to bend sth until it breaks; ~ **una ventana a pedradas** to break a window by throwing stones at it **2.** (*negociaciones, relaciones*) to break off; (*contrato, promesa*) to break; ~ **el silencio/el encanto** to break the silence/the spell; ~ **el hilo del discurso** to interrupt the speech; ~ **(las) filas** MIL to break ranks **3.** (*iniciar*) ~ **el fuego** to open fire; **los pájaros rompen vuelo** the birds take to flight ▶**de rompe y rasga** determined; **una persona de rompe y rasga** a very determined person **III.** *vr:* ~**se** **1.** (*hacerse pedazos*) to break **2.** (*fracturarse*) to break; ~**se la pierna** to break one's leg; ~**se la cabeza** *fig* to rack one's brains ▶**¿qué tripa se te ha roto?** *inf* what are you so upset about?
rompiente *m* reef
rompimiento *m* (*rotura*) breaking; (*de negociaciones, relaciones*) breakdown
rompope *m AmC, Ecua, Méx* GASTR eggnog
ron *m* rum
roncar <c→qu> *vi* (*persona*) to snore; (*gamo*) to bellow; (*viento*) to howl; (*olas*) to roar; (*suelo*) to creak
roncear *vt Arg, Chile, Méx* to move by levering
roncha *f* **1.** (*hinchazón*) swilling; (*cardenal*) bruise; (*picadura*) sting **2.** (*loncha*) slice; **una** ~ **de chorizo** a slice of sausage
ronco, **-a** *adj* (*afónico*) voiceless; (*áspero*) hoarse
roncón, **-ona** *m, f Col, Ven* bragging
ronda *f* **1.** (*de vigilancia*) round; **hacer una** ~ **de inspección por la fábrica** to do an inspection tour of the factory **2.** (*de copas*) round; **pagar una** ~ to buy a round **3.** POL round (*of voting*) **4.** (*jóvenes*) group of serenaders; (*serenata*) serenade; **andar de** ~ (*tocar música*) to go serenading; (*buscar aventura*) to go courting **5.** (*avenida*) ring road *Brit,* beltway *Am*
rondalla *f* **1.** (*música*) street music **2.** (*conjunto musical*) street musicians
rondar **I.** *vi* **1.** (*vigilar*) to be on patrol **2.** (*andar paseando de noche*) to prowl about **II.** *vt* **1.** (*a las mujeres*) to court **2.** (*rodear*) to surround; **las mariposas nocturnas rondan la luz** moths are drawn to the light; **lo ronda a todas horas para conseguir el empleo** he/she pesters him night and day to try and get the job; **anda rondando los setenta años** he/she is about seventy years old
rondín *m* **1.** *Bol, Ecua, Perú* (*armónica*) harmonica **2.** *Bol, Chile* (*vigilante*) watchman
ronquera *f* hoarseness
ronquido *m* (*de una persona*) snore; (*del viento*) howl; (*del mar*) roar; (*de la sierra*) buzz; (*del suelo*) creak; (*del gamo*) bellow
ronronear *vi* (*gato*) to purr

ronzar <z→c> **I.** *vi* to crunch **II.** *vt* (*mascar*) to crunch

roña *f* **1.** (*mugre*) filth **2.** (*mezquindad*) meanness; (*tacañería*) stinginess **3.** (*orín*) rust **4.** (*sarna de carneros*) scab

roñería *f* **1.** (*mezquindad*) meanness **2.** (*tacañería*) stinginess

roñoso, **-a** *adj* **1.** (*tacaño*) mean, tight **2.** (*sucio*) filthy **3.** (*sarnoso*) scabby **4.** (*oxidado*) rusty

ropa *f* **1.** (*géneros de tela*) ~ **blanca** white wash *pl*, whites *Brit*; ~ **de color** colored wash *pl*, coloureds *Brit*; ~ **delicada** delicates *pl*; ~ (**interior**) underwear; **cambiar la ~ de cama** to change the bedclothes **2.** (*vestidos, traje*) clothes *pl*; **~s hechas** ready-made clothes; **cambiar(se) la ~** to change one's clothes; **estar en ~s menores** to be in one's underwear; **poner(se) la ~** to get dressed; **ponerse ~ de abrigo** to put on warm clothing; **ligero de ~** lightly dressed ►**de buena ~** of good family; **de poca ~** insignificant; **a quema ~** point-blank; **disparar a quema ~** to shoot at close range; **¡cuidado que hay ~ tendida!** be careful what you say!; **no tocar la ~ a alguien** not to touch a hair of sb's head

ropaje *m* **1.** (*ropas*) clothing **2.** (*ropa elegante*) finery

ropero *m* **1.** (*armario*) wardrobe **2.** (*asociación benéfica*) *charity which distributes clothing*

roque *m* **1.** (*ajedrez*) rook, castle **2.** (*dormido*) **quedarse ~** to fall fast asleep

roqueño, **-a** *adj* **1.** (*rocoso*) rocky **2.** (*duro*) rock hard

roquero, **-a I.** *adj* **1.** (*de rocas*) rocky; **castillo ~** mountain castle **2.** MÚS rock **II.** *m, f* (*fan*) rock fan; (*músico*) rock musician

rosa I. *adj* pink **II.** *f* BOT rose; ~ **de azafrán** saffron crocus; **color de ~** pink; **esencia de ~s** rose essence ►**no hay ~ sin espinas** *prov* every rose has its thorn *prov*; ~ **náutica** compass rose

rosáceo, **-a** *adj* rosy

rosado, **-a** *adj* (*color*) pink; **vino ~** rosé (wine)

rosal *m* rosebush

rosaleda *f* rose garden

rosario *m* **1.** REL rosary; **rezar el ~** to say the rosary **2.** (*serie*) string; **un ~ de coches/de injurias** a string of cars/of insults ►**acabar como el ~ de la aurora** to end in confusion; **tener el ~ al cuello y el diablo en el cuerpo** to be a complete hypocrite

rosbif <rosbifs> *m* roast beef

rosca *f* **1.** TÉC thread; **el tornillo se pasó de ~** the screw broke the thread **2.** (*forma de espiral*) coil; **hecho una ~** rolled up into a ball; **hacerse ~** (*gato, serpiente*) to roll up into a ball **3.** (*forma de anillo*) ring; (*bollo*) (ring-shaped) bread roll; (*torta*) sponge ring; ~ **de Reyes** *Méx* Christmas cake eaten on Epiphany ►**no comerse una ~** not to get off with anyone; **hacer la ~ a alguien** to suck up to sb; **pasarse de ~** to go too far; **tirarse una ~** to fail

rosco *m* (ring-shaped) bread roll; ~ **de viento** *type of doughnut*

roscón *m* sponge ring; ~ **de Reyes** Christmas cake eaten on Epiphany

rosedal *m Arg, Urug* BOT rosebed

rosetón *m* ARQUIT rose window

rosquete *adj, m Perú, vulg* queer

rosquilla *f* doughnut ►**venderse como ~s** to sell like hot cakes

rosticería *f Chile, Méx: shop that sells roast chicken, beef and other dishes*

rostro *m* **1.** (*cara*) face **2.** (*pico*) beak ►**tener mucho ~** to have a lot of nerve

rotación *f* rotation; ~ **de cultivos** AGR crop rotation; ~ **del capital** capital movement; ~ **de mercancías** stock turnover

rotativo *m* newspaper

rotativo, **-a** *adj* rotary; **impresión rotativa** TIPO rotary printing

rotatorio, **-a** *adj* rotating

rotería *f Chile* **1.** (*acción*) inconsiderate act **2.** (*plebe*) the masses, rabble *pej*

rotisería *f Arg: shop that sells roast chicken, beef and other dishes*

roto *m* (*desgarrón*) tear; (*agujero*) hole

roto, **-a I.** *pp de* **romper II.** *adj* **1.** (*despedazado*) broken; **un vestido ~** a torn dress; **un florero/un cristal ~** a broken vase/glass **2.** (*andrajoso*) wretched **3.** (*licencioso*) debauched **4.** (*destrozado*) destroyed

rotonda *f* AUTO roundabout *Brit*, traffic circle *Am*

rotoso, **-a I.** *adj AmL* tattered **II.** *m, f* wretch

rótula *f* **1.** ANAT knee joint **2.** TÉC ball-and-socket joint

rotulador *m* felt-tip pen

rotuladora *f* labelling *Brit* [*o* labeling *Am*] machine

rotular *vt* (*letreros*) to make; (*mercancías*) to label; CINE to subtitle

rótulo *m* sign; (*encabezamiento*) heading; (*etiqueta*) ticket; (*letrero*) sign; (*anuncio público*) notice; CINE subtitle; ~ **de población** town sign

rotundamente *adv* **1.** (*sin rodeos*) directly **2.** (*terminantemente*) emphatically; **negar ~** to flatly deny

rotundo, **-a** *adj* **1.** (*terminante*) emphatic; **un éxito ~** a resounding success; **una negativa rotunda** a flat refusal **2.** (*lleno y sonoro*) sonorous; **palabras rotundas** resounding words

rotura *f* (*acción*) breaking; (*parte quebrada*) break; ~ **de hueso** fracture; ~ **de ligamento** torn ligament

roturar *vt* AGR to plough *Brit*, to plow *Am*

rouge *m Arg, Chile* (*colorete*) blusher, rouge

roya *f* rust

roza *f*, **rozado** *m Arg* AGR cleared ground

rozadura *f* scratch; (*de la piel*) graze

rozamiento *m* **1.** (*fricción*) rubbing **2.** (*roce*) brush **3.** (*desavenencias*) friction

rozar <z→c> **I.** *vi* to rub; **rozar (por) los cincuenta** *fig* to be pushing fifty **II.** *vt* **1.** *t. fig* (*tocar ligeramente*) to brush; ~ **la ridiculez** *fig* to border on the ridiculous **2.** (*frotar*) to rub **3.** AGR to clear; (*animales*) to graze **III.** *vr:* **~se 1.** (*restregarse*) to rub **2.** (*relacionarse*) to rub shoulders

rte. *abr de* **remitente** sender

RTVE *f abr de* **Radio Televisión Española** Spanish state broadcasting corporation

rúa *f* street

ruana *f AmS* (*poncho*) poncho

rubéola *f sin pl* MED German measles

rubí *m* MIN ruby

rubicundo, **-a** *adj* **1.** (*pelo*) reddish **2.** (*rostro*) ruddy

rubio, **-a I.** *adj* fair; **tabaco** ~ Virginia tobacco **II.** *m, f* blond; (*mujer*) blonde

rublo *m* (*moneda*) rouble

rubor *m* **1.** (*color*) bright red; (*de vergüenza*) blush **2.** (*vergüenza*) shame; (*bochorno*) embarrassment; **lo confieso con el ~ de mi cara** my blushing face leaves me no choice but to confess; **el ~ le quema la cara** he has turned red with shame/embarrassment

ruborizado, **-a** *adj* blushing

ruborizar <z→c> **I.** *vt* to cause to blush **II.** *vr:* **~se** to blush

ruboroso, **-a** *adj* **1.** (*vergonzoso*) ashamed; (*de bochorno*) embarrassed **2.** (*ruborizado*) blushing

rúbrica *f* **1.** (*firma*) signature; (*después del nombre*) flourish **2.** (*epígrafe*) heading

rubricar <c→qu> *vt* **1.** (*firmar*) to sign; (*ratificar*) to endorse **2.** (*sellar*) to seal

rubro *m AmL* **1.** (*título*) heading, title **2.** COM (*asiento, partida*) area

ruca *f Arg, Chile* (*choza*) shack

rucio, **-a** *adj* (*animales*) grey *Brit,* gray *Am;* **caballo ~** grey

ruco, **-a** *adj AmC* old

rudeza *f* **1.** (*brusquedad*) rudeness **2.** (*tosquedad*) coarseness **3.** (*torpeza*) stupidity

rudimentario, **-a** *adj* rudimentary

rudo, **-a** *adj* **1.** (*material*) rough; (*sin trabajar*) raw **2.** (*persona tosca*) coarse; (*brusca*) rude; (*torpe*) clumsy; (*poco inteligente*) stupid **3.** (*penoso*) harsh

rueda *f* **1.** (*que gira*) wheel; (*de mueble*) castor; **~ de aspas** wheel (*of windmill*)*;* **~ de paletas** paddle wheel; **~ de repuesto** spare tyre; **vapor de ~s** paddle steamer; **hacer la ~** DEP to do a cartwheel; **el pavo hace la ~** the peacock spreads its tail; **hacer la ~ a una mujer** to court a woman **2.** (*de personas*) ring; **~ de prensa** press conference; **~ de identificación** (*sospechosos*) police line-up **3.** (*rodaja*) slice; **una ~ de salami** a slice of salami **4.** (*orden sucesivo*) ring ►**comulgar con ~s de molino** to be very gullible; **todo marcha sobre ~s** everything is going smoothly

ruedo *m* **1.** (*contorno*) ring **2.** (*borde*) edge; (*del vestido*) hem **3.** TAUR bullring **4.** (*estera*) (round) mat ►**echarse al ~** to enter the fray

ruego *m* request ►**~s y preguntas** POL any other business; **no valen ~s ni súplicas** there is no point pleading

rufián *m* **1.** (*chulo*) pimp **2.** (*granuja*) scoundrel

rugby *m* DEP rugby

rugido *m* **1.** (*del león*) roar **2.** (*del viento*) howl **3.** (*de las tripas*) rumble

rugir <g→j> **I.** *vi* **1.** (*león*) to roar; (*viento*) to howl **2.** (*estómago*) to rumble, to growl; **sus tripas rugen** his/her stomach is rumbling **3.** (*persona*) **este hombre está que ruge** this man is beside himself with rage **II.** *vimpers* to become known; **rugía que…** it became known that …

rugoso, **-a** *adj* **1.** (*arrugado*) wrinkled **2.** (*áspero*) rough **3.** (*ondulado*) wavy

ruibarbo *m* rhubarb

ruido *m* **1.** (*sonido*) *t.* ELEC noise; **~s parásitos** interference, static **2.** (*estrépito*) noise; **nivel de ~** noise level; **~ de fondo** background noise ►**mucho ~ y pocas nueces** much ado about nothing; **hacer ~** to cause a stir; **querer ~** to be looking for trouble; **quitarse de ~s** to keep out of trouble

ruidoso, **-a** *adj* noisy; *fig* sensational; **una carcajada ruidosa** a loud guffaw

ruin *adj* **1.** (*malvado*) wicked; (*vil*) despicable **2.** (*tacaño*) mean

ruina *f* **1.** (*destrucción*) destruction; **este hombre está hecho una ~** *fig* this man is a wreck **2.** ARQUIT ruin; **las ~s de un castillo** the ruins of a castle **3.** *pl* (*escombros*) ruins *pl;* **convertir una ciudad en ~s** to raze a city to the ground; **declarar una casa en ~s** to condemn a house **4.** (*perdición*) downfall; **causar la ~ de alguien** to cause sb's downfall; **estar en la ~** to be bankrupt; **salvar a alguien de la ~** to save sb from disaster

ruindad *f* **1.** (*maldad*) wickedness **2.** (*tacañería*) meanness

ruinoso, **-a** *adj* **1.** (*edificios*) dilapidated **2.** (*perjudicial*) disastrous; ECON ruinous

ruiseñor *m* nightingale

rulenco, **-a** *adj Chile* weak; (*raquítico*) stunted

rulero *m AmS* hair curler, roller

ruleta *f* (*juego*) roulette

ruletear *vi AmC, Méx* (*conducir un taxi*) to drive a taxi

ruletero, **-a** *m, f AmC, Méx* (*conductor*) taxi driver

rulo *m* **1.** (*del cabello*) curl **2.** (*rizador*) *t.* TÉC roller

rulota *f* (*caravana*) caravan *Brit,* trailer *Am*

ruma *f AmS* (*montón*) **una ~ de…** a pile of …; **~s de…** lots of …

Rumania *f,* **Rumanía** *f* Romania

rumano, **-a** *adj, m, f* Romanian

rumba *f* MÚS rumba

rumbo *m* **1.** (*dirección*) direction; *t. fig* AVIAT, NÁUT course; **tomar ~ a un puerto** to head for a port; **con ~ a** bound [*o* headed] for; **dar otro ~ a la conversación** to change the topic of the conversation; **no tengo ~ fijo** I'm not going anywhere in particular; **la negociación está tomando un ~ favorable** the negotiation is taking a turn for the better; **tomar otro ~** POL to change course **2.** (*pompa*) lavishness; **de ~** lavish; **una fiesta con mucho ~** a spectacular party

rumboso, -a *adj* **1.** (*generoso*) generous **2.** (*pomposo*) lavish

rumiante *m* ruminant

rumiar *vt* **1.** (*vacas*) to ruminate **2.** *inf* (*cavilar*) to think over **3.** *inf* (*refunfuñar*) to grumble about

rumor *m* **1.** (*chisme*) rumour *Brit,* rumor *Am;* **a título de ~** as a rumour *Brit* [*o* rumor *Am*]; **poner un ~ en circulación** to spread a rumour *Brit,* to start a rumor (going) *Am;* **corren ~es de que...** it is rumoured that ... **2.** (*ruido*) murmur; (*del viento*) whistle; (*del bosque*) rustle; **~ de voces** buzz of conversation

rumorearse *vr* **se rumorea que...** it is rumoured *Brit* [*o* rumored *Am*] that ...

rumoroso, -a *adj* murmuring; (*viento*) whistling; (*bosque*) rustling

runa *f* rune

runcho *m Col* ZOOL opossum

rundún *m Arg* **1.** (*pájaro mosca*) tiny hummingbird **2.** (*juguete*) bull-roarer

runrún *m inf* **1.** (*ruido*) buzz; (*murmullo*) murmur **2.** (*chisme*) rumour *Brit,* rumor *Am*

rupestre *adj* rock; **pintura ~** cave painting

rupia *f* (*moneda*) rupee

ruptura *f* breaking; (*de relaciones*) breaking-off

rural **I.** *adj* rural; **vida ~** country life **II.** *m* **1.** *AmL, t. pey* (*rústico*) yokel **2.** *pl, Méx* (*policía*) rural police

Rusia *f* Russia

ruso, -a **I.** *adj* Russian; **ensaladilla rusa** Russian salad (*potato salad with carrots, eggs and tuna*)*;* **filete ~** breaded hamburger steak **II.** *m, f* Russian

rústico, -a **I.** *adj* **1.** (*campestre*) rural; **finca rústica** farmhouse **2.** (*tosco*) rough; **en rústica** TIPO paperback **II.** *m, f* peasant; *pey* yokel

rustidera *f* roasting pan

ruta *f* **1.** (*camino*) route; **~ federal** *AmL* federal highway *Am;* **~ de itinerario** itinerary; **~ de vuelo** flight path **2.** (*conducta*) **tienes que cambiar de ~** you'll have to change your ways

rutina *f* **1.** (*costumbre*) routine; **~ cotidiana** daily routine **2.** INFOR routine

rutinario, -a *adj* routine; **un hombre ~** (*de costumbres*) a man of habit; (*aburrido*) an unimaginative man

S

S, s *f* S, s; **~ de Soria** S for Sugar

S. *abr de* **San** St

S.A. *f* **1.** *abr de* **Sociedad Anónima** plc **2.** *abr de* **Su Alteza** Your Highness

sábado *m* **1.** (*día*) Saturday; *v.t.* **lunes** **2.** (*judaísmo*) sabbath

sabana *f* savanna(h)

sábana *f* sheet; **~ ajustable** fitted sheet; **~ encimera/bajera** top/bottom sheet; **se me han pegado las ~s** *inf* I've overslept

sabandija *f* **1.** (*insecto*) bug **2.** *pey* (*persona*) wretch; **¡qué ~s!** little wretches!

sabanear *vi AmL* to ride the plains

sabañón *m* chilblain; **comer como un ~** *inf* to eat like a horse

sabático, -a *adj* **1.** (*judaísmo*) sabbatical **2.** (*universidad*) **un año ~** a sabbatical year

sabelotodo *mf inv, inf* know-all *Brit,* know-it--all *Am*

saber *irr* **I.** *vt* **1.** (*estar informado*) to know; **¿se puede ~ si... ?** could you tell me if ...?; **¿se puede ~ dónde/cómo/quién...?** can sb tell me where/how/who ...?; **sin ~lo yo** without my knowing; **se sabe que...** it is known that ...; **¡cualquiera sabe!** who knows?; **vete tú/vaya usted a ~** it's anyone's guess; **¡véte tu a ~ si es cierto!** your guess is as good as mine!; **(al menos) que yo sepa** as far as I know; **para que lo sepas** for your information; **¡pues no sé qué te diga!** I wouldn't be so sure!; **tener (un) no sé qué de raro** to have sth strange about one; **¡no sé ni por dónde ando!** *inf* I don't know whether I'm coming or going!; **¡y qué sé yo!** how should I know! **2.** (*tener habilidad*) **él sabe (hablar) ruso** he can speak Russian; **no ~(se) la poesía** not to know the poem by heart **3.** (*conocer*) to know; **¿sabes mi nombre?** do you know my name?; **~ de algo** to know about sth; **~ mucho de literatura** to know a lot about literature **4.** (*noticia*) to find out; **lo supe por mi hermano** I heard about it from my brother; **lo supe por el periódico** I read it in the papers; **la prensa hizo ~ anoche la noticia** the papers gave out the news last night; **¡va a ~ quién soy yo!** he/she will find out who he/she is dealing with! ▶**a** ~ namely **II.** *vi* **1.** (*tener sabor*) **~ a algo** to taste of sth; **sabe mal** it tastes bad; **(me) supo a quemado** it tasted burnt; **sabe a traición** it sounds like treachery; **~ a gloria** to taste [*o* be] divine; **~ a cuerno quemado** to be fishy **2.** (*agradar*) **la conferencia me supo a poco** the conference was really good but it should have been longer; **me supo mal aquella respuesta** that reply upset me **3.** (*tener noticia*) to have news; **no sé nada de mi hermano** I have no news of my brother **4.** (*tener la habilidad*) **~ de algo** to know how to do sth; **él no sabe resolver ni los ejercicios**

más fáciles he can't do even the simplest exercises **III.** *vr* **sabérselas todas** *inf* she knows all the tricks **IV.** *m sin pl* knowledge ►**el ~ no ocupa lugar** *prov* you can't know too much

sabichoso, -a *adj Cuba, PRico* pedantic; (*sabiondo*) know-all *Brit,* know-it-all *Am*

sabido, -a *adj* **1.** (*conocido*) known; **es cosa sabida** it's well known; **dar por ~** to take for granted **2.** (*leído*) learned

sabiduría *f* **1.** (*conocimientos*) knowledge **2.** (*sensatez*) wisdom **3.** (*erudición*) learning

sabiendas a ~ knowingly; **lo hizo a ~ de que me molestaba** he/she did it knowing full well that it annoyed me

sabihondo, -a *m, f* know-all *Brit,* know-it-all *Am;* (*niño*) smart-aleck, smarty pants

sabio, -a I. *adj* wise **II.** *m, f* scholar ►**errar es de ~s** *prov* to err is human

sabiondo, -a *m, f v.* **sabihondo**

sablazo *m* **1.** (*golpe*) sable stroke; (*herida*) sable wound **2.** *inf* **dar a alguien un ~** to sponge off sb

sable *m* sabre *Brit,* saber *Am*

sablear *vi inf* to scrounge

sabor *m* taste; **tiene (un) ~ a naranja** it tastes of orange; **de ~ romántico** with a romantic flavour *Brit* [*o* flavor *Am*]; **dejar un mal ~ de boca** to leave a nasty taste in the mouth

saborear *vt* to savour *Brit,* to savor *Am;* (*triunfo*) to relish

sabotaje *m* sabotage

sabotear *vt* to sabotage

sabroso, -a *adj* **1.** (*sazonado*) tasty **2.** (*gracioso*) racy **3.** (*salado*) slightly salty

sabueso *m* **1.** ZOOL bloodhound **2.** *fig* sleuth

saca *f* **1.** (*saco*) sack; **~ de correos** mailbag **2.** (*extracción*) withdrawal **3.** (*exportación*) export **4.** (*copia*) authorized copy

sacabocados *m inv* TÉC punch; (*papel, billete*) hole [*o* ticket] punch

sacabuche *m* **1.** MÚS sackbut **2.** NÁUT hand pump **3.** *Méx* (*navaja*) pointed knife

sacacorchos *m inv* corkscrew

sacamanchas *m inv* stain remover

sacamuelas *mf inf* dentist

sacapuntas *m inv* pencil sharpener

sacar <c→qu> **I.** *vt* **1.** (*de un sitio*) to take out, to remove; (*agua, espada*) to draw; (*diente*) to pull (out); **~ a bailar** to invite to dance; **~ a alguien de la cama/de la cárcel** to get sb out of bed/of jail; **~ a pasear** to take out for a walk; **sácalo del garage** take it out of the garage; **saca las plantas al balcón** put the plants out on the balcony; **¿de dónde lo has sacado?** where did you get it from?; **recién sacado del horno** freshly baked; **¡te voy a ~ los ojos!** *fig* I'll teach you (to do that)! **2.** (*de una situación*) to get; **~ adelante** (*persona*) to look after; (*negocio*) to run; (*niño*) to bring up; **~ a alguien del atolladero** to get sb out of a jam; **~ a alguien de la pobreza** to rescue sb from poverty **3.** (*solucionar*) to solve **4.** (*reconocer*) to recognize **5.** (*entrada*) to get **6.** (*obtener*) to obtain; (*premio, votos*) to get; **~ las consecuencias** to come to conclusions; **~ en claro (de)** to gather (from); **no ~ ni para vivir** not to make enough to live on; **~ a alguien 10 euros** to get 10 euros off sb **7.** MIN to extract **8.** (*parte del cuerpo*) to stick out **9.** *inf* (*foto*) to take; (*dibujo*) to do; **¡sácame una foto!** take a photo of me!; **el pintor te sacó muy bien** the painter got a good likeness of you **10.** (*mancha*) to remove **11.** (*producto*) to bring out; **~ a la venta** to put on sale [*o* the market]; (*libro*) to publish; **~ un apodo a alguien** to give sb a nickname **12.** (*mostrar*) to show; (*desenterrar*) to unearth; **~ en hombros** to carry out shoulder-high; **~ algo a relucir** to bring out the dirty linen **13.** (*ventaja*) **el ganador me sacó dos minutos** the winner was two minutes quicker than me; **mi hermana me saca tres años** my sister is three years older than I am **II.** *vi* (*tenis*) to serve; (*fútbol: portero*) to take a goal kick; (*fútbol: saque de banda*) to take a throw-in **III.** *vr* **se sacó una pestaña del ojo** he/she took an eyelash out of his/her eye

sacarina *f sin pl* saccharin

sacerdote *m* priest

sacho *m* **1.** (*para sachar*) weeder **2.** *Chile* (*ancla*) anchor

saciado, -a *adj* satiated

saciar I. *vt* (*hambre, curiosidad*) to satisfy; (*instintos sexuales*) to satiate; (*sed*) to quench **II.** *vr:* **~se** *t. fig* to satiate oneself; **me sacié de salchichas** I ate my fill of sausages

saciedad *f sin pl* satiation; **repetir hasta la ~** to repeat over and over

saco *m* **1.** (*bolsa*) bag; (*costal*) sack; **~ de trigo** sack of wheat; **~ de dormir** sleeping bag **2.** (*prenda*) jacket **3.** (*saqueo*) sacking; **entrar a ~** to loot **4.** DEP (*boxeo*) punchball *Brit,* punching bag *Am* ►**en el mismo ~** in the same boat; **caer en ~ roto** to fall on deaf ears; **no echar algo en ~ roto** to take note of sth

sacón, -ona *m, f Méx, inf* (*miedica*) chicken

sacramento *m* sacrament; **el ~ de la Eucaristía** the Blessed Sacrament; **administrar a alguien los últimos ~s** to give sb the last rites; **con todos los ~s** *fig* without forgetting anything

sacrificar <c→qu> **I.** *vt* **1.** (*ofrecer*) to sacrifice; *t. fig* to give up **2.** (*animal*) to slaughter **II.** *vr* **~se por algo/alguien** to sacrifice oneself for sth/sb

sacrificio *m* sacrifice; **el Santo Sacrificio** Holy Communion

sacrilegio *m* sacrilege

sacrílego, -a *adj* sacrilegious; **acción sacrílega** act of sacrilege

sacristán *m* sacristan ►**¡ése es un buen ~!** *inf* he's a right one!

sacristía *f* vestry, sacristy

sacro, -a *adj* **1.** (*sagrado*) sacred **2.** ANAT **hueso ~** sacrum

sacrosanto, **-a** *adj* most holy; *fig* sacrosanct

sacudida *f* shake; ~ **eléctrica** electric shock; ~ **sísmica** earthquake; **el coche pegaba ~s** the car was jolting; **dale una ~ a la alfombra** shake the carpet [*o* rug]

sacudir **I.** *vt* **1.** (*agitar*) to shake; (*moscas*) to brush off; ~ **el rabo** to swish its tail; ~ **a alguien por los hombros** to shake sb by the shoulders; **un estremecimiento le sacudió todo el cuerpo** a shiver ran all through his/her body **2.** (*pegar*) to belt **II.** *vr:* **~se** to shake oneself; **~se la duda** to dispel the doubt; **~se el yugo** to shake off the yoke; **~se a alguien de encima** *fig* to get rid of sb

sádico, **-a** **I.** *adj* sadistic **II.** *m, f* sadist

sadismo *m sin pl* sadism

sadomasoquismo *m sin pl* sadomasochism

sadomasoquista **I.** *adj* sadomasochistic **II.** *mf* sadomasochist

saeta *f* **1.** (*flecha*) arrow **2.** (*reloj*) hand; (*brújula*) magnetic needle **3.** MÚS *pious song in flamenco style typically sung in the religious processions in Spain during Easter week*

safari *m* safari

sagacidad *f sin pl* astuteness

sagaz *adj* astute

Sagitario *m* Sagittarius

sagrado, **-a** <sacratísimo> *adj* sacred

sagrario *m* (*para las hostias*) tabernacle

sagú *m AmC* **1.** (*planta*) arrowroot **2.** (*harina*) sago starch

Sáhara *m* **el** ~ the Sahara

sahumar *vt* (*incienso*) to perfume; (*humo*) to smoke

sahumerio *m* smoking

sainete *m* **1.** TEAT one-act farce **2.** (*comida*) titbit

sajón, **-ona** *adj, m, f* Saxon

Sajonia *f* Saxony; **Baja** ~ Lower Saxony

sal *f* **1.** (*condimento*) salt; ~ **común** table salt; **poner demasiada ~ a algo** to put too much salt in sth; ~ **marina** sea [*o* bay] salt; ~ **gorda** coarse [*o* rock] salt **2.** *pl* (*perfume*) smelling salts *pl;* **~es de baño** bath salts **3.** (*gracia*) wit; (*encanto*) charm; **la ~ de la vida** the spice of life **4.** *AmL* (*mala suerte*) bad luck ►**tener poca ~ en la mollera** *inf* to be a bit dim

sala *f* **1.** (*habitación*) room; (*grande*) hall; ~ **de espera** waiting room; ~ **de estar** living room; ~ **de fiestas** dance hall **2.** JUR courtroom; **Sala de lo Civil/Penal** Civil/Criminal Court

salado, **-a** *adj* **1.** (*comida*) salty **2.** (*gracioso*) witty; (*encantador*) charming **3.** *AmL* (*infortunado*) unfortunate

saladura *f* salting

salamanca *f* **1.** *Arg* ZOOL *flat-headed salamander* **2.** *CSur* (*cueva natural*) natural cave

salamandra *f* salamander; ~ **acuática** newt

salamanquesa *f* gecko; ~ **de agua** newt

salame *adj Arg, inf* (*tonto*) fool

salami *m* salami

salar *vt* **1.** (*condimentar*) to add salt to; ~ **algo demasiado** to put too much salt in sth **2.** (*para conservar*) to salt **3.** *AmL* (*echar a perder*) to spoil

salarial *adj* wage

salario *m* wages *pl;* ~ **en especie** payment in kind

salazón *m* **1.** (*saladura*) salting **2.** *pl* (*carne*) salted meat

salchicha *f* sausage; **perro** ~ *inf* (*dachshund*) sausage dog *Brit,* hotdog *Am*

salchichón *m salami-type cured sausage*

saldar *vt* **1.** (*cuenta*) to pay; (*deuda*) to pay off; **todavía no hemos saldado nuestras diferencias** we still haven't settled our differences **2.** (*mercancía*) to sell off

saldo *m* **1.** (*diferencia*) balance; (*pago*) payment; ~ **acreedor** credit balance; ~ **de la cuenta** account balance **2.** *pl* (*rebajas*) sales *pl*

salero *m* **1.** (*objeto*) salt cellar *Brit,* salt shaker *Am* **2.** (*gracia*) wit; (*encanto*) charm

saleroso, **-a** *adj inf* (*ingenioso*) witty; (*encantador*) charming

salida *f* **1.** (*puerta*) way out; ~ **para coches** car exit; **a la ~ del teatro** coming out of the theatre *Brit* [*o* theater *Am*]; **callejón sin ~** dead end; ~ **de emergencia** emergency exit **2.** (*de un tren, avión*) departure; (*de un barco*) sailing **3.** (*astr*) rising; ~ **del sol** sunrise **4.** DEP start; **dar la** ~ to start the race **5.** COM sale; (*partida*) consignment; **este producto no tiene** ~ there is no market for this product; ~ **de capital** capital outflow **6.** *inf* (*ocurrencia*) witty remark; ~ **de tono** inappropriate remark; **¡menuda ~!** what a crazy idea! **7.** (*pretexto*) pretext **8.** (*solución*) way out; **en este asunto no hay** ~ there is no way out of this

salido, **-a** *adj inf* randy, horny; **más ~ que la punta de una plancha** randier than a rooster in the henhouse

salidor(a) *adj AmL* party-loving; **es muy** ~ he likes to go out a lot

saliente *adj* **1.** (*excelente*) outstanding **2.** (*ojos*) protruding **3.** (*ministro*) outgoing

salina *f* **1.** (*instalación*) salt works **2.** (*mina*) salt mine

salinidad *f sin pl* salinity

salino, **-a** *adj* saline

salir *irr* **I.** *vi* **1.** (*ir al exterior*) to go out; (*ir fuera*) to go away; ~ **a dar una vuelta** to go out for a stroll [*o* walk]; ~ **con alguien** *inf* to go out with sb; ~ **adelante** to make progress; ~ **mal con alguien** to fall out with sb **2.** (*de viaje*) to leave; (*avión*) to depart; ~ **del cascarón** [*o* **del huevo**] to come out of the egg; **para ~ de dudas le pregunté directamente** to clear up any doubts I asked him/her directly; ~ **ileso** [*o* **bien librado**] to come out unscathed; ~ **ganando/perdiendo** to come out the better/the worse **3.** (*flores, fuente*) to come out; (*sol*) to rise; ~ **a la luz** to come to light; ~ **en la tele** to be on TV **4.** (*convertirse*) to turn into; **salió un buen artista** he became a good artist **5.** (*parecerse*) ~ **a alguien** to look like sb; **este niño ha salido a su padre** the boy takes after his father **6.** INFOR ~ **de un programa** to exit a program **7.** DEP to start **8.** (*costar*) to cost; **nos sale a 4 euros el metro** it costs us 4 euros per metre *Brit* [*o* meter *Am*] ►~ **pitando** *inf* to beat it; **salga lo que salga** whatever happens **II.** *vr:* ~**se 1.** (*de un recipiente*) to spill; (*líquido*) to overflow; (*leche*) to boil over; (*vasija*) to leak; **el río se salió** (**de madre**) the river burst its banks **2.** (*de una organización*) ~**se de la Iglesia** to leave the Church ►~**se con la suya** to get one's own way

salitre *m* saltpetre *Brit,* saltpeter *Am*

saliva *f* saliva; **gastar** ~ **en balde** *fig* to waste one's breath; **tragar** ~ *fig* to conceal one's feelings

salivadera *f Arg, Urug* (*escupidera*) spittoon

salmantino, -a I. *adj* of/from Salamanca **II.** *m, f* native/inhabitant of Salamanca

salmo *m* psalm; **cantar a alguien el** ~ *fig* to tell sb a few home truths

salmón I. *adj* salmon-pink **II.** *m* salmon

salmonete *m* red mullet

salmuera *f* brine

salobre *adj* salty; (*agua*) brackish

salón *m* **1.** (*de casa*) living-room **2.** (*local*) hall; ~ **de actos** assembly hall; ~ **de baile** dancehall **3.** (*feria*) show

salpicadera *f Méx* AUTO mudguard

salpicadero *m* AUTO dashboard

salpicadura *f* **1.** (*acción*) splashing **2.** (*mancha*) fleck, spatter

salpicar <c→qu> *vt* **1.** (*rociar*) to sprinkle; (*con pintura*) to splash; ~ **la mesa de flores** to decorate the table with flowers **2.** (*manchar*) to spatter **3.** (*con chistes*) to pepper

salpicón *m* **1.** GASTR ≈ salmagundi (*chopped seafood or meat with oil, vinegar and seasoning*) **2.** *Col, Ecua* (*bebida*) cold drink of fruit juice **3.** (*mancha*) spatter

> In **Colombia** and **Ecuador** the **salpicón** is a cold fruit drink. In Spain, however, **salpicón** is a cold meat, fish or seafood dish.

salpimentar <e→ie> *vt* to season, to add salt and pepper; ~ **algo con algo** *fig* to liven sth up with sth

salsa *f* **1.** GASTR sauce; (*caldo*) gravy; ~ **mayonesa** mayonnaise; ~ **verde** parsley sauce; ~ **de tomate** (*de aderezo*) ketchup, catsup *Am;* (*para cocinar*) tomato sauce **2.** (*gracia*) humour *Brit,* humor *Am;* **este libro tiene mucha** ~ this book is very amusing; **esa es la** ~ **de la vida** she is the spice of life **3.** MÚS salsa ►**la** ~ **de San Bernardo** a healthy appetite; **estar en su propia** ~ to be in one's element

salsamentaría *f Col* COM delicatessen

salsera *f* gravy boat

saltado, -a *adj* **1.** (*desprendido*) missing **2.** (*saltón*) protruding

saltador *m* (*comba*) skipping rope

saltador(a) I. *adj* jumping **II.** *m(f)* **1.** (*atleta*) jumper; ~ **de altura** high-jumper; ~ **de longitud** long-jumper; ~ **de pértiga** pole-vaulter **2.** (*saltimbanqui*) acrobat

saltamontes *m inv* grasshopper

saltaperico *m Cuba* BOT manyroot

saltar I. *vi* **1.** (*botar*) to jump; (*chispas*) to fly up; ~ **por los aires** to blow up; *fig* to get furious; ~ **de alegría** to jump for joy; ~ **a la cuerda** to skip; ~ **a la pata coja** to hop (on one leg); ~ **en pedazos** to break into pieces; **los jugadores** ~**on al terreno de juego** the players ran out onto the pitch [*o* the field *Am*] **2.** (*lanzarse*) to jump; ~ **al agua** to jump into the water; ~ **con paracaídas** to make a parachute jump **3.** (*explotar*) to explode; (*costura*) to burst; (*los plomos*) to blow **4.** (*picarse*) to explode **5.** (*irrumpir*) to come out **6.** (*trabajo*) to be promoted rapidly; (*ser destituido*) to be kicked out **7.** (*desprenderse*) to come off ►**estar a la que salta** to look out for an opportunity **II.** *vt* **1.** (*movimiento*) to jump (over) **2.** (*animal*) to cover **III.** *vr:* ~**se 1.** (*ley, norma*) to break **2.** (*línea, párrafo*) to miss out, to skip **3.** (*desprenderse*) to come off; **se me saltó un botón** one of my buttons came off; **se me** ~**on las lágrimas** my eyes filled with tears

saltarín, -ina I. *adj* **1.** (*inquieto*) restless **2.** (*inestable*) shaky **II.** *m, f* **1.** (*bailarín*) dancer **2.** (*zarandillo*) active person

salteador(a) *m(f)* holdup man *m,* holdup woman *f*

saltear *vt* **1.** (*asaltar*) to hold up **2.** GASTR to sauté **3.** (*interrumpir*) to do in fits and starts

saltimbanqui *m* acrobat

salto *m* **1.** (*bote*) jump; **de** [*o* **en**] **un** ~ with one jump; **apartarse de un** ~ to jump away; **dar un** ~ to jump; *fig* to jump with fright; **dar** ~**s de alegría** to jump for joy; **dar un** ~ **atrás** to jump backwards; **me pegó un** ~ **el corazón** my heart pounded; **moverse a** ~**s** to jump along **2.** DEP jump; ~ **de altura** high jump; ~ **de longitud** long jump; ~ **mortal** somersault; ~ **con pértiga** pole vault; ~ **del potro** vault; **a** ~**s** in leaps and bounds **3.** (*trabajo*) rapid promotion **4.** (*bata*) ~ **de cama** negligée **5.** INFOR ~ **de línea** line break; ~ **de página** page break **6.** (*omisión*) gap, omission ►~ **de agua** waterfall; **a** ~ **de mata** *inf* (*repentinamente*) suddenly; (*superficialmente*) carelessly; **vivir a** ~ **de mata** *inf* to live from hand to mouth

saltón, -ona *adj* **1.** (*saltarín*) restless **2.** (*sobresaliente*) protruding; **ojos saltones** bulging eyes

salubre *adj* <salubérrimo> (*saludable*) healthy; (*curativo*) curative

salubridad *f sin pl* healthiness; *AmL* (*higiene*) hygiene

salud *f sin pl* (*estado físico*) health; **¡~!** (*al estornudar*) bless you!; (*al brindar*) good health!; **beber a la** ~ **de...** to drink to the health of …; **rebosante de** ~ bursting with health; **¡~, dinero y amor!** *inf* cheers!; **curarse en** ~ *fig* to take precautions; **gastar** ~ to be in good health; **lo juro por la** ~ **de mis hijos** I swear on the Bible

saludable *adj* **1.**(*sano*) healthy **2.**(*provechoso*) beneficial

saludar *vt* **1.**(*al encontrar*) to greet; (*con la mano*) to wave; MIL to salute; **le saluda atentamente su…** *form* yours faithfully …; **he ido a** ~ **a mis padres** I went to visit my parents; **estos ya ni se saludan** they don't even speak to each other now **2.**(*recibir*) to welcome **3.**(*mandar saludos*) to send regards to

saludo *m* **1.**(*palabras*) greeting; **con un cordial** ~ *form* yours sincerely; **¡déle ~s de mi parte!** give him/her my regards; **tu madre te manda ~s** your mother sends her love; **muchos ~s a tu hermano de mi parte** give my warmest regards to your brother **2.**(*recibimiento*) welcome

salutación *f* greeting; (*recibimiento*) welcome; (*oración*) Hail Mary

salva *f* salvo; ~ **de aplausos** round of applause

salvación *f* rescue; REL salvation; **Ejército de Salvación** Salvation Army

salvado *m* bran

salvador(a) **I.** *adj* saving; REL salvational; (*curativo*) curative **II.** *m(f)* rescuer; REL saviour *Brit*, savior *Am*

Salvador *m* El ~ El Salvador

> The Republic of **El Salvador** lies in the north--eastern part of Central America. The capital is **San Salvador**. The official language of the country is Spanish and the monetary unit of **El Salvador** is the **colón**. The country is the smallest and most densely populated in Central America.

salvadoreño, -a *adj, m, f* Salvadoran

salvaguardar *vt* to safeguard; (*derechos, intereses*) to protect

salvaguardia *f* **1.**(*protección*) safeguard; (*de intereses*) safekeeping **2.**(*salvoconducto*) safe-conduct

salvajada *f* savage deed, atrocity

salvaje **I.** *adj* (*planta, animal*) wild; (*persona*) uncivilized; (*acto*) savage; **huelga** ~ wildcat strike **II.** *mf* savage; (*persona ruda*) barbarian

salvajismo *m sin pl* **1.**(*animal*) wild nature **2.**(*gamberrismo*) vandalism **3.**(*crueldad*) savagery

salvamanteles *m inv* table mat, place mat *Am*

salvamento *m* salvation; (*accidente, naufragio*) rescue

salvar **I.** *vt* **1.** *t.* REL (*del peligro*) to save; ~ **del peligro** to save from danger **2.**(*foso*) to jump across; (*distancia*) to cover; (*obstáculo*) to get round; (*problema*) to overcome; ~ **las apariencias** to keep up appearances **II.** *vr:* **~se** to save oneself; (*en sentido religioso*) to be saved; **¡sálvese quien pueda!** every man for himself!; **~se por los pelos** to have a narrow escape

salvavidas *m inv* (*cinturón*) lifebelt; **bote** ~ lifeboat; **chaleco** ~ lifejacket

salvavidas *mf* lifeguard

salvedad *f* **1.**(*excepción*) exception **2.**(*condición*) reservation; **con la** ~ **de que…** with the proviso that …

salvia *f* sage

salvilla *f Chile* cruet

salvo *prep* except; ~ **que** +*subj* unless; ~ **error u omisión** *form* errors and omissions excepted; ~ **aviso en contrario** *form* unless otherwise informed

salvo, -a *adj* safe; **poner a** ~ to put in a safe place; **sano y** ~ safe and sound

salvoconducto *m* safe-conduct

samba *f* samba

sambenito *m* **colgar un** ~ **a alguien** to give sb a bad name; (*culpar*) to put the blame on sb

sambumbia *f* **1.** *Col* (*cosa desmoronada*) **volver algo** ~ to smash sth to pieces **2.** *Cuba* GASTR *drink of cane syrup, water and peppers* **3.** *Méx* GASTR pineapple cordial

san *adj* Saint

sanar **I.** *vi* ~ **de algo** to recover from sth **II.** *vt* to cure

sanatorio *m* sanatorium

sanción *f* **1.**(*multa*) penalty; ECON sanction **2.**(*ley*) passing **3.**(*autorización*) endorsement

sancionable *adj* punishable

sancionar *vt* **1.**(*castigar*) to punish; ECON (*aplicar sanciones*) to impose sanctions on **2.**(*aprobar*) to authorize; JUR to ratify

sancochar *vt AmL* (*rehogar*) to parboil

sancocho *m* **1.** *AmC, PRico, Ven* (*lío*) fuss **2.** *And, Ven* parboiled meat

sandalia *f* sandal

sándalo *m* **1.**(*árbol*) sandalwood tree **2.**(*madera*) sandalwood

sandez *f* stupid action; **no decir más que sandeces** to say nothing but foolish things

sandía *f* watermelon

sandinista *adj, mf Nic* Sandinista

sandunga *f inf* **1.**(*gracia*) charm **2.** *Col, Chile, PRico* celebration

sándwich *m* GASTR toasted sandwich; **día** ~ *Arg, inf: day taken as vacation between two public holidays*

saneado, -a *adj* (*renta, haber*) debt-free

saneamiento *m* **1.**(*de un edificio*) repair; (*de un terreno*) drainage **2.**(*de economía*) reform **3.** JUR compensation

sanear *vt* **1.**(*edificio*) to clean up; (*tierra*) to drain **2.**(*economía*) to reform; ~ **un vicio** to break a bad habit **3.** JUR to compensate

Sanfermines *mpl Pamplona bull-running festival*

sangrante *adj* bleeding; **un ejemplo** ~ *fig* a flagrant example

S

sangrar I. *vi* to bleed; **estar sangrando por la nariz** to have a nosebleed; **estar sangrando** *fig* to be very fresh II. *vt* 1. MED to bleed 2. (*dinero*) to bleed dry 3. (*agua, resina*) to drain off 4. TIPO to indent

sangre *f* 1. (*líquido*) blood; **a ~ fría** in cold blood; **de ~ azul** blue-blooded; **animales de ~ caliente/fría** warm/cold-blooded animals; (**caballo de**) **pura ~** thoroughbred (horse); **chupar la ~** (**de las venas**) **a alguien** *inf* to bleed sb dry; **conservar la ~ fría** *fig* to keep one's cool; **dar** [*o* **donar**] **~** to give [*o* donate] blood; **dar la ~ de sus venas** *fig* to give everything one has; **hacer ~** (*en una pelea, lucha*) to draw blood; **aportar ~ nueva a algo** to inject new blood [*o* life] into sth; **llevar algo en la ~** to have sth in the blood; (*de familia*) to run in the family; **le hierve la ~** *fig* his/her blood boils; **la ~ se me heló en las venas** my blood ran cold; **se le subió la ~ a la cabeza** he/she saw red 2. (*linaje*) lineage ▸**la letra con ~ entra** *prov* spare the rod and spoil the child; **no llegar la ~ al río** not to have disastrous results; **hacerse mala ~** to get bitter; **sudar ~** to go through hardships; **tener mala ~** to be bad-tempered; **la ~ tira** blood is thicker than water *prov*

sangría *f* 1. MED bleeding; **una ~ de votos** a continuous loss of votes 2. (*brazo*) inner angle of the elbow 3. (*aguas*) irrigation channel 4. TIPO indentation 5. (*bebida*) sangria ▸**lo mismo son ~s que ventosas** that won't make any difference

> **Sangría** is a punch made from red wine, water, sugar, lemon and orange. It is normally served in a **jarra de barro** (earthenware jug).

sangriento, **-a** *adj* bloody; (*injusticia*) cruel; **hecho ~** bloody event

sangriligero, **-a** *adj AmC* friendly, nice

sangripesado, **-a** *adj AmC* unpleasant, disagreeable

sangrón, **-ona** *adj Méx, inf* boring; **su novio es un ~, no lo soporto** her boyfriend is a bore, I can't stand him

sanguaraña *f* 1. *Ecua, Perú* (*circunloquio*) evasion; **déjate de ~s** stop beating about the bush 2. *Perú: popular Peruvian dance*

sanguijuela *f* 1. ZOOL leech 2. *pey* (*persona*) bloodsucker

sanguinario, **-a** *adj* (*persona, animal*) blood-thirsty; (*hecho*) cruel

sanguíneo, **-a** *adj* 1. MED blood; **rojo ~** blood-red; **grupo ~** blood type [*o* group] 2. (*temperamento*) sanguine

sanguinolento, **-a** *adj* bloody; (*color*) blood-red; (*ojos*) bloodshot

sanidad *f sin pl* health; **~ (pública)** public health

sanitario *m* (*wáter*) toilet

sanitario, **-a** I. *adj* health; (*aparatos, medidas*) sanitary II. *m, f* health worker

sano, **-a** *adj* 1. (*robusto, saludable*) healthy; **~ de juicio** of sound mind; **cortar por lo ~** to take extreme measures; **estar más ~ que una manzana** to be as sound as a bell; **salir ~ y salvo** to emerge safe and sound 2. (*no roto*) intact 3. (*sincero*) wholesome

santanderino, **-a** I. *adj* of/from Santander II. *m, f* native/inhabitant of Santander

santería *f AmL: shop selling religious items*

santero, **-a** I. *adj pey* (*beato*) pious; **ese es muy ~** he's very fond of the saints II. *m, f* 1. *pey* (*beato*) Holy Joe 2. (*guardián*) shrine keeper

Santiago *m* ~ (**de Chile**) Santiago

santiaguino, **-a** I. *adj* of/from Santiago (in Chile) II. *m, f* native/inhabitant of Santiago (in Chile)

santiamén *m* **en un ~** in a jiffy

santidad *f* holiness; **Su Santidad** His Holiness, the Pope

santificar <c→qu> *vt* 1. (*consagrar*) to consecrate 2. (*canonizar*) to sanctify 3. (*respetar*) to glorify

santiguar <gu→gü> I. *vt* 1. (*signarse*) to make the sign of the cross over 2. *inf* (*maltratar*) to hit II. *vr:* **~se** to cross oneself

santo, **-a** I. *adj* sacred, holy; (*piadoso*) saintly; (*inviolable*) consecrated; **la Santa Sede** the Holy See; **el Santo Oficio** HIST the Inquisition; **campo ~** cemetery; **Jueves Santo** Maundy Thursday; **Semana Santa** Holy Week, Easter; **Viernes Santo** Good Friday; **¿qué haces en Semana Santa?** what are you doing over Easter?; **se pasó todo el ~ día haciendo...** he/she spent the whole blessed day doing ...; **¡y santas pascuas!** and that's that! II. *m, f* 1. (*personaje*) saint; **día de Todos los Santos** All Saint's Day 2. (*fiesta*) saint's day, name day; **el día de mi ~** my saint's day 3. (*imagen*) (religious) illustration; **ver los ~s de un libro** to look at the pictures in a book ▸**hoy tengo el ~ de cara/espalda** I'm in/out of luck today; **se le fue el ~ al cielo** he/she forgot what he/she was going to say; **no ser ~ de la devoción de alguien** to not be particularly fond of sb; **alzarse con el ~ y la limosna** to clear off with everything; **ser mano de ~** to be good at everything; **~ y seña** password; **¡ésta se come los ~s!** *inf* she's very religious!; **desnudar a un ~ para vestir a otro** to rob Peter to pay Paul; **dormirse como un ~** (**bendito**) to sleep like a baby; **llegar y besar el ~** (*sin esfuerzo*) to pull it off at the first attempt; (*fácil*) like taking candy from a baby; **quedarse para vestir ~s** (*mujer*) to be left on the shelf, to remain an old maid; **no sé a ~ de qué me dijo eso** I don't know why on earth he/she told me that

santuario *m* 1. (*templo*) shrine; (*capilla*) chapel 2. (*refugio*) sanctuary, refuge 3. *Col* (*tesoro*) buried treasure

santurrón, **-ona** I. *adj* sanctimonious; (*hipócrita*) hypocritical II. *m, f* sanctimonious individual; (*hipócrita*) hypocrite
saña *f* 1. (*ira*) anger 2. (*rencor*) viciousness; **lo hizo con toda la mala** ~ he/she did it with great cruelty
sapaneco, **-a** *adj Hond* chubby
sapiencia *f sin pl* 1. (*conocimientos*) wisdom 2. (*sensatez*) good sense
sapo *m* 1. ZOOL toad 2. (*persona*) nasty bit of work 3. *inf* (*bicho*) small animal ►**pisar el** ~ to have a lie-in, to sleep late
saponaria *f* soapwort
saque *m* DEP (*fútbol*) goal kick, throw-in; (*fútbol americano*) kick-off; (*tenis*) serve; ~ **de esquina** corner kick ►**tener buen** ~ to have a hearty appetite
saquear *vt* to loot
saqueo *m* looting
sarampión *m sin pl* MED measles
sarao *m* (*fiesta*) evening party; **¡menudo ~ se armó allí!** what a to-do that was!
sarape *m Méx* blanket
sarasa *m pey* lilac, pansy
sarazo, **-a** *adj Col, Cuba, Méx, Ven* (*Mais*) ripening
sarcasmo *m sin pl* sarcasm
sarcástico, **-a** *adj* sarcastic
sarcófago *m* sarcophagus; (*tumba*) tomb
sarcoma *m* MED sarcoma
sardana *f* MÚS *typical Catalan dance*
sardina *f* sardine; **~s en aceite** sardines in oil; **entierro de la** ~ *festival to mark the beginning of Lent;* (**estar**) **como ~s en lata** to be packed like sardines
sardo, **-a** *adj, m, f* Sardinian
sardónico, **-a** *adj* sardonic
sargenta *f fig* bossy woman
sargento *m* sergeant
sargo *m* sea bream, sheepshead
sarmentoso, **-a** *adj* (*extremidades*) gnarled; (*plant*) climbing
sarmiento *m* (*tallo*) vine shoot
sarna *f sin pl* MED scabies; (*de los animales*) mange ►**~ con gusto no pica**(**, pero mortifica**) *prov* if you like sth you'll do it whatever the cost; **ser más viejo que la** ~ *inf* to be as old as the hills
sarpullido *m* MED (*irritación*) rash
sarracina *f* quarrel
sarro *m* 1. MED (*de los dientes*) tartar; (*en la lengua*) fur 2. (*poso*) deposit
sarta *f* 1. (*hilo*) string 2. (*serie*) row; **una ~ de mentiras** a string [*o* pack] of lies
sartén *f* frying pan ►**saltar de la ~ y dar en las brasas** to jump from the frying pan into the fire; **tener la ~ por el mango** to have the whip [*o* upper] hand
sastre, **-a** *m, f* tailor; **traje** ~ tailor-made suit; **de eso, será lo que tase un** ~ *inf* that's more than doubtful
sastrería *f* tailor's shop; (*oficio*) tailoring
satánico, **-a** *adj* satanic
satélite *m* ASTR, TÉC satellite; (**país**) ~ satellite (state)
satén *m* satin
satinado, **-a** *adj* shiny, glossy; **papel** ~ shiny paper
sátira *f* LIT satire
satírico, **-a** I. *adj* satirical II. *m, f* satirist
satirizar <z→c> *vt* to satirize
sátiro *m* satyr; (*hombre lascivo*) lecher
satisfacción *f* 1. (*estado*) satisfaction; (*alegría*) happiness; **a mi entera** ~ to my complete satisfaction 2. (*pago*) settlement 3. REL fulfilment *Brit,* fulfillment *Am*
satisfacer *irr como hacer* I. *vt* 1. (*pagar*) to honour *Brit,* to honor *Am;* ~ **la penitencia por sus pecados** to do penitence for one's sins 2. (*deseo, curiosidad, hambre*) to satisfy; (*sed*) to quench; (*demanda*) to settle; ~ **todos los caprichos de sus hijos** to gratify all one's children's whims 3. (*requisitos*) to meet 4. (*agravio*) ~ **algo** to make amends for sth II. *vr:* **~se** 1. (*contentarse*) to satisfy oneself 2. (*agravio*) to obtain redress
satisfactorio, **-a** *adj* (*solución*) satisfactory; **no ser** ~ to be unsatisfactory; **resulta ~ comprobar que...** it is pleasing to confirm that ...
satisfecho, **-a** I. *pp de* **satisfacer** II. *adj* (*contento*) contented; (*exigencias, deseo sexual*) satisfied; ~ **de sí mismo** self-satisfied; **estar** ~ (*harto*) to have had enough
saturación *f* saturation
saturar *vt* to saturate
sauce *m* willow; ~ **llorón** weeping willow
saúco *m* elder tree
saudí <saudíes>, **saudita** I. *adj* Saudi; **Arabia Saudí** Saudi Arabia II. *mf* Saudi
sauna *f* sauna
savia *f* 1. (*de árbol*) sap 2. (*energía*) vitality
saxofón *m,* **saxófono** *m* saxophone
saya *f* (*de mujer*) petticoat; (*falda*) skirt
sayo *m inf* smock ►**cortar a alguien un** ~ to speak ill of sb in his/her absence
sazón *f* 1. (*condimento*) flavour *Brit,* flavor *Am* 2. (*madurez*) ripeness; **estar en** ~ to be ripe ►**fuera de** ~ out of season; **a la** ~ at that time; **en** ~ opportunely
sazonado, **-a** *adj* 1. (*comida*) seasoned 2. (*fruta*) ripe 3. (*frase*) witty
sazonar *vt* 1. (*comida*) to season 2. (*madurar*) to ripen
se *pron pers* 1. *forma reflexiva: m sing* himself; *f sing* herself; *de cosa* itself; *pl* themselves; *de Ud.* yourself; *de Uds.* yourselves 2. *objeto indirecto: m sing* to him; *f sing* to her; *a una cosa* to it; *pl* to them; *a Ud., Uds.* to you; **mi hermana ~ lo prestó a su amiga** my sister lent it to her friend 3. (*oración impers*) you; ~ **aprende mucho en esta clase** you learn a lot in this class 4. (*oración pasiva*) ~ **confirmó la sentencia** the sentence was confirmed
sé *1. pres de* **saber**
SE *abr de* **sudeste** SE
SEBC *abr de* **Sistema Europeo de Bancos**

Centrales European System of Central Banks
sebo *m* grease; (*vela*) tallow; **hacer** ~ *Arg, inf* to idle
seborrea *f* MED seborrhoea *Brit,* seborrhea *Am*
seboso, **-a** *adj* greasy
seca *f* **1.**(*sequía*) drought; *AmL* (*temporada*) dry season **2.**(*banco de arena*) dry sandbank
secadero *m* **1.**(*local*) drying shed **2.**(*recinto*) *place where fruit is placed to dry*
secado *m* drying
secador *m* hair dryer
secadora *f* tumble dryer, spin dryer
secano *m* **1.**(*tierra*) dry land; **cultivo de** ~ crop which can be grown in dry areas; **ése es de** ~ *inf* he's not one for drink **2.**(*isleta*) small sandy island
secante[1] **I.** *adj* drying; **línea** ~ secant; **papel** ~ blotting paper **II.** *m* **1.**(*pintura*) paint dryer **2.**(*papel*) blotting paper
secante[2] *f* MAT secant
secar <c→qu> **I.** *vt* **1.**(*deshumedecer*) to dry **2.**(*enjugar*) to wipe **3.**(*agostar*) to wither **4.**(*cicatrizar*) to heal **II.** *vr:* **~se 1.**(*deshumedecer*) to dry up **2.**(*enjugar*) to wipe up **3.**(*desecarse*) to dry up; (*fuente*) to run dry; (*agostarse*) to wither away **4.**(*curarse*) to heal up **5.**(*enflaquecer*) to get thin **6.**(*insensibilizarse*) to become hardened **7.**(*estar sediento*) to be very thirsty; **~se de sed** to have a raging thirst
sección *f* **1.**(*cortadura, perfil*) cross-section **2.**(*parte*) section **3.**(*departamento*) branch
seccionar *vt* to divide into sections
secesión *f* (*separación*) split; (*fracción de Estado*) secession
seco, **-a** *adj* **1.**(*sin agua*) dry; **golpe** ~ dull blow; **estar** ~ to be very thirsty; **limpiar en** ~ to dry clean **2.**(*desecado*) dried up; **frutos ~s** dried fruit and nuts **3.**(*río*) dried up **4.**(*marchito*) withered **5.**(*flaco*) skinny **6.**(*cicatriz*) healed **7.**(*tajante*) curt **8.**(*vino*) dry **9.**(*pasmado*) **dejar** ~ **a alguien** to dumbfound sb; (*matar*) to kill sb; **quedarse** ~ to be dumbfounded ►**a secas** on its own; **en** ~ suddenly; **frenar en** ~ to pull up sharply
secreción *f* **1.**(*sustancia*) secretion **2.**(*el segregar*) segregation
secretar *vt* to secrete
secretaría *f* **1.**(*oficina*) secretary's office **2.**(*cargo*) secretaryship **3.** *AmL* (*ministerio*) ministry **4.**(*organismo*) secretariat
secretariado *m* **1.**(*oficina*) secretary's office **2.**(*cargo*) secretaryship **3.**(*carrera*) profession of secretary **4.**(*organismo*) secretariat
secretario, **-a** *m, f* **1.**(*de oficina*) secretary **2.** *AmL* (*ministro*) minister
secretear *vi inf* to exchange secrets
secreter *m* (*mueble*) writing desk
secreto *m* **1.**(*misterio*) secret; ~ **profesional** trade secret; ~ **a voces** open secret; **en** ~ in secret; **mantener en** ~ to keep secret; **guardar un** ~ to keep a secret; ~ **de confesión** REL seal of confession **2.**(*reserva*) secrecy **3.**(*lugar*) secret drawer
secreto, **-a** *adj* **1.**(*oculto*) secret **2.**(*callado*) secretive
secta *f* (*grupo*) sect
sectario, **-a** **I.** *adj* **1.**(*de secta*) sectarian **2.**(*fanático*) fanatical **II.** *m, f* **1.**(*de una secta*) member of a sect **2.**(*fanático*) fanatic
sector *m* **1.** *t.* MAT sector; ~ **económico** economic sector; ~ **hotelero** hotel [*o* hospitality] industry; ~ **de la informática** computing sector; ~ **de inicialización** INFOR initialization sector; ~ **multimedia** multimedia sector; ~ **servicios** service sector **2.**(*grupo*) group
secuaz *mf pey* henchman
secuela *f* consequence; ~ (**de una enfermedad**) after-effect (of an illness); **dejar ~s** to have after-effects
secuencia *f* **1.**(*serie*) *t.* CINE sequence; ~ **de caracteres** *t.* INFOR series of characters **2.**(*orden de las palabras*) word order
secuestrador(**a**) *m(f)* kidnapper
secuestrar *vt* **1.**(*raptar*) to kidnap **2.**(*embargar*) to confiscate
secuestro *m* **1.**(*rapto*) kidnapping **2.**(*bienes*) confiscation **3.**(*embargo*) seizure
secular *adj* secular; *fig* age-old
secundar *vt* to second
secundario, **-a** *adj* (*segundo*) secondary; (*cargo*) minor; **papel** ~ CINE, TEAT supporting role; **esto es** ~ that's of minor importance
sed *f* **1.**(*falta de agua*) thirst **2.**(*de plantas*) dryness; **tener** ~ to be thirsty **3.**(*afán*) ~ **de algo** longing for sth; ~ **de amor** hunger for love; ~ **de poder** thirst for power
seda *f* **1.** ZOOL bristle **2.**(*tela, hilo*) silk; **de** ~ **natural** of pure silk; **como una** ~ (*tacto*) as smooth as silk; (*persona*) sweet-tempered; (*sin tropiezos*) smoothly
sedal *m* (fishing) line
sedante **I.** *adj* (**de efecto**) ~ soothing **II.** *m* sedative
sedar *vt* to sedate
sedativo, **-a** *adj* sedative
sede *f* (*residencia*) seat; (*empresa*) headquarters *pl;* **la Santa Sede** the Holy See
sedentario, **-a** *adj* sedentary
sedente *adj* seated
sedición *f* sedition
sedicioso, **-a** **I.** *adj* seditious; **acto** ~ act of sedition **II.** *m, f* troublemaker
sediento, **-a** *adj* thirsty; ~ **de algo** thirsty for sth; ~ **de poder** eager for power
sedimentación *f* sedimentation
sedimentar **I.** *vt* (*sosegar*) to calm; (*sedimento*) to deposit **II.** *vr:* **~se 1.**(*depositarse*) to settle **2.**(*sosegarse*) to calm down
sedimento *m* sediment, deposit
sedoso, **-a** *adj* silky, silken
seducción *f* **1.**(*persuasión*) seduction **2.**(*tentación*) fascination
seducir *irr como traducir vt* **1.**(*persuadir*) to seduce **2.**(*fascinar*) to charm
seductor(**a**) **I.** *adj* seductive; **artes ~as** wiles;

(*idea*) captivating; (*tentador*) tempting **II.** *m(f)* (*que seduce*) seducer; (*que encanta*) charmer

sefardí, **sefardita** **I.** *adj* Sephardic **II.** *mf* Sephardi, Sephardic Jew *m*, Sephardic Jewess *f*

> A **sefardí** is the descendant of a Jewish person who originated from Spain or Portugal. The language is also called **sefardí** (or **ladino**). The **sefardíes** were driven out of the Iberian Peninsula at the end of the 15th century. They subsequently settled in North Africa and some European countries.

segador(a) **I.** *adj* reaping **II.** *m(f)* reaper

segadora *f* mower

segar *irr como fregar vt* **1.** (*cortar*) to reap; (*hierba*) to mow; ~ **algo en flor** *fig* to mow sth down **2.** (*frustrar*) to dash

seglar *adj* lay, secular

segmentar *vt* to divide into segments

segmento *m* (*parte*) segment; (*motor*) piston rings *pl*

segoviano, **-a**, **segoviense** **I.** *adj* of/from Segovia **II.** *m* native/inhabitant of Segovia

segregación *f* segregation

segregar <g→gu> *vt* to segregate

seguido, **-a** *adj* **1.** (*continuo*) consecutive; **un año** ~ a whole year **2.** (*en línea recta*) straight; **todo** ~ straight on

seguidor(a) *m(f)* follower, supporter; DEP fan

seguimiento *m* (*persecución*) chase; (*sucesión*) continuation; (*estudio*) follow-up

seguir *irr* **I.** *vt* **1.** (*suceder, ser adepto*) to follow **2.** (*perseguir*) to chase **3.** (*acompañar, cursar*) to follow; ~ **un curso de informática** to take a computing course **4.** (*continuar*) ~ **adelante** to carry on; **¡que sigas bien!** I hope you keep well! **II.** *vi* **sigue por esta calle** follow this street **III.** *vr:* ~**se** to ensue

según **I.** *prep* according to; ~ **eso** according to that; ~ **la ley** in accordance with the law; ~ **tus propias palabras/tu sonrisa** judging by your own words/your smile **II.** *adv* **1.** (*como*) as; ~ **lo convenido** as we agreed **2.** (*mientras*) while; **podemos hablar** ~ **vamos andando** we can talk as we walk **3.** (*eventualidad*) ~ (**y como**) it depends; ~ **el trabajo iré o no** I'll go if work permits

segunda *f* AUTO second gear; FERRO second class ►**con** ~**s** with veiled meaning

segundero *m* second hand

segundo *m* (*tiempo*) second

segundo, **-a** **I.** *adj* second; **primo** ~ second cousin; **segunda intención** implied second meaning; **vivir en el** ~ to live on the second floor **II.** *m, f* second (one); *v.t.* **octavo**

segundón, **-ona** *m, f* second son *m*, second daughter *f*

seguramente *adv* **1.** (*de modo seguro*) certainly **2.** (*probablemente*) probably

seguridad *f* **1.** (*protección*) security; **Seguridad Social** ADMIN Social Security; **agente de** ~ security guard **2.** (*certeza*) certainty; **para mayor** ~ to be sure of it **3.** (*firmeza*) confidence; **habla con mucha** ~ he/she speaks with great self-confidence **4.** (*garantía*) surety **5.** (*confiabilidad*) trustworthiness

seguro **I.** *m* **1.** (*contrato*) insurance; ~ **médico** medical [*o* health] insurance; ~ **de protección jurídica** legal insurance; ~ **a riesgo parcial** AUTO third-party insurance; ~ **a todo riesgo** AUTO comprehensive insurance **2.** (*mecanismo*) safety device **II.** *adv* for sure; **a buen** [*o* **de**] ~ surely; **sobre** ~ on safe ground; **en** ~ in a safe place; **tener** ~ **algo** to have sth firmly fastened

seguro, **-a** *adj* **1.** (*exento de peligro*) safe **2.** (*firme*) secure **3.** (*sólido*) solid **4.** (*convencido*) certain; ~ **de sí mismo** confident; **¿estás** ~**?** are you sure?

seis *adj inv, m* six; *v.t.* **ocho**

seisavo, **-a** *adj* sixth; *v.t.* **octavo**

seiscientos, **-as** *adj* six hundred; *v.t.* **ochocientos**

seísmo *m* (*temblor*) tremor; (*terremoto*) earthquake

selección *f* selection; ~ **nacional** national team; ~ **natural** natural selection

seleccionador(a) *m(f)* DEP selector

seleccionar *vt* to select

selectividad *f* UNIV *university entrance exam*

> The **selectividad** is a state school leaving exam, which all pupils must successfully sit after having completed the **bachillerato**, if they wish to enrol at a Spanish university.

selectivo, **-a** *adj* selective; **método** ~ selective criterion

selecto, **-a** *adj* select; (*ambiente*) exclusive

selector *m* selector; ~ **de cambio de marcha** gear lever [*o* stick]

self-service *m sin pl* self-service

sellado, **-a** *adj* (*timbrado*) stamped; (*precinto*) sealed

sellar *vt* **1.** (*timbrar*) to stamp **2.** (*dejar huella*) to leave a mark **3.** (*concluir*) to end **4.** (*precintar*) to seal; (*cerrar*) to close; ~ **los labios** to seal one's lips

sello *m* **1.** (*instrumento, marca*) stamp; ~ **de garantía** mark [*o* seal] of guarantee; ~ **oficial** official stamp **2.** (*correo*) (postage) stamp **3.** (*precinto*) seal; **cerrar con un** ~ to seal **4.** (*distintivo*) stamp, hallmark; **esta película lleva el** ~ **de su director** this film carries the stamp of its director **5.** (*anillo*) signet ring **6.** MED capsule

selva *f* (*bosque*) forest; (*tropical*) jungle; ~ **virgen** virgin forest

selvático, **-a** *adj* **1.** (*de la selva*) woodland; (*de jungla*) jungle **2.** (*salvaje*) wild

semáforo *m* **1.** (*de circulación*) traffic lights *pl* **2.** (*telégrafo*) signal

semana *f* week; **Semana Santa** Easter, Holy Week; **fin de** ~ weekend; **durante** ~**s** (**enteras**) for weeks (on end); **entre** ~ during the week
semanal *adj* weekly; **revista** ~ weekly magazine
semanario *m* weekly (magazine)
semanario, **-a** *adj* weekly
semántica *f sin pl* LING semantics
semblante *m* **1.** (*cara*) face **2.** (*expresión*) appearance; **tener un** ~ **alegre** to look cheerful; **componer el** ~ to regain one's composure
semblanza *f* **1.** (*parecido*) similarity **2.** (*bosquejo biográfico*) biographical sketch
sembrar <e→ie> *vt* **1.** (*plantar*) to sow **2.** (*esparcir*) to scatter; ~ **una calle de flores** to strew a street with flowers; ~ **para el futuro** to sow for the future; ~ **el terror** to spread terror ►**quien** mal **siembra, mal coge** *prov* as you sow, so shall you reap
semejante **I.** *adj* **1.** (*similar*) similar **2.** (*tal*) such; ~ **persona** such a person **II.** *m* fellow man
semejanza *f* **1.** (*similitud*) similarity; (*físico*) resemblance **2.** MED mimosis
semejar **I.** *vi* to resemble **II.** *vr:* ~**se** to look alike; ~**se a alguien** to look like sb
semen *m* **1.** (*espermatozoide*) semen **2.** (*semilla*) seed
semental **I.** *adj* **1.** AGR sowing **2.** ZOOL breeding; **caballo** ~ stud **II.** *m* stud
sementar <e→ie> *vt* to sow
sementera *f* **1.** (*siembra*) sowing **2.** (*sembrado*) sown field **3.** (*cosa sembrada*) crop **4.** (*tiempo*) sowing season
semestral *adj* half-yearly
semestre *m* six-month period; UNIV semester
semiautomático, **-a** *adj* semi-automatic **semicírculo** *m* semicircle **semiconductor** *m* semiconductor **semiconsciente** *adj* half-conscious **semidesnatado**, **-a** *adj* semi-skimmed **semidiós**, **-osa** *m, f* demigod **semidormido**, **-a** *adj* half-asleep **semifinal** *f* semi-final; **pasar a la** ~ to get through to the semi-final
semifusa *f* MÚS hemidemisemiquaver
semilla *f* seed
semillero *m* **1.** (*sementera*) seedbed **2.** (*origen*) breeding ground
semilunar *adj* semicircular
seminal *adj* seminal
seminario *m* **1.** ENS, REL seminary **2.** (*sementera*) seedbed
seminuevo, **-a** *adj* almost new
semioscuridad *f* half-darkness
semiótica *f* LING semiotics
semiprecioso, **-a** *adj* **piedra semipreciosa** semi-precious stone **semirrecto**, **-a** *adj* **ángulo** ~ 45° angle
semiseco, **-a** *adj* medium-dry
semita **I.** *adj* Semitic **II.** *mf* Semite
semivocal *f* semivowel
sémola *f* semolina
sempiterno, **-a** *adj* everlasting
Sena *m* Seine
senado *m* senate
senador(**a**) *m(f)* senator
sencillamente *adv* simply
sencillez *f* **1.** (*simplicidad*) simplicity **2.** (*naturalidad*) naturalness **3.** (*sinceridad*) sincerity **4.** (*candidez*) straightforwardness
sencillo, **-a** *adj* **1.** (*simple*) simple; (*fácil*) easy **2.** (*natural*) natural; **gente sencilla** unaffected people **3.** (*sincero*) straightforward **4.** (*cándido*) ingenuous
senda *f*, **sendero** *m* **1.** (*camino*) path; ~ **del jardín** garden path **2.** (*método*) way
senderismo *m* hillwalking, hiking
sendos, **-as** *adj* each of two; **llegamos en** ~ **coches** we both arrived by car
senectud *f* old age
senegalés, **-esa** *adj, m, f* Senegalese
senil *adj* senile
senilidad *f* (*decrepitud*) senility
sénior **I.** *adj* senior **II.** *mf* senior
seno *m* **1.** (*concavidad*) hollow; **un fregadero de dos** ~**s** a two-basin sink, a double sink **2.** ANAT, MAT sinus; ~ **frontal** frontal sinus **3.** (*matriz*) womb **4.** (*pecho*) breast **5.** (*de organización*) heart
sensación *f* **1.** (*sentimiento*) feeling **2.** (*novedad*) sensation **3.** (*reacción*) **causar** ~ to cause a sensation
sensacional *adj* sensational
sensacionalismo *m sin pl* sensationalism
sensacionalista *adj* sensationalist; **prensa** ~ gutter [*o* tabloid] press
sensatez *f* good sense
sensato, **-a** *adj* sensible
sensibilidad *f* sensitivity
sensibilizar <z→c> *vt* to sensitize
sensible *adj* **1.** (*sensitivo*) sensitive; (*impresionable*) impressionable; ~ **a los cambios de tiempo** sensitive to changes in the weather; ~ **a la luz** sensitive to light **2.** (*perceptible*) noticeable
sensiblemente *adv* **1.** (*perceptible*) perceptibly **2.** (*evidente*) markedly
sensiblería *f* (over-)sentimentality, mawkishness
sensiblero, **-a** *adj* (over)sentimental
sensitiva *f* mimosa
sensitivo, **-a** *adj* **1.** (*sensorial*) sensory; **tacto** ~ sense of touch **2.** (*sensible*) sensitive **3.** (*sensual*) sensual
sensor *m* sensor
sensorial *adj* sensory; **órgano** ~ sense organ
sensorio *m* sensorium
sensorio, **-a** *adj v.* **sensorial**
sensual *adj* sensual
sensualidad *f sin pl* sensuality
sentada *f* sit-in, sit-down protest; **hacer una** ~ to organize a sit-in; **hacer algo de una** ~ to do sth in one sitting
sentado, **-a** **I.** *pp de* **sentar** **II.** *adj* (*sensato*) sensible ►**dar algo por** ~ to take sth for

granted

sentador(a) *adj Arg, Chile* (*prenda de vestir*) becoming, well-fitting

sentar <e→ie> **I.** *vi* (*ropa*) to suit; ~ **bien/mal a alguien** (*comida*) to agree/disagree with sb; ~ **como un tiro** to be as welcome as a hole in the head; **esa chaqueta me siente bien/mal** that jacket suits/doesn't suit me **II.** *vt* to sit; **estar sentado** to be sitting down; **estar bien sentado** *fig* to be well established **III.** *vr:* ~**se 1.** (*asentarse*) to sit down; **¡siéntese!** have a seat! **2.** (*establecerse*) to settle down **3.** (*estabilizarse*) to stabilize

sentencia *f* **1.** (*proverbio*) maxim **2.** JUR sentence; **dictar** ~ to pronounce sentence; ~ **de divorcio** decree of divorce

sentenciar *vt* **1.** (*decidir*) ~ **algo** to give one's opinion on [*o* about] sth **2.** (*condenar*) to sentence

sentido *m* **1.** (*facultad, significado*) sense; ~ **común** common sense; ~ **del deber** sense of duty; ~ **del humor** sense of humour *Brit* [*o* humor *Am*]; **doble** ~ (*significado*) double meaning; (*dirección*) two-way; **costar un** ~ to cost the earth; **estar con los cinco ~s en el asunto** to be totally absorbed in the subject; **estar sin** ~ to be unconscious; **perder el** ~ to lose consciousness; **sexto** ~ intuition, sixth sense **2.** (*dirección*) direction; **en el** ~ **de la flecha** in the direction of the arrow; **en el** ~ **de las agujas del reloj** clockwise; ~ **único** one-way **3.** (*significado*) meaning

sentido, -a *adj* **1.** (*conmovido*) deeply felt **2.** (*sensible*) sensitive; **ser muy** ~ to be easily hurt

sentimental *adj* sentimental

sentimentalismo *m* sentimentality

sentimiento *m* **1.** (*emoción*) feeling; **sin ~s** unfeeling **2.** (*pena*) sorrow; **le acompaño en el** ~ please accept my condolences

sentir *irr* **I.** *vt* **1.** (*percibir*) to feel; ~ **frío** to feel cold; **sin** ~ without noticing **2.** (*lamentar*) to be sorry for; **lo siento mucho** I am very sorry; **siento que** +*subj* I'm sorry that **II.** *vr:* ~**se 1.** (*estar*) to feel; ~**se bien/mal** to feel good/bad **2.** (*padecer*) ~**se de algo** to suffer from sth **III.** *m* **1.** (*opinión*) opinion; ~ **popular** public opinion; **en mi** ~ in my view **2.** (*sentimiento*) feeling

seña *f* **1.** (*gesto*) sign; **hacer ~s** to make signs, to signal; **hablar por ~s** to use [*o* talk in] sign language **2.** (*particularidad*) distinguishing mark; **las ~s son mortales** the signs are unmistakable; **por más ~s** to be more specific **3.** *pl* (*dirección*) address

señal *f* **1.** (*particularidad*) distinguishing mark **2.** (*signo*) sign; ~ **de tráfico** road sign; **en** ~ **de** as a sign [*o* token] of; **dar ~es de vida** *fig* to show oneself **3.** (*teléfono*) tone; ~ **de comunicar** engaged tone *Brit,* busy signal *Am* **4.** (*huella*) mark; **ni** ~ no trace **5.** (*cicatriz*) scar **6.** (*adelanto*) deposit; **paga y** ~ first payment; **dejar una** ~ to leave a deposit

señalado, -a *adj* **1.** (*famoso*) distinguished **2.** (*importante*) special

señalar **I.** *vt* **1.** (*anunciar*) to announce **2.** (*marcar*) to mark **3.** (*estigmatizar*) to mark (for life) **4.** (*mostrar*) to show **5.** (*indicar*) to point out **6.** (*fijar*) to fix **II.** *vr* ~**se por algo** to distinguish oneself by sth

señalización *f* signposting

señalizar <z→c> *vt* to signpost

señero, -a *adj* **1.** (*único*) unequalled *Brit,* unequaled *Am;* (*importante*) outstanding **2.** (*solitario*) isolated

señor(a) **I.** *adj inf* **1.** (*noble*) lordly **2.** (*enorme*) huge **II.** *m(f)* **1.** (*dueño*) owner **2.** (*hombre*) (gentle)man; (*mujer*) wife; (*dama*) lady; ~**a de compañía** companion; **¡~as y ~es!** ladies and gentlemen! **3.** (*título*) Mister *m,* Mr *f;* **el ~/la ~a García** Mr/Mrs García; **los ~es García** the Garcías; **muy** ~ **mío:** Dear Sir; **¡no, ~!** not a bit of it!; **¡sí, ~!** it certainly is! **4.** REL **el Señor** Our Lord; **nuestra Señora** Our Lady; **descansar en el Señor** to rest in peace

señorear **I.** *vt* **1.** (*dominar*) to control **2.** (*sobresalir*) to soar above **II.** *vr:* ~**se** to seize control

señoría *f* rule; **Su Señoría** Your Lordship

señori(a)l *adj* lordly; **casa** ~ stately home

señorío *m* **1.** (*dominio*) rule **2.** (*territorio*) domain **3.** (*dignidad*) stateliness **4.** (*personas*) distinguished people *pl*

señorita *f* **1.** (*tratamiento*) Miss **2.** (*chica*) young lady

señorito *m* young gentleman

señuelo *m* decoy; *fig* lure

separación *f* **1.** (*desunión*) separation **2.** (*espacio*) distance

separado *adv* **por** ~ separately; **contar por** ~ to count one by one

separar **I.** *vt* **1.** (*desunir*) to separate; ~ **algo de algo** to separate sth from sth **2.** (*apartar*) to remove **3.** (*destituir*) to dismisss **II.** *vr:* ~**se** (*person*) to separate

separo *m Méx* (*celda*) cell

sepelio *m elev* religious funeral, Christian burial

sepia *f* cuttlefish; **de color** ~ sepia

septentrión *m elev* (*norte*) north; (**viento**) ~ north wind

septentrional *adj elev* northern

septicemia *f* MED blood poisoning, septicaemia *Brit,* septicemia *Am*

septiembre *m* September; *v.t.* **marzo**

séptimo, -a *adj, m, f* seventh; *v.t.* **octavo**

septuagésimo, -a *adj* seventieth; *v.t.* **octavo**

séptuplo, -a *adj* sevenfold

sepulcral *adj* sepulchral; **silencio** ~ deathly silence

sepulcro *m* **1.** (*tumba*) tomb; **es un** ~ *fig* he/she can keep a secret **2.** (*relicario*) reliquary

sepultar **I.** *vt* **1.** *t. fig* (*inhumar*) to bury **2.** (*cubrir*) to conceal **II.** *vr:* ~**se** (*sumergir*) to hide away

sepultura *f* **1.** (*sepelio*) burial **2.** (*tumba*) grave; **dar ~ a alguien** to bury sb; **estar cavando su propia ~** to be digging one's own grave

sepulturero, -a *m, f* gravedigger

sequedad *f* **1.** (*aridez*) dryness **2.** (*descortesía*) bluntness; **con ~** curtly

sequía *f* drought

séquito *m* retinue

ser *irr* **I.** *aux* **1.** (*construcción de la pasiva*) **las casas fueron vendidas** the houses were sold; **el triunfo fue celebrado** the triumph was celebrated **2.** (*en frases pasivas*) **era de esperar** it was to be expected; **es de esperar que** +*subj* it is to be hoped that **II.** *vi* **1.** (*absoluto, copulativo, existir, constituir*) to be; **cuatro y cuatro son ocho** four and four make eight; **éramos cuatro** there were four of us; **¿quién es?** (*puerta*) who is it?; (*teléfono*) who's calling?; **soy Pepe** (*a la puerta*) it's me, Pepe; (*al teléfono*) this is Pepe; **es de noche** it's night time; **son las cuatro** it's four o'clock; **el que fue director del teatro** the former theatre *Brit* [*o* theater *Am*] director **2.** (*tener lugar*) **el examen es mañana** the exam is tomorrow; **el concierto es en el pabellón** the concert is in the pavillion; **eso fue en 2000** that was in 2000 **3.** (*costar*) **¿a cuánto es el pollo?** how much is the chicken?; **¿cuánto es todo?** how much is everything? **4.** (*estar*) **el cine es en la otra calle** the cinema is in the next street **5.** (*convertirse en*) **¿qué quieres ~ de mayor?** what do you want to be when you grow up?; **¿qué es de él?** what's he doing now?; **¿qué ha sido de ella?** whatever happened to her?; **llegó a ~ ministro** he became a minister **6.** (*depender*) **todo es que se decida pronto** everything depends on a quick decision **7.** (*con 'de': posesión*) **¿de quién es esto?** whose is this?; **el paquete es de él** the parcel belongs to him; **el anillo es de plata** the ring is made of silver; **el coche es de color azul** the car is blue; **~ de Escocia** to be from Scotland; **~ de 2 euros** to cost 2 euros; **es de 30 años** he/she is thirty years old; **lo que ha hecho es muy de ella** that's typical of her; **esta manera de hablar no es de un catedrático** that's no way for a lecturer to talk; **es de lo más guay** it's really great; **eres de lo que no hay** there's nobody like you; **es de un cobarde que no veas** he's a terrible coward **8.** (*con 'para'*) **este estilo no es para ti** that's not your style; **¿para quién es el vino?** who is the wine for?; **la película no es para niños** it's not a film for children; **no es para ponerse así** there's no need to get so angry; **es como para no hablarte más** it's enough to never speak to you again **9.** (*con 'que'*) **esto es que no lo has visto bien** you can't have seen it properly; **es que ahora no puedo** the thing is I can't at the moment; **si es que merece la pena** if it's worthwhile; **¡y es que tenía unas ganas de acabarlo!** I was longing to finish it! **10.** (*oraciones enfáticas, interrogativas*) **¡esto es!** (*así se hace*) that's the way!; (*correcto*) that's right!; **¿pero qué es esto?** what's this then?; **¿cómo es eso?** how is that possible?; **¡como debe ~!** that's as it should be!; **¡no puede ~!** that can't be!; **¿no puede ~?** isn't that possible?; **¡eso es cantar!** that's what I call singing! **11.** (*en futuro*) **¿~á capaz?** will he/she be up to it?; **¡~á capaz!** trust him/her!; **~á lo que sea** we can't change things now **12.** (*en infinitivo*) **manera de ~** manner; **razón de ~** raison d'être; **a no ~ que** +*subj* unless; **todo puede ~** everything is possible; **quizá ganemos el campeonato – todo puede ~** we may yet win the championship – all is not over; **por lo que pueda ~** just in case **13.** (*en indicativo, condicional*) **es más** what is more; **siendo así** that being so; **y eso es todo** and that's that; **~ más/menos que alguien** to be better/worse than sb; **es igual** (*no importa*) it doesn't matter; **yo soy de los que piensan que...** I'm one of those who think that ...; **de no haber sido por ti** if it hadn't been for you; **no es lo que tú piensas** it's not what you think; **con el carisma que tiene sería un buen líder** (**de un partido**) with his charisma he'd be a fine leader **14.** (*en subjuntivo*) **si yo fuera tú** if I were you; **si no fuera por eso...** if it weren't for that ...; **si por mí fuera** if it were up to me; **me tratas como si fuera un niño** you treat me like a child; **sea lo que sea** whatever it is; **lo que sea ~á** whatever will be will be; **hazlo sea como sea** do it whatever; **sea quien sea** whoever it is; **dos reales, o sea, 50 céntimos** two reals, that is 50 cents; **el color que quieras, pero que no sea rojo** any colour *Brit* [*o* color *Am*] you like apart from red; **cómprame un chupa-chups o lo que sea** buy me a lollipop or sth; **por listo que sea...** however clever he is ...; **cualquiera que sea el día** whatever day it is **III.** *m* **1.** (*criatura*) being; **~ vivo** living creature; **~ humano** human being **2.** (*esencia*) essence **3.** FILOS life

serba *f* service tree fruit

Serbia *f* Serbia

serbio, -a **I.** *adj* Serb, Serbian **II.** *m, f* Serb

serenar **I.** *vt* (*calmar*) to calm **II.** *vi, vr:* **~se** (*calmarse*) to calm down; (*tiempo*) to clear up

serenata *f* MÚS serenade

serenidad *f sin pl* **1.** (*sosiego*) calmness **2.** (*príncipe*) **Su Serenidad** His Serene Highness

sereno *m* **1.** (*humedad*) night dew; **al ~** out in the open **2.** (*vigilante*) night watchman

sereno, -a *adj* **1.** (*sosegado*) calm **2.** (*sin nubes*) clear

serial *m* RADIO, TV serial

serie *f* **1.** (*sucesión*) series *inv;* **asesino en ~** serial killer; **~ televisiva** TV series *inv;* **fuera de ~** out of order; *fig* outstanding, special **2.** *t.* MAT (*gran cantidad*) set; **fabricar en ~** to mass produce **3.** DEP competition

seriedad *f sin pl* seriousness; **falta de** ~ irresponsibility

serigrafía *f* TIPO serigraphy

serio, **-a** *adj* **1.** (*grave*) serious **2.** (*severo*) solemn **3.** (*formal*) reliable **4.** (*responsable*) trustworthy **5.** (*sin burla*) serious; **esto va en** ~ this is in earnest; **¿en ~?** are you serious?

sermón *m* sermon; **echar un** ~ **a alguien** to give sb a ticking off, to preach to sb

sermonear **I.** *vi* to sermonize **II.** *vt inf* to lecture

seropositivo, **-a** *adj* HIV-positive

serosidad *f* serosity

serpear *vi* to creep

serpenteante *adj* winding; **carretera** ~ winding road

serpentear *vi* to creep; *fig* to wind

serpenteo *m* creeping

serpentina *f* (*de papel*) streamer

serpiente *f* snake; ~ **de cascabel** rattlesnake; ~ **de vidrio** slow worm; ~ **de verano** *fig* made-up story

serrado, **-a** *adj* serrated

serraduras *fpl* sawdust

serranía *f* mountainous area

serrano, **-a** *adj* highland; **jamón** ~ cured ham

serrar <e→ie> *vt* to saw

serrín *m* sawdust

serruchar *vt Arg, Chile, PRico* to saw

serrucho *m* (*sierra*) handsaw

servible *adj* serviceable

servicial *adj* obliging

servicio *m* **1.** (*acción de servir*) service; ~ **civil sustitutorio** community service; ~ **a domicilio** home delivery; ~ **de información telefónica** telephone answering service; ~ **en línea** online service; ~ **militar** military service; ~ **postal express** express delivery service; ~ **posventa** aftersales service; **estar de** ~ to be on duty; **hacer el** ~ to do military service; **hacer un** ~ **a alguien** to do sb a service; **hacer un flaco** ~ **a alguien** to do sb more harm than good **2.** (*servidumbre*) (domestic) service; **entrada de** ~ tradesman's entrance *Brit*, service entrance *Am* **3.** (*culto*) service **4.** (*cubierto*) set; ~ **de té** tea set **5.** (*retrete*) lavatory **6.** DEP serve **7.** MED sanitation

servidor *m* INFOR server

servidor(**a**) *m(f)* (*criado*) servant; **un** ~ yours truly; **¿quién es el último? –** ~ who is the last in the queue *Brit* [*o* line *Am*] ? – I am

servidumbre *f* **1.** (*personal*) servants *pl* **2.** (*esclavitud*) servitude **3.** (*trabajo de siervo*) slave labour *Brit*, slave labor *Am* **4.** (*sujeción*) compulsion **5.** JUR obligation

servil **I.** *adj* servile **II.** *m* crawler

servilismo *m sin pl* servility

servilleta *f* napkin; **doblar la** ~ *fig, inf* to kick the bucket

servilletero *m* napkin holder; (*aro*) napkin ring

servir *irr como pedir* **I.** *vi* **1.** (*ser útil*) to be of use; **no sirve de nada** it's no use; **no sirve para nada** it's useless [*o* no use at all] **2.** (*ser soldado, criado*) to serve **3.** (*ayudar*) to assist; **¿en qué puedo ~le?** can I help you?; **¡para ~le!** at your service! **4.** (*atender a alguien*) to serve **5.** DEP to serve **6.** (*suministrar*) to supply **7.** (*poner en el plato*) to serve; (*en el vaso*) to pour out **II.** *vr:* **~se** **1.** (*utilizar*) to make use **2.** (*dignarse*) **sírvase cerrar la ventana** please close the window

servoasistido, **-a** *adj* power-assisted **servodirección** *f* AUTO power steering

sésamo *m* **1.** BOT sesame **2.** TV **barrio** ~ Sesame Street ►**¡ábrete,** ~**!** open sesame!

sesear *vi to pronounce the Spanish 'c' and 'z' before 'e' and 'i' as 's'*

sesenta *adj inv, m* sixty; *v.t.* **ochenta**

seseo *m pronunciation of the Spanish 'c' and 'z' as 's' before 'e' and 'i'*

sesera *f inf* **1.** (*cerebro*) brainpan **2.** (*cabeza*) brains *pl;* (*inteligencia*) intelligence

sesgar <g→gu> *vt* **1.** (*cortar*) to cut down **2.** (*torcer*) to slant **3.** TÉC to bevel **4.** (*estudio*) to bias

sesgo *m* **1.** (*oblicuidad*) slant; **al** ~ aslant **2.** (*orientación*) direction **3.** (*opinión, estudio*) bias

sesión *f* **1.** (*reunión*) session; ~ **a puerta cerrada** private session; **abrir/levantar la** ~ to open/close [*o* adjourn] the meeting **2.** (*representación*) show(ing); ~ **de noche** night showing; ~ **de tarde** matinée

seso *m* **1.** ANAT brain **2.** (*inteligencia*) brains *pl;* **beber**(**se**) **los ~s** *fig* to drive (oneself) mad; **calentarse los ~s** *inf* to rack one's brains **3.** *pl* GASTR brains *pl* ►**tener sorbido el** ~ **a alguien** *inf* to have complete control over sb

sesudo, **-a** *adj* **1.** (*inteligente*) brainy **2.** (*sensato*) sensible

set *m* <sets> **1.** DEP set **2.** (*conjunto*) service

seta *f* mushroom; (*no comestible*) toadstool; **crecer como ~s** to mushroom

setecientos, **-as** *adj* seven hundred; *v.t.* **ochocientos**

setenta *adj inv, m* seventy; *v.t.* **ochenta**

setiembre *m v.* **septiembre**

seto *m* fence; ~ **vivo** hedge

seudónimo *m* pseudonym; (*escritor*) pen name

Seúl *m* Seoul

severidad *f sin pl* severity; (*brusquedad*) roughness; (*rigurosidad*) strictness

severo, **-a** *adj* harsh; (*brusco*) rough; (*riguroso*) strict; (*austero*) austere; (*grave*) serious

Sevilla *f* Seville

sevillano, **-a** *adj, m, f* Sevillian

sexagésimo, **-a** *adj* sixtieth; *v.t.* **octavo**

sexismo *m* sexism, gender bias

sexista **I.** *adj* sexist **II.** *mf* sexist; (*machista*) male chauvinist

sexo *m* **1.** (*individuos, actividad*) sex **2.** (*órganos*) sex organs *pl*

sextante *m* sextant

sexteto *m* MÚS sextet

sexto, **-a** *adj, m, f* sixth; *v.t.* **octavo**
séxtuplo, **-a** I. *adj* sixfold II. *m, f* sextuplet
sexual *adj* sexual; **órganos ~es** sex organs
sexualidad *f sin pl* sexuality
shock *m* shock
short *m* shorts *pl*
si I. *conj* 1. (*condicional*) if; ~ **acaso** maybe; ~ **no** if not, otherwise; **por ~...** in case ...; **por ~ acaso** just in case 2. (*en preguntas indirectas*) whether, if; **¿y si ...?** what if ...? 3. (*en oraciones concesivas*) ~ **bien** although 4. (*comparación*) **como ~...** +*subj* as if ...; **el padre está más nervioso que ~ fuera él mismo a dar a luz** the father is as nervous as if he were going to give birth himself 5. (*en frases desiderativas*) **¡~ hiciera un poco más de calor!** if only it were a little warmer! 6. (*protesta, sorpresa*) but; **¡pero ~ ella se está riendo!** but she's laughing! 7. (*énfasis*) **fíjate ~ es tonto que...** he's so stupid that ... II. *m* MÚS B; **en Si bemol mayor** in B flat major
sí I. *adv* yes; **¡~, señor!** yes sir!; **¡~ que está buena la tarta!** the cake tastes really good!; **¡(claro) que ~!** of course!; **creo que ~** I think so; **¡eso ~ que no!** certainly not!; **por ~ o por no** in any case; **porque ~** (*es así*) because that's the way it is; (*lo digo yo*) because I say so; **volver en ~** to regain consciousness II. *pron pers: m sing* himself; *f sing* herself; *cosa, objeto* itself; **a ~ mismo** to himself; **de ~** in itself; **dar de ~** to be extensive; (*tela*) to give; **el tema da mucho de ~** it's a wide subject; **en** [*o* **de por**] **~** separately; **estar fuera de ~** to be beside oneself; **hablar entre ~** to talk among themselves; **por ~** in itself; **mirar por ~** to be selfish III. *m* consent; **dar el ~** to agree; (*casamiento*) to accept the proposal; **tener el ~ de la madre** to have the mother's consent; **no hay entre ellos ni un ~ ni un no** they get on extremely well
siamés, **-esa** *adj* Siamese; **gato ~** Siamese cat; **hermanos siameses** Siamese twins
sibarita I. *adj* sybaritic II. *mf* sybarite, pleasure seeker
Siberia *f* Siberia
siberiano, **-a** *adj, m, f* Siberian
sibilino, **-a** *adj* cryptic
sicalíptico, **-a** *adj* saucy
sicario *m* hired assassin [*o* gunman]
Sicilia *f* Sicily
siciliano, **-a** *adj, m, f* Sicilian
sicología *f v.* **(p)sicología**
sida, **SIDA** *m abr de* **síndrome de inmunodeficiencia adquirida** Aids, AIDS
siderurgia *f* iron and steel industry
siderúrgico, **-a** *adj* iron and steel
sidoso, **-a** I. *adj* Aids; **enfermo ~** Aids sufferer II. *m, f* Aids sufferer
sidra *f* cider
siega *f* 1. (*el segar*) reaping 2. (*tiempo*) harvest time 3. (*mieses*) cornfields *pl*
siembra *f* 1. (*el sembrar*) sowing 2. (*tiempo*) sowing time 3. (*terreno*) sown field
siempre *adv* always; **de ~** always; **a la hora de ~** at the usual time; **una amistad de ~** a lifelong friendship; **eso es así desde ~** that's always been so; **~ pasa lo mismo** the same thing always happens; **¡hasta ~!** see you!; **por ~** for ever; **por ~ jamás** for ever and ever; **~ que** +*subj* provided that, as long as
sien *f* ANAT temple
sierpe *f* 1. snake; **tener una lengua de ~** *fig* to have a sharp tongue 2. (*persona feroz*) fierce person; (*colérica*) bad-tempered person; (*fea*) ugly person
sierra *f* 1. (*herramienta*) saw; **~ continua** chainsaw; **~ mecánica** power saw 2. (*lugar*) sawmill 3. GEO mountain range; **~ de peñascos cortados** ridge
siervo, **-a** *m, f* 1. (*esclavo*) slave; **~ de la gleba** serf 2. (*servidor*) servant
siesta *f* 1. (*descanso*) siesta; **echar** [*o* **dormir**] **la ~** to have a nap 2. (*hora de calor*) hottest part of the day
siete I. *adj inv* seven II. *m* 1. (*número*) seven; *v.t.* **ocho** 2. *inf* (*rasgón*) rent 3. (*carpintería*) G-clamp 4. *AmS, Méx, vulg* (*ano*) arse *Brit,* ass *Am*
sietemesino, **-a** I. *adj* **niño ~** baby born 2 months premature II. *m, f* 1. (*prematuro*) baby born 2 months premature 2. *inf* (*chico presumido*) little squirt
sífilis *f* syphilis
sifón *m* 1. TÉC (*tubo, tubería*) trap 2. (*botella*) siphon 3. (*soda*) soda, club soda *Am*
siga *f Chile* chase
sigilar *vt* 1. (*ocultar*) to conceal 2. (*sellar*) to stamp
sigilo *m* 1. (*discreción*) discretion; **~ profesional** client confidentiality 2. (*secreto*) stealth; **~ sacramental** secrecy of the confessional, seal of confession 3. (*sello*) stamp
sigla *f* 1. (*letra inicial*) initial 2. (*rótulo de siglas*) acronym; **~ de fabricante** manufacturer's mark
siglo *m* century; **Siglo de las Luces** Age of Enlightment; **el ~ XXI** the 21st century; **el Siglo de Oro** the Golden Age; **por los ~s de los ~s** for ever and ever; **hace un ~ que no te veo** I haven't seen you for ages; **retirarse del ~** to withdraw from the world
signar I. *vt* 1. (*marcar*) to put one's mark on 2. (*firmar*) to sign 3. REL to make the sign of the cross over II. *vr:* **~se** to cross oneself
signatario, **-a** I. *adj* signatory; **poder ~** JUR power of attorney II. *m, f* signatory
signatura *f* 1. (*firma*) *t.* TIPO signature 2. (*en biblioteca*) catalogue *Brit* [*o* catalog *Am*] number
significación *f* 1. (*importancia*) significance 2. (*sentido*) meaning
significado *m* meaning
significar <c→qu> I. *vt, vi* to mean; **¿qué significa eso?** what's the meaning of this? II. *vr* **~se por algo** to become known for sth
significativo, **-a** *adj* (*importante*) significant;

(*con significado*) meaningful

signo *m* 1. *t.* LING, MAT (*señal*) sign; ~ **de enfermedad** sign of illness; ~ **de más/menos** plus/minus sign; ~ **de la multiplicación** multiplication sign; ~ **de puntuación** punctuation mark 2. (*escrito*) mark 3. (*destino*) fate

siguiente I. *adj* following; **de la ~ manera** in the following way II. *mf* next; **¡el ~!** next please!

sílaba *f* syllable; ~ **aguda** stressed syllable; **de dos ~s** two-syllable

silba *f* hissing

silbar *vi, vt* 1. (*persona*) to whistle; (*serpiente*) to hiss; (*sirena*) to blow; (*una flecha, bala*) to whizz 2. (*abuchear*) to boo

silbatina *f AmS* hissing

silbato *m* whistle

silbido *m* whistle; (*serpiente*) hiss; (*sirena*) blast; (*viento*) whistling; ~ **de los oídos** ringing in the ears

silbo *m* 1. (*silbido*) whistle 2. (*voz, serpiente*) hiss; (*viento*) whistling

silenciador *m* silencer

silenciar *vt* 1. (*suceso*) to hush up 2. (*persona*) to silence

silencio *m* 1. silence; **en** ~ in silence; **guardar** ~ to remain silent; **guardar ~ sobre algo** to keep silent about sth; **imponer** ~ to impose silence; **pasar algo en** ~ to pass over sth in silence; **romper el** ~ to break the silence; **entregar algo al** ~ *fig* to cast sth into oblivion; **¡~!** quiet! 2. MÚS rest

silencioso, **-a** I. *adj* 1. (*poco hablador*) quiet 2. (*callado*) silent 3. (*sin ruido*) soundless; (*motor*) noiseless II. *m, f* silencer

Silesia *f* Silesia

silesio, **-a** *adj, m, f* Silesian

silicio *m* silicon

silicona *f* silicone

silla *f* 1. *t.* REL (*asiento*) chair; ~ **de manos** litter; ~ **de lona** deckchair; ~ **giratoria** swivel chair; ~ **plegable** folding chair; ~ **de ruedas** wheelchair 2. (*montura*) saddle

sillín *m* saddle, seat *Am*

sillón *m* (*butaca*) armchair

silueta *f* silhouette; **cuidar la** ~ to look after one's figure; **la ~ de Nueva York** the New York skyline

silvestre *adj* wild

silvicultura *f* forestry

sima *f* GEO abyss

simbólico, **-a** *adj* symbolic

simbolismo *m* symbolism

simbolizar <z→c> *vt* to symbolize

símbolo *m* symbol; ~ **de prestigio** status symbol

simetría *f* symmetry

simétrico, **-a** *adj* symmetrical

simiente *f* seed

símil I. *adj* similar II. *m* simile

similar *adj* similar

similitud *f* similarity; (*física*) resemblance

simio *m* ape

simpatía *f* 1. (*agrado*) liking; **sentir ~ por algo** to be attracted to sth; **tener ~ por alguien** to have a liking for sb 2. (*carácter*) friendliness

simpático, **-a** *adj* friendly; **hacerse el** ~ to ingratiate oneself

simpatizante *mf* sympathizer

simpatizar <z→c> *vi* 1. (*congeniar*) to get on *Brit*, to get along *Am* 2. (*identificarse con*) to sympathize

simple <simplísimo *o* simplicísimo> I. *adj* 1. (*sencillo*) simple 2. (*fácil*) easy, straightforward 3. (*mero*) pure; **a ~ vista** with the naked eye 4. (*mentecato*) simple II. *m* 1. (*persona*) simpleton 2. (*tenis*) singles *inv*

simplemente *adv* simply

simpleza *f* 1. (*bobería*) simpleness 2. (*tontería*) silly thing 3. (*insignificancia*) trifle

simplicidad *f sin pl* 1. (*sencillez*) simplicity 2. (*ingenuidad*) simpleness

simplicísimo, **-a** *adj superl de* **simple**

simplificar <c→qu> *vt* 1. (*facilitar*) to simplify 2. MAT to break down

simposio *m* symposium

simulación *f* simulation; (*fingir*) feigning

simulacro *m* 1. (*apariencia*) simulacrum; ~ **de incendio** fire drill 2. (*acción simulada*) sham

simulador *m* TÉC simulator; ~ **de vuelo** flight simulator

simulador(a) *m(f)* faker

simular *vt* to simulate

simultanear *vt* to do simultaneously

simultaneidad *f sin pl* simultaneity

simultáneo, **-a** *adj* simultaneous; **interpretación simultánea** simultaneous interpreting

sin I. *prep* without; ~ **dormir** without sleep; ~ **querer** unintentionally; ~ **más** nothing more; ~ **más ni más** without thinking about it, without further ado; **estar ~ algo** to be out of sth II. *adv* ~ **embargo** however

sinagoga *f* REL synagogue

sincerarse *vr* (*exculparse*) ~ **ante alguien** to justify oneself to sb; (*abrirse*) to be completely honest with sb

sinceridad *f* sincerity; **con toda** ~ in all sincerity

sincero, **-a** *adj* sincere; **seré ~ contigo** I'll be honest with you

síncopa *f* MÚS syncopation

sincrónico, **-a** *adj* synchronous

sincronizador(a) *m(f)* synchro

sincronizar <z→c> *vt* to synchronize

sindical *adj* union

sindicalismo *m* 1. (*movimiento*) trade unionism 2. (*doctrina*) syndicalism

sindicalista I. *adj* (*sindical*) union II. *mf* (*miembro*) trade unionist

sindicar <c→qu> I. *vt* 1. (*obreros*) to unionize 2. (*delatar*) to betray 3. (*poner bajo sospecha*) to place under suspicion II. *vr:* **~se** to join a union

sindicato *m* trade union *Brit,* labor union *Am*
síndico *m* **1.** (*administrador de la quiebra*) official receiver **2.** (*representante*) trustee
síndrome *m* syndrome; ~ **de abstinencia** withdrawal symptoms; ~ **de Estocolmo** Stockholm syndrome
sinfín *m* huge number
sinfonía *f* symphony
sinfónico, -a *adj* symphonic; **orquesta sinfónica** symphony orchestra
Singapur *m* Singapore
singular I. *adj* **1.** (*único*) singular; **ejemplar** ~ unique example **2.** (*excepcional*) outstanding; **en** ~ in the singular; *fig* in particular **3.** (*extraño*) peculiar **II.** *m* LING singular; **¡habla en ~!** *fig* speak for yourself!
singularidad *f* **1.** (*unicidad*) singularity **2.** (*excepcionalidad*) exceptional nature **3.** (*distinción*) peculiarity
singularizar <z→c> **I.** *vt* (*particularizar*) to single out **II.** *vr:* **~se** to stand out
singularmente *adv* especially
siniestro *m* (*accidente*) accident; (*catástrofe*) natural disaster; (*incendio*) fire
siniestro, -a *adj elev* **1.** (*maligno*) evil; **un personaje** ~ a sinister character **2.** (*funesto*) disastrous **3.** (*izquierdo*) left; **a diestra y siniestra** right and left
sinnúmero *m* huge number
sino I. *m* fate **II.** *conj* **1.** (*al contrario*) but **2.** (*solamente*) **no espero ~ que me creas** I only hope that you believe me **3.** (*excepto*) except
sinónimo *m* synonym
sinónimo, -a *adj* synonymous
sinopsis *f inv* **1.** (*resumen*) synopsis **2.** (*esquema*) diagram
sinóptico, -a *adj* **1.** (*resumido*) synoptic **2.** (*esquemático*) diagrammatic
sinrazón *f* injustice; (*absurdo*) unreasonableness
sinsabor *m* **1.** (*cosa desagradable*) unpleasantness **2.** (*disgusto*) sorrow
sinsentido *m* absurdity
sinsonte *m AmL* ZOOL mockingbird
sintáctico, -a *adj* syntactic
sintaxis *f inv* syntax
síntesis *f inv* synthesis; **en** ~ in a word
sintético, -a *adj* synthetic
sintetizador *m* MÚS synthesizer
sintetizar <z→c> *vt* **1.** QUÍM to synthesize **2.** (*resumir*) to summarize
síntoma *m* symptom
sintomático, -a *adj* symptomatic
sintomatología *f* symptomatology
sintonía *f* **1.** (*adecuación*) tuning **2.** (*señal sonora, melodía*) signature tune **3.** (*entendimiento*) **estar en ~ (con alguien)** to be on the same wavelength (as sb)
sintonizador *m* (*aparato*) tuner; (*botón, dial*) tuning knob
sintonizar <z→c> **I.** *vt* to tune in to; ~ **una emisora** to pick up a radio station **II.** *vi* to tune in
sinuosidad *f* **1.** (*curvación*) sinuosity **2.** (*concavidad*) curve
sinuoso, -a *adj* **1.** (*curvado*) winding **2.** (*retorcido*) devious
sinvergüenza I. *adj* shameless **II.** *mf pey* rotter
sionismo *m* Zionism
síquico, -a *adj v.* **(p)síquico**
siquiera I. *adv* at least; **ni** ~ not even **II.** *conj* + *subj* even if
sirena *f* **1.** (*bocina*) siren **2.** (*mujer pez*) mermaid
sirga *f* towrope
Siria *f* Syria
sirio, -a *adj, m, f* Syrian
siroco *m* METEO sirocco
sirope *m AmC, Col* (*jarabe*) syrup
sirviente *mf* (*criado*) servant
sisa *f* **1.** (*corte*) armhole **2.** (*dinero*) petty theft
sisar *vt* **1.** (*cortar una sisa*) to take in **2.** (*hurtar*) to pilfer
sisear *vt* to hiss
siseo *m* hissing
sisirisco *m Méx* **1.** (*ano*) anus **2.** (*miedo*) fright
sísmico, -a *adj* seismic; **movimiento** ~ earth tremor
sismo *m* (*temblor*) tremor; (*terremoto*) earthquake
sismógrafo *m* seismograph
sistema *m* system; ~ **antibloqueo de frenos** AUTO antilocking brake system; ~ **de alarma** alarm system; **Sistema Europeo de Bancos Centrales** European System of Central Banks; ~ **inmunitario** immune system; **Sistema Monetario Europeo** European Monetary System; ~ **montañoso** mountain range; ~ **operativo** INFOR operating system; ~ **periódico** QUÍM periodic table; ~ **planetario** ASTR solar system; **por** ~ on principle
sistemático, -a *adj* systematic
sistematizar <z→c> *vt* to systematize
sitiar *vt* to besiege; *fig* to surround
sitio *m* **1.** (*lugar*) place; (*espacio*) room; ~ **de veraneo** holiday resort; **en cualquier** ~ anywhere; **en ningún** ~ nowhere; **en todos los ~s** everywhere; **guardar el ~ a alguien** to keep sb's place; **hacer** ~ to make room; **ocupar mucho** ~ to take up a lot of room; **poner a alguien en su** ~ *fig* to put sb in his/her place; **quedarse en su** ~ *fig* to be dead on the spot *Brit,* to drop dead *Am* **2.** MIL siege **3.** *Méx* ~ **(de taxis)** taxi stand
sito, -a *adj* ~ **en** situated in
situación *f* **1.** (*ubicación*) location **2.** (*estado*) situation; **estar en ~ desahogada** to be comfortably off
situado, -a *adj* situated; **estar** ~ to be financially secure; **estar bien** ~ (*trabajo*) to have a good job
situar <*1. pres:* sitúo> **I.** *vt* (*colocar*) to place; (*emplazar*) to locate **II.** *vr:* **~se**

1. (*ponerse en un lugar*) to situate oneself 2. (*abrirse paso*) to make one's way

siútico, -a *adj Chile, inf* 1. (*de mal gusto*) vulgar 2. (*de nuevo rico*) affected

S.M. *mf abr de* **Su Majestad** H.M.

SME *m abr de* **Sistema Monetario Europeo** EMS

smog *m sin pl* smog; ~ **electrónico** e-smog

s/n *abr de* **sin número** no number

so I. *interj* whoa! II. *prep* under; ~ **pena de...** on pain of ...; ~ **pretexto de que...** under the pretext of ... III. *m inf* ¡~ **imbécil!** you idiot!

SO *abr de* **sudoeste** SW

soba *f inf* 1. (*a persona*) pawing, touching up *Brit*, feel-up *Am* 2. (*de un objeto*) handling, fingering 3. (*zurra*) hiding

sobaco *m* armpit

sobado *m* pawing

sobado, -a *adj* 1. (*objetos*) worn 2. (*papel*) dog-eared 3. (*tema*) well worn

sobajar *vt* 1. (*manosear con fuerza*) to paw 2. *Méx* (*humillar*) to humiliate

sobandero *m Col* bonesetter

sobaquina *f* underarm odour *Brit* [*o* odor *Am*]

sobar *vt* 1. *inf* (*a persona*) to paw, to touch up *Brit*, to feel up *Am* 2. (*un objeto*) to handle, to finger 3. (*ablandar*) to knead 4. (*pegar*) to wallop 5. (*molestar*) to pester 6. *inf* (*dormir*) to sleep, to kip *Brit*

soberanamente *adv* (*extremadamente*) supremely; **divertirse** ~ to have a whale of a time

soberanía *f* sovereignty

soberano, -a I. *adj* 1. POL sovereign 2. (*excelente*) supreme 3. *inf* (*enorme*) really big II. *m, f* (*monarca*) sovereign

soberbia *f* 1. (*orgullo*) pride 2. (*suntuosidad*) magnificence 3. (*ira*) anger

soberbio, -a *adj* 1. (*orgulloso*) proud 2. (*suntuoso*) magnificent 3. *inf* (*enorme*) really big

sobón, -ona *adj* 1. (*impertinente*) over familiar 2. *inf* (*vago*) lazy

sobornar *vt* to bribe

soborno *m* 1. (*acción*) bribery 2. (*dinero*) bribe; (*regalo*) gift (*given as a bribe*)

sobra *f* 1. (*exceso*) surplus; **de** ~ (*en abundancia*) more than enough; (*inútilmente*) in the way; **saber algo de** ~ to know sth only too well 2. *pl* (*desperdicios*) leftovers *pl*; (*restos*) remnants *pl*

sobradamente *adv* amply

sobrado I. *m* garret II. *adv* extremely

sobrado, -a *adj* 1. (*demasiado*) more than enough; **estar** ~ **de algo** to have more than enough of sth 2. (*atrevido*) bold 3. (*rico*) wealthy

sobrador(a) *m(f) Arg, Urug* conceited person

sobrante I. *adj* 1. (*que sobra*) spare; COM, FIN surplus 2. (*de más*) excess II. *m* (*que sobra*) remainder; (*superávit*) surplus; (*saldo*) balance in hand

sobrar *vi* 1. (*quedar*) to remain; **nos sobra bastante tiempo** we have plenty of time 2. (*abundar*) to be more than enough; **me sobran cinco kilos** I've got five kilos left over; (*perder peso*) I've got to lose five kilos; **aquí sobran las palabras** nothing more needs to be said 3. (*estar de más*) to be superfluous; **creo que sobras aquí** I think you're in the way [*o* not needed] here

sobrasada *f sausage spread, typical of the Balearic Islands*

sobre I. *m* 1. (*para una carta*) envelope; ~ **monedero** special delivery envelope; ~ **de ventanilla** window envelope; **un** ~ **de levadura** a packet of yeast 2. *inf* (*cama*) bed; **irse al** ~ to go off to bed II. *prep* 1. (*por encima de*) on; **deja el periódico** ~ **la mesa** leave the newspaper on the table; **marchar** ~ **la ciudad** to march on the town; **estar** ~ **alguien** to keep constant watch on sb 2. (*cantidad aproximada*) **pesar** ~ **los cien kilos** to weigh about a hundred kilos 3. (*aproximación temporal*) **llegar** ~ **las tres** to arrive at about three o'clock; **irse de vacaciones** ~ **el 20** to go on holiday on about the 20th 4. (*tema, asunto*) about; ~ **ello** about it 5. (*reiteración*) on top of; **le caía lágrima** ~ **lágrima** he/she shed tear after tear 6. (*además de*) as well as 7. (*superioridad*) **el boxeador triunfó** ~ **su adversario** the boxer triumphed over his opponent; **destacar** ~ **alguien por su estatura** to tower over sb 8. (*porcentajes*) out of; **tres** ~ **cien** three out of a hundred 9. FIN **un préstamo** ~ **una casa** a loan on a house; **préstame cien dólares** ~ **este anillo** lend me a hundred dollars on this ring

sobreabundancia *f* superabundance, overabundance

sobreabundar *vi* to overabound, to be very abundant

sobrealimentación *f* overfeeding

sobrealimentar *vt* 1. ELEC to supercharge 2. (*animales*) to overfeed

sobrecama *f* bedspread

sobrecarga *f* excess; (*persona*) added burden; ELEC overload; COM surcharge

sobrecargar I. *vt* (*por peso*) to overload; (*por esfuerzo*) to overburden II. *vr:* ~**se** to overload oneself; ~**se de trabajo** to take on too much work

sobrecoger I. *vt* 1. (*sorprender*) to take by surprise 2. (*espantar*) to frighten II. *vr:* ~**se** 1. (*asustarse*) to be startled 2. (*sorprenderse*) ~**se de algo** to be surprised by sth

sobrecubierta *f* outer cover; (*de libro*) jacket, dust cover

sobredicho, -a *adj* aforementioned, above-mentioned

sobredorar *vt* 1. (*con oro*) to gild 2. (*con palabras*) to gloss over

sobredosis *f inv* overdose

sobreentender <e→ie> I. *vt* 1. (*adivinar*) to infer; **de todo ello sobreentendemos que...** we understand from all this that ...

2. (*presuponer*) to presuppose II. *vr:* **~se** (*ser evidente*) to be obvious; **aquí queda sobreentendido que...** (*implicado*) it is implied here that ...
sobreestimar *vt* to overestimate
sobreexceder I. *vt* to surpass II. *vr:* **~se** to lead a dissipated life
sobreexcitar I. *vt* (*órgano*) to overexcite II. *vr:* **~se** to get overexcited
sobreexpuesto, -a *adj* 1. FOTO overexposed 2. (*arriba mencionado*) discussed above
sobrehilado *m* 1. (*acción*) tacking *Brit*, basting *Am* 2. (*puntada*) tacking stitch *Brit*, basting stitch *Am*
sobrehilar *vt* to tack *Brit*, to baste *Am*
sobrehumano, -a *adj* superhuman
sobrellevar *vt* 1. (*aguantar*) to bear; **~ mal** to take badly; **~ bien** to take well 2. (*peso*) **~ algo a alguien** to help sb with sth
sobremanera *adv* exceedingly
sobremesa *f* 1. (*mantel*) table cover 2. (*postre*) dessert 3. (*tras la comida*) **de ~** after-dinner; INFOR desktop; **conversación de ~** table talk; **programa de ~** TV afternoon programme *Brit* [*o* program *Am*]; **estar de ~** to be gathered after a meal
sobrenadar *vi* to float
sobrenatural *adj* 1. (*fenómenos*) supernatural; **ciencias ~es** occult sciences; **la vida ~** life after death 2. (*extraordinario*) incredible
sobrenombre *m* 1. (*calificativo*) epithet 2. (*apodo*) nickname
sobrentender <e→ie> *vt, vr v.* **sobreentender**
sobreparto *m* confinement; **dolores de ~** afterpains *pl;* **morir de ~** to die in childbirth
sobrepasar *vt* 1. (*en cantidad*) to surpass; (*límite*) to exceed; **~ su ámbito de responsabilidades** to go beyond one's powers 2. (*aventajar*) to pass; (*un récord, el mejor*) to beat 3. (*adelantar*) to overtake
sobreponer *irr como poner* I. *vt* 1. (*encima de algo*) to superimpose, to put on top; (*cubierta, funda*) cover; (*añadir*) to add 2. (*en consideración, rango*) **~ a algo/alguien** to place above sth/sb; (*anteponer*) to prefer to sth/sb; **~ a alguien a todos los demás** to put sb before everyone else II. *vr:* **~se** 1. (*calmarse*) to pull oneself together 2. (*al enemigo, a una enfermedad*) to overcome; (*al miedo, a un susto*) to recover from
sobreprecio *m* surcharge
sobrepujar *vt* **~ en algo** to outdo in sth
sobresaliente I. *adj* 1. (*excelente*) outstanding 2. ENS (*en títulos superiores*) first class; (*nota: nine or better on a scale of one to ten*) excellent II. *m* ENS (*nota*) distinction
sobresalir *irr como salir vi* 1. *t.* ARQUIT (*por tamaño, estatura*) **~ de algo** to stand out from sth 2. (*distinguirse*) to stand out 3. (*ser excelente*) **~ en algo** to be outstanding at sth
sobresaltar I. *vi* to start II. *vt* to startle III. *vr* **~se con** [*o* **de**] **algo** to be startled at sth
sobresalto *m* 1. (*susto*) scare 2. (*turbación*) sudden shock; **con ~** shocked; **de ~** suddenly
sobreseer *irr como leer* I. *vt* (*dejar*) to stop; (*aplazar*) to suspend; (*interrumpir*) to stay II. *vi* to desist; **~ en los pagos** to interrupt payment
sobreseimiento *m* JUR stay of proceedings; (*aplazamiento*) discontinuance; (*renuncia*) dismissal
sobrestante *m* (*capataz*) foreman; **~ de turno** foreman on duty
sobrestimar *vt* to overestimate
sobresueldo *m* extra pay [*o* wage]
sobretasa *f* (*suplemento*) surcharge; **~ por retraso** surcharge for delayed payment
sobretodo *m* (*abrigo*) overcoat; (*mono*) overall
sobrevenir *irr como venir vi* (*epidemia*) to ensue; (*desgracia, guerra*) to happen unexpectedly; (*tormenta*) to break; **le sobrevino una sensación de gran tristeza** a feeling of deep sadness took [*o* came over] him/her
sobreviviente *mf* survivor
sobrevivir *vi* (*acontecimientos*) to survive; (*a alguien*) to outlive; **pero ella sigue sobreviviendo en mi recuerdo** but she lives on in my memory
sobrevolar <o→ue> *vt* to fly over
sobrexceder *vt, vr v.* **sobreexceder**
sobrexcitar *vt, vr v.* **sobreexcitar**
sobriedad *f sin pl* 1. (*sin beber*) soberness 2. (*moderación*) moderation 3. (*prudencia*) restraint 4. (*estilo*) plainness
sobrino, -a *m, f* nephew *m*, niece *f*
sobrinonieto, -a *m, f* great-nephew *m*, great-niece *f*
sobrio, -a *adj* 1. (*no borracho*) sober 2. (*moderado*) moderate 3. (*prudente*) restrained; **~ de palabras** of few words 4. (*estilo*) plain
soca *f AmL* AGR ratoon
socaire *m* NÁUT lee; **al ~** to leeward; **al ~ de** (*protección*) protected by; (*pretexto*) under the pretext that; **estar al ~** (*vaguear*) to shirk
socaliña *f* (*astucia*) cunning
socar <c→qu> I. *vt AmC* to compress II. *vr:* **~se** *AmC* to get drunk
socarrar I. *vt* to scorch; (*tela*) to singe II. *vr:* **~se** to char
socarrón, -ona I. *adj* 1. (*sarcástico*) ironic 2. (*astuto*) crafty II. *m, f* 1. (*pícaro*) rogue 2. (*taimado*) sly devil
socavar *vt* to dig under; *fig* to undermine
socavón *m* 1. MIN subsidence 2. (*en el suelo*) hole
sociable *adj* 1. (*tratable*) sociable; (*que no discute*) easy-going 2. (*afable*) friendly
social *adj* 1. (*relativo a la sociedad*) society; (*a la convivencia*) social 2. (*por parte del estado*) **asistencia ~** social work; **asistente ~** social worker; **Estado Social** Welfare State 3. JUR, ECON company, corporate; **razón ~** company name
socialdemócrata I. *adj* social-democratic

II. *mf* social democrat

socialismo *m sin pl* socialism

socialista *adj, mf* socialist

socializar <z→c> *vt* to socialize

sociedad *f* 1. (*población, humanidad*) society; ~ **del bienestar** welfare society [*o* state] 2. (*trato*) company; **la ~ con la que tratas** the company you keep 3. (*empresa*) company; ~ **anónima** corporation 4. (*asociación*) association; ~ **protectora (de animales)** society for the prevention of cruelty to animals 5. JUR ~ **conyugal** property held jointly by spouses 6. (*mundo elegante*) society; **la buena** [*o* **alta**] ~ high society

socio, -a *m, f* 1. (*de una asociación*) member 2. (*en sociedad comercial*) partner; ~ **comercial** business partner 3. *inf* (*compañero*) mate

socioeconómico, -a *adj* socioeconomic

sociología *f sin pl* sociology

sociólogo, -a *m, f* sociologist

sociopolítico, -a *adj* sociopolitical

socolar *vt Col, Ecua, Hond, Nic* to clear land

socollón *m AmC, Cuba* jolt

socorrer *vt* to help, to come to the aid of

socorrido, -a *adj* 1. (*útil*) useful 2. (*que ayuda*) helpful 3. (*comprobado*) tried and tested 4. (*común*) ordinary; (*trillado*) well worn

socorrismo *m* live-saving

socorrista *mf* (*de playas*) lifeguard; (*en piscinas*) pool attendant

socorro *m* 1. (*ayuda*) help; (*salvamento*) rescue; **pedir** ~ to ask for help; **puesto de** ~ first-aid post; **señal de** ~ distress signal, S.O.S. 2. (*dinero*) money towards sth

socoyote *m Méx* (*benjamín*) youngest child

soda *f* (*bebida*) soda water

sódico, -a *adj* sodium

sodio *m* sodium

soez *adj* crude, coarse

sofá <sofás> *m* sofa

sofá-cama <sofás-cama> *m* sofa-bed

sofisticación *f* sophistication

sofisticado, -a *adj* 1. (*afectado*) affected 2. TÉC sophisticated

sofisticar <c→qu> *vt* 1. (*refinar*) to over-refine 2. (*falsificar*) to adulterate

sofocación *f* 1. (*ahogo*) suffocation 2. (*calor*) heat 3. (*bochorno*) stifling atmosphere

sofocado, -a *adj* **estar** ~ to be stifled

sofocante *adj* 1. (*asfixiante*) stifling; (*ambiente, aire*) suffocating; **hace un calor** ~ the heat is stifling 2. (*avergonzante*) shameless

sofocar <c→qu> I. *vt* 1. (*asfixiar*) to suffocate 2. (*impedir que progrese*) to stifle; (*fuego*) to put out; (*revolución*) to crush; (*epidemia*) to stop 3. (*avergonzar*) to embarrass 4. (*enojar*) to upset II. *vr:* **~se** 1. (*sonrojar*) to blush 2. (*excitarse*) to get worked up; (*enojarse*) to get angry 3. (*ahogarse*) to suffocate

sofoco *m* 1. (*ahogo*) suffocation; (*después de un esfuerzo*) panting 2. (*excitación*) shock 3. (*calor*) heat flush

sofocón *m inf* 1. (*enojo*) annoyance 2. (*excitación*) shock

sofreír *irr como reír vt* to fry lightly

soga *f* rope; (*para ahorcar*) noose; **dar** ~ to pay out rope; **dar ~ a alguien** (*mofarse*) to make fun of sb; (*llevar la corriente*) to humour sb *Brit,* to humor sb *Am;* **Pedro está con la ~ al cuello** *fig* Pedro has his back to the wall

sois *2. pres pl de* **ser**

soja *f* soya *Brit,* soy *Am;* ~ **transgénica** GM soya; **semilla de** ~ soya bean *Brit,* soybean *Am*

sojuzgar <g→gu> *vt* to subdue

sol *m* 1. (*astro*) sun; (*luz*) sunlight; **al ~ puesto** at dusk; **de ~ a ~** from dawn to dusk; **día de** ~ sunny day; **ponerse al** ~ (*tumbarse*) to lie in the sun; (*sentarse*) to sit in the sun; **tomar el** ~ to sunbathe; **hoy hace** ~ it's sunny today 2. (*bebida*) ~ **y sombra** brandy and anisette 3. (*moneda*) sol 4. *inf* (*alabanza*) **es un** ~ he/she is an angel 5. MÚS G; ~ **mayor** G major ▸**no dejar a alguien ni a ~ ni a sombra** not to leave sb alone; **arrimarse al ~ que más calienta** to know which side one's bread is buttered on

solamente *adv* 1. (*únicamente*) only 2. (*expresamente*) expressly

solana *f* 1. (*en edificios*) suntrap; (*en montañas*) south-facing slope 2. (*galería*) sun gallery

solano *m* east wind

solapa *f* 1. (*chaqueta*) lapel 2. (*libro*) flap

solapado, -a *adj* underhand *Brit,* underhanded *Am*

solapar I. *vi* to overlap II. *vt* 1. (*cubrir*) to cover up 2. (*chaqueta, vestido*) to put lapels on 3. (*disimular*) to conceal

solar I. *adj* solar; **plexo** ~ solar plexus II. *m* 1. (*terreno*) plot; ~ **para edificaciones** building site 2. (*casa*) family seat 3. (*linaje*) line; **venir del ~ de...** to come from the ... family 4. *AmC* (*patio*) yard III. <o→ue> *vt* 1. (*pavimentar*) to tile 2. (*calzado*) to sole

solariego, -a I. *adj* 1. (*de linaje noble*) of noble birth 2. (*propiedad*) manorial; **casa solariega** family seat II. *m, f* 1. (*noble*) landowner 2. (*propiedad*) estate

solaz *m* 1. (*recreo*) recreation; (*esparcimiento*) relaxation 2. (*consuelo*) solace

solazar <z→c> I. *vt* 1. (*recrear*) to allow to relax 2. (*entretener*) to amuse 3. (*consolar*) to comfort II. *vr:* **~se** 1. (*recrearse*) to relax 2. (*divertirse*) to enjoy oneself; (*entretenerse*) to amuse oneself

soldada *f* (*salario*) salary; MIL service pay

soldado, -a *m, f* 1. MIL soldier; ~ **de infantería** infantryman, foot soldier; ~ **de caballería** cavalryman; ~ **raso** private 2. (*defensor*) defender

soldador *m* TÉC soldering iron [*o* gun]

soldador *mf* welder

soldadura *f* TÉC 1. (*trabajo*) welding 2. (*punto de unión*) soldered [*o* welded] joint 3. (*material*) solder

S

soldar <o→ue> **I.** *vt* (*con metal fundido*) to weld; (*unir*) to join **II.** *vr:* ~**se** (*herida*) to heal; (*huesos*) to knit together

soleado, **-a** *adj* sunny

solear I. *vt* to put out in the sun; (*blanquear*) to bleach **II.** *vr:* ~**se** to bleach

soledad *f* (*estado*) solitude; (*sentimiento*) loneliness

solemne *adj* **1.** (*ceremonioso*) solemn; **discurso** ~ formal speech **2.** (*mentira*) monstrous; (*error*) monumental

solemnidad *f* **1.** (*cualidad*) solemnity **2.** REL (*festividad*) religious ceremony **3.** *pl* (*formalidades*) formalities *pl*

solemnizar <z→c> *vt* to celebrate

soler <o→ue> *vi* ~ **hacer** to be in the habit of doing; **en España se suelen celebrar los santos** in Spain saints' days are usually celebrated; **suele ocurrir que...** it often occurs that ...; **solemos coger el tren** we usually catch the train; **solíamos coger el tren, pero ya no** we used to catch the train, but not any more

solera *f* **1.** (*puntal*) support **2.** (*del molino*) lower millstone **3.** (*del vino*) *mature wine mixed with younger wine to give it flavour* **4.** (*abolengo*) tradition; **con mucha** ~ with a lot of character

solfa *f* **1.** MÚS (*signos*) musical notation; (*arte de solfear*) sol-fa; (*melodía*) music; **estar (escrito) en** ~ to be in musical notation **2.** *inf* (*zurra*) hiding ►**poner algo en** ~ (*ridiculizar*) to hold sth up to mockery; (*con arte y orden*) to put sth in order

solfear *vt* **1.** MÚS to practise sol-fa *Brit,* to practice sol-fa *Am* **2.** (*pegar*) to tan **3.** *inf* (*reprender*) to tell off

solfeo *m* **1.** MÚS (*acción*) solfeggio, singing of scales; (*fragmento*) sol-fa **2.** *inf* (*zurra*) hiding

solicitación *f* **1.** (*petición*) request **2.** (*para un trabajo*) application

solicitante *mf* **1.** (*de una petición*) petitioner; ~ **de asilo** asylum seeker **2.** (*para un trabajo*) applicant

solicitar *vt* **1.** (*pedir*) to ask for; (*gestionar*) to solicit; (*un trabajo*) to apply for; ~ **un médico** to call for a doctor **2.** (*compañía, atención*) to seek; ~ **la mano de una mujer** to ask for a woman's hand in marriage; **te solicitan en todas partes** you're in great demand

solícito, **-a** *adj* (*diligente*) diligent; (*cuidadoso*) solicitous

solicitud *f* **1.** (*diligencia*) diligence; (*cuidado*) solicitude **2.** (*petición*) request; (*formal*) petition; ~ **de empleo** job application

solidaridad *f sin pl* solidarity; **por** ~ **con** out of solidarity with

solidario, **-a** *adj* shared; **hacerse** ~ **de alguien** to sympathize with sb

solidarizarse <z→c> *vr* to feel solidarity with; **me solidarizo con tu opinión** I share your view

solidez *f* solidity; (*estabilidad*) firmness

solidificación *f* FÍS solidification

solidificar <c→qu> **I.** *vt* to solidify; *fig* to harden **II.** *vr:* ~**se** to solidify

sólido *m* **1.** FÍS solid **2.** (*geometría*) solid shape

sólido, **-a** *adj t.* FÍS solid; (*colores*) fast; (*ingreso*) steady; (*precios*) stable; (*voz*) strong

soliloquio *m* monologue; TEAT soliloquy

solio *m* throne; ~ **pontificio** papacy

solista *mf* MÚS soloist

solitaria *f* ZOOL tapeworm

solitario *m* **1.** (*diamante*) solitaire **2.** (*cartas*) patience *Brit,* solitaire *Am*

solitario, **-a I.** *adj* **1.** (*sin compañía*) alone; (*abandonado*) lonely; **en** ~ single-handed **2.** (*lugar*) isolated **II.** *m, f* loner

soliviantar *vt* **1.** (*incitar*) to stir up **2.** (*enojar*) to anger **3.** (*encandilar*) to arouse **4.** (*inquietar*) to worry; **los celos le tienen soliviantado** he is consumed with jealousy

sollozar <z→c> *vi* to sob

sollozo *m* sob

solo *m* **1.** *t.* MÚS (*baile*) solo **2.** (*cartas*) patience *Brit,* solitaire *Am*

solo, **-a** *adj* **1.** (*sin compañía*) alone; (*sin familia*) orphaned; (*solitario*) lonely; **a solas** alone; **por sí** ~ on one's own; **lo hace como ella sola** she does it as only she can **2.** (*único*) only; **ni una sola vez** not once **3.** (*sin añadir nada*) on its own; (*café*) black; (*alcohol*) straight, neat; **comer el pan** ~ to eat plain bread ►**estar más** ~ **que la una** to be completely on one's own; **más vale** ~ **que mal acompañado** better to be alone than in bad company

sólo *adv* **1.** (*únicamente*) only; ~ **que...** except that ...; **tan** ~ just; **aunque** ~ **sean 10 minutos de deporte al día** even if it's only 10 minutes sport a day **2.** (*expresamente*) expressly

solomillo *m* sirloin

solsticio *m* solstice

soltar *irr* **I.** *vt* **1.** (*dejar de sujetar*) to let go of; (*liberar*) to free; (*dejar caer*) to drop; **no** ~ **prenda** not to say a word about sth, to give nothing away; **¡suéltame!** let me go!, let go of me! **2.** (*nudo*) to untie **3.** (*expresión, grito*) to let out; (*tacos*) to come out with; ~ **una carcajada** to burst out laughing **4.** (*golpe*) ~ **un golpe** to strike; ~ **una bofetada a alguien** to cuff [*o* slap] sb **5.** (*puesto*) to give up **6.** (*lágrimas*) to shed **7.** AUTO (*embrague*) to let out; (*frenos*) to release; (*cinturón*) to undo **8.** (*gases*) ~ **un pedo** *inf* to let out a fart **9.** *inf* (*dinero*) to cough up; ~ **la mosca** to fork out **II.** *vr:* ~**se 1.** (*liberarse*) to escape; (*de unas ataduras*) to free oneself; ~**se de la mano** to let go of sb's hand **2.** (*un nudo*) to come undone; (*un tiro*) to go off **3.** (*al hablar*) to let oneself go; (*una palabra, expresión*) to let out; **se me soltó la lengua** I found my tongue **4.** (*desenvoltura*) to become expert; ~**se a hacer algo** to become expert at sth **5.** (*para independizarse*) to achieve independence

soltero, **-a** I. *adj* single II. *m, f* bachelor *m,* unmarried woman *f;* **apellido de soltera** maiden name; **de solteras solíamos salir mucho** we used to go out a lot before we all married

solterón *m* confirmed bachelor

solterona *f* old maid, spinster

soltura *f* 1. (*de una cuerda, del pelo*) looseness 2. (*de forma relajada*) ease; (*al hablar*) fluency

soluble *adj* 1. (*líquido*) soluble; ~ **en agua** water-soluble; **café** ~ instant coffee 2. (*problema*) solvable

solución *f* 1. (*líquido*) solution; ~ **anticongelante** antifreeze 2. (*de un problema*) solution; **este problema no tiene** ~ there's no solution to this problem; **no hay más** ~ there's nothing more to be done 3. (*interrupción*) ~ **de continuidad** break in continuity

solucionar *vt* to solve

solvencia *f* 1. FIN solvency 2. (*responsabilidad*) trustworthiness; ~ **moral** character; **de toda** ~ **moral** of excellent character

solventar *vt* 1. (*problema*) to resolve; (*asunto*) to settle; (*desavenencia*) to end 2. (*deuda, cuenta*) to pay

solvente I. *adj* 1. FIN solvent 2. (*sin deudas*) free of debts 3. (*reputación*) respectable II. *m* solvent

somatada *f AmC* blow

sombra *f* 1. (*proyección*) shadow; ~**s chinescas** shadow play; ~ **de ojos** (*producto cosmético*) eyeshadow; **se ha convertido en mi** ~ he/she follows me everywhere; **no es** ~ **de lo que era** he/she is a shadow of his/her former self 2. (*contrario de sol*) shade; **hacer** ~ to give shade; **hacer** ~ **a alguien** *fig* to put sb in the shade; **dar** (**una**) **buena** ~ to give good shade; **sentarse a la** ~ **de un árbol** to sit in the shade of a tree; **quita de ahí que me haces** ~ move over, you're blocking my light; **no ver más que** ~**s a su alrededor** to be pessimistic about everything; **no fiarse ni de su** (**propia**) ~ to be extremely suspicious 3. *pl* (*oscuridad*) darkness 4. (*clandestinidad*) **trabajar en la** ~ to work illegally 5. ARTE shading 6. (*cantidad mínima*) trace; **esto no tiene la más mínima** ~ **de verdad** there's not the slightest truth in this; **una** ~ **de tristeza** a trace of sadness; ~ **de duda** shadow of doubt 7. (*de un difunto*) ghost 8. (*defecto*) stain 9. *inf* (*cárcel*) **a la** ~ in the nick *Brit,* in the slammer *Am;* **poner a la** ~ to lock up ►**tener** **buena** ~ (*tener chiste*) to be witty; (*ser simpático*) to have charm; (*tener suerte*) to be lucky; **tener mala** ~ (*ser antipático*) to be a nasty bit of work; (*tener mala suerte*) to be unlucky; **¡vete por la** ~**!** watch how you go!; **ni por** ~ not in the least

sombreado *m* shading

sombrear *vt* 1. (*dar sombra*) to shade; (*a alguien*) to cast a shadow over; ~ **los ojos** to put eyeshadow on 2. ARTE to shade

sombrero *m* (*prenda*) hat; ~ **de copa** top hat; ~ **hongo** bowler (hat) *Brit,* derby *Am;* **quitarse el** ~ **ante algo** to take one's hat off to sth

sombrilla *f* parasol

sombrío, **-a** *adj* 1. (*en la sombra*) shady; (*oscuro*) dark 2. (*triste*) sad; (*pesimista*) gloomy

somero, **-a** *adj* 1. (*superficial*) superficial; (*vago*) imprecise 2. (*aguas*) shallow

someter I. *vt* 1. (*dominar*) to force to submit; (*subyugar*) to conquer; ~ **la voluntad** to subjugate one's will 2. (*proyecto, ideas, a un tratamiento*) to submit 3. (*encomendar*) **el asunto es sometido a los tribunales** the matter is referred to the courts 4. (*subordinar*) to subordinate; **todo está sometido a tu decisión** everything is subject to your decision II. *vr:* ~**se** 1. (*en una lucha*) to give in 2. (*a una acción, un tratamiento*) ~**se a algo** to undergo sth 3. (*a una decisión, opinión*) to bow; ~**se a las órdenes/la voluntad de alguien** to bow to sb's orders/will

somier <somieres> *m* bed base; (*de muelles*) bedsprings *pl;* (*de láminas*) slats *pl*

somnífero *m* sleeping pill

somnífero, **-a** *adj* sleep-inducing

somnolencia *f* (*sueño*) drowsiness

somnoliento, **-a** *adj* (*con sueño*) drowsy; (*al despertarse*) half asleep

somos *1. pres pl de* **ser**

son I. *m* 1. (*sonido*) sound 2. (*rumor, voz*) rumour *Brit,* rumor *Am;* **corre el** ~ **de que...** rumour *Brit* [*o* rumor *Am*] has it that ... 3. (*en actitud*) **venir en** ~ **de paz** to come in peace; **en** ~ **de broma** as a joke ►**bailar al** ~ **que tocan** to toe the line; **hacer algo a su** ~ to do sth one's own way; **¿a** ~ **de qué?**, **¿a qué** ~**?** why?; **sin** ~ for no reason at all II. *3. pres pl de* **ser**

sonado, **-a** *adj* 1. (*corriente*) common; (*famoso*) famous; (*escandaloso*) scandalous; (*sensacional*) sensational 2. *inf* (*loco*) crazy 3. (*boxeador*) punch drunk [*o* happy]

sonajero *m* (baby's) rattle

sonambulismo *m sin pl* sleepwalking

sonámbulo, **-a** I. *adj* sleepwalking II. *m, f* sleepwalker

sonante *adj* **dinero contante y** ~ (hard) cash

sonar <o→ue> I. *vi* 1. (*timbre, teléfono, campana*) to ring; (*instrumento*) to be heard; **me suenan las tripas** my stomach is rumbling 2. *t.* LING, MÚS (*parecerse*) to sound; ~ **a algo** to sound like sth; ~ **a hueco** to sound hollow; **esto me suena** this sounds familiar; (**tal y**) **como suena** as I'm telling you; **lo que sea** ~**á** what will be, will be II. *vt* 1. (*instrumento*) to play 2. (*la nariz*) to blow; ~ **la nariz a un niño** to blow a child's nose III. *vr:* ~**se** to blow one's nose

sonata *f* sonata

sonda *f* 1. (*acción*) sounding 2. MED probe, catheter 3. NÁUT lead; ~ **acústica** echo-sounder

S

sondar *vt* **1.** MED to probe **2.** NÁUT to sound **3.** MIN ~ **algo** to bore into sth **4.** (*explorar*) to explore, to investigate

sondear *vt* **1.** (*una persona*) to sound out **2.** *v.* **sondar**

sondeo *m* **1.** MED probing **2.** MIN boring **3.** NÁUT sounding **4.** (*averiguación*) investigation; ~ **de mercado** ECON market survey; ~ **de la opinión pública** public opinion survey

soneto *m* LIT sonnet

songa-songa *AmC, Chile, Ecua* **a la** ~ underhand

songo, **-a** *adj Col, Méx* **1.** (*tonto*) stupid **2.** (*taimado*) sly

sonido *m* **1.** (*ruido*) sound **2.** *t.* MÚS (*manera de sonar*) tone **3.** FÍS resonance **4.** RADIO sound; ~ **estereofónico** stereo sound

sonoridad *f t.* MÚS (*características*) sonority; (*agradable*) sonorousness

sonorizar <z→c> *vt* **1.** CINE to set to music, to record the soundtrack **2.** LING to voice

sonoro, **-a** *adj* **1.** (*que puede sonar*) resonant; (*acústico*) acoustic; (*bóveda*) echoing **2.** (*fuerte*) loud; (*agradable*) sonorous; **una voz sonora/poco sonora** a rich/thin voice **3.** LING voiced **4.** FÍS resonant **5.** CINE **banda sonora** soundtrack; **película sonora** talkie

sonreír *irr como reír* **I.** *vi, vr:* **~se** (*reír levemente*) to smile; ~ **a alguien** to smile at sb; ~ **maliciosamente** to smile maliciously; ~ **de felicidad** to beam with happiness **II.** *vi* (*la vida, la suerte*) to smile; **le sonríe la fortuna** fortune smiles on him/her

sonrisa *f* (*leve*) smile; (*maliciosa*) smirk; ~ **de oreja a oreja** (broad) grin

sonrojar **I.** *vt* to make blush **II.** *vr:* **~se** to blush

sonrojo *m* **1.** (*acción*) blushing **2.** (*rubor*) blush **3.** (*causa*) naughty remark

sonrosar **I.** *vt* to make pink **II.** *vr:* **~se** to turn pink

sonsacar <c→qu> *vt* **1.** (*indagar*) ~ **a alguien** to find out from sb; (*secreto*) to worm [*o* wheedle] out from sb **2.** (*empleado*) to pump for information

sonsear *vi CSur* (*tontear*) to behave stupidly

sonsera *f Arg* foolishness

sonso, **-a** *m, f CSur* (*tonto*) stupid

sonsonete *m* **1.** (*golpecitos*) tapping; (*lluvia*) dripping **2.** (*de mofa*) mocking tone **3.** (*monotonía*) same old story

soñado, **-a** *adj* (*con que se sueña*) dreamt-of; **el hombre** ~ Mr Right

soñador(a) **I.** *adj* dreamy **II.** *m(f)* dreamer

soñar <o→ue> *vi, vt* to dream; ~ **con algo** to dream of sth; ~ **despierto** to daydream; **¡ni ~lo!** no way!; **siempre he soñado con ser médico** I've always dreamt of being a doctor; **sueño con volver a verte** I dream of seeing you again; **¡sueña** [*o* que sueñes] **con los angelitos!** sweet dreams!

soñoliento, **-a** *adj* drowsy

sopa *f* **1.** (*caldo*) soup **2.** *pl* (*pan*) **~s de leche** bread and milk ►**ése os da ~s con <u>honda</u> a todos vosotros** he's streets ahead of all of you; **poner a alguien como la ~ de <u>Pascua</u>** to give sb a ticking off; **comer la** [*o* **andar a la**] ~ **<u>boba</u>** to live off other people; **<u>estar</u>** ~ to be tight; **<u>ver</u> hasta en la** ~ to see everywhere; **<u>como</u>** [*o* **<u>hecho</u>**] **una** ~ (*mojado*) soaked to the skin

sopapo *m* **1.** (*puñetazo*) punch **2.** *inf* (*bofetada*) slap; **dar un ~ a alguien** to slap sb

sopera *f* soup tureen

sopero, **-a** **I.** *adj* soup; **ser muy** ~ to be very fond of soup **II.** *m, f* soup plate

sopesar *vt* to try the weight of; *fig* to weigh up

sopetón *m* punch; **de** ~ unexpectedly

soplar **I.** *vi* to blow ►~ **y <u>beber</u>, no puede ser** *prov* you can't have your cake and eat it too; **¡sopla!** well I'm blowed! **II.** *vt* **1.** (*con la boca*) to blow on; (*apartar*) to blow away; (*velas*) to blow out; (*hinchar*) to blow up; (*fuego*) to blow on; **soplado a boca** (*vidrio*) hand-blown **2.** (*en un examen*) to whisper; TEAT to prompt **3.** *inf* (*delatar*) to inform [*o* squeal] on; (*entre alumnos*) to tell on **4.** *inf* (*hurtar*) to nick *Brit,* to swipe; (*cobrar*) to sting for **5.** (*golpe*) to deal **6.** (*inspirar*) to inspire **III.** *vr:* **~se** *inf* **1.** (*comer*) to wolf down; (*beber*) to knock back **2.** (*engreírse*) to get conceited

soplete *m* blow lamp *Brit,* blow torch; ~ **soldador** welding torch

soplillo *m* fan; **orejas de** ~ stick-out ears, Dumbo ears

soplo *m* **1.** (*acción*) puff; **apagar las velas de un** ~ to blow out the candles with one puff **2.** (*viento leve*) breeze; ~ **de viento** breath of wind **3.** (*tiempo*) **como un** ~ like a flash **4.** (*denuncia*) tip-off **5.** (*sonido*) murmur; (*corazón*) heart murmur

soplón, **-ona** *m, f* **1.** (*de la policía*) informer **2.** TEAT prompter **3.** (*entre alumnos*) talebearer *Brit,* tattletale *Am*

soponcio *m* **1.** (*desmayo*) fainting fit **2.** (*mareo*) dizzy spell

sopor *m* lethargy

soporífero *m* sleeping pill

soporífero, **-a** *adj* **1.** (*que da sueño*) sleep-inducing **2.** (*aburrido*) soporific, dull

soportable *adj* bearable

soportal *m* **1.** (*entrada*) porch **2.** *pl* (*arcos*) arcade

soportar *vt* **1.** (*sostener*) to support **2.** (*aguantar*) to stand

soporte *m* **1.** *t. fig* (*apoyo*) support **2.** (*pilar*) support pillar; (*de madera*) beam; ~ **para bicicletas** bike rack **3.** INFOR ~ **físico** hardware; ~ **lógico** software

soprano[1] *m* MÚS (*voz*) soprano

soprano[2] *f* MÚS soprano

soquete *m AmL* (*calcetín*) (short) sock, anklet

sor *f* REL sister

sorber *vt* **1.** (*con los labios*) to sip; (*por una pajita*) to suck; (*por la nariz*) to sniff; MED to inhale; ~ **tabaco** to take snuff **2.** (*empaparse de*) to soak up **3.** (*escuchar*) to drink in

sorbete *m* GASTR sorbet *Brit,* sherbet *Am*

sorbo *m* (*cantidad, trago*) sip; **beber a ~s** to sip; **tomar de un ~** to drink in one go; **échame otro ~** give me another drop

sordera *f* **1.** (*privación*) deafness **2.** (*disminución*) loss of hearing

sordidez *f* sordidness

sórdido, -a *adj* sordid

sordina *f* MÚS (*instrumento de viento*) mute; (*piano*) damper

sordo, -a I. *adj* **1.** (*que no oye*) deaf; ~ **de un oído** deaf in one ear; **hacer oídos ~s** to turn a deaf ear; ~ **como una tapia** as deaf as a post, stone deaf; **quedarse ~** to go deaf **2.** (*que oye mal*) hard of hearing **3.** (*algo que no hace ruido*) noiseless; **a sordas, a lo ~** on the quiet **4.** (*de timbre oscuro*) dull; **un golpe ~** a dull thud **5.** (*que no presta atención*) inattentive **6.** (*sentimiento, pasión*) repressed **7.** LING voiceless **II.** *m, f* deaf person; **los ~s** the deaf, deaf people; **hacerse el ~** to pretend not to hear; **predicar a los ~s** to preach to the deaf; **no hay peor ~ que el que no quiere oír** *prov* there are none so deaf as those who will not hear

sordomudo, -a I. *adj* deaf and dumb **II.** *m, f* deaf mute

sorgo *m* sorghum

soriano, -a I. *adj* of/from Soria **II.** *m, f* native /inhabitant of Soria

sorna *f* **1.** (*al obrar*) slyness; **con ~** slyly **2.** (*al hablar*) sarcasm; **con ~** sarcastically

sorprendente *adj* **1.** (*inesperado*) unexpected; (*desarrollo, evolución*) surprising; (*asombroso*) amazing; **es ~ que** +*subj* it's surprising that **2.** (*que salta a la vista*) striking; **poseer una estatura ~** to be surprisingly tall **3.** (*extraordinario*) incredible; **no es ~ que** +*subj* it's hardly surprising that

sorprender I. *vt* **1.** (*coger desprevenido*) to take by surprise; (*asombrar*) to startle, to amaze; (*extrañar*) to surprise; **no me ~ía que viniera** I wouldn't be surprised if he/she came; **durante un momento me quedé sorprendida** I was surprised for a moment **2.** (*descubrir algo*) to come across **3.** (*pillar*) to catch (in the act) **4.** MIL (*atacar*) to surprise **II.** *vr:* **~se 1.** (*asombrarse*) **~se de algo** to be amazed at sth **2.** (*extrañarse*) to be surprised

sorpresa *f* **1.** (*acción*) surprise; **coger a alguien de** [*o* **por**] ~ to take sb by surprise **2.** (*efecto*) suddenness; (*asombro*) amazement; (*extrañeza*) surprise

sorpresivo, -a *adj* **1.** (*inesperado*) surprising; (*asombroso*) amazing **2.** (*repentino*) sudden

sortear *vt* **1.** (*decidir*) to draw lots for; (*destino*) to toss up for; (*rifar*) to raffle **2.** (*esquivar*) to avoid

sorteo *m* **1.** (*decisión*) drawing of lots; (*rifa*) raffle; (*lotería*) draw **2.** (*esquivación*) avoidance

sortija *f* **1.** (*joya*) ring; (*con sello*) signet ring **2.** (*rizo*) curl

sortilegio *m* **1.** (*brujería*) sorcery **2.** (*vaticinio*) prediction; **hacer un ~ a alguien** (*vaticinar*) to tell sb's fortune; (*hechizar*) to cast a spell on sb

sosegado, -a *adj* **1.** (*apacible*) peaceful **2.** (*tranquilo*) calm

sosegar *irr como fregar* **I.** *vt* (*calmar*) to calm **II.** *vi, vr:* **~se** (*descansar*) to rest **III.** *vr:* **~se** (*calmarse*) to calm down

sosegate *m Arg, Urug* **dar** [*o* **pegar**] **un ~ a alguien** to give sb a telling-off

sosería *f* dullness; **esto es una ~** this is boring

sosia *m elev* double

sosiego *m* calm; **hacer algo con ~** to do sth calmly

soslayar *vt* **1.** (*objeto*) to put sideways **2.** (*evitar*) to avoid

soslayo, -a *adj* sideways; **mirar a alguien de ~** to look at sb out of the corner of one's eye; **pasar de ~ por la casa de la abuela** to drop in at grandma's house; **pasar por un tema de** [*o* **al**] ~ to touch on a subject

soso, -a *adj* **1.** (*sin sal*) unsalted; (*sin sabor*) tasteless, insipid **2.** (*persona*) dull

sospecha *f* **1.** (*suposición*) supposition **2.** (*desconfianza*) mistrust **3.** (*de un crimen*) suspicion; (*contra alguien concreto*) accusation; **bajo ~ de asesinato** suspected of murder

sospechar I. *vt* **1.** (*creer posible*) to suppose; **¡ya lo sospechaba!** I thought as much! **2.** (*recelar*) to suspect **II.** *vi* to be suspicious

sospechoso, -a I. *adj* suspicious; **me resulta ~ que** +*subj* I find it suspicious that **II.** *m, f* suspect

sostén *m* **1.** *t. fig* (*apoyo*) support; **pilar de ~** support pillar **2.** (*prenda*) bra **3.** (*de familia*) support; (*alimentos*) sustenance

sostener *irr como tener* **I.** *vt* **1.** (*sujetar*) to support **2.** (*aguantar*) to bear; (*por debajo*) to hold up **3.** (*afirmar*) to maintain; (*idea, teoría*) to stick to **4.** (*persona*) to support **5.** (*lucha, velocidad, posición*) to keep up; ~ **una larga conversación** to have a long conversation **II.** *vr:* **~se 1.** (*sujetarse*) to hold oneself up **2.** (*aguantarse*) to keep going **3.** (*en pie*) to stand up **4.** (*económicamente*) **apenas me puedo ~** I can hardly support myself **5.** (*en opinión*) **~se en algo** to insist on sth

sostenido *m* MÚS sharp; **poner un ~** to raise by a semitone

sostenido, -a *adj* **1.** (*esfuerzo*) sustained **2.** MÚS sharp; **fa ~** F sharp

sostenimiento *m* **1.** (*acción*) support **2.** (*apoyo*) holding up **3.** (*manutención*) maintenance **4.** (*mantenimiento*) upkeep

sota *f* (*naipe*) jack

sotana *f* cassock, soutane

sótano *m* **1.** (*piso*) basement **2.** (*habitación*) cellar

sotavento *m* leeward

soterrar <e→ie> *vt* **1.**(*enterrar*) to bury **2.**(*esconder*) to hide away; (*sentimientos*) to conceal
sotreta *adj Arg, Bol, Urug* **1.**(*caballo*) old and useless **2.**(*holgazán*) idle; (*no fiable*) untrustworthy
soturno, **-a** *adj Ven* (*taciturno*) taciturn
soy *1. pres de* **ser**
spaguetti *mpl* spaghetti
sponsorizar <z→c> *vt* to sponsor
spot *m* <spots> TV commercial
spray *m* <sprays> spray
sprint *m* <sprints> sprint; **hacer un** ~ to sprint
sprintar *vt* DEP to sprint
squash *m sin pl* DEP squash
Sr. *abr de* **señor** Mr; (*en direcciones*) Esquire
Sra. *abr de* **señora** Mrs
S.R.C. *abr de* **se ruega contestación** R.S.V.P.
Srta. *f abr de* **señorita** Miss
Sta. *f abr de* **santa** St
stand *m* <stands> stand
standing *m* **de alto** ~ high-ranking; (*calidad*) de luxe, luxury
status *m inv* status
stick *m* DEP stick
Sto. *abr de* **santo** St.
stock *m* COM stock
stop *m* **1.**(*acción*) stop **2.**(*autobús*) bus stop **3.**(*señal*) stop sign
su *adj* (*de él*) his; (*de ella*) her; (*de cosa, animal*) its; (*de ellos*) their; (*de Ud., Uds.*) your; (*de uno*) one's; ~ **familia** his/her/their family
suampo *m AmC* (*ciénaga*) swamp
suave *adj* **1.**(*superficie, piel*) smooth; (*jersey, cabello, droga*) soft; (*viento, noche*) gentle; (*sopa, salsa*) mild **2.**(*aterrizaje*) smooth; (*curva, subida*) gentle; (*temperatura, tabaco*) mild **3.**(*carácter*) docile; (*maneras*) refined; (*palabras*) kind
suavidad *f sin pl* **1.**(*de superficie, piel*) smoothness; (*de jersey, cabello*) softness; (*de viento, noche, temperatura*) gentleness; (*de sopa*) mildness **2.**(*de aterrizaje*) smoothness; (*de caricia, subida*) gentleness **3.**(*de carácter*) docility; (*de palabras*) kindness
suavizante **I.** *adj* **crema** ~ conditioner **II.** *m* **1.**(*para la ropa*) fabric softener **2.**(*para el cabello*) conditioner
suavizar <z→c> *vt* **1.**(*hacer suave*) to smooth; (*pelo, piel*) to soften; (*superficie*) to smooth out; (*navaja*) to strop **2.**(*expresión*) to soften; (*situación*) to relax, to ease **3.**(*persona*) to mollify **4.**(*recorrido, trabajo*) to make easy; (*velocidad*) to moderate
suba *f Arg* (*alza*) rise
subalimentación *f* undernourishment
subalimentado, **-a** *adj* undernourished
subalterno, **-a** **I.** *adj* secondary **II.** *m, f* (*empleado*) subordinate
subarrendar <e→ie> *vt* (*ceder: piso*) to sublet; (*finca*) to sublease
subarriendo *m* (*cesión: de piso*) subletting; (*de finca*) sublease
subasta *f* **1.**(*venta*) auction; ~ **forzada** forced auction; **sacar a** ~ **pública** to put up for auction **2.**(*de contrato público*) tender
subastador(a) *m(f)* auctioneer
subastar *vt* **1.**(*vender*) to auction **2.**(*contrato público*) to put out to tender
subcampeón, **-ona** *m, f* runner-up; ~ **mundial** world number two
subconsciencia *f* subconscious
subconsciente *adj* subconscious
subcontinente *m* subcontinent
subcontratante *mf* subcontractor
subcontratar *vt, vi* to subcontract
subcultura *f* subculture
subcutáneo, **-a** *adj* subcutaneous
subdesarrollado, **-a** *adj* underdeveloped
subdirector(a) *m(f)* subdirector, assistant director [*o* manager]
súbdito, **-a** *m, f* **1.**(*sometido*) vassal **2.** POL (*de un rey*) subject; (*ciudadano*) citizen
subdividir *vt* to subdivide
subdivisión *f* subdivision
subempleo *m* underemployment
subestimar **I.** *vt* to underestimate; (*propiedad*) to undervalue **II.** *vr:* **~se** to underestimate oneself
subida *f* **1.**(*de una calle, un río*) rise **2.**(*cuesta*) slope; **la calle hace** ~ the street is on a slope **3.**(*de precios, temperaturas, costes*) increase **4.**(*acción de subir*) ascent; (*en coche, teleférico*) climb **5.** POL ~ **al poder** rise to power; ~ **al trono** ascent to the throne
subido, **-a** *adj* **1.**(*color*) bright; (*olor*) strong; **rojo** ~ bright red **2.** *inf* (*persona*) vain; (*tono*) proud **3.**(*precio*) high
subinquilino, **-a** *m, f* subtenant
subir **I.** *vi* **1.**(*ascender: calle, cuesta*) to go up; (*sol, pastel, globo, río*) to rise; ~ **a la cima** to climb to the peak; ~ **a primera** DEP to go up to the first division; **la marea ha subido** the tide has come in **2.**(*andando*) to go up; **sube a por tus cosas** go up and get your things **3.**(*aumentar*) ~ **en algo** to increase by sth; **la gasolina ha subido** petrol *Brit* [*o* gas *Am*] has gone up **4.**(*montar: al coche*) to get in; (*al caballo, tren, a la bici*) to get on; ~ **a un árbol** to climb a tree **II.** *vt* **1.**(*precio*) to raise; **hacer** ~ **los precios** to put up the prices **2.**(*música*) to turn up; (*voz*) to raise **3.**(*en coche*) to go up; (*montaña*) to climb **4.**(*poner más alto: brazos*) to lift up; (*cortina, persiana*) to raise; (*cuello de abrigo*) to turn up; (*cabeza, pesas*) to lift; ~ **a un niño en brazos** to lift up a child **5.**(*llevar*) to take up; ~ **al tercer piso** to go up to the third floor **6.**(*pared*) to build **III.** *vr:* **~se** (*al coche*) to get in; (*al tren, a la bici*) to get on; **~se a un árbol/a una silla** to climb a tree/onto a chair; **se me ha subido el vino a la cabeza** the wine has gone to my head
súbito *adv* suddenly; **de** ~ (*repentinamente*) suddenly; (*inesperadamente*) unexpectedly
súbito, **-a** *adj* **1.**(*repentino*) sudden; **muerte**

súbita MED sudden death; (*de bebés*) crib death **2.** (*inesperado*) unexpected **3.** (*carácter, genio*) irritable
subjefe, **-a** *m, f* assistant manager
subjetividad *f sin pl* subjectivity
subjetivizar <z→c> *vt* to subjectivize
subjetivo, **-a** *adj* subjective
subjuntivo *m* subjunctive
sublevación *f* uprising
sublevar **I.** *vt* **1.** (*amotinar*) to rouse to revolt **2.** (*irritar*) to upset **II.** *vr:* **~se** to revolt
sublimación *f* **1.** (*de alguien*) praise **2.** PSICO, QUÍM sublimation
sublimar *vt* **1.** (*a alguien*) to praise **2.** PSICO, QUÍM to sublimate
sublime *adj* sublime
subliminal *adj* subliminal
submarinismo *m sin pl* scuba-diving, skin-diving; **hacer ~** to go scuba-diving [*o* skin-diving]
submarinista *mf* scuba diver
submarino *m* submarine
submarino, **-a** *adj* submarine; (*vida*) underwater
subnormal **I.** *adj* subnormal **II.** *mf* (*persona*) subnormal person; **¡eres un ~!** *pey* you moron!
subordinación *f* subordination; (*obediencia*) obedience
subordinado, **-a** **I.** *adj* **1.** (*en el trabajo*) subordinate **2.** LING **oración subordinada** subordinate clause **II.** *m, f* (*en el trabajo*) subordinate
subordinar *vt* to subordinate
subproducto *m* by-product
subrayado *m* underlining
subrayar *vt* **1.** (*con raya*) to underline **2.** (*recalcar*) to emphasize
subrepticio, **-a** *adj* surreptitious
subrogante *adj Chile* (*interino*) substitute
subrogar <g→gu> *vt* **1.** (*a alguien: temporalmente*) to substitute; (*definitivamente*) to replace **2.** (*algo*) to replace
subsanar *vt* **1.** (*falta*) to make up for **2.** (*error*) to rectify; (*defecto*) to repair; (*mal*) to remedy **3.** (*dificultad*) to overcome
subscripción *f v.* **suscripción**
subsecretario, **-a** *m, f* **1.** POL undersecretary **2.** (*en oficina*) assistant
subseguir *irr como seguir vi, vr:* **~se** **1.** (*seguir*) **~ a alguien** to follow immediately behind sb **2.** (*deducirse*) **~ de algo** to deduce from sth
subsidiar *vt* to subsidize
subsidiariedad *f* subsidiarity
subsidiario, **-a** *adj* **1.** (*de subsidio*) subsidiary; **órgano ~** (*institución*) subsidiary company **2.** (*secundario*) complementary
subsidio *m* subsidy; **~ de paro** [*o* **de desempleo**] unemployment benefit *Brit,* unemployment compensation *Am*
subsiguiente *adj* subsequent
subsistencia *f* **1.** (*hecho*) subsistence **2.** *pl* (*alimentos*) sustenance **3.** (*material*) support
subsistente *adj* (*existente*) surviving
subsistir *vi* **1.** (*vivir*) to subsist **2.** (*perdurar*) to endure; (*creencia*) to exist; (*empresa*) to survive
substancia *f v.* **sustancia**
substantivo *adj, m v.* **sustantivo**
substitución *f v.* **sustitución**
substraer *irr como traer vt v.* **sustraer**
subsuelo *m* subsoil
subte *m Arg, inf* (*metro*) underground *Brit,* subway *Am*
subterfugio *m* (*evasiva*) subterfuge; (*pretexto*) pretext
subterráneo, **-a** *adj* underground, subterranean
subtitular *vt* CINE to subtitle; **película subtitulada en inglés** film with English subtitles
subtítulo *m t.* CINE subtitle
subtropical *adj* subtropical
suburbano, **-a** *adj* suburban; **línea suburbana** suburban line
suburbio *m* **1.** (*alrededores*) (poor) suburb; **vivir en los ~s de París** to live on the edge of Paris **2.** (*barrio*) slum area
subvención *f* grant; POL subsidy
subvencionar *vt* to aid; POL to subsidize; ADMIN to finance with a grant
subvenir *irr como venir vi* **~ a las necesidades de alguien** to provide for sb's needs; **~ a los gastos** to meet expenses
subversión *f* subversion
subversivo, **-a** *adj* subversive
subvertir *irr como sentir vt* **1.** (*sistema, gobierno*) to overthrow **2.** (*valor moral*) to undermine **3.** (*orden social*) to disrupt
subyacente *adj elev* **1.** (*capa*) underlying **2.** (*problema*) hidden
subyugar <g→gu> *vt* **1.** (*oprimir*) to subjugate **2.** (*sugestionar*) to dominate
succión *f* suction; **efecto de ~** suction effect
succionar *vt* to suck; (*tierra, esponja*) to soak up
sucedáneo *m* substitute; (*imitación*) imitation
sucedáneo, **-a** *adj* substitute
suceder **I.** *vi* **1.** (*seguir*) to succeed **2.** (*ocurrir*) to happen; **¿qué sucede?** what's happening?; **por lo que pueda ~** just in case; **suceda lo que suceda** whatever happens; **lo más que puede ~ es que** *+subj* the worst thing that can happen is; **sucede que...** the thing is that ... **3.** (*en cargo*) to follow on **II.** *vt* (*heredar*) to inherit; (*seguir*) to succeed; **~ al rey** to succeed the king
sucedido *m* happening
sucesión *f* **1.** (*acción*) succession **2.** (*serie*) series *inv* **3.** (*cargo, trono*) succession **4.** (*herencia*) inheritance **5.** (*descendencia*) issue
sucesivo, **-a** *adj* following; **en lo ~** henceforth; **hicimos el examen en dos días ~s** we did the exam on two consecutive days
suceso *m* **1.** (*hecho*) event; (*repentino*) inci-

S

dent **2.** (*transcurso*) outcome **3.** (*crimen*) crime; **página** [*o* **sección**] **de ~s** PREN accident and crime reports

sucesor(a) *m(f)* **1.** (*a un cargo*) successor **2.** (*heredero*) heir

sucesorio, -a *adj* succession; **comunidad sucesoria** inherited property

suche **I.** *adj Ven* (*agrio*) bitter **II.** *m Chile* **1.** (*subalterno*) assistant **2.** (*rufián*) pimp

suciedad *f* **1.** (*cualidad*) dirtiness **2.** (*porquería*) dirt **3.** (*jugada*) dirty act

sucinto, -a *adj* succinct

sucio *adv* **jugar ~** to play dirty

sucio, -a *adj* dirty; (*jugada*) foul; **tengo los apuntes en ~** I've got the notes in rough; **hacer el trabajo ~** to do the dirty work

Sucre *m* Sucre

sucucho *m AmL* (*vivienda miserable*) hovel

suculento, -a *adj* **1.** (*sabroso*) tasty **2.** (*nutritivo*) nutritious **3.** (*jugoso*) juicy, succulent

sucumbir *vi* **1.** (*rendirse*) to succumb; JUR to lose; **Agassi sucumbió ante Pete Sampras** Agassi succumbed to Pete Sampras **2.** (*morir*) to die

sucursal *f* **1.** (*de empresa*) subsidiary; (*de banco, negocio*) branch **2.** (*negociado*) department

sucusumucu *adv Col, Cuba, PRico* **a lo ~** (*fingiéndose tonto*) playing dumb *inf*

sudaca *mf pey: pejorative term used to refer to a South American*

sudadera *f* sweatshirt

sudado, -a *adj* sweaty

Sudáfrica *f* South Africa

sudafricano, -a *adj, m, f* South African

Sudamérica *f* South America

sudamericano, -a *adj, m, f* South American

Sudán *m* Sudan

sudanés, -esa *adj, m, f* Sudanese

sudar **I.** *vi, vt* to sweat; **me sudan los pies** my feet are sweating; **estoy sudando a chorros** I'm dripping with sweat **II.** *vi inf* (*trabajar*) to sweat it out **III.** *vt* **1.** (*camisa*) to make sweaty **2.** (*conseguir*) **gano mucho pero lo sudo** I earn good money but I have to work for it ►**me la suda** *vulg* I don't give a fuck

sudario *m* shroud

sudeste *m* south-east

sudoeste *m* south-west

sudor *m* (*de la piel*) sweat; **con el ~ de mi frente** with the sweat of my brow; **me costó ~es** *inf* I had to slog my guts out

sudoroso, -a *adj* sweaty

Suecia *f* Sweden

sueco, -a **I.** *adj* Swedish **II.** *m, f* Swede ►**hacerse el ~** to pretend not to hear [*o* see]

suegro, -a *m, f* father-in-law *m*, mother-in-law *f*; **los ~s** the in-laws

suela *f* sole; **echar las medias ~s** to patch up; **tú no me llegas a la ~ del zapato** *fig* you can't hold a candle to me; **de siete ~s** out-and--out; **es un tonto de siete ~s** *inf* he's a total idiot; **como la ~ de un zapato** tough as an old boot [*o* as shoe-leather]

suelazo *m Chile, Col, Ecua, Ven* hard fall

sueldo *m* pay; (*mensual*) salary; (*semanal*) wage; **~ base** basic salary; **~ fijo** regular wage; **un aumento de ~** a pay rise *Brit*, a pay raise *Am*; **¿qué ~ ganas?** how much do you earn?

suelo *m* **1.** (*de la tierra*) ground; **~ natal** native soil; **poner una maleta en el ~** to put a suitcase on the ground; **dar consigo en el ~** to hit the ground; **besar el ~** to kiss the ground; **está muy hondo, no toco (el) ~** it's very deep, I can't reach the bottom; **no toca con los pies en el ~ de contento** *fig* he's overjoyed **2.** (*de casa*) floor; **~ de tarima** wood flooring, floorboards *pl* **3.** (*terreno*) land; **~ edificable** building land **4.** (*de vasija*) bottom **5.** (*poso*) dregs *pl* **6.** DEP **ejercicios de ~** floor exercises ►**no te dejes arrastrar por el ~** don't let them run you down; **estar por los ~s** (*deprimido*) to feel very down; (*de precio*) to be dirt cheap; **irse al ~** to fail; **poner algo/a alguien por el ~** to speak badly of sth/sb

suelto *m* **1.** (*dinero*) loose change **2.** (*artículo*) short item

suelto, -a *adj* **1.** (*desenganchado: tornillo, lana*) loose **2.** (*desatado: cordón, pelo, perro*) loose; (*broche*) unfastened; (*arroz*) fluffy; **dinero ~** ready money; **no dejar ni un cabo ~** to leave no loose ends; **un prisionero anda ~** a prisoner is on the loose; **voy ~ de vientre** *fig* I have diarrhoea *Brit* [*o* diarrhea *Am*] **3.** (*separado*) separate; **pieza suelta** individual piece **4.** (*vestido*) loose-fitting **5.** (*incontrolado*) **tener la lengua suelta** to have a ready tongue **6.** (*estilo*) free; (*lenguaje*) fluent; **dibujar con mano suelta** to draw free-hand **7.** (*no envasado*) loose **8.** *inf* (*no agarrotado*) free; **eso lo hago yo fácil y ~** I'll do that in a jiffy

sueño *m* **1.** (*acto de dormir*) sleep; **me cogió el ~** sleep overcame me; **descabezar** [*o* **echarse**] **un ~** to have a nap; **entre ~s** half asleep; **tener el ~ ligero/pesado** to be a light/heavy sleeper **2.** (*ganas de dormir*) sleepiness; **tener ~** to be sleepy; **entrar ~ a uno** to get sleepy [*o* drowsy]; **caerse de ~** to be falling asleep; **me quita el ~** it keeps me awake **3.** (*fantasía*) dream; **ni en** [*o* **por**] **~s** not even in your wildest dreams; **un coche que es un ~** a dream car; **los ~s, ~s son** dreams are dreams; **~ húmedo** wet dream

suero *m* **1.** (*de leche*) whey **2.** MED serum

suerte *f* **1.** (*fortuna*) luck; **¡(buena) ~!** good luck!; **estar de ~** to be in luck; **no estar de ~** to be out of luck; **tener buena/mala ~** to be lucky/unlucky; **traer/dar buena/mala ~** to bring/give good/bad luck; **por ~** fortunately; **probar ~** to try one's luck; **ser cuestión de ~** to be a matter of luck; **tener una ~ loca** to be amazingly lucky; **¡deséame ~!** wish me luck!; **la ~ está echada** the die is cast **2.** (*destino*) fate; **echar algo a ~(s)** to draw lots for sth; **¿quién sabe la ~ que te espera?** who knows what fate awaits you? **3.** (*casualidad*) chance **4.** (*manera*) way; **de ~ que...** in such a way that ...; **de esta ~** in this way **5.** (*tipo*) kind; **tratar con toda ~ de gente** to deal with all sorts of people **6.** (*condición*) state; **de tal ~ que** so that

suertero, **-a** **I.** *adj Ecua, Hond, Perú* lucky **II.** *m, f Perú* lottery ticket seller

suéter *m* sweater

suficiencia *f* **1.** (*lo bastante*) sufficiency **2.** (*presunción*) self-importance, smugness; **decir con aires de ~** to say with a superior air **3.** (*pedantería*) pedantry **4.** (*aptitud*) competence

suficiente **I.** *adj* **1.** (*bastante*) enough; **ser ~** to be sufficient; **~ que conozco eso yo** I know that well enough **2.** (*presumido*) self-important, smug **3.** (*pedante*) pedantic **II.** *m* ENS (*nota*) pass

sufijo *m* suffix

suflé *m* GASTR soufflé

sufragar <g→gu> **I.** *vt* **1.** (*ayudar*) to aid **2.** (*costear: gastos*) to meet; (*tasa*) to pay; (*beca*) to finance **II.** *vi AmL* (*votar*) **~ por alguien** to vote for sb

sufragio *m* **1.** (*voto*) vote **2.** (*derecho*) suffrage; **~ universal** universal suffrage **3.** (*sistema*) election **4.** REL suffrage

sufrible *adj* bearable

sufrido, **-a** *adj* **1.** (*persona*) patient, uncomplaining; **eres demasiado ~** you're too long-suffering **2.** (*color*) fast; **una tela sufrida** a hard-wearing material **3.** (*marido*) complaisant

sufrimiento *m* **1.** (*acción*) suffering **2.** (*moral*) tolerance; (*físico*) toughness

sufrir *vt* **1.** (*aguantar*) to bear; (*peso*) to support; (*a alguien*) to put up with **2.** (*padecer*) to suffer; **~ de celos** to suffer from jealousy; **~ de la espalda** to have back trouble; **~ persecuciones** to be persecuted; **~ quejas** to receive complaints; **~ las consecuencias** to suffer the consequences **3.** (*experimentar: cambio*) to undergo; (*examen*) to take; (*desengaño, accidente*) to have; (*pena*) to be stricken with; **~ una operación** to have an operation

sugerencia *f* **1.** (*propuesta*) suggestion **2.** (*recomendación*) recommendation **3.** (*inspiración*) inspiration

sugerir *irr como sentir vt* **1.** (*proponer*) to suggest **2.** (*insinuar*) to hint **3.** (*evocar*) to prompt **4.** (*inspirar*) to inspire

sugestión *f* **1.** (*de sugestionar*) hypnotic power **2.** (*propuesta*) suggestion **3.** (*inspiración*) inspiration

sugestionar **I.** *vt* (*influenciar*) to influence; (*dominar*) to dominate **II.** *vr:* **~se** to indulge in autosuggestion

sugestivo, **-a** *adj* **1.** (*que sugiere*) evocative **2.** (*que influencia*) thought-provoking **3.** (*plan*) attractive

suiche *m Méx* (*botón*) switch; (*de un coche*) ignition key

suicida **I.** *adj* suicidal **II.** *mf* **1.** (*muerto*) person who has committed suicide **2.** (*loco*) suicidal person

suicidarse *vr* to commit suicide

suicidio *m* suicide; **intento de ~** suicide attempt

suite *f* suite; **~ nupcial** bridal suite

Suiza *f* Switzerland

suizo *m* GASTR sweet bun

suizo, **-a** **I.** *adj* Swiss; **chocolate ~** Swiss chocolate **II.** *m, f* Swiss

suje *m inf* bra

sujeción *f* **1.** (*dominio*) domination; (*sometimiento*) subjection; (*dependencia*) dependency **2.** (*agarre*) hold **3.** (*aseguramiento*) support **4.** (*a un convenio, una promesa*) binding

sujetador *m* **1.** (*sostén*) bra **2.** (*del bikini*) fastener

sujetapapeles *m inv* paperclip

sujetar **I.** *vt* **1.** (*agarrar*) **~ por algo** to seize by sth **2.** (*dominar*) to dominate **3.** (*someter*) to subject **4.** (*asegurar*) to support; (*pelo*) to hold in place; (*con clavos*) to nail down; (*con tornillos*) to screw down **II.** *vr:* **~se** **1.** (*agarrarse*) to subject oneself **2.** (*a reglamento*) **~se a algo** to abide by sth

sujeto *m* **1.** (*tema*) subject **2.** *pey* (*individuo*) individual

sujeto, **-a** *adj* (*expuesto a*) subject; **~ a comprobación** subject to checking; **~ a la inflación** affected by inflation; **estar ~ a fluctuaciones** to be subject to fluctuation

sulfato *m* sulphate *Brit,* sulfate *Am*

sulfurar **I.** *vt* **1.** (*con azufre*) to sulphurate *Brit,* to sulfurate *Am* **2.** (*exasperar*) to infuriate **II.** *vr* **~se por algo/alguien** to get mad about sth/at sb

sulfúrico, **-a** *adj* sulphuric *Brit,* sulfuric *Am*

sulfuro *m* sulphide *Brit,* sulfide *Am*

sultán, **-ana** *m, f* sultan *m,* sultana *f*

suma *f* **1.** MAT (*acción*) adding (up); (*resultado*) total; **~ y sigue** (*cuenta*) carried forward; *fig* it's still going on; **en ~** in short **2.** (*cantidad*) sum **3.** (*esencia*) summary

sumamente *adv* extremely

sumar **I.** *vt* **1.** MAT to add (up) **2.** (*una obra*) to gather; (*hechos*) to summarize **II.** *vr:* **~se** (*a una manifestación, a una idea*) to join; (*a una discusión*) to participate in

sumario *m* **1.** JUR committal proceedings *pl* **2.** (*resumen*) summary

sumario, **-a** *adj* **1.** (*explicación*) concise **2.** JUR **juicio ~** summary trial

sumergible **I.** *adj* **1.** (*reloj*) waterproof **2.** (*submarino*) submersible **II.** *m* submarine

sumergir <g→j> **I.** *vt* to submerge **II.** *vr:* **~se** to submerge

sumidero *m* (*rejilla*) drain; (*de la calle*) sewer

sumiller *m* wine waiter

suministrador(a) *m(f)* supplier

suministrar *vt* **1.** *t.* COM (*datos, información*) to supply **2.** (*abastecer*) to stock **3.** (*facilitar*) to supply

suministro *m* **1.** *t.* COM (*de datos, infor-*

mación) supply **2.** (*abastecimiento*) stock **3.** *pl* MIL supplies *pl*

sumir I. *vt* (*hundir*) to sink; ~ **en la miseria a alguien** to plunge sb into poverty **II.** *vr:* ~**se** to sink; ~**se en el trabajo** to become absorbed in one's work

sumisión *f* **1.** (*acción*) submission **2.** (*carácter*) submissiveness **3.** (*obediencia*) obedience

sumiso, -a *adj* **1.** (*que se somete*) submissive **2.** (*que no rechista*) uncomplaining

sumo, -a *adj* **1.** (*más alto*) high(est); ~ **sacerdote** high priest; **a lo** ~ at most; **en grado** ~ highly **2.** (*mayor*) great

sunco, -a I. *adj Chile* (*de un brazo*) one-armed; (*de una mano*) one-handed **II.** *m, f Chile* (*de un brazo*) one-armed person; (*de una mano*) one-handed person

sungo, -a *adj Col* (*de raza negra*) Black

suntuario, -a *adj* sumptuary

suntuosidad *f* **1.** (*lujo*) sumptuousness **2.** (*opulencia*) lavishness **3.** (*aparatosidad*) magnificence

suntuoso, -a *adj* **1.** (*lujoso*) sumptuous **2.** (*opulento*) lavish **3.** (*aparatoso*) magnificent

supeditar I. *vt* **1.** (*subordinar*) to subordinate **2.** (*someter*) to subdue **3.** (*condicionar*) to condition **II.** *vr:* ~**se** to submit

súper[1] **I.** *adj inf* super **II.** *m* supermarket

súper[2] *f* four-star petrol *Brit,* Premium (gas) *Am*

superable *adj* **1.** (*récord*) beatable **2.** (*situación*) surmountable

superabundancia *f* (*en cantidad*) superabundance; (*en diversidad*) great variety

superabundante *adj* superabundant; (*negativo*) excessive

superación *f* **1.** (*de récord*) improvement **2.** (*de situación*) surmounting

superar I. *vt* **1.** (*sobrepasar: a alguien*) to surpass; (*límite*) to exceed; (*récord*) to beat; ~ **todo lo que se había visto hasta ahora** to go beyond anything seen before **2.** (*prueba*) to pass **3.** (*situación*) to overcome **II.** *vr:* ~**se** to excel oneself

superávit *m* <superávit(s)> surplus

superchería *f* (*engaño*) fraud; (*mentira*) deceit

superdotado, -a *adj* extremely gifted

superferolítico, -a *adj inf* affected

superficial *adj* superficial; (*detalle*) minor; **herida** ~ flesh wound

superficialidad *f* superficiality

superficie *f* **1.** (*parte externa*) surface; ~ **cultivable** arable area; **salir a la** ~ (*submarino*) to surface; (*minero*) to come to the surface; *fig* to come to light **2.** MAT surface; (*área*) surface area **3.** (*apariencia*) external appearance

superfluo, -a *adj* superfluous; (*gastos*) unnecessary

superhombre *m* superman

superintendente *mf* supervisor; (*de policía*) superintendent

superior *adj* **1.** (*más alto*) higher; **el curso** ~ **de un río** the upper course of a river; **el piso** ~ **al mío** the flat *Brit* [*o* the apartment *Am*] above mine **2.** (*en calidad*) better; (*en inteligencia, rango*) superior **3.** (*excelente*) excellent; **mujer** ~ superwoman

superior(a) *m(f)* superior

superioridad *f* superiority; ~ **sobre alguien** superiority over sb; **hablar con un tono de** ~ to speak in a superior tone of voice

superlativo *m* LING superlative

superlativo, -a *adj t.* LING superlative

supermercado *m* supermarket

supermoderno, -a *adj* ultra-modern

supernumerario, -a I. *adj* **1.** (*número*) surplus **2.** (*funcionario*) supernumerary **II.** *m, f* supernumerary

superpetrolero *m* supertanker

superpoblación *f* overpopulation

superponer *irr como poner vt* **1.** (*dos cosas*) to superimpose; ~ **algo a algo** to superimpose sth on sth **2.** (*dar prioridad*) to give more importance to

superpotencia *f* superpower

superproducción *f* **1.** COM overproduction **2.** CINE big-budget movie

supersónico, -a *adj* supersonic

superstición *f* superstition

supersticioso, -a *adj* superstitious

supervalorar *vt* to overvalue

superventas *m inv* bestseller; **lista de** ~ MÚS charts *pl*

supervisar *vt* to supervise; (*en un examen*) to invigilate

supervisión *f* **1.** (*vigilancia*) supervision **2.** (*en examen*) invigilation

supervisor(a) *m(f)* supervisor; (*funcionario*) inspector

supervivencia *f* survival

superviviente I. *adj* surviving **II.** *mf* survivor

supino, -a *adj* **1.** (*posición*) supine **2.** (*excesivo*) **ignorancia supina** abject ignorance

suplantar *vt* **1.** (*en el trabajo*) to supplant **2.** (*escrito*) to forge

suplementario, -a *adj* supplementary; **tomo** ~ additional volume

suplementero *m Chile* newspaper vendor

suplemento *m* **1.** (*complemento*) supplement **2.** (*tomo*) supplementary volume **3.** (*de periódico*) ~ **en color** colour supplement *Brit,* color supplement *Am* **4.** (*precio*) extra charge; (*del tren*) excess fare; (*plus*) bonus; ~ **por turnos** shift bonus

suplencia *f* substitution

suplente I. *adj* substitute; **maestro** ~ supply teacher *Brit,* substitute teacher *Am* **II.** *mf t.* DEP substitute

supletorio *m* TEL extension

supletorio, -a *adj* supplementary; **cama supletoria** extra [*o* spare] bed

súplica *f* plea; (*escrito*) request; JUR petition

suplicar <c→qu> *vt* **1.** (*rogar*) to implore; ~

algo de rodillas to beg on one's knees for sth **2.** JUR ~ **algo** to appeal against sth

suplicio *m* **1.** (*tortura*) torture **2.** (*tormento*) torment; **el viaje fue un** ~ we had a terrible journey

suplir *vt* **1.** (*completar*) to make up for **2.** (*sustituir*) to substitute; ~ **el bolígrafo por un lápiz** to change the pen for a pencil **3.** (*en el trabajo*) to replace

supo *3. pret de* **saber**

suponer *irr como poner vt* **1.** (*dar por sentado*) to suppose; **vamos a** ~ **que...** let's suppose that ...; **se supone que...** it is assumed that ...; **suponiendo que...** supposing that ...; **supongamos que...** let us assume that ...; **dar algo por supuesto** to take sth for granted **2.** (*figurar*) to imagine; **supongo que vendrá Gema, no? – supongo que sí** I imagine Gema will come, won't she? – I suppose so; **no supongo que** *+subj* I don't imagine; **puedes** ~ **que...** you can imagine that ...; **¿estás suponiendo que...?** are you assuming that ...? **3.** (*atribuir*) **le supongo unos 40 años** I imagine him/her to be about 40; **no le suponía tan fuerte** I didn't realize he/she was so strong **4.** (*significar*) to mean; ~ **un duro golpe para alguien** to be a real blow for sb; **esto me supone 60 euros al mes** this amounts to 60 euros a month for me; **no** ~ **molestia alguna** to be no trouble

suposición *f* supposition; (*presunción*) assumption

supositorio *m* MED suppository

supremacía *f* **1.** (*superioridad*) supremacy **2.** (*prioridad*) priority

supremo, **-a** *adj* (*altísimo*) highest; *fig* supreme; **el instante** ~ the culminating moment; **el Tribunal Supremo** the Supreme Court

supresión *f* **1.** (*eliminación*) suppression; (*de fronteras*) elimination; (*de obstáculos*) removal; (*de una regla*) abolition **2.** (*omisión*) omission

suprimir *vt* **1.** (*poner fin*) to suppress; (*fronteras*) to eliminate; (*controles, obstáculos, amenaza*) to remove; (*regla*) to abolish **2.** (*omitir*) to omit **3.** (*silenciar*) to silence

supuesto *m* **1.** (*suposición*) assumption, supposition **2.** (*hipótesis*) hypothesis

supuesto, **-a** *adj* (*ladrón, asesino*) alleged; (*testigo, nombre*) assumed; (*causa*) supposed; **por** ~ of course; **dar algo por** ~ to take sth for granted; (*pretendido*) so-called; ~ **que** since, as

supurar *vi* MED to suppurate

sur *m* **1.** (*punto*) south; **el** ~ **de España** the south of Spain **2.** (*viento*) south wind

surafricano, **-a** *adj, m, f* South African

surazo *m Arg, Bol* (*viento*) strong southerly wind

surcar <c→qu> *vt* **1.** (*tierra*) to plough *Brit,* to plow *Am* **2.** *elev* (*mar*) ~ **el mar** to sail the seas

surco *m* **1.** (*en tierra*) furrow **2.** (*arruga*) wrinkle **3.** (*en disco*) groove

sureste *m* south-east

surf *m* DEP *sin pl* surfing; **hacer** ~ to windsurf

surfear *vi* to windsurf; INFOR to surf

surfista *mf* surfer; INFOR Internet surfer

surgir <g→j> *vi* **1.** (*agua*) to gush **2.** (*aparecer: dificultad, posibilidad*) to arise; (*pregunta*) to come up; (*persona*) to appear unexpectedly **3.** (*edificio*) to rise up

suroeste *m* south-west

surrealismo *m sin pl* ARTE surrealism

surrealista *adj, mf* surrealist

surtido *m* selection, assortment

surtido, **-a** *adj* **1.** (*mezclado*) mixed; **galletas surtidas** assorted biscuits **2.** (*variado*) varied **3.** (*bien provisto*) well-stocked

surtidor *m* **1.** (*lugar*) petrol [*o* filling] station *Brit,* gas station *Am* **2.** (*aparato*) petrol pump *Brit,* gas pump *Am* **3.** (*chorro*) jet; (*fuente*) fountain

surtir **I.** *vt* **1.** (*proveer*) ~ **de algo** to supply with sth **2.** (*tener*) ~ **efecto** (*palabras*) to have the desired effect; (*medicamento*) to work **II.** *vi* to spout **III.** *vr* ~**se de algo** to provide oneself with sth

suruco *m CSur, vulg* shit, crap

surumbo, **-a** *adj Guat, Hond* stunned

surupa *f Ven* (*cucaracha*) cockroach

susceptibilidad *f* (*sensibilidad*) *t.* MED susceptibility

susceptible *adj* **1.** (*cosa*) ~ **de mejora** capable of improvement; **materiales** ~**s de ser reutilizados** material which can be reused **2.** (*persona: sensible*) sensitive; (*irritable*) touchy

suscitar *vt* (*sospecha, discordia*) to cause; (*discusión*) to start; (*escándalo, comentarios*) to provoke; (*odio, conflicto*) to stir up; (*problema*) to raise; (*antipatías, curiosidad*) to arouse

suscribir *irr como escribir* **I.** *vt* **1.** (*escrito*) to sign **2.** (*opinión*) to endorse **3.** (*acciones*) to take out an option on **II.** *vr* ~**se a una revista** to subscribe to a magazine

suscripción *f* **1.** (*firma*) signature **2.** (*de acciones*) taking up **3.** (*a una revista*) subscription

suscri(p)tor(a) *m(f)* **1.** (*firmante*) signatory **2.** (*de acciones*) subscriber **3.** (*de una revista*) subscriber

susodicho, **-a** *adj* (*dicho arriba*) above-mentioned; (*dicho antes*) aforementioned

suspender *vt* **1.** (*tener en el aire*) ~ **de algo** to hang from sth **2.** (*trabajador, deportista*) to suspend **3.** (*en un examen*) to fail; **he suspendido matemáticas** I've failed maths *Brit,* I've flunked math *Am* **4.** (*interrumpir: sesión*) to adjourn; (*tratamiento*) to break off; (*embargo*) to lift; (*servicio*) to discontinue; ~ **las disputas** to end the dispute; **se ha suspendido la función de esta noche** tonight's show has been called off **5.** (*embelesar*) to astonish

suspense *m* suspense; **una película/novela de** ~ a thriller

suspensión *f* **1.**(*acción de colgar*) suspension **2.**(*interrupción: de sesión*) adjournment; (*de tratamiento*) interruption; (*de disputas*) end; (*de producción*) break; (*de embargo*) lifting; ~ **de armas** truce; ~ **de la pena** annulment of the penalty; ~ **de pagos** temporary receivership, suspension of payment

suspensivo, **-a** *adj* **puntos ~s** suspension points

suspenso *m* **1.** ENS fail; **sacar un** ~ to fail, to flunk *Am* **2.** *AmL v.* **suspense**

suspenso, **-a** *adj* (*perplejo*) perplexed

suspensores *mpl AmL* (*tiradores*) braces *pl Brit,* suspenders *pl Am*

suspensorio *m* DEP athletic support, jockstrap

suspicacia *f* suspicion

suspicaz *adj* suspicious

suspirado, **-a** *adj* longed-for

suspirar *vi* **1.**(*dar suspiros*) to sigh **2.**(*anhelar*) ~ **por algo** to long for sth

suspiro *m* (*de persona*) sigh; (*del viento*) breath

sustancia *f* **1.**(*materia, esencia*) substance; ~ **activa** active ingredient; ~ **gris** ANAT grey matter *Brit,* gray matter *Am;* **en** ~ in essence; **este ensayo no tiene** ~ this essay is lacking in substance **2.**(*de alimentos*) stock **3.**(*juicio*) **un fundamento sin** ~ an unconvincing reason; **decir cosas sin** ~ to say superficial things; **un comentario sin** ~ a shallow commentary

sustancial *adj* **1.**(*esencial*) vital; (*fundamental*) essential **2.**(*comida*) substantial **3.**(*libro*) meaty

sustancioso, **-a** *adj* **1.**(*comida*) substantial **2.**(*libro*) meaty

sustantivo *m* noun

sustantivo, **-a** *adj* **1.**(*esencial*) vital; (*fundamental*) essential **2.** LING nominal

sustentáculo *m* sustenance

sustentar **I.** *vt* **1.**(*una cosa*) to hold up; (*columna*) to support **2.**(*esperanza*) to sustain **3.**(*familia*) to feed **II.** *vr:* **~se** **1.**(*alimentarse*) to sustain oneself **2.**(*aguantarse*) **~se en algo** to rely on sth

sustento *m* **1.**(*mantenimiento*) maintenance **2.**(*apoyo*) support

sustitución *f* replacement; (*temporal*) substitution

sustituir *irr como huir vt t.* DEP to substitute; ~ **a alguien** (*temporalmente*) to stand in for sb; (*definitivamente*) to replace sb

sustitutivo *m* substitute

sustitutivo, **-a** *adj* substitute

sustituto, **-a** *m, f* substitute, replacement

susto *m* scare; **poner cara de** ~ to look scared; **darle un** ~ **a alguien** to give sb a fright; **pegarse** [*o* **llevarse**] **un** ~ to get scared; **pegarle un** ~ **a alguien** to scare sb; **no ganar para ~s** to have one problem after another

sustraer *irr como traer* **I.** *vt* **1.**(*restar*) to subtract **2.**(*robar*) to steal **3.**(*privar*) to remove **4.**(*separar*) to abduct **II.** *vr* **~se de algo** to get away from sth; **~se de los periodistas** to avoid the journalists

susurrar **I.** *vi* **1.**(*hablar bajo*) to whisper; (*no claro*) to mutter; ~ **algo a alguien** to whisper sth to sb **2.**(*viento*) to murmur **II.** *vr:* **~se** to be rumoured *Brit,* to be rumored *Am* **III.** *vimpers* **se susurra que...** it is rumoured that ... *Brit,* it is rumored that ... *Am*

susurro *m* **1.**(*al hablar: bajo*) whisper; (*no claro*) mutter **2.**(*del viento*) murmur

sutil *adj* **1.**(*velo, hilo*) delicate; (*rebanada*) thin **2.**(*sabor*) subtle; (*aroma*) delicate **3.**(*diferencia, ironía*) fine; (*jugada, sistema*) refined **4.**(*persona*) sharp

sutileza *f,* **sutilidad** *f* **1.**(*de velo, hilo*) delicacy **2.**(*de sabor*) subtlety; (*de aroma*) delicacy **3.**(*de diferencia, ironía*) fineness; (*de jugada, sistema*) refinement **4.**(*de persona*) sharpness

sutilizar <z→c> *vt* **1.**(*hacer sutil*) to refine **2.**(*diferencia*) to quibble about; (*jugada*) to perfect **3.**(*discurrir*) to analyse *Brit,* to analyze *Am*

sutura *f* MED suture; **punto de** ~ stitch

suturar *vt* to stitch

suyo, **-a** *adj, pron* (*de él*) his; (*de ella*) hers; (*de cosa, animal*) its; (*de ellos*) theirs; (*de Ud., Uds.*) yours; (*de uno*) one's; **este encendedor es** ~ this lighter is his/hers; **siempre habla de los ~s** he/she is always talking about his/her family; ~ **afectísimo** yours truly; **darle a alguien lo** ~ to give sb what belongs to him/her; *fig* to give sb what he/she deserves; **ya ha hecho otra de las suyas** *inf* he/she has been up to his/her tricks again; **leer Hamlet tiene lo** ~ (*es difícil*) reading Hamlet is not easy; (*es interesante*) reading Hamlet is rewarding; **el problema es ya de** ~ **difícil de resolver** (by its nature) the problem is hard to solve; **hacer suyas las quejas de los alumnos** to echo the pupils' complaints; **Albert es muy** ~ Albert keeps to himself; **eso es muy** ~ that's typical of him/her; **ir a lo** ~ to go one's own way

swazilandés, **-esa** **I.** *adj* of/from Swaziland **II.** *m, f* native/inhabitant of Swaziland

Swazilandia *f* Swaziland

T

T, t *f* T, t; ~ **de Tarragona** T for Tommy *Brit,* T for Tare *Am*

taba *f* **1.** ANAT anklebone; **menear las ~s** *inf* (*andar*) to get a move on; *fig* to shake a leg **2.**(*juego*) **jugar a las tabas** to play jacks

tabacal *m AmL* tobacco plantation

tabacalero, **-a** **I.** *adj* tobacco brown **II.** *m, f* tobacco grower

tabaco *m* **1.**(*planta, producto*) tobacco; **de color** ~ tobacco; ~ **rubio** Virginia tobacco; ~ **de mascar** chewing tobacco **2.**(*cigarrillo*) cigarettes *pl;* (*cigarro, puro*) cigar; **¿tienes ~?** do you have any cigarettes?

tabalear I. *vt, vr:* **~se** to rock to and fro **II.** *vi* to drum (with the fingers)

tabanco *m AmC* (*desván*) attic

tábano *m* **1.** ZOOL horsefly **2.**(*persona*) nuisance

tabaquera *f* tobacco pouch

tabardo *m* tabard

tabarra *f inf* nuisance; **dar la** ~ to pester, to bug

taberna *f* tavern, bar

tabernáculo *m* (*sagrario*) tabernacle

tabernario, -a *adj* **1.**(*de la taberna*) tavern **2.** *pey* coarse

tabernero, -a *m, f* (*dueño*) landlord; (*camarero*) barman, tavernkeeper *liter*

tabicar <c→qu> **I.** *vt* to partition **II.** *vr:* **~se** to get stopped up

tabique *m* partition; ~ **nasal** nasal septum

tabla *f* **1.**(*plancha*) board; ~ **de cocina** cutting board; ~ **de planchar** ironing board; **ser la única** ~ **de salvación** *fig* to be the last resort; ~ **de surf** surfboard; ~ **de windsurf** sailboard **2.**(*de libro*) table of contents **3.**(*lista*) list; (*cuadro*) table; **las Tablas de la Ley** the Tables of the Law; **decir la** ~ to recite the multiplication table **4.**(*de vestido*) pleat **5.**(*pintura*) panel **6.** AGR (*para plantas*) garden patch; (*más grande*) plot **7.** *pl* DEP draw, tie **8.** *pl* TEAT stage **9.** *pl* (*experiencia*) **un político con muchas ~s** an experienced politician ►**a raja** ~ to the letter; **hacer** ~ **rasa de algo** to wipe the slate clean

tablada *f* **1.** *CSur* (*lugar*) stockyard **2.** *Par* (*matadero*) slaughterhouse

tablado *m* **1.**(*suelo*) plank floor **2.**(*entarimado*) wooden platform **3.**(*del escenario*) stage

tablao *m* **1.**(*escenario*) stage **2.**(*sitio*) *bar or place where a Flamenco show is performed*

tablear *vt* **1.**(*madero*) to cut into boards **2.**(*tela*) to pleat **3.**(*terreno*) to level **4.**(*tierra*) to divide into plots

tablero *m* **1.**(*de madera*) board; ~ **de anuncios** notice board *Brit,* bulletin board *Am* **2.**(*pizarra*) blackboard **3.** DEP ~ **de ajedrez** chess board; ~ **de damas** draught board *Brit,* checkers board *Am* **4.**(*de mesa*) table top **5.** AUTO dashboard **6.** AVIAT ~ **de mandos** instrument panel **7.**(*ábaco*) abacus

tableta *f* **1.**(*de chocolate*) bar **2.** MED tablet **3.**(*papel*) (writing) pad, notepad

tabletear *vi* (*puerta*) to rattle; (*máquina*) to clack

tabloide *m AmL* tabloid

tablón *m* **1.**(*de andamio*) plank; (*de anuncios*) notice board *Brit,* bulletin board *Am* **2.** *inf* (*borrachera*) **coger** [*o* **agarrar**] **un** ~ to get smashed **3.** *AmL* (*para plantas*) patch; (*más grande*) plot

tabú *m* <tabúes> taboo

tabuco *m pey* hovel

tabulador *m* (*tecla*) tab

tabular *vt* (*listar*) to tabulate

taburete *m* stool

tacada *f* **1.**(*golpe*) shot; **de una** ~ all in one go **2.**(*carambolas*) break

tacañear *vi* to be stingy

tacañería *f* stinginess, miserliness

tacaño, -a I. *adj* stingy, mean *Brit* **II.** *m, f* miser, tightwad *Am, inf*

tacataca *m* baby-walker

tacha *f* **1.**(*defecto*) blemish; **sin** ~ flawless; **es un joven sin** ~ he is an upright young man; **una reputación sin** ~ an untarnished reputation; **un diamante sin** ~ a flawless diamond **2.**(*tachuela*) large tack

tachadura *f* **1.**(*acción*) crossing out **2.**(*tachón*) correction, erasure

tachar *vt* **1.**(*rayar*) to cross out **2.**(*atribuir*) ~ **de algo** to brand as sth **3.**(*acusar*) to accuse; **le ~on de incompetente** they accused him of being incompetent

tachero *m Arg, inf* (*taxista*) taxi driver

tacho *m* **1.** *AmL* (*vasija*) metal basin **2.** *AmL* (*hojalata*) tin **3.** *AmL* (*cubo*) dustbin *Brit,* garbage can *Am* **4.** *Arg, inf* (*taxi*) taxi ►**irse al** ~ *Arg, inf* to collapse

tachón *m* **1.**(*borrón*) crossing out **2.**(*tachuela*) large stud

tachonado, -a *adj* ~ **de estrellas** star-studded

tachonar *vt* **1.**(*clavetear*) to stud **2.**(*adornar*) to dot

tachuela *f* (*clavo*) tack; (*ropa*) stud

tácito, -a *adj* tacit

taciturno, -a *adj* **1.**(*callado*) taciturn **2.**(*melancólico*) melancholy, glum

taco *m* **1.**(*pedazo*) piece; **~s de salida** DEP starting block **2.**(*de arma*) wad **3.**(*de billar*) cue **4.**(*de bota*) stud; ~ **de rosca** screw-in stud **5.**(*de papel*) pad; (*calendario*) tear-off desk, calendar; (*fajo*) wad **6.**(*de jamón*) cube; (*bocado*) bite to eat **7.** TÉC plug; (*para tornillo*) Rawlplug® **8.** *inf* (*palabrota*) swearword, four-letter word; **decir** [*o* **soltar**] **~s** to swear **9.** *inf* (*lío*) mess; **estar hecho un** ~ to be all mixed up **10.** *AmL* (*tacón*) heel **11.** *pl inf* (*años*) years; **¡ya tengo mis 40 ~s!** I'm already past 40!

tacómetro *m* TÉC tachometer

tacón *m* heel; ~ **de aguja** spike heel; **zapatos de** ~ **alto** high-heel(ed) shoes

taconear *vi* **1.**(*suelo*) to tap one's heel **2.**(*arrogantemente*) to strut

taconeo *m* heel clicking; (*andar*) noisy walking

táctica *f* tactic(s); **ir con** ~ to move strategically

táctico, -a I. *adj* tactical **II.** *m, f* tactician

táctil *adj* tactile

tacto *m* **1.** (*sentido*) sense of touch; **al** ~ to the touch; **ser áspero al** ~ to feel rough **2.** (*contacto*) touch **3.** (*habilidad*) tact; **no tener** ~ to be tactless

tacuache *m Cuba, Méx* ZOOL (*Solenodon*) almique

tacuaco, -a *adj Chile* (*rechoncho*) chubby

tafetán *m* (*tela*) taffeta

tahona *f* (*panadería*) bakery

tahonero, -a *m, f* baker

tahúr *m* cardsharp; (*tramposo*) cheat

taifa *f geopolitical unit during Muslim domination of Spain*

tailandés, -esa *adj, m, f* Thai

Tailandia *f* Thailand

taimado, -a *adj* (*maligno*) sly, crafty

taita *m* **1.** *CSur* expert **2.** *Arg* (*matón*) bully, tough **3.** *Ven* (*jefe de familia*) head of the family

Taiwán *m* Taiwan

taiwanés, -esa *adj, m, f* Taiwanese

tajada *f* **1.** (*porción*) slice; **llevarse la mejor** ~ to take the lion's share; **sacar** ~ **de algo** to get something out of sth **2.** *inf* (*ronquera*) **tener una** ~ to be hoarse **3.** *inf* (*borrachera*) **anoche pilló una buena** ~ last night he/she got smashed **4.** (*corte*) cut

tajamar *m* **1.** (*espolón*) dike [*o* dyke] **2.** (*de puente*) cutwater

tajante *adj* **1.** (*respuesta*) categorical; (*actitud*) dogmatic; (*medidas*) unequivocal **2.** (*absoluto*) in no uncertain terms **3.** (*cortante*) sharp

tajar *vt* **1.** (*cortar*) to cut; (*en lonchas*) to slice; (*trocear*) to chop **2.** *AmL* (*afilar*) to sharpen

tajo *m* **1.** (*corte*) cut; **darse un** ~ **en el dedo** to cut one's finger **2.** GEO gorge **3.** (*filo*) cutting edge **4.** *inf* (*trabajo*) work; **ir al** ~ to go to work **5.** (*de carnicero*) butcher's block; (*para decapitar*) executioner's block **6.** (*min*) face **7.** (*taburete*) three-legged stool

tal I. *adj* **1.** (*igual*) such; ~ **día hace un año** a day like this a year ago; **en** ~ **caso** in that case; **no digas** ~ **cosa** don't say any such thing; **no he dicho nunca** ~ **cosa** I never said anything of the kind **2.** (*tanto*) so; **la distancia es** ~ **que...** it's so far away that ..., it's such a long way that ... **3.** (*cierto*) certain; **un** ~ **Pérez... llamó...** somebody called Perez phoned ... **II.** *pron* **1.** (*alguien*) ~ **habrá que piense así** there's bound to be sb who thinks so; **el** ~ that fellow; ~ **o cual** someone or other; **¡ése es otro que** ~**!** he's another one! **2.** (*cosa*) **no haré** ~ I won't do anything of the sort; **¡no hay** ~**!** there's no such thing!; **hablar de** ~ **y cual** to talk about one thing and another; **... y** ~ **y cual** (*enumeración*) and so on and so forth **III.** *adv* **1.** (*así*) so **2.** (*de la misma manera*) just; **es** ~ **cual lo buscaba** it's just what I was looking for; **son** ~ **para cual** they're two of a kind, they're made for each other; **estar** ~ **cual** to be just as it was; **lo dejé** ~ **cual** I left it just as I found it; ~ **y como** just as; ~ **y como suena** just as I'm telling you **3.** (*cómo*) **¿qué** ~ **(te va)?** how are things?; **¿qué** ~ **el viaje?** how was the trip?; **¿qué** ~ **te lo has pasado?** did you have a good time?; **¿qué** ~ **si tomamos una copa?** why don't we have sth to drink?; **¿qué** ~ **es tu nuevo jefe?** what's your new boss like?; ~ **y como están las cosas** the way things are now **IV.** *conj* **con** ~ **de** +*infin*, **con** ~ **de que** +*subj* (*mientras*) as long as; (*condición*) provided; ~ **vez** (*quizás*) perhaps, maybe

tala *f* **1.** (*de árboles*) felling **2.** (*destrucción*) destruction

taladradora *f* pneumatic drill

taladrar *vt* **1.** (*con taladro*) to drill **2.** (*oídos*) to pierce; **un ruido que taladra los oídos** an ear-splitting noise

taladro *m* drill; (*agujero*) (drill) hole

tálamo *m* **1.** ANAT thalamus **2.** *elev* (*lecho*) nuptial bed

talamoco, -a *adj Ecua* albino

talante *m* **1.** (*modo*) disposition **2.** (*humor*) mood; **de buen/mal** ~ good-/ill-tempered **3.** (*gana*) **de buen** ~ willingly

talar I. *adj* **túnica** ~ full-length tunic **II.** *vt* **1.** (*árboles*) to fell **2.** (*destruir*) to lay waste

talco *m* **1.** (*mineral*) talc **2.** (*polvos*) talcum powder

talega *f* **1.** (*bolsa*) bag **2.** *inf* (*dinero*) dosh *Brit,* bread

talego *m* **1.** (*talega*) sack **2.** *inf* (*persona*) fat person **3.** *inf* (*cárcel*) nick *Brit,* slammer *Am*

talento *m* (*capacidad*) talent; **de gran** ~ very talented; **tener** ~ **para los idiomas** to have a gift for languages

talentoso, -a *adj* talented

talero *m Arg, Chile, Urug* whip

Talgo *m abr de* **Tren Articulado Ligero Goicoechea Oriol** *high speed light articulated train of Spanish invention for intercity passenger transportation*

talismán *m* talisman, lucky charm

talla *f* **1.** (*de diamante*) cutting **2.** (*en madera*) carving; (*en piedra*) sculpting **3.** (*estatura*) height; **ser de poca** ~ to be short; **no dar la** ~ MIL not to be qualified; *fig* not to be good enough **4.** (*medidor*) measuring stick **5.** (*de vestido*) size; **un abrigo de la** ~ **42** a size 42 coat **6.** (*moral, intelectual*) stature

tallaje *m* sizes *pl,* sizing

tallar *vt* **1.** (*diamante*) to cut **2.** (*madera*) to carve; (*en piedra*) to sculpt **3.** (*la estatura*) to measure the height of **4.** (*en juego*) to deal

tallarín *m* noodle

talle *m* **1.** (*cintura, del vestido*) waist **2.** (*figura*) figure

taller *m* **1.** TÉC workshop; ~ **artesanal** craft workshop; ~**es gráficos** printing works **2.** (*seminario*) seminar **3.** (*estudio*) studio **4.** (*auto*) garage

tallo *m* **1.** BOT stem, stalk **2.** (*renuevo*) shoot, sprout

talludo, -a *adj* **1.** BOT tall **2.** (*mayor*) grown-up

3. (*espigado*) lanky
talón *m* 1. (*del pie, zapato, calcetín*) heel; **pisar a alguien los talones** *inf* (*perseguir*) to be hot on sb's heels; (*emular*) to follow in sb's footsteps; ~ **de Aquiles** Achilles' heel; *fig* weak point 2. (*cheque*) cheque *Brit,* check *Am;* **hazme un ~ de 10.000 pts.** make me out a cheque for 10000 pesetas; ~ **sin fondos** bad [*o* bounced] cheque 3. (*resguardo*) voucher; (*recibo*) receipt
talonario *m* 1. (*de cheques*) chequebook *Brit,* checkbook *Am* 2. (*de recibos*) receipt book
talud *m* slope
tamal *m AmC, Méx* tamale (*dish made of cornmeal, meat or chicken, and chili wrapped in corn husks or banana leaves*)
tamalada *f Méx* GASTR tamale party
tamango *m CSur* (*calzado*) coarse leather shoe
tamaño *m* 1. (*medida*) size; **de ~ natural** life size; **¿de qué ~ es?** what size is it?, how big is it?; **de gran~** large 2. (*formato*) size; **en ~ grande** large size; **en ~ bolsillo** pocket size
tamaño, -a *adj* 1. (*grande*) such a big, so big a 2. (*pequeño*) such a small, so small a 3. (*semejante*) such a; **tamaña tontería** such a stupid thing; **sólo a tí se te ocurre ~ disparate** only you would think of such an absurd idea
tamarindo *m* tamarind
tambache *m Méx, inf* bundle; **un ~ de ropa/de hojas de papel** a pile of clothes/of papers; **hacer ~ a alguien** to play a dirty trick on sb
tambalear *vi, vr:* **~se** to stagger; *fig* to totter
tambarria *f Perú* (*fiesta*) party
tambembe *m Chile* (*trasero*) bottom, butt *inf*
tambero, -a I. *adj Arg* dairy; **vaca tambera** milking cow II. *m, f Arg* (*ganado manso*) tame livestock; (*vaca lechera*) milk cow
también *adv* also, as well, too; **yo lo ví ~** I also saw him, I saw him too [*o* as well]
tambocha *f Col, Ven* (*hormiga*) poisonous red-headed ant
tambor *m* 1. (*cilindro, instrumento*) drum; **tocar el ~** to play the drum; **proclamar algo a ~ batiente** to proclaim sth triumphantly 2. (*músico*) drummer 3. ANAT eardrum
tamboril *m* MÚS small drum
tamborilear *vi* 1. (*tocar*) to play the drum 2. (*con dedos*) to drum, to tap
Támesis *m* **el ~** the Thames
tamiz *m* sieve, sifter; **pasar por el ~** to sift
tamizar <z→c> *vt* to sift, to sieve; *fig* to screen
tampoco *adv* not either, nor, neither; **ni puedo ni ~ quiero** I neither can nor do I want to; **~ me gusta éste** I don't like this one either; **si tú no lo haces yo ~** if you don't do it, neither will I
tampón *m* 1. (*de tinta*) ink pad 2. (*para la mujer*) tampon
tamuga *f* 1. *AmC* (*fardo*) bundle; (*mochila*) knapsack 2. *AmL* (*marihuana*) joint, reefer *inf*
tan *adv* so; **~... como...** as ... as ...; **~ es así que no he podido hacerlo** so much so that I haven't been able to do it; **de ~ simpático me resulta insoportable** he/she is so nice I find him/her unbearable; **~ siquiera una vez** just once; **ni ~ siquiera** not even; **ni ~ siquiera han llamado** they haven't even called
tanate *m* 1. *AmC, Méx* (*cesto*) pannier 2. *AmC* (*fardo*) bundle 3. *pl, Méx, vulg* (*testículos*) balls *pl* 4. *pl, AmC* (*cachivaches*) gear, stuff
tanatorio *m* funeral parlour *Brit,* funeral parlor *Am*
tanda *f* 1. (*turno*) shift, turn; **estar en la ~ de día** to be on the day shift; **¿me puedes guardar la ~?** will you keep my place for me? 2. (*serie*) series *inv;* **por ~s** in batches; **en ~s de ocho** (*en filas*) in rows of eight; (*en grupos*) in groups of eight; **~ de palos** thrashing 3. (*de trabajo, capa*) layer 4. (*trabajo*) job, task
tándem *m* tandem
tanga *m* tanga, G-string
tangente *f* tangent; **salirse** [*o* **irse**] **por la ~** *fig* to go off on a tangent
Tánger *m* Tangier(s)
tangerino, -a *adj, m, f* Tangerine
tangible *adj* tangible; *fig* concrete
tango *m* MÚS tango
tanino *m* QUÍM tannin
tano, -a *adj, m, f Arg, Urug, inf* (*italiano*) Italian
tanque *m* 1. MIL tank 2. (*cisterna*) tanker 3. (*vehículo*) road-tanker 4. *inf* (*de cerveza*) large glass 5. *vulg* (*gordo*) fatso 6. *AmL* (*estanque*) pool
tanquear *vi Col* (*echar gasolina*) to get some petrol [*o* gas *Am*]
tantán *m* tom-tom
tantara(n)tán *m* 1. (*onomatopeya*) rat-a-tat-tat 2. (*golpe*) heavy punch, bang
tanteador *m* 1. (*aparato*) scoreboard 2. (*persona*) scorekeeper
tantear *vt* 1. (*calcular: cantidad*) to calculate; (*tamaño, volumen*) to gauge, to weigh up; (*a ojo*) to size up; (*precio*) to estimate 2. (*probar*) to try out; (*persona: sondear*) to sound out; **~ el terreno** *fig* to get the lay of the land 3. (*dibujo*) to sketch 4. DEP (*puntos*) to keep the score of; (*goles*) to score 5. (*ir a tientas*) to grope; **tuvimos que bajar la escalera tanteando** we had to feel our way down the stairs
tanteo *m* 1. (*cálculo: cantidad*) calculation; (*de tamaño, volumen*) weghing up; (*a ojo*) sizing up, gauging; (*de precio*) estimate; **al** [*o* **por**] **~** by trial and error 2. (*sondeo*) sounding out 3. DEP (*de puntos*) score; (*de goles*) scoring; **~ final** final score
tanto I. *m* 1. (*cantidad*) certain amount; COM rate; **~ alzado** lump sum basis; **~ por ciento** percentage; **me pagan a ~ la hora** I'm paid so much the hour; **costar otro ~** to cost as much again; **un ~** a bit; **estar un ~ harto de algo** to be rather fed up with sth; **estoy un ~ sorprendido** I'm somewhat surprised 2. (*punto*)

T

point; (*gol*) goal; **un ~ a favor de algo** a point in sb's favour *Brit* [*o* favor *Am*]; **apuntarse un ~ a favor** to score a point ►**estar al ~ de algo** to be up to date on sth **II.** *adv* **1.** (*de tal modo*) so much, to such an extent; **no es para ~** there's no need to make such a fuss; **pensé que vendrías; ~ es así que no salí de casa** I thought you'd come; in fact, I was so sure, I stayed home **2.** (*en tal cantidad*) **no me das ni ~ así de pena** I don't feel the least bit sorry for you **3.** (*de duración*) so long; **tu respuesta tardó ~ que...** your answer took so long that ... **4.** (*comparativo*) **~ mejor/peor** so much the better/worse; **~ como** as much as; **eso era ~ como no decir nada** that was the same as not saying anything; **~ cuanto necesito para vivir** all I need to live on; **~ si llueve como si no...** whether it rains or not ... ►**¡ni ~ ni tan calvo!** neither one extreme nor the other!; **~...como...** both ... and ...; **~ él como su hermano juegan al baloncesto** both he and his brother play basketball; **en ~** (**que** +*subj*) (*mientras*) as long as, provided; **entre ~** meanwhile, in the meantime; **por** (**lo**) **~** therefore, so; **por lo ~ mejor callar** so best keep quiet

tanto, **-a I.** *adj* **1.** (*comparativo*) as much, as many; **no tengo ~ dinero como tú** I don't have as much money as you; **tenemos ~s días de vacación como ellos** we have as many vacation days as they do **2.** (*tal cantidad, ponderativo*) so much; **tantas posibilidades** so many possibilities; **¡hace ~ tiempo!** such a long time ago!; **¡hace ~ tiempo que no te veo!** I haven't seen you for so long!; **~ gusto en conocerle** a pleasure to meet you; **¿a qué se debe tanta risa?** what's so funny? **3.** *pl* (*número indefinido*) **en mil novecientos ochenta y ~s** in nineteen eighty-something; **uno de ~s** one of many; **a ~s de enero** on such and such a day of January; **tener 40 y ~s años** to be 40-odd years old; **a las tantas de la madrugada** *inf* in the wee hours of the morning; **quedarse despierto hasta las tantas** to stay up until all hours ►**~ tienes, ~ vales** *prov* a man's worth is the worth of his land **II.** *pron dem* **~s** as many; **coge ~s como quieras** take as many as you like; **no llego a ~** I won't go that far; **no me imaginaba que iba a llegar a ~** I never thought it would come to that; **jamás podré llegar a ~** I'll never be able to go so far

Tanzania *f* Tanzania

tanzano, **-a** *adj, m, f* Tanzanian

tañer <*3. pret:* tañó> **I.** *vt* **1.** (*instrumento*) to play **2.** (*campanas*) to ring **II.** *vi* to toll

tañido *m* sound

taoísmo *m* Taoism

taoísta *adj, mf* Taoist

tapa *f* **1.** (*cubierta*) lid; **~ de rosca** screw-top; **libro de ~s duras** hardback; **levantar** [*o* **saltar**] **a alguien la ~ de los sesos** *inf* to blow sb's brains out **2.** (*de zapato*) heelpiece **3.** GASTR tapa; **una ~ de aceitunas** a small dish of olives **4.** (*carne*) **tapa de ternera** round of beef

> **Tapa** is the synonym for **pincho**, i.e. a snack or a bite to eat between meals. In **Andalucía**, however, a **tapa** consists exclusively of **embutido y/o jamón** (cured sausage and/or ham), which is served with wine or beer.

tapacubos *m inv* hubcap

tapada *f And, inf* save, stop

tapadera *f* **1.** (*de vasija*) lid **2.** (*negocio*) cover

tapadillo *m* **de ~** secretly

tapado *m Arg* (*abrigo*) coat

tapado, **-a** *adj AmL* (*animal*) all one colour *Brit* [*o* colored *Am*]

tapaporos *m inv* (*pintura*) sealer, primer

tapar I. *vt* **1.** (*cuerpo*) to cover; (*cazuela*) to put a lid on; (*en cama*) to cover up **2.** (*puerta*) to wall up; (*desagüe*) to obstruct; (*agujero*) to fill in; (*botella*) to put the cap on **3.** (*vista*) **¿te tapo?** am I blocking your view?; **la pared nos tapa el viento** the wall protects us from the wind **4.** (*ocultar*) to hide **II.** *vr:* **~se 1.** (*con ropa*) to wrap up; (*en cama*) to cover up; (*completamente*) to hide; (*con velo*) to shroud **2.** (*oídos, nariz*) to get blocked; **~se la cara/los ojos** to cover one's face/eyes

taparrabo(**s**) *m* (*inv*) **1.** (*de Tarzán*) loincloth **2.** (*bañador*) swimming trunks *pl*

tapayagua *f Hond* drizzle

tape *m* **1.** *Arg, Urug* (*aindiado*) *Indian-looking person* **2.** *Cuba, PRico* (*tapa*) lid **3.** *RíoPl* (*cinta de video*) tape

tapeo *m* **ir de ~** to go barhopping (*to go round the bars for beer or wine and tapas*)

tapete *m* table runner; **~ verde** card table; **estar sobre el ~** *fig* to be under consideration; **poner sobre el ~** *fig* to bring up

tapia *f* wall; (*de jardín*) garden wall; **estar más sordo que una ~** to be as deaf as a post

tapiar *vt* **1.** (*cerrar*) to wall up **2.** (*rodear*) to wall in

tapicería *f* **1.** (*tapices*) tapestries *pl,* wall--hangings *pl* **2.** (*tienda: de tapices*) tapestry shop; (*de muebles*) upholstery; (*taller*) upholsterer's **3.** (*arte*) tapestry-making **4.** (*tela*) upholstery material; **muebles de ~** upholstered furniture

tapicero, **-a** *m, f* **1.** (*de sillones*) upholsterer **2.** (*de paredes*) tapestry maker

tapisca *f AmC* AGR maize harvest *Brit,* corn harvest *Am*

tapiz *m* tapestry, wall-hanging; (*en el suelo*) rug

tapizar <z→c> *vt* (*muebles*) to upholster; (*acolchar*) to quilt

tapón *m* **1.** (*obturador*) stopper; (*cilindro, de fregadero*) drain plug; (*de corcho*) cork; (*de cuba*) bung; AUTO oil drain plug **2.** *inf* (*persona*) short stubby person **3.** MED tampon;

(*para el oído*) earplug **4.** (*cerumen*) wax in the ear **5.** (*de tráfico*) traffic jam

taponar *vt* **1.** (*cerrar*) to plug; (*con corcho*) to cork; (*de plástico*) to seal; (*cuba*) to bung; (*desagüe*) to clog **2.** (*herida*) to plug

tapujarse *vr inf* to muffle oneself up

tapujo *m* **1.** (*embozo*) muffler **2.** *inf* (*disimulo*) false pretext; **andar con ~s** (*obrar*) to behave deceitfully; **no andarse con ~s** (*hablar*) to speak plainly

taquear **I.** *vi AmL* **1.** *inf* (*jugar*) to shoot pool **2.** (*arma*) to ram **3.** (*llenar*) to stuff **II.** *vr:* **~se** *AmL* to tap one's heels

taquería *f* **1.** *Cuba* (*descaro*) cheek **2.** *Méx* (*tacos*) taco stand

taquicardia *f* MED tachycardia

taquigrafía *f* shorthand, stenography

taquigrafiar <*1. pres:* taquigrafío> *vt* to take down in shorthand

taquígrafo, **-a** *m, f* shorthand writer

taquilla *f* **1.** TEAT, CINE box office; DEP gate money; FERRO ticket window; (*de apuestas*) tote window; **éxito de ~** box-office hit **2.** (*recaudación*) receipts *pl*, takings *pl* **3.** (*armario*) locker; (*archivador*) filing cabinet

taquillero, **-a** **I.** *adj* **una artista ~** a crowd-puller; **una película taquillera** a box-office draw **II.** *m, f* **1.** FERRO ticket clerk, ticket seller **2.** TEAT, CINE ticket agent

taquimecanógrafo, **-a** *m, f* shorthand typist

tara *f* **1.** (*defecto*) defect **2.** COM (*peso*) tare

tarabilla *f* **1.** *inf* (*parlanchín*) chatter box; **hablar como una ~ descompuesta** to talk nine to the dozen *Brit,* to talk a blue streak *Am* **2.** (*palabra*) jabbering **3.** (*de ventana*) latch

taracea *f* marquetry, inlay

taracear *vt* to inlay

tarado, **-a** **I.** *adj* **1.** (*objeto*) defective, imperfect **2.** (*alocado*) crazy; (*imbécil*) stupid **II.** *m, f* (*loco*) nitwit

tarambana *mf inf* disaster

tarantín <tarantines> *m* **1.** *Ven* (*tenducha*) stall **2.** *pl, AmC, Cuba, PRico* (*cachivaches*) odds *pl* and ends

tarántula *f* tarantula

tarará *m v.* **tararí**

tararear *vt* to la-la-la, to croon; (*con labios cerrados*) to hum

tararí **I.** *adj* **estar ~** *inf* to be batty **II.** *m* (*de trompeta*) sound of trumpet

tarascón *m AmS* (*mordedura*) bite; (*herida*) bite wound

tardanza *f* delay; **perdona la ~ en escribirte** forgive me for taking so long to write

tardar *vi* to take time; **~ en llegar** to take a long time to arrive; FERRO to be late arriving; **~ en responder** to take a long time to answer; **~on tres semanas en contestar** it took them three weeks to answer; **~on mucho en arreglarlo** it took them a long time to fix it; **no tardo nada** I won't be long; **no ~é en volver** I'll be right back; **¡no tardes!** don't be gone long!; **a más ~** at the latest; **sin ~** without taking long

tarde **I.** *f* **1.** (*primeras horas*) afternoon; **por la ~** in the afternoon; **¡buenas ~s!** good afternoon! **2.** (*últimas horas*) evening; **¡buenas ~s!** good evening!; (**todos**) **los viernes por la ~** Friday evenings **II.** *adv* late; **~ o temprano** sooner or later; **de ~ en ~** now and then, occasionally; **se me hace ~** it's getting late ►**más vale ~ que <u>nunca</u>** *prov* better late than never *prov*

tardío, **-a** *adj* **1.** (*atrasado*) late; **es un consejo ~** a belated piece of advice **2.** (*lento*) slow

tardo, **-a** *adj* slow; **~ de oído** hard of hearing

tardón, **-ona** **I.** *adj* **1.** (*lento*) slow **2.** (*tonto*) dense **II.** *m, f* **1.** (*lento*) slowcoach *Brit,* slowpoke *Am;* **es un ~** he/she's a slowcoach **2.** (*tardo*) dullard

tarea *f* **1.** (*faena*) task **2.** (*trabajo*) job; **~s de la casa** housework **3.** *pl* ENS homework; **¿has hecho tus ~s?** have you done your homework?

tareco *m Cuba, Ecua, Ven* **1.** (*herramienta*) tool of trade **2.** (*trasto*) old thing

tarifa *f* rate; (*transporte*) fare; **¿cuál es su ~?** how much does he/she charge?

tarima *f* platform

tarja *f* **1.** HIST (*escudo*) shield **2.** *AmL* (*tarjeta de visita*) visiting card ►**<u>beber</u> sobre ~** to drink on credit

tarjar *vt Chile* to cross out

tarjeta *f* **1.** card; **~ de crédito** credit card; **~ de embarque** AVIAT boarding pass; **~ postal** postcard; **~ de visita** visiting-card *Brit,* calling-card *Am* **2.** INFOR **~ de gráficos** graphics card; **~ de memoria** memory chip; **~ de sonido** sound card

tarjetero *m* card case

tarquín *m* mud, silt

tarraconense **I.** *adj* of/from Tarragona **II.** *mf* native/inhabitant of Tarragona

tarro *m* **1.** (*envase*) pot; (*de cristal*) jar; (*de metal*) tin, can **2.** *inf* (*cabeza*) head; **comer el ~ a alguien** to brainwash sb; **¿estás mal del ~?** are you off your head?; **comerse el ~** to think hard on sth

tarso *m* ANAT tarsus

tarta *f* cake; (*pastel*) pie

tartajear *vi* to stammer, to stutter

tartamudear *vi* to stammer, to stutter

tartamudo, **-a** **I.** *adj* stammering, stuttering **II.** *m, f* stammerer, stutterer

tartera *f* **1.** (*para tartas*) cake pan **2.** (*fiambrera*) lunchbox

tarugo *m* **1.** (*trozo*) chunk **2.** (*clavija*) wooden peg **3.** (*pan*) hunk of stale bread **4.** *inf* (*persona*) blockhead

tarumba *adj inf* confused; **estar ~** to be crazy; **volver a alguien ~** to drive sb mad [*o* crazy]

tasa *f* **1.** (*valoración*) valuation **2.** (*precio, derechos*) fee; (*de impuesto*) tax **3.** (*de joya*) appraisal **4.** (*porcentaje*) rate; **~ de desempleo** unemployment rate; **~ de interés** inter-

est rate; ~ **impositiva** tax rate; ~ **de natalidad** birth rate
tasación *f* 1. (*de producto*) fixing of a price; (*de impuesto*) tax regulation 2. (*de joya*) appraisement
tasajear *vt AmL* 1. (*tajear*) to cut 2. (*carne*) to jerk
tasajo *m* 1. (*trozo*) piece of meat 2. (*salado*) jerked meat
tasar *vt* 1. (*precio*) to fix the price of; (*impuesto*) to tax 2. (*valorar*) to value; (*trabajo*) to regulate; ~ **en exceso** to overrate 3. (*tabaco, comida*) to ration; (*libertad*) to limit
tasca *f* (*taberna*) bar
tata[1] *f inf* (*niñera*) nanny
tata[2] *m AmL* (*papá*) daddy
tatarabuelo, -a *m, f* great-great-grandfather
tataranieto, -a *m, f* great-great-grandson
tate *interj* 1. (*cuidado*) watch out!, look out!, be careful! 2. (*despacito*) easy does it! 3. (*sorpresa*) good heavens! 4. (*comprensión*) so that's it!, I see!
tatuaje *m* tattoo
tatuar <*1. pres:* tatúo> *vt* to tattoo
tauca *f* 1. *Bol, Chile, Ecua* (*montón*) heap; **una ~ de papeles** a pile of papers 2. *Chile* (*talega grande*) large bag
taumaturgia *f* thaumaturgy, miracle-working
taumaturgo, -a *m, f* thaumaturge, miracle-worker
taurino, -a *adj* 1. (*del toro*) taurine 2. (*de la corrida*) bullfighting
Tauro *m* Taurus
tauromaquia *f sin pl* art of bullfighting
taxativo, -a *adj* restrictive; (*categórico*) precise; **de forma taxativa** in a categorical way
taxi *m* taxi, taxicab
taxímetro *m* taximeter
taxista *mf* taxi driver *Brit*, cabdriver *Am*
taza *f* 1. (*de café*) cup; **una ~ de café** (*con café*) a cup of coffee; (*para el café*) coffee cup 2. (*grande*) mug 3. (*del wáter*) toilet bowl 4. (*de fuente*) basin 5. (*medida*) cupful
tazón *m* (*taza grande*) large cup; (*cuenco*) bowl
te I. *f* **la letra ~** the letter t II. *pron pers* (*objeto directo, indirecto*) you; **¡míra~!** look at yourself! III. *pron reflexivo* ~ **vistes** you get dressed; ~ **levantas** you get up; **no ~ hagas daño** don't hurt yourself; **¿~ has lavado los dientes?** have you brushed your teeth?
té *m* tea; **dar a alguien el ~** *fig* to bore sb to tears
tea *f* 1. (*astillas*) firelighter; (*antorcha*) torch 2. *inf* (*borrachera*) **coger una ~** to get plastered
teatral *adj* theatre; (*efecto, experiencia, autor*) stage; *fig* theatrical
teatralidad *f* drama, theatrics *pl; pey* staginess
teatro *m* 1. (*t. fig*) TEAT theatre *Brit,* theater *Am;* **obra de ~** play; **el ~ de Calderón** Calderon's plays; **hacer ~** to work in the theatre *Brit* [*o* theater *Am*]; *fig* to playact; (*exagerar*) to exaggerate 2. (*escenario*) stage
tebeo *m* comic; **esto está más visto que el ~** *inf* this is as old as the hills
teca *f* teak
techado *m* roof
techar *vt* to roof
techo *m* 1. (*de habitación*) ceiling 2. (*de casa*) roof; **vivir bajo el mismo ~** to live under the same roof 3. (*tope*) maximum; (*de evolución*) peak
techumbre *f* 1. (*techo*) roof 2. (*estructura*) roofing; ~ **de paja** thatching
tecla *f* 1. (*de piano, ordenador*) key; ~ **de mayúsculas** shift key; ~ **de retroceso** backspace key; ~ **de intro** enter key; **tocar una ~** (*piano, ordenador*) to press a key; **dar en la ~** *inf* to hit the nail on the head; **hay que tocar muchas ~s para averiguar eso** a lot of strings will have to be pulled to find that out; **tocar demasiadas ~s** *fig* to do too many things at once 2. (*materia*) weak point; **tocar la ~ sensible** to touch a nerve
teclado *m* keyboard; **tocar los ~s en un grupo** to play the keyboards in a group
teclear *vi* 1. (*piano*) to play; (*ordenador*) to type 2. (*dedos*) to drum
técnica *f* 1. (*método*) technique 2. (*tecnología*) technology
técnicamente *adv* technically
tecnicismo *m* 1. (*término*) technical term 2. (*detalle*) technicality
técnico, -a I. *adj* 1. (*de la técnica*) technical 2. (*de especialidad*) technical; **término ~** technical term II. *m, f* 1. TÉC technician; (*de lavadoras*) repairman, engineer 2. (*especialista*) expert, specialist 3. DEP trainer, coach
tecnicolor *m* Technicolor®
tecnócrata I. *adj* technocratic II. *mf* technocrat
tecnología *f* 1. TÉC, ECON technology; ~ **punta** leading-edge technology 2. (*técnica*) technique
tecnológico, -a *adj* 1. TÉC technological; (*desarrollo*) technological; **parque ~** technology park 2. (*técnico*) technical
tecolote *m AmC, Méx* ZOOL (*búho*) owl
tedio *m* boredom
tedioso, -a *adj* tedious, wearisome
teína *f* QUÍM theine
teísmo *m* theism
teísta I. *adj* theistic II. *mf* theist
teja *f* 1. (*del tejado*) roof tile; **de color ~** brownish-orange 2. (*sombrero*) shovel hat ►**pagar a toca ~** to pay cash on the nail; **de ~s (para) abajo** in this world; **de ~s (para) arriba** in heaven
tejado *m* roof; **empezar la casa por el ~** *fig* to put the cart before the horse; **la pelota sigue en el ~** *fig* it is still in the air; **tirar piedras sobre su propio ~** *fig* to foul one's own nest ►**quien tiene el ~ de vidrio, no tire**

piedras al de su vecino *prov* people who live in glass houses shouldn't throw stones *prov*

tejano, -a I. *adj* 1. (*de Tejas*) Texan 2. (*ropa*) denim; **pantalón** ~ jeans II. *m, f* Texan

tejanos *mpl* jeans

tejar I. *vt* to tile II. *m* tile works *pl*

tejaván *m AmL* 1. (*cobertizo*) shed 2. (*corredor*) corridor 3. (*alero*) eaves *pl* 4. (*casa*) rustic house with tiled roof

tejedor(a) *m(f)* 1. weaver 2. ZOOL water strider

tejemaneje *m inf* 1. (*actividad*) to-do; **traerse un ~ increíble con los papeles** to make such a fuss with the papers 2. (*intriga*) scheming; **se deben de traer algún ~** they must be up to sth

tejer *vt* 1. (*tela*) to weave; (*tricotar*) to knit; **~ y destejer** *fig* to blow hot and cold 2. (*cestos, trenzas*) to plait 3. ZOOL (*araña*) to spin 4. (*intrigas, plan*) to plot

tejido *m* 1. *t.* ANAT (*textura*) tissue 2. (*tela*) fabric; **los ~s** textiles *pl*

tejo *m* 1. (*disco*) disk; **tirar los ~s a alguien** *inf* to flirt with sb 2. BOT yew tree 3. (*juego*) hopscotch

tejón *m* badger

tejuelo *m* TIPO book label

tela *f* 1. (*tejido*) material, fabric; **~ de araña** spider's web *Brit,* spiderweb *Am;* **~ metálica** wire screen; **~ de punto** knit; **~ de saco** sackcloth, burlap; **lo cubrieron con una ~ blanca** they covered it with a white cloth 2. (*en leche*) film; **llegar a las ~s del corazón** *fig* to pull heartstrings 3. *inf* (*asunto*) matter; **hay ~ para rato** (*para discutir*) there's plenty to talk about; (*para trabajar*) there's a lot to be done; **este asunto trae ~** it's a complicated matter; **este problema tiene ~** this isn't an easy problem 4. (*lienzo*) canvas; **una ~ de Barceló** a painting by Barcelo 5. *inf* (*dinero*) dough ▸**poner algo en ~ de juicio** (*dudar*) to question sth; (*tener reparos*) to raise objections about sth

telar *m* (*máquina*) loom

telaraña *f* cobweb *Brit,* spiderweb *Am;* **mirar las ~s** *fig* to have one's head in the clouds; **tener ~s en los ojos** *fig* to be blind to what is going on

tele *f inf abr de* **televisión** TV, telly *Brit;* **ver la ~** to watch TV

teleadicto, -a *adj inf* telly addict *Brit,* couch potato

telebanca *f* e-bank

telebanking *m sin pl* e-banking

telebasura *f* junk TV

telecabina *f* cable car

telecomedia *f* 1. (*serie*) sitcom, TV comedy show 2. (*película*) TV film

telecompra *f sin pl* teleshopping

telecomunicación *f* 1. (*sistema*) telecommunication; **ingeniero de Telecomunicaciones** telecommunications engineer 2. *pl* (*empresa*) telecommunications *pl*

teleconcurso *m* game show

teleconferencia *f* COM teleconference, video-phone conference

telecontrol *m* remote control

telediario *m* TV news; **el ~ de las 3** the 3 o'clock news

teledifusión *f* telecast

teledirigido, -a I. *adj* remote-controlled II. *m, f* (*juguete*) remote-controlled car

teledirigir <g→j> *vt* to operate by remote control

teléf. *abr de* **teléfono** tel.

teleférico *m* cable car

telefilm *m* TV film, made-for-TV movie *Am*

telefonazo *m inf* ring; **dar un ~ a alguien** to give sb a ring

telefonear I. *vt* 1. (*comunicar*) to telephone, to phone, to call 2. *inf* (*a alguien*) to ring II. *vi* to telephone

telefonía *f* telephony

Telefónica *f national telephone company in Spain*

telefónico, -a *adj* 1. (*de teléfono*) telephone; **cabina telefónica** phone box; **guía telefónica** telephone directory, phone book; **llamada telefónica** phonecall 2. (*de telefonía*) telephonic

telefonista *mf* telephone operator

teléfono *m* 1. (*sistema, aparato*) telephone; **~ móvil** mobile phone, cellphone *Am;* **~ público** public phone; **~ rojo** *fig* hotline; **~ de tarjeta** card phone; **por ~** over the phone; **hablar por ~** to talk on the phone; **llamar por ~** to telephone 2. (*número*) phone number 3. *pl* (*compañía*) telephone company

telegrafía *f* telegraphy

telegrafiar <*3. pret:* telegrafió> *vt, vi* to telegraph

telegráfico, -a *adj* 1. (*por telégrafo*) telegraph 2. (*relativo a la telegrafía*) telegraphic

telégrafo *m* 1. (*aparato*) telegraph 2. *pl* (*administración*) post office

telegrama *m* telegram

teleimpresor *m* teleprinter

telele *m inf* fit; **como me digas que no, me da un ~** if you say 'no', I'll have a fit

telemando *m* remote control; (*de la televisión*) remote control

telemarujeo *m pey: women's TV programmes*

telemática *f* telematics *pl*

telémetro *m* 1. FOTO rangefinder 2. TÉC telemeter

telenovela *f* TV soap opera

telenque I. *adj* 1. *Chile* (*temblón*) shaking; (*enfermizo*) sickly 2. *ElSal* (*torcido*) crooked II. *m Guat* (*cachivache*) junk

teleobjetivo *m* FOTO telephoto lens

telepatía *f sin pl* telepathy

telepático, -a *adj* telepathic

telequinesia *f* telekinesis

telera *f* 1. (*travesaño*) transom 2. (*de un arado, carro*) plough pin *Brit,* plow pin *Am*

3. (*de una prensa*) jaw
telescópico, -a *adj* telescopic
telescopio *m* telescope
telesilla *f* chair-lift
telespectador(a) *m(f)* TV viewer
telesquí *m* ski-lift
teletexto *m* teletext
teletienda *f* TV shop
teletipo *m* teletype®
teletrabajo *m* teleworking (from home)
televidente *mf v.* **telespectador**
televisar *vt* to televise, to broadcast; (*en directo*) to televise live
televisión *f* 1. (*sistema, organización*) television; ~ **digital** digital television; ~ **de pago** pay-television 2. *inf* (*televisor*) television, TV set; ~ **en color** colour TV *Brit,* color TV *Am*
televisivo, -a *adj* 1. (*relativo a*) television 2. (*apto para*) telegenic
televisor *m* television set
télex *m* telex
telón *m* curtain; **el ~ de acero** the iron curtain; ~ **de fondo** backdrop
tema *m t.* MÚS, LIT theme; **cada loco con su ~** to each his own; **ése es el ~ de mi sermón** *fig* that's just what I'm always saying; **alejarse del ~** to stray from the issue; **~s de actualidad** current issues
temario *m* 1. (*lista de temas*) programme *Brit,* program *Am* 2. (*para un examen*) list of topics 3. (*de una conferencia*) agenda
temática *f* subjects *pl*
temático, -a *adj* thematic
temblar <e→ie> *vi* to tremble; ~ **de miedo** to tremble with fear; ~ **por alguien** to fear for sb; **dejar temblando** (*comer*) to polish off; ~ **de frío** to shiver (with cold); ~ **de pensarlo** to shudder just to think of it; ~ **como un flan** to shake like a leaf; **me tiembla el ojo** my eye is twitching
tembleque *m inf* 1. (*temblor*) shaking; **me dio un ~** I got the shakes 2. (*persona*) weakling
temblequear *vi inf* to shake
temblón *m* (**álamo**) ~ quaking aspen
temblón, -ona *adj inf* trembling
temblor *m* (*tembleque*) tremor; (*escalofrío*) shiver; ~ **de frío** shivers; ~ (**de tierra**) earthquake
tembloroso, -a *adj* shaky
temer I. *vt* 1. (*sentir temor*) to fear 2. (*sospechar*) to be afraid II. *vi* to be afraid; ~ **por alguien** to fear for sb III. *vr:* **~se** to be afraid; **me temo que sí/no** I'm afraid so/not
temerario, -a *adj* 1. (*imprudente*) reckless 2. (*sin fundamento*) rash
temeridad *f sin pl* 1. (*imprudencia*) recklessness 2. (*insensatez*) rashness
temeroso, -a *adj* 1. (*medroso*) fearful; ~ **de Dios** God-fearing; ~ **de que...** +*subj* fearful that ... 2. (*temible*) dreadful
temible *adj* fearsome
temor *m* 1. (*miedo*) fear; **por ~ a lo que diga la gente** for fear of what people will say 2. (*sospecha*) suspicion
témpano *m* 1. (*pedazo*) chunk; (*de hielo*) ice floe; **quedarse como un ~** to be chilled to the bone; **tener las manos como un ~** to have ice-cold hands; **él es como un ~** *fig* he is as cold as stone 2. (*tambor*) kettledrum; (*piel*) drumhead
temperamental *adj* 1. (*del temperamento*) temperamental; **característica ~** characteristic of one's nature 2. (*persona*) spirited
temperamento *m* (*carácter, vivacidad*) temperament; **tener mucho ~** to have a strong character
temperante I. *adj AmS* (*abstemio*) abstemious, teetotalling II. *mf AmS* teetotaller *Brit,* teetotaler *Am*
temperar I. *vt* to temper; MED to calm II. *vr:* **~se** to warm up
temperatura *f* temperature; (*de una persona*) temperature; (*fiebre*) fever; **el niño tiene mucha ~** the boy's running a very high temperature; **tengo algo de ~** I have a slight fever
tempestad *f* (*tormenta*) storm; (*marejada*) gale; (*agitación*) turmoil; ~ **de aplausos** tumultuous applause; ~ **de injurias** storm of insults; ~ **de silbidos** outburst of whistling; **levantar ~es** to produce turmoil; **levantar una ~ de protestas** to raise a storm of protest; **una ~ en un vaso de agua** a storm in a teacup
tempestivo, -a *adj elev* timely, opportune
tempestuoso, -a *adj* tempestuous; (*ambiente*) stormy
templado, -a *adj* 1. (*tibio*) lukewarm 2. (*temperado*) tempered 3. (*moderado*) moderate; **ser ~ en la bebida** to drink with moderation 4. (*sereno*) composed 5. (*valiente*) courageous 6. *inf* (*bebido*) tipsy; **estar ~** to be drunk 7. MÚS tuned
templanza *f* 1. (*moderación*) temperateness 2. (*clima, temperatura*) mildness 3. (*virtud*) temperance
templar I. *vt* 1. (*moderar*) to moderate; (*suavizar*) to soften; (*calmar*) to calm down 2. (*calentar*) to warm up 3. (*entibiar*) to cool down 4. MÚS (*afinar*) to tune; ~ **a alguien la gaita** *fig* to calm sb down 5. (*apretar*) to tighten 6. (*mezclar*) to blend 7. (*acero*) to temper II. *vr:* **~se** 1. (*moderarse*) to control oneself 2. (*calentarse*) to get warm; (*enfriarse*) to cool off 3. *AmL* (*enamorarse*) to fall in love 4. *Col, Perú* (*emborracharse*) to get drunk
temple *m* 1. (*valentía*) courage 2. (*carácter*) disposition; (*humor*) mood; **estar de buen/mal ~** to be in a good/bad mood 3. (*temperatura*) temperature; (*tiempo*) weather 4. (*del acero: proceso*) tempering; (*dureza*) hardness 5. MÚS tuning 6. ARTE tempera
templete *m* bandstand
templo *m* temple; (*iglesia*) church; **una verdad como un ~** *inf* the naked truth

temporada *f* (*tiempo*) season; (*época*) period; ~ **alta** high season; ~ **baja** low season; ~ **de caza/pesca** hunting/fishing season; **fruta de** ~ seasonal fruit; **están pasando por una** ~ **difícil** they're going through a difficult period; **llevo una** ~ **que salgo poco** I've been going out very little lately

temporal I. *adj* 1. (*relativo al tiempo*) stormy 2. (*no permanente*) temporary, provisional; (*no eterno*) temporal; **contrato** ~ temporary contract 3. (*secular*) worldly 4. ANAT **hueso** ~ temporal II. *m* 1. (*tormenta*) storm; (*marejada*) stormy seas *pl*; **capear el** ~ *fig* to weather the storm 2. ANAT temporal bone

temporario, -a *adj AmL* temporary

temporero, -a I. *adj* seasonal; **trabajador** ~ seasonal worker II. *m, f* seasonal worker, migrant worker; AGR seasonal worker

tempranero, -a I. *adj* 1. (*anticipado*) premature; (*fruta*) early 2. (*madrugador*) **ser** ~ to be an early riser; **¡qué** ~ **estás hoy!** you're up early today! II. *m, f* early riser, earlybird

temprano *adv* 1. (*a primera hora*) early; ~ **por la mañana** early in the morning 2. (*antes*) early; **llegar** (**demasiado**) ~ to arrive (too) early

temprano, -a *adj* early; **a edad temprana** at an early age

tenacidad *f sin pl* 1. (*persona*) tenacity; (*porfía*) perseverance 2. (*material*) resilience 3. (*dolor*) persistence; (*mancha*) stubbornness

tenacillas *fpl* tongs *pl*; (*para rizar*) curling iron; (*para depilar*) tweezers *pl*

tenaz *adj* 1. (*perserverante*) persevering; (*cabezota*) stubborn; **ser** ~ **en sus decisiones** to be firm in his/her decisions 2. (*resistente*) resistent 3. (*persistente*) persistent; (*niebla*) clinging

tenaza(**s**) *f*(*pl*) pliers *pl*

tenca *f* tench

tencha *f Guat* (*cárcel*) jail

tendajo *m inf* small tumble-down shop

tendajón *m Méx* small shop

tendal *m* (*toldo*) awning

tendear *vi Méx* to windowshop

tendedero *m* 1. (*lugar*) drying place 2. (*armazón*) clothes horse; (*cuerdas*) clothes line

tendencia *f* 1. (*inclinación*) tendency; **tener** ~ **a** to have a tendency to 2. (*dirección*) trend; ~ **alcista** upward [*o* bullish] trend; ~ **al alza/a la baja** upward/downward trend, bullish/bearish; **las últimas** ~**s de la moda** the latest fashion trends 3. (*aspiración*) ~ **a algo** drift toward sth; ~**s autonomistas** trend toward self-government

tendencioso, -a *adj pey* tendentious

tender <e→ie> I. *vt* 1. (*desdoblar, esparcir*) ~ **sobre algo** to spread over sth; ~ **la cama** *AmL* to make the bed; ~ **la mesa** *AmL* to lay the table 2. (*tumbar*) to lay; (*de golpe*) to throw down 3. (*colocar: ropa*) to hang out; (*cuerda*) to stretch; (*puente*) to build; (*línea, vía*) to lay 4. (*aproximar*) to hold out; ~ **la mano a alguien** *fig* to give sb a hand II. *vi* 1. (*inclinarse, aspirar*) to tend; **tu cabello tiende a rojizo** your hair is slightly reddish; **tiendo a ser optimista** I tend to be optimistic 2. MAT to tend toward III. *vr:* ~**se** 1. (*tumbarse*) to stretch out 2. (*abandonarse*) to let oneself go

tenderete *m* COM stall, stand

tendero, -a *m, f* 1. (*dueño*) shopkeeper *Brit,* storekeeper *Am* 2. (*dependiente*) shop assistant

tendido *m* 1. (*de un cable*) laying 2. (*cables*) cables *pl,* wiring 3. (*ropa*) washing *Brit,* wash *Am* 4. TAUR *front rows of seats* 5. *AmL* (*de la cama*) bed linen

tendido, -a *adj* (*galope*) at full gallop; **largo y** ~ long and hard

tendón *m* ANAT tendon

tenebroso, -a *adj t. fig* (*oscuro*) dark; (*tétrico*) gloomy

tenedor *m* (*para comer*) fork

tenedor(**a**) *m*(*f*) 1. (*propietario*) holder; ~ **de tierras** landowner 2. FIN ~ **de libros** bookkeeper

teneduría *f* bookkeeping

tenencia *f* JUR possession; ~ **ilícita de armas** illegal possession of arms

tener *irr* I. *vt* 1. (*poseer, disfrutar, sentir, padecer*) to have; ~ **los ojos azules** to have blue eyes; ~ **29 años** to be 29 years old; ~ **hambre/sed/calor/sueño** to be hungry/thirsty/hot/sleepy; ~ **poco de tonto** to be no fool; **no** ~ **nada de especial** to be nothing special; **¿**(**con que**) **ésas tenemos?** so that's the way it is?; ~**la tomada con alguien** *inf* to have it in for sb; **no** ~**las todas consigo** not to be sure of something; **no** ~ **nada que perder** to have nothing to lose; **no** ~ **precio** to be priceless; ~ **cariño a alguien** to be fond of sb; ~ **la culpa de algo** to be to blame for sth; **¿tienes frío?** are you cold?; **le tengo lástima** I feel sorry for him/her; ~ **sueño** to be sleepy 2. (*considerar*) ~ **por algo** to consider sth; ~ **a alguien en menos/mucho** to think all the less/more of sb; **ten por seguro que...** rest assured that ...; **tengo para mí que...** I think that ... 3. (*guardar*) to keep 4. (*contener*) to have; **el frasco ya no tiene miel** there's no honey left in the jar 5. (*coger*) to take; **ten esto** take this 6. (*sujetar*) to hold; ~ **a alguien por el brazo** to hold sb by the arm 7. (*recibir*) to have; ~ **un niño** to have a baby 8. (*hacer sentir*) **me tienes preocupada** I'm worried about you; **me tienes loca** you're driving me mad! 9. (*cumplir*) ~ **su palabra** to keep one's word II. *vr:* ~**se** 1. (*considerarse*) ~**se por algo** to consider oneself sth; ~**se en mucho** to think highly of oneself 2. (*sostenerse*) to stand; ~**se de pie** to stand; ~**se firme** to stand upright; *fig* to stand firm; **estoy que no me tengo** I'm exhausted 3. (*dominarse*) to control oneself 4. (*atenerse*) to adhere III. *aux* 1. (*con participio concordante*) ~ **pensado**

T

hacer algo to plan to do sth; **ya tengo comprado todo** I've bought everything already; ~**se algo callado** to keep quiet about sth; **ya me lo tenía pensado** I had already thought of that **2.** (*obligación, necesidad*) ~ **que** to have to; ~ **mucho que hacer** to have a lot to do; **¿qué tiene que ver esto conmigo?** what does this have to do with me?

Tenerife *m* Tenerife

tenia *f* tapeworm

tenida *f Chile* meeting; (*traje*) suit; (*uniforme*) uniform

teniente *m* MIL lieutenant; ~ **coronel** lieutenant-colonel

tenis *m sin pl* tennis; ~ **de mesa** table tennis

tenista *mf* tennis player

tenor *m* **1.** *t.* MÚS (*contenido*) tenor; **a este** ~ at this rate; **a** ~ **de** according to **2.** (*constitución*) constitution

tenorio *m* Don Juan, womanizer

tensar *vt* (*músculo*) to tense; (*cuerda*) to tighten

tensión *f* **1.** FÍS tension **2.** (*estado: cosa*) stress; (*cuerda, piel*) tautness; (*nervios, músculos*) tension; (*impaciencia*) anxiety; **película de** ~ thriller; **estar en** ~ (*nervioso*) to be nervous; (*impaciente*) to be anxious **3.** MED ~ **arterial** blood pressure **4.** ELEC voltage **5.** *pl* (*conflicto*) strained relations *pl*

tenso, **-a** *adj* (*cosa, situación*) tense; (*cuerda, piel*) taut; (*músculos, nervios*) tense; (*impaciente*) anxious

tentación *f* temptation; **me dan tentaciones de...** I'm tempted to ...; **caer en la** ~ to succumb [*o* give in] to the temptation

tentáculo *m* tentacle

tentador(a) **I.** *adj* tempting **II.** *m(f)* tempter *m*, temptress *f*

tentar <e→ie> *vt* **1.** (*palpar*) to feel; (*reconocer*) to probe **2.** (*atraer*) to tempt; (*seducir*) to entice; **no me tientes** don't tempt me

tentativa *f* attempt; ~ **de robo** attempted robbery

tentempié *m inf* (*refrigerio*) bite to eat

tenue *adj* **1.** (*delgado*) fine; (*delicado*) delicate **2.** (*sutil*) subtle; (*débil*) weak; **luz** ~ faint light **3.** (*sencillo*) simple

teñir *irr como ceñir vt, vr:* ~**se** to dye; ~(**se**) **de rojo** to dye red; ~**se el cabello de negro** to dye one's hair black; ~ **de tristeza** to tinge with sadness

teología *f* theology

teológico, **-a** *adj* theological

teólogo, **-a** **I.** *adj* theologic **II.** *m, f* theologian; (*estudiante*) divinity student

teorema *m* theorem

teoría *f* theory; ~ **del caos** the chaos theory; **en** ~ in theory

teórica *f* theoretics *pl*

teórico, **-a** **I.** *adj* theoretical **II.** *m, f* theorist, theoretician

teorizar <z→c> *vi, vt* to theorize

tepache *m Méx* GASTR tepache (*drink made of pulque, water, pineapple and cloves*)

tequesquite *m Méx* rock salt

tequiche *m Ven* GASTR *dish made with toasted maize, coconut milk and butter*

tequila *m* tequila

tequio *m AmC, Méx* **1.** (*molestia*) bother **2.** (*daño*) harm

tequioso, **-a** *adj AmC* **1.** (*travieso*) mischievous; (*niño*) trying **2.** (*molesto*) bothersome

TER *m abr de* **Tren Español Rápido** express train (*Spanish intercity high-speed train*)

terapeuta *mf* therapist

terapéutica *f* therapeutics *pl*

terapéutico, **-a** *adj* therapeutic(al)

terapia *f* therapy; ~ **en** [*o* de] **grupo** group therapy

tercena *f Ecua* butcher's shop

tercer *adj v.* **tercero**

tercera *f* **1.** AUTO third gear **2.** MÚS third **3.** FERRO third-class

tercería *f* (*mediación*) mediation

tercermundista *adj* third-world, underdeveloped

Tercer Mundo *m sin pl* Third World

tercero **I.** *m* **1.** *t.* JUR third party **2.** (*alcahuete*) procurer **II.** *adv* third

tercero, **-a** **I.** *adj* (*delante de un sustantivo masculino: tercer*) third; **terceras personas** third parties; **en tercer lugar** thirdly; **ser** ~ to be the odd man out; **viven en el** ~ they live on the third floor; **tercera edad** senior citizens, retirement years ►**a la tercera va la vencida** *prov* third time lucky *prov* **II.** *m, f* third; *v.t.* **octavo**

terceto *m* LIT tercet, triplet; MÚS trio

tercia *f* REL tierce

terciar **I.** *vt* **1.** (*dividir*) to divide into three parts **2.** (*atravesar*) to place diagonally across **3.** (*la carga*) to balance **4.** *AmL* (*aguar*) to water down **II.** *vi* **1.** (*intervenir*) to intervene **2.** (*mediar*) to have a word **3.** (*participar*) to take part; ~ **en un juego** to join in a game **III.** *vr, vimpers:* ~**se** **1.** (*ocurrir*) to arise; **si se tercia** should the occasion arise; **prepararse por lo que se pueda** ~ to get ready for what may happen **2.** (*ponerse*) to make up the number

terciario *m* GEO Tertiary period

terciario, **-a** *adj t.* GEO Tertiary

tercio *m* (*parte*) third; *v.t.* **octavo** ►**hacer buen/mal** ~ **a alguien** to do sb a good/bad turn

terciopelo *m* velvet; **lazo de** ~ velvet bow

terco, **-a** **I.** *adj* **1.** (*persona*) stubborn, obstinate **2.** (*niño*) unruly **3.** (*animal*) balky **4.** (*cosa*) tough **II.** *m, f* stubborn person

tereque *m Col, Dom, PRico, Ven* (*cachivache*) utensil

tergal® *m type of synthetic fabric*

tergiversar *vt* (*hechos*) to misrepresent; (*la verdad*) to distort; (*palabras*) to twist

termal *adj* thermal; **aguas** ~**es** hot springs

termas *fpl* (*baños*) hot baths *pl;* (*de los*

romanos) thermae

termes *m inv* termite

térmico, -a *adj* thermal, thermic; **central térmica** power station

terminación *f* **1.**(*acción*) termination; (*de un proyecto*) completion; (*producción*) finish; (*de un plazo*) end **2.**(*final*) end; (*borde*) end, edge

terminal[1] **I.** *adj* terminal; **parte** ~ final part; **un enfermo** ~ a terminally ill patient **II.** *m* INFOR terminal

terminal[2] *f* **1.**(*estación*) terminal, terminus; FERRO station **2.**(*de* (*aero*)*puerto*) terminal; ~ **aérea** air terminal

terminante *adj* **1.**(*claro*) clear **2.**(*definitivo*) categorical

terminar **I.** *vt* **1.**(*finalizar*) to finish; (*proyecto*) to complete; **¿cuándo terminas?** when will you be done? **2.**(*producir*) to finish; **¿cuándo van a ~ el puerto?** when are they going to finish the port?; **estar bien terminado** to be well finished **3.**(*consumir*) to finish up; (*beber*) to drink up; (*comer*) to eat up **II.** *vi* **1.**(*tener fin*) to finish, to end; (*plazo, contrato*) to end; ~ **bien/mal** to have a happy/unhappy ending; ~ **en punta** to end in a point; ~ **de construir** to finish building; ~ **de hacer/coser/comer** to finish doing/sewing/eating; **cuando termines de comer...** when you finish eating ...; **¿cuándo termina la película?** what time does the film end?; **la escuela termina a las dos** school is out at 2 pm **2.**(*acercarse al final*) to be ending; **ya termina la película** the film is almost over **3.**(*poner fin*) to put an end to **4.**(*destruir*) to do away; **el tabaco va a ~ contigo** tobacco is going to be the end of you! **5.**(*separarse*) to break up **6.**(*llegar a*) ~ **por hacer algo** to end up doing sth; **terminaron peleándose** they wound up fighting **7.**(*haber hecho*) ~ **de hacer algo** to have just done sth **III.** *vr:* **~se 1.**(*aproximarse al final*) to be almost over **2.**(*no haber más*) (for) there to be no more; **se me está terminando la paciencia** I'm running out of patience; **se terminaron las galletas** there aren't any more biscuits (left)

término *m* **1.**(*fin*) end; **dar ~ a algo** to finish sth off; **llevar a ~** to carry out; **poner ~ a algo** to put an end to sth; **sin ~** endless; **me bajé en el ~** I got off at the terminus; **he llegado al ~ de mi paciencia** I've reached the end of my patience **2.**(*plazo*) period; **en el ~ de quince días** within 15 days **3.**(*linde*) boundary **4.** ADMIN district; ~ **municipal** township **5.**(*vocablo*) word; (*especial*) term; **en buenos ~s** on good terms; **en otros ~s** in other words; **contestar en malos ~s** to answer rudely **6.**(*parte*) term **7.** *pl* (*de un contrato*) terms *pl,* conditions *pl* ►**estar en buenos/malos ~s** to be on good/bad terms; **separarse en buenos/malos ~s** to separate on good/bad terms; **en ~s generales** generally speaking; ~ **medio** compromise; **en medios ~s** with vague half-answers; **en primer ~** first of all; **en último ~** as a last resort; **por ~ medio** on the average

terminología *f* terminology

terminológico, -a *adj* terminological; **diccionario ~** specialized dictionary

termita *f* termite

termo *m* thermos

termodinámica *f* thermodynamics *pl*

termómetro *m* thermometer; ~ **clínico** clinical thermometer

termonuclear *adj* thermonuclear

termosifón *m* (*calentador*) boiler

termostato *m,* **termóstato** *m* thermostat, thermal switch

termotecnia *f* thermotechnics *pl,* heat engineering

terna *f* (*candidatos*) short list (*a list of three candidates for a job o position*)

ternario, -a *adj* ternary; (*de tres unidades*) three-part

terne **I.** *adj* **1.** *inf* (*bravucón*) bullying **2.** *inf* (*cabezota*) bullheaded **3.**(*recio*) husky **II.** *m inf* (*bravucón*) bully

ternejo, -a *adj Ecua, Perú* (*persona*) lively

ternera *f* (*carne*) beef, veal

ternero, -a *m, f* calf

terneza *f v.* **ternura**

ternilla *f* gristle

terno *m* **1.**(*conjunto*) set of three **2.**(*traje*) three-piece suit **3.**(*juramento*) swearword; **echar ~s** to curse

ternura *f* **1.**(*cariño*) tenderness **2.**(*dulzura*) sweetness **3.**(*blandura, suavidad*) softness **4.**(*delicadeza, sensibilidad*) gentleness **5.** *Chile, Ecua, Guat* (*inmadurez*) greenness

terquedad *f* **1.**(*testarudez*) stubbornness, obstinacy **2.**(*porfía*) willfulness **3.**(*de un niño*) unruliness **4.**(*de un animal*) balkiness

terracota *f* terracotta

terrado *m* flat roof; (*terraza*) terrace

terral **I.** *adj* land **II.** *m* METEO land wind

Terranova *f* Newfoundland

terraplén *m* **1.**(*montón*) mound; (*protección*) rampart **2.**(*desnivel*) slope; ~ **de un ferrocarril** railway embankment

terráqueo, -a **I.** *adj* terrestrial, terraqueous; **globo ~** globe **II.** *m, f* terraquean

terrario *m* terrarium

terrateniente *mf* landowner, landholder

terraza *f* **1.**(*jardín*) terrace; (*balcón*) balcony; (*azotea*) flat roof **2.**(*of a café*) terrace (*area outside a bar or café where tables are placed to serve customers in good weather*)

terregal *m Méx* loose topsoil

terremoto *m* earthquake

terrenal *adj* worldly; **paraíso ~** earthly paradise

terreno *m* **1.**(*suelo*) land; GEO terrain; ~ **arcilloso** clayey ground **2.**(*espacio*) lot; (*parcela*) plot of land; (*campo*) field; DEP playing field; ~ **de fútbol** football pitch *Brit,* soccer field *Am;* ~ **edificable** buildable land; **vehí-**

T

culo todo ~ all-terrain vehicle **3.** (*esfera*) sphere; ~ **desconocido** unfamiliar territory; **estar en su propio** ~ to be on one's own ground ►**ceder** ~ to give up ground; **explorar el** ~ to see how the land lies; **ganar/perder** ~ to gain/lose ground; **minar el** ~ **a alguien** to undermine sb's plans; **preparar el** ~ **para algo** to pave the way for sth; **saber uno el** ~ **que pisa** to know what one's doing; **ser** ~ **abonado para...** to be ideal for ...; **sobre el** ~ on the spot

terreno, **-a** *adj* earthly

terrera *f* lark

terrestre **I.** *adj* **1.** (*de la Tierra*) terrestrial; **globo** ~ globe **2.** (*en la tierra*) earthly; **animal** ~ land animal; **transporte** ~ ground transport **3.** (*terrenal*) earthly **II.** *mf* terrestrial

terrible *adj* terrible; **hace un frío** ~ it's terribly cold; **tener un hambre** ~ to be terribly hungry

terrícola *mf* earthling, earth dweller

terrífico, **-a** *adj* terrifying

territorial *adj* territorial; **división** ~ territorial division

territorio *m* **1.** (*región*) territory; POL region/district; JUR district; ~ **jurisdiccional** jurisdictional territory; **en todo el** ~ **nacional** over the whole country, nationwide **2.** ZOOL territory

terrón *m* **1.** (*masa*) lump; ~ (**de azúcar**) lump; ~ (**de tierra**) clod; **azúcar de** ~ lump sugar **2.** *(pl), inf* (*campo*) land

terror *m* **1.** (*miedo*) terror; **película de** ~ horror film; **las arañas me dan** ~ I'm terrified of spiders; **me domina el** ~ I'm terrified **2.** (*que provoca miedo*) terror **3.** POL terror; **reino de** ~ reign of terror

terrorífico, **-a** *adj* terrifying

terrorismo *m sin pl* terrorism

terrorista **I.** *adj* terrorist; **organización** ~ terrorist organization **II.** *mf* terrorist

terroso, **-a** *adj* earthy; (*color*) earth-coloured *Brit*, earth-colored *Am*

terruño *m* **1.** (*trozo*) clod **2.** (*comarca*) region; (*patria*) native land **3.** (*terreno*) piece of land; AGR soil

terso, **-a** *adj* **1.** (*liso*) smooth; (*tirante*) taut **2.** (*limpio*) clean; (*transparente*) clear; (*brillante*) shiny **3.** (*sencillo*) easy; (*fluido*) flowing

tertulia *f* **1.** (*reunión*) gathering; **estar de** ~ to talk; **hacer** ~ to meet informally to talk; ~ **literaria** literary circle **2.** (*para jugar*) games room

tesina *f* project; UNIV (*trabajo*) minor thesis

tesis *f inv* **1.** (*proposición*) theory **2.** (*trabajo*) thesis; ~ **doctoral** doctorate [*o* doctoral] thesis

tesitura *f* **1.** (*disposición*) frame of mind **2.** MÚS range

tesón *m* tenacity; **trabajar con** ~ to work diligently

tesonero, **-a** *adj AmL* **1.** (*perseverante*) persevering **2.** (*tenaz*) tenacious

tesorería *f* **1.** (*cargo*) treasury **2.** *t.* FIN (*despacho*) treasurer's office

tesorero, **-a** *m, f* treasurer

tesoro *m* **1.** (*de gran valor*) treasure; **ser un** ~ **de una persona** to be a real treasure; **valer un** ~ to be worth a fortune **2.** (*fortuna*) fortune; ~ (**público**) Exchequer, Treasury **3.** (*cariño*) dear

test *m* test

testa *f* **1.** (*cabeza*) head; ~ **dura** hard head; ~ **de ferro** figurehead **2.** (*frente*) forehead **3.** *inf* (*sensatez*) brains *pl*

testaferro *m* man of straw

testamentario, **-a** **I.** *adj* testamentary **II.** *m, f* executor *m*, executrix *f*

testamento *m* will, testament; ~ **abierto** nuncupative will; **hacer** ~ to make one's will

testar *vi* to make a will

testarada *f* bump on the head; **darse una** ~ to bump one's head; **darse una** ~ **con alguien** *t. fig* to bump heads

testarudez *f* **1.** (*cualidad*) pigheadedness **2.** (*acción*) an act of stubbornness

testarudo, **-a** **I.** *adj* pigheaded **II.** *m, f* stubborn person

testera *f* **1.** (*de la cabeza*) forehead **2.** (*parte*) front part; (*fachada*) facade

testículo *m* ANAT testicle

testificar <c→qu> **I.** *vt* **1.** (*declarar*) to testify; (*testigo*) to witness **2.** (*afirmar: testigo*) to attest; (*documento*) to bear witness **3.** (*demostrar*) to give evidence **II.** *vi* to testify

testigo[1] *mf t.* JUR witness; ~ **de cargo/de descargo** witness for the prosecution/defence *Brit* [*o* defense *Am*]; ~ **de matrimonio** witness at sb's wedding; ~ **ocular** eyewitness; **fui** ~ **del accidente** I witnessed the accident; **examinar ~s** to examine witnesses; **poner a alguien por** ~ to cite sb as witness; **a Dios pongo por testigo** I swear to God

testigo[2] *m* **1.** (*prueba*) proof; **ser** ~ **de algo** to bear witness to sth **2.** DEP baton

testimonial *adj* **1.** (*que afirma*) attesting; **declaración** ~ testimony **2.** (*que prueba*) testificatory

testimoniar **I.** *vt* **1.** (*declarar*) to testify **2.** (*afirmar*) to attest **3.** (*dar muestra*) to show **4.** (*probar*) to be proof of **II.** *vi* to testify

testimonio *m* **1.** (*declaración*) testimony; **dar** ~ to testify; **no levantarás falso** ~ thou shalt not bear false witness **2.** (*afirmación*) affidavit **3.** (*muestra*) evidence **4.** (*prueba*) proof

testosterona *m* **1.** (*hormona*) testosterone **2.** *inf* (*violencia brutal*) **es una película con mucha** ~ it's a film with a lot of violence

testuz *m o f* **1.** (*frente*) forehead **2.** (*nuca*) nape

teta *f* **1.** *inf* (*pecho*) breast; **niño de** ~ *inf* babe-in-arms; **dar la** ~ to breast-feed; **quitar la** ~ to wean **2.** (*ubre*) udder **3.** (*pezón: mujer*) nipple; (*animal*) teat

tétano(**s**) *m* (*inv*) MED tetanus

tetera *f* **1.** (*para té*) teapot; (*para hervir*) kettle **2.** *AmL* (*tetilla*) nipple **3.** *AmL v.* **tetero**

tetero *m AmL* baby's bottle

tetilla *f* **1.** (*biberón*) nipple **2.** (*animal*) teat **3.** (*queso*) cone-shaped cheese (*type of cheese made in Galicia*)

tetrabrik® *m* carton; **un ~ de leche/zumo** a carton of milk/juice

tétrico, -a *adj* dismal

tetuda *adj vulg* big-breasted

textil I. *adj* textile; **planta ~** textile mill **II.** *m* textile

texto *m* text; (*pasaje*) extract; (**libro de**) **~** textbook

textual *adj* **1.** (*relativo al texto*) textual; (*escrito*) written **2.** (*conforme al texto*) textual; (*literal*) word-for-word; (*exacto*) exact; **con las palabras ~es** with those exact words

textura *f* **1.** (*tejido*) weave **2.** (*estructura*) structure; GEO, QUÍM texture

tez *f* complexion; **de ~ morena** dark

ti *pron pers* **a ~** (*objeto directo, indirecto*) you; **de ~** from you; **de ~ para mí** from you for me; **para ~** for you; **por ~** for you

tía *f* **1.** (*pariente*) aunt; **~ abuela** great-aunt; **¡(cuéntaselo a) tu ~!** *inf* tell that to the marines!; **no hay tu ~** *inf* nothing doing! **2.** *inf* (*mujer*) woman; **ser una ~ buena** to be a good-looking woman; **¡qué ~ más buena!** what a babe!; **vaya ~ más tonta** what a stupid woman!; **pero ~, ¿qué te pasa?** hey, girl, what's the matter with you?

tianguis *m inv, Méx* (*rastro indígena*) street market

tiarrón, -ona *m, f inf* big guy

tibetano, -a *adj, m, f* Tibetan

tibia *f* ANAT tibia, shinbone *inf*

tibiarse *vr AmC, Ven* (*irritarse*) to get cross

tibiera *f Ven* **1.** (*molestia*) irritation **2.** (*fastidio*) nuisance

tibieza *f* lukewarmness; (*apatía*) lack of enthusiasm; (*frialdad en el trato*) coolness

tibio, -a *adj* **1.** (*temperatura*) lukewarm **2.** (*carácter, sentimiento*) unenthusiastic **3.** *AmL, inf* (*enfadado*) angry ▸**poner ~ a alguien** to lay in to sb; **ponerse ~** (**de comida**) to stuff oneself

tibor *m* **1.** (*vasija*) vase **2.** *AmL* (*orinal*) chamber pot

tiburón *m* **1.** ZOOL shark **2.** FIN raider

tic I. *interj* tick **II.** *m* <tics> tic; (*manía*) habit

tico, -a *adj, m, f AmL, inf* (*costarricense*) Costa Rican

tictac I. *interj* tick-tock; **hacer ~** to tick **II.** *m sin pl* ticking

tiempo *m* **1.** (*momento, duración, periodo*) time; **~ libre/de ocio** spare/leisure time; **al poco ~** shortly after; **~ de pago** payday; **los buenos ~s** the good old days; **a ~** in time; **a ~ parcial** part-time; **a su ~** in due course; **todo a su ~** all in good time; **cada cosa a su ~** there is a time for everything; **al** (**mismo**) **~, a un ~** at the same time; **al ~ que...** while ...; **antes de ~** early; **llegar antes de ~** to arrive ahead of time; **andando el ~** in the course of time; **con ~** in good time; **llegué a la estación con ~** I reached the station early; **hazlo con ~** don't leave it for the last minute; **de ~ en ~** from time to time; **desde hace mucho ~** for a long time; **durante cierto ~** for some time; **en estos ~s** nowadays; **en ~s de paz** in peacetime; **en ~s de Franco** in the Franco era; **en mis ~s** in my time [*o* day]; **en otros ~s** in the past; **el ~ pasa volando** time flies; **amanecerán ~s mejores** better days are coming; **dar ~ al ~** to give it time; **este problema ya viene de ~** this problem goes way back; **hace ~ que...** it's a long time since ...; **hace ~ que no voy al cine** I haven't been to the cinema for a long time; **¡cuánto ~ sin verte!** long time no see!; **les faltó ~ para decirlo a todos** it didn't take them long to tell everyone; **hay ~** there's time; **matar el/hacer ~** to kill time; **mucho/demasiado ~** long/too long; **perder el ~** to waste time; **sin perder ~** losing no time; **si me da ~...** if I have enough time; **ya es ~ que** +*subj* it's about time; **tomarse ~** to take one's time **2.** (*época*) time; (*estación*) season **3.** METEO weather; **cerveza del ~** beer at room temperature; **~ de perros** filthy weather; **el ~ amenaza lluvia** it's threatening rain; **si el ~ no lo impide** weather permitting; **hoy hace mal ~** the weather is bad today **4.** LING tense; **~ presente** present tense **5.** (*edad*) age; **¿cuánto ~ tiene el niño?** how old is the child? **6.** DEP (**medio**) **~** half-time; **~ muerto** time out **7.** MÚS time, beat; (*parte*) movement; TÉC stroke; **motor de dos ~s** two-stroke engine ▸**a(l) mal ~ buena cara** *prov* you have to look on the bright side of things *prov;* **el ~ es oro** *prov* time is money *prov;* **el ~ no perdona** *prov* time and tide wait for no man *prov*

tienda *f* **1.** (*establecimiento*) shop, store; **~ de comestibles** grocer's *Brit,* grocery store *Am;* **ir de ~s** to go shopping **2.** (*alojamiento*) **~** (**de campaña**) tent; **montar/desmontar una ~** to put up [*o* pitch]/take down a tent

tienta *f* **1.** MED probe **2.** (*astucia*) cleverness ▸**andar a ~s** to feel one's way

tiento *m* **1.** (*acción*) touch; **a ~** gropingly **2.** (*prueba*) try; **dar un ~ a la botella** *inf* to take a swig from the bottle **3.** (*examen*) check; **dar un ~** to test; **dar un ~ al melón** to see if the melon is ripe **4.** (*tacto*) tact; (*cautela*) caution; **con ~** carefully; (*cuidado*) care **5.** (*de un ciego*) blindman's cane **6.** (*tentáculo*) tentacle **7.** (*pulso*) sureness of hand; **con ~** with a steady hand

tierno, -a I. *adj* **1.** (*blando*) soft; (*pan, dulces*) fresh **2.** (*suave, delicado, sensible*) tender; **a tierna edad** at a tender age; **desde mi más tierna edad...** since I was very young ...; **en mi más tierna niñez** in early childhood; **¡qué ~!** how tender! **3.** (*cariñoso*) affectionate **4.** *Chile, Ecua, Guat* (*inmaduro*) green **II.** *m, f Guat, Nic* newborn or very young child

tierra *f* **1.** (*materia, superficie, planeta*) earth; **~ vegetal** humus; **toma de ~** ELEC earth *Brit,* ground *Am;* **bajo** ~ MIN underground; **estar bajo** ~ to be buried; ~ **de nadie** no-man's-land; ~**s altas/bajas** highlands/lowlands; **dar en** ~ to fall; **caer por** ~ *fig* to crumble; **echar** ~ **a algo** *fig* to cover sth up; **echar por** ~ to knock down; *fig* to ruin; **me falta** ~ *fig* I'm not sure; **¡trágame, ~!** *inf* I wish the ground would open up and swallow me!; **parece que se lo ha tragado la** ~ *inf* it is as if he had vanished off the face of the earth **2.** (*firme*) mainland; ~ **adentro** inland; **poner** ~ **por medio** to make oneself scarce; **tomar** ~ AVIAT to land, to touch down; NÁUT to land; **como no lleguemos pronto a la estación, nos vamos a quedar en** ~ if we don't get to the station soon, the train will leave without us **3.** (*región*) land; **Tierra Santa** Holy Land; ~ (**natal**) native land **4.** (*hacienda*) property; ~ **de labor** agricultural land; ~ **de pastos** grazing land; **poseer** ~**s** to own land; **aquí, como en toda la** ~ **de garbanzos...** *inf* here, like everywhere in the world

tierral *m AmL* (*polvareda*) cloud of dust

tieso *adv* firmly

tieso, -a *adj* **1.** (*rígido*) stiff; **dejar** ~ **a alguien** *inf* (*matar*) to bump sb off; (*sorprender*) to dumbfound; **quedarse** ~ (*de frío*) to be frozen stiff; (*miedo*) to be scared stiff; (*morirse*) to croak; (*dormirse*) to fall asleep **2.** (*erguido*) erect; (*orejas*) pricked up **3.** (*terco*) unbending; **tenérselas tiesas** to hold firm **4.** (*serio*) stiff **5.** (*engreído*) conceited; **no te pongas** ~ don't act so stuck up **6.** (*tirante*) taut **7.** (*valiente*) brave **8.** (*robusto*) robust; (*sano*) fit

tiesto *m* **1.** (*maceta*) flowerpot **2.** *Chile* (*vasija*) pot, bowl

tiesura *f* stiffness

tifoideo, -a *adj* typhoid; **fiebre tifoidea** typhoid fever

tifón *m* **1.** (*huracán*) typhoon **2.** (*tromba*) waterspout

tifus *m inv* MED typhus

tigre, -a *m, f AmL* ZOOL jaguar

tigre(sa) *m(f)* **1.** ZOOL tiger *m,* tigress *f;* **oler a** ~ *inf* to stink **2.** (*persona*) tiger

tijera *f* **1.** *(pl)* (*utensilio, con esta forma*) scissors *pl;* (*más grandes*) shears *pl;* **silla de** ~ folding chair; **echar** ~ **a algo** *inf* to start cutting sth **2.** (*persona*) gossip **3.** DEP scissor-kick

tijereta *f* earwig

tijeretada *f,* **tijeretazo** *m* snip

tijeretear **I.** *vt* to snip **II.** *vi* **1.** (*cortar*) to cut **2.** *inf* (*entrometerse*) to meddle

tila *f* **1.** (*tilo*) linden tree **2.** (*flor*) linden-blossom **3.** (*té*) linden-blossom tea

tildar *vt* **1.** (*con acento*) to put an accent on **2.** (*la ñ*) to put a tilde over **3.** (*a alguien*) ~ **de algo** to brand as sth **4.** (*tachar*) to cross out

tilde *f* **1.** (*acento*) accent **2.** (*de la ñ*) tilde **3.** (*tacha*) flaw **4.** (*cosa mínima*) jot

tiliches *mpl AmC, Méx* (*trastos*) junk

tilín *m sin pl* (*sonido*) tinkle; **¡~!** ting-a-ling! ►hacer ~ to appeal; **el pastel no me hace** ~ I don't like the cake much

tilingo, -a *adj* **1.** *CSur, Méx* (*atolondrado*) silly **2.** *Arg* (*demente*) soft in the head

tilo *m* linden

timador(a) *m(f)* swindler

timar **I.** *vt* to con **II.** *vr:* ~**se** (*hacerse guiños*) to make eyes at each other; (*tontear*) to flirt

timba *f inf* **1.** (*partida*) game **2.** (*lugar*) gambling den **3.** *AmL* (*barriga*) belly

timbal *m* **1.** MÚS small drum; (*grande*) kettledrum **2.** GASTR meat pie

timbrar *vt* (*pegar*) to put a stamp on; (*estampar*) to postmark

timbrazo *m* loud ring

timbre *m* **1.** (*aparato*) bell; (*de la puerta*) doorbell; **han tocado el** ~ somebody rang the bell **2.** *t.* MÚS (*sonido*) timbre **3.** (*sello que se pega*) stamp; (*que se estampa*) seal **4.** (*acción*) action to one's credit; ~ **de gloria** mark of honour *Brit,* mark of honor *Am;* **ser un** ~ **de gloria para alguien** to be a credit to sb

timidez *f* shyness

tímido, -a *adj* shy, timid

timo *m* **1.** (*fraude*) con; **dar un** ~ **de 5.000 ptas a alguien** to swindle sb out of 5000 pesetas **2.** (*glándula*) thymus

timón *m* rudder; **llevar el** ~ **de una empresa** *inf* to be at the helm of a business

timonel *mf* helmsman

timorato, -a *adj* **1.** (*tímido*) timid **2.** (*de Dios*) God-fearing; *pey* spineless

tímpano *m* **1.** ANAT (*membrana*) eardrum **2.** (*instrumento*) kettledrum

tina *f* vat; *AmL* (*bañera*) bathtub

tinaja *f* large earthenware jar

tincanque *m Chile, inf* flip

tincar <c→qu> *vt* **1.** *Chile* (*presentir*) to have a hunch **2.** *Arg, Chile* (*pelota*) to drive

tincazo *m Arg, Ecua, inf* flick

tinerfeño, -a **I.** *adj* of/from Tenerife **II.** *m, f* native/inhabitant of Tenerife

tinga *f Méx* (*alboroto*) uproar

tinglado *m* **1.** (*cobertizo*) shed **2.** *inf* (*lío*) tangle **3.** (*artimaña*) intrigue; **manejar el** ~ to pull the strings **4.** (*tablado*) platform

tingo *Méx* **del** ~ **al tango** from pillar to post

tiniebla *f* darkness

tino *m* **1.** (*puntería*) aim **2.** (*destreza*) skill **3.** (*moderación*) moderation; **a buen** ~ by guesswork; **sin** ~ recklessly; **estar a** ~ to be guessing; **sacar de** ~ **a alguien** to exasperate sb **4.** (*tina*) vat

tinoso, -a *adj Col, Ven* **1.** (*hábil*) skilful *Brit,* skillful *Am* **2.** (*sensato*) sensible

tinta *f* **1.** (*para escribir*) ink; ~ **china** Indian ink; ~ **de imprenta** printer's ink; **a dos** ~**s** in two colours *Brit* [*o* colors *Am*]; **cargar las** ~**s** to exaggerate; **saber algo de buena** ~ to know sth from a reliable source; **sudar** ~ to sweat blood; **sobre este asunto han corrido ríos de** ~ much has been written about this matter **2.** (*color*) hue; **medias** ~**s** half-tones;

fig half measures
tintar *vt* to dye
tinte *m* **1.** (*teñidura*) dye **2.** (*colorante*) colouring *Brit,* coloring *Am* **3.** (*tintorería*) dry cleaner's **4.** (*matiz*) tinge; (*apariencia*) touch; **un cierto ~ de escepticismo** a certain touch of scepticism *Brit* [*o* skepticism *Am*]; **tus palabras tenían un cierto ~ de ironía** his words were tinged with irony
tinterillo *m pey* **1.** (*chupatintas*) penpusher **2.** *AmL* (*picapleitos*) shyster lawyer
tintero *m* inkwell; **dejar(se) algo en el ~** *fig* to leave sth unsaid
tintín *m* clinking
tintin(e)ar *vi* to clink
tinto, **-a** *adj* (*rojo oscuro*) dark red; (*uvas*) red; **vino ~** red wine
tintorería *f* dry cleaner's
tintorro *m inf* cheap red wine, plonk *Brit*
tintura *f* **1.** (*tinte*) tint **2.** (*colorante*) dye **3.** (*maquillaje*) rouge **4.** MED tincture
tiña *f* **1.** MED ringworm **2.** *inf* (*miseria*) poverty
tiñoso, **-a** *adj* **1.** MED scabby **2.** *inf* (*mísero*) poor **3.** (*tacaño*) stingy
tío *m* **1.** (*pariente*) uncle; **~ abuelo** great-uncle; **mis ~s** my aunt and uncle; **tener un ~ en América** to have a rich friend or relative **2.** *inf* (*hombre*) bloke *Brit,* guy; **¡oye ~!** hey, man!; **ser un ~ bueno** to be a good-looking guy
tiovivo *m* merry-go-round, carrousel *Am;* **dar más vueltas que un ~** *inf* to go all over the place
tipear *vi AmC, AmS* to type
tipejo *m pey* twerp
típico, **-a** *adj* typical; **plato ~** local or traditional dish
tipificar *vt* **1.** (*normalizar*) to standardize **2.** (*caracterizar*) to typify
tipismo *m* local colour *Brit,* local color *Am,* picturesqueness
tiple[1] *mf* MÚS (*persona*) soprano
tiple[2] *m* MÚS (*voz*) soprano
tipo *m* **1.** (*modelo*) model **2.** (*muestra*) sample; (*espécimen*) type; **un impreso/una carta ~** a standard form/letter **3.** (*cuerpo*) build; **aguantar el ~** to hold out; **arriesgar el ~** *inf* to risk one's neck; **mover el ~** *inf* to get moving; **tener buen ~** to have a good figure; **él tiene buen ~** he's well-built **4.** (*clase*) type, kind **5.** FIN rate; **~ de cambio** exchange rate **6.** TIPO type
tipo, **-a** *m, f* **1.** *inf* guy *m,* woman *f* **2.** *pey* character; **~ raro** weirdo; **no soporto esa tipa** I can't stand that bitch
tipografía *f* (*impresión*) printing; (*taller*) printing press
tipográfico, **-a** *adj* printing
tipógrafo, **-a** *m, f* printer
tiquear *vt* **1.** *AmC, PRico, Col* (*chequear*) to check **2.** *Chile* (*perforar*) to punch
tiquet *m* <tiquets> (*de viaje, de espectáculos*) ticket; (*de compra*) sales slip, receipt
tiquismiquis[1] *mf inv* (*remilgado*) fusspot
tiquismiquis[2] *mpl* **1.** (*remilgo*) silly scruples *pl* **2.** (*ñoñería*) finickiness
tira *f* **1.** (*banda*) strip, band; **~ cómica** comic strip; **hacer ~s algo** to tear sth to shreds **2.** *inf* (*mucho*) **esto me ha gustado la ~** I really liked this a lot
tirabuzón *m* **1.** (*rizo*) ringlet, curl **2.** (*sacacorchos*) corkscrew
tirachinas *m inv* catapult *Brit,* slingshot *Am*
tirada *f* **1.** (*edición*) print run; **el periódico local tiene una ~ de 10.000 ejemplares** the local paper has a circulation of 10,000 copies; **de una ~** *fig* without stopping **2.** (*distancia*) stretch
tiradero *m Méx* (*vertedero*) rubbish dump
tirado, **-a** **I.** *adj* **1.** *estar inf* (*barato*) dirt cheap; **dejar ~ a alguien** (*decepcionar*) to let sb down; (*en situación difícil*) to leave in the lurch **2.** *ser pey* (*descuidado*) slovenly **3.** *estar inf* (*fácil*) very easy; **ese ejercicio está ~** that exercise is dead easy **II.** *m, f inf* nohoper
tirador *m* **1.** (*agarradero*) handle, knob **2.** (*cordón*) pull chain **3.** (*tirachinas*) catapult *Brit,* slingshot *Am*
tirador(a) *m(f)* (*disparador*) shot, marskman
tiragomas *m inv* catapult *Brit,* slingshot *Am*
tiralevitas *mf inv* bootlicker
tiralíneas *m inv* ruling pen
tiranía *f* tyranny; **someterse a la ~ de la moda** to be a slave to fashion
tiránico, **-a** *adj* tyrannical
tiranizar <z→c> *vt* to tyrannize
tirano, **-a** **I.** *adj* tyrannic **II.** *m, f* tyrant, despot
tirante **I.** *adj* **1.** (*tieso*) taut; **el pantalón me está ~** the trousers *Brit* [*o* pants *Am*] are tight on me **2.** (*conflictivo*) tense; **estar ~ con alguien** to have strained relations with sb **II.** *m* **1.** (*travesaño*) strut; **se me caen los ~s de este vestido** the straps on this dress keep slipping; **~s (elásticos)** braces *pl Brit,* suspenders *pl Am* **2.** (*de caballería*) trace
tirantez *f* **1.** (*tensión*) tension, strain **2.** (*extensión*) stretch
tirar **I.** *vi* **1.** (*arrastrar*) **~ de algo** to pull on sth; **tira y afloja** give and take; **a todo ~** at the most; **~ de la lengua a alguien** to draw sb out **2.** (*atraer*) to attract; **no me tiran los libros** I'm not very interested in books **3.** (*sacar*) **~ de algo** to pull out sth **4.** (*chimenea*) to draw **5.** (*colores*) **~ a rojo** to tend toward red **6.** (*vestidos*) **esta camisa me tira de los hombros** this shirt is tight in the shoulders **7.** (*querer lograr*) **~ para director** to be aiming at being director **8.** (*parecerse*) to take after; **él tira a su padre** he takes after his father **9.** (*torcer*) to turn; **aquí cada uno tira por su lado** here everyone takes his/her own turning **10.** (*disparar*) to shoot; **~ al blanco** to target shoot ▶**¿qué tal? – vamos tirando** *inf* how are you? – we're managing **II.** *vt* **1.** (*lanzar*) to throw; **~ piedras a alguien** to throw stones at sb **2.** (*malgastar*) to waste **3.** (*de-

sechar) to throw away **4.** (*disparar*) to shoot; (*bombas*) to drop; (*cohetes*) to launch **5.** (*derribar*) to knock down; (*árbol*) to fell; (*edificio*) to pull down **6.** (*trazar*) to draw **7.** (*imprimir*) to print **8.** (*extender*) to stretch **9.** FOTO to take **10.** (*derramar*) to spill **III.** *vr:* **~se 1.** (*lanzarse*) to throw oneself **2.** (*echarse*) to lie down **3.** *inf* (*pasar*) to spend; **~se una hora esperando** to spend an hour waiting **4.** (*acometer*) to throw oneself **5.** *vulg* (*copular*) **~se a alguien** to lay sb

tirita *f* plaster *Brit,* Band Aid®

tiritar *vi* to shiver; **se me ha quedado la cuenta del banco tiritando** there isn't much left in my bank account

tiritón *m* shiver; **dar tiritones** to shiver

tiro *m* **1.** (*lanzamiento, disparo*) shot; **~ a portería** shot at goal; **~ al aire** warning shot; **barraca de ~ al blanco** shooting range; **~ con arco** archery; **a ~** in range; *fig* accessible; **a ~ limpio** guns blazing; **dar un ~** to fire a shot; **estar a un ~ de piedra** to be a stone's throw away; **¡que le den un ~!** *inf* somebody shoot him!; **pegarse un ~** to shoot oneself; **no van por ahí los ~s** *inf* that's not the way the wind is blowing; **me salió el ~ por la culata** *inf* it backfired on me **2.** (*munición*) round **3.** (*daño*) injury **4.** (*alcance*) range **5.** (*arrastre*) pull **6.** (*caballerías*) team **7.** (*arreos*) trace; **poner el ~ a los caballos** to harness the horses **8.** (*corriente de aire*) draught *Brit,* draft *Am* **9.** *inf* (*heroína*) heroin ►**a ~ <u>hecho</u>** deliberately; **de ~s <u>largos</u>** all dressed up, dressed to kill; **<u>sentar</u> a alguien como un ~** (*comida*) to disagree with sb; (*noticia*) to upset sb; **<u>ni</u> a ~s** not on a long shot

tiroides **I.** *adj inv* ANAT **glándula ~** thyroid gland **II.** *m inv* MED thyroid

tirolés, -esa **I.** *adj* Tyrolese **II.** *m, f* Tyrolean

tirón *m* (*acción*) snatch; **de un ~** (*bruscamente*) suddenly; (*de una vez*) without stopping, in one go *Brit;* **no lo sacan de aquí ni a (dos) tirones** not for a million years will they get him out of here

tironear *vt* to tug at

tirotear **I.** *vt* to shoot at **II.** *vr:* **~se 1.** (*disparar*) to shoot at each other **2.** (*disputar*) to quarrel

tiroteo *m* shooting

tirria *f inf* dislike; **tener ~ a alguien** to have a grudge against sb

tisana *f* herbal tea

tísico, -a **I.** *adj* MED tubercular **II.** *m, f* consumptive person

tisis *f inv* MED tuberculosis

tisú *m* tissue

titán *m* Titan

titánico, -a *adj* titanic

titanio *m* QUÍM titanium

titeo *m Arg, Bol, Urug* **1.** (*burla*) mocking **2.** (*tomadura de pelo*) teasing; **tomar a alguien para el ~** to make fun of sb

títere *m* **1.** *t. fig* (*muñeco*) puppet; **no dejar ~ con cabeza** to spare no one **2.** (*tipejo*) weakling **3.** *pl* (*espectáculo*) puppet show

titilar *vi* **1.** (*temblar*) to quiver **2.** (*centellear*) to twinkle

titipuchal *m Méx, inf* (*tropel*) throng

titiritero, -a *m, f* **1.** (*persona que maneja los títeres*) puppeteer **2.** (*acróbata*) acrobat

tito, -a *m, f inf diminutivo de* **tío**

titubear *vi* **1.** (*vacilar*) to waver; *fig* to hesitate **2.** (*balbucear*) to stutter

titubeo *m* **1.** (*vacilación*) tottering; *fig* hesitation; **deja a un lado tus ~s** put your doubts aside **2.** (*balbuceo*) stammering

titulación *f* (*denominación*) title; (*académica*) qualifications *pl*

titulado, -a **I.** *adj* titled **II.** *m, f* degree holder; **~ (universitario)** university graduate

titular[1] **I.** *adj* **profesor ~** full professor **II.** *mf* holder; **~ de acciones** shareholder

titular[2] **I.** *m* headline; **aparecer en los ~es** to appear in the newspaper headlines; **ocupar los ~es** to be in all the newspapers **II.** *vt* (*poner título*) to title **III.** *vr:* **~se** to be entitled; **el libro se titula...** the book is titled ...

titularidad *f* ownership

título *m* **1.** (*rótulo, dignidad*) title; **~ de crédito** credits **2.** (*diploma*) diploma; **~ universitario** university degree **3.** (*motivo*) reason; **¿a ~ de qué hace Ud. eso?** why are you doing that?; **a justo ~** rightly **4.** (*en calidad de*) **a ~ de** by way of; **a ~ de devolución** as a refund; **a ~ gratuito** for free; **a ~ de prueba** as a trial **5.** (*valor comercial*) bond **6. ~ de propiedad** (property) deeds *pl*

tiza *f* chalk

tizate *m Guat, Hond, Nic* chalk

tiznado, -a *adj AmC* drunk

tiznar **I.** *vt* **1.** (*ennegrecer*) to blacken **2.** (*desacreditar*) to sully **II.** *vr:* **~se** (*entiznarse*) to get dirty

tizne *m o f* (*hollín*) soot

tiznón *m* smudge

tizón *m* **1.** (*palo*) partly-burned stick; **más negro que un ~** as black as coal **2.** (*deshonra*) stain

tlachique *m Méx* GASTR unfermented pulque

tlacote *m Méx* MED **1.** (*absceso*) boil **2.** (*tumor*) tumour *Brit,* tumor *Am*

tlapalería *f Méx* (*ferretería*) ironmonger's *Brit,* hardware store *Am*

toalla *f* towel; **~ de lavabo/baño** hand/bath towel; **arrojar la ~** *fig* to throw in the towel

toallero *m* towel rail, towel rack *Am*

toallita *f* small towel, towelette; **~s húmedas** wet wipes

toba *f* **1.** (*piedra*) tufa **2.** (*sarro*) tartar **3.** (*capa*) crust

tobera *f* nozzle

tobillera *f* ankle support

tobillo *m* ankle

tobo *m Ven* (*cubo*) bucket

tobogán *m* **1.** (*deslizadero*) slide **2.** (*pista*) chute **3.** (*trineo*) toboggan, sledge *Brit,* sled

Am

toca *f* headdress

tocadiscos *m inv* record player

tocado *m* **1.**(*peinado*) hairdo **2.**(*complemento*) headdress

tocado, -a *adj* **1.**(*perturbado*) slightly touched; **estar ~ (de la cabeza)** to be not all there **2.**(*lesionado*) injured **3.**(*medio podrido*) going bad **4.**(*cubierto en la cabeza*) **ir ~ de un sombrero** to be wearing a hat

tocador *m* **1.**(*mueble*) dressing table **2.**(*habitación*) ladies' dressing room; (*servicios*) ladies' room **3.**(*estuche*) vanity case

tocador(a) *m(f)* MÚS **~ de guitarra** guitarist

tocamiento *f* feeling, fondling

tocante *adj* **~ a** concerning

tocar <c→qu> **I.** *vt* **1.**(*contacto*) to touch, to feel; **tócame la frente (y dime si está caliente)** feel my forehead (and tell me if it's hot); **~ de cerca algo** *fig* to hit home; **~ fondo** to hit bottom; **¡no lo toques!** don't touch it! **2.** MÚS to play; (*campana*) to ring; (*tambor*) to beat; **~ la bocina** to blow the horn; **~ alarma** to sound the alarm; **~ a fuego** to sound the fire alarm; **~ a misa** to ring the bell for mass; **~ a muerto** to toll (a death knell); **el reloj tocó las tres** the clock struck three; **~ el timbre** to ring the doorbell; **~ a la puerta** to knock at the door **3.**(*modificar*) to change **4.**(*chocar*) to run into **5.**(*afectar*) to affect; **~ en el corazón** to touch one's heart **6.**(*peinar*) to comb **II.** *vi* **1.**(*corresponder*) **te toca a ti decidir** it's up to you to decide; **te toca jugar** it's your turn; **hoy me toca salir** today I have to go out **2.**(*obligación*) **me toca barrer el patio todas las mañanas** I have to sweep the courtyard every morning **3.**(*llegar el momento oportuno*) to be time; **toca ir a la compra** it's time to do the shopping **4.**(*caer en suerte*) to fall; **le tocó a él hacerlo** it fell to him to do it; **le tocó el premio gordo** he/she won the grand prize **5.**(*estar muy cerca*) to verge on **6.**(*ser parientes*) to be related **III.** *vr:* **~se 1.**(*estar en contacto*) to touch **2.**(*peinarse*) to do one's hair **3.**(*cubrirse la cabeza*) **~se con un sombrero** to wear a hat; **~se con un pañuelo** to cover one's head with a scarf ►**los extremos se tocan** *prov* extremes meet *prov;* **tocárselas** *inf* to beat it

tocateja a ~ cash

tocayo, -a *m, f* namesake

tocho *m* **1.**(*hierro*) iron ingot **2.** *inf* (*libro*) thick book

tocho, -a *adj* **1.**(*tosco*) coarse **2.**(*necio*) foolish

tocineta *f Col v.* **tocino**

tocino *m* (*lardo*) pork fat; (*carne*) bacon; **confundir la velocidad con el ~** *inf* to mix up two completely different things

tocología *f sin pl* MED obstetrics *pl*

tocólogo, -a *m, f* MED obstetrician

tocón *m* stump

todavía *adv* **1.**(*aún*) still; **~ no** not yet; **es ~ más caro que...** it is even more expensive than ... **2.**(*sin embargo*) **pero ~** however

todo I. *pron indef* all; **~ lo que..., ~ cuanto...** all ...; **(o) ~ o nada** all or nothing; **~ lo más** at the most; **es ~ uno** it's all one and the same; **ante [*o* sobre] ~** above all; **~ lo contrario** quite the contrary; **antes que ~** first of all; **después de ~** *inf* after all; **con ~** nevertheless; **en ~ y por ~** absolutely; **y ~** and all; **estar en ~** *inf* to be on the ball, not to miss a thing; **me invitaron a comer y ~** they even invited me to eat (and all); **para ~** all-purpose; **me es ~ uno** it's all the same to me **II.** *adv inf* all, completely **III.** *m sin pl* (*la totalidad*) the whole; **del ~** completely; **no del ~** not entirely; **jugarse el ~ por el ~** to risk all; **ser el ~** to be the chief

todo, -a *art indef* **1.**(*entero*) all; **toda la familia** the whole family; **toda España** all Spain; **en toda Europa** all over Europe; **a toda prisa, a ~ correr** as fast as possible **2.**(*cada*) every; **a toda costa** at all cost; **~ Dios [*o* quisqui]** *inf* absolutely everyone; **toda precaución es poca** there are never too many precautions taken **3.** *pl* all; **día de Todos los Santos** All Saints' Day; **a ~s los niños les gusta el chocolate** all children like chocolate; **~s los niños de la clase tomaron chocolate** all of the children in the class had chocolate; **~s y cada uno** each and every one; **a todas horas** at all hours; **en todas partes** everywhere; **de ~s modos** anyway **4.**(*intensificación*) **su cara es toda nariz** his face is all nose; **ser ~ nervios** to be a bundle of nerves

todopoderoso, -a *adj* almighty

todoterreno I. *adj inv* all-purpose, versatile **II.** *m* AUTO all-terrain vehicle; **ser un ~** *fig* to be a Jack-of-all-trades

toga *f* robe; (*romana*) toga

Togo *m* Togo

togolés, -esa *adj, m, f* Togolese

toldillo *m Col* mosquito net

toldo *m* **1.**(*marquesina*) marquee; (*en un balcón*) canopy; (*en una tienda*) awning *Brit,* sunshade *Am* **2.**(*de carro*) tarpaulin

tole *m* **1.**(*bulla*) hubbub; **se armó un ~ tremendo** there was a tremendous commotion **2.**(*rumor*) rumour *Brit,* rumor *Am* **3.** *inf* (*irse*) **tomar el ~** to beat it

toledano, -a I. *adj* Toledan; **noche toledana** *fig* sleepless night **II.** *m, f* Toledan

tolerancia *f* **1.**(*indulgencia*) tolerance **2.**(*resistencia*) tolerance

tolerante *adj* tolerant

tolerar *vt* **1.**(*soportar*) to bear, to tolerate; (*alimentos, medicinas*) to be able to take **2.**(*permitir*) **~ algo** to be lenient with sth, to allow sth; **una película tolerada para menores** a film suitable for children **3.**(*aceptar*) tolerate

tolete *m* **1.** *AmL* (*garrote*) bludgeon **2.** *Col, Cuba* (*trozo*) piece

tolvanera *f AmC, Méx* (*polvareda*) cloud of dust

toma *f* **1.** (*adquisición*) taking; ~ **de conciencia** awareness; ~ **de declaración** taking of evidence; ~ **de datos** INFOR data acquisition; ~ **de decisiones** decision making; ~ **de poder** takeover; ~ **de posesión** taking office; ~ **de rehenes** taking of hostages **2.** (*conquista*) capture; ~ **por asalto** to take by storm **3.** (*dosis*) dose **4.** TÉC inlet; ~ **de tierra** ground **5.** (*grabación*) take **6.** (*ingesta*) intake **7.** FOTO shot

tomacorriente *m* **1.** *AmL* (*colector*) collector **2.** *Arg, Perú* (*enchufe*) socket, plug

tomadura *f* taking; ~ **de pelo** (*burla*) joke; (*timo*) rip-off; (*engaño*) hoax

tomar I. *vi* to turn; ~ **por la derecha** to take a right **II.** *vt* **1.** (*coger, quitar, llevar*) to take; (*préstamo*) to borrow; (*aliento*) to catch; (*fuerzas*) to gather; ~ **las armas** to take up arms; ~ **una decisión** to make a decision; ~ **medidas** to take measures **2.** (*beber*) to have, to drink; ~ **café** to have coffee; **no tomes ese agua** don't drink that water **3.** (*to eat*) to have, to eat **4.** (*interpretar*) to take; ~ **a la ligera** to take lightly; ~ **algo a mal** to take offence at sth *Brit*, to take offense at sth *Am*; ~ **muy a pecho** to take to heart; ~ **a risa** to take as a joke; ~ **en serio** to take seriously; ~ **a alguien por ladrón** to take sb for a thief; **¿por quién me tomas?** what do you take me for? **5.** (*adquirir*) to take; ~ **conciencia de algo** to become aware of sth **6.** (*sentir*) to take; ~ **cariño/odio a alguien** to take a like/dislike to sb; ~ **confianza a alguien** to treat sb as a friend **7.** (*conquistar*) to take, to capture **8.** (*copiar*) to copy **9.** (*contratar*) to hire; ~ **un abogado** to hire a lawyer **10.** (*alquilar*) to rent **11.** (*adoptar*) adopt; ~ **una actitud de...** to adopt an attitude of ... **12.** (*hacerse cargo*) to take over; ~ **sobre sí** to take upon oneself **13.** (*filmar*) to shoot **14.** (*sobrevenir*) to come over **15.** (*transporte*) to take **16.** (*medir*) to take; **le ~ron la tensión** they measured [*o* took] his/her blood pressure **17.** *AmL* (*beber alcohol*) to drink; **no debes ~ ni fumar** you shouldn't drink or smoke; **~la** (*emborracharse*) to get drunk **18.** ZOOL (*copular*) to cover; **¡vete a ~ por culo!** *vulg* fuck off! ►**¡toma castaña!** well, that will serve you right!; **~la con algo/alguien** to take it out on sth/sb; **¡toma!** well! **III.** *vr:* **~se 1.** (*coger*) to take; **~se libertades** to take liberties; **~se unas vacaciones** to take a vacation **2.** (*beber*) to drink, to have; **me he tomado un vaso de leche** I had a glass of milk **3.** (*comer*) to eat, to have **4.** (*ponerse la voz ronca*) **se me ha tomado la voz** I'm hoarse **5.** *AmL* (*emborracharse*) **tomársela** to get drunk **6.** *inf* (*expresión*) **¡tómate esa!** take that!

tomate *m* **1.** BOT tomato **2.** *inf* (*agujero*) hole **3.** *inf* (*situación poco clara*) **tener** ~ to be difficult ►**ponerse rojo como un** ~ to turn as red as a beetroot

tomatera *f* tomato plant

tomavistas¹ *m inv* FOTO film camera *Brit*, movie camera *Am*

tomavistas² *mf inv* FOTO (*operador*) camera(man)

tómbola *f* tombola, charity raffle

tomillo *m* thyme

tomo *m* (*volumen*) volume; **de cuatro ~s** in four volumes ►**de ~ y lomo** out-and-out

tomografía *f* MED tomography; **tomografía axial computerizada** (**TAC**) computerized axial tomograph (CAT)

ton *inf* **sin ~ ni son** for no particular reason

tonada *f* **1.** (*canción*) song **2.** (*melodía*) tune, melody **3.** *AmL* (*tonillo*) accent

tonalidad *f* **1.** LING intonation **2.** MÚS tonality, tone; ~ **menor** minor key **3.** ARTE shade

tonel *m* **1.** (*barril*) barrel **2.** *inf* (*persona gorda*) fatso

tonelada *f* (*peso*) ton

tonelaje *m* tonnage

tonelero *m* cooper

tongo *m* DEP fixing; **hubo** ~ it was rigged

tónica *f* **1.** MÚS tonic, keynote **2.** (*bebida*) tonic water **3.** (*tono general*) general trend

tónico *m* **1.** MED tonic **2.** (*para el rostro*) toner; (*para el cabello*) hair tonic

tónico, -a *adj* **1.** LING stressed **2.** MÚS tonic; **nota tónica** keynote **3.** MED tonic

tonificar <c→qu> *vt* to tone up

tonillo *m* **1.** (*deje*) accent, lilt **2.** (*habla monótona*) monotonous tone **3.** (*retintín*) sarcastic tone

tonina *f Arg, Urug* ZOOL dolphin

tono *m* **1.** (*altura*) tone, pitch; ~ **agudo/grave** high/low pitch **2.** (*señal*) tone; ~ **de marcar** TEL dialling tone *Brit*, dialtone *Am* **3.** (*intensidad*) **bajar el** ~ to lower one's voice **4.** (*deje, estilo*) tone; **en ~ de reproche** reproachfully; **bajar el** ~ to tone down; **dar el** ~ to set the tone; **darse** ~ to put on airs; **fuera de** ~ out of place; **estar a ~ con algo** to be in tune with sth; **subirse de** ~ to become heated **5.** (*atmósfera*) tone **6.** (*maneras*) **el buen** ~ refinement; **de buen** ~ tasteful; **de mal** ~ vulgar **7.** MED tone **8.** MÚS (*modo*) key; ~ **mayor/menor** major/minor key; **~s y semitonos** whole tones and halftones

tontaina *mf inf* ninny

tontear *vi* **1.** (*bobear*) to fool around **2.** *inf* to flirt

tontera *f* foolishness

tontería *f* **1.** (*memez*) stupidity, foolishness **2.** (*nadería*) trifle

tonto, -a I. *adj* silly; **ser más ~ que Picio** *inf* to be as dumb as they come; **hacer algo a tontas y a locas** to do sth without thinking; **ponerse** ~ *inf* to get silly; **ser ~ del culo** *inf* to be a complete idiot; **ser ~ perdido** to be dead from the neck up **II.** *m, f* fool; **hacer el** ~ to clown around; **le gusta más que a un ~ un lápiz** he/she is crazy about it; **hacerse el** ~ to play dumb; **el ~ del pueblo** the village idiot

topacio *m* MIN topaz

topadora *f Arg, Méx, Urug* (*buldózer*) bulldozer

topar I. *vi* 1. (*chocar*) ~ **con algo** to run into sth; ~ **contra algo** to bump against [*o* into] sth 2. (*hallar*) ~ **con alguien** to bump into sb 3. (*consistir*) to lie 4. *inf* (*salir bien*) to work 5. (*en el juego*) to take a bet II. *vt* 1. (*chocar*) to butt 2. (*hallar: algo*) to come across; (*a alguien*) to bump into III. *vr:* ~**se** 1. (*chocar*) ~**se con algo** to run into sth; ~**se contra algo** to bump against [*o* into] sth 2. (*hallar*) ~**se con alguien** to bump into sb

tope I. *adj* top, maximum; **fecha** ~ latest date, at the latest II. *m* 1. (*extremo*) end; **estar hasta el** ~ (*lleno*) to be jam-packed; (*harto*) to be fed up; **estoy a** ~ **de trabajo** I'm swamped with work 2. (*parachoques*) buffer; AUTO bumper 3. (*para impedir un movimiento*) check; (*puerta*) doorstop 4. (*obstáculo*) obstacle

topera *f* molehill

topetada *f* butt

topetar *vi, vt* to butt

topetazo *m* collision

topetear *vi, vt* to bump into

tópico *m* 1. (*lugar común*) commonplace 2. (*estereotipo*) cliché 3. MED **uso** ~ external application

tópico, **-a** *adj* 1. (*trivial*) trite 2. (*local*) local 3. MED for external application; **de uso** ~ for external use only

topinambur *m Arg, Bol* BOT Jerusalem artichoke

topless *m* **en** ~ topless

topo *m* 1. (*roedor, espía*) mole; **ver menos que un** ~ *inf* to be as blind as a bat; **ser un** ~ *inf* to be a bumbler 2. (*persona torpe*) clumsy clot 3. (*lunar*) polka dot

topocho, **-a** *adj Ven* plump

topografía *f* topography, surveying

topógrafo, **-a** *m, f* surveyor, topographer

topón *m* 1. *Chile, Col, Hond* (*topetazo*) butt 2. *Col* (*puñetazo*) punch

topónimo *m* place name

toposo, **-a** *adj Ven* 1. (*entrometido*) meddlesome 2. (*pedante*) pretentious

toque *m* 1. (*roce*) touch 2. (*golpe*) tap; **dar un** ~ **en la puerta** to tap on the door 3. (*sonido*) ~ **de campanas** ringing of bells; ~ **de queda** curfew; ~ **de tambor** drumbeat; ~ **de atención** warning note; **dáme un** ~ **más tarde** give me a ring later 4. (*advertencia*) warning 5. (*matiz*) touch; **el** ~ **femenino** a woman's touch 6. (*modificación*) touch up; **dar los últimos** ~**s a algo** to put the finishing touches to [*o* on *Am*] sth 7. (*pincelada*) dab 8. (*ensayo*) test; **piedra de** ~ touchstone 9. (*lo principal*) crux 10. (*aplicación medicinal*) painting of throat

toquetear *vt inf* to fiddle with, to finger

toquilla *f* (*pañuelo*) shawl

tora *f* REL Torah

torada *f* herd of bulls

tórax *m inv* thorax

torbellino *m* whirlwind; **ser un** ~ *inf* to be a bundle of energy

torcaz *adj* **paloma** ~ wood pigeon

torcedura *f* MED sprain

torcer *irr como cocer* I. *vi* to turn; ~ **a la izquierda** to turn left II. *vt* 1. (*encorvar*) to bend 2. (*dar vueltas, desviar*) to wind; ~ **el cuello a alguien** to wring sb's neck; ~ **las intenciones de alguien** to foil sb's plans; ~ **las manos** to wring one's hands; ~ **la vista** to squint 3. (*referente al gesto*) ~ **el gesto** to scowl III. *vr:* ~**se** 1. (*encorvarse*) to bend; **la madera se ha torcido con la humedad** the dampness has warped the wood 2. (*dislocarse*) to sprain; **me he torcido el pie** I've twisted my ankle 3. (*corromperse*) to go astray; (*fracasar*) to go wrong 4. (*agriarse*) to go sour

torcida *f* wick

torcido, **-a** *adj* 1. (*ladeado*) lopsided 2. (*encorvado*) crooked 3. (*artero*) devious

tordo *m* thrush

tordo, **-a** I. *adj* 1. (*color*) **yegua torda** dapple-grey mare *Brit,* dapple-gray mare *Am* 2. (*torpe*) dim II. *m, f* dapple-grey horse *Brit,* dapple-gray horse *Am*

torear I. *vi* (*lidiar*) to fight; (*toros*) to bullfight II. *vt* 1. (*lidiar*) to fight; (*toros*) to bullfight 2. (*evitar*) to dodge 3. (*engañar*) to string along 4. (*tomar el pelo*) to tease

toreo *m* 1. (*tauromaquia*) bullfighting 2. (*lidia*) fighting 3. (*burla*) covert mockery

torera *f* bolero (jacket)

torero, **-a** I. *adj inf* bullfighting; **valor** ~ outstanding figure in bullfighting II. *m, f* bullfighter, matador; **saltarse algo a la torera** *inf* to blatantly ignore sth; **tener más suerte que un** ~ *inf* to have the luck of the devil

toril *m* bullpen

tormenta *f* 1. *t. fig* (*temporal*) storm 2. (*agitación*) turmoil; **una** ~ **de celos** a fit of jealousy; ~ **de ideas** brainstorm; **una** ~ **en un vaso de agua** a storm in a teacup

tormento *m* 1. (*castigo*) torment; **potro de** ~ torture rack; **dar** ~ **a alguien** to torture sb 2. (*congoja*) anguish

tormentoso, **-a** *adj* stormy; (*situación*) turbulent

torna *f* 1. (*devolución*) restitution 2. (*regreso*) return ►**se han cambiado las** ~**s** the boot's *Brit* [*o* shoe's *Am*] on the other foot; **volver las** ~**s a alguien** to turn the tables on sb; **volverse las** ~**s** to turn the tables; **se han vuelto las** ~**s y ahora mando yo** the tables have turned and now I'm calling the tune

tornadizo, **-a** *adj* changeable

tornado *m* METEO tornado

tornar I. *vi* to return; ~ **en sí** to regain consciousness; ~ **a hacer algo** to do sth again II. *vt* 1. (*devolver*) to return 2. (*cambiar*) to make; ~ **triste** to make sad III. *vr:* ~**se** to turn;

T

~**se azul** to turn blue
tornasol *m* **1.** (*girasol*) sunflower **2.** (*reflejo*) iridescence **3.** QUÍM litmus
torneado, -a *adj* shapely
tornear I. *vi* **1.** (*dar vueltas*) to spin **2.** (*en un torneo*) to joust **3.** (*cavilar*) to ponder **II.** *vt* (*metal*) to work; (*madera*) to turn
torneo *m* tournament
tornero, -a *m, f* (*de metal*) machinist; (*de madera*) lathe operator
tornillo *m* **1.** (*clavo con rosca*) screw; **apretar un** ~ to tighten a screw; **apretar los** ~**s a alguien** *fig* to put pressure on sb; **te falta un** ~ *inf* you have a screw loose; **beso de** ~ French kiss **2.** *inf* (*deserción*) desertion **3.** (*abrazadera*) clamp; ~ **de banco** vice *Brit,* vise *Am*
torniquete *m* **1.** (*puerta*) turnstile **2.** MED tourniquet
torniscón *m inf* **1.** (*bofetón*) slap **2.** (*pellizco*) pinch
torno *m* **1.** (*máquina, para madera*) lathe; (*de alfarero*) potter's wheel; (*de banco*) vice *Brit,* vise *Am* **2.** (*cabrestante*) winch **3.** (*giro*) turn **4.** (*freno*) brake **5.** (*de un río*) bend in a river ►en ~ **a** about; **en** ~ **a ese tema** with regard to this subject
toro *m* **1.** (*animal*) bull; ~ **bravo** [*o* **de lidia**] *bull raised to fight in the bullring;* **coger el** ~ **por los cuernos** *fig* to take the bull by the horns; **fuerte como un** ~ strong as an ox; **¡otro** ~**!** *fig* change the subject! **2.** *pl* (*toreo*) bullfighting; **ir a los** ~**s** to go to bullfights; **ver los** ~**s desde la barrera** *fig* to watch sth from the sidelines **3.** (*hombre*) strong man
toronja *f* **1.** (*naranja*) bitter orange **2.** (*pomelo*) grapefruit
toronjil *m* lemon [*o* garden] balm
torpe *adj* **1.** (*inhábil*) clumsy **2.** (*pesado*) sluggish **3.** (*obsceno*) lewd
torpedear *vt* to torpedo
torpedo *m* torpedo
torpeza *f* **1.** (*pesadez*) heaviness **2.** (*inhabilidad*) clumsiness **3.** (*obscenidad*) baseness **4.** (*tontería*) stupidity **5.** (*error*) blunder
torrar *vt* to roast
torre *f* tower; ~ **de alta tensión** electricity plyon; ~ **de extracción** [*o* **de perforación**] derrick; ~ **de mando** control tower; ~ **del homenaje** donjon; ~ **de marfil** *fig* ivory tower; (*buque*) turret; (*campanario*) bell tower; (*ajedrez*) rook, castle
torrefacción *f* roasting
torrefacto, -a *adj* dark roasted
torreja *f AmL* GASTR ≈ French toast
torrencial *adj* **lluvia** ~ torrential rains
torrente *m* **1.** (*corriente*) torrent **2.** (*multitud*) flood
torrentoso, -a *adj AmL* (*lluvia*) torrential; (*caudal*) fast-flowing
torrero, -a *m, f* watchtower keeper; (*de un faro*) lighthouse keeper
torrezno *m* fried bacon
tórrido, -a *adj elev* torrid
torrija *f* ≈ French toast
torsión *f* (*desviación*) torsion; ~ **hacia la izquierda** twisting to the left
torso *m* torso; ARTE bust
torta *f* **1.** (*tarta*) cake; *AmL* (*pastel*) pie **2.** *inf* (*bofetada*) slap; (*golpe*) punch; **darse una** ~ to bang oneself **3.** *inf* (*borrachera*) drunkenness ►**ser** ~**s y pan pintado** *inf* to be child's play; **no saber ni** ~ *inf* not to know a thing
tortazo *m inf* **1.** (*bofetada*) slap; **acabar a** ~ **limpio** *inf* to end up in a fight **2.** (*choque*) crash; **darse un** ~ to come a cropper
tortícolis *f inv* MED torticollis, stiff neck
tortilla *f* (*de huevos*) ≈ omelette *Brit,* ≈ omelet *Am; AmL* (*de harina*) tortilla ►**dar la vuelta a la** ~ to change things completely; **se ha vuelto la** ~ the tables have turned; **hacer** ~ **a alguien** to flatten sb

> **Tortilla** is a type of Spanish omelette. A **tortilla de patatas** is an omelette with potatoes and onions, but there are also **tortillas** made from other ingredients, such as spinach, tuna, asparagus, etc. In Latin America, particularly in Mexico, a **tortilla** is a flat pancake prepared with maize and is one of the staple foods of this region.

tortillera *m vulg* dyke
tórtola *f* turtledove
tórtolo *m* **1.** (*ave*) lovebird **2.** (*hombre*) lover-boy **3.** *pl* (*enamorados*) lovebirds *pl*
tortuga *f* turtle; **a paso de** ~ to walk at a snail's pace
tortuoso, -a *adj* **1.** (*sinuoso*) winding **2.** (*astuto*) tortuous
tortura *f* (*suplicio*) torture; **sufrir** ~**s** to be tortured
torturar *vt* to torture
torvo, -a *adj* fierce; (*mirada*) baleful
torzal *m* cord
tos *f* cough; ~ **ferina** whooping cough
tosco, -a *adj* rough, coarse
tosedera *f AmL* nagging cough
toser *vi* to cough; **no hay quien te tosa** *inf* nobody can compete with you
tostada *f* **1.** (*para desayuno*) toast **2.** *Méx: fried tortilla* ►**olerse la** ~ *inf* to smell a rat
tostadero *m* roasting room
tostador *m* toaster
tostar <o→ue> **I.** *vt* **1.** (*torrar*) to roast; (*pan*) to toast **2.** (*curtir*) to brown **II.** *vr:* ~**se** to tan
tostón *m* **1.** (*persona pesada*) drag; (*molestia*) nuisance **2.** (*cochinillo*) roast suckling pig **3.** (*de pan*) crouton
total I. *adj* total; **importe** ~ total amount; **en** ~ in all; **un cambio** ~ a complete change; **¡ha sido** ~**!** *inf* it was great! **II.** *m* MAT sum **III.** *adv* so, in the end
totalidad *f sin pl* totality, whole; **en su** ~ in its

entirety
totalitario, **-a** *adj* **1.** (*completo*) total **2.** (*dictatorial*) totalitarian
totalizar <z→c> *vt* to total
totalmente *adv* entirely, totally
totora *f AmS* BOT (*junco*) reed
toxicidad *f* toxicity
tóxico *m* toxic substance
tóxico, **-a** *adj* toxic
toxicomanía *f sin pl* drug addiction
toxicómano, **-a** **I.** *adj* addicted to drugs **II.** *m, f* drug addict, substance abuser
toxina *f* toxin
tozudo, **-a** **I.** *adj* obstinate **II.** *m, f* stubborn person
traba *f* **1.** (*trabamiento*) tie **2.** (*cuerda*) hobble **3.** (*obstáculo*) hindrance; **poner ~s a…** to put obstacles in the way of … **4.** *AmL, inf* (*marihuana*) grass; (*efecto*) high
trabajado, **-a** *adj* **1.** (*cansado*) worn-out **2.** (*con esmero*) well-crafted
trabajador(a) **I.** *adj* hard-working **II.** *m(f)* worker
trabajar **I.** *vi* to work; **~ de vendedora** to work as a saleswoman; **en edad de ~** of working age; **~ como un condenado** to work like a slave; **~ en balde** to work in vain; **~ por horas** to be paid by the hour; **~ por cuenta propia** to be self-employed; **~ a tiempo completo/parcial** to work full-time/part-time **II.** *vt* **1.** (*tratar*) to work; (*caballo*) to train **2.** (*perfeccionar*) to work on; **tienes que ~ el acento** you have to work on your accent **3.** (*inquietar*) to disturb **4.** (*amasar*) to knead **5.** (*máquina*) to run, to operate **III.** *vr:* **~se** to work
trabajo *m* (*acción*) work; (*puesto*) job; **~ en cadena** assembly-line work; **~ a destajo** piecework; **~ estacional** seasonal work; **~s manuales** handicrafts *pl;* **~s forzados** hard labour *Brit,* hard labor *Am;* **con/sin ~** employed/unemployed; **~ en equipo** team-work; **~ perdido** wasted effort; **puesto de ~** post/job; **~ de chinos** intricate laborious work; **~ fijo** steady job; **~ cualificado** skilled work; **~ de campo** field work; **~ negro** illegal work; **~ eventual** temporary [*o* casual] work; **~ intelectual** brainwork; **hacer un buen ~** to do a good job; **almuerzo de ~** working lunch; **tener ~ atrasado** to have a backlog; **¡buen ~!** well done!; **quedarse sin ~** to be let go; **mucha gente se quedó sin ~ cuando instalaron la nueva maquinaria** many people were made redundant when the new machinery was installed; **costar ~** to be difficult; **tomarse el ~ de hacer algo** to take the trouble to do sth; **ahorrarse el ~ de hacer algo** to spare oneself the trouble of doing sth
trabajoso, **-a** *adj* hard
trabalenguas *m inv* tongue twister
trabar **I.** *vt* **1.** (*juntar*) to join **2.** (*coger*) to seize **3.** (*atar*) to tie **4.** (*impedir*) to impede **5.** (*espesar*) to thicken **6.** (*comenzar*) to start; (*contactos*) to strike up **7.** (*embargar bienes*) to put a lien on **II.** *vi* to take hold **III.** *vr:* **~se** to get stuck; **~se la lengua** to get tongue-tied
trabazón *f* **1.** (*enlace*) connection **2.** (*el espesar*) consistency
trabilla *f* belt loop; (*en la pernera*) foot strap
trabucar <c→qu> **I.** *vt* to jumble up **II.** *vr:* **~se** (*al hablar*) to get tongue-tied; (*al escribir*) to get all mixed up
trácala *f* **1.** *Ecua* (*multitud*) mob **2.** *Méx, PRico* (*fullería*) fraud **3.** *Méx* (*persona tramposa*) trickster
tracalada *f* **1.** *AmC, AmS* (*multitud*) crowd, lot **2.** *Méx* (*fullería*) trickery
tracalero, **-a** *m, f Méx, PRico* cheat
tracción *f* **1.** (*tirar*) pulling **2.** (*accionar*) drive, traction; **~ a cuatro ruedas** four-wheel drive; **~ delantera/trasera** front/rear-wheel drive
tractor *m* tractor
tradición *f* tradition
tradicional *adj* traditional
traducción *f* translation; **~ al/del inglés** translation into/from English; **~ automática** machine [*o* automatic] translation; **~ directa/inversa** translation from/into a foreign language; **~ libre** free translation; **~ simultánea** simultaneous translation
traducir *irr vt* to translate
traductor(a) **I.** *adj* translating **II.** *m(f)* translator; **~ de bolsillo** pocket-size electronic translating device; **~ jurado** sworn translator
traer *irr* **I.** *vt* **1.** (*llevar: a alguien*) to bring along; (*consigo*) to bring; (*vestido*) to wear; **tengo una carta para ti – trae** I have a letter for you – give it to me; **¿has traído la carta?** did you bring the letter?; **lo traigo en la cartera** I've got it in my briefcase; **~ a alguien arrastra(n)do** to drag sb; **¿qué te trae por aquí?** what brings you here?; **el jefe me trae de aquí para allí todo el día** my boss has me running all day; **me la trae floja** *vulg* I don't give a damn; **me trae sin cuidado** I couldn't care less **2.** (*ir a por*) to fetch **3.** (*atraer*) to attract **4.** (*ocasionar*) to cause **5.** (*implicar*) involve **6.** (*más adjetivo*) **~ convencido a alguien** to have sb convinced; **~ preocupado a alguien** to have sb worried; **~ de cabeza a alguien** *inf* to be driving sb mad; **esta mujer me trae perdido** this woman will be my ruin **7.** (*más sustantivo*) **~ retraso** to be late; **~ prisa** to be in a hurry; **~ hambre** to be hungry; **traes cara de circunstancias** *inf* you look very serious **8.** (*razones, ejemplos*) to adduce **9.** (*más 'a'*) **~ a colación** to bring up; **~ a cuento** to mention; **~ a alguien a razones** to get sb to listen to reason; **~ a la memoria** to bring to mind **II.** *vr:* **~se 1.** (*llevar a cabo*) **~se algo entre manos** to be up to something **2.** (*vestirse*) **~se bien** to dress well **3.** (*ser difícil, intenso*) **este examen se las trae** the exam is really tough; **hace un frío que se las trae** it's really cold

T

traficante *mf* dealer, trader; (*de drogas*) drug dealer; (*de personas, coches*) smuggler
traficar <c→qu> *vi* to deal; (*con drogas*) to traffic; (*con personas*) to smuggle
tráfico *m* **1.** (*de vehículos*) traffic; ~ **por carretera** road traffic **2.** COM trade; (*de drogas*) traffic; (*de personas, coches*) smuggling; ~ **de contrabando** smuggling; ~ **de blancas** white-slave traffic; ~ **de influencias** peddling of political favours *Brit* [*o* favors *Am*]
tragaderas *fpl* **1.** (*faringe*) throat; **tener buenas** ~ *inf* to be a walking dustbin *Brit* [*o* garbage can *Am*]; *fig* to be ready to put up with a lot **2.** *inf* (*credulidad*) **tener** ~ to be very gullible **3.** *inf* (*tolerancia*) **tener buenas/malas** ~ to be very tolerant/intolerant
tragaldabas *mf inv* glutton
tragaluz *m* (*grande*) skylight; (*pequeño*) transom
traganíqueles *f inv, Nic, inf* (*tragaperras*) slot machine
tragaperras *f inv* vending machine; (*de juego*) slot machine
tragar <g→gu> **I.** *vt, vr:* ~**se** (*comida, bebida, crítica*) to swallow; (*historia, mentira*) to fall for; **tuve que** ~**me el enfado** I had to hold back my anger; **ése se lo traga todo** *fig* he believes everything you tell him; **¡trágame tierra!** I wish the ground would open up and swallow me! **II.** *vt* **1.** (*soportar*) **no** ~ **a alguien** to not be able to stand sb **2.** (*consumir*) to down; (*absorber*) to soak up **3.** (*aguantar*) **tuvimos que** ~ **toda la conferencia** we had to sit through the whole conference; ~ **saliva** to eat crow
tragedia *f* tragedy
trágico, **-a I.** *adj* tragic; **no te pongas** ~ don't get all melodramatic **II.** *m, f* TEAT, LIT tragedian *m,* tragedienne *f*
trago *m* **1.** (*de bebida*) swig; **a** ~**s cortos** in sips; **a** ~**s largos** in long drinks; **de un** ~ in one gulp **2.** (*bebida*) drink; **tomar un** ~ **de más** *inf* to have one drink too many **3.** (*vicio*) bottle, drink **4.** (*experiencia*) experience; **pasar un mal** ~ to have a bad time of it
tragón, **-ona** *m, f inf* glutton
traición *f* **1.** (*acto desleal*) treachery, betrayal **2.** JUR treason; **matar a** ~ to kill treacherously
traicionar *vt* to betray; (*adulterio*) to be unfaithful; **la memoria me traiciona** my memory fails me; **le traicionó su acento** his/her accent gave him/her away
traicionero, **-a I.** *adj* (*persona*) perfidious; (*acción*) traitorous; (*memoria*) unreliable; (*animal*) dangerous **II.** *m, f* traitor
traída *f* ~ **de aguas** water supply
traidor(**a**) **I.** *adj* traitorous; (*falso*) deceitful **II.** *m(f)* traitor
traigo *1. pres de* **traer**
traílla *f* **1.** (*correa*) leash **2.** (*dos perros*) team **3.** AGR harrow
traje *m* **1.** (*vestidura*) dress; ~ **de baño** bathing suit; ~ **de luces** bullfighter's costume **2.** (*de hombre*) suit; ~ **de etiqueta** formal dress; ~ **hecho a la medida** custom-made suit; ~ **de confección** ready-to-wear suit **3.** (*de mujer*) outfit; ~ **de noche** evening dress; ~ (**de**) **chaqueta** suit **4.** (*popular*) regional costume **5.** (*de época*) period costume
trajeado, **-a** *adj* **ir bien/mal** ~ to be well/badly dressed
trajín *m* **1.** (*de mercancías*) haulage **2.** (*ajetreo*) rush; **el** ~ **de la ciudad** the hustle and bustle of the city; **había un gran** ~ there was a lot of commotion
trajinar I. *vt* to transport **II.** *vi* to rush about; **llevo todo el día trajinando** I've been on the go all day
trajinera *f Méx* (*canoa*) ≈ canoe (*small boat typical for canals that carries up to 15 people and is moved with the help of a long stick*)
tralla *f* **1.** (*cuerda*) rope **2.** (*látigo*) lash
trama *f* **1.** (*de hilos*) weft **2.** LIT plot **3.** (*intriga*) scheme
tramar *vt* **1.** (*traición*) to plot; (*intriga, plan*) to scheme; **¿qué estarán tramando?** what are they up to?; **aquí se está tramando algo** something's cooking here **2.** (*tejidos*) to weave
tramitar *vt* **1.** (*asunto*) to attend to; (*negocio*) to transact; **está tramitando el divorcio** he/she has started divorce proceedings **2.** (*expediente*) to process
trámite *m* **1.** (*diligencias*) ~ **burocrático** administrative proceedings; **pasar por todos los** ~**s** to go through the whole procedure **2.** (*formalidad*) formality; **estar en** ~**s de hacer algo** to be in the process of doing sth; **esto es puro** ~ this is just a formality; **¿has hecho los** ~**s para el pasaporte?** have you taken the necessary steps to obtain your passport?
tramo *m* **1.** (*de camino*) stretch; FERRO section **2.** (*de escalera*) flight
tramoya *f* **1.** TEAT stage machinery **2.** (*engaño*) scheme, scam
trampa *f* **1.** (*para personas, animales*) trap; ~ **mortal** death trap; **caer en la** ~ (*animal*) to be caught in the snare; (*persona*) to fall into the trap; **poner una** ~ **a un animal/a alguien** to set a trap for an animal/for sb **2.** (*trampilla*) trapdoor **3.** (*del mostrador*) hinged section of a counter **4.** (*engaño*) trick; (*en los juegos*) cheating; **hacer** ~ (*engañar*) to cheat; (*en el deporte*) fixing **5.** *inf* (*deuda*) bad debt ▸**sin** ~ **ni cartón** with no catches; **hecha la ley hecha la** ~ *prov* laws are made to be broken *prov*
trampear *vi* **1.** *inf* (*estafar*) to swindle **2.** (*de penuria*) to get by **3.** (*ir tirando*) to manage
trampilla *f* **1.** (*en habitación*) trapdoor **2.** (*portezuela*) oven door **3.** AUTO hatch
trampolín *m* (*de piscina*) diving board; (*de gimnasia*) trampoline; (*de esquí*) ski jump
tramposo, **-a I.** *adj* cheating **II.** *m, f* **1.** (*estafador*) swindler **2.** (*en los juegos*) cheat

tranca *f* **1.** (*palo*) cudgel; (*de la puerta*) crossbar **2.** *inf* (*borrachera*) binge; **coger una ~** *inf* to get plastered ►**a ~s y barrancas** through fire and water

trance *m* **1.** (*momento*) **pasar un ~ difícil** to go through a difficult time **2.** (*hipnótico*) trance **3.** (*situación*) **estar en ~ de hacer algo** to be on the point of doing sth; **estar en ~ de muerte** to be at death's door ►**hacer algo a todo ~** to do sth at any cost

tranco *m* **1.** (*paso*) stride; **andar a ~s** to stride; **subir una escalera a ~s** to go up the stairs two at a time **2.** (*umbral*) threshold ►**a ~s** in a hurry

tranque *m Chile* (*embalse*) reservoir

tranqui *adj inf* **¡oye, ~!** hey, cool it!

tranquilamente *adv* calmly

tranquilidad *f* **1.** (*calma, serenidad*) tranquility; (*del mar*) calm; **para mayor ~** to be on the safe side; **~ de conciencia** ease of mind; **trabajar con ~** to work calmly; **debo decirte para tu ~ que...** I must tell you, to put your mind at rest, that ... **2.** (*autocontrol*) calmness **3.** (*despreocupación*) lack of concern

tranquilizante *m* tranquillizer *Brit,* tranquilizer *Am*

tranquilizar <z→c> **I.** *vt* to calm down; (*con palabras*) to reassure **II.** *vr:* **~se** to calm down

tranquilla *f* **1.** (*pasador*) bolt **2.** (*para desorientar*) red herring

tranquillo *m* **coger el ~ a algo** to get the knack of sth

tranquilo, -a *adj* **1.** (*no agitado, mar*) calm; **¡déjame ~!** leave me alone!; **mientras no te digan nada, tú ~** as long as they don't mention anything to you, don't worry **2.** (*persona: serena*) serene; (*con autocontrol*) calm; (*despreocupada*) unconcerned; **tú ~, que no pasará nada** don't worry, everything will be all right

transa *f* **1.** *AmL* (*espíritu de compromiso*) committedness **2.** *Méx* (*engaño*) deceit **3.** *RíoPl* (*transacción*) transaction; (*tráfico de droga*) drug dealing

transacción *f* **1.** JUR settlement **2.** POL agreement **3.** COM deal **4.** FIN transaction

transalpino, -a *adj* transalpine

transandino, -a *adj* trans-Andean

transar *vi AmL* (*transigir*) to compromise; **no pienso ~ en eso** I'm not giving in on that

transatlántico *m* ocean liner

transatlántico, -a *adj* transatlantic; **barco ~** ocean liner

transbordador *m* **1.** NÁUT ferry **2.** AVIAT shuttle

transbordar **I.** *vt* **1.** (*por río*) to ferry across **2.** (*mercancías*) to transfer; (*en grandes cantidades*) to transload; (*entre barcos*) to transship **II.** *vi* to change, to transfer

transbordo *m* **1.** (*cambio*) change; **hay que hacer ~ en Barajas** you have to change [*o* transfer] planes at Barajas airport **2.** (*mercancías*) transfer

transcendental *adj v.* **trascendental**

transcender <e→ie> *vi v.* **trascender**

transcribir *irr como escribir vt* **1.** (*copiar*) to transcribe **2.** *t.* MÚS (*transliterar*) to transpose

transcripción *f* (*acción*) transcription; (*resultado*) transcript

transcultural *adj* cross-cultural

transcurrir *vi* **1.** (*el tiempo*) to elapse, to pass **2.** (*acontecer*) to take place

transcurso *m* course; **en el ~ del día** during the course of the day

transeúnte **I.** *adj* transient; (*habitante*) temporary **II.** *mf* **1.** (*peatón*) passer-by, pedestrian **2.** (*habitante*) **los ~s** transients, temporary residents

transferencia *f* **1.** (*traslado*) transfer **2.** FIN transfer; **a través de una ~ bancaria** by bank draft **3.** (*de propiedad*) transfer **4.** PSICO transference

transferir *irr como sentir vt* **1.** (*trasladar*) to transfer **2.** (*posponer*) to postpone **3.** FIN to make over **4.** (*propiedad, derecho*) to transfer

transfigurar *vt* to transfigure

transformación *f* transformation; (*de costumbres*) change

transformador *m* ELEC transformer

transformar *vt* to transform; (*costumbres*) to change; **desde el accidente está transformado** he/she has changed completely since the accident

tránsfuga *mf* **1.** (*fugitivo*) fugitive **2.** MIL deserter **3.** POL turncoat

transfundir *vt* (*líquido*) to transfuse

transfusión *f t.* MED transfusion

transgénico, -a *adj* genetically engineered

transgredir *irr como abolir vt* (*ley*) to violate, to break; (*orden*) to disobey

transgresión *f* (*ley*) transgression, violation; (*orden*) disobedience

transición *f* transition

transido, -a *adj elev* **~ de dolor** racked with pain; **~ de emoción** overcome with emotion; **~ de hambre** weak with hunger; **~ de miedo** panic-stricken

transigencia *f* **1.** (*condescendencia*) obligingness **2.** (*tolerancia*) tolerance **3.** POL compromise

transigente *adj* **1.** (*condescendiente*) broad-minded **2.** (*tolerante*) tolerant **3.** POL compromising

transigir <g→j> *vi* **1.** (*ceder*) to yield **2.** (*tolerar*) **~ con algo** to tolerate sth **3.** JUR, POL to compromise; **~ sobre algo** to reach a settlement on sth

transistor *m* ELEC transistor

transitable *adj* (*en coche*) open to traffic; (*a pie*) passable

transitar *vi* **~ por algo** (*en coche*) to go along sth; (*por un túnel*) to go through sth; (*a pie*) to walk along sth; **una calle muy transitada** a very busy street; **nadie transitaba por la calle** there was no one on the streets

transitivo, -a *adj* LING transitive

T

tránsito *m* **1.** (*circulación*) traffic; **de mucho** ~ very busy; **el** ~ **por esta calle es algo complicado** transit along this road is rather complicated **2.** (*de personas*) transit; COM transit

transitorio, -a *adj* **1.** (*temporal*) temporary; (*ley, periodo, disposición*) transitional **2.** (*pasajero*) fleeting, transitory

translúcido, -a *adj* translucent

transmigrar *vi* **1.** (*personas*) to migrate **2.** REL to transmigrate

transmisible *adj* transmissible

transmisión *f* **1.** (*de noticia*) broadcast; ~ **en directo/diferida** live/pre-recorded transmission [*o* broadcast] **2.** TV, AUTO, INFOR transmission **3.** (*enfermedad*) transmission **4.** TÉC drive; (*mecanismo*) transmission; (*propulsión*) drive **5.** JUR transfer **6.** (*por herencia*) descent

transmisor *m* TÉC transmitter

transmisor(a) *adj* **estación** ~**a** transmitter, radio/TV station

transmitir *vt* **1.** (*noticia*) to broadcast **2.** TV, RADIO, TÉC to transmit **3.** (*enfermedad*) to give **4.** (*por herencia*) to pass on **5.** FÍS to transmit

transmutar *vt* to transmute

transparencia *f* **1.** (*calidad*) transparency **2.** (*de intención*) openness **3.** FOTO slide **4.** (*para un proyector*) overhead transparency

transparentar **I.** *vt* to reveal **II.** *vi, vr:* ~**se** (*ser transparente*) to be transparent **III.** *vr:* ~**se** (*dejarse ver, adivinar*) to show through

transparente **I.** *adj* **1.** (*material*) transparent **2.** (*intenciones*) clear **II.** *m* curtain, blind

transpiración *f* (*persona*) perspiration

transpirar *vi* (*persona*) to perspire

transponer *irr como poner* **I.** *vt* (*persona, cosa*) to move; (*trasplantar*) to transplant **II.** *vr:* ~**se** **1.** (*persona*) to move **2.** (*sol*) to go out of sight **3.** (*dormirse*) to doze off

transportar **I.** *vt* **1.** (*trasladar*) to transport; (*en brazos*) to carry; (*en un vehículo*) to take; ~ **por barco** to ship **2.** MÚS to transpose **II.** *vr:* ~**se** to be transported

transporte *m* **1.** COM transport; *t.* TÉC (*de personas*) carriage; ~ **aéreo/marítimo** air/sea transport; ~ **por carretera** road transport; **compañía de** ~**s** transport company **2.** (*vehículo*) ~**s públicos** public transportation; **¿qué** ~ **utilizas para ir a la ciudad?** how do you get into town? **3.** *pl* (*conjunto*) carriage **4.** (*exaltación*) rapture **5.** MÚS transposition

transportista *mf* (*empresa, agente*) carrier, transporter

transpuesto, -a **I.** *pp de* **transponer** **II.** *adj* **quedarse** ~ to doze off

transversal *adj* (*atravesado, perpendicular*) transverse, crosswise; **calle** ~ cross street

transverso, -a *adj v.* **transversal**

transvestido *m* transvestite

tranvía *m* tram *Brit,* streetcar *Am*

trapa *m o f* **1.** (*de los pies*) stamping of feet **2.** (*vocerío*) uproar

trapacear *vi* to cheat

trapacería *f* racket

trapacero, -a *m, f* cheating

trapajoso, -a *adj* **1.** (*en el vestir*) shabby **2.** (*en el hablar*) **tener una lengua trapajosa** to speak thickly

trápala[1] *f* **1.** (*de gente*) hubbub **2.** (*de caballo*) clatter of hooves **3.** *inf* (*embuste*) scam

trápala[2] *m inf* jabbering

trápala[3] *mf* **1.** (*trapacero*) trickster **2.** (*parlanchín*) chatterbox

trapalear *vi* **1.** (*caballo*) to clatter **2.** (*hablar*) to chatter

trapatiesta *f inf* **1.** (*riña: verbal*) row; (*con puñetazos*) brawl **2.** (*jaleo*) ruckus

trapear *vt AmL* (*limpiar*) to mop

trapecio *m* **1.** (*de circo*) trapeze **2.** MAT trapezium *Brit,* trapezoid *Am* **3.** ANAT (*hueso*) trapezium; (*músculo*) trapezius

trapecista *mf* trapeze artist

trapero, -a *m, f* ragman

trapiche *m AmL* (*exprimidor de caña*) sugar mill

trapichear *vi* **1.** *inf* (*enredos*) to be mixed up in shady business; (*intrigar*) to scheme; (*artimaña*) to contrive; ~ **en los negocios** to have crooked dealings **2.** (*comerciar*) to buy and sell small scale

trapicheo *m inf* **1.** (*enredo*) jiggery-pokery; (*negocio*) dealing **2.** (*intriga*) scheming; (*artimaña*) contriving; **ha habido** ~**s en las elecciones** there's been some tampering in the elections

trapío *m* **1.** (*de mujer*) gracefulness **2.** TAUR spirit and good looks

trapisonda *f* **1.** (*riña, alboroto*) squabble **2.** (*intriga*) schemery

trapo *m* **1.** (*tela*) rag **2.** (*para limpiar*) cleaning cloth; ~ **de cocina** tea towel, dish towel *Am;* **pasar el** ~ **por algo** to wipe sth off **3.** *pl, inf* (*vestidos*) clothes *pl* **4.** NÁUT sails *pl;* **a todo** ~ under full sail; *inf* (*a toda velocidad*) at top speed; **el coche iba a todo** ~ *inf* the car was going at full speed; **poner la música a todo** ~ *inf* to put music on full blast **5.** TEAT curtain ►**tener lengua de** ~ to mumble; **tener manos de** ~ to be a butterfingers; **estar hecho un** ~ to be worn out; **sacar los** ~**s sucios a relucir** to wash one's dirty linen in public; **entrar al** ~ to fall into the trap; **poner a alguien como un** ~ to give sb a good telling off; **soltar el** ~ (*reír*) to burst out laughing; (*llorar*) to burst into tears; **tratar a alguien como un** ~ to treat sb like dirt

tráquea *f* ANAT trachea, windpipe *inf*

traquetear **I.** *vi* (*chapa, vajilla*) to clatter; (*motor, ametralladora*) to rattle; (*sillas, carro*) to jolt **II.** *vt* to shake

traqueteo *m* banging; (*chapa, vajilla*) clattering; (*ametralladora, motor*) rattling; (*de sillas, carro*) jolting

traquido *m* (*pistola*) report; (*madera*) crack

tras **I.** *prep* **1.** (*temporal*) after; **día** ~ **día** day after day **2.** (*espacial: detrás de*) behind;

(*orden*) after; **voy ~ tuyo** (*en la cola*) I'm behind you, I'm after you; (*en el coche*) behind; **ir ~ alguien** (*perseguir*) to go after sb **3.** (*con movimiento*) after; **ponerse uno ~ otro** to put one after the other **4.** (*además de*) besides; **~ de ser de pésima calidad es caro** it's not just terrible quality but it's expensive too **II.** *m inf* bottom **III.** *interj* **¡~ ~!** knock knock!

trasatlántico *m v.* **transatlántico**

trasatlántico, -a *adj v.* **transatlántico, -a**

trasbocar <c→qu> *vt AmC, AmS* to throw up

trasbordar *vt, vi v.* **transbordar**

trascendencia *f* (*importancia*) consequence; **no tener ~** to be of little importance; **un incidente sin más ~** an insignificant incident

trascendental *adj* **1.** (*importante*) important **2.** FILOS transcendental

trascender <e→ie> *vi* **1.** (*hecho, noticia*) to become known **2.** (*efecto, consecuencias*) **~ a algo** to have a wide effect on sth **3.** (*ir más allá*) **~ de algo** to go beyond sth **4.** (*olor*) to smell **5.** (*extenderse*) to spread; **el discurso transciende a fascismo** the speech reeks of fascism

trascurrir *vi v.* **transcurrir**

trasegar *irr como fregar vt* **1.** (*objetos: desordenar*) to turn upside down; (*cambiar*) to switch around **2.** (*líquidos*) to decant; (*de garrafa a botella*) to transfer **3.** (*alcohol*) to swill, to guzzle

trasera *f* back

trasero *m* **1.** (*animal*) hindquarters *pl* **2.** *inf* (*persona*) bottom, backside

trasero, -a *adj* back; **asiento ~** back seat; **luz trasera** rear light; **parte trasera** rear; **propulsión trasera** rear-wheel drive; **rueda trasera** rear wheel

trasferir *irr como sentir vt v.* **transferir**

trasfigurar *vt* to transfigure

trasfondo *m* background

trasiego *m* **1.** (*de objetos: desorden*) clutter **2.** (*cambio*) shuffling **3.** (*de líquidos*) decanting; (*a botella*) transfer

traslación *f* (*de cosas*) transfer; (*de cuerpo*) moving; (*de tropa*) transfer

trasladar I. *vt* **1.** (*cosas*) to move; (*cuerpo*) to go; (*tropa, tienda*) to relocate; (*prisionero: a otra prisión*) to transfer; (*a otra comisaría*) to move **2.** (*funcionario*) to transfer **3.** (*fecha*) to postpone **4.** (*idea, obra*) **~ al papel** to put on paper; **~ a la pantalla** to make into a film **5.** (*orden, medida*) to notify **6.** (*escrito*) to copy **II.** *vr:* **~se 1.** (*mudarse*) to move **2.** (*ir a*) to go to; **~se en coche** to drive

traslado *m* **1.** (*de cosas, cuerpo*) movement; (*tropa*) relocation; (*prisionero: de prisión*) transfer; (*de comisaría*) move **2.** (*de funcionario*) transfer **3.** (*de fecha*) postponement **4.** (*mudanza*) removal **5.** (*copia*) copy **6.** (*de orden, medida*) notification

traslucir *irr como lucir* **I.** *vt* (*cara*) to reveal; **dejar ~ algo** (*alguien*) to hint at sth **II.** *vr:* **~se 1.** (*ser translúcido*) to be translucent **2.** (*verse, notarse*) to show through **3.** (*hecho, intención*) to become evident

trasluz *m* diffused or reflected light; **mirar algo al ~** to hold sth up to the light

trasmano no puedo cogerlo, me pilla a ~ I can't get it, it's out of my reach; **su casa cae tan a ~ que apenas lo visito** his house is so far out of the way that I seldom visit him

trasmigrar *vi v.* **transmigrar**

trasmitir *vt v.* **transmitir**

trasmutar *vt* to transmute

trasnochado, -a *adj* **1.** (*comida*) stale **2.** (*idea, plan*) outdated **3.** (*persona*) drawn

trasnochador(a) *m(f) fig* night owl

trasnochar I. *vi* **1.** (*no dormir*) to spend a sleepless night; (*ir de juerga*) to have a night out; (*trabajando*) to sleep on sth **2.** (*acostarse tarde*) to stay up late **3.** (*pernoctar*) to spend the night **II.** *vt* to sleep on

traspapelar I. *vt* to misplace, to mislay **II.** *vr:* **~se** to get mislaid

trasparentar *vt, vr:* **~se** *v.* **transparentar**

traspasar *vt* **1.** (*atravesar: arma, rayos*) to go through; (*penetrar, perforar*) to pierce; (*líquido*) to soak through; (*calle, río*) to cross **2.** (*pasar a*) to transfer; FIN to make over; **se traspasa tienda** shop for sale **3.** (*sentidos*) **~ el corazón** to break sb's heart **4.** (*límite*) to go beyond; (*ley*) to break

traspaso *m* **1.** (*de piso, negocio, dinero*) transfer **2.** (*de límite*) exceeding; (*ley*) infringement **3.** (*de arma, rayos*) passage; (*de líquido*) soaking through; (*de calle, río*) crossing

traspatio *m AmL* backyard

traspié(s) *m* (*inv*) stumble; *fig* slip-up; **dar un ~** (*tropezar*) to stumble; (*resbalar*) to slip; (*meter la pata*) to slip up; (*en sociedad*) to make a faux pas

trasplantar I. *vt* **1.** (*planta*) to transplant **2.** (*personas*) to transfer **3.** MED to transplant **II.** *vr:* **~se** to migrate

trasplante *m* **1.** (*de plantas*) transplanting **2.** (*de persona*) transfer **3.** MED transplant

trasponer *irr como poner vt, vr:* **~se** *v.* **transponer**

trasportar *vt, vr:* **~se** *v.* **transportar**

trasquilar *vt* **1.** (*animal*) to shear **2.** (*persona*) to crop; **salir trasquilado** *fig, inf* to get fleeced **3.** *inf* (*cosa*) to cut down

trastabillar *vi* **1.** (*dar traspiés*) to stumble **2.** (*tambalear*) to stagger **3.** (*tartamudear*) to stutter

trastada *f* **1.** *inf* (*travesura*) prank; **hacer una ~ a alguien** to play a prank on sb **2.** (*mala pasada*) dirty trick

trastazo *m inf* bump; **pegarse un ~** to come a cropper; **pegarse un ~ contra algo** to bang into sth

traste *m* **1.** (*de guitarra*) fret **2.** *AmL* (*trasto*) piece of junk ►**dar al ~ con algo** to spoil sth;

irse **al** ~ to fall through

trastear I. *vt* ~ **a alguien** *inf* to twist sb around one's little finger II. *vi* (*trastos*) to rummage through

trastero, -a *adj* **cuarto** ~ lumber room

trastienda *f* 1. (*de tienda*) back room 2. *inf* (*astucia*) **tener mucha** ~ to be very crafty; (*reserva*) to be a dark horse

trasto *m* 1. (*mueble*) piece of furniture; (*utensilio*) utensil; **tirarse los ~s a la cabeza** to have a knock down drag out fight 2. *pl* (*herramientas*) gear 3. *pl* (*para tirar*) junk 4. *inf* (*persona*) **mi hijo es un** ~ my son is a holy terror; **tratar como un** ~ to treat like a dog

trastornado, -a *adj* (*confundido*) confused; (*sicológicamente*) disturbed; (*loco*) mad, crazy

trastornar I. *vt* 1. (*cosa*) to disarrange; (*de arriba abajo*) to turn upside down 2. (*orden, plan, ideas*) disrupt; (*orden público*) to disturb 3. (*psicológicamente*) to traumatize; (*por amor*) to lose one's head over sb; **la muerte de su marido la trastornó** she was traumatized by her husband's death 4. (*encantar*) **me trastornan los coches** I'm crazy about cars II. *vr:* **~se** 1. (*enloquecer*) to go mad 2. (*estropearse*) to fall through 3. (*turbarse*) to get upset

trastorno *m* 1. (*desorden*) disorder 2. (*del orden público*) disturbance; **~s políticos** political upheaval; **ocasionar ~s** to disrupt 3. (*sicológicamente*) disorder 4. MED disorder; **~s estomacales** stomach problems

trastrocar <c→qu> *vt* 1. (*el orden*) to invert 2. (*de sitio*) to switch around 3. (*el sentido*) to change 4. (*el estado*) to transform

trasunto *m* 1. (*escrito*) copy 2. (*imitación*) imitation; **ser un ~ de algo** (*reflectar*) to be a reflection of sth

trasvase *m* transfer; (*de río*) diversion

trasvasijar *vt Chile* (*trasvasar*) to pour from one container to another, to decant

trata *f* ~ **de blancas** white slave trade

tratable *adj* sociable

tratadista *mf* (treatise) writer, essayist

tratado *m* 1. *t.* POL treaty; ~ **de no agresión** non-aggression treaty; ~ **comercial** trade agreement 2. (*científico*) ~ **de algo** treatise on sth

tratamiento *m* 1. *t.* MED, QUÍM (*de asunto*) treatment 2. *t.* INFOR (*elaboración*) processing; ~ **de texto** word processing; ~ **de agua potable** drinking-water processing 3. (*de cortesía*) form of address; **el ~ de usted** the polite 'you' form; **¿qué ~ se le da a un cardenal?** what is the correct way to address a cardinal?

tratante *mf* dealer

tratar I. *vt* 1. (*manejar, portarse*) to deal with; **no es una persona fácil de** ~ he/she is not an easy person to deal with 2. MED, QUÍM to treat 3. *t.* INFOR (*elaborar, agua, minerales*) to process 4. (*dar tratamiento*) to address; ~ **de tú/usted** to adress sb in an informal/formal manner using tú/usted; ~ **a alguien de loco** to treat sb as if he/she were mad 5. (*tema, asunto*) to discuss II. *vi* 1. (*libro, película*) ~ **de** [*o* **sobre**] **algo** to be about sth, to deal with sth 2. (*intentar*) to try; **trata de concentrarte** try to concentrate 3. (*con alguien*) to have contact with 4. COM to deal III. *vr:* **~se** 1. (*tener trato*) to have to do; **no me trato con él** I don't have anything to do with him 2. (*ser cuestión de*) to be a question; **¿de qué se trata?** what's it about?; **tratándose de ti...** in your case ...

tratativas *fpl Arg, Par* (*negociación*) negotiations *pl;* **siguen en** ~ they are still discussing terms

trato *m* 1. (*manejo, comportamiento*) treatment; **malos ~s** ill-treatment, abuse; **recibir un buen** ~ to be well-treated 2. (*contacto*) contact; ~ **carnal** sexual relations; **tener ~ de gentes** to have a way with people; **romper el ~ con alguien** to break off relations with sb; **no querer ~s con alguien** to want nothing to do with sb; **es una señora de un ~ exquisito** she is a lady of exquisite manners 3. (*pacto*) agreement; (*negocio*) deal; **cerrar un ~ con alguien** to close a deal with sb; **entrar en ~s con alguien** to open negotiations with sb; **¡~ hecho!** it's a deal!

trauma *m* trauma

traumático, -a *adj* traumatic

traumatismo *m* injury; ~ **cervical** whiplash injury; MED traumatism

traumatología *f* orthopedic surgery, orthopedics *pl*

través I. *m* 1. (*inclinación*) slant 2. (*contratiempo*) setback ▸**dar al ~ con algo** to hit sth broadsides; (*arruinar*) to ruin sth; **mirar a alguien de** ~ to look at sb out of the corner of one's eye; **de** ~ crossways, crosswise II. *prep* **a ~ de** (*de un lugar*) across; (*de la radio*) on; (*de una persona*) from, through

travesaño *m* 1. ARQUIT crosspiece 2. DEP crossbar 3. (*de una escalera*) rung

travesía *f* 1. (*por aire*) flight; (*por mar*) crossing 2. (*distancia*) distance 3. (*calle*) cross street

travesti *mf,* **travestí** *mf,* **travestido, -a** *m, f* transvestite

travesura *f* prank

traviesa *f* 1. FERRO sleeper 2. (*de poste*) crossbar

travieso, -a *adj* 1. (*de través*) across; **correr a campo traviesa** to run cross-country 2. (*niño*) mischievous, naughty; **Daniel el Travieso** Dennis the Menace 3. (*adulto*) dissolute

trayecto *m* (*trecho*) distance; (*ruta*) route; (*recorrido*) itinerary; **final de** ~ end of the line

trayectoria *f* 1. (*de cuerpo*) path; ~ **de la Luna** the moon's trajectory 2. (*profesional*) career

traza *f* 1. *t.* ARQUIT (*plan*) plan 2. (*habilidad*) ability; **tener ~ para escribir** to be good at writing; **tener ~ para hablar** to have a knack for speaking **3.** (*aspecto*) appearance; **por las ~s** from the look of things; **lleva todas las ~s de acabar mal** it clearly looks as though it isn't going to turn out well **4.** (*rastro*) trace

trazado *m* **1.** *t.* ARQUIT (*de plan*) design **2.** (*recorrido*) route; FERRO line **3.** (*dirección*) direction **4.** (*disposición*) layout

trazado, -a *adj* **bien ~** nice-looking; **mal ~** unattractive

trazar <z→c> *vt* **1.** (*líneas*) to trace; (*esquemáticamente*) to outline; (*dibujos*) to sketch **2.** *t.* ARQUIT (*plan*) to draw up **3.** (*describir*) to describe

trazo *m* **1.** (*de bolígrafo, lápiz*) mark; **dibujar al ~** to outline **2.** (*de escritura*) stroke **3.** (*dibujo*) sketch **4.** (*de la cara*) **de ~s suaves** with soft features

trébede(s) *f(pl)* trivet

trebejo *m* utensil; **~s de pesca** fishing gear

trébol *m* **1.** (*planta*) clover; (*hoja*) clover leaf; (*emblema nacional de Irlanda*) shamrock **2.** (*cartas*) clubs

trece **I.** *adj inv* thirteen; **seguir en sus ~** to stand firm; **en el siglo ~** in the thirteenth century; **martes y ~** ≈ Friday the thirteenth **II.** *m* thirteen; *v.t.* **ocho**

trecho *m* **1.** (*distancia*) distance, way **2.** (*tramo*) stretch **3.** (*tiempo*) period, spell **4.** (*trozo*) piece; **de ~ a** [*o* **en**] **~** every so often; **a ~s** at intervals; **hacer algo a ~s** to do sth in fits and starts

tregua *f* **1.** MIL truce **2.** (*descanso*) respite; **dar ~s** (*dolor*) to let up now and then; **la muela le daba ~s** his/her toothache would come and go; **sin ~** relentlessly

treinta *adj inv, m* thirty; *v.t.* **ochenta**

treintavo, -a *adj* thirtieth; *v.t.* **ochentavo**

treintena *f* **1.** (*treinta unidades*) **una ~** thirty; **una ~ de años** about thirty years; **aún están en la ~** they are still in their thirties **2.** (*parte*) thirtieth

tremebundo, -a *adj* terrible

tremendista *adj* alarmist; (*exagerado*) sensationalist

tremendo, -a *adj* **1.** (*temible*) frightful **2.** (*enorme*) tremendous **3.** (*niño*) full of mischief **4.** (*respetable*) imposing ►**conseguir algo por la tremenda** to want to get sth by whatever means; **tomar las cosas a la tremenda** to make such a fuss over things

trementina *f* turpentine

tremolar *vi* to wave, to flutter

tremolina *f* **1.** (*del viento*) whistling **2.** (*bulla*) uproar

trémulo, -a *adj elev* tremulous; (*luz*) flickering

tren *m* **1.** FERRO train; **~ interurbano** intercity train; **~ de juguete** toy train; **~ rápido** express train; **~ de cercanías** suburban train; **~ de alta velocidad** high-speed train; **~ directo** through train; **coger el ~** to catch [*o* take] the train; **ir en ~** to go by train; **todas quieren subirse al ~** *fig* everyone wants to get in on it, everyone wants to climb on the bandwagon; **perder el último ~** *fig* to miss the boat **2.** TÉC **~ de lavado** carwash **3.** (*lujo*) **~ de vida** lifestyle; **llevar un gran ~ de vida** to live in style **4.** (*ritmo*) **imponer un fuerte ~ en la carrera** to set a fast pace in the race **5.** *inf* (*muy bien*) **estar como un ~** (*persona*) to be very good-looking **6.** *inf* (*en abundancia*) **hay sangría como para parar un ~** there's plenty of sangria

trena *f inf* clink *Brit,* slammer *Am*

trenca *f* (*abrigo*) duffle coat

trenza *f* **1.** (*de pelo*) plait *Brit,* braid *Am* **2.** (*de cintas*) braid

trenzar <z→c> *vt* **1.** (*pelo*) to plait *Brit,* to braid *Am* **2.** (*fibras*) to plait

trepa[1] *f* (*astucia*) cunning

trepa[2] *m pey, inf* climber; **esta oficina esta llena de ~s luchando por llegar a la cima** this office is full of ambitious go-getters scrambling to reach the top

trepador(a) **I.** *adj* **planta ~a** climbing plant **II.** *m(f)* (*arribista*) social climber, go-getter

trepar **I.** *vi, vt* **1.** (*al árbol*) to climb **2.** (*planta*) to creep **II.** *vt* to climb

trepe *m CRi* (*regaño*) scolding; **echar un ~ a alguien por algo** to give sb a telling-off for sth

trepidar *vi* **1.** (*temblar*) to vibrate **2.** *AmL* (*vacilar*) to hesitate

treque *adj Ven* **1.** (*ingenioso*) witty **2.** (*chistoso*) funny

tres **I.** *adj inv* three; **esta traducción no me sale ni a la de ~** I just can't do this translation no matter how I try; **como ~ y dos son cinco** as sure as you are born; **de ~ al cuarto** two-bit; **~ en raya** (*juego*) noughts and crosses *Brit,* tic-tac-toe *Am* **II.** *m inv* three; *v.t.* **ocho**

trescientos, -as *adj* three hundred; *v.t.* **ochocientos**

tresillo *m* **1.** (*mueble*) three-piece living room suite **2.** MÚS triplet

treta *f* trick

tría *f* sorting

tríada *f* triad

triangular *adj* triangular

triángulo *m* **1.** (*figura*) triangle **2.** MÚS triangle **3.** (*sentimental*) **~ amoroso** eternal triangle

triar <*1. pres:* trío> *vt* to sort

triates *mpl Méx* (*trillizos*) triplets *pl*

tribu *f* tribe

tribulación *f* **1.** tribulation; (*pena*) grief **2.** (*sufrimiento*) suffering **3.** (*adversidad*) hardship

tribuna *f* **1.** (*en parlamento*) rostrum **2.** (*en desfile, estadio*) stand **3.** JUR **~ de jurados** jury box **4.** **~ de la prensa** press box

tribunal *m* **1.** JUR court; **Tribunal de Cuentas** National Audit Office; **Tribunal Europeo de Cuentas** European Court of Auditors; **Tribunal de Justicia Europeo** European Court of Justice; **llevar a los ~es** to take to court **2.** (*comisión*) **~ examinador** board of examiners

tributación *f* **1.** (*acción*) payment **2.** (*tributo*) taxation; ~ **por utilidades** income tax **3.** (*sistema*) tax system
tributar *vt* **1.** (*impuestos*) to pay **2.** (*honor*) to render; (*respeto*) to show; ~ **un homenaje a alguien** to pay tribute to sb
tributario, **-a** *adj* tributary; (*imponible*) tax; **agencia tributaria** Inland Revenue
tributo *m* **1.** (*impuesto*) tax **2.** (*homenaje*) tribute; **pagar** ~ to pay tribute
triciclo *m* tricycle
tricolor *adj* tricolour *Brit,* tricolor *Am*
tricota *f AmL* (*chaqueta*) sweater
tricotar *vt* to knit
tridimensional *adj* three-dimensional
trienal *adj* **1.** (*duración*) three-year **2.** (*cada 3 años*) triennial
trifásico, **-a** *adj* three-phase
trifulca *f inf* rumpus
trigal *m* wheat field
trigésimo, **-a** *adj* thirtieth; *v.t.* **octavo**
trigo *m* **1.** (*planta*) wheat **2.** (*grano*) wheat; **no ser** ~ **limpio** *fig* not to be totally above board
trigueño, **-a** **I.** *adj* light brown; (*pelo*) dark blond; (*piel*) olive-skinned; *AmL* (*persona*) coloured *Brit,* colored *Am* **II.** *m, f AmL* coloured person
trilingüe *adj* trilingual
trilla *f* **1.** (*acción*) threshing **2.** (*época*) threshing season **3.** *AmL, inf* (*paliza*) thrashing **4.** (*trillo*) thresher
trillado, **-a** *adj inf* (*asunto*) over-worked
trilladora *f* threshing machine
trillar *vt* **1.** (*grano*) to thresh **2.** (*usar*) to overuse **3.** *AmL, inf* (*golpear*) to beat
trillizo *m* triplet
trillo *m* **1.** AGR (*máquina*) thresher **2.** *AmC* (*senda*) narrow path
trillón *m* trillion
trimestral *adj* **1.** (*duración*) three-month **2.** (*cada tres meses*) three-monthly, quarterly
trimestre *m* **1.** (*período*) three-month period **2.** (*educación*) term *Brit,* semester *Am* **3.** (*paga*) quarterly payment; (*alquiler*) quarter's rent
trinar *vi* **1.** (*persona*) to sing; (*pájaro*) to warble **2.** *inf* (*rabiar*) to fume; **está que trina** he/she is hopping mad **3.** MÚS to trill
trinca *f* **1.** (*tres*) threesome **2.** *And, CSur* (*pandilla*) gang **3.** *AmL, inf* (*embriaguez*) drunkenness **4.** *CSur* (*canicas*) game of marbles
trincar <c→qu> **I.** *vt* **1.** (*con cuerdas*) to tie up **2.** (*detener*) to nab **3.** (*romper*) to break up; (*papel*) to tear up **4.** *inf* (*robar*) to steal **5.** *inf* (*matar*) to bump off **6.** *AmL* (*apretar*) to be too tight **II.** *vr:* ~**se** **1.** *inf* (*emborracharse*) to get plastered **2.** *vulg* (*copular*) to screw
trinchar *vt* (*carne*) to carve
trinchera *f* **1.** MIL trench; **guerra de** ~**s** trench warfare **2.** (*gabardina*) trench coat
trineo *m* sledge *Brit,* sled *Am*
trinidad *f* trinity; **la Santísima Trinidad** the Holy Trinity
trinitaria *f* **1.** BOT (*pensamiento*) pansy **2.** *Col, PRico, Ven* BOT bougainvillea
trino *m* **1.** MÚS trill **2.** (*pájaro*) warble
trinquete *m* **1.** TÉC pawl **2.** (*mástil*) foremast
trío *m* trio
tripa *f* **1.** (*intestino*) intestine, gut; **quitar las** ~**s a un pez** to gut a fish **2.** *pl* (*vísceras*) entrails *pl,* innards *pl;* (*comestibles*) tripe; **me suenan las** ~**s** my stomach's rumbling; **echar las** ~**s** *inf* (*vomitar*) to throw up; **hacer de** ~**s corazón** *inf* to pluck up courage, to grin and bear it; **¿qué** ~ **se te ha roto?** *inf* what's up with you?; **se me revuelven las** ~**s** it turns my stomach; **¡te voy a sacar las** ~**s!** *inf* I'm going to tear you to pieces!; **tener malas** ~**s** *inf* to be cruel **3.** (*vientre*) tummy; **echar** ~ *inf* to get a paunch; **llenar**(**se**) **la** ~ *inf* to eat one's fill; **estar con** ~ (*embarazada*) to be in the family way; **dejar con** ~ *inf* to get sb pregnant **4.** *pl* (*interior*) insides *pl;* (*de fruta*) core
tripi *m inf* dose of LSD
triple **I.** *adj* triple; (*de tres capas*) three-ply **II.** *m* (*cantidad*) triple; **ser el** ~ **de grande** to be three times as large
triplicado, **-a** *adj* triplicate; **por** ~ (*acta*) in triplicate
triplicar <c→qu> **I.** *vt* to triple, to treble **II.** *vr:* ~**se** to triple, to treble
trípode *m* FOTO tripod
tripón, **-ona** **I.** *adj inf* pot-bellied **II.** *m, f* **1.** *Méx, inf* little boy or girl; **los tripones** the kids **2.** *inf* (*persona gorda*) fatty
tríptico *m* (*documento*) three-page leaflet
triptongo *m* LING triphthong
tripudo, **-a** **I.** *adj inf* big-bellied **II.** *m, f* fatty
tripulación *f* (*avión, barco*) crew
tripulante *m* crew member
tripular *vt* **1.** (*proveer de tripulación*) to man **2.** (*conducir: coche*) to drive; (*avión, barco*) to pilot
tripulina *f Chile* hubbub, rumpus
triquiñuela *f* trick
triquitraque *m* **1.** (*ruido*) clatter **2.** (*tira*) string of firecrackers
tris *m inv* **1.** (*ruido*) crack **2.** (*porción pequeña*) bit **3.** (*momento*) trice; **estar en un** ~ to be in a jiffy; **estar en un** ~ **de hacer algo** to be within an inch of doing sth; **por un** ~ by the skin of one's teeth
trisca *f* **1.** (*crujido*) crunch **2.** (*jaleo*) racket **3.** *AmC* (*mofa*) surreptitious sneer
triscar <c→qu> **I.** *vi* **1.** (*patalear*) to stamp **2.** (*jugar*) to romp **II.** *vt* **1.** (*mezclar*) to mingle **2.** (*confundir*) to mix up **3.** *AmC* (*mofar*) to make fun of
triste *adj* sad; (*mustio, pálido*) gloomy; (*descolorido*) dreary; (*paisaje*) dismal; (*flor*) withered; **un** ~ **sueldo** a sorry salary; **aún no he comido ni un** ~ **bocadillo** I haven't even had a measly sandwich yet; **aún no he ganado ni una** ~ **peseta** I've yet to earn a single peseta; **es** ~ **que no podamos ir** it's a

pity that we can't go; **el caballero de la ~ figura** (**Don Quijote**) the knight of the sad countenance
tristeza *f* sadness, sorrow
tristón, **-ona** *adj* gloomy
tristura *f AmL* sadness
tritón *m* newt, triton
trituradora *f* TÉC crusher; (*de la cocina*) grinder; ~ **de carne** meat grinder; ~ **de forraje** forrage chopper; ~ **de papel** paper shredder; ~ **de basura** waste-disposal unit; ~ **de hielo** ice crusher
triturar *vt* **1.** (*desmenuzar*) to chop; (*moler*) to grind; (*al masticar*) to chew **2.** (*maltratar*) to beat to a pulp; (*destruir*) to pulverize **3.** (*criticar*) to tear to pieces
triunfador(a) *m(f)* winner
triunfal *adj* triumphal, triumphant; **canto ~** song of triumph
triunfar *vi* **1.** (*salir triunfador*) to triumph **2.** (*ganar*) ~ **en algo** to win at sth; (*tener éxito*) to succeed; ~ **en la vida** to succeed in life **3.** (*exultar*) ~ **de algo** to exult over sth **4.** (*naipes*) to trump; (*jugar un triunfo*) to play a trump; **triunfan corazones** hearts are trumps
triunfo *m* **1.** (*victoria*) triumph, victory; (*éxito*) success; **arco de ~** victory arch; **costar un ~** to be no easy task **2.** (*naipe*) trump
trivial *adj* trivial
trivialidad *f* **1.** (*cualidad*) triviality, pettiness **2.** (*dicho*) trite remark
trivializar <z→c> *vt* **1.** (*restar importancia*) to trivialize **2.** (*simplificar*) to play down
triza *f* shred; **estar hecho ~s** to feel washed out; **hacer ~s** to tear into shreds; (*papel*) to shred; (*película*) to tear to pieces; **hacerse ~s** to smash to bits; (*jarrón*) to shatter; **hacer ~s a alguien** to tear sb apart
trocar *irr como volcar* **I.** *vt* **1.** (*cambiar*) ~ **por algo** to exchange for sth, to barter for sth; (*palabras*) to interchange **2.** (*dinero*) to change **3.** (*confundir*) to confuse **4.** (*vomitar*) to vomit **5.** *CSur* (*vender*) to sell **II.** *vr:* **~se** (*cambiar*) to change; (*transformarse*) to turn
trocear *vt* to cut up
trocha *f* **1.** (*senda*) trail; (*atajo*) shortcut **2.** *AmL* FERRO gauge
trochemoche a ~ (*sin orden*) helter-skelter; (*desparramado*) all over the place
trofeo *m* **1.** (*señal*) trophy; ~ **de guerra** war trophy **2.** (*victoria*) victory, triumph; (*éxito*) success
troglodita I. *adj* **1.** (*cavernícola*) cave-dwelling **2.** *inf* (*burdo*) brutish **II.** *m* **1.** (*cavernícola*) troglodyte, cave-dweller **2.** *inf* (*burdo*) lout
trola *f inf* (*mentira*) lie, whopper
trole *m* ELEC trolley pole
trolebús *m* trolley bus
trolero *m inf* (*mentiroso*) liar
tromba *f* METEO ~ (**de agua**) water spout; (*aguacero*) downpour; ~ (**terrestre**) whirlwind; **en ~** en masse
trombón *m* MÚS **1.** (*instrumento*) trombone **2.** (*músico*) trombonist
trombosis *f inv* MED thrombosis
trompa¹ *f* **1.** ZOOL (*elefante*) trunk; (*insectos*) proboscis; ~ **de Falopio** Fallopian tube **2.** *inf* (*nariz*) conk **3.** *AmL, inf* (*labios*) lips *pl;* **¡cierra la ~!** shut your trap! **4.** MÚS (*instrumento*) horn **5.** (*peonza*) top **6.** *inf* (*borrachera*) drunkenness; **coger una ~** to get smashed; **estar ~** to be drunk **7.** METEO *v.* **tromba**
trompa² *mf* **1.** (*músico*) horn player **2.** *CSur, inf* (*patrón*) boss
trompada *f*, **trompazo** *m* (*porrazo*) bash; (*choque*) crash; (*puñetazo*) punch
trompear I. *vt AmL, inf* to punch **II.** *vr:* **~se** *inf* **1.** (*emborracharse*) to get plastered **2.** *AmL* (*pelearse*) to fight
trompeta¹ *mf* (*músico*) trumpet player
trompeta² *f* (*instrumento*) trumpet
trompicar <c→qu> *vi* to stumble
trompicón *m* **1.** (*tropezón*) stumble; **a trompicones** in fits and starts **2.** *AmC* (*puñetazo*) punch
trompis *m inv, Arg, Urug* (*trompada*) punch; **agarrarse a ~** to start punching each other
trompiza *f AmS* fight
trompo *m* spinning top
trompudo, **-a** *adj AmL* thick-lipped
tronada *f* METEO thunderstorm
tronado, **-a** *adj* **1.** (*desgastado*) worn **2.** *inf* (*loco*) **estar ~** to be cracked; (*arruinado*) to be broke; *AmL* (*drogado*) to be high on drugs
tronar <o→ue> **I.** *vimpers* METEO to thunder **II.** *vi* **1.** (*ruido*) to thunder; (*gritar*) to roar **2.** (*oponerse*) to denounce violently, to thunder
troncal *adj* (*principal*) main; **asignaturas troncales** ENS core subjects
troncar *vt* to truncate
troncha *f Arg, Chile, Perú* (*lonja*) slice
tronchar I. *vt* **1.** (*tronco*) to cut down; (*rama*) to snap **2.** (*vida*) to cut short; (*esperanzas*) to shatter **II.** *vr:* **~se** to split; **~se de risa** *inf* to split one's sides laughing
troncho *m* **1.** BOT stem; (*de hortaliza*) stalk **2.** *CSur* (*trozo*) chunk
tronco *m* **1.** (*árbol*) trunk; (*flor*) stem; (*hortaliza*) stalk; (*de un árbol talado*) stump; (*leño*) log; **dormir como un ~** *inf* to sleep like a log **2.** (*cuerpo*) torso, trunk **3.** (*de familia*) stock **4.** *inf* (*amigo*) mate *Brit,* buddy; **tranqui ~** cool it, pal **5.** (*conducto*) main line
tronera¹ *f* **1.** (*ventana*) dormer; (*en el tejado*) small skylight **2.** MIL crenel **3.** (*billar*) pocket **4.** *Méx* (*chimenea*) chimney
tronera² *mf* (*tarambana*) harebrained person
trono *m* **1.** (*asiento*) throne; **ser leal al ~** to be loyal to the crown; **subir al ~** to come to the throne; **sucesor al ~** heir to the throne **2.** *inf* (*inodoro*) loo *Brit,* John *Am*
tropa *f* **1.** (*multitud*) crowd; *pey* (*grupo*) horde; **se presentaron Pepe y Clara y toda la ~** Pepe and Clara and the whole crew

T

showed up; **en ~** in disorganized groups **2.** MIL troop
tropear *vi Arg* (*conducir el ganado*) to herd
tropecientos, -as *adj inf* hundreds; **había ~ coches aparcados por todas partes** there were hundreds and hundreds of cars parked all over the place
tropel *m* **1.** (*mucha gente*) throng; **en ~** in a mad rush; **salieron en ~ del estadio** they came pouring out of the stadium **2.** (*prisa*) rush **3.** (*desorden*) jumble
tropelía *f* **1.** (*abuso de autoridad*) abuse of authority; (*acto violento*) violent act **2.** (*prisa*) haste
tropero *m Arg* (*vaquero*) cowboy
tropezar *irr como empezar* **I.** *vi* **1.** (*con los pies*) to trip **2.** (*topar*) to come across **3.** (*cometer un error*) to make a mistake; (*moralmente*) to go astray **4.** (*reñir*) to quarrel **II.** *vr:* **~se** (*encontrarse*) to run into
tropezón *m* **1.** (*acción*) stumble; **dar un ~** to trip; **a tropezones** by fits and starts; *fig* falling and rising; **hablaba a tropezones** he/she spoke falteringly **2.** (*error*) mistake; (*desliz*) lapse **3.** (*persona*) run-in **4.** (*en sopas, legumbres*) small chunks of meat, vegetables or seafood
tropical *adj* tropical; **clima ~** tropical climate; **fantasías ~es** exotic fantasies
trópico *m* tropic; **~ de Cáncer** Tropic of Cancer; **pasar los ~s** *AmC, fig* to have a hard time
tropiezo *m* **1.** (*en el camino*) stumbling block; **dar un ~** to trip **2.** (*error*) blunder; (*moralmente*) moral lapse **3.** (*revés*) setback **4.** (*desgracia*) misfortune; (*en el amor*) thwarting **5.** (*discusión*) quarrel
tropilla *f CSur* drove
troquel *m* die
trotamundos *mf inv* globetrotter
trotar *vi* **1.** (*caballos*) to trot; (*jinete*) to trot **2.** (*con prisas*) to hustle
trote *m* **1.** (*caballos*) trot; **ir al ~** to trot **2.** (*con prisa*) bustle; **a(l) ~** quickly **3.** (*ropa*) **para todo ~** for everyday use; **ser de mucho ~** to be very durable **4.** *inf* (*actividad*) **es demasiado viejo, ya no está para estos ~s** he's too old and is not up to that sort of thing any more
trova *f* (*verso*) verse; (*poema*) poem; (*canción*) ballad
trovador *m* troubadour
trozo *m* **1.** (*pedazo*) piece, bit; **a ~s** in pieces; **la pared se está cayendo a ~s** the wall is falling apart bit by bit **2.** LIT, MÚS excerpt, passage
trucaje *m* **1.** (*con trampa*) rigging **2.** CINE (*método*) trick photograply, special effects; FOTO touching up
trucar *vt* **1.** (*amañar*) to fix, to rig; FOTO to alter **2.** *inf* AUTO to soup up
trucha *f* **1.** (*pez*) trout; **~ asalmonada** salmon trout **2.** *AmC* COM (*caseta*) stand
trucho, -a *adj Arg, Col* (*astuto*) crafty, rascally
truco *m* trick; **esto tiene ~** there's a trick [*o* a catch] to this; **ése tiene muchos ~s** he's full of tricks ►**coger el ~ a algo** to get the hang of sth; **coger el ~ a alguien** to catch on to sb
truculento, -a *adj* **1.** (*cruel*) cruel **2.** (*terrible*) gruesome
trueno *m* **1.** (*ruido*) clap of thunder **2.** *inf* (*juerguista*) madcap; (*alborotador*) wild youth; **ir de ~** to go on a spree
trueque *m* exchange; COM (*sin dinero*) barter; **a ~ de** in exchange for
trufa *f* **1.** *t.* BOT truffle **2.** (*mentira*) lie; (*embuste*) hoax; (*fanfarronada*) bluster **3.** (*bombón*) (chocolate) truffle
trufar **I.** *vi* (*mentir*) to lie; (*engañar*) to deceive; (*fanfarronear*) to bluster **II.** *vt* (*rellenar*) to stuff
truhán *m* (*estafador*) rogue; (*charlatán*) mountebank
trullo *m inf* (*prisión*) clink *Brit,* slammer *Am*
truncado, -a *adj* (*incompleto*) cut short, truncated
truncar <c→qu> *vt* **1.** (*cortar*) to truncate; (*la cabeza*) to cut off **2.** (*texto*) to abridge; (*significado*) to destroy; (*cita*) to mutilate **3.** (*desarrollo*) to stunt; (*esperanzas, ilusiones*) to shatter
trusa *f Méx, Perú* (*faja*) girdle
tu *art pos* your; **~ padre/blusa/libro** your father/blouse/book; **~s hermanos/hermanas** your brothers/sisters
tú *pron pers* you; **yo que ~** if I were you; **tratar de ~** to address in the familiar manner using 'tú'; **de ~ a ~** on equal footing
tuba *f* tuba
tubérculo *m* **1.** BOT tuber **2.** *t.* MED (*bulto*) tubercle
tuberculosis *f inv* tuberculosis
tubería *f* **1.** (*tubo*) pipe **2.** (*conjunto*) pipes *pl*
tubo *m* **1.** (*para fluidos, gases*) tube; **~ de chimenea** flue; **~ digestivo** alimentary canal; **~ de ensayo** test tube; **~ de escape** exhaust pipe *Brit,* tailpipe *Am;* **~ de respiración** breathing tube; **tienes que pasar por el ~** *inf* you have to knuckle under; **fue como por un ~** *inf* it was a cinch; **alucinar por un ~** *inf* to really flip; **tenemos trabajo por un ~** *inf* we have loads of work to do **2.** RADIO, TV tube **3.** (*recipiente*) tube; **~ de pasta de dientes** tube of toothpaste **4.** *AmL* TEL (*auricular*) receiver **5.** *inf* (*metro*) tube *Brit,* metro
tubular *adj* tubular, tube-shaped
tucán *m* toucan
tuerca *f* nut; **~ mariposa** wing nut
tuerto, -a **I.** *adj* **1.** (*de sólo un ojo*) one-eyed **2.** (*torcido*) crooked, twisted **II.** *m, f* injustice
tueste *m* toasting; (*café*) roasting
tuétano *m* **1.** (*médula*) marrow **2.** (*corazón, esencia*) core, heart; **hasta los ~s** through and through; **enamorado hasta los ~s** head over heels in love; **llegar al ~ de un asunto** to get to the crux of a matter; **calado hasta los ~s** soaked to the skin

tufarada *f* strong smell; **¡qué ~ a cerveza echaba!** he/she reeked of beer!
tufillas *mf inf* irascible person
tufillo *m* **~ a algo** slight smell of sth; **este libro tiene un cierto ~ nostálgico** *fig* this book has an air of nostalgia about it
tufo *m* **1.** (*olor malo*) foul smell; (*de cuerpo*) body odour *Brit*, body odor *Am*; (*halitosis*) bad breath; (*a alcohol*) reek; (*a cerrado*) stuffy **2.** (*vapor*) fume **3.** (*rizo*) curl **4.** *pl* (*vanidad*) airs *pl*; **tener ~** *inf* to be conceited
tugurio *m* **1.** (*chabola*) hovel; (*cuartucho*) small room **2.** *pl* (*barrio*) slums *pl* **3.** *pey* (*bar*) joint
tuición *f* JUR custody, protection; **bajo la ~ de** sponsored by
tul *m* tulle
tulipa *f* tulip-shaped lampshade
tulipán *m* tulip
tullido, -a **I.** *adj* (*persona*) disabled; *pey* crippled; (*brazo*) maimed **II.** *m, f* cripple
tullir <*3. pret:* tulló> *vt* **1.** (*maltratar*) to maltreat **2.** (*herir*) to injure; (*lisiar*) to cripple; **te voy a ~ a palos** I'm going to beat you to a pulp **3.** (*paralizar*) to paralyze **4.** (*agotar*) to wear out, to exhaust
tumba *f* **1.** (*sepulcro*) grave, tomb; **ser (como) una ~** (*callado*) to keep quiet; **soy una ~** my lips are sealed; **llevar a alguien a la ~** to carry sb off; **hablar a ~ abierta** to speak openly; **lanzarse a ~ abierta en algo** to go headlong into sth; **tu abuelo se revolvería en su ~** your grandfather would turn in his grave; **cavar su propia ~** to drive a nail into one's own coffin **2.** (*voltereta*) somersault **3.** *AmL* (*tala*) felling of trees; (*claro*) tree clearing
tumbar **I.** *vt* **1.** (*tirar*) to knock down; (*pegando*) to flatten; **el campeón le tumbo en el tercer asalto** the champ knocked him out in the third round; *inf* (*matar*) to bump off; **estar tumbado** to be lying down **2.** *inf* ENS (*suspender*) to fail, to flunk *Am* **3.** *inf* (*perturbar, impresionar*) to bowl over **4.** *AmL* (*árboles*) to fell; (*tierra*) to clear **5.** *vulg* (*copular*) to screw **II.** *vr:* **~se** **1.** (*acostarse*) to lie down; **~se en la cama** to lie down on the bed **2.** (*desistir*) to give up **3.** *inf* (*en el trabajo*) to ease up
tumbo *m* **1.** (*caída*) fall, tumble **2.** (*vaivén*) roll; **dar un ~** to jolt; **ir por la vida dando ~s** to go through life moving from one hardship to another **3.** (*voltereta*) somersault
tumbón, -ona **I.** *adj* **1.** (*astuto*) cunning **2.** (*vago*) lazy **II.** *m, f* **1.** (*persona astuta*) sly person **2.** (*vago*) idler, loafer
tumbona *f* deck chair
tumefacción *f* MED swelling
tumor *m* MED tumour *Brit*, tumor *Am*
tumulto *m* tumult; **un ~ de gente** a crowd of people
tuna *f* **1.** MÚS tuna **2.** (*vida picaresca*) **correr la ~** to live it up

The **tuna** is a group of students who get together to sing and play music. Up until recently, only male students were admitted to **tunas**, but in the last few years new **tunas** have been formed for female students. In order to become a member of a **tuna**, certain initiation rites involving trials of courage have to be successfully completed.

tunante *mf v.* **tuno**
tunda *f* **1.** (*paliza*) beating **2.** (*esfuerzo*) exhausting effort; **darse una ~** to wear oneself out **3.** (*de paños*) clipping
tundir *vt* **1.** (*pegar*) to thrash **2.** (*paños*) to clip **3.** (*hierba*) to mow, to cut
tunecino, -a *adj, m, f* Tunisian
túnel *m* tunnel; **~ aerodinámico** wind tunnel; **~ de lavado** car wash; **salir del ~** *fig* to see the light at the end of the tunnel
Túnez *m* **1.** (*país*) Tunisia **2.** (*capital*) Tunis
túnica *f* **1.** (*vestidura*) tunic, robe **2.** (*membrana*) tunica
tuno, -a **I.** *adj* **1.** (*astuto*) cunning **2.** (*pícaro*) roguish **II.** *m, f* **1.** (*truhán*) rogue **2.** (*astuto*) crook **3.** (*niño*) scamp **4.** (*de la tuna*) member of a student 'tuna'
tuntún *m inf* **al (buen) ~** any old way; **juzgar al buen ~** to jump to conclusions
tupé *m* **1.** (*cabello*) quiff *Brit*, pompadour *Am* **2.** (*frescura*) cheek
tupí *mf AmL* (*aborigen del Brasil*) Tupi
tupido, -a **I.** *adj* **1.** (*denso*) thick; **correr un ~ velo** to draw a veil over sth; *fig* to keep sth quiet **2.** *AmL* (*obstruido*) blocked **3.** *Méx* (*frecuente*) frequent **4.** (*con tesón*) persistently **II.** *adv* (*a menudo*) often
tupir **I.** *vt* **1.** (*apretar*) to pack tightly; (*tapar agujeros*) to fill in **2.** (*obstruir*) to obstruct **II.** *vr:* **~se** **1.** (*comer mucho*) to gorge oneself; (*beber mucho*) to guzzle down **2.** *AmL* (*obstruirse*) to get blocked up
turba *f* **1.** (*materia*) peat **2.** *v.* **turbamulta**
turbación *f* **1.** (*disturbio*) disturbance **2.** (*alarma*) concern **3.** (*vergüenza*) embarrassment **4.** (*confusión*) confusion
turbamulta *f* crowd; *pey* mob
turbante *m* turban
turbar **I.** *vt* **1.** (*perturbar*) to disturb **2.** (*alarmar*) to worry **3.** (*avergonzar*) to embarrass **4.** (*desconcertar*) to unsettle **5.** (*agua*) to stir up **II.** *vr:* **~se** **1.** (*ser disturbado*) to be disturbed **2.** (*alarmarse*) to get worried **3.** (*avergonzarse*) to get embarrassed **4.** (*desconcertarse*) to become confused **5.** (*agua*) to get stirred up
turbina *f* turbine
turbio, -a *adj* (*líquido*) cloudy; (*asunto*) turbid, shady; (*sin transparencia, carácter*) opaque; (*negocio*) shady; (*vista*) blurry, unclear
turbión *m* **1.** (*aguacero*) downpour; (*devastador*) hurricane **2.** (*todo a la vez*) sweep; **~ de**

T

balas hail of bullets
turbo *m t.* AUTO turbo
turborreactor *m* turbojet
turbulencia *f* **1.** (*agua, aire*) turbulence **2.** (*alboroto*) commotion; (*confusión*) turmoil **3.** (*sin transparencia*) turbidness
turbulento, **-a** *adj* **1.** (*agua, aire*) turbulent **2.** (*alborotado*) stormy; (*confuso*) confused **3.** (*rebelde*) disorderly **4.** (*turbio*) cloudy
turco, **-a** **I.** *adj* Turkish **II.** *m, f* Turk; **cabeza de** ~ *fig* scapegoat
turgencia *f* (*hinchazón*) swelling; (*firmeza*) turgidness
turgente *adj* **1.** (*hinchado*) swollen **2.** (*abultado*) protuberant; (*pechos*) firm
turismo *m* **1.** (*viajar*) tourism; ~ **verde** eco-tourism; **industria del** ~ tourist trade; **oficina de** ~ visitors' bureau; **hacer** ~ to travel as a tourist **2.** AUTO private car
turista *mf* tourist
turístico, **-a** *adj* tourist; **viaje** ~ sightseeing trip
turnar *vi, vr:* ~**se** to take turns
turno *m* **1.** (*en la fábrica*) shift; **cambio de** ~ shift change; **estar de** ~ to be on duty; **trabajar por** ~**s** to work shifts; ~ **de día/noche** day/night shift **2.** (*orden*) turn; **a** [*o* **por**] ~**s** by turns; **es tu** ~ it's your turn; **pedir** ~ to ask who is last in line; **aguardar su** ~ to wait one's turn; ~ **de preguntas** question and answer session; **hacer algo por** ~**s** to take turns doing sth; **de** ~ current; **apareció con la novia de** ~ he showed up with his latest girlfriend
turolense **I.** *adj* of/from Teruel **II.** *mf* native/inhabitant of Teruel
turón *m* polecat
turquesa[1] **I.** *adj* turquoise **II.** *m* (*color*) turquoise blue
turquesa[2] *f* MIN (*piedra*) turquoise
Turquía *f* Turkey
turrón *m* **1.** (*dulce*) ≈ nougat **2.** (*puesto*) cushy job; **comer del** ~ *fig* to fill a government post

> Like the British Christmas cake, **turrón** is a must in Spain at Christmas. The traditional **turrón** is either a soft or hard bar, rather like nougat, containing nuts or honey-coated almonds. The **turrón** is made particularly in **Levante**, and especially in **Jijona** and **Alicante**.

turulato, **-a** *adj inf* dazed, stunned; **dejar a alguien** ~ to leave sb flabbergasted
tusar **I.** *vi Guat* (*murmurar*) to murmur **II.** *vt AmL* (*cortar mal el pelo*) to scalp *inf*
tuso, **-a** *adj* **1.** *Col, PRico* (*pelón*) cropped, shorn **2.** *Col, Ven* (*picado de viruelas*) pock-marked **3.** *PRico* (*rabón*) tailless, bobtailed
tute *m* **1.** (*juego*) *Spanish card game* **2.** *inf* (*trabajo*) **darse un** ~ to work one's fingers to the bone
tutear **I.** *vt* to address in the familiar manner using 'tú' **II.** *vr:* ~**se** to be on familiar terms
tutela *f* **1.** (*cargo*) guardianship; **poner bajo** ~ to place in ward **2.** (*amparo*) protection; **estar bajo la** ~ **de alguien** to be under the protection of sb
tutelaje *m CSur, Guat, Méx* (*tutela*) guardianship, protection
tutelar **I.** *adj* **1.** JUR tutelary; **juez** ~ tutelary judge **2.** (*protector*) protective, guardian **II.** *vt* **1.** (*ejercer la tutela*) to have the charge of **2.** (*proteger*) to protect, to guard **3.** (*velar*) to supervise
tuteo *m* familiar use of 'tú'
tutilimundi *m* **1.** (*mundonuevo*) cosmorama **2.** *AmL, inf* everybody
tutiplén *adv inf* galore; **a** ~ in abundance; **comer a** ~ to eat like there's no tomorrow
tutor(a) *m(f)* **1.** JUR guardian; **firma/consentimiento del padre o** ~ signature/consent of parent or guardian **2.** (*protector*) protector **3.** (*profesor*) teacher **4.** ENS, UNIV tutor
tutoría *f* **1.** JUR guardianship, tutelage **2.** UNIV tutorship; (*class*) tutorial
tuyo, **-a** *pron pos* **1.** (*propiedad*) **el perro es** ~ the dog is yours; **la botella/la casa es tuya** the bottle/the house is yours; **¡ya es** ~**!** all yours! **2.** (*tras artículo*) **el** ~**/la tuya/lo** ~ yours; **mi coche está roto, vamos en el** ~ my car isn't working, let's take yours; **no cojas mi lápiz, tienes el** ~ don't take my pencil, you have your own; **los** ~**s** yours; (*parientes*) your family; **ésta es la tuya** *fig* this is your chance; **una de las tuyas** (*travesura*) one of your tricks **3.** (*tras substantivo*) of yours; **una amiga tuya** a friend of yours; **una hermana tuya** one of your sisters; **es culpa tuya** it's your fault **4.** (*tras impersonal 'lo'*) **lo** ~ what is yours; **tú a lo** ~ you mind your own business; **esto no es lo** ~ this isn't your strong point
TVE *f abr de* **Televisión Española** *the Spanish state-owned television broadcasting company*
txacolí, **txakolí** *m type of white wine from the Basque country*

U

U, **u** *f* <úes> U, u; ~ **de Uruguay** U for Uncle
U *abr de* **University** U., Univ.
u *conj placed before words beginning with 'o' or 'ho'* or; **diez u once** ten or eleven
ubérrimo, **-a** *adj* very fertile
ubicación *f* **1.** (*lugar*) location; (*de una empresa*) site **2.** (*situación*) situation **3.** (*empleo*) position **4.** *AmL* (*colocación*) placing
ubicar <c→qu> **I.** *vi* to be (situated) **II.** *vt AmL* (*situar*) to situate; (*guardar*) to place **III.** *vr:* ~**se** to be (situated)
ubicuo, **-a** *adj* ubiquitous

ubre *f* udder

UC *f abr de* **Unión de Consumidores** *Consumers Association*

UCI *abr de* **Unidad de Cuidados Intesivos** ICU

Ucrania *f* Ukraine

ucrani(an)o, -a *adj, m, f* Ukrainian

Ud(s). *abr de* **usted(es)** you

UE *f abr de* **Unión Europea** EU

UEFA *f abr de* **Unión de Asociaciones Europeas de Fútbol** UEFA

UEME *abr de* **Unión Económica y Monetaria Europea** EEMU

UEO *f abr de* **Unión Europea Occidental** WEU

uf *interj* **1.** (*de asco, fastidio*) ugh **2.** (*de cansancio, alivio*) phew

ufanarse *vr* to boast; ~ **de algo** to brag about sth

ufanía *f* **1.** (*orgullo*) pride **2.** (*engreimiento*) conceit; (*arrogancia*) arrogance **3.** (*satisfacción*) complacency

ufano, -a *adj* **1.** (*orgulloso*) proud **2.** (*engreído*) conceited; (*arrogante*) arrogant **3.** (*satisfecho*) complacent; **va muy ~ con su nueva moto** he is very smug about his new motorbike **4.** (*planta*) lush, luxuriant

ufología *f sin pl* ufology

ugandés, -esa *adj, m, f* Ugandan

UGT *f abr de* **Unión General de Trabajadores** *socialist trade union, one of the two main TUs in Spain.*

ujier *m* **1.** (*de un tribunal*) usher **2.** (*de un palacio*) gatekeeper

úlcera *f* MED ulcer; (*pupa*) sore

ulcerar *vt, vr:* **~se** to ulcerate, to fester

ulterior *adj* (*posterior*) later, subsequent; (*más*) further

ulteriormente *adv* later, subsequently

ultimación *f* completion, conclusion

últimamente *adv* **1.** (*recientemente, hace poco*) recently, lately **2.** (*por último*) lastly, finally

ultimar *vt* **1.** (*proyecto, obra*) to finish, to complete; (*acuerdo*) to conclude **2.** *AmL* (*matar*) to murder

ultimátum *m sin pl* ultimatum; **dar el ~ a alguien** to give sb an ultimatum

último, -a *adj* **1.** (*en orden*) last; **el ~ de cada mes** the last day of each month; **a ~s de mes** at the end of the month; **soy el ~ de la clase** I'm the worst student in the class; **fue el ~ en firmar** he was the last to sign; **siempre llega el ~** he/she is always the last to arrive; **por última vez** for the last time; **hacia la última parte la película mejora** the film gets better towards the end; **la última moda** the lastest fashion; **por ~** lastly, finally; **¿quién es el ~?** (*en una cola*) who is last in the queue? *Brit,* who's the last in line? *Am;* **unos estudian ciencias, otros letras; los ~s...** some study science, others Arts; the latter ... **2.** (*espacio*) **la última fila** the last row; **en el ~ piso** on the top floor; **ocupar la última posición de la tabla** to be at the bottom of the chart; **el ~ rincón del mundo** *inf* the back of beyond *Brit,* the boondocks *pl Am* ►**estar en las últimas** (*muriéndose*) to be at death's door; (*arruinado*) to be on one's last legs; **ser lo ~** (*lo mejor*) to be great; (*lo peor*) to be the end

ultra **I.** *adj* extreme **II.** *mf* extreme right-winger, neo-fascist **III.** *adv* extremely

ultracongelado, -a *adj* deep-frozen

ultracongelar *vt* to deep-freeze

ultraconservador(a) *adj* ultraconservative

ultrafino, -a *adj* exceedingly fine

ultrajar *vt* **1.** (*insultar*) to insult; (*monumento*) to spoil; ~ **de palabra** to revile **2.** (*humillar*) to humiliate **3.** (*ajar*) to crumple

ultraje *m* abuse; **un ~ a la bandera** a dishonour *Brit* [*o* dishonor *Am*] to the flag

ultramar *m sin pl* foreign parts *pl;* **pasé mi infancia en ~** I spent my childhood in foreign parts [*o* overseas]; **han venido de ~** they have come from overseas **ultramarino, -a** *adj* overseas **ultramarinos** *mpl* **1.** (*tienda*) grocer's *Brit,* grocery store *Am* **2.** (*víveres*) groceries *pl* **ultramoderno, -a** *adj* extremely modern

ultranza **1.** (*a muerte*) **el padre defendió el honor de su familia a ~** the father defended the honour of his family with his life; **luchar a ~** to fight to the death **2.** (*resueltamente*) **ser de izquierda a ~** to be an out-and-out left-winger; **ser un ecologista a ~** to be a radical ecologist

ultrarrápido, -a *adj* extra fast; **tren ~** a high-speed train **ultrasecreto, -a** *adj* top secret **ultrasensible** *adj* ultrasensitive **ultrasónico, -a** *adj* ultrasonic **ultrasonido** *m sin pl* ultrasound **ultratumba** *f* **la vida de ~** the next life **ultravioleta** *adj inv* ultraviolet; **rayos ~** ultraviolet rays

ulular *vi* **1.** (*animal, viento*) to howl; (*búho*) to hoot **2.** (*persona*) to shriek

umbilical *adj* umbilical

umbráculo *m* pergola

umbral *m* **1.** (*de puerta*) threshold; **atravesar los ~es de una casa** to set foot in a house **2.** (*principio*) beginning, outset **3.** ECON ~ **de rentabilidad** break even point

umbrío, -a *adj* shady

umbroso, -a *adj* shady

UME *f abr de* **Unión Monetaria Europea** EMU

un, una <unos, -as> **I.** *art indef* **1.** (*no determinado*) a; (*before a vowel or initial silent h*) an; **un perro** a dog; **una chica** a girl; **un elefante** an elephant; **¡tiene una jeta!** he/she's got a nerve! **2.** *pl* (*algunos*) some, a few **3.** *pl* (*aproximadamente*) approximately, about; **unos 30 euros** about 30 euros **II.** *adj v.* **uno, -a**

unánime *adj* (*opinión, decisión*) unanimous

unanimidad *f* (*de opinión, decisión*) unanimity; **aprobar algo por ~** to approve sth

U

unanimously
unción *f* anointing
uncir <c→z> *vt* to yoke
undécimo, **-a** *adj* eleventh; *v.t.* **octavo**
undulación *f* wave, ripple
undular *vi, vt* to wave
UNED *f abr de* **Universidad Nacional de Educación a Distancia** ≈ OU
ungir <g→j> *vt t.* REL to anoint
ungüento *m* **1.** MED ointment **2.** (*remedio*) salve
únicamente *adv* only, solely
unicameral *adj* single-chamber **unicelular** *adj* unicellular
unicidad *f* uniqueness
único, **-a** *adj* **1.** (*solo*) only; **hijo** ~ only child; **heredero** ~ sole heir; **calle de dirección única** one-way street; **hoy hay plato** ~ today there is only one main course **2.** (*extraordinario*) unique
unicornio *m* unicorn
unidad *f* **1.** *t.* MIL, MAT unit; ~ **familiar** family unit; **Unidad de Cuidados Intensivos** intensive care unit; ~ **de medida** unit of measure; ~ **monetaria** currency unit **2.** LIT unity **3.** TÉC (*aparato*) unit; ~ **de control** control unit; ~ **externa de disco duro** INFOR external hard disc unit [*o* drive]; ~ **de visualización** visual display unit; ~ **periférica** peripheral (device); TV, RADIO mobile unit
unidimensional *adj* one-dimensional
unido, **-a** *adj* united; **estamos muy ~s** we are very close; **mantenerse ~s** to stay together
unifamiliar *adj* single-family; **una casa** ~ a detatched house
unificación *f* **1.** (*unión*) unification; **la** ~ **política** political unification **2.** (*uniformización*) standardization
unificar <c→qu> *vt* **1.** (*pueblos, esfuerzos*) to unite; ~ **posiciones** to unify positions **2.** (*uniformar*) to standardize
uniformar *vt* **1.** (*hacer unitario, impreso*) to standardize **2.** (*vestir*) ~ **a alguien** to put sb into uniform; **ir uniformado** to be dressed in uniform
uniforme **I.** *adj* (*igual, de la misma forma*) uniform, same; (*movimiento*) steady **II.** *m* uniform; **vestir de** ~ to wear a uniform
uniformidad *f* **1.** (*constancia*) regularity; (*movimiento*) steadiness **2.** (*similaridad*) uniformity
uniformizar <z→c> *vt* to standardize; (*mezclar*) to blend
unigénito, **-a** *adj* only-begotten; **ser** ~ to be an only child
unilateral *adj* (*visión*) one-sided; POL unilateral
unión *f* **1.** *t.* TÉC (*de dos elementos*) joint; **no hay muchos puntos de** ~ **entre nosotros** we haven't much in common **2.** *t.* ECON, POL (*territorial*) union; **Unión Europea** European Union; ~ **monetaria** monetary union; **en** ~ **con** (together) with **3.** (*matrimonio*) marriage **4.** COM merger **5.** (*armonía*) unity, closeness ►**la** ~ **hace la fuerza** *prov* united we stand
unipersonal *adj* **1.** (*de una persona*) one-person; (*de un hombre*) one-man; (*de una mujer*) one-woman **2.** (*individual*) single, individual **3.** LING *applying to a verb used only in the infinitive form or the 3rd person singular*
unir **I.** *vt* **1.** *t.* TÉC (*dos elementos*) to join **2.** (*territorios, familia*) to unite; **nos une una gran amistad** there is a great bond of affection between us **3.** (*ingredientes*) to mix **4.** (*esfuerzos*) to combine **II.** *vr:* **~se** (*territorios, dos personas*) to join together, to unite; ECON to merge; **~se en matrimonio** to marry
unisex *adj* unisex; **moda** ~ unisex fashion; **peluquería** ~ unisex hairdresser's
unísono *m* MÚS unison; **protestaron al** ~ they unanimously protested; **trabajar al** ~ to work in harmony; **actuar al** ~ to act in complete agreement
unísono, **-a** *adj* **1.** (*de un solo tono*) unisonal **2.** (*de una sola voz*) in unison
unitario, **-a** *adj* unitary
universal *adj* **1.** (*del universo*) universal; **receptor** ~ RADIO universal receiver **2.** (*del mundo*) worldwide; **de renombre** ~ internationally known; **historia** ~ world history; **de fama** ~ world famous **3.** (*general, amplio*) widespread; **regla** ~ general rule **4.** TÉC (*máquina*) multi-purpose machine; **detergente** ~ all-purpose detergent
universalidad *f* (*de regla*) universality
universalizar <z→c> *vt* to make universal
universalmente *adv* **1.** (*en todo el mundo*) universally; ~ **conocido** known all over the world **2.** (*generalmente*) generally
universidad *f* university; **ir a la** ~ to be at university; **¿a qué** ~ **vas?** which university do you go to?
universitario, **-a** **I.** *adj* university; **estudiante** ~ university student; **profesor** ~ university teacher; **tener estudios ~s** to have studied at university **II.** *m, f* **1.** (*estudiante*) university student **2.** (*no licenciado*) undergraduate; (*licenciado*) graduate
universo *m* (*cosmos*) universe
unívoco, **-a** *adj* unanimous
uno *m* one
uno, **-a** **I.** *adj* **1.** (*número*) one; **a la una** (*hora*) at one o'clock; **¡(a la) una, (a las) dos y (a las) tres!** ready, steady, go! *Brit,* ready, set, go!; **fila** ~ front row **2.** (*único*) **sólo hay una calle** there's only one street ►**andar a una** to agree **II.** *pron indef* **1.** (*alguno*) one, somebody; **cada** ~ each (one), every one; **~s cuantos** some, a few; **~..., el otro...** one ..., the other ...; ~ **de tantos** one of many; **aquí hay** ~ **que pregunta por ti** there's sb here asking for you; **una de dos, o... o...** the choice is simple, either ... or ....; **una que otra vez** once in a while; **de** ~ **en** ~ one by one, one at a time; **cantar a una** to sing all together; **luchar todos a una** to fight as one; **no acierto una** I

can't do anything right; **me ha dejado pero me he quedado el piso, lo ~ por lo otro** he left me but I've kept the flat, what you lose on the swings you gain on the roundabouts *Brit* **2.** *pl* (*algunos*) some **3.** (*indeterminado*) one, you

untar **I.** *vt* **1.** (*con mantequilla*) to spread **2.** (*mojar*) to dip **3.** (*con grasa*) to grease; (*con aceite*) to oil; (*el cuerpo*) to smear **4.** (*sobornar*) to bribe **II.** *vr* **1.** (*mancharse*) to smear; **~se de algo** to become smeared with sth **2.** (*crema*) **~se con/de algo** to rub sth in **3.** (*dinero*) to line one's pocket

unto *m* **1.** (*grasa*) grease **2.** MED ointment **3.** *Chile* (*betún*) shoe-polish

unt(u)oso, -a *adj* **1.** (*pegajoso*) sticky **2.** (*jabón*) slippery **3.** (*pingüe*) greasy

untura *f* **1.** MED ointment **2.** (*grasa*) grease

uña *f* **1.** (*de persona*) nail; **~ encarnada** ingrowing nail *Brit,* ingrown nail *Am;* (*de gato*) claw; **~s de los pies** toenails *pl;* **afilarse las ~s** *fig* to sharpen one's claws; **limarse las ~s** to file one's nails; **fue a la peluquería a hacerse las ~s** she went to the hairdresser's to have her nails done; **comerse las ~s** to bite one's nails; *fig* to become furious; **estar de ~s con alguien** *inf* to be at loggerheads with sb; **enseñar las ~s** (*mostrarse agresivo*) to show on's teeth; **para triunfar se dejó las ~s en el trabajo** *fig* to triumph at work he/she wore his/her fingers to the bone **2.** (*pezuña*) hoof **3.** (*del alacrán*) sting ►**ser ~ y carne** to be inseparable; **defenderse con ~s y dientes** to fight tooth and nail to defend oneself; **ser largo de ~s** to be light-fingered

uñada *f* **1.** (*arañazo*) scratch **2.** (*señal*) nail mark

uñero *m* **1.** (*inflamación*) whitlow **2.** (*uña*) ingrowing nail *Brit,* ingrown nail *Am*

upa **I.** *interj inf* upsy-daisy [*o* upsadaisy]; **llevar a ~ un niño** to carry a child **II.** *adj Ecua, Perú* (*tonto*) idiot

upar *vt inf* to lift up

uperizado, -a *adj* **leche uperizada** UHT milk

Urales *mpl* Urals *pl*

uralita® *f* asbestos (cement)

uranio *m* uranium

urbanidad *f* urbanity, courtesy

urbanismo *m* (*planificación*) town planning

urbanístico, -a *adj* town-planning; **desarrollo ~** urban development; **plan ~** development plan

urbanización *f* **1.** (*acción*) urbanization **2.** (*de casas*) housing estate [*o* development]

urbanizar <z→c> **I.** *vt* to urbanize **II.** *vt, vr:* **~se** (*de personas*) to become civilized

urbano *m* traffic policeman

urbano, -a *adj* **1.** (*de la ciudad*) urban; **conferencia urbana** TEL local call; **un hombre ~** a city man; **planificación urbana** town [*o* city] planning **2.** (*cortés*) urbane, courteous

urbe *f* large city, metropolis

urdir *vt* (*conspiración*) to scheme; **~ intrigas** to plot a scheme

uréter *m* ANAT ureter

uretra *f* ANAT urethra

urgencia *f* **1.** (*cualidad*) urgency **2.** (*caso*) emergency; **llamada de ~** pressing/urgent call; **en caso de ~** if case of emergency; **tratar algo con la debida ~** to handle sth with due speed **3.** *pl* (*en hospital*) casualty room *Brit,* emergency room *Am;* **servicio de ~s** (*en ambulatorio*) emergency service

urgente *adj* urgent, pressing; (*carta, telegrama, pedido*) express; **un pedido ~** a rush order; **¿es ~?** is it urgent?

urgir <g→j> *vi* to be urgent, to be pressing

urinario *m* urinal, public lavatory

urinario, -a *adj* urinary; **aparato ~** MED urinary tract

urna *f* **1.** (*caja de cristal*) glass case **2.** (*para cenizas*) urn **3.** POL ballot box; **acudir a las ~s** to go and vote, to go to the polls

uro *m* aurochs *inv*

urogallo *m* capercaillie

urología *f* urology

urraca *f* **1.** ZOOL magpie **2.** (*cotorra*) chatter-box; **hablar más que una ~** to talk nineteen to the dozen *Brit,* to talk a blue streak *Am*

URSS *f abr de* **Unión de Repúblicas Socialistas Soviéticas** USSR

urticaria *f* MED hives *pl,* skin rash

Uruguay *m* Uruguay

> **Uruguay** (official title: **República Oriental del Uruguay**) lies in the southeastern part of South America. The capital and the most important city in Uruguay is **Montevideo**. The official language of the country is Spanish and the monetary unit is the **peso uruguayo**.

uruguayo, -a *adj, m, f* Uruguayan

usado, -a *adj* **1.** (*no nuevo*) secondhand; (*sello*) used **2.** (*gastado*) worn; (*expresión*) common, everyday

usanza *f* usage, custom

usar **I.** *vt* **1.** (*utilizar*) **~ algo** to use sth, to make use of sth; (*palabra*) to speak; (*libro*) to consult, to look up; (*ropa, gafas*) to wear; **~ la razón** to reason; **tuve que ~ (de) mis influencias** I had to use all my influence; **de ~ y tirar** disposable; **sin ~** brand new **2.** (*cargo*) to hold; (*oficio*) to discharge **II.** *vr* **1.** (*utilizar*) to use; **esta palabra ya no se usa** this word is no longer in use **2.** (*ropa*) top be in fashion; **los escotes ya no se usan** low necklines are out of fashion

usina *f AmL* (*de gas*) gasworks; (*de electricidad*) power plant

uso *m* **1.** (*utilización*) use; (*gramática*) usage; **~ ilegal** MED illegal use; **de ~ externo** MED for external application; **hacer ~ de algo** to make use of sth; **hacer ~ de la palabra** (*en parla-*

mento, senado) to take the floor, to speak; **una expresión de ~ corriente** an everyday expression; **tener muchos ~s** to have many uses; **en buen ~** *inf* in good condition; **desde que tengo ~ de razón...** since I have been old enough to reason ...; **estar en pleno ~ de sus facultades** to be sound of mind **2.** (*moda*) fashion **3.** (*costumbre*) custom, usage; **métodos al ~** methods; **al ~ francés** French style; **el dedal todavía está en ~** the thimble is still used; **encalar las fachadas está fuera de ~** whitewashing the outside of houses is no longer done

usted *pron* **1.** *sing* you; **~es** you; **tratar de ~ a alguien** to address sb courteously; **gracias – a ~** thank you – you're welcome **2.** *pl, AmL* (*vosotros*) you

usual *adj* **1.** (*de siempre*) usual **2.** (*común*) common **3.** (*tradicional*) customary

usuario, **-a** *m, f t.* INFOR user

usura *f* usury; **pagar con ~ un favor** to pay back a favour *Brit* [*o* favor *Am*] on unequal terms

usurario, **-a** *adj* usurious

usurero, **-a** *m, f* usurer

usurpador(a) **I.** *adj* usurping **II.** *m(f)* usurper

usurpar *vt* to usurp; (*derecho*) to encroach on sth

utensilio *m* utensil; (*herramienta*) tool; **~s de pintor** painter's materials

uterino, **-a** *adj* ANAT, MED uterine; **furor ~** nymphomania; **hermano ~** *a brother born of the same mother*

útero *m* uterus, womb; **el cuello del ~** the cervix

útil **I.** *adj* **1.** (*objeto*) useful, handy **2.** (*persona*) useful; **ser declarado ~** MIL to be fit for military service **3.** (*ayuda*) helpful; **¿en qué puedo serle ~?** can I be of any help to you? **4.** (*inversión*) profitable **II.** *mpl* tools *pl*, implements *pl*

utilidad *f* **1.** *t.* INFOR (*de objeto*) utility; **ser de ~** to be useful **2.** (*de persona*) usefulness **3.** (*de inversión*) profit

utilitario *m* **1.** (*calidad de útil*) utility **2.** (*coche*) small car

utilitario, **-a** *adj* (*edificio*) utilitarian; (*coche, tela*) utility; (*persona, punto de vista*) practical; **pensamiento ~** utilitarian thinking

utilizable *adj* usable; (*terreno*) available; (*restos*) reusable

utilización *f* utilization; (*de un derecho*) application; (*de una persona*) employment

utilizar <z→c> **I.** *vt* to use; (*derecho, hospitalidad*) to avail oneself of sth; (*tiempo, a alguien*) to make use of sth **II.** *vr:* **~se** to be used

utillaje *m* tackle

utopía *f* utopia

utópico, **-a** *adj* utopian

uva *f* grape; **~ pasa** raisin ▶**de ~s a peras** *inf* once in a blue moon; **estar de mala ~** *inf* to be in a bad mood; **tener mala ~** *inf* to be bad-tempered

> It is custumary in Spain on New Year's Eve at exactely twelve seconds to midnight to eat one (white) **uva** (grape) for every **campanada** (chime of the bell), which can be heard on television at intervals of one second. This is supposed to bring good fortune for the coming year.

uve *f* v; **~ doble** w

UVI *f abr de* **Unidad de Vigilancia Intensiva** ICU

úvula *f* ANAT uvula

Uzbekistán *m* Uzbekistan

uzbeko, **-a** *adj, m, f* Uzbek

V

V, **v** *f* V, v; **~ de Valencia** V for Victor

vaca *f* **1.** ZOOL cow; **~ marina** manatee; **~ de San Antón** ladybird *Brit*, ladybug *Am;* **síndrome de las ~s locas** mad cow disease; **~s gordas/flacas** *fig* prosperous/lean period; **ponerse como una ~** to get as fat as a cow [*o* pig] **2.** (*carne*) beef **3.** (*cuero*) cowhide

vacaciones *fpl* holidays *pl Brit*, vacation *Am;* **estar de ~** to be on holiday *Brit*, to be on vacation *Am;* **irse de ~ a Tenerife** to go on holiday to Tenerife; **~ a la sombra** *inf* time served in jail

vacante **I.** *adj* vacant **II.** *f* vacancy; (*puesto*) unfilled post; **cubrir (las) ~s** to fill (the) vacancies

vaciado *m* **1.** (*molde*) cast **2.** (*ahuecamiento*) hollowing out **3.** (*de datos*) extraction of information **4.** INFOR dumping

vaciar <*1. pres:* vacío> *vt* **1.** (*dejar vacío*) to empty; (*con bomba de agua*) to pump out **2.** (*verter*) to pour **3.** (*hueco*) to hollow out **4.** (*escultura*) to cast **5.** (*afilar*) to sharpen **6.** (*información*) to extract **7.** *Col, inf* (*vituperar*) to give a dressing-down

vaciedad *f sin pl* **1.** (*vacío*) emptiness **2.** *fig* silliness

vacilación *f* hesitation; **sin vacilaciones** unhesitatingly

vacilada *f Méx, inf* (*borrachera*) binge, spree; (*chiste*) joke; (*chiste verde*) dirty joke; (*timo*) rip-off; **me dieron una ~** they really ripped me off

vacilante *adj* **1.** (*persona*) hesitant **2.** (*estructura*) unsteady **3.** (*voz*) faltering

vacilar *vi* **1.** (*balancearse: objeto*) to sway; (*borracho*) to stagger; (*llama*) to flicker **2.** (*dudar*) to hesitate **3.** *inf* (*tomar el pelo*) **~ a alguien** to have sb on, to pull sb's leg; **¡no me vaciles!** don't give me that!

vacío *m sin pl* **1.** (*espacio, ausencia*) emptiness; FÍS vacuum; (*hueco*) gap; (*abismo*) void;

~ **legal** gap in the law, legal void; ~ **de poder** political vacuum; **envasado al** ~ vacuum-packed; **hacer el** ~ FÍS to make a vacuum; **hacer el** ~ **a alguien** to give sb the cold shoulder; **la propuesta cayó en el** ~ the proposal fell flat **2.** ANAT side

vacío, **-a** *adj* **1.** (*sin contenido, sin gente*) empty; (*hueco*) hollow; **peso en** ~ unladen weight; **con las manos vacías** emptyhanded; **volver de** ~ *fig* to come back empty-handed **2.** (*insustancial*) insubstantial; (*superficial*) superficial

vacuidad *f sin pl* **1.** (*vacío*) emptiness **2.** (*superficial*) vacuity

vacuna *f* **1.** (*substancia*) vaccine; ~ **anticolérica** cholera vaccine **2.** (*vacunación*) vaccination; **poner una** ~ to vaccinate; ~ **antirrábica** rabies vaccination; **eso te servirá de** ~ *fig* that should teach you a lesson **3.** (*de las vacas*) cowpox

vacunación *f* vaccination; **cartilla de** ~ vaccination certificate

vacunar **I.** *vt* to vaccinate **II.** *vr:* ~**se** to get vaccinated; **se ha vacunado contra la gripe** he/she got vaccinated against flu

vacuno *m* cattle

vacuno, **-a** *adj* cow, bovine; (**carne de**) ~ beef; **ganado** ~ cattle

vacuo, **-a** *adj* vacuous

vade *m* satchel

vadeable *adj* **1.** (*río*) fordable **2.** (*dificultad*) surmountable

vadear *vt* **1.** (*río*) to ford **2.** (*dificultad*) to overcome **3.** (*a pie*) to wade across

vado *m* **1.** (*río*) ford **2.** AUTO ~ **permanente** no parking (garage entrance), keep clear ►**tentar el** ~ to examine possible solutions

vagabundear *vi* **1.** (*vagar*) to wander **2.** (*gandulear*) to lay about **3.** *pey* to be a tramp [*o* bum]

vagabundo, **-a** **I.** *adj* wandering; (*perro*) stray; *fig, pey* vagrant **II.** *m, f* wanderer; *fig* tramp, bum

vagancia *f sin pl* laziness; JUR vagrancy

vagar **I.** <g→gu> *vi* **1.** (*vagabundear*) to wander **2.** (*descansar*) to be idle **II.** *m* leisure, free time

vagido *m* wail

vagina *f* ANAT vagina

vago, **-a** **I.** *adj* **1.** (*perezoso*) lazy **2.** (*impreciso*) vague **3.** (*vagante*) vagrant **II.** *m, f* **1.** (*vagabundo*) tramp **2.** (*holgazán*) layabout, lazybones; **hacer el** ~ to laze [*o* loaf] about

vagón *m* (*de pasajeros*) coach *Brit,* car *Am;* (*de mercancías*) goods wagon *Brit,* freight car *Am;* ~ **de cola** guard's van *Brit,* caboose *Am;* ~ **restaurante** dining car

vaguada *f* watercourse

vaguear *vi* **1.** (*holgazanear*) to laze about **2.** (*vagar*) to wander

vaguedad *f* **1.** (*imprecisión*) vagueness **2.** (*palabras*) vague remark

vaharada *f* **1.** (*aliento*) puff **2.** (*olor*) whiff

vahído *m* dizzy spell; **me dio un** ~ I felt dizzy

vaho *m* **1.** (*vapor*) vapour *Brit,* vapor *Am* **2.** (*aliento*) breath **3.** *pl* inhalation

vaina[1] *f* **1.** (*de la espada*) sheath **2.** BOT pod

vaina[2] *m pey* twit *Brit,* dork *Am*

vainica *f CRi* (*judía verde*) string bean

vainilla *f* vanilla; ~ **azucarada** vanilla sugar

vaivén *m* (*balanceo*) swaying; (*sacudida*) lurch; **los vaivenes de la vida** life's ups and downs

vajilla *f* crockery, dishes *pl*

vale *m* voucher; FIN promissory note; (*pagaré*) IOU *inf*

valedero, **-a** *adj* (*válido*) valid; (*vigente*) in force; **ser** ~ **por seis meses** to be valid for six months

valedor(a) *m(f)* (*que protege*) protector; (*que favorece*) patron

valedura *f Méx* (*favor*) favour *Brit,* favor *Am;* (*protección*) protection; (*ayuda*) help

valencia *f* QUÍM valency

valenciana *f* **1.** *CSur* (*encaje*) fine cotton lace **2.** *Méx* (*del pantalón*) turn-up *Brit,* cuff *Am*

valenciano, **-a** *adj, m, f* Valencian

valentía *f* **1.** (*valor*) bravery **2.** (*hazaña*) brave deed

valentón, **-ona** **I.** *adj pey* boastful **II.** *m, f pey* braggart

valer *irr* **I.** *vt* **1.** (*costar*) to cost **2.** (*equivaler*) to equal **3.** (*producir*) to earn **4.** (*proteger*) to protect ►**valga la <u>expresión</u>** so to speak; **vale tanto <u>oro</u> como pesa** it/he/she is worth its/his/her weight in gold; **<u>hacer</u>** ~ **sus derechos** to assert one's rights; **vale <u>más</u> que te olvides de él** you'd best forget him; **¡vale <u>ya</u>!** that's enough!; **¡vale!** OK! **II.** *vi* **1.** (*ropa*) to be of use **2.** (*tener validez*) to be valid; **no vale** it's no good **3.** (*funcionar*) to be of use; **esta vez no te valdrán tus excusas** your excuses won't help you this time; **no sé para qué vale este trasto** I don't know what this piece of junk is for; **esta vez no hay peros que valgan** this time, no ifs, ands or buts! **4.** (*tener mérito*) to be worthy; **no** ~ **nada** to be worthless; ~ **poco** to be worth little **5.** (*estar permitido*) to be allowed; **¡eso no vale!** that's not allowed!, that's not fair! **III.** *vr:* ~**se** **1.** (*servirse*) to make use; ~**se de los servicios de alguien** to avail oneself of sb's services; ~**se de sus contactos** to take advantage of one's contacts **2.** (*desenvolverse*) to manage; **ya no puede** ~**se** he/she can't fend for him/herself any longer

valeriana *f* valerian

valeroso, **-a** *adj* brave

valía *f sin pl* worth

validar *vt* to validate

validez *f sin pl* validity; **dar** ~ **a algo** to validate sth; **tener** ~ to be valid; (*ley*) to be in force; **no tener** ~ to be invalid; (*ley*) to be inapplicable

válido, **-a** *adj* valid; **no ser** ~ to be invalid

valiente *adj* brave; **¡**~ **amigo tienes!** *irón* a

fine friend you've got!

valija *f* case; (*del cartero*) mailbag; ~ **diplomática** diplomatic bag

valioso, **-a** *adj* valuable

valla *f* **1.** (*tapia*) wall; (*barrera*) barrier; (*alambrada*) fence; (*defensa*) barricade **2.** (*publicitaria*) hoarding *Brit,* billboard *Am* **3.** DEP hurdle

vallado *m* fence

vallar *vt* to fence in; ~ **con un muro** to put a wall around

valle *m* valley; ~ **de lágrimas** vale of tears; **lirio del** ~ (*muguet*) lily-of-the-valley

vallunco, **-a** *adj AmC* **1.** (*rústico*) rustic **2.** (*campesino*) peasant

valona *f Méx* **hacer a alguien la** ~ *inf* to put in a good word for sb

valor *m* **1.** (*valentía*) bravery; ~ **cívico** civil duty; **armarse de** ~ to pluck up courage **2.** (*desvergüenza*) cheek **3.** (*valía*) *t.* COM, MÚS value; (*cuantía*) amount; ~ **nutritivo/alimenticio** nutritional/food value; ~ **adquisitivo** purchasing power; ~ **nominal** face value; ~ **probatorio** JUR value as evidence **4.** (*significado*) meaning; ~ **actual** current meaning **5.** *pl* FIN securities *pl;* **~es bursátiles** stock exchange securities; **~es inmuebles** real estate **6.** *pl* (*ética*) **~es morales** moral principles; **escala de ~es** scale of values

valoración *f* valuation; (*del precio*) value; (*análisis*) assessment

valorar *vt* ~ **en algo** to value at sth; **valoro muchísimo tu generosidad** I greatly appreciate your generosity

valorizar <z→c> *vt v.* **valorar**

vals *m* MÚS waltz

valsar *vi* to waltz

valse *m AmL v.* **vals**

valuar <*1. pres:* valúo> *vt* ~ **en algo** to value at sth

valva *f* valve

válvula *f* ANAT, TÉC valve; ~ **de seguridad** safety valve

vampiresa *f* vamp, femme fatale

vampiro *m* vampire; *fig* bloodsucker

vanagloriarse *vr* to boast

vanaglorioso, **-a** *adj* boastful

vanamente *adv* vainly

vandalismo *m sin pl* vandalism

vándalo, **-a** I. *adj* HIST Vandal II. *m, f* HIST Vandal; *fig* vandal, hooligan

vanguardia *f* **1.** MIL van **2.** (*movimiento*) forefront; LIT avant-garde; **de** ~ ultra-modern

vanguardista I. *adj* ultra-modern II. *mf* ultra-modern individual; *fig* pioneer

vanidad *f* vanity

vanidoso, **-a** *adj* vain

vano *m* ARQUIT space

vano, **-a** *adj* **1.** (*ineficaz*) vain, useless; **en** ~ in vain **2.** (*infundado*) groundless; **es una vana ilusión** it's a mere illusion

vánova *f Arg* bedspread

vapor *m* (*vaho*) vapour *Brit,* vapor *Am;* (*de agua*) steam; (**barco de**) ~ steamer; **cocer al** ~ to steam

vaporizador *m* vaporizer; (*perfume*) atomizer

vaporizar <z→c> I. *vt* **1.** (*evaporar*) to vaporize **2.** (*perfume*) to spray II. *vr:* **~se** to vaporize

vaporizo *m Méx, PRico* **1.** (*vaho*) vapour *Brit,* vapor *Am;* (*para inhalar*) inhalation **2.** (*calor*) sultry heat

vaporoso, **-a** *adj* **1.** (*tela*) light, diaphanous *liter* **2.** (*humeante*) steamy

vapulear *vt* **1.** (*zurrar*) to beat; (*zarandear*) to shake **2.** (*criticar*) to slate *Brit,* to slam *Am*

vapuleo *m* **1.** (*paliza*) beating **2.** (*crítica*) tongue-lashing

vaquería *f AmS* (*explotación*) cattle-rearing; (*lechería*) dairy

vaquero, **-a** I. *adj* cattle II. *m, f* cowherd; (*americano*) cowboy *m,* cowgirl *f*

vaquero(s) *m(pl)* jeans *pl*

vaqueta *f* cowhide

vaquetón, **-ona** *adj Méx* **1.** *inf* (*lento*) sluggish **2.** (*vago*) shiftless **3.** (*descarado*) shameless

vaquilla *f,* **vaquillona** *f Arg, Chile, Nic, Perú* heifer

vara *f* **1.** (*rama*) branch; (*palo*) stick; ~ **mágica** magic wand **2.** (*medida*) ≈ yard (*approximately*) **3.** ADMIN wand (of office); **tener alta** ~ to have authority [*o* influence]; **doblar la** ~ **de la justicia** to pervert the course of justice **4.** TÉC (*bastón de mando*) rod **5.** (*del trombón*) slide **6.** TAUR pike

varadero *m* NÁUT dry dock

varado, **-a** *adj* (*anclado*) stranded

varal *m* long pole; (*de un carro*) shaft

varapalo *m* **1.** (*rapapolvo*) dressing-down; **dar un** ~ **a alguien** to give sb a ticking off **2.** (*golpe*) blow; (*paliza*) beating **3.** (*palo*) stick

varar I. *vi* **1.** (*encallar*) to run aground; *fig* to get bogged down **2.** *AmL* (*coche*) to break down II. *vt* to beach

varear *vt* **1.** (*fruta*) to knock down **2.** (*lana*) to sell by the yard

varejón *m* **1.** *AmS, Nic* (*verdasca*) switch **2.** *Col* BOT type of yucca

variable I. *adj* variable; (*carácter*) changeable II. *f* MAT variable

variación *f* **1.** MAT, MÚS variation **2.** (*cambio*) change; (*oscilación*) oscillation

variado, **-a** *adj* (*no siempre igual*) varied; (*distinto*) mixed, assorted; (*colores*) variegated

variante *f* **1.** (*variedad*) variety; (*versión*) version **2.** (*diferencia*) variation **3.** (*carretera*) bypass **4.** LING variant

variar <*1. pres:* varío> I. *vi* **1.** (*modificarse*) to vary **2.** (*cambiar*) to change; ~ **de comida** to vary one's diet; ~ **de peinado** to change one's hairstyle II. *vt* **1.** (*cambiar*) to change **2.** (*dar variedad*) to vary; **y para ~...** and for a change ...

varicela *f sin pl* MED chickenpox

variedad *f* **1.** (*clase*) variety **2.** (*pluralidad*)

variation; **una gran ~ de ofertas** a wide range of offers **3.** *pl* (*espectáculo*) variety show; **teatro de ~es** music hall ▸**en la ~ está el gusto** *prov* variety is the spice of life
vario, -a *adj pl* **1.** (*diferente*) several; **asuntos ~s** other business **2.** (*algunos*) some; **varias veces** several times
variopinto, -a *adj* **1.** (*diverso*) diverse **2.** (*color*) colourful *Brit,* colorful *Am*
variz *f* MED varicose vein
varón *m* **1.** (*hombre*) male; (*niño*) boy; **santo ~** *fig* extremely kind and patient man **2.** NÁUT rudder chain
varonil *adj* (*hombre*) manly, virile; **voz ~** deep voice; (*mujer*) mannish
Varsovia *f* Warsaw
vasallo, -a *m, f* HIST vassal
vasco, -a **I.** *adj* Basque; **País Vasco** Basque Country **II.** *m, f* Basque
Vascongadas *fpl* Basque Provinces *pl*
vascongado, -a *adj, m, f* Basque
vascuence *m* **1.** (*lengua*) Basque **2.** *inf* (*incomprensible*) Greek
vasectomía *f* MED vasectomy
vaselina® *f* Vaseline®
vasija *f* (*recipiente*) container
vaso *m* **1.** (*recipiente*) glass; **un ~ de agua** a glass of water; **~ de papel** paper cup **2.** ANAT vessel
vástago *m* **1.** BOT shoot **2.** *fig* (*hijo*) scion *liter;* **~s** offspring **3.** TÉC rod
vasto, -a *adj* vast; (*saber*) wide
vate *m* **1.** (*adivino*) seer **2.** *elev* (*poeta*) bard
váter *m* toilet
vaticano, -a *adj* Vatican
Vaticano *m* Vatican; **la Ciudad del ~** the Vatican City
vaticinador(a) *m(f)* prophet
vaticinar *vt* to predict, to prophesy
vaticinio *m* prediction, prophecy
vatio *m* watt; **una bombilla de 100 ~s** a 100-watt bulb
Vd. *pron pers abr de* **usted** you
vda. *abr de* **viuda** widow
Vds. *pron pers abr de* **ustedes** you
V.E. *abr de* **Vuestra Excelencia** Your Excellency
vecinal *adj* local; **camino ~** country road
vecindad *f* neighbourhood *Brit,* neighborhood *Am;* **chisme de ~** neighbours' gossip *Brit,* neighbors' gossip *Am*
vecindario *m* **1.** (*vecindad*) neighbourhood *Brit,* neighborhood *Am;* (*ciudadanos*) neighbours *pl Brit,* neighbors *pl Am;* (*comunidad*) local community **2.** (*padrón*) residence
vecino, -a **I.** *adj* **1.** (*cercano*) **~ de algo** near sth; **pueblo ~** next village **2.** (*parecido*) **~ a algo** similar to sth **II.** *m, f* **1.** (*que vive cerca*) neighbour *Brit,* neighbor *Am* **2.** (*habitante*) inhabitant; **José García, ~ de Villavieja** José García, a Villavieja resident ▸**cada hijo de ~** *inf* anyone
vector *m* vector
veda *f* **1.** (*prohibición*) prohibition; **levantar la ~ de animales de caza** to open the hunting season **2.** (*temporada*) close season
vedado *m* reserve *Brit,* preserve *Am;* **~ de caza** game reserve *Brit,* game preserve *Am;* **cazar/pescar en ~** to poach
vedar *vt* to prohibit, to ban
vedette *f* (music hall) star
vedija *f* (*de lana*) tuft; (*de pelo*) mat
vega *f* **1.** (*de un río*) fertile plain **2.** *Cuba* (*tabacal*) tobacco plantation **3.** *Chile* (*terreno pantanoso*) marshland
vegetación *f* **1.** BOT vegetation **2.** *pl* ANAT adenoids *pl*
vegetal **I.** *adj* plant; **aceite ~** vegetable oil; **carbón ~** charcoal **II.** *m* vegetable
vegetar *vi* **1.** BOT to grow **2.** (*enfermo*) to be like a vegetable **3.** *pey* (*persona*) to vegetate
vegetariano, -a *adj, m, f* vegetarian
vehemencia *f sin pl* **1.** (*ímpetu*) impetuosity **2.** (*entusiasmo*) eagerness **3.** (*fervor*) vehemence
vehemente *adj* **1.** (*impetuoso*) impetuous **2.** (*ardiente*) passionate **3.** (*persona*) forceful
vehículo *m* **1.** (*transporte*) vehicle; **~ de motor** motor vehicle **2.** (*medio*) vehicle; MED carrier
veinte *adj inv* twenty; *v.t.* **ochenta**
veintena *f* (*unidades*) about twenty; **una ~ de personas** about twenty people
veintitantos *adj inv* twenty-odd
vejación *f,* **vejamen** *m* **1.** (*molestia*) annoyance **2.** (*humillación*) humiliation
vejar *vt* **1.** (*molestar*) to annoy **2.** (*humillar*) to humiliate
vejatorio, -a *adj* **1.** (*molesto*) annoying **2.** (*humillante*) humiliating
vejestorio, -a *m, f pey* old crock [*o* geezer]
vejete *m inf* old-timer
vejez *f sin pl* **1.** (*ancianidad*) old age; **pasar su ~ en Mallorca** to spend one's old age in Mallorca **2.** (*envejecimiento*) ageing *Brit,* aging *Am* ▸**a la ~, viruelas** *prov* there's no fool like an old fool *prov*
vejiga *f* **1.** ANAT bladder **2.** (*ampolla*) blister
vela *f* **1.** NÁUT sail; **~ cuadra** squaresail; **~ mayor** mainsail; **alzar ~s** to raise the sails; *fig* to prepare to depart; **a toda ~** at full sail; *fig* energetically; **ser un aficionado a la ~** to be a sailing enthusiast; **recoger ~s** *fig* to back down **2.** (*luz*) candle; **se está acabando la ~** the candle is coming to an end; **derecho como una ~** *fig* straight as a ramrod ▸**poner una ~ a San Miguel y otra al diablo** to have a foot in both camps; **¿a ti quién te ha dado ~ en este entierro?** who gave you any say in this matter?; **pasar la noche en ~** to have a sleepless night; **estar a dos ~s** to be broke
velación *f* wake, vigil
velada *f* evening gathering; LIT, MÚS, TEAT soirée
velador *m* **1.** (*mesita*) pedestal table **2.** (*candelero*) candlestick
veladora *f AmL* (*vela*) candlestick

V

velamen *m* NÁUT canvas

velar I. *vi* 1. (*no dormir*) to stay awake; (*trabajar*) to work late 2. (*cuidar*) ~ **por algo** to watch over sth; ~ **bien por sus intereses** to look after one's interests II. *vt* 1. (*vigilar*) to keep watch over; ~ **al enfermo** to sit up with an ill person; ~ **a un muerto** to hold a wake 2. (*ocultar*) to hide; (*tapar*) to veil III. *vr:* ~**se** (*ocultarse*) to hide; (*foto*) to blur

velatorio *m* wake, vigil

veleidad *f* (*inconstancia*) fickleness; (*capricho*) whim

veleidoso, -a *adj* (*inconstante*) fickle; (*caprichoso*) capricious

velero *m* NÁUT sailing ship

veleta[1] *f* (*para el viento*) weather vane, weathercock *Brit*

veleta[2] *mf* (*persona*) changeable person; **ser un** ~ to blow hot and cold

veliz *m Méx* (*de cuero*) valise; (*de metal*) case

vello *m sin pl* 1. (*corporal*) (body) hair; ~ **de las axilas** hair under the armpits 2. BOT, ZOOL down, fuzz

vellón *m* (*piel*) fleece

velloso, -a *adj* BOT, ZOOL downy; (*corporal*) hairy

velludo, -a *adj* hairy

velo *m* 1. (*tela, prenda*) veil; **correr un (tupido)** ~ **sobre** *fig* to draw a veil over; **descorrer el** ~ **sobre** to reveal; **tomar el** ~ to take the veil 2. ANAT ~ **del paladar** soft palate

velocidad *f* 1. *t.* FÍS, INFOR speed; ~ **de crucero** cruising speed; ~ **de obturación** FOTO shutter speed; ~ **de transmisión de datos** INFOR data transfer rate; **exceso de** ~ speeding; **a gran** ~ at high speed; **a toda** ~ at full speed 2. (*marcha*) gear; **cambio de** ~**es** gearchange

velocímetro *m* speedometer

velódromo *m* cycle track

velón *m* (*lámpara*) oil lamp

velorio *m* 1. (*velatorio*) wake, vigil 2. (*fiesta*) party

veloz *adj* swift; **raudo y** ~ in a flash

vena *f* 1. ANAT vein; ~ **yugular** jugular vein 2. BOT vein 3. (*filón*) lode; ~ **de agua** underground stream 4. (*inspiración*) talent 5. *inf* (*disposición*) mood; **dar la** ~ **a alguien** to take it into one's head

venablo *m* javelin; **echar** ~**s** *fig* to explode in anger

venado *m* 1. (*ciervo*) deer 2. (*carne*) venison 3. (*caza mayor*) big game

venal *adj* 1. ANAT venous 2. (*vendible*) saleable *Brit,* salable *Am* 3. (*sobornable*) corrupt

venalidad *f sin pl* corruptness

vencedor(a) I. *adj* winning; **equipo** ~ winning team II. *m(f)* winner

vencejo *m* swift

vencer <c→z> I. *vi* 1. (*ganar*) to win 2. (*plazo*) to expire II. *vt* 1. (*ganar*) to win; (*enemigos*) to defeat; **¡no te dejes ~!** don't let them beat you! 2. (*obstáculo, sueño*) to overcome; (*dificultad*) to get round; **me venció el sueño** sleep overcame me 3. (*bajo peso*) to break ►**a la tercera va la vencida** *prov* third time lucky III. *vr:* ~**se** to collapse

vencimiento *m* COM expiry

venda *f* MED bandage; **tener una** ~ **en los ojos** to have a bandage over one's eyes; *fig* to be blinkered; **caérse a uno la** ~ **de los ojos** to see the truth

vendaje *m* bandaging

vendar *vt* to bandage

vendaval *m* (*viento*) strong wind; (*huracán*) hurricane

vendedor(a) *m(f)* seller; (*comerciante*) salesman *m,* saleswoman *f;* ~ **ambulante** hawker; ~ **a domicilio** door-to-door salesman

vender I. *vt* to sell II. *vr:* ~**se** 1. COM to sell, to be for sale; **se vende** for sale; ~**se al por menor/mayor** to sell (at) retail/wholesale; **se ha vendido todo** everything has been sold; ~**se muy caro** *fig* to play hard to get 2. (*persona*) to give oneself away; **estar vendido** *inf* to be in a real fix

vendible *adj* saleable *Brit,* salable *Am*

vendimia *f* grape harvest

vendimiar *vi* to harvest grapes

Venecia *f* Venice

veneciano, -a *adj, m, f* Venetian

veneno *m* poison

venenoso, -a *adj* poisonous; **serpiente venenosa** poisonous snake

venera *f* 1. (*concha*) scallop shell 2. (*insignia*) scallop, *decoration worn by knights;* **no se te cae la** ~ *fig* it's not going to kill you

venerable *adj* venerable

veneración *f sin pl* (*adoración*) worship; (*respeto*) veneration

venerar *vt* 1. (*adorar*) to worship 2. (*respetar*) to venerate

venéreo, -a *adj* MED venereal

venero *m* 1. (*manantial*) spring; *t. fig* source 2. (*yacimiento*) lode

venezolano, -a *adj, m, f* Venezuelan

Venezuela *f* Venezuela

> **Venezuela** (official title: **República de Venezuela**) borders both the Caribbean Sea and the Atlantic Ocean to the north, Guyana to the east, Brazil to the south and Colombia to the west. The capital is **Caracas**. Spanish is the official language of the country and the monetary unit is the **bolívar**.

vengador(a) I. *adj* (*que se venga*) avenging; (*propenso a*) vindictive II. *m(f)* avenger

venganza *f* vengeance; **deseo de** ~ thirst for vengeance

vengar <g→gu> I. *vt* to avenge; ~ **la muerte de alguien** to avenge sb's death II. *vr:* ~**se** to take revenge

vengativo, -a *adj* 1. (*vengador*) avenging 2. (*rencoroso*) vindictive, vengeful

venia *f sin pl, elev* permission

venial *adj* (*pecado*) venial
venida *f* **1.** (*llegada*) arrival; (*vuelta*) return **2.** (*de un río*) floodwater
venidero, **-a** *adj* future; **en años venideros** in years to come
venir *irr* **I.** *vi* **1.** (*trasladarse*) to come; (*llegar*) to arrive; **vengo (a) por la leche** I've come to fetch the milk **2.** (*ocurrir*) to happen; **vino la guerra** the war came **3.** (*proceder*) to come; **el dinero me viene de mi padre** I inherited the money from my father; ~ **de una familia muy rica** to come from a very rich family **4.** (*idea, ganas*) to come; **me vinieron ganas de reír** I felt like laughing; **no sé por qué me vino eso a la memoria** I don't know why that came to my mind **5.** (*tiempo*) to come; (*seguir*) to follow; **el mes que viene** next month; **ya viene la primavera** spring is on its way **6.** (*figurar*) to appear; **no viene en la guía** it's not in the guide **7.** (*prenda*) to suit **8.** (*aproximadamente*) **vienen a ser unas 3000 pesetas para cada uno** it works out at about 3000 pesetas each **9.** *elev* (*servir para*) **aquel suceso vino a turbar nuestra tranquilidad** that event served to destroy our peace **10.** (*terminar por*) **vino a dar con sus huesos en la cárcel** *inf* he/she ended up in jail; **viene a querer decir que...** it amounts to saying that ... **11.** (*persistir*) to keep on; **ya te lo vengo advirtiendo hace mucho tiempo** I've been warning you for a long time ▸**el dinero me viene muy bien** the money comes in very handy; **¿te viene bien mañana después de comer?** would tomorrow after lunch suit you?; **el que venga detrás, que arree** every man for himself; **me viene mal darte la clase por la tarde** teaching you in the afternoon doesn't suit me; **es una familia venida a menos** that family has come down in the world; **a mí eso ni me va ni me viene** to me that's neither here nor there; **¿a qué viene ahora hacerme esos reproches?** why reproach me like that now? **II.** *vr:* **~se 1.** (*volver*) to come back **2.** (*hundirse*) **~se abajo** to collapse; *fig* to fail
venoso, **-a** *adj* venous
venta *f* **1.** COM sale; ~ **callejera** street sale; ~ **a domicilio** door-to-door selling; ~ **al contado** cash sale; ~ **al por menor/mayor** retail/wholesale; ~ **por catálogo** mail order; ~ **a plazos** hire purchase; **precio de ~ al público** retail price; **volumen de ~s** sales volume; **en ~** for sale; **estar a la [*o* en] ~** to be for sale; **poner a la [*o* en] ~** to put sth up for sale **2.** (*posada*) inn
ventaja *f t.* DEP advantage; ~ **competitiva** competitive advantage; **sacar ~ de la debilidad del contrincante** to take advantage of the opponent's weakness; **tener ~ sobre alguien** to have an advantage over sb; **dar 300 metros de ~** to give 300 metres start *Brit,* to give 300 meters head start *Am*
ventajista **I.** *adj* unscrupulous **II.** *mf* unscrupulous individual
ventajoso, **-a** *adj* advantageous; (*negocio*) profitable
ventana *f* **1.** (*abertura*) window; ~ **corrediza** sliding window; ~ **de doble cristal** double-glazed window; ~ **de guillotina** sash window **2.** ANAT ~ **de la nariz** nostril ▸**echar la casa por la ~** to go to great expense
ventanal *m* large window
ventanilla *f* **1.** (*ventana*) small window; (*de coche*) side window; **sobre con ~** window envelope **2.** (*taquilla*) ticket office **3.** (*mostrador*) counter
ventear **I.** *vt* **1.** (*olfatear*) to sniff; *fig* to pry into **2.** (*airear*) to air **II.** *vi fig* to poke about **III.** *vimpers* **ventea** it's windy
ventilación *f* ventilation
ventilador *m* **1.** (*aparato*) fan **2.** (*conducto*) ventilator (shaft)
ventilar **I.** *vt* **1.** (*airear*) to ventilate **2.** (*resolver*) to clear up **II.** *vr:* **~se** (*persona*) to get some air
ventisca *f* blizzard
ventisquero *m* snowdrift
ventolera *f* **1.** (*viento*) gust of wind; **le ha dado la ~ de...** *fig* he/she has taken it into his/her head to ... **2.** (*juguete*) windmill
ventosa *f* **1.** (*objeto*) suction cup, sucker **2.** ZOOL sucker **3.** (*abertura*) vent
ventosear *vi* to break wind
ventosidad *f* fart
ventoso, **-a** *adj* windy; (*persona*) flatulent
ventral *adj* ventral
ventrículo *m* ANAT ventricle
ventrílocuo, **-a** *m, f* ventriloquist
ventrudo, **-a** *adj* pot-bellied
ventura *f* (good) fortune; **mala ~** ill luck; **a la (buena) ~** with no fixed plan; **echar la buena ~ a alguien** to tell sb's fortune; **por ~** fortunately; **probar ~** to try one's luck ▸**viene ~ a quien la procura** *prov* God helps those who help themselves
venturero, **-a** **I.** *adj* **1.** (*casual*) casual **2.** (*irregular*) irregular **II.** *m, f* wanderer
venturoso, **-a** *adj* fortunate
veo-veo *m* **jugar al ~** to play I-spy
ver *irr* **I.** *vi, vt* **1.** (*con los ojos*) to see; **no se ve ni torta** you can't see a thing; **véase la página dos** see page two; **¡que se vean los forzudos!** let's see what you're made of!; **lo nunca visto** something unheard of; **¡habráse visto!** did you ever!; **como vimos ayer en la conferencia** as we saw in the lecture yesterday; **no veas lo contenta que se puso** you should have seen how happy she was; **si no lo veo, no lo creo** if I hadn't seen it with my own eyes, I wouldn't have believed it; **a ~** let's see **2.** (*con la inteligencia*) to see, to understand; **a mi modo de ~** as I see it; **¿no ves que...?** don't you see that ...?; **quiero hacerte ~ esto** I want you to understand this; **veo bien que te cases** I approve of your getting married; **ya lo veo** I can see that; **bueno, ya ~emos** well,

V

we'll see **3.** (*observar*) to watch; (*documentos, información*) to examine **4.** (*visitar*) to see; (*encontrarse*) to meet; **es de** ~ *inf* you can see that **5.** (*comprobar*) to check **6.** (*algo desagradable*) to see; **te veo venir** *fig* I know what you're up to; **veo que hoy me tocará a mí** I can see that it'll be my turn today; **~ás como al final te engaña** he/she will trick you in the end, you'll see **7.** JUR (*causa*) to hear **8.** (*relación*) **tener que ~ con alguien/algo** to have to do with sb/sth **9.** (*duda*) **eso está por ~** that remains to be seen; **estoy por ~ si me dan el crédito** I'll have to see if they give me credit; **habrá que ~ si eso es verdad** it remains to be seen whether that's true **10.** (*intentar*) **~é de hablarle** I'll try to speak to him/her ►**tengo un hambre/un sueño que no veo** I'm really tired/hungry; **no haberlas visto nunca más gordas** to never have been in such a spot; **si te he visto, no me acuerdo** out of sight, out of mind *prov;* **no veas la que se armó allí** there was a tremendous row; **¡hay que ~!** it just goes to show!; **hay que ~ lo tranquilo que es Pedro** Pedro is such a quiet fellow; **¡vamos a ~!** let's see!; **¡a ~, escuchadme todos!** come on, listen to me everybody!; **a ~, venga** come on, hurry up; **a ~ cómo lo hacemos** let's see how we can do this; **¡para que veas!** so there!; **luego ya ~emos** we'll see about that later; **~emos,...** let me see, ...; **veamos,...** let me see, ...; **¡~ás!** just you wait! **II.** *vr:* **~se 1.** (*encontrarse*) to meet **2.** (*estado*) to be; **~se apurado** to be in a jam; **se ve enfermo** he thinks he's ill; **~se negro** to be in a fix; **~se pobre** to feel poor **3.** (*imaginarse*) to imagine; **me lo estoy viendo de médico** I can just see him as a doctor **4.** (*parecer*) **se ve que no tienen tiempo** it seems they have no time **5.** *AmL* (*tener aspecto*) to look **III.** *m* **1.** (*aspecto*) appearance; **tener buen ~** to be good-looking **2.** (*opinión*) opinion; **a mi ~** in my view

vera *f* **1.** (*orilla*) bank; **~ de un río** river bank **2.** (*lado*) edge; **a la ~ de** beside

veracidad *f* truthfulness; (*de una declaración*) veracity

veraneante *mf* holidaymaker *Brit,* vacationer *Am*

veranear *vi* **~ en Ibiza** to spend the summer in Ibiza

veraneo *m* summer holiday *Brit,* summer vacation *Am;* **lugar de ~** holiday resort *Brit,* vacation spot *Am;* **estar de ~** to be on one's summer holiday

veraniego, -a *adj* summer

veranillo *m* **~ de San Miguel** [*o* **de San Juan** *AmL*] Indian summer

verano *m* summer

veras *fpl* **de ~** (*de verdad*) really; (*en serio*) in earnest; **esto va de ~** this is serious

veraz *adj* **1.** (*hechos*) true **2.** (*persona*) truthful

verbal *adj* **1.** (*del verbo*) verbal; **frase ~** verb phrase **2.** (*oral*) oral

verbalizar <z→c> *vt* (*expresar*) to verbalize

verbena *f* **1.** (*fiesta*) street party **2.** BOT verbena

verbigracia *adv* for example

verbo *m* **1.** (*expresa acción*) verb; **~ auxiliar** auxiliary verb **2.** (*palabra*) curse

verborrea *f,* **verbosidad** *f* **1.** (*locuacidad*) verbosity; *pey* verbal diarrhoea **2.** (*palabras*) verbiage

verboso, -a *adj* verbose

verdad *f* truth; **una ~ a medias** a half truth; **a la ~** in truth; **bien es ~ que...** it is certainly true that ...; **bueno, a decir ~, ...** well, to tell you the truth, ...; **¡de ~!** really!; **¡es ~!** it's true!; **faltar a la ~** to be untruthful; **hay una parte de ~ en esto** there's some truth in this; **la ~ lisa y llana** the plain and simple truth; **pues la ~, no lo sé** I don't know, to tell you the truth; **si bien es ~ que...** although it's true that ...; **un héroe de ~** a real hero; **¿~?** isn't it?, aren't you?; **¿~ que no fuiste tú?** it wasn't you, was it?; **la ~ es que hace frío** it certainly is cold ►**~ de Perogrullo** truism; **~es como puños** self-evident truths; **decir cuatro ~es a alguien** to give sb a piece of one's mind; **la ~, toda la ~, y nada más que la ~** the truth, the whole truth, and nothing but the truth

verdaderamente *adv* truly

verdadero, -a *adj* **1.** (*cierto*) true **2.** (*real*) real **3.** (*persona*) truthful

verde **I.** *adj* **1.** (*color*) *t.* POL green; **~ oliva** olive-green **2.** (*fruta*) unripe, green; (*leña*) green **3.** (*chistes, canciones*) dirty **4.** (*personas*) randy; **viejo ~** *inf* dirty old man ►**estar ~ de envidia** to be green with envy; **poner ~ a alguien** to have a go at sb *Brit,* to badmouth sb *Am* **II.** *m* **1.** (*color*) green **2.** (*hierba*) green grass; (*pienso*) green fodder **3.** (*del árbol*) foliage **4.** *inf* (*billete*) thousand-peseta note **5.** *CSur* (*pasto*) pasture **6.** *CSur* (*mate*) maté **7.** *CSur* (*ensalada*) salad **8.** *AmC, Méx* (*campo*) countryside

verdear *vi* **1.** (*mostrarse verde*) to look green **2.** (*tirar a verde*) to be greenish **3.** (*ponerse verde*) to turn green **4.** *CSur* (*beber*) to drink maté

verdecer *irr como crecer vi* to turn green

verderón *m* greenfinch

verdín *m* **1.** (*del cobre*) verdigris **2.** (*verde*) fresh green **3.** (*musgo*) moss

verdor *m* **1.** (*verde*) greenness, verdure *form* **2.** BOT lushness **3.** (*juventud*) youth

verdoso, -a *adj* greenish

verdugo *m* **1.** (*de ejecuciones*) executioner **2.** (*tirano*) slave driver; (*atormentador*) tormentor **3.** (*tormento*) torment **4.** (*látigo*) lash **5.** (*hematoma*) weal **6.** BOT shoot **7.** (*gorro*) balaklava

verdugón *m* **1.** (*hematoma*) weal **2.** BOT shoot

verdulera *f pey* fishwife

verdulero, -a *m, f* greengrocer

verdura *f* **1.** (*hortalizas*) vegetable, greens *pl* **2.** (*verdor*) greenness **3.** (*obscenidad*) smuttiness

verdusco, -a *adj* dark green

vereda *f* **1.** (*sendero*) path **2.** *AmL* (*acera*) pavement *Brit,* sidewalk *Am* ►**entrar en** ~ to start to lead an orderly life; **hacer entrar en ~ a alguien** to make sb toe the line; **ir por la** ~ to do the right thing

veredicto *m* JUR verdict; ~ **de culpabilidad/inculpabilidad** guilty/not guilty verdict

verga *f* **1.** (*vara*) rod **2.** *vulg* (*pene*) cock

vergajo *m* **1.** (*verga del toro*) pizzle **2.** *vulg* (*pene*) cock **3.** (*látigo*) whip **4.** *And, vulg* (*canalla*) bastard, son of a bitch

vergel *m elev* orchard

vergonzante *adj* **1.** (*acción*) shameful **2.** (*persona*) shamefaced

vergonzoso, -a *adj* **1.** (*persona*) bashful; (*tímido*) shy **2.** (*acción*) disgraceful

vergüenza *f* **1.** (*rubor*) shame; **se me cae la cara de** ~ I feel so ashamed; **me da ~...** I'm ashamed to ...; **¿no te da ~?** aren't you ashamed?; **pasar** ~ to feel embarrassed; **¡qué ~!** shame on you!; **tener poca** ~ to have no shame, to be shameless; **pasar ~ ajena** to be embarrassed for sb else **2.** (*pundonor*) shyness; **perder la** ~ to lose one's shyness **3.** (*persona, acción*) timidity; (*escándalo*) disgrace; **sacar a alguien a la** ~ (**pública**) to disgrace sb publicly **4.** (*cortedad*) modesty; (*sexual*) (sexual) shame; **le da ~ al hablar** he/she is embarrassed to speak **5.** *pl* ANAT private parts *pl*

vericueto *m* rough terrain

verídico, -a *adj* **1.** (*verdadero*) true **2.** (*muy probable*) credible **3.** (*sincero*) truthful

verificación *f* **1.** (*inspección*) inspection **2.** (*prueba*) testing **3.** (*realización*) realization **4.** (*de una profecía*) fulfilment *Brit,* fulfillment *Am*

verificar <c→qu> **I.** *vt* **1.** (*comprobar*) to check **2.** (*controlar*) to verify **3.** (*realizar*) to carry out; (*ceremonia*) to perform **II.** *vr:* **~se 1.** (*acto solemne*) to be held **2.** (*una profecía*) to come true; (*deseos*) to be fulfilled; (*temores*) to be realized

verja *f* (*rejas*) grating; (*cerca*) grille; (*puerta*) iron gate

vermú *m,* **vermut** *m* <vermús> **1.** (*licor*) vermouth **2.** *And, CSur* TEAT early performance

vernáculo, -a *adj* vernacular; **lengua vernácula** vernacular

vero *m* sable

verónica *f* TAUR *a type of pass with the cape*

verosímil *adj* **1.** (*probable*) likely **2.** (*creíble*) credible

verosimilitud *f* likelihood

verraco *m* **1.** (*para procrear*) boar **2.** *AmC, CSur* (*jabalí*) wild boar

verraquera *f inf* **1.** (*llanto*) crying spell **2.** *AmC, Col* (*borrachera*) drunken bout

verruga *f* wart; *fig* defect

verrugoso, -a *adj* warty

versado, -a *adj* ~ **en algo** expert in sth

versal I. *adj* **letra** ~ capital letter **II.** *f* capital

versalita TIPO **I.** *adj* **letra** ~ small capital letter **II.** *f* small capital

versar *vi* **1.** (*tratar*) ~ **sobre algo** to deal with sth; **la conferencia ~á sobre las vacunas** the lecture is about vaccines **2.** (*dar vueltas*) to turn, to go round **3.** *AmC* (*escribir*) to versify **4.** *AmC* (*charlar*) to chat **5.** *Méx* (*bromear*) to crack jokes

versátil *adj* **1.** (*persona*) versatile **2.** (*que se dobla*) flexible

versatilidad *f* **1.** (*inconstancia*) changeableness **2.** (*flexibilidad*) versatility

versículo *m* REL verse

versificar <c→qu> **I.** *vt* to put into verse **II.** *vi* to write verses

versión *f* **1.** (*interpretación*) version; (*descripción*) account; ~ **resumida** abridged version **2.** (*traducción*) translation **3.** CINE ~ **original** in the original language

verso *m* **1.** (*palabras*) line; **en** ~ in verse **2.** (*género*) verse **3.** (*poema*) poem

vértebra *f* ANAT vertebra

vertebrado *m* vertebrate

vertebral *adj* vertebral; **columna** ~ spinal column

vertedero *m* (*escombrero*) rubbish tip *Brit,* garbage dump *Am*

verter <e→ie> **I.** *vt* **1.** (*vaciar*) to empty; (*líquido*) to pour; (*sin querer*) to spill; (*basura*) to dump; ~ **el café en las tazas** to pour the coffee into the cups **2.** (*traducir*) to translate **3.** (*ideas, conceptos*) to transfer **II.** *vi* to flow

vertical *adj, f* vertical

vértice *m* vertex

vertiente *f* **1.** (*declive*) slope; (*lado*) side **2.** (*punto de vista*) perspective **3.** *And, CSur, Méx* (*fuente*) fountain

vertiginoso, -a *adj* **1.** (*que marea*) giddy **2.** (*velocidad*) excessive

vértigo *m* **1.** (*mareo*) dizziness; (*por las alturas*) vertigo; **causar ~(s)** to cause dizziness; **de** ~ *inf* (*jaleo*) tremendous; (*increíble*) extraordinary; (*fantástico*) wonderful; (*velocidad*) giddy **2.** (*desmayo*) fainting fit **3.** (*frenesí*) frenzy; (*locura*) fit of madness

vesania *f* **1.** (*locura*) rage **2.** (*ira*) fury

vesícula *f* ANAT vesicle; (*en la epidermis*) blister; ~ **biliar** gall bladder

vespa® *f* motor scooter

vespasiana *f Arg, Chile* public toilet

vespertino, -a *adj* evening, crepuscular *liter*

vespino® *m* moped

vestíbulo *m* (*de un piso*) hall; (*de un hotel*) lobby; TEAT foyer; (*atrio*) atrium

vestido *m* **1.** (*prenda*) item of clothing; (*de mujer*) dress **2.** (*ropa*) clothing; ~ **de etiqueta** [*o* **noche**] evening [*o* formal] dress

vestidor *m* dressing room

vestidura *f* **1.** *elev* (*ropa*) apparel **2.** *pl* REL vestments *pl* ►**rasgarse las ~s** to make a great show of being shocked

V

vestigio *m* **1.** (*huella*) vestige **2.** (*señal*) trace
vestimenta *f* clothing
vestir *irr como pedir* **I.** *vt* **1.** (*cuerpo, persona*) to dress; ~ **de algo** to dress in sth; (*estatua*) to cover in sth; (*pared*) to hang with sth; (*adornar*) to adorn with sth; **estar vestido de pirata** (*disfrazado*) to be dressed as a pirate; ~ **a alguien con un abrigo** to dress sb in a coat **2.** (*llevar*) to wear; (*ponerse*) to put on **3.** (*confeccionar*) to make; **¿qué sastre le viste?** which tailor makes your clothes? **4.** (*expresión*) ~ **el rostro de seriedad** to put on a serious expression ►**vísteme despacio que tengo prisa** *prov* make haste slowly **II.** *vi* to dress; ~ **de blanco** to dress in white; ~ **de uniforme** to wear a uniform; ~ **siempre muy bien** to always be very well-dressed; **de** ~ (*elegante*) formal; (*para una ocasión*) for special occasions; ~ **mucho** to be dressy ►**el mismo que viste y calza** the self-same **III.** *vr:* ~**se 1.** (*la ropa*) to get dressed; (*cubrirse*) to cover oneself; ~**se a la moda** to dress according to fashion; ~**se de azul** to dress in blue; **los árboles se visten de verde** the trees are coming out in leaf; **los campos se visten de blanco** the fields are turning white with snow; ~**se en Milán** (*comprar*) to buy one's clothes in Milan **2.** (*estado de ánimo*) ~**se de cierta actitud** to adopt a certain attitude; ~**se de severidad** to adopt a severe tone
vestón *m Chile* (*chaqueta*) jacket
vestuario *m* **1.** (*conjunto*) clothes *pl;* (*de una misma person*) wardrobe **2.** (*lugar*) TEAT dressing room; DEP changing room
veta *f* **1.** MIN seam **2.** (*en madera*) grain; (*en mármol*) vein
vetar *vt* to veto
vetarro, -a *adj Méx, inf* old; **ya estan muy** ~**s** they're getting on a bit
vetazo *m Ecua* whiplash
vetear *vt* **1.** (*como la madera*) to grain **2.** (*como el mármol*) to streak
veterano *m* MIL veteran
veterano, -a I. *adj* **1.** MIL veteran **2.** (*experimentado*) experienced **II.** *m, f* **1.** MIL veteran **2.** (*experto*) old hand
veterinaria *f sin pl* veterinary science
veterinario, -a *m, f* vet *inf,* veterinary surgeon *Brit,* veterinarian *Am*
veto *m* veto; (**inter**)**poner** (**su**) ~ **a algo** to veto sth
vetusto, -a *adj elev* **1.** (*persona*) venerable **2.** (*cosa*) very old; *pey* ancient
vez *f* **1.** (*acto repetido*) time; **a la** ~ at the same time; **a veces** sometimes; **alguna que otra** ~ ocasionally; **cada** ~ **me gusta menos** I like him/it less and less; **cada** ~ **que...** each time that ...; **de una** ~ (*en un solo acto*) in one go; (*sin interrupción*) without a break; (*definitivamente*) once and for all; **de** ~ **en cuando** from time to time; **dilo otra** ~ say it again; **acabemos de una** ~ let's get it over with; **por primera** ~ for the first time; **aquella** ~ on that occasion; **esta** ~ this time; **alguna** ~ sometimes; **muchas veces** many times; **¿cuántas veces ...?** how many times ...?, how often ...?; **repetidas veces** over and over again; **otra** ~ **será** it'll have to wait for another occasion; **pocas veces, rara** ~ seldom; **tal** ~ perhaps; **una y otra** ~ time and time again; **de una** ~ **por todas** once and for all; **una** ~ **que haya terminado, ...** once it is over, ...; **érase una** ~**...** once upon a time ... **2.** (*con número*) time; **una** ~ once; **dos veces** twice; **una y mil veces** a thousand times; **3 veces 9** MAT 3 times 9; **dos veces más que** twice as much as; **por enésima** ~ for the umpteenth time **3.** (*turno*) **cuando llegue mi** ~**...** when it's my turn ...; **él a su** ~ **no respondió** he didn't reply in his turn; **en** ~ **de** instead of; **hacer las veces de alguien** to take sb's place; **ceder la** ~ **en una cola** to give up one's place in a queue *Brit* [*o* line *Am*] ►**una** ~ **al año no hace daño** *prov* once won't do any harm
vía *f* **1.** (*camino*) road; (*calle*) street; ~ **aérea** (*correos*) airmail; ~ **láctea** Milky Way; ~ **pública** public thoroughfare; **por** ~ **aérea** by air; (*correos*) by air mail; **¡**~ **libre!** make way!; **la tradición está en** ~**s de recuperación** the tradition is being recovered **2.** (*ruta*) via; **a Madrid** ~ **París** to Madrid via Paris **3.** (*carril*) line; FERRO track; ~ **férrea** railway *Brit,* railroad *Am;* **por** ~ **férrea** by rail; ~ **muerta** siding; **de** ~ **estrecha** narrow gauge; *fig* narrow-minded; **de** ~ **única** single track **4.** ANAT passage; ~**s digestivas** digestive tract; ~**s respiratorias** breathing passage; ~**s urinarias** urinary tract; **por** ~ **oral** by mouth **5.** (*procedimiento*) proceedings *pl;* **por** ~ **judicial** by legal means **6.** INFOR track
viable *adj* viable
vía crucis *m inv* Stations *pl* of the Cross; *fig* terrible ordeal
viada *f And* speed
viaducto *m* viaduct
viajante *mf* travelling salesman *Brit,* traveling salesman *Am;* COM commercial traveller *Brit,* commercial traveler *Am*
viajar *vi* to travel; ~ **por Italia** to travel round Italy; ~ **en avión** to travel by plane
viaje *m* **1.** (*general*) travel; **estar de** ~ to be away (on a trip); **irse de** ~ to go on a trip; ~ **de negocios** business trip; ~ **de novios** honeymoon; ~ **organizado** package tour; ~ **de ida** outgoing trip; ~ **de ida y vuelta** return trip *Brit,* round trip *Am;* **cheque de** ~ traveller's cheque *Brit,* traveler's check *Am;* **¡buen** ~**!** bon voyage!, have a good trip! **2.** (*carga*) load; (*recorrido*) trip; **un** ~ **de leña** a load of firewood; **hacer la mudanza en cinco** ~**s** to move house in five trips; **de un** ~ *AmC, fig* in one go **3.** *inf* (*drogas*) trip
viajero, -a I. *adj* travelling *Brit,* traveling *Am;* ZOOL migratory; **ave viajera** migratory bird **II.** *m, f* traveller *Brit,* traveler *Am;* (*pasajero*) passenger; ~ **diario** commuter

vial I. *adj* (*caminos*) road; FERRO rail; **circulación** ~ road traffic; **fluidez** ~ traffic flow; **reglamento** ~ rules of the road II. *m* avenue
vianda *f elev* (*alimento*) provisions *pl;* (*comida*) food
viandante *mf* (*peatón*) pedestrian, passer-by
viaraza *f AmL* (*rapto de ira*) fit of rage; **me dio la** ~ I just felt like it
viático *m* 1. REL viaticum 2. (*subvención*) travel allowance
víbora *f* 1. ZOOL viper 2. *pey* (*persona*) snake; **lengua de** ~ *fig* venomous tongue; **nido de ~s** *fig* nest of vipers
viborear *vi* 1. *AmL, inf* (*murmurar*) to backbite 2. *CSur* (*serpentear*) to snake, to twist and turn
vibración *f* 1. (*vaivén*) vibration 2. (*sentimiento*) vibe *inf,* vibration; **ese tío me da buenas/malas vibraciones** that guy gives me good/bad vibes
vibrador *m* vibrator
vibrante *adj* 1. (*sonoro*) resonant 2. (*entusiasta*) vibrant; (*emoción*) quivering
vibrar I. *vi* 1. (*oscilar*) to vibrate 2. (*voz*) to quiver II. *vt* (*agitar*) to shake
vicario *m* vicar
vicedirector(a) *m(f)* 1. COM deputy manager 2. ENS deputy head teacher *Brit,* vice principal *Am*
vicenal *adj* 1. (*que dura*) lasting 20 years 2. (*que se repite*) occurring every 20 years
vicepresidente, -a *m, f* POL vice-president; (*en juntas*) vice-chairperson
vicerrector(a) *m(f)* UNIV vice-chancellor *Brit,* vice-president *Am*
vicetiple *f* chorus girl
viceversa *adv* vice versa
vichar *vt Arg, Urug* 1. (*espiar*) to spy on 2. (*ver*) to peep at 3. (*buscar con la mirada*) to look around for
viciado, -a *adj* (*aire*) stuffy
viciar I. *vt* 1. (*falsear*) to falsify; (*deformar*) to distort 2. (*anular*) to invalidate II. *vr:* **~se** 1. (*costumbres*) to deteriorate; (*persona*) to get a bad habit 2. (*ser adicto*) **~se con algo** to become addicted to sth; **~se con la televisión** to get hooked on television 3. (*deformarse*) to warp; (*romperse*) to break
vicio *m* 1. (*mala costumbre*) bad habit; **el ~ de siempre** the same old bad habit; **hacer algo por** ~ to do sth for the hell of it; **tener el ~ de comerse las uñas** to have the bad habit of biting one's nails 2. (*adicción*) vice; **no poder quitarse el ~ de fumar** to be unable to kick the smoking habit 3. (*objeto*) defect 4. JUR (*error*) flaw 5. (*capricho*) whim; **quejarse de** ~ to complain out of sheer habit 6. BOT **tener mucho** ~ to grow abundantly
vicioso, -a I. *adj* 1. (*carácter*) dissolute 2. (*que produce vicio*) habit-forming 3. (*defecto*) defective 4. (*consentido*) spoilt 5. BOT luxuriant II. *m, f* **en lo que respecta a la bebida es un** ~ he drinks too much
vicisitud *f* 1. (*acontecimiento*) important event; (*desgracia*) mishap 2. (*cambio*) change 3. *pl* (*alternancia*) ups *pl* and downs
víctima *f* victim; (*afectado*) person affected; **ser ~ de un fraude** to be the victim of fraud; **no hubo que lamentar ~s** fortunately there were no casualties; ~ **propiciatoria** scapegoat
victimar *vt AmL* 1. (*herir*) to injure 2. (*matar*) to kill
victimario, -a *m, f* 1. (*el que daña*) victimizer 2. *AmL* (*el que mata*) killer, murderer
victoria *f* victory; ~ **por puntos** victory on points; **cantar** ~ to count one's chickens
victorioso, -a *adj* victorious
vid *f* (*parra*) (grape)vine
vida *f* 1. (*existencia, actividad*) life; ~ **íntima** private life; ~ **perra** dog's life; **amargar la ~ a alguien** to make sb's life miserable; (**grape**)**¿cómo te va la ~?** how's life treating you?; **complicarse la** ~ to make life difficult for oneself; **costo de la** ~ cost of living; **dar ~ a** TEAT, CINE to portray; (*animar*) to enliven; **dejarse la ~ en algo** to dedicate one's life to sth; **esperanza de** ~ life expectancy; **estar aún con** ~ to still be alive; **este material es de corta** ~ this material doesn't last; **hacer ~ marital** to live together; **llevar una ~ miserable** to lead a wretched existence; **me va la ~ en este asunto** this is a matter of life or death for me; **partir de esta** ~ to depart this life; **pasar a mejor** ~ to pass away; **pasarse la ~ haciendo algo** to spend one's life doing sth; **perder la** ~ to lose one's life; **¿qué es de tu ~?** what have you been up to lately?; **quitar la ~ a alguien** to take sb's life; **quitarse la** ~ to take one's own life; **salir con** ~ to survive; **tener siete ~s** to have the nine lives of a cat; **tren de** ~ lifestyle 2. (*sustento*) livelihood; **buscarse la** ~ to get by on one's own 3. (*biografía*) life; **de toda la** ~ all my life; **la ~ y milagros de alguien** sb's life story; **la otra** ~ afterlife 4. (*placer*) pleasure; **este sol es** ~ this sun is a delight 5. (*alegría*) joy 6. (*cariño*) **¡mi ~!** my darling! 7. (*prostituta*) **mujer de la** ~ prostitute; **hacer la** ~ *inf* to be on the game ►**estar entre la ~ y la muerte** to be fighting for one's life; (*a punto de morir*) to be at death's door; **darse la ~ padre** to live the life of Riley; **hacer por la** ~ *inf* to eat; **de por** ~ for life; **¡en ~!** not on your life!
videncia *f* clairvoyance
vidente *mf* (*que ve*) sighted person; (*que adivina*) clairvoyant
vídeo *m* 1. (*aparato*) video (cassette) recorder, VCR *Am;* **cámara de** ~ video camera; **editar en** ~ to edit on video; **grabar en** ~ to record on video 2. (*película*) video
videocámara *f* video camera
videocasete *m* videocassette
videoclip *m* music video
videoconferencia *f* INFOR video conference
videojuego *m* video game
videoteléfono *m* videophone

V

videotexto *m* teletext

vidorria *f* 1. *Chile, RíoPl* (*vida fácil*) easy life 2. *Col, PRico, Ven* (*vida dura*) dog's life

vidriado *m* 1. (*barniz*) glaze 2. (*loza*) (piece of) glazed pottery

vidriar I. *vt* (*loza*) to glaze II. *vr:* ~**se** (*hacerse transparente*) to become clear

vidriera *f* 1. (*ventana*) stained-glass window; **puerta** ~ glazed door 2. *AmL* (*escaparate*) shop window

vidriero, **-a** *m, f* glazier

vidrio *m* 1. (*material*) glass; ~ **de color** coloured glass *Brit,* colored glass *Am;* **¡~!** (*frágil*) fragile – handle with care 2. (*placa*) sheet of glass; (*de una ventana*) window pane 3. (*objeto*) piece of glassware; (*productos*) glassware ►**pagar los ~s rotos** *inf* to carry the can *Brit,* to take the rap *Am*

vidrioso, **-a** *adj* 1. (*como vidrio*) glassy; (*mirada*) glazed 2. (*transparente*) like glass; **ojos ~s** glassy eyes 3. (*frágil*) fragile 4. (*superficie*) slippery 5. (*persona*) easily discouraged 6. (*asunto*) delicate

vidurria *f Arg, inf* (*vidorra*) life of leisure

viejales *m inv, inf* old boy *Brit,* old coot *Brit*

viejera *f PRico* 1. (*vejez*) old age 2. (*cosa inservible*) old piece of junk

viejo, **-a** I. *adj* old; (*usado*) used; (*gastado*) worn-out; **hacerse** ~ to grow [*o* get] old; **Noche Vieja** New year's Eve ►**tan ~ como Canalillo** *inf* as old as Moses II. *m, f* old man *m,* old woman *f;* **mi** ~ my old man; **mi vieja** my old lady; **mis ~s** *AmL* (*padres*) my folks, my parents

Viena *f* Vienna

vienés, **-esa** *adj, m, f* Viennese

viento *m* 1. (*corriente*) wind; **~s alisios** trade winds; ~ **ascendente** rising wind; ~ **de cola** tail wind; ~ **de frente** head wind; ~ **huracanado** hurricane; **instrumento de** ~ wind instrument; **hace** ~ it's windy; **como el** ~ like the wind; **corre un poquito de** ~ there's a slight breeze; **un pequeño soplo de** ~ a gentle breeze; **estar lleno de** ~ (*vacío*) to be full of (hot) air; (*vanidoso*) to be vain 2. NÁUT (*rumbo*) course; (*dirección*) direction; **a los cuatro ~s** in all directions; **pregonar algo a los cuatro ~s** to shout sth from the rooftops 3. *inf* (*irse*) **tomar** ~ to be off; **¡vete a tomar ~!** *inf* get lost! 4. (*olor*) scent; (*olfato*) sense of smell; **me da el ~ que...** I have a feeling that ... 5. *AmC* MED flatulence ►**contra ~ y marea** against all odds, come hell or high water; **el negocio va ~ en popa** business is going well; **quien siembra ~s, recoge tempestades** *prov* sow the wind and reap the whirlwind *prov;* **echar a alguien con ~ fresco** to tell sb to get lost; **corren malos ~s para...** it's a bad time for ...; **beber los ~s por algo** to crazy about sth

vientre *m* 1. (*abdomen*) abdomen; **hacer de** ~ to have a bowel movement 2. (*barriga*) belly; **danza del** ~ belly-dancing 3. (*matriz*) womb

viernes *m inv* Friday; **Viernes Santo** Good Friday; *v.t.* **lunes** ►**la semana que no tenga ~** when pigs fly

vietnamita *adj, mf* Vietnamese

viga *f* (*de madera*) beam; (*de metal*) girder

vigencia *f* validity; **estar en** ~ to be valid; **entrar en** ~ to come into effect; **perder** ~ to become invalid

vigente *adj* valid

vigésimo, **-a** *adj* twentieth; *v.t.* **octavo**

vigía[1] *f* watchtower

vigía[2] *mf* lookout

vigilancia *f* 1. (*cuidado*) vigilance 2. (*observación*) surveillance; (*servicio*) security service; **tener a alguien bajo** ~ to have sb under surveillance

vigilante I. *adj* (*despierto*) awake; (*en alerta*) alert II. *mf* 1. (*guardián*) guard; (*de cárcel*) warder *Brit,* warden; (*en tienda*) night watchman; (*en museo*) attendant; ~ **nocturno** night watchman; ~ **de seguridad** security guard 2. *CSur* (*policía*) policeman *m,* policewoman *f*

vigilar I. *vt* to guard; (*niños*) to watch II. *vi* ~ **por algo** to keep watch over sth

vigilia *f* 1. (*no dormir*) wakefulness 2. (*falta de sueño*) insomnia 3. (*víspera*) vigil 4. (*sin comer*) abstinence; (*comida*) meal without meat; **día de** ~ day of abstinence; **comer de** ~ to eat without meat 5. (*en el trabajo*) late-night work

vigor *m* 1. (*fuerza*) vigour *Brit,* vigor *Am;* (*energía*) energy; **con** ~ vigorously; **sin** ~ without vigour *Brit* [*o* vigor *Am*] 2. (*vitalidad*) vitality; (*empuje*) drive 3. (*vigencia*) validity; **entrar en** ~ to come into effect; **poner en** ~ to bring into effect

vigorizar <z→c> *vt* 1. (*fortalecer*) to strengthen 2. (*revitalizar*) to invigorate 3. (*animar*) to encourage

vigoroso, **-a** *adj* 1. (*fuerte*) vigorous; (*resistente*) tough 2. (*animado*) lively; (*vital*) energetic 3. (*protesta*) strong

viguería *f* (*de madera*) beams *pl;* (*de metal*) girderwork

vigués, **-esa** I. *adj* of/from Vigo II. *m, f* native/inhabitant of Vigo

vigueta *f* tie-beam

VIH *m sin pl abr de* **virus de inmunodeficiencia humana** HIV

vil *adj* (*malo*) vile; (*bajo*) base; (*infame*) despicable

vileza *f* 1. (*cualidad*) vileness 2. (*acción*) vile act

vilipendiar *vt* 1. (*despreciar*) to revile; (*tratar*) to humiliate 2. (*insultar*) to vilify

villa *f* 1. HIST (*población*) town 2. (*casa*) villa

Villadiego *m* **tomar las de** ~ *inf* to take to one's heels

villancico *m* ~ (**de Navidad**) (Christmas) carol

villanía *f* 1. (*bajeza*) vile act 2. (*expresión*) obscenity

villano, **-a** I. *adj* 1. (*bajo*) villainous 2. (*rús-*

tico) HIST peasant; (*expresión*) obscene **II.** *m, f* **1.** *pey* (*grosero*) rogue **2.** HIST villein; (*campesino*) peasant

villorrio *m pey, inf* one-horse town

vilo *adv* **en ~** suspended; *fig* in suspense; **tener en ~** to keep in suspense; **estar en ~** to be up in the air

vinagre *m* **1.** (*condimento*) vinegar **2.** (*persona*) disagreeable person

vinagrera *f* **1.** (*recipiente*) vinegar bottle **2.** *pl* (*para la mesa*) cruet set **3.** *AmL* (*ardor*) indigestion

vinagreta *f* vinaigrette

vincha *f AmS* (*cinta*) hairband

vinchuca *f Arg, Chile, Par* ZOOL barbeiro, assassin bug

vinculación *f* link

vincular *vt* **1.** (*ligar*) to link; (*unir*) to join; **~ a** [*o* **con**] **algo** to link to sth **2.** (*obligar*) to bind

vínculo *m* **1.** (*unión*) tie; **el ~ conyugal** the bond of matrimony; **~s familiares** family ties; **~s naturales** blood relations; **los ~s con el extranjero** links with foreign countries **2.** (*obligación*) bond

vindicación *f* **1.** (*venganza*) vengeance **2.** (*justificación*) vindication **3.** (*reivindicación*) claim

vindicar <c→qu> *vt* **1.** (*vengar*) to avenge **2.** (*justificar*) to vindicate **3.** (*reivindicar*) to claim

vinería *f And, CSur* (*vinatería*) wineshop

vinícola **I.** *adj* wine; (*cultivo*) wine-growing **II.** *mf* wine-grower

vinicultor(a) *m(f)* wine producer

vinicultura *f* wine production

vino *m* **1.** wine; **~ rosado** rosé wine; **~ tinto** red wine; **~ caliente** hot punch; **~ de mesa** table wine; **~ de Jerez** sherry; **~ generoso** full-bodied wine; **~ de la casa** house wine; **~ de Oporto** port; **~ espumoso** [*o* **de aguja**] sparkling wine; **~ peleón** cheap wine, plonk *Brit* **2.** (*recepción*) reception; **~ de honor** reception ►**echar agua al ~** to tone things down; **tener buen ~** to hold one's drink well; **tiene mal ~** he/she can't hold his/her drink

viña *f* **1.** (*monte*) vineyard **2.** (*planta*) vine ►**de todo hay en la ~ del Señor** *prov* it takes all sorts to make a world; **ser una ~** to be useful; **tener una ~ con algo** to have a goldmine in sth

viñador(a) *m(f)* vineyard worker

viñatero, -a *m, f Arg, Perú* winegrower

viñedo *m* **1.** (*monte*) vineyard **2.** (*planta*) vine

viola *f* **1.** MÚS viola **2.** BOT violet

violáceo, -a *adj* purplish

violación *f* **1.** (*infracción*) violation; (*de una ley*) breaking; **~ de contrato** breach of contract **2.** (*de una mujer*) rape **3.** (*invasión*) invasion

violado, -a *adj* (*color*) violet

violar *vt* **1.** (*mujer*) to rape **2.** (*ley, principio, sepultura*) to violate; (*contrato*) to break

violencia *f* **1.** (*condición*) violence; (*fuerza*) force; **no ~** non-violence; **con ~** by force; **sin ~** peacefully **2.** (*acción*) violent action

violentar **I.** *vt* **1.** (*obligar*) to force; (*sexualmente*) to assault **2.** (*una casa*) to break into; (*un banco*) to rob **3.** (*principio*) to break **4.** (*al interpretar*) to distort **II.** *vr:* **~se** (*obligarse*) to force oneself

violento, -a *adj* **1.** (*impetuoso*) impetuous; (*esfuerzo*) violent; (*discusión*) heated; (*temperamento*) fiery **2.** (*brutal*) aggressive; (*con violencia*) violent; **acto ~** act of violence **3.** (*persona*) violent **4.** (*postura*) unnatural **5.** (*acto*) embarrassing; (*cohibido*) embarrassed; (*duro*) difficult; **me es muy ~ tener que aceptarlo** I'm embarrassed to have to accept it; **me resulta ~ decirle que no** I find it very hard to say no to him/her **6.** (*tergiversado*) distorted **7.** *AmL* (*de repente*) suddenly

violeta *adj, f* violet

violín *m* MÚS violin, fiddle *inf*

violinista *mf* violinist

violón *m* MÚS double bass ►**tocar el ~** to talk nonsense

violoncelista *mf* MÚS cellist

violonc(h)elo *m* MÚS cello

vip, VIP *m abr de* **Very Important Person** VIP; **sala ~** VIP lounge

Viracocha *m And* **1.** (*dios inca*) *Incan god of creation* **2.** (*apelativo de conquistadores*) conquistador (*name applied to the Spanish conquistadors by the Incans*)

viraje *m* **1.** (*giro*) turn; (*curva*) bend; **~ en horquilla** hairpin bend; **hacer** [*o* **dar**] **un ~** to swerve **2.** (*cambio*) switch; (*de opinión*) shift; (*de dirección*) change **3.** NÁUT tack

virar **I.** *vi* **1.** (*girar*) to turn; (*curva*) to bend; **~ en redondo** *t. fig* to retrace one's steps; **el coche viró a la izquierda** the car swerved to the left **2.** (*cambiar*) to switch, to change; (*de opinión*) to shift **3.** NÁUT to tack **II.** *vt* (*girar*) to turn

virgen **I.** *adj* virgin; *fig* pure; (*cinta*) blank; (*tierras*) virgin **II.** *f* REL **la Virgen** the Virgin; **la Santísima Virgen María** the Blessed Virgin Mary; **¡Santísima Virgen!** *inf* my goodness! ►**ser de la Virgen del puño** *inf* to be tight-fisted; **aparecérsele a uno la Virgen** *inf* to hit the jackpot; **ser un viva la Virgen** *inf* to be happy-go-lucky

virginal *adj* (*inmaculado*) virginal; (*puro*) pure

virginidad *f sin pl* virginity

Virgo *m* Virgo

viril *adj* **1.** (*masculino*) virile; **edad ~** adulthood **2.** (*enérgico*) vigorous

virilidad *f sin pl* **1.** (*masculinidad*) virility **2.** (*energía*) vigour *Brit,* vigor *Am* **3.** (*potencia*) strength **4.** (*edad*) adulthood

viringo, -a *adj Col* (*sin ropa*) naked; (*sin piel*) skinned; (*sin pelo*) hairless

virola *f* ferrule

virrey, -reina *m, f* viceroy *m,* vicereine *f*

virtual *adj* virtual

V

virtud *f* **1.** (*en las personas*) virtue; **en ~ de** by virtue of **2.** (*poder*) power; **tener la ~ de aliviar** to bring relief
virtuoso, **-a** *adj* **1.** (*con gran habilidad*) virtuoso **2.** (*lleno de virtudes*) virtuous
viruela *f* MED **1.** (*enfermedad*) smallpox; **~ loca** scarlet fever **2.** (*pústula*) pustule; **picado de ~s** pockmarked; **señales de (la) ~** marks of smallpox
virulento, **-a** *adj* **1.** MED virulent **2.** (*maligno*) infected
virus *m inv* MED, INFOR virus
viruta *f* shaving; **un ~s** *irón* (*carpintero*) a carpenter; **echando ~s** *inf* very fast
vis *f* **~ cómica** comic effect
visa *m o f AmL,* **visado** *m* visa; **~ de entrada/de salida** entry/exit visa
visaje *m* (*mueca*) (funny) face; **hacer ~s** to make [*o* pull] faces
visar *vt* (*pasaporte*) to put a visa in
vísceras *fpl* entrails *pl,* viscera *pl*
viscosa *f* QUÍM viscose
viscosidad *f* **1.** (*consistencia*) thickness **2.** (*mucosidad*) viscosity
viscoso, **-a** *adj* **1.** (*espeso*) thick **2.** (*glutinoso*) viscous; (*blando*) soft
visera *f* **1.** HIST, MIL visor **2.** (*de una gorra*) peak
visibilidad *f* (*cualidad*) visibility
visible *adj* **1.** (*perceptible*) visible **2.** (*obvio*) clear **3.** (*persona*) striking **4.** *inf* (*presentable*) presentable
visillo *m* net curtain
visión *f* **1.** (*vista*) sight, vision; **perder la ~ de un ojo** to lose the sight in one eye **2.** (*aparición*) vision; **ver visiones** *fig* to be seeing things; **me quedé (como) viendo visiones** *fig* I was stunned **3.** (*punto de vista*) view; **~ de conjunto** overview; **~ del mundo** view of the world **4.** *pey, inf* (*mamarracho*) sight; **ir hecho una ~** to look a sight
visionario, **-a** **I.** *adj* **1.** (*con imaginación*) visionary **2.** (*adivinatorio*) prophetic **3.** (*soñador*) idealistic, dreamy *pej* **II.** *m, f* **1.** (*con imaginación*) vision **2.** (*adivinador*) prophet **3.** (*soñador*) idealist; *pey* dreamer
visita *f* **1.** (*visitante*) visitor **2.** (*acción*) visit; **~ del médico** doctor's call; **~ de médico** *fig* flying visit; **~ guiada** guided tour; **~ oficial** POL official visit; **estar de ~ en casa de alguien** to be staying with sb; **ir de ~** to go visiting; **rendir ~ a alguien** to pay sb a visit; **tener (a alguien de) ~** to have visitors
visitante **I.** *adj* visiting; **comisión ~** visiting commission **II.** *mf* visitor
visitar *vt* **1.** (*ir a ver*) to visit **2.** MED to call (on)
vislumbrar *vt* (*ver*) to make out, to distinguish
vislumbre *f* **1.** (*resplandor*) glimmer **2.** (*idea*) sign
viso *m* **1.** (*resplandor*) glow; (*irisación*) sheen; **hacer ~s** to be irridescent **2.** (*aspecto*) sign; **esto tiene ~s de no acabar nunca** this shows no sign of ever ending; **tiene ~s de llover** it looks like rain
visón *m* mink
visor *m* **1.** MIL sights *pl;* **~ de luz infrarroja** infrared sights **2.** FOTO (*cámara*) viewfinder; (*para diapositivas*) slide viewer
víspera *f* (*noche anterior*) night before, eve; (*día anterior*) day before; **en ~s de** just before; **estar en ~s de hacer algo** to be on the point of doing sth
vista *f* **1.** (*visión*) sight, vision; **tener la ~ cansada** to have eye strain; (*mirada*) look; **~ de lince** eyes like a hawk; **aguzar la ~** to keep one's eyes skinned *Brit* [*o* peeled *Am*]; **al alcance de la ~** within view; **fuera del alcance de la ~** out of sight; **a la ~** (*al parecer*) from what can be seen; (*visible*) visible; (*previsible*) in full view; **a la ~ de todos** in full view of everyone; **a la ~ está** anyone can see that; **alzar/bajar la ~** to look up/down; **apartar la ~** to look away; **no apartar la ~ de alguien** not to take one's eyes off sb; **no perder de ~ a alguien/algo** not to lose sight of sb/sth; **a primera ~** at first sight; **a simple ~** just by looking; *fig* superficially; **comerse a alguien con la ~** to devour sb with one's eyes; **con la ~ puesta en algo** with one's sights set on sth; **con ~s a...** with a view to ...; **corto de ~** short-sighted; **dejar vagar la ~** to let one's eyes wander; **dirigir la ~ a algo** to look towards sth; **a Paco no hay quien le eche la ~ encima** Paco's nowhere to be seen; **de ~** by sight; **en ~ de que...** in view of ...; **está a la ~ quién va a ganar** it's obvious who's going to win; **¡fuera de mi ~!** get out of my sight!; **¡hasta la ~!** see you!; **hasta donde alcanza la ~** as far as the eye can see; **se me nubló la ~** my eyes clouded over; **no perder de ~** not to lose sight of; **pagadero a la ~** COM due on demand; **perder de ~** to lose sight of; **quedar a la ~** to remain in sight; **saltar a la ~** to be patently obvious; **tener buena ~** to have good eyesight; **volver la ~ (atrás)** to look back **2.** (*panorama*) view; **~ panorámica** panoramic view; (*mirador*) viewpoint; **con ~s al mar** with sea views, overlooking the sea **3.** (*imagen, perspectiva*) image; FOTO picture; **~ aérea** aerial view; ARQUIT perspective; **~ general** overall view **4.** (*aspecto*) appearance; **tener buena ~** to look good **5.** JUR hearing; **~ oral** hearing ► **~ de pájaro** bird's-eye view; **ver algo a ~ de pájaro** to have a bird's-eye view of sth; **hacer la ~ gorda** to turn a blind eye; **tener ~** to be shrewd
vistazo *m* look; **de un ~** at a glance; **echar [*o* dar] un ~ a algo** to have a (quick) look at sth
visto, **-a** **I.** *pp de* **ver** **II.** *adj* **1.** (*poco original*) common; **está muy ~** that's been seen before, that's old hat **2.** (*obvio*) **está ~ que no puede ser de otra forma** it's clear that things can't be otherwise **3.** JUR **~ para sentencia** conclusion of the trial ► **nunca ~** unknown; (*inaudito*) unheard of; **el pastel desapareció ~ y no ~** the cake disappeared in a flash; **por**

lo ~ apparently III. *conj* ~ **que...** since ...
visto bueno *m* ADMIN, JUR approval; **dar el ~ a algo** to give sth the go-ahead
vistoso, -a *adj* (*atractivo*) colourful *Brit,* colorful *Am;* (*llamativo*) striking; (*hermoso*) attractive
visual I. *adj* visual; **campo ~** field of vision II. *f* line of sight
visualización *f* visualization; (*display*) *t.* INFOR visual display
visualizador *m* INFOR display (screen)
visualizar <z→c> *vt* 1. (*representar*) to visualize 2. *AmL* (*divisar*) to make out 3. INFOR to display
vital *adj* 1. *t.* MED vital; **constantes ~es** vital signs, basic functions; **fuerza ~** life force 2. (*necesario*) essential 3. (*vivaz*) lively
vitalicio, -a *adj* ADMIN, FIN life; **renta vitalicia** life pension; **seguro ~** life insurance
vitalidad *f sin pl* 1. (*alegría de vivir*) vitality 2. (*importancia*) vital importance
vitalizar <z→c> *vt* 1. (*vivificar*) to revitalize 2. (*fortalecer*) to strengthen
vitamina *f* vitamin; **pobre/rico en ~s** low/rich in vitamins
vitaminar *vt* to enrich with vitamins
vitícola *adj* vine growing
viticultor(a) *m(f)* vine grower
viticultura *f* viticulture
vítor *m* cheer, hurrah; **prorrumpir en ~es** to cheer
vitorear *vt* to cheer
vitoriano, -a I. *adj* of/from Vitoria II. *m, f* native/inhabitant of Vitoria
vítreo, -a *adj* 1. (*de vidrio*) glass 2. (*similar al vidrio*) vitreous; (*vidrioso*) glassy
vitrina *f* glass cabinet; *AmL* (*escaparate*) shop window
vituallas *fpl* MIL provisions *pl,* victuals *pl liter*
vituperable *adj* 1. (*inmoral*) reproachable 2. (*censurable*) reprehensible 3. (*despreciable*) despicable
vituperación *f* 1. (*reprobación*) condemnation 2. (*censura*) censure 3. (*injuria*) vituperation *liter*
vituperar *vt* 1. (*reprobar*) to condemn 2. (*censurar*) to censure 3. (*injuriar*) **~ a alguien** to vituperate against sb
vituperio *m* 1. (*censura*) criticism 2. (*injuria*) vituperation *liter*
viudedad *f* 1. (*viudez*) widowhood 2. (*pensión: de viuda*) widow's pension; (*de viudo*) widower's pension
viudez *f* widowhood
viudo, -a I. *adj* widowed; **quedarse ~** to be widowed II. *m, f* widower *m,* widow *f*
viva I. *interj* hurray!; **¡~ el rey!** long live the King!; **¡~n los novios!** three cheers for the bride and groom! II. *m* cheer; **dar ~s a alguien** to cheer sb; **recibir con ~s** to welcome with cheers
vivacidad *f sin pl* 1. (*viveza*) vivacity 2. (*energía*) vigour *Brit,* vigor *Am* 3. (*agilidad*) liveliness 4. (*agudeza*) sharpness
vivales *m inv, inf* wide boy, punk *Am*
vivar I. *m* 1. (*conejera*) warren 2. (*criadero*) nursery, breeding place; (*de peces*) hatchery II. *vt AmL* (*vitorear*) to cheer
vivaracho, -a *adj* 1. (*vivo*) vivacious 2. (*despierto*) bright
vivaz *adj* 1. BOT perennial 2. (*vivaracho*) vivacious 3. (*enérgico*) lively 4. (*despierto*) bright
vivencia *f* experience
víveres *mpl* provisions *pl;* MIL supplies *pl*
vivero *m* 1. (*de plantas*) nursery 2. (*de peces*) hatchery; (*en un restaurante*) holding tank
viveza *f* 1. (*celeridad*) swiftness; (*agilidad*) liveliness 2. (*energía*) vigour *Brit,* vigor *Am* 3. (*agudeza*) sharpness 4. (*de colores*) brightness
vívido, -a *adj* vivid
vivienda *f* 1. (*residencia*) residence; (*casa*) house; (*piso*) flat *Brit,* apartment *Am;* **sin ~** homeless; **el problema de la ~** the housing problem 2. *AmL* (*modo de vida*) way of life
viviente *adj* living; **seres ~s** living beings; **ni alma ~** *fig* not a living soul; **todo bicho ~** every living creature
vivificar <c→qu> *vt* 1. (*vitalizar*) to revitalize 2. (*animar*) to invigorate
vivir I. *vi* 1. (*estar vivo*) to be alive; **~ al día** to live from day to day; **~ a lo grande** to live it up; **~ como un rey** to live like a lord; **~ de rentas** to live off the rent; **¡~ para ver!** (*asombro*) who would believe it!, live and learn; **no dejar ~ a alguien** not to leave sb alone; **no ~ de preocupación** to be worried to death; **¿quién vive?** MIL who goes there? 2. (*habitar*) to live 3. (*durar*) to last; (*perdurar*) to live on II. *vt* to live; **~ su (propia) vida** to live one's own life III. *m* life; (*modo de vida*) way of life; **gente de mal ~** (*vicio*) dissolute characters; (*delincuencia*) shady characters
vivo *m* 1. (*borde*) edge, trim 2. (*tira*) strip
vivo, -a *adj* 1. (*viviente*) alive; **cal viva** quicklime; **ser ~** living being; **a fuego ~** GASTR on a high heat; **a lo ~** vividly; **al rojo ~** red-hot; **en ~** MÚS live; **estar ~** to be alive; **tener el ~ deseo de que** +*subj* to really hope that; **herir en lo más ~** to cut to the quick; **ser la viva imagen de alguien** to be the spitting image of sb; **~ o muerto** dead or alive 2. (*vivaz*) lively 3. (*enérgico*) vigorous; **de genio ~** quick-tempered 4. (*color*) bright 5. (*actual*) current; (*presente*) present; (*duradero*) lasting 6. (*vívido*) vivid 7. (*avispado*) sharp; *pey* crafty
vizcaíno, -a I. *adj* of/from Biscay II. *m, f* native/inhabitant of Biscay
Vizcaya *f* Biscay
V.O. *abr de* **versión original** original version
vocablo *m* word, term
vocabulario *m* 1. (*léxico*) vocabulary; **~ especializado** technical vocabulary; **tener un buen ~** to have a wide vocabulary 2. (*lista*) vocabulary (list)
vocación *f* vocation; **~ artística** artistic

vocation; **por** ~ from a sense of vocation; **sentir** ~ to feel an inclination; **tener** ~ to have a calling

vocal[1] I. *adj* MÚS vocal II. *f* LING vowel

vocal[2] *mf* 1. (*de consejo, tribunal*) member 2. (*portavoz*) spokesperson, spokesman *m,* spokeswoman *f*

vocalizar <z→c> *vt* to vocalize

voceador(a) I. *adj* shouting II. *m(f)* 1. (*pregonero*) town crier 2. *AmL* (*de periódicos*) news hawker

vocear I. *vi* to shout II. *vt* 1. (*manifestar*) to express 2. (*llamar*) to call 3. (*pregonar*) to cry 4. (*divulgar*) to spread 5. (*aclamar*) to acclaim 6. (*presumir*) ~ **algo** to boast of sth

vocerío *m* (*griterío*) clamour *Brit,* clamor *Am*

vocero, -a *m, f AmL* (*portavoz*) spokesperson, spokesman *m,* spokeswoman *f*

vociferar I. *vi* to yell II. *vt* 1. (*gritar*) to shout 2. *pey* (*proclamar*) to shout from the rooftops

vocinglero, -a *adj pey* loudmouthed; **ser** ~ to be a loudmouth

vodka *m o f* vodka

vol. *abr de* **volumen** vol.

volado, -a *adj* 1. ARQUIT projecting 2. *inf* (*loco*) crazy 3. TIPO superior 4. *AmL* (*ausente*) absent-minded; (*enamorado*) lovesick 5. *CSur* ~ **de genio** *inf* quick-tempered 6. (*inquieto*) uneasy

volador(a) *adj* flying

voladura *f* blowing-up

volandas *fpl* **en** ~ (*en el aire*) up in the air; (*deprisa*) in a rush; **llevar en** ~ to carry shoulder-high

volandero, -a *adj* 1. (*volantón*) fledgling 2. (*móvil*) loose 3. *fig* (*inquieto*) fickle

volante I. *adj* (*móvil*) flying; **rueda** ~ band wheel; **platillo** ~ flying saucer II. *m* 1. AUTO steering wheel; **ir al** ~ to be at the wheel; **ponerse al** ~ to take the wheel 2. TÉC flywheel; (*manual*) handwheel 3. (*del reloj*) balance wheel 4. (*adorno*) flounce 5. (*escrito*) leaflet 6. MED referral note 7. DEP shuttlecock 8. *AmL* (*conductor*) racing driver; DEP winger

volantón *m* 1. (*sedal*) fishing line 2. *AmL* (*cometa*) kite 3. *AmL* (*voltereta*) somersault; (*acrobacia*) acrobatics *pl*

volar <o→ue> I. *vi* 1. (*en el aire*) to fly; **echar a** ~ to fly off; **el tiempo vuela** time flies; **las malas noticias vuelan** bad news travels fast, no news is good news 2. (*desaparecer*) to disappear; **el dinero ha volado** the money has vanished 3. (*apresurarse*) to dash; **¡voy volando!** I'm on my way!; ~ **a hacer algo** to rush off to do sth 4. *inf* (*con drogas*) to be high II. *vt* 1. (*hacer explotar*) to blow up 2. (*enfadar*) to drive mad 3. (*hacer volar*) to fly; (*ave*) to frighten off; **hacer** ~ **una cometa** to fly a kite 4. TIPO to write in superscript III. *vr:* ~**se** 1. (*huir*) to run away 2. (*desaparecer*) to vanish 3. *AmL* (*enfadarse*) to get mad 4. (*hacer novillos*) to bunk off (school) *Brit,* to play hooky *Am*

volatería *f* (*pájaros*) fowl *pl*

volátil I. *adj* 1. (*volador*) flying 2. QUÍM volatile 3. (*inconstante*) unpredictable II. *m* poultry

volatilizar <z→c> *vt, vr:* ~**se** QUÍM to volatilize

volcán *m* 1. GEO volcano; **un** ~ **activo/inactivo** an active/dormant volcano; **ser un** ~ **de pasión** *fig* to be afire with passion 2. *AmL, fig* (*montón*) loads *pl*

volcánico, -a *adj* 1. GEO volcanic 2. (*ardiente*) fiery

volcar *irr* I. *vi* (*tumbarse*) to overturn; (*barco*) to capsize II. *vt* 1. (*hacer caer*) to knock over; (*verter*) to spill 2. (*dar la vuelta*) to turn over III. *vr:* ~**se** 1. (*darse la vuelta*) to overturn; (*caer*) to get knocked over; (*dar una voltereta*) to turn a somersault 2. (*esforzarse*) to make an effort; ~**se en** [*o* **con**] **alguien** to be extremely kind to sb; ~**se en algo** to throw oneself into sth

volea *f v.* **voleo**

volear I. *vi, vt* (*dep*) to volley II. *vt* (*semillas*) scatter

voleibol *m* DEP volleyball

voleiplaya *m* DEP beach volleyball

voleo *m* DEP volley; **a** ~ on the volley; *fig* at random

volován *m* vol-au-vent

volquete *m* dumper [*o* tip] truck *Brit,* dump truck *Am*

voltaje *m* voltage

voltario, -a *adj Chile* 1. (*gastador*) spendthrift; (*dadivoso*) generous 2. (*obstinado*) self-willed

volteado *m Méx, inf* (*homosexual*) bender *Brit,* fag *Am*

voltear I. *vi* 1. (*dar vueltas: persona*) to roll over; (*cosa*) to spin; (*campana*) to peal 2. (*volcar*) to overturn 3. *AmL* (*torcer*) to turn; (*girarse*) to turn around; ~ **a hacer algo** to do sth again 4. *AmL* (*pasear*) to go for a walk II. *vt* 1. (*invertir*) to turn over; (*volver del revés*) to turn the right way up 2. (*hacer girar*) to spin; ~ **las campanas** to ring the bells 3. *AmL* (*volcar*) to knock over; (*volver*) to turn; ~ **la espalda a alguien** to turn one's back on sb 4. *AmL* (*lanzar al aire*) to throw into the air; (*el lazo*) to swing III. *vr:* ~**se** 1. (*dar vueltas*) to turn over 2. (*cambiar de ideas*) to change one's ideas 3. *AmL* (*volcar*) to overturn; (*darse la vuelta*) to turn around

voltereta *f* 1. (*cabriola*) handspring; (*en el aire*) somersault; **dar una** ~ to do a handspring; (*en el aire*) to turn a somersault 2. (*vuelco*) (sudden) change

voltio *m* volt

volubilidad *f* 1. QUÍM instability 2. (*inconstancia*) fickleness; (*imprevisibilidad*) changeableness

voluble *adj* 1. QUÍM unstable 2. (*inconstante*) fickle; (*imprevisible*) changeable 3. BOT climbing

volumen *m* 1. (*tamaño*) size; *t.* FÍS, MAT volume 2. (*cantidad*) amount; (*del pelo*) body; ~

de ventas turnover; **de gran** ~ large, bulky **3.** (*de sonido*) volume; **a todo** ~ (at) full volume; **poner la música a todo** ~ to put the music on full blast **4.** (*tomo*) volume; **en dos/varios volúmenes** in two/several volumes

voluminoso, -a *adj* sizeable; (*poco manejable*) bulky; (*grueso*) thick; (*corpulento*) heavy

voluntad *f* **1.** (*intención*) will; (*fuerza de voluntad*) will-power; ~ **de vivir** will to live; **buena** ~ goodwill; **mala** ~ evil intent; **a** ~ at one's discretion; **con buena** ~ with good intentions; **con mucha/poca** ~ willingly/unwillingly; **contra su** ~ against one's will; **de última** ~ as a last wish; **hacer su santa** ~ to do exactly as one pleases; **poner** ~ **en algo** to put one's heart into sth; **por causas ajenas a nuestra** ~ for reasons beyond our control; **por propia** ~ of one's own free will; **quitar a alguien la** ~ **de algo** to stop sb feeling like doing sth; **tener mucha/poca** ~ to have a lot of/not very much will-power; **última** ~ JUR last will **2.** (*cariño*) affection; **ganarse la** ~ **de alguien** to win sb's affection

voluntariedad *f* **1.** (*carácter voluntario*) voluntary nature; JUR intent **2.** (*arbitrariedad*) arbitrary nature **3.** (*fuerza de voluntad*) willingness; (*perseverancia*) persistence

voluntario, -a **I.** *adj* **1.** (*libre*) voluntary **2.** (*arbitrario*) arbitrary **II.** *m, f* volunteer; **ofrecerse** ~ **para algo** to volunteer for sth

voluntarioso, -a *adj* willing; (*perseverante*) persistent; (*caprichoso*) self-willed

voluptuosidad *f* voluptuousness

voluptuoso, -a *adj* voluptuous

volver *irr* **I.** *vi* **1.** (*dar la vuelta*) to go back; ~ **atrás** to turn back **2.** (*regresar*) to return; ~ **a casa** to go home; **al** ~ **a casa me acosté** when I got home I went to bed; **al** ~ **compra el pan** buy the bread on the way back; **al** ~ **me llamó** he/she called me when he/she got back; **he vuelto por la autopista** I came back on the motorway; ~ **en sí** to come round [*o* to]; ~ **sobre sí** to turn round; **volviendo al tema** to come back to the subject **3.** (*repetir*) ~ **a hacer algo** to do sth again; **he vuelto a cometer el mismo error** I've made the same mistake again; **he vuelto a casarme** I've remarried **II.** *vt* **1.** (*dar la vuelta*) to turn over; ~ **la espalda a alguien** *t. fig* to turn one's back on sb; ~ **la vista a algo** to look back at sth **2.** (*poner del revés*) to turn inside out; (*manga*) to roll up **3.** (*transformar*) to make; ~ **furioso** to make mad; ~ **a su estado original** to revert to its original state; ~ **loco a alguien** to drive sb crazy **4.** (*devolver*) to return; ~ **algo a su sitio** to put sth back in its place; ~ **a la vida** to revive **III.** *vr:* **~se** **1.** (*darse la vuelta*) **~se a** [*o* **hacia**] **algo** to turn around towards sth **2.** (*dirigirse*) **~se a** [*o* **hacia**] **algo** to turn towards sth; **~se contra alguien** to turn against sb; **~se (para) atrás** to retrace one's steps; *fig* to back out; **no tengo dónde ~me** I've got no place to go **3.** (*regresar*) to return **4.** (*convertirse*) to become; (*ponerse*) to grow; **~se viejo** to grow old; **~se rico** to get rich

vomitar **I.** *vi* to vomit, to be sick *Brit;* **es para** ~ *vulg* it's enough to make you sick; **este salchichón me da ganas de** ~ this sausage makes me feel sick **II.** *vt* **1.** (*comida*) to bring up; *fig* to spew out; (*insultos*) to hurl; (*sangre*) to cough up **2.** *fig* (*desembuchar*) to spit out

vomitivo, -a *adj* **1.** MED emetic **2.** *inf* (*asqueroso*) revolting; **ese es** ~ that's disgusting

vómito *m* (*acción*) vomiting; (*lo vomitado*) vomit; ~ **de sangre** coughing up of blood; **provocar ~s a alguien** to make sb throw up *inf*

voracidad *f* voraciousness; (*avaricia*) greed

vorágine *f* **1.** (*remolino*) whirlpool **2.** (*confusión*) whirl, vortex

voraz *adj t. fig* voracious; (*hambriento*) ravenous; **apetito** ~ voracious appetite; (*avaro*) greedy

vórtice *m* (*de agua*) whirlpool; (*de viento*) whirlwind; (*de un ciclón*) eye

vos *pron pers* **1.** *AmL* (*tú*) you; **esto es para** ~ this is for you; **voy con** ~ I'll go with you **2.** HIST (*usted*) thou

> The term **vosear** means to address someone in a familiar way using '**vos**' instead of '**tu**'. This is very common practice in **Argentina** and other Spanish-speaking countries of Latin America.

vosotros, -as *pron pers, pl* you; ~ **sois muy listos** you are very clever; **esto es para** ~ this is for you

votación *f* vote; ~ **a mano alzada** vote by show of hands; **someter algo a** ~ to put sth to the vote

votar **I.** *vi* (*elegir*) to vote; ~ **a** [*o* **por**] **alguien/algo** to vote for sb/sth **II.** *vt* (*decidir*) ~ **a alguien** to vote for sb; ~ **un presupuesto** to approve a budget

voto *m* **1.** POL (*opinión*) vote; (*acción*) voting; ~ **afirmativo** [*o* **a favor**] vote in favour *Brit,* vote in favor *Am;* ~ **de castigo** protest vote; ~ **en blanco** unmarked ballot (paper) (*as a protest*); ~ **de censura** vote of no confidence; ~ **por correo** postal vote *Brit,* mail vote *Am;* ~ **negativo** [*o* **en contra**] vote against; **derecho a** ~ right to vote; **dar su** ~ **a algo** to vote for sth; **emitir su** ~ to cast one's vote; **tener (derecho a)** ~ to have the (right to) vote **2.** REL (*promesa*) vow; **hacer ~s por** +*infin,* **hacer ~s por que** +*subj t. fig* to vow to

voy *1. pres de* **ir**

voz *f* **1.** (*sonido, facultad, voto*) voice; ~ **afeminada** effeminate voice; ~ **aguardentosa** gravelly voice; ~ **cantante** melody line; ~ **de mando** voice of command; **a dos/cuatro voces** MÚS for two/four voices; **aclarar la** ~ to clear one's throat; **ahuecar la** ~ to deepen

V

one's voice; **levantar/bajar la** ~ to raise/lower one's voice; **levantar la** ~ **a alguien** to raise one's voice to sb; **a media** ~ in a whisper; **de viva** ~ in person; **hablar en** ~ **alta/baja** to speak loudly/softly; **leer en** ~ **alta** to read aloud; **hacer oír su** ~ to make one's voice heard; **no tener ni** ~ **ni voto** to have no right to vote; *fig* to have no say in the matter; **se me quebró la** ~ I lost my voice; *fig* words failed me; **tener** ~ **en algo** to have a say in sth **2.** (*grito*) shouting; **voces** shouts; **a voces** in a loud voice; **a** ~ **en grito** at the top of one's voice; **dar una** ~ **a alguien** to give a shout to sb; **dar voces** to shout; **dar la** ~ **de alarma** to raise the alarm; **pegar** (**cuatro**) **voces** to shout; **pedir algo a voces** to cry out for sth **3.** (*sonido*) tone **4.** (*rumor*) rumour *Brit,* rumor *Am;* **corre la** ~ **de que...** rumour *Brit* [*o* rumor *Am*] has it that ... **5.** (*vocablo*) word; ~ **técnica** technical term **6.** LING ~ **activa/pasiva** active/passive voice ►**llevar la** ~ **cantante** to call the tune

vozarrón *m* booming voice

vudú *m* voodoo

vuelco *m* **1.** (*tumbo*) turning over; (*voltereta*) somersault **2.** (*cambio*) drastic change; **dar un** ~ to overturn; *fig* to change completely ►**me dio un** ~ **el corazón** my heart missed a beat

vuelo *m* **1.** (*en el aire*) flight; ~ **acrobático** acrobatic flight; ~ **en globo** balloon flight; ~ **sin motor** gliding; ~ **nacional/internacional** domestic/international flight; ~ **rasante** low-level flight; ~ **regular** scheduled flight; **levantar** [*o* **alzar**] **el** ~ (*pájaro*) to fly off; (*avión*) to take off; **al** ~ in flight; *fig* quickly; **tomar** ~ to take flight; (*fig*) to leave **2.** (*de la ropa*) looseness; **falda de** ~ full skirt ►**oír el** ~ **de una mosca** to hear a pin drop; **de altos** ~**s** high-powered; **cogerlas al** ~ to be very quick on the uptake; **cortar los** ~**s a alguien** to clip sb's wings

vuelta *f* **1.** (*giro*) turn; **el camión dio una** ~ **de campana** the lorry *Brit* [*o* truck *Am*] turned over; **andar a** ~**s con algo** *inf* to be working on sth; **a la** ~ **de** (*lugar*) near; (*tiempo*) after; **a la** ~ **de la esquina** around the corner; **dar la** ~ (*rodear*) to go around; (*volver*) to turn back; (*poner cabeza abajo*) to put face down; (*llave*) to turn; **darse la** ~ to turn over; **dar media** ~ to turn around; **dar una** ~ to have a walk around; **dar** ~**s a algo** to turn sth over; **dar mil** ~**s a alguien** to run rings around sb; **no dar más** ~**s al tema** to stop worrying about sth; **la cabeza me da** ~**s** my head is spinning **2.** (*regreso*) return; (*viaje*) trip; ~ **atrás** return (trip); *fig* look back; CINE, LIT flashback; **a la** ~ **pasaremos por vuestra casa** we'll pass by your house on the way back; **a la** ~ **empezaré a trabajar** I'll start work when I get back; **de** ~ **a casa** back home; **estar de** ~ to be back; **la** ~ **al cole**(**gio**) back to school **3.** (*curva*) bend; **dar** ~**s y revueltas** to turn this way and that **4.** (*dinero*) change; **dar la** ~ to give change **5.** (*cambio*) change; **la vida da muchas** ~**s** life has many ups and downs; **¡las** ~**s que da la vida!** how things change! **6.** DEP lap; ~ **ciclista** cycle race; **partida de** ~ return match **7.** POL round **8.** (*devolución*) refund **9.** (*reverso*) back **10.** (*de la ropa*) facing ►**a** ~ **de correo** by return of post; **esto no tiene** ~ **de hoja** (*está claro*) there's no doubt about it; (*no hay otra solución*) it's the only way; **poner a alguien de** ~ **y media** to tear sb off a strip *Brit,* to tell sb off *Am;* **estar de** ~ **de todo** to have seen it all before; **buscar las** ~**s a alguien** to try to catch sb out; **dar muchas** ~**s a algo** to think over sth again and again

vuelto *m AmL* (*cambio*) change; **dar el** ~ to give change

vuelto, **-a** *pp de* **volver**

vuestro, **-a** **I.** *adj* your; ~ **coche** your car; **vuestra hija** your daughter; ~**s libros** your books **II.** *pron pos* **1.** (*de vuestra propiedad*) yours; **¿es** ~**?** is this yours? **2.** (*tras artículo*) **el** ~ yours; **los** ~**s** yours; (*parientes*) your family; **mi radio no funciona, ¿me dejáis la vuestra?** my radio doesn't work, can I borrow yours? **3.** (*tras substantivo*) (of) yours; **un amigo** ~ a friend of yours; (**no**) **es culpa vuestra** it's not your fault ►**ésta es la vuestra** *inf* this is your chance

vulcanizadora *f Méx* vulcanizer

vulgar *adj* **1.** (*común*) common **2.** (*ordinario*) vulgar **3.** (*ramplón*) coarse

vulgaridad *f* **1.** (*normalidad*) ordinariness **2.** *pey* (*grosería*) vulgarity **3.** (*ramplonería*) coarseness

vulgarizar <z→c> **I.** *vt* **1.** (*simplificar*) to vulgarize **2.** (*popularizar*) to popularize **II.** *vr:* ~**se** **1.** *pey* (*persona*) to become vulgar **2.** (*trivializarse*) to become trivial **3.** (*popularizarse*) to become popular

vulgo *m* **1.** (*mayoría*) public; *pey* (*masa*) masses *pl* **2.** (*pueblo, profanos*) ordinary [*o* common] people *pl*

vulnerabilidad *f* vulnerability; (*de la salud*) delicate nature; (*de máquinas*) poor quality

vulnerable *adj* vulnerable

vulneración *f* violation

vulnerar *vt* (*persona*) to hurt; (*derecho*) to violate

vulva *f* ANAT vulva

W

W, **w** *f* W, w; ~ **de Washington** W for William

walkie-talkie *m* walkie-talkie

walkman® *m* Walkman®

wampa *f Méx* (*ciénaga*) swamp

warrant <warrants> *m* FIN warrant

wáter *m* toilet

waterpolo *m* DEP water polo

watt *m* ELEC watt
W.C. *m abr de* **water-closet** toilet
web *m o f* INFOR web
wélter I. *adj AmL* DEP **peso** ~ welterweight II. *m AmL* DEP welterweight
whisky *m* whisky
windsurf *m* 1. DEP windsurfing 2. (*tabla*) windsurfer
windsurfing *m sin pl* windsurfing
wing *m AmL* 1. (*extremo delantero*) winger 2. (*extrema delantera*) wing
WWW *abr de* **World Wide Web** WWW

X

X, x *f* 1. (*letra*) X, x; ~ **de xilófono** X for Xmas *Brit,* X for X *Am;* **rayos** ~ X-rays *pl;* **en (forma de)** ~ X-shaped 2. MAT x; ~ **veces** x times 3. *fig* (*indeterminado*) x; **le presté x libras** I lent him/her x pounds 4. (*numeración romana*) ten
xenofobia *f* xenophobia
xenófobo, -a *adj* xenophobic
xerografía *f* xerography
xilófono *m* MÚS xylophone
xilografía *f* xylography
xirgo, -a *adj Méx* 1. (*desaseado*) untidy 2. (*hirsuto*) hairy
xocoyote *m Méx* (*benjamín*) youngest child

Y

Y, y *f* Y, y; ~ **de yema** Y for Yellow *Brit,* Y for Yoke *Am*
y *conj* and; **días ~ días** days and days; **¿~ qué?** so what?; **me voy de vacaciones – ¿~ tu trabajo?** I'm going on holiday – what about your job?; **¿~ tu marido(, qué tal?)** and how is your husband?; **¿~ mi monedero? – en el coche** where's my purse? – it's in the car; **¿~ este paquete? – de mis padres** whose is this packet? – it's my parents'; ~ **eso que...** despite that, ...; **¡~ tanto!** you bet!, you can say that again!
ya I. *adv* 1. (*en el pasado*) already; ~ **es hora de que cambies** it's time you changed; ~ **en 1800** as early as 1800 2. (*pronto*) soon, right away; **¡~ voy!** coming!; ~ **verás** you'll see 3. (*ahora*) now; ~ **falta poco para Navidades** Christmas is near now 4. (*negación*) ~ **no fumo** I don't smoke any more; ~ **no... sino...** not only ..., but ... 5. (*afirmación*) yes; **~, ~** all right, OK; *irón* oh, sure!; **¡ah ~!** I get it now!; **¡anda ~!** come off it!; **¡pues ~!** right now! II. *conj* 1. (*porque*) ~ **que** since, as 2. (*aprovechando que*) ~ **que estás aquí...** now that you're here ...; ~ **que lo mencionas...** now that you mention it ... 3. (*o*) ~ **por...,** ~ **por...** either by ... or ... III. *interj* that's it!
yacaré *m Arg, Bol, Par, Urug* ZOOL alligator
yacer *irr vi elev* 1. (*estar echado*) to lie; **aquí yace el conde** here lies the count 2. (*acostarse*) to lie down 3. (*estar*) to be
yacija *f* 1. *pey* (*cama*) rough bed, pallet *liter;* (*de paja*) straw bed 2. (*sepultura*) grave
yacimiento *m* GEO, MIN deposit; (*capa*) layer
yagua *f* 1. *AmL* BOT royal palm 2. (*fibras*) royal palm fibre
yagual *m AmC* padded ring (*for carrying heavy loads on the head*)
yaguré *m AmL* ZOOL skunk
yak *m* yak
yámbico, -a *adj* LIT iambic
yambo *m* LIT iambus
yanqui I. *adj* Yankee II. *mf* Yank
yapa *f AmL* 1. (*a un precio*) bonus 2. (*objeto*) extra; **de** ~ as an addition
yapar *vt AmL* 1. (*el precio*) ~ **algo** to give sth as a bonus 2. (*un objeto*) ~ **algo** to add sth as an extra
yarda *f* (*medida*) yard
yate *m* yacht
yayo, -a *m, f inf* grandpa *m,* grandma *f*
yazco, yazgo *1. pres de* **yacer**
ye *f* letter Y
yedra *f* ivy
yegua *f* 1. ZOOL mare 2. *AmC* (*colilla*) cigar stub

> The term **yeísmo** signifies the pronounciation of the 'll' as a 'y', e.g. '**gayo**' instead of '**gallo**'. The **yeísmo** is very widespread, particularly amongst city dwellers.

yelmo *m* helmet
yema *f* 1. (*de un huevo*) yolk 2. (*de un dedo*) fingertip 3. GASTR egg yolk 4. BOT young shoot 5. (*parte mejor*) best part; **~s de espárrago** asparagus tips
Yemen *m* Yemen
yemení, yemenita I. *adj* of/from Yemen II. *mf* native/inhabitant of Yemen
yendo *gerundio de* **ir**
yerba *f* 1. (*planta*) grass; ~ **mate** *AmS* maté herb 2. (*césped*) lawn; (*pasto*) pasture; (*seco*) dry grass
yerbal *m RíoPl* maté plantation
yerbatal *m Arg* (*yerbal*) maté plantation
yerbatero, -a I. *adj AmL* maté II. *m, f AmS* 1. (*curandero*) folk healer 2. (*vendedor: de hierbas*) herbalist; (*de forraje*) person who sells fodder; (*de mate*) grower of maté
yerbear *vi AmL* to drink maté
yerbera *f RíoPl* maté container
yerbero, -a *m, f Méx* (*curandero*) herb doctor
yergo *1. pres de* **erguir**
yermo *m* 1. (*terreno*) waste land 2. AGR uncultivated land

yermo, **-a** *adj* 1.(*inhabitado*) uninhabited 2. AGR uncultivated; **dejar** ~ to leave uncultivated

yerno *m* son-in-law

yernocracia *f inf* old-boy network

yero *m* vetch

yerra *f RíoPl* branding

yerro *m* 1.(*equivocación*) confusion 2.(*falta*) mistake

yérsey *m*, **yersí** *m AmC, AmS* jersey

yerto, **-a** *adj* stiff; **quedar** ~ (**de un susto**) to be scared stiff

yesca *f* tinder

yeso *m* 1.(*material*) plaster; **dar de** ~ **una pared** to plaster a wall 2. GEO gypsum

yesquero *m* tinder-box

yeta *f Arg, Urug* bad luck

yé-yé *adj inf* cool; **hoy vas muy** ~ you look very hip today

yira *f Arg, pey, inf* slut

yo I. *pron pers* I; ~ **que tú...** if I were you ...; **esto queda entre tú y** ~ this is between you and me; **¿quién lo hizo? – ~ no** who did it? – not me; **soy ~, Susan** it's me, Susan; ~ **mismo** myself II. *m t.* PSICO ego

yocalla *m Bol* 1.(*niño callejero*) street urchin 2.(*niño mestizo*) half-breed

yod *f* LING yod

yodado, **-a** *adj* iodized; **sal yodada** iodized salt

yodo *m* iodine

yoga *m* yoga

yogui *mf* yogi

yogur *m* 1. GASTR yogurt; ~ **natural** plain yogurt; ~ **desnatado** low-fat yogurt 2. *inf* (*genio*) **estar de mal** ~ to be like a bear with a sore head; **tener muy mal** ~ to be very hot-tempered

yolo *m Méx, inf* (*corazón*) darling; **¡~ mío!** my darling!

yonqui *mf inf* (*drogata*) junkie

yóquei *m*, **yoqui** *m* DEP jockey

yoyó *m* yoyo

yuca *f* yucca

yudo *m* judo

yugo *m* 1. *t.* AGR (*dominio*) yoke; **someterse al** ~ to bow to the yoke 2.(*de la campana*) bell cage

Yugoslavia *f* Yugoslavia

yugoslavo, **-a** I. *adj* Yugoslav(ian) II. *m, f* Yugoslav

yugular[1] *f* ANAT jugular vein

yugular[2] I. *vt* 1.(*decapitar*) to decapitate 2.(*detener*) to break off II. *adj* jugular

yunga *mf Bol, Chile, Ecua, Perú* valley native (*native or resident of the warm valleys on either side of the Andes*)

yungas *fpl Bol, Chile, Ecua, Perú* warm valleys *pl*

yunque *m t.* ANAT anvil

yunta *f* 1.(*par*) yoke (of oxen), couple 2. *pl, PRico, Urug, Ven* cufflinks *pl*

yuppy *mf* yuppy

yute *m* jute

yuxtaponer *irr como poner* I. *vt* (*a otra cosa*) to join; (*dos cosas*) to juxtapose II. *vr:* ~**se** to join together

yuxtaposición *f* juxtaposition

yuxtapuesto, **-a** *adj* juxtaposed

yuyal *m CSur* weed-covered ground

yuyero, **-a** *m, f Arg, CSur* herbalist

yuyo *m* 1. *CSur* (*yerbajo*) weed 2. *pl, Col, Ecua* (*condimento*) seasoning 3. *pl, Perú* (*verdura*) herbs *pl* 4. *AmC* (*ampolla*) blister

Z

Z, z *f* Z, z; ~ **de Zaragoza** Z for Zebra

zabuir *vi PRico* (*zambullir*) to plunge

zacatal *m AmC, Méx* pasture

zacate *m AmL* (*paja*) hay

zafacoca *f* 1. *AmC, AmS* (*pelea*) row, quarrel 2. *Chile* (*alboroto*) commotion 3. *Méx* (*reyerta*) brawl

zafacón *m PRico, RDom* (*cubo de la basura*) rubbish bin *Brit*, trash can *Am*

zafado, **-a** *adj Arg* (*descarado*) cheeky *Brit*, sassy *Am*

zafadura *f AmL* MED (*luxación*) dislocation

zafar I. *vt* NÁUT to free II. *vr:* ~**se** 1.(*de una persona*) to get away; **el ladrón se zafó del policía** the thief gave the policeman the slip 2.(*de un compromiso*) ~**se de** to get out of 3. TÉC (*correa*) to come off 4. *AmL* (*dislocarse*) to dislocate

zafarrancho *m* 1. NÁUT clearing of the decks 2. *inf* (*limpieza*) clearing up 3. *inf* (*riña*) quarrel 4. *inf* (*destrozo*) mess

zafio, **-a** *adj* 1.(*grosero*) rude 2.(*tosco*) rough, uncouth

zafiro *m* MIN sapphire

zafo *adv AmL* (*salvo*) except

zafo, **-a** *adj* 1. NÁUT free 2.(*indemne*) unhurt; **salir** ~ to escape unscathed

zafra *f* 1.(*cosecha*) sugar harvest 2.(*fabricación*) sugar production 3.(*tiempo*) sugar season 4.(*jarra*) oil jar

zaga *f* 1.(*parte posterior*) rear; **ir a la ~ de alguien** to be behind sb; **el vicepresidente no le va a la ~ al presidente** the vicepresident is a match for the president 2. DEP defence

zagal(a) *m(f)* (*muchacho*) boy, lad *Brit;* (*muchacha*) girl, lass *Brit*

zaguán *m* 1.(*vestíbulo*) hall 2.(*exterior*) entrance

zaguero *m* DEP (*en pelota*) deep ball; (*en fútbol*) defender

zaguero, **-a** *adj* rear

zahareño, **-a** *adj* wild

zaherir *irr como sentir vt* 1.(*reprender*) to reprimand 2.(*mortificar*) to humiliate

zahorí <zahoríes> *m* 1.(*vidente*) seer

2. (*perspicaz*) very perceptive person 3. (*buscar agua*) water diviner
zaino, -a *adj* 1. (*persona*) treacherous; **mirar a lo** ~ to look shifty 2. (*res*) black; (*caballo*) chestnut
zaireño *adj, m, f* Zairean
zalamería *f* flattery
zalamero, -a I. *adj* flattering II. *m, f* flatterer
zalema *f* 1. (*reverencia*) deep bow 2. (*zalamería*) flattery
zamacuco, -a *m, f* (*zoquete*) dolt; (*astuto*) sly devil
zamarra *f* 1. (*de pastor*) shepherd's waistcoat 2. (*chaqueta*) sheepskin jacket 3. (*piel*) sheepskin
zamarro *m* 1. (*chaqueta*) sheepskin jacket 2. (*piel*) sheepskin 3. (*rústico*) yokel 4. (*bribón*) sly individual 5. *pl, AmL* (*pantalones*) breeches *pl*
Zambia *f* Zambia
zambiano, -a I. *adj* Zambian II. *m, f* Zambian
zambo, -a *adj* (*piernas*) knock-kneed, bow-legged
zambomba *f* MÚS *drum-like instrument played by rubbing a stick through the center of the drumskin*
zambombazo *m inf* 1. (*porrazo*) blow 2. (*explosión*) blast
zambra *f* 1. (*bulla*) racket; (*riña*) quarrel 2. HIST (*fiesta gitana*) gypsy festivity
zambucar <c→qu> *vt inf* to hide away
zambullir <*3. pret:* zambulló> I. *vt* to submerge II. *vr:* **~se** 1. (*en el agua*) to dive 2. (*en un asunto*) **~se en algo** to plunge into sth 3. (*ocultarse*) to hide; (*cubrirse*) to cover oneself
zambullón *m AmS* (*zambullida*) dip, dive
Zamora *f* Zamora ►**~ no se ganó en una hora** *prov* Rome was not built in a day
zamorano, -a I. *adj* of/from Zamora II. *m, f* native/inhabitant of Zamora
zampabollos *mf inv, inf* greedyguts *Brit*
zampar I. *vt* 1. (*comer*) to scoff *Brit,* to scarf down *Am* 2. (*ocultar*) to whip out of sight 3. (*tirar*) to dash (to the ground) II. *vr:* **~se** 1. (*comer*) to scoff 2. (*en un lugar*) to crash 3. *pey* (*invitarse*) to gatecrash
zampatortas *mf inv, inf* scoffer *Brit,* foodie
zampón, -ona I. *adj inf* greedy II. *m, f inf* glutton
zampoña *f* MÚS rustic flute
zamuro *m Ven* (*buitre*) turkey vulture
zanahoria[1] *f* BOT carrot
zanahoria[2] *m RíoPl* (*imbécil*) idiot
zanca *f* 1. (*del ave*) shank 2. *inf* (*del hombre*) long leg
zancada *f* stride; **dar ~s** to stride; **se recorrió la ciudad en dos ~s** he/she walked round the town in no time
zancadilla *f* **poner la ~ a alguien** to trip sb up; *fig* to ruin sb's chances
zancadillear *vt* **~ a alguien** to trip sb up; *fig* to ruin sb's chances
zanco *m* stilt
zancón, -ona *adj* 1. (*zancudo*) long-legged 2. *Col, Guat, Méx* (*demasiado corto*) too short; **el vestido le queda ~** the dress is too short on her
zancudo *m AmL* 1. (*insecto*) mosquito 2. (*ave*) wader
zancudo, -a *adj* long-legged
zanganear *vi inf* to idle
zángano *m* 1. (*vago*) idler 2. *t.* ZOOL drone 3. (*torpe*) bore
zanja *f* 1. (*excavación*) ditch 2. *AmL* (*arroyada*) watercourse
zanjar *vt* 1. (*abrir zanjas*) to dig ditches 2. (*asunto*) to settle; (*disputa*) to end
zanjón *m* 1. (*zanja*) gully, ditch 2. *AmL* (*despeñadero*) gorge
zanquilargo, -a *adj inf* long-legged
zapa *f* 1. (*pala*) hoe 2. MIL sap; **labor de ~** *fig* scheming
zapallo *m* 1. *AmL* (*calabaza*) pumpkin 2. *Arg, Chile* (*chiripa*) fluke
zapar *vi* (*cavar*) to dig ditches
zapata *f* TÉC shoe; (*arandela*) washer; **~ de freno** brake shoe
zapatear I. *vt* (*golpear*) to kick II. *vi* 1. (*bailando*) to tap dance 2. (*velas*) to flap violently
zapatería *f* 1. (*tienda*) shoeshop 2. (*fábrica*) shoe factory 3. (*taller*) cobbler's 4. (*oficio*) shoemaking
zapatero *m* (*mueble*) shoe rack
zapatero, -a I. *adj* (*patatas*) hard II. *m, f* shoemaker ►**~ a tus zapatos** *prov* cobbler, stick to your last *prov;* (*no meterse*) mind your own business
zapatilla *f* 1. (*para casa*) slipper 2. (*de deporte*) trainer, sneaker *Am;* **~s de clavos** spiked shoes; **~s de tenis** tennis shoes
zapato *m* shoe; **~ de salón** court shoe *Brit,* pump *Am;* **~s de tacón** high-heeled shoes; **un par de ~s** a pair of shoes ►**tú no me llegas a la suela del ~** you can't hold a candle to me; **saber dónde aprieta el ~** to know which side one's bread is buttered on; **meter a alguien en un ~** to intimidate sb
zape *interj* 1. (*animal*) shoo! 2. (*peligro*) look out!
zapear *vt* 1. (*espantar*) to scare away 2. *inf* TV to channel-hop, to zap (channels)
zapotazo *m Méx, inf* thump
zapote *m AmC, Méx* BOT sapodilla
zapping *m* channel-hopping
zar, zarina *m, f* tsar *m,* tsarina *f*
zaragozano, -a I. *adj* of/from Zaragoza II. *m, f* native/inhabitant of Zaragoza
zaramullo *m Perú, Ven* silly thing
zarandajas *fpl* trifles *pl*
zarandear I. *vt* 1. (*sacudir*) to shake hard 2. (*ajetrear*) to keep busy 3. (*cribar*) to sieve 4. *AmL* (*ridiculizar*) to mock II. *vr:* **~se** 1. (*ajetrearse*) to busy oneself 2. (*burlarse*) to make fun
zarcillo *m* 1. (*pendiente*) earring 2. BOT ten-

dril

zarco, **-a** *adj* light blue

zarina *f v.* **zar**

zarpa *f* **1.** (*del león*) paw; *inf* (*del hombre*) huge hand, mitt; **echar la ~** (*animal*) to claw; *inf* (*persona*) to grab **2.** (*barco*) weighing anchor

zarpar *vi* NÁUT to set sail

zarrapastroso, **-a** *adj inf* dirty

zarza *f* bramble, blackberry bush

zarzal *m* bramble patch

zarzamora *f* blackberry

zarzo *m Col* loft ►**ser caído del ~** *inf* to be a sucker

zarzuela *f* **1.** MÚS zarzuela (*Spanish musical comedy or operetta*) **2.** GASTR *dish made of fish and shellfish*

zas *interj* **1.** (*de rapidez*) whoosh! **2.** (*de golpe*) bang!

zascandil *m* **1.** (*casquivano*) scatterbrained **2.** (*entrometido*) busybody

zascandilear *vi* **1.** (*tontear*) to do foolish things **2.** (*entrometerse*) to meddle

zenit *m* zenith

zepelín *m* zeppelin

zeta *f* zed

zigzag *m* <zigzagues *o* zigzags> zigzag

zigzaguear *vi* to zigzag

Zimbabue *m* Zimbabwe

zimbabuo, **-a** **I.** *adj* Zimbabwean **II.** *m, f* Zimbabwean

zinc *m* <cines *o* zines> zinc; **óxido de ~** zinc oxide

zíngaro, **-a** *m, f* gipsy *Brit,* (Hungarian) gypsy *Am*

zíper *m Méx* (*cremallera*) zip fastener

zipizape *m inf* set-to

zócalo *m* **1.** ARQUIT pedestal **2.** (*de pared*) skirting board **3.** *Méx* (*plaza*) (town) square

zodíaco *m* zodiac; **signos del ~** signs of the Zodiac

zombi *m* **1.** (*muerto*) zombie **2.** (*atontado*) **estar ~** to be like a zombie

zona *f* **1.** *t.* POL, GEO, METEO (*general*) zone; (*terreno*) belt; (*área*) region; **~ de ensanche** area to be built up; **~ franca** (duty-)free zone; **~ de influencia** area of influence; **~ peatonal** pedestrian precinct; **~ urbana** urban area; **~ verde** green belt **2.** DEP (*baloncesto: área*) area; (*defensa*) zone defender; (*falta*) zone fault

zoncera *f AmL,* **zoncería** *f* (*tontería*) foolishness

zonzo, **-a** *adj* **1.** (*aburrido*) dull **2.** *AmL* (*tonto*) stupid

zoo *m* zoo

zoología *f sin pl* zoology

zoológico, **-a** *adj* zoological; **parque ~** zoo

zoólogo, **-a** *m, f* zoologist

zopenco, **-a** **I.** *adj* oafish **II.** *m, f* dolt

zopilote *m Méx* ZOOL turkey vulture

zopo, **-a** *adj* lame

zoquete *m* **1.** (*madera*) block **2.** (*tonto*) blockhead **3.** *Arg* (*calcetín*) sock

zorra *f* **1.** ZOOL vixen **2.** *inf* (*prostituta*) whore; (*insulto*) bitch **3.** *inf* (*borrachera*) drunkenness

zorrera *f* **1.** (*de zorros*) earth **2.** (*habitación*) smoky room **3.** (*modorra*) drowsiness

zorrería *f* craftiness

zorrillo *m AmL* (*mofeta*) skunk

zorro *m* **1.** ZOOL fox **2.** (*piel*) foxskin **3.** *inf* (*astuto*) crafty fellow ►**hacerse el ~** to act stupid; **estar hecho unos ~s** to be dead beat; **poner a alguien hecho unos ~s** to tire sb to death

zorzal *m* **1.** ZOOL thrush **2.** (*listo*) shrewd person **3.** *AmL* (*papanatas*) simpleton

zote **I.** *adj* foolish **II.** *mf* fool

zozobra *f* anxiety

zozobrar **I.** *vi* **1.** (*barco*) to capsize **2.** (*plan*) to fail **3.** (*persona*) to hesitate **II.** *vt* **1.** (*barco*) to sink **2.** (*plan*) to spoil

zueco *m* clog

zumba *f* **1.** (*cencerro*) mule bell **2.** (*juguete*) rattle **3.** (*burla*) teasing **4.** *AmL* (*paliza*) beating

zumbado, **-a** *adj* **estar ~** *inf* to be barmy *Brit,* to be nuts

zumbador *m* ELEC buzzer

zumbar **I.** *vi* **1.** (*abejorro, máquina*) to buzz; **salir zumbando** to rush [*o* zoom] off **2.** (*oídos*) to hum **II.** *vt* **1.** (*golpe*) to deal **2.** *AmL* (*arrojar*) to throw; (*expulsar*) to chuck out **3.** (*guasear*) to mock **III.** *vr:* **~se** to make fun

zumbido *m* **1.** (*ruido*) hum; **~ de los oídos** ringing in the ears **2.** *inf* (*golpe*) clout

zumbón, **-ona** *m, f inf* joker

zumo *m* **1.** (*de frutas*) juice **2.** *fig* (*utilidad*) profit; **sacar ~ de algo** to get benefit from sth

zuncho *m* ring

zupay *m AmL* (*demonio*) devil

zurcir <c→z> *vt* to mend; **¡que te zurzan!** *inf* to hell with you!

zurda *f* left hand; **hacer algo a ~s** to do sth with the left hand; *fig* to do sth the wrong way

zurdo, **-a** **I.** *adj* left-handed **II.** *m, f* left-handed person

zurra *f* **1.** (*de la piel*) tanning **2.** (*paliza*) hiding; **dar una ~ a alguien** to give sb a hiding

zurrapa *f* **1.** (*poso*) dregs *pl* **2.** *inf* (*cosa*) muck; (*persona*) weak and ugly person

zurraposo, **-a** *adj* full of dregs, muddy

zurrar *vt* **1.** (*pieles*) to tan **2.** *inf* (*apalizar*) to beat **3.** *inf* (*criticar*) to knock

zurriagar <g→gu> *vt* to whip

zurriagazo *m* **1.** (*latigazo*) lash **2.** (*desgracia*) bad blow **3.** (*desdén*) snub

zurriago *m* (*látigo*) whip

zurribanda *f inf* **1.** (*tunda*) beating **2.** (*riña*) fight

zurrumbanco, **-a** *adj CRi, Méx* half-drunk, light-headed

zurullo *m inf* **1.** (*grumo*) lump **2.** (*excremento*) turd

zutano, **-a** *m, f* **fulano y ~** Tom, Dick and Harry; **fulano y ~ se han casado** what's-his-name and you-know-who have got married (*when you can't remember sb's name*)

Apéndice I

Supplement I

Correspondencia privada
Private correspondence

A la oficina de turismo: solicitud de folletos informativos

Sr. Silvinio Pérez
Pza. Padre Silverio, 35
09001 Burgos

Dirección General de Turismo de Tarragona
Rambla Nova, 46
43004 Tarragona

Burgos, a 13 de febrero de 2002

Distinguidos señores:

Me gustaría pasar las vacaciones con mi familia en agosto en la costa de Tarragona. Por este motivo les agradecería que fueran tan amables de enviarme prospectos de los lugares turísticos y de los hoteles de esta zona.

Sin otro particular y agradeciéndoles por adelantado su respuesta, les saluda atentamente,

Silvinio Pérez

Me gustaría pasar las vacaciones en…	*I wish to spend my holidays in …*
enviarme prospectos	*send me details*

Note: Spanish writers put both their name and address at the top left of the page, with the name and address of the other person below and to the left.

Tourist office: asking for information

65 Rogers Road,
Rickland
GN8 4BY

2 February 2002

England Tourist Board
New Park
Southbridge
Kent
XP1 7TU

Dear Sirs,

My family and I wish to spend our holidays in the South-East during July.

Could you kindly send me details of places of interest and hotels.

With thanks,

Yours faithfully,

John Roberts

¡Atención! En una carta inglesa el nombre no suele aparecer en el membrete. La dirección del remitente se pone arriba a la derecha, la dirección del destinatario a la izquierda.

Reservar una habitación de hotel

Distinguidos señores:

Les agradezco las molestias que se han tomado al enviarme folletos informativos sobre las condiciones de estancia en su hotel.

Les agradecería que reservaran para mi señora, para mí mismo y nuestros dos hijos dos habitaciones dobles con ducha, una con dos camas y la otra con una de matrimonio, en régimen de media pensión del 2 al 15 de julio.

Les agradezco por adelantado su confirmación.

Sin otro particular, les saluda atentamente,

José Otero

folletos informativos	*your leaflet giving details*
Les agradecería que reservaran…	*I would like to book …*

Booking a room in a hotel

Dear Sirs,

Thank you for your leaflet giving details about your hotel.

I would like to book two double rooms with bathroom at half-board from 2 to 15 July inclusive, one for my wife and myself with double bed, and one with twin beds for my two daughters.

I would be grateful if you could confirm this booking.

Yours sincerely,

Tim Smith

Pedir información sobre un apartamento para las vacaciones

Distinguidos señores:

La Oficina de Turismo me ha enviado la lista y la descripción de los chalets y apartamentos que se alquilan para las vacaciones en su ciudad y en los alrededores.

Me interesaría particularmente el apartamento amueblado que ustedes me recomiendan. Desearía alquilarlo por un período de un mes a partir del 1 de julio. Quisiera, no obstante, antes de tomar la decisión, que me dieran alguna información más.

¿Podrían precisarme si los gastos suplementarios (de gas, electricidad u otros) están incluidos en el precio de alquiler y cuál sería la cantidad del depósito a pagar? ¿Disponen las camas de sábanas y mantas? Y, por último, ¿se admiten animales?

Esperando su respuesta y sin otro particular, les saluda atentamente,

Juan Ibáñez

la lista y la descripción de los chalets y apartamentos	*a detailed list of holiday lettings*
apartamento amueblado	*furnished apartment*
por un período de un mes a partir del 1 de julio	*for one month from 1 July*
¿Podrían precisarme si…?	*Could you tell me if …*
el precio de alquiler	*the rent*
la cantidad del depósito	*the deposit*
¿Disponen las camas de sábanas y mantas?	*Is bedding provided?*

Information about a holiday apartment

Dear Sir,

The tourist office has sent me details of holiday lettings in and around your town and I am particularly interested in your furnished apartment. I would like to rent it for one month from 1 July. However I should be grateful for some further details before making a final decision.

Could you tell me if bills (gas, electricity and any taxes) are included in the rent? What deposit do you require? Is bedding provided? And finally, are pets welcome?

Yours sincerely,

John Roberts

Alquilar un apartamento para las vacaciones

Apreciados señores:

En primer lugar quisiera agradecerles su rápida respuesta.

Una vez obtenida la información adicional que han tenido la amabilidad de comunicarnos, les confirmo la decisión de alquilar el apartamento del 1 al 30 de julio, ambos incluidos.

Les adjunto un cheque de 200 euros en concepto de depósito. El resto del alquiler, es decir, 375 euros, les será entregado el día de nuestra llegada, el 1 de julio.

Sin otro particular, les saluda atentamente,

Silvia Gómez

P.S.: ¿Podrían precisarnos, por favor, dónde podemos recoger las llaves el día de nuestra llegada?

...que han tenido la amabilidad de comunicarnos	*... that you have kindly sent*
les confirmo la decisión de alquilar	*I confirm that we have decided to rent*
en concepto de depósito	*as a deposit*
El resto del alquiler les será entregado...	*We will pay the balance ...*
¿Podrían precisarnos, por favor, dónde...?	*Kindly let us know where ...*

Booking a holiday apartment

Dear Mr Hill,

Thank you for answering my letter so quickly.

I have read through the information and I can now confirm that we have decided to rent your apartment from 1 to 30 July inclusive.

I enclose a cheque for £150; and we will pay the balance of £700 on our arrival on 1 July.

Yours sincerely,

Steven Roberts

PS: Kindly let us know where to pick up the keys to the apartment on the day of our arrival.

Carta desde el lugar de vacaciones

Querido Mario, querida Inés:
Un gran saludo desde la isla de Cuba donde desde hace una semana disfrutamos del sol y de las playas a la sombra de un cocotero. Hemos degustado ya todas las especialidades culinarias de la isla. ¿Y qué decir del delicioso ron de aquí? En una palabra: unas vacaciones de ensueño, y eso que el hotel, aunque confortable, es bastante ruidoso. Espero que los dos estéis bien y que no sufráis demasiado con el frío invernal de la capital.
Un abrazo muy fuerte,
Juan y Christina

Familia Martinez
c/Ruiseñor 24

08034 Barcelona

Holiday postcard

Here we are in Barbados. There's plenty of sun, sand and palm trees. The beach suits me fine, but Peter keeps trying to tempt me off the beach to join him for some water-skiing. The hotel is good and the food is delicious, but the disco can be rather noisy if you want an early night! We have another week here before we head back home to a British winter. We hope that you're both well and we'll see you soon.
Love from
Maggie and Peter

Gemma and John Roberts
65 Rogers Road
Rickland
GN8 4BY

Felicitación de Navidad (registro informal)

Querido Pedro, querida María:

Muchas gracias por vuestra felicitación de Navidad.

Igualmente queremos desearos una feliz Navidad y un próspero Año Nuevo y que el 2003 os traiga toda la felicidad del mundo.

Hasta pronto, en Madrid o en Cambridge.

Besos,

Marga y David

Christmas Greetings (informal register)

Dear Julia and Robert,

Wishing you both a very Merry Christmas and an excellent New Year, hoping that it brings you all the joy and success you wish for.

Hope to see you soon over here or back home in the States.

Love from

Maddie and Neil

Felicitación de Navidad (registro formal)

SR. D. SERGIO LÓPEZ

Presidente de la Cámara de Comercio regional

Les deseo a usted y a su familia

una feliz Navidad y un próspero Año Nuevo

Atentamente,

Sergio Moreno

Christmas Greetings (formal register)

A very Happy Christmas and good wishes for the New Year

from

Elaine Goodman

Goodman and Hart
Solicitors
48 High Street
Rickland
GN8 4SK

Felicitación de cumpleaños

Querida Ángeles:

13 de diciembre: un año más... Pero qué importa eso, tú siempre serás joven.

Te deseo de todo corazón un feliz cumpleaños.

Si no fuera porque vivo tan lejos te habría llevado personalmente un pequeño regalo: Correos se encargará de ello. Espero que llegue a tiempo. Una cosa más: ¡que tengas un buen día!

Un abrazo muy fuerte,

Carmen

Te deseo de todo corazón un feliz cumpleaños. *I wish you a very happy birthday.*

Birthday card

Dear Simon,

Happy Birthday! But I can't believe it's a year since the last one!

It's far too long since we got together and it's a real shame that we won't be around for the celebrations. We hope you like our little present and that you'll have a good time on the day.

Love from

Sophie and Mike

Tarjeta de pésame

Los Srs. García

enterados de la cruel pérdida que han sufrido
quieren expresarles su más sincero pésame

su más sincero pésame — *our sincere condolences*

Condolences

We were deeply saddened to hear of your sad loss and wish to offer our sincere condolences

With our deepest sympathy,

James and Barbara Thornton

Invitación

Queridos amigos:

Hace un mes ya que nos hemos instalado en nuestra nueva casa de Orio, un pequeño y pintoresco pueblo del norte de España.

Estaríamos encantados si os pudiéramos recibir el fin de semana de Carnaval. El sábado por la noche celebraremos el estreno de la casa con todos los amigos. Nos gustaría que estuvierais presentes.

Os adjuntamos un plano para que podáis encontrar la casa.

Esperando una respuesta afirmativa por vuestra parte os enviamos un cordial saludo,

Belén y Ramón

celebramos el estreno de la casa	*we're throwing a house-warming party*
Os adjuntamos un plano	*We have enclosed a map*
Esperando una respuesta afirmativa...	*Hoping that you can make it ...*

Invitation

Dear Angela and Martin,

It's just over a month since we moved into our new house at Bennington. We like it here in the north of England, and it's very picturesque.

Would you be able to come and stay with us for the holiday weekend? We're throwing a house-warming party on Saturday night and would be very happy if you could be there.

We have enclosed a map so that you don't get lost.

Hoping that you can make it.

With warm regards,

Elizabeth and Paul

Aceptar una invitación

Queridos amigos:

Con gran placer queremos comunicaros que aceptamos vuestra amable invitación. Nos encantará poder volver a veros.

Llegaremos el viernes por la noche y nos quedaremos hasta el lunes por la mañana. Gracias por el plano.

Aprovechamos esta breve respuesta para felicitaros por vuestra nueva casa.

Saludos afectuosos,

Sinda y Miguel

Nos encantará poder volver a veros.	*We're really looking forward to seeing you again.*

Accepting an invitation

Dear Elizabeth and Paul,

Of course we would be delighted to accept your kind invitation and we're really looking forward to seeing you again.

We should get there early on Friday evening we'll be off again on Monday morning. Thanks for the map.

Congratulations on your new home.

With warmest regards

Angela and Martin

Rechazar una invitación

Queridos amigos:

Vuestra amable invitación nos ha satisfecho mucho y os la agradecemos sinceramente. Desgraciadamente tenemos ya compromisos familiares que nos impedirán estar libres ese fin de semana. ¡Cuánto lo sentimos!

Nos hubiera encantado volver a veros; quizás se presente dentro de poco otra ocasión para podernos ver.

Os enviamos un afectuoso saludo,

Laura y Javier

Desgraciadamente tenemos ya compromisos familiares.	*We already have family commitments.*

Dear Elizabeth and Paul,

We were delighted to receive your kind invitation and would like to thank you very much.

We're terribly sorry but we already have family commitments that prevent us getting away on that weekend. Shame! It would have been great to get out into the country for a break.

We're terribly sorry we won't be seeing you, let's hope there'll be another chance to get together in the near future.

With our best wishes,

Angela and Martin

Agradecer a alguien su hospitalidad

Estimados señores:

Queremos por la presente agradecer sinceramente la acogida tan amable y calurosa que nos dispensaron.

No olvidaremos jamás los maravillosos momentos pasados en su compañía. Gracias a todas las excursiones que tuvieron la gentileza de organizarnos hemos podido descubrir su ciudad, su región y también otra manera de vivir.

Díganles a sus vecinos, los Sres. Alcántara, que guardamos un muy grato recuerdo de las partidas de mus que echamos con ellos.

Dándoles de nuevo las gracias por todo y esperando tener pronto el placer de enseñarles nuestro país cuando se presente la ocasión, les saludamos muy atentamente,

Susana y Roberto

la acogida tan amable y calurosa que nos dispensaron	*the warm welcome you gave us*
los maravillosos momentos pasados en su compañía	*the wonderful time we spent with you*
guardamos un muy grato recuerdo de…	*we won't forget …*

Thanks after staying in someone's home

Dear Mr and Mrs Shaw,

We would like to say a big thank you for the warm welcome you gave us.

We had a wonderful time while we were with you. We have many happy memories of our outings in Exeter and its surroundings and I hope you'll enjoy the photographs we took.

Would you please thank all your friends, especially Bob and Sandra Carter from the tennis club, who did so much to make our stay enjoyable.

It was a holiday to remember and I hope it will not be too long before we are able to welcome you to our country.

Yours sincerely,

Eric and Mary

Anuncio de boda

D. Abelino Pérez y señora
y
D. Juan Carrascal y señora

tienen el placer de comunicarles la boda

de sus hijos,

Carmen y Javier.

El enlace tendrá lugar en la iglesia parroquial
el 11 de septiembre de 2002 a las 11 horas.

Se recibirá a los invitados tras la ceremonia religiosa
en la finca „Los Pinos“ de Úbeda (Jaén)

Se agradecerá confirmación.

tras la ceremonia religiosa	*following the ceremony*
Se agracederá confirmación.	*R.S.V.P.*

Marriage announcement

Mr and Mrs Henry Grant

request the pleasure of your company at the marriage of their daughter
Christine to Mr Robin Davies

at St Anne's Church, Lewes on Saturday 17 June at 11 a.m.

and at the reception afterwards at

Hollyoak Manor, Kingston

R.S.V.P

Invitación de boda

Querida Isabel, querido Antonio:

He cogido la pluma más bonita que tengo para anunciaros una gran novedad: ¡María se casa! Pero seguramente ya lo habréis leído en la tarjeta que va incluida en esta carta.

Espero de todo corazón que nos complaceréis asistiendo a la boda. Estaríamos encantados de teneros entre nosotros ese día. Será una oportunidad para vernos de nuevo y celebrar la fiesta juntos. Contamos con vuestra presencia.

En cuanto al alojamiento, no os preocupéis, ¡todo está preparado!

Esperando veros pronto, os enviamos un saludo muy cordial.

Teresa y Manuel

Espero de todo corazón que nos complaceréis asistiendo a la boda.	*I really hope that you will be able to come to the wedding.*
Será una oportunidad para vernos de nuevo.	*It will be good to see each other again.*
Contamos con vuestra presencia.	*We are counting on you.*

Wedding invitation

Dear Helen and Mark,

I've got some news for you: Christine is getting married! You'll be getting the invitation card in the post soon.

We really hope that you can come to the wedding. We would be delighted to have you with us. It would be good to see each other again and celebrate together. We are counting on you.

Don't worry about where to stay, we'll take care of everything.

We hope to see you again soon,

With our very best wishes,

Lorna and Henry Grant

Aceptar la invitación a una boda

Querida Matilde, querido Juan:

Nos ha emocionado mucho recibir la amable invitación a la boda de vuestra hija María, invitación que aceptamos con sumo gusto. Estaremos encantados de poder felicitar personalmente a la joven pareja.

Os agradecemos sinceramente que hayáis pensado en nosotros y nos alegramos de poder volver a veros tras todos estos meses en los que no hemos dado señales de vida. Pero, como sabéis, nuestra profesión nos absorbe por completo y las semanas pasan volando.

Sin otro particular y esperando que vosotros y los vuestros gocéis de buena salud os saludamos hasta muy pronto.

Un abrazo,

Isabel y Antonio

P.S.: Quizás podríais sugerirnos un regalo de bodas que pudiera agradar a los recién casados. Gracias por adelantado.

...que aceptamos con mucho gusto	*... which we are delighted to accept*
tras todos estos meses	*after so many months*
nuestra profesión nos absorbe por completo	*our professional lives keep us so busy*
sugerir un regalo de bodas que pudiera agradar a los recién casados	*suggest a wedding gift that the newlyweds would like*

Acceptance of a wedding invitation

Dear Lorna and Henry

We were very so pleased to hear about Christine's wedding, and delighted to get your invitation. Of course we shall be coming and look forward to seeing the young couple and giving them our best wishes.

Things have been terribly busy at work over the past few months. Time passes too quickly and it's easy to lose touch with our friends, so it will be lovely to see you all again.

We hope that everyone is keeping well and we will see you soon.

With warmest regards,

Helen and Mark

P.S. Do you have any ideas for a wedding gift that Christine and Robin might like? We'd be very grateful for suggestions.

Agradecer un regalo de bodas

> *Queridos amigos:*
>
> *¿Cómo os podemos agradecer el fantástico regalo que habéis tenido la gentileza de hacernos con motivo de nuestro enlace?*
>
> *Nos ha encantado, de verdad, lo que habéis hecho y nos sentimos realmente agasajados.*
>
> *Gracias de nuevo y sabed que siempre tendréis en nosotros a unos sinceros amigos.*
>
> *Isabel y Diego*

el fantástico regalo que habéis tenido la gentileza de hacernos	*the wonderful present that you gave us*
Nos ha encantado de verdad.	*It was really too much.*

Thanks for a wedding gift

> *Dear Helen and Mark*
>
> *Thank you so much for the wonderful present that you gave us for our wedding.*
>
> *We were very touched by your kindness. It was really too much.*
>
> *Thank you once again.*
>
> *With our love,*
>
> *Christine and Robin*

Agradecer un regalo de cumpleaños

Querida Antonia, querido Francisco:

Recibí vuestro regalo el mismo día de mi cumpleaños. Miles de gracias. Pero de verdad que es demasiado. Me habéis puesto casi en una situación embarazosa. Sabéis que no hay nada que me pueda satisfacer más y nunca dejáis pasar una ocasión para demostrar vuestro afecto que, como sabréis, es recíproco.

Una vez más, muchas gracias y hasta muy pronto. Un abrazo muy fuerte.

Sonia

Miles de gracias.	*Thank you so much.*
Me habéis puesto casi en una situación embarazosa.	*I'm almost overwhelmed.*

Thanks for a birthday present

Dear Sophie and Mike,

You always remember my birthday – even though I'd rather forget about it now!

Thank you so much your present – really you shouldn't have. It made my day: you certainly know what I like! It will remind me of you, but don't think I really need any reminder. I could never forget good friends like you.

Thanks once again, and I hope it won't be too long before we see each other.

Love

Simon

Correspondencia comercial
Business correspondence

Carta de pedido

Pastelería RAMOS
Plaza de la Libertad, 21
34005 Zamora

Turrones, S.A.
c/Gijón, 13
46003 Valencia

Ref.: pedido n° 111

Zamora, a 18 de octubre de 2002

Estimados Sres.:

Hace quince días recibimos su envío de muestras, además de la lista correspondiente de precios. La relación precio-calidad de sus productos nos ha parecido sumamente interesante. De hecho creemos que también convencerá a nuestros clientes.

Por ello deseamos tomen nota del pedido que especificamos a continuación:

Cantidad/Unidades	Producto	Precio
30 cajas de 50 u.	Turrón duro	70 euros/caja
10 cajas de 50 u.	Turrón blando	70 euros/caja
10 cajas de 50 u.	Turrón Nata Nuez	80 euros/caja
10 cajas de 50 u.	Turrón Yema Tostada	80 euros/caja

Rogamos nos hagan llegar el envío antes del 1 de noviembre.

Como ya habíamos acordado por teléfono, el envío se efectuará a través de la empresa de transportes 'La Liebre', por supuesto con portes pagados. El pago, con una letra de cambio a 30 días.

En espera de sus prontas noticias, les saludamos muy atentamente,

Marcos Ruíz Pérez

(Encargado Pastelería RAMOS)

46, Ambrose Crescent
Silhurst
CW3 8DS

Hitchfield Electronics
Chingleford
QN4 6RT

10 March 2002

Dear Sir,

Re. Printer supplies

Further to our telephone conversation this morning, I would like to confirm my order for the following items:

Type	Quantity
Printer cable, code HX398	1
Inkjet cartridges, black, code HW 546	2
Colour cartridge, code HW 756	1

Please debit my credit card, no. 1111 2222 3333 4444, expiry date 02/04

I understand that you deliver within three working days.

Yours faithfully,

Ronald Grieves

Acusar recibo de un pedido

Almacenes Guadalquivir
Ciudad Expo, bloque 22, bajo C
41927 Mairena del Aljarafe
(Sevilla)

Supermercados MERCAMIL
c/Torres Quevedo, 1, bajo
45004 Toledo

Sevilla, a 2 de julio de 2002

Distinguidos señores:

Ante todo, gracias por su pedido nº 32 del 15 del mes corriente que acabamos de recibir. Tengan la seguridad de que pondremos nuestro mayor esmero en llevarlo a cabo.

Aceptamos sus condiciones de entrega y de pago, a saber:

Entrega: antes del 12 de mayo, portes pagados, por camión.
Pago: 60 días fecha factura, sin descuento.

Condiciones particulares: les reconocemos, a partir de ahora, el derecho a rechazar los artículos que no les sean entregados antes del 12 de mayo.

Estando en todo momento a su disposición, aprovecho la oportunidad para saludarles atentamente,

Diego Blanco Novoa

(Gerente Almacenes GUADALQUIVIR)

Confirming receipt of an order

PWP Ceramics
15, Highbridge Road
Mingley
WP9 7SA
Tel.: 024 4825 3147

Hailingbury plc
11, Foghard Way
Hocksmore
TQ3 6BV

18 April 2002

Dear Sirs,

Thank you for your order number 32 dated 15 April.

This order will be dealt with and shipped as soon as possible

Our standard payment and delivery conditions apply, i.e.

Delivery: by 12 May, carriage paid, by courier service.
Payment: within 60 days of the billing date, without discount.

All goods should be inspected on delivery.

Yours faithfully,

A Black

Anne Black
Sales Department

Carta de reclamación

Manuel Gómez Marcos
c/Ruiseñor, 24–3 °C
08084 Barcelona

PRICAR, S.L.
Paseo Gaudí, 33
08080 Barcelona

Barcelona, a 11 de noviembre de 2002

Muy señores míos:

Hace dos días, es decir el sábado, día 9 de noviembre, adquirí en su establecimiento del Paseo Gaudí una antena parabólica de la casa 'Télix'. Cuál fue mi sorpresa cuando al llegar a mi domicilio y comenzar su instalación comprobé que faltaba el cable. Ruego me lo hagan llegar a la mayor brevedad a través de su servicio técnico.

Sin otro particular, atentamente,

Manuel Gómez Marcos

Complaint

38, Swinburne Avenue
Hawdrey
MY7 9PL

20 April 2002

Dear Madam,

I have received the items ordered by letter dated 22 March.

However, further inspection has revealed a defect in the cooler unit, part reference PL-00274/B and this prevents its use in the manufacturing process.

I would therefore be grateful if you would supply a replacement unit a.s.a.p. Please advise us when you will be able to deliver and collect the defective item from us.

Yours faithfully,

C Benson

Charles Benson

Carta de solicitud de empleo

Carmen Bermúdez Díaz
c/Reyes Católicos, 42, 3° G
10002 Cáceres

IBERIA, L.A.E.
c/Henri Dunant, 2
28036 Madrid

Cáceres, a 28 de mayo de 2002

(Ref. 1324 Trip. Cab.)

Estimados señores:

Con fecha del 26 de mayo he leído su anuncio en el diario 'El País' en el que solicitan auxiliares de vuelo (tripulantes de cabina de pasajeros).

Entre mis aspiraciones profesionales siempre me atrajo un puesto como el que ofrecen en la presente convocatoria. De hecho creo reunir los requisitos que demandan.

En la actualidad tengo 24 años, domino tres idiomas y además cuento con otras aptitudes, adquiridas especialmente durante mi permanencia en la agencia de viajes HALCÓN.

En el currículum vitae que les adjunto describo con más detalle todos estos datos y otros que pudieran serles de interés.

Si ustedes lo estiman oportuno y creen ver en mí un posible candidato, estoy a su disposición para una entrevista personal.

Muy atentamente,

Carmen Bermúdez Díaz

Anexos: C.V., fotografía reciente

Application letter

Sonia Gómez Ruiz
c/Santa Fé, 34–2 °C
08084 Barcelona

3 November 2002

Dear Sir or Madam,

Re: Application for post of Secretary/Personal Assistant

With reference to your advertisement in today's *Guardian*, I would like to apply for the position of Secretary/Personal Assistant to the Sales Manager.

I am currently looking for full-time work that will allow me to develop my organizational skills and to use my Spanish (mother tongue), English and German which I have been able to practise during several visits and training programmes abroad. My current position has enabled me to acquire sound computing skills.

I enclose my curriculum vitae.

Please do not hesitate to contact me to arrange a suitable time for an interview.

Yours faithfully,

Sonia Gómez

Carta de solicitud de empleo al azar

Laura Roberts
65 Rogers Road,
Rickland
GN8 4BY

Rickland, a 1 de mayo de 2002

Distinguido señor Director:

La reputación de su empresa va a la par con la calidad de sus productos y de su dinamismo. Me he enterado de que están a punto de adoptar una nueva política de marketing, área en la que tengo un particular interés.

En la empresa donde actualmente trabajo he organizado el departamento de publicidad que en tres años ha multiplicado su importancia por dos (ver currículum vitae adjunto).

Mi experiencia profesional, mis cualidades en concepto de rigor y de organización y también mi creatividad me hacen creer que reúno las condiciones para un puesto de trabajo en su equipo.

Si esta solicitud fuera de su interés estaría a su disposición para mantener en un próximo futuro un encuentro personal.

Esperando su respuesta, aprovecho la ocasión para saludarle afectuosamente,

Laura Roberts

Unsolicited application letter

Carmen Rodríguez Santos
c/Serafín, 53, 2°, 3ª
08014 Barcelona

1 September 2002

Dear Sir,

I have been following the performance of your company and have been particularly interested by press reports that you are currently overhauling your overseas marketing strategy.

Over the past three years I have been closely involved in the restructuring of our advertising department, which has led to an 80 % increase in public awareness of our brands at home, and a 50 % increase in overseas sales. You will find full details of my work and responsibilities in the enclosed CV.

I am proud of my achievements and I believe that my professionalism, creativity and discipline could be a major asset to your organization.

I hope that we will be able to meet and discuss this further.

Yours faithfully,

Carmen Rodriguez

Currículum vitae

I. DATOS PERSONALES

Apellidos	Iglesias Vieira
Nombre	Ana María
Dirección particular	c/Martínez Sueiro, 114, 1° M 37004 Salamanca Tel. (988) 222225
Fecha de nacimiento	27.05.1970
Lugar de nacimiento	Celanova (Orense)
Estado civil	soltera
Nacionalidad	española

II. TITULACIÓN ACADÉMICA

Octubre 1989 – junio 1994	Licenciatura en Filología Inglesa, Universidad de Salamanca
Octubre 1994 – junio 1997	Diplomatura en Ciencias Empresariales, Universidad de Salamanca

III. FORMACIÓN PROFESIONAL

Octubre 1996 – junio 1997	Master en Comunidades Europeas y Derechos Humanos, Universidad Pontificia de Salamanca
Octubre 1997 – enero 1998	Master en Marketing, Universidad Politécnica de Alcalá de Henares

IV. EXPERIENCIA PROFESIONAL

Enero 1998 – diciembre 2000	Clases de inglés comercial en la Cámara de Comercio de Salamanca
Agosto de 1999 – presente	Caja de Ahorros de Salamanca y Soria, Responsable del Dpto. de Marketing

V. IDIOMAS

Excelente dominio del inglés y del portugués
Conocimientos de alemán, francés e italiano

VI. OTROS CONOCIMIENTOS

Conocimientos de informática a nivel de usuario

Ann Roberts
65 Rogers Road,
Rickland
GN8 4BY

Date of Birth: 02/07/1970
British
Single

EDUCATION & TRAINING

1991	BA – International Business
1990	Highfield Tertiary College (shorthand and typing)
1988	A Levels (English, Spanish, Maths, Economics)

PROFESSIONAL EXPERIENCE

Since October 1999	Personal assistant to the Export Director of a software company.	
	Responsibilities:	Follow-up of orders Contacts with subsidiaries abroad Canvassing foreign clients
April – August 1999	Trainee at Publicat, press agency in Madrid, in the office of the director's secretary (learning computer page layout techniques)	
October 1997 – March 1998	Trainee at Sama in Salamanca, in Customer Relations, dealing with telephone enquiries in three languages	

LANGUAGES

Trilingual: Spanish, English, German
6 months as a trainee for Sama in Spain

OTHER INTERESTS

Volunteer helper with a local disabled group
Sports: gymnastics, judo

Fórmulas útiles para la correspondencia

Useful expressions in letters

EL ENCABEZAMIENTO EN UNA CARTA – AT THE BEGINNING OF A LETTER

When you're writing ...	Escribes...
... to someone you know or to a friend Querida Sandra: Querido Pablo: ¡Hola Silvia!	**...a un conocido o a un amigo** Dear Mark, Dear Janet,
... to someone you know or to business contacts Estimada Srta. Hernández: Estimada Sra. Gómez: Estimado Sr. González:	**...a alguien a quien conoces a nivel personal o profesional** Dear Mrs Arnold, Dear Mr Arnold,
... to companies or organizations Muy señores míos: Estimados Sres:/Estimados señores:	**...a una empresa o a una persona cuyo nombre desconoces** Dear Sir or Madam, Dear Sirs,
... to someone whose title you know Distinguido/Estimado Dr. Pedro Santos: Distinguida/Estimada Catedrática D.ª Cristina Suárez:	**...a una persona cuyo título o grado académico conoces** Dear Sir, Dear Madam, Dear Doctor, *(dirigiéndose a un médico)*

LA DESPEDIDA EN UNA CARTA – ENDING A LETTER

Informally	Menos formal o familiar
Un abrazo muy fuerte, Un fuerte abrazo, Besos,	Love, (With) warmest regards,
Un cordial saludo, Un afectuoso saludo,	(With) kind regards, With best wishes,
Saludos ¡Hasta pronto!	Regards, Yours, Yours ever, Yours, with best wishes

Formal	Formal
Atentamente, Muy atentamente,	Yours sincerely, *(Si la carta comienza con "Dear Mr/Mrs ...")* Yours faithfully, *(Si la carta comienza con "Dear Sir/Madam")*

Very formal	Muy respetuoso
Sin otro particular, aprovechamos la oportunidad para saludarles muy atentamente/muy cordialmente.	Yours faithfully, (*a alguien cuyo nombre desconoces*)
Sin otro particular, le saludo atentamente.	Yours sincerely, *(Si la carta comienza con "Dear Mr/Mrs ...")*
Quedando en todo momento a su disposición, aprovecho la oportunidad para saludarles muy atentamente.	Yours faithfully, *(Si la carta comienza con "Dear Sir/Madam")*

Expresiones útiles / Useful phrases

La hora / Time

La hora	Time
¿Qué hora es?	What time is it?
¿Me puede decir qué hora es, por favor?	Could you tell me the time please?
Es la una en punto.	It's one o'clock exactly.
Son casi…	It's nearly …
las tres.	three o'clock.
las tres y cinco.	five past three.
las tres y cuarto.	quarter past three.
las tres y veinticinco.	twenty-five minutes past three.
las tres y media.	half past three.
las cuatro menos veinticinco.	twenty-five minutes to four.
las cuatro menos cuarto.	quarter to four.
las doce del mediodía/de la noche.	twelve o'clock midday/midnight.
Son más de las cuatro./Son las cuatro pasadas.	It's already after four (o'clock).
Ven entre las cuatro y las cinco.	Come between four and half past (four).

Saludos, presentaciones, despedidas / Greetings, Introductions, Farewell

Saludos, presentaciones, despedidas	Greetings, Introductions, Farewell
¡Buenos días!	Good morning!
¡Buenos días! *(until 2 pm)* ¡Buenas tardes! *(from 2 pm onwards)*	Hello!/Good day! (*Aus*)
¡Buenas tardes! *(until 9 pm)* ¡Buenas noches! *(from 9 pm onwards)*	Good evening!
¡Hola!	Hello!
Hola, ¿qué tal?	Hi!
Me llamo Chris.	My name is Chris.
¿Cómo está(n) usted(es)/estás? ¿Cómo le(s)/te va?	How are you?
¿Qué hay? ¿Qué tal? ¿Cómo te va?	How are you?
Bien, gracias, ¿y usted(es)/tú?	Fine, thanks! And you?
¡Adiós!	Goodbye!
¡Hasta luego!	Bye! See you later!
¡Hasta mañana!	Until tomorrow/Goodnight!
¡Que te lo pases/os lo paséis bien!	Enjoy yourself!/Have fun!
¡Buenas noches!	Goodnight!
Salude(n)/Saluda a la señora Gómez de mi parte.	Say hello to Ms Gómez for me.

Citas	**Appointments**
¿Le(s)/Te puedo invitar a comer?	May I invite you to a meal?
¿Tiene(n)/Tienes/Tenéis algo planeado para mañana?	Do you already have plans for tomorrow?
¿A qué hora quedamos?	When are we meeting?
¿Le(s)/Te/Os puedo pasar a recoger?	Can I pick you up?
Nos encontramos a las nueve delante del cine.	Let's meet in front of the cinema at nine o'clock.

Por favor y gracias	**Please and Thank-You Expressions**
Sí, gracias.	Yes, please.
No, gracias.	No, thanks.
¡Gracias!	Thank you!
¡Gracias, igualmente!	Thanks, same to you!
¿Me podría ayudar?	Can you help me please?
Gracias. De nada.	My pleasure!
Muchas gracias.	Many thanks!
No es nada.	It's not worth mentioning.

Pedir perdón, expresiones de lamento	**Apologies, Regrets**
¡Perdón!	Excuse me!
Debo disculparme.	I must apologise!
Lo siento mucho.	I am very sorry!
No era esa mi intención.	I did not mean it like that!
¡Qué lástima!	Pity!
¡Qué pena!	That is sad!

Felicitaciones en distintas ocasiones	**Wishes and congratulations**
¡Felicidades!	Congratulations!
¡Mucha suerte!	Good luck!
¡Que se mejore/te mejores pronto!	Get well soon!
¡Que pase(s)/paséis unas buenas vacaciones!	Have a great holiday!
¡Felices Pascuas!	Happy Easter!
¡Feliz Navidad y próspero Año Nuevo!	Merry Christmas and a Happy New Year!
¡Feliz cumpleaños!	Happy birthday!
Te deseo mucha suerte.	I'll keep my fingers crossed for you.

Preguntar por el camino, por la dirección / Asking Directions

Perdone, ¿cómo puedo ir a...?	Excuse me, how do I get to ...?
¿Me podría decir cómo puedo ir a...?	Can you tell me, how I get to the ...?
Todo recto hasta...	Straight ahead until ...
Cuando llegue al semáforo gire a la derecha.	Turn right at the traffic lights.
Siga las indicaciones.	Follow the signs.
No se puede perder.	You cannot miss it.
¿Qué autobús va a...?	Which bus goes to ...?
¿Es este el autobús que va a...?	Is this the right bus to ...?
¿Está muy lejos?	How far is it?
Por aquí no es.	You are at the wrong place.
Debe(n) volver hasta...	You need to go back to ...

En el restaurante / In a Restaurant

Quisiera reservar una mesa para cuatro personas.	I would like to reserve a table for four people.
Una mesa para dos, por favor.	A table for two, please.
¿Está libre esta mesa/este asiento?	Is this table/place free?
Tomaré...	I will take ...
¿Nos podría traer un poco más de pan?	Could we have some more bread please?
La cuenta, por favor.	I'd like to pay.
Todo junto.	All together please.
Cuentas separadas, por favor.	Seperate bills please.

De compras / Shopping

¿Dónde puedo encontrar...?	Where can I find ...?
Me podría recomendar una tienda de repostería/ de alimentación?	Can you recommend a delicatessen/food-store?
¿Le atienden?	Are you beeing served?
Gracias, solo quiero mirar.	Thanks, I'm just looking around.
¿Qué desea?	What would you like?
Póngame, por favor...	Could I please have ...
Quisiera...	I would like ...
¿Algo más?	Would you like anything else?
¿Aceptan tarjetas de crédito?	Do you accept credit cards?
¿Me lo puede envolver?	Could you wrap it up for me?

En el banco / At the Bank

Quisiera cambiar 50 euros en dólares.	I would like to exchange 50 euros into dollars.
Quisiera cobrar este cheque de viaje.	I would like to cash this travellers cheque.
¿Cuál es importe máximo al que puedo extender el talón?	What is the maximum limit on the cheque?
Quisiera sacar 200 euros de mi cuenta.	I would like to withdraw 200 euros from my account.
¿Me enseña su carnet, por favor?	My I see your ID?
Firme, por favor.	Your signature please!

En Correos / At the Post Office

¿Dónde está el buzón más cercano/la oficina de correos más cercana?	Where is the nearest postbox/postoffice?
¿Cuánto vale una carta para España?	How much is a letter to Spain?
Tres sellos de 1 euro, por favor	Three 1 euro stamps please.
Quisiera enviar un telegrama.	I would like to send a telegram.
Quisiera una tarjeta telefónica.	I would like a telephone card.
¿Puedo enviar desde aquí un fax a Londres?	Can I send a fax to London from here?

Llamar por teléfono / Making a Phone Call

¿Dónde está la cabina de teléfonos más cerca?	Where is the nearest telephone box?
¿Cuál es el prefijo de España?	What's the international dialling code for Spain?
Quisiera hacer una llamada a cobro revertido.	I would like to make a reverse-charge call.
¿Sí?, ¿con quién hablo?	Hello, who's speaking?
Quisiera hablar con la señora Clear.	May I please speak to Ms Clear?
Le pongo.	Connecting now!
Espere, no cuelge.	Please hold the line.
Lo siento pero no está.	I am sorry, she is not here.
¿Quiere dejar un mensaje?	Would you like to leave a message?
Volveré a llamar más tarde.	I'll call again later.
Este abonado ha cambiado de número.	The number you have called has not been recognised.

A

A, a [eɪ] *n* **1.** (*letter*) A, a *f*, ~ *for Andrew; Brit* ~ *for Abel; Am* A de Antonio; **to get from ~ to B** ir de un lugar a otro; **from ~ to Z** de cabo a rabo **2.** MUS (*note*) la *m* **3.** SCHOOL ≈ sobresaliente *m* **4.** *Brit* SCHOOL ~ **level** ≈ bachillerato *m*
a [ə, *stressed:* eɪ] *indef art before consonant,* **an** [ən, *stressed:* æn] *before vowel* **1.** (*in general*) un, una; ~ **car** un coche; ~ **house** una casa; **in ~ day or two** en unos días **2.** (*not translated*) **do you have ~ car?** ¿tienes coche?; **he is an Englishman** es inglés; **she is ~ teacher** es maestra; **a hundred days** cien días **3.** (*to express prices, rates*) **£2 ~ dozen** 2 libras la docena; **£6 ~ week** 6 libras por semana **4.** (*before person's name*) ~ **Mr Robinson** un tal Sr. Robinson
A *n abbr of* **answer** R
AA [ˌeɪ'eɪ] **1.** *abbr of* **Alcoholics Anonymous** AA **2.** *Brit* AUTO *abbr of* **Automobile Association** ≈ RACE *m*
AAA **1.** *Brit abbr of* **Amateur Athletics Association** *federación británica de atletismo aficionado* **2.** *Am* AUTO *abbr of* **American Automobile Association** ≈ RACE *m*
AB *Am abbr of* **Artium Baccalaureus** **1.** (*person*) ldo., -a. *m, f* en Letras **2.** (*degree*) licenciatura *f* en Letras
aback [ə'bæk] *adv* **to take sb ~** coger a alguien de improviso; **to be taken ~ (by sth)** quedarse desconcertado (por algo)
abacus ['æbəkəs] *n* ábaco *m*
abandon [ə'bændən] **I.** *vt* **1.** (*vehicle, place, person*) abandonar, dejar; **to ~ ship** evacuar el barco; **to ~ sb to his/her fate** abandonar a alguien a su suerte **2.** (*give up: plan*) renunciar a; (*game*) suspender **3.** (*lose self-control*) **to ~ oneself to sth** entregarse a algo **II.** *n no pl* abandono *m;* **with (wild) ~** con desenfreno
abandoned [ə'bændənd] *adj* **1.** (*place, vehicle*) abandonado, -a **2.** (*person*) desamparado, -a
abashed [ə'bæʃt] *adj* avergonzado, -a; **to be ~ at sth** avergonzarse de algo
abate [ə'beɪt] *vi* **1.** (*noise, anger*) disminuir **2.** (*wind*) amainar
abatement *n no pl* disminución *f*
abattoir ['æbətwɑːʳ, *Am:* -twɑːr] *n* matadero *m*
abbess ['æbes, *Am:* -əs] *n* REL abadesa *f*
abbey ['æbi] *n* abadía *f*
abbot ['æbət] *n* REL abad *m*
abbreviate [ə'briːvieɪt] *vt* abreviar
abbreviation [əˌbriːvɪ'eɪʃən] *n* abreviatura *f*
ABC¹ [ˌeɪbiː'siː] *n Am: pl* **1.** (*alphabet*) abecedario *m* **2.** (*rudiments*) abecé *m*, nociones *fpl* básicas
ABC² [ˌeɪbiː'siː] *n* **1.** *Aus* TV *abbr of* **Australian Broadcasting Corporation** *compañía australiana de radiotelevisión* **2.** *Am* TV *abbr of* **American Broadcasting Company** *compañía estadounidense de radiotelevisión*
abdicate ['æbdɪkeɪt] **I.** *vi* abdicar **II.** *vt* (*right*) renunciar a; (*throne*) abdicar (de)
abdication [ˌæbdɪ'keɪʃən] *n no pl* **1.** (*of right*) renuncia *f* **2.** (*of throne*) abdicación *f*
abdomen ['æbdəmən] *n* abdomen *m*
abdominal [æb'dɒmɪnl, *Am:* -'dɑːmə-] *adj* abdominal
abduct [æb'dʌkt] *vt* secuestrar, plagiar *AmL*
abduction [æb'dʌkʃən] *n* secuestro *m*, plagio *m AmL*
aberration [ˌæbə'reɪʃən] *n* aberración *f*
abet [ə'bet] <-tt-> *vt* instigar, incitar; **to aid and ~ sb** ser cómplice de alguien
abeyance [ə'beɪəns] *n no pl* **to fall into ~** caer en desuso
abhor [əb'hɔːʳ, *Am:* æb'hɔːr] <-rr-> *vt* aborrecer
abhorrence [əb'hɒrəns, *Am:* æb'hɔːr-] *n no pl* aborrecimiento *m*
abhorrent *adj* aborrecible
abide [ə'baɪd] <-d *o* abode, -d *o* abode> *vt* soportar; **I can't ~ her** no la soporto
◆**abide by** *vt* **1.** (*rule, decision*) atenerse a **2.** (*promise*) cumplir
abiding *adj* duradero, -a
ability [ə'bɪləti, *Am:* -əṭi] <-ies> *n* **1.** *no pl* (*capability*) capacidad *f;* **to the best of one's ~** lo mejor que uno pueda **2.** *no pl* (*talent*) aptitud *f* **3.** *pl* (*skills*) dotes *fpl*
abject ['æbdʒekt] *adj* **1.** (*wretched*) abyecto, -a **2.** (*absolute: poverty, failure*) absoluto, -a
ablaze [ə'bleɪz] *adj* en llamas; *fig* resplandeciente
able ['eɪbl] *adj* **1.** (*capable: person*) capaz; **to be ~ to do sth** (*have ability, manage*) poder hacer algo; (*have knowledge*) saber hacer algo **2.** (*piece of work*) logrado, -a
able-bodied [ˌeɪbl'bɒdɪd, *Am:* -'bɑːdɪd] *adj* sano, -a y fuerte; ~ **seaman** marinero *m* de primera
ABM *n abbr of* **anti-ballistic missile** misil *m* antibalístico
abnormal [æb'nɔːml, *Am:* -'nɔːr-] *adj* **1.** (*feature*) anómalo, -a **2.** (*person*) anormal
abnormality [ˌæbnə'mælɪti, *Am:* -nɔːrmæləṭi] <-ies> *n* **1.** (*abnormal feature*) anomalía *f* **2.** *no pl* (*unusualness*) anormalidad *f*
aboard [ə'bɔːd, *Am:* ə'bɔːrd] **I.** *adv* a bordo; **all ~!** ¡pasajeros a bordo! **II.** *prep* a bordo de; **to go ~ a boat** subir a una barca; **to go ~ plane** embarcar en el avión, subir al avión
abode [ə'bəʊd, *Am:* ə'boʊd] **I.** *vi pt, pp of* **abide** **II.** *n form* domicilio *m;* **of no fixed ~** sin domicilio fijo
abolish [ə'bɒlɪʃ, *Am:* -ɑːl-] *vt* abolir
abolition [əbəl'ɪʃən] *n no pl* abolición *f*
abominable [ə'bɒmɪnəbl, *Am:* ə'bɑːm-] *adj* abominable
abominate [ə'bɒmɪneɪt, *Am:* ə'bɑːm-] *vt* abominar (de)
abomination [əˌbɒmɪ'neɪʃən, *Am:*

ə'bɑːm-] *n* **1.** (*abominable thing*) abominación *f* **2.** (*disgust*) aversión *f*

aboriginal [ˌæbə'rɪdʒənl] **I.** *adj* aborigen **II.** *n* aborigen *mf* (de Australia)

Aborigine [ˌæbə'rɪdʒɪni] *n* aborigen *mf* (de Australia)

abort [ə'bɔːt, *Am:* ə'bɔrt] **I.** *vt* **1.** MED abortar **2.** *a.* INFOR abandonar **II.** *vi* **1.** MED abortar **2.** (*fail*) fracasar

abortion [ə'bɔːʃən, *Am:* ə'bɔr-] *n* MED aborto *m* (provocado); **to have an ~** abortar, tener un aborto

abortive [ə'bɔːtɪv, *Am:* ə'bɔːrt̬ɪv] *adj* malogrado, -a

abound [ə'baʊnd] *vi* abundar

about [ə'baʊt] **I.** *prep* **1.** (*on subject of*) sobre, acerca de; **a book ~ football** un libro sobre fútbol; **what is the film ~?** ¿de qué trata la película?; **to talk ~ cinema** hablar sobre cine; **while he is ~ it** *Brit, inf* mientras esté haciendo eso **2.** (*surrounding*) alrededor de; **the garden ~ the house** el jardín alrededor de la casa **3.** (*in and through*) por; **to go ~ a place** andar por un lugar **4.** (*characteristic of*) **that's what I like ~ him** eso es lo que me gusta de él **5.** *Brit* (*with*) **I have no money ~ me** no llevo dinero encima ►**how ~ that!** ¡vaya!; **what ~ it?** (*suggestion*) ¿quieres/queréis?; (*so what?*) ¿y qué?; **what ~ a drink?** ¿qué tal si tomamos algo? **II.** *adv* **1.** (*around*) **all ~** por todas partes; **to leave things lying ~ somewhere** dejar cosas tiradas por un sitio; **to be the other way ~** ser exactamente al revés; **is Paul ~?** ¿está Paul por ahí? **2.** (*approximately*) aproximadamente; **~ my size** más o menos de mi tamaño; **round ~ 5 km** cerca de 5 kilómetros; **~ here** más o menos aquí; **~ 5 years ago** hace unos cinco años; **~ twenty** unos veinte; **to be somewhere ~** estar por aquí; **to have had just ~ enough of sth** estar harto de algo; **that's ~ it for today** eso es todo por hoy **3.** (*almost*) casi; **to be (just) ~ ready** estar casi listo **4.** (*willing to*) **not to be ~ to do sth** no estar dispuesto a hacer algo **5.** (*on the point of*) **to be ~ to do sth** estar a punto de hacer algo

about-face [ə'baʊtfeɪs] *n Am, Aus,* **about-turn** [ə'baʊttɜːn, *Am:* -tɜːrn] *n Aus, Brit* **1.** MIL media vuelta *f* **2.** (*opinion*) cambio *m* drástico de opinión; (*position*) cambio *m* drástico de postura

above [ə'bʌv] **I.** *prep* **1.** (*on the top of*) encima de **2.** (*over*) sobre; **~ suspicion** por encima de toda sospecha **3.** (*greater than, superior to*) por encima de; **~ 3** más de 3; **those ~ the age of 70** los mayores de 70 años; **he is not ~ lying** es muy capaz de mentir; **~ all** sobre todo; **to shout ~ the noise** tener que gritar porque hay ruido; **it's ~ me** no lo entiendo **4.** GEO (*upstream*) más arriba de; (*north of*) al norte de **II.** *adv* encima, arriba; **the floor ~** la planta de arriba; **up ~ sth** por encima de algo; **up ~ in the sky** arriba en el cielo; **from ~** de las alturas; **see ~** (*in text*) véase más arriba **III.** *adj* susodicho, -a **IV.** *n* **the ~** lo antedicho

aboveboard *adj* legítimo, -a

above-mentioned *adj* anteriormente mencionado, -a

abrasion [ə'breɪʒən] *n* MED abrasión *f*

abrasive [ə'breɪsɪv] **I.** *adj* **1.** (*rough*) abrasivo, -a **2.** (*manner*) agresivo, -a **II.** *n* abrasivo *m*

abreast [ə'brest] *adv* **1.** (*side by side*) **two/three ~** en fila de a dos/tres **2.** (*up to date*) **to be/keep ~ of sth** estar/mantenerse al corriente de algo

abridge [ə'brɪdʒ] *vt* abreviar; **an ~ed version** una versión abreviada

abridgement *n,* **abridgment** [ə'brɪdʒmənt] *n* **1.** (*version*) compendio *m* **2.** *no pl* (*action*) abreviación *f*

abroad [ə'brɔːd, *Am:* ə'brɑːd] *adv* **1.** (*in foreign country*) en el extranjero; **from ~** del extranjero; **to be ~** estar en el extranjero; **to go ~** ir al extranjero; **at home and ~** dentro y fuera del país **2.** *form* (*outside*) fuera; **the news quickly spread ~** la noticia se divulgó rápidamente

abrupt [ə'brʌpt] *adj* **1.** (*sudden*) repentino, -a; (*change*) brusco, -a; (*end*) inesperado, -a **2.** (*brusque*) brusco, -a **3.** (*steep*) abrupto, -a

ABS [ˌeɪbiː'es] *n abbr of* **anti-lock braking system** ABS *m*

abscess ['æbses] *n* absceso *m*

abscond [əb'skɒnd, *Am:* -'skɑːnd] *vi* fugarse; **to ~ with sb/sth** fugarse con alguien/algo

abseil ['æbsaɪl] *vi Aus, Brit* hacer rappel

absence ['æbsəns] *n no pl* **1.** (*of person, thing*) ausencia *f*; **in the ~ of** en ausencia de; **on leave of ~** MIL de permiso **2.** (*of money, information*) carencia *f*; **in the ~ of** a falta de ►**~ makes the heart grow fonder** *prov* la ausencia es al amor lo que el fuego al aire: que apaga el pequeño y aviva el grande *prov*

absent[1] ['æbsənt] *adj* **1.** (*not present*) ausente; **~ without leave** MIL ausente sin permiso **2.** (*lacking*) que falta; **to be ~ in sth** no estar presente en algo **3.** (*distracted*) ausente, distraído, -a

absent[2] [əb'sent] *vt form* **to ~ oneself (from sth)** ausentarse (de algo)

absentee [ˌæbsən'tiː] *n* ausente *mf*

absenteeism *n no pl* absentismo *m*

absentee landlord *n* propietario, -a *m, f* absentista (*que apenas reside en su propiedad*) **absentee voting** *n Am* voto *m* por correo

absent-minded [ˌæbsənt'maɪndɪd] *adj* despistado, -a, volado, -a *AmL*

absolute ['æbsəluːt] **I.** *adj* **1.** (*total, not relative*) *a.* POL absoluto, -a; (*denial*) rotundo, -a; (*trust, power, confidence*) pleno, -a; (*disaster*) absoluto, -a, completo, -a **2.** CHEM puro, -a **II.** *n* **the ~** PHILOS lo absoluto

absolutely *adv* **1.** (*comprehensively*) absolutamente; **~!** *inf* ¡claro que sí!; **~ not!** ¡de ninguna manera! **2.** (*very*) totalmente
absolution [ˌæbsəˈluːʃən] *n no pl* REL absolución *f*
absolutism [ˈæbsəluːtɪzəm, *Am:* -səluːt̬-] *n no pl* POL absolutismo *m*
absolve [əbˈzɒlv, *Am:* -ˈzɑːlv] *vt* absolver
absorb [əbˈsɔːb, *Am:* -ˈsɔːrb] *vt* **1.** (*liquid*) absorber; (*shock*) amortiguar **2.** (*understand*) asimilar **3.** (*engross*) ocupar; **to get ~ed in sth** estar completamente absorbido por algo; **to be ~ed in one's thoughts** estar abstraído [*o* absorto] en sus pensamientos
absorbent [əbˈsɔːbənt, *Am:* -ˈsɔːrb-] *adj* absorbente
absorbing *adj* (*book, story*) absorvente, apasionante
absorption [əbˈsɔːpʃən] *n no pl* **1.** (*of liquid*) absorción *f* **2.** (*in book, story*) concentración *f* **3.** (*in work*) dedicación *f* absoluta
abstain [əbˈsteɪn] *vi a.* POL abstenerse; **to ~ from (doing) sth** abstenerse de (hacer) algo
abstemious [əbˈstiːmɪəs] *adj* mesurado, -a, comedido, -a
abstention [əbˈstenʃən] *n no pl a.* POL abstención *f*
abstinence [ˈæbstɪnəns] *n no pl* abstinencia *f*
abstract¹ [ˈæbstrækt] **I.** *adj* abstracto, -a; **~ art/painting** arte abstracto/pintura abstracta **II.** *n* **1.** (*not concrete*) abstracto *m*; **in the ~** en abstracto **2.** (*summary*) extracto *m*
abstract² [əbˈstrækt] *vt* **1.** *a.* CHEM extraer **2.** (*summarize*) resumir **3.** (*steal*) robar
abstracted [æbˈstræktɪd] *adj* distraído, -a
abstraction [əbˈstrækʃən] *n* **1.** (*abstract concept*) abstracción *f* **2.** *no pl* (*abstracted state*) distracción *f*
abstruse [əbˈstruːs] *adj* abstruso, -a
absurd [əbˈsɜːd, *Am:* -ˈsɜːrd] *adj* absurdo, -a
absurdity [əbˈsɜːdəti, *Am:* -ˈsɜːrdət̬i] <-ies> *n* **1.** *no pl* (*absurd state*) absurdo *m;* (*of idea, situation*) ridiculez *f* **2.** (*absurd thing*) disparate *m,* candinga *f Chile*
abundance [əˈbʌndəns] *n no pl* abundancia *f*
abundant [əˈbʌndənt] *adj* abundante
abuse¹ [əˈbjuːs] *n* **1.** *no pl* (*insults*) insultos *mpl,* insultadas *fpl AmL;* **to hurl ~ at sb** lanzar improperios a alguien **2.** *no pl* (*mistreatment*) maltrato *m* **3.** *no pl* (*misuse*) abuso *m;* **sexual ~** abuso sexual **4.** (*infringement*) infracción *f;* **~ of human rights** violación de los derechos humanos
abuse² [əˈbjuːz] *vt* **1.** (*insult*) insultar **2.** (*mistreat*) maltratar **3.** (*sexually*) abusar de **4.** (*misuse*) abusar de **5.** (*infringe*) infringir
abusive [əˈbjuːsɪv] *adj* **1.** (*language*) insultante, ofensivo, -a **2.** (*person*) agresivo, -a
abut [əˈbʌt] <-tt-> **I.** *vt* lindar con **II.** *vi* **to ~ on** lindar con
abysmal [əˈbɪzməl] *adj* pésimo, -a
abyss [əˈbɪs] *n a. fig* abismo *m*
AC [ˌeɪˈsiː] *n abbr of* **alternating current** CA *f*
a/c [ˌeɪˈsiː] *abbr of* **account** c/, cta.
academic [ˌækəˈdemɪk] **I.** *adj* **1.** UNIV académico, -a; SCHOOL escolar **2.** (*intellectual*) erudito, -a **3.** (*theoretical*) teórico, -a; (*argument*) especulativo **4.** (*irrelevant*) irrelevante **II.** *n* académico, -a *m, f*
academy [əˈkædəmi] <-ies> *n* **1.** (*training school*) academia *f* **2.** *Am, Scot* (*school*) instituto *m* (*de enseñanza secundaria*) **3.** CINE **the Academy Awards** los Óscars
ACAS [ˈeɪˌkæs] *n Brit abbr of* **Advisory, Conciliation and Arbitration Service** Instituto *m* de Mediación, Arbitraje y Conciliación
accede [ækˈsiːd] *vi* **1.** (*agree*) **to ~ to sth** acceder a algo **2.** (*to a position*) acceder a; **to ~ to the throne** subir al trono
accelerate [əkˈseləreɪt] **I.** *vi* (*car*) acelerar; (*growth*) acelerarse **II.** *vt* acelerar
acceleration [əkˌseləˈreɪʃən] *n no pl* aceleración *f*
accelerator [əkˈseləreɪtəʳ, *Am:* -eɪt̬ɚ] *n* **1.** (*in vehicle*) acelerador *m,* chancleta *f Ven, Col* **2.** *a.* PHYS acelerador *m*
accent¹ [ˈæksənt, *Am:* -sent] *n* **1.** LING acento *m* **2.** LIT, MUS énfasis *m inv*
accent² [ækˈsent] *vt* **1.** LIT, MUS acentuar **2.** (*emphasize*) enfatizar
accentuate [əkˈsentʃʊeɪt] *vt* acentuar
accept [əkˈsept] **I.** *vt* **1.** (*take when offered*) aceptar **2.** (*approve*) aprobar **3.** (*believe*) creer en **4.** (*acknowledge*) reconocer **5.** (*include socially*) acoger, dar acogida a **II.** *vi* aceptar
acceptable *adj* (*behaviour, suggestion*) aceptable; (*explanation*) admisible
acceptance [əkˈseptəns] *n* **1.** *no pl* (*of gift, help*) aceptación *f* **2.** (*approval*) aprobación *f*
accepted *adj* aceptado, -a; **the ~ procedure** el procedimiento habitual
access [ˈækses] **I.** *n no pl* entrada *f,* aproches *mpl AmL; a.* INFOR acceso *m;* **~ privileges** INFOR autorización de acceso; **~ road** vía *f* de acceso; **Internet ~** INFOR acceso a Internet; **to gain ~ to sth** acceder a algo; **to have ~ to sth** tener acceso a algo; **easy/difficult of ~** asequible/inasequible **II.** *vt* INFOR entrar en, acceder a
accessibility [ækˌsesəˈbɪləti, *Am:* -ət̬i] *n no pl* **1.** accesibilidad *f* **2.** *fig* carácter *m* accesible
accessible [əkˈsesəbl] *adj* **1.** (*place, work of art*) accesible **2.** (*person*) tratable, accesible
accession [ækˈseʃən] *n no pl* ascenso *m*
accessory [əkˈsesəri] <-ies> *n* **1.** (*for outfit*) complemento *m,* accesorio *m* **2.** (*for machine, toy*) accesorio *m* **3.** LAW cómplice *mf*
accident [ˈæksɪdənt] *n* accidente *m;* **~ insurance** seguro *m* contra accidentes; **by ~** (*accidentally*) sin querer; (*by chance*) por casualidad; **more by ~ than design** más por casualidad que por otra cosa; **~s will happen** son cosas que pasan
accidental [ˌæksɪˈdentəl, *Am:* -t̬əl] *adj*

1. (*unintentional*) casual, accidental; LAW (*death*) accidental **2.** (*discovery*) fortuito, -a
acclaim [ə'kleɪm] **I.** *vt* aclamar; **to ~ sb king** proclamar a alguien rey; **critically ~ed** elogiado por la crítica **II.** *n no pl* aclamación *f*
acclamation [ˌæklə'meɪʃən] *n no pl* aclamación *f*
acclimate ['æklɪmeɪt, *Am:* -lə-] *vt, vi Am s.* **acclimatize**
acclimation [ˌæklaɪ'meɪʃən] *n Am,* **acclimatization** [əˌklaɪmətaɪ'zeɪʃən, *Am:* -mət̬ə'zeɪʃən] *n no pl* aclimatación *f*
acclimatize [ə'klaɪmətaɪz] **I.** *vi* aclimatarse **II.** *vt* aclimatar
accolade ['ækəleɪd] *n* elogio *m*
accommodate [ə'kɒmədeɪt, *Am:* -'kɑː-] *vt* **1.** (*give place to stay*) alojar, hospedar; (*have room for*) albergar, alojar **2.** *form* (*adapt*) adaptar, acomodar; **to ~ oneself to sth** adaptarse a algo **3.** (*satisfy*) complacer
accommodating [ə'kɒmədeɪtɪŋ, *Am:* ə'kɑːmədeɪt̬ɪŋ] *adj* servicial
accommodation [əˌkɒmə'deɪʃən, *Am:* -kɑː-] *n* **1.** *no pl, Aus, Brit* (*place to stay*) alojamiento *m* **2.** *pl, Am* (*lodgings*) alojamiento *m* **3.** (*on vehicle, plane*) asientos *mpl* **4.** *form* (*compromise*) acuerdo *m*
accompaniment [ə'kʌmpənɪmənt] *n a.* MUS acompañamiento *m*
accompanist [ə'kʌmpənɪst] *n* MUS acompañante *mf*
accompany [ə'kʌmpəni] <-ie-> *vt a.* MUS (*go with*) acompañar; **to ~ sb on the violin** acompañar a alguien al violín
accomplice [ə'kʌmplɪs, *Am:* -'kɑːm-] *n* cómplice *mf*
accomplish [ə'kʌmplɪʃ, *Am:* -'kɑːm-] *vt* **1.** (*achieve*) efectuar **2.** (*finish*) concluir; **to ~ a task** realizar una tarea
accomplished [ə'kʌmplɪʃt, *Am:* -'kɑːm-] *adj* consumado, -a
accomplishment *n* **1.** (*achievement*) logro *m* **2.** *no pl* (*completion*) conclusión *f;* **~ of a task** realización *f* de una tarea **3.** (*skill*) talento *m*
accord [ə'kɔːd, *Am:* -'kɔːrd] **I.** *n* **1.** (*treaty*) convenio *m* **2.** *no pl* (*agreement, harmony*) acuerdo *m;* **with one ~** de común acuerdo; **of one's own ~** espontáneamente; **to be in ~ with** estar de acuerdo con **II.** *vt form* conceder **III.** *vi* **to ~ with sth** concordar con algo
accordance [ə'kɔːdəns, *Am:* -'kɔːrd-] *prep* **in ~ with** de conformidad con, conforme a
accordingly *adv* **1.** (*appropriately*) como corresponde **2.** (*therefore*) por consiguiente
according to [ə'kɔːdɪŋ tʊ, *Am:* ə'kɔːrdɪŋ tə] *prep* **1.** (*as told by*) según; **~ her/what I read** según ella/lo que leí; **to go ~ plan** salir según lo previsto **2.** (*as basis*) con arreglo a; **~ the law** con arreglo a la ley; **~ the recipe** según la receta
accordion [ə'kɔːdɪən, *Am:* -'kɔːrd-] *n* acordeón *m,* filarmónica *f Méx*
accost [ə'kɒst, *Am:* -'kɑːst] *vt form* abordar
account [ə'kaʊnt] **I.** *n* **1.** (*with bank*) cuenta *f* **2.** (*bill*) factura *f;* **to settle an ~** liquidar una cuenta **3.** *pl* (*financial records*) cuentas *fpl;* **to keep ~s** llevar las cuentas; **to keep an ~ of sth** llevar la cuenta de algo **4.** (*customer*) cliente *mf* **5.** (*description*) relato *m;* **an ~ of sth** un relato [*o* una relación] de algo; **to give an ~ of sth** informar sobre algo; **by all ~s** a decir de todos; **by her own ~** según ella misma **6.** *no pl* (*consideration*) **to take sth into ~** tomar [*o* tener] algo en cuenta; **to take no ~ of sth** no tomar [*o* tener] en cuenta algo, no hacer caso de; **on ~ of sth** por causa de algo; **on no ~** de ninguna manera **7.** *no pl, form* (*importance*) **of little/no ~** de poca/ninguna importancia **8.** *no pl* (*responsibility*) responsabilidad *f;* **on one's own ~** por cuenta propia; **on sb's ~** a cuenta de alguien ▸**to give a good ~ of oneself** lucirse; **to be called to ~ (for sth)** tener que rendir cuentas (de algo); **to settle ~s with sb** ajustar cuentas con alguien; **to turn sth to ~** sacar provecho de algo **II.** *vt form* considerar
◆**account for** *vt* **1.** (*explain*) explicar **2.** (*constitute*) representar
accountability [əˌkaʊntə'bɪlɪti, *Am:* -kaʊnt̬ə'bɪlət̬i] *n no pl* responsabilidad *f*
accountable [ə'kaʊntəbl, *Am:* -t̬ə-] *adj* responsable
accountancy [ə'kaʊntənsi, *Am:* -'kaʊnt̬nsi] *n no pl* contabilidad *f*
accountant [ə'kaʊntənt] *n* contable *mf,* contador(a) *m(f) And*
account(s) book *n* libro *m* de contabilidad [*o* de cuentas]
accredit [ə'kredɪt] *vt* **1.** (*recognize*) certificar **2.** POL acreditar **3.** (*credit*) atribuir
accrue [ə'kruː] *vi* **1.** **to ~ to sb** corresponder a alguien; **to ~ from** proceder de **2.** (*increase*) aumentar; (*interés*) acumularse
accumulate [ə'kjuːmjʊleɪt] **I.** *vt* acumular **II.** *vi* acumularse
accumulation [əˌkjuːmjʊ'leɪʃən] *n* **1.** *no pl* (*process*) acumulación *f* **2.** (*quantity*) cúmulo *m,* montón *m*
accumulator [ə'kjuːmjʊleɪtə^r] *n Aus, Brit* ELEC acumulador *m*
accuracy ['ækjərəsi, *Am:* -jɚəsi] *n no pl* precisión *f,* exactitud *f*
accurate ['ækjərət, *Am:* -jɚət] *adj* **1.** (*on target*) certero, -a **2.** (*correct*) preciso, -a, exacto, -a
accusation [ˌækjuː'zeɪʃən] *n* acusación *f*
accusative [ə'kjuːzətɪv, *Am:* -t̬ɪv] **I.** *n* acusativo *m* **II.** *adj* acusativo, -a
accusatory [ækjuː'zeitəri, *Am:* ə'kjuːzətɔːri] *adj form* acusador(a)
accuse [ə'kjuːz] *vt* acusar; **she stands ~d of ...** se la acusa de...
accused [ə'kjuːzd] *n* **the ~** el acusado, la acusada
accustom [ə'kʌstəm] *vt* acostumbrar

accustomed [ə'kʌstəmd] *adj* **1.** (*used*) acostumbrado, -a; **to be ~ to doing sth** estar acostumbrado a hacer algo; **to grow ~ to doing sth** acostumbrarse a hacer algo **2.** (*usual*) usual
AC/DC [ˌeɪsiː'diːsiː] *n* ELEC *abbr of* **alternating current/direct current** corriente *f* alterna/corriente *f* continua
ace [eɪs] **I.** *n* **1.** (*playing card*) as *m* **2.** *inf* (*expert*) as *m*, experto, -a *m, f* ►**to come within an ~ of doing sth** estar a punto de hacer algo **II.** *adj* **1.** *inf* (*expert*) experto, -a **2.** *inf* (*excellent*) genial; **~!** ¡genial!, ¡estupendo!
acetate ['æsɪteɪt] *n no pl* acetato *m*
acetic [ə'siːtɪk, *Am:* ə'siːt̬ɪk] *adj* acético, -a
acetylene [ə'setəliːn, *Am:* ə'set̬ə-] *n no pl* acetileno *m*
ache [eɪk] **I.** *n* dolor *m;* **~s and pains** dolores y achaques **II.** *vi* doler; **I am aching to see her again** me muero de ganas de volver a verla
achieve [ə'tʃiːv] *vt* (*aim, objective*) lograr; (*task*) llevar a cabo; (*victory*) conseguir; (*success*) alcanzar
achievement *n* **1.** (*feat*) hazaña *f;* (*success*) éxito *m*, logro *m* **2.** *no pl* (*achieving*) realización *f*
acid ['æsɪd] **I.** *n* **1.** CHEM ácido *m* **2.** *no pl, inf* (*LSD*) ácido *m* **II.** *adj* **1.** CHEM ácido, -a **2.** (*sarcastic*) mordaz
acid house *n* MUS música *f* acid
acidic [ə'sɪdɪk] *adj* ácido, -a
acidify [ə'sɪdɪfaɪ] <-ie-> **I.** *vt* acidificar **II.** *vi* acidificarse
acidity [ə'sɪdəti, *Am:* -ət̬i] *n no pl* **1.** CHEM acidez *f* **2.** *fig* mordacidad *f*
acid rain *n* lluvia *f* ácida **acid test** *n* prueba *f* de fuego
acknowledge [ək'nɒlɪdʒ, *Am:* -'nɑːlɪdʒ] *vt* **1.** (*admit*) admitir; (*guilt*) confesar **2.** (*recognize*) reconocer; (*letter*) acusar recibo de; (*favour*) agradecer
acknowledg(e)ment *n* **1.** *no pl* (*admission*) admisión *f;* (*of guilt*) confesión *f* **2.** *no pl* (*recognition*) reconocimiento *m* **3.** (*reply*) acuse *m* de recibo **4.** *pl* (*in book*) agradecimientos *mpl*
acne ['ækni] *n no pl* acné *m*
acorn ['eɪkɔːn, *Am:* -kɔrn] *n* bellota *f*
acoustic [ə'kuːstɪk] **I.** *adj* acústico, -a **II.** *npl* acústica *f*
acoustic coupler ['kʌplər] *n* acoplador *m* acústico **acoustic guitar** *n* guitarra *f* acústica **acoustic nerve** *n* ANAT nervio *m* auditivo
acquaint [ə'kweɪnt] *vt* **1.** (*know*) **to be/become ~ed with sb** conocer a alguien **2.** (*familiarize*) familiarizar; **to be ~ed with sth** estar al corriente de algo
acquaintance [ə'kweɪntəns] *n* **1.** (*person*) conocido, -a *m, f* **2.** *no pl* (*relationship*) relación *f;* **to make sb's ~** conocer a alguien **3.** *no pl* (*knowledge*) conocimiento *m*
acquiesce [ˌækwɪ'es] *vi form* **to ~ in sth** estar conforme con algo
acquiescence [ˌækwɪ'esns] *n no pl, form* conformidad *f*, aquiescencia *f*
acquiescent [ˌækwɪ'esnt] *adj form* conforme, aquiescente
acquire [ə'kwaɪər, *Am:* -'kwaɪɚ] *vt* adquirir
acquisition [ˌækwɪ'zɪʃən] *n* adquisición *f*
acquisitive [ə'kwɪzətɪv, *Am:* -ət̬ɪv] *adj* codicioso, -a
acquit [ə'kwɪt] <-tt-> *vt* **1.** LAW absolver; **to ~ sb of a charge** absolver a alguien de una acusación **2. to ~ oneself well/badly** salir bien/mal parado
acquittal [ə'kwɪtəl, *Am:* -'kwɪt̬-] *n no pl* absolución *f*
acre ['eɪkər, *Am:* 'eɪkɚ] *n* acre *m;* **~s of space** *inf* un montón de espacio
acreage ['eikrədʒ] *n no pl* superficie (en acres) *f*
acrid ['ækrɪd] *adj* **1.** (*smell, taste*) acre **2.** *fig* áspero, -a
acrimonious [ˌækrɪ'məʊnɪəs, *Am:* -'moʊnɪ-] *adj* (*remark*) mordaz; (*debate*) reñido, -a
acrimony ['ækrɪməni, *Am:* -moʊni] *n no pl, form* acrimonia *f*
acrobat ['ækrəbæt] *n* acróbata *mf*
acrobatic [ˌækrə'bætɪk, *Am:* -'bæt̬ɪk] *adj* acrobático, -a
acronym ['ækrəʊnɪm, *Am:* -rə-] *n* acrónimo *m*
across [ə'krɒs, *Am:* ə'krɑːs] **I.** *prep* **1.** (*on other side of*) al otro lado de; **just ~ the street** justo al otro lado de la calle; **~ from sb/sth** enfrente de alguien/algo **2.** (*from one side to other*) a través de; **to walk ~ the bridge** cruzar el puente andando; **the bridge ~ the river** el puente que cruza el río; **to go ~ the sea to France** ir a Francia cruzando el mar ►**~ the board** general, global **II.** *adv* de un lado a otro; **to run/swim ~** cruzar corriendo/a nado; **to be 2m ~** tener 2 m de ancho
act [ækt] **I.** *n* **1.** (*action*) acto *m;* **~ of charity** obra *f* de caridad; **an ~ of God** LAW un caso de fuerza mayor; **the A~s of the Apostles** REL los Hechos de los Apóstoles; **to catch sb in the ~** coger a alguien con las manos en la masa **2.** (*performance*) número *m;* **a hard ~ to follow** un número difícil de repetir **3.** (*pretence*) fingimiento *m* **4.** THEAT acto *m* **5.** LAW ley *f* ►**to get one's ~ together** *inf* arreglárselas; **to get in on the ~** lograr tomar parte en el asunto **II.** *vi* **1.** (*take action*) actuar; **to ~ for sb** representar a alguien **2.** (*behave*) portarse **3.** (*take effect*) dar resultados **4.** THEAT actuar **5.** (*pretend*) fingir **III.** *vt* THEAT representar; **to ~ the part of sb** hacer el papel de alguien; **to ~ the fool** hacer el tonto
◆**act on** *vt* obrar de acuerdo con
◆**act out** *vt* (*scene*) representar
◆**act up** *vi inf* **1.** (*person*) hacer de las suyas **2.** (*machine*) fallar, no funcionar

acting ['æktɪŋ] **I.** *adj* en funciones **II.** *n no pl* THEAT arte *m* dramático

action ['ækʃən] *n* **1.** *no pl* (*activeness*) acción *f*; **to be out of ~** (*person*) estar inactivo; (*machine*) no funcionar; **to put sth out of ~** inutilizar algo; **to swing into ~** ponerse en marcha; **to take ~** tomar medidas; **to take no ~** no hacer nada **2.** *no pl* MIL acción *f*; **to see ~** servir; **to go into ~** entrar en combate; **killed in ~** muerto en acto de servicio **3.** (*mechanism*) mecanismo *m* **4.** (*motion*) movimiento *m* **5.** LAW (*case*) demanda *f*; **civil ~** demanda civil; **to bring an ~ against sb** entablar una demanda contra alguien **6.** *no pl, inf* (*exciting events*) bullicio *m*; (*fun*) jarana *f* ►**~s speak louder than words** *prov* hechos son amores y no buenas razones *prov*, obras son amores y no buenas razones *prov*

action-packed *adj* de acción

action replay *n Brit* TV repetición *f*

activate ['æktɪveɪt] *vt a.* CHEM activar

active ['æktɪv] *adj* **1.** (*lively, not passive*) activo, -a; **to be ~ in sth** participar en algo; **to take an ~ part in sth** participar activamente en algo **2.** (*energetic*) enérgico, -a

actively *adv* **1.** (*lively*) activamente **2.** (*energetically*) enérgicamente

activist ['æktɪvɪst] *n* POL activista *mf*

activity [æk'tɪvəti, *Am:* -əţi] <-ies> *n* **1.** *no pl* (*state*) actividad *f* **2.** *pl* (*pursuits*) actividades *fpl*

actor ['æktəʳ, *Am:* -tɚ] *n* actor *m*

actress ['æktrɪs] *n* actriz *f*

actual ['æktʃʊəl] *adj* **1.** (*real*) verdadero, -a; **in ~ fact** en realidad **2.** (*precise*) exacto, -a; **what were her ~ words?** ¿cuáles fueron sus palabras exactas?

actually ['æktʃʊli] *adv* **1.** (*in fact*) en realidad **2.** (*by the way*) **~ I saw her yesterday** pues la vi ayer

actuate ['æktʃʊeɪt] *vt* **1.** (*set going: mechanism*) accionar **2.** *form* (*motivate*) estimular

acumen ['ækjʊmən, *Am:* ə'kjuːmən] *n* perspicacia *f*; **business ~** perspicacia para los negocios

acupuncture ['ækjʊpʌŋktʃəʳ, *Am:* -tʃɚ] *n no pl* acupuntura *f*

acute [ə'kjuːt] **I.** *adj* **1.** (*serious*) agudo, -a; (*anxiety*) extremo, -a; (*embarrassment*) hondo, -a; (*difficulties*) grande; (*shortage*) fuerte **2.** (*shrewd*) listo, -a **3.** MAT (*angle*) agudo, -a **II.** *n* LING acento *m* agudo

acutely *adv* extremadamente; **to be ~ aware of sth** ser plenamente consciente de algo

ad [æd] *n inf abbr of* **advertisement** anuncio *m*

AD [ˌeɪ'diː] *abbr of* **anno Domini** d. (de) C.

adage ['ædɪdʒ] *n* refrán *m*

adagio [ə'dɑːdʒɪəʊ, *Am:* ə'dɑːdʒoʊ] **I.** *adv* pausadamente **II.** *n* adagio *m*

Adam ['ædəm] *n* Adán *m* ►**not to know sb from ~** no conocer a alguien en absoluto

adamant ['ædəmənt] *adj* firme, categórico, -a

Adam's apple *n* ANAT nuez *f*, bocado *m* de Adán

adapt [ə'dæpt] **I.** *vt* adaptar; **to ~ oneself** adaptarse **II.** *vi* adaptarse

adaptable *adj* adaptable

adaptation [ˌædæp'teɪʃən] *n* **1.** THEAT, MUS, CINE, LIT adaptación *f*, versión *f* **2.** *no pl* (*act of adapting*) adaptación *f*

adapter *n*, **adaptor** [ə'dæptəʳ, *Am:* ə'dæptɚ] *n* ELEC adaptador *m*; (*for several plugs*) ladrón *m*

add [æd] *vt* **1.** (*put with*) añadir, agregar *AmL* **2.** (*say*) añadir, agregar **3.** MAT sumar

◆**add up** **I.** *vi* sumar; **to ~ to ...** ascender a...; **it doesn't ~ to much** *fig* no significa mucho **II.** *vt* sumar

addendum [ə'dendəm] <-da> *n* adenda *f*

adder ['ædəʳ, *Am:* 'ædɚ] *n* víbora *f*

addict ['ædɪkt] *n* **1.** MED adicto, -a *m, f*; **drug ~** drogadicto *m* **2.** *fig* partidario, -a *m, f*; **to be a cinema ~** ser un apasionado del cine

addicted [ə'dɪktɪd] *adj* adicto, -a; **~ to drugs** drogadicto, -a; **to be ~ to sth** ser adicto a algo; *fig* ser muy aficionado a algo

addiction [ə'dɪkʃən] *n no pl* adicción *f*; **drug ~** drogadicción *f*

addictive [ə'dɪktɪv] *adj* adictivo, -a

addition [ə'dɪʃən] *n* **1.** *no pl* MAT suma *f* **2.** *no pl* (*act of adding*) adición *f*; **in ~** además; **in ~ to ...** además de... **3.** (*added thing*) añadido *m*, añadidura *f*; **an ~ to the family** uno más en la familia

additional [ə'dɪʃənl] *adj* adicional

additionally [ə'dɪʃənəli] *adv* por añadidura; **and ~** y además

additive ['ædɪtɪv, *Am:* -əţɪv] *n* aditivo *m*

address [ə'dres, *Am:* 'ædres] **I.** *n* **1.** *a.* INFOR dirección *f* **2.** (*speech*) discurso *m* **3.** (*title*) **form of ~** tratamiento *m* **II.** *vt* **1.** (*write address on*) dirigir; **to be wrongly ~ed** llevar la dirección equivocada **2.** (*speak to*) dirigirse a **3.** (*use title*) **to ~ sb** (**as sth**) dar a alguien el tratamiento (de algo) **4.** (*deal with*) abordar

addressee [ˌædre'siː] *n* destinatario, -a *m, f*

adenoids ['ædɪnɔɪdz, *Am:* 'ædnɔɪdz] *npl* ANAT vegetaciones *fpl*, adenoides *fpl*

adept ['ædept, *Am:* ə'dept] *adj* experto, -a; **to be ~ at sth** ser hábil para algo

adequacy ['ædɪkwəsi] *n no pl* **1.** (*being enough*) suficiencia *f* **2.** (*being good enough*) idoneidad *f*

adequate ['ædɪkwət] *adj* **1.** (*sufficient*) suficiente **2.** (*good enough*) adecuado, -a

adhere [əd'hɪəʳ, *Am:* -'hɪr] *vi* **1.** *form* adherirse **2.** to **~ to** (*rule*) observar; (*belief*) aferrarse a

adherence [əd'hɪərəns, *Am:* -'hɪrns] *n no pl* (*to rule*) observancia *f*; (*to belief*) adhesión *f*

adherent [əd'hɪərənt] *n form* partidario, -a *m, f*

adhesive [əd'hiːsɪv] **I.** *adj* adhesivo, -a **II.** *n no pl* adhesivo *m*

A

ad hoc [ˌæd'hɒk, *Am:* -'hɑːk] *adj* ad hoc
adipose tissue ['ædɪpəʊsˌtɪʃuː, *Am:* -poʊzˌtɪʃuː] *n* tejido *m* adiposo
adjacent [ə'dʒeɪsnt] *adj* contiguo, -a; MAT adyacente
adjectival [ˌædʒɪk'taɪvl] *adj* adjetivo, -a, adjetival
adjective ['ædʒɪktɪv] *n* adjetivo *m*
adjoin [ə'dʒɔɪn] **I.** *vt* lindar con **II.** *vi* colindar
adjoining *adj* colindante
adjourn [ə'dʒɜːn, *Am:* -'dʒɜːrn] **I.** *vt* aplazar, posponer **II.** *vi* **1.** (*pause: meeting*) aplazarse **2.** *form* (*go to*) **to ~ to another room** trasladarse a otra habitación
adjudicate [ə'dʒuːdɪkeɪt] **I.** *vt* juzgar **II.** *vi* actuar como árbitro
adjust [ə'dʒʌst] **I.** *vt* **1.** *a.* TECH ajustar, regular **2.** (*rearrange*) arreglar; **to ~ a seam** (*take it in*) meter el dobladillo; (*let it out*) sacar el dobladillo **3.** (*change*) modificar **4.** (*adapt*) adaptar **II.** *vi* adaptarse; **to ~ to sth** adaptarse a algo
adjustable *adj* ajustable
adjustable spanner *n Aus, Brit* llave *f* inglesa
adjustment *n* **1.** (*mechanical*) ajuste *m* **2.** (*mental*) adaptación *f*
adjutant ['ædʒʊtənt] *n* ayudante *mf*
ad-lib [ˌæd'lɪb] <-bb-> **I.** *adv* improvisando **II.** *vi, vt* improvisar
adman ['ædmæn] <-men> *n* ECON publicista *m*
admin ['ædmɪn] *abbr of* **administration** admón.
administer [əd'mɪnɪstəʳ, *Am:* -stɚ] *vt* **1.** *a.* POL (*manage: funds, estate*) administrar; **to ~ sth** estar al cargo de algo **2.** (*dispense: punishment*) aplicar; (*medicine*) administrar; **to ~ aid** [*o* **relief**] **to sb** asistir a alguien; **to ~ first aid to sb** prestar primeros auxilios a alguien; **to ~ a severe blow to sb** dar un palo a alguien; **to ~ an oath** tomar juramento
administration [ədˌmɪnɪ'streɪʃən] *n* **1.** *no pl* (*organization*) administración *f;* (*management*) gerencia *f;* **the ~** la dirección **2.** *Am* (*time in power*) mandato *m* **3.** POL gobierno *m* **4.** *no pl* (*dispensing: of medicine*) administración *f;* **the ~ of an oath** la toma de un juramento
administrative [əd'mɪnɪstrətɪv] *adj* administrativo, -a
administrator [əd'mɪnɪstreɪtəʳ, *Am:* -tɚ] *n* **1.** (*of organization, institution*) administrador(a) *m(f)* **2.** LAW albacea *mf*
admirable ['ædmərəbl] *adj* admirable
admiral ['ædmərəl] *n* almirante *m*
Admiralty ['ædmərəlti, *Am:* -t̬i] *n no pl, Brit* HIST Almirantazgo *m*
admiration [ˌædmə'reɪʃən] *n no pl* admiración *f;* **in ~** lleno de admiración
admire [əd'maɪəʳ, *Am:* əd'maɪɚ] *vt* admirar; **to ~ sb for sth** admirar a alguien por algo; **to ~ sb from afar** embobarse con alguien desde lejos
admirer [əd'mɪərəʳ, *Am:* -ɚ] *n* admirador(a) *m(f)*
admissible [əd'mɪsəbl] *adj* admisible
admission [əd'mɪʃən] *n* **1.** *no pl* (*entry: to place, building*) entrada; (*to college, organization*) ingreso *m,* admisión *f* **2.** (*entrance fee*) entrada *f* **3.** (*acknowledgement*) confesión *f;* **by** [*o* **on**] **his own ~, ...** por confesión propia...
admit [əd'mɪt] <-tt-> **I.** *vt* **1.** (*acknowledge: error*) reconocer; (*crime*) confesar; **to ~ that ...** reconocer que... **2.** (*allow entrance to*) dejar entrar **3.** (*permit*) admitir **II.** *vi* **to ~ to sth** confesarse culpable de algo
admittance [əd'mɪtns] *n no pl* entrada *f;* **to refuse sb ~** negar la entrada a alguien; **no ~** se prohíbe la entrada
admittedly [əd'mɪtɪdli, *Am:* -'mɪt̬ɪdli] *adv* **~, ...** es cierto que...
admonish [əd'mɒnɪʃ, *Am:* -'mɑːnɪʃ] *vt* amonestar
admonishment *n,* **admonition** [ˌædmə'nɪʃən] *n* amonestación *f*
ado [ə'duː] *n no pl* **1.** (*commotion*) embrollo *m* **2.** (*delay*) demora *f;* **without more** [*o* **further**] **~** sin más preámbulos ▸**much ~ about nothing** mucho ruido y pocas nueces
adolescence [ˌædə'lesns] *n no pl* adolescencia *f*
adolescent [ˌædə'lesnt] **I.** *adj* **1.** (*relating to adolescence*) adolescente **2.** (*immature*) inmaduro, -a **II.** *n* adolescente *mf*
adopt [ə'dɒpt, *Am:* -'dɑːpt] *vt* **1.** (*child, strategy*) adoptar **2.** (*candidate*) nombrar
adoption [ə'dɒpʃən, *Am:* -'dɑːp-] *n* **1.** (*of child, strategy*) adopción *f* **2.** (*of candidate*) nombramiento *m*
adorable [ˌə'dɔːrəbl] *adj* encantador(a); **just ~** irresistible
adoration [ˌædə'reɪʃən] *n no pl* adoración *f;* **the ~ of the Virgin Mary** REL el culto a la virgen María
adore [ə'dɔːʳ, *Am:* -'dɔːr] *vt* **1.** (*love strongly*) adorar **2.** REL venerar
adoring [ə'dɔːrɪŋ] *adj* cariñoso, -a
adorn [ə'dɔːn, *Am:* -'dɔːrn] *vt form* adornar
adornment *n form* adorno *m*
adrenalin(e) [ə'drenəlɪn] *n no pl* adrenalina *f*
Adriatic [ˌeɪdri'ætɪk] *n* **the ~** (**Sea**) el (mar) Adriático
adrift [ə'drɪft] *adv* a la deriva; **to cut sth ~** cortar las amarras de algo; **to come** [*o* **go**] **~** *Brit, fig* fallar
adroit [ə'drɔɪt] *adj* mañoso, -a; (*mentally*) hábil; **to be ~ at sth** ser diestro en algo; **to be ~ at doing sth** ser habilidoso haciendo algo
adulation [ˌædjʊ'leɪʃən, *Am:* ˌædʒə-] *n no pl* adulación *f*
adult ['ædʌlt, *Am:* ə'dʌlt] **I.** *n* (*person*) adulto, -a *m, f;* (*animal*) animal *m* adulto **II.** *adj* **1.** (*fully grown*) adulto, -a **2.** (*mature*) maduro, -a; **let's try to be ~ about this problem** sea-

mos razonables con este problema **3.** (*explicit*) para adultos
adult education *n no pl* educación *f* para adultos
adulterate [əˈdʌltəreɪt, *Am:* -t̬əreɪt] *vt* adulterar
adulterer [əˈdʌltərəʳ, *Am:* -t̬ɚɚ] *n* adúltero *m*
adulteress [əˈdʌltərɪs, *Am:* -t̬ɚ-] <-es> *n* adúltera *f*
adulterous [əˈdʌltərəs, *Am:* -t̬ɚ-] *adj* adúltero, -a
adultery [əˈdʌltəri, *Am:* -t̬ɚi] <-ies> *n no pl* adulterio *m;* **to commit** ~ cometer adulterio
adulthood [ˈædʌlthʊd] *n* edad *f* adulta
advance [ədˈvɑːns, *Am:* -ˈvæːns] **I.** *vi* avanzar; **to** ~ **on sb/sth** avanzar hacia alguien/algo **II.** *vt* **1.** (*cause to move forward*) avanzar; (*interest, cause*) promover, fomentar **2.** (*pay in advance*) anticipar **III.** *n* **1.** (*forward movement*) avance *m,* progreso *m;* **in** ~ de antemano **2.** FIN anticipo *m* **3.** *pl* (*sexual flirtation*) insinuaciones *fpl;* **unwelcome ~s** molestias *fpl;* **to reject sb's ~s** rechazar las insinuaciones de alguien **IV.** *adj* avanzado, -a; **without** ~ **warning** sin previo aviso
advance booking *n* reserva *f* anticipada
advanced [ədˈvɑːnst, *Am:* -ˈvæːnst] *adj* (*country, pupil*) avanzado, -a; (*level*) superior
advancement [ədˈvɑːnsmənt, *Am:* -ˈvæːnsmənt] *n* **1.** (*improvement*) avance *m* **2.** *no pl* (*promotion*) fomento *m;* **an opportunity for** ~ una oportunidad para mejorar
advance notice *n no pl* aviso *m* (previo)
advance payment *n* anticipo *m*
advantage [ədˈvɑːntɪdʒ, *Am:* -ˈvæːnt̬ɪdʒ] *n a.* SPORTS ventaja *f;* ~ **Jackson** ventaja para Jackson; **to have an** ~ **over sb** tener ventaja sobre alguien; **to take** ~ **of sb/sth** aprovecharse de alguien/algo
advantageous [ˌædvənˈteɪdʒəs, *Am:* -vænˈ-] *adj* ventajoso, -a
advent [ˈædvənt] *n no pl* **1.** (*coming*) llegada *f* **2.** REL **Advent** Adviento *m*
adventure [ədˈventʃəʳ, *Am:* -tʃɚ] *n* aventura *f;* **to look for** ~ buscar el riesgo
adventurer *n* **1.** (*seeker of excitement*) aventurero, -a *m, f* **2.** (*opportunist*) aprovechado, -a *m, f*
adventurous [ədˈventʃərəs] *adj* (*person*) aventurero, -a; (*decision*) arriesgado, -a
adverb [ˈædvɜːb, *Am:* -vɜːrb] *n* adverbio *m*
adverbial [ædˈvɜːbɪəl, *Am:* -ˈvɜːr-] *adj* adverbial
adversary [ˈædvəsəri, *Am:* -vɚseri] <-ies> *n* adversario, -a *m, f*
adverse [ˈædvɜːs, *Am:* -vɜːrs] *adj* (*decision, criticism, effect*) adverso, -a; (*conditions*) adverso, -a, desfavorable; (*reaction*) hostil
adversity [ədˈvɜːsəti, *Am:* -ˈvɜːrsət̬i] <-ies> *n* adversidad *f;* **in** ~ en situaciones adversas
advert [ˈædvɜːt, *Am:* -vɜːrt] *n s.* **advertisement**
advertise [ˈædvətaɪz, *Am:* -vɚ-] **I.** *vt* anunciar **II.** *vi* hacer publicidad
advertisement [ədˈvɜːtɪsmənt, *Am:* ˌædvərˈtaɪzmənt] *n* COM anuncio *m,* aviso *m AmL;* **to be a good/bad** ~ **for sth** *fig* decir/no decir mucho en favor de algo; **job** ~ oferta *f* de empleo
advertiser [ˈædvətaɪzəʳ, *Am:* -vɚtaɪzɚ] *n* anunciante *mf*
advertising [ˈædvəˌtaɪzɪŋ, *Am:* -vɚˌtaɪzɪŋ] *n* publicidad *f*
advertising agency <-ies> *n* agencia *f* de publicidad **advertising campaign** *n* campaña *f* publicitaria
advice [ədˈvaɪs] *n no pl* **1.** (*suggestion, opinion*) consejo *m;* **a piece of** ~ un consejo; **to ask for** ~ pedir consejo; **to ask sb for** ~ **on sth** pedir consejo a alguien sobre algo; **to give some good** ~ dar buenos consejos; **on sb's** ~ siguiendo el consejo de alguien **2.** COM aviso *m*
advisable [ədˈvaɪzəbl] *adj* aconsejable; **it is (not)** ~ (no) es recomendable [*o* aconsejable]
advise [ədˈvaɪz] **I.** *vt* aconsejar; (*specialist*) asesorar; **to** ~ **sb against sth** desaconsejar algo a alguien; **to** ~ **sb on sth** aconsejar a alguien sobre algo; **to** ~ **sb of sth** informar a alguien sobre algo **II.** *vi* dar un consejo; **to** ~ **against sth** desaconsejar algo; **to** ~ **on sth** asesorar en algo
adviser *n,* **advisor** [ədˈvaɪzəʳ, *Am:* -zɚ] *n* asesor(a) *m(f)*
advisory [ədˈvaɪzəri] *adj* consultivo, -a; **in an** ~ **capacity** en calidad de asesor; ~ **committee** comité consultivo
advocate¹ [ˈædvəkeɪt] *vt* recomendar; **to** ~ **doing sth** recomendar hacer algo
advocate² [ˈædvəkət] *n* abogado, -a *m, f* defensor(a)
AEC *n Am abbr of* **Atomic Energy Commission** CEA *f*
Aegean [iːˈdʒiːən] *n* **the** ~ **(Sea)** el (mar) Egeo
aegis [ˈiːdʒɪs] *n no pl* **under the** ~ **of ...** bajo los auspicios de...
aeon [ˈiːən, *Am:* -ɑːn] *n Brit* **1.** (*period of time*) eón *m* **2.** *fig* eternidad *f*
aerate [ˈeəreɪt, *Am:* ˈereɪt] *vt* **1.** (*expose to air*) airear **2.** (*drink*) oxigenar
aerial [ˈeərɪəl, *Am:* ˈerɪ-] **I.** *adj* aéreo,-a; ~ **photography** fotografía *f* aérea **II.** *n* antena *f*
aerobatic [ˌeərəʊˈbætɪk, *Am:* ˌeroʊˈbæt̬-] *adj* de acrobacia aérea
aerobatics *npl* acrobacia *f* aérea
aerobics [eəˈrəʊbɪks, *Am:* erˈoʊ-] *n + sing/pl vb* aeróbic *m,* aerobic *m;* **to do** ~ hacer aeróbic
aerodrome [ˈeərədrəʊm, *Am:* ˈerədroʊm] *n Brit* aeródromo *m*
aerodynamic [ˌeərəʊdaɪˈnæmɪk, *Am:* ˌeroʊ-] *adj* aerodinámico, -a
aerodynamics *n + sing vb* aerodinámica *f*
aeronautic [ˌeərəˈnɔːtɪk, *Am:* ˌerəˈnɑːt̬ɪk] *adj* aeronáutico, -a

aeronautics [ˌeərəˈnɔːtɪks, *Am:* ˌerəˈnɑːt̬ɪks] *n + sing vb* aeronáutica *f*

aeroplane [ˈeərəpleɪn, *Am:* ˈerə-] *n Aus, Brit* avión *m*

aerosol [ˈeərəsɒl, *Am:* ˈerəsɑːl] *n* aerosol *m*

aerospace industry [ˈeərəʊspeɪs ˈɪndəstri, *Am:* ˈeroʊ-] *n* industria *f* aeroespacial

aesthetic [iːsˈθetɪk(l), *Am:* esˈθet̬-] *adj* estético, -a

aesthetics [iːsˈθetɪks, *Am:* esˈθet̬-] *n + sing vb* estética *f*

afar [əˈfɑːʳ, *Am:* -ˈfɑːr] *adv form* lejos; **from ~** desde lejos

affable [ˈæfəbl] *adj* afable

affair [əˈfeəʳ, *Am:* -ˈfer] *n* **1.** (*matter*) asunto *m;* **~s of state** asuntos de estado; **financial ~s** asuntos financieros; **to meddle in sb's ~s** meterse en los asuntos de alguien; **it's his own ~** eso es asunto suyo **2.** (*controversial situation*) episodio *m;* (*scandal*) escándalo *m* **3.** (*sexual relationship*) aventura *f* (amorosa); **to have an ~ (with sb)** tener una aventura (con alguien) **4.** (*event, occasion*) acontecimiento *m*

affect [əˈfekt] *vt* **1.** (*have affect on*) afectar; **to be ~ed by sth** (*be moved*) conmoverse por algo **2.** (*influence: decision*) afectar a, influir en **3.** (*simulate*) fingir

affectation [ˌæfekˈteɪʃən] *n* afectación *f,* amaneramiento *m*

affected [əˈfektɪd] *adj* (*behaviour, accent*) afectado, -a, amanerado, -a; (*emotion*) fingido, -a; (*smile*) falso, -a; (*style*) forzado, -a

affection [əˈfekʃən] *n* afecto *m,* cariño *m;* **to have a deep ~ for sb** tener mucho cariño a alguien

affectionate [əˈfekʃənət] *adj* afectuoso, -a, cariñoso, -a

affidavit [ˌæfɪˈdeɪvɪt] *n* declaración *f* jurada

affiliate [əˈfɪlɪeɪt] **I.** *vt* afiliar; **to be ~d to** [*o* **with**] **sb/sth** estar afiliado a alguien/algo **II.** *n a.* ECON filial *f*

affiliation [əˌfɪlɪˈeɪʃən] *n* afiliación *f*

affinity [əˈfɪnəti, *Am:* -ət̬i] <-ies> *n* afinidad *f*

affirm [əˈfɜːm, *Am:* -ˈfɜːrm] *vt* afirmar

affirmation [ˌæfəˈmeɪʃən, *Am:* -ɚ-] *n* afirmación *f*

affirmative [əˈfɜːmətɪv, *Am:* -ˈfɜːrmət̬ɪv] **I.** *adj* afirmativo, -a **II.** *n* **to answer** [*o* **reply**] **in the ~** contestar afirmativamente, dar una respuesta afirmativa; **~ action** discriminación *f* positiva

affix¹ [əˈfɪks] *vt* (*attach*) poner; (*stick on*) pegar; (*clip on*) clavar

affix² [æˈfɪks] *n* <-es> LING afijo *m*

afflict [əˈflɪkt] *vt* afligir; **to be ~ed with sth** padecer de algo

affliction [əˈflɪkʃən] *n* aflicción *f*

affluence [ˈæflʊəns] *n no pl* riqueza *f*

affluent [ˈæflʊənt] *adj* rico, -a; **an ~ way of life** una vida acomodada; **~ society** sociedad opulenta

afford [əˈfɔːd, *Am:* -ˈfɔːrd] *vt* **1.** (*have money, time for*) permitirse; **to be able to ~ sth** poder permitirse algo; **he can ill ~ it** a duras penas se lo puede permitir **2.** (*provide*) proporcionar, dar; **to ~ protection** ofrecer protección

affordable [əˈfɔːdəbl, *Am:* -ˈfɔːr-] *adj* (*price, purchase*) asequible

afforestation [əˌfɒrɪˈsteɪʃən, *Am:* -ˌfɔːrə-] *n no pl* forestación *f*

affront [əˈfrʌnt] **I.** *n* afrenta *f;* **an ~ to sb's dignity** una afrenta [*o* ofensa] a la dignidad de alguien **II.** *vt* afrentar; **to be ~ed at** [*o* **by**] **sth** ofenderse por algo

Afghan [ˈæfgæn] **I.** *n* **1.** (*person*) afgano, -a *m, f* **2.** LING afgano *m* **3.** (*dog*) galgo *m* afgano **II.** *adj* afgano, -a

Afghanistan [æfˈgænɪstæn, *Am:* -ə-] *n* Afganistán *m*

afield [əˈfiːld] *adv* **far ~** muy lejos; **further ~** más lejos

afloat [əˈfləʊt, *Am:* -ˈfloʊt] *adj* a flote; **to keep** [*o* **stay**] **~** *a. fig* mantenerse a flote

afoot [əˈfʊt] *adj* **there's sth ~** se está tramando algo

aforementioned [əˌfɔːˈmenʃnd, *Am:* -ˌfɔːr-ˌ], **aforesaid** [əˌfɔːsed, *Am:* -ˌfɔːr-ˌ] *form* **I.** *adj* (*in text*) anteriormente mencionado, -a; (*in conversation*) dicho, -a **II.** *n inv* **the ~** el mencionado/la mencionada; (*of person mentioned in conversation*) el susodicho/la susodicha

afraid [əˈfreɪd] *adj* **1.** (*scared*) **to be ~** tener miedo; **to be ~ of doing** [*o* **to do**] **sth** tener miedo de hacer algo; **to be ~ of sb/sth** tener miedo a algo/alguien **2.** (*sorry*) **I'm ~ so** lo siento, pero así es; **I'm ~ not** lo siento pero no; **I haven't got the time, I'm ~** me temo que no tengo tiempo

afresh [əˈfreʃ] *adv* de nuevo; **to start ~** empezar de nuevo

Africa [ˈæfrɪkə] *n no pl* África *f*

African [ˈæfrɪkən] **I.** *n* africano, -a *m, f* **II.** *adj* africano, -a

African-American [ˌæfrɪkənəˈmerɪkən] *adj, n s.* **Afro-American**

Afrikaans [ˌæfrɪˈkɑːns] *n* LING africaans *m inv*

Afro-American [ˌæfrəʊəˈmerɪkən, *Am:* -roʊ-] **I.** *adj* afroamericano, -a **II.** *n* afroamericano, -a *m, f*

Afro-Caribbean [ˌæfrəʊkærɪˈbiːən, *Am:* -roʊker-] **I.** *adj* afrocaribeño, -a **II.** *n* afrocaribeño, -a *m, f*

after [ˈɑːftəʳ, *Am:* ˈæftɚ] **I.** *prep* **1.** (*at later time*) después de; **~ two days** al cabo de dos días; **(shortly) ~ breakfast** (poco) después de desayunar **2.** (*behind*) detrás de; **to run ~ sb** correr detrás de alguien **3.** (*following*) después de; **D comes ~ C** la D viene después [*o* detrás] de la C; **to have quarrel ~ quarrel** tener pelea tras pelea **4.** (*about*) por; **to ask ~ sb** preguntar por alguien **5.** (*despite*) **~ all** después de todo **6.** (*in the style of*) **a drawing ~ Picasso** un dibujo al estilo de Picasso **7.** (*in *honour of*) **to name sth/sb ~ sb** llamar a algo/alguien a como alguien **II.** *adv* después; **soon ~** poco después; **the day ~** el día después **III.** *conj* después de que +*subj;* **he spoke ~ she went out** habló después de que ella se fuera; **I'll call him** (**straight**) **~ I've taken a shower** le llamaré tan pronto (como) me haya duchado

aftercare ['ɑːftəkeəʳ, *Am:* 'æftɚker] *n no pl* MED asistencia *f* postoperatoria

after-dinner *adj* de sobremesa

after-effects ['ɑːftərɪˌfektz, *Am:* 'æftɚ-] *npl* (*of drugs, treatment*) efectos *mpl* secundarios; (*of accident*) secuelas *fpl*

afterlife ['ɑːftəlaɪf, *Am:* 'æftɚ-] *n no pl* vida *f* más allá de la muerte; **the ~** el más allá

aftermath ['ɑːftəmɑːθ, *Am:* 'æftɚmæθ] *n no pl* secuelas *fpl*

afternoon [ˌɑːftə'nuːn, *Am:* ˌæftɚ-] **I.** *n* tarde *f;* **this ~** esta tarde; **in the ~** por la tarde; **all ~** toda la tarde; **tomorrow/yesterday ~** mañana/ayer por la tarde; **4 o'clock in the ~** las 4 de la tarde; **good ~!** ¡buenas tardes! **II.** *adj* de la tarde; **~ nap** siesta *f*

after-sales service [ˌɑːftə'seilz, *Am:* ˌæftɚ-'seilz] *n no pl* servicio *m* postventa

aftershave ['ɑːftəʃeɪv, *Am:* 'æftɚ-] *n* loción *f* para depués del afeitado

aftertaste ['ɑːftəteɪst, *Am:* 'æftɚ-] *n a. fig* regusto *m*

afterthought ['ɑːftəθɔːt, *Am:* 'æftɚθɑːt] *n* idea *f* tardía

afterward *adv Am,* **afterwards** ['ɑːftəwədz, *Am:* 'æftɚwɚdz] *adv* (*later*) más tarde; (*after something*) después; **shortly ~** poco después

again [ə'gen] *adv* **1.** (*as a repetition*) otra vez; (*one more time*) de nuevo; **never ~** nunca más; **once ~** otra vez; **then ~** por otra parte; **yet ~** una vez más; **~ and ~** una y otra vez **2.** (*anew*) de nuevo

against [ə'genst] **I.** *prep* **1.** (*in opposition to*) (en) contra (de); **to be ~ sth/sb** estar en contra de algo/alguien; **~ what he said** en contra de lo que dijo; **~ my will** en contra de mi voluntad **2.** (*as protection from*) contra; **to protect oneself ~ rain** protegerse de la lluvia **3.** (*in contact with*) contra; **to lean ~ a tree** apoyarse en un árbol; **to run ~ a wall** estrellarse contra una pared **4.** (*in front of*) **~ the light** a contraluz **5.** (*in competition with*) **~ time/the clock** contra el tiempo/el reloj **6.** (*in comparison with*) **the dollar rose/fell ~ the euro** el dólar subió/bajó respecto al euro **7.** (*in exchange for*) **payment ~ invoice** pago *m* contra recibo **II.** *adv a.* POL en contra; **there were 10 votes ~** hubo 10 votos en contra

agate ['ægət] *n* ágata *f*

age [eɪdʒ] **I.** *n* **1.** (*of person, object*) edad *f;* **old ~** vejez *f;* **what is your age?** ¿qué edad tienes?; **when I was her ~** cuando tenía su edad; **to be seven years of ~** tener siete años; **to be under ~** ser menor de edad; **to improve with ~** mejorar con los años [*o* la edad] **2.** (*era*) época *f;* **in this day and ~** en estos tiempos **3.** (*long time*) siglos *mpl;* **I haven't seen you in ~s!** ¡hace siglos que no te veo! **II.** *vi* **1.** (*become older*) envejecer **2.** GASTR (*mature*) madurar **III.** *vt* **1.** (*make older*) envejecer **2.** GASTR (*mature*) madurar

age bracket *n s.* **age group**

aged[1] [eɪdʒd] *adj* (*with age of*) de…años de edad; **this game is for children ~ 8 to 12** este juego es para niños de entre 8 y 12 años de edad

aged[2] ['eɪdʒɪd] **I.** *adj* (*old*) viejo, -a **II.** *n* **the ~** los ancianos

age group *n* grupo *m* de edad

ageing **I.** *adj* envejecido, -a **II.** *n* envejecimiento *m;* **the ~ process** el proceso de envejecimiento

ageless ['eɪdʒlɪs] *adj* eterno, -a

age limit *n* límite *m* de edad

agency ['eɪdʒənsi] <-ies> *n* **1.** COM agencia *f;* **travel ~** agencia de viajes **2.** ADMIN agencia *f,* organismo *m;* **government ~** agencia [*o* organismo] gubernamental **3.** *no pl, form* **through the ~ of** por acción de

agenda [ə'dʒendə] *n* (*for meeting*) orden *m* del día; **to be at the top of the ~** *fig* ser un asunto prioritario

agent ['eɪdʒənt] *n* agente *mf;* **secret ~** agente secreto

agglomerate [ə'glɒməreɪt, *Am:* -'glɑː-] *n,* **agglomeration** [əˌglɒmə'reɪʃən, *Am:* -ˌglɑːmə-] *n* aglomeración *f*

aggravate ['ægrəveɪt] *vt* **1.** (*make worse*) agravar **2.** *inf* (*annoy*) fastidiar

aggravating *adj* (*annoying*) molesto, -a

aggravation [ˌægrə'veɪʃən] *n no pl, inf* fastidio *m*

aggregate ['ægrɪgɪt] **I.** *n* **1.** FIN, ECON conglomerado *m;* (*sum total*) suma *f* total; (*total value*) valor *f* total **2.** *no pl* MAT suma *f* **II.** *adj* FIN, ECON total **III.** *vt* FIN, ECON sumar

aggression [ə'greʃən] *n no pl* **1.** (*feelings*) agresividad *f* **2.** (*violence*) agresión *f;* **an act of ~** una agresión

aggressive [ə'gresɪv] *adj* agresivo, -a

aggressor [ə'gresəʳ, *Am:* -ɚ] *n* agresor(a) *m(f)*

aggrieved [ə'griːvd] *adj* ofendido, -a

aghast [ə'gɑːst, *Am:* -'gæst] *adj* horrorizado, -a; **to be ~ at sth** estar horrorizado por algo

agile ['ædʒaɪl, *Am:* 'ædʒl] *adj* ágil

agility [ə'dʒɪləti, *Am:* -t̬i] *n no pl* agilidad *f*

aging *adj s.* **ageing**

agitate ['ædʒɪteɪt] **I.** *vt* **1.** (*make nervous*) inquietar; **to become ~d** inquietarse, ponerse inquieto **2.** (*shake*) agitar **II.** *vi* **to ~ for/against sth** hacer campaña en favor de/en contra de algo

agitation [ˌædʒɪ'teɪʃən] *n no pl a.* POL agitación *f*

agitator ['ædʒɪteɪtəʳ, *Am:* -t̬ɚ] *n* agitador(a)

m(f), violentista *mf Chile*

AGM [ˌeɪdʒiː'em] *n abbr of* **annual general meeting** junta *f* general anual

agnostic [æg'nɒstɪk, *Am:* -'nɑːstɪk] **I.** *n* agnóstico, -a *m, f* **II.** *adj* agnóstico, -a

ago [ə'gəʊ, *Am:* -'goʊ] *adv* **a minute/a year ~** hace un minuto/un año; **a long time ~, long ~** hace mucho tiempo; **how long ~ was that?** ¿cuánto tiempo hace de eso?

agog [ə'gɒg, *Am:* -'gɑːg] *adj* **to watch/listen ~** mirar/escuchar con avidez

agonize ['ægənaɪz] *vi* atormentarse; **to ~ about whether to do sth** atormentarse respecto a hacer o no hacer algo; **an ~d cry** un grito de angustia

agonizing ['ægənaɪzɪŋ] *adj* **1.** (*pain*) atroz; **to die an ~ death** tener una muerte espantosa **2.** (*delay, decision*) angustiante

agony ['ægəni] <-ies> *n* agonía *f;* **to be in ~** sufrir fuertes dolores; **to prolong the ~** (**of sth**) prolongar la agonía (de algo)

agony aunt *n* PUBL consultora *f* sentimental

agree [ə'griː] **I.** *vi* **1.** (*hold same opinion*) estar de acuerdo; **to ~ on sth** (*be in agreement*) estar de acuerdo en algo; (*reach agreement*) acordar algo; **to ~ to do sth** (*reach agreement*) acordar hacer algo; (*consent*) acceder a hacer algo; **to ~ to a suggestion** aceptar una sugerencia; **we don't ~ on many things** no estamos de acuerdo en muchas cosas; **they can't ~** no pueden ponerse de acuerdo; **to ~ to differ** estar en desacuerdo amistoso **2.** (*be good for*) **to ~ with sb** sentar bien a alguien **3.** (*match up*) casar, concordar **4.** LING concordar **II.** *vt* **1.** (*concur*) acordar; **it is ~d that ...** se ha acordado que...; **at the ~d time** a la hora fijada **2.** *Brit* (*accept*) acceder a

agreeable *adj* **1.** *form* (*acceptable*) aceptable; **is that ~ to you?** ¿está de acuerdo? **2.** (*pleasant*) agradable; **he's quite an ~ guy** es un tipo muy agradable **3.** (*consenting*) **to be ~** (**to sth**) estar conforme (con algo)

agreement *n* **1.** *no pl* (*shared opinion*) acuerdo *m;* **to be in ~ with sb** estar de acuerdo con alguien; **to reach ~** llegar a un acuerdo **2.** (*contract, arrangement*) acuerdo *m;* **to break an ~** romper un acuerdo **3.** LING concordancia *f*

agribusiness ['ægrɪˌbɪznɪs] *n no pl* industria *f* agropecuaria

agricultural [ˌægrɪ'kʌltʃərəl] *adj* agrícola; **~ science** agronomía *f*

agriculture ['ægrɪkʌltʃəʳ, *Am:* -tʃɚ] *n no pl* agricultura *f;* **subsistence ~** agricultura de subsistencia

agrotourism [ægrəʊ'tʊərɪzəm, *Am:* ægroʊ'tʊrɪ-] *n no pl* agroturismo

aground [ə'graʊnd] *adv* NAUT **to run ~** encallar; *fig* fracasar

ah [ɑː] *interj* ah

aha [ɑː'hɑː] *interj* ajá

ahead [ə'hed] *adv* **1.** (*in front*) delante; **the road ~ was blocked** había atascos en la carretera delante de nosotros **2.** (*advanced position, forwards*) adelante; **to go ~** adelantarse; **to move ~ quickly** avanzar rápidamente; **to press ~ with the plan** tirar adelante con el plan **3.** (*in the future*) **to look ~** anticiparse; **to plan ~** hacer planes con antelación

ahead of *prep* **1.** (*in front of*) delante de; **to walk ~ sb** caminar delante de alguien; (**way**) **~ sb/sth** (muy) por delante de alguien/algo **2.** (*before*) antes de; **to decide/arrive ~ time** decidir/llegar antes de tiempo **3.** (*more advanced than*) **to be a minute ~ sb** llevar un minuto de ventaja sobre alguien; **to be ~ one's time** anticiparse a su época **4.** (*informed about*) **to keep ~ sth** mantenerse al tanto de algo

ahem [ə'həm] *interj* ejem

ahoy [ə'hɔɪ] *interj* **land/ship ~!** ¡tierra/barco a la vista!; **~ there!** ¡ah del barco!

AI [ˌeɪ'aɪ] *n no pl* **1.** INFOR *abbr of* **artificial intelligence** IA **2.** MED, BIO *abbr of* **artificial insemination** inseminación *f* artificial

aid [eɪd] **I.** *n* **1.** *no pl* (*assistance, support*) ayuda *f;* **to be in ~ of sb/sth** ser en beneficio de alguien/algo; **to come/go to the ~ of sb** ir en ayuda de alguien; **with the ~ of sb/sth** con (la) ayuda de alguien/algo **2.** *no pl* POL, ECON ayuda *f;* **emergency ~** ayuda de emergencia; **financial ~** asistencia *f* financiera **3.** (*device*) ayuda *f;* **hearing ~** audífono *m;* **slimming ~** producto de adelgazamiento ►**what's all this in ~ of?** *Brit, inf* ¿a qué viene todo eso? **II.** *vt* ayudar; **to ~ and abet sb** ser cómplice de alguien

AID *n* **1.** *abbr of* **Agency for International Development** AID *f* **2.** *abbr of* **artificial insemination by donor** inseminación *f* artificial con donante

aid convoy *n* convoy *m* humanitario

aide [eɪd] *n* asistente *mf*

AIDS [eɪdz] *n no pl abbr of* **Acquired Immune Deficiency Syndrome** sida *m*

ail [eɪl] *form* **I.** *vi* estar enfermo, -a **II.** *vt* afligir; **what ~s you?** *a. iron* ¿qué te pasa?

aileron ['eɪlərɒn, *Am:* -rɑːn] *n* AVIAT alerón *m*

ailing ['eɪlɪŋ] *adj* **1.** (*person*) enfermo, -a **2.** (*company, economy*) debilitado, -a

ailment ['eɪlmənt] *n* dolencia *f*

aim [eɪm] **I.** *vi* **1.** (*point: weapon*) apuntar; **to ~ at sb/sth** apuntar a alguien/algo **2.** (*plan to achieve*) **to ~ at** [*o* **for**] **sth** tener algo como objetivo; **to ~ to do sth** poner como objetivo hacer algo **II.** *vt* **1.** (*point a weapon*) apuntar; **to ~ sth at sb/sth** apuntar algo hacia alguien/algo **2.** (*direct at*) **to ~ sth at sb** dirigir algo hacia alguien **3.** *fig* **to be ~ed at doing sth** ir encaminado a hacer algo **III.** *n* **1.** *no pl* (*ability*) puntería *f;* **to take ~** apuntar **2.** (*goal*) objetivo *m,* meta *f;* **his ~ was to make fun of us** su objetivo era burlarse de nosotros; **sb's ~ in life** la meta de alguien en la vida; **with the ~ of doing sth** con el objetivo de hacer algo

aimless ['eɪmlɪs] *adj* sin objetivo(s)

A

ain't [eɪnt] *inf* **1.** (*to be*) *s.* **am not, are not, is not 2.** (*to have*) *s.* **have not, has not**

air [eəʳ, *Am:* er] **I.** *n* **1.** *no pl* (*earth's atmosphere*) aire *m* **2.** *no pl* (*space overhead, sky*) aire *m;* **put your hands in the ~!** ¡manos arriba!; **to fire into the ~** disparar al aire; **to be up in the ~** *fig* estar en el aire **3.** *no pl* AVIAT **by ~** por avión; **to travel by ~** viajar en avión **4.** *no pl* TV, RADIO, CINE **to be on (the) ~** estar en antena [*o* en el aire]; **to be taken off the ~** ser retirado de antena **5.** *no pl* (*aura, quality*) aire *m;* **he has a unbearable ~ of arrogance** tiene un aire de arrogancia insoportable **6.** MUS aire *m,* tonada *f* ►**~s and graces** *pej* melindres *mpl;* **out of thin ~** de la nada; **to disappear into thin ~** desaparecer como por arte de magia **II.** *adj* aéreo, -a **III.** *vt* **1.** TV, RADIO emitir; **the programme will be ~ed on Saturday** el programa se emitirá el sábado **2.** (*expose to air*) airear **3.** (*publicize*) **to ~ one's grievances** ventilar sus quejas **IV.** *vi* **1.** *Am* TV, RADIO airear, emitirse **2.** (*be exposed to air*) ventilarse

air ambulance *n* avión *m* ambulancia **air bag** *n* airbag *m* **airbase** *n* base *f* aérea

airborne ['eəbɔːn, *Am:* 'erbɔːrn] *adj* **1.** (*transported by aircraft*) aerotransportado, -a **2.** (*in the air*) **to be ~** volar; **to get ~** (*plane*) despegar

air brake *n* freno *m* neumático **air bubble** *n* burbuja *f* de aire **air-conditioned** *adj* climatizado, -a **air conditioner** *n* acondicionador *m* de aire **air conditioning** *n no pl* aire *m* acondicionado, climatización *f;* **to turn the ~ down/up** bajar/subir el aire acondicionado **air-cooled** *adj* enfriado, -a por aire **air corridor** *n* corredor *m* aéreo

aircraft ['eəkrɑːft, *Am:* 'erkræft] *n* (*in general*) aeronave *f;* (*aeroplane*) avión *m* **aircraft carrier** *n* porta(a)viones *m inv* **aircraft industry** *n no pl* industria *f* aeronáutica

aircrew ['eəkruː, *Am:* 'er-] *n + sing/pl vb* tripulación *f* de vuelo **air cushion** *n* cojín *m* de aire **airfield** *n* aeródromo *m* **air filter** *n* filtro *m* de aire **air force** *n* fuerza *f* aérea **air freight** *n no pl* carga *f* aérea **air gun** *n* pistola *f* de aire comprimido **air hole** *n* respiradero *m*

airing cupboard ['eərɪŋ ˌcʌbəd, *Am:* 'erɪŋ ˌcʌbɚd] *n* armario *m* (para orear la ropa)

airless ['eələs, *Am:* 'er-] *n* (*room*) mal ventilado, -a; (*day*) sin viento

air lift **I.** *n* puente *m* aéreo **II.** *vt* aerotransportar **airline** *n* línea *f* aérea, aerolínea *f AmL* **airliner** *n* avión *m* de pasajeros **airmail** *n no pl* correo *m* aéreo **airman** <-men> *n* **1.** (*pilot*) aviador *m;* (*crew member*) tripulante *mf* **2.** MIL soldado *m* de las fuerzas aéreas **airplane** *n Am* avión *m* **air pollutant** *n* agente *m* contaminante (del aire) **air pollution** *n* contaminación *f* atmosférica **airport** *n* aeropuerto *m* **air quality** *n* calidad *f* del aire **air raid** *n* ataque *m* aéreo **airsick** *adj* mareado, -a; **to get ~** marearse (en avión) **air space** *n no pl* espacio *m* aéreo **air stewardess** *n* azafata *f* **airstrip** *n* pista *f* de aterrizaje **air terminal** *n* terminal *f* aérea **air ticket** *n* billete *m* de avión

airtight ['eətaɪt, *Am:* 'er-] *adj* hermético, -a

air traffic *n no pl* tráfico *m* aéreo **air-traffic controller** *n* controlador(a) *m(f)* aéreo, -a

airway ['eəweɪ, *Am:* 'er-] *n* **1.** ANAT vía *f* respiratoria **2.** (*path or route of aircraft*) vía *f* aérea

airworthy ['eəˌwɜːði, *Am:* 'erˌwɜːr-] *adj* en condiciones para el vuelo

airy ['eəri, *Am:* 'er-] *adj* **1.** ARCHIT espacioso, -a **2.** (*light*) ligero, -a; **with an ~ step** con un paso grácil **3.** (*lacking substance*) etéreo, -a

airy-fairy ['eərɪ'feəri, *Am:* 'erɪ'feri] *adj inf* fantasioso, -a

aisle [aɪl] *n* pasillo *m;* (*in church*) nave *f* lateral ►**to have sb rolling in the ~s** tener a alguien riéndose a carcajadas; **to take sb down the ~** llevar al altar a alguien

ajar [ə'dʒɑːʳ, *Am:* -'dʒɑːr] *adj* entreabierto, -a

a.k.a. *abbr of* **also known as** alias

akimbo [ə'kɪmbəʊ, *Am:* -boʊ] *adj* **(with) arms ~** (con) los brazos en jarras

akin [ə'kɪn] *adj* **~ to** parecido a

à la carte [æ lə 'kɑːt, *Am:* ɑː lə 'kɑːrt] *adj, adv* a la carta

alacrity [ə'lækrəti, *Am:* -t̬i] *n no pl* prontitud *f*

alarm [ə'lɑːm, *Am:* -'lɑːrm] **I.** *n* **1.** *no pl* (*worry*) alarma *f;* **to cause sb ~** alarmar a alguien **2.** (*warning*) alarma *f;* **fire ~** alarma contra incendios; **burglar ~** dispositivo *m* antirrobo; **a false ~** una falsa alarma; **to give the ~** dar la (voz de) alarma; *a. fig* alertar **3.** (*clock*) reloj *m* despertador **II.** *vt* alarmar; **to be ~ed** estar alarmado

alarm clock *n* reloj *m* despertador

alarming *adj* alarmante

alarmist [ə'lɑːmɪst, *Am:* -'lɑːr-] **I.** *adj* alarmista **II.** *n* alarmista *mf*

Albania [æl'beɪnɪə] *n* Albania *f*

Albanian **I.** *n* **1.** (*person*) albanés, -esa *m, f* **2.** LING albanés *m* **II.** *adj* albanés, -esa

albatross ['ælbətrɒs, *Am:* -trɑːs] *n* albatros *m*

albeit [ɔːl'biːɪt] *conj* aunque

albino [æl'biːnəʊ, *Am:* -'baiːnoʊ] **I.** *adj* albino, -a, ruaco, -a *Ven* **II.** *n* albino, -a *m, f*

album ['ælbəm] *n a.* MUS álbum *m;* **the family ~** el álbum de la familia

> **Alcatraz** es una antigua cárcel situada en la Isla de Alcatraz, que a su vez se encuentra en la bahía de San Francisco. Dado que la isla se erige sobre una base de cinco hectáreas de rocosos acantilados, la cárcel recibe el sobrenombre de '**La Roca**'. Allí eran confinados presos considerados especialmente peligrosos.

alcohol ['ælkəhɒl, *Am:* -hɑːl] *n no pl* alcohol *m*
alcohol-free *adj* sin alcohol
alcoholic [ˌælkə'hɒlɪk, *Am:* -'hɑːlɪk] I. *n* alcohólico, -a *m, f* II. *adj* alcohólico, -a
alcoholism *n no pl* alcoholismo *m*
alcove ['ælkəʊv, *Am:* -koʊv] *n* nicho *m* (*para estantería o cama*)
alder ['ɔːldəʳ, *Am:* -dɚ] *n* aliso *m*
alderman ['ɔːldəmən, *Am:* -dɚ-] <-men> *n* POL 1. *Brit* HIST concejal(a) *m(f)* 2. *Am, Aus, Can* (*elected city government member*) regidor(a) *m(f)*
ale [eɪl] *n* cerveza *f*
alert [ə'lɜːt, *Am:* -'lɜːrt] I. *adj* despierto, -a; **to keep** ~ mantenerse alerta II. *n* 1. (*alarm*) alarma *f* 2. *no pl* (*period of watchfulness*) alerta *f;* **state of** ~ estado *m* de alerta; **to be on the** ~ estar alerta III. *vt* (*notify*) alertar
A-level ['eilevəl] *n Brit abbr of* **Advanced-level** ≈ bachillerato *m*

El **A-Level** es un tipo de examen final que realizan los alumnos al finalizar la enseñanza secundaria. La mayoría de los alumnos elige tres asignaturas de examen, pero también es posible examinarse de una sola asignatura. Aprobar los **A-Levels** le da al alumno la posibilidad de acceder a los estudios universitarios.

alga ['ælgə] *n* alga *f*
algal bloom ['ælgəlˌbluːm] *n* marea *f* de algas
algebra ['ældʒɪbrə] *n no pl* álgebra *f*
algebraic [ˌældʒɪ'breɪɪk] *adj* algebraico, -a
Algeria [æl'dʒɪərɪə, *Am:* -'dʒɪ-] *n* Argelia *f*
Algerian I. *n* argelino, -a *m, f* II. *adj* argelino, -a
Algiers [æl'dʒɪəz, *Am:* -'dʒɪrz] *n* Argel *m*
alias ['eɪlɪəs] I. *n* alias *m inv* II. *conj* alias
alibi ['ælɪbaɪ] *n* coartada *f*
alien ['eɪlɪən] I. *adj* 1. (*foreign*) extranjero, -a 2. (*strange*) extraño, -a; ~ **to sb** ajeno a alguien; **an** ~ **idea** una idea poco normal II. *n* 1. *form* (*foreigner*) extranjero, -a *m, f;* **illegal** ~ extranjero ilegal 2. (*extra-terrestrial creature*) extraterrestre *mf*
alienate ['eɪlɪəneɪt] *vt* 1. (*person*) distanciar; **to** ~ **sb from sb/sth** hacer que alguien se distancie de alguien/algo 2. LAW (*property*) enajenar
alienation [ˌeɪlɪə'neɪʃən] *n no pl* 1. (*of people*) distanciamiento *m* 2. LAW (*of property*) enajenación *f*
alight¹ [ə'laɪt] *adj* 1. (*on fire*) quemando; **to be** ~ estar ardiendo; **to set sth** ~ prender fuego a algo 2. *fig* (*with enthusiasm, joy*) resplandeciente; **to set sb's imagination** ~ despertar la imaginación a alguien
alight² [ə'laɪt] *vi form* 1. (*from vehicle*) apearse 2. (*on branch*) posarse
◆**alight on** *vi* **to** ~ **sth** dar con [*o* encontrar] algo
align [ə'laɪn] *vt* 1. (*two things*) poner en línea (recta); (*wheels*) alinear 2. *fig* **to** ~ **oneself with sb/sth** alinearse con alguien/algo
alignment *n no pl* alineación *f;* **to be out of** ~ no estar alineado
alike [ə'laɪk] I. *adj* 1. parecido, -a; **to look** ~ parecerse 2. **Clara and Clive** ~ **...** (*both*) tanto Clara como Clive... II. *adv* (*similarly*) de un modo parecido; **to think** ~ pensar de forma parecida
alimony ['ælɪməni, *Am:* -moʊ-] *n no pl* pensión *f* alimenticia
aline [ə'laɪn] *vt s.* **align**
alive [ə'laɪv] *adj* 1. (*not dead*) vivo, -a; **to be** ~ estar vivo; **to be buried** ~ ser enterrado vivo; **to keep sb** ~ mantener a alguien con vida; **to keep hope** ~ mantener vivas las esperanzas 2. (*active*) activo, -a; **to make sth come** ~ dar vida a algo 3. (*aware*) **to be** ~ **to sth** ser consciente de algo
alkali ['ælkəlaɪ, *Am:* -kəlaɪ] I. <-s *o* -es> *n* álcali *m* II. *adj* alcalino, -a
alkaline ['ælkəlaɪn, *Am:* -kəlaɪn] *adj* alcalino, -a
all [ɔːl] I. *adj* todo, -a; ~ **the butter** toda la mantequilla; ~ **the wine** todo el vino; ~ **my sisters** todas mis hermanas; **with** ~ **possible speed** con la máxima velocidad posible II. *pron* 1. (*everybody*) todos, -as; ~ **aboard!** ¡todos a bordo!; ~ **but him** todos menos él; **he's got four daughters,** ~ **blue-eyed** tiene cuatro hijas, todas con ojos azules; **once and for** ~ de una vez por todas 2. (*everything*) todo; ~ **but ...** todo menos...; **most of** ~ sobre todo; **the best of** ~ **would be ...** lo mejor de todo sería...; **for** ~ **I know** que yo sepa; **for** ~ **he may think** a pesar de lo que pueda pensar 3. (*the whole quantity*) todo, -a; **they took/drank it** ~ se lo tomaron/bebieron todo; ~ **of France** toda Francia 4. (*the only thing*) todo, -a; ~ **I want is ...** lo único que quiero es...; **I am** ~ **the family she has** soy toda la familia que ella tiene 5. SPORTS **two** ~ dos a dos; **to draw two** ~ empatar a dos III. *adv* totalmente; ~ **round** completo; **not as stupid as** ~ **that** no del todo estúpido; **it's** ~ **the same** me da igual
Allah ['ælə] *n* Alá *m*
all-around *adj Am s.* **all-round**
allay [ə'leɪ] *vt* (*fear*) calmar; (*doubt*) despejar
all clear [ˌɔːl'klɪəʳ, *Am:* -'klɪr] *n* cese *m* de alarma; **to give/hear the** ~ dar/oír el cese de alarma; **to give sth the** ~ *fig* dar la luz verde a algo
allegation [ˌælɪ'geɪʃən] *n* acusación *f;* **to make an** ~ **against sb** acusar a alguien
allege [ə'ledʒ] *vt* afirmar; **she is ~d to have stolen the money** se dice que ha robado el dinero; **it is ~d that ...** se dice que...
alleged [ə'ledʒd] *adj* supuesto, -a
allegedly [ə'ledʒɪdli] *adv* (según) se dice

allegiance [ə'liːdʒəns] *n no pl* lealtad *f;* **to pledge ~ to sb/sth** jurar lealtad a alguien/algo

allegoric(al) [ˌælɪ'gɒrɪk(əl), *Am:* -'gɔːr-] *adj* alegórico, -a

allegory ['ælɪgəri, *Am:* -gɔːri] <-ies> *n* alegoría *f*

alleluia [ˌælɪ'luːjə] **I.** *interj* aleluya **II.** *n* aleluya *f*

allergen ['ælədʒən, *Am:* -ɚ-] *n* alergeno *m,* alérgeno *m*

allergenic [ælə'dʒenɪk, *Am:* -ɚ-] *adj* alergénico, -a

allergic [ə'lɜːdʒɪk, *Am:* -'lɜːr-] *adj* alérgico, -a; **~ reaction** reacción *f* alérgica

allergy ['ælədʒi, *Am:* -ɚ-] <-ies> *n* alergia *f;* **to trigger an ~** provocar una alergia

alleviate [ə'liːvɪeɪt] *vt* aliviar

alley ['æli] *n* **1.** (*between buildings*) callejón *m;* **blind ~** callejón sin salida **2.** (*in garden*) paseo *m*

alley cat *n* gato *m* callejero

All Fools' Day [ˌɔːl'fuːlzdeɪ] *n* ≈ Día *m* de los Santos Inocentes (*en Gran Bretaña el 1 de abril*)

alliance [ə'laɪəns] *n* alianza *f;* **to form an ~** formar una alianza; **to be in ~ with sth/sb** estar aliado con algo/alguien

allied ['ælaɪd] *adj* **1.** *a.* MIL aliado, -a; **the Allied forces** las fuerzas aliadas **2.** (*combined*) **~ with** [*o* **to**] **sth** unido a algo

alligator ['ælɪgeɪtəʳ, *Am:* -t̬ɚ] *n* caimán *m*

all-in [ɔːl'ɪn] *adj* todo incluido; **~ rate** precio *m* con todo incluido

all-inclusive [ˌɔːlɪŋ'kluːsɪv, *Am:* -ɪn'-] *adj* todo incluido

all-in wrestling *n* lucha *f* libre

allocate ['æləkeɪt] *vt* **1.** (*assign*) asignar **2.** (*distribute*) repartir; **to ~ blame for sth to sb** echar las culpas a alguien de algo

allocation [ˌælə'keɪʃən] *n no pl* **1.** (*assignment*) asignación *f* **2.** (*act of distributing*) distribución *f*

allot [ə'lɒt, *Am:* -'lɑːt] <-tt-> *vt* asignar

allotment *n* **1.** (*assignment*) asignación *f* **2.** (*distribution*) distribución *f* **3.** *Brit* (*plot of land*) ≈ huerto *m* particular (*en las afueras de la ciudad*)

all-out [ɔːl'aʊt] *adj* total; **to make an ~ effort** hacer un esfuerzo supremo; **~ attack** ataque *m* total

allow [ə'laʊ] *vt* **1.** (*permit*) permitir; **to ~ access** permitir el acceso; **to ~ sb to do sth** dejar a alguien hacer algo; **~ me** *form* permíta(n)me; **will you ~ me?** ¿me permite(n)?; **please ~ me through** *form* déje(n)me pasar, por favor; **smoking is not ~ed** se prohíbe fumar **2.** (*allocate*) asignar; **please ~ 7 days for delivery** entrega en un plazo máximo de 7 días **3.** (*admit*) **to ~ that ...** reconocer que...
◆**allow for** *vt* tener en cuenta

allowable *adj* **1.** (*error*) permisible **2.** (*expenses*) deducible

allowance [ə'laʊəns] *n* **1.** (*permitted amount*) cantidad *f* permitida; **baggage ~** equipaje *m* no sujeto a tasas; **tax ~** desgravación *f* fiscal **2.** *Am* (*money*) dinero *m* de bolsillo **3.** (*preparation*) **to make ~(s) for sth** tener algo en cuenta **4.** (*excuse*) **to make ~s for sb** ser indulgente con alguien; **to make ~s for sth** tolerar algo

alloy ['ælɔɪ] **I.** *n* aleación *f;* **~ wheels** llantas *fpl* de aleación **II.** *vt form* empañar

all-purpose [ɔːl'pɜːpəs, *Am:* -'pɜːr-] *adj* universal, multiuso

all right **I.** *adv* **1.** (*o.k.*) bien; **that's ~** (*after thanks*) de nada; (*after excuse*) no pasa nada; **what do you think of the book? – it was ~ nothing special** ¿qué te parece el libro? – ah, pasable, nada del otro mundo; **she's a bit of ~!** *Brit, inf* ¡está buenísima!; **to be ~ with sb** comportarse bien con alguien **2.** (*healthy*) bien; **to be ~** estar bien (de salud); (*safe*) estar sano y salvo; **to get home ~** llegar a casa sin ningún percance **II.** *interj* (*expressing agreement*) de acuerdo **III.** *adv* **1.** (*well*) bien **2.** (*certainly*) con (toda) seguridad **3.** (*in answer*) vale

all-round [ˌɔːl'raʊnd] *adj* completo, -a; **~ talent** talento *m* para todo

all-rounder [ɔːl'raʊndəʳ, *Am:* -dɚ] *n Aus, Brit* persona *f* con talento en varias disciplinas; SPORTS deportista *mf* completo, -a (*que puede jugar en cualquier posición*)

All Saints' Day *n no pl* día *m* de Todos los Santos

All Souls' Day *n* día *m* de (los) Difuntos

all-time high [ˌɔːlˌtaɪm'haɪ] *n* máximo *m* histórico **all-time low** *n* mínimo *m* histórico

allude [ə'luːd] *vi* **to ~ to sth** aludir a algo

allure [ə'lʊəʳ, *Am:* -'lʊr] **I.** *n no pl* (*attractiveness*) atractivo *m;* (*charm*) encanto *m;* **sexual ~** atractivo sexual **II.** *vt* atraer

alluring [ə'lʊərɪŋ, *Am:* -'lʊrɪŋ] *adj* (*attractive*) atractivo, -a; (*enticing*) tentador(a)

allusion [ə'luːʒən] *n* alusión *f*

all-weather [ˌɔːl'weðəʳ] *adj* para todo tiempo

ally ['ælaɪ] **I.** <-ies> *n* **1.** (*country*) aliado, -a *m, f* **2.** (*supporter*) partidario, -a *m, f* **II.** <-ie-> *vt* **to ~ oneself with sb** POL aliarse con alguien

almanac ['ɔːlmənæk] *n* almanaque *m*

almighty [ɔːl'maɪti, *Am:* -t̬i] **I.** *adj inf* todopoderoso, -a **II.** *n* **the Almighty** el Todopoderoso

almond ['ɑːmənd] *n* **1.** (*nut*) almendra *f* **2.** (*tree*) almendro *m*

almost ['ɔːlməʊst, *Am:* -moʊst] *adv* casi; **~ half** casi la mitad; **we're ~ there** casi hemos llegado

alms [ɑːmz] *npl* limosna *f*

aloe vera [ˌæləʊ'vɪərə, *Am:* -oʊ'vɪrə] *n* áloe *m* vera

alone [ə'ləʊn, *Am:* -'loʊn] **I.** *adj* **1.** (*without others*) solo, -a; **to do sth ~** hacer algo solo; **to**

go it ~ *inf* hacerlo por su cuenta; **to leave sb** ~ dejar a alguien en paz; **to leave sth** ~ dejar algo como está **2.** (*unique*) **to be** ~ **in doing sth** ser el único/los únicos en hacer algo; **Jane** ~ **can do that** Jane es la única que puede hacerlo ►**let** ~ **...** mucho menos... **II.** *adv* solamente, sólo

along [ə'lɒŋ, *Am:* -'lɑːŋ] **I.** *prep* por; **all** ~ a lo largo de; ~ **the road** por la carretera; **all** ~ **the river** a lo largo del río; **I lost it** ~ **the way** lo perdí por el camino; **it's** ~ **here** está por aquí **II.** *adv* **all** ~ todo el tiempo; **to bring/take sb** ~ traer/llevar a alguien; **to go** ~ seguir adelante; **he will be** ~ **in an hour** llegará en una hora; **come** ~**!** ¡ven con nosotros!

alongside [əˌlɒŋ'saɪd, *Am:* ə'lɑːŋsaɪd] **I.** *prep* **1.** (*next to*) junto a; **to draw up** ~ **sb/sth** pararse al lado de alguien/algo; ~ **each other** uno junto al otro; **to fight** ~ **sb** luchar al lado de alguien **2.** NAUT al costado de **II.** *adv* al lado; NAUT de costado

aloof [ə'luːf] *adj* distante; **to keep** ~ **from sth** mantenerse alejado de algo

aloud [ə'laʊd] *adv* en voz alta; **to think** ~ pensar en voz alta

alpha ['ælfə] *n* **1.** (*Greek letter*) alfa *f* **2.** *Brit* (*student mark*) ≈ sobresaliente *m*

alphabet ['ælfəbet] *n* alfabeto *m*

alphabetical [ˌælfə'betɪkl, *Am:* -'bet̬-] *adj* alfabético, -a; **in** ~ **order** en orden alfabético

alphanumeric [ˌælfənjuː'merɪk, *Am:* -nuː-] *adj* alfanumérico, -a

alpha particle *n* partícula *f* alfa **alpha ray** *n* rayo *m* alfa

alpine ['ælpaɪn] **I.** *adj* alpino, -a **II.** *n* planta *f* alpestre

Alps [ælps] *npl* **the** ~ los Alpes

already [ɔːl'redi] *adv* ya

alright [ɔl'raɪt] *adv s.* **all right**

Alsace [æl'sæs] *n* Alsacia *f*

Alsatian [æl'seɪʃən] **I.** *n* **1.** (*person*) alsaciano, -a *m, f* **2.** (*dog*) pastor *m* alemán **II.** *adj* alsaciano, -a

also ['ɔːlsəʊ, *Am:* 'ɔːlsoʊ] *adv* también

altar ['ɔːltəʳ, *Am:* -t̬ɚ] *n* altar *m*

altar boy *n* monaguillo *m*

alter ['ɔːltəʳ, *Am:* -t̬ɚ] **I.** *vt* **1.** (*change: text, plan*) cambiar; (*option*) cambiar de; (*paint*) retocar **2.** *Am* (*castrate*) castrar **II.** *vi* cambiarse

alterable ['ɔːltərəbl, *Am:* -t̬ɚəbl] *adj* modificable

alteration [ˌɔːltə'reɪʃən, *Am:* -t̬ə-] *n* **1.** (*change*) modificación *f;* (*in house*) reforma *f* **2.** *no pl* (*act of changing*) modificación *f*

altercation [ˌɔːltə'keɪʃən, *Am:* -t̬ɚ-] *n* altercado *m*

alternate¹ ['ɔːltəneɪt, *Am:* 'ɔːlt̬ɚ-] *vi, vt* alternar

alternate² [ɔː'lɜːnət, *Am:* -'t̬ɜːr-] *adj* **1.** (*by turns*) alterno, -a; **on** ~ **days** en días alternos **2.** *Am* (*alternative*) alternativo, -a

alternating ['ɔːltəneɪtɪŋ, *Am:* -t̬ɪŋ] *adj* alterno, -a

alternative [ɔː'lɜːnətɪv, *Am:* -'tɜːrnət̬ɪv] **I.** *n* alternativa *f;* **to have no** ~ **but to do sth** no tener otra alternativa que hacer algo **II.** *adj* alternativo, -a

alternatively *adv* **1.** (*on the other hand*) si no **2.** (*as a substitute*) en lugar de esto

alternator ['ɔːltəneɪtəʳ, *Am:* -tɚneɪt̬ɚ] *n* alternador *m*

although [ɔːl'ðəʊ, *Am:* -'ðoʊ] *conj* aunque; **he is mean** ~ **he is rich** es tacaño a pesar de que es rico; ~ **it's snowing ...** aunque está nevando...

altimeter ['æltɪmiːtəʳ, *Am:* æl'tɪmət̬ɚ] *n* altímetro *m*

altitude ['æltɪtjuːd, *Am:* -tətuːd] *n* altitud *f*

alto ['æltəʊ, *Am:* -toʊ] *n* **1.** (*woman*) contralto *f* **2.** (*man*) contralto *m*

altogether [ˌɔːltə'geðəʳ, *Am:* -ɚ] **I.** *adv* **1.** (*completely*) totalmente; **not** ~ no del todo **2.** (*in total*) en total **II.** *n* **in the** ~ en cueros

alto saxophone *n* saxofón *m* alto

altruism ['æltruːɪzəm] *n no pl* altruismo *m*

altruist ['æltruːɪst] *n* altruista *mf*

altruistic [ˌæltruː'ɪstɪk] *adj* altruista

aluminium [ˌæljʊ'mɪnɪəm] *n no pl* aluminio *m*

aluminium foil *n* papel *m* de plata **aluminium oxide** *n* alúmina *f*

aluminum [ə'luːmɪnəm] *n Am s.* **aluminium**

always ['ɔːlweɪz] *adv* **1.** (*at all times*) siempre **2.** (*alternatively*) siempre, en todo caso

am [əm, *stressed:* æm] *vi 1. pers sing of* **be**

a.m. [ˌeɪ'em] *abbr of* **ante meridiem** a.m.

amalgam [ə'mælgəm] *n* amalgama *f*

amalgamate [ə'mælgəmeɪt] **I.** *vt* **1.** (*metals*) amalgamar **2.** COM fusionar **II.** *vi* **1.** (*metals*) amalgamarse **2.** COM fusionarse

amalgamation [əˌmælgə'meɪʃən] *n no pl* **1.** (*process*) amalgamación *f* **2.** COM fusión *f*

amass [ə'mæs] *vt* (*money*) amasar; (*information*) acumular

amateur ['æmətəʳ, *Am:* -tʃɚ] **I.** *n* **1.** (*not professional*) aficionado, -a *m, f* **2.** (*lacking skill*) chapucero, -a *m, f* **II.** *adj* aficionado, -a; ~ **sport** deporte *m* de aficionados

amateurish ['æmətərɪʃ, *Am:* ˌæmə'tɜːrɪʃ] *adj* chapucero, -a

amaze [ə'meɪz] *vt* **1.** (*astound*) asombrar; **to be** ~**d that ...** quedar asombrado porque...; **to be** ~**d by sth** estar asombrado por algo **2.** (*surprise*) sorprender; **to be** ~**d by sth** estar sorprendido por algo

amazement *n no pl* asombro *m;* **to stare at sth in** ~ quedarse boquiabierto mirando algo; **to my** ~ para mi gran asombro

amazing *adj* asombroso, -a, sorpresivo, -a *AmL;* **truly** ~ realmente increíble

Amazon ['æməzən, *Am:* -zɑːn] *n* **1.** (*female warrior*) amazona *f* **2.** (*river*) **the** ~ el Amazonas

ambassador [æm'bæsədəʳ, *Am:* -dɚ] *n* embajador(a) *m(f)*

amber ['æmbəʳ, *Am:* -bɚ] **I.** *n* ámbar *m* **II.** *adj* ambarino, -a; **the traffic light is at ~** *Brit* el semáforo está en amarillo

ambidextrous [ˌæmbɪ'dekstrəs] *adj* ambidextro, -a

ambiguity [ˌæmbɪ'gjuːəti, *Am:* -bə'gjuːət̬i] <-ies> *n* ambigüedad *f*

ambiguous [æm'bɪgjʊəs] *adj* ambiguo, -a

ambition [æm'bɪʃən] *n* ambición *f;* **she lacks ~** no es nada ambiciosa

ambitious [æm'bɪʃəs] *adj* ambicioso, -a; **to be ~ for sb** tener grandes ambiciones para alguien; **to be ~ to do sth** tener la ambición de hacer algo

ambivalent [æm'bɪvələnt] *adj* ambivalente; **to feel ~ about** [*o* **towards**] **sth/sb** tener sentimientos encontrados hacia algo/alguien

amble ['æmbl] **I.** *vi* andar [*o* pasear] tranquilamente **II.** *n no pl* **1.** (*stroll*) **to go for an ~** pasear sin prisas **2.** (*of horse*) ambladura *f*

ambulance ['æmbjʊləns] *n* ambulancia *f*

ambush ['æmbʊʃ] **I.** *vt* **to ~ sb** tender una emboscada a alguien **II.** *n* <-es> emboscada *f;* **to lie in ~ for sb** aguardar emboscado a alguien

ameba [ə'miːbə] <-s *o* -bae> *n Am s.* **amoeba**

amebic *adj Am s.* **amoebic**

ameliorate [ə'miːlɪəreɪt] *vt form* mejorar

amelioration [əˌmiːlɪə'reɪʃən] *n no pl, form* mejora *f*

amen [ɑː'men, *Am:* eɪ'men] *interj* amén; **~ to that!** ¡así es!

amenable [ə'miːnəbl] *adj* receptivo, -a; **to be ~ to sth** mostrarse receptivo a (aceptar) algo; **to be ~ to reason** estar dispuesto a entrar en razón

amend [ə'mend] *vt* (*text, constitution*) enmendar; (*plan*) modificar

amendment *n* (*to text, constitution*) enmienda *f;* (*to plan*) modificación *f*

amends *npl* **to make ~ for sth** reparar algo

amenities [ə'miːnətɪz, *Am:* -'menət̬ɪz] *npl* comodidades *fpl;* (**public**) **~** instalaciones públicas

America [ə'merɪkə] *n* América *f* (del Norte); **the ~s** las Américas

American [ə'merɪkən] **I.** *n* **1.** (*person from USA*) estadounidense *mf,* americano, -a *m, f* **2.** (*person from American continent*) americano, -a *m, f* **3.** LING inglés *m* americano **II.** *adj* americano, -a

American football *n* fútbol *m* americano

American Indian *n* amerindio, -a *m, f*

Americanism *n* americanismo *m*

Americanize *vt* americanizar

amethyst ['æmɪθɪst] **I.** *n* **1.** (*stone*) amatista *f* **2.** (*colour*) amatista *m* **II.** *adj* amatista

amiability [ˌeɪmiə'bɪləti, *Am:* -t̬i] *n no pl* amabilidad *f*

amiable ['eɪmiəbl] *adj* amable

amicable ['æmɪkəbl] *adj* amistoso, -a; **to reach an ~ settlement** llegar a un arreglo amistoso

amid(st) [ə'mɪd(st)] *prep* en medio de, entre

amino acid [ə'miːnəʊ'æsɪd, *Am:* -noʊ-] *n* aminoácido *m*

amiss [ə'mɪs] **I.** *adj* **there's something ~** algo va mal **II.** *adv* **to take sth ~** tomar algo a mal; **a little courtesy would not go ~** no vendría mal un poco de cortesía

ammeter ['æmɪtəʳ, *Am:* -t̬ɚ] *n* amperímetro *m*

ammonia [ə'məʊnɪə, *Am:* -'moʊnjə] *n no pl* **1.** (*gas*) amoniaco *m,* amoníaco *m* **2.** (*liquid*) amoniaco *m* (líquido), amoníaco *m* (líquido)

ammunition [ˌæmjʊ'nɪʃən, *Am:* -jə-] *n no pl* **1.** (*for guns*) municiones *fpl* **2.** *fig* argumentos *mpl*

ammunition depot *n,* **ammunition dump** *n* depósito *m* de municiones

amnesia [æm'niːzɪə, *Am:* -ʒə] *n no pl* amnesia *f*

amnesty ['æmnəsti] <-ies> *n* amnistía *f*

amoeba [ə'miːbə] <-bas *o* -bae> *n* ameba *f*

amoebic [ə'miːbɪk] *adj* amébico, -a

amoebic dysentery *n* amebiasis *f inv,* disentería *f* amebiana

amok [ə'mɒk] *adv* de forma descontrolada; **to run ~** descontrolarse

among(st) [ə'mʌŋ(st)] *prep* entre; **~ friends** entre amigos; (**just**) **one ~ many** (sólo) uno entre muchos; **~ Scots** entre los escoceses; **to divide sth up ~ us** dividir algo entre nosotros; **~ the flowers/the pupils** entre las flores/los alumnos; **~ other things** entre otras cosas

amoral [ˌeɪ'mɒrəl, *Am:* -'mɔːr-] *adj* amoral

amorous ['æmərəs] *adj* amoroso, -a; **to make ~ advances to sb** insinuarse a alguien

amorphous [ə'mɔːfəs, *Am:* -'mɔːr-] *adj* amorfo, -a

amortization [əˌmɔːtɪ'zeɪʃən, *Am:* æmˌɔːrt̬ə-] *n* amortización *f*

amortize [ə'mɔːtaɪz, *Am:* æm'ɔːr-] *vt* amortizar

amount [ə'maʊnt] **I.** *n* **1.** cantidad *f;* **any ~ of** grandes cantidades de; **any ~ of people** mucha gente; **a certain ~ of difficulty** alguna [*o* cierta] dificultad **2.** (*of money*) suma *f,* importe *m;* **a check in the ~ of ...** *Am* un cheque por valor de...; **~ carried forward** traslado a cuenta nueva **II.** *vi* **1.** (*add up to*) **to ~ to sth** ascender a algo; **that ~s to a refusal** eso viene a ser una negativa **2.** (*be successful*) **to ~ to sth** llegar a algo; **he will never ~ to much** nunca llegará a nada

amp. *abbr of* **ampere** amp.

ampere ['æmpeəʳ, *Am:* -pɪr] *n* amperio *m*

amphetamine [æm'fetəmiːn] *n* anfetamina *f*

amphibian [æm'fɪbɪən] **I.** *adj* anfibio, -a **II.** *n* **1.** ZOOL anfibio *m* **2.** AUTO vehículo *m* anfibio

amphibious [æm'fɪbɪəs] *adj* anfibio, -a

amphitheater *n Am,* **amphitheatre** ['æmpfɪˌθɪətəʳ, *Am:* -fəˌθiːət̬ɚ] *n Aus, Brit* anfiteatro *m*

ample ['æmpl] *adj* **1.**(*plentiful*) abundante **2.**(*large*) amplio, -a **3.**(*enough*) suficiente

amplification [ˌæmplɪfɪ'keɪʃən] *n no pl* **1.** MUS amplificación *f* **2.**(*increased detail*) ampliación *f;* **to say sth in ~ of sth** *form* decir algo como aclaración de algo

amplifier ['æmplɪfaɪəʳ, *Am:* -ɚ] *n* amplificador *m*

amplify ['æmplɪfaɪ] <-ie-> **I.** *vt* **1.** MUS amplificar **2.**(*enlarge upon: statement*) ampliar; (*idea*) desarrollar; (*remark*) aclarar **II.** *vi* **to ~ upon sth** extenderse sobre algo

amplitude ['æmplɪtjuːd, *Am:* -tuːd] *n no pl* amplitud *f*

ampoule *n Brit,* **ampule** ['æmpuːl] *n Am* MED ampolla *f*

amputate ['æmpjʊteɪt] *vt* amputar

amputation [ˌæmpjʊ'teɪʃən] *n* amputación *f*

amputee [ˌæmpjʊ'tiː] *n* mutilado, -a *m, f*

amuck [ə'mʌk] *adv s.* **amok**

amulet ['æmjʊlɪt] *n* amuleto *m,* cábula *f Arg, Par*

amuse [ə'mjuːz] *vt* **1.**(*entertain*) entretener; **to ~ oneself** distraerse; **to keep sb ~d** entretener a alguien **2.**(*cause laughter*) divertir, hacer gracia; **I'm not ~d** no me hace gracia

amusement [ə'mjuːzmənt] *n* **1.** *no pl* (*entertainment*) entretenimiento *m,* entretención *f AmL;* **for one's own ~** para entretenerse **2.**(*mirth*) diversión *f;* (**much**) **to my ~** con (gran) regocijo por mi parte; **he looked on in ~** miró divertido **3.**(*laughter*) risa *f;* **to conceal one's ~** aguantarse la risa

amusement arcade *n Brit* sala *f* de juegos recreativos **amusement park** *n* parque *m* de atracciones

amusing *adj* divertido, -a, gracioso, -a

an [ən, *stressed:* æn] *indef art before vowel s.* **a**

anabolic steroid [ænə'bɔlik 'sterɔid] *n* esteroide *m* anabolizante

anachronism [ə'nækrənɪzəm] *n* anacronismo *m*

anachronistic [əˌnækrə'nɪstɪk] *adj* anacrónico, -a

anaconda [ˌænə'kɒndə, *Am:* -'kɑːn-] *n* anaconda *f*

anaemia [ə'niːmɪə] *n no pl* anemia *f*

anaemic [ə'niːmɪk] *adj* anémico, -a

anaesthesia [ˌænɪs'θiːzɪə] *n no pl* anestesia *f*

anaesthetic [ˌænɪs'θetɪk] **I.** *adj* anestésico, -a **II.** *n* anestésico *m;* **to be under ~** estar bajo los efectos de la anestesia; **to give sb an ~** anestesiar a alguien

anaesthetist [ˌænɪs'θetɪst] *n* anestesista *mf*

anaesthetize [ə'niːsθətaɪz] *vt* anestesiar

anagram ['ænəgræm] *n* anagrama *m*

anal ['eɪnəl] *adj* anal

analgesic [ˌænæl'dʒiːsɪk] **I.** *adj* analgésico, -a **II.** *n* analgésico *m*

analog ['ænəlɒg] *n Am s.* **analogue**

analogous [ə'næləgəs] *adj* análogo, -a; **to be ~ to sth** ser análogo a algo

analogue ['ænəlɒg] *n Brit* equivalente *m*

analogue computer *n* ordenador *m* analógico, computadora *f* analógica *AmL*

analogy [ə'nælədʒi] <-ies> *n* analogía *f;* **to draw an ~ between** establecer una analogía entre; **by ~ with sth** por analogía con algo

analyse ['ænəlaɪz] *vt Aus, Brit* analizar; PSYCH psicoanalizar

analysis [ə'næləsɪs] <-ses> *n* **1.**(*examination*) análisis *m inv* **2.**(*psychoanalysis*) psicoanálisis *m inv;* **to be in ~** *Am* seguir un tratamiento de psicoanálisis ▶**in the final** [*o* **last**] **~** a fin de cuentas

analyst ['ænəlɪst] *n* **1.**(*analyzer*) analista *mf;* **food ~** analista de alimentos; **financial ~** analista de inversiones **2.** PSYCH psicoanalista *mf*

analytic(**al**) [ˌænə'lɪtɪk(əl), *Am:* -'lɪt̬-] *adj* analítico, -a

analyze ['ænəlaɪz] *vt Am s.* **analyse**

anarchic(**al**) [ə'nɑːkɪk(əl), *Am:* æn'ɑːr-] *adj* anárquico, -a

anarchism ['ænəkɪzəm, *Am:* -ɚ-] *n no pl* anarquismo *m*

anarchist ['ænəkɪst, *Am:* -ɚ-] **I.** *adj* anarquista **II.** *n* anarquista *mf*

anarchistic [ˌænə'kɪstɪk, *Am:* -ɚ-] *adj* anarquista

anarchy ['ænəki, *Am:* -ɚ-] *n no pl* anarquía *f*

anathema [ə'næθəmə] *n no pl* **1.** REL anatema *m* **2.** *fig* **the very idea was ~ to her** la sola idea le resultaba odiosa

anatomical [ˌænə'tɒmɪkl, *Am:* -'tɑː-] *adj* anatómico, -a

anatomy [ə'nætəmi, *Am:* -'næt̬-] <-ies> *n* **1.** *no pl* BIO anatomía *f* **2.** *iron* (*body*) anatomía *f,* cuerpo *m* **3.** *no pl* (*analysis*) análisis *m inv*

ancestor ['ænsestəʳ, *Am:* -sestɚ] *n* **1.**(*of person*) antepasado, -a *m, f* **2.**(*of idea, organization*) precursor(a) *m(f)*

ancestral [æn'sestrəl] *adj* ancestral; **the ~ home** la casa solariega

ancestry ['ænsestri] <-ies> *n* ascendencia *f;* **she is of Polish ~** es de ascendencia polaca

anchor ['æŋkəʳ, *Am:* -kɚ] **I.** *n* **1.** NAUT ancla *f,* sacho *m Chile;* **to be at ~** estar anclado; **to drop/weigh ~** echar/levar anclas **2.** *fig* sostén *m* **II.** *vt* **1.** NAUT anclar **2.**(*rope, tent*) sujetar **3.** RADIO, TV **to ~ a radio/TV programme** presentar un programa de radio/de televisión **III.** *vi* NAUT echar anclas

anchorage ['æŋkərɪdʒ] *n* **1.**(*place*) fondeadero *m* **2.**(*charge*) anclaje *m*

anchorman ['æŋkəmæn, *Am:* -kɚ-] <-men> *n* **1.** RADIO, TV presentador *m* **2.** *fig* hombre *m* clave

anchorwoman ['æŋkəˌwʊmən, *Am:* -kɚ-] <-men> *n* **1.** RADIO, TV presentadora *f* **2.** *fig* mujer *f* clave

anchovy ['æntʃəvi, *Am:* -tʃoʊ-] <-ies> *n* (*fresh*) boquerón *m;* (*tinned, smoked*) anchoa *f*

ancient ['eɪnʃənt] **I.** *adj* **1.** *a.* HIST antiguo, -a; **since ~ times** desde tiempos remotos; **in ~ days** hace muchísimo tiempo; **~ history** historia antigua; **to be ~ history** *iron* haber pasado a la historia **2.** *inf* (*very old*) prehistórico, -a, del año de la pera; **I feel pretty ~** me siento viejísimo **II.** *n* **the ~s** los antiguos

ancillary [æn'sɪləri, *Am:* 'ænsəleri] *adj* **1.** (*staff*) auxiliar **2.** (*road*) secundario, -a; **to be ~ to sth** estar subordinado a algo

and [ən, ənd, *stressed:* ænd] *conj* **1.** (*also*) y; (*before 'i' or 'hi'*) e; **black ~ white** blanco y negro; **food ~ drink** comida y bebida; **parents ~ children** padres e hijos **2.** MAT y; **2 ~ 3 is 5** 2 más 3 son 5; **four hundred ~ twelve** cuatrocientos doce **3.** (*then*) **she went ~ opened the window** fue y abrió la ventana **4.** (*increase*) **more ~ more** cada vez más; **better ~ better** cada vez mejor **5.** (*repetition*) **I tried ~ tried** lo intenté una y otra vez [*o* repetidas veces] **6.** (*continuation*) **he cried ~ cried** lloraba sin parar ►**~ so on** [*o* **forth**] etcétera

Andalusia [ˌændə'lu:siə, *Am:* -'luʒə] *n* Andalucía *f*

Andalusian **I.** *adj* andaluz(a) **II.** *n* **1.** (*person*) andaluz(a) *m(f)* **2.** LING andaluz *m*

Andean ['ændɪən] *adj* andino, -a

Andes ['ændi:z] *npl* Andes *mpl*

Andorra [æn'dɔ:rə] *n* Andorra *f*

Andorran **I.** *adj* andorrano, -a **II.** *n* andorrano, -a *m, f*

androgynous [æn'drɒdʒənəs] *adj* andrógino, -a

android ['ændrɔɪd] *n* androide *m*

anecdotal [ˌænɪk'dəʊtəl, *Am:* -'doʊt̬əl] *adj* anecdótico, -a

anecdote ['ænɪkdəʊt, *Am:* -doʊt] *n* anécdota *f*

anemia [ə'ni:mɪə] *n Am s.* **anaemia**

anemic [ə'ni:mɪk] *adj Am s.* **anaemic**

anemone [ə'neməni] *n* anémona *f*

anesthesia [ˌænɪs'θi:ʒə] *n Am s.* **anaesthesia**

anesthetic [ˌænɪs'θet̬ɪk] *adj, n Am s.* **anaesthetic**

anesthetist [ˌænɪs'θet̬ɪst] *n Am s.* **anaesthetist**

anesthetize [ə'nesθətaɪz] *vt Am s.* **anaesthetize**

anew [ə'nju:, *Am:* -'nu:] *adv* de nuevo; **to begin ~** volver a empezar (de nuevo)

angel ['eɪndʒl] *n* ángel *m;* **~ of death** ángel exterminador; **be an ~ and buy me these shoes** sé bueno y cómprame estos zapatos; **to be no ~** no ser ningún ángel

angelic [æn'dʒelɪk] *adj* angelical

anger ['æŋgəʳ, *Am:* -gɚ] **I.** *n no pl* enfado *m,* enojo *m AmL;* (*stronger*) ira *f,* cólera *f;* **to speak in ~** hablar indignado **II.** *vt* enfadar, enojar *AmL*

angina [æn'dʒaɪnə] *n* angina *f;* **~ pectoris** angina de pecho

angle¹ ['æŋgl] **I.** *n* **1.** *a.* MAT ángulo *m;* **at an ~ of x degrees** en ángulo de x grados; **to be at an ~ (to sth)** formar un ángulo (con algo); **the picture was hanging at an ~** el cuadro estaba torcido; **he wore his hat at an ~** llevaba el sombrero ladeado **2.** (*perspective*) perspectiva *f;* **to have a different ~** tener un modo diferente de enfocar la cuestión; **what is the best news ~ for this story?** ¿cuál es el mejor enfoque informativo para esta historia? **3.** (*opinion*) punto *m* de vista; **what's your ~ on this issue?** ¿qué opina(s) sobre esta cuestión? **4.** *inf* (*scheme, ploy*) **she knows all the ~s** se las sabe todas **II.** *vt* **1.** (*shot*) ladear **2.** (*information*) dirigir; **this article is ~d towards teenagers** este artículo se dirige a los adolescentes

angle² ['æŋgl] *vi* **1.** (*to fish*) pescar (con caña) **2.** *fig* **to ~ for sth** *inf* tratar de pescar algo

angler ['æŋgləʳ, *Am:* -glɚ] *n* pescador(a) *m(f)* de caña

Anglican ['æŋglɪkən] **I.** *adj* anglicano, -a **II.** *n* anglicano, -a *m, f*

Anglican Church *n* Iglesia *f* anglicana

Anglicanism ['æŋglɪkənɪzəm] *n* anglicanismo *m*

anglicise ['æŋglɪsaɪz] *vt Aus, Brit s.* **anglicize**

anglicism ['æŋglɪsɪzəm] *n* anglicismo *m*

anglicist ['æŋglɪsɪst] *n* anglicista *mf*

anglicize ['æŋglɪsaɪz] *vt* anglicanizar

angling ['æŋglɪŋ] *n* pesca *f* (con caña); **to go ~** ir a pescar

Anglo-American [ˌæŋgləʊə'merɪkən, *Am:* -gloʊ] *Am* **I.** *n* angloamericano, -a *m, f* **II.** *adj* angloamericano, -a

anglophile [ˌæŋgləʊfaɪl, *Am:* -gloʊ] *n* anglófilo, -a *m, f*

anglophobe [ˌæŋgləʊ'fəʊb, *Am:* -glə-] *n* anglófobo, -a *m, f*

Anglo-Saxon [ˌæŋgləʊ'sæksən, *Am:* -gloʊ] **I.** *adj* anglosajón, -ona **II.** *n* **1.** (*person*) anglosajón, -ona *m, f* **2.** LING anglosajón *m*

Angola [æŋ'gəʊlə, *Am:* -'goʊ-] *n* Angola *f*

Angolan **I.** *adj* angoleño, -a **II.** *n* angoleño, -a *m, f*

angora [æŋ'gɔ:rə, *Am:* -'gɔ:rə] *n no pl* (*fabric*) angora *f*

angora cat *n* gato *m* de angora

angry ['æŋgri] *adj* **1.** (*person*) enfadado, -a, enojado, -a *AmL;* (*crowd*) enfurecido, -a; (*sky*) tormentoso, -a; (*sea*) embravecido, -a; **to make sb ~** enfadar [*o* enojar *AmL*] a alguien; **to get ~ with sb** enfadarse con alguien, enojarse con alguien *AmL;* **to get ~ about sth** enfadarse por algo, enojarse por algo *AmL;* **to exchange ~ words** intercambiar palabras llenas de ira **2.** MED inflamado, -a

angst [æŋst] *n no pl* angustia *f*

anguish ['æŋgwɪʃ] *n no pl* angustia *f;* **to be**

in ~ (at sth) estar angustiado (por algo); **to cause sb** ~ angustiar a alguien

angular ['æŋgjʊlə^r, *Am:* -lɚ] *adj* (*shape*) angular; (*face*) anguloso, -a

animal ['ænɪml] **I.** *n* **1.** ZOOL animal *m;* ~ **fat** grasa *f* animal **2.** *fig* (*person*) animal *m,* bestia *mf* **II.** *adj* (*instincts*) animal; (*desires*) carnal

animal husbandry *n no pl* cría *f* de animales **animal kingdom** *n no pl* reino *m* animal **animal rights** *npl* derechos *mpl* de los animales

animate ['ænɪmeɪt] **I.** *adj* animado, -a **II.** *vt* animar

animated *adj* animado, -a; **to become** ~ animarse

animated cartoon *n* dibujos *mpl* animados

animation [ˌænɪ'meɪʃən] *n no pl* animación *f;* **computer** ~ animación por ordenador [*o* computadora *AmL*]

animator ['ænɪmeɪtə^r, *Am:* -t̬ɚ] *n* animador(a) *m(f)*

animosity [ˌænɪ'mɒsəti, *Am:* -'mɑːsət̬i] *n no pl* animosidad *f*

animus ['ænɪməs] *n* rencor *m,* animosidad *f*

anise ['ænɪs] *n no pl* (planta *f* de) anís *m*

aniseed ['ænɪsiːd] *n no pl* (semilla *f* de) anís

ankle ['æŋkl] *n* tobillo *m*

anklebone ['æŋklbəʊn] *n* hueso *m* del tobillo

ankle-deep *adj* **to be** ~ **in sth** estar metido hasta los tobillos en algo

ankle sock *n Brit* calcetín *m* corto, soquete *m CSur*

anklet ['æŋklɪt] *n* **1.** (*chain*) pulsera *f* tobillera **2.** *Am* (*short sock*) calcetín *m* corto

annals ['ænlz] *npl* anales *mpl*

annex ['æneks] **I.** *vt* **1.** (*territory*) anexionar **2.** (*document*) adjuntar (como anexo); (*clause*) añadir **II.** *n* <-es> *Am s.* **annexe**

annexation [ˌænek'seɪʃən] *n no pl* anexión *f*

annexe ['æneks] *n Brit, Aus* **1.** (*of building*) edificio *m* anexo **2.** (*of document*) anexo *m,* apéndice *m*

annihilate [ə'naɪəleɪt] *vt a. fig* aniquilar

annihilation [əˌnaɪə'leɪʃən] *n a. fig* aniquilación *f*

anniversary [ˌænɪ'vɜːsəri, *Am:* -'vɜːr-] <-ies> *n* aniversario *m;* **wedding** ~ aniversario de bodas

annotate ['ænəteɪt] *vt* anotar; ~**d edition** edición *f* comentada

annotation [ˌænə'teɪʃən] *n* **1.** *no pl* (*act of writing*) anotación *f* **2.** (*note*) anotación *f,* nota *f*

annotator ['ænəteɪtə^r, *Am:* -t̬ɚ] *n* anotador(a) *m(f)*

announce [ə'naʊns] *vt* anunciar; (*result*) comunicar

announcement *n* anuncio *m;* **official** ~ comunicado *m* oficial; **to make an** ~ **about sth** anunciar algo

announcer [ə'naʊnsə^r, *Am:* -sɚ] *n* locutor(a) *m(f);* **sports** ~ comentarista *mf* deportivo, -a

annoy [ə'nɔɪ] *vt* molestar, fastidiar, embromar *AmL,* enchilar *AmC;* **it ~s me to think that ...** me da rabia pensar que...; **to get ~ed with sb** enfadarse [*o* enojarse *AmL*] con alguien

annoyance [ə'nɔɪəns] *n* **1.** (*irritation*) fastidio *m,* enojo *m AmL;* **much to my ~, she won** me fastidia que haya ganado **2.** (*irritating thing*) molestia *f,* fastidio *m*

annoying *adj* (*noise, fact*) molesto, -a, chocante *AmL;* (*person*) pesado, -a; (*habit*) fastidioso, -a; **the ~ thing about it is that ...** lo que me da rabia es que... +*subj;* **how ~!** ¡qué fastidio!

annual ['ænjʊəl] **I.** *adj* anual **II.** *n* **1.** (*book*) anuario *m* **2.** BOT planta *f* anual

annual general meeting *n Brit* junta *f* general anual

annually ['ænjʊəli] *adv* anualmente

annuity [ə'njuːəti, *Am:* -'nuːət̬i] <-ies> *n* renta *f* anual

annul [ə'nʌl] <-ll-> *vt* anular

annulment [ə'nʌlmənt] *n* anulación *f*

Annunciation [əˌnʌnsɪ'eɪʃən] *n* **the** ~ la Anunciación

anode ['ænəʊd, *Am:* -oʊd] *n* ánodo *m*

anodyne ['ænədaɪn, *Am:* -oʊ-] **I.** *adj* anodino, -a **II.** *n* MED analgésico *m*

anoint [ə'nɔɪnt] *vt* untar; (*oil*) ungir

anointing *n* unción *f*

anomalous [ə'nɒmələs, *Am:* -'nɑː-] *adj* anómalo, -a

anomaly [ə'nɒməli, *Am:* -'nɑː-] <-ies> *n* anomalía *f*

anonymity [ˌænə'nɪməti, *Am:* -t̬i] *n no pl* anonimato *m*

anonymous [ə'nɒnɪməs, *Am:* -'nɑːnə-] *adj* anónimo, -a; ~ **letter** anónimo *m;* **to remain** ~ permanecer en el anonimato

anorak ['ænəræk] *n Brit* anorak *m*

anorexia [ˌɑnə'reksɪə] *n no pl* anorexia *f*

anorexia nervosa *n no pl* anorexia *f* nerviosa

anorexic [ˌænər'eksɪk] *adj* anoréxico, -a

another [ə'nʌðə^r, *Am:* -ɚ] **I.** *pron* **1.** (*one more*) otro, -a; **what with one thing and ~, ...** entre unas cosas y otras,... **2.** (*mutual*) **one** ~ uno a otro; **they love one** ~ se quieren **II.** *adj* otro, -a; ~ **cake?** ¿otro pastel?; ~ **£30** otras 30 libras; **could he be ~ Mozart?** ¿podría ser otro Mozart?

answer ['ɑːnsə^r, *Am:* 'æːnsɚ] **I.** *n* **1.** (*reply*) respuesta *f,* contestación *f;* **to have an ~ for everything** tener respuesta para todo; **in ~ to your question** como respuesta a tu pregunta; **I called but there was no** ~ llamé pero no contestaron; **the short ~ is 'no'** en una palabra: no **2.** (*solution*) solución *f* **3.** LAW contestación *f* **4.** (*equivalent*) **to be the French ~ to the Beatles** ser el equivalente francés de los Beatles **II.** *vt* **1.** (*respond to*) contestar a; **to ~ the telephone** contestar al teléfono; **to ~ the door** abrir la puerta **2.** (*fit, suit: description*)

responder a; (*need*) satisfacer; (*prayers*) escuchar **III.** *vi* contestar, responder
◆**answer back** *vi* contestar, replicar; **don't ~!** ¡no repliques!
◆**answer for** *vt* (*action, situation*) responder de; (*person*) responder por; **to have a lot to ~** tener mucha culpa
◆**answer to** *vt* **1.**(*obey*) obedecer a **2.**(*fit: description*) corresponder a **3.**(*be named*) **to ~ the name of Billy** responder al nombre de Billy
answerable ['ɑːnsərəbl, *Am:* 'æn-] *adj* **1.**(*responsible*) **to be ~ for sth** ser responsable de algo **2.**(*accountable*) **to be ~ to sb** tener que rendir cuentas a alguien; **to be ~ to nobody** no tener que rendir cuentas a nadie
answering machine *n* contestador *m* automático **answering service** *n* servicio *m* de mensajes
ant [ænt] *n* hormiga *f* ▶**to have ~s in one's pants** *inf* ser un polvorilla, ser un manojo de nervios
antagonism [æn'tægənɪzəm] *n* **1.**(*towards someone*) animadversión *f;* (*between people*) rivalidad *f* **2.** *pl* (*of ideas, systems*) antagonismo *m*
antagonistic [æn,tægə'nɪstɪk] *adj* **1.**(*person, attitude*) antagónico, -a **2.** ANAT antagonista
antagonize [æn'tægənaɪz] *vt* enfadar, enojar *AmL*
Antarctic [æn'tɑːktɪk, *Am:* -'tɑːrk-] **I.** *adj* antártico, -a **II.** *n* **the ~** el Antártico
Antarctica [ænt'ɑːktɪkə] *n* la Antártida
Antarctic Circle *n* círculo *m* polar antártico **Antarctic Ocean** *n* Océano *m* Antártico **Antarctic Peninsula** *n* península *f* Antártica
ante ['ænti] *n* apuesta *f;* **to raise the ~** subir la apuesta
anteater ['ænt,iːtə^r, *Am:* -tɚ] *n* oso *m* hormiguero
antecedent [,æntɪ'siːdnt] **I.** *n* **1.**(*forerunner*) antecedente *m,* precedente *m* **2.** *pl* (*past history*) antecedentes *mpl* **II.** *adj form* antecedente, precedente
antechamber ['æntɪʃeɪmbə^r, *Am:* -t̬ɪtʃeɪmbɚ] *n* antecámara *f*
antediluvian [,æntɪdɪ'luːvɪən, *Am:* -t̬ɪdə-] *adj a. fig* antediluviano, -a
antelope ['æntɪləʊp, *Am:* -t̬loʊp] <-(s)> *n* antílope *m*
antenatal [,æntɪ'neɪtəl, *Am:* -t̬ɪ-] *adj* prenatal; **~ clinic** clínica *f* de asistencia prenatal
antenna [æn'tenə] <-nae *o* -s> *n* antena *f*
anterior [æn'tɪərɪə^r, *Am:* -'tɪrɪɚ] *adj* anterior
anteroom ['æntɪrʊm, *Am:* -t̬ɪruːm] *n* antesala *f*
anthem ['ænθəm] *n* himno *m*
anthill ['ænthɪl] *n* hormiguero *m*
anthology [æn'θɒlədʒi, *Am:* -'θɑːlə-] <-ies> *n* antología *f*
anthracite ['ænθrəsaɪt] *n no pl* antracita *f*
anthropoid ['ænθrəpɔɪd] **I.** *n* antropoide *mf* **II.** *adj* antropoide
anthropological [,ænθrəpə'lɒdʒɪkl] *adj* antropológico, -a
anthropologist [,ænθrəpə'lɒdʒɪst] *n* antropólogo, -a *m, f*
anthropology [,ænθrə'pɒlədʒi, *Am:* -'pɑːlə-] *n no pl* antropología *f*
anti ['ænti, *Am:* 'ænt̬i] **I.** *adj* en contra; **to be ~** estar en contra **II.** *prep* en contra de
anti-abortion [,æntiə'bɔːʃən, *Am:* -t̬iə'bɔːr-] *adj* antiabortista, contrario al aborto
anti-abortionist *n* antiabortista *mf*
anti-aircraft [,æntɪ'eəkrɑːft, *Am:* -t̬ɪ'erkræft] *adj* antiaéreo, -a
antibiotic [,æntɪbaɪ'ɒtɪk, *Am:* -t̬ɪbaɪ'ɑːt̬ɪk] **I.** *n* antibiótico *m* **II.** *adj* antibiótico, -a
antibody ['æntɪbɒdi, *Am:* -t̬ɪbɑːdi] <-ies> *n* anticuerpo *m*
Antichrist ['æntɪkraɪst, *Am:* -t̬ɪ-] *n* **the ~** el Anticristo
anticipate [æn'tɪsɪpeɪt, *Am:* -ə-] *vt* **1.**(*expect, foresee*) prever; **to ~ doing/being sth** tener previsto hacer/ser algo **2.**(*look forward to*) esperar (con ilusión) **3.**(*act in advance of*) anticiparse a; **to ~ one's inheritance** gastarse de antemano la herencia
anticipation [æn,tɪsɪ'peɪʃən, *Am:* æn,tɪsə-] *n no pl* **1.**(*foresight*) previsión *f;* **in ~ of** en previsión de **2.**(*funds*) anticipo *m* **3.**(*realization in advance*) **to thank sb in ~** dar las gracias a alguien de antemano **4.**(*excitement*) ilusión *f;* **to wait in ~** esperar con gran ilusión
anticipatory [æn,tɪsɪ'peɪtəri, *Am:* æn'tɪsɪpətɔːr-] *adj* previsor(a)
anticlerical [,æntɪ'klerɪkl, *Am:* -t̬ɪ-] *adj* anticlerical
anticlimactic [,æntɪ'klaɪmæktɪk, *Am:* -t̬ɪ-] *adj* decepcionante
anticlimax [,æntɪ'klaɪmæks, *Am:* -t̬ɪ-] <-es> *n* anticlímax *m inv;* (*disappointment*) decepción *f*
anti-clockwise [,æntɪ'klɒkwaɪz, *Am:* -t̬ɪ'klɑːk-] *adv Aus, Brit* en sentido contrario a las agujas del reloj
anticoagulant [,æntɪkəʊ'ægjʊlənt, *Am:* -t̬ɪkoʊ'ægjə-] **I.** *n* anticoagulante *m* **II.** *adj* anticoagulante
anticorrosive [,æntɪkə'rəʊsɪv] **I.** *adj* anticorrosivo, -a **II.** *n* anticorrosivo *m*
antics ['æntɪks, *Am:* -t̬ɪks] *npl* **1.**(*foolish behaviour*) payasadas *fpl* **2.**(*tricks*) travesuras *fpl*
anticyclone [,æntɪ'saɪkləʊn, *Am:* -t̬ɪ'saɪkloʊn] *n* anticiclón *m*
antidazzle [,æntɪ'dæzl] *adj* antideslumbrante
antidepressant [,æntɪdɪ'presnt] **I.** *adj* antidepresivo, -a **II.** *n* antidepresivo *m*
antidote ['æntɪdəʊt, *Am:* -t̬ɪdoʊt] *n* antídoto *m;* **an ~ to sth** un antídoto contra algo
antifreeze ['æntɪfriːz, *Am:* -t̬ɪ-] *n no pl* anticongelante *m*

antigen ['æntɪdʒən, *Am:* -t̬ɪ-] *n* antígeno *m*

Antigua and Barbuda [æn'ti:gə ən bɑ:'bju:də] *n* Antigua y Barbuda

Antiguan [æn't:gən] **I.** *adj* antigano, -a **II.** *n* antigano, -a *m, f*

anti-hero [æntɪ'hɪərəʊ, *Am:* æntɪ̬'hɪroʊ] <-es> *n* antihéroe *m*

antihistamine [ˌæntɪ'hɪstəˌmi:n, *Am:* -t̬ɪ-] *n* antihistamínico *m*

anti-inflationary [ˌæntɪɪn'fleɪʃnri, *Am:* -t̬ɪ-] *adj* antiinflacionista, antiinflacionario, -a

antiknock [ˌæntɪ'nɒk, *Am:* 'ænt̬ɪ'nɑ:k] *adj* antidetonante

Antilles [æn'tɪli:z] *npl* **the ~** las Antillas

antilock braking system [æntɪ'lɒk 'breɪkɪŋ 'sɪstəm] *n* AUTO sistema *m* antibloqueo de frenos

antimatter ['æntɪmætəʳ, *Am:* -t̬ɪmæt̬ɚ] *n no pl* antimateria *f*

antimissile [ˌæntɪ'mɪsaɪl, *Am:* -t̬ɪ'mɪsl] *adj* antimisil

antioxidant [ˌæntɪ'ɒksɪdənt, *Am:* -t̬ɪ'ɑ:k-] *n* antioxidante *m*

antipathy [æn'tɪpəθi] <-ies> *n* antipatía *f*

antiperspirant [ˌæntɪ'pɜ:spərənt, *Am:* -t̬ɪ'pɜ:rspɚ-] *n* antitranspirante *m*

antipodean [æn'tɪpə'di:ən] **I.** *adj* de las antípodas; *iron* australiano, -a **II.** *n* habitante *mf* de las antípodas; *iron* australiano, -a *m, f*

antipodes [æn'tɪpədi:z] *npl* antípodas *fpl;* **the Antipodes** *Brit* Australia y Nueva Zelanda

antiquarian [ˌæntɪ'kweərɪən, *Am:* -t̬ə'kwerɪ-] **I.** *n* (*dealer*) anticuario, -a *m, f;* (*collector*) coleccionista *mf* de antigüedades **II.** *adj* antiguo, -a

antiquarian bookseller *n* librero, -a *m, f* especializado, -a en libros antiguos **antiquarian bookshop** *n* librería *f* de libros antiguos

antiquary ['æntɪkwəri, *Am:* -t̬əkwər-] <-ies> *n s.* **antiquarian**

antiquated ['æntɪkweɪtɪd, *Am:* -t̬əkweɪt̬ɪd] *adj* anticuado, -a

antique [æn'ti:k] **I.** *n* (*object, piece of furniture*) antigüedad *f; pej, iron* antigualla *f* **II.** *adj* antiguo, -a; *pej* anticuado, -a

antique dealer *n* anticuario, -a *m, f* **antique shop** *n* tienda *f* de antigüedades, anticuario *m*

antiquity [æn'tɪkwəti, *Am:* -t̬i] <-ies> *n* **1.** *no pl* (*ancient times*) antigüedad *f* **2.** *pl* (*relics*) antigüedades *fpl*

anti-rust [ˌæntɪ'rʌst] *adj* antioxidante

anti-Semite [ˌæntɪ'si:maɪt, *Am:* -t̬ɪ'semaɪt] *n* antisemita *mf*

anti-Semitic [ˌæntɪsɪ'mɪtɪk, *Am:* -t̬ɪsə'mɪt̬-] *adj* antisemita

anti-Semitism [æntɪ'semɪtɪsm, *Am:* -t̬ɪ'semə-] *n no pl* antisemitismo *m*

antiseptic [ˌæntɪ'septɪk, *Am:* -t̬ə-] **I.** *n* antiséptico *m* **II.** *adj* **1.** MED antiséptico, -a **2.** *fig, pej* aséptico, -a

antisocial [ˌæntɪ'səʊʃl, *Am:* -t̬ɪ'soʊ-] *adj* antisocial

antistatic [ˌæntɪ'stætɪk, *Am:* -t̬ɪ'stæt̬-] *adj* antiestático, -a

antitank [ˌæntɪ'tæŋk, *Am:* -t̬ɪ-] *adj* antitanque

antithesis [æn'tɪθəsɪs] <-ses> *n* antítesis *f inv*

antithetic(al) [ˌæntɪ'θetɪk(əl), *Am:* -t̬ə'θet̬-] *adj* antitético, -a

antitoxin [ˌæntɪ'tɒksɪn, *Am:* -tɪ'tɑ:k-] *n* antitoxina *f*

anti-virus [ˌæntɪ'vaɪrəs, *Am:* -t̬ɪ-] *adj* antivirus *inv;* **~ programme** (programa *m*) antivirus *m inv*

anti-war [ˌæntɪ'wɔ:r, *Am:* -t̬ɪ-] *adj* antibelicista

anti-wrinkle cream [ˌæntɪ'rɪŋklˌkri:m] *n* crema *f* antiarrugas

antler ['æntləʳ, *Am:* -lɚ] *n* cuerno *m;* **~s** cornamenta *f*

antonym ['æntənɪm, *Am:* -tnɪm] *n* antónimo *m*

Antwerp ['æntwɜ:p] *n* Amberes *m*

anus ['eɪnəs] *n* ano *m*

anvil ['ænvɪl, *Am:* -vl] *n a.* ANAT yunque *m*

anxiety [æŋ'zaɪəti, *Am:* -t̬i] *n* **1.** (*concern*) inquietud *f;* PSYCH ansiedad *f;* **a source of ~** una fuente de preocupación **2.** (*desire*) ansia *f;* **~ to do sth** ansias de hacer algo; **~ for sth** ansia de [*o* por] algo

anxiety attack *n* ataque *m* de ansiedad

anxious ['æŋkʃəs] *adj* **1.** (*concerned*) preocupado, -a; (*look*) de inquietud; **to keep an ~ eye on sth** no quitar los ojos de encima a algo; **to be ~ about sth** estar preocupado por algo; **an ~ moment** un momento de preocupación **2.** (*eager*) ansioso, -a, chingo, -a *Ven;* **to be ~ to do sth** estar ansioso por hacer algo; **to be ~ for sth** estar ansioso por algo

any ['eni] **I.** *adj* **1.** (*some*) algún, alguna; **~ books** algunos libros; **do they have ~ money?** ¿tienen dinero?; **do you want ~ more soup?** ¿quieres más sopa? **2.** (*not important which*) cualquier; **come at ~ time** ven cuando quieras; **in ~ case** en cualquier caso **3.** (*negative sense*) ningún, ninguna; **I haven't ~ money** no tengo dinero; **there aren't ~ cars** no hay ningún coche **II.** *adv* **1.** (*not*) **~ more** no más; **she does not come ~ more** ya no viene más **2.** (*at all*) **does she feel ~ better?** ¿se siente algo mejor?; **it doesn't help him ~** *inf* no le ayuda para nada **III.** *pron* **1.** (*some*) alguno, alguna; **~ of you** alguno de vosotros; **~ but him would have gone** cualquier otro habría ido **2.** (*negative sense*) ninguno, ninguna; **not ~** ninguno; **he ate two cakes and I didn't eat ~** él se comió dos pasteles y yo ninguno

anybody ['enɪbɒdi, *Am:* -bɑ:di] *pron indef* **1.** (*someone*) alguien, alguno; **did you hear ~?** ¿has oído a alguien? **2.** (*not important which*) cualquiera; **~ but him** cualquiera menos él; **~ else would have done it** cualquier otro lo hubiese hecho; ~ **will do** cualquiera sirve; **she's not just** ~ no es cualquiera **3.** (*no one*) nadie, ninguno; **I've not seen** ~ **like that** no he visto a nadie así; **more than** ~ más que nadie

anyhow ['enɪhaʊ] *adv* **1.** (*in any case*) de todas maneras, de todos modos **2.** (*well*) bueno; ~**, as I was saying …** bueno, como iba diciendo… **3.** (*in a disorderly way*) de cualquier manera; **she dumped the tools into the box just** ~ metió las herramientas en la caja de cualquier manera

anyone ['enɪwʌn] *pron indef s.* **anybody**

anyplace ['enɪpleɪs] *adv Am s.* **anywhere**

anything ['enɪθɪŋ] *pron indef* **1.** (*something*) algo; ~ **else?** ¿algo más?; **is there** ~ **new?** ¿alguna novedad? **2.** (*each thing*) cualquier cosa; **they can choose** ~ **they like** pueden escoger cualquier cosa que quieran; **it is** ~ **but funny** es todo menos gracioso; ~ **and everything** cualquier cosa; **to be as fast as** ~ *inf* ser rapidísimo **3.** (*nothing*) nada; **hardly** ~ casi nada; **I didn't find** ~ **better** no encontré nada mejor; **I was afraid, if** ~ estaba asustado, si acaso; **for** ~ (**in the world**) por nada del mundo ▶ ~ **but!** ¡lo que sea menos eso!

anytime ['enitaɪm] *adv Am* = **any time**

anyway ['enɪweɪ] *adv,* **anyways** ['enɪweɪz] *adv Am, inf* **1.** (*in any case*) de todas maneras, de todos modos **2.** (*well*) bueno; ~**, as I was saying …** bueno, como iba diciendo…

anywhere ['enɪweəʳ, *Am:* -wer] *adv* **1.** (*interrogative*) en alguna parte; **have you seen my glasses** ~**?** ¿has visto mis gafas en alguna parte?; **are we** ~ **near finishing yet?** *inf* ¿nos queda mucho para terminar? **2.** (*positive sense*) en cualquier parte [*o* sitio]; **I can sleep** ~ puedo dormir en cualquier sitio; ~ **else** en cualquier otro sitio; (*negative sense*) en ningún otro sitio; **to live miles from** ~ *inf* vivir en el quinto pino; **its value is** ~ **between £25 and £30** *inf* vale entre las 25 y las 30 libras **3.** (*negative sense*) en ninguna parte; **you won't see this** ~ no verás esto en ningún sitio; **he isn't** ~ **near as popular as he used to be** *inf* no es ni la mitad de popular de lo que era

> El **Anzac Day** (**A**ustralian and **N**ew **Z**ealand **A**rmed **C**orps) se celebra el 25 de abril y es un día de luto en Australia y Nueva Zelanda. Con misas y marchas fúnebres se conmemora el desembarco de las **Anzacs** en la península griega de Gallipoli que tuvo lugar el día 25 de abril de 1915, durante el transcurso de la I Guerra Mundial. Las **Anzacs** fueron derrotadas posteriormente. El significado simbólico de este acontecimiento radica en que los australianos luchaban por primera vez como ejército australiano fuera de sus fronteras.

a.o.b. *abbr of* **any other business** ruegos *mpl* y preguntas

aorta [eɪ'ɔːtə, *Am:* -'ɔːrt̬ə] *n* aorta *f*

apace [ə'peɪs] *adv* aprisa

apart [ə'pɑːt, *Am:* -'pɑːrt] *adv* **1.** (*separated*) aparte; **to be 20 km** ~ estar a 20 km de distancia; **far** ~ lejos; **to live** ~ vivir separados; **to move** ~ apartarse **2.** (*aside*) **to be** ~ **from sth** estar apartado de algo; **to set** ~ apartar; **to stand** ~ mantenerse apartado **3.** (*into pieces*) **to come** ~ desprenderse; **to take sth** ~ desmontar algo **4.** (*separately*) **to consider each case** ~ considerar cada caso por separado **5.** (*except for*) **you and me** ~ excepto [*o* salvo] tú y yo; **joking** ~ bromas aparte

apart from *prep* **1.** (*except for*) excepto, salvo; ~ **that** excepto [*o* salvo] eso **2.** (*in addition to*) aparte de, además de **3.** (*separate from*) **to live** ~ **sb** vivir separado de alguien; **to live** ~ **each other** vivir separados el uno del otro

apartheid [ə'pɑːtheɪt, *Am:* -'pɑːrteɪt] *n no pl* apartheid *m*

apartment [ə'pɑːtmənt, *Am:* -'pɑːrt-] *n Am* apartamento *m,* piso *m,* departamento *m AmL;* **holiday** ~ apartamento *m*

apartment building *n Am,* **apartment house** *n Am* edificio *m* de apartamentos, bloque *m* de pisos, edificio *m* de departamentos *AmL*

apathetic [ˌæpə'θetɪk, *Am:* -'θet̬-] *adj* apático, -a

apathy ['æpəθi] *n no pl* apatía *f;* ~ **about sth** apatía respecto a algo

ape [eɪp] **I.** *n* mono *m,* simio *m* ▶ **to go** ~ *inf* volverse loco **II.** *vt* imitar

aperitif [əˌperə'tiːf] *n* aperitivo *m*

aperture ['æpətʃəʳ, *Am:* -ɚtʃʊr] *n* **1.** (*crack*) rendija *f* **2.** PHOT abertura *f*

apex ['eɪpeks] <-es *o* apices> *pl n* **1.** (*top*) ápice *m* **2.** *fig* cumbre *f,* cima *f* **3.** MAT vértice *m*

aphid ['eɪfɪd] *n* áfido *m,* afídido *m*

aphorism ['æfərɪzəm, *Am:* -ɚ-] *n* aforismo *m*

aphrodisiac [ˌæfrə'dɪziæk] **I.** *n* afrodisíaco *m,* afrodisiaco *m* **II.** *adj* afrodisíaco, -a, afrodisiaco, -a

apiarist ['eɪpɪərɪst] *n* apicultor(a) *m(f)*

apiary ['eɪpɪəri, *Am:* -eri] <-ies> *n* colmenar *m*

apiculture ['eɪpɪkʌltʃəʳ, *Am:* -tʃɚ] *n* apicultura *f*

apiece [ə'piːs] *adv* cada uno; (*per person*) por persona; **they cost £5** ~ cuestan 5 libras cada uno

aplenty [ə'plenti] *adv* en abundancia; **there was beer** ~ había cerveza en abundancia

aplomb [ə'plɒm] *n* aplomo *m*

apocalypse [ə'pɒkəlɪps, *Am:* -'pɑːkə-] *n no pl* apocalipsis *m inv;* **the Apocalypse** REL el Apocalipsis

apocalyptic [əˌpɒkə'lɪptɪk, *Am:* -ˌpɑːkə-]

adj apocalíptico, -a

apogee ['æpədʒiː, *Am:* -ə-] *n no pl a.* ASTR apogeo *m*

apologetic [əˌpɒlə'dʒetɪk, *Am:* -ˌpɑːlə'dʒet̬-] *adj* (*tone, look, smile*) de disculpa; **to be ~ about sth** disculparse por algo

apologetically *adv* disculpándose, excusándose; **to say sth ~** decir algo disculpándose

apologize [ə'pɒlədʒaɪz, *Am:* -'pɑːlə-] *vi* disculparse; **to ~ to sb for sth** pedir perdón a alguien por algo; **I do ~ if my voice is a little low** *form* pido disculpas si mi tono de voz es bajo

apology [ə'pɒlədʒi, *Am:* -'pɑːlə-] <-ies> *n* disculpa *f;* **to make an ~** disculparse; **please accept my apologies** le ruego (que) me disculpe; **an ~ for a breakfast** una birria de desayuno

apoplectic [ˌæpə'plektɪk] *adj* **1.** MED apopléjico, -a, apoplético, -a **2.** *fig* furioso, -a; **to be ~ with fury** estar hecho una furia

apoplectic stroke *n* apoplejía *f*

apostle [ə'pɒsl, *Am:* -'pɑːsl] *n* apóstol *m*

apostolic [ˌæpəs'tɒlɪk] *adj* apostólico, -a

apostrophe [ə'pɒstrəfi, *Am:* -'pɑːstrə-] *n* apóstrofo *m*

appal [ə'pɔːl] <-ll-> *vt* horrorizar; **to be ~led at sth** estar horrorizado de [*o* por] algo

Appalachian Mountains [ˌæpə'leɪʃən] *npl* Montes *mpl* Apalaches

appall [ə'pɔːl] *vt Am s.* **appal**

appalling *adj* **1.** (*shocking*) asombroso, -a **2.** (*terrible*) horroroso, -a; **an ~ headache** un terrible dolor de cabeza; **~ luck** suerte pésima; **an ~ trip** un viaje espantoso

apparatus [ˌæpə'reɪtəs, *Am:* -ə'ræt̬-] *n* **1.** (*equipment*) equipo *m;* **climbing ~** equipo *m* de montañismo; **a piece of ~** un aparato **2.** (*organization*) aparato *m*

apparel [ə'pærəl, *Am:* -'per-] *n no pl, form* indumentaria *f;* **sports ~** ropa *f* deportiva

apparent [ə'pærənt, *Am:* -'pernt] *adj* **1.** (*clear*) evidente; **to become ~ that ...** hacerse evidente que...; **it is ~ to me that ...** me parece evidente que... +*subj* **2.** (*seeming*) aparente; **for no ~ reason** sin motivo aparente

apparition [ˌæpə'rɪʃən] *n* aparición *f,* espectro *m,* azoro *m AmC*

appeal [ə'piːl] **I.** *vi* **1.** (*attract*) atraer; **the idea doesn't ~ to me** no me atrae la idea **2.** LAW apelar; **to ~ against sth** apelar contra algo **3.** (*plead*) **to ~ to sb for sth** pedir algo a alguien; **to ~ for donations/help** solicitar donaciones/ayuda; **she ~ed for silence** rogó silencio **II.** *n* **1.** (*attraction*) atractivo *m;* **to have ~** tener gancho *inf;* **to lose one's ~** perder su atractivo **2.** LAW apelación *f;* **court of ~** tribunal *m* de apelación; **to lodge an ~ (against sth)** interponer una apelación (contra algo) **3.** (*request*) petición *f;* **an ~ to sb for sth** una solicitud de algo a alguien; **to launch an ~ to do sth** hacer un llamamiento para hacer algo

appealing [ə'piːlɪŋ] *adj* **1.** (*attractive: smile*) atractivo, -a; (*idea*) tentador(a) **2.** (*beseeching: eyes*) suplicante

appealingly *adv* **1.** (*dress*) con estilo **2.** (*look*) de manera suplicante; (*speak*) con tono suplicante

appear [ə'pɪəʳ, *Am:* -'pɪr] *vi* **1.** (*be seen*) aparecer **2.** (*newspaper*) salir; (*book*) publicarse, aparecer; (*film*) estrenarse **3.** LAW **to ~ in court/before a magistrate** comparecer ante un tribunal/ante un juez **4.** (*seem*) **to ~ to be ...** parecer ser...; **it ~s to me that ...** me parece que...; **so it ~s** eso parece; **it would ~ that ...** parecería que...

appearance [ə'pɪərəns, *Am:* -'pɪrəns] *n* **1.** (*instance of appearing*) aparición *f;* **to make an ~** aparecer **2.** LAW comparecencia *f* **3.** *no pl* (*looks*) aspecto *m* **4.** *pl* (*outward signs*) apariencias *fpl;* **to** [*o* **from** *Am*] **all ~s** según parece; **to keep up ~s** guardar las apariencias **5.** (*performance*) actuación *f;* **stage ~** aparición *f* en escena ►**~s can be deceptive** *prov* las apariencias engañan *prov*

appease [ə'piːz] *vt form* **1.** (*pacify: person*) apaciguar; POL contemporizar con **2.** (*relieve: hunger, suspicion*) aplacar; (*pain*) mitigar

appeasement *n no pl* **1.** (*conciliation*) apaciguamiento *m;* **policy of ~** POL política *f* de contemporización **2.** (*relief: of anger*) aplacamiento *m;* (*of pain*) mitigación

appellant [ə'pelənt] *n* apelante *mf*

appellation [ˌæpə'leɪʃən] *n* título *m;* (*of wine*) denominación *f* de origen

append [ə'pend] *vt form* (*document, note*) adjuntar; (*signature*) añadir

appendage [ə'pendɪdʒ] *n* apéndice *m,* añadidura *f*

appendicitis [əˌpendɪ'saɪtɪs] *n no pl* apendicitis *f inv*

appendix [ə'pendɪks] *n* **1.** <-es> ANAT apéndice *m* **2.** <-dices *o* -es> TYPO apéndice *m*

appertain [ˌæpə'teɪn] *vi* **to ~ to** (*person*) relacionarse con; (*matter*) tener que ver con

appetite ['æpɪtaɪt, *Am:* -ə-] *n* **1.** (*for food*) apetito *m,* antojo *m Méx;* **to have a healthy ~** tener buen apetito **2.** *fig* afán *m*

appetite suppressant *n* inhibidor *m* del apetito

appetizer ['æpɪtaɪzəʳ, *Am:* -ətaɪzɚ] *n* **1.** (*snack*) aperitivo *m,* botana *f Méx,* pasabocas *m inv Col* **2.** *Am* (*first course*) entrante *m*

appetizing ['æpɪtaɪzɪŋ, *Am:* -ə-] *adj* apetitoso, -a

applaud [ə'plɔːd, *Am:* -'plɑːd] **I.** *vi* aplaudir **II.** *vt a. fig* aplaudir

applause [ə'plɔːz, *Am:* -'plɑːz] *n no pl* aplauso *m;* **a round of ~ for the singer** un aplauso para el cantante; **loud ~** fuerte aplauso

apple ['æpl] *n* manzana *f* ►**an ~ a day keeps the doctor away** *prov* a diario una manzana es cosa sana; **to be the ~ of sb's eye** ser la niña de los ojos de alguien; **the Big Apple** *inf* Nueva York

applecart ['æplkɑːt, *Am:* -kɑːrt] *n* **to upset the ~** desbaratar los planes

apple juice *n* zumo *m* de manzana **apple pie** *n* pastel *m* de manzana **apple sauce** *n* compota *f* de manzana **apple tart** *n* tarta *f* de manzana **apple tree** *n* manzano *m,* manzanero *m Ecua*

appliance [ə'plaɪəns] *n* aparato *m;* **electrical ~** electrodoméstico *m*

applicability [ˌæplɪkə'bɪlɪti] *n* aplicabilidad *f*

applicable ['æplɪkəbl] *adj* aplicable; **delete where not ~** táchese lo que no proceda; **those rules are not ~ any more** esas normas ya no están vigentes

applicant ['æplɪkənt] *n* (*for money, support*) solicitante *mf;* (*for job*) candidato, -a *m, f;* **an ~ for a job** un candidato a un puesto de trabajo

application [ˌæplɪ'keɪʃən] *n* **1.** (*request*) solicitud *f;* **on ~** mediante solicitud **2.** (*coating*) aplicación *f* **3.** (*use*) aplicación *f,* uso *m* **4.** *no pl* (*perseverance*) diligencia *f* **5.** INFOR aplicación *f*

application form *n* (hoja *f* de) solicitud *f*

applied [ə'plaɪd] *adj* aplicado, -a

appliqué [æ'pliːkeɪ, *Am:* ˌæplɪ'keɪ] *n* bordado *m* sobrepuesto

apply [ə'plaɪ] **I.** *vi* **1.** (*request*) presentarse; **to ~ to sb** dirigirse a alguien; **to ~ to sb for sth** solicitar algo a alguien; **to ~ for a job** presentarse a [*o* solicitar] un puesto de trabajo; **to ~ in writing** dirigirse por escrito **2.** (*be relevant*) **to ~ to sb** concernir a alguien **II.** *vt* **1.** (*coat*) aplicar **2.** (*use*) aplicar, usar; **to ~ force** hacer uso de la fuerza; **to ~ pressure to sth** ejercer presión sobre algo; **to ~ sanctions** aplicar sanciones; **to ~ common sense** usar el sentido común **3.** (*persevere*) **to ~ oneself to sth** dedicarse a algo

appoint [ə'pɔɪnt] *vt* **1.** (*select*) nombrar; **to ~ sb as heir** nombrar a alguien heredero **2.** *form* (*designate*) **to ~ a date** fijar una fecha; **at the ~ed time** a la hora señalada

appointed *adj form* (*equipped*) equipado, -a

appointee [əpɔɪn'tiː] *n* persona *f* nombrada

appointment *n* **1.** (*selection*) nombramiento *m* **2.** (*meeting*) cita *f;* **dental ~** cita *f* con el dentista; **to have an ~ at the hairdresser's** tener hora en la peluquería; **to keep an ~** acudir a una cita; **by ~ only** sólo con cita previa **3.** *pl* (*furniture*) mobiliario *m* ►**by ~ to the Queen** proveedores de la reina

appointment book *n* libro *m* de visitas

apportion [ə'pɔːʃən] *vt* repartir

apposite ['æpəzɪt] *adj form* apropiado, -a; (*observation*) pertinente

apposition [ˌæpə'zɪʃən] *n* aposición *f*

appraisal [ə'preɪzl] *n* **1.** (*evaluation*) evaluación *f;* (*of performance, evidence*) valoración *f;* (*of property*) tasación *f;* **to carry out an ~ of sth** efectuar una evaluación de algo **2.** (*estimation*) estimación *f*

appraise [ə'preɪz] *vt* **1.** (*evaluate*) evaluar; (*performance, evidence*) valorar; (*property*) tasar; **to ~ sb's needs** valorar las necesidades de alguien **2.** (*estimate*) estimar

appreciable [ə'priːʃəbl] *adj* apreciable; (*change*) notorio, -a; (*progress*) considerable

appreciate [ə'priːʃɪeɪt] **I.** *vt* **1.** (*value*) apreciar **2.** (*understand*) comprender **3.** (*be grateful for*) agradecer **II.** *vi* FIN (*price*) subir; (*property, shares*) revalorizarse

appreciation [əˌpriːʃɪ'eɪʃən] *n no pl* **1.** (*gratitude*) agradecimiento *m* **2.** (*understanding*) aprecio *m;* **she has no ~ of my work** no sabe apreciar mi trabajo **3.** FIN (*of price*) subida *f;* (*of property, shares*) revalorización *f*

appreciative [ə'priːʃɪətɪv] *adj* agradecido, -a; **an ~ audience** un público que sabe apreciar

apprehend [ˌæprɪ'hend] *vt form* **1.** (*arrest*) detener **2.** (*comprehend*) entender; **to ~ the importance of doing sth** darse cuenta de la importancia de hacer algo **3.** (*fear*) temer

apprehension [ˌæprɪ'henʃən] *n no pl* **1.** *form* (*arrest*) detención *f* **2.** *no pl, form* (*comprehension*) comprensión *f;* **~ of reality** percepción *f* de la realidad **3.** *no pl* (*fear*) aprensión *f;* **~ about sth** temor *m* por algo

apprehensive [ˌæprɪ'hensɪv] *adj* aprensivo, -a, flatoso, -a *AmL;* **to be ~ about sth** estar preocupado por algo; **to be ~ that** temer que +*subj*

apprentice [ə'prentɪs, *Am:* -t̬ɪs] **I.** *n* aprendiz(a) *m(f)*, peón, -ona *m, f Méx* **II.** *vt* **to ~ sb (to sb)** colocar a alguien de aprendiz (de alguien)

apprenticeship [ə'prentɪʃɪp, *Am:* -t̬əsʃɪp] *n* aprendizaje *m*

approach [ə'prəʊtʃ, *Am:* -'proʊtʃ] **I.** *vt* **1.** (*get close to*) acercarse a **2.** (*ask*) dirigirse a; **to ~ sb (about sth)** dirigirse a alguien (para pedir algo) **3.** (*deal with*) abordar **II.** *vi* acercarse **III.** *n* **1.** (*coming*) aproximación *f;* **at the ~ of winter** al acercarse el invierno **2.** (*access*) acceso *m* **3.** (*proposition*) propuesta *f;* (*for help*) petición *f;* **to make ~es to sb** dirigirse a alguien **4.** (*methodology*) enfoque *m*

approachable [ə'prəʊtʃəbl, *Am:* -'proʊ-] *adj* (*person, place*) accesible

approach road *n* (carretera *f* de) acceso *m,* aproches *mpl AmL*

approbation [ˌæprə'beɪʃən] *n no pl, form* aprobación *f*

appropriate[1] [ə'prəʊprɪət, *Am:* -'proʊ-] *adj* apropiado, -a, adecuado, -a; **~ to the occasion** apropiado [*o* adecuado] para la ocasión

appropriate[2] [ə'prəʊprɪeɪt, *Am:* -'proʊ-] *vt form* **1.** (*take*) apropiarse de **2.** FIN asignar; **to ~ funds (for sth)** destinar fondos (a algo)

appropriation [əˌprəʊprɪ'eɪʃən, *Am:* -ˌproʊ-] *n* **1.** (*taking*) apropiación *f* **2.** FIN asignación *f*

A

approval [ə'pruːvl] *n no pl* aprobación *f;* **to meet with sb's** ~ obtener la aprobación de alguien; **to nod one's** ~ asentir con la cabeza; **on** ~ ECON a prueba
approve [ə'pruːv] **I.** *vi* estar de acuerdo; **to** ~ **of sth** estar de acuerdo con [*o* aprobar] algo; **she doesn't** ~ **of smoking** no le parece bien que se fume **II.** *vt* aprobar
approved *adj* **1.** (*agreed*) aprobado, -a **2.** (*authorized*) autorizado, -a; **an** ~ **qualification** un título homologado
approving [ə'pruːvɪŋ] *adj* de aprobación
approvingly [ə'pruːvɪŋli] *adv* con aprobación; **to smile** ~ sonreír en señal de aprobación
approx. [ə'prɒks, *Am:* -'prɑːk-] *n abbr of* **approximately** aprox.
approximate[1] [ə'prɒksɪmət, *Am:* -'prɑːk-] *adj* aproximado, -a
approximate[2] [ə'prɒksɪmeɪt, *Am:* -'prɑːk-] **I.** *vt form* aproximarse a **II.** *vi form* **to** ~ **to sth** aproximarse a algo
approximately [ə'prɒksɪmətli] *adv* aproximadamente
approximation [əˌprɒksɪ'meɪʃən, *Am:* -ˌprɑːk-] *n form* aproximación *f*
APR [ˌeɪpiː'ɑːʳ, *Am:* -'ɑːr] *n abbr of* **annual percentage rate** TAE *f*
apricot ['eɪprɪkɒt, *Am:* -kɑːt] **I.** *n* **1.** BOT albaricoque *m,* chabacano *m Méx,* damasco *m AmS* **2.** *no pl* (*colour*) (color *m*) albaricoque *m* **II.** *adj* (de color) albaricoque
apricot tree *n* albaricoquero *m,* chabacano *m Méx,* damasco *m AmS*
April ['eɪprəl] *n* abril *m;* **in** ~ en abril; **every** ~ todos los meses de abril; **the month of** ~ el mes de abril; **at the beginning/end of** ~ a principios/finales de abril; **on** ~ **the fourth** el cuatro de abril
April Fools' Day *n no pl* ≈ Día *m* de los Santos Inocentes (*en Gran Bretaña, el 1 de abril*)
a priori [ˌeɪpraɪ'ɔraɪ] *adv* a priori
apron ['eɪprən] *n* **1.** (*clothing*) delantal *m* **2.** AVIAT pista *f* de estacionamiento **3.** THEAT proscenio *m*
apron strings *n pl* cordeles *mpl* del delantal ►**to be <u>tied</u> to one's mother's** ~ estar pegado a las faldas de la madre
apropos, **a propos** [ˌæprə'əʊ, *Am:* -'poʊ] **I.** *prep* ~ **of** a propósito de **II.** *adv* a propósito **III.** *adj* apropiado, -a
apse [æps] *n* ábside *m*
apt [æpt] *adj* **1.** (*appropriate*) apropiado, -a; (*comment*) oportuno, -a; (*description*) adecuado, -a **2.** (*clever*) inteligente **3.** (*likely*) **to be** ~ **to do sth** tener tendencia a hacer algo
APT *n abbr of* **advanced passenger train** *tren de alta velocidad*
aptitude ['æptɪtjuːd, *Am:* -tuːd] *n* aptitud *f*
aptitude test *n* prueba *f* de aptitud
aquaculture ['ækwəˌkʌltʃəʳ, *Am:* 'ɑːkwəˌkʌltʃɚ] *n* acuicultura *f*
aqualung ['ækwəlʌŋ] escafandra *f* autónoma
aquamarine [ˌækwəmə'riːn, *Am:* ˌɑːkwə-] **I.** *n* **1.** (*stone*) aguamarina *f* **2.** *no pl* (*colour*) color *m* verde mar **II.** *adj* de color verde mar
aquaplaning [ˌækwə'pleɪnɪŋ, *Am:* ˌɑːkwə-] *n* **1.** SPORTS ≈ esquí *m* acuático **2.** AUTO aquaplaning *m*
Aquarian [əkwɛərɪən] *n* acuario *mf*
aquarium [ə'kweərɪəm, *Am:* -'kwerɪ-] <-s *o* -ria> *n* acuario *m,* acuárium *m*
Aquarius [ə'kweərɪəs, *Am:* -'kwerɪ-] *n* Acuario *m*
aquarobics [ˌækwə'rɔbɪks] *npl* aeróbic *m* en el agua
aquatic [ə'kwætɪk, *Am:* -'kwæt̬-] *adj* acuático, -a
aqueduct ['ækwɪdʌkt] *n* acueducto *m*
aquifer ['ækwɪfər] *n* acuífero *m*
aquiline ['ækwɪlaɪn, *Am:* -lən] *adj* aquilino, -a; ~ **nose** nariz *f* aguileña
Arab ['ærəb, *Am:* 'er-] **I.** *adj* árabe; **the** (**United**) ~ **Emirates** los Emiratos Árabes (Unidos) **II.** *n* árabe *mf*
arabesque [ˌærə'besk, *Am:* ˌer-] *n* arabesco *m*
Arabia [ə'reɪbɪə] *n* Arabia *f*
Arabian *adj* árabe, arábigo, -a
Arabic ['ærəbɪk, *Am:* 'er-] *n* LING árabe *m*
arable ['ærəbl, *Am:* 'er-] *adj* cultivable
arachnid [ə'ræknɪd] *n* arácnido *m*
arbiter ['ɑːbɪtəʳ, *Am:* 'ɑːrbɪtɚ] *n* árbitro, -a *m, f*
arbitrage [ˌɑːbɪtrɑːʒ] *n* arbitraje *m* (financiero)
arbitrariness ['ɑːbɪtrərɪnɪs] *n* arbitrariedad *f*
arbitrary ['ɑːbɪtrəri, *Am:* 'ɑːrbətreri] *adj* arbitrario, -a
arbitrate ['ɑːbɪtreɪt, *Am:* 'ɑːrbə-] **I.** *vt* arbitrar, mediar en; **to** ~ **an argument** mediar en una disputa **II.** *vi* arbitrar, mediar; **to** ~ **between ...** mediar entre...
arbitration [ˌɑːbɪ'treɪʃən, *Am:* ˌɑːrbə-] *n no pl* arbitraje *m,* mediación *f;* **to go to** ~ recurrir al arbitraje
arbitrator ['ɑːbɪtreɪtəʳ, *Am:* 'ɑːrbə-] *n* árbitro, -a *m, f*
arbor ['ɑːrbɚ] *n Am, Aus s.* **arbour**

> Con motivo del **Arbor Day** se plantan árboles en los EE.UU. En algunos estados es, incluso, un día festivo. La fecha exacta del **Arbor Day** varía en cada uno de los distintos estados, ya que la época apropiada para plantar árboles no es la misma en todos los sitios.

arboriculture ['ɑːbərɪˌkʌltʃəʳ, *Am:* 'ɑːrbɚɪˌkʌltʃɚ] *n* arboricultura *f*
arbour ['ɑːbəʳ] *n Aus, Brit* cenador *m*
arc [ɑːk, *Am:* ɑːrk] **I.** *n* arco *m* **II.** *vi* arquearse
arcade [ɑː'keɪd, *Am:* ɑːr-] *n* **1.** (*of shops*) galería *f* comercial **2.** (*around square*) soportales *mpl*

arch[1] [ɑːtʃ, *Am:* ɑːrtʃ] **I.** *n* arco *m* **II.** *vi* arquearse **III.** *vt* arquear; **to ~ one's eyebrows** arquear las cejas

arch[2] [ɑːtʃ, *Am:* ɑːrtʃ] <-er, -est> *adj* burlón, -ona

archaeological [ˌɑːkɪəˈlɒdʒɪkl, *Am:* ˌɑːrkɪəˈlɑːdʒɪ-] *adj* arqueológico, -a

archaeologist [ˌɑːkɪˈɒlədʒɪst, *Am:* ˌɑːrkɪˈɑːlə-] *n* arqueólogo, -a *m, f*

archaeology [ˌɑːkɪˈɒlədʒi, *Am:* ˌɑːrkɪˈɑːlə-] *n no pl* arqueología *f*

archaic [ɑːˈkeɪɪk, *Am:* ɑːr-] *adj* arcaico, -a

archangel [ˈɑːkeɪndʒl, *Am:* ˈɑːr-] *n* arcángel *m*

archbishop [ˌɑːtʃˈbɪʃəp, *Am:* ˌɑːrtʃ-] *n* arzobispo *m*

archdeacon [ˌɑːtʃˈdiːkən, *Am:* ˌɑːrtʃ-] *n* arcediano *m*

archdiocese [ˌɑːtʃˈdaɪəsɪs, *Am:* ˌɑːrtʃ-] *n* archidiócesis *f inv*

arch enemy <-ies> *n* archienemigo, -a *m, f*

archeological [ˌarkiəˈlɑːdʒɪkəl] *adj Am s.* **archaeological**

archeologist [ˌɑːrkiˈɑːləʒɪst] *n Am s.* **archaeologist**

archeology [ˌɑːrkiˈɑːləʒi] *n Am s.* **archaeology**

archer [ˈɑːtʃəʳ, *Am:* ˈɑːrtʃɚ] *n* arquero, -a *m, f*

archery [ˈɑːtʃəri, *Am:* ˈɑːr-] *n no pl* tiro *m* con arco

archetype [ˈɑːkɪtaɪp, *Am:* ˈɑːr-] *n* arquetipo *m*

archipelago [ˌɑːkɪˈpeləgəʊ, *Am:* ˌɑːrkəˈpeləgoʊ] <-(e)s> *n* archipiélago *m*

architect [ˈɑːkɪtekt, *Am:* ˈɑːrkə-] *n* **1.** (*of building*) arquitecto, -a *m, f* **2.** *fig* artífice *mf*

architecture [ˈɑːkɪtektʃəʳ, *Am:* ˈɑːrkətektʃɚ] *n no pl* arquitectura *f*

archive [ˈɑːkaɪv, *Am:* ˈɑːr-] *n a.* INFOR archivo *m*

archivist [ˈɑːkɪvɪst, *Am:* ˈɑːrkaɪ-] *n* archivero, -a *m, f,* archivista *mf Méx*

archway [ˈɑːtʃweɪ, *Am:* ˈɑːrtʃ-] *n* (*entrance*) arco *m;* (*passageway*) pasadizo *m* abovedado

arc lamp *n,* **arc light** *n* arco *m* voltaico

Arctic [ˈɑːktɪk, *Am:* ˈɑːrk-] *no pl* **I.** *n* **the ~** el Ártico **II.** *adj* **1.** ártico, -a **2.** (*extremely cold*) glacial

Arctic Circle *n* Círculo *m* Polar Ártico **Arctic Ocean** *n* Océano *m* Glacial Ártico

arc welding *n* soldadura *f* por arco

ardent [ˈɑːdnt, *Am:* ˈɑːr-] *adj* ferviente; (*desire, plea*) vehemente

ardor *n Am,* **ardour** [ˈɑːdəʳ, *Am:* ˈɑːrdɚ] *n no pl, Brit* fervor *m*

arduous [ˈɑːdjʊəs, *Am:* ˈɑːrdʒu-] *adj* arduo, -a; (*task*) trabajoso, -a

are [əʳ, *stressed:* ɑːʳ, *Am:* ɚ, *stressed:* ɑːr] *vi s.* **be**

area [ˈeərɪə, *Am:* ˈerɪ-] *n* **1.** *a.* MAT, SPORTS área *f;* **in the ~ of** alrededor de **2.** (*field*) campo *m;* **~ of competence/knowledge** ámbito *m* de competencia(s)/conocimiento(s)

area code *n Am, Aus* prefijo *m*

arena [əˈriːnə] *n a. fig* arena *f*

Argentina [ˌɑːdʒənˈtiːnə, *Am:* ˌɑːr-] *n* Argentina *f*

Argentine [ˈɑːdʒəntaɪn, *Am:* ˈɑːrdʒən-], **Argentinian** [ˌɑːdʒənˈtɪnɪən, *Am:* ˌɑːr-] **I.** *adj* argentino, -a **II.** *n* argentino, -a *m, f*

arguable [ˈɑːgjuəbl, *Am:* ˈɑːrg-] *adj* discutible

arguably *adv* posiblemente

argue [ˈɑːgjuː, *Am:* ˈɑːrg-] **I.** *vi* **1.** (*disagree*) discutir, alegar *AmL* **2.** (*reason*) razonar; **to ~ against/for sth** abogar contra/a favor de algo **II.** *vt* **1.** (*debate*) sostener; **to ~ that ...** sostener que... **2.** (*persuade*) **to ~ sb into doing sth** persuadir a alguien de hacer algo; **to ~ sb out of doing sth** persuadir a alguien para que abandone la idea de hacer algo

argument [ˈɑːgjʊmənt, *Am:* ˈɑːrgjə-] *n* **1.** (*disagreement*) discusión *f* **2.** (*reasoning*) argumento *m;* **suppose for ~'s sake that ...** supongamos por caso que...

argumentative [ˌɑːgjʊˈmentətɪv, *Am:* ˌɑːrgjəˈmen̬t̬ət̬ɪv] *adj* discutidor(a)

aria [ˈɑːrɪə] *n* MUS aria *f*

arid [ˈærɪd, *Am:* ˈer-] *adj* árido, -a

Aries [ˈeəriːz, *Am:* ˈeriːz] *n* Aries *m*

arise [əˈraɪz] <arose, arisen> *vi* **1.** (*come about*) surgir; **to ~ from** surgir de; **should the need ~** si fuera necesario; **should doubt ~** en caso de presentarse la duda **2.** *form* (*rise up*) alzarse

arisen [əˈrɪzn] *pp of* **arise**

aristocracy [ˌærɪˈstɒkrəsi, *Am:* ˌerəˈstɑːkrə-] <-ies> *n + sing/pl vb* aristocracia *f*

aristocrat [ˈærɪstəkræt, *Am:* əˈrɪs-] *n* aristócrata *mf*

aristocratic [ˌærɪstəˈkrætɪk, *Am:* eˌrɪstəˈkræt̬ɪk] *adj* aristocrático, -a

arithmetic [əˈrɪθmətɪk, *Am:* ˌerɪθˈmet̬ɪk] **I.** *n no pl* aritmética *f* **II.** *adj* aritmético, -a

arithmetical [ˌærɪθˈmetɪkl, *Am:* ˌerɪθˈmet̬ɪkl] *adj* aritmético, -a

ark [ɑːk, *Am:* ɑːrk] *n no pl* arca *f;* **Noah's ark** el Arca de Noé

arm[1] [ɑːrm] *n* **1.** ANAT, GEO brazo *m;* **to put one's ~s round sb** abrazar a alguien; **to hold sb in one's ~s** tener a alguien en brazos; **~ in ~** (agarrados) del brazo **2.** (*sleeve*) manga *f* **3.** (*division*) sección *f* ►**the (long) ~ of the law** el brazo de la ley; **to cost an ~ and a leg** *inf* costar un ojo de la cara; **to keep sb at ~'s length** *fig* mantener a alguien a distancia

arm[2] [ɑːm, *Am:* ɑːrm] MIL **I.** *vt* **1.** (*supply with weapons*) armar; **to ~ oneself against sth** armarse contra algo **2.** (*prepare for detonation*) activar; (*rocket*) cebar **II.** *n* (*weapon*) arma *f;* **under ~s** en armas; **to lay down one's ~s** rendir las armas; **to present ~s** presentar armas; **to take up ~s (against sb/sth)** tomar las armas (contra alguien/algo) ►**to be up in ~s about ...** poner el grito en el cielo

A

contra…
armaments ['ɑːməməntz, *Am:* 'ɑːr-] *npl* armamento *m*
armature ['ɑːmətʃʊəʳ, *Am:* 'ɑːrmətʃɚ] *n* 1. TECH, ZOOL, BOT armadura *f* 2. ELEC inducido *m*
armband ['ɑːmbænd, *Am:* 'ɑːrm-] *n* brazalete *m*
armchair [ˌɑːm'tʃeəʳ, *Am:* 'ɑːrmtʃer] *n* sillón *m*
armed [ɑːmd, *Am:* ɑːrmd] *adj* armado, -a
armed forces *npl* **the** ~ las fuerzas armadas
Armenia [ɑː'miːniə, *Am:* ɑːr-] *n* Armenia *f*
Armenian I. *n* 1. (*person*) armenio, -a *m, f* 2. LING armenio *m* II. *adj* armenio, -a
armful ['ɑːmfʊl, *Am:* 'ɑːrm-] *n* brazada *f*
armhole ['ɑːmhəʊl, *Am:* 'ɑːrmhoʊl] *n* sisa *f*
arming ['ɑːmɪŋ] *n* aprovisionamiento *m* de armas
armistice ['ɑːmɪstɪs, *Am:* 'ɑːrmə-] *n* armisticio *m*
armor ['ɑːməʳ, *Am:* 'ɑːrmɚ] *n Am s.* **armour**
armored ['ɑːməd, *Am:* 'ɑːrmɚd] *adj Am s.* **armoured**
armor-plated ['ɑːmə'pleɪtɪd] *adj Am s.* **armour-plated**
armour ['ɑːməʳ, *Am:* 'ɑːrmɚ] *n no pl, Brit* 1. (*protective covering*) blindaje *m* 2. *a.* MIL, ZOOL armadura *f* 3. (*tanks*) carros *mpl* blindados
armoured ['ɑːməd, *Am:* 'ɑːrmɚd] *adj Brit* (*car*) blindado, -a; (*train*) acorazado, -a
armour-plated ['ɑːmə'pleɪtɪd] *adj Brit* blindado, -a
armpit ['ɑːmpɪt, *Am:* 'ɑːrm-] *n* axila *f*
armrest ['ɑːmrest, *Am:* 'ɑːrm-] *n* descansabrazos *m inv*
arms control *n*, **arms limitation** *n* MIL control *m* de armamentos **arms race** *n* **the** ~ la carrera armamentista **arms reduction** *n* reducción *f* de armamentos
army ['ɑːmi, *Am:* 'ɑːr-] <-ies> *n* 1. MIL ejército *m;* **to join the** ~ alistarse 2. *fig* multitud *f*
aroma [ə'rəʊmə, *Am:* -'roʊ-] *n* aroma *m*
aromatherapy [əˌrəʊmə'θerəpi, *Am:* -ˌroʊ-] *n no pl* aromaterapia *f*
aromatic [ˌærə'mætɪk, *Am:* ˌerə'mæt̬-] *adj* aromático, -a
arose [ə'rəʊz, *Am:* ə'roʊz] *pt of* **arise**
around [ə'raʊnd] I. *prep* 1. (*surrounding*) alrededor de; **all** ~ **sth** por todas partes; **the earth goes** ~ **the sun** la tierra gira alrededor del sol; **to go** ~ **the corner** doblar la esquina 2. (*here and there within*) por; **to drive** ~ **France** viajar (en coche) por Francia; **to go** ~ **a museum** visitar un museo; **to go all** ~ **the world** viajar por el mundo; **to sit** ~ **the room** sentarse en la habitación 3. (*approximately*) más o menos, alrededor de; ~ **May 10** alrededor del 10 de mayo; **somewhere** ~ **here** en algún lugar por aquí II. *adv* 1. (*round about*) alrededor; **all** ~ en todas partes; **for 50 m** ~ en un radio de 50 m; **for miles** ~ en millas a la redonda 2. (*aimlessly*) **to walk** ~ dar una vuelta; **to stand/hang** ~ estar/andar por ahí; **to have been** ~ haber visto mundo; (*be experienced*) tener mucha experiencia 3. (*near by*) por ahí; **is he** ~**?** ¿está por ahí?; **to be still** ~ seguir todavía ahí
arouse [ə'raʊz] *vt* 1. (*stir*) suscitar; (*anger*) provocar 2. (*sexually excite*) excitar
arr. *abbr of* **arrival** llegadas *fpl*
arrange [ə'reɪndʒ] I. *vt* 1. (*organize*) organizar; **to** ~ **a date** acordar una cita 2. (*put in order*) *a.* MUS arreglar II. *vi* disponer; **to** ~ **for sth** disponer algo; **to** ~ **to do sth** quedar en hacer algo
arrangement *n* 1. *pl* (*preparations*) preparativos *mpl;* **to make** ~**s** (**for sth**) hacer los preparativos (de algo) 2. (*agreement*) acuerdo *m;* **to come to an** ~ llegar a un acuerdo 3. (*method of organizing sth*) *a.* MUS arreglo *m*
array [ə'reɪ] I. *n* 1. (*display*) colección *f* 2. *form* (*clothes*) atavío *m* 3. MIL formación *f* II. *vt* 1. (*display*) colocar, exponer 2. *form* (*clothes*) ataviar 3. MIL desplegar
arrears [ə'rɪəz, *Am:* -'rɪrz] *npl* FIN atraso *m;* **to be in** ~ **on sth** estar atrasado en el pago de algo; **to pay in** ~ pagar con atraso
arrest [ə'rest] I. *vt* 1. LAW detener 2. *form* (*put a stop to*) detener 3. (*attract*) **to** ~ **sb's attention** captar la atención de alguien II. *n* detención *f;* **to be under** ~ estar detenido; **to put sb under** ~ detener a alguien
arresting *adj* llamativo, -a; (*account*) cautivante; (*performance*) impresionante
arrival [ə'raɪvl] *n* 1. (*at destination*) llegada *f;* **on his** ~ a su llegada 2. (*person*) persona *f* que llega; **new** ~ recién llegado *m*
arrive [ə'raɪv] *vi* 1. (*come*) llegar; **to** ~ **at a conclusion** llegar a una conclusión 2. *inf* (*establish one's reputation*) llegar a ser alguien 3. (*be born*) nacer
arriviste [ˌæriː'viːst, *Am:* ˌer-] *n* arribista *mf*
arrogance ['ærəgəns, *Am:* 'er-] *n no pl* arrogancia *f*
arrogant ['ærəgənt, *Am:* 'er-] *adj* arrogante
arrow ['ærəʊ, *Am:* 'eroʊ] *n* flecha *f*, jara *f Guat, Méx*
arrowhead *n* punta *f* de flecha
arse [ɑːs, *Am:* ɑːrs] *n Aus, Brit, vulg* culo *m*, siete *m AmS, Méx* ►**get your** ~ **in gear!** ¡espabílate!; **to make an** ~ **out of oneself** quedar como un gilipollas; **move your** ~**!** ¡muévete!; **to work one's** ~ **off** trabajar como un burro
arsenal ['ɑːsənl, *Am:* 'ɑːr-] *n* arsenal *m*
arsenic ['ɑːsnɪk, *Am:* 'ɑːr-] *n no pl* arsénico *m*
arson ['ɑːsn, *Am:* 'ɑːr-] *n* incendio *m* provocado
art [ɑːt, *Am:* ɑːrt] *n* arte *m*
art collection *n* colección *f* de arte **art critic** *n* crítico *m* de arte **art dealer** *n* marchante *mf* de arte

artefact [ˈɑːtɪfækt, *Am:* ˈɑːrt̬ə-] *n Brit* artefacto *m*

arterial [ɑːˈtɪərɪəl, *Am:* ɑːrˈtɪrɪ-] *adj* **1.** ANAT arterial **2.** AUTO, RAIL principal

arteriosclerosis [ɑːˌtɪərɪəʊskləˈrəʊsɪs, *Am:* ɑːrˌtɪrɪoʊskləˈroʊsəs] *n* arteriosclerosis *f inv*

artery [ˈɑːtəri, *Am:* ˈɑːrt̬ɚ] <-ies> *n* arteria *f*

artesian well [ɑːˈtiːzɪənˈwel, *Am:* ɑːrˈtiːʒənˈwel] *n* pozo *m* artesiano

artful [ˈɑːtfəl, *Am:* ˈɑːrt-] *adj* hábil, ingenioso, -a

art gallery *n* (*for public exhibitions*) museo *m* de arte; (*for sale of paintings*) galería *f* de arte

arthritic [ɑːˈθrɪtɪk, *Am:* ɑːrˈθrɪt̬-] *adj* artrítico, -a

arthritis [ɑːˈθraɪtɪs, *Am:* ɑːrˈθraɪt̬əs] *n no pl* artritis *f inv*

artichoke [ˈɑːtɪtʃəʊk, *Am:* ˈɑːrt̬ətʃoʊk] *n* alcachofa *f*

article [ˈɑːtɪkl, *Am:* ˈɑːrt̬ɪ-] *n* **1.** (*object*) artículo *m*, objeto *m;* ~ **of clothing** prenda *f* de vestir **2.** *a.* LAW, LING, TYPO artículo *m*

articulate[1] [ɑːˈtɪkjʊlət, *Am:* ɑːrˈtɪkjə-] *adj* **1.** (*person*) que se expresa con claridad; (*speech*) claro, -a **2.** TECH articulado, -a

articulate[2] [ɑːˈtɪkjʊleɪt, *Am:* ɑːrˈtɪkjə-] *vt form* **1.** (*express*) expresar claramente; **to ~ an idea** articular una idea **2.** (*pronounce*) articular

articulated lorry *n Brit* camión *m* articulado

articulation [ɑːˌtɪkjʊˈleɪʃən, *Am:* ɑːrˌtɪkjə-] *n no pl* (*of idea, feeling*) expresión *f*

artifact [ˈɑːtɪfækt, *Am:* ˈɑːrt̬ə-] *n Am* artefacto *m*

artifice [ˈɑːtɪfɪs, *Am:* ˈɑːrt̬ə-] *n form* artificio *m*

artificial [ˌɑːtɪˈfɪʃl, *Am:* ˌɑːrt̬ə-] *adj* artificial

artificial insemination *n* inseminación *f* artificial **artificial intelligence** *n* inteligencia *f* artificial

artillery [ɑːˈtɪləri, *Am:* ɑːr-] *n no pl* artillería *f*

artilleryman [ɑːˈtɪlərɪmən, *Am:* ɑːrˈtɪlrɪmen] *n* artillero *m*

artisan [ˌɑːtɪˈzæn, *Am:* ˈɑːrt̬əzn] *n* artesano, -a *m, f*

artist [ˈɑːtɪst, *Am:* ˈɑːrt̬əst-] *n* artista *mf*

artiste [ɑːˈtiːst, *Am:* ɑːr-] *n* THEAT artista *mf*

artistic [ɑːˈtɪstɪk, *Am:* ɑːr-] *adj* artístico, -a

artistry [ˈɑːtɪstri, *Am:* ˈɑːrt̬ə-] *n no pl* arte *m o f*

artless [ˈɑːtlɪs, *Am:* ˈɑːrt-] *adj* **1.** (*simple*) sencillo, -a **2.** (*clumsy*) torpe

artwork [ˈɑːtwɜːk, *Am:* ˈɑːrtwɜːrk] *n no pl* material *m* gráfico, ilustraciones *fpl*

arty [ˈɑːti, *Am:* ˈɑːrt̬i] <-ier, -iest> *adj inf* (*person*) pseudoartístico, -a; (*film*) pretencioso, -a

Aryan [ˈeərɪən, *Am:* ˈerɪ-] HIST **I.** *n* ario, -a *m, f* **II.** *adj* ario, -a

as [əz, *stressed:* æz] **I.** *prep* como; **dressed ~ a clown** vestido de payaso; **the king, ~ such** el Rey, como tal; ~ **a baby, I was ...** de bebé, yo era...; **to use sth ~ a lever** utilizar algo como palanca **II.** *conj* **1.** (*in comparison*) como; **the same name ~ sth/sb** el mismo nombre que algo/alguien; ~ **fast ~ sth/sb** tan rápido como algo/alguien; **to eat ~ much ~ sb** comer tanto como alguien; ~ **soon ~ possible** lo antes posible, tan pronto como sea posible **2.** (*like*) (tal) como; ~ **it is** tal como es; **I came ~ promised** vine, como (lo) prometí; **she was dressed ~ he was** llevaba la misma ropa que él; ~ **if it were true** como si fuese verdad **3.** (*because*) como; ~ **he is here I'm going** como él está aquí, yo me voy **4.** (*while*) mientras **5.** (*although*) (~) **fine ~ the day is, ...** aunque el día está bien,...; **try ~ I would, I couldn't** por más que me esforzara, no podía ► ~ far ~ (*to the extent that*) en la medida en que; (*concerning*) respecto a **III.** *adv* ~ **well** también; ~ **long as** mientras que *+subj;* ~ **much as** tanto como; ~ **soon as** en cuanto, tan pronto

a.s.a.p. [ˌeɪeseɪˈpiː] *abbr of* **as soon as possible** lo antes posible, tan pronto como sea posible

asbestos [æzˈbestɒs, *Am:* -təs] *n no pl* asbesto *m*

asbestosis [ˌæsbesˈtəʊsɪs, *Am:* -ˈtoʊ-] *n no pl* asbestosis *f inv*

ascend [əˈsend] **I.** *vt form* (*steps*) subir; (*mountain*) ascender; **to ~ the throne** subir al trono **II.** *vi* ascender; **in ~ing order** en orden ascendente

ascendancy [əˈsendəntsi] *n no pl* ascendencia *f;* (*supremacy*) supremacía *f*

ascendant [əˈsendənt] **I.** *n no pl, form* **1.** (*position of power*) **to be in the ~** estar en alza **2.** ASTR ascendente *m* **II.** *adj* ascendente

ascendency [əˈsendəntsi] *n s.* **ascendancy**

ascendent [əˈsendənt] *n, adj s.* **ascendant**

ascension [əˈsenʃən] *n* **1.** (*going up*) ascensión *f* **2.** REL **the Ascension** la Ascensión

Ascension Day *n no pl* día *m* de la Ascensión

ascent [əˈsent] *n* **1.** *form* (*climb*) ascensión *f* **2.** (*slope*) pendiente *f*

ascertain [ˌæsəˈteɪn, *Am:* -ɚ-] *vt form* **1.** (*find out*) averiguar **2.** (*make sure*) comprobar

ascetic [əˈsetɪk, *Am:* -ˈset̬-] **I.** *n* asceta *mf* **II.** *adj* ascético, -a

asceticism [əˈsetɪsɪzəm, *Am:* -ˈset̬ə-] *n no pl* ascetismo *m*

ASCII [ˈæskiː] *abbr of* **American Standard Code for Information Interchange** ASCII

Ascot es el nombre de una pequeña localidad en Berkshire en la que se encuentra un hipódromo construido en 1711 por expreso deseo de la Reina Anne. Con el nombre de

Royal Ascot se conocen unas jornadas hípicas, de cuatro días de duración, que se celebran con carácter anual durante el mes de Junio y a las que la reina suele acudir casi siempre.

ascribe [ə'skraɪb] *vt* **to ~ sth to sb** atribuir algo a alguien
ascription [ə'skrɪpʃən] *n* atribución *f*
asexual [ˌeɪ'sekʃʊəl, *Am:* -ʃuəl] *adj* **1.** (*reproduction*) asexual **2.** (*person*) asexuado, -a
ash¹ [æʃ] *n no pl* (*powder*) ceniza *f*
ash² [æʃ] *n* **1.** (*tree*) fresno *m* **2.** *no pl* (*wood*) (madera *f* de) fresno *m*
ashamed [ə'ʃeɪmd] *adj* avergonzado, -a; **to feel ~** estar avergonzado; **to be ~ of oneself** avergonzarse de uno mismo
ashcan ['æʃkæn] *n Am* cubo *m* de basura, bote *m* de basura *Méx*
ashore [ə'ʃɔːʳ] **I.** *adj* en tierra **II.** *adv* a tierra; **to go ~** desembarcar; **to run ~** encallar
ashtray ['æʃˌtreɪ] *n* cenicero *m*
Ash Wednesday *n* Miércoles *m* de Ceniza
Asia ['eɪʃə, *Am:* -ʒə] *n no pl* Asia *f*
Asia Minor *n* Asia *f* Menor
Asian ['eɪʃən, *Am:* -ʒən] **I.** *n* asiático, -a *m, f* **II.** *adj* asiático, -a
Asiatic [ˌeɪʃi'ætɪk] **I.** *adj* asiático, -a **II.** *n* asiático, -a *m, f*
aside [ə'saɪd] **I.** *n* **1.** (*in a speech*) digresión *f* **2.** (*in a conversation*) comentario *m* aparte **3.** THEAT aparte *m* **II.** *adv* a un lado; **to stand ~** hacerse a un lado; **to leave sth ~** dejar algo a un lado
aside from *prep* aparte de; **to turn ~ sb/sth** alejarse de alguien/algo
ask [ɑːsk, *Am:* æsk] **I.** *vt* **1.** (*request information*) preguntar; **to ~ sb sth** preguntar algo a alguien; **to ~ (sb) a question about sth** hacer (a alguien) una pregunta acerca de algo; **don't ~ me** ni me preguntes; **if you ~ me ...** en mi opinión... **2.** (*request*) pedir; **to ~ advice/a favour** pedir consejo/un favor **3.** (*invite*) invitar; **to ~ sb to do sth** invitar a alguien a hacer algo **4.** (*demand a price*) pedir; **to ~ 100 euros for sth** pedir 100 euros por algo **5.** (*expect*) **to ~ too much of sb** pedir demasiado de alguien **II.** *vi* **1.** (*request information*) preguntar **2.** (*make a request*) pedir
◆**ask for** *vt* **1.** (*request*) pedir **2.** (*inquire about*) preguntar por **3.** (*deserve*) **to ~ trouble** buscar complicaciones
askance [ə'skæns] *adv* con recelo; **to look ~ (at sb/sth)** mirar con recelo (a alguien/algo)
askew [ə'skjuː] *adj* torcido, -a, ladeado, -a
asking ['ɑːskɪŋ, *Am:* 'æskɪŋ] *n no pl* petición *f*; **it's yours for the ~** lo tienes a pedir de boca
asleep [ə'sliːp] *adj* dormido, -a; **to be ~** estar dormido; **to fall ~** quedarse dormido
asparagus [ə'spærəgəs, *Am:* -'sper-] *n* **1.** (*vegetable*) espárrago *m* **2.** (*plant*) esparraguera *f*
ASPCA [ˌeɪesˌpiːsiː'eɪ] *n abbr of* **American Society for Prevention of Cruelty to Animals** *asociación americana protectora de los animales*
aspect ['æspekt] *n* **1.** (*point of view*) punto *m* de vista **2.** (*feature*) faceta *f* **3.** (*direction*) orientación *f* **4.** (*appearance*) aspecto *m* **5.** *no pl* ASTR aspecto *m* **6.** LING aspecto *m*
aspen ['æspən] *n* álamo *m* temblón
asperity [æ'sperəti, *Am:* -əţi] <-ies> *n form no pl* aspereza *f*
aspersion [ə'spɜːʃən, *Am:* -'spɜːrʒən] *n form* calumnia *f*; **to cast ~ on sb** calumniar a alguien
asphalt ['æsfælt, *Am:* -faːlt] **I.** *n* asfalto *m*, asfaltado *m AmL* **II.** *vt* asfaltar
asphyxia [æs'fɪksɪə] *n no pl* asfixia *f*
asphyxiate [əs'fɪksɪeɪt] **I.** *vi form* asfixiarse **II.** *vt* asfixiar
asphyxiation [əsˌfɪksɪ'eɪʃən] *n no pl* asfixia *f*
aspirant [ə'spaɪərənt, *Am:* 'æspɚnt] *n form* aspirante *mf*; (*to job, position*) candidato, -a *m, f*
aspiration [ˌæspə'reɪʃən] *n* aspiración *f*
aspire [ə'spaɪəʳ, *Am:* -'spaɪɚ] *vi* **to ~ to sth** aspirar a algo
aspirin® ['æsprɪn] *n no pl* aspirina® *f*
aspiring [ə'spaɪərɪŋ, *Am:* -'spaɪɚ-] *adj* en ciernes
ass [æs] <-es> *n* **1.** (*donkey*) asno *m* **2.** *inf* (*stupid person*) burro, -a *m, f*; **to make an ~ of oneself** hacer el burro **3.** *Am, vulg* (*bottom*) culo *m*, siete *m AmS, Méx*
assail [ə'seɪl] *vt* **1.** (*attack*) atacar **2.** (*attack verbally*) insultar **3.** (*torment*) abrumar
assailant *n* asaltante *mf*, agresor(a) *m(f)*
assassin [ə'sæsɪn, *Am:* -ən] *n* asesino, -a *m, f*; **paid ~** asesino a sueldo
assassinate [ə'sæsɪneɪt] *vt* asesinar
assassination [əˌsæsɪ'neɪʃən] *n no pl* asesinato *m*
assault [ə'sɔːlt] **I.** *n* **1.** (*attack*) ataque *m*, fajada *f Ant*; **to make an ~ on sth/sb** asaltar algo/a alguien **2.** (*attempted climb*) asalto *m* **II.** *vt* atacar
assault and battery *n* lesiones *fpl* **assault course** *n* pista *f* americana
assemble [ə'sembl] **I.** *vi* congregarse **II.** *vt* **1.** (*collect: people, things*) reunir **2.** (*put together*) armar
assembly [ə'sembli] <-ies> *n* **1.** (*meeting*) reunión *f* **2.** *no pl* TECH montaje *m*
assembly line *n* línea *f* de montaje
assent [ə'sent] **I.** *n no pl, form* consentimiento *m* **II.** *vi* **to ~ to sth** asentir a algo
assert [ə'sɜːt, *Am:* -'sɜːrt] *vt* afirmar; **to ~ oneself** imponerse
assertion [ə'sɜːʃən, *Am:* -'sɜːr-] *n* afirmación *f*
assertive [ə'sɜːtɪv, *Am:* -'sɜːrţɪv] *adj* confiado, -a
assertiveness *n no pl* autoafirmación *f*

assess [ə'ses] *vt* **1.** (*evaluate*) evaluar **2.** (*tax*) calcular

assessment *n* **1.** (*calculation*) valoración *f* **2.** *no pl* (*evaluation*) evaluación *f* **3.** (*taxation*) cálculo *m* de los ingresos imponibles

assessor [ə'sesəʳ, *Am:* -'sesɚ] *n* **1.** (*evaluator*) evaluador(a) *m(f)* **2.** (*legal advisor*) asesor(a) *m(f)*; **legal ~** asesor jurídico **3.** *Am* (*tax evaluator*) tasador(a) *m(f)*

asset ['æset] *n* **1.** (*benefit*) ventaja *f*; (*person*) persona *f* valiosa; **he is an ~ to the team** es una valiosa aportación al equipo **2.** *pl* FIN activo *m*; **liquid ~s** activos *mpl* líquidos

assiduous [ə'sɪdjʊəs, *Am:* -'sɪdʒu-] *adj* **1.** (*hardworking*) diligente **2.** (*keen*) asiduo, -a

assign [ə'saɪn] *vt* **1.** (*task, resources*) asignar, apropiar *AmL*; **to ~ sb to a position** destinar a alguien a un puesto; **to ~ sb to do sth** asignar a alguien la tarea de hacer algo; **to ~ the blame for sth to sb** atribuir la culpa de algo a alguien **2.** LAW ceder

assignment *n* **1.** (*task*) tarea *f*; **foreign ~** cargo *m* en el extranjero; **diplomatic ~** misión *f* diplomática; **to send sb on an ~** mandar a alguien a una misión; **an ~ to do sth** un encargo de hacer algo **2.** *no pl* (*attribution*) asignación *f*

assimilate [ə'sɪməleɪt] **I.** *vt* asimilar **II.** *vi* asimilarse

assimilation [əˌsɪmə'leɪʃən] *n no pl* asimilación *f*

assist [ə'sɪst] **I.** *vt* ayudar; **to ~ sb with sth** ayudar a alguien con algo **II.** *vi* ayudar; **to ~ with sth** ayudar en algo

assistance [ə'sɪstəns] *n no pl* asistencia *f*; **to be of ~** ser de ayuda; **can I be of any ~?** ¿puedo ayudar en algo?

assistant [ə'sɪstənt] *n* **1.** (*helper*) ayudante *mf*, suche *m Chile* **2.** INFOR asistente *m*

assistant manager *n* subdirector, -a *m, f*

assizes [ə'saɪzɪz] *npl Brit* LAW ≈ audiencia *f* provisional (*sesiones que solían celebrar los tribunales superiores en Gales e Inglaterra*)

associate[1] [ə'səʊʃiət, *Am:* -'soʊʃɪit] **I.** *n* asociado, -a *m, f*; **business ~** socio, -a *m, f* **II.** *adj Am* UNIV adjunto, -a *m, f*

associate[2] [ə'səʊʃiəɪt, *Am:* -'soʊ-] **I.** *vt* asociar; **to ~ oneself with sth** relacionarse con algo **II.** *vi* relacionarse

associate professor *n* profesor *m* adjunto, profesora *f* adjunta

association [əˌsəʊsɪ'eɪʃən, *Am:* -ˌsoʊ-] *n* **1.** (*organization*) asociación *f* **2.** *no pl* (*involvement*) colaboración *f* **3.** (*mental connection*) asociación *f*

assorted [ə'sɔːtɪd, *Am:* -'sɔːrt̬ɪd] *adj* (*mixed*) surtido, -a; (*goods*) variado, -a

assortment [ə'sɔːtmənt, *Am:* -'sɔːrt-] *n* surtido *m*; **a motley ~** una mezcolanza; **a rich ~** una rica variedad

assuage [ə'sweɪdʒ] *vt* (*pain*) aliviar; (*anger*) aplacar

assume [ə'sjuːm, *Am:* -'suːm] *vt* **1.** (*regard as true*) suponer, asumir *AmL*; **let's ~ that ...** supongamos que... **2.** (*adopt*) adoptar **3.** (*undertake*) asumir; (*power*) tomar

assumed [ə'sjuːmd, *Am:* -'suːmd] *adj* supuesto, -a; **under an ~d name** bajo un nombre falso

assumption [ə'sʌmpʃən] *n* **1.** (*supposition*) supuesto *m*; **on the ~ that ...** en el supuesto de que...; **to act on the ~ that ...** actuar suponiendo que... **2.** *no pl* (*hypothesis*) suposición *f* **3.** *no pl* (*taking over*) toma *f* **4.** REL **the Assumption** la Asunción

assurance [ə'ʃʊərəns, *Am:* 'ʃʊrns] *n* **1.** (*self-confidence*) seguridad *f*; **to have ~** tener confianza **2.** (*promise*) garantía *f*; **to give an ~ of sth** dar garantías de algo **3.** *Brit* (*insurance*) seguro *m*

assure [ə'ʃʊəʳ, *Am:* -'ʃʊr] *vt* **1.** (*guarantee*) asegurar **2.** (*promise*) garantizar; **to ~ sb of sth** asegurar algo a alguien **3.** *Brit* FIN asegurar

assured *adj* seguro, -a

assuredly [ə'ʃʊərɪdli, *Am:* -'ʃʊr-] *adv* **1.** (*confidently*) seguramente **2.** (*certainly*) ciertamente

asterisk ['æstərɪsk] *n* asterisco *m*

astern [ə'stɜːn, *Am:* -'stɜːrn] *adv* **1.** NAUT hacia popa; **to go ~** ir atrás **2.** (*behind*) **~ of** detrás de **3.** (*backwards*) hacia atrás

asteroid ['æstərɔɪd] *n* asteroide *m*

asthma ['æsmə, *Am:* 'æz-] *n no pl* asma *m*

asthma attack *n* ataque *m* de asma

asthmatic [æs'mætɪk, *Am:* æz'mæt̬-] **I.** *n* asmático, -a *m, f* **II.** *adj* asmático, -a

astonish [ə'stɒnɪʃ, *Am:* -'stɑːnɪʃ] *vt* asombrar; **to be ~ed** asombrarse

astonishing *adj* asombroso, -a

astonishment *n no pl* asombro *m*; **to her ~** para gran sorpresa suya

astound [ə'staʊnd] *vt* asombrar; **to be ~ed** quedarse atónito

astounding *adj* asombroso, -a

astray [ə'streɪ] *adv* **to go ~** (*letter*) extraviarse; (*person*) desencaminarse; **to lead sb ~** llevar a alguien por mal camino

astride [ə'straɪd] **I.** *prep* a horcajadas [*o* a caballo] sobre **II.** *adv* a horcajadas

astringent [ə'strɪndʒənt] **I.** *n* astringente *m* **II.** *adj* **1.** MED astringente **2.** *fig* cáustico, -a

astrologer [ə'strɒlədʒəʳ, *Am:* -'strɑːlədʒɚ] *n* astrólogo, -a *m, f*

astrological [ˌæstrə'lɒdʒɪkl, *Am:* -'lɑːdʒɪkl] *adj* astrológico, -a

astrology [ə'strɒlədʒi, *Am:* -'strɑːlə-] *n no pl* astrología *f*

astronaut ['æstrənɔːt, *Am:* -nɑːt] *n* astronauta *mf*

astronomer [ə'strɒnəməʳ, *Am:* -'strɑːnəmɚ] *n* astrónomo, -a *m, f*

astronomical [ˌæstrə'nɒmɪkl, *Am:* -'nɑːmɪkl] *adj a. fig* astronómico, -a

astronomy [ə'strɒnəmi, *Am:* -'strɑːnə-] *n no pl* astronomía *f*

Asturian [æs'tʊəriən, *Am:* ə'stʊri-] **I.** *adj*

asturiano, -a **II.** *n* (*person*) asturiano, -a *m, f*
astute [ə'stjuːt, *Am:* -'stuːt] *adj* astuto, -a
astuteness *n no pl* astucia *f*
asylum [ə'saɪləm] *n* **1.** (*protection*) asilo *m* **2.** (*institution*) asilo *m;* **mental** ~ manicomio *m*
asylum seeker *n* solicitante *mf* de asilo
asymmetrical [ˌeɪsɪ'metrɪkəl] *adj* asimétrico, -a
at[1] [ət] *prep* **1.** (*place*) en; ~ **the dentist's** en el dentista; ~ **home/school** en casa/la escuela; ~ **the table/office** en la mesa/oficina; ~ **the window** a la ventana **2.** (*time*) ~ **Easter** en Pascua; ~ **night** por la noche; ~ **once** en seguida; **all** ~ **once** de repente; ~ **present** en este momento; ~ **the time** en el momento; ~ **the same time** al mismo tiempo; ~ **three o'clock** a las tres; **while I am** ~ **it** mientras lo estoy haciendo **3.** (*towards*) **to laugh** ~ **sb** reírse de alguien; **to look/aim** ~ **sth/sb** mirar/apuntar a algo/alguien; **to point** ~ **sb** señalar a alguien; **to rush** ~ **sb/sth** abalanzarse sobre alguien/algo **4.** (*in reaction to*) ~ **sb's request** a petición de alguien; **to be astonished/annoyed** ~ **sth** estar asombrado/molesto por algo **5.** (*in amount of*) ~ **all** para nada; **to sell sth** ~ **£10 a kilo** vender algo a 10 libras el kilo; ~ **120 km/h** a 120 km/h **6.** (*in state of*) ~ **best/worst** en el mejor/peor de los casos; ~ **first** al principio; ~ **least** al menos; ~ **war/peace** en guerra/paz; ~ **20** a los 20 (años); **I feel** ~ **ease** me siento tranquilo; **to be** ~ **a loss** estar sin saber qué hacer; **to be** ~ **lunch** estar en el almuerzo; **a child** ~ **play** un niño jugando **7.** (*in ability to*) **to be good/bad** ~ **French** ser bueno/malo en francés; **to be** ~ **an advantage** estar en ventaja **8.** (*repeatedly do*) en; **to be mad** ~ **sb** estar enfadado con alguien; **to pull** ~ **sb's hair** tirar de los pelos a alguien; **to tug** ~ **the rope** tirar de la cuerda; **to be unhappy** ~ **sth** no estar feliz con algo; **to wear** ~ **sb's nerves** poner los nervios de punta a alguien ► ~ **all** en realidad; **did you know the film** ~ **all?** ¿conocías la película?; **not** ~ **all!** ¡para nada!, ¡en absoluto!; (*as answer to thanks*) ¡de nada!; **nobody** ~ **all** nadie en absoluto; **to hardly do sth** ~ **all** apenas hacer algo
at[2] [ɑːt, æt] (*in email address*) arroba *f*
atavistic [ˌætə'vɪstɪk, *Am:* ˌæt̬-] *adj* atávico, -a
ATC [ˌeɪtiː'siː] *n Brit abbr of* **Air Training Corps** *cuerpo militar de formación de aviadores*
ate [et, *Am:* eɪt] *pt of* **eat**
atheism ['eɪθiɪzəm] *n no pl* ateísmo *m*
atheist ['eɪθiɪst] **I.** *n* ateo, -a *m, f* **II.** *adj* ateísta
atheistic [ˌeɪθɪ'ɪstɪk] *adj* ateísta
Athens ['æθənz] *n* Atenas *f*
athlete ['æθliːt] *n* atleta *mf*
athletic [æθ'letɪk, *Am:* -'let̬-] *adj* atlético, -a
athletics [æθ'letɪks, *Am:* -'let̬-] *npl* atletismo *m*
Atlantic [ət'læntɪk, *Am:* -t̬ɪk] **I.** *n no pl* **the** ~ **(Ocean)** el (Océano) Atlántico **II.** *adj* atlántico, -a
atlas ['ætləs] <-es> *n* atlas *m inv*
ATM [ˌeɪtiː'em] *n Am abbr of* **automated teller machine** cajero *m* automático
atmosphere ['ætməsfɪəʳ, *Am:* -fɪr] *n* **1.** *a.* PHYS atmósfera *f* **2.** *fig* ambiente *m*
atmospheric [ˌætməs'ferɪk] *adj* **1.** METEO atmosférico, -a **2.** *fig* evocador(a)
atoll ['ætɒl, *Am:* -ɑːl] *n* atolón *m*
atom ['ætəm, *Am:* 'æt̬-] *n a. fig* átomo *m*
atom bomb *n* bomba *f* atómica
atomic [ə'tɒmɪk, *Am:* -'tɑːmɪk] *adj* atómico, -a
atomic energy *n* energía *f* atómica
atomize ['ætəmaɪz, *Am:* 'æt̬-] *vt* atomizar; *fig* pulverizar
atomizer ['ætəmaɪzəʳ, *Am:* 'æt̬əmaɪzɚ] *n* atomizador *m*
atone for [ə'təʊn, *Am:* -'toʊn] *vi* (*sin*) expiar; (*mistake*) reparar
atonement *n no pl, form* expiación *f*
atrocious [ə'trəʊʃəs, *Am:* -'troʊ-] *adj* atroz
atrocity [ə'trɒsəti] <-ies> *n* atrocidad *f*
atrophy ['ætrəfi] <-ies> *vi* atrofiarse
at-sign *n* INFOR arroba *f*
attach [ə'tætʃ] **I.** *vt* **1.** (*fix*) fijar; (*label*) pegar; **to** ~ **sth to sth** fijar [*o* pegar] una cosa a otra **2.** (*connect*) ligar **3.** INFOR adjuntar **4.** (*join*) unir; **to** ~ **oneself to sb** unirse a alguien **5.** (*assign*) destinar; **to be ~ed to sth** estar destinado a algo **6.** (*associate*) vincular; **to** ~ **importance to sth** dar importancia a algo **II.** *vi form* acompañar; **no blame ~es to you** tú no tienes ninguna culpa
attaché [ə'tæʃeɪ, *Am:* ˌæt̬ə'ʃeɪ] *n* agregado, -a *m, f*
attaché case *n* cartera *f,* attaché *m,* portafolio *m AmL*
attachment [ə'tætʃmənt] *n* **1.** (*fondness*) apego *m;* **to form an** ~ **to sb** coger cariño a alguien **2.** *no pl* (*support*) adhesión *f* **3.** *no pl* (*union*) fijación *f* **4.** (*attached device*) accesorio *m* **5.** LAW incautación *f* **6.** INFOR attachment *m,* anexo *m*
attack [ə'tæk] **I.** *n* ataque *m;* **to be on the** ~ emprender una ofensiva; **to come under** ~ ser atacado **II.** *vt* **1.** (*use violence*) atacar, cachorrear *Col* **2.** (*tackle: problem*) afrontar **3.** (*eat greedily*) devorar **III.** *vi* atacar
attain [ə'teɪn] *vt form* alcanzar; (*independence*) lograr; **to** ~ **one's majority** LAW alcanzar la mayoría de edad
attainable *adj form* alcanzable
attainment *n* **1.** *form* logro *m* **2.** *pl* conocimientos *mpl*
attempt [ə'tempt] **I.** *n* **1.** (*try*) intento *m;* **to make an** ~ **at doing sth** intentar hacer algo **2.** (*attack*) atentado *m* **II.** *vt* intentar
attempted murder *n* intento *m* de asesinato

attend [ə'tend] **I.** *vt* **1.** (*be present at*) asistir a **2.** (*take care of*) atender **II.** *vi* **1.** (*be present*) asistir **2.** *form* (*listen carefully*) atender

attendance [ə'tendəns] *n* **1.** *no pl* (*presence*) asistencia *f;* **to be in** ~ estar presente **2.** (*people present*) concurrencia *f* **3.** (*care*) asistencia *f*

attendant [ə'tendənt] **I.** *n* **1.** (*servant*) encargado, -a *m, f* **2.** (*helper*) asistente, -a *m, f* **II.** *adj* relacionado, -a, asociado, -a

attention [ə'tenʃən] *n no pl* **1.** (*maintenance*) cuidado *m* **2.** (*care, notice*) atención *f;* **for the** ~ **of** *form* a la atención de; **to pay** ~ prestar atención; **to turn one's** ~**s to sth** dirigir la atención hacia algo **3.** *no pl* MIL **to stand at** ~ cuadrarse; ~**!** ¡firmes!

attention span *n* capacidad *f* de concentración

attentive [ə'tentɪv, *Am:* -t̬ɪv] *adj* atento, -a; **to be** ~ **to sb** ser atento con alguien; **to be** ~ **to sb's needs** preocuparse por las necesidades de alguien

attenuate [ə'tenjʊeɪt] *vt form* atenuar

attest [ə'test] **I.** *vt* **1.** (*demonstrate*) testimoniar **2.** (*authenticate*) atestiguar **II.** *vi* testimoniar

Att-Gen [ˌæt'dʒen] *n Am abbr of* **Attorny-General** fiscal *mf* general del Estado

attic ['ætɪk, *Am:* 'æt̬-] *n* desván *m,* tabanco *m AmC,* entretecho *m CSur*

attire [ə'taɪəʳ, *Am:* -taɪɚ] *n* atavío *m*

attitude ['ætɪtju:d, *Am:* 'æt̬ətu:d] *n* **1.** (*opinion*) actitud *f;* **a change of** ~ un cambio de actitud; **to have the** ~ **that ...** ser de la opinión de que...; **an** ~ **towards sb/sth** una actitud hacia alguien/algo **2.** (*position*) postura *f;* **to adopt an** ~ adoptar una postura **3.** ART posición *f*

attorney [ə'tɜ:ni, *Am:* -'tɜ:r-] *n Am* abogado, -a *m, f;* **criminal** ~ abogado penalista; **legal** ~ apoderado *m* legal

attract [ə'trækt] *vt* atraer, jalar *AmL;* **to** ~ **attention/support** atraer la atención/conseguir el apoyo; **to** ~ **sb's notice** atraer la atención de alguien; **to be** ~**ed by sb/sth** sentirse atraído por alguien/algo

attraction [ə'trækʃən] *n* **1.** (*force, place of enjoyment*) atracción *f;* **tourist** ~ atracción turística **2.** *no pl* (*appeal*) atractivo *m;* **to feel an** ~ **to sb** sentirse atraído por alguien

attractive [ə'træktɪv] *adj* atractivo, -a

attribute[1] [ə'trɪbju:t] *vt* **1.** (*ascribe*) atribuir; **to** ~ **the blame to sb** achacar la culpa a alguien; **to** ~ **importance to sth** dar importancia a algo **2.** (*give credit for*) **to** ~ **sth to sb** atribuir algo a alguien

attribute[2] ['ætrɪbju:t] *n* atributo *m*

attributive [ə'trɪbjʊtɪv, *Am:* -jət̬ɪv] *adj* atributivo, -a

attrition [ə'trɪʃən] *n no pl* **1.** (*wearing down*) desgaste *m;* **war of** ~ guerra *f* de desgaste **2.** *Am, Aus* ECON reducción *f* **3.** REL atrición *f*

aubergine ['əʊbəʒi:n, *Am:* 'oʊbɚ-] *n Brit* berenjena *f*

auburn ['ɔ:bən, *Am:* 'ɑ:bɚn] *adj* castaño, -a

auction ['ɔ:kʃən, *Am:* 'ɑ:kʃən] **I.** *n* subasta *f;* **to hold an** ~ presidir una subasta; **to be sold at** [*o* **by** *Brit*] ~ ser vendido en [*o* por] subasta; **to put sth up for** ~ subastar algo **II.** *vt* **to** ~ **sth** (**off**) subastar algo

auctioneer [ˌɔ:kʃə'nɪəʳ, *Am:* ˌɑ:kʃə'nɪr] *n* subastador(a) *m(f)*

audacious [ɔ:'deɪʃəs, *Am:* ɑ:-] *adj* **1.** (*bold*) audaz **2.** (*impudent*) descarado, -a

audacity [ɔ:'dæsəti, *Am:* ɑ:'dæsət̬i] *n no pl* **1.** (*boldness*) audacia *f* **2.** (*impudence*) descaro *m*

audible ['ɔ:dəbl, *Am:* 'ɑ:-] *adj* perceptible

audience ['ɔ:dɪəns, *Am:* 'ɑ:-] *n* **1.** (*spectators*) público *m;* TV, RADIO audiencia *f;* (*of book*) lectores *mpl* **2.** (*formal interview*) audiencia *f*

audio [ˌɔ:dɪəʊ, *Am:* ˌɑ:dɪoʊ] *adj inv* de sonido

audio cassette *n* casete *m o f*

audit[1] ['ɔ:dɪt, *Am:* 'ɑ:-] FIN **I.** *n* auditoría *f* contable **II.** *vt* auditar

audit[2] ['ɔ:dɪt, *Am:* 'ɑ:-] *vt* UNIV **to** ~ **a course** asistir de oyente a un curso

audition [ɔ:'dɪʃən, *Am:* ɑ:-] THEAT **I.** *n* audición *f* **II.** *vi* hacer una prueba **III.** *vt* **to** ~ **sb** hacer una prueba a alguien

auditor ['ɔ:dɪtəʳ, *Am:* 'ɑ:dət̬ɚ] *n* **1.** COM auditor(a) *m(f)* **2.** *Am* UNIV oyente *mf*

auditorium [ˌɔ:dɪ'tɔ:rɪəm, *Am:* ˌɑ:də-] <-s *o* auditoria> *n* auditorio *m*

augment [ɔ:g'ment, *Am:* ɑ:g-] *vt form* aumentar; **to** ~ **one's income** aumentar sus ingresos

augur ['ɔ:gəʳ, *Am:* 'ɑ:gɚ] **I.** *vi* **to** ~ **badly/well** ser de mal/buen agüero **II.** *vt* augurar

august [ɔ:'gʌst, *Am:* ɑ:-] *adj form* augusto, -a

August ['ɔ:gəst, *Am:* 'ɑ:-] *n* agosto *m; s. a.* **April**

aunt [ɑ:nt, *Am:* ænt] *n* tía *f*

au pair [ˌəʊ'peəʳ, *Am:* oʊ'per] **I.** *n* au pair *f* **II.** *adj* ~ **girl** chica au pair

aura ['ɔ:rə] *n* aura *f*

aural ['ɔ:rəl] *adj* auditivo, -a

auricle ['ɔ:rɪkl] *n* (*of heart*) aurícula *f*

auricular [ɔ:'rɪkjʊləʳ, *Am:* -jəlɚ] *adj* **1.** (*relating to hearing*) auditivo, -a **2.** (*concerning the heart*) auricular

aurora [ɔ:'rɔ:rə] *n* aurora *f*

auspices ['ɔ:spɪsɪz, *Am:* 'ɑ:-] *n pl* auspicios *mpl;* **under the** ~ **of** bajo los auspicios de

auspicious [ɔ:'spɪʃəs, *Am:* ɑ:-] *adj form* propicio, -a

austere [ɔ:'stɪəʳ, *Am:* ɑ:'stɪr] *adj* austero, -a

austerity [ɔ:'sterəti, *Am:* ɑ:'sterət̬i] <-ies> *n* austeridad *f;* ~ **programme** ECON programa *m* de austeridad

Australia [ɒ'streɪlɪə, *Am:* ɑ:'streɪlʒə] *n* Australia *f*

El **Australia Day**, 26 de enero, conmemora la fundación del primer asentamiento británico en 1788 en Sydney Cove. Para los **Aborigines**, los primeros habitantes de Australia, es el día de la invasión de su país. Durante ese día tienen lugar distintos acontecimientos de tipo multicultural que suelen reunir a australianos de todas las procedencias.

Australian [ɒ'streɪlɪən, *Am:* ɑː'streɪlʒən] **I.** *n* australiano, -a *m, f* **II.** *adj* australiano, -a
Austria ['ɒstrɪə, *Am:* 'ɑː-] *n* Austria *f*
Austrian ['ɒstrɪən, *Am:* 'ɑː-] **I.** *n* austriaco, -a *m, f* **II.** *adj* austriaco, -a
AUT *n Brit abbr of* **Association of University Teachers** *asociación británica de profesores de universidad*
authentic [ɔː'θentɪk, *Am:* ɑː'θent̬ɪk] *adj* auténtico, -a; ~ **leather** cuero genuino; **an ~ Goya painting** un Goya auténtico
authenticate [ɔː'θentɪkeɪt, *Am:* ɑː'θent̬ɪ-] *vt* autentificar
authentication [ɔːˌθentɪ'keɪʃən, *Am:* ɑːˌθent̬ɪ-] *n no pl* autentificación *f*
authenticity [ˌɔːθən'tɪsəti, *Am:* ˌɑːθən'tɪsət̬i] *n no pl* autenticidad *f*
author ['ɔːθəʳ, *Am:* 'ɑːθɚ] **I.** *n* **1.** (*writer*) autor *m* **2.** *fig* creador(a) *m(f)* **II.** *vt* escribir
authoress ['ɔːθərɪs, *Am:* 'ɑːθɚ-] *n* autora *f*
authoritarian [ɔːˌθɒrɪ'teərɪən, *Am:* əːˌθɔːrə'terɪ-] **I.** *n* autoritario, -a *m, f* **II.** *adj* autoritario, -a
authoritative [ɔː'θɒrɪtətɪv, *Am:* əː'θɔːrəteɪt̬ɪv] *adj* **1.** (*assertive*) autoritario, -a **2.** (*reliable*) autorizado, -a
authority [ɔː'θɒrəti, *Am:* əː'θɔːrət̬i] <-ies> *n* **1.** *no pl* (*right to control*) autoridad *f;* **to be in ~** tener autoridad **2.** *no pl* (*permission*) autorización *f* **3.** *no pl* (*control*) control *m* **4.** (*knowledge*) **with ~** con conocimiento de causa; **to be an ~ on sth** ser una autoridad en algo **5.** (*organization*) autoridad *f;* **the authorities** las autoridades ▸**to have sth on good ~** saber algo de buena tinta; **to have sth on sb's ~** saber algo a través de alguien
authorization [ˌɔːθəraɪ'zeɪʃən, *Am:* ˌɑːθɚɪ-] *n no pl* autorización *f;* **to give one's ~ for sth** dar la autorización para hacer algo
authorize ['ɔːθəraɪz, *Am:* 'ɑː-] *vt* autorizar; **to ~ sb to do sth** autorizar a alguien para hacer algo
authorship ['ɔːθəʃɪp, *Am:* 'ɑːθɚ-] *n no pl* autoría *f;* **the article is of unknown ~** el artículo es de autor desconocido
autistic [ɔː'tɪstɪk] *adj* autista
auto ['ɔːtəʊ, *Am:* 'ɑːt̬oʊ] *n Am* coche *m*, carro *m AmL*
autobiographical [ˌɔːtəbaɪə'græfɪkl, *Am:* ˌɑːt̬ə-] *adj* autobiográfico, -a
autobiography [ˌɔːtəbaɪ'ɒgrəfi, *Am:* ˌɑːt̬əbaɪ'ɑːgrə-] *n* autobiografía *f*
autocracy [ɔː'tɒkrəsi, *Am:* ɑː'tɑːkrə-] *n* autocracia *f*
autocrat ['ɔːtəkræt, *Am:* 'ɑːt̬ə-] *n* autócrata *mf*
autocratic [ˌɔːtə'krætik, *Am:* ˌɑːt̬ə'kræt̬-] *adj* autocrático, -a
autocue® ['ɔːtəˌkjuː, *Am:* 'ɑːt̬oʊ-] *n Brit* TV autocue® *m*
autograph ['ɔːtəgrɑːf, *Am:* 'ɑːt̬əgræf] **I.** *n* autógrafo *m* **II.** *vt* firmar
automate ['ɔːtəmeɪt, *Am:* 'ɑːt̬ə-] *vt* automatizar
automated ['ɔːtəmeɪtɪd, *Am:* 'ɑːt̬əmeɪt̬ɪd] *adj* automatizado, -a
automated teller machine *n* cajero *m* automático
automatic [ˌɔːtə'mætɪk, *Am:* ˌɑːt̬ə'mæt̬-] **I.** *n* **1.** (*machine*) máquina *f* **2.** (*car*) coche *m* automático **3.** (*pistol*) pistola *f* automática; (*rifle*) metralleta *f* **II.** *adj* automático, -a
automatic pilot *n* piloto *m* automático
automation [ˌɔːtə'meɪʃən, *Am:* ˌɑːt̬ə-] *n no pl* automatización *f*
automaton [ɔː'tɒmətən, *Am:* ɑː'tɑːmə-] <automata> *n a. fig* autómata *m*
automobile ['ɔːtəməbiːl, *Am:* 'ɑːt̬əmoʊ-] *n Am* automóvil *m;* ~ **accident/industry** accidente de coche/industria del automóvil
automotive [ˌɔːtə'məʊtɪv, *Am:* ˌɑːt̬ə'moʊt̬ɪv] *adj inv* automovilístico, -a
autonomous [ɔː'tɒnəməs, *Am:* ɑː'tɑːnə-] *adj* autónomo, -a; **to be ~ of sth** ser independiente de algo
autonomy [ɔː'tɒnəmi, *Am:* ɑː'tɑːnə-] *n no pl* autonomía *f*
autopsy ['ɔːtɒpsi, *Am:* 'ɑːtɑːp-] <-ies> *n* autopsia *f*
autumn ['ɔːtəm, *Am:* 'ɑːt̬əm] *n* otoño *m;* **in (the) ~** en (el) otoño; ~ **colours** colores *mpl* otoñales
autumnal [ɔː'tʌmnəl, *Am:* ɑː-] *adj* otoñal
auxiliary [ɔːg'zɪlɪəri, *Am:* ɑːg'zɪljri] <-ies> **I.** *n* **1.** HIST (*soldier*) soldado *m* auxiliar **2.** (*nurse*) auxiliar *mf* **3.** LING auxiliar *m* **II.** *adj* auxiliar; ~ **staff** personal *m* auxiliar
AV *abbr of* **audiovisual** audiovisual
av. *abbr of* **average** media *f*
Av. *abbr of* **avenue** Avda.
avail [ə'veɪl] **I.** *n* provecho *m;* **to no ~** en vano **II.** *vt* **to ~ oneself of sth** aprovecharse de algo
available [ə'veɪləbl] *adj* **1.** (*obtainable*) disponible; **to make sth ~ to sb** poner algo a la disposición [*o* al alcance] de alguien **2.** (*free*) libre; **to be ~ to do sth** tener tiempo para hacer algo **3.** (*free for romantic involvement*) **to be ~** estar sin compromiso
avalanche ['ævəlɑːnʃ, *Am:* -æntʃ] *n* **1.** (*of snow*) alud *m*, avalancha *f* **2.** *fig* torrente *m*
avant-garde [ˌævɒŋ'gɑːd, *Am:* ˌɑːvɑːnt'gɑːrd] **I.** *n* vanguardia *f* **II.** *adj* vanguardista, de vanguardia
avarice ['ævərɪs] *n no pl, form* avaricia *f*
avaricious [ˌævə'rɪʃəs] *adj form* ávaro, -a
Ave. *n abbr of* **Avenue** Avda.

avenge [ə'vendʒ] *vt* vengar; **to ~ oneself on sb** vengarse de alguien

avenue ['ævənju:, *Am:* -nu:] *n* **1.** (*street*) avenida *f*, carrera *f AmL* **2.** (*possibility*) camino *m;* **to explore an ~** explorar una vía

average ['ævərɪdʒ] **I.** *n* MAT promedio *m*, media *f;* **above/below ~** por encima/por debajo de la media; **on ~** por término medio **II.** *adj* **1.** MAT medio, -a; **~ rainfall** precipitación media **2.** (*mediocre*) mediocre **III.** *vt* **1.** (*have mean value*) promediar **2.** (*calculate mean value of*) sacar la media de

averse [ə'vɜ:s, *Am:* -'vɜ:rs] *adj* **to be ~ to sth** ser contrario a algo; **I'm not ~ to the occasional glass of wine** no me opongo a tomar un vino de vez en cuando

aversion [ə'vɜ:ʃən, *Am:* -'vɜ:rʒən] *n* **1.** (*dislike*) aversión *f;* **to have an ~ to sth/sb** sentir aversión hacia algo/alguien **2.** (*object of dislike*) fobia *f*

avert [ə'vɜ:t, *Am:* -'vɜ:rt] *vt* **1.** (*prevent*) prevenir **2.** (*turn away*) **to ~ one's eyes from sth** desviar la mirada de algo; **to ~ one's thoughts from sth** apartar sus pensamientos de algo

aviary ['eɪvɪəri, *Am:* -er-] *n* pajarera *f*

aviation [ˌeɪvɪ'eɪʃən] *n no pl* aviación *f*

aviation industry *n* industria *f* aeronáutica

avid ['ævɪd] *adj* ávido, -a

avidity [ə'vɪdəti, *Am:* -t̬i] *n no pl* avidez *f*

avocado [ˌævə'kɑ:dəʊ, *Am:* -doʊ] <-s *o* -es> *n* aguacate *m*, abocado *m AmL*, ahuacatl *m Méx*

avoid [ə'vɔɪd] *vt* (*person, thing*) evitar; (*when moving*) esquivar; **to ~ doing sth** evitar hacer algo; **to ~ paying taxes** evadir impuestos

avoidable *adj* evitable

avoidance *n no pl* evasión *f;* **tax ~** evasión de impuestos

avow [ə'vaʊ] *vt form* **1.** (*admit*) admitir **2.** (*declare*) declarar

avowal [ə'vaʊəl] *n form* declaración *f*

avowedly [ə'vaʊɪdli] *adv* abiertamente

AWACS ['eɪwæks] *n abbr of* **airborne warning and control system** sistema *m* AWACS

await [ə'weɪt] *vt* aguardar; **eagerly ~ed** esperado con ansiedad

awake [ə'weɪk] <awoke, awoken *o* -d, awoken *Am*> **I.** *vi* despertarse; **to ~ to sth** *fig* darse cuenta de algo **II.** *vt* despertar **III.** *adj* **1.** (*not sleeping*) despierto, -a; **to stay ~** mantenerse despierto; **to keep sb awake** mantener a alguien despierto; **to lie ~** quedarse despierto **2.** *fig* alerta; **to be ~ to sth** estar alerta ante algo

awaken [ə'weɪkən] **I.** *vt form* despertar; **to ~ sb to sth** *fig* abrir los ojos a alguien sobre algo **II.** *vi fig* darse cuenta

awakening [ə'weɪknɪŋ] *n no pl* despertar *m;* **she's in for a rude ~** le espera una sorpresa desagradable

award [ə'wɔ:d, *Am:* -'wɔ:rd] **I.** *n* **1.** (*prize*) premio *m* **2.** (*reward*) recompensa *f* **3.** MIL condecoración *f* **II.** *vt* otorgar; **to ~ sth to sb** conferir algo a alguien; **to ~ damages** indemnizar por daños y perjuicios; **to ~ sb a grant** conceder a alguien una beca

aware [ə'weəʳ, *Am:* -'wer] *adj* **1.** (*knowing*) **to be ~ that ...** saber que...; **as far as I'm ~ ...** por lo que yo sé...; **not that I'm ~ of** no, que yo sepa **2.** (*sense*) **to be ~ of sth** ser consciente de algo

awareness [ə'weənɪs, *Am:* -'wer-] *n no pl* conciencia *f*

awash [ə'wɒʃ, *Am:* -wɑ:ʃ] *adj* inundado, -a; **to be ~ with money** estar forrado de dinero

away [ə'weɪ] *adv* **1.** (*distant*) **10 km ~** a 10 km; **as far ~ as possible** lo más lejos posible; **to be miles ~** *fig* no prestar atención **2.** (*absent*) fuera; **to be ~ on holiday** estar de vacaciones **3.** (*in future time*) **to be only a week ~** no faltar más que una semana; **right ~!** ¡enseguida! **4.** (*continuously*) **to write ~** escribir sin cesar

away from *prep* **1.** (*at distance from*) **~ the town** lejos del pueblo; **~ each other** alejados el uno del otro; **to stay ~ sth/sb** mantenerse alejado de algo/alguien **2.** (*in other direction from*) **to go ~ sth** alejarse de algo

away game *n* partido *m* fuera de casa

awe [ɔ:, *Am:* ɑ:] *n no pl* respeto *m;* **to hold sb in ~** tener un gran respeto por alguien; **to stand in ~ of sb** imponer alguien respeto a uno

awe-inspiring ['ɔ:ɪnspaɪərɪŋ, *Am:* 'ɑ:-] *adj* imponente

awesome ['ɔ:səm, *Am:* 'ɑ:-] *adj* **1.** (*impressive*) imponente **2.** (*fearsome*) temible **3.** (*daunting*) intimidatorio, -a **4.** *Am, inf* (*very good*) estupendo, -a

awestricken ['ɔ:ˌstrɪkən, *Am:* 'ɑ:-] *adj*, **awestruck** ['ɔ:strʌk, *Am:* 'ɑ:-] *adj* atemorizado, -a

awful ['ɔ:fəl, *Am:* 'ɑ:-] *adj* **1.** (*bad*) terrible **2.** (*as intensifier*) **an ~ lot** mucho

awfully ['ɔ:fəli, *Am:* 'ɑ:-] *adv* **1.** (*badly*) terriblemente **2.** (*very*) **~ clever/stupid** muy inteligente/tonto; **I'm ~ sorry** lo siento muchísimo; **not to be ~ good at sth** no ser muy bueno para algo

awhile [ə'hwaɪl] *adv* **to wait ~** esperar un rato

awkward ['ɔ:kwəd, *Am:* 'ɑ:kwɚd] *adj* **1.** (*difficult*) difícil; **an ~ customer** *inf* un tipo difícil; **to make things ~ for sb** crear problemas a alguien **2.** (*embarrassed*) incómodo, -a; **an ~ silence** un silencio perturbador; **an ~ question** una pregunta delicada; **to feel ~** sentirse incómodo **3.** (*inconvenient*) **an ~ time** una hora inoportuna **4.** (*clumsy*) torpe **5.** *Brit* (*uncooperative*) terco, -a

awning ['ɔ:nɪŋ, *Am:* 'ɑ:-] *n* toldo *m*

awoke [ə'wəʊk, *Am:* -'woʊk] *pt of* **awake**

awoken [ə'wəʊkən, *Am:* -'woʊ-] *pp of* **awake**

AWOL ['eɪwɒl, *Am:* -wɑːl] MIL *abbr of* **absent without (official) leave** ausente sin permiso; **to go ~** *inf* desaparecer así como así
awry [ə'raɪ] *adj* **to go ~** salir mal
ax *n Am,* **axe** [æks] **I.** *n* hacha *f* ►**to get the ~** *inf* (*worker*) ser despedido; (*project*) ser anulado; **to have an ~ to grind** tener un interés personal **II.** <axing> *vt* recortar; **to ~ jobs** reducir los puestos de trabajo
axiom ['æksɪəm] *n form* axioma *m*
axis ['æksɪs] *n a.* MAT, POL eje *m*
axle ['æksl] *n* eje *m,* cardán *m AmC, Ven, Col;* **back/front ~** eje trasero/frontal
ayatollah [,aɪjə'tɔlə, *Am:* ,aɪə'toʊlə-] *n* ayatolá *m*
aye [aɪ] **I.** *n* POL **the ~s** los votos a favor **II.** *interj Scot* sí
azalea [ə'zeɪlɪə, *Am:* -'zeɪljə] *n* azalea *f*
Azerbaijan [,æzəbaɪ'dʒɑːn, *Am:* ,ɑːzɚ-] *n* Azerbaiyán *m*
Azerbaijani **I.** *adj* azerbaiyano, -a **II.** *n* azerbaiyano, -a *m, f*
Aztec ['æztɛk] **I.** *adj* azteca **II.** *n* azteca *mf*
azure ['æʒəʳ, *Am:* 'æʒɚ] **I.** *n* azul *m* celeste **II.** *adj* azul celeste

B

B, b [biː] *n* **1.** (*letter*) B, b *f;* **~ for Benjamin** *Brit,* **~ for Baker** *Am* B de Barcelona **2.** MUS si *m* **3.** SCHOOL notable *m*
b & b *n,* **B & B** [,biːənd'biː] *n abbr of* **bed and breakfast** pensión *f* familiar
BA [,biː'eɪ] *n* **1.** *abbr of* **Bachelor of Arts** Ldo., -a *m, f* (en Filosofía y Letras) **2.** *abbr of* **British Airways** BA *f*
baa [bɑː, *Am:* bæ] **I.** *n* balido *m* **II.** <-ed> *vi* balar
babble ['bæbl] **I.** *n no pl* **1.** (*of a baby*) balbuceo *m* **2.** (*of a stream*) murmullo *m* **II.** *vi* (*baby*) balbucear; (*adult*) parlotear
babe [beɪb] *n* **1.** *form* (*baby*) bebé *m inf;* **~ in arms** niño, -a *m, f* de pecho **2.** *Am, inf* (*term of address*) muñeca *f*
babel ['beɪbl] *n no pl* babel *m o f*
baboon [bə'buːn, *Am:* bæb'uːn] *n* babuino *m*
baby ['beɪbi] **I.** *n* **1.** (*child*) bebé *m;* **to expect/have a ~** esperar/tener un bebé **2.** (*youngest person*) benjamín *m* **3.** *inf* (*term of address*) nene, -a *m, f* ►**to throw out the ~ with the bathwater** tirar las frutas frescas con las pochas, actuar con exceso de celo **II.** *adj* **1.** (*person*) infantil **2.** (*tomato, carrot*) pequeño, -a **III.** *vt* mimar
baby carriage *n Am* coche *m* de bebé, carriola *f Méx* **baby food** *n no pl* comida *f* para bebés
babyhood ['beɪbɪhʊd] *n no pl* niñez *f*
babyish ['beɪbiɪʃ] *adj* infantil
babysitter ['beɪbɪ,sɪtəʳ, *Am:* -,sɪt̬ɚ] *n* canguro *mf,* nana *f Méx*
bachelor ['bætʃələʳ, *Am:* -lɚ] *n* **1.** (*man*) soltero *m* **2.** UNIV licenciado, -a *m, f;* **Bachelor of Arts** Licenciado, -a *m, f* en Filosofía y Letras; **Bachelor of Science** Licenciado, -a *m, f* en Ciencias

> El **Bachelor's degree** es el título que obtienen los estudiantes después de haber cursado carreras universitarias de tres años (en algunos casos, de cuatro o cinco años). Este título recibe varios nombres según las disciplinas. Los títulos más importantes son: **BA** (**Bachelor of Arts**) en las disciplinas de humanidades, **BSc** (**Bachelor of Science**) en las disciplinas científicas, **BEd** (**Bachelor of Education**) en las disciplinas de tipo pedagógico, **LLB** (**Bachelor of Laws**) para los estudiantes de Derecho y **BMus** para los estudiantes de Musicología.

bacillus [bə'sɪləs] *n* <-li> bacilo *m*
back [bæk] **I.** *n* **1.** (*opposite of front*) parte *f* trasera; (*of a hand*) dorso *m;* (*of a chair*) respaldo *m;* (*reverse side*) revés *m;* (*of a piece of paper, envelope*) dorso *m;* **~ to front** al revés; **to know sth ~ to front** saberse algo al derecho y al revés **2.** (*end: of a book*) final *m* **3.** ANAT espalda *f;* (*of an animal*) lomo *m;* **to be on one's ~** estar boca arriba; **to break one's ~** *inf* deslomarse; **to do sth behind sb's ~** *a. fig* hacer algo a espaldas de alguien; **to turn one's ~ on sb** *a. fig* dar la espalda a alguien **4.** SPORTS defensa *mf* ►**to know sth like the ~ of one's hand** conocer algo al dedillo *inf;* **to make a rod for one's own ~** *Brit* cavarse la propia tumba; **to have one's ~ against the wall** estar entre la espada y la pared; **to break the ~ of sth** *Aus, Brit* hacer la peor parte de algo; **you scratch my ~ and I'll scratch yours** hoy por ti, mañana por mí; **to stab sb in the ~** dar a alguien una puñalada por la espalda **II.** *adj* **1.** (*rear*) trasero, -a **2.** MED dorsal **III.** *adv* **1.** **to be ~** estar de vuelta; **to come ~** volver; **to want sb ~** querer que alguien vuelva; **I want the money ~ (from them)** quiero que me devuelvan el dinero; **to bring ~ memories** traer viejos recuerdos a la memoria **2.** (*to the rear, behind*) detrás, atrás; **~ and forth** atrás y adelante; **to look ~** mirar hacia atrás; **to sit ~** recostarse **3.** (*in return*) de vuelta **4.** (*into the past*) atrás **IV.** *vt* apoyar
◆**back away** *vi* echarse atrás
◆**back down** *vi* retirar(se)
◆**back on to** *vt* **the building backs on to the garden** la parte trasera del edificio da al jardín
◆**back out of** *vt* salir de; *fig* retirarse de
◆**back up** *vt* **1.** (*reverse*) dar marcha atrás **2.** INFOR **to ~ data/files** hacer copias de seguridad de datos/archivos **3.** (*support*) respaldar

back-bencher [ˌbækˈbentʃəʳ, *Am:* -tʃɚ] *n Brit* POL *diputado sin cargo específico ni en el gobierno ni en la oposición*

backbiting [ˈbækˌbaɪtɪŋ, *Am:* -t̬ɪŋ] *n no pl* murmureo *m,* viboreo *m Méx*

backbone [ˈbækbəʊn, *Am:* -boʊn] *n* **1.**(*spine*) columna *f* vertebral **2.** *fig* pilar *m* **3.** *no pl* (*strength of character*) coraje *m*

backchat [ˈbæktʃæt] *n* réplicas *fpl*

backcloth [ˈbækˌklɒθ, *Am:* -klɑːθ] *n Brit, a. fig* telón *m* de fondo

back door [ˌbækˈdɔːʳ] *n* puerta *f* trasera

backdrop [ˈbækdrɒp, *Am:* -drɑːp] *n a. fig* telón *m* de fondo

backer [ˈbækəʳ, *Am:* -ɚ] *n* partidario, -a *m, f;* **financial** ~ patrocinador *m* financiero

backfire [ˌbækˈfaɪəʳ, *Am:* -ˈfaɪɚ] *vi* **1.**(*go wrong*) fallar; **his plans ~d** sus planes fracasaron **2.** AUTO petardear, detonar *AmL*

backgammon [bækˈgæmən] *n no pl* backgamon *m*

background [ˈbækgraʊnd] *n* **1.**(*rear view*) fondo *m;* **in the** ~ *fig* en segundo plano **2.**(*education, family*) educación *f* **3.**(*training*) formación *f;* **to have a ~ in mathematics** tener una formación en matemáticas **4.**(*circumstances*) antecedentes *mpl*

background music *n* música *f* de fondo

backhand [ˈbækhænd] *n no pl* revés *m*

backhander [ˌbækˈhændəʳ, *Am:* -ɚ] *n inf* soborno *m,* mordida *f Méx,* coima *f AmS*

backing [ˈbækɪŋ] *n no pl* **1.**(*support, aid*) apoyo *m* **2.** FASHION refuerzo *m* **3.** MUS acompañamiento *m*

backlash [ˈbæklæʃ] *n* reacción *f*

backlog [ˈbæklɒg, *Am:* -lɑːg] *n* atraso *m*

back number *n* número *m* atrasado

backpack [ˈbækpæk] **I.** *n* mochila *f* **II.** *vi* viajar con mochila

backpacker *n* mochilero, -a *m, f*

back pay *n* atrasos *mpl* de sueldo

back seat *n* asiento *m* trasero

backside [ˈbæksaɪd] *n inf* trasero *m*

backslash [ˈbækslæʃ] *n* barra *f* inversa

backspace (**key**) *n* tecla *f* de retroceso

backstage [bækˈsteɪdʒ] **I.** *adj* **1.** THEAT de bastidores **2.** *fig* subrepticio, -a **II.** *adv* THEAT tras bambalinas, entre bastidores

backstroke [ˈbækstrəʊk, *Am:* -stroʊk] *n no pl* (estilo *m*) espalda *f,* nado *m* de dorso *AmL*

backtalk [ˈbæktɔːk] *n* réplicas *fpl*

backtrack [ˈbæktræk] *vi* **1.** retroceder **2.** *fig* dar marcha atrás; **to ~ on one's statement** retirar lo dicho

backup [ˈbækʌp] *n* **1.** INFOR copia *f* de seguridad **2.**(*support*) apoyo *m*

backward [ˈbækwəd, *Am:* -wɚd] **I.** *adj* **1.**(*to the rear*) hacia atrás **2.**(*slow in learning*) retrasado, -a **3.**(*underdeveloped*) atrasado, -a **II.** *adv* hacia atrás

backwards [ˈbækwədz, *Am:* -wɚdz] *adv* **1.**(*towards the back*) hacia atrás **2.**(*in reverse order*) al revés **3.**(*from better to worse*) de mal en peor **4.**(*into the past*) atrás en el tiempo ►**to bend over** ~ (**to help sb**) hacer lo imposible (por alguien); **to lean over** ~ **to do sth** desvivirse por hacer algo

backwater [ˈbækˌwɔːtəʳ, *Am:* -ˌwɑːt̬ɚ] *n* **1.**(*river*) remanso *m* **2.** *pej* lugar *m* atrasado

backwoods [ˈbækwʊdz] *npl* **the** ~ el interior

backwoodsman [ˈbækwʊdzmən] *n* <-men> *fig* patán *m*

back yard *n Brit* (*yard*) patio *m* trasero; *Am* (*garden*) jardín *m* trasero

bacon [ˈbeɪkən] *n* beicon *m,* tocino *m AmL* ►**to bring home the** ~ *inf* ganar los garbanzos; **to save sb's** ~ salvar la vida a alguien

bacteria [bækˈtɪərɪə] *n pl of* **bacterium**

bacteriologist [bækˌtɪərɪˈɒlədʒɪst, *Am:* -ˌtɪrɪˈɑːlə-] *n* bacteriólogo, -a *m, f*

bacterium [bækˈtɪərɪəm] *n* <-ria> bacteria *f*

bad [bæd] <worse, worst> **I.** *adj* **1.**(*not good*) malo, -a; **to have a ~ marriage** tener un matrimonio difícil; **to feel** ~ sentirse mal; **to look** ~ tener mal aspecto; **too ~!** ¡qué lástima!; ~ **dream** pesadilla *f;* (**to act**) **in ~ faith** actuar de mala fe; ~ **habits** malas costumbres; **to use ~ language** decir palabrotas; ~ **luck** mala suerte, macacoa *f PRico;* **a ~ name** una mala reputación; **in ~ taste** de mal gusto; **to have a ~ temper** tener mal carácter; ~ **times** tiempos *mpl* difíciles **2.**(*harmful*) dañino, -a; **to be ~ for sth/sb** ser perjudicial para algo/alguien **3.**(*spoiled*) malo, -a; **to go** ~ echarse a perder **4.**(*unhealthy*) enfermo, -a; **to have a ~ heart/back** estar mal del corazón/de la espalda **5.**(*serious: accident, mistake*) grave **6.**(*severe: pain*) fuerte ►**to go from ~ to worse** ir de mal en peor **II.** *adv inf* mal **III.** *n no pl* **the** ~ lo malo; **to go to the** ~ echarse a perder

badge [bædʒ] *n* insignia *f,* placa *f Méx*

badger [ˈbædʒəʳ, *Am:* -ɚ] **I.** *n* tejón *m* **II.** *vt* importunar

badly [ˈbædli] <worse, worst> *adv* **1.**(*poorly*) mal; **this house is ~ built** esta casa está mal construida **2.**(*in a negative way*) mal; **to think ~ of sb** pensar mal de alguien; **to come out of sth** ~ salir mal parado de algo **3.**(*very much*) desesperadamente; **to be ~ in need of sth** necesitar algo desesperadamente; **he was ~ defeated** fue derrotado estrepitosamente

badminton [ˈbædmɪntən] *n no pl* bádminton *m*

baffle [ˈbæfl] **I.** *vt* **1.**(*confuse*) desconcertar **2.**(*hinder*) impedir **II.** *n* TECH deflector *m,* bafle *m Méx*

baffling *adj* desconcertante

bag [bæg] **I.** *n* **1.**(*container*) bolsa *f,* busaca *f Col, Ven;* (*handbag*) bolso *m;* (*sack*) saco *m;* **to pack one's ~s** hacer las maletas; *fig* marcharse **2.**(*swollen skin*) **to have ~s under one's eyes** tener ojeras **3.** *inf* (*grumpy* *woman*) bruja *f* **4.** (*catch*) presa *f* ►**to be a ~ of bones** *inf* estar en los huesos; **the whole ~ of tricks** *inf* todas las mañas; **a mixed ~** un grupo heterogéneo; **~s of** *inf* un montón de; **to have ~s of money/space/time** *inf* tener montones de dinero/espacio/tiempo **II.** *vt* <-gg-> **1.** (*put in bag*) ensacar **2.** *inf* (*obtain*) obtener **3.** (*hunt*) cazar

bagel ['beɪgəl] *n tipo de rosca de pan*

baggage ['bægɪdʒ] *n no pl* **1.** (*luggage*) equipaje *m;* **excess ~** exceso *m* de equipaje **2.** (*army equipment*) bagaje *m* **3.** *pej* (*unpleasant woman*) bruja *f*

baggage allowance *n* límite *m* de equipaje **baggage car** *n Am, Aus* vagón *m* de equipaje, breque *m Ecua, Perú, RíoPl* **baggage check** *n Am* documentación *f* del equipaje **baggage claim** *n* recogida *f* del equipaje

baggy ['bægi] *adj* holgado, -a

bag lady *n inf* vagabunda *f*

bagpiper ['bægpaɪpəʳ, *Am:* -ɚ] *n* gaitero, -a *m, f*

bagpipes ['bægpaɪps] *npl* gaita *f*

Bahamas [bə'hɑːməz] *npl* **the ~** las (Islas) Bahamas

Bahamian [bə'eɪmiən] **I.** *adj* de las Bahamas **II.** *n* habitante *mf* de las Bahamas

Bahrain [bɑː'reɪn] *n* Bahrein *m*

bail [beɪl] **I.** *n* fianza *f;* **on ~** bajo fianza; **to post ~ for sb** *Am* dar fianza por alguien **II.** *vi* achicar **III.** *vt* **1.** (*remove: water*) achicar **2.** (*guarantee*) afianzar

◆**bail out** *vt* **to bail sb out** sacar a alguien de apuros

bailiff ['beɪlɪf] *n* **1.** *Brit* (*landlord's agent*) administrador(a) *m(f)* **2.** *Am* (*court official*) alguacil *mf*

bait [beɪt] **I.** *n* **1.** (*for fish*) cebo *m* **2.** *fig* señuelo *m;* **to swallow the ~** *inf* morder el anzuelo **II.** *vt* **1.** (*put bait on*) cebar **2.** (*harass*) acosar

bake [beɪk] **I.** *vi* **1.** (*cook*) cocerse **2.** *inf* (*be hot*) achicharrarse **II.** *vt* **1.** (*cook*) hornear **2.** (*harden*) endurecer

baker ['beɪkəʳ, *Am:* -kɚ] *n* panadero, -a *m, f*

bakery ['beɪkəri] *n* panadería *f*

baking *adj* **it's ~ hot** hace un calor achicharrante

baking powder *n* levadura *f*

balance ['bæləns] **I.** *n* **1.** (*device*) balanza *f* **2.** *no pl, a. fig* equilibrio *m;* **to lose one's ~** perder el equilibrio **3.** (*state of equality*) equidad *f* **4.** (*amount in bank account*) saldo *m* **5.** (*difference between amount paid and owed*) balance *m* **II.** *vi* equilibrarse **III.** *vt* **1.** (*compare*) contrapesar; **to ~ sth against sth** comparar algo con algo **2.** (*keep in a position*) estabilizar **3.** (*achieve equilibrium*) equilibrar; **to ~ the books** hacer cuadrar los libros de cuentas

balanced *adj* equilibrado, -a

balance of trade *n* balanza *f* comercial **balance sheet** *n* balance *m*

balcony ['bælkəni] *n* balcón *m*

bald [bɔːld] *adj* **1.** (*lacking hair*) calvo, -a, pelón, -ona *Méx;* **to go ~** quedarse calvo **2.** (*plain*) escueto, -a

baldly [bɔːldli] *adv* francamente

baldness ['bɔːldnɪs] *n no pl* calvicie *f,* pelada *f CSur*

bale [beɪl] **I.** *n* fardo *m* **II.** *vt* embalar

Balearic Islands *n* **the ~** las Islas Baleares

Balearics [ˌbæli'ærɪks, *Am:* ˌbɑːli'-] *n* **the ~** las Baleares

baleen whale [bə'liːn 'hweɪl] *n* misticeto *m*

baleful [beɪlfʊl] *adj* siniestro, -a

balk [bɔːk] **I.** *n* viga *f* **II.** *vi* **to ~ at sth** resistirse a algo

Balkans ['bɔlkəns] *n* **the ~** los Balcanes

ball [bɔːl] *n* **1.** (*for golf, tennis*) pelota *f;* (*for football, basketball*) balón *m,* pelota *f;* **to play ~** jugar a la pelota; *fig* cooperar **2.** (*round form*) bola *f* **3.** (*dance*) baile *m* ►**to have a ~** divertirse; **to get the ~ rolling** poner las cosas en marcha

ballad ['bæləd] *n* balada *f*

balladeer [ˌbælə'dɪəʳ, *Am:* -'dɪr] *n* cantautor(a) *m(f)*

ballast ['bæləst] *n no pl* **1.** NAUT lastre *m* **2.** (*gravel*) balasto *m*

ball bearing *n* cojinete *m*

ballerina [ˌbælər'iːnə, *Am:* -ə'riː-] *n* bailarina *f*

ballet dancer ['bæleɪˌdɑːntsəʳ, *Am:* 'bæleɪˌdæːntsɚ] *n* bailarín, -ina *m, f*

ball game *n Am* partido *m* de béisbol ►**that's a whole new ~** eso es completamente distinto

ballistic [bə'lɪstɪk] *adj* balístico, -a ►**to go ~** *inf* enfurecerse

balloon [bə'luːn] **I.** *n* globo *m* ►**to go down like a lead ~** fracasar estrepitosamente **II.** *vi* inflarse

balloonist *n* ascensionista *mf,* aeronauta *mf*

ballot ['bælət] **I.** *n* **1.** (*process*) votación *f* **2.** (*election*) sufragio *m* **3.** (*paper*) papeleta *f* **II.** *vi* invitar a votar **III.** *vt* consultar por votación

ballot box *n* urna *f* **ballot paper** *n* papeleta *f*

ball park *n* **1.** estadio *m* de béisbol **2.** *fig* **a ~ figure** una cifra aproximada **ball player** *n* jugador(a) *m(f)* de béisbol

ballpoint (**pen**) [ˌbɔːlpɔɪnt (pen)] *n* bolígrafo *m,* birome *m RíoPl*

ballroom ['bɔːlrʊm] *n* salón *m* de baile

ballroom dancing *n no pl* baile *m* de salón

balls-up ['bɔːlzʌp] *n Brit, vulg* lío *m*

balm [bɑːm] *n* **1.** (*ointment*) bálsamo *m* **2.** *fig* consuelo *m*

balmy ['bɑːmi] <-ier, -iest> *adj* (*weather*) templado, -a; (*breeze*) suave

Baltic ['bɔːltɪk] *n* **the ~** (**Sea**) el (Mar) Báltico

balustrade [ˌbælə'streɪd, *Am:* 'bæl-] *n* balaustrada *f,* barandilla *f Méx*

bamboo [bæm'buː] *n no pl* bambú *m*

bamboozle [bæm'bu:zl] *vt inf* **1.** (*confuse*) enredar **2.** (*trick*) engatusar
ban [bæn] **I.** *n* prohibición *f;* **to put** [*o* **place**] **a ~ on sth** prohibir algo **II.** *vt* <-nn-> prohibir; **she was ~ned from driving** le prohibieron conducir
banal [bə'nɑ:l] *adj* banal
banality [bə'nælәti, *Am:* -әṱi] *n* <-ies> banalidad *f*
banana [bә'nɑ:nә, *Am:* -'nænә] *n* plátano *m,* banana *f AmL* ►**to go ~s** *inf* enfurecerse
banana republic *n pej* república *f* bananera
banana tree *n* platanero *m,* banano *m*
band¹ [bænd] *n* **1.** (*strip: of cloth, metal*) banda *f* **2.** (*stripe*) franja *f* **3.** (*ribbon*) cinta *f;* **head ~** cinta *f* de pelo; **waist ~** faja *f* **4.** (*range*) *a.* TEL banda *f* **5.** (*ring*) anillo *m;* **wedding ~** alianza *f*
band² [bænd] *n* **1.** MUS grupo *m;* **brass ~** charanga *f* **2.** (*of friends*) pandilla *f;* (*of robbers*) banda *f*
◆**band together** *vi* agruparse
bandage ['bændɪdʒ] **I.** *n* vendaje *m* **II.** *vt* vendar
band-aid ['bændeɪd] *n* tirita *f*
bandit ['bændɪt] *n* bandido, -a *m, f,* carrilano, -a *m, f Chile*
bandsman ['bændzmәn] *n* <-men> músico *m* (de banda)
bandstand ['bændstænd] *n* quiosco *m* (de música)
bandwagon ['bændwægәn] *n* **to jump on the ~** *fig* subirse al carro
bandwidth *n* INFOR ancho *m* de banda
bandy¹ ['bændi] <-ier, -iest> *adj* patizambo, -a
bandy² ['bændi] *vt* <-ies, -ied> (*insults, words*) intercambiar
◆**bandy about** *vt* **it was bandied about that ...** se rumoreaba que...
bang [bæŋ] **I.** *n* **1.** (*noise, blow*) golpe *m;* (*explosion*) detonación *f* **2.** *pl, Am* (*fringe*) flequillo *m,* pollina *f PRico, Ven* ►**to go (off) with a ~** *inf* tener éxito **II.** *adv* **1.** *inf* (*exactly*) directamente; **~ in the middle of the road** justo en medio de la carretera **2.** (*make noise*) **to go ~** estallar **III.** *interj* bang **IV.** *vi* (*make noise*) dar golpes; (*exploding noise*) estallar; (*slam*) cerrarse de golpe; **to ~ on sth** dar golpes en algo **V.** *vt* (*hit*) golpear; **to ~ one's head against/on sth** darse un golpe en la cabeza contra/en algo
◆**bang about** *vi inf* hacer ruido
banger ['bæŋә', *Am:* -ɚ] *n* **1.** *Brit, inf* (*car*) coche *m,* cacharro *m* **2.** (*firework*) petardo *m* **3.** *Brit, inf* (*sausage*) salchicha *f*
Bangladesh [bæŋglә'deʃ] *n* Bangladesh *m*
Bangladeshi [bæŋglә'deʃi] **I.** *n* bangladesí *mf* **II.** *adj* bangladesí
bangle ['bæŋgl] *n* ajorca *f*
banish ['bænɪʃ] *vt a. fig* desterrar; **to ~ sth from one's mind** disipar algo de su mente
banishment *n no pl* destierro *m*
banister ['bænɪstә', *Am:* -әstɚ] *n* pasamano *m*
banjo ['bændʒәʊ] *n* <-(oe)s> banjo *m*
bank¹ [bæŋk] **I.** *n* **1.** FIN banco *m;* (*in games*) banca *f;* **to break the ~** hacer saltar la banca **2.** (*storage place*) depósito *m;* **blood ~** banco *m* de sangre; **data ~** banco *m* de datos ►**to laugh all the way to the ~** *inf* ganar mucha pasta **II.** *vi* **to ~ with Barclays** tener una cuenta en el banco Barclays **III.** *vt* depositar
bank² [bæŋk] **I.** *n* (*edge: of river*) orilla *m* **II.** *vi* AVIAT ladearse
bank³ [bæŋk] *n* (*of earth*) terraplén *m;* (*of fog*) banco *m;* (*of cloud*) montón *m;* (*of switches*) batería *f*
◆**bank up I.** *vi* amontonarse **II.** *vt* amontonar
bank account *n* cuenta *f* bancaria **bank balance** *n* balance *m* bancario **bank book** *n* libreta *f* bancaria **bank charges** *n* gastos *mpl* bancarios **bank clerk** *n* empleado, -a *m, f* de banco
banker ['bæŋkә', *Am:* -kɚ] *n* banquero, -a *m, f*
bank holiday *n Am, Brit* día *m* festivo
banking *n no pl* banca *f*
banking hall *n* sala *f* de ventanillas **banking hours** *npl* horario *m* bancario
bank manager *n* gerente *mf* de banco **banknote** *n* billete *m* de banco **bank rate** *n* tipo *m* bancario **bank robber** *n* ladrón, -ona *m, f* de banco
bankrupt ['bæŋkrʌpt] **I.** *n* quebrado *m* **II.** *vt* llevar a la bancarrota **III.** *adj* **1.** (*bust*) insolvente; **to be ~** estar en quiebra; **to go ~** quebrar **2.** *fig* **to be morally ~** estar moralmente destrozado
bankruptcy ['bæŋkrәptsi] *n* <-ies> bancarrota *f*
bank statement *n* estado *m* de cuentas
bank transfer *n* transferencia *f* bancaria
banner ['bænә', *Am:* -ɚ] *n* **1.** (*flag*) bandera *f;* **under the ~ of ...** bajo la bandera de... **2.** (*placard*) pancarta **3.** (*in Internet*) anuncio *m*
banns [bænz] *npl* **to publish the ~** correr las amonestaciones
banquet ['bæŋkwɪt, *Am:* -kwәt] **I.** *n* banquete *m* **II.** *vi* banquetear
bantam ['bæntәm, *Am:* -ṱәm] *n* gallina *f* de Bantam
banter ['bæntә', *Am:* -ṱɚ] **I.** *n* bromas *fpl* **II.** *vi* bromear
baptise [bæp'taɪz] *vt Aus, Brit s.* **baptize**
baptism ['bæptɪzәm] *n* bautismo *m;* **~ of fire** bautismo de fuego
baptismal ['bæptɪzmәl] *adj* bautismal
baptismal font *n* pila *f* baptismal
Baptist ['bæptɪst] *n* bautista *mf;* **John the ~** Juan el Bautista; **the Baptist Church** la iglesia bautista
baptize [bæp'taɪz, *Am:* 'bæp-] *vt* bautizar; **I was ~d Clara** me bautizaron con el nombre de Clara

B

bar¹ [bɑːʳ, *Am:* bɑːr] **I.** *n* **1.** (*of metal, wood*) barra *f;* (*of a cage, prison*) reja *f;* (*of chocolate*) tableta *f;* (*of gold*) lingote *m;* (*of soap*) pastilla *f;* **to be behind ~s** *inf* estar entre rejas **2.** (*band of colour*) franja *f* **3.** MUS compás *m* **4.** MIL barra *f* **5.** (*sandbank*) banco *m* de arena **6.** (*restriction*) obstáculo *m* **7.** (*place to drink*) bar *m;* (*counter*) barra *f,* mostrador *m* **8.** INFOR barra *f;* **task/scroll/space ~** barra de tareas/desplazamiento/espacio **II.** *vt* <-rr-> **1.** (*fasten: door, window*) atrancar **2.** (*obstruct*) obstruir; **to ~ sb's way/path** obstaculizar el camino/paso a alguien **3.** (*prohibit*) prohibir; **to ~ sb from doing sth** prohibir a alguien hacer algo **4.** (*exclude*) excluir

bar² [bɑːʳ, *Am:* bɑːr] *prep Brit* excepto; **~ none** sin excepción

Bar [bɑːʳ, *Am:* bɑːr] *n* **the ~** (*group of lawyers*) el Colegio de Abogados; (*profession*) el foro, la Barra *Méx*

barb [bɑːb, *Am:* bɑːrb] *n* **1.** ZOOL púa *f* **2.** (*insult*) observación *f* aguda

Barbadian [bɑːˈbeɪdiən, *Am:* bɑːr-] **I.** *adj* de Barbados **II.** *n* habitante *mf* de Barbados

Barbados [bɑːˈbəɪdɒs, *Am:* bɑːrˈbəɪdoʊs] *n* Barbados *m*

barbarian [bɑːˈbeərɪən, *Am:* bɑːrˈberɪ-] *n* bárbaro, -a *m, f*

barbaric [bɑːˈbærɪk, *Am:* bɑːrˈber-] *adj* bárbaro, -a

barbarity [bɑːˈbærəti, *Am:* bɑːrˈberət̬i] *n* <-ies> crueldad *f*

barbarous [ˈbɑːbərəs, *Am:* ˈbɑːr-] *adj* bárbaro, -a

barbecue [ˈbɑːbɪkjuː, *Am:* ˈbɑːr-] *n* **1.** (*grill*) parrilla *f* **2.** (*event*) barbacoa *f,* parrillada *f Col, Ven,* asado *m Chile*

barbed [bɑːbd, *Am:* bɑːrbd] *adj* **1.** (*with barbs*) de púas **2.** *fig* (*comment, criticism*) mordaz

barbed wire *n* alambre *m* de púas

barber [ˈbɑːbəʳ, *Am:* ˈbɑːrbɚ] *n* barbero *m*

barbershop [ˈbɑːbəʃɒp, *Am:* ˈbɑːrbɚʃɑːp] *n no pl* barbería *f*

barbiturate [bɑːˈbɪtjʊrɪt, *Am:* bɑːrˈbɪtʃrət] *n* barbitúrico *m*

bar chart *n* gráfico *m* de barras **bar code** *n* código *m* de barras

bard [bɑːd, *Am:* bɑːrd] *n* bardo *m;* **the Bard** Shakespeare

bare [beəʳ, *Am:* ber] **I.** *adj* **1.** (*without any clothes*) desnudo, -a; (*uncovered*) descubierto, -a; **with one's ~ hands** con las propias manos; **to fight with one's ~ hands** luchar sin armas **2.** (*empty*) vacío, -a; (*without plants, leaves*) desnudo, -a; **to be ~ of sth** estar desprovisto de algo **3.** (*unadorned*) **to tell sb the ~ facts** [*o* **truth**] decir a alguien la pura verdad **4.** (*little*) **the ~ minimum** lo mínimo; **the ~ necessities** las necesidades básicas **II.** *vt* desnudar; **to ~ one's head** decrubrirse; **to ~ one's teeth** enseñar los dientes; **to ~ one's heart/soul to sb** abrir su corazón/alma a alguien

bareback [ˈbeəbæk, *Am:* ˈber-] *adv* a pelo

barefaced [ˈbeəfeɪst, *Am:* ˈber-] *adj* descarado, -a

barefoot [ˈbeəfʊt, *Am:* ˈber-] *adv,* **barefooted** [ˌbeəˈfʊtɪd, *Am:* ˌberˈfʊt̬-] *adv* descalzo, -a

barely [ˈbeəli, *Am:* ˈber-] *adv* **1.** (*hardly*) apenas, agatas *Arg, Urug, Par* **2.** (*scantily*) escasamente

barf [bɑːf, *Am:* bɑːrf] *vi Am, inf* vomitar

bargain [ˈbɑːgɪn, *Am:* ˈbɑːr-] **I.** *n* **1.** (*agreement*) trato *m;* **to drive a hard ~** saber regatear; **to strike a ~** cerrar un trato **2.** (*item*) ganga *f,* pichincha *f Arg, Bol, Par, Urug,* mamada *f AmC, Bol, Chile, Perú* ▸**into the ~** por añadidura **II.** *vi* (*negotiate*) negociar; (*haggle*) regatear; **to ~ away sth** malvender algo

◆**bargain for** *vi,* **bargain on** *vi* contar con; **to get more than one bargained for** *fig* recibir más de lo que uno se esperaba

bargain basement *n* sección *f* de ofertas **bargain price** *n* precio *m* de oferta **bargain sale** *n* rebajas *fpl*

barge [bɑːdʒ, *Am:* bɑːrdʒ] **I.** *n* barcaza *f* **II.** *vt inf* empujar; **to ~ one's way through sth** abrirse paso por algo

◆**barge in** *vi* **1.** (*intrude*) entrar sin pedir permiso **2.** *fig* (*interrupt*) **sorry to ~** disculpe si me entrometo

◆**barge into** *vi* **to ~ sb** chocar con alguien

◆**barge through** *vi* abrirse paso a empujones

baritone [ˈbærɪtəʊn, *Am:* ˈberətoʊn] **I.** *n* barítono *m* **II.** *adj* barítono, -a

bark¹ [bɑːk, *Am:* bɑːrk] **I.** *n* (*of a dog*) ladrido *m* ▸**his ~ is worse than his bite** perro ladrador poco mordedor *prov* **II.** *vi* ladrar; (*person*) gritar **III.** *vt* gritar

◆**bark out** *vt* gritar

bark² [bɑːk, *Am:* bɑːrk] *n no pl* (*of a tree*) corteza *f*

barkeeper [ˈbɑːkiːpəʳ, *Am:* ˈbɑːrkiːpɚ] *n* (*owner*) tabernero, -a *m, f;* (*barperson*) camarero, -a *m, f*

barley [ˈbɑːli, *Am:* ˈbɑːr-] *n no pl* cebada *f*

barmaid [ˈbɑːmeɪd, *Am:* ˈbɑːr-] *n* camarera *f*

barman [ˈbɑːmən, *Am:* ˈbɑːr-] *n* <-men> camarero *m*

barmy [ˈbɑːmi, *Am:* ˈbɑːr-] *adj inf* chiflado, -a

barn [bɑːn, *Am:* bɑːrn] *n* granero *m*

barnacle [ˈbɑːnəkl, *Am:* ˈbɑːr-] *n* bálano *m*

barn yard *n* corral *m*

barometer [bəˈrɒmɪtəʳ, *Am:* -ˈrɑːmət̬ɚ] *n* barómetro *m*

baron [ˈbærən, *Am:* ˈber-] *n* **1.** (*aristocrat*) barón *m* **2.** *fig* magnate *m*

baroness [ˈbærənɪs, *Am:* ˈbernəs] *n* baronesa *f*

baronet [ˈbærənɪt, *Am:* ˈbernət] *n* baronet *m*

baronial [bəˈrəʊnɪəl, *Am:* -ˈroʊ-] *adj* baro-

nial
baroque [bə'rɒk, *Am:* -'roʊk] *adj a. fig* barroco, -a
barrack ['bærək, *Am:* 'ber-] *vt* abuchear
barracks ['bærəks, *Am:* 'ber-] *npl* cuartel *m*
barrage ['bærɑːʒ, *Am:* bə'rɑːʒ] *n* **1.** MIL cortina *f* de fuego **2.** *fig* (*of questions, complaints*) aluvión *m* **3.** *Brit* (*barrier*) barrera *f*
barrel ['bærəl, *Am:* 'ber-] **I.** *n* **1.** (*container*) barril *m*, tonel *m* **2.** (*measure: of oil*) barril *m* **3.** (*of a gun*) cañón *m* ►**to be a ~ of fun** ser divertido; **to have sb over a ~** tener a alguien en un puño; **to scrape (the bottom of) the ~** tener que recurrir a lo peor **II.** *vi* <*Brit:* -ll-, *Am:* -l-> *inf* correr **III.** *vt* <*Brit:* -ll-, *Am:* -l-> embarrilar
barrel organ *n* organillo *m*
barren ['bærən, *Am:* 'ber-] *adj* **1.** (*infertile*) estéril; (*landscape*) árido, -a **2.** (*unproductive*) improductivo, -a; **~ years** años perdidos
barricade [ˌbærɪ'keɪd, *Am:* ˌberə-] **I.** *n* barricada *f* **II.** *vt* cerrar con barricadas; **she ~d herself into her room** se atrincheró en su habitación
barrier ['bærɪəʳ, *Am:* 'berɪɚ] *n* barrera *f*; **language ~** barrera lingüística
barring ['bɑːrɪŋ] *prep* (*except for*) excepto; (*if there are no*) a menos que *+subj*; **~ accidents** si Dios quiere; **~ complications** a menos que se presenten complicaciones; **~ delays** a menos que se produzcan retrasos
barrister ['bærɪstəʳ, *Am:* 'berɪstɚ] *n Aus, Brit* abogado, -a *m, f*
barrow ['bærəʊ, *Am:* 'beroʊ] *n* (*wheelbarrow*) carretilla *f*; (*cart*) carreta *f*
bartender ['bɑːtendəʳ, *Am:* 'bɑːrtendɚ] *n* camarero, -a *m, f*
barter ['bɑːtəʳ, *Am:* 'bɑːrt̬ɚ] **I.** *n no pl* trueque *m* **II.** *vi* comerciar **III.** *vt* **to ~ sth for sth** trocar [*o* cambiar] algo por algo
basalt ['bæsɔːlt, *Am:* bə'sɔːlt] *n no pl* basalto *m*
base¹ [beɪs] **I.** *n* **1.** (*lower part*) base *f* **2.** (*bottom*) fondo *m* **3.** (*source of support*) apoyo *m* **4.** (*basis*) fundamento *m* **5.** MIL base **6.** (*of a company*) sede *f* ►**to be off ~** *Am, inf* estar equivocado; **to touch ~** tocar fondo **II.** *vt* **1.** (*found*) basar; **to be ~d on** basarse en **2.** MIL estacionar **3.** (*stay*) **to be ~d in London** (*company*) tener su sede en Londres; (*person*) trabajar en Londres; **which hotel are you ~d at?** ¿en qué hotel vives?
base² [beɪs] *adj* **1.** (*not honourable*) vil **2.** (*not pure: metal*) impuro, -a
baseball ['beɪsbɔːl] *n* béisbol *m*
base camp *n* campamento *m* base
Basel ['bɑːzl] *n* Basilea *f*
baseless ['beɪslɪs] *adj* sin fundamento; (*accusation*) infundado, -a
base rate ['beisreit] *n Brit* tipo *m* de interés base
bash [bæʃ] **I.** *n* **1.** (*blow*) porrazo *m* **2.** *inf* (*party*) fiesta *f* **II.** *vt* (*hit hard: thing*) golpear; (*person*) pegar; **to have a ~ at doing sth** *inf* intentar hacer algo
◆**bash into** *vi insep* estrellarse contra
bashful ['bæʃfəl] *adj* tímido, -a
basic ['beɪsɪk] **I.** *adj* básico, -a; **~ idea** idea *f* principal; **~ requirements** requisitos mínimos; **to have a ~ command of sth** tener conocimientos básicos de algo **II.** *npl* **the ~s** lo básico
BASIC ['beɪsɪk] *n* INFOR *abbr of* **Beginner's All-purpose Symbolic Instruction Code** BASIC *m*
basically *adv* básicamente
basic vocabulary *n* vocabulario *m* básico
basic wage *n* salario *m* mínimo
basil ['bæzəl, *Am:* 'beɪzəl] *n* albahaca *f*
basilica [bə'zɪlɪkə, *Am:* -'sɪl-] *n* ARCHIT basílica *f*
basin ['beɪsn] *n* **1.** (*for cooking*) cuenco *m*; (*for washing hands*) lavabo *m* **2.** GEO cuenca *f*
basis ['beɪsɪs] *n* <bases> base *f*; **on a weekly ~** semanalmente; **to be the ~ for sth** ser el fundamento de algo; **on the ~ of sth** sobre la base de algo
bask [bɑːsk, *Am:* bæsk] *vi* **to ~ in the sun** tomar el sol; **to ~ in sb's favour** gozar del favor de alguien
basket ['bɑːskɪt, *Am:* 'bæskət] *n* **1.** (*container*) cesto *m*; (*two handled*) canasta *f* **2.** (*amount in basket*) canastada *f* **3.** SPORTS canasta *f*
basketball ['bɑːskɪtbɔːl, *Am:* 'bæskətbɔːl] *n* baloncesto *m*
basket case *n inf* **to be a ~** ser un fracaso
basking shark *n* tiburón *m* peregrino
Basque [bæsk] **I.** *adj* vasco, -a; **~ Country** País *m* Vasco **II.** *n* **1.** vasco, -a *m, f* **2.** *no pl* LING euskera *m*
bass¹ [beɪs] *n* **1.** (*voice*) bajo *m* **2.** (*instrument: classical*) contrabajo *m*; (*electric*) bajo *m*
bass² [bæs] *n* ZOOL lubina *f*
bass clef *n* clave *f* de fa
bass drum *n* bombo *m*
bassoon [bə'suːn] *n* fagot *m*
bastard ['bɑːstəd, *Am:* 'bæstɚd] *n* **1.** (*child*) bastardo, -a *m, f* **2.** *vulg* cabrón, -ona *m, f*
baste [beɪst] *vt* **1.** GASTR pringar **2.** *Am, Aus* (*tack*) hilvanar
bastion ['bæstɪən, *Am:* -tʃən] *n a. fig* baluarte *m*
bat¹ [bæt] *n* murciélago *m* ►**to have ~s in the belfry** *inf* estar chiflado; **to be as blind as a ~** no ver tres en un burro
bat² [bæt] *vt* **to ~ one's eyelids** pestañear; **to ~ one's eyelids at sb** guiñar un ojo a alguien; **he/she didn't ~ an eyelid when ...** *fig* permaneció indiferente cuando...
bat³ [bæt] **I.** *n* **1.** (*in baseball, cricket*) bate *m* **2.** (*blow*) golpe *m* ►**right off the ~** *Am* al instante; **to do sth off one's own ~** *Brit, inf* hacer algo por su propia cuenta **II.** *vt, vi* <-tt-> SPORTS batear

batch [bætʃ] *n* <-es> tanda *f;* COM, INFOR lote *m;* (*of cakes*) hornada *f*
batch file *n* INFOR fichero *m* por lotes **batch processing** *n* INFOR procesamiento *m* por lotes
bated ['beɪtɪd, *Am:* 'bæt̬-] *adj* **with ~ breath** con ansiedad
bath [bɑ:θ, *Am:* bæθ] **I.** *n* **1.** (*container*) bañera *f,* tina *f AmL,* bañadera *f Arg* **2.** (*action*) baño *m,* bañada *f Méx;* **to have** [*o* **take**] **a ~** bañarse **II.** *vi* bañarse **III.** *vt* bañar
bathe [beɪð] **I.** *vi* bañarse **II.** *vt* (*wound, eyes*) lavar; (*person, animal*) bañar; **to be ~d in sweat/tears** estar bañado en sudor/lágrimas **III.** *n no pl* baño *m;* **to have a ~** bañarse
bather ['beɪðəʳ, *Am:* -ðɚ] *n* bañista *mf*
bathing *n no pl* **~ prohibited** prohibido bañarse
bathing cap *n* gorro *m* de baño **bathing costume** *n Aus, Brit,* **bathing suit** *n Am* bañador *m,* malla *f* (de baño) *RíoPl,* vestido *m* de baño *Col* **bathing trunks** *npl* bañador *m*
bathrobe ['bɑ:θrəʊb] *n* albornoz *m*
bathroom ['bɑ:θru:m] *n* **1.** (*room with bath*) (cuarto *m* de) baño *m* **2.** *Am, Aus* (*lavatory*) baño *m,* servicio *m*
bath towel *n* toalla *f* de baño
bathtub ['bɑ:θtʌb, *Am:* 'bæθ-] *n* bañera *f,* tina *f AmL,* bañadera *f Arg*
baton ['bætən, *Am:* bə'tɑ:n] *n* **1.** MUS batuta *f;* MIL bastón *m* **2.** (*of a policeman*) porra *f* **3.** SPORTS testigo *m;* **~ change** relevo *m*
batsman ['bætsmən] <-men> *n* bateador *m*
battalion [bə'tælɪən, *Am:* -jən] *n* batallón *m*
batten ['bætn] **I.** *n* **1.** ARCHIT (*for a door, wall*) listón *m;* (*for flooring*) tabla *f* **2.** NAUT (*for a sail*) sable *m;* (*for a hatch*) listón *m,* barra *f* de cierre **3.** THEAT guía *f* **II.** *vt* reforzar con listones **III.** *vi* **to ~ on sb** vivir a costa de alguien
◆**batten down** *vt* **to ~ the hatches** *fig* atarse los machos
batter ['bætəʳ, *Am:* 'bæt̬ɚ] **I.** *n* **1.** GASTR (*for fried food*) rebozado *m;* (*for a pancake, cake*) masa *f* **2.** *Am* SPORTS bateador(a) *m(f)* **II.** *vt* **1.** (*assault*) maltratar, pegar **2.** (*hit*) golpear; **to ~ the door in** [*o* **down**] derribar la puerta **3.** GASTR rebozar **III.** *vi* **to ~ at the door** aporrear la puerta; **the waves ~ed against the rocks** las olas azotaban las rocas
battered ['bætəd, *Am:* -ɚd] *adj* **1.** (*injured*) maltratado, -a **2.** (*damaged: hat, clothes*) estropeado, -a; (*reputation, image*) maltrecho, -a **3.** GASTR rebozado, -a
battering ['bætərɪŋ, *Am:* 'bæt̬-] *n* paliza *f;* **to give sb a ~** dar una paliza a alguien
battering ram ['bætəriŋræm, *Am:* 'bæt̬-] *n* HIST, MIL ariete *m*
battery ['bætəri, *Am:* 'bæt̬-] <-ies> *n* **1.** (*for a radio, torch*) pila *f;* (*for a car*) batería *f* **2.** (*large number*) serie *f;* **a ~ of questions** una sarta de preguntas **3.** MIL batería *f* **4.** LAW agresión *f*
battery charger *n* cargador *m* de pilas; AUTO cargador *m* de baterías
battery hen *n Aus, Brit* gallina *f* de criadero
battle ['bætl, *Am:* 'bæt̬-] **I.** *n* **1.** MIL batalla *f* **2.** (*struggle*) lucha *f* ►**that's half the ~** eso es la parte más difícil, con eso ya hay medio camino andado; **to fight a losing ~** luchar por una causa perdida **II.** *vi* (*fight*) pelear; (*non-violently*) luchar **III.** *vt* combatir; **to ~ one's way to the top** abrirse paso hasta la cima
battleax *n Am,* **battleaxe** ['bætlæks, *Am:* 'bæt̬-] *n Aus, Brit* **1.** HIST hacha *f* de guerra **2.** *pej, inf* (*woman*) sargenta *f,* sisebuta *f RíoPl*
battle cry *n* grito *m* de guerra **battledress** *n no pl* traje *m* de campaña **battlefield** *n* campo *m* de batalla **battleground** *n* campo *m* de batalla
battlements ['bætlmənts, *Am:* 'bæt̬-] *npl* almenas *fpl*
battleship ['bætlʃɪp, *Am:* 'bæt̬-] *n* acorazado *m*
baud [bɔ:d, *Am:* bɑ:d] *n* INFOR baudio *m*
baud rate *n* INFOR velocidad *f* de transmisión
baulk [bɔ:k, *Am:* bɑ:k] *vi s.* **balk**
bauxite ['bɔ:ksaɪt, *Am:* 'bɑ:k-] *n no pl* bauxita *f*
bawdy ['bɔ:di, *Am:* 'bɑ:-] <-ier, -iest> *adj* (*scene*) subido, -a de tono; (*joke*) verde, colorado, -a *Méx*
bawl [bɔ:l, *Am:* bɑ:l] **I.** *vi* **1.** (*bellow*) vociferar; **to ~ at sb** gritar a alguien **2.** (*weep*) berrear **II.** *vt* gritar; **to ~ sb out** echar la bronca a alguien; **to ~ one's eyes out** desgañitarse
bay¹ [beɪ] *n* GEO bahía *f*
bay² [beɪ] *n* laurel *m*
bay³ [beɪ] *n* **1.** ARCHIT (*between columns*) intercolumnio *m;* (*in a church*) crujía *f;* (*of a factory*) nave *f;* (*in a house*) saliente *m* **2.** *Brit* (*marked-off space*) **parking ~** plaza *f* de estacionamiento
bay⁴ [beɪ] *n* ZOOL caballo *m* zaino
bay⁵ [beɪ] **I.** *vi* aullar **II.** *n no pl* (*howling*) aullido *m* ►**to be at ~** estar acorralado; **to bring sth/sb to ~** acorralar algo/a alguien; **to hold sth/sb at ~** mantener algo/a alguien a raya
bay leaf *n* hoja *f* de laurel
Bay of Biscay *n* Golfo *m* de Vizcaya
bayonet ['beɪənɪt, *Am:* ˌbeɪə'net] **I.** *n* bayoneta *f* **II.** *vt* (*wound*) herir con una bayoneta; (*kill*) matar con una bayoneta
bay window *n* mirador *m*
bazaar [bə'zɑ:ʳ, *Am:* -'zɑ:r] *n* **1.** bazar *m* **2.** (*event*) venta *f* benéfica, bazar *m Col*
BBC ['bi:bi:'si:] *n abbr of* **British Broadcasting Corporation** BBC *f*
BC [ˌbi:'si:] **I.** *Can abbr of* **British-Columbia** Columbia *f* Británica **II.** *adv abbr of* **before Christ** a.C.
BCG [ˌbi:si:'dʒi:] *abbr of* **bacillus of Calmette and Guérin** vacuna *f* de la tuberculosis
be [bi:] <was, been> **I.** *vi* **1.** + *n/adj* (*permanent state, quality, identity*) ser; **she's a cook** es cocinera; **she's Spanish** es española; **to ~ good** ser bueno; **to ~ able to do sth** ser capaz

de hacer algo; **what do you want to ~ when you grow up?** ¿qué quieres ser de mayor?; **to ~ married/single** estar [*o* ser *CSur*] casado/soltero; **to ~ a widow** ser viuda **2.** + *adj* (*mental and physical states*) estar; **to ~ fat** estar gordo; **to ~ hungry** tener hambre; **to ~ happy** estar contento **3.** (*age*) tener; **I'm 21** tengo 21 años **4.** (*indicates sb's opinion*) **to ~ for/against sth** estar a favor/en contra de algo **5.** (*calculation, cost*) **two and two is four** dos y dos son cuatro; **these glasses are £2 each** estos vasos cuestan 2 libras cada uno; **how much is that?** ¿cuánto es? **6.** (*measurement*) medir; (*weight*) pesar; **to ~ 2 metres long** medir 2 metros de largo **7.** (*exist, live*) **there is/are ...** hay...; **to let sth/sb ~** dejar en paz algo/a alguien; **I think, therefore I am** pienso, luego existo; **to ~ or not to ~** ser o no ser **8.** (*location, situation*) estar; **to ~ in Rome** estar en Roma; **to ~ in a bad situation** estar en una mala situación **9.** *pp* (*go, visit*) **I've never ~en to Mexico** nunca he estado en Méjico; **the plumber hasn't ~en yet** el fontanero todavía no ha venido **10.** (*take place*) ser, tener lugar; **the meeting is next Tuesday** la reunión es el próximo martes **11.** (*circumstances*) **to ~ on the pill** tomar la píldora; **to ~ on vacation** estar de vacaciones; **to ~ on a diet** estar a régimen **12.** (*in time expressions*) **don't ~ too long** no tardes mucho **13.** (*expresses possibility*) **can it ~ that ...?** *form* ¿puede ser que... +*subj*?; **what are we to do?** ¿qué podemos hacer? ►**~ that as it may** sea como fuere; **so ~ it** así sea **II.** *impers vb* (*expressing physical conditions, circumstances*) **it's cloudy** está nublado; **it's sunny** hace sol; **it's two o'clock** son las dos; **it's ~en so long!** ¡cuánto tiempo!; **it's ten minutes by bus to the market** el mercado está a diez minutos en autobús; **it was Anne who drank it** fue Anne quien se lo bebió **III.** *aux vb* **1.** (*expresses continuation*) estar; **to ~ doing sth** estar haciendo algo; **don't sing while I'm reading** no cantes mientras estoy leyendo [*o* mientras leo]; **you're always complaining** siempre te estás quejando; **she's leaving tomorrow** se va mañana **2.** (*expresses passive*) ser; **to ~ discovered by sb** ser descubierto por alguien; **he was left speechless** lo dejaron sin palabras; **he was asked ...** le preguntaron... **3.** (*expresses future*) **we are to visit Peru in the winter** vamos a ir a Perú en invierno **4.** (*expresses future in past*) **she was never to see her brother again** nunca más volvería a ver a su hermano **5.** (*expresses subjunctive possibility in conditionals*) **if he was to work harder, he'd get better grades** si trabajara más, tendría mejores notas; **were I to refuse, they'd ~ very annoyed** si me negara, se enfadarían mucho **6.** (*expresses obligation*) **you are to come here right now** tienes que venir aquí ahora mismo **7.** (*in question tags*) **she is tall, isn't she?** es alta, ¿no?

beach [biːtʃ] **I.** *n* playa *f* **II.** *vt* hacer embarrancar, varar

beach ball *n* balón *m* de playa

beachhead ['biːtʃhed] *n* cabeza *f* de playa

beachwear ['biːtʃweəʳ, *Am:* -wer] *n no pl* ropa *f* playera

beacon ['biːkən] *n* **1.** (*signal*) baliza *f* **2.** (*lighthouse*) faro *m* **3.** (*fire*) almenara *f* **4.** *fig* (*guide*) luz *f*

bead [biːd] *n* **1.** (*ball: of glass*) abalorio *m*, cuenta *f*; (*of wood*) viruta *f* **2.** (*drop*) gota *f*; **~s of sweat** gotas *fpl* de sudor **3.** *pl* REL rosario *m*; **to tell one's ~s** rezar el rosario **4.** (*on a gun*) punto *m* de mira; **to draw a ~ on sb/sth** apuntar a alguien/algo **5.** (*on a tyre*) talón *m*

beading ['biːdɪŋ] *n* ARCHIT moldura *f*

beady ['biːdi] <-ier, -iest> *adj* **~ eyes** *ojos redondos, pequeños y brillantes;* **to cast a ~ eye on** [*o* **over**] **sth** mirar algo con lupa

beak [biːk] *n* **1.** ZOOL pico *m* **2.** *inf* (*nose*) napia *f*, naso *m RíoPl* **3.** *Brit, inf* (*magistrate*) juez *mf*

beaker ['biːkəʳ, *Am:* -kɚ] *n* **1.** (*cup*) jarra *f* **2.** CHEM vaso *m* de precipitados

be-all ['biːˈɔːl] *n* **the ~** (**and end-all**) la única cosa que importa

beam [biːm] **I.** *n* **1.** (*ray*) rayo *m*; (*light*) haz *m* de luz; **full ~** luces *fpl* largas, luces *fpl* altas *Chile* **2.** ARCHIT viga *f* **3.** SPORTS barra *f* sueca ►**to be off ~** *inf* estar equivocado **II.** *vt* transmitir; **to ~ a smile at sb** dedicar una sonrisa a alguien **III.** *vi* brillar; (*smile*) sonreír (abiertamente)

beaming *adj* **to be ~** estar radiante

bean [biːn] *n* **1.** (*seed*) semilla *f*; **coffee ~** grano *m* de café **2.** (*plant*) judía *f* **3.** (*vegetable: fresh*) judía *f* verde, ejote *m Méx*, chaucha *f RíoPl*, poroto *m* verde *Chile*, vainita *f Ven*; (*dried*) alubia *f*; **baked ~s** alubias *fpl* en salsa de tomate ►**to be full of ~s** *inf* estar lleno de vida; **old ~!** *inf* ¡viejo!; **to not have a ~** *inf* estar pelado; **to spill the ~s** *inf* descubrir el pastel, levantar la perdiz *RíoPl*

beanfeast ['biːnfiːst] *n Aus, Brit, inf* fiestorro *m*, festichola *f RíoPl*, fiestoca *f Chile* **bean sprout** *n* brote *m* de soja

bear¹ [beəʳ, *Am:* ber] *n* **1.** ZOOL oso, -a *m, f*; **to be like a ~ with a sore head** *fig, inf* estar de mala leche **2.** FIN bajista *mf*

bear² [beəʳ, *Am:* ber] <bore, borne> **I.** *vt* **1.** (*carry*) llevar; **to ~ arms** *form* portar armas **2.** (*display*) **to ~ a resemblance to ...** parecerse a... **3.** (*have, possess*) tener **4.** (*conduct*) **to ~ oneself** comportarse **5.** (*support: weight*) aguantar **6.** (*accept: cost*) correr con; (*responsibility*) cargar con **7.** (*endure: hardship, pain*) soportar; (*blame*) cargar con **8.** (*be fit for*) **what might have happened doesn't ~ thinking about** da miedo sólo de pensar lo que podía haber pasado; **he said something so awful that it doesn't ~ repeating** dijo algo tan horrible que no es como para repetirlo **9.** (*tolerate*) soportar, aguantar **10.** (*harbour*)

to ~ sb a grudge tener [*o* guardar] rencor a alguien; **she ~s him no ill will** no le desea ningún mal **11.** (*keep*) **to ~ sth/sb in mind** tener algo/a alguien presente **12.** (*give birth to*) dar a luz a; **she bore him a daughter** tuvo una hija con él **13.** AGR, BOT (*fruit*) dar **14.** FIN, ECON (*interest*) devengar **15.** (*give*) **to ~ testimony** [*o* **witness**] **to sth** atestiguar algo **II.** *vi* (*tend*) **to ~ east** dirigirse al este; **to ~ left/right** torcer a la izquierda/a la derecha

◆**bear down on** *vt* avanzar hacia; **the train was bearing down on her** el tren se le venía encima

◆**bear off** *vt* llevarse

◆**bear on** *vt* **1.** (*be relevant to*) tener que ver con **2.** (*have affect on*) afectar a **3.** (*pressurize*) hacer presión sobre

◆**bear up** *vi* aguantar

◆**bear with** *vi* tener paciencia con

bearable ['beərəbl, *Am:* 'berə-] *adj* soportable

beard [bɪəd, *Am:* bɪrd] **I.** *n* **1.** (*hair*) barba *f;* **to shave off one's ~** afeitarse la barba **2.** ZOOL barbas *fpl* **II.** *vt* HIST desafiar

bearded *adj* barbudo, -a

beardless ['bɪədləs, *Am:* 'bɪrd-] *adj* lampiño, -a; **to be ~** ser imberbe

bearer ['beərəʳ, *Am:* 'berɚ] *n* portador(a) *m(f)*

bearing ['beərɪŋ, *Am:* 'berɪŋ] *n* **1.** NAUT rumbo *m;* **to get one's ~s** *a. fig* orientarse; **to lose one's ~s** *a. fig* desorientarse **2.** (*behaviour*) comportamiento *m* **3.** (*posture*) porte *m* **4.** TECH cojinete *m* **5.** ARCHIT soporte *m* ►**to have some ~ on sth** tener que ver con algo

bearskin ['beəskɪn, *Am:* 'ber-] *n* **1.** (*bear fur*) piel *f* de oso **2.** (*military hat*) gorro *m* militar de piel de oso

beast [bi:st] *n* **1.** (*animal*) bestia *f;* **~ of burden** animal *m* de carga **2.** *inf* (*person*) animal *m;* **to be a ~ to sb** portarse como un animal con alguien **3.** *fig, inf* **a ~ of a day** un día asqueroso

beastly ['bi:stli] <-ier, -iest> *adj inf* horroroso, -a; **to be ~ to sb** portarse muy mal con alguien

beat [bi:t] <beat, beaten> **I.** *n* **1.** (*pulsation: of the heart*) latido *m;* (*of the pulse*) pulsación *f;* (*of a hammer*) martilleo *m* **2.** MUS (*stress*) tiempo *m;* (*stroke of the hand*) compás *m;* (*rhythm*) ritmo *m* **3.** *no pl* (*of a police officer*) ronda *f;* **to walk one's ~** hacer la ronda **II.** *adj inf* reventado, -a; **to be dead ~** *Brit* estar reventado [*o* molido] **III.** *vt* **1.** (*strike*) golpear; (*metal*) batir; (*carpet*) sacudir, festejar *Méx;* **to ~ sb black and blue** dar una paliza soberana a alguien; **to ~ a confession out of sb** hacer confesar a alguien a base de palos; **to ~ sb to death** matar a alguien a golpes **2.** (*wings*) batir **3.** GASTR batir **4.** (*cut through*) **to ~ a path through sth** abrirse paso en [*o* a través de] algo **5.** (*defeat*) derrotar, ganar; **Mary always ~s me at chess** Mary siempre me gana al ajedrez **6.** (*surpass: record*) batir **7.** (*arrive before*) **she ~ me to the door** llegó antes que yo a la puerta **8.** (*be better than*) superar; **to ~ sb for sth** superar a alguien en algo; **taking the bus sure ~s walking there** *inf* es mucho mejor coger el autobús que ir caminando **9.** MUS (*drum*) tocar ►**if you can't ~ them, join them** *prov* si no puedes con ellos, únete a ellos; **that ~s everything** *inf* ¡eso es el colmo!; **~ it!** *inf* ¡lárgate!, ¡mándate mudar! *RíoPl;* **it ~s me how/why ...** no llego a comprender cómo/por qué... **IV.** *vi* **1.** (*pound: rain*) caer; (*sea*) batir; (*person*) golpear **2.** (*pulsate, vibrate: heart, pulse*) latir; (*wings*) batir; (*drum*) redoblar; (*hammer*) martillear

◆**beat about** *vi,* **beat around** *vi Am* **to ~ the bush** andarse con rodeos, firuletear *Arg, Urug*

◆**beat back** *vt* rechazar

◆**beat down** **I.** *vi* (*hail, rain*) caer con fuerza; (*sun*) picar **II.** *vt* **1.** (*haggle*) **to beat the price down** bajar el precio; **I managed to beat him down to 50 pence** conseguí que me lo dejara por 50 peniques **2.** (*flatten: door*) derribar

◆**beat off** *vt* rechazar

◆**beat up** **I.** *vt* dar una paliza a **II.** *vi Am* **to ~ on sb** dar una paliza a alguien

beaten ['bi:tn, *Am:* 'bi:t̬n] **I.** *pp of* **beat** **II.** *adj* **1.** (*metal*) batido, -a **2.** **to be off the ~ track** [*o* **path** *Am*] (*isolated*) estar aislado

beater ['bi:təʳ, *Am:* 'bi:t̬ɚ] *n* **1.** GASTR batidora *f;* (*for carpets*) sacudidor *m* **2.** (*in hunting*) batidor(a) *m(f)*

beatific [bɪə'tɪfɪk] *adj liter* beatífico, -a

beatification [bɪˌætɪfɪ'keɪʃən, *Am:* -ˌæt̬ə-] *n* beatificación *f*

beatify [bɪ'ætɪfaɪ, *Am:* -'æt̬ə-] *vt* beatificar

beating ['bi:tɪŋ, *Am:* 'bi:t̬ɪŋ] *n* **1.** (*assault*) paliza *f,* cueriza *f AmL,* zumba *f AmL,* biaba *f Arg, Urug,* batida *f Perú, PRico,* fajada *f Arg;* **to give sb a ~** dar una paliza a alguien **2.** (*defeat*) derrota *f;* **to take a ~** recibir una paliza; **her time will take some ~** va a ser difícil superar su marca **3.** (*of the heart*) latido *m*

beautician [bju:'tɪʃən] *n* esteticista *mf*

beautiful ['bju:tɪfəl, *Am:* -t̬ə-] *adj* hermoso, -a, precioso, -a; (*sight, weather*) estupendo, -a; **small is ~** lo bueno viene en frascos pequeños

beautify ['bju:tɪfaɪ, *Am:* -t̬ə-] *vt* embellecer

beauty ['bju:ti, *Am:* -t̬i] <-ies> *n* **1.** *no pl* (*property*) belleza *f* **2.** (*beautiful woman*) belleza *f* **3.** *inf* (*specimen*) preciosidad *f,* maravilla *f* **4.** *inf* (*advantage*) **the ~ of ...** lo bueno de... ►**~ is in the eye of the beholder** *prov* todo depende del color del cristal con que se mira; **~ is only skin-deep** *prov* la belleza está en el interior

beauty contest *n,* **beauty pageant** *n* concurso *m* de belleza **beauty parlour** *n,* **beauty salon** *n,* **beauty shop** *n Am* salón *m* de belleza **beauty spot** *n* **1.** (*location*) lugar *m* pintoresco **2.** (*on the skin*) lunar *m*

beaver [ˈbiːvəʳ, *Am:* -vɚ] **I.** *n* **1.** ZOOL castor *m* **2.** *no pl* (*fur*) piel *f* de castor **3.** *fig, inf* (*person*) (**eager**) ~ persona *f* trabajadora **4.** *Am, vulg* (*female genitals*) coño *m*, panocha *f Col, Méx*, cola *f RíoPl* **II.** *vi inf* **to ~ away** trabajar como una hormiguita

becalmed [bɪˈkɑːmd] *adj* **to be ~** estar inmóvil (a causa de la falta de viento)

became [bɪˈkeɪm] *pt of* **become**

because [bɪˈkɒz, *Am:* -ˈkɑːz] **I.** *conj* porque; **just ~ he smiles doesn't mean he is in love** *inf* sólo porque sonríe no significa que esté enamorado; **~ I said that, I had to leave** como dije eso, tuve que irme; **not ~ I am sad but ...** no es porque esté triste, pero... **II.** *prep* **~ of** a causa de; **~ of me** por mi culpa; **~ of illness** por enfermedad; **~ of the fine weather** debido al buen tiempo

beck [bek] *n* **to be at sb's ~ and call** estar siempre a entera disposición de alguien

beckon [ˈbekən] **I.** *vt* llamar por señas; **to ~ sb over** hacer señas a alguien para que se acerque; **I ~ed her to follow** (**me**) le hice señas para que me siguiera **II.** *vi* **to ~ to sb** hacer señas a alguien; **I have to go because work ~s** me tengo que ir porque el trabajo me llama

become [bɪˈkʌm] <became, become> **I.** *vi* (+ *adj*) volverse; (+ *n*) llegar a ser; **to ~ angry** enfadarse; **to ~ famous/old** hacerse famoso/viejo; **to ~ sad/happy** ponerse triste/feliz; **to ~ convinced that ...** convencerse de que...; **to ~ interested in sth/sb** interesarse por algo/alguien **II.** *vt* **1.** (*suit*) favorecer **2.** (*befit*) ser apropiado para

becoming [bɪˈkʌmɪŋ] *adj* **1.** (*clothes, haircut*) favorecedor(a), sentador(a) *Arg, Chile* **2.** (*behaviour*) apropiado, -a

bed [bed] **I.** *n* **1.** (*furniture*) cama *f*; **to get out of ~** levantarse de la cama; **to go to ~** acostarse; **to go to ~ with sb** acostarse con alguien; **to make the ~** hacer la cama; **to put sb to ~** acostar a alguien **2.** (*flower patch*) arriate *m*, cantero *m RíoPl* **3.** (*base*) base *f* **4.** (*bottom: of the sea*) fondo *m*; (*of a river*) lecho *m* **5.** (*layer*) capa *f* ►**a ~ of <u>nails</u>** un calvario; **a ~ of <u>roses</u>** un lecho de rosas; **to get out of** [*o* **up on** *Am*] **the wrong <u>side</u> of the ~** levantarse con el pie izquierdo; **you have made your ~ and now you must <u>lie</u> in it** quien mal cama hace en ella se yace *prov*; **<u>early</u> to ~ and early to rise** (**makes a man healthy, wealthy and wise**) *prov* a quien madruga, Dios le ayuda *prov* **II.** <-dd-> *vt* **1.** (*embed*) asentar **2.** *form* (*have sex with*) acostarse con

◆**bed down** *vi* acostarse

BEd [biːˈed] *abbr of* **Bachelor of Education** Ldo., -a *m, f* en Magisterio

bed and breakfast *n* (*hotel*) pensión *f* familiar; (*service*) alojamiento *m* y desayuno

bedbug [ˈbedbʌg] *n* chinche *f*

bedclothes [ˈbedkləʊðz] *npl* ropa *f* de cama, cobijas *fpl AmL*

bedding [ˈbedɪŋ] *n no pl* **1.** (*bed clothes*) ropa *f* de cama **2.** (*for an animal*) cama *f*

bedecked [bɪˈdekt] *adj* **to be ~ with ...** estar adornado con...

bedevil [bɪˈdevəl] <*Brit:* -ll-, *Am:* -l-> *vt* **to be ~ed with** [*o* **by**] **problems** estar plagado de problemas

bedfellow [ˈbedˌfeləʊ, *Am:* -oʊ] *n* **to make strange ~s** hacer una extraña pareja

bedlam [ˈbedləm] *n no pl* alboroto *m*

bedlinen [ˈbedˌlɪnɪn, *Am:* -ən] *n* ropa *f* de cama

Bedouin [ˈbedʊɪn] **I.** *adj* beduino, -a **II.** <-(s)> *n* beduino, -a *m, f*

bedraggled [bɪˈdrægld] *adj* **1.** (*wet*) empapado, -a **2.** (*dishevelled: person, appearance*) desaliñado, -a; (*hair*) despeinado, -a

bedridden [ˈbedˌrɪdn] *adj* postrado, -a en cama

bedrock [ˈbedrɒk, *Am:* -rɑːk] *n no pl* **1.** GEO roca *f* firme **2.** *fig* cimientos *mpl*, base *f*

bedroom [ˈbedrʊm, *Am:* -ruːm] *n* dormitorio *m*, recámara *f Méx*

bedside [ˈbedsaɪd] *n no pl* cabecera *f*

bedside lamp *n* lámpara *f* de noche **bedside rug** *n* alfombrilla *f* de cama **bedside table** *n* mesita *f* de noche, nochero *m Col, Chile, Urug*, búro *m Méx*

bedsit [ˈbedsɪt] *n Brit*, **bed-sitting room** *n Brit* habitación *f* de alquiler

bedsore [ˈbedsɔːʳ, *Am:* -sɔːr] *n* escara *f*, úlcera *f* de decúbito

bedspread [ˈbedspred] *n* cubrecama *m*, colcha *f*

bedstead [ˈbedsted] *n* armazón *m o f* de cama, catre *m CSur*

bedtime [ˈbedtaɪm] *n no pl* hora *f* de acostarse; **it's** (**way**) **past your ~** hace rato que deberías estar durmiendo

bee [biː] *n* **1.** ZOOL abeja *f* **2.** *Am, Aus* (*group*) círculo *m*; **sewing ~** círculo de costura ►**to have a ~ in one's <u>bonnet</u> about sth** tener algo metido entre ceja y ceja; **the ~s' <u>knees</u>** *Brit, inf* el no va más; **to be a <u>busy</u> ~** *iron* estar muy atareado

beech [biːtʃ] *n* haya *f*

beechnut [ˈbiːtʃnʌt] *n* hayuco *m*

beef [biːf] **I.** *n no pl* **1.** GASTR carne *f* de ternera [*o* de res *AmC, Méx*]; **minced ~** carne de ternera picada; **roast ~** rosbif *m* **2.** *inf* (*complaint*) queja *f* **II.** *vi inf* **to ~ about sth** quejarse de algo

beefburger [ˈbiːfˌbɜːgəʳ, *Am:* -ˌbɜːrgɚ] *n* hamburguesa *f*

beefcake [ˈbiːfkeɪk] *n inf* machote *m*, cachas *m inv*

beefeater [ˈbiːfˌiːtəʳ, *Am:* -t̬ɚ] *n* alabardero *m* de la Torre de Londres

beefsteak [ˌbiːfˈsteɪk] *n* bistec *m*, churrasco *m AmS*, bife *m RíoPl*

beefy [ˈbiːfi] <-ier, -iest> *adj inf* fornido, -a, cachas

beehive [ˈbiːhaɪv] *n* colmena *f*

beekeeper ['biː,kiːpəʳ, *Am:* -pɚ] *n* apicultor(a) *m(f)*

beeline ['biːlaɪn] *n no pl, inf* **to make a ~ for sth/sb** ir derechito a algo/alguien

been [biːn, *Am:* bɪn] *pp of* **be**

beep [biːp] **I.** *n* pitido *m* **II.** *vi* pitar

beeper ['biːpəʳ, *Am:* -pɚ] *n* localizador *m*, busca *m inf*

beer [bɪəʳ, *Am:* bɪr] *n* cerveza *f*

beer garden *n* terraza *f* de verano **beer mat** *n* posavasos *m inv*

beery ['bɪəri, *Am:* 'bɪr-] *adj* de cerveza

beeswax ['biːzwæks] *n* cera *f* de abeja

beet [biːt] *n* **1.** (*sugar beet*) remolacha *f* (azucarera) **2.** *Am* (*beetroot*) remolacha *f*, betabel *f Méx*

beetle ['biːtl, *Am:* -t̬l] *n* escarabajo *m*
 ◆**beetle off** *vi inf* marcharse

beetroot ['biːtruːt] *n* remolacha *f*, betabel *f Méx;* **to go** [*o* **turn**] **as red as a ~** ponerse rojo como un tomate **beet sugar** *n* azúcar *m* de remolacha

befit [bɪ'fɪt] <-tt-> *vt form* corresponder a; **as ~s a princess** como corresponde a una princesa

befitting *adj form* conveniente

before [bɪ'fɔːʳ, *Am:* -'fɔːr] **I.** *prep* **1.** (*earlier*) antes de; **to leave ~ sb** salir antes que alguien; **~ doing sth** antes de hacer algo; **to wash one's hands ~ lunch** lavarse las manos antes de la comida **2.** (*in front of*) delante de; **~ my house** delante de mi casa; **to bow ~ sb** inclinarse ante alguien; **~ our eyes** ante nuestros ojos **3.** (*preceding*) **C comes ~ D** la C va delante de la D; **just ~ the bus stop** justo antes de la parada del autobús **4.** (*having priority*) antes que; **~ everything** antes que nada; **to put sth ~ sth else** anteponer algo a algo **5.** (*as future task*) **to have sth ~ one** tener algo ante sí **II.** *adv* **1.** (*previously*) antes; **I've seen it ~** lo he visto anteriormente; **the day ~** el día anterior; **two days ~** dos días antes; **as ~** como antes **2.** (*in front*) **this word and the one ~** esta palabra y la anterior **III.** *conj* antes de que *+subj;* **he spoke ~ she went out** habló antes de que ella se fuera; **he had a glass ~ he went** se tomó una copa antes de irse; **it was a week ~ he came** pasó una semana antes de que llegara; **he'd die ~ he'd tell the truth** preferiría morir a decir la verdad

beforehand [bɪ'fɔːhænd, *Am:* -'fɔːr-] *adv* de antemano

befriend [bɪ'frend] *vt* hacerse amigo de

beg [beg] <-gg-> **I.** *vt* (*request*) suplicar, rogar; **to ~ sb to do sth** suplicar a alguien que haga algo; **to ~ sb's pardon** pedir disculpas a alguien; **I ~ your pardon!** ¡disculpe!; **I ~ to inform you that ...** *form* tengo el gusto de comunicarle que... **II.** *vi* **1.** (*seek charity*) pedir (limosna); **to ~ on the streets** mendigar por las calles; **to ~ for sth** pedir algo **2.** (*request*) implorar; **I ~ of you** ¡te lo imploro!; **to ~ for clemency** implorar clemencia; **I ~ to differ** *form* no estoy de acuerdo **3.** (*sit up and request: dog*) pedir ▶**there are jobs going ~ging** *inf* hay trabajos a patadas

began [bɪ'gæn] *pt of* **begin**

beget [bɪ'get] <begot, begotten> *vt form* engendrar

beggar ['begəʳ, *Am:* -ɚ] **I.** *vt* **to ~ belief** parecer absolutamente inverosímil; **to ~ description** resultar indescriptible **II.** *n* **1.** (*poor person*) mendigo, -a *m, f*, limosnero, -a *m, f AmL* **2.** (*rascal*) pilluelo, -a *m, f* ▶**~s can't be choosers** *prov* a buen hambre no hay pan duro *prov*

begin [bɪ'gɪn] <began, begun> **I.** *vt* empezar, comenzar; **to ~ a conversation** entablar una conversación; **to ~ doing sth** empezar a hacer algo; **to ~ work** empezar a trabajar **II.** *vi* empezar, comenzar; **the film ~s at eight** la película comienza a las ocho; **to ~ with ...** al principio...; (*enumeration*) primero...; **"well" he began ...** "bueno", comenzó...

beginner [bɪ'gɪnəʳ, *Am:* -ɚ] *n* principiante *mf;* **~s' class** curso *m* para principiantes; **~'s luck** la suerte del principiante

beginning **I.** *n* **1.** (*start*) principio *m*, comienzo *m*, empiezo *m Arg, Col, Ecua, Guat;* **at** [*o* **in**] **the ~** al principio; **from ~ to end** de principio a fin **2.** (*origin*) origen *m;* **the ~s of humanity** los albores de la humanidad **II.** *adj* inicial; **~ stage** fase *f* inicial

begonia [bɪ'gəʊniə, *Am:* -'goʊnjə] *n* begoña *f*

begot [bɪ'gɒt, *Am:* -'gɑːt] *pt, pp of* **beget**

begotten [bɪ'gɒtn, *Am:* -'gɑːt̬n] *pp of* **beget**

begrudge [bɪ'grʌdʒ] *vt* **1.** (*envy*) tener envidia a **2.** (*resent*) **to ~ doing sth** hacer algo de mala gana

begun [bɪ'gʌn] *pp of* **begin**

behalf [bɪ'hɑːf, *Am:* -'hæf] *n no pl* **on ~ of sb/sth** (*for*) en beneficio de alguien/algo; (*from*) de parte de alguien/algo

behave [bɪ'heɪv] *vi* **1.** (*act*) comportarse; (*in a proper manner*) conducirse; **to ~ badly/well** portarse mal/bien; **~!** ¡pórtate bien! **2.** (*function*) funcionar

behavior *n no pl, Am, Aus,* **behaviour** [bɪ'heɪvjəʳ, *Am:* -vjɚ] *n no pl, Aus, Brit* comportamiento *m;* **to be on one's best ~** portarse lo mejor posible

behavioral *adj Am, Aus,* **behavioural** *adj Aus, Brit* de la conducta

behaviorism *n Am, Aus,* **behaviourism** [bɪ'heɪvjərɪzəm] *n no pl, Aus, Brit* conductismo *m*

behaviour pattern *n* patrón *m* de conducta

behead [bɪ'hed] *vt* decapitar

behind [bɪ'haɪnd] **I.** *prep* **1.** (*to the rear of*) detrás de; **right ~ sb/sth** justo detrás de alguien/algo; **he walks ~ me** camina detrás de mí; **~ the wheel** al volante; **a face ~ a mask** un rostro detrás de una máscara **2.** *fig* **who is ~ that scheme?** ¿quién está detrás de ese plan?; **there is somebody ~ this** hay alguien detrás de todo esto **3.** (*in support of*) **to be ~ sb/sth** (**all the way**) estar con alguien/algo (hasta el final) **4.** (*late for*) **~ time** retrasado; **to be ~ schedule** ir con retraso **5.** (*less advanced*) **to be ~ sb/the times** estar atrasado con respecto a alguien/la época **II.** *adv* **1.** (*at the back*) por detrás; **to fall ~** (*be slower*) quedarse atrás; (*in work, studies*) atrasarse; **to come from ~** venir desde atrás; **a blow from ~** un golpe por detrás; **to leave sb ~** dejar a alguien atrás; **to stay ~** quedarse atrás **2.** (*overdue*) **to be ~** retrasarse; **he is a long way ~** está muy retrasado; **to be ~** (**in sth**) estar atrasado (en algo) **III.** *n inf* trasero *m;* **to get off one's ~** mover el culo

behindhand [bɪˈhaɪndhænd] *adv* atrasado, -a; **to be ~** estar atrasado

behold [bɪˈhəʊld, *Am:* -ˈhoʊld] *vt* contemplar

beige [beɪʒ] *adj* beige

being [ˈbiːɪŋ] **I.** *n* **1.** (*creature*) ser *m* **2.** (*life*) vida *f;* **to come into ~** nacer **3.** (*soul*) alma *f* **II.** *pres p of* **be III.** *adj after n* **for the time ~** por el momento

Belarus [beləˈrʌs] *n* Bielorrusia *f*

belated [bɪˈleɪtɪd, *Am:* -t̬ɪd] *adj* tardío, -a

belch [beltʃ] **I.** *n* eructo *m* **II.** *vi* eructar **III.** *vt* vomitar; **to ~ clouds of smoke** arrojar nubes de humo

beleaguered [bɪˈliːgəʳd, *Am:* -gɚd] *adj* (*city*) asediado, -a; (*person, government*) acosado, -a

belfry [ˈbelfri] *n* campanario *m*

Belgian [ˈbeldʒən] **I.** *adj* belga **II.** *n* belga *mf*

Belgium [ˈbeldʒəm] *n* Bélgica *f*

belie [bɪˈlaɪ] *irr vt* **1.** (*disprove*) desmentir **2.** (*conceal*) ocultar

belief [bɪˈliːf] *n* **1.** REL creencia *f* **2.** (*conviction*) opinión *f;* **it is my firm ~ that ...** creo firmemente que...; **to the best of my ~** *Brit* que yo sepa; **to be beyond ~** ser increíble; **in the ~ that ...** con la convicción de que...

believable [bɪˈliːvəbl] *adj* creíble

believe [bɪˈliːv] **I.** *vt* creer; **~ you me!** ¡créeme!; **would you ~ it?** ¡no lo puedo creer!; **she couldn't ~ her eyes** no podía dar crédito a sus ojos; **I can't ~ how ...** me cuesta creer cómo...; **I'll ~ it when I see it!** ¡lo creeré cuando lo vea!; **~ it or not, ...** aunque parezca mentira... **II.** *vi* creer; **to ~ in sth** creer en algo; (*support*) ser partidario de algo

believer [bɪˈliːvəʳ, *Am:* -vɚ] *n* **1.** REL creyente *mf* **2.** (*supporter*) partidario, -a *m, f;* **to be a ~ in sth** ser partidario de algo

belittle [bɪˈlɪtl, *Am:* -ˈlɪt̬-] *vt* menospreciar

Belize [bəˈliːz] *n* Belice *m*

Belizean [bəˈliːzɪən] **I.** *adj* beliceño, -a **II.** *n* beliceño, -a *m, f*

bell [bel] *n* **1.** (*of a church*) campana *f;* (*handbell*) campanilla *f;* (*on a hat, cat*) cascabel *m;* (*of a bicycle, door*) timbre *m* **2.** (*signal*) campanada *f;* **to give sb a ~** *Brit, inf* llamar a alguien (por teléfono) ►**as clear as a ~** más claro que el agua; **as sound as a ~** fuerte como un roble; **his name/face rings a ~** me suena su nombre/cara

belladonna [ˌbeləˈdɒnə, *Am:* -ˈdɑːnə] *n no pl* belladona *f*

bellboy [ˈbelbɔɪ] *n* botones *m inv*

bellicose [ˈbelɪkəʊs, *Am:* -koʊs] *adj* belicoso, -a; **to be in a ~ mood** tener ganas de pelear

belligerent [bɪˈlɪdʒərənt] *adj* beligerante

bell jar *n* campana *f* de vidrio

bellow [ˈbeləʊ, *Am:* -oʊ] **I.** *vt* gritar **II.** *vi* bramar **III.** *n* grito *m;* **to give a ~ of pain** lanzar un grito de dolor

bellows [ˈbeləʊz, *Am:* -oʊz] *npl* fuelle *m;* **a pair of ~** un fuelle

bell push *n Brit* pulsador *m* de timbre

belly [ˈbeli] <-ies> *n inf* barriga *f,* guata *f Chile* ►**to have fire in one's ~** tener mucho celo idealista; **to go** [*o* **turn** *Am*] **~ up** *inf* quebrar

bellyache *inf* **I.** *n* dolor *m* de barriga; **to have a ~** tener dolor(es) de barriga **II.** *vi* quejarse

belly button *n inf* ombligo *m* **belly dancer** *n* bailarina *f* de la danza del vientre **bellyflop** *n* panzazo *m*

belong [bɪˈlɒŋ, *Am:* -ˈlɑːŋ] *vi* **1.** (*be property of, be from*) **to ~ to sb/sth** pertenecer a alguien/algo **2.** (*be a member of*) **to ~ to** (*club*) ser socio de; (*party*) estar afiliado a **3.** (*have a place*) **where do these spoons ~?** ¿dónde pongo estas cucharas?; **this doesn't ~ here** esto no va aquí; **I feel I don't ~ here** no me encuentro a gusto aquí **4.** (*should be*) deber estar **5.** (*match*) **they ~ together** están hechos el uno para el otro

belongings *npl* pertenencias *fpl*

Belorussian [beləˈrʌʃən] **I.** *adj* bielorruso, -a **II.** *n* **1.** (*person*) bielorruso, -a *m, f* **2.** *no pl* LING bielorruso *m*

beloved[1] [bɪˈlʌvɪd] *n no pl* amado, -a *m, f*

beloved[2] [bɪˈlʌvd] *adj* amado, -a; **her ~ husband** su amado marido; **to be ~ by sb** ser amado por alguien

below [bɪˈləʊ, *Am:* -ˈloʊ] **I.** *prep* **1.** (*lower than, underneath*) debajo de, bajo; **~ the table/surface** debajo de la mesa/superficie; **~ us** debajo de nosotros; **~ sea level** por debajo del nivel del mar; **the sun sinks ~ the horizon** el sol se hunde bajo el horizonte; **to bend ~ sth** agacharse bajo algo **2.** GEO **London is ~ Oxford** Londres está debajo de Oxford; **the river ~ the town** el río abajo del pueblo **3.** (*less than*) **~ average** por debajo de la media; **~ freezing** bajo cero; **it's 4 degrees ~ zero** estamos a 4 grados bajo cero; **children ~ the age of twelve** menores de doce años **4.** (*inferior to*) **to be ~ sb in rank** tener un rango por debajo de alguien; **to work ~ sb** trabajar bajo (las órdenes de) alguien **5.** (*of a lower standard than*) **to be ~ sb** no ser digno de alguien; **to marry ~ oneself** casarse por debajo de sus expectativas **II.** *adv* abajo; **the family** ~ la familia de abajo; **from** ~ desde abajo; **see** ~ (*in a text*) ver más adelante

belt [belt] **I.** *n* **1.** FASHION cinturón *m;* **to fasten one's** ~ abrocharse el cinturón **2.** TECH correa *f* **3.** (*area*) zona *f* **4.** *inf* (*punch*) golpe *m* ►**to tighten one's** ~ apretarse el cinturón; **to have some experience under one's** ~ tener algo de experiencia a sus espaldas **II.** *vt* **1.** (*secure with a belt*) ceñir **2.** *inf* (*hit*) zurrar **III.** *vi inf* correr a todo tren; **to** ~ **along** ir como una bala

◆**belt out** *vt inf* **to** ~ **a song** cantar una canción a pleno pulmón

◆**belt up** *vi* **1.** AUTO abrocharse el cinturón **2.** *inf* ~**!** ¡cierra el pico!

bemoan [bɪ'məʊn, *Am:* -'moʊn] *vt form* lamentar; **to** ~ **one's fate** quejarse de su destino

bemused [bɪ'mju:zd] *adj* desconcertado, -a; **a** ~ **look** una mirada de desconcierto

bench [bentʃ] *n* **1.** (*seat*) banco *m* **2.** SPORTS **the** ~ el banquillo **3.** LAW **the** ~ la judicatura; **to serve on the** ~ actuar como juez **4.** *pl, Brit* POL escaños *mpl* **5.** *Aus* (*worktop*) encimera *f*

benchmark ['bentʃma:k, *Am:* -ma:rk] *n* punto *m* de referencia

bend [bend] <bent, bent> **I.** *n* **1.** (*of a river, road*) curva *f;* (*of a pipe*) codo *m;* **to take a** ~ tomar una curva **2.** *pl, inf* (*illness*) apoplejía *f* por descompresión ►**to go/be round the** ~ *inf* volverse/estar loco **II.** *vi* **1.** (*move*) doblarse **2.** (*change direction*) hacer una curva **III.** *vt* **1.** (*move: arms, legs*) doblar; (*head*) inclinar **2.** (*change*) **to** ~ **sb to one's will** doblar a alguien a su voluntad **3.** (*interpret*) **to** ~ **the rules** interpretar las reglas a su manera

◆**bend back** *vt* doblar hacia atrás

◆**bend down** *vi* inclinarse

◆**bend over** *vi* inclinarse

bended ['bendɪd] *adj form* doblado, -a; **on** ~ **knee** de rodillas; **to go down on** ~ **knee** arrodillarse

beneath [bɪ'ni:θ] **I.** *prep* **1.** (*lower than, underneath*) debajo de, bajo; ~ **the table/surface** debajo de la mesa/superficie; ~ **us** debajo de nosotros; **the sun sinks** ~ **the horizon** el sol se hunde bajo el horizonte **2.** (*inferior to*) **to be** ~ **sb in rank** tener un rango por debajo de alguien **3.** (*lower standard than*) **to marry** ~ **one's self** casarse por debajo de sus expectativas; **to be** ~ **sb** no ser digno de alguien **II.** *adv* abajo

benediction [ˌbenɪ'dɪkʃən] *n form* bendición *f*

benefactor ['benɪfæktəʳ] *n* benefactor *m*

benefactress ['benɪfæktrɪs] *n* benefactora *f*

beneficence [bɪ'nefɪsns] *n no pl* beneficencia *f*

beneficent [bɪ'nefɪsnt] *adj form* (*benign*) benéfico, -a; (*charitable*) caritativo, -a

beneficiary [ˌbenɪ'fɪʃəri] *n* <-ies> beneficiario, -a *m, f*

benefit ['benɪfɪt] **I.** *n* **1.** (*profit*) beneficio *m;* **to derive (much)** ~ **from sth** sacar (mucho) provecho a algo; **I didn't derive much** ~ **from school** no aprendí gran cosa en la escuela; **for the** ~ **of sb** a beneficio de alguien; **to the** ~ **of sth/sb** para beneficio de algo/alguien **2.** (*welfare payment*) subsidio *m* **II.** <-t- *o* -tt-> *vi* **to** ~ **from sth** beneficiarse de algo **III.** <-t- *o* -tt-> *vt* beneficiar

Benelux ['benɪlʌks] *n* **the** ~ **countries** los países del Benelux

Bengali [beŋ'gɔ:li] **I.** *adj* bengalí **II.** *n* bengalí *mf*

Benin [ben'i:n] *n* Benín *m*

Beninese [beni'ni:z] **I.** *adj* de Benín **II.** *n* habitante *mf* de Benín

bent [bent] **I.** *pt, pp of* **bend** **II.** *n* **1.** (*aptitude*) inclinación *f;* **to have a** ~ **for sth** tener una inclinación por algo; **to follow one's** ~ obrar de acuerdo a sus inclinaciones **2.** (*preference*) afición *f* **III.** *adj* **1.** (*not straight*) torcido, -a **2.** (*determined*) **to be** ~ **on (doing) sth** estar empeñado en (hacer) algo **3.** *inf* (*corrupt*) corrupto, -a

benzene ['benzi:n] *n no pl* benceno *m*

benzine ['benzi:n] *n* bencina *f*

bequeath [bɪ'kwi:ð] *vt* legar

bequest [bɪ'kwest] *n* legado *m*

berate [bɪ'reɪt] *vt form* regañar

bereave [bɪ'ri:v] *vt* **he has recently been** ~**d of his son** acaba de perder a su hijo

bereaved *n* **the** ~ la familia del difunto

bereavement [bɪ'ri:vmənt] *n* muerte *f* (de un familiar); **to suffer a** ~ sufrir la pérdida de un familiar

bereft [bɪ'reft] *adj form* **to be** ~ **of sth** estar privado de algo; **to feel** ~ sentirse desolado

beret ['bereɪ, *Am:* bə'reɪ] *n* boina *f*

Bermuda [bɜ:'mju:də, *Am:* bɚ-] *n* las Bermudas

Bermuda shorts [bɜ:'mju:dəʃɔ:ts, *Am:* bɚ- ʃɔ:rts] *n* bermudas *fpl*

Bern [bɜ:n, *Am:* bɜ:rn] *n* Berna *f*

berry ['beri] <-ies> *n* baya *f*

berserk [bə'sɜ:k, *Am:* bɚ'sɜ:rk] *adj* **1.** (*frantic*) enloquecido, -a *inf* **2.** (*angry*) furioso, -a; **to go** ~ enfurecerse

berth [bɜ:θ, *Am:* bɜ:rθ] **I.** *n* **1.** (*on a ship*) camarote *m* **2.** (*on a train*) litera *f* **3.** (*in a harbour*) amarradero *m* **4.** *fig* **to give sb a wide** ~ evitar a alguien **II.** *vt, vi* NAUT atracar

beseech [bɪ'si:tʃ] <beseeched, besought> *vt form* **to** ~ **sb to do sth** suplicar a alguien que haga algo

beseeching *adj* suplicante

beset [bɪ'set] <beset, beset> *vt* acosar; **to be** ~ **by sth** estar acosado por algo; ~ **by worries** atormentado por las preocupaciones

beside [bɪ'saɪd] *prep* **1.** (*next to*) al lado de; **right** ~ **sb/sth** justo al lado de alguien/algo **2.** (*together with*) ~ **sb** junto a alguien **3.** (*in comparison to*) frente a **4.** (*overwhelmed*) **to be** ~ **oneself** estar fuera de sí **5.** (*irrelevant to*) **to be** ~ **the point** no venir al caso

besides [bɪ'saɪdz] I. *prep* 1. (*in addition to*) además de 2. (*except for*) excepto II. *adv* 1. (*in addition*) además 2. (*else*) **nothing** ~ nada más

besiege [bɪ'siːdʒ] *vt* 1. (*city*) sitiar 2. (*with questions, complaints*) acosar

besmirch [bɪ'smɜːtʃ, *Am:* -'smɜːrtʃ] *vt liter* manchar; **to ~ sb's good name** mancillar el buen nombre de alguien

besotted [bɪ'sɒtɪd, *Am:* 'sɑːṯɪd] *adj* enamorado, -a; **to be ~ with sth** estar obsesionado con algo; **to be ~ with sb** estar chalado por alguien *inf*

besought [bɪ'sɔːt, *Am:* -'sɑːt] *pt, pp of* **beseech**

best [best] I. *adj superl of* **good** mejor; **the ~** el/la mejor; **the ~ days of my life** los mejores días de mi vida; **the ~ part** (*the majority*) la mayor parte; **may the ~ man win** que gane el mejor; **with the ~ will** con la mejor voluntad II. *adv superl of* **well** mejor; **the ~** lo mejor; **we'd ~ stay here** lo mejor es quedarse aquí; **as ~ you can** lo mejor que puedas; **do as you think ~** haz lo que te parezca mejor III. *n no pl* 1. (*the finest*) **all the ~!** *inf* (*congratulation*) ¡felicidades!; (*end of letter*) un abrazo; **to be the ~ of friends** ser los mejores amigos; **to bring out the ~ in sb** sacar lo mejor de alguien; **to turn out for the ~** ir para bien; **to wear one's Sunday ~** llevar el traje de los domingos; **to the ~ of my knowledge** que yo sepa; **at ~** como mucho, a lo mucho *Méx* 2. SPORTS récord *m* IV. *vt form* vencer

bestial ['bestɪəl, *Am:* -tʃl] *adj* bestial

bestiality [ˌbestɪ'æləti, *Am:* -tʃi'æləṯi] *n no pl* 1. (*behaviour*) bestialidad *f* 2. LAW (*sexual*) zoofilia *f*

bestir [bɪ'stɜːʳ, *Am:* -'stɜːr] <-rr-> *vt form* **to ~ oneself to do sth** avivarse para hacer algo

best man *n* padrino *m* de boda

bestow [bɪ'stəʊ, *Am:* -'stoʊ] *vt form* **to ~ sth on sb** otorgar algo a alguien; **to ~ a favour on sb** conceder un favor a alguien

bestowal [bɪ'stəʊəl, *Am:* -'stoʊ-] *n no pl, form* concesión *f*

bestseller ['bestseləʳ, *Am:* -ɚ] *n* éxito *m* de ventas

bet [bet] <bet *o* -ted, bet *o* -ted> I. *n* apuesta *f;* **it is a fair** [*o* **safe**] **~ that ...** es casi seguro que... *+subj;* **to be the best ~** ser la mejor opción; **to make a ~ with sb** hacer una apuesta con alguien; **to place a ~ on sth** apostar por algo ►**to hedge one's ~s** cubrirse contra un riesgo II. *vt* apostar; **I ~ you don't!** ¡a que no lo haces! III. *vi* apostar; **to ~ on sth** apostar por algo; **I wouldn't ~ on it** yo no estaría tan seguro ►**I'll ~!** ¡seguro!; **you ~!** *inf* ¡ya lo creo!

beta ['biːtə, *Am:* 'beɪṯə] *n* beta *f;* **~ version of a programme** INFOR versión *f* beta de un programa

betablocker ['biːtɜ'blɒkəʳ, *Am:* 'beɪːṯə'blɑːkɚ] *n* MED betabloqueador *m*, betabloqueante *m*

beta testing *n* INFOR pruebas *fpl* beta **beta version** *n* INFOR versión *f* beta

betray [bɪ'treɪ] *vt* 1. (*be disloyal to*) traicionar; **to ~ a promise** romper una promesa; **to ~ sb's trust** defraudar la confianza de alguien; **to be ~ed by sb** ser traicionado por alguien; **he ~ed his wife** engañó a su esposa 2. (*reveal*) delatar; **to ~ sth to sb** revelar algo a alguien; **to ~ one's ignorance** demostrar ignorancia

betrayal [bɪ'treɪəl] *n* 1. (*disloyalty*) traición *f;* **an act of ~** una traición 2. (*revelation*) revelación *f*

better[1] ['betəʳ, *Am:* 'beṯɚ] I. *adj comp of* **good** mejor; **to be ~** MED estar mejor; **~ than nothing** mejor que nada; **to appeal to sb's ~ nature** apelar a la bondad de alguien; **~ luck next time** mejor suerte la próxima vez; **it's ~ that way** es mejor así II. *adv comp of* **well** mejor; **I like this ~** me gusta más esto; **there is nothing I like ~ than ...** nada me gusta más que...; **It'll be ~ to tell her** más vale decírselo; **you had ~ go** mejor que te vayas; **to think ~ of sth** cambiar de opinión respecto a algo; **or ~ still ...** o mejor... III. *n no pl* 1. el/la mejor; **not to have seen ~** no haber visto nada mejor; **to change for the ~** cambiar para bien; **the sooner, the ~** cuanto antes, mejor; **so much the ~** tanto mejor 2. *pl* **my ~s** mis superiores ►**for ~ or (for) worse** para bien o para mal; **to get the ~ of sb** vencer a alguien IV. *vt* vencer; **to ~ oneself** prosperar; (*further one's knowledge*) superarse

better[2] *n*, **bettor** ['betəʳ, *Am:* 'beṯɚ] *n Am* apostador(a) *m(f)*

betterment ['betəmənt] *n no pl* mejoramiento *m*

betting ['betɪŋ] *n no pl* apuestas *fpl* ►**the ~ is that ...** lo más probable es que... *+subj*

betting office *n*, **betting shop** *n Brit* agencia *f* de apuestas

between [bɪ'twiːn] I. *prep* entre; **to eat ~ meals** comer entre horas; **~ now and tomorrow** entre hoy y mañana; **~ the two of us** entre nosotros dos; **a misunderstanding ~ the couple** un malentendido entre la pareja; **nothing will come ~ them** nada se interpondrá entre ellos; **the 3 children have £10 ~ them** entre los 3 niños tienen 10 libras; **the mule is a cross ~ a donkey and a horse** la mula es un cruce entre un burro y un caballo II. *adv* (**in**) **~** en medio de; (*time*) a mitad de

betwixt [bɪ'twɪkst] *adv* **between and ~** entre lo uno y lo otro

bevel ['bevl] I. <*Brit:* -ll-, *Am* -l-> *vt* biselar II. *n* bisel *m*

beverage ['bevərɪdʒ] *n form* bebida *f;* **alcoholic ~s** bebidas alcohólicas

bevy ['bevi] *n Brit* (*of birds*) bandada *f; inf* (*of people*) grupo *m*

bewail [bɪ'weɪl] *vt form* lamentar

beware [bɪ'weəʳ, *Am:* 'wer] *vi* tener cuidado;

B

~! ¡ten cuidado!; **~ of pickpockets!** ¡cuidado con los carteristas!
bewilder [bɪ'wɪldəʳ, *Am:* -dɚ] *vt* desconcertar
bewildered *adj* desconcertado, -a
bewildering *adj* desconcertante
bewilderment *n no pl* desconcierto *m,* azoro *m Méx, Perú, PRico*
bewitch [bɪ'wɪtʃ] *vt* **1.** (*place magic charm on*) hechizar **2.** (*fascinate*) fascinar
bewitching *adj* fascinante
beyond [bɪ'jɒnd, *Am:* -'ɑːnd] **I.** *prep* **1.** (*on the other side of*) más allá de; **~ the mountain** al otro lado de la montaña; **don't go ~ the line!** ¡no traspases la línea!; **~ the wall** más allá del muro; **the regions ~ the sea** las regiones más allá del mar; **from ~ the grave** desde el más allá **2.** (*after*) después de; (*more than*) más de; **~ 8:00** después de las 8:00; **to stay ~ a week** quedarse más de una semana; **~ lunchtime** después del almuerzo **3.** (*further than*) más allá de; **to see/go (way) ~ sth** ver/ir (mucho) más allá de algo; **it goes ~ a joke** va más allá de una broma; **~ the reach of sb** fuera del alcance de alguien; **~ belief/hope** más allá de cualquier creencia/esperanza; **he is ~ help** *a. iron* es un caso perdido; **~ the shadow of a doubt** sin lugar a dudas; **to go ~ the point of no return** ir más allá de todo regreso **4.** (*too difficult for*) **to be ~ sb** (*theory, idea*) ser demasiado difícil de entender para alguien; **that is ~ me** se me escapa; **this is ~ my abilities** esto sobrepasa mis capacidades **5.** (*above*) por encima de; **to live ~ one's means** vivir por encima de sus posibilidades; **to value sth above and ~ all else** valorar algo por encima de todo **6.** *with neg or interrog* (*except for*) fuera de, excepto **II.** *adv* **1.** (*past*) **the house ~** la casa de más allá **2.** (*future*) **the next ten years and ~** los próximos diez años y más **III.** *n* **the ~** REL el más allá
biannual [ˌbaɪ'ænjʊəl] *adj* semestral
bias ['baɪəs] **I.** *n* **1.** (*prejudice*) prejuicio *m;* **to have ~es against sb/sth** ser parcial contra alguien/algo **2.** *no pl* (*one-sidedness*) parcialidad *f;* **without ~** imparcial **3.** (*tendency*) tendencia *f;* **to have a ~ towards sth** sentir inclinación por algo **4.** *no pl* (*in sewing*) sesgo *m* **II.** <*Brit:* -ss-, *Am:* -s> *vt* influir; **to ~ sb towards/against sb** predisponer a alguien a favor de/en contra de alguien
biased *adj Am,* **biassed** *adj Brit* parcial; **~ in sb's favour** predispuesto a favor de alguien; **~ opinions** opiniones parciales
bib [bɪb] *n* babero *m*
Bible ['baɪbl] *n* **the ~** la Biblia
biblical ['bɪblɪkl] *adj* bíblico, -a
bibliographer [ˌbɪblɪ'ɒgrəfəʳ, *Am:* -'ɑːgrəfɚ] *n* bibliógrafo, -a *m, f*
bibliographic(al) [ˌbɪblɪɒ'græfɪk(l)] *adj* bibliográfico, -a
bibliography [ˌbɪblɪ'ɒgrəfi, *Am:* -'ɑːgrə-] <-ies> *n* bibliografía *f*
bibliophile ['bɪblɪəfaɪl] *n form* bibliófilo, -a *m, f*
bicarbonate [ˌbaɪ'kɑːbənət, *Am:* -'kɑːr-] *n no pl* bicarbonato *m*
bicarbonate of soda *n* bicarbonato *m* de soda
bicentenary [ˌbaɪsen'tiːnəri, *Am:* baɪ'sentner-] <-ies> *n,* **bicentennial** *Am* **I.** *n* bicentenario *m* **II.** *adj* bicentenario, -a; **~ celebration** celebración *f* del bicentenario
biceps ['baɪseps] *n inv* bíceps *m inv*
bicker ['bɪkəʳ, *Am:* -ɚ] *vi* reñir
bickering *n no pl* riñas *fpl*
bicycle ['baɪsɪkl] *n* bicicleta *f;* **to ride a ~** montar en bicicleta; **by ~** en bicicleta
bicycle lane *n* carril *m* de bicicletas
bid[1] [bɪd] <bid *o* bade, bid *o* bidden> *vt form* **1.** (*greet*) **to ~ sb farewell** decir adiós a alguien; **to ~ sb good morning** desear buenos días a alguien; **to ~ sb welcome** dar la bienvenida a alguien **2.** (*command*) ordenar **3.** (*invite*) invitar
bid[2] [bɪd] **I.** *n* **1.** (*offer*) oferta *f;* **hostile takeover ~** COM oferta hostil de adquisición; **to make a ~ to do sth** concursar para hacer algo; **to make a ~ for sth** hacer una oferta sobre [*o* por] algo **2.** (*attempt*) intento *m* **II.** <bid, bid> *vi* **1.** (*at an auction*) pujar **2.** COM hacer una oferta; **to ~ for a contract** concursar por un contrato **III.** <bid, bid> *vt* pujar
bidden ['bɪdn] *pp of* **bid**[1]
bidder ['bɪdəʳ, *Am:* -ɚ] *n* postor(a) *m(f);* **to the highest ~** al mejor postor
bidding ['bɪdɪŋ] *n no pl* **1.** FIN puja *f* **2.** (*command*) orden *f;* **to do sb's ~** cumplir las órdenes de alguien; **at sb's ~** a las órdenes de alguien
bide [baɪd] *vt* **to ~ one's time** esperar el momento oportuno
bidet ['biːdeɪ, *Am:* bɪ'deɪ] *n* bidé *m*
biennial [baɪ'enɪəl] **I.** *adj a.* BOT bienal **II.** *n* planta *f* bienal
bier [bɪəʳ, *Am:* bɪr] *n* andas *fpl*
bifocal [baɪ'fəʊkl, *Am:* 'baɪˌfoʊ-] *adj* bifocal
bifocals [baɪ'fəʊklz, *Am:* 'baɪˌfoʊ-] *npl* gafas *fpl* bifocales, anteojos *mpl* bifocales *AmL*
big [bɪg] <-ger, -gest> *adj* **1.** (*in size, amount*) grande; (*before singular nouns*) gran; **a ~ book** un libro grande; **a ~ budget film** una película de gran presupuesto; **a ~ house** una casa grande; **~ letters** mayúsculas *fpl;* **to be a ~ spender** *inf* ser un derrochador; **~ words** *inf* palabras *fpl* altisonantes; **the ~ger the better** cuanto más grande mejor **2.** (*grown-up*) mayor; **~ boy/girl** chico/chica mayor; **~ sister/brother** hermana/hermano mayor **3.** (*significant*) gran(de); **a ~ day** *inf* un día importante; **this group is ~ in Spain** este grupo es muy popular en España **4.** (*on a large scale*) a gran escala ►**to make it ~** *inf* triunfar a lo grande; **to think ~** tener grandes aspiraciones

bigamist ['bɪgəmɪst] *n* bígamo, -a *m, f*
bigamy ['bɪgəmi] *n no pl* bigamia *f*
Big Apple *n* the ~ Nueva York *f*

> El **Big Ben** era, originariamente, el sobrenombre de una gran campana, fundida en 1856, que se encontraba en la torre de las **Houses of Parliament**. Sir Benjamin Hall, entonces **Chief Commissioner of Works**, es el que la bautizó con este nombre. Hoy en día, por **Big Ben**, se conocen tanto la campana como la torre. Las campanadas con las que el **Big Ben** da la hora se pueden oír en los telediarios de algunas cadenas de radio y televisión.

big business *n* el gran capital **Big Easy** *n* the ~ Nueva Orleans *f* **big game** *n no pl* caza *f* mayor
bigot ['bɪgət] *n* intolerante *mf;* REL fanático, -a *m, f*
bigoted *adj* intolerante; REL fanático, -a
bigotry ['bɪgətri] *n no pl* fanatismo *m;* REL intolerancia *f*
big shot *n inf* pez *m* gordo **big toe** *n* dedo *m* gordo del pie **big top** *n* carpa *f* de circo **big wheel** *n* noria *f* **bigwig** *n inf* pez *m* gordo
bike [baɪk] *n inf* **1.** (*bicycle*) bici *f;* **to get on a ~** montar en una bici **2.** (*motorcycle*) moto *f*
biker ['baɪkəʳ, *Am:* -kɚ] *n inf* motociclista *mf*
bikini [bɪ'ki:ni] *n* bikini *m*
bilateral [ˌbaɪ'lætərəl, *Am:* -'læt̬ɚl] *adj* bilateral
bilberry ['bɪlbəri, *Am:* -ber-] <-ies> *n* arándano *m*
bile [baɪl] *n* **1.** *no pl* ANAT bilis *f* **2.** *fig* mal genio *m*
bilharzia [bɪl'hɑ:zɪə, *Am:* -'hɑ:rzɪ-] *n* MED esquistosomiasis *f inv*
bilingual [baɪ'lɪŋgwəl] *adj* bilingüe
bilingual secretary *n* secretaria *f* bilingüe
bilious ['bɪliəs, *Am:* -jəs] *adj* **1.** MED bilioso, -a **2.** *fig* (*angry*) bilioso, -a; (*unpleasant*) asqueroso, -a
bill[1] [bɪl] **I.** *n* **1.** (*invoice*) factura *f;* **phone ~** factura del teléfono; **to foot the ~** pagar la cuenta; **the ~, please** la cuenta, por favor **2.** *Am* (*banknote*) billete *m* **3.** POL, LAW proyecto *m* de ley; **to pass a ~** aprobar un proyecto de ley **4.** (*poster, placard*) cartel *m* ▶**to give sth/sb a clean ~ of health** dar a algo/alguien el visto bueno; **to fit the ~** convenir **II.** *vt* **to ~ sb** pasar la cuenta a alguien; **to ~ sb for sth** facturar algo a alguien
bill[2] [bɪl] **I.** *n* (*of a bird*) pico *m* **II.** *vi* **to ~ and coo** *inf* estar como dos tortolitos
billboard ['bɪlbɔ:d, *Am:* -bɔ:rd] *n* valla *f* publicitaria
billet ['bɪlɪt, *Am:* -ət] MIL **I.** *n* acantonamiento *m* **II.** *vt* acantonar
billfold ['bɪlfəʊld, *Am:* -foʊld] *n Am* cartera *f*
billiard ball *n* bola *f* de billar
billiards ['bɪliədz, *Am:* '-jɚdz] *n no pl* billar *m*
billiard table *n* mesa *f* de billar
billing *n* **to be given top ~** encabezar el reparto
billion ['bɪliən, *Am:* -jən] *n* mil millones *mpl*
billow ['bɪləʊ, *Am:* -oʊ] **I.** *vi* (*clothes, sails*) hincharse **II.** *n* **a ~ of smoke** una nube de humo
billowy *adj* (*waves, clouds*) ondulante; (*sail*) ondeante
billposter ['bɪlˌpəʊstəʳ, *Am:* -ˌpoʊstɚ] *n,* **billsticker** ['bɪlstɪkəʳ, *Am:* -kɚ] *n* cartelero *m*
billy ['bɪli] <-ies> *n,* **billycan** *n Aus, Brit* cacerola *f*
billy goat *n* macho *m* cabrío
bimbo ['bɪmbəʊ, *Am:* -boʊ] <-(e)s> *n pej, inf: mujer joven y guapa, pero tonta*
bi-monthly [ˌbaɪ'mʌnθli] **I.** *adj* **1.** (*twice a month*) quincenal **2.** (*every two months*) bimestral **II.** *adv* **1.** (*twice a month*) quincenalmente **2.** (*once every two months*) bimestralmente
bin [bɪn] **I.** *n* **1.** *Aus, Brit* (*for waste*) cubo *m* de basura, basurero *m Méx;* **to consign sth to the ~** tirar algo a la basura; *fig* desechar algo **2.** (*for storage*) recipiente *m* **II.** *vt Brit* tirar
binary ['baɪnəri] *adj* INFOR binario, -a
binary code *n* INFOR código *m* binario
bind [baɪnd] **I.** *n no pl, Brit, inf* apuro *m;* **to be in a ~** estar en un apuro **II.** <bound, bound> *vi* unirse **III.** <bound, bound> *vt* **1.** (*tie together*) atar; **to be bound hand and foot** estar atado de pies y manos **2.** (*unite*) **to ~** (**together**) unir; **to be bound to sb** estar ligado a alguien **3.** (*commit*) vincular **4.** (*sew*) ribetear **5.** (*book*) encuadernar **6.** (*oblige*) **to ~ sb to do sth** obligar a alguien a hacer algo; **to ~ sb to a contract** comprometer a alguien contractualmente
binder ['baɪndəʳ, *Am:* -dɚ] *n* (*cover*) carpeta *f*
bindery ['baɪndəri] <-ies> *n* taller *m* de encuadernación, encuadernadora *f Méx*
binding ['baɪndɪŋ] **I.** *n no pl* **1.** TYPO encuadernación *f* **2.** FASHION ribete *m* **II.** *adj* vinculante
bindweed ['baɪndwi:d] *n no pl* correhuela *f*
binge [bɪndʒ] *inf* **I.** *n* (*of drinking*) borrachera *f,* vacilada *f Méx;* (*of eating*) comilona *f;* **to go on a ~** ir de farra, ir de parranda **II.** *vi* atiborrarse
bingo ['bɪŋgəʊ, *Am:* -goʊ] **I.** *n no pl* bingo *m* **II.** *interj inf* bingo
binoculars [bɪ'nɒkjʊləz, *Am:* -'nɑ:kjəlɚz] *npl* prismáticos *mpl,* binoculares *mpl AmL;* **a pair of ~** unos prismáticos
binomial [baɪ'nəʊmɪəl, *Am:* -'noʊ-] **I.** *n* MAT binomio *m* **II.** *adj* MAT binomial
biochemical [ˌbaɪəʊ'kemɪkl, *Am:* -oʊ-] *adj* bioquímico, -a

biochemist [ˌbaɪəʊ'kemɪst, *Am:* -oʊ-] *n* bioquímico, -a *m, f* **biochemistry** [ˌbaɪəʊ'kemɪstri, *Am:* -oʊ-] *n no pl* bioquímica *f*
biodegradable [ˌbaɪəʊdɪ'greidəbl, *Am:* -oʊ-] *adj* biodegradable
biodegrade [ˌbaɪəʊdɪ'greid, *Am:* -oʊ-] *vi* biodegradarse
biodiversity [ˌbaɪəʊdaɪ'vɜːsəti, *Am:* -oʊdɪ'vɜːrsət̬i] *n no pl* biodiversidad *f*
bioengineering [ˌbaɪəʊendʒɪ'nɪərɪŋ, *Am:* -oʊendʒɪ'nɪrɪŋ] *n no pl* ingeniería *f* biológica
biofeedback [ˌbaɪəʊ'fiːdbæk, *Am:* -oʊ-] *n no pl* retroalimentación *f* biológica
biofuel ['baɪəʊˌfjuːl] *n* combustible *m* biológico
biogas ['baɪəʊˌgæs] *n no pl* biogás *m*
biographer [baɪ'ɒgrəfəʳ, *Am:* -'ɑːgrəfɚ] *n* biógrafo, -a *m, f*
biographical [ˌbaɪəʊ'græfɪkəl] *adj* biográfico, -a
biography [baɪ'ɒgrəfi, *Am:* -'ɑːgrə-] <-ies> *n* biografía *f*
biological [ˌbaɪə'lɒdʒɪkəl, *Am:* -'lɑːdʒɪ-] *adj* biológico, -a; ~ **cycle/rhythm** ciclo/ritmo biológico
biological control *n* control *m* biológico **biological indicator** *n* indicador *m* biológico
biologist [baɪ'ɒlədʒɪst, *Am:* -'ɑːlə-] *n* biólogo, -a *m, f*
biology [baɪ'ɒlədʒi, *Am:* -'ɑːlə-] *n no pl* biología *f*
biomass [ˌbaiəmæs] *n* BIO biomasa *f*
biopsy ['baɪɒpsi, *Am:* -ɑːp-] *n* MED biopsia *f*
biorhythm ['baɪəriðəm, *Am:* -oʊ-] *n* biorritmo *m*
biosphere ['baɪəsfiːəʳ, *Am:* -sfir] *n no pl* biosfera *f*
biotechnology [ˌbaɪəʊtek'nɒlədʒi, *Am:* -oʊtek'nɑːlə-] *n no pl* biotecnología *f*
biotope ['baɪətəʊp, *Am:* -toʊp] *n* biótopo *m*
bipartisan [ˌbaɪpɑːtɪ'zæn, *Am:* -'pɑːrt̬əzən] *adj* POL bipartidista
biped ['baɪped] *n* BIO bípedo *m*
biplane ['baɪpleɪn] *n* biplano *m*
bipolar [ˌbaɪ'pəʊləʳ, *Am:* -'poʊlɚ] *adj* ELEC, PHYS bipolar
birch [bɜːtʃ, *Am:* bɜːrtʃ] **I.** *n* **1.** (*tree*) abedul *m* **2.** *no pl* (*for punishment*) palo *m* **II.** *vt* castigar con el palo
bird [bɜːd, *Am:* bɜːrd] *n* **1.** ZOOL pájaro *m;* (*larger*) ave *f;* **a flock of ~s** una bandada de pájaros; **to feel as free as a** ~ sentirse libre como un pájaro **2.** *inf* (*person*) **a strange** [*o* **queer**] ~ un bicho raro **3.** *Aus, Brit, inf* (*girl, woman*) chica *f,* chava *f Méx,* piba *f RíoPl* ►~**s of a feather flock together** *prov* Dios los cría y ellos se juntan *prov;* **a** ~ **in the hand is worth two in the bush** *prov* más vale pájaro en mano que ciento volando *prov;* **to kill two ~s with one stone** matar dos pájaros de un tiro *fig;* **it's the early** ~ **that catches the worm** *prov* al que madruga, Dios le ayuda *prov;* **to give sb the** ~ *inf* abuchear a alguien
birdcage *n* pajarera *f*
birdie ['bɜːdi, *Am:* 'bɜːr-] *n* **1.** *childspeak* pajarito *m;* **watch the** ~ PHOT ¡mira el pajarito! **2.** (*in golf*) birdie *m*
Bird of Paradise *n* ave *f* del paraíso
birdseed ['bɜːdsiːd, *Am:* 'bɜːrd-] *n no pl* alpiste *m*
bird's-eye view [ˌbɜːdzaɪ'vjuː, *Am:* ˌbɜːrdz-] *n no pl* vista *f* panorámica
bird table *n Brit* comedero *m* de aves **birdwatching** *n no pl* observación *f* de aves
biro® ['baɪərəʊ, *Am:* -roʊ] *n* bolígrafo *m,* birome *m RíoPl*
birth [bɜːθ, *Am:* bɜːrθ] *n* **1.** nacimiento *m,* paritorio *m Cuba, Ven;* MED parto *m;* **at** ~ al nacer; **by** ~ de nacimiento; **from** ~ de nacimiento; **date/place of** ~ fecha/lugar de nacimiento; **to give** ~ **to a child** dar a luz a un bebé **2.** *no pl* (*descent, beginning*) origen *m;* **to be of low/noble** ~ ser de origen humilde/noble
birth certificate *n* certificado *m* de nacimiento **birth control** *n* control *m* de natalidad
birthday ['bɜːθdeɪ, *Am:* 'bɜːrθ-] *n* cumpleaños *m inv* **happy ~!** ¡feliz cumpleaños!
birthday cake *n* tarta *f* de cumpleaños, pastel *m* de cumpleaños *AmL* **birthday card** *n* tarjeta *f* de cumpleaños **birthday party** *n* fiesta *f* de cumpleaños **birthday present** *n* regalo *m* de cumpleaños **birthday suit** *n inf* **in one's** ~ en cueros
birthmark ['bɜːθmɑːk, *Am:* 'bɜːrθmɑːrk] *n* marca *f* de nacimiento **birthplace** *n* lugar *m* de nacimiento **birth rate** *n* tasa *f* de natalidad; **falling/rising** ~ natalidad decreciente/creciente **birthright** *n* derecho *m* de nacimiento; *fig* patrimonio *m*
Biscay ['bɪskeɪ] *n* Vizcaya *f*
biscuit ['bɪskɪt] *n* **1.** *Aus, Brit* galleta *f* **2.** *Am* (*soft cake*) bizcocho *m* ►**that** (**really**) **takes the ~!** *inf* ¡eso es el colmo!

> Con la expresión **biscuits and gravy** se designa un desayuno típico de los EE.UU. procedente de los estados del sur. Los **biscuits** son una clase de panecillos planos servidos con **gravy** (un tipo de salsa de asado). En algunas zonas, este tipo de desayuno sólo se sirve en **truck stops** (locales frecuentados por camioneros).

bisect [baɪ'sekt, *Am:* 'baɪsekt] *vt* MAT bisecar
bisection [baɪ'sekʃən] *n* MAT bisección *f*
bisexual [ˌbaɪ'sekʃʊəl, *Am:* -ʃʊəl] **I.** *n* bisexual *mf* **II.** *adj* bisexual
bishop ['bɪʃəp] *n* **1.** REL obispo *m* **2.** (*chess piece*) alfil *m*
bishopric ['bɪʃəprɪk] *n* obispado *m*
bison ['baɪsən] *n* bisonte *m*

bit[1] [bɪt] *n* 1. *inf* (*small piece*) trozo *m*, pedazo *m;* (*of glass*) fragmento *m;* **a ~ of paper** un trozo de papel; **little ~s** pedacitos *mpl;* **to smash sth to ~s** romper algo en pedazos 2. (*some*) **a ~ of** un poco de; **a ~ of luck** un poco de suerte; **a ~ of news** una noticia; **a ~ of trouble** un problemilla 3. (*part*) parte *f;* **the difficult ~ of sth** la parte difícil de algo; **~ by ~** poco a poco; **to do one's ~** *inf* hacer su parte 4. *pl, inf* (*things*) **~s and pieces** cosas *fpl* 5. *inf* (*short time*) momento *m;* **for a ~** por un momento; **hold on a ~** espera un momento 6. (*somewhat*) **a ~** algo; **a ~ stupid** un poco tonto; **quite a ~** bastante; **not a ~** en absoluto

bit[2] [bɪt] *n* 1. (*for horses*) bocado *m* 2. (*for drill*) broca *f* ►**to chafe** [*o* **champ**] **at the ~** impacientarse, comer ansias *Méx*

bit[3] [bɪt] *n* INFOR bit *m*

bit[4] [bɪt] *pt of* **bite**

bitch [bɪtʃ] I. *n* 1. ZOOL perra *f* 2. *inf* (*complaint*) queja *f;* **to have a good ~** quejarse 3. *inf* (*woman*) zorra *f*, tusa *f AmL, Cuba;* **you ~!** ¡lagarta! II. *vi inf* quejarse; **to ~ about sb/sth** quejarse de alguien/algo

bitchy ['bɪtʃi] *adj* malicioso, -a

bite [baɪt] I. <bit, bitten> *vt* morder; (*insect*) picar; **to ~ one's nails/lips** morderse las uñas/los labios; **what's biting you?** *inf* ¿qué mosca te ha picado? II. <bit, bitten> *vi* 1. (*dog, person*) morder; (*insect, fish*) picar 2. (*have effect*) surtir efecto ►**once bitten twice shy** *prov* el gato escaldado del agua fría huye *prov* III. *n* 1. (*of a dog, person*) mordisco *m;* (*of an insect*) picadura *f;* **~ mark** marca *f* de mordedura; (*of an insect*) picadura *f;* **a dog's ~** una mordedura de un perro; **to give sb a ~** dar un mordisco a alguien; **to take a ~ of sth** tomar un bocado de algo 2. (*mouthful*) bocado *m* 3. *no pl, fig* (*sharpness*) mordacidad *f;* **to have (real) ~** tener (verdadera) garra

biting ['baɪtɪŋ, *Am:* -t̬ɪŋ] *adj* (*wind*) cortante; (*criticism*) mordaz

bitten ['bɪtn] *pp of* **bite**

bitter ['bɪtə^r, *Am:* 'bɪt̬ɚ] I. *adj* <-er, -est> 1. (*acrid*) agrio, -a; (*fruit*) amargo, -a 2. (*painful*) amargo, -a; **to be ~ about sth** estar amargado por algo; **to carry on to the ~ end** seguir hasta el final 3. (*intense*) acérrimo, -a; (*dispute*) encarnizado, -a; (*disappointment*) agudo, -a; (*wind*) cortante II. *n Aus, Brit* (*beer*) cerveza *f* (amarga)

bitterly *adv* 1. (*resentfully*) con rencor; **to weep ~** llorar a lágrima viva 2. (*intensely*) intensamente; **to condemn sth ~** condenar algo firmemente

bitterness *n no pl* 1. (*animosity*) amargura *f;* (*resentment*) resentimiento *m;* **~ towards sb** resentimiento contra alguien 2. (*taste*) amargor *m*

bitumen ['bɪtjʊmən, *Am:* bɪ'tu:mən] *n no pl* betún *m*

bituminous [bɪ'tju:mɪnəs, *Am:* -'tu:-] *adj* bituminoso, -a

bivalve ['baivælv] *n* bivalvo *m*

bivouac ['bɪvʊæk, *Am:* -uæk] I. *n* vivaque *m*, vivac *m* II. <-k-> *vi* vivaquear

biweekly [ˌbaɪ'wi:kli] I. *adj* 1. (*every two weeks*) quincenal 2. (*twice a week*) bisemanal II. *adv* 1. (*every two weeks*) quincenalmente 2. (*twice a week*) bisemanalmente

bizarre [bɪ'zɑ:^r, *Am:* -'zɑ:r] *adj* (*behaviour, person*) extraño, -a; (*clothes*) estrafalario, -a

blab [blæb] <-bb-> *vi inf* 1. (*talk too much*) irse de la lengua 2. *inf* (*inform*) cantar

black [blæk] I. *adj* 1. (*colour*) negro, -a; **~ man** negro *m;* **~ woman** negra *f* 2. *fig* (*extreme*) negro, -a; **~ despair** negra desesperación 3. (*dark*) oscuro, -a 4. (*very dirty*) mugriento, -a, mugroso, -a *Méx* ►**to beat sb ~ and blue** *inf* moler a alguien a palos; **he is not as ~ as he is painted** no es tan malo como lo pintan II. *vt* 1. (*make black*) ennegrecer; **to ~ one's face** pintarse la cara de negro; **to ~ sb's eye** poner a alguien el ojo morado [*o* a la funerala] 2. *Brit* (*boycott*) boicotear III. *n* 1. (*colour*) negro *m;* **in ~** de negro; **in ~ and white** CINE, PHOT en blanco y negro 2. (*person*) negro, -a *m, f* 3. FIN **in the ~** con saldo positivo
◆**black out** I. *vi* perder el conocimiento II. *vt* 1. o(b)scurecer 2. (*censure*) censurar

blackball ['blækbɔ:l] *vt* (*vote*) votar en contra de; (*reject*) dar bola negra a

blackberry ['blækbəri, *Am:* -ˌber-] <-ies> *n* (*fruit*) zarzamora *f;* (*plant*) zarza *f*

blackbird ['blækbɜ:d, *Am:* -bɜ:rd] *n* mirlo *m*

blackboard ['blækbɔ:d, *Am:* -bɔ:rd] *n* pizarra *f*

black book *n* **to be in sb's ~(s)** figurar en la lista negra de alguien **black box** *n* AVIAT caja *f* negra

blackcurrant [ˌblæk'kʌrənt, *Am:* 'blækˌkɜ:r-] *n* casis *m inv*, grosella *f* negra

blacken ['blækən] I. *vt* 1. (*make black*) ennegrecer 2. (*slander*) desacreditar; **to ~ sb's name** manchar la reputación de alguien II. *vi* ennegrecerse

black eye *n* ojo *m* morado

blackguard ['blægɑ:d, *Am:* -ɑ:rd] *n* sinvergüenza *m*

blackhead ['blækhed] *n* barrillo *m* **black hole** *n* agujero *m* negro **black ice** *n* *hielo invisible en la carretera*

blacking ['blækɪŋ] *n no pl* betún *m*

blackish ['blækɪʃ] *adj* negruzco, -a

blackjack ['blækˌdʒæk] *n* 1. GAMES veintiuna *f* 2. *Am* (*cosh*) (cachi)porra *f*

blackleg ['blækleg] *n Brit* esquirol(a) *m(f)*

blacklist ['blæklɪst] I. *vt* poner en la lista negra II. *n* lista *f* negra

blackmail ['blækmeɪl] I. *n* chantaje *m* II. *vt* chantajear; **to ~ sb into doing sth** chantajear a alguien para que haga algo

blackmailer ['blækmeɪlə^r, *Am:* -ɚ] *n* chantajista *mf*

black mark *n* punto *m* en contra **black market** *n* mercado *m* negro **black mar-**

keteer *n* estraperlista *mf*
blackness ['blæknɪs] *n no pl* (*colour*) negrura *f;* (*darkness*) oscuridad *f*
blackout ['blækaʊt] *n* **1.** (*faint*) desmayo *m;* **to have a ~** sufrir un desmayo **2.** (*censorship*) bloqueo *m;* **news ~** bloqueo informativo **3.** ELEC apagón *m*
black pudding *n Brit* morcilla *f,* moronga *f Méx* **Black Sea** *n* Mar *m* Negro **black sheep** *n a. fig* oveja *f* negra
blacksmith ['blæksmɪθ] *n* herrero *m*
bladder ['blædəʳ, *Am:* -ɚ] *n* ANAT vejiga *f*
blade [bleɪd] **I.** *n* (*of a tool, weapon*) hoja *f;* (*of an oar*) pala *f;* **~ of grass** brizna *f* de hierba **II.** *vi inf* patinar (en línea)
blah [blɑː] *interj inf* **~, ~,** (~) blabla
blame [bleɪm] **I.** *vt* culpar; **to ~ sb for sth, to ~ sth on sb** echar a alguien la culpa de algo; **to be to ~ for sth** tener la culpa de algo; **I don't ~ you** te comprendo **II.** *n no pl* culpa *f;* **to bear the ~** tener la culpa; **to lay the ~ for sth on sb** echar a alguien la culpa de algo; **to take the ~** declararse culpable
blameless ['bleɪmlɪs] *adj* libre de culpa; **~ life** vida *f* intachable
blameworthy ['bleɪmwɜːði, *Am:* -wɜːr-] *adj form* censurable
blanch [blɑːntʃ, *Am:* blænʃ] **I.** *vi* palidecer **II.** *vt* **1.** blanquear **2.** GASTR escaldar; **~ed almonds** almendras peladas
blancmange [blə'mɒnʒ, *Am:* 'mɑːnʒ] *n no pl flan de harina de maíz y leche*
bland [blænd] *adj* **1.** (*mild*) suave **2.** (*insipid*) soso, -a
blandishments ['blændɪʃmənts] *npl* halagos *mpl*
blank [blæŋk] **I.** *adj* **1.** (*empty*) en blanco; **~ page/space** página *f* /espacio *m* en blanco; **~ tape** cinta *f* virgen; **~ cheque** cheque *m* en blanco; **to go ~** quedarse en blanco; **my mind went ~** me quedé con la mente en blanco; **the screen went ~** la pantalla se quedó negra **2.** (*unemotional: look*) sin expresión **3.** (*complete*) absoluto, -a; (*despair*) completo, -a; **to be met by a ~ refusal** encontrarse con un rechazo absoluto **II.** *n* **1.** (*space*) espacio *m* **2.** (*cartridge*) cartucho *m* de salvas ►**to <u>draw</u> a** (**complete**) **~** no encontrar nada
blanket ['blæŋkɪt] **I.** *n* **1.** (*cover*) manta *f,* frisa *f RDom, PRico,* cobija *f Méx; fig* cobertura *f* **2.** (*of snow*) capa *f* **II.** *vt* cubrir; **to ~ sth in sth** cubrir algo con algo **III.** *adj* general; LING (*term*) genérico, -a
blankly *adv* (*without expression*) inexpresivamente; (*without understanding*) sin comprender
blare [bleəʳ, *Am:* bler] **I.** *vi* resonar **II.** *n no pl* estruendo *m;* (*of a trumpet*) trompetazo *m*
blaspheme [blæs'fiːm, *Am:* 'blæsfiːm] *vi* blasfemar
blasphemer [blæs'fiːməʳ, *Am:* 'blæsfiːmɚ] *n* blasfemo, -a *m, f*
blasphemous ['blæsfəməs] *adj* blasfemo, -a
blasphemy ['blæsfəmi] *n no pl* blasfemia *f*
blast [blɑːst, *Am:* blæst] **I.** *vt* **1.** (*with an explosive*) volar **2.** (*criticize*) criticar duramente **II.** *n* **1.** (*detonation*) explosión *f* **2.** (*gust of wind*) ráfaga *f* **3.** (*noise*) toque *m;* (*of a trumpet*) trompetazo *m;* **to blow a ~ on a trumpet** dar un trompetazo **4.** *Am, inf* (*party*) fiesta *f,* tambarria *f AmC, AmS,* guateque *m CRi* **5.** (**at**) **full ~** (*volume*) al máximo (de volúmen); (*speed*) a toda marcha **III.** *interj inf* maldición; **~ it!** ¡maldita sea!
blasted *adj inf* (*damned*) maldito, -a
blast furnace *n* alto horno *m*
blast-off ['blɑːstɒf, *Am:* 'blæstɑːf] *n* despegue *m*
blast wave *n* onda *f* expansiva
blatant ['bleɪtnt] *adj* descarado, -a
blaze [bleɪz] **I.** *vi* resplandecer, brillar; (*fire*) arder; **to ~ with anger** echar chispas **II.** *vt* **to ~ a trail** abrir camino **III.** *n* **1.** (*fire*) fuego *m;* (*flames*) llamarada *f* **2.** (*light, colour*) resplandor *m* **3.** (*display*) **a ~ of glory** un rayo de gloria; **a ~ of publicity** una campaña de publicidad a bombo y platillo; **~ of anger** arranque *m* de ira
◆**blaze away** *vi* **1.** (*burn*) arder **2.** (*shoot*) disparar rápidamente
◆**blaze up** *vi* encenderse vivamente
blazer ['bleɪzəʳ, *Am:* -zɚ] *n* chaqueta *f;* **school ~** chaqueta escolar
blazing ['bleɪzɪŋ] *adj* **1.** resplandeciente; (*heat*) abrasador(a); (*sunshine*) esplendoroso, -a; (*light*) brillante; (*fire*) vivo, -a **2.** (*argument*) violento, -a
bleach [bliːtʃ] **I.** *vt* blanquear **II.** *n* lejía *f;* (*for hair*) decolorante *m*
bleachers ['bliːtʃəz, *Am:* -tʃɚz] *n pl, Am* gradería *f*
bleak [bliːk] *adj* (*future*) sombrío, -a; (*weather*) gris; (*landscape*) desolador(a); (*smile*) triste
bleary ['blɪəri, *Am:* 'blɪri] *adj* <-ier, -iest> (*person*) cansado, -a; (*eyes*) lagañoso, -a
bleary-eyed [ˌblɪəri'aɪd, *Am:* 'blɪriaɪd] *adj* **to be ~** estar medio dormido
bleat [bliːt] **I.** *vi* **1.** (*sheep*) balar; (*calf*) mugir **2.** (*complain*) quejarse **II.** *n* **1.** (*of sheep*) balido *m* **2.** (*complaint*) quejido *m*
bled [bled] *pt, pp of* **bleed**
bleed [bliːd] <bled, bled> **I.** *vi* sangrar; **to ~ to death** morir desangrado; **my heart ~s** *iron* lo siento mucho **II.** *vt* **1.** hacer una sangría a; **to ~ sb dry** *inf* dejar seco a alguien **2.** TECH, AUTO purgar
bleeder ['bliːdəʳ, *Am:* -ɚ] *n Brit, inf* cabrón *m*
bleeding **I.** *adj Brit, inf* puñetero, -a **II.** *n* **1.** MED sangría *f* **2.** TECH, AUTO purgamiento *m*
bleep [bliːp] **I.** *n* pitido *m* **II.** *vi* pitar **III.** *vt* llamar (con un localizador)
bleeper ['blɪːpəʳ, *Am:* -pɚ] *n* localizador *m,* busca *m inf*
blemish ['blemɪʃ] **I.** *n a. fig* mancha *f;* **a reputation without ~** una reputación inta-

B

chable **II.** *vt a. fig* manchar

blemish-free *adj* sin defectos

blench [blentʃ] *vi* recular; **to ~ at a thought** retroceder ante un pensamiento

blend [blend] **I.** *n* mezcla *f* **II.** *vt* mezclar **III.** *vi* armonizar; **to ~ in** no desentonar

blender [blendəʳ, *Am:* -dɚ] *n* licuadora *f*

bless [bles] *vt* bendecir ►**~ him/her!** ¡bendito sea!; **~ you!** (*on sneezing*) ¡Jesús!

blessed ['blesɪd] *adj* **1.** (*holy*) bendito, -a; (*ground*) santo, -a; **the Blessed Virgin** la Santísima Virgen; **~ are the meek ...** bienaventurados los humildes... **2.** *inf* dichoso, -a; **the whole ~ day** todo el santo día

blessing ['blesɪŋ] *n* **1.** (*benediction*) bendición *f*; **to give one's ~ to sth** dar su aprobación a algo **2.** (*benefit*) beneficio *m;* (*advantage*) ventaja *f* ►**it's a ~ in disguise** no hay mal que por bien no venga *prov;* **to count one's ~s** apreciar lo que uno tiene

blew [blu:] *pt of* **blow**

blight [blaɪt] **I.** *vt* AGR *a. fig* arruinar **II.** *n* **1.** AGR añublo *m* **2.** *fig* ruina *f;* **to cast a ~ on sth** arruinar algo

blighter ['blaɪtəʳ, *Am:* -ţɚ] *n Brit, inf* canalla *m*

blimey ['blaɪmi] *interj Brit, inf* caray

blind [blaɪnd] **I.** *n* **1.** *pl* (*person*) **the ~** los ciegos **2.** (*window shade*) persiana *f* **3.** (*cover*) pantalla *f* **II.** *vt* **1.** ANAT, MED cegar **2.** (*dazzle*) deslumbrar **III.** *adj* **1.** (*unable to see*) ciego, -a; **to be ~ in one eye** ser tuerto; **to be ~ to sth** no ver algo **2.** (*without reason*) sin razón; (*acceptance, devotion*) apasionado, -a **3.** (*hidden: corner*) de poca visibilidad **4.** *Brit, inf* (*as intensifier*) **not to take a ~ bit of notice of sth** no conceder la más mínima importancia a algo **IV.** *adv* **to be ~ drunk** estar más borracho que una cuba; **to swear ~ that ...** jurar y perjurar que...

blind alley <-s> *n a. fig* callejón *m* sin salida

blinder ['blaɪndəʳ, *Am:* -ɚ] *n inf* SPORTS partido *m* excepcional

blindfold ['blaɪndfəʊld, *Am:* -foʊld] **I.** *n* venda *f* **II.** *vt* vendar los ojos a **III.** *adj* con los ojos vendados; **to be able to do sth ~** poder hacer algo con los ojos cerrados

blinding *adj* (*dazzling*) cegador(a)

blind man's buff *n no pl* gallina *f* ciega

blindness *n* ceguera *f*

blind spot *n* punto *m* ciego

blink [blɪŋk] **I.** *vt* parpadear; **to ~ one's eyes** parpadear **II.** *vi* pestañear; **to ~ back one's tears** contener las lágrimas; **she didn't even ~** ni se inmutó **III.** *n* parpadeo *m* ►**in the ~ of an eye** en un abrir y cerrar de ojos; **to be on the ~** *inf* estar averiado

blinker ['blɪŋkəʳ, *Am:* -kɚ] *n* anteojera *f*

blinkered *adj* estrecho, -a de miras

blinking *adj Brit, inf* maldito, -a

bliss [blɪs] *n no pl* dicha *f;* **marital ~** felicidad *f* conyugal

blissful ['blɪsfəl] *adj* **1.** (*happy*) bienaventurado, -a **2.** (*enjoyable*) maravilloso, -a

blister ['blɪstəʳ, *Am:* -tɚ] **I.** *n* **1.** ANAT ampolla *f* **2.** (*bubble*) burbuja *f* **II.** *vt* ampollar **III.** *vi* ampollarse

blistering *adj* (*very hot*) abrasador(a)

blithering ['blɪðərɪŋ] *adj* **~ idiot!** ¡imbécil!

blitz [blɪts] **I.** *n no pl* bombardeo *m* aéreo; **the Blitz** *el bombardeo alemán de Londres en 1940–41* **II.** *vt* bombardear desde el aire

blizzard ['blɪzəd] *n* ventisca *f*

bloated ['bləʊtɪd, *Am:* 'bloʊţɪd] *adj* **1.** (*swollen*) hinchado, -a **2.** (*excessive*) excesivo, -a

blob [blɒb, *Am:* blɑ:b] *n* goterón *m*

bloc [blɒk] *n* POL bloque *m*

block [blɒk, *Am:* blɑ:k] **I.** *n* **1.** (*solid lump*) bloque *m;* (*of wood*) zoquete *m;* (*for executions*) tajo *m;* **to be sent to the ~** ser condenado a ser decapitado **2.** INFOR bloque *m* **3.** (*tall building*) edificio *m;* (*group of buildings*) manzana *f,* cuadra *f AmL;* **~ of flats** *Brit* bloque *m* de viviendas **4.** (*barrier*) barrera *f;* (*impediment*) obstrucción *f* **5.** (*child's toy*) cubo *m* **6.** SPORTS taco *m* de salida **II.** *vt* **1.** (*road, pipe*) bloquear; (*sb's progress*) obstaculizar **2.** INFOR **to ~ and copy** seleccionar y copiar

◆**block off** *vt* cortar

◆**block up** **I.** *vt* cerrar, tapar **II.** *vi* atascarse, atorozarse *AmC;* MED taparse

blockade [blɒ'keɪd, *Am:* blɑ:'keɪd] **I.** *n* bloqueo *m* **II.** *vt* bloquear; (*block off*) cortar

blockage ['blɒkɪdʒ, *Am:* 'blɑ:kɪdʒ] *n* obstrucción *f*

block capitals *n* letra *f* de imprenta

blockhouse ['blɒkhaʊs, *Am:* 'blɑ:k-] *n* blocao *m*

bloke [bləʊk] *n Brit, inf* tío *m*

blond(e) [blɒnd, *Am:* blɑ:nd] **I.** *adj* (*hair*) rubio, -a, güero, -a *Méx, Guat, Ven* **II.** *n* rubio, -a *m, f,* güero, -a *Méx, Guat, Ven*

blood [blʌd] *n no pl* sangre *f;* **to be of the same ~** ser parientes ►**to have ~ on one's hands** tener las manos manchadas de sangre *fig;* **~ is thicker than water** la sangre siempre tira; **bad ~** mala sangre; **in cold ~** a sangre fría; **her ~ ran cold** se le heló la sangre; **it makes my ~ boil** hace que me hierva la sangre; **to make sb's ~ curdle** [*o* **freeze**] hacer que a alguien se le hiele la sangre; **to smell ~** oler la sangre; **to sweat ~** sudar tinta; **to be after sb's ~** tener un odio mortal a alguien

blood bank *n* banco *m* de sangre

bloodbath ['blʌdbɑ:θ, *Am:* -bæθ] *n* baño *m* de sangre

blood clot *n* coágulo *m* de sangre

bloodcurdling ['blʌdˌkɜ:dlɪŋ, *Am:* -ˌkɜ:rdlɪŋ] *adj* espeluznante **blood donor** *n* donante *mf* de sangre **blood group** *n* grupo *m* sanguíneo

bloodhound ['blʌdhaʊnd] *n a. fig* sabueso *m*

B

bloodless ['blʌdlɪs] *adj* 1. (*face, lips*) exangüe 2. (*coup*) incruento, -a 3. (*emotionless: film, style*) soso, -a

blood poisoning *n no pl* septicemia *f* **blood pressure** *n no pl* tensión *f* arterial **blood relation** *n*, **blood relative** *n* pariente, -a *m, f* consanguíneo, -a

bloodshed ['blʌdʃed] *n no pl* derramamiento *m* de sangre

bloodshot ['blʌdʃɒt, *Am:* -ʃɑːt] *adj* inyectado, -a de sangre; (*eyes*) rojo, -a **blood sport** *n* (*hunting*) deporte *m* cinegético

bloodstained ['blʌdsteɪnd] *adj* manchado, -a de sangre

bloodstock ['blʌdstɒk, *Am:* -stɑːk] *n no pl* caballos *mpl* de raza

bloodstream ['blʌdstriːm] *n* corriente *f* sanguínea

bloodsucker ['blʌdˌsʌkəʳ, *Am:* -ɚ] *n* sanguijuela *f*

blood sugar *n no pl* azúcar *m* de la sangre **blood test** *n* análisis *m inv* de sangre

bloodthirsty ['blʌdˌθɜːsti, *Am:* -ˌθɜːr-] *adj* sanguinario, -a

blood transfusion *n* transfusión *f* de sangre **blood type** *n* grupo *m* sanguineo **blood vessel** *n* vaso *m* sanguíneo

bloody ['blʌdi] <-ier, -iest> I. *adj* 1. (*with blood*) ensangrentado, -a 2. *Aus, Brit, inf* (*for emphasis*) puñetero, -a; (**what the**) ~ **hell!** ¡(qué) coño! II. *adv Aus, Brit, inf* 1. (*very*) muy; **to be ~ useless** no servir para nada 2. (*for emphasis*) **I don't ~ know** no tengo ni puñetera idea

bloody-minded [ˌblʌdi'maɪndɪd] *adj* terco, -a

bloom [bluːm] I. *n no pl, a. fig* flor *f;* **to come into ~** florecer; **in the full ~ of youth** en la flor de la juventud II. *vi* 1. (*produce flowers*) florecer 2. (*peak*) prosperar

bloomer ['bluːməʳ, *Am:* -mɚ] *n Brit, inf* (*gaffe*) metedura *f* de pata; **to make a ~** meter la pata

blooming[1] ['bluːmɪŋ] *adj* floreciente

blooming[2] *adj*, **bloomin'** ['bluːmɪŋ] *adj Brit, inf* puñetero, -a

blossom ['blɒsəm, *Am:* 'blɑːsəm] I. *n* flor *f;* **in ~** en flor; **orange ~** azahar *m* II. *vi* 1. (*flower*) florecer 2. (*mature*) madurar

blot [blɒt, *Am:* blɑːt] I. *n* 1. (*mark*) borrón *m* 2. (*on sb's reputation*) mancha *f* II. *vt* 1. (*mark*) emborronar 2. (*dry*) secar

blotch [blɒtʃ, *Am:* blɑːtʃ] *n* borrón *m;* (*on the skin*) mancha *f*

blotchy ['blɒtʃi, *Am:* 'blɑːtʃi] <-ier, -iest> *adj* lleno, -a de manchas

blotter ['blɒtəʳ, *Am:* 'blɑːt̬ɚ] *n* hoja *f* de papel secante

blotting paper ['blɒtɪŋˌpeɪpəʳ, *Am:* 'blɑːt̬ɪŋˌpeɪpɚ] *n no pl* papel *m* secante

blotto ['blɒtəʊ, *Am:* 'blɑːt̬oʊ] *adj inf* **to be ~** estar como una cuba

blouse [blaʊz] *n* blusa *f*

blow[1] [bləʊ, *Am:* bloʊ] *n* 1. (*hit*) golpe *m*, zuque *m Col;* (*with the fist*) puñetazo *m;* **to come to ~s** llegar a las manos 2. (*setback*) disgusto *m*

blow[2] [bləʊ, *Am:* bloʊ] I. <blew, blown> *vi* 1. (*expel air*) soplar 2. (*fuse*) fundirse 3. (*tyre*) reventar II. *vt* 1. (*instrument*) tocar 2. (*clear*) **to ~ one's nose** sonarse la nariz 3. (*burn through*) fundir; (*burst*) reventar 4. *inf* (*spend*) despilfarrar ►~ **it!** *inf* ¡al diablo!

◆**blow away** *vt* 1. (*wind*) arrancar, llevar 2. *inf* (*kill*) liquidar

◆**blow down** I. *vi* caerse II. *vt* derribar

◆**blow off** *vt* quitar soplando; (*wind*) llevarse

◆**blow out** I. *vt* apagar II. *vi* apagarse

◆**blow over** *vi* (*scandal*) pasar al olvido; (*argument, dispute*) calmarse

◆**blow up** I. *vi* (*storm, gale*) levantarse II. *vt* 1. (*fill with air*) inflar 2. PHOTO ampliar 3. (*explode*) volar

blow-by-blow [ˌbləʊbaɪ'bləʊ, *Am:* ˌbloʊbaɪ'bloʊ] *adj* **a ~ account** una descripción con todo lujo de detalles

blow-dry ['bləʊˌdraɪ, *Am:* 'bloʊ-] *vt* secar con secador

blower ['bləʊəʳ, *Am:* 'bloʊɚ] *n Aus, Brit, inf* teléfono *m*

blowfly ['bləʊflaɪ, *Am:* 'bloʊ-] <-ies> *n* moscarda *f*

blowhole ['bləʊhəʊl, *Am:* 'bloʊhoʊl] *n* orificio *m* nasal

blowjob ['bləʊdʒɒb, *Am:* 'bloʊdʒɑːb] *n vulg* mamada *f*

blowlamp ['bləʊlæmp, *Am:* 'bloʊ-] *n* soplete *m*

blown [bləʊn, *Am:* 'bloʊn] *vt, vi pp of* **blow**

blowout ['bləʊaʊt, *Am:* 'bloʊ-] *n inf* 1. *Brit* (*huge meal*) comilona *f* 2. (*burst tyre*) reventón *m*

blowpipe ['bləʊpaɪp, *Am:* 'bloʊ-] *n* (*weapon*) cerbatana *f*

blowtorch ['bləʊtɔːtʃ, *Am:* 'bloʊtɔːrtʃ] *n* soplete *m*

blow-up ['bləʊʌp] *n* PHOTO ampliación *f*

blub [blʌb] <-bb-> *vi s.* **blubber**[1]

blubber[1] ['blʌbəʳ, *Am:* -ɚ] *vi* lloriquear

blubber[2] ['blʌbəʳ, *Am:* -ɚ] *n* grasa *f* (de ballena)

bludgeon ['blʌdʒən] I. *n* porra *f*, tolete *m AmC, AmS* II. *vt* aporrear

blue [bluː] I. *adj* 1. (*colour*) azul *m;* **light/dark ~** azul claro/oscuro; **pale/deep ~** azul pálido/intenso 2. (*sad*) triste; **to feel ~** sentirse triste II. *n* azul *m;* **sky ~** azul cielo; **the door is painted ~** la puerta está pintada de azul ►**out of the ~** cuando menos se espera

bluebell ['bluːbel] *n* campánula *f* azul

blueberry ['bluːbəri, *Am:* -ˌber-] <-ies> *n* arándano *m*

bluebottle ['bluːˌbɒtl, *Am:* -ˌbɑːt̬l] *n* mosca *f* azul

blue chip *adj* puntero, -a **blue collar** *adj*

(*union, background*) obrero, -a; (*job*) manual
blueprint ['blu:prɪnt] *n* plano *m;* (*programme*) programa *m*
blues [blu:z] *npl* **1.** melancolía *f* **2.** MUS blues *m*
blue whale *n* ballena *f* azul
bluff[1] [blʌf] **I.** *vi* tirarse un farol **II.** *vt* engañar **III.** *n* farol *m,* bluff *m AmL;* **to call sb's ~** descubrir a alguien la farolada
bluff[2] [blʌf] *n* (*steep bank*) risco *m;* (*cliff*) acantilado *m*
bluff[3] [blʌf] <-er, -est> *adj* campechano, -a
bluffer ['blʌfə^r, *Am:* -ɚ] *n* farolero, -a *m, f*
bluish ['blu:ɪʃ] *adj* azulado, -a
blunder ['blʌndə^r, *Am:* -dɚ] **I.** *n* error *m* garrafal, embarrada *f AmL* **II.** *vi* **1.** (*make a mistake*) cometer un error garrafal **2.** (*move clumsily*) **to ~ into sth** tropezar con algo
◆**blunder about** *vi* andar dando tropezones
blunt [blʌnt] **I.** *adj* **1.** (*not sharp*) desafilado, -a, pompo, -a *Ecua, Col* **2.** (*direct*) directo, -a **II.** *vt* despuntar; *fig* suavizar
bluntly *adv* sin rodeos; **to put it ~, ...** para decirlo sin rodeos,...
bluntness *n no pl* **1.** (*of a blade*) falta *f* de filo **2.** (*directness*) franqueza *f*
blur [blɜ:^r, *Am:* blɜ:r] **I.** *vi* <-rr-> desdibujarse **II.** *vt* <-rr-> desdibujar; (*picture*) desenfocar **III.** *n no pl* (*shape*) contorno *m* borroso; (*memory*) vago recuerdo *m*
blurb [blɜ:b, *Am:* blɜ:rb] *n no pl, inf* propaganda *f* publicitaria
blurred [blɜ:d, *Am:* blɜ:rd] *adj* indistinto, -a; (*photograph, picture*) borroso, -a
blurt out [blɜ:t'aʊt, *Am:* blɜ:rt'aʊt] *vt* soltar
blush [blʌʃ] **I.** *vi* ruborizarse **II.** *n* rubor *m*
blusher ['blʌsə^r, *Am:* -ɚ] *n* colorete *m,* rouge *m Chile*
blushing *adj* ruboroso, -a
bluster ['blʌstə^r, *Am:* -tɚ] **I.** *vi* **1.** (*speak*) bravuconear **2.** (*blow*) rugir **II.** *n no pl* bravuconería *f*
BMA *abbr of* **British Medical Association** *colegio de médicos británico*
BO [ˌbi:'əʊ, *Am:* -'oʊ] *n abbr of* **body odour** olor *m* corporal
boa ['bəʊə, *Am:* 'boʊə] *n* boa *f*
boar [bɔ:^r, *Am:* bɔ:r] *n* (*male pig*) cerdo *m* macho; (**wild**) ~ jabalí *m*
board [bɔ:d, *Am:* bɔ:rd] **I.** *n* **1.** (*wood*) tabla *f* **2.** (*blackboard*) pizarra *f;* (*notice board*) tablero *m* **3.** GAMES tablero *m* **4.** ADMIN consejo *m* de administración, junta *f;* ~ (**of directors**) junta directiva; **Board of Trade** *Am* Cámara *f* de Comercio **5.** (*in a hotel*) **full ~** pensión *f* completa; **half ~** media pensión *f* **6.** NAUT **on ~** a bordo ►**to let sth go by the ~** dejar algo a un lado; **to sweep the ~** llevarse todos los premios; (*in gambling*) limpiar la mesa; **to take sth on ~** adoptar algo; **to tread the ~s** THEAT salir a escena; **across the ~** en general **II.** *vt* (*get on: ship*) subir a bordo de; (*bus, train*) subir a **III.** *vi* (*stay*) alojarse; (*in school*) estar interno; **to ~ with sb** hospedarse en casa de alguien
◆**board up** *vt* entablar
boarder ['bɔ:də^r, *Am:* 'bɔ:rdɚ] *n* SCHOOL interno, -a *m, f*
board game *n* juego *m* de mesa
boarding card *n Brit* tarjeta *f* de embarque
boarding house *n* pensión *f*
boarding pass *n* tarjeta *f* de embarque
boarding school *n* internado *m*
board meeting *n* reunión *f* de la junta directiva **boardroom** *n* sala *f* de juntas
boardwalk ['bɔ:dwɔ:k, *Am:* 'bɔ:rdwɔ:k] *n Am: paseo marítimo entablado*
boast [bəʊst, *Am:* boʊst] **I.** *vi* alardear; **to ~ about/of sth** vanagloriarse sobre/de algo **II.** *vt* (*have*) tener; (*be proud of*) enorgullecerse de **III.** *n* alarde *m*
boastful ['bəʊstfəl, *Am:* 'boʊst-] *adj* fanfarrón, -ona, bocatero, -a *AmL*
boat [bəʊt, *Am:* boʊt] *n* barco *m;* (*small*) barca *f,* bote *m;* (*large*) buque *m;* **to go by ~** ir en barco ►**to be in the same ~** estar en la misma situación; **to burn one's ~s** (**behind one**) quemar las naves; **to miss the ~** perder la oportunidad; **to push the ~ out** *Brit* tirar la casa por la ventana; **to rock the ~** *inf* hacer olas
boat hook *n* bichero *m* **boat house** *n* cobertizo *m*
boating ['bəʊtɪŋ, *Am:* 'boʊt̬ɪŋ] *n no pl* **to go ~** dar un paseo en barca
boatman ['bəʊtmən, *Am:* 'boʊt-] *n* barquero *m*
boat people *npl* refugiados *mpl* del mar
boat race *n* regata *f;* **the Boat Race** *Brit: carrera anual de remo entre Oxford y Cambridge*

La anual **Boat Race** (competición de remo) se celebra un sábado de marzo en el río **Thames** (Támesis). Ocho remeros de las universidades de Oxford y Cambridge compiten en dicha carrera. Es un acontecimiento nacional muy importante seguido por 460 millones de espectadores de todo el mundo.

boatswain ['bəʊsən, *Am:* 'boʊ-] *n* contramaestre *m*
boat train *n* tren *m* que enlaza con un barco
boat trip *n* viaje *m* en barco
bob[1] [bɒb, *Am:* ba:b] *n* (*hairstyle*) pelo *m* a lo garçon
bob[2] [bɒb, *Am:* ba:b] <-bb-> **I.** *vi* **to ~ (up and down)** agitarse **II.** *n* meneo *m*
bob[3] [bɒb, *Am:* ba:b] *n Brit* (*shilling*) chelín *m*
bobbin ['bɒbɪn, *Am:* 'ba:bɪn] *n* bobina *f*
bobble hat ['bɒblˌhæt, *Am:* 'ba:bl-] *n* gorro *m* con pompón
bobby ['bɒbi, *Am:* 'ba:bi] <-ies> *n Brit, inf* poli *mf*
bobsled ['bɒbsled, *Am:* 'ba:b-] *n,*

bobsleigh ['bɒbsleɪ, *Am:* 'bɑːb-] *n* SPORTS bobsleigh *m*

bobtail ['bɒbteɪl, *Am:* 'bɑːb-] *n* **1.** (*docked tail*) cola *f* cortada **2.** (*animal*) animal *m* rabicorto

bode [bəʊd, *Am:* boʊd] **I.** *vi* **to ~ well/ill** ser una buena/mala señal **II.** *vt* presagiar

bodice ['bɒdɪs, *Am:* 'bɑːdɪs] *n* (*of a dress*) canesú *m;* (*underwear*) corpiño *m*

bodily ['bɒdəli] **I.** *adj* corpóreo, -a; (*harm, injury*) corporal; (*functions, needs*) fisiológico, -a **II.** *adv* (*in person*) en persona; (*as a whole*) en conjunto

body ['bɒdi, *Am:* 'bɑːdi] <-ies> *n* **1.** *a.* ANAT, ASTR, CHEM cuerpo *m* **2.** (*person*) **a cheerful old ~** un tipo alegre **3.** ADMIN, POL unidad *f;* (*governing*) organismo *m;* (*group*) grupo *m;* **in a ~** en bloque **4.** (*amount*) cantidad *f;* (*of water*) masa *f* **5.** AUTO caja *f,* carrocería *f* **6.** (*dead corpse*) cadáver *m* ►**to keep ~ and soul together** sobrevivir; **to throw oneself ~ and soul into sth** entregarse a algo en cuerpo y alma; **over my dead ~** ¡por encima de mi cadáver!; **to sell one's ~** prostituirse

body bag *n* bolsa *f* para cadáveres

bodybuilding *n no pl* culturismo *m*

bodyguard ['bɒdigɑːd, *Am:* 'bɑːdigɑːrd] *n* guardaespaldas *mf inv,* espaldero *m Ven*

body language *n no pl* lenguaje *m* corporal **body lotion** *n* loción *f* corporal **body politic** *n no pl* POL estado *m* **body search** *n* cacheo *m*

bodysuit *n* body *m*

bodywork ['bɒdiwɜːk, *Am:* 'bɑːdiwɜːrk] *n* carrocería *f*

bog [bɒg, *Am:* bɑːg] *n* **1.** (*wet ground*) ciénaga *f,* estero *m Bol, Col, Ven;* **peat ~** turbera *f* **2.** *Aus, Brit, inf* (*toilet*) retrete *m*

◆**bog down** <-gg-> *vt* **to get bogged down in sth** quedar atascado en algo; *fig* atrancarse en algo

bogey ['bəʊgi, *Am:* 'boʊ-] *n* **1.** (*unreasoned fear*) coco *m* **2.** *inf* (*snot*) moco *m* seco **3.** (*golf score*) bogey *m*

boggle ['bɒgl, *Am:* 'bɑːgl] **I.** *vi* quedarse atónito **II.** *vt* **to ~ the mind** ser increíble

boggy ['bɒgi, *Am:* 'bɑːgi] <-ier, -iest> *adj* pantanoso, -a

bogie ['boʊgi] *n Am s.* **bogey**

bogus ['bəʊgəs, *Am:* 'boʊ-] *adj* (*document*) falso, -a; (*argument*) falaz; (*person*) presuntuoso, -a

bogy ['bəʊgi, *Am:* 'boʊ-] *n s.* **bogey**

bohemian [bəʊ'hiːmiən, *Am:* boʊ-] **I.** *n* bohemio, -a *m, f* **II.** *adj* bohemio, -a

boil [bɔɪl] **I.** *vi, vt a. fig* hervir; **a (hard/soft) ~ed egg** un huevo duro/pasado por agua **II.** *n* **1.** *no pl* **to bring sth to the ~** calentar algo hasta que hierva; **to be on the ~** estar hirviendo; *fig* (*person*) estar furioso; **to go off the ~** dejar de hervir **2.** MED furúnculo *m*

◆**boil away** *vi* evaporarse

◆**boil down** **I.** *vi* reducirse por cocción **II.** *vt* reducir

◆**boil down to** *vt fig* reducirse a

◆**boil over** *vi* **1.** GASTR rebosar **2.** (*person*) perder el control; (*situation*) estallar

◆**boil up** *vt* hervir

boiler ['bɔɪləʳ, *Am:* -lɚ] *n* caldera *f*

boilerhouse *n* edificio *m* de la caldera **boiler room** *n* sala *f* de calderas **boiler suit** *n Aus, Brit* mono *m*

boiling *adj* **1.** hirviendo **2.** *fig* (*day, weather*) abrasador(a); (*angry: person*) enfadadísimo, -a; **I am ~** (*feeling hot*) me estoy asando; **it's ~ (hot) today** hace un calor achicharrante

boiling point *n* punto *m* de ebullición; **to reach ~** *fig* ponerse al rojo vivo

boisterous ['bɔɪstərəs] *adj* **1.** (*person, party*) bullicioso, -a **2.** (*sea*) enfurecido, -a

bold [bəʊld, *Am:* boʊld] <-er, -est> *adj* **1.** (*brave, audacious*) audaz **2.** (*strong: colour*) llamativo, -a **3.** INFOR, TYPO **~ (type)** negrita *f;* **in ~** en negrita **4.** (*not shy*) atrevido, -a; (*cheeky*) descarado, -a

boldness *n* audacia *f*

bole [bəʊl, *Am:* boʊl] *n* tronco *m*

bolero [bə'leərəʊ, *Am:* -'leroʊ] <-s> *n* **1.** (*short jacket*) torera *f* **2.** MUS bolero *m*

Bolivia [bə'lɪvɪə] *n* Bolivia *f*

Bolivian [bə'lɪvɪən] **I.** *adj* boliviano, -a **II.** *n* boliviano, -a *m, f*

bollard ['bɒlɑːd, *Am:* 'bɑːlɚd] *n Brit* baliza *f*

bolster ['bəʊlstəʳ, *Am:* 'boʊlstɚ] **I.** *n* cabezal *m* **II.** *vt* **1.** (*support*) reafirmar **2.** (*encourage*) alentar **3.** (*increase*) levantar

bolt [bəʊlt, *Am:* boʊlt] **I.** *vi* fugarse **II.** *vt* **1.** GASTR engullir **2.** (*lock*) echar el pestillo a **3.** (*fix*) atornillar **III.** *n* **1.** (*on a door*) pestillo *m* **2.** (*screw*) tornillo *m* **3.** (*of lightning*) rayo *m* **4.** (*roll: of cloth*) rollo *m* **5.** (*arrow*) flecha *f* ►**to make a ~ for it** fugarse; **a ~ from the blue** un acontecimiento inesperado **IV.** *adv* **~ upright** rígido, derecho

bolt hole *n* refugio *m*

bomb [bɒm, *Am:* bɑːm] **I.** *n* **1.** (*explosive*) bomba *f* **2.** *Brit, inf* **to cost/be worth a ~** costar/valer un dineral ►**to go like a ~** *Brit, inf* (*go well*) marchar a las mil maravillas; (*go very quickly*) ir como un bólido; (*be a success*) ser un exitazo **II.** *vt* bombardear **III.** *vi inf* estrellarse

bombard [bɒm'bɑːd, *Am:* bɑːm'bɑːrd] *vt* bombardear; **to ~ sb with questions** acribillar a alguien a preguntas

bombardment [bɒm'bɑːdmənt, *Am:* bɑːm'bɑːrd-] *n* bombardeo *m*

bombast ['bɒmbæst, *Am:* 'bɑːm-] *n no pl* grandilocuencia *f*

bombastic [bɒm'bæstɪk, *Am:* bɑːm-] *adj* grandilocuente; (*style*) rimbombante

bomb crater *n* cráter *m* de bomba **bomb disposal unit** *n* brigada *f* de bombas

bombed [bɒmd] *adj* **1.** bombardeado, -a **2.** *Am, inf* (*on drugs*) colocado, -a

bomber ['bɒməʳ, *Am:* 'bɑːmɚ] *n* **1.** AVIAT

bombardero *m* **2.** (*terrorist*) terrorista *mf* (que coloca bombas)
bombing *n* **1.** MIL bombardeo *m* **2.** (*by terrorists*) atentado *m* (con bomba)
bombproof *adj* a prueba de bombas
bombshell ['bɒmʃel, *Am:* 'bɑːm-] *n* **1.** MIL obús *m* **2.** (*woman*) mujer *f* despampanante **3.** (*surprise*) bombazo *m inf*
bona fide [ˌbəʊnə'faɪdi, *Am:* ˌboʊ-] *adj* **1.** (*genuine*) genuino, -a; (*agreement, alibi*) auténtico, -a **2.** (*serious*) serio, -a
bonanza [bə'nænzə] **I.** *n a. fig* bonanza *f* **II.** *adj* próspero, -a
bond [bɒnd, *Am:* bɑːnd] **I.** *n* **1.** (*connection*) vínculo *m;* (*of friendship, love*) lazo *m;* **to break one's** ~ romper sus cadenas *fig* **2.** (*obligation*) obligación *f* **3.** FIN bono *m;* **to place goods in** ~ poner mercancías en el almacén aduanero **4.** LAW garantía *f; Am* (*bail*) fianza *f* **5.** *pl, liter* (*chains*) cadenas *fpl* **6.** (*joint*) junta *f* **II.** *vt* **1.** (*stick*) pegar **2.** (*unite emotionally*) **to** ~ (**together**) vincular **3.** COM depositar bajo fianza **III.** *vi* adherirse
bondage ['bɒndɪdʒ, *Am:* 'bɑːn-] *n no pl* **1.** *liter* (*slavery*) esclavitud *f;* **to be in** ~ **to sb/sth** estar esclavo de alguien/algo **2.** (*for sexual pleasure*) bondage *m*
bonded *adj* **1.** COM en depósito aduanero **2.** FIN garantizado, -a por obligación escrita
bonded debt *n* FIN deuda *f* consolidada
bonded warehouse *n* COM almacén *m* aduanero
bondholder *n* FIN titular *mf* de bonos
bone [bəʊn, *Am:* boʊn] **I.** *n* ANAT hueso *m;* (*of a fish*) espina *f* ►~ **of contention** manzana *f* de la discordia; **to work one's fingers to the** ~ trabajar como un esclavo; **close to the** ~ fuera de tono; **to cut sth to the** ~ reducir algo a lo esencial; **to feel sth in one's** ~**s** tener un presentimiento de algo; **to make no** ~**s about sth** no ocultar algo; **to have a** ~ **to pick with sb** *inf* tener que ajustar cuentas con alguien **II.** *adj* de hueso **III.** *vt* (*piece of meat*) deshuesar; (*fish*) quitar las espinas a
bonehead ['bəʊnhed, *Am:* 'boʊn-] *n inf* estúpido, -a *m, f*
bone idle *adj,* **bone lazy** *adj inf* vago, -a
bone marrow *n no pl* médula *f* ósea **bonemeal** *n no pl* harina *f* de huesos
boneshaker ['bəʊnˌʃeɪkə^r, *Am:* 'boʊnˌʃeɪkɚ] *n inf* carraca *f*
bonfire ['bɒnfaɪə^r, *Am:* 'bɑːnfaɪɚ] *n* hoguera *f*
bonkers ['bɒŋkəz, *Am:* 'bɑːŋkɚz] *adj inf* loco, -a; **to go** ~ volverse loco
bonnet ['bɒnɪt, *Am:* 'bɑːnɪt] *n* **1.** (*hat*) sombrero *m;* (*baby's*) gorrito *m* **2.** *Aus, Brit* AUTO capote *m*
bonny ['bɒni, *Am:* 'bɑːni] *adj Scot* hermoso, -a
bonus ['bəʊnəs, *Am:* 'boʊ-] *n* **1.** (*money*) prima *f,* abono *m AmL;* (*for Christmas*) bonificación *f;* **productivity** ~ plus *m* **2.** (*advantage*) ventaja *f*
bony ['bəʊni, *Am:* 'boʊ-] *adj* <-ier, -iest> **1.** (*with prominent bones*) huesudo, -a; (*fish*) con muchas espinas **2.** (*like bones*) óseo, -a
boo [buː] **I.** *interj inf* bu **II.** *vi* abuchear, pifiar *Chile, Méx* **III.** *vt* abuchear; **he was ~ed off the stage** lo abuchearon hasta que abandonó el escenario
boob [buːb] **I.** *n* **1.** *inf* (*breast*) teta *f* **2.** *Brit, inf* (*blunder*) metedura *f* de pata **3.** *Am* (*fool*) bobo, -a *m, f* **II.** *vi Brit, inf* meter la pata
booby ['buːbi] *n* bobo, -a *m, f*
booby prize *n* premio *m* al peor **booby trap** *n* trampa *f*
book [bʊk] **I.** *n* **1.** libro *m;* **the Good Book** la Biblia **2.** (*of stamps*) taco *m;* (*of tickets*) talonario *m* **3.** (*register*) registro *m* **4.** COM, FIN **the** ~**s** las cuentas ►**to be in sb's bad** ~**s** estar en la lista negra de alguien; **to be a closed** ~ (**to sb**) ser un misterio (para alguien); **to be in sb's good** ~**s** gozar de las simpatías de alguien; **to bring sb to** ~ pedir cuentas a alguien; **to cook the** ~**s** *inf* amañar las cuentas; **to be able to read sb like a** ~ conocer a alguien a fondo; **to suit sb's** ~ convenir a alguien; **to throw the** ~ **at sb** castigar duramente a alguien, cantar las cuarenta a alguien; **in my** ~ en mi opinión **II.** *vt* **1.** (*reserve*) reservar **2.** (*register*) fichar **III.** *vi* reservar
◆**book in I.** *vi* inscribirse **II.** *vt* **to book sb in** (*register*) registrar a alguien; (*make a reservation for*) reservar una habitación para alguien
◆**book up** *vt* **to be booked up** estar completo
bookable ['bʊkəbl] *adj* ~ **in advance** *que se puede reservar por adelantado*
bookbinder ['bʊkˌbaɪndə^r, *Am:* -dɚ] *n* encuadernador(a) *m(f)*
bookbinding *n no pl* encuadernación *f*
bookcase ['bʊkkeɪs] *n* estantería *f*
book club *n* club *m* de lectores
bookend ['bʊkend] *n* sujetalibros *m inv*
bookie ['bʊki] *n inf* corredor(a) *m(f)* de apuestas
booking ['bʊkɪŋ] *n* reserva *f;* **to make/cancel a** ~ hacer/cancelar una reserva
booking clerk *n* taquillero, -a *m, f* **booking office** *n* **1.** (*theatre*) taquilla *f* **2.** (*station*) ventanilla *f* de venta de billetes
bookish ['bʊkɪʃ] *adj* libresco, -a; *pej* pedante
bookkeeper ['bʊkˌkiːpə^r, *Am:* -pɚ] *n* contable *mf*
bookkeeping ['bʊk ˌkiːpɪŋ] *n no pl* contabilidad *f*
booklet ['bʊklɪt] *n* folleto *m*
bookmaker ['bʊkˌmeɪkə^r, *Am:* -kɚ] *n* corredor(a) *m(f)* de apuestas
bookmark ['bʊkmaːk, *Am:* -maːrk] *n a.* INFOR marcador *m*
bookplate ['bʊkpleɪt] *n* ex libris *m*
book review *n* crítica *f* de libros **book reviewer** *n* crítico, -a *m, f* de libros
bookseller ['bʊkˌselə^r, *Am:* -ɚ] *n* (*person*)

librero, -a *m, f;* (*shop*) librería *f*
bookshelf ['bʊkʃelf] <-shelves> *n* estante *m*
bookshop ['bʊksɒp, *Am:* -ʃɑːp] *n* librería *f*
bookstall ['bʊkstɔːl, *Am:* -stɔːl] *n* quiosco *m*
bookstore ['bʊkstɔːʳ, *Am:* -stɔːr] *n Am* librería *f*
book token *n* vale *m* cancejable por libros
book trade *n no pl* comercio *m* de libros
bookworm ['bʊkwɜːm, *Am:* -wɜːrm] *n* ratón *m* de biblioteca
boom¹ [buːm] ECON **I.** *vi* estar en auge **II.** *n* boom *m* **III.** *adj* en alza; **a ~ time** un período de prosperidad; **a ~ town** una ciudad próspera
boom² [buːm] **I.** *n* (*sound*) estruendo *m* **II.** *vi* **to ~** (**out**) tronar; (*voice*) resonar **III.** *vt* tronar
boom³ [buːm] *n* **1.** (*floating barrier*) barrera *f* **2.** NAUT botavara *f* **3.** (*for a microphone*) jirafa *f*
boomerang ['buːməræŋ] **I.** *n* bumerán *m* **II.** *vi* **it ~ed on her/him** le salió el tiro por la culata *inf*
boon [buːn] *n no pl* beneficio *m;* **to be a ~** (**to sb**) ser de gran ayuda (para alguien); **~ companion** *liter* amigo, -a *m, f* del alma
boor [bʊəʳ, *Am:* bʊr] *n* grosero, -a *m, f*
boorish ['bɔːrɪʃ, *Am:* 'bʊrɪʃ] *adj* grosero, -a
boost [buːst] **I.** *n no pl* incentivo *m;* **to give a ~ to sth, to give sth a ~** estimular algo **II.** *vt* **1.** (*increase*) aumentar, incrementar; (*morale*) reforzar; (*process*) estimular **2.** *inf* (*promote*) promover; (*image, ego*) potenciar
booster [buːstəʳ, *Am:* -stɚ] *n* **1.** (*improvement*) mejora *f* **2.** MED vacuna *f* de refuerzo
booster rocket *n* TECH cohete *m* propulsor
booster seat *n* AUTO booster *m*
boot [buːt] **I.** *n* **1.** (*footwear*) bota *f;* **ankle ~** botín *m;* **wellington ~** bota *f* de goma **2.** *inf* (*kick*) patada *f*, puntapié *m;* **to put the ~ in** *inf* emplear la violencia; *fig* obrar decisivamente **3.** INFOR arranque *m*, inicialización *f;* **warm/cold ~** arranque en frío/en caliente **4.** *Brit, Aus* AUTO maletero *m*, cajuela *f Méx*, baúl *m Arg* ►**the ~'s on the other <u>foot</u>** se ha vuelto la tortilla; **to be too <u>big</u> for one's ~s** *inf* tener muchos humos; **to <u>get</u> the ~** *inf* ser despedido; **to <u>give</u> sb the ~** *inf* echar a alguien; **to <u>lick</u> sb's ~s** hacer la pelota a alguien; **to <u>shake</u> in one's ~s** *inf* temblar de miedo **II.** *vt inf* **1.** (*kick*) dar un puntapié a **2.** INFOR arrancar ►**<u>to</u> ~** además, por si fuera poco
◆**boot out** *vt inf* poner de patitas en la calle
bootblack ['buːtblæk] *n* limpiabotas *mf inv*
bootee ['buːtiː, *Am:* -t̬i] *n* patuco *m*
booth [buːð] *n* **1.** (*cubicle*) cubículo *m;* (*telephone*) cabina *f;* (*polling*) casilla *f* **2.** (*at a fair, market*) caseta *f*
bootlace ['buːtleɪs] *n* cordón *m*
bootleg ['buːtleg] <-gg-> *adj* **1.** (*alcohol, cigarettes*) de contrabando **2.** (*recording, software*) pirata
bootlicker ['buːtlɪkəʳ] *n inf* lameculos *m inv*, olfa *mf Arg, Par, Urug*
bootmaker *n* fabricante *mf* de zapatos
booty ['buːti, *Am:* -t̬i] *n* botín *m*
booze [buːz] **I.** *n inf* bebida *f;* **to go out on the ~** salir de juerga **II.** *vi inf* empinar el codo, chupar *AmL*
boozer ['buːzəʳ, *Am:* -ɚ] *n inf* **1.** *Brit* (*pub*) bar *m* **2.** (*person*) borrachín, -ina *m, f*
boozy ['buːzi] <-ier, -iest> *adj inf* borrachín, -ina
border ['bɔːdəʳ, *Am:* 'bɔːrdɚ] **I.** *n* **1.** (*frontier*) frontera *f* **2.** (*edge, boundary*) borde *m* **3.** FASHION cenefa *f* **4.** (*in a garden*) arriate *m* **II.** *adj* fronterizo, -a **III.** *vt* limitar con
◆**border on** *vi* **1.** (*share border with*) limitar con **2.** *fig* rayar en
bordering *adj* limítrofe
borderland ['bɔːdəlænd, *Am:* 'bɔːrdɚ-] *n* zona *f* fronteriza
borderline ['bɔːdəlaɪn, *Am:* 'bɔːrdɚ-] **I.** *n no pl* frontera *f* **II.** *adj* (*candidate, case*) dudoso, -a
bore¹ [bɔːʳ, *Am:* bɔːr] **I.** *n* **1.** (*thing*) aburrimiento *m;* (*task*) lata *f*, fastidio *m;* **what a ~!** ¡qué lata! **2.** (*person*) pesado, -a *m, f* **II.** <bored> *vt* aburrir; **to ~ sb to death** *inf* aburrir a alguien como una ostra
bore² [bɔːʳ, *Am:* bɔːr] **I.** *n* (*of a pipe*) alma *f;* (*of a gun*) calibre *m* **II.** *vt* perforar; **to ~ a hole** abrir un agujero
bore³ [bɔːʳ, *Am:* bɔːr] *pp of* **bear**
bored *adj* aburrido, -a
boredom ['bɔːdəm, *Am:* 'bɔːr-] *n no pl* aburrimiento *m*
boric ['bɔːrɪk] *adj* bórico, -a; **~ acid** ácido bórico
boring ['bɔːrɪŋ] *adj* aburrido, -a, cansador(a) *Arg, Chile, Urug,* fome *Chile;* **to find sth ~** encontrar algo pesado
born [bɔːn, *Am:* bɔːrn] *adj* **1.** (*brought into life*) nacido, -a; **to be ~** nacer; **where were you ~?** ¿dónde naciste?; **he was ~ in the year 1975** nació en el año 1975; **he was ~ blind** es ciego de nacimiento **2.** (*ability*) nato, -a; (*quality, sympathy*) innato, -a ►**I wasn't ~ <u>yesterday</u>** *inf* no nací ayer
born-again ['bɔːnəgen, *Am:* ˌbɔːrn-] *adj* renacido, -a; **~ Christian** cristiano convertido
borne [bɔːn, *Am:* bɔːrn] *pt of* **bear**
borough ['bʌrə, *Am:* 'bɜːroʊ] *n* municipio *m*
borrow ['bɒrəʊ, *Am:* 'bɑːroʊ] *vt* **1.** (*be given temporarily*) tomar prestado; (*ask for*) pedir prestado; **may I ~ your bag?** ¿me prestas tu bolso? **2.** LING tomar
borrower *n* prestatario, -a *m, f*
borrowing *n no pl* préstamo *m;* **public ~** oferta *f* pública
Bosnia ['bɒzniə, *Am:* 'bɑːz-] *n* Bosnia *f*
Bosnia-Herzegovina ['bɒzniəˌhɜːzə'gɒvɪnə, *Am:* 'bɑːzniəˌhertsəgoʊviːnə] *n* Bosnia *f* Herzegovina
Bosnian ['bɒznɪən, *Am:* 'bɑːz-] **I.** *adj* bosnio, -a **II.** *n* bosnio, -a *m, f*
bosom ['bʊzəm] *n no pl* **1.** pecho *m* **2.** *fig*

B

seno *m;* **in the ~ of one's family** en el seno de su familia

bosom buddy *n* amigo *m* del alma

boss[1] [bɒs, *Am:* bɑːs] **I.** *n* (*person in charge*) jefe, -a *m, f;* (*owner*) patrón, -ona *m, f;* **to be one's own ~** ser su propio jefe **II.** *vt inf* **to ~ sb about** mandonear a alguien

boss[2] [bɒs, *Am:* bɑːs] *adj Am, inf* chulo, -a

bossy ['bɒsi, *Am:* 'bɑːsi] <-ier, -iest> *adj* mandón, -ona

bossy boots *n inf* mandón, -ona *m, f*

bosun ['bəʊsən, *Am:* 'boʊ-] *n* contramaestre *m*

botanical [bə'tænɪkəl] *adj* botánico, -a

botanist ['bɒtənɪst, *Am:* 'bɑːtnɪst] *n* botánico, -a *m, f*

botany ['bɒtəni, *Am:* 'bɑːtni] *n no pl* botánica *f*

botch [bɒtʃ, *Am:* bɑːtʃ] **I.** *n* chapuza *f;* **to make a ~ of sth** hacer una chapuza de algo **II.** *vt* **to ~ sth** (**up**) hacer una chapuza de algo

botch-up ['bɒtʃʌp, *Am:* 'bɑːtʃ-] *Aus, Brit s.* **botch I.**

both [bəʊθ, *Am:* boʊθ] **I.** *adj, pron* los dos, las dos, ambos, ambas; **~ of them** ellos dos, ellas dos; **~ of us** nosotros dos, nosotras dos; **~** (**the**) **brothers** los dos hermanos; **on ~ sides** en ambos lados **II.** *adv* **~ Mathilde and Sara** tanto Mathilde como Sara; **to be ~ sad and pleased** estar a la vez triste y satisfecho

bother ['bɒðə^r, *Am:* 'bɑːðɚ] **I.** *n* molestia *f,* friega *f AmL;* **it is no ~** no es ninguna molestia; **not to want to be a ~** no querer molestar; **it is not worth the ~** no vale la pena; **to get into a spot of ~** *Brit, inf* meterse en un lío **II.** *vi* molestarse; (**not**) **to ~ to do sth** (no) molestarse en hacer algo; **why ~?** ¿para qué molestarse? **III.** *vt* **1.** (*annoy*) molestar **2.** (*worry*) preocupar; **he doesn't seem to be ~ed by ...** no parece que le preocupa...; **what ~s me is ...** lo que me preocupa es...

bothersome ['bɒðəsəm, *Am:* 'bɑːðɚ-] *adj* molesto, -a, tequioso, -a *AmC,* espeso, -a *Perú, Ven*

Botswana [ˌbɒt'swɑːnə, *Am:* bɑːt-] *n* Botsuana *f*

Botswanan [ˌbɒt'swɑːnən] **I.** *adj* botsuano, -a **II.** *n* botsuano, -a *m, f*

bottle ['bɒtl, *Am:* 'bɑːt̬l] **I.** *n* **1.** (*container*) botella *f;* (*of ink, perfume*) frasco *m;* (*baby's*) biberón *m* **2.** *no pl, inf* (*alcohol*) **the ~** la bebida; **to hit the ~** empinar el codo **3.** *no pl, Brit, inf* (*courage*) agallas *fpl* **II.** *vt Brit* embotellar

bottle bank *n* contenedor *m* de recogida de vidrio **bottle brush** *n* limpiabotellas *m inv*

bottled ['bɒtld, *Am:* 'bɑːt̬ld] *adj* embotellado, -a; (*beer, gas*) de botella

bottle-feeding ['bɒtlˌfiːdɪŋ] *n no pl* alimentación *f* con biberón **bottle-green** *adj* verde botella

bottleneck ['bɒtlnek, *Am:* 'bɑːt̬l-] *n a. fig* cuello *m* de botella

bottle opener *n* abrebotellas *m inv*

bottom ['bɒtəm, *Am:* 'bɑːt̬əm] **I.** *n no pl* **1.** (*of sea, street, glass*) fondo *m;* (*of chair*) asiento *m;* (*of stairs, page*) pie *m;* **to touch ~** (*reach bottom of water*) llegar al fondo; *fig* tocar fondo **2.** (*lower part*) parte *f* inferior; **from top to ~** de arriba a abajo **3.** (*buttocks*) trasero *m* ▶**from the ~ of one's heart** de todo corazón; **~s up!** ¡al centro y para adentro!; **to get to the ~ of sth** llegar al fondo de algo; **at ~** en el fondo; **to be at the ~ of sth** ser el motivo de algo **II.** *adj* (*lower*) más bajo; **the ~ half of society** la clase media-baja; **in ~ gear** en primera; **the ~ end of the table** la mitad inferior de la mesa

bottomless ['bɒtəmləs, *Am:* 'bɑːt̬əm-] *adj* **1.** (*without limit*) sin fondo **2.** (*very deep*) infinito, -a; **a ~ pit** *fig* un pozo sin fondo; **she is a ~ pit** tiene la solitaria

bottom line *n* **the ~** *fig* lo fundamental

botulism ['bɒtjʊlɪzəm, *Am:* 'bɑːtʃə-] *n no pl* botulismo *m*

bough [baʊ] *n liter* rama *f*

bought [bɔːt, *Am:* bɑːt] *vt pt of* **buy**

boulder ['bəʊldə^r, *Am:* 'boʊldɚ] *n* roca *f*

boulevard ['buːləvɑːd, *Am:* 'bʊləvɑːrd] *n* bulevar *m*

bounce [baʊnts] **I.** *vi* **1.** (*rebound*) (re)botar; **to ~ against sth** botar contra algo; **to ~ an idea off sb** pedir la opinión a alguien; **to ~ sb into doing sth** presionar a alguien para hacer algo **2.** (*jump or spring up and down*) dar brincos **3.** *inf* COM ser devuelto **II.** *vt* **1.** (*cause to rebound*) hacer (re)botar; **to ~ a baby** hacer el caballito a un niño **2.** *inf* COM **to ~ a cheque** devolver un cheque **III.** *n* **1.** (*rebound*) (re)bote *m* **2.** *no pl* (*spring*) bote *m* **3.** *no pl* (*vitality*) vitalidad *f;* (*energy*) energía *f* **4.** *Am, inf* **to give sb the ~** poner a alguien de patitas en la calle

◆**bounce back** *vi* recuperarse

bouncer ['baʊntsə^r, *Am:* -sɚ] *n inf* gorila *m*

bouncing *adj* robusto, -a

bouncy ['baʊntsi] *adj* **1.** (*ball*) que rebota **2.** (*lively*) animado, -a

bound[1] [baʊnd] **I.** *vi* **1.** (*leap*) saltar **2.** (*bounce: ball*) botar, rebotar *AmL* **II.** *n* salto *m;* **with one ~** de un salto

bound[2] [baʊnd] *vt* **to be ~ed by sth** estar rodeado por algo

bound[3] [baʊnd] *adj* **to be ~ for ...** ir rumbo a...; **where is this ship ~ for?** ¿a dónde se dirige este barco?

bound[4] [baʊnd] **I.** *pt, pp of* **bind II.** *adj* **1.** (*sure*) **she's ~ to come** seguro que viene; **it's ~ to be cheap** seguro que es barato; **it was ~ to happen sooner or later** tarde o temprano tenía que suceder **2.** (*obliged*) **to be ~ to do sth** estar obligado a hacer algo ▶**to be ~ and determined** *Am* tener intenciones firmes

boundary ['baʊndri] <-ies> *n* **1.** *a. fig* (*line*) límite *m;* **to blur the boundaries** *fig* desdibujar los límites; **to transgress the boundaries of good taste** transgredir los límites del buen gusto **2.** (*border*) frontera *f*; **to cross a ~** cruzar una frontera; **to mark a ~ (between two places)** establecer una frontera (entre dos lugares) **3.** SPORTS banda *f*

boundless ['baʊndlɪs] *adj* (*love, patience*) sin límites; (*energy*) ilimitado, -a, inagotable; (*universe*) infinito, -a

bounds [baʊndz] *n pl* límites *mpl*; **to know no ~** no conocer límites; **to be beyond the ~ of possibility** no ser posible; **to be outside the ~ of acceptable behaviour** estar lejos de ser un comportamiento aceptable; **this area is out of ~ to civilians** los civiles tienen prohibido la entrada en esta zona; **within ~** dentro de ciertos límites; **to be within the ~ of the law** estar dentro de los límites legales

bounty ['baʊnti, *Am:* -t̬i] <-ies> *n* **1.** (*reward*) recompensa *f* **2.** (*gift*) regalo *m* **3.** *no pl, liter* (*generosity*) munificencia *f*

bouquet [bʊ'keɪ, *Am:* boʊ-] *n* **1.** (*of flowers*) ramo *m* **2.** (*smell, aroma*) aroma *m*; (*of wine*) bouquet *m* **3.** (*compliment*) elogio *m*

bourbon ['bɜːbən, *Am:* 'bɜːr-] *n* bourbon *m*

bourgeois ['bɔːʒwɑː, *Am:* 'bʊrʒ-] *adj* burgués, -esa

bout [baʊt] *n* **1.** (*of illness*) ataque *m*; **~ of coughing** ataque *m* de tos; **~ of insanity** período *m* de locura; **drinking ~** borrachera *f* **2.** SPORTS (*in boxing, wrestling*) combate *m*; (*in fencing*) asalto *m*

boutique [buː'tiːk] *n* boutique *f*

bovine ['bəʊvaɪn, *Am:* 'boʊ-] *adj* **1.** (*of cows*) bovino, -a **2.** *fig* (*stupid*) tonto, -a

bovver boy ['bɒvəʳ,bɔɪ] *n inf* gamberro *m*

bow¹ [bəʊ, *Am:* boʊ] *n* **1.** (*weapon*) *a.* MUS arco *m* **2.** (*slip-knot*) lazo *m*, moño *m AmL*, moña *f Urug*, rosa *f Chile* ►**to have more than one string to one's ~** ser una persona de recursos

bow² [baʊ] *n* NAUT proa *f*

bow³ [baʊ] **I.** *vi* **1.** (*greet*) hacer una reverencia; *fig* ceder; **to ~ to sb** hacer una reverencia ante alguien **2.** (*yield*) **to ~ to sth** someterse a algo ►**to ~ and scrape** hacer la pelota, hacer la barba *Méx* **II.** *vt* (*one's head*) inclinar, agachar; (*body*) doblegar **III.** *n* reverencia *f*, venia *f CSur, Col*, caravana *f Méx*; **to take a ~** recibir un aplauso

◆**bow out** *vi* retirarse

bowdlerise *vt Aus, Brit*, **bowdlerize** ['baʊdləraɪz, *Am:* 'boʊdləraɪz] *vt* expurgar

bowel ['baʊəl] *n* MED intestino *m* grueso; **to move one's ~s** hacer de vientre, mover el vientre *RíoPl*

bowel movement *n* evacuación *f* (intestinal)

bowl¹ [bəʊl, *Am:* boʊl] *n* **1.** (*dish*) bol *m*; (*for soup*) plato *m* hondo; (*of toilet*) taza *f*; (*for washing*) palangana *f*; (*of pipe*) cazoleta *f*; (*of fountain*) pila *f*; **fruit ~** frutero *m*, frutera *f CSur* **2.** *Am* (*stadium*) estadio *m* **3.** (*hollow*) hondonada *f*

bowl² [bəʊl, *Am:* boʊl] SPORTS **I.** *vi* **1.** (*in cricket, bowling*) lanzar **2.** (*play bowls, go bowling*) jugar a los bolos **II.** *vt* lanzar **III.** *n* **1.** (*in bowls, bowling*) bola *f*, bocha *f* **2.** *pl juego semejante a la petanca o las bochas que se juega sobre el césped*

◆**bowl out** *vt* eliminar

◆**bowl over** *vt* **1.** (*knock over*) tumbar **2.** (*astonish*) dejar atónito; **to be bowled over** estar desconcertado

bow-legged [,bəʊ'legd, *Am:* boʊ-] *adj* (*person*) patizambo, -a, cascorvo, -a *Col*; (*table*) de patas arqueadas

bowler ['bəʊləʳ, *Am:* 'boʊlɚ] *n* **1.** (*in cricket*) lanzador(a) *m(f)* **2.** (*at bowling, bowls*) jugador(a) *m(f)* **3.** (*hat*) bombín *m*

bowling *n no pl* **1.** (*game*) bolos *mpl* **2.** (*in cricket*) lanzamiento *m*

bowling alley *n* bolera *f* **bowling green** *n pista donde se juega a los bolos*

bowman ['bəʊmən, *Am:* 'boʊ-] *n* arquero *m*

bowstring ['bəʊstrɪŋ, *Am:* 'boʊ-] *n* MUS cuerda *f* del arco

bow tie *n* pajarita *f*, corbatín *m Col*, moñita *f Urug*

bow window *n* mirador *m*

box¹ [bɒks, *Am:* bɑːks] **I.** *vi* SPORTS boxear **II.** *vt* **1.** SPORTS boxear con [*o* contra] **2. to ~ sb's ears** dar un sopapo a alguien **III.** *n* sopapo *m*; **to give sb a ~ on the ears** dar un sopapo a alguien

box² [bɒks, *Am:* bɑːks] **I.** *n* **1.** (*container*) caja *f*; **cardboard ~** caja de cartón; **tool ~** caja de herramientas **2.** (*rectangular space*) casilla *f*; (*in soccer, baseball*) área *f*; (*at road junction*) parrilla *f*; (**penalty**) **~** (*in soccer*) área (de castigo); (*in ice hockey*) banquillo *m* **3.** (*small space*) agujero *m*; **their new house is just a ~** su nueva casa es un agujero **4.** THEAT palco *m*; (*booth*) cabina *f*; **sentry ~** garita *f*; **witness ~** estrado *m* **5.** *Aus, Brit* SPORTS (*protector*) protector *m*, concha *f Méx* **6.** *inf* (*television*) **the ~** la caja tonta **7.** *no pl* (*tree*) boj *m* **8.** INFOR **dialogue ~** cuadro *m* de diálogo **II.** *vt* poner en una caja

◆**box in** *vt* acorralar; **to ~ a car** cerrar el paso a un coche; **to feel boxed in** *fig* sentirse limitado

◆**box off** *vt* compartimentar

◆**box up** *vt* poner en una caja

boxer ['bɒksəʳ, *Am:* 'bɑːksɚ] *n* **1.** (*dog*) bóxer *mf* **2.** (*person*) boxeador(a) *m(f)*

boxer shorts *npl* calzoncillos *mpl*

boxing ['bɒksɪŋ, *Am:* 'bɑːksɪŋ] *n no pl* boxeo *m*, box *m AmL*

El **Boxing Day** se celebra el 26 de diciembre. El nombre de este día proviene de cuando los aprendices de un oficio, el día después de Navidad, recogían en **boxes** (cajas) las propinas que los clientes del taller de su maestro les daban. Antiguamente se denominaba **Christmas box** a la paga navideña que recibían los empleados.

boxing glove *n* guante *m* de boxeo **boxing match** *n* partido *m* de boxeo **boxing ring** *n* ring *m*

box number *n* (*at a newspaper*) (número *m* de) referencia *f;* (*at the post office*) apartado *m* de correos, apartado *m* postal *Méx,* casilla *f* postal *CSur* **box office** *n* taquilla *f,* boletería *f AmL*

boy [bɔɪ] **I.** *n* **1.** (*child*) niño *m* **2.** (*young man*) chico *m,* muchacho *m,* chamaco, -a *m, f Méx,* pibe *m Arg* **3.** (*son*) hijo *m,* chico *m* **4.** (*servant*) criado *m,* mozo *m* **5.** (*boyfriend*) novio *m* ►**the old ~ network** el amiguismo; **the ~s in blue** *inf* la policía; **~s will be ~s** así son los chicos [*o* niños] **II.** *interj* (**oh**) **~!** ¡vaya!

boycott ['bɔɪkɒt, *Am:* -kɑːt] **I.** *vt* boicotear **II.** *n* boicot *m*

boyfriend ['bɔɪfrend] *n* novio *m*

boyhood ['bɔɪhʊd] *n no pl* niñez *f*

boyish ['bɔɪɪʃ] *adj* (*woman*) de chico; (*enthusiasm*) de niño

Boy Scout *n* boy scout *m*

Bq *abbr of* **becquerel** Bq

BR [ˌbiːˈɑr, *Am:* -ˈɑːr] *n abbr of* **British Rail** *compañía ferroviaria británica*

bra [brɑː] *n* sujetador *m,* brasier *m Col, Méx,* corpiño *m RíoPl*

brace [breɪs] **I.** *vt* **1.** (*prepare*) **to ~ oneself for sth** prepararse para algo **2.** (*support: wall*) reforzar **II.** *n* **1.** (*for teeth*) aparato(s) *m(pl)* **2.** (*for the back*) aparato *m* ortopédico **3.** *pl, Aus, Brit* (*suspenders*) tirantes *mpl,* tiradores *mpl RíoPl* **4.** *pl, Am* (*callipers*) corrector *m*

bracelet ['breɪslɪt] *n* pulsera *f*

bracken ['brækn] *n no pl* helechos *mpl*

bracket ['brækɪt] **I.** *n pl* TYPO (*round*) paréntesis *m inv;* **in ~s** entre paréntesis; **angled ~** corchete *m* agudo; **curly ~** llave *f;* **square ~** corchete *m* **II.** *n* **1.** (*category*) categoría *f;* **age ~** grupo *m* etario; **income ~** nivel *m* de ingresos; **tax ~** banda *f* impositiva **2.** (*for a shelf*) soporte *m* **III.** *vt* **1.** TYPO poner entre paréntesis **2.** (*include*) agrupar; **to ~ sb with sb else** equiparar a alguien con alguien

brackish ['brækɪʃ] *adj* salobre

brag [bræg] <-gg-> *inf* **I.** *vi* fanfarronear; **to ~ about sth** alardear de algo **II.** *vt* **to ~ that ...** hacer alarde [*o* jactarse] de que...

braid [breɪd] **I.** *n* **1.** *no pl* FASHION galón *m* **2.** *Am* (*plait*) trenza *f,* chongo *m Méx,* chapeca *f Arg* **II.** *vt, vi Am* (*plait*) trenzar

Braille [breɪl] *n no pl* braille *m*

brain [breɪn] **I.** *n* **1.** (*organ*) cerebro *m* **2.** *pl* (*substance*) sesos *mpl* **3.** (*intelligence*) cerebro *m;* **to have ~s** ser inteligente **4.** *inf* (*intelligent person*) cerebro *m,* lumbrera *f;* **the best ~s** los mejores cerebros ►**to beat one's ~s out** *inf* estrujarse el cerebro; **to blow sb's ~s out** *inf* levantar la tapa de los sesos a alguien; **to have sth on the ~** *inf* estar obsesionado con algo; **to pick sb's ~s** *inf* hacer preguntas a alguien; **to rack one's ~** devanarse los sesos **II.** *vt inf* romper la crisma a

brainchild ['breɪntʃaɪld] *n no pl* creación *f*

brain damage *n* lesión *f* cerebral **brain-dead** *adj* **1.** MED clínicamente muerto, -a **2.** *fig* subnormal **brain death** *n* muerte *f* clínica [*o* cerebral] **brain drain** *n no pl* fuga *f* de cerebros

brainless ['breɪnləs] *adj* estúpido, -a

brain scan *n* exploración *f* cerebral mediante escáner

brainstorm ['breɪnstɔːm, *Am:* -stɔːrm] **I.** *vi* hacer un brainstorming **II.** *vt* hacer un brainstorming sobre [*o* de] **III.** *n* **1.** *Brit, inf* (*confusion*) **she had a ~** se le cruzaron los cables **2.** *Am* (*great idea*) idea *f* brillante

brainstorming ['breɪnˌstɔːmɪŋ, *Am:* -ˌstɔːr-] *n no pl* brainstorming *m*

brains trust *n* grupo *m* de peritos

brain tumor *n Am,* **brain tumour** *n* tumor *m* cerebral

brainwash ['breɪnwɒʃ, *Am:* -wɑːʃ-] *vt* lavar el cerebro a

brainwashing ['breɪnwɒʃɪŋ, *Am:* -wɑːʃ-] *n no pl* lavado *m* de cerebro

brainwave ['breɪnweɪv] *n inf* idea *f* brillante, lamparazo *m Col;* **she had a ~** tuvo una idea genial, tuvo un lamparazo *Col,* se le prendió el foco *Méx,* se le prendió la lamparilla *RíoPl*

brainwork *n* trabajo *m* intelectual

brainy ['breɪni] <-ier, -iest> *adj* inteligente

braise [breɪz] *vt* estofar

brake [breɪk] **I.** *n* freno *m;* **to apply the ~s** frenar; **to put a ~ on sth** *fig* poner freno a algo **II.** *vi* frenar

brake block *n* pastilla *f* del freno **brake fluid** *n* AUTO líquido *m* de frenos **brake shoe** *n* AUTO zapata *f* del freno

braking *n no pl* frenado *m*

braking distance *n* distancia *f* de frenado

bramble ['bræmbl] *n* **1.** (*bush*) zarza *f* **2.** (*fruit*) zarzamora *f*

bran [bræn] *n no pl* salvado *m*

branch [brɑːntʃ, *Am:* bræntʃ] **I.** *n* **1.** (*of a tree*) rama *f* **2.** (*of a railway, river, road*) ramal *m* **3.** (*office: of a company, bank, library*) sucursal *f;* (*of a union, government department*) delegación *f* **4.** (*subdivision*) rama *f;* **the ~es of learning** las ramas del saber **II.** *vi* **1.** (*tree*) echar ramas **2.** (*river, road*) bifurcarse

◆**branch off** *vi* **1.** (*start*) bifurcarse **2.** (*digress*) **to ~ from a subject** salirse de un tema

◆**branch out** *vi* diversificarse; **to ~ on one's own** establecerse por su cuenta

branch line *n* ramal *m* **branch office** *n* sucursal *f*

brand [brænd] **I.** *n* **1.** COM marca *f* **2.** *fig* clase *f;* **do you like his ~ of humour?** ¿te gusta su tipo de humor? **3.** (*mark*) hierro *m* **II.** *vt* **1.** (*label*) **to ~ sth/sb (as) sth** tachar algo/a alguien de algo; **to ~ sb a liar** tildar a alguien de mentiroso **2.** (*cattle, slave*) marcar con hierro candente

brandish ['brændɪʃ] *vt* blandir

brand name ['brændneɪm] *n* marca *f*

brand-new [ˌbrænd'nju:] *adj inv* completamente nuevo, -a; **~ baby** recién nacido *m*

brandy ['brændi] <-ies> *n* brandy *m*; **French ~** coñac *m*

brandy snap *n barquillo dulce que a veces se sirve relleno de nata*

brash [bræʃ] *adj* **1.** (*cocky: attitude*) chulo, -a **2.** (*gaudy: colours*) chillón, -ona

brass [brɑ:s, *Am:* bræs] *n* **1.** *no pl* (*metal*) latón *m* **2.** (*engraving: in a church*) placa *f* conmemorativa (*de latón*) **3.** + *pl/sing vb* MUS **the ~** los metales

brass band *n* banda *f* de música, orfeón *m* *Chile* **brass plate** *n* placa *f* conmemorativa **brass section** *n* MUS **the ~** los metales

brassware *n no pl* latonería *f*

brassy ['brɑ:si, *Am:* 'bræsi] <-ier, -iest> *adj* **1.** (*of brass*) de latón; **~ colour** color *m* dorado **2.** (*voice*) estridente **3.** (*cocky*) ordinario, -a

brat [bræt] *n inf* mocoso, -a *m, f*; **he is a spoilt ~** es un niño mimado, es un sute *Col, Ven*

bravado [brə'vɑ:dəʊ, *Am:* -doʊ] *n no pl* bravuconada *f*

brave [breɪv] **I.** *adj* valiente **II.** *vt* afrontar

bravery ['breɪvəri] *n no pl* valentía *f*

brawl [brɔ:l, *Am:* brɑ:l] **I.** *n* pelea *f*, bulla *f* *AmL* **II.** *vi* pelearse

brawling *n no pl* alboroto *m*

brawn [brɔ:n, *Am:* brɑ:n] *n no pl* **1.** (*physical strength*) fuerza *f* muscular **2.** *Aus, Brit* GASTR cabeza *f* de jabalí

brawny ['brɔ:ni, *Am:* brɑ:-] <-ier, -iest> *adj* musculoso, -a

bray [breɪ] **I.** *vi* rebuznar; **~ing laugh** risa *f* estridente **II.** *n* rebuzno *m*

brazen ['breɪzn] *adj* descarado, -a; **~ lie** mentira *f* descarada

◆**brazen out** *vt* **to brazen it out** defenderse con argumentos descarados

brazier ['breɪziə^r^, *Am:* -ʒɚ] *n* brasero *m*

Brazil [brə'zɪl] *n* Brasil *m*

Brazilian [brə'zɪliən, *Am:* -jən] **I.** *n* brasileño, -a *m, f* **II.** *adj* brasileño, -a

Brazil nut *n* coquito *m* del Brasil

breach [bri:tʃ] **I.** *n* **1.** (*infraction: of a regulation*) infracción *f*, violación *f*; (*of an agreement*) ruptura *f*; (*of confidence*) abuso *m*; (*of a contract*) incumplimiento *m*; **to be in ~ of the law** infringir la ley **2.** (*estrangement*) ruptura *f* **3.** (*opening*) brecha *f* **II.** *vt* **1.** (*break: law*) infringir, violar; (*agreement*) romper; (*contract*) incumplir; (*security*) poner en peligro **2.** (*infiltrate*) abrir una brecha en

breach of the peace *n no pl* alteración *f* del orden público

bread [bred] *n* **1.** pan *m*; **a loaf of ~** un pan **2.** *inf* (*money*) pasta *f* ►**to cast one's ~ upon the waters** *form* hacer el bien sin mirar a quien; **to want one's ~ buttered on both sides** querer el oro y el moro, querer la chancha y los cinco reales *RíoPl*; **to earn one's (daily) ~** *form* ganarse el pan (de cada día)

bread and butter *n no pl* sustento *m*; **~ issues** asuntos *mpl* básicos

breadbasket *n* **1.** (*container*) panera *f* **2.** (*region*) granero *m* **breadbin** *n* panera *f*

breadcrumb ['bredkrʌm] *n* **1.** (*small fragment*) miga *f* (de pan) **2.** *pl* GASTR pan *m* rallado

breadth ['bretθ] *n no pl* **1.** anchura *f*; **to be 5 metres in ~** tener 5 metros de ancho **2.** *fig* amplitud *f*

breadwinner ['bredˌwɪnə^r^, *Am:* -ɚ] *n* sostén *m*

break [breɪk] **I.** *n* **1.** (*crack, gap*) grieta *f* **2.** (*escape*) fuga *f* **3.** (*interruption*) interrupción *f*; (*commercial*) pausa *f* **4.** (*rest period*) descanso *m* **5.** *Brit* (*pause in school*) recreo *m* **6.** (*vacation*) vacaciones *fpl* **7.** **the ~ of day** el amanecer **8.** (*divergence*) ruptura *f* **9.** (*opportunity*) oportunidad *f* **10.** SPORTS saque *m* ►**to make a clean ~** cortar por lo sano; **give me a ~!** ¡déjame en paz! **II.** <broke, broken> *vt* **1.** (*shatter, damage, fracture*) romper; **to ~ sth into pieces** hacer algo añicos; **to ~ the sonic [*o* sound] barrier** AVIAT romper la barrera del sonido **2.** (*interrupt: circuit*) cortar; (*silence*) romper **3.** (*put an end to: deadlock, impasse*) salir de; (*peace, silence*) romper; (*strike*) poner fin a; (*give up: habit*) dejar; **to ~ sb of a habit** quitar a alguien una costumbre **4.** (*in tennis*) **to ~ sb's service** romper el servicio a alguien **5.** (*violate: agreement*) incumplir; (*date*) no acudir a; (*treaty*) violar **6.** (*decipher*) descifrar **7.** (*make public*) revelar **8.** (*tell*) decir; **to ~ the news to sb** dar la noticia a alguien; **~ it to me gently!** *iron* ¡dímelo con tacto! **9.** (*make change for*) cambiar; **to ~ a bill** cambiar un billete **10.** MIL **to ~ formation** romper filas **III.** <broke, broken> *vi* **1.** (*shatter or separate*) romperse; **to ~ into pieces** hacerse añicos **2.** (*interrupt*) **shall we ~ (off) for lunch?** ¿paramos para comer? **3.** (*strike: wave*) romper **4.** (*change of voice*) **the boy's voice is ~ing** la voz del niño está cambiando **5.** (*under the strain*) **her voice broke (with emotion)** se le entrecortó la voz (de la emoción) **6.** METEO (*weather*) cambiar; (*dawn, day*) romper, despuntar **7.** (*in pool, snooker*) abrir el juego **8.** (*giving birth*) **her waters broke on the way to hospital** rompió aguas en el camino al hospital ►**to ~ even** salir sin ganar ni perder; **to ~ free** liberarse; **to ~ loose** soltarse

◆**break away** *vi* (*piece, from friends*) desprenderse; (*boat*) soltarse; POL (*faction, region*) escindirse

◆**break down** **I.** *vi* **1.** (*stop working*) dejar

de funcionar; (*car, machine*) averiarse **2.** (*marriage*) romperse; (*negotiation*) fracasar **3.** (*physically, psychologically*) derrumbarse **4.** (*decompose*) descomponerse **II.** *vt* **1.** (*door*) echar abajo **2.** (*opposition, resistance*) acabar con **3.** CHEM descomponer **4.** (*separate into parts: sentence*) separar, dividir; (*process*) dividir

◆**break forth** *vi* **to ~ into song** ponerse a cantar

◆**break in I.** *vi* **1.** (*enter: burglar*) entrar (para robar) **2.** (*butt in, interrupt*) interrumpir; **to ~ on sb** interrumpir a alguien **II.** *vt* **1.** (*make comfortable: shoes*) ablandar **2.** *Am* AUTO hacer el rodaje de **3.** (*tame*) domar

◆**break into** *vi* **1.** (*enter: car*) entrar (para robar) **2.** (*start doing*) **to ~ laughter/tears** echarse a reir/llorar; **to ~ song** ponerse a cantar **3.** (*get involved in: business*) introducirse en

◆**break off I.** *vt* **1.** (*detach*) partir **2.** (*end: relationship*) romper **II.** *vi* **1.** (*become detached*) desprenderse **2.** (*stop speaking*) callarse

◆**break out** *vi* **1.** (*escape*) escaparse; (*of a prison*) fugarse **2.** (*begin: war, storm, laughing*) estallar **3. to ~ in a sweat** empezar a sudar; **she broke out in a rash** le salió un sarpullido; **he broke out in spots** le salieron granos

◆**break through I.** *vi* penetrar; (*sun*) salir **II.** *vt* atravesar; **to ~ a crowd** abrirse paso entre una multitud

◆**break up I.** *vt* **1.** (*end: meeting, strike*) terminar; **break it up, you two!** *inf* ¡vosotros dos, basta ya! **2.** (*split up: coalition, union*) disolver; (*collection*) dividir; (*family*) separar; (*gang, monopoly, cartel*) desarticular **3.** *Am* (*make laugh*) **to break sb up** hacer reír a alguien **II.** *vi* **1.** (*end a relationship*) separarse **2.** (*come to an end: marriage*) fracasar; (*meeting*) terminar **3.** (*fall apart: coalition*) fracasar; (*ship*) irse a pique **4.** *Brit* SCHOOL terminar

breakable ['breɪkəbl] *adj* frágil

breakage ['breɪkɪdʒ] *n* roturas *fpl;* **all ~s must be paid for** el cliente debe pagar lo que se rompa

breakaway ['breɪkəweɪ] *adj* POL disidente

breakdown ['breɪkdaʊn] *n* **1.** (*collapse: of negotiations, relationship*) ruptura *f* **2.** TECH avería *f* **3.** (*division*) división *f* **4.** (*decomposition*) descomposición *f* **5.** PSYCH (**nervous**) ~ crisis *f inv* nerviosa

breakdown lorry *n Brit* grúa *f* **breakdown service** *n* servicio *m* de asistencia en carretera

breaker ['breɪkəʳ, *Am:* -kɚ] *n* **1.** (*wave*) gran ola *f* **2.** *inf* RADIO radioaficionado, -a *m, f*

breakfast ['brekfəst] **I.** *n* desayuno *m;* **to have ~** desayunar **II.** *vi form* desayunar

breaking and entering *n* allanamiento *m* de morada **breaking point** *n* límite *m;* **to reach ~** llegar al límite

breakneck ['breɪknek] *adj* vertiginoso, -a; **at ~ speed** a una velocidad vertiginosa

breakout ['breɪkaʊt] *n* fuga *f*

breakthrough ['breɪkθruː] *n* **1.** (*in science*) adelanto *m* **2.** MIL avance *m*

breakup ['breɪkʌp] *n* (*of marriage*) separación *f;* (*of group, empire*) disolución *f;* (*of talks*) fracaso *m;* (*of family, physical structure*) desintegración *f*

breakwater ['breɪkwɔːtəʳ, *Am:* -ˌwɑːt̬ɚ] *n* rompeolas *m inv,* molo *m Chile*

breast [brest] *n* **1.** ANAT pecho *m* **2.** GASTR pechuga *f*

breastbone ['brestbəʊn, *Am:* -boʊn] *n* **1.** ANAT esternón *m* **2.** GASTR hueso *m* de la pechuga

breast cancer *n no pl* cáncer *m* de mama

breastfeed ['brestfiːd] *vt* amamantar

breast pocket *n* bolsillo *m* superior

breaststroke ['breststrəʊk, *Am:* -stroʊk] *n no pl* (estilo *m*) braza *f;* **to do** (**the**) ~ nadar a braza

breath [breθ] *n* aliento *m;* **to be out of ~** estar sin aliento; **to be short of ~** ahogarse; **to catch one's ~** (*stop breathing*) quedarse sin respiración; (*return to normal breathing*) volver a respirar; **to draw ~** respirar; **to hold one's ~** *a. fig* contener la respiración; **to mutter sth under one's ~** decir algo entre dientes; **to take a deep ~** respirar hondo; **to go out for a ~ of fresh air** salir para que le dé a uno el aire; **there wasn't a ~ of air** no había ni un soplo de viento ▶**in the <u>same</u> ~** a continuación; **to <u>take</u> sb's ~ <u>away</u>** dejar a alguien sin habla

breathalyse *vt Aus, Brit,* **breathalyze** ['breθəlaɪz] *vt Am* hacer la prueba de la alcoholemia a

breathalyser® *n,* **breathalyzer®** *n* alcoholímetro *m*

breathe [briːð] **I.** *vi* respirar; **to ~ again** [*o* **easily**] respirar tranquilo; **to ~ through one's nose** respirar por la nariz; **to let a wine ~** dejar respirar un vino **II.** *vt* **1.** (*exhale*) **to ~ alcohol** echar aliento a alcohol; **to ~ smoke on sb** echar el humo a alguien **2.** (*whisper*) musitar **3.** (*let out: sigh*) dejar escapar

breather ['briːðəʳ, *Am:* -ðɚ] *n* descanso *m,* respiro *m;* **to take a ~** descansar

breathing *n no pl* respiración *f*

breathing apparatus *n* respirador *m* **breathing room** *n no pl,* **breathing space** *n no pl* respiro *m*

breathless ['breθlɪs] *adj* (*person*) sin aliento; (*words*) entrecortado, -a

breathtaking ['breθteɪkɪŋ] *adj* imponente, impresionante

breath test *n* prueba *f* de la alcoholemia

bred [bred] *pt, pp of* **breed**

breech [briːtʃ] *n* recámara *f*

breeches ['brɪtʃɪz] *npl* **1.** (*knee-length trousers*) pantalones *mpl* bombachos; **riding ~** pantalones *mpl* de montar, zamarros *mpl*

Col, Ecua, Ven **2.** *inf* (*trousers*) pantalones *mpl*

breed [bri:d] **I.** *vt* <bred, bred> **1.** criar **2.** (*disease, violence*) engendrar, generar **II.** *vi* <bred, bred> reproducirse; (*violence*) generarse **III.** *n* **1.** ZOOL raza *f;* BOT variedad *f* **2.** *inf* (*type of person*) tipo *m;* **a dying ~** una especie en vías de extinción

breeder ['bri:dəʳ, *Am:* -dɚ] *n* (*of animals*) criador(a) *m(f);* (*of plants*) cultivador(a) *m(f)*

breeding *n no pl* **1.** (*of animals*) cría *f* **2.** *fig* (*upbringing*) educación *f*

breeding ground *n fig* caldo *m* de cultivo

breeze [bri:z] **I.** *n* **1.** (*wind*) brisa *f* **2.** *inf* (*easy task*) **to be a ~** ser pan comido, ser un bollo *RíoPl* **3.** *no pl* (*cinders*) cisco *m* de carbón y leña **II.** *vi Am* **to ~ into the room** entrar en la habitación como Pedro por su casa

breeze block [brɪ:z blɒk] *n Brit* bloque *m* de cemento

breezy ['bri:zi] <-ier, -iest> *adj* **1.** (*windy*) ventoso, -a; **it is ~** hace aire **2.** (*jovial*) alegre

breve [bri:v] *n* MUS breve *f*

breviary ['bri:vɪəri] <-ies> *n* breviario *m*

brevity ['brevəti, *Am:* -t̬i] *n no pl* **1.** (*shortness*) brevedad *f* **2.** (*conciseness*) concisión *f*

brew [bru:] **I.** *n* **1.** (*mixture*) brebaje *m* **2.** *Brit, inf* **to have a ~** tomar un té **II.** *vi* **1.** (*beer*) fermentar **2.** (*tea*) hacerse; **to let the tea ~** dejar reposar el té **3.** (*storm, trouble*) avecinarse; **there's something ~ing** se está cociendo algo **III.** *vt* (*beer*) elaborar; (*tea*) hacer

◆**brew up** *vi* **1.** *Brit, inf* (*make tea*) hacer un té **2.** (*develop: storm, trouble*) avecinarse

brewer ['bru:əʳ, *Am:* -ɚ] *n* cervecero, -a *m, f*

brewery ['brʊəri, *Am:* 'bru:ɚi] <-ies> *n* **1.** (*company*) cervecería *f,* cervecera *f Méx* **2.** (*place*) fábrica *f* de cerveza

briar ['braɪəʳ, *Am:* 'braɪɚ] *n* brezo *m*

bribe [braɪb] **I.** *vt* sobornar; **to ~ sb into doing sth** sobornar a alguien para que haga algo **II.** *n* soborno *m;* **to take a ~** dejarse sobornar, aceptar un soborno

bribery ['braɪbəri] *n no pl* soborno *m,* coima *f Perú, CSur,* mordida *f Méx*

bric-a-brac ['brɪkəbræk] *n no pl* baratijas *fpl*

brick [brɪk] *n* **1.** (*block*) ladrillo *m* **2.** *inf* **~s and mortar** inmueble *m;* **to invest in ~s and mortar** invertir en bienes inmuebles ►**you can't make ~s without __straw__** *prov* sin paja no hay ladrillos

◆**brick in** *vt* tapiar

◆**brick up** *vt* tapiar

brickie ['brɪki] *n Aus, Brit, inf,* **bricklayer** ['brɪkˌleɪəʳ, *Am:* -ɚ] *n* albañil *mf*

brick wall *n* pared *f* (de ladrillos) ►**to be banging one's __head__ against a ~** *inf* llevar todas las de perder

brickwork ['brɪkwɜ:k, *Am:* -wɜ:rk] *n no pl* enladrillado *m*

brickworks *n,* **brickyard** ['brɪkjɑ:d, *Am:* -jɑ:rd] *n* fábrica *f* de ladrillos

bridal ['braɪdəl] *adj* (*suite*) nupcial; (*shop*) para novias; (*gown*) de novia

bride ['braɪd] *n* novia *f*

bridegroom ['braɪdgrʊm, *Am:* -gru:m] *n* novio *m*

bridesmaid ['braɪdzmeɪd] *n* dama *f* de honor

bridge [brɪdʒ] **I.** *n* **1.** *a.* ARCHIT, MED, MUS puente *m* **2.** ANAT caballete *m* **3.** NAUT puente *m* (de mando) **4.** *no pl* GAMES bridge *m* **II.** *vt* **1.** (*build a bridge over*) construir un puente sobre **2.** (*decrease the difference*) salvar

bridging loan ['brɪdʒɪŋ'ləʊn, *Am:* -'loʊn] *n Aus, Brit* préstamo *m* puente, crédito *m* puente

bridle ['braɪdl] **I.** *n* brida *f* **II.** *vt* (*horse*) embridar **III.** *vi* **to ~ at sth** molestarse por algo

bridle path *n,* **bridleway** *n* camino *m* de herradura

brief [bri:f] **I.** *adj* **1.** (*short*) corto, -a **2.** (*concise*) conciso, -a, sucinto, -a; **be ~!** ¡sé breve!; **in ~** en resumen **II.** *n* **1.** *Aus, Brit* (*instructions*) instrucciones *fpl* **2.** LAW escrito *m* **3.** *pl* (*underpants: man's*) calzoncillos *mpl,* slip *m;* (*woman's*) bragas *fpl* **III.** *vt* **1.** (*inform*) informar **2.** (*give instructions to*) dar instrucciones a

briefcase ['bri:fkeɪs] *n* maletín *m*

briefing *n* **1.** (*instructions*) instrucciones *fpl* **2.** (*information session*) reunión *f* informativa

briefly *adv* **1.** (*for short time*) por poco tiempo **2.** (*concisely*) brevemente; **~, ...** en resumen,...

briefness *n no pl* brevedad *f*

brier ['braɪəʳ, *Am:* 'braɪɚ] *n* brezo *m*

brigade [brɪ'geɪd] *n* MIL brigada *f*

brigadier [ˌbrɪgə'dɪəʳ] *n Brit,* **brigadier general** [ˌbrɪgədɪr'dʒenərəl] *n Am* MIL general *m* de brigada

bright [braɪt] **I.** *adj* **1.** (*light*) brillante, fuerte; (*room*) con mucha luz; (*star*) brillante; **a ~ day** un día soleado **2.** (*colour*) vivo, -a, fuerte; **to go ~ red** ponerse como un tomate **3.** (*intelligent: person*) inteligente; (*idea*) brillante **4.** (*cheerful, happy*) vivaracho, -a **5.** (*promising: future*) prometedor(a) ►**to look on the ~ __side__ of sth** mirar [*o* ver] el lado bueno de algo; **to get up ~ and __early__** levantarse tempranito **II.** *n pl, Am* AUTO (luces *fpl*) largas *fpl,* (luces *fpl*) altas *fpl And*

◆**brighten** (**up**) ['braɪtən('ʌp)] **I.** *vt* **1.** (*make brighter*) iluminar **2.** (*become cheerful*) alegrar, animar **II.** *vi* **1.** (*become brighter*) hacerse más brillante; (*weather*) mejorar **2.** (*become cheerful*) animarse, alegrarse; (*eyes, face*) iluminarse **3.** (*become more promising*) mejorar

brightness *n no pl* **1.** brillo *m;* (*of sound*) claridad *f* **2.** (*cheerfulness*) alegría *f* **3.** (*cleverness*) inteligencia *f*

brill[1] ['brɪl] *adj Aus, Brit* genial

brill[2] ['brɪl] *n* rodaballo *m* menor

brilliance ['brɪlɪəns] *n no pl* **1.** (*cleverness*) brillantez *f* **2.** (*brightness*) resplandor *m*

B

brilliant ['brɪlɪənt, *Am:* -jənt] **I.** *adj* **1.**(*shining: colour*) brillante; (*sunlight, smile*) radiante; (*water*) resplandeciente **2.**(*clever*) brillante; (*idea*) genial **3.** *Brit, inf*(*excellent*) fantástico, -a; ~ **success** gran éxito **II.** *interj Brit, inf* genial

brim [brɪm] **I.** *n* **1.**(*of a hat*) ala *f* **2.**(*of a vessel*) borde *m;* **to fill sth to the** ~ llenar algo hasta el borde **II.** *vi* <-mm-> **to** ~ **with happiness/energy** rebosar de felicidad/energía

◆**brim over** *vi a. fig* rebosar

brimful [ˌbrɪm'fʊl] *adj* repleto, -a; (*of life, confidence*) rebosante

brine [braɪn] *n no pl* GASTR salmuera *f;* (*sea water*) agua *f* salada [*o* de mar]

bring [brɪŋ] <brought, brought> *vt* **1.**(*come with, carry*) traer; ~ **her here!** ¡tráela aquí!; **to** ~ **sb in** hacer pasar a alguien; **to** ~ **sth in** entrar algo; **to** ~ **news** traer noticias **2.**(*take*) llevar; **this subject ~s me to the second part** este tema me lleva a la segunda parte; **to** ~ **sth/sb with oneself** llevar algo/a alguien consigo **3.**(*cause to come, cause to happen*) causar, traer; **to** ~ **poverty/fame to a town** traer pobreza/fama a un pueblo; **to** ~ **sb luck** traer suerte a alguien **4.** LAW interponer; **to** ~ **an action** (**against sb**) interponer una demanda (contra alguien); **to** ~ **a complaint against sb** formular un queja contra alguien **5.**(*force*) **to** ~ **oneself to do sth** resignarse a hacer algo **6.** FIN dar

◆**bring about** *vt* **1.**(*cause to happen*) provocar **2.**(*achieve*) lograr

◆**bring along** *vt* traer

◆**bring back** *vt* **1.**(*reintroduce*) volver a introducir **2.**(*call to mind*) recordar **3.**(*return*) devolver

◆**bring down** *vt* **1.**(*reduce: benefits, level*) reducir; (*temperature*) hacer bajar **2.**(*fell: tree*) talar; (*person*) derribar; (*dictator, government*) derrocar **3.**(*knock down*) tirar, echar abajo **4.**(*make sad*) deprimir

◆**bring forth** *vt insep, form* procrear, dar a luz

◆**bring forward** *vt* **1.**(*reschedule for an earlier date*) adelantar **2.**(*present for discussion*) presentar **3.** FIN (*carry over*) transferir

◆**bring in** *vt* **1.**(*introduce*) introducir; (*bill*) presentar **2.**(*call in*) llamar **3.** FIN (*earn*) **to** ~ **a profit** reportar un beneficio **4.**(*reap*) cosechar **5.** LAW (*produce*) **to** ~ **a verdict of not guilty** pronunciar un veredicto de inocente

◆**bring off** *vt inf* lograr

◆**bring on** *vt* **1.**(*cause to occur*) provocar; (*shame, dishonour, discredit*) causar, acarrear; **to bring sth on oneself** buscarse algo uno mismo **2.**(*improve*) mejorar

◆**bring out** *vt* **1.** COM introducir (en el mercado); (*book*) publicar **2.**(*reveal*) **to** ~ **sth in sb** realzar algo de alguien **3.** *Aus, Brit* (*encourage*) **to bring sb out** hacer que alguien pierda la timidez

◆**bring over** *vt* **1.**(*person*) convertir, convencer **2.**(*take with*) traer

◆**bring round** *vt* **1.** MED hacer volver en sí **2.**(*persuade*) convencer

◆**bring to** *vt always sep* reanimar

◆**bring up** *vt* **1.**(*child*) criar; **to bring sb up to be/to do sth** educar a alguien para que sea/haga algo **2.**(*mention*) sacar **3.** *inf*(*vomit*) vomitar ►**to bring sb up short** dejar helado a alguien

brink [brɪŋk] *n no pl* borde *m;* **to drive sb to the** ~ **of sth** llevar a alguien al borde de algo; **to be on the** ~ **of bankruptcy/war** estar al borde de la bancarrota/la guerra

briny ['braɪni] **I.** <-ier, -iest> *adj liter* salobre **II.** *n iron* **the** ~ el mar

briquet(te) [brɪ'ket] *n* briqueta *f*

brisk [brɪsk] *adj* **1.**(*fast: pace*) rápido, -a; (*walk*) a paso ligero **2.**(*refreshing: breeze*) fresco, -a **3.**(*manner, voice*) enérgico, -a

briskness *n no pl* (*of pace*) brío *m;* (*of trading*) dinamismo *m;* (*of business*) eficiencia *f*

bristle ['brɪsl] **I.** *n* (*of an animal*) cerda *f;* (*on the face*) barba *f* **II.** *vi* **1.**(*fur, hair*) erizarse, ponerse de punta **2.** *fig* **to** ~ **with anger** enfurecerse

bristly ['brɪsli] <-ier, -iest> *adj* hirsuto, -a

Brit [brɪt] *n inf* británico, -a *m, f*

Britain ['brɪtən] *n* Gran Bretaña *f*

British ['brɪtɪʃ, *Am:* 'brɪt̬-] **I.** *adj* británico, -a; ~ **English** inglés *m* británico **II.** *n pl* **the** ~ los británicos

British Columbia *n* Columbia *f* Británica

British Isles *n* **the** ~ las Islas Británicas

Briton ['brɪtn] *n* británico, -a *m, f*

Brittany ['brɪtæni] *n* Bretaña *f*

brittle ['brɪtl, *Am:* 'brɪt̬-] *adj* **1.**(*fragile*) quebradizo, -a **2.**(*irritable*) susceptible

broach [brəʊtʃ, *Am:* broʊtʃ] **I.** *vt* (*mention*) mencionar **II.** *n Am* broche *m*

broad [brɔːd, *Am:* brɑːd] **I.** *adj* **1.**(*wide*) ancho, -a **2.**(*spacious*) amplio, -a **3.**(*obvious*) **a** ~ **hint** una clara indirecta **4.**(*general*) general **5.**(*wide-ranging*) amplio, -a; ~ **interests** intereses diversos **6.**(*liberal*) liberal; **a** ~ **mind** una mente abierta **7.**(*strong: accent*) cerrado, -a **II.** *n Am, inf* tipa *f*

broad bean *n* haba *f*

broadcast ['brɔːdkɑːst, *Am:* 'brɑːdkæst] **I.** *n* RADIO programa *m* (de radio); TV programa *m* (de televisión); (*of a concert*) emisión *f* **II.** *vi,v t* <broadcast *Am:* broadcasted, broadcast *Am:* broadcasted> transmitir, emitir **III.** *vt* <broadcast *Am:* broadcasted, broadcast *Am:* broadcasted> TV transmitir; RADIO emitir; (*rumour*) difundir

broadcaster *n* (*person*) locutor(a) *m(f);* (*station*) emisora *f*

broadcasting *n no pl* TV transmisión *f;* RADIO radiodifusión *f*

broadcasting station *n* emisora *f*

broaden ['brɔːdn, *Am:* 'brɑː-] **I.** *vi* (*interests*) ampliarse; (*valley*) ensancharse **II.** *vt* (*horizons*) ampliar; **to** ~ **the mind** abrir la

mente
broadly ['brɔːdli] *adv* **1.** (*generally*) en líneas generales **2.** (*widely: smile*) de oreja a oreja
broad-minded [ˌbrɔːd'maɪndɪd, *Am:* ˌbrɑːd-] *adj* con mentalidad abierta
broadsheet ['brɔːdʃiːt, *Am:* ˌbrɑːd-] *n Aus, Brit: periódico de formato grande*
broadside ['brɔːdsaɪd, *Am:* ˌbrɑːd-] *n* **1.** NAUT, MIL andanada *f* **2.** (*verbal attack*) invectiva *f*, ataque *m* verbal

> **Broadway** es el nombre que recibe una larga calle de New York City. En esta calle se localiza el conocido barrio de **Broadway** famoso por su intensa actividad teatral. Prácticamente todas las piezas dramáticas americanas de importancia se representan allí. Aquellas que, bien por tratarse de producciones baratas, bien por ser de carácter experimental no se representan, reciben el nombre de **off-Broadway plays**

brocade [brə'keɪd, *Am:* broʊ-] *n no pl* brocado *m*
broccoli ['brɒkəli, *Am:* 'brɑːkl-] *n no pl* bróculi *m*, brécol *m*
brochure ['brəʊʃəʳ, *Am:* broʊ'ʃʊr] *n* folleto *m*
brogue¹ [brəʊg, *Am:* broʊg] *n* (*shoe*) *zapato bajo y resistente, normalmente para hombre*
brogue² [brəʊg, *Am:* broʊg] *n* LING acento *m* irlandés
broil [brɔɪl] *vt Am* asar a la parrilla
broiler ['brɔɪləʳ, *Am:* -lɚ] *n* **1.** (*chicken*) pollo *m* para asar, pollo *m* parrillero *RíoPl*, broiler *m Chile* **2.** *Am* (*grill*) parrilla *f*, grill *m*
broke [brəʊk, *Am:* broʊk] **I.** *pt of* **break** **II.** *adj inf* pelado, -a, planchado, -a *Chile* ▶**to go ~** *inf* arruinarse; **to go for ~** *inf* jugarse el todo por el todo
broken ['brəʊkən, *Am:* 'broʊ-] **I.** *pp of* **break** **II.** *adj* **1.** (*damaged*) roto, -a; **~ heart** corazón destrozado **2.** LING **in ~ English** en un inglés incorrecto **3.** (*interrupted*) interrumpido, -a
broken-down [ˌbrəʊkən'daʊn, *Am:* ˌbroʊ-] *adj* **1.** TECH averiado, -a, en pana *Chile*, varado, -a *Col* **2.** (*dilapidated: building*) ruinoso, -a
broken-hearted [ˌbrəʊkən'hɑːtɪd, *Am:* ˌbroʊkən'hɑrt̬ɪd] *adj* destrozado, -a, deshecho, -a; **to die ~** morir de pena
broker ['brəʊkəʳ, *Am:* 'broʊkɚ] **I.** *n* **1.** FIN corredor(a) *m(f)* de bolsa **2.** (*of an agreement, marriage*) agente *mf* **II.** *vt* **1.** FIN hacer corretaje de **2.** (*agreement*) negociar
brokerage ['brəʊkərɪdʒ, *Am:* 'broʊ-] *n no pl* FIN **1.** (*commission*) corretaje *m* **2.** (*business*) agencia *f* de corredores de bolsa
brolly ['brɒli, *Am:* 'brɑːli] *n Aus, Brit, inf* paraguas *m inv*
bromide ['brəʊmaɪd, *Am:* 'broʊ-] *n* **1.** CHEM bromuro *m* **2.** (*platitude*) lugar *m* común, tópico *m*
bromine ['brəʊmiːn, *Am:* 'broʊ-] *n no pl* bromo *m*
bronchi ['brɒŋkaɪ] *npl* bronquios *mpl*
bronchial ['brɒŋkɪəl, *Am:* 'brɑːŋ-] *adj* bronquial
bronchitis [brɒŋ'kaɪtɪs, *Am:* brɑːŋ'kaɪt̬ɪs] *n no pl* bronquitis *f*
bronze [brɒnz, *Am:* brɑːnz] **I.** *n* bronce *m* **II.** *adj* de bronce; (*hair*) dorado, -a; (*skin*) bronceado, -a
Bronze Age **I.** *n* **the ~** la Edad de Bronce **II.** *adj* de la Edad de Bronce **bronze medal** *n* medalla *f* de bronce
brooch [brəʊtʃ, *Am:* broʊtʃ] *n* broche *m*
brood [bruːd] **I.** *n* **1.** (*of mammals*) camada *f*; (*of birds*) nidada *f* **2.** *iron* (*children*) prole *f* **II.** *vi* **1.** (*reflect at length*) **to ~ over sth** dar vueltas a algo **2.** (*hatch*) empollar
broody ['bruːdi] <-ier, -iest> *adj* **1.** (*hen*) clueco, -a **2.** (*motherly*) con sentimientos maternales **3.** (*gloomy*) melancólico, -a
brook¹ [brʊk] *n* arroyo *m*
brook² [brʊk] *vt form* (*tolerate*) tolerar
broom [bruːm] *n* **1.** (*brush*) escoba *f* **2.** *no pl* BOT retama *f*, hiniesta *f* ▶**a new ~ sweeps clean** *prov* escoba nueva barre bien *prov*
broomstick ['bruːmstɪk] *n* palo *m* de escoba
broth [brɒθ, *Am:* brɑːθ] *n no pl* caldo *m*
brothel ['brɒθl, *Am:* 'brɑːθl] *n* burdel *m*
brother ['brʌðəʳ, *Am:* -ɚ] *n* **1.** hermano *m* **2.** *Am, inf* (*male friend*) colega *m*
brotherhood ['brʌðəhʊd, *Am:* '-ɚ-] *n + pl/sing vb* **1.** (*fellowship*) fraternidad *f* **2.** (*organization*) hermandad *f* **3.** REL cofradía *f*
brother-in-law ['brʌðərɪnlɔː, *Am:* -ɚɪnlɑː] <brothers-in-law *Brit:* brother-in-laws> *n* cuñado *m*, concuño *m AmL*
brotherly ['brʌðəli, *Am:* -ɚli] *adj* fraternal
brought [brɔːt, *Am:* brɑːt] *pp, pt of* **bring**
brow [braʊ] *n* **1.** *no pl, liter* (*forehead*) frente **2.** (*of a hill*) cima *f*
browbeat ['braʊbiːt] <browbeat, browbeaten> *vt* intimidar; **to ~ sb into doing sth** intimidar a alguien para que haga algo
brown [braʊn] **I.** *n* marrón *m* **II.** *adj* marrón; (*eyes, hair*) castaño, -a **III.** *vi* (*leaves*) amarillearse; (*person*) broncearse; GASTR dorarse **IV.** *vt* broncear; GASTR dorar
◆**brown off** *vt* **to be browned off** *inf* estar hasta las narices
brown bread *n* pan *m* integral
brownie ['braʊni] *n Am* bizcocho *m* de chocolate y nueces
brownish ['braʊnɪʃ] *adj* pardusco, -a
brown paper ['braʊn'peɪpəʳ, *Am:* -ɚ] *n no pl* papel *m* de estraza **brown rice** *n no pl* arroz *m* integral
brownstone ['braʊnstəʊn, *Am:* -stoʊn] *n Am* **1.** (*sandstone*) piedra *f* rojiza **2.** (*house*) casa *f* de piedra rojiza
browse [braʊz] **I.** *vi* **1.** (*skim*) **to ~ through**

sth echar un vistazo a algo; (*book, magazine*) hojear algo **2.** (*look around*) mirar **3.** (*graze*) pastar **II.** *n no pl* **1.** (*act of looking around*) **to go for a ~ around the shops** ir de tiendas **2.** (*act of skimming*) ojeada *f,* vistazo *m;* **to have a ~ through sth** echar una ojeada [*o* un vistazo] a algo; (*book, magazine*) hojear algo

browser [braʊzə, *Am:* -ɚ] *n* INFOR navegador *m*

bruise [bruːz] **I.** *n* morado *m,* moretón *m;* (*on fruit*) magulladura *f;* **to be covered in ~s** estar lleno de morados **II.** *vt* (*person*) contusionar; (*fruit*) magullar; *fig* (*hurt*) herir; **to ~ one's arm** hacerse morados [*o* un morado] en el brazo; **to ~ sb's feelings** herir los sentimientos de alguien **III.** *vi* (*fruit*) magullarse; **she ~s easily** le salen morados con mucha facilidad

bruiser ['bruːzəʳ, *Am:* -zɚ] *n iron, inf* bestia *f*

brunch [brʌntʃ] *n* desayuno-almuerzo *m*

Brunei ['bruːnaɪ] *n* Brunei *m*

brunette [bruː'net] *n* morena *f,* morocha *f CSur*

brunt [brʌnt] *n no pl* (*impact*) impacto *m;* **to bear the ~ of sth** aguantar lo más duro de algo

brush [brʌʃ] **I.** *n* **1.** (*for hair*) cepillo *m* **2.** (*broom*) escoba *f* **3.** (*for painting*) pincel *m;* (*bigger*) brocha *f* **4.** (*action*) cepilladura *f;* **to give one's teeth a brush** lavarse los dientes **5.** *no pl* (*stroke*) pincelada *f* **6.** (*encounter*) roce *m* **7.** *no pl, Am* (*brushwood*) maleza *f* **8.** (*fox's tail*) cola *f* **II.** *vt* **1.** (*clean: teeth, hair*) cepillar; (*floor*) barrer **2.** (*remove*) **to ~ sth off** quitar algo con un cepillo **3.** (*graze, touch lightly*) rozar

◆**brush against** *vt* rozar

◆**brush aside** *vt* **1.** (*push to one side*) apartar **2.** (*disregard*) hacer caso omiso de; (*criticism*) pasar por alto

◆**brush away** *vt* quitar

◆**brush off** *vt* (*person*) no hacer caso a; (*criticism*) pasar por alto

◆**brush up** **I.** *vt* dar un repaso a **II.** *vi* **to ~ on sth** dar un repaso a algo

brush-off ['brʌʃɒf, *Am:* -ɑːf] *n inf* **to give sb the ~** dar calabazas a alguien; **to get the ~ from sb** recibir calabazas de alguien

brushwood ['brʌʃwʊd] *n no pl* maleza *f*

brusque [bruːsk, *Am:* brʌsk] *adj* brusco, -a

brusqueness *n no pl* brusquedad *f*

Brussels ['brʌsəlz] *n* Bruselas *f*

Brussels sprout *n* col *f* de Bruselas

brutal ['bruːtəl, *Am:* -t̬əl] *adj* **1.** (*cruel, savage: attack*) brutal; (*words*) cruel **2.** (*harsh: honesty, truth*) crudo, -a

brutality [bruː'tæləti, *Am:* -əṯi] *n* (*cruelty: of an attack*) brutalidad *f;* (*of words*) crueldad *f;* (*harshness*) crudeza *f*

brutalize ['bruːtəlaɪz, *Am:* -t̬əl-] *vt* **1.** (*treat cruelly*) tratar con crueldad **2.** (*make brutal*) brutalizar

brute [bruːt] **I.** *n* **1.** (*brutal person*) bestia *f,* bruto, -a *m, f* **2.** (*animal*) bestia *f* **II.** *adj* **~ force** fuerza *f* bruta

brutish ['bruːtɪʃ, *Am:* -t̬ɪʃ] *adj* **1.** (*cruel*) brutal, salvaje **2.** (*coarse*) bruto, -a **3.** (*like an animal*) animal

BSc [ˌbiːes'siː] *abbr of* **Bachelor of Science** Ldo., -a *m, f* (en Ciencias)

BSE [ˌbiːes'iː] *n abbr of* **bovine spongiform encephalopathy** encefalopatía *f* espongiforme bovina

BST [ˌbiːes'tiː] *abbr of* **British Summer Time** *horario de verano británico, adelantado una hora respecto al meridiano 0*

bubble ['bʌbl] **I.** *n* burbuja *f;* (*in cartoons*) bocadillo *m;* **to blow a ~** hacer una burbuja ►**to burst sb's ~** desengañar a alguien; **the ~ has burst** se ha roto el encanto **II.** *vi* **1.** (*boil*) hervir **2.** (*make boiling sound*) borbotear

◆**bubble over with** *vi* **to ~ joy** no caber en sí de alegría

bubble bath *n* espuma *f* de baño **bubble gum** *n* chicle *m* **bubblejet** (**printer**) *n* INFOR impresora *f* de inyección de burbujas

bubbly ['bʌbli] **I.** *n inf* champán *m* **II.** *adj* **1.** (*full of bubbles*) burbujeante **2.** *fig* (*lively*) animado, -a

bubonic plague [bjuːˌbɒnɪk'pleɪg, *Am:* -ˌbɑːnɪk'pleɪg] *n no pl* peste *f* bubónica

buccaneer [ˌbʌkə'nɪəʳ, *Am:* -'nɪr] *n* bucanero *m*

buck¹ [bʌk] <-(s)> **I.** *n* **1.** (*male: deer*) ciervo *m* (macho); (*rabbit*) conejo *m;* (*hare*) liebre *f* macho **2.** *liter* (*man*) galán *m* **II.** *vi* corcovear **III.** *vt* ir contra; **to ~ the trend** invertir la tendencia

buck² [bʌk] *n Am, Aus, inf* (*dollar*) dólar *m;* **to make a fast ~** hacer dinero fácil

buck³ [bʌk] *n no pl, inf* **to pass the ~** escurrir el bulto; **the ~ stops here** *prov* yo soy el responsable

◆**buck up** *inf* **I.** *vi* **1.** (*cheer up*) levantar el ánimo; **~!** ¡arriba ese ánimo! **2.** (*hurry up*) darse prisa **II.** *vt* **1.** (*cheer up*) **to buck sb up** levantar el ánimo a alguien **2.** **to ~ one's ideas** espabilarse

bucket ['bʌkɪt] *n* **1.** (*pail*) cubo *m* **2.** *pl, inf* (*a lot*) **to rain ~s** llover a cántaros; **to weep ~s** llorar a moco tendido ►**to kick the ~** *inf* estirar la pata

bucketful ['bʌkɪtfʊl] <-s *o* bucketsful> *n* cubo *m* (lleno)

> El **Buckingham Palace** es la residencia londinense de la familia real británica. El palacio dispone de unas 600 habitaciones y fue construido por John Nash por expreso deseo del rey George IV entre los años 1821–1830. El edificio fue inaugurado en 1837 con motivo de la subida al trono de la reina Victoria.

buckle ['bʌkl] **I.** *n* hebilla *f* **II.** *vt* **1.** (*fasten: belt, shoes*) abrochar **2.** (*bend*) torcer **III.** *vi*

1.(*fasten*) abrocharse 2.(*bend*) torcerse; (*knees*) doblarse

buckshot ['bʌkʃɒt, *Am:* -ʃɑːt] *n no pl* perdigón *m*

buckskin ['bʌkskɪn] **I.** *n no pl* gamuza *f* **II.** *adj* de gamuza

buckwheat ['bʌkwiːt] *n no pl* alforfón *m*, trigo *m* sarraceno

bud [bʌd] **I.** *n* (*of leaf, branch*) brote *m;* (*of a flower*) capullo *m;* **to be in** ~ tener brotes **II.** *vi* <-dd-> echar brotes

Buddhism ['bʊdɪzəm, *Am:* 'buːdɪ-] *n no pl* budismo *m*

Buddhist **I.** *n* budista *mf* **II.** *adj* budista

budding ['bʌdɪŋ] *adj* en ciernes

buddy ['bʌdi] *n Am, inf* colega *m*, cuate *m Méx*

budge [bʌdʒ] **I.** *vi* **1.**(*move*) moverse; ~ **over!** ¡córrete un poquito! **2.**(*change opinion*) **to** ~ (**from sth**) cambiar de opinión (en algo) **II.** *vt* **1.**(*move*) mover **2.**(*cause to change opinion*) hacer cambiar de opinión a

budgerigar ['bʌdʒərɪgɑːʳ, *Am:* -gɑːr] *n* periquito *m*

budget ['bʌdʒɪt] **I.** *n* presupuesto *m* **II.** *vt* presupuestar; (*wages, time*) administrar **III.** *vi* **to** ~ **for sth** presupuestar algo **IV.** *adj* (*travel, prices*) económico, -a

budgetary ['bʌdʒɪtəri] *adj* presupuestario, -a

budget deficit *n* déficit *m inv* presupuestario

budgie ['bʌdʒi] *n inf* periquito *m*

buff [bʌf] **I.** *n* **1.**(*leather*) gamuza *f* **2.** *inf* (*person*) entusiasta *mf;* **film** ~ cinéfilo, -a *m, f* ►**in the** ~ *inf* en cueros **II.** *adj* color de ante **III.** *vt* (*metal*) pulir; (*shoes*) sacar brillo a

buffalo ['bʌfələʊ, *Am:* -əloʊ] <-(es)> *n* búfalo *m*

buffer[1] ['bʌfəʳ, *Am:* -ɚ] **I.** *n* **1.**(*of a car*) parachoques *m inv;* (*of a train*) tope *m* **2.** INFOR memoria *f* intermedia **3.** CHEM regulador *m* **II.** *vt* proteger

buffer[2] ['bʌfəʳ, *Am:* -ɚ] *n Brit, inf* (*person*) **old** ~ carca *m*

buffer zone *n* zona *f* de protección

buffet[1] ['bʊfeɪ, *Am:* bə'feɪ] *n* **1.**(*meal*) buffet *m* **2.**(*bar*) cafetería *f*

buffet[2] ['bʌfɪt] *vt* zarandear, sacudir

buffet car *n Brit* vagón *m* restaurante

buffet lunch *n* buffet *m*

buffoon [bə'fuːn] *n* bufón, -ona *m, f;* **to play the** ~ hacer el payaso, hacer payasadas

bug [bʌg] **I.** *n* **1.** ZOOL chinche *f;* (*any insect*) bicho *m* **2.** MED virus *m inv* **3.** INFOR error *m* **4.** TEL micrófono *m* oculto **5.** *no pl, inf* (*enthusiasm*) fiebre *f*, entusiasmo *m;* **she's caught the travel** ~ le ha picado el gusanillo de viajar ►**to be** [*o* **feel**] **snug as a** ~ **in a rug** estar muy cómodo **II.** *vt* <-gg-> **1.**(*tap: telephone*) pinchar; (*conversation*) escuchar clandestinamente; (*room*) ocultar micrófonos en; ~**ging operation** vigilancia secreta **2.** *inf* (*annoy*) fastidiar

bugbear ['bʌgbeəʳ, *Am:* -ber] *n* pesadilla *f*

bugger ['bʌgəʳ, *Am:* -ɚ] **I.** *n inf* (*person*) gilipollas *mf inv;* **poor** ~ pobre desgraciado **II.** *interj Aus, Brit, vulg* (*damn*) mierda ►~ **it** ¡mierda! **III.** *vt vulg* cometer sodomía con

◆**bugger off** *vi vulg* ~! ¡vete a la mierda!

◆**bugger up** *vt vulg* joder

buggery ['bʌgəri] *n no pl* sodomía *f*

buggy ['bʌgi] *n* **1.** *Brit* (*pushchair*) sillita *f* de paseo **2.** *Am* (*pram*) cochecito *m* (de niño) **3.**(*carriage*) calesa *f*

bugle ['bjuːgl] *n* clarín *m*

bugler ['bjuːgləʳ] *n* corneta *mf*

build [bɪld] **I.** *vt* <built, built> **1.**(*make: house*) construir; (*fire*) hacer; (*car*) fabricar **2.**(*establish: trust*) cimentar; (*relationship*) establecer **II.** *vi* <built, built> **1.**(*construct*) edificar **2.**(*increase*) aumentar **III.** *n* complexión *f*

◆**build in** *vt* incorporar

◆**build on** *vt* **to build sth on sth** agregar algo a algo

◆**build up** **I.** *vt* **1.**(*increase*) acrecentar **2.**(*accumulate*) acumular **3.**(*strengthen*) fortalecer **4.**(*develop*) desarrollar **5.**(*praise*) **to build sb up** poner a alguien por las nubes **II.** *vi* **1.**(*increase*) ir en aumento **2.**(*accumulate*) acumularse

builder ['bɪldəʳ, *Am:* -dɚ] *n* (*company*) constructor(a) *m(f);* (*worker*) albañil *mf*

building *n* edificio *m*

building contractor *n* contratista *mf* (de obras) **building site** *n* obra *f* **building society** *n Aus, Brit* sociedad *f* de crédito hipotecario

build-up ['bɪldʌp] *n* **1.**(*accumulation*) acumulación *f;* (*of pressure*) aumento *m* **2.**(*publicity*) propaganda *f*

built [bɪlt] **I.** *pp, pt of* **build** **II.** *adj* **1.**(*house*) **well** ~ bien construido **2.**(*person*) **slightly** ~ menudo; **well** ~ de complexión robusto

built-in ['bɪlt'ɪn, *Am:* 'bɪltɪn] *adj* **1.**(*cupboard*) empotrado, -a **2.**(*feature*) incorporado, -a **3.**(*advantage*) intrínseco, -a

built-up ['bɪltʌp] *adj* **1.**(*area*) edificado, -a **2.**(*heels, shoes*) con alza

bulb [bʌlb] *n* **1.** BOT bulbo *m;* ~ **of garlic** cabeza *f* de ajo **2.**(*of a thermometer*) cubeta *f* **3.** ELEC bombilla *f*, bombillo *m AmL*

bulbous ['bʌlbəs] *adj* bulboso, -a; ~ **nose** nariz *f* protuberante

Bulgaria [bʌl'geərɪə, *Am:* -'gerɪ-] *n* Bulgaria *f*

Bulgarian [bʌl'geərɪən, *Am:* -'gerɪ-] **I.** *adj* búlgaro, -a **II.** *n* **1.**(*person*) búlgaro, -a *m, f* **2.** *no pl* LING búlgaro *m*

bulge [bʌldʒ] **I.** *vi* sobresalir; **her eyes ~d in surprise** su sorpresa fue tal que los ojos se le salían de las órbitas; **to** ~ (**with sth**) estar repleto (de algo) **II.** *n* **1.**(*swelling*) bulto *m* **2.**(*in a statistical trend*) alza *f*

bulging *adj* abultado, -a; (*bag, box*) repleto, -a; ~ **eyes** ojos *mpl* saltones

bulimia [bʊlɪ:miə, *Am:* bju:'-] *n no pl* MED bulimia *f*
bulk [bʌlk] **I.** *n* **1.** *no pl* (*magnitude*) volumen *m* **2.** *no pl* (*mass*) mole *f* **3.** *no pl* (*quantity*) **in ~** a granel; ECON al por mayor; **to ~ buy sth, to buy (sth) in ~** comprar (algo) en grandes cantidades; ECON comprar (algo) al por mayor **4.** (*largest part*) **the ~ of** la mayor parte de **II.** *vi* **to ~ large** ser importante
bulk buying *n* ECON *no pl* compra *f* al por mayor
bulkhead ['bʌlkhed] *n* NAUT mamparo *m*
bulky ['bʌlki] <-ier, iest> *adj* (*large*) voluminoso, -a; (*heavy*) pesado, -a; (*person*) corpulento, -a
bull[1] [bʊl] *n* **1.** (*male bovine*) toro *m* **2.** (*male animal*) macho *m;* **~ elephant** elefante *m;* **~ whale** ballena *f* macho ▶**like a ~ in a china shop** como un elefante en una cacharrería; **to take the ~ by the horns** coger [*o* agarrar *AmL*] el toro por los cuernos; **to be like a red rag to a ~ to sb** poner furioso a alguien
bull[2] [bʊl] *n* **1.** *no pl, inf* (*nonsense*) chorradas *fpl,* macanas *fpl RíoPl* **2.** FIN alcista *m;* **~ market** mercado *m* alcista **3.** *Brit* SPORTS diana *f*
bulldog ['bʊldɒg, *Am:* -dɑ:g] *n* bulldog *m*
bulldoze ['bʊldəʊz, *Am:* -doʊz] *vt* **1.** ARCHIT demoler **2.** *fig* **to ~ sth through** conseguir algo a la fuerza; **to ~ sb into doing sth** forzar a alguien a hacer algo
bulldozer ['bʊldəʊzəʳ, *Am:* -doʊzɚ] *n* bulldozer *m,* topadora *f Arg, Méx, Urug*
bullet ['bʊlɪt] *n* MIL bala *f;* **to fire a ~** disparar una bala ▶**to bite the ~** *inf* apretar los dientes, hacer de tripas corazón
bulletin ['bʊlətɪn, *Am:* -ət̬ɪn] *n* boletín *m;* (**news**) **~** TV, CINE boletín (informativo)
bulletin board *n Am a.* INFOR tablón *m* de anuncios
bulletproof ['bʊlɪtpru:f] *adj* a prueba de balas; **~ glass** vidrio *m* antibalas
bulletproof vest *n* chaleco *m* antibalas
bullfight ['bʊlfaɪt] *n* corrida *f* de toros
bullfighter ['bʊlfaɪtəʳ, *Am:* -t̬ɚ] *n* torero, -a *m, f*
bullfinch ['bʊlfɪntʃ] *n* pinzón *m*
bullion ['bʊlɪən, *Am:* -jən] *n no pl* **gold/silver ~** oro *m*/plata *f* en lingotes
bullock ['bʊlək] *n* buey *m*
bullring ['bʊlrɪŋ] *n* plaza *f* de toros
bull's-eye ['bʊlzaɪ] *n* blanco *f;* **to hit the ~** *a. fig* dar en el blanco
bullshit ['bʊlʃɪt] **I.** *n no pl, inf* gilipolleces *fpl;* **don't give me that ~!** ¡no me vengas con hostias! *vulg* **II.** *interj inf* y una mierda *vulg* **III.** <-tt-> *vi inf* decir gilipolleces
bully ['bʊli] **I.** <-ies> *n* (*person*) matón, -ona *m, f* **II.** <-ie-> *vt* intimidar; **to ~ sb into doing sth** intimidar a alguien a hacer algo **III.** *interj inf* **~ for you!** ¡qué bien!; *iron* ¡bravo!
bully beef *n* carne *f* de vaca enlatada
bulrush ['bʊlrʌʃ] <-es> *n* anea *f*
bulwark ['bʊlwək, *Am:* -wɚk] *n* **1.** baluarte *m* **2.** NAUT macarrón *m*
bum [bʌm] **I.** *n* **1.** *Am* (*lazy person*) vago, -a *m, f* **2.** *Am* (*tramp*) vagabundo, -a *m, f* **3.** *Aus, Brit, inf* (*bottom*) culo *m* ▶**to give sb the ~'s rush** *Am, inf* echar a alguien a patadas **II.** *adj inf* (*bad, useless*) malo, -a; **a ~ job** una porquería de trabajo **III.** <-mm-> *vt inf* **to ~ sth off sb** gorronear algo a alguien **IV.** *vi inf* **1. to ~ about** [*o* **around**] vagabundear **2. to ~ off sb** gorronear a alguien
bumble ['bʌmbl] *vi* andar a tropezones
bumblebee ['bʌmblbi:] *n* abejorro *m*
bumbling *adj* torpe
bumf [bʌmf] *n no pl, Aus, Brit, inf* **1.** (*printed matter*) papeles *mpl* **2.** (*paperwork*) papeleo *m*
bump [bʌmp] **I.** *n* **1.** (*lump*) bulto *m;* (*on head*) chichón *m;* (*on road*) bache *m* **2.** *inf* (*blow*) porrazo *m* **3.** (*thud*) golpe *m* **4.** (*collision*) topetazo *m* **II.** *vt* chocar contra; **to ~ one's head on/against sth** darse un golpe en la cabeza con/contra algo
◆**bump into** *vt insep* **1.** (*collide with*) chocar contra **2.** (*meet*) topar con
◆**bump off** *vt inf* **to bump sb off** cargarse a alguien
bumper ['bʌmpəʳ, *Am:* -pɚ] **I.** *n Brit, Aus* AUTO parachoques *m inv,* paragolpes *m inv AmL,* defensa *f Méx;* **the traffic is ~ to ~** hay un atasco **II.** *adj* **1.** (*crop*) abundante **2.** (*edition*) especial
bumper car *n* auto *m* de choque, carrito *m* chocón *Méx, Ven,* carro *m* loco *Col* **bumper sticker** *n* pegatina *f*
bumph [bʌmpf] *n no pl s.* **bumf**
bumpkin ['bʌmpkɪn] *n inf* (**country**) **~** paleto, -a *m, f*
bumptious ['bʌmpʃəs] *adj* engreído, -a
bumpy ['bʌmpi] <-ier, iest> *adj* (*surface*) desigual; (*road*) lleno, -a de baches; (*journey*) zarandeado, -a
bun [bʌn] *n* **1.** (*pastry*) bollo *m* **2.** *Am* (*roll*) panecillo *m,* pancito *m CSur* **3.** (*knot of hair*) moño *m,* chongo *m Méx*
bunch [bʌntʃ] <-es> **I.** *n* **1.** (*of bananas, grapes*) racimo *m;* (*of carrots, radishes, keys*) manojo *m;* (*of flowers*) ramo *m* **2.** (*group: of people*) grupo *m;* (*of friends*) pandilla *f* **3.** *Am* (*a lot*) **a ~ of problems** un montón de problemas **4.** *pl, Brit* (*hair style*) coletas *fpl* ▶**to be the best of the ~** ser lo mejor **II.** *vt* agrupar **III.** *vi* **to ~** (**together**) amontonarse
bundle ['bʌndl] **I.** *n* (*of clothes*) fardo *m;* (*of money*) fajo *m;* (*of sticks*) haz *f* ▶**to be a ~ of joy** *inf* ser un cascabel; **to be a ~ of laughs** ser muy divertido; **to be a ~ of nerves** ser un manojo de nervios; **to go a ~ on sth** *Brit, inf* volverse loco por algo **II.** *vt* **to ~ sb into a car** meter a alguien a empujones en un coche
◆**bundle up** **I.** *vt* atar, liar **II.** *vi* (*dress warmly*) abrigarse

bung [bʌŋ] **I.** *n Brit* tapón *m* **II.** *vt* **1.** *Brit* (*close*) taponar **2.** *Aus, Brit, inf* (*throw*) tirar; (*put*) poner

bungalow ['bʌŋgələʊ, *Am:* -oʊ] *n* bungaló *m*, bóngalo *m AmL*

bungee jumping ['bʌndʒɪˌdʒʌmpɪŋ] *n no pl* puenting *m*

bungle ['bʌŋgl] *vt* chapucear

bungler *n* chapucero, -a *m, f*

bungling *adj* torpe

bunk [bʌŋk] *n* NAUT litera *f*, cucheta *f RíoPl* ►**to do a ~** *Aus, Brit, inf* poner pies en polvorosa

◆**bunk down** *vi inf* echarse a dormir

bunk bed *n* litera *f*

bunker ['bʌŋkəʳ, *Am:* -kɚ] *n* búnker *m*

bunkum ['bʌŋkəm] *n* chorradas *fpl*

bunny (rabbit) ['bʌni ('ræbɪt)] *n childspeak* conejito *m*

bunsen burner [ˌbʌntsən'bɜːnəʳ, *Am:* 'bʌntsɪnˌbɜːrnɚ] *n* mechero *m* Bunsen

bunting ['bʌntɪŋ, *Am:* -t̬ɪŋ] *n no pl* banderitas *fpl*

buoy [bɔɪ] *n* boya *f*

◆**buoy up** *vt* **1.** (*cause to float*) mantener a flote **2.** *fig* (*cause to rise*) aumentar **3.** *fig* **to buoy sb up** animar a alguien

buoyancy ['bɔɪənsi, *Am:* -jən-] *n no pl* **1.** *a.* NAUT capacidad *f* para flotar **2.** (*cheerfulness*) optimismo *m*

buoyant ['bɔɪənt, *Am:* -jənt] *adj* **1.** (*able to float*) flotante **2.** (*cheerful*) optimista; **to be in a ~ mood** estar de buen humor **3.** FIN **a ~ currency** una moneda fuerte

burble ['bɜːbl, *Am:* 'bɜːr-] *vi* **1.** (*make burbling noise*) borbotar **2.** (*talk nonsense*) parlotear

burden ['bɜːdən, *Am:* 'bɜːr-] **I.** *n* **1.** (*load*) carga *f* **2.** *fig* carga *f*; (*responsibility*) responsabilidad *f*; **tax ~** ECON gravamen *m*; **the ~ of proof** LAW la carga de la prueba; **to be a ~ on [*o* to] sb** ser una carga para alguien **II.** *vt* **1.** (*load*) cargar **2.** *fig* estorbar; **I don't want to ~ you with my problems** no quiero preocuparte con mis problemas

burdensome ['bɜːdənsəm, *Am:* 'bɜːr-] *adj form* oneroso, -a

bureau ['bjʊərəʊ, *Am:* 'bjʊroʊ] <-x *Am, Aus:* -s> *n* **1.** *Am* (*government department*) departamento *m*; (*office*) agencia *f*; **employment ~** oficina *f* de empleo **2.** *Brit* (*desk*) escritorio *m* **3.** *Am* (*chest of drawers*) cómoda *f*

bureaucracy [bjʊə'rɒkrəsi, *Am:* bjʊ'rɑːkrə-] *n* burocracia *f*

bureaucrat ['bjʊərəkræt, *Am:* 'bjʊrə-] *n* burócrata *mf*

bureaucratic [ˌbjʊərə'krætɪk, *Am:* ˌbjʊrə'kræt̬-] *adj* burocrático, -a

burgeoning ['bɜːdʒənɪŋ, *Am:* 'bɜːr-] *adj* creciente

burger ['bɜːgəʳ, *Am:* 'bɜːrgɚ] *n inf abbr of* **hamburger** hamburguesa *f*

burglar ['bɜːgləʳ, *Am:* 'bɜːrglɚ] *n* ladrón, -ona *m, f*

burglar alarm *n* alarma *f* antirrobo

burglarize ['bɜːgləraɪz, *Am:* 'bɜːrglə-] *vt Am s.* **burgle**

burglary ['bɜːgləri, *Am:* 'bɜːr-] <-ies> *n* robo *m*

burgle ['bɜːgl, *Am:* 'bɜːr-] *vt* robar; **five houses have been ~d** han entrado a robar en cinco casas

burial ['berɪəl] *n* entierro *m*

burial ground *n* cementerio *m* **burial service** *n* funerales *mpl*

Burkinabe ['bɜːkiːneɪb] **I.** *adj* de Burkina Faso **II.** *n* habitante *mf* de Burkina Faso

Burkina Faso [bɜːˌkiːnə'fæsəʊ] *n* Burkina *f* Faso

burlesque [bɜː'lesk, *Am:* 'bɜːr-] **I.** *n* parodia *f* **II.** *adj* burlesco, -a

burly ['bɜːli, *Am:* 'bɜːr-] <-ier, -iest> *adj* (*person*) fornido, -a; (*arm, leg*) musculoso, -a

Burma ['bɜːmə, *Am:* 'bɜr-] *n* Birmania *f*

burn¹ [bɜːn, *Am:* bɜːrn] *n Scot* (*stream*) arroyo *m*

burn² [bɜːn, *Am:* bɜːrn] **I.** <burnt *o* -ed, burnt *o* -ed> *vi* **1.** (*be in flames: house*) arder; (*coal, wood*) quemarse **2.** (*be hot*) arder; **his forehead was ~ing** la frente le ardía **3.** (*be switched on*) estar encendido, -a; **he left all the lights ~ing** dejó todas las luces encendidas **4.** (*long*) **to be ~ing to do sth** estar deseando hacer algo **5.** (*feel emotion strongly*) **to ~ with sth** arder de algo; **to ~ with desire** desear ardientemente **6.** (*be red*) **his face ~ed with anger/shame** se puso rojo de furia/vergüenza **II.** <burnt *o* -ed, burnt *o* -ed> *vt* (*paper, rubbish, food*) quemar; (*building*) incendiar; (*throat, tongue*) quemar, escaldar; **to be ~ed** (*by the sun*) quemarse; (*injured*) sufrir quemaduras; **to ~ calories/fat** quemar calorías/grasa; **this machine ~s electricity** esta máquina funciona con electricidad; **we ~ a lot of gas** consumimos mucho gas **III.** *n* quemadura *f*, quemada *f Méx*; **severe/minor ~s** quemaduras graves/leves

◆**burn away I.** *vi* (*forest*) quemarse; (*candle*) consumirse **II.** *vt* quemar

◆**burn down I.** *vt* incendiar **II.** *vi* (*house*) incendiarse; (*fire, candle*) apagarse

◆**burn out I.** *vi* (*engine*) quemarse; (*fire, candle*) apagarse; (*light bulb*) fundirse **II.** *vt* **to burn oneself out** agotarse, quemarse

◆**burn up I.** *vt inf* (*fuel*) consumir; (*calories*) quemar **II.** *vi* abrasarse; **you're burning up!** *inf* (*have fever*) ¡estás ardiendo!

burner ['bɜːnəʳ, *Am:* 'bɜːrnɚ] *n* fogón *m*; TECH quemador *m*

burning ['bɜːnɪŋ, *Am:* 'bɜːrnɪŋ] *adj* **1.** (*hot*) ardiente; (*sun*) abrasador; **to be ~ hot** estar ardiendo; **a ~ sensation** una quemazón **2.** (*issue, question*) candente; (*desire, hatred*) ardiente

La **Burns Night** tiene lugar el 25 de enero. En este día se conmemora el nacimiento del poeta escocés Robert Burns (1759-1796). A la celebración acuden entusiastas de la obra de Burns, no sólo de Escocia sino de todas las partes del mundo. En ese día se sirve una comida especial llamada **Burns Supper** que se compone de **haggis** (una especie de asado de carne picada hecha de vísceras especiadas de oveja, mezclado con avena y cebolla. Todo ello es cocido dentro de la tripa de la oveja y después dorado al horno), **neeps** (nabos) y **mashed tatties** (puré de patatas).

burnt [bɜːnt, *Am:* 'bɜːrnt] **I.** *pt, pp of* **burn II.** *adj* quemado, -a; **a ~ smell/taste** un olor/sabor a quemado

burp [bɜːp, *Am:* bɜːrp] **I.** *n* eructo *m;* **to let out a ~** soltar un eructo **II.** *vi* eructar **III.** *vt* **to ~ a baby** hacer eructar a un bebé

burr [bɜːʳ, *Am:* bɜːr] *n* **1.** BOT abrojo *m* **2.** (*noise*) zumbido *m* **3.** LING sonido *m* gutural

burrow ['bʌrəʊ, *Am:* 'bɜːroʊ] **I.** *n* madriguera *f;* **rabbit ~** conejera *f* **II.** *vi* (*dig a hole*) excavar un agujero; (*a tunnel*) excavar un túnel; (*a home*) excavar una madriguera; **to ~ into sth** horadar algo; *fig* hurgar en algo **III.** *vt* excavar

bursar ['bɜːsəʳ, *Am:* 'bɜːrsɚ] *n* tesorero, -a *m, f*

bursary ['bɜːsəri, *Am:* 'bɜːr-] *n Brit* beca *f*

burst [bɜːst, *Am:* bɜːrst] **I.** *n* **1.** (*explosion*) explosión *f* **2.** MIL (*of fire*) ráfaga *f* **3.** (*brief period*) **a ~ of laughter** una carcajada; **a ~ of applause** una salva de aplausos; **a ~ of anger** un arranque de cólera **II.** <burst *Am:* bursted, burst *Am:* bursted> *vi* **1.** (*balloon, tyre*) reventar; (*storm*) desatarse; **to ~ into tears** romper a llorar **2.** (*move suddenly*) **to ~ into a place** irrumpir en un lugar; **to ~ open** abrirse de golpe **3.** *fig* **to be ~ing to do sth** morirse de ganas de hacer algo; **to be ~ing with health** rebosar de salud; **to be ~ing with curiosity** morirse de curiosidad **III.** <burst *Am:* bursted, burst *Am:* bursted> *vt* reventar; **to ~ its banks** (*river*) desbordarse

◆**burst forth** *vi* brotar

◆**burst in** *vi* entrar de sopetón

◆**burst out** *vi* **1.** (*exclaim*) saltar **2.** (*break out*) **to ~ laughing/crying** echarse a reír/llorar

Burundi [bʊ'rʊndi] *n* Burundi *m*

bury ['beri] <-ie-> *vt* **1.** (*put underground*) enterrar **2.** (*hide*) ocultar; **to ~ oneself in sth** enfrascarse en algo; **to be buried in thought** estar ensimismado; **to ~ one's head in one's hands** ocultar el rostro en las manos

bus [bʌs] **I.** <-es> *n* (*local*) autobús *m,* colectivo *m Arg, Ven,* guagua *f Cuba,* omnibús *m Perú, Urug;* **school ~** autobús escolar; **to catch/miss the ~** coger/perder el autobús; **to go by ~** ir en autobús ►**to miss the ~** perder el (último) tren **II.** <-ss-> *vt* llevar en autobús **III.** <-ss-> *vi* ir en autobús

bus driver *n* conductor(a) *m(f)* de autobús

bush [bʊʃ] <-es> *n* **1.** BOT arbusto *m;* **a ~ of hair** una mata de pelo **2.** *no pl* (*land*) **the ~** el monte ►**to beat about the ~** andarse con rodeos; **to beat the ~es for sth** *Am* buscar algo por todas partes

bushel ['bʊʃl] *n* fanega *f* (*en Gran Bretaña, esta medida equivale a 36,4 l; en Estados Unidos a 35,2 l.*) ►**to hide one's light under a ~** ocultar sus talentos

bushman ['bʊʃmən] <-men> *n* bosquimano *m*

bushy ['bʊʃi] <-ier, -iest> *adj* (*hair*) tupido, -a; (*beard, moustache*) espeso, -a; (*eyebrows*) poblado, -a

busily *adv* afanosamente

business ['bɪznɪs] *n* **1.** *no pl* (*trade, commerce*) negocios *mpl;* **to be away on ~** estar de viaje de negocios; **to do ~ with sb** hacer negocios con alguien; **to get down to ~** empezar a trabajar; **to go out of ~** cerrar; **to set up in ~** montar un negocio; **to set up in ~ as a lawyer** establecerse como abogado; **to work in ~** dedicarse a los negocios; **~ is booming** el negocio va muy bien; **once we get the computer installed, we'll be in ~** *inf* una vez que hayamos instalado el ordenador podremos empezar **2.** <-es> (*sector*) industria *f;* **the frozen food ~** la industria de los congelados; **what line of ~ are you in?** ¿en qué ramo trabajas? **3.** <-es> (*firm*) empresa *f;* **to start up/run a ~** poner/llevar un negocio **4.** *no pl* (*matter*) asunto *m;* **an unfinished ~** un asunto pendiente; **it's none of your ~!** *inf* ¡no es asunto tuyo!; **mind your own ~!** *inf* ¡no te metas donde no te llaman!; **to have no ~ doing sth** no tener derecho a hacer algo; **I make it my ~ to do that** me encargo de hacer eso; **it's a time-consuming ~** requiere mucho tiempo ►**~ before pleasure** *prov* antes es la obligación que el placer; **~ as usual** *prov* todo sigue igual; **to (not) be in the ~ of doing sth** (no) tener por costumbre hacer algo; **to mean ~** hablar en serio; **like nobody's ~** *inf* como loco

business address *n* dirección *f* comercial **business card** *n* tarjeta *f* comercial **business class** *n* clase *f* preferente **business expenses** *npl* gastos *mpl* comerciales **business hours** *n* horas *fpl* de oficina **business letter** *n* carta *f* comercial

businesslike ['bɪznɪslaɪk] *adj* **1.** (*serious*) formal **2.** (*efficient*) eficiente

businessman ['bɪznɪsmæn] <-men> *n* hombre *m* de negocios

business park *n* parque *m* de negocios **business trip** *n* viaje *m* de negocios

businesswoman ['bɪznɪsˌwʊmən] <-women> *n* mujer *f* de negocios

busk [bʌsk] *vi Aus, Brit: tocar un instrumento en la calle*

busker ['bʌskəʳ, *Am:* -ɚ] *n Aus, Brit* músico, -a *m, f* ambulante

busload ['bʌsləʊd, *Am:* -loʊd] *n* **~s of tourists** autobuses *mpl* llenos de turistas

bus service *n* servicio *m* de autobuses **bus station** *n* estación *f* de autobuses **bus stop** *n* parada *f* de autobús

bust¹ [bʌst] *n* busto *m*

bust² [bʌst] **I.** *adj inf* **1.** (*broken*) destrozado, -a **2.** (*bankrupt*) en bancarrota; **to go ~** quebrar **II.** <bust *Am:* busted, bust *Am:* busted> *vt inf* **1.** (*break*) destrozar **2.** (*raid*) realizar una redada en

bustle ['bʌsl] **I.** *vi* **to ~ about** ir y venir; **to ~ with activity** rebosar de actividad **II.** *n* **1.** *no pl* ajetreo *m;* **hustle and ~** bullicio *m* **2.** HIST (*dress part*) polisón *m*

bustling *adj* (*town, street*) animado, -a

bust-up ['bʌstʌp] *n Aus, Brit, inf* riña *f;* **to have a (big) ~ with sb** partir peras con alguien

busy¹ ['bɪzi] <-ier, -iest> *adj* **1.** (*occupied*) atareado, -a; **to be ~ doing sth** estar muy ocupado haciendo algo; **to be ~ with sth** estar ocupado con algo; **to get ~** empezar a trabajar **2.** (*full of activity*) activo, -a; (*exhausting*) agotador(a); **~ street** calle *f* concurrida; **~ seaport** puerto *m* marítimo de gran actividad; **a ~ time** un tiempo de actividad frenética; **I've had a ~ day** he tenido un día ajetreado **3.** *Am* TEL **to be ~** estar comunicando

busy² ['bɪzi] <-ie-> *vt* **to ~ oneself with sth** ocuparse de algo

busybody ['bɪzi,bɒdi, *Am:* -,bɑːdi] <-ies> *n inf* entrometido, -a *m, f;* **to be a ~** ser un metomentodo

but [bʌt] **I.** *prep* excepto; **all ~ one** todos excepto uno; **anything ~ ...** lo que sea menos...; **nothing ~ ...** nada más que...; **no one ~ he** nadie salvo él; **~ for that I'd have had an accident** si no fuera por eso habría tenido un accidente; **there is nothing for it ~ to go in** no hay nada que hacer excepto entrar **II.** *conj* pero; **I'm not an Englishman ~ a Scot** no soy inglés sino escocés; **he has paper ~ no pen** tiene papel pero no una pluma; **it is not red ~ pink** no es rojo sino rosa **III.** *adv* sólo; **he is ~ a baby** no es más que un bebé; **I can ~ hope she wins** solamente puedo esperar que gane; **I can't help ~ cry** no puedo evitar llorar **IV.** *n* pero *m;* **there are no ~s about it!** ¡no hay peros que valgan!

butane ['bjuːteɪn] *n no pl* butano *m*

butch [bʊtʃ] *adj* **1.** (*man*) macho **2.** (*woman*) marimacho

butcher ['bʊtʃəʳ, *Am:* -ɚ] **I.** *n* carnicero, -a *m, f* **II.** *vt* **1.** (*slaughter*) matar **2.** (*murder*) asesinar (brutalmente), masacrar **3.** *fig* **to ~ a language** mutilar una lengua

butchery ['bʊtʃəri] *n no pl* **1.** (*of an animal*) matanza *f* **2.** (*killing*) carnicería *f*

butler ['bʌtləʳ, *Am:* -lɚ] *n* mayordomo *m*

butt [bʌt] **I.** *n* **1.** (*of rifle*) culata *f* **2.** (*of cigarette*) colilla *f* **3.** (*blow: with the head*) cabezada *f* **4.** (*target*) **to be the ~ of sth** ser el blanco de algo **5.** (*container*) tonel *m* **6.** *Am, inf* (*buttocks*) culo *m* **II.** *vt* (*with the horns*) topetar; (*with the head*) dar una cabezada contra

butter ['bʌtəʳ, *Am:* 'bʌt̬ɚ] **I.** *n no pl* mantequilla *f* ►**he/she looks as if ~ wouldn't melt in his/her mouth** parece que no haya roto un plato en su vida **II.** *vt* untar con mantequilla

◆**butter up** *vt* dar jabón a, cepillar *AmL*

buttercup ['bʌtəkʌp, *Am:* 'bʌt̬ɚ-] *n* ranúnculo *m*

butter dish *n* recipiente *m* para mantequilla

butterfingers ['bʌtə,fɪŋgəz, *Am:* 'bʌt̬ɚ-,fɪŋgɚz] *n inv* manazas *mf inv*

butterfly ['bʌtəflaɪ, *Am:* 'bʌt̬ɚ-] <-ies> *n* **1.** ZOOL mariposa *f; fig* (*person*) persona *f* frívola **2.** TECH calón *m* **3.** *no pl* SPORTS mariposa *f* ►**to have butterflies in one's stomach** estar con los nervios a flor de piel

buttermilk ['bʌtəmɪlk, *Am:* 'bʌt̬ɚ-] *n no pl* suero *m* de leche

buttery ['bʌtəri, *Am:* 'bʌt̬-] <-ier, -iest> *adj* de mantequilla

buttock ['bʌtək, *Am:* 'bʌt̬-] *n* nalga *f*

button ['bʌtən] **I.** *n* botón *m;* **start ~** botón de inicio; **right/left mouse ~** botón derecho/izquierdo del ratón; **to push a ~** apretar un botón; **at the push of a ~** con sólo pulsar un botón ►**to be (as) bright as a ~** ser más listo que el hambre; **to be right on the ~** *Am* estar en lo cierto **II.** *vi* abrocharse **III.** *vt* abrochar ►**to ~ it** *Am, inf* no decir ni esta boca es mía

◆**button up** *vt* abrochar

buttonhole ['bʌtənhəʊl, *Am:* -hoʊl] **I.** *n* **1.** FASHION ojal *m* **2.** *Brit* (*flower*) *flor que se lleva en el ojal* **II.** *vt* obligar a escuchar

buttress ['bʌtrɪs] <-es> *n* ARCHIT contrafuerte *m; fig* apoyo *m*

buxom ['bʌksəm] *adj* pechugona

buy [baɪ] **I.** *n* compra *f;* **a good ~** una ganga **II.** <bought, bought> *vt* **1.** (*purchase*) comprar; **to ~ sth from [*o* off] sb** *inf* comprar algo a alguien; **to ~ sb's silence** comprar el silencio de alguien **2.** *inf* (*believe*) creer; **did the teacher ~ your excuse?** ¿se tragó el profesor tu excusa?

◆**buy back** *vt* volver a comprar

◆**buy in** *vt always sep, Brit* aprovisionarse de

◆**buy off** *vt always sep* sobornar

◆**buy out** *vt* COM comprar la parte de

◆**buy up** *vt insep* acaparar

buyer ['baɪəʳ, *Am:* -ɚ] *n* **1.** (*purchaser*) comprador(a) *m(f)* **2.** (*buying agent*) encargado, -a *m, f* de compras

buyout ['baɪaʊt] *n* FIN compra *f* (*de la totalidad de las acciones*)**; management/worker ~** compra de una empresa por los gerentes/empleados

buzz [bʌz] I. *vi* 1. (*hum*) zumbar; (*bell*) sonar; **my ears were ~ing** me zumbaban los oídos; **the village was ~ing with rumours** el pueblo era un hervidero de rumores 2. *Am, inf* (*be tipsy*) ir borracho II. *vt inf* TEL llamar III. *n* 1. (*humming noise*) zumbido *m;* (*low noise*) rumor *m;* (*of a doorbell*) llamada *f;* **the ~ of conversation** el rumor de la conversación 2. *no pl, inf* (*telephone call*) llamada *f;* **to give sb a ~** llamar a alguien 3. *no pl, inf* (*feeling*) excitación *f;* (*of alcohol*) subidón *m;* **I get a ~ from** [*o* **out of**] **surfing** el surf me entusiasma; **sb gets a ~ from sth** algo excita a alguien; **I get a ~ from champagne** el champán se me sube a la cabeza

◆**buzz off** *vi inf* largarse

buzzard ['bʌzəd, *Am:* -ɚd] *n* 1. *Brit* (*hawk*) ratonero *m* común 2. *Am* (*turkey vulture*) gallinazo *m* común

buzzer ['bʌzəʳ, *Am:* -ɚ] *n* timbre *m*

buzz word *n* palabra *f* de moda

by [baɪ] I. *prep* 1. (*near*) cerca de; **close** [*o* **near**] **~ ...** cerca de...; **to be/lie/stand ~ ...** estar/yacer/permanecer cerca de...; **~ the sea** junto al mar 2. (*at*) junto a; **to remain ~ sb for two days** quedarse junto a alguien durante dos días 3. (*during*) **~ day/night** durante el día/la noche; **~ moonlight** a la luz de la luna 4. (*at the latest time*) para; **~ tomorrow/midnight** para mañana/la medianoche; **~ then/now** para entonces/este momento 5. (*cause*) por; **a novel ~ Joyce** una novela de Joyce; **to be killed ~ sth/sb** ser matado por algo/alguien; **surrounded ~ dogs** rodeado de perros 6. (*through means of*) **~ rail/plane/tram** en tren/avión/tranvía; **made ~ hand** hecho a mano; **to hold sb ~ the arm** tomar a alguien por el brazo; **to go in ~ the door** entrar por la puerta; **~ doing sth** haciendo algo 7. (*through*) **~ chance/mistake** por suerte/error 8. (*under*) **to call sb/sth ~ their/it's name** llamar a alguien/algo por su nombre; **what does he mean ~ that?** ¿a qué se refiere con eso? 9. (*alone*) **to be ~ oneself** estar solo; **to do sth ~ oneself** hacer algo solo 10. (*as promise to*) **to swear ~ God/sth** jurar por Dios/algo 11. (*in measurement, arithmetic*) **to buy ~ the kilo/dozen** comprar por kilo/docenas; **to divide ~ 6** dividir entre 6; **to increase ~ 10%** aumentar en un 10%; **to multiply ~ 4** multiplicar por 4; **paid ~ the hour/day** pagado por hora/día; **4 metres ~ 6** 4 metros por 6; **one ~ one** uno a uno 12. (*from the perspective of*) **to judge ~ appearances** juzgar por las apariencias; **all right ~ me** *inf* por mí, de acuerdo II. *adv* 1. (*near*) cerca; **to put/lay sth ~** poner/dejar algo a mano 2. (*in a while*) **~ and ~** dentro de poco 3. (*past*) **to go/pass ~** pasar ►**~ and large** en general

bye [baɪ] *interj,* **bye-bye** [ˌbaɪ'baɪ] *interj inf* adiós

bye-law ['baɪlɔː] *n Brit s.* **by-law**

by-election ['baɪɪəlekʃən] *n Brit* elección *f* parcial

bygone ['baɪgɒn, *Am:* -gɑːn] I. *adj inv* pasado, -a II. *n* **let ~s be ~s** lo pasado pasado está

by-law ['baɪlɔː, *Am:* -lɑː] *n* 1. (*regional law*) reglamento *m* local 2. (*organization's rule*) estatuto *m*

> El **BYO-restaurant** (**B**ring **Y**our **O**wn) se encuentra en Australia. Es un tipo de restaurante que no tiene licencia para servir bebidas alcohólicas. Por ello, si los clientes desean consumir esta clase de bebidas, deben de traerlas ellos mismos.

by-pass ['baɪpɑːs, *Am:* -pæs] I. *n* 1. AUTO carretera *f* de circunvalación 2. ELEC desviación *f* 3. MED by-pass *m* II. *vt* 1. (*make a detour*) evitar 2. *fig* (*act without permission of*) **to ~ sb** actuar sin el consentimiento de alguien 3. *fig* (*avoid*) evitar

byplay ['baɪpleɪ] *n no pl* THEAT acción *f* de segundo plano

by-product ['baɪprɒdʌkt, *Am:* -prɑːdəkt] *n* subproducto *m; fig* derivado *m*

by-road ['bəɪrəʊd, *Am:* -roʊd] *n* carretera *f* secundaria

bystander ['baɪstændəʳ, *Am:* -dɚ] *n* espectador(a) *m(f)*

byte [baɪt] *n* byte *m*

byway ['baɪweɪ] *n* camino *m* poco concurrido

byword ['baɪwɜːd, *Am:* -wɜːrd] *n* ejemplo *m;* **to be a ~ for sth** ser sinónimo de algo

C

C, c [siː] *n* 1. (*letter*) C, c *f;* **~ for Charlie** C de Carmen 2. MUS do *m* 3. SCHOOL ≈ suficiente *m*

C *after n abbr of* **Celsius** C

c. 1. *abbr of* **circa** (*by numbers*) aprox.; (*by dates*) hacia 2. *abbr of* **cent** cent 3. *abbr of* **century** s.

ca. *abbr of* **circa** 1. (*by numbers*) aprox. 2. (*by dates*) hacia

CAA [ˌsiːeɪ'eɪ] *n abbr of* **Civil Aviation Authority** (autoridades *fpl* de) Aviación *f* Civil

cab [kæb] *n* 1. (*vehicle's driver area*) cabina *f* 2. *Am, Aus* (*taxi*) taxi *m;* **by ~** en taxi 3. HIST (*horse-drawn vehicle*) carruaje *m*

CAB [ˌsiːeɪ'biː] *n* 1. *abbr of* **Citizens' Advice Bureau** Oficina *f* de Atención al Ciudadano 2. *Am abbr of* **Civil Aeronautics Board** Oficina *f* de Aviación Civil

cabaret ['kæbəreɪ, *Am:* ˌkæbə'reɪ] *n* cabaret *m*

cabbage ['kæbɪdʒ] *n* 1. GASTR col *f* 2. ZOOL **~ white** mariposa *f* de la col 3. *Brit* (*person*) vegetal *m*

cabbie *n,* **cabby** ['kæbi] *n,* **cabdriver** [kæbˌdraɪvəʳ, *Am:* -vɚ] *n Am* taxista *mf*

cabin ['kæbɪn] *n* **1.** (*in a vehicle*) cabina *f* **2.** (*simple wooden house*) cabaña *f*

cabin class *n* AVIAT clase *f* de compartimento

cabin cruiser *n* yate *m* de motor

cabinet ['kæbɪnɪt] *n* **1.** (*storage place*) armario *m;* (*glass-fronted*) vitrina *f;* **filing** ~ archivador *m* **2.** + *sing/pl vb* (*group of ministers*) gabinete *m,* consejo *m* de ministros

cabinet maker *n* ebanista *mf*

cable ['keɪbl] **I.** *n* **1.** (*wire rope*) cable *m;* **coil of** ~ rollo *m* de cable **2.** *no pl* TV televisión *f* por cable **3.** HIST (*electrically transmitted message*) cablegrama *m;* **to send sth by** ~ cablegrafiar algo **II.** *vt* HIST cablegrafiar

cable car *n* teleférico *m* **cable network** *n* cableado *m* **cable railway** *n Am* funicular *m* **cable stitch** *n no pl* punto *m* trenzado **cable television** *n no pl,* **cable TV** *n no pl* televisión *f* por cable

caboodle [kə'buːdl] *n Am, inf* **the whole** (**kit and**) ~ toda la pesca

cab rank *n,* **cab stand** *n Am* (*taxi rank*) parada *f* de taxis

cabriolet ['kæbriəʊleɪ, *Am:* ˌkæbriə'leɪ] *n* descapotable *m*

cacao [kə'kɑːəʊ, *Am:* -oʊ] *n no pl* cacao *m;* ~ (**bean**) (semilla *f* de) cacao *m*

cache [kæʃ] *n* **1.** (*hiding place*) escondite *m;* (*secret stockpile*) alijo *m;* ~ **of weapons** alijo de armas **2.** INFOR caché *m;* ~ **memory** memoria *f* caché

cachet ['kæʃeɪ, *Am:* kæʃ'eɪ] *n no pl* distinción *f,* prestigio *m*

cackle ['kækl] **I.** *vi* **1.** (*hen*) cacarear **2.** *fig* (*laugh*) reírse escandalosamente **3.** (*talk*) cotorrear **II.** *n* **1.** *no pl* (*of hen*) cacareo *m* **2.** (*laugh*) risotada *f* ►**cut the** ~**!** *Brit, Aus, iron* ¡corta el rollo!

cacophony [kæ'kɒfəni, *Am:* kə'kɑːfə-] *n no pl* (*loud discord*) cacofonía *f;* (*noise*) estrépito *m*

cactus ['kæktəs] <-es *o* cacti> *n* cactus *m inv,* ulala *f Bol*

CAD [kæd] *n abbr of* **Computer-Aided Design** DAO *m,* DAC *m AmL*

cadaver [kə'deɪvəʳ, *Am:* -'dævɚ] *n* MED cadáver *m*

CAD/CAM ['kædkæm] *n abbr of* **computer-aided design and manufacture** CAD/CAM *m*

caddie, caddy ['kædi] <-ies> **I.** *n* caddie *mf,* caddy *mf* **II.** <caddied, caddied, caddying> *vi* **to** ~ **for sb** hacer de caddy de alguien

cadence ['keɪdns] *n* cadencia *f*

cadet [kə'det] *n a.* MIL cadete *mf*

cadge [kædʒ] **I.** *vt inf* **to** ~ **sth** (**off sb**) (*get by begging*) obtener algo (de alguien) mendigando; (*get for free*) gorronear algo (a alguien) **II.** *vi inf* (*get by begging*) obtener mendigando; (*get something for free*) gorronear

cadger ['kædʒəʳ, *Am:* -ɚ] *n* gorrón, -ona *m, f*

cadmium ['kædmjəm] *n no pl* cadmio *m*

cadre ['kɑːdəʳ, *Am:* 'kædriː] *n* **1.** (*elite trained group*) cuadro *m* **2.** (*group member*) (miembro *mf* del) cuadro *m*

Caesar ['siːzəʳ, *Am:* -zɚ] *n* César *m;* **Julius** ~ HIST Julio César

caesarean [si'zeəriən, *Am:* si'zeri] *n* ~ (**section**) cesárea *f*

caesium ['sɪːzjəm] *n no pl, Brit* cesio *m*

cafe *n,* **café** ['kæfeɪ, *Am:* kæf'eɪ] *n* café *m*

cafeteria [ˌkæfɪ'tɪəriə, *Am:* -'tɪri-] *n* restaurante *m* autoservicio, self-service *m*

caffeine ['kæfiːn, *Am:* kæf'iːn] *n no pl* cafeína *f*

cage [keɪdʒ] **I.** *n* jaula *f* **II.** *vt* enjaular

cagey ['keɪdʒi] <-ier, -iest> *adj inf* reservado, -a; **to be** ~ **about sth** ocultar [*o* reservarse] información sobre algo

cahoots [kə'huːts] *npl inf* **to be in** ~ (**with sb**) estar compinchado (con alguien)

cairn [keən, *Am:* kern] *n* mojón *m* (de piedras)

Cairo ['keərəʊ, *Am:* 'keroʊ] *n* El Cairo

cajole [kə'dʒəʊl, *Am:* -'dʒoʊl] **I.** *vt* engatusar; **to** ~ **sb into/out of doing sth** engatusar a alguien para que haga/no haga algo **II.** *vi* engatusar, camelar *inf*

cake [keɪk] **I.** *n* **1.** GASTR pastel *m;* (*small*) pasta *f;* **iced** ~ tarta *f* helada; **sponge** ~ bizcocho *m,* queque *m AmL* **2.** (*of soap*) pastilla *f;* (*of chocolate*) barra *f* ►**to sell like hot** ~**s** *inf* venderse como rosquillas; **to want to have one's** ~ **and eat it** quererlo todo **II.** *vt* (*cover with*) **his boots were** ~**d with mud** sus botas estaban cubiertas de barro **III.** *vi* (*dry*) endurecerse

cal. *n abbr of* **calorie** cal *f*

calamity [kə'læməti, *Am:* -əṱi] <-ies> *n* calamidad *f*

calciferous [kæl'sɪfərəs] *adj* calizo, -a

calcify ['kælsɪfaɪ] <-ie-> **I.** *vt* calcificar **II.** *vi* calcificarse

calcium ['kælsɪəm] *n no pl* calcio *m*

calculable ['kælkjʊləbl, *Am:* -kjə-] *adj* MAT, ECON calculable; **the total damage is** ~ **at £15,000** los daños totales se estiman en 15.000 libras

calculate ['kælkjʊleɪt, *Am:* -kjə-] **I.** *vt* calcular; **to** ~ **sth at ...** calcular algo en... **II.** *vi* calcular

calculated *adj* calculado, -a; **to be** ~ **to do sth** estar pensado para hacer algo

calculating *adj* calculador(a)

calculation [ˌkælkjʊ'leɪʃən, *Am:* -kjə-] *n* **1.** MAT cálculo *m; no pl* (*figures*) cómputo *m* **2.** (*foreseeing*) cálculo *m* **3.** *no pl* (*selfish planning*) premeditación *f*

calculator ['kælkjʊleɪtəʳ, *Am:* -kjəleɪṱɚ] *n* calculadora *f*

calculus ['kælkjʊləs, *Am:* -kjə-] *n no pl* cálculo *m*

calendar ['kælɪndəʳ, *Am:* -dɚ] **I.** *n* calendario *m*, exfoliador *m Chile, Méx* **II.** *adj* ~ **year** año *m* civil
calendar month <-es> *n* mes *m*
calf¹ [kɑːf, *Am:* kæf] <calves> *n* **1.** (*young cow or bull*) ternero, -a *m, f;* **to be in** ~ estar preñada **2.** *no pl* (*leather*) piel *f* de becerro ▸**to kill the** __**fatted**__ ~ echar la casa por la ventana (para celebrar la llegada de alguien)
calf² [kɑːf, *Am:* kæf] <calves> *n* (*lower leg*) pantorrilla *f*
calf-love *n no pl* amor *m* de adolescente
caliber ['kæləbɚ] *n no pl, Am s.* **calibre**
calibrate ['kælɪbreɪt] *vt* calibrar
calibre ['kælɪbəʳ, *Am:* -əbɚ] *n* calibre *m;* **to be of (a) high** ~ ser de grueso calibre
calico ['kælɪkəʊ, *Am:* -koʊ] *n no pl* calicó *m*, percal *m*
California [ˌkælɪ'fɔːniə, *Am:* -ə'fɔrnjə] *n* California *f*
call [kɔːl] **I.** *n* **1.** (*telephone*) llamada *f* **2.** (*visit*) visita *f;* **to be on a** ~ estar haciendo una visita; **to be on** ~ estar de guardia; **to pay a** ~ **on sb** hacer una visita a alguien **3.** (*shout*) grito *m;* **to give a** ~ pegar un grito **4.** (*animal cry*) grito *m;* (*bird*) canto *m* **5.** *a.* POL llamamiento *m;* **a** ~ **for help** una llamada de socorro **6.** *no pl a.* ECON requerimiento *m;* **money on** ~ dinero *m* a la vista; **there is not much** ~ **for sth** no hay demasiada demanda de algo **7.** *form* (*need*) **to have no** ~ **for sth** no tener ninguna necesidad de algo; **you had no** ~ **to say that** no tenías por qué decir eso ▸**to have a** __**close**__ ~ salvarse por los pelos **II.** *vt* **1.** (*name, address as*) llamar; **to** ~ **sb names** insultar a alguien; **what's that actor ~ed?** ¿cómo se llama ese actor?; **what's his new film ~ed?** ¿cómo se titula su nueva película?; **she's ~ed by her second name, Jane** la llaman por su segundo nombre, Jane **2.** (*telephone*) llamar, telefonear *AmL;* **to** ~ **sb collect** *Am* llamar a alguien a cobro revertido **3.** (*make noise to attract*) **to** ~ **sb's attention** llamar la atención de alguien; **I ~ed you to come to eat ten minutes ago** te he llamado para que vinieras a comer hace diez minutos **4.** (*ask to come*) reclamar; **she was ~ed to a meeting in London** fue convocada para una reunión en Londres **5.** (*ask for quiet*) **to** ~ **for order** pedir orden **6.** (*reprimand*) amonestar; **to** ~ **sth to mind** (*recall*) acordarse de algo; (*remember*) recordar algo **7.** (*regard as*) **to** ~ **sth one's own** poder decir que algo es de uno; **you** ~ **this a party?** ¿a esto llamas fiesta?; **I'm not ~ing you a liar** no digo que seas un mentiroso; **I don't know exactly how much you owe me, but let's** ~ **it £10** no sé cuánto me debes exactamente, ¿lo dejamos en 10 libras?; **he has very few ideas that he can genuinely** ~ **his own** tiene muy pocas ideas realmente propias **8.** (*decide to have*) **to** ~ **a meeting** convocar una reunión; **to** ~ **a halt to sth** suspender algo; **to** ~ **a strike** declarar una huelga **III.** *vi* **1.** (*telephone*) llamar **2.** (*drop by*) pasar **3.** (*shout*) gritar
◆**call at** *vt insep* **1.** (*place*) pasar por **2.** (*port*) hacer escala en
◆**call away** *vt* **he was called away** tuvo que salir; **he was called away on business** tuvo que irse por negocios
◆**call back I.** *vt* **1.** (*telephone*) volver a llamar **2.** (*ask to return*) hacer volver **3.** ECON requerir; **the company has called back a type of toy** la empresa ha pedido la devolución de un tipo de juguete **II.** *vi* (*phone again*) volver a llamar
◆**call down on** *vt* **he called curses down on his boss** puso verde a su jefe
◆**call for** *vi insep* **1.** (*come to get*) pasar a recoger **2.** (*ask*) pedir **3.** (*demand, require*) exigir; (*require*) requerir; **this calls for a celebration** esto hay que celebrarlo
◆**call forth** *vi form* suscitar
◆**call in** *vt* **1.** (*ask to come*) llamar **2.** FIN **to** ~ **a loan** pedir la devolución de un préstamo
◆**call off** *vt* **1.** (*cancel*) suspender **2.** (*order back*) **he called off his dog** llamó a su perro
◆**call on** *vt insep* **1.** (*appeal to*) **to** ~ **sb (to do sth)** apelar a alguien (para que haga algo); **to** ~ **a witness** citar a un testigo; **I now** ~ **everyone to raise a glass to our friend** *form* propongo un brindis por nuestro amigo **2.** (*visit*) visitar
◆**call out I.** *vt* (*shout*) gritar **II.** *vi* **1.** (*shout*) gritar **2.** *fig* (*demand*) **to call out for sth** exigir algo
◆**call up** *vt* **1.** *Am* (*telephone*) llamar **2.** INFOR **to** ~ **sth** sacar algo en pantalla **3.** (*order to join the military*) **to call sb up** llamar a alguien a filas **4.** (*conjure up*) conjurar
call box <-es> *n* cabina *f* telefónica
caller ['kɔːləʳ, *Am:* -lɚ] *n* **1.** (*person on the telephone*) persona *f* que llama por teléfono; **hold the line please,** ~ espere, por favor **2.** (*visitor, guest*) visita *f;* **they don't get many ~s at the shop** no tienen muchos clientes en la tienda
call girl *n* prostituta *f*
calligraphy [kə'lɪgrəfi] *n no pl* caligrafía *f*
call-in *n* RADIO, TV *programa con llamadas del público*
calling ['kɔːlɪŋ] *n form* vocación *f*
calling card *n Am* **1.** (*telephone credit card*) tarjeta *f* telefónica **2.** (*card with one's name*) tarjeta *f* de visita
callous ['kæləs] *adj* (*heartless*) cruel; (*insensitive*) insensible
call-sign ['kɔːlsaɪn] *n* distintivo *m* de llamada
call-up ['kɔːlʌp] *n* MIL llamamiento *m* a filas
callus ['kæləs] <-es> *n* MED callo *m*
calm [kɑːm] **I.** *adj* **1.** (*not nervous*) tranquilo, -a; **to keep** ~ mantenerse tranquilo **2.** (*peaceful*) pacífico, -a **3.** (*not windy*) sin viento **4.** (*not wavy*) sin olas **II.** *n* tranquilidad *f;* **the** ~ **before the storm** *fig* la calma que precede a la

tormenta **III.** *vt* tranquilizar; **to ~ oneself** calmarse

calmness *n no pl* **1.** (*lack of agitation*) tranquilidad *f* **2.** (*of the sea*) calma *f*

caloric ['kælərɪk, *Am:* kə'lɔːr-] *adj* calórico, -a

calorie ['kæləri] *n* caloría *f*

calorific [ˌkælər'ɪfək] *adj* calorífico, -a

calumny ['kæləmni] *n no pl, form* calumnia *f*

Calvary ['kælvəri] *n no pl* Calvario *m*

calve [kɑːv, *Am:* kæv] *vi* parir

Calvinism ['kælvɪnɪzəm] *n no pl* REL calvinismo *m*

Calvinist ['kælvɪnɪst] REL **I.** *n* calvinista *mf* **II.** *adj* calvinista

CAM [kæm] *n abbr of* **computer assisted manufacture** FAO *f*

cam [kæm] *n* TECH leva *f*

camaraderie [ˌkæmə'rɑːdəri, *Am:* -'rædər-] *n no pl* compañerismo *m*

camber ['kæmbəʳ, *Am:* -bɚ] *n* (*of road*) peralte *m*

Cambodia [kæm'bəʊdɪə, *Am:* -'boʊ-] *n* Camboya *f*

Cambodian [kæm'bəʊdɪən, *Am:* -'boʊ-] **I.** *adj* camboyano, -a **II.** *n* camboyano, -a *m, f*

camcorder ['kæmkɔdəʳ] *n* videocámara *f*

came [keɪm] *vi pt of* **come**

camel ['kæml] **I.** *n* **1.** ZOOL camello *m* **2.** (*colour*) beige *m* **II.** *adj* **1.** (*camel-hair*) de pelo de camello **2.** (*colour*) beige

camel-hair ['kæməlheəʳ, *Am:* -her] *n no pl* pelo *m* de camello

cameo ['kæmɪəʊ, *Am:* -oʊ] *n* **1.** (*jewellery*) camafeo *m* **2.** CINE, TV aparición *f* breve, papel *m* corto

camera ['kæmərə] *n* **1.** PHOT máquina *f* fotográfica; CINE cámara *f;* **to be on ~** estar en imagen **2.** LAW **in ~** a puerta cerrada; *fig* en secreto

camera angle *n* ángulo *m* de cámara **cameraman** <-men> *n* cámara *m* **camera-ready copy** <-ies> *n* TYPO material *m* preparado para la cámara **camera shot** *n* CINE toma *f* **camera-shy** *adj* **to be ~** no ser muy amigo de las fotografías **camerawoman** <-women> *n* cámara *f*

Cameroon [ˌkæmə'ruːn] *n* Camerún *m*

Cameroonian [ˌkæmə'ruːnɪən, *Am:* -'roʊ-] **I.** *adj* camerunés, -esa **II.** *n* camerunés, -esa *m, f*

camomile ['kæməmaɪl, *Am:* -miːl] *n* camomila *f;* **~ tea** manzanilla *f*

camouflage ['kæməˌflɑːʒ] **I.** *n no pl* camuflaje *m* **II.** *vt* camuflar; **to ~ oneself** camuflarse

camp¹ [kæmp] **I.** *n* **1.** (*encampment*) campamento *m;* **army ~** campamento militar; **summer ~** *Am* campamento de verano; **to break ~** levantar el campamento; **to pitch ~** acampar **2.** (*group*) bando *m;* **to go over to the other ~** pasarse al otro bando; **to have a foot in both ~s** estar en ambos bandos, nadar entre dos aguas **II.** *vi* acampar; **to ~ out** acampar; **to go ~ing** ir de cámping, campear *AmL*

camp² [kæmp] **I.** *n no pl* (**high**) ~ amaneramiento *m* **II.** *adj* (*affected*) afectado, -a; (*effeminate*) amanerado, -a **III.** *vt* **to ~ it up** actuar con afectación

campaign [kæm'peɪn] **I.** *n* campaña *f;* **~ trail** campaña *f* electoral **II.** *vi* hacer campaña; **to ~ for sth/sb** hacer campaña a favor de algo/alguien

campaigner [kæm'peɪnəʳ, *Am:* -ɚ] *n* **1.** (*election worker*) partidario, -a *m, f* **2.** (*person who campaigns*) defensor(a) *m(f);* **a ~ for sth** un luchador a favor de algo

camp bed *n Brit, Aus* cama *f* plegable **camp chair** *n Brit, Aus* silla *f* plegable

camper ['kæmpəʳ, *Am:* -pɚ] *n* **1.** (*person*) campista *mf* **2.** AUTO caravana *f*

campfire *n* fogata *f;* **~ song** canción *f* de hoguera

camp follower *n* **1.** (*civilian worker*) trabajador(a) *m(f)* civil **2.** (*supporter*) simpatizante *mf*

camphor ['kæmfəʳ, *Am:* -fɚ] *n no pl* MED alcanfor *m*

camping ['kæmpɪŋ] *n no pl* cámping *m;* **to go ~** ir de acampada

camping ground *n Aus,* **camping site** *n Brit* (terreno *m* de) cámping *m* **camping van** *n* autocaravana *f*

campsite ['kæmpsait] *n* cámping *m; Am* (*for one tent*) parcela *f* de cámping **camp stool** *n Brit* silla *f* plegable

campus ['kæmpəs] <-es> *n* campus *m inv*

camshaft ['kæmʃɑːft, *Am:* -ʃæft] *n* TECH árbol *m* de levas

can¹ [kæn] **I.** *n* **1.** (*container*) lata *f;* (*of oil*) bidón *m* **2.** *Am, inf* (*prison*) trullo *m* **3.** *Am, inf* (*toilet*) trono *m* ►**a ~ of worms** un problema peliagudo; **to open (up) a ~ of worms** abrir la caja de los truenos; **to carry the ~** *Brit, inf* pagar el pato **II.** <-nn-> *vt* **1.** (*put in cans*) enlatar **2.** *Am, inf* (*stop*) **~ it!** ¡basta ya!

can² [kən] <could, could> *aux* **1.** (*be able to*) poder; **if I could** si pudiera; **I think she ~ help you** creo que ella te puede ayudar; **I could have kissed her** hubiera podido besarla **2.** *inf* (*be permitted to*) poder; **you can't go** no puedes ir; **could I look at it?** ¿podría verlo? **3.** (*know how to*) saber; **~ you swim?** ¿sabes nadar?

Canada ['kænədə] *n* Canadá *m*

Canadian [kə'neɪdɪən] **I.** *n* canadiense *mf* **II.** *adj* canadiense

canal [kə'næl] *n* canal *m*

canalization [ˌkænəlaɪ'zeɪʃən, *Am:* -ɪ'-] *n no pl* canalización *f*

canalize ['kænəlaɪz] *vt* **1.** (*provide with canals*) *a. fig* encauzar **2.** (*convert into a canal*) canalizar

canary [kə'neəri, *Am:* -'neri] **I.** <-ies> *n* **1.** ZOOL canario *m* **2. to sing like a ~** *Brit, inf* chivarse **II.** *adj* **~ yellow** amarillo canario

Canary Islands *n* Islas *fpl* Canarias

canary seed *n* alpiste *m*

C

canasta [kəˈnæstə] *n* GAMES canasta *f*
cancel [ˈkænsl] <-ll-, *Am:* -l-> **I.** *vt* **1.** (*reservation, meeting*) cancelar; (*party, concert*) suspender; (*result, licence*) anular; (*payment*) retirar **2.** MAT **to ~ each other out** anularse mutuamente **3.** INFOR cancelar **II.** *vi* (*reservation*) cancelar una reserva; (*meeting*) cancelar una reunión
cancellation [ˌkænsəˈleɪʃən] *n* (*of reservation, meeting*) cancelación *f;* (*of party, concert*) suspensión *f;* (*of licence*) anulación *f;* (*of contract*) rescisión *f*
cancer [ˈkænsəʳ, *Am:* -sɚ] *n* MED *no pl* cáncer *m,* cangro *m Col, Guat;* ~ **specialist** oncólogo, -a *m, f;* ~ **cell** célula *f* cancerígena
Cancer [ˈkænsəʳ, *Am:* -sɚ] *n* Cáncer *m*
cancer check-up *n* MED control *m* oncológico **cancer clinic** *n* MED clínica *f* oncológica
cancerous [ˈkænsərəs] *adj* MED canceroso, -a
cancer research *n no pl* MED investigación *f* oncológica
candelabra [ˌkændəlˈɑːbrə] <-(s)> *n* candelabro *m,* candil *m AmL*
candid [ˈkændɪd] *adj* franco, -a; (*talks*) sincero, -a; (*picture*) natural
candidacy [ˈkændɪdəsi] *n no pl* candidatura *f*
candidate [ˈkændɪdət] *n* **1.** POL (*competitor*) candidato, -a *m, f* **2.** (*possible choice*) aspirante *mf*
candidature [ˈkændɪdətʃəʳ, *Am:* -dədətʃʊr] *n no pl, Brit s.* **candidacy**
candid camera *n* cámara *f* indiscreta
candied [ˈkændɪd] *adj* confitado, -a
candle [ˈkændl] *n* **1.** (*light*) vela *f* **2.** BOT castaña *f* de Indias ►**to burn one's ~ at both ends** hacer de la noche día; **she can't hold a ~ to him** no le llega ni a la suela del zapato
candlelight [ˈkændllaɪt] *n no pl* luz *f* de una vela; **to do sth by ~** hacer algo a la luz de una vela
Candlemas [ˈkændlməs] *n no pl* REL Candelaria *f*
candle-power [ˈkændlpaʊəʳ, *Am:* -paʊɚ] *n no pl* bujía *f*
candlestick [ˈkændlstɪk] *n* candelero *m*
candlewick [ˈkændlwɪk] *n no pl* (*textile*) chenilla *f*
candor *n Am,* **candour** [ˈkændəʳ, *Am:* -dɚ] *n no pl, Brit, Aus, form* franqueza *f*
candy [ˈkændi] **I.** <-ies> *n Am* (*sweets*) golosinas *fpl* **II.** *vt* escarchar
candy bar *n Am* tableta *f* de chocolate **candyfloss** *n no pl, Brit* algodón *m* de azúcar **candy store** *n Am* tienda *f* de golosinas
cane [keɪn] **I.** *n* **1.** *no pl* (*dried plant stem*) caña *f* **2.** *no pl* (*furniture*) mimbre *m* **3.** (*stick*) bastón *m;* (*for punishment*) palmeta *f* **II.** *vt* dar palmetazos
cane chair *n* silla *f* de mimbre **cane sugar** *n no pl* azúcar *m* de caña
canine [ˈkeɪnaɪn] **I.** *n* **1.** ZOOL canino *m* **2.** (*tooth*) colmillo *m* **II.** *adj* canino, -a
canister [ˈkænɪstəʳ, *Am:* -əstɚ] *n* (*metal*) lata *f;* (*plastic*) bote *m*
cannabis [ˈkænəbɪs] *n no pl* (*plant*) cannabis *f;* (*drug*) marihuana *f*
canned [kænd] *adj* **1.** (*in metal containers*) enlatado, -a; (*fruit, vegetables*) en conserva; (*food, meat, beer*) de lata **2.** MUS, TV ~ **music** música *f* enlatada; ~ **laughter** risas *fpl* grabadas **3.** *inf* (*drunk*) mamado, -a; **to get ~** acabar borracho como una cuba
cannery [ˈkænəri] <-ies> *n* fábrica *f* de conservas
cannibal [ˈkænɪbl] *n* caníbal *mf*
cannibalism [ˈkænɪbəlɪzəm] *n no pl* canibalismo *m*
cannibalize [ˈkænɪbəlaɪz] *vt* AUTO desguazar
canning [ˈkænɪŋ] *n no pl* enlatado *m;* ~ **factory** fábrica *f* de conservas
cannon [ˈkænən] **I.** *n* cañón *m* **II.** *vi* **to ~ into sb/sth** chocar contra alguien/algo
cannon ball *n* bala *f* de cañón **cannon fodder** *n no pl* carne *f* de cañón
cannot [ˈkænɒt, *Am:* -ɑːt] *aux* = **can not** *s.* **can²**
canny [ˈkæni] <-ier, -iest> *adj* (*clever*) astuto, -a
canoe [kəˈnuː] *n* canoa *f; Brit* (*kayak*) piragua *f* ►**to paddle one's own ~** arreglárselas solo
canoeing *n no pl* piragüismo *m*
canoeist [kəˈnuːɪst] *n* piragüista *mf*
canon [ˈkænən] *n* **1.** REL, MUS canon *m* **2.** (*person*) canónigo *m* **3.** LIT obra *f* (literaria)
canonization [ˌkænənaɪˈzeɪʃən, *Am:* -nɪˈ-] *n* canonización *f*
canonize [ˈkænənaɪz] *vt* canonizar
can opener [ˈkænˌəʊpənəʳ, *Am:* -oʊpnɚ] *n* abrelatas *m inv*
canopy [ˈkænəpi] <-ies> *n* **1.** (*roof-like covering*) toldo *m* **2.** AVIAT cubierta *f* transparente **3.** ARCHIT baldaquín *m* **4.** *form* (*sky*) bóveda *f* celeste
cant¹ [kænt] *n no pl* **1.** (*insincere talk*) hipocresía *f* **2.** LING jerga *f*
cant² [kænt] **I.** *n* inclinación *f* **II.** *vt* inclinar **III.** *vi* inclinarse, ladearse
can't [kɑːnt, *Am:* kænt] = **cannot**
cantankerous [kænˈtæŋkərəs] *adj* intratable
cantata [kænˈtɑːtə, *Am:* kənˈtɑːt̬ə] *n* MUS cantata *f*
canteen¹ [kænˈtiːn] *n* (*cafetería*) cantina *f*
canteen² [kænˈtiːn] *n* **1.** ~ **of cutlery** juego de cubiertos **2.** MIL (*drink container*) cantimplora *f*
canter [ˈkæntəʳ, *Am:* -t̬ɚ] **I.** *n* medio galope *m* **II.** *vi* ir a medio galope
cantilever [ˈkæntɪliːvəʳ, *Am:* -t̬əliːvɚ] *n* viga *f* voladiza; ~ **bridge** puente *m* voladizo
Cantonese [ˌkæntəˈniːz] **I.** *adj* cantonés, -esa **II.** *n* **1.** (*language*) cantonés *m* **2.** (*person*) cantonés, -esa *m, f*
canvas [ˈkænvəs] <-es> *n* **1.** *no pl* (*cloth*)

lona *f;* NAUT velamen *m;* **under** ~ (*in a tent*) en una tienda de campaña **2.** ART lienzo *m,* holán *m AmC*

canvass ['kænvəs] **I.** *vt* **1.** (*gather opinion*) sondear; **to** ~ **sth** hacer una encuesta de algo **2.** POL (*votes*) solicitar **II.** *vi* POL hacer campaña

canvasser ['kænvəsəʳ, *Am:* -ɚ] *n* POL *persona que va de puerta en puerta solicitando votos para un determinado partido político*

canvassing *n* POL solicitación *f* de votos

canyon ['kænjən] *n* cañón *m*

CAP [ˌsiːeɪ'piː] *n abbr of* Common Agricultural Policy PAC *f*

cap¹ [kæp] **I.** *n* **1.** (*without peak*) gorro *m* **2.** (*with peak*) gorra *f;* ~ **and gown** UNIV toga *f* y birrete **3.** (*cover*) tapón *m;* PHOT tapa *f;* **screw-on** ~ casquete *m* **4.** (*of tooth*) funda *f* **5.** (*limit*) tope *m;* **salary** ~ *Am* salario *m* máximo **6.** (*contraceptive*) diafragma *m* **7.** (*in toy gun*) fulminante *m* ►**to go ~ in hand** mendigar; **to put on one's thinking** ~ *inf* hacer uso de la materia gris; **if the ~ fits, wear it** *Brit, prov* el que se pica, ajos come *prov;* **to set one's ~ at sb** poner los ojos en alguien **II.** <-pp-> *vt* **1.** (*limit*) limitar **2.** SPORTS **he has been ~ped two times for Spain** ha integrado dos veces la selección española **3.** (*cover*) tapar; (*tooth*) enfundar **4.** (*outdo*) coronar; **to ~ it all** para colmo

cap² [kæp] *n abbr of* **capital** (**letter**) mayúscula *f*

capability [ˌkeɪpə'bɪləti, *Am:* -t̬i] <-ies> *n* **1.** *no pl* (*ability*) capacidad *f;* (*power*) poder *m* **2.** (*skill*) aptitud *f*

capable ['keɪpəbl] *adj* **1.** (*competent*) competente **2.** (*able*) capaz; **to be ~ of doing sth** ser capaz de hacer algo

capacity [kə'pæsəti, *Am:* -t̬i] <-ies> *n* **1.** *no pl* (*volume*) cabida *f,* capacidad *f;* **to be full to** ~ estar completamente lleno; **filled to** ~ completamente lleno **2.** *no pl* (*ability*) capacidad *f;* (*mental*) aptitud *f* **3.** (*amount*) capacidad *f;* **seating** ~ aforo *m* **4.** (*output*) rendimiento *m;* **to work at full** ~ trabajar a pleno rendimiento **5.** (*role*) calidad *f*

cape¹ [keɪp] *n* GEO cabo *m*

cape² [keɪp] *n* (*cloak*) capa *f*

caper¹ ['keɪpəʳ, *Am:* -ɚ] **I.** *n* **1.** (*joyful leaping movement*) cabriola *f;* **to cut ~s** hacer cabriolas **2.** (*dubious activity*) travesura *f* **II.** *vi* dar brincos

caper² ['keɪpəʳ, *Am:* -pɚ] *n* BOT alcaparra *f*

Cape Town ['keɪptaʊn] *n* Ciudad *f* del Cabo

Cape Verde ['keɪpvɜːd, *Am:* -vɜːrd] *n* Cabo *m* Verde

capillary [kə'pɪləri, *Am:* 'kæpəler-] <-ies> *n* vaso *m* capilar

capital ['kæpɪtl, *Am:* -ət̬l] **I.** *n* **1.** (*principal city*) capital *f* **2.** TYPO mayúscula *f;* **small ~s** versalitas *fpl* **3.** ARCHIT capitel *m* **4.** FIN capital *m;* **to make** ~ (**out**) **of sth** *fig* sacar partido de algo **II.** *adj* **1.** (*principal*) primordial; ~ **city** capital *f* **2.** TYPO (*letter*) mayúscula **3.** LAW capital; ~ **punishment** pena *f* capital [*o* de muerte] **4.** *Brit* (*very good*) estupendo, -a

capital assets *npl* FIN activo *m* fijo **capital crime** *n* LAW crimen *m* capital **capital gains tax** <-es> *n* impuesto *m* sobre la plusvalía **capital investment** *n* FIN inversión *f* de capital **capital investment company** <-ies> *n* sociedad *f* inversora

C

capitalism ['kæpɪtəlɪzəm, *Am:* 'kæpət̬-] *n no pl* capitalismo *m*

capitalist ['kæpɪtəlɪst, *Am:* 'kæpət̬əl-] **I.** *n* capitalista *mf* **II.** *adj* capitalista

capitalistic [ˌkæpɪtə'lɪstɪk, *Am:* -ət̬ə'lɪs-] *adj* capitalista

capitalization [ˌkæpɪtəlaɪ'zeɪʃən, *Am:* ˌkæpət̬lɪ-] *n* capitalización *f*

capitalize ['kæpɪtəlaɪz, *Am:* 'kæpət̬əlaɪz] *vt* **1.** TYPO escribir en mayúsculas **2.** *a.* FIN capitalizar

capital letter ['kæpɪtl 'letəʳ, *Am:* -ət̬l 'let̬ɚ] *n* mayúscula *f;* **in ~s** con mayúsculas **capital punishment** *n no pl* pena *f* de muerte

capitulate [kə'pɪtʃʊleɪt, *Am:* -'pɪtʃə-] *vi* **1.** MIL **to ~ to sth/sb** capitular ante algo/alguien **2.** (*give way*) ceder

capitulation [kəˌpɪtʃʊ'leɪʃən, *Am:* -'pɪtʃə-] *n* capitulación *f;* ~ **to sb/sth** capitulación ante alguien/algo

cappuccino [ˌkæpʊ'tʃiːnəʊ, *Am:* ˌkæpə'tʃiːnoʊ] *n* capuchino *m*

caprice [kə'priːs] *n liter* capricho *m*

capricious [kə'prɪʃəs] *adj* caprichoso, -a

Capricorn ['kæprɪkɔːn, *Am:* -rəkɔːrn] *n* Capricornio *m*

Caps. *n abbr of* **capitals** mayúsculas *fpl*

capsize [kæp'saɪz, *Am:* 'kæpsaɪz] **I.** *vt* NAUT hacer zozobrar; *fig* volcar **II.** *vi* NAUT zozobrar; *fig* volcar

capstan ['kæpstən] *n* NAUT cabrestante *m*

capsule ['kæpsjuːl, *Am:* -sl] *n* cápsula *f*

captain ['kæptɪn] **I.** *n* capitán, -ana *m, f* **II.** *vt* capitanear

captaincy ['kæptɪnsi] *n no pl* capitanía *f*

caption ['kæpʃən] *n* **1.** TYPO, PUBL (*heading*) título *m;* (*for cartoon*) leyenda *f* **2.** CINE subtítulo *m*

captivate ['kæptɪveɪt, *Am:* -tə-] *vt* cautivar

captive ['kæptɪv] **I.** *n* cautivo, -a *m, f* **II.** *adj* cautivo, -a; **to hold sb** ~ tener prisionero a alguien

captivity [kæp'tɪvəti, *Am:* -t̬i] *n no pl* cautiverio *m;* **to be in** ~ estar en cautividad

capture ['kæptʃəʳ, *Am:* -tʃɚ] **I.** *vt* **1.** (*take prisoner*) prender **2.** (*take possession of*) capturar; (*city*) conquistar; (*ship*) apresar; (*votes*) conseguir **3.** (*gain*) captar; **to ~ the market** COM hacerse con el mercado **4.** ART captar; **to ~ sth on film** reproducir algo en una película **5.** INFOR recoger **II.** *n* captura *f;* (*of city*) conquista *f;* (*of ship*) presa *f*

car [kɑːʳ, *Am:* kɑːr] *n* **1.** AUTO coche *m,* carro *m AmL,* auto *m Arg, Chile, Urug* **2.** RAIL vagón *m* **3.** (*in airship, balloon*) barquilla *f*

car accessories *npl* accesorios *mpl* para el coche **car aerial** *n* antena *f* del coche
carafe ['kærəf] *n* garrafa *f*
caramel ['kærəmel, *Am:* 'kɑːrml] **I.** *n* **1.** *no pl* (*burnt sugar*) azúcar *m* quemado **2.** (*sweet*) caramelo *m* **II.** *adj* de caramelo; ~ **cream** flan *m*
carat ['kærət, *Am:* 'ker-] <-(s)> *n* quilate *m*
caravan ['kærəvæn, *Am:* 'ker-] *n* **1.** *Brit* (*vehicle*) caravana *f;* **gypsy** ~ carromato *m* de gitanos **2.** (*group of travellers*) caravana *f*
caravansary [ˌkærə'vænsəri, *Am:* ˌker-] *n,* **caravanserai** [ˌkærə'vænsəraɪ, *Am:* ˌker-] *n* caravasar *m*
caraway ['kærəweɪ, *Am:* 'ker-] *n no pl* alcaravea *f*
caraway seed *n* carvi *m*
carbide ['kɑːbaɪd, *Am:* 'kɑːr-] *n* carburo *m*
carbine ['kɑːbaɪn, *Am:* 'kɑːrbiːn] *n* carabina *f*
car body ['kɑːbɒdi, *Am:* 'kɑːrbɑː-] <-ies> *n* chasis *m inv* del automóvil
carbohydrate [ˌkɑːbəʊ'haɪdreɪt, *Am:* ˌkɑːrboʊ-] *n* hidrato *m* de carbono; ~ **content** contenido *m* de carbohidratos
carbolic [kɑː'bɒlɪk, *Am:* kɑːr'bɑːlɪk] *adj* ~ **acid** ácido *m* fénico
car bomb ['kɑːbɒm, *Am:* 'kɑːrbɑːm] *n* coche *m* bomba
carbon ['kɑːbən, *Am:* 'kɑːr-] **I.** *n* **1.** *no pl* CHEM carbono *m* **2.** (*copy*) copia *f* al carbón **3.** (*paper*) papel *m* de calco **II.** *adj* de carbono
carbon copy <-ies> *n* copia *f* en papel de calco **carbon-copy crime** *n* crimen *m* calcado **carbon dating** *n no pl* datación *f* por C-14 **carbon dioxide** *n no pl* dióxido *m* de carbono
carbonic [kɑː'bɒnɪk, *Am:* kɑːr'bɑːnɪk] *adj* ~ **acid** ácido *m* carbónico
carbonize ['kɑːbənaɪz, *Am:* 'kɑːr-] **I.** *vt* carbonizar **II.** *vi* carbonizarse
carbon monoxide *n no pl* monóxido *m* de carbono **carbon paper** *n no pl* papel *m* de calco
car-boot sale ['kɑːbuːtˌseɪl] *n Brit: venta de objetos expuestos en los maleteros de los coches*
carbuncle ['kɑːbʌŋkl, *Am:* 'kɑːr-] *n* **1.** MED furúnculo *m* **2.** (*gem*) carbúnculo *m*
carburet ['kɑːbjʊˌret] *vt* mezclar con carbono
carburetor *n Am,* **carburettor** [ˌkɑːbjə'retəʳ, *Am:* 'kɑːrbəreɪt̬ɚ] *n* carburador *m*
carcass ['kɑːkəs, *Am:* 'kɑːr-] <-es> *n* **1.** (*of animal*) cadáver *m* de animal **2.** (*of vehicle*) armazón *m* **3.** (*of cooked chicken*) huesos *mpl*
carcinogen ['kɑːsɪnəˌdʒen, *Am:* kɑːr'sɪn-] *n* MED (agente *m*) carcinógeno *m*
carcinogenic [ˌkɑːsɪnəʊ'dʒenɪk, *Am:* ˌkɑːrsənoʊ'-] *adj* MED cancerígeno, -a
carcinoma [ˌkɑːsɪ'nəʊmə, *Am:* kɑːrsn'oʊ-] *n* MED carcinoma *m*
card¹ [kɑːd, *Am:* kɑːrd] **I.** *n* **1.** *no pl a.* FIN, INFOR tarjeta *f* **2.** (*postcard*) postal *f* **3.** GAMES carta *f,* naipe *m;* **pack of** ~**s** baraja *f;* **to play** ~**s** jugar a las cartas **4.** SPORTS (*programme*) programa *m* **5.** (*index* ~) ficha *f* **6.** (*proof of identity*) carnet *m;* **membership** ~ carnet de socio **7.** *Brit, inf* **to give sb his/her** ~**s** echar a alguien; **to get one's** ~**s** ser despedido ►**to hold one's** ~**s close to one's chest** no soltar prenda; **to have a** ~ **up one's sleeve** tener un as en la manga; **to put one's** ~**s on the table** poner las cartas sobre la mesa; **to have all the** ~**s** controlar la situación; **to hold all the** ~**s** tener todas las de ganar; **to play one's** ~**s right** hacer una buena jugada **II.** *vt Am, inf* pedir la documentación
card² [kɑːd, *Am:* kɑːrd] *n inf* cómico, -a *m, f,* persona *f* chusca
card³ [kɑːd, *Am:* kɑːrd] **I.** *n* carda *f* **II.** *vt* cardar
cardboard ['kɑːdbɔːd, *Am:* 'kɑːrdbɔːrd] *n no pl* cartón *m*
cardiac ['kɑːdɪæk, *Am:* 'kɑːr-] *adj* MED cardíaco, -a; (*disease*) cardiovascular
cardigan ['kɑːdɪgən, *Am:* 'kɑːr-] *n* cárdigan *m;* (*for women*) rebeca *f*
cardinal ['kɑːdɪnl, *Am:* 'kɑːr-] **I.** *n* **1.** REL, ZOOL cardenal *m* **2.** (*number*) cardinal *m* **II.** *adj* (*importance: rule*) fundamental; (*error*) grave; (*sin*) capital
cardinal number *n* número *m* cardinal **cardinal points** *npl* puntos *mpl* cardinales
card index ['kɑːdˌɪndeks, *Am:* 'kɑːrd-] <-es> *n* fichero *m*
cardiogram ['kɑːdɪəʊgræm, *Am:* 'kɑːrdɪoʊ-] *n* MED cardiograma *m*
car door ['kɑːdɔːʳ, *Am:* 'kɑːr] *n* puerta *f* del coche
cardphone ['kɑːdfəʊn, *Am:* 'kɑːrdfoʊn] *n* teléfono *m* de tarjeta **cardpunch** *n Brit* INFOR perforadora *f* de tarjetas **card reader** *n* lector *m* de tarjetas perforadas **card table** *n* tapete *m* verde
care [keəʳ, *Am:* ker] **I.** *n* **1.** (*attention*) cuidado *m;* **to take** ~ **of** cuidar de; (*object*) guardar; (*situation*) encargarse de; **take** ~ (**of yourself**)! ¡cuídate!; **to do sth with** ~ hacer algo con cuidado; **that takes** ~ **of that!** ¡eso ya está!; **handle with** ~ frágil **2.** (*worry*) preocupación *f;* **to not have a** ~ **in the world** no tener ninguna preocupación; **to be free from** ~ no tener problemas **II.** *vi* **1.** (*be concerned*) preocuparse; **to** ~ **about sb/sth** preocuparse por alguien/algo; **as if I** ~**d!** ¿y a mí qué?; **for all I** ~ (*as far as I'm concerned*) por mí; **who** ~**s?** ¿qué más da? **2.** (*feel affection*) importar **3.** (*want*) **to** ~ **to do sth** estar dispuesto a hacer algo
CARE [keəʳ, *Am:* ker] *n abbr of* **Cooperative for American Relief Everywhere** *cooperativa de auxilio estadounidense en cualquier parte del mundo*
career [kə'rɪəʳ, *Am:* -'rɪr] **I.** *n* **1.** (*profession*) profesión *f* **2.** (*working life*) carrera *f* profe-

sional **II.** *vi* ir a toda velocidad; **to ~ out of control** (*car*) perder el control
careerist [kəˈrɪərɪst, *Am:* -ˈrɪrɪst] **I.** *n* ambicioso, -a *m, f*, arribista *mf* **II.** *adj* ambicioso, -a
careers officer *n* consejero, -a *m, f* de orientación profesional
career woman <-women> *n* mujer *f* dedicada por completo a su profesión
carefree [ˈkeəfriː, *Am:* ˈker-] *adj* despreocupado, -a
careful [ˈkeəfəl, *Am:* ˈker-] *adj* **1.** (*cautious*) cuidadoso, -a; (*driver*) prudente; **to be ~ of sth** tener cuidado con algo; **to be ~ to do sth** procurar hacer algo **2.** (*painstaking, meticulous*) meticuloso, -a; (*worker*) esmerado, -a
carefulness *n no pl* **1.** (*caution*) cuidado *m* **2.** (*meticulousness*) meticulosidad *f*
careless [ˈkeələs, *Am:* ˈker-] *adj* **1.** (*lacking attention*) distraído, -a **2.** (*unthinking*) irreflexivo, -a, despistado, -a **3.** (*not painstaking*) descuidado, -a, imprudente **4.** (*carefree*) despreocupado, -a
carelessness *n no pl* **1.** (*lack of attention*) falta *f* de atención **2.** (*lack of concern*) despreocupación *f*
carer *n persona que cuida a una persona anciana o enferma, sin recebir remuneración alguna*
caress [kəˈres] **I.** <-es> *n* caricia *f* **II.** *vi, vt* acariciar, barbear *AmC*
caretaker [ˈkeəˌteɪkəʳ, *Am:* ˈkerˌteɪkɚ] *n* **1.** *Brit* (*janitor*) conserje *mf* **2.** *Am* (*job*) portero, -a *m, f*
careworn [ˈkeəwɔːn, *Am:* ˈkerwɔːrn] *adj* agobiado, -a por las preocupaciones
car ferry <-ies> *n* NAUT transbordador *m*
cargo [ˈkɑːgəʊ, *Am:* ˈkɑːrgoʊ] <-(e)s> *n* **1.** *no pl* (*goods*) carga *f* **2.** (*load*) cargamento *m*
cargo aircraft *n* avión *m* de carga **cargo boat** *n* carguero *m* **cargo plane** *n* avión *m* de carga **cargo ship** *n* barco *m* de carga **cargo vessel** *n* carguero *m*
car hire [ˈkɑːˌhaɪəʳ, *Am:* ˈkɑːrˌhaɪr] *n no pl* alquiler *m* de coches
Caribbean [ˌkærɪˈbiːən, *Am:* ˌkerɪˈbiː-] **I.** *n* **the ~** el Caribe **II.** *adj* caribeño, -a, caribe *AmL*
caricature [ˈkærɪkətjʊəʳ, *Am:* ˈkerəkətjʊr] **I.** *n a.* ART caricatura *f* **II.** *vt* LIT caricaturizar
caricaturist [ˈkærɪkətʃʊərɪst, *Am:* ˈkerəkətʃʊrɪst] *n* ART caricaturista *mf*
caries [ˈkeəriːz, *Am:* ˈkeriːz] *n no pl* MED caries *f inv*
caring *adj* compasivo, -a
car insurance *n no pl* seguro *m* de vehículos
carjacking *n Am* robo *m* de coche
car license *n Brit* permiso *m* de circulación
carnage [ˈkɑːnɪdʒ, *Am:* ˈkɑːr-] *n no pl* matanza *f*
carnal [ˈkɑːnl, *Am:* ˈkɑːr-] *adj* carnal
carnation [kɑːˈneɪʃən, *Am:* kɑːr-] **I.** *n* **1.** BOT clavel *m* **2.** (*colour*) rosa *m* vivo **II.** *adj* rosa vivo
carnival [ˈkɑːnɪvl, *Am:* ˈkɑːrnə-] *n* carnaval *m*, chaya *f Arg, Chile*
carnivore [ˈkɑːnɪvɔːʳ, *Am:* ˈkɑːrnəvɔːr] *n* carnívoro, -a *m, f*
carnivorous [kɑːˈnɪvərəs, *Am:* kɑːr-] *adj* carnívoro, -a
carol [ˈkærəl, *Am:* ˈker-] *n* villancico *m*
carol singer *n* persona *f* que canta villancicos
carotene [ˈkærətiːn] *n no pl* BIO caroteno *m*
carousel [ˌkærəˈsel] *n* **1.** (*merry-go-round*) tiovivo *m* **2.** (*baggage return*) cinta *f* transportadora
car owner [ˈkɑːrəʊnəʳ, *Am:* -oʊnɚ] *n* propietario, -a *m, f* de un coche
carp[1] [kɑːp, *Am:* kɑːrp] *n* <-(s)> carpa *f*
carp[2] [kɑːp, *Am:* kɑːrp] *vi* criticar por criticar; **to ~ about sth/sb** quejarse de algo/alguien sin motivo
car park [ˈkɑːpɑːk, *Am:* ˈkɑːrpɑːrk] *n Brit, Aus* aparcamiento *m*, párking *m*
carpenter [ˈkɑːpəntəʳ, *Am:* ˈkɑːrpnt̬ɚ] *n* carpintero, -a *m, f*
carpentry [ˈkɑːpəntri, *Am:* ˈkɑːrpn-] *n no pl* carpintería *f*
carpet [ˈkɑːpɪt, *Am:* ˈkɑːrpət] **I.** *n* (*fitted*) moqueta *f*, alfombra *f AmL*; (*not fitted*) alfombra *f* ►**to sweep sth under the ~** correr un velo sobre algo; **to be on the ~** *inf* tener que aguantar una bronca **II.** *vt* **1.** (*cover floor*) moquetar, alfombrar *AmL* **2.** *inf* (*reprimand*) **to ~ sb** (**for sth**) echar un rapapolvo a alguien (por algo)
carpet-bag [ˈkɑːpɪtbæg, *Am:* ˈkɑːrpət-] *n maletín o bolso de tejido de alfombra*
carpetbagger [ˈkɑːpɪtˌbægəʳ, *Am:* ˈkɑːrpətˌbægɚ] *n Am: persona que intenta entrar en el mundo de la política lejos de su lugar de origen porque piensa que así tiene más posibilidades de triunfar*
carpeting [ˈkɑːpɪtɪŋ, *Am:* ˈkɑːrpət̬ɪŋ] *n no pl* alfombrado *m*
carpet sweeper *n* cepillo *m* mecánico para alfombras
car pool [ˈkɑːpuːl, *Am:* ˈkɑːr-] *n grupo de personas que comparten el mismo coche para desplazarse al trabajo*
carriage [ˈkærɪdʒ, *Am:* ˈker-] *n* **1.** (*horse-drawn vehicle*) carruaje *m* **2.** *Brit* (*train wagon*) vagón *m* **3.** (*posture*) andares *mpl* **4.** (*part of typewriter*) carro *m* **5.** *no pl, Brit* (*transport costs*) porte *m*
carriage-return *n* TYPO retorno *m* del carro
carriageway [ˈkærɪdʒˈweɪ, *Am:* ˈker-] *n Brit* calzada *f*; **dual ~** autovía *f*
carrier [ˈkærɪəʳ] *n* **1.** (*person who carries*) transportista *mf*; (*messenger*) mensajero, -a *m, f* **2.** MIL (*vehicle*) vehículo *m* transportador; **aircraft ~** portaviones *m inv* **3.** MED portador(a) *m(f)* **4.** (*transport company*) empresa *f* de transportes **5.** *Brit, inf* bolsa *f*
carrier bag *n Brit* bolsa *f*
carrion [ˈkærɪən, *Am:* ˈker-] *n no pl* carroña *f*
carrion crow *n* corneja *f*

carrot ['kærət, *Am:* 'ker-] *n* **1.** (*vegetable*) zanahoria *f* **2.** *inf* (*reward*) incentivo *m;* **the ~ and stick approach** la política de incentivos y amenazas

carroty ['kærəti, *Am:* 'kerət̬i] <-ier, -iest> *adj* color zanahoria

carry ['kæri, *Am:* 'ker-] <-ies, -ied> **I.** *vt* **1.** (*transport in hands or arms*) llevar; (*take*) traer **2.** (*transport*) transportar, acarrear **3.** (*have on one's person*) llevar encima **4.** MED (*transmit*) transmitir **5.** (*support*) soportar **6.** *Am* (*sell*) vender **7.** (*win: position*) conquistar; **to ~ conviction** ser convincente; **to ~ all before one** arrasar **8.** (*approve*) aprobar **9.** PUBL **to ~ an article** publicar un artículo **10.** (*develop*) **to ~ consequences** tener consecuencias; **to ~ an argument to its (logical) conclusion** desarrollar un argumento hacia su conclusión (lógica) **11.** (*be pregnant*) **to ~ a child** esperar un hijo ▸**to ~ sb back to sth** recordar algo a alguien **II.** *vi* **1.** (*be audible*) oírse **2.** (*fly*) volar

◆**carry along** *vt* llevar; (*water*) arrastrar

◆**carry away** *vt* **1.** (*remove*) arrastrar **2. to be carried away (by sth)** (*be overcome by*) dejarse llevar (por algo); (*be enchanted by*) entusiasmarse (con algo); **to get carried away** exaltarse

◆**carry forward** *vt* FIN transferir

◆**carry off** *vt* **1.** llevarse; (*win: prize*) ganar; **to ~ sth** hacerse con algo **2.** (*succeed*) **to carry sth off** salir airoso de algo

◆**carry on I.** *vt insep* continuar con; **~ the good work!** ¡sigue con el buen trabajo! **II.** *vi* **1.** (*continue*) seguir; **to ~ doing sth** continuar haciendo algo **2.** *inf* (*make a fuss*) montar un número

◆**carry out** *vt* (*repairs*) hacer; (*plan, attack*) llevar a cabo; (*job*) realizar; (*order*) cumplir

◆**carry over I.** *vt* **1.** (*bring forward*) pasar a cuenta nueva; FIN transferir **2.** (*postpone*) posponer **II.** *vi* **1. to ~ into sth** (*have an effect on*) influir en algo **2.** (*remain*) quedar

◆**carry through** *vt* **1.** (*support*) sostener **2.** (*complete successfully*) llevar a término

carry-all ['kæriɔːl] *n Am* bolso *m* grande

carry-cot ['kærɪˌkɒt, *Am:* 'kerɪkaːt] *n* cuna *f* portátil **carrying agent** *n* agente *mf* de carga **carrying capacity** <-ies> *n* capacidad *f* de carga **carrying-on** <carryings-on> *n inf* **1.** *no pl* (*dubious affair*) enredos *mpl* **2.** (*dubious activity*) líos *mpl* **carry-over** *n* **1.** FIN *pérdida trasladada al ejercicio siguiente* **2.** (*remnant*) remanente *m*

cart [kaːt, *Am:* kaːrt] **I.** *n* **1.** (*vehicle*) carreta *f*, carro *m* **2.** *Am* (*supermarket trolley*) carrito *m* ▸**to put the ~ before the horse** empezar la casa por el tejado **II.** *vt* (*transport*) acarrear; (*carry*) cargar

carte blanche [ˌkaːt'blɑ̃ːntʃ, *Am:* ˌkaːrt-'blaːnʃ] *n no pl* carta *f* blanca

cartel [kaː'tel, *Am:* kaːr-] *n* cartel *m*

carter ['kaːtəʳ, *Am:* 'kaːrt̬ɚ] *n* carretero *m*

carthorse ['kaːtˌhɔːs, *Am:* 'kaːrthɔːrs] *n* caballo *m* de tiro

cartilage ['kaːtɪlɪdʒ, *Am:* 'kaːrt̬lɪdʒ] *n no pl* cartílago *m*

cartload ['kaːtˌləʊd, *Am:* 'kaːrtloʊd] *n* carretada *f;* **~s of rubbish** montones *mpl* de basura

cartographer [kaː'tɒgrəfəʳ, *Am:* kaːr'taː-grəfɚ] *n* cartógrafo, -a *m, f*

cartography [kaː'tɒgrəfi, *Am:* kaːr'taːgrə-] *n no pl* cartografía *f*

carton ['kaːtn, *Am:* 'kaːr-] *n* (*box*) caja *f* de cartón; (*of juice, milk*) envase *m* de cartón

cartoon [kaː'tuːn, *Am:* kaːr-] *n* **1.** ART viñeta *f* **2.** CINE dibujos *mpl* animados

cartoonist *n* dibujante *mf*

cartridge ['kaːtrɪdʒ, *Am:* 'kaːr-] *n* **1.** (*for ink, ammunition, cassette*) cartucho *m*, cachimba *f AmL* **2.** (*pick-up head*) cápsula *f*

cartridge case *n* cartucho *m* **cartridge paper** *n no pl* papel *m* de dibujo

cartwheel ['kaːthwiːl, *Am:* 'kaːrt-] **I.** *n* **1.** (*wheel*) rueda *f* de carro **2.** (*playing*) rueda *f;* **to do a ~** hacer la rueda **II.** *vi* hacer ruedas

carve [kaːv, *Am:* kaːrv] **I.** *vt* **1.** (*cut*) cortar; **to ~ (out) a name for oneself** *fig* hacerse un nombre **2.** (*stone, wood*) tallar **3.** (*cut meat*) trinchar **II.** *vi* cortar

carver ['kaːvəʳ, *Am:* 'kaːrvɚ] *n* **1.** ART escultor(a) *m(f)* **2.** *pl* GASTR trinchantes *mpl*

carvery ['kaːvəʳi, *Am:* 'kaːrvɚi] <-ies> *n* asador *m*

carving *n* ART **1.** *no pl* (*art of cutting*) arte *m* de esculpir **2.** (*ornamental figure*) escultura *f;* (*of wood*) talla *f*

carving knife <knives> *n* cuchillo *m* de trinchar

car wash <-es> *n* túnel *m* de lavado

cascade [kæ'skeɪd] **I.** *n* **1.** (*waterfall*) cascada *f* **2.** *liter* (*flowing mass*) torrente *m* **II.** *vi* **to ~ from sth** caer en cascada de algo

case[1] [keɪs] *n* **1.** *a.* MED caso *m;* **in any ~** en cualquier caso; **just in ~** por si acaso; **in ~ it rains** en caso de que llueva; **as the ~ stands** tal como está el caso **2.** LING caso *m* **3.** LAW caso *m;* **to close the ~** cerrar el caso; **to lose one's ~** perder el caso **4.** (*argument*) **to make out a ~ for sth** argumentar a favor de algo

case[2] [keɪs] *n* **1.** *Brit* (*suitcase*) maleta *f;* (*chest*) arcón *m*, veliz *m Méx* **2.** (*container*) caja *f;* (*for jewels, spectacles*) estuche *m;* (*for camera, musical instrument*) funda *f;* **glass ~** vitrina *f*

case book *n* diario *m;* MED registro *m* **case law** *n no pl* LAW jurisprudencia *f* **case study** <-ies> *n* monografía *f*

cash [kæʃ] **I.** *n no pl* dinero *m* en efectivo; **~ in advance** adelanto *m;* **to be strapped for ~** *inf* andar corto de dinero **II.** *vt* cobrar; (*cheque*) cambiar; **to ~ sth in** canjear algo; **to ~ in (one's chips)** *inf* (*die*) palmarla

◆**cash down** *vt*, **cash over** *vt Am, inf* pagar al contado

◆**cash in** I. *vt insep* canjear II. *vi* **to ~ on sth** sacar provecho de algo

cash-and-carry [ˌkæʃənd'kæri, *Am:* -ənd-'ker-] I. <-ies> *n* tienda *f* de venta al por mayor II. *adj* de venta al por mayor III. *adv* al por mayor

cash balance *n* saldo *m* de caja **cash box** <-es> *n* caja *f* del dinero **cash card** *n Brit* tarjeta *f* del cajero automático **cash crop** *n* cultivo *m* comercial **cash dispenser** *n Brit* cajero *m* automático

cashew ['kæʃuː] *n*, **cashew nut** *n* anacardo *m*, acajú *m Cuba, Méx, PRico, RDom*

cash flow ['kæʃˌfləʊ, *Am:* -ˌfloʊ] *n* FIN flujo *m* de caja

cashier¹ [kæ'ʃɪəʳ, *Am:* kæʃɪr] *n* cajero, -a *m, f*

cashier² [kæ'ʃɪəʳ, *Am:* kæʃɪr] *vt* MIL destituir

cash machine *n* cajero *m* automático

cashmere ['kæʃmɪə, *Am:* 'kæʒmɪr] *n* cachemir *m*

cash payment ['kæʃˌpeɪmənt] *n* pago *m* al contado **cashpoint** *n Brit* cajero *m* automático **cash register** *n* caja *f* registradora **cash sale** *n* venta *f* al contado

casing ['keɪsɪŋ] *n* cubierta *f;* (*of machine*) carcasa *f;* (*of cable*) tubo *m* de revestimiento

casino [kə'siːnəʊ, *Am:* -noʊ] *n* casino *m*

cask [kɑːsk, *Am:* kæsk] *n* tonel *m;* (*of wine*) barril *m*

casket ['kɑːskɪt, *Am:* 'kæskɪt] *n* 1. (*box*) cofre *m;* (*for jewels*) joyero *m* 2. *Am* (*coffin*) ataúd *m*

Caspian Sea ['kæspiən] *n* Mar *m* Caspio

casserole ['kæsərəʊl, *Am:* -əroʊl] I. *n* 1. (*cooking vessel*) cazuela *f;* (*of iron*) cacerola *f* 2. GASTR guiso *m* II. *vt* guisar (en una cazuela)

cassette [kə'set] *n* casete *m o f;* **video ~** videocasete *m*

cassette deck *n* platina *f* **cassette player** *n*, **cassette recorder** *n* casete *m*

cast [kɑst, *Am:* kæst] I. *n* 1. THEAT, CINE reparto *m;* **supporting ~** reparto secundario 2. (*mould*) molde *m* 3. MED escayola *f* 4. (*of worm*) rastro *m* II. <cast, cast> *vt* 1. (*throw*) lanzar; (*fishing line*) arrojar 2. (*direct*) **to ~ doubt on sth** poner algo en duda; **to ~ a shadow on sth** ensombrecer algo; **to ~ light on sth** proyectar luz sobre algo; *fig* echar luz sobre algo; **to ~ an eye over sth** echar una ojeada a algo; **to ~ one's mind back** hacer un esfuerzo de memoria 3. (*allocate roles*) asignar; **to ~ sb as sb/sth** dar a alguien el papel de alguien/algo; **to ~ sb in a role** elegir a alguien para un papel 4. (*give*) dar; (*vote*) emitir 5. (*make in a mould*) vaciar

◆**cast about** *vi*, **cast around** *vi* **to ~ for sth** ir a por algo

◆**cast aside** *vt*, **cast away** *vt* (*rid oneself of*) dejar de lado; (*free oneself of*) desechar

◆**cast down** *vt* **to be ~** estar deprimido

◆**cast off** I. *vt* 1. (*stitch*) cerrar 2. (*throw off*) desechar II. *vi* 1. NAUT soltar amarras 2. (*in knitting*) terminar

◆**cast on** I. *vt* (*in knitting: stitch*) echar II. *vi* (*in knitting*) montar los puntos

◆**cast out** *vt* arrojar; (*demons, ideas*) echar fuera de sí; (*person*) expulsar

◆**cast up** *vt* echar

castanets [kæstə'nets] *npl* castañuelas *fpl*

castaway ['kɑːstəweɪ, *Am:* 'kæstə-] *n* 1. (*survivor from a ship*) náufrago, -a *m, f* 2. (*discarded object*) trasto *m*

caste [kɑːst, *Am:* kæst] *n* (*social class*) casta *f;* **~ system** sistema *m* de castas

caster ['kɑːstəʳ, *Am:* 'kæstɚ] *n* ruedecita *f*

castigate ['kæstɪgeɪt, *Am:* -tə-] *vt form* fustigar; **to ~ sb for sth** censurar a alguien por algo

castigation [ˌkæstɪ'geɪʃən, *Am:* -ə'-] *n no pl* censura *f;* (*rebuke*) reprobación *f*

casting ['kɑːstɪŋ, *Am:* 'kæstɪŋ] *n* 1. (*forming in a mould*) vaciado *m* 2. THEAT reparto *m* de papeles

casting vote *n* voto *m* de calidad

cast iron [ˌkɑːst'aɪən] I. *n no pl* hierro *m* fundido II. *adj* 1. (*made of cast iron*) de hierro fundido 2. *fig* (*evidence*) irrefutable; (*alibi*) a toda prueba; (*promise*) firme

castle ['kɑːsl, *Am:* 'kæsl] I. *n* 1. (*building*) castillo *m* 2. (*chess piece*) torre *f* ►**to build ~s in the air** construir castillos en el aire II. *vi* (*in chess*) enrocar

cast-off [ˌkɑːst'ɒf, *Am:* 'kæstɑːf] I. *n* (*garment*) prenda *f* desechada [*o* vieja]; **~s** ropa *f* desechada [*o* vieja] II. *adj* (*clothes, shoes*) desechado, -a, viejo, -a

castor ['kɑːstəʳ, *Am:* 'kæstɚ] *n* ruedecita *f*

castor oil *n no pl* aceite *m* de ricino **castor stand** *n Am* puesto *m* de los espolvoreadores **castor sugar** *n no pl, Brit* azúcar *m* blanco muy fino

castrate [kæ'streɪt] *vt* castrar, componer *AmL*

casual ['kæʒʊəl, *Am:* 'kæʒuː-] *adj* 1. (*relaxed*) relajado, -a 2. (*not permanent*) casual; (*sex*) ocasional 3. (*not serious*) despreocupado, -a; (*glance*) al azar; (*remark*) a la ligera; (*meeting*) fortuito, -a 4. (*not habitual*) de vez en cuando 5. (*informal*) informal; (*clothes*) deportivo, -a

casual labour *n no pl*, **casual work** *n no pl* trabajo *m* temporal

casual labourer *n*, **casual worker** *n* trabajador(a) *m(f)* temporero, -a

casually *adv* de forma relajada

casualty ['kæʒʊəlti, *Am:* 'kæʒuː-] <-ies> *n* 1. (*accident victim*) víctima *f;* (*injured person*) herido, -a *m, f;* MIL (*dead person*) baja *f* 2. (*negative result*) pérdidas *fpl* 3. *no pl* (*hospital department*) urgencias *fpl*

cat [kæt] *n* gato, -a *m, f* ►**to let the ~ out of the bag** descubrir el pastel; **to not have a ~ in hell's chance** *inf* no tener la más mínima posibilidad; **to fight like ~ and dog** llevarse como (el) perro y (el) gato; **to rain ~s and dogs** llover a cántaros; **to put the ~ among the pigeons** armar un revuelo; **there's not**

C

enough room to swing a ~ no cabe ni un alfiler; **to look like something the** ~ **brought in** ir hecho un pordiosero

CAT [kæt] *n* **1.** INFOR *abbr of* **computer-assisted translation** TAO *f* **2.** MED *abbr of* **computerized axial tomography** TAC *m o f;* ~ **scan** (escáner *m*) TAC *m*

cataclysmic [ˌkætəˈklɪzmɪk, *Am:* ˌkæt̬əˈ-] *adj* desastroso, -a

catacombs [ˈkætəkuːmz, *Am:* ˈkæt̬əkoʊm] *npl* catacumbas *fpl*

Catalan [ˌkætəˈlæn, *Am:* ˈkæt̬əlæn] **I.** *adj* catalán, -ana **II.** *n* **1.** (*habitant*) catalán, -ana *m, f* **2.** (*language*) catalán *m*

catalog *Am,* **catalogue** [ˈkætəlɒg, *Am:* ˈkæt̬əlɑːg] *Brit* **I.** *n* catálogo *m;* (*repeated events*) serie *f;* **a** ~ **of mistakes** *fig* un error detrás de otro **II.** *vt* catalogar

Catalonia [ˌkætələʊniə, *Am:* -ˈloʊ-] *n* Cataluña *f*

Catalonian [ˌkætələʊniən, *Am:* -ˈloʊ-] *adj, n s.* **Catalan**

catalysis [kəˈtæləsɪs] *n no pl* catálisis *f inv*

catalyst [ˈkætəlɪst, *Am:* ˈkæt̬-] *n a. fig* catalizador *m*

catalytic [kætəˈlɪtɪk] *adj* catalítico, -a; ~ **converter** AUTO catalizador *m*

catamaran [ˌkætəməˈræn, *Am:* ˌkæt̬-] *n* catamarán *m*

catapult [ˈkætəpʌlt, *Am:* ˈkæt̬-] **I.** *n* tirachinas *m inv;* HIST catapulta *f* **II.** *vt* catapultar

cataract¹ [ˈkætərækt, *Am:* ˈkæt̬ərækt] *n* MED catarata *f*

cataract² [ˈkætərækt, *Am:* ˈkæt̬ərækt] *n* (*waterfall*) catarata *f*

catarrh [kəˈtɑːʳ, *Am:* kəˈtɑːr] *n no pl* catarro *m*

catastrophe [kəˈtæstrəfi] *n* catástrofe *f*

catastrophic [ˌkætəˈstrɒfɪk, *Am:* ˌkæt̬əˈstrɑːfɪk] *adj* catastrófico, -a

catcall [ˈkætkɔːl] *n* (*booing*) abucheo *m;* (*whistling*) silbido *m*

catch [kætʃ] <-es> **I.** *n* **1.** *no pl* (*fish caught*) pesca *f* **2.** (*fastening device*) pestillo *m;* (*on window*) cierre *m* **3.** *inf* (*suitable partner*) **he's a good** ~ es un buen partido **4.** (*trick*) trampa *f* **II.** <caught, caught> *vt* **1.** (*hold moving object*) agarrar; (*person*) atrapar; **to** ~ **sb at a bad moment** pillar a alguien en un mal momento **2.** (*entangle*) involucrar; **to get caught in sth** quedar atrapado en algo; **to get caught up in sth** quedar involucrado en algo; **to get caught on sth** engancharse a algo **3.** (*collect*) acumular; (*liquid*) recoger **4.** (*capture an expression*) percibir; (*hear*) oír **5.** (*attract*) atraer **6.** (*get*) coger, tomar *AmL;* **to** ~ **the bus** coger el bus **7.** (*discover*) descubrir **8.** (*notice*) darse cuenta de; (*by chance*) pillar por casualidad **9.** (*discover by surprise*) **to** ~ **sb (doing sth)** sorprender [*o* pillar] a alguien (haciendo algo); **to** ~ **sb red handed** *fig* coger [*o* pillar] a alguien con las manos en la masa; **to** ~ **sb with their trousers down, to** ~ **sb napping** *fig* coger [*o* pillar] a alguien desprevenido **10.** MED (*become infected*) contagiarse de **11.** (*start burning: fire*) prender

◆**catch at** *vi* tratar de coger

◆**catch on** *vi* **1.** (*be popular*) ponerse de moda **2.** *inf* (*understand*) entender

◆**catch out** *vt* **1.** (*discover wrongdoing*) **to catch sb out** pescar [*o* sorprender] a alguien; **we were caught out by his reaction** su reacción nos cogió desprevenidos **2.** (*ask trick questions*) pillar, engañar

◆**catch up** **I.** *vi* **to** ~ **with sb** alcanzar el nivel de alguien; **to** ~ **with sth** (*make up lost time*) ponerse al corriente de algo; (*equal the standard*) igualarse a algo **II.** *vt* **to catch sb up** *Brit, Aus* alcanzar a alguien

catchall [ˈkætʃɔːl] *adj* comodín

catcher [ˈkætʃəʳ, *Am:* -ɚ] *n* SPORTS receptor(a) *m(f)*

catching [ˈkætʃɪŋ] *adj a. fig, inf* contagioso, -a

catchment [ˈkætʃmənt] *n* captación *f*

catchphrase [ˈkætʃfreɪz] *n* eslogan *m*

catch question *n* pregunta *f* capciosa

catchup [ˈkætʃəp] *n* ketchup *m*

catchword [ˈkætʃˌwɜːd, *Am:* -ˌwɜːrd] *n* eslogan *m*

catchy [ˈkætʃi] <-ier, -iest> *adj* pegadizo, -a

catechism [ˈkætɪkɪzəm, *Am:* ˈkæt̬-] *n* **1.** (*instruction*) catequesis *f inv* **2.** (*book*) catecismo *m*

categorical [ˌkætɪˈgɒrɪkl, *Am:* ˌkæt̬əˈgɔːr-] *adj* (*denial, refusal*) categórico, -a

categorise *vt Brit, Aus,* **categorize** [ˈkætəgəraɪz, *Am:* ˈkæt̬əgəraɪz] *vt Am* clasificar

category [ˈkætəgəri, *Am:* ˈkæt̬əgɔːr-] <-ies> *n* categoría *f*

cater [ˈkeɪtəʳ, *Am:* -t̬ɚ] *vi* encargarse del servicio de comidas

caterer [ˈkeɪtərəʳ, *Am:* ˈkeɪt̬ɚɚ] *n* encargado, -a *m, f* del servicio de comidas

catering [ˈkeɪtərɪŋ] *n no pl* restauración *f;* (*service*) servicio *m* de comidas

caterpillar [ˈkætəpɪləʳ, *Am:* ˈkæt̬ɚpɪlɚ] *n* **1.** ZOOL oruga *f* **2.** (*on vehicle wheels*) rodado *m* de oruga **3.** (*vehicle*) tractor *m* oruga

caterpillar tractor *n* tractor *m* oruga

caterwaul [ˈkætəwɔːl, *Am:* ˈkæt̬ɚ-] **I.** *n* aullido *m* **II.** *vi* aullar

catgut [ˈkætgʌt] *n no pl* cuerda *f* de tripa; MED catgut *m*

cathartic [kəˈθɑːtɪk, *Am:* kəˈθɑːrt̬ɪk] *adj* catártico, -a

cathedral [kəˈθiːdrəl] *n* catedral *f;* ~ **city** ciudad *f* episcopal

catherine wheel [ˈkæθərɪnˌhwiːl] *n* (*firework*) girándula *f*

catheter [ˈkæθɪtəʳ, *Am:* -ət̬ɚ] *n* MED catéter *m*

cathode [ˈkæθəʊd, *Am:* -oʊd] *n* ELEC cátodo *m*

cathode ray *n* rayo *m* catódico

Catholic [ˈkæθəlɪk] REL **I.** *n* católico, -a *m, f*

II. *adj* católico, -a

catholic ['kæθəlɪk] *adj* variado, -a

Catholicism [kə'θɒləsɪzəm, *Am:* -'θɑ:lə-] *n no pl* catolicismo *m*

catkin ['kætkɪn] *n* amento *m*

cat litter *n no pl* arena *f* higiénica

catnap ['kæt͵næp] **I.** *n inf* siestecita *f;* **to have a ~** echar una cabezada **II.** <-pp-> *vi inf* echar una siestecita

cat's cradle [͵kæts'kreɪdl] *n* juego *m* de la cuna

cat's eye ['kætsaɪ] *n Brit, Aus* ojo *m* de gato

catsup ['kætsəp] *n Am* ketchup *m*

cattle ['kætl, *Am:* 'kæţ-] *npl* (*bovines*) ganado *m;* **beef ~** ganado vacuno; **dairy ~** vacas *fpl* lecheras

cattle-breeder *n* ganadero, -a *m, f* **cattle-breeding** *n no pl* ganadería *f* **cattle-car** *n Am* RAIL vagón *m* de ganado **cattle-thief** <-thieves> *n* ladrón, -ona *m, f* de ganado

catty ['kæti, *Am:* 'kæţ-] <-ier, -iest> *adj* (*hurtful*) malicioso, -a; (*remark*) intencionado, -a

cat-walk ['kæt͵wɔ:k, *Am:* -wɑ:k] *n* **1.** THEAT puente *m* de trabajo **2.** *Brit* FASHION pasarela *f*

Caucasian [kɔ:'keɪzɪən, *Am:* kɑ:'keɪʒən] *form* **I.** *n* **1.** (*white*) blanco, -a *m, f* **2.** (*European*) caucásico, -a *m, f* **3.** (*languages*) caucásico *m* **II.** *adj* **1.** (*white*) blanco, -a **2.** (*European*) caucásico, -a **3.** (*of the Caucasus*) caucasiano, -a; (*language*) caucásico, -a

caucus ['kɔ:kəs, *Am:* 'kɑ:-] **I.** *n* <-es> **1.** (*group*) comité *m* **2.** (*members*) camarilla *f* **3.** *Am* (*meeting*) reunión *f* del comité de un partido **II.** *vi* celebrar una reunión del comité del partido

caught [kɔ:t, *Am:* kɑ:t] *pt, pp of* **catch**

cauldron ['kɔ:ldrən, *Am:* 'kɑ:l-] *n* caldero *m; fig* hervidero *m*

cauliflower ['kɒlɪflaʊəʳ, *Am:* 'kɑ:lɪ͵flaʊɚ] *n* coliflor *f*

caulk [kɔ:k, *Am:* kɑ:k] *vt* enmasillar; NAUT calafatear

causal ['kɔ:zl, *Am:* 'kɑ:-] *adj a.* LING causal; (*relationship*) de causa-efecto

causality [kɔ:'zæləti, *Am:* kɑ:'zæləţi] *n no pl, form* causalidad *f*

causative ['kɔ:zətɪv, *Am:* 'kɑ:zəţɪv] *adj form* **1.** (*acting as a cause*) causante **2.** LING causativo, -a

cause [kɔ:z] **I.** *n* **1.** (*a reason for*) causa *f,* motivo *m;* **he is the ~ of all her woes** él es el causante de todas sus penas; **this is no ~ for ...** esto no justifica... **2.** *no pl* (*objective*) causa *f* **3.** (*principle*) causa *f;* **to do sth in the ~ of sth** hacer algo en pro de algo **4.** LAW pleito *m* **II.** *vt* causar; (*an accident*) provocar; **to ~ sb/sth to do sth** hacer que alguien/algo haga algo; **to ~ sb harm** ocasionar daños a alguien; **this medicine may ~ dizziness and nausea** este medicamento puede provocar mareos y náuseas

causeway ['kɔ:z͵weɪ, *Am:* 'kɑ:z-] *n* **1.** (*road bridge*) carretera *f* elevada **2.** (*pathway*) paso *m* elevado

caustic ['kɔ:stɪk, *Am:* 'kɑ:-] *adj a. fig* cáustico, -a; (*lime*) vivo, -a; (*remark*) mordaz; (*tongue*) viperino, -a

cauterise *vt Brit, Aus,* **cauterize** ['kɔ:təraɪz, *Am:* 'kɑ:ţəraɪz] *vt a. fig* cauterizar

caution ['kɔ:ʃən, *Am:* 'kɑ:-] **I.** *n no pl* **1.** (*carefulness*) cautela *f;* **~ is advised** se recomienda prudencia; **to throw ~ to the winds** jugársela; **to treat sth with ~** tratar algo con cuidado **2.** (*warning*) advertencia *f;* **a note of ~** un aviso; **~!** ¡cuidado! **3.** *Brit* LAW fianza *f;* **to let sb off with a ~** dejar a alguien en libertad bajo fianza **II.** *vt form* **1.** (*warn*) prevenir a; **to ~ sb to do sth** aconsejar a alguien que haga algo **2.** *Brit* (*reprimand*) amonestar a; **to ~ sb about sth** llamar la atención a alguien por algo

cautionary ['kɔ:ʃənəri, *Am:* 'kɑ:ʃəner-] *adj* aleccionador(a); **a ~ tale** un cuento con moraleja

cautious ['kɔ:ʃəs, *Am:* 'kɑ:-] *adj* cauto, -a; (*optimism*) moderado, -a; **to be ~ in sth** ser prudente en algo

cavalcade [͵kævl'keɪd] *n* **1.** (*procession*) cabalgata *f* **2.** (*succession*) desfile *m;* (*of memories*) sucesión *f*

cavalier [͵kævəl'ɪəʳ, *Am:* -əlɪr] **I.** *n* HIST caballero *m* **II.** *adj* arrogante; **a ~ attitude** una actitud desdeñosa

cavalry ['kævəlri] *n pl vb* MIL caballería *f*

cavalryman ['kævəlrimən] <-men> *n* **1.** HIST (*mounted*) caballero *m* **2.** MIL (*in armoured vehicles*) soldado *m* de caballería

cave¹ [keɪv] *n* **to keep ~** vigilar

cave² [keɪv] **I.** *n* (*natural*) cueva *f;* (*man-made*) caverna *f* **II.** *vi* **1.** (*hollow out*) cavar **2.** *Brit* SPORTS hacer espeleología

◆**cave in** *vi* ceder

caveat ['kæviæt] *n* **1.** (*warning*) advertencia *f* **2.** LAW *anotación provisional para asegurar el cumplimiento de la resolución judicial*

cavedweller *n* cavernícola *mf*

cave-in *n* derrumbamiento *m*

caveman ['keɪvmæn] <-men> *n* **1.** (*prehistoric man*) hombre *m* de las cavernas **2.** *inf* (*socially underdeveloped*) bruto *m inf,* troglodita *m* **cave painting** *n* pintura *f* rupestre

caver ['keɪvəʳ, *Am:* -ɚ] *n Brit, Aus* espeleólogo, -a *m, f*

cavern ['kævən, *Am:* -ɚn] *n* caverna *f*

cavernous ['kævənəs, *Am:* -ɚn-] *adj* cavernoso, -a; (*hole, room*) oscuro, -a; (*pit*) profundo, -a; (*eyes*) hundido, -a

caviar(e) ['kævɪɑ:ʳ, *Am:* -ɑ:r] *n no pl* caviar *m*

cavity ['kævɪti, *Am:* -ţi] <-ies> *n* **1.** *a.* ANAT cavidad *f;* **nasal ~** fosa *f* nasal **2.** MED caries *f inv*

caw [kɔ:, *Am:* kɑ:] **I.** *n* graznido *m* **II.** *vi* graznar

cayenne [keɪ'en, *Am:* kaɪ-] *n,* **cayenne**

pepper *n no pl* (pimienta *f* de) cayena *f*
Cayman Islands ['keɪmən,aɪləndz] *n* Islas *fpl* Cayman
CB [,siː'biː] *n no pl abbr of* **Citizen's Band** banda *f* ciudadana
CBI [,siːbiː'aɪ] *n Brit abbr of* **Confederation of British Industry** ≈ CEOE *f*
CBT *abbr of* **Computer Based Training** CBT
CBW *n abbr of* **chemical and biological warfare** guerra *f* bioquímica
cc [,siː'siː] *abbr of* **cubic centimetres** cc
CCTV [,siːsiːtiː'viː] *n abbr of* **closed-circuit television** circuito *m* cerrado de televisión
ccw. *adj, adv abbr of* **counterclockwise** en sentido contrario a las agujas del reloj
CD [,siː'diː] *n abbr of* **compact disc** CD *m*
CDI [,siːdiː'aɪ] *n* INFOR *abbr of* **compact disk interactive** CDI *m*
CD-player *n abbr of* **compact disc player** reproductor *m* de CD
CD-R *n abbr of* **Compact Disc Recordable** CD-R *m*
CD-ROM [,siːdiː'rɒm, *Am:* -'rɑːm] *n abbr of* **compact disc read-only memory** CD-ROM *m;* **on ~** en CD-ROM
CD-ROM drive *n* unidad *f* de CD-ROM
CD-ROM player *n* lector *m* de CD-ROM
CD-ROM writer *n* grabador *m* de CD-ROM
CD-RW *n abbr of* **Compact Disc Rewritable Unit** CD-RW *m*
cease [siːs] *form* **I.** *n no pl* **without ~** sin cesar **II.** *vi* cesar; **to ~ from sth** cesar de (hacer) algo **III.** *vt* suspender; **it never ~s to amaze me** nunca deja de sorprenderme; **~ firing!** MIL ¡alto el fuego!
cease-fire [,siːs'faɪəʳ, *Am:* -'faɪɚ] *n* MIL alto *m* el fuego, cese *m* del fuego *AmL*
ceaseless ['siːslɪs] *adj* incesante
cedar ['siːdəʳ, *Am:* -dɚ] *n* **1.** (*tree*) cedro *m* **2.** *no pl* (*wood*) (madera *f* de) cedro *m*
cede [siːd] *vt form* ceder
ceiling ['siːlɪŋ] *n* **1.** ARCHIT, AVIAT techo *m* **2.** (*upper limit*) tope *m;* (*on prices*) límite *m;* **to impose a ~ on sth** poner un tope a algo **3.** METEO cielo *m* (raso) ▶**to hit the ~** *inf* subirse por las paredes
celebrate ['selɪbreɪt] **I.** *vi* celebrar; **let's ~!** ¡vamos a celebrarlo! **II.** *vt* celebrar; (*anniversary of death*) conmemorar; **they ~d him as a hero** lo agasajaron como a un héroe
celebrated *adj* célebre
celebration [,selɪ'breɪʃən] *n* **1.** (*party*) fiesta *f* **2.** (*of an occasion*) celebración *f;* (*of an event*) conmemoración *f;* **to throw a party in ~ of sth** dar una fiesta para celebrar algo; **this calls for a ~!** ¡esto hay que celebrarlo!
celebratory [,selə'breɪtəri, *Am:* 'seləbrətɔːri] *adj* **we went for a ~ dinner** fuimos a cenar para celebrarlo
celebrity [sɪ'lebrəti, *Am:* sə'lebrəṭi] *n* **1.** <-ies> (*person*) famoso, -a *m, f* **2.** *no pl* (*fame*) celebridad *f*
celeriac [sə'lerɪæk] *n no pl* apio *m* nabo
celery ['seləri] *n no pl* apio *m,* panul *m CSur*
celestial [sɪ'lestɪəl, *Am:* -tʃl] *adj a. fig* celestial
celestial body <-ies> *n* cuerpo *m* celeste
celibacy ['selɪbəsi] *n no pl* **1.** *a.* REL celibato *m* **2.** (*being single*) soltería *f*
celibate ['selɪbət] **I.** *n* célibe *mf* **II.** *adj* **1.** *a.* REL (*refraining from sex*) célibe **2.** (*unmarried*) soltero, -a
cell [sel] *n* **1.** (*in prison*) celda *f,* separo *m Méx* **2.** BIO, POL célula *f;* **a single ~ animal** un animal unicelular; **grey ~s** materia *f* gris *inf* **3.** ELEC pila *f*
cellar ['seləʳ, *Am:* -ɚ] *n* **1.** (*basement*) sótano *m;* (*for wine*) bodega *f* **2.** *Am* SPORTS último lugar *m*
cellist ['tʃelɪst] *n* MUS violoncelista *mf*
cell nucleus ['sel,njuːklɪəs, *Am:* -nuː-] <-clei *o* -es> *n* núcleo *m* celular
cello ['tʃeləʊ, *Am:* -oʊ] <-s *o* -li> *n* MUS violoncelo *m*
cellophane® ['seləfeɪn] *n* celofán *m*
cellular ['seljʊləʳ, *Am:* -lɚ] *adj* **1.** BIO celular **2.** (*porous*) poroso, -a
cellular phone *n,* **cellphone** ['selfəʊn, *Am:* -foʊn] *n* téléfono *m* móvil
cellulite ['seljəlaɪt] *n no pl* celulitis *f inv*
celluloid ['seljʊlɔɪd] **I.** *n no pl* celuloide *m* **II.** *adj* de celuloide
cellulose ['seljʊləʊs, *Am:* -loʊs] *n no pl* celulosa *f*
Celsius ['selsiəs] *adj* PHYS Celsius
Celt [kelt, selt] *n* HIST celta *mf*
Celtic ['keltik, 'seltɪk] **I.** *adj* céltico, -a; (*language*) celta **II.** *n* celta *m*
cement [sɪ'ment] **I.** *n no pl* **1.** ARCHIT cemento *m* **2.** (*glue*) cola *f* **3.** MED empaste *m* **4.** (*uniting idea*) aglutinante *m* **II.** *vt* **1.** (*cover with cement*) revestir de cemento; **to ~ over sth** revestir algo de cemento **2.** (*stabilize*) fortalecer; (*a friendship*) consolidar **3.** MED empastar
cement mixer *n* hormigonera *f*
cemetery ['semətri, *Am:* -teri] <-ies> *n* cementerio *m,* panteón *m AmL*
censer ['sensəʳ, *Am:* -sɚ] *n* REL incensario *m*
censor ['sensəʳ, *Am:* -sɚ] **I.** *n* **1.** (*official*) censor(a) *m(f)* **2.** PSYCH censura *f* **II.** *vt* censurar
censorious [sen'sɔːrɪəs, *Am:* -'sɔːrɪ-] *adj* censurador(a); (*comments*) de reprobación; **to be ~ about** [*o* **of**] **sth/sb** censurar algo/a alguien
censorship ['sentsəʃɪp, *Am:* -sɚ-] *n no pl* censura *f*
censure ['sentʃɚ] *vt* censurar
census ['sensəs] <-es> *n* censo *m*
cent [sent] *n Am* centavo *m* ▶**to not have a red ~** *Am, inf* no tengo ni un céntimo; **I don't care a ~** me importa un bledo
centenarian [,sentɪ'neərɪən, *Am:* -tnerɪ-] *n* centenario, -a *m, f*
centenary [sen'tiːnəri, *Am:* 'sentner-]

I. <-ies> *n* centenario *m* **II.** *adj* (*once every century*) secular; ~ **year** año *m* del centenario

centennial [sen'tenɪəl] *n, adj Am s.* **centenary**

center ['sent̬ɚ] *n, vt Am s.* **centre**

centerpiece ['sent̬ɚ'piːs] *n Am s.* **centrepiece**

centigrade ['sentɪgreɪd, *Am:* -t̬ə-] *adj* centígrado, -a

centigram(me) ['sentɪgræm, *Am:* -t̬ə-] *n* centigramo *m*

centimeter *n Am,* **centimetre** ['sentɪˌmiːtəʳ, *Am:* -t̬əˌmiːt̬ɚ] *n Brit, Aus* centímetro *m*

centipede ['sentɪpiːd, *Am:* -t̬ə-] *n* ciempiés *m inv*

central ['sentrəl] *adj* **1.** (*at the middle*) central; (*street*) céntrico, -a; **in ~ Madrid** en el centro de Madrid **2.** (*important: issue*) fundamental; **to be ~ to sth** ser vital para algo; **to be of ~ importance (to sb)** ser de una importancia primordial (para alguien); **the ~ character** el protagonista **3.** (*from a main point: bank, heating*) central; AUTO (*locking*) centralizado, -a; ~ **processing unit** INFOR unidad *f* central de procesamiento

Central African **I.** *adj* centroafricano, -a **II.** *n* centroafricano, -a *m, f*

Central African Republic *n* República *f* Centroafricana

Central Bank *n* Banco *m* Central

centralization [ˌsentrəlaɪ'zeɪʃən, *Am:* -lɪ'-] *n no pl* centralización *f*

centralize ['sentrəlaɪz] *vt* centralizar

centre ['sentəʳ] *Brit* **I.** *n* **1.** (*focus*) **a.** PHYS, POL, SPORTS centro *m;* ~ **party** partido *m* de centro **2.** (*of population*) núcleo *m* **3.** (*building*) centro *m* **4.** SPORTS (*in football*) centro *m* **II.** *vt* **1. a.** SPORTS, TYPO centrar **2.** (*efforts*) concentrar

◆**centre around** *vi* girar en torno a; **his life centres around his family** su vida se centra en su familia

◆**centre on** *vi* concentrarse en

centrepiece ['sentəpiːs, *Am:* -t̬ɚ-] *n Brit* eje *m;* **racial integration was the ~ of the party's proposals** la integración racial era el aspecto fundamental de las propuestas del partido

centrifugal [sen'trɪfjʊgl, *Am:* -jəgl] *adj* PHYS centrífugo, -a

centrifuge ['sentrɪfjuːdʒ, *Am:* -trə-] *n* MED, TECH centrifugadora *f*

centripetal [sen'trɪpɪtl, *Am:* -pət̬l] *adj* PHYS centrípeto, -a

century ['sentʃəri] <-ies> *n* **1.** (*100 years*) siglo *m;* **the twentieth ~** el siglo veinte; **a centuries-old custom** una costumbre secular **2.** SPORTS (*cricket*) cien carreras *fpl*

CEO [ˌsiːiː'əʊ, *Am:* -'oʊ] *n abbr of* **chief executive officer** director(a) *m(f)* general

ceramic [sɪ'ræmɪk, *Am:* sə-] *adj* de cerámica

ceramics *n pl* cerámica *f*

cereal ['sɪərɪəl, *Am:* 'sɪrɪ-] **I.** *n* **1.** *no pl* (*cultivated grass*) cereal *m* **2.** (*breakfast food*) cereales *mpl* **II.** *adj* cereal

cerebellum [ˌserɪ'beləm, *Am:* ˌserə-] <-s *o* -la> *n* cerebelo *m*

cerebral ['serɪbrəl, *Am:* ˌserə-] *adj* cerebral; ~ **palsy** parálisis *f inv* cerebral

cerebrum ['serɪbrəm, *Am:* ˌserə-] <-(bra)> *n* cerebro *m*

ceremonial [ˌserɪ'məʊnɪəl, *Am:* -ə'moʊ-] **I.** *n form* ceremonial *m* **II.** *adj* ceremonial; (*event*) solemne; (*uniform*) de gala

ceremonious [ˌserɪ'məʊnɪəs, *Am:* -ə-'moʊ-] *adj* ceremonioso, -a

ceremony ['serɪməni, *Am:* -əmoʊ-] <-ies> *n* ceremonia *f;* **to stand on ~** ser muy ceremonioso; **to go through the ~ of sth** *fig* cumplir con todas las formalidades de algo

cert [sɜːt, *Am:* sɜːrt] *n Brit, inf abbr of* **certainty that's a (dead) ~** *inf* eso está claro

certain ['sɜːtn, *Am:* 'sɜːr-] **I.** *adj* **1.** (*sure*) seguro, -a; **it is quite ~ (that) ...** es muy probable que... +*subj;* **to be ~ about sb** confiar en alguien; **to be ~ about sth** estar convencido de algo; **to make ~ of sth** asegurarse de algo; **it is not yet ~ ...** todavía no se sabe con certeza...; **to feel ~ (that ...)** estar convencido (de que...); **to make ~ (that ...)** asegurarse (de que...); **please make ~ that he has answered** por favor, asegúrate de que ha respondido; **I don't know yet for ~** todavía no lo sé a ciencia cierta; **one thing is (for) ~ ...** de lo que no cabe duda es...; **for ~** con certeza **2.** (*undeniable*) cierto, -a; **it is ~ that ...** es cierto que...; **the disaster seemed ~** el desastre parecía inevitable **3.** (*specified*) cierto, -a; **a ~ Steve Rukus** un tal Steve Rukus; **to a ~ extent** hasta cierto punto **II.** *pron* cierto, -a

certainly *adv* **1.** (*surely*) por supuesto; **she ~ is a looker, isn't she?** es guapa, ¿verdad?; **she ~ had a friend called Mark** está claro que tenía un amigo que se llamaba Mark; **he is ~ strong** desde luego es fuerte **2.** (*gladly*) desde luego; **~, Sir!** ¡por supuesto, señor!; **~ not!** ¡desde luego que no!

certainty ['sɜːtənti, *Am:* 'sɜːr-] <-ies> *n* certeza *f;* **Joan is a ~ to win** está claro que Joan ganará; **with ~** a ciencia cierta

certifiable [ˌsɜːtɪ'faɪəbl, *Am:* 'sɜːrt̬ə-] *adj* **1.** (*declared*) certificable **2.** PSYCH (*mentally ill*) demente; **he is ~!** *inf* ¡está para que lo encierren!

certificate [sə'tɪfɪkət, *Am:* sɚ-] *n* **1.** (*document*) certificado *m;* (*of baptism, birth, death*) partida *f;* (*of ownership*) título *m* **2.** SCHOOL título *m*

certification [ˌsɜːtɪfɪ'keɪʃən, *Am:* ˌsɜːrt̬ə-] *n no pl* **1.** (*process*) certificación *f* **2.** (*document*) certificado *m*

certify ['sɜːtɪfaɪ, *Am:* -t̬ə-] <-ie-> *vt* certificar; **certified copy** copia *f* legalizada; **this is to ~ that ...** *form* por la presente certifico que...; **he is certified to practise medicine**

está habilitado para ejercer la medicina; **to ~ sb (as) mad** declarar a alguien demente

certitude ['sɜːtɪtjuːd, *Am:* 'sɜːrt̬ətuːd] *n no pl* certidumbre *f*

cervical ['sɜːvɪkl, sɜː'vaɪkl, *Am:* 'sɜːrvɪ-] *adj* **1.** (*neck*) cervical; ~ **collar** collarín *m;* ~ **vertebra** vértebra *f* cervical **2.** (*cervix*) del cuello del útero

cervix ['sɜːvɪks, *Am:* 'sɜːr-] <-es *o* -vices> *n* **1.** (*neck*) cerviz *f* **2.** (*womb*) cuello *m* del útero

cesarean [sɪ'zeəriən, *Am:* sə'zeri-] *n* **a ~ section** una cesárea

cesium ['siːziəm] *n Am s.* **caesium**

cessation [se'seɪʃən] *n no pl, form* (*end*) cesación *f;* (*of hostilities*) cese *m*

cesspit ['sespɪt] *n,* **cesspool** ['sespuːl] *n* **1.** (*for excrements*) pozo *m* negro **2.** (*unpleasant area*) cloaca *f*

CET *n abbr of* **Central European Time** horario *m* de Centroeuropa

Ceylon [sɪ'lɒn, *Am:* -'lɑːn] *n no pl* **1.** HIST (*Sri Lanka*) Ceilán *m* **2.** (*Ceylon tea*) té *m* de Ceilán

Ceylonese [sɪlɒ'niːz, *Am:* ˌsiːlə'niːz] **I.** *n* ceilanés, -esa *m, f* **II.** *adj* HIST ceilanés, -esa

cf. *abbr of* **confer** cf.

CFC [ˌsiːef'siː] *n abbr of* **chlorofluorocarbon** clorofluorocarbono *m*

c/h *n abbr of* **central heating** calef. *f*

Chad [tschæd] *n no pl* Chad *m*

Chadian **I.** *adj* chadiano, -a **II.** *n* chadiano, -a *m, f*

chafe [tʃeɪf] **I.** *vi* **1.** (*sore*) rozar; (*worn*) desgastarse **2.** *fig* (*irritated*) irritarse; **to ~ at sth** enfadarse por algo; **to ~ to do sth** estar impaciente por algo **II.** *vt* **1.** (*rub sore*) irritar **2.** (*rub*) rozar; (*rub for warmth*) frotar **3.** *fig* enfadar

chafer ['tʃeɪfəʳ, *Am:* -fɚ] *n* abejorro *m*

chaff¹ [tʃɑːf, *Am:* tʃæf] *n no pl* AGR **1.** (*husks*) granza *f* **2.** (*cut grass*) forraje *m* **3.** (*worthless material*) paja *f*

chaff² [tʃɑːf, *Am:* tʃæf] **I.** *n no pl* broma *f* **II.** *vt* tomar el pelo a

chaffinch ['tʃæfɪntʃ] <-es> *n* pinzón *m*

chagrin ['ʃægrɪn, *Am:* ʃə'grɪn] **I.** *n no pl* irritación *f* **II.** *vt* irritar

chain [tʃeɪn] **I.** *n* **1.** cadena *f;* ~ **gang** cuerda *f* de presos; **to be in ~s** estar encadenado **2.** (*restrictions*) cadenas *fpl* **3.** (*series*) cadena *f;* (*of mishaps*) sucesión *f* **II.** *vt* encadenar; **to ~ sth/sb (up) to sth** encadenar algo/a alguien a algo; **to be ~ed to a desk** *fig* estar encerrado en un despacho

chain letter *n* carta *f* en cadena (*que debe ser copiada y remitida a varias personas*) **chainmail** *n no pl* cota *f* de malla **chain reaction** *n* reacción *f* en cadena; **to set off a ~** provocar una reacción en cadena **chain saw** *n* motosierra *f* **chainsmoker** *n* fumador(a) *m(f)* empedernido, -a

chain store *n* tienda *f* de una cadena

chair [tʃeəʳ, *Am:* tʃer] **I.** *n* **1.** (*seat*) silla *f;* **take [*o* have] a ~ please** siéntese, por favor **2.** (*head*) presidente, -a *m, f;* **to be ~ of a department** ser jefe de un departamento; **to be in the ~** ocupar la presidencia **3.** (*position*) cargo *m* **4.** *Am* (*electric chair*) silla *f* eléctrica **5.** UNIV cátedra *f;* **to hold a ~ in sth** ocupar una cátedra de algo **II.** *vt* (*a meeting*) presidir

chair lift *n* telesilla *m*

chairman ['tʃeəmən, *Am:* 'tʃer-] <-men> *n* presidente *m*

chairmanship ['tʃeəmənʃɪp, *Am:* 'tʃer-] *n* presidencia *f*

chairperson ['tʃeəˌpɜːsən, *Am:* 'tʃerˌpɜːr-] *n* presidente, -a *m, f* **chairwoman** <-women> *n* presidenta *f*

chalet ['ʃæleɪ, *Am:* ʃæl'eɪ] *n* chalet *m*

chalk [tʃɔːk] **I.** *n no pl* **1.** GEO (*stone*) caliza *f* **2.** (*stick*) tiza *f,* gis *m Méx* ►**to be as different as ~ and <u>cheese</u>** ser (como) la noche y el día; **to be as alike as ~ and <u>cheese</u>** parecerse una cosa a otra como un huevo a una castaña; **to not know ~ from <u>cheese</u>** no distinguir lo blanco de lo negro; **she is the most intelligent by a <u>long</u> ~** es la más inteligente con mucho; **not by a <u>long</u> ~** ni mucho menos **II.** *vt* (*write*) escribir con tiza; (*draw*) dibujar con tiza

◆**chalk out** *vt* marcar con tiza

◆**chalk up** *vt* **1.** (*write with chalk*) escribir con tiza **2.** (*make an achievement*) apuntar; (*a victory*) anotarse; **to ~ sth to sb** anotar algo en la cuenta de alguien; **never mind, chalk it up to experience** no importa, es una experiencia más

chalkboard ['tʃɔːkbɔːd, *Am:* -bɔːrd] *n* pizarra *f*

chalky ['tʃɔːki] <-ier, -iest> *adj* **1.** (*made of chalk*) cretáceo, -a; (*water*) calcáreo, -a **2.** (*dusty*) **to be all ~** estar lleno de tiza **3.** (*chalk-like*) terroso, -a **4.** (*pale*) apagado, -a

challenge ['tʃælɪndʒ] **I.** *n* **1.** (*a call to competition*) desafío *m;* **to be faced with a ~** enfrentarse a un reto; **to present sb (with) a ~** enfrentar a alguien con un reto; **to pose a ~ to sth** poner algo en tela de juicio **2.** *a.* MIL alto *m* **3.** LAW recusación *f* **II.** *vt* **1.** (*ask to compete*) desafiar; **to ~ sb to a duel** retar a alguien a duelo **2.** (*question*) cuestionar, poner en tela de juicio **3.** (*test*) poner a prueba; **that's a matter that ~s attention** es una cuestión que requiere atención **4.** *a.* MIL dar el alto; **I was ~ed by the new security guard** me paró el nuevo guardia de seguridad **5.** LAW recusar

challenger ['tʃælɪndʒəʳ, *Am:* -ɚ] *n* desafiador(a) *m(f);* (*for a title*) aspirante *mf*

challenging *adj* (*book, movie*) que hace pensar; (*look, smile*) desafiante; (*work*) estimulante

chamber ['tʃeɪmbəʳ, *Am:* -bɚ] *n* **1.** (*room*) cámara *f;* **torture ~** sala *f* de torturas **2.** ANAT, POL cámara *f;* ~ **of Deputies** cámara de los diputados; **Upper/Lower** ~ cámara alta/baja **3.** ECON ~ **of commerce** cámara de comercio **4.** *pl* LAW (*barrister's office*) bufete *m;* **the case will be heard in** ~**s** la vista será a puerta cerrada **5.** TECH (*of a gun*) recámara *f;* **combustion** ~ cámara de combustión

chamberlain ['tʃeɪmbəlɪn, *Am:* -bɚ-] *n* HIST chambelán *m*

chambermaid ['tʃeɪmbəmeɪd, *Am:* -bɚ-] *n* camarera *f*

chamber music *n no pl* música *f* de cámara

chamber pot *n* orinal *m,* escupidera *f AmL,* tibor *m Cuba*

chameleon [kə'miːlɪən] *n a. fig* camaleón *m*

chamois ['ʃæmwɑ, *Am:* 'ʃæmi] <- *o* chamoix> *n inv* gamuza *f*

champ [tʃæmp] **I.** *n inf* campeón, -ona *m, f* **II.** *vi* morder ►**to** ~ **at the bit** estar impaciente **III.** *vt* morder

champagne [ʃæm'peɪn] **I.** *n no pl* champán *m* **II.** *adj* **1.** (*colour*) champán **2.** (*expensive*) **he has** ~ **tastes** tiene gustos caros

champion ['tʃæmpiən] **I.** *n* **1.** SPORTS campeón, -ona *m, f* **2.** (*supporter*) defensor(a) *m(f);* **to be a** ~ **of sth** ser un paladín de algo **II.** *vt* defender; **to** ~ **a cause** abogar por una causa **III.** *adj* **1.** SPORTS campeón, -ona **2.** *Brit, inf* estupendo, -a **IV.** *adv Brit, inf* de primera

championship ['tʃæmpiənʃɪp] *n* **1.** (*competition*) campeonato *m* **2.** *no pl* (*supporting*) defensa *f*

chance [tʃɑːns, *Am:* tʃæns] **I.** *n* **1.** *no pl* (*random force*) casualidad *f;* **a** ~ **encounter** un encuentro casual; ~ **was against me** la suerte me fue contraria; **a game of** ~ un juego de azar; **to leave nothing to** ~ no dejar nada al azar; **by** ~ por casualidad **2.** *no pl* (*likelihood*) probabilidad *f;* **there's not much of a** ~ **of my coming to the party** no es muy probable que vaya a la fiesta; **the** ~**s are that she's already gone** lo más probable es que ya se haya marchado; **to be in with a** ~ tener posibilidades; **to do sth on the off** ~ **that ...** hacer algo con la esperanza de que...; **to stand a** ~ **of doing sth** *inf* tener posibilidades de hacer algo; **to not stand a** ~ **with sb** tenerlo muy difícil con alguien; **it's a long** ~ es poco probable; **not a** ~**!** *inf* ¡ni en broma! **3.** (*opportunity*) oportunidad *f;* **the** ~ **of a lifetime** la oportunidad de la vida; **to give sb a** ~ (**to do sth**) dar a alguien una oportunidad (de hacer algo); **given half a** ~ **...** a la menor ocasión...; **to have the** ~ (**to do sth**) tener la ocasión (de hacer algo); **to jump at the** ~ no dejar escapar la oportunidad; **to miss one's** ~ (**to do sth**) desperdiciar la ocasión (de hacer algo); **to not have a** ~ **in hell** no tener ninguna posibilidad; **you must take your** ~**s when they arise** cuando se presenta una oportunidad debes aprovecharla **4.** (*hazard*) riesgo *m;* **to run a** ~ correr un riesgo; **to take a** ~ arriesgarse **II.** *vi* **to** ~ (**up**) **on sth/sb** encontrarse algo/a alguien por casualidad; **they** ~**ed to be in the restaurant just when I arrived** justamente estaban en el restaurante cuando llegué **III.** *vt* arriesgar; **to** ~ **one's luck** probar suerte; **to** ~ **it, to** ~ **one's arm** arriesgarse

chancellor ['tʃɑːnsələʳ, *Am:* 'tʃæn-] *n* **1.** POL (*head of state*) canciller *mf;* ~ **of the Exchequer** ministro, -a *m, f* de Hacienda; **Lord** ~ presidente *m* de la Cámara de los Lores **2.** (*head of a university*) rector(a) *m(f)*

chancellory ['tʃɑːnsəlri, *Am:* 'tʃæn-] <-ies> *n* cancillería *f*

chancy ['tʃɑːnsi, *Am:* 'tʃæn-] <-ier, -iest> *adj* arriesgado, -a

chandelier [ʃændə'lɪəʳ, *Am:* -'lɪr] *n* araña *f*

change ['tʃeɪndʒ] **I.** *n* **1.** (*alteration*) cambio *m;* **a** ~ **of clothes** una muda; **the** ~ (**of life**) *inf* la menopausia; **for a** ~ para variar; **that would make a** (**nice**) ~ no estaría mal hacer eso para variar; **to ring the** ~**s** *fig* hacer una cosa de todas las formas posibles **2.** *no pl* (*coins*) cambio *m,* sencillo *m AmL,* feria *f Méx;* **small** ~ calderilla *f inf;* **five pounds in** ~ cinco libras en monedas; **have you got** ~ **for** [*o* **of**] **a twenty-dollar bill?** ¿tienes cambio de 20 dólares?; **how much do you have in** ~**?** ¿cuánto dinero suelto llevas? **3.** *no pl* (*money returned*) cambio *m,* vuelto *m AmL;* **no** ~ **given** se ruega importe exacto **4.** *no pl* (*exact amount*) **to have the correct** ~ tener el importe exacto **5.** (*travel connection*) transbordo *m* **II.** *vi* **1.** (*alter*) cambiar; **to** ~ **into sth** convertirse en algo; **the traffic light** ~**d back to red** el semáforo se puso en rojo **2.** (*get off a train and board another*) hacer transbordo **3.** (*put on different clothes*) cambiarse **4.** (*change speed*) cambiar de marcha **III.** *vt* **1.** (*exchange*) cambiar; **to** ~ **places with sb** *fig* ponerse en el lugar de alguien; **to** ~ **sth/sb into sth** convertir algo/a alguien en algo **2.** (*give coins for bills*) **to** ~ **a dollar/a pound** cambiar un dólar/una libra **3.** (*get off a train and board another*) **to** ~ **trains** cambiar de tren **4.** (*alter speed*) **to** ~ **gear**(**s**) cambiar de marcha

◆**change down** *vi* reducir (de marcha)

◆**change up** *vi* aumentar (de marcha)

changeable ['tʃeɪndʒəbl] *adj* cambiante; (*weather*) inestable

changeover ['tʃeɪndʒəʊvəʳ, *Am:* -ˌoʊvɚ] *n* **1.** (*transition*) cambio *m* **2.** (*in a race*) relevo *m*

changing ['tʃeɪndʒɪŋ] *adj* cambiante; ~ **room** SPORTS vestuario *m;* (*in a shop*) probador *m*

channel ['tʃænl] **I.** *n* **1.** TV canal *m* **2.** (*waterway*) canal *m;* **The** (**English**) **Channel** el Canal de la Mancha; **irrigation** ~ acequia *f* **3.** (*means*) conducto *m;* **distribution** ~ canal de distribución; **through diplomatic** ~**s** por la vía diplomática **II.** <*Brit:* -ll-, *Am:* -l-> *vt* canalizar; *fig* encauzar

Channel Islands *n* Islas *fpl* Normandas

Channel Tunnel *n no pl* túnel *m* del Canal

C

de la Mancha

chant [tʃɑːnt, *Am:* tʃænt] **I.** *n* **1.** REL canto *m;* (*singing*) salmodia *f;* **gregorian** ~ canto gregoriano **2.** (*utterance*) consigna *f* **II.** *vi* **1.** REL (*intone*) salmodiar **2.** (*repeat*) gritar al unísono **III.** *vt* **1.** REL (*sing*) cantar; (*speak in a monotone*) salmodiar **2.** (*repeat*) repetir al unísono

chanterelle [ˌtʃæntəˈrel, *Am:* ˌtʃænt̬ə-] *n* mízcalo *m*

Chanukah [ˈhɑːnuːkɑː, *Am:* ˈhɑːnəkə] *n* REL Januká *m*

chaos [ˈkeɪɒs, *Am:* -ɑːs] *n no pl* caos *m inv*

Chaos Theory *n no pl* PHYS teoría *f* del caos

chaotic [keɪˈɒtɪk, *Am:* -ˈɑːt̬ɪk] *adj* caótico, -a

chap¹ [tʃæp] *n* (*fellow, friend*) tío *m*

chap² [tʃæp] <-pp-> **I.** *vi* agrietarse, pasparse *RíoPl* **II.** *vt* agrietar

chap. *n abbr of* **chapter** cap. *m*

chapel [ˈtʃæpl] *n* **1.** (*room*) capilla *f;* **funeral** ~ capilla ardiente **2.** *Brit* (*church*) templo *m* **3.** (*service*) servicio *m* religioso

chaperon(e) [ˈʃæpərəʊn, *Am:* -əroʊn] *n* carabina *f;* (*supervisor*) acompañante *f*

chaplain [ˈtʃæplɪn] *n* REL capellán *m*

chapter [ˈtʃæptəʳ, *Am:* -tɚ] *n* **1.** *a. fig* capítulo *m;* **to quote** ~ **and verse** citar textualmente **2.** *Am* (*local branch*) sección *f* **3.** *Brit, Aus, form* (*series of disasters*) **their trip was a** ~ **of accidents** sufrieron toda una serie de desgracias durante el viaje ▸**to give** ~ **and verse for sth** contar algo con pelos y señales

chapter-house *n* **1.** *Am* (*fraternity*) sala *f* capitular **2.** *Am* (*chapter*) sala *f* de reuniones

char [tʃɑːʳ, *Am:* tʃɑːr] <-rr-> **I.** *n* **1.** (*charwoman*) asistenta *f* **2.** (*charcoal*) carbón *m* de leña **II.** *vi* (*be burned black*) carbonizarse **III.** <-rr-> *vt* (*burn black*) carbonizar

character [ˈkærəktəʳ, *Am:* ˈkerəkt̬ɚ] *n* **1.** *no pl* (*qualities*) carácter *m;* **to be in/out of** ~ **with sb/sth** ser/no ser típico de alguien/algo **2.** (*moral integrity*) reputación *f;* ~ **reference** referencias *fpl;* **to be a bad** ~ tener mala reputación; **of dubious** ~ de dudosa reputación; **of irreprochable** ~ de reputación intachable **3.** (*unique person*) personaje *mf* **4.** (*representation*) personaje *m,* carácter *m Col, Méx;* **in the** ~ **of ...** en el papel de... **5.** TYPO carácter *m*

character actor *n* actor *m* de carácter

characteristic [ˌkærəktəˈrɪstɪk, *Am:* ˌker-] **I.** *n* característica *f* **II.** *adj* característico, -a; **with her** ~ **dignity** con la dignidad que le caracteriza

characteristically [ˌkærəktəˈrɪstɪkli, *Am:* ˌker-] *adv* característicamente

characterization [ˌkærəktəraɪˈzeɪʃən, *Am:* ˌkerəktɚɪ-] *n* caracterización *f*

characterize [ˈkærəktəraɪz, *Am:* ˈkerək-] *vt* **1.** *a.* CINE, THEAT caracterizar **2.** (*outline*) describir; **to** ~ **sth/sb as sth** calificar algo/a alguien de algo

charade [ʃəˈrɑːd, *Am:* -ˈreɪd] *n* **1.** *pl* GAMES charada *f* **2.** (*pretence*) farsa *f*

charcoal [ˈtʃɑːkəʊl, *Am:* ˈtʃɑːrkoʊl] **I.** *n no pl* **1.** (*fuel*) carbón *m* vegetal **2.** ART (*for drawing*) carboncillo *m,* carbonilla *f RíoPl;* **to draw in** ~ dibujar al carboncillo **II.** *adj* **1.** (*of charcoal*) ~ **drawing** dibujo *m* al carboncillo **2.** (*dark grey*) ~ **grey** gris marengo

charcoal-burner *n* quemador *m* de carbón

charge [tʃɑːdʒ, *Am:* tʃɑːrdʒ] **I.** *n* **1.** (*load*) carga *f* **2.** (*cost*) precio *m;* **overhead** ~**s** gastos *mpl* generales; **scale of** ~**s** tarifa *f* de precios; **travel** ~**s** gastos *mpl* de viaje; **at no extra** ~ sin cargo adicional; **free of** ~ gratis **3.** LAW (*accusation*) cargo *m;* **to bring** ~**s against sb** presentar cargos contra alguien **4.** (*attack: of a bull*) embestida *f;* MIL carga *f;* SPORTS ofensiva *f* **5.** *no pl* (*authority*) responsabilidad *f;* **in the** ~ **of sb** a cargo de alguien; **to be in** ~ **of sb/sth** tener algo/a alguien a su cargo; **who is in** ~ **here?** ¿quién es el responsable aquí? **6.** *no pl* ELEC carga *f* **II.** *vi* **1.** FIN cobrar **2.** (*attack*) **to** ~ **at sb/sth** arremeter contra alguien/algo; MIL cargar contra alguien/algo; ~**!** ¡al ataque! **3.** ELEC cargarse **III.** *vt* **1.** FIN (*ask a price*) cobrar; **to** ~ **sth to sb's account** cargar algo en la cuenta de alguien **2.** LAW (*accuse*) acusar; **she's been** ~**d with murder** se le acusa de asesinato; **the crimes with which he is** ~**d** los delitos que se le imputan *form* **3.** MIL cargar contra **4.** ELEC cargar

chargeable [ˈtʃɑːdʒəbl, *Am:* ˈtʃɑːr-] *adj* FIN ~ **to the customer** a cargo del cliente; **to be** ~ **to tax** estar sujeto a impuestos

charge account *n Am* cuenta *f* de crédito

charge card *n* tarjeta *f* de pago

charged *adj* cargado, -a

chargé d'affaires [ˌʃɑːʒeɪdæˈfeəʳ, *Am:* ʃɑːrʒeɪdəˈfer] <chargés d'affaires> *n* encargado, -a *m, f* de negocios

chariot [ˈtʃæriət] *n* HIST carro *m*

charisma [kəˈrɪzmə] *n no pl* carisma *m*

charitable [ˈtʃærɪtəbl, *Am:* ˈtʃer-] *adj* **1.** (*with money*) generoso, -a; (*with kindness*) bueno, -a **2.** (*concerning charity*) caritativo, -a; (*gifts, donation*) benéfico, -a; (*organisation*) de beneficencia

charity [ˈtʃærəti, *Am:* ˈtʃerət̬i] <-ies> *n* **1.** *no pl* (*generosity of spirit*) caridad *f* **2.** (*compassion*) compasión *f;* **to depend on** ~ depender de limosnas **3.** (*organization*) institución *f* benéfica

charity organisation *n* organización *f* benéfica

charity shop *n* tienda *f* de una organización benéfica

charlatan [ˈʃɑːlətən, *Am:* ˈʃɑːrlətən] *n* charlatán *m*

Charles [tʃɑːlz, *Am:* tʃɑːrlz] *n* Carlos *m;* ~ **the Fifth** (**of Spain**) Carlos V (de España)

Charlie [tʃɑːli, *Am:* tʃɑːrli] *n inf* Carlitos

charm [tʃɑːm, *Am:* tʃɑːrm] **I.** *n* **1.** (*quality*) encanto *m;* **she used all her** ~**s** usó todos sus encantos **2.** (*bangle*) colgante *m* **3.** (*talisman*) amuleto *m,* payé *m CSur* **II.** *vt* cautivar; **to** ~ **sb into doing sth** embelesar a alguien para que haga algo ►**to ~ the** **pants** **off** (**of**) **sb** *inf* llevarse a alguien de calle

charmed *adj* afortunado, -a; **to lead a ~ existence** tener una vida afotunada

charmer ['tʃɑːməʳ, *Am:* 'tʃɑːrmɚ] *n* persona *f* encantadora

charming ['tʃɑːmɪŋ, *Am:* 'tʃɑːr-] *adj* encantador(a); **oh, that's just ~!** ¡es de lo más encantador!

charred *adj* carbonizado, -a

chart [tʃɑːt, *Am:* tʃɑːrt] **I.** *n* **1.** (*display of information*) tabla *f;* **weather ~** mapa *m* meteorológico **2.** *pl* MUS **the ~s** la lista de éxitos; **to top the ~s** llegar al número uno de la lista **II.** *vt* **1.** *a. fig* trazar; **the map ~s the course of the river** el mapa reproduce gráficamente el curso del río **2.** (*observe*) seguir atentamente

charter ['tʃɑːtəʳ, *Am:* 'tʃɑːrt̬ɚ] **I.** *n* **1.** (*government statement*) estatutos *mpl* **2.** (*document stating aims*) carta *f* **3.** (*exclusive right*) privilegio *m* **4.** (*founding document*) escritura *f* de constitución **5.** *no pl* COM fletamiento *m* **6.** COM contrato *m* de fletamento **II.** *vt* **1.** (*sign founding papers*) estatuir **2.** COM fletar

charter company <-ies> *n* compañía *f* de vuelos chárter

chartered ['tʃɑːtəd, *Am:* 'tʃɑːrt̬ɚd] *adj* **1.** COM fletado, -a **2.** *Brit, Aus* (*qualified*) jurado, -a

charterer ['tʃɑːtərəʳ, *Am:* 'tʃɑːrt̬ɚɚ] *n* COM fletador *m*

charter flight *n* vuelo *m* chárter

chase [tʃeɪs] **I.** *n* **1.** (*pursual*) persecución *f;* **to give ~ to sb** salir en busca de alguien **2.** (*hunt*) *a. fig* caza *f* **II.** *vi* (*rollick about*) **they ~ed after her** fueron en busca de ella **III.** *vt* **1.** (*pursue: dreams*) perseguir; (*women*) andar detrás de **2.** (*scare away*) **to ~ away sth** ahuyentar algo **3.** *Brit, inf* (*follow up on*) **to ~ sb** (**up**) **to do sth** recordar a alguien que haga algo

chasm ['kæzəm] *n* **1.** (*deep cleft*) abismo *m* **2.** (*omission*) hueco *m* **3.** *fig* (*great discrepancy*) diferencias *fpl;* **to bridge a ~** salvar las diferencias

chassis ['ʃæsi] *n inv* chasis *m inv*

chaste [tʃeɪst] *adj form* casto, -a

chasten ['tʃeɪsn] *vt* **1.** (*admonish*) reprender **2.** (*punish*) castigar

chastise [tʃæ'staɪz, *Am:* 'tʃæstaɪz] *vt* reprender

chastity ['tʃæstəti, *Am:* -tət̬i] *n no pl* castidad *f;* **vow of ~** voto *m* de castidad

chat [tʃæt] **I.** *n* **1.** charla *f* **2.** *no pl* (*gossip*) parloteo *m* **II.** *vi* <-tt-> **1.** (*informally*) charlar, versar *AmC* **2.** (*animatedly*) **to ~ away** estar de cháchara **3.** (*idly*) hablar sin ton ni son

chateau ['ʃætəʊ, *Am:* ʃæt'oʊ] *n* casa *f* señorial

chat room *n* foro *m* de chat **chat show** *n* programa *m* de entrevistas

chatter ['tʃætəʳ, *Am:* 'tʃæt̬ɚ] **I.** *n no pl* cháchara *f;* (*of birds*) cotorreo *m* **II.** *vi* **1.** (*converse superficially*) **to ~ about sth** charlar sobre algo; **they ~ed about everything and nothing** chacharearon de todo y de nada **2.** (*make clacking noises: machines*) tabletear; (*birds*) cotorrear; (*teeth*) castañear

chatty ['tʃæti, *Am:* 'tʃæt̬-] <-ier, -iest> *adj inf* **1.** (*friendly person*) hablador(a) **2.** LIT (*informal*) informal; (*style*) llano, -a

chauffeur ['ʃəʊfəʳ, *Am:* 'ʃɑːfɚ] **I.** *n* chófer *mf* **II.** *vt* **to ~ sb around** *a. fig* hacer de chófer de alguien

chauvinism ['ʃəʊvɪnɪzəm, *Am:* 'ʃoʊ-] *n no pl* chovinismo *m*

chauvinist *n* chovinista *mf*

chauvinistic [ˌʃəʊvɪ'nɪstɪk, *Am:* ʃoʊ-] *adj* chovinista

cheap [tʃiːp] *adj* **1.** (*inexpensive*) barato, -a; (*ticket*) económico, -a; **dirt ~** tirado, -a **2.** (*exploited*) **~ labour** mano *f* de obra barata **3.** (*worthless*) regalado, -a **4.** (*inexpensive but bad quality*) ordinario, -a **5.** (*miserly*) chapucero, -a **6.** (*sexually easy*) fácil ►**~ and** **cheerful** *Brit, Aus, inf* bueno, bonito y barato; **~ and** **nasty** *inf* ordinario, -a; **on** **the ~** *inf* barato; **to buy something on the ~** *inf* comprar algo por poco dinero

cheapen ['tʃiːpən] *vt* **1.** (*lower price of*) rebajar **2.** (*reduce morally*) degradar

cheap labour *n* mano *f* de obra barata

cheaply *adv* de forma barata

cheapness ['tʃiːpnɪs] *n no pl* **1.** (*low price*) baratura *f* **2.** (*vulgarity*) ordinariez *f*

cheapskate ['tʃiːpˌskeɪt] *inf* **I.** *n* tacaño, -a *m, f* **II.** *adj* tacaño, -a, agarrado, -a

cheat [tʃiːt] **I.** *n* **1.** (*dishonest person*) estafador(a) *m(f)* **2.** (*trick*) trampa *f* **II.** *vi* **to ~ at sth** hacer trampa en algo; **to ~ in a test** copiar en un examen **III.** *vt* engañar; **to ~ the taxman** timar a Hacienda

check [tʃek] **I.** *n* **1.** (*inspection*) control *m;* **security ~** control de seguridad; **to keep sth in ~** mantener algo bajo control **2.** MED chequeo *m* **3.** (*a look*) vistazo *m* **4.** (*search for information*) verificación *f;* **to run a ~** realizar una inspección **5.** *Am* (*deposit receipt*) resguardo *m* **6.** (*textile*) tela *f* de cuadros **7.** GAMES jaque *m;* **to be in ~** estar en jaque **8.** *Am* (*tick*) marca *f,* visto *m* **9.** *Am* cheque *m;* **open ~** cheque al portador; **to make out a blank ~** hacer un cheque en blanco; *fig* dar carta blanca; **to pay by ~** pagar con cheque **10.** *Am, Scot* (*bill*) cuenta *f* **II.** *adj* a cuadros **III.** *vt* **1.** (*inspect for problems*) comprobar, chequear *AmL* **2.** (*prevent*) frenar **3.** (*temporarily deposit*) dejar en consigna; AVIAT facturar **4.** GAMES dar jaque a **5.** *Am* (*make a mark*) marcar **IV.** *vi* **1.** (*examine*) revisar **2.** (*ask*) consultar **3.** *Am* (*be in accordance with*) coincidir

◆**check in** *vi* **1.** (*at airport*) facturar **2.** (*at hotel*) registrarse

◆**check off** *vt* verificar (haciendo marcas)

◆**check out** **I.** *vi* **to ~ of a room** dejar libre

una habitación **II.** *vt Am* investigar
◆check up on *vt* controlar; (*person*) hacer averiguaciones sobre
checkbook ['tʃek,bʊk] *n Am* talonario *m* de cheques
checked *adj* a cuadros
checkerboard ['tʃekəʳ,bɔːd, *Am:* -ɚ,bɔːrd] *n Am* (*chessboard for draughts*) tablero *m* de ajedrez
checkered ['tʃekəʳd, *Am:* -ɚd] *adj Am* **1.** (*patterned with squares*) a cuadros **2.** (*inconsistent*) accidentado, -a; **to have a ~ past** tener un pasado con altibajos
checkers ['tʃekəz, *Am:* -ɚz] *n + sing vb* GAMES damas *fpl*
check-in ['tʃekɪn] *n* facturación *f*
check-in counter *n,* **check-in desk** *n* mostrador *m* de facturación
checking account *n Am* cuenta *f* corriente
check-in time *n* hora *f* de facturación
checklist ['tʃeklɪst] *n* lista *f* **checkmate I.** *n no pl* **1.** GAMES jaque *m* mate; **to be ~** estar en jaque mate **2.** (*defeat*) fracaso *m* **II.** *vt* **1.** GAMES dar jaque mate a **2.** (*win a victory over*) ganar
checkout ['tʃekaʊt] *n* caja *f*
checkout counter *n* caja *f*
checkpoint ['tʃekpɔɪnt] *n* punto *m* de control **check room** *n Am* **1.** (*for coats*) guardarropa *m* **2.** (*for luggage*) consigna *f*
checkup ['tʃekʌp] *n* comprobación *f;* MED chequeo *m* médico
cheddar ['tʃedəʳ, *Am:* -ɚ] *n no pl* queso *m* de cheddar
cheek [tʃiːk] *n* **1.** (*soft skin connecting jaws*) mejilla *f* **2.** *no pl* (*impertinence*) descaro *m,* empaque *m AmL;* **to have a ~** ser un caradura; **to have the ~ to do sth** tener la caradura de hacer algo ►**to go ~ by jowl** ir codo con codo; **to turn the other ~** poner la otra mejilla
cheekbone ['tʃiːkbəʊn, *Am:* -boʊn] *n* pómulo *m*
cheeky ['tʃiːki] <-ier, -iest> *adj* descarado, -a, fregado, -a *AmL;* **to be ~ to sb** ser descarado con alguien
cheep [tʃiːp] **I.** *n* (*of bird*) pío *m;* **to not get a ~ out of sb** no sacarle ni una palabra a alguien; **to not hear a ~ out of sb** no decir alguien esta boca es mía **II.** *vi* piar
cheer [tʃɪəʳ, *Am:* tʃɪr] **I.** *n* **1.** (*exuberant shout*) ovación *f;* **three ~s for the champion!** ¡tres hurras por el campeón!; **to give a ~** vitorear **2.** *no pl* (*joy*) alegría *f;* **to be of good ~** estar animado **II.** *interj pl* **1.** (*said when drinking*) salud **2.** *Brit* (*thanks*) gracias **III.** *vi* **to ~ for sb** animar a alguien
cheerful ['tʃɪəfʊl, *Am:* 'tʃɪr-] *adj* **1.** (*happy*) alegre; (*with a positive attitude*) jovial **2.** (*colour*) vivo, -a **3.** (*encouraging*) alentador(a)
cheerfulness *n no pl* alegría *f*
cheeriness *n no pl* **1.** (*happiness*) alegría *f* **2.** (*brightness*) jovialidad *f*
cheering I. *n no pl* aplausos *mpl* **II.** *adj* alentador(a)
cheerio [,tʃɪərɪ'əʊ, *Am:* ,tʃɪrɪ'oʊ] *interj Brit, inf* hasta luego, chao *AmL*
cheerleader ['tʃɪə,liːdəʳ, *Am:* 'tʃɪr,liːdɚ] *n Am* animadora *f*

> Con el nombre de **cheerleaders** se designa en los EE.UU. a aquellas chicas jóvenes que animan a un equipo deportivo. Su labor consiste fundamentalmente en guiar las canciones y gritos de ánimo de los fans y entretener al público asistente con pequeñas coreografías en las que utilizan los característicos **pompoms**. Su vestuario suele consistir en un vestido corto o falda y blusa además de calcetines y zapatos de cuero, todo ello en los colores de su equipo o colegio.

cheery ['tʃɪəri, *Am:* 'tʃɪr-] <-ier, -iest> *adj* alegre
cheese [tʃiːz] *n no pl* queso *m;* **hard ~** queso curado; **melted ~** queso fundido ►**hard ~** *inf* mala pata; **say ~!** ¡decid patata!
cheeseburger ['tʃiːz,bɜːgəʳ, *Am:* -,bɜːrgɚ] *n* hamburguesa *f* con queso
cheesecake ['tʃiːzkeɪk] *n* pastel *m* de queso
cheesecloth ['tʃiːzklɒθ, *Am:* -klɑːθ] <-es> *n no pl* estopilla *f*
cheesed off *adj Brit, Aus, inf* **to be ~ with sb** estar hasta la coronilla de alguien
cheeseparing ['tʃiːz,peərɪŋ, *Am:* -,perɪŋ] *n no pl* tacaño, -a *m, f*
cheesy ['tʃiːzi] <-ier, -iest> *adj* **1.** (*like cheese*) como queso **2.** *inf* (*cheap and shoddy*) chungo, -a
cheetah ['tʃiːtə, *Am:* -t̬ə] *n* guepardo *m*
chef [ʃef] *n* jefe, -a *m, f* de cocina, chef *mf*
chemical ['kemɪkl] **I.** *n* (*atoms*) sustancia *f* química; (*additive*) aditivo *m* **II.** *adj* químico, -a
chemist ['kemɪst] *n* **1.** (*person*) químico, -a *m, f* **2.** *Brit, Aus* (*store*) farmacia *f;* (*person*) farmacéutico, -a *m, f*
chemistry ['kemɪstri] *n no pl* química *f*
chemotherapy [,kiːmə'θerəpi, *Am:* ,kiː-moʊ-] *n no pl* quimioterapia *f;* **to undergo ~** seguir un tratamiento de quimioterapia
cheque [tʃek] *n Brit, Aus s.* **check**
chequeaccount *n* cuenta *f* corriente
cheque book *n Brit, Aus* talonario *m* de cheques
chequered ['tʃekəd, *Am:* -ɚd] *adj Brit, Aus s.* **checkered**
cherish ['tʃerɪʃ] *vt* (*hold dear*) apreciar; (*remember fondly*) recordar
cheroot [ʃə'ruːt] *n* puro *m* (*cortado por ambos extremos*)
cherry ['tʃeri] <-ies> **I.** *n* **1.** (*fruit*) cereza *f* **2.** (*tree*) cerezo *m* **II.** *adj* (de) color rojo cereza
cherry-blossom *n* flor *f* de cerezo **cherry brandy** *n no pl* aguardiente *m* de cerezas
cherub ['tʃerəb] <-s *o* -im> *n* querubín *m*
chervil ['tʃɜːvɪl, *Am:* 'tʃɜːr-] *n no pl* perifollo *m*

chess [tʃes] *n no pl* ajedrez *m*
chessboard ['tʃesbɔːd, *Am:* -bɔːrd] *n* tablero *m* de ajedrez
chessman ['tʃesmæn] <-men> *n* pieza *f* de ajedrez
chest [tʃest] *n* **1.** (*human torso*) pecho *m;* ~ **pains** dolores *mpl* pectorales; **to fold one's arms across one's** ~ cruzarse de brazos **2.** (*breasts*) senos *mpl* **3.** (*trunk*) baúl *m,* petaca *f AmL;* **medicine** ~ botiquín *m* ►**to get sth off one's** ~ desahogarse confesando algo
chestnut ['tʃesnʌt] **I.** *n* **1.** (*fruit*) castaña *f* **2.** (*joke*) chiste *m* viejo **3.** (*horse*) caballo *m* castaño ►**to pull sb's ~s out of the fire** sacarle a alguien las castañas del fuego **II.** *adj* castaño, -a
chesty ['tʃesti] <-ier, -iest> *adj* pectoral; ~ **cough** tos *f* de pecho; **to get** ~ *Brit* coger un resfriado (de pecho)
chew [tʃuː] **I.** *n* **1.** (*bite*) bocado *m* **2.** (*candy*) mascada *f* **II.** *vt* masticar
chewing gum ['tʃuːɪŋgʌm] *n no pl* chicle *m*
chewy ['tʃuːi] <-ier, -iest> *adj* masticable; (*meat*) duro, -a
chic [ʃiːk] **I.** *n* chic *m* **II.** *adj* chic, a la moda
chicane [ʃɪ'kein] *n* chicane *f*
chicanery [ʃɪ'keɪnəri] *n no pl* artimaña *f*
chick [tʃɪk] *n* **1.** (*baby chicken*) pollito, -a *m, f* **2.** (*young bird*) polluelo, -a *m, f* **3.** *inf* (*young woman*) tía *f*
chicken ['tʃɪkɪn] *n* **1.** (*farm bird*) pollo, -a *m, f* **2.** *no pl* (*meat*) carne *f* de pollo; **fried/roasted** ~ pollo frito/asado; **grilled** ~ pollo a la brasa **3.** *inf* (*person*) gallina *m,* rajado *m,* rajón, -ona *m, f Cuba, Méx* ►**it's a** ~ **and egg situation** es como aquello de la gallina y el huevo; **to not be a (spring)** ~ ya no ser ningún crío
chicken broth *n no pl* sopa *f* de pollo **chicken farm** *n* granja *f* de pollos **chickenfeed** *n no pl* **1.** (*food*) pienso *m* **2.** (*small amount of money*) calderilla *f* **chicken-hearted** *adj* cobarde **chickenpox** *n no pl* varicela *f* **chicken-run** *n* gallinero *m*
chickpea ['tʃɪkpiː] *n* garbanzo *m*
chicory ['tʃɪkəri] *n no pl* **1.** BOT endivia *f,* endibia *f* **2.** (*in coffee*) achicoria *f,* radicheta *f Arg, Urug*
chief [tʃiːf] **I.** *n* **1.** (*boss*) jefe, -a *m, f* **2.** (*of a tribe*) jerarca *m* **II.** *adj* **1.** (*top*) primero, -a **2.** (*major*) principal
chief clerk *n* encargado, -a *m, f* **chief editor** *n* editor(a) *m(f)* jefe **chief executive** *n,* **chief executive officer** *n Am* director(a) *m(f)* general **chief justice** *n* presidente, -a *m, f* del Tribunal Supremo
chiefly *adv* principalmente
chieftain ['tʃiːftən] *n* cacique *m*
chiffon ['ʃɪfɒn, *Am:* ʃɪ'fɑːn] *n no pl* chifón *m,* chiffon *m*
chilblain ['tʃɪlbleɪn] *n* sabañón *m*
child [tʃaɪld] <children> *pl n* **1.** (*person who's not fully grown*) niño, -a *m, f;* **unborn** ~ feto *m* **2.** (*offspring*) hijo, -a *m, f;* **illegitimate** ~ hijo bastardo; **to be a** ~ **of the eighties** *fig* ser un producto de los (años) ochenta ►**spare the rod and spoil the** ~ *prov* quien bien te quiere te hará llorar *prov*
child abuse ['tʃaildəbjuːs] *n no pl* abuso *m* (sexual) de los niños **childbearing** *n no pl* maternidad *f;* **women of** ~ **age** mujeres *fpl* en edad de tener hijos **child benefit** *n Brit* subvención *f* familiar por hijos **childbirth** *n no pl* parto *m,* parición *f AmL* **childcare** *n no pl* cuidado *m* de los niños **childhood** *n no pl* infancia *f*
childish ['tʃaɪldɪʃ] *adj pej* infantil, achiquillado, -a *Méx;* **don't be** ~**!** ¡no seas niño!
childless ['tʃaɪldlɪs] *adj* sin hijos
childlike ['tʃaɪldlaɪk] *adj* infantil
childminder ['tʃaɪldˌmaɪndəʳ, *Am:* -dɚ] *n Brit* canguro *mf* **childproof** *adj* a prueba de niños; ~ **lock** cerradura *f* de seguridad para niños
children ['tʃɪldrən] *n pl of* **child**
child-resistant *adj form* a prueba de niños
child's play *n fig* juego *m* de niños
child support *n no pl* subsidio *m* de maternidad
Chile ['tʃɪli] *n* Chile *m*
Chilean ['tʃɪlɪən, *Am:* tʃɪ'lɪː-] **I.** *adj* chileno, -a **II.** *n* chileno, -a *m, f*
chili ['tʃɪli] <-es> *n Am s.* **chilli**
chill [tʃɪl] **I.** *n* **1.** (*coldness*) frío *m;* **to catch a** ~ resfriarse; **to take the** ~ **off of something** calentar algo un poco **2.** (*shiver*) escalofrío *m;* **to send a** ~ **down someone's spine** hacer entrar escalofríos a alguien **II.** *adj* (*cold*) frío, -a; (*frightening*) estremecedor(a) **III.** *vt* enfriar; **to be ~ed to the bone** estar como un témpano
chilli ['tʃɪli] <-es> *n* chile *m,* ají *m* (picante) *AmS, Ant*
chill(i)ness *n no pl* frío *m; fig* frialdad *f*
chilling *adj* terrorífico, -a
chilly ['tʃɪli] <-ier, -iest> *adj a. fig* frío, -a; **to feel** ~ tener frío
chime [tʃaɪm] **I.** *n* repique *m;* **wind ~s** carillón *m* **II.** *vi* repicar **III.** *vt* **to** ~ **eleven** dar las once
chimney ['tʃɪmni] *n* **1.** (*in a building*) chimenea *f,* tronera *f Méx* **2.** (*in rock*) cañón *m*
chimneypot *n* cañón *m* de la chimenea **chimneystack** *n Brit* fuste *m* de chimenea **chimneysweep** *n,* **chimneysweeper** *n a.* HIST deshollinador(a) *m(f)*
chimpanzee [ˌtʃɪmpæn'ziː, *Am:* tʃɪm'pænziː] *n* chimpancé *m*
chin ['tʃɪn] *n* barbilla *f* ►**to keep one's** ~ **up** no desanimarse
china ['tʃaɪnə] *n no pl* **1.** (*porcelain*) porcelana *f* **2.** (*crockery*) vajilla *f*
China ['tʃaɪnə] *n* China *f*
chinchilla [tʃɪn'tʃɪlə] *n* chinchilla *f*
Chinese [tʃaɪ'niːz] **I.** *adj* chino, -a **II.** *n*

1. (*person*) chino, -a *m, f* 2. LING chino *m*
Chinese cabbage *n* col *f* china **Chinese lantern** *n* farolillo *m* **Chinese restaurant** *n* restaurante *m* chino
chink [tʃɪŋk] I. *n* 1. (*thin opening*) hendidura *f*; **the ~ in sb's armour** *fig* el punto débil de alguien 2. (*clinking noise*) tintineo *m* II. *vi* tintinear
chintz [tʃɪnts] *n no pl* chintz *m*
chip [tʃɪp] I. *n* 1. (*flake*) pedazo *m*; (*stone*) lasca *f*; (*wood*) astilla *f* 2. *pl, Brit* (*French fries*) patatas *fpl* fritas, papas *fpl* fritas *AmL*; *Am* (*crisp potato snack*) patatas *fpl* fritas (de churrería), papas *fpl* fritas (de churrería) *AmL* 3. INFOR chip *m* 4. (*money token for gambling*) ficha *f*; **bargaining ~** moneda *f* de cambio ►**he's a ~ off the old block** *inf* de tal palo tal astilla; **to have a ~ on one's shoulder** *inf* estar resentido; **when the ~s are down** *Brit, inf* a la hora de la verdad II. *vt* <-pp-> desportillar III. *vi* <-pp-> desportillarse
chip-basket *n Brit* envase *m* de patatas
chipmunk ['tʃɪpmʌŋk] *n* ardilla *f* listada
chip-pan *n Brit* freidora *f*
chipped ['tʃɪpt] *adj* desportillado, -a
chipping ['tʃɪpɪŋ] *n pl, Brit* gravilla *f*
chippy ['tʃɪpi] <-ies> *n* 1. *Brit, inf* tienda *f* de comida rápida (*donde se venden fritos*) 2. *Am, inf* (*prostitute*) fulana *f*
chiropodist [kɪ'rɒpədɪst, *Am:* kɪ'rɑːpə-] *n* podólogo, -a *m, f*
chiropody [kɪ'rɒpədi, *Am:* kɪ'rɑːpə-] *n no pl* podología *f*
chiropractic ['kaɪrəpræktɪk] *n no pl* quiropráctica *f*
chiropractor ['kaɪrəpræktəʳ, *Am:* ˌkaɪroʊpræktɚ] *n* quiropráctico, -a *m, f*
chirpy ['tʃɜːpi, *Am:* 'tʃɜːr-] <-ier, -iest> *adj* animado, -a
chirrup ['tʃɪrəp], **chirp** I. *n* gorjeo *m* II. *vi* gorjear III. *vt* decir alegremente
chisel ['tʃɪzl] I. *n* cincel *m* II. <-ll-, *Am* -l-> *vt* 1. (*cut*) esculpir 2. *Am, inf* (*get by trickery*) estafar
chit [tʃɪt] *n* 1. (*note*) nota *f* 2. (*voucher*) vale *m*
chit-chat ['tʃɪtˌtʃæt] I. *n no pl, inf* cháchara *f* II. *vi inf* **to ~ about sth** estar de palique sobre algo
chivalrous ['ʃɪvlrəs] *adj* caballeroso, -a
chivalry ['ʃɪvlri] *n no pl* 1. (*gallant behavior*) caballerosidad *f* 2. HIST caballería *f*
chives [tʃaɪvz] *npl* cebollinos *mpl*
chloride ['klɔːraɪd] *n no pl* cloruro *m*
chlorinate ['klɔːrɪneɪt] *vt* clorar
chlorine ['klɔːriːn] *n no pl* cloro *m*
chlorofluorocarbon ['klɔːrəˌfluːərəˌkɑːbən, *Am:* ˌklɔːroʊˌflɔːroʊˌkɑːr-] *n* clorofluorocarbono *m*
chloroform ['klɒrəfɔːm, *Am:* 'klɔːrəfɔːrm] I. *n no pl* cloroformo *m* II. *vt* cloroformizar
chlorophyll ['klɒrəfɪl, *Am:* 'klɔːrə-] *n no pl* clorofila *f*
chlorous ['klɔːrəs] *adj* cloroso, -a
choc-ice ['tʃɒkˌaɪs, *Am:* 'tʃɑːk-] *n Brit* bombón *m* helado
chock [tʃɒk, *Am:* 'tʃɑːk] *n* cuña *f*
chock-a-block [ˌtʃɒkə'blɒk, *Am:* ˌtʃɑːkə'blɑːk] *adj* ~ **with people** abarrotado de gente **chock-full** *adj* **to be ~ of sth** estar abarrotado de algo; **~ of calories** cargado de calorías
chocolate ['tʃɒklət, *Am:* 'tʃɑːk-] *n* 1. *no pl* (*sweet*) chocolate *m*; **dark ~** chocolate negro; **a bar of ~** una tableta de chocolate 2. (*piece of chocolate candy*) bombón *m*
choice ['tʃɔɪs] I. *n* 1. *no pl* (*possibility of selection*) elección *f*; **to make a ~** elegir; **to have no ~** no tener alternativa; **she didn't have much ~** no tenía muchas opciones 2. *no pl* (*selection*) selección *f*; **a wide ~ of sth** un amplio surtido de algo 3. (*selected person or thing*) preferencia *f* II. *adj* 1. (*top quality*) selecto, -a 2. *fig* (*bitingly angry*) furioso, -a
choir ['kwaɪəʳ, *Am:* 'kwaɪɚ] *n* coro *m*
choirmaster ['kwaɪəˌmɑːstəʳ, *Am:* 'kwaɪɚˌmæstɚ] *n* director(a) *m(f)* de coro **choir stalls** *npl* coro *m*
choke [tʃəʊk, *Am:* tʃoʊk] I. *vi* sofocarse; **to ~ to death** morir asfixiado II. *n* AUTO estárter *m* III. *vt* 1. (*deprive of air*) estrangular 2. (*block*) obstruir; **~d with leaves** atascado de hojas
◆**choke back** *vt* ahogar; **to ~ tears** contener las lágrimas
◆**choke down** *vt* ahogar
◆**choke off** *vt* cortar; **to choke sb off** *inf* echar un rapapolvo a alguien
◆**choke up** *vt* obstruir
choker ['tʃəʊkəʳ, *Am:* 'tʃoʊkɚ] *n* gargantilla *f*
cholera ['kɒlərə, *Am:* 'kɑːlɚ-] *n no pl* cólera *m*
choleric ['kɒlərɪk, *Am:* 'kɑːlɚ-] *adj* colérico, -a
cholesterol [kə'lestərɒl, *Am:* kə'lestərɑːl] *n no pl* colesterol *m*
cholesterol level *n no pl* nivel *m* de colesterol
choose [tʃuːz] <chose, chosen> I. *vt* elegir; (*prefer*) preferir, decidirse por II. *vi* elegir; **to have to ~ between** tener que elegir entre; **I cannot ~ but** no tengo más remedio que
choos(e)y ['tʃuːzi] <-ier, -iest> *adj inf* quisquilloso, -a
chop [tʃɒp, *Am:* tʃɑːp] I. *vt* <-pp-> cortar; (*wood*) partir; (*meat*) picar II. *vi* <-pp-> **to ~ and change** (*vacillate*) cambiar constantemente de opinión; (*switch jobs*) cambiar constantemente de trabajo III. *n* 1. GASTR chuleta *f* 2. (*blow*) golpe *m*; **to get the ~** *inf* ser despedido
◆**chop away** *vt* cortar
◆**chop down** *vt* talar
◆**chop off** I. *vt* tronchar II. *vi* (*wind*) cambiar repentinamente de dirección
chop-chop [ˌtʃɒp'tʃɒp, *Am:* ˌtʃɑːp'tʃɑːp]

interj inf ¡vamos, de prisa!
chopper ['tʃɒpəʳ, *Am:* 'tʃɑːpɚ] *n* **1.** (*tool*) hacha *f* **2.** *inf* AVIAT helicóptero *m*
chopping block *n* tajo *m* **chopping board** *n* tabla *f* de cortar
choppy ['tʃɒpi, *Am:* 'tʃɑːpi] <-ier, -iest> *adj* **1.** NAUT agitado, -a **2.** (*words, sentences*) entrecortado, -a
chopsticks ['tʃɒpstɪks, *Am:* 'tʃɑːp-] *npl* palillos *mpl* (para comer comida oriental)
chop suey [ˌtʃɒp'suːi, *Am:* ˌtʃɑːp-] *n* chop suey *m*
choral ['kɔːrəl] *adj* coral; ~ **society** coral *f*
chord ['kɔːd, *Am:* 'kɔːrd] *n* MUS acorde *m* ►**to strike a** ~ (**with sb**) tocar la fibra sensible (a alguien)
chore [tʃɔːʳ, *Am:* tʃɔːr] *n* **1.** (*routine job*) tarea *f;* **household** ~**s** quehaceres *mpl* domésticos **2.** (*tedious task*) lata *f*
choreograph ['kɒriəgrɑːf, *Am:* 'kɔːriəgræf] *vi, vt* coreografiar
choreographer [ˌkɒrɪ'ɒgrəfəʳ, *Am:* ˌkɔːrɪ'ɑːgrəfɚ] *n* coreógrafo, -a *m, f*
choreography [ˌkɒrɪ'ɒgrəfi, *Am:* ˌkɔːrɪ'ɑːgrə-] *n no pl* coreografía *f*
chorister ['kɒrɪstəʳ, *Am:* 'kɔːrɪstɚ] *n* corista *mf*
chorus ['kɔːrəs, *Am:* 'kɔːrəs] **I.** <-es> *n* **1.** (*refrain*) estribillo *m;* **to join in the** ~ cantar el estribillo **2.** + *sing/pl vb* (*group of singers*) coral *f* **3.** + *sing/pl vb* (*supporting singers*) coro *m;* ~ **girl** corista *f;* **in** ~ a coro **II.** *vi, vt* corear
chose [tʃəʊz, *Am:* tʃoʊz] *pt of* **choose**
chosen ['tʃəʊzn, *Am:* 'tʃoʊ-] *pp of* **choose**
chow [tʃaʊ] *n inf* (*food*) manduca *f,* lata *f Col,* morfi *m CSur*
chow chow *n* chow-chow *mf*
chowder ['tʃaʊdəʳ, *Am:* -dɚ] *n no pl sopa espesa o guiso de pescado o verduras*
Christ [kraɪst] **I.** *n* Cristo *m* **II.** *interj inf* ¡Dios!, ¡Jesús!; **for** ~**'s sake** ¡por amor de Dios!
christen ['krɪsən] *vt* **1.** (*baptise*) bautizar **2.** (*give name to*) **they** ~**ed their second child Sara** a su segundo bebé le pusieron Sara **3.** (*use for first time*) estrenar
Christendom ['krɪsəndəm] *n no pl* HIST cristiandad *f*
christening ['krɪsənɪŋ] *n,* **christening ceremony** *n* bautismo *m,* bautizo *m*
Christian ['krɪstʃən] **I.** *n* cristiano, -a *m, f* **II.** *adj* **1.** (*of Christ's teachings*) cristiano, -a **2.** (*kind*) amable **3.** (*decent*) honrado, -a
Christian burial *n* cristiana sepultura *f*
Christianity [ˌkrɪstɪ'ænəti, *Am:* -tʃɪ'ænəṭi] *n no pl* cristianismo *m*
Christianize ['krɪstʃənaɪz] *vt* cristianizar
Christian name *n Brit* nombre *m* de pila
Christmas ['krɪstməs, *Am:* 'krɪs-] <-es *o* -ses> *n no pl* Navidad *f;* **at** ~ en Navidad; **Merry** [*o* **Happy**] ~**!** ¡Feliz Navidad!; **Father** ~ Papá *m* Noel, viejo *m* Pascuero *Chile*

En Gran Bretaña el envío de **Christmas cards** (postales de Navidad) comienza a principios del mes de diciembre. Esta costumbre surgió a mediados del siglo XIX. Otra de las tradiciones navideñas británicas consiste en colgar los **Christmas stockings** (unos grandes calcetines) o fundas de almohadas para que aparezcan llenas de regalos a la mañana siguiente. Este ritual navideño es llevado a cabo por los niños durante el **Christmas Eve** (día de Nochebuena) que es día laborable en Gran Bretaña. La comida tradicional del **Christmas Day** consiste en pavo acompañado de patatas salteadas y de postre **Christmas pudding** o **plum pudding** que es un pastel hecho al vapor con diversos tipos de pasas, entre otras, pasas sultanas y de Corinto. Los **Christmas crackers** (otro invento británico de mediados del siglo XIX) son unos pequeños cilindros de cartón muy decorados que contienen en su interior un pequeño regalo, un proverbio y una corona de papel. Este cilindro de cartón se abre durante la comida de Navidad tirando dos personas de él simultáneamente, una por por cada lado.

Christmas carol *n* villancico *m* **Christmas cracker** *n* sorpresa *f* de Navidad **Christmas Day** *n* día *m* de Navidad, día *m* de Pascua *Perú, Chile* **Christmas Eve** *n* Nochebuena *f* **Christmas pudding** *n* pudín *m* de Navidad (con frutas confitadas y coñac) **Christmas tree** *n* árbol *m* de Navidad
Christopher ['krɪstəfəʳ, *Am:* -fɚ] *n* Cristóbal *m;* ~ **Columbus** HIST Cristóbal Colón
chromatic [krəʊ'mætɪk, *Am:* kroʊ'mæṭɪk] *adj* cromático, -a
chrome [krəʊm, *Am:* kroʊm] *n no pl* cromo *m*
chrome-plated *adj* cromado, -a
chromosome ['krəʊməsəʊm, *Am:* 'kroʊməsoʊm] *n* cromosoma *m*
chronic ['krɒnɪk, *Am:* 'krɑːnɪk] *adj* **1.** (*lasting a long time*) crónico, -a **2.** (*habitual: liar*) empedernido, -a **3.** *Brit, Aus, inf* (*extremely bad*) malísimo, -a, terrible
chronicle ['krɒnɪkl, *Am:* 'krɑːnɪ-] **I.** *vt* registrar **II.** *n* crónica *f*
chronicler ['krɒnɪkləʳ, *Am:* 'krɑːnɪklɚ] *n* cronista *mf*
chronological [ˌkrɒnə'lɒdʒɪkl, *Am:* ˌkrɑːnə'lɑːdʒɪ-] *adj* cronológico, -a; **in** ~ **order** en orden cronológico
chronology [krə'nɒlədʒi, *Am:* krə'nɑːlə-] *n no pl* cronología *f*
chrysalis ['krɪsəlɪs] <-es> *n* crisálida *f*
chrysanthemum [krɪ'sænθəməm] *n* crisantemo *m*
chubby ['tʃʌbi] <-ier, -iest> *adj* (*fingers, legs, face*) regordete, -a; (*child*) gordinflón,

-ona, rechoncho, -a, tacuaco, -a *Chile*

chuck [tʃʌk] **I.** *n* **1.** (*playful touch*) palmadita *f* **2.** (*device for holding tool*) portabrocas *m inv* **3.** (*beef cut*) *corte de carne vacuna del cuarto delantero* **II.** *vt* **1.** *inf* (*throw*) tirar **2.** *inf* (*give up*) dejar; **to ~ sb** cortar con alguien **3.** (*touch playfully*) **to ~ sb under the chin** tocarle la barbilla a alguien

◆**chuck away** *vt inf* **1.** (*money*) derrochar, despilfarrar **2.** (*old things*) tirar

◆**chuck out** *vt* **1.** (*throw away*) tirar **2.** (*force sb to leave*) echar, zumbar *AmL*

◆**chuck up** **I.** *vt* abandonar **II.** *vi inf* devolver, guacarear *Méx*

chucker-out [ˌtʃʌkər'aʊt] <chuckers-out> *n Brit, inf* gorila *m* (de una discoteca)

chuckle ['tʃʌkl] **I.** *n* risita *f* **II.** *vi* reírse

chug [tʃʌg] **I.** <-gg-> *vi* resoplar **II.** *n* resoplido *m*

chum [tʃʌm] *n inf* amigo, -a *m, f,* colega *mf,* cuate *m Méx*

◆**chum around** <-mm-> *vi,* **chum up** <-mm-> *vi Brit, inf* **to ~ with sb** hacerse amigo de alguien

chummy ['tʃʌmi] <-ier, -iest> *adj inf* (*friendly*) simpático, -a; **to get ~ with sb** hacerse amigo de alguien

chump [tʃʌmp] *n Brit, inf* (*likeable fool*) tontorrón, -ona *m, f* ►**to go off one's ~** *Brit, inf* volverse medio chiflado

chunk [tʃʌŋk] *n* **1.** (*thick lump: of cheese, bread, meat*) pedazo *m,* trozo *m,* troncho *m CSur* **2.** *inf* (*large part*) buena parte *f*

chunky ['tʃʌŋki] <-ier, -iest> *adj* (*clothes*) grueso, -a; (*person*) fornido, -a, macizo, -a

Chunnel ['tʃʌnl] *n inf* **the ~** el Eurotúnel, el túnel del Canal de la Mancha

church [tʃɜːtʃ, *Am:* tʃɜːrtʃ] **I.** *n* iglesia *f;* **to go to ~** ir a misa; **to enter the ~** hacerse sacerdote; (*become a nun*) meterse a monja **II.** *adj* **1.** (*of the organization: parade, fête*) religioso, -a **2.** (*of a building*) de iglesia

churchgoer ['tʃɜːtʃˌgəʊəʳ, *Am:* 'tʃɜːrtʃˌgoʊɚ] *n* practicante *mf*

churchwarden [ˌtʃɜːtʃ'wɔːdn, *Am:* ˌtʃɜːrtʃ'wɔːr-] *n Brit* **1.** REL coadjutor(a) *m(f)* **2.** (*pipe*) *pipa de arcilla de cañón largo*

churchyard [ˌtʃɜːtʃ'jɑːd, *Am:* ˌtʃɜːrtʃjɑːrd] *n* cementerio *m*

churlish ['tʃɜːlɪʃ, *Am:* 'tʃɜːr-] *adj* grosero, -a, maleducado, -a

churn [tʃɜːn, *Am:* tʃɜːrn] **I.** *n* **1.** (*for milk*) lechera *f* **2.** (*for butter*) mantequera *f* **II.** *vt* batir; *fig* agitar **III.** *vi* (*liquid*) arremolinarse; (*wheels*) girar rápidamente; **my stomach was ~ing** tenía un nudo en el estómago

chute [ʃuːt] *n* **1.** (*sloping tube*) rampa *f;* **rubbish ~** *Brit,* **garbage ~** *Am* vertedero *m* de basuras **2.** (*swimming pool slide*) tobogán *m* (de agua) **3.** *inf* AVIAT paracaídas *m inv*

chutney ['tʃʌtni] *n* chutney *m* (*conserva agridulce que se come con carnes, queso, etc.*)

CIA [ˌsiːaɪ'eɪ] *n Am abbr of* **Central Intelligence Agency** CIA *f*

CID [ˌsiːaɪ'diː] *n Brit abbr of* **Criminal Investigation Department** departamento *m* de Investigación Criminal

cider ['saɪdəʳ, *Am:* -dɚ] *n* **1.** *Brit* (*alcoholic apple drink*) sidra *f* **2.** *Am* (*unfermented apple juice*) **sweet ~** zumo *m* de manzana

cigar [sɪ'gɑːʳ, *Am:* -gɑːr] *n* puro *m*

cigarbox <-es> *n,* **cigarcase** *n* cigarrera *f*

cigar-cutter *n* cortapuros *m inv*

cigarette [ˌsɪgə'ret] *n* cigarrillo *m;* **to light a ~** encender un cigarrillo

cigarette case *n* pitillera *f* **cigarette end** *n* colilla *f* **cigarette holder** *n* boquilla *f* **cigarette paper** *n* papel *m* de fumar, mortaja *f AmL*

cigarillo [sɪgə'rɪləʊ, *Am:* -oʊ] *n* purito *m*

cilantro [sɪ'lɑntrəʊ, *Am:* -roʊ] *n no pl* cilantro *m*

cinch [sɪntʃ] <-es> *n* **it's a ~** *inf* está tirado [*o* chupado]

cinder ['sɪndəʳ, *Am:* -dɚ] *n* **1.** (*burnt residue*) carbonilla *f,* carboncillo *m* **2.** *pl* (*ashes*) ceniza *f;* **to burn sth to a ~** carbonizar algo

Cinderella [ˌsɪndə'relə] *n* Cenicienta *f*

cine-camera ['sɪniˌkæmərə] *n* filmadora *f;* (*professional*) cámara *f* cinematográfica

cine-film ['sɪnifɪlm] *n* película *f*

cinema ['sɪnəmə] *n* cine *m,* biógrafo *m Arg, Chile, Urug*

cinemagoer ['sɪnəməˌgəʊəʳ, *Am:* -goʊɚ] *n* cinéfilo, -a *m, f*

cinematic [ˌsɪnə'mætɪk, *Am:* -'mæṯ-] *adj* cinematográfico, -a

cine-projector ['sɪnɪprəˌdʒektəʳ, *Am:* -tɚ] *n* proyector *m* de cine

cinnamon ['sɪnəmən] *n no pl* canela *f;* **a ~ stick** un trozo de canela en rama

CIO *n Am abbr of* **Congress of Industrial Organizations** Congreso *m* de Organizaciones Industriales

cipher *n,* **cypher** ['saɪfəʳ, *Am:* -fɚ] *n* **1.** (*code*) clave *f;* **in ~** en clave **2.** (*unimportant person*) cero *m* a la izquierda **3.** *Am* (*zero*) cero *m*

cipher code *n no pl* clave *f*

circa ['sɜːkə, *Am:* 'sɜːr-] *prep* hacia; **~ 1850** hacia (el año) 1850

circle ['sɜːkl, *Am:* 'sɜːr-] **I.** *n* **1.** *a.* MAT círculo *m;* **to go round in ~s** dar vueltas; **to run round in ~s** *fig* dar vueltas y más vueltas a algo; **to have ~s under one's eyes** tener ojeras **2.** *no pl* THEAT anfiteatro *m* ►**to come full ~** volver al punto de partida; **to square the ~** intentar la cuadratura del círculo **II.** *vt* trazar un círculo alrededor de; (*move in a circle*) dar vueltas alrededor de, rodear **III.** *vi* dar vueltas; (*aircraft*) volar en círculos

circuit ['sɜːkɪt, *Am:* 'sɜːr-] *n* **1.** ELEC circuito *m* **2.** SPORTS pista *f* **3.** (*circular route*) vuelta *f* **4.** (*district under circuit judge*) distrito *m,* territorio *m* jurisdiccional

circuit board *n* placa *f* base

circuit breaker *n* cortacircuitos *m inv*

circuitous [sɜː'kjuːɪtəs, *Am:* sɚ'kjuːət̬əs] *adj* (*route*) tortuoso, -a

circular ['sɜːkjʊləʳ, *Am:* 'sɜːrkjəlɚ] **I.** *adj* circular **II.** *n* circular *f*

circular letter *n* circular *f* **circular saw** *n* sierra *f* circular **circular tour** *n*, **circular trip** *n* circuito *m*

circulate ['sɜːkjʊleɪt, *Am:* 'sɜːrkjə-] **I.** *vt* hacer circular, divulgar; (*card*) enviar una circular a **II.** *vi* circular

circulating library <-ies> *n* biblioteca *f* itinerante

circulation [ˌsɜːkjʊ'leɪʃən, *Am:* ˌsɜːr-] *n no pl* circulación *f*; **to be out of ~** estar fuera de circulación

circulatory [ˌsɜːkjʊ'leɪtəri, *Am:* 'sɜːrkjələtɔːri] *adj* circulatorio, -a

circumcise ['sɜːkəmsaɪz, *Am:* 'sɜːr-] *vt* circuncidar

circumcision [ˌsɜːkəm'sɪʒən, *Am:* ˌsɜːr-] *n* circuncisión *f*

circumference [sə'kʌmfərəns, *Am:* sɚ-] *n* **1.** (*circle's boundary line*) circunferencia *f* **2.** (*perimeter*) perímetro *m*

circumlocution [ˌsɜːkəmlə'kjuːʃən, *Am:* ˌsɜːr-] *n form* **1.** *no pl* (*expression*) circunlocución *f* **2.** (*way of speaking*) circunloquio *m*

circumnavigate [ˌsɜːkəm'nævɪgeɪt, *Am:* ˌsɜːr-] *vt form* circunnavegar

circumnavigation [ˌsɜːkəmˌnævɪ'geɪʃən, *Am:* ˌsɜːr-] *n form* circunnavegación *f*

circumscribe ['sɜːkəmskraɪb, *Am:* 'sɜːr-] *vt form* circunscribir

circumscription [ˌsɜːkəm'skrɪpʃən, *Am:* ˌsɜːr-] *n no pl* **1.** circunscripción *f* **2.** (*on coin*) grafila *f*

circumspect ['sɜːkəmspekt, *Am:* 'sɜːr-] *adj form* circunspecto, -a

circumstance ['sɜːkəmstəns, *Am:* 'sɜːrkəmstæns] *n* circunstancia *f*; **in no ~s** bajo ningún concepto, bajo ninguna circunstancia

circumstantial [ˌsɜːkəm'stænʃl, *Am:* ˌsɜːr-] *adj* circunstancial

circumvent [ˌsɜːkəm'vent, *Am:* ˌsɜːr-] *vt form* (*regulations*) burlar; (*obstacle*) sortear, salvar

circus ['sɜːkəs, *Am:* 'sɜːr-] **I.** <-es> *n* circo *m* **II.** *adj* de circo

cirrhosis [sɪ'rəʊsɪs, *Am:* sə'roʊ-] *n no pl* cirrosis *f inv*

cirrus ['sɪrəs] *n* METEO cirro *m*, cirrus *m inv*

CIS [ˌsiːaɪ'es] *n abbr of* **Commonwealth of Independent States** CEI *f*

cissy ['sɪsi] *inf* **I.** <-ies> *n* marica *m* **II.** <-ier, -iest> *adj* mariquita

cistern ['sɪstən, *Am:* -tɚn] *n* cisterna *f*, jagüel *m AmL*

citadel ['sɪtədəl, *Am:* 'sɪt̬-] *n* ciudadela *f*

citation [saɪ'teɪʃən] *n* **1.** (*written quotation*) cita *f* **2.** *Am* MIL mención *f*

cite [saɪt] *vt form* **1.** (*offer as proof*) alegar **2.** (*quote*) citar **3.** *Am* MIL **to be ~ed** recibir una mención

citizen ['sɪtɪzn, *Am:* 'sɪt̬-] *n* **1.** (*subject*) ciudadano, -a *m, f* **2.** (*resident of town*) habitante *mf*

Citizens' Band *n s.* **CB** banda *f* ciudadana

citizenship ['sɪtɪzənʃɪp, *Am:* 'sɪt̬] *n no pl* ciudadanía *f*

citric ['sɪtrɪk] *adj* cítrico, -a

citrus ['sɪtrəs] <citrus *o* citruses> **I.** *n* cítrico *m* **II.** *adj* cítrico, -a

city ['sɪti, *Am:* 'sɪt̬-] <-ies> **I.** *n* ciudad *f* **II.** *adj* (*scape*) urbano, -a; (*life*) ciudadano, -a

Muchas **cities** (grandes ciudades) americanas son conocidas entre sus ciudadanos por sus sobrenombres. Así **New York** es conocida como **Gotham** o **The Big Apple**. **Los Angeles** como **The Big Orange** o como **The City of the Angels**. De la misma manera **Chicago** es conocida como **The Windy City**. La expresión **The City of Brotherly Love** se usa para referirse a **Philadelphia**. **Denver**, debido a su situación, es conocida como **The Mile-High City** y **Detroit**, a causa de su industria automovilística, como **Motor City**.

city father *n* mandatario *m* municipal **city hall** *n Am* ayuntamiento *m*

civic ['sɪvɪk] <inv> *adj* (*authorities*) civil; (*education*) cívico, -a

civies ['sɪviz] *npl* traje *m* de paisano

civil ['sɪvl] *adj* **1.** civil **2.** (*courteous*) cortés; **to not have a ~ word to say for sb** hablar mal de alguien

civil action *n* procedimiento *m* civil **civil court** *n* sala *f* de lo Civil **civil defence** *n* defensa *f* civil **civil disobedience** *n* resistencia *f* pasiva **civil engineer** *n* ingeniero, -a *m, f* de caminos

civilian [sɪ'vɪliən, *Am:* -jən] <inv> **I.** *n* civil *mf* **II.** *adj* (*clothes*) de paisano, -a; (*population*) civil

civility [sɪ'vɪləti, *Am:* -t̬i] <-ies> *n* **1.** *no pl* (*formality*) urbanidad *f* **2.** (*formal remarks*) cumplido *m*

civilization [ˌsɪvəlaɪ'zeɪʃən, *Am:* ˌsɪvəlɪ-] *n* civilización *f*

civilize ['sɪvəlaɪz] *vt* civilizar

civil law ['sɪvl'lɔː, *Am:* -'lɑː] *n* derecho *m* civil **civil liberties** *npl* derechos *mpl* civiles **civil marriage** *n* matrimonio *m* civil **civil population** *n* población *f* civil **civil rights** *npl* derechos *mpl* civiles **civil servant** *n* funcionario, -a *m, f* **Civil Service** *n* Administración *f* Pública

En Gran Bretaña el **Civil Service** forma parte de la administración central del país. Dentro de él se encuentran el cuerpo diplomático, **Inland Revenue** (Hacienda), la Seguridad Social y los centros de enseñanza estatales. Los **civil servants** (funcionarios) son fijos y, dado que su puesto no es político, no se ven afectados por los cambios de gobierno.

civil war *n* guerra *f* civil
civvies ['sɪvɪz] *npl inf* **in ~** de paisano
ckw. *adj, adv abbr of* **clockwise** en sentido de las agujas del reloj
clack [klæk] **I.** *vi* **1.** (*heels*) taconear; (*typewriter*) teclear **2.** (*talk rapidly*) parlotear **II.** *n* (*with heels*) taconeo *m;* (*continual rapid talk*) parloteo *m*
clad [klæd] *adj a. iron* vestido, -a
claim [kleɪm] **I.** *n* **1.** (*assertion*) afirmación *f* **2.** (*written demand*) demanda *f;* (*insurance*) reclamación *f;* **to put in a ~ (for sth)** presentar una demanda (por algo) **3.** (*right*) derecho *m;* **to lay ~ to sth** reivindicar algo **II.** *vt* **1.** (*assert*) asegurar, afirmar; (*right, responsibility*) reivindicar **2.** (*declare ownership*) reclamar; (*reward, title*) reivindicar; (*diplomatic immunity*) solicitar **3.** (*require: time*) llevar, requerir **4.** (*demand in writing*) reclamar; **to ~ damages** reclamar daños y perjuicios **III.** *vi* **to ~ for sth** reclamar algo
claimant ['kleɪmənt] *n* solicitante *mf;* (*to a throne*) pretendiente, -a *m, f*
clairvoyance [ˌkleə'vɔɪənts, *Am:* ˌkler-] *n no pl* clarividencia *f*
clairvoyant [ˌkleə'vɔɪən, *Am:* ˌkler-] **I.** *n* clarividente *mf* **II.** *adj* extrasensorial; **to be ~** ser clarividente
clam [klæm] *n* almeja *f* ▶**to shut up like a ~** quedarse como una tumba
◆**clam up** <-mm-> *vi* (*not say anything*) no abrir la boca
clamber ['klæmbəʳ, *Am:* -bɚ] **I.** *vi* trepar **II.** *n* ascensión *f*
clam chowder ['klæmˌtʃaʊdəʳ, *Am:* -dɚ] *n* sopa *f* de almejas
clammy ['klæmi] <-ier, -iest> *adj* (*feet*) sudoroso, -a; (*weather*) bochornoso, -a
clamor ['klæmɚ] *n Am s.* **clamour**
clamorous ['klæmərəs] *adj* **1.** (*vociferous*) vociferante **2.** (*loud, noisy*) ruidoso, -a
clamour ['klæməʳ, *Am:* -ɚ] *Brit* **I.** *vi* (*demand loudly*) pedir a gritos, clamar **II.** *n* clamor *m*
clamp [klæmp] **I.** *n* **1.** ARCHIT abrazadera *f;* **wheel ~** *Brit* cepo *m* **2.** TECH tornillo *m* de banco **II.** *vt* **1.** (*fasten together*) sujetar con abrazaderas **2.** (*impose forcefully*) imponer **3.** *Brit* (*immobilise a vehicle*) **to ~ a car** poner el cepo a un coche
◆**clamp down** *vi* **to ~ on sth** tomar medidas drásticas contra algo
clan [klæn] *n + sing/pl vb, Scot* clan *m*
clandestine [klæn'destɪn] *adj form* clandestino, -a
clang [klæŋ] **I.** *vi* (*bells*) repicar **II.** *vt* **to ~ sth shut** cerrar algo con estruendo **III.** *n* sonido *m* metálico fuerte; **the ~ of the bell** el repiqueteo de la campana
clanger ['klæŋgəʳ, *Am:* -ɚ] *n Brit, inf* metedura *f* de pata; **to drop a ~** meter la pata
clangor *n Am,* **clangour** ['klæŋəʳ, *Am:* 'klæŋgɚ] *n no pl* sonido *m* metálico fuerte
clank [klæŋk] **I.** *vi* hacer ruido **II.** *vt* hacer sonar **III.** *n* ruido *m* metálico
clap [klæp] **I.** <-pp-> *vt* **1.** (*slap palms together*) **to ~ one's hands (together)** batir palmas, dar palmadas **2.** (*applaud*) aplaudir **3.** (*place quickly*) poner **II.** <-pp-> *vi* **1.** (*slap palms together*) dar palmadas **2.** (*applaud*) aplaudir **III.** *n* **1.** (*slap*) palmada *f* **2.** (*applause*) aplauso *m;* **to give sb a ~** aplaudir a alguien **3.** (*noise*) ruido *m;* **a ~ of thunder** un trueno
clapped-out [ˌklæpt'aʊt] *adj Brit, Aus, inf* (*machine, car*) destartalado, -a; (*person*) hecho, -a polvo, reventado, -a
clapper ['klæpəʳ, *Am:* -ɚ] *n* badajo *m;* **like the ~s** como una bala
claptrap ['klæptræp] *n no pl, inf* tonterías *fpl*
claret ['klærət, *Am:* 'kler-] *n* **1.** (*wine*) burdeos *m inv* **2.** (*colour*) granate *m*
clarification [ˌklærɪfɪ'keɪʃən, *Am:* ˌkler-] *n no pl* aclaración *f*
clarify ['klærɪfaɪ, *Am:* 'kler-] <-ie-> *vt* **1.** (*make clearer*) aclarar **2.** (*explain*) explicar **3.** (*purify*) clarificar
clarinet [ˌklærɪ'net, *Am:* ˌkler-] *n* clarinete *m*
clarity ['klærəti, *Am:* 'klerət̬i] *n no pl* claridad *f*
clash [klæʃ] **I.** *vi* **1.** (*fight*) tener un enfrentamiento; (*argue*) discutir; **to ~ over sth** discutir sobre algo **2.** (*compete against*) enfrentarse **3.** (*contradict: views*) contradecirse **4.** (*not match: colours*) desentonar **5.** *Brit, Aus* (*coincide inconveniently*) coincidir **6.** (*make loud noise*) sonar fuerte **II.** *vt* **1.** (*strike*) golpear con estruendo **2.** (*produce sound*) tocar **III.** <-es> *n* **1.** (*hostile encounter*) enfrentamiento *m* **2.** (*contest*) contienda *f* **3.** (*conflict*) conflicto *m* **4.** (*incompatibility*) choque *m* **5.** *Brit, Aus* (*coincidence*) coincidencia *f* **6.** (*loud harsh noise*) estruendo *m*
clasp [klɑːsp, *Am:* klæsp] **I.** *n* **1.** (*firm grip: of hands*) apretón *m* **2.** (*fastening device*) broche *m*, cierre *m* **II.** *vt* **1.** (*grip*) agarrar, sujetar; **to ~ one's hands** darse un apretón de manos; **to ~ sb in one's arms** estrechar a alguien entre sus brazos **2.** (*fasten: belt*) apretar
clasp knife <knives> *n* navaja *f*
class [klɑːs, *Am:* klæs] **I.** <-es> *n* **1.** clase *f* **2.** *Brit, Aus* (*type of degree*) **a first/second ~ honours degree** licenciatura *f* superior con sobresaliente/notable ▶**the <u>chattering</u> ~es** *Brit, pej* los intelectualoides **II.** *adj* (*excellent*) de primera clase **III.** *vt* catalogar; **to ~ sb as sth** catalogar a alguien de algo; **to ~ sb among sth** considerar a alguien como algo
class-conscious ['klɑːsˌkɒntʃəs, *Am:* 'klæsˌkɑːntʃəs] *adj* con conciencia de clase; (*classist*) clasista

classic ['klæsɪk] I. *adj* 1. clásico, -a; (*typical*) típico, -a 2. *inf* (*joke, story*) genial II. *n* 1. (*work*) clásico *m* 2. (*garment*) prenda *f* clásica
classical ['klæsɪkl] *adj* clásico, -a
classicism ['klæsɪsɪzəm] *n no pl* clasicismo *m*
classicist ['klæsɪsɪst] *n* clasicista *mf*
classics ['klæsɪks] *n* 1. *pl* **the ~** (*great literature*) los clásicos 2. + *sing vb* (*Greek and Roman studies*) clásicas *fpl inf*
classification [ˌklæsɪfɪ'keɪʃən, *Am:* ˌklæsə-] *n* clasificación *f*
classified ['klæsɪfaɪd] <inv> *adj* clasificado, -a; (*confidential*) confidencial, secreto, -a
classify ['klæsɪfaɪ] <-ie-> *vt* clasificar; (*designate as secret*) clasificar como secreto
classless ['klɑːslɪs, *Am:* 'klæs-] *adj* (*society*) sin clases
classmate *n* compañero, -a *m, f* de clase **classroom** *n* clase *f*, aula *f* **class struggle** *n,* **class war** *n* lucha *f* de clases
classy ['klɑːsi, *Am:* 'klæsi] <-ier, -iest> *adj* con estilo, con clase
clatter ['klætəʳ, *Am:* 'klæt̬ɚ] I. *vi* 1. (*make rattling noise*) hacer ruido 2. (*walk noisily*) chacolotear II. *n* estruendo *m;* (*of hooves*) chacoloteo *m*
clause [klɔːz, *Am:* klɑːz] *n* cláusula *f;* LING oración *f*
claustrophobia [ˌklɔːstrə'fəʊbɪə, *Am:* ˌklɑːstrə'foʊ-] *n* claustrofobia *f*
claustrophobic *adj* claustrofóbico, -a
clavicle ['klævɪkl] *n* clavícula *f*
claw [klɔː, *Am:* klɑː] I. *n* garra *f;* (*of sea creatures*) pinza *f;* **to show one's ~s** *fig* sacar [*o* enseñar] las uñas II. *vt* arañar
clay [kleɪ] I. *n no pl* 1. arcilla *f; fig, liter* barro *m* 2. SPORTS tierra *f* batida II. *adj* de arcilla
clay pigeon *n* plato *m* de tiro
clean [kliːn] I. *adj* 1. (*free of dirt*) limpio, -a; (**as**) **~ as a new pin** limpio como una patena 2. (*free from bacteria*) desinfectado, -a 3. (*fair*) honrado, -a 4. (*morally acceptable*) decente; (*reputation*) sin tacha; (*driving licence*) sin sanciones; **~ police record** registro *m* de antecedentes penales limpio 5. (*smooth: cut*) limpio, -a; (*design*) elegante 6. (*complete*) **to make a ~ break with sth** romper por completo con algo 7. (*blank: piece of paper*) en blanco II. *n* limpieza *f* III. *adv* completamente; **to ~ forget that ...** olvidarse por completo de que... IV. *vt* limpiar V. *vi* hacer la limpieza; **the coffee stain ~ed off easily** la mancha de café salió fácilmente
◆**clean down** *vt* limpiar
◆**clean out** *vt* 1. (*clean thoroughly*) limpiar; (*with water*) lavar 2. (*make penniless*) dejar sin blanca a
◆**clean up** I. *vt* 1. (*make clean*) limpiar; (*tidy up*) ordenar; **to ~ the city** limpiar la ciudad; **to clean oneself up** asearse 2. (*remove illegal*) acabar con II. *vi* 1. (*make clean*) limpiar 2. *Am, inf* (*make profit*) hacer un buen negocio
clean-cut [ˌkliːn'kʌt] *adj* (*straight*) preciso, -a; (*features*) perfilado, -a; (*person*) de buen parecer
cleaner ['kliːnəʳ, *Am:* -nɚ] *n* 1. (*person*) asistente, -a *m, f* 2. *no pl* (*substance*) producto *m* de limpieza
cleaning [kliːnɪŋ] *n no pl* limpieza *f*
cleaning lady <-ies> *n,* **cleaning woman** <women> *n* mujer *f* de la limpieza
cleanliness ['klenlɪnɪs] *n no pl* aseo *m*
cleanly ['klenli] *adv* limpiamente
cleanse ['klenz] *vt* 1. (*make clean*) limpiar 2. (*make morally pure*) purificar
cleanser ['klenzəʳ, *Am:* -ɚ] *n* leche *f* limpiadora
clean-shaven ['kliːn'ʃeɪvn] *adj* bien afeitado, -a
cleansing cream *n no pl* leche *f* limpiadora
cleansing tissue *n* toallita *f* desmaquilladora
clean-up ['kliːnʌp] *n* limpieza *f*
clear [klɪəʳ, *Am:* klɪr] I. *n* **to be in the ~** estar fuera de peligro II. *adv* claramente; **to get ~ of sth** deshacerse de algo; **to stand ~** (**of sth**) mantenerse a distancia (de algo) III. *adj* 1. (*transparent*) claro, -a; (*air*) transparente; (*picture*) nítido, -a; **to make oneself ~** explicarse con claridad; **as ~ as day** más claro que el agua 2. (*certain*) evidente 3. (*free from guilt: conscience*) tranquilo, -a; **to be ~ of debt** estar libre de deudas 4. (*complete*) completo, -a; **three ~ months** tres meses enteros 5. (*net*) neto, -a IV. *vt* 1. (*remove obstacles*) limpiar; (*empty*) desocupar 2. (*remove blockage*) desatascar; **to ~ the way** abrir el camino 3. (*remove doubts*) aclarar; **to ~ one's head** despejar la cabeza 4. (*acquit*) absolver 5. (*net*) sacar beneficio de 6. (*jump*) saltar por encima de 7. (*give official permission*) autorizar V. *vi* (*water*) aclararse; (*weather*) despejarse
◆**clear away** I. *vt* quitar II. *vi* irse
◆**clear off** I. *vi inf* largarse, jalar *Bol, PRico, Urug* II. *vt* liquidar
◆**clear out** I. *vt* limpiar; (*throw away*) vaciar II. *vi* irse
◆**clear up** I. *vt* aclarar; (*tidy*) ordenar II. *vi* despejarse
clearance ['klɪərəns, *Am:* 'klɪr-] *n no pl* 1. (*act of clearing*) despeje *m* 2. (*space*) espacio *m* libre 3. (*permission*) autorización *f*
clearance sale *n* liquidación *f*
clear-cut ['klɪə'kʌt, *Am:* ˌklɪr'kʌt] I. *adj* bien definido, -a; *fig* claro, -a II. *vt* cortar de forma neta **clear-headed** *adj* perspicaz
clearing ['klɪərɪŋ, *Am:* 'klɪrɪŋ] *n* claro *m*
clearing bank *n Brit* banco *m* de compensación **clearing house** *n Brit* cámara *f* de compensación **clearing office** *n Brit* cámara *f* de compensación
clearly ['klɪəli, *Am:* 'klɪr-] *adv* 1. (*distinctly*) claramente 2. (*obviously*) evidentemente;

C

(*undoubtedly*) sin duda

clearness ['klɪənɪs, *Am:* 'klɪr-] *n* claridad *f*

clear-sighted [ˌklɪə'saɪtɪd] *adj* clarividente

cleavage ['kli:vɪdʒ] *n* **1.** *no pl* (*in a dress*) escote *m* **2.** *form* (*division*) división *f*

cleave [kli:v] <-ed *Am:* clove, -ed *Am:* cloven> **I.** *vi liter* henderse **II.** *vt* partir

cleaver ['kli:və^r, *Am:* -vɚ] *n* cuchilla *f*

clef [klef] *n* clave *f*

cleft [kleft] **I.** <inv> *adj* dividido, -a; (*lip*) partido, -a **II.** *n* grieta *f*

clematis ['klemətɪs, *Am:* 'kleməţəs] *n inv* clemátide *f*

clemency ['klemənsi] *n no pl, form* clemencia *f*

clement ['klemənt] *adj* **1.** *form* (*mild*) benigno, -a **2.** *form* (*merciful*) clemente

clench [klentʃ] *vt* presionar; (*one's fist*) apretar

Cleopatra [ˌkliə'pætrə, *Am:* ˌklioʊpætrə] *n* Cleopatra *f*

clergy ['klɜ:dʒi, *Am:* 'klɜ:r-] *n + sing/pl vb* clero *m*

clergyman ['klɜ:dʒɪmən, *Am:* 'klɜ:r-] <-men> *n* sacerdote *m;* (*protestant*) pastor *m*

clergywoman ['klɜ:dʒɪˌwʊmən, *Am:* 'klɜ:r-] <-women> *n* pastora *f*

cleric ['klerɪk] *n* clérigo *m*

clerical ['klerɪkl] *adj* **1.** (*of the clergy*) clerical **2.** (*of offices*) de oficina; ~ **worker** oficinista *mf*

clerical error *n* error *m* administrativo

clerical staff *n* personal *m* de oficina

clerical work *n no pl* trabajo *m* de oficina

clerk [klɑ:k, *Am:* klɜ:rk] *n* **1.** (*in office*) oficinista *mf* **2.** *Am* (*in hotel*) recepcionista *mf;* (*in shop*) dependiente *mf;* **sales** ~ vendedor(a) *m(f)*

clever ['klevə^r, *Am:* -ɚ] *adj* **1.** (*intelligent*) inteligente **2.** (*skilful*) hábil; (*invention*) ingenioso, -a **3.** *pej* astuto, -a; **to be too ~ by half** pasarse de listo

clever clogs *n,* **clever dick** *n Brit* sabelotodo *mf*

cleverness *n no pl* **1.** (*intelligence*) inteligencia *f* **2.** (*skill*) habilidad *f*

cliché ['kli:ʃeɪ, *Am:* kli:'ʃeɪ] *n* **1.** cliché *m* **2.** (*platitude*) tópico *m*

click [klɪk] **I.** *n* clic *m;* (*of one's heels*) taconeo *m;* (*of one's tongue*) chasquido *m* **II.** *vi* **1.** (*make short, sharp sound*) chasquear **2.** INFOR hacer clic; **to ~ on a symbol** hacer clic en un símbolo **3.** (*become friendly*) congeniar; (*become popular*) tener éxito **4.** (*become clear*) caer en la cuenta **III.** *vt* **1.** (*make short, sharp sound: tongue*) chasquear; (*heels*) taconear **2.** (*press button on mouse*) pulsar

◆**click on** *vi* INFOR pulsar, hacer clic

client ['klaɪənt] *n* cliente *mf*

clientele [ˌkli:ɒn'tel, *Am:* ˌklaɪən-] *n* clientela *f*

cliff [klɪf] *n* precipicio *m;* (*on coast*) acantilado *m*

cliffhanger ['klɪfˌhæŋə^r, *Am:* -ɚ] *n* situación *f* de suspense

climacteric [klaɪ'mæktərɪk, *Am:* -tɚ-] *n form* climaterio *m*

climactic [ˌklaɪ'mæktɪk] *adj* culminante

climate ['klaɪmɪt] *n* **1.** (*weather*) clima *m* **2.** (*general conditions*) ambiente *m;* **the ~ of opinion** la opinión general

climatic [klaɪ'mætɪk] *adj* climático, -a

climatologist [ˌklaɪmə'tɔlədʒist, *Am:* -'tɑ:lə-] *n* climatólogo, -a *m, f*

climatology [ˌklaɪmə'tɒlədʒi, *Am:* -'tɑ:lə-] *n no pl* climatología *f*

climax ['klaɪmæks] **I.** <-es> *n* clímax *m inv;* (*sexual*) orgasmo *m* **II.** *vi* llegar a un punto culminante; (*sexual*) llegar al orgasmo

climb [klaɪm] **I.** *n* subida *f;* (*to power*) ascenso *m* **II.** *vt* (*stairs*) subir; (*tree*) trepar a; (*mountain*) escalar **III.** *vi* subir; **to ~ to a height of ...** AVIAT ascender a una altura de...

◆**climb down** *vi* bajar; *fig* volverse atrás

climbdown ['klaɪmdaʊn] *n* vuelta *f* atrás

climber ['klaɪmə^r, *Am:* -mɚ] *n* **1.** (*of mountains*) alpinista *mf,* andinista *mf AmL;* (*of rock faces*) escalador(a) *m(f)* **2.** (*plant*) enredadera *f* **3.** *inf* (*striver for higher status*) arribista *mf*

climbing ['klaɪmɪŋ] **I.** *n no pl* **1.** (*ascending mountains*) alpinismo *m,* andinismo *m AmL* **2.** (*ascending rock faces*) escalada *f* **II.** *adj* (*plant*) trepador(a); (*boots*) de montaña

climbing irons *npl* crampones *mpl*

clinch [klɪntʃ] **I.** <-es> *n* abrazo *m* **II.** *vt* **1.** (*settle decisively*) resolver; (*a deal*) cerrar **2.** *inf* (*embrace*) abrazar **3.** (*secure a nail*) remachar

clincher ['klɪntʃə^r, *Am:* -ɚ] *n inf* argumento *m* decisivo

cling [klɪŋ] <clung, clung> *vi* **1.** (*embrace*) abrazarse **2.** (*hold*) agarrarse; *fig* aferrarse **3.** (*stick*) adherirse **4.** (*stay close*) pegarse **5.** (*follow closely*) no separarse de

clingfilm ['kliŋfilm] *n no pl, Brit* papel *m* de plástico para envolver

clinging *adj* **1.** (*clothes*) ajustado, -a, ceñido, -a **2.** (*person*) pegajoso, -a

clingy ['klɪŋi] <-ier, -iest> *adj* pegajoso, -a

clinic ['klɪnɪk] *n* clínica *f*

clinical ['klɪnɪkl] *adj* **1.** clínico, -a **2.** (*emotionless*) frío, -a

clinician [klɪ'nɪʃən] *n* médico, -a *m, f* especializado, -a

clink [klɪŋk] **I.** *vt* hacer tintinear; (*glasses*) chocar **II.** *vi* tintinear **III.** *n no pl* **1.** tintineo *m;* (*of glasses*) choque *m* **2.** *inf* (*prison*) chirona *f*

clinker ['klɪŋkə^r, *Am:* -kɚ] *n no pl* escoria *f*

clip¹ [klɪp] **I.** *n* **1.** (*fastener*) clip *m;* (*for paper*) sujetapapeles *m inv,* broche *m AmL;* (*for hair*) horquilla *f* **2.** (*gun part*) cargador *m* **3.** (*jewellery*) broche *m* **II.** <-pp-> *vt* sujetar

clip² [klɪp] <-pp-> **I.** *vt* **1.** (*cut*) recortar; (*hair, nails*) cortar; (*sheep*) esquilar; (*ticket*) picar **2.** (*reduce*) abreviar; (*words*) comerse **3.** (*attach*) sujetar **4.** (*hit*) dar una bofetada a

II. *n* 1. (*trim*) recorte *m* 2. (*extract*) fragmento *m* 3. (*hit*) bofetada *f*

clipboard ['klɪpbɔːd, *Am:* -bɔːrd] *n* tablilla *f* con sujetapapeles

clipped *adj* cortado, -a

clipper ['klɪpəʳ, *Am:* -ɚ] *n* NAUT clíper *m*

clipping ['klɪpɪŋ] *n* recorte *m*

clique [kliːk] *n* pandilla *f*

cliquey ['kliːki] <cliquier, cliquiest> *adj*, **cliquish** ['kliːkɪʃ] *adj* exclusivista

clitoris ['klɪtərəs, *Am:* 'klɪţɚəs] <-es> *n* clítoris *m inv*

cloak [kləʊk, *Am:* kloʊk] I. *n* 1. *a. fig* capa *f* 2. *no pl* (*covering*) manto *m;* **under the ~ of darkness** al amparo de la oscuridad II. *vt* encapotar; (*hide*) encubrir

cloakroom ['kləʊkrʊm, *Am:* 'kloʊkruːm] *n* 1. (*for coats*) guardarropa *m* 2. *Brit* (*toilet*) lavabo *m*

clobber ['klɒbəʳ, *Am:* 'klɑːbɚ] I. *vt inf* dar una paliza a II. *n no pl, Brit, Aus, inf* bártulos *mpl*

clock [klɒk, *Am:* klɑːk] I. *n* 1. (*for time*) reloj *m;* **alarm ~** despertador *m;* **round the ~** las 24 horas; **to run against the ~** correr contra reloj 2. (*speedometer*) velocímetro *m;* (*mileometer*) cuentakilómetros *m inv* II. *vt* 1. (*take amount of time*) cronometrar 2. (*measure time*) registrar; **this car can ~ 150mph** este coche alcanza una velocidad de 150 millas por hora 3. *inf* (*hit*) dar un bofetón a

◆**clock in** *vi* 1. (*record time*) fichar 2. *inf* (*arrive*) llegar al trabajo

◆**clock out** *vi* 1. (*record time*) fichar 2. *inf* (*leave work*) salir del trabajo

◆**clock up** *vt insep* (*attain*) alcanzar; (*travel*) recorrer

clockface *n* esfera *f* del reloj **clock radio** *n* radiodespertador *m* **clock timer** *n* temporizador *m* **clock-watcher** *n inf: persona que mira el reloj ansiando salir del trabajo*

clockwise *adj, adv* en el sentido de las agujas del reloj

clockwork *n no pl* mecanismo *m* de relojería; **to go like ~** salir todo bien; **as regular as ~** como un reloj

clod [klɒd, *Am:* klɑːd] *n* 1. (*earth*) terrón *m* 2. (*person*) zopenco, -a *m, f*

clog [klɒg, *Am:* klɑːg] I. *n* zueco *m*, zueca *f* II. <-gg-> *vi* atascarse III. <-gg-> *vt* atascar

◆**clog up** *vt* atascar

clog-dance ['klɒgdɑːns] *n baile en el que se usan zuecos para seguir el ritmo de la música*

cloister ['klɔɪstəʳ, *Am:* -stɚ] *n pl* claustro *m*

clone [kləʊn, *Am:* kloʊn] I. *n* 1. BIO clon *m* 2. INFOR clónico *m* II. *vt* clonar

cloning ['kləʊniŋ, *Am:* 'kloʊn-] *n no pl* clonación *f*

close¹ [kləʊs, *Am:* kloʊs] I. *adj* 1. (*near in location*) cercano, -a; **~ combat** combate *m* cuerpo a cuerpo 2. (*intimate*) íntimo, -a; **~ relatives** parientes *mpl* cercanos 3. (*almost even*) exacto, -a 4. (*similar*) parecido, -a 5. (*unwilling to be frank*) reservado, -a 6. (*airless*) sofocado, -a; (*stuffy*) cargado, -a II. *adv* 1. (*near in location*) cerca; **to move ~** acercarse 2. (*near in time*) casi

close² [kləʊz, *Am:* kloʊz] I. *n* 1. *no pl* (*end*) fin *m;* (*finish*) final *m;* **to bring sth to a ~** terminar algo 2. *Brit* (*cul-de-sac road*) callejón *m* sin salida II. *vt* 1. (*shut*) cerrar; **to ~ ranks** cerrar filas 2. (*end*) terminar; (*bring to an end*) concluir; **to ~ a deal** cerrar un trato III. *vi* 1. (*shut*) cerrarse 2. (*end*) terminarse

◆**close down** I. *vi* cerrarse (definitivamente) II. *vt* cerrar (definitivamente)

◆**close in** *vi* 1. (*surround*) rodear 2. (*get shorter*) acortarse

◆**close off** *vt* cerrar

◆**close up** I. *vi* 1. (*people*) arrimarse 2. (*wound*) cicatrizar II. *vt* cerrar del todo

closed *adj* cerrado, -a; **behind ~ doors** a puerta cerrada

closed-door *adj* a puerta cerrada **close-down** *n* cierre *m* **close-knit** *adj* unido, -a

closely ['kləʊsli, *Am:* 'kloʊs-] *adv* 1. (*near*) de cerca 2. (*intimately*) estrechamente 3. (*carefully*) atentamente

closeness ['kləʊsnɪs, *Am:* 'kloʊs-] *n* 1. *no pl* (*nearness*) proximidad *f* 2. *no pl* (*intimacy*) intimidad *f* 3. (*airlessness*) bochorno *m*

close season *n Am* veda *f*

closet ['klɒzɪt, *Am:* 'klɑːzɪt] I. *n Am* (*cupboard*) armario *m;* (*for clothes*) ropero *m;* (*for food*) alacena *f* ►**to <u>come out</u> of the ~** declararse homosexual II. *adj* secreto, -a III. *vt* **to be ~ed with sb** estar reunido con alguien a puerta cerrada

close to I. *prep* 1. (*near*) cerca de; **to be ~ the beginning/end of sth** estar cerca del comienzo/final de algo; **to live ~ the airport** vivir cerca del aeropuerto 2. (*almost*) **~ tears/death** a punto de llorar/morir; **~ doing sth** cerca de hacer algo; **~ three metres** cerca de tres metros 3. (*in friendship with*) **to be ~ sb** estar unido a alguien II. *adv* (*almost*) **~ finished/complete** casi terminado/completo

close-up ['kləʊsʌp, *Am:* 'kloʊs-] *n* CINE primer plano *m*

closing I. *adj* último, -a; (*speech*) de clausura II. *n no pl* 1. (*ending*) conclusión *f;* (*act*) clausura *f* 2. COM cierre *m*

closing date *n* fecha *f* límite **closing down** *n no pl* cierre *m* **closing-down sale** *n* liquidación *f* **closing price** *n* cotización *f* de cierre **closing time** *n Brit*, **closing hour** *n* hora *f* de cierre

closure ['kləʊʒəʳ, *Am:* 'kloʊʒɚ] *n* (*closing*) cierre *m;* (*end*) fin *m;* (*in Parliament*) clausura *f*

clot [klɒt, *Am:* klɑːt] I. *n* 1. MED coágulo *m;* **~ of blood** coágulo *m* sanguíneo 2. *Brit, inf* (*person*) bobo, -a *m, f* II. <-tt-> *vi* cuajar; (*blood*) coagular

cloth [klɒθ, *Am:* klɑːθ] I. *n* 1. (*material*) tela *f;* (*for cleaning*) trapo *m* 2. (*clergy*) clero *m;* **a**

man of the ~ un clérigo **II.** *adj* de tela

clothe [kləʊð, *Am:* kloʊð] *vt* vestir; *fig* revestir de

clothes [kləʊðz, *Am:* kloʊðz] *npl* vestidos *mpl;* (*collectively*) ropa *f* **clothes-hanger** *n* percha *f* **clothes horse** *n* tendedero *m* plegable **clothes line** *n* cuerda *f* para tender la ropa **clothes-moth** *n* polilla *f* **clothes peg** *n Brit,* **clothes pin** *n Am* pinza *f* (para la ropa)

clothing ['kləʊðɪŋ, *Am:* 'kloʊ-] *n no pl* ropa *f;* **article of** ~ prenda *f* de vestir

clothing industry <-ies> *n* industria *f* textil

cloud [klaʊd] **I.** *n* nube *f* ►**every** ~ **has a silver lining** *prov* no hay mal que por bien no venga *prov;* **to be on** ~ **nine** estar en el séptimo cielo; **to be under a** ~ estar bajo sospecha **II.** *vt a. fig* anublar

◆**cloud over** *vi* **1.** METEO nublarse **2.** (*become gloomy*) ensombrecerse; (*face*) entristecerse **3.** (*become misty: eyes*) empañarse

cloud bank *n* banco *m* de niebla **cloudburst** *n* chaparrón *m* **cloud-capped** *adj* envuelto, -a en nubes **cloud-chamber** *n* PHYS cámara *f* de niebla **cloud-cuckooland** *n* Babia *f;* **to live in** ~ estar en Babia

clouded ['klaʊdɪd] *adj* **1.** (*cloudy*) nublado, -a **2.** (*not transparent: liquid*) turbio, -a **3.** (*confused: mind*) confuso, -a

cloudless ['klaʊdlɪs] *adj* despejado, -a

cloudy ['klaʊdi] <-ier, -iest> *adj* **1.** (*overcast*) nublado, -a **2.** (*not transparent: liquid*) turbio, -a

clout [klaʊt] **I.** *n* **1.** *inf* (*hit*) tortazo *m* **2.** *no pl* (*power*) influencia *f* ►**ne'er cast a** ~ **till May is out** *prov* hasta el cuarenta de mayo no te quites el sayo *prov* **II.** *vt inf* dar un tortazo a

clove¹ [kləʊv, *Am:* kloʊv] *n* clavo *m;* (*of garlic*) diente *m*

clove² [kləʊv, *Am:* kloʊv] *pt of* **cleave**

cloven ['kləʊvn, *Am:* 'kloʊ-] **I.** *pp of* **cleave** **II.** *adj* hendido, -a

clover ['kləʊvəʳ, *Am:* 'kloʊvɚ] *n no pl* trébol *m* ►**to live in** ~ vivir a cuerpo de rey

cloverleaf *n* <-leaves> hoja *f* de trébol

clown [klaʊn] **I.** *n* payaso, -a *m, f* **II.** *vi* **to** ~ **around** hacer el payaso

clownish ['klaʊnɪʃ] *adj* torpe; (*behaviour*) grosero, -a

cloying [klɔɪɪŋ] *adj* empalagoso, -a

cloyingly *adv* de manera empalagosa; ~ **sweet** empalagoso, -a

club [klʌb] **I.** *n* **1.** (*group*) asociación *f* **2.** (*team*) club *m* **3.** SPORTS palo *m* de golf **4.** (*weapon*) cachiporra *f* **5.** (*playing card*) trébol *m;* (*in Spanish cards*) basto *m* **6.** (*disco*) sala *f* de fiestas, club *m* **II.** <-bb-> *vt* aporrear

◆**club together** *vi* reunirse

clubbing *vi* **to go** ~ salir por la noche (a las discotecas)

club car *n Am* coche *m* salón **club foot** <feet> *n* pie *m* zopo **club-house** *n* sede *f* de un club **club member** *n* socio, -a *m, f* de un club **club sandwich** <-es> *n Am* bocadillo *m* vegetal con pollo y bacon **club soda** *n Am* soda *f*

cluck [klʌk] *vi* cloquear; *fig* parlotear

clue [klu:] *n* **1.** (*evidence*) indicio *m;* (*hint*) pista *f* **2.** (*secret*) clave *f* **3.** (*idea*) idea *f;* **I haven't a** ~ *inf* no tengo ni idea

◆**clue up** *vt Aus* **to clue sb up** (**on sth**) informar a alguien (de algo)

clueless ['klu:lɪs] *adj inf* despistado, -a

clump [klʌmp] **I.** *vt* **to** ~ **sth together** agrupar algo **II.** *vi* **1.** (*group*) **to** ~ **together** agruparse **2.** (*walk noisily*) caminar haciendo ruido **III.** *n* **1.** (*thick group: of trees*) grupo *m;* (*of flowers*) macizo *m* **2.** (*lump*) terrón *m*

clumsiness ['klʌmzɪnɪs] *n no pl* torpeza *f*

clumsy ['klʌmzi] <-ier, -iest> *adj* pesado, -a; (*bungling*) torpe

clung [klʌŋ] *pp, pt of* **cling**

clunk [klʌŋk] *n* sonido *m* metálico

cluster ['klʌstəʳ, *Am:* -tɚ] **I.** *n* (*of people*) grupo *m;* (*of fruits*) racimo *m* **II.** *vi* agruparse

cluster bomb *n* bomba *f* de dispersión

clutch [klʌtʃ] **I.** *vi* **to** ~ **at sth** agarrarse a algo **II.** *vt* agarrar **III.** *n* **1.** AUTO embrague *m* **2.** (*set: of eggs*) nidada *f* **3.** (*control*) **to be in the** ~**s of sb/sth** estar en las garras de alguien/algo

clutch bag *n* bolso *m* de mano **clutch hitter** *n* bateador(a) *m(f)* clave

clutter ['klʌtəʳ, *Am:* 'klʌt̬ɚ] **I.** *n no pl* desorden *m* **II.** *vt* desordenar

◆**clutter up** *vt* atestar

cluttered *adj* desordenado, -a; *fig* confuso, -a; **to be** ~ **with** estar atestado de

cm *inv abbr of* **centimetre** cm

c'mon *inf* = **come on**

CND [ˌsi:en'di:] *abbr of* **Campaign for Nuclear Disarmament** Campaña *f* pro Desarme Nuclear

CO [ˌsi:'əʊ, *Am:* -'oʊ] *abbr of* **Commanding Officer** oficial *mf* al mando

Co [kəʊ, *Am:* koʊ] **1.** *abbr of* **company** Cía. **2.** *Am, Brit* GEO *abbr of* **county** condado *m* **3.** CHEM *abbr of* **cobalt** Co

c/o *abbr of* **care of** a/c

coach [kəʊtʃ, *Am:* koʊtʃ] **I.** <-es> *n* **1.** (*private bus*) autocar *m* **2.** (*horse-drawn carriage*) coche *m* de caballos, diligencia *f* **3.** (*railway carriage*) vagón *m* **4.** (*teacher*) profesor(a) *m(f)* particular; SPORTS entrenador(a) *m(f)* **II.** *vt* **to** ~ **sb** (**in sth**) enseñar (algo) a alguien **III.** *vi* dar clases particulares

coachbuilder ['kəʊtʃbɪldəʳ] *n Brit* carrocero, -a *m, f*

coaching *n no pl* preparación *f*

coaching staff *n + sing/pl vb* personal *m* de entrenamiento

coachman ['kəʊtʃmən, *Am:* 'koʊtʃ-] <-men> *n* cochero *m*

coach station *n Brit* estación *f* de autocares

coachwork *n no pl, Brit* carrocería *f*

coagulate [kəʊ'ægjʊleɪt, *Am:* koʊ'ægjə-] **I.** *vi* (*blood*) coagularse; (*sauce*) ligarse **II.** *vt* (*blood*) coagular; (*sauce*) ligar

coagulation [kəʊˌægjʊ'leɪʃən, *Am:* koʊˌægjə-] *n no pl* coagulación *f*

coal [kəʊl, *Am:* koʊl] *n no pl* carbón *m;* **piece of ~** hulla *f* ►**to carry ~s to Newcastle** echar agua en el mar

coal-bed *n* estrato *m* de carbón **coal black** *adj* negro, -a como el carbón **coal-box** <-es> *n* coquera *f* **coal bunker** *n* carbonera *f*

coalesce [kəʊə'les, *Am:* koʊə-] *vi form* (*to merge*) fundirse; (*to unit in coalition*) unirse

coalescence [kəʊə'lesnts, *Am:* koʊə-] *n no pl, form* (*merger*) fusión *f;* (*coalition*) unión *f*

coal face *n* frente *m* de arranque del carbón **coal field** *n* yacimiento *m* de carbón **coal-fired** *adj* que quema carbón

coalition [ˌkəʊə'lɪʃən, *Am:* ˌkoʊə-] *n* coalición *f*

coal mine *n* mina *f* de carbón **coal miner** *n* minero *m* de carbón **coal mining** *n no pl* explotación *f* hullera **coal scuttle** *n* cubo *m* para el carbón **coal tar** *n no pl* alquitrán *m* mineral

coarse [kɔːs, *Am:* kɔːrs] <-r, -st> *adj* **1.** (*rough*) basto, -a; (*sand*) grueso, -a; (*skin*) áspero, -a **2.** (*vulgar*) grosero, -a; (*joke*) verde

coarsely *adv* toscamente

coarsen ['kɔːsn, *Am:* 'kɔːr-] **I.** *vt* curtir **II.** *vi* curtirse

coarseness ['kɔːsnɪs, *Am:* 'kɔːrs-] *n no pl* **1.** (*roughness*) tosquedad *f* **2.** (*rudeness*) grosería *f*

coast [kəʊst, *Am:* koʊst] **I.** *n* costa *f* ►**the ~ is clear** *inf* no hay moros en la costa **II.** *vi* avanzar sin esfuerzo

coastal ['kəʊstl, *Am:* 'koʊ-] *adj* costero, -a, abajeño, -a *AmL;* **~ traffic** cabotaje *m*

coaster ['kəʊstəʳ, *Am:* 'koʊstɚ] *n* **1.** (*boat*) barco *m* de cabotaje **2.** (*mat*) salvamanteles *m inv* **3.** (*dripmat*) posavasos *m inv*

coastguard ['kəʊstgɑːd, *Am:* 'koʊstgɑːrd] *n* guardacostas *mf inv* **coastline** *n no pl* litoral *m* **coast-to-coast** *adj* de costa a costa

coat [kəʊt, *Am:* koʊt] **I.** *n* **1.** (*overcoat*) abrigo *m,* tapado *m AmS;* (*jacket*) chaqueta *f* **2.** (*animal's skin*) pelaje *m* **3.** (*layer*) capa *f;* (*of paint*) mano *f;* (*of chocolate*) baño *m* ►**to cut one's ~ according to one's cloth** vivir según sus posibilidades **II.** *vt* **to ~ sth in sth** cubrir algo de algo

coated ['kəʊtɪd, *Am:* 'koʊt-] *adj* cubierto, -a; (*tongue*) saburral

coat-hanger *n* percha *f* **coat-hook** *n* colgador *m*

coati [kəʊ'ɑti] *n* coatí *m*

coating ['kəʊtɪŋ, *Am:* 'koʊt-] *n s.* **coat**

coat of arms <coats of arms> *n* escudo *m* de armas **coat peg** *n Brit* colgador *m* **coat-tails** *npl* faldones *mpl* (*de un frac, etc.*) ►**to ride on sb's ~** salir adelante gracias al favor de alguien

co-author [kəʊ'ɔːθəʳ, *Am:* koʊ'ɑːθɚ] **I.** *n* coautor(a) *m(f)* **II.** *vt* escribir conjuntamente

coax [kəʊks, *Am:* koʊks] *vt* convencer; **to ~ sth out of sb** sonsacarle algo a alguien

coaxing **I.** *n no pl* persuasión *f* **II.** *adj* persuasivo, -a

coaxingly *adv* persuasivamente

cobalt ['kəʊbɔːlt, *Am:* 'koʊbɔːlt] *n no pl* cobalto *m*

cobalt blue *n* azul *m* cobalto

cobble[1] ['kɒbl, *Am:* 'kɑːbl] **I.** *n* adoquín *m* **II.** *vt* adoquinar

cobble[2] ['kɒbl, *Am:* 'kɑːbl] *vt* (*repair*) remendar

◆**cobble together** *vt* improvisar

cobbled *adj* **~ streets** calles *fpl* adoquinadas

cobbler ['kɒbləʳ, *Am:* 'kɑːblɚ] *n* zapatero *m* remendón ►**the ~ should stick to his last** *prov* zapatero, a tus zapatos *prov*

cobblestone ['kɒblstəʊn, *Am:* 'kɑːblstoʊn] *n* adoquín *m*

cobnut ['kɒbnʌt, *Am:* 'kɑːb-] *n* avellana *f*

cobol *n,* **COBOL** ['kəʊbɒl, *Am:* 'koʊbɔːl] *n* INFOR *abbr of* **common business-oriented language** COBOL *m*

cobra ['kəʊbrə, *Am:* 'koʊbrə] *n* cobra *f*

cobweb ['kɒbweb, *Am:* 'kɑːb-] *n* telaraña *f*

coca ['kəʊkə, *Am:* 'koʊ-] *n* coca *f*

Coca-Cola® [ˌkəʊkə'kəʊlə, *Am:* ˌkoʊkə'koʊ-] *n* Coca-Cola® *f*

cocaine [kəʊ'keɪn, *Am:* koʊ-] *n no pl* cocaína *f*

coccyx ['kɒksɪks, *Am:* 'kɑːk-] <-es *o* coccyges> *n* coxis *m inv*

cochineal [ˌkɒtʃɪ'niːl, *Am:* 'kɑːtʃəniːl] *n no pl* cochinilla *f*

cochlea ['ɒkliə, *Am:* 'kaːk-] <-e *o* -s> *n* cóclea *f*

cock [kɒk, *Am:* kɑːk] **I.** *n* **1.** (*male chicken*) gallo *m* **2.** *vulg* (*penis*) polla *f,* pichula *f Chile* **3.** *Brit, inf* (*form of address*) macho *m* **II.** *vt* **1.** (*turn*) ladear **2.** (*ready gun*) amartillar **III.** *adj* (*in ornitology*) macho

cockade [kɒ'keɪd, *Am:* kɑː'keɪd] *n* escarapela *f*

cock-a-doodle-doo [ˌkɒkəˌduːdl'duː, *Am:* ˌkɑːk-] *n childspeak* quiquiriquí *m* **cock-a-hoop** *adj Brit, inf* **to be ~** estar más contento que unas pascuas **cock-a-leekie** *n* caldo *m* de pollo y puerros **cock-and-bull story** <-ies> *n* cuento *m* chino

cockatoo [ˌkɒkə'tuː, *Am:* 'kɑːkə-] <-(s)> *n* cacatúa *f*

cockchafer ['kɒktʃeɪfəʳ, *Am:* 'kɑːktʃeɪfɚ] *n* abejorro *m*

cockcrow ['kɒkkrəʊ, *Am:* 'kɑːkkroʊ] *n* canto *m* del gallo; **at ~** al amanecer

cocked *adj* **~ hat** sombrero *m* de tres picos

cocker ['kɒkəʳ, *Am:* 'kɑːkɚ] *n,* **cocker spaniel** *n* cócker *mf*

cockerel ['kɒkərəl, *Am:* 'kɑːkɚ-] *n* gallo *m* joven

cockeyed ['kɒkaɪd, *Am:* 'kɑːk-] *adj* **1.** *inf*

(*not straight*) torcido, -a **2.** (*ridiculous*) disparatado, -a

cock fight *n* pelea *f* de gallos

cockiness ['kɒkɪnɪs] *n no pl* presunción *f*

cockle ['kɒkl, *Am:* 'kɑːkl] *n* berberecho *m*

cockney ['kɒkni, *Am:* 'kɑːk-] *n* **1.** (*person*) *londinense de un barrio de clase obrera* **2.** (*dialect*) cockney *m* (*dialecto de un barrio del East End londinense*)

Cockney rhyming slang *n jerga en la que se sustituyen palabras o frases por rimas*

cockpit ['kɒkpɪt, *Am:* 'kɑːk-] *n* **1.** (*pilot's area*) cabina *f* **2.** (*area of fighting*) campo *m* de batalla

cockroach ['kɒkrəʊtʃ, *Am:* 'kɑːkroʊtʃ] <-es> *n* cucaracha *f*, surupa *f Ven*

cockscomb ['kɒkskəʊm, *Am:* 'kɑːkskoʊm] *n* cresta *f* de gallo

cocksure [ˌkɒk'ʃʊəʳ, *Am:* ˌkɑːk'ʃʊr] *adj inf* engreído, -a

cocktail ['kɒkteɪl, *Am:* 'kɑːk-] *n* **1.** (*drink*) cóctel *m*, copetín *m Arg* **2.** *inf* (*mixture*) mezcla *f*

cocktail cabinet *n* mueble-bar *m* **cocktail dress** <-es> *n* vestido *m* de cóctel **cocktail lounge** *n* salón *m* de cóctel **cocktail stick** *n* palillo *m* de cóctel

cock-up ['kɒkʌp, *Am:* 'kɑːk-] *n inf* lío *m*

cocky ['kɒki, *Am:* 'kɑːki] <-ier, -iest> *adj inf* engreído, -a

cocoa ['kəʊkəʊ, *Am:* 'koʊkoʊ] *n no pl* **1.** (*chocolate powder*) cacao *m* **2.** (*hot drink*) chocolate *m*

cocoa butter *n* manteca *f* de cacao

coconut ['kəʊkənʌt, *Am:* 'koʊ-] *n* coco *m*

coconut butter *n no pl* manteca *f* de coco **coconut matting** *n no pl* estera *f* de (fibras de) coco **coconut milk** *n no pl* leche *f* de coco **coconut oil** *n no pl* aceite *m* de coco **coconut palm** *n* cocotero *m* **coconut shy** <-ies> *n Brit* (*game*) tiro *m* al coco

cocoon [kə'kuːn] **I.** *n* capullo *m* **II.** *vt a. fig* arropar

cod [kɒd, *Am:* kɑːd] *n inv* bacalao *m*

COD [ˌsiːəʊ'diː, *Am:* -oʊ'-] *abbr of* **cash on delivery** pago *m* contra reembolso

coda ['kəʊdə, *Am:* 'koʊ-] *n* MUS coda *f*

coddle ['kɒdl, *Am:* 'kɑːdl] *vt* **1.** (*cook gently*) cocer a fuego lento **2.** (*treat tenderly*) mimar

code [kəʊd, *Am:* koʊd] **I.** *n* **1.** (*ciphered language*) clave *f* **2.** LAW código *m* **II.** *vt* cifrar

coded *adj* codificado, -a

codeine [kəʊdiːn, *Am:* koʊ-] *n no pl* codeína *f*

code name *n* nombre *m* en clave **code-named** *adj* **the mission is ~ 'Dolores'** la misión tiene el nombre en clave de 'Dolores' **code number** *n* prefijo *m* **code of conduct** *n* código *m* de conducta **code of practice** *n* código *m* deontológico

co-determination [ˌkəʊdɪtɜːmɪ'neɪʃən, *Am:* ˌkoʊdɪtɜːr-] *n no pl* codeterminación *f*

code word *n* palabra *f* en clave

codex ['kəʊdeks, *Am:* 'koʊ-] <codices> *n* códice *m*

codger ['kɒdʒəʳ] *n iron* vejete *m*

codices ['kəʊdɪsiːz, *Am:* 'koʊdəsiːz] *n pl of* **codex**

codicil ['kəʊdɪsɪl] *n* codicilo *m*

codify ['kəʊdɪfaɪ, *Am:* 'kɑː-] <-ie-> *vt* codificar

codling ['kɒdlɪŋ, *Am:* 'kɑːd-] *n* bacalao *m* pequeño

codling moth *n* gusano *m* de la manzana

cod-liver oil *n* aceite *m* de hígado de bacalao

codpiece ['kɒdpiːs, *Am:* 'kɑːd-] *n* bragueta *f*

codswallop ['kɒdzˌwɒləp, *Am:* 'kɑːzˌwɑːləp] *n no pl, Aus, Brit, inf* tonterías *fpl*

co-ed ['kəʊed, *Am:* 'koʊed] **I.** *adj inf* mixto, -a **II.** *n inf* alumna *f* de un colegio mixto

co-education [ˌkəʊedʒʊ'keɪʃən, *Am:* ˌkoʊ-] *n no pl* educación *f* mixta

co-educational [ˌkəʊedʒʊ'keɪʃənəl, *Am:* ˌkoʊedʒə'-] *adj* mixto, -a

coefficient [ˌkəʊɪ'fɪʃnt, *Am:* ˌkoʊ-] *n* coeficiente *m*

coequal [ˌkəʊ'iːkwl, *Am:* ˌkoʊ-] **I.** *n form* igual *mf* **II.** *adj form* igual

coerce [kəʊ'ɜːs, *Am:* koʊ'ɜːrs] *vt form* coaccionar

coercion [kəʊ'ɜːʃən, *Am:* koʊ'ɜːrʒən] *n no pl* coacción *f*

coercive [kəʊ'ɜːsɪv, *Am:* koʊ'ɜːr-] *adj* coactivo, -a

coeval [kəʊ'iːvl, *Am:* koʊ-] *form* **I.** *n* coetáneo, -a *m, f* **II.** *adj* coetáneo, -a

coexist [ˌkəʊɪg'zɪst, *Am:* ˌkoʊ-] *vi* coexistir

coexistence [ˌkəʊɪg'zɪstəns, *Am:* ˌkoʊ-] *n no pl* coexistencia *f*

coexistent [ˌkəʊɪg'zɪstənt, *Am:* ˌkoʊ-] *adj* coexistente

C of E [ˌsiːəv'iː] *abbr of* **Church of England** Iglesia *f* Anglicana

coffee ['kɒfi, *Am:* 'kɑːfi] *n* café *m*

coffee bar *n* café *m* **coffee bean** *n* grano *m* de café

coffee break *n* pausa *f* para tomar café

coffee cake *n Aus, Brit* pastel *m* de café

coffee-coloured *adj* de color café

coffee cup *n* taza *f* de café **coffee-grinder** *n* molinillo *m* de café **coffee grounds** *n pl* poso *m* **coffee house** *n* café *m* **coffee klatch** <-es> *n Am* tertulia *f* **coffee machine** *n* máquina *f* de café, greca *f AmL* **coffee mill** *n* molinillo *m* de café **coffee morning** *n Brit* tertulia *f* para tomar el café por la mañana **coffeepot** *n* cafetera *f* **coffee shop** *n* cafétería *f* **coffee table** *n* mesa *f* baja **coffee-table book** *n* libro *m* de gran formato

coffer ['kɒfəʳ, *Am:* 'kɑːfɚ] *n* **1.** (*storage place*) cofre *m* **2.** *pl* (*money reserves*) fondos *mpl*

coffin ['kɒfɪn, *Am:* 'kɔːfɪn] *n Aus, Brit* ataúd *m*

cog [kɒg, *Am:* kɑːg] *n* TECH diente *m;* (*wheel*)

rueda *f* dentada; **to be a ~ in a machine** ser una pieza más de una organización
cogency [ˈkəʊdʒəntsi, *Am:* ˈkoʊ-] *n no pl, form* fuerza *f*
cogent [ˈkəʊdʒənt, *Am:* ˈkoʊ-] *adj form* fuerte; (*argument*) convincente
cogently *adv form* convincentemente
cogitate [ˈkɒdʒɪteɪt, *Am:* ˈkɑːdʒə-] *vi* reflexionar
cogitation [ˌkɒdʒɪˈteɪʃən, *Am:* ˌkɑːdʒə-] *n* reflexión *f*
cognac [ˈkɒnjæk, *Am:* ˈkoʊnjæk] *n* coñac *m*
cognate [ˈkɒgneɪt, *Am:* ˈkɑːg-] *adj* afín
cognition [kɒgˈnɪʃən, *Am:* kɑːg-] *n form* **1.** (*thought*) percepción *f* **2.** (*mental processes*) cognición *f*
cognitive [ˈkɒgnɪtɪv, *Am:* ˈkɑːgnət̬ɪv] *adj* cognitivo, -a
cognitive psychology *n no pl* psicología *f* cognitiva **cognitive therapy** <-ies> *n* terapia *f* cognitiva
cognizance [ˈkɒgnɪznts, *Am:* ˈkɑːgnə-] *n no pl* LAW competencia *f;* **to take ~ of sth** tener algo en cuenta
cognizant [ˈkɒgnɪznt, *Am:* ˈkɑːgnə-] *adj* conocedor(a); LAW competente
cognomen [kɒgˈnəʊmən, *Am:* kɑːgˈnoʊ-] *n* **1.** (*nickname*) apodo *m* **2.** HIST apellido *m*
cognoscenti [ˌkɒnjəʊˈʃenti, *Am:* ˌkɑːgnəˈʃenti] *npl* expertos *mpl*
cogwheel [ˈkɒgwiːl, *Am:* ˈkɑːg-] *n* rueda *f* dentada
cohabit [kəʊˈhæbɪt, *Am:* koʊ-] *vi* cohabitar
cohabitant [kəʊˈhæbɪtænt, *Am:* koʊ-] *n* cohabitante *mf*
cohabitation [kəʊˌhæbɪˈteɪʃən, *Am:* koʊˌhæb-] *n no pl* cohabitación *f*
cohabitee [ˌkəʊhæbɪˈtiː, *Am:* ˌkoʊ-] *n form s.* **cohabitant**
cohere [kəʊˈhɪəʳ, *Am:* koʊˈhɪr] *vi* ser coherente
coherence [kəʊˈhɪərəns, *Am:* koʊˈhɪr-] *n no pl* coherencia *f*
coherent [ˈkəʊˈhɪərənt, *Am:* ˈkoʊˈhɪr-] *adj* coherente
coherently *adv* coherentemente
cohesion [kəʊˈhiːʒən, *Am:* koʊ-] *n no pl* cohesión *f*
cohesive [kəʊˈhiːsɪv, *Am:* koʊ-] *adj* cohesivo, -a
cohesiveness *n no pl* cohesión *f*
cohort [ˈkəʊhɔːt, *Am:* ˈkoʊhɔːrt] *n* cohorte *f*
COI *n Brit abbr of* **Central Office of Information** oficina *f* central de información
coil [kɔɪl] **I.** *n* **1.** rollo *m* **2.** ELEC bobina *f* **3.** MED espiral *f* (intrauterina) **II.** *vi* enrollarse **III.** *vt* enrollar
coiled *adj* enrollado, -a
coin [kɔɪn] **I.** *n* moneda *f;* **to toss a ~** echar una moneda al aire **II.** *vt* acuñar ►**to ~ a phrase ...** como se suele decir...
coinage [ˈkɔɪnɪdʒ] *n* **1.** *no pl* (*system*) sistema *m* monetario **2.** (*act*) acuñación *f*
coin-box telephone *n* teléfono *m* público de monedas
coincide [ˌkəʊɪnˈsaɪd, *Am:* ˌkoʊ-] *vi* coincidir; (*agree*) estar de acuerdo
coincidence [kəʊˈɪnsɪdəns, *Am:* koʊ-] *n* coincidencia *f;* (*chance*) casualidad *f*
coincident [kəʊˈɪnsɪdənt, *Am:* koʊ-] *adj* coincidente
coincidental [kəʊˌɪnsɪˈdentəl, *Am:* koʊˌɪnsɪˈdent̬əl] *adj* coincidente
coincidentally *adv* por casualidad
coitus [ˈkəʊɪtəs, *Am:* ˈkoʊət̬əs] *n no pl, form* coito *m*
coitus interruptus *n* coitus *m inv* interruptus
coke [kəʊk, *Am:* koʊk] *n no pl* **1.** (*fuel*) coque *m* **2.** *inf* coca *f,* pichicata *f Arg*
Coke® [kəʊk, *Am:* koʊk] *n* Coca-Cola® *f*
col [kɒl, *Am:* kɑːl] *n abbr of* **column** columna *f*
Col *n abbr of* **colonel** coronel *m*
COL *n abbr of* **computer-oriented language** COL *m*
cola [ˈkəʊlə, *Am:* ˈkoʊ-] *n* Coca-Cola® *f*
colander [ˈkɒləndəʳ, *Am:* ˈkʌləndɚ] *n* colador *m*
cold [kəʊld, *Am:* koʊld] **I.** *adj* frío, -a; **to be ~** tener frío; **to go ~** (*soup, coffee*) enfriarse; **to get ~** (*person*) tener frío; **it's bitterly ~** hace un frío que pela ►**to leave sb ~** dejar frío a alguien **II.** *n* **1.** METEO frío *m* **2.** MED resfriado *m;* **to catch a ~** acatarrarse; **to have a ~** estar acatarrado ►**to leave sb out in the ~** dejar a alguien al margen
cold bag *n Brit* nevera *f* portátil **cold-blooded** *adj* (*animal*) de sangre fría; (*person*) cruel **cold call** *n estilo de venta que consiste en llamar a la puerta del potencial cliente o llamarle por teléfono* **cold comfort** *n* poco consuelo *m* **cold cream** *n* crema *f* para el cutis **cold cuts** *npl* fiambres *mpl* **cold-eyed** *adj* hostil **cold frame** *n* vivero *m* de plantas **cold front** *n* frente *m* frío **cold-hearted** *adj* insensible
coldish [ˈkəʊldɪʃ, *Am:* ˈkoʊl-] *adj* fresquito, -a
coldness [ˈkəʊldnɪs, *Am:* ˈkoʊld-] *n no pl* frialdad *f*
cold shower *n a. fig* ducha *f* fría **cold snap** *n* ola *f* de frío **cold sore** *n* MED boquera *f* **cold start** *n* AUTO, INFOR arranque *m* en frío **cold storage** *n no pl* conservación *f* en cámara frigorífica **cold store** *n* cámara *f* frigorífica **cold sweat** *n* sudor *m* frío **cold truth** *n* **the ~** la cruda verdad **cold turkey** *n no pl, Am, Aus, inf* mono *m* **cold war** *n* guerra *f* fría **cold wave** *n* ola *f* de frío
coleslaw [ˈkəʊlslɔː, *Am:* ˈkoʊlslɑː] *n no pl* ensalada *f* de col con salsa
coley [ˈkəʊli, *Am:* ˈkoʊ-] <-(s)> *n* abadejo *m*
colic [ˈkɒlɪk, *Am:* ˈkɑːlɪk] *n no pl* cólico *m*
collaborate [kəˈlæbəreɪt] *vi* colaborar
collaboration [kəˌlæbəˈreɪʃən] *n* colaboración *f*

collaborationist [kəˌlæbəˈreɪʃnɪst] *adj* colaboracionista *mf*
collaborative [kəˈæbərətɪv] *adj* de colaboración; (*effort*) común
collaborator [kəˈlæbəreɪtəʳ, *Am:* -t̬ɚ] *n* 1. colaborador(a) *m(f)* 2. *pej* colaboracionista *mf*
collage [ˈkɒlɑːʒ, *Am:* kəlɑːʒ] *n* collage *m*
collagen [ˈkɒlədʒən, *Am:* ˈkɑːlə-] *n no pl* colágeno *m*
collagen implant *n*, **collagen injection** *n* implante *m* de colágeno
collapse [kəˈlæps] I. *vi* 1. MED sufrir un colapso 2. (*fall down: buildings*) derrumbarse; (*people*) hundirse 3. (*fail*) fracasar II. *n* 1. MED colapso *m* 2. (*act of falling down*) derrumbamiento *m*; (*of people*) hundimiento *m* 3. (*failure*) fracaso *m*
collapsible [kəˈlæpsɪbl] *adj* plegable
collar [ˈkɒləʳ, *Am:* ˈkɑːlɚ] I. *n* 1. FASHION cuello *m* 2. (*of a dog, cat*) collar *m*; *Brit* (*leash*) correa *f* ►**to get** (**all**) **hot under the** ~ acalorarse II. *vt inf* coger por el cuello; *fig* capturar
collar bone *n* clavícula *f*
collate [kəˈleɪt] *vt* 1. (*analyze*) cotejar 2. (*arrange in order*) ordenar
collateral [kəˈlætərəl, *Am:* -ˈlæt̬-] I. *n* FIN garantía *f* subsidiaria II. *adj* colateral
collateral damage *n* daño *m* colateral **collateral loan** *n* FIN préstamo *m* pignoraticio
collaterally [kəˈlætərəli, *Am:* -ˈlæt̬-] *adv* colateralmente
colleague [ˈkɒliːg, *Am:* ˈkɑːliːg] *n* colega *mf*
collect [kəˈlekt, *Am:* ˈkɑːl-] I. *vi* 1. (*gather*) reunirse 2. (*money: contributions*) hacer una colecta; (*money: payments due*) cobrar II. *n* REL colecta *f* III. *adj Am* TEL a cobro revertido IV. *vt* 1. (*gather*) reunir; (*money*) recaudar; (*stamps*) coleccionar 2. (*pick up*) recoger 3. *form* (*regain control*) **to** ~ **oneself** reponerse; **to** ~ **one's thoughts** poner en orden sus ideas
♦**collect up** *vt* recoger
collectable [kəˈlektəbl] I. *adj* coleccionable II. *n* coleccionable *m*
collect call *n Am* llamada *f* a cobro revertido
collected [kəˈlektɪd] *adj* sosegado, -a
collectible [kəˈlektəbl] I. *adj* coleccionable II. *n* coleccionable *m*
collection [kəˈlekʃən] *n* 1. (*money gathered*) recaudación *f*; REL colecta *f* 2. (*object collected*) colección *f* 3. (*large number*) montón *m* 4. (*act of getting*) recogida *f*
collective [kəˈlektɪv] I. *adj* colectivo, -a II. *n* colectivo *m*
collective bargaining *n* negociación *f* colectiva **collective farm** *n* granja *f* colectiva
collectively *adv* colectivamente
collective noun *n* nombre *m* colectivo
collectivism [kəˈlektɪvɪzm, *Am:* -tə-] *n no pl* colectivismo *m*
collector [kəˈlektəʳ, *Am:* -ɚ] *n* 1. (*one who gathers objects*) coleccionista *mf* 2. (*one who collects payments*) cobrador(a) *m(f)*
collector's item *n*, **collector's piece** *n* pieza *f* de coleccionista
colleen [ˈkɒliːn, *Am:* ˈkɑliːn] *n Irish* muchacha *f*
college [ˈkɒlɪdʒ, *Am:* ˈkɑːlɪdʒ] *n* 1. (*school*) colegio *m* 2. (*university*) universidad *f*

> El término **college** designa el tiempo necesario en la universidad para alcanzar el **bachelor's degree**, aproximadamente 4-5 años. Las universidades en las que los estudiantes sólo pueden obtener el **bacherlor's degree** se llaman **colleges**, el mismo nombre reciben algunas escuelas profesionales. Las universidades, en sentido estricto, son aquellas que ofrecen también **higher degrees** (títulos superiores) como por ejemplo, **master's degrees** y **doctorates**. En los **junior colleges** se pueden cursar los dos primeros años de estudios universitarios o capacitarse para aprender una profesión técnica.

college graduate *n Am* licenciado, -a *m, f*
collegiate [kəˈliːdʒɪət, *Am:* -dʒɪt] *adj* colegiado, -a; *Am* universitario, -a
collide [kəˈlaɪd] *vi* chocar
collie [ˈkɒli, *Am:* ˈkɑːli] *n* collie *m*
collier [ˈkɒlɪəʳ, *Am:* ˈkɑːljɚ] *n form* 1. MIN minero, -a *m, f* de carbón 2. (*ship*) barco *m* carbonero
colliery [ˈkɒlɪəri, *Am:* ˈkɑːljɚ] <-ies> *n* mina *f* de carbón
collision [kəˈlɪʒən] *n* choque *m*
collocate [ˈkɒləʊkeɪt, *Am:* ˈkɑːlə-] I. *vi* LING **to** ~ **with sth** aparecer en combinación con algo II. *n* LING colocación *f*
collocation [ˌkɒləʊkeɪʃən, *Am:* ˌkɑːləˈ-] *n* colocación *f*
colloquial [kəˈləʊkwɪəl, *Am:* -ˈloʊ-] *adj* familiar; (*language*) coloquial
colloquialism *n* expresión *f* coloquial
colloquy [ˈkɒləkwi, *Am:* ˈkɑːlə-] *n* coloquio *m*
collude [kəˈluːd] *vi form* confabularse
collusion [kəˈluːʒən] *n no pl, form* confabulación *f*
collusive [kəˈluːsiv] *adj form* colusorio, -a
collywobbles [ˈkɒliˌwɒblz, *Am:* ˈkɑːliˌwɑː-] *npl iron* ruido *m* de tripas; (*nervousness*) nervios *mpl*
cologne [kəˈləʊn, *Am:* -loʊn] *n no pl, Am* (*perfume*) colonia *f*
Colombia [kəˈlʌmbɪə] *n* Colombia *f*
Colombian [kəˈlʌmbɪən] I. *adj* colombiano, -a II. *n* colombiano, -a *m, f*
colon [ˈkəʊlən, *Am:* ˈkoʊ-] *n* 1. ANAT colon *m* 2. LING dos puntos *mpl*
colon cancer *n* cáncer *m* de colon
colonel [ˈkɜːnl, *Am:* ˈkɜːr-] *n* coronel *mf*

colonial [kə'ləʊniəl, *Am:* -'loʊ-] I. *adj* colonial II. *n* colono, -a *m, f*
colonialism [kə'ləʊniəlɪzəm, *Am:* -'loʊ-] *n no pl* colonialismo *m*
colonialist I. *n* colonialista *mf* II. *adj* colonialista
colonial mentality *n no pl* mentalidad *f* colonial
colonisation ['kɒlənaɪzeɪʃən, *Am:* 'kɑːl-] *n Aus, Brit* colonización *f*
colonise ['kɒlənaɪz, *Am:* 'kɑːlənaɪz] *vt Aus, Brit* colonizar
colonist ['kɒlənɪst, *Am:* 'kɑːlə-] *n* 1. (*foreigner*) colonizador(a) *m(f)* 2. (*former inhabitant*) colono, -a *m, f*
colonization [ˌkɒlənaɪ'zeɪʃən, *Am:* ˌkɑːlənɪ-] *n no pl, Am* colonización *f*
colonize ['kɒlənaɪz, *Am:* 'kɑːlə-] *vt* colonizar
colonizer ['kɒlənaɪzəʳ, *Am:* 'kɑːlənaɪzɚ] *n* colonizador(a) *m(f)*
colony ['kɒləni, *Am:* 'kɑːlə-] <-ies> *n a.* ZOOL colonia *f*
color ['kʌləʳ, *Am:* -ɚ] *n, adj, vi, vt Am s.* **colour**
Colorado beetle [ˌkɒlə'rɑːdəʊ'biːtl, *Am:* ˌkɑːlə'rædoʊ'biːt̬l] *n,* **Colorado potato beetle** *n* escarabajo *m* de la patata
coloration [ˌkʌlə'reɪʃən] *n no pl* coloración *f*
colored *adj Am s.* **coloured**
colorful *adj Am s.* **colourful**
coloring *n Am s.* **colouring**
colorless *adj Am s.* **colourless**
color line *n Am* barrera *f* racial
colossal [kə'lɒsl, *Am:* -'lɑːsl] *adj* colosal
colossus [kə'lɒsəs] *n* <-es *o* colossi> coloso *m*
colour ['kʌləʳ, *Am:* -ɚ] I. *n* 1. (*appearance*) color *m;* **primary** ~ color primario; **what ~ is your dress?** ¿de qué color es tu vestido?; **to have ~ in one's cheeks** tener las mejillas sonrosadas 2. (*vigour*) colorido *m* 3. (*dye*) tinte *m* 4. *pl* SCHOOL, UNIV (*sports honour*) colores *mpl* del equipo 5. *pl* POL, MIL (*official flag*) bandera *f;* **to call to ~s** llamar a filas 6. (*character*) **to show one's true ~s** mostrar el verdadero rostro; **to see sb in their true ~s** ver a alguien tal como es II. *vt* 1. (*change colour of*) colorear, pintar; **to ~ a room blue** pintar una habitación de azul 2. (*dye*) teñir 3. (*distort*) alterar III. *vi* sonrojarse
colour bar *n Brit* barrera *f* racial
colour blind *adj* daltónico, -a
colour blindness *n no pl* daltonismo *m*
coloured *adj* coloreado, -a; (*pencil, people*) de color
colour-fast ['kʌləfɑːst, *Am:* -ɚfæst] *adj* no desteñible
colour filter *n* PHOT filtro *m* de color
colourful ['kʌləfəl, *Am:* -ɚ-] *adj* 1. (*full of colour: paintings, clothing*) lleno, -a de colorido 2. (*lively*) vivo, -a; (*countryside*) pintoresco, -a; ~ **part of town** zona *f* animada de la ciudad
colouring ['kʌlərɪŋ] *n no pl* 1. (*complexion*) color *m* 2. (*chemical*) colorante *m*
colourless ['kʌləlɪs, *Am:* -ɚ-] *adj Brit* 1. (*having no colour*) incoloro, -a 2. (*bland*) soso, -a; **a grey, ~ city** una ciudad gris, apagada
colour scheme *n* combinación *f* de colores
colour slide *n* diapositiva *f* de color
colour television *n* televisión *f* en color
cols *n abbr of* **columns** columnas *fpl*
colt [kəʊlt, *Am:* koʊlt] *n* potro *m,* potranco *m AmL*
Columbia [kə'lʌmbiə] *n* **the District of ~** el distrito de Columbia
Columbus Day [kə'lʌmbəsˌdeɪ] *n no pl, Am* día *m* de la Hispanidad, día *m* de la Raza *AmL*

Columbus Day es el día en el que se conmemora que Colón descubrió el Nuevo Mundo el 12 de octubre de 1492. Desde 1971 este día se celebra siempre el segundo lunes del mes de octubre.

column ['kɒləm, *Am:* 'kɑːləm] *n a.* ARCHIT, ANAT, TYPO columna *f;* **spinal ~** columna vertebral; **to march in ~s** MIL, NAUT marchar en filas
columnist ['kɒləmnɪst, *Am:* 'kɑːləm-] *n* columnista *mf*
coma ['kəʊmə, *Am:* 'koʊ-] *n* coma *m;* **to go into a ~** entrar en coma; **to wake up out of one's ~** salir del coma
comatose ['kəʊmətəʊs, *Am:* 'koʊmətoʊs] *adj* comatoso, -a; ~ **state** estado *m* de coma
comb [kəʊm, *Am:* koʊm] I. *n* 1. (*hair device*) peine *m* 2. ZOOL cresta *f* de gallo II. *vt* 1. (*tidy with a comb*) **to ~ one's hair** peinarse el pelo 2. (*search thoroughly*) **to ~ an apartment for clues** rastrear un apartamento en busca de pruebas
◆**comb out** *vt* (*a knot, tangles, lice*) desenredar
combat ['kɒmbæt, *Am:* 'kɑːm-] I. *n* 1. *no pl* (*wartime fighting*) combate *m;* **hand-to-hand ~** combate cuerpo a cuerpo 2. (*battle*) lucha *f* II. *vt* luchar contra; (*crime*) combatir; (*a desire*) resistirse a
combat aircraft *n* avión *m* de combate
combatant ['kɒmbətənt, *Am:* kəm'bæt-] *n* combatiente *mf*
combative ['kɒmbətɪv, *Am:* kəm'bæt̬ɪv] *adj* combativo, -a
combination [ˌkɒmbɪ'neɪʃən, *Am:* ˌkɑːmbə-] *n* 1. (*mixture*) combinación *f* 2. (*sequence of numbers*) combinación *f;* **in ~** (*together*) en combinación
combine [kəm'baɪn, *Am:* 'kɑːmbaɪn] I. *vt* combinar; **to ~ family life with a career** compaginar la vida familiar con una carrera profesional; **to ~ ingredients** mezclar ingredientes; **to ~ forces against sb/sth** reunir fuerzas contra alguien/algo II. *vi* asociarse
combined [kəm'baɪnd, *Am:* 'kɑːm-] *adj*

C

combinado, -a; (*efforts*) conjunto, -a
combine harvester *n* cosechadora *f*
combustible [kəm'bʌstəbl] *adj form* **1.**(*highly flammable*) combustible **2.**(*easily angry*) excitable
combustion [kəm'bʌstʃən] *n no pl* combustión *f*
combustion chamber *n* cámara *f* de combustión
come [kʌm] <came, come, coming> *vi* **1.**(*move towards*) venir; **to ~ towards sb** venir hacia alguien **2.**(*go*) venirse; **are you coming to the pub with us?** ¿te vienes al pub con nosotros? **3.**(*arrive*) llegar; **January ~s before February** enero precede a febrero; **the year to ~** el próximo año; **to ~ to an agreement** llegar a un acuerdo; **to ~ to a decision** llegar a una decisión; **to ~ home** volver a casa; **to ~ to sb's rescue** socorrer a alguien; **to ~ first/second/third** *Aus, Brit* ser primero/segundo/tercero **4.**(*happen*) pasar; **to ~ to pass** suceder, ocurrir; **~ what may** pase lo que pase; **how ~?** *inf* ¿cómo es?; **nothing came of it** todo quedó en nada **5.**(*behave like*) **to ~ the poor little innocent** hacerse el pobre niño inocente **6.**(*become*) hacerse, llegar a; **my dream has ~ true** mi sueño se ha hecho realidad; **I like it as it ~s** me gusta tal cual; **to ~ open** abrirse; **to ~ in red** haberlo en rojo **7.** *vulg* (*have an orgasm*) correrse, acabar *AmL* ▶ **~ <u>again</u>?** *inf* ¿cómo?; **to ~ <u>clean</u>** (**about sth**) ser sincero (acerca de algo); **<u>everything</u> ~s to him who <u>waits</u>** *prov* con paciencia y esperar se gana el cielo *prov;* **<u>don't</u> ~ it** (**with me**)! ¡(a mí) no me vengas con ésas!; **to <u>have</u> it coming** tenerlo merecido
◆**come about** *vi* suceder
◆**come across** **I.** *vt insep* encontrarse con, dar con; **to ~ a problem** topar con un problema **II.** *vi* **1.**(*be evident*) ser entendido **2.**(*create an impression*) dar una imagen
◆**come along** *vi* **1.**(*hurry*) darse prisa; **~!** ¡date prisa! **2.**(*go too*) venir también **3.**(*progressing*) progresar
◆**come apart** *vi* separarse
◆**come around** *vi s.* **come round**
◆**come at** *vt insep* **1.**(*attack*) atacar **2.**(*arrive*) llegar a
◆**come away** *vi* **1.**(*leave*) irse **2.**(*become detached*) separarse; **to ~ from sth** desprenderse de algo
◆**come back** *vi* **1.**(*return*) regresar **2.**(*be remembered*) volver (a la memoria) **3.**(*return to fashion*) volver **4.** SPORTS contraatacar
◆**come by** **I.** *vt insep* **1.** dar con; (*a problem*) topar con **2.**(*obtain by chance*) recibir **II.** *vi* pasar (por)
◆**come down** *vi* **1.**(*move down*) bajar; (*move down in rank: people*) descender **2.**(*drop: roof*) venirse abajo **3.**(*land*) aterrizar **4.**(*fall: rain, snow*) caer **5.**(*visit southern place*) viajar al sur **6.**(*become less: prices, cost, inflation*) reducirse; (*lower one's price*) rebajarse
◆**come forward** *vi* **1.**(*advance*) avanzar **2.**(*offer assistance*) ofrecerse (voluntariamente); **to ~ to do sth** ofrecerse para hacer algo
◆**come from** *vt* ser de; (*a family*) descender de; **where do you ~?** ¿de dónde eres?; **to ~ a good family** ser de buena familia
◆**come in** *vi* **1.**(*enter*) entrar **2.**(*arrive*) llegar **3.**(*become fashionable*) ponerse de moda **4.**(*be useful*) servir **5.**(*be*) resultar **6.**(*participate in*) tomar parte en **7.** *Am* (*be positioned*) **to ~ first** situarse primero
◆**come into** *vt insep* **1.**(*enter*) entrar en; (*power*) tomar; **to ~ office** tomar posesión de un cargo; **to ~ fashion** ponerse de moda; **to ~ sb's life** entrar en la vida de alguien **2.**(*inherit*) heredar
◆**come off** **I.** *vi* **1.** *inf* (*succeed*) tener éxito **2.**(*end up*) terminar **3.**(*become detached*) desprenderse **4.**(*fall*) caerse **II.** *vt insep* **1.**(*fall*) **to ~ the bike** caerse de la bici **2.** *Am* (*complete*) terminar; **to ~ an injury** MED recuperarse de una herida ▶ **~ <u>it</u>!** *inf* ¡anda ya!
◆**come on** **I.** *vi* **1.**(*improve*) progresar **2.** THEAT, CINE (*actor, performer*) aparecer **3.**(*begin: film, programme*) empezar; **what time does the news ~?** ¿a qué hora dan las noticias? **4.**(*start gradually*) **I've got a headache coming on** me está cogiendo dolor de cabeza **II.** *vt insep* encontrar **III.** *interj* (*hurry*) ¡date prisa!, ¡ándale! *Méx;* (*encouragement*) ¡ánimo!, ¡órale! *Méx;* (*annoyance*) ¡venga ya!
◆**come out** *vi* **1.**(*express opinion*) **to ~ in favour of/against sth** pronunciarse a favor/en contra de algo **2.**(*end up*) **how did your painting ~?** ¿cómo quedó tu cuadro? **3.** + *n* **to ~ a mess** resultar un desastre **4.** + *adj* **to ~ wrong/right** salir mal/bien **5.**(*go out socially*) presentarse en sociedad **6.**(*become known*) darse a conocer; **to ~ that ...** revelarse que... **7.**(*reveal one's homosexuality*) declararse homosexual **8.** *Brit* (*strike*) declararse en huelga **9.**(*be removed*) salir, quitarse **10.**(*become available: stamp, book, magazine*) publicarse **11.**(*appear in sky: moon, stars, sun*) aparecer **12.**(*open: flowers*) florecer
◆**come over** **I.** *vi* **1.**(*come nearer*) acercarse **2.**(*visit sb's home*) visitar **3.** *Aus, Brit* (*feel*) sentir **II.** *vt* **to ~ sb** apoderarse de alguien
◆**come round** *vi* **1.**(*change one's mind*) cambiar de opinión; **to ~ to sb's point of view** adoptar el punto de vista de alguien **2.** MED volver en sí **3.**(*visit sb's home*) pasarse **4.**(*arrive: a holiday, letter*) llegar
◆**come through** **I.** *vi* **1.**(*show: one's nervousness, excitement, charm*) mostrar **2.** *Aus, Brit* (*arrive: results, visa, call*) llegar **3.**(*survive*) sobrevivir **II.** *vt insep* superar
◆**come to** **I.** *vt insep* **1.**(*reach*) llegar a; **to come down to sth** bajar a algo; **to come up**

to sth subir a algo; to ~ rest irse a dormir; to ~ nothing quedarse en nada 2. (*amount to*) subir a II. *vi* MED volver en sí

◆**come under** *vt no pl* 1. (*be listed under*) aparecer bajo 2. (*be dealt with*) ser competencia de 3. (*be subjected to*) **to ~ criticism** ser objeto de crítica

◆**come up** *vi* 1. (*be mentioned*) mencionarse 2. (*happen*) suceder

◆**come upon** *vt no pl* encontrarse con

comeback ['kʌmbæk] *n* 1. vuelta *f;* SPORTS recuperación *f* 2. (*retort*) réplica *f*

Comecon ['kɒmɪkɒn, *Am:* 'kɑːmɪkɑːn] *n abbr of* **Council for Mutual Economic Assistance** COMECON *m*

comedian [kə'miːdɪən] *n* 1. (*person telling jokes*) cómico, -a *m, f* 2. (*funny person*) payaso, -a *m, f*

comedienne [kəˌmiːdi'ən] *n* 1. (*female comedian*) cómica *f* 2. (*funny female*) payasa *f*

comedown ['kʌmdaʊn] *n no pl, inf* 1. (*anti-climax*) revés *m* 2. (*decline in status*) humillación *f*

comedy ['kɒmədi, *Am:* 'kɑːmə-] <-ies> *n* 1. CINE, THEAT, LIT comedia *f* 2. (*funny situation*) comicidad *f*

comeliness ['kʌmlɪnɪs] *n no pl* encanto *m*

comely ['kʌmli] <-ier, -iest> *adj* (*woman*) atractiva

come-on ['kʌmɒn, *Am:* -ɑːn] *n Am, inf* 1. (*expression of sexual interest*) invitación *f;* **to give sb the ~** tirar los tejos a alguien 2. (*enticement*) reclamo *m*

comet ['kɒmɪt, *Am:* 'kɑːmɪt] *n* cometa *m*

come-uppance [kʌm'ʌpənts] *n* merecido *m;* **he got his ~ in the end** al final se llevó su merecido

comfort ['kʌmfət, *Am:* -fɚt] I. *n* 1. (*comfortable feeling*) comodidad *f* 2. (*consolation*) consuelo *m;* **to be a ~ to sb** ser un consuelo para alguien 3. (*pleasurable things in life*) bienestar *m;* **the ~s of life** las cosas agradables de la vida II. *vt* consolar

comfortable ['kʌmftəbl, *Am:* 'kʌmfɚt̬ə-] *adj* 1. (*offering comfort*) cómodo, -a; **to make oneself ~** ponerse cómodo 2. (*financially stable*) acomodado, -a; **~ life** vida *f* holgada 3. SPORTS (*substantial*) fácil

comfortably ['kʌmftəbli, *Am:* 'kʌmfɚt̬ə-] *adv* 1. (*in a comfortable manner: sit, lie*) cómodamente 2. (*easily*) fácilmente 3. (*in financially stable manner*) **to live ~** vivir de forma acomodada

comforter ['kʌmfətəʳ, *Am:* -fɚt̬ɚ] *n Am* (*duvet*) edredón *m*

comforting ['kʌmfətɪŋ, *Am:* -fɚt̬ɪŋ] *adj* (*thought, words*) reconfortante

comfortless ['kʌmfətlɪs, *Am:* -fɚt-] *adj form* incómodo, -a

comfort station *n Am* (*public toilet*) servicios *mpl* públicos

comfy ['kʌmfi] <-ier, -iest> *adj inf* (*furniture, clothes*) cómodo, -a

comic ['kɒmɪk, *Am:* 'kɑːmɪk] I. *n* 1. (*cartoon magazine*) cómic *m* 2. (*person*) cómico, -a *m, f* II. *adj* cómico, -a; **~ play** comedia *f*

comical ['kɒmɪkl, *Am:* 'kɑːmɪ-] *adj* cómico, -a; (*idea*) divertido, -a

comic book *n Am* (*comic*) tebeo *m* **comic strip** *n* tira *f* cómica

coming ['kʌmɪŋ] I. *adj* 1. (*next*) próximo, -a; **the ~ year** el año que viene 2. (*approaching*) venidero, -a II. *n* llegada *f;* **~s and goings** idas y venidas

comma ['kɒmə, *Am:* 'kɑːmə] *n* coma *f*

command [kə'mɑːnd, *Am:* -'mænd] I. *vt* 1. (*order*) **to ~ sb to do sth** ordenar a alguien que haga algo; **to ~ that** mandar que +*subj* 2. (*have command over*) estar al mando de 3. (*have at one's disposal*) disponer de 4. (*overlook: view*) tener 5. (*respect*) imponer; (*sympathy*) inspirar II. *n* 1. (*order*) mandato *m;* **to obey a ~** acatar una orden; **to take ~ of** asumir el mando de; **to have ~ over a fleet** estar al mando de una flota; **at sb's ~** a la disposición de alguien; **under sb's ~** bajo las órdenes de alguien 2. (*control*) mando *m;* **to be in ~ of sth** estar al mando de algo 3. MIL comandancia *f* 4. INFOR orden *f* 5. *no pl* (*knowledge*) dominio *m* 6. *no pl, form* (*view*) vista *f*

commandant [ˌkɒmən'dænt, *Am:* 'kɑː-məndænt] *n* MIL comandante *mf*

commandeer [ˌkɒmən'dɪəʳ, *Am:* ˌkɑːmən-'dɪr] *vt* apropriarse de

commander [kə'mɑːndəʳ, *Am:* -'mændɚ] *n* 1. MIL (*officer in charge*) comandante *mf* 2. *Brit* MIL, NAUT (*naval officer*) capitán *m* de fragata

commanding [kə'mɑːndɪŋ, *Am:* -'mæn-] *adj* 1. (*authoritative*) dominante; (*voice*) imponente 2. (*dominant: position*) dominante 3. (*considerable*) abrumador(a)

command key *n* INFOR tecla *f* de comando

commandment [kə'mɑːndmənt, *Am:* -'mænd-] *n liter* orden *f*

Commandment [kə'mɑːndmənt, *Am:* -'mænd-] *n* **the Ten ~s** REL los diez mandamientos

command module *n* AVIAT módulo *m* de maniobra y mando

commando [kə'mɑːndəʊ, *Am:* -'mændoʊ] <-s *o* -es> *n* MIL 1. (*group of soldiers*) comando *m* 2. (*member of commando*) miembro *mf* de un comando

command post *n* MIL puesto *m* de mando

command prompt *n* INFOR línea *f* de comandos

commemorate [kə'meməreɪt] *vt* conmemorar

commemoration [kəˌmemə'reɪʃən] *n no pl* conmemoración *f;* **in ~ of ...** en conmemoración de...

commemorative [kə'memərətɪv, *Am:* -t̬ɪv] *adj* conmemorativo, -a

commence [kə'ments] *vi form* empezar; **to**

~ **speaking** comenzar un discurso

commencement [kəˈmentsmənt] *n form* **1.** (*beginning*) inicio *m* **2.** *Am* SCHOOL, UNIV ceremonia *f* de graduación

commend [kəˈmend] *vt* **1.** (*praise*) elogiar; **to ~ sth/sb** (**on sth**) alabar algo/a alguien (por algo) **2.** (*entrust*) encomendar; **to ~ sth to sb** encomendar algo a alguien **3.** (*recommend*) recomendar

commendable [kəˈmendəbl] *adj* recomendable; ~ **bravery** valor *m* loable

commendation [ˌkɒmenˈdeɪʃən, *Am:* ˌkɑːmen-] *n* **1.** (*praise*) elogio *m* **2.** (*recommendation*) recomendación *f*

commendatory [kəˈmendətəri, *Am:* -tɔːri] *adj* loable

commensurable [kəˈmenʃərəbl, *Am:* -sɚ-] *adj* conmensurable

commensurate [kəˈmenʃərət, *Am:* -sɚ-] *adj form* proporcionado, -a

comment [ˈkɒment, *Am:* ˈkɑːment] **I.** *n* comentario *m;* **no ~** sin comentarios; **to make a ~** hacer una observación **II.** *vi* comentar; **to ~ that ...** observar que…

commentary [ˈkɒməntəri, *Am:* ˈkɑːmənter-] <-ies> *n* comentario *m;* **colour ~** reportaje *m* en color; **literary ~** crítica *f* literaria

commentate [ˈkɒmənteɪt, *Am:* ˈkɑːmən-] *vi* TV, RADIO **to ~ on sth** hacer un reportaje sobre algo

commentator [ˈkɒmənteɪtəʳ, *Am:* ˈkɑːmənteɪt̬ɚ] *n* TV, RADIO comentarista *mf*

commerce [ˈkɒmɜːs, *Am:* ˈkɑːmɜːrs] *n no pl* comercio *m*

commercial [kəˈmɜːʃl, *Am:* -ˈmɜːr-] **I.** *adj* **1.** (*relating to commerce*) comercial **2.** RADIO, TV publicitario, -a **II.** *n* RADIO, TV anuncio *m*, comercial *m AmL*

commercialism [kəˈmɜːʃəlɪzəm, *Am:* -ˈmɜːr-] *n no pl* comercialismo *m*

commercialization [kəˌmɜːʃəlaɪˈzeɪʃən] *n no pl, Am* comercialización *f*

commercialize [kəˈmɜːʃəlaɪz, *Am:* -ˈmɜːr-] *vt Am* comercializar

commercialized *adj* comercializado, -a

commiserate [kəˈmɪzəreɪt] *vi* mostrar conmiseración

commiseration [kəˌmɪzəˈreɪʃən] *n* conmiseración *f;* ~**s for failing the exam** siento que suspendieras el examen

commission [kəˈmɪʃən] **I.** *vt* **1.** (*order*) encargar **2.** MIL (*appoint*) **to ~ sb as sth** nombrar a alguien algo; ~**ed officer** oficial *mf* **II.** *n* **1.** (*order*) encargo *m* **2.** (*system of payment*) comisión *f;* **to be on ~** estar a comisión **3.** (*investigative body*) comisión *f* **4.** MIL (*appointment*) nombramiento *m;* **to resign one's ~** dimitir del cargo **5.** *no pl* LAW (*perpetration*) perpetración *f* **6.** NAUT, AVIAT **out of ~** fuera de servicio

commissionaire [kəˌmɪʃəˈneəʳ, *Am:* -ˈer] *n Brit* conserje *mf*

commissioned officer *n* oficial *m* en activo

commissioner [kəˈmɪʃənəʳ, *Am:* -ɚ] *n* comisario, -a *m, f;* ~ **for oaths** notario, -a *m, f* público, -a

commit [kəˈmɪt] <-tt-> *vt* **1.** (*carry out*) cometer; **to ~ suicide** suicidarse; **to ~ an error** incurrir en un error **2.** (*bind*) **to ~ oneself** (**to sth**) comprometerse (a algo); **to ~ soldiers to the defence of a region** enviar soldados a defender la región **3.** (*institutionalize*) **to ~ sb to prison** encarcelar a alguien; **to ~ sb to hospital** internar a alguien en un hospital **4.** (*entrust*) **to ~ sth to memory** memorizar algo; **to ~ sth to paper** poner algo por escrito

commitment [kəˈmɪtmənt] *n* **1.** (*dedication*) dedicación *f* **2.** (*obligation*) obligación *f;* **family ~s** compromisos *mpl* familiares; **to make a ~** hacer una promesa

committed *adj* comprometido, -a

committee [kəˈmɪti, *Am:* -ˈmɪt̬-] *n* comité *m;* **to appoint a ~** nombrar un comité; **to be** [*o* **sit**] **on a ~** ser miembro de un comité

commode [kəˈməʊd, *Am:* -ˈmoʊd] *n* **1.** (*chest of drawers*) cómoda *f* **2.** (*toilet*) silla *f* con orinal

commodious [kəˈməʊdɪəs, *Am:* -ˈmoʊ-] *adj* amplio, -a, espacioso, -a

commodity [kəˈmɒdəti, *Am:* -ˈmɑːdət̬i] <-ies> *n* **1.** (*product*) mercancía *f;* ~ **markets** mercados *mpl* de mercancías **2.** *pl* (*raw material*) materia *f* prima

commodore [ˈkɒmədɔːʳ, *Am:* ˈkɑːmədɔːr] *n* comodoro *m*

common [ˈkɒmən, *Am:* ˈkɑːmən] **I.** *adj* **1.** (*ordinary*) corriente; (*usual*) usual; (*widespread*) frecuente; **a ~ disease** una enfermedad común; **to be ~ knowledge** ser de dominio público; **a ~ name** un nombre común; **the ~ man** el hombre medio **2.** (*shared*) común; ~ **property** propiedad *f* comunal; **by ~ assent** por unanimidad; **for the ~ good** en beneficio de todos **3.** (*vulgar*) vulgar **II.** *n* **1.** (*land*) ejido *m* **2.** *Am* UNIV comedor *m*

common denominator *n* denominador *m* común

commoner [ˈkɒmənəʳ, *Am:* ˈkɑːmənɚ] *n* plebeyo, -a *m, f*

common ground *n no pl* puntos *mpl* en común; **to be on ~ with sb** coincidir con alguien **common land** *n* ejido *m* **common law** *n no pl* ≈ derecho *m* consuetudinario **common-law wife** <wives> *n* mujer *f* en una pareja de hecho

commonly *adv* (*often*) frecuentemente; (*usually*) normalmente

common-or-garden [ˌkɒmənɔːˈgɑːdən, *Am:* ˌkɑːmənɔːrˈgɑːr-] *adj* normal y corriente

commonplace [ˈkɒmənpleɪs, *Am:* ˈkɑːmən-] **I.** *adj* corriente; **it is ~ to see that ...** es frecuente ver que… **II.** *n* lugar *m* común

common room *n Brit* sala *f* de reuniones (de un colegio) **common sense** *n no pl* sentido *m* común; **a ~ solution** una solución lógica **common stock** *n Am* FIN acciones *fpl* ordinarias

Commonwealth ['kɒmənwelθ, *Am:* 'kɑːmən-] *n* **the ~** la Commonwealth

> La **Commonwealth of Nations** (antiguamente la **British Commonwealth**) es una organización libre de estados independientes, que se ha ido desarrollando a partir del antiguo **British Empire**. Fue fundada oficialmente en 1931 a partir de los **Statute of Westminster**. En aquel momento, Canadá, Australia, Sudáfrica y Nueva Zelanda ya habían alcanzado la independencia y junto con el Reino Unido fueron los primeros miembros. La mayoría de los países que formaban el antiguo Imperio Británico al alcanzar la independencia han ido engrosando la lista de los países pertenecientes a dicha organización. Hoy en día esta organización trabaja en la línea de la colaboración económica y cultural. Los jefes de estado de los países integrantes de la **Commonwealth** se reúnen dos veces al año.

commotion [kə'məʊʃən, *Am:* -'moʊ-] *n* alboroto *m*

communal ['kɒmjʊnl, *Am:* kə'mjuː] *adj* comunal

commune [kə'mjuːn] *n* comuna *f*

communicable [kə'mjʊːnikəbl] *adj* **1.** (*information*) comunicable **2.** MED transmisible

communicate [kə'mjuːnɪkeɪt] **I.** *vt* **1.** (*information*) comunicar **2.** MED transmitir **II.** *vi* **1.** (*give information*) comunicar(se); **I'm afraid we just don't ~** creo que simplemente no conectamos **2.** (*connect*) comunicar(se); **the bedroom ~s with the hall** el dormitorio comunica con el recibidor

communication [kəˌmjuːnɪ'keɪʃən] *n* **1.** *no pl* (*process*) comunicación *f* **2.** (*missive*) comunicación *f* **3.** *pl* (*means*) comunicaciones *fpl*

communicative [kə'mjuːnɪkətɪv, *Am:* -nəkeɪt̬ɪv] *adj* comunicativo, -a

communion [kə'mjuːnɪən, *Am:* -njən] *n no pl* comunión *f;* **to take ~** comulgar

communiqué [kə'mjuːnɪkeɪ, *Am:* kəˌmjuːnɪ'keɪ] *n* comunicado *m*

communism ['kɒmjʊnɪzəm, *Am:* 'kɑːmjə-] *n no pl* comunismo *m*

communist ['kɒmjʊnɪst, *Am:* 'kɑːmjə-] **I.** *n* comunista *mf* **II.** *adj* comunista

community [kə'mjuːnəti, *Am:* -nət̬i] <-ies> *n* **1.** (*of people*) comunidad *f;* **the local ~** el vecindario **2.** (*of animals, plants*) colonia *f* **3.** (*togetherness*) colectividad *f*

community centre *n* centro *m* social

community home *n* centro *m* de reeducación **community service** *n* trabajo *m* social **community singing** *n no pl* canto *m* colectivo **community worker** *n* asistente *mf* social

commutable [kə'mjuːtəbl, *Am:* -t̬ə-] *adj* conmutable

commutation [ˌkɒmjuː'teɪʃən, *Am:* ˌkɑːmjə-] *n* conmutación *f*

commutation ticket *n Am* abono *m* de temporada

commute [kə'mjuːt] **I.** *vi* viajar (diariamente) al lugar de trabajo **II.** *n inf* viaje *m* (diario) al trabajo **III.** *vt* **1.** (*change, convert*) convertir **2.** FIN, LAW conmutar

commuter [kɒ'mjuːtəʳ, *Am:* -t̬ɚ] *n persona que debe viajar diariamente para ir al trabajo*

commuter belt *n* barrios *mpl* periféricos **commuter train** *n* tren *m* de cercanías

Comoran ['kɒmərən, *Am:* 'kɑːm-] **I.** *adj* comorano, -a **II.** *n* comorano, -a *m, f*

Comoros ['kɒmərəʊz, *Am:* 'kɑːməroʊz] *npl* **the ~** las Islas Comoras

compact¹ ['kɒmpækt, *Am:* 'kɑːm-] **I.** *adj* (*small*) compacto, -a; (*material*) apretado, -a **II.** *vt* condensar **III.** *n* **1.** *Am, Aus* AUTO utilitario *m* **2.** (*powder*) polvera *f*

compact² ['kɒmpækt, *Am:* 'kɑːm-] *n* acuerdo *m*

compact disc *n* compact *m,* disco *m* compacto

compact disc player *n* reproductor *m* de discos compactos

compactness [kəm'pæktnɪs, *Am:* kəm-] *n no pl* compresión *f*

companion [kəm'pænjən] *n* **1.** (*person, animal*) compañero, -a *m, f;* **travelling ~** compañero de viaje **2.** (*guidebook*) guía *f*

companionable [kəm'pænjənəbl] *adj* simpático, -a

companionship *n no pl* compañerismo *m*

companionway [kəm'pænjənweɪ] *n* NAUT escalerilla *f*

company ['kʌmpəni] <-ies> *n* **1.** (*firm, enterprise*) empresa *f;* **Duggan and Company** Duggan y Compañía; **~ union** *Am* sindicato *m* de empresa **2.** *no pl* (*companionship*) compañía *f;* **you are in good ~** estás en buena compañía; **to keep sb ~** hacer compañía a alguien; **he's been keeping bad ~** va con malas compañías; **Margaret stayed for a week as ~ for my mother** Margaret se quedó una semana para hacer compañía a mi madre **3.** (*group*) *a.* MIL compañía *f* ▸**two's ~ (three's a crowd)** *prov* dos son compañía, tres son multitud

comparable ['kɒmpərəbl, *Am:* 'kɑːm-] *adj* comparable; **~ to** equiparable a

comparative [kəm'pærətɪv, *Am:* -'perət̬ɪv] **I.** *n* comparativo *m* **II.** *adj* comparativo, -a; **~ literature** literatura *f* comparada

comparatively *adv* (*by comparison*) comparativamente; (*relatively*) relativamente

compare [kəm'peəʳ, *Am:* -'per] **I.** *vt* comparar; **to ~ sth/sb to** [*o* **with**] **sth/sb** comparar algo/a alguien con algo/alguien; **instant**

coffee can't be ~d with an expresso el café instantáneo no puede compararse con un expreso; **to ~ notes on sth** hacer un intercambio de impresiones sobre algo **II.** *vi* compararse; **to ~ favourably with sth** ser mejor que algo; **last year's weather just doesn't ~** el tiempo del año pasado no puede compararse

comparison [kəm'pærɪsn, *Am:* -'per-] *n* comparación *f;* **to make a ~** hacer una comparación; **by ~ with sb/sth** en comparación con alguien/algo; **there's no ~ between the two restaurants** no hay ni punto de comparación entre los dos restaurantes

compartment [kəm'pɑːtmənt, *Am:* -'pɑːrt-] *n* **1.** RAIL compartimiento *m* **2.** (*section*) departamento *m*

compass ['kʌmpəs] <-es> *n* **1.** *a.* NAUT brújula *f* **2.** *no pl, form* (*range*) alcance *m;* (*area*) ámbito *m;* **to be beyond the ~ of sb's knowledge** sobrepasar los límites de los conocimientos de alguien

compassion [kəm'pæʃən] *n no pl* compasión *f*

compassionate [kəm'pæʃənət] *adj* compasivo, -a

compatibility [kəm,pætə'bɪləti, *Am:* -,pæt̬ə'bɪlət̬i] *n no pl* compatibilidad *f*

compatible [kəm'pætəbl, *Am:* -'pæt̬-] *adj* **1.** *a.* MED, INFOR compatible **2.** (*consistent*) conciliable

compatriot [kəm'pætrɪət, *Am:* -'peɪtrɪ-] *n* **1.** (*countryman*) compatriota *mf* **2.** *Am* (*companion*) colega *mf*

compel [kəm'pel] <-ll-> *vt* **1.** (*force*) obligar; **the new circumstances ~led a change in policy** las nuevas circunstancias exigían un cambio de política **2.** (*produce*) imponer

compelling *adj* (*reason*) imponente; (*film*) convincente

compendium [kəm'pendɪəm] <-s *o* -dia> *n* compendio *m*

compensate ['kɒmpənseɪt, *Am:* 'kɑːm-] **I.** *vt* (*make up for*) compensar; (*for loss, damage*) indemnizar **II.** *vi* **to ~ for sth** (*reward*) compensar algo

compensation [,kɒmpen'seɪʃən, *Am:* ,kɑːm-] *n no pl* **1.** (*award*) compensación *f;* (*for loss, damage*) indemnización *f;* **to claim ~** reclamar una indemnización; **in ~ for sth** en compensación por algo **2.** (*recompense*) recompensa *f;* **in ~** como recompensa

compere ['kɒmpeəʳ, *Am:* 'kɑːmper] *Brit* **I.** *n* presentador(a) *m(f)* **II.** *vt* presentar

compete [kəm'piːt] *vi* **1.** (*strive*) competir; **to ~ for sth** competir por algo; **the new shop will have a tough time competing with the two supermarkets** la nueva tienda lo tendrá difícil si quiere competir con los dos supermercados; **turn the music down – I'm not competing with that noise** baja la música – no pienso gritar para que me puedas oír **2.** (*take part*) participar; **to ~ in an event** participar en un acontecimiento

competence ['kɒmpɪtənts, *Am:* 'kɑːm-] *n,* **competency** *n no pl* competencia *f*

competent ['kɒmpɪtənt, *Am:* 'kɑːmpɪt̬ənt] *adj* competente; **to be ~ at sth** ser competente en algo

competition [,kɒmpə'tɪʃən, *Am:* ,kɑːm-] *n* **1.** (*state of competing*) competencia *f* **2.** (*rivalry*) rivalidad *f* **3.** (*contest*) concurso *m;* **beauty ~** concurso de belleza; **to enter a ~** presentarse a un concurso

competitive [kəm'petətɪv, *Am:* -'pet̬ət̬ɪv] *adj* competitivo, -a; **~ spirit** espíritu *m* competitivo; **~ sports** deportes *mpl* de competición; **their prices are very ~** sus precios son muy competitivos

competitiveness [kəm'petətivnəs] *n no pl* competitividad *f*

competitor [kəm'petɪtəʳ, *Am:* -'pet̬ət̬ɚ] *n* **1.** *a.* ECON competidor(a) *m(f)* **2.** SPORTS rival *mf;* (*participant*) participante *mf*

compilation [,kɒmpɪ'leɪʃən, *Am:* ,kɑːmpə-] *n* **1.** (*act of compiling*) compilación *f* **2.** (*collection*) recopilación *f*

compile [kəm'paɪl] *vt* **1.** *a.* INFOR compilar **2.** (*collect*) recopilar

compiler [,kɒm'pɪləʳ, *Am:* -ɚ] *n* **1.** (*person*) recopilador(a) *m(f)* **2.** *a.* INFOR compilador *m*

complacence [kəm'pleɪsənts] *n,* **complacency** *n no pl* complacencia *f* (excesiva)

complacent [kəm'pleɪsənt] *adj* satisfecho, -a de sí mismo, -a

complain [kəm'pleɪn] *vi* quejarse; **to ~ about** [*o* **of**] **sth** quejarse de algo

complainant [kəm'pleɪnənt] *n* LAW demandante *mf*

complaint [kəm'pleɪnt] *n* **1.** (*expression of displeasure*) queja *f;* **to have cause for ~** tener motivo de queja; **to make a ~ about sb/sth** quejarse de alguien/algo; **to lodge a ~** formular una queja **2.** LAW querella *f* **3.** (*illness*) enfermedad *f*

complaisance [kəm'pleɪzəns, *Am:* -səns] *n no pl, form* complacencia *f*

complaisant [kəm'pleɪzənt, *Am:* -sənt] *adj form* complaciente

complement ['kɒmplɪmənt, *Am:* 'kɑːm-] *vt* complementar

complementary [,kɒmplɪ'mentəri, *Am:* ,kɑːmplə'ment̬ɚi] *adj* complementario, -a

complete [kəm'pliːt] **I.** *vt* **1.** (*add what is missing*) completar **2.** (*finish*) terminar; **to ~ doing sth** terminar de hacer algo **3.** (*fill out entirely*) rellenar **II.** *adj* completo, -a, entero, -a; **~ coverage** cobertura *f* total; **in ~ darkness** en la más absoluta oscuridad; **~ paralysis** parálisis *f inv* total; **he wore the whole rabbit, ~ with teeth** llevaba el conejo entero, con dientes y todo; **the man's a ~ fool!** ¡el hombre es un loco de remate!; **are we ~?** ¿estamos todos?

completely *adv* totalmente

completeness *n no pl* totalidad *f*

completion [kəm'pliːʃən] *n no pl* finalización *f;* **to be nearing** ~ estar a punto de terminarse; **you'll be paid on** ~ **of the project** cobrarás cuando se haya terminado el proyecto

complex ['kɒmpleks, *Am:* 'kɑːm-] **I.** *adj* complejo, -a **II.** <-es> *n* **1.** PSYCH complejo *m;* **guilt/inferiority** ~ complejo de culpabilidad/inferioridad; **to have a** ~ **about sth** estar acomplejado por algo; **to give sb a** ~ acomplejar a alguien; **I've got a real** ~ **about spiders** tengo verdadera fobia a las arañas **2.** ARCHIT complejo

complexion [kəm'plekʃən] *n* **1.** (*skin*) cutis *m inv;* (*colour*) tez *f;* **a healthy** ~ un cutis sano **2.** (*character*) cariz *m;* (*of people*) aspecto *m;* **MPs of all** ~**s have mounted this campaign** diputados de todos los colores han organizado esta campaña; **that puts a different** ~ **on things** eso le da un cariz nuevo a las cosas

complexity [kəm'pleksəti, *Am:* -səṱi] *n no pl* complejidad *f*

compliance [kəm'plaɪənts] *n no pl* obediencia *f;* (*agreement*) conformidad *f;* **in** ~ **with the law** conforme a la ley; **to act in** ~ **with sth** actuar de acuerdo con algo

compliant [kəm'plaɪənt] *adj form* (*obedient*) obediente; (*overly obedient*) sumiso, -a

complicate ['kɒmplɪkeɪt, *Am:* 'kɑːmplə-] *vt* complicar; (*make worse*) empeorar; **his breathing problem has been** ~**d by the flu** su problema respiratorio se ha visto agravado por una gripe

complicated *adj* complicado, -a

complication [ˌkɒmplɪ'keɪʃən, *Am:* ˌkɑːmplə-] *n* complicación *f;* **if any** ~**s arise, let me know and I'll help** si surge alguna dificultad, avísame y te ayudaré

complicity [kəm'plɪsəti, *Am:* -əṱi] *n no pl* complicidad *f*

compliment ['kɒmplɪmənt, *Am:* 'kɑːmplə-] **I.** *n* **1.** (*expression of approval*) cumplido *m;* (*flirt*) piropo *m;* **to pay sb a** ~ hacer un cumplido a alguien; **to repay a** ~ devolver un cumplido; **I take it as a** ~ **that ...** me halaga que... **2.** *pl* saludos *mpl;* **to present one's** ~**s** *form* presentar sus respetos; **to send** ~**s** enviar saludos; **with** ~**s** con un atento saludo ▶**to fish for** ~**s** buscar elogios **II.** *vt* **to** ~ **sb on sth** felicitar a alguien por algo

complimentary [ˌkɒmplɪ'mentəri, *Am:* ˌkɑːmplə'menṱɚi] *adj* **1.** (*praising*) positivo, -a; **to be** ~ **about sth** hablar en términos muy favorables de algo **2.** (*free*) gratuito, -a

compliments slip *n* tarjeta *f* comercial

comply [kəm'plaɪ] <-ie-> *vi* cumplir; **to refuse to** ~ negarse a obedecer; **to** ~ **with the law/the rules** acatar la ley/las normas

component [kəm'pəʊnənt, *Am:* -'poʊ-] *n* componente *m;* **key** ~ pieza *f* clave

component parts *npl* piezas *fpl*

compose [kəm'pəʊz, *Am:* -'poʊz] **I.** *vi* (*write music, poetry*) componer **II.** *vt* **1.** (*music, poetry*) componer **2.** (*write*) redactar **3.** (*make up*) **to be** ~**d of sth** constar de algo; **the committee is** ~**d of experts** el comité está formado por expertos **4.** (*calm*) **to** ~ **oneself** calmarse; **she tried hard to** ~ **her features into a smile** se esforzó mucho para mostrar una sonrisa; **to** ~ **one's thoughts** ordenar sus pensamientos **5.** TYPO componer

composed [kəm'pəʊzd, *Am:* -'poʊzd] *adj* tranquilo, -a

composer [kəm'pəʊzəʳ, *Am:* -'poʊzɚ] *n* compositor(a) *m(f)*

composite ['kɒmpəzɪt, *Am:* kəm'pɑː-] *adj* compuesto, -a

composition [ˌkɒmpə'zɪʃən, *Am:* ˌkɑːm-] *n* **1.** composición *f* **2.** LAW arreglo *m* **3.** *no pl* (*make-up: of a group*) formación *f*

compositor [kəm'pɒzɪtəʳ, *Am:* -'pɑːzɪṱɚ] *n* TYPO cajista *m, f*

compost ['kɒmpɒst, *Am:* 'kɑːmpoʊst] **I.** *n no pl* abono *m* orgánico **II.** *vt* **1.** (*turn into fertilizer*) convertir en abono **2.** (*fertilize*) abonar

composure [kəm'pəʊʒəʳ, *Am:* -'poʊʒɚ] *n no pl* compostura *f;* **to lose/regain one's** ~ perder/recobrar la compostura

compound ['kɒmpaʊnd, *Am:* 'kɑːm-] **I.** *vt* **1.** (*make worse*) agravar **2.** (*mix*) combinar **3.** (*make up*) **to be** ~**ed of sth** constar de algo **II.** *n* **1.** (*combination*) mezcla *f* **2.** CHEM compuesto *m* **3.** (*enclosure*) recinto *m*

compound fracture *n* fractura *f* múltiple

compound interest *n* interés *m* compuesto

comprehend [ˌkɒmprɪ'hend, *Am:* ˌkɑːm-] *vi, vt* comprender

comprehensible [ˌkɒmprɪ'hensəbl, *Am:* ˌkɑːm-] *adj* comprensible

comprehension [ˌkɒmprɪ'henʃən, *Am:* ˌkɑːm-] *n no pl* comprensión *f;* **beyond** ~ incomprensible; **he has no** ~ **of the size of the problem** no es consciente de la envergadura del problema

comprehensive [ˌkɒmprɪ'hensɪv, *Am:* ˌkɑːmprə-] **I.** *adj* (*exhaustive*) exhaustivo, -a; (*global*) completo, -a; ~ **coverage** cobertura *f* global; ~ **list** lista *f* detallada **II.** *n Brit* SCHOOL *escuela para niños mayores de once años en la que no hay separación de alumnos según su nivel de aptitud*

> La **comprehensive school** es una escuela integrada para chicos de edades comprendidas entre los 11-18 años. La **comprehensive school** es el resultado de la unificación de la **secondary modern school** y la **grammar school** (para alumnos que habían aprobado el **eleven-plus examination**), producida en los años 60 y 70.

compress [kəm'pres] **I.** *vt* **1.** *a.* INFOR comprimir **2.** (*make shorter*) condensar; **I had to** ~ **ten pages of notes into four paragraphs** tuve que resumir diez páginas de apuntes en cuatro párrafos **II.** <-es> *n* compresa *f*

compressed [kəm'prest] *adj* comprimido, -a

compression [kəm'preʃən] *n a.* INFOR compresión *f*

compressor [kəm'presəʳ, *Am:* -ɚ] *n* compresor *m*

comprise [kəm'praɪz] *vt* **1.** (*include*) comprender **2.** (*consist of*) constar de, componerse de

compromise ['kɒmprəmaɪz, *Am:* 'kɑːm-] **I.** *n* **1.** (*concession*) transigencia *f;* **to agree to a ~** consentir en transigir; **to make a ~** hacer una concesión **2.** (*agreement*) arreglo *m;* **to reach a ~** llegar a un acuerdo **II.** *vi* transigir **III.** *vt* **1.** (*betray*) comprometer; **to ~ one's beliefs/principles** dejar de lado sus creencias/principios **2.** (*endanger*) poner en peligro; **to ~ one's reputation** poner en entredicho su reputación

compromising *adj* comprometido, -a

comptroller [kən'trəʊləʳ, *Am:* -'troʊlɚ] *n* interventor(a) *m(f)*, contralor(a) *m(f) AmL*

compulsion [kəm'pʌlʃən] *n no pl* obligación *f;* **to be under no ~ to do sth** no estar obligado a hacer algo; **he seems to have a constant ~ to eat** parece que tiene una obsesión constante por la comida

compulsive [kəm'pʌlsɪv] *adj* compulsivo, -a

compulsory [kəm'pʌlsəri] *adj* obligatorio, -a; **~ purchase** expropiación *f;* **~ by law** preceptivo por ley

compunction [kəm'pʌŋkʃən] *n no pl* remordimiento *m;* **to have no ~ about sth** no tener reparo en algo

computation [ˌkɒmpjʊ'teɪʃən, *Am:* ˌkɑːm-pjə-] *n* cómputo *m;* INFOR computación *f*

compute [kəm'pjuːt] *vt* computar

computer [kəm'pjuːtəʳ, *Am:* -ɚ] *n* ordenador *m*, computador(a) *m(f) AmL;* **to do sth by ~** hacer algo con el ordenador

computer-aided *adj* asistido, -a por ordenador

computer centre *n* centro *m* de informática **computer game** *n* videojuego *m* **computer graphics** *n + sing/pl vb* gráficos *mpl* por ordenador [*o* computadora *AmL*]

computerization [kəmˌpjuːtəraɪ'zeɪʃən, *Am:* -t̬ɚɪ-] *n no pl* **1.** (*computer storage*) computerización *f* **2.** (*equipping with computers*) instalación *f* de equipo informático

computerize [kəm'pjuːtəraɪz, *Am:* -t̬ə-raɪz] **I.** *vt* **1.** (*store on computer*) informatizar, computerizar **2.** (*equip with computers*) instalar ordenadores [*o* computadoras *AmL*] en **II.** *vi* informatizarse

computer network *n* red *f* de ordenadores [*o* computadoras *AmL*] **computer programmer** *n* programador(a) *m(f)* **computer science** *n no pl* informática *f;* **~ course** curso *m* de informática **computer scientist** *n* informático, -a *m, f* **computer search** <-es> *n* búsqueda *f* por ordenador [*o* computadora *AmL*] **computer virus** <-es> *n* virus *m inv* informático **computer workstation** *n* terminal *m* de trabajo

computing *n no pl* informática *f*

comrade ['kɒmreɪd, *Am:* 'kɑːmræd] *n* **1.** (*friend*) compañero, -a *m, f* **2.** POL camarada *mf*

comradeship ['kɒmreɪdʃɪp, *Am:* 'kɑːm-ræd-] *n no pl* camaradería *f;* **there's a great sense of ~ among the team** hay mucho compañerismo en el grupo

COMSAT ['kɒmsæt, *Am:* 'kɑːm-] *n Am abbr of* **communications satellite** COMSAT *m*

con[1] [kɒn, *Am:* kɑːn] <-nn-> *vt inf* engañar; **to ~ sb** (**into doing sth**) engañar a alguien (para que haga algo); **to ~ sb into believing that ...** hacer creer a alguien que...; **to ~ sb out of sth** estafar algo a alguien

con[2] [kɒn, *Am:* kɑːn] *n* contra *m;* **the pros and ~s of sth** los pros y los contras de algo

con artist [ˌkɒn'ɑːtɪst, *Am:* ˌkɑːn'ɑːrt̬əst] *n inf* estafador(a) *m(f)*

concatenation [kɒnˌkætɪ'neɪʃən, *Am:* kən-ˌkæt̬ə-] *n* concatenación *f*

concave ['kɒnkeɪv, *Am:* kɑːn-] *adj* cóncavo, -a

concavity [kən'kævɪti, *Am:* kɑːn'kævət̬i] <-ies> *n* concavidad *f*

conceal [kən'siːl] *vt* esconder; (*a surprise*) contener; (*the truth*) encubrir

concealment [kən'siːlmənt] *n no pl* (*of information, evidence*) encubrimiento *m;* (*of feelings*) disimulación *f;* **to watch sth from a place of ~** ver algo desde un escondrijo

concede [kən'siːd] **I.** *vt* **1.** (*acknowledge*) conceder; (*defeat*) aceptar; **to ~ that ...** admitir que... **2.** (*surrender*) ceder; **to ~ sth to sb** otorgar algo a alguien **3.** (*permit*) acceder a **4.** (*allow to score*) **to ~ a goal** encajar un gol **II.** *vi* darse por vencido

conceit [kən'siːt] *n* **1.** *no pl* (*vanity*) vanidad *f;* **to be full of ~** tener muchas presunciones **2.** *liter* (*elaborate comparison*) concepto *m*

conceited [kən'siːtɪd, *Am:* -t̬ɪd] *adj* vanidoso, -a; **without wishing to sound ~** sin querer parecer presuntuoso

conceivable [kən'siːvəbl] *adj* concebible; **it's ~** es verosímil

conceive [kən'siːv] **I.** *vt* **1.** (*imagine, become pregnant with*) concebir **2.** (*devise*) idear; (*arrange*) preparar **II.** *vi* **1.** (*think*) **to ~ of sb/sth** formarse un concepto de alguien/algo; **other people may influence how we ~ of ourselves** los demás pueden influir en el concepto que tenemos de nosotros mismos **2.** (*devise*) imaginar(se) **3.** (*become pregnant*) concebir

concentrate ['kɒnsəntreɪt, *Am:* 'kɑːn-] **I.** *vi* **1.** (*focus one's thoughts*) concentrarse; **to ~ on sth** concentrarse en algo **2.** (*gather*) reunirse **II.** *vt* **1.** (*focus*) concentrar; (*search*) centrar **2.** (*accumulate*) reunir; (*population*) concentrar **3.** (*not dilute*) concentrar **III.** *n* concentrado *m*

concentrated *adj a. fig* concentrado, -a; (*attack*) conciso, -a

concentration [ˌkɒnsn'treɪʃən, *Am:* ˌkɑːn-] *n no pl* **1.** concentración *f;* ~ **on sth** concentración en algo; **to lose (one's)** ~ perder la concentración **2.** (*accumulation*) acumulación *f;* (*of troops*) concentración *f*

concentration camp *n* campo *m* de concentración

concentric [kən'sentrɪk] *adj* concéntrico, -a

concept ['kɒnsept, *Am:* 'kɑːn-] *n* concepto *m;* **to grasp a** ~ coger una idea

conception [kən'sepʃən] *n* **1.** (*notion*) noción *f;* (*idea*) idea *f;* (*creation*) concepción *f* **2.** *no pl* BIO concepción *f*

conceptual [kən'septʃuəl] *adj* conceptual

conceptualise *Aus, Brit,* **conceptualize** [kən'septʃuəlaɪz] *Am* **I.** *vi* formarse un concepto **II.** *vt* conceptualizar

concern [kən'sɜːn, *Am:* -'sɜːrn] **I.** *vt* **1.** (*apply to*) referirse a; **to** ~ **oneself about sth** interesarse por algo; **there's no need for you to** ~ **yourself with this matter** no tienes porqué meterte en este asunto **2.** (*affect*) incumbir; **to whom it may** ~ a quien le corresponda **3.** (*be about*) tener que ver con; **to be ~ed with sth** ocuparse de algo; **as far as I'm ~ed** por lo que a mí respecta; **I'd like to thank everyone ~ed** me gustaría dar las gracias a todos los que han colaborado; **I'm not very good where money is ~ed** no soy muy bueno en cuestiones de dinero; **her job is something ~ed with computers** su trabajo tiene que ver con los ordenadores **4.** (*worry*) preocuparse; **to be ~ed about sth** estar preocupado por algo **II.** *n* **1.** (*matter of interest*) asunto *m;* **a major** ~ una grave preocupación; **it's no** ~ **of mine** eso no es de mi incumbencia; **what's happening? – that's none of your** ~ ¿qué ocurre? – no es asunto tuyo; **to be of** ~ **to sb** interesar a alguien **2.** (*worry*) preocupación *f;* **a matter of** ~ un asunto de interés; **the** ~ **for sth** la inquietud por algo; **his** ~ **to appear sophisticated amused her** sus esfuerzos para parecer sofisticado le hacían gracia **3.** (*company*) empresa *f;* **a going** ~ una empresa próspera

concerning *prep* acerca de

concert ['kɒnsət, *Am:* 'kɑːnsɚt] *n* **1.** (*musical performance*) concierto *m;* ~ **hall** sala *f* de conciertos; ~ **pianist** pianista *mf;* ~ **tour** gira *f* de conciertos **2. in** ~ (*performing live*) en concierto; *form* (*all together*) conjuntamente; **in** ~ **with sb** conjuntamente con alguien; **to act in** ~ actuar de común acuerdo

concerted [kən'sɜːtɪd] *adj* **1.** (*joint*) concertado, -a; (*action*) conjunto, -a; (*exercise*) acordado, -a **2.** (*resolute*) resuelto, -a; (*effort*) enérgico, -a

concert grand ['kɒnsət grænd, *Am:* 'kɑːnsɚt-] *n* piano *m* de cola

concertina [ˌkɒnsə'tiːnə, *Am:* ˌkɑːnsɚ-] **I.** *n* concertina *f* **II.** *vi Aus, Brit* colisionar en cadena **III.** *vt Aus, Brit* **it wasn't possible to** ~ **the three meetings into one afternoon** fue imposible concentrar las tres reuniones en una tarde

concertmaster [ˌkɒnsət'mæstəʳ, *Am:* ˌkɑːnsɚt'mæstɚ] *n Am* concertino *m*

concerto [kən'tʃeətəʊ, *Am:* -'tʃertoʊ] <-s *o* -ti> *n* concierto *m*

concert pitch *n* MUS diapasón *m* ▶**to be at** ~ estar preparado

concession [kən'seʃən] *n* **1.** (*tax compensation*) desgravación *f* **2.** (*compromise*) concesión *f;* ~ **to sell goods** licencia *f* para vender productos

conciliate [kən'sɪlɪeɪt] **I.** *vi* conciliarse **II.** *vt* **1.** (*placate*) apaciguar **2.** (*reconcile*) conciliar

conciliation [kənˌsɪlɪ'eɪʃən] *n no pl, form* conciliación *f*

conciliation board *n* equipo *m* de conciliación

conciliatory [kən'sɪlɪətəri, *Am:* -tɔːri] *adj* conciliador(a)

concise [kən'saɪs] *adj* conciso, -a

conciseness *n no pl,* **concision** [kən'sɪʒən] *n no pl* concisión *f*

conclave ['kɒnkleɪv, *Am:* 'kɑːn-] *n form* **1.** (*private meeting*) reunión *f* a puerta cerrada **2.** REL (*gathering of cardinals*) cónclave *m*

conclude [kən'kluːd] **I.** *vi* concluir **II.** *vt* **1.** (*finish*) finalizar; **to** ~ **by doing sth** terminar haciendo algo **2.** (*decide*) resolver; **we talked all night, but nothing was ~d** hablamos toda la noche, pero no llegamos a ninguna conclusión **3.** (*infer*) **to** ~ **(from sth) that ...** deducir (de algo) que... **4.** (*ratify*) pactar; (*a contract*) firmar; (*a peace treaty*) ratificar

concluding *adj* final; (*chapter*) último, -a

conclusion [kən'kluːʒən] *n* **1.** (*end*) conclusión *f;* (*of a story*) final *m* **2.** (*decision*) decisión *f* **3.** (*inference*) conclusión *f;* **to come to a** ~ llegar a una conclusión **4.** (*ratification*) ratificación *f;* (*of a contract*) firma *f* **5.** (*lastly*) **in** ~ en conclusión; **in ~, I should like to say that ...** para terminar, me gustaría decir que...

conclusive [kən'kluːsɪv] *adj* **1.** (*convincing*) concluyente; ~ **arguments** argumentos *mpl* irrefutables **2.** (*decisive*) decisivo, -a

concoct [kən'kɒkt, *Am:* -'kɑːkt] *vt* **1.** (*create by mixing ingredients: a dish*) preparar **2.** (*devise*) tramar; (*a plan*) maquinar **3.** (*fabricate*) inventar

concoction [kən'kɒkʃən, *Am:* -'kɑːk-] *n* (*dish*) mezcla *f;* (*drink*) brebaje *m;* **is this dish of your ~, Paul?** *iron* ¿este plato es invento tuyo, Paul?

concourse ['kɒŋkɔːs, *Am:* 'kɑːnkɔːrs] *n* vestíbulo *m*

concrete ['kɒnkriːt, *Am:* 'kɑːn-] **I.** *n no pl* hormigón *m* **II.** *adj* de hormigón **III.** *vt* revestir de hormigón

concrete mixer *n* hormigonera *f*

concubine ['kɒŋkjʊbaɪn, *Am:* 'kɑːŋ-] *n* HIST concubina *f*

concur [kən'kɜːʳ, *Am:* -'kɜːr] <-rr-> *vi form* **1.** (*agree*) coincidir; **to** ~ **with sb (in sth)** estar de acuerdo con alguien (en algo) **2.** (*happen*

simultaneously) concurrir
concurrence [kən'kʌrəns] *n no pl, form* 1.(*agreement*) conformidad *f* **2.**(*simultaneous occurrence*) concurrencia *f*
concurrent [kən'kʌrənt] *adj* concurrente
concuss [kən'kʌs] *vt* **to be ~ed** tener una conmoción cerebral
concussed *adj* que padece una conmoción cerebral
concussion [kən'kʌʃən] *n no pl* conmoción *f* cerebral; **to suffer** (**from**) ~ padecer una conmoción cerebral
condemn [kən'dem] *vt* 1.(*reprove*) condenar; **to ~ sb for sth** censurar a alguien por algo **2.**(*sentence*) **to be ~ed to death** ser condenado a muerte **3.**(*pronounced unsafe: building*) declarar en ruina; (*food*) declarar no apto para el consumo
condemnation [ˌkɒndem'neɪʃən, *Am:* ˌkɑːn-] *n* 1.(*reproof*) condena *f* **2.**(*reason to reprove*) motivo *m* de crítica
condensation [ˌkɒnden'seɪʃən, *Am:* ˌkɑːn-] *n no pl* 1.(*process of changing to liquid*) condensación *f* **2.**(*reducing in size*) abreviación *f*
condense [kɒn'dens] **I.** *vt* **1.**(*shorten*) sintetizar **2.**(*concentrate*) **to ~ a liquid** condensar un líquido **3.**(*form droplets from*) **the air was ~d into clouds** el aire formó nubes por condensación **II.** *vi* condensarse
condenser [kɒn'densəʳ, *Am:* -sɚ] *n* condensador *m*
condescend [ˌkɒndɪ'send, *Am:* ˌkɑːn-] *vi* **to ~ to do sth** rebajarse [*o* condescender] a hacer algo
condescending [ˌkɒndɪ'sendɪŋ, *Am:* ˌkɑːn-] *adj* con aires de superioridad
condescension [ˌkɒdɪ'senʃən, *Am:* ˌkɑːn-] *n no pl* aires *mpl* de superioridad
condiment ['kɒndɪmənt, *Am:* 'kɑːndə-] *n form* condimento *m;* ~ **set** aliño *m*
condition [kən'dɪʃən] **I.** *n* **1.**(*state*) condición *f;* **in perfect ~** en perfecto estado; **in peak ~** en condiciones óptimas; **in a terrible ~** en un estado deplorable; **to be out of ~** (*person*) estar en baja forma; (*thing*) estar en mal estado; **to be in no ~ to do sth** no estar en condiciones de hacer algo; **for a man of sixty-three, Jim's in pretty good ~** para tener sesenta y tres, Jim está en plena forma **2.**(*mental or physical state*) estado *m;* **heart ~** afección *f* cardíaca **3.**(*circumstances*) **~s** *pl* condiciones *fpl* **4.**(*stipulation*) condición *f;* **to make a ~** poner una condición; **on the ~ that** con la condición de que *+subj;* **under the ~s of sth** según los términos de algo **II.** *vt* **1.**(*train*) preparar; (*influence*) condicionar **2.**(*treat hair*) acondicionar
conditional [kən'dɪʃənl] **I.** *adj* (*provisory*) condicional; ~ **on sth** condicionado a algo **II.** *n* LING **the ~** el condicional
conditionally [kən'dɪʃənəli] *adv* con reservas
conditioned [kən'dɪʃənd] *adj* (*trained*) preparado, -a; (*place, air*) acondicionado, -a; (*reflex*) condicionado, -a
conditioner [kən'dɪʃənəʳ, *Am:* -ɚ] *n* **1.**(*for hair*) acondicionador *m* **2.**(*for clothes*) suavizante *m*
conditioning *n no pl* condicionamiento *m*
condo [ˌkɒndəʊ, *Am:* ˌkɑːndoʊ] *n Am, inf s.* **condominium**
condolence [kən'dəʊləns, *Am:* -'doʊ-] *n no pl* **~s** pésame *m;* **to offer one's ~s** (**to sb**) *form* dar el pésame (a alguien)
condom ['kɒndəm, *Am:* 'kɑːn-] *n* condón *m*
condominium [ˌkɒndə'mɪnɪəm, *Am:* ˌkɑːn-] *n* **1.** *Am* (*apartment building*) propiedad *f* horizontal, condominio *m AmL* **2.** *Am* (*unit*) piso *m* **3.** POL condominio *m*
condone [kən'dəʊn, *Am:* -'doʊn] *vt* **1.**(*approve*) aprobar **2.**(*forgive*) condonar
conducive [kən'djuːsɪv, *Am:* -'duː-] *adj* propicio, -a; **to be ~ to sth** ser apropiado para algo
conduct [kən'dʌkt, *Am:* 'kɑːn-] **I.** *vt* **1.**(*carry out*) llevar a cabo **2.**(*direct*) dirigir; **to ~ a business** conducir un negocio; **to ~ the religious service** dirigir el oficio religioso; (*guide*) guiar **3.**(*behave*) **to ~ oneself** comportarse **4.** ELEC, PHYS (*transmit*) conducir **II.** *vi* MUS llevar la batuta **III.** *n no pl* **1.**(*management*) dirección *f* **2.**(*behaviour*) conducta *f;* **sb's ~ towards sb** el comportamiento de alguien hacia alguien
conductive [kən'dʌktɪv] *adj* ELEC, PHYS conductor(a)
conductor [kən'dʌktəʳ, *Am:* -tɚ] *n* **1.**(*director*) director(a) *m(f)* **2.** PHYS, ELEC conductor *m* **3.**(*fare collector*) cobrador *m;* (*of train*) revisor *m*
conductress [kən'dʌktrɪs] <-es> *n* cobradora *f;* (*of train*) revisora *f*
conduit ['kɒndjuɪt, *Am:* 'kɑːnduɪt] *n* conducto *m*
cone [kəʊn, *Am:* koʊn] *n* **1.** *a.* MAT cono *m* **2.**(*cornet for ice cream*) cucurucho *m* **3.**(*fruit*) piña *f*
confection [kən'fekʃən] *n form* **1.** COM confección *f* **2.** GASTR dulce *m;* (*sweet*) golosina *f*
confectioner [kən'fekʃnəʳ, *Am:* -ɚ] *n* confitero, -a *m, f*
confectionery [kən'fekʃənəri, *Am:* -eri] *n no pl* confitería *f*
confederacy [kən'fedərəsi] <-ies> *n* **1.** + *pl/sing vb* (*union*) confederación *f;* **the Confederancy** *Am* HIST la Confederación **2.**(*plot*) complot *m*
confederate [kən'fedərət] **I.** *n* cómplice *mf* **II.** *adj* POL, HIST confederado, -a
confederation [kənˌfedə'reɪʃən] *n + pl/sing vb* POL confederación *f*

> El **Confederation Day** o **Canada Day** es la fiesta nacional de Canadá que se celebra el día 1 de julio.

confer [kən'fɜːʳ, *Am:* -'fɜːr] <-rr-> **I.** *vi* consultar **II.** *vt* otorgar

conference ['kɒnfərəns, *Am:* 'kaːnfɚ-] *n* conferencia *f;* **to be in ~ (with sb)** estar reunido (con alguien)

confess [kən'fes] **I.** *vi* confesarse; **to ~ to a crime** confesarse de un crimen **II.** *vt* confesar; **I must ~ that I'm a little bit confused** tengo que admitir que estoy un poco confuso

confessedly *adv* con franqueza

confession [kən'feʃən] *n* **1.** (*admission*) confesión *f;* **I have a ~ to make** tengo que hacer una confesión **2.** (*profession*) profesión *f;* **~ of faith** profesión de fe

confessional [kən'feʃənl] *n* confesionario *m*

confessor [kən'fesəʳ, *Am:* -'fesɚ] *n* confesor *m*

confetti [kən'feti, *Am:* -'fet̬-] *n no pl* confeti *m;* **to shower sb in ~** tirar confeti a alguien

confidant [ˌkɒnfɪ'dænt, *Am:* ˌkaːnfə-] *n* confidente *m*

confidante [ˌkɒnfɪ'dænt, *Am:* ˌkaːnfə-] *n* confidente *f*

confide [kən'faɪd] *vt* confiar; **to ~ (to sb) that ...** decir (a alguien) en confidencia que...

confidence ['kɒnfɪdəns, *Am:* 'kaːnfə-] *n* **1.** (*trust*) confianza *f;* **to have every ~ in sb** tener toda la confianza en alguien; **to place one's ~ in sb/sth** poner la confianza en alguien/algo; **to take sb into one's ~** confiar en alguien; **to win sb's ~** ganarse la confianza de alguien; **he certainly doesn't lack ~** desde luego no le falta confianza en sí mismo **2.** *no pl* (*secrecy*) **~s** confidencia *f*

confident ['kɒnfɪdənt, *Am:* 'kaːnfə-] *adj* **1.** (*sure*) seguro, -a; **to be ~ about oneself** tener confianza en uno mismo; **to be ~ about sth** estar seguro de algo **2.** (*self-assured*) confiado, -a

confidential [ˌkɒnfɪ'denʃl, *Am:* ˌkaːnfə-] *adj* confidencial

confidentially [ˌkɒnfɪ'denʃəli, *Am:* ˌkaːnfə-] *adv* confidencialmente

confiding [kən'faɪdɪŋ] *adj* confiado, -a

configuration [kənˌfɪgə'reɪʃən, *Am:* kənˌfɪgjə'-] *n a.* INFOR configuración *f*

confine ['kɒnfaɪn, *Am:* 'kaːn-] **I.** *vt* **1.** (*limit*) **to ~ sth to sth** restringir algo a algo; **to be ~d to doing sth** limitarse a hacer algo **2.** (*imprison*) confinar **3.** (*shut in: person*) recluir; (*animal*) encerrar; **to be ~d to quarters** MIL estar retenido en los barracones **II.** *n pl* **the ~s** los confines; **beyond the ~s of sth** más allá de los límites de algo

confined *adj* (*prisoner*) recluido, -a; (*space*) reducido, -a

confinement [kən'faɪnmənt] *n no pl* **1.** (*act of being confined*) reclusión *f;* (*state of being confined*) confinamiento *m;* **his ~ to bed really annoyed him** le resultaba especialmente fastidioso tener que quedar en cama **2.** (*childbirth*) parto *m*

confines *n pl* límites *mpl*

confirm [kən'fɜːm, *Am:* -'fɜːrm] **I.** *vt* **1.** (*verify*) verificar **2.** REL **to ~ sb's faith** confirmar la fe de alguien **II.** *vi* confirmarse

confirmation [ˌkɒnfə'meɪʃən, *Am:* ˌkaːnfɚ-] *n a.* REL confirmación *f*

confirmed [kən'fɜːmd, *Am:* -'fɜːrmd] *adj* **1.** (*established*) firme **2.** (*chronic*) **~ alcoholic** alcohólico *m* empedernido **3.** (*proved*) confirmado, -a

confiscate ['kɒnfɪskeɪt, *Am:* 'kaːnfə-] *vt* confiscar

conflict[1] ['kɒnflɪkt, *Am:* 'kaːn-] *n* **1.** (*clash*) conflicto *m;* **to come into ~ with sb** entrar en conflicto con alguien **2.** (*battle*) discrepancia *f*

conflict[2] [kən'flɪkt] *vi* **to ~ with sb** chocar con alguien

conflicting [kən'flɪktɪŋ] *adj* opuesto, -a; (*evidence*) contradictorio, -a; (*interest*) encontrado, -a

confluence ['kɒnfluːəns, *Am:* 'kaːn-] *n* confluencia *f*

conform [kən'fɔːm, *Am:* -'fɔːrm] *vi* conformarse; **to ~ to the law** ser conforme a la ley

conformist [kən'fɔːmɪst, *Am:* -'fɔːr-] **I.** *n* conformista *mf* **II.** *adj* conformista

conformity [kən'fɔːmɪti, *Am:* -'fɔːrmət̬i] *n no pl* conformidad *f;* **in ~ with sth** conforme con algo

confound [kən'faʊnd] *vt* confundir

confounded *adj inf* maldito, -a

confront [kən'frʌnt] *vt* (*a danger*) enfrentarse a; (*the enemy*) plantar cara a

confrontation [ˌkɒnfrʌn'teɪʃən, *Am:* ˌkaːnfrən-] *n* confrontación *f*

confrontational [ˌkɒnfrʌn'teɪʃnəl, *Am:* ˌkaːnfrən-] *adj* contencioso, -a; (*of opinions*) polémico, -a

confuse [kən'fjuːz] *vt* **1.** (*perplex*) desconcertar **2.** (*put into disarray*) turbar **3.** (*mix up*) confundir

confused [kən'fjuːzd] *adj* (*perplexed*) confundido, -a; (*disordered*) confuso, -a

confusing [kən'fjuːzɪŋ] *adj* confuso, -a

confusion [kən'fjuːʒən] *n no pl* **1.** (*perplexity*) desconcierto *m* **2.** (*mix up*) confusión *f* **3.** (*disorder*) desorden *m*

congeal [kən'dʒiːl] *vi* (*sauce*) espesarse; (*fat*) cuajar; (*blood*) coagular(se)

congenial [kən'dʒiːnɪəl, *Am:* -njəl] *adj* placentero, -a; (*people*) agradable

congenital [kən'dʒenɪtəl, *Am:* -ət̬əl] *adj* congénito, -a

congested [kən'dʒestɪd] *adj* **1.** (*overcrowded*) congestionado, -a; (*people*) abarrotado, -a **2.** MED (*blocked*) congestionado, -a

congestion [kən'dʒestʃən] *n no pl* (*overcrowding*) congestión *f;* (*on roads, freeways*) caravana *f*

conglomerate [kən'glɒmərət, *Am:* -'glaːmɚ-] *n* conglomerado *m*

conglomeration [kənˌglɒmə'reɪʃən, *Am:* -ˌglaːmə-] *n* conglomeración *f*

Congo ['kɒŋgəʊ, *Am:* 'kaːŋgoʊ] **I.** *n* **the ~**

el Congo II. *adj* del Congo

Congolese [ˌkɒŋgəʊ'liːz, *Am:* ˌkɑːŋgə'-] I. *adj* congoleño, -a II. *n* congoleño, -a *m, f*

congratulate [kən'grætʃʊleɪt, *Am:* -'grætʃə-] *vt* felicitar; **to ~ sb (on sth)** felicitar a alguien (por algo)

congratulation [kənˌgrætʃʊ'leɪʃən, *Am:* -ˌgrætʃə-] *n* felicitación *f;* **~s!** ¡felicitaciones!; **a note of ~** una postal de felicitación

congregate ['kɒŋgrɪgeɪt, *Am:* 'kɑːŋ-] *vi* congregarse

congregation [ˌkɒŋgrɪ'geɪʃən, *Am:* ˌkɑːŋ-] *n* congregación *f*

congregational [ˌkɒŋgrɪ'geɪʃənl, *Am:* ˌkɑːŋ-] *adj* congregacionalista

congress ['kɒŋgres, *Am:* 'kɑːŋ-] *n* congreso *m*

congressional [kən'greʃənəl, *Am:* kəŋ-] *adj Am* congresista

congressman ['kɒŋgresmən, *Am:* 'kɑːŋ-] *n* <-men> *Am* congresista *m* **congresswoman** *n* <-women> *Am* congresista *f*

congruence ['kɒngrʊəns, *Am:* 'kɑːŋ-] *n no pl a.* MAT congruencia *f*

congruent ['kɒŋgrʊənt, *Am:* 'kɑːŋ-] *adj a.* MAT congruente

conical ['kɒnɪkl, *Am:* 'kɑːnɪ-] *adj* cónico, -a

conifer ['kɒnɪfəʳ, *Am:* 'kɑːnəfɚ] *n* conífera *f*

coniferous [kə'nɪfərəs, *Am:* koʊ'-] *adj* conífero, -a

conjectural [kən'dʒektʃərəl] *adj* conjetural

conjecture [kən'dʒektʃəʳ, *Am:* -tʃɚ] I. *n* conjetura *f* II. *vi* conjeturar

conjugal ['kɒndʒʊgl, *Am:* 'kɑːndʒə-] *adj form* conyugal; **~ bed** lecho *m* conyugal

conjugate ['kɒndʒʊgeɪt, *Am:* 'kɑːndʒə-] *vt* conjugar

conjugation [ˌkɒndʒʊ'geɪʃən, *Am:* ˌkɑːndʒə-] *n* conjugación *f*

conjunction [kən'dʒʌŋkʃən] *n a.* LING conjunción *f;* **in ~ with** conjuntamente con

conjunctivitis [kənˌdʒʌŋktɪ'vaɪtɪs, *Am:* -tə'vaɪt̬ɪs] *n* conjuntivitis *f inv*

conjure ['kʌndʒəʳ, *Am:* -dʒɚ] I. *vi* hacer magia II. *vt* conjurar; *fig* evocar

◆conjure up *vt* hacer aparecer; **to ~ an image** evocar una imagen

conjurer ['kʌndʒəʳəʳ, *Am:* -dʒɚ] *n* mago, -a *m, f*

conjuring *n no pl* ilusionismo *m*

conjuring trick *n* truco *m* de magia

conjuror ['kʌndʒərəʳ, *Am:* -ɚɚ] *n* mago, -a *m, f*

conk [kɒŋk, *Am:* kɑːŋk] I. *n Brit, Aus, iron* narizota *f* II. *vt iron, inf* **to ~ one's head on sth** darse un porrazo (en la cabeza) contra algo

◆conk out *vi inf* 1. (*break down: machine, vehicle*) averiarse 2. (*become exhausted*) quedarse hecho polvo

conker ['kɒŋkəʳ, *Am:* 'kɑːŋkɚ] *n Brit, childspeak* castaña *f* de Indias

con man ['kɒnˌmæn, *Am:* 'kɑːn-] *n abbr of* **confidence man** estafador *m*

connect [kə'nekt] I. *vi* conectar(se); **to ~ to the Internet** conectarse a internet II. *vt* 1. (*join*) conectar 2. (*associate*) **to ~ sth/sb with sth** asociar algo/a alguien con algo 3. (*join by telephone*) poner en contacto 4. (*in tourism*) enlazar

connected *adj* 1. (*joined together*) conectado, -a 2. (*having ties*) **to be ~d to sb** tener relación con alguien

connecting *adj* comunicado, -a; **~ link** enlace *m* de conexión

connection *n,* **connexion** [kə'nekʃən] *n* 1. *a.* ELEC, INFOR conexión *f* 2. (*relation*) relación *f*

connector *n* conector *m*

connivance [kə'naɪvənts] *n no pl* connivencia *f*

connive [kə'naɪv] *vi* **to ~ with sb** confabularse con alguien

connoisseur [ˌkɒnə'sɜːʳ, *Am:* ˌkɑːnə'sɜːr] *n* entendido, -a *m, f;* **art/wine ~** experto, -a *m, f* en arte/vino

connotation [ˌkɒnə'teɪʃən, *Am:* ˌkɑːnə-] *n* connotación *f*

conquer ['kɒŋkəʳ, *Am:* 'kɑːŋkɚ] *vt* 1. *a.* HIST conquistar 2. (*a problem*) acabar con

conqueror ['kɒŋkərəʳ, *Am:* 'kɑːŋkɚɚ] *n* 1. *a.* HIST conquistador(a) *m(f)* 2. (*in a competition*) vencedor(a) *m(f)*

conquest ['kɒŋkwəst, *Am:* 'kɑːn-] *n no pl, a. iron* conquista *f*

conscience ['kɒnʃəns, *Am:* 'kɑːn-] *n* conciencia *f;* **a clear ~** una conciencia limpia; **a guilty ~** remordimientos *mpl* de conciencia; **to prey on sb's ~** *fig* pesar en la conciencia de alguien; **to prick sb's ~** *fig* hacer sentir culpable a alguien; **in all** [*o* **good** *Am*] **~** en conciencia

conscientious [ˌkɒntʃi'entʃəs, *Am:* ˌkɑːn-] *adj* concienzudo, -a

conscientiousness *n no pl* escrupulosidad *f*

conscientious objector *n* objetor *m* de conciencia

conscious ['kɒnʃəs, *Am:* 'kɑːn-] *adj* 1. (*deliberate*) expreso, -a 2. (*aware*) consciente; **fashion ~** preocupado por la moda; **to be ~ of sth** ser consciente de algo; **to become ~ of sth** darse cuenta de algo

consciousness ['kɒnʃəsnɪs, *Am:* 'kɑːn-] *n no pl* 1. MED (*state of being conscious*) conocimiento *m* 2. (*awareness*) conciencia *f;* **political/social ~** conciencia política/social; **to raise one's ~** concienciarse

conscript [kən'skrɪpt, *Am:* 'kɑːn-] I. *n* MIL recluta *mf* II. *adj* MIL reclutado, -a III. *vt* MIL reclutar

conscription [kən'skrɪpʃən] *n no pl* MIL servicio *m* militar, conscripción *f AmL*

consecrate ['kɒnsɪkreɪt, *Am:* 'kɑːnsə-] *vt* consagrar

consecration [ˌkɒnsɪ'kreɪʃən, *Am:* ˌkɑːnsə-] *n no pl* REL consagración *f*

consecutive [kən'sekjʊtɪv, *Am:* -jət̬ɪv] *adj*

consecutivo, -a

consecutively *adv* consecutivamente

consensus [kən'sensəs] *n no pl* consenso *m*

consent [kən'sent] I. *n form* consentimiento *m;* **by common ~** de común acuerdo II. *vi* (*agree*) **to ~ to do sth** consentir en hacer algo

consequence ['kɒntsɪkwənts, *Am:* 'kɑːnt-] *n* consecuencia *f;* **as a ~** como consecuencia; **in ~** por consiguiente; **nothing of ~** nada importante

consequent ['kɒntsɪkwənt, *Am:* 'kɑːnt-] *adj,* **consequential** [ˌkɒntsɪ'kwentʃəl, *Am:* ˌkɑːnt-] *adj* consiguiente

consequently *adv* por consiguiente

conservation [ˌkɒntsə'veɪʃən, *Am:* ˌkɑːntsɚ-] *n* conservación *f;* **environment ~** preservación *f* del medio ambiente

conservationist [ˌkɒntsə'veɪʃənɪst, *Am:* ˌkɑːntsɚ-] *n* conservacionista *mf*

conservation technology <-ies> *n* tecnología *f* para la conservación del medio ambiente

conservatism [kən'sɜːvətɪzəm, *Am:* -'sɜːr-] *n no pl* conservadurismo *m*

conservative [kən'sɜːvətɪv, *Am:* -'sɜːrvət̬ɪv] *adj* 1. a. POL (*opposed to change*) conservador(a) 2. (*cautious*) cauteloso, -a; **~ estimate** estimación *f* prudente

conservatoire [kən'sɜːvətwɑːʳ, *Am:* -'sɜːrvətwɑːr] *n,* **conservatory** [kən'sɜːvətri, *Am:* -'sɜːrvətɔːri] *n* conservatorio *m*

conserve [kən'sɜːv, *Am:* -sɜːrv] *vt* conservar; **to ~ energy** ahorrar energía; **to ~ strength** reservar energías

consider [kən'sɪdəʳ, *Am:* -ɚ] *vt* 1. (*contemplate*) considerar 2. (*look attentively at*) examinar 3. (*show regard for*) tener en cuenta 4. (*regard as*) **to be ~ed to be the best** ser considerado el mejor; **to ~ that ...** creer que...

considerable [kən'sɪdərəbl] *adj* considerable

considerate [kən'sɪdərət] *adj* considerado, -a

consideration [kənˌsɪdə'reɪʃən] *n no pl* consideración *f;* **to take sth into ~** tener algo en cuenta; **the project is under ~** el proyecto se está estudiando; **for a small ~** *iron* por una módica cantidad

considered [kən'sɪdəd, *Am:* -ɚd] *adj* considerado, -a; **highly ~** muy bien considerado

considering [kən'sɪdərɪŋ] I. *prep* teniendo en cuenta; **~ the weather** en vista del tiempo II. *adv* a pesar de todo III. *conj* **~ (that)** ... ya que..., teniendo en cuenta que...

consignment [kən'saɪnmənt] *n* 1. (*instance of consigning*) envío *m* 2. ECON remesa *f;* **goods on ~** mercancías *fpl* en consignación

consist [kən'sɪst] *vi* **to ~ of sth** consistir en algo

consistency [kən'sɪstəntsi] *n no pl* 1. (*degree of firmness*) consistencia *f* 2. (*being coherent*) coherencia *f*

consistent [kən'sɪstənt] *adj* 1. (*keeping to same principles*) consecuente; **to be ~ with sth** ser consecuente con algo 2. (*not varying*) estable

consolation [ˌkɒnsə'leɪʃən, *Am:* ˌkɑːn-] *n no pl* consuelo *m;* **it was ~ to him to know that ...** le reconfortó saber que...; **if it's of any ~ ...** si te sirve de consuelo...

consolation prize *n* premio *m* de consolación

consolatory [kən'sɒlətəri, *Am:* -'sɑːlətɔːri] *adj* consolador(a); **~ words** palabras *fpl* reconfortantes

console[1] ['kɒnsəʊl, *Am:* 'kɑːnsɔʊl] *vt* (*comfort*) consolar

console[2] [kən'səʊl, *Am:* -'sɔʊl] *n* (*switch panel*) consola *f*

consolidate [kən'sɒlɪdeɪt, *Am:* -'sɑːlə-] I. *vi* 1. (*reinforce*) consolidarse 2. (*unite*) fusionarse II. *vt* consolidar

consolidated *adj* consolidado, -a

consolidation [kənˌsɒlɪ'deɪʃən, *Am:* -ˌsɑːlə-] *n no pl* 1. (*becoming stronger*) fortalecimiento *m* 2. ECON consolidación *f*

consommé [kən'sɒmeɪ, *Am:* ˌkɑːn'sə'meɪ] *n no pl* consomé *m*

consonance ['kɒnsənəns, *Am:* 'kɑːn-] *n* MUS consonancia *f*

consonant ['kɒnsənənt, *Am:* 'kɑːn-] *n no pl* consonante *f*

consort [kən'sɔːt, *Am:* -'sɔːrt] I. *vi* **to ~ with sb** tratar con alguien II. *n* consorte *mf;* **prince ~** príncipe *m* consorte

consortium [kən'sɔːtɪəm, *Am:* -'sɔːrt̬-] *n* <consortiums *o* consortia> consorcio *m;* **~ of companies** grupo *m* de empresas

conspicuous [kən'spɪkjʊəs] *adj* conspicuo, -a; (*beauty*) destacable; (*figure*) llamativo, -a; **to be ~ by one's absence** *iron* brillar por su ausencia

conspicuous consumption *n* consumo *m* destinado a la ostentación

conspiracy [kən'spɪrəsi] <-ies> *n* conspiración *f;* **a ~ against sb** un complot contra alguien

conspirator [kən'spɪrətəʳ, *Am:* -t̬ɚ] *n* conspirador(a) *m(f)*

conspire [kən'spaɪəʳ, *Am:* -'spaɪɚ] *vi* conspirar; **to ~ to do sth** conspirar para hacer algo

constable ['kʌnstəbl, *Am:* 'kɑːn-] *n Brit* policía *mf*

constabulary [kən'stæbjʊləri, *Am:* -jəler-] *n Brit* cuerpo *m* de policía

constancy ['kɒnstəntsi, *Am:* 'kɑːn-] *n no pl, form* constancia *f*

constant ['kɒnstənt, *Am:* 'kɑːn-] I. *n* constante *f* II. *adj* 1. (*continuous*) constante; (*noise*) continuo, -a; (*surveillance*) incesante 2. (*unchanging*) inalterable; (*love*) fiel; (*friend*) leal; (*temperature*) constante 3. (*frequent*) asiduo, -a; **~ use** uso *m* frecuente; **to be in ~ trouble** meterse en problemas constantemente

constantly *adv* constantemente

constellation [ˌkɒnstəˈleɪʃən, *Am:* ˌkɑːn-] *n* constelación *f*
consternation [ˌkɒnstəˈneɪʃən, *Am:* ˌkɑːnstɚ-] *n no pl* consternación *f*
constipate [ˈkɒnstɪpeɪt, *Am:* ˈkɑːnstə-] *vt* MED estreñir
constipated *adj* estreñido, -a
constipation [ˌkɒnstɪˈpeɪʃən, *Am:* ˈkɑːnstə-] *n* MED estreñimiento *m,* prendimiento *m CSur*
constituency [kənˈstɪtjuəntsi, *Am:* -ˈstɪtʃu-] *n* **1.** (*electoral district*) distrito *m* electoral **2.** (*body of voters in this area*) electorado *m* **3.** (*seat*) escaño *m*
constituent [kənˈstɪtjuənt, *Am:* -ˈstɪtʃu-] **I.** *n* **1.** (*voter*) elector(a) *m(f)* **2.** CHEM, PHYS (*component*) constituente *m* **II.** *adj* constituente
constitute [ˈkɒnstɪtjuːt, *Am:* ˈkɑːnstətuːt] *vt* constituir
constitution [ˌkɒnstɪˈtjuːʃən, *Am:* ˌkɑːnstəˈtuː-] *n* constitución *f*
constitutional [ˌkɒnstɪˈtjuːʃənl, *Am:* ˌkɑːnstəˈtuː-] **I.** *adj* constitucional; ~ **law** derecho político **II.** *n iron* paseo *m*
constrain [kənˈstreɪn] *vt* **1.** (*restrict*) constreñir **2.** LAW (*imprison*) encarcelar
constraint [kənˈstreɪnt] *n* **1.** *no pl* (*compulsion*) coacción *f;* **under** ~ bajo coacción **2.** (*limit*) restricción *f;* **to impose ~s on sb/sth** imponer limitaciones a alguien/algo
constrict [kənˈstrɪkt] *vt* constreñir
constriction [kənˈstrɪkʃən] *n* constricción *f*
constrictor *n* constrictor(a) *m(f)*
construct [kənˈstrʌkt] **I.** *n* construcción *f* **II.** *vt* construir
construction [kənˈstrʌkʃən] *n* **1.** *no pl* (*act of making or building*) construcción *f* **2.** (*building*) edificio *m* **3.** LING construcción *f* **4.** (*interpretation*) interpretación *f;* **to put a ~ on sth** interpretar algo
constructional [kənˈstrʌkʃnl] *adj* estructural
constructive [kənˈstrʌktɪv] *adj* constructivo, -a
constructor [kənˈstrʌktəʳ, *Am:* -tɚ] *n* constructor(a) *m(f)*
construe [kənˈstruː] *vt* interpretar
consul [ˈkɒnsl, *Am:* ˈkɑːn-] *n* cónsul *mf*
consular [ˈkɒnsjʊləʳ, *Am:* ˈkɑːn-] *adj* consular
consulate [ˈkɒnsjʊlət, *Am:* ˈkɑːn-] *n* consulado *m*
consulate general *n* consulado *m* general
consul general *n* cónsul *mf* general
consult [kənˈsʌlt] **I.** *vi* consultar **II.** *vt* **1.** (*seek information or advice*) consultar **2.** (*examine*) tener en cuenta; **to ~ one's feelings** considerar sus sentimientos
consultancy [kənˈsʌltəntsi] <-ies> *n* asesoría *f*
consultant [kənˈsʌltənt] *n* **1.** ECON asesor(a) *m(f);* **management ~** asesor de gestión; **tax ~** asesor fiscal **2.** *Brit* MED especialista *mf*
consultation [ˌkɒnsʌlˈteɪʃən, *Am:* ˌkɑːn-] *n* consulta *f*
consultative [kənˈsʌltətɪv, *Am:* -t̬ət̬ɪv] *adj* consultivo, -a
consulting [kənˈsʌltɪŋ, *Am:* -t̬ɪŋ] *adj* ~ **engineer/lawyer** ingeniero *m* asesor/abogado *m* asesor
consume [kənˈsjuːm, *Am:* -ˈsuːm] *vt* consumir; **to be ~d by sth** estar consumido por algo; **to be ~d by anger** estar corroído por la ira; **to be ~d by envy** estar muerto de envidia; **to ~ all the money** gastar todo el dinero
consumer [kənˈsjuːməʳ, *Am:* -ˈsuːmɚ] *n* consumidor(a) *m(f);* ~ **credit** crédito *m* al consumidor; ~ **demand** demanda *f* de consumo; ~ **society** sociedad *f* de consumo
consumerism [kənˈsjuːmərɪzəm, *Am:* -ˈsuːmɚɪ-] *n no pl* **1.** (*protection*) defensa *f* del consumidor **2.** *pej* (*exaggerated purchasing*) consumismo *m*
consummate [ˈkɒnsəmeɪt, *Am:* ˈkɑːn-] *adj form* consumado, -a; ~ **happiness** felicidad *f* completa; ~ **skill** suma habilidad *f*
consummation [ˌkɒnsəˈmeɪʃən, *Am:* ˌkɑːnsə-] *n no pl, form* consumación *f*
consumption [kənˈsʌmpʃən] *n no pl* **1.** consumo *m* **2.** HIST, MED tisis *f inv*
consumptive [kənˈsʌmptɪv] *adj* HIST, MED tísico, -a
contact [ˈkɒntækt, *Am:* ˈkɑːn-] **I.** *n* **1.** *no pl* (*state of communication*) contacto *m* **2.** (*connection*) relación *f;* **to have ~s** tener contactos **3.** (*act of touching*) *a.* ELEC contacto *m;* **physical ~** contacto físico; **to come into ~ with sth** entrar en contacto con algo **II.** *vt* contactar con
contact-breaker *n* ELEC, TECH interruptor *m*
contact lens *n* lentilla *f* **contact man** *n* intermediario *m* **contact print** *n* contacto *m*
contagion [kənˈteɪdʒən] *n form* contagio *m*
contagious [kənˈteɪdʒəs] *adj a. fig* contagioso, -a
contain [kənˈteɪn] *vt* contener
container [kənˈteɪnəʳ, *Am:* -nɚ] *n* **1.** (*vessel*) recipiente *m;* **unbreakable ~** envase *m* irrompible **2.** (*for transport*) contenedor *m*
containerize [kənˈteɪnəraɪz] *vt* poner en contenedores
container ship *n* buque *m* contenedor
containment [kənˈteinmənt] *n no pl* contención *f*
contaminate [kənˈtæmɪneɪt] *vt* contaminar
contamination [kənˌtæmɪˈneɪʃən] *n no pl* contaminación *f*
contemplate [ˈkɒntempleɪt, *Am:* ˈkɑːnt̬em-] *vt* **1.** (*gaze at*) contemplar **2.** (*consider*) reflexionar acerca de **3.** (*intend*) **to ~ doing sth** tener la intención de hacer algo; **to ~ suicide** pensar suicidarse
contemplation [ˌkɒntemˈpleɪʃən, *Am:* ˌkɑːnt̬em-] *n no pl* contemplación *f*

contemplative [kən'templətɪv, *Am:* -t̬ɪv] *adj* **1.** (*reflective*) contemplativo, -a **2.** (*meditative*) meditativo, -a

contemporary [kən'tempərəri, *Am:* -pərer-] **I.** *n* contemporáneo, -a *m, f* **II.** *adj* contemporáneo, -a

contempt [kən'tempt] *n no pl* desprecio *m;* **to be beneath** ~ ser despreciable; **to hold sth/sb in** ~ despreciar algo/a alguien

contemptible [kən'temptəbl] *adj* despreciable

contemptuous [kən'temptʃuəs] *adj* desdeñoso, -a; (*look*) de desprecio; **to be** ~ **of sb** menospreciar a alguien

contend [kən'tend] **I.** *vi* **1.** (*compete*) competir; **to** ~ **for sth** competir por algo **2.** (*struggle*) luchar, contender; **to** ~ **against sb/sth** contender contra alguien/algo; **to have sb/sth to** ~ **with** tener que enfrentarse a alguien/algo **II.** *vi* **to** ~ **that ...** afirmar que...

contender *n* aspirante *mf*

content[1] ['kɒntent, *Am:* 'kɑːn-] *n* contenido *m*

content[2] [kən'tent] **I.** *vi* (*satisfy*) contentarse; **to** ~ **oneself with sth** contentarse con algo **II.** *vt* satisfacer **III.** *adj* contento, -a; **to one's heart's** ~ a más no poder; **to be** ~ **with sth** estar satisfecho con algo; **to be** ~ **to do sth** estar contento de hacer algo

contented *adj* satisfecho, -a

contention [kən'tenʃən] *n no pl* **1.** (*disagreement*) controversia *f;* **teams in** ~ grupos *mpl* rivales **2.** (*opinion*) opinión *f* **3.** (*competition*) **to be in** ~ **for sth** competir por algo; **to be out of** ~ **for sth** no tener posibilidades de algo

contentious [kən'tenʃəs] *adj* conflictivo, -a

contentment [kən'tentmənt] *n no pl* satisfacción *f*

contents ['kɒntents, *Am:* 'kɑːntents] *n pl* contenido *m;* (*index*) índice *m*

contest [kən'test, *Am:* 'kɑːn-] **I.** *n* **1.** (*competition*) concurso *m;* **beauty** ~ certamen *m* de belleza; **sports** ~ competición *f* deportiva **2.** (*dispute*) controversia *f* **II.** *vt* **1.** (*challenge*) rebatir; (*claims, a will*) impugnar; (*a decision*) cuestionar **2.** (*compete for*) presentarse como candidato a

contestant [kən'testənt] *n* (*match*) contrincante *mf;* (*election*) candidato, -a *m, f;* (*contest*) concursante *mf*

context ['kɒntekst, *Am:* 'kɑːn-] *n* contexto *m*

contextual [kən'tekstjuəl, *Am:* kən'tekstʃu-] *adj form* contextual

contextualize [kən'tekstjuəlaɪz, *Am:* kən'tekstʃu-] *vt* contextualizar

continent[1] ['kɒntɪnənt, *Am:* 'kɑːntnənt] *n* **1.** (*landmass*) continente *m* **2.** *Brit* **the Continent** el continente europeo

continent[2] ['kɒntɪnənt, *Am:* 'kɑːntnənt] *adj a.* MED continente

continental [ˌkɒntɪ'nentl, *Am:* ˌkɑːntn'ent̬l] **I.** *adj* **1.** (*relating to a continent*) continental; ~ **drift** movimiento *m* de los continentes; ~ **shelf** plataforma *f* continental **2.** *Brit* (*of mainland Europe*) de Europa continental **II.** *n* europeo, -a *m, f* continental

continental breakfast *n desayuno de café o té con bollería y mermelada*

contingency [kən'tɪndʒəntsi] <-ies> *n form* (*possibility*) contingencia *f;* (*event*) acontecimiento *m* fortuito

contingent [kən'tɪndʒənt] **I.** *n* **1.** (*part of a larger group*) representación *f* **2.** MIL contingente *m* **II.** *adj* **1.** (*liable to happen*) eventual **2.** (*dependent*) **to be** ~ **on sth** depender de algo **3.** (*incidental*) **risks** ~ **to a profession** riesgos derivados de una profesión

continual [kən'tɪnjuəl] *adj* continuo, -a

continually *adv* continuamente

continuation [kənˌtɪnju'eɪʃən] *n no pl* continuación *f*

continue [kən'tɪnjuː] **I.** *vi* **1.** (*persist*) continuar; **he** ~**d by saying that ...** prosiguió diciendo que...; **to** ~ **to do** [*o* **doing**] **sth** seguir haciendo algo **2.** (*remain unchanged*) seguir; **to** ~ (**on**) **one's way** seguir su camino; **to be** ~**d** continuará **II.** *vt* **1.** (*go on*) seguir con **2.** (*lengthen*) prolongar **3.** LAW aplazar

continued *adj* **to be** ~ continuará

continuity [ˌkɒntɪ'njuːəti, *Am:* ˌkɑːntən'uːət̬i] *n no pl* **1.** (*fact of continuing*) continuidad *f* **2.** RADIO, TV (*between two programs*) intervalo *m* hablado [*o* musical] **3.** CINE, TV (*scenario*) guión *m;* ~ **boy/girl** secretario, -a *m, f* de rodaje

continuous [kən'tɪnjuəs] *adj* continuo, -a

contort [kən'tɔːt, *Am:* -'tɔːrt] **I.** *vi* crisparse; **his face had** ~**ed with bitterness and rage** tenía el rostro desencajado por la amargura y la rabia **II.** *vt* torcer; **to** ~ **sb's words** deformar las palabras de alguien

contortion [kən'tɔːʃən, *Am:* -'tɔːr-] *n* contorsión *f;* **bodily** ~**s** contorsiones *fpl;* **a** ~ **of reality** una deformación de la realidad

contortionist [kən'tɔːʃənɪst, *Am:* -'tɔːr-] *n a. fig* contorsionista *mf*

contour ['kɒntʊəʳ, *Am:* 'kɑːntʊr] **I.** *n* contorno *m;* (*face*) perfil *m* **II.** *vt* perfilar

contour line *n* GEO curva *f* de nivel **contour map** *n* GEO mapa *m* topográfico

contraband ['kɒntrəbænd, *Am:* 'kɑːn-] **I.** *n no pl* contrabando *m* **II.** *adj* de contrabando

contraception [ˌkɒntrə'sepʃən, *Am:* ˌkɑːn-] *n no pl* anticoncepción *f*

contraceptive [ˌkɒntrə'septɪv, *Am:* ˌkɑːn-] *n* anticonceptivo *m*

contract[1] [kən'trækt] **I.** *vi* contraerse **II.** *vt* **1.** (*make shorter*) contraer **2.** (*catch*) **to** ~ **smallpox/AIDS/a cold** contraer la viruela/el SIDA/un resfriado

contract[2] ['kɒntrækt, *Am:* 'kɑːn-] **I.** *n* contrato *m;* ~ **of employment** contrato laboral; **temporary** ~ contrato temporal; **to**

sign/enter into a ~ firmar/celebrar un contrato **II.** *vi* **to** ~ **with sb** celebrar un contrato con alguien **III.** *vt* contratar
◆**contract in** *vt* tomar parte en
◆**contract out** *vi Brit* **to** ~ **of sth** optar por no participar en algo
contraction [kən'trækʃən] *n* contracción *f*
contractor [kən'træktəʳ, *Am:* 'kɑːntræktɚ] *n* contratista *mf*
contractual [kən'træktʃʊəl, *Am:* -tʃu-] *adj* contractual; ~ **conditions** condiciones *fpl* de contrato; ~ **terms** términos *mpl* del contrato; **to be under a** ~ **obligation to sb** tener un contrato con alguien
contradict [ˌkɒntrə'dɪkt, *Am:* ˌkɑːn-] **I.** *vi* contradecirse **II.** *vt* contradecir; **to** ~ **oneself** contradecirse; **everything I say you want to** ~ quieres contradecir todo lo que digo; **don't** ~ **me!** ¡no me contradigas!
contradiction [ˌkɒntrə'dɪkʃən, *Am:* ˌkɑːn-] *n* contradicción *f;* **a** ~ **in terms** un contrasentido
contradictory [ˌkɒntrə'dɪktəri, *Am:* ˌkɑːn-] *adj* contradictorio, -a
contralto [kən'træltəʊ, *Am:* -'træltoʊ] *n no pl* MUS **1.** (*voice*) contralto *m* **2.** (*person*) contralto *mf*
contraption [kən'træpʃən] *n* artilugio *m;* **don't ask me how to use this** ~ no me preguntes cómo funciona este chisme
contrary ['kɒntrəri, *Am:* 'kɑːntrɚ-] **I.** *n no pl* **the** ~ lo contrario; **on the** ~ al contrario; **quite the** ~**!** ¡todo lo contrario!; **to the** ~ en contra **II.** *adj* contrario, -a; **to be** ~ **to ...** ser contrario a...
contrary to *prep* al contrario de; ~ **what he says** al contrario de lo que dice; ~ **to all our expectations** contra todo pronóstico
contrast [kən'trɑːst, *Am:* -'træst] **I.** *n* contraste *m;* **to be a** ~ **to sb/sth** contrastar con alguien/algo; **by** [*o* **in**] ~ por contraste; **in** ~ **to** [*o* **with**] **sb/sth** a diferencia de alguien/algo **II.** *vt* contrastar
contrast control *n* TV control *m* del contraste
contrasting *adj* contrastante
contravene [ˌkɒntrə'viːn, *Am:* ˌkɑːn-] *vt* contravenir
contravention [ˌkɒntrə'venʃən, *Am:* ˌkɑːn-] *n* contravención *f;* **to act in** ~ **of the regulations** obrar en contravención de las normas
contribute [kən'trɪbjuːt] **I.** *vi* **1.** (*money, time*) contribuir; **to** ~ **towards sth** contribuir en algo; **to** ~ **to a fund** hacer aportaciones [*o* aportes *AmL*] a un fondo **2.** (*participate*) intervenir **3.** PUBL colaborar **II.** *vt* **1.** (*money*) contribuir; **to** ~ (**sth**) **to sth** contribuir (con algo) a algo; **to** ~ **sth towards ...** aportar algo a... **2.** (*article*) escribir; (*information*) aportar
contribution [ˌkɒntrɪ'bjuːʃən, *Am:* ˌkɑːn-] *n* **1.** (*something contributed*) contribución *f* **2.** (*money*) aportación *f;* **a** ~ **to social security fund** una cotización a la Seguridad Social **3.** (*text or article for publication*) colaboración *f;* **a** ~ **for the autumn issue of a magazine** un artículo para el número de otoño de una revista
contributor [kən'trɪbjuːtəʳ, *Am:* -'trɪbjət̬ɚ] *n* contribuyente *mf*
contributory [kən'trɪbjʊtəri, *Am:* -jətɔːri] *adj* contributivo, -a
contrite ['kɒntraɪt, *Am:* kən'-] *adj* contrito, -a; ~ **expression** expresión *f* de arrepentimiento
contrition [kən'trɪʃən] *n no pl* contrición *f*
contrivance [kən'traɪvəns] *n* **1.** (*act of contriving*) artimaña *f* **2.** (*device*) artilugio *m* **3.** (*inventive capacity*) ingenio *m*
contrive [kən'traɪv] *vt* **1.** (*plan*) ingeniar; (*a meeting*) arreglar; (*a plan*) idear **2.** (*manage*) **to** ~ **to do sth** ingeniárselas para hacer algo; **she** ~**d to make it happen** se las ingenió para que ocurriera
contrived *adj* artificial
control [kən'trəʊl, *Am:* -'troʊl] **I.** *n* **1.** control *m;* **to bring sth under** ~ controlar algo; **to go out of** ~ descontrolarse; **to have the** ~ **over sb** tener el control sobre alguien; **to lose** ~ **over sth** perder el control de algo; **to lose** ~ **of oneself** perder el control de uno mismo **2.** (*leadership*) mando *m;* **to be in** ~ mandar; **to be under the** ~ **of sb** estar bajo el dominio de alguien **3.** AVIAT estación *f* de control **4.** *pl* TECH mandos *mpl;* **to be at the** ~**s** llevar los mandos **II.** *vt* <-ll-> **1.** (*have power over*) controlar; (*vehicle*) manejar **2.** (*restrain: anger*) dominar; (*temper, urge*) controlar **3.** (*stop: epidemic, disease*) controlar **4.** ECON, FIN controlar
control board *n* tablero *m* de mando **control centre** *n* centro *m* de control **control column** *n* palanca *f* de mando **control desk** *n* consola *f*
controllable *adj* controlable
controlled [kən'trəʊld, *Am:* -'troʊld] *adj* controlado, -a
controller [kən'trəʊləʳ, *Am:* -'troʊlɚ] *n* (*person in charge*) director(a) *m(f);* FIN, ECON director(a) *m(f)* financiero, -a
control panel *n* tablero *m* de control
control point *n* punto *m* de control **control tower** *n* torre *f* de control **control unit** *n* INFOR unidad *f* de control
controversial [ˌkɒntrə'vɜːʃəl, *Am:* ˌkɑːntrə'vɜːr-] *adj* polémico, -a
controversy ['kɒntrəvɜːsi, *Am:* 'kɑːntrəvɜːr-] *n* <-ies> polémica *f;* **to be beyond** ~ ser incuestionable
contusion [kən'tjuːʒən, *Am:* -'tuː-] *n* contusión *f*
conundrum [kə'nʌndrəm] *n* acertijo *m*
conurbation [ˌkɒnɜː'beɪʃən, *Am:* ˌkɑːnɜːr-] *n* conurbación *f*
convalesce [ˌkɒnvə'les, *Am:* ˌkɑːn-] *vi* convalecer; **to** ~ **from sth** convalecer [*o* recupe-

rarse] de algo

convalescence [ˌkɒnvəˈlesns, *Am:* ˌkɑːn-] *n* convalecencia *f*

convalescent [ˌkɒnvəˈlesnt, *Am:* ˌkɑːn-] **I.** *n* convaleciente *mf* **II.** *adj* convaleciente; **a long ~ period** un largo período de convalecencia

convection [kənˈvekʃən] *n* convección *f*

convection oven *n* horno *m* de convección

convector [kənˈvektəʳ, *Am:* -tɚ] *n,* **convector heater** *n* estufa *f* de convección

convene [kənˈviːn] **I.** *vi form* reunirse **II.** *vt form* citar; (*meeting*) convocar

convener [kənˈviːnəʳ, *Am:* -ɚ] *n Brit* convocador(a) *m(f)*

convenience [kənˈviːnɪəns, *Am:* -ˈviːnjəns] *n no pl* **1.** conveniencia *f* **2.** (*practicality*) comodidad *f;* (*advantage*) ventaja *f;* **for ~'s sake** por comodidad; **at your ~** cuando le venga(n) bien **3.** (*toilet*) servicio *m*

convenience store *n Am: tienda que abre temprano y cierra tarde*

convenient [kənˈviːnɪənt, *Am:* -ˈviːnjənt] *adj* **1.** (*handy*) útil **2.** (*suitable*) conveniente **3.** (*practical*) práctico, -a **4.** (*easily accessible*) bien situado, -a

convenor [kənˈviːnəʳ, *Am:* -ɚ] *n* convocador(a) *m(f)*

convent [ˈkɒnvənt, *Am:* ˈkɑːn-] *n* convento *m*

convention [kənˈvenʃən] *n* **1.** (*custom*) convención *f;* **~ dictates that** es costumbre que +*subj* **2.** (*general agreement*) convenio *m;* (*of human rights*) convención *f* **3.** (*large meeting*) congreso *m*

conventional [kənˈventʃənəl] *adj* convencional; (*wisdom*) ortodoxo, -a; (*medicine*) tradicional

conventionally *adv* de manera convencional

converge [kənˈvɜːdʒ, *Am:* -ˈvɜːrdʒ] *vi a. fig* converger; (*persons*) reunirse

convergence [kənˈvɜːdʒəns, *Am:* -ˈvɜːr-] *n* convergencia *f*

convergent [kənˈvɜːdʒent, *Am:* -ˈvɜːr-] *adj* convergente

conversant [kənˈvɜːsnt, *Am:* -ˈvɜːr-] *adj* versado, -a; **to be ~ with sth** ser versado en algo

conversation [ˌkɒnvəˈseɪʃən, *Am:* ˌkɑːnvɚ-] *n* (*word exchange*) conversación *f,* plática *f AmL;* **to strike up a ~ with sb** entablar conversación con alguien

conversational [ˌkɒnvəˈseɪʃənəl, *Am:* ˌkɑːnvɚ-] *adj* familiar; (*tone*) coloquial; (*skills*) conversacional

conversationally *adv* en tono familiar

converse[1] [kənˈvɜːs, *Am:* -ˈvɜːrs] *vi form* **to ~ with sb** conversar con alguien, platicar con alguien *AmL*

converse[2] [ˈkɒnvɜːs, *Am:* ˈkɑːnvɜːrs] **I.** *n* **the ~** lo opuesto **II.** *adj form* inverso, -a

conversely *adv* a la inversa

conversion [kənˈvɜːʃən, *Am:* -ˈvɜːrʒən] *n* conversión *f*

conversion rate *n* precio *m* de conversión

convert [kənˈvɜːt, *Am:* -ˈvɜːrt] **I.** *n* converso, -a *m, f* **II.** *vi* convertirse **III.** *vt* convertir

converter [kənˈvɜːtəʳ, *Am:* -ˈvɜːrt̬ɚ] *n* **1.** (*person*) convertidor(a) *m(f)* **2.** ELEC transformador *m* **3.** TECH convertidor *m*

convertible [kənˈvɜːtəbl, *Am:* -ˈvɜːrt̬ə-] **I.** *n* AUTO descapotable *m* **II.** *adj a.* FIN, ECON convertible; **~ sofa** sofá-cama *m,* convertible *m AmL*

convex [ˈkɒnveks, *Am:* ˈkɑːn-] *adj* convexo, -a

convey [kənˈveɪ] *vt* **1.** (*transport*) transportar; (*electricity*) conducir **2.** (*communicate*) transmitir; **to ~ how ...** expresar cómo...; **to ~ sth to sb** dar a entender algo a alguien

conveyance [kənˈveɪənts] *n* **1.** (*act of carrying*) transporte *m;* **these pipes are used for the ~ of water** estas tuberías sirven para conducir agua **2.** (*communication*) transmisión *f* **3.** (*vehicle*) vehículo *m;* **form of ~** medio *m* de transporte **4.** LAW traspaso *m;* (*document*) escritura *f* de traspaso

conveyancing *n no pl* LAW traspaso; (*document*) redacción *f* de una escritura de traspaso

conveyor [kənˈveɪəʳ, *Am:* -ɚ] *n* transportador *m;* (*belt*) cinta *f* transportadora, banda *f* transportadora *Méx*

convict [ˈkɒnvɪkt, *Am:* ˈkɑːn-] **I.** *n* presidiario, -a *m, f* **II.** *vt* condenar

conviction [kənˈvɪkʃən] *n* **1.** LAW condena *f* **2.** (*firm belief*) convicción *f;* **to have a ~ about sth** estar convencido de algo

convince [kənˈvɪnts] *vt* convencer; **I'm not ~d** no estoy convencido

convincing [kənˈvɪntsɪŋ] *adj* convincente

convoluted *adj* enrevesado, -a

convoy [ˈkɒnvɔɪ, *Am:* ˈkɑːn-] **I.** *n* convoy *m;* **in** [*o* **under**] **~** en caravana **II.** *vt* escoltar

convulse [kənˈvʌls] **I.** *vi* tener convulsiones; **to ~ in laughter** desternillarse de risa; **to ~ in pain** retorcerse de dolor **II.** *vt* convulsionar; **to be ~d with anger** descomponerse de ira

convulsion [kənˈvʌlʃən] *n* **1.** (*violent motion*) convulsión *f;* **she went into ~s** le dio un ataque convulsivo; (*uncontrolled laughter*) le dio un ataque de risa **2.** (*violent natural occurrence*) conmoción *f*

convulsive [kənˈvʌlsɪv] *adj* convulsivo, -a

coo [kuː] **I.** *vi* arrullar **II.** *vt* susurrar

cook [kʊk] **I.** *n* cocinero, -a *m, f* ►**too many ~s spoil the broth** *prov* muchas manos en un plato hacen mucho garabato *prov* **II.** *vi* hacerse; **how long does this cake take to ~?** ¿cuánto tarda en cocerse este pastel? ►**what's ~ing?** *inf* ¿qué pasa? **III.** *vt* cocinar; (*meat*) asar; **to ~ lunch** hacer la comida

cookbook [ˈkʊkbʊk] *n* libro *m* de cocina

cooker [ˈkʊkəʳ, *Am:* -ɚ] *n* **1.** *Brit* (*stove*) cocina *f,* estufa *f Col, Méx* **2.** *Brit* (*cooking apple*) manzana *f* para cocinar

cookery [ˈkʊkəri] *n no pl* cocina *f*

cookery book *n Brit* libro *m* de recetas

cookie ['kʊki] *n Am* **1.** (*biscuit*) galleta *f* **2.** *inf* (*person*) tipo *m* **3.** INFOR cookie *m* ▸**that's the way the ~ crumbles** *inf* ¡así es la vida!

cooking ['kʊkɪŋ] *n no pl* **to do the ~** hacer la comida

cool [ku:l] **I.** *adj* **1.** (*slightly cold*) fresco, -a; (*color*) frío, -a **2.** (*calm*) tranquilo, -a; **keep ~** tómatelo con calma **3.** *inf* (*impudent*) fresco, -a; **to be a ~ one** ser un fresco **4.** (*unfriendly*) frío, -a **5.** *inf* (*fashionable*) **to be ~** estar en la onda; **that disco is very ~** esa discoteca está muy de moda **II.** *interj inf* ¡genial! **III.** *n no pl* **1.** (*coolness*) fresco *m* **2.** (*calm*) calma *f* **IV.** *vt* enfriar; **just ~ it** *inf* ¡calma! **V.** *vi* (*become colder*) enfriarse; **to ~ down** [*o* **off**] (*become cooler*) enfriarse; (*become calmer*) calmarse

cooler ['ku:ləʳ, *Am:* -lɚ] *n* **1.** (*box*) refrigerador *m* **2.** (*drink*) refresco *m*

coolheaded [ˌku:l'hedɪd] *adj* sereno, -a

cooling ['ku:lɪŋ] *adj* refrescante; (*breeze*) fresco, -a

cooling tower *n* torre *f* de refrigeración

coolly ['ku:li] *adv* **1.** (*calmly*) con serenidad **2.** (*coldly*) fríamente

coolness ['ku:lnɪs] *n no pl* **1.** METEO frescor *m* **2.** (*unfriendliness*) frialdad *f*

coop [ku:p] **I.** *n* gallinero *m* **II.** *vt* encerrar

◆**coop up** *vt* encerrar

co-op ['kəʊɒp, *Am:* 'koʊɑ:p] *n abbr of* **cooperative** cooperativa *f*

cooper ['ku:pəʳ, *Am:* -pɚ] **I.** *n* tonelero, -a *m, f* **II.** *vi* (*make barrels*) fabricar barriles; (*repair barrels*) reparar barriles

cooperate [kəʊ'ɒpəreɪt, *Am:* koʊ'ɑ:pəreɪt] *vi* cooperar; **to ~ with sb** colaborar con alguien

cooperation [kəʊˌɒpə'reɪʃən, *Am:* koʊˌɑ:pə-] *n* cooperación *f*

cooperative [kəʊ'ɒpərətɪv, *Am:* koʊ'ɑ:pɚət̬ɪv] **I.** *n* ECON cooperativa *f*; **~ society** sociedad *f* cooperativa **II.** *adj* cooperativo, -a

co-opt [kəʊ'ɒpt, *Am:* koʊ'ɑ:pt] *vt* **1.** (*make sb a member*) **to ~ sb onto sth** nombrar a alguien para algo **2.** (*absorb into larger unit*) **to be ~ed into sth** ser incorporado a algo

coordinate [ˌkəʊ'ɔ:dɪneɪt, *Am:* ˌkoʊ'ɔ:r-] **I.** *n* coordenada *f* **II.** *vi* **1.** (*work together effectively*) coordinar(se) **2.** (*match*) combinar **III.** *vt* coordinar **IV.** *adj* **1.** (*equal*) igualitario, -a **2.** (*involving coordination*) coordinado, -a

coordination [ˌkəʊˌɔ:dɪ'neɪʃən, *Am:* ˌkoʊˌɔ:rdə'neɪ-] *n no pl* coordinación *f*

coordinator *n* coordinador(a) *m(f)*

coot [ku:t] *n* **1.** ZOOL fúlica *f* **2.** *inf* (*rather dim person*) bobo, -a *m, f*

cop [kɒp, *Am:* kɑ:p] **I.** *n* **1.** *inf* (*police officer*) poli *mf*; **to play ~s and robbers** jugar a policías y ladrones **2.** *Brit, inf* (*poor quality*) **to not be much ~** no valer gran cosa **II.** <-pp-> *vt* **1.** (*grab*) coger; **to ~ a (quick) look at sth** echar una ojeada a algo **2.** *Am* LAW **to ~ a plea** declararse culpable

co-partner ['kəʊ'pɑ:tnəʳ, *Am:* 'koʊˌpɑ:rtnɚ] *n* copartícipe *mf*

copartnership ['kəʊ'pɑ:tnəʃɪp, *Am:* 'koʊˌpɑ:rtnɚ-] *n* coparticipación *f*

cope [kəʊp, *Am:* koʊp] *vi* **1.** (*master a situation*) aguantar **2.** (*deal with*) poder con; (*situation*) enfrentarse; (*problem*) hacer frente; (*pain*) soportar

Copenhagen [ˌkəʊpən'heɪgən, *Am:* 'koʊpənˌheɪ-] *n* Copenhague *m*

copier ['kɒpɪəʳ, *Am:* 'kɑ:pɪɚ] *n* copiadora *f*

co-pilot ['kəʊ'paɪlət, *Am:* 'koʊˌpaɪ-] *n* copiloto *mf*

copious ['kəʊpɪəs, *Am:* 'koʊ-] *adj* copioso, -a; (*amount*) abundante

copper ['kɒpəʳ, *Am:* 'kɑ:pɚ] **I.** *n* **1.** *no pl* (*metal*) cobre *m* **2.** *Brit, inf* (*police officer*) poli *mf* **3.** *pl, Brit, inf* (*coin*) calderilla *f* **II.** *adj* (*colour*) cobrizo, -a

copper beech <-es> *n* haya *f* roja **copper-ore** *n* mineral *m* de cobre **copperplate** **I.** *n* **1.** *no pl* (*handwriting*) caligrafía *f* **2.** (*metal plaque*) lámina *f* de cobre **II.** *adj* caligrafiado, -a **copper-smith** *n* calderero, -a *m, f*

coppice ['kɒpɪs, *Am:* 'kɑ:pɪs] **I.** *n* bosquecillo *m* **II.** *vt* talar

copulate ['kɒpjʊleɪt, *Am:* 'kɑ:pjə-] *vi* copular

copulation [ˌkɒpjʊ'leɪʃən, *Am:* ˌkɑ:pjə-] *n no pl* cópula *f*

copy ['kɒpi, *Am:* 'kɑ:pi] **I.** <-ies> *n* **1.** (*facsimile*) copia *f*; (*of a book*) ejemplar *m*; ART imitación *f*; **to be a carbon ~ of sb** ser idéntico a alguien; **an exact ~** una reproducción exacta **2.** INFOR copia *f*; **hard ~** copia en el disco duro; **to make a ~** hacer una copia **3.** (*text to be published*) original *m*; (*advertisement text*) texto *m* publicitario **4.** (*topics for articles*) tema *m* **II.** <-ie-> *vt* **1.** *a.* INFOR, MUS copiar **2.** (*imitate*) imitar **III.** *vi* SCHOOL copiar

copybook ['kɒpibʊk, *Am:* 'kɑ:pi-] **I.** *adj* **1.** (*exemplary*) modélico, -a **2.** (*unoriginal*) convencional **II.** *n* cuaderno *m* de escritura ▸**to blot one's ~** manchar su reputación

copycat **I.** *n childspeak, inf* copión, -ona *m, f* **II.** *adj* **~ version** imitación *f*; **a ~ crime** un crimen inspirado en otro **copy desk** *n Am* mesa *f* de redacción **copy editor** *n* corrector(a) *m(f)* de originales

copying ink *n no pl* tinta *f* de copiar **copying paper** *n* papel *m* de calcar

copy-protection *n* INFOR protección *f* contra escritura **copyright** *n* derechos *mpl* de autor; **to hold the ~ of sth** tener los derechos de autor de algo; **protected under ~** protegido según los derechos de la propiedad intelectual; **~ reserved** reservado el derecho de reproducción **copywriter** *n* escritor(a) *m(f)* de textos publicitarios

coral ['kɒrəl, *Am:* 'kɔ:r-] **I.** *n no pl* coral *m*; **made of ~** de coral **II.** *adj* (*reddish colour*) coralino, -a

coral island *n* isla *f* coralina **coral reef** *n* arrecife *m* de coral

cord [kɔːd, *Am:* kɔːrd] *n* **1.** (*rope*) cuerda *f,* piola *f AmS;* ELEC cable *m;* **spinal** ~ médula *f* espinal; **umbilical** ~ cordón *m* umbilical **2.** (*corduroy*) pana *f;* **a** ~ **shirt** una camisa de pana

cordial [ˈkɔːdɪəl, *Am:* ˈkɔːrdʒəl] **I.** *adj* **1.** (*friendly*) cordial; (*relations*) amistoso, -a **2.** *form* (*strong*) de corazón **II.** *n no pl, Brit, Aus: bebida con sabor a fruta a la que se le añade agua*

cordiality [ˌkɔːdɪˈæləti, *Am:* ˌkɔːrdʒɪˈæləṱi] <-ies> *n form* cordialidad *f*

cordless [ˈkɔːdləs, *Am:* ˈkɔːrd-] *adj* inalámbrico, -a

cordon [ˈkɔːdn, *Am:* ˈkɔːr-] **I.** *n* **1.** (*line*) cordón *m;* **police** ~ cordón policial **2.** (*fruit tree*) enredadera *f* **II.** *vt* acordonar

cords *npl* pantalón *m* de pana

corduroy [ˈkɔːdərɔɪ, *Am:* ˈkɔːr-] *n no pl* pana *f*

core [kɔːʳ, *Am:* kɔːr] **I.** *n* **1.** (*centre*) centro *m;* **to the** ~ *fig* hasta la médula; **to be rotten to the** ~ *fig* estar podrido hasta la médula, estar completamente corrompido; **to be at the** ~ **of a problem** llegar al quid de la cuestión **2.** (*sample of strata*) muestra *f* **3.** (*centre with seeds*) corazón *m* **4.** PHYS núcleo *m* **5.** ELEC eje *m* **II.** *adj* **the** ~ **issue** la cuestión principal **III.** *vt* deshuesar

CORE [kɔːʳ, *Am:* kɔːr] *n Am abbr of* **Congress of Racial Equality** Congreso *m* de la Igualdad Racial

core subject *n* tema *m* central

coriander [ˌkɒriˈændəʳ, *Am:* ˈkɔːriædɚ] *n* cilantro *m*

cork [kɔːk, *Am:* kɔːrk] **I.** *n* **1.** *no pl* corcho *m* **2.** (*stopper*) tapón *m* **II.** *vt* **1.** (*put stopper in*) taponar **2.** (*blacken*) **to** ~ **one's face** taparse la cara **3.** (*spoiled wine*) **the wine is** ~**ed** el vino sabe a corcho

corkage [ˈkɔkədʒ, *Am:* ˈkɔːr-] *n no pl,* **cork charge** *n precio que algunos restaurantes hacen pagar por servir vino comprado en otro lugar*

corkscrew [ˈkɔːkskruː, *Am:* ˈkɔːrk-] **I.** *n* sacacorchos *m inv* **II.** *adj* en espiral; ~ **curls** tirabuzones *mpl*

corn[1] [kɔːn, *Am:* kɔːrn] *n no pl* **1.** *Brit* (*cereal*) cereal *m* **2.** *Am* (*maize*) maíz *m,* choclo *m AmS,* abatí *m Arg;* ~ **on the cob** mazorca *f* de maíz **3.** *Am, inf* (*something trite*) sensiblería *f*

corn[2] [kɔːn, *Am:* kɔːrn] *n* MED callo *m* ►**to <u>tread</u> on sb's** ~**s** herir los sentimientos de alguien

corncob *n* mazorca *f* de maíz

cornea [ˈkɔːnɪə, *Am:* ˈkɔːr-] *n* córnea *f*

corner [ˈkɔːnəʳ, *Am:* ˈkɔːrnɚ] **I.** *n* **1.** (*junction of two roads*) esquina *f;* **to cut a** ~ doblar una esquina; **to be round the** ~ estar a la vuelta de la esquina; **to turn the** ~ doblar la esquina; *fig* salir de un apuro **2.** (*of a room*) rincón *m;* **to put sb in the** ~ *a.* SCHOOL arrinconar a alguien **3.** (*place*) **a distant** ~ **of the globe** un rincón remoto de la tierra; **the four** ~**s of the world** todas las partes del mundo **4.** (*manoevre in sport*) córner *m* **5.** SPORTS (*assistants*) recogepelotas *m inv* **6.** (*difficult position*) **to be in a tight** ~ estar en un aprieto; **to drive sb into a** (**tight**) ~ poner a alguien entre la espada y la pared **7.** (*domination*) **to have a** ~ **of the market** controlar una parte del mercado **8.** (*periphery*) **out of the** ~ **of one's eye** con el rabillo del ojo; **out of the** ~ **of sb's mouth** en la comisura de los labios ►**to <u>cut</u>** ~**s** ahorrar esfuerzos **II.** *vt* **1.** (*hinder escape*) acorralar; *iron* abordar; **to get sb** ~**ed** *fig* acorralar a alguien **2.** ECON **to** ~ **the market** acaparar el mercado **III.** *vi* (*auto*) tomar una curva

cornered [ˈkɔːnəd, *Am:* ˈkɔːrnɚd] *adj* acorralado, -a

corner house *n* casa *f* que hace esquina **corner seat** *n* asiento *m* en la esquina **corner shop** *n* tienda *f* de la esquina **cornerstone** *n a. fig* piedra *f* angular

cornet [ˈkɔːnɪt, *Am:* kɔːrˈnet] *n* **1.** (*brass instrument*) corneta *f* **2.** (*wafer cone*) cucurucho *m*

cornflakes [ˈkɔːnfleɪks, *Am:* ˈkɔːrn-] *npl* copos *mpl* de maíz; **a bowl of** ~ un tazón de cereales

cornflour [ˈkɔːnflaʊəʳ, *Am:* ˈkɔːrnflaʊɚ] *n no pl, Brit, Aus* harina *f* de maíz

cornflower [ˈkɔːnflaʊəʳ, *Am:* ˈkɔːrnflaʊɚ] **I.** *n* aciano *m* **II.** *adj* ~ **blue** azul aciano

cornice [ˈkɔːnɪs, *Am:* ˈkɔːr-] *n* ARCHIT cornisa *f*

corn-poppy <-ies> *n* amapola *f*

Cornwall [ˈkɔːrnwɔːl] *n* Cornualles *m*

corny [ˈkɔːni, *Am:* ˈkɔːr-] <-ier, -iest> *adj* **1.** *inf* viejo, -a; (*joke*) gastado, -a **2.** (*emotive*) sensiblero, -a

corollary [kəˈrɒləri, *Am:* ˈkɔːrəler-] <-ies> *n form* corolario *m*

coronary [ˈkɒrənəri, *Am:* ˈkɔːrəner-] **I.** *n* infarto *m* de miocardio; **when he got the bill he nearly had a** ~ *iron* cuando le dieron la cuenta casi le coge un infarto **II.** *adj* coronario, -a

coronation [ˌkɒrəˈneɪʃən, *Am:* ˌkɔːr-] **I.** *n* coronación *f* **II.** *adj* de coronación

coroner [ˈkɒrənəʳ, *Am:* ˈkɔːrənɚ] *n funcionario encargado de investigar muertes no naturales*

Corp **1.** *Am abbr of* **corporation** sociedad *f* anónima **2.** MIL *abbr of* **corporal** cabo *m*

corporal [ˈkɔːpərəl, *Am:* ˈkɔːr-] **I.** *n* MIL cabo *mf* **II.** *adj form* corporal; **a** ~ **oath** HIST juramento *m* a la corona

corporate [ˈkɔːpərət, *Am:* ˈkɔːr-] *adj* **1.** (*shared by group*) colectivo, -a **2.** (*of corporation*) corporativo, -a, empresarial; ~ **capital** capital *m* social; ~ **law** derecho *m* de sociedades; ~ **policy** política *f* de cooperación

corporation [ˌkɔːpəˈreɪʃən, *Am:* ˌkɔːrpə-] *n*

C

+ *sing/pl vb* **1.** (*business*) sociedad *f* anónima; **multinational** ~ empresa *f* multinacional, empresa transnacional *AmL;* **a public** ~ *Brit* una empresa pública **2.** (*local council*) ayuntamiento *m;* **municipal** ~ corporación *f* municipal

corporation tax <-es> *n* impuesto *m* de sociedades

corps [kɔːʳ, *Am:* kɔːr] *n* + *sing/pl vb* **1.** MIL (*unit*) cuerpo *m* **2.** (*group*) equipo *m*

corps de ballet [ˌkɔːdəˈbæleɪ, *Am:* ˌkɔːr-] *n* cuerpo *m* de baile

corpse [kɔːps, *Am:* kɔːrps] *n* cadáver *m*

corpus [ˈkɔːpəs, *Am:* ˈkɔːr-] <-pora *o* -es> *n* **1.** LIT (*collection*) colección *f* **2.** LING corpus *m inv* **3.** ECON capital *m*

Corpus Christi [ˌkɔːpəsˈkrɪsti, *Am:* ˌkɔːr-] *n* REL Corpus *m inv*

corpuscle [ˈkɔːpʌsl, *Am:* ˈkɔːr-] *n* corpúsculo *m*

corral [kəˈrɑːl, *Am:* -ˈræl] **I.** *n* caballeriza *f* **II.** <-ll-> *vt* estabular

correct [kəˈrekt] **I.** *vt* (*put right*) corregir; ~ **me if I'm wrong but ...** corrígeme si me equivoco, pero... **II.** *adj* correcto, -a; **that is** ~ *form* así es

correction [kəˈrekʃən] *n* **1.** corrección *f;* **subject to** ~ sujeto a enmienda **2.** *no pl* (*improvememt*) rectificación *f*

correction fluid *n* líquido *m* corrector

corrective [kəˈrektɪv] **I.** *adj* correctivo, -a **II.** *n* medida *f* correctiva

correctly [kəˈrektli] *adv* correctamente

correctness [kəˈrektnɪs] *n no pl* corrección *f*

correlate [ˈkɒrəleɪt, *Am:* ˈkɔːrə-] **I.** *vt* correlacionar **II.** *vi* (*relate*) poner en correlación; *fig* estar en relación

correlation [ˌkɒrəˈleɪʃən, *Am:* ˌkɔːrə-] *n* (*connection*) correlación *f;* (*relationship*) relación *f;* **there is a** ~ **between smoking and lung cancer** el tabaco y el cáncer de pulmón están relacionados entre sí

correspond [ˌkɒrɪˈspɒnd, *Am:* ˌkɔːrə-] *vi* **1.** (*be equal to*) corresponder a **2.** (*write*) cartearse

correspondence [ˌkɒrɪˈspɒndəns, *Am:* ˌkɔːrəˈspɑːn-] *n no pl* correspondencia *f;* **business** ~ correspondencia comercial; **to enter into** ~ **with sb** *form* cartearse con alguien

correspondent [ˌkɒrɪˈspɒndənt, *Am:* ˌkɔːrəˈspɑːn-] *n* **1.** (*writer of letters*) remitente *mf* **2.** (*journalist*) corresponsal *mf;* **special** ~ enviado, -a *m, f* especial

corresponding [ˌkɒrɪˈspɒndɪŋ, *Am:* ˌkɔːrə-] *adj* correspondiente

corridor [ˈkɒrɪdɔːʳ, *Am:* ˈkɔːrədɚ] *n* **1.** (*passage*) pasillo *m* **2.** (*land*) corredor *m*

corrie [ˈkɒri, *Am:* ˈkɔːr-] *n* GEO circo *m*

corroborate [kəˈrɒbəreɪt, *Am:* -ˈrɑːbə-] *vt* corroborar

corroboration [kəˌrɒbəˈreɪʃən, *Am:* -ˌrɑːbə-] *n* corroboración *f;* **in** ~ **of sth** de conformidad con algo

corroborative [kəˈrɒbərətɪv, *Am:* -ˈrɑːbɚət̬ɪv] *adj* corroborable

corrode [kəˈrəʊd, *Am:* -ˈroʊd] **I.** *vi* corroerse **II.** *vt* corroer; *fig* menoscabar

corrosion [kəˈrəʊʒən, *Am:* -ˈroʊ-] *n no pl* **1.** corrosión *f* **2.** *fig* (*deterioration*) deterioro *m*

corrosive [kəˈrəʊsɪv, *Am:* -ˈroʊ-] **I.** *adj* **1.** (*destructive*) corrosivo, -a **2.** *fig* (*harmful*) destructivo, -a; ~ **attack** *fig* ataque *m* con malicia **II.** *n* corrosivo *m*

corrugated [ˈkɒrəgeɪtɪd, *Am:* -t̬ɪd] *adj* **1.** (*furrowed*) ondulado, -a **2.** (*rutted: road*) de curvas

corrupt [kəˈrʌpt] **I.** *vt* **1.** (*debase*) corromper **2.** (*influence by bribes*) sobornar **3.** (*document*) dañar **II.** *vi* corromper **III.** *adj* **1.** (*influenced by bribes*) corrupto, -a; ~ **practices** prácticas *fpl* corruptas **2.** (*document*) dañado, -a

corruption [kəˈrʌpʃən] *n no pl* **1.** (*debasement*) corrupción *f* **2.** (*bribery*) soborno *m*

corset [ˈkɔːsɪt, *Am:* ˈkɔːr-] *n* corsé *m*

Corsica [ˈkɔːsɪkə, *Am:* ˈkɔːr-] *n* Córcega *f*

Corsican [ˈkɔːsɪkən, *Am:* ˈkɔːr-] **I.** *adj* corso, -a **II.** *n* **1.** (*person*) corso, -a *m, f* **2.** LING corso *m*

cos [kɒs, *Am:* kɑːs] MAT *abbr of* **cosine** cos

cosec [ˈkəʊsek, *Am:* ˈkoʊ-] MAT *abbr of* **cosecant** cosec

cosignatory [ˌkəʊˈsɪgnətəri, *Am:* ˌkoʊˈsɪgnətɔːri] <-ies> *n* cosignatario, -a *m, f*

cosine [ˈkəʊsaɪn, *Am:* ˈkoʊ-] *n* coseno *m*

cosiness [ˈkəʊzɪnɪs, *Am:* ˈkoʊ-] *n no pl* comodidad *f*

cos lettuce [ˈkɒsˌletɪs, *Am:* ˈkɑːsˌlet̬-] *n Brit, Aus* lechuga *f*

cosmetic [kɒzˈmetɪk, *Am:* kɑːzˈmet̬-] **I.** *n* cosmético *m;* ~**s** cosméticos *mpl* **II.** *adj* **1.** cosmético, -a; ~ **cream** crema *f* cosmética **2.** (*superficial*) superficial

cosmetician [ˌkɒzməˈtɪʃən] *n* esteticista *mf*

cosmic [ˈkɒzmɪk, *Am:* ˈkɑːz-] *adj fig* cósmico, -a; **of** ~ **proportions** de proporciones astronómicas

cosmology [kɒzˈmɒlədʒi, *Am:* kɑːzˈmɑːlə-] *n* cosmología *f*

cosmonaut [ˈkɒzmənɔːt, *Am:* ˈkɑːzmənɑːt] *n* cosmonauta *mf*

cosmopolitan [ˌkɒzməˈpɒlɪtən, *Am:* ˌkɑːzməˈpɑːlɪ-] **I.** *adj* cosmopolita **II.** *n* cosmopolita *mf*

cosmos [ˈkɒzmɒs, *Am:* ˈkɑːzmoʊs] *n no pl* cosmos *m inv*

cost [kɒst, *Am:* kɑːst] **I.** *vt* **1.** <cost, cost> (*amount to*) valer; **to** ~ **a packet** *inf* costar un ojo de la cara **2.** <cost, cost> (*cause the loss of*) costar; **to** ~ **sb dear** salir caro a alguien **3.** <costed, costed> (*calculate price*) calcular el precio de **II.** *n* **1.** (*price*) precio *m;* **at no extra** ~ sin costes adicionales; **to cut the** ~ recortar costes; **to defray the** ~ **of sth** *form* costear algo **2.** *pl* (*expence*) costes *mpl;* LAW costas *fpl;* **to cut ~s** recortar costes **3.** *fig* (*sacrifice*) **to count the ~(s)** (**of sth**) (*consider effects*) valorar el riesgo (de algo); (*suffer*) padecer las consecuencias (de algo); (**only**) **at the ~ of doing sth** (sólo) a costa de hacer algo; **to one's ~** a expensas de uno; **at all ~(s)** a toda costa

co-star [ˌkəʊ'stɑːʳ, *Am:* 'koʊstɑːr] **I.** *n* coprotagonista *mf* **II.** <-rr-> *vt* coprotagonizar **III.** <-rr-> *vi* **to ~ with sb** protagonizar con alguien

Costa Rica [ˌkɒstə'riːkə, *Am:* ˌkoʊstə-] *n* Costa Rica *f*

Costa Rican [ˌkɒstə'riːkən, *Am:* ˌkoʊstə-] **I.** *adj* costarricense **II.** *n* costarricense *mf*

costly ['kɒstli, *Am:* 'kɑːst-] <-ier, -iest> *adj* costoso, -a; (*mistake*) caro, -a; **to prove ~** *a. fig* resultar muy caro

cost price ['kɒstˌpraɪs, *Am:* 'kɑːst-] *n* **at ~** a precio de coste

costume ['kɒstjuːm, *Am:* 'kɑːstuːm] *n* **1.** (*national dress*) traje *m;* **to dress in ~** ir trajeado **2.** (*decorative dress*) disfraz *m*

cosy ['kəʊzi, *Am:* 'koʊ-] **I.** <-ier, -iest> *adj* **1.** (*comfortable*) cómodo, -a; (*place*) acogedor(a); (*chat*) agradable **2.** *pej* (*convenient*) de conveniencia **II.** <-ies> *n* tapadera *f*

cot [kɒt, *Am:* kɑːt] *n* **1.** (*baby's bed*) cuna *f* **2.** *Am* (*camp bed*) cama *f* plegable

cotangent ['kəʊˌtændʒənt, *Am:* ˌkoʊ'tæn-] *n* cotangente *f*

cot death *n* muerte *f* súbita infantil

cottage ['kɒtɪdʒ, *Am:* 'kɑːt̬ɪdʒ] *n* **country ~** casa *f* de campo; **thatched ~** casa *f* con techo de paja

cottage cheese *n no pl* requesón *m* **cottage industry** <-ies> *n* industria *f* familiar

cot(**an**) MAT *abbr of* **cotangent** cot

cotton ['kɒtn, *Am:* 'kɑːtn] **I.** *n* **1.** (*plant*) algodón *m* **2.** *no pl* (*material*) algodón *m* **3.** *no pl* (*thread*) hilo *m* de coser **II.** *vi* **to ~ on** (**to sth**) caer en la cuenta (de algo)

cotton bud *n* bastoncillo *m* de algodón **cotton-grower** *n* cultivador(a) *m(f)* de algodón **cotton mill** *n* fábrica *f* de algodón **cottonseed** *n* semilla *f* de algodón **cotton wool** *n no pl* **1.** (*common use*) algodón *m* en rama **2.** *Am* MED algodón *m* hidrófilo ►**to wrap sb in ~** criar a alguien entre algodones

couch [kaʊtʃ] <-es> **I.** *n* canapé *m;* **psychiatrist's ~** diván *m* **II.** *vt* expresar

couchette [kuː'ʃet] *n* litera *f*

couch potato <- -es> *n* teleadicto, -a *m, f*

cough [kɒf, *Am:* kɑːf] **I.** *n* tos *f;* **chesty ~** tos seca **II.** *vi* **1.** toser **2.** (*auto*) rugir **III.** *vt* **to ~ blood** escupir sangre

◆**cough up** **I.** *vi inf* apoquinar **II.** *vt inf* **1.** (*bring up: blood*) escupir; MED expectorar **2.** (*give back*) devolver **3.** *inf* (*pay*) apoquinar

cough drop *n* pastilla *f* para la tos **cough medicine** *n,* **cough mixture** *n no pl* medicina *f* para la tos

could [kʊd] *pt, pp* **can²**

council ['kaʊntsəl] *n + sing/pl vb* ADMIN **city ~** ayuntamiento *m;* MIL consejo *m;* **local ~** consejo local; **the United Nations Security Council** el Consejo de Seguridad de las Naciones Unidas

council estate *n Brit* ≈ urbanización *f* de protección oficial **council flat** *n,* **council house** *n Brit* ≈ piso *m* de protección oficial **council housing** *n Brit* ≈ viviendas *fpl* de protección oficial

council(**l**)**or** ['kaʊntsələʳ, *Am:* -ɚ] *n* concejal(a) *m(f)*

Council of Economic and Finance Ministers *n* Consejo *m* de Ministros de Economía y Finanzas **Council of Europe** *n* Consejo *m* de Europa **Council of Ministers** *n* Consejo *m* de Ministros **Council of the European Union** *n* Consejo *m* de la Unión Europea

council tax <-es> *n Brit* impuesto *m* municipal

counsel ['kaʊntsəl] **I.** <*Brit* -ll-, *Am* -l-> *vt* (*advise*) aconsejar; **to ~ sb against sth** *form* prevenir a alguien de algo **II.** *n* **1.** *no pl, form* (*advice*) consejo *m;* **a ~ of perfection** un ideal imposible; **to take ~ from sb** aconsejarse por alguien **2.** (*lawyer*) abogado, -a *m, f;* **~ for the defence** abogado defensor; **~ for the prosecution** fiscal *mf* ►**to keep one's own ~** guardar silencio

counsel(**l**)**ing** **I.** *n no pl* asesoramiento *m* **II.** *adj* de orientación

counsel(**l**)**or** ['kaʊntsələʳ, *Am:* -ɚ] *n* **1.** (*adviser*) asesor(a) *m(f);* **marriage guidance ~** consejero, -a *m, f* matrimonial **2.** *Am* (*lawyer*) abogado, -a *m, f*

count¹ [kaʊnt] *n* conde *m*

count² [kaʊnt] **I.** *n* **1.** (*totalling up*) total *m;* **final ~** suma *f* final **2.** (*measured amount*) recuento *m* **3.** (*act of counting*) cuenta *f;* **to keep ~ of sth** contar algo; **to lose ~ of sth** perder la cuenta de algo **4.** LAW acusación *f* **5.** (*opinion*) opinión *f;* **to be angry with sb on several ~s** estar enfadado con alguien por varios motivos ►**to be out for the ~** estar durmiendo **II.** *vt* **1.** (*number*) contar; **to ~ one's change** contar el cambio; **to ~ heads** contar uno por uno **2.** (*consider*) considerar; **to ~ sth a success/failure** considerar algo un éxito/fracaso; **to ~ sb as a friend** tener a alguien como amigo **III.** *vi* **1.** (*number*) contar; **that's what ~s** eso es lo que importa; **this doesn't ~ for anything** esto no cuenta para nada **2.** (*be considered*) **to not ~** no tener ni voz ni voto

◆**count down** *vi* hacer la cuenta atrás

◆**count out** *vt always sep* **1.** (*money*) contar **2.** *inf* (*leave out*) **to count sb out** no contar con alguien

countable noun [ˌkaʊntəbl'naʊn] *n* nombre *m* contable

count-down ['kaʊntdaʊn] *n* cuenta *f* atrás

countenance ['kaʊntɪnəns, *Am:* -tənəns] **I.** *n no pl* **1.** *form* (*facial expression*) rostro *m;*

to be of noble ~ tener rasgos nobles **2.** (*approval*) aprobación *f;* **to give ~ to sth** dar el visto bueno a algo **3.** (*composure*) compostura *f;* **to keep one's ~** *form* guardar la compostura **II.** *vt form* aprobar

counter ['kaʊntəʳ, *Am:* -t̬ɚ] **I.** *n* **1.** (*service point*) mostrador *m;* **over the ~** sin receta médica; **under the ~** *fig* subrepticiamente **2.** (*person who counts*) cajero, -a *m, f* **3.** (*machine*) caja *f;* TECH contador *m* **4.** (*disc*) ficha *f* **II.** *vt* contrarrestar **III.** *vi* **1.** (*oppose*) oponerse **2.** (*react by scoring*) contraatacar **IV.** *adv* en contra; **to act ~ to sth** actuar contrariamente a algo; **to run ~ to sth** oponerse a algo

counteract [ˌkaʊntər'ækt, *Am:* -t̬ɚ-] *vt* contrarrestar; **to ~ the effects of sth** neutralizar los efectos de algo; **~ inflation** combatir la inflación

counteractive [ˌkaʊntər'æktɪv, *Am:* -t̬ɚ-] *adj* **1.** (*working against*) que contrarresta **2.** (*neutralizing*) neutralizador(a)

counterattack ['kɑːʊntərətæk, *Am:* 'kaʊnt̬ɚ-] **I.** *n* contraataque *m* **II.** *vt* contraatacar **III.** *vi* (*attack in return*) contraatacar

counterbalance ['kaʊntəbæləns, *Am:* -t̬ɚ-] **I.** *n* contrapeso *m; fig* compensación *f* **II.** *vt* (*balance out*) contrapesar; *fig* compensar

countercharge ['kaʊntətʃɑːdʒ, *Am:* -t̬ɚ-tʃɑːrdʒ] **I.** *n* LAW reconvención *f* **II.** *vt* LAW reconvenir

countercheck ['kauntətʃek] **I.** *n* **1.** (*restraint*) obstáculo *m;* **to put a ~ on sth** *fig* poner trabas a algo **2.** (*second check*) segunda comprobación *f* **II.** *vt* volver a comprobar

counterclockwise [ˌkaʊntə 'klɒkwaɪz, *Am:* -t̬ɚ 'klɑːkwaɪz] *adj Am* en sentido opuesto a las agujas del reloj

counterespionage [ˌkaʊntər'espiənɑːʒ, *Am:* -t̬ɚ-] *n no pl* contraespionaje *m*

counterespionage service *n* servicio *m* de contraespionaje

counterfeit ['kaʊntəfɪt, *Am:* -t̬ɚ-] **I.** *adj* falsificado, -a; (*money*) falso, -a **II.** *vt* falsificar **III.** *n* falsificación *f*

counterfoil ['kaʊntəfɔɪl, *Am:* -t̬ɚ-] *n Brit* FIN talón *m*

counterintelligence [ˌkaʊntər ɪn'telɪdʒəns, *Am:* -t̬ɚ-] *n no pl* contraespionaje *m*

countermand [ˌkaʊntə'mɑːnd, *Am:* -t̬ɚ-'mænd] *vt* contramandar; MIL contradecir

countermeasure ['kaʊntəmeʒəʳ, *Am:* -t̬ɚmeʒɚ] *n* medida *f* en contra

counterpart ['kaʊntəpɑːt, *Am:* -t̬ɚpɑːrt] *n* contrapartida *f;* POL homólogo, -a *m, f*

counterpoint ['kaʊntəpɔɪnt, *Am:* -t̬ɚ-] *n* MUS contrapunto *m*

counterpoise ['kaʊntəpɔɪz, *Am:* -t̬ɚ-] *form* **I.** *n* contrapeso *m; fig* compensación *f* **II.** *vt* contrapesar; *fig* compensar

counterproductive [ˌkaʊntəprə'dʌktɪv, *Am:* -t̬ɚ-] *adj* contraproducente

counter-revolution [ˌkaʊntəˌrevə'luːʃən, *Am:* -t̬ɚ-] *n* contrarrevolución *f*

countersign ['kaʊntəsaɪn, *Am:* -t̬ɚ-] *vt* refrendar

countersink ['kaʊntəsɪŋk, *Am:* -t̬ɚ-] *irr vt* avellanar

counter-terrorism [ˌkaʊntə'terərɪzəm, *Am:* -t̬ɚ'terɚ-] *n no pl* acción *f* contra el terrorismo

countess ['kaʊntɪs, *Am:* -t̬ɪs] *n* condesa *f*

countless ['kaʊntlɪs] *adj* incontable

country ['kʌntri] **I.** *n* **1.** *no pl* (*rural area*) campo *m* **2.** <-ies> (*political unit*) país *m;* (*native land*) patria *f* **3.** (*area of land*) territorio *m* **4.** MUS country *m* **II.** *adj* **1.** (*rural*) del campo; (*life, manners*) rural **2.** MUS (*music*) country

country bumpkin *n Brit* pueblerino, -a *m, f* **country club** *n* club *m* de campo **country dance** *n Brit* danza *f* folclórica **country-folk** *n + pl vb* gente *f* de campo **country house** *n* casa *f* solariega

countryman ['kʌntrɪmən] <-men> *n* **1.** (*same nationality*) compatriota *m* **2.** (*from rural area*) campesino *m*

country music *n* música *f* country

country road *n* camino *m* rural

countryside ['kʌntrɪsaɪd] *n no pl* campo *m*, verde *m AmC, Méx*

countrywide ['kʌntrɪwaɪd] *adj* a escala nacional

countrywoman ['kʌntrɪwʊmən] <-women> *n* **1.** (*same nationality*) compatriota *f* **2.** (*from rural area*) campesina *f*

county ['kaʊnti, *Am:* -t̬i] **I.** <-ies> *n* condado *m* **II.** *adj* **to be ~** *Brit* ser pijo

county borough *n Brit* HIST municipio *m* **county council** *n Brit* delegación *f* de gobierno en un condado **county court** *n Brit* juzgado *m* comarcal **county seat** *n Am,* **county town** *n Brit* capital *f* del condado

coup [kuː] <coups> *n* golpe *m*

coup de grâce [ˌkuːdə'grɑːs] *n* golpe *m* de gracia **coup d'état** <coups d'état> *n* golpe *m* de Estado

coupé ['kuːpeɪ] *n* cupé *m*

couple ['kʌpl] **I.** *n* **1.** *no pl* (*a few*) par *m;* **the first ~ of weeks** las primeras dos semanas **2.** *+ sing/pl vb* (*two people*) pareja *f;* (*married*) matrimonio *m* **II.** *vt* **1.** RAIL, AUTO enganchar **2.** (*connect*) conectar **3.** (*link*) unir **III.** *vi* HIST aparearse

couplet ['kʌplɪt] *n* dístico *m;* (*rhyming*) pareado *m*

coupling ['kʌplɪŋ] *n* **1.** RAIL, AUTO enganche *m* **2.** (*linking*) combinación *f* **3.** (*sexual intercourse: of people*) apareamiento *m;* (*of animals*) cópula *f*

coupon ['kuːpɒn, *Am:* -pɑːn] *n* **1.** (*voucher*) vale *m* **2.** (*return-slip of advert*) cupón *m* **3.** *Brit* SPORTS boleto *m*

courage ['kʌrɪdʒ] *n* coraje *m;* **to show great ~** mostrar gran valor; **to take one's ~ in both hands** hacer de tripas corazón

courageous [kəˈreɪdʒəs] *adj* (*person*) valiente; (*act*) valeroso, -a

courgette [kʊəˈʒet, *Am:* kʊr-] *n* calabacín *m*

courier [ˈkʊrɪəʳ, *Am:* ˈkʊrɪɚ] **I.** *n* **1.** (*tour guide*) guía *mf* **2.** (*delivers post*) mensajero, -a *m, f* **II.** *adj* ~ **service** servicio *m* de mensajería

course [kɔːs, *Am:* kɔːrs] **I.** *n* **1.** (*direction*) recorrido *m;* (*of a river*) curso *m;* **to be off** ~ *a. fig* desviarse; **to set** ~ **for sth** poner rumbo hacia algo; **your best** ~ **would be …** lo mejor que podrías hacer sería… **2.** (*development*) transcurso *m;* **in the** ~ **of time** con el tiempo **3.** (*treatment*) tratamiento *m* **4.** SPORTS (*area*) pista *f;* (*golf*) campo *m* **5.** (*part of meal*) plato *m* **6.** (*layer*) hilada *f* ►**to let sth run its** ~ dejar que algo siga su curso; **to stay the** ~ aguantar hasta el final; **of** ~ claro; **of** ~ **not** desde luego que no **II.** *vi* correr

coursebook *n* libro *m* de texto **courseware** *n no pl* INFOR material *m* de enseñanza informatizado

court [kɔːt, *Am:* kɔːrt] **I.** *n* **1.** (*room for trials*) juzgado *m* **2.** (*judicial body*) tribunal *m* **3.** (*marked out area for playing*) cancha *f;* (*tennis*) pista *f* **4.** (*yard*) patio *m* **5.** (*road*) calle *f* **6.** *Brit* (*apartment buildings*) apartamentos *mpl* **7.** HIST palacio *m* **8.** (*sovereign*) corte *f* ►**to hold** ~ recibir en audiencia; **to laugh sb out of** ~ reírse de alguien **II.** *vt* (*woman*) cortejar; (*danger*) exponerse a **III.** *vi* (*couple*) salir

courteous [ˈkɜːtɪəs, *Am:* ˈkɜːrt̬ɪ-] *adj* cortés

courtesy [ˈkɜːtəsi, *Am:* ˈkɜːrt̬ə-] <-ies> *n* **1.** (*politeness*) gentileza *f,* cortesía *f* **2.** *no pl* (*decency*) decencia *f* **3.** (*permission*) (**by**) ~ **of** por gentileza de

courtesy bus *n* autobús *m* de cortesía **courtesy light** *n* AUTO luz *f* interior **courtesy title** *n* tratamiento *m* de cortesía

court hearing *n* vista *f* judicial

courthouse [ˈkɔːthaʊs, *Am:* ˈkɔːrt-] *n Am* juzgado *m*

courtier [ˈkɔːtɪəʳ, *Am:* ˈkɔːrt̬ɪɚ] *n* cortesano, -a *m, f*

court martial **I.** <court martials> *n* consejo *m* de guerra **II.** <-ll-, *Am:* -l-> *vt* someter a consejo de guerra **court of appeal** *n* tribunal *m* de apelación

Court of Auditors *n* Tribunal *m* de Cuentas

Court of Justice *n* Tribunal *m* de Justicia

courtroom [ˈkɔːtrʊm, *Am:* ˈkɔːrtruːm] *n* sala *f* de tribunal **courtship** *n* noviazgo *m; a.* ZOOL cortejo *m* **courtyard** *n* patio *m*

cousin [ˈkʌzn] *n* primo, -a *m, f*

couture [kuːˈtjʊəʳ, *Am:* kuːˈtʊr] *n* FASHION costura *f;* **haute** ~ alta costura

cove [kəʊv, *Am:* koʊv] *n* cala *f*

covenant [ˈkʌvənənt, *Am:* -ænt] **I.** *n* **1.** (*agreement*) contrato *m* **2.** *Brit* (*donation*) donación *f* **II.** *vt* contratar

Coventry [ˈkɒvntri, *Am:* ˈkʌv-] *n* **to send sb to** ~ hacer el vacío a alguien

cover [ˈkʌvəʳ, *Am:* -ɚ] **I.** *n* **1.** (*top*) tapa *f* **2.** (*outer sheet: of a book*) cubierta *f;* (*of a magazine*) portada *f* **3.** (*bedding*) cubrecama *m* **4.** (*envelope*) sobre *m* **5.** (*concealment*) abrigo *m;* **to break** ~ salir al descubierto **6.** (*shelter*) refugio *m* **7.** (*insurance*) cobertura *f* **8.** (*provision*) suplencia *f* **9.** (*at table*) cubierto *m* **II.** *vt* **1.** (*hide: eyes, ears*) tapar; (*head*) cubrir **2.** (*put over*) tapar; (*book*) forrar **3.** (*keep warm*) abrigar **4.** (*travel*) recorrer **5.** (*deal with*) contemplar **6.** (*include*) incluir **7.** (*report on*) informar acerca de **8.** (*insure*) asegurar **9.** (*give armed protection*) cubrir **10.** MUS (*song*) versionar **III.** *vi* sustituir

◆**cover over** *vt* cubrir

◆**cover up** **I.** *vt* (*protect*) cubrir **II.** *vi* **to** ~ **for sb** encubrir a alguien

coverage [ˈkʌvərɪdʒ] *n no pl* **1.** (*reporting*) cobertura *f* **2.** (*dealing with*) contemplación *f*

coveralls [ˈkʌvərɔːlz] *npl* mono *m*

cover charge [ˈkʌvətʃɑːdʒ, *Am:* -ɚtʃɑːrdʒ] *n dinero extra que se paga en un restaurante o discoteca para cubrir algunos gastos de éstos*

covered *adj* **1.** (*roofed over*) cubierto, -a **2.** (*insured*) asegurado, -a

cover girl [ˈkʌvəgɜːl, *Am:* -ɚgɜːrl] *n* modelo *f* de portada

covering *n* capa *f*

covering letter *n* carta *f* adjunta

cover note [ˈkʌvənəʊt, *Am:* -ɚnoʊt] *n Am, Aus* (*covering note*) seguro *m* provisional

covers [ˈkʌvəz, *Am:* -ɚz] *n* mantas *fpl*

cover story <-ies> *n* noticia *f* de primera página

covert[1] [ˈkʌvət, *Am:* ˈkoʊvɜːrt] *adj* encubierto, -a

covert[2] [ˈkʌvət, *Am:* ˈkʌvɚt] *n* espesura *f*

cover-up [ˈkʌvərʌp, *Am:* -ɚ-] *n* encubrimiento *m*

covet [ˈkʌvɪt] *vt* desear

cow[1] [kaʊ] *n* **1.** (*female ox*) vaca *f* **2.** (*female mammal*) hembra *f* **3.** *Brit, pej* (*woman*) tía *f;* **stupid** ~**!** ¡imbécil! ►**until the** ~**s come home** hasta que las ranas críen pelo

cow[2] [kaʊ] *vt* intimidar

coward [ˈkaʊəd, *Am:* ˈkaʊɚd] *n* cobarde *mf*

cowardice [ˈkaʊədɪs, *Am:* ˈkaʊɚ-] *n no pl* cobardía *f*

cowardly [ˈkaʊədli, *Am:* ˈkaʊɚd-] *adj* **1.** (*fearful*) cobarde **2.** (*nasty*) mezquino, -a

cowboy [ˈkaʊbɔɪ] **I.** *n* **1.** (*cattle hand*) vaquero *m,* cowboy *m,* tropero *m Arg* **2.** *inf* (*dishonest tradesperson*) pirata *mf* **II.** *adj* vaquero, -a

cower [ˈkaʊəʳ, *Am:* ˈkaʊɚ] *vi* encogerse de miedo

cowherd [ˈkaʊhɜːd, *Am:* -hɜːrd] *n* vaquero, -a *m, f* **cowhide** **I.** *n no pl* cuero *m* **II.** *adj* de cuero

cowl [kaʊl] *n* **1.** (*hood*) capucha *f* **2.** (*hood on chimney*) sombrerete *m* **3.** (*engine hood*) cubierta *f*

cowling *n* cubierta *f* de proa

cowman [ˈkaʊmən] <-men> *n* **1.** (*male*

cowherd) vaquero *m* **2.** *Aus* (*cattle farm manager*) ganadero *m*

co-worker [ˌkəʊ'wɜːkəʳ, *Am:* 'koʊˌwɜːrkɚ] *n* colaborador(a) *m(f)*

cowshed ['kaʊʃed] *n* establo *m*

cowslip ['kaʊslɪp] *n* prímula *f*

cox ['kɒks, *Am:* 'kɑːks] <-es> *n*, **coxswain** ['kɒksən, *Am:* 'kɑːk-] *n form* timonel *mf*

coy [kɔɪ, *Am:* -ɚ] <-er, -est> *adj* **1.** (*secretive*) tímido, -a **2.** (*flirtatiously shy*) coqueto, -a

coyote [kɔɪ'əʊt, *Am:* kaɪ'oʊt̬i] *n* coyote *m*

cozy ['kəʊzi, *Am:* 'koʊ-] *adj Am s.* **cosy**

CP *n abbr of* **Communist Party** PC *m*

CPU [ˌsiːpiː'juː] *n* INFOR *abbr of* **central processing unit** CPU *f*

crab[1] [kræb] *n* **1.** (*sea animal*) cangrejo *m*, jaiba *f AmL* **2.** ASTR Cáncer *m*

crab[2] [kræb] <-bb-> *vi* rezongar

crab (**apple**) ['kræb(ˌæpl)] *n* **1.** (*fruit*) manzana *f* silvestre **2.** (*tree*) manzano *m* silvestre

crabbed ['kræbɪd] *adj* **1.** (*handwriting*) apretado, -a **2.** (*mood*) refunfuñón, -ona

crabby ['kræbi] <-ier, -iest> *adj inf* rezongón, -ona

crab louse *n* ladilla *f*

crack [kræk] **I.** *n* **1.** (*fissure*) grieta *f* **2.** (*sharp sound: of a rifle*) estallido *m;* (*of a breaking branch*) crujido *m;* (*of the whip*) chasquido *m* **3.** *inf* (*drug*) crack *m* **4.** (*joke*) chiste *m* **5.** *inf* (*attempt*) intento *m* ►**the ~ of dawn** el amanecer; **to give sb a fair ~ of the whip** dar a alguien las mismas posibilidades **II.** *adj* de primera **III.** *vt* **1.** (*break*) romper **2.** (*open: an egg*) cascar; (*nuts*) partir; (*safe*) forzar; (*code*) descifrar **3.** (*resolve*) resolver **4.** (*hit*) pegar; (*knuckles*) hacer crujir; (*whip*) hacer chasquear; **to ~ a joke** contar un chiste **IV.** *vi* **1.** (*break*) romperse; (*paintwork*) agrietarse **2.** (*break down*) sufrir una crisis nerviosa **3.** (*make a sharp noise*) chasquear ►**to get ~ing** poner manos a la obra

◆**crack down** *vi* **to ~ on sb/sth** tomar medidas enérgicas contra alguien/algo

◆**crack up** *vi* **1.** MED sufrir un colapso nervioso **2.** (*break down: car*) averiarse; (*business*) fallar

crackdown ['krækdaʊn] *n* ofensiva *f*

cracked [krækt] *adj* **1.** (*having fissures*) rajado, -a; (*lips*) agrietado, -a **2.** (*crazy*) chiflado, -a

cracker ['krækəʳ, *Am:* -ɚ] *n* **1.** (*dry biscuit*) galleta *f* **2.** *Brit* (*device*) sorpresa *f* **3.** INFOR cracker *mf* **4.** *inf* (*excellent thing*) fenómeno *m;* (*woman*) pimpollo *m*

crackers ['krækəz, *Am:* -ɚz] *adj* lelo, -a; **to be ~** estar chiflado

crackle ['krækl] **I.** *vi* (*of paper*) crujir; (*telephone line*) hacer ruido; (*burning logs*) crepitar **II.** *vt* hacer crujir **III.** *n* (*of paper*) crujido *m;* (*of a telephone line*) ruido *m;* (*of burning wood*) chisporroteo *m*

crackling ['kræklɪŋ] *n* **1.** (*sound: of a fire*) crujido *m;* (*of a radio*) ruido *m* **2.** (*pork skin*) chicharrón *m*

crackpot ['krækpɒt, *Am:* -pɑːt] **I.** *n inf* chiflado, -a *m, f* **II.** *adj inf* chalado, -a

crack-up ['krækʌp] *n inf* **1.** (*mental breakdown*) colapso *m* **2.** (*car crash*) choque *m*

cradle ['kreɪdl] **I.** *n* **1.** (*baby's bed*) cuna *f;* **from the ~ to the grave** durante toda la vida **2.** (*framework*) andamio *m* **II.** *vt* acunar

craft [krɑːft, *Am:* kræft] **I.** *n* **1.** (*means of transport*) nave *f* **2.** *no pl* (*special skill*) arte *m* **3.** (*trade*) oficio *m* **4.** *no pl* (*ability*) destreza *f* **II.** *vt* construir

craftiness *n no pl* astucia *f*

craft shop *n* tienda *f* de artesanía

craftsman ['krɑːftsmən, *Am:* 'kræfts-] <-men> *n* artesano *m*

crafty ['krɑːfti, *Am:* 'kræf-] <-ier, -iest> *adj* astuto, -a

crag [kræg] *n* peñasco *m*

craggy ['krægi] <-ier, -iest> *adj* escarpado, -a; (*features*) marcado, -a

cram [kræm] <-mm-> **I.** *vt* meter; **to ~ sth with** llenar algo de **II.** *vi* memorizar

cramfull [ˌkræm'fʊl] *adj* atestado, -a

crammer ['kræməʳ, *Am:* -ɚ] *adj inf: escuela o libro para aprender rápidamente*

cramp [kræmp] **I.** *vt* poner obstáculos a; **to ~ sb's style** cortar las alas a alguien **II.** *n Brit, Aus* calambre *m*

cramped *adj* apretujado, -a

crampon ['kræmpɒn, *Am:* -pɑːn] *n* crampón *m*

cranberry ['krænbəri, *Am:* -ˌber-] <-ies> *n* arándano *m*

crane [kreɪn] **I.** *n* **1.** (*vehicle for lifting*) grúa *f* **2.** ZOOL grulla *f* **II.** *vt* **to ~ one's neck** estirar el cuello **III.** *vi* **to ~ forward** inclinarse estirando el cuello

crane fly <-ies> *n* típula *f*

cranium ['kreɪnɪəm] <craniums *o* crania> *n* cráneo *m*

crank[1] ['kræŋk] **I.** *n inf* maniático, -a *m, f* **II.** *adj* raro, -a

crank[2] [kræŋk] *n* cigüeñal *m*

crankcase ['kræŋkkeɪs] *n* cárter *m* (del cigüeñal)

crankshaft ['kræŋkʃɑːft, *Am:* -ʃæft] *n* eje *m* (del cigüeñal)

cranky ['kræŋki] <-ier, -iest> *adj Am, Aus, inf* maniático, -a

cranny ['kræni] <-ies> *n* ranura *f;* **in every nook and ~** en el último rincón

crap [kræp] **I.** <-pp-> *vi vulg* cagar **II.** *n vulg* **1.** (*excrement*) mierda *f* **2.** *no pl* (*nonsense*) estupidez *f* **III.** *adj* de mierda

crape [kreɪp] *n* crespón *m*

crappy ['kræpi] <-ier, -iest> *adj inf* malo, -a

crash [kræʃ] **I.** *n* <-es> **1.** (*accident*) accidente *m;* (*of a car*) choque *m* **2.** (*noise*) estrépito *m* **3.** COM crac *m* **4.** INFOR caída *f* (del sistema) **II.** *vi* **1.** (*have an accident*) chocar; (*plane*) estrellarse **2.** (*make loud noise*) retumbar **3.** (*break noisily*) derrumbarse **4.** COM colapsar **5.** INFOR colgarse **III.** *vt* **1.** (*damage in accident*) chocar **2.** (*make noise*) hacer ruido ▶**to ~ a party** colarse en una fiesta

crash barrier *n Brit, Aus* barrera *f* de protección **crash course** *n* curso *m* intensivo **crash diet** *n* dieta *f* intensiva **crash helmet** *n* casco *m* protector

crashing *adj* **to be a ~ bore** ser un verdadero muermo

crash-land [ˌkræʃˈlænd, *Am:* ˈkræʃlænd] *vi* aterrizar forzosamente

crash-landing *n* aterrizaje *m* forzoso **crash programme** *n* SCHOOL curso *m* intensivo

crass [kræs] *adj* **1.** (*gross*) flagrante **2.** (*coarse: comment*) grosero, -a

crate [kreɪt] **I.** *n* **1.** (*open box*) cajón *m* **2.** *inf* (*old car*) carraca *f* **II.** *vt* embalar en cajones

crater [ˈkreɪtəʳ, *Am:* -t̬ɚ] *n* cráter *m*

cravat [krəˈvæt] *n* fular *m*

crave [kreɪv] *vt* ansiar; (*attention*) reclamar

craving [ˈkreɪvɪŋ] *n* ansia *f*

crawl [krɔːl, *Am:* krɑːl] **I.** *vi* **1.** (*go on all fours*) gatear **2.** (*move slowly*) arrastrarse **3.** *inf* (*be obsequious*) **to ~ (up) to sb** hacer la pelota a alguien **4.** *inf* (*become infested*) **to be ~ing with sth** estar plagado de algo **II.** *n no pl* **1.** (*go very slowly*) arrastramiento *m* **2.** (*style of swimming*) crol *m;* **to do the ~** nadar crol

crawler [ˈkrɔːləʳ, *Am:* ˈkrɑːlɚ] *n* **1.** TECH tractor *m* de oruga **2.** (*baby*) bebé *mf* **3.** *inf* (*flatterer*) adulador(a) *m(f)*

crawler lane *n Brit* carril *m* para vehículos lentos

crawlers [ˈkrɔːləz, *Am:* ˈkrɑːlɚz] *npl* pijama *m* de cuerpo entero para bebés

crayfish [ˈkreɪfɪʃ] *n inv* **1.** (*Astacus*) cangrejo *m* de río **2.** GASTR (*in sea*) langosta *f*

crayon [ˈkreɪən, *Am:* -ɑːn] **I.** *n* lápiz *m* de color **II.** *vt* colorear **III.** *vi* dibujar

craze [kreɪz] *n* manía *f*

crazed [kreɪzd] *adj* de loco, -a; (*expression*) enloquecido, -a

craziness *n no pl* locura *f*

crazy [ˈkreɪzi] <-ier, -iest> *adj* loco, -a, tarado, -a *AmL;* **to go ~** volverse loco

creak [kriːk] **I.** *vi* (*door*) chirriar; (*bones*) crujir **II.** *n* (*of door*) chirrido *m;* (*of bones*) crujido *m*

creaky [ˈkriːki] <-ier, -iest> *adj* **1.** (*squeaky*) chirriante **2.** (*badly made*) poco firme **3.** (*unsafe*) inestable

cream [kriːm] **I.** *n* **1.** *no pl* (*milk fat*) nata *f;* **single ~** *Brit* crema *f* de leche; **double ~** *Brit* nata *f* para montar **2.** (*cosmetic product*) crema *f* **3.** (*the best*) flor y nata *f* **II.** *adj* **1.** (*containing cream*) cremoso, -a **2.** (*off-white colour*) de color crema **III.** *vt* (*butter*) batir; (*milk*) desnatar; **to ~ coffee** añadir crema al café

cream cheese *n no pl* queso *m* para untar

cream-colo(u)red *adj* de color crema

creamery [ˈkriːməri] <-ies> *n* lechería *f*

creamy [ˈkriːmi] <-ier, -iest> *adj* **1.** (*smooth*) cremoso, -a; (*skin*) hidratado, -a **2.** (*off-white*) de color hueso

crease [kriːs] **I.** *n* **1.** (*fold*) arruga *f;* (*hat*) pliegue *m* **2.** (*cricket*) línea *f* **II.** *vt* arrugar **III.** *vi* arrugarse

create [kriːˈeɪt] **I.** *vt* **1.** (*produce new*) crear **2.** (*produce skillfully*) posibilitar **3.** (*cause*) causar; (*impression*) provocar; (*sensation*) hacer; (*scandal*) motivar **4.** (*appoint*) nombrar **II.** *vi Brit, Aus, inf* armar jaleo

creation [kriːˈeɪʃən] *n* **1.** *no pl* (*making*) creación *f* **2.** (*product*) producción *f* **3.** FASHION modelo *m*

creative [kriːˈeɪtɪv, *Am:* -t̬ɪv] *adj* creativo, -a; (*imagination*) original

creator [kriːˈeɪtəʳ, *Am:* -t̬ɚ] *n* creador(a) *m(f)*

creature [ˈkriːtʃəʳ, *Am:* -tʃɚ] *n* **1.** (*being*) criatura *f* **2.** (*person being discussed*) individuo, -a *m, f;* **to be a ~ of habit** ser un animal de costumbres; **poor ~!** ¡pobrecito! **3.** (*pawn*) títere *m*

creature comforts *npl inf* bienestar *m* material

creche [kreɪʃ] *n Brit, Aus* guardería *f*

credence [ˈkriːdns] *no pl n form* crédito *m*

credentials [krɪˈdenʃlz] *npl* credenciales *fpl*

credibility [ˌkredɪˈbɪləti, *Am:* -əˈbɪlət̬i] *n no pl* credibilidad *f*

credible [ˈkredəbl] *adj* verosímil; (*witness*) creíble

credit [ˈkredɪt] **I.** *n* **1.** (*belief*) crédito *m;* **to give ~ to sth** dar crédito a algo **2.** (*honour*) honor *m;* (*recognition*) mérito *m;* **to be a ~ to sb** ser un orgullo [*o* honor] para alguien; **to sb's ~** en favor de alguien; **to take (the) ~ for sth** atribuirse el mérito de algo; **~ where ~'s due** el honor a quien le corresponda **3.** FIN crédito *m;* **to buy sth on ~** comprar algo a plazos; **to give sb ~** abrir crédito a alguien **4.** *no pl* COM haber *m;* **to be in ~** *Brit* tener saldo positivo **5.** *pl* CINE títulos *mpl* de crédito, créditos *mpl* **II.** *vt* **1.** (*believe*) creer **2.** FIN **to ~ sb with 2000 euros** abonar 2000 euros en cuenta a alguien **3.** (*attribute*) **he is ~ed with ...** se le atribuye...

creditable [ˈkredɪtəbl, *Am:* -t̬ə-] *adj* **1.** (*believable*) digno, -a de crédito **2.** (*commendable*) digno, -a de elogio

credit card *n* tarjeta *f* de crédito **credit facilities** *npl* facilidades *fpl* de pago **credit limit** *n* límite *m* de crédito **credit note** *n Aus, Brit* nota *f* de crédito

creditor [ˈkredɪtəʳ, *Am:* -t̬ɚ] *n* acreedor(a) *m(f)*

creditor bank *n* banco *m* acreedor

credit rating *n* clasificación *f* de solvencia

credits *npl* CINE créditos *mpl*

credit side *n* COM haber *m* **credit terms** *npl* condiciones *fpl* de un crédito

creditworthy [ˈkredɪtˌwɜːði, *Am:* -wɜːr-] *adj* solvente

credulity [krɪˈdjuːləti, *Am:* krəˈduːlə-] *n no*

C

pl credulidad *f*

credulous ['kredjʊləs, *Am:* 'kredjə-] *adj* crédulo, -a

creed [kri:d] *n* credo *m;* **the Creed** el Credo

creek [kri:k] *n* **1.** *Brit* (*narrow bay*) cala *f* **2.** *Am, Aus* (*stream*) riachuelo *m* ▸**to be up the ~** (**without a paddle**) *inf* estar en un aprieto

creep [kri:p] **I.** <crept, crept> *vi* **1.** (*crawl*) arrastrarse; (*snake*) reptar; (*baby*) andar a gatas; (*plant*) trepar **2.** (*move imperceptibly*) deslizarse **3.** (*move slowly*) moverse lentamente **II.** *n* **1.** (*act of creeping*) deslizamiento *m* **2.** *inf* (*sycophant*) pelotillero, -a *m, f,* lambiscón, -ona *m, f Méx,* lambón, -ona *m, f Col* **3.** (*pervert*) pervertido, -a *m, f* ▸**to give sb the ~s** *inf* poner a alguien la carne de gallina
◆**creep into** *vt insep* entrar sigilosamente en
◆**creep up** *vi* **to ~ on sb** acercarse sigilosamente a alguien

creeper ['kri:pəʳ, *Am:* -pɚ] *n* **1.** (*rope*) trepador *m* **2.** BOT enredadera *f* **3.** ZOOL ave *f* trepadora **4.** *pl, Am* (*babywear*) pelele *m* **5.** *pl, Am* zapatillas *f pl* deportivas

creeping *adj* progresivo, -a

creepy ['kri:pi] <-ier, -iest> *adj inf* espeluznante

creepy crawlie *n a. childspeak* bicho *m*

cremate [krɪ'meɪt, *Am:* kri:'meɪt] *vt* incinerar

cremation [krɪ'meɪʃən] *n* incineración *f*

crematorium [ˌkremə'tɔ:rɪəm, *Am:* ˌkri:mə'tɔ:ri-] <-s *o* -ria> *n* crematorio *m*

crematory ['kremətəri] **I.** *n Am* (*crematorium*) crematorio *m* **II.** *adj* crematorio, -a

crème de la crème [ˌkremdəlɑ:'krem] *n* **the ~** la flor y nata

crepe [kreɪp] *n* crepé *f,* crêpe *f*

crept [krept] *pp, pt of* **creep**

crescendo [krɪ'ʃendəʊ, *Am:* -doʊ] *n* crescendo *m*

crescent ['kresnt] **I.** *n* **1.** (*shape*) media luna *f* **2.** (*curved street*) *calle en forma de media luna* **II.** *adj* creciente

cress [kres] *n no pl* berro *m*

crest [krest] **I.** *n* **1.** (*peak*) cima *f;* (*of wave, bird*) cresta *f* **2.** (*helmet decoration*) cimera *f* **3.** ARCHIT caballete *m* **II.** *vt* coronar **III.** *vi* (*wave*) encresparse

crestfallen ['krestˌfɔ:lən] *adj* cabizbajo, -a

Crete [kri:t] *n* Creta *f*

cretin ['kretɪn, *Am:* 'kri:tn] *n inf* cretino, -a *m, f*

crevasse ['krɪvæs, *Am:* krə'væs] *n* grieta *f* en un glaciar

crevice ['krevɪs] *n a. fig* grieta *f*

crew¹ [kru:] **I.** *n* + *pl/sing vb* **1.** NAUT, AVIAT tripulación *f;* RAIL personal *m;* **ground/flight ~** personal de tierra/de vuelo; **two ~** dos miembros de la tripulación **2.** (*team*) equipo *m* **3.** *inf* (*gang*) banda *f* **II.** *vt* **to ~ a boat** formar parte de la tripulación de una embarcación **III.** *vi* **to ~ for sb** formar parte de la tripulación del barco de alguien

crew² [kru:] *Brit pp, pt of* **crow²**

crew cut *n* corte *m* de pelo al rape

crewman <-men> *n* miembro *m* de la tripulación

crewmember *n* miembro *mf* de la tripulación

crib [krɪb] **I.** *n* **1.** *Am, Brit* (*baby's bed*) cuna *f* **2.** (*nativity scene*) belén *m* **3.** *inf* (*plagiarized work*) plagio *m* **4.** *inf* SCHOOL chuleta *f,* acordeón *m Méx,* machete *m RíoPl* **II.** <-bb-> *vt inf* **1.** (*plagiarize*) plagiar **2.** SCHOOL copiar; **to ~ sth from a book** copiar algo de un libro **III.** <-bb-> *vi inf* **1.** (*plagiarize*) plagiar **2.** SCHOOL copiar; **to ~ from sb** copiar de alguien

cribbage ['krɪbɪdʒ] *n* GAMES *especie de juego de naipes*

crick [krɪk] **I.** *n* (*in the neck*) tortícolis *f inv;* (*in the back*) lumbago *m;* **to have a ~ in one's neck/back** tener tortícolis/lumbago **II.** *vt* **I have ~ed my neck/back** me ha dado tortícolis/lumbago

cricket¹ ['krɪkɪt] *n no pl* SPORTS cricket *m* ▸**that's not ~** ¡eso no es jugar limpio!

cricket² ['krɪkɪt] *n* ZOOL grillo *m,* siripita *f Bol*

cricket bat *n* bate *m* de cricket

cricketer ['krɪkɪtəʳ, *Am:* -t̬ɚ] *n* jugador(a) *m(f)* de cricket

cricket field *n,* **cricket ground** *n,* **cricket pitch** <-es> *n* campo *m* de cricket

crier ['kraɪəʳ, *Am:* -ɚ] *n* pregonero, -a *m, f*

crikey ['kraɪki] *interj inf* ¡santo Dios!

crime [kraɪm] *n* **1.** LAW (*illegal act*) delito *m;* (*more serious*) crimen *m;* **a ~ against humanity** un crimen contra la humanidad; **~ of passion** crimen pasional; **to accuse sb of a ~** imputar un delito a alguien; **to commit a ~** cometer un delito; **the scene of the ~** la escena del crimen; **it would be a ~** *inf* sería un pecado **2.** (*criminal activity*) delincuencia *f;* **~ rate** índice *m* de criminalidad; **organized ~** crimen organizado

crime prevention *n no pl* prevención *f* de la delincuencia **crime-ridden** *adj* con un alto índice de criminalidad **crime wave** *n* ola *f* de delincuencia

criminal ['krɪmɪnl] **I.** *n* (*offender*) delincuente *mf;* (*more serious*) criminal *mf* **II.** *adj* **1.** (*illegal*) delictivo, -a; (*more serious*) criminal **2.** LAW penal; **~ court** juzgado *m* de lo penal; **~ lawyer** abogado, -a *m, f* penalista; **~ record** antecedentes *mpl* penales **3.** *fig* (*shameful*) vergonzoso, -a; **to be ~ to do sth** ser un crimen hacer algo

criminality [ˌkrɪmɪ'næləti, *Am:* -ə'nælət̬i] *n no pl* criminalidad *f*

criminologist [krɪmɪ'nɒlədʒɪst, *Am:* -'nɑ:lə-] *n* criminólogo, -a *m, f*

criminology [ˌkrɪmɪ'nɒlədʒi, *Am:* -'nɑ:lə-] *n no pl* criminología *f*

crimp [krɪmp] *vt* **1.** (*press into folds, frill*) plisar **2.** (*make wavy*) ondular; (*make curly*) rizar

crimson ['krɪmzn] **I.** *n no pl* carmesí *m* **II.** *adj*

1. (*colour*) carmesí 2. (*red-faced*) colorado, -a; **to blush ~** ponerse como un tomate

cringe [krɪndʒ] *vi* 1. *inf* (*shrink*) encogerse; **to ~ with embarrassment at sth** morirse de vergüenza por algo 2. (*lower*) humillarse; **to ~ before sb** arrastrarse ante alguien

crinkle ['krɪŋkl] I. *vt* (*wrinkle*) arrugar; (*wave*) ondular II. *vi* **to ~** (**up**) (*wrinkle*) arrugarse; (*ripple*) ondularse III. *n* arruga *f;* (*in hair*) rizo *m*

crinkly ['krɪŋkli] <-ier, -iest> *adj* 1. (*wrinkled*) arrugado, -a 2. (*wavy*) ondulado, -a; (*curly*) rizado, -a

cripple ['krɪpl] I. *n* lisiado, -a *m, f* II. *vt* 1. (*disable*) lisiar; (*machine, object*) inutilizar 2. (*paralyse*) paralizar

crippling *adj fig* terrible

crisis ['kraɪsɪs] <crises> *n* crisis *f inv;* **a ~ over sth** una crisis provocada por algo; **~ in** [*o* **of**] **confidence** crisis de confianza; **to go through a ~** atravesar una crisis

crisis management *n no pl* gestión *f* de crisis

crisp [krɪsp] I. <-er, -est> *adj* 1. (*snow, bacon*) crujiente 2. (*apple, lettuce*) fresco, -a 3. (*shirt, trousers*) recién planchado, -a; (*banknote*) nuevo, -a 4. (*air*) vivificante 5. (*sharp*) nítido, -a 6. (*lively*) animado, -a 7. (*quick and precise*) escueto, -a; (*manner*) seco, -a; (*style*) conciso, -a II. *n Brit pl* (*thin fried potatoes*) patatas *fpl* de churrero, papas *fpl* fritas *AmL* III. *vt* 1. (*make crisp*) tostar ligeramente 2. (*curl*) encrespar

crispbread ['krɪsbred] *n galleta crujiente de centeno*

crispy ['krɪspi] <-ier, -iest> *adj* crujiente

criss-cross ['krɪskrɒs, *Am:* -krɑːs] I. *vt* entrecruzar II. *vi* entrecruzarse III. *adj* entrecruzado, -a IV. <-es> *n* 1. entramado *m* 2. *fig* enredo *m*

criterion [kraɪ'tɪəriən, *Am:* -'tɪrɪ-] <-ria> *n* criterio *m*

critic ['krɪtɪk, *Am:* 'krɪţ-] *n* crítico, -a *m, f*

critical ['krɪtɪkl, *Am:* 'krɪţ-] *adj* 1. (*disapproving*) crítico, -a; **to be ~ of sth/sb** criticar algo/a alguien; **to be highly ~ of sth** criticar duramente algo 2. (*decisive*) fundamental; **to be ~ to sth** ser de vital importancia para algo; **to be in a ~ condition** *a.* MED estar en estado crítico

criticism ['krɪtɪsɪzəm, *Am:* 'krɪţ-] *n* crítica *f;* **to take ~** admitir la crítica; **I have a few ~s of what you say** tengo algunas críticas que hacer respecto a eso que dices

criticize ['krɪtɪsaɪz, *Am:* 'krɪţ-] *vt, vi* criticar

critique [krɪ'tiːk] *n* crítica *f*

croak [krəʊk, *Am:* kroʊk] I. *vi* 1. (*crow*) graznar; (*frog*) croar; (*person*) gruñir 2. *inf* (*die*) estirar la pata II. *vt* decir con voz ronca III. *n* (*crow*) graznido *m;* (*frog*) croar *m;* (*person*) gruñido *m*

Croat ['krəʊæt, *Am:* 'kroʊ-] *n* croata *mf*

Croatia [krəʊ'eɪʃɪə, *Am:* kroʊ-] *n* Croacia *f*

Croatian [krəʊ'eɪʃɪən, *Am:* kroʊ-] I. *adj* croata II. *n* croata *mf*

crochet ['krəʊʃeɪ, *Am:* kroʊ'ʃeɪ] I. *n no pl* ganchillo *m,* croché *m* II. *vi* hacer ganchillo III. *vt* hacer a ganchillo

crochet hook *n,* **crochet needle** *n* aguja *f* de ganchillo [*o* de croché]

crock [krɒk, *Am:* krɑːk] *n* 1. (*clay container*) vasija *f* de barro 2. *iron* **old ~** (*person*) carcamal *m inf;* (*thing*) cacharro *m inf* 3. *Am, inf* **a ~ of shit** (*nonsense*) una chorrada

crockery ['krɒkəri, *Am:* 'krɑːkɚ-] *n no pl* vajilla *f*

crocodile ['krɒkədaɪl, *Am:* 'krɑːkə-] <-(s)> *n* 1. ZOOL cocodrilo *m* 2. *Brit, inf* (*line of pupils*) fila *f* de a dos

crocodile tears *npl* lágrimas *fpl* de cocodrilo; **to shed ~** llorar lágrimas de cocodrilo

crocus ['krəʊkəs, *Am:* 'kroʊ-] <-es> *n* azafrán *m*

croft [krɒft, *Am:* krɑːft] *n Scot* (*small farm*) granja *f* pequeña

crofter ['krɒftəʳ, *Am:* 'krɑːftɚ] *n Scot* propietario, -a *m, f* de una granja pequeña

croissant ['krwɑːsɒŋ, *Am:* kwɑː'sɑ-] *n* croissant *m,* cruasán *m*

crony ['krəʊni, *Am:* 'kroʊ-] <-ies> *n iron, inf* amigote *mf*

crook [krʊk] I. *n* 1. (*criminal*) delincuente *mf* 2. *inf* (*rogue*) sinvergüenza *mf* 3. (*of elbow*) pliegue *m;* (*of leg*) corva *f* 4. (*curve*) recodo *m* 5. (*staff: of shepherd*) cayado *m;* (*of bishop*) báculo *m* II. *adj Aus, inf* 1. (*ill*) **to feel ~** encontrarse mal 2. (*angry*) **to go ~** (**at sb**) ponerse furioso (con alguien) 3. (*out of order*) estropeado, -a 4. (*unsatisfactory*) malo, -a III. *vt* doblar; **to ~ one's finger at sb** hacer señas con el dedo a alguien

crooked ['krʊkɪd] *adj* 1. (*not straight: nose, legs*) torcido, -a; (*back*) encorvado, -a; (*path*) tortuoso, -a 2. *inf* (*dishonest*) deshonesto, -a

croon [kruːn] I. *vt, vi* canturrear II. *n* canturreo *m*

crooner ['kruːnəʳ, *Am:* -ɚ] *n iron, inf* cantante *mf* melódico, -a

crop [krɒp, *Am:* krɑːp] I. *n* 1. AGR (*plant*) cultivo *m;* (*harvest*) cosecha *f* 2. (*group: of people*) montón *m;* (*of things*) sarta *f;* **a ~ of lies** una sarta de mentiras 3. (*haircut*) corte *m* de pelo muy corto; **to wear one's hair in a ~** llevar el pelo muy corto 4. (*of bird*) buche *m* 5. (*whip*) fusta *f* II. <-pp-> *vt* 1. AGR cultivar 2. (*cut*) recortar; (*tail*) cortar; (*hair*) cortar muy corto; (*plant*) podar 3. (*graze*) pacer III. *vi* AGR darse; (*land*) rendir

◆**crop out** *vi* GEO aflorar

◆**crop up** *vi* surgir

cropper ['krɒpəʳ, *Am:* 'krɑːpɚ] *n no pl* 1. (*person*) agricultor(a) *m(f)* 2. (*plant*) cultivo *m;* **to be a good/bad ~** tener buen/mal rendimiento ►**to come a ~** *inf* (*have a bad accident*) darse un porrazo; (*fail miserably*) fracasar abiertamente; (*in an exam*) catear

crop rotation *n* rotación *f* de cultivos

croquet ['krəʊkeɪ, *Am:* kroʊ'keɪ] *n no pl* croquet *m*

cross [krɒs, *Am:* krɑːs] **I.** *vt* **1.** (*go across: road, threshold*) cruzar; (*desert, river, sea*) atravesar **2.** (*lie across*) **the bridge ~es the river** el puente cruza el río **3.** (*place crosswise*) **to ~ one's legs** cruzar las piernas; **to ~ one's arms** cruzarse de brazos; **to ~ one's fingers** *a. fig* cruzar los dedos **4.** BIO (*crossbreed*) cruzar **5.** REL **to ~ oneself** hacerse la señal de la cruz **6.** (*oppose*) contrariar **7.** (*mark with a cross*) marcar con una cruz **8.** (*draw a line across*) cruzar, rayar; **to ~ a cheque** *Aus, Brit* cruzar un cheque ►**I'll ~ that bridge when I come to it** me ocuparé de ello cuando llegue el momento; **~ my heart and hope to die** que me muera si no es verdad; **to ~ one's mind** ocurrírsele a alguien; **to ~ swords with sb** habérselas con alguien **II.** *vi* **1.** (*intersect*) cruzarse **2.** (*go across*) cruzar **III.** *n* **1.** *a.* REL cruz *f;* **the sign of the ~** la señal de la cruz; **to bear one's ~** cargar con su cruz; **Maltese ~** cruz de Malta **2.** (*crossing: of streets, roads*) cruce *m* **3.** BIO cruce *m,* cruza *f AmL* **4.** (*mixture*) mezcla *f* **IV.** *adj* enfadado, -a; **to be ~ about sth** estar enfadado por algo; **to get ~ with sb** enfadarse con alguien

◆**cross off** *vt,* **cross out** *vt* tachar

◆**cross over** *vi, vt* cruzar

crossbar ['krɒsbɑːʳ, *Am:* 'krɑːsbɑːr] *n* travesaño *m;* (*of goal*) larguero *m;* (*of bicycle*) barra *f* **crossbeam** *n* viga *f* transversal **cross-border** *adj* transfronterizo, -a **crossbow** *n* ballesta *f* **crossbreed** *n* BIO cruce *m,* cruza *f AmL* **cross-channel** *adj* **~ ferry** (*across the English channel*) ferry *m* del canal de la Mancha **crosscheck I.** *n* comprobación *f* adicional **II.** *vt* volver a comprobar **cross-country I.** *adj* a campo traviesa; **~ race** cross *m;* **~ skiing** esquí *m* nórdico **II.** *adv* a campo traviesa **III.** *n* competición *f* a campo a través **cross-current** *n* contracorriente *f* **cross-examination** *n* LAW interrogatorio *m* cruzado **cross-examine** *vt* contrainterrogar **cross-eyed** *adj* bizco, -a **cross-fertilization** *n no pl* BIO fecundación *f* cruzada **crossfire** *n no pl* fuego *m* cruzado; **to be caught in the ~** *fig* estar entre dos fuegos **cross-grained** *adj* (*wood*) de fibras cruzadas

crossing ['krɒsɪŋ, *Am:* 'krɑːsɪŋ] *n* **1.** (*place to cross*) paso *m;* **level ~** RAIL paso *m* a nivel; **border ~** paso fronterizo; **pedestrian ~** paso de peatones **2.** (*crossroads*) cruce *m* **3.** ARCHIT crucero *m* **4.** (*journey*) paso *m;* (*across the sea*) travesía *f;* **the ~ of the Alps** el paso de los Alpes

cross-legged [ˌkrɒs'legd, *Am:* ˌkrɑːs'legəd] *adj* con las piernas cruzadas **crossover** *n* paso *m;* **a ~ of popular and classical music** una fusión de música popular y clásica **cross-purposes** *npl* **to be talking at ~** estar hablando de cosas distintas **cross-reference** *n* remisión *f* **crossroads** *n inv* **1.** cruce *m* **2.** *fig* encrucijada *f;* **to be at a ~** estar en una encrucijada **cross-section** *n* **1.** sección *f* transversal **2.** *fig* muestra *f* representativa **crosstalk** *n no pl* **1.** TEL cruce *m* de líneas; RADIO interferencia *f* **2.** *Brit* (*repartee*) *intercambio de réplicas ocurrentes* **crosswalk** *n Am* (*pedestrian crossing*) paso *m* de peatones **crossways** *adv* transversalmente **crosswind** *n* viento *m* de costado **crosswise** *adv* transversalmente **crossword** (**puzzle**) *n* crucigrama *m*

crotch [krɒtʃ, *Am:* krɑːtʃ] <-es> *n* entrepierna *f*

crotchet ['krɒtʃɪt, *Am:* 'krɑːtʃət] *n* MUS negra *f*

crotchety ['krɒtʃɪti, *Am:* 'krɑːtʃət̬i] *adj inf* (*bad-tempered*) malhumorado, -a

crouch [kraʊtʃ] **I.** *vi* **to ~** (**down**) agacharse; **to be ~ing** estar en cuclillas **II.** *n* **to lower oneself into a ~** agacharse

croup [kruːp] *n no pl* **1.** (*rump*) grupa *f* **2.** MED crup *m,* garrotillo *m*

croupier ['kruːpɪeɪ, *Am:* -eɪ] *n* crupier *mf*

crow¹ [krəʊ, *Am:* kroʊ] *n* ZOOL cuervo *m* ►**to eat ~** *Am, inf* tener que reconocer un error; **as the ~ flies** en línea recta

crow² [krəʊ, *Am:* kroʊ] <crowed *Brit:* crew, crowed *Brit:* crew> **I.** *n* **1.** (*call of a cock*) cacareo *m* **2.** (*cry of pleasure*) grito *m* de alegría; (*of baby*) gorjeo *m* **II.** *vi* **1.** (*cock*) cacarear **2.** (*cry out happily*) gritar de entusiasmo; (*baby*) gorjear **3.** (*boast*) alardear; **to ~ over sth** jactarse de algo

crowbar ['krəʊbɑːʳ, *Am:* 'kroʊbɑːr] *n* palanca *f*

crowd [kraʊd] **I.** *n + pl/sing vb* **1.** (*throng*) multitud *f;* **there was quite a ~** había mucha gente **2.** *inf* (*group*) grupo *m;* **the usual ~** los de siempre **3.** *inf* (*large number*) montón *m;* **a ~ of things** un montón de cosas **4.** (*common people*) **the ~** el vulgo **5.** (*masses*) masas *fpl;* **to stand out from the ~** *fig* destacar(se); **to follow the ~** *fig* dejarse llevar por los demás **6.** (*audience*) público *m,* espectadores *mpl* **II.** *vi* aglomerarse; **to ~ into a place** entrar en tropel en un sitio; **to ~ round sb/sth** apiñarse alrededor de alguien/algo **III.** *vt* **1.** (*fill*) llenar; **to ~ the streets/a stadium** abarrotar las calles/un estadio **2.** (*cram*) amontonar **3.** *inf* (*pressure*) atosigar

◆**crowd out** *vt* **1.** (*exclude*) excluir **2.** (*fill*) **to be crowded out** estar lleno de gente

crowded *adj* lleno, -a; **~ together** amontonados; **the bar was ~** había mucha gente en el bar; **the drawer is ~ with useless things** el cajón está atiborrado de cosas inservibles

crowd-puller *n* gran atracción *f*

crown [kraʊn] **I.** *n* **1.** corona *f;* **the Crown** (*monarchy*) la Corona **2.** (*top part: of hill, mountain*) cima *f;* (*of hat, tree*) copa *f;* (*of head*) coronilla *f;* (*of road*) centro *m;* (*of roof*) caballete *m* **3.** ZOOL (*of bird*) cresta *f* **4.** (*culmi-*

nation) culminación *f* **5.** (*of tooth*) funda *f* **II.** *vt* **1.** (*coronate*) coronar; **to ~ sb queen** coronar reina a alguien **2.** (*complete*) rematar; **the church is ~ed by a golden dome** una cúpula dorada corona la iglesia; **the prize ~ed his career** el premio fue la culminación de su carrera **3.** *inf* (*hit on head*) dar un golpe en la cabeza **4.** MED (*tooth*) poner una funda en ►**to ~ it all** *Aus, Brit* para rematarlo todo; (*misfortune*) para colmo de desgracias

crown cap *n* cápsula *f* **crown colony** <-ies> *n* colonia *f* de la Corona **crown cork** *n* cápsula *f*

crowning *adj* supremo, -a

crown jewels *n a. fig, iron* joyas *fpl* de la Corona **crown prince** *n* príncipe *m* heredero

crow's feet ['krəʊzfiːt, *Am:* 'kroʊz-] *npl* patas *fpl* de gallo **crow's nest** *n* NAUT torre *f* de vigía

CRT [ˌsiːɑːr'tiː, *Am:* -ɑːr'-] *n abbr of* **cathoderay tube** TRC *m*

crucial ['kruːʃl] *adj* (*decisive*) decisivo, -a; (*moment*) crucial; **to be ~ to sth** ser decisivo para algo; **it is ~ that ...** es de vital importancia que... *+subj*

crucible ['kruːsɪbl] *n a. fig* crisol *m*

crucifix [ˌkruːsɪ'fɪks] <-es> *n* crucifijo *m*

crucifixion [ˌkruːsɪ'fɪkʃən] *n* crucifixión *f*

crucify ['kruːsɪfaɪ] <-ie-> *vt* **1.** (*execute*) crucificar **2.** *fig* martirizar; **if she ever finds out, she'll ~ me** si alguna vez lo descubre, me matará

cruddy ['krʌdi] <-ier, -iest> *adj inf* asqueroso, -a; **a ~ book** una porquería de libro

crude [kruːd] **I.** *adj* **1.** (*rudimentary*) rudimentario, -a; (*letter*) tosco, -a **2.** (*unrefined*) bruto, -a; (*oil*) crudo, -a **3.** (*unfinished, undeveloped*) mal acabado, -a **4.** (*vulgar*) basto, -a; (*manners*) grosero, -a **II.** *n* crudo *m*

cruel [krʊəl] <-(l)ler, -(l)lest> *adj* cruel; **to be ~ to sb** ser cruel con alguien ►**to be ~ to be kind** *prov* hacer sufrir a alguien por su bien

cruelty ['krʊəlti, *Am:* -ṭi] <-ies> *n* crueldad *f;* **~ to sb** crueldad con alguien; **society for the prevention of ~ to animals** sociedad *f* protectora de los animales

cruise [kruːz] **I.** *n* crucero *m;* **~ ship** transatlántico *m;* **to go on a ~** hacer un crucero **II.** *vi* **1.** NAUT (*take a cruise*) hacer un crucero **2.** (*travel at constant speed*) ir a una velocidad de crucero; (*aeroplane*) volar a una velocidad constante **3.** (*police car*) patrullar **4.** *inf* (*drive around aimlessly*) dar una vuelta en coche **5.** *inf* (*look for casual sex*) buscar plan

cruise missile *n* MIL misil *m* de crucero

cruiser ['kruːzəʳ, *Am:* -ɚ] *n* **1.** (*warship*) crucero *m* **2.** (*pleasure boat*) embarcación *f* de recreo **3.** (*squad car*) coche *m* patrulla

cruise ship *n* transatlántico *m*

cruising *adj* (*speed*) de crucero

crumb [krʌm] *n* **1.** (*of bread*) miga *f* **2.** (*small amount*) pizca *f;* **a small ~ of ...** un poco de...; **a ~ of hope** algo de esperanza **3.** *inf* (*worthless person*) mequetrefe *mf*

crumble ['krʌmbl] **I.** *vt* **1.** (*bread, biscuit*) desmigajar **2.** (*stone, cheese*) desmenuzar **II.** *vi* (*cliff*) derrumbarse; (*plaster, stone*) desmenuzarse; (*empire*) desmoronarse; (*resistance, opposition*) venirse abajo **III.** *n Brit: postre de fruta cubierto de una pasta desmenuzada de azúcar, mantequilla y harina*

crumbly ['krʌmbli] <-ier, -iest> *adj* (*bread, cake*) que se desmigaja; (*cheese*) desmenuzable; (*house, wall*) desmoronadizo, -a

crummy ['krʌmi] <-ier, -iest> *adj inf* (*film, idea, car*) de pena; (*furniture, house*) cutre; (*place*) de mala muerte; **a ~ salary** un sueldo miserable

crumpet ['krʌmpɪt] *n* **1.** *Brit: panecillo blando que se come tostado* **2.** *Brit, inf* (*sexually attractive woman*) tía *f* buena

crumple ['krʌmpl] **I.** *vt* (*clothes, paper*) arrugar; (*metal*) abollar; **to ~ a piece of paper into a ball** hacer una pelota con un papel **II.** *vi* **1.** (*become dented: mudguard*) abollarse **2.** (*become wrinkled: fabric, face*) arrugarse **3.** (*collapse*) desplomarse

crunch [krʌntʃ] **I.** *vt* **1.** (*in the mouth*) masticar (haciendo ruido) **2.** (*grind*) hacer crujir **II.** *vi* crujir **III.** <-es> *n* **1.** (*crushing sound*) crujido *m* **2.** *no pl, inf* (*important moment*) momento *m* decisivo; **when it comes to the ~** *inf* a la hora de la verdad

crunchy [krʌntʃi] <-ier, -iest> *adj* crujiente

crusade [kruː'seɪd] **I.** *n* **1.** REL, HIST cruzada *f* **2.** *fig* campaña *f;* **a ~ for/against sth** una campaña a favor/en contra de algo **II.** *vi* **1.** HIST, REL participar en una cruzada **2.** *fig* hacer una campaña; **to ~ for sth** hacer una cruzada en pro de algo

crusader [kruː'seɪdəʳ, *Am:* -dɚ] *n* **1.** REL, HIST cruzado *m* **2.** *fig* defensor(a) *m(f);* **a ~ against sth** un detractor de algo

crush [krʌʃ] **I.** *vt* **1.** (*compress*) aplastar; (*paper*) estrujar; (*dress*) arrugar; (*person*) apretujar; **to be ~ed to death** morir aplastado **2.** (*grind: garlic*) machacar; (*grapes, olives*) prensar; (*stone*) triturar; (*ice*) picar **3.** (*extract by pressing*) **to ~ the juice from an orange** exprimir una naranja **4.** (*shock severely*) abatir **5.** (*defeat, suppress*) aplastar; (*rebellion, revolution*) reprimir; (*opponent*) derrotar; (*one's hopes*) frustrar; (*rumour*) acallar **II.** *vi* **1.** (*clothes, paper*) arrugarse **2.** (*people*) apretujarse **III.** <-es> *n* **1.** *no pl* (*act of crushing*) aplastamiento *m* **2.** *no pl* (*throng*) muchedumbre *f;* **there was a great ~** había una gran aglomeración **3.** *inf* (*temporary infatuation*) enamoramiento *m;* **to have a ~ on sb** encapricharse de alguien **4.** *Brit* (*crushed ice drink*) **orange ~** naranjada *f*

◆**crush up** *vt* triturar

crush barrier *n Brit* valla *f* de contención

crushing **I.** *n* aplastamiento *m* **II.** *adj* (*defeat*) aplastante; (*reply, argument*) contundente

crust [krʌst] **I.** *n* **1.** GASTR, BOT corteza *f;* (*dry bread*) mendrugo *m;* ~ **of the Earth** GEO corteza terrestre **2.** (*hard external layer*) capa *f;* **a ~ of ice/dirt** una capa de hielo/suciedad **3.** ZOOL caparazón *m* **4.** MED costra *f* **5.** (*deposit from wine*) poso *m* **II.** *vi* formar una costra **III.** *vt* **to be ~ed with mud** tener una capa de barro

crustacean [krʌ'steɪʃən] *n* crustáceo *m*

crusty ['krʌsti] <-ier, -iest> *adj* **1.** GASTR crujiente **2.** (*grumpy, surly*) malhumorado, -a

crutch [krʌtʃ] <-es> *n* **1.** MED muleta *f;* **to be on ~es** andar con muletas **2.** *fig* (*source of support*) apoyo *m* **3.** ANAT horcajadura *f*

crux [krʌks] *n no pl* punto *m* clave; **the ~ of sth** lo esencial de algo; **the ~ of the matter** el quid de la cuestión

cry [kraɪ] **I.** <-ie-> *vi* **1.** (*weep*) llorar; **to ~ for joy** llorar de alegría **2.** (*shout*) gritar; (*animal*) aullar; **to ~ for help** pedir ayuda a gritos **II.** <-ie-> *vt* **1.** (*shed tears*) llorar **2.** (*shout*) gritar **3.** (*announce publicly*) pregonar ▸**to ~ one's eyes out** llorar a lágrima viva; **to ~ foul at sth** mostrarse indignado por algo; **to ~ wolf** dar una falsa alarma **III.** *n* **1.** *no pl* (*weeping*) llanto *m;* **to have a ~** llorar **2.** (*shout*) grito *m;* **to give a ~** dar un grito; **a ~ for help** una llamada de socorro **3.** (*slogan*) lema *m* **4.** ZOOL aullido *m* ▸**to be a far ~ from sth** tener poco que ver con algo, ser muy distinto de algo; **to be in full ~ after sth** perseguir algo

◆**cry down** *vt* **1.** (*decry*) despreciar **2.** (*disparage*) desacreditar

◆**cry for** *vt insep* pedir

◆**cry off** *vi inf* echarse atrás; **to ~ a deal** romper un trato

◆**cry out I.** *vi* gritar; **to ~ against sth** clamar contra algo; **to ~ for sth** pedir algo a gritos; **for crying out loud!** *inf* ¡por el amor de Dios! **II.** *vt* gritar

crying ['kraɪɪŋ] **I.** *n no pl* lloro *m* **II.** *adj* (*need*) apremiante; (*injustice*) que clama al cielo; **a ~ shame** *inf* una verdadera vergüenza

crypt [krɪpt] *n* cripta *f*

cryptic ['krɪptɪk] *adj* críptico, -a; (*comment, remark*) ambiguo, -a; (*smile*) enigmático, -a

crystal ['krɪstl] **I.** *n* cristal *m* **II.** *adj* **1.** cristalino, -a **2.** (*made of crystal*) de cristal

crystal ball *n* bola *f* de cristal **crystal clear** *adj* **1.** (*transparent: water*) cristalino, -a; (*image*) nítido, -a **2.** (*obvious*) obvio, -a; **it is ~ (that)** está más claro que el agua (que +*subj*)

crystalline ['krɪstəlaɪn] *adj* cristalino, -a

crystallization [ˌkrɪstəlaɪ'zeɪʃən, *Am:* -ɪ'-] *n no pl* cristalización *f*

crystallize ['krɪstəlaɪz] **I.** *vi* cristalizarse **II.** *vt* **1.** cristalizar; (*plan, thought*) materializar **2.** GASTR escarchar

CSCE *n abbr of* **Conference on Security and Cooperation in Europe** CSCE *f*

CSE [ˌsiːes'iː] *n Brit abbr of* **Certificate of Secondary Education** *título de formación secundaria*

ct. 1. *abbr of* **cent** centavo *m* **2.** *abbr of* **carat** quilate *m*

CTC *n Brit abbr of* **city technology college** *instituto de tecnología*

cub [kʌb] *n* **1.** ZOOL cachorro *m* **2.** (*person*) novato, -a *m, f*

Cuba ['kjuːbə] *n* Cuba *f*

Cuban ['kjuːbən] **I.** *adj* cubano, -a **II.** *n* cubano, -a *m, f*

cubby-hole ['kʌbɪhəʊl, *Am:* -hoʊl] *n* cuchitril *m*

cube [kjuːb] **I.** *n* cubo *m;* (*of cheese*) dado *m;* (*of sugar*) terrón *m;* **ice ~** cubito *m* de hielo; **~ root** MAT raíz *f* cúbica **II.** *vt* **1.** GASTR cortar en dados **2.** MAT elevar al cubo; **2 ~d** 2 (elevado) al cubo

cubic ['kjuːbɪk] *adj* **1.** (*cube-shaped*) cúbico, -a; **~ centimetre/metre** centímetro *m* cúbico/metro *m* cúbico **2.** MAT de tercer grado; **~ equation** ecuación *f* de tercer grado

cubicle ['kjuːbɪkl] *n* **1.** (*changing room*) probador *m* **2.** (*sleeping compartment*) cubículo *m*

cuckoo ['kʊkuː, *Am:* 'kuːkuː] **I.** *n* cuco *m* **II.** *adj inf* chiflado, -a

cuckoo clock *n* reloj *m* de cuco

cucumber ['kjuːkʌmbəʳ, *Am:* -bɚ] *n* pepino *m* ▸**(as) cool as a ~** *inf* más fresco que una lechuga

cud [kʌd] *n no pl* **to chew the ~** *a. fig, inf* rumiar

cuddle ['kʌdl] **I.** *vt* abrazar **II.** *vi* abrazarse **III.** *n* abrazo *m;* **to give sb a ~** abrazar a alguien

cuddly <-ier, -iest> *adj* mimoso, -a; **~ toy** juguete *m* de peluche

cudgel ['kʌdʒəl] **I.** *n* **1.** (*short thick stick*) garrote *m* **2.** (*weapon*) porra *f* ▸**to take up (the) ~s for sb/sth** *Aus, Brit* romper una lanza por alguien/algo **II.** <-ll-, *Am:* -l-> *vt* (*with a cudgel*) dar garrotazos a; (*with a weapon*) golpear

cue [kjuː] *n* **1.** THEAT pie *m;* **to miss one's ~** no salir a escena en el momento debido **2.** MUS entrada *f* **3.** (*billiards*) taco *m;* **~ ball** bola *f* blanca ▸**to take one's ~ from sb** seguir el ejemplo de alguien; **(right) on ~** en el momento justo

cuff [kʌf] **I.** *n* **1.** (*end of sleeve*) puño *m* **2.** *Am, Aus* (*turned-up trouser leg*) vuelta *f,* valenciana *f Méx* **3.** (*slap*) cachete *m* **4.** *pl, inf* (*handcuffs*) esposas *fpl* ▸**off the ~** improvisado, -a **II.** *vt* **1.** (*slap playfully*) dar un cachete a **2.** *inf* (*handcuff*) esposar

cuff links *npl* gemelos *mpl,* mellizos *mpl AmL,* mancuernas *fpl AmC, Méx, Ven, Fili,* colleras *f Chile, Col*

cuisine [kwɪ'ziːn] *n no pl* cocina *f*

cul-de-sac ['kʌldəsæk] <-s *o* **culs-de-sac**> *n a. fig* callejón *m* sin salida

culinary ['kʌlɪneri, *Am:* -əner-] *adj* culinario, -a

cull [kʌl] **I.** *vt* **1.** ZOOL sacrificar (*de forma* *selectiva*) **2.** (*choose*) seleccionar; **to ~ sth from sth** entresacar algo de algo **II.** *n* matanza *f* (selectiva)

culminate ['kʌlmɪneɪt] *vi* culminar; **to ~ in sth** culminar en algo

culmination [ˌkʌlmɪ'neɪʃən] *n no pl* culminación *f*

culottes [kju:'lɒts, *Am:* 'ku:lɑ:ts] *npl* falda *f* pantalón, pollera *f* pantalón *AmL;* **a pair of ~** una falda pantalón

culpable ['kʌlpəbl] *adj form* culpable; **to hold sb ~ for sth** considerar a alguien culpable de algo

culprit ['kʌlprɪt] *n* culpable *mf*

cult [kʌlt] *n* **1.** (*worship*) culto *m;* **fitness ~** culto al cuerpo **2.** (*sect*) secta *f*

cult figure *n* ídolo *m*

cultivate ['kʌltɪveɪt, *Am:* -t̬ə-] *vt a. fig* cultivar

cultivated *adj* **1.** AGR cultivado, -a **2.** (*person*) culto, -a

cultivation [ˌkʌltɪ'veɪʃən, *Am:* -t̬ə-] *n no pl* **1.** AGR cultivo *m;* **to be under ~** estar en cultivo **2.** (*of a person*) cultura *f*

cultivator ['kʌltɪveɪtə^r, *Am:* -t̬əveɪt̬ɚ] *n* AGR **1.** (*tool, machine*) cultivador *m* **2.** (*person*) cultivador(a) *m(f)*

cultural ['kʌltʃərəl] *adj* cultural

culture ['kʌltʃə^r, *Am:* -tʃɚ] **I.** *n* **1.** (*way of life*) cultura *f;* **enterprise ~** cultura de empresa **2.** *no pl* (*arts*) cultura *f* **3.** AGR cultivo *m* **II.** *vt* cultivar

cultured ['kʌltʃəd, *Am:* -tʃɚd] *adj* **1.** AGR cultivado, -a **2.** (*intellectual*) culto, -a; (*taste*) refinado, -a **3.** BIO de cultivo

culture vulture *n Brit* intelectualoide *mf*

cumbersome ['kʌmbəsəm, *Am:* -bɚ-] *adj,* **cumbrous** ['kʌmbrəs] *adj* **1.** (*unwieldly*) engorroso, -a; (*heavy*) pesado, -a; (*big*) voluminoso, -a **2.** (*awkward*) torpe

cumin ['kʌmɪn] *n no pl* comino *m*

cumulative ['kju:mjʊlətɪv, *Am:* -mjələt̬ɪv] *adj* **1.** (*increasing*) acumulativo, -a **2.** (*accumulated*) acumulado, -a

cumulus ['kjumjʊləs, *Am:* -mjə-] <-li> *n* cúmulo *m*

cunning ['kʌnɪŋ] **I.** *adj* **1.** (*ingenious: person*) astuto, -a; (*device, idea, plan*) ingenioso, -a **2.** (*sly*) taimado, -a **3.** *Am* (*cute, attractive*) lindo, -a, mono, -a **II.** *n no pl* astucia *f*

cunt [kʌnt] *n* **1.** *vulg* coño *m* **2.** *vulg* (*despicable person*) cabrón, -a *m, f*

cup [kʌp] **I.** *n* **1.** (*container*) taza *f;* **coffee/tea ~** taza de café/té; **egg ~** huevera *f;* **a ~ of flour/chocolate** una taza de harina/chocolate **2.** SPORTS (*trophy*) copa *f;* **the World Cup** la copa del mundo **3.** BOT, REL cáliz *m* **4.** (*part of bra*) copa *f;* **a C ~** una copa de la talla C ▸**he isn't my ~ of tea** *inf* no es santo de mi devoción; **it's not my ~ of tea** no es plato de mi gusto; **to be in one's ~s** estar borracho **II.** <-pp-> *vt* **to ~ one's hands** ahuecar las manos; **to ~ one's hands to one's mouth** hacer bocina con las manos

cupboard ['kʌbəd, *Am:* -ɚd] *n* armario *m;* **built-in ~** armario empotrado; **kitchen ~** armario de cocina

cup final *n Brit* final *f* de la copa

cupful ['kʌpfʊl] <-s, *Am:* cupsful> *n* taza *f;* **a ~ of sugar** una taza de azúcar

cupola ['kju:pələ] *n* ARCHIT cúpula *f*

cuppa ['kʌpə] *n Brit, inf* (taza *f* de) té *m*

cup tie *n* SPORTS partido *m* de copa **cup winner** *n* SPORTS ganador(a) *m(f)* de la copa

cur [kɜ:^r, *Am:* kɜ:r] *n* **1.** (*dog*) perro *m* callejero **2.** (*person*) canalla *m*

curable ['kjʊərəbl, *Am:* 'kjʊr-] *adj* curable

curate ['kjʊərət, *Am:* 'kjʊrət] *n* coadjutor *m*

curator [kjʊə'reɪtə^r, *Am:* 'kjʊreɪt̬ɚ] *n* director(a) *m(f)* (*de museo o galería*)

curb [kɜ:b, *Am:* kɜ:rb] **I.** *vt* (*anger, passion*) dominar; (*inflation, appetite*) controlar; (*expenditure*) frenar **II.** *n* **1.** (*control*) freno *m;* **to keep a ~ on sth** refrenar algo; **to put a ~ on sth** poner freno a algo **2.** (*obstacle*) estorbo *m* **3.** *Am* (*at roadside*) bordillo *m*

curb bit *n* freno *m* de las caballerías

curbstone ['kɜ:bstəʊn, *Am:* 'kɜ:rbstoʊn] *n Am* bordillo *m*

curd [kɜ:d, *Am:* kɜ:rd] *n* cuajada *f;* **~ cheese** requesón *m*

curdle [kɜ:dl, *Am:* kɜ:r-] **I.** *vi* cuajar(se); (*sauce*) cortarse **II.** *vt* cuajar; (*sauce*) cortar

cure ['kjʊə^r, *Am:* 'kjʊr] **I.** *vt* **1.** MED, GASTR curar **2.** (*problem*) remediar **3.** (*leather*) curtir **II.** *vi* curar; (*meat, fish*) curarse **III.** *n* **1.** MED, GASTR cura *f;* **to be past ~** no tener curación; *fig* no tener remedio **2.** (*return to health*) curación *f* **3.** (*solution*) remedio *m* **4.** (*of leather*) curtido *m*

cure-all ['kjʊərɔ:l, *Am:* 'kjʊrɑ:l] *n* curalotodo *m;* **a ~ for sth** una panacea para algo

curfew ['kɜ:fju:, *Am:* 'kɜ:r-] *n* (toque *m* de) queda *f*

curiosity [ˌkjʊərɪ'ɒsəti, *Am:* ˌkjʊrɪ'ɑ:sət̬i] <-ies> *n* **1.** *no pl* (*desire to know*) curiosidad *f* **2.** (*strange thing*) curiosidad *f* ▸**~ killed the cat** *prov* no seas tan curioso

curious ['kjʊərɪəs] *adj* curioso, -a; **to be ~ to see sth/sb** tener curiosidad por ver algo/a alguien; **to be ~ about sth** tener curiosidad por algo; **it is ~ that** es curioso que *+subj*

curl [kɜ:l, *Am:* kɜ:rl] **I.** *n* **1.** (*loop of hair*) rizo *m* **2.** (*sinuosity*) serpenteo *m* **3.** (*spiral*) espiral *f;* **~ of smoke** voluta *f* de humo **4.** (*of the lips*) mueca *f* de desprecio **II.** *vi* (*hair*) rizarse; (*paper*) ondularse; (*path*) serpentear; (*smoke*) hacer volutas **III.** *vt* (*hair*) rizar; **to ~ oneself up** acurrucarse ▸**to ~ one's lip** hacer una mueca de desprecio

curler ['kɜ:lə^r, *Am:* 'kɜ:rlɚ] *n* rulo *m*

curlew ['kɜ:lju:, *Am:* 'kɜ:rlu:] *n* zarapito *m*

curling ['kɜ:lɪŋ, *Am:* 'kɜ:r-] *n no pl* **1.** (*of hair*) rizado *m* **2.** SPORTS curling *m*

curling iron *n,* **curling tongs** *npl* tenacillas *fpl* de rizar

curly ['kɜːli, *Am:* 'kɜːr-] <-ier, -iest> *adj* (*hair*) rizado, -,a; (*path*) sinuoso, -a

currant ['kʌrənt, *Am:* 'kɜːr-] *n* **1.** (*dried grape*) pasa *f* de Corinto **2.** (*berry*) grosella *f*

currency ['kʌrənsi, *Am:* 'kɜːr-] <-ies> *n* **1.** FIN moneda *f;* **foreign** ~ divisas *fpl;* ~ **conversion** reforma *f* monetaria; ~ **market** mercado *m* de divisas; ~ **unit** unidad *f* monetaria **2.** *no pl* (*acceptance*) difusión *f;* **to enjoy wide** ~ tener una amplia difusión; **to gain** ~ extenderse

current ['kʌrənt, *Am:* 'kɜːr-] **I.** *adj* **1.** (*present*) actual; (*year, month*) en curso; **in** ~ **use** en uso **2.** (*latest*) último, -a; **the** ~ **issue** (*of magazine*) el último número; **the** ~ **craze** el último grito **3.** (*prevalent: use*) generalizado, -a; (*practice*) común **4.** (*valid*) vigente **II.** *n* **1.** *a.* ELEC corriente *f* **2.** (*tendency: of fashion*) tendencias *fpl* ►**to drift with the** ~ dejarse llevar por la corriente; **to swim against the** ~ nadar contra corriente

current account *n Brit* cuenta *f* corriente

current affairs *npl,* **current events** *npl* sucesos *mpl* de actualidad **current expenses** *npl* gastos *mpl* corrientes

currently *adv* **1.** (*at present*) actualmente **2.** (*commonly*) comúnmente

current opinion *n* opinión *f* generalizada

current rate *n* tipo *m* actual

curriculum vitae [kəˌrɪkjələm'viːtaɪ] <-s *o* curricula vitae> *n* currículum *m* (vitae)

curry¹ ['kʌri, *Am:* 'kɜːr-] **I.** <-ies> *n* curry *m;* **chicken** ~ pollo *m* al curry; **vegetable** ~ curry de verduras **II.** *vt* preparar con curry

curry² ['kʌri, *Am:* 'kɜːr-] *vt* **1.** (*groom: horse*) almohazar **2.** (*leather*) curtir ►**to** ~ **favour with sb** buscar el favor de alguien

curse [kɜːs, *Am:* kɜːrs] **I.** *vi* **1.** (*swear*) soltar palabrotas **2.** (*blaspheme*) blasfemar **II.** *vt* **1.** (*swear at*) insultar **2.** (*damn*) maldecir; ~ **it!** ¡maldito sea! **III.** *n* **1.** (*oath*) palabrota *f;* **to let out a** ~ soltar un taco **2.** (*evil spell*) maldición *f;* **to put a** ~ **on sb** echar una maldición a alguien **3.** (*affliction*) **the** ~ **of racism** la lacra del racismo; **to be the** ~ **of sb's life** ser la cruz de alguien

cursed ['kɜːsɪd, *Am:* 'kɜːr-] *adj* maldito, -a

cursor ['kɜːsəʳ, *Am:* 'kɜːrsɚ] *n* INFOR cursor *m*

cursory ['kɜːsəri, *Am:* 'kɜːr-] *adj* (*glance, reading*) rápido, -a; (*check, examination*) superficial; (*remark*) somero, -a

curt [kɜːt, *Am:* kɜːrt] *adj* **1.** (*brief*) conciso, -a **2.** (*laconic*) lacónico, -a **3.** (*rudely brief*) seco, -a; (*refusal*) tajante

curtail [kɜː'teɪl, *Am:* kɚ-] *vt* **1.** (*limit, reduce: right, freedom*) restringir; (*expenses*) reducir **2.** (*shorten*) abreviar

curtailment *n* **1.** (*of spending*) reducción *f;* (*of right, freedom*) restricción *f* **2.** (*cutting short*) acortamiento *m*

curtain ['kɜːtn, *Am:* 'kɜːrtn] **I.** *n* **1.** *a. fig* cortina *f;* **lace** ~ visillo *m;* **to draw the** ~**s** correr las cortinas; **a** ~ **of rain** una cortina de lluvia **2.** THEAT telón *m;* **to raise/lower the** ~ subir/bajar el telón ►**it's** ~**s for you** estás acabado **II.** *vt* poner cortinas en; **to** ~ **off** separar con una cortina

curtain call *n* THEAT salida *f* a escena para saludar; **to take a** ~ salir al escenario a saludar

curtain raiser *n* THEAT pieza *f* preliminar

curts(e)y ['kəːtsi, *Am:* 'kɜːrt-] **I.** *vi* hacer una reverencia **II.** *n* reverencia *f;* **to make a** ~ **to sb** hacer una reverencia a alguien

curvature ['kɜːvətʃəʳ, *Am:* 'kɜːrvətʃɚ] *n no pl* curvatura *f;* MED desviación *f*

curve [kɜːv, *Am:* kɜːrv] **I.** *n* curva *f* **II.** *vi* estar curvado; (*path, road*) hacer una curva; **to** ~ **round to the left** (*path*) torcer a mano izquierda **III.** *vt* curvar

cushion ['kʊʃən] **I.** *n* **1.** cojín *m* **2.** TECH colchón *m;* **a** ~ **of air** un colchón de aire **3.** (*in billiards*) banda *f* **II.** *vt* **1.** (*furnish with cushions*) poner cojines en **2.** (*pad*) almohadillar **3.** (*ease the effects of*) amortiguar **4.** (*protect*) proteger

cushy ['kʊʃi] <-ier, -iest> *adj inf* fácil; **a** ~ **job** un chollo; **to be on to a** ~ **number** *Brit* haber encontrado una ganga

cuss [kʌs] *inf* **I.** *vi* **1.** (*swear*) decir palabrotas **2.** (*curse*) despotricar **II.** *n* **1.** (*rude word*) palabrota *f* **2.** (*person*) tipo, -a *m, f*

custard ['kʌstəd, *Am:* -tɚd] *n no pl* ≈ natillas *fpl*

custodial [kʌs'təʊdiəl, *Am:* -'toʊ-] *adj* **1.** LAW carcelario, -a **2.** (*care*) protectivo, -a

custodian [kʌ'stəʊdɪən, *Am:* kʌs'toʊ-] *n* **1.** (*keeper, conservator*) custodio, -a *m, f;* (*of morals, of a castle*) guardián, -ana *m, f* **2.** *Am* (*of a building*) portero, -a *m, f* **3.** (*of a museum*) conservador(a) *m(f)*

custody ['kʌstədi] *n no pl* **1.** (*care*) cuidado *m;* **in the** ~ **of sb** al cuidado de alguien **2.** (*guardianship*) custodia *f;* **to award** ~ **of sb to sb** conceder a alguien la custodia de alguien **3.** LAW (*detention*) detención *f;* **to take sb into** ~ detener a alguien

custom ['kʌstəm] *n* **1.** (*tradition*) costumbre *f;* **an ancient** ~ una antigua tradición; **according to** ~ según la costumbre; **it is his** ~ **to do sth** tiene por costumbre hacer algo **2.** LAW derecho *m* consuetudinario **3.** *no pl* (*clientele*) clientela *f* **4.** *pl* (*place*) aduana *f;* (*tax*) aranceles *mpl;* **to get through** ~**s** pasar por la aduana; **to pay** ~**s** (**on sth**) pagar derechos de aduana (por algo)

customary ['kʌstəməri, *Am:* -mer-] *adj* **1.** (*traditional*) tradicional; **it is** ~ **to** +*infin* es costumbre +*infin* **2.** (*usual*) habitual

custom-built ['kʌstəmˌbɪlt] *adj* (*car*) hecho, -a de encargo

custom clothes *npl Am* ropa *f* hecha a la medida

customer ['kʌstəməʳ, *Am:* -mɚ] *n* COM, ECON **1.** (*buyer, patron*) cliente, -a *m, f;* **regular** ~ cliente habitual **2.** *inf* (*person*) tío, -a *m, f*

customer number *n* número *m* de cliente

customer services *n pl* atención *f* al

cliente

customise ['kʌstəmaɪz] *vt Aus, Brit* adaptar (según las necesidades del cliente); *a.* INFOR personalizar

customised *adj Aus, Brit* personalizado, -a

customize ['kʌstəmaɪz] *vt Am s.* **customise**

customized *adj Am s.* **customised**

custom-made ['kʌstəm'meɪd, *Am:* 'kʌstəmˌmeɪd] *adj* (*clothes*) hecho, -a a medida; (*car, furniture*) hecho, -a de encargo

customs barrier ['kʌstəmz'bærɪə^{r}, *Am:* -'berɪɚ] *n* barrera *f* arancelaria

customs clearance *n* trámites *mpl* de aduana **customs declaration** *n* declaración *f* de aduana **customs dues** *npl,* **customs duties** *npl* derechos *mpl* arancelarios; **to pay ~** pagar derechos de aduana **customs examination** *n* inspección *f* aduanera **custom(s) house** *n* aduana *f* **customs officer** *n,* **customs official** *n* oficial *mf* de aduana **customs union** *n* unión *f* aduanera

cut [kʌt] **I.** *n* **1.** (*incision*) *a.* FASHION corte *m;* **to make a ~** hacer un corte; **the ~ of a shirt** el corte de una camisa **2.** (*gash, wound*) herida *f,* cortada *f AmL;* **a deep ~** un corte profundo; **to get a ~** cortarse **3.** (*action: with a knife*) cuchillada *f;* (*with a whip*) latigazo *m* **4.** (*portion*) parte *f;* (*slice*) tajada *f;* **to take one's ~ of sth** *inf* sacar tajada de algo **5.** (*part*) trozo *m;* **cold ~s** fiambres *mpl* **6.** (*decrease*) reducción *f;* **a ~ in production** una disminución de la producción; **a ~ in staff** una reducción de plantilla; **wage/budget ~** recorte *m* salarial/presupuestario **7.** (*part taken out*) *a.* CINE trozo *m* omitido, corte *m;* **to make a ~ in a film** cortar una secuencia de una película **8.** GAMES **who's ~ is it?** ¿quién corta? **9.** *inf* (*absence*) ausencia *f* ►**the ~ and thrust** la lucha; **to be a ~ above sb/sth** ser superior a alguien/algo **II.** *adj* cortado, -a; (*glass, diamond*) tallado, -a **III.** <cut, cut, -tt-> *vt* **1.** (*make an incision*) cortar; **to ~ oneself** cortarse; **to ~ sth open** abrir algo con un corte; **to ~ sth in half** partir algo por la mitad; **to ~ sth to pieces** trocear algo; **to have one's hair ~** cortarse el pelo; **to ~ the lawn** cortar el césped; **who's going to ~ the cards?** GAMES ¿quién corta? **2.** (*saw down: trees*) talar **3.** (*reap: corn*) segar **4.** (*cause moral pain*) herir **5.** (*decrease size, amount, length*) reducir; (*costs, budget*) recortar; (*prices*) rebajar; (*wages, workforce*) hacer recortes en; **to ~ sth (a bit) fine** calcular algo muy justo **6.** (*divide: benefits*) repartir **7.** (*hollow out*) **to ~ a hole** hacer un agujero **8.** shorten; (*speech*) acortar; CINE, TV editar **9.** (*shape precisely: diamond*) tallar **10.** *Am, inf* (*skip: school, class*) faltar a **11.** TECH (*turn off: motor, lights*) apagar **12.** MUS (*record, CD*) grabar **13.** (*cease*) dejar de; **~ all this noise!** ¡basta ya de hacer ruido! ►**to ~ sb dead** negar el saludo a alguien **IV.** <cut, cut, -tt-> *vi* **1.** (*slice*) cortar(se); **this knife ~s well** este cuchillo corta bien; **this cheese ~s easily** este queso se corta con facilidad **2.** GAMES cortar; **let's ~ to see who starts** vamos a cortar para ver quién sale **3.** CINE **~!** ¡corten! **4.** (*change direction suddenly*) **to ~ to the right** torcer a mano derecha **5.** (*morally wound: remark, words*) herir ►**to ~ both ways** ser un arma de doble filo; **to ~ and run** salir pitando *inf*

◆**cut across** *vt insep* **1.** (*take short cut*) tomar un atajo a través de **2.** (*transcend*) trascender

◆**cut away** *vt* cortar

◆**cut back** **I.** *vt* **1.** (*trim down*) recortar; (*bushes, branches*) podar **2.** (*reduce: production*) reducir; **to ~ (on) sth** hacer recortes en algo; **to ~ (on) costs** recortar costes **II.** *vi* CINE **to ~ to ...** volver a..., retroceder a...

◆**cut down** **I.** *vt* **1.** (*tree*) talar **2.** (*reduce: production*) reducir; **to ~ expenses** recortar gastos **3.** (*destroy, kill*) destruir; **he was ~ in his prime** murió en la flor de la vida **4.** (*remodel, shorten: garment*) acortar **II.** *vi* **to ~ on sth** reducir el consumo de algo; **to ~ on smoking** fumar menos

◆**cut in** **I.** *vi* **1.** (*interrupt*) **to ~ (on sb)** interrumpir (a alguien); **to ~ on a conversation** interrumpir una conversación; **may I ~?** (*in dance*) ¿me permite? **2.** AUTO meterse delante; **to ~ on sb** meterse delante de alguien, cerrar el paso a alguien **II.** *vt* **1.** (*divide profits with*) **to cut sb in on sth** hacer partícipe a alguien en los beneficios de algo **2.** (*include when playing*) **to cut sb in on the game** dejar entrar a alguien en el juego

◆**cut into** *vt insep* **1.** (*start cutting: cake*) empezar a cortar **2.** (*interrupt*) interrumpir **3.** AUTO meterse delante de

◆**cut off** *vt* **1.** (*sever*) *a.* ELEC, TEL cortar **2.** (*amputate*) amputar **3.** (*stop talking*) interrumpir **4.** (*separate, isolate*) aislar; **to cut oneself off (from sb)** aislarse (de alguien); **to be ~ by the snow** estar incomunicado por la nieve

◆**cut out** **I.** *vt* **1.** (*slice out of*) cortar, recortar **2.** (*suppress: sugar, fatty food*) eliminar; **to cut a scene out of a film** suprimir una escena de una película; **to cut sb out of one's will** desheredar a alguien **3.** (*exclude*) **to cut sb out (of sth)** no contar con alguien (para algo); **you can cut me out!** *Brit* ¡no cuentes conmigo! **4.** *inf* (*stop*) dejar; **to ~ smoking** dejar de fumar; **~ all this nonsense** ¡déjate de tonterías!; **cut it out!** ¡basta ya! **II.** *vi* TECH (*engine*) pararse; (*machine*) apagarse

◆**cut short** *vt* acortar

◆**cut up** **I.** *vt* **1.** (*slice into pieces*) cortar en pedazos; (*meat*) trinchar **2.** (*hurt*) herir; **to be badly ~** tener heridas graves **3.** *Brit* (*cause to suffer*) **to be ~ (about sth)** estar sufriendo (por algo) **II.** *vi Am* (*misbehave*) hacer el tonto

cut-and-dried [ˌkʌtən'draɪd] *adj* **1.** (*fixed in advance*) decidido, -a de antemano **2.** (*not original*) preparado, -a de antemano; (*idea*)

preconcebido, -a
cut-and-paste [ˌkʌtənd'peɪst] *adj a.* INFOR de cortar y pegar
cutback ['kʌtbæk] *n* **1.** (*reduction*) reducción *f;* ~ **in expenditure** recorte *m* de los gastos **2.** CINE flashback *m*
cute [kju:t] *adj* **1.** (*sweet: baby*) mono, -a *inf* **2.** (*remark, idea*) ingenioso, -a
cut(e)y ['kju:ti, *Am:* -t̬i] <-ies> *n Am, inf s.* **cutie**
cuticle ['kju:tɪkl, *Am:* -t̬ə-] *n* cutícula *f*
cutie ['kju:ti, *Am:* -t̬i] *n,* **cutiepie** ['kju:tipaɪ, *Am:* -t̬i-] *n Am, inf* (*woman*) bombón *m;* (*child*) monada *f*
cutlass ['kʌtləs] <-es> *n* MIL alfanje *m*
cutlery ['kʌtləri] *n no pl* cubiertos *fpl*
cutlet ['kʌtlɪt] *n* chuleta *f*
cut-off ['kʌtɒf, *Am:* 'kʌt̬ɑ:f] *n* **1.** TECH corte *m,* cierre *m;* ~ **date** fecha *f* límite; ~ **point** tope *m* **2.** *Am* (*short cut*) atajo *m* **cut-out** *n* **1.** (*design prepared for cutting*) recortable *m* **2.** ELEC cortacircuitos *m inv* **3.** TECH válvula *f* de escape **cut-price** *adj* a precio reducido **cut-rate** *adj* rebajado, -a **cut-sheet feed** *n* INFOR alimentación *f* por hojas sueltas
cutter ['kʌtəʳ, *Am:* 'kʌt̬ɚ] *n* **1.** (*tool which cuts*) cuchilla *f;* (*for metal*) cizalla *f;* (*for glass*) diamante *m* **2.** (*person*) cortador(a) *m(f);* (*of precious stones*) tallista *mf* **3.** NAUT cúter *m*
cut-throat ['kʌtθrəʊt, *Am:* -θroʊt] **I.** *n* **1.** (*murderer*) asesino, -a *m, f* **2.** (*razor*) navaja *f* barbera **II.** *adj* salvaje; (*competition*) feroz
cutting ['kʌtɪŋ, *Am:* 'kʌt̬-] **I.** *n* **1.** (*act*) corte *m* **2.** (*piece*) recorte *m;* (*of cloth*) retal *m* **3.** BOT esqueje *m,* gajo *m Arg* **4.** (*for road, railway*) zanja *f* **5.** CINE montaje *m* **II.** *adj* (*blade*) cortante; *fig* (*remark, comment*) hiriente
cutting-edge *adj* puntero, -a
cuttlefish ['kʌtlfɪʃ, *Am:* 'kʌt̬-] *n inv* sepia *f*
CV [ˌsi:'vi:] *n abbr of* **curriculum vitae** CV *m*
cwt. *abbr of* **hundredweight** *unidad de peso de 45.36 kg. en EE.UU. y de 50.80 kg. en el Reino Unido*
cyanide ['saɪənaɪd] *n no pl* cianuro *m*
cybercafé ['saɪbəˌkæfeɪ] *n* cibercafé *m*
cybercash ['saɪbəˌkæʃ] *no pl n* dinero *m* electrónico
cybernaut [ˌsaɪbə'nɔ:t] *n* cibernauta *mf*
cybernetics [ˌsaɪbə'netɪks, *Am:* -bɚ'net̬-] *n + sing vb* cibernética *f*
cybersex ['saɪbəseks, *Am:* -bɚ-] *n no pl* cibersexo *m* **cyberspace** *n no pl* ciberespacio *m*
cyclamen ['sɪkləmən, *Am:* 'saɪklə-] *n* ciclamen *m*
cycle¹ ['saɪkl] **I.** *n* bicicleta *f* **II.** *vi* ir en bicicleta
cycle² ['saɪkl] *n* **1.** (*of life, seasons*) ciclo *m* **2.** ASTR órbita *f*
cyclic ['saɪklɪk] *adj,* **cyclical** *adj* cíclico, -a
cycling *n no pl* SPORTS ciclismo *m;* ~ **shorts** pantalones *mpl* de ciclista
cyclist ['saɪklɪst] *n* SPORTS ciclista *mf*
cyclone ['saɪkləʊn, *Am:* -kloʊn] *n* METEO ciclón *m*
cygnet ['sɪgnɪt] *n* pollo *m* de cisne
cylinder ['sɪlɪndəʳ, *Am:* -dɚ] *n* **1.** MAT, AUTO, TECH cilindro *m* **2.** (*container: of gas*) bombona *f,* garrafa *f Arg, Urug;* (*of water*) tanque *m*
cylinder block *n* TECH bloque *m* de cilindros
cylinder capacity *n no pl* TECH cilindrada *f*
cylinder head *n* TECH culata *f*
cylindrical [sɪ'lɪndrɪkl] *adj* cilíndrico, -a
cymbal ['sɪmbl] *n* MUS platillo *m*
cynic ['sɪnɪk] **I.** *n* cínico, -a *m, f,* valemadrista *mf Méx* **II.** *adj* cínico, -a, valemadrista *Méx*
cynical ['sɪnɪkl] *adj* cínico, -a
cynicism ['sɪnɪsɪzəm] *n no pl* cinismo *m*
cypher ['saɪfəʳ, *Am:* -fɚ] *n s.* **cipher**
cypress ['saɪprəs] <-es> *n* ciprés *m*
Cypriot ['sɪprɪət] **I.** *adj* chipriota **II.** *n* chipriota *mf*
Cyprus ['saɪprəs] *n* GEO Chipre *m*
cyst [sɪst] *n* MED quiste *m*
cystitis [sɪs'taɪtɪs, *Am:* -t̬ɪs] *n no pl* MED cistitis *f inv*
czar [zɑ:ʳ, *Am:* zɑ:r] *n Am* zar *m*
czarina [zɑ:'ri:nə] *n Am* zarina *f*
Czech [tʃek] **I.** *n* **1.** (*person*) checo, -a *m, f* **2.** (*language*) checo *m* **II.** *adj* checo, -a
Czech Republic *n* República *f* Checa

D

D, d [di:] *n* **1.** (*letter*) D, d *f;* ~ **for David** *Brit,* ~ **for dog** *Am* D de Dolores **2.** MUS re *m*
d. **1.** *abbr of* **day** d. **2.** *abbr of* **diameter** d. **3.** *abbr of* **died** murió
DA [ˌdi:'eɪ] *n Am abbr of* **District Attorney** fiscal *mf* del distrito
dab [dæb] **I.** <-bb-> *vt* tocar ligeramente; **he ~bed the stain from the dress** quitó la mancha frotando suavemente el vestido **II.** <-bb-> *vi* **to ~ at sth** dar ligeros toques a algo **III.** *n* **1.** (*pat*) toque *m;* **to give sth a ~ (with sth)** dar a algo un toque (de algo) **2.** (*tiny bit*) pizca *f;* (*of liquid*) gota *f;* **a ~ of paint** un toque de pintura **IV.** *adj* **he's a ~ hand at darts** es un hacha con los dardos
dabble ['dæbl] **I.** <-ling> *vi* **1.** (*play in water*) chapotear **2.** (*work*) **to ~ in sth** interesarse superficialmente por algo **II.** <-ling> *vt* salpicar; **to ~ sth (in sth)** mojar algo (en algo)
dad ['dæd] *n inf* papá *m*
daddy ['dædi] *n childspeak, inf* papaíto *m,* tata *m AmL*
daddy-longlegs [ˌdædɪ'lɒŋlegz, *Am:* -'lɑ:ŋ-] *inv n* **1.** *Brit, inf* (*crane fly*) típula *f* **2.** *Am* (*spider-like insect*) segador *m*
daemon ['di:mən] *n* demonio *m*
daffodil ['dæfədɪl] *n* narciso *m*
daft [dɑ:ft, *Am:* dæft] *adj Brit, inf* (*idiotic*)

tonto, -a; **to be ~ about sth/sb** estar loco por algo/alguien

dagger ['dægəʳ, *Am:* -ɚ] *n* (*small knife*) puñal *m* ►**to be at ~s drawn** odiarse a muerte; **to look ~s at sb** fulminar a alguien con la mirada

dahlia ['deɪliə, *Am:* 'dæljə] *n* dalia *f*

> El **Dáil** es la cámara baja del **Oireachtas**, parlamento de la **Irish Republic**. Tiene 166 diputados, elegidos democráticamente para un mandato de cinco años. La cámara alta, el **Seanad** (senado), consta de 60 senadores, de los cuales, 11 son nombrados por el **taoiseach** (primer ministro), 6 por las universidades irlandesas y otros 43 son nombrados de forma que todos los intereses profesionales, culturales y económicos estén representados.

daily ['deɪli] **I.** *adj* (*each day*) diario, -a; **~ dozen** ejercicios *mpl* matinales; **on a ~ basis** por días; **to earn one's ~ bread** *inf* ganarse el pan **II.** *adv* a diario; **twice ~** dos veces al día **III.** <-ies> *n* **1.** PUBL diario *m* **2.** *Brit, inf* (*cleaning person*) asistente, -a *m, f*

daintiness *n no pl* **1.** (*delicacy*) delicadeza *f* **2.** (*affectation*) remilgos *mpl*

dainty ['deɪnti, *Am:* -t̬i] <-ier, -iest> *adj* **1.** (*delicate: flowers, painting*) delicado, -a; (*manners*) refinado, -a **2.** (*delicious*) exquisito, -a **3.** (*scrupulous*) escrupuloso, -a **4.** (*affected*) remilgado, -a

dairy ['deəri, *Am:* 'deri] **I.** *n* **1.** (*shop*) lechería *f* **2.** *Am* (*farm*) vaquería *f*, tambo *m Arg* **II.** *adj* **1.** (*made from milk*) lácteo, -a **2.** (*producing milk*) lechero, -a; (*farm, herd*) de vacas; **~ industry** industria láctea

dairy cattle *npl* vacas *fpl* lecheras **dairyman** *n* lechero *m* **dairy produce** *n* productos *mpl* lácteos

dais ['deɪɪs] *n* ARCHIT tarima *f*

daisy ['deɪzi] <-ies> *n* margarita *f* ►**to fell as fresh as a ~** sentirse tan fresco como una rosa; **to push up (the) daisies** *inf* criar malvas

daisy wheel *n* margarita *f*; **~ printer** impresora *f* de margarita

dally ['dæli] <-ie-> *vi* **1.** (*dawdle*) perder el tiempo; **to ~ about** entretenerse; **to ~ over sth** perder el tiempo haciendo algo **2.** (*play*) jugar; **to ~ with sb/sth** coquetear con alguien/algo; **to ~ with an idea** dar vueltas a una idea

dam [dæm] **I.** *n* **1.** (*barrier*) presa *f* **2.** (*reservoir*) embalse *m* **II.** <-mm-> *vt* **1.** (*river*) represar **2.** (*emotions, feelings*) contener

damage ['dæmɪdʒ] **I.** *vt* **1.** (*harm, hurt: building, objects*) dañar; (*environment, health, reputation*) perjudicar; **to be badly ~d** sufrir daños de consideración **2.** (*spoil*) estropear **II.** *n no pl* **1.** (*harm: to objects*) daño *m;* (*to pride, reputation*) perjuicio *m;* **to do ~ to sb/sth** hacer daño a alguien/algo; **to cause serious ~ to sb's reputation** perjudicar seriamente la reputación de alguien **2.** *pl* LAW daños *mpl* y prejuicios ►**the ~ is done** el daño ya está hecho; **what's the ~?** *iron, inf* ¿cuánto le debo?

damage limitation *n no pl* POL *táctica para minimizar el impacto negativo de una decisión*

Damascus [də'mæskəs] *n* Damasco *m*

damask ['dæməsk] **I.** *n no pl* damasco *m* **II.** *adj* de damasco

dame [deɪm] *n* **1.** *Brit* (*title of honor*) dama *f* (*título honorífico concedido a mujeres*) **2.** *Am, inf* (*woman*) tía *f*, tipa *f AmL* **3.** *Brit* THEAT *papel de anciana que representa un hombre*

damn [dæm] *inf* **I.** *interj* mierda **II.** *adj* **1.** (*blasted*) maldito, -a **2.** (*great*) **to be a ~ fool** ser tonto de remate; **to be a ~ shame** ser una verdadera lástima; **to be a ~ sight better** ser mucho mejor **III.** *vt* **1.** (*curse, be irritated with*) maldecir; **~ him! he's borrowed my bike without asking!** ¡ese idiota se ha llevado mi bicicleta sin pedirme permiso! **2.** REL condenar ►**well, I'll be ~ed!** ¡mecachis!; **I'll be ~ed if I know** que me cuelguen si lo sé **IV.** *adv* muy; **to be ~ lucky** tener una suerte increíble ►**~ all** *Brit* absolutamente nada; **I know ~ all about it** no tengo ni idea de eso **V.** *n no pl* **I don't give a ~ what he says!** ¡me importa un comino lo que diga!

damnable ['dæmnəbl] *adj inf* deplorable

damnation [dæm'neɪʃən] **I.** *n no pl* condenación *f* **II.** *interj* maldición

damned **I.** *adj inf* **1.** (*blasted*) maldito, -a **2.** (*damnable*) detestable **II.** *npl* REL **the ~** los condenados

damning *adj* **~ evidence** prueba *f* irrecusable

damp [dæmp] **I.** *adj* húmedo, -a **II.** *n no pl, Brit, Aus* humedad *f* **III.** *vt* **1.** (*wet slightly*) humedecer **2.** *a. fig* PHYS, TECH amortiguar; MUS (*sound*) apagar **3.** (*extinguish*) **to ~ (down)** (*flames, fire*) sofocar; (*enthusiasm*) enfriar; **to ~ down sb's spirits** desalentar a alguien

damp-course *n* ARCHIT membrana *f* aislante

dampen ['dæmpən] *vt* **1.** (*make wet*) humedecer **2.** (*lessen enthusiasm*) desanimar; **to ~ sb's enthusiasm** apagar el entusiasmo de alguien; **to ~ sb's expectations** frustrar las esperanzas de alguien **3.** *a. fig* PHYS, TECH amortiguar; MUS (*sound*) apagar

damper ['dæmpəʳ, *Am:* -pɚ] *n inf* sordina *f;* **to put a ~ on things** aguar la fiesta *inf;* **to put a ~ on one's enthusiasm** apagar el entusiasmo de uno

dampness *n no pl* humedad *f*

dance [dɑːnts, *Am:* dænts] **I.** <-cing> *vi* **1.** (*move around to music*) bailar; **to ~ to sth** bailar al compás de algo; **shall we ~?** ¿bailas?; **to go dancing** ir a bailar **2.** (*move energetically*) saltar; **to ~ with joy** dar saltos de alegría **3.** (*bob*) agitarse; **the daffodils were ~ing in the breeze** los narcisos se mecían con la brisa

►**to ~ to sb's tune** estar a las órdenes de alguien *fig* **II.** <-cing> *vt* bailar; **to ~ the night away** bailar toda la noche ►**to ~ attendance on sb** desvivirse por alguien **III.** *n* baile *m;* **end-of-term ~** baile de fin de curso; **to have a ~ with sb** bailar con alguien; **the band played a slow ~** la orquesta tocaba una (canción) lenta

dance band *n* orquesta *f* de baile **dance music** *n no pl* música *f* de baile

dancer ['dɑːntsəʳ, *Am:* 'dæntsɚ] *n* bailarín, -ina *m, f*

dancing *n no pl* baile *m*

dancing master *n* profesor, -a *m, f* de baile **dancing partner** *n* pareja *f* de baile **dancing shoes** *npl* zapatillas *fpl* de baile

dandelion ['dændɪlaɪən, *Am:* -də-] *n* diente *m* de león

dandruff ['dændrʌf, *Am:* -drəf] *n no pl* caspa *f*

dandy ['dændi] **I.** <-ies> *n* dandi *m* **II.** <-ier, -iest> *adj Am* estupendo, -a

Dane [deɪn] *n* danés, -esa *m, f*

danger ['deɪndʒəʳ, *Am:* -dʒɚ] *n* **1.** *no pl* (*peril*) peligro *m;* **to be in ~** correr peligro; **there's no ~ of him knowing that** no hay peligro de que lo sepa; **a ~ to sth/sb** un peligro para algo/alguien; **to be out of ~** estar fuera de peligro **2.** (*perilous aspect*) riesgo *m;* **the ~s of sth** los peligros de algo

danger area *n* zona *f* peligrosa **danger money** *n Brit, Aus* plus *m* de peligrosidad

dangerous ['deɪndʒərəs] *adj* peligroso, -a, riesgoso, -a *AmL*

dangle ['dæŋgl] **I.** <-ling> *vi* colgar; **to ~ from** [*o* **off**] **sth** colgar de algo; **to ~ after sb** ir detrás de alguien **II.** <-ling> *vt* **1.** (*cause to hang down*) hacer oscilar **2.** (*tempt with*) **to ~ sth before sb** tentar a alguien con algo

Danish ['deɪnɪʃ] **I.** *adj* danés, -esa **II.** *n* **1.** (*person*) danés, -esa *m, f* **2.** LING danés *m*

dank [dæŋk] *adj* (*air, building*) húmedo, -a

Danube ['dænjuːb] *n* GEO Danubio *m*

dapper ['dæpəʳ, *Am:* -ɚ] *adj* (*man*) atildado, -a; **a ~ appearance** un aspecto pulcro

dapple ['dæpl] *vt* motear

dare [deəʳ, *Am:* der] **I.** <-ring> *vt* **1.** (*risk doing*) **to ~ to do sth** atreverse a hacer algo; **not ~ to do sth** no atreverse a hacer algo; **I ~ not go there** no me atrevo a ir **2.** (*face*) desafiar; **to ~ sb (to do sth)** retar a alguien (a hacer algo) ►**don't you ~!** ¡ni se te ocurra!; **I ~ say** me lo imagino; **how ~ you speak to me like that?** ¿cómo se atreve a hablarme de esa forma? **II.** <-ring> *vi* atreverse; **just you ~!** ¡atrévete y verás! **III.** *n* desafío *m;* **to take a ~** aceptar un reto

dare-devil ['deəˌdevəl, *Am:* 'der-] *inf* **I.** *n* atrevido, -a *m, f* **II.** *adj* temerario, -a

daring ['deərɪŋ, *Am:* 'derɪŋ] **I.** *adj* **1.** (*courageous*) temerario, -a **2.** (*provocative: dress*) atrevido, -a **II.** *n no pl* osadía *f*

dark [dɑːk, *Am:* dɑːrk] **I.** *adj* **1.** (*without light, black*) oscuro, -a; **~ blue** azul oscuro; **~ chocolate** *Am, Aus* chocolate *m* sin leche **2.** (*not pale: complexion, hair*) moreno, -a **3.** (*tragic, depressing*) sombrío, -a; **a ~ chapter** un capítulo oscuro; **to have a ~ side** tener un lado oscuro; **to look on the ~ side of things** ver el lado malo de las cosas **4.** (*bad, mean, evil*) tenebroso, -a **5.** (*unknown, secret*) oculto, -a; **the ~ side of sth** la cara oculta de algo **II.** *n no pl* **1.** (*darkness*) oscuridad *f;* **to be in the ~** estar a oscuras; **to be afraid of the ~** tener miedo de la oscuridad **2. at ~** al caer la noche; **to do sth before/after ~** hacer algo antes/después de que anochezca ►**to keep sb in the ~ about sth** ocultar algo a alguien

Dark Ages *npl* HIST **the ~** la Alta Edad Media; *fig* la prehistoria **Dark Continent** *n* GEO, HIST **the ~** el Continente Negro

darken ['dɑːkən, *Am:* 'dɑːr-] **I.** *vi* oscurecerse; (*sky*) nublarse; *fig* ensombrecerse **II.** *vt* (*make darker*) oscurecer; *fig* ensombrecer

dark horse *n* SPORTS, POL **1.** *Brit, Aus* (*unknown candidate*) competidor(a) *m(f)* desconocido **2.** *Am* (*unexpected victor*) ganador(a) *m(f)* sorpresa

darkly *adv* **1.** (*mysteriously*) misteriosamente **2.** (*gloomily*) tristemente; **to look at sb ~** mirar a alguien con aire sombrío

darkness *n no pl* **1.** (*dark*) oscuridad *f;* **to plunge sth into ~** sumir algo en la oscuridad **2.** *fig* (*lack of knowledge*) tinieblas *fpl*

darkroom ['dɑːkrʊm, *Am:* 'dɑːrkruːm] *n* PHOT cámara *f* oscura

dark-skinned *adj* de piel oscura

darling ['dɑːlɪŋ, *Am:* 'dɑːr-] **I.** *n* **1.** (*beloved person*) amor *m* **2.** (*form of address*) cariño *mf* **II.** *adj* **1.** (*beloved*) querido, -a; **my ~ John** mi querido John **2.** (*cute*) mono, -a; **a ~ little room** una monada de habitación

darn[1] [dɑːn, *Am:* dɑːrn] **I.** *vt* zurcir **II.** *n* zurcido *m*

darn[2] [dɑːn, *Am:* dɑːrn] *vt inf* **~ it!** ¡maldita sea!; **I'll be ~ed if I'll do it!** ¡no lo hago ni que me maten!

darning *n no pl* zurcido *m*

darning needle *n* aguja *f* de zurcir

dart [dɑːt, *Am:* dɑːrt] **I.** *n* **1.** (*type of weapon*) dardo *m;* **to fire a ~ at sb/sth** disparar un dardo a alguien/algo **2.** *pl* (*pub game*) dardos *mpl;* **to play ~s** jugar a los dardos; **a game of ~s** una partida de dardos **3.** (*quick run*) movimiento *m* rápido; **to make a ~ for sb/sth** precipitarse hacia alguien/algo **4.** FASHION pinza *f* **II.** *vi* **to ~ (for sth)** precipitarse (hacia algo); **to ~ away** salir disparado; **I ~ed behind the sofa** corrí a esconderme detrás del sofá **III.** *vt* **1.** (*send quickly: look*) lanzar **2.** (*stick out quickly*) sacar; **the lizard ~ed out its tongue** la largatija disparó la lengua

dartboard ['dɑːtbɔːd, *Am:* 'dɑːrtbɔːrd] *n* diana *f*

dash [dæʃ] **I.** <-es> *n* **1.** (*rush*) carrera *f;* **to make a ~ for** precipitarse hacia; **to make a ~**

for it huir precipitadamente **2.** (*pinch*) poquito *m;* (*of salt*) pizca *f;* **a ~ of colour** una nota de color **3.** TYPO guión *m* **4.** (*flair*) brío *m* **5.** (*Morse*) raya *f* **II.** *vi* **1.** (*hurry*) precipitarse **2.** (*slam into*) **to ~ against sth** romperse contra algo **III.** *vt* **1.** (*shatter*) romper **2.** (*hopes*) defraudar

dashboard ['dæʃbɔːd, *Am:* -bɔːrd] *n* salpicadero *m*

dashing ['dæʃɪŋ] *adj* gallardo, -a

dastardly ['dæstədli, *Am:* 'dæstɚdli] *adj liter* (*crime, act*) ruin

DAT [dæt] *n abbr of* **digital audio tape** DAT *m*

data ['deɪtə, *Am:* 'deɪt̬ə] *npl + sing/pl vb a.* INFOR datos *mpl*

data bank *n* banco *m* de datos **database** *n* base *f* de datos **data file** *n* archivo *m* de datos **dataglove** *n* INFOR guante *m* de datos **data processing** *n no pl* procesamiento *m* de datos **data protection** *n no pl, Brit* protección *m* de datos

date[1] [deɪt] **I.** *n* **1.** (*calendar day*) fecha *f;* **expiry ~, expiration ~** *Am* fecha *f* de vencimiento; **what ~ is it today?** ¿cuál es la fecha de hoy?; **to be out of ~** FASHION estar pasado de moda; GASTR estar caducado **2.** (*appointment*) cita *f;* **to have a ~** tener una cita; **to make a ~ with sb** quedar con alguien **3.** FIN plazo *f* **4.** *Am, inf* (*person*) novio, -a *m, f* **II.** *vt* **1.** (*recognize age of*) fechar; **to ~ sth at ...** fechar algo en... **2.** (*give date to sth*) asignar una fecha a algo **3.** *Am, inf* (*have relationship with*) **to ~ sb** salir con alguien **III.** *vi* **1.** (*go back to*) **to ~ back to** remontarse a **2.** (*go out of fashion*) pasar de moda

date[2] [deɪt] *n* (*fruit*) dátil *m;* (*tree*) palmera *f* datilera

dated ['deɪtɪd, *Am:* -t̬ɪd] *adj* anticuado, -a

dateline ['deɪtlaɪn] *n* línea *f* de cambio de fecha

date-stamp ['deɪtstæmp] *n* fechador *m*

dative ['deɪtɪv, *Am:* -t̬ɪv] **I.** *n no pl* dativo; **to be in the ~** estar en dativo **II.** *adj* dativo, -a

daub [dɔːb, *Am:* dɑːb] **I.** *vt* **1.** (*smear*) **to ~ sth with sth** manchar algo de algo **2.** (*paint unskilfully*) pintarrajear **II.** *n* **1.** (*smear*) mancha *f* **2.** (*painting*) pintarrajo *m*

daughter ['dɔːtə^r, *Am:* 'dɑːt̬ɚ] *n* hija *f*

daughter-in-law ['dɔːtə^rɪnlɔː, *Am:* 'dɑːt̬ɚɪnlɑː] <daughters-in-law> *n* nuera *f*

daunt [dɔːnt, *Am:* dɑːnt] *vt* **1.** (*intimidate*) intimidar; **nothing ~ed** *Brit* sin inmutarse **2.** (*discourage*) desalentar

daunting *adj* amedrentador(a)

dauntless ['dɔːntləs, *Am:* 'dɑːnt-] *adj* intrépido, -a

dawdle ['dɔːdl, *Am:* 'dɑː-] *vi* holgazanear

dawdler ['dɔːdlə^r, *Am:* 'dɑːdlɚ] *n* persona *f* lenta

dawn [dɔːn, *Am:* dɑːn] **I.** *n* **1.** *no pl* alba *m,* amanezca *f Méx;* **from ~ to dusk** de sol a sol; **at ~** al alba **2.** *fig* (*beginning*) nacimiento *m* **II.** *vi* amanecer; *fig* (*era*) nacer; **it ~ed on him that ...** cayó en la cuenta de que...

day [deɪ] *n* **1.** día *m;* **~ after ~** día tras día; **~ by ~** día a día; **all ~ (long)** todo el día; **any ~ now** cualquier día de estos; **by ~** de día; **by the ~** diariamente; **for a few ~s** durante algunos días; **from that ~ on(wards)** desde ese día; **from this ~ forth** de aquí en adelante; **from one ~ to the next** de un día para otro; **one ~** algún día; **two ~s ago** hace dos días; **the ~ before yesterday** anteayer; **the ~ after tomorrow** pasado mañana; **in the (good) old ~s** en los buenos tiempos; **the examination is ten ~s from now** el examen es dentro de diez días **2.** (*working period*) jornada *f;* **to take a ~ off** tomarse un día de descanso ▶**in this ~ and age** en estos tiempos nuestros; **Day of Judgement** día *m* del Juicio Final; **to have seen better ~s** haber conocido tiempos mejores; **to call it a ~** dejarlo para otro día; **to carry the ~** salir victorioso; **~ in ~ out** un día sí y otro también

daybreak ['deɪbreɪk] *n no pl* alba *m*

daycare ['deɪkeə^r] *n* **1.** (*for children*) servicio *m* de guardería **2.** (*for old people*) atención *f* geriátrica de día

daydream ['deɪdriːm] **I.** *vi* soñar despierto **II.** *n* ensueño *m*

daylight ['deɪlaɪt] *n no pl* luz *f* del día; **in broad ~** a plena luz del día ▶**to scare the living ~s out of sb** *inf* dar un susto de muerte a alguien **day nursery** <-ies> *n* guardería *f* **day return** *n Brit* billete *m* de ida y vuelta **day shift** *n* turno *m* de día

daytime ['deɪtaɪm] *n* día *m;* **in the ~** de día

day-to-day [ˌdeɪtə'deɪ, *Am:* -t̬ə-] *adj* cotidiano, -a **day trip** *n* excursión *f* (de un día)

daze [deɪz] **I.** *n no pl* aturdimiento *m;* **to be in a ~** estar aturdido **II.** *vt* aturdir

dazed *adj* aturdido, -a

dazzle ['dæzl] **I.** *vt* deslumbrar **II.** *n no pl* deslumbramiento *m*

dazzled *adj* deslumbrado, -a

dB *n abbr of* **decibel** dB

DC [ˌdiː'siː] *n* **1.** *abbr of* **direct current** CC **2.** *abbr of* **District Commissioner** comisario, -a *m, f* de distrito **3.** *abbr of* **District of Colombia** DC *m*

DD [ˌdiː'diː] *n abbr of* **Doctor of Divinity** Dr. en Teología

D-Day ['diːdeɪ] *n* el día D

DDT [ˌdiːdiː'tiː] *n no pl abbr of* **dichloro-diphenyl-trichloroethane** DDT *m*

deacon ['diːkən] *n* diácono *m*

deaconess [ˌdiːkə'nes, *Am:* 'diːkənəs] *n* diaconisa *f*

dead [ded] **I.** *adj* **1.** (*no longer alive*) muerto, -a; **to be ~ on arrival** ingresar cadáver (en el hospital) **2.** (*inactive*) parado, -a; (*fire*) apagado, -a **3.** (*quiet, boring*) muerto, -a; (*town*) desierto, -a **4.** (*numb*) dormido, -a **5.** (*silence*) profundo, -a; **to be a ~ loss** ser un desastre total; **to come to a ~ stop** pararse en seco ▶**as**

D

~ **as a doornail** muerto y bien muerto; **to be a ~ duck** ser un fracaso seguro; ~ **men tell no tales** *Am, prov* los muertos no hablan; **she wouldn't be seen ~ wearing that** *inf* por nada del mundo se pondría eso **II.** *n* **the ~** los muertos ►**in the ~ of night/winter** en plena noche/pleno invierno **III.** *adv* **1.** *inf* (*totally*) completamente; ~ **beat** completamente rendido; **to be ~ set against sth** estar completamente en contra de algo; **to be ~ set on sth** estar completamente decidido a algo **2.** (*directly*) justo; ~ **ahead** justo al frente

deadbeat [ˌded'biːt] *adj Am, inf* rendido, -a

dead centre *n* punto *m* muerto

deaden ['dedən] *vt* (*pain*) aliviar; (*noise*) amortiguar

dead-end [ˌded'end] **I.** *n* callejón *m* sin salida **II.** *adj* sin salida; ~ **job** trabajo *m* sin porvenir

dead heat *n* empate *m*

deadline ['dedlaɪn] *n* plazo *m* límite; **to meet/to miss the ~** cumplir/incumplir el plazo

deadlock ['dedlɒk, *Am:* -lɑːk] *n no pl* punto *m* muerto *inv;* **to reach ~** llegar a un punto muerto

deadly ['dedli] **I.** <-ier, -iest> *adj* **1.** (*capable of killing*) mortal **2.** *inf* (*very boring*) aburridísimo, -a **II.** <-ier, -iest> *adv* extremadamente; ~ **pale** blanco como la cera

deadpan ['dedpæn] *adj* inexpresivo, -a

Dead Sea *n* Mar *m* Muerto

deadwood ['dedwʊd] *n no pl* **1.** (*branch, tree*) madera *f* seca **2.** *inf* (*person*) persona *f* inútil; (*people*) gente *f* inútil; (*thing*) cosa *f* inútil

deaf [def] **I.** *adj* sordo, -a; ~ **in one ear** sordo de un oído; **to go ~** volverse sordo; **to be ~ to sth** hacer oídos sordos a algo **II.** *npl* **the ~** los sordos

deaf aid *n* audífono *m*

deafen ['defən] *vt* ensordecer

deafening *adj* ensordecedor(a)

deaf-mute [ˌdef'mjuːt] *n* sordomudo, -a *m, f*

deafness *n no pl* sordera *f*

deal¹ [diːl] *n no pl* (*large amount*) cantidad *f;* **a great ~** una gran cantidad; **a great ~ of effort** mucho esfuerzo

deal² [diːl] <dealt, dealt> **I.** *n* **1.** COM negocio *m;* **a big ~** un negocio importante **2.** (*agreement*) pacto *m;* **to do a ~ (with sb)** hacer un trato (con alguien) **3.** GAMES (*of cards*) reparto *m;* **it's your ~** te toca dar a ti ►**big ~!** *iron, inf* ¡gran cosa!; **it's no big ~!** *inf* ¡no es para tanto! **II.** *vi* **1.** (*do business*) negociar; **to ~ with sb** hacer negocios con alguien; **to ~ in sth** comerciar con algo **2.** GAMES repartir **III.** *vt* **1.** GAMES (*cards*) repartir **2.** (*give*) dar; **to ~ sb a blow** propinar un golpe a alguien

◆**deal out** *vt* repartir

◆**deal with** *vt* **1.** (*take care of: problem*) ocuparse de; (*person*) tratar con **2.** (*be about: book*) tratar de **3.** (*punish*) castigar

dealer ['diːlə^r, *Am:* -lɚ] *n* **1.** COM negociante *mf;* **drug ~** traficante *mf* de drogas; **he's a ~ in antiquities** es un marchante de antiguedades **2.** GAMES (*in cards*) mano *mf*

dealership ['diːləʃɪp, *Am:* -lɚ-] *n* COM concesión *f*

dealing ['diːlɪŋ] *n* **1.** COM comercio *m* **2.** *pl* FIN transacciones *fpl* **3.** *pl* (*relations*) relaciones *fpl;* **to have ~s with sb** tratar con alguien **4.** GAMES reparto *m*

dealt [delt] *pt, pp of* **deal**

dean [diːn] *n* **1.** UNIV decano, -a *m, f* **2.** REL deán *m*

dear [dɪə^r, *Am:* dɪr] **I.** *adj* **1.** (*much loved*) querido, -a; **it is ~ to me** le tengo mucho cariño **2.** (*in letters*) estimado, -a; **Dear Sarah** Querida Sarah; **Dear Sir** Muy señor mío **3.** (*expensive*) caro, -a **II.** *adv* caro **III.** *interj inf* **oh ~!** ¡Dios mío! **IV.** *n* encanto *m;* **she is a ~** es encantadora

dearly *adv* **1.** mucho; **I love her ~** la quiero mucho **2.** *fig* caro; **he paid ~ for his success** su éxito le costó caro

dearness *n no pl* alto precio *m*

dearth [dɜːθ, *Am:* dɜːrθ] *n no pl* escasez *f;* **to suffer from a ~ of sth** sufrir la escasez de algo

deary *n,* **dearie** ['dɪəri, *Am:* 'dɪri] *n inf* querido, -a *m, f*

death [deθ] *n* muerte *f;* **frightened to ~** muerto de miedo; **to die a natural ~** morir de muerte natural; **to put sb to ~** matar a alguien; **to catch one's ~ of cold** coger una gripe de muerte ►**to be at ~'s door** estar a las puertas de la muerte; **to be bored to ~ with sth** morirse de aburrimiento con algo; **to dice with ~** jugar con la muerte; **to laugh oneself to ~** morirse de la risa

deathbed ['deθbed] *n* lecho *m* de muerte

death-blow *n* golpe *m* mortal **death-certificate** *n* certificado *m* de defunción **death duties** *npl Brit, inf* impuesto *m* de sucesiones

deathly ['deθli] **I.** *adv* de muerte; ~ **pale** pálido como un muerto **II.** *adj* mortífero, -a

death penalty *n* pena *f* de muerte **death-rate** *n* tasa *f* de mortalidad **death row** *n Am* corredor *m* de la muerte **death sentence** *n* pena *f* de muerte **death squad** *n* escuadrón *m* de la muerte **death trap** *n* trampa *f* mortal

debacle [deɪ'bɑːkl, *Am:* dɪ-] *n* debacle *f*

debar [dɪ'bɑː^r, *Am:* -'bɑːr] <-rr-> *vt* excluir; **to ~ sb from doing sth** privar a alguien de hacer algo

debase [dɪ'beɪs] *vt* (*reduce in quality or value*) degradar; ECON devaluar

debatable [dɪ'beɪtəbl, *Am:* dɪ'beɪţə-] *adj* discutible

debate [dɪ'beɪt] **I.** *n no pl* debate *m;* **a ~ over sth** un debate sobre algo **II.** *vt* debatir **III.** *vi* debatir; **to ~ about sth** debatir acerca de algo

debater [dɪ'beɪtə^r, *Am:* -ţɚ] *n* polemista *mf*

debauch [dɪ'bɔːtʃ, *Am:* -'bɑːtʃ] **I.** *vt* corromper **II.** *n* orgía *f*

debauchery [dɪˈbɔːtʃəri, *Am:* ˈbɑː-] *n no pl* vicio *m*
debenture [dɪˈbentʃəʳ, *Am:* -ˈbentʃɚ] *n Brit* FIN obligación *f*
debilitate [dɪˈbɪlɪteɪt] *vt* debilitar
debilitating *adj* debilitante
debility [dɪˈbɪləti, *Am:* dɪˈbɪləṱi] *n no pl* debilidad *f*
debit [ˈdebɪt] **I.** *n* débito *m;* **to be in** ~ estar en números rojos **II.** *vt* **the bank ~ed the rent to my account** el banco cargó la renta a mi cuenta bancaria
debit card *n* tarjeta *f* de débito **debit column** *n,* **debit-side** *n* debe *m*
debonair [ˌdebəˈneəʳ, *Am:* -ˈner] *adj form* refinado, -a
debris [ˈdeɪbriː, *Am:* dəˈbriː] *n no pl* escombros *mpl*
debt [det] *n* deuda *f;* **to be in** ~ tener deudas; **to pay off a** ~ pagar una deuda; **to be out of** ~ estar libre de deudas
debt-collector *n* cobrador(a) *m(f)* de deudas
debtor [ˈdetəʳ, *Am:* ˈdeṱɚ] *n* deudor(a) *m(f)*
debtor country *n,* **debtor nation** *n* país *m* deudor
debt servicing *n no pl* pago *m* de una deuda
debug [ˌdiːˈbʌg] <-gg-> *vt* INFOR depurar
debunk [diːˈbʌŋk] *vt* desacreditar
debut [ˈdeɪbjuː, *Am:* -ˈ-] **I.** *n* **1.** (*first public appearance*) debut *m;* **to make one's** ~ debutar **2.** (*introduction into society*) presentación en sociedad **II.** *vi* debutar; **to** ~ **in/as sth** debutar en/como algo
debutante [ˈdebjuːtɑːnt] *n* (*young woman who is introduced into society*) debutante *f;* **a ~'s ball** un baile de debutantes
decade [ˈdekeɪd] *n* década *f*
decadence [ˈdekədəns] *n no pl* decadencia *f*
decadent [ˈdekədənt] *adj* decadente
decaf [ˈdiːkæf] *adj, n inf abbr of* **decaffeinated** descafeinado
decaffeinated [ˌdiːˈkæfɪneɪtɪd] **I.** *adj* descafeinado, -a **II.** *n inf* descafeinado *m*
decamp [dɪˈkæmp] *vi inf* (*leave secretly*) fugarse, rajarse *AmL;* (*run away*) huir; (*set off*) irse
decant [dɪˈkænt] *vt* decantar
decanter [dɪˈkæntəʳ, *Am:* -ṱɚ] *n* licorera *f*
decapitate [dɪˈkæpɪteɪt] *vt* decapitar
decapitation [dɪˌkæpɪˈteɪʃən] *n no pl* decapitación *f*
decathlete [dɪˈkæθliːt] *n* decatleta *mf*
decathlon [dɪˈkæθlən, *Am:* -lɑːn] *n* decatlón *m*
decay [dɪˈkeɪ] **I.** *n no pl* (*of food*) descomposición *f;* (*of building, intellect*) deterioro *m;* (*dental*) caries *f inv;* (*of civilization*) decadencia *f;* **to be in an advanced state of** ~ estar en avanzado estado de descomposición **II.** *vi* (*food*) pudrirse; (*building, intellect*) deteriorarse; (*teeth*) cariarse **III.** *vt* descomponer
decease [dɪˈsiːs] *n no pl* fallecimiento *m*
deceased [dɪˈsiːst] **I.** *n* difunto, -a *m, f* **II.** *adj* difunto, -a
deceit [dɪˈsiːt] *n* engaño *m,* transa *f Méx*
deceitful [dɪˈsiːtfəl] *adj* engañoso, -a
deceive [dɪˈsiːv] *vt* engañar; **to** ~ **oneself** engañarse a sí mismo ►**appearances** ~ *prov* las apariencias engañan *prov*
deceiver [dɪˈsiːvəʳ, *Am:* -ɚ] *n* impostor(a) *m(f)*
decelerate [diːˈseləreɪt] **I.** *vi* desacelerarse; (*vehicle, driver*) aminorar la velocidad **II.** *vt* desacelerar
December [dɪˈsembəʳ, *Am:* -bɚ] *n* diciembre *m; s. a.* **April**
decency [ˈdiːsəntsi] *n* **1.** *no pl* (*respectability*) decencia *f* **2.** *pl* (*approved behaviour*) buenas costumbres *fpl*
decent [ˈdiːsənt] *adj* **1.** (*socially acceptable*) decente; **are you ~?** *iron* ¿estás visible? **2.** *inf* (*kind*) amable
decentralization [diːˌsentrəlaɪˈzeɪʃən, *Am:* -ɪˈ-] *n no pl* descentralización *f*
decentralize [diːˈsentrəlaɪz] *vt* descentralizar
decentralized *adj* descentralizado, -a
deception [dɪˈsepʃən] *n* engaño *m;* **to practise** ~ **on sb** engañar a alguien
deceptive [dɪˈseptɪv] *adj* engañoso, -a
decibel [ˈdesɪbel] *n* decibel(io) *m*
decide [dɪˈsaɪd] **I.** *vi* decidirse; **to** ~ **on sth** decidirse [*o* optar] por algo **II.** *vt* decidir
decided [dɪˈsaɪdɪd] *adj* (*person, manner*) decidido, -a; (*improvement*) indudable
deciduous [dɪˈsɪdjʊəs, *Am:* -ˈsɪdʒʊ-] *adj* caducifolio, -a
decimal [ˈdesɪml] **I.** *n* decimal *m* **II.** *adj* decimal
decimalize [ˈdesɪməlaɪz] *vt* aplicar el sistema decimal a
decimate [ˈdesɪmeɪt] *vt* diezmar
decipher [dɪˈsaɪfəʳ, *Am:* -fɚ] *vt* descifrar
decision [dɪˈsɪʒən] *n* **1.** (*choice, resolution*) decisión *f;* **to make a** ~ tomar una decisión **2.** LAW fallo *m* **3.** *no pl* (*resoluteness*) resolución *f*
decision-making [dɪˈsɪʒənˌmeɪkɪŋ] *n no pl* ~ **process** proceso *m* decisorio
decisive [dɪˈsaɪsɪv] *adj* (*factor*) decisivo, -a; (*manner*) categórico, -a
deck [dek] **I.** *n* **1.** (*of ship*) cubierta *f;* **to go below ~s** ir bajo cubierta **2.** (*of bus*) piso *m* **3.** *Am* (*cards*) baraja *f* **4.** MUS, ELEC platina *f* ►**to clear the ~s** prepararse para algo; **to hit the** ~ *inf* caerse al suelo **II.** *vt* ~ **out** adornar; **to be ~ed (out) in one's best** ir de tiros largos
deckchair [ˈdektʃeəʳ, *Am:* -tʃer] *n* tumbona *f,* reposera *f Arg*
declaim [dɪˈkleɪm] *vi, vt* declamar
declamation [ˌdekləˈmeɪʃən] *n no pl* declamación *f*
declamatory [dɪˈklæmətəri, *Am:* dɪˈklæmətɔːri] *adj form* declamatorio, -a
declaration [ˌdekləˈreɪʃən] *n* declaración *f*

declare [dɪˈkleəʳ, *Am:* dɪˈkler] I. *vt* declarar; **to ~ war on sb** declarar la guerra a alguien; **to ~ goods** declarar mercancías; **to ~ oneself** (**to be**) **bankrupt** declararse en bancarrota II. *vi* declararse

decline [dɪˈklaɪn] I. *vi* 1. (*price*) bajar; (*power, influence*) disminuir; (*civilization*) decaer; **to ~ in value** disminuir de valor 2. MED debilitarse 3. (*refuse*) rehusar II. *n no pl* 1. (*of price, power, influence*) disminución *f*; (*of civilization*) decadencia *f*; **to be in ~** estar en declive 2. MED debilitación *f* III. *vt* 1. (*refuse*) rehusar 2. LING declinar

declutch [ˌdiːˈklʌtʃ] *vi* desembragar

decode [ˌdiːˈkəʊd, *Am:* -ˈkoʊd] *vi, vt* descodificar

decoder *n* descodificador *m*

decolonization [ˌdiːˌkɒlɪnaɪˈzeɪʃən, *Am:* -ˌkɑːlənɪˈ-] *n no pl* descolonización *f*

decompose [ˌdiːkəmˈpəʊz, *Am:* -ˈpoʊz] I. *vi* descomponerse II. *vt* descomponer

decomposition [ˌdiːkɒmpəˈzɪʃən, *Am:* ˌdiːkɑːm-] *n no pl* descomposición *f*

decompress [ˌdiːkəmˈpres] *vt* descomprimir

decompression [ˌdiːkəmˈpreʃən] *n no pl* descompresión *f*

decompression chamber *n* cámara *f* de descompresión

decontaminate [ˌdiːkənˈtæmɪneɪt] *vt* descontaminar

decontamination [ˌdiːkənˌtæmɪˈneɪʃən] *n no pl* descontaminación *f*

decontrol [ˌdiːkənˈtrəʊl, *Am:* -ˈtroʊl] <-ll-> *vt* liberalizar

decor [ˈdeɪkɔːʳ, *Am:* ˈdeɪkɔːr] *n* decorado *m*

decorate [ˈdekəreɪt] I. *vt* 1. (*adorn*) decorar 2. (*add new paint*) pintar; (*wallpaper*) empapelar 3. (*honour*) condecorar II. *vi* 1. (*add new paint*) pintar 2. (*wallpaper*) empapelar

decoration [ˌdekəˈreɪʃən] *n* 1. (*ornament*) adorno *m* 2. (*act of decorating*) decoración *f* 3. (*medal*) condecoración *f*

decorative [ˈdekərətɪv, *Am:* -t̬ɪv] *adj* decorativo, -a; **just sit there and look ~** *iron* siéntate y estate calladito

decorator [ˈdekəreɪtəʳ, *Am:* -t̬ɚ] *n Brit* 1. (*one who plans interior design*) decorador(a) *m(f)* 2. (*painter*) pintor(a) *m(f)* 3. (*paperhanger*) empapelador(a) *m(f)*

decorous [ˈdekərəs, *Am:* -ɚəs] *adj form* decoroso, -a

decorum [dɪˈkɔːrəm] *n no pl, form* decoro *m*

decoy [ˈdiːkɔɪ] I. *n a. fig* señuelo *m*; **to act as a ~** hacer de señuelo II. *vt* atraer con un señuelo

decrease [dɪˈkriːs, *Am:* ˈdiːkriːs] I. *vi* disminuir; (*prices*) bajar II. *vt* disminuir III. *n* disminución *f*

decree [dɪˈkriː] I. *n* 1. (*command*) decreto *m*; **to issue a ~** promulgar un decreto 2. LAW sentencia *f* II. *vt* decretar

decree nisi [dɪˈkriː ˈnaɪsaɪ] *n* sentencia *f* provisional de divorcio

decrepit [dɪˈkrepɪt] *adj* (*in bad condition*) deteriorado, -a; (*house*) destartalado, -a; (*person*) decrépito, -a

decrepitude [dɪˈkrepɪtjuːd, *Am:* -tuːd] *n no pl* deterioro *m*; (*of person*) decrepitud *f*

decriminalize [ˌdiːˈkrɪmɪnəlaɪz] *vt* despenalizar

decry [dɪˈkraɪ] *vt form* censurar

dedicate [ˈdedɪkeɪt] *vt* 1. (*devote*) **to ~ oneself to sth** dedicarse a algo 2. (*do in sb's honour*) **to ~ sth to sb** dedicar algo a alguien 3. *form* (*formally open*) inaugurar; (*a church*) dedicar

dedicated *adj* dedicado, -a

dedication [ˌdedɪˈkeɪʃən] *n* 1. (*devotion*) dedicación *f* 2. (*inscription*) dedicatoria *f* 3. (*official opening*) inauguración *f*; (*of a church*) dedicación *f*

deduce [dɪˈdjuːs, *Am:* dɪˈduːs] *vt* (*infer*) deducir

deducible [dɪˈdjuːsəbl, *Am:* dɪˈduː-] *adj* deducible

deduct [dɪˈdʌkt] *vt* deducir

deductable *adj Aus*, **deductible** *adj* deducible

deduction [dɪˈdʌkʃən] *n* deducción *f*; **£1000 after ~s** 1000 libras netas

deductive [dɪˈdʌktɪv] *adj* deductivo, -a

deed [diːd] *n* 1. (*act*) acto *m*; (*remarkable feat*) hazaña *f*; **in word and ~** de palabra y obra 2. LAW escritura *f*

deed poll *n* **to do sth by ~** hacer algo por escritura unilateral

deem [diːm] *vt form* considerar; **he was ~ed to be of sound mind** se juzgó que estaba en plenas facultades mentales

deep [diːp] I. *adj* 1. (*not shallow*) profundo, -a 2. (*full*) **to take a ~ breath** respirar hondo 3. (*extending back*) **the wardrobe is 60 cm ~** el armario tiene 60 cm de fondo 4. (*extreme: regret, disappointment*) gran(de); **in ~ mourning** de luto riguroso; **to be in ~ trouble** estar metido en un buen lío *inf* 5. (*absorbed by*) **to be in ~ thought** estar absorto en sus pensamientos 6. *inf* (*hard to understand*) difícil de entender 7. (*low in pitch*) grave 8. (*dark*) oscuro, -a; **~ red** rojo intenso II. *adv* 1. (*far down*) **to dig ~** *fig* cavar hondo; **~ in the forest** en lo más profundo del bosque 2. (*extremely*) mucho; **to be ~ in debt** estar cargado de deudas ►**to go ~ into sth** ahondar en algo III. *n liter* **the ~** el piélago; **in the ~ of winter** en lo más crudo del invierno

deepen [ˈdiːpən] I. *vt* 1. (*make deeper*) hacer más profundo 2. (*increase*) aumentar; (*knowledge*) ampliar II. *vi* 1. (*become deeper*) hacerse más profundo 2. (*increase*) aumentar 3. (*become lower in pitch*) volverse grave 4. (*color*) intensificarse

deep-freeze *n* congelador *m* **deep-frozen** *adj* ultracongelado, -a **deep-fry** *vt* freír en aceite abundante

deeply *adv* profundamente; (*breathe*) hondo; **to be ~ interested in sth** sentir un profundo interés por algo

deepness *n* profundidad *f*

deep-rooted [ˌdiːpˈruːtɪd, *Am:* -t̬ɪd] *adj* **1.** (*well-established*) profundamente arraigado, -a **2.** BOT de raíces profundas **deep-sea animal** *n* animal *m* de las profundidades marinas **deep-seated** *adj* profundamente arraigado, -a; (*hatred*) de raíces profundas **deep space** *n* AVIAT espacio *m* interplanetario

deer [dɪəʳ, *Am:* dɪr] *n inv* ciervo *m*

deerstalker [ˈdɪəˌstɔːkəʳ, *Am:* ˈdɪrˌstɔːkɚ] *n* gorra *f* de cazador

deface [dɪˈfeɪs] *vt* (*damage the appearance of*) afear; (*a wall*) pintarrajear; (*a stamp*) matar

defamation [ˌdefəˈmeɪʃən] *n no pl* difamación *f*

defamatory [dɪˈfæmətəri, *Am:* -tɔːri] *adj* difamatorio, -a

defame [dɪˈfeɪm] *vt* difamar

default [dɪˈfɔːlt, *Am:* dɪˈfɑːlt] **I.** *vi* **1.** FIN no pagar; **to ~ on a payment** estar en mora en un pago **2.** LAW estar en rebeldía **3.** SPORTS no presentarse **II.** *n* **1.** omisión *f;* FIN mora *f* **2.** LAW **judgement by ~** sentencia *f* en rebeldía; **to win a case by ~** ganar un caso en rebeldía del adversario **3.** *no pl* (*pre-selected option*) **by ~** por defecto **4.** *form* (*absence*) **in ~ of any better alternative ...** a falta de una alternativa mejor...

default value *n* INFOR valor *m* por defecto

defeat [dɪˈfiːt] **I.** *vt* derrotar; (*hopes*) frustrar; (*a proposal*) rechazar **II.** *n* **1.** (*by an opponent*) derrota *f;* **to admit ~** darse por vencido **2.** (*of plans*) fracaso *m*

defeatism [dɪˈfiːtɪzəm, *Am:* dɪˈfiːt̬ɪ-] *n* derrotismo *m*

defeatist *adj* derrotista

defecate [ˈdefəkeɪt] *vi* MED defecar

defecation [ˌdefəˈkeɪʃən] *n no pl* MED defecación *f*

defect¹ [ˈdiːfekt] *n a.* TECH, MED defecto *m*

defect² [dɪˈfekt] *vi* POL (*from a country*) huir; (*from the army*) desertar

defection [dɪˈfekʃən] *n* defección *f;* MIL deserción *f*

defective [dɪˈfektɪv] *adj* defectuoso, -a; **mentally ~** deficiente *mf* mental

defence [dɪˈfents] *n Aus, Brit* **1.** defensa *f;* **to rush to sb's ~** acudir en defensa de alguien **2.** LAW **the ~** la defensa; **counsel for the ~** abogado(a) *m(f)* defensor(a) **3.** SPORTS **to play in** [*o* **on** *Am*] **~** jugar en la defensa **4.** MED **the body's ~s** las defensas del organismo **5.** PSYCH **~ mechanism** mecanismo *m* de defensa

defenceless [dɪˈfentsləs] *adj* indefenso, -a

defence minister *n* ministro, -a *m, f* de defensa

defend [dɪˈfend] **I.** *vt* **1.** (*protect*) defender; **to ~ oneself (from sb/sth)** defenderse (de alguien/algo) **2.** *a.* LAW defender **3.** SPORTS (*a title*) defender **II.** *vi* **1.** LAW **who is ~ing in that case?** ¿quién actúa por la defensa en esa causa? **2.** SPORTS **the team we were playing against ~ed badly** el equipo contrario no era bueno en la defensa

defendant [dɪˈfendənt] *n* LAW (*in a civil case*) demandado, -a *m, f;* (*in a criminal case*) acusado, -a *m, f*

defense [dɪˈfents] *n Am s.* **defence**

defensible [dɪˈfentsəbl] *adj* **1.** (*capable of being defended*) defendible **2.** (*justifiable*) justificable

defensive [dɪˈfentsɪv] **I.** *adj* (*intended for defence*) defensivo, -a; **she's rather ~ about her family background** se pone a la defensiva cuando se le habla de su situación familiar **II.** *n* **to be/go on the ~** estar/ponerse a la defensiva

defer [dɪˈfɜːʳ, *Am:* dɪˈfɜːr] <-rr-> *vt* aplazar

deference [ˈdefərənts] *n no pl* deferencia *f*

deferential [ˌdefəˈrentʃəl] *adj* respetuoso, -a

deferred payment *n* pago *m* aplazado

defiance [dɪˈfaɪənts] *n no pl* desafío *m;* **in ~ of sth** a despecho de algo

defiant [dɪˈfaɪənt] *adj* **1.** (*person*) rebelde **2.** (*attitude*) desafiante; **to be in a ~ mood** mostrar una actitud desafiante

deficiency [dɪˈfɪʃəntsi] *n* **1.** (*shortage*) escasez *f* **2.** COM déficit *m* **3.** MED deficiencia *f*

deficient [dɪˈfɪʃənt] *adj* deficiente; **to be ~ in sth** carecer de algo

deficit [ˈdefɪsɪt] *n* déficit *m*

defile [dɪˈfaɪl] **I.** *vt form* **1.** (*spoil*) corromper; (*reputation*) mancillar **2.** (*desecrate*) profanar **II.** *n* desfiladero *m*

define [dɪˈfaɪn] *vt* **1.** (*give definition of*) definir **2.** (*explain*) determinar; (*rights*) formular **3.** (*characterize*) caracterizar **4.** (*clearly show*) **the outline of the castle was clearly ~d against the sky** el contorno del castillo se recortaba claramente contra el cielo

definite [ˈdefɪnət] *adj* **1.** (*final*) definitivo, -a **2.** (*certain*) seguro, -a; (*date*) confirmado, -a; (*opinion*) claro, -a; **to be ~ about sth** ser categórico respecto a algo; **it's ~ that ...** no hay duda de que...

definite article *n* artículo *m* determinado

definitely *adv* definitivamente; **to ~ decide sth** decidir algo de forma definitiva

definition [ˌdefɪˈnɪʃən] *n* definición *f;* **to give ~ to sth** realzar algo; **her ideas lack ~** sus ideas no son muy claras

definitive [dɪˈfɪnətɪv, *Am:* -t̬ɪv] *adj* **1.** (*final*) definitivo, -a, rajante *Arg* **2.** (*best*) de mayor autoridad

deflate [dɪˈfleɪt] **I.** *vt* **1.** (*reduce*) reducir; (*hopes*) frustrar **2.** (*cause to lose confidence*) deprimir **3.** (*let air out of*) desinflar **4.** ECON, FIN provocar la deflación de **II.** *vi* desinflarse

deflation [dɪˈfleɪʃən] *n no pl* **1.** ECON, FIN deflación *f* **2.** (*act of deflating*) desinflamiento *m* **3.** (*reduction*) caída *f*

D

deflationary *adj* deflacionario, -a
deflect [dɪ'flekt] I. *vt* desviar II. *vi* (*change direction of*) **to ~ off sth** desviarse de algo
deflection [dɪ'flekʃən] *n* desviación *f*
defoliant [ˌdiː'fəʊliənt, *Am:* -'foʊ-] *n* defoliante *m*
defoliate [ˌdiː'fəʊlieɪt, *Am:* -'foʊ-] *vt* defoliar
deforest [ˌdiː'fɒrɪst, *Am:* -'fɔːr-] *vt* deforestar
deforestation [diːˌfɒrɪ'steɪʃən, *Am:* diːˌfɔːr-] *n no pl* deforestación *f*
deform [dɪ'fɔːm, *Am:* dɪ'fɔːrm] I. *vt* deformar; (*person*) desfigurar II. *vi* deformarse; (*person*) desfigurarse
deformation [ˌdiːfɔː'meɪʃən, *Am:* ˌdiːfɔːr-] *n no pl* deformación *f;* (*of a person*) desfiguración *f*
deformed *adj* deformado, -a
deformity [dɪ'fɔːməti, *Am:* dɪ'fɔːrməṭi] *n* deformidad *f*
defraud [dɪ'frɔːd, *Am:* dɪ'frɑːd] *vt* estafar; **to ~ one's creditors** defraudar a sus acreedores; **to ~ sb** (**of sth**) estafar (algo) a alguien
defray [dɪ'freɪ] *vt form* costear
defrost [ˌdiː'frɒst, *Am:* -'frɑːst] I. *vt* deshelar; (*a fridge*) descongelar; (*the windscreen*) desempañar II. *vi* deshelarse; (*fridge, food*) descongelarse
deft [deft] *adj* hábil; **to be ~ at sth** ser diestro en algo
defunct [dɪ'fʌŋkt] *adj* (*dead*) difunto, -a; (*idea*) caduco, -a; (*institution*) extinto, -a
defy [dɪ'faɪ] *vt* 1. (*challenge*) desafiar 2. (*resist*) resistirse a; **it defies description** es indescriptible 3. (*disobey*) desobedecer
deg. *abbr of* **degree** grado *m*
degenerate¹ [dɪ'dʒenəreɪt] *vi* (*lose quality*) degenerar; (*health*) deteriorarse; **to ~ into sth** degenerar en algo
degenerate² [dɪ'dʒenərət] I. *adj* degenerado, -a II. *n* degenerado, -a *m, f*
degeneration [dɪˌdʒenə'reɪʃən] *n no pl* degeneración *f*
degrade [dɪ'greɪd] I. *vt* 1. *a.* CHEM degradar; **to ~ oneself** rebajarse 2. (*destroy: the environment*) destruir II. *vi* ELEC distorsionarse
degree [dɪ'griː] *n* 1. MAT, METEO grado *m;* **5 ~s below zero** 5 grados bajo cero; **first/second ~ murder** LAW homicidio en primer/segundo grado; **first/second ~ burns** MED quemaduras de primer/segundo grado 2. (*amount*) nivel *m* 3. (*extent*) **I agree with you to some ~** estoy de acuerdo contigo hasta cierto punto; **by ~s** gradualmente; **to the last ~** en grado sumo 4. UNIV título *m;* **to have a ~ in sth** ser licenciado en algo; **she's got a physics ~ from Oxford** es licenciada en física por la universidad de Oxford; **to have a master's ~ in sth** tener un máster en algo; **to do a ~ in chemistry** estudiar la carrera de química
degree course *n* carrera *f* (universitaria)
dehumanise *vt Brit, Aus,* **dehumanize** [ˌdiː'hjuːmənaɪz] *vt* deshumanizar
dehydrate [ˌdiːhaɪ'dreɪt] I. *vt* deshidratar II. *vi* MED deshidratarse
dehydrated *adj* deshidratado, -a; (*milk*) en polvo; **to become ~** deshidratarse
dehydration [ˌdiːhaɪ'dreɪʃən] *n no pl* MED deshidratación *f*
de-ice [ˌdiː'aɪs] *vt* deshelar
deign [deɪn] *vi* **to ~ to do sth** dignarse a hacer algo
deism ['deɪɪzəm, *Am:* 'diː-] *n no pl* deísmo *m*
deity ['deɪɪti, *Am:* 'diːəṭi] *n* deidad *f*
deject [dɪ'dʒekt] *vt* desanimar
dejected *adj* desanimado, -a
dejection [dɪ'dʒekʃən] *n no pl* desánimo *m*
delay [dɪ'leɪ] I. *vt* aplazar; **to be ~ed** retrasarse; **to ~ doing sth** posponer el momento de hacer algo II. *vi* tardar; **to ~ in doing sth** dejar algo para más tarde; **don't ~!** ¡no te entretengas! III. *n* tardanza *f;* **without ~** sin dilación; **a two-hour ~** un retraso de dos horas
delayed-action *adj* de efecto retardado; **~ bomb** bomba de efecto retardado
delaying *adj* **~ tactics** tácticas dilatorias
delectable [dɪ'lektəbl] *adj* (*taste*) delicioso, -a; (*person*) encantador, -a
delectation [ˌdiːlek'teɪʃən] *n no pl* delectación *f;* **for the public's ~** para deleite del público
delegate¹ ['delɪgət] *n* delegado, -a *m, f*
delegate² ['delɪgeɪt] *vt* delegar
delegation [ˌdelɪ'geɪʃən] *n* delegación *f*
delete [dɪ'liːt] *vt* 1. borrar; **please ~ as appropriate** táchese lo que no corresponda 2. INFOR suprimir; (*file*) eliminar
deletion [dɪ'liːʃən] *n* 1. (*act of erasing*) eliminación *f* 2. (*removal*) supresión *f*
deli ['deli] *n inf s.* **delicatessen**
deliberate¹ [dɪ'lɪbərət] *adj* 1. (*intentional*) deliberado, -a 2. (*cautious: decision*) meditado, -a 3. (*unhurried*) lento, -a; (*movement*) pausado, -a
deliberate² [dɪ'lɪbəreɪt] I. *vi* **to ~ on sth** reflexionar sobre algo; **to ~ on a case** deliberar sobre una causa II. *vt* deliberar sobre
deliberately *adv* 1. (*intentionally*) adrede 2. (*unhurriedly*) pausadamente
deliberation [dɪˌlɪbə'reɪʃən] *n* 1. *no pl* (*formal discussion*) deliberación *f* 2. (*consideration*) reflexión *f;* **after due ~** después de pensarlo bien 3. (*unhurried manner*) parsimonia *f*
delicacy ['delɪkəsi] *n* 1. *no pl* (*tact*) delicadeza *f* 2. (*trickiness*) **the ~ of the situation** lo delicado de la situación 3. (*food*) manjar *m*
delicate ['delɪkət] *adj* 1. (*fragile*) frágil 2. (*tricky: situation*) delicado, -a 3. (*highly sensitive*) muy sensible 4. (*fine*) primoroso, -a; (*balance*) delicado, -a 5. (*easily injured*) **to be in ~ health** estar delicado (de salud) 6. (*soft*) suave; (*aroma*) exquisito, -a
delicatessen [ˌdelɪkə'tesən] *n* delicatessen *m*
delicious [dɪ'lɪʃəs] *adj* delicioso, -a
delight [dɪ'laɪt] I. *n* placer *m;* **to do sth with**

~ hacer algo a gusto; **to take ~ in sth** disfrutar con algo; **the children squealed in ~** los niños gritaron de júbilo **II.** *vt* deleitar; **to be ~ed with sth** estar encantado con algo
◆delight in *vi* **to ~ doing sth** deleitarse haciendo algo

delighted *adj* encantado, -a

delightful [dɪˈlaɪtfəl] *adj* delicioso, -a; (*person*) encantador(a)

delimit [dɪˈlɪmɪt] *vt* delimitar

delineate [dɪˈlɪnieɪt] *vt* **1.**(*draw*) delinear **2.**(*describe: plan*) trazar; (*character*) perfilar

delinquency [dɪˈlɪŋkwəntsi] *n* delincuencia *f*

delinquent [dɪˈlɪŋkwənt] **I.** *n* LAW delincuente *mf* **II.** *adj* **1.**(*behaviour*) delictivo, -a **2.** *Am* (*debtor*) moroso, -a

delirious [dɪˈlɪriəs] *adj* **1.** MED **to be ~** delirar **2.**(*ecstatic*) **to be ~ with joy** estar delirante de alegría

deliriously *adv* **1.**(*in a delirious manner*) delirantemente; **she raves ~** desvaría en su delirio **2.**(*extremely*) locamente; **she was ~ happy** estaba loca de alegría *inf*

delirium [dɪˈlɪriəm] *n no pl* delirio *m*

deliver [dɪˈlɪvəʳ, *Am:* dɪˈlɪvɚ] **I.** *vt* **1.**(*hand over*) entregar; (*to addressee*) repartir a domicilio **2.**(*recite: lecture*) dar; (*speech, verdict*) pronunciar **3.**(*direct*) **to ~ a blow to sb's head** asestar a alguien un golpe en la cabeza; **he ~ed a sharp rebuke to his son** dirigió una severa reprimenda a su hijo **4.** SPORTS (*throw*) lanzar **5.**(*give birth to*) **to ~ a baby** asistir al parto de un niño; **to be ~ed of a baby** dar a luz a un niño **6.**(*save*) librar **7.**(*produce*) **to ~ a promise** cumplir una promesa; **to ~ the goods** cumplir lo prometido **II.** *vi* COM **we ~** se entrega a domicilio
◆deliver of *vr* **to deliver oneself of sth** expresar algo

deliverance [dɪˈlɪvərənts] *n no pl* liberación *f*

deliverer *n* libertador(a) *m(f)*

delivery [dɪˈlɪvəri] *n* **1.**(*act of distributing goods*) reparto *m;* **~ charges** gastos *mpl* de envío; **~ man** repartidor *m;* **~ woman** repartidora *f;* **to pay on ~** pagar contra reembolso; **to take ~ of sth** recibir algo **2.**(*manner of speaking*) pronunciación *f* **3.** SPORTS lanzamiento *m* **4.**(*birth*) parto *m*

delivery note *n* albarán *m* **delivery room** *n,* **delivery suite** *n,* **delivery unit** *n* sala *f* de partos **delivery service** *n* servicio *m* de reparto a domicilio **delivery van** *n* furgoneta *f* de reparto

delta [ˈdeltə, *Am:* -t̬ə] *n* GEO delta *m*

delta wing *n* AVIAT ala *f* delta

delude [dɪˈluːd] *vt* engañar; **to ~ sb into believing sth** hacer creer algo a alguien

deluge [ˈdeljuːdʒ] **I.** *n* **1.**(*downpour*) diluvio *m;* (*flood*) inundación *f* **2.** *a. fig* (*inundation*) avalancha *f;* (*of complaints*) aluvión *m* **II.** *vt a. fig* inundar; **to be ~d with tears** estar bañado en lágrimas; **she is ~d with offers** le llueven las ofertas

delusion [dɪˈluːʒən] *n* **1.**(*wrong idea*) error *m;* **to labour under a ~** estar equivocado **2.** PSYCH alucinación *f;* **~s of grandeur** megalomanía *f* **3.**(*deceit*) engaño *m*

de luxe [dəˈlʌks, *Am:* dɪˈlʌks] *adj* de lujo

delve [delv] *vi* **1.**(*explore*) **to ~ into sth** ahondar en algo **2.**(*rummage*) hurgar

demagog [ˈdeməgɑːg] *n Am s.* **demagogue**

demagogic [ˌdeməˈgɒgɪk, *Am:* -ˈgɑːdʒɪk] *adj* demagógico, -a

demagogue [ˈdeməgɒg, *Am:* -gɑːg] *n* demagogo, -a *m, f*

demagoguery [ˌdeməˈgɒgəri, *Am:* -ˈgɑːdʒɚ-] *n,* **demagogy** [ˈdeməgɒgi, *Am:* -gɑːdʒi] *n no pl* demagogia *f*

demand [dɪˈmɑːnd, *Am:* dɪˈmænd] **I.** *vt* **1.**(*ask for forcefully*) exigir; (*a right*) reclamar; **to ~ that...** exigir que... *+subj;* **she demanded to see the person in charge** insistió en ver a la persona responsable **2.**(*require*) requerir **II.** *n* **1.**(*insistent request*) exigencia *f;* **~ for independence** reivindicación *f* de independencia; **to make a ~ on sth** exigir algo; **to make a ~ that ...** hacer una petición de que... *+subj;* **to make heavy ~s on sb's time** ocupar gran parte del tiempo de alguien; **to meet a ~ for sth** satisfacer las exigencias de algo; **by popular ~** a petición del público **2.** *Brit* (*request for payment*) reclamación *f* de un pago **3.** COM demanda *f;* **to be in ~** (*object*) tener mucha demanda; (*person*) estar muy solicitado

demanding [dɪˈmɑːndɪŋ, *Am:* dɪˈmæn-] *adj* exigente

demand note *n Am* título *m* pagadero a la vista

demarcate [ˈdiːmɑːkeɪt, *Am:* diːˈmɑːr-] *vt* demarcar

demarcation [ˌdiːmɑːˈkeɪʃən, *Am:* -mɑːrˈ-] *n* demarcación *f*

demarcation line *n* MIL, POL línea *f* de demarcación

demean [dɪˈmiːn] *vt* degradar; **to ~ oneself** rebajarse

demeaning *adj* degradante

demeanor *n Am, Aus,* **demeanour** [dɪˈmiːnəʳ, *Am:* dɪˈmiːnɚ] *n Brit, Aus no pl, form* (*behaviour*) conducta *f;* (*bearing*) porte *m*

demented [dɪˈmentɪd, *Am:* -ˈment̬ɪd] *adj inf* **1.**(*insane*) demente **2.** *fig, inf* (*extremely worried*) histérico, -a; **to drive sb ~** volver loco a alguien

demerit [ˌdiːˈmerɪt, *Am:* dɪˈmer-] *n* **1.**(*fault*) desmerecimiento *m* **2.** *Am* SCHOOL punto *m* negativo

demesne [dɪˈmeɪn] *n* **1.**(*possession of property as one's own*) propiedad *f* **2.**(*domain*) esfera *f* de actividad

demigod [ˈdemigɒd, *Am:* -gɑːd] *n* semidiós

m

demilitarize [ˌdiːˈmɪlɪtəraɪz, *Am:* -t̬əraɪz] *vt* desmilitarizar

demise [dɪˈmaɪz] *n no pl* **1.** (*death*) deceso *m* **2.** *fig* (*end*) desaparición *f;* (*of a company*) cierre *m*

demist [ˌdiːˈmɪst] *vt Brit* (*window*) desempañar

demister [ˌdiːˈmɪstəʳ] *n Brit* AUTO dispositivo *m* anti-vaho

demobilize [ˌdiːˈməʊbəlaɪz, *Am:* -ˈmoʊbəlaɪz] **I.** *vt* desmovilizar **II.** *vi* desmovilizarse

democracy [dɪˈmɒkrəsi, *Am:* dɪˈmɑː-] *n* democracia *f*

democrat [ˈdeməkræt] *n* demócrata *mf*

democratic [ˌdeməˈkrætɪk, *Am:* -ˈkræt̬-] *adj* democrático, -a

democratisation *n Brit, Aus,* **democratization** [dɪˌmɒkrətaɪˈzeɪʃən, *Am:* dɪˌmɑːkrət̬ɪˈ-] *n no pl* democratización *f*

democratize [dɪˈmɒkrətaɪz, *Am:* dɪˈmɑːkrə-] *vt Am* democratizar

demolish [dɪˈmɒlɪʃ, *Am:* dɪˈmɑːlɪʃ] *vt* (*a building*) demoler; (*a car*) destrozar; *fig* (*argument*) echar por tierra

demolition [ˌdeməˈlɪʃən] *n* (*of a building*) demolición *f; fig* destrucción *f*

demon [ˈdiːmən] *n* **1.** (*evil spirit*) demonio *m* **2.** (*naughty child*) diablillo *m* ►**to be a ~ at sth** *inf* ser un hacha haciendo algo; **to work like a ~** trabajar como una fiera; **to be a ~ for work, to be a ~ worker** *inf* ser una fiera para el trabajo

demoniac [dɪˈməʊniæk, *Am:* dɪˈmoʊ-] *adj,* **demonic** [dɪˈmɒnɪk, *Am:* dɪˈmɑːnɪk] *adj* **1.** (*devilish*) demoníaco, -a **2.** (*evil*) diabólico, -a

demonstrable [dɪˈmɒntstrəbl, *Am:* dɪˈmɑːnt-] *adj* demostrable

demonstrate [ˈdemənstreɪt] **I.** *vt* (*show clearly*) mostrar; (*prove*) demostrar; **to ~ that ...** demostrar que... **II.** *vi* POL manifestarse

demonstration [ˌdemənˈstreɪʃən] *n* **1.** (*act of showing*) demostración *f;* **she gave him a kiss as a ~ of her affection** le dio un beso como muestra de su afecto **2.** (*march*) manifestación *f;* **to hold a ~** manifestarse

demonstration model *n* modelo *m* de muestra

demonstrative [dɪˈmɒntstrətɪv, *Am:* dɪˈmɑːnstrət̬ɪv] *adj* **1.** (*illustrative*) concluyente **2.** (*expressing feelings*) efusivo, -a

demonstrator [ˈdemənstreɪtəʳ, *Am:* -t̬ɚ] *n* **1.** (*person who demonstrates a product*) demostrador(a) *m(f)* **2.** (*protester*) manifestante *mf*

demoralize [dɪˈmɒrəlaɪz, *Am:* -ˈmɔːr-] *vt Am* desmoralizar

demote [dɪˈməʊt, *Am:* -ˈmoʊt] *vt* bajar de categoría; MIL degradar

demure [dɪˈmjʊəʳ, *Am:* -ˈmjʊr] *adj* **1.** (*sedate*) recatado, -a **2.** (*affectedly modest*) remilgado, -a

den [den] *n* **1.** (*lair*) guarida *f* **2.** *Am* (*small room*) estudio *m* **3.** *iron* (*place for vice*) antro *m;* **a ~ of thieves** una guarida de ladrones

denationalize [ˌdiːˈnæʃənəlaɪz] *vt* privatizar

denial [dɪˈnaɪəl] *n* **1.** (*act of refuting*) negación *f* **2.** (*refusal*) negativa *f* **3.** *no pl* (*of a right*) denegación *f* **4.** (*rejection*) desmentido *m;* **to issue a ~ of sth** desmentir algo

denigrate [ˈdenɪgreɪt] *vt* denigrar

denim [ˈdenɪm] *n* **1.** *no pl* (*cloth*) tela *f* vaquera **2.** *pl, inf* (*clothes*) mono *m*

denim jacket *n* chaqueta *f* vaquera **denim shirt** *n* camisa *f* vaquera

denizen [ˈdenɪzən] *n liter* morador(a) *m(f)*

Denmark [ˈdenmɑːk, *Am:* ˈdenmɑːrk] *n* Dinamarca *f*

denomination [dɪˌnɒmɪˈneɪʃən, *Am:* -ˌnɑːmə-] *n* **1.** (*religious group*) confesión *f* **2.** (*unit of value*) denominación *f*

denominational [dɪˌnɒmɪˈneɪʃənl, *Am:* -ˌnɑːmə-] *adj* confesional

denominator [dɪˈnɒmɪneɪtəʳ, *Am:* -ˈnɑːməneɪt̬ɚ] *n* denominador *m*

denotation [ˌdiːnəʊˈteɪʃən, *Am:* -noʊˈ-] *n* denotación *f*

denote [dɪˈnəʊt, *Am:* -ˈnoʊt] *vt* **1.** (*indicate*) denotar **2.** (*show: displeasure*) mostrar

denouement [deɪˈnuːmɑ̃ːŋ] *n* desenlace *m*

denounce [dɪˈnaʊnts] *vt* **1.** (*condemn*) censurar **2.** (*give information against*) denunciar

dense [dents] *adj* **1.** (*thick*) espeso, -a **2.** (*closely packed*) denso, -a; (*compact*) compacto, -a; (*print*) apiñado, -a **3.** (*complex*) difícil **4.** *inf* (*stupid*) duro, -a de mollera

densely *adv* densamente

density [ˈdentsɪti, *Am:* -sət̬i] *n* **1.** (*compactness*) densidad *f;* **to be high/low in ~** ser de alta/baja densidad **2.** (*complexity*) impenetrabilidad *f*

dent [dent] **I.** *n* **1.** (*mark*) abolladura *f* **2.** (*adverse effect*) mella *f* **II.** *vt* **1.** (*put a dent in*) abollar **2.** (*have adverse effect on: confidence*) hacer mella en

dental [ˈdentəl] *adj* dental

dental practitioner *n,* **dental surgeon** *n,* **dentist** [ˈdentɪst, *Am:* -t̬ɪst] *n* dentista *mf*

dentistry [ˈdentɪstri, *Am:* -t̬ɪ-] *n no pl* odontología *f*

dentition [denˈtɪʃən] *n* dentición *f*

dentures [ˈdentʃəz, *Am:* ˈdentʃɚz] *npl* dentadura *f* postiza

denude [dɪˈnjuːd, *Am:* -ˈnuːd] *vt* (*surface*) denudar; **the sheep have denuded the field of grass** *fig* las ovejas han despojado el campo de hierba

denunciation [dɪˌnʌntsiˈeɪʃən] *n* **1.** (*condemnation*) censura *f* **2.** (*accusation*) denuncia *f*

deny [dɪˈnaɪ] *vt* **1.** (*declare untrue*) negar; (*report*) desmentir; **to ~ having done sth** negar haber hecho algo; **she denies that she**

saw it niega haberlo visto **2.** (*refuse*) denegar; **to ~ sb a privilege** negar a alguien un privilegio; **you cannot ~ me my right to free speech** no me puedes privar de mi derecho a la libertad de expresión **3.** (*do without things*) **to ~ oneself sth** privarse de algo **4.** (*disown*) renegar de

deodorant [di'əʊdərənt, *Am:* -'oʊ-] *n* desodorante *m*

deodorise *vt Aus, Brit,* **deodorize** [di'əʊdəraɪz, *Am:* -'oʊdəraɪz] *vt Am* desodorizar

dep. *abbr of* **department** dpto.

depart [dɪ'pɑːt, *Am:* dɪ'pɑːrt] **I.** *vi* (*person*) partir; (*plane*) despegar; (*train*) salir; (*ship*) zarpar **II.** *vt* **to ~ this life** dejar de existir

◆**depart from** *vi* desviarse de

departed **I.** *adj* **1.** (*dead*) difunto, -a **2.** (*past: triumph*) pasado, -a **II.** *n pl* **the ~** los difuntos; **to mourn the ~** llorar por las almas

department [dɪ'pɑːtmənt, *Am:* dɪ'pɑːrt-] *n* **1.** (*division: of a university, company*) departamento *m;* (*of a shop*) sección *f* **2.** ADMIN, POL ministerio *m;* **~ of Health and Social Security** Ministerio *m* de Sanidad y Seguridad Social **3.** *inf* (*domain*) ramo *m*

departmental [ˌdiːpɑːt'mentəl, *Am:* -pɑːrt'menţəl] *adj* departamental

department store *n* grandes almacenes *mpl,* tienda *f* por departamentos *AmS*

departure [dɪ'pɑːtʃəʳ, *Am:* dɪ'pɑːrtʃɚ] *n* **1.** (*act of leaving*) partida *f;* (*of vehicle*) salida *f;* (*of plane*) despegue *m;* **~ from politics** alejamiento *m* de la política; **to take one's ~** marcharse **2.** (*deviation*) desviación *f;* (*new undertaking*) nuevo rumbo *m;* **to be a new ~ for sb/sth** ser una novedad para alguien/algo

departure gate *n* puerta *f* de embarque

departure lounge *n* AVIAT sala *f* de embarque

departure time *n* AVIAT hora *f* de salida

depend [dɪ'pend] *vi* **1.** (*be determined by*) **to ~ on sth** depender de algo; **~ing on the weather...** según el tiempo que haga... **2.** (*rely on for aid*) **she depends on her father for money** depende del dinero de su padre **3.** (*trust*) **to ~ on sb/sth** confiar en alguien/algo

dependability [dɪˌpendə'bɪləti, *Am:* dɪˌpendə'bɪləţi] *n no pl* (*reliability*) seriedad *f*

dependable [dɪ'pendəbl] *adj* (*thing*) seguro, -a; (*person*) serio, -a

dependant [dɪ'pendənt] *n* familiar *m* dependiente

dependence [dɪ'pendənts] *n no pl* dependencia *f*

dependency *n* **1.** *no pl* (*overreliance*) dependencia *f* **2.** (*dependent state*) posesión *f;* **Puerto Rico is a U.S. ~** Puerto Rico es una posesión de EE.UU.

dependent [dɪ'pendənt] **I.** *adj* **1.** (*conditional*) **to be ~ on sth** depender de algo **2.** (*in need of*) dependiente; **to be ~ on sth** depender de algo; **to be ~ on drugs** ser drogadicto; **she has two ~ children** tiene dos niños a su cargo **II.** *n Am s.* **dependant**

depict [dɪ'pɪkt] *vt* representar

depiction [dɪ'pɪkʃən] *n* representación *f*

depilatory [dɪ'pɪlətəri, *Am:* -tɔːri] **I.** *n* depilatorio *m* **II.** *adj* depilatorio, -a

depilatory cream *n* crema *f* depilatoria

deplete [dɪ'pliːt] *vt* reducir

depleted *adj* agotado, -a

depletion [dɪ'pliːʃən] *n* (*of resources*) agotamiento *m;* (*of money*) merma *f;* **~ of the ozone layer** reducción *f* de la capa de ozono

deplorable [dɪ'plɔːrəbl] *adj* deplorable

deplore [dɪ'plɔːʳ, *Am:* -'plɔːr] *vt* deplorar; **it is to be ~d** *Aus, Brit* es lamentable

deploy [dɪ'plɔɪ] *vt* (*resources*) desplegar; (*skills*) demostrar

deployment [dɪ'plɔɪmənt] *n no pl* despliegue *m*

depopulate [ˌdiː'pɒpjəleɪt, *Am:* -'pɑːpjə-] *vt* despoblar

deport [dɪ'pɔːt, *Am:* dɪ'pɔːrt] *vt* deportar

deportation [ˌdiːpɔː'teɪʃən, *Am:* -pɔːr'-] *n* deportación *f*

deportee [ˌdiːpɔː'tiː, *Am:* -pɔːr'-] *n* deportado, -a *m, f*

deportment [dɪ'pɔːtmənt, *Am:* dɪ'pɔːrt-] *n no pl* porte *m*

depose [dɪ'pəʊz, *Am:* dɪ'poʊz] *vt* destituir

deposit [dɪ'pɒzɪt, *Am:* dɪ'pɑːzɪt] **I.** *vt* **1.** (*leave*) depositar; (*eggs*) poner; (*luggage*) guardar en consigna; **the bus ~ed me in the middle of nowhere** el bus me dejó donde Cristo perdió el gorro **2.** FIN (*store, pay into account*) ingresar; **to ~ £1000** dejar 1000 libras en depósito **II.** *n* **1.** (*sediment*) sedimento *m* **2.** GEO yacimiento *m* **3.** (*payment made as pledge*) depósito *m;* **to make a ~** efectuar un depósito; **to leave a ~** dejar un depósito; **to leave sth as a ~** dejar algo en garantía; **on ~** en depósito

deposit account *n Brit* cuenta *f* de depósitos a plazo

deposition [ˌdepə'zɪʃən] *n* **1.** *no pl* (*removal from power*) destitución *f;* (*of a dictator*) derrocamiento *f* **2.** (*formal written statement*) declaración *f;* **to file a ~** dar testimonio

depositor [dɪ'pɒzɪtəʳ, *Am:* dɪ'pɑːzəţɚ] *n* cuentahabiente *mf*

depot ['depəʊ, *Am:* 'diːpoʊ] *n* **1.** (*storehouse*) almacén *m; Brit* (*for vehicles*) cochera *f* **2.** (*station*) estación *f*

deprave [dɪ'preɪv] *vt* pervertir

depraved *adj* depravado, -a

depravity [dɪ'prævəti, *Am:* dɪ'prævəţi] *n no pl* depravación *f*

deprecate ['deprəkeɪt] *vt* **1.** (*show disapproval of*) desaprobar **2.** (*belittle*) menospreciar

deprecating *adj* **1.** (*strongly disapproving*) de desaprobación **2.** (*belittling*) de menosprecio

deprecation [ˌdeprə'keɪʃən] *n no pl* **1.** (*disapproving*) desaprobación *f* **2.** (*belittling*)

menosprecio *m*
deprecatory ['deprəkətəri, *Am:* 'deprəkə-tɔːri] *adj s.* **deprecating**
depreciate [dɪ'priːʃieɪt] **I.** *vi* depreciarse **II.** *vt* depreciar
depreciation [dɪˌpriːʃi'eɪʃən] *n no pl* depreciación *f*
depredation [ˌdeprə'deɪʃən] *n* estragos *fpl*
depress [dɪ'pres] *vt* **1.** (*sadden*) deprimir; **it ~es me that ...** me deprime que... *+subj* **2.** (*reduce activity of*) disminuir; (*the economy*) paralizar; (*earnings*) reducir; (*prices*) bajar **3.** (*press down*) presionar; (*a pedal*) apretar
depressant I. *n* sedante *m* **II.** *adj* deprimente
depressed *adj* **1.** (*sad*) deprimido, -a, apolismado, -a *Méx, Ven;* **to feel ~** sentirse abatido **2.** (*impoverished: period*) de depresión; (*area*) deprimido, -a; (*economy*) en crisis
depressing [dɪ'presɪŋ] *adj* deprimente
depression [dɪ'preʃən] *n* **1.** *a.* METEO, FIN depresión *f* **2.** (*hollow*) hoyo *m*
depressive [dɪ'presɪv] **I.** *n* depresivo, -a *m, f* **II.** *adj* depresivo, -a
deprivation [ˌleprɪ'veɪʃən] *n* privación *f*
deprive [dɪ'praɪv] *vt* (*of dignity*) despojar; (*of sleep*) quitar; **to ~ sb of sth** privar a alguien de algo
deprived *adj* desvalido, -a
depth [depθ] *n* **1.** *a. fig* profundidad *f;* **in the ~ of her heart** en lo más hondo de su corazón; **in the ~ of winter** en pleno invierno **2.** (*intensity*) intensidad *f* **3.** *no pl* (*low sound*) gravedad *f* ▶**to get out of one's ~** perder pie; **to sink to a ~** degenerar mucho; **in ~** en detalle
depth charge *n* carga *f* de profundidad
deputation [ˌdepjə'teɪʃən] *n + pl/sing vb* delegación *f*
depute [dɪ'pjuːt] *vt* **1.** (*appoint*) comisionar **2.** (*delegate*) **to ~ sth to sb** delegar algo en alguien
deputise *vi Aus, Brit,* **deputize** ['depjətaɪz] *vi* **to ~ for sb** suplir a alguien
deputy ['depjəti, *Am:* -t̬i] *n* delegado, -a *m, f;* **~ manager** subdirector(a) *m(f)*
derail [dɪ'reɪl] **I.** *vt* hacer descarrilar **II.** *vi* descarrilar
derailment [dɪ'reɪlmənt] *n* descarrilamiento *m*
derange [dɪ'reɪndʒ] *vt* perturbar
deranged *adj* trastornado, -a
derangement *n no pl* trastorno *m* mental
derby ['dɑːbi, *Am:* 'dɜːr-] *n* **1.** *Brit* derby (*partido entre equipos locales*) **2.** *Am* (*hat*) hongo *m*
Derby ['dɑːbi, *Am:* 'dɑːrb-] *n no pl* (*horse race*) Derby *m*
deregulation [ˌdɪregjə'leɪʃən] *n no pl* deregulación *f*
derelict ['derəlɪkt] **I.** *adj* (*building*) abandonado, -a; (*site*) baldío, -a **II.** *n* (*tramp*) desposeído, -a *m, f*
dereliction [ˌderə'lɪkʃən] *n* **1.** *no pl* (*dilapidation*) abandono *m* **2.** (*deliberate neglect*) negligencia *f*
deride [dɪ'raɪd] *vt* burlarse de; **to ~ sb for doing sth** ridiculizar a alguien por hacer algo
derision [dɪ'rɪʒən] *n no pl* burla *f;* **to meet sth with ~** hacer burla de algo
derisive [dɪ'raɪsɪv] *adj* burlón, -ona
derisory [dɪ'raɪsəri] *adj* (*amount*) irrisorio, -a
derivation [ˌderɪ'veɪʃən] *n* (*origin*) origen *m;* (*process of evolving*) derivación *f*
derivative [dɪ'rɪvətɪv, *Am:* dɪ'rɪvət̬ɪv] **I.** *adj pej* poco original **II.** *n* derivado *m*
derive [dɪ'raɪv] **I.** *vt* (*get from*) **to ~ sth from sth** obtener algo de algo; **I ~ a lot of pleasure from working with children** disfruto mucho trabajando con niños **II.** *vi* (*come from*) **to ~ from sth** derivar de algo
dermatitis [ˌdɜːmə'taɪtɪs, *Am:* ˌdɜːrmə-'taɪt̬əs] *n no pl* dermatitis *f*
dermatologist *n* dermatólogo, -a *m, f*
dermatology [ˌdɜːmə'tɒlədʒi, *Am:* ˌdɜːr-mə'tɑːlə-] *n no pl* dermatología *f*
derogate ['derəʊgeɪt, *Am:* 'derə-] *vi* (*detract from*) **to ~ from sth** atentar contra algo
derogation [ˌderəʊ'geɪʃən, *Am:* ˌderə'-] *n no pl* **1.** (*lessening*) menosprecio *m* **2.** (*abolition*) abolición *f*
derogatory [dɪ'rɒgətəri, *Am:* dɪ'rɑːgətɔːri] *adj* desdeñoso, -a
derrick ['derɪk] *n* **1.** (*crane*) grúa *f* **2.** (*framework*) torre *f* de perforación
DES [ˌdiːiː'es] *n Brit abbr of* **Department of Education and Science** MEC *m*
desalinate [ˌdiː'sælɪneɪt] *vt* desalinizar
desalination [diːˌsælɪ'neɪʃən] *n no pl* desalinización *f*
desalination plant *n* planta *f* desalinizadora
descale [ˌdiː'skeɪl] *vt* desincrustar
descant ['deskænt, *Am:* 'deskænt] *n* MUS contrapunto *m*
descend [dɪ'send] **I.** *vi* **1.** (*go down*) descender; (*fall*) caer **2.** (*lower oneself*) **to ~ to stealing** rebajarse a robar **3. to ~ from sb/sth** provenir de alguien/algo **II.** *vt* descender; (*a ladder*) bajar
descendant [dɪ'sendənt] *n* descendiente *mf*
descent [dɪ'sent] *n* **1.** (*landing approach*) descenso *m;* (*way down*) bajada *f* **2.** (*decline*) declive *m* **3.** *no pl* (*ancestry*) origen *m;* **of Irish ~** de ascendencia irlandesa
describe [dɪ'skraɪb] *vt* **1.** (*tell in words*) describir; (*an experience*) relatar; **to ~ sb as stupid** calificar a alguien de tonto **2.** (*draw*) trazar
description [dɪ'skrɪpʃən] *n* **1.** (*account*) descripción *f;* **to answer a ~ of sb/sth** corresponder a una descripción de alguien/algo **2.** (*sort*) clase *f;* **of every ~** de todo tipo
descriptive [dɪ'skrɪptɪv] *adj* descriptivo, -a
desecrate ['desɪkreɪt] *vt* profanar
desecration [ˌdesɪ'kreɪʃən] *n no pl* profana-

ción *f*

desegregate [ˌdiːˈsegrɪgeɪt] *vt* desegregar

desegregation [ˌdiːˈsegrɪgeɪʃən, *Am:* diː-ˌsegrɪˈgeɪʃən] *n no pl* desegregación *f*

desensitize [ˌdiːˈsensɪtaɪz] *vt Am a.* MED insensibilizar

desert[1] [dɪˈzɜːt, *Am:* -ˈzɜːrt] **I.** *vi* MIL desertar **II.** *vt* **1.** MIL desertar de **2.** (*abandon*) abandonar; (*one's post*) retirarse de; **luck ~ed me** la suerte me abandonó; **to ~ sb** (**for sb else**) dejar a alguien (por otra persona)

desert[2] [ˈdezət, *Am:* -ɚt] *n* desierto *m;* **~ plant/animal** planta/animal del desierto

deserted *adj* **1.** (*place*) desierto, -a **2.** (*person*) abandonado, -a

deserter *n* MIL desertor(a) *m(f);* POL tránsfuga *mf*

desertification [dɪˌzɜːtɪfɪˈkeɪʃən, *Am:* dɪˌzɜːrt̬ə-] *n no pl* desertificación *f*

desertion [dɪˈzɜːʃən, *Am:* dɪˈzɜːr-] *n* MIL deserción *f;* (*act of leaving*) abandono *m*

deserts [dɪˈzɜːts, *Am:* dɪˈzɜːrts] *npl* merecido *m;* **to get one's ~** tener su merecido

deserve [dɪˈzɜːv, *Am:* dɪˈzɜːrv] *vt* merecer; **what have I done to ~ (all) this?** ¿qué he hecho para merecer (todo) esto?

deservedly *adv* merecidamente

deserving *adj* meritorio, -a; **to be ~ of sth** ser digno de algo

design [dɪˈzaɪn] **I.** *vt* **1.** (*plan*) **to ~ sth** (**for sb**) planear algo (para alguien) **2.** (*intend*) **to ~ sth for sb/sth** concebir algo para alguien/algo; **this dictionary is ~ed for advanced learners** este diccionario está dirigido a estudiantes de nivel avanzado; **these measures are ~ed to reduce criminality** estas medidas buscan reducir la criminalidad **II.** *vi* hacer diseños **III.** *n* **1.** (*plan*) diseño *m* **2.** (*sketch*) bosquejo *m* **3.** (*pattern*) dibujo *m* **4.** *no pl* (*intention*) propósito *m;* **to do sth by ~** hacer algo adrede **5.** *pl, inf* (*dishonest intentions*) malas intenciones *fpl;* **to have ~s on a championship** pretender un campeonato **IV.** *adj* de diseño

designate [ˈdezɪgneɪt] **I.** *vt* **1.** (*name for a duty*) nombrar; **to ~ sb to do sth** designar a alguien para hacer algo **2.** (*indicate*) señalar **II.** *adj* electo, -a; **the Governor ~** el gobernador electo

designation [ˌdezɪgˈneɪʃən] *n* **1.** (*appointment*) nombramiento *m* **2.** (*act of indicating*) señalamiento *m*

designedly *adv* a propósito

designer [dɪˈzaɪnəʳ, *Am:* dɪˈzaɪnɚ] **I.** *n* diseñador(a) *m(f)* **II.** *adj* de marca

designing **I.** *n* (*art*) diseño *m* **II.** *adj pej* intrigante

desirable [dɪˈzaɪərəbl, *Am:* dɪˈzaɪ-] *adj* **1.** (*necessary*) conveniente; **it is ~ that ...** sería deseable que... +*subj* **2.** (*sexually attractive*) deseable **3.** (*popular or fashionable: area, job*) codiciado, -a

desire [dɪˈzaɪəʳ, *Am:* dɪˈzaɪɚ] **I.** *vt* **1.** (*want*) desear; **I ~ you to leave** le ruego que se vaya **2.** (*request*) **to ~ that ...** desear que... +*subj* **3.** (*be sexually attracted to*) **to ~ sb** desear a alguien **II.** *n* **1.** (*craving*) deseo *m* **2.** (*request*) petición *f* **3.** (*sensual appetite*) apetencia *f* sexual; **to be the object of sb's ~** ser el objeto de deseo de alguien

desired *adj* deseado, -a

desirous [dɪˈzaɪərəs, *Am:* dɪˈzaɪrəs] *adj* deseoso, -a; **to be ~ of sth** estar deseoso de algo

desist [dɪˈsɪst] *vi form* desistir

desk [desk] *n* **1.** (*table*) escritorio *m* **2.** (*counter*) mostrador *m* **3.** (*section of a newspaper*) sección *f*

desk lamp *n* lámpara *f* de escritorio

desktop [ˈdesktɒp, *Am:* -tɑːp] *n* INFOR **~ (computer)** microordenador *m* de mesa

desktop publishing *n* autoedición *f*

desolate[1] [ˈdesələt] *adj* **1.** (*barren*) solitario, -a; (*landscape, prospect*) desierto, -a **2.** (*sad*) desolado, -a; **to feel ~** sentirse desconsolado

desolate[2] [ˈdesəleɪt] *vt* asolar

desolation [ˌdesəˈleɪʃən] *n no pl* **1.** (*barrenness*) desolación *f* **2.** (*sadness*) aflicción *f*

despair [dɪˈspeəʳ, *Am:* dɪˈsper] **I.** *n no pl* (*feeling of hopelessness*) desesperación *f;* **to be in ~ about sth** estar desesperado por algo; **to drive sb to ~** desesperar a alguien; **to the ~ of sb** para desesperanza de alguien ►**to be the ~ of sb** tener loco a alguien **II.** *vi* desesperarse; **to ~ of sb/sth** perder las esperanzas con alguien/algo

despairing *adj* desesperado, -a; (*glance*) de desesperación

despatch [dɪˈspætʃ] *n, vt s.* **dispatch**

desperado [ˌdespəˈrɑːdəʊ, *Am:* -doʊ] <-(e)s> *n* criminal *mf* peligroso, -a

desperate [ˈdespərət] *adj* **1.** (*risking all on a small chance*) temerario, -a; (*violent*) encarnizado, -a; (*measure, solution*) desesperado, -a **2.** (*serious*) grave; (*poverty*) extremo, -a; (*situation*) difícil; **to be in ~ straits** estar en grandes apuros **3.** (*great*) extremo, -a; **to be in a ~ hurry** estar muy apurado; **to be in ~ need of help** tener necesidad extrema de ayuda **4.** (*having great need or desire*) **to be ~ for sth** necesitar algo con suma urgencia; **I'm ~ for a drink!** *iron* ¡me muero por un trago!

desperation [ˌdespəˈreɪʃən] *n no pl* desesperación *f;* **in ~** a la desesperada; **to drive sb to ~** desesperar a alguien

despicable [dɪˈspɪkəbl] *adj* despreciable

despise [dɪˈspaɪz] *vt* despreciar; **to ~ sb for sth** menospreciar a alguien por algo

despite [dɪˈspaɪt] *prep* a pesar de

despoil [dɪˈspɔɪl] *vt* saquear

despondent [dɪˈspɒndənt, *Am:* -ˈspɑːn-] *adj* desalentado, -a; **to feel ~ about sth** sentirse desanimado por algo

despot [ˈdespɒt, *Am:* -pət] *n* déspota *mf*

despotic [dɪˈspɒtɪk, *Am:* desˈpɑːt̬ɪk] *adj* despótico, -a

despotism ['despətɪzəm] *n no pl* despotismo *m*
dessert [dɪ'zɜːt, *Am:* -'zɜːrt] *n* postre *m;* **there's apple pie for ~** hay pastel de manzana de postre
dessertspoon [dɪ'zɜːtˌspuːn, *Am:* -'zɜːrt] *n* **1.** (*spoon for dessert*) cuchara *f* de postre **2.** (*dessertspoonful*) cucharadita *f*
destabilization [ˌdiːˈsteɪbəlaɪz'eɪʃən, *Am:* -bəlɪ'zeɪ-] *n no pl* desestabilización *f*
destabilize [ˌdiː'steɪbəlaɪz] *vt* desestabilizar
destination [ˌdestɪ'neɪʃən] *n* destino *m*
destiny ['destɪni] *n* destino *m;* **to be a victim of ~** ser una víctima del destino; **to fight against ~** luchar contra el destino; **to shape one's ~** hacerse su propio destino
destitute ['destɪtjuːt, *Am:* -tuːt] **I.** *adj* necesitado, -a **II.** *n* **the ~** *pl* los indigentes
destitution [ˌdestɪ'tjuːʃən, *Am:* -'tuː-] *n no pl* **1.** (*deprivation of office*) destitución *f* **2.** (*poverty*) miseria *f*
destroy [dɪ'strɔɪ] *vt* **1.** (*demolish*) destruir **2.** (*kill*) matar; (*animal*) sacrificar **3.** (*ruin*) arruinar
destroyer [dɪ'strɔɪəʳ, *Am:* dɪ'strɔɪɚ] *n* NAUT destructor *m*
destructible [dɪ'strʌktəbl] *adj* destructible
destruction [dɪ'strʌkʃən] *n no pl* destrucción *f;* **mass ~** destrucción en masa; **to leave a trail of ~** dejar una estela de destrucción
destructive [dɪ'strʌktɪv] *adj* destructivo, -a
destructiveness *n no pl* destructividad *f*
desulphurization [diːˌsʌlfəraɪ'zeɪʃən] *n no pl* desulfurización *f*
desultory ['desəltəri, *Am:* -tɔːri] *adj* (*disconnected*) inconexo, -a; (*lacking plan*) desordenado, -a
Det *n abbr of* **Detective** detective *mf*
detach [dɪ'tætʃ] *vt* separar
detachable *adj* separable
detached *adj* **1.** (*separated*) separado, -a; **~ house** chalet *m* **2.** (*aloof*) indiferente **3.** (*impartial*) imparcial
detachment [dɪ'tætʃmənt] *n* **1.** *no pl* (*separation*) separación *f* **2.** *no pl* (*disinterest*) desinterés *m* **3.** (*group of soldiers*) destacamento *m*
detail ['diːteɪl, *Am:* dɪ'teɪl] **I.** *n* **1.** (*item of information*) detalle *m;* **in ~** en detalle **2.** (*unimportant item*) minucia *f;* **gory ~s** *iron* intimidades *fpl;* **to go into ~** entrar en detalles **3.** (*small feature*) elemento *m* **4.** MIL (*group*) destacamento *m* **II.** *vt* **1.** (*explain fully*) detallar **2.** (*tell, mention*) pormenorizar **3.** (*assign a duty to*) **to ~ sb to do sth** destacar a alguien para que haga algo
detailed *adj* detallado, -a; (*report, study*) pormenorizado, -a
detain [dɪ'teɪn] *vt* **1.** (*hold as prisoner*) detener **2.** (*delay*) entretener; (*keep waiting*) retener
detainee [ˌdiːteɪ'niː] *n* detenido, -a *m, f*
detect [dɪ'tekt] *vt* **1.** (*discover*) descubrir **2.** (*note*) advertir; (*sense presence of*) percibir; (*a mine*) hallar
detectable [dɪ'tektəbl] *adj* (*able to be found*) averiguable; (*discernible*) perceptible
detection [dɪ'tekʃən] *n no pl* descubrimiento *m*
detective [dɪ'tektɪv] *n* detective *mf*
detective inspector *n* comisario, -a *m, f*
detective novel *n* novela *f* policíaca
detective story *n* novela *f* policíaca
detective superintendent *n* superintendente *mf* general
detector [dɪ'tektəʳ, *Am:* -tɚ] *n* detector *m*
detention [dɪ'tenʃən] *n* **1.** (*being held as a prisoner*) arresto *m* **2.** (*act*) detención *f* **3.** (*school punishment*) castigo *f*
detention centre *n* **1.** (*for youths*) correccional *m* **2.** (*for refugees*) campo *m* de refugiados
deter [dɪ'tɜːʳ, *Am:* -'tɜːr] <-rr-> *vt* disuadir
detergent [dɪ'tɜːdʒənt, *Am:* -'tɜːr] *n* detergente *m*
deteriorate [dɪ'tɪərɪəreɪt, *Am:* -'tɪrɪ-] *vi* **1.** (*wear out*) deteriorarse **2.** (*become worse*) empeorar
deterioration [dɪˌtɪərɪə'reɪʃən, *Am:* -'tɪrɪ-] *n no pl* **1.** (*wearing out*) deterioro *m* **2.** (*worsening*) empeoramiento *m*
determinable [dɪ'tɜːmɪnəbl, *Am:* -'tɜːr-] *adj* determinable
determinant [dɪ'tɜːmɪnənt, *Am:* -'tɜːr-] **I.** *n* determinante *m* **II.** *adj* determinante
determinate [dɪ'tɜːmɪnət, *Am:* -'tɜːr-] *adj* **1.** (*limited*) definido, -a **2.** (*of specific scope*) determinado, -a
determination [dɪˌtɜːmɪ'neɪʃən, *Am:* -ˌtɜːr-] *n no pl* **1.** (*firmness of purpose*) resolución *f* **2.** (*decision*) determinación *f*
determine [dɪ'tɜːmɪn, *Am:* -'tɜːr-] **I.** *vi* **1.** (*decide*) **to ~ on sth** decidirse por algo **2.** LAW expirar **II.** *vt* **1.** (*decide*) decidir **2.** (*settle*) establecer **3.** (*find out*) fijar **4.** (*influence*) influir **5.** LAW (*terminate*) rescindir
determined [dɪ'tɜːmɪnd, *Am:* -'tɜːr-] *adj* decidido, -a; **to be ~ to do sth** estar resuelto a hacer algo
deterrence [dɪ'terəns] *n no pl* disuasión *f*
deterrent [dɪ'terənt] **I.** *n* (*obstacle*) freno *m;* **to act as a ~ to sb** disuadir a alguien **II.** *adj* disuasivo, -a
detest [dɪ'test] *vt* detestar
detestable [dɪ'testəbl] *adj* detestable
detestation [ˌdiːte'steɪʃən] *n no pl* aborrecimiento *m*
dethrone [ˌdiː'θrəʊn, *Am:* dɪ'θroʊn] *vt* destronar
detonate ['detəneɪt] **I.** *vi* detonar **II.** *vt* hacer detonar
detonation [ˌdetə'neɪʃən] *n* detonación *f*
detonator ['detəneɪtəʳ, *Am:* -t̬ɚ] *n* detonador *m*
detour ['diːtʊəʳ, *Am:* 'diːtʊr] *n* desvío *m;* **to**

make a ~ desviarse

detoxify [dɪ'tɒksɪfaɪ, *Am:* diː'tɑːk-] *vt* desintoxicar

detract [dɪ'trækt] *vi* **1.** (*devalue*) **to ~ from sth** quitar mérito a algo **2.** (*take away*) apartar

detractor [dɪ'træktəʳ, *Am:* -tɚ] *n* detractor(a) *m(f)*

detriment ['detrɪmənt] *n no pl* perjuicio *m;* **to the ~ of sth** en detrimento de algo; **without ~ to sth** sin perjuicio de algo

detrimental [ˌdetrɪ'mentəl, *Am:* -t̬l] *adj* nocivo, -a

detritus [dɪ'traɪtəs, *Am:* -t̬əs] *n no pl* **1.** (*small fragments*) detrito *m* **2.** (*debris*) escombros *mpl*

deuce [djuːs, *Am:* duːs] *n no pl* **1.** (*in cards*) dos *m* **2.** (*in tennis*) empate *m*

devaluate [ˌdiː'væljueɪt] *vt s.* **devalue**

devaluation [ˌdiːvælju'eɪʃən] *n* devaluación *f*

devalue [ˌdiː'væljuː] *vt* devaluar

devastate ['devəsteɪt] *vt* devastar

devastating *adj* **1.** (*causing great destruction*) desolador(a); (*powerful*) devastador(a) **2.** (*with great effect*) abrumador(a); (*beauty*) arrollador(a); (*charm*) irresistible

devastation [ˌdevə'steɪʃən] *n no pl* devastación *f*

develop [dɪ'veləp] **I.** *vi* (*grow*) desarrollarse; (*become more advanced*) progresar; **to ~ into sth** transformarse en algo **II.** *vt* **1.** (*expand*) desarrollar; (*improve*) ampliar **2.** (*create*) crear **3.** (*begin to show*) revelar; (*catch*) empezar a tener; (*an illness*) contraer **4.** (*build*) construir; (*build on*) urbanizar **5.** PHOT revelar **6.** MUS elaborar

developed *adj* desarrollado, -a

developer [dɪ'veləpəʳ, *Am:* -pɚ] *n* **1.** (*one who develops*) promotor(a) *m(f)* inmobiliario, -a; (*company*) inmobiliaria *f* **2.** PHOT revelador *m*

developing *adj* de desarrollo

development [dɪ'veləpmənt] *n* **1.** (*process*) desarrollo *m;* (*growth*) crecimiento *m* **2.** (*growth stage*) avance *m;* (*of skills*) evolución *f* **3.** (*progress*) progreso *m;* (*of products*) explotación *m* **4.** (*event*) acontecimiento *m* **5.** (*building of*) construcción *f;* **housing ~** construcción de viviendas **6.** (*building on: of land*) urbanización *f* **7.** (*industrialization*) industrialización *f* **8.** MUS (*elaboration*) elaboración *f*

deviant ['diːviənt] *adj* (*behaviour*) que se aparta de la norma, desviado, -a; (*sexually*) pervertido, -a

deviate ['diːvieɪt] *vi* apartarse; **to ~ from sth** desviarse de algo

deviation [ˌdiːvi'eɪʃən] *n* desviación *f*

deviationist [ˌdiːvi'eɪʃənɪst] *n* desviacionista *mf*

device [dɪ'vaɪs] *n* **1.** (*mechanism*) dispositivo *m;* **sound ~** INFOR dispositivo *m* de sonido; **input/output ~** INFOR dispositivo *m* de entrada/salida **2.** (*method*) estrategia *f;* **literary/rhetorical ~** recurso *m* literario/retórico **3.** (*bomb*) artefacto *m;* **nuclear ~** ingenio *m* nuclear ►**to leave sb to their own ~s** abandonar a alguien a su suerte

devil ['devəl] *n* **1.** (*Satan*) diablo *m,* mandinga *m;* **to be possessed by the Devil** estar poseído por el demonio **2.** (*evil spirit*) espíritu *m* maligno **3.** *inf* (*wicked person*) diablo *m* **4.** (*mischievous person*) **to be a ~** ser malo; **go on, be a ~!** *inf* ¡venga, pórtate mal!; **lucky ~!** ¡qué suerte!; **the poor ~!** ¡pobre diablo! **5.** (*difficult thing*) **to have the ~ of a job doing sth** costar Dios y ayuda hacer algo **6.** (*feisty energy*) arrojo *m* **7.** (*machine*) máquina *f* deshilachadora ►**~ take the hindmost** camarón que se duerme se lo lleva la corriente *prov;* **between the ~ and the deep blue sea** entre la espada y la pared; **to sell one's soul to the ~** vender el alma al diablo; **better the ~ you know (than the devil you don't)** más vale malo conocido que bueno por conocer *prov;* **to go to the ~** irse al infierno; **there'll be the ~ to pay** se formará un lío de todos los diablos; **to play the ~ with sth** estropear algo; **speak of the ~** hablando del rey de Roma, por la puerta asoma; **how/who/what/where the ~ ...?** ¿cómo/quién/qué/dónde diablos...?; **like the ~** como el demonio

devilish ['devəlɪʃ] *adj* **1.** (*evil*) diabólico, -a **2.** (*mischievous*) malvado, -a **3.** (*extreme*) muy difícil; (*terrible*) extremo, -a **4.** (*very clever*) ingenioso, -a

devil-may-care [ˌdevəlmeɪ'keəʳ, *Am:* -'ker] *adj* irresponsable

devilment ['devəlmənt] *n,* **devilry** ['devəlri] *n no pl* diablura *f*

devious ['diːviəs] *adj* **1.** (*dishonest*) insincero, -a **2.** (*winding*) tortuoso, -a; (*route*) intrincado, -a

devise [dɪ'vaɪz] **I.** *n* legado *m* **II.** *vt* **1.** (*plan, think out*) idear; (*a plot*) diseñar; (*a scheme*) trazar **2.** (*leave property via a will*) legar

devoid [dɪ'vɔɪd] *adj* **to be ~ of sth** estar desprovisto de algo

devolution [ˌdiːvə'luːʃən, *Am:* ˌdevə'luː-] *n no pl* **1.** POL (*decentralisation of power*) delegación *f* **2.** (*progression through stages*) transferencia *f* **3.** (*transference of wealth*) traspaso *m*

devolve [dɪ'vɒlv, *Am:* dɪ'vɑːlv] **I.** *vi* recaer **II.** *vt* (*transfer*) transferir; (*powers*) delegar

devote [dɪ'vəʊt, *Am:* -'voʊt] *vt* dedicar; **to ~ oneself to sth** dedicarse a algo

devoted [dɪ'vəʊtɪd, *Am:* -'voʊt̬ɪd] *adj* dedicado, -a; (*husband, mother*) devoto, -a; **to be ~ to sb/sth** estar consagrado a alguien/algo

devotee [ˌdevə'tiː, *Am:* -ə'tiː] *n* (*supporter*) partidario, -a *m, f;* (*admirer*) fanático, -a *m, f;* (*advocate*) devoto, -a *m, f*

devotion [dɪ'vəʊʃən, *Am:* dɪ'voʊ-] *n no pl* **1.** (*loyalty*) lealtad *f;* (*affection*) afecto *m;*

D

(*admiration*) fervor *m;* (*great attachment*) dedicación *f;* **to inspire** ~ inspirar devoción **2.** REL devoción *f* **3.** (*devoutness*) piedad *f*
devotional [dɪ'vəʊʃənəl, *Am:* dɪ'voʊ-] *adj* (*attitude*) devoto, -a; (*music, practices*) piadoso, -a
devour [dɪ'vaʊəʳ, *Am:* dɪ'vaʊɚ] *vt* **1.** (*eat eagerly*) tragar **2.** (*engulf*) devorar **3.** (*consume quickly*) consumir **4.** (*feel strongly*) **to be ~ed by jealousy** estar consumido por los celos
devouring *adj* devorador(a)
devout [dɪ'vaʊt] *adj* **1.** REL devoto, -a **2.** (*compulsive*) fervoroso, -a
dew [dju:, *Am:* du:] *n no pl* rocío *m*
dewdrop ['dju:drɒp, *Am:* 'du:drɑ:p] *n* gota *f* de rocío
dewy ['dju:i, *Am:* 'du:-] *adj* cubierto, -a de rocío
dexterity [ˌdek'sterəti, *Am:* -əṱi] *n no pl* (*skilful handling*) agilidad *f*
dexterous ['dekstərəs] *adj* diestro, -a
dextrose ['dekstrəʊs, *Am:* -stroʊs] *n no pl* dextrosa *f*
dextrous ['dekstrəs] *adj s.* **dexterous**
diabetes [ˌdaɪə'bi:ti:z, *Am:* -ṱəs] *n no pl* diabetes *f*
diabetic [ˌdaɪə'betɪk, *Am:* -'beṱ-] **I.** *n* diabético, -a *m, f* **II.** *adj* (*who has diabetes*) diabético, -a
diabolic(**al**) [ˌdaɪə'bɒlɪk(əl), *Am:* -'bɑ:lɪk-] *adj* **1.** (*of Devil*) diabólico, -a **2.** (*evil*) malvado, -a **3.** *inf* (*very bad*) maligno, -a
diadem ['daɪədem] *n* (*crown*) diadema *f*
diagnose ['daɪəgnəʊz, *Am:* ˌdaɪəg'noʊs] **I.** *vi* hacer un diagnóstico **II.** *vt* diagnosticar
diagnosis [ˌdaɪəg'nəʊsɪs, *Am:* -'noʊ-] <-ses> *n* **1.** (*of a disease*) diagnóstico *m* **2.** (*science*) diagnosis *f inv*
diagnostic [ˌdaɪəg'nɒstɪk, *Am:* -'nɑ:stɪk] **I.** *n* diagnóstico *m* **II.** *adj* diagnóstico, -a
diagonal [daɪ'ægənl] **I.** *n* diagonal *f* **II.** *adj* diagonal
diagram ['daɪəgræm] **I.** *n* **1.** (*drawing*) diagrama *f;* (*plan*) esquema *f* **2.** (*chart*) gráfico *m* **3.** (*figure*) figura *f* **II.** <-mm-> *vt* diagramar
dial ['daɪəl] **I.** *n* **1.** (*clock face*) esfera *f* **2.** (*part of scale*) cuadrante *m* **3.** (*movable disc on a telephone*) disco *m* **4.** *Brit, inf* (*face*) cara *f* **II.** <*Brit:* -ll-, *Am:* -l-> *vi* marcar un número, discar *Arg, Perú, Urug* **III.** *vt* **1.** TEL marcar; **to ~ direct** hacer una llamada directa **2.** RADIO sintonizar
dialect ['daɪəlekt] *n* dialecto *m*
dialectal [ˌdaɪə'lektəl] *adj* dialectal
dialectical [ˌdaɪə'lektɪkəl] *adj* dialéctico, -a
dialling *n no pl* (*telephone*) marcación *f,* discado *m Arg, Perú, Urug*
dialog *n Am,* **dialogue** ['daɪəlɒg, *Am:* -lɑ:g] *n* **1.** (*conversation*) diálogo *m* **2.** POL interlocución *f;* **to engage in** ~ dialogar
dial-up service *n* INFOR servicio *m* de marcado
dialysis [daɪ'æləsɪs] *n no pl* diálisis *f*
diameter [daɪ'æmɪtəʳ, *Am:* -əṱɚ] *n* diámetro *m*
diametrically [ˌdaɪə'metrɪkəli] *adv* **1.** (*as a diameter*) diametralmente **2.** (*completely*) en su totalidad
diamond ['daɪəmənd] *n* **1.** (*precious stone*) diamante *m;* **the ace/king of ~s** GAMES el as/rey de diamantes **2.** (*rhombus*) rombo *m* **3.** (*tool for cutting glass*) cortavidrios *m inv* **4.** (*baseball field*) diamante *m;* (*infield*) cuadro *m* ►**a rough** ~ un diamante en bruto; ~ **cut** ~ *Brit* tal para cual
diamond cutter *n* diamantista *mf* **diamond wedding** *n* bodas *fpl* de diamante
diaper ['daɪəpəʳ, *Am:* -pɚ] *n Am* pañal *m*
diaphanous [daɪ'æfənəs] *adj liter* diáfano, -a; (*cloth*) transparente
diaphragm ['daɪəfræm] *n* diafragma *m*
diarist ['daɪərɪst] *n* diarista *mf*
diarrhea *n,* **diarrhoea** [ˌdaɪə'rɪə, *Am:* -'ri:ə] *n no pl* diarrea *f*
diary ['daɪəri] *n* **1.** (*journal*) diario *m* **2.** (*planner*) agenda *f*
diatonic [ˌdaɪə'tɒnɪk, *Am:* -'tɑ:nɪk] *adj* MUS diatónico, -a
diatribe ['daɪətraɪb] *n* diatriba *f*
dice [daɪs] **I.** *npl* **1.** (*cubes with spots*) dados *mpl;* **to roll the** ~ echar los dados **2.** (*game with dice*) juego *m* de dados **3.** (*food in small cubes*) tacos *mpl* ►**no** ~ *Am, inf* de ninguna manera **II.** *vi* jugar a los dados **III.** *vt* cortar en tacos
dicey ['daɪsi] <-ier, -iest> *adj Brit, Aus, inf* peligroso, -a
dichotomy [daɪ'kɒtəmi, *Am:* -'kɑ:ṱə-] *n* dicotomía *f*
dick [dɪk] *n* **1.** *vulg* (*penis*) polla *f,* pija *f AmL,* paloma *f Méx, Ven,* pajarito *m RíoPl* **2.** *vulg* (*stupid person*) gilipollas *mf inv*
dickens ['dɪkɪnz] *npl inf* **what the ~ ...?** ¿qué diablos...?
dicky ['dɪki] *n Brit, inf* **a ~ heart** una debilidad cardiaca
dictaphone® ['dɪktəfəʊn, *Am:* -foʊn] *n* dictáfono *m*
dictate[1] ['dɪkteɪt] *n* dictado *m*
dictate[2] [dɪk'teɪt, *Am:* 'dɪkteɪt] **I.** *vi* **1.** (*command*) mandar **2.** (*state sth exactly*) dictar; **to ~ to sb** dictar a alguien **II.** *vt* **1.** (*give orders*) ordenar **2.** (*make necessary*) influir; (*state exactly*) imponer
dictation [dɪk'teɪʃən] *n no pl* SCHOOL dictado *m*
dictator [dɪk'teɪtəʳ, *Am:* 'dɪkteɪṱɚ] *n* POL dictador(a) *m(f)*
dictatorial [ˌdɪktə'tɔ:riəl] *adj* dictatorial
dictatorship [dɪk'teɪtəʃɪp, *Am:* -ṱɚ-] *n* dictadura *f*
diction ['dɪkʃən] *n no pl* dicción *f*
dictionary ['dɪkʃənəri, *Am:* -eri] *n* diccionario *m*
did [dɪd] *pt of* **do**

didactic [dɪ'dæktɪk, *Am:* daɪ-] *adj* didáctico, -a
diddle ['dɪdl] *vt inf* timar; **to ~ sb out of sth** estafar algo a alguien
didn't [dɪdənt] = **did not** *s.* **do**
die¹ [daɪ] *n* **1.** dado *m* **2.** TECH molde *m* ►**as straight as a ~** más derecho que una vela; **the ~ is cast** la suerte está echada
die² [daɪ] <dying, died> *vi* **1.** (*cease to live*) morir; **to ~ a violent/natural death** morir de muerte violenta/natural; **to ~ by one's own hand** suicidarse **2.** (*end*) desaparecer; **the secret will ~ with her** se llevará el secreto a la tumba **3.** (*stop functioning*) dejar de servir; **the engine just ~d** *Am* el motor se ha muerto **4.** (*go out, fade away*) extinguirse ►**to ~ hard** persistir; **never say ~!** ¡nunca te rindas!; **to do or ~** vencer o morir; **to ~ to do sth** tener muchas ganas de hacer algo; **I'm dying for a cup of tea** me muero por una taza de té
◆**die away** *vi* desaparecer; (*sobs, anger*) calmarse; (*enthusiasm*) decaer; (*wind*) amainar; (*sound*) apagarse
◆**die back** *vi* secarse
◆**die down** *vi* apagarse
◆**die off** *vi* (*species*) extinguirse; (*customs*) desaparecer
◆**die out** *vi* extinguirse
dieback ['daɪˌbæk] *n* muerte *f* de los bosques (*a causa de la polución del medio ambiente*)
diehard ['daɪhɑːd, *Am:* -hɑːrd] *n* intransigente *mf;* **a ~ conservative** un conservador recalcitrante
diesel ['diːzəl, *Am:* -səl] *n no pl* diesel *m*
diesel engine *n* motor *m* diesel **diesel oil** *n* aceite *m* diesel
diet¹ ['daɪət] **I.** *n* dieta *f;* **staple ~** dieta básica; **to be on a ~** estar a dieta; **to put sb on a ~** poner a alguien a dieta; **to go on a ~** seguir una dieta **II.** *vi* estar a dieta **III.** *vt* **to ~ sb** poner a alguien a dieta
diet² ['daɪət] *n* (*legislative body*) asamblea *f* legislativa
dietary ['daɪətəri, *Am:* 'daɪəter-] *adj* (*food*) dietético, -a; (*habit*) de alimentación
dietary fibre *n* fibra *f* dietética
dietetic [ˌdaɪə'tetɪk, *Am:* -'teṭ-] *adj* dietético, -a
dietetics *n no pl* dietética *f*
dietician *n,* **dietitian** [ˌdaɪə'tɪʃən] *n* dietista *mf*
differ ['dɪfəʳ, *Am:* -ɚ] *vi* **1.** (*be unlike*) ser diferente; **to ~ from sth** ser distinto de algo **2.** (*disagree*) no estar de acuerdo; **to ~ about sth** (*persons*) discrepar en algo
difference ['dɪfərənts] *n* **1.** (*state of being different*) diferencia *f* **2.** (*distinction*) distinción *f;* **that makes all the ~** eso cambia todo; **to make a ~** importar; **to not make any ~** ser igual **3.** (*new feature*) singularidad *f* **4.** (*amount left*) **to pay the ~** pagar la diferencia **5.** (*disagreement*) discrepancia *f;* **to put aside ~s** apartar las diferencias; **to settle ~s** resolver diferencias; **to sink one's ~s** olvidar las diferencias
different ['dɪfərənt] *adj* **1.** (*not the same*) diferente **2.** (*distinct*) distinto, -a **3.** (*unusual*) raro, -a; **to do something ~** romper la rutina ►**to be as ~ as chalk and cheese** *Brit, Aus,* **to be as ~ as night and day** *Am* ser la noche y el día
differential [ˌdɪfə'rentʃəl] **I.** *n* **1.** *a.* MAT diferencial *m* **2.** (*difference in pay*) **pay ~s** diferencia *f* de sueldo **II.** *adj* **1.** (*different*) diferente **2.** MAT diferencial
differentiate [ˌdɪfə'rentʃieɪt] **I.** *vi* distinguir **II.** *vt* **to ~ one wine from another** distinguir un vino de otro
differentiation [ˌdɪfərentʃi'eɪʃən] *n* diferenciación *f*
difficult ['dɪfɪkəlt] *adj* **1.** (*not easy*) difícil; **she is said to be a very ~ person** dicen que es una persona muy difícil **2.** (*troublesome*) duro, -a
difficulty ['dɪfɪkəlti, *Am:* -ṭi] <-ies> *n* **1.** *no pl* (*being difficult*) dificultad *f;* **with ~** difícilmente **2.** (*problem*) obstáculo *m;* **to be in difficulties** estar en apuros; **to be in difficulties with sb** tener problemas con alguien; **to encounter difficulties** encontrar dificultades; **to have ~ doing sth** tener problemas para hacer algo
diffident ['dɪfɪdənt] *adj* (*shy*) tímido, -a; (*modest*) modesto, -a
diffract [dɪ'frækt] *vt* difractar
diffuse¹ [dɪ'fjuːz] **I.** *vi* difundirse **II.** *vt* difundir
diffuse² [dɪ'fjuːs] *adj* **1.** (*spread out*) dilatado, -a **2.** (*imprecise*) difuso, -a **3.** (*verbose*) verboso, -a
diffusion [dɪ'fjuːʒən] *n no pl* **1.** (*process of diffusing*) difusión *f* **2.** CHEM, PHYS dispersión *f*
dig [dɪg] **I.** *n* **1.** (*excavation*) excavación *f* **2.** (*poke*) empujón *m* **3.** (*sarcastic remark*) pulla *f;* **to have ~s at sb** meterse con alguien **II.** <-gg-, dug, dug> *vi* **1.** (*turn over ground*) escarbar; **to ~ deeper** ahondar **2.** (*poke*) empujar **III.** *vt* **1.** (*move ground*) cavar; (*a well, canal*) abrir **2.** (*excavate*) excavar **3.** (*stab, poke*) clavar; **to dig one's elbow into sb's ribs** dar un codazo en las costillas a alguien; **to dig one's spurs into a horse** hincar las espuelas en un caballo **4.** *inf* (*like*) gustar ►**to ~ one's own grave** cavarse su propia tumba
◆**dig in I.** *vi inf* (*start eating*) atacar **II.** *vt* **1.** enterrar **2.** (*dig trenches*) atrincherarse **3.** (*establish oneself*) instalarse; (*settle in*) asentarse
◆**dig into I.** *vi* clavar ►**to dig (deeper) into one's pockets** buscar en los bolsillos **II.** *vt always sep inf* atacar ►**to dig oneself into a hole** meterse en un problema
◆**dig out** *vt* (*hole*) excavar; (*buried object*) extraer
◆**dig up** *vt* **1.** (*retrieve from ground*) desen-

terrar **2.** (*excavate*) remover **3.** (*find out*) descubrir

digest[1] ['daɪdʒest] *n* **1.** (*summary of laws*) digesto *m* **2.** (*summary of report*) resumen *m*

digest[2] [daɪ'dʒest] **I.** *vi* (*food*) digerirse; (*break down food*) digerir la comida **II.** *vt* **1.** (*break down: food*) digerir **2.** (*understand*) asimilar **3.** (*decompose*) descomponer **4.** (*classify*) clasificar

digestible [daɪ'dʒestəbl] *adj* digerible

digestion [daɪ'dʒestʃən] *n* digestión *f*

digestive [daɪ'dʒestɪv] *adj* digestivo, -a

digger ['dɪgəʳ, *Am:* -ɚ] *n* **1.** (*machine for digging*) excavadora *f* **2.** (*person*) cavador(a) *m(f); Aus* (*gold miner*) minero, -a *m, f* **3.** *Aus, inf* (*soldier*) australiano, -a *m, f*

digit ['dɪdʒɪt] *n* **1.** (*number from 0 to 9*) dígito *m* **2.** (*finger, toe*) dedo *m*

digital ['dɪdʒɪtl, *Am:* -t̬l] *adj* digital

digitalize ['dɪdʒɪtəlaɪz, *Am:* -t̬əlaɪz] *vt* digitalizar

digitize ['dɪdʒɪtaɪz] *vt* INFOR digitalizar

digitizer ['dɪdʒɪtaɪzəʳ, *Am:* -ɚ] *n* INFOR digitalizador *m*

dignified ['dɪgnɪfaɪd] *adj* **1.** (*worthy of respect*) digno, -a **2.** (*solemn*) solemne

dignify ['dɪgnɪfaɪ] <-ie-> *vt* dignificar

dignitary ['dɪgnɪtəri, *Am:* -nəter-] <-ies> *n* dignatario, -a *m, f*

dignity ['dɪgnəti, *Am:* -t̬i] *n no pl* **1.** (*composed style*) decoro *m* **2.** (*state worthy of respect*) dignidad *f* **3.** (*respect*) respeto *m;* **to be beneath sb's** ~ no ser digno de alguien

digress [daɪ'gres] *vi* **1.** (*wander*) hacer una digresión **2.** (*deviate*) desviarse; **to** ~ **from sth** salirse de algo

digressive [daɪ'gresɪv] *adj* digresivo, -a

dike [daɪk] *n* dique *m*

dilapidated [dɪ'læpɪdeɪtɪd, *Am:* -t̬ɪd] *adj* (*house*) derruido, -a; (*car*) destartalado, -a

dilate [daɪ'leɪt, *Am:* 'daɪleɪt] **I.** *vi* dilatarse **II.** *vt* dilatar

dilation [daɪ'leɪʃən] *n no pl* dilatación *f*

dilatory ['dɪlətəri, *Am:* -tɔːri] *adj* **1.** (*slow*) lento, -a **2.** LAW dilatorio, -a

dilemma [dɪ'lemə, daɪ'lemə] *n* dilema *m;* **to be in a** ~ estar en un dilema; **to face a** ~ enfrentarse a un dilema

dilettante [ˌdɪlɪ'tænti, *Am:* -ə'tɑːnt] *n* <-s *o* -ti> diletante *mf*

diligence ['dɪlɪdʒəns] *n no pl* (*effort, care*) diligencia *f*

diligent ['dɪlɪdʒənt] *adj* (*careful*) concienzudo, -a; (*hard-working*) diligente; **he is** ~ **about his work** es diligente en su trabajo

dill [dɪl] *n no pl* eneldo *m*

dillydally ['dɪlɪdæli] *vi* **1.** *inf* (*dawdle*) perder el tiempo **2.** *inf* (*vacillate*) vacilar

dilute [daɪ'ljuːt, *Am:* -'luːt] **I.** *vt* diluir **II.** *vi* diluirse **III.** *adj* diluido, -a

dilution [daɪ'ljuːʃən, *Am:* -'luː-] *n no pl, a. fig* disolución *f*

dim [dɪm] **I.** <-mm-> *vi* (*colour*) apagarse **II.** *vt* apagar **III.** <-mm-> *adj* **1.** (*not bright*) tenue **2.** (*unclear*) borroso, -a **3.** (*stupid*) lerdo, -a **4.** (*unfavourable*) sombrío, -a

dime [daɪm] *n* moneda *f* de diez centavos ►**a** ~ **a dozen** del montón

dimension [ˌdaɪ'mentʃən, *Am:* dɪ'mentʃən] **I.** *n* dimensión *f* **II.** *vt Am* dimensionar

dimensional [ˌdaɪ'mentʃənəl, *Am:* dɪ'mentʃən-] *adj* dimensional

diminish [dɪ'mɪnɪʃ] **I.** *vi* disminuir; **to** ~ **(greatly) in value** perder mucho valor **II.** *vt* **1.** (*make less*) disminuir **2.** (*damage sb's reputation*) rebajar

diminution [ˌdɪmɪ'njuːʃən, *Am:* -ə'nuː-] *n* disminución *f*

diminutive [dɪ'mɪnjʊtɪv, *Am:* -jət̬ɪv] **I.** *n* LING diminutivo *m* **II.** *adj* (*very small*) diminuto, -a

dimmer ['dɪməʳ, *Am:* -ɚ] *n,* **dimmer switch** *n* potenciómetro *m*

dimness *n no pl* penumbra *f*

dimple ['dɪmpl] **I.** *n* hoyuelo *m* **II.** *vt* formar hoyuelos en

din [dɪn] *n no pl* estrépito *m*

dine [daɪn] *vi* cenar

diner ['daɪnəʳ, *Am:* -nɚ] *n* **1.** (*person*) comensal *mf* **2.** *Am* (*restaurant at the side of the road*) restaurante *m* de carretera

dinghy ['dɪŋgi, *Am:* 'dɪŋi] *n* <-ies> bote *m*

dingo ['dɪŋgəʊ, *Am:* -goʊ] *n* <-es> dingo *m*

dingy ['dɪndʒi] <-ier, -iest> *adj* deslustrado, -a

dining car *n no pl* (*car*) vagón *m* restaurante **dining room** *n* comedor *m*

dinky[1] ['dɪŋki] <-ies> *n abbr of* **double income no kids** *pareja con dos sueldos y sin hijos*

dinky[2] ['dɪŋki] *adj* **1.** (*dainty*) mono, -a **2.** *Am* (*insignificant*) pobre

dinner ['dɪnəʳ, *Am:* -ɚ] *n* (*evening meal*) cena *f;* (*lunch*) almuerzo *m;* **to make** ~ hacer la cena

dinner jacket *n* esmoquin *m* **dinner party** *n* cena *f* **dinner service** *n,* **dinner set** *n* vajilla *f* **dinner table** *n* mesa *f* de comedor

dinnertime *n no pl* hora *f* de cenar

dinosaur ['daɪnəsɔːʳ, *Am:* -sɔːr] *n* **1.** (*extinct reptile*) dinosaurio *m* **2.** *fig* (*old-fashioned object*) antigualla *f*

dint [dɪnt] *n* **by** ~ **of sth** a fuerza de algo

diocese ['daɪəsɪs] *n* diócesis *f*

dioxide [daɪ'ɒksaɪd, *Am:* -'ɑːk-] *n no pl* dióxido *m*

dioxin [daɪ'ɒksɪn, *Am:* -'ɑːk-] *n* dioxina *f*

dip [dɪp] **I.** *n* **1.** (*instance of dipping*) baño *m* **2.** (*sudden drop*) caída *f;* (*of a road*) hondonada *f* **3.** (*liquid*) salsa *f* **4.** (*brief swim*) chapuzón *m* **5.** (*depression of horizon, ground*) depresión *f* **6.** (*angle made by magnetic field*) inclinación *f* **II.** *vi* **1.** (*drop down*) descender **2.** (*slope down*) inclinarse **3.** (*submerge and re-emerge*) zambullirse **III.** *vt* **1.** (*immerse*) sumergir; *a.* GASTR mojar **2.** (*put into*) meter

3. (*lower*) bajar 4. (*dye*) teñir 5. (*wash*) desinfectar

◆**dip into** I. *vt always sep* (*put*) meter II. *vi* (*look at casually*) hojear

Dip *abbr of* **Diploma** D

diphtheria [dɪfˈθɪəriə, *Am:* -ˈθɪri-] *n* MED difteria *f*

diphthong [ˈdɪfθɒŋ, *Am:* -θɑːŋ] *n* LING diptongo *m*

diploma [dɪˈpləʊmə, *Am:* -ˈploʊ-] *n* (*certificate*) diploma *m*; **a ~ in sth** un diploma de algo

diplomacy [dɪˈpləʊməsi, *Am:* -ˈploʊ-] *n no pl* 1. (*managing relationships between countries*) diplomacia *f* 2. (*tact*) tacto *m*

diplomat [ˈdɪpləmæt] *n* 1. (*of country*) diplomático, -a *m, f* 2. (*tactful person*) persona *f* diplomática

diplomatic [ˌdɪpləˈmætɪk, *Am:* -ˈmæt̬-] *adj* diplomático, -a

diplomatist [dɪˈpləʊmətɪst, *Am:* -ˈploʊmət̬ɪst] *n s.* **diplomat**

dipper [ˈdɪpəʳ, *Am:* -ɚ] *n* mirlo *m* acuático

dipsomania [ˌdɪpsəʊˈmeɪniə, *Am:* -səˈ-] *n no pl* MED dipsomanía *f*

dipsomaniac [ˌdɪpsəʊˈmeɪniæk, *Am:* -səˈ-] *n* MED dipsómano, -a *m, f*

dipstick [ˈdɪpstɪk] *n* varilla *f* de medir

dip-switch [ˈdɪpswɪtʃ] *n* AUTO conmutador *m* de luces

dire [ˈdaɪəʳ, *Am:* ˈdaɪɚ] *adj* 1. (*terrible*) horrendo, -a 2. (*serious*) grave 3. (*extreme*) extremo, -a

direct [dɪˈrekt] I. *vi* MUS dirigir II. *vt* 1. dirigir; **to ~ sth at sb** dirigir algo a alguien 2. (*command*) ordenar 3. (*indicate*) **to ~ sb to a place** indicar a alguien el camino hacia un sitio III. *adj* 1. (*straight*) directo, -a 2. (*exact*) exacto, -a; **the ~ opposite of sth** exactamente lo contrario de algo IV. *adv* 1. (*with no intermediary*) directamente 2. (*by a direct way*) recto

direct action *n* acción *f* directa **direct current** *n no pl* corriente *f* continua **direct debit** *n* domiciliación *f* bancaria **direct dial** *n* marcación *f* directa, discado *m* directo *Arg, Perú, Urug,* marcado *m* automático *Méx* **direct hit** *n* impacto *m* en la diana

direction [dɪˈrekʃən] *n no pl* 1. (*supervision*) dirección *f* 2. (*movement*) **in the ~ of sth** en dirección a/hacia algo; **sense of ~** sentido *m* de la orientación 3. *pl* (*information*) instrucciones *fpl;* **can you give me directions?** ¿me puedes indicar el camino?

directional [dɪˈrekʃənəl] *adj* direccional

directive [dɪˈrektɪv] *n* directriz *f,* directiva *f AmL*

directly [dɪˈrektli] I. *adv* 1. (*frankly*) directamente 2. (*immediately*) inmediatamente; (*right after*) inmediatamente después 3. (*shortly*) pronto 4. (*exactly*) exactamente II. *conj* en cuanto

direct object *n* objeto *m* directo

director [dɪˈrektəʳ, *Am:* dɪˈrektɚ] *n* 1. ECON (*manager*) director(a) *m(f)* 2. (*board member*) miembro *m* del consejo; **board of ~s** consejo *m* de administración

directorate [dɪˈrektərət] *n* 1. (*responsible department*) directiva *f* 2. (*board of directors*) junta *f* directiva

directorship [dɪˈrektəʃɪp, *Am:* dɪˈrektɚ-] *n* dirección *f*

directory [dɪˈrektəri] *n* 1. (*book*) guía *f,* directorio *m Méx;* **to look sth up in a ~** buscar algo en una guía 2. INFOR directorio *m;* **~ structure** estructura *f* de directorios

directory enquiries *n Brit* servicio *m* de información telefónica

dirt [dɜːt, *Am:* dɜːrt] *n no pl* 1. (*unclean substance*) suciedad *f* 2. (*earth, soil*) tierra *f* 3. (*foul language*) obscenidad *f* 4. (*scandal*) trapos *mpl* sucios *fig* 5. (*excrement*) excremento *mpl* 6. (*worthless thing*) porquería *f;* **to treat sb like ~** tratar a alguien como basura ►**to eat ~** tragar quina

dirt cheap *adj inf* tirado, -a, botado, -a *Méx*

dirt road *n Brit, Aus,* **dirt track** *n* pista *f* de tierra, camino *m* de terracería *Méx*

dirty [ˈdɜːti, *Am:* ˈdɜːrt̬i] I. *n Brit, Aus* **to do the ~ on sb** hacer una mala pasada a alguien II. *vt* ensuciar; **to ~ one's hands** ensuciarse las manos III. <-ier, -iest> *adj* 1. (*unclean*) sucio, -a, chancho, -a *AmL* 2. (*mean, nasty*) bajo, -a 3. (*lewd*) obsceno, -a; (*joke*) verde; (*look*) lascivo, -a; **~ old man** viejo verde 4. (*unpleasant*) sucio, -a; **to do the ~ work** hacer el trabajo sucio IV. *adv Brit* suciamente; **to play ~** jugar sucio

disability [ˌdɪsəˈbɪləti, *Am:* -ət̬i] *n* 1. (*incapacity*) discapacidad *f,* invalidez *f AmL* 2. *no pl* (*condition of incapacity*) incapacidad *f*

disable [dɪˈseɪbl] *vt* 1. incapacitar 2. MED lisiar

disabled I. *npl* **the ~** los discapacitados II. *adj* incapacitado, -a

disablement *n no pl* incapacitación *f;* MED minusvalía *f*

disabuse [ˌdɪsəˈbjuːz] *vt* **to ~ sb of sth** desengañar a alguien de algo

disadvantage [ˌdɪsədˈvɑːntɪdʒ, *Am:* -ˈvænt̬ɪdʒ] I. *n* desventaja *f;* **to be at a ~** estar en desventaja II. *vt* perjudicar

disadvantaged *adj* desfavorecido, -a

disadvantageous [ˌdɪsˌædvənˈteɪdʒəs, *Am:* ˌdɪsˌædvænˈ-] *adj* desventajoso, -a

disaffected [ˌdɪsəˈfektɪd] *adj* 1. (*disloyal*) desleal 2. (*estranged*) desafecto, -a

disaffection [ˌdɪsəˈfekʃən] *n no pl* desafección *f*

disagree [ˌdɪsəˈgriː] *vi* 1. (*not agree*) discrepar; **to ~ on sth** no estar de acuerdo en algo 2. (*differ*) diferir; **the answers ~** las respuestas no concuerdan 3. (*have bad effect*) sentar mal; **spicy food ~s with me** la comida picante me sienta mal

disagreeable [ˌdɪsəˈgriːəbl] *adj* desagra-

D

dable

disagreement [ˌdɪsəˈgriːmənt] *n no pl* 1. (*lack of agreement*) desacuerdo *m* 2. (*argument*) discusión *f* 3. (*discrepancy*) discrepancia *f*

disallow [ˌdɪsəˈlaʊ] *vt* (*not allow*) rechazar; *a.* LAW, SPORTS anular

disappear [ˌdɪsəˈpɪəʳ, *Am:* -ˈpɪr] *vi* desaparecer; **to ~ from sight** desaparecer de la vista; **to ~ without a trace** desaparecer sin dejar rastro; **to have all but ~ed** haber casi desaparecido

disappearance [ˌdɪsəˈpɪərənts, *Am:* -ˈpɪr-] *n no pl* desaparición *f*

disappoint [ˌdɪsəˈpɔɪnt] *vt* decepcionar, enchilar *AmC*

disappointed *adj* decepcionado, -a; **to be ~ in sb** estar decepcionado con alguien

disappointing *adj* decepcionante

disappointment [ˌdɪsəˈpɔɪntmənt] *n* decepción *f*

disapprobation [ˌdɪsæprəʊˈbeɪʃən, *Am:* ˌdɪsˌæprəˈ-] *n no pl* desaprobación *f*

disapproval [ˌdɪsəˈpruːvəl] *n no pl* desaprobación *f*

disapprove [ˌdɪsəˈpruːv] *vi* desaprobar

◆**disapprove of** *vt* desaprobar

disarm [dɪsˈɑːm, *Am:* -ɑːrm] I. *vi* (*stop holding weapons*) deponer las armas II. *vt* 1. (*take weapons away*) desarmar 2. (*remove fuse*) desactivar 3. (*placate*) apaciguar

disarmament [dɪsˈɑːməmənt, *Am:* -ɑːr-] *n no pl* desarme *m*

disarming [dɪsˈɑːmɪŋ, *Am:* -ɑːrmɪŋ] *adj* 1. MIL que quita las defensas 2. (*person*) encantador(a)

disarrange [ˌdɪsəˈreɪndʒ] *vt* desarreglar

disarray [ˌdɪsəˈreɪ] *n no pl* (*disorder*) desorden *m;* (*confusion*) confusión *f*

disaster [dɪˈzɑːstəʳ, *Am:* dɪˈzæstɚ] *n* 1. (*great misfortune*) desastre *m;* **~ area** zona *f* catastrófica 2. (*failure*) fiasco *m*

disastrous [dɪˈzɑːstrəs, *Am:* dɪˈzæstrəs] *adj* 1. (*causing disaster*) desastroso, -a 2. (*very unsuccessful*) catastrófico, -a

disband [dɪsˈbænd] *vt* disolver

disbelief [ˌdɪsbɪˈliːf] *n no pl* incredulidad *f*

disbelieve [ˌdɪsbɪˈliːv] *vt* no creer

disbeliever *n* incrédulo, -a *m, f*

disburse [dɪsˈbɜːs, *Am:* -ˈbɜːrs] *vt* desembolsar

disbursement [dɪsˈbɜːsmənt, *Am:* -ˈbɜːrs-] *n* desembolso *m*

disc [dɪsk] *n* disco *m*

discard¹ [ˈdɪskɑːd, *Am:* -kɑːrd] *n* descarte *m*

discard² [dɪˈskɑːd, *Am:* -skɑːrd] *vt* 1. (*get rid of*) desechar 2. *a.* GAMES descartar

disc brake *n* freno *m* de disco

discern [dɪˈsɜːn, *Am:* dɪˈsɜːrn] *vt* 1. (*perceive*) percibir; (*distinguish*) distinguir 2. (*make out*) discernir

discernable *adj,* **discernible** [dɪˈsɜːnəbl, *Am:* dɪˈsɜːr-] *adj* (*with senses*) perceptible; (*mentally*) discernible

discerning [dɪˈsɜːnɪŋ, *Am:* dɪˈsɜːr-] *adj* (*discriminating*) exigente; (*acute*) perspicaz

discernment [dɪˈsɜːnmənt, *Am:* dɪˈsɜːrn-] *n no pl* (*good judgement*) criterio *m;* (*clear perception*) discernimiento *m*

discharge¹ [ˈdɪstʃɑːdʒ, *Am:* ˈdɪstʃɑːrdʒ] *n no pl* 1. (*release*) liberación *f* 2. (*release papers*) alta *f* 3. (*firing off*) disparo *m* 4. (*emission*) emisión *f* 5. (*of liquid*) secreción *f* 6. (*debt payment*) liquidación *f* 7. (*performing of a duty*) desempeño *m* 8. (*energy release*) descarga *f*

discharge² [dɪsˈtʃɑːdʒ, *Am:* -ˈtʃɑːrdʒ] I. *vi* 1. (*ship*) descargar 2. (*produce liquid*) secretar; (*wound*) supurar II. *vt* 1. LAW liberar 2. MIL, ECON (*dismiss*) despedir 3. (*let out*) emitir 4. (*utter*) gritar 5. (*perform*) **to ~ one's duty** cumplir con sus obligaciones 6. (*pay: debt*) liquidar 7. (*cancel*) cancelar 8. (*release*) liberar 9. (*unload*) descargar

disciple [dɪˈsaɪpl] *n* 1. (*follower*) seguidor(a) *m(f)* 2. *a.* REL (*pupil*) discípulo, -a *m, f*

disciplinary [ˌdɪsəˈplɪnəri, *Am:* ˈdɪsəplɪner-] *adj* disciplinario, -a

discipline [ˈdɪsəplɪn] I. *n* 1. *no pl* (*obedience*) disciplina *f* 2. *no pl* (*self-punishment*) auto-castigo *m* II. *vt* 1. (*punish*) castigar; **to ~ oneself to do sth** obligarse a hacer algo 2. (*train*) disciplinar

disciplined *adj* disciplinado, -a

disc jockey *n* disc jockey *mf,* pinchadiscos *mf inv*

disclaim [dɪsˈkleɪm] *vt* 1. (*deny*) negar 2. (*give up right to*) renunciar a

disclaimer [dɪsˈkleɪməʳ, *Am:* -mɚ] *n* 1. (*denial*) descargo *m* de responsabilidad 2. (*repudiating a claim*) repudio *m*

disclose [dɪsˈkləʊz, *Am:* -ˈkloʊz] *vt* 1. (*make public*) divulgar 2. (*uncover*) desvelar

disclosure [dɪsˈkləʊʒəʳ, *Am:* -ˈkloʊʒɚ] *n* 1. (*act of making public*) divulgación *f* 2. (*revelation*) revelación *f*

disco [ˈdɪskəʊ, *Am:* -koʊ] *n* 1. *no pl* (*music*) música *f* disco 2. (*place*) discoteca *f*

discolor *Am, Aus,* **discolour** [dɪˈskʌləʳ, *Am:* -ˈskʌlɚ] I. *vi* desteñirse II. *vt* decolorar; **my blue shirt has ~d the curtains** mi camisa azul ha desteñido en las cortinas

discomfit [dɪˈskʌmpfɪt] *vt* desconcertar

discomfiture [dɪˈskʌmpfɪtʃəʳ, *Am:* -tʃɚ] *n no pl* (*uneasiness*) turbación *f;* (*confusion*) desconcierto *m*

discomfort [dɪˈskʌmpfət, *Am:* -fɚt] *n* 1. *no pl* (*uneasiness*) malestar *m;* **~ at sth** malestar respecto a algo 2. (*inconvenience*) molestia *f*

disconcert [ˌdɪskənˈsɜːt, *Am:* -ˈsɜːrt] *vt* desconcertar

disconnect [ˌdɪskəˈnekt] *vt* 1. (*phone*) desconectar 2. (*customer*) cortar el suministro a 3. (*unfasten*) separar

disconnected *adj* 1. (*cut off*) desconectado, -a 2. (*incoherent*) inconexo, -a

disconsolate [dɪ'skɒntsələt, *Am:* -skɑːnt-] *adj* desconsolado, -a
discontent [ˌdɪskən'tent] **I.** *n no pl* descontento *m* **II.** *adj* descontento, -a
discontented *adj* descontento, -a
discontentment *n no pl s.* **discontent**
discontinue [ˌdɪskən'tɪnjuː] **I.** *vi* desistir **II.** *vt* suspender
discontinuity [ˌdɪsˌkɒntɪ'njuːəti, *Am:* ˌdɪs-kɑːntən'uːət̬i] <-ies> *n* **1.** (*lack of continuity*) discontinuidad *f* **2.** (*gap*) laguna *f*
discontinuous [ˌdɪskən'tɪnjuəs] *adj* (*without continuity*) discontinuo, -a; (*broken*) interrumpido, -a
discord ['dɪskɔːd, *Am:* -kɔːrd] *n no pl* **1.** (*disagreement*) discordia *f* **2.** (*clashing noise*) discordancia *f* **3.** (*lack of harmony*) disonancia *f*
discordant [dɪ'skɔːdənt, *Am:* -'skɔːr-] *adj* **1.** (*disagreeing*) discordante **2.** (*not in harmony*) disonante
discotheque ['dɪskətek] *n* discoteca *f*
discount[1] ['dɪskaʊnt] *n* descuento *m;* **at a** ~ con descuento
discount[2] [dɪ'skaʊnt] *vt* **1.** (*reduce selling price*) descontar **2.** (*disregard*) no hacer caso de **3.** (*leave out*) dejar de lado
discount store *n* tienda *f* de descuento
discourage [dɪ'skʌrɪdʒ, *Am:* -'skɜːr-] *vt* **1.** (*dishearten*) desanimar **2.** (*dissuade*) **to** ~ **sb from doing sth** disuadir a alguien de hacer algo **3.** (*oppose*) desaprobar
discouragement [dɪ'skʌrɪdʒ, *Am:* -'skɜːr-] *n* **1.** *no pl* (*feeling discouraged*) desaliento *m* **2.** (*deterrent*) impedimento *m*
discouraging *adj* desalentador(a)
discourse[1] ['dɪskɔːs, *Am:* -kɔːrs] *n* discurso *m;* (*written*) tratado *m;* **a** ~ **about** [*o* **on**] **sth** un discurso sobre algo; (*written*) un tratado sobre algo
discourse[2] [dɪ'skɔːs, *Am:* -'skɔːrs] *vi* hablar; **to** ~ **upon sth** conversar sobre algo, platicar sobre algo *AmL*
discourteous [dɪs'kɜːtiəs, *Am:* -kɜːrt̬i-] *adj* descortés
discourtesy [dɪs'kɜːtəsi, *Am:* -kɜːrt̬ə-] <-ies> *n* **1.** *no pl* (*rudeness*) descortesía *f* **2.** (*act of rudeness*) grosería *f*
discover [dɪ'skʌvəʳ, *Am:* -ɚ] *vt* **1.** (*find out*) descubrir **2.** (*find*) hallar
discoverer *n* descubridor(a) *m(f)*
discovery [dɪ'skʌvəri] <-ies> *n* descubrimiento *m*
Discovery Day *n no pl, Can* Día *m* del Descubrimiento (de América)
discredit [dɪ'skredɪt] **I.** *n no pl* **1.** (*disrepute*) desprestigio *m* **2.** (*disgrace*) vergüenza *f;* **she is a** ~ **to her school** es una vergüenza para su escuela **3.** (*doubt*) duda *f* **II.** *vt* desacreditar
discreditable [dɪ'skredɪtəbl, *Am:* -t̬ə-] *adj* deshonroso, -a
discreet [dɪ'skriːt] *adj* discreto, -a
discrepancy [dɪ'skrepəntsi] <-ies> *n* discrepancia *f*
discrete [dɪ'skriːt] *adj* separado, -a
discretion [dɪ'skreʃən] *n no pl* **1.** (*discreet behaviour*) discreción *f;* **to leave sth to sb's** ~ dejar algo a discreción de alguien **2.** (*good judgment*) criterio *m* **3.** LAW (*of court*) arbitrio *m*
discriminate [dɪ'skrɪmɪneɪt] **I.** *vi* **1.** (*see a difference*) discernir **2.** (*treat unfairly*) **to** ~ **against sb** discriminar a alguien **II.** *vt* distinguir
discriminating *adj* **1.** (*able to discern*) discerniente **2.** (*palate, taste*) exigente
discrimination [dɪˌskrɪmɪ'neɪʃən] *n no pl* **1.** (*unfair treatment*) discriminación *f* **2.** (*good judgement*) criterio *m* **3.** (*ability to differentiate*) discernimiento *m*
discriminatory [dɪ'skrɪmɪnətəri, *Am:* -tɔːri] *adj* discriminatorio, -a
discursive [dɪ'skɜːsɪv, *Am:* -'skɜːr-] *adj* digresivo, -a
discus ['dɪskəs] *n* SPORTS disco *m*
discuss [dɪ'skʌs] *vt* **1.** (*exchange ideas about*) discutir **2.** (*consider*) tratar sobre
discussion [dɪ'skʌʃən] *n* discusión *f,* argumento *m AmL;* ~ **group** grupo *m* de discusión
disdain [dɪs'deɪn] **I.** *n no pl* desdén *m* **II.** *vt* desdeñar; **to** ~ **to do sth** no dignarse a hacer algo; **powerful men** ~ **the weak** los poderosos desdeñan al débil
disdainful [dɪs'deɪnfəl] *adj* desdeñoso, -a
disease [dɪ'ziːz] *n a. fig* enfermedad *f;* **to catch a** ~ contraer una enfermedad
diseased *adj a. fig* enfermo, -a
disembark [ˌdɪsɪm'bɑːk, *Am:* -'bɑːrk] *vi* desembarcar
disembarkation [ˌdɪsˌɪmbɑː'keɪʃən, *Am:* -bɑːr'-] *n* desembarque *m*
disembodied [ˌdɪsɪm'bɒdid, *Am:* -bɑːdid] *adj* incorpóreo, -a
disenchant [ˌdɪsɪn'tʃɑːnt, *Am:* -'tʃænt] *vt* desencantar
disenchanted *adj* desencantado, -a
disenfranchise [ˌdɪsɪn'fræntʃaɪz] *vt* **1.** (*deprive of vote*) privar del voto **2.** (*deprive of rights*) privar de derechos
disengage [ˌdɪsɪn'geɪdʒ] **I.** *vi* **1.** (*become detached*) separarse **2.** (*make a fencing move*) fintar **II.** *vt* **1.** (*uncouple*) separar **2.** (*detach*) desconectar; (*a clutch*) quitar **3.** MIL retirar
disengagement [ˌdɪsɪn'geɪdʒmənt] *n no pl* desconexión *m*
disentangle [ˌdɪsɪn'tæŋgl] **I.** *vi* desenredarse **II.** *vt* **1.** (*untangle*) desenredar **2.** *fig* (*unravel*) desembrollar
disfavor *Am, Aus,* **disfavour** [ˌdɪs'feɪvəʳ, *Am:* -vɚ] **I.** *n no pl* desaprobación *f;* **to fall into** ~ caer en desgracia **II.** *vt* desfavorecer
disfigure [dɪs'fɪgəʳ, *Am:* -jɚ] *vt* desfigurar
disfigurement *n no pl* desfiguración *f*
disfranchise [dɪs'fræntʃaɪz] *s.* **disenfranchise**

D

disgorge [dɪs'gɔːdʒ, *Am:* -'gɔːrdʒ] *vt* arrojar; *fig* vomitar

disgrace [dɪs'greɪs] **I.** *n no pl* **1.** (*loss of honour*) deshonra *f* **2.** (*shameful thing or person*) vergüenza *f* **II.** *vt* deshonrar

disgraced *adj* deshonrado, -a

disgraceful [dɪs'greɪsfəl] *adj* vergonzoso, -a

disgruntled [dɪs'grʌntld, *Am:* -t̬ld] *adj* contrariado, -a; **to be ~ at sth** estar descontento de algo

disguise [dɪs'gaɪz] **I.** *n* disfraz *m;* **to be in ~** estar disfrazado **II.** *vt* **1.** (*change appearance*) disfrazar; **to ~ oneself as sth** disfrazarse de algo **2.** (*hide*) encubrir

disgust [dɪs'gʌst] **I.** *n no pl* **1.** (*repugnance*) asco *m;* **to turn away from sth in ~** alejarse con repugnancia de algo **2.** (*indignation*) indignación *f;* **~ at sth** indignación por algo **II.** *vt* **1.** (*sicken*) dar asco, repugnar, chocar *AmL* **2.** (*revolt*) indignar

disgusted *adj* **1.** (*sickened*) asqueado, -a **2.** (*indignant*) indignado, -a

disgusting [dɪs'gʌstɪŋ] *adj* **1.** (*repulsive*) repugnante, chocante *AmL* **2.** (*unacceptable*) indignante

dish [dɪʃ] **I.** <-es> *n* **1.** (*for food*) plato *m;* **oven-proof ~** plato térmico; **to do the ~es** fregar los platos **2.** (*equipment*) (antena *f*) parabólica *f* **3.** *inf* (*sexually attractive person*) bombón *m* **II.** *vt inf* **1.** (*serve*) servir **2.** (*spoil*) arruinar

◆**dish out** *vt* **1.** (*distribute too liberally*) repartir a diestro y siniestro **2.** (*serve*) servir

◆**dish up** *vt inf* **1.** (*serve*) servir **2.** (*offer*) ofrecer

dish aerial *n Brit* (antena) parabólica *f*

disharmonious [ˌdɪshɑː'məʊniəs, *Am:* -hɑːrmoʊ-] *adj* discordante

disharmony [dɪs'hɑːməni, *Am:* -'hɑːr-] *n no pl* falta *f* de armonía

dishcloth ['dɪʃklɒθ, *Am:* -klɑːθ] *n* trapo *m* de cocina, repasador *m Arg, Urug*

dishearten [dɪs'hɑːtən, *Am:* -'hɑːr-] *vt* descorazonar

disheveled *adj Am,* **dishevelled** [dɪ'ʃevəld] *adj* desaliñado, -a; **with ~ hair** despeinado

dishonest [dɪ'sɒnɪst, *Am:* -'sɑːnɪst] *adj* deshonesto, -a; **to be ~ about sth** ser falso acerca de algo

dishonesty [dɪ'sɒnɪsti, *Am:* -'sɑːnə-] *n no pl* **1.** (*lack of honesty*) falta *f* de honestidad **2.** (*dishonest act*) fraude *m*

dishonor [dɪ'sɑːnɚ] *n Am s.* **dishonour**

dishonorable [dɪ'sɑːnɚəbl] *adj Am s.* **dishonourable**

dishonour [dɪ'sɒnəʳ, *Am:* -'sɑːnɚ] **I.** *n no pl* deshonor *m;* **to bring ~ on sb** traer la deshonra a alguien **II.** *vt* **1.** (*disgrace*) deshonrar **2.** (*not keep*) incumplir

dishonourable [dɪ'sɒnərəbl, *Am:* -'sɑːnɚ-] *adj* deshonroso, -a

dishtowel ['dɪʃtaʊəl] *n Am* paño *m* de cocina **dishwasher** *n* **1.** (*machine*) lavavajillas *f inv;* **to run the ~** poner el lavaplatos *m* **2.** (*person*) lavaplatos *mf* **dishwater** *n no pl* agua *f* de lavar platos

disillusion [ˌdɪsɪ'luːʒən] **I.** *vt* desilusionar **II.** *n no pl* desilusión *f*

disillusioned *adj* desilusionado, -a; **to be ~ with sth** estar desilusionado con algo; **to be ~ with sb** estar desilusionado de alguien

disillusionment *n no pl* desilusión

disinclination [ˌdɪsɪnklɪ'neɪʃən] *n no pl* renuencia *f*

disinclined [ˌdɪsɪn'klaɪnd] *adj* renuente; **to be ~ to do sth** tener pocas ganas de hacer algo

disinfect [ˌdɪsɪn'fekt] *vt* desinfectar

disinfectant [ˌdɪsɪn'fektənt] **I.** *n* desinfectante *m* **II.** *adj no pl* desinfectante

disinfection [ˌdɪsɪn'fekʃən] *n no pl* desinfección *f*

disingenuous [ˌdɪsɪn'dʒenjuəs] *adj* insincero, -a

disinherit [ˌdɪsɪn'herɪt] *vt* desheredar

disintegrate [dɪ'sɪntɪgreɪt, *Am:* -t̬ə-] **I.** *vi* desintegrarse **II.** *vt* desintegrar

disintegration [dɪˌsɪntɪ'greɪʃən, *Am:* -t̬ə'-] *n no pl* desintegración *f*

disinterested [dɪ'sɪntrəstɪd, *Am:* -'sɪntrɪstɪd] *adj* **1.** (*impartial*) imparcial **2.** (*uninterested*) desinteresado, -a

disjointed [dɪs'dʒɔɪntɪd, *Am:* -t̬ɪd] *adj* inconexo, -a

disk [dɪsk] *n* INFOR disco *m;* **hard ~** disco duro; **floppy ~** disquete *m;* **installation ~** disco de instalación; **start-up ~** disco de arranque; **high density ~** disquete de alta densidad; **compact laser ~** laserdisc *m*

disk drive *n* disquetera *f*

diskette [dɪs'kæt] *n* disquete *m*

dislike [dɪs'laɪk] **I.** *vt* tener aversión a **II.** *n no pl* aversión *f;* **to take a ~ to sb/sth** tomar aversión a alguien/algo

dislocate ['dɪsləkeɪt, *Am:* dɪ'sloʊ-] *vt* **1.** (*put out of place*) desplazar **2.** MED **he dislocated his shoulder** se dislocó el hombro **3.** *fig* (*disturb the working of*) trastornar

dislocation [ˌdɪslə'keɪʃən, *Am:* -loʊ'-] *n* **1.** (*displacement*) desplazamiento *m* **2.** MED dislocación *f* **3.** *no pl, fig* (*disturbance*) trastorno *m*

dislodge [dɪ'slɒdʒ, *Am:* -'slɑːdʒ] *vt* desalojar

disloyal [dɪ'slɔɪəl] *adj* desleal; **to be ~ to sb/sth** ser desleal a alguien/algo

dismal ['dɪzməl] *adj* **1.** (*depressing*) deprimente **2.** *inf* (*awful*) terrible; (*truth*) triste

dismantle [dɪ'smæntl, *Am:* dɪ'smænt̬l] *vt* desmontar; (*system*) desmantelar

dismay [dɪ'smeɪ] **I.** *n no pl* consternación *f;* **to sb's (great) ~** para (gran) consternación de alguien **II.** *vt* consternar

dismayed *adj* consternado, -a

dismember [dɪ'smembəʳ, *Am:* -bɚ] *vt a. fig* desmembrar

dismiss [dɪ'smɪs] *vt* **1.** (*not consider*) descartar **2.** (*let go*) dejar ir **3.** (*from job*) despedir; **to be ~ed from one's job** ser despedido del trabajo **4.** LAW desestimar

dismissal [dɪ'smɪsəl] *n no pl* **1.** (*disregarding*) descarte *m* **2.** (*from job*) despido *m*

dismissive [dɪ'smɪsɪv] *adj* **she was dismissive about the idea** no daba crédito a la idea

dismount [dɪ'smaʊnt] *vi* desmontar(se)

disobedience [ˌdɪsəʊ'biːdiənts, *Am:* -ə'-] *n no pl* desobediencia *f*

disobedient [ˌdɪsəʊ'biːdiənt, *Am:* -ə'-] *adj* desobediente

disobey [ˌdɪsəʊ'beɪ, *Am:* -ə'-] *vi, vt* desobedecer

disoblige [ˌdɪsə'blaɪdʒ] *vt* disgustar

disobliging *adj* desatento, -a

disorder [dɪ'sɔːdə^r, *Am:* -'sɔːrdɚ] *n* **1.** *no pl* (*lack of order*) desorden *m*, desparramo *m* *CSur* **2.** (*sickness*) trastorno *m*

disordered *adj* desordenado, -a

disorderly [dɪ'sɔːdəli, *Am:* -'sɔːrdɚ-] *adj* **1.** (*untidy*) desordenado, -a **2.** (*unruly*) escandaloso, -a; ~ **conduct** alteración *f* del orden público

disorganized [dɪ'sɔːgənaɪzd, *Am:* dɪ'sɔːr-] *adj* desorganizado, -a

disorient [dɪ'sɔːriənt, *Am:* -ent] *vt Am*, **disorientate** [dɪ'sɔːriənteɪt] *vt* desorientar; **to get ~ed** desorientarse

disoriented *adj* desorientado, -a

disown [dɪ'səʊn, *Am:* dɪ'soʊn] *vt* repudiar

disparage [dɪ'spærɪdʒ, *Am:* -'sper-] *vt* menospreciar

disparagement *n no pl* menosprecio *m*

disparaging *adj* (*disdainful*) despreciativo, -a; (*remark*) desdeñoso, -a

disparate ['dɪspərət] *adj* dispar

disparity [dɪ'spærəti, *Am:* -'perət̬i] *n* disparidad *f*

dispassionate [dɪ'spæʃənət] *adj* desapasionado, -a

dispatch [dɪ'spætʃ] **I.** <-es> *n* **1.** *no pl* (*sending*) despacho *m*; **I have just received the latest ~ of our war correspondent** acabo de recibir el último despacho de nuestro corresponsal de guerra **2.** (*something sent*) envío *m* **II.** *vt a. fig* despachar

dispel [dɪ'spel] <-ll-> *vt* (*fears, doubts*) disipar; (*a rumour*) desmentir

dispensable [dɪ'spensəbl] *adj* prescindible

dispensary [dɪ'spensəri] *n Brit* dispensario *m*

dispensation [ˌdɪspen'seɪʃən] *n* **1.** (*special permission*) dispensa *f* **2.** (*distributing*) administración *f*

dispense [dɪ'spens] *vt* **1.** (*give out*) repartir **2.** MED (*medicine*) administrar

◆**dispense with** *vi* prescindir de

dispenser [dɪ'spensə^r, *Am:* -ɚ] *n* **1.** (*device*) máquina *f* expendedora; **cash ~** cajero *m* automático **2.** (*one who distributes*) distribuidor(a) *m(f)*

dispersal [dɪ'spɜːsl, *Am:* -'spɜːr-] *n no pl* (*dispersing*) dispersión *f*

disperse [dɪ'spɜːs, *Am:* -'spɜːrs] **I.** *vt* dispersar **II.** *vi* dispersarse

dispersion [dɪ'spɜːʃən, *Am:* -'spɜːrʒən] *n no pl* dispersión *f*

dispirited [dɪ'spɪrɪtɪd, *Am:* -t̬ɪd] *adj* desanimado, -a

displace [dɪs'pleɪs] *vt* **1.** (*eject*) desplazar **2.** (*take the place of*) reemplazar

displacement [dɪs'pleɪsmənt] *n no pl* desplazamiento *m*

display [dɪ'spleɪ] **I.** *vt* **1.** (*arrange for showing*) exhibir; **to ~ sth in a shop window** exhibir algo en un escaparate **2.** (*show*) demostrar **II.** *n* **1.** (*arrangement*) exposición *f*; **firework ~** *Am, Aus* exhibición *f* pirotécnica **2.** *no pl* (*demonstration*) demostración *f* **3.** INFOR pantalla *f*; **liquid crystal ~** pantalla de cristal líquido

display case *n* estuche *m* **display window** *n* escaparate *m*

displease [dɪ'spliːz] *vt* disgustar; **to be ~d by sth** estar disgustado con algo

displeasing *adj* desagradable

displeasure [dɪ'spleʒə^r, *Am:* -ɚ] *n no pl* disgusto *m*

disposable [dɪ'spəʊzəbl, *Am:* -'spoʊ-] *adj* desechable

disposable income *n* renta *f* disponible

disposal [dɪ'spəʊzl, *Am:* dɪ'spoʊ-] *n* **1.** *no pl* (*getting rid of*) eliminación *f* **2.** *Am* (*grinding machine*) trituradora *f* ►**to be at sb's ~** estar a disposición de alguien

dispose [dɪ'spəʊz, *Am:* -'spoʊz] **I.** *vt* **1.** (*place*) disponer **2.** (*incline*) predisponer **II.** *vi* **to ~ of sth** (*throw away*) desechar algo; (*get rid of*) deshacerse de algo

disposed *adj* **to be well ~ towards sb** estar bien dispuesto hacia alguien

disposition [ˌdɪspə'zɪʃən] *n* disposición *f*; **to have a happy ~** mostrar una buena disposición

dispossess [ˌdɪspə'zes] *vt* desposeer

disproportionate [ˌdɪsprə'pɔːʃənət, *Am:* -'pɔːr-] *adj* desproporcionado, -a

disprove [dɪ'spruːv] *vt* refutar

disputable [dɪ'spjuːtəbl, *Am:* dɪ'spjuːt̬ə-] *adj* discutible

disputation [ˌdɪspjʊ'teɪʃən, *Am:* -pjuː'-] *n* debate *m*

disputatious [ˌdɪspjʊ'teɪʃəs, *Am:* -pjuː'-] *adj* disputador(a)

dispute [dɪ'spjuːt] **I.** *vt* **1.** (*argue*) discutir **2.** (*doubt*) poner en duda **II.** *vi* **to ~** (**with sb**) **over sth** discutir (con alguien) sobre algo **III.** *n* discusión *f*; **a ~ over sth** una discusión sobre algo

disqualification [dɪˌskwɒlɪfɪ'keɪʃən, *Am:* dɪˌskwɑːlə-] *n* **1.** *no pl* SPORTS descalificación *f* **2.** (*incapacity*) incapacidad *f*

disqualify [dɪ'skwɒlɪfaɪ, *Am:* dɪ'skwɑːlə-] <-ie-> *vt* descalificar; **to ~ sb from an event**

descalificar a alguien de un evento
disquiet [dɪ'skwaɪət] **I.** *n no pl* inquietud *f*; ~ **over sth** inquietud acerca de algo **II.** *vt* inquietar
disquieting *adj* inquietante
disregard [ˌdɪsrɪ'gɑːd, *Am:* -rɪ'gɑːrd] **I.** *vt* desatender **II.** *n no pl* despreocupación *f*
disrepair [ˌdɪsrɪ'peəʳ, *Am:* -rɪ'per] *n no pl* deterioro *m*; **to be in a state of** ~ estar en mal estado
disreputable [dɪs'repjətəbl, *Am:* -jət̬ə-] *adj* de mala fama
disrepute [ˌdɪsrɪ'pjuːt] *n* desprestigio *m*
disrespect [ˌdɪsrɪ'spekt] *n no pl* falta *f* de respeto; **to show** ~ mostrar descortesía
disrespectful [ˌdɪsrɪ'spektfəl] *adj* descortés
disrupt [dɪs'rʌpt] *vt* (*interrupt*) interrumpir; (*disturb*) trastornar
disruption [dɪs'rʌpʃən] *n* (*interruption*) interrupción *f*; (*disturbance*) perturbación *f*; *fig* (*disorder*) desorganización *f*
disruptive [dɪs'rʌptɪv] *adj* que trastorna
dissatisfaction [dɪsˌsætɪs'fækʃən, *Am:* ˌdɪssæt̬əs'-] *n no pl* insatisfacción *f*
dissatisfied [dɪs'sætɪsfaɪd, *Am:* -'sæt̬əs-] *adj* insatisfecho, -a
dissect [dɪ'sekt] *vt* **1.** (*cut open*) diseccionar **2.** *fig* (*examine*) examinar
dissection [dɪ'sekʃən] *n* disección *f*
dissemble [dɪ'sembl] *vi, vt* disimular
disseminate [dɪ'semɪneɪt] *vt* diseminar
dissemination [dɪˌsemɪ'neɪʃən] *n no pl* diseminación *f*
dissension [dɪ'sentʃən] *n* disensión *f*; **to sow** ~ sembrar la discordia
dissent [dɪ'sent] **I.** *n no pl* disidencia *f* **II.** *vi* **1.** (*not agree with*) disentir; **to** ~ **from sth** disentir de algo **2.** (*reject a doctrine*) disidir
dissenter *n* disidente *mf*
dissertation [ˌdɪsə'teɪʃən, *Am:* -ɚ'-] *n* **1.** (*long piece of writing*) disertación *f* **2.** UNIV tesis *f*
disservice [ˌdɪs'sɜːvɪs, *Am:* -'sɜːr-] *n no pl* perjuicio *m*; **to do sth/sb a** ~ perjudicar a algo/a alguien
dissident ['dɪsɪdənt] **I.** *n* disidente *mf* **II.** *adj* disidente
dissimilar [ˌdɪs'sɪmɪləʳ, *Am:* -lɚ] *adj* diferente, disímbolo, -a *Méx*; **to be** ~ **to sb/sth** ser distinto de alguien/algo
dissimilarity [ˌdɪsˌsɪmɪ'lærəti, *Am:* -'lerət̬i] <-ies> *n* desemejanza *f*
dissimulation [ˌdɪsˌsɪmjə'leɪʃən] *n* disimulo *m*
dissipate ['dɪsɪpeɪt] **I.** *vi* **1.** (*disperse*) disiparse **2.** *fig* (*engage in frivolous pleasures*) llevar una vida disoluta **II.** *vt* disipar
dissipated *adj* disipado, -a
dissipation [ˌdɪsɪ'peɪʃən] *n* **1.** (*wasting frivolously*) desperdicio *m*; (*of money*) derroche *m* **2.** (*damaging indulgence in pleasure*) disipación *f*
dissociate [dɪ'səʊʃieɪt, *Am:* -'soʊ-] *vt* **to** ~ **carbon from sth** disociar el carbono de algo; **to** ~ **oneself from sb/sth** disociarse de alguien/algo
dissociation [dɪˌsəʊʃi'eɪʃən, *Am:* -ˌsoʊ-] *n no pl* disociación *f*
dissolute ['dɪsəluːt] *adj liter* disoluto, -a
dissolution [ˌdɪsə'luːʃən] *n no pl* disolución *f*
dissolve [dɪ'zɒlv, *Am:* -'zɑːlv] **I.** *vi* **1.** (*become part of a liquid*) disolverse **2.** *fig* (*collapse*) deshacerse; **to** ~ **into tears** deshacerse en lágrimas **3.** *fig* (*disappear*) desvanecerse **II.** *vt* disolver; **to** ~ **a society** disolver una sociedad
dissonance ['dɪsənənts] *n no pl* disonancia *f*
dissonant ['dɪsənənt] *adj* disonante; *fig* discordante
dissuade [dɪ'sweɪd] *vt* disuadir
distance ['dɪstənts] **I.** *n* **1.** (*space*) distancia *f*; **his house is within walking** ~ se puede ir andando a su casa; **to keep one's** ~ guardar las distancias **2.** (*space far away*) lejanía *f* **II.** *vt* **to** ~ **oneself from sb/sth** distanciarse de alguien/algo
distant ['dɪstənt] *adj* **1.** (*far away*) distante **2.** (*not closely related*) lejano, -a
distantly *adv* **1.** (*in the distance*) de lejos **2.** *fig* (*in an unfriendly manner*) distantemente
distaste [dɪ'steɪst] *n no pl* aversión *f*
distasteful [dɪ'steɪstfəl] *adj* desagradable
distemper [dɪ'stempəʳ, *Am:* -pɚ] *n* **1.** (*animal disease*) moquillo *m* **2.** (*type of paint*) temple *m* **3.** (*bad temper*) malhumor *m*
distend [dɪ'stend] *vi* distenderse
distension [dɪ'stentʃən] *n no pl* distensión *f*
distil [dɪ'stɪl] <-ll-> *vt*, **distill** *vt Am, Aus* destilar
distillation [ˌdɪstɪ'leɪʃən] *n no pl* destilación *f*
distiller [dɪ'stɪləʳ, *Am:* dɪ'stɪlɚ] *n* **1.** (*company*) destilería *f* **2.** (*person*) destilador(a) *m(f)*
distillery [dɪ'stɪləri] *n* destilería *f*
distinct [dɪ'stɪŋkt] *adj* **1.** (*separate*) distinto **2.** (*marked*) definido, -a **3.** (*noticeable*) nítido, -a
distinction [dɪ'stɪŋkʃən] *n* **1.** (*difference*) distinción *m* **2.** *no pl* (*eminence*) distinción *m*; **of great** ~ de gran renombre **3.** *Brit* (*excellent marks*) sobresaliente *m*
distinctive [dɪ'stɪŋktɪv] *adj* característico, -a
distinguish [dɪ'stɪŋgwɪʃ] **I.** *vi* distinguir **II.** *vt* **1.** (*tell apart*) distinguir **2.** (*be excellent in*) **to** ~ **oneself in sth** destacar en algo
distinguishable [dɪ'stɪŋgwɪʃəbl] *adj* distinguible
distinguished *adj* **1.** (*celebrated*) eminente **2.** (*stylish*) distinguido, -a
distort [dɪ'stɔːt, *Am:* -'stɔːrt] *vt* torcer; (*facts, the truth*) tergiversar
distortion [dɪ'stɔːʃən, *Am:* -'stɔːr-] *n* (*of the truth, facts*) distorsión *f*; (*of a face*) contorsión

f

distract [dɪ'strækt] *vt* distraer

distracted *adj* distraído, -a

distraction [dɪ'strækʃən] *n* **1.** (*disturbing factor*) distracción *f* **2.** (*pastime*) entretenimiento *m* **3.** *no pl* (*confused agitation*) aturdimiento *m*

distraught [dɪ'strɔːt, *Am:* -'strɑːt] *adj* turbado, -a

distress [dɪ'stres] **I.** *n no pl* **1.** (*extreme pain*) aflicción *f* **2.** (*anguish*) congoja *f* **3.** (*state of danger*) apuro *m* **II.** *vt* afligir

distressed *adj* **1.** (*unhappy*) afligido, -a **2.** (*in difficulties*) apurado, -a

distressful [dɪ'stresfəl] *adj Am*, **distressing** *adj* **1.** (*causing great worry*) angustioso, -a **2.** (*painful*) doloroso, -a

distribute [dɪ'strɪbjuːt] *vt* **1.** (*share*) repartir **2.** (*spread over space*) distribuir; **to be widely ~d** estar ampliamente repartido

distribution [ˌdɪstrɪ'bjuːʃən] *n no pl* **1.** (*giving out*) reparto *m* **2.** (*spread*) distribución

distribution area *n* ECON área *f* de distribución **distribution channel** *n* ECON canal *m* de distribución **distribution rights** *npl* derechos *mpl* de distribución

distributive [dɪ'strɪbjətɪv, *Am:* -jət̬ɪv] *adj* distributivo, -a

distributor [dɪ'strɪbjətəʳ, *Am:* -t̬ɚ] *n* **1.** (*person*) distribuidor(a) *m(f)* **2.** (*device*) distribuidor *m*

district ['dɪstrɪkt] *n* **1.** (*defined area*) distrito *m*, intendencia *f CSur* **2.** (*region*) región *f*

district attorney *n Am* fiscal *m* de distrito **district council** *n Brit* ayuntamiento *m* de distrito **district court** *n Am* tribunal *m* federal

distrust [dɪ'strʌst] **I.** *vt* desconfiar de **II.** *n no pl* desconfianza *f*

distrustful [dɪ'strʌstfəl] *adj* desconfiado, -a

disturb [dɪ'stɜːb, *Am:* -'stɜːrb] *vt* **1.** (*bother*) molestar **2.** (*worry*) preocupar **3.** (*move around*) perturbar

disturbance [dɪ'stɜːbənts, *Am:* -'stɜːr-] *n* **1.** (*bother*) molestia *f* **2.** (*public incident*) disturbio *m*

disturbed *adj* **1.** (*restless*) inquieto, -a **2.** (*moved around*) perturbado, -a

disturbing *adj* **1.** (*annoying*) molesto, -a **2.** (*worrying*) preocupante

disunite [ˌdɪsjuː'naɪt] *vt* desunir

disunity [dɪ'sjuːnəti, *Am:* -t̬i] *n no pl* desunión *f*

disuse [dɪ'sjuːs] *n no pl* desuso *m*

disused [dɪ'sjuːzd] *adj* en desuso

ditch [dɪtʃ] **I.** <-es> *n* **1.** zanja *f*; (*road*) cuneta *f*; **irrigation ~** acequia *f* **2.** (*for defense*) foso *m* **II.** *vt* **1.** (*discard*) deshacerse de; (*car*) abandonar; (*idea*) descartar **2.** (*escape from*) zafarse de **3.** *inf* (*end a relationship*) cortar con **4.** (*land in water*) **to ~ a plane** hacer un amaraje forzoso **III.** *vi* abrir zanjas

dither ['dɪðəʳ, *Am:* -ɚ] **I.** *n no pl* **to be in a ~** estar hecho un flan **II.** *vi inf* **1.** (*be indecisive*) vacilar; **to ~ over whether to do sth** vacilar sobre si hacer algo **2.** (*behave nervously*) ponerse nervioso

ditto ['dɪtəʊ, *Am:* 'dɪt̬oʊ] **I.** *n* (*mark indicating repetition*) comillas *fpl* **II.** *adv* (*so do I*) ídem; *Am* (*same for me*) lo mismo

ditty ['dɪti, *Am:* 'dɪt̬-] <-ies> *n* cancioncilla *f*

diurnal [daɪ'ɜːnəl, *Am:* -'ɜːr-] *adj* diurno, -a

divan [dɪ'væn] *n* diván *m*

dive [daɪv] **I.** *n* **1.** (*jump into water*) salto *m* de cabeza **2.** (*plunge*) inmersión *f* **3.** *a. fig* (*sudden decline*) descenso *m* en picado; **to take a ~** caer en picado **4.** *inf* (*undesirable establishment*) antro *m* **II.** *vi* <dived *o Am:* dove, dived *o Am:* dove> **1.** (*plunge into water*) zambullirse; **to ~ under sth** bucear por debajo de algo; **to ~ to a depth of ...** sumergirse a una profundidad de... **2.** (*jump head first into water*) tirarse de cabeza **3.** (*go sharply downwards*) bajar en picado **4.** (*move towards*) precipitarse; **to ~ for cover** buscar abrigo precipitadamente

diver ['daɪvəʳ, *Am:* -vɚ] *n* **1.** (*person who dives*) buceador(a) *m(f)* **2.** (*person working under water*) buzo *m*

diverge [daɪ'vɜːdʒ, *Am:* -'vɜːrdʒ] *vi* divergir; **to ~ from sth** apartarse de algo

divergence [daɪ'vɜːdʒəns, *Am:* dɪ'vɜːr-] *n no pl* divergencia *f*

divergent [daɪ'vɜːdʒənt, *Am:* dɪ'vɜːr-] *adj* **1.** (*differing*) divergente **2.** (*different*) distinto, -a

diverse [daɪ'vɜːs, *Am:* dɪ'vɜːrs] *adj* **1.** (*varied*) variado, -a **2.** (*not alike*) diverso, -a

diversification [daɪˌvɜːsɪfɪ'keɪʃən, *Am:* dɪˌvɜːr-] *n no pl* diversificación *f*

diversify [daɪ'vɜːsɪfaɪ, *Am:* dɪˌvɜːr-] <-ie-> **I.** *vi* diversificarse **II.** *vt* diversificar

diversion [daɪ'vɜːʃən, *Am:* dɪ'vɜːr-] *n* **1.** *no pl* (*changing of direction*) desviación *f*; (*of railway, river*) desvío *m* **2.** (*distraction*) entretenimiento *m* **3.** (*activity*) diversión *f*

diversity [daɪ'vɜːsəti, *Am:* dɪ'vɜːrsət̬i] *n no pl* diversidad *f*

divert [daɪ'vɜːt, *Am:* dɪ'vɜːrt] *vt* **1.** (*change direction*) desviar **2.** (*distract*) distraer **3.** (*amuse*) divertir

diverting [daɪ'vɜːtɪŋ, *Am:* dɪ'vɜːrt̬ɪŋ] *adj* divertido, -a

divest [daɪ'vest, *Am:* dɪ-] **I.** *vt* despojar de **II.** *vi* **1.** *Am* (*sell*) vender **2.** (*get rid of involvement in*) **to ~ from sth** renunciar a algo
◆**divest of** *vr fig* (*take from*) despojarse de

divide [dɪ'vaɪd] **I.** *n* **1.** (*gulf*) separación *f* **2.** *Am* (*watershed*) punto *m* de inflexión **II.** *vt* **1.** *a.* MAT dividir; **to ~ sth into three groups** dividir algo en tres grupos; **the party is ~d** *fig* el partido está dividido **2.** (*allot*) repartir **III.** *vi* **1.** (*split*) dividirse; **their paths ~d** sus caminos se separaron **2.** *Brit* (*vote for or against*) votar
►**~ and rule** divide y vencerás

◆**divide off** *vt always sep* dividir

◆**divide out**, **divide up** *vt always sep* (re)partir

divided *adj* **1.**(*undecided*) **to be ~ between two options** encontrarse en un dilema entre dos opciones **2.**(*in disagreement*) dividido, -a

dividend ['dɪvɪdend] *n* MAT, FIN dividendo *m*

dividing line *n* línea *f* divisoria

divination [ˌdɪvɪ'neɪʃən] *n no pl* adivinación *f*

divine [dɪ'vaɪn] **I.** *adj* **1.**(*of or from God*) divino, -a **2.**(*wonderful*) sublime **II.** *vt* (*guess correctly*) adivinar; (*the future*) predecir **III.** *vi* hacer pronósticos

diviner *n* adivinador(a) *m(f)*; (*of future events*) vidente *mf*

diving *n no pl* **1.**(*jumping*) zambullida *f* **2.**(*swimming*) buceo *m*

diving bell *n* campana *f* de buzo **diving board** *n* trampolín *m* **diving-suit** *n* escafandra *f*

divining-rod [dɪ'vaɪnɪŋˈrɒd, *Am:* -ˈrɑːd] *n* varilla *f* de zahorí

divinity [dɪ'vɪnəti, *Am:* -ət̬i] <-ies> *n* **1.** *no pl* (*state*) divinidad *f* **2.** *pl* (*god*) deidad *f* **3.** *no pl* (*study*) teología *f*

divisible [dɪ'vɪzəbl] *adj* divisible

division [dɪ'vɪʒən] *n* **1.** *a.* MIL, MAT, SPORTS división *f* **2.** *no pl* (*splitting up*) repartimiento *m* **3.**(*disagreement*) discordia *f* **4.**(*gulf*) separación *f* **5.** *Brit* (*voting*) votación *f*

divisive [dɪ'vaɪsɪv] *adj* divisivo, -a

divorce [dɪ'vɔːs, *Am:* -'vɔːrs] **I.** *n* divorcio *m*; *fig* separación *f* **II.** *vt* **1.**(*break marriage*) **to get ~d** (**from sb**) divorciarse (de alguien); **he ~d her for infidelity** se divorció de ella por infidelidad **2.** *fig* (*separate*) separar **III.** *vi* divorciarse

divorced *adj* divorciado, -a

divorcee *n*, **divorcée** [dɪˌvɔː'siː, *Am:* dɪˌvɔːr'seɪ] *n* divorciado, -a *m, f*

divulge [daɪ'vʌldʒ, *Am:* dɪ-] *vt* divulgar

DIY [ˌdiːaɪ'waɪ] *abbr of* **do-it-yourself** bricolaje *m*

dizziness *n no pl* (*feeling of spinning round*) mareo *m*; (*because of height*) vértigo *m*

dizzy ['dɪzi] <-ier, -iest> *adj* **1.**(*having a spinning sensation*) mareado, -a **2.**(*causing a spinning sensation*) vertiginoso, -a **3.** *inf* (*silly*) tonto, -a

DJ [ˌdiː'dʒeɪ, *Am:* 'diːdʒeɪ] *n* **1.** *abbr of* **dinner jacket** chaqué *m* **2.** *abbr of* **disc jockey** DJ *m*

Djibouti [dʒɪ'buːti] *n* Yibuti *m*

Djiboutian [dʒɪ'buːtiən] **I.** *adj* de Yibuti **II.** *n* habitante *mf* de Yibuti

DNA [ˌdiːen'eɪ] *n no pl abbr of* **deoxyribonucleic acid** ADN *m*

do [duː] **I.** *n* **1.** *Brit, inf* (*treatment of people*) trato *m*; **a poor ~** un mal trato **2.** *Brit, Aus, inf* (*party*) fiesta *f* **II.** <does, did, done> *aux* **1.**(*word to form questions*) **~ you own a dog?** ¿tienes un perro? **2.**(*word to form negatives*) **Frida ~esn't like olives** a Frida no le gustan las aceitunas **3.**(*word to form imperatives*) **~ your homework!** ¡haz los deberes!; **~ come in!** ¡pero pasa, por favor! **4.**(*word used for emphasis*) **~ go to the party!** ¡ve a la fiesta!; **he ~es get on my nerves** me saca de quicio, la verdad; **he did ~ it** sí que lo hizo **5.**(*replaces a repeated verb*) **so ~ I** yo también; **neither ~ I** yo tampoco; **she speaks more fluently than he ~es** ella habla con mayor fluidez que él **6.**(*word requesting affirmation*) ¿verdad?; **you ~n't want to answer, ~ you?** no quieres contestar, ¿no? **III.** <does, did, done> *vt* **1.**(*carry out*) hacer; **to ~ nothing but ...** hacer sólo...; **to ~ one's best** emplearse a fondo; **to ~ justice** hacer justicia; **to ~ everything possible** hacer todo lo posible; **what on earth are you ~ing** (**there**)? ¿que diablos haces (ahí)?; **what is to be ~ne about that?** ¿qué se puede hacer al respecto?; **~n't just stand there, ~ something!** ¡no te quedes ahí plantado, haz algo! **2.**(*undertake*) realizar **3.**(*place somewhere*) poner **4.**(*help*) **to ~ something for sb/sth** hacer algo por alguien/algo **5.**(*act*) actuar; **to ~ as others ~** hacer como hacen los demás **6.**(*deal with*) encargarse de; **if you ~ the washing up, I'll ~ the drying** si tú lavas los platos yo los secaré **7.**(*construct*) producir **8.**(*learn*) estudiar **9.**(*figure out*) resolver **10.**(*finish*) terminar **11.**(*put in order*) ordenar; (*clean*) limpiar; **to ~ one's nails** (*varnish*) pintarse las uñas; (*cut*) cortarse las uñas; **to ~ one's shoes** limpiarse los zapatos; **to ~ one's teeth** lavarse los dientes **12.**(*make neat*) arreglar **13.**(*tour*) visitar **14.**(*go at a speed of*) **to ~ Barcelona to Geneva in seven hours** cubrir el trayecto de Barcelona a Ginebra en siete horas **15.**(*be satisfactory*) **"I only have beer – will that ~ you?"** "sólo tengo cerveza – ¿te va bien?" **16.**(*sell*) vender; (*offer*) servir **17.**(*cook*) cocer; **to ~ sth for sb** cocinar algo para alguien **18.**(*cause*) **to ~ sb credit** decir mucho a favor de alguien; **to ~ sb a good turn** echar una mano a alguien; **to ~ sb good** sentar bien a alguien **19.** *Brit* (*offer good service*) **to ~ sb well** tratar bien a alguien **20.**(*act*) desempeñar **21.** *inf* (*burglarize*) allanar **22.** *inf* (*swindle*) estafar **23.** *Brit, inf* (*make suffer*) amargar **24.** *inf* (*take drugs*) chutarse ►**just ~ it!** ¡hazlo!; **what's ~ne is ~ne** a lo hecho, pecho; **that ~es it** eso es el colmo **IV.** <does, did, done> *vi* **1.**(*finish with*) **to have ~ne with sb/sth** haber terminado con algo/alguien **2.**(*be satisfactory*) **this behaviour just won't ~!** ¡no se puede tolerar este comportamiento! **3.**(*function as*) **it'll ~ for a spoon** servirá de cuchara **4.** *inf* (*going on*) **to be ~ing** suceder **5.**(*manage*) salir adelante; **mother and baby are ~ing well** la madre y el bebé se encuentran bien; **many shops are ~ing well** muchas tiendas van prosperando; **how are you ~ing?** ¿qué tal estás?; **to ~ well for one-**

self darse una buena vida **6.** *Brit* (*clean house*) **to ~ for sb** trabajar como criada para alguien **7.** *Brit, Aus* (*treat*) **to ~ badly/well by sb** tratar bien/mal a alguien **8.** *Brit, inf* (*beat up*) **to ~ for sb** acabar con alguien **9.** *inf* (*serve prison time*) cumplir condena ►**that will never ~** eso no sirve; **~ unto others as you would have them ~ unto you** *prov* no quieras para los otros lo que no quieras para ti; **~ as you would be ~ne by** *Brit, prov* trata a los demás como te gustaría que te trataran a ti; **that will ~!** ¡ya basta!

◆**do away with** *vi* **1.** (*dispose of*) suprimir **2.** *inf* (*kill*) **to ~ sb** liquidar a alguien

◆**do down** *vt* **1.** (*humiliate*) humillar **2.** (*cheat*) estafar

◆**do in** *vt always sep* **1.** (*murder*) **to do sb in** acabar con alguien **2.** *fig* (*make exhausted*) agotar

◆**do out** *vt always sep* **1.** *Brit, inf* (*tidy up*) arreglar **2.** (*adorn*) decorar **3.** (*cheat*) **to do sb out of sth** quitar una cosa a alguien por engaño

◆**do over** *vt always sep* **1.** *Am, inf* (*redo*) **to do sth over again** volver a hacer algo **2.** *Am, inf* (*redecorate*) redecorar **3.** (*burglarize*) robar **4.** *Brit, Aus, inf* (*beat up*) **to do sb over** dar una paliza a alguien

◆**do up** *vt* **1.** (*fasten: button*) abrochar; (*tie*) hacer el nudo; (*shoes*) atar; (*zip*) cerrar **2.** (*restore*) renovar; (*a house*) restaurar; (*one's hair*) arreglarse; **to do oneself up** acicalarse **3.** (*wrap*) envolver

◆**do with** *vi* **1.** (*be related to*) **to have to do with sth** (*book*) tratar de algo; (*person*) tener que ver con algo; **to not have anything to do with sb** no tener tratos con alguien **2.** *Brit, inf* (*need*) **I could do with a drink** me hace falta tomar algo; **I can't do with pop music** no soporto la música pop

◆**do without** *vi* apañarse sin

DOA [ˌdiːəʊˈeɪ] *abbr of* **dead on arrival** ingresó cadáver

docile [ˈdəʊsaɪl, *Am:* ˈdɑːsəl] *adj* dócil

docility [dəʊˈsɪləti, *Am:* dɑːˈsɪləṭi] *n no pl* docilidad *f*

dock[1] [dɒk, *Am:* dɑːk] **I.** *n* **1.** (*wharf*) desembarcadero *m* **2.** (*enclosed part of port*) dársena *f;* **the car is in ~** *Brit, Aus* el coche está en el taller **3.** *Am* (*pier*) dique *m* **II.** *vi* **1.** NAUT atracar **2.** (*spacecraft*) acoplarse **III.** *vt* NAUT atracar

dock[2] [dɒk, *Am:* dɑːk] *n no pl, Brit* **to be in the ~** estar en el banquillo; *fig* estar en apuros

dock[3] [dɒk, *Am:* dɑːk] *vt* **1.** (*take away*) deducir **2.** (*cut tail off*) descolar

dock[4] [dɒk, *Am:* dɑːk] *n no pl* BOT romaza *f*

docker [ˈdɒkəʳ, *Am:* ˈdɑːkɚ] *n inf* estibador *m*

docket [ˈdɒkɪt, *Am:* ˈdɑːkɪt] **I.** *n* **1.** *Brit, Aus* (*document*) cédula *f* **2.** *Am* LAW (*list of cases*) registro *m* de sumarios de causas **3.** *Am* (*business agenda*) agenda *f;* (*in a meeting*) orden *m* del día **II.** *vt* registrar

docking [ˈdɒkɪŋ, *Am:* ˈdɑːk-] *n no pl* **1.** NAUT amarre *m* **2.** (*joining of spacecraft*) acoplamiento *m* **3.** (*cutting*) reducción *f;* (*of wages*) reajuste *m*

dockyard [ˈdɒkjɑːd, *Am:* ˈdɑːkjɑːrd] *n* astillero *m*

doctor [ˈdɒktəʳ, *Am:* ˈdɑːktɚ] **I.** *n* **1.** (*physician*) médico, -a *m, f;* **to be at the ~'s** estar en la consulta; **to go to the ~'s** ir al médico; **this hot bath is just what the ~ ordered** *fig* este baño caliente es justo lo que necesitaba **2.** UNIV doctor(a) *m(f)* **II.** *vt* **1.** (*illegally alter*) falsear **2.** *Brit* (*add poison*) envenenar **3.** *Am* (*adulterate*) adulterar **4.** *Brit, Aus, inf* (*animal*) castrar

doctorate [ˈdɒktərət, *Am:* ˈdɑːk-] *n* doctorado *m*

> El **doctorate** o **doctor's degree** en una disciplina es el título académico más alto que se puede obtener en una universidad. En las universidades anglosajonas los doctorados reciben diversas denominaciones según las materias. El doctorado más común es el **PhD**, también llamado **Dphil** (**Doctor of Philosophy**). Este título se concede tras la realización de una tesis doctoral en cualquier materia exceptuando Derecho y Medicina. Otros títulos de doctorado son: **Dmus** (**Doctor of Music**), **MD** (**Doctor of Medicine**), **LLD** (**Doctor of Laws**) y **DD** (**Doctor of Divinity**, Doctor en Teología). Las universidades también pueden conceder el título de doctor a aquellas personalidades de alto rango que han destacado por su contribución a la investigación científica, su trabajo o sus importantes publicaciones. Este tipo de doctorado se denomina doctorado Honoris Causa. A esta modalidad pertenecen el **Dlitt** (**Doctor of Letters**) o el **DSc** (**Doctor of Science**).

doctrinaire [ˌdɒktrɪˈneəʳ, *Am:* ˌdɑːktrəˈner] *adj* doctrinario, -a

doctrine [ˈdɒktrɪn, *Am:* ˈdɑːk-] *n* doctrina *f;* **military ~** credo *m* militar

document [ˈdɒkjʊmənt, *Am:* ˈdɑːkjə-] **I.** *n* documento *m* **II.** *vt* documentar

documentary [ˌdɒkjʊˈmentəri, *Am:* ˌdɑːkjəˈmenṭɚ-] **I.** <-ies> *n* documental *m* **II.** *adj* documental

documentation [ˌdɒkjʊmenˈteɪʃən, *Am:* ˌdɑːkjə-] *n no pl* documentación *f*

docusoap *n* docudrama *m*

DOD *n Am abbr of* **Department of Defense** Departamento *m* de Defensa

doddery [ˈdɒdəri, *Am:* ˈdɑːdɚ-] <-ier, -iest> *adj* chocho, -a

dodge [dɒdʒ, *Am:* dɑːdʒ] **I.** *vt* (*avoid by moving aside*) esquivar; (*a question*) eludir; **to ~ doing sth** escaquearse de hacer algo **II.** *vi* SPORTS regatear **III.** *n inf* truco *m;* **tax ~** evasión *f* de impuestos

dodger [ˈdɒdʒəʳ, *Am:* -ɚ] *n pej* granuja *mf*

dodgy [ˈdɒdʒi, *Am:* ˈdɑːdʒi] <-ier, -iest>

D

adj Brit, Aus, inf **1.** (*of person*) tramposo, -a; **to sound** ~ sonar a timo **2.** (*of situation*) delicado, -a **3.** (*of weather*) variable

doe [dəʊ, *Am:* doʊ] *n* **1.** (*female deer*) cierva *f*, venada *f AmL* **2.** (*female rabbit*) coneja *f*

DoE *n Brit abbr of* **Department of the Environment** Departamento *m* de Medioambiente

doer ['du:əʳ, *Am:* -ɚ] *n* **1.** (*person acting*) hacedor(a) *m(f)* **2.** (*active person*) persona *f* dinámica

does [dʌz] *vt, vi, aux 3. pers sing of* **do**

doeskin ['dəʊskɪn, *Am:* 'doʊ-] *n* ante *m*

doesn't ['dʌznt] = **does not** *s.* **do**

dog [dɒg, *Am:* dɑ:g] **I.** *n* (*animal*) perro, -a *m, f*; **hunting** ~ perro de caza; **pet** ~ perro mascota; **the** (**dirty**) ~**!** *inf* ¡el muy canalla! ►**a** ~**'s breakfast** *inf* un revoltijo; **he hasn't a** ~**'s chance** *inf* no tiene la más remota posibilidad; **every** ~ **has its day** *prov* a cada uno le llega su momento de gloria; **to be done up like a** ~**'s dinner** estar hecho un adefesio; **to lead a** ~**'s life** llevar una vida de perros; **to be a** ~ **in the manger** ser como el perro del hortelano; **to give a** ~ **a bad name** *Brit, prov* por un perro que maté, mataperros me llamaron *prov;* **to go to the** ~**s** ir de capa caída; **to put on the** ~ darse pisto **II.** <-gg-> *vt* (*pursue*) seguir; *fig* acosar

dog biscuit *n* canil *m* **dog collar** *n* collar *m* de perro; *iron* alzacuello *m* **dog days** *n pl* canícula *f* **dog-eared** *adj* (*book*) **to be** ~ tener las puntas dobladas

dogged ['dɒgɪd, *Am:* 'dɑ:gɪd] *adj* obstinado, -a

doggerel ['dɒgərəl, *Am:* 'dɑ:gɚ-] *n no pl* poesía *f* barata

doghouse ['dɒghaʊs, *Am:* 'dɑ:g-] *n Am* perrera *f;* **to be in the** ~ estar en desgracia

dogma ['dɒgmə, *Am:* 'dɑ:g-] *n* dogma *m*

dogmatic [dɒg'mætɪk, *Am:* dɑ:g'mæt̬-] *adj* dogmático, -a

dogmatism ['dɒgmətɪzəm, *Am:* 'dɑ:g-] *n no pl* dogmatismo *m*

dogsbody ['dɒgzˌbɒdi, *Am:* 'dɑ:gzˌbɑ:di] *n Brit, Aus, inf* burro *m* de carga

dog-tired [ˌdɒg'taɪəd, *Am:* ˌdɑ:g'taɪɚd] *adj inf* hecho, -a polvo

doing ['du:ɪŋ] *n no pl* actividad *f;* **to be** (**of**) **sb's** ~ ser asunto de alguien; **to take some** ~ requerir esfuerzo

doings ['du:ɪŋz] *n pl* **1.** *Brit, inf* (*thing needed*) chisme *m* **2.** (*activities*) actividades *fpl*

do-it-yourself ['du:ɪtjɔ:'self, *Am:* ˌdu:ɪtjɚ'-] *n no pl* bricolaje *m*

doldrums ['dɒldrəmz, *Am:* 'doʊl-] *npl* GEO zona *f* de las calmas ecuatoriales; **to be in the** ~ (*person*) estar deprimido; (*business*) estar estancado

dole [dəʊl, *Am:* doʊl] *n* subsidio *m* de desempleo; **to be on the** ~ estar cobrando el paro

◆**dole out** *vt* (*money, food*) repartir

doleful ['dəʊlfəl, *Am:* 'doʊl-] *adj* (*person*) triste; (*expression*) compungido, -a; (*cry*) lastimero, -a

doll [dɒl, *Am:* dɑ:l] *n* **1.** (*toy*) muñeco, -a *m, f;* ~**'s house** casa *f* de muñecas **2.** *Am, inf* (*term of address*) muñeca *f*

◆**doll up** *vt* emperifollar; **to** ~ **oneself up** ponerse de punta en blanco

dollar ['dɒləʳ, *Am:* 'dɑ:lɚ] *n* dólar *m* ►**to feel/look like a million** ~**s** sentirse/verse a las mil maravillas

dollop ['dɒləp, *Am:* 'dɑ:ləp] *n* (*amount*) porción *f;* (*spoonful*) cucharada *f*

dolly ['dɒli, *Am:* 'dɑ:li] <-ies> *n* **1.** *childspeak* (*doll*) muñequita *f* **2.** CINE travelín *m*

dolly bird *n Brit, inf* (*attractive girl*) barbie *f*

dolphin ['dɒlfɪn, *Am:* 'dɑ:l-] *n* delfín *m,* bufeo *m Perú*

dolt [dəʊlt, *Am:* doʊlt] *n* imbécil *mf*

domain [dəʊ'meɪn, *Am:* doʊ-] *n* **1.** POL, INFOR dominio *m;* (*lands*) propiedad *f* **2.** (*sphere of activity*) ámbito *m;* **to be in the public** ~ ser de dominio público; **that is outside my** ~ eso está fuera de mi campo

dome [dəʊm, *Am:* doʊm] *n* **1.** (*rounded roof*) cúpula *f* **2.** (*rounded ceiling*) bóveda *f* **3.** *inf* (*bald head*) calva *f*

domestic [də'mestɪk] **I.** *adj* **1.** (*of the house*) doméstico, -a **2.** (*home-loving*) casero, -a **3.** *a.* ECON, FIN, POL (*produce, flight, news*) nacional; (*market, trade, policy*) interior; **gross** ~ **product** producto *m* interior bruto **II.** *n* doméstico *m*

domestic appliance *n* electrodoméstico *m*

domesticate [də'mestɪkeɪt] *vt* (*animal*) domesticar; (*plant*) aclimatar; (*person*) volver casero; **he is a very** ~**d man** es un hombre muy de su casa

domesticated *adj* domesticado, -a

domesticity [ˌdəʊmes'tɪsəti, *Am:* ˌdoʊmes'-] *n* domesticidad *f*

domestic science *n* economía *f* doméstica

domicile ['dɒmɪsaɪl, *Am:* 'dɑ:mə-] **I.** *n* domicilio *m* **II.** *vt* domiciliar; **to be** ~**d in** residir en

dominance ['dɒmɪnənts, *Am:* 'dɑ:mə-] *no pl n* **1.** (*rule*) dominación *f* **2.** MIL supremacía *f*

dominant ['dɒmɪnənt, *Am:* 'dɑ:mə-] *adj* dominante

dominate ['dɒmɪneɪt, *Am:* 'dɑ:mə-] *vi, vt* dominar

domination [ˌdɒmɪ'neɪʃən, *Am:* ˌdɑ:mə-] *no pl n* dominación *f*

domineer [ˌdɒmɪ'nɪəʳ, *Am:* ˌdɑ:mə'nɪr] *vi* dominar; **to** ~ **over sb** tiranizar a alguien

domineering *adj* dominante; **a** ~ **management style** una forma de dirigir muy tiránica

Dominica [ˌdɒmɪ'ni:kə, *Am:* ˌdɑ:mɪ'ni:-] *n* Dominica *f*

Dominican [də'mɪnɪkən, *Am:* doʊ'mɪn-] **I.** *adj* (*from Dominican Republic*) dominicano, -a **II.** *n* **1.** (*nationality*) dominicano, -a *m, f* **2.** REL dominico, -a *m, f*

Dominican Republic *n* República *f* Dominicana
dominion [də'mɪnjən] *n* dominio *m;* **to have ~ over sb/sth** tener a alguien/algo bajo su dominio
domino ['dɒmɪnəʊ, *Am:* 'dɑːmənoʊ] <-es> *n* **1.** *pl* (*games*) dominó *m;* **to play ~es** jugar al dominó **2.** (*piece*) ficha *f* de dominó
domino effect *n no pl* efecto *m* dominó
don [dɒn, *Am:* dɑːn] **I.** *n* UNIV profesor(a) *m(f)* **II.** *vt* (*of clothing*) ponerse
donate [dəʊ'neɪt, *Am:* 'doʊneɪt] *vt* donar
donation [dəʊ'neɪʃən, *Am:* doʊ'neɪ-] *n* **1.** (*contribution*) donativo *m* **2.** *no pl* (*act*) donación *f*
done [dʌn] *pp of* **do**
donkey ['dɒŋki, *Am:* 'dɑːŋ-] *n a. fig* burro *m,* burra *f*
donkey jacket *n Brit* chaqueta *f* de obrero **donkey work** *no pl n inf* trabajo *m* pesado
donor ['dəʊnəʳ, *Am:* 'doʊnɚ] *n* donante *mf*
don't [dəʊnt, *Am:* doʊnt] = **do not** *s.* **do**
donut ['dəʊnʌt, *Am:* 'doʊ-] *n Am, Aus* donut *m*
doodle ['duːdl] **I.** *vi* garabatear **II.** *n* garabato *m*
doom [duːm] **I.** *n* **1.** (*destiny*) suerte *f* **2.** (*death*) muerte *f* **II.** *vt* condenar
doomed *adj* condenado, -a; **to be ~ to failure** estar condenado al fracaso; **~ to die** condenado a muerte
doomsday ['duːmzdeɪ] *no pl n* día *m* del juicio final
door [dɔːʳ, *Am:* dɔːr] *n* **1.** puerta *f;* **main/back ~** puerta principal/trasera; **revolving/sliding ~** puerta giratoria/corredera; **to knock at** [*o* **on**] **the ~** llamar a la puerta; **there's someone at the ~** llaman a la puerta; **to answer the ~** abrir la puerta; **to see sb to the ~** acompañar a alguien hasta la puerta; **to live next ~** (**to sb**) vivir al lado (de alguien); **to show sb the ~** echar a alguien; **out of ~s** al aire libre; **behind closed ~s** a puerta cerrada; **to close the ~ on sb** cerrar la puerta a alguien; **to leave the ~ open to sb** dejar la puerta abierta a alguien; **~ to ~** puerta a puerta **2.** (*doorway*) entrada *f* ▶**to slam the ~ in sb's <u>face</u>** dar a alguien con la puerta en las narices; **to never <u>darken</u> sb's ~s again** *liter* no volver a poner los pies en casa de alguien; **to <u>lay</u> sth at sb's ~** echar a alguien la culpa de algo
doorbell ['dɔːbel, *Am:* 'dɔːr-] *n* timbre *m* **doorframe** *n* marco *m* de la puerta **doorkeeper** *n s.* **doorman doorknob** *n* pomo *m* de la puerta **doorman** <-men> *n* portero *m* **doormat** *n* felpudo *m* **doornail** *n inf* **as dead as a ~** muerto y bien muerto **doorplate** *n* placa *f* (*que se pone en la puerta de una casa*) **doorstep** *n* peldaño *m* (*de la puerta de entrada*) ▶**to be <u>right</u> on the ~** estar a la vuelta de la esquina
door-to-door [ˌdɔːtə'dɔːʳ, *Am:* ˌdɔːrt̬ə'dɔːr] **I.** *adj* de puerta a puerta; **~ selling** venta *f* a domicilio **II.** *adv* de puerta a puerta
doorway ['dɔːweɪ, *Am:* 'dɔːr-] *n* entrada *f*
dope [dəʊp, *Am:* doʊp] **I.** *n* **1.** *no pl, inf* (*drugs*) drogas *fpl;* (*marijuana*) marihuana *f* **2.** SPORTS doping *m;* **~ test** control *m* antidoping **3.** *inf* (*stupid person*) idiota *mf* **4.** *no pl, inf* (*information*) información *f;* **to give sb the ~ on** [*o* **about**] **sth** pasar informes a alguien sobre algo **II.** *vt* (*drug*) drogar; SPORTS dopar
dope dealer *n,* **dope peddler** *n,* **dope pusher** *n inf* camello *mf*
dopey *adj,* **dopy** ['dəʊpi, *Am:* 'doʊ-] *adj* <-ier, -iest> **1.** (*drowsy*) atontado, -a, abombado, -a *AmS* **2.** (*stupid*) tonto, -a
dormant ['dɔːmənt, *Am:* 'dɔːr-] *adj* (*volcano*) inactivo, -a; (*animal*) aletargado, -a; (*law*) inaplicado, -a; (*idea*) latente; **to lie ~** permanecer latente
dormer (**window**) *n* buhardilla *f*
dormitory ['dɔːmɪtəri, *Am:* 'dɔːrmətɔːri] <-ies> *n* **1.** dormitorio *m;* **~ town** ciudad *f* dormitorio **2.** *Am* UNIV residencia *f* de estudiantes
Dormobile® ['dɔːməbiːl, *Am:* 'dɔːr-] *n* autocaravana *f*
dormouse ['dɔːmaʊs, *Am:* 'dɔːr-] <-mice> *n* lirón *m*
dorsal ['dɔːsəl, *Am:* 'dɔːr-] *adj* dorsal
DOS [dɒs, *Am:* dɑːs] *n no pl abbr of* **disk operating system** DOS *m*
dosage ['dəʊsɪdʒ, *Am:* 'doʊ-] *n* dosis *f inv*
dose [dəʊs, *Am:* doʊs] **I.** *n a. fig* dosis *f inv;* **a ~ of bad news** una mala noticia; **a nasty ~ of flu** una gripe muy fuerte **II.** *vt* administrar una dosis a; **to ~ oneself with** medicarse con
doss [dɒs, *Am:* dɑːs] *vi Brit, Aus, inf* **1.** (*sleep*) sobar, apolillar *RíoPl;* **to ~ down on the sofa** apañarse para dormir en el sofá **2.** (*do nothing*) hacer el vago; **he's just ~ing** (**around**) sólo está haciendo el vago
dosser *n Brit, inf* **1.** (*tramp*) vagabundo, -a *m, f* **2.** (*lazy*) vago, -a *m, f*
dosshouse ['dɒshaʊs, *Am:* 'dɑːs-] *n Brit, inf* albergue *m* de acogida
dossier ['dɒsieɪ, *Am:* 'dɑːsieɪ] *n* expediente *m;* **to keep a ~ on sb/sth** llevar un expediente sobre alguien/algo
dot [dɒt, *Am:* dɑːt] **I.** *n* **1.** punto *m;* **on the ~** en punto; **she arrived at half past three on the ~** llegó a las tres y media en punto **2.** *pl* TYPO puntos *mpl* suspensivos **II.** <-tt-> *vt* **1.** (*mark with a dot*) puntuar **2.** (*put a dot on*) poner el punto en **3.** (*scatter*) esparcir ▶**to ~ one's i's and <u>cross</u> one's t's** poner los puntos sobre las íes
dote on [ˌdəʊt'ɒn, *Am:* ˌdoʊt̬'ɑːn] *vt,* **dote upon** *vt* adorar
doting *adj* muy cariñoso, -a; **we saw photos of the ~ father with the baby** le vimos en unas fotos, hecho todo un padrazo con el bebé
dot-matrix printer [ˌdɒtmeɪtrɪks'prɪntəʳ, *Am:* ˌdɑːt'meɪtrɪksprɪnt̬ɚ] *n* impresora *f* matricial

dotty ['dɒti, *Am:* 'dɑːt̬i] *adj* <-ier, -iest> (*person*) chiflado, -a; (*idea*) descabellado, -a

double ['dʌbl] **I.** *adj* **1.** (*twice as much/many*) doble; **a ~ door** una puerta de dos hojas; **a ~ whisky** un whisky doble; **it is ~ that** es el doble de eso; **to have a ~ meaning** tener un doble sentido; **to lead a ~ life** llevar una doble vida **2.** (*composed of two*) **in ~ figures** más de diez; **the number of deaths has now reached double figures** la cifra de muertos ya ha pasado de diez; **a ~ 's'** dos eses; **his number is ~ two five three five six** su número es el dos dos cinco tres cinco seis **3.** (*for two*) **~ mattress** colchón *m* de matrimonio; **~ room** habitación *f* doble **II.** *adv* doble; **to see ~** ver doble; **to fold sth ~** doblar algo por la mitad; **~ four is eight** el doble de cuatro es ocho; **he's ~ your age** te dobla la edad; **to be bent ~** estar encorvado **III.** *vt* (*increase*) doblar; (*efforts*) redoblar; **we have ~d our profits** hemos duplicado los beneficios **IV.** *vi* duplicarse; **to ~ for sb** CINE, THEAT doblar a alguien **V.** *n* **1.** (*double quantity*) doble *m* **2.** (*person*) doble *mf;* **sb's ~** el/la doble de alguien **3.** *pl* SPORTS dobles *m;* **to play ~s** jugar una partida de dobles ▶**at** [*o* **on**] **the ~** *inf* inmediatamente

◆**double back** *vi* (*person, animal*) volver sobre sus pasos; (*path, river*) describir una curva

◆**double up** *vi* **1.** (*bend over*) retorcerse; **to ~ with laughter** troncharse de risa; **to ~ with pain** retorcerse de dolor **2.** (*share room*) compartir habitación

double-barrelled [ˌdʌbl'bærld, *Am:* -'ber-] *adj* **1.** (*shotgun*) de dos cañones **2.** *Am, Aus* (*having two purposes*) de doble efecto **3.** *Brit* (*surname*) compuesto, -a

double bass <-es> *n* contrabajo *m* **double bed** *n* cama *f* de matrimonio

double-breasted [ˌdʌbl'brestɪd] *adj* (*of jacket*) cruzado, -a

double-check [ˌdʌbl'tʃek] *vt* comprobar dos veces

double chin *n* papada *f*

double-click *vi* INFOR hacer doble clic; **to ~ on the left mouse button** hacer doble clic con el botón izquierdo del ratón **double-cross** **I.** *vt* traicionar **II.** <-es> *n* traición *f*

double-crosser [ˌdʌbl'krɒsəʳ, *Am:* -'krɑːsɚ] *n* traidor(a) *m(f)* **double-dealer** *n* embustero, -a *m, f* **double-dealing** *n* engaño *m* **double-decker** *n* **1.** (*bus*) autobús *m* de dos pisos **2.** (*sandwich*) sandwich *m* doble **double Dutch** *no pl n Brit, inf* (*incomprehensible language*) chino *m fig;* **to talk ~** hablar en chino

double-edged [ˌdʌbl'edʒd] *adj a. fig* de doble filo

double-entry bookkeeping *n* contabilidad *f* por partida doble **double feature** *n* programa *m* doble

double-glaze [ˌdʌbl'gleɪz] *vt* **to ~ a window** instalar doble aislamiento en

double-glazing [ˌdʌbl'gleɪzɪŋ] *no pl n* doble acristalamiento *m*

double-jointed [ˌdʌbl'dʒɔɪntɪd, *Am:* -t̬ɪd] *adj* con articulaciones dobles

double-park [ˌdʌbl'pɑːk, *Am:* -'pɑːrk] *vi, vt* aparcar en doble fila

double-quick [ˌdʌbl'kwɪk] **I.** *adv* (*very quickly*) a paso ligero; **to get home ~** llegar a casa en un momento **II.** *adj* (*step*) ligero, -a; **in ~ time** volando

doublespeak ['dʌblspiːk] *n no pl* palabras *fpl* ambiguas

double standard *n* **to have ~s** no medir con el mismo rasero **double take** *n* reacción *f* retardada; **to do a ~** tardar en reaccionar **double-talk** *n no pl s.* **double-speak** **double-think** *n no pl* aceptación *f* de principios contradictorios **double time** *no pl n* **1.** COM, ECON paga *f* doble **2.** MIL paso *m* ligero

doubly ['dʌbli] *adv* doblemente; **to make ~ sure that ...** asegurarse bien de que... +*subj*

doubt [daʊt] *no pl* **I.** *n* duda *f;* **to be in ~ whether to ...** dudar si...; **without the shadow of a ~** sin sombra de duda; **no ~** sin duda; **without a ~** sin duda alguna; **he will no ~ come at Christmas** seguramente vendrá en Navidad; **there is no ~ about it** no cabe la menor duda; **to have one's ~s about sth** tener sus dudas respecto a algo; **the future of the project is in ~** no se sabe si el proyecto seguirá adelante; **beyond all reasonable ~** más allá de toda duda fundada; **to raise ~s about sth** hacer dudar de algo; **to cast ~ on sth** poner algo en tela de juicio **II.** *vt* **1.** (*be unwilling to believe*) dudar de; **to ~ sb's word** dudar de la palabra de alguien **2.** (*call into question: capability, sincerity*) poner en duda **3.** (*feel uncertain*) dudar; **to ~ that** dudar que +*subj;* **to ~ if** [*o* **whether**] **...** dudar si...; **I very much ~ it** lo dudo mucho **III.** *vi* dudar

doubtful ['daʊtfəl] *adj* **1.** (*uncertain, undecided*) indeciso, -a; **to be ~ whether to ...** dudar si...; **to be ~ about going** estar indeciso respecto a si ir o no **2.** (*unlikely*) incierto, -a **3.** (*questionable*) dudoso, -a

doubtless ['daʊtlɪs] *adv* sin duda

dough [dəʊ, *Am:* doʊ] *n* **1.** GASTR masa *f* **2.** *Am, inf* (*money*) pasta *f,* plata *f AmS*

doughnut ['dəʊnʌt, *Am:* 'doʊ-] *n Brit* donut *m*

doughy ['dəʊi, *Am:* 'doʊ-] *adj* pastoso, -a

dour [dʊəʳ, *Am:* dʊr] *adj* (*manner*) adusto, -a; (*appearance*) austero, -a

douse [daʊs] *vt* **1.** (*throw liquid on*) mojar; **to ~ sth in petrol** mojar algo con gasolina **2.** (*extinguish: light, candle*) apagar

dove¹ [dʌv] *n* ZOOL paloma *f*

dove² [dəʊv, *Am:* doʊv] *Am pt of* **dive**

dovecot(e) ['dʌvkəʊt, *Am:* -kɑːt] *n* palomar *m*

Dover ['dəʊvəʳ, *Am:* 'doʊvɚ] *n* Dover *m*

dovetail ['dʌvteɪl] **I.** *n* TECH cola *f* de milano

II. *vi* encajar III. *vt* 1. TECH ensamblar a cola de milano 2. (*fit*) **to ~ into/with sth** encajar en/con algo

dowager ['daʊədʒəʳ, *Am:* -dʒɚ] *n* viuda *f* de un noble; ~ **duchess** duquesa *f* viuda

dowdy ['daʊdi] *adj* <-ier, -iest> poco atractivo, -a; **to wear ~ clothes** vestir con poca gracia

dowel ['daʊəl] *n* TECH espiga *f*

down[1] [daʊn] *n* (*feathers*) plumón *m;* (*hairs*) pelusa *f;* (*on body*) vello *m;* (*on face*) bozo *m*

down[2] [daʊn] I. *adv* 1. (*movement*) abajo; **to fall ~** caerse; **to lie ~** acostarse 2. (*from another point*) **to go ~ to Brighton/the sea** bajar a Brighton/al mar; ~ **South** hacia el sur 3. (*less volume or intensity*) **to be worn ~** estar gastado; **the wind died ~** el viento se calmó; **the sun is ~** se ha puesto el sol; **the fire is burning ~** el fuego se está consumiendo; **the tyres are ~** los neumáticos están desinflados; **the price is ~** el precio ha bajado 4. (*temporal*) **from 1900 ~ to the present** desde 1900 hasta el presente; ~ **through the ages** a través de la historia 5. (*in writing*) **to write/get sth ~** escribir/anotar algo ▶**to be ~ on sb** tener manía a alguien; ~ **with the dictator!** ¡abajo el dictador! II. *prep* 1. (*lower*) **to go ~ the stairs** bajar las escaleras; **to run ~ the slope** correr cuesta abajo 2. (*along*) **to go ~ the street** ir por la calle

down and out, **down-and-out** [ˌdaʊnənd'aʊt] I. *adj* **to be ~** no tener donde caerse muerto II. *n* vagabundo, -a *m, f*

downcast ['daʊnkɑːst, *Am:* 'daʊnkæst] *adj* alicaído, -a

downfall ['daʊnfɔːl] *n* (*of government*) caída *f;* (*of organization, firm*) derrumbamiento *m;* (*of person*) perdición *f;* **that will be his ~** eso será su ruina

downgrade [ˌdaʊn'greɪd] I. *vt* 1. (*lower category of*) bajar de categoría 2. (*disparage*) minimizar; **to ~ the importance of sth** minimizar la importancia de algo II. *n* bajada; **to be on the ~** *fig* ir cuesta abajo

downhearted [ˌdaʊn'hɑːtɪd, *Am:* -'hɑːrt̬ɪd] *adj* descorazonado, -a

downhill [ˌdaʊn'hɪl] I. *adv* cuesta abajo; **to go ~** ir cuesta abajo; *fig* ir de mal en peor II. *adj* (*path*) cuesta abajo; **it's all ~ from now on** (*easy*) ya lo tenemos chupado *inf*

download [ˌdaʊn'ləʊd, *Am:* 'daʊnloʊd] *vt* INFOR bajar

downmarket [ˌdaʊn'mɑːkɪt, *Am:* 'daʊnˌmɑːr-] I. *adj* (*neighbourhood, newspaper*) popular; (*shop, store*) barato, -a; (*programme*) de masas II. *adv* **to move ~** perder prestigio; (*intentionally*) dirigirse a un sector popular del público

down payment *n* entrada *f,* cuota *f* inicial *AmL;* **to make a ~ on sth** dar la entrada para comprar algo

downplay [ˌdaʊn'pleɪ, *Am:* 'daʊnpleɪ] *vt* restar importancia a

downpour ['daʊnpɔːʳ, *Am:* -pɔːr] *n* chaparrón *m*

downright ['daʊnraɪt] I. *adj* (*refusal, disobedience*) completo, -a; (*lie*) abierto, -a; (*liar*) redomado, -a; (*fool*) de remate; **it is a ~ disgrace** es una auténtica vergüenza; **that's ~ stupid** eso es una solemne tontería II. *adv* completamente; **to be ~ difficult** ser dificilísimo; **to refuse ~** *Am* negarse rotundamente

downside ['daʊnsaɪd] *n no pl* inconveniente *m;* **on the ~, it is far from the village** tiene el inconveniente de que está lejos del pueblo

downsize [ˌdaʊn'saɪz, *Am:* 'daʊnsaɪz] *vt* reducir

downsizing *n no pl* reducción *f*

Down's Syndrome ['daʊnz'sɪndrəʊm, *Am:* -ˌsɪndroʊm] *n no pl* síndrome *m* de Down

downstairs [ˌdaʊn'steəz, *Am:* -'sterz] I. *adv* abajo; **to go ~** bajar; **to run ~** bajar corriendo (las escaleras) II. *adj* (del piso) de abajo III. *n no pl* planta *f* baja

downstream [ˌdaʊn'striːm] *adv* río abajo; **it is another few miles ~ from here** eso está a unas millas más abajo de aquí; **to paddle downstream** remar río abajo

downtime ['daʊntaɪm] *n no pl* INFOR, TECH tiempo *m* improductivo

down-to-earth [ˌdaʊntə'ɜːθ, *Am:* -'ɜːrθ] *adj* (*explanation*) realista; (*person*) práctico, -a

downtown ['daʊntaʊn, *Am:* ˌdaʊn'-] I. *n no pl, Am* centro *m* (de la ciudad) II. *adv Am* **to go ~** ir al centro; **to live ~** vivir en el centro III. *adj Am* (*situated in the central section*) céntrico, -a; (*related to the central section*) del centro de la ciudad; ~ **Los Angeles** el centro de Los Ángeles

downtrodden ['daʊntrɒdn, *Am:* -trɑːdn] *adj* (*grass*) pisoteado, -a; (*person*) oprimido, -a

downturn ['daʊntɜːn, *Am:* -tɜːrn] *n* empeoramiento *m;* **a ~ in sth** un giro negativo en algo; **to take a ~** dar un bajón; **an economic ~** un empeoramiento de la situación económica

downward ['daʊnwəd, *Am:* -wɚd] I. *adj* (*movement*) descendente; (*direction*) hacia abajo; (*path*) cuesta abajo; (*tendency, prices*) a la baja; **inflation is on a ~ trend** la inflación está disminuyendo II. *adv* **Am** *s.* **downwards**

downwards ['daʊnwədz, *Am:* -wɚdz] *adv* hacia abajo

downy ['daʊni] *adj* aterciopelado, -a

dowry ['daʊəri] <-ies> *n* dote *f*

dowse[1] [daʊs] *vi* buscar con una varilla de zahorí; **to ~ for water** buscar agua con una varilla de zahorí

dowse[2] [daʊs] *vt s.* **douse**

dowser *n* zahorí *mf*

dowsing *n no pl búsqueda de agua o metales con una varilla de zahorí*

dowsing rod *n* varilla *f* de zahorí

doyen ['dɔɪən] *n* decano *m*

D

doyenne ['dɔɪen] *n* decana *f*
doz. *abbr of* **dozen** docena *f*
doze [dəʊz, *Am:* doʊz] **I.** *vi* dormitar; **to ~ off** dormirse **II.** *n* cabezada *f*; **to have a ~** echar un sueño
dozen ['dʌzn] *n* **1.** (*twelve*) docena *f*; **half a ~** media docena; **two ~ eggs** dos docenas de huevos **2.** (*many*) **~s of times** montones de veces; **by the ~** por docenas ►**it's six of one and half a ~ of the other** da lo mismo; **to talk nineteen to the ~** hablar por los codos
dozy ['dəʊzi, *Am:* 'doʊ-] *adj* <-ier, -iest> **1.** (*drowsy, sleepy*) soñoliento, -a **2.** *Brit, inf* (*stupid*) tonto, -a, abombado, -a *AmL*
DP **1.** *abbr of* **data processing** PD *m* **2.** *abbr of* **displaced person** desplazado, -a *m, f*
DPhil *n abbr of* **Doctor of Philosophy** doctor(a) *m(f)* en Filosofía
Dr *abbr of* **Doctor** Dr. *m*, Dra. *f*
drab [dræb] *adj* <drabber, drabbest> (*food*) soso, -a; (*colour*) apagado, -a; (*existence*) monótono, -a
drachma ['drækmə] *n* dracma *f*
draconian [drə'kəʊnɪən, *Am:* -'koʊ-] *adj* draconiano, -a
draft [drɑːft, *Am:* dræft] **I.** *n* **1.** (*drawing*) boceto *m* **2.** (*preliminary version*) borrador *m*; (*of novel, speech*) primera versión *f*; (*of contract*) minuta *f*; **~ bill** LAW anteproyecto *m* de ley **3.** *no pl, Am* MIL reclutamiento *m* **4.** *Brit* FIN, ECON letra *f* de cambio **II.** *vt* **1.** (*prepare a preliminary version*) hacer un borrador de; (*novel*) redactar la primera versión de; (*plan*) trazar; (*contract*) redactar la minuta de **2.** *Am* MIL llamar a filas
draft dodger *n Am* MIL prófugo *m*
draftee [drɑː'ftiː, *Am:* 'dræf-] *n Am* MIL recluta *mf*
draftsman ['drɑːftsmən, *Am:* 'dræfts-] <-men> *n Am, Aus* TECH *s.* **draughtsman**
drafty ['dræfti] *adj Am s.* **draughty**
drag [dræg] <-gg-> **I.** *vt* **1.** (*pull*) arrastrar; **to ~ oneself somewhere** arrastrarse hasta un sitio; **to ~ one's heels** arrastrar los pies; *fig* dar largas a un asunto; **to ~ sb's name through the mud** dejar a alguien por los suelos **2.** (*in water*) dragar **II.** *vi* **1.** (*trail along*) arrastrarse por el suelo **2.** (*time*) pasar lentamente; (*meeting, conversation*) hacerse interminable **3.** (*lag behind*) rezagarse **III.** *n* **1.** (*device*) draga *f* **2.** *no pl* PHYS resistencia *f* al avance; AVIAT resistencia *f* aerodinámica **3.** *no pl* (*hindrance*) estorbo *m*; **to be a ~ on sb** ser una carga para alguien **4.** *no pl, inf* (*boring experience*) lata *f*; **what a ~!** ¡qué rollo! **5.** *no pl, inf* (*boring person*) pelmazo *m* **6.** *no pl, inf* (*women's clothes*) disfraz *m* de mujer; **to be in ~** ir vestido de mujer **7.** *inf* (*inhalation*) calada *f*; **to take a ~** dar una calada ►**the main ~** *Am, Aus, inf* la calle principal
◆**drag along** *vt* arrastrar con dificultad
◆**drag away** *vt* arrancar
◆**drag behind** *vi* seguir con atraso
◆**drag down** *vt* **1.** (*force to a lower level*) arrastrar hacia abajo **2.** (*make depressed*) hundir; (*make weak*) debilitar
◆**drag in** *vt* (*person*) involucrar; (*subject*) traer por los pelos
◆**drag on** *vi* (*meeting, film*) hacerse interminable
◆**drag out** <-gg-> *vt* (*meeting, conversation*) alargar
◆**drag up** *vt* sacar a relucir
drag lift *n Brit* telearrastre *m*
dragon ['drægən] *n* **1.** (*mythical creature*) dragón *m* **2.** (*fierce woman*) arpía *f*
dragonfly ['drægənflaɪ] <-ies> *n* libélula *f*, alguacil *m RíoPl*
dragoon [drə'guːn] *n* MIL dragón *m*
drain [dreɪn] **I.** *vt* **1.** AGR, MED drenar; (*pond*) vaciar; (*river*) desaguar; (*food*) escurrir; (*machine*) purgar **2.** (*empty by drinking: glass, cup*) apurar; (*bottle*) acabar **3.** (*exhaust, tire out: person*) dejar agotado; (*resources*) agotar; **to ~ sb's energies** consumir las energías de alguien; **war ~s the nation of its youth and its wealth** la guerra mina la juventud y la riqueza de una nación **II.** *vi* (*dishes*) escurrirse **III.** *n* **1.** (*conduit*) canal *m* de desagüe **2.** (*sewer*) alcantarilla *f*, resumidero *m AmL*; **the ~s** el alcantarillado **3.** (*plughole*) desagüe *m*; **to throw sth down the ~** tirar algo por la borda; **to throw** [*o* **to pour**] **money down the ~** tirar el dinero por la ventana **4.** (*constant outflow*) fuga *f*; **brain ~** fuga de cerebros; **to be a ~ on sb's resources** consumir los recursos de alguien ►**to laugh like a ~** *Brit, inf* reírse a mandíbula batiente
◆**drain away** *vi* (*water*) irse; (*energy*) agotarse; (*tension*) disiparse
◆**drain off** *vt* (*liquid*) extraer
drainage ['dreɪnɪdʒ] *n no pl* **1.** AGR, MED drenaje *m* **2.** TECH desagüe *m*; **~ system** alcantarillado *m*
drainage basin *n* cuenca *f* hidrográfica
draining board ['dreɪnɪŋ'bɔːd, *Am:* -ˌbɔːrd] *n* escurridero *m*
drainpipe ['dreɪnpaɪp] *n* **1.** (*pipe*) tubo *m* de desagüe **2.** *pl* (*trousers*) pantalones *mpl* pitillo
drainpipe trousers *npl* pantalones *mpl* pitillo
drake [dreɪk] *n* pato (macho) *m*
dram [dræm] *n Scot* (*of whisky, liquor*) copita *f*
drama ['drɑːmə] *n* **1.** LIT drama *m* **2.** THEAT arte *m* dramático; **~ teacher** profesor(a) *m(f)* de arte dramático ►**high ~** *inf* follón padre
drama school *n* escuela *f* de arte dramático
dramatic [drə'mætɪk, *Am:* -'mæt̬-] *adj* **1.** THEAT dramático, -a; (*artist, production*) teatral **2.** (*very noticeable: rise*) espectacular; (*effect, discovery*) notable
dramatics [drə'mætɪks, *Am:* -'mæt̬-] *npl* **1.** + *sing vb* THEAT teatro *m*; **amateur ~** teatro amateur **2.** *pej* (*behaviour*) teatralidad *f*

dramatis personae [ˌdræmətɪspɜːˈsəʊnaɪ, *Am:* ˌdrɑːmət̬ɪspɚˈsoʊ-] *npl* THEAT personajes *mpl* (*de una obra de teatro*)

dramatist [ˈdræmətɪst, *Am:* ˈdrɑːmət̬ɪst] *n* THEAT dramaturgo, -a *m, f*

dramatization [ˌdræmətaɪˈzeɪʃən, *Am:* ˌdrɑːmət̬ɪ-] *n* dramatización *f*

dramatize [ˈdræmətaɪz, *Am:* ˈdrɑːmə-] *vt* **1.** THEAT adaptar al teatro **2.** (*exaggerate*) dramatizar

drank [dræŋk] *pt of* **drink**

drape [dreɪp] **I.** *vt* **1.** (*hang*) cubrir; **to ~ sth (in a flag)** cubrir algo (con una bandera) **2.** (*place*) colocar; **she ~d the scarf around her shoulders** se puso el chal sobre las espaldas; **to lie ~d over sth** estar tendido sobre algo **II.** *vi* colgar; **to ~ well** (*clothes*) tener caída **III.** *n* **1.** *no pl* (*loose*) caída *f* **2.** (*fold*) pliegue *m* **3.** *pl, Am, Aus* (*curtains*) cortinas *fpl*

draper [ˈdreɪpəʳ, *Am:* -pɚ] *n Brit* pañero, -a *m, f*, mercero, -a *m, f AmL*

drapery [ˈdreɪpəri] <-ies> *n* **1.** *no pl* (*hangings*) ropaje *m* **2.** *no pl, Brit* (*cloths, fabrics*) pañería *f* **3.** *pl, Am, Aus* (*curtains*) cortinas *fpl*

drastic [ˈdræstɪk] *adj* (*measure*) drástico, -a; (*change*) radical

drat [dræt] *interj* maldita sea

draught [drɑːft, *Am:* dræft] **I.** *n* **1.** (*air current*) corriente *f* de aire; **to feel the ~** *fig* sufrir las consecuencias **2.** (*drink*) trago *m;* **to take at one ~** apurar de un trago **3.** MED dosis *f inv* **4.** GASTR **on ~** de barril **5.** NAUT calado *m* **6.** *pl* GAMES damas *fpl* **II.** *adj* **1.** (*beer*) de barril **2.** (*horse*) de tiro

draught board *n* tablero *m* de damas

draughtsman [ˈdrɑːftsmən, *Am:* ˈdræfts-] <-men> *n* delineante *m*

draughty [ˈdrɑːfti, *Am:* ˈdræf-] *adj* <-ier, -iest> lleno, -a de corrientes de aire; **it's ~ here with the door open** hace corriente con la puerta abierta

draw [drɔː, *Am:* drɑː] **I.** <drew, drawn> *vt* **1.** ART dibujar; (*line*) trazar; (*character*) perfilar; (*diagram*) representar; **to ~ sth to scale** reproducir algo a escala **2.** (*pull, haul: cart, wagon*) arrastrar; **to ~ the curtains** correr las cortinas; **to ~ sb aside** llevarse a alguien aparte; **to ~ sb into (an) ambush** meter a alguien en una emboscada; **I was soon drawn into the argument** pronto me vi envuelto en la discusión **3.** (*attract*) atraer; **to ~ applause** arrancar aplausos; **to be ~n toward(s) sb** sentirse atraído por alguien; **to ~ attention to** llamar la atención sobre; **to ~ criticism** suscitar críticas **4.** (*elicit, evoke*) **to ~ sth (from sb/sth)** conseguir algo (de alguien/algo); **to ~ a confession from sb** sacar una confesión a alguien; **to ~ a reply** obtener una respuesta; **to ~ laughter** provocar risa **5.** (*formulate, perceive*) **to ~ an analogy** establecer una analogía; **to ~ a conclusion** sacar una conclusión; **to ~ an inference** inferir **6.** (*take out*) sacar; (*money*) retirar; **to ~ a card (from the deck)** GAMES escoger una carta (de la baraja); **to ~ blood** *fig* hacer sangrar **7.** (*obtain*) obtener; (*salary*) ganar; (*pension*) cobrar **8.** (*lottery*) sortear **9.** SPORTS, GAMES empatar **10.** GASTR **to ~ a beer** poner una cerveza de barril **11.** FIN, ECON (*write out a bill, cheque or draft*) **to ~ a cheque on sb** extender un cheque a cargo de alguien; **to ~ a bill on sb** girar una letra a cargo de alguien **12.** NAUT **the boat ~s 1.5 metres** el barco tiene un calado de 1,5 metros **13.** SPORTS **to ~ a bow** tensar un arco **II.** <drew, drawn> *vi* **1.** ART dibujar **2.** (*move, procede*) **to ~ ahead** adelantarse; **to ~ away** apartarse; **~ up here and he'll get into the car** para aquí y podrá subir en el coche; **to ~ level with sb/sth** *Brit* alcanzar a alguien/algo **3.** (*approach*) acercarse; **to ~ to a close** finalizar; **to ~ to an end** concluir **4.** (*draw lots*) echar a suertes **5.** SPORTS, GAMES empatar **III.** *n* **1.** (*attraction*) atracción *f* **2.** SPORTS, GAMES empate *m* **3.** (*drawing of lots*) sorteo *m* **4.** (*act of drawing a gun*) **to be quick on the ~** ser rápido en sacar la pistola; *fig* pescarlas al vuelo

◆**draw apart** *vi* distanciarse

◆**draw aside** *vt always sep* (*person*) apartar; (*curtain*) correr

◆**draw away** **I.** *vi* **1.** (*move off*) alejarse **2.** (*move ahead*) **to ~ from sb** dejar atrás a alguien **3.** (*move away*) apartarse **II.** *vt* apartar

◆**draw down** *vt* bajar; **to wear a hat drawn down over one's ears** llevar un gorro calado hasta las orejas

◆**draw in** **I.** *vi* **1.** (*car, bus, train*) llegar **2.** (*days*) acortarse **II.** *vt* **1.** (*breath*) tomar **2.** (*attract*) atraer

◆**draw off** *vt* (*boots*) quitarse; (*liquid*) vaciar

◆**draw on** **I.** *vt* **1.** (*make use of*) usar; **to ~ sb's own resources** utilizar sus propios recursos; **to ~ the stocks** tirar de existencias **2.** (*put on*) ponerse **II.** *vi* **1.** (*continue: time, day*) seguir su curso **2.** (*approach*) acercarse

◆**draw out** **I.** *vt* **1.** (*prolong*) alargar **2.** (*elicit*) sacar; **to be highly skilled at drawing out information** ser muy hábil para sonsacar información; **to ~ feelings and memories** hacer aflorar sentimientos y recuerdos; **to draw sb out (of himself)** hacer que alguien se desinhiba **3.** FIN, ECON, COM retirar **II.** *vi* **1.** (*car, bus, train*) salir **2.** (*day*) hacerse más largo

◆**draw together** **I.** *vt* juntar **II.** *vi* acercarse

◆**draw up** **I.** *vt* **1.** (*draft*) redactar; (*list*) hacer; (*guidelines, plan*) trazar; **to ~ a constitution** LAW redactar una constitución **2.** (*pull toward one*) arrimar **3.** (*raise*) levantar; **to draw oneself up** erguirse **II.** *vi* (*vehicle*) pararse

drawback [ˈdrɔːbæk, *Am:* ˈdrɑː-] *n* desventaja *f* **drawbridge** *n* puente *m* levadizo

drawer [ˈdrɔːʳ, *Am:* ˈdrɔːr] *n* cajón *m*

drawing *n* ART dibujo *m;* **pencil ~** dibujo a lápiz

drawing board *n* tablero *m* de delineación;

back to the ~! ¡vuelta a empezar! **drawing pin** *n Brit, Aus* chincheta *f* **drawing room** *n* salón *m*

drawl [drɔːl, *Am:* drɑːl] **I.** *n* habla *f* lenta **II.** *vi* hablar arrastrando las vocales

drawn [drɔːn, *Am:* drɑːn] **I.** *pp of* **draw** **II.** *adj* **1.** (*face*) demacrado, -a; **you look tired and ~** se te ve cansado y ojeroso **2.** GASTR deretido, -a

dread [dred] **I.** *vt* temer; **I ~ to think ...** me da miedo pensar... **II.** *n no pl* terror *m;* **to fill sb with ~** aterrorizar a alguien **III.** *adj liter* aterrador(a)

dreadful ['dredfəl] *adj* **1.** (*terrible*) atroz; (*mistake*) terrible; (*atrocity*) espantoso, -a **2.** (*of very bad quality*) fatal **3.** (*very great*) horroroso, -a; **I feel ~ about it** me da mucha pena

dreadfully ['dredfəli] *adv* **1.** (*in a terrible manner*) terriblemente **2.** (*very poorly*) fatal **3.** (*extremely*) enormemente

dream [driːm] **I.** *n* **1.** sueño *m;* **a bad ~** una pesadilla **2.** (*daydream*) ensueño *m;* (*fantasy*) ilusión *f;* **to be in a ~** estar en las nubes; **like a ~** como un sueño; **he cooks like a ~** cocina de maravilla; **to go like a ~** ir como la seda; **a ~ come true** un sueño hecho realidad; **in your ~s!** ¡ni lo sueñes! **II.** <dreamt *o* dreamed, dreamt *o* dreamed> *vi* soñar; **to ~ of (doing) sth** soñar con (hacer) algo; **~ on!** *inf* ¡ni de coña!; **I would not ~ of (doing) that** no se me pasaría por la cabeza (hacer) eso **III.** <dreamt *o* dreamed, dreamt *o* dreamed> *vt* soñar; **I never ~t that ...** nunca se me había ocurrido que... *+condicional* **IV.** *adj* ideal; **his ~ house** la casa de sus sueños; **to be (living) in a ~ world** vivir en las nubes

♦**dream away** *vt* **to ~ the day** pasarse el día soñando

♦**dream up** *vt* idear

dreamer ['driːməʳ, *Am:* -mɚ] *n* soñador(a) *m(f); pej* iluso, -a *m, f*

dreamland *n inf* país *m* de los sueños

dreamless *adj* sin sueños

dreamlike *adj* de ensueño

dreamt [dremt] *pt, pp of* **dream**

dreamy ['driːmi] *adj* <-ier, -iest> **1.** (*dreamlike*) de ensueño **2.** (*daydreaming*) soñador(a) **3.** *inf* (*wonderful*) maravilloso, -a

dreary ['drɪəri, *Am:* 'drɪr-] *adj* <-ier, -iest> (*life*) deprimente; (*place*) lóbrego, -a; (*weather*) gris

dredge[1] [dredʒ] **I.** *n* TECH red *f* de arrastre **II.** *vt* TECH dragar

dredge[2] [dredʒ] *vt* GASTR espolvorear

dredger[1] ['dredʒəʳ, *Am:* -ɚ] *n* TECH draga *f*

dredger[2] ['dredʒəʳ, *Am:* -ɚ] *n* GASTR espolvoreador *m*

dregs [dregz] *npl* **1.** (*sediment*) poso *m* **2.** (*undesirable part*) **the ~ of society** la escoria de la sociedad

drench [drentʃ] *vt* empapar; **to be ~ed with** estar calado de

dress [dres] **I.** *n* <-es> vestido *m;* **strapless/sleeveless ~** vestido sin tirantes/sin mangas; **evening ~** (*for woman*) vestido de noche; (*for man*) traje *m* de etiqueta **II.** *vi* vestirse; **to ~ in blue** vestir de azul; **to ~ smartly for sth** ponerse elegante para algo **III.** *vt* **1.** (*put clothes on*) vestir **2.** GASTR (*greens, salad*) aliñar **3.** MED (*wound*) vendar **4.** (*decorate*) adornar; (*hair*) peinar; **to ~ shop windows** decorar escaparates **IV.** *adj* de gala; **a ~ suit** traje *m* de gala

♦**dress down** **I.** *vi* vestir informal **II.** *vt Brit, inf* regañar

♦**dress up** **I.** *vi* ponerse elegante; **to ~ as** disfrazarse de **II.** *vt* **1.** (*put on formal clothes*) poner elegante **2.** (*disguise*) disfrazar; **to dress sb up as** disfrazar a alguien de **3.** (*embellish*) adornar

dress circle *n* THEAT piso *m* principal **dress coat** *n* frac *m*

dresser ['dresəʳ, *Am:* -ɚ] *n* **1.** FASHION **to be a very stylish ~** vestir con mucho estilo **2.** THEAT encargado, -a *m, f* de vestuario **3.** (*sideboard*) aparador *m; Am, Can* (*dressing table*) tocador *m*

dressing ['dresɪŋ] *n* **1.** *no pl* FASHION el vestir *m* **2.** GASTR aliño *m* **3.** MED vendaje *m*

dressing-down *n Brit* reprimenda *f* **dressing gown** *n* (*garment worn inside the house*) bata *f;* (*towel*) albornoz *m* **dressing room** *n* vestidor *m;* THEAT camerino *m* **dressing table** *n* tocador *m*

dressmaker ['dresˌmeɪkəʳ, *Am:* -kɚ] *n* modisto, -a *m, f*

dressmaking **I.** *n no pl* costura *f* **II.** *adj* **~ course** curso *m* de corte y confección; **~ and tailoring shop** sastrería *f*

dress rehearsal *n* ensayo *m* general **dress shirt** *n* camisa *f* de etiqueta **dress suit** *n* vestido *m* de gala **dress uniform** *n* uniforme *m* de gala

dressy ['dresi] *adj* <-ier, -iest> (*clothing*) elegante

drew [druː] *pt of* **draw**

dribble ['drɪbl] **I.** *vi* **1.** (*person*) babear **2.** (*water*) gotear **3.** SPORTS regatear con; **to ~ past a defender** driblar a un defensa **II.** *vt* **1.** (*water*) dejar caer gota a gota **2.** SPORTS regatear con **III.** *n* **1.** *no pl* (*saliva*) baba *f* **2.** (*water*) chorrito *m* **3.** SPORTS dribling *m*

driblet ['drɪblɪt] *n* trocito *m;* **in ~s** en pequeñas cantidades

dribs [drɪbz] *npl* **in ~ and drabs** poco a poco

dried [draɪd] **I.** *pt, pp of* **dry** **II.** *adj* seco, -a; **~ meat** cecina *f;* **~ milk** leche *f* en polvo

dried-up [ˌdraɪd'ʌp] *adj,* **dried up** *adj* seco, -a

drier *adj,* **dryer** ['draɪəʳ, *Am:* -ɚ] *adj comp of* **dry**

drift [drɪft] **I.** *vi* **1.** (*on water*) dejarse llevar por la corriente; (*in air*) dejarse llevar por el viento; **to ~ out to sea** ir a la deriva **2.** (*move* *aimlessly*) dejarse llevar **3.**(*progress aimlessly*) vivir sin rumbo **4.** METEO (*sand, snow*) amontonarse **II.** *n* **1.** NAUT deriva *f* **2.** *fig* (*movement*) movimiento *m* **3.**(*trend*) tendencia *f* **4.** METEO montón *m;* **a sand ~** un montón de arena **5.**(*sense*) significado *m;* **to catch sb's ~** caer en la cuenta de lo que alguien quiere decir

◆drift apart *vi* (*people*) distanciarse (progresivamente)

◆drift off *vi* dormirse lentamente

drifter ['drɪftəʳ, *Am:* -tɚ] *n* vagabundo, -a *m, f*

drift-ice *n no pl* hielo *m* flotante

drifting *adj* **~ fog banks** bancos *mpl* de niebla empujados por la corriente

driftwood *n no pl madera que flota en el mar arrastrada por la corriente*

drill¹ [drɪl] **I.** *n* TECH taladro *m;* (*dentist's*) fresa *f;* **~ bit** broca *f* **II.** *vt* TECH perforar; **to ~ a hole** hacer un agujero **III.** *vi* TECH perforar

drill² [drɪl] **I.** *n* MIL, SCHOOL ejercicios *fpl;* **to do spelling ~s** hacer ejercicios de ortografía ▶**to know the ~** *inf* saber lo que hay que hacer; **what's the ~?** *inf* ¿cómo se hace? **II.** *vt* **1.** SCHOOL instruir; **to ~ sth into sb** inculcar algo a alguien **2.** MIL enseñar la instrucción a **III.** *vi* **1.**(*go through exercise*) hacer ejercicios **2.** MIL hacer la instrucción **IV.** *adj* MIL de instrucción

drilling rig ['drɪlɪŋ,rɪg] *n* torre *f* de perforación

drink [drɪŋk] **I.** <drank, drunk> *vi* beber; **to ~ heavily** beber en exceso; **to ~ in moderation** beber con moderación; **to ~ to sb** brindar por alguien; **to ~ like a fish** beber como una esponja **II.** <drank, drunk> *vt* beber; **to ~ a toast** (**to sb/sth**) brindar (por alguien/algo); **to ~ sb under the table** tener mucho más aguante que alguien **III.** *n* bebida *f;* (*alcoholic beverage*) copa *f;* **to have a ~** tomar algo; **to drive sb to ~** llevar a alguien a la bebida; **the ~** *inf* el agua

◆drink in *vt* beber; (*words*) estar pendiente de

drinkable [drɪŋkəbl] *adj* potable

drinker *n* bebedor(a) *m(f)*

drinking *n no pl* (*act*) el beber *m;* (*drunkenness*) bebida *f;* **no ~ allowed in these premises** se prohíbe el consumo de bebidas alcohólicas

drinking fountain *n* fuente *f* de agua potable **drinking song** *n* canción *f* de taberna **drinking straw** *n* caña *f*

drinking water *no pl n* agua *f* potable **drinking-water supply** *n* abastecimiento *m* de agua potable

drip [drɪp] **I.** <-pp-> *vi* gotear **II.** <-pp-> *vt* dejar caer gota a gota **III.** *n* **1.** *no pl* (*act of dripping*) goteo *m* **2.**(*drop*) gota *f* **3.** MED gota a gota *m* **4.** *inf* (*person*) pánfilo, -a *m, f*

drip-dry [,drɪp'draɪ] <-ie-> *adj* de lava y pon

dripping ['drɪpɪŋ] **I.** *adj* **1.**(*tap*) que gotea **2.**(*extremely wet*) chorreante **II.** *adv* **to be ~ wet** estar empapado **III.** *n Am: pl* pringue *m*

drive [draɪv] **I.** <drove, driven> *vt* **1.** AUTO conducir, manejar *AmL;* **to ~ sb home** llevar a alguien a casa (en coche); **to ~ a race car** (*operate*) pilotar un coche de carreras; **to ~ a sports car** tener un coche deportivo **2.**(*urge*) empujar; **to ~ sb to (do) sth** forzar a alguien a (hacer) algo **3.**(*cattle*) guiar **4.**(*render, make*) volver; **to ~ sb mad** sacar a alguien de quicio **5.**(*ball*) golpear; (*tunnel*) abrir; (*road*) construir; **to ~ a passage** abrir un camino **6.** TECH mover **II.** <drove, driven> *vi* AUTO **1.**(*steer*) conducir, manejar *AmL* **2.**(*travel*) ir en coche **3.**(*function*) funcionar **III.** *n* **1.** AUTO paseo *m;* (*journey*) viaje *m;* **to go for a ~** ir a dar una vuelta en coche **2.**(*driveway*) entrada *f* **3.** *no pl* TECH transmisión *f;* **front-wheel ~** tracción delantera; **all-wheel ~** tracción a las cuatro ruedas **4.** *no pl* PSYCH impulso *m;* **to have ~** ser emprendedor; **sex ~** apetito *m* sexual **5.**(*campaign*) campaña *f;* **to be on an economy ~** estar en una economía restrictiva; **a fund-raising ~** campaña para recaudar fondos **6.** SPORTS golpe *m* fuerte **7.** INFOR unidad *f* de disco; **to insert a floppy disk into the disk ~** insertar un disquete en la disquetera

◆drive at *vt inf* insinuar

◆drive in **I.** *vi* entrar (en coche) **II.** *vt* (*nail*) clavar

◆drive off **I.** *vt always sep* ahuyentar **II.** *vi* irse (en coche)

◆drive out *vt* expulsar

◆drive up *vi* **to ~ (somewhere)** acercarse (a algún sitio)

drive-in ['draɪvɪn] **I.** *adj Am, Aus* **~ cinema** autocine *m* **II.** *n Am, Aus* (*drive-in restaurant*) *restaurante donde se sirve a los clientes en su propio coche;* (*drive-in cinema*) autocine *m*

drive-in bank *n Am, Aus* autobanco *m*

drive-in cinema *n,* **drive-in movie** *n Am, Aus* autocine *m*

drivel ['drɪvəl] *n no pl* tonterías *fpl*

driven ['drɪvən] *pp of* **drive**

driver ['draɪvəʳ, *Am:* -vɚ] *n* **1.** AUTO conductor(a) *m(f);* **truck ~** camionero, -a *m, f;* **taxi ~** taxista *mf;* **~'s license** *Am* carné *m* de conducir, brevete *m Perú;* **to be in the ~'s seat** *fig* llevar las riendas de algo **2.** INFOR driver *m*

> Las **Drive through bottle shops** son un tipo de tiendas que se pueden encontrar por toda Australia. Generalmente pertenecen a hoteles y por su aspecto se parecen a un garaje abierto o a un granero en el que se puede entrar con el coche. A este tipo de tiendas también se las conoce como **liquor barns**. En ellas, sin tener que apearse del vehículo, se puede comprar vino, cerveza y cualquier bebida alcohólica. El cliente es servido directamente en la ventanilla de su coche.

driveway ['draɪvweɪ] *n* camino de entrada *m*

D

driving I. *n* conducción *f*, manejo *m AmL* II. *adj* 1. AUTO, TECH de conducir 2. METEO (*rain*) torrencial 3. (*powerful: ambition, force*) impulsor(a)

driving ban *n* retirada *f* del carné de conducir **driving force** *n no pl* fuerza *f* motriz **driving instructor** *n* profesor(a) *m(f)* de autoescuela **driving lessons** *npl* prácticas *fpl* de conducir **driving licence** *n Brit* carné *m* de conducir **driving pool** *n* flota *f* de automóviles **driving school** *n* autoescuela *f* **driving test** *n* examen *m* de conducir

drizzle ['drɪzl] I. *n no pl* METEO llovizna *f*, garúa *f AmL*, chipichipi *m Méx* II. *vi* METEO lloviznar, garuar *AmL*

drizzly ['drɪzli] *adj* **it was a grey ~ afternoon** la tarde era gris y lloviznaba

droll [drəʊl, *Am:* droʊl] *adj* divertido, -a

dromedary ['drɒmədəri, *Am:* 'drɑːməder-] <-ies> *n* dromedario *m*

drone [drəʊn, *Am:* droʊn] I. *n no pl* 1. ZOOL zángano *m* 2. (*person*) vago, -a *m, f* 3. (*tone*) zumbido *m* II. *vi* 1. (*make a monotonous sound*) zumbar 2. (*speak in a monotonous tone*) hablar con monotonía

drool [druːl] I. *vi* babear; **to ~ over sth/sb** *fig* caérse a uno la baba con algo/alguien II. *n no pl* baba *f*

droop [druːp] I. *vi* 1. (*fall*) colgar 2. (*flowers*) marchitarse 3. (*person*) desanimarse; (*mood, spirits*) decaer II. *vt* inclinar

drop [drɒp, *Am:* drɑːp] I. *n* 1. (*of liquid*) gota *f*; **~ by ~** gota a gota 2. (*vertical distance*) declive *f*; **a sheer ~** un profundo precipicio 3. (*decrease*) disminución *f*; (*of temperature*) descenso *m* 4. (*fall*) caída *f*; (*distribution by aircraft*) lanzamiento *m*; **~ of medical supplies** aprovisionamiento *m* aéreo de suministros médicos 5. *inf* (*of drink*) sorbo *m*; **just a ~** sólo un poco; **to have had a ~ too much** (**to drink**) llevar una copa de más; **to take a ~** tomar un trago 6. (*sweet*) pastilla *f* 7. (*secret collection point*) escondrijo *m* ▶**at the ~ of a hat** en seguida; **it's a ~ in the ocean** es una gota de agua en el mar II. <-pp-> *vt* 1. (*allow to fall*) dejar caer; **to ~ anchor** echar el ancla; **to ~ a bomb** lanzar una bomba; **to ~ ballast** soltar lastre 2. (*lower*) bajar; **to ~ prices** reducir los precios; **to ~ one's voice** bajar la voz 3. *inf* (*send*) enviar; **to ~ a letter into a mailbox** *Am* echar una carta al correo 4. *inf* (*express*) soltar; **to ~ a hint** soltar una indirecta; **to ~ a word in sb's ear** decir una palabra al oído a alguien 5. (*dismiss*) despedir 6. (*abandon, give up*) renunciar a; **to ~ a demand** retirar una demanda; **to ~ sb** romper con alguien 7. (*leave out*) omitir; **to ~ one's aitches** *Brit, Aus* no pronunciar las haches ▶**to ~ a brick**, **to ~ a clanger** *Brit* meter la pata III. <-pp-> *vi* 1. (*descend*) bajar 2. (*go to*) **to ~ into a bar/a shop** pasarse por un bar/una tienda 3. (*go lower: prices*) bajar 4. *inf* (*become exhausted*) estar agotado, -a; **to ~ with exhaustion** caer rendido; **he is ready to ~** está que no se tiene; **to ~ (down) dead** caerse muerto; **~ dead!** *inf* ¡muérete! ▶**to let it ~** dejarlo; **to let it ~ that ...** dar a entender que...

◆**drop across** *vt insep, inf* encontrarse con

◆**drop behind** *vi* quedarse atrás; **to ~ in sth** rezagarse en algo

◆**drop down** *vi* caer

◆**drop in** I. *vi inf* entrar un momento; **to ~ on sb** ir a ver a alguien; (*unexpectedly*) visitar a alguien inesperadamente II. *vt* **to drop sb right in it** *inf* meter a alguien en problemas

◆**drop off** I. *vt inf* (*passenger*) dejar II. *vi* 1. (*decrease*) disminuir 2. *inf* (*fall asleep*) quedarse dormido 3. (*become separated*) desprenderse

◆**drop out** *vi* 1. (*person*) darse de baja; **to ~ of a course** darse de baja de un curso 2. LING omitir

drop-down menu *n* INFOR menú *m* desplegable

drop kick *n* SPORTS bote pronto *m*

droplet ['drɒplət, *Am:* 'drɑːp-] *n* gotita *f*

dropout ['drɒpaʊt, *Am:* 'drɑːp-] *n* 1. (*person who lives in an unusual way*) automarginado, -a *m, f* 2. UNIV, SCHOOL persona *f* que ha abandonado los estudios

dropper ['drɒpəʳ, *Am:* 'drɑːpɚ] *n* cuentagotas *m inv*, gotero *m AmL*

droppings ['drɒpɪŋz, *Am:* 'drɑːpɪŋz] *npl* excremento *m*

drop shot *n* SPORTS dejada *f*

dross [drɒs, *Am:* drɑːs] *n no pl, Brit* escoria *f*

drought [draʊt] *n* sequía *f*

drove[1] [drəʊv, *Am:* droʊv] I. *vt* modelar con cincel II. *n* 1. (*chisel*) cincel *m* 2. (*of animals*) rebaño *m* 3. *pl, inf* (*large group of people*) multitud *f*; **in ~s** en tropel

drove[2] [drəʊv, *Am:* droʊv] *pt of* **drive**

drover ['drəʊvəʳ, *Am:* 'droʊvɚ] *n* pastor(a) *m(f)*

drown [draʊn] I. *vt* 1. (*cause to die*) ahogar; **to look like a ~ed rat** *inf* estar calado hasta los huesos 2. (*engulf in water*) anegar 3. (*make inaudible*) apagar ▶**to ~ one's sorrows in drink** ahogar las penas en alcohol II. *vi* 1. (*die through submersion*) ahogarse 2. *inf* (*have too much*) **to be ~ing in work** estar hasta arriba de trabajo

drowning *n* ahogo *m*

drowse [draʊz] *vi* dormitar

drowsy ['draʊzi] <-ier, -iest> *adj* soñoliento, -a

drudge [drʌdʒ] I. *n* esclavo, -a *m, f* del trabajo II. *vi* trabajar como un esclavo

drudgery ['drʌdʒəri] *n no pl* trabajo *m* penoso

drug [drʌg] I. *n* 1. MED fármaco *m* 2. (*narcotic*) droga *f*; **to take ~s** tomar drogas II. <-gg-> *vt* drogar

drug abuse *n* toxicomanía *f* **drug addict** *n* toxicómano, -a *m, f* **drug addiction** *n* drogadicción *f* **drug dealer** *n* traficante *mf* de drogas **drug dependency** *n* drogodependencia *f* **drug manufacturer** *n* fabricante *mf* de drogas sintéticas **drug pusher** *n inf* camello *mf* **drug squad** *n,* **drugs squad** *n Brit* brigada *f* de estupefacientes

drugstore ['drʌgstɔ:ʳ, *Am:* -stɔ:r] *n Am* farmacia *f* (*donde suelen venderse otros artículos, además de productos farmacéuticos*)

drug taking *n* consumo *m* de drogas **drug traffic** *n* tráfico *m* de drogas **drug trafficker** *n* narcotraficante *mf* **drug trafficking** *n* narcotráfico *m*

druid ['dru:ɪd] *n* druida *m*

drum [drʌm] **I.** *n* **1.** MUS, TECH tambor *m* **2.** *pl* (*in a band*) batería *f* **3.** (*for oil*) bidón *m* **4.** ANAT tímpano *m* **II.** <-mm-> *vi* (*play percussion*) tocar el tambor; (*with fingers*) tamborilear con los dedos; **to ~ on sth** tamborilear con los dedos sobre algo **III.** *vt inf* **to ~ sth into sb** meter a alguien algo en la cabeza

drumbeat ['drʌmbi:t] *n* redoble *m*

drum brake *n* freno *m* de tambor

drumhead ['drʌmhed] *n* parche *m* de tambor

drum major *n* tambor *m* mayor

drummer ['drʌməʳ, *Am:* -ɚ] *n* (*in a band*) tambor *m;* (*in a group*) batería *f*

drumstick ['drʌmstɪk] *n* **1.** MUS palillo *m* **2.** GASTR pierna *f* de pollo

drunk [drʌŋk] **I.** *vt, vi pp of* **drink II.** *adj* **1.** (*inebriated*) borracho, -a, jumo, -a *AmL,* ido, -a *AmC,* bota *Méx;* **to be ~** estar borracho; **to get ~** emborracharse **2.** *fig* (*very much affected*) **to be ~ with joy** estar ebrio de alegría **III.** *n* borracho, -a *m, f*

drunkard ['drʌŋkəd, *Am:* -kɚd] *n* borracho, -a *m, f*

drunken ['drʌŋkən] *adj* borracho, -a; **a ~ brawl** una reyerta de borrachos; **~ driving** *Am* conducción *f* en estado de embriaguez

drunkenness ['drʌŋkənɪs] *n no pl* embriaguez *f,* bomba *f AmL*

dry [draɪ] **I.** <-ier *o* -er, -iest *o* -est> *adj* **1.** (*not wet*) seco, -a; **to go ~** secarse; **~ red wine** vino tinto seco **2.** (*climate, soil*) árido, -a **3.** (*bread*) sin mantequilla **4.** (*without alcohol: state*) prohibicionista **5.** (*uninteresting*) aburrido, -a **6.** (*brief*) lacónico, -a; **~** (**sense of**) **humour** (sentido del) humor agudo ►**to bleed sb ~** sacar a alguien hasta el útimo céntimo; **to run ~** agotarse **II.** <-ie-> *vt* secar; (*tears*) enjugarse **III.** <-ie-> *vi* secarse; **to put sth out to ~** sacar algo para que se seque

◆**dry up I.** *vi* **1.** (*become dry*) secarse **2.** (*dry the dishes*) secar los platos **3.** (*stop talking*) callarse; (*on stage*) quedarse en blanco **4.** (*run out*) agotarse **5.** *inf* (*become silent*) enmudecer **II.** *vt* secar

dryad ['draɪæd] *n* dríade *f*

dry cell *n* ELEC pila *f* seca

dry cell battery *n* batería *f* de pila seca

dry-clean [ˌdraɪ'kli:n] *vt* limpiar en seco

dry cleaner's *n no pl* tintorería *f*

dry cleaning *n* limpieza *f* en seco

dry dock *n* dique *m* seco

dryer ['draɪəʳ, *Am:* -ɚ] *n* **1.** (*for hair*) secador *m* **2.** (*machine for drying clothes*) secadora *f*

dry goods *npl Am* mercería *f* **dry ice** *n* nieve *f* carbóica **dry land** *n* (*not sea*) tierra *f* firme **dry measure** *n* medida *f* para áridos

dryness ['draɪnəs] *n no pl, a. fig* sequedad *f*

dry rot *n* putrefacción *f* de la madera **dry-shod** *adj, adv* a pie enjuto

drystone wall *n Brit* muro *m* seco

DS *n abbr of* **Detective Sergeant** comisario *m*

DSc *abbr of* **Doctor of Science** doctor(a) *m(f)* en Ciencias

DTP [ˌdi:ti:'pi:] *n abbr of* **desktop publishing** DTP *m*

dual ['dju:əl, *Am:* 'du:-] *adj inv* doble; **~ ownership** ECON condominio *m*

dual carriageway *n Brit* autovía *f,* autocarril *m Bol, Chile, Nic* **dual-currency period** *n* período *m* de convivencia de dos monedas

dualism ['djʊəlɪzəm, *Am:* 'du:-] *n no pl* dualismo *m*

dub[1] [dʌb] <-bb-> *vt* **1.** (*confer knighthood*) armar caballero **2.** (*give sb a nickname*) apodar

dub[2] [dʌb] <-bb-> *vt* (*film*) doblar; **to be ~bed into English/French** estar doblado en inglés/francés

dubbing ['dʌbɪŋ] *n* doblaje *m*

dubious ['dju:bɪəs, *Am:* 'du:-] *adj* **1.** (*doubtful*) dudoso, -a **2.** (*untrustworthy*) sospechoso, -a

Dubliner ['dʌblɪnəʳ] *n* dublinés, -esa *m, f*

duchess ['dʌtʃɪs] *n* duquesa *f*

duchy ['dʌtʃi] *n* ducado *m*

duck[1] [dʌk] *n Brit, inf* cariño *mf*

duck[2] [dʌk] **I.** *n* **1.** (*bird*) pato *m* **2.** SPORTS cero *m;* **to be out for a ~** ser eliminado a cero ►**to take to sth like a ~ to water** *inf* sentirse como pez en el agua con/en algo **II.** *vi* **1.** (*dip head*) agachar la cabeza **2.** (*go under water*) chapuzarse **3.** (*hide*) agacharse; **to ~ out of sth** escabullirse de algo **III.** *vt* **1.** (*lower suddenly*) **to ~ one's head** agachar la cabeza; **to ~ one's head under water** sumergir la cabeza dentro del agua **2.** (*avoid*) esquivar; *fig* eludir; **to ~ an issue** eludir un tema

duckboards ['dʌkbɔ:dz, *Am:* -bɔ:rdz] *npl* pasadera *f*

duckling ['dʌklɪŋ] *n* patito *m*

ducky ['dʌki] *n inf* cariño *m*

duct [dʌkt] *n* **1.** (*pipe*) conducto *m;* **air ~** conducto del aire **2.** ANAT canal *m;* **ear ~** canal auditivo

dud [dʌd] **I.** *n* **1.** (*person*) persona *f* inútil **2.** (*bomb*) bomba *f* que no estalla **3.** (*failure*) fallo *m* **II.** *adj* **1.** (*useless, worthless*) falso, -a **2.** (*forged*) falsificado, -a; **~ cheque** cheque *m* sin fondos

dude [dju:d] *n Am, inf* (*guy*) individuo *m;* (*smartly dressed*) figurín *m*

due [dju:, *Am:* du:] **I.** *adj* **1.** (*payable*)

D

pagadero, -a; (*owing*) debido, -a; ~ **date** fecha *f* de vencimiento; **the loan is now ~ for repayment** hay que devolver el préstamo; **to fall ~** vencer **2.** (*appropriate*) conveniente; **with (all) due respect** con el debido respeto; **in ~ course** a su debido tiempo **3.** *after n, Brit, Aus* (*appropriate, owing*) **to treat sb with the respect ~ to him/her** tratar a alguien con el respeto que se merece **4.** (*expected*) esperado, -a; **I'm ~ in Berlin this evening** esta noche me esperan en Berlín **5.** (*owing to, because of*) **~ to** debido a; **~ to circumstances beyond our control ...** por circunstancias ajenas a nuestra voluntad... **II.** *n* **1.** (*fair treatment*) merecido *m;* **to give sb his/her ~** dar a alguien lo que se merece **2.** (*debts*) deuda *f; pl* (*obligations*) deberes *mpl;* **to pay one's ~s** (*meet obligations/duties*) cumplir con sus obligaciones/deberes; (*meet debts*) pagar las deudas **3.** *pl* (*regular payment*) cuota *f* **III.** *adv before adv* exactamente; **~ north/south** derecho hacia el norte/sur

duel ['djuːəl, *Am:* 'duː-] **I.** *n* duelo *m;* **to fight a ~** batirse en duelo **II.** *vi* <*Brit:* -ll-, *Am:* -l-> HIST batirse en duelo

duet [dju'et, *Am:* du-] *n* dúo *m;* **to play a ~** interpretar un dueto

duffel bag ['dʌfəlˌbæg] *n* NAUT bolsa *f* de lona **duffel coat** *n* trenca *f*

duffer ['dʌfəʳ, *Am:* -ɚ] *n* zoquete *m*

dug[1] [dʌg] *pt, pp of* **dig**

dug[2] [dʌg] *n* (*of mammal*) teta *f;* (*of cow*) ubre *f*

dugout ['dʌgaʊt] *n* **1.** MIL refugio *m* subterráneo **2.** SPORTS banquillo *m* **3.** NAUT piragua *f* (*hecha de un tronco*)

duke [djuːk, *Am:* duːk] *n* duque *m*

dull [dʌl] **I.** *adj* **1.** (*boring*) aburrido, -a; (*life*) monótono, -a; **as ~ as ditchwater** más aburrido que un entierro de tercera **2.** (*not bright: surface*) deslustrado, -a; (*sky*) gris; (*weather*) desapacible; (*colour*) apagado, -a; (*light*) pálido, -a **3.** (*muffled, muted*) callado, -a; (*ache, thud*) sordo, -a **4.** *Am* (*blunt, unsharpened*) desafilado, -a **II.** *vt* **1.** (*alleviate*) aliviar **2.** (*desensitize*) insensibilizar

dullard ['dʌləd, *Am:* -ɚd] *n* zoquete *m*

dullness ['dʌlnɪs] *n no pl* **1.** (*lack of excitement*) insipidez *f* **2.** (*tediousness*) pesadez *f*

duly ['djuːli, *Am:* 'duː-] *adv* **1.** (*appropriately*) debidamente **2.** (*on time*) a su debido tiempo

dumb [dʌm] *adj* **1.** (*mute*) mudo, -a; **deaf and ~** sordomudo, -a; **to be struck ~** quedarse mudo de asombro **2.** *inf* (*stupid*) estúpido, -a; **to play ~** hacerse el tonto

dumbbell ['dʌmbel] *n* **1.** (*weight*) pesa *f* **2.** *Am, inf* (*person*) bobo, -a *m, f*

dumbfound [ˌdʌm'faʊnd, *Am:* 'dʌmfaʊnd] *vt* dejar mudo (de asombro)

dumbfounded *adj* mudo, -a de asombro

dumbshow ['dʌmʃəʊ, *Am:* -ʃoʊ] *n Brit, inf* pantomima *f;* **to use ~** emplear la mímica

dumbstricken ['dʌmˌstrɪkən] *adj,* **dumbstruck** ['dʌmstrʌk] *adj* mudo, -a (de asombro)

dumb waiter *n* montaplatos *m*

dumfound [ˌdʌm'faʊnd, *Am:* 'dʌmfaʊnd] *vt s.* **dumbfound**

dummy ['dʌmi] **I.** <-ies> *n* **1.** (*mannequin*) maniquí *m* **2.** (*duplicate*) imitación *f* **3.** *Brit, Aus* (*for baby*) chupete *m* **4.** (*fool*) tonto, -a **II.** *adj* (*duplicate*) copiado, -a; (*false*) falso, -a; **~ run** prueba *f;* (*tryout*) ensayo *m* **III.** *vi Am, inf* **to ~ up** callarse como un muerto

dump [dʌmp] **I.** *n* **1.** (*for waste*) vertedero *m,* botadero *m Ven* **2.** (*nasty place*) tugurio *m* **3.** MIL depósito *m;* **ammunition ~** almacén *m* de municiones **II.** *vt* **1.** (*drop carelessly*) verter; (*get rid of*) deshacerse de **2.** (*abandon*) abandonar **3.** *inf* (*end relationship with*) dejar **4.** INFOR volcar **III.** *vi Am, inf* **to ~ on sb** pagarla con alguien

dumper ['dʌmpəʳ, *Am:* -pɚ] *n* dúmper *m*

dumping *n* dúmping *m*

dumping ground *n* vertedero *m*

dumpling ['dʌmplɪŋ] *n bolita de masa que puede estar rellena de carne o bien de fruta*

dumpy ['dʌmpi] <-ier, -iest> *adj* regordete, -a

dun[1] [dʌn] *adj* pardo, -a

dun[2] [dʌn] **I.** <-nn-> *vt* **to ~ sb** apremiar a alguien para que pague lo que debe **II.** *n* petición *f* de reembolso

dunce [dʌns] *n* burro, -a *mf*

dune [djuːn, *Am:* duːn] *n* duna *f*

dung [dʌŋ] *n no pl* excrementos *mpl,* estiércol *m*

dungarees [ˌdʌŋgə'riːz] *npl Brit* (*overall*) peto *m; Am* (*denim clothes*) mono *m*

dungeon ['dʌndʒən] *n* mazmorra *f*

dunghill ['dʌŋhɪl] *n* estercolero *m*

dunk [dʌŋk] *vt* mojar

duo ['djuːəʊ, *Am:* 'duːoʊ] *n* dúo *m;* **comedy ~** pareja cómica

duodenum [ˌdjuːə'diːnəm, *Am:* ˌduː-] <-na *o* -s> *n* duodeno *m*

dup. *n abbr of* **duplicate** dup.

dupe [djuːp, *Am:* duːp] **I.** *n* inocentón, -ona *m, f* **II.** *vt* **to be ~d** ser engañado

duplex ['djuːpleks, *Am:* 'duː-] **I.** *n* **1.** *Am* (*apartment*) dúplex **2.** *Aus* (*house*) casa *f* adosada **II.** *adj* doble

duplicate ['djuːplɪkət, *Am:* 'duː-] **I.** *vt* **1.** (*replicate*) duplicar; (*repeat*) repetir **2.** (*copy*) copiar; **to ~ a device** hacer una réplica de un dispositivo **II.** *adj inv* duplicado, -a; **~ key** duplicado *m* de una llave **III.** *n* duplicado *m*

duplicator ['djuːplɪkeɪtəʳ, *Am:* 'duːplɪkeɪt̬ɚ] *n* multicopista *f*

duplicity [djuː'plɪsəti, *Am:* duː'plɪsət̬i] *n no pl* duplicidad *f*

durability [ˌdjʊərə'bɪləti, *Am:* ˌdʊrə'bɪlət̬i] *n no pl* **1.** (*permanence, persistency*) durabilidad *f* **2.** (*life of a product*) duración *f*

durable ['djʊərəbl, *Am:* 'dʊrə-] *adj* **1.** (*hard-wearing*) resistente **2.** (*long-lasting*) duradero, -a
duration [djʊ'reɪʃən, *Am:* dʊ-] *n no pl* duración *f;* **a stay of two years'** ~ una estancia de dos años de duración; **for the** ~ hasta que se acabe
duress [djʊ'res, *Am:* dʊ-] *n no pl* coacción *f;* **under** ~ bajo coacción
during ['djʊərɪŋ, *Am:* 'dʊrɪŋ] *prep* durante; ~ **work/the week** durante el trabajo/la semana
dusk [dʌsk] *n no pl* crepúsculo *m;* **at** ~ al atardecer
dusky ['dʌski] <-ier, iest> *adj* **1.** (*dark*) oscuro, -a **2.** *a. pej* (*dark-skinned*) moreno, -a
dust [dʌst] **I.** *n no pl* polvo *m;* **coal** ~ cisco *m* ►**to bite the** ~ morder el polvo; **to wait till the** ~ **has settled** dejar que se aclare la atmósfera; **to throw** ~ **in the eyes of sb** engañar a alguien con falsas apariencias; **to turn to** ~ *liter* convertirse en polvo **II.** *vt* **1.** (*clean*) quitar el polvo a **2.** (*spread over*) salpicar; **to** ~ **sth with insecticide** espolvorear insecticida sobre la superficie de algo **III.** *vi* quitar el polvo
dustbin ['dʌstbɪn] *n Brit* cubo *m* de (la) basura **dustcart** *n Brit* camión *m* de la basura **dust-coat** *n* sobretodo *m* **dust cover** *n* **1.** (*for furniture*) guardapolvo *m* **2.** (*on book*) forro *m*
duster ['dʌstəʳ, *Am:* -tɚ] *n* trapo *m*
dust jacket *n* (*of a book*) sobrecubierta *f* **dustman** <-men> *n Brit* basurero *m* **dustpan** *n* recogedor *m;* ~ **and brush** recogedor y escoba **dust storm** *n* vendaval *m* de polvo
dust-up ['dʌstʌp] *n inf* **1.** (*physical clash*) pelea *f* **2.** (*dispute*) enfrentamiento *m*
dusty ['dʌsti] <-ier, -iest> *adj* **1.** (*covered in dust*) polvoriento, -a **2.** (*of greyish colour*) ceniciento, -a; ~ **brown** marrón grisáceo
Dutch [dʌtʃ] **I.** *adj* holandés, -esa **II.** *n* **1.** *pl* (*people*) **the** ~ los holandeses **2.** LING holandés ►**to go** ~ pagar a escote
Dutchman ['dʌtʃmən] <-men> *n* holandés *m* ►**if ... I'm a** ~ *Brit* que me maten si...
Dutchwoman ['dʌtʃ,wʊmən] <-women> *n* holandesa *f*
dutiable ['dju:tiəbl, *Am:* 'du:ţi-] *adj* sujeto, -a a derechos de aduana
dutiful ['dju:tɪfəl, *Am:* 'du:ţɪ-] *adj* obediente
duty ['dju:ti, *Am:* 'du:ţi] <-ies> *n* **1.** (*moral*) deber *m;* (*obligation*) obligación *f;* **it's my** ~ es mi deber; **to do sth out of** ~ hacer algo por compromiso; **to do one's** ~ cumplir con su obligación **2.** (*task, function*) función *f* **3.** *no pl* (*work*) tarea *f;* **to do** ~ **for sb** sustituir a alguien; **to be suspended from** ~ ser suspendido del servicio; **to be on/off** ~ estar/no estar de servicio **4.** (*tax*) impuesto *m;* (*revenue on imports*) derechos *mpl* de aduana; **customs duties** arancel *m;* **to pay** ~ **on sth** pagar derechos de aduana por algo
duty call *n* visita *f* de cumplido
duty-free [,dju:ti'fri:, *Am:* ,du:ţi-] **I.** *adj* libre de impuestos **II.** *n* bien *m* libre de impuestos
duty roster *n* lista *f* de guardias
duvet ['dju:veɪ, *Am:* du:'veɪ] *n Brit* edredón *m* nórdico
DVD *n inv* INFOR *abbr of* **Digital Versatile Disk** DVD *m*
DVLA *n Brit abbr of* **Driver and Vehicle Licensing Authority** ≈ DGT *f*
dwarf [dwɔ:f, *Am:* dwɔ:rf] **I.** <-s *o* -ves> *n* enano, -a *m, f* **II.** *vt* empequeñecer
dwell [dwel] <dwelt *o* -ed, dwelt *o* -ed> *vi* **1.** (*live*) morar **2.** (*give attention to*) **to** ~ **on sth** insistir en algo; **to** ~ **on a subject** explayarse en un tema
dweller *n* morador(a) *m(f)*
dwelling ['dwelɪŋ] *n* morada *f*
dwelling house *n* casa *f* particular
dwelt [dwelt] *pp, pt of* **dwell**
dwindle ['dwɪndl] *vi* menguar
dye [daɪ] **I.** *vt* teñir **II.** *n* tinte *m*
dyed-in-the-wool [,daɪdɪnðə'wʊl] *adj* convencido, -a; ~ **opinions** opiniones *fpl* firmes
dye-works ['daɪwɜ:ks, *Am:* -wɜ:rks] *n* tintorería *f*
dying ['daɪɪŋ] *adj* **1.** (*approaching death*) moribundo, -a **2.** (*manifested before death: words*) último, -a
dyke[1] [daɪk] *n* **1.** *a. fig* dique *m* **2.** (*channel*) acequia *f*
dyke[2] [daɪk] *n inf* (*lesbian*) tortillera *f*
dynamic [daɪ'næmɪk] *adj* dinámico, -a
dynamics [daɪ'næmɪks] *n* **1.** PHYS dinámica *f;* (*development*) desarrollo *m* **2.** MUS (*alterations of volume*) crecimiento *m*
dynamite ['daɪnəmaɪt] **I.** *n no pl* dinamita *f* **II.** *vt* dinamitar
dynamo ['daɪnəməʊ, *Am:* -moʊ] <-s> *n* dinamo *f*
dynasty ['dɪnəsti, *Am:* 'daɪnə-] <-ies> *n* dinastía *f*
dysentery ['dɪsəntəri, *Am:* -teri] *n no pl* MED disentería *f*
dysfunctional [dɪs'fʌŋkʃənəl] *adj* disfuncional
dyslexia [dɪ'sleksiə] *n no pl* dislexia *f*
dyslexic [dɪ'sleksɪk] *adj* disléxico, -a
dyspepsia [dɪ'spepsiə] *n* MED dispepsia *f*

E

E, e [i:] *n* **1.** (*letter*) E, e *f;* ~ **for Edward** E de España **2.** MUS mi *m* **3.** SCHOOL ≈ insuficiente *m*
E *abbr of* **east** E
each [i:tʃ] **I.** *adj* cada; ~ **one of you** cada uno de vosotros; ~ **and every house** cada casa sin excepción **II.** *pron* cada uno, cada una; ~ **of them could beat you** cada uno de ellos podría ganarte; **£70** ~ £70 cada uno; **he gave**

us £10 ~ nos dió a cada uno £10; **I'll take one kilo of** ~ tomaré un kilo de cada (uno)

each other *pron* uno a otro, una a la otra; **they are always arguing with** ~ siempre discuten entre ellos; **to help** ~ ayudarse mutuamente; **to be made for** ~ estar hechos el uno para el otro

eager ['iːgəʳ, *Am:* -gɚ] *adj* ansioso, -a; **to be** ~ **for sth** ansiar algo; **to be** ~ **for revenge** tener sed de venganza; **to be** ~ **to start** estar ansioso por empezar

eager beaver *n inf* **he is an** ~ se esmera mucho en su trabajo

eagerness *n no pl* entusiasmo *m;* ~ **to please** deseo *m* de agradar

eagle ['iːgl] *n* águila *f*

eagle-eyed ['iːglaɪd] *adj* **to be** ~ tener ojos de lince

ear[1] [ɪəʳ, *Am:* ɪr] *n* ANAT oído *m;* (*outer part*) oreja *f;* ~, **nose and throat specialist** otorrinolaringólogo, -a *m, f;* **to have a good** ~ tener buen oído; **to have an** ~ **for music** tener buen oído para la música; **to smile from** ~ **to** ~ sonreír de oreja a oreja ▸**to be up to one's** ~**s in debt** *inf* estar endeudado hasta la camisa; **to have one's** ~ **to the ground** *inf* mantenerse al corriente; **to be all** ~**s** *inf* ser todo oídos; **to keep one's** ~**s open** *inf* abrir los oídos; **he'll be out on his** ~ *inf* lo van a poner de patitas en la calle; **his** ~**s must be burning** *inf* le deben de estar zumbando los oídos; **to turn a deaf** ~ (**to sth**) hacer oídos sordos (a algo); **to give sb a thick** ~ *inf* pegar una paliza a alguien; **to bend sb's** ~ *inf* fastidiar a alguien; **to close one's** ~**s to sth** hacer oídos sordos a algo; **sb's** ~**s are flapping** *inf* alguien tiene puesta la antena; **it goes in one** ~ **and out the other** *inf* por un oído le entra y por el otro le sale; **to have the** ~ **of sb** gozar de la confianza de alguien

ear[2] [ɪəʳ, *Am:* ɪr] *n* BOT espiga *f*

earache ['ɪəreɪk, *Am:* 'ɪr-] *n* dolor *m* de oído **eardrum** *n* tímpano *m* **ear infection** *n* infección *f* de oído

earl [ɜːl, *Am:* ɜːrl] *n* conde *m*

earlobe ['ɪələʊb] *n* lóbulo *m* de la oreja

early ['ɜːli, *Am:* 'ɜːr-] **I.** <-ier, -iest> *adj* **1.** (*ahead of time, near the beginning*) temprano, -a; **to be** ~ llegar temprano; ~ **retirement** jubilación *f* anticipada; **to take** ~ **retirement** jubilarse anticipadamente; **an** ~ **death** una muerte prematura; **the** ~ **hours** la madrugada; **in the** ~ **morning** de madrugada; **in the** ~ **afternoon** a primera hora de la tarde; **at an** ~ **age** a una edad temprana; **he is in his** ~ **twenties** tiene poco más de veinte años; **in the** ~ **15th century** a principios del siglo XV; ~ **education** primera enseñanza *f;* **to have an** ~ **night** acostarse temprano; **the** ~ **stages** las primeras etapas; **the** ~ **days/years of sth** los primeros tiempos de algo **2.** *form* (*prompt: reply*) rápido, -a; **at your earliest convenience** tan pronto como le sea posible **3.** (*first*) primero, -a **II.** *adv* **1.** (*ahead of time*) temprano; **to get up** ~ madrugar; ~ **in the morning** por la mañana temprano; ~ **in the year** a principios de año; **to be half an hour** ~ llegar media hora antes **2.** (*soon*) pronto; **as** ~ **as possible** tan pronto como sea posible; **reply** ~ respondan cuanto antes; **book your tickets** ~ compren sus entradas con tiempo **3.** (*prematurely*) prematuramente; **to die** ~ morir joven

Early Church *n* **the** ~ la iglesia de los primeros cristianos

earmark ['ɪəmɑːk, *Am:* 'ɪrmɑːrk] **I.** *vt* **1.** (*animal*) marcar en la oreja; (*document*) marcar **2.** (*put aside*) reservar; (*funds*) destinar **II.** *n* marca *f* en la oreja; *fig* marca *f* distintiva

earmuffs ['ɪəmʌfs, *Am:* 'ɪr-] *npl* orejeras *fpl*

earn [ɜːn, *Am:* ɜːrn] **I.** *vt* **1.** (*be paid*) ganar; **to** ~ **one's daily bread** ganarse el pan; **to** ~ **a living** ganarse la vida **2.** (*bring in*) dar; (*interest*) devengar **3.** (*obtain*) **to** ~ **money from sth** obtener dinero de algo; **coffee exports** ~ **Brasil many millions of pounds** Brasil obtiene muchos millones de libras de la exportación de café **4.** (*deserve*) merecer, ganarse; **his decision** ~**ed him the confidence of his boss** su decisión le valió la confianza de su jefe **II.** *vi* trabajar

earned income *n* ingresos *mpl* en concepto de salario

earner *n* asalariado, -a *m, f*

earnest ['ɜːnɪst, *Am:* 'ɜːr-] **I.** *adj* **1.** (*serious*) serio, -a **2.** (*sincere*) sincero, -a; (*attempt*) concienzudo, -a; (*desire*) ferviente **II.** *n no pl* seriedad *f;* **in** ~ en serio; **school has now begun in** ~ ahora ha empezado de verdad el colegio; **to be in** (**deadly**) ~ hablar (completamente) en serio

earnestly *adv* **1.** (*speak*) seriamente **2.** (*desire*) de todo corazón

earning capacity *n Brit,* **earning power** *n Am* potencial *m* de ingresos

earnings ['ɜːnɪŋz, *Am:* 'ɜːr-] *npl* **1.** (*of a person*) ingresos *mpl* **2.** (*of a company*) beneficios *mpl,* utilidades *fpl AmL*

earnings-related *adj* proporcional al sueldo

earphones ['ɪəfəʊnz, *Am:* 'ɪrfoʊnz] *npl* auriculares *mpl*

earpiece ['ɪəpiːs, *Am:* 'ɪr-] *n* **1.** (*of a phone*) auricular *m* **2.** (*of glasses*) patilla *f*

earplug ['ɪəplʌg, *Am:* 'ɪr-] *n pl* tapón *m* para el oído

earring ['ɪərɪŋ, *Am:* 'ɪrɪŋ] *n* pendiente *m,* caravana *f CSur,* candonga *f Col;* **a pair of** ~**s** unos pendientes

earshot ['ɪəʃɒt, *Am:* 'ɪrʃɑːt] *n no pl* alcance *m* del oído; **in/out of** ~ al alcance/fuera del alcance del oído

earth [ɜːθ, *Am:* ɜːrθ] **I.** *n no pl* **1.** (*planeta*) tierra *f;* **on** ~ en el mundo; **you look like nothing** (**else**) **on** ~ estás espantoso **2.** (*animal's hole*) madriguera *f* **3.** ELEC toma *f* de tierra ▸**to bring sb back** (**down**) **to** ~ hacer bajar de las nubes a alguien; **to come back**

(**down**) **to** ~ bajar de las nubes; **to cost the** ~ costar un ojo de la cara; **to go to** ~ esconderse; **to promise the** ~ prometer el oro y el moro; **what/who/where/why on** ~ **...?** *inf* ¿qué/quién/dónde/por qué diablos...? **II.** *vt* conectar a tierra

earthbound ['ɜːθbaʊnd, *Am:* 'ɜːrθ-] *adj* **1.** terrestre **2.** *fig* prosaico, -a

earthenware ['ɜːθnweəʳ, *Am:* 'ɜːrθnwer] **I.** *n* objetos *mpl* de barro **II.** *adj* de barro

earthiness ['ɜːθɪnɪs] *n no pl* **1.** (*directness*) llaneza *f* **2.** (*coarseness*) grosería *f*

earthling ['ɜːθlɪŋ, *Am:* 'ɜːrθ-] *n* terrícola *mf*

earthly ['ɜːθli, *Am:* 'ɜːrθ-] *adj* **1.** (*concerning life on earth*) terreno, -a; (*existence, paradise*) terrenal; **her** ~ **belongings** *form* todo lo que posee en este mundo; ~ **remains** restos *mpl* mortales **2.** *inf* (*possible*) **to be of no** ~ **use** no servir absolutamente para nada ►**to not have an** ~ (**chance**) *Brit, inf* no tener ninguna posibilidad

earthquake ['ɜːθkweɪk, *Am:* 'ɜːrθ-] *n* **1.** terremoto *m*, temblor *m AmL* **2.** *fig* conmoción *f*

earth-shattering *adj* extraordinario, -a

earthwork *n* **1.** *pl* MIL terraplén *m* **2.** (*work*) trabajos *mpl* de preparación del terreno

earthworm *n* lombriz *f*

earthy ['ɜːθi, *Am:* 'ɜːr-] <-ier, -iest> *adj* **1.** (*with earth*) terroso, -a **2.** (*direct*) llano, -a **3.** (*vulgar*) grosero, -a

earwax ['ɪəwæks, *Am:* 'ɪr-] *n* cerumen *m*

earwig ['ɪəwɪg, *Am:* 'ɪr-] *n* tijereta *f*

ease [iːz] **I.** *n* **1.** (*without much effort*) facilidad *f*; **for** ~ **of access** para facilitar el acceso; **to do sth with** ~ hacer algo con facilidad **2.** (*comfort, uninhibitedness*) comodidad *f*; **to live a life of** ~ vivir con desahogo; **to feel at** (**one's**) ~ sentirse cómodo; **to be ill at** ~ estar molesto; **to be at** (**one's**) ~ estar a sus anchas; **to put sb at** (**his/her**) ~ hacer que alguien se relaje; (**stand**) **at** ~**!** MIL ¡descansen! **II.** *vt* **1.** (*relieve: pain*) aliviar; (*tension*) hacer disminuir; **to** ~ **one's conscience** descargarse la conciencia; **to** ~ **sb's mind** tranquilizar a alguien **2.** (*burden*) aligerar; (*screw*) aflojar **III.** *vi* (*pain*) aliviarse; (*tension, prices*) disminuir; (*wind*) amainar

◆**ease off** *vi*, **ease up** *vi* (*pain*) aliviarse; (*fever, sales*) bajar; (*tension*) disminuir; (*person*) relajarse; ~ **or you will have a nervous breakdown** si no te relajas tendrás una crisis nerviosa

easel ['iːzl] *n* caballete *m*

easily ['iːzəli] *adv* **1.** (*without difficulty*) fácilmente; **to be** ~ **impressed** ser fácil de impresionar; **to win** ~ ganar sin dificultades; **I get tired very** ~ me canso en seguida **2.** + *superl* (*clearly*) **to be** ~ **the best** ser con mucho el mejor **3.** (*probably*) perfectamente; **his guess could** ~ **be wrong** es fácil que se equivoque

easiness ['iːzɪnɪs] *n no pl* facilidad *f*

east ['iːst] **I.** *n* este *m*; **to lie 5 km to the** ~ **of Bath** quedar a 5 km al este de Bath; **to go/drive to the** ~ ir/conducir hacia el este; **further** ~ más hacia el este; **in the** ~ **of France** en el este de Francia; **Far East** Extremo *m* Oriente; **Middle East** Oriente *m* Medio **II.** *adj* del este; ~ **wind** viento *m* de Levante; ~ **coast** costa *f* del este; **East Indies** Indias *fpl* Orientales

eastbound ['iːstbaʊnd] *adj* que va en dirección este

Easter ['iːstəʳ, *Am:* -stɚ] *n* **1.** (*holiday*) Pascua *f* **2.** (*season*) Semana *f* Santa; **at** ~ en Semana Santa

> **At Easter** (En Semana Santa) es costumbre en Gran Bretaña consumir dos tipos de dulce: los **hot cross buns**, por un lado, panecillos especiados que tienen una cruz en la parte de arriba hecha con la misma masa, y el **simnel cake**, por otro lado, un denso pastel de pasas, que se decora con mazapán. Durante estos días es costumbre que los niños jueguen a arrojar huevos cocidos cuesta abajo para ver cuál es el huevo que llega más lejos. Hoy en día con el término de **Easter egg** (huevo de Pascua) se denomina al huevo de chocolate relleno de dulces y golosinas que se suele regalar durante estos días.

Easter Day *n*, **Easter Sunday** *n* Domingo *m* de Pascua **Easter egg** *n* huevo *m* de Pascua **Easter holidays** *npl* vacaciones *fpl* de Semana Santa **Easter Island** *npl* Isla *f* de Pascua

easterly ['iːstəli, *Am:* -stɚ-] **I.** *adj* (*wind*) del este; **in an** ~ **direction** en dirección este **II.** *adv* **1.** (*towards the east*) hacia el este **2.** (*from the east*) del este **III.** *n* viento *m* del este

Easter Monday *n* lunes *m* de Pascua

eastern ['iːstən, *Am:* -stɚn] *adj* del este, oriental

easterner ['iːstənəʳ, *Am:* -tɚnɚ] *n Am* habitante *mf* del nordeste de los Estados Unidos

easternmost ['iːstənməʊst, *Am:* -stɚnmoʊst] *adj* más oriental; **the** ~ **zone** la zona más oriental

East Germany [ˌiːst'dʒɜːməni] *n* HIST Alemania *f* oriental

eastward ['iːstwəd, *Am:* -wɚd] **I.** *adj* **in an** ~ **direction** en dirección este **II.** *adv* hacia el este

eastwards ['iːstwədz, *Am:* -wɚdz] *adv* hacia el este

easy ['iːzi] <-ier, -iest> **I.** *adj* **1.** (*simple*) fácil; ~ **money** *inf* dinero *m* fácil; **the hotel is within** ~ **reach of the beach** el hotel está muy cerca de la playa; **to be far from** ~ no ser fácil en absoluto; ~ **to get on with** de trato fácil; **to take the** ~ **way out** optar por el camino más fácil; **to be as** ~ **as anything** *inf* estar tirado; **to be the easiest thing in the world** ser lo más fácil del mundo; **that's**

easier said than done *inf* es más fácil decirlo que hacerlo **2.** (*comfortable, carefree*) cómodo, -a; **I'm** ~ *inf* me da lo mismo; **to feel** ~ **about sth** estar tranquilo por algo; **she won't be** ~ **in her mind until I call her** no se quedará tranquila hasta que la llame **3.** (*relaxed: manners*) natural; **at an** ~ **pace** sin prisa; **to be on** ~ **terms with sb** estar en confianza con alguien **4.** (*undemanding*) indulgente; **to be** ~ **on sb** ser poco severo con alguien **5.** (*pleasant*) ~ **on the ear/eye** agradable al oído/a la vista **6.** FIN (*price, interest rate*) bajo, -a; **on** ~ **terms** con facilidades de pago; (*loan*) con condiciones favorables **II.** *adv* **1.** (*cautiously*) con cuidado; ~ **does it** *inf* despacito y buena letra **2.** (*leniant*) **to go** ~ **on sb** *inf* no ser demasiado severo con alguien **3.** *inf* (*less actively*) **to take things** ~ tomarse las cosas con calma; **take it** ~**!** ¡cálmate! ►~ **come,** ~ **go** *inf* tan fácil como viene, se va

easy-care *adj* que no necesita plancha **easy chair** *n* poltrona *f* **easy-going** *adj* (*person*) de trato fácil; (*attitude*) tolerante **easy-peasy** *adj Brit, childspeak* chupado, -a *inf*

eat [i:t] **I.** <ate, eaten> *vt* comer; **to** ~ **breakfast** tomar el desayuno; **to** ~ **lunch/supper** comer/cenar; **to** ~ **one's fill** comer bien; **to** ~ **in** comer en casa ►**what is** ~**ing him?** *inf* ¿qué mosca le ha picado? **II.** *vi* comer

◆**eat away** *vt* (*acid*) corroer; (*termites*) carcomer

◆**eat away at** *vt*, **eat into** *vt* corroer

◆**eat out** *vi* comer fuera

◆**eat up** *vt* comerse, terminar

eatable ['i:təbl, *Am:* -t̬ə-] *adj* comestible

eatables ['i:təblz, *Am:* -t̬ə-] *npl* comestibles *mpl*

eat-by date ['i:tbaɪˌdeɪt] *n* fecha *f* de caducidad

eaten ['i:tn, *Am:* -t̬ən] *pp of* **eat**

eater ['i:tə^r, *Am:* -t̬ɚ] *n* **1.** (*person*) **to be a big** ~ ser comilón; **to be a small eater** no ser de mucho comer **2.** *Brit, inf* (*apple*) manzana *f* de mesa

eatery ['i:təri, *Am:* -t̬ɚ-] *n inf* restaurante *m*

eating ['i:tɪŋ, *Am:* -t̬ɪŋ] *n* comer *m;* **to be good** ~ ser sabroso

eating apple *n* manzana *f* de mesa **eating disorder** *n* trastorno *m* alimenticio **eating habits** *npl* hábitos *mpl* alimenticios **eating house** *n* restaurante *m*

eau de Cologne [ˌəʊ də kə'ləʊn, *Am:* ˌoʊ də kə'loʊn] *n* (agua *f* de) colonia *f*

eaves [i:vz] *npl* ARCHIT alero *m,* tejaván *m AmL*

eavesdrop ['i:vzdrɒp, *Am:* -drɑ:p] <-pp-> *vi* **to** ~ **on sth/sb** escuchar algo/a alguien a escondidas

eavesdropper ['i:vzdrɒpə^r, *Am:* -drɑ:pɚ] *n* escuchón, -ona *m, f*

ebb [eb] **I.** *vi* **1.** (*tide*) bajar **2.** *fig* decaer **II.** *n no pl* **1.** (*tide*) reflujo *m;* **the tide is on the** ~ la marea está bajando **2.** *fig* **the** ~ **and flow of sth** los altibajos de algo; **to be at a low** ~ estar en un punto bajo; (*person*) estar deprimido **III.** *adj* ~ **tide** marea *f* menguante

ebony ['ebəni] *n* ébano *m*

ebullient [ɪ'bʌlɪənt, *Am:* -'bʊljənt] *adj* vivaz; **to be in an** ~ **mood** estar exaltado

EC [ˌi:'si:] *n abbr of* **European Community** CE *f*

e-car ['i:kɑ:^r, *Am:* -kɑ:r] *n* automóvil *m* eléctrico

e-cash ['i:kæʃ] *n* dinero *m* electrónico

ECB [ˌi:si:'bi:] *n abbr of* **European Central Bank** BCE *m*

eccentric [ɪk'sentrɪk] **I.** *n* excéntrico, -a *m, f* **II.** *adj* excéntrico, -a

eccentricity [ˌeksen'trɪsəti, *Am:* -ət̬i] *n* <-ies> excentricidad *f*

ecclesiastic [ɪˌkli:zɪ'æstɪk] **I.** *n form* eclesiástico *m* **II.** *adj form* eclesiástico, -a

ecclesiastical [ɪˌkli:zɪ'æstɪkl] *adj form* eclesiástico, -a

ECG [ˌi:si:'dʒi:] *n abbr of* **electrocardiogram** electrocardiograma *m*

echelon ['eʃəlɒn, *Am:* -lɑ:n] *n* **1.** (*strata*) nivel *m;* (*of society*) capa *f;* **the highest** ~**s of sth** el más alto grado de algo **2.** MIL escalón *m*

echo ['ekəʊ, *Am:* -oʊ] **I.** <-es> *n* eco *m* ►**to cheer sb to the** ~ ovacionar a alguien **II.** <-es, -ing, -ed> *vi* resonar **III.** <-es, -ing, -ed> *vt* **1.** (*reflect*) repetir; **the mountains** ~**ed** (**back**) **his voice** las montañas le devolvían el eco de su voz **2.** (*second*) hacerse eco de **3.** (*resemble*) parecerse a

echo chamber *n* cámara *f* de resonancia **echo sounder** *n* sonda *f* acústica

eclectic [ek'lektɪk] **I.** *n form* ecléctico, -a *m, f* **II.** *adj form* ecléctico

eclipse [ɪ'klɪps] **I.** *n* eclipse *m;* **solar/lunar** ~ eclipse solar/de luna; **total/partial** ~ **of the sun** eclipse solar total/parcial; **to go into** ~ entrar en eclipse; **to be in** ~ *a. fig* estar eclipsado **II.** *vt* eclipsar

ECOFIN ['ekəʊfɪn] *n abbr of* **Economic and Finance Ministers Council** ECOFIN *m*

ecological [ˌi:kə'lɒdʒɪkl, *Am:* -'lɑ:dʒɪ-] *adj* ecológico, -a

ecologically [ˌɪ:kə'lɒdʒɪkli, *Am:* -'lɑ:dʒɪ-] *adv* ecológicamente; ~ **friendly** ecológico, -a; ~ **harmful** perjudicial para el medio ambiente

ecologist [i:'kɒlədʒɪst, *Am:* -'kɑ:lə-] *n* **1.** (*expert*) ecólogo, -a *m, f* **2.** POL ecologista *mf*

ecology [i:'kɒlədʒi, *Am:* -'kɑ:lə-] *n no pl* ecología *f*

ecology movement *n* movimiento *m* ecologista **ecology party** *n* partido *m* ecologista

e-commerce ['i:kɒmɜ:s, *Am:* -kɑ:mɜ:rs] *n* comercio *m* electrónico

economic [ˌi:kə'nɒmɪk, *Am:* -'nɑ:mɪk] *adj* **1.** POL, ECON económico, -a **2.** (*profitable*) rentable

economical [ˌi:kə'nɒmɪkl, *Am:* -'nɑ:mɪ-] *adj* económico, -a ►**to be** ~ **with the truth**

iron decir verdades a medias

Economic and Monetary Unit *n* Unión *f* Económica y Monetaria

economics [ˌiːkəˈnɒmɪks, *Am:* -ˈnɑːmɪks] *npl* **1.** + *sing vb* (*discipline*) economía *f;* **School of Economics** Facultad *f* de Ciencias Económicas **2.** + *pl vb* (*matter*) aspecto *m* económico; **the ~ of the agreement** la rentabilidad del acuerdo

economist [ɪˈkɒnəmɪst, *Am:* -ˈkɑːnə-] *n* economista *mf*

economize [ɪˈkɒnəmaɪz, *Am:* -ˈkɑːnə-] *vi* ahorrar; **to ~ on sth** economizar en algo

economy [ɪˈkɒnəmi, *Am:* -ˈkɑːnə-] <-ies> *n* **1.** (*frugality*) ahorro *m;* **for the purposes of ~** por ahorro; **to make economies, to practise ~** ahorrar **2.** (*monetary assets*) economía *f;* **the state of the ~** la situación económica; **capitalist/market/planned ~** economía capitalista/de mercado/planificada

economy class *n* AVIAT clase *f* turista **economy drive** *n* campaña *f* para reducir gastos **economy size** *n* tamaño *m* familiar

ecosystem *n* ecosistema *m* **ecotourism** *n* ecoturismo *m* **eco-tourist** *n* ecoturista *mf* **ecowarrior** *n* ecologista *mf* militante

ecstasy [ˈekstəsi] <-ies> *n* éxtasis *m inv;* **to go into ecstasies** extasiarse

ecstatic [ɪkˈstætɪk, *Am:* ekˈstæt̬-] *adj* extático, -a; (*rapturous*) eufórico, -a; **to be ~ about sth** estar entusiasmado con algo

ECT [ˌiːsiːˈtiː] *n abbr of* **electroconvulsive therapy** terapia *f* de electroshock

ecu, ECU [ˈekjuː, *Am:* ˈeɪkuː] *n abbr of* **European Currency Unit** ecu *m,* ECU *m*

Ecuador [ˈekwədɔːʳ, *Am:* -dɔːr] *n* Ecuador *m*

Ecuadorian [ˌekwəˈdɔːrɪən] **I.** *n* ecuatoriano, -a *m, f* **II.** *adj* ecuatoriano, -a

ecumenical [ˌiːkjuːˈmenɪkl, *Am:* ˌekjʊˈ-] *adj* ecuménico, -a

eczema [ˈeksɪmə, *Am:* -sə-] *n no pl* eczema *m*

ed. **1.** *abbr of* **editor** editor(a) *m(f)* **2.** *abbr of* **edition** ed. **3.** *abbr of* **edited** editado, -a

eddy [ˈedi] **I.** <-ie-> *vi* arremolinarse **II.** <-ies> *n* remolino *m*

Eden [ˈiːdn] *n no pl* Edén *m;* **the garden of ~** el jardín del Edén

edge [edʒ] **I.** *n sing* **1.** (*limit*) borde *m;* (*of a lake, pond*) orilla *f;* (*of a mountain*) cresta *f;* (*of a page*) margen *m;* (*of a table, coin*) canto *m;* **to bring sth to the ~ of disaster** llevar algo hasta el límite del desastre; **to take the ~ off one's appetite/hunger** calmar el apetito/hambre; **to take the ~ off an argument** restar fuerza a un argumento **2.** (*cutting part*) filo *m;* **to put an ~ on sth** afilar algo **3.** *no pl* (*anger*) **to be on ~** tener los nervios a flor de piel; **there's a definite ~ in her voice** hay un tono áspero en su voz **4.** SPORTS ventaja *f;* **to have the ~ over sb** tener ventaja sobre alguien ►**to be (balanced) on a razor's ~** pender de un hilo; **to set sb's teeth on ~** poner nervioso a alguien; **to give sb the sharp ~ of one's tongue** echar una bronca a alguien **II.** *vt* **1.** (*border*) bordear **2.** (*in sewing*) ribetear **3.** (*move slowly*) **to ~ one's way through sth** ir abriéndose paso por algo; **shes's edging her party towards extremism** está acercando su partido hacia el extremismo **III.** *vi* **to ~ closer to sth** ir acercándose a algo; **to ~ away from the danger** ir alejándose del peligro; **to ~ forward** ir avanzando

edgeways [ˈedʒweɪz] *adv,* **edgewise** *adv Am* de lado

edging [ˈedʒɪŋ] *n* borde *m;* (*of a ribbon*) ribete *m*

edgy [ˈedʒi] <-ier, -iest> *adj inf* nervioso

edible [ˈedɪbl] *adj* comestible

edict [ˈiːdɪkt] *n* **1.** HIST edicto *m* **2.** (*order*) mandato *m*

edification [ˌedɪfɪˈkeɪʃən] *n no pl, form* edificación *f*

edifice [ˈedɪfɪs] *n* **1.** *form* (*building*) edificio *m* **2.** *fig* (*of ideas*) estructura *f*

edify [ˈedɪfaɪ] <-ie-> *vt form* edificar

edifying *adj form* edificante

Edinburgh [ˈedɪnbrə, *Am:* -bʌrə] *n* Edimburgo *m*

> Desde 1947 tiene lugar cada año en **Edinburgh**, la capital de Escocia, el **Edinburgh International Festival**. Se celebra en torno a mediados de agosto y dura tres semanas. En el marco de este festival tienen lugar numerosos espectáculos de tipo cultural: teatro, música, ópera y baile. Al mismo tiempo se celebran un **Film Festival**, un **Jazz Festival** y un **Book Festival**. Paralelamente al **Festival** oficial se ha ido desarrollando un **Festival Fringe** con alrededor de 1.000 espectáculos diferentes que se caracteriza por su vivacidad y su capacidad de innovación.

edit [ˈedɪt] *vt* **1.** (*correct*) corregir; (*articles*) editar **2.** (*newspaper*) dirigir **3.** CINE montar **4.** INFOR editar

◆**edit out** *vt* suprimir

edition [ɪˈdɪʃən] *n* edición *f;* (*set of books*) tirada *f;* **paperback ~** encuadernación *f* en rústica; **limited ~** edición limitada

editor [ˈedɪtəʳ, *Am:* -t̬ɚ] *n* **1.** (*of book*) editor(a) *m(f);* (*of article*) redactor(a) *m(f);* (*of a newspaper*) director(a) *m(f);* **chief ~** redactor(a) *m(f)* jefe; **sports ~** redactor(a) *m(f)* de deportes **2.** CINE montador(a) *m(f)* **3.** INFOR editor *m*

editorial [ˌedɪˈtɔːrɪəl, *Am:* -əˈ-] **I.** *n* editorial *m* **II.** *adj* editorial; **~ staff** redacción *f*

editor-in-chief [ˌedɪtəʳɪnˈtʃiːf, *Am:* -t̬ɚ-] *n* redactor(a) *m(f)* jefe

EDP [ˌiːdiːˈpiː] *n abbr of* **electronic data processing** PED *m*

educate [ˈedʒʊkeɪt] *vt* **1.** (*bring up*) educar **2.** (*teach*) instruir; **to ~ the ear** educar el oído

3. (*inform*) concienciar; **to ~ sb in sth** concienciar a alguien de algo

educated ['edʒʊkeɪtɪd, *Am:* -t̬ɪd] *adj* culto, -a; **highly ~** cultivado, -a; **to be Oxford ~** haber estudiado en Oxford

education [ˌedʒʊ'keɪʃən] *n no pl* **1.** SCHOOL educación *f;* **primary/secondary ~** enseñanza *f* primaria/secundaria; **Ministry of Education** Ministerio *m* de Educación **2.** (*training*) formación *f;* **science/literary ~** formación científica/literaria **3.** (*teaching*) enseñanza *f;* (*study of teaching*) pedagogía *f* **4.** (*culture*) cultura *f*

educational [ˌedʒʊ'keɪʃənl] *adj* **1.** SCHOOL (*system*) educativo, -a; (*establishment*) docente; (*method*) pedagógico, -a; **for ~ purposes** con fines educativos **2.** (*instructive*) instructivo, -a **3.** (*raising awareness*) de concienciación

education(al)ist [ˌedʒʊ'keɪʃən(əl)ɪst] *n* pedagogo, -a *m, f*

educator ['edʒʊkeɪtəʳ, *Am:* -t̬ɚ] *n Am* educador(a) *m(f)*

Edwardian [ed'wɔdiən, *Am:* -'wɔːr-] *adj* eduardiano, -a

EEC [ˌiːiː'siː] *n no pl* HIST *abbr of* **European Economic Community** CEE *f*

EEG [ˌiːiː'dʒiː] *n abbr of* **electroencephalogram** electroencefalograma *m*

eel [iːl] *n* anguila *f* ►**to be slippery as an ~** ser escurridizo

EEMU *n abbr of* **European Economic and Monetary Union** UEME *f*

eerie ['ɪəri, *Am:* 'ɪri] *adj,* **eery** <-ier, -iest> *adj* espeluznante

efface [ɪ'feɪs] *vt* **1.** *a. fig* borrar **2.** (*be humble*) **to ~ oneself** intentar pasar inadvertido

effect [ɪ'fekt] **I.** *n* **1.** (*consequence*) efecto *m;* **to have an ~ on sth** afectar a algo; **to have a disastrous ~ on** [*o* **upon**] **sth** tener consecuencias nefastas para algo; **to have no ~ on sb** no hacer ningún efecto a alguien **2.** (*result*) resultado *m;* **to be of little/no ~** dar poco/no dar resultado; **to take ~** surtir efecto; (*medicine, alcohol*) hacer efecto; **to the ~ that ...** con el propósito de...; **to no ~** en vano **3.** *no pl* LAW vigencia *f;* **to come into** [*o* **to take**] **~** entrar en vigor; **to remain/be in ~** permanecer/estar vigente **4.** (*gist*) **to the same ~** por el estilo; **he disapproved of our idea and wrote to us to that ~** no estaba de acuerdo con nuestra idea y nos escribió para manifestarlo **5.** (*impression*) impresión *f;* **the overall ~** la impresión general; **for ~** para llamar la atención **6.** *pl* (*belongings*) efectos *mpl;* **personal ~s** efectos personales ►**in ~** en efecto **II.** *vt* realizar; (*payment*) efectuar; (*cure*) lograr

effective [ɪ'fektɪv] *adj* **1.** (*giving result*) efectivo, -a; (*medicine*) eficaz; **he was an ~ speaker** tenía grandes dotes de orador **2.** (*real*) real; **~ control** control efectivo **3.** (*operative*) vigente; **to become ~** entrar en vigor **4.** (*striking*) impresionante

effectively *adv* **1.** (*giving result*) eficazmente **2.** (*really*) realmente **3.** (*strikingly*) de manera impresionante

effectiveness *n no pl* **1.** (*efficiency*) efectividad *f;* (*of a plan*) eficacia *f* **2.** (*of a rule*) vigencia *f*

effectual [ɪ'fektʃʊəl, *Am:* -tʃuː-] *adj* **1.** (*efficient*) efectivo, -a **2.** (*operative*) válido, -a

effectuate [ɪ'fektʃʊeɪt, *Am:* -tʃuː-] *vt* efectuar

effeminacy [ɪ'femɪnəsi] *n no pl* afeminación *f,* afeminamiento *m*

effeminate [ɪ'femɪnət] **I.** *adj* afeminado, -a **II.** *n* afeminado *m*

effervesce [ˌefə'ves, *Am:* -ɚ'-] *vi* **1.** (*bubble*) burbujear **2.** *fig* (*person*) estar eufórico, -a

effervescence [ˌefə'vesns, *Am:* -ɚ'-] *n no pl* efervescencia *f*

effervescent [ˌefə'vesnt, *Am:* -ɚ'-] *adj* **1.** efervescente **2.** *fig* eufórico, -a

effete [ɪ'fiːt] *adj* **1.** (*enfeebled*) debilitado, -a **2.** (*decadent*) decadente **3.** (*effeminate*) amanerado, -a

efficacious [ˌefɪ'keɪʃəs] *adj form* eficaz; **an ~ medicine** un medicamento efectivo

efficacy ['efɪkəsi] *n no pl, form* eficacia *f*

efficiency [ɪ'fɪʃnsi] *n no pl* **1.** (*of a person*) eficiencia *f;* (*of a method*) eficacia *f* **2.** (*of a machine*) rendimiento *m*

efficient [ɪ'fɪʃnt] *adj* (*person*) eficiente; (*machine, system*) de buen rendimiento

effigy ['efɪdʒi] *n* efigie *f*

effluent ['eflʊənt] *n* **1.** efluente *m* **2.** (*liquid waste*) vertidos *mpl*

effort ['efət, *Am:* -ɚt] *n* **1.** *a.* PHYS esfuerzo *m;* **to be worth the ~** valer la pena; **to make an ~ to do sth** esforzarse [*o* hacer un esfuerzo] para hacer algo; **to spare no ~** no escatimar esfuerzos; **without ~** sin esfuerzo **2.** (*attempt*) tentativa *f;* **please make an ~ to ...** por favor, intenten... **3.** (*work*) obra *f*

effortless ['efətləs, *Am:* -ɚt-] *adj* fácil; **an ~ movement** un movimiento sin esfuerzo aparente; **an ~ grace** una gracia natural

effrontery [ɪ'frʌntəri, *Am:* e'frʌn-] *n no pl, form* descaro *m;* **to have the ~ to do sth** tener la desfachatez de hacer algo

effusion [ɪ'fjuːʒən] *n a. fig* efusión *f*

effusive [ɪ'fjuːsɪv] *adj form* efusivo, -a

EFL [ˌiːef'el] *n,* **Efl** *n abbr of* **English as a foreign language** inglés *m* como idioma extranjero

eft [eft] *n* tritón *m*

EFT *abbr of* **electronic funds transfer** servicio *m* de pagos electrónico

EFTA ['eftə] *n,* **Efta** *n abbr of* **European Free Trade Association** EFTA *f*

e.g. [ˌiː'dʒiː] *abbr of* **exempli gratia** (= **for example**) p.ej.

egalitarian [ɪˌgælɪ'teəriən, *Am:* -teri-] *adj* igualitario, -a

e-generation [iːˌdʒenə'reɪʃən] *n* generación

f de internet

egg [eg] *n* huevo *m;* **fried/boiled ~s** huevos fritos/pasados por agua; **hard-boiled ~** huevo duro; **scrambled ~s** huevos revueltos ▶**to put all one's ~s in one basket** jugárselo todo a una carta; **they had ~ on their faces** *inf* quedaron en ridículo; **to be a bad ~** *inf* ser un sinvergüenza

◆**egg on** *vt* incitar

egg cell *n* óvulo *m* **egg cup** *n*, **eggcup** *n* huevera *f* **egghead** *n inf* cerebro *m* **eggplant** *n Am, Aus* berenjena *f* **eggshell** *n* cáscara *f* de huevo **egg timer** *n* temporizador *m* para huevos **egg yolk** *n* yema *f* de huevo

ego ['egəʊ, *Am:* 'iːgoʊ] *n* <-s> **1.** PSYCH ego *m;* **to bolster sb's ~** reforzar el ego de alguien **2.** (*self-esteem*) amor *m* propio

egocentric [ˌegəʊ'sentrɪk, *Am:* ˌiːgoʊ-] *adj* egocéntrico, -a

egoism ['egəʊɪzəm, *Am:* 'iːgoʊ-] *n no pl* egoísmo *m*

egoist ['egəʊɪst, *Am:* 'iːgoʊ-] *n* egoísta *mf*

egoistic(al) [ˌegəʊ'ɪstɪk(l), *Am:* ˌiːgoʊ-] *adj* egoísta

egotism ['egəʊtɪzəm, *Am:* 'iːgoʊ-] *n no pl* egotismo *m*

egotist ['egəʊtɪst, *Am:* 'iːgoʊ-] *n* egotista *mf*

egotistic(al) [ˌegə'tɪstɪk(l), *Am:* ˌiːgoʊ'-] *adj* **1.** (*selfish*) egoísta **2.** (*self-important*) egotista

ego trip ['egəʊtrɪp, *Am:* 'iːgoʊ-] *n* **to be on an ~** darse autobombo

egregious [ɪ'griːdʒəs] *adj* escandaloso, -a

Egypt ['iːdʒɪpt] *n* Egipto *m*

Egyptian [ɪ'dʒɪpʃən] **I.** *n* egipcio, -a *m, f* **II.** *adj* egipcio, -a

eh [eɪ] *interj inf* (*asking for repetition*) ¿eh?; (*expressing surprise*) ¿qué?; (*inviting response*) ¿no?; **that's good, ~?** está bueno, ¿no?

eider ['aɪdəʳ, *Am:* -dɚ] *n* eider *m*

eiderdown ['aɪdədaʊn, *Am:* -dɚ-] *n* edredón *m*

Eiffel tower [ˌaɪfl'taʊər, *Am:* -'taʊɚ] *n* **the ~** la torre Eiffel

eight [eɪt] **I.** *adj* ocho *inv;* **there are ~ of us** somos ocho; **~ and a quarter/half** ocho y cuarto/medio; **~ o'clock** las ocho; **it's ~ o'clock** son las ocho; **it's half past ~** son las ocho y media; **at ~ twenty/thirty** a las ocho y veinte/media **II.** *n* ocho *m* ▶**to have had one over the ~** *Brit, inf* llevar una copa de más

eighteen [ˌeɪ'tiːn] **I.** *adj* dieciocho **II.** *n* dieciocho *m; s. a.* **eight**

eighteenth [ˌeɪ'tiːnθ] **I.** *adj* decimoctavo, -a **II.** *n* **1.** (*order*) decimoctavo, -a *m, f* **2.** (*date*) ocho *m* **3.** (*fraction*) dieciochoavo *m;* (*part*) decimoctava parte *f; s. a.* **eighth**

eighth [eɪtθ] **I.** *adj* octavo, -a; **~ note** *Am* corchea *f* **II.** *n no pl* **1.** (*order*) octavo, -a *m, f;* **to be ~ in a race** quedar de octavo en una carrera **2.** (*date*) ocho *m;* **the ~** el día ocho; **the ~ of December, December the ~** el ocho de diciembre **3.** (*fraction*) octavo *m;* (*part*) octava parte *f* **III.** *adv* (*in lists*) octavo

eight-hour day *n* jornada *f* de ocho horas

eightieth ['eɪtɪəθ, *Am:* -t̬ɪəθ] **I.** *adj* octogésimo, -a **II.** *n no pl* (*order*) octogésimo, -a *m, f;* (*fraction*) octogésimo *m;* (*part*) octogésima parte *f; s. a.* **eighth**

eighty ['eɪti, *Am:* -t̬i] **I.** *adj* ochenta *inv;* **he is ~ (years old)** tiene ochenta años; **a man of about ~ years of age** un hombre de alrededor de ochenta años **II.** *n* <-ies> **1.** (*number*) ochenta *m;* **to do ~** *inf* ir a 80 km por hora **2.** (*age*) **a woman in her eighties** una mujer en sus ochenta **3.** (*decade*) **the eighties** los (años) ochenta

Eire ['æərə, *Am:* 'erə] *n* Eire *m*

EIS [ˌiːaɪ'es] *n* **1.** INFOR *abbr of* **executive information system** EIS *m* **2.** SCHOOL *abbr of* **Education Insitute of Scotland** *sindicato de profesores*

either ['aɪðəʳ, *Am:* 'iːðɚ] **I.** *adj* **1.** (*one of two*) **I'll do it ~ way** lo haré de una manera u otra; **I don't like ~ dress** no me gusta ninguno de los dos vestidos **2.** (*each*) cada; **on ~ side of the river** a cada lado del río **II.** *pron* cualquiera (de los dos); **which one? – ~** ¿cuál? – cualquiera **III.** *adv* tampoco; **if he doesn't go, I won't go ~** si él no va, yo tampoco **IV.** *conj* **~ ... or ...** o... o...; **~ buy it or rent it** cómpralo o alquílalo; **I can ~ stay or leave** puedo quedarme o irme

ejaculate [ɪ'dʒækjʊleɪt] *vt* **1.** (*semen*) eyacular **2.** (*blurt out*) exclamar

ejaculation [ɪˌdʒækjʊ'leɪʃən] *n* **1.** (*of semen*) eyaculación *f* **2.** (*sudden outburst*) exclamación *f*

eject [ɪ'dʒekt] **I.** *vt* echar, expulsar; (*liquid, gas*) expeler **II.** *vi* eyectarse

ejector seat [ɪ'dʒektəʳ siːt, *Am:* -tɚ] *n* asiento *m* de eyección

eke out [iːk aʊt] *vt* (*money, food*) hacer durar; **to ~ one's salary** estirar su sueldo *inf;* **to ~ a living** ganarse la vida a duras penas

elaborate [ɪ'læbərət] **I.** *adj* (*complicated*) complicado, -a; (*very detailed: plan*) minucioso, -a; (*style*) trabajado, -a; (*excuse*) rebuscado, -a; (*meal*) de muchos platos **II.** *vt* elaborar; (*plan*) idear **III.** *vi* entrar en detalles; **to refuse to ~** negarse a dar más detalles; **to ~ on an idea** explicar una idea con más detalles

elaboration [ɪˌlæbə'reɪʃən] <-(s)> *n* **1.** (*of a theory*) elaboración *f;* (*of texts*) explicación *f;* **without any ~s** sin entrar en demasiados detalles **2.** *no pl* (*complexity*) complicación *f*

elapse [ɪ'læps] *vi form* transcurrir

elastic [ɪ'læstɪk] **I.** *adj* elástico, -a **II.** *n* **1.** (*material*) elástico *m* **2.** (*garter*) liga *f*

elastic band *n Brit* gomita *f*

elasticity [ˌelæ'stɪsəti, *Am:* -t̬i] *n no pl, a. fig* elasticidad *f*

elate [ɪ'leɪt] *vt* regocijar; **to be ~d at sth** estar eufórico por algo

elated *adj* eufórico, -a

E

elation [ɪ'leɪʃən] *n no pl* regocijo *m*
Elba ['elbə] *n* Elba *f*
elbow ['elbəʊ, *Am:* -boʊ] **I.** *n* **1.** (*of people*) codo *m;* (*of animals*) codillo *m* **2.** (*in a pipe*) codo *m;* (*in a road, river*) recodo *m* ►**out at the ~s** (*clothing*) raído, -a; (*person*) desharrapado, -a; **to be at one's ~** estar al alcance de la mano; **to give sb the ~** deshacerse de alguien; **to rub ~s with sb** codearse con alguien **II.** *vt* dar un codazo a; **to ~ one's way through the crowd** abrirse paso a codazos entre la multitud
elbow grease *n no pl, inf* fuerza *f;* **to put some ~ into sth** poner empeño en algo
elbow room *n no pl* **1.** (*space*) espacio *m* **2.** (*freedom*) libertad *f* de acción
elder[1] ['eldəʳ, *Am:* -dɚ] **I.** *n* **1.** (*older person*) mayor *mf;* **she is my ~ by three years** es tres años mayor que yo **2.** (*senior person*) anciano, -a *m, f* **II.** *adj* mayor; **Pliny the Elder** Plinio el Viejo; **~ statesman/stateswoman** POL veterano, -a *m, f* de la política
elder[2] ['eldəʳ, *Am:* -dɚ] *n* saúco *m*
elderberry ['eldəberi, *Am:* -dɚ-] <-ies> *n* **1.** (*berry*) baya *f* del saúco **2.** BOT saúco *m*
elderly ['eldəli, *Am:* -dɚ-] **I.** *adj* anciano, -a; **an ~ woman** una señora mayor **II.** *n no pl* **the ~** los ancianos
eldest ['eldɪst] *adj superl of* **old** mayor; **the ~** el/la mayor; **her ~ (child) is nearly 14** su hijo mayor tiene casi 14 años
elect [ɪ'lekt] **I.** *vt* **1.** (*by vote*) elegir **2.** (*not by vote*) decidir; **to ~ to resign** optar por dimitir **II.** *n no pl* REL **the ~** los elegidos **III.** *adj* **the president ~** el presidente electo, la presidente electa
election [ɪ'lekʃən] *n* **1.** (*event*) elecciones *fpl;* **to call/hold an ~** convocar/celebrar elecciones; **to stand for an ~** presentarse a las elecciones **2.** *no pl* (*action*) elección *f*
election address *n,* **election speech** *n* discurso *m* electoral **election booth** *n s.* **polling booth** **election campaign** *n* campaña *f* electoral **election day** *n,* **Election Day** *n Am* jornada *f* electoral **election defeat** *n* derrota *f* electoral
electioneer [ɪˌlekʃə'nɪəʳ, *Am:* -'nɪr] *vi* hacer campaña electoral
electioneering [ɪˌlekʃə'nɪərɪŋ, *Am:* -'nɪr-] *n no pl* campaña *f* electoral; *pej* promesas *fpl* electoralistas
election manifesto *n* manifiesto *m* electoral **election meeting** *n* mitin *m* electoral **election platform** *n,* **election programme** *n* programa *m* electoral **election poster** *n* cartel *m* de propaganda electoral **election results** *npl,* **election returns** *npl* resultados *mpl* electorales
elective [ɪ'lektɪv] **I.** *adj* **1.** *form* (*appointed by election*) electivo, -a; (*based on voting*) electoral **2.** (*optional*) optativo, -a **3.** (*selective*) **~ affinity** afinidad electiva **II.** *n Am* SCHOOL, UNIV optativa *f*
elector [ɪ'lektəʳ, *Am:* -t̬ɚ] *n* **1.** (*voter*) elector(a) *m(f)* **2.** *Am* (*member of electoral college*) miembro *mf* de un colegio electoral
electoral [ɪ'lektərəl] *adj* electoral; **~ college** colegio *m* electoral; **~ register** [*o* **roll**] censo *m* electoral
electorate [ɪ'lektərət] *n* electorado *m*
electric [ɪ'lektrɪk] *adj* **1.** ELEC eléctrico, -a; (*fence*) electrificado, -a; **~ blanket** manta eléctrica; **~ chair** silla eléctrica; **~ cooker** cocina eléctrica; **~ current** corriente eléctrica; **~ fire** estufa eléctrica; **~ light** luz eléctrica; **~ shock** descarga eléctrica; **~ windows** AUTO elevalunas eléctrico **2.** *fig* electrizante; (*atmosphere*) cargado, -a de electricidad
electrical [ɪ'lektrɪkl] *adj* eléctrico, -a; **~ tape** cinta *f* aislante; **~ engineering** ingeniería *f* eléctrica, electrotecnia *f*
electrician [ɪˌlek'trɪʃən] *n* electricista *mf*
electricity [ɪˌlek'trɪsəti] *n no pl* electricidad *f;* **powered by ~** eléctrico, -a; **to run on ~** funcionar con electricidad
electricity board *n Brit* compañía *f* eléctrica
electrification [ɪˌlektrɪfɪ'keɪʃən] *n no pl* electrificación *f*
electrify [ɪ'lektrɪfaɪ] *vt* electrificar; *fig* electrizar
electroanalysis [ɪˌlektrəʊə'nælɪsɪs] *n* electroanálisis *m*
electrocardiogram [ɪˌlektrəʊ'kɑːdɪəʊgræm, *Am:* -troʊ'kɑːrdɪə-] *n* electrocardiograma *m*
electroconvulsive [ˈˌlektrəʊkən'vʌlsɪv, *Am:* -troʊ-] *adj* **~ therapy** electroterapia *f*
electrocute [ɪ'lektrəkjuːt] *vt* electrocutar
electrocution [ɪˌlektrə'kjuːʃən] *n* electrocución *f*
electrode [ɪ'lektrəʊd, *Am:* -troʊd] *n* electrodo *m*
electroencephalogram [ɪˌlektrəʊen'sefələˌgræm, *Am:* -troʊen'sefəloʊ-] *n* electroencefalograma *m*
electrolysis [ɪˌlek'trɒləsɪs, *Am:* -'trɑːlə-] *n no pl* electrólisis *f*
electromagnet [ɪ'lektrəʊ'mægnɪt, *Am:* -troʊ'-] *n* electroimán *m*
electromagnetic [ɪˌlektrəʊmæg'netɪk, *Am:* -troʊmæg'net̬-] *adj* electromagnético, -a
electron [ɪ'lektrɒn, *Am:* -trɑːn] *n* electrón *m*
electronic [ˌɪlek'trɒnɪk, *Am:* ɪˌlek'trɑːnɪk] *adj* electrónico, -a; **~ data processing** procesamiento electrónico de datos; **~ fund transfer** transferencia electrónica de fondos; **~ mail** correo electrónico
electronics [ˌɪlek'trɒnɪks, *Am:* ɪˌlek'trɑːnɪks] *n + sing vb* electrónica *f;* **the ~ industry** la industria electrónica
electron microscope *n* microscopio *m* electrónico
electroplate [ɪ'lektrəʊpleɪt, *Am:* ɪ'lektroʊpleɪt] *vt* galvanizar
electroscope [ɪ'lektrəʊˌskəʊp, *Am:* -troʊˌskoʊp] *n* electroscopio *m* **electrotherapy** *n* electroterapia *f*

elegance ['elɪgəns, *Am:* '-ə-] *n no pl* elegancia *f*

elegant ['elɪgənt, *Am:* '-ə-] *adj* elegante

elegiac [ˌelɪ'dʒaɪək] **I.** *adj* elegíaco, -a **II.** *n pl* versos *mpl* elegíacos

elegy ['elədʒi] *n* elegía *f*

element ['elɪmənt, *Am:* '-ə-] *n* **1.** *a.* CHEM, MAT elemento *m;* **the four ~s** los cuatro elementos; **he's in his ~** está en su elemento **2.** (*factor*) factor *m;* **an ~ of luck** algo de suerte; **the ~ of surprise** el factor sorpresa; **there's an ~ of truth in what they say** hay algo de verdad en lo que dicen **3.** ELEC resistencia *f* **4.** *pl* (*rudiments*) rudimentos *mpl* **5.** *pl* METEO **the ~s** los elementos

elemental [ˌelɪ'mentl, *Am:* -ə'menţl] *adj* elemental; (*forces*) de la naturaleza; (*feelings, needs*) primario, -a

elementary [ˌelɪ'mentəri, *Am:* -ə'menţɚ-] *adj* elemental; (*course*) básico, -a; **~ school** *Am* escuela *f* (de enseñanza) primaria

elephant ['elɪfənt] *n* elefante *m*

elephantiasis [ˌelɪfən'taɪəsɪs] *n* MED elefantiasis *f inv*

elephantine [ˌelɪ'fæntaɪn] *adj* **1.** (*huge*) colosal **2.** (*clumsy*) torpe

elevate ['elɪveɪt] *vt* **1.** (*raise*) elevar; (*prices*) aumentar; **to ~ the mind** ser edificante **2.** REL alzar **3.** (*in rank*) ascender

elevated ['elɪveɪtɪd, *Am:* -ţɪd] *adj* **1.** (*raised: part*) elevado, -a **2.** (*important*) alto, -a; (*position*) importante

elevation [ˌelɪ'veɪʃən] *n* **1.** (*rise*) elevación *f;* (*of person*) ascenso *m* **2.** (*height*) altura *f* **3.** GEO elevación *f* (del terreno) **4.** ARCHIT alzado *m*

elevator ['elɪveɪtə^r, *Am:* -ţɚ] *n Am* (*for people*) ascensor *m,* elevador *m AmL;* (*for goods*) montacargas *m inv*

eleven [ɪ'levn] **I.** *adj* once **II.** *n* once *m; s. a.* **eight**

elevenses [ɪ'levnzɪz] *npl Brit, inf* **to have ~** tomar las once

eleventh [ɪ'levnθ] **I.** *adj* undécimo, -a **II.** *n no pl* **1.** (*order*) undécimo, -a *m, f* **2.** (*date*) once *m* **3.** (*fraction*) onceavo *m;* (*part*) onceava parte *f; s. a.* **eighth**

elf [elf] <elves> *n* (*folklore*) duende *m;* (*mythology*) elfo *m*

elicit [ɪ'lɪsɪt] *vt* **1.** (*obtain*) obtener **2.** (*provoke: criticism*) suscitar

eligibility [ˌelɪdʒə'bɪləti, *Am:* -ţi] *n no pl* elegibilidad *f*

eligible ['elɪdʒəbl] *adj* **1.** elegible; **~ to vote** con derecho a voto **2.** (*desirable*) deseable; **to be ~ for** [*o* **to**] **the job** reunir los requisitos necesarios para el puesto; **an ~ bachelor** un soltero codiciado; **an ~ young man/woman** un buen partido

eliminate [ɪ'lɪmɪneɪt] *vt* **1.** (*eradicate*) eliminar **2.** (*exclude from consideration*) descartar

elimination [ɪˌlɪmɪ'neɪʃən] *n no pl* eliminación *f;* **by a process of ~** por eliminación

elimination contest *n* prueba *f* eliminatoria

elite [eɪ'liːt] **I.** *n* élite *f* **II.** *adj* de élite

elitism [ei'liːtɪsm] *n no pl* elitismo *m*

elitist [ei'liːtɪst] *adj* elitista

elixir [ɪ'lɪksə^r, *Am:* -sɚ] *n* elixir *m*

elk [elk] <-(s)> *n* (*European*) alce *m;* (*American*) uapití *m*

ellipse [ɪ'lɪps] *n* elipse *f*

elliptic(al) [ɪ'lɪptɪk(l)] *adj* elíptico, -a

elm [elm] *n* olmo *m*

elocution [ˌelə'kjuːʃən] *n no pl* dicción *f;* (*art*) elocución *f*

elongate ['iːlɒŋgeɪt, *Am:* ɪ'lɑːŋ-] **I.** *vt* alargar **II.** *vi* alargarse

elongated *adj* alargado, -a

elope [ɪ'ləʊp, *Am:* -'loʊp] *vi* fugarse

elopement [ɪ'ləʊpmənt, *Am:* -'loʊp] *n* fuga *f*

eloquent ['eləkwənt] *adj* elocuente

El Salvador [el'sælvəˌdɔːr, *Am:* -dɔːr] *n* El Salvador

else [els] *adv* **1.** (*in addition*) más; **anyone/anything ~** cualquier otra persona/cosa; **anywhere ~** en cualquier otro lugar; **anyone ~?** ¿alquien más?; **anything ~?** ¿algo más?; **everybody ~** (todos) los demás; **I can't remember anything/anybody ~** no puedo recordar nada/a nadie más; **everything/all ~** todo lo demás; **someone/something ~** otra persona/cosa; **it's something ~!** ¡es algo fuera de serie!; **how ~?** ¿de qué otra forma?; **what/who ~?** ¿qué/quién más? **2.** (*otherwise*) **or ~** si no; **come here or ~!** ¡ven, o ya verás!; **shut up, or else!** ¡como no te calles!

elsewhere [ˌels'weə^r, *Am:* 'elswer] *adv* en otro sitio; **let's go ~!** ¡vamos a otra parte!

ELT [ˌiːel'tiː] *n abbr of* **English language teaching** *enseñanza de inglés*

elucidate [ɪ'luːsɪdeɪt] *form* **I.** *vt* dilucidar; (*mystery*) esclarecer **II.** *vi* **I don't understand, you'll have to ~** no lo entiendo, tendrás que aclarármvelo

elude [ɪ'luːd] *vt* eludir; (*blow*) esquivar

elusive [ɪ'luːsɪv] *adj* **1.** (*evasive*) evasivo, -a; (*personality*) esquivo, -a; **memory** fugaz **2.** (*slippery*) escurridizo, -a **3.** (*difficult to obtain*) difícil de conseguir

elves [elvz] *n pl of* **elf**

emaciated [ɪ'meɪʃɪeɪtɪd, *Am:* -ţɪd] *adj form* demacrado, -a, jalado, -a *AmL*

e-mail ['iːmeɪl] *n abbr of* **electronic mail** e-mail *m*

e-mail address *n* dirección *f* de correo electrónico

emanate ['eməneɪt] **I.** *vi form* (*originate*) proceder; (*radiate*) emanar **II.** *vt* emanar

emancipate [ɪ'mænsɪpeɪt] *vt* emancipar

emancipated *adj* emancipado, -a; (*not constrained by tradition*) liberado, -a; (*ideas*) progresista

emancipation [ɪˌmænsɪ'peɪʃən] *n no pl* emancipación *f*

embalm [ɪm'bɑːm, *Am:* em-] *vt* embalsamar
embankment [ɪm'bæŋkmənt, *Am:* em-] *n* (*of a road*) terraplén *m;* (*by river*) dique *m*
embargo [ɪm'bɑːgəʊ, *Am:* em'bɑːrgoʊ] **I.** <-goes> *n* embargo *m;* **trade** ~ embargo comercial; **to be under** ~ estar sujeto a embargo; **to put** [*o* **lay**] **an** ~ **on a country** imponer un embargo sobre un país **II.** *vt* prohibir; LAW embargar
embark [ɪm'bɑːk, *Am:* em'bɑːrk] **I.** *vi* embarcar(se); **to** ~ **on** [*o* **upon**] **sth** emprender algo **II.** *vt* embarcar
embarkation [ˌembɑː'keɪʃən, *Am:* -bɑːr'-] *n* embarque *m*
embarrass [ɪm'bærəs, *Am:* em'ber-] *vt* **1.** (*make feel uncomfortable*) avergonzar **2.** (*disconcert*) desconcertar
embarrassed *adj* avergonzado, -a; (*silence*) violento, -a; **to be** ~ pasar vergüenza; **I felt** ~ **about saying that** me daba vergüenza decir eso; **to be financially** ~ tener problemas económicos
embarrassing *adj* embarazoso, -a
embarrassment [ɪm'bærəsment, *Am:* em'ber-] *n* **1.** (*shame*) vergüenza *f* **2.** (*trouble, nuisance*) molestia *f;* **to be an** ~ (**to sb**) ser un estorbo (para alguien)
embassy ['embəsi] <-ies> *n* embajada *f*
embed [ɪm'bed, *Am:* em-] <-dd-> *vt* **1.** (*fix*) hincar; (*in rock*) incrustar; (*in memory*) grabar **2.** LING insertar
embellish [ɪm'belɪʃ, *Am:* em-] *vt* adornar
embers ['embəʳz, *Am:* -bɚz] *npl* ascuas *fpl*
embezzle [ɪm'bezl] <-ing> *vt* desfalcar
embezzlement [ɪm'bezlmənt] *n no pl* desfalco *m;* ~ **of public funds** malversación *f* de fondos púiblicos
embezzler [ɪm'bezləʳ, *Am:* em'bezlɚ] *n* desfalcador(a) *m(f)*
embitter [ɪm'bɪtəʳ, *Am:* em'bɪt̬ɚ] *vt* amargar
emblem ['embləm] *n* emblema *m*
embodiment [ɪm'bɒdɪmənt, *Am:* em'bɑːdɪ-] *n no pl* **1.** (*personification*) encarnación *f;* **the** ~ **of virtue** la virtud personificada **2.** (*inclusion*) incorporación *f*
embody [ɪm'bɒdi, *Am:* em'bɑːdɪ-] *vt* **1.** (*convey: theory, idea*) expresar **2.** (*personify*) personificar **3.** (*include*) incorporar
embolism ['embəlɪsm] *n* MED embolia *f*
emboss [ɪm'bɒs, *Am:* em'bɑːs] *vt* **1.** (*design, letters*) grabar en relieve **2.** (*leather, metal*) repujar; **~ed writing paper** papel *m* de carta con membrete en relieve
embrace [ɪm'breɪs, *Am:* em-] **I.** *vt* **1.** (*hug*) abrazar **2.** (*accept: offer*) aceptar; (*ideas, religion*) incorporarse a **3.** (*include*) abarcar **II.** *vi* abrazarse **III.** *n* abrazo *m*
embrocation [ˌembrə'keɪʃən, *Am:* -broʊ'-] *n* cataplasma *f*
embroider [ɪm'brɔɪdəʳ, *Am:* em'brɔɪdɚ] **I.** *vi* bordar **II.** *vt* bordar; *fig* adornar
embroidery [ɪm'brɔɪdəri, *Am:* em-] *n* **1.** bordado *m;* ~ **frame** bastidor *m* **2.** *no pl, fig* florituras *fpl*
embroil [ɪm'brɔɪl] *vt* embrollar
embryo ['embrɪəʊ, *Am:* -oʊ] *n* embrión *m*
embryonic [ˌembrɪ'ɒnɪk, *Am:* -'ɑːnɪk] *adj* embrionario, -a; *fig* en estado embrionario
emcee [ɛm'siː] *n Am* presentador(a) *m(f)*
emend [ɪ'mend] *vt form* enmendar
emerald ['emərəld] **I.** *n* esmeralda *f* **II.** *adj* de esmeraldas; (*colour*) esmeralda
emerge [ɪ'mɜːdʒ, *Am:* -'mɜːrdʒ] *vi* (*come out*) salir; (*secret*) revelarse; (*ideas*) surgir; **they ~d from the bushes** salieron de entre los arbustos; **new ideas ~d from the meeting** a partir de la reunión surgieron nuevas ideas
emergence [ɪ'mɜːdʒəns, *Am:* -'mɜːr-] *n no pl* salida *f;* (*of a secret*) revelación *f;* (*appearance*) aparición *f*
emergency [ɪ'mɜːdʒənsi, *Am:* -'mɜːr-] **I.** <-ies> *n* **1.** (*dangerous situation*) emergencia *f;* **in an** [*o* **in case of**] ~ en caso de emergencia; **to provide for emergencies** prevenirse contra cualquier eventualidad **2.** MED urgencia *f;* ~ **room** sala *f* de urgencias **3.** POL crisis *f inv;* **national** ~ crisis nacional; **to declare a state of** ~ declarar el estado de excepción **II.** *adj* (*exit*) de emergencia; (*services*) de urgencia; (*brake*) de seguridad; (*landing*) forzoso, -a; (*rations*) de reserva; ~ **cord** *Am* timbre de alarma; ~ **exit** salida de emergencia; ~ **landing** aterrizaje forzoso; ~ **service** servicio de urgencia
emergent [ɪ'mɜːdʒənt, *Am:* -'mɜːr-] *adj* emergente; (*democracy, nation*) joven
emerging *adj* emergente
emery ['eməri] *n no pl* esmeril *m*
emery board *n* lima *f* de esmeril **emery paper** *n* papel *m* de lija
emetic [ɪ'metɪk, *Am:* -'met̬-] **I.** *adj* emético, -a, vomitivo, -a **II.** *n* emético *m,* vomitivo *m*
EMI [ˌiːem'aɪ] *n s.* **European Monetary Institute** IME *m*
emigrant ['emɪgrənt] *n* emigrante *mf*
emigrate ['emɪgreɪt] *vi* emigrar
emigration [ˌemɪ'greɪʃən] *n* emigración *f*
eminence ['emɪnəns] *n no pl* eminencia *f;* **Your Eminence** REL Vuestra Eminencia
eminent ['emɪnənt] *adj* eminente
eminently *adv* sumamente
emissary ['emɪsəri, *Am:* -ser-] <-ies> *n* emisario, -a *m, f*
emission [mɪʃən] *n* emisión *f*
emit [ɪ'mɪt] <-tt-> *vt* (*radiation, light*) emitir; (*heat*) desprender; (*odour*) despedir; (*smoke*) echar; (*cry*) dar
emoluments [ɪ'mɒljʊməntz, *Am:* -'mɑːl-] *npl Brit, form* emolumentos *mpl*
emoticon *n* INFOR emoticón *m*
emotion [ɪ'məʊʃən, *Am:* -'moʊ-] *n* **1.** (*feeling*) sentimiento *m* **2.** (*affective state*) emoción *f*
emotional [ɪ'məʊʃənl, *Am:* -'moʊ-] *adj*

1. (*relating to the emotions*) emocional; (*involvement, link*) afectivo, -a 2. (*moving*) conmovedor(a) 3. (*governed by emotion*) emocionado, -a; **to get** ~ emocionarse 4. (*determined by emotion: decision*) impulsivo, -a

emotionless *adj* impasible

emotive [ɪ'məʊtɪv, *Am:* -'moʊt̬ɪv] *adj* emotivo, -a

empathy ['empəθi] *n no pl* empatía *f*

emperor ['empərəʳ, *Am:* -ɚɚ] *n* emperador *m*

emphasis ['emfəsɪs] <emphases> *n* 1. LING acento *m* 2. (*importance*) énfasis *m inv;* **to put** [*o* **lay**] **great** ~ **on punctuality** hacer especial hincapié en la punctualidad

emphasize ['emfəsaɪz] *vt* 1. LING acentuar 2. (*insist on*) poner énfasis en, enfatizar *AmL;* (*fact*) hacer hincapié en

emphatic [ɪm'fætɪk, *Am:* em'fæt̬-] *adj* (*forcibly expressive*) enfático, -a; (*strong*) enérgico, -a; (*assertion*) categórico, -a; (*refusal*) rotundo, -a; **to be** ~ **about sth** hacer hincapié en algo

emphatically *adv* (*expressively*) con énfasis; (*strongly*) enérgicamente; (*forcefully*) categóricamente

empire ['empaɪəʳ, *Am:* -paɪɚ] *n* imperio *m*

empirical [ɪm'pɪrɪkl, *Am:* em-] *adj* empírico, -a

employ [ɪm'plɔɪ, *Am:* em-] *vt* 1. (*person*) emplear; **to** ~ **sb to do sth** contratar a alguien para hacer algo 2. (*object*) utilizar

employee [ˌɪmplɔɪ'iː, *Am:* 'em-] *n* empleado, -a *m, f*

employer [ɪm'plɔɪəʳ, *Am:* em'plɔɪɚ] *n* empresario, -a *m, f;* ~**s' organization** organización *f* patronal

employment [ɪm'plɔɪmənt, *Am:* 'em-] *n no pl* 1. (*of a person*) empleo *m;* **to be in** ~ *Brit, form* tener trabajo 2. (*of an object*) utilización *f*

employment agency *n* agencia *f* de empleo

emporium [ɪm'pɔːrɪəm, *Am:* em-] <-s *o* emporia> *n* emporio *m*

empower [ɪm'paʊəʳ, *Am:* em'paʊɚ] *vt* **to** ~ **sb to do sth** (*give ability to*) capacitar a alguien para hacer algo; (*authorise*) autorizar a alguien a hacer algo

empowerment [ɪm'paʊəmənt, *Am:* em'paʊɚ-] *n no pl* autorización *f*

empress ['emprɪs] *n* emperatriz *f*

emptiness ['emptɪnɪs] *n no pl* vacío *m; fig* vacuidad *f*

empty ['empti] I. <-ier, -iest> *adj* 1. (*with nothing inside*) vacío, -a; (*lorry, ship, train*) sin carga; (*house*) desocupado, -a 2. (*useless*) inútil; (*words*) vano, -a; ~ **phrase** frase vacía II. <-ie-> *vt* (*pour*) verter; (*deprive of contents*) vaciar III. <-ie-> *vi* vaciarse; (*river*) desembocar; **to** ~ **into the Nile** desembocar en el Nilo IV. <-ies> *n pl* envases *mpl* (vacíos)

◆**empty out** *vt* vaciar

empty-handed [ˌemptɪ'hændɪd] *adj* con las manos vacías **empty-headed** *adj* casquivano, -a **empty weight** *n* tara *f*

EMS [ˌiːem'es] *n abbr of* **Economic and Monetary System** SME *m*

emu ['iːmjuː] *n* emú *m*

EMU [ˌiːem'juː] *n abbr of* **Economic and Monetary Union** UME *f*

emulate ['emjʊleɪt] *vt* emular

emulation [ˌemjʊ'leɪʃən] *n no pl* emulación *f;* ~ **of sb** imitación *f* de alguien

emulsifier [ɪ'mʌlsifaɪəʳ, *Am:* -ɚ] *n* emulsionante *m*

emulsify [ɪ'mʌlsɪfaɪ] <-ie-> I. *vt* emulsionar II. *vi* emulsionarse

emulsion [ɪ'mʌlʃən] *n* 1. *a.* PHOT emulsión *f* 2. (*paint*) pintura *f* emulsionada

enable [ɪ'neɪbl] *vt* 1. **to** ~ **sb to do sth** permitir a alguien que haga algo 2. INFOR activar

enact [ɪ'nækt] *vt* 1. (*carry out*) llevar a cabo 2. THEAT representar 3. (*law*) promulgar; **to** ~ **that ...** decretar que...

enactment *n* 1. *no pl* (*carrying out*) puesta *f* en práctica; (*of legislation*) promulgación *f* 2. THEAT representación *f*

enamel [ɪ'næml] I. *n* esmalte *m* II. <-ll-, *Am:* -l-> *vt* esmaltar

enamored *adj Am,* **enamoured** [ɪ'næməʳd, *Am:* -ɚd] *adj Brit* **to be** ~ **of sb** estar enamorado de alguien; **to be** ~ **with sth** estar entusiasmado con algo

enc. *s.* **enc(l)**.

encamp [ɪn'kæmp, *Am:* en-] *vi Brit* acampar

encampment *n* campamento *m*

encapsulate [ɪn'kæpsjəleɪt] *vt* encapsular; *fig* resumir

encase [ɪn'keɪs, *Am:* en-] *vt* encerrar

encephalitis [ˌensefə'laɪtɪs, *Am:* enˌsefə'laɪt̬ɪs] *n* encefalitis *f inv*

enchant [ɪn'tʃɑːnt, *Am:* en'tʃænt] *vt* 1. (*charm*) encantar 2. (*bewitch*) hechizar

enchanted *adj* (*charmed*) encantado, -a; (*bewitched*) hechizado, -a

enchanter *n* hechicero *m*

enchanting *adj* encantador(a)

enchantment *n* 1. (*spell*) hechizo *m* 2. (*charm*) encanto *m*

enchantress *n* (*witch*) hechicera *f;* (*alluring woman*) mujer *f* encantadora

encipher [ɪn'saɪfəʳ, *Am:* en'saɪfɚ] *vt* codificar

encircle [ɪn'sɜːkl, *Am:* en'sɜːr-] *vt* rodear; **to** ~ **the enemy** rodear al enemigo

encirclement *n* cerco *m;* MIL envolvimiento *m*

enc(l). *abbr of* **enclosure** recinto *m*

enclave ['enkleɪv] *n* enclave *m*

enclose [ɪn'kləʊz, *Am:* en'kloʊz] *vt* 1. (*surround*) cercar; **to** ~ **sth in brackets** poner algo entre paréntesis; **to** ~ **the monument with a park** rodear el monumento con el parque 2. (*include*) adjuntar, adosar *AmL*

enclosed [ɪn'kləʊzd, *Am:* en'kloʊzd] *adj*

1. (*confined*) cerrado, -a; (*garden*) vallado, -a; ~ **order** REL orden *f* de clausura 2. (*included*) adjunto, -a

enclosure [ɪn'kləʊʒəʳ, *Am:* en'kloʊʒɚ] *n* 1. (*enclosed area*) recinto *m;* (*for animals*) corral *m* 2. (*action*) cercamiento *m* 3. (*letter*) documento *m* adjunto

encode [ɪn'kəʊd, *Am:* en'koʊd] *vt a.* INFOR codificar; LING cifrar

encompass [ɪn'kʌmpəs, *Am:* en-] *vt* 1. (*surround*) rodear 2. (*include*) abarcar

encore ['ɒŋkɔːʳ, *Am:* 'ɑːnkɔːr] **I.** *n* repetición *f;* **as** [*o* **for**] **an** ~ como bis **II.** *interj* otra

encore marriage *n* segundo matrimonio *m*

encounter [ɪn'kaʊntəʳ, *Am:* en'kaʊnt̬ɚ] **I.** *vt* encontrar; **to** ~ **sb** encontrarse con alguien (por casualidad) **II.** *n* encuentro *m*

encourage [ɪn'kʌrɪdʒ, *Am:* en'kɜːr-] *vt* 1. (*give confidence*) alentar; (*give hope*) dar ánimos a; **to** ~ **sb to do sth** animar a alguien a hacer algo 2. (*support*) fomentar

encouragement [ɪn'kʌrɪdʒmənt, *Am:* en'kɜːr-] *n no pl* estímulo *m;* **to give** ~ **to sth** fomentar algo

encouraging *adj* alentador(a); **an** ~ **prospect** una perspectiva de futuro halagüeña

encroach [ɪn'krəʊtʃ, *Am:* en'kroʊtʃ] *vi* **to** ~ **on** [*o* **upon**] **sth** (*intrude*) invadir algo; *fig* usurpar algo

encroachment *n* 1. (*intrusion*) invasión *f* 2. *fig* usurpación *f;* **an** ~ **on human rights** una violación de los derechos humanos

encryption [ɪn'krɪpʃən] *n* INFOR codificación *f*

encumber [ɪn'kʌmbəʳ, *Am:* en'kʌmbɚ] *vt* **to be** ~**ed with sth** tener que cargar con algo; (*impede*) ser estorbado por algo

encyclop(a)edia [ɪnˌsaɪklə'piːdɪə, *Am:* en-] *n* enciclopedia *f*

encyclop(a)edic [ɪnˌsaɪklə'piːdɪk, *Am:* en-] *adj* enciclopédico, -a

end [end] **I.** *n* 1. (*last, furthest point*) final *m* 2. (*finish*) fin *m* 3. (*extremities*) extremo *m* 4. *pl* (*aims*) fin *m;* (*purpose*) intención *f;* **to achieve one's** ~**s** conseguir los propios objetivos; **for commercial** ~**s** con fines comerciales 5. (*death*) muerte *f;* **he is nearing his** ~ está a punto de morir 6. (*piece remaining*) resto *m* 7. SPORTS lado *m* 8. INFOR tecla *f* de fin ▸**to reach the** ~ **of the line** [*o* **road**] llegar al final; **the** ~ **justifies the means** *prov* el fin justifica los medios *prov;* ~ **of story** punto y final; **you deserved to be punished,** ~ **of story** merecías ser castigado, y punto; **to be at the** ~ **of one's tether** [*o* **rope** *Am*] no poder más; **it's not the** ~ **of the world** no es el fin del mundo; **to come to a bad** [*o* **sticky**] ~ acabar mal; **to go off the deep** ~ *inf* subirse por las paredes; **this is just the** ~ esto (ya) es el colmo; **to hold** [*o* **keep**] **one's** ~ **up** defenderse bien; **to make** ~**s meet** llegar a fin de mes; **to meet one's** ~ encontrar la muerte; **to play both** ~**s against the middle** *Am* oponer a dos contrincantes en beneficio propio; **to put an** ~ **to oneself** [*o* **it all**] acabar con su vida; **in the** ~ a fin de cuentas; **to this** ~ para ello **II.** *vt* 1. (*finish*) acabar 2. (*bring to a stop: reign, war*) poner fin a **III.** *vi* acabar; **to** ~ **in sth** terminar en algo

◆**end up** *vi* terminar; **to** ~ **in love with sb** acabar enamorándose de alguien; **to** ~ **a rich man** acabar siendo un hombre rico; **to** ~ **penniless** acabar sin dinero; **to** ~ **in prison** acabar en la cárcel; **to** ~ **doing sth** terminar haciendo algo

endanger [ɪn'deɪndʒəʳ, *Am:* en'deɪndʒɚ] *vt* poner en peligro; **an** ~**ed species** una especie en peligro de extinción

endear [ɪn'dɪəʳ, *Am:* en'dɪr] *vt* **to** ~ **oneself to sb** hacerse querer por alguien

endearing *adj* entrañable; **an** ~ **smile** una sonrisa agradable

endearment *n* ternura *f;* **terms of** ~ palabras *fpl* cariñosas; **to whisper** ~**s to each other** susurrarse tiernas palabras

endeavor *Am,* **endeavour** [ɪn'devəʳ, *Am:* en'devɚ] *Brit* **I.** *vi* **to** ~ **to do sth** esforzarse por hacer algo **II.** *n* esfuerzo *m;* **to make every** ~ **to do sth** hacer todo lo posible para conseguir algo

endemic [en'demɪk] *adj* endémico, -a

ending ['endɪŋ] *n* fin *m;* LING terminación *f*

endive ['endɪv, *Am:* 'endaɪv] *n Am* endibia *f*

endless ['endlɪs] *adj* interminable, inacabable

endorse [ɪn'dɔːs, *Am:* en'dɔːrs] *vt* 1. (*declare approval for*) aprobar; (*product*) promocionar 2. FIN endosar 3. *Brit* LAW **to** ~ **a driving licence** dejar constancia de sanción en un permiso de conducir

endorsee [ɪnˌdɔː'siː, *Am:* -dɔːr-] *n* endosatario, -a *m, f*

endorsement *n* 1. (*support: of a plan*) aprobación *f;* (*recommendation*) recomendación *f* 2. FIN endoso *m* 3. *Brit* LAW nota *f* de sanción

endorser *n* endosante *mf*

endow [ɪn'daʊ, *Am:* en-] *vt* dotar; **to be** ~**ed with sth** estar dotado de algo

endowment *n* 1. FIN dotación *f* 2. (*talent*) talento *m* 3. BIO **genetic** ~ dotación *f* genética

endpaper ['endpeɪpəʳ, *Am:* -pɚ] *n* guarda *f*

end product *n* producto *m* final **end result** *n* resultado *m* final

endurable [ɪn'djʊərəbl, *Am:* en'dʊrə-] *adj* soportable

endurance [ɪn'djʊərəns, *Am:* en'dʊrəns] *n no pl* resistencia *f*

endure [ɪn'djʊəʳ, *Am:* en'dʊr] **I.** *vt* 1. (*tolerate*) soportar, aguantar 2. (*suffer*) resisitir **II.** *vi form* durar

enduring *adj* duradero, -a

ENE *abbr of* **east-northeast** ENE

enema ['enɪmə, *Am:* -ə-] <-s *o* enemata> *n* enema *m*

enemy ['enəmi] **I.** *n* enemigo, -a *m, f* **II.** *adj* enemigo, -a

energetic [ˌenə'dʒetɪk, *Am:* -ɚ'dʒet̬-] *adj*

enérgico, -a; (*active*) activo, -a

energize ['enədʒaɪz, *Am:* -ɚ-] *vt* **1.** ELEC activar **2.** *fig* dar energía a

energy ['enədʒi, *Am:* -ɚ-] <-ies> *n* energía *f;* **to be full of ~** estar lleno de energía; **to have the ~ to do sth** tener energías para hacer algo

energy crisis *n* asdl asldj asldj crisis *f inv* energética **energy resources** *npl* fuentes *fpl* energéticas [*o* de energía] **energy saving** *n* ahorro *m* de energía

enervate ['enəveɪt, *Am:* -ɚ-] *vt liter* enervar

enervating *adj liter* enervador(a)

enfeeble [ɪn'fiːbl, *Am:* en-] *vt form* debilitar

enforce [ɪn'fɔːs, *Am:* en'fɔːrs] *vt* aplicar; (*law*) hacer cumplir; (*regulation*) poner en vigor

enforceable *adj* ejecutable; (*law*) que se puede hacer cumplir

enforcement [ɪn'fɔːsmənt, *Am:* en'fɔːrs-] *n no pl* (*of a law*) aplicación *f;* (*of a regulation*) ejecución *f*

enfranchise [ɪn'fræntʃaɪz, *Am:* en-] *vt form* conceder el derecho a voto a

engage [ɪn'geɪdʒ, *Am:* en-] **I.** *vt* **1.** *form* (*hold interest*) atraer; **to ~ sb's attention** llamar la atención de alguien **2.** (*put into use*) activar **3.** *Brit, form* (*employ*) contratar **4.** TECH (*cogs*) engranar; **to ~ the clutch** embragar **II.** *vi* **1.** MIL trabar batalla **2.** TECH engranar

engaged *adj* **1.** (*occupied*) ocupado, -a; **to be ~** (*telephone*) estar comunicando **2.** (*to be married*) prometido, -a; **to get ~** (**to sb**) comprometerse (con alguien)

engagement [ɪn'geɪdʒmənt, *Am:* en-] *n* **1.** (*appointment*) compromiso *m* **2.** MIL combate *m* **3.** (*marriage*) compromiso *m*

engagement book *n,* **engagement diary** *n* agenda *f* **engagement ring** *n* anillo *m* de compromiso

engaging *adj* atractivo, -a

engender [ɪn'dʒendəʳ, *Am:* en'dʒendɚ] *vt form* engendrar

engine ['endʒɪn] *n* **1.** (*motor*) motor *m;* **diesel/petrol ~** motor diesel/gasolina; **jet ~** motor a reacción **2.** *Brit* RAIL máquina *f*

engineer [ˌendʒɪ'nɪəʳ, *Am:* -'nɪr] **I.** *n* **1.** (*with a degree*) ingeniero, -a *m, f;* **civil ~** ingeniero de caminos **2.** (*technician*) técnico, -a *m, f* **3.** *Am* RAIL maquinista *mf* **II.** *vt* construir; *fig* maquinar

engineering [ˌendʒɪ'nɪərɪŋ, *Am:* -'nɪr-] *n no pl* ingeniería *f;* **~ works** obras *fpl* de ingeniería

England ['ɪŋglənd] *n* Inglaterra *f*

English ['ɪŋglɪʃ] **I.** *n inv* **1.** (*language*) inglés *m* **2.** *pl* (*people*) **the ~** los ingleses **II.** *adj* inglés, -esa; **an ~ film** una película inglesa; **an ~ class** una clase de inglés

English breakfast *n* desayuno *m* inglés **English Channel** *n* Canal *m* de la Mancha **Englishman** <-men> *n* inglés *m* **English-speaker** *n* persona *f* de habla inglesa **English-speaking** *adj* de habla inglesa **Englishwoman** <-women> *n* inglesa *f*

engrave [ɪn'greɪv, *Am:* en-] *vt* grabar; **to be ~ed on the memory** estar grabado en la memoria

engraver [en'greɪvɚ] *n* grabador(a) *m(f)*

engraving [ɪn'greɪvɪŋ, *Am:* en-] *n* grabado *m*

engross [ɪn'grəʊs, *Am:* en'groʊs] *vt* **1.** (*absorb the attention of*) absorber; **to be ~ed in sth** estar absorto en algo **2.** LAW copiar

engulf [ɪn'gʌlf, *Am:* en-] *vt* hundir

enhance [ɪn'hɑːns, *Am:* -'hæns] *vt* realzar; (*improve or intensify: chances*) aumentar; (*memory*) refrescar

enigma [ɪ'nɪgmə] *n* enigma *m*

enigmatic(al) [ˌenɪg'mætɪk(əl), *Am:* -'mæt̬-] *adj* enigmático, -a

enjoy [ɪn'dʒɔɪ, *Am:* en-] **I.** *vt* **1.** (*get pleasure from*) disfrutar de; **to ~ doing sth** disfrutar haciendo algo; **~ yourselves!** ¡que lo paséis bien! **2.** (*have: health*) poseer; **to ~ sb's confidence** tener la confianza de alguien; **to ~ good health** gozar de buena salud **II.** *vi Am* pasarlo bien

enjoyable [ɪn'dʒɔɪəbl, *Am:* en-] *adj* agradable; (*film, book, play*) divertido, -a

enjoyment [ɪn'dʒɔɪmənt, *Am:* en-] *n no pl* disfrute *m;* **to get real ~ out of doing sth** disfrutar realmente haciendo algo

enlarge [ɪn'lɑːdʒ, *Am:* en'lɑːrdʒ] **I.** *vt* **1.** (*make bigger*) agrandar; (*expand*) extender; **to ~ one's vocabulary** ampliar su léxico **2.** PHOT ampliar **II.** *vi* extenderse

enlargement *n* aumento *m;* (*expanding*) extensión *f;* PHOT ampliación *f*

enlighten [ɪn'laɪtn, *Am:* en-] *vt* **1.** REL iluminar **2.** (*explain*) instruir; **to ~ the public of sth** informar al público de algo

enlightened *adj* (*person*) progresista; REL iluminado, -a; (*age*) ilustrado, -a

enlightenment [ɪn'laɪtnmənt, *Am:* en-] *n no pl* **1.** REL iluminación *f* **2.** PHILOS **the** (**Age of**) **Enlightenment** el Siglo de las Luces **3.** (*explanation*) aclaración *f;* **to give sb ~ on sth** hacer una aclaración a alguien sobre algo

enlist [ɪn'lɪst, *Am:* en-] **I.** *vi* MIL alistarse **II.** *vt* MIL alistar; (*support*) conseguir

enliven [ɪn'laɪvn, *Am:* en-] *vt* avivar; (*person*) animar

en masse [ɑ̃ːm'mæs, *Am:* ɑːn-] *adv* en masa

enmesh [ɪn'meʃ, *Am:* en-] *vt* coger en una red; **to be ~ed in sth** *a. fig* estar enredado en algo; **to get ~ed in sth** *a. fig* enredarse en algo

enmity ['enməti] <-ies> *n* enemistad *f*

ennoble [ɪ'nəʊbl, *Am:* e'noʊbl] *vt* ennoblecer

enormity [ɪ'nɔːməti, *Am:* -'nɔːrmət̬i] <-ies> *n* (*of damage*) magnitud *f;* (*of a task, mistake*) enormidad *f;* (*of a crime*) atrocidad *f*

enormous [ɪ'nɔːməs, *Am:* -'nɔːr-] *adj* enorme; **~ difficulties** grandes dificultades *fpl*

enough [ɪ'nʌf] **I.** *adj* (*sufficient*) suficiente, bastante **II.** *adv* bastante; **to be experienced ~** (**to do sth**) tener la suficiente experiencia (para hacer algo); **to have seen** ~ haber visto demasiado; **she was kind** [*o* **friendly**] ~ **to help me** tuvo la amabilidad de ayudarme; **bad ~, but his brother is worse** si él es malo, peor es su hermano; **oddly** [*o* **strangely**] ~ por extraño que parezca **III.** *interj* basta **IV.** *pron* bastante; **to have ~ to eat and drink** tener lo suficiente para comer y beber; **I know ~ about it** sé lo suficiente acerca de ello; **that should be** ~ eso debería ser suficiente; **more than** ~ más que suficiente; **it is ~ for me to know ...** me basta con saber...; **to have had** ~ (**of sb/sth**) estar harto (de alguien/algo); **as if that wasn't** ~ por si fuera poco; **that's** (**quite**) **~!** ¡basta ya!; ~ **is** ~ basta y sobra

enquire [ɪn'kwaɪəʳ, *Am:* en'kwaɪɚ] **I.** *vi* **1.** (*ask*) preguntar; **to ~ for sb** preguntar por alguien; **to ~ about sth** pedir información sobre algo; **to ~ after sb's health** preguntar por la salud de alguien **2.** (*investigate*) investigar; **to ~ into a matter** indagar en un asunto; **to ~ of sb whether ...** *form* preguntar a alguien si... **II.** *vt* preguntar; **to ~ the reason** preguntar por qué

enquiry [ɪn'kwaɪəri, *Am:* en'kwaɪri] <-ies> *n* **1.** (*question*) pregunta *f;* **to make an ~ into sth** indagar en algo **2.** (*investigation*) investigación *f;* **an ~ into sth** una investigación sobre algo; **to hold an** ~ llevar a cabo una investigación

enrage [ɪn'reɪdʒ, *Am:* en-] *vt* enfurecer

enraged [ɪn'reɪdʒd, *Am:* en-] *adj* enfurecido, -a

enrapture [ɪn'ræptʃəʳ, *Am:* en'ræptʃɚ] *vt* embelesar

enrich [ɪn'rɪtʃ, *Am:* en-] *vt* enriquecer

enrol *Brit,* **enroll** [ɪn'rəʊl, *Am:* en'roʊl] *Am, Aus* **I.** *vi* inscribirse; **to ~ for/on a course** matricularse para/en un curso **II.** *vt* inscribir; (*on a course*) matricular

enrollment *n Am,* **enrolment** [ɪn'rəʊlmənt, *Am:* en'roʊl-] *n* inscripción *f;* (*on a course*) matriculación *f*

en route [ˌɒn'ruːt, *Am:* ˌɑːn-] *adv* en el camino

ensemble [ɒn'sɒmbl, *Am:* ɑːn'sɑːm-] *n* **1.** MUS, THEAT grupo *m* **2.** FASHION conjunto *m*

ensign ['ensən] *n* MIL **1.** enseña *f* **2.** (*standard-bearer*) abanderado *m*

enslave [ɪn'sleɪv, *Am:* en-] *vt* esclavizar; **to be ~d by sth** ser dominado por algo

ensnare [ɪn'sneəʳ, *Am:* en'sner] *vt liter* atrapar, coger en una trampa; **to be ~d in sth** estar atrapado en algo

ensue [ɪn'sjuː, *Am:* en'suː] *vi form* seguirse; **to ~ from sth** resultar de algo

ensuing *adj* siguiente

en suite bathroom [ɑ̃ːnswiːt'bɑːθrʊm, *Am:* ˌɑːnswiːt'bæθruːm] *n* baño *m* incorporado

ensure [ɪn'ʃʊəʳ, *Am:* en'ʃʊr] *vt* asegurar; (*guarantee*) garantizar

ENT *abbr of* **ear, nose and throat** otorrinolaringología *f*

entail [ɪn'teɪl, *Am:* en-] *vt* **1.** (*involve*) acarrear; **to ~ some risk** entrañar algún riesgo **2.** (*necessitate*) **to ~ doing sth** implicar hacer algo

entangle [ɪn'tæŋgl, *Am:* en-] *vt* enredar; **to ~ oneself** enredarse; **to get ~d in sth** quedar enredado en algo; *fig* verse envuelto en algo; **to get ~d with sb** meterse en un lío con alguien

entanglement *n* enredo *m;* (*situation*) embrollo *m;* **emotional ~s** aventuras *fpl* amorosas

enter ['entəʳ, *Am:* -t̬ɚ] **I.** *vt* **1.** (*go into*) entrar en; (*penetrate*) penetrar **2.** (*insert*) introducir; (*into a register*) inscribir **3.** (*join*) hacerse socio de; **to ~ school** ingresar en la escuela **4.** (*make known*) anotar; (*claim*) presentar; (*plea*) formular **II.** *vi* THEAT entrar

◆**enter into** *vi* (*form part of*) tomar parte en; **to ~ a marriage** contraer matrimonio; **to ~ conversation** entablar una conversación; **to ~ discussion** meterse en una discusión; **to ~ negotiations** iniciar negociaciones ►**to ~ the spirit of sth** tomar parte en algo con entusiasmo

◆**enter up** *vt* asentar; (*in accounts*) registrar

◆**enter upon** *vi* emprender

enter key *n* INFOR clave *f* de acceso

enterprise ['entəpraɪz, *Am:* -t̬ɚ-] *n* **1.** (*business firm*) empresa *f;* **to start an** ~ abrir un negocio **2.** (*initiative*) iniciativa *f;* **to show ~ in doing sth** mostrar un espíritu emprendedor para hacer algo

enterprise culture *n no pl* cultura *f* empresarial

enterprising *adj* emprendedor(a)

entertain [ˌentə'teɪn, *Am:* -t̬ɚ-] **I.** *vt* **1.** (*amuse*) entretener **2.** (*guests*) recibir **3.** (*consider*) considerar; **to ~ doubts** abrigar dudas; **to ~ an idea/a plan** estudiar una idea/un proyecto **II.** *vi* (*invite guests*) recibir en casa

entertainer [ˌentə'teɪnəʳ, *Am:* -t̬ɚ'teɪnɚ] *n* artista *mf*

entertaining *adj no pl* entretenido, -a; (*person*) divertido, -a

entertainment [ˌentə'teɪnmənt, *Am:* -t̬ɚ-] *n* **1.** *no pl* (*amusement*) diversión *f;* **to provide some** ~ proporcionar entretenimiento **2.** (*show*) espectáculo *m*

enthral <-ll-> *vt,* **enthrall** [ɪn'θrɔːl, *Am:* en'θrɔːl] *vt Am* cautivar

enthrone [ɪn'θrəʊn, *Am:* en'θroʊn] *vt form* entronizar

enthuse [ɪn'θjuːz, *Am:* en'θuːz] **I.** <-sing> *vi* **to ~ about sth** entusiasmarse muchísimo con algo **II.** <-sing> *vt* **to ~ sb** (**with sth**) entusiasmar a alguien (con algo)

enthusiasm [ɪn'θjuːzɪæzəm, *Am:* en'θuː-] *n* entusiasmo *m;* ~ **for sth** entusiasmo por algo

enthusiast [ɪn'θjuːzɪæst] *n* entusiasta *mf*

enthusiastic [ɪnˌθjuːzɪ'æstɪk, *Am:* enˌθuː-] *adj* entusiasta; **to be ~ about sth** estar entusiasmado con algo

entice [ɪn'taɪs, *Am:* en-] *vt* tentar; **to ~ sb to do sth** tentar a alguien a hacer algo; **to ~ sb away from sth** inducir con maña a alguien para que deje algo

enticement *n* tentación *f*

enticing *adj* tentador(a); (*smile*) atractivo, -a

entire [ɪn'taɪə^r, *Am:* en'taɪɚ] *adj* **1.** (*whole*) todo, -a; (*total*) total; **the ~ world** el mundo entero; **the ~ day** todo el día **2.** (*complete*) entero, -a

entirely *adv* enteramente; **to be ~ sb's fault** ser toda la culpa de alguien; **to agree ~** estar completamente de acuerdo; **to disagree ~** estar del todo en desacuerdo

entirety [ɪn'taɪə^rəti, *Am:* en'taɪrət̬i] *n* **in its ~** en su totalidad

entitle [ɪn'taɪtl, *Am:* en'taɪt̬l] *vt* **1.** (*give right*) autorizar; **to ~ sb to act** autorizar a alguien para actuar; **to ~ sb to a holiday** dar a alguien derecho a vacaciones **2.** (*book*) titular

entitled *adj* **1.** (*person*) autorizado, -a **2.** (*book*) titulado, -a

entitlement [ɪn'taɪtlmənt, *Am:* en'taɪt̬l-] *n no pl* autorización *f;* (*claim*) derecho *m*

entity ['entəti, *Am:* -t̬ət̬i] <-ies> *n form* entidad *f;* **legal ~** persona *f* jurídica; **a single/separate ~** un ente único/separado

entomology [ˌentə'mɒlədʒi, *Am:* -t̬ə'mɑːlə-] *n no pl* entomología *f*

entourage ['ɒntʊrɑːʒ, *Am:* ˌɑːntʊ'rɑːʒ] *n* séquito *m form*

entrails ['entreɪlz] *npl* entrañas *fpl*

entrance¹ ['entrəns] *n* **1.** (*way in*) entrada *f;* (*door*) puerta *f;* **front ~** entrada *f* principal; **the ~ to sth** la entrada de algo; **to refuse ~** negar el acceso **2.** THEAT entrada *f* en escena

entrance² [ɪn'trɑːns, *Am:* en'træns] *vt* encantar

entrance examination ['entrəns ɪgˌzæmɪ'neɪʃən] *n* examen *m* de ingreso **entrance fee** *n* cuota *f* de entrada [*o* de inscripción] **entrance form** *n* formulario *m* de inscripción **entrance hall** *n* vestíbulo *m* **entrance requirement** *n* requisito *m* de entrada

entrant ['entrənt] *n* participante *mf*

entreat [ɪn'triːt, *Am:* en-] *vt* **to ~ sb to do sth** suplicar a alguien que haga algo

entreaty [ɪn'triːti, *Am:* en'triːt̬i] <-ies> *n* ruego *m*

entrench [ɪn'trentʃ, *Am:* en-] *vt passive* **1. to become ~ed** (*idea*) arraigarse **2. to ~ oneself** MIL atrincherarse

entrenched *adj* **1.** (*idea*) arraigado, -a **2.** MIL atrincherado, -a

entrepreneur [ˌɒntrəprə'nɜː^r, *Am:* ˌɑːntrəprə'nɜːr] *n* empresario, -a *m, f*

entrepreneurial spirit [ˌɒntrəprə'nɜːriəl 'spɪrɪt, *Am:* ˌɑːn-] *n no pl* espíritu *m* empresarial

entrust [ɪn'trʌst, *Am:* en-] *vt* confiar; **to ~ sth to sb** confiar algo a alguien; **to ~ sth into sb's care** dejar algo al cuidado de alguien

entry ['entri] <-ies> *n* **1.** (*act of entering*) entrada *f;* (*joining an organization*) ingreso *m* **2.** (*entrance*) acceso *m*

entry fee *n* cuota *f* de entrada **entry form** *n* formulario *m* de inscripción **entry permit** *n* permiso *m* de entrada **entryphone** *n Brit* portero *m* automático **entry regulations** *n* normativa *f* de entrada **entry test** *n* prueba *f* de acceso

entwine [ɪn'twaɪn, *Am:* en-] *vt* (*weave*) entretejer; (*twist*) entrelazar; (*plants*) enredar; **to be ~d** (**together**) *fig* estar entrelazados

E-number ['iːnʌmbə^r, *Am:* -bɚ] *n* número *m* E

enumerate [ɪ'njuːməreɪt, *Am:* -'nuː-] *vt* enumerar

enumeration [ɪˌnjuːmə'reɪʃən, *Am:* -ˌnuː-] *n* enumeración *f*

enunciate [ɪ'nʌnsɪeɪt] *vt* **1.** (*sound*) pronunciar, articular **2.** (*theory*) enunciar

envelop [ɪn'veləp, *Am:* en-] *vt* envolver

envelope ['envələʊp, *Am:* -loʊp] *n* sobre *m,* cierro *m Chile*

enviable ['envɪəbl] *adj* envidiable

envious ['envɪəs] *adj* envidioso, -a; **to be ~ of sb/sth** tener envidia de alguien/algo

environment [ɪn'vaɪərənmənt, *Am:* en'vaɪ-] *n* entorno *m;* **the ~** ECOL el medio ambiente; **home/professional ~** entorno familiar/profesional; **working ~** ambiente *m* de trabajo

environmental [ɪnˌvaɪərən'mentl, *Am:* enˌvaɪrən'ment̬l] *adj* ambiental; ECOL medioambiental; **~ damage** daños *mpl* ecológicos; **~ impact** impacto *m* sobre el medio ambiente; **~ pollution** contaminación *f* ambiental; **~ stress** electrosmog *m*

environmentalist [ɪnˌvaɪərən'mentəlɪst, *Am:* enˌvaɪrən'ment̬əl-] *n* ecologista *mf*

environmentally-friendly [ɪnˌvaɪərən'mentəli'frendli, *Am:* enˌvaɪrən'ment̬əl-] *adj* ecológico, -a

environs [ɪn'vaɪərənz, *Am:* en'vaɪ-] *npl form* alrededores *mpl*

envisage [ɪn'vɪzɪdʒ, *Am:* en-] *vt,* **envision** [ɪn'vɪʒən, *Am:* en-] *vt Am* **1.** (*expect*) prever **2.** (*imagine*) formarse una idea de; **to ~ that ...** prever [*o* calcular] que...

envoy ['envɔɪ, *Am:* 'ɑːn-] *n* enviado, -a *m, f*

envy ['envi] **I.** *n no pl* envidia *f;* **the car is the ~ of my brother** mi hermano me envidia el coche; **she feels ~ towards her sister** le tiene envidia a su hermana ►**to be green with ~** reconcomerse de envidia **II.** <-ie-> *vt* envidiar

enzyme ['enzaɪm] *n* enzima *f*

EOC *n Brit abbr of* **Equal Opportunities Commission** *comisión para la igualdad de oportunidades*

EOF *n* INFOR *abbr of* **end of file** fin *m* de archivo

EP [ˌiː'piː] *abbr of* **extended play** duración *m* ampliada

E

EPA [ˌiːpiːˈeɪ] *Am abbr of* **Environmental Protection Agency** Agencia *f* del Medio Ambiente
ephemeral [ɪˈfemərəl, *Am:* -ɚ-] *adj a.* BIO efímero, -a
epic [ˈepɪk] **I.** *n* epopeya *f* **II.** *adj* épico, -a; ~ **poetry** poesía épica; **an** ~ **journey** un viaje que es toda una epopeya
epicenter *n Am,* **epicentre** [ˈepɪsentəʳ, *Am:* -t̬ɚ] *n Brit, Aus* epicentro *m*
epicycle [ˈepɪsaɪkl, *Am:* ˈ-ə-] *n* MAT, ASTR epiciclo *m*
epidemic [ˌepɪˈdemɪk, *Am:* -əˈ-] **I.** *n* epidemia *f* **II.** *adj* epidémico, -a; ~ **proportions** proporciones gigantescas
epidermis [ˌepɪˈdɜːmɪs, *Am:* -əˈdɜːr-] <-mes> *n* epidermis *f inv*
epigram [ˈepɪgræm, *Am:* ˈ-ə-] *n* epigrama *m*
epilepsy [ˈepɪlepsi] *n no pl* epilepsia *f*
epileptic [ˌepɪˈleptɪk] **I.** *n* epiléptico, -a *m, f* **II.** *adj* epiléptico, -a; ~ **fit** ataque epiléptico
epilog *n Am,* **epilogue** [ˈepɪlɒg, *Am:* -əlɑːg] *n Brit* epílogo *m*
Epiphany [ɪˈpɪfəni] <-ies> *n* Epifanía *f*
episcopacy [ɪˈpɪskəpəsi] <-ies> *n* episcopado *m*
episcopal [ɪˈpɪskəpl] *adj* episcopal
Episcopalian [ɪˌpɪskəˈpeɪlɪən] **I.** *adj* episcopaliano, -a **II.** *n* episcopaliano, -a *m, f*
episode [ˈepɪsəʊd, *Am:* -əsoʊd] *n* episodio *m*
episodic [ˌepɪˈsɒdɪk, *Am:* -əˈsɑːdɪk] *adj* **1.** (*occasional*) episódico, -a **2.** LIT (*consisting of episodes*) por episodios [*o* capítulos]
epistle [ɪˈpɪsl] *n* epístola *f*
epistolary [ɪˈpɪstələri, *Am:* -eri] *adj* epistolar
epitaph [ˈepɪtɑːf, *Am:* -ətæf] *n* epitafio *m*
epithet [ˈepɪθet] *n* LING epíteto *m*
epitome [ɪˈpɪtəmi, *Am:* -ˈpɪt̬-] *n* **1.** (*embodiment*) personificación *f* **2.** (*example*) arquetipo *m;* **the** ~ **of poor taste** el colmo del mal gusto
epitomise *vt Aus, Brit,* **epitomize** [ɪˈpɪtəmaɪz, *Am:* -ˈpɪt̬-] *vt* personificar
epoch [ˈiːpɒk, *Am:* ˈepək] *n form* era *f;* **historical** ~ época *f* histórica
epoch-making [ˈiːpɒkˌmeɪkɪŋ, *Am:* ˈepək-] *adj* ~ **discovery** descubrimiento *m* que hace época
eponymous [ɪˈpɒnɪməs, *Am:* ɪˈpɑːnə-] *adj* epónimo, -a
equable [ˈekwəbl] *adj* (*temperament*) ecuánime; (*climate*) templado, -a; **to have an** ~ **disposition** ser de talante tranquilo
equal [ˈiːkwəl] **I.** *adj* **1.** (*the same*) igual; (*treatment*) equitativo, -a; **to have** ~ **reason to do sth** tener las mismas razones para hacer algo; **of** ~ **size** de la misma medida; **on** ~ **terms** en igualdad de condiciones **2.** (*able to do*) **to be** ~ **to a task** ser capaz de realizar una tarea **II.** *n* igual *mf;* **it has no** ~ no hay nada parecido **III.** <*Brit:* -ll-, *Am:* -l-> *vt* **1.** *pl* MAT ser igual a **2.** (*match*) igualar
equality [ɪˈkwɒləti, *Am:* -ˈkwɑːlət̬i] *n no pl* igualdad *f*
equalization [ˌiːkwəlaɪˈzeɪʃən, *Am:* -ɪˈ-] *n* nivelización *f*
equalize [ˈiːkwəlaɪz] **I.** *vt* nivelar **II.** *vi Aus, Brit* SPORTS empatar
equalizer [ˈiːkwəlaɪzəʳ, *Am:* -zɚ] *n Aus, Brit* SPORTS tanto *m* del empate; **to score an** ~ marcar el empate
equally [ˈiːkwəli] *adv* igualmente; **to contribute** ~ **to sth** contribuir por igual a algo; **to divide sth** ~ dividir algo equitativamente
equal opportunities *npl Brit,* **equal opportunity** *n Am* igualdad *f* de oportunidades **equal(s) sign** *n* MAT signo *m* de igual
equanimity [ˌekwəˈnɪməti, *Am:* -ət̬i] *n no pl* ecuanimidad *f;* **to receive sth with** ~ recibir algo serenamente
equate [ɪˈkweɪt] **I.** *vt* equiparar **II.** *vi* **to** ~ **to sth** ser equivalente [*o* igual] a algo
equation [ɪˈkweɪʒən] *n* ecuación *f*
equator [ɪˈkweɪtəʳ, *Am:* -t̬ɚ] *n* ecuador *m*
equatorial [ˌekwəˈtɔːrɪəl] *adj* ecuatorial
Equatorial Guinea *n* Guinea *f* Ecuatorial
equestrian [ɪˈkwestrɪən] **I.** *adj* ecuestre; ~ **events** pruebas hípicas; ~ **statue** estatua *f* ecuestre **II.** *n* (*man*) jinete *m;* (*woman*) amazona *f*
equidistant [ˌiːkwɪˈdɪstənt] *adj* equidistante
equilateral [ˌiːkwɪˈlætərəl, *Am:* -ˈlæt̬-] *adj* MAT equilátero, -a
equilibrium [ˌiːkwɪˈlɪbrɪəm] *n no pl* equilibrio *m*
equinoctial [ˌiːkwɪˈnɒkʃl, *Am:* -ˈnɑːk-] *adj* equinoccial
equinox [ˈiːkwɪnɒks, *Am:* -nɑːks] <-es> *n* equinoccio *m;* **autumn** ~ equinoccio de otoño
equip [ɪˈkwɪp] <-pp-> *vt* **1.** (*fit out*) equipar; **to** ~ **sb with sth** proveer a alguien de algo **2.** (*prepare*) preparar
equipment [ɪˈkwɪpmənt] *n no pl* equipo *m;* **camping** ~ accesorios *mpl* de cámping; **office** ~ material *m* de oficina
equitable [ˈekwɪtəbl, *Am:* -t̬ə-] *adj* equitativo, -a
equity [ˈekwəti, *Am:* -t̬i] <-ies> *n no pl* **1.** (*fairness*) equidad *f* **2.** *pl, Brit* FIN acciones *fpl* ordinarias
eq(uiv). *abbr of* **equivalent** equivalente
equivalence [ɪˈkwɪvələns] *n no pl* equivalencia *f*
equivalent [ɪˈkwɪvələnt] **I.** *adj* equivalente; **to be** ~ **to sth** equivaler a algo **II.** *n* equivalente *m*
equivocal [ɪˈkwɪvəkl] *adj* equívoco, -a
equivocate [ɪˈkwɪvəkeɪt] *vi form* hablar de forma equívoca
equivocation [ɪˌkwɪvəˈkeɪʃən] *n no pl* ambigüedad *f*
ER [ˌiːˈɑːʳ, *Am:* -ˈɑːr] *n abbr of* **Elizabeth Regina** Reina *f* Isabel
era [ˈɪərə, *Am:* ˈɪrə] *n* era *f;* **communist** ~ era comunista; **post-war** ~ época *f* de la pos-

guerra; **to usher in an ~** marcar el cominezo de una era
eradicate [ɪˈrædɪkeɪt] *vt* erradicar
erase [ɪˈreɪz, *Am:* -ˈreɪs] *vt a.* INFOR borrar; **to ~ a deficit** eliminar un déficit
eraser [ɪˈreɪzəʳ, *Am:* -ˈreɪsɚ] *n Am* goma *f* de borrar
erasure [ɪˈreɪʒəʳ, *Am:* -ʃɚ] *n Am* borradura *f*
ere [eəʳ] **I.** *prep liter* antes de; **~ long** dentro de poco **II.** *conj liter* antes de que
erect [ɪˈrekt] **I.** *adj* erguido, -a; ANAT erecto, -a **II.** *vt* eregir; (*construct*) construir; (*put up*) levantar
erectile [ɪˈrektaɪl, *Am:* -təl] *adj* ANAT eréctil
erection [ɪˈrekʃən] *n* **1.** *no pl* ARCHIT construcción *f* **2.** ANAT erección *f*
erg [ɜːg, *Am:* ɜːrg] *n* PHYS ergio *m*
ergonomic [ˌɜːgəˈnɒmɪk, *Am:* ˌɜːrgəˈnɑːmɪk] *adj* ergonómico, -a
ergonomics *n* ergonomía *f*
ERM [ˌiːɑːrˈem] *abbr of* **Exchange Rate Mechanism** SME *m*
ermine [ˈɜːmɪn, *Am:* ˈɜːr-] *n* armiño *m*
erode [ɪˈrəʊd, *Am:* -ˈroʊd] **I.** *vt* erosionar **II.** *vi* erosionarse
erogenous [ɪˈrɒdʒənəs, *Am:* -ˈrɑːdʒɪ-] *adj* erógeno, -a
erosion [ɪˈrəʊʒən, *Am:* -ˈroʊ-] *n no pl* erosión *f*
erotic [ɪˈrɒtɪk, *Am:* -ˈrɑːt̬ɪk] *adj* erótico, -a
eroticism [ɪˈrɒtɪsɪzəm, *Am:* -ˈrɑːt̬ə-] *n no pl* erotismo *m*
err [ɜːʳ, *Am:* ɜːr] *vi* errar; **to ~ on the side of sth** pecar (por exceso) de algo; **to ~ on the side of caution** pecar de cauteloso ▸**to ~ is human** *prov* errar es humano *prov*
errand [ˈerənd] *n* recado *m;* **to run an ~** (salir a) hacer un recado; **an ~ of mercy** *form* una misión de caridad
errand boy *n* chico *m* de los recados
errant [ˈerənt] *adj* **1.** *form* descarriado, -a **2.** *iron* (*unfaithful*) infiel
erratic [ɪˈrætɪk, *Am:* -ˈræt̬-] *adj* **1.** GEO errático, -a **2.** MED (*pulse*) irregular
erratum [eˈrɑːtəm, *Am:* -t̬əm] <-ta> *n form* errata *f*
erroneous [ɪˈrəʊnɪəs, *Am:* əˈroʊ-] *adj* erróneo, -a; **~ assumption** suposición equivocada
error [ˈerəʳ, *Am:* -ɚ] *n* error *m;* **to do sth in ~** hacer algo por equivocación; **human ~** error humano ▸**to see the ~ of one's ways** darse cuenta de lo mal que uno ha actuado; **to show sb the ~ of his/her ways** demostrar a alguien lo equivocado de su actuación
error message *n* INFOR mensaje *m* de error
error-prone *adj* propenso, -a a errores **error rate** *n* porcentaje *m* de errores
erudite [ˈeruːdaɪt, *Am:* -jə-] *adj* erudito, -a
erudition [ˌeruːˈdɪʃən, *Am:* -juːˈ-] *n no pl* erudición *f*
erupt [ɪˈrʌpt] *vi* **1.** (*explode: volcano*) entrar en erupción; *fig* estallar **2.** MED salir
eruption [ɪˈrʌpʃən] *n* erupción *f; fig* estallido *m*
escalate [ˈeskəleɪt] **I.** *vi* (*increase*) aumentar; (*incidents*) intensificarse; **to ~ into sth** terminar en algo **II.** *vt* intensificar
escalation [ˌeskəˈleɪʃən] *n* escalada *f;* **~ of tension** escalada de la tensión
escalator [ˈeskəleɪtəʳ, *Am:* -t̬ɚ] *n* escalera *f* mecánica
escalope [ˈeskələp, *Am:* ˌeskəˈloʊp] *n* escalope *m*
escapade [ˌeskəˈpeɪd] *n* aventura *f;* (*mischievous*) travesura *f*
escape [ɪˈskeɪp] **I.** *vi* escaparse; (*person*) huir de; **to ~ from** escaparse de; **to ~ from a program** INFOR salir de un programa **II.** *vt* escapar a; (*avoid*) evitar; **to ~ sb('s attention)** pasar desapercibido a alguien; **nothing ~s his attention** no se le escapa ni una; **the word ~s me** se me ha ido la palabra (de la cabeza); **a cry ~d him** se le escapó un grito **III.** *n* **1.** (*act*) fuga *f;* **to have a narrow ~** salvarse por muy poco **2.** (*outflow*) escape *m* **3.** LAW **~ clause** cláusula *f* de excepción
escapee [ɪˌskeɪˈpiː] *n* fugitivo, -a *m, f*
escapism [ɪˈskeɪpɪzəm] *n no pl* escapismo *m*
escapist **I.** *n* escapista *mf* **II.** *adj* escapista; **~ literature** literatura *f* de evasión
escarpment [ɪˈskɑːpmənt, *Am:* eˈskɑːrp-] *n* escarpa *f*
ESCB *n s.* **European System of Central Banks** SEBC *m*
eschew [ɪˈstʃuː, *Am:* es-] *vt form* evitar
escort [ˈeskɔːt, *Am:* -kɔːrt] **I.** *vt* acompañar; (*politician*) escoltar **II.** *n* **1.** (*companion*) acompañante *mf* **2.** (*paid companion*) señorito, -a *m, f* de compañía **3.** *no pl* (*guard*) escolta *f*
escutcheon [ɪˈskʌtʃən] *n* blasón *m* ▸**a blot on sb's ~** una mancha en el honor de alguien
ESE *n abbr of* **east-southeast** ESE *m*
Eskimo [ˈeskɪməʊ, *Am:* -kəmoʊ] <-s> *n* **1.** (*person*) esquimal *mf* **2.** *no pl* LING esquimal *m*
ESL [ˌiːesˈel] *n abbr of* **English as a second language** inglés *m* como segunda lengua
ESN [ˌiːesˈen] *abbr of* **educationally subnormal** impedido, -a para aprender
esophagus [iːˈsɒfəgəs, *Am:* ɪˈsɑːfə-] *n Am* esófago *m*
esoteric [ˌesəʊˈterɪk, *Am:* ˌesəˈ-] *adj* esotérico, -a
ESP [ˌiːesˈpiː] *n abbr of* **extrasensory perception** percepción *f* extrasensorial
esp. *abbr of* **especially** especialmente
espadrille [ˈespədrɪl] *n* alpargata *f*
especial [ɪˈspeʃl] *adj* especial
especially [ɪˈspeʃəli] *adv* **1.** (*particularly*) especialmente; **I bought this ~ for you** lo compré expresamente para ti **2.** (*in particular*) en particular
espionage [ˈespɪənɑːʒ] *n no pl* espionaje *m;*

E

industrial ~ espionaje industrial

esplanade [ˌespləˈneɪd, *Am:* ˈesplənɑːd] *n* paseo *m* marítimo

espousal [ɪˈspaʊzl] *n no pl, form* apoyo *m*

espouse [ɪˈspaʊz] *vt* apoyar

espresso [eˈspresəʊ, *Am:* -oʊ] <-s> *n* café *m* exprés

Esq. *abbr of* **Esquire** Sr.

Esquire [ɪˈskwaɪəʳ, *Am:* ˈeskwaɪɚ] *n Brit* (*special title*) Señor *m*

essay¹ [eˈseɪ] *n* **1.** LIT ensayo *m* **2.** SCHOOL redacción *f;* **an ~ on sth** una redacción sobre algo

essay² [ˈeseɪ] *vt* **1.** (*try*) intentar hacer **2.** (*test*) probar

essayist *n* ensayista *mf*

essence [ˈesns] *n* **1.** *no pl* esencia *f;* **time is of the ~ here** el tiempo es de vital importancia aquí **2.** (*in food*) esencia *f*, extracto *m*

essential [ɪˈsenʃl] **I.** *adj* esencial; (*difference*) fundamental; **to be ~ to sb/sth** ser esencial para alguien/algo **II.** *n pl* **the ~s** los elementos básicos [*o* esenciales]; **the bare ~s** lo justamente necesario

essentially [ɪˈsenʃəli] *adv* esencialmente

est. 1. *abbr of* **estimated** est. **2.** *abbr of* **established** fundado, -a

establish [ɪˈstæblɪʃ] **I.** *vt* **1.** (*found*) fundar; (*commission, hospital*) crear; (*dictatorship*) instaurar **2.** (*begin: relationship*) entablar **3.** (*set: precedent*) sentar; (*priorities, norm*) establecer **4.** (*secure*) asegurar; (*order*) imponer; **he ~ed his authority over the workers** afirmó su autoridad sobre los obreros; **to ~ a reputation as a pianist** hacerse un nombre como pianista **5.** (*demonstrate*) **to ~ sb as sth** acreditar a alguien como algo **6.** (*determine*) determinar, establecer; (*facts*) verificar; (*truth*) comprobar; **to ~ whether/where ...** determinar si/dónde...; **to ~ that ...** comprobar que... **7.** ADMIN **to ~ residence** fijar la residencia **II.** *vi* establecerse

established [ɪˈstæblɪʃt] *adj* **1.** (*founded*) fundado, -a **2.** (*fact*) comprobado, -a; (*procedures*) establecido, -a

establishment [ɪˈstæbliʃmənt] *n* **1.** (*business*) empresa *f;* **family ~** empresa *f* familiar **2.** (*organization*) establecimiento *m;* **educational ~** centro *m* educativo; **financial ~** institución *f* financiera; **the Establishment** POL la clase dirigente

estate [ɪˈsteɪt] *n* **1.** (*piece of land*) finca *f;* **country ~** finca *f*, hacienda *f AmL* **2.** LAW patrimonio *m;* **housing ~** urbanización *f;* **industrial ~** polígono *m* industrial; **council ~** viviendas *fpl* de protección oficial **3.** *Brit* (*car*) coche *m* familiar

estate agent *n Brit* agente *mf* de la propiedad inmobiliaria **estate car** *n Brit* coche *m* familiar **estate duty** <-ies> *n*, **estate tax** *n* impuesto *m* sobre sucesiones

esteem [ɪˈstiːm] **I.** *n no pl* estima *f;* **to fall/rise in sb's ~** perder/ganarse la estima de alguien; **to hold sb in high/low ~** tener a alguien en gran/poca estima **II.** *vt* **1.** (*respect*) apreciar, valorar **2.** (*consider*) considerar, estimar; **to ~ it an honour to do sth** considerar un honor (poder) hacer algo

esteemed *adj* apreciado, -a, valorado, -a; **highly ~** muy apreciado

esthetic [iːsˈθetɪk] *adj* estético, -a

esthetics *n* estética *f*

estimable [ˈestɪməbl] *adj form* estimable

estimate [ˈestɪmeɪt, *Am:* -mɪt] **I.** *vt* calcular; **to ~ that ...** calcular que... **II.** *n* cálculo *m* (aproximado); **rough ~** *inf* cálculo aproximado; **at a rough ~** aproximadamente

estimated [ˈestɪmeɪtɪd, *Am:* -t̬ɪd] *adj* estimado, -a

estimation [ˌestɪˈmeɪʃən] *n no pl* opinión *f;* **in my ~** a mi juicio

Estonia [esˈtəʊniə, *Am:* esˈtoʊ-] *n* Estonia *f*

Estonian [esˈtəʊniən, *Am:* esˈtoʊ-] **I.** *adj* estonio, -a **II.** *n* **1.** (*person*) estonio, -a *m, f* **2.** LING estonio *m*

estrange [ɪˈstreɪndʒ] *vt* **to ~ sb from sb/sth** distanciar a alguien de alguien/algo

estranged *adj* (*distance*) distanciado, -a; (*state*) separado, -a

estrangement [ɪˈstreɪndʒmənt] *n* distanciamiento *m*

estrogen [ˈiːstrəʊdʒən, *Am:* ˈestrədʒən] *n Am s.* **oestrogen**

estuary [ˈestʃʊəri, *Am:* ˈestʃuːeri] <-ies> *n* estuario *m*

ETA [ˌiːtiːˈeɪ] *abbr of* **estimated time of arrival** hora *f* prevista de llegada

et al. [etˈæl] *abbr of* **et alii** et al

etc. *abbr of* **et cetera** etc.

et cetera [ɪtˈsetərə, *Am:* -ˈset̬ɚ-] *adv* etcétera

etch [etʃ] *vt* **1.** grabar (al agua fuerte) **2.** *fig* **to be ~ed on sb's memory** estar grabado en la memoria de alguien

etcher *n* aguafuertista *mf*

etching *n* aguafuerte *m*

ETD *abbr of* **estimated time of departure** hora *f* prevista de salida

eternal [ɪˈtɜːnl, *Am:* -ˈtɜːr-] *adj* **1.** (*lasting forever*) eterno, -a **2.** (*constant*) constante, incesante ► **~ triangle** *Brit* triángulo amoroso

eternally [ɪˈtɜːnəli, *Am:* -ˈtɜːr-] *adv* **1.** (*forever*) eternamente **2.** (*constantly*) constantemente, incesantemente

eternity [ɪˈtɜːnəti, *Am:* -ˈtɜːrnət̬i] *n no pl* eternidad *f;* **to seem like an ~** parecer una eternidad; **to wait an ~ for sb** esperar una eternidad a alguien

ether [ˈiːθəʳ, *Am:* -θɚ] *n no pl* éter *m*

ethereal [ɪˈθɪərɪəl, *Am:* -ˈθɪrɪ-] *adj* etéreo, -a

ethic [ˈeθɪk] *n* **work ~** ética del trabajo *f*

ethical *adj* ético, -a

ethics *n + sing vb* ética *f*

Ethiopia [ˌiːθɪˈəʊpɪə, *Am:* -ˈoʊ-] *n no pl* Etiopía *f*

Ethiopian [ˌiːθɪˈəʊpɪən, *Am:* -ˈoʊ-] **I.** *n* etíope *mf* **II.** *adj* etíope

ethnic ['eθnɪk] *adj* étnico, -a; ~ **cleaning** limpieza étnica; ~ **costumes** trajes *mpl* tradicionales

ethnology [eθ'nɒlədʒi, *Am:* -'nɑ:lə-] *n no pl* etnología *f*

ethos ['i:θɒs, *Am:* -θɑ:s] *n no pl* espiritú *m;* **the working-class** ~ los valores de la clase trabajadora

ethyl alcohol ['eθɪl 'ælkəhɒl, *Am:* 'eθəl 'ælkəhɑ:l] *n* alcohol *m* etílico

etiquette ['etɪket, *Am:* 'et̬ɪkɪt] *n no pl* etiqueta *f;* **court** ~ etiqueta de palacio

etymological [ˌetɪmə'lɒdʒɪkl, *Am:* ˌet̬ɪmə'lɑ:dʒɪkl] *adj* etimológico, -a

etymology [ˌetɪ'mɒlədʒi, *Am:* ˌet̬ɪ'mɑ:lə-] *n no pl* etimología *f*

EU [ˌi:'ju:] *n abbr of* **European Union** UE *f*

eucalyptus [ˌju:kə'lɪptəs] <-es *o* -ti> *n* eucalipto *m*

eucalyptus oil *n no pl* bálsamo *m* de eucalipto

Eucharist ['ju:kərɪst] *n no pl* REL **the** ~ la Eucaristía

eulogize ['ju:lədʒaɪz] **I.** *vt form* elogiar **II.** *vi form* **to ~ over sth/sb** elogiar algo/a alguien

eulogy ['ju:lədʒi] <-ies> *n form* **1.** (*high praise*) elogio *m* **2.** LIT panegírico *m;* **to deliver a** ~ hacer un panegírico

eunuch ['ju:nək] *n* eunuco *m*

euphemism ['ju:fəmɪzəm] *n* eufemismo *m*

euphemistic [ˌju:fə'mɪstɪk] *adj* eufemístico, -a

euphony ['ju:fəni] *n no pl, form* eufonía *f*

euphoria [ju:'fɔ:rɪə] *n no pl* euforia *f*

euphoric [ju:'fɒrɪk, *Am:* -'fɔ:rɪk] *adj* eufórico, -a

EUR *n s.* **Euro** EUR *m*

Eurasia [jʊə'reɪʒə, *Am:* jʊ'-] *n no pl* Eurasia *f*

Eurasian [jʊə'reɪʒən, *Am:* jʊ'-] **I.** *adj* euroasiático, -a **II.** *n* euroasiático, -a *m, f*

Euratom [jʊə'rætəm, *Am:* jʊ'ræt̬-] *n abbr of* **European Atomic Energy Community** Euratom *f*

eurhythmics [ju:'rɪðmɪks, *Am:* jʊ'-] *n Brit,* **eurythmics** *n Am + sing vb* euritmia *f*

euro ['jʊərəʊ, *Am:* 'jʊroʊ] *n* euro *m*

euro cent *n* céntimo *m* de euro

Eurocheque ['jʊrətʃek, *Am:* 'jʊroʊ-] *n* eurocheque *m*

euro coins *npl* monedas *fpl* de euro

Eurocrat ['jʊərəʊkræt, *Am:* 'jʊrə-] *n* eurócrata *mf*

eurocurrency *n* eurodivisa *f* **Eurodollar** *n* eurodólar *m* **euro notes** *npl* billetes *mpl* de euro

Europe ['jʊərəp, *Am:* 'jʊrəp] *n no pl* Europa *f*

European [ˌjʊərə'pɪən, *Am:* ˌjʊrə-] **I.** *adj* europeo, -a **II.** *n* europeo, -a *m, f*

European Central Bank *n* Banco *m* Central Europeo **European Commission** *n* Comisión *f* Europea **European Community** *n* Comunidad *f* Europea **European Council** *n* Consejo *m* Europeo **European Court of Auditors** *n* Tribunal *m* Europeo de Cuentas **European Court of Justice** *n* Tribunal *m* de Justicia Europeo **European Economic and Monetary Union** *n* Unión *f* Económica y Monetaria Europea **European Investment Bank** *n* Banco *m* Europeo de Inversiones **European Monetary Institute** *n* Instituto *m* Monetario Europeo **European Monetary System** *n* Sistema *m* Monetario Europeo **European Parliament** *n* Parlamento *m* Europeo **European Single Market** *n* Mercado *m* Único Europeo **European System of Central Banks** *n* Sistema *m* Europeo de Bancos Centrales **European Union** *n* Unión *f* Europea

euthanasia [ˌju:θə'neɪzɪə, *Am:* -ʒə] *n no pl* eutanasia *f*

evacuate [ɪ'vækjʊeɪt] *vt* (*people*) evacuar; (*building*) desocupar

evacuation [ɪˌvækjʊ'eɪʃən] *n* evacuación *f;* ~ **of the bowels** MED evacuación *f*

evacuee [ɪˌvækju:'i:] *n* evacuado, -a *m, f*

evade [ɪ'veɪd] *vt* (*responsibility, person*) eludir; (*police*) escaparse de; (*taxes*) evadir; **to ~ doing sth** evitar hacer algo

evaluate [ɪ'væljʊeɪt] *vt* (*value*) tasar; (*result*) evaluar; (*person*) examinar

evaluation [ɪˌvæljʊ'eɪʃən] *n* evaluación *f;* (*of an experience*) valoración *f;* (*of a book*) crítica *f*

evangelical [ˌi:væn'dʒelɪkl] **I.** *n* evangélico, -a *m, f* **II.** *adj* evangélico, -a

evangelist [ɪ'vændʒəlɪst] *n* evangelista *mf*

evangelize [ɪ'vændʒəlaɪz] **I.** *vt* evangelizar **II.** *vi* evangelizar

evaporate [ɪ'væpəreɪt] **I.** *vt* evaporar; **~d milk** leche evaporada **II.** *vi* evaporarse; *fig* desaparecer

evaporation [ɪˌvæpə'reɪʃən] *n* evaporación *f*

evasion [ɪ'veɪʒən] *n* **1.** (*of tax, responsability*) evasión *f* **2.** (*avoidance*) evasiva *f*

evasive [ɪ'veɪsɪv] *adj* evasivo, -a

eve [i:v] *n no pl* víspera *f;* **on the ~ of** en vísperas de; **Christmas Eve** Nochebuena *f;* **New Year's Eve** Nochevieja *f*

Eve [i:v] *n* Eva *f*

even ['i:vn] **I.** *adv* **1.** (*indicates the unexpected*) incluso; **not ~** ni siquiera **2.** (*despite*) **~ if ...** aunque...; **~ so ...** aun así...; **~ though ...** aunque... **3.** (*used to intensify*) hasta **4.** + *superl* (*all the more*) aún; **it will be ~ colder** hará incluso más frío **II.** *adj* **1.** (*level*) llano, -a; (*surface*) liso, -a **2.** (*equalized*) igualado, -a; **the chances are about ~** hay casi las mismas posibilidades; **to be on ~ terms** estar en las mismas condiciones; **to get ~ with sb** ajustar cuentas con alguien **3.** (*of same size, amount*) igual **4.** (*constant, regular*) uniforme; (*rate*) constante **5.** (*fair*) ecuánime **6.** MAT par **III.** *vt* **1.** (*make level*) nivelar; (*surface*) allanar **2.** (*equalize*) igualar

◆**even out** **I.** *vi* (*prices*) nivelarse **II.** *vt* igua-

lar
◆**even up** *vt* igualar
evening ['i:vnɪŋ] *n* (*early*) tarde *f;* (*late*) noche *f;* **good** ~! ¡buenas tardes/noches!; **in the** ~ por la tarde/noche; **that** ~ esa noche; **the previous** ~ la noche anterior; **every Monday** ~ cada lunes por la noche; **on Monday** ~ el lunes por la noche; **during the** ~ durante la noche; **one July** ~ una noche de julio; **8 o'clock in the** ~ las 8 de la noche; **at the end of the** ~ al final de la noche; **all** ~ toda la noche
evening class *n* clase *f* nocturna **evening dress** *n* traje *m* de noche; **to wear** ~ ir de etiqueta **evening edition** *n* edición *f* vespertina **evening gown** *n* traje *m* de noche **evening meal** *n* cena *f* **evening (news)paper** *n* periódico *m* de la tarde **evening performance** *n* función *f* de noche **evening prayer** *n* oración *f* de la tarde **evening service** *n* misa *f* vespertina **evening star** *n* estrella *f* vespertina
evenly ['i:vənli] *adv* **1.** (*calmly*) apaciblemente; **to state sth** ~ decir algo sin alterarse **2.** (*equally*) igualmente; **to divide sth** ~ dividir algo de forma equitativa
evenness ['i:vnnɪs] *n no pl* **1.** uniformidad *f* **2.** (*calmness*) serenidad *f*
evens *adj Brit* **the chances are** ~ las posibilidades son del cincuenta por ciento
event [ɪ'vent] *n* **1.** (*happening*) evento *m;* **sporting** ~ acontecimiento *m* deportivo; **to be swept along by the tide of** ~**s** dejarse llevar por los acontecimientos **2.** (*case*) caso *m;* **in any** ~, **at all** ~**s** *Brit* en cualquier caso; **in the** ~ **(that) it rains** en caso de que llueva; **in either** ~ en cualquier caso
even-tempered ['i:vən'tempəd] *adj* ecuánime
eventful [ɪ'ventfəl] *adj* accidentado, -a
eventual [ɪ'ventʃʊəl] *adj* final
eventuality [ɪˌventʃʊ'æləti, *Am:* -t̬i] <-ies> *n inv* eventualidad *f*
eventually [ɪ'ventʃʊəli] *adv* **1.** (*finally*) finalmente **2.** (*some day*) con el tiempo
ever ['evəʳ, *Am:* -ɚ] *adv* **1.** (*on any occasion*) alguna vez; **have you** ~ **been to Barcelona?** ¿has estado alguna vez en Barcelona?; **for the first time** ~ por primera vez; **the hottest day** ~ el día mas caliente; **better than** ~ mejor que nunca; **have you** ~ **seen such a thing!** ¡habráse visto semejante cosa!; **would you** ~ **dye your hair?** te teñerías el pelo? **2.** (*in negative statements*) nunca, jamás; **nobody has** ~ **heard of him** nadie ha oído nunca hablar de él; **never** ~ nunca jamás; **hardly** ~ casi nunca; **nothing** ~ **happens** nunca pasa nada; **don't you** ~ **do that again!** no se te ocurra volve **3.** (*always*) ~ **after** desde entonces; **as** ~ como siempre; ~ **since ...** desde que...; ~ **since** (*since then*) desde entonces **4.** *Brit, inf* (*very*) **I'm** ~ **so grateful** se lo agradezco profundamente; **your're** ~ **so kind!** ¡usted es (siempre) tán amable!; **I am** ~ **so sorry** lo siento muchísimo; **it's** ~ **so hot** hace muchísimo calor; **thank you** ~ **so much** muchísimas gracias **5.** (*used to intensify*) **who** ~ **was that woman?** ¿quién demonios era esa mujer?; **all he** ~ **does is** +*infin* lo único que hace es +*infin;* **don't you** ~ **come here again!** ¡no se te ocurra volver a venir aquí!
everglade ['evəgleɪd, *Am:* -ɚ-] *n Am: tierra baja pantanosa cubierta de altas hierbas*
evergreen ['evəgri:n, *Am:* -ɚ-] **I.** *n* árbol *m* de hoja perenne **II.** *adj* de hoja perenne; *fig* imperecedero, -a
everlasting [ˌevə'lɑ:stɪŋ, *Am:* -ɚ'læstɪŋ] *adj* **1.** (*undying*) imperecedero, -a; (*gratitude*) eterno, -a *f* **2.** (*incessant*) interminable
evermore [ˌevə'mɔ:ʳ, *Am:* -ɚ'mɔ:r] *adv liter* eternamente; **for** ~ por siempre jamás
every ['evri] *adj* **1.** (*each*) cada; ~ **time** cada vez; **her** ~ **wish** su más mínimo deseo; **not** ~ **book can be borrowed** no todo libro puede ser tomado en préstamo **2.** (*all*) todo, -a; ~ **one of them** todos y cada uno de ellos; **in** ~ **way** de todas las maneras **3.** (*repeated*) ~ **other week** en semanas alternas; ~ **now and then** [*o* **again**] de vez en cuando ►~ <u>**little**</u> **helps** *prov* cualquier ayuda es buena
everybody ['evriˌbɒdi, *Am:* -ˌbɑ:di] *pron indef, sing* todos, todo el mundo; ~ **but Paul** todos menos Paul; ~ **else** todos los demás; ~ **who agrees** todos los que están de acuerdo
everybody else *pron* todos los demás
everyday ['evrɪdeɪ] *adj* diario, -a; (*clothes*) de diario; (*event*) ordinario, -a; (*language*) corriente; (*life*) cotidiano, -a
everyone ['evrɪwʌn] *pron s.* **everybody**
everything ['evrɪθɪŋ] *pron indef, sing* todo; **is** ~ **all right?** ¿está todo bien?; ~ **they drink** todo lo que beben; **to be** ~ **to sb** serlo todo para alguien; **to do** ~ **necessary/one can** hacer todo lo necesario/lo posible; **time is** ~ el tiempo lo es todo; **wealth isn't** ~ la riqueza no lo es todo
everywhere ['evrɪweəʳ, *Am:* -wer] *adv* en todas partes; ~ **else** en cualquier otro sitio; **to look** ~ **for sth** buscar algo por todas partes; **to travel** ~ viajar a todas partes
evict [ɪ'vɪkt] *vt* desahuciar
eviction [ɪ'vɪkʃən] *n* desahucio *m*
evidence ['evɪdəns] *n* **1.** *no pl* (*sign*) indicios *mpl* **2.** (*proof*) prueba *f* **3.** (*testimony*) testimonio *m;* **on the** ~ **of those present** según las declaraciones de los presentes; **to give** ~ **(on sth/against sb)** prestar declaración (sobre algo/contra alguien); **to turn Queen's** ~ *Brit* delatar a los cómplices; **to turn state's** ~ **against sb** *Am* delatar a alguien **4.** (*view*) evidencia *f;* **to be (much) in** ~ ser (muy) manifiesto
evident ['evɪdənt] *adj* evidente; **to be** ~ ser evidente; **to be** ~ **to sb** ser evidente para alguien; **to be** ~ **in sth** manifestarse en algo; **it is** ~ **that ...** está claro que...

evidently *adv* evidentemente

evil [ˈiːvl] I. *adj* malo, -a; **the** ~ **day** *iron* el día crítico; ~ **eye** mal *m* de ojo; ~ **spirit** espíritu maligno; **to have an** ~ **tongue** tener una lengua afilada II. *n* mal *m;* **social** ~ lacra *f* social; **an aura of** ~ un aura de maldad; **good and** ~ el bien y el mal; **the lesser of two** ~**s** el menor de dos males

evil-doer [ˌiːvlˈduːəʳ, *Am:* -ɚ] *n* malhechor(a) *m(f)* **evil-minded** *adj* malintencionado, -a **evil-tempered** *adj* de muy mal genio; **to be** ~ tener muy mal genio

evince [ɪˈvɪns] *vt form* dar señales de; **to** ~ **interest** mostrar interés

evocation [ˌevəˈkeɪʃən] *n form* evocación *f*

evocative [ɪˈvɒkətɪv, *Am:* -ˈvɑːkət̬ɪv] *adj* evocador(a); **an** ~ **image** una imagen sugerente; **to be** ~ **of sth** evocar algo

evoke [ɪˈvəʊk, *Am:* -ˈvoʊk] *vt* evocar

evolution [ˌiːvəˈluːʃən, *Am:* ˌevə-] *n no pl* evolución *f; fig* desarrollo *m*

evolve [ɪˈvɒlv, *Am:* -ˈvɑːlv] I. *vi* (*gradually develop*) desarrollarse; (*animals*) evolucionar; **to** ~ **into sth** convertirse en algo II. *vt* desarrollar; **to** ~ **new forms of life** crear nuevas formas de vida

ewe [juː] *n* oveja *f*

ewer [ˈjuːəʳ, *Am:* -ɚ] *n* aguamanil *m*

ex [eks] <-es> *n inf* ex *mf*

exacerbate [ɪgˈzæsəbeɪt, *Am:* -ɚ-] *vt* exacerbar

exact [ɪgˈzækt] I. *adj* exacto, -a; **to be** ~ **in one's reporting** ser muy preciso al informar; **the** ~ **opposite** justo el contrario II. *vt* exigir; **to** ~ **sth from sb** exigir algo a alguien

exacting *adj* exigente

exactitude [ɪgˈzæktɪtjuːd, *Am:* -tətuːd] *n no pl* exactitud *f*

exactly [ɪgˈzæktli] *adv* exactamente; ~ **like ...** justo como...; **how/what/where** ~ **...** cómo/qué/dónde exactamente...; **I don't** ~ **agree to that** no estoy del todo de acuerdo en eso; **not** ~ no precisamente; ~**!** ¡exacto!

exactness [ɪgˈzæktnɪs] *n no pl* exactitud *f*

exaggerate [ɪgˈzædʒəreɪt] *vi, vt* exagerar; **let's not** ~**!** ¡no exageremos!

exaggerated [ɪgˈzædʒəreɪtɪd, *Am:* -t̬ɪd] *adj* exagerado, -a; **greatly** ~ muy exagerado

exaggeration [ɪgˌzædʒəˈreɪʃən] *n* exageración *f;* **it's no** ~ **to say that ...** no es exagerado decir que...

exalt [ɪgˈzɔːlt] *vt* 1. (*praise*) exaltar; (*honour*) ensalzar; **to** ~ **sth as a virtue** elevar algo a la categoría de virtud 2. (*raise rank*) ascender

exaltation [ˌegzɔːlˈteɪʃən] *n no pl* exaltación *f*

exalted [ɪgˈzɔːltɪd, *Am:* -t̬ɪd] *adj* 1. (*elevated*) elevado, -a; ~ **rank** alto rango 2. (*jubilant*) exaltado, -a

exam [ɪgˈzæm] *n* examen *m*

examination [ɪgˌzæmɪˈneɪʃən] *n* 1. (*exam*) examen *m* 2. (*investigation*) investigación *f;* **medical** ~ reconocimiento *m* médico 3. LAW interrogatorio *m*

examination paper *n* hoja *f* de examen **examination results** *n* resultados *m pl* del examen

examine [ɪgˈzæmɪn] *vt* 1. (*test*) **to** ~ **sb** (**in sth**) examinar a alguien (de algo); **to be** ~**d** examinarse 2. (*study*) estudiar; **to** ~ **credentials** comprobar las credenciales; **to** ~ **the effects of sth** estudiar los efectos de algo 3. LAW interrogar 4. MED hacer un reconocimiento médico de

examinee [ɪgˌzæmɪˈniː] *n* examinando, -a *m, f*

examiner [ɪgˈzæmɪnəʳ, *Am:* -ɚ] *n* examinador(a) *m(f)*

examining board *n* junta *f* examinadora

example [ɪgˈzɑːmpl, *Am:* ɪgˈzæm-] *n* 1. (*sample, model*) ejemplo *m;* **for** ~ por ejemplo; **to be a shining** ~ **of sth** ser un ejemplo magnífico de algo; **to follow sb's** ~ seguir el ejemplo de alguien; **to give** (**sb**) **an** ~ (**of sth**) dar (a alguien) un ejemplo (de algo); **to set a good** ~ dar un buen ejemplo 2. (*copy*) ejemplar *m*

exasperate [ɪgˈzɑːspəreɪt] *vt* exasperar; **he** ~**s me** me saca de quicio

exasperating [ɪgˈzɑːspəreɪtɪŋ, *Am:* -t̬ɪŋ] *adj* irritante

exasperation [ɪgˌzɑːspəˈreɪʃən] *n no pl* exasperación *f*

excavate [ˈekskəveɪt] *vt* 1. (*expose*) desenterrar 2. (*hollow*) excavar

excavation [ˌekskəˈveɪʃən] *n* excavación *f*

excavator [ˈekskəveɪtəʳ, *Am:* -t̬ɚ] *n Aus, Brit* excavadora *f*

exceed [ɪkˈsiːd] *vt* exceder; (*outshine*) sobrepasar

exceedingly *adv* excesivamente

excel [ɪkˈsel] <-ll-> I. *vi* sobresalir; **to** ~ **at sth** destacar en algo II. *vt* **to** ~ **oneself** lucirse

excellence [ˈeksələns] *n no pl* excelencia *f*

Excellency [ˈeksələnsi] *n* Excelencia *f;* **His** ~ Su Excelencia; (**Your**) ~ (Su/Vuestra) Excelencia

excellent [ˈeksələnt] *adj* excelente

except [ɪkˈsept] I. *prep* ~ (**for**) excepto, salvo, zafo *AmL;* **to do nothing** ~ **wait** no hacer nada más que esperar II. *vt form* exceptuar; **to** ~ **sth/sb from sth** excluir algo/a alguien de algo

excepting *prep* excepto, salvo

exception [ɪkˈsepʃən] *n* excepción *f;* **to be an** ~ ser una excepción; **to make an** ~ hacer una excepción; **with the** ~ **of ...** con excepción de...; **to take** ~ (**to sth**) ofenderse (por algo); **I take great** ~ **to your last comment** me ha molestado mucho tu último comentario ►**the** ~ **proves the rule** *prov* la excepción confirma la regla *prov*

exceptional [ɪkˈsepʃənl] *adj* excepcional

exceptionally [ɪkˈsepʃnəli] *adv* excepcionalmente; **to be** ~ **clever** ser especialmente listo

excerpt [ˈeksɜːpt, *Am:* -sɜːrpt] *n* extracto *m*

E

excess [ɪk'ses] <-es> *n* exceso *m;* **to eat to ~** comer en exceso; **to carry sth to ~** llevar algo al exceso; **in ~ of** superior a

excess amount *n* cantidad *f* excedente **excess baggage** *n,* **excess luggage** *n* exceso *m* de equipaje **excess charge** *n* suplemento *m* **excess expenditure** *n* gastos *mpl* adicionales **excess fare** *n* suplemento *m*

excessive [ɪk'sesɪv] *adj* excesivo, -a; (*claim*) exagerado, -a; (*violence*) gratuito, -a

excess production *n* excedente *m* de producción **excess supply** *n* exceso *m* de oferta

exchange [ɪks'tʃeɪndʒ] **I.** *vt* **1.** (*trade for the equivalent*) cambiar **2.** (*interchange*) intercambiar; **to ~ blows** pegarse; **to ~ words** discutir **II.** *n* **1.** (*interchange, trade*) intercambio *m;* **in ~ for sth** a cambio de algo; **~ of (gun)fire** tiroteo *m* **2.** FIN, ECON cambio *m;* **foreign ~** divisas *fpl* **3.** (*verbal interchange*) **~ of threats** intercambio *m* de amenzas

exchangeable *adj* cambiable; (*goods*) canjeable; **~ currency** divisa *f;* **~ token** cupón *m* canjeable; **to be ~ for sth** ser intercambiable por algo

exchange broker *n,* **exchange dealer** *n* corredor(a) *m(f)* de bolsa **exchange conditions** *n* condiciones *fpl* de cambio **exchange control** *n* control *m* de divisas **exchange course mechanism** *n* ECON, FIN mecanismo *m* complementario de cambio **exchange market** *n* mercado *m* de divisas **exchange rate** *n* tipo *m* de cambio **exchange regulations** *npl* ECON, FIN normativa *f* cambiaria **exchange restrictions** *n* ECON, FIN control *m* de divisas **exchange stability** *n* ECON, FIN estabilidad *f* cambiaria **exchange student** *n* estudiante *mf* de intercambio **exchange teacher** *n* profesor(a) *m(f)* de intercambio **exchange value** *n* contravalor *m*

exchequer [ɪks'tʃekəʳ, *Am:* -ɚ] *n no pl* erario *m;* **the Exchequer** Hacienda

excise¹ ['eksaɪz] *n no pl* FIN impuestos *mpl* interiores; **~ on alcohol** impuestos especiales sobre el alcohol

excise² [ek'saɪz] *vt form* **1.** quitar; (*tumour*) extraer **2.** *fig* eliminar, suprimir

excitable [ɪk'saɪtəbl, *Am:* -t̬əbl] *adj* excitable

excite [ɪk'saɪt] *vt* **1.** (*move*) emocionar; **to ~ an audience** entusiasmar al público; **to be ~d about an idea** estar entusiasmado ante una idea **2.** (*stimulate*) estimular; **to ~ sb's curiosity** despertar la curiosidad de alguien

excited [ɪk'saɪtɪd, *Am:* -t̬ɪd] *adj* emocionado, -a

excitement [ɪk'saɪtmənt] *n* emoción *f;* **to be in a state of ~** estar emocionado; **what ~!** ¡qué emoción!

exciting [ɪk'saɪtɪŋ, *Am:* -t̬ɪŋ] *adj* emocionante

excl. **1.** *abbr of* **exluding** excepto, salvo **2.** *abbr of* **exclusive** exclusive

exclaim [ɪk'skleɪm] *vi, vt* exclamar; **to ~ in delight** exclamar de placer

exclamation [ˌekskləˈmeɪʃən] *n* exclamación *f*

exclamation mark *n* signo *m* de exclamación

exclude [ɪk'sklu:d] *vt* **1.** (*shut out*) expulsar; **to be ~d from school** ser expulsado de la escuela **2.** (*leave out*) excluir; (*possibility*) descartar

excluding [ɪk'sklu:dɪŋ] *prep* excepto, salvo

exclusion [ɪk'sklu:ʒən] *n* exclusión *f;* **to the ~ of** con exclusión de

exclusive [ɪks'klu:sɪv] **I.** *adj* exclusivo, -a; **~ interview** entrevista *f* en exclusiva; **in ~ circles** en círculos selectos; **to be ~ to sb** ser exclusivo de alguien; **~ of** sin; **to be ~ of** not incluir **II.** *n* exclusiva *f* **III.** *adv* **from 5 to 10 ~** del 5 al 10 exclusive

exclusively *adv* exclusivamente

excommunicate [ˌekskəˈmju:nɪkeɪt] *vt* excomulgar

excommunication [ˌekskəˌmju:nɪˈkeɪʃən] *n* excomunión *f*

excrement ['ekskrəmənt] *n no pl* excremento *m*

excrescence [ɪk'skresns] *n* **1.** MED excrecencia *f* **2.** *fig* (*ugly object*) adefesio *m*

excreta [ɪk'skri:tə, *Am:* -t̬ə] *n no pl, form* excrementos *mpl*

excrete [ɪk'skri:t] *vi, vt form* excretar

excretion [ɪk'skri:ʃən] *n form* excreción *f*

excruciating [ɪk'skru:ʃɪeɪtɪŋ, *Am:* -t̬ɪŋ] *adj* agudísimo, -a; (*pain*) atroz, insoportable

excursion [ɪk'skɜ:ʃən, *Am:* -'skɜ:rʒən] *n* excursión *f;* **to go on an ~** ir de excursión

excursion ticket *n* billete *m* de excursión **excursion train** *n* tren *m* de recreo

excusable [ɪk'skju:zəbl] *adj* perdonable

excuse [ɪk'skju:z] **I.** *vt* **1.** (*justify: behaviour*) justificar; (*lateness*) disculpar; **to ~ sb for sth** excusar a alguien por algo **2.** (*forgive*) perdonar; **~ me!** ¡perdone! **3.** (*allow not to attend*) **to ~ sb from sth** dispensar a alguien de algo **4.** (*leave*) **after an hour she ~d herself** después de una hora se disculpó y se fue **II.** *n* **1.** (*explanation*) excusa *f,* agarradera *f* *AmL* **2.** (*pretext*) pretexto *m;* **poor ~** mal pretexto; **to make ~s for sb** justificar a alguien

ex-directory [ˌeksdɪ'rektəri] *adj Aus, Brit* **to be ~** no figurar en la guía

execrable ['eksɪkrəbl] *adj* execrable; (*meal*) abominable

execrate ['eksɪkreɪt] *vt form* execrar

execute ['eksɪkju:t] *vt* **1.** (*carry out*) realizar; (*manoeuvre*) efectuar; (*plan*) llevar a cabo; (*order*) cumplir; **to ~ sb's will** otorgar el testamento de alguien **2.** (*put to death*) ejecutar

execution [ˌeksɪ'kju:ʃən] *n* **1.** *no pl* (*carrying out*) realización *f;* **to put a plan into ~** llevar a cabo un plan **2.** (*putting to death*) ejecución *f*

executioner [ˌeksɪˈkjuːʃnər, *Am:* -ɚ] *n* verdugo *m*
executive [ɪɡˈzekjʊtɪv, *Am:* -t̬ɪv] **I.** *n* **1.** (*senior manager*) ejecutivo, -a *m, f* **2.** + *sing/pl vb* POL poder *m* ejecutivo; ECON órgano *m* ejecutivo **II.** *adj* ejecutivo, -a; ~ **branch** poder ejecutivo
executor [ɪɡˈzekjʊtər, *Am:* -t̬ɚ] *n* albacea *mf*
exemplary [ɪɡˈzempləri] *adj* ejemplar
exemplification [ɪɡˌzemplɪfɪˈkeɪʃən, *Am:* -plə-] *n* ejemplificación *f;* (*of an idea*) ilustración *f*
exemplify [ɪɡˈzemplɪfaɪ] <-ie-> *vt* ejemplificar; (*strategy*) mostrar
exempt [ɪɡˈzempt] **I.** *vt* eximir **II.** *adj* exento, -a; **to be ~ from sth** estar exento de algo
exemption [ɪɡˈzempʃən] *n no pl* exención *f*
exercise [ˈeksəsaɪz, *Am:* -sɚ-] **I.** *vt* **1.** (*muscles*) ejercitar; (*dog*) llevar de paseo; (*horse*) entrenar; **to ~ one's muscles/memory** ejercitar los músculos/la memoria **2.** (*apply: authority, control*) ejercer; **to ~ caution** proceder con cautela; **to ~ common sense** hacer uso del sentido común; **to ~ discretion** actuar con discreción; **to ~ self-discipline** imponerse autodisciplina **II.** *vi* hacer ejercicio **III.** *n* **1.** (*physical training*) ejercicio *m;* **physical ~** gimnasia *f;* **to do ~s** hacer ejercicios **2.** SCHOOL, UNIV ejercicio *m;* **written ~s** ejercicios *mpl* escritos **3.** MIL maniobras *fpl* **4.** *no pl* (*action, achievement*) acción *f* **5.** *no pl* (*use*) uso *m* **6.** *pl, Am* ceremonia *f*
exercise bike *n* bicicleta *f* de ejercicio **exercise book** *n* cuaderno *m*
exerciser [ˈeksəsaɪzər, *Am:* -sɚsaɪzɚ] *n* máquina *f* de ejercicios
exercise studio *n* gimnasio *m*
exert [ɪɡˈzɜːt, *Am:* -ˈzɜːrt] *vt* ejercer; (*apply*) emplear; **to ~ oneself** esforzarse
exertion [ɪɡˈzɜːʃən, *Am:* -ˈzɜːr-] *n* **1.** *no pl* (*application*) aplicación *f* **2.** (*physical effort*) esfuerzo *m*
exfoliant [ɪksˈfəʊlɪənt] *n* exfoliante *m*
exfoliating cream [eksˌfəʊlɪˈeɪtɪŋˌkriːm, *Am:* -ˌfoʊlɪˈeɪt̬ɪŋ-] *n* crema *f* exfoliante
exfoliation [eksˌfəʊlɪˈeɪʃən, *Am:* -ˌfoʊ-] *n no pl* exfoliación *f*
exhalation [ˌekshəˈleɪʃən] *n* exhalación *f*
exhale [eksˈheɪl] **I.** *vt* espirar; (*gases, scents*) despedir **II.** *vi* espirar
exhaust [ɪɡˈzɔːst, *Am:* -ˈzɑː-] **I.** *vt a. fig* agotar; **to ~ oneself** agotarse **II.** *n* **1.** *no pl* AUTO (*gas*) gases *mpl* de escape **2.** *Aus, Brit* (*pipe*) tubo *m* de escape
exhausted *adj* agotado, -a
exhaust fumes *npl* gases *mpl* de escape
exhausting *adj* agotador(a)
exhaustion [ɪɡˈzɔːstʃən, *Am:* -ˈzɑː-] *n no pl* agotamiento *m;* **to suffer from ~** estar agotado
exhaustive [ɪɡˈzɔːstɪv, *Am:* -ˈzɑː-] *adj* exhaustivo, -a
exhaust pipe *n* tubo *m* de escape **exhaust system** *n* sistema *m* de escape
exhibit [ɪɡˈzɪbɪt] **I.** *n* **1.** (*display*) objeto *m* expuesto **2.** LAW documento *m* **II.** *vt* **1.** (*show*) enseñar; (*work*) presentar **2.** (*display character traits*) mostrar; (*rudeness*) manifestar
exhibition [ˌeksɪˈbɪʃən] *n* (*display*) exposición *f;* (*performance*) exhibición *f* ►**to make an ~ of oneself** ponerse en ridículo
exhibitionism [ˌeksɪˈbɪʃnɪzəm] *n no pl* exhibicionismo *m*
exhibitionist [ˌeksɪˈbɪʃnɪst] *n* exhibicionista *mf*
exhibitor [ɪɡˈzɪbɪtər, *Am:* -t̬ɚ] *n* expositor(a) *m(f)*
exhilarating [ɪɡˈzɪləreɪtɪŋ, *Am:* -t̬ɪŋ] *adj* estimulante; **an ~ walk** un paseo vivificante
exhilaration [ɪɡˈzɪləreɪʃən] *n no pl* regocijo *m;* **the ~ of liberty/speed** la sensación estimulante de la libertad/velocidad; **the ~ of doing sth** la alegría de hacer algo
exhort [ɪɡˈzɔːt, *Am:* -ˈzɔːrt] *vt form* **to ~ sb to do sth** exhortar a alguien a hacer algo; **she ~ed him to keep working** le exhortó a que siguiera trabajando
exhortation [ˌeksɔːˈteɪʃən, *Am:* ˌeɡzɔːr-] *n no pl* exhortación *f*
exhumation [ˌekshjuːˈmeɪʃən] *n no pl* exhumación *f*
exhume [eksˈhjuːm, *Am:* eɡzˈuːm] *vt* exhumar
ex-husband *n* ex marido *m*
exigence [ˈeksɪdʒəns] *n,* **exigency** [ˈekzɪdʒənsi] <-ies> *n* **1.** *no pl* (*extreme urgency*) emergencia *f* **2.** *pl* (*urgent demands*) exigencias *fpl*
exigent [ˈeksɪdʒənt] *adj form* **1.** (*urgent*) apremiante; **an ~ issue** una cuestión urgente; **an ~ environmental problem** un problema medioambiental inaplazable **2.** (*demanding*) exigente
exiguous [eɡˈzɪɡjʊəs] *adj form* exiguo, -a
exile [ˈeksaɪl] **I.** *n* **1.** *no pl* (*banishment*) exilio *m;* **political ~** exilio político; **to be in ~** estar en el exilio; **to go into ~** exiliarse **2.** (*person*) exiliado, -a *m, f* **II.** *vt* exili(a)r; **to ~ sb to Siberia** exiliar a alguien a Siberia
exist [ɪɡˈzɪst] *vi* **1.** (*be*) existir **2.** (*live*) vivir; **to ~ on sth** vivir de algo; **to ~ without sth** sobrevivir sin algo
existence [ɪɡˈzɪstəns] *n* **1.** *no pl* (*being*) existencia *f;* **to be in ~** existir; **to come into ~** nacer **2.** (*life*) vida *f*
existent [ˌeɡˈzɪstent] *adj* existente; **the only ~ copy** la única copia que existe
existential [ˌeɡzɪˈstenʃl] *adj* existencial
existentialism [ˌeɡzɪˈstenʃəlɪzəm] *n no pl* existencialismo *m*
existing [ɪɡˈzɪstɪŋ] *adj* existente; **the ~ laws** la actual legislación
exit [ˈeksɪt] **I.** *n* salida *f;* (*of road*) desvío *m;* **to make an ~** salir **II.** *vt* salir de **III.** *vi* **1.** *a.* INFOR (*leave*) salir **2.** THEAT hacer mutis

exit visa *n* visado *m* de salida
exodus ['eksədəs] *n* éxodo *m*
ex officio [ˌeks ə'fɪʃɪəʊ, *Am:* -oʊ] **I.** *adv* ADMIN oficialmente; **to act ~** actuar de oficio **II.** *adj* ADMIN de oficio
exonerate [ɪg'zɒnəreɪt, *Am:* -'zɑːnə-] *vt form* exonerar
exoneration [ɪgˌzɒnə'reɪʃən, *Am:* -ˌzɑːnə-] *n no pl, form* exoneración *f*
exorbitance [ɪg'zɔːbɪtəns, *Am:* -'zɔːrbət̬əns] *n no pl* exorbitancia *f*
exorbitant [ɪg'zɔːbɪtənt, *Am:* -'zɔːrbət̬ənt] *adj* exorbitante; (*demand*) excesivo, -a; (*price*) desorbitado, -a
exorcism ['eksɔːsɪzəm, *Am:* -sɔːr-] *n no pl* exorcismo *m*
exorcist ['eksɔːsɪst, *Am:* -sɔːr-] *n* exorcista *mf*
exorcize ['eksɔːsaɪz, *Am:* -sɔːr-] *vt* exorcizar
exotic [ɪg'zɒtɪk, *Am:* -'zɑːt̬ɪk] *adj* exótico, -a
expand [ɪk'spænd] **I.** *vi* **1.** (*increase*) expandirse; (*trade*) desarrollarse **2.** (*spread*) extenderse **3.** PHYS dilatarse **II.** *vt* **1.** (*make larger*) ampliar; (*wings*) extender; (*trade*) desarrollar **2.** PHYS dilatar **3.** (*elaborate*) desarrollar
expandable [ɪk'spændəbl] *adj* expansible
expanse [ɪk'spæns] *n* **1.** (*large area*) extensión *f* **2.** (*expansion*) expansión *f*
expansion [ɪk'spænʃən] *n* **1.** *no pl* (*spreading out*) expansión *f;* (*of a metal*) dilatación *f* **2.** (*elaboration*) desarrollo *m*
expansionism [ɪk'spænʃənɪzəm] *n no pl* expansionismo *m;* **policy of ~** política *f* expansionista
expansive [ɪk'spænsɪv] *adj* **1.** (*sociable*) expansivo, -a **2.** (*broad, vast*) amplio, -a **3.** (*elaborated*) extenso, -a
expatriate [eks'pætrɪeɪt, *Am:* -'peɪ-] **I.** *n* expatriado, -a *m, f* **II.** *vt* expatriar
expect [ɪk'spekt] *vt* esperar; (*imagine*) imaginarse; **to ~ to do sth** esperar hacer algo; **to ~ sb to do sth** esperar que alguien haga algo; **you are ~ed to return books on time** debes devolver los libros puntualmente; **to ~ sth of sb** esperar algo de alguien; **to be ~ing (a baby)** esperar un bebé; **I ~ed as much** ya me lo esperaba; **I ~ed better of you than that** esperaba algo más de ti que eso; **I ~ you are hungry** supongo que estaréis hambrientos; **I ~ so** me lo imagino; **to ~ that** esperar que *+subj*
expectancy [ɪk'spektəntsi] *n no pl* esperanza *f;* **life ~** esperanza *f* de vida
expectant [ɪk'spektənt] *adj* expectante; (*look*) de esperanza; **~ mother** futura madre
expectation [ˌekspek'teɪʃən] *n* **1.** (*hope*) esperanza *f* **2.** (*anticipation*) expectativa *f;* **in ~ of sth** en espera de algo
expectorate [ɪk'spektəreɪt] *vi form* expectorar
expedience *n,* **expediency** [ɪk'spiːdiəntsi] *n no pl* **1.** (*advisability*) conveniencia *f;* **as a matter of ~ we will not be taking on any new staff this year** no nos conviene contratar a más personal este año **2.** (*self-interest*) oportunismo *m;* **to operate on the basis of ~** actuar por conveniencia
expedient [ɪk'spiːdɪənt] **I.** *adj* **1.** (*advantageous*) conveniente; **it is ~ to do sth** es oportuno hacer algo *form* **2.** (*necessary*) necesario, -a; (*measure*) oportuno, -a; **to be ~ that** ser conveniente que *+subj* **II.** *n* recurso *m;* **they took the ~ of asking advice** tomaron la precaución de informarse
expedite ['ekspɪdaɪt] *vt form* acelerar
expedition [ˌekspɪ'dɪʃən] *n* expedición *f;* **to be on an ~** estar de expedición; **to go on an ~** ir de expedición; **to go on a shopping ~** *iron* ir de compras
expeditious [ˌekspɪ'dɪʃəs] *adj form* expeditivo, -a
expel [ɪk'spel] <-ll-> *vt* expeler, arrojar; (*person*) expulsar
expend [ɪk'spend] *vt form* dedicar; (*money*) gastar; **to ~ time on sth** dedicar tiempo a algo
expenditure [ɪk'spendɪtʃə^r, *Am:* -tʃɚ] *n no pl* (*money*) gasto *m;* **public ~** gasto público; **the ~ on cleaning** la cantidad dedicada a la limpieza
expense [ɪk'spens] *n* gasto(s) *m(pl);* **all ~(s) paid** con todos los gastos pagados; **at great ~** gastando mucho dinero; **at sb's ~** *a. fig* a costa de alguien; **at the ~ of sth** *a. fig* a costa de algo; **to go to ~** meterse en gastos; **to go to the ~ of** meterse en gastos para; **to spare no ~** no reparar en gastos
expense account *n* cuenta *f* de gastos de representación
expensive [ɪk'spensɪv] *adj* caro, -a; **this was an ~ mistake for the ministry** este error le ha salido caro al ministerio
experience [ɪk'spɪərɪəns, *Am:* -'spɪrɪ-] **I.** *n* experiencia *f;* **to have ~ of translating** tener experiencia en traducir; **from ~** por experiencia; **to know sth from ~** saber algo por experiencia; **to learn by ~** aprender a través de la experiencia **II.** *vt* experimentar; **to ~ happiness/pain** sentir alegría/dolor; **to ~ difficulty in passing an exam** tener dificultades para aprobar un examen; **to ~ a loss** sufrir una pérdida
experienced [ɪk'spɪərɪənst, *Am:* -'spɪrɪ-] *adj* experimentado, -a; **to be ~ at organising** tener experiencia en organización
experiment [ɪk'sperɪmənt] **I.** *n* experimento *m;* **as an ~** como experimento; **by ~** experimentando **II.** *vi* experimentar; **to ~ on a patient** hacer experimentos con un paciente; **to ~ with mice** hacer experimentos con ratones
experimental [ɪkˌsperɪ'mentl, *Am:* ekˌsper-] *adj* experimental; **~ psychology** psicología *f* experimental; **to be still at the ~ stage** estar todavía en fase experimental
experimentation [ɪkˌsperɪmen'teɪʃən] *n no pl* experimentación *f*
expert ['ekspɜːt, *Am:* -spɜːrt] **I.** *n* experto, -a

m, f; **gardening** ~ experto en jardinería; **to be an ~ at training athletes** ser un experto en el entrenamiento de atletas; **to be an ~ in** [*o* **on**] **computing** ser un experto en informática **II.** *adj* **1.** (*skilful*) experto, -a; **she's an ~ swimmer** es una experta nadadora **2.** LAW pericial; ~ **report** informe *m* pericial

expert advice *n* **to seek ~** asesorarse con un experto

expertise [ˌekspɜːˈtiːz, *Am:* -spɜːr-] *n no pl* pericia *f;* (*knowledge*) conocimientos *mpl*

expert knowledge *n* conocimientos *mpl* de experto **expert opinion** *n* dictamen *m* pericial **expert system** *n* INFOR sistema *m* experto **expert witness** *n* perito, -a *m, f*

expiate [ˈekspɪeɪt] *vt form* expiar

expiation [ˌekspɪˈeɪʃən] *n form* expiación *f*

expiration [ˌekspɪˈreɪʃən, *Am:* -spə-] *n no pl* terminación *f;* COM vencimiento *f,* caducidad *f*

expire [ɪkˈspaɪəʳ, *Am:* -ˈspaɪɚ] **I.** *vi* **1.** (*terminate*) finalizar; (*contract, licence*) expirar; (*passport, food*) caducar **2.** (*die*) expirar **II.** *vt* espirar

expiry [ɪkˈspaɪəri, *Am:* -ˈspaɪ-] *n no pl s.* **expiration**

expiry date *n* vencimiento *m* de un plazo

explain [ɪkˈspleɪn] **I.** *vt* explicar; **to ~ a text to a pupil** explicar un texto a un alumno; **to ~ how/what/where/why ...** explicar cómo/qué/dónde/por qué...; **to ~ oneself** explicarse; **that ~s everything!** ¡eso lo aclara todo!; **to ~ away sth** justificar algo **II.** *vi* explicar

◆**explain away** *vt* justificar

explanation [ˌekspləˈneɪʃən] *n* explicación *f;* **to give an ~ for an incident** dar una explicación de [*o* sobre] un incidente; **to offer no ~ for the delay** no dar explicaciones sobre el retraso; **by way of ~** como explicación

explanatory [ɪkˈsplænətri, *Am:* -ətɔːri] *adj* explicativo, -a

expletive [ɪkˈspliːtɪv, *Am:* ˈəkspləṯɪv] *n* palabrota *f;* **to let out a string of ~s** soltar una sarta de tacos

explicable [ekˈsplɪkəbl] *adj* explicable

explicate [ˈeksplɪkeɪt] *vt form* explicar

explicit [ɪkˈsplɪsɪt] *adj* explícito, -a; ~ **directions** instrucciones explícitas; ~ **film** película *f* no apta para menores; **he was very ~ about the plans** era muy categórico en cuanto a los planes

explode [ɪkˈspləʊd, *Am:* -ˈsploʊd] **I.** *vi* **1.** (*blow up*) explotar; (*bomb*) estallar; (*tyre*) reventar; **to ~ with anger** montar en cólera **2.** (*grow rapidly*) dispararse **II.** *vt* **1.** (*blow up: bomb*) hacer explotar; (*ball*) reventar **2.** (*discredit: rumours*) desmentir; (*theory*) refutar; (*myth*) destruir

exploit [ˈeksplɔɪt] **I.** *vt* explotar, pilotear *Chile* **II.** *n* hazaña *f*

exploitation [ˌeksplɔɪˈteɪʃən] *n no pl* explotación *f*

exploration [ˌeksplәˈreɪʃən, *Am:* -splɔːˈ-] *n* **1.** *a.* MED exploración *f;* **voyage of ~** viaje *m* de exploración; **to make an ~ of sth** explorar algo **2.** (*examination*) estudio *m*

exploratory [ɪkˈsplɒrətəri, *Am:* -ˈsplɔːrətɔːri] *adj* (*voyage*) de exploración; (*test*) de sondeo; (*meeting*) preliminar

explore [ɪkˈsplɔːʳ, *Am:* -ˈsplɔːr] **I.** *vt* **1.** *a.* MED, INFOR explorar **2.** (*examine*) analizar; **to ~ sb's past** investigar sobre el pasado de alguien **II.** *vi* explorar

explorer [ɪkˈsplɔːrəʳ, *Am:* -ɚ] *n* explorador(a) *m(f)*

explosion [ɪkˈspləʊʒən, *Am:* -ˈsploʊ-] *n* explosión *f;* **gas ~** explosión de gas; **an ~ of applause** una gran ovación; **population ~** explosión demográfica; **there has been an ~ in demand for computers in the last few years** la demanda de ordenadores se ha disparado en los últimos años

explosive [ɪkˈspləʊsɪv, *Am:* -ˈsploʊ-] **I.** *adj* explosivo, -a; ~ **device** artefacto explosivo; **an ~ situation** una situación delicada; **an ~ issue** un asunto espinoso; **to have an ~ temper** tener un genio muy vivo **II.** *n* explosivo *m*

exponent [ɪkˈspəʊnənt, *Am:* -ˈspoʊ-] *n* **1.** (*person*) exponente *mf;* **a leading ~ of neoclassicism** un máximo exponente del neoclasicismo **2.** MAT exponente *m*

export [ɪkˈspɔːt, *Am:* -ˈspɔːrt] **I.** *vt* exportar **II.** *n* **1.** (*product*) artículo *m* de exportación **2.** *no pl* (*selling*) exportación *f;* ~ **duties** aranceles *mpl* de exportación

exportable [ɪkˈspɔːtəbl, *Am:* -ˈspɔːrṯə-] *adj* exportable

exportation [ˌekspɔːˈteɪʃən, *Am:* -spɔːr-] *n no pl* exportación *f*

export business *n* **1.** (*business which sells abroad*) negocio *m* de exportación **2.** *no pl* (*special branch*) exportación *f;* **to be in the ~** dedicarse a la exportación

exporter [ikˈspɔːtəʳ, *Am:* -ˈspɔːrṯɚ] *n* exportador(a) *m(f)*

export goods *npl* productos *mpl* de exportación **export licence** *n* licencia *f* de exportación **export marketing** *n no pl* marketing *m* de exportación **export regulations** *npl* normativa *f* de exportación **export surplus** *n no pl* excedente *m* de exportación **export trade** *n no pl* comercio *m* de exportación

expose [ɪkˈspəʊz, *Am:* -ˈspoʊz] *vt* **1.** (*uncover*) enseñar **2.** (*leave vulnerable to*) exponer; **to ~ sb to ridicule** poner a alguien en ridículo **3.** (*reveal: person*) descubrir; (*plot*) desvelar; (*secret*) sacar a la luz; **to ~ a business as a fraud** revelar un negocio como un fraude

exposed [ɪkˈspəʊzd, *Am:* -ˈspoʊzd] *adj* **1.** (*vulnerable*) expuesto, -a **2.** (*uncovered*) descubierto, -a **3.** (*unprotected*) desprotegido, -a

exposition [ˌekspəˈzɪʃən, *Am:* -pə-] *n* exposición *f*

expostulate [ɪkˈspɒstjʊleɪt, *Am:*

E

-'spɑːstʃə-] *vi form* protestar; **to ~ with the waiter about the bill** reconvenir al camarero sobre la factura

exposure [ɪk'spəʊʒəʳ, *Am:* -'spoʊʒɚ] *n* **1.** (*contact*) exposición *f*; **~ to the sun** exposición al sol; **~ to new ideas** contacto *m* con nuevas ideas **2.** *no pl* MED hipotermia *f*; **to die of ~** morir de frío **3.** *a.* PHOT revelación *f* **4.** (*revelation*) descubrimiento *m* **5.** *no pl* (*media coverage*) publicidad *f*

exposure meter *n* PHOT exposímetro *m*

expound [ɪk'spaʊnd] **I.** *vi form* hablar; **to ~ (at length) on** [*o* **about**] **sth** hablar (largo y tendido) sobre algo **II.** *vt form* exponer

express [ɪk'spres] **I.** *vt* **1.** (*convey: thoughts, feelings*) expresar; **to ~ oneself** expresarse; **to ~ oneself through music** expresarse a través de la música; **I would like to ~ my thanks for ...** querría expresar mi agradecimiento por... **2.** *inf* (*send quickly*) enviar por correo urgente; **to ~ sth to sb** enviar algo a alguien por correo urgente **3.** *form* (*squeeze out*) exprimir **II.** *adj* **1.** (*rapid*) rápido, -a; **by ~ delivery** por correo urgente; **~ train** tren expreso **2.** (*precise*) explícito, -a; **by ~ order** por orden expresa; **~ wish** deseo expreso **III.** *n* **1.** (*train*) expreso *m* **2.** *no pl* (*service*) **by ~** por correo urgente **IV.** *adv* **to send sth ~** enviar algo por correo urgente

expression [ɪk'spreʃən] *n* expresión *f*; (*of love, solidarity*) demostración *f*; **as an ~ of thanks** en señal de agradecimiento; **to give ~ to sth** expresar algo; **to find ~ in music** expresarse a través de la música

expressionism [ɪk'spreʃənɪzəm] *n* expresionismo *m*

expressionist [ɪk'spreʃənɪst] *n* expresionista *mf*

expressionless [ɪk'spreʃənlɪs] *adj* inexpresivo, -a

expressive [ɪk'spresɪv] *adj* expresivo, -a; **to be ~ of sadness** *form* denotar tristeza

expressly [ɪk'spresli] *adv* **1.** (*clearly*) claramente **2.** (*especially*) expresamente

expressway [ɪk'spresweɪ] *n Am, Aus* autopista *f*

ex-prisoner *n* ex prisionero, -a *m*

expropriate [eks'prəʊprɪeɪt, *Am:* -'proʊ-] *vt* expropiar

expropriation [eks'prəʊ prɪeɪʃən, *Am:* -'proʊ-] *n* expropiación *f*

expulsion [ɪk'spʌlʃən] *n* expulsión *f*

exquisite ['ekskwɪzɪt] *adj* **1.** (*delicate*) exquisito, -a; **an ~ piece of china** una delicada pieza de porcelana **2.** (*intense*) intenso, -a

ex-serviceman [ˌeks'sɜːvɪsmən, *Am:* -'sɜːr-] <-men> *n* excombatiente *m*

ext. TEL *abbr of* **extension** Ext.

extant [ek'stænt, *Am:* 'ekstənt] *adj form* (todavía) existente; **to be still ~** existir todavía

extemporaneous [ekˌstempə'reɪnɪəs] *adj form* improvisado, -a

extempore [ek'stempəri] *form* **I.** *adj* improvisado, -a **II.** *adv* improvisadamente; **to perform ~** improvisar; **to speak ~** improvisar un discurso

extemporise *vi Aus, Brit,* **extemporize** [ɪk'stempəraɪz] *vi form* improvisar

extend [ɪk'stend] **I.** *vi* extenderse; **to ~ beyond the river** extenderse más allá del río; **to ~ to una discussion** llegar a una discusión **II.** *vt* **1.** (*enlarge: house*) ampliar; (*street*) alargar **2.** (*prolong: deadline*) prorrogar; (*holiday*) prolongar **3.** (*offer*) ofrecer; **to ~ an invitation to sb** cursar una invitación a alguien; **to ~ one's hand as a greeting** tender la mano para saludar; **to ~ one's thanks to sb** dar las gracias a alguien; **to ~ a warm welcome to sb** dar una calurosa bienvenida a alguien **4.** FIN (*credit*) conceder

extended *adj* extenso, -a; **~ family** clan *m* familiar; **an ~ holiday** unas vacaciones prolongadas

extension [ɪk'stenʃən] *n* **1.** (*increase*) extensión *f*; (*of rights*) ampliación *f*; **by ~** por extensión **2.** (*of a deadline*) prórroga *f* **3.** (*appendage*) apéndice *m* **4.** TEL extensión *f*, supletorio *m AmL*, anexo *m Chile*

extension cable *n* ELEC extensión *f* **extension cord** *n Am s.* **extension lead extension ladder** *n* escalera *f* extensible **extension lead** *n* alargador *m*, alargue *m RíoPl*

extensive [ɪk'stensɪv] *adj* **1.** *a. fig* extenso, -a; (*knowledge*) exhaustivo, -a; (*experience*) amplio, -a **2.** (*large: repair*) importante; **~ damage** daños *mpl* de consideración **3.** AGR (*farming*) extensivo, -a

extensively *adv* intensamente

extent [ɪk'stent] *n no pl* **1.** (*size*) extensión *f*; **to its fullest ~** en toda su extensión **2.** (*degree*) alcance *m*; **to go to the ~ of striking sb** llegar al extremo de golpear a alguien; **to a great ~** en gran parte; **to the same ~ as ...** en la misma medida que...; **to some ~** hasta cierto punto; **to such an ~ that ...** hasta tal punto que...; **to that ~** hasta ese punto; **to what ~ ...?** ¿hasta qué punto...?

extenuate [ɪk'stenjʊeɪt] *vt form* atenuar

extenuating *adj form* atenuante

extenuation [ɪkˌstenjʊ'eɪʃən] *n no pl, form* atenuación *f*; **in ~ of sth** como atenuante de algo

exterior [ɪk'stɪərɪəʳ, *Am:* -'stɪrɪɚ] **I.** *adj* exterior; **~ angle** MAT ángulo externo **II.** *n* **1.** (*outside surface*) exterior *m* **2.** (*outward appearance*) aspecto *m* **3.** CINE exteriores *mpl*

exterminate [ɪk'stɜːmɪneɪt, *Am:* -'stɜːr-] *vt* exterminar

extermination [ɪkˌstɜːmɪ'neɪʃən, *Am:* -ˌstɜːr-] *n no pl* exterminio *m*, exterminación *f*; **~ of a plague** exterminación *f* de una plaga

external [ɪk'stɜːnl, *Am:* -'stɜːr-] **I.** *adj* **1.** (*exterior*) externo, -a; (*influence*) del exterior; (*wall*) exterior; **~ world** mundo *m* exterior; **to be ~ to the problem** ser ajeno al problema **2.** (*foreign*) exterior **3.** MED tópico, -a

II. *npl* las apariencias
externalize [ɪk'stɜːnəlaɪz, *Am:* -'stɜːr-] *vt* exteriorizar
external world *n no pl* mundo *m* exterior
exterritorial [ˌeksˌterɪ'tɔːrɪəl] *adj* extraterritorial
extinct [ɪk'stɪŋkt] *adj* (*practice*) extinto, -a; (*volcano*) apagado, -a; **to become ~** extinguirse
extinction [ɪk'stɪŋkʃən] *n no pl* extinción *f*
extinguish [ɪk'stɪŋgwɪʃ] *vt* (*candle, cigar*) apagar; (*love, passion*) extinguir; (*life, memory*) apagar; (*debt*) amortizar
extinguisher [ɪk'stɪŋgwɪʃəʳ, *Am:* -ɚ] *n* extintor *m*
extirpate ['ekstəpeɪt, *Am:* -stɚ-] *vt form* extirpar; **to ~ an evil** erradicar un mal
extol <-ll-> *vt*, **extoll** [ɪk'stəʊl, *Am:* -'stoʊl] *vt Am* alabar; **to ~ the virtues of yoga** ensalzar las virtudes del yoga
extort [ɪk'stɔːt, *Am:* -'stɔːrt] *vt* extorsionar; (*confession*) arrancar
extortion [ɪk'stɔːʃən, *Am:* -'stɔːr-] *n no pl* extorsión *f*; **that's sheer ~!** ¡esto es un robo!
extortionate [ɪk'stɔːʃənət, *Am:* -'stɔːr-] *adj* excesivo, -a; **~ demands** peticiones desmesuradas; **~ prices** precios *mpl* exorbitantes
extra ['ekstrə] I. *adj* adicional; **to work an ~ two hours** trabajar dos horas más; **~ clothes** ropa *f* de repuesto; **it costs an ~ £2** cuesta dos libras más; **meals are ~** el precio no incluye las comidas II. *adv* (*more*) más; (*extraordinarily*) extraordinariamente; **they pay her ~ to work nights** le pagan más por trabajar por la noche; **I'll try ~ hard this time** esta vez voy a poner más empeño; **£10 ~** diez libras más; **to charge ~ for sth** cobrar algo aparte III. *n* 1. ECON suplemento *m;* AUTO extra *m* 2. CINE extra *mf*
extra charge *n* recargo *m*
extract [ɪk'strækt] I. *vt* 1. (*remove*) extraer 2. (*obtain: information*) sacar 3. MAT (*square root*) sacar II. *n* 1. (*concentrate*) extracto *m* 2. (*excerpt*) fragmento *m*
extraction [ɪk'strækʃən] *n* 1. (*removal*) extracción *f* 2. (*descent*) origen *m;* **he's of American ~** es de origen americano
extracurricular [ˌekstrəkə'rɪkjʊləʳ, *Am:* -jələ̆] *adj* extraescolar
extradite ['ekstrədaɪt] *vt* extraditar
extradition [ekstrə'dɪʃən] *n no pl* extradición *f*
extramarital [ˌekstrə'mærɪtl, *Am:* -'merət̬l] *adj* extramatrimonial
extramural [ˌekstrə'mjʊərəl, *Am:* -'mjʊrəl] *adj Brit* (*course*) para estudiantes externos
extraneous [ɪk'streɪnɪəs] *adj* extraño, -a; **to be ~ to sth** no tener relación con algo
extranet ['ekstrənet] *n* INFOR extranet *f*
extraordinary [ɪk'strɔːdənəri, *Am:* -'strɔːrdəner-] *adj* 1. *a.* POL extraordinario, -a 2. (*astonishing*) asombroso, -a
extra pay ['ekstrəˌpeɪ] *n no pl* paga *f* extra
extrapolate [ek'stræpəleɪt] I. *vt form* extrapolar II. *vi form* **to ~ from sth** hacer una extrapolación de algo
extrasensory [ˌekstrə'sensəri] *adj* extrasensorial; **~ perception** percepción *f* extrasensorial
extraterrestrial ['ekstrətɪ'restrɪəl, *Am:* -tə'-] *adj* extraterrestre
extraterritorial [ˌekstrəˌterɪ'tɔːrɪəl] *adj* extraterritorial
extra time ['ekstrətaɪm] *n no pl, Aus, Brit* SPORTS prórroga *f;* **to play ~** jugar la prórroga
extravagance [ɪk'strævəgəns] *n no pl* 1. (*wastefulness*) derroche *m* 2. (*luxury*) lujo *m* 3. (*elaborateness*) extravagancia *f*
extravagant [ɪk'strævəgənt] *adj* 1. (*wasteful*) despilfarrador(a) 2. (*luxurious*) lujoso, -a; **an ~ lifestyle** un tren de vida lujoso 3. (*exaggerated: praise*) excesivo, -a; **~ price** precio *m* exorbitante 4. (*elaborate*) extravagante
extravaganza [ɪkˌstrævə'gænzə] *n* (*spectacle*) **a film ~** una película espectacular
extreme [ɪk'striːm] I. *adj* extremo, -a; **an ~ case** un caso excepcional; **with ~ caution** con sumo cuidado; **~ difficulties** grandes dificultades; **~ pain** dolor agudo; **in the ~ north** en la zona más septentrional; **~ sport** deporte de alto riesgo; **to be ~ in sth** ser extremista en algo II. *n* extremo *m;* **a man of ~s** un extremista; **at the ~** *fig* en el peor de los casos; **in the ~** sumamente; **to go from one ~ to the other** pasar de un extremo a otro; **to go to ~s** llegar a extremos
extremely *adv* extremadamente; **to be ~ sorry** estar muy arrepentido
extremism [ɪk'striːmɪzəm] *n no pl* extremismo *m*
extremist [ɪk'striːmɪst] I. *adj* extremista; **~ tendencies** tendencias extremistas II. *n* extremista *mf*
extremity [ɪk'streməti, *Am:* -t̬i] *n* 1. (*furthest point*) extremo *m;* **at the ~ of his endurance** al extremo de su resistencia 2. (*situation*) situación *f* extrema; **to be driven to the ~ of leaving the country** tener que llegar al extremo de abandonar el país 3. *pl* ANAT extremidades *fpl*
extricate ['ekstrɪkeɪt] *vt form* sacar; **to ~ oneself from sth** lograr salir de algo
extrovert ['ekstrəvɜːt, *Am:* -vɜːrt] I. *n* extrovertido, -a *m, f* II. *adj* extrovertido, -a
extrude [eks'truːd] I. *vt* 1. TECH extruir 2. (*force out*) expulsar II. *vi* sobresalir
exuberance [ɪg'zjuːbərəns, *Am:* -'zuː-] *n no pl* 1. (*abundance*) exuberancia *f* 2. (*liveliness*) exaltación *f*
exuberant [ɪg'zjuːbərənt, *Am:* -'zuː-] *adj* 1. (*luxuriant*) exuberante 2. (*energetic*) desbordante; **young and ~** joven y lleno de energía
exude [ɪg'zjuːd, *Am:* -'zuːd] I. *vt* 1. exudar; **to ~ pus** supurar 2. *fig* rezumar; **to ~ confidence** irradiar confianza II. *vi* exudar

exult [ɪg'zʌlt] *vi form* regocijarse; **to ~ at** [*o* **in**] **the prize** regocijarse con [*o* de] [*o* en] el premio

exultant [ɪg'zʌltənt] *adj form* regocijado, -a, exultante; **~ shout** grito *m* de júbilo

exultation [ˌegzʌl'teɪʃən, *Am:* ˌeksʌl'-] *n no pl, form* regocijo *m,* exultación *f;* **~ at sth** regocijo *m* por algo

eye [aɪ] **I.** *n* **1.** ANAT ojo *m;* **to blink one's ~s** parpadear; **to keep an ~ on sth/sb** *inf* echar un ojo a algo/alguien; **to roll one's ~s** poner los ojos en blanco; **to rub one's ~s** restregarse los ojos; **to set ~s on sb/sth** poner los ojos en alguien/algo; **visible to the naked ~** visible a simple vista; **her ~s flashed with anger** sus ojos echaban chispas; **his ~s** (**nearly**) **popped** (**out of his head**) (casi) se le salieron los ojos de las órbitas; **he couldn't take his ~s off the girl** *inf* no le quitaba ojo a la chica **2.** BOT yema *f* ►**to have ~s in the back of one's head** *inf* tener ojos en la nuca; **to have ~s too big for one's stomach** *iron* llenar antes los ojos que la barriga; **an ~ for an ~, a tooth for a tooth** *prov* ojo por ojo y diente por diente; **to be up to one's ~s in work** *inf* estar muy agobiado con el trabajo; **to be all ~s** ser todo ojos; **to give sb a black ~** poner a alguien un ojo a la funerala; **to turn a blind ~** (**to sth**) hacer la vista gorda (a algo); **as far as the ~ can see** hasta donde alcanza la vista; **to have a good ~ for sth** tener (buen) ojo para algo; **there's more to this than meets the ~** las apariencias engañan; **to be one in the ~ for sb** *Brit, inf* dejar a alguien con un palmo de narices; **to keep one's ~s open** mantener los ojos abiertos; **to do sth with one's ~s open** *inf* hacer algo sabiendo muy bien lo que se hace; **to keep one's ~s peeled for sth** *inf* estar ojo avizor; **to go around with one's ~s shut** *inf* andar siempre distraído; **to be able to do sth with one's ~s shut** *inf* poder hacer algo con los ojos cerrados; (**right**) **before** [*o* **under**] **my very ~s** delante de mis propios ojos; **to not believe one's ~s** no dar crédito a sus ojos; **to catch sb's ~** llamar la atención de alguien; **to give sb the ~** *inf,* **to make ~s at sb** *inf* echar miraditas a alguien; **to open sb's ~s** abrir los ojos a alguien; **to run one's ~ over sth** dar una ojeada a algo; **to** (**not**) **see ~ to ~ with sb** (no) estar de acuerdo con alguien; **in my ~s** en mi opinión **II.** <-ing> *vt* mirar; (*observe*) observar; **to ~ sb up and down** mirar a alguien de arriba abajo

eyeball ['aɪbɔːl] **I.** *n* globo *m* ocular ►**to meet ~ to ~ with sb** *inf* enfrentarse cara a cara con alguien **II.** *vt Am, inf* mirar de arriba abajo

eyebrow *n* ceja *f;* **bushy ~s** cejas pobladas; **to raise one's ~s at sth** asombrarse ante algo **eyebrow pencil** *n* lápiz *m* de cejas

eye-catching ['aɪˌkætʃɪŋ] *adj* llamativo, -a

eye contact *n* contacto *m* ocular **eyedrops** *npl* gotas *f* para los ojos *pl* **eyeful** *n* **to be an ~** *inf* estar de buen ver; **get an ~ of this!** *inf* ¡echa un vistazo a esto!; **I got an ~ of dust** me ha entrado polvo en el ojo **eyeglass** *n* **1.** monóculo *m* **2.** *pl Am* gafas *f* **eyelash** <-es> *n* pestaña *f;* **false ~es** pestañas *fpl* postizas **eyelet** *n* ojete *m* **eyelid** *n* párpado *m* **eyeliner** *n no pl* lápiz *m* de ojos **eye-opener** *n* revelación *f;* **it was a real ~ for me** me hizo abrir los ojos **eyepiece** *n* ocular *m* **eyeshadow** *n* sombra *f* de ojos **eyesight** *n no pl* vista *f;* **keen ~** vista aguda; **his ~ is failing** le está fallando la vista **eyesore** *n* **to be an ~** ofender a la vista **eyestrain** *n no pl* vista *f* cansada; **to cause ~** cansar la vista **eyetooth** <-teeth> *n* colmillo *m* ►**I'd give my eyeteeth for that** daría cualquier cosa por eso **eyewash** *n* **1.** *no pl* MED colirio *m* **2.** *no pl, inf* (*nonsense*) disparate *m;* **it's a lot of ~** eso es un cuento chino **eyewitness** <-es> *n* testigo *mf* ocular

eyrie ['aɪəri, *Am:* 'eri] *n* aguilera *f*

e-zine ['iːziːn] *n* revista *f* electrónica

F

F, f [ef] *n* **1.** (*letter*) F, f *f;* **~ for Frederick** *Brit,* **~ for Fox** *Am* F de Francia **2.** MUS fa *m*

f 1. *abbr of* **folio** f **2.** *abbr of* **feminine** f

F *abbr of* **Fahrenheit** F

FA [ˌef'eɪ] *n Brit abbr of* **Football Association** *federación inglesa de fútbol*

fable ['feɪbl] *n* **1.** (*story*) fábula *f* **2.** (*lie*) cuento *m*

fabled ['feɪbld] *adj* legendario, -a

fabric ['fæbrɪk] *n* **1.** *no pl* (*cloth, textile*) tejido *m;* **cotton ~** tela *f* de algodón; **woollen ~** género *m* de lana **2.** *no pl* (*of building*) estructura *f;* **the ~ of society** el tejido social

fabricate ['fæbrɪkeɪt] *vt* **1.** (*manufacture*) fabricar **2.** *fig* (*invent*) **to ~ an excuse** inventar(se) una excusa **3.** (*forge*) falsificar

fabulous ['fæbjʊləs, *Am:* -jə-] *adj* fabuloso, -a; **to look absolutely ~** estar estupendo; **a ~ bargain** una ganga increíble

facade [fə'sɑːd] *n a. fig* fachada *f*

face [feɪs] **I.** *n* **1.** *a.* ANAT cara *f;* **a happy/sad ~** una cara de felicidad/de tristeza; **a smiling ~** un rostro sonriente; **to dare** (**to**) **show one's ~** atreverse a dar la cara; **to have a puzzled expression on one's ~** tener un semblante preocupado; **to keep a smile on one's ~** no perder la sonrisa; **to keep a straight ~** mantenerse impávido; **to laugh in sb's ~** reírse en la cara de alguien; **to pull a ~** (**at sb**) hacer una mueca (a alguien); **to tell sth to sb's ~** decir algo a la cara de alguien; **her ~ was a picture** *Brit* había que ver la cara que puso **2.** (*front: of building*) fachada *f;* (*of coin*) cara *f;* (*of clock*) esfera *f,* carátula *f Méx;* (*of* *mountain*) pared *f* **3.** (*respect, honour*) prestigio *m;* **to lose ~** desprestigiarse; **to save ~** guardar las apariencias ▶**to have a ~ like thunder** tener una cara de pocos amigos; **to put a brave ~ on sth** poner al mal tiempo buena cara; **to be brought ~ to ~ with sth** tener que enfrentarse a algo; **to make a long ~** poner cara larga; **his ~ fell when he opened the letter** le mudó el semblante cuando abrió la carta; **if your ~ fits you will get the job** *Brit, inf* si les caes bien conseguirás el trabajo; **to fly in the ~ of logic/reason** oponerse abiertamente a la lógica/razón; **on the ~ of it** a primera vista **II.** *vt* **1.** (*turn towards*) mirar hacia; **to ~ the audience** volverse hacia el público; **please ~ me when I'm talking to you** por favor, mírame cuando te estoy hablando **2.** (*confront*) hacer frente a; **the two teams will ~ each other next week** los dos equipos se enfrentarán la próxima semana; **to ~ the facts** enfrentarse a los hechos; **to ~ one's fears/problems** afrontar los miedos/problemas de uno; **to be ~d with sth** verse frente a algo; **I can't ~ doing that** no me atrevo a hacer eso; **we are ~d by financial problems** estamos pasando por graves problemas financieros; **she can't ~ seeing him so soon after their breakup** no podría soportar verlo tan poco tiempo después de romper **3.** ARCHIT recubrir **4.** FASHION forrar ▶**to ~ the music** *inf* afrontar las consecuencias **III.** *vi* **to ~ towards the street** dar a la calle; **about ~!** ¡media vuelta!

◆**face up to** *vi* **to ~ sth** hacer frente a algo; **you must ~ the fact that ...** debes aceptar que...

facecloth ['feɪsklɒθ, *Am:* 'feɪsklɑːθ] *n* toallita *f* **face cream** *n no pl* crema *f* facial **facelift** *n* lifting *m* **facepack** *n* mascarilla *f* **face powder** *n no pl* polvos *mpl* (para la cara)

facet ['fæsɪt] *n a. fig* faceta *f*

facetious [fə'siːʃəs] *adj* chistoso, -a, faceto, -a *Méx;* **stop being so ~** deja de hacerte el gracioso

face-to-face [ˌfeɪstə'feɪs, *Am:* -t̬ə-] *adv* cara a cara; **to come ~ with sth/sb** encontrarse frente a frente con algo/alguien; **to discuss sth ~ with sb** discutir algo con alguien cara a cara

face value *n* **1.** ECON valor *m* nominal **2.** *fig* **to take sth at ~** creer algo a pie juntillas; **to take sb at ~** fiarse de alguien

facial ['feɪʃl] **I.** *adj* facial **II.** *n* mascarilla *f* facial

facile ['fæsaɪl, *Am:* -ɪl] *adj* **1.** (*remark, argument*) simplista **2.** (*victory*) fácil

facilitate [fə'sɪlɪteɪt] *vt* facilitar

facilitator [fə'sɪlɪteɪtəʳ, *Am:* -t̬ɚ] *n* promotor(a) *m(f)*

facility [fə'sɪləti, *Am:* -t̬i] *n* <-ies> **1.** (*services*) servicio *m;* **credit facilities** facilidades *fpl* de pago; **transport facilities** medios *mpl* de transporte **2.** (*ability, feature*) facilidad *f;* **~ for doing sth** facilidad para hacer algo **3.** (*building for a special purpose*) complejo *m;* **research ~** centro *m* de investigación; **sports ~** complejo *m* deportivo

facing ['feɪsɪŋ] *n* **1.** ARCHIT revestimiento *m* **2.** *no pl* (*cloth strip*) vuelta *f*

facsimile [fæk'sɪməli] *n* **1.** (*exact copy*) facsímil *m* **2.** (*fax*) fax *m*

facsimile machine *n* máquina *f* de fax

fact [fækt] *n* hecho *m;* **the bare ~s** los hechos concretos; **to stick to the ~s** atenerse a los hechos ▶**~s and figures** *inf* información *f* detallada; **a ~ of life** ley de vida; **the ~s of life** los detalles de la reproducción; **as a matter of ~ ...** de hecho...; **the ~ of the matter is that ...** la verdad es que...; **in ~** de hecho

fact-finding ['fæktfaɪndɪŋ] *adj* investigador(a); **~ committee** comisión *f* de investigación

faction ['fækʃən] *n* POL facción *f*

factor ['fæktəʳ, *Am:* -tɚ] *n* factor *m;* **to be a contributing ~ in sth** contribuir a algo; **to be a crucial ~ in sth** ser de vital importancia para algo; **rhesus ~** factor *m* rhesus

factory ['fæktəri] <-ies> *n* fábrica *f;* **car ~** fábrica de coches

factory farm *n* granja *f* industrial **factory worker** *n* obrero, -a *m, f* de fábrica

factotum [fæk'təʊtəm, *Am:* -'toʊt̬əm] *n form* factótum *m*

factual ['fæktʃʊəl, *Am:* -tʃuːəl] *adj* basado, -a en hechos reales; **a ~ error** un error de hecho

faculty ['fæklti, *Am:* -t̬i] <-ies> *n* **1.** UNIV facultad *f* **2.** *no pl, Am* UNIV (*teachers*) cuerpo *m* docente **3.** (*ability*) facultad *f;* **to have a ~ for sth** tener facilidad para algo

fad [fæd] *n inf* **1.** (*fashion*) moda *f;* **a passing ~** una moda pasajera **2.** (*obsession*) manía *f*

faddish ['fædɪʃ] *adj inf s.* **faddy**

faddy ['fædi] *adj inf* maniático, -a, mañoso, -a *AmL*

fade [feɪd] **I.** *vi* **1.** (*lose colour*) desteñirse **2.** (*lose intensity: light*) apagarse; (*sound*) debilitarse; (*smile*) borrarse; (*interest*) decaer; (*hope, optimism, memory*) desvanecerse; (*plant, beauty*) marchitarse; (*life*) apagarse **3.** (*disappear*) desaparecer; **to ~ from sight** perderse de vista; **to ~ from the scene** desaparecer del mapa **4.** CINE, TV fundirse **II.** *vt* desteñir

◆**fade away** *vi* (*hope, memory*) desvanecerse; (*sound, love, grief*) apagarse; (*beauty*) marchitarse; (*person*) consumirse

◆**fade in I.** *vi* (*picture*) aparecer progresivamente; (*sound*) subir gradualmente **II.** *vt* (*picture*) hacer aparecer progresivamente; (*sound*) subir gradualmente

◆**fade out** *vi* (*picture*) desaparecer gradualmente; (*sound*) desvanecerse

faeces ['fiːsiːz] *npl form* heces *fpl*

fag [fæg] **I.** *n inf* **1.** (*cigarette*) pitillo *m* **2.** *no pl, Brit, Aus* (*bother*) fastidio *m;* **to be a ~** ser

F

una lata **3.** *Am, pej* (*homosexual*) marica *m* **II.** <-gg-> *vt inf* fatigar; **I can't be ~ed** paso; **to be ~ed out** estar rendido, -a

fag end *n* **1.** (*cigarette butt*) colilla *f* **2.** (*of film, conversation*) final *m*

faggot ['fægət] *n* **1.** (*bundle of sticks*) haz *m* de leña **2.** *Am, pej* (*homosexual*) marica *m* **3.** *Brit* (*meatball*) albóndiga *f*

fagot ['fægət] *n Am s.* **faggot**

Fahrenheit ['færnhaɪt, *Am:* 'fern-] *n* Fahrenheit *m*

fail [feɪl] **I.** *vi* **1.** (*not succeed: person*) fracasar; (*attempt, plan, operation*) fallar; **if all else ~s** como último recurso; **to ~ to do sth** no conseguir hacer algo; **to never ~ to do sth** siempre salirse con la suya; **to ~ to appreciate sth** no saber apreciar algo; **to ~ in one's duty** no cumplir con las obligaciones de uno; **I ~ to see why that matters** no veo qué importancia tiene **2.** SCHOOL, UNIV (*in exam*) suspender, ser reprobado *AmL* **3.** TECH, AUTO (*brakes, steering*) fallar; (*engine*) averiarse; (*eyesight, hearing, heart*) fallar **4. the light was ~ing** iba oscureciendo **5.** FIN, COM (*go bankrupt*) quebrar **6.** AGR, BOT perderse **II.** *vt* **1.** (*not pass: exam, pupil*) suspender **2.** (*not help*) **her courage ~ed her** le abandonó el coraje; **his nerve ~ed him** perdió el valor **III.** *n* SCHOOL, UNIV suspenso *m*, reprobado *m AmL* ►**without ~** (*definitely*) sin falta; (*always*) sin excepción

failing ['feɪlɪŋ] **I.** *adj* (*health*) débil; **in the ~ light** al anochecer **II.** *n* (*of mechanism*) defecto *m;* (*of person*) debilidad *f* **III.** *prep* a falta de

fail-safe ['feɪlseɪf] *adj* infalible

fail-safe device *n* mecanismo *m* de seguridad

failure ['feɪljəʳ, *Am:* 'feɪljɚ] *n* **1.** *no pl* (*lack of success*) fracaso *m;* **crop ~** AGR pérdida *f* de la cosecha; **to be doomed to ~** estar destinado al fracaso; **the ~ to answer** el incumplimiento de responder **2.** TECH, ELEC (*breakdown*) fallo *m* **3.** COM quiebra *f*

faint [feɪnt] **I.** *adj* **1.** (*scent, odour, taste*) leve; (*sound, murmur*) apenas perceptible; (*light, glow*) ténue; (*line, outline, scratch*) apenas visible; (*memory*) confuso, -a; (*smile*) ligero, -a **2.** (*slight: resemblance, sign, suspicion*) vago, -a; (*chance, hope, possibility*) ligero, -a; **not to make the ~est attempt to do sth** no mostrar la menor intención de hacer algo; **not to have the ~est idea** *inf* no tener ni idea **3.** (*weak*) **to be ~ with hunger** estar desfallecido por hambre; **to feel ~** sentirse mareado **II.** *vi* desmayarse **III.** *n* desmayo *m;* **to fall down in a faint** *Brit* caer desmayado

faint-hearted [ˌfeɪnt'hɑːtɪd, *Am:* -'hɑːrt̬ɪd] *adj* (*person*) pusilánime

faintly *adv* (*barely perceptibly*) débilmente; (*remember*) vagamente; (*slightly*) ligeramente

fair¹ [feəʳ, *Am:* fer] **I.** *adj* **1.** (*just: society, trial, wage*) justo, -a; (*price*) razonable; **a ~ share** una parte equitativa; **~ enough** está bien; **it's only ~ that she should be told** lo justo es decírselo **2.** *inf* (*quite large: amount*) bastante; **it's a ~ size** es bastante grande **3.** (*reasonably good: chance, prospect*) bueno, -a **4.** (*not bad*) aceptable **5.** (*light in colour: skin*) blanco, -a, güero, -a *AmL;* (*hair*) rubio, -a **6.** METEO **~ weather** tiempo *m* agradable ►**~ go** *Aus* sé razonable; **by ~ means or foul** con métodos ortodoxos o sin ellos; **it's set ~** *Brit* la situación es favorable; **~'s ~** *inf* lo justo es justo **II.** *adv* **to play ~** jugar limpio ►**~ and square** (*following the rules*) con todas las de la ley; (*directly*) de lleno

fair² [feəʳ] *n* feria *f;* **trade ~** feria comercial

fair copy <-ies> *n* copia *f* en limpio **fair game** *no pl n* caza *f* legal; *fig* objeto *m* legítimo

fairground ['feəgraʊnd, *Am:* 'fer-] *n* parque *m* de atracciones

fair-haired [ˌfeə'heəd, *Am:* ˌfer'herd] *adj* rubio, -a

fairly ['feəli, *Am:* 'fer-] *adv* **1.** (*quite*) bastante **2.** (*justly*) con imparcialidad **3.** *liter* (*almost*) prácticamente ►**~ and squarely** *Brit, Aus* de lleno

fair-minded [ˌfeə'maɪndɪd, *Am:* ˌfer-] *adj* imparcial

fairness *n no pl* **1.** (*justice*) justicia *f;* **in (all) ~ ...** para ser justo... **2.** (*of skin*) blancura *f;* (*of hair*) lo rubio

fair play *n no pl* juego *m* limpio

fairway ['feəweɪ, *Am:* 'fer-] *n* **1.** (*in golf*) calle *f* **2.** NAUT canal *m* navegable

fairy ['feəri, *Am:* 'feri] <-ies> *n* **1.** (*creature*) hada *f* **2.** *pej, inf* (*homosexual*) mariquita *m*

fairy-lights *npl* bombillas *fpl* de colores

fairytale *n* cuento *m* de hadas; *fig* cuento *m* chino; **a ~ ending** un final feliz

faith [feɪθ] *n* fe *f;* **to have/lose ~ in sb/sth** tener/perder la fe en alguien/algo; **to put one's ~ in sb/sth** confiar en alguien/algo; **to renounce one's ~** renunciar a sus creencias; **to keep the ~** mantener la fe

faithful ['feɪθfəl] **I.** *adj* fiel **II.** *n* **the ~** los fieles

faithfully *adv* **1.** (*loyally: serve*) lealmente; **to promise ~ to do sth** prometer sinceramente hacer algo; **Yours ~** *Brit, Aus* (le saluda) atentamente **2.** (*exactly: copy, translate*) fielmente

faith healer *n* curandero, -a *m, f*

faithless ['feɪθləs] *adj* REL infiel; (*disloyal*) desleal

fake [feɪk] **I.** *n* **1.** (*painting, jewel*) falsificación *f* **2.** (*person*) impostor(a) *m(f)* **II.** *adj* **~ fur** piel sintética; **~ jewel** joya falsa; **a ~ tan** un bronceado artificial **III.** *vt* **1.** (*counterfeit*) falsificar **2.** (*pretend to feel*) fingir **IV.** *vi* fingir

fakir ['feɪkɪəʳ, *Am:* fɑː'kɪr] *n* faquir *m*

falcon ['fɔːlkən, *Am:* 'fæl-] *n* halcón *m*

Falkland Islands ['fɔːklædˌaɪləndz] *npl* **the ~** las (Islas) Malvinas

fall [fɔːl] <fell, fallen> **I.** *vi* **1.** (*drop down*) caerse; (*rain, snow*) caer; (*tree*) venirse abajo;

THEAT (*curtain*) caer; **to ~ flat** (*joke*) no tener gracia; (*plan, suggestion*) no tener éxito; **to ~ down the stairs** caerse por las escaleras; **to ~ (down) dead** caer muerto; **to ~ flat on one's face** caerse de morros **2. to ~ to one's knees** arrodillarse **3.** (*land: bomb, missile*) caer **4.** (*accent, stress*) recaer **5.** (*decrease: prices*) bajar; (*demand*) descender; **to ~ sharply** caer de forma acusada **6.** (*temperature*) descender **7.** (*league table, charts*) bajar **8.** (*be defeated*) caer; **to ~ under sb's power** caer bajo el dominio de alguien; **the prize fell to him** le tocó el premio **9.** *liter* (*die in battle*) caer **10.** REL pecar **11.** (*occur*) **to ~ on a Monday** caer en lunes **12.** (*happen*) **night was ~ing** anochecía **13.** (*belong*) **to ~ into a category** pertenecer a una categoría **14.** (*hang down: hair, cloth*) colgar **15.** (*go down: cliff, ground, road*) descender **16.** + *adj* (*become*) **to ~ asleep** dormirse; **to ~ due** tocar (pagar); **to ~ foul of a law** infringir la ley; **to ~ foul of sb** tener desavenencias con alguien; **to ~ ill** caer enfermo; **to ~ vacant** quedar vacante **17.** (*enter a particular state*) **to ~ madly in love** (**with sb/sth**) enamorarse perdidamente (de alguien/algo); **to ~ out of favour** perder popularidad; **to ~ under the influence of sb/sth** entrar bajo la influencia de alguien/algo **II.** *n* **1.** (*drop from a height*) caída *f* **2.** (*decrease*) disminución *f*; **~ in temperature** descenso *m* de la temperatura **3.** (*defeat*) caída *f* **4.** *Am* (*autumn*) otoño *m* **5.** *pl* (*waterfall*) cascada *f*; **the Niagara Falls** las cataratas del Niágara **6.** *no pl* REL **the Fall** la Caída **III.** *adj Am* (*occuring in autumm*) en otoño; (*of autumn*) otoñal

◆**fall about** *vi Brit, Aus, inf* troncharse, partirse; **to ~ (laughing)** morirse de risa

◆**fall away** *vi* **1.** (*become detached: plaster, rock*) desprenderse **2.** (*slope downward*) caer en declive **3.** *Brit, Aus* (*decrease: attendance, support*) decaer; **to ~ sharply** irse a pique **4.** (*disappear: feeling*) desvanecerse

◆**fall back** *vi* **1.** (*move backwards: crowd*) quedarse atrás **2.** (*retreat: army*) replegarse **3.** SPORTS (*runner*) perder posiciones **4.** *Brit, Aus* (*decrease: production, prices*) reducirse

◆**fall back on** *vt*, **fall back upon** *vt* echar mano de

◆**fall behind** *vi* **1.** (*become slower*) quedarse atrás **2.** (*achieve less: team, country*) quedarse rezagado **3.** (*fail to do sth on time*) retrasarse **4.** SPORTS quedarse atrás

◆**fall down** *vi* **1.** (*person*) caerse; (*building*) derrumbarse; **to be falling down** estar viniéndose abajo **2.** (*be unsatisfactory: person, plan*) fallar; **to ~ on the job** *inf* no servir para el trabajo

◆**fall for** *vt* **to ~ sb** enamorarse de alguien; **to ~ a trick** caer en la trampa

◆**fall in** *vi* **1.** (*into water, hole*) caerse **2.** (*collapse: roof, ceiling*) venirse abajo **3.** MIL formar filas

◆**fall in with** *vt insep* **1.** (*agree to*) aceptar **2.** (*become friendly with*) **to ~ sb** juntarse con alguien

◆**fall off** *vi* **1.** (*become detached*) desprenderse **2.** (*decrease*) reducirse

◆**fall on** *vt insep* **1.** (*date*) caer en **2.** (*attack*) echarse encima de; **to ~ sb** (*cuts*) recaer sobre alguien **3.** *liter* (*embrace*) abrazar

◆**fall out** *vi* **1.** (*drop out: of container*) caer; (*teeth, hair*) caerse **2.** *inf* (*quarrel*) pelearse **3.** MIL romper filas

◆**fall over I.** *vi insep* caerse **II.** *vt* tropezarse con; **to fall over oneself to do sth** *inf* desvivirse por hacer algo

◆**fall through** *vi* fracasar

◆**fall to** *vt insep* **1.** (*be responsibility of*) tocar a **2.** (*fail*) **to ~ pieces** (*plan, relationship*) terminar en nada; (*person*) venirse abajo

◆**fall upon** *vt s.* **fall on**

fallacious [fə'leɪʃəs] *adj form* falaz

fallacy ['fæləsi] <-ies> *n* falacia *f*

fallen ['fɔːlən] *adj* caído, -a; **~ arches** MED pies *mpl* planos; **a ~ dictator** un dictador derrocado; **a ~ woman** una mujer perdida

fall guy *n Am, inf* cabeza *f* de turco

fallible ['fæləbl] *adj* falible; **we are all ~** errar es humano

falling star *n* estrella *f* fugaz

fall-off ['fɔːlɒf, *Am:* -ɑːf] *n* COM baja *f*; (*lessening*) empeoramiento *m*

Fallopian tube [fə'ləʊpɪən'tjuːb, *Am:* fə'loʊpɪən'tuːb] *n* trompa *f* de Falopio

fallout ['fɔːlaʊt] *n no pl* **1.** PHYS lluvia *f* radiactiva **2.** *fig* secuelas *fpl*

fallout shelter *n* refugio *m* antinuclear

fallow ['fæləʊ, *Am:* -oʊ] **I.** *adj* **1.** (*ground, field*) en barbecho **2.** (*period, time*) improductivo, -a **II.** *adv* **to lie ~** estar en barbecho

fallow deer ['fæləʊdɪəʳ, *Am:* -oʊdɪr] *n inv* gamo *m*

false [fɔːls] **I.** *adj* **1.** (*untrue: idea, information*) falso, -a; **a ~ dawn** una señal errónea; **~ economy** falso ahorro *m*; **~ move** movimiento *m* en falso; **to take a ~ step** dar un paso en falso; **a ~ pregnancy** MED, PSYCH embarazo *m* psicológico; **to give a ~ impression** dar una impresión equivocada; **to raise ~ hopes** levantar falsas esperanzas **2.** (*artificial: beard, eyelashes*) postizo, -a; **a ~ bottom** un doble fondo **3.** (*name, address, identity*) falso, -a; **to give ~ evidence in court** LAW dar falso testimonio en un juicio; **~ accounting** LAW, FIN falsificación *f* de la contabilidad; **under ~ colours** *liter* aparentando lo que no es; **under ~ pretences** con engaños **4.** (*insincere: smile, laugh, manner*) falso, -a; **to put on a ~ front** ser hipócrita; **~ modesty** falsa modestia *f* **5.** *liter* (*disloyal*) **a ~ friend** un amigo traicionero **II.** *adv* **to play sb ~** traicionar a alguien

false alarm *n* falsa alarma *f* **false friend** *n* LING falso amigo *m*

falsehood ['fɔːlshʊd] *n* **1.** *no pl* (*untruth*)

falsedad *f* **2.** (*lie*) mentira *f*
false imprisonment *n* detención *f* ilegal
falseness *n no pl* **1.** (*inaccuracy*) inexactitud *f* **2.** (*insincerity*) falsedad *f*
false start *n* SPORTS salida *f* nula **false teeth** *npl* dientes *mpl* postizos
falsetto [fɔːl'setəʊ, *Am:* fɔːl'set̬oʊ] **I.** *n* falsete *m;* ~ **voice** voz *f* de falsete **II.** *adv* **to sing** ~ cantar en falsete
falsification [ˌfɔːlsɪfɪ'keɪʃən] *n no pl* falsificación *f;* ~ **of evidence** falseamiento *m* de las pruebas
falsify ['fɔːlsɪfaɪ] *vt* falsificar
falsity ['fɔːlsəti, *Am:* -t̬i] *n no pl* **1.** (*inaccuracy*) inexactitud *f* **2.** (*insincerity*) falsedad *f*
falter ['fɔːltəʳ, *Am:* -t̬ɚ] *vi* (*person*) vacilar; (*conversation*) decaer; (*courage, negotiations*) tambalearse
faltering ['fɔːltərɪŋ, *Am:* -t̬ɚ-] *adj* (*voice, speech*) entrecortado, -a; (*steps*) indeciso, -a
fame [feɪm] *n no pl* fama *f;* **to rise to** ~ hacerse famoso
famed ['feɪmd] *adj* famoso, -a
familiar [fə'mɪliəʳ, *Am:* -jɚ] *adj* **1.** (*well-known*) familiar; (*face*) conocido, -a **2.** (*acquainted*) familiarizado, -a **3.** (*friendly*) de familiaridad; ~ **form of address** LING forma *f* de trato informal; **to be on** ~ **terms** (**with sb**) tener un trato de confianza (con alguien)
familiarity [fəˌmɪli'ærəti, *Am:* -'erət̬i] *n no pl* **1.** (*intimacy*) familiaridad *f;* (*inappropriate friendliness*) confianza *f* excesiva **2.** (*knowledge*) conocimiento *m*
familiarize [fə'mɪliəraɪz, *Am:* -jəraɪz] *vt* acostumbrar; **to** ~ **oneself with sth** familiarizarse con algo
family ['fæməli] <-ies> **I.** *n* familia *f;* **to be** ~ ser familia; **to be** (**like**) **one of the** ~ ser como uno más de la familia; **to run in the** ~ venir de familia; **to start a** ~ formar una familia **II.** *adj* familiar
family allowance *n Brit* subsidio *m* familiar **family doctor** *n Brit* médico *m* de cabecera **family man** *n* (*enjoying family life*) hombre *m* casero; (*with wife and family*) padre *m* de familia **family name** *n* apellido *m* **family planning** *n no pl* planificación *f* familiar **family tree** *n* árbol *m* genealógico
famine ['fæmɪn] *n* hambruna *f*
famished ['fæmɪʃt] *adj inf* **to be** ~ estar muerto de hambre
famous ['feɪməs] *adj* famoso, -a; **to become** ~ **for sth** hacerse célebre por algo
famously *adv* **to get on** ~ llevarse divinamente
fan[1] [fæn] **I.** *n* **1.** (*hand-held*) abanico *m* **2.** (*electrical*) ventilador *m* **II.** <-nn-> *vt* **1.** (*cool with fan*) abanicar; **to** ~ **oneself** abanicarse **2.** *fig* (*heighten: passion, interest*) avivar; **to** ~ **the flames** *fig* echar leña al fuego
fan[2] [fæn] *n* (*of person*) admirador(a) *m(f);* (*of team*) hincha *mf;* (*of music*) fan *mf*
fanatic [fə'nætɪk, *Am:* -'næt̬ɪk] *n* **1.** entusiasta *mf* **2.** *pej* fanático, -a *m, f*
fanatical *adj* fanático, -a; **to be** ~ **about sth** estar ciego por algo
fanaticism [fə'nætɪsɪzəm, *Am:* -'næt̬-] *n no pl* fanatismo *m*
fan belt *n* AUTO correa *f* del ventilador
fancied *adj* favorito, -a
fancier *n* **pigeon** ~ criador(a) *m(f)* de palomas
fanciful ['fæntsɪfəl] *adj* **1.** (*idea, notion*) descabellado, -a **2.** (*design, style*) imaginativo, -a
fan club *n* club *m* de fans
fancy ['fæntsi] **I.** <-ie-> *vt* **1.** *Brit* (*want, like*) **to** ~ **doing sth** tener ganas de hacer algo **2.** *Brit* (*be attracted to*) **he fancies you** le gustas; **to** ~ **oneself** ser un creído; **to** ~ **oneself as sth** dárselas de algo **3.** (*imagine*) **to** ~ (**that**) ... imaginarse (que)...; ~ (**that**)! ¡lo que son las cosas!; **...,** **I** ~ *Brit* ...,me parece; ~ **shouting at him!** ¡cómo se te (etc.) ocurre gritarle!; ~ **meeting here!** ¡qué casualidad encontrarnos aquí! **II.** *n* <-ies> **1.** *no pl* (*liking*) **to take a** ~ **to sth/sb** quedarse prendado de algo/alguien; **to take sb's** ~ dejar fascinado a alguien; **it tickled his** ~ le hizo gracia **2.** *no pl* (*imagination*) fantasía *f* **3.** (*whimsical idea*) capricho *m;* **whenever the** ~ **takes you** cuando se te antoje **III.** *adj* <-ier, -iest> **1.** (*elaborate: decoration, frills*) de adorno; **the speech was all** ~ **phrases** el discurso estaba lleno de florituras **2.** (*whimsical: ideas, notions*) extravagante **3.** *inf* (*expensive*) carísimo, -a; ~ **hotel** hotel *m* de lujo; ~ **prices** precios *mpl* exorbitantes
fancy dress *n no pl, Brit, Aus* disfraz *m*
fancy-free [ˌfætsi'friː] *adj* libre
fancy goods *npl* artículos *mpl* de regalo **fancy man** <-men> *n inf* amante *m*
fanfare ['fænfeəʳ, *Am:* -fer] *n* fanfarria *f*
fang [fæŋ] *n* (*of dog, lion*) colmillo *m;* (*of snake*) diente *m*
fanlight ['fænlaɪt] *n* montante *m* (*de ventana*)
fan mail *n no pl* cartas *fpl* de admiradores
fanny ['fæni] *n* **1.** *Brit, vulg* coño *m* **2.** *Am, inf* culo *m*
fantasize ['fæntəsaɪz, *Am:* -t̬ə-] *vi* **to** ~ **about sth** fantasear sobre algo
fantastic [fæn'tæstɪk] *adj* **1.** (*excellent*) fantástico, -a **2.** (*unbelievable: coincidence*) increíble; (*notion, plan*) absurdo, -a
fantasy ['fæntəsi, *Am:* -t̬ə-] <-ies> *n* fantasía *f*
fanzine ['fænziːn] *n* fanzine *m*
FAO *n abbr of* **Food and Agriculture Organization** OAA *f*
FAQ *n* INFOR *abbr of* **frequently asked questions** FAQ *f*
far [fɑːʳ, *Am:* fɑːr] <farther, farthest *o* further, furthest> **I.** *adv* **1.** (*a long distance*) lejos; **how** ~ **is it from Boston to Maine?** ¿qué distancia hay entre Boston y Maine?; ~ **away** muy lejos; ~ **distant** *liter* muy lejos; ~ **from doing sth** lejos de hacer algo; ~ **from it**

todo lo contrario **2.** (*distant in time*) **as ~ back as I remember …** hasta donde me alcanza la memoria…; **to be not ~ off sth** rondar algo; **so ~** hasta ahora **3.** (*in progress*) **to not get very ~ with sb/sth** no llegar muy lejos con alguien/algo; **he will go ~** llegará lejos; **to go too ~** ir demasiado lejos **4.** (*much*) **~ better** mucho mejor; **~ nicer** mucho más bonito; **to be the best by ~** ser el/la mejor con diferencia; **to be ~ too expensive** ser demasiado caro **5.** (*connecting adverbial phrase*) **as ~ as I know …** que yo sepa…; **as ~ as you can** en (todo) lo que puedas; **as ~ as possible** en lo posible; **as ~ as I'm concerned …** en lo que a mí se refiere…; **the essay is OK as ~ as it goes** la redacción es aceptable ►**so ~ so good** hasta ahora todo va bien; **~ and wide** por todas partes **II.** *adj* **1.** (*distant*) lejano, -a; **in the ~ distance** a lo lejos; **a ~ country** *liter* un país lejano **2.** (*further away*) **the ~ bank of the river** el otro lado de la orilla; **the ~ left/right** (**of a party**) la extrema izquierda/derecha (de un partido)

faraway ['fɑːrəweɪ] *adj* **a ~ land** una tierra lejana; **to have a ~ expression** estar abstraído

farce [fɑːs, *Am:* fɑːrs] *n* **1.** THEAT farsa *f* **2.** *fig* follón *m*

farcical ['fɑːsɪkl, *Am:* 'fɑːr-] *adj* absurdo, -a

fare [feəʳ, *Am:* fer] **I.** *n* **1.** (*for journey*) tarifa *f;* **single/return ~** billete sencillo/de ida y vuelta **2.** (*taxi passenger*) pasajero, -a *m, f* **3.** *no pl* GASTR comida *f;* **traditional British ~** comida tradicional británica **II.** *vi* **to ~ badly/well** salir mal/bien parado; **how did you ~ at the interview?** ¿qué tal te fue la entrevista?

Far East *n* **the ~** el Extremo Oriente

farewell [ˌfeə'wel, *Am:* ˌfer-] **I.** *interj form* adiós; **to bid ~ to sb/sth** despedirse de alguien/algo **II.** *n* despedida *f* **III.** *adj* de despedida

far-fetched [ˌfɑː'fetʃt, *Am:* ˌfɑːr-] *adj* inverosímil

far-flung [ˌfɑː'flʌŋ, *Am:* ˌfɑːr-] *adj liter* **1.** (*spread over wide area*) extenso, -a **2.** (*remote*) lejano, -a

farm [fɑːm, *Am:* fɑːrm] **I.** *n* (*small*) granja *f,* hacienda *f AmL,* chacra *f CSur, Perú;* (*large*) hacienda *f* **II.** *vt* cultivar **III.** *vi* cultivar la tierra
◆**farm out** *vt* **to ~ work** subcontratar; **to ~ children to sb** pedir a alguien que cuide de los niños

farmer ['fɑːməʳ, *Am:* 'fɑːrmɚ] *n* granjero, -a *m, f,* hacendado, -a *m, f,* chacarero, -a *m, f CSur, Perú*

farmhand *n* mozo *m* de labranza **farmhouse** *n* <-s> casa *f* de labranza **farmland** *n* terreno *m* agrícola **farmstead** *n Am: edificios de una granja* **farmyard** *n* corral *m*

far-off [ˌfɑː'rɒf, *Am:* ˌfɑːr'ɑːf] *adj* (*place, country*) lejano, -a; (*time*) remoto, -a

far-reaching [ˌfɑː'riːtʃɪŋ, *Am:* ˌfɑːr-] *adj* de grandes repercusiones

far-seeing [ˌfɑː'siːɪŋ, *Am:* ˌfɑːr-] *adj* (*decision, policy*) con visión de futuro; (*person*) previsor(a)

far-sighted [ˌfɑː'saɪtɪd, *Am:* ˌfɑːr'saɪt̬ɪd] *adj Brit, Aus* (*decision, policy*) con visión de futuro; (*person*) previsor(a)

fart [fɑːt, *Am:* fɑːrt] *inf* **I.** *n* pedo *m;* **to do a ~** tirarse un pedo **II.** *vi* tirarse un pedo

farther ['fɑːðəʳ, *Am:* 'fɑːrðɚ] **I.** *adv comp of* **far 1.** (*distance*) más allá; **~ away from …** más lejos de…; **~ down/up** más abajo/arriba **2.** (*time*) **~ back in time** más atrás en el tiempo **3.** (*additional*) *s.* **further II.** *adj comp of* **far** más lejano, -a

farthest ['fɑːðɪst, *Am:* 'fɑːr-] **I.** *adv superl of* **far** más lejos **II.** *adj superl of* **far** (*distance*) más lejano, -a; (*time*) más remoto, -a

farthing ['fɑːðɪŋ, *Am:* 'fɑːr-] *n* (*coin*) cuarto *m* de penique

fascia ['feɪʃə] *n* **1.** *Brit* (*dashboard*) tablero *m* de mandos **2.** (*board above shop window*) letrero *m* **3.** ARCHIT faja *f*

fascinate ['fæsɪneɪt, *Am:* -əneɪt] *vt* fascinar

fascinating ['fæsɪneɪtɪŋ, *Am:* -t̬ɪŋ] *adj* fascinante

fascination [ˌfæsɪ'neɪʃən, *Am:* -ə'-] *n no pl* fascinación *f;* **to listen in ~** escuchar fascinado

fascism *n,* **Fascism** ['fæʃɪzəm] *n no pl* fascismo *m*

fascist, **Fascist** ['fæʃɪst] **I.** *n* fascista *mf* **II.** *adj* fascista

fashion ['fæʃən] **I.** *n* **1.** (*popular style*) moda *f;* **to be in ~** estar de moda; **to be out of ~** estar pasado de moda; **to come into ~** ponerse de moda; **to be all the ~** estar muy de moda; **the latest ~** la última moda **2.** (*manner*) manera *f;* **in the usual ~** como de costumbre; **after a ~** si se le puede llamar así **II.** *vt form* dar forma a; (*create*) crear

fashionable ['fæʃənəbl] *adj* (*clothes, style*) moderno, -a; (*nightclub, restaurant*) de moda; (*person, set*) a la moda

fashion designer *n* diseñador(a) *m(f)* de moda **fashion parade** *n* desfile *m* de moda **fashion show** *n* desfile *m* de moda

fast¹ [fɑːst, *Am:* fæst] **I.** <-er, -est> *adj* **1.** rápido, -a; **the ~ lane** el carril de adelantamiento; **~ train** tren *m* expreso; **to be a ~ worker** trabajar rápido **2.** (*clock*) **to be ~** ir adelantado **3.** (*firmly fixed*) fijo, -a; **to make ~** NAUT amarrar firmemente; **to make sth ~** (**to sth**) fijar algo (a algo) **4.** (*immoral*) **~ woman** mujer *f* lanzada **II.** *adv* **1.** (*quickly*) rápidamente; **not so ~!** ¡no tan rápido! **2.** (*firmly*) firmemente; **to hold ~ to sth** agarrarse bien a algo; **to stand ~** mantenerse firme **3.** (*deeply*) profundamente; **to be ~ asleep** estar profundamente dormido

fast² [fɑːst, *Am:* fæst] **I.** *vi* ayunar **II.** *n* ayuno *m*

fasten ['fɑːsən, *Am:* 'fæsən] *vt* **1.** (*do up*) atar **2.** (*fix securely*) fijar **3.** **to ~ sth onto sth** atar firmemente algo a algo; **to ~ one's eyes on sth** fijar la mirada en algo; **to ~ sth**

F

together (*with paper clip*) unir algo; (*with string*) atar algo

◆**fasten down** *vt* sujetar

◆**fasten on I.** *vt* fijarse en; **to ~ an idea** aferrarse a una idea **II.** *vi* **to ~ to sb** pegarse a alguien

◆**fasten up** *vi, vt Brit, Aus* abrochar(se)

fastener ['fɑːsənəʳ, *Am:* 'fæsənɚ] *n* cierre *m;* **snap ~** cierre *m* automático; **zip ~** cremallera *f*

fast food *n no pl* comida *f* rápida

fast-forward [ˌfɑːst'fɔːwəd, *Am:* ˌfæst'fɔːrwɚd] **I.** *vt* hacer avanzar rápidamente **II.** *vi* avanzar rápidamente **III.** *n no pl* botón *m* de avance

fastidious [fə'stɪdɪəs] *adj* escrupuloso, -a

fastness ['fɑːstnɪs, *Am:* 'fæst-] <-es> *n* **1.** MIL fortaleza *f* **2.** *liter* (*stronghold*) refugio *m*

fat [fæt] **I.** *adj* **1.** gordo, -a; **to get ~** engordar **2.** (*thick*) grueso, -a **3.** (*large*) grande; **a ~ cheque** un cheque sustancioso ▶**~ chance!** *inf* ¡para nada!, ¡ni soñarlo! **II.** *n* **1.** *no pl* (*meat tissue*) carnes *fpl* **2.** (*fatty substance*) grasa *f;* **vegetable ~** grasa vegetal ▶**the ~ is in the fire** aquí se va a armar la gorda; **to live off the ~ of the land** vivir a cuerpo de rey; **to chew the ~ with sb** *inf* estar de palique [*o* de cháchara] con alguien

fatal ['feɪtəl, *Am:* -t̬əl] *adj* **1.** (*causing death*) mortal **2.** (*disastrous*) desastroso, -a **3.** *liter* (*consequences*) funesto, -a

fatalism ['feɪtəlɪzəm, *Am:* -t̬əl-] *n no pl* fatalismo *m*

fatalist *n* fatalista *mf*

fatality [fə'tæləti, *Am:* -t̬i] <-ies> *n* fatalidad *f*

fatally *adv* **1.** (*causing death*) mortalmente; **~ ill** enfermo de muerte **2.** (*disastrously*) desastrosamente; **~ damaged** dañado de forma irreparable

fat cat *n inf* pez *m* gordo

fate [feɪt] *n no pl* (*destiny*) destino *m;* (*one's end*) suerte *f;* **to leave sb to his ~** dejar a alguien a su suerte; **to meet one's ~** hallar su destino; **to seal sb's ~** determinar el destino de alguien; **to share the same ~** compartir la misma suerte; **to tempt ~** tentar a la suerte; **a ~ worse than death** un destino peor que la muerte; **it must be ~** debe ser el destino

fated ['feɪtɪd, *Am:* -t̬ɪd] *adj* predestinado, -a; **to be ~ to do sth** estar predestinado a hacer algo; **it was ~ that ...** estaba escrito que...

fateful ['feɪtfəl] *adj* fatídico, -a

fat-free *adj* sin grasas

fathead ['fæthed] *n inf* imbécil *mf*

father ['fɑːðəʳ, *Am:* -ðɚ] **I.** *n* **1.** (*parent*) padre *m;* **from ~ to son** de padre a hijo; **to be like a ~ to sb** ser como un padre para alguien; **on your ~'s side** por parte paterna **2.** (*founder*) fundador *m* **3.** *pl, liter* (*ancestors*) antepasados *mpl* ▶**like ~, like son** de tal palo tal astilla **II.** *vt* (*child*) engendrar; (*idea*) crear

Father Christmas *n Brit* Papá *m* Noel

father figure *n* figura *f* paterna

fatherhood ['fɑːðəhʊd, *Am:* -ðɚ-] *n no pl* paternidad *f*

father-in-law ['fɑːðərɪnlɔː, *Am:* -ðɚɪnlɑː] <fathers-in-law *o* father-in-laws> *n* suegro *m*

fatherland ['fɑːðəlænd, *Am:* -ðɚ-] *n* patria *f*

fatherless ['fɑːðələs, *Am:* -ðɚ-] *adj* huérfano, -a de padre

fatherly ['fɑːðəli, *Am:* -ðɚli] *adj* paternal

Father's Day *n no pl* Día *m* del Padre

fathom ['fæðəm] **I.** *n* NAUT braza *f* **II.** *vt* (*mystery*) desentrañar

fathomless *adj liter* **1.** (*too deep to measure*) insondable **2.** (*impossible to understand*) incomprensible

fatigue [fə'tiːg] **I.** *n* **1.** *no pl* (*tiredness*) cansancio *m,* fatiga *f;* **to suffer from ~** estar cansado **2.** TECH fatiga *f* **3.** MIL faena *f;* (*uniform*) uniforme *m* de faena **II.** *vt* **1.** *form* (*tire*) cansar **2.** TECH (*weaken*) debilitar

fatigue dress *n,* **fatigues** *npl* MIL traje *m* de faena

fatten ['fætən] *vt* engordar

fattening *adj* que hace engordar

fatty ['fæti, *Am:* 'fæt̬-] **I.** *adj* **1.** (*food*) graso, -a **2.** (*tissue*) adiposo, -a **II.** <-ies> *n inf* gordinflón, -ona *m, f*

fatuous ['fætʃʊəs, *Am:* 'fætʃu-] *adj* fatuo, -a

faucet ['fɔːsɪt, *Am:* 'fɑː-] *n Am* grifo *m,* bitoque *m Méx, RíoPl;* **to turn a ~ on/off** abrir/cerrar el grifo

fault [fɔːlt] **I.** *n* **1.** *no pl* (*responsibility*) culpa *f;* **it's not my ~** yo no tengo la culpa; **to be sb's ~ (that ...)** ser culpa de alguien (que ...); **to be at ~** tener la culpa; **to find ~ with sb** criticar a alguien **2.** (*character weakness*) debilidad *f;* **to have its ~s** tener sus defectos; **to be generous to a ~** ser demasiado generoso **3.** (*defect*) fallo *m;* **electrical/technical ~** fallo eléctrico/técnico **4.** GEO falla *f* **5.** SPORTS falta *f;* **double ~** doble falta; **foot ~** falta de pie; **to call a ~** pitar una falta **II.** *vt* encontrar defectos en

fault-finding ['fɔːltˌfaɪndɪŋ] **I.** *n no pl* **1.** (*criticism*) crítica *f* **2.** ELEC detección *f* de averías **II.** *adj* criticón, -ona

faultless ['fɔːltləs] *adj* impecable

faulty ['fɔːlti, *Am:* -t̬i] *adj* defectuoso, -a; **~ logic** lógica *f* imperfecta

faun [fɔːn, *Am:* fɑːn] *n* fauno *m*

fauna ['fɔːnə, *Am:* 'fɑː-] *n* fauna *f*

favor ['feɪvəʳ, *Am:* -vɚ] *n, vt Am, Aus s.* **favour**

favorable ['feɪvərəbl] *adj Am, Aus s.* **favourable**

favored *adj Am, Aus s.* **favoured**

favorite ['feɪvərɪt] *adj, n Am, Aus s.* **favourite**

favoritism *n Am, Aus s.* **favouritism**

favour ['feɪvəʳ, *Am:* -vɚ] *Brit, Aus* **I.** *n* **1.** *no pl* (*approval*) favor *m,* aprobación *f;* **to be in ~**

of sb/sth estar a favor de alguien/algo; **to decide/vote in ~ of (doing) sth** decidir/votar a favor de (hacer) algo; **to come down in ~ of (doing) sth** ponerse a favor de (hacer) algo; **to be in ~** tener mucha aceptación; **to be in ~ with sb** tener el apoyo de alguien; **to be out of ~** no tener aceptación; **to reject sth in ~ of sth else** rechazar algo por otra cosa; **to find in ~ of sb** LAW fallar a favor de alguien; **to find ~ with sb** caer en gracia a alguien; **to gain** [*o* **win**] **sb's ~** ganarse la simpatía de alguien; **to show ~ to sb** *form* favorecer a alguien **2.** *no pl* (*advantage*) **to be in sb's ~** apoyar a alguien; **to have sth in one's ~** tener algo a favor; **to have the wind in one's ~** tener el viento a favor **3.** (*helpful act*) favor *m*, valedura *f Méx;* **to ask sb a ~** pedir un favor a alguien; **to do sb a ~** hacer un favor a alguien; **do me a ~!** *Brit, inf* ¡hazme el favor! **4.** *Am* (*small gift*) detalle *m* **II.** *vt* **1.** (*prefer*) preferir **2.** (*give advantage to*) favorecer **3.** (*show partiality towards*) mostrar parcialidad por **4.** *form* (*graciously give*) **to ~ sb with sth** dar algo a alguien

favourable ['feɪvərəbl] *adj* **1.** (*approving*) favorable; **to make a ~ impression (on sb)** causar una impresión favorable (a alguien) **2.** (*advantageous*) ventajoso, -a; **~ to sth/sb** ventajoso para algo/alguien

favoured ['feɪvəd, *Am:* -vɚd] *adj* predilecto, -a

favourite ['feɪvərɪt] **I.** *adj* (*most liked*) favorito, -a; **~ son** *Am* POL hijo *m* predilecto **II.** *n* favorito, -a *m, f*

favouritism *n no pl* favoritismo *m*

fawn[1] [fɔːn, *Am:* fɑːn] **I.** *n* **1.** (*young deer*) cervato *m* **2.** (*colour*) beige *m* **II.** *adj* beige

fawn[2] [fɔːn, *Am:* fɑːn] *vi* **to ~ on sb** elogiar a alguien

fawning ['fɔːnɪŋ, *Am:* 'fɑː-] *adj* adulador(a)

fax [fæks] **I.** *n no pl* fax *m;* **to send something by ~** enviar algo por fax **II.** *vt* mandar por fax; **to ~ sth through to sb** pasar algo por fax a alguien

fax machine *n* fax *m*

FBI [ˌefbiː'aɪ] *n abbr of* **Federal Bureau of Investigation** FBI *m*

FCO [ˌefsiː'əʊ, *Am:* -'oʊ] *n Brit* POL *abbr of* **Foreign and Commonwealth Office** *ministerio de asuntos exteriores y de la Commonwealth*

fear [fɪəʳ, *Am:* fɪr] **I.** *n* miedo *m;* **to have a ~ of sth** tener miedo de algo; **~ of heights** miedo a las alturas; **for ~ of doing sth** por miedo a hacer algo; **for ~ that** por temor a; **to be in ~ of sth** temer algo; **to go in ~ of sth** temer por algo; **no ~!** *Brit, Aus, inf* ¡no temas!; **there's no ~ of death** no hay peligro de muerte; **to put the ~ of God into sb** dar un susto de muerte a alguien; **without ~ or favour** imparcialmente **II.** *vt* **1.** (*be afraid of*) tener miedo de; **to have nothing to ~** no tener nada que temer; **to ~ to do sth** tener miedo de hacer algo **2.** *form* (*feel concern*) **to ~ (that ...)** temer (que ...) **III.** *vi liter* tener miedo; **to ~ for one's life** temer por la vida de uno; **never ~!** *iron* ¡no hay cuidado!

fearful ['fɪəfəl, *Am:* 'fɪr-] *adj* **1.** (*anxious*) temeroso, -a; **~ of doing sth** temeroso de hacer algo **2.** (*terrible: pain, accident*) terrible **3.** *inf* (*very bad: noise, mess*) horrendo, -a

fearless ['fɪələs, *Am:* 'fɪr-] *adj* intrépido, -a

fearsome ['fɪəsəm, *Am:* 'fɪr-] *adj* temible

feasibility [ˌfiːzə'bɪləti, *Am:* -t̬i] *n no pl* viabilidad *f*

feasibility study *n* estudio *m* de viabilidad

feasible ['fiːzəbl] *adj* **1.** (*plan*) factible **2.** (*story*) plausible

feast [fiːst] **I.** *n* **1.** (*meal*) banquete *m;* **a ~ for the eye** una fiesta para los ojos; **a ~ for the ear** un deleite para el oído **2.** REL festividad *f* **II.** *vi* **to ~ on sth** darse un banquete con algo **III.** *vt* preparar un banquete para ►**to ~ one's eyes on sth** regalarse la vista con algo

feat [fiːt] *n* hazaña *f;* **~ of agility** proeza *f* de agilidad; **~ of engineering** logro *m* de la ingeniería

feather ['feðəʳ, *Am:* -ɚ] **I.** *n* pluma *f;* **a ~ quilt** un edredón de plumas ►**to be a ~ in sb's cap** ser un triunfo para alguien; **as light as a ~** tan ligero como una pluma; **you could have knocked me down with a ~** *Brit, Aus, inf* casi me caigo de espaldas; **to rufle sb's ~s** buscar las cosquillas a alguien **II.** *vt* **to ~ one's own nest** barrer hacia dentro

featherbed ['feðəbed, *Am:* '-ɚ-] *vt* subvencionar (demasiado)

featherbrained ['feðəbreɪnd, *Am:* '-ɚ-] *adj* casquivano, -a

featherweight ['feðəweɪt, *Am:* '-ɚ-] *n* SPORTS peso *m* pluma

feathery ['feðəri] *adj* (*clouds, leaves*) ligero, -a (como una pluma); (*feel, texture*) plumoso, -a

feature ['fiːtʃəʳ, *Am:* -tʃɚ] **I.** *n* **1.** (*distinguishing attribute*) característica *f;* (*speciality*) peculiaridad *f;* **sb's/sth's best ~** lo mejor de alguien/algo; **a distinguishing ~** un rasgo distintivo; **a physical ~** un rasgo físico; **to make a ~ of sth** hacer de algo un rasgo distintivo **2.** *pl* (*facial attributes*) facciones *fpl;* **to have regular/strong ~s** tener las facciones normales/muy marcadas **3.** (*article*) reportaje *m* **4.** CINE largometraje *m* **II.** *vt* **1.** (*have as performer, star*) presentar; **a film ~ing sb as ...** una película que presenta a alguien en el papel de... **2.** (*give special prominence to*) ofrecer (como atracción principal); **to ~ sth** (*article, report*) destacar algo; (*product*) ofrecer la prestación de algo **3.** (*include*) incluir **III.** *vi* **1.** (*appear*) constar; **to ~ in ...** constar en... **2.** (*be an actor in*) figurar; **to ~ in ...** figurar en...

feature film *n* largometraje *m*

featureless *adj* sin rasgos distintivos

feature story *n* reportaje *m*

febrile ['fi:braɪl, *Am:* -brɪl] *adj liter* febril
February ['febrʊəri, *Am:* -eri] *n* febrero *m;* *s. a.* **April**
feces ['fi:si:z] *npl Am s.* **faeces**
feckless ['feklɪs] *adj form* irreflexivo, -a
Fed *abbr of* **federal** fed.
federal ['fedərəl] *adj* federal; ~ **republic** república *f* federal
federalism ['fedərəlɪzəm] *n no pl* federalismo *m*
federalist ['fedərəlɪst] *n* federalista *mf*
federate ['fedəreɪt] *vi, vt* federar(se)
federation [ˌfedə'reɪʃən] *n* federación *f*
fed up [ˌfed'ʌp] *adj inf* harto, -a; **to be ~ with sth/sb** estar harto de algo/alguien; **to be ~ to the back teeth with sb/sth** *Brit, Aus* estar hasta el gorro de alguien/algo
fee [fi:] *n* (*for doctor, lawyer*) honorarios *mpl;* (*membership*) cuota *f* de miembro; (*for school, university*) tasas *fpl* de matrícula; **to charge/receive a ~ for sth** cobrar/recibir unos honorarios por algo
feeble ['fi:bl] *adj* (*person, attempt*) débil; (*performance*) flojo, -a
feeble-minded [ˌfi:bl'maɪndɪd] *adj* lelo, -a
feebleness *n no pl* debilidad *f*
feed [fi:d] <fed> **I.** *vt* **1.** (*give food to: person, animal*) alimentar; (*plant*) nutrir; (*baby*) amamantar; **to ~ the fire** avivar el fuego **2.** (*provide food for: family, country*) dar de comer a **3.** (*supply*) proporcionar; **to ~ the data from a scanner into the computer** introducir datos de un escáner al ordenador; **to ~ sb a line** THEAT apuntar a alguien **II.** *vi* alimentarse; (*baby*) amamantar **III.** *n* **1.** *no pl* (*for farm animals*) pienso *m;* **cattle ~** pienso para ganado; **to be off its ~** no tener apetito **2.** *inf* (*meal*) comida *f* **3.** TECH tubo *m* de alimentación
◆**feed back** *vt* proporcionar
◆**feed in** *vt* alimentar; (*information*) introducir
◆**feed on** *vt insep, a. fig* alimentarse de
◆**feed up** *vt* (*person*) alimentar; (*animal*) cebar
feedback ['fi:dbæk] *n* **1.** *no pl* (*information*) reacción *f;* **positive/negative ~** reacción *f* positiva/negativa **2.** *no pl* ELEC realimentación *f*
feeder *n* **1.** TECH alimentador *m* **2.** (*river*) afluente *m;* **~ road** carretera *f* de acceso
feeding bottle *n* biberón *m*
feel [fi:l] <felt> **I.** *vi* **1.** + *adj/n* (*sensation or emotion*) sentir; **to ~ well** sentirse bien; **to ~ hot/cold** tener calor/frío; **to ~ hungry/thirsty** tener hambre/sed; **to ~ certain/convinced** estar seguro/convencido; **to ~ as if ...** sentirse como si... +*subj;* **to ~ like a biscuit/a coffee** tener ganas de una galleta/un café; **to ~ like a walk** tener ganas de dar un paseo; **to ~ free to do sth** sentirse libre para hacer algo; **to ~ one's age** notar el peso de los años; **it ~s wonderful/awful** me parece maravilloso/fatal; **how do you ~ about him?** ¿qué opinas de él?; **how would you ~ if ...?** ¿qué te parece si...? **2.** + *adj* (*seem*) parecer **3.** (*search*) **to ~ for sth** buscar algo; **to ~ (around) somewhere** buscar palpando por algún sitio **II.** *vt* **1.** (*experience*) experimentar; **not to ~ a thing** no sentir nada; **to ~ the cold/heat** sentir frío/calor; **to ~ something/nothing for sb** sentir algo/no sentir nada por alguien; **to ~ it in one's bones (that ...)** sentir en la propia piel (que...) **2.** (*think, believe*) **to ~ (that) ...** creer (que)...; **to ~ it appropriate/necessary to do sth** considerar adecuado/necesario hacer algo **3.** (*touch*) tocar; (*pulse*) tomar **III.** *n* **1.** *no pl* (*texture*) textura *f;* **the ~ of sth** el tacto de algo **2.** *no pl* (*act of touching*) tacto *m;* **to have a ~ of sth** tocar algo **3.** *no pl* (*character, atmosphere*) ambiente *m;* **a ~ of mystery** una atmósfera de misterio **4.** *no pl* (*natural talent*) talento *m* natural; **to have a ~ for sth** tener talento natural para algo; **to get the ~ of sth** acostumbrarse a algo
◆**feel about** *vi* buscar palpando; **to ~ for sth** buscar algo a tientas
◆**feel for** *vt* **to ~ sb** sentirlo por alguien, compadecer a alguien
feeler ['fi:lə^r, *Am:* -lɚ] *n* ZOOL antena *f* ►**to put <u>out</u> ~s** tantear el terreno
feelgood ['fi:lgʊd] *adj* que hace sentir bien; **~ factor** sensación *f* de bienestar
feeling ['fi:lɪŋ] *n* **1.** (*emotion*) sentimiento *m;* **mixed ~s** sentimientos entremezclados; **to hurt sb's ~s** herir los sentimientos de alguien **2.** (*sensation*) sensación *f;* **a dizzy ~** una sensación de vértigo **3.** (*impression*) impresión *f;* **to have the ~ (that) ...** tener la impresión (de que)... **4.** (*opinion*) opinión *f;* **to have strong ~s about sth** tener firmes convicciones sobre algo **5.** *no pl* (*strong emotion*) sentimiento *m;* **to say sth with ~** decir algo con emoción **6.** *no pl* (*physical sensation*) sensibilidad *f;* **lose the ~ in one's leg** perder la sensibilidad de la pierna **7.** (*natural talent*) **to have a ~ for sth** tener un talento innato para algo
feet [fi:t] *n pl of* **foot**
feign [feɪn] *vt liter* fingir; **to ~ madness** fingir estar loco
feigned ['feɪnd] *adj liter* fingido, -a
feint [feɪnt] **I.** *vi* hacer una finta; **to ~ left** fintar a la izquierda; **to ~ to do sth** simular la intención de hacer algo **II.** *n* SPORTS finta *f*
felicitous [fə'lɪsɪtəs, *Am:* -t̬əs] *adj* feliz
felicity [fə'lɪsəti, *Am:* -t̬i] <-ies> *n no pl, liter* felicidad *f*
feline ['fi:laɪn] **I.** *adj* **1.** ZOOL felino, -a **2.** (*cat-like*) de gato **II.** *n* felino *m*
fell[1] [fel] *pt of* **fall**
fell[2] [fel] *vt* **1.** (*cut down*) cortar **2.** (*knock down*) hundir
fell[3] [fel] *n* (*mountain*) montaña *f*
fell[4] [fel] *adj* HIST feroz ►**at one ~ <u>swoop</u>** de un solo golpe
fellow ['feləʊ, *Am:* -oʊ] **I.** *n* **1.** *inf* (*man*) tío

m; **an odd ~** un tipo raro **2.** UNIV profesor(a) *m(f)* **3.** *form* (*colleague*) compañero, -a *m, f* **II.** *adj* **~ student** compañero, -a *m, f* de clase

fellow being *n* prójimo *m* **fellow citizen** *n* conciudadano, -a *m, f* **fellow countryman** *n* compatriota *m* **fellow feeling** *n* compañerismo *m* **fellow member** *n* consocio *mf* **fellow passenger** *n* compañero, -a *m, f* de viaje

fellowship ['feləʊʃɪp, *Am:* -oʊ-] *n* **1.** *no pl* (*comradely feeling*) compañerismo *m* **2.** (*group*) asociación *f* **3.** UNIV **research ~** beca *f* de investigación

fellow traveller *n* compañero, -a *m, f* de viaje **fellow worker** *n* compañero, -a *m, f* de trabajo

felon ['felən] *n* criminal *mf*

felonious [fɪ'ləʊnɪəs, *Am:* fə'loʊ-] *adj* criminal

felony ['feləni] <-ies> *n Am* crimen *m*

felt[1] [felt] *pt, pp of* **feel**

felt[2] [felt] **I.** *n no pl* fieltro *m* **II.** *adj* de fieltro

felt-tip (**pen**) [ˌfelt'tɪp (pen)] *n* rotulador *m*

female ['fiːmeɪl] **I.** *adj* femenino, -a; ZOOL, TECH hembra **II.** *n* (*woman*) mujer *f;* ZOOL hembra *f*

feminine ['femənɪn] **I.** *adj* femenino, -a **II.** *n* LING **the ~** el femenino

femininity [ˌfemə'nɪnəti, *Am:* -t̬i] *n no pl* feminidad *f*

feminism ['femɪnɪzəm] *n no pl* feminismo *m*

feminist ['femɪnɪst] **I.** *n* feminista *mf* **II.** *adj* feminista

femur ['fiːməʳ, *Am:* -mɚ] <-s *o* -mora> *n* fémur *m*

fen [fen] *n* pantano *m*

fence [fens] **I.** *n* **1.** (*barrier*) cerca *f* **2.** *inf* (*person*) perista *mf* ▸ **to mend one's ~s** mejorar su reputación; **to sit on the ~** nadar entre dos aguas **II.** *vi* **1.** SPORTS esgrimir **2.** *form* **to ~** (**with sb**) enfrentarse (a alguien) **III.** *vt* (*enclose*) cercar

fencer *n* esgrimidor(a) *m(f)*

fencing *n no pl* esgrima *f*

fend for ['fendˌfɔːʳ, *Am:* 'fendˌfɔːr] *vt* **to ~ oneself** arreglárselas

◆**fend off** *vt* apartar; **to ~ a question** esquivar una pregunta

fender ['fendəʳ, *Am:* -dɚ] *n* **1.** (*around fireplace*) guardafuego *m* **2.** *Am* AUTO parachoques *m inv,* bómper *m AmL,* defensa *f Méx* **3.** NAUT defensa *f*

fennel ['fenl] *n no pl* hinojo *m*

ferment[1] [fə'ment, *Am:* fɚ-] **I.** *vt* **1.** CHEM hacer fermentar **2.** *form* (*stir up*) agitar **II.** *vi* **1.** CHEM fermentar **2.** *form* (*develop*) desarrollarse

ferment[2] ['fɜːment, *Am:* 'fɜːr-] *n* **1.** *no pl, form* (*state of excitement*) agitación *f;* **to be in ~** estar conmocionado **2.** *no pl* (*fermentation*) fermentación *f*

fermentation [ˌfɜːmen'teɪʃən, *Am:* ˌfɜːr-] *n no pl* fermentación *f*

fern [fɜːn, *Am:* fɜːrn] *n* helecho *m*

ferocious [fə'rəʊʃəs, *Am:* -'roʊ-] *adj* (*battle, criticism*) feroz; (*competition*) duro, -a; (*heat*) tremendo, -a; (*temper*) violento, -a

ferocity [fə'rɒsəti, *Am:* -'rɑːsət̬i] *n no pl* (*of animal, person*) ferocidad *f;* (*of attack*) violencia *f;* (*of storm, wind*) intensidad *f*

ferret ['ferɪt] **I.** *n* hurón *m* **II.** *vi* **1.** (*search*) **to ~ around** [*o* **about**] **for sth** husmear en algo **2.** (*hunt with ferrets*) **to go ~ing** ir a cazar con hurones

Ferris wheel ['ferɪsˌhwiːl] *n* noria *f*

ferrous ['ferəs] *adj* ferroso, -a

ferry ['feri] <-ies> **I.** *n* (*ship*) ferry *m;* (*smaller*) balsa *f;* **car ~** ferry de coches **II.** *vt* **1.** (*in boat*) llevar en barca **2.** *inf* (*by car*) llevar en coche

ferry boat *n* ferry *m* **ferryman** <-men> *n* barquero *m*

fertile ['fɜːtaɪl, *Am:* 'fɜːrt̬l] *adj a. fig* fértil; **to be ~ ground for sth** *fig* ser terreno propicio para algo

fertility [fə'tɪləti, *Am:* fɚ'tɪlət̬i] *n no pl* fertilidad *f*

fertilization [ˌfɜːtəlaɪ'zeɪʃən, *Am:* ˌfɜːrt̬lɪ-] *n no pl* fertilización *f*

fertilize ['fɜːtəlaɪz, *Am:* 'fɜːrt̬ə-] *vt* **1.** BIO fertilizar **2.** AGR abonar

fertilizer ['fɜːtəlaɪzəʳ, *Am:* 'fɜːrt̬əl-] *n* fertilizante *m*

fervent ['fɜːvənt, *Am:* 'fɜːr-] *adj,* **fervid** ['fɜːvɪd, *Am:* 'fɜːr-] *adj form* ferviente

fervor *n Am,* **fervour** ['fɜːvəʳ, *Am:* 'fɜːrvɚ] *n Aus, Brit no pl* fervor *m*

fester ['festəʳ, *Am:* -tɚ] *vi* (*wound, quarrel*) enconarse

festival ['festɪvəl] *n* **1.** REL festividad *f* **2.** (*special event*) festival *m;* **a film/music ~** una fiesta de cine/música

festive ['festɪv] *adj* festivo, -a; **to be in ~ mood** estar muy alegre

festivity [fe'stɪvəti, *Am:* -t̬i] <-ies> *n* **1.** *pl* (*festive activities*) festejos *mpl* **2.** (*festival*) fiesta *f*

festoon [fe'stuːn] **I.** *n* guirnalda *f* **II.** *vt* adornar

fetal ['fiːtl, *Am:* -t̬l] *adj Am s.* **foetal**

fetch [fetʃ] **I.** *vt* **1.** (*bring back*) traer; **to ~ the police** ir a por la policía; **to ~ sb sth** (**from somewhere**) traer algo a alguien (de algún sitio) **2.** (*be sold for*) venderse por **3.** *inf* (*blow*) **to ~ sb a blow** dar un golpe a alguien **II.** *vi* **to ~ and carry** ir de acá para allá; **to ~ and carry for sb** ser el esclavo de alguien

fetching ['fetʃɪŋ] *adj* atractivo, -a

fête [feɪt] **I.** *n Brit, Aus* (*fair*) fiesta *f* **II.** *vt* festejar

fetid ['fetɪd, *Am:* 'fet̬-] *adj form* fétido, -a

fetish ['fetɪʃ, *Am:* 'fet̬-] *n* fetiche *m;* **to make a ~ of sth** hacer que algo se convierta en una obsesión

fetishism ['fetɪʃɪzəm, *Am:* 'fet̬-] *n no pl* fetichismo *m*

fetishist ['fetɪʃɪst, *Am:* 'fet̬-] *n* fetichista *mf*

fetter ['fetəʳ, *Am:* 'fet̬ɚ] *vt* **1.** (*chain up*) **to ~ sb** (**to sth**) encadenar a alguien (a algo); **to ~ a horse** atar a un caballo **2.** *liter* (*restrict freedom*) atar

fettle ['fetl, *Am:* 'fet̬-] *n no pl, inf* **to be in fine ~** estar lleno de vitalidad

fetus ['fi:təs, *Am:* -t̬əs] *n Am s.* **foetus**

feud [fju:d] **I.** *n* enemistad *f* (heredada); **a ~ between sb and sb** una enemistad de sangre entre alguien y alguien; **a ~ over sth** un odio de sangre por algo; **a family ~** una enemistad entre familias **II.** *vi* pelearse

feudal ['fju:dəl] *adj* HIST feudal

feudalism ['fju:dəlɪzəm] *n no pl* feudalismo *m*

fever ['fi:vəʳ, *Am:* -vɚ] *n* **1.** MED fiebre *f;* **to have** [*o* **run**] **a ~** tener fiebre **2.** (*excited state*) emoción *f;* **a ~ of excitement** un estado de emoción; **football ~** fiebre *f* de fútbol

feverish ['fi:vərɪʃ] *adj* **1.** MED con fiebre **2.** (*frantic*) febril

few [fju:] <-er, -est> **I.** *adj det* **1.** (*small number*) pocos, pocas; **there are ~ things that please him** hay pocas cosas que le agradan; **one of her ~ friends** uno de sus pocos amigos; **quite a ~ people** bastante gente; **not ~er than 100 people** no menos de 100 personas; **the takings are ~** las ganancias son pocas; **to be ~ and far between** ser poquísimos, ser contadísimos **2.** (*some*) algunos, algunas; **they left a ~ boxes** dejaron algunas cajas **II.** *pron* pocos, pocas; **a ~** unos pocos; **I'd like a ~ more** quisiera un poco más; **the ~ who have the book** los pocos que tienen el libro; **the happy/lucky ~** los pocos felices/afortunados

fewer ['fju:əʳ, *Am:* -ɚ] *adj, pron* menos; **no ~ than** nada menos que

fewest ['fju:ɪst] *adj, pron* los menos, las menos

ff *abbr of* **the following** sigs.

fiancé [fɪ'ɒnseɪ, *Am:* ˌfi:ɑ:n'seɪ] *n* prometido *m*

fiancée [fɪ'ɒnseɪ, *Am:* ˌfi:ɑ:n'seɪ] *n* prometida *f*

fiasco [fɪ'æskəʊ, *Am:* -koʊ] <-cos *o* -coes> *n* fiasco *m*

fib [fɪb] <-bb-> *inf* **I.** *vi* decir mentirijillas; **to ~** (**to sb**) **about sth** decir mentirijillas (a alguien) sobre algo **II.** *n* mentirijilla *f,* pepa *f And;* **to tell a ~** (**about sth/sb**) decir una mentirijilla (sobre algo/alguien)

fibber ['fɪbəʳ, *Am:* -ɚ] *n* mentirosillo, -a *m, f*

fiber *n Am,* **fibre** ['faɪbəʳ, *Am:* -bɚ] *n* **1.** fibra *f* **2.** *fig* carácter *m*

fibreglass ['faɪbəglɑ:s, *Am:* -bɚglæs] *n* fibra *f* de vidrio

fibre optic cable *n* cable *m* de fibra óptica **fibre optics** *n + sing vb* transmisión *f* por fibra óptica

fibula ['fɪbjʊlə, *Am:* -jə-] <-s *o* -ae> *n* peroné *m*

fickle ['fɪkl] *adj* inconstante

fiction ['fɪkʃən] *n* **1.** *no pl a.* LIT ficción *f;* **~ writer** escritor(a) *m(f)* de novelas de ficción **2.** (*false statement*) invención *f*

fictional ['fɪkʃənl] *adj* ficticio, -a

fictitious [fɪk'tɪʃəs] *adj* **1.** (*false, untrue*) falso, -a **2.** (*imaginary*) ficticio, -a; **~ character** personaje *m* de ficción

fiddle ['fɪdl] **I.** *vt Brit, inf* (*fraudulently change*) falsificar **II.** *vi* **1.** *inf* (*play the violin*) tocar el violín **2. to ~ with sth** (*fidget with*) juguetear con algo; (*try to repair*) intentar arreglar algo **III.** *n inf* **1.** *Brit* (*fraud*) trampa *f;* **to be on the ~** trapichear **2.** (*violin*) violín *m;* **to play the ~** tocar el violín **3.** *Brit* (*difficult task*) tarea *f* difícil; **it's a ~ to do it** resulta difícil hacerlo ▶**to be** (**as**) **fit as a ~** *inf* estar en plena forma; **to play second ~** desempeñar un papel secundario

fiddler ['fɪdləʳ, *Am:* -lɚ] *n inf* **1.** (*violinist*) violinista *mf* **2.** *Brit* (*fraudster*) tramposo, -a *m, f*

fiddling ['fɪdlɪŋ] **I.** *adj* trivial; **~ restrictions** restricciones *fpl* insignificantes **II.** *n no pl* trampas *fpl*

fiddly ['fɪdli] <-ier, -iest> *adj inf* difícil

fidelity [fɪ'deləti, *Am:* -t̬i] *n no pl* fidelidad *f*

fidget ['fɪdʒɪt] **I.** *vi* agitarse (nerviosamente) **II.** *n* persona *f* inquieta; **to have the ~s** ponerse inquieto

fidgety ['fɪdʒɪti] *adj* inquieto, -a

fiefdom ['fi:fdəm] *n* feudo *m*

field [fi:ld] **I.** *n* **1.** *a.* ELEC, AGR, SPORTS campo *m;* (*meadow*) prado *m* **2.** *+ sing/pl vb* (*contestants*) competidores *mpl;* **to lead the ~** ir en cabeza; **to play the ~** *fig* tantear el terreno **3.** (*sphere of activity*) esfera *f;* **to be outside sb's ~** estar fuera del ámbito de alguien; **it's not my ~** no es de mi competencia **4.** INFOR campo *m* **II.** *vt* **1.** (*return*) **to ~ the ball** recoger la pelota; **to ~ a question** sortear una pregunta **2.** (*candidate*) presentar

field day *n* **1.** MIL maniobras *fpl* **2.** SPORTS día *m* de competición ▶**to have a ~** divertirse muchísimo

fielder ['fi:ldəʳ, *Am:* -dɚ] *n* SPORTS fildeador(a) *m(f)*

field event *n* SPORTS prueba *f* de atletismo **field glasses** *n* prismáticos *mpl* **field mouse** *n* ratón *m* de campo **field sports** *n* *la caza y la pesca*

fieldwork ['fi:ldwɜ:k, *Am:* -wɜ:rk] *n* trabajo *m* de campo

fieldworker *n* investigador(a) *m(f)* de campo

fiend [fi:nd] *n* **1.** (*brute*) demonio *m* **2.** *inf* (*enthusiast*) entusiasta *mf;* **a chess ~** un fanático del ajedrez

fiendish ['fi:ndɪʃ] *adj* **1.** (*cruel*) diabólico, -a **2.** *Brit* (*exceptional*) extraordinario, -a

fierce [fɪəs, *Am:* fɪrs] *adj* <-er, -est> **1.** (*animal*) salvaje **2.** (*love, jealousy*) ardiente; (*hate*) profundo, -a; (*competition, opposition*) intenso, -a; (*debate, discussion*) acalorado, -a; (*fighting*) encarnizado, -a; (*wind*) fuerte **3.** *Am, inf* (*hard*) difícil

fierceness ['fɪəsnɪs, *Am:* 'fɪrs-] *n no pl* **1.** (*wildness*) furia *f* **2.** (*of competition, opposition*) intensidad *f;* (*of emotions*) fogosidad *f* **3.** (*of wind*) ferocidad *f*

fiery ['faɪəri, *Am:* 'faɪri] <-ier, -iest> *adj* **1.** (*heat*) abrasador(a) **2.** (*passionate*) apasionado, -a **3.** (*intensely spiced*) muy picante

FIFA ['fi:fə] *n abbr of* **Federation of International Football Association** FIFA *f*

fife [faɪf] *n* pífano *m*

fifteen [ˌfɪf'ti:n] **I.** *adj* quince **II.** *n* quince *m; s. a.* **eight**

fifteenth **I.** *adj* decimoquinto, -a **II.** *n* **1.** (*order*) decimoquinto, -a *m, f* **2.** (*date*) quince *m* **3.** (*fraction*) quinceavo *m;* (*part*) decimaquinta parte *f; s. a.* **eighth**

fifth [fɪfθ] **I.** *adj* quinto, -a **II.** *n* **1.** (*order*) quinto, -a *m, f* **2.** (*date*) cinco *m* **3.** (*fraction*) quinto *m;* (*part*) quinta parte *f; s. a.* **eighth**

fiftieth ['fɪftiəθ] **I.** *adj* quincuagésimo, -a **II.** *n no pl* (*order*) quincuagésimo, -a *m, f;* (*fraction*) quincuagésimo *m;* (*part*) quincuagésima parte *f; s. a.* **eighth**

fifty ['fɪfti] **I.** *adj* cincuenta **II.** <-ies> *n* cincuenta *m; s. a.* **eighty**

fig [fɪg] *n* **1.** (*fruit*) higo *m* **2.** (*tree*) higuera *f* ►**I don't give** [*o* **care**] **a ~ about it!** !me importa un comino!; **to be not worth a ~** no valer nada

fig. **I.** *n abbr of* **figure** fig. **II.** *adj abbr of* **figurative** fig.

fight [faɪt] **I.** *n* **1.** (*physical*) pelea *f;* (*argument*) disputa *f;* **to put up a ~** defenderse bien **2.** MIL combate *m* **3.** (*struggle*) lucha *f;* **the ~ against AIDS** la lucha contra el SIDA **4.** *no pl* (*spirit*) combatividad *f;* **to show some ~** enseñar los dientes **II.** <fought, fought> *vi* **1.** (*exchange blows*) pelear; MIL combatir; **to ~ with each other** pelearse; **to ~ with sb** (*against*) luchar contra alguien; (*on same side*) luchar junto a alguien **2.** (*dispute*) discutir; **to ~ over sth** discutir por algo; **to ~ about sth** discutir sobre algo **3.** (*struggle to overcome*) luchar; **to ~ for/against sth** luchar por/contra algo **III.** *vt* **1.** (*exchange blows with, argue with*) pelearse con **2.** (*wage war, do battle*) luchar con; **to ~ a battle** librar una batalla; **to ~ a duel** batirse en duelo **3.** (*struggle to overcome*) combatir; **to ~ a case** LAW negar una acusación **4.** (*struggle to obtain*) **to ~ one's way through the crowd** hacerse paso entre la multitud; **to ~ one's way to the top** hacerse camino luchando hasta la cima

◆**fight back** **I.** *vi* (*counter-attack*) contraatacar; (*defend oneself*) defenderse **II.** *vt* **to ~ one's tears** contener las lágrimas

◆**fight off** *vt* (*repel*) rechazar; (*master, resist*) resistir; **to ~ the cold/depression** luchar por no sucumbir ante el frío/la depresión

◆**fight on** *vi* seguir luchando

fighter ['faɪtə^r, *Am:* -t̬ɚ] *n* **1.** (*person*) luchador(a) *m(f)* **2.** AVIAT caza *m*

fighting ['faɪtɪŋ, *Am:* -t̬ɪŋ] **I.** *n no pl* lucha *f;* (*battle*) combate *m* **II.** *adj* combativo, -a; **~ spirit** espirítu *m* de lucha ►**there's a ~ chance that ...** existen grandes posibilidades de que... *+subj*

figment ['fɪgmənt] *n* **a ~ of the imagination** un producto de la imaginación

figurative ['fɪgjərətɪv, *Am:* -jɚət̬ɪv] *adj* **1.** LING figurado, -a **2.** ART figurativo, -a

figuratively *adv* en sentido figurado

figure ['fɪgə^r, *Am:* -jɚ] **I.** *n* **1.** (*shape*) figura *f;* **mother ~** figura materna; **a fine ~ of a man** un hombre de físico imponente; **to cut a fine ~** causar buena impresión; **to cut a sorry ~** parecer ridículo; **to keep one's ~** guardar la línea **2.** ART estatua *f;* (*human being*) figura *f* **3.** (*digit*) dígito *m;* (*numeral*) cifra *f;* **column of ~s** columna *f* de números; **to have a head for ~s** ser bueno para los números; **to be good at ~s** saber de aritmética; **in round ~s** en cifras redondas; **single ~s** cifras de un sólo dígito; **double ~s** cifras de dos dígitos **4.** (*price*) precio *m;* **a high ~** una gran suma de dinero **5.** (*diagram*) figura *f;* (*illustration*) ilustración *f* **II.** *vt* **1.** *Am* (*think*) figurarse; **to ~ that ...** figurarse que... **2.** (*in diagram*) representar **3.** (*calculate*) calcular **III.** *vi* (*feature*) figurar; **to ~ in sth** figurar en algo; **to ~ as sth/sb** figurar como algo/alguien; **that ~s** *Am* es natural

◆**figure out** *vt* (*comprehend*) entender; (*work out*) resolver; **to ~ why ...** explicarse por qué...

figurehead ['fɪgəhed, *Am:* -jɚ-] *n* **1.** NAUT mascarón *m* de proa **2.** *fig* testaferro *m*

figure skater *n* patinador(a) *m(f)* artístico, -a

figure skating *n* patinaje *m* artístico

Fiji ['fi:dʒi:] *n* **the ~ Islands** las Islas Fiji

Fijian [fɪ'dʒi:ən] **I.** *adj* de Fiji **II.** *n* habitante *mf* de (las Islas) Fiji

filament ['fɪləmənt] *n* filamento *m*

filch [fɪltʃ] *vt inf* birlar

file[1] [faɪl] **I.** *n* **1.** (*folder*) carpeta *f* **2.** (*record*) expediente *m;* **to open a ~** abrir un expediente; **to keep sth on ~** guardar algo archivado **3.** INFOR fichero *m,* archivo *m* **4.** (*row*) fila *f;* **in single ~** en fila india **II.** *vt* **1.** (*record*) archivar, failear *AmC, RíoPl* **2.** (*present: claim, complaint*) presentar; **to ~ a petition** interponer una demanda **III.** *vi* **1.** LAW **to ~ for bankruptcy** declararse en quiebra; **to ~ for divorce** presentar una demanda de divorcio **2.** (*move in line*) desfilar

◆**file away** *vt* archivar

file[2] [faɪl] **I.** *n* (*tool*) lima *f* **II.** *vt* limar; **to ~ one's nails** limarse las uñas **III.** *vi* **~ down sth** limar algo; **to ~ through sth** partir algo con una lima

◆**file in** *vi* entrar en fila

◆**file out** *vi* salir en fila

file manager *n* administrador *m* de ficheros **file name** *n* nombre *m* de fichero

filial ['fɪliəl] *adj form* filial

filibuster ['fɪlɪbʌstəʳ, *Am:* -tɚ] *vi* POL usar maniobras obstruccionistas

filigree ['fɪlɪgriː] *n no pl* filigrana *f*

filing ['faɪlɪŋ] *n* **1.** *no pl* (*archiving*) clasificación *f* **2.** LAW presentación *f* **3.** *pl* (*bits of metal*) limaduras *fpl*

filing cabinet *n* archivador *m*

Filipino [fɪlɪ'piːnəʊ, *Am:* -noʊ] **I.** *adj* filipino, -a **II.** *n* filipino, -a *m, f*

fill [fɪl] **I.** *vt* **1.** (*make full*) llenar; (*space*) ocupar; **to ~ a vacancy** cubrir una vacante; **to ~ a vacuum** llenar un vacío; **to ~ a need** satisfacer una necesidad; **to ~ a need in the market** satisfacer una demanda del mercado **2.** (*seal*) empastar, emplomar *AmL* **3.** GASTR rellenar **4.** (*fulfil: order, requirement*) cumplir **II.** *vi* llenarse **III.** *n* **to drink/eat one's ~** hartarse de beber/comer; **to have one's ~ of sth** estar harto de algo

◆**fill in** **I.** *vt* **1.** (*seal opening*) llenar; **to ~ a hole** tapar un agujero **2.** (*document*) rellenar **3.** (*colour in*) colorear **4.** (*infor*) informar; **to fill sb in on the details** poner a alguien al corriente de los detalles **5.** (*time*) ocupar **II.** *vi* **to ~ (for sb)** hacer las veces (de alguien)

◆**fill out** **I.** *vt* (*document*) rellenar **II.** *vi* (*put on weight*) engordar

◆**fill up** **I.** *vt* llenar; (*completely*) colmar; **to fill oneself up** llenarse el estómago **II.** *vi* llenarse

filler ['fɪləʳ, *Am:* -ɚ] *n* **1.** (*sealing material*) masilla *f* **2.** TV relleno *m*

fillet ['fɪlɪt] **I.** *n* filete *m* **II.** *vt* cortar en filetes; **to ~ a fish** cortar un pescado en filetes

fillet steak *n* solomillo *m*

filling **I.** *n* **1.** (*substance*) relleno *m* **2.** (*in tooth*) empaste *m*, emplomadura *f AmL* **II.** *adj* sólido, -a; **to be ~** llenar el estómago

filling station *n* gasolinera *f*, bencinera *f Chile*, grifo *m Perú*

fillip ['fɪlɪp] *n* estímulo *m;* **to provide a ~ to sb** estimular a alguien; **to give sb a (big) ~** dar un (gran) estímulo a alguien

film [fɪlm] **I.** *n* **1.** PHOT película *f;* **to make a ~** hacer una película; **to see [*o* watch] a ~** ver una película **2.** (*fine coating*) capa *f;* **a ~ of oil** una película de aceite **II.** *vt* filmar **III.** *vi* rodar

film buff *n* cinéfilo, -a *m, f* **film camera** *n* cámara *f* cinematográfica **film director** *n* director(a) *m(f)* de cine **film star** *n* estrella *f* de cine **film studio** *n* estudio *m* de cine

filter ['fɪltəʳ, *Am:* -t̬ɚ] **I.** *n* filtro *m;* **traffic ~** *Brit* semáforo *m* con flecha verde de giro **II.** *vt* filtrar **III.** *vi* filtrarse

◆**filter out** **I.** *vi* llegar a saberse **II.** *vt* quitar filtrando

◆**filter through** *vi* filtrarse

filter bed *n* lecho *m* de filtración **filter lane** *n* carril *m* de giro **filter paper** *n* papel *m* de filtro **filter tip** *n* filtro *m*

filth [fɪlθ] *n no pl* **1.** (*dirt*) mugre *f;* (*excrement*) excrementos *mpl* **2.** (*obscenity*) obscenidad *f*

filthy ['fɪlθi] **I.** *adj* **1.** (*very dirty*) inmundo, -a; (*weather*) asqueroso, -a **2.** *inf* (*obscene*) obsceno, -a **II.** *adv inf* **to be ~ rich** estar forrado

filtration [fɪl'treɪʃən] *n no pl* filtración *f*

fin [fɪn] *n* aleta *f*

final ['faɪnl] **I.** *adj* **1.** (*last*) final; **~ instalment** último plazo *m* **2.** (*irrevocable*) definitivo, -a; **to have the ~ say (on sth)** tener la última palabra (sobre algo); **and that's ~** *inf* y sanseacabó **II.** *n* **1.** SPORTS final *f;* **to get (through) to the ~** llegar a la final **2.** *pl* UNIV examen *m* de fin de carrera; **to take one's ~s** hacer los exámenes de fin de carrera

finale [fɪ'nɑːli, *Am:* -'næli] *n* final *m;* **grand ~** gran escena final

finalist ['faɪnəlɪst] *n* finalista *mf*

finality [faɪ'næləti, *Am:* -t̬i] *n no pl* **1.** (*irreversibility*) finalidad *f* **2.** (*determination*) resolución *f*

finalize ['faɪnəlaɪz] *vt* ultimar

finally ['faɪnəli] *adv* **1.** (*at long last*) finalmente; (*expressing impatience*) por fin **2.** (*in conclusion*) en conclusión **3.** (*irrevocably*) definitivamente; (*decisively*) de forma decisiva

finance ['faɪnænts] *vt* financiar

finance company *n,* **finance house** *n* sociedad *f* financiera

finances ['faɪnæntsɪz] *npl* finanzas *fpl*

financial [faɪ'næntʃəl] *adj* financiero, -a; (*problem*) monetario, -a; **sb's ~ affairs** los asuntos financieros de alguien

financial adviser *n* asesor(a) *m(f)* financiero **financial year** *n* año *m* fiscal

financier [faɪ'næntsiəʳ, *Am:* fɪ'næntsiɚ] *n* financiero, -a *m, f*, financista *mf AmL*

finch [fɪntʃ] *n* pinzón *m*

find [faɪnd] **I.** <found, found> *vt* **1.** (*lost object, person*) encontrar **2.** (*locate*) localizar, hallar; **to ~ support** encontrar apoyo; **to ~ happiness with sb** descubrir la felicidad con alguien; **to ~ oneself somewhere** encontrarse en algún sitio; **to be nowhere to be found** no encontrarse por ningún sitio; **to ~ no reason why ...** no hallar razón alguna por la que...; **to ~ (the) time** sacar tiempo; **to ~ excuses** buscar pretextos; **to ~ the strength (to do sth)** hallar las fuerzas (para hacer algo); **to ~ (enough) money** conseguir (suficiente) dinero **3.** (*experience*) sentir; **to ~ oneself alone** sentirse solo **4.** (*conclude*) **to ~ sb guilty/innocent** declarar a alguien culpable/inocente **5.** (*discover*) descubrir **II.** *n* hallazgo *m*

◆**find out** **I.** *vt* descubrir; (*dishonesty*) desenmascarar; **to ~ when/where/who ...** averiguar cuándo/dónde/quién... **II.** *vi* **to ~ about sth/sb** informarse sobre algo/alguien

finder ['faɪndəʳ, *Am:* -dɚ] *n* (*of sth*

unknown) descubridor(a) *m(f)*; (*of sth lost*) persona *f* que encuentra

finding ['faɪndɪŋ] *n* **1.** LAW fallo *m* **2.** (*recommendation*) recomendación *f* **3.** (*discovery*) descubrimiento *m*

fine[1] [faɪn] **I.** *adj* **1.** (*slender, light*) fino, -a; (*feature*) delicado, -a; (*nuance*) sutil **2.** (*good*) bueno, -a; (*satisfactory*) satisfactorio, -a; ~ **weather** buen tiempo *m*; **to be ~ by sb** estar bien para alguien; **that's all very ~, but ...** está todo muy bien, pero... **3.** (*excellent*) excelente; **the ~st wines in the world** los vinos más selectos del mundo; **to have a ~ time doing sth** pasarlo bien haciendo algo; ~ **words** *iron* palabras *fpl* valientes; **to appeal to sb's ~r feelings** apelar a los mejores sentimientos de alguien **4.** (*deep*) profundo, -a **II.** *adv* **1.** (*all right*) muy bien; **to feel ~** sentirse bien; **to work ~** funcionar bien **2.** (*fine-grained*) fino, -a ►**to cut it ~** dejar algo para el último momento

fine[2] [faɪn] **I.** *n* multa *f*, boleta *f AmS* **II.** *vt* multar

fine arts *n* bellas artes *fpl*

fineness *n no pl* (*lightness*) fineza *f*; (*delicacy, ornateness*) delicadeza *f*

finery ['faɪnəri] *n no pl* **in all one's ~** con las mejores galas

finesse [fɪ'nes] *n no pl* **1.** (*elegance*) fineza *f* **2.** (*skill*) habilidad *f*

fine-tooth comb [ˌfaɪntuːθ'kəʊm, *Am:* ˌfaɪntuːθ'koʊm] *n* **to go through sth with a ~** revisar algo a fondo

finger ['fɪŋgəʳ, *Am:* -gɚ] **I.** *n* dedo *m*; **little ~** dedo meñique ►**to be able to be counted on the ~s of one hand** poderse contar con los dedos de una mano; **to have a ~ in every pie** meter baza en todo; **to have one's ~ on the pulse** estar al tanto de lo que pasa; **to put one's ~ on the spot** poner el dedo en la llaga; **to be all ~s and thumbs** *Brit, Aus* ser terriblemente desmañado; **to catch sb with their ~s in the till** pillar a alguien robando (en la empresa); **to get/have one's ~s burnt** pillarse los dedos *fig*; **to have sb wrapped round one's little ~** hacer que alguien baile al son que le tocan; **to get one's ~ out** *inf* espabilarse; **to keep one's ~s crossed** tener los dedos cruzados; **to lay a ~ on sb** poner la mano encima a alguien; **to not lift a ~** no mover ni un dedo **II.** *vt* **1.** (*handle*) manosear **2.** *inf* (*reveal*) delatar; **to ~ sb to the police** denunciar a alguien a la policía

fingering ['fɪŋgərɪŋ] *n no pl* digitación *f*

fingermark ['fɪŋgəmaːk, *Am:* -gɚmaːrk] *n* huella *f* (dactilar) **fingernail** *n* uña *f* **fingerprint** **I.** *n* huella *f* dactilar **II.** *vt* **to ~ sb** tomar las huellas dactilares a alguien **fingertip** *n* punta *f* del dedo; **to have sth at one's ~s** tener algo a mano; *fig* saber(se) algo al dedillo

finicky ['fɪnɪki] *adj* **1.** (*person*) melindroso, -a **2.** (*job*) delicado, -a

finish ['fɪnɪʃ] **I.** *n* **1.** (*end*) final *m*, fin *m*; SPORTS meta *f*; **to be in at the ~** estar presente en la conclusión **2.** (*sealing, varnishing: of fabric*) acabado *m*; (*of furniture*) pulido *m* **II.** *vi* terminar(se), acabar(se); **to ~ doing sth** terminar de hacer algo; **to ~ by saying that ...** concluir diciendo que... **III.** *vt* **1.** (*bring to end*) terminar, acabar; **to ~ school** terminar los estudios; **to ~ a sentence** completar una oración **2.** (*make final touches to*) acabar

◆**finish off** **I.** *vt* **1.** (*end*) terminar, acabar **2.** (*defeat*) acabar con **3.** *Am, inf* (*murder*) liquidar **II.** *vi* concluir

◆**finish up** **I.** *vi* **to ~ at** ir a parar en **II.** *vt* (*food, drink*) terminar

◆**finish with** *vt* terminar con; **to ~ sb** romper con alguien; **to ~ politics** abandonar la política

finished *adj* **1.** (*product*) terminado, -a, acabado, -a **2.** *inf* (*tired*) hecho, -a polvo

finishing line *n*, **finishing post** *n* línea *f* de meta

finite ['faɪnaɪt] *adj a.* LING finito, -a

Finland ['fɪnlənd] *n* Finlandia *f*

Finn [fɪn] *n* finlandés, -esa *m, f*

Finnish ['fɪnɪʃ] **I.** *adj* finlandés, -esa **II.** *n* finlandés *m*

fiord [fɪ'ɔːd, *Am:* fjɔːrd] *n* fiordo *m*

fir [fɜːʳ, *Am:* fɜːr] *n* abeto *m*

fir cone *n Brit* piña *f*

fire ['faɪəʳ, *Am:* 'faɪɚ] **I.** *n* **1.** (*flames*) fuego *m*; (*in fireplace*) lumbre *f*; (*accidental*) incendio *m*; **to set sth on ~** prender fuego a algo; **to catch ~** encenderse; **forest ~** incendio forestal **2.** TECH calefacción *f*; (*stove*) hornillo *m* **3.** MIL **to open ~ on sb** abrir fuego contra alguien; **to be under ~** MIL estar en la línea de fuego; *fig* ser criticado **4.** (*passion*) pasión *f* ►**there's no smoke without ~** *prov* cuando el río suena, agua lleva *prov*; **to go through ~ and water** afrontar todos los peligros; **to set the world on ~** hacerse famoso; **to hang ~** suspender operaciones; **to play with ~** jugar con fuego **II.** *vt* **1.** (*set fire to*) encender; (*ceramics*) cocer **2.** (*weapon*) disparar; **to ~ questions at sb** bombardear a alguien con preguntas **3.** *inf* (*dismiss*) despedir, botar *AmL*, fletar *Arg* **4.** (*inspire*) inspirar **III.** *vi* **1.** (*with gun*) disparar; **to ~ at sb** disparar contra alguien **2.** AUTO encenderse

◆**fire away** *vi inf* seguir adelante

◆**fire off** *vt* (*letter, reply*) despachar enseguida

fire alarm *n* alarma *f* contra incendios **firearm** *n* arma *f* de fuego **fireball** *n* bola *f* de fuego **firebrand** *n* **1.** (*torch*) tea *f* **2.** *fig* revoltoso, -a *m, f* **firebreak** *n* cortafuegos *m inv* **firebrick** *n* ladrillo *m* refractario **fire brigade** *n Brit* cuerpo *m* de bomberos **firecracker** *n* petardo *m* **fire department** *n Am* cuerpo *m* de bomberos **fire-eater** *n* tragafuegos *mf inv* **fire engine** *n* bomba *m* de incendios **fire escape** *n* escalera *f* de incen-

F

dios **fire exit** *n* salida *f* de incendios **fire extinguisher** *n* extintor *m* de incendios **firefighter** *n* bombero *mf* **firefly** *n* luciérnaga *f*, cocuyo *m AmL* **fireguard** *n* guardafuegos *m inv* **fire house** *n Am* parque *m* de bomberos **fire insurance** *n* seguro *m* contra incendios **fire irons** *npl* utensilios *mpl* de chimenea **fireman** <-men> *n* bombero *m* **fireplace** *n* chimenea *f*, hogar *m*

fireproof ['faɪəʳpruːf, *Am:* 'faɪɚ-] *adj* a prueba de incendios

fire-raiser *n Brit* pirómano, -a *m, f* **fire--raising** *n Brit* piromanía *f* **fireside** *n* hogar *m* **fire station** *n* parque *m* de bomberos **fire wall** *n* muro *m* cortafuegos **firewater** *n no pl, inf* aguardiente *m* **firewoman** <-women> *n* mujer *f* bombero **firewood** *n no pl* leña *f* **firework** *n* **1.** fuego *m* artificial **2.** *pl, fig* explosión *f* (de cólera)

firing ['faɪərɪŋ, *Am:* 'faɪɚ-] *n* **1.** MIL disparo *m* **2.** (*of ceramic*) cocción *f*

firing line *n* línea *f* de fuego **firing squad** *n* pelotón *m* de fusilamiento

firm¹ [fɜːm, *Am:* fɜːrm] **I.** *adj* **1.** (*secure*) firme; (*strong*) fuerte; **a ~ offer** una oferta en firme **2.** (*dense, solid*) duro, -a **3.** (*resolute*) decidido, -a **4.** (*strict*) estricto, -a **II.** *adv* firmemente; **to stand ~** mantenerse firme

firm² [fɜːm, *Am:* fɜːrm] *n* (*company*) empresa *f*; **~ of lawyers** bufete *m* de abogados

firmament ['fɜːməmənt, *Am:* 'fɜːr-] *n no pl* firmamento *m*

firmness ['fɜːmnɪs, *Am:* 'fɜːrm-] *n no pl* **1.** (*hardness*) dureza *f* **2.** (*strictness*) firmeza *f*

first [fɜːst, *Am:* fɜːrst] **I.** *adj* (*earliest*) primero, -a; **for the ~ time** por primera vez; **at ~ sight** a primera vista; **the ~ December** el primero de diciembre ►**~ and foremost** ante todo **II.** *adv* primero; (*firstly*) en primer lugar; **~ of all** ante todo; **at ~** al principio; **to go head ~** meterse de cabeza ►**~ come ~ served** *inf* por orden de llegada **III.** *n* **1. the ~** el primero, la primera; **from the** (**very**) **~** desde el principio **2.** *Brit* UNIV *nota más alta que se puede obtener al final de los estudios universitarios*

first aid *n* primeros auxilios *mpl* **first aid box** *n* botiquín *m* de primeros auxilios

first-born ['fɜːstbɔːn, *Am:* 'fɜːrstbɔːrn] **I.** *adj* primogénito, -a **II.** *n* primogénito, -a *m, f*

first-class **I.** *adj* de primera clase **II.** *adv* **to travel ~** viajar en primera

first cousin *n* primo, -a *m, f* hermano **first floor** *n Aus, Brit* primer piso *m*; *Am* planta *f* baja

first-hand [ˌfɜːst'hænd, *Am:* ˌfɜːrst-] **I.** *adj* de primera mano **II.** *adv* directamente

first lady *n Am* **the ~** la Primera Dama

firstly ['fɜːstli, *Am:* 'fɜːrst-] *adv* en primer lugar

first name *n* nombre *m* (de pila) **first night** *n* noche *f* de estreno **first offender** *n persona que comete un delito por primera vez* **first person** *n* LING primera persona *f*

first-rate [ˌfɜːst'reɪt, *Am:* ˌfɜːrst-] *adj* de primer orden

first strike *n* primer golpe *m*

firth [fɜːθ, *Am:* fɜːrθ] *n Scot* estuario *m*

fiscal ['fɪskl] *adj* fiscal

fish [fɪʃ] **I.** <-(es)> *n* **1.** ZOOL pez *m* **2.** *no pl* GASTR pescado *m*; **~ and chips** pescado frito con patatas fritas ►**to be a big ~ in a small pond** ser un pez gordo (en un sitio pequeño); **there are plenty more ~ in the sea** hay mucho más donde elegir; (**like**) **a ~ out of water** como pez fuera del agua; **to have bigger ~ to fry** tener cosas más importantes que hacer; **an odd ~** un tipo raro **II.** *vi* pescar; **to ~ for information** ir a la caza de información **III.** *vt* pescar

fishbone ['fɪʃbəʊn, *Am:* -boʊn] *n* espina *f* de pescado

fishcake ['fɪʃkeɪk] *n* croqueta *f* de pescado

fisherman ['fɪʃəmən, *Am:* -ɚ-] <-men> *n* pescador *m*

fishery ['fɪʃəri] *n* pesquería *f*

fishfinger *n* palito *m* de merluza **fish-hook** *n* anzuelo *m*

fishing **I.** *n no pl* pesca *f* **II.** *adj* pesquero, -a

fishing grounds *npl* zona *f* de pesca **fishing line** *n* sedal *m* **fishing rod** *n Brit, Aus* caña *f* de pescar **fishing tackle** *n* avío *m* de pesca

fishmonger ['fɪʃmʌŋgəʳ, *Am:* -gɚ] *n Brit* pescadero, -a *m, f*

fishpond ['fɪʃpɒnd, *Am:* -pɑːnd] *n* estanque *m* para peces

fishy ['fɪʃi] <-ier, -iest> *adj* **1.** (*taste*) que sabe a pescado; (*smell*) que huele a pescado **2.** *inf* (*dubious*) dudoso, -a ►**to smell ~** oler a chamusquina

fissile ['fɪsaɪl, *Am:* -ɪl] *adj* físil

fission ['fɪʃən] *n no pl* PHYS fisión *f*; BIO escisión *f*

fissure ['fɪʃəʳ, *Am:* -ɚ] *n* fisura *f*

fist [fɪst] *n* puño *m*; **to clench one's ~s** cerrar los puños; **to shake one's ~ at sb** amenazar a alguien con el puño

fit¹ [fɪt] **I.** <-tt-> *adj* **1.** (*apt, suitable*) apto, -a, apropiado, -a; (*competent*) capaz; **~ to eat** bueno para comer; **it's not ~ to eat** no se puede comer **2.** (*ready*) listo, -a **3.** SPORTS en forma **4.** MED sano, -a ►**to be ~ to be tied** *Am* estar fuera de sí **II.** <-tt-> *vt* **1.** (*adapt*) ajustar; **to ~ the key in the lock** meter la llave en la cerradura **2.** (*clothes*) sentar bien **3.** (*facts*) corresponder con **4.** TECH caber en, encajar en **III.** *vi* <-tt-> **1.** (*be correct size*) ir bien **2.** (*correspond*) corresponder **IV.** *n no pl* ajuste *m*

◆**fit in** **I.** *vi* **1.** (*conform*) encajar **2.** (*get on well*) llevarse bien **II.** *vt* tener tiempo para

◆**fit out** *vt* equipar

◆**fit together** *vi* encajar

◆**fit up** *vt* equipar

fit² [fɪt] *n* **1.** MED ataque *m*; **coughing ~** acceso *m* de tos **2.** *inf* (*outburst of rage*) arranque *m*; **they were in ~s of laughter** se morían de (la) risa; **in ~s and starts** a empujones

fitful ['fɪtfəl] *adj* espasmódico, -a; (*breath*) entrecortado, -a; (*gusts*) intermitente; (*sleep*) irregular

fitment ['fɪtmənt] *n Brit* mueble *m*

fitness ['fɪtnɪs] *n no pl* **1.** (*competence, suitability*) conveniencia *f* **2.** (*good condition*) (buena) condición *f* física; (*health*) (buena) salud *f*

fitted ['fɪtɪd, *Am:* 'fɪt̬-] *adj* (*adapted, suitable*) idóneo, -a; (*tailor-made*) a medida; ~ **kitchen** cocina *f* empotrada

fitter ['fɪtəʳ, *Am:* 'fɪt̬ɚ] *n* técnico, -a *m, f*

fitting ['fɪtɪŋ, *Am:* 'fɪt̬-] **I.** *n* **1.** *pl* (*fixtures*) accesorios *mpl* **2.** (*of clothes*) prueba *f* **II.** *adj* apropiado, -a

five [faɪv] **I.** *adj* cinco **II.** *n* cinco *m;* **gimme ~!** *Am, inf* ¡choca esos cinco!; *s. a.* **eight**

fivefold *adj* quíntuple

fiver ['faɪvəʳ, *Am:* -vɚ] *n Brit, inf* billete *m* de 5 libras; *Am, inf* billete *m* de 5 dólares

fix [fɪks] **I.** *vt* **1.** (*fasten*) sujetar; **to ~ sth in one's mind** grabar algo en la memoria; **to ~ sb with one's eyes** fijar los ojos en alguien **2.** (*determine*) fijar; **to ~ a date** fijar una fecha **3.** (*arrange*) arreglar; **to ~ one's face** *inf* maquillarse **4.** (*repair*) arreglar **5.** *Am, inf* (*food*) preparar **6.** *inf* (*manipulate: election, result*) amañar **7.** *inf* (*take revenge on*) ajustar las cuentas con; **I'll ~ him** me las pagará **8.** PHYS, PHOT (*colour*) fijar **II.** *n* **1.** *inf* (*dilemma*) aprieto *m;* **to be in a ~** estar en un aprieto **2.** *inf* (*shot*) chute *m,* pichicata *f Arg* **3.** AVIAT, AUTO posición *f*

◆**fix on** *vt* **1.** (*choose*) escoger **2.** (*make definite*) fijar

◆**fix up** *vt* **1.** (*supply with*) **to fix sb up (with sth)** proveer a alguien (de algo) **2.** (*arrange*) organizar **3.** (*repair*) arreglar

◆**fix upon** *vt s.* **fix on**

fixation [fɪk'seɪʃən] *n* fijación *f*

fixed *adj* fijo, -a; **to be of no ~ abode** LAW no tener domicilio permanente

fixedly ['fɪksɪdli] *adv* fijamente

fixer *n inf* chanchullero, -a *m, f*

fixing bath *n* baño *m* fijador

fixity ['fɪksəti, *Am:* -əṯi] *n no pl, form* fijeza *f*

fixture ['fɪkstʃəʳ, *Am:* -tʃɚ] *n* **1.** (*furniture*) instalación *f* fija; **~s and fittings** muebles *mpl* y accesorios **2.** *Brit, Aus* SPORTS partido *m*

fizz [fɪz] **I.** *vi* burbujear **II.** *n no pl* **1.** (*bubble, frothiness*) efervescencia *f* **2.** *inf* (*champagne*) champán *m* **3.** *Am, Aus* (*sweet lemonade*) gaseosa *f*

fizzle ['fɪzl] *vi* chisporrotear

fizzy ['fɪzi] <-ier, -iest> *adj* (*bubbly*) efervescente; (*carbonated*) gaseoso, -a

fjord [fɪ'ɔːd, *Am:* fjɔːrd] *n* fiordo *m*

flabbergast ['flæbəgɑːst, *Am:* -ɚgæst] *vt inf* dejar sin habla

flabby ['flæbi] <-ier, -iest> *adj pej* **1.** (*body*) fofo, -a **2.** (*weak*) débil

flaccid ['flæksɪd] *adj* flácido, -a; *fig* flojo, -a

flag¹ [flæg] **I.** *n* **1.** (*national*) bandera *f;* (*pennant*) estandarte *m;* **to raise a ~** izar una bandera; **to fly the ~** *fig* hacer acto de presencia; **to keep the ~ flying** *fig* resisitir **2.** (*marker*) señalizador *m* **II.** <-gg-> *vt* (*mark*) señalar; (*label computer data*) etiquetar **III.** <-gg-> *vi* flaquear

flag² [flæg] *n* (*stone*) losa *f*

flag day *n Brit: día de recaudación de fondos;* **Flag Day** *Am* Día *m* de la Bandera

flagellate ['flædʒəleɪt] *vt* flagelar

flagon ['flægən] *n* jarro *m*

flagpole ['flægpəʊl, *Am:* -poʊl] *n* asta *f*

flagrant ['fleɪgrənt] *adj* descarado, -a

flagship ['flægʃɪp] *n* buque *m* insignia

flagstaff ['flægstɑːf, *Am:* -stæf] *n s.* **flagpole**

flail [fleɪl] *vi* **to ~ (about)** agitarse

flair [fleəʳ, *Am:* fler] *n no pl* **1.** (*genius*) don *m* **2.** (*style*) estilo *m*

flak [flæk] *n* **1.** MIL fuego *m* antiaéreo **2.** (*criticism*) críticas *fpl*

flake [fleɪk] **I.** *vi* (*skin*) pelarse; (*paint*) desconcharse; (*wood*) astillarse; (*plaster*) descascararse **II.** *n* (*peeling*) hojuela *f;* (*shaving, sliver*) viruta *f;* (*of paint, wood*) lámina *f;* (*of plaster*) placa *f;* (*of skin*) escama *f;* (*of snow*) copo *m*

◆**flake out** *vi inf* caer rendido

flaky ['fleɪki] <-ier, -iest> *adj* **1.** (*skin*) escamoso, -a; (*paint*) de láminas **2.** *inf* (*strange*) chiflado, -a

flaky pastry *n* hojaldre *m*

flamboyant [flæm'bɔɪənt] *adj* (*manner, person*) exuberante; (*air, clothes*) vistoso, -a

flame [fleɪm] **I.** *n* **1.** llama *f;* **to be in ~s** arder en llamas; **to go up in ~s** ser presa de las llamas; **to burst into ~** estallar en llamas **2.** (*lover*) **(old) ~** antiguo amor *m* **II.** *vi* (*blaze, burn*) llamear; (*glare*) brillar

flaming ['fleɪmɪŋ] *adj* **1.** (*burning*) en llamas **2.** *fig* (*quarrel*) acalorado, -a **3.** *Brit, inf* (*as intensifier*) condenado, -a

flamingo [flə'mɪŋgəʊ, *Am:* -goʊ] <-(e)s> *n* flamenco *m*

flammable ['flæməbl] *adj Am* inflamable

flan [flæn] *n* tarta *f* (de frutas)

Flanders ['flɑːndəz] *n* Flandes *m*

flange [flændʒ] *n* pestaña *f*

flank [flæŋk] **I.** *n* (*of person*) costado *m;* (*of animal*) ijada *f,* verija *f AmL;* (*of hill*) lado *m;* MIL flanco *m* **II.** *vt* flanquear

flannel ['flænl] **I.** *n* **1.** (*material*) franela *f* **2.** *Brit* (*facecloth*) toallita *f* **3.** *pl* (*trousers*) pantalones *mpl* de franela **II.** <-ll-> *vt Brit, Aus, inf* lisonjear **III.** <-ll-> *vi Brit, Aus, inf* hablar con rodeos

flap [flæp] **I.** <-pp-> *vt* (*wings*) batir; (*shake*) sacudir **II.** <-pp-> *vi* **1.** (*wings*) aletear; (*sails*) gualdrapear; (*flag*) ondear **2.** *inf* (*become nervous*) agitarse; **don't ~!** ¡con calma! **III.** *n* **1.** (*of cloth*) faldón *m;* (*of skin*) colgajo *m;* (*of pocket, envelope*) solapa *f;* (*of table*) hoja *f*

F

2. AVIAT flap *m* **3.** (*of wing*) aleteo *m* **4.** *inf* (*panic*) **to get in a ~** ponerse nervioso

flapjack ['flæpdʒæk] *n* **1.** *Brit, Aus* galleta *f* de avena **2.** *Am* (*pancake*) torta *f*, panqueque *m AmL*

flare [fleəʳ, *Am:* fler] **I.** *n* **1.** (*blaze*) llamarada *f;* (*of light*) resplandor *m* **2.** (*signal*) cohete *m* de señales **3.** MIL bengala *f* **4.** (*of clothes*) vuelo *m* **II.** *vi* **1.** (*blaze*) llamear; (*light*) resplandecer **2.** (*trouble*) estallar **3.** (*skirt*) acampanarse **III.** *vt* **to ~ one's nostrils** resoplar

flare-up ['fleəʳʌp, *Am:* 'fler-] *n* estallido *m fig*

flash [flæʃ] **I.** *vt* **1.** (*shine: light*) enfocar; **to ~ a light in sb's eyes** dirigir un rayo de luz a los ojos de alguien **2.** (*show quickly*) mostrar (rápidamente); **to ~ sth on the screen** proyectar algo en la pantalla muy rápidamente **3.** (*communicate*) transmitir; (*smile, look*) lanzar **II.** *vi* **1.** (*lightning*) relampaguear; *fig* (*eyes*) brillar **2.** *inf* (*expose genitals*) exhibirse **3.** (*move swiftly*) **to ~ by** pasar como un rayo **III.** *n* **1.** (*burst*) destello *m;* **~ of inspiration** momento *m* de inspiración; **~ of light(ning)** relámpago *m* **2.** PHOT flash *m* ▶**a ~ in the <u>pan</u>** flor de un día; **<u>like</u> a ~** como un relámpago; **<u>in</u> a ~** en un instante **IV.** <-er, -est> *adj inf* llamativo, -a

◆**flash back** *vi* volver atrás

flashback ['flæʃbæk] *n* CINE, LIT, THEAT escena *f* retrospectiva, flashback *m*

flashbulb ['flæʃbʌlb] *n* bombilla *f* de flash

flasher ['flæʃəʳ, *Am:* -ɚ] *n Brit, inf* exhibicionista *m*

flashgun ['flæʃgʌn] *n* disparador *m* de flash

flashlight ['flæʃlaɪt] *n* linterna *f* eléctrica

flash point *n* **1.** CHEM punto *m* de inflamación **2.** *fig* punto *m* crucial

flashy ['flæʃi] <-ier, -iest> *adj inf* ostentoso, -a, llamativo, -a

flask [flɑːsk, *Am:* flæsk] *n* CHEM matraz *m;* (*thermos*) termo *m;* **hip ~** petaca *f*

flat¹ [flæt] **I.** *adj* <-tt-> **1.** (*surface*) llano, -a, plano, -a; **~ as a pancake** *inf* liso como la palma de la mano **2.** (*unexciting*) deslustrado, -a **3.** (*drink*) sin gas **4.** (*tyre*) desinflado, -a **5.** *Aus, Brit* (*battery*) descargado, -a **6.** (*absolute: refusal, rejection*) categórico, -a; **and that's ~** y no hay más de qué hablar **7.** COM (*fixed*) fijo, -a **8.** MUS desafinado, -a **II.** <-tt-> *adv* **1.** (*level*) horizontalmente; **to lie ~ on one's back** estar boca arriba **2.** *inf* (*absolutely*) completamente ▶**to be ~ <u>broke</u>** no tener ni un centavo; **to <u>fall</u> ~** resultar un fracaso; **<u>in</u> five minutes ~** *inf* en sólo cinco minutos **III.** *n* **1.** (*level surface: of sword, knife*) plano *m;* **the ~ of the hand** la palma de la mano **2.** (*low level ground*) llanura *f;* **salt ~s** salinas *fpl* **3.** *Aus, Brit* (*tyre*) pinchazo *m* **4.** MUS bemol *m*

flat² [flæt] *n Aus, Brit* (*apartment*) piso *m*, apartamento *m Ven, Col,* departamento *m Méx, CSur*

flat feet *npl* pies *mpl* planos

flatfish ['flætfɪʃ] <-(es)> *n* pez *m* pleuronecto

flat-footed [ˌflæt'fʊtɪd, *Am:* -'fʊt̬-] *adj* de pies planos

flatlet ['flætlɪt] *n Brit* piso *m* pequeño, apartamentico *m Ven*

flatly *adv* (*deny, refuse*) rotundamente

flatmate ['flætmeɪt] *n Aus, Brit* compañero, -a *m, f* de piso

flatness *n no pl* **1.** (*of surface*) llanura *f* **2.** (*lack of excitement*) aburrimiento *m*

flatten ['flætn] *vt* **1.** (*make level*) allanar; **to ~ oneself against sth** pegarse contra algo **2.** MUS bajar el tono

flatter ['flætəʳ, *Am:* 'flæt̬ɚ] *vt* **1.** (*gratify vanity*) adular **2.** (*make attractive*) favorecer **3.** (*be proud of*) **to ~ oneself on sth** enorgullecerse de algo

flatterer *n* adulador(a) *m(f)*

flattering *adj* **1.** (*clothes, portrait*) que favorece **2.** (*remark, description*) halagador(a)

flattery ['flætəri, *Am:* 'flæt̬-] *n no pl* adulación *f;* **~ will get you nowhere** adulando no conseguirás tu propósito

flatulence ['flætjʊləns, *Am:* 'flætʃə-] *n no pl, form* flatulencia *f*

flaunt [flɔːnt, *Am:* flɑːnt] *vt* hacer alarde de

flautist ['flɔːtɪst, *Am:* 'flɑːt̬ɪst] *n* flautista *mf*

flavor ['fleɪvəʳ, *Am:* -vɚ] *Am* **I.** *n, vt s.* **flavour II.** *n s.* **flavouring**

flavour ['fleɪvəʳ, *Am:* -vɚ] *Brit, Aus* **I.** *n* **1.** (*taste*) gusto *m;* (*ice cream, fizzy drink*) sabor *m* **2.** *fig* sabor *m;* **a novel with a romantic ~** una novela con sabor romántico **II.** *vt* sazonar

flavouring ['fleɪvərɪŋ] *n Brit, Aus* condimento *m;* (*in industry*) aromatizante *m*

flaw [flɔː, *Am:* flɑː] **I.** *n* (*in machine*) defecto *m;* (*in argument, character*) fallo *m;* (*in cloth*) imperfección *f* **II.** *vt* dañar

flawless ['flɔːlɪs, *Am:* 'flɑː-] *adj* intachable; **~ performance** ejecución *f* perfecta

flax [flæks] *n no pl* lino *m*

flaxen ['flæksn] *adj liter* muy rubio, -a

flay [fleɪ] *vt* **1.** (*animal*) desollar **2.** *fig* despellejar

flea [fliː] *n* pulga *f* ▶**to send sb away with a ~ in his/her <u>ear</u>** echar un buen rapapolvo a alguien

fleabite ['fliːbaɪt] *n* picadura *f* de pulga

fleabitten *adj Brit, inf* miserable

flea market *n* rastrillo *m*

fleck [flek] **I.** *n* (*of colour*) mota *f;* (*of paint*) salpicadura *f* **II.** *vt* salpicar

fled [fled] *pp of* **flee**

fledged [fledʒd] *adj* plumado, -a

fledgeling, fledgling ['fledʒlɪŋ] **I.** *n* (*young bird*) volandero *m* **II.** *adj* (*inexperienced*) inexperto, -a

flee [fliː] <fled> **I.** *vt* (*run away from*) huir de **II.** *vi* (*run away*) escaparse; *liter* desaparecer

fleece [fliːs] **I.** *n* **1.** (*of sheep*) vellón *m* **2.** (*clothing*) borreguillo *m* **II.** *vt* **1.** (*a sheep*) esquilar **2.** *inf* (*cheat*) despojar

fleet[1] [fliːt] *n* 1. NAUT flota *f;* **the British** ~ la armada británica 2. (*of aeroplanes*) escuadrón *m;* **car** ~ parque *m* móvil

fleet[2] [fliːt] <-er, -est> *adj* veloz

fleeting ['fliːtɪŋ, *Am:* -t̬ɪŋ] *adj* (*encounter, romance*) pasajero, -a; (*glance, impression, smile*) efímero, -a; (*moment, opportunity, time*) breve; (*idea*) fugaz

Flemish ['flemɪʃ] *adj* flamenco, -a

flesh [fleʃ] *n no pl* (*body tissue*) carne *f;* (*pulp*) pulpa *f;* **to put** ~ **on an argument/idea** dar cuerpo a un argumento/idea ►**to be** (**only**) ~ **and blood** ser (sólo) de carne y hueso; **it made my** ~ **crawl** se me puso la piel de gallina; **in the** ~ en persona

flesh-coloured *adj Aus, Brit* de color carne

fleshpot ['fleʃpɒt, *Am:* -pɑːt] *n* antro *m* de placer

flesh wound *n* herida *f* superficial

fleshy ['fleʃi] <-ier, -iest> *adj* 1. (*voluminous: person, limb*) gordo, -a; (*fruit*) carnoso, -a 2. (*colour*) de carne

flew [fluː] *pp, pt of* **fly**

flex [fleks] I. *vt* flexionar ►**to** ~ **one's muscles** medir sus fuerzas II. *n* ELEC cable *m*

flexibility [ˌfleksə'bɪləti, *Am:* -t̬i] *n no pl* 1. (*of material*) elasticidad *f* 2. (*of person, approach*) flexibilidad *f*

flexible ['fleksəbl] *adj* 1. (*pliable: material, tubing*) flexible 2. (*arrangement, policy, schedule*) adaptable

flexitime ['fleksɪtaɪm] *n no pl* horario *m* flexible

flick [flɪk] I. *vt* (*with finger*) chasquear; **to** ~ **out one's tongue** lengüetear; **to** ~ **the light switch on/off** encender/apagar la luz; **to** ~ **channels** cambiar los canales II. *n* 1. (*sudden movement, strike*) golpecito *m* 2. **the** ~**s** *pl, inf* (*cinema*) el cine

flicker ['flɪkəʳ, *Am:* -ɚ] I. *vi* parpadear II. *n* parpadeo *m*

flick knife *n Aus, Brit* navaja *f* automática

flier ['flaɪəʳ, *Am:* -ɚ] *n* 1. (*air traveller*) aviador(a) *m(f)* 2. (*leaflet*) folleto *m*

flight [flaɪt] *n* 1. (*act*) vuelo *m;* **the** ~ **of time** el paso del tiempo 2. (*group: of birds*) bandada *f;* (*of aircraft*) escuadrilla *f* 3. (*retreat*) escape *m;* ~ **of investment** fuga *f* de inversión; **to take** ~ darse a la fuga; **to put sb to** ~ poner a alguien en fuga 4. (*series: of stairs*) tramo *m* ►**a** ~ **of fancy** una fantasía

flight attendant *n* auxiliar *mf* de vuelo **flight controller** *n* controlador(a) *m(f)* aéreo, -a **flight deck** *n* 1. (*cockpit*) cabina *f* de pilotaje 2. (*on aircraft carrier*) cubierta *f* de aterrizaje **flight engineer** *n* mecánico *m* de vuelo

flightless *adj* incapaz de volar

flight number *n* número *m* de vuelo **flight path** *n* trayectoria *f* de vuelo

flighty ['flaɪti, *Am:* -t̬i] <-ier, -iest> *adj pej* (*woman*) frívolo, -a

flimsiness ['flɪmzɪnɪs] *n no pl* debilidad *f*

flimsy ['flɪmzi] <-ier, -iest> *adj* 1. (*light: dress, blouse*) ligero, -a 2. (*construction*) débil 3. (*argument, excuse*) poco sólido, -a

flinch [flɪntʃ] *vi* (*in pain*) rechistar; **to** ~ **from doing sth** resistirse a hacer algo

fling [flɪŋ] <flung> I. *vt* (*throw*) lanzar; **to** ~ **oneself in front of a train** arrojarse al tren; **to** ~ **sb into prison** echar a alguien a la cárcel; **to** ~ **accusations at sb** lanzar acusaciones a alguien II. *n inf* 1. (*short pleasant time*) rato *m* de juerga 2. (*relationship*) aventura *f* (amorosa) 3. (*try*) **to have a** ~ **at sth** intentar algo

◆**fling away** *vt* desechar

◆**fling off** *vt* **to** ~ **one's clothes** desvestirse con prisa

◆**fling on** *vt inf* **to** ~ **one's clothes** vestirse de prisa

◆**fling open** *vt* abrir de golpe

◆**fling out** *vt inf* (*throw out*) tirar

flint [flɪnt] *n* pedernal *m*

flip [flɪp] <-pp-> I. *vt* (*turn over quickly*) dar la vuelta a; **to** ~ **a coin** echar a cara o cruz II. *vi* 1. (*turn quickly*) **to** ~ **over** dar una vuelta de campana 2. *inf* (*go mad*) perder la chaveta III. *n* (*toss in the air*) ~ **of a coin** lanzamiento *m* de una moneda

flip chart *n* rotafolio *m*

flip-flop ['flɪpflɒp, *Am:* -flɑːp] *n* chancla *f*

flippancy ['flɪpəntsi] *n no pl* falta *f* de seriedad

flippant ['flɪpənt] *adj* poco serio, -a

flipper ['flɪpəʳ, *Am:* -ɚ] *n* aleta *f*

flipping *adj, adv Brit, inf* (*as intensifier*) maldito, -a

flip side *n* 1. MUS (*of record*) cara *f* B 2. (*of policy, situation*) **the** ~ la otra cara de la moneda

flirt [flɜːt, *Am:* flɜːrt] I. *n* (*woman*) coqueta *f;* (*man*) galanteador *m* II. *vi* 1. (*be sexually attracted*) flirtear 2. (*toy with*) **to** ~ **with sth** jugar con algo

flirtation [flɜː'teɪʃən, *Am:* flɜːr'-] *n* flirteo *m*

flirtatious [flɜː'teɪʃəs, *Am:* flɜːr'-] *adj* (*woman*) coqueta; (*man*) galanteador

flit [flɪt] <-tt-> I. *vi* **to** ~ (**about**) (*bats*) revolotear; (*bees*) volar; (*people*) moverse II. *n Brit, inf* **to do a** (**moonlight**) ~ huir a escondidas

float [fləʊt, *Am:* floʊt] I. *vi* 1. (*in liquid, air*) flotar, boyar *AmL;* **to** ~ **to the surface** salir a la superficie 2. (*move aimlessly*) moverse sin rumbo 3. ECON fluctuar II. *vt* 1. (*keep afloat*) poner a flote 2. ECON, FIN **to** ~ **a business/company** lanzar una empresa/compañía a bolsa 3. (*air*) **to** ~ **an idea/a plan** sugerir una idea/un plan III. *n* 1. NAUT flotador *m;* (*for people*) salvavidas *m inv* 2. (*vehicle*) carroza *f* 3. *Aus, Brit* (*cash*) fondo *m*

◆**float about** *vi,* **float around** *vi inf* (*circulate*) circular; (*people*) moverse sin rumbo; (*rumour*) correr

◆**float off** *vi* irse a la deriva

floatation [fləʊ'teɪʃən, *Am:* floʊ-] *n s.* **flo-**

tation
floating ['fləʊtɪŋ, *Am:* 'floʊt̬ɪŋ] *adj* flotante
flock [flɒk, *Am:* flɑːk] **I.** *n* **1.** (*group: of goats, sheep*) rebaño *m;* (*of birds*) bandada *f,* parvada *f AmL;* (*of people*) multitud *f* **2.** REL grey *f* **II.** *vi* congregarse
floe [fləʊ, *Am:* floʊ] *n* témpano *m*
flog [flɒg, *Am:* flɑːg] <-gg-> *vt* **1.** (*punish*) azotar; *fig* flagelar **2.** *Brit, inf* (*sell*) vender ►**to ~ sth to death** *inf* repetir algo hasta la saciedad
flogging *n* azotaina *f*
flood [flʌd] **I.** *vt* inundar; **the calls for tickets ~ed the switchboard** el aluvión de peticiones de entradas colapsó la centralita; **to ~ an engine** AUTO ahogar un motor **II.** *vi* METEO (*town*) inundarse; (*river*) desbordarse; **refugees have been ~ing in** un aluvión de refugiados ha estado llegando **III.** *n* **1.** METEO inundación *f* **2.** REL **the Flood** el Diluvio **3.** (*outpouring*) torrente *m;* **~ of tears** mar *m* de lágrimas; **~ of products** productos *mpl* a raudales; **~ of abuse** aluvión *m* de insultos; **to let out a ~ of abuse** soltar una retahíla de insultos; **~ of complaints** lluvia *f* de quejas
floodgate ['flʌdgeɪt] *n fig* **to open the ~s to sth** abrir las puertas a algo
floodlight ['flʌdlaɪt] **I.** *n* foco *m* **II.** *vt irr* iluminar (con focos)
floor [flɔːʳ, *Am:* flɔːr] **I.** *n* **1.** (*of room*) suelo *m;* **dance ~** pista *f* de baile; **to take the ~** (*in debate*) tomar la palabra; (*start dancing*) salir a bailar **2.** (*level in building*) piso *m;* **sea ~** fondo *m* del mar ►**to wipe the ~ with sb** hacer trizas a alguien; **to go through the ~** (*prices*) estar por los suelos **II.** *vt* (*knock down*) tumbar; **the question ~ed her** la pregunta la dejó sin respuesta
floorboard ['flɔːbɔːd, *Am:* 'flɔrːbɔːrd] *n* tabla *f* del suelo
flooring *n no pl* solado *m;* **wooden ~** entablado *m*
floor lamp *n Am* lámpara *f* de pie **floor polish** *n* cera *f* para el suelo **floor show** *n* espectáculo *m* de cabaret **floor-walker** *n Am* vigilante *m*
flop [flɒp, *Am:* flɑːp] <-pp-> **I.** *vi* **1.** (*fall*) dejarse caer **2.** *inf* (*fail*) fracasar **II.** *n inf* (*failure*) fracaso *m*
floppy ['flɒpi, *Am:* 'flɑːpi] **I.** <-ier, -iest> *adj* (*ears*) caído, -a; (*hat*) flexible **II.** <-ies> *n* diskette *m*
floppy disk *n* diskette *m*
flora ['flɔːrə] *n no pl* flora *f;* **~ and fauna** flora y fauna
floral ['flɔːrəl] *adj* floral
florid ['flɒrɪd, *Am:* 'flɔːr-] *adj* **1.** (*style*) florido, -a; (*prose, rhetoric*) ornamentado, -a **2.** *form* (*ruddy*) rojizo, -a
Florida ['flɒrɪdə, *Am:* 'flɔːr-] *n* Florida *f*
florist ['flɒrɪst, *Am:* 'flɔːr-] *n* florista *mf;* **the ~'s** la floristería
flotation [fləʊ'teɪʃən, *Am:* floʊ-] *n* ECON, FIN salida *f* a Bolsa
flotilla [flə'tɪlə, *Am:* floʊ-] *n* MIL, NAUT flotilla *f*
flotsam ['flɒtsəm, *Am:* 'flɑːt-] *n no pl* restos *mpl* flotantes; **~ and jetsam** desechos *mpl*
flounce[1] [flaʊnts] *vi* **to ~ about** moverse violentamente; **to ~ in/out** entrar/salir indignado
flounce[2] [flaʊnts] *n* (*decoration*) volante *m,* arandela *f Méx, Perú*
flounder[1] ['flaʊndəʳ, *Am:* -dɚ] *vi* **1.** (*struggle*) sufrir **2.** (*fail*) ir(se) a pique
flounder[2] ['flaʊndəʳ, *Am:* -dɚ] *n* (*flatfish*) platija *f*
flour ['flaʊəʳ, *Am:* -ɚ] **I.** *n no pl* harina *f* **II.** *vt* enharinar
flourish ['flʌrɪʃ, *Am:* 'flɜːr-] **I.** *vi* florecer **II.** *vt* hacer gala de **III.** *n* **with a ~** con un gesto ceremonioso
flourishing *adj* (*place*) esplendoroso, -a; (*business, market, trade*) próspero, -a
flour-mill *n* molino *m* de harina
floury ['flaʊəri] <-ier, -iest> *adj* harinoso, -a
flout [flaʊt] *vt* **to ~ a law/rule** incumplir una ley/regla; **to ~ tradition** no hacer caso de la tradición
flow [fləʊ, *Am:* floʊ] **I.** *vi* fluir, correr **II.** *n no pl* (*of water, ideas*) flujo *m;* (*of goods*) circulación *f;* **~ of oil/water** chorro *m* de aceite/agua; **~ of blood** derrame *m* de sangre ►**in full ~** en pleno discurso; **to go against the ~** ir contra la corriente; **to go with the ~** seguir la corriente
flowchart *n,* **flow diagram** *n* organigrama *m*
flower ['flaʊəʳ, *Am:* 'flaʊɚ] **I.** *n* **1.** (*plant*) flor *f;* **to be in ~** estar en flor **2.** *liter* (*best*) **the ~** la flor y nata **II.** *vi* florecer, florear *AmL; fig* desarrollarse
flower arrangement *n* arreglo *m* floral **flowerbed** *n* arriate *m* de flores **flower garden** *n* jardín *m* de flores **flower pot** *n* maceta *f*
flowery ['flaʊəri] <-ier, -iest> *adj* **1.** (*material*) floreado, -a **2.** (*style, language*) florido, -a
flowing *adj* (*hair, robes*) suelto, -a
flown [fləʊn, *Am:* floʊn] *pp of* **fly**[1]
flu [fluː] *n no pl* gripe *f,* gripa *f Col*
fluctuate ['flʌktʃʊeɪt] *vi* fluctuar
fluctuation [ˌflʌktʃʊ'eɪʃən] *n* fluctuación *f*
flue [fluː] *n* cañón *m* de chimenea
fluency ['fluːəntsi] *n no pl* fluidez *f*
fluent ['fluːənt] *adj* (*style, movement*) con fluidez; **to speak ~ English** hablar inglés con soltura
fluff [flʌf] **I.** *n no pl* **1.** (*furry piece*) lanilla *f;* (*dust*) pelusa *f* **2.** *Am* (*trifle*) nimiedad *f* **II.** *vt inf* (*fail*) hacer mal
fluffy ['flʌfi] <-ier, -iest> *adj* (*furry: animal*) peludo, -a; (*toy*) de peluche; (*clothes*) lanudo, -a; GASTR (*light*) esponjoso, -a
fluid ['fluːɪd] **I.** *n* fluido *m* **II.** *adj* **1.** (*liquid*) líquido, -a **2.** (*situation*) inestable

fluid ounce *n* onza *f* fluida (*unidad de capacidad equivalente a 28,42 milímetros*)
flung [flʌŋ] *pp, pt of* **fling**
flunk [flʌŋk] *vt Am, inf* suspender
fluorescence [flʊə'resns, *Am:* flɔː-] *n no pl* fluorescencia *f*
fluorescent [flʊə'resnt, *Am:* flɔː-] *adj* fluorescente; ~ **tube** tubo *m* fluorescente
fluoride ['flʊəraɪd, *Am:* 'flɔːraɪd] *n no pl* fluoruro *m*
fluorine ['flʊəriːn, *Am:* 'flɔːriːn] *n no pl* flúor *m*
fluorocarbon [ˌflʊərə'kɑːbən, *Am:* ˌflɔːrə-'kɑːr-] *n* fluorocarburo *m*
flurry ['flʌri, *Am:* 'flɜːr-] <-ies> *n* agitación *f;* (*of snow*) ráfaga *f;* **a ~ of excitement** un frenesí; **a ~ of speculation** una ola de especulación
flush[1] [flʌʃ] **I.** *vi* (*blush*) ruborizarse **II.** *vt* **to ~ the toilet** tirar de la cadena **III.** *n* **1.** *no pl* (*blush*) rubor *m;* ~ **of anger** sonrojo *m* de rabia **2.** (*toilet*) cisterna *f*
flush[2] [flʌʃ] *adj* **1.** (*level*) llano, -a **2.** *inf* (*rich*) **to be ~ with money** andar bien de dinero
◆flush out *vt* hacer salir
flushed ['flʌʃt] *adj* emocionado, -a; ~ **with anger** rojo de rabia; ~ **with joy** pletórico de alegría; ~ **with success** emocionado con el éxito
fluster ['flʌstəʳ, *Am:* -tɚ] **I.** *vt* **to ~ sb** poner nervioso a alguien **II.** *n no pl* **to be in a ~** estar nervioso
flute [fluːt] *n* MUS flauta *f*
fluting *n* acanalado *m*
flutist ['fluːtɪst, *Am:* -t̬ɪst] *n Am s.* **flautist**
flutter ['flʌtəʳ, *Am:* 'flʌt̬ɚ] **I.** *n* **1.** *no pl, Aus, Brit, inf* (*bet*) apuesta *f;* **to have a ~** apostar **2.** (*sound*) revoloteo *m* **3.** *fig* (*nervousness*) agitación *f;* **to put sb in a ~** poner nervioso a alguien; **to be all of a ~** ser un manojo de nervios **II.** *vi* **1.** (*quiver*) temblar; **to make hearts ~** *fig* hacer palpitar los corazones **2.** (*flap*) agitarse **III.** *vt* (*flap*) agitar; **to ~ one's wings** aletear; **to ~ one's eyelashes** pestañear
fluvial ['fluːvɪəl] *adj* fluvial
flux [flʌks] *n no pl* **1.** (*change*) cambio *m* continuo; **to be in a state of ~** estar continuamente cambiando **2.** MED flujo *m*
fly[1] [flaɪ] <flew, flown> **I.** *vi* **1.** (*through air*) volar; (*travel by aircraft*) viajar en avión **2.** (*move rapidly*) lanzarse; **to ~ at sb** precipitarse sobre alguien **3.** (*leave*) salir corriendo ►**to ~ high** *Am* volar muy alto **II.** *vt* **1.** (*aircraft*) pilotar **2.** (*make move through air*) hacer volar; **to ~ a flag** enarbolar una bandera; **to ~ a kite** hacer volar una cometa
fly[2] [flaɪ] *n* (*insect*) mosca *f* ►**he wouldn't harm a ~** sería incapaz de matar una mosca; **to drop (off)** [*o* **die**] **like flies** *inf* caer como moscas; **a ~ in the ointment** la única pega
◆fly away *vi* irse volando
◆fly in *vi* **to ~ from somewhere** llegar (en avión) desde algún sitio
◆fly off *vi* irse volando
flyaway ['flaɪəweɪ] *adj* suelto, -a
fly-by-night ['flaɪbaɪnaɪt] *adj inf* nada serio, -a
flycatcher ['flaɪˌkætʃəʳ, *Am:* -ɚ] *n* papamoscas *m*
flyer ['flaɪəʳ, *Am:* -ɚ] *n* **1.** (*air traveller*) aviador(a) *m(f)* **2.** (*leaflet*) folleto *m*
flying ['flaɪɪŋ] *n no pl* el volar
flying boat *n* hidroavión *m* **flying fish** *n* pez *m* volador **flying fox** *n* panique *m* **flying saucer** *n* platillo *m* volante **flying squad** *n* brigada *f* móvil **flying start** *n* SPORTS salida *f* lanzada; **to get off to a ~** entrar con buen pie **flying time** *n* horas *fpl* de vuelo **flying visit** *n inf* visita *f* relámpago
flyleaf ['flaɪliːf] <flyleaves> *n* guarda *f*
flyover ['flaɪˌəʊvəʳ, *Am:* -ˌoʊvɚ] *n* **1.** *Brit* paso *m* elevado **2.** *Am* desfile *m* aéreo
flypaper ['flaɪˌpeɪpəʳ, *Am:* -pɚ] *n* papel *m* matamoscas
flypast ['flaɪpɑːst, *Am:* -pæst] *n* MIL desfile *m* aéreo
flysheet *n Brit* doble techo *m* (*de una tienda de campaña*)
fly-trap *n* atrapamoscas *m*
flyweight ['flaɪweɪt] *n* SPORTS peso *m* mosca
flywheel ['flaɪhwiːl] *n* TECH volante *m*
FM [ˌef'em] PHYS *abbr of* **frequency modulation** FM
FO [ˌef'əʊ, *Am:* -oʊ] *n Brit abbr of* **Foreign Office** Ministerio *m* de Asuntos Exteriores
foal [fəʊl, *Am:* foʊl] **I.** *n* potro, -a *m, f;* **to be in ~** estar preñada **II.** *vi* parir
foam [fəʊm, *Am:* foʊm] **I.** *n no pl* (*bubbles, foam rubber*) espuma *f;* **shaving ~** espuma de afeitar **II.** *vi* **to ~ with rage** echar espuma de (pura) rabia
foam bath *n* baño *m* de espuma **foam rubber** *n* goma espuma *f*
foamy ['fəʊmi, *Am:* 'foʊm-] <-ier, -iest> *adj* espumoso, -a
fob [fɒb, *Am:* fɑːb] *n* cadena *f* de reloj
focal ['fəʊkl, *Am:* 'foʊ-] *adj* focal; ~ **point** punto *m* central
focus ['fəʊkəs, *Am:* 'foʊ-] <-es *o* foci> **I.** *n* **1.** foco *m;* **to be in/out of ~** estar enfocado/desenfocado **2.** (*centre*) centro *m;* ~ **of interest** centro de interés; **the ~ of a programme** el enfoque de un programa; **to bring sth into ~** *fig* destacar algo **II.** <-s- *o* -ss-> *vi* enfocar; **to ~ on sth** (*concentrate*) concentrarse en algo **III.** *vt* enfocar; **to ~ one's attention on sth** centrar la atención en algo
fodder ['fɒdəʳ, *Am:* 'fɑːdɚ] *n no pl* **1.** (*animal food*) forraje *m;* ~ **crop** cereal-pienso *m* **2.** *fig, inf* pasto *m*
foe [fəʊ, *Am:* foʊ] *n* enemigo, -a *m, f*
foetal ['fiːtəl, *Am:* -t̬əl] *adj* BIO fetal
foetus ['fiːtəs, *Am:* -t̬əs] *n* feto *m*
fog [fɒg, *Am:* fɑːg] *n* niebla *f;* **to be in a ~** *fig* estar confundido
fog bank *n* banco *m* de niebla

fogbound ['fɒgbaʊnd, *Am:* 'fɑ:g-] *adj* inmovilizado, -a por la niebla
fogey ['fəʊgi, *Am:* 'foʊ-] *n pej, inf* persona *f* chapada a la antigua; **old** ~ carroza *mf;* **young** ~ joven *mf* de ideas anticuadas
foggy ['fɒgi, *Am:* 'fɑ:gi] <-ier, -iest> *adj* nebuloso, -a ▶**to not have the foggiest** (**idea**) no tener la más remota idea
foghorn ['fɒghɔ:n, *Am:* 'fɑ:ghɔ:rn] *n* sirena *f* de niebla; **to have a voice like a** ~ tener una voz chillona
foglamp *n,* **foglight** *n* faro *m* antiniebla
fogy ['fɒgi, *Am:* 'fɑ:gi] <-ies> *n inf s.* **fogey**
foible ['fɔɪbl] *n* debilidad *f*
foil[1] [fɔɪl] *n* **1.** (*metal paper*) papel *m* de aluminio **2.** (*sword*) florete *m* **3.** *fig* **to act as a** ~ **to sth** servir de contraste con algo
foil[2] [fɔɪl] *vt* frustrar
foist (**up**)**on** [ˌfɔɪst(ə'p)ɒn, *Am:* ˌfɔɪst(ə'p)ɑ:n] *vt* **to foist sth** (**up**)**on sb** hacer que alguien se encargue de algo
fold[1] [fəʊld, *Am:* foʊld] **I.** *vt* **1.** (*bend*) plegar; **to** ~ **sth back/down** plegar algo **2.** (*wrap*) **to** ~ **sth** (**in sth**) envolver algo (en algo) **II.** *vi* **1.** (*bend over*) doblarse **2.** (*fail, go bankrupt*) fracasar **III.** *n* pliegue *m*
fold[2] [fəʊld, *Am:* foʊld] *n* (*sheep pen*) redil *m;* **to return to the** ~ *fig* volver al hogar
◆**fold up** *vt* doblar
folder ['fəʊldəʳ, *Am:* 'foʊldɚ] *n a.* INFOR carpeta *f,* fólder *m Col, Méx*
folding ['fəʊldɪŋ, *Am:* 'foʊld-] *adj* plegable; ~ **door** puerta *f* plegadiza; ~ **money** *Am* billetes *mpl* de banco
foliage ['fəʊlɪɪdʒ, *Am:* 'foʊ-] *n no pl* follaje *m*
folio ['fəʊliəʊ, *Am:* 'foʊlioʊ] *n* folio *m*
folk [fəʊk, *Am:* foʊk] *npl* pueblo *m;* **farming** ~ gente *f* de campo; **the old** ~ los viejos; **ordinary** ~ gente *f* corriente; (~ *memory*) memoria *f* colectiva; ~ **wisdom** sabiduría *f* popular
folk dance *n* baile *m* popular
folklore ['fəʊklɔ:ʳ, *Am:* 'foʊklɔ:r] *n no pl* folklore *m*
folk music *n* música *f* folk **folk song** *n* canción *f* popular
folksy ['fəʊksi, *Am:* 'foʊk-] <-ier, -iest> *adj* (*friendly*) amigable
folk tale *n* cuento *m* popular
foll. *abbr of* **followed, following** sig.
follow ['fɒləʊ, *Am:* 'fɑ:loʊ] **I.** *vt* **1.** (*take same route as*) seguir **2.** (*happen next*) **to** ~ **sth** suceder a algo **3.** **to** ~ **ancient traditions** seguir las antiguas tradiciones **4.** (*understand*) **to** ~ **sb/sth** seguir a alguien/algo **5.** (*have an interest in*) **to** ~ **sth** interesarse por algo **II.** *vi* **1.** (*take same route as*) seguir **2.** (*happen next*) suceder **3.** (*result*) resultar; **to** ~ **from sth** ser consecuencia de algo
◆**follow on** *vi* seguir
◆**follow through I.** *vt* **1.** (*study*) investigar **2.** (*see through to end*) terminar **II.** *vi* SPORTS terminar
◆**follow up** *vt* **1.** (*consider, investigate*) investigar **2.** (*do next*) **to** ~ **sth by** [*o* **with**] **...** hacer algo después de...
follower *n* seguidor(a) *m(f)*
following I. *n inv* **1. I'd say the** ~ diría lo siguiente; **my idea was the** ~ mi idea era la siguiente **2.** (*supporters: of idea*) partidarios, -as *m, f pl;* (*of doctrine*) seguidores, -as *m, f pl* **II.** *adj* **1.** (*next*) siguiente; **the** ~ **ideas** las siguientes ideas **2.** (*from behind*) ~ **wind** viento de cola [*o* de popa] **III.** *prep* después de; ~ **the dinner/your letter** después de la cena/tu carta
follow-up ['fɒləʊʌp, *Am:* 'fɑ:loʊ-] *n* seguimiento *m*
folly ['fɒli, *Am:* 'fɑ:li] *n* **1.** (*foolishness*) locura *f;* **it's sheer** ~**!** ¡es una locura! **2.** *Brit* ARCHIT capricho *m*
fond [fɒnd, *Am:* fɑ:nd] <-er, -est> *adj* **1.** (*with liking for*) **to be** ~ **of sb** tener cariño a alguien; **he is** ~ **of ...** le gusta... **2.** (*loving*) cariñoso, -a; ~ **memories** tiernos recuerdos *mpl* **3.** (*hope*) vano, -a
fondle ['fɒndl, *Am:* 'fɑ:n-] <-ling> *vt* acariciar
fondness ['fɒndnɪs, *Am:* 'fɑ:nd-] *n no pl* cariño *m;* **to have a** ~ **for sth** tener una afición por algo
font [fɒnt, *Am:* fɑ:nt] *n* **1.** (*receptacle*) pila *f* (bautismal) **2.** TYPO fuente *f*
food [fu:d] *n* comida *f* ▶**to give sb** ~ **for thought** dar a alguien algo en que pensar; **to be off one's** ~ estar desganado
food chain *n* cadena *f* alimentaria **food poisoning** *n no pl* envenenamiento *m* por alimentos **food processor** *n* procesador *m* de alimentos **foodstuff** *n* artículo *m* alimenticio
fool [fu:l] **I.** *n* idiota *mf;* **to be** ~ **enough to do sth** ser bastante idiota como para hacer algo; **to act the** ~ hacer el tonto; **to make a** ~ **of sb** poner a alguien en ridículo; **any** ~ cualquiera **II.** *vt* engañar; **you could have** ~**ed me!** *inf* ¡no me lo puedo creer! **III.** *vi* (*joke*) bromear **IV.** *adj Am, inf* (*silly*) tonto, -a
◆**fool about** *vi* hacer payasadas
foolhardy ['fu:lhɑ:di, *Am:* -hɑ:r-] *adj* temerario, -a
foolish ['fu:lɪʃ] *adj* tonto, -a
foolproof ['fu:lpru:f] *adj* a toda prueba
foolscap ['fu:lskæp] *n no pl* papel *m* tamaño folio
foot [fʊt] **I.** <feet> *n* **1.** (*of person*) pie *m;* (*of animal*) pata *f* **2.** (*unit of measurement*) pie *m* (*30,48 cm*) **3.** (*bottom or lowest part*) **at the** ~ **of one's bed** al pie de la cama; **at the** ~ **of the page** a pie de página ▶**to get a** ~ **in the door** abrirse una brecha; **to have one** ~ **in the grave** estar con un pie en la tumba; **to have both feet on the ground** ser realista; **to set** ~ **on dry land** poner los pies en tierra firme; **to be back on one's feet** estar recuperado; **to have/get cold feet** estar/ponerse

nervioso; **to catch sb on the wrong ~** pillar a alguien desprevenido; **to fall on one's feet** caer de pie; **to find one's feet** acostumbrarse al ambiente; **to put one's ~ down** acelerar; **to put one's ~ in it** [*o* **in your mouth**] *Am* meter la pata; **to set ~ in sth** pisar algo; **I'll never set ~ in his house again** no volveré a pisar su casa; **to be under sb's feet** estar siempre pegado a alguien **II.** *vt inf* **to ~ the bill** pagar

footage ['fʊtɪdʒ, *Am:* 'fʊt̬-] *n no pl* CINE, TV secuencias *fpl,* imágenes *fpl*

foot-and-mouth disease [ˌfʊtənd'maʊθ-dɪˌziːz] *n* fiebre *f* aftosa

football ['fʊtbɔːl] *n no pl* **1.** *Brit* (*soccer*) fútbol *m* **2.** *Am* (*American football*) fútbol *m* americano **3.** (*ball*) balón *m*

football hooligan *n* hooligan *mf* **football player** *n* futbolista *mf* **football pools** *npl* quinielas *fpl*

foot board *n* AUTO estribo *m*

footbridge ['fʊtbrɪdʒ] *n* puente *m* peatonal

footer ['fʊtəʳ, *Am:* 'fʊt̬ɚ] *n* pie *m* de página

foothills ['fʊthɪlz] *n* estribaciones *fpl*

foothold ['fʊthəʊld, *Am:* -hoʊld] *n* asidero *m* para el pie; **to gain a ~** *fig* lograr establecerse

footing ['fʊtɪŋ, *Am:* 'fʊt̬-] *n no pl* **1. to lose one's ~** resbalar **2.** (*basis*) posición *f;* **on a war ~** en pie de guerra; **on an equal ~** en un mismo pie de igualdad

footlights ['fʊtlaɪts] *npl* candilejas *fpl*

footling ['fuːtlɪŋ] *adj* trivial

footloose ['fʊtluːs] *adj* libre ►**to be ~ and fancy-free** estar soltero y sin compromiso

footman ['fʊtmən] <-men> *n* lacayo *m*

footnote ['fʊtnəʊt, *Am:* -noʊt] *n* nota *f* a pie de página

footpath ['fʊtpɑːθ, *Am:* -pæθ] *n* sendero *m*

footprint ['fʊtprɪnt] *n* huella *f*

footrest ['fʊtrest] *n* reposapiés *m inv*

footsie ['fʊtsi] *n no pl, inf* **to play ~ with sb** acariciar a alguien con el pie

footslog ['fʊtslɒg] <-gg-> *vi inf* andar hasta acabar rendido

footsore ['fʊtsɔːʳ, *Am:* -sɔːr] *adj liter* **to be ~** tener los pies cansados

footstep ['fʊtstep] *n* paso *m*

footstool ['fʊtstuːl] *n* reposapiés *m inv*

footwear ['fʊtweəʳ, *Am:* -wer] *n no pl* calzado *m*

footwork ['fʊtwɜːk, *Am:* -wɜːrk] *n no pl* juego *m* de piernas

for [fɔːʳ, *Am:* fɔːr] **I.** *prep* **1.** (*destined for*) para; **this is ~ you** esto es para ti; **a present ~ my mother** un regalo para mi madre **2.** (*to give to*) por; **to do sth ~ sb** hacer algo por alguien **3.** (*intention, purpose*) **~ sale/rent** en venta/alquiler; **sth ~ a headache** algo para el dolor de cabeza; **it's time ~ lunch** es hora del almuerzo; **it's time ~ sleep** es hora de dormir; **to invite sb ~ dinner** invitar a alguien para cenar; **to wait ~ sb** esperar a alguien; **to go ~ a walk** ir a dar un paseo; **fit ~ nothing** bueno para nada; **what ~?** ¿para qué?; **what's that ~?** ¿para qué es eso?; **it's ~ cutting cheese** es para cortar queso; **~ this to be possible** para que esto sea posible; **to look ~ a way to do sth** buscar una manera de hacer algo **4.** (*to acquire*) **eager ~ power** ávido de poder; **to search ~ sth** buscar algo; **to ask/hope ~ news** pedir/esperar noticias; **to apply ~ a job** solicitar un trabajo; **to shout ~ help** gritar pidiendo ayuda **5.** (*towards*) **the train ~ Glasgow** el tren hacia Glasgow; **to make ~ home** dirigirse hacia casa; **to run ~ safety** correr a ponerse a salvo **6.** (*distance*) **to walk ~ 8 km** caminar durante 8 km **7.** (*time*) **~ now** por ahora; **~ a while/a time** por un rato/un momento; **to last ~ hours** durar horas y horas; **I'm going to be here ~ three weeks** voy a estar aquí durante tres semanas; **I haven't been there ~ three years** hace tres años que no estoy allí; **I have known her ~ three years** la conozco desde hace tres años **8.** (*on date of*) **to have sth finished ~ Sunday** acabar algo para el domingo; **to set the wedding ~ May 4** fijar la boda para el 4 de mayo **9.** (*in support of*) **is he ~ or against it?** ¿está a favor o en contra?; **to fight ~ sth** luchar por algo **10.** (*employed by*) **to work ~ a company** trabajar para una empresa **11.** (*the task of*) **it's ~ him to say/do ...** le toca a él decir/hacer... **12.** (*in substitution*) **the substitute ~ the teacher** el substituto del maestro; **say hello ~ me** dile hola de mi parte **13.** (*price*) **a cheque ~ £100** un cheque de £100; **I paid £10 ~ it** pagué £10 por ello **14.** (*concerning*) **as ~ me/that** en cuanto a mí/eso; **two are enough ~ me** dos son suficientes para mí; **sorry ~ doing that** perdón por hacer eso; **the best would be ~ me to go** lo mejor sería que me fuese **15.** (*in reference to*) **what's the Chinese ~ 'book'?** ¿cómo se dice 'libro' en chino? **16.** (*cause*) **excuse me ~ being late** discúlpame por llegar tarde; **as the reason ~ one's behaviour** como razón por su comportamiento; **~ lack of reasons** por falta de motivos **17.** (*because of*) **to do sth ~ love** hacer algo por amor; **~ fear of doing sth** por miedo a hacer algo; **to cry ~ joy** gritar de alegría; **he can't talk ~ laughing** no puede hablar de la risa **18.** (*despite*) **~ all that/her money** a pesar de todo eso/de su dinero; **~ all I know** por lo que yo sepa **19.** (*as*) **~ example** por ejemplo; **he ~ one** empezando por él ►**she's ~ it!** ¡se la va a cargar!; **that's kids ~ you!** ¡así son los niños! **II.** *conj form* pues

forage ['fɒrɪdʒ, *Am:* 'fɔːr-] **I.** *vi* **to ~** (**about**) **for sth** buscar algo **II.** *n no pl* (*fodder*) forraje *m*

foray ['fɒreɪ, *Am:* 'fɔːr-] *n* (*raid*) correría *f;* **to make a ~** (**into sth**) hacer una incursión (en algo)

forbad(e) [fə'bæd, *Am:* fɚ-] *pt of* **forbid**

forbear [fɔː'beəʳ, *Am:* fɔːr'ber] <forbore, forborne> *vi form* (*abstain, refrain*) contenerse; **to ~ from doing sth** abstenerse de hacer algo

forbearance [fɔːˈbeərəns, *Am:* fɔːrˈberəns] *n no pl, form* **1.** paciencia *f* **2.** (*self-control*) dominio *m* de sí mismo

forbid [fəˈbɪd, *Am:* fɚ-] <forbade, forbidden> *vt* prohibir; **to ~ sb from doing sth** prohibir a alguien hacer algo; **to ~ sb sth** *form* prohibir algo a alguien

forbidden [fəˈbɪdn, *Am:* fɚ-] *pp of* **forbid**

forbidding [fəˈbɪdɪŋ, *Am:* fɚ-] *adj* **1.** (*impressive*) imponente **2.** (*severe*) severo, -a

forbore [fɔːˈbɔːʳ, *Am:* fɔːrˈbɔːr] *pt of* **forbear**

forborne [fɔːˈbɔːn, *Am:* fɔːrˈbɔːrn] *pp of* **forbear**

force [fɔːs, *Am:* fɔːrs] **I.** *n* **1.** fuerza *f;* **by sheer ~ of numbers** por superioridad numérica; **~ of gravity** PHYS fuerza de la gravedad; **to combine ~s** unir esfuerzos **2.** (*large numbers*) **in ~** en grandes cantidades **3.** (*influence*) influencia *f;* **by ~ of circumstance** debido a las circunstancias; **by ~ of habit** por costumbre; **the ~s of nature** *liter* las fuerzas de la naturaleza **4.** (*validity*) validez *f;* **to come into ~** entrar en vigor **5.** MIL **police ~** cuerpo *m* de policía; **Air Force** Fuerzas Aéreas; **armed ~s** fuerzas *fpl* armadas **II.** *vt* **1.** (*use power*) forzar; **to ~ a door** forzar una puerta **2.** (*oblige to do*) obligar; **to ~ sb to do sth** obligar a alguien a hacer algo; **to ~ a smile** sonreír forzadamente; **to ~ words out of sb** hacer hablar a alguien **3.** (*cause to grow faster*) hacer madurar temprano

◆**force into** *vt* **to force sb into (doing) sth** forzar a alguien a (hacer) algo

◆**force off** *vt* quitar por la fuerza

◆**force on** *vt* **to force sth on sb** imponer algo a alguien

◆**force out** *vt* hacer salir

◆**force upon** *vt s.* **force on**

forced *adj* (*smile, friendliness*) forzado, -a; **~ landing** aterrizaje *m* forzoso

force-feed [ˌfɔːsˈfiːd, *Am:* ˈfɔːrsfiːd] *vt* dar de comer a la fuerza

forceful [ˈfɔːsfəl, *Am:* ˈfɔːrs-] *adj* enérgico, -a

forceps [ˈfɔːseps, *Am:* ˈfɔːr-] *npl* MED fórceps *mpl;* **a pair of ~** unos fórceps

forceps delivery *n* MED parto *m* con fórceps

forcible [ˈfɔːsəbl, *Am:* ˈfɔːr-] *adj* a la fuerza

forcibly *adv* a la fuerza

ford [fɔːd, *Am:* fɔːrd] **I.** *n* vado *m,* botadero *m Méx* **II.** *vt* vadear

fore [fɔːʳ, *Am:* fɔːr] **I.** *adj* anterior; **~ and aft** de popa a proa **II.** *n no pl* **to be to the ~** ir delante; **to come to the ~** destacar

forearm¹ [ˈfɔːrɑːm, *Am:* -ɑːrm] *n* antebrazo *m*

forearm² [ˌfɔːrˈɑːm, *Am:* -ˈɑːrm] *vt liter* **to ~ oneself (against sth)** prevenirse (contra algo)

forebears [ˈfɔːbeəz, *Am:* ˈfɔːrberz] *npl form* antepasados *mpl*

forebode [fɔːˈbəʊd, *Am:* fɔːrˈboʊd] *vt liter* presagiar

foreboding [fɔːˈbəʊdɪŋ, *Am:* fɔːrˈboʊ-] *n liter* presentimiento *m;* **to have a ~ (that) ...** tener una corazonada (de que)...

forecast [ˈfɔːkɑːst, *Am:* ˈfɔːrkæst] <forecast *o* forecasted> **I.** *n* predicción *f;* **weather ~** previsión *f* meteorológica **II.** *vt* pronosticar

forecaster *n* ECON pronosticador(a) *m(f);* **weather ~** meteorólogo, -a *m, f*

forecastle [ˈfəʊksl, *Am:* ˈfoʊk-] *n* NAUT castillo *m* de proa

foreclose [fɔːˈkləʊz, *Am:* fɔːrˈkloʊz] **I.** *vt* **to ~ a possibility** descartar una posibilidad **II.** *vi* FIN extinguir; **to ~ on a loan** liquidar un préstamo

forecourt [ˈfɔːkɔːt, *Am:* ˈfɔːrkɔːrt] *n* explanada *f*

forefathers [ˈfɔːˌfɑːðəʳ, *Am:* ˈfɔːrˌfɑːðɚ] *npl liter* antepasados *mpl*

forefinger [ˈfɔːfɪŋgəʳ, *Am:* ˈfɔːrfɪŋgɚ] *n* índice *m*

forefront [ˈfɔːfrʌnt, *Am:* ˈfɔːr-] *n no pl* primer plano *m;* **to be at the ~ of sth** estar en la vanguardia de algo

forego [fɔːˈgəʊ, *Am:* fɔːrˈgoʊ] <forewent, foregone> *vt s.* **forgo**

foregoing [ˈfɔːgəʊɪŋ, *Am:* ˈfɔːrgoʊ-] **I.** *adj form* anterior **II.** *n no pl* **the ~** *form* el anterior

foregone [fɔːˈgɒn, *Am:* fɔːrˈgɑːn] *pp of* **forego**

foreground [ˈfɔːgraʊnd, *Am:* ˈfɔːr-] **I.** *n no pl* **1.** ART **the ~** el primer plano; **in the ~** en primer término **2.** (*prominent position*) **to put oneself in the ~** ponerse al frente **II.** *vt* destacar

forehand [ˈfɔːhænd, *Am:* ˈfɔːr-] *n* (*tennis shot*) derechazo *m*

forehead [ˈfɒrɪd, *Am:* ˈfɔːred] *n* frente *f*

foreign [ˈfɒrɪn, *Am:* ˈfɔːr-] *adj* **1.** (*from another country*) extranjero, -a; **~ soil** *form* suelo *m* extranjero **2.** (*involving other countries*) exterior; **~ relations** relaciones *fpl* exteriores; **~ trade** comercio *m* exterior **3.** (*unknown*) extraño, -a; (*uncharacteristic*) impropio, -a; **to be ~ to sb** ser extraño para alguien; **to be ~ to one's nature** no ser propio de la naturaleza de uno **4.** (*not belonging*) ajeno, -a; **a ~ body** un cuerpo extraño

foreign affairs *npl* asuntos *mpl* exteriores; **Ministry of Foreign Affairs** Ministerio *m* de Asuntos Exteriores **foreign correspondent** *n* corresponsal *mf* en el extranjero **foreign currency** *n* divisa *f*

foreigner [ˈfɒrɪnəʳ, *Am:* ˈfɔːr-] *n* extranjero, -a *m, f*

foreign exchange *n no pl* **1.** (*system*) cambio *m* de divisas **2.** (*currency*) divisa *f* **foreign minister** *n* ministro, -a *m, f* de Asuntos Exteriores, canciller *mf AmL* **Foreign Office** *n no pl, Brit* Ministerio *m* de Asuntos Exteriores **foreign policy** *n* política *f* exterior **Foreign Secretary** *n Brit* ministro, -a *m, f* de Asuntos Exteriores

foreknowledge [ˌfɔː'nɒlɪdʒ, *Am:* ˌfɔːr'nɑː-lɪdʒ] *n no pl* presciencia *f;* **to have ~ of sth** saber algo de antemano

foreman ['fɔːmən, *Am:* 'fɔːr-] <-men> *n* **1.** (*in factory*) capataz *m* **2.** LAW (*head of jury*) presidente *m* (del jurado)

foremost ['fɔːməʊst, *Am:* 'fɔːrmoʊst] *adj* **1.** (*most important*) principal; **to be ~ among ...** ser el más importante entre... **2.** (*furthest forward*) delantero, -a

forename ['fɔːneɪm, *Am:* 'fɔːr-] *n form* nombre *m* (de pila)

forensic [fə'rensɪk] *adj* forense; **~ medicine** medicina *f* forense

foreordain [ˌfɔːrɔː'deɪn, *Am:* -ɔːr'-] *vt form* predeterminar; **to be ~ed** (**to do sth**) estar predestinado (a hacer algo)

foreplay ['fɔːpleɪ, *Am:* 'fɔːr-] *n no pl* juegos *mpl* eróticos preliminares

forerunner ['fɔːrʌnəʳ, *Am:* 'fɔːrˌrʌnɚ] *n* precursor(a) *m(f)*

foresail ['fɔːseɪl, *Am:* 'fɔːr-] *n* NAUT trinquete *m*

foresee [fɔː'siː, *Am:* fɔːr-] *irr vt* prever

foreseeable *adj* previsible; **in the ~ future** en el futuro inmediato

foreshadow [fɔː'ʃædəʊ, *Am:* fɔːr'ʃædoʊ] *vt* anunciar

foresight ['fɔːsaɪt, *Am:* 'fɔːr-] *n* previsión *f;* **lack of ~** falta *f* de previsión

foreskin ['fɔːskɪn, *Am:* 'fɔːr-] *n* prepucio *m*

forest ['fɒrɪst, *Am:* 'fɔːr-] **I.** *n* (*wood*) bosque *m;* (*tropical*) selva *f* **II.** *adj* forestal

forestall [fɔː'stɔːl, *Am:* fɔːr-] *vt* anticiparse a; **to ~ criticism** adelantarse a las críticas

forester ['fɒrɪstəʳ, *Am:* 'fɔːr-] *n* guardabosques *mf*

forest fire *n* incendio *m* forestal **forest ranger** *n Am* guarda *mf* forestal

forestry ['fɒrɪstri, *Am:* 'fɔːr-] *n no pl* silvicultura *f*

foretaste ['fɔːteɪst, *Am:* 'fɔːr-] *n no pl* anticipo *m*

foretell [fɔː'tel, *Am:* fɔːr-] <foretold> *vt* predecir

forever [fə'revəʳ, *Am:* fɔːr'evɚ] *adv,* **for ever** *adv Brit* **1.** (*for all time*) para siempre **2.** *inf* (*continually*) continuamente; **to be ~ doing sth** estar haciendo algo sin cesar

forewarn [fɔː'wɔːn, *Am:* fɔːr'wɔːrn] *vt* prevenir ►**~ed is forearmed** *prov* hombre prevenido vale por dos

forewent [fɔː'went, *Am:* fɔːr-] *pp of* **forego**

foreword ['fɔːwɜːd, *Am:* 'fɔːrwɜːrd] *n* prefacio *m*

forfeit ['fɔːfɪt, *Am:* 'fɔːr-] **I.** *vt* **1.** (*lose*) perder **2.** (*renounce*) perder el derecho a **II.** *n* **1.** (*penalty*) multa *f;* **to pay a ~** pagar una multa **2.** *pl* (*game*) **to play ~s** jugar a las prendas **3.** *form* (*penalty*) pena *f* **III.** *adj* **her property was ~** sus bienes fueron confiscados

forfeiture ['fɔːfɪtʃəʳ, *Am:* 'fɔːrfə-] *n no pl* pérdida *f*

forgather [fɔː'gæðəʳ, *Am:* fɔːr'gæðɚ] *vi form* reunirse

forgave [fə'geɪv, *Am:* fɚ-] *n pt of* **forgive**

forge [fɔːdʒ, *Am:* fɔːrdʒ] **I.** *vt* **1.** (*make illegal copy*) falsificar **2.** (*metal*) forjar **3.** *fig* **to ~ a bond** forjar un vínculo; **to ~ a career** forjarse un porvenir **II.** *vi* **to ~ into the lead** adelantarse mucho **III.** *n* **1.** (*furnace*) fragua *f* **2.** (*smithy*) herrería *f*

◆**forge ahead** *vi* **1.** (*make progress*) avanzar rápidamente **2.** (*move into lead*) ponerse en cabeza

forger ['fɔːdʒəʳ, *Am:* 'fɔːrdʒɚ] *n* falsificador(a) *m(f)*

forgery ['fɔːdʒəri, *Am:* 'fɔːr-] <-ies> *n* falsificación *f*

forget [fə'get, *Am:* fɚ-] <forgot, forgotten> **I.** *vt* **1.** (*not remember*) olvidar; **to ~ to do sth** olvidarse de hacer algo; **to ~** (**that**) ... olvidar (que)... **2.** (*leave behind*) **to ~ sth** dejarse algo; **to ~ one's keys** dejarse las llaves **3.** (*stop thinking about*) **to ~ sth/sb** dejar de pensar en algo/alguien; **to ~ one's quarrels** olvidar las rencillas; **to ~ one's dignity** dejar la dignidad de uno a un lado; **it's best forgotten** sería mejor olvidarlo **4.** (*give up*) **to ~ sth** dejar algo; **~ it** olvídalo **5. to ~ oneself** (*behave badly*) propasarse **II.** *vi* **1.** (*not remember*) olvidarse; **to ~ about sth/sb** olvidarse de algo/alguien; **to ~ about doing sth** olvidarse de hacer algo **2.** (*stop thinking about*) **to ~ about sth/sb** dejar de pensar en algo/alguien; **to ~ about a plan** abandonar un plan; **let's ~ about it!** ¡pelillos a la mar!

forgetful [fə'getfəl, *Am:* fɚ-] *adj* olvidadizo, -a

forget-me-not [fə'getminɒt, *Am:* fɚ'get-minɑːt] *n* nomeolvides *f inv*

forgive [fə'gɪv, *Am:* fɚ-] <forgave, forgiven> **I.** *vt* **1.** (*pardon*) perdonar; **to ~ sb** (**for**) **sth** perdonar algo a alguien; **to ~ sb for doing sth** perdonar a alguien por hacer algo **2.** *form* (*pardon*) **~ me** discúlpeme; **~ my ignorance/language** disculpe mi ignorancia/lenguaje; **~ me** (**for**) **mentioning it** perdone que lo mencione **II.** *vi* perdonar; **to ~ and forget** perdonar y olvidar

forgiven *pp of* **forgive**

forgiveness *n* perdón *m*

forgiving *adj* misericordioso, -a

forgo [fɔː'gəʊ, *Am:* fɔːr'goʊ] *irr vt* privarse de

forgot [fə'gɒt, *Am:* fɚ'gɑːt] *pt of* **forget**

forgotten [fə'gɒtn, *Am:* fɚ'gɑːtn] **I.** *pp of* **forget II.** *adj* olvidado, -a

fork [fɔːk, *Am:* fɔːrk] **I.** *n* **1.** (*cutlery*) tenedor *m* **2.** (*tool*) horca *f* **3.** (*in road*) bifurcación *f* **4.** *pl* (*on bicycle*) horquilla *f* **II.** *vt* coger con tenedor, agarrar con tenedor *AmL* **III.** *vi* bifurcarse

forked *adj* bifurcado, -a

forked lightning *n* relámpago *m* en zigzag

fork-lift (**truck**) [ˌfɔːklɪft(ˈtrʌk), *Am:* ˌfɔːrk-lɪft(ˈtrʌk)] *n* carretilla *f* elevadora

forlorn [fəˈlɔːn, *Am:* fɔːrˈlɔːrn] *adj* (*person*) triste; (*place*) abandonado, -a; (*hope*) vano, -a

form [fɔːm, *Am:* fɔːrm] **I.** *n* **1.** (*type, variety*) tipo *m;* ~ **of exercise** tipo de ejercicio; ~ **of government** sistema *m* de gobierno; ~ **of transport** medio *m* de transporte; ~ **of persuasion** medida *f* de persuasión; **a** ~ **of disease** un tipo de enfermedad; **in any** (**shape or**) ~ de cualquier modo; **in the** ~ **of sth** en forma de algo; **to take the** ~ **of sth** adoptar la forma de algo **2.** (*outward shape*) forma *f;* (*of an object*) bulto *m;* **to take** ~ tomar forma; **in liquid/solid** ~ en estado líquido/sólido **3.** LING (*of word*) forma *f;* **the singular** ~ la forma singular **4.** (*document*) formulario *m;* **an application/entry** ~ un formulario de solicitud/admisión; **to fill in a** ~ rellenar un formulario **5.** *no pl* SPORTS forma *f;* **to be in** ~ estar en forma; **to be out of** ~ estar en baja forma **6.** *no pl* (*correct procedure*) **in due** ~ de la debida forma; **a matter of** ~ una cuestión de forma; **for** ~**'s sake** para salvar las apariencias; **to be bad** ~ ser de mal gusto **7.** *Brit* (*class*) clase *f* **8.** *Brit* (*bench*) banco *m* **9.** (*mould*) molde *m* **II.** *vt* **1.** (*make*) formar; **to** ~ **part of sth** formar parte de algo; **to** ~ **the basis of sth** constituir la base de algo; **to** ~ **a queue** formar una cola; **to** ~ **the impression** tener la impresión; **to** ~ **an opinion** formarse una opinión; **to** ~ **a habit** adquirir un hábito **2.** (*mould*) moldear **3.** (*set up*) establecer; **to** ~ **a committee/government** formar un comité/gobierno; **to** ~ **a relationship** iniciar una relación; **to** ~ **an alliance with sb** establecer una alianza con alguien **III.** *vi* formarse

formal [ˈfɔːməl, *Am:* ˈfɔːr-] *adj* (*official, ceremonious*) formal; ~ **dress** traje *m* de etiqueta; ~ **procedures** procedimientos *mpl* oficiales; ~ **interest** interés *m* sólo de palabra

formaldehyde [fɔːˈmældɪhaɪd, *Am:* fɔːr-] *n no pl* formaldehído *m*

formality [fɔːˈmæləti, *Am:* -t̬i] <-ies> *n* formalidad *f;* **to be merely a** ~ ser una pura formalidad

formalize [ˈfɔːməlaɪz, *Am:* ˈfɔːr-] *vt* formalizar; **to** ~ **one's thoughts** dar forma a los pensamientos de uno

formally *adv* formalmente

format [ˈfɔːmæt, *Am:* ˈfɔːr-] **I.** *n* formato *m* **II.** <-tt-> *vt* INFOR formatear

formation [fɔːˈmeɪʃən, *Am:* fɔːr-] *n* formación *f;* **rock** ~ formación *f* rocosa; **in battle** ~ en orden de batalla

formation flying *n no pl* vuelo *m* en formación

formative [ˈfɔːmətɪv, *Am:* ˈfɔːrmət̬ɪv] *adj* formativo, -a; **the** ~ **years** los años de formación

formatting *n* INFOR formateo *m*

former [ˈfɔːməʳ, *Am:* ˈfɔːrmɚ] *adj* **1.** (*previous*) anterior; **in a** ~ **life** en una vida anterior **2.** (*first of two*) primero, -a

formerly *adv* antes

form feed *n* INFOR avance *m* de página

formic acid [ˌfɔːmɪkˈæsɪd, *Am:* ˌfɔːr-] *n* ácido *m* fórmico

formidable [ˈfɔːmɪdəbl, *Am:* ˈfɔːrmə-] *adj* (*person*) extraordinario, -a; (*opponent, task*) difícil

formless [ˈfɔːmlɪs, *Am:* ˈfɔːrm-] *adj* amorfo, -a

formula [ˈfɔːmjʊlə] <-s *o* -lae> *pl pl n* **1.** MAT *a. fig* fórmula *f* **2.** COM (*recipe for product*) receta *f;* **the** ~ **for success** la fórmula del éxito **3.** (*form of words*) expresión *f* **4.** *no pl, Am* (*milk*) leche *f* para lactantes

formulate [ˈfɔːmjʊleɪt, *Am:* ˈfɔːr-] *vt* **1.** (*draw up*) formular **2.** (*express in words*) expresar

formulation [ˌfɔːmjʊˈleɪʃən, *Am:* ˈfɔːr-] *n no pl* formulación *f*

fornicate [ˈfɔːnɪkeɪt, *Am:* ˈfɔːr-] *vi* fornicar

forsake [fəˈseɪk, *Am:* fɔːr-] <forsook, forsaken> *vt* (*abandon*) abandonar; (*give up*) renunciar a

forsaken [fəˈseɪkən, *Am:* fɔːr-] **I.** *pp of* **forsake II.** *adj* abandonado, -a

forsook [fəˈsʊk, *Am:* fɔːr-] *pt of* **forsake**

forswear [fɔːˈsweəʳ, *Am:* fɔːrˈswer] <forswore, forsworn> *vt liter* renunciar a

fort [fɔːt, *Am:* fɔːrt] *n* fortaleza *f*

forte[1] [ˈfɔːteɪ, *Am:* fɔːrt] *n no pl* (*strong point*) fuerte *m*

forte[2] [ˈfɔːteɪ, *Am:* fɔːrt-] *adv* MUS forte *m*

forth [fɔːθ, *Am:* fɔːrθ] *adv form* **to go** ~ irse; **back and** ~ de acá para allá; **from that day** ~ de ese día en adelante

forthcoming [ˌfɔːθˈkʌmɪŋ, *Am:* ˌfɔːrθ-] *adj* **1.** (*happening soon*) venidero, -a; (*book*) de próxima aparición; (*film*) de próximo estreno **2.** (*available*) **to be** ~ (**from sb**) venir (de alguien) **3.** (*informative*) **to be** ~ (**about sth**) estar dispuesto a hablar (de algo)

forthright [ˈfɔːθraɪt, *Am:* ˈfɔːrθ-] *adj* directo, -a

forthwith [ˌfɔːθˈwɪθ, *Am:* ˌfɔːrθ-] *adv form* en el acto

fortieth [ˈfɔːtɪəθ, *Am:* ˈfɔːrt̬ɪ-] **I.** *adj* cuadragésimo, -a **II.** *n* (*order*) cuadragésimo, -a *m, f;* (*fraction*) cuadragésimo *m;* (*part*) cuadragésima parte *f; s. a.* **eighth**

fortification [ˌfɔːtɪfɪˈkeɪʃən, *Am:* ˌfɔːrt̬ə-] *n no pl* fortificación *f*

fortify [ˈfɔːtɪfaɪ, *Am:* ˈfɔːrt̬ə-] <-ie-> *vt* **1.** MIL fortificar **2.** **to** ~ **oneself** (**with sth**) fortalecerse (con algo)

fortitude [ˈfɔːtɪtjuːd, *Am:* ˈfɔːrt̬ətuːd] *n no pl, form* fortaleza *f*

fortnight [ˈfɔːtnaɪt, *Am:* ˈfɔːrt-] *n no pl, Brit, Aus* quince días *mpl;* (*business*) quincena *f;* **in a** ~**'s time** dentro de una quincena

fortnightly [ˈfɔːtnaɪtli, *Am:* ˈfɔːrt-] **I.** *adj* quincenal **II.** *adv* cada quince días

fortress ['fɔːtrɪs, *Am:* 'fɔːr-] *n* fortaleza *f*
fortuitous [fɔː'tjuːɪtəs, *Am:* fɔːr'tuːət̬əs] *adj form* fortuito, -a
fortunate ['fɔːtʃənət, *Am:* 'fɔːr-] *adj* afortunado, -a; **to be ~ to do sth** tener la suerte de hacer algo; **to be ~ in sth** tener suerte en algo; **it is ~ for her that ...** tiene la suerte de que...
fortunately *adv* afortunadamente
fortune ['fɔːtʃuːn, *Am:* 'fɔːrtʃən] *n* **1.**(*money*) fortuna *f;* **a small ~** una pequeña fortuna; **to be worth a ~** valer una fortuna; **to cost a ~** costar un dineral; **to make a ~** hacer una fortuna **2.** *no pl, form* (*luck*) suerte *f;* **good/ill ~** buena/mala suerte; **to have the good ~ to do sth** tener la suerte de hacer algo; **to tell sb's ~** decir la buenaventura a alguien **3.** *no pl, liter* (*luck personified*) **~ smiled on him** la fortuna le sonrió **4.** *pl* (*fate*) peripecias *fpl*
fortune hunter *n* cazafortunas *mf* **fortune teller** *n* adivino, -a *m, f*
forty ['fɔːti, *Am:* 'fɔːrt̬i] **I.** *adj* cuarenta **II.** <-ies> *n* cuarenta *m; s. a.* **eighty**
forum ['fɔːrəm] *n* foro *m*
forward ['fɔːwəd, *Am:* 'fɔːrwɚd] **I.** *adv* **1.**(*towards the front*) hacia adelante; **to lean ~** inclinarse hacia adelante; **a step ~** *fig* un paso hacia adelante **2.** *form* (*onwards in time*) en adelante; **from that day/time ~** de ese día/momento en adelante; **to put one's watch/the clock ~** adelantar el reloj **II.** *adj* **1.**(*towards the front*) hacia adelante; **~ movement** movimiento *m* hacia adelante; **~ gear** AUTO marcha *f* adelante **2.**(*in a position close to front*) en la parte delantera; **to be ~ of sth** estar en la parte de delante de algo **3.**(*near front of plane*) delantero, -a; (*ship*) de proa **4.** MIL (*close to enemy*) de avance **5.**(*relating to the future*) **~ buying** compra *f* a plazos; **~ look** mirada *f* hacia el futuro; **~ planning** planes *mpl* de futuro **6.**(*over-confident*) descarado, -a **III.** *n* SPORTS delantero, -a *m, f;* **centre ~** delantero centro **IV.** *vt* **1.**(*send*) remitir; **please ~** por favor, hacer seguir **2.** *form* (*help to progress*) promover
forwarding address *n* dirección *f* (*para enviar el correo*) **forwarding agent** *n* agente *mf* de tránsito
forward-looking *adj* con miras al futuro
forwardness *n no pl* precocidad *f*
forwards ['fɔːwədz, *Am:* 'fɔːrwɚdz] *adv s.* **forward**
forwent [fɔː'went, *Am:* fɔːr-] *pt of* **forgo**
fossil ['fɒsəl, *Am:* 'fɑːsəl] *n* **1.** GEO fósil *m* **2.** *inf* (*person*) carca *mf*
fossil fuel *n* combustible *m* fósil
fossilized ['fɒsəlaɪzd, *Am:* 'fɑːsə-] *adj* **1.** GEO fosilizado, -a **2.** *inf* (*outdated*) anticuado, -a
foster ['fɒstə^r, *Am:* 'fɑːstɚ] *vt* **1.**(*look after*) acoger **2.**(*encourage*) fomentar
foster brother *n* hermano *m* acogido **foster child** *n* hijo, -a *m, f* acogido, -a **foster father** *n* padre *m* de acogida **foster home** *n* casa *f* de acogida **foster mother** *n* madre *f* de acogida **foster sister** *n* hermana *f* acogida
fought [fɔːt, *Am:* fɑːt] *pt, pp of* **fight**
foul [faʊl] **I.** *adj* (*disgusting: taste*) asqueroso, -a; (*air*) sucio, -a; (*smell*) fétido, -a; (*weather*) pésimo, -a; (*language*) ordinario, -a; (*mood, temper*) insoportable; **to be ~ to sb** ser insoportable con alguien **II.** *n* SPORTS falta *f,* penal *m AmL* **III.** *vt* **1.**(*pollute*) ensuciar; (*dog*) hacer sus necesidades en **2.** SPORTS **to ~ sb** cometer una falta contra alguien **3.**(*tangle*) liar
foul-mouthed [ˌfaʊl'maʊðd] *adj* malhablado, -a
foulness ['faʊlnəs] *n no pl* **1.**(*dirtiness*) suciedad *f* **2.**(*unpleasantness*) lo desagradable **3.**(*coarseness*) basteza *f*
foul play *n* SPORTS juego *m* sucio
found[1] [faʊnd] *pt, pp of* **find**
found[2] [faʊnd] *vt* **1.**(*establish*) fundar **2.**(*base*) basar; **to ~ a statement/a case on sth** basar una declaración/un caso en algo **3.**(*build*) **to be ~ed on sth** estar construido sobre algo
found[3] [faʊnd] *vt* MIN fundir
foundation [faʊn'deɪʃən] *n* **1.** *pl* (*of building*) cimientos *mpl;* **to lay the ~(s) (of sth)** poner los cimientos (de algo); **to shake sth to its ~s** remover algo hasta los cimientos **2.** *fig* (*basis*) base *f;* **to lay the ~(s) of sth** establecer la(s)base(s) de algo **3.** *no pl* (*evidence*) fundamento *m;* **to have no ~** no tener fundamento alguno **4.** *no pl* (*establishment*) establecimiento *m* **5.**(*organization*) fundación *f* **6.** *no pl* (*make-up*) maquillaje *m* de base
foundation cream *n no pl* maquillaje *m* de base **foundation stone** *n* piedra *f* fundamental
founder[1] ['faʊndə^r, *Am:* -dɚ] *n* fundador(a) *m(f)*
founder[2] ['faʊndə^r, *Am:* -dɚ] *vi* **1.**(*sink*) hundirse **2.** *fig* (*fail*) fracasar; **to ~ on sth** fracasar en algo
Founding Fathers *npl* **the ~** *los fundadores de la nación americana*
foundry ['faʊndri] <-ries> *n* fundición *f,* fundidora *AmS*
fount [faʊnt] *n a. fig, form* fuente *f;* **to be the ~ of all knowledge/wisdom** ser la fuente del conocimiento/de la sabiduría
fountain ['faʊntɪn, *Am:* -tən] *n* fuente *f*
fountain pen *n* pluma *f* estilográfica
four [fɔː^r, *Am:* fɔːr] **I.** *adj* cuatro **II.** *n* **1.** cuatro *m* **2.**(*group of four*) cuarteto *m* ►**to go on all ~s** andar a gatas; *s. a.* **eight**
four-by-four *n Am* AUTO cuatro por cuatro *m*
four-door car *n* coche *m* de cuatro puertas
fourfold ['fɔːfəʊld, *Am:* 'fɔːrfoʊld] **I.** *adj* cuádruple **II.** *adv* **to increase ~** aumentar en cuatro veces
four-footed [ˌfɔː'fʊtɪd, *Am:* ˌfɔːr'fʊt̬-] *adj* cuadrúpedo, -a
four-handed *adj* **1.**(*involving four people*)

F

de cuatro jugadores **2.** (*for two pianists*) para dos pianistas

four-leaf clover *n*, **four-leaved clover** *n* trébol *m* de cuatro hojas **four-letter word** *n* palabrota *f*

foursome ['fɔːsəm, *Am:* 'fɔːr-] *n* grupo *m* de cuatro personas; **to make up a ~** hacer un grupo de cuatro

four-square [ˌfɔː'skweəʳ, *Am:* ˌfɔːr'swer] *adj* **1.** (*building*) firme **2.** (*person*) resoluto, -a; **to stand ~ behind sb** apoyar decididamente a alguien

fourteen [ˌfɔː'tiːn, *Am:* ˌfɔːr-] **I.** *adj* catorce **II.** *n* catorce *m; s. a.* **eight**

fourteenth **I.** *adj* decimocuarto, -a **II.** *n* **1.** (*order*) decimocuarto, -a *m, f* **2.** (*date*) quatorce *m* **3.** (*fraction*) catorceavo *m;* (*part*) catorceava parte *f; s. a.* **eighth**

fourth [fɔːθ, *Am:* fɔːrθ] **I.** *adj* cuarto, -a **II.** *n* **1.** (*order*) cuarto, -a *m, f* **2.** (*date*) ocho *m* **3.** (*fraction*) cuarto *m;* (*part*) cuarta parte *f* **4.** MUS cuarta *f; s. a.* **eighth**

fourth gear *n* AUTO cuarta marcha *f*

Fourth of July *n no pl, Am* Día *m* de la Independencia de Estados Unidos

> El **Fourth of July** o **Independence Day** es el día de fiesta americano no confesional más importante. En este día se conmemora la **Declaration of Independence** (declaración de independencia), mediante la cual las colonias americanas se declaran independientes de Gran Bretaña. Esto ocurrió el 4 de julio de 1776. Esta festividad se celebra con meriendas campestres, fiestas familiares y partidos de baseball. Como broche de oro el día se cierra con unos vistosos fuegos artificiales.

four-wheel drive [ˌfɔːhwiːl'draɪv, *Am:* ˌfɔːr-] *n* tracción *f* a cuatro ruedas

fowl [faʊl] <-(s)> *n* ave *f* de corral

fowlpest ['faʊlpest] *n no pl* enfermedad *f* de aves de corral

fox [fɒks, *Am:* fɑːks] **I.** *n* **1.** (*animal*) zorro *m* **2.** *no pl* (*fur*) piel *f* de zorro **3.** *inf* (*cunning person*) **an old ~** un viejo zorro **4.** *Am, inf* (*sexy woman*) tía *f* buena **II.** *vt* **1.** (*mystify*) mistificar **2.** (*trick*) engañar

foxglove ['fɒksglʌv, *Am:* 'fɑːks-] *n* dedalera *f*

foxhunt ['fɒkshʌnt, *Am:* 'fɑːks-] *n* cacería *f* del zorro **fox terrier** *n* fox terrier *mf*

foxtrot ['fɒkstrɒt, *Am:* 'fɑːkstrɑːt] <-tt-> **I.** *n* foxtrot *m* **II.** *vi* bailar un foxtrot

foxy ['fɒksi, *Am:* 'fɑːk-] <-ier, -iest> *adj* **1.** (*crafty*) taimado, -a **2.** *Am, inf* (*sexy*) sexy

foyer ['fɔɪeɪ, *Am:* -ɚ] *n* **1.** (*entrance hall*) vestíbulo *m* **2.** *Am* (*hall of house*) recibidor *m*

fracas ['frækɑː, *Am:* 'freɪkəs] <-(ses)> *n* gresca *f*

fractal ['fræktl] *n* MAT fractal *m*

fraction ['frækʃən] *n* fracción *f*

fractional ['frækʃənl] *adj* **1.** MAT fraccionario, -a **2.** (*difference*) mínimo, -a

fractious ['frækʃəs] *adj* díscolo, -a

fracture ['fræktʃəʳ, *Am:* -tʃɚ] **I.** *vt* **1.** MED fracturar; **to ~ one's leg** fracturarse la pierna **2.** (*break*) romper; **to ~ an agreement** romper un acuerdo **II.** *vi* fracturarse **III.** *n* MED fractura *f*

fragile ['frædʒaɪl, *Am:* -əl] *adj* delicado, -a; (*object, peace*) frágil; **to feel ~** sentirse débil

fragility [frə'dʒɪləti, *Am:* -ţi] *n no pl* fragilidad *f*

fragment ['frægmənt, *Am:* 'frægment] **I.** *n* fragmento *m;* **to smash sth (in)to ~s** hacer algo añicos **II.** *vi* **1.** (*break into pieces*) fragmentarse **2.** *fig* (*break up*) romperse **III.** *vt* **1.** (*break into pieces*) fragmentar **2.** *fig* (*break up*) romper

fragmentary ['frægməntri] *adj* fragmentario, -a

fragrance ['freɪgrəns] *n* fragancia *f*

fragrant ['freɪgrənt] *adj* fragante

frail [freɪl] *adj* (*person*) endeble; (*thing*) frágil

frailty ['freɪlti, *Am:* -ţi] <-ies> *n* **1.** *no pl* (*weakness: of person*) flaqueza *f;* (*of thing*) fragilidad *f* **2.** (*moral flaw*) defecto *m* moral

frame [freɪm] **I.** *n* **1.** (*for door, picture*) *a.* INFOR marco *m* **2.** *pl* (*spectacles*) montura *f* **3.** (*supporting structure*) armazón *m o f* **4.** (*body*) cuerpo *m* **5.** CINE, TV fotograma *m* **II.** *vt* **1.** (*picture*) enmarcar **2.** (*act as a surround to*) servir de marco **3.** (*put into words*) formular **4.** *inf* (*falsely incriminate*) incriminar dolosamente

frame-up ['freɪmʌp] *n inf* montaje *m* (*para inculpar a alguien*)

framework ['freɪmwɜːk, *Am:* -wɜːrk] *n* **1.** (*supporting structure*) armazón *m o f* **2.** *fig* (*set of rules, principles*) sistema *m*

franc [fræn] *n* franco *m*

France [frɑːns, *Am:* fræns] *n* Francia *f*

franchise ['fræntʃaɪz] **I.** *n* franquicia *f* **II.** *vt* conceder en franquicia

Franciscan [fræn'sɪskən] **I.** *n* REL franciscano, -a *m, f* **II.** *adj* REL franciscano, -a

Franco- ['fræŋkəʊ, *Am:* -koʊ] *in compounds* franco-

frank [fræŋk] **I.** *adj* franco, -a; **to be ~, ...** sinceramente,... **II.** *vt* franquear

frankfurter ['fræŋkfɜːtəʳ, *Am:* -fɜːrţɚ] *n* salchicha *f* de Frankfurt

frankincense ['fræŋkɪnsents] *n no pl* incienso *m*

franking machine *n* (máquina *f*) franqueadora

frankly *adv* sinceramente

frantic ['fræntɪk, *Am:* -ţɪk] *adj* (*hurry, activity*) frénetico, -a; **to be ~ with rage** estar furioso; **to be ~ with worry** andar loco de inquietud; **to drive sb ~** sacar a alguien de quicio

fraternal [frə'tɜːnl, *Am:* -'tɜːr-] *adj* **1.** (*brotherly*) fraternal **2.** *fig* (*friendly*) amical

fraternity [frə'tɜːnəti, *Am:* -'tɜːrnəţi] <-ies> *n* **1.** *no pl* (*brotherly feeling*) fraternidad *f* **2.** (*group of people*) cofradía *f* **3.** *Am* UNIV club *m* de estudiantes

fraternize ['frætənaɪz, *Am:* '-ɚ-] *vi* fraternizar

fratricide ['frætrɪsaɪd, *Am:* -rə-] *n* (*crime*) fratricidio *m*

fraud [frɔːd, *Am:* frɑːd] *n* **1.** *no pl a.* LAW fraude *m* **2.** (*trick*) trampa *f* **3.** (*person*) impostor(a) *m(f)*

fraudulence ['frɔːdjʊləns, *Am:* 'frɑːdʒə-] *n no pl* **1.** (*financial dishonesty*) fraude *m* **2.** (*of claim, behaviour*) fraudulencia *f*

fraudulent ['frɔːdjʊlənt, *Am:* 'frɑːdʒə-] *adj* fraudulento, -a

fraught [frɔːt, *Am:* frɑːt] *adj* tenso, -a; **to be ~ with difficulties/problems** estar lleno de dificultades/problemas

fray[1] [freɪ] *vi* (*rope, cloth*) deshilacharse; **tempers were beginning to ~** la gente estaba perdiendo la paciencia

fray[2] [freɪ] *n* **the ~** la lucha; **to enter the ~** pasar a la lucha

freak [friːk] **I.** *n* **1.** (*abnormal person, thing*) monstruo *m;* **a ~ of nature** un fenómeno de la naturaleza **2.** (*enthusiast*) fanático, -a *m, f* **II.** *adj* anormal **III.** *vi s.* **freak out I**

◆**freak out I.** *vi* flipar **II.** *vt* **to freak sb out** alucinar a alguien

freckle ['frekl] *n pl* peca *f*

freckled ['frekld] *adj* pecoso, -a

free [friː] **I.** <-r, -est> *adj* **1.** (*not constrained: person, country, elections*) libre; **to break ~ (of sth)** soltarse (de algo); **to break ~ of sb** despegarse de alguien; **to go ~** salir en libertad; **to set sb ~** poner en libertad a alguien; **to be ~ to do sth** no tener reparos para hacer algo; **~ press** prensa *f* independiente **2.** (*not affected by*) **to be ~ of sth** no estar afectado por algo; **to be ~ of a disease** no estar afectado por una enfermedad **3.** (*not attached*) **to get sth ~** liberar algo **4.** (*not busy*) **to be ~ to do sth** estar libre para hacer algo; **to leave sb ~ to do sth** dejar a alguien que haga algo **5.** (*not occupied*) libre; **to leave sth ~** dejar algo libre **6.** (*costing nothing*) gratis; **~ ticket** billete *m* gratis; **~ of charge** gratis; **~ sample** muestra *f* gratuita; **~ on board** franco a bordo; **to be ~ of customs/tax** estar libre de aranceles/impuestos; **to be ~ to sb** ser gratis para alguien **7.** (*generous*) **to be ~ with sth** dar algo en abundancia; **to make ~ with sth** *pej* usar algo como si fuera cosa propia **8.** (*translation, verse*) libre ▸**~ and easy** despreocupado **II.** *adv* gratis; **~ of charge** gratis; **for ~** *inf* gratis **III.** *vt* **1.** (*release: person*) poner en libertad **2.** (*make available*) permitir; **to ~ sb to do sth** dar libertad a alguien para que haga algo

freebie ['friːbiː] *n* obsequio *m*

freebooter ['friːbuːtəʳ, *Am:* -t̬ɚ] *n* filibustero *m*

freedom ['friːdəm] *n* **1.** (*of person, country*) libertad *f;* **to have the ~ to do sth** tener la libertad de hacer algo; **~ of action/movement** libertad *f* de acción/movimiento; **~ of the press** libertad *f* de prensa; **~ of speech/thought** libertad *f* de expresión/pensamiento; **to have ~ from interference** no sufrir intromisiones **2.** (*right*) derecho *m* **3.** (*room for movement*) soltura *f* **4.** (*unrestricted use*) usufructo *m;* **to have the ~ of sb's house** tener el usufructo de la casa de alguien

free enterprise *n no pl* libre empresa *f* **free fall** *n no pl* caída *f* libre; **to go into ~** FIN caer en picado

free-for-all ['friːfəʳ,ɔːl, *Am:* 'friːfɚɔːl] *n* gresca *f*

freehold ['friːhəʊld, *Am:* -hoʊld] **I.** *n* plena propiedad *f* **II.** *adj* de plena propiedad **III.** *adv* en propiedad absoluta

freeholder *n* propietario, -a *m, f* absoluto, -a

free kick *n* SPORTS tiro *m* libre

freelance ['friːlɑːns, *Am:* 'friːlæns] **I.** *n* freelance *mf* **II.** *adj* autónomo, -a **III.** *adv* por cuenta propia **IV.** *vi* trabajar por cuenta propia

freeload ['friːləʊd, *Am:* -loʊd] *vi Am, Aus, pej* gorronear; **to ~ off sb** gorronear a alguien

freeloader *vi pej* gorrón, -ona *m, f*

freely *adv* **1.** (*unrestrictedly*) sin límite; **to be ~ available** poder obtenerse sin trabas **2.** (*without obstruction*) libremente **3.** (*frankly*) francamente **4.** (*generously*) generosamente

freeman ['friːmən] <-men> *n* **1.** HIST (*not slave*) hombre *m* libre **2.** (*honorary citizen*) ciudadano *m* de honor

free market *n* libre mercado *m*

Freemason ['friː,meɪsən] *n* francmasón, -ona *m, f*

Freephone [,friːfəʊn, *Am:* -foʊn] *n Brit* número *m* gratuito

free port *n* puerto *m* franco

free-range [,friː'reɪndʒ] *adj* de granja **free-range chicken** *n* pollo *m* de corral **free-range egg** *n* huevo *m* de granja

free speech *n no pl* libertad *f* de expresión

free-spoken [,friː'spəʊkən, *Am:* -'spoʊ-] *adj* que habla sin reservas

free-standing [,friː'stændɪŋ] *adj* independiente

freestyle ['friːstaɪl] *n no pl* estilo *m* libre

freethinker [,friː'θɪŋkəʳ, *Am:* -kɚ] *n* librepensador(a) *m(f)*

freethinking *adj* librepensador(a)

free trade *n no pl* librecambio *m* **freeware** *n* programa *m* de libre distribución **freeway** *n Am, Aus* autopista *f*

freewheel [,friː'hwiːl, *Am:* 'friːhwiːl] *vi* ir en punto muerto

free will *n no pl* libre albedrío *m*

freeze [friːz] <froze, frozen> **I.** *vi* **1.** (*liquid*) helarse; (*food*) congelarse **2.** (*become totally still*) quedarse completamente rígido, -a **II.** *vt* (*liquid*) helar; (*food, prices*) congelar **III.** *n* **1.** METEO ola *f* de frío **2.** ECON congelación *f*

◆**freeze up** *vi* helarse

freezer *n* congelador *m,* congeladora *f AmS*

freezing I. *adj* glacial; **it's** ~ hiela; **I'm** ~ estoy helado II. *n no pl* congelación *f*

freezing point *n* punto *m* de congelación

freight [freɪt] *no pl* I. *n* 1. (*type of transportation*) flete *m* 2. (*goods*) mercancías *fpl* 3. (*charge*) porte *m* 4. *Am* RAIL tren *m* de mercancías II. *adv* por flete III. *vt* fletar

freight car *n Am* RAIL vagón *m* de mercancías

freighter ['freɪtəʳ, *Am:* -t̬ɚ] *n* 1. (*ship*) buque *m* de carga 2. (*plane*) avión *m* de mercancías

freight train *n Am* tren *m* de mercancías

French [frentʃ] I. *adj* francés, -esa; ~ **speaker** francófono, -a *m, f* II. *n* 1. (*person*) francés, -esa *m, f* 2. (*language*) francés *m*

French bean *n Brit* judía *f* verde **French chalk** *n no pl* jabón *m* de sastre **French doors** *npl* puertaventana *f* **French dressing** *n no pl* vinagreta *f* **French fried potatoes** *npl*, **French fries** *npl* patatas *fpl* fritas **French horn** *n* trompa *f* de llaves **French letter** *n Brit, Aus, inf* (*condom*) condón *m* **Frenchman** <-men> *n* francés *m* **French windows** *npl Am s.* **French doors** **Frenchwoman** <-women> *n* francesa *f*

frenetic [frə'netɪk, *Am:* -'net̬-] *adj* frenético, -a

frenzied *adj* frenético, -a

frenzy ['frenzi] *n no pl* frenesí *m*

frequency ['fri:kwəntsi] <-cies> *n no pl* frecuencia *f*

frequency band *n* banda *f* de frecuencia **frequency modulation** *n* frecuencia *f* modulada

frequent¹ ['fri:kwənt] *adj* frecuente, tupido, -a *Méx*

frequent² [frɪ'kwent] *vt* frecuentar

frequently ['fri:kwəntli] *adv* con frecuencia

fresco ['freskəʊ, *Am:* -koʊ] <-s *o* -es> *n* fresco *m*

fresh [freʃ] *adj* 1. (*not stale: air, water, food*) fresco, -a; (*bread*) recién hecho, -a 2. (*new*) nuevo, -a; (*snow*) virgen; **to make a** ~ **start** volver a empezar; ~ **from the oven/the factory** recién salido del horno/de fábrica 3. (*cool: breeze*) fresco, -a 4. (*not tired*) como nuevo, -a 5. *inf* (*disrespectful*) descarado, -a

freshen ['freʃən] I. *vt* refrescar II. *vi* (*wind*) soplar más recio

freshman ['freʃmən] <-men> *n* UNIV novato *m*, estudiante *m* de primer año

Con el nombre de **Freshman** se conoce en los EE.UU. a un alumno de la clase novena, con el de **Sophonmore** a uno de la décima, con el de **Junior** al alumno de la decimoprimera clase y con el de **Senior** al de la decimosegunda. Estos términos se utilizan corrientemente para los alumnos de secundaria, aun incluso en el caso de aquellas **High Schools** en las que los alumnos sólo se incorporan a partir de la décima clase. Esta terminología es empleada también por los alumnos universitarios durante sus cuatro años de college.

freshness *n no pl* 1. (*of air, water, food*) frescura *f* 2. (*of ideas, approach*) novedad *f*

fresh water *n* agua *f* dulce

fret¹ [fret] I. <-tt-> *vi* inquietarse II. *n* **to be in a** ~ estar muy inquieto

fret² [fret] *n* MUS traste *m*

fretful ['fretfəl] *adj* (*person, tone*) quejoso, -a

fretsaw ['fretsɔ:, *Am:* -sɑ:] *n* sierra *f* de calados

fretwork ['fretwɜ:k, *Am:* -wɜ:rk] *n no pl* calado *m*

friar ['fraɪəʳ, *Am:* -ɚ] *n* fraile *m*

fricative ['frɪkətɪv, *Am:* -t̬ɪv] LING I. *adj* fricativo, -a II. *n* fricativa *f*

friction ['frɪkʃən] *n no pl* 1. (*rubbing*) fricción *f* 2. *fig* (*disagreement*) desavenencia *f*

Friday ['fraɪdi] *n* viernes *m inv;* **on** ~**s** los viernes; **every** ~ todos los viernes; **this (coming)** ~ este (próximo) viernes; **on** ~ **mornings** los viernes por la mañana; **on** ~ **night** el viernes por la noche; **last/next** ~ el viernes pasado/que viene; **every other** ~ un viernes sí y otro no; **on** ~ **we are going on holiday** el viernes nos vamos de vacaciones

fridge [frɪdʒ] *n* nevera *f*, refrigeradora *f AmS*

fried [fraɪd] *adj* frito, -a

fried chicken *n* pollo *m* frito **fried egg** *n* huevo *m* frito

friend [frend] *n* amigo, -a *m, f;* **to be** ~**s** ser amigos; **to make** ~**s** (**with sb**) hacerse amigo (de alguien); **a** ~ **of mine/his/hers/yours** un amigo mío/suyo/tuyo

friendless ['frendləs] *adj* sin amigos

friendly ['frendli] I. <-ier, -iest> *adj* 1. (*person*) simpático, -a, entrador(a) *Arg;* (*house, environment*) acogedor(a); (*nation*) cordial; **to be on** ~ **terms with sb** estar a bien con alguien; **to be** ~ **towards sb** mostrarse amable con alguien; **to be** ~ **with sb** llevarse bien con alguien 2. SPORTS (*not competitive*) amistoso, -a II. *n* SPORTS partido *m* amistoso

friendly society *n Brit* FIN sociedad *f* de socorro mutuo

friendship ['frendʃɪp] *n* amistad *f*

fries [fraɪz] *npl inf* patatas *fpl* fritas

frieze [fri:z] *n* friso *m*

frigate ['frɪgət] *n* fragata *f*

fright [fraɪt] *n* 1. (*feeling of fear*) terror *m;* **to take** ~ (**at sth**) asustarse (por algo) 2. *no pl* (*frightening experience*) susto *m*, jabón *m Arg, Méx, Prico;* **to get a** ~ llevarse un susto; **to give sb a** ~ dar un susto a alguien 3. *inf* (*unattractive sight*) adefesio *m;* **to look a** ~ tener un aspecto horrible

frighten ['fraɪtən] I. *vt* asustar II. *vi* asustarse ◆**frighten away** *vt* espantar

frightened *adj* asustado, -a

frightening *adj* aterrador(a)

frightful ['fraɪtfəl] *adj* espantoso, -a

frigid ['frɪdʒɪd] *adj* **1.** (*sexually*) frígido, -a **2.** (*unfriendly*) frío, -a **3.** (*very cold*) glacial

frigidity [frɪ'dʒɪdəti, *Am:* -t̬i] *n* **1.** (*sexual*) frigidez *f* **2.** (*unfriendliness*) frialdad *f*

frill [frɪl] *n* **1.** (*cloth*) volante *m* **2. no ~s** sin excesos

frilly ['frɪli] *adj* (*dress*) de volantes; (*style*) recargado, -a

fringe [frɪndʒ] **I.** *n* **1.** (*decorative edging*) flecos *mpl* **2.** *Brit, Aus* (*hair*) flequillo *m,* pava *f AmC, And* **3.** (*edge*) margen *m* **II.** *vt* rodear **III.** *adj no pl* secundario, -a

fringe benefits *npl* ECON beneficios *mpl* complementarios **fringe group** *n* grupo *m* marginal **fringe theatre** *n no pl* teatro *m* experimental

frippery ['frɪpəri] <-ies> *n pl* perifollos *mpl*

frisk [frɪsk] **I.** *vi* juguetear **II.** *vt* cachear

frisky ['frɪski] <-ier, -iest> *adj* **1.** (*lively, energetic*) retozón, -ona; (*horse*) fogoso, -a **2.** *inf* (*sexually*) juguetón, -ona

fritter[1] ['frɪtəʳ, *Am:* 'frɪt̬ɚ] *n* buñuelo *m,* picarón *m AmL*

fritter[2] ['frɪtəʳ, *Am:* 'frɪt̬ɚ] *vt* **to ~ (away)** desperdiciar

frivolity [frɪ'vɒləti, *Am:* -'vɑːlət̬i] <-ties> *n* frivolidad *f*

frivolous ['frɪvələs] *adj* frívolo, -a; (*not serious*) poco formal

frizzy ['frɪzi] *adj* (*hair*) encrespado, -a

fro [frəʊ, *Am:* froʊ] *adv* **to and ~** de un lado a otro

frock [frɒk, *Am:* frɑːk] *n* vestido *m*

frog[1] [frɒg, *Am:* frɑːg] *n* ZOOL rana *f* ►**to have a ~ in one's throat** tener carraspera

frog[2] [frɒg, *Am:* frɑːg] *n pej* (*French person*) gabacho, -a *m, f*

frogman ['frɒgmən, *Am:* 'frɑːg-] <-men> *n* hombre-rana *m*

frogmarch ['frɒgmɑːtʃ, *Am:* 'frɑːgmɑːrtʃ] *vt* llevar a la fuerza

frogspawn ['frɒgspɔːn, *Am:* 'frɑːgspɑːn] *n no pl* huevos *mpl* de rana

frolic ['frɒlɪk, *Am:* 'frɑːlɪk] **I.** <-ck-> *vi* juguetear **II.** *n* jolgorio *m*

frolicsome ['frɒlɪksəm, *Am:* 'frɑːlɪk-] *adj* juguetón, -ona

from [frɒm, *Am:* frɑːm] *prep* **1.** (*as starting point*) de; **where is he ~?** ¿de dónde es?; **the flight ~ London** el vuelo procedente de Londres; **to fly ~ New York to Tokyo** volar de Nueva York a Tokio; **to appear ~ among the trees** aparecer de entre los árboles; **shirts ~ £5** camisas desde £5; **~ inside** desde dentro; **to drink ~ a cup/the bottle** beber de una taza/la botella **2.** (*temporal*) **~ day to day** día tras día; **~ time to time** de vez en cuando; **~ his childhood** desde su infancia; **~ that date on(wards)** desde esa fecha **3.** (*at distance to*) **100 metres ~ the river** 100 metros del río; **far ~ doing sth** lejos de hacer algo **4.** (*one to another*) **to go ~ door to door** ir de puerta en puerta; **to tell good ~ evil** distinguir el bien del mal **5.** (*originating in*) **a card ~ Paul/Corsica** una tarjeta de Paul/Córcega; **~ my point of view** en mi opinión **6.** (*in reference to*) **~ what I heard** según lo que he escuchado; **translated ~ the English** traducido del inglés; **quotations ~ Joyce** citas de Joyce; **~ 'War and Peace'** de 'Guerra y Paz'; **to judge ~ appearances** juzgar según las aparencias; **different ~ the others** diferente de los demás **7.** (*caused by*) **~ experience** por experiencia; **weak ~ hunger** débil de [*o* por] hambre; **to die ~ thirst** morir de sed **8.** (*removed*) **to steal/take sth ~ sb** robar/quitar algo a alguien; **to prevent sb ~ doing sth** evitar que alguien haga algo; **to keep sth ~ sb** mantener algo alejado de alguien; **to shade ~ the sun** protegerse del sol; **4 (subtracted) ~ 7 equals 3** MAT 4 restado de 7 es igual a 3

front [frʌnt] **I.** *n* **1.** *no pl* (*forward-facing part*) frente *f;* (*of building*) fachada *f* **2.** (*outside cover*) cubierta *f* exterior; (*first pages*) principio *m* **3.** (*front area*) parte *f* delantera; **in ~** delante; **in ~ of** delante de **4.** THEAT auditorio *m* **5.** (*deceptive appearance*) apariencias *fpl;* **he's/she's putting on a bold ~** la procesión va por dentro **6.** MIL frente *m;* **on the domestic/work ~** en el terreno doméstico/laboral **7.** POL frente *m;* **a united ~** un frente común **8.** *no pl* (*promenade*) paseo *m* marítimo **9.** METEO frente *m* **II.** *adj* **1.** (*at the front*) delantero, -a **2.** (*first*) primero, -a **III.** *vt* **1.** (*be head of*) liderar **2.** TV presentar **IV.** *vi* estar enfrente de; **the flat ~s north** el piso da al norte; **to ~ for** servir de fachada [*o* tapadera]

frontage ['frʌntɪdʒ, *Am:* -t̬ɪdʒ] *n* fachada *f*

frontal ['frʌntəl, *Am:* -t̬əl] *adj* ANAT, METEO frontal; (*attack*) de frente

front bench *n Brit* POL *los ministros del gobierno o sus homólogos en la oposición* **front door** *n* puerta *f* principal **front-end** *n* INFOR frontal *m*

frontier [frʌn'tɪəʳ, *Am:* frʌn'tɪr] *n* **1.** (*border*) *a. fig* frontera *f* **2.** *Am* (*outlying areas*) **the ~** los límites

frontiersman <-men> *n Am* HIST hombre *m* de la frontera **frontier station** *n* puesto *m* fronterizo

frontispiece ['frʌntɪspiːs, *Am:* -t̬ɪs-] *n* frontispicio *m*

front line *n* primera línea *f* **front page** *n* primera página *f* **front-page** *adj* de primera plana **front runner** *n* líder *mf* **front-wheel drive** *n* tracción *f* delantera

frost [frɒst, *Am:* frɑːst] **I.** *n* escarcha *f;* **12 degrees of ~** 12 grados bajo cero **II.** *vt* **1.** (*cover with frost*) cubrir de escarcha **2.** *Am* (*cover with icing*) escarchar

frostbite ['frɒstbaɪt, *Am:* 'frɑːst-] *n no pl* congelación *f*

frostbitten *adj* congelado, -a

frostbound *adj* helado, -a

frosted *adj* **1.** *Am* (*covered with icing*) es-

carchado, -a **2.** (*opaque*) esmerilado, -a
frosting *n no pl, Am* (*icing*) azúcar *m* glaseado
frosty ['frɒsti, *Am:* 'frɑːsti] <-ier, -iest> *adj* **1.** (*with frost*) escarchado, -a **2.** (*unfriendly*) frío, -a
froth [frɒθ, *Am:* frɑːθ] **I.** *n no pl* **1.** (*bubbles*) espuma *f* **2.** *fig* banalidad *f* **II.** *vi* echar espuma **III.** *vt* espumar
frothy ['frɒθi, *Am:* 'frɑːθi] <-ier, -iest> *adj* espumoso, -a
frown [fraʊn] **I.** *vi* fruncir el ceño; **to ~ at sb/sth** mirar con el ceño fruncido a alguien/algo **II.** *n* ceño *m* fruncido
frowsy *adj,* **frowzy** ['fraʊzi] <-ier, -iest> *adj inf* desaliñado, -a
froze [frəʊz, *Am:* froʊz] *pt of* **freeze**
frozen ['frəʊzn, *Am:* 'froʊzn] **I.** *pp of* **freeze** **II.** *adj* congelado, -a
frugal ['fruːgl] *adj* frugal
frugality [fruː'gæləti, *Am:* -t̬i] *n no pl* frugalidad *f*
fruit [fruːt] **I.** *n* **1.** *no pl* (*for eating*) fruta *f;* (*on tree, product*) fruto *m* **2.** (*results*) fruto *m* ►**to bear ~** dar fruto; *fig* dar resultado **II.** *vi* dar fruto
fruitcake ['fruːtkeɪk] *n* **1.** *no pl* (*cake*) tarta *f* de frutas **2.** *Brit, Aus, inf* (*person*) chiflado, -a *m, f*
fruitful ['fruːtfəl] *adj* **1.** (*productive*) provechoso, -a; (*discussion*) productivo, -a **2.** *liter* (*fertile*) fructuoso, -a
fruition [fruː'ɪʃən] *n no pl* **to bring sth to ~** llevar algo a buen término; **to come to ~** realizarse
fruit knife *n* cuchillo *m* de la fruta
fruitless ['fruːtləs] *adj* infructuoso, -a
fruit salad *n no pl* macedonia *f*
fruity ['fruːti, *Am:* -t̬i] <-ier, -iest> *adj* **1.** afrutado, -a **2.** *inf* (*joke*) verde
frumpish ['frʌmpɪʃ] *adj pej* anticuado, -a
frustrate [frʌs'treɪt, *Am:* 'frʌstreɪt] <-ting> *vt* frustrar
frustrated *adj* frustrado, -a
frustrating *adj* frustrante
frustration [frʌs'treɪʃən] *n* frustración *f*
fry[1] [fraɪ] <-ie-> **I.** *vt* freír **II.** *vi* **1.** (*be cooked*) freírse **2.** *inf* (*get burnt*) quemarse
fry[2] [fraɪ] *n Am,* **fry-up** *n Brit* fritada *f*
frying pan *n* sartén *f,* paila *f AmL* ►**to jump out of the ~ into the fire** salir de Guatemala y meterse en Guatepeor
ft *abbr of* **foot, feet** pie
FT [,ef'tiː] INFOR *abbr of* **formula translation** TF
fuchsia ['fjuːʃə] **I.** *n* fucsia *m* **II.** *adj* fucsia
fuck [fʌk] *vulg* **I.** *vt* joder, coger *AmL;* **~ you!** ¡jódete!; **~ that idea** ¡a la mierda esa idea! **II.** *vi* joder, coger *AmL* **III.** *n no pl* polvo *m* **IV.** *interj* joder
◆**fuck off** *vi* **~!** ¡vete a la mierda!
fucker ['fʌkər, *Am:* -ɚ] *n vulg* gilipollas *mf inv*
fuddled ['fʌdld] *adj* **1.** (*confused*) aturdido, -a **2.** (*drunk*) borracho, -a
fuddy-duddy ['fʌdi,dʌdi] **I.** <-ies> *n pej, inf* persona *f* chapada a la antigua **II.** *adj pej, inf* chapado, -a a la antigua
fudge [fʌdʒ] **I.** *n* **1.** *no pl* (*sweet*) dulce *m* de azúcar **2.** (*compromise*) apaño *m* **II.** <-ging> *vt* (*issue*) esquivar **III.** <-ging> *vi* quedar indeciso, -a
fuel ['fjuːəl] **I.** *n no pl* combustible *m* **II.** <*Brit:* -ll-, *Am:* -l-> *vt* **1.** (*provide with fuel*) aprovisionar de combustible **2.** (*increase: tension, controversy*) avivar
fuel consumption *n no pl* AUTO consumo *m* de gasolina **fuel gauge** *n* indicador *m* del nivel de gasolina **fuel-injection engine** *n* motor *m* de inyección **fuel pump** *n* bomba *f* de combustible **fuel rod** *n* varilla *f* de combustible
fug [fʌg] *n no pl* aire *m* viciado
fuggy ['fʌgi] <-ier, -iest> *adj* cargado, -a
fugitive ['fjuːdʒətɪv, *Am:* -t̬ɪv] **I.** *n* fugitivo, -a *m, f* **II.** *adj* (*escaping*) fugitivo, -a
fugue [fjuːg] *n* MUS fuga *f*
fulfil <-ll-> *vt Brit,* **fulfill** [fʊl'fɪl] *vt Am, Aus* (*ambition, task*) realizar; (*condition, requirement*) cumplir; (*need*) satisfacer; (*function, role*) desempeñar; **to ~ oneself** realizarse
fulfilment *n Brit,* **fulfillment** *n Am, Aus no pl* (*of condition, requirement*) cumplimiento *m;* (*of function, role*) desempeño *m;* (*satisfaction*) realización *f*
full [fʊl] **I.** <-er, -est> *adj* **1.** (*container, space*) lleno, -a; (*vehicle*) completo, -a **2.** (*total: support*) total; (*recovery*) completo, -a; (*member*) numerario, -a; **to be in ~ dress** estar de gala; **to be in ~ flow** estar en pleno discurso; **to be in ~ swing** estar en pleno apogeo **3.** (*maximum: marks*) máximo, -a; (*employment*) pleno, -a; **to be on ~ beam** (*car light*) tener puesta la larga; **at ~ speed** a toda velocidad; **at ~ stretch** al máximo **4.** (*busy and active*) ocupado, -a **5.** (*rounded*) redondo, -a **6.** (*wide*) amplio, -a; (*skirt*) holgado, -a **7.** (*wine*) con cuerpo **II.** *adv* **1.** (*completely*) completamente **2.** (*directly*) directamente **3.** (*very*) muy; **to know ~ well (that ...)** saber muy bien (que...) **III.** *n* **in ~** sin abreviar; **to the ~** al máximo
fullback ['fʊlbæk] *n* defensa *mf*
full-blooded [,fʊl'blʌdɪd] *adj* **1.** (*wholehearted*) entusiasta **2.** (*animal*) de raza
full-blown [,fʊl'bləʊn, *Am:* -'bloʊn] *adj* (*disaster, scandal*) auténtico, -a
full board *n* pensión *f* completa
full-bodied [,fʊl'bɒdɪd, *Am:* -'bɑːdɪd] *adj* (*taste*) fuerte; (*wine*) con mucho cuerpo
full-cream milk *n* leche *f* entera
full-fledged [,fʊl'fledʒd] *adj Am s.* **fully-fledged**
full-frontal **I.** *adj* desenfrenado, -a **II.** *n* desnudo *m* visto de frente **full-grown** *adj* crecido, -a **full-length** *adj* **1.** (*for entire body*) de cuerpo entero **2.** (*not short*) extenso,

-a **full moon** *n* luna *f* llena
fullness *n no pl* **1.** (*being full*) plenitud *f;* **in the ~ of time** a su debido tiempo **2.** (*roundedness*) redondez *f* **3.** (*richness*) riqueza *f*
full-page *adj* de página entera **full-scale** *adj* **1.** (*original size*) de tamaño natural **2.** (*all-out*) a gran escala **full stop** *Brit, Aus* **I.** *n* punto *m;* **to come to a ~** *fig* paralizarse **II.** *adv* y punto **full time** *n* SPORTS fin *m* del partido **full-time** *adj* de horario completo
fully ['fʊli] *adv* **1.** (*completely*) completamente **2.** (*in detail*) detalladamente **3.** (*at least*) al menos
fully-fledged [ˌfʊli'fledʒd] *adj Brit* (*bird*) plumado; (*person*) hecho, -a y derecho, -a
fulminate ['fʌlmɪneɪt] *vi* **to ~** (**against sth**) tronar (contra algo)
fulsome ['fʊlsəm] *adj pej* (*praise*) exagerado, -a; (*person, manner*) servil
fumble ['fʌmbl] **I.** *vi* **to ~ around for sth** buscar algo a tientas; **to ~ for words** titubear buscando las palabras **II.** *vt* SPORTS **to ~ the ball** dejar caer la pelota
fumbler ['fʌmbləʳ, *Am:* -blɚ] *n* torpe *mf*
fume [fjuːm] *vi* **1.** (*be angry*) estar furioso, -a; **to ~ at sb** echar pestes de alguien **2.** (*emit fumes*) humear
fumigate ['fjuːmɪgeɪt] *vt* fumigar
fun [fʌn] **I.** *n no pl* diversión *f;* **it was good ~** fue muy agradable; **full of ~** pletórico de alegría; **to do sth for ~** hacer algo por placer; **to do sth in ~** hacer algo en broma; **to have** (**a lot of**) **~** divertirse (mucho); **have ~ on your weekend!** ¡pásalo bien de fin de semana!; **have ~!** ¡diviértete!; **to have ~ at sb's expense** reírse a costa de alguien; **to get a lot of ~ out of** [*o* **from**] **sth** pasarlo bien con algo; **to make ~ of sb, to poke ~ at sb** reírse de alguien; **what ~!** ¡qué divertido! ►**~ and games** *pej* odisea *f;* **it's not all ~ and games** no todo el monte es orégano **II.** *adj Am, Aus* **1.** (*enjoyable*) agradable **2.** (*funny*) divertido, -a; **she's a real ~ person** *inf* es una persona divertidísima
function ['fʌŋkʃən] **I.** *n* **1.** *a.* MAT función *f;* **in my ~ as mayor, ...** como alcalde,... **2.** (*formal ceremony*) ceremonia *f;* (*formal social event*) acto *m* **II.** *vi* funcionar
functional ['fʌŋkʃənl] *adj* **1.** *a.* LING funcional **2.** (*operational, working*) práctico, -a
functionary ['fʌŋkʃənəri, *Am:* -eri] <-ies> *n* funcionario, -a *m, f*
function key *n* INFOR tecla *f* de función
fund [fʌnd] **I.** *n* fondo *m;* **to be short of ~s** ir mal de fondos; **to have a ~ of knowledge about sth** saber mucho de algo **II.** *vt* financiar
fundamental [ˌfʌndə'mentəl, *Am:* -t̬əl] **I.** *adj* fundamental; (*difference*) esencial; (*principles*) básico, -a; **to be of ~ importance** ser de vital importancia **II.** *n* **the ~s** los principios básicos
fundamentalism [ˌfʌndə'mentəlɪzəm, *Am:* -t̬əl-] *n no pl* fundamentalismo *m*
fundamentalist **I.** *n* integrista *mf* **II.** *adj* integrista
fundamentally *adv* **1.** (*basically*) fundamentalmente **2.** (*in the most important sense*) esencialmente
funding *n* (*act*) financiación *f;* (*resources*) fondos *mpl*
fundraising ['fʌndˌreɪzɪŋ] *n* recaudación *f* de fondos
funeral ['fjuːnərəl] *n* entierro *m;* **to attend a ~** asistir a un funeral ►**that's your/his ~** *inf* eso es tu/su problema
funeral director *n* director(a) *m(f)* de funeraria **funeral march** <-es> *n* márcha *f* fúnebre **funeral parlour** *n* funeraria *f* **funeral pyre** *n* pira *f*
funereal [fjuːˈnɪəriəl, *Am:* -'nɪri-] *adj* fúnebre
funfair ['fʌnfeəʳ, *Am:* -fer] *n Brit* **1.** (*amusement park*) parque *m* de atracciones **2.** (*fair*) feria *f*
fungicide ['fʌŋgɪsaɪd, *Am:* 'fʌndʒɪ-] *n* fungicida *m*
fungus ['fʌŋgəs] *n* (*wild mushroom*) hongo *m;* (*mould*) moho *m*
fun house *n Am* pasaje *m* del terror
funicular [fjuː'nɪkjələʳ, *Am:* -juːlɚ] *n,* **funicular railway** *n* funicular *m*
funk [fʌŋk] *n no pl* **1.** *Am, Aus* (*depression*) abatimiento *m fig* **2.** *Brit, inf* (*fear*) **to be in a blue ~** estar paralizado por el miedo **3.** (*music*) funk *m*
funky ['fʌŋki] <-ier, -iest> *adj inf* **1.** (*cool*) genial **2.** (*music*) funky
fun-loving *adj* marchoso, -a
funnel ['fʌnəl] **I.** *n* **1.** (*implement*) embudo *m* **2.** NAUT chimenea *f* **II.** <*Brit:* -ll-, *Am:* -l-> *vt* canalizar
funnies ['fʌniz] *npl* **the ~** las tiras cómicas
funny ['fʌni] <-ier, -iest> *adj* **1.** (*amusing*) divertido, -a; **to see the ~ side of a situation** observar lo curioso de una situación **2.** (*odd, peculiar*) raro, -a; **to have a ~ feeling that ...** tener la extraña sensación de que...; **to have ~ ideas** tener ideas de bombero **3.** (*slightly ill*) **to feel ~** no encontrarse bien **4.** *Brit, inf* (*witty*) gracioso, -a; **to try to be ~** *inf* hacerse el gracioso
funny bone *n inf* hueso *m* de la alegría
fur [fɜːʳ, *Am:* fɜːr] **I.** *n* **1.** (*animal hair*) piel *f* **2.** *no pl* CHEM, MED sarro *m* **II.** <-rr-> *vi* **to ~ up** (*kettle, pipes*) cubrirse de sarro
fur coat *n* abrigo *m* de piel
furious ['fjʊərɪəs, *Am:* 'fjʊrɪ-] *adj* **1.** (*very angry*) furioso, -a, enchilado, -a *Méx,* caribe *Ant;* **to be ~ about sth** estar furioso por algo; **a ~ outburst** un acceso de furia **2.** (*intense, violent*) violento, -a; **at a ~ pace** a un ritmo vertiginoso
furl [fɜːl, *Am:* fɜːrl] *vt* (*flag, sail*) recoger
furlong ['fɜːlɒŋ, *Am:* 'fɜːrlɑːŋ] *n Brit: medida de longitud equivalente a 200 metros aproximadamente*

furlough ['fɜːləʊ, *Am:* 'fɜːrloʊ] *n* MIL permiso *m;* **to be on** ~ estar de permiso

furnace ['fɜːnɪs, *Am:* 'fɜːr-] *n a. fig* horno *m*

furnish ['fɜːnɪʃ, *Am:* 'fɜːr-] *vt* **1.** (*supply*) proporcionar; **to** ~ **sb with sth** suministrar algo a alguien; **to be** ~**ed with sth** estar provisto de algo **2.** (*provide furniture*) amueblar

furnished ['fɜːnɪʃt, *Am:* 'fɜːr-] *adj* amueblado, -a

furnishings ['fɜːnɪʃɪŋz, *Am:* 'fɜːr-] *npl* muebles *mpl*

furniture ['fɜːnɪtʃəʳ, *Am:* 'fɜːrnɪtʃɚ] *n no pl* mobiliario *m;* **piece of** ~ mueble *m*

furniture van *n* camión *m* de mudanzas

furore [fjʊə'rɔːri, *Am:* 'fjʊrɔːr] *n* furor *m*

furrier ['fʌriəʳ, *Am:* 'fɜːriɚ] *n* peletero, -a *m, f*

furrow ['fʌrəʊ, *Am:* 'fɜːroʊ] **I.** *n* **1.** (*groove*) ranura *f* **2.** (*wrinkle*) arruga *f* **II.** *vt* arrugar; **to** ~ **one's brow** fruncir el ceño

furry ['fɜːri] <-ier, -iest> *adj* **1.** peludo, -a **2.** (*looking like fur*) peloso, -a; ~ **toy** peluche *m*

further ['fɜːðəʳ, *Am:* 'fɜːrðɚ] **I.** *adj comp of* **far 1.** (*greater distance*) más lejano; **nothing could be** ~ **from his mind** estará pensando en cualquier cosa menos en eso **2.** (*additional*) otro, -a; **if you have any** ~ **problems ...** si tienes más problemas...; **until** ~ **notice** hasta nuevo aviso **II.** *adv comp of* **far 1.** (*greater distance*) más lejos; **we didn't get much** ~ no llegamos mucho más allá; ~ **on** más adelante; ~ **and** ~ cada vez más lejos; **to go** ~ **with sth** hacer progresos con algo **2.** (*more*) más; **I have nothing** ~ **to say** no tengo (nada) más que decir ►**to not go** __**any**__ ~ no ir más allá; **this musn't go** __**any**__ ~ esto debe quedar entre nosotros **III.** *vt* fomentar; **to** ~ **sb's interests** favorecer los intereses de alguien

furtherance ['fɜːðərəns, *Am:* 'fɜːr-] *n no pl, form* fomento *m*

furthermore [ˌfɜːðə'mɔːʳ, *Am:* 'fɜːrðɚmɔːr] *adv* además

furthermost ['fɜːðəməʊst, *Am:* 'fɜːrðɚmoʊst] *adj* más lejano, -a

furthest ['fɜːðɪst, *Am:* 'fɜːr-] **I.** *adj* **1.** *superl of* **far 2.** (*greatest*) mayor; **prices have fallen/risen** ~ **in the south** los precios han bajado/subido más en el sur **3.** (*at the greatest distance*) más lejano, -a; **the** ~ **island from the mainland** la isla más apartada de tierra firme **II.** *adv* **1.** *superl of* **far 2.** (*greatest distance*) más lejos; **that's the** ~ **I can go** eso es lo más lejos que puedo ir

furtive ['fɜːtɪv, *Am:* 'fɜːrt̬ɪv] *adj* furtivo, -a

furtiveness *n no pl* furtivismo *m*

fury ['fjʊəri, *Am:* 'fjʊri] *n no pl* furor *m;* **fit of** ~ ataque *m* de furia; **I've been working like** ~ he estado trabajando con frenesí

fuse [fjuːz] **I.** *n* **1.** ELEC fusible *m;* **the** ~ **has gone** *Brit, Aus* han saltado los plomos **2.** (*ignition device, detonator*) espoleta *f;* (*string*) mecha *f* ►**to have a** __**short**__ ~ tener mucho genio; **to** __**light**__ **the** ~ encender la mecha **II.** *vi* **1.** ELEC fundirse **2.** (*join together*) fusionarse **III.** *vt* **1.** ELEC fundir **2.** (*join*) fusionar

fuse box <-es> *n* caja *f* de fusibles

fuselage ['fjuːzəlɑːʒ, *Am:* -səlɑːʒ] *n* fuselaje *m*

fusion ['fjuːʒən] *n* **1.** (*joining together*) fusión *f* **2.** *no pl* PHYS fusión *f;* **nuclear** ~ fusión nuclear

fusion bomb *n* bomba *f* termonuclear

fusion reactor *n* reactor *m* nuclear

fuss [fʌs] **I.** *n* alboroto *m;* **it's a lot of** ~ **about nothing** mucho ruido y pocas nueces; **to make a** ~ armar un escándalo **II.** *vi* preocuparse; **to** ~ **over sth** preocuparse en exceso por algo **III.** *vt* molestar

fusspot ['fʌspɒt, *Am:* -pɑːt] *n inf* quisquilloso, -a *m, f*

fussy ['fʌsi] <-ier, -iest> *adj* **1.** (*over-particular*) puntilloso, -a; **I'm not** ~ *Brit, inf* no me importa **2.** (*quick to criticize*) quisquilloso, -a **3.** (*overdone, overdecorated*) recargado, -a

fusty ['fʌsti] <-ier, -iest> *adj pej* **1.** (*smelling damp and stale*) rancio, -a; (*room*) que huele a cerrado **2.** (*old-fashioned*) anticuado, -a

futile ['fjuːtaɪl, *Am:* -t̬əl] *adj* inútil; ~ **attempt** intento *m* en vano

futility [fjuː'tɪləti, *Am:* -t̬i] *n no pl* inutilidad *f*

future ['fjuːtʃəʳ, *Am:* -tʃɚ] **I.** *n* **1.** *a.* LING futuro *m;* **to have plans for the** ~ tener planes de futuro; **in the** ~ **tense** en futuro; **the distant/near** ~ el futuro lejano/próximo; **what the** ~ **will bring** lo que depara el futuro **2.** (*prospects*) porvenir *m;* **she has a great** ~ **ahead of her** tiene un gran porvenir **II.** *adj* futuro, -a

future perfect *n* LING futuro *m* perfecto

futures market *n* mercado *m* de futuros

futuristic [ˌfjuːtʃə'rɪstɪk] *adj* futurista

fuze [fjuːz] *Am* **I.** *n* (*ignition device, detonator*) espoleta *f;* (*string*) mecha *f* **II.** *vt* molestar

fuzz [fʌz] *n no pl* **1.** (*fluff*) pelusa *f* **2.** (*fluffy hair*) pelo *m* crespo **3.** (*short growing hair*) vello *m;* **peach** ~ *fig* piel *f* de melocotón **4.** *inf* (*police*) **the** ~ la pasma

fuzzy ['fʌzi] *adj* **1.** (*unclear*) borroso, -a **2.** (*hair*) (*short, soft*) velloso, -a; (*curly*) rizado, -a

f-word ['efˌwɜːd, *Am:* -wɜːrd] *n forma de evitar el uso de la palabra 'fuck'*

G

G, g [dʒiː] *n* G, g *f;* ~ **for George** G de Granada

g *abbr of* **gram** g.

gab [gæb] **I.** <-bb-> *vi inf* estar de palique **II.** *n* cháchara *f;* **to have the gift of the** ~ tener mucha labia

gabardine [ˌgæbə'diːn, *Am:* 'gæbɚdiːn] *n*

no pl gabardina *f*

gabble ['gæbl] **I.** *vi* (*talk inarticulately*) farfullar; (*talk quickly*) hablar atropelladamente **II.** *vt* (*utter too quickly*) decir atropelladamente; (*utter indistinctly*) pronunciar de modo ininteligible **III.** *n no pl* (*inarticulate speech*) farfulla *f;* (*quick speech*) habla *f* atropellada

gable ['geɪbl] *n* ARCHIT aguilón *m;* ~ **roof** tejado *m* de dos aguas

Gabon [gæ'bɒn, *Am:* -'boʊn] *n* Gabón *m*

Gabonese [ˌgæbɒn'iːz, *Am:* -'boʊn] **I.** *adj* de Gabón **II.** *n* habitante *mf* de Gabón

gad [gæd] <-dd-> *vi inf* **to** ~ **about** callejear

gadabout ['gædəbaʊt] *n* trotacalles *mf inv*

gadfly ['gædflaɪ] <-flies> *n* (*insect*) tábano *m*

gadget ['gædʒɪt] *n* artilugio *m;* ~**s** chismes *mpl*

gadgetry ['gædʒɪtri] *n no pl* chismes *mpl*

Gaelic ['geɪlɪk] **I.** *n* gaélico *m* **II.** *adj* gaélico, -a

gaff [gæf] *n* arpón *m* ►**to blow the** ~ *Brit, inf* descubrir el pastel

gaffe [gæf] *n* metedura *f* de pata; **to make a** ~ meter la pata

gaffer ['gæfəʳ, *Am:* -ɚ] *n* **1.** *Brit, inf* (*foreman*) capataz *m; fig* jefe *m* **2.** (*head electrician on a film*) iluminista *mf* **3.** *Brit, inf* (*old man*) viejo, -a *m, f*

gag [gæg] **I.** *n* **1.** (*cloth*) mordaza *f* **2.** (*joke*) chiste *m* **3.** THEAT morcilla *f* **II.** <-gg-> *vt* amordazar; (*silence*) hacer callar **III.** <-gg-> *vi* (*to joke*) contar chistes; THEAT meter morcillas

gaga ['gɑːgɑː] *adj inf* chocho, -a; **to go** ~ chochear

gage [geɪdʒ] *n, vt Am s.* **gauge**

gagging order *n inf* bloqueo *m* informativo

gaggle ['gægl] *n a. iron* manada *f*

gaiety ['geɪəti, *Am:* -t̬i] *n no pl* alegría *f*

gaily ['geɪli] *adv* alegremente

gain [geɪn] **I.** *n* **1.** (*increase*) aumento *m;* ~ **in weight** aumento de peso **2.** ECON, FIN (*profit*) beneficio *m;* **net** ~ beneficio neto **3.** *fig* (*advantage*) ventaja *f* **II.** *vt* **1.** (*obtain*) ganar **2.** (*acquire*) adquirir **3.** (*catch up*) alcanzar; **to** ~ **success** conseguir el éxito **4.** (*increase: velocity*) adquirir; **to** ~ **weight** engordar ►**to** ~ **the upper hand** tomar ventaja **III.** *vi* (*increase*) aumentar; (*prices, numbers*) subir; (*clock, watch*) adelantarse; **once she went off the diet she started ~ing again** cuando dejó la dieta volvió a engordar

gainful ['geɪnfəl] *adj* lucrativo, -a

gait [geɪt] *n a.* SPORTS paso *m*

gaiter ['geɪtəʳ, *Am:* -t̬ɚ] *n pl* polaina *f*

gala ['gɑːlə, *Am:* 'geɪ-] **I.** *n* **1.** (*special public entertainment*) gala *f* **2.** *Brit* (*sports competition*) competición *f* **II.** *adj* (*festive*) de gala; ~ **night** noche *f* de gala

galactic [gə'læktɪk] *adj* galáctico, -a

Galapagos Islands [gə'læpəgəs 'aɪlənd] *npl* Islas *fpl* Galápagos

galaxy ['gæləksi] <-ies> *n* **1.** (*space*) galaxia *f* **2.** *fig* constelación *f*

gale [geɪl] *n* tormenta *f;* **a ~-force wind** un vendaval; ~**s of laughter** carcajadas *fpl*

gale warning *n* aviso *m* de tormenta

Galicia [gə'lɪsiə] *n* Galicia *f*

Galician **I.** *adj* gallego, -a **II.** *n* gallego, -a *m, f*

gall [gɔːl] **I.** *n* **1.** (*bile*) bilis *f inv* **2.** (*impertinence*) impertinencia *f;* **to have the** ~ **to do sth** tener agallas para hacer algo; *pej* tener la cara de hacer algo **II.** *vt* mortificar

gall. *abbr of* **gallon** gal.

gallant ['gælənt] **I.** *adj* **1.** (*chivalrous*) galante **2.** (*brave*) valiente **II.** *n* HIST galán *m*

gallantry ['gæləntri] *n* **1.** *no pl* (*chivalry*) cortesía *f* **2.** *no pl* (*courage*) valentía *f* **3.** <-tries> (*act of courtly politeness*) galanterías *fpl*

gall bladder *n* vesícula *f* biliar

galleon ['gælɪən] *n* galeón *m*

gallery ['gæləri] <-ries> *n* **1.** (*for displaying art*) museo *m;* (*for paintings*) galería *f* **2.** ARCHIT, THEAT tribuna *f*

galley ['gæli] *n* **1.** NAUT, AVIAT (*kitchen*) cocina *f* **2.** HIST (*ship*) galera *f*

galley-proof *n* galerada *f*

gallivant [ˌgælɪ'vænt, *Am:* -ə'-] *vi inf* **to** ~ **about** callejear

gallon ['gælən] *n* galón *m* (*Brit: 4,55 l, Am: 3,79 l*)

gallop ['gæləp] **I.** *vi* galopar **II.** *vt* (*cause to gallop*) hacer galopar **III.** *n* galope *m;* **to break into a** ~ echar a galopar; **at a** ~ *fig* al galope

gallows ['gæləʊz, *Am:* -oʊz] *npl* **the** ~ la horca; **to send sb to the** ~ mandar a alguien al patíbulo

gallstone ['gɔːlstəʊn, *Am:* -stoʊn] *n* cálculo *m* biliar

Gallup poll ['gæləp pəʊl, *Am:* -poʊl] *n* sondeo *m* de la opinión pública

galore [gə'lɔːʳ, *Am:* -'lɔːr] *adj* en cantidad

galoshes [gə'lɒʃɪz, *Am:* -'lɑːʃ-] *npl* chanclos *mpl*

galumph [gə'lʌmf] *vi inf* moverse torpemente

galvanize ['gælvənaɪz] *vt a. fig* galvanizar; **to** ~ **sb into sth** forzar a alguien a algo

Gambia ['gæmbɪə] *n no pl* Gambia *f*

Gambian **I.** *adj* gambiano, -a **II.** *n* gambiano, -a *m, f*

gambit ['gæmbɪt] *n* **1.** (*chess move*) gambito *m* **2.** (*tactic*) táctica *f;* **opening** ~ estrategia *f* inicial

gamble ['gæmbl] **I.** *n* jugada *f;* **business** ~ riesgo *m* comercial **II.** *vi* jugar; **to** ~ **on sth** confiar en algo; **to** ~ **on the stock market** jugar a la bolsa **III.** *vt* (*money*) jugar; (*one's life*) arriesgar; **to** ~ **one's fortune/future/money** jugarse la fortuna/el futuro/el dinero

gambler ['gæmbləʳ, *Am:* -blɚ] *n* jugador(a) *m(f)*

gambling *n no pl* juego *m* **gambling den** *n* timba *f*

gambol ['gæmbl] <*Brit:* -ll-, *Am:* -l-> *vi liter* brincar

game¹ [geɪm] **I.** *n* **1.**(*unit of sports*) juego *m* **2.**(*unit of play*) partida *f;* **board** ~ juego de mesa; ~ **of chance** juego de azar; **a** ~ **of chess** una partida de ajedrez **3.** SPORTS (*skill level*) **to be off one's** ~ *a. fig* estar en baja forma **4.**(*tactic*) **the** ~ **is up** todo se acabó; **what's your** ~? ¿qué pretendes? **5.** *pl, Brit* (*organized school sports*) educación *f* física; **the Olympic Games** los juegos olímpicos ►**to give the** ~ **away** descubrir las cartas; **two can play at that** ~ donde las dan las toman; **to beat sb at his/her own** ~ ganar a alguien a sus propias cartas; **to play the** ~ *Brit* jugar limpio; **to be on the** ~ *Brit, inf* hacer la calle **II.** *adj* **1.** *inf* (*willing*) animoso, -a; **to be** ~ (**to do sth**) animarse (a hacer algo); **to be** ~ **for anything** no tener miedo a nada **2.** *inf* (*lame*) lisiado, -a

game² [geɪm] *n no pl* (*in hunting*) caza *f;* **big** ~ caza mayor

game-cock ['geɪmkɒk, *Am:* -'kɑːk] *n* gallo *m* de pelea **gamekeeper** *n* guardabosque *mf* **game show** *n* concurso *m* de televisión

gaming ['geɪmɪŋ] *n no pl* juego *m;* ~ **house** casa *f* de juego

gaming table *n* tablero *m* de juego

gamma radiation *n no pl,* **gamma rays** *npl* rayos *mpl* gamma

gammon ['gæmən] *n no pl* jamón *m*

gammy ['gæmi] <-ier, -iest> *adj Brit, inf* lisiado, -a

gamut ['gæmət] *n* gama *f*

gander ['gændəʳ, *Am:* -dɚ] *n* **1.**(*male goose*) ganso *m* **2.** *inf* (*look*) **to take a** ~ echar una ojeada

gang [gæŋ] **I.** *n* **1.**(*criminal group*) banda *f* **2.**(*organized group*) cuadrilla *f;* (*of workers*) brigada *f;* **chain** ~ grupo *m* de presidiarios encadenados **3.** *inf* (*group of friends*) pandilla *f,* barra *f AmL,* trinca *f And, CSur* **II.** *vi* **to** ~ **up on** unirse contra

ganger ['gæŋəʳ] *n Brit* capataz *mf*

gangling ['gæŋglɪŋ] *adj* larguirucho, -a

ganglion ['gæŋglɪən] <-s *o* -glia> *n* ANAT **1.**(*group of nerves*) ganglio *m* **2.**(*swelling*) protuberancia *f*

gangly ['gæŋgli] <-ier, -iest> *adj* desgarbado, -a

gangplank ['gæŋplæŋk] *n* plancha *f*

gangrene ['gæŋgriːn] *n no pl* gangrena *f*

gangrenous ['gæŋgrɪnəs, *Am:* -grə-] *adj* gangrenoso, -a

gangster ['gæŋstəʳ, *Am:* -stɚ] *n* gángster *m*

gang warfare *n no pl* guerra *f* entre bandas

gangway ['gæŋweɪ] **I.** *n* **1.** NAUT (*gangplank*) pasarela *f;* (*ladder*) escalerilla *f* **2.** *Brit* (*aisle*) pasillo *m* **II.** *interj inf* abran paso

gantry ['gæntri] <-ies> *n* caballete *m;* (*crane*) pórtico *m;* AVIAT torre *f* de lanzamiento

gaol [dʒeɪl] *n Brit s.* **jail**

gap [gæp] *n* **1.**(*opening*) abertura *f;* (*empty space*) hueco *m;* (*in text*) laguna *f;* **to fill a** ~ llenar un espacio en blanco **2.**(*break in time*) intervalo *m* **3.**(*difference*) diferencia *f;* **age** ~ diferencia de edad

gape [geɪp] **I.** *vi* abrirse; (*person*) quedarse boquiabierto **II.** *n* (*look*) mirada *f* pasmada; (*yawn*) bostezo *m*

gaping *adj* (*hole*) enorme; (*person*) boquiabierto, -a

garage ['gærɑːʒ, *Am:* gə'rɑːʒ] **I.** *n* **1.**(*of house*) garaje *m* **2.** *Brit, Aus* (*petrol station*) gasolinera *f* **3.**(*for repair*) taller *m* **II.** *vt* **to** ~ **a car** dejar un coche en el garaje

garb [gɑːb, *Am:* gɑːrb] **I.** *n no pl* vestidura *f* **II.** *vt* **to be** ~**ed as** ir vestido de

garbage ['gɑːbɪdʒ, *Am:* 'gɑːr-] *n no pl, Am, Aus* basura *f;* **to take the** ~ **out** sacar la basura

garbage can *n Am* (*dustbin*) cubo *m* de la basura, tacho *m AmL* **garbage chute** *n Am* (*rubbish chute*) vertedero *m* de basuras **garbage collector** *n Am* (*dustman*) basurero *m* **garbage disposal** *n,* **garbage disposer** *n Am* (*rubbish disposer*) triturador *m* de basuras **garbage dump** *n Am* (*rubbish dump*) vertedero *m* **garbage truck** *n Am, Aus* camión *m* de la basura

garble ['gɑːbl, *Am:* 'gɑːr-] *vt* **1.**(*confuse*) confundir **2.**(*distort*) distorsionar

garbled *adj* **1.**(*confused*) confuso, -a **2.**(*distorted*) distorsionado, -a

garden ['gɑːdn, *Am:* 'gɑːr-] **I.** *n* **1.** jardín *m;* **vegetable** ~ huerto *m;* ~ **furniture** muebles *mpl* de jardín **2.** *pl* (*ornamental grounds*) parque *m;* **botanical** ~ jardín *m* botánico **II.** *vi* (*flowers*) trabajar en el jardín; (*vegetables*) cultivar un huerto

garden centre *n* vivero *m* (de plantas)

garden city <-ies> *n* ciudad *f* jardín

gardener ['gɑːdnəʳ, *Am:* 'gɑːrdnɚ] *n* **1.**(*of flowers*) jardinero, -a *m, f* **2.**(*of vegetables*) hortelano, -a *m, f*

gardenia [gɑː'diːnɪə, *Am:* gɑːr-] *n* gardenia *f*

gardening ['gɑːdnɪŋ, *Am:* 'gɑːr-] *n no pl* (*of flowers*) jardinería *f;* (*of vegetables*) horticultura *f*

garden party <-ies> *n* fiesta *f* al aire libre

gargantuan [gɑː'gæntjʊən, *Am:* gɑːr-'gæntʃu-] *adj liter* colosal

gargle ['gɑːgl, *Am:* 'gɑːr-] **I.** *vi* hacer gárgaras **II.** *n* gárgaras *fpl*

gargoyle ['gɑːgɔɪl, *Am:* 'gɑːr-] *n* gárgola *f*

garish ['geərɪʃ, *Am:* 'ger-] *adj* chillón, -ona

garland ['gɑːlənd, *Am:* 'gɑːr-] **I.** *n* guirnalda *f* **II.** *vt* adornar con guirnaldas

garlic ['gɑːlɪk, *Am:* 'gɑːr-] *n no pl* ajo *m;* **clove of** ~ diente *m* de ajo; ~ **sauce** ajiaceite *m*

garlic press <-es> *n* triturador *m* de ajos

garment ['gɑːmənt, *Am:* 'gɑːr-] *n* prenda *f* de vestir

garnet ['gɑːnɪt, *Am:* 'gɑːr-] *n* granate *m*

garnish ['gɑːnɪʃ, *Am:* 'gɑːr-] **I.** *vt* adornar; GASTR aderezar **II.** <-es> *n* adorno *m;* GASTR

aderezo *m*
garret ['gærət, *Am:* 'ger-] *n* ARCHIT buhardilla *f;* (*attic room*) desván *m*
garrison ['gærɪsn, *Am:* 'gerə-] **I.** *n* guarnición *f* **II.** *adj* de guarnición; ~ **town** ciudad *f* con guarnición **III.** *vt* (*troops*) poner en guarnición, acuartelar; (*place*) guarnecer
garrulous ['gærələs, *Am:* 'ger-] *adj* gárrulo, -a
garter ['gɑːtəʳ, *Am:* 'gɑːrt̬ɚ] *n* liga *f;* **the Order of the Garter** *Brit* la orden de la Jarretera
garter stitch <-es> *n* punto *m* de media
gas [gæs] **I.** <-s(s)es> *n* **1.** *a.* MED, CHEM gas *m;* **natural** ~ gas natural; **to cut off the** ~ cerrar el gas **2.** *no pl, Am* (*fuel*) gasolina *f;* **leaded/unleaded** ~ gasolina con plomo/sin plomo; **to step on the** ~ acelerar **II.** <-ss-> *vt* asfixiar con gas **III.** <-ss-> *vi inf* charlar
gasbag ['gæsbæg] *n inf* loro *mf*
gas chamber *n* cámara *f* de gas **gas cooker** *n Brit* cocina *f* de gas
gaseous ['gæsɪəs] *adj* gaseoso, -a
gas field *n* yacimiento *m* de gas **gas fire** *n Brit* estufa *f* de gas **gas-fitter** *n Brit* técnico, -a *m, f* de la compañía del gas
gas gauge *n Am* (*petrol gauge*) medidor *m* del nivel de gasolina
gash [gæʃ] **I.** <-es> *n* (*deep cut*) raja *f;* (*wound*) cuchillada *f* **II.** *vt* rajar; (*wound*) acuchillar
gas heating *n* calefacción *f* de gas **gasholder** *n* gasómetro *m*
gasket ['gæskɪt] *n* junta *f*
gas lamp *n* lámpara *f* de gas **gas lighter** *n* mechero *m* de gas **gasman** <-men> *n Brit, inf* técnico *m* de la compañía del gas **gasmask** *n* máscara *f* antigás **gas meter** *n* contador *m* del gas
gasoline, **gasolene** ['gæsəliːn] *n Am* (*petrol*) gasolina *f,* nafta *f CSur* **gasoline tank** *n Am* depósito *m* de gasolina **gasometer** *n* gasómetro *m* **gas-oven** *n* horno *m* de gas
gasp [gɑːsp, *Am:* gæsp] **I.** *vi* **1.** (*breathe*) jadear; **to** ~ **for air** hacer esfuerzos para respirar; **I** ~**ed in amazement** di un grito ahogado de asombro **2.** (*speak*) hablar con voz entrecortada **3.** *Brit, inf* **to be** ~**ing for sth** morirse por algo **II.** *vt* **to** ~ **out sth** decir algo con voz entrecortada **III.** *n* jadeo *m;* **he gave a** ~ **of astonishment** dio un grito ahogado de asombro ▸**to be at one's last** ~ estar en las últimas; **to do sth at the last** ~ hacer algo en el último momento
gas pedal *n* acelerador *m* **gas pipe** *n* tubería *f* de gas **gas pump** *n Am, Can* (*petrol pump*) surtidor *m* de gasolina **gas ring** *n Brit* hornillo *m* de gas **gas station** *n Am* (*petrol station*) gasolinera *f* **gas station operator** *n Am* (*petrol station operator*) empleado, -a *m, f* de una gasolinera **gas stove** *n* cocina *f* de gas
gassy ['gæsi] <-ier, -iest> *adj* **1.** (*full of gas*) gaseoso, -a **2.** *inf* (*pointless, verbose*) rimbombante
gastric ['gæstrɪk] *adj* gástrico, -a
gastritis [gæ'straɪtɪs, *Am:* -t̬əs] *n no pl* gastritis *f inv*
gastroenteritis [ˌgæstrəʊˌentə'raɪtɪs, *Am:* -troʊˌent̬ə'raɪt̬əs] *n no pl* gastroenteritis *f inv*
gastronomic [ˌgæstrə'nɒmɪk, *Am:* -'nɑːmɪk] *adj* gastronómico, -a
gastronomy [gæ'strɒnəmi, *Am:* -'strɑːnə-] *n no pl* gastronomía *f*
gastroscopy [ˌgæs'trəʊskɒpi] <-ies> *n* MED endoscopia *f*
gasworks ['gæswɜːks, *Am:* -wɜːrks] *n* + *sing vb* fábrica *f* de gas, usina *f AmL*
gate [geɪt] **I.** *n* **1.** (*entrance barrier*) puerta *f;* RAIL barrera *f* **2.** SPORTS entrada *f* **3.** AVIAT puerta *f* de embarque **4.** NAUT compuerta *f* **II.** *vt Brit* **to be** ~**d** SCHOOL estar castigado sin salir
gatecrash ['geɪtkræʃ] **I.** *vt* colarse en **II.** *vi* colarse
gatecrasher *n* intruso, -a *m, f*
gatehouse *n* casa *f* del guarda
gatekeeper *n* portero, -a *m, f;* RAIL guardabarrera *mf*
gate-legged table *n,* **gate-leg table** ['geɪtleg 'teɪbl] *n* mesa *f* plegable
gate money *n no pl, Brit, Aus* recaudación *f*
gatepost *n* poste *m* ▸**between you and me and the** ~ entre tú y yo, que no salga de estas cuatro paredes
gateway *n* **1.** (*entrance*) entrada *f* **2.** (*means of access*) puerta *f*
gateway drug *n* primer droga *f* (*que lleva a una posterior adicción*)
gather ['gæðəʳ, *Am:* -ɚ] **I.** *vt* **1.** (*collect together*) juntar; (*flowers*) recoger; (*information*) reunir; (*harvest*) cosechar **2.** (*increase*) **to** ~ **speed** ganar velocidad **3.** (*accumulate*) acumular; **to** ~ **one's strength** cobrar fuerzas **4.** (*infer*) deducir; **to** ~ **that ...** sacar la conclusión de que... **II.** *vi* juntarse; (*people*) reunirse; (*things*) amontonarse; (*storm*) amenazar
gathering *n* reunión *f*
GATT [gæt] *n abbr of* **General Agreement on Tariffs and Trade** GATT *m*
gauche [gəʊʃ, *Am:* goʊʃ] *adj* torpe; (*shy*) poco seguro, -a de sí mismo, -a
gaudy[1] ['gɔːdi, *Am:* 'gɑː-] <-ier, -iest> *adj* llamativo, -a
gaudy[2] ['gɔːdi] <-ies> *n Brit* fanfarrón, -ona *m, f*
gauge [geɪdʒ] **I.** *n* **1.** (*measure*) medida *f* **2.** (*instrument*) indicador *m* **3.** RAIL ancho *m* de vía **4.** *fig* medidor *m,* indicador *m* **II.** *vt* **1.** (*measure*) medir **2.** (*assess*) determinar; **it's difficult to** ~ **what he will answer** resulta difícil determinar qué responderá
gaunt [gɔːnt, *Am:* gɑːnt] *adj* **1.** (*very thin*) flaco, -a; (*too thin*) demacrado, -a **2.** (*desolate*) lúgubre
gauntlet ['gɔːntlɪt, *Am:* 'gɑːnt-] *n* guante *m;*

HIST guantelete *m;* **to take up/throw down the ~** *fig* recoger/arrojar el guante ►**to run the ~** MIL, HIST correr baquetas
gauze [gɔːz, *Am:* gɑːz] *n no pl a.* MED gasa *f*
gauzy ['gɔːzi, *Am:* 'gɑːz-] <-ier, -iest> *adj* diáfano, -a
gave [geɪv] *pt of* **give**
gavel ['gævl] **I.** *n* mazo *m* **II.** <*Brit:* -ll-, *Am:* -l-> *vt* golpear
gawk [gɔːk, *Am:* gɑːk] *vi inf* papar moscas; **to ~ at** mirar tontamente
gawky ['gɔːki, *Am:* 'gɑː-] *adj* torpe; (*tall, awkward*) desgarbado, -a
gay [geɪ] **I.** *adj* **1.** (*homosexual*) gay **2.** (*cheerful*) alegre **II.** *n* gay *mf*
gaze [geɪz] **I.** *vi* mirar; **to ~ at sth** mirar algo fijamente **II.** *n* mirada *f* fija; **to be exposed to the public ~** estar expuesto para contemplación del público
gazelle [gə'zel] *n* gacela *f*
gazette [gə'zet] *n* gaceta *f*
gazetteer [ˌgæzə'tɪəʳ, *Am:* -'tɪr] *n* índice *m* geográfico
gazump [gə'zʌmp] *vt Brit, Aus, inf: vender un inmueble a alguien que ofrece más dinero, sin tener en cuenta un acuerdo de venta anterior*
GB [ˌdʒiː'biː] *n* **1.** *no pl abbr of* **Great Britain** GB **2.** INFOR *abbr of* **gigabyte** GB
GBH [ˌdʒiːbiː'eɪtʃ] *Brit abbr of* **grievous bodily harm** daño *m* personal grave
GCE [ˌdʒiːsiː'iː] *n Brit abbr of* **General Certificate of Education** GCE *m* (*título que permite el acceso a los estudios universitarios*)
GCHQ [ˌdʒiːsiːeɪtʃ'kjuː] *n Brit abbr of* **Government Communications Headquarters** Centro *m* Gubernamental de Comunicaciones
GCSE [ˌdʒiːsiːes'iː] *n Brit abbr of* **General Certificate of Secondary Education** GCSE *m* (*título de enseñanza secundaria que se consigue dos años antes que el GCE*)

> Para obtener el **GCSE** (**General Certificate of Secondary Education**), antiguamente **O-level** (**Ordinary Level**), los alumnos ingleses, galeses y nordirlandeses de 16 años deben realizar un examen. Es posible examinarse de una única asignatura, pero la mayoría de los alumnos prefieren examinarse de siete u ocho. En Escocia este examen se conoce como **Standard Grade**.

Gdns *abbr of* **Gardens** Jardines *fpl*
GDP [ˌdʒiːdiː'piː] *n abbr of* **gross domestic product** PIB *m*
gear [gɪəʳ, *Am:* gɪr] *n* **1.** TECH engranaje *m* **2.** AUTO marcha *f* **3.** *no pl* (*equipment*) equipo *m* **4.** *no pl* (*clothes*) ropa *f*
gearbox ['gɪəbɒks, *Am:* 'gɪrbɑːks] <-es> *n*, **gearcase** *n* caja *f* de cambios
gearing *n no pl* engranaje *m*
gear lever *n Brit, Aus,* **gearshift** ['gɪəʃɪft, *Am:* 'gɪr-] *n Am* palanca *f* de cambio
gearwheel *n* rueda *f* dentada
gee ['dʒiː] *interj Am, inf* caramba
geezer ['giːzəʳ, *Am:* -zɚ] *n inf* tío *m;* **old ~** vejete *m*
geisha (**girl**) ['geɪʃə] *n* geisha *f*
gel [dʒel] *n* gel *m*
gelatin(**e**) ['dʒelətɪn] *n no pl* gelatina *f*
gelatinous [dʒɪ'lætɪnəs, *Am:* -ənəs] *adj* gelatinoso, -a
geld [geld] *vt* castrar
gelding ['geldɪŋ] *n* caballo *m* castrado
gem [dʒem] *n* **1.** (*jewel*) piedra *f* preciosa **2.** (*person*) joya *f fig*
Gemini ['dʒemɪni] *n* Géminis *mf*
gen [dʒen] *n no pl, Brit, inf* información *f;* **to give sb the ~ on sth** poner a alguien al corriente de algo
◆**gen up** <-nn-> *vi Brit, inf* **to ~ on sth** informarse acerca de algo
gender ['dʒendəʳ, *Am:* -dɚ] *n* **1.** (*sexual identity*) sexo *m* **2.** LING género *m*
gene [dʒiːn] *n* gen *m*
genealogical [ˌdʒiːnɪə'lɒdʒɪkl, *Am:* -'lɑːdʒɪ-] *adj* genealógico, -a
genealogist [ˌdʒiːnɪ'ælədʒɪst] *n* genealogista *mf*
genealogy [ˌdʒiːnɪ'ælədʒi] *n no pl* genealogía *f*
gene bank *n* banco *m* de genes
general ['dʒenrəl] **I.** *adj* general; **to be of ~ interest** ser de interés general; **as a ~ rule** por regla general; **to talk in ~ terms** hablar en términos generales **II.** *n* **1.** MIL general *mf;* **~ lieutenant** teniente *mf* general **2.** (*servant*) chica *f* para todo
general agency <-ies> *n* organismo *m* general **general agent** *n Brit* agente *mf* general **general anaesthetic** *n* anestesia *f* general **general assembly** <-ies> *n* asamblea *f* general **general delivery** *n no pl, Am, Can* (*poste restante*) lista *f* de correos **general director** *n* director(a) *m(f)* general **general editor** *n* editor(a) *m(f)* jefe **general election** *n* elecciones *fpl* generales **general endorsement** *n* aprobación *f* general **general headquarters** *n + sing vb* cuartel *m* general
generality [ˌdʒenə'rælәti, *Am:* -t̬i] <-ies> *n* generalidad *f*
generalization [ˌdʒenərəlaiz'eɪʃən, *Am:* -ɪ'-] *n* generalización *f*
generalize ['dʒenərəlaɪz] *vi, vt* generalizar
generally ['dʒenrəli] *adv* **1.** (*usually*) generalmente **2.** (*mostly*) en general **3.** (*widely, extensively*) por lo general; **~ speaking** hablando en términos generales
general management *n no pl* dirección *f* general **general manager** *n* director(a) *m(f)* general **general partnership** *n* sociedad *f* regular colectiva **General Post Office** *n* Administración *f* de Correos **general practitioner** *n Brit, Aus, Can* médico, -a *m, f* de cabecera **general staff** *n*

no pl MIL estado *m* mayor **general store** *n Am* tienda *f* **general strike** *n* huelga *f* general **general view** *n no pl* opinión *f* general; **I do not subscribe to the ~ that ...** no estoy de acuerdo con la opinión general de que...

generate ['dʒenəreɪt] *vt* generar

generating station ['dʒenəreɪtɪŋ ˌsteɪʃən, *Am:* -t̬ɪŋ ˌsteɪʃən] *n* central *f* generadora

generation [ˌdʒenə'reɪʃən] *n* generación *f;* **for ~s** durante generaciones

generative ['dʒenərətɪv, *Am:* -t̬ɪv] *adj* generativo, -a

generator ['dʒenəreɪtəʳ, *Am:* -t̬ɚ] *n a.* ELEC generador *m*

generic [dʒɪ'nerɪk] **I.** *adj* genérico, -a **II.** *n* genérico *m*

generosity [ˌdʒenə'rɒsəti, *Am:* -'rɑːsət̬i] *n no pl* generosidad *f*

generous ['dʒenərəs] *adj* **1.** (*magnanimous*) generoso, -a, rangoso, -a *AmS* **2.** (*ample*) abundante **3.** (*better than deserved*) espléndido, -a

genesis ['dʒenəsɪs] *n no pl* génesis *f inv*

gene therapy [ˌdʒiːn'θerəpi] *n no pl* terapia *f* génica

genetic [dʒɪ'netɪk, *Am:* -'net̬ɪk] *adj* genético, -a; **~ disease** enfermedad *f* genética

geneticist [dʒɪ'netɪsɪst, *Am:* -'net̬ə-] *n* genetista *mf*

genetics *n + sing vb* genética *f*

Geneva [dʒə'niːvə] *n* Ginebra *f*

genial ['dʒiːnɪəl] *adj* afable

geniality [ˌdʒiːnɪ'æləti, *Am:* -t̬i] *n no pl* afabilidad *f*

genie ['dʒiːni] <-nii *o* -ies> *n* genio *m*

genitalia [dʒenɪ'teɪliə] *npl,* **genitals** ['dʒenɪtəlz, *Am:* -ət̬əlz] *npl* genitales *mpl*

genitive ['dʒenətɪv, *Am:* -ət̬ɪv] **I.** *adj* genitivo, -a **II.** *n* genitivo *m*

genius ['dʒiːnɪəs] *n* <-ses> *no pl* genio *m*

genocide ['dʒenəsaɪd] *n no pl* genocidio *m*

genre ['ʒɑ̃ːnrə] *n a.* LIT género *m*

genre painting *n* pintura *f* de género

gent [dʒent] *n Brit, Aus, inf, iron* caballero *m;* **he is a true ~** es todo un caballero; **the ~s** el servicio de caballeros

genteel [dʒen'tiːl] *adj* distinguido, -a

gentian ['dʒenʃən] *n* genciana *f*

Gentile ['dʒentaɪl] **I.** *adj* gentil **II.** *n* gentil *mf*

gentle ['dʒentl] *adj* **1.** (*kind*) amable; (*calm*) suave; **to be as ~ as a lamb** ser manso como un cordero **2.** (*moderate*) moderado, -a **3.** (*high-born*) **to be of ~ birth** ser de alcurnia; **~ reader** apreciado lector

gentlefolk ['dʒentlfəʊk, *Am:* -t̬lfoʊk] *npl* gente *f* de buena familia

gentleman ['dʒentlmən, *Am:* -t̬l-] <-men> *n* **1.** (*man*) señor *m;* **ladies and ~** señoras y señores **2.** (*well-behaved man*) caballero *m*

gentlemanly ['dʒentlmənli, *Am:* -t̬l-] *adj* caballeroso, -a

gentleness ['dʒentlnɪs] *n no pl* delicadeza *f*

gentlewoman ['dʒentlwʊmən, *Am:* -t̬l-] <-women> *n* dama *f*

gentry ['dʒentri] *n no pl, Brit* alta burguesía *f*

genuine ['dʒenjʊɪn] *adj* **1.** (*not fake*) genuino, -a **2.** (*real, sincere*) verdadero, -a

genus ['dʒiːnəs] <-nera> *n* BIO género *m*

geocentric [ˌdʒiːəʊ'sentrɪk, *Am:* -oʊ'-] *adj* geocéntrico, -a

geodesic [ˌdʒɪːəʊ'desɪk, *Am:* -ə'-] *adj* geodésico, -a

geographer [dʒɪ'ɒgrəfəʳ, *Am:* -'ɑːgrəfɚ] *n* geógrafo, -a *m, f*

geographic(**al**) [ˌdʒɪə'græfɪk(l), *Am:* -ə'-] *adj* geográfico, -a

geography [dʒɪ'ɒgrəfi, *Am:* -'ɑːgrə-] *n no pl* geografía *f*

geological [ˌdʒiəʊ'lɒdʒɪkəl, *Am:* -ə-'lɑːdʒɪk-] *adj* geológico, -a

geologist [dʒɪ'ɒlədʒɪst, *Am:* -'ɑːlə-] *n* geólogo, -a *m, f*

geology [dʒɪ'ɒlədʒi, *Am:* -'ɑːlə-] *n no pl* geología *f*

geometric(**al**) [ˌdzɪə'metrɪk(l), *Am:* -ə'-] *adj* geométrico, -a

geometry [dʒɪ'ɒmətri, *Am:* -'ɑːmətri] *n no pl* geometría *f*

geophysical [ˌdʒɪə'fɪzɪkl, *Am:* -oʊ'-] *adj* geofísico, -a

geophysics [ˌdʒiːəʊ'fɪzɪks, *Am:* -oʊ'-] *n + sing vb* geofísica *f*

> La **George Cross** y la **George Medal** son dos condecoraciones británicas introducidas en 1940 que reciben su nombre del Rey George VI. Con estas condecoraciones se distingue a aquellos civiles que han sobresalido por su valentía.

Georgia ['dʒɔːdʒə, *Am:* 'dʒɔːr-] *n* Georgia *f*

geothermal [ˌdʒiːəʊ'θɜːməl, *Am:* -oʊ'θɜːr-] *adj* geotérmico, -a

geranium [dʒə'reɪnɪəm] *n* geranio *m,* malvón *m Arg, Méx, Par, Urug*

geriatric [ˌdʒeri'ætrɪk] *adj* anciano, -a

geriatrician [ˌdʒeriə'trɪʃən] *n* geriatra *mf*

geriatrics *n + sing vb* geriatría *f*

germ [dʒɜːm, *Am:* dʒɜːrm] *n* **1.** (*causes disease*) microbio *m* **2.** (*plant, principle*) germen *m*

German ['dʒɜːmən, *Am:* 'dʒɜːr-] **I.** *n* **1.** (*person*) alemán, -ana *m, f* **2.** (*language*) alemán *m* **II.** *adj* alemán, -ana

germane [dʒə'meɪn, *Am:* dʒɚ-] *adj form* relacionado, -a

Germanic [dʒə'mænɪk, *Am:* dʒɚ-] *adj* germánico, -a

German measles *n + sing vb* rubeola *f*

German shepherd (**dog**) *n Am* pastor *m* alemán

Germany ['dʒɜːməni, *Am:* 'dʒɜːr-] *n* Alemania *f*

germ-free *adj* esterilizado, -a

germicidal [ˌdʒɜːmɪ'saɪdəl, *Am:* ˌdʒɜːrmə'-]

adj germicida

germicide ['dʒɜːmɪsaɪd, *Am:* 'dʒɜːrmə-] *n* germicida *m*

germinal ['dʒɜːmɪnəl, *Am:* 'dʒɜːrmə-] *adj* germinal

germinate ['dʒɜːmɪneɪt, *Am:* 'dʒɜːrmə-] *vi, vt* germinar

germination [ˌdʒɜːmɪ'neɪʃən, *Am:* ˌdʒɜːrmə-] *n no pl* germinación *f*

germ warfare *n no pl* guerra *f* bacteriana

gerontologist [ˌdʒerɒn'tɒlədʒɪst, *Am:* ˌdʒern'tɑːlə-] *n* gerontólogo, -a *m, f*

gerontology [ˌdʒerɒn'tɒlədʒi, *Am:* ˌdʒern'tɑːlə-] *n no pl* gerontología *f*

gerrymander ['dʒerɪmændəʳ, *Am:* -dɚ] *vi* POL falsificar elecciones

gerund ['dʒerənd] *n* gerundio *m*

gestation [dʒe'steɪʃən] *n no pl* gestación *f*

gesticulate [dʒe'stɪkjʊleɪt, *Am:* -jə-] *vi form* gesticular

gesticulation [dʒeˌstɪkjʊ'leɪʃən, *Am:* -jə'-] *n form* gesticulación *f*

gesture ['dʒestʃəʳ, *Am:* -tʃɚ] **I.** *n* **1.** (*body movement*) gesto *m* **2.** (*act*) muestra *f*; **a ~ towards sb** un detalle con alguien **II.** *vi* hacer un ademán **III.** *vt* indicar con un ademán

get [get] **I.** <got, got, *Am, Aus:* gotten> *vt inf* **1.** (*obtain*) obtener; (*secure*) conseguir; (*gain*) ganar; (*buy*) comprar; (*find*) encontrar; (*take*) coger; **to ~ the door** *Am, inf* abrir la puerta; **to ~ the telephone** *Am, inf* coger el teléfono; **to ~ a surprise** llevarse una sorpresa; **to ~ pleasure out of sth** disfrutar con algo; **to ~ the impression that ...** tener la impresión de que...; **to ~ a meal/drinks** *Am, inf* comer/tomar algo **2.** (*catch: plane, train*) coger **3.** *inf* (*hear, understand*) comprender; (*message*) captar; (*picture*) entender; **to ~ sth/sb wrong** entender algo/a alguien mal **4.** (*prepare: meal*) preparar **5.** (*cause to be*) **to ~ sth done** hacer algo; **to ~ sb to do sth** hacer que alguien haga algo **6.** *inf* (*irk*) fastidiar; (*make emotional*) afectar **7.** *inf* (*start*) **to ~ going** poner en marcha; **to ~ cracking** poner manos a la obra **II.** *vi* **1.** + *n/adj* (*become*) volverse; **to ~ married** casarse; **to ~ upset** enfadarse; **to ~ used to sth** acostumbrarse a algo; **to ~ to be sth** llegar a ser algo; **to ~ to like sth** coger afición a algo **2.** (*have opportunity*) **to ~ to do sth** llegar a hacer algo; **to ~ to see sb** lograr ver a alguien **3.** (*travel*) llegar; **to ~ home** llegar a casa

◆**get about** *vi* **1.** desplazarse **2.** (*travel*) viajar mucho

◆**get across** *vt* hacer pasar; **to ~ a message to sb** comunicar un mensaje a alguien

◆**get along** *vi* **1.** (*good relationship*) llevarse bien **2.** (*manage*) arreglárselas

◆**get around** **I.** *vt insep* (*avoid*) evitar **II.** *vi* **1.** (*spread*) llegar a **2.** (*travel*) viajar mucho

◆**get at** *vt insep, inf* **1.** (*suggest*) apuntar a **2.** *Aus, Brit* (*criticize*) meterse con **3.** (*influence illegally*) sobornar **4.** (*reach*) llegar a

◆**get away** *vi* marcharse

◆**get back** **I.** *vt* recuperar **II.** *vi* volver

◆**get behind** **I.** *vi* quedarse atrás **II.** *vt insep* quedarse detrás de

◆**get by** *vi* (*manage*) arreglárselas

◆**get down** *vt always sep* **1.** (*disturb*) deprimir **2.** (*swallow*) tragar

◆**get in** **I.** *vt* **1.** (*say*) decir **2.** (*bring inside*) llevar dentro **II.** *vi* **1.** (*become elected*) ser elegido **2.** (*enter*) entrar **3.** (*arrive*) llegar a casa

◆**get into** *vt insep* **1.** (*become interested in*) interesarse por **2.** (*involve*) meter; **to get sb into trouble** meter a alguien en problemas **3.** (*enter*) entrar en

◆**get off** **I.** *vi* **1.** (*start sleeping*) dormirse **2.** (*avoid punishment*) librarse **3.** (*depart*) marcharse **II.** *vt always sep* **1.** (*help avoid punishment*) librarse de **2.** (*remove from*) sacar **3.** (*send*) enviar

◆**get on** *vi* **1.** (*be friends*) llevarse bien **2.** (*manage*) arreglárselas **3.** (*get older*) envejecer **4.** (*to get late*) **time's getting on** se está haciendo tarde

◆**get out** **I.** *vt* sacar **II.** *vi* salir

◆**get over** *vt insep* **1.** (*recover from*) recuperarse de; (*illness*) reponerse de; (*difficulty*) superar **2.** (*forget about*) **to ~ sb/sth** olvidarse de alguien/algo

◆**get round** *vt* **1.** (*avoid*) evitar **2.** *Brit* (*persuade*) persuadir

◆**get through** **I.** *vi* **to ~ to sth/sb** comunicarse con algo/alguien **II.** *vt* **1.** (*make understood*) **to get it through to sb that ...** hacer que alguien entienda que... **2.** (*survive*) pasar; (*exam*) aprobar

◆**get together** **I.** *vi* reunirse **II.** *vt* reunir

◆**get up** **I.** *vt* **1.** (*organize*) organizar **2.** *inf* (*dress*) ataviar **3.** *always sep, Brit, inf* (*wake*) levantar **4.** *insep* (*climb*) subir **II.** *vi* **1.** (*get out of bed*) levantarse **2.** (*rise*) subir

◆**get up to** *vt* llegar a

get-at-able [ˌget'ætəbl, *Am:* ˌgeţ'æţ-] *adj inf* accesible

getaway ['getəweɪ, *Am:* 'geţ-] *n inf* fuga *f*; **to make a ~** fugarse

get-together ['gettə'geðəʳ, *Am:* -ɚ] *n inf* reunión *f*

get-up ['getʌp, *Am:* 'geţ-] *n inf* atuendo *m*

geyser ['giːzəʳ, *Am:* -zɚ] *n* **1.** (*hot spring*) géiser *m* **2.** *Brit* (*water heater*) calentador *m* de agua

Ghana ['gɑːnə] *n* Ghana *f*

Ghanaian [gɑː'neɪən, *Am:* -'niː-] **I.** *adj* ghanés, -esa **II.** *n* ghanés, -esa *m, f*

ghastly ['gɑːstli, *Am:* 'gæst-] <-ier, -iest> *adj inf* **1.** (*frightful*) horroroso, -a **2.** (*unpleasant*) desagradable **3.** *liter* (*pallid*) **~ white/pale** blanco, -a/pálido, -a (como la cera)

Ghent [gent] *n* Gante *m*

gherkin ['gɜːkɪn, *Am:* 'gɜːr-] *n* pepinillo *m*

ghetto ['getəʊ, *Am:* 'geţoʊ] **I.** <-s *o* -es> *n*

gueto *m* **II.** *adj* (*life*) de [*o* en un] gueto; (*conditions*) de marginación

ghetto blaster *n inf* radio *f* portátil de gran frecuencia

ghost [gəʊst, *Am:* goʊst] **I.** *n a. fig* (*spirit*) fantasma *m,* espanto *m AmL,* azoro *m AmC;* **to believe in ~s** creer en fantasmas; **to be haunted by ~s** haber fantasmas; **the ~ of the past** los fantasmas del pasado ►**to give up the ~** (*to die*) exhalar el último suspiro; (*to stop working*) dejar de funcionar **II.** *vt* escribir para otro; **his speech was ~ed** el discurso no lo escribió él **III.** *vi* hacer de negro

ghostly ['gəʊstli] <-ier, -iest> *adj* **1.** (*ghostlike*) fantasmal **2.** (*spooky*) escalofriante

ghost town *n* pueblo *m* fantasma **ghostwriter** *n* negro, -a *m, f* (*persona que escribe para otra*)

ghoul [gu:l] *n* (*evil spirit*) espíritu *m* demoníaco

g.I. *n,* **G.I.** [ˌdʒi:'aɪ] *n inf* soldado *m* norteamericano (*especialmente en la II Guerra Mundial*)

GI *abbr of* **government issue** propiedad *f* del Estado

giant ['dʒaɪənt] **I.** *n* gigante *m;* **a political ~** un coloso de la política **II.** *adj* gigantesco, -a

giantess ['dʒaɪəntes, *Am:* -t̬əs] *n* **1.** (*female giant*) giganta *f* **2.** (*influential female*) colosa *f*

gibber ['dʒɪbəʳ, *Am:* -ɚ] *vi* farfullar; **to ~ with rage** hablar atropelladamente de rabia

gibberish ['dʒɪbərɪʃ] *n no pl* galimatías *m inv*

gibbet ['dʒɪbɪt] *n* horca *f*

gibbon ['gɪbən] *n* gibón *m*

gibe [dʒaɪb] **I.** *n* burla *f* **II.** *vi* **to ~ at sb/sth** burlarse de alguien/algo

giblets ['dʒɪblɪts] *npl* menudillos *mpl*

Gibraltar [dʒɪ'brɔ:ltəʳ, *Am:* -'brɑ:ltɚ] *n* Gibraltar *m*

giddy ['gɪdi] <-ier, -iest> *adj* mareado, -a

gift [gɪft] *n* **1.** (*present*) regalo *m;* **to bear ~s** traer [*o* llevar] regalos; **to be a ~ from the Gods** ser un regalo caído del cielo **2.** *inf* (*bargain*) **£100 for this bicycle? it's a ~!** ¿100 libras por esta bicicleta? ¡Está tirada! **3.** (*talent*) don *m;* **to have a ~ for languages** tener talento para los idiomas; **to have the ~ of the gab** *inf* tener mucha labia

gift certificate *n Am* vale *m* de [*o* por un] regalo

gifted *adj* **1.** (*talented*) de (gran) talento **2.** (*intellectually bright*) brillante; **~ child** niño *m* superdotado

gift horse *n* **never look a ~ in the mouth** *prov* a caballo regalado, no le mires el dentado *prov* **gift shop** *n* tienda *f* de regalos **gift token** *n,* **gift voucher** *n* vale *m* de [*o* por un] regalo

gig¹ [gɪg] **I.** *n inf* (*musical performance*) concierto *m;* **to do a ~** dar un concierto **II.** *vi* <-gg-> (*do a gig*) dar un concierto

gig² [gɪg] *n* calesín *m*

gigabyte ['gɪgəbaɪt] *n* gigabyte *m*

gigantic [dʒaɪ'gæntɪk, *Am:* -t̬ɪk] *adj* gigantesco, -a

giggle ['gɪgl] **I.** *vi* reír(se) tontamente **II.** *n* **1.** (*laugh*) risita *f;* **she got the ~s** le dio la risa tonta **2.** *no pl, Aus, Brit, inf* (*joke*) broma *f;* **to do sth for a ~** hacer algo para reírse [*o* divertirse] un rato **3.** *pl* **the ~s, to get** (**a fit of**) **the ~s** tener un ataque de risa

gild [gɪld] *vt* **1.** (*cover with gold*) dorar **2.** (*light up*) iluminar ►**to ~ the lily** rizar el rizo

gilded *adj* dorado, -a

gill¹ [gɪl] *n* (*of a fish*) agalla *f* ►**to be green about the ~s** *iron* estar pálido como la cera; **to be packed to the ~s** estar a tope (de lleno); **to be stuffed to the ~s** estar a tope (de comida); **to the ~s** *inf* a tope

gill² [dʒɪl] *n* (*measure*) ≈ cuartillo *m*

gilt [gɪlt] **I.** *adj* dorado, -a **II.** *n no pl* dorado *m*

gilt-edged [ˌgɪlt'edʒd] *adj* (*securities, stocks*) de máxima garantía

gimcrack ['dʒɪmkræk] *adj* (*ideas*) de pacotilla; (*architecture*) de baja calidad

gimlet ['gɪmlɪt] *n* **1.** (*tool*) barrena *f* **2.** *Am* (*alcoholic drink*) cóctel *m* de zumo de lima y vodka o ginebra

gimlet-eyed *adj* penetrante; **to be ~** tener una mirada penetrante

gimmick ['gɪmɪk] *n* **1.** (*commercial*) truco *m* (*para vender más*) **2.** (*attention-getter*) truco *m* efectista (*para atraer la atención*)

gimmicky ['gɪmɪki] *adj* efectista

gin¹ [dʒɪn] *n* ginebra *f;* **~ and tonic** gin tonic *m*

gin² [dʒɪn] *n* **1.** (*trap*) trampa *f* **2.** AGR desmotadora *f* de algodón

ginger ['dʒɪndʒəʳ, *Am:* -dʒɚ] **I.** *n no pl* **1.** (*root spice*) jengibre *m* **2.** (*reddish-yellow*) rojo *m* anaranjado **3.** *s.* **ginger ale II.** *adj* rojizo, -a; (*hair*) pelirrojo, -a

ginger ale, **ginger beer** *n* ginger ale *m,* refresco *m* de jengibre

gingerbread ['dʒɪndʒəbred, *Am:* -dʒɚ] *n no pl* pan *m* de jengibre

ginger group *n Aus, Brit* POL grupo *m* de presión

ginger-haired *adj* pelirrojo, -a

gingerly ['dʒɪnʒəli, *Am:* -dʒɚli] *adv* con cautela

ginger nut *n Aus, Brit,* **ginger snap** *n Am* galleta *f* de jengibre

gingivitis [ˌdʒɪndʒɪ'vaɪtɪs, *Am:* -dʒə'vaɪt̬əs] *n no pl* gingivitis *f inv*

ginseng ['dʒɪnseŋ] *n no pl* ginseng *m*

gipsy ['dʒɪpsi] *n s.* **gypsy**

giraffe [dʒɪ'rɑ:f, *Am:* dʒə'ræf] *n* <-(s)> jirafa *f*

girder ['gɜ:dəʳ, *Am:* 'gɜ:rdɚ] *n* viga *f* (*de metal u hormigón*)

girdle ['gɜ:dl, *Am:* 'gɜ:r-] **I.** *n* **1.** *a. fig* (*belt*) cinturón *m* **2.** (*corset*) faja *f* **II.** *vt a. fig* (*surround*) rodear

girl [gɜ:l, *Am:* gɜ:rl] *n* **1.** (*child*) niña *f;* (*young* *woman*) joven *f*, piba *f Arg* **2.** (*daughter*) hija *f* **3. the ~s** *pl* (*at work*) las compañeras; (*friends*) las amigas

girl Friday *n* chica *f* para todo

girlfriend ['gɜːlfrend, *Am:* 'gɜːrl-] *n* **1.** (*of woman*) amiga *f* **2.** (*of man*) novia *f*, polola *f And*

girl guide *n Brit* guía *f*

girlhood ['gɜːlhʊd, *Am:* 'gɜːrl-] *n no pl* juventud *f*

girlie ['gɜːli, *Am:* 'gɜːr-] *adj* de destape

girlie magazine *n* revista *f* de chicas desnudas

girlish ['gɜːlɪʃ, *Am:* 'gɜːr-] *adj* de [*o* como una] niña

girl scout *n Am* exploradora *f*

giro ['dʒaɪrəʊ, *Am:* -roʊ] *n* **1.** *no pl* (*credit transfer system*) giro *m* bancario; **to transfer by ~** enviar mediante giro (bancario) **2.** *Brit* (*social benefit cheque*) cheque *m* del subsidio (*que se recibe del Estado por desempleo o ayuda social*)

giro account *n* cuenta *f* de giros **giro system** *n* sistema *m* de giro bancario **giro transfer** *n* transferencia *f* bancaria

girth [gɜːθ, *Am:* gɜːrθ] *n* **1.** *no pl* (*circumference*) circunferencia *f* **2.** *no pl, iron* (*obesity*) obesidad *f* **3.** <-es> (*strap around horse*) cincha *f*

gist [dʒɪst] *n* **the ~** lo esencial; **to give sb the ~ (of sth)** contar a alguien lo fundamental (sobre algo); **to get the ~ of sth** entender lo básico de algo

give [gɪv] **I.** *vt* <gave, given> **1.** (*offer*) dar, ofrecer; (*kiss, signal*) dar; (*a seat*) ceder; **to ~ sb an excuse for sth** dar una excusa a alguien para algo; **given the choice ...** si pudiera elegir...; **to ~ sb something to eat/drink** dar a alguien algo de comer/beber; **to not ~ much for sth** *fig* no dar mucho por algo; **to ~ sb full life imprisonment** condenar a alguien a cadena perpetua; **don't ~ me that!** *inf* ¡venga ya, tú me la quieres dar con queso!; **~ me a break!** ¡déjame en paz!; **I don't ~ a damn** *inf* me importa un bledo; **to ~ notice** avisar, hacer saber; **to ~ sb the creeps** producir a alguien escalofríos; **to ~ (it) one's all** [*o* **best** *Am*] dar todo de sí mismo; **to ~ anything for sth/to do sth** dar cualquier cosa por algo/por hacer algo; **to ~ one's life to sth** dedicar la vida de uno a algo; **to ~ sb what for** *inf* echar a alguien un rapapolvo **2.** (*lecture, performance*) dar; (*speech*) pronunciar; (*noise*) hacer; (*strange look*) echar; (*headache, trouble*) producir, dar; **to ~ sb a call** llamar a alguien (por teléfono); **to ~ sth a go** intentar algo; **to ~ sb to understand sth** *form* dar a entender algo a alguien **3.** (*organize*) dar, organizar **4.** (*pass on*) contagiar **II.** *vi* <gave, given> **1.** (*offer*) dar, ofrecer; **to ~ as good as one gets** devolver golpe por golpe; **to ~ of one's money** hacer una aportación (monetaria); **to ~ of one's best** dar todo de sí **2.** (*stretch*) estirarse, dar de sí; **something will have to ~** *fig* algo tendrá que cambiar **3. what ~s?** *Am, inf* ¿qué hay? ►**it is better to ~ than to receive** *prov* es mejor dar que recibir *prov* **III.** *n* elasticidad *f*

◆**give away** *vt* **1.** (*reveal*) revelar; **to give the game away** tirar de la manta; **to give sb away** delatar a alguien **2.** (*offer for free*) regalar **3.** *form* (*bride*) entregar en matrimonio

◆**give back** *vt* devolver, regresar *Méx*

◆**give in I.** *vi* rendirse; **to ~ to sth** acceder (finalmente) a algo **II.** *vt* **1.** (*hand in*) entregar **2.** SPORTS **to give the ball in** *Brit* dar la pelota como buena

◆**give off** *vt* emitir; (*smell*) despedir; (*heat*) producir

◆**give out I.** *vi* **1.** (*run out*) acabar(se) **2.** (*machine*) estropearse; (*legs*) ceder **II.** *vt* **1.** (*distribute*) repartir **2.** (*announce*) anunciar **3.** (*produce*) producir; (*noise*) emitir **4.** SPORTS (*disallow*) **to give the ball out** *Brit* dar la pelota como mala

◆**give over** *vi Brit, inf* **1.** (*cease criticizing*) dejar de hacer; **he told me to ~** me dijo que parara ya **2. ~!** ¡venga ya!

◆**give up I.** *vt* **1.** (*resign*) renunciar **2.** (*quit*) **to ~ doing sth** dejar de hacer algo; **to ~ smoking** dejar de fumar **3.** (*lose hope*) **to give sb up** (*patient*) desahuciar a alguien; (*missing person*) dar a alguien por desaparecido **4.** (*stop being friendly towards*) romper (la amistad); **to ~ one's friends** terminar (la amistad) con los amigos de uno **5.** (*hand over*) entregar; **to give oneself up (to the police)** entregarse (a la policía) **II.** *vi* **1.** (*quit*) dejar **2.** (*cease trying to guess*) rendirse

give-and-take [ˌgɪvən'teɪk] *n* (*compromise*) toma *m* y daca

give-away ['gɪvəweɪ] **I.** *n* **1.** *no pl, inf* (*exposure*) prueba *f* (que delata algo) **2.** (*free gift*) regalo *m* **II.** *adj* **1.** (*very low*) **~ price** precio *m* de saldo **2.** (*free*) gratis; **~ newspaper** periódico *m* gratuito

given ['gɪvn] **I.** *n Am* dato *m* conocido; **to take sth as a ~** dar algo por sentado **II.** *adj* **1.** (*arranged*) determinado, -a, acordado, -a; **in a ~ time** en un tiempo determinado **2. to be ~ to do sth** ser dado a hacer algo **III.** *pp of* **give IV.** *prep* **~ that** dado que +*subj*, en el caso de que +*subj*; **~ the chance I would go to Paris** si tuviese la oportunidad iría a París

given name *n Am, Scot* nombre *m* de pila

giver ['gɪvəʳ, *Am:* -ɚ] *n* donante *mf*

glacé ['glæseɪ, *Am:* glæs'eɪ] *adj*, **glacéed** *adj Am inv* glaseado, -a; **~ fruit** fruta *f* confitada

glacial ['gleɪsiəl, *Am:* 'gleɪʃəl] *adj* GEO glacial; **~ epoch/look** época *f*/mirada *f* glacial

glacier ['glæsiəʳ, *Am:* 'gleɪʃɚ] *n* glaciar *m*

glad [glæd] <gladder, gladdest> *adj* contento, -a; **to be ~ about sth** alegrarse de algo; **I'd be ~ to go with you** me encantaría ir contigo; **I'm ~ of your help** agradezco tu

ayuda
gladden ['glædn] *vt* alegrar
glade [gleɪd] *n* claro *m* (de un bosque)
gladiator ['glædɪeɪtə^r, *Am:* -t̬ɚ] *n* gladiador *m*
gladiolus [ˌglædɪ'əʊləs, *Am:* -'oʊ-] <-es *o* -li> *n* gladiolo *m*
gladly ['glædli] *adv* con mucho gusto
gladness ['glædnɪs] *n no pl* alegría *f*
glad rags *n no pl, iron* **to put on one's ~** ponerse las mejores galas
glamor ['glæmə^r, *Am:* -ɚ] *n no pl, Am, Aus s.* **glamour**
glamorise *vt,* **glamorize** ['glæməraɪz] *vt* hacer más atractivo; **this film ~s violence** esta película exalta la violencia
glamorous ['glæmərəs] *adj* glamoroso, -a, atractivo, -a; (*traje*) con glamour, sofisticado, -a
glamour ['glæmə^r, *Am:* -ɚ] *n no pl, Aus, Brit* glamour *m,* encanto *m,* atractivo *m*
glamour boy *n* guapo *m*
glamour girl *n* guapa *f*
glance [glɑːns, *Am:* glæns] **I.** *n* mirada *f;* **to take a ~ at sth** echar una mirada [*o* un vistazo] a algo; **at first ~** a primera vista; **at a ~** de un vistazo **II.** *vi* **1.** (*look cursorily*) **to ~ up** (**from sth**) levantar la mirada (de algo); **to ~ around sth** mirar alrededor de algo; **to ~ over sth** echar un vistazo a algo **2.** (*shine*) brillar
◆glance off *vi* (chocar y) rebotar
gland [glænd] *n* glándula *f*
glandular ['glændjʊlə^r, *Am:* -dʒəlɚ] *adj* glandular
glandular fever *n* mononucleosis *f inv* infecciosa
glare [gleə^r, *Am:* gler] **I.** *n* **1.** (*mean look*) mirada *f* (fulminadora); **to give sb a ~** fulminar a alguien con la mirada **2.** *no pl* (*reflection*) resplandor *m;* **to give off ~** deslumbrar; **to be dazzled by the ~ of sth** quedar deslumbrado por el resplandor de algo **II.** *vi* **1.** (*look*) fulminar con la mirada **2.** (*shine*) resplandecer; **the sun ~s down on my eyes** el sol me da directamente a los ojos
glaring *adj* **1.** (*which blinds*) deslumbrante **2.** (*obvious*) que salta a la vista; **~ weakness** debilidad *f* manifiesta; **~ injustice** injusticia *f* que clama al cielo
glass [glɑːs, *Am:* glæs] <-es> *n* **1.** *no pl* (*material*) vidrio *m,* cristal *m;* **pane of ~** hoja *f* de vidrio; **under ~** en invernadero **2.** *no pl* (*glassware*) cristalería *f* **3.** (*for drinks*) vaso *m* **4.** (*drink*) copa *f* **5.** (*mirror*) espejo *m* **6.** *pl* gafas *fpl,* lentes *fpl AmL* **7.** *pl* (*binoculars*) prismáticos *mpl*
glass-blower ['glɑːsˌbləʊə^r, *Am:* 'glæsˌbloʊɚ] *n* soplador(a) *m(f)* **glass-cutter** *n* cortador *m* de vidrio
glass fiber *n Am,* **glass fibre** *n Brit* fibra *f* de vidrio
glassful ['glɑːsfʊl, *Am:* 'glæs-] *n* vaso *m;* **a ~ of orange juice** un vaso (lleno) de zumo de naranja
glasshouse ['glɑːshaʊs, *Am:* 'glæs-] *n* invernadero *m* **glassware** *n no pl* cristalería *f* **glassworks** *npl* fábrica *f* de vidrio
glassy ['glɑːsi, *Am:* 'glæsi] <-ier, -iest> *adj* **1.** *liter* (*as glass*) vítreo, -a **2.** (*eyes*) vidrioso, -a
Glaswegian [glæz'wiːdʒən, *Am:* glæs-] *n* habitante *mf* de Glasgow
glaucoma [glɔː'kəʊmə, *Am:* glɑː'koʊ-] *n* glaucoma *m*
glaucous ['glɔːkəs, *Am:* 'glɑː-] *adj* **1.** (*greenish-blue*) glauco, -a **2.** BOT (*with bloom*) cubierto, -a de una pelusilla verdosa
glaze [gleɪz] **I.** *n a.* GASTR glaseado *m;* (*paper*) glaseado *m;* (*painting*) barniz *m;* (*pottery*) vidriado *m* **II.** *vt* **1.** (*paper*) glasear **2.** (*window*) poner vidrios a
glazier ['gleɪzɪər] *n* vidriero, -a *m, f,* cristalero, -a *m, f*
gleam [gliːm] **I.** *n* reflejo *m,* destello *m;* **~ of hope** rayo *m* de esperanza **II.** *vi* brillar, relucir
glean [gliːn] *vt* **to ~ sth from sb** deducir algo (de las palabras) de alguien
gleanings *npl* información *f* recogida
glee [gliː] *n no pl* júbilo *m;* **to do sth with ~** hacer algo con gran alegría
gleeful ['gliːfəl] *adj* eufórico, -a
glen [glen] *n Scot* valle *m*
glib [glɪb] <glibber, glibbest> *adj* simplista
glide [glaɪd] **I.** *vi* **1.** (*move smoothly*) deslizarse **2.** AVIAT planear; **to take sb gliding** llevar a alguien a volar con planeador **II.** *n* **1.** (*sliding movement*) deslizamiento *m* **2.** AVIAT planeo *m;* **with a ~** con un movimiento deslizante
glider ['glaɪdə^r, *Am:* -dɚ] *n* planeador *m*
glider pilot *n* piloto *mf* de planeador
gliding ['glaɪdɪŋ] *n no pl* vuelo *m* sin motor
gliding club *n* club *m* de vuelo sin motor
glimmer ['glɪmə^r, *Am:* -ɚ] **I.** *vi* brillar tenuemente **II.** *n* (*light*) luz *f* tenue; **~ of hope** atisbo *m* de esperanza
glimpse [glɪmps] **I.** *vt* (*signs*) vislumbrar **II.** *n* **to catch a ~ of** vislumbrar; **to catch a ~ of sb's life** captar algo de la vida de alguien
glint [glɪnt] **I.** *vi* destellar; **to ~ with sth** brillar por causa de algo **II.** *n* destello *m*
glisten ['glɪsn] *vi* brillar, relucir
glitch [glɪtʃ] <-es> *n inf* fallo *m*
glitter ['glɪtə^r, *Am:* 'glɪt̬ɚ] **I.** *vi* brillar, relucir **II.** *n no pl* **1.** (*sparkling*) brillo *m,* destello *m* **2.** (*excitement*) esplendor *m* **3.** (*shiny material*) purpurina *f*
glittering *adj* **1.** (*sparkling, impressive*) brillante **2.** (*exciting*) esplendoroso, -a
glitz [glɪts] *n no pl* ostentosidad *f*
glitzy ['glɪtsi] <-ier, -iest> *adj* ostentoso, -a; **~ car** cochazo *m* imponente
gloat [gləʊt, *Am:* gloʊt] **I.** *vi* disfrutar con regocijo; **to ~ over sth** manifestar (gran) satisfacción por algo; **to ~ at sth** regodearse con algo **II.** *n* regocijo *m*
global ['gləʊbl, *Am:* 'gloʊ-] *adj* **1.** (*worldwide*) a nivel mundial **2.** (*complete*) global
global warming *n* calentamiento *m* de la

atmósfera terrestre

globe [gləʊb, *Am:* gloʊb] *n* 1. (*map of world*) globo *m* terráqueo 2. (*object*) globo *m* 3. *Aus* (*light bulb*) bombilla *f*

globetrotter ['gləʊbˌtrɒtəʳ, *Am:* 'gloʊbˌtrɑːt̬ɚ] *n* trotamundos *mf inv*

globule ['glɒbjuːl, *Am:* 'glɑːbjuːl] *n* glóbulo *m*

gloom [gluːm] *n no pl* 1. (*hopelessness*) pesimismo *m*, melancolía *f*; ~ **and doom** profunda desesperación; ~ **and despondency** pesimismo y abatimiento 2. (*darkness*) oscuridad *f*

gloominess ['gluːmɪnəs] *n no pl* 1. (*hopelessness*) pesimismo *m* 2. (*darkness*) oscuridad *f*

gloomy ['gluːmi] <-ier, -iest> *adj* 1. (*dismal*) abatido, -a; (*thoughts*) melancólico, -a; **to be ~ about sth** ser pesimista respecto a algo; **to turn ~** abatirse 2. (*dark*) oscuro, -a

glorification [ˌglɔːrɪfɪ'keɪʃən, *Am:* ˌglɔːrəfə'-] *n no pl* 1. (*honouring, praising*) alabanza *f* 2. (*seem more splendid*) glorificación *f*

glorify ['glɔːrɪfaɪ, *Am:* ˌglɔːrə-] <-ie-> *vt* 1. (*make seem better*) glorificar 2. (*honour*) alabar; **to ~ God/Allah** REL alabar a Dios/Alá

glorious ['glɔːrɪəs] *adj* 1. (*honourable, illustrious*) glorioso, -a 2. (*splendid: day, weather*) espléndido, -a 3. *iron* (*extreme*) enorme; **this bedroom is one ~ mess** esta habitación es un completo desorden

glory ['glɔːri] I. *n no pl* 1. (*honour*) gloria *f*; **to bathe in ~** bañarse de gloria; **to cover oneself in ~** cubrirse de gloria; **to deserve/get all the ~ for sth** merecer/conseguir toda la gloria por algo 2. (*splendour*) esplendor *m*; **in all her ~** en todo su esplendor 3. (*state of delight*) **to be in one's ~** estar en la gloria 4. (*adoration, praise*) adoración *f* 5. REL (*heaven*) cielo *m*; **to be in ~** estar en la gloria; **to go to ~** *inf* ir al cielo ▶ **~ be!** (*thank God!*) ¡gracias a Dios! II. <-ie-> *vi* vanagloriarse; **to ~ in sth** vanagloriarse de algo

glory-hole *n inf* leonera *f*

gloss¹ [glɒs, *Am:* glɑːs] I. *n no pl* 1. (*shine*) brillo *m*, lustre *m*; **high ~** mucho brillo *m* 2. (*shiny substance*) sustancia *f* abrillantadora 3. (*shiny finish*) acabado *m* brillante 4. (*shiny paint*) pintura *f* esmalte 5. (*lip moisturizer*) brillo *m* para labios ▶ **to take the ~ off sth** desmejorar algo, quitar la gracia a algo II. *adj* de brillo

gloss² [glɒs, *Am:* glɑːs] I. <-es> *n* glosa *f* II. *vt* glosar

◆**gloss over** *vt* pasar por alto

glossary ['glɒsəri, *Am:* 'glɑːsər-] <-ies> *n* PUBL, LIT glosario *m*

gloss paint *n no pl* pintura *f* esmalte

glossy ['glɒsi, *Am:* 'glɑːsi] I. <-ier, -iest> *adj* 1. (*shiny*) brillante, lustroso, -a; (*paper*) satinado, -a; (*magazine*) elegante, de lujo 2. (*superficially attractive*) superficialmente atractivo, -a II. <-ies> *n* 1. *Am, Aus* PHOT fotografía *f* brillante 2. PUBL revista *f* (*impresa en papel satinado*)

glottal stop ['glɒtl'stɒp, *Am:* 'glɑːt̬əl'stɑːp] *n* LING oclusión *f* glotal

glottis ['glɒtɪs, *Am:* 'glɑːt̬əs] <-es> *n* ANAT, MED glotis *f inv*

glove [glʌv] I. *n* guante *m*; **leather/wool ~s** guantes *mpl* de piel/lana; **a pair of ~s** unos guantes; **to put on/take off one's ~s** ponerse/sacarse los guantes ▶ **to fit sb like a ~** venir a alguien como anillo al dedo, quedar a alguien como un guante II. *vt Am* 1. (*dress in gloves*) **to ~ one's hands** ponerse los guantes 2. (*catch*) atrapar

glove box *n*, **glove compartment** *n* AUTO guantera *f*

glover ['glʌvəʳ, *Am:* -ɚ] *n* guantero, -a *m, f*

glow [gləʊ, *Am:* gloʊ] I. *n* 1. (*light*) luz *f* 2. (*warmth and redness*) calor *m* 3. (*good feeling*) sensación *f* grata; **~ of happiness** sensación *f* de felicidad; **~ of pride** sentimiento *m* de orgullo; **~ of satisfaction** sensación *f* de satisfacción II. *vi* 1. (*illuminate*) brillar 2. (*be red and hot*) arder 3. (*look radiant*) estar radiante

glower ['glaʊəʳ, *Am:* -ɚ] I. *vi* mirar con el ceño fruncido; **to ~ at sb** mirar con el ceño fruncido a alguien; **large black rain clouds ~ in the sky** *fig* LIT grandes nubes negras de lluvia amenazan en el cielo II. *n* mirada *f* furiosa

glowing *adj* ardiente; (*report, praise*) efusivo, -a

glow-lamp *n*, **glowlight** *n* lámpara *f* incandescente **glow-worm** *n* luciérnaga *f*, candelilla *f CRi, Chile, Hond*

glucose ['gluːkəʊs, *Am:* -koʊs] *n no pl* glucosa *f*; **~ syrup** jarabe *m* de glucosa

glue [gluː] I. *n no pl* cola *f*, pegamento *m*; **to fix sth with ~** fijar algo con cola; **to sniff ~** esnifar pegamento II. *vt* encolar; **to ~ sth together** pegar algo; **to ~ sth on** encolar algo; **to be ~d to sth** *fig* estar pegado a algo; **to keep one's eyes ~d to sth/sb** *fig* mantener los ojos pegados a algo/alguien

glue-sniffing ['gluːˌsnɪfɪŋ] *n* inhalación *f* de pegamento

glue stick *n* pegamento *m*

glum [glʌm] <glummer, glummest> *adj* 1. (*morose, downcast*) taciturno, -a; **to be/feel ~** (**about sth**) ser/sentirse melancólico (por algo) 2. (*drab*) monótono, -a

glut [glʌt] I. *n* ECON exceso *m* de oferta; **a ~ of sth** una superabundancia de algo II. <-tt-> *vt* ECON inundar

gluten ['gluːtən] *n no pl* gluten *m*

glutinous ['gluːtɪnəs, *Am:* -tnəs] *adj* glutinoso, -a

glutton [glʌtn] *n* 1. (*overeater*) glotón, -ona *m, f* 2. *inf* (*enthusiast*) entusiasta *mf*

gluttonous ['glʌtənəs] *adj* glotón, -ona, angurriento, -a *AmL*

gluttony ['glʌtəni] *n no pl* glotonería *f*

glycerin ['glɪsərɪn] *n Am,* **glycerine** ['glɪsəri:n] *n Brit, Aus,* **glycerol** ['glɪsərɒl, *Am:* -rɑ:l] *n no pl* glicerina *f*

glycol ['glaɪkɒl, *Am:* -kɑ:l] *n no pl* glicol *m*

GMT [ˌdʒi:em'ti:] *abbr of* **Greenwich Mean Time** hora *f* de Greenwich

gnarled [nɑ:ld, *Am:* nɑ:rld] *adj* (*knobby and twisted*) retorcido, -a; (*knotted*) nudoso, -a

gnash [næʃ] *vt* hacer rechinar; **to ~ one's teeth about sth** rechinar los dientes por algo

gnat [næt] *n* BIO mosquito *m,* jején *m AmS*

gnaw [nɔ:, *Am:* nɑ:] **I.** *vi* **1.** (*chew*) **to ~ at** [*o* **on**] **sth** roer algo **2.** *fig* (*deplete*) reducir; **to ~ away at sth** agotar algo **3.** (*bother*) molestar; **to ~ at sb** molestar a alguien **II.** *vt* **1.** (*chew*) roer **2.** *fig* (*pursue*) **to be ~ed by doubt/fear/guilt** ser asaltado por las dudas/el miedo/el sentimiento de culpa

◆gnaw away *vt* roer

gnawing **I.** *adj* persistente; (*pain*) punzante; (*doubt*) que atormenta **II.** *n no pl* roedura *f;* (*stomach*) retortijón *m*

gneiss [naɪs] *n no pl* GEO gneis *m*

gnome [nəʊm, *Am:* noʊm] *n* gnomo *m*

GNP [ˌdʒi:en'pi:] *no pl abbr of* **Gross National Product** PNB

gnu [nu:] <-(s)> *n* BIO ñu *m*

go [gəʊ, *Am:* goʊ] **I.** <went, gone> *vi* **1.** (*proceed*) ir; **to ~ (and) do sth** ir a hacer algo; **to ~ home** irse a casa **2.** (*travel*) viajar; **to ~ on a cruise** ir de crucero; **to ~ on holiday** irse de vacaciones; **to ~ on a trip** irse de viaje **3.** (*adopt position*) **when I ~ like this, my back hurts** cuando hago esto, me duele la espalda **4.** (*leave*) marcharse; **to have to ~** tener que irse; **when does the bus ~?** ¿a qué hora sale el autobús? **5.** (*do*) hacer; **to ~ biking** salir en bicicleta; **to ~ camping/fishing/shopping** ir de camping/pesca/compras; **to ~ jogging** hacer footing; **to ~ swimming** ir a nadar **6.** (*attend*) asistir; **to ~ to a concert** ir a un concierto; **to ~ to a movie** ir a ver una película; **to ~ to a party** ir a una fiesta **7.** + *adj or n* (*become*) volverse; **to ~ senile** volverse viejo; **to ~ bankrupt** caer en bancarrota; **to ~ public** hacerse público; **to ~ communist** volverse comunista; **to ~ adrift** fallar; (*be stolen*) ser robado; **to ~ bald** quedarse calvo; **to ~ haywire** volverse loco; **to ~ missing** *Aus, Brit* desaparecer; **to ~ to sleep** dormirse; **to ~ wrong** salir mal **8.** + *adj* (*exist*) **to ~ hungry/thirsty** pasar hambre/sed; **to ~ unmentioned/unsolved** no ser mencionado/no solucionarse; **to ~ unnoticed** pasar desapercibido; **as prices ~ ...** considerando los precios actuales... **9.** (*happen*) **to ~ badly/well** ir mal/bien; **to ~ from bad to worse** ir de mal en peor; **the way things are ~ing** tal como van las cosas **10.** (*pass*) pasar; **time seems to ~ faster as you get older** parece que pasa el tiempo más rápido a medida que envejeces **11.** (*begin*) empezar; **ready, steady, ~** preparados, listos, ya **12.** (*fail*) **to ~ downhill** ir de capa caída **13.** (*belong*) pertenecer; **I'll put it where it ~es** lo pondré en su sitio **14.** (*fit*) quedar bien; **that old picture would ~ well on that wall** ese viejo cuadro quedaría bien en aquella pared; **two ~es into eight four times** MAT ocho entre dos da cuatro **15.** (*lead*) conducir; **this road ~es to Barcelona** esta carretera lleva a Barcelona **16.** (*extend*) extenderse; **those numbers ~ from 1 to 10** esos números van del 1 al 10 **17.** (*function*) funcionar; **to ~ slow** ir despacio; **to get sth to ~** hacer que algo funcione; **to keep a conversation ~ing** mantener una conversación **18.** (*be sold*) venderse; **the painting went for a lot more than was expected** el cuadro se vendió mucho más caro de lo esperado; **to ~ for £50** venderse por 50 libras; **to ~ like hot cakes** *fig* venderse como rosquillas **19.** (*contribute*) contribuir; **love and friendship ~ to make a lasting relationship** el amor y la amistad contribuyen a hacer duradera una relación **20.** (*sound*) sonar; **the ambulance had sirens ~ing** la ambulancia hacía sonar las sirenas **21.** (*be told*) **as the saying ~es** como dice el refrán; **the text ~es that ...** reza el texto que... **22.** GAMES tocar; **I ~ now** ahora me toca a mí **23.** *inf* (*use the toilet*) **do any of the kids have to ~?** ¿alguno de los niños tiene que ir al lavabo? **24.** (*express annoyance*) **~ jump in a lake!** *inf* ¡vete a freír espárragos! ►**what he <u>says</u> ~es** lo que él dice va a misa; **<u>anything</u> ~es** cualquier cosa vale; **<u>here</u> ~!** ¡vamos a ver! **II.** <went, gone> *vt* **1.** (*travel*) **to ~ it some** *inf* ir a toda pastilla **2.** *inf* (*say*) decir; **ducks ~ 'quack'** los patos hacen 'cuac' **3.** (*bid*) apostar; **to ~ nap** *Brit* jugárselo todo **4.** (*make*) hacer; **to ~ it alone** hacerlo solo; **to ~ it** *inf* correrla; (*work*) darle duro **III.** <-es> *n* **1.** (*turn*) turno *m;* **I'll have a ~ at driving if you're tired** ahora conduciré yo si estás cansado; **it's my ~** me toca a mí **2.** (*attempt*) intento *m;* **all in one ~** todo de un tirón; **to have a ~ at sth** intentar algo; **to have a ~ at sb about sth** tomarla con alguien por algo **3.** (*a success*) éxito *m;* **to be no ~** ser imposible; **to make a ~ of sth** tener éxito en algo **4.** (*energy*) energía *f;* **she's full of ~ today** hoy está pletórica de energía **5.** (*activity*) actividad *f;* **to be on the ~** trajinar; **to keep sb on the ~** hacer que alguien siga trabajando **6.** *inf* (*business*) asunto *m;* **a rum ~** un asunto extraño **7.** MED caso *m* ►**from the <u>word</u> ~** desde el principio **IV.** *adj* AVIAT listo, -a

◆go about **I.** *vt insep* **1.** (*proceed with*) ocuparse de; **to ~ one's business** ocuparse de sus asuntos **2.** (*perform a task*) llevar a cabo **II.** *vi* andar (de un sitio para otro)

◆go abroad *vi* **1.** (*rumour*) correr **2.** (*travel*) viajar al extranjero

◆go after *vt insep* **1.** (*follow*) seguir; **to ~ sb** ir detrás de alguien **2.** (*chase*) perseguir **3.** (*try to get*) intentar conseguir

◆go against *vt insep* **1.** (*contradict*)

G

contradecir **2.** (*oppose*) ir en contra de, oponerse a **3.** (*disobey*) desobedecer a
◆**go ahead** *vi* **1.** (*begin*) empezar **2.** (*go before*) ir adelante **3.** (*proceed*) seguir adelante; **~!** ¡sigue!; **all preparations have finished but they can't ~** todos los preparativos están listos pero no pueden sacarlo adelante
◆**go along** *vi* **1.** (*move onward*) ir hacia delante **2.** (*proceed*) proceder a
◆**go around** *vi* **1.** (*move around*) andar (de un lado para otro) **2.** (*move in a curve*) girar **3.** (*visit*) **to ~ to sb's** visitar a alguien; **to ~ and see sb** ir a ver a alguien **4.** (*rotate*) rotar **5.** (*be in circulation*) estar circulando; **it's going around that ...** se dice que...
◆**go at** *vt insep* **1.** (*attack*) acometer, lanzarse sobre **2.** (*work hard*) **to ~ it** trabajar mucho
◆**go away** *vi* **1.** (*travel*) viajar **2.** (*leave*) marcharse **3.** (*disappear*) desaparecer
◆**go back** *vi* **1.** (*move backwards*) retroceder **2.** (*return*) volver, regresarse *AmL* **3.** (*date back*) remontarse
◆**go between** *vi* interponerse
◆**go beyond** *vt* **1.** (*proceed past*) sobrepasar **2.** (*exceed*) superar
◆**go by** *vi* **1.** (*move past*) pasar (junto a) **2.** (*pass*) transcurrir; **in days gone by** *form* en tiempos pasados; **to let sth ~** no aprovechar algo **3.** (*be guided by*) guiarse por
◆**go down** **I.** *vt insep* bajar, descender; **to ~ a mine** MIN bajar a una mina **II.** *vi* **1.** (*set*) ponerse; (*ship*) hundirse; (*plane*) estrellarse; **to ~ on all fours** ponerse a gatas **2.** (*collapse*) derrumbarse **3.** (*decrease*) disminuir; FIN ir a la baja **4.** (*decrease in quality*) empeorar; **to ~ in sb's estimation** bajar en la estima de alguien **5.** (*decrease in size*) empequeñecer **6.** (*break down*) estropearse **7.** (*lose*) perder; **to ~ to sb/sth** ser derrotado por alguien/algo; SPORTS perder frente a alguien/algo; **to ~ without a fight** rendirse sin luchar **8.** (*proceed*) proceder; *Brit* (*visit quickly*) hacer una visita rápida **9.** (*travel southward*) ir hacia el sur **10.** (*extend*) extenderse **11.** (*be received*) ser recibido; **to ~ well/badly (with sb)** ser bien/mal recibido (por alguien) **12.** (*be recorded*) quedar registrado; **to ~ in writing** quedar registrado por escrito **13.** *Brit* UNIV acabar la universidad
◆**go far** *vi* **1.** (*have success*) llegar lejos **2.** (*contribute*) **to ~ towards sth** contribuir de forma significativa a algo; **not to ~** no estirarse
◆**go for** *vt insep* **1.** (*fetch*) ir a por, ir a buscar; **could you ~ oranges?** ¿puedes ir a buscar naranjas? **2.** (*try to achieve*) intentar conseguir; (*try to grasp*) intentar alcanzar; **~ it!** ¡a por ello! **3.** (*choose*) elegir **4.** (*attack*) atacar; **to ~ sb with sth** atacar a alguien con algo **5.** (*sell for*) venderse por **6.** *inf* (*like*) gustar; (*believe*) creer en
◆**go in** *vi* **1.** (*enter*) entrar; (*go to work*) empezar a trabajar **2.** (*belong in*) ir en; **those forks ~ the drawer** esos tenedores van en el cajón **3.** (*go behind a cloud*) esconderse **4.** *inf* (*be understood*) ser entendido
◆**go into** *vt insep* **1.** (*enter*) entrar en **2.** (*fit into*) encajar en; **does two ~ six?** ¿seis es divisible por dos? **3.** (*begin*) empezar; **to ~ a coma** MED entrar en coma; **to ~ a trance** entrar en trance; **to ~ action** pasar a la acción; **to ~ effect** entrar en vigor **4.** (*begin*) **to ~ politics** dedicarse a la política; **to ~ production** empezar a producirse **5.** (*examine and discuss*) examinar; **to ~ detail** entrar en detalles **6.** (*be used in*) ser utilizado en **7.** (*join*) unirse; **to ~ a group/an organization** unirse a un grupo/una organización **8.** (*crash into*) dar de lleno contra
◆**go off** *vi* **1.** (*leave*) irse; (*disappear*) desaparecer **2.** (*spoil*) estropearse **3.** (*ring*) dispararse **4.** (*explode*) estallar **5.** *Brit, Aus* (*decrease in quality*) perder calidad; (*diminish*) disminuir; GASTR (*rot*) pasarse **6.** (*stop liking*) dejar de gustar **7.** (*happen*) pasar; **to ~ badly/well** salir mal/bien **8.** (*digress*) salirse; **to ~ the subject** salirse del tema **9.** (*fall asleep*) quedarse dormido
◆**go on** **I.** *vi* **1.** (*move on*) seguir su camino, seguir adelante **2.** (*continue*) seguir; (*continue speaking*) seguir hablando **3.** (*go further*) ir más allá; **to ~ ahead** seguir adelante **4.** (*extend*) extenderse **5.** (*pass*) pasar **6.** (*happen*) suceder **7.** (*start*) empezar; (*begin functioning*) empezar a funcionar; THEAT, MUS salir (a escena) **II.** *vt insep* basarse en **III.** *interj* (*as encouragement*) vamos; (*express disbelief*) anda ya
◆**go out** *vi* **1.** (*leave*) salir; **to ~ to dinner** salir a cenar; **to ~ with sb** salir con alguien **2.** (*stop working*) dejar de funcionar; (*light*) apagarse **3.** RADIO, TV ser emitido **4.** (*recede*) retirarse **5.** (*become unfashionable*) pasar de moda
◆**go over** **I.** *vt insep* **1.** (*examine*) examinar **2.** (*cross*) atravesar; **to ~ a mountain** subir y bajar una montaña; **to ~ a border/river/street** cruzar una frontera/un río/una calle **3.** (*exceed*) exceder; **to ~ a budget/limit** exceder un presupuesto/límite **4.** (*attack*) atacar brutalmente **II.** *vi* **to ~ to** (*visit*) visitar a; (*change party*) pasarse a
◆**go through** *vt insep* **1.** (*pass*) pasar por **2.** (*experience*) experimentar; (*operation*) sufrir **3.** (*practice, perform*) practicar; (*review, discuss*) repasar **4.** (*be approved*) ser aprobado **5.** (*use up*) gastar **6.** (*look through*) examinar **7.** (*wear through*) gastar
◆**go to** *vt insep* visitar; **to ~ the country** ir a elecciones generales; **to ~ court** acudir a los tribunales; **to ~ expense** gastar
◆**go together** *vi* **1.** (*harmonize*) **to ~ (with sth)** armonizar (con algo) **2.** (*go with*) ir juntos
◆**go under** *vi* **1.** NAUT (*sink*) hundirse **2.** (*move below*) ir por debajo de **3.** (*fail*) fracasar; (*be defeated*) ser derrotado **4.** (*be known by*) ser conocido como

◆**go up** *vi* **1.**(*move higher*) subir **2.**(*increase*) aumentar; FIN, ECON ascender **3.**(*approach*) **to ~ to sb/sth** acercarse a alguien/algo **4.**(*travel*) subir, viajar hacia el norte; **to ~ to London** ir a Londres **5.**(*be built*) ser construido **6.**(*burn up*) arder; **to ~ in flames** arder en llamas **7.** *Brit* UNIV (*begin*) entrar en la universidad; (*return*) volver a la universidad

◆**go with** *vt insep* **1.**(*accompany*) acompañar a **2.**(*harmonize*) armonizar con, hacer juego con **3.**(*agree with*) estar de acuerdo en; **to ~ sb on sth** coincidir con alguien en algo **4.**(*follow*) seguir **5.**(*date*) salir con

◆**go without** *vt insep* pasar sin, prescindir de

goad [gəʊd, *Am:* goʊd] **I.** *vt* **1.**(*spur*) incitar; (*curiosity*) despertar **2.**(*tease*) fastidiar **II.** *n* **1.**(*motivating factor*) estímulo *m* **2.** AGR aguijada *f*

go-ahead ['gəʊəhed, *Am:* 'goʊ-] **I.** *n no pl* (*permission*) luz *f* verde; **to give/receive the ~** dar/recibir luz verde **II.** *adj Aus, Brit* emprendedor(a)

goal [gəʊl, *Am:* goʊl] *n* **1.**(*aim*) objetivo *m*, meta *f*; **to achieve a ~** conseguir un objetivo; **to pursue a ~** perseguir un fin; **to set a ~** fijar un objetivo **2.** SPORTS (*scoring area*) portería *f*; **to keep ~** defender la portería; **to play in ~** *Brit* ser portero **3.** SPORTS (*point*) gol *m*; **to score a ~** marcar un gol; **a penalty ~** un gol de penalty

goalie ['gəʊli, *Am:* 'goʊ-] *n inf,* **goalkeeper** ['gəʊlˌkiːpəʳ, *Am:* 'goʊlˌkiːpɚ] *n* SPORTS portero, -a *m, f*

goal line *n* SPORTS línea *f* de la portería **goalpost** *n* SPORTS poste *m* de la portería ►**to move the ~s** *inf* cambiar las reglas del juego

goat [gəʊt, *Am:* goʊt] *n* **1.** ZOOL cabra *f*; **~'s milk** leche *f* de cabra; **~'s cheese** queso *m* de cabra; **mountain ~** cabra montesa; **to act the ~** *Brit, inf* hacer el imbécil **2.** *inf* (*man*) viejo *m* verde ►**to separate the sheep from the ~s** separar el grano de la paja; **to get sb's ~** sacar de quicio a alguien

goatee [gəʊ'tiː, *Am:* goʊ-] *n* perilla *f*

gobble ['gɒbl, *Am:* 'gɑːbl] **I.** *vi* **1.** *inf* (*eat*) jalar **2.**(*make turkey noise*) gluglutear **II.** *vt inf* jalar **III.** *n* gluglú *m*

gobbledegook, gobbledygook ['gɒbldiˌguːk, *Am:* 'gɑːbl-] *n no pl, inf* galimatías *m; inv*

go-between ['gəʊbɪtwiːn, *Am:* 'goʊbə-] *n* medianero, -a *m, f*; **to act as a ~** hacer de intermediario

goblet ['gɒblɪt, *Am:* 'gɑːblət] *n* cáliz *m*

goblin ['gɒblɪn, *Am:* 'gɑːblɪn] *n* duende *m*

go-cart ['gəʊkɑːt, *Am:* 'goʊkɑːrt] *n Am* AUTO, SPORTS kart *m*

god [gɒd, *Am:* gɑːd] *n* **1.** REL **God** Dios; **God bless** que Dios te/le... bendiga; **God forbid** no lo permita Dios; **God knows** quien sabe; **please God!** ¡Dios lo quiera!; **for God's sake!** ¡por el amor de Dios! **2.** REL **Greek/Roman ~s** dioses *mpl* griegos/romanos **3.**(*idolized person*) ídolo *m*

god-awful ['gɒd'ɔːfəl, *Am:* ˌgɑːd'ɑː-] *adj inf* horrible **godchild** *n* ahijado, -a *m, f* **goddam(ned)** *adj inf* maldito, -a **goddaughter** *n* ahijada *f*

goddess ['gɒdɪs, *Am:* 'gɑːdɪs] <-es> *n* **1.** REL diosa *f* **2.**(*idolized woman*) ídolo *m*

godfather ['gɒdˌfɑːðəʳ, *Am:* 'gɑːdˌfɑːðɚ] *n* padrino *m* **god-fearing** *adj* temeroso, -a de Dios **god-forsaken** *adj* dejado, -a de la mano de Dios **godhead** *n,* **Godhead** ['gɒdhed, *Am:* 'gɑːd-] *n no pl* divinidad *f*

godless ['gɒdlɪs, *Am:* 'gɑːd-] *adj* **1.** REL impío, -a; (*without God*) sin Dios **2.**(*evil*) demoníaco, -a

godlike ['gɒdlaɪk, *Am:* 'gɑːd-] *adj* divino, -a

godly ['gɒdli, *Am:* 'gɑːd-] *adj* piadoso, -a; **to lead a ~ life** llevar una vida piadosa

godmother ['gɒdˌmʌðəʳ, *Am:* 'gɑːdˌmʌðɚ] *n* madrina *f* **godparents** *npl* padrinos *mpl* **godsend** *n inf* cosa *f* llovida del cielo; **to be a ~ (to sb)** ser un regalo celestial (para alguien) **godson** *n* ahijado *m*

goer ['gəʊəʳ, *Am:* 'goʊɚ] *n* **1.** *inf* (*party person*) juergista *mf*; (*promiscuous person*) calentón, -ona *m, f vulg* **2.** ECON proyecto *m* viable

goes [gəʊz, *Am:* goʊz] *3rd pers sing of* **go**

go-getter [ˌgəʊ'getəʳ] *n* persona *f* emprendedora

go-getting [ˌgəʊ'getɪŋ] *adj* emprendedor(a)

goggle ['gɒgl, *Am:* 'gɑːgl] **I.** *vi inf* **to ~ at sb/sth** mirar con ojos desorbitados a alguien/algo **II.** *n pl* (*glasses*) gafas *fpl*; **safety ~s** gafas de protección; **ski/swim ~s** gafas de esquiar/natación

goggle-box ['gɒglbɒks, *Am:* 'gɑːglbɑːks] <-es> *n Brit, inf* caja *f* boba

goggle-eyed ['gɒglaɪd, *Am:* 'gɑːgl-] *adj inf* con ojos desorbitados; (*person*) con [*o* de] ojos saltones

go-go dancer ['gəʊgəʊ'dɑːnsəʳ, *Am:* 'goʊgoʊ'dænsɚ] *n* gogó *mf*

go-go dancing *n no pl* baile *m* de gogós

going ['gəʊɪŋ, *Am:* 'goʊ-] **I.** *n* **1.**(*act of leaving*) ida *f*; (*departure*) salida *f* **2.**(*conditions*) **easy/rough ~** condiciones *fpl* favorables/adversas; **while the ~ is good** mientras las condiciones lo permitan **3.**(*progress*) progreso *m* ►**when the ~ gets tough (the tough get ~)** cuando las cosas se ponen feas (los fuertes entran en acción) **II.** *adj* **1.**(*available*) disponible **2.**(*in action*) en funcionamiento; **to get sth ~** poner algo en funcionamiento **3.**(*current*) actual **III.** *vi aux* **to be ~ to do sth** ir a hacer algo

going price *n* **1.**(*market price*) precio *m* de mercado **2.**(*current price*) precio *m* actual

goings-on [ˌgəʊɪŋz'ɒn, *Am:* ˌgoʊɪŋz'ɑːn] *npl* **1.**(*events*) sucesos *mpl* **2.**(*activities*) tejemanejes *mpl*

goiter *n Am,* **goitre** ['gɔɪtəʳ, *Am:* -t̬ɚ] *n Brit, Aus no pl* MED bocio *m*

go-kart ['gəʊkɑːt, *Am:* 'goʊkɑːrt] *n Brit, Aus* AUTO, SPORTS kart *m*

gold [gəʊld, *Am:* goʊld] **I.** *n no pl* **1.** (*metal*) oro *m;* **to pan for** ~ lavar oro; **to strike** ~ encontrar oro; **to be dripping with** ~ *fig* llevar puestas muchas joyas de oro **2.** SPORTS medalla *f* de oro ►**to be worth one's weight in** ~ valer su peso en oro; **to be good as** ~ portarse como un ángel; **all that glitters is not** ~ *prov* no es oro todo lo que reluce *prov* **II.** *adj* de oro; **a** ~ **ring** un anillo de oro

gold brick **I.** *n inf* **1.** (*sham*) estafa *f* **2.** *Am* (*person*) gandul(a) *m(f)* **II.** *vt* estafar **III.** *vi Am* escurrir el bulto **gold bullion** *n no pl* oro *m* en lingotes **gold coin** *n* moneda *f* de oro **gold content** *n no pl* contenido *m* de oro **gold digger** *n* **1.** (*gold miner*) buscador(a) *m(f)* de oro **2.** (*money-seeker*) cazafortunas *mf inv* **gold dust** *n no pl* oro *m* en polvo; **to be like** ~ *fig* ser muy cotizado

golden ['gəʊldən, *Am:* 'goʊl-] *adj* **1.** de oro; ~ **anniversary** bodas *fpl* de oro **2.** (*colour*) dorado, -a; ~ **brown** tostado, -a; (*skin*) bronceado, -a **3.** (*very good*) excelente; ~ **oldies** MUS melodías *fpl* de ayer; *iron* viejas cantinelas *fpl*

golden age *n* edad *f* de oro **golden goose** *n* gallina *f* de los huevos de oro **golden mean** *n no pl* justo medio *m* **golden triangle** *n no pl* **the** ~ el Triángulo Dorado **golden wedding** *n* bodas *fpl* de oro

goldfinch ['gəʊldfɪntʃ, *Am:* 'goʊld-] <-es> *n* jilguero *m* **goldfish** *n inv* pez *m* de colores **gold foil** *n no pl* lámina *f* de oro **gold leaf** *n no pl* hoja *f* de oro **gold medal** *n* SPORTS medalla *f* de oro **goldmine** *n* **1.** (*mine*) mina *f* de oro **2.** FIN filón *m* **gold nugget** *n* pepita *f* de oro **gold plating** *n no pl* **1.** (*layer*) baño *m* de oro **2.** (*production process*) chapado *m* de oro **gold reserve** *n* reserva *f* de oro **goldsmith** *n* orfebre *m* **gold standard** *n* FIN patrón *m* oro

golf [gɒlf, *Am:* gɑːlf] **I.** *n no pl* golf *m;* **to play** ~ jugar al golf; **crazy** ~ minigolf *m* **II.** *vi* jugar al golf

golf ball *n* pelota *f* de golf

golf-ball typewriter *n* máquina *f* de escribir a bola

golf club *n* **1.** (*stick*) palo *m* de golf **2.** (*sports association*) club *m* de golf **golf course** *n* campo *m* de golf

golfer ['gɒlfəʳ, *Am:* 'gɑːlfɚ] *n* golfista *mf*

golf links *npl* campo *m* de golf

Goliath [gə'laɪəθ] *n* Goliat *m;* **a David and** ~ **battle** *fig* una batalla entre David y Goliat

golliwog *n,* **gollywog** ['gɒlɪwɒg, *Am:* 'gɑːlɪwɔːg] *n Brit, Aus: muñeco negro de trapo; la expresión en inglés puede considerarse ofensiva*

golly ['gɒli, *Am:* 'gɑːli] *interj inf* caramba; **by** ~ ¡vaya!

goloshes [gə'lɒʃɪz, *Am:* -'lɑːʃ-] *npl* chanclos *mpl;* **rubber** ~ chanclos de goma

gondola ['gɒndələ, *Am:* 'gɑːn-] *n* góndola *f*

gondolier [ˌgɒndə'lɪəʳ, *Am:* ˌgɑːndə'lɪr] *n* gondolero, -a *m, f*

gone [gɒn, *Am:* gɑːn] **I.** *pp of* **go** **II.** *prep Brit* después de **III.** *adj* **1.** (*no longer there*) ausente **2.** (*dead*) muerto, -a **3.** *inf* (*pregnant*) embarazada **4.** *inf* (*absorbed*) ido, -a **5.** *inf* (*infatuated*) **to be** ~ **on sb** estar loco, -a por alguien

goner ['gɒnəʳ, *Am:* 'gɑːnɚ] *n* **to be a** ~ (*bound to die*) ser hombre muerto; (*broken*) estar para tirar

gong [gɒŋ, *Am:* gɑːŋ] *n* **1.** (*flat bell*) gong *m* **2.** *Brit, Aus, inf* (*an award*) medalla *f;* **to win a** ~ (**for sth**) ganar una condecoración (por algo)

gonorrh(o)ea [ˌgɒnə'rɪə, *Am:* ˌgɑːnə'-] *n no pl* gonorrea *f*

goo [guː] *n no pl* **1.** *inf* (*substance*) sustancia *f* viscosa **2.** (*sentimentality*) sentimentalismo *m*

good [gʊd] **I.** <better, best> *adj* **1.** (*of high quality*) bueno, -a; ~ **ears** buen oído; ~ **eyes** buena vista; ~ **thinking!** ¡buena idea!; **to be a** ~ **catch** ser un buen partido; **to do a** ~ **job** hacer un buen trabajo; **to have the** ~ **sense to do sth** tener el sentido común para hacer algo; **to be in** ~ **shape** estar en buena forma; **to be/to be not** ~ **enough** ser/no ser lo suficientemente bueno **2.** (*skilled*) capacitado, -a; **to be** ~ **at** [*o* **in**] **sth/doing sth** estar capacitado para algo/hacer algo; **to be** ~ **at sth** dársele bien algo; **to be** ~ **with one's hands** ser bueno con las manos **3.** (*pleasant*) placentero, -a; **to have a** ~ **day/evening** tener un buen día/pasar una velada placentera; **to have a** ~ **time** pasar(se)lo bien **4.** (*appealing to senses*) **to feel** ~ sentirse bien; **to have** ~ **looks** ser guapo; **to look** ~ tener buen aspecto; **to smell** ~ oler bien **5.** (*favourable*) **the** ~ **life** la buena vida; ~ **luck** (**in sth**) buena suerte (en algo); **a** ~ **omen** un buen presagio; ~ **times** buenos tiempos; **to be a** ~ **thing** [*o* **job** *Brit*] **that ...** ser bueno que... +*subj;* **to be/sound too** ~ **to be true** ser demasiado bueno/sonar demasiado bien para ser verdad **6.** (*beneficial*) beneficioso, -a; **a** ~ **habit** una buena costumbre; **to be** ~ **for sb/sth** ser bueno para alguien/algo; **to be** ~ **for business** ser bueno para el negocio **7.** (*useful*) útil **8.** (*appropriate*) adecuado, -a; (*choice, decision*) correcto, -a; **to be in a** ~ **position to do sth** estar en buena posición para hacer algo; **a** ~ **time to do sth** un buen momento para hacer algo **9.** (*kind*) amable; ~ **deeds/works** buenas obras **10.** (*moral*) **the Good Book** la Biblia; **a** ~ **name/reputation** un buen nombre/una buena reputación; **to be** ~ **as one's word** cumplir su palabra **11.** (*well-behaved*) de buenos modales; **a** ~ **loser** un buen perdedor; **to be on** ~ **behaviour** comportarse bien **12.** (*thorough*) completo, -a; **a** ~ **beating** una paliza **13.** (*valid*) válido, -a; (*not forged*) auténtico, -a; (*useable*) útil, provechoso, -a; **to**

make sth ~ (*pay for*) pagar por algo; (*do successfully*) cumplir algo; **to be** ~ **for nothing** ser completamente inútil **14.** (*substantial*) sustancial; **a** ~ **few/many** unos pocos/muchos **15.** GASTR en su punto **16.** (*almost, virtually*) **it's as** ~ **as done** está prácticamente terminado; **to be as** ~ **as new** estar como nuevo **17.** (*said to emphasize*) **to be** ~ **and ready** estar listo **18.** (*said to express affection*) **the** ~ **old days** los buenos tiempos ►**to give as** ~ **as one gets** devolver golpe por golpe **II.** *n no pl* **1.** (*moral force, not evil*) bien *m;* **to be no** ~ ser inútil; **to be up to no** ~ estar tramando algo **2.** (*profit, benefit*) beneficio *m;* **this soup will do you** ~ esta sopa te sentará bien; **for one's own** ~ en beneficio propio; **to do** ~ hacer bien; **to do more harm than** ~ hacer más daño que bien; **to be not much** ~ no valer mucho **3.** *pl* (*moral people*) **the** ~ la gente buena ►**for** ~ definitivamente **III.** *adv* **1.** *dial, inf* (*well*) bien **2.** (*thoroughly*) totalmente **IV.** *interj* **1.** (*to express approval*) bien **2.** (*to express surprise, shock*) ~ **God!** ¡Dios mío!; ~ **gracious!** ¡Dios mío!; ~ **grief!** ¡madre mía! **3.** (*said as greeting*) ~ **afternoon,** ~ **evening** buenas tardes; ~ **morning** buenos días; ~ **night** buenas noches **4.** *Brit* (*said to accept order*) **very** ~ entendido

goodbye, **goodby** *Am* **I.** *interj* adiós **II.** *n* **1.** (*departing word*) adiós *m;* **to say** ~ **(to sb)** decir adiós (a alguien); **to say** ~ despedirse **2.** *inf* (*loss*) **to say** ~ **to sth** olvidarse definitivamente de algo; **to kiss sth** ~ despedirse de algo

good-for-nothing ['gʊdfəˌnʌθɪŋ, *Am:* -fɚˌ-] **I.** *n* inútil *mf* **II.** *adj* inútil

Good Friday *n* Viernes *m* Santo

good-humoured, **good-humored** [ˌgʊd'hjuːməd, *Am:* -mɚd] *adj Am* afable

good-looking [ˌgʊd'lʊkɪŋ] <better-looking, best-looking> *adj* guapo, -a

good looks *n no pl* buen parecer *m*

goodly ['gʊdli] <-ier, -iest> *adj* agradable

good-natured <better-natured, best-natured> *adj* **1.** (*pleasant*) afable **2.** (*inherently good*) bonachón, -ona

goodness ['gʊdnɪs] **I.** *n no pl* **1.** (*moral virtue*) bondad *f* **2.** (*kindness*) amabilidad *f* **3.** (*quality*) buena calidad *f* **4.** (*said for emphasis*) ~ **knows** quién sabe; **for** ~**' sake** ¡por Dios!; **thank** ~**!** ¡gracias a Dios!; **to wish** [*o* **to hope**] **to** ~ ojalá Dios quiera **II.** *interj* ~ **gracious (me)!** (*surprise*) ¡Dios mío!; (*annoyance*) ¡vaya por Dios!

goods [gʊdz] *npl* **1.** (*freight*) mercancías *fpl;* ~ **lorry** camión *m* de carga; ~ **depot** depósito *m* de mercancías; ~ **train** tren *m* de mercancías **2.** (*wares*) productos *mpl;* **manufactured** ~ bienes *mpl* elaborados **3.** (*personal belongings*) pertenencias *fpl;* ~ **and chattels** bienes *mpl* muebles **4.** (*desired things*) artículos *mpl* pedidos; **to deliver the** ~ entregar la mercancía; *fig* dar la talla

good-sized [ˌgʊd'saɪzd] <better-sized, best-sized> *adj* bastante grande

goods station *n* RAIL estación *f* de mercancías **goods traffic** *n no pl* tránsito *m* de mercancías **goods train** *n Brit* tren *m* de mercancías

good-tempered [ˌgʊd'tempəd, *Am:* -pɚd] <better-tempered, best-tempered> *adj irr* afable

goodwill [ˌgʊd'wɪl] *n no pl* buena voluntad *f;* ~ **towards sb** buenas intenciones con alguien; **a gesture of** ~ un gesto de buena voluntad

goody ['gʊdi] **I.** <-ies> *n* **1.** *childspeak* GASTR golosina *f* **2.** THEAT, CINE bueno, -a *m, f;* **the goodies** los buenos **II.** *interj childspeak* qué bien

gooey ['guːi] <gooier, gooiest> *adj* (*sticky*) pegajoso, -a; GASTR empalagoso, -a

goof [guːf] **I.** *vi inf* pifiarla **II.** *n inf* **1.** (*mistake*) error *m* **2.** (*silly person*) bobo, -a *m, f*

◆**goof up** *vt inf* fastidiar

goofy ['guːfi] <-ier, -iest> *adj Am, inf* bobo, -a

goolies ['guːliːz] *npl Brit, inf* cataplines *mpl*

goon [guːn] *n inf* **1.** (*stupid person*) imbécil *mf* **2.** *Am* gángster *m* a sueldo

goose [guːs] <geese> *n* ganso, -a *m, f* ►**to kill the** ~ **that lays the golden eggs** matar la gallina de los huevos de oro; **to cook someone's** ~ *inf* hacer la pascua a alguien; **to not say boo to a** ~ *pej* no decir ni mu

gooseberry ['gʊzbəri, *Am:* 'guːsberi] <-ies> *n* grosella *f* espinosa ►**to play** ~ *Brit, inf* hacer de carabina **goose-flesh** *n no pl,* **goose-pimples** *npl* carne *f* de gallina **goose-pimply** *adj inf* **to go** [*o* **get**] **(all)** ~ ponerse a uno la carne de gallina **goosestep** **I.** <-pp-> *vi* marchar a paso de oca **II.** *n no pl* paso *m* de oca

goos(e)y ['guːsi] <-ier, -iest> *adj Aus s.* **goose-pimply**

gore[1] [gɔːʳ, *Am:* gɔːr] *n* sangre *f* derramada

gore[2] [gɔːʳ, *Am:* gɔːr] *vt* cornear

gore[3] [gɔːʳ, *Am:* gɔːr] *n* (*clothing*) godet *m*

gorge [gɔːdʒ, *Am:* gɔːrdʒ] **I.** *n* **1.** GEO cañón *m* **2.** ANAT garganta *f;* **my** ~ **rises** me da asco **3.** *inf* (*large feast*) banquete *m* **II.** *vi* engullir **III.** *vt* **to** ~ **oneself on sth** atracarse de algo

gorgeous ['gɔːdʒəs, *Am:* 'gɔːr-] **I.** *adj* **1.** (*beautiful*) precioso, -a **2.** (*pleasurable*) maravilloso, -a **II.** *n* **hello** ~**!** ¡hola ricura!

gorilla [gə'rɪlə] *n* gorila *m*

gormless ['gɔːmlɪs, *Am:* 'gɔːrm-] *adj Brit, inf* idiota

gorse [gɔːs, *Am:* gɔːrs] *n no pl* aulaga *f*

gory ['gɔːri] <-ier, -iest> *adj* sangriento, -a

gosh [gɒʃ, *Am:* gɑːʃ] *interj inf* dios mío

gosling ['gɒzlɪŋ, *Am:* 'gɑːz-] *n* ansarino *m*

go-slow ['gəʊsləʊ, *Am:* 'goʊsloʊ] *n Brit* huelga *f* de celo

gospel ['gɒspl, *Am:* 'gɑːs-] *n* **1.** REL evangelio *m;* **to spread/preach the** ~ extender/predicar el evangelio; ~ **singer** cantante *mf* de gospel **2.** (*principle*) principio *m*

gossamer ['gɒsəməʳ, *Am:* 'gɑːsəmɚ] **I.** *n* hilo *m* de telaraña **II.** *adj* sutil

gossip ['gɒsɪp, *Am:* 'gɑːsəp] **I.** *n* **1.** *no pl* (*rumour*) chismorreo *m;* **idle** ~ rumor *m* infundado; **the latest** ~ los últimos chismes; ~ **columnist** periodista *mf* de prensa rosa **2.** (*person*) chismoso, -a *m, f* **3.** (*conversation*) cotilleo *m;* **to have a** ~ **about sb** cotillear sobre alguien **II.** *vi* **1.** (*spread rumors*) chismorrear; **to** ~ **about sb** cotillear acerca de alguien **2.** (*chatter*) contar chismes

gossip column *n* columna *f* de cotilleo

gossipy ['gɒsɪpi, *Am:* 'gɑːsəp-] *adj* **1.** (*rumour-spreading*) chismoso, -a, lenguón, -ona *AmL* **2.** (*containing gossip*) de cotilleo

got [gɒt, *Am:* gɑːt] *pt, Brit: pp of* **get**

Gothic ['gɒθɪk, *Am:* 'gɑːθɪk] **I.** *adj* **1.** ARCHIT, LIT gótico, -a; ~ **architecture** arquitectura *f* gótica **2.** (*of Goths*) godo, -a **3.** TYPO ~ **script** escritura *f* gótica **II.** *n no pl* **1.** LING gótico *m* **2.** TYPO letra *f* gótica

gotten ['gɒtən, *Am:* 'gɑːtən] *Am, Aus pp of* **get**

gouge [gaʊdʒ] **I.** *vt* **1.** (*pierce*) excavar; **to** ~ **a hole into sth** hacer un agujero en algo **2.** *Am, inf* (*overcharge*) cobrar de más **II.** *n* gubia *f*

goulash ['guːlæʃ, *Am:* -lɑːʃ] *n no pl* puchero *m* (húngaro)

gourd [gʊəd, *Am:* gɔːrd] *n* calabaza *f* (*para beber*)

gourmand ['gʊəmənd, *Am:* 'gʊrmɑːnd] *n* glotón, -ona *m, f*

gourmet ['gʊəmeɪ, *Am:* 'gʊr-] GASTR **I.** *n* gastrónomo, -a *m, f* **II.** *adj* de gastrónomo, -a

gout [gaʊt] *n no pl* gota *f*

Gov. *abbr of* **Governor** gobernador(a) *m(f)*

govern ['gʌvn, *Am:* -ɚn] **I.** *vt* **1.** POL, ADMIN (*country*) gobernar; (*organization*) dirigir **2.** LAW (*regulate*) regular; (*contract*) regir; **to** ~ **how/when/what ...** regular cómo/cuándo/qué... **3.** (*control*) controlar **4.** BIO **to be** ~**ed by sth** ser determinado por algo **5.** LING regir **II.** *vi* POL, ADMIN gobernar; **to be fit/unfit to** ~ tener/no tener las cualidades para gobernar

governess ['gʌvənɪs, *Am:* -ɚnəs] <-es> *n* institutriz *f*, gobernanta *f AmL*

governing *adj* directivo, -a

government ['gʌvənmənt, *Am:* -ɚn-] *n* **1.** (*ruling body*) gobierno *m,* administración *f Arg;* ~ **organization** organización *f* gubernamental; ~ **policy** política *f* estatal; ~ **bond/paper** FIN bono *m*/título *m* del Estado; ~ **securities** FIN valores *mpl* del Estado; **Government House** *Brit* residencia *f* del Gobernador **2.** (*administration*) administración *f;* **to form a** ~ formar gobierno **3.** *no pl* (*governing*) **to be in** ~ *Aus, Brit* estar en el gobierno

governmental [ˌgʌvən'mentəl, *Am:* -ɚn-'men t̬əl] *adj* gubernamental

governor ['gʌvənəʳ, *Am:* -ɚnɚ] *n* **1.** (*of area*) gobernador(a) *m(f)* **2.** *Brit* (*of organization*) director(a) *m(f);* **the board of** ~**s** el consejo de dirección **3.** *Brit, inf* (*boss*) jefe *m;* (*father*) viejo *m* **4.** TECH regulador *m*

Govt. *abbr of* **Government** gobno.

gown [gaʊn] *n* **1.** (*evening dress*) traje *m;* **ball** ~ vestido *m* de baile **2.** MED bata *f;* **surgical** ~ bata de cirujano **3.** UNIV toga *f*

GP [ˌdʒiː'piː] *n Brit, Aus abbr of* **general practitioner** médico, -a *m, f* de cabecera

GPO [ˌdʒiːpiː'əʊ, *Am:* -'oʊ] *n Brit* ADMIN *abbr of* **General Post Office** Administración *f* General de Correos

grab [græb] **I.** *n* **to make a** ~ **for sth** hacerse con algo; **to be up for** ~**s** *inf* estar libre **II.** <-bb-> *vt* **1.** (*snatch*) quitar; **to** ~ **sth** (**away**) **from sb** arrebatar algo a alguien; **to** ~ **sth out of sb's hands** quitar algo a alguien de las manos **2.** (*take hold of*) coger, hacerse con; **to** ~ **hold of sth** hacerse con algo **3.** (*arrest*) detener **4.** *inf* (*get, acquire*) conseguir; **to** ~ **some sleep** dormir un rato; **to** ~ **a chance** aprovechar una oportunidad; **to** ~ **sb's attention** captar la atención de alguien; **how does this** ~ **you?** *inf* ¿qué te parece esto? **III.** <-bb-> *vi* **1.** (*snatch*) arrebatar **2.** (*hold on*) asir

grace [greɪs] **I.** *n* **1.** *no pl* (*movement*) elegancia *f,* gracia *f* **2.** *no pl* (*elegant proportions*) elegancia *f* **3.** *no pl* REL gracia *f;* **divine** ~ gracia divina; **by the** ~ **of God** por la gracia de Dios; **to be in a state of** ~ estar en estado de buena esperanza; **the year of** ~ *form* el año de gracia **4.** (*favour*) favor *m;* **to be in/get into sb's good** ~**s** congraciarse con alguien; **to fall from** ~ caer en desgracia **5.** *no pl* (*politeness*) cortesía *f;* **to do sth with good/bad** ~ hacer algo de buen grado/a regañadientes; **to have the** (**good**) ~ **to do sth** tener la cortesía de hacer algo **6.** (*prayer*) bendición *f* (de la mesa); **to say** ~ bendecir la mesa **7.** (*leeway*) demora *f* **8.** (*Highness*) **Your/His/Her Grace** su Excelencia **9.** (*sister goddesses*) **the Graces** las Gracias **II.** *vt* **1.** (*honour*) honrar **2.** (*make beautiful*) embellecer

graceful ['greɪsfəl] *adj* **1.** (*moving*) grácil; ~ **movements** movimientos *mpl* garbosos **2.** (*elegant*) elegante **3.** (*polite*) educado, -a

graceless ['greɪslɪs] *adj* **1.** (*lacking smooth elegance*) desgarbado, -a **2.** (*impolite*) descortés

gracious ['greɪʃəs] **I.** *adj* **1.** (*warm and kind*) afable **2.** (*elegant*) elegante **3.** (*merciful*) clemente **II.** *interj* (**good**) ~ (**me**) ¡Dios mío!

gradation [grə'deɪʃən, *Am:* greɪ'-] *n* gradación *f*

grade [greɪd] **I.** *n* **1.** (*rank*) rango *m* **2.** *Am* SCHOOL curso *m;* **to skip a** ~ perder un curso **3.** (*mark*) nota *f;* **good/bad** ~**s** buenas/malas notas **4.** (*level of quality*) clase *f,* calidad *f;* **high/low** ~ alta/baja calidad **5.** *Am* GEO pendiente *f;* **gentle/steep** ~ pendiente suave/pronunciada ►**to be on the down** ~ ir cuesta abajo; **to be on the up** ~ prosperar; **to make**

the ~ dar la talla **II.** *vt* **1.** SCHOOL, UNIV (*evaluate*) evaluar; **to ~ up/down** subir/bajar la nota **2.** (*categorize*) clasificar
grade crossing *n Am* paso *m* a nivel
grade school *n Am* SCHOOL escuela *f* primaria
gradient ['greɪdɪənt] *n* GEO, AUTO pendiente *f*
grading ['greɪdɪŋ] *n* **1.** (*gradation*) gradación *f* **2.** (*classification*) clasificación *f*

El sistema de calificación que se utiliza en los EE.UU. recibe el nombre de **grading system**. Este sistema emplea las siguientes letras para expresar las distintas calificaciones: A, B, C, D, E y F. La letra E, sin embargo, no se suele utilizar. La A representa la máxima calificación, mientras que la F (**Fail**) significa suspenso. Las notas además pueden ir matizadas por un más o un menos. Quien obtiene una A+ es que ha tenido un rendimiento verdaderamente sobresaliente.

gradual ['grædʒʊəl] *adj* **1.** (*not sudden*) gradual **2.** (*not steep*) suave
gradually ['grædʒʊli] *adv* **1.** (*not steeply*) gradualmente **2.** (*not suddenly*) progresivamente, paulatinamente
graduate[1] ['grædʒʊət] *n* **1.** UNIV licenciado, -a *m, f;* **university ~** licenciado *m* universitario **2.** *Am* SCHOOL graduado, -a *m, f* **3.** (*postgraduate*) pos(t)graduado, -a *m, f;* **~ school** escuela *f* de pos(t)grado
graduate[2] ['grædʒʊeɪt] **I.** *vi* **1.** UNIV licenciarse; *Am* SCHOOL graduarse; **to ~ cum laude** graduarse cum laude **2.** (*move to a higher level*) subir de categoría; **to ~ to ...** ascender a... **3.** (*calibrate*) calibrar **II.** *vt Am* graduar
graduated *adj* graduado, -a
graduation [ˌgrædʒʊ'eɪʃən, *Am:* ˌgrædʒu'-] *n* **1.** SCHOOL, UNIV graduación *f*, egreso *m Arg, Chile* **2.** (*promotion*) ascenso *m* **3.** (*marks of calibration*) calibrado *m*
graffiti [grə'fi:ti, *Am:* -t̬i] *npl* graffiti *m;* **a ~ artist** un artista de graffiti
graft [grɑ:ft, *Am:* græft] **I.** *n* **1.** BOT, AGR, MED injerto *m;* **a skin ~** un injerto de piel **2.** POL corrupción *f* **3.** *Brit, inf* (*work*) trabajo *m* duro **II.** *vt* **1.** BOT, AGR, MED injertar **2.** (*add on*) añadir **III.** *vi* **1.** POL trampear **2.** *Brit, inf* (*work hard*) currar mucho
grafter ['grɑ:ftəʳ, *Am:* 'græftɚ] *n* **1.** BOT, AGR persona *f* que realiza injertos **2.** *Brit, inf* (*hard worker*) persona *f* que trabaja duro
Grail [greɪl] *n* **the Holy ~** el Santo Grial
grain [greɪn] **I.** *n* **1.** (*smallest piece*) grano *m;* **~ of sand/salt** grano de arena/sal **2.** *no pl* (*cereal*) cereal *m* **3.** (*direction of fibres*) fibra *f;* **wood ~** hebra *f* de madera **4.** GASTR veta *f;* **meat ~** veta de carne; **it goes against the ~ (for me)** *fig* se me hace cuesta arriba *inf* **5.** (*smallest quantity*) pizca *f;* **a ~ of hope** una pequeña esperanza; **a ~ of truth** una pizca de verdad ▸**to take sth with a ~ of salt** no creerse algo del todo **II.** *vt* **1.** (*granulate*) granular **2.** (*remove hair from*) pelar
grain elevator *n* elevador *m* de granos
grain export *n* exportación *f* de grano
grain market *n* mercado *m* de cereales
grammar ['græməʳ, *Am:* -ɚ] *n no pl* gramática *f*
grammar book *n* libro *m* de gramática
grammarian [grə'meərɪən, *Am:* -'merɪ-] *n* gramático, -a *m, f*
grammar school *n* **1.** *Am* (*elementary school*) colegio *m* **2.** *Brit* HIST (*upper level school*) *colegio de enseñanza secundaria al cual se accede por medio de un examen*

Las antiguas **grammar schools** (que más o menos se corresponden con los institutos) fueron fundadas hace muchos siglos en Gran Bretaña para el estudio del latín. Hacia 1950 el alumno que quería acceder a esta escuela debía aprobar el **eleven-plus examination**. Pero sólo un 20% del alumnado aprobaba este examen. El resto continuaba su intinerario educativo en una **secondary modern school** (escuela secundaria de grado inferior). Estos dos tipos de escuela fueron reorganizados durante los años 60 y 70 como **comprehensive schools** (escuelas integradas).

grammatical [grə'mætɪkl, *Am:* -'mæt̬ɪ-] *adj* gramatical
gram(me) [græm] *n* gramo *m*
gramophone ['græməfəʊn, *Am:* -foʊn] *n* gramófono *m*, vitrola *f AmL*
grampus ['græmpəs] <-es> *n* **1.** ZOOL orca *f* **2.** *Brit, inf* (*person*) abuelo *m*
gran [græn] *n inf abbr of* **grandmother** abuela *f*
granary ['grænəri] AGR **I.** <-ies> *n* **1.** (*silo*) granero *m* **2.** (*grain region*) región *f* de cereales **II.** *adj* granero, -a
granary bread *n no pl,* **granary loaf** <-loaves> *n Brit* pan *m* con granos enteros
grand [grænd] **I.** *adj* **1.** (*splendid*) magnífico, -a; **in ~ style** de estilo sublime; **a ~ opening** una gran apertura; **to make a ~ entrance** hacer una entrada triunfal; **the Grand Canyon** el Gran Cañón **2.** *inf* (*excellent*) sublime **3.** (*far-reaching*) importante; **~ ambitions/ideas** grandes ambiciones/ideas **4.** (*large*) grande; **on a ~ scale** a gran escala **5.** (*overall*) **the ~ total** el importe total **6.** (*of upper class*) **~ duke** gran duque *m* **II.** *n* **1.** *inv, inf* (*dollars*) mil dólares *mpl;* (*pounds*) mil libras *fpl* **2.** MUS piano *m* de cola
grandchild <-children> *n* nieto, -a *m, f*
grand(d)ad *n* **1.** *inf* (*grandfather*) abuelito *m* **2.** (*old man*) viejo *m* **granddaughter** *n* nieta *f*
grandee [græn'di:] *n* grande *m*, pez *m* gordo
grandeur ['grændʒəʳ, *Am:* -dʒɚ] *n no pl* **1.** (*imposing splendor*) magnificencia *f* **2.** (*nobility*) nobleza *f*

G

grandfather *n* abuelo *m*
grandiloquent [græn'dɪləkwənt] *adj* grandilocuente
grandiose ['grændɪəʊs, *Am:* -oʊs] *adj* **1.** (*extremely grand*) grandioso, -a **2.** (*excessively splendid*) pomposo, -a
grand jury <- -ies> *n Am* LAW gran jurado *m*
grand larceny *n no pl* hurto *m* mayor
grandly *adv* majestuosamente
grandma *n inf* abuelita *f* **grandmaster** *n* GAMES (*chess pro*) gran maestro *m* **grandmother** *n* abuela *f* ▶**you can't teach your ~ to suck eggs** ¡a mí me lo vas a decir! **grandpa** *n inf* abuelito *m* **grandparents** *npl* abuelos *mpl* **grand piano** *n* piano *m* de cola **grandson** *n* nieto *m* **grandstand** *n* tribuna *f;* ~ **seat** asiento *m* de tribuna; ~ **ticket** entrada *f* de tribuna; **a ~ view** *fig* una vista que abarca todo el panorama **grand sum**, **grand total** *n* importe *m* total
grange [greɪndʒ] *n Brit* casa *f* solariega
granite ['grænɪt] *n no pl* granito *m*
grannie, **granny** ['græni] *n inf* abuelita *f*
grant [grɑːnt, *Am:* grænt] **I.** *n* **1.** UNIV beca *f;* **research ~** subvención *f* a una investigación; **to be on a ~** disfrutar de una beca; **to give sb a ~** conceder una beca a alguien **2.** (*a government grant*) subvención *f* **3.** (*from authority*) concesión *f;* **federal ~** ayuda *f* estatal; **maternity ~** subsidio *m* por maternidad; **to apply for a ~** solicitar una subvención **4.** LAW cesión *f* **II.** *vt* **1.** (*allow*) otorgar; **to ~ sb a permit/visa** conceder a alguien un permiso/visado **2.** (*transfer legally*) ceder; (*asylum*) dar; **to ~ sb a pardon** conceder un indulto a alguien **3.** *form* (*consent to fulfil*) **to ~ sb sth** conceder algo a alguien; **to ~ sb a favour** hacer un favor a alguien; **to ~ sb a request** acceder a la petición de alguien; **to ~ sb a wish** conceder un deseo a alguien **4.** (*admit to*) reconocer, admitir; **~ed** de acuerdo; **~ed, it's not easy ...** de acuerdo, no es fácil...; **I ~ you, ...** estoy de acuerdo contigo,...; **to ~ that ...** estar de acuerdo en que... *+subj* ▶**to take sth for ~ed** dar algo por sentado; **to take sb for ~ed** no valorar a alguien como se merece
granular ['grænjʊləʳ, *Am:* -jələ˞] *adj* granular
granulated ['grænjʊleɪtɪd, *Am:* -jəleɪt̬ɪd] *adj* **1.** (*in grains*) granulado, -a; ~ **sugar** azúcar *m* cristalizado **2.** (*raised*) rugoso, -a
granule ['grænjuːl] *n* gránulo *m;* **~s** granos *mpl;* **instant coffee ~s** granos de café instantáneo
grape [greɪp] *n* **1.** (*fruit*) uva *f;* **a bunch of ~s** un racimo de uvas **2.** *iron* (*wine*) **the ~** el vino ▶**it's just sour ~s** es pura envidia
grapefruit ['greɪpfruːt] *n inv* pomelo *m*
grape juice *n no pl* mosto *m*
grapevine *n* vid *f;* (*climbing plant*) parra *f* ▶**to hear sth on the ~** saber algo por los rumores que corren; **I heard it on the ~ that he is marrying** corren rumores de que se va a casar
graph[1] [grɑːf, *Am:* græf] *n* gráfica *f;* (*diagram*) gráfico *m;* **temperature ~** gráfico de temperaturas
graph[2] [grɑːf, *Am:* græf] *n* LING grafía *f*
graphic ['græfɪk] *adj* gráfico, -a; **to describe sth in ~ detail** describir algo de forma gráfica; **~ works** (**of an artist**) trabajos gráficos (de un artista)
graphic design *n no pl* diseño *m* gráfico
graphics *n + sing vb* **1.** (*drawings*) artes *fpl* gráficas **2.** (*presentation*) gráficos *mpl* **3.** INFOR gráficos *mpl;* **computer ~** gráficos de ordenador
graphics card *n* tarjeta *f* gráfica **graphics screen** *n* pantalla *f* gráfica
graphite ['græfaɪt] *n* grafito *m*
graphologist [græ'fɒlədʒɪst, *Am:* grə'fɑːlə-] *n* grafólogo, -a *m, f*
graphology [græ'fɒlədʒi, *Am:* grə'fɑːlə-] *n no pl* grafología *f*
grapple ['græpl] *vi* **to ~ for/with sth** luchar a brazo partido por/con algo
grappling iron *n,* **grappling hook** *n* arpeo *m*
grasp [grɑːsp, *Am:* græsp] **I.** *n no pl* **1.** (*grip*) agarre *m* **2.** (*attainability*) alcance *m;* **to be beyond sb's ~** estar fuera del alcance de alguien **3.** (*understanding*) comprensión *f;* (*knowledge*) conocimiento *m* ▶**his reach exceeds his ~** alarga más el brazo que la manga **II.** *vt* **1.** (*take firm hold*) agarrar; **to ~ sb by the arm/hand** coger a alguien del brazo/de la mano **2.** (*understand*) entender **III.** *vi* **1.** (*try to hold*) intentar coger **2.** *fig* (*take advantage*) **to ~ at** sacar provecho de; **to ~ at the chance** aprovechar la oportunidad
grasping *adj* avaro, -a
grass [grɑːs, *Am:* græs] **I.** <-es> *n* **1.** hierba *f;* **wild ~es** hierbas silvestres **2.** *no pl* (*area of grass*) prado *m;* (*lawn*) césped *m;* **to cut the ~** cortar el césped; **to put a garden down to ~** poner césped en un jardín **3.** *no pl* (*pasture*) pasto *m;* **to be at ~** pastar; **to put cattle out to ~** sacar a pastar el ganado; **to put sb out to ~** *inf* jubilar a alguien **4.** *no pl, inf* (*marijuana*) hierba *f inf,* traba *f AmL, inf* **5.** *Brit, inf* (*an informer*) soplón, -ona *m, f* ▶**to let the ~ grow under one's feet** perder el tiempo; **the ~ is** (**always**) **greener on the other side** (**of the fence**) *prov* (siempre) parece mejor lo de los demás **II.** *vt* cubrir de hierba **III.** *vi Aus, Brit, inf* dar el chivatazo; **to ~ on sb** (**to sb**) delatar a alguien (diciéndoselo a alguien)
grasshopper ['grɑːshɒpəʳ, *Am:* 'græshɑːpə˞] *n* saltamontes *m inv,* chapulín *m AmC, Méx,* saltagatos *m inv AmC, Méx* ▶**to be knee-high to a ~** ser un renacuajo **grassland** *n* pastos *mpl;* (*savannah*) sabana *f* **grassroots I.** *npl* (*ordinary people*) pueblo *m;* (*of a party, organization*) base *f* popular **II.** *adj* básico, -a; ~ **opinion** opinión *f* del pueblo; ~ **politics** política *f* que trata los problemas de la vida diaria **grass-snake** *n* cule-

bra *f* de collar **grass widow** *n mujer cuyo marido está ausente* **grass widower** *n* ≈ Rodríguez *m inf* (*marido cuya mujer está ausente*)

grassy ['grɑːsi, *Am:* 'græsi] <-ier, -iest> *adj* cubierto, -a de hierba, pastoso, -a *AmL*

grate[1] [greɪt] *n* **1.** (*grid in fireplace*) rejilla *f* de la chimenea **2.** (*fireplace*) chimenea *f*

grate[2] [greɪt] **I.** *vi* **1.** (*annoy: noise*) rechinar; **to ~ on sb** molestar a alguien **2.** (*rub together*) rozar; **to ~ against each other** rozar uno con otro **II.** *vt* GASTR rallar

grateful ['greɪtfəl] *adj* agradecido, -a; **to be ~ (to sb) for sth** agradecer algo (a alguien); **I'd be most ~ if you ...** *form* te agradecería mucho que... +*subj*

grater ['greɪtəʳ, *Am:* -t̬ɚ] *n* rallador *m*

gratification [ˌgrætɪfɪ'keɪʃən, *Am:* ˌgræt̬ə-] *n* gratificación *f;* (*of a wish*) satisfacción *f;* **sexual ~** placer *m* sexual; **with (some) ~** con (cierta) satisfacción

gratify ['grætɪfaɪ, *Am:* 'græt̬ə-] <-ie-> *vt* **1.** (*please*) gratificar; **to be gratified at sth** estar complacido por algo **2.** (*satisfy*) satisfacer

gratifying *adj* gratificante

grating ['greɪtɪŋ, *Am:* -t̬ɪŋ] **I.** *n* rejilla *f* **II.** *adj* **1.** (*scraping*) que rasca; (*squeaking*) chirriante **2.** (*annoyingly harsh*) áspero, -a; **~ voice** voz *f* rasgada

gratis ['greɪtɪs, *Am:* 'græt̬əs] **I.** *adj* gratuito, -a **II.** *adv* gratis

gratitude ['grætɪtjuːd, *Am:* 'græt̬ətuːd] *n no pl, form* gratitud *f,* reconocimiento *m;* **as a token of my ~** como muestra de mi gratitud

gratuitous [grə'tjuːɪtəs, *Am:* -'tuːət̬əs] *adj* **1.** (*free*) gratuito, -a **2.** (*without justification*) innecesario, -a

gratuity [grə'tjuːəti, *Am:* -'tuːət̬i] <-ies> *n* **1.** *form* (*tip*) propina *f* **2.** *Brit* MIL (*monetary reward for service*) pensión *f* militar **3.** *Am* (*bribe*) **illegal ~** soborno *m*

grave[1] [greɪv] *n* tumba *f,* sepultura *f;* **mass ~** fosa *f* común; **to go to one's ~** irse a la tumba; **beyond the ~** más allá de la sepultura; **from beyond the ~** desde el más allá

grave[2] [greɪv] *adj* **1.** (*seriously bad*) grave; (*serious*) serio, -a; (*be taken seriously*) importante; (*worrying*) preocupante; **a ~ mistake/risk** un grave error/riesgo; **~ news** noticias *fpl* alarmantes **2.** (*momentous*) trascendental **3.** (*solemn*) **a ~ ceremony** una ceremonia solemne; **a ~ person/face** una persona/cara seria

grave-digger ['greɪvˌdɪgəʳ, *Am:* -ɚ] *n* sepulturero, -a *m, f*

gravel ['grævəl] *n* **1.** (*small stones*) gravilla *f;* GEO grava *f;* **a ~ path** un camino de grava **2.** MED arenilla *f*

gravel-pit *n* gravera *f* **gravel-stone** *n* arenilla *f*

grave mound *n* túmulo *m* de una tumba **grave robber** *n* ladrón, -ona *m, f* de tumbas

gravestone *n* lápida *f* sepulcral **graveyard** *n* cementerio *m*

graving dock ['greɪvɪŋˌdɒk, *Am:* -dɑːk] *n* dique *m* seco [*o* de carena]

gravitate ['grævɪteɪt] *vi* gravitar; **to ~ towards sth/sb** tender hacia algo/alguien

gravitation [ˌgrævɪ'teɪʃən] *n no pl* **1.** (*movement*) gravitación *f;* (*tendency*) tendencia *f;* **the ~ of people to/towards the cities** la emigración de la gente a/hacia las ciudades **2.** (*attracting force*) atracción *f*

gravitational [ˌgrævɪ'teɪʃənl] *adj* gravitacional; **~ force** fuerza *f* gravitatoria

gravity ['grævəti, *Am:* -t̬i] *n no pl* gravedad *f;* **the law of ~** la ley de la gravedad

gravure [grə'vjʊəʳ, *Am:* -'vjʊr] *n* fotograbado *m*

gravy ['greɪvi] *n no pl* **1.** GASTR *salsa hecha con el jugo de la carne* **2.** *Am, inf* (*easy money*) ganga *f;* **the ~ train** un chollo; **to make some ~** conseguir un chollo

gravy boat *n* salsera *f*

gray [greɪ] *adj Am s.* **grey**

grayish ['greɪɪʃ] *adj Am s.* **greyish**

graze[1] [greɪz] **I.** *n* roce *m* **II.** *vt* rozar; **the bullet just ~ed his arm** la bala sólo le rozó el brazo

graze[2] [greɪz] **I.** *vi* pastar **II.** *vt* apacentar

grease [griːs] **I.** *n* **1.** (*fat*) grasa *f* **2.** (*lubricant*) lubricante *m* **II.** *vt* engrasar; (*in mechanics*) lubricar

grease gun *n* pistola *f* de engrase **grease mark** *n* mancha *f* de grasa **greasepaint** *n* maquillaje *m* teatral **greaseproof paper** *n* papel *m* encerado **grease spot** *n* mancha *f* de grasa

greasy ['griːsi] <-ier, -iest> *adj* grasiento, -a

great [greɪt] **I.** *n* grande *mf;* **the ~ and the good** *Brit* los grandes y los buenos; **Alexander the ~** Alejandro *m* Magno **II.** *adj* **1.** (*very big*) enorme; **a ~ amount** una gran cantidad; **a ~ deal of time/money** muchísimo tiempo/dinero; **a ~ joy/sadness** una gran alegría/pena; **a ~ many people** muchísima gente; **the ~ majority of people** la gran mayoría (de la gente); **it gives me ~ pleasure to announce ...** *form* es un gran placer para mí anunciar...; **it is with ~ sorrow that I tell you of ...** lamento mucho comunicarles que... **2.** (*famous and important*) famoso, -a; **the ~est boxer** el boxeador más destacado; **~ minds think that ...** las mentes más prestigiosas creen que... **3.** (*wonderful*) magnífico, -a; **to be ~ at doing sth** *inf* ser bueno en algo; **she's ~ at playing tennis** *inf* a ella se le da muy bien el tenis; **to be a ~ one for doing sth** encantar a uno hacer algo; **it's ~ to be back home again** es maravilloso estar de nuevo en casa; **the ~ thing about sth/sb is (that)** lo mejor de algo/alguien es (que); **I had a ~ time with you** lo he pasado fenomenal contigo; **~!** ¡estupendo! **4.** (*very healthy*) sano, -a; **to feel not all that ~** no sentirse demasido bien **5.** (*for* *emphasis*) **you ~ idiot!** ¡pedazo de idiota!; **they're ~ friends** son muy amigos; **~ big** muy grande **6.** (*good*) excelente; **Peter is a ~ organiser** Peter es un magnífico organizador

great-aunt *n* tía *f* abuela

Great Bear *n* Osa *f* Mayor **Great Britain** *n* Gran Bretaña *f*

> **Great Britain** (Gran Bretaña) se compone del reino de Inglaterra, el de Escocia y el principado de Gales. (El rey Eduardo I de Inglaterra se anexionó Gales en 1282 y en 1301 nombró a su único hijo **Prince of Wales**. El rey Jacobo VI de Escocia heredó en 1603 la corona inglesa convirtiéndose en Jacobo I y en 1707 se unieron los parlamentos de ambos reinos). Estos países forman, junto con Irlanda del Norte, el **United Kingdom** (Reino Unido). El concepto geográfico de **British Isles** (Islas Británicas) incluye no sólo a la isla mayor que es Gran Bretaña, sino también a Irlanda, la Isla de Man, las Hébridas, Orkney, Shetland, las Islas Scilly y las **Channel Islands** (Islas del Canal de la Mancha).

greatcoat *n* sobretodo *m* **Great Depression** *n* Gran Depresión *f*

Greater London *n la ciudad de Londres y su área metropolitana*

great-grandchild *n* bisnieto, -a *m, f* **great-grandparents** *npl* bisabuelos *mpl* **great-great-grandparents** *npl* tatarabuelos *mpl*

Great Lakes *n* Grandes Lagos *mpl*

greatly ['greɪtli] *adv form* sumamente; **to improve ~** mejorar mucho; **to ~ regret sth** lamentar algo muchísimo; **to be ~ impressed** estar muy impresionado

great-nephew *n* sobrino *m* nieto

greatness ['greɪtnɪs] *n no pl* grandeza *f*

great-niece *n* sobrina *f* nieta **great-uncle** *n* tío *m* abuelo

Grecian ['gri:ʃən] *adj* griego, -a

Greece [gri:s] *n* Grecia *f*

greed [gri:d] *n no pl* codicia *f;* (*for food*) gula *f;* (*for money*) avaricia *f;* **~ for power** ansia *f* de poder

greediness ['gri:dɪnɪs] *n no pl s.* **greed**

greedy ['gri:di] <-ier, -iest> *adj* (*wanting too much*) codicioso, -a; (*wanting food*) glotón, -ona; (*wanting money, things*) avaricioso, -a; **~ for success/victory** ávido de éxito/victoria; **~ -guts** *Aus, Brit, childspeak* comilón, -ona; **this plant's ~ for water** esta planta necesita agua

Greek [gri:k] **I.** *n* **1.** (*person*) griego, -a *m, f* **2.** LING griego *m* **II.** *adj* griego, -a ►**it's all ~ to me** eso me suena a chino

green [gri:n] **I.** *n* **1.** (*colour*) verde *m* **2.** *pl* (*green vegetables*) verduras *fpl* **3.** ECOL, POL verde *mf* **4.** (*lawn*) césped *m* **5.** SPORTS pista *f;* **bowling ~** pista de bolos **II.** *adj* **1.** *a.* ECOL, POL verde; **to turn ~** (*traffic lights*) ponerse en verde **2.** (*unripe*) verde, tierno, -a *Chile, Ecua, Guat* **3.** (*inexperienced*) novato, -a; (*naive*) ingenuo, -a **4.** (*covered with plants*) cubierto, -a de vegetación **5.** *fig* (*jealous*) **~ with envy** muerto, -a de envidia ►**to have ~ fingers** *Brit, Aus,* **to have ~ thumbs** *Am* tener habilidad para la jardinería

greenback *n Am, inf* billete *m* (de banco) **green belt** *n* zona *f* verde (*zona en las afueras de las ciudades en la que no se permite construir*) **green card** *n* **1.** *Brit* AUTO carta *f* verde **2.** *Am* (*residence and work permit*) permiso *m* de residencia y de trabajo **green consumerism** *n actitud consumista que respecta la protección del medioambiente*

greenery ['gri:nəri] *n no pl* vegetación *f*

green-eyed [ˌgri:n'aɪd, *Am:* 'gri:naɪd] *adj* **1.** (*with green eyes*) de ojos verdes **2.** *fig* (*jealous*) celoso, -a

greenfly <-ies> *n* pulgón *m*

greengage *n* ciruela *f* claudia; **~ jam** mermelada *f* de ciruelas verdes; **~ tree** ciruelo *m*

greengrocer [-ˌgroʊsɚ] *n Brit* verdulero, -a *m, f;* **at the ~'s** en la verdulería **greenhorn** *n Am* novato, -a *m, f* **greenhouse** *n* invernadero *m* **greenhouse effect** *n no pl* **the ~** el efecto invernadero

greenish ['gri:nɪʃ] *adj* verdoso, -a

green issue *n* cuestión *f* medioambiental

Greenland ['gri:nlənd] *n* Groenlandia *f*

Greenlander ['gri:nləndə^r] *n* groenlandés, -esa *m, f*

greenness ['gri:nnɪs] *n no pl* verdor *m*

green pepper [ˌgri:n'pepə^r, *Am:* -ɚ] *n* pimiento *m* verde

green politics *n + sing vb* política *f* del medioambiente

Greenwich ['grɪnɪtʃ, *Am:* 'gren-] *n* Greenwich *m;* **~ mean time** hora *f* de Greenwich

> El **Royal Observatory** (observatorio astronómico) de **Greenwich** fue construido en 1675 para obtener datos exactos sobre la posición de las estrellas con vista a la creación de cartas de navegación. El **Greenwich meridian** (meridiano de Greenwich) no se fijó oficialmente como el grado cero de longitud con validez universal hasta 1884. Las 24 franjas horarias del planeta se fijan a partir de la hora local del meridiano que es conocida como **Greenwich Mean Time** o **Universal Time**.

greenwood ['gri:nwʊd] *n* bosque *m* caducifolio

greeny <-ier, -iest> *adj* verdoso, -a

greet [gri:t] *vt* **1.** (*welcome*) saludar; (*receive*) recibir; **to ~ each other** saludarse; **to ~ sb by shaking hands/with a smile** saludar a alguien con un apretón de manos/con una sonrisa **2.** (*react*) **to ~ sth** reaccionar ante algo; **to ~ sth with anger/applause**

recibir algo con enfado/un aplauso; **to ~ sth with delight** sentir gran placer ante algo **3.** *fig* (*make itself noticeable*) presentarse; **a scene of joy ~ed us** se mostró ante nosotros una escena de alegría

greeting *n* saludo *m;* (*receiving*) recepción *f*

gregarious [grɪ'geərɪəs, *Am:* -'gerɪ-] *adj* **1.** (*liking company*) sociable **2.** ZOOL (*living in groups*) gregario, -a

Grenada [grə'neɪdə] *n* Granada *f*

Grenadan **I.** *adj* granadino, -a **II.** *n* granadino, -a *m, f*

grenade [grɪ'neɪd] *n* granada *f;* **hand ~** granada de mano

grenadier [ˌgrenə'dɪəʳ, *Am:* -'dɪr] *n* **1.** HIST (*soldier*) granadero *m* **2.** (*member of regiment*) soldado *m* granadero; **the Grenadiers** *Brit* los Granaderos

grew [gru:] *pt of* **grow**

grey [greɪ] **I.** *n no pl* **1.** (*colour*) gris *m* **2.** (*regiment*) **the** (**Royal Scots**) **Greys** los Grises (Reales Escoceses) **3.** (*white horse*) rucio *m* **II.** *adj* **1.** (*coloured grey*) gris; **~ weather** tiempo *m* gris **2.** (*grey-haired*) canoso, -a; **to go ~** encanecer; **he has started to go ~** empieza a tener canas **3.** (*white colour of horse*) rucio, -a **4.** (*pale*) pálido, -a **5.** *fig* (*sad*) triste

greybeard ['greɪˌbɪəd, *Am:* -bɪrd] *n* anciano *m* **greyhound** *n* galgo *m*

greying *adj* con canas

greyish ['greɪɪʃ] *adj* grisáceo, -a; (*hair*) entrecano, -a

grey matter *n inf* materia *f* gris

grid [grɪd] *n* parrilla *f;* SPORTS parrilla de salida

griddle ['grɪdl] **I.** *n* GASTR plancha *f,* burén *m Cuba* **II.** *vt* **to ~ food** asar comida a la plancha

gridiron ['grɪdaɪən, *Am:* -aɪɚn] *n* **1.** (*metal grid*) parrilla *f* **2.** *Am* (*American football field*) campo *m* de fútbol **3.** NAUT (*framework*) carenero *m* **4.** THEAT peine *m* **gridlock** *n no pl* paralización *f* del tráfico; *fig* inactividad *f* **grid square** *n* cuadrícula *f*

grief [gri:f] *n no pl* (*extreme sadness*) aflicción *f;* (*individual mournful feelings*) pesar *m;* (*pain*) dolor *m;* **to cause ~** *inf* dar pena; **to cause sb ~** causar aflicción a alguien; **to give sb** (**a lot of**) **~** hacer sentir (muy) mal a alguien ►**to <u>come</u> to ~** (*fail*) fracasar; (*have an accident*) sufrir un percance

grievance ['gri:vns] *n* **1.** (*complaint*) queja *f,* reivindicación *f;* **to harbour a ~ against sb** presentar una queja contra alguien **2.** (*sense of injustice*) injusticia *f*

grieve [gri:v] **I.** *vi* sufrir; **to ~ for sth/sb** llorar por algo/alguien **II.** *vt* **1.** (*distress*) causar dolor; (*make sad*) afligir; **it ~s me to see your situation** me da pena ver tu situación **2.** (*annoy*) molestar; **it ~s me to see that you don't do anything to solve it** me molesta que no hagas nada para solucionarlo

grievous ['gri:vəs] *adj form* (*pain*) fuerte; (*danger*) serio, -a; (*error*) craso, -a; (*injuries*) considerable; (*news*) lamentable; **a ~ crime** un crimen grave

grievous bodily harm *n no pl* graves daños *mpl* corporales

griffin ['grɪfɪn] *n,* **griffon** ['grɪfən] *n* grifo *m*

grill [grɪl] **I.** *n* **1.** (*part of cooker*) parrilla *f;* (*grid over fire*) parrilla *f,* grill *m* **2.** *Am* (*informal restaurant*) asador *m* **II.** *vt* (*cook*) asar a la parrilla

grille [grɪl] *n* rejilla *f;* (*of windows*) reja *f;* (*of doors*) verja *f*

grilling ['grɪlɪŋ] *n inf* interrogatorio *m;* **to give sb a** (**good**) **~** interrogar a alguien (muy) intensamente

grim [grɪm] *adj* **1.** (*very serious*) severo, -a **2.** (*unpleasant*) desagradable; (*horrible*) horrible; **~ outlook** mirada *f* inexorable; **to feel ~** sentirse muy mal ►**to hang on like ~ <u>death</u>** (*dog*) no soltar la presa; (*person*) no cejar en el empeño

grimace [grɪ'meɪs, *Am:* 'grɪməs] **I.** *n* (*facial expression*) mueca *f;* **to make a ~ of disgust/pain/hatred** hacer una mueca de disgusto/dolor/odio **II.** *vi* hacer muecas; **to ~ with pain** hacer muecas de dolor

grime [graɪm] **I.** *n* (*ingrained dirt*) mugre *f;* (*soot*) hollín *m* **II.** *vt* **to be ~d with soot** estar manchado de hollín

grimy ['graɪmi] <-ier, -iest> *adj* mugriento, -a; (*sooty*) sucio, -a

grin [grɪn] **I.** *n* ancha sonrisa *f* **II.** *vi* (*smile widely*) sonreír de oreja a oreja; (*beam*) sonreír alegremente; **to ~ impishly at sb** dirigir una sonrisa traviesa a alguien ►**to ~ and <u>bear</u> it** poner al mal tiempo buena cara

grind [graɪnd] **I.** *n inf* **1.** (*tiring work*) trabajo *m* pesado; **to be a real ~** ser un trabajo durísimo **2.** (*boring work*) rutina *f;* **the daily ~** la rutina diaria **II.** <ground, ground> *vt* **1.** (*crush*) aplastar; (*mill*) moler; **to ~ sth** (**in**)**to flour/a powder** reducir algo a harina/polvo **2.** *Am, Aus* (*chop finely: meat*) picar **3.** (*press firmly and twist*) **to ~ a cigarette into an ashtray** apagar un cigarrillo en un cenicero **4.** (*sharpen*) afilar

◆**grind down** *vt* **1.** (*file*) pulir **2.** (*mill*) moler **3.** (*wear*) desgastar **4.** (*oppress*) oprimir; (*treat cruelly*) maltratar; **to grind sb down** destrozar a alguien

◆**grind out** *vt* (*produce continuously*) producir mecánicamente

grinder ['graɪndəʳ, *Am:* -dɚ] *n* **1.** (*crushing machine*) molinillo *m;* **a hand/electric ~** una picadora manual/eléctrica **2.** (*sharpener*) afiladora *f* **3.** (*person who sharpens things*) afilador(a) *m(f);* **knife/scissor ~** afilador(a) *m(f)* de cuchillos/tijeras

grindstone ['graɪndstəʊn, *Am:* -stoʊn] *n* muela *f,* piedra *f* de amolar ►**to keep one's <u>nose</u> to the ~** *inf* trabajar como un enano

gringo ['grɪŋgəʊ, *Am:* -goʊ] *n* gringo, -a *m, f*

grip [grɪp] **I.** *n* **1.** (*hold*) agarre *m; fig* control *m;* **to keep a firm ~ on the bag** agarrar fuertemente la bolsa; **to be in the ~ of sth** estar en poder de algo; **the economy is in the ~ of a crisis** la economía está atravesando una crisis **2.** (*way of holding*) asidero *m* **3.** (*bag*) maletín *m* ▶**to get to ~s with sth** enfrentarse con algo; **to get a ~ on oneself** controlarse **II.** <-pp-> *vt* **1.** (*hold firmly*) agarrar **2.** (*overwhelm*) **to be ~ped by emotion** estar embargado por la emoción; **he was ~ped by fear** el miedo le invadió **3.** (*interest deeply*) absorber la atención de **III.** *vi* agarrarse

gripe [graɪp] **I.** *n inf* queja *f* **II.** *vi inf* quejarse

gripping ['grɪpɪŋ] *adj* **1.** (*exciting*) emocionante **2.** (*stabbing*) punzante

grisly ['grɪzli] <-ier, -iest> *adj* (*repellant*) espeluznante; *fig, inf* asqueroso, -a

grist [grɪst] *n* **it's all ~ to the mill** se puede sacar provecho de todo

gristle ['grɪsl] *n no pl* cartílago *m*

grit [grɪt] **I.** *n no pl* **1.** (*small stones*) arenilla *f* **2.** (*courage*) valor *m* **II.** <-tt-> *vt* **1. to ~ a road** echar grava a un camino **2.** (*press together*) **to ~ one's teeth** *a. fig* apretar los dientes

gritty ['grɪti, *Am:* 'grɪṱi] <-ier, -iest> *adj* con arenilla; (*plucky*) valiente

grizzle ['grɪzl] *vi inf* **1.** (*cry continually: baby, small child*) gimotear **2.** (*complain*) quejarse

grizzled *adj* **1.** (*greying*) grisáceo, -a **2.** (*grey*) gris **3.** (*grey-haired*) de pelo canoso; **a ~ man** un hombre canoso

grizzly ['grɪzli] **I.** <-ier, iest> *adj* gris **II.** <-ies> *n* oso *m* pardo americano

groan [grəʊn, *Am:* groʊn] **I.** *n* gemido *m* **II.** *vi* **1.** (*make a noise: people*) gemir; (*floorboards, hinges*) crujir; **to ~ in pain** gemir de dolor **2.** (*speak unhappily*) decir gimiendo; **to ~ inwardly** lamentarse para sus adentros **3.** *inf* (*complain*) quejarse; **to ~ about sth** quejarse de algo; **why are you moaning and ~ing about that?** ¿por qué te quejas de eso? **4.** (*bear a load*) llevar una carga a cuestas

grocer ['grəʊsəʳ, *Am:* 'groʊsɚ] *n* **1.** (*shopkeeper*) tendero, -a *m, f* **2.** (*food shop*) tienda *f* de ultramarinos

grocery ['grəʊsəri, *Am:* 'groʊ-] **I.** *adj* de ultramarinos **II.** <-ies> *n* tienda *f* de ultramarinos

grog [grɒg, *Am:* grɑːg] *n* grog *m,* ponche *m*

groggy ['grɒgi, *Am:* 'grɑːgi] <-ier -iest> *adj* grogui

groin¹ [grɔɪn] *n* ingle *f;* (*male sex organs*) genitales *mpl*

groin² [grɔɪn] *n Am* arista *f*

groom [gruːm] **I.** *n* **1.** (*person caring for horses*) mozo *m* de cuadra **2.** (*bridegroom*) novio *m* **II.** *vt* **1.** (*clean: an animal*) cuidar; (*a horse*) almohazar **2.** (*prepare: a person*) preparar

groove [gruːv] *n* ranura *f;* MUS surco *m; fig* onda *f* ▶**to be in a ~** estar metido en una rutina

groovy ['gruːvi] <-ier, -iest> *adj inf* guay

grope [grəʊp, *Am:* groʊp] **I.** *vi* ir a tientas; **to ~ for sth** buscar algo a tientas; **to ~ for the right words** buscar las palabras **II.** *vt* **1. to ~ one's way** ir a tientas **2.** *inf* (*touch sexually*) sobar

gropingly ['grəʊpɪŋli, *Am:* 'groʊp-] *adv* a tientas

gross¹ [grəʊs, *Am:* groʊs] <-sses> *n* gruesa *f;* **by the ~** en gruesas

gross² [grəʊs, *Am:* groʊs] **I.** *adj* **1.** LAW grave; (*neglect*) serio, -a; (*negligence*) grave **2.** (*very fat*) muy gordo, -a **3.** *Am* (*extremely offensive*) grosero, -a; (*revolting*) asqueroso, -a **4.** (*total*) total; (*without deductions*) bruto **II.** *vt* FIN (*earn before taxes*) ganar en bruto

gross cash flow *n* flujo *m* de caja bruto **gross domestic product** *n* producto *m* interior bruto **gross income** *n* ingreso *m* bruto

grossly *adv* (*in a gross manner*) groseramente; (*extremely*) enormemente; **to be ~ unfair** ser completamente injusto

gross national product *n* producto *m* nacional bruto **gross negligence** *n* imprudencia *f* temeraria **gross pay** *n* paga *f* íntegra **gross profit** *n* ganancia *f* bruta **gross tonnage** *n* tonelaje *m* bruto **gross weight** *n* peso *m* total

grotesque [grəʊ'tesk, *Am:* groʊ-] *n a.* ART, LIT grotesco, -a

grotto ['grɒtəʊ, *Am:* 'grɑːṱoʊ] <-oes *o* -os> *n* gruta *f*

grotty ['grɒti, *Am:* 'grɑːṱi] <-ier, -iest> *adj Brit, inf* chungo, -a

grouch [graʊtʃ] **I.** *n* **1.** (*grudge*) rencor *m;* (*complaint*) queja *f* **2.** (*grumpy person*) refunfuñón, -ona *m, f,* cascarrabias *mf inv* **II.** *vi* refunfuñar; **to ~ about sth/sb** quejarse de algo/alguien

grouchy ['graʊtʃi] <-ier, -iest> *adj* malhumorado, -a

ground¹ [graʊnd] **I.** *n* **1.** *no pl* (*the Earth's surface*) tierra *f;* **above/below ~** sobre el nivel del suelo/bajo tierra **2.** *no pl* (*soil*) suelo *m* **3.** (*area of land*) terreno *m;* **breeding ~** zona *f* de cría; **fishing ~s** pesquería *f;* **waste ~** tierra *f* baldía **4.** SPORTS campo *m* **5.** *no pl* (*bottom of the sea*) fondo *m* del mar; **to touch ~** (*ship*) varar **6.** *no pl* (*area of knowledge*) tema *m;* **to be on one's own ~** estar en su elemento; **to give ~** ceder terreno; **to stand one's ~** mantenerse firme **7.** (*reason*) motivo *m;* **to have ~s to do sth** tener motivos para hacer algo; **on the ~s that ...** porque... **II.** *vt* **1.** AVIAT no dejar despegar; **to be ~ed** no poder despegar **2.** (*unable to move*) **to be ~ed** estar encallado, -a **3.** *Am, Aus, fig, inf* no dejar salir

ground² [graʊnd] **I.** *vt pt of* **grind** **II.** *adj* (*cristal*) deslustrado, -a **III.** *n pl* sedimentos *mpl;* **coffee ~s** poso *m* de café

groundbreaking ['graʊnd,breɪkɪŋ] *adj*

pionero, -a

ground control *n* control *m* de [*o* desde] tierra **ground crew** *n + sing/pl vb* personal *m* de tierra **ground floor** *n Brit* planta *f* baja; **on the ~** en la planta baja, en el primer piso *AmS;* **~ apartment** entresuelo *m* ►**to go in on the ~** empezar desde abajo **ground fog** *n* niebla *f* baja **ground frost** *n no pl* escarcha *f*

grounding ['graʊndɪŋ] *n no pl* rudimentos *mpl*, base *f*

groundkeeper *n* cuidador(a) *m(f)* del terreno de juego

groundless ['graʊndlɪs] *adj* infundado, -a

groundnut *n* cacahuete *m*, maní *m AmS* **ground personnel** *n + pl vb* AVIAT personal *m* de tierra **ground rules** *npl* directrices *fpl* **groundsheet** *n* tela *f* impermeable **groundskeeper** *n Am s.* **groundkeeper** **groundsman** <-men> *n Brit, Aus* encargado *m* de campo **ground staff** *n + pl vb* **1.** (*maintenance at sports ground*) personal *m* de mantenimiento **2.** (*non-flying staff at airport*) personal *m* de tierra **ground-station** *n* RADIO, TV estación *f* terrena **groundswell** *n no pl* **1.** NAUT (*heavy sea*) mar *m o f* de fondo **2.** (*opinion*) sentimiento *m* acusado **ground-to-air missile** *n* misil *m* tierra-aire **ground water** *n no pl* aguas *fpl* subterráneas

groundwork ['graʊndwɜːk, *Am:* -wɜːrk] *n no pl* trabajo *m* preliminar; (*for further study*) trabajo *m* preparatorio; **to lay the ~ for sth** *fig* establecer las bases de algo

group [gruːp] **I.** *n* **1.** *a.* CHEM grupo *m;* **~ photo** foto *f* de grupo; **~ of trees** arboleda *f;* **in ~s** en grupos; **to get into ~s** hacer grupos **2.** (*specially assembled*) colectivo *m* **3.** (*business association*) agrupación *f* **4.** (*musicians*) conjunto *m* musical **II.** *vt* agrupar **III.** *vi* agruparse; **to ~ together round sb** agruparse en torno a alguien

group booking *n* reserva *f* para grupos **group captain** *n Brit* MIL jefe *m* de escuadrilla **group dynamics** *npl* dinámica *f* de grupo

groupie ['gruːpi] *n inf* groupie *mf*

grouping ['gruːpɪŋ] *n* agrupamiento *m*

group practice ['gruːpˌpræktɪs] *n* práctica *f* colectiva **group therapy** <-ies> *n* terapia *f* de grupo **group ticket** *n* AUTO billete *m* de grupo

grouse[1] [graʊs] *n* **black ~** gallo *m* lira; **red ~** urogallo *m* escocés

grouse[2] [graʊs] **I.** *n* **1.** (*complaint*) queja *f* **2.** (*complaining person*) cascarrabias *mf inv* **II.** *vi* quejarse; **to ~ at sb** quejarse de alguien

grove [grəʊv, *Am:* groʊv] *n* (*group of trees*) arboleda *f;* (*orchard*) plantación *f;* **olive ~** olivar *m;* **orange ~** naranjal *m*

grovel ['grɒvl, *Am:* 'grɑːvl] <*Brit:* -ll-, *Am:* -l-> *vi* **1.** (*behave obsequiously*) **to ~** (**before sb**) humillarse (ante alguien) **2.** (*crawl*) arrastrarse; **to ~ in the dust** *fig* morder el polvo

grow [grəʊ, *Am:* groʊ] <grew, grown> **I.** *vi* **1.** (*increase in size*) crecer; (*flourish*) florecer; **to ~ taller** crecer en estatura **2.** (*increase*) aumentar; **to ~ by 2%** aumentar un 2% **3.** (*develop*) desarrollarse **4.** (*become*) volverse; **to ~ old** hacerse viejo; **to ~ to like sth** llegar a querer algo **II.** *vt* **1.** (*cultivate*) cultivar **2.** (*let grow*) dejar crecer; **to ~ a beard** dejarse crecer la barba; **some animals ~ a thicker coat in winter** algunos animales desarrollan una piel más gruesa en invierno

◆**grow away from** *vt* irse alejando de

◆**grow into** *vt insep* llegar a ser; *fig* acostumbrarse a

◆**grow out of** *vt insep* **1.** (*become too big*) **she has grown out of her clothes** se le ha quedado la ropa pequeña **2.** (*habit*) perder

◆**grow up** *vi* **1.** (*become adult*) crecer; (*behave like an adult*) madurar; **when I grow up I'd like to ...** cuando sea mayor me gustaría... **2.** (*develop*) desarrollarse

grower ['grəʊəʳ, *Am:* 'groʊ-] *n* **1.** (*gardener*) cultivador(a) *m(f)* **2.** (*plant*) **this plant is a good ~** esta planta crece rápido

growing ['grəʊɪŋ, *Am:* 'groʊ-] **I.** *n no pl* crecimiento *m* **II.** *adj* **1.** (*developing*) **a ~ boy/girl** un chico/una chica que está creciendo **2.** ECON que se expande **3.** (*increasing*) que aumenta

growing pains *npl* **1.** (*pains in the joints*) dolores *mpl* del crecimiento **2.** (*adolescent emotional problems*) problemas *mpl* de la adolescencia

growl [graʊl] **I.** *n* **1.** (*low throaty sound: of a dog*) gruñido *m;* (*of a person*) refunfuño *m* **2.** (*rumble*) ruido *m* sordo **II.** *vi* (*dog*) gruñir; (*person*) refunfuñar

grown [grəʊn, *Am:* groʊn] **I.** *adj* adulto, -a **II.** *pp of* **grow**

grown-up ['grəʊnʌp, *Am:* 'groʊn-] *n a. childspeak* adulto, -a *m, f*

growth [grəʊθ, *Am:* groʊθ] *n* **1.** *no pl* (*increase in size*) crecimiento *m* **2.** (*stage of growing*) madurez *f;* **to reach full ~** alcanzar su plenitud **3.** *no pl* (*increase*) aumento *m;* **rate of ~** tasa *f* de crecimiento **4.** (*development*) desarrollo *m* **5.** (*growing part of plant*) brote *m* **6.** (*whiskers*) crecimiento *m;* **to have a three days' ~ on one's chin** tener barba de tres días **7.** (*caused by disease*) bulto *m*

growth industries *n pl* sectores *mpl* en expansión **growth rate** *n* ECON tasa *f* de crecimiento **growth stock** *n* ECON acciones *fpl* con perspectivas de valorización

groyne [grɔɪn] *n* rompeolas *m inv*

grub [grʌb] **I.** *n* **1.** (*larva*) larva *f* **2.** *no pl, Brit, inf* GASTR rancho *m;* **~ up!** ¡la comida está servida! **II.** <-bb-> *vi* cavar; **to ~ about** (**for sth**) remover la tierra (buscando algo) **III.** *vt* **to ~ up** arrancar

grubby ['grʌbi] <-ier, -iest> *adj inf* roñoso, -a

grudge [grʌdʒ] **I.** *n* rencor *m*, roña *f Cuba,*

Méx, PRico; **to have a ~ against sb** guardar rencor a alguien **II.** *vt* **to ~ sb sth** envidiar algo a alguien

grudging *adj* poco generoso, -a

grudgingly ['grʌdʒɪŋli] *adv* de mala gana

gruel ['gru:əl] *n no pl* gachas *fpl*

gruelling ['gru:əlɪŋ, *Am:* 'gru:lɪŋ] *adj* duro, -a, penoso, -a

gruesome ['gru:səm] *adj* horripilante

gruff [grʌf] *adj* brusco, -a; **a ~ voice** una voz bronca

grumble ['grʌmbl] **I.** *n* (*complaint*) queja *f* **II.** *vi* (*person*) quejarse; (*stomach*) hacer ruido; **to ~ about sth/sb** quejarse de algo/alguien

grumpy ['grʌmpi] <-ier, -iest> *adj inf* (*bad tempered*) gruñón, -ona; (*annoyed*) cabreado, -a

grunt [grʌnt] **I.** *n* (*snort*) gruñido *m;* (*groan*) resoplido *m* **II.** *vi* **1.** (*snort*) gruñir **2.** (*groan*) resoplar

G-string ['dʒi:strɪŋ] *n* **1.** (*musical instrument*) cuerda *f* para la nota Sol **2.** (*underwear*) tanga *m*

guarantee [ˌgærən'ti:, *Am:* ˌger-] **I.** *n* **1.** (*a promise*) promesa *f;* **to give sb one's ~** hacer una promesa a alguien **2.** (*repair or replacement*) garantía *f* **3.** (*document*) certificado *m* de garantía **4.** (*certainty*) seguridad *f;* **there's no ~ that** no es seguro que *+subj* **5.** (*responsibility for debt*) aval *m* **6.** (*security*) prenda *f* **II.** *vt* **1.** (*promise*) prometer **2.** (*promise to correct faults*) ofrecer una garantía; **to be ~d for three years** tener una garantía de tres años **3.** (*make certain*) **to ~ that** asegurar que *+subj* **4.** (*another's debt*) avalar

guarantor [ˌgærən'tɔ:ʳ, *Am:* 'gerən'tɔ:r] *n* garante *mf*

guaranty ['gærənti, *Am:* 'gerənṱi] <-ies> *n* **1.** (*acceptance of debt*) garantía *f* **2.** (*thing offered as security*) prenda *f*

guard [gɑ:d, *Am:* gɑ:rd] **I.** *n* **1.** (*person*) guardia *mf;* **prison ~** *Am* carcelero, -a *m, f;* **security ~** guardia de seguridad; **to be on ~** estar de guardia; **to be on one's ~** (**against sth/sb**) estar en alerta (contra algo/alguien); **to be under ~** estar bajo guardia y custodia; **to drop one's ~** bajar la guardia; **to keep ~ over sth/sb** vigilar algo/a alguien; **to post ~s** designar las guardias **2.** SPORTS defensa *f* **3.** (*protective device*) resguardo *m* **4.** *Brit* (*railway official*) jefe, -a *m, f* de tren **5.** MIL **the Guards** la Guardia **II.** *vt* **1.** (*protect*) proteger; (*prevent from escaping*) vigilar **2.** (*keep secret*) guardar
◆**guard against** *vt always sep* (*protect from*) **to guard sth/sb against sth/sb** proteger algo/a alguien de algo/alguien

> A las **Household Troops** de la monarquía británica pertenecen siete regimientos de los **Guards** (Guardia). Dos regimientos de **Household Cavalry** (caballería): los **Life Guards** y los **Blues and Royals**. Y cinco regimientos de infantería: los **Grenadier Guards**, los **Coldstream Guards**, los **Scots Guards**, los **Irish Guards** y los **Welsh Guards**. La ceremonia del cambio de guardia tiene lugar cada dos días a las 11:30 en el **Buckingham Palace**.

guard dog *n* perro *m* guardián **guard duty** <-ies> *n* guardia *f*

guarded ['gɑ:dɪd, *Am:* 'gɑ:rd-] *adj* cauteloso, -a

guardhouse *n* cuartel *m* de la guardia

guardian ['gɑ:dɪən, *Am:* 'gɑ:r-] *n* **1.** (*responsible person*) guardián, -ana *m, f* **2.** *form* (*protector*) protector(a) *m(f)*

guardian angel *n a. fig* ángel *m* de la guardia

guardianship *n no pl* **1.** (*being a guardian*) custodia *f* **2.** *form* (*care*) cuidado *m;* **to be in the ~ of sb** estar bajo la tutela de alguien

guardrail ['gɑ:dreɪl, *Am:* 'gɑ:rd-] *n* (*in bridge*) pretil *m;* (*in staircase*) barandilla *f*

guardroom *n* cuarto *m* de guardia

guardsman <-men> *n* guardia *m*

Guatemala [ˌgwɑ:tɪ'mɑ:lə, *Am:* -ṱə'-] *n* Guatemala *f*

Guatemala City *n* ciudad *f* de Guatemala

Guatemalan [ˌgwɑ:tɪ'mɑ:lən, *Am:* -ṱə'-] **I.** *adj* guatemalteco, -a **II.** *n* guatemalteco, -a *m, f*

guerilla [gə'rɪlə] *n s.* **guerrilla**

Guernsey ['gɜ:nzi, *Am:* 'ɜ:rn-] *n* (**the island of**) ~ (la isla de) Guernesey *m*

guerrilla [gə'rɪlə] *n* guerrilla *f*

guerrilla warfare *n* guerra *f* de guerrillas

guess [ges] **I.** *n* conjetura *f;* **a lucky ~** un acierto afortunado; **to have a ~, to take a ~** *Am* adivinar; **to make a wild ~** hacer una conjetura al azar; **at a ~** por decir algo; **your ~ is as good as mine!** ¡vaya Vd. a saber! ►**it's anybody's ~** ¿quién sabe? **II.** *vi* **1.** (*conjecture*) conjeturar; **to ~ right/wrong** adivinar/equivocarse; **~ what I'm doing now?** ¿adivinas qué estoy haciendo ahora?; **to ~ that ...** imaginar que...; **how did you ~?** ¿cómo lo has adivinado? **2.** *Am* (*believe, suppose*) suponer; (*suspect*) sospechar; **I ~ you're right** supongo que estás en lo cierto **III.** *vt* adivinar ►**to keep sb ~ing** tener a alguien en suspense; **~ what?** ¿sabes qué?

guessing game ['gesɪŋˌgeɪm] *n a. fig* adivinanza *f*

guesstimate *n,* **guestimate** ['gestɪmət] *n inf* estimación *f*

guesswork ['geswɜ:k, *Am:* -wɜ:rk] *n no pl* conjeturas *fpl*

guest [gest] **I.** *n* **1.** (*invited person*) invitado, -a *m, f;* **paying ~** (*person renting*) inquilino, -a *m, f;* (*lodger*) huésped *mf* **2.** (*hotel customer*) cliente *mf* ►**be my ~** *inf* ¡adelante! **II.** *vi a.* TV aparecer como invitado

guesthouse *n* casa *f* de huéspedes **guest-**

room *n* habitación *f* de invitados

guffaw [gə'fɔː, *Am:* -'fɑː] **I.** *n* carcajada *f* **II.** *vi* reírse a carcajadas

guidance ['gaɪdns] *n no pl* (*help and advice*) consejo *m;* (*direction*) orientación *f;* ~ **system** *a.* MIL sistema *m* de dirección

guide [gaɪd] **I.** *n* **1.** (*person*) guía *mf;* **tour/mountain** ~ guía turístico/de montaña **2.** (*book*) guía *f* **3.** (*help*) orientación *f* **4.** (*indication*) indicación *f* **5.** (*girls' association*) **the Guides** las exploradoras **II.** *vt* **1.** (*show*) guiar **2.** (*instruct*) orientar; **the manual will** ~ **you to ...** el manual te dará instrucciones para... **3.** (*steer, influence*) dirigir; **to be ~d by one's emotions** dejarse llevar por los sentimientos

guidebook *n* guía *f*

guided ['gaɪdɪd] *adj* **1.** (*led by a guide*) dirigido, -a; **~ed tour** excursión *f* con guía **2.** (*automatically steered*) teledirigido, -a; ~ **missile** MIL misil *m* teledirigido

guide dog *n* perro-guía *m* **guideline** *n* directriz *f;* (*figure*) pauta *f*

guiding hand ['gaɪdɪŋ 'hænd] *n fig* mano *f* amiga **guiding principle** *n* principio *m* director

guild [gɪld] *n* (*of merchants*) corporación *f;* (*of craftsmen*) gremio *m;* **Writers' Guild** asociación *f* de escritores

guilder ['gɪldəʳ, *Am:* -dɚ] *n* florín *m* holandés

guile [gaɪl] *n no pl, form* astucia *f*

guileful ['gaɪlfəl] *adj form* astuto, -a

guileless ['gaɪllɪs] *adj* inocente

guillotine ['gɪlətiːn] *n* guillotina *f*

guilt [gɪlt] *n no pl* **1.** (*shame for wrongdoing*) culpabilidad *f* **2.** (*responsibility for crime*) culpa *f;* **to admit one's** ~ confesarse culpable; **to establish sb's** ~ determinar la culpabilidad de alguien

guiltless ['gɪltləs] *adj* inocente

guilt-ridden *adj* atormentado, -a por un sentido de culpabilidad

guilty ['gɪlti, *Am:* -t̬i] <-ier, -iest> *adj* culpable; **to be** ~ **of a crime/murder** ser culpable de un delito/asesinato; **to have a** ~ **conscience** tener un sentimiento de culpabilidad; **to feel** ~ **about sth** sentirse culpable por algo; **to plead** ~ **to sth** declararse culpable de algo; **to prove sb** ~ demostrar la culpabilidad de alguien

guinea ['gɪni] *n Brit* guinea *f*

Guinea ['gɪni] *n* Guinea *f*

guinea fowl *n* gallina *f* de Guinea

Guinean **I.** *adj* guineano, -a **II.** *n* guineano, -a *m, f*

guinea pig *n* conejillo *m* de Indias, cuy *m AmS*

guise [gaɪz] *n no pl* **1.** (*style*) guisa *f* **2.** (*appearance*) apariencia *f;* **it's an old idea in new** ~ se trata de una antigua idea pero con un nuevo aspecto **3.** (*pretence*) pretensión *f;* **under the** ~ **of sth** bajo el disfraz de algo

guitar [gɪ'tɑːʳ, *Am:* -'tɑːr] *n* guitarra *f;* **to play the** ~ tocar la guitarra

guitarist [gɪ'tɑːrɪst] *n* guitarrista *mf*

gulch [gʌltʃ] <-es> *n Am* (*gully*) barranco *m*

gulf [gʌlf] *n* **1.** (*area of sea*) golfo *m;* **the Gulf of Mexico** el Golfo de Méjico; **the Gulf of Suez** el Golfo de Suez; **the** (**Persian**) **Gulf** el Golfo (Pérsico) **2.** (*chasm*) abismo *m* **3.** (*difference of opinion*) diferencias *fpl;* **to bridge a** ~ llenar un vacío

gull¹ [gʌl] *n* gaviota *f*

gull² [gʌl] *vt* **to** ~ **sb** estafar a alguien; **I was ~ed into believing that it was a great chance** me hicieron creer que era una gran oportunidad

gullet ['gʌlɪt] *n* **1.** (*food pipe*) esófago *m* **2.** (*throat*) garganta *f*

gullible ['gʌləbl] *adj* crédulo, -a

gully ['gʌli] <-ies> *n* (*narrow gorge*) barranco *m;* (*channel*) hondonada *f*

gulp [gʌlp] **I.** *n* trago *m;* **a** ~ **of air** una bocanada de aire; **to take a** ~ **of milk/tea** beber un trago de leche/té; **in one** ~ de un trago **II.** *vt* tragar; (*liquid*) beber; (*food*) engullir **III.** *vi* **1.** (*swallow with emotion*) tragar saliva **2.** (*breath*) **to** ~ **for air** respirar hondo

gum¹ [gʌm] *n* ANAT encía *f*

gum² [gʌm] **I.** *n* **1.** *no pl* (*soft sticky substance*) goma *f;* BOT resina *f* **2.** *no pl* (*glue*) pegamento *m;* (*on envelope flaps*) cola *f* **3.** (*type of sweet*) gominola *f;* **chewing** ~ chicle *m* **II.** *vt* pegar

◆**gum up** *vt* estropear ▶**to** ~ **the works** (*stop operation*) paralizar los trabajos; (*interfere*) estropearlo todo

gumboil ['gʌmbɔɪl] *n* MED flemón *m*

gumdrop ['gʌmdrɒp, *Am:* -drɑːp] *n* pastilla *f* de goma

gummy ['gʌmi] <-ier, -iest> *adj* (*sticky*) pegajoso, -a; (*with glue on*) engomado, -a

gumption ['gʌmpʃən] *n no pl, inf* **1.** (*courage*) valor *m;* **to have the** ~ **to do sth** tener valor para hacer algo **2.** (*intelligence*) seso *m*

gumshield ['gʌmʃiːld] *n* protector *m* de dientes

gumshoe ['gʌmʃuː] *n* **1.** (*overshoe*) chanclo *m* **2.** *Am, inf* (*detective*) detective *mf*

gumtree ['gʌmtriː] *n* árbol *m* de caucho, gomero *m AmL* ▶**to be up a** ~ *inf* estar en un aprieto

gun [gʌn] **I.** *n* **1.** (*weapon*) arma *f* de fuego; (*cannon*) cañón *m;* (*pistol*) pistola *f;* (*revolver*) revólver *m;* (*rifle*) fusil *m;* **to carry a** ~ llevar pistola **2.** SPORTS pistoletazo *m* **3.** (*device*) pistola *f* inyectora **4.** *Am* (*person*) pistolero, -a *m, f;* **a hired** ~ un pistolero a sueldo ▶**to jump the** ~ SPORTS salir antes de tiempo; **to stick to one's ~s** mantenerse en sus trece **II.** <-nn-> *vi* (*vehicle*) acelerar a fondo

gun barrel *n* cañón *m* de un arma **gunboat** *n* cañonera *f* **gunfight** *n* tiroteo *m* **gunfire** *n no pl* **1.** (*gunfight*) tiroteo *m;* (*shots*) dis-

G

paros *mpl* 2. (*cannonfire*) cañoneo *m* **gun-licence** *n* licencia *f* de armas **gunman** <-men> *n* pistolero *m*

gunner ['gʌnəʳ, *Am:* -ɚ] *n* artillero *m*

gunpoint *n no pl* **at ~** a punto de pistola **gunpowder** *n no pl* pólvora *f* **gun-runner** *n* traficante *mf* de armas **gun-running** *n no pl* contrabando *m* de armas

gunshot ['gʌnʃɒt, *Am:* -ʃɑːt] *n* disparo *m*

gunshot wound *n* herida *f* de bala

gunslinger ['gʌnˌslɪŋəʳ] *n* HIST pistolero, -a *m, f*

gurgle ['gɜːgl, *Am:* 'gɜːr-] I. *n* (*happy noise*) gorjeo *m;* (*noise of water*) borboteo *m* II. *vi* 1. (*baby*) gorjear; **to ~ with pleasure/with delight** gorjear de felicidad/regocijo 2. (*water*) borbotear

guru ['gʊru, *Am:* 'guːruː] *n* gurú *mf*

gush [gʌʃ] I. <-es> *n* chorro *m; fig* efusión *f;* **a ~ of water** un chorro de agua II. *vi* 1. (*any liquid*) chorrear 2. *inf* (*praise excessively*) deshacerse en elogios III. *vt* derramar a borbollones

gusher ['gʌʃəʳ, *Am:* -ɚ] *n* pozo *m* petrolífero

gushing *adj* excesivamente efusivo, -a; (*enthusiastically*) efusivo, -a

gushy ['gʌʃi] <-ier, -iest> *adj* extremo, -a, efusivo, -a

gusset ['gʌsɪt] *n* escudete *m*

gust [gʌst] I. *n* (*of wind*) ráfaga *f;* (*of rain*) chaparrón *m* II. *vi* soplar

gusto ['gʌstəʊ, *Am:* -toʊ] *n no pl* entusiasmo *m*

gusty ['gʌsti] <-ier -iest> *adj* borrascoso, -a

gut [gʌt] I. *n* 1. (*intestine*) intestino *m;* **a ~ feeling/reaction** un instinto/una reacción visceral 2. (*string from animal intestine*) tripa *f* 3. *pl, inf* (*bowels*) entrañas *fpl* 4. *pl* (*courage*) valor *m;* (*strength of character*) determinación *f;* **it takes ~s** se necesita valor ►**to have sb's ~s for garters** *Brit, iron* romper la cabeza a alguien; **to bust a ~** *inf* echar los bofes II. <-tt-> *vt* 1. (*remove the innards*) destripar 2. (*destroy by fire*) **to be ~ed** estar destruido 3. (*emotional suffering*) destrozar

gutless [gʌtlɪs] *adj inf* (*lacking courage*) cobarde; (*lacking enthusiasm*) apático, -a

gutsy ['gʌtsi] <-ier, -iest> *adj* 1. (*brave*) valiente; (*adventurous*) atrevido, -a 2. (*powerful*) vigoroso, -a

gutter ['gʌtəʳ, *Am:* 'gʌt̬ɚ] *n* (*drainage channel: at the roadside*) alcantarilla *f;* (*on the roof*) canalón *m; fig* barrio *m* marginal

gutter journalism *n no pl* periodismo *m* sensacionalista **gutter press** *n no pl, Brit* prensa *f* amarilla

guttural ['gʌtərəl, *Am:* 'gʌt̬-] *adj a.* LING gutural

guy [gaɪ] *n inf* 1. (*man*) tío *m;* **hi ~s** *Am, Aus* ¿qué hay, colegas? 2. *Brit* (*effigy of Guy Fawkes*) *nombre que se les da a unos muñecos que se queman en hogueras la noche del 5 de noviembre en memoria de Guy Fawkes* 3. (*rope to fix a tent, guy rope*) viento *m*

Guyana [gaɪ'ænə] *n* Guyana *f*

Guyanese [ˌgaɪə'niːz] I. *adj* guyanés, -esa II. *n* guyanés, -esa *m, f*

guzzle ['gʌzl] I. *vt inf* (*eat*) jalar; (*drink*) tragar II. *vi* zampar

gym [dʒɪm] *n inf* 1. *no pl* (*gymnastics*) gimnasia *f* 2. (*gymnasium*) gimnasio *m*

gymkhana [dʒɪm'kɑːnə] *n Brit* gincana *f;* SPORTS carrera *f* de obstáculos

gymnasium [dʒɪm'neɪzɪəm] *n* gimnasio *m*

gymnast ['dʒɪmnæst] *n* gimnasta *mf*

gymnastic [dʒɪm'næstɪk] *adj* gimnástico, -a

gymnastics [dʒɪm'næstɪks] *npl* gimnasia *f*

gym shoes *n* zapatillas *fpl* de deporte

gynaecological *adj Brit,* **gynecological** [ˌgaɪnəkə'lɒdʒɪkəl, *Am:* -'lɑːdʒɪ-] *adj Am, Aus* ginecológico, -a

gynaecologist *n Brit,* **gynecologist** *n Am, Aus* ginecólogo, -a *m, f*

gynaecology *n Brit,* **gynecology** [ˌgaɪnə'kɒlədʒi, *Am:* -'kɑːlə-] *n Am, Aus no pl* ginecología *f*

gyp [dʒɪp] *n Aus, Brit, inf* 1. (*pain*) dolor *m* 2. (*ticking off*) bronca *f*

gypsum ['dʒɪpsəm] *n no pl* yeso *m*

gypsy ['dʒɪpsi] <-ies> I. *n* gitano, -a *m, f* II. *adj* gitano, -a; **~ encampment** campamento *m* de gitanos

gyrate [ˌdʒaɪ'reɪt] *vi* girar

gyration [ˌdʒaɪ'reɪʃən] *n* giro *m; fig* vuelco *m*

gyrocompass ['dʒaɪrəʊ'kɒmpəs, *Am:* -roʊˌkʌm-] *n* brújula *f* giroscópica

gyroscope ['dʒaɪrəskəʊp, *Am:* -skoʊp] *n* NAUT, AVIAT giroscopio *m*

H

H, h [eɪtʃ] *n* H, h *f;* **~ for Harry** *Brit,* **~ for How** *Am* H de Huelva

ha [hɑː] *interj a. iron* ¡ajá!

habeas corpus [ˌheɪbɪəs'kɔːpəs, *Am:* -'kɔːr-] *n no pl* LAW hábeas corpus *m;* **Habeas Corpus Act** Ley *f* de Hábeas Corpus

haberdasher ['hæbədæʃəʳ, *Am:* -ɚdæʃɚ] *n* 1. *Brit* mercero, -a *m, f* 2. *Am* camisero, -a *m, f*

haberdashery [ˌhæbə'dæʃəri, *Am:* 'hæbɚdæʃɚ-] <-ies> *n* 1. *no pl, Brit* (*wares*) artículos *mpl* de mercería 2. *Brit* (*shop*) mercería *f* 3. *no pl, Am* (*clothing*) ropa *f* de caballero 4. (*shop*) camisería *f*

habit ['hæbɪt] *n* 1. (*customary practice*) hábito *m,* costumbre *f;* **to be in the ~ of doing sth** tener por costumbre hacer algo; **by sheer force of ~** por pura costumbre; **to do sth out of ~** hacer algo por costumbre; **to get**

into the ~ (of doing sth) acostumbrarse (a hacer algo); **to get out of the ~ of doing sth** perder la costumbre de hacer algo; **a bad ~** una mala costumbre; **to break a ~** quitarse una costumbre; **don't make a ~ of it** no lo hagas por costumbre **2.** (*dress*) hábito *m;* **riding ~** traje *m* de montar **3.** (*addiction*) adicción *f;* **to have a heroin ~** ser adicto a la heroína

habitable ['hæbɪtəbl, *Am:* -t̬ə-] *adj* habitable

habitat ['hæbɪtæt, *Am:* '-ə-] *n* hábitat *m*

habitation [ˌhæbɪ'teɪʃən] *n* **1.** *no pl* (*occupancy*) **unfit for human ~** inhabitable **2.** (*dwelling*) morada *f* **3.** (*settlement*) asentamiento *m*

habitual [hə'bɪtʃuəl] *adj* **1.** (*usual*) habitual; **~ drug use** consumo frecuente de drogas **2.** (*describing person*) empedernido, -a

habituate [hə'bɪtʃueɪt] *vt* habituar; **to ~ oneself to do sth** habituarse a hacer algo

hack¹ [hæk] **I.** *vt* **1.** *Brit* (*football*) dar una patada a **2.** (*chop violently*) cortar a tajos; **to ~ to death** matar a cuchilladas; **to ~ sth to pieces** hacer algo trizas **3.** *Am, Aus, inf* (*cope with*) aguantar **II.** *vi* hacer tajos; **to ~ at sth** cortar algo a tajos **III.** *n* **1.** (*journalist*) periodista *mf* de pacotilla **2.** (*politician*) politicucho, -a *m, f* **3.** (*writer*) escritorzuelo, -a *m, f*

hack² [hæk] *vt* INFOR **to ~ (into) a system** introducirse ilegalmente en un sistema

hack³ [hæk] **I.** *vi* montar a caballo **II.** *n* **1.** (*rural horse-ride*) paseo *m* a caballo **2.** *Am, inf* (*taxi car*) taxi *m* **3.** (*driver*) taxista *mf*

hacker [hækəʳ, *Am:* -ɚ] *n* INFOR hacker *mf*

hackles ['hæklz] *npl* (*on dogs' backs*) pelo *m* erizado; (*on birds' necks*) collar *m* ►**to <u>get</u> one's ~ <u>up</u>** enfurecerse; **to <u>make</u> sb's ~ rise** poner furioso a alguien; **to <u>raise</u> ~** levantar ampollas

hackney ['hækni] *n,* **hackney carriage** *n* **1.** (*carriage*) coche *m* de alquiler **2.** (*taxi*) taxi *m*

hackneyed ['hæknɪd] *adj* (*argument, theme*) trillado, -a

hacksaw ['hæksɔː, *Am:* -sɑː] *n* sierra *f* para metales

had [həd, *stressed:* hæd] *pt, pp of* **have**

haddock ['hædək] *n* eglefino *m*

hadn't ['hædnt] = **had not** *s.* **have**

haematite ['hemətaɪt] *n* MIN hematites *f inv*

haemoglobin [ˌhiːmə'gləʊbɪn, *Am:* 'hiːməgloʊ-] *n no pl, Brit, Aus* hemoglobina *f*

haemophilia [ˌhiːmə'fɪlɪə, *Am:* ˌhiːmoʊ'-] *n no pl, Brit, Aus* hemofilia *f*

haemophiliac [ˌhiːməʊ'fɪlɪæk, *Am:* ˌhiːmoʊ'-] *n Brit, Aus* hemofílico, -a *m, f*

haemorrhage ['hemərɪdʒ, *Am:* -ɚɪdʒ] **I.** *n* hemorragia *f;* **brain ~** derrame *m* cerebral **II.** *vi Brit, Aus* tener una hemorragia

haemorrhoids ['hemərɔɪdz] *npl* hemorroides *fpl*

haft [hɑːft, *Am:* hæft] *n* (*of a knife*) mango *m;* (*of a sword*) empuñadura *f*

hag [hæg] *n* (*ugly old woman*) bruja *f*

haggard ['hægəd, *Am:* -ɚd] *adj* macilento, -a

haggis ['hægɪs] *n no pl plato escocés a base de vísceras de cordero*

haggle ['hægl] *vi* regatear; **to ~ over sth** regatear el precio de algo

Hague [heɪg] *n* **the ~** la Haya

haha *interj,* **ha-ha** ['hɑːhɑː] *interj,* **ha ha** *interj iron* ¡ja, ja!

hail¹ [heɪl] **I.** *n no pl* METEO granizo *m;* (*of stones, insults*) lluvia *f* **II.** *vi* granizar; **to ~ down on sb/sth** *a. fig* llover sobre alguien/algo

hail² [heɪl] **I.** *vt* **1.** (*call*) llamar; **to ~ a taxi** parar un taxi **2.** (*acclaim*) aclamar **3.** (*welcome*) acoger; **she ~ed the news with joy** recibió la noticia con alegría **II.** *vi* **to ~ from** (*person*) ser de; (*thing*) proceder de

hail-fellow-well-met [ˌheɪlˌfeləʊˌwel'met, *Am:* ˌ-oʊˌ-] *n* (demasiado) campechano, -a

hair [heəʳ, *Am:* her] *n* **1.** (*on the skin of an animal or a person*) pelo *m;* (*on human head*) cabello *m;* **to do one's ~** arreglarse el pelo (en una peluquería); **to have one's ~ cut** cortarse el pelo; **to wash one's ~** lavarse el pelo; **to wear one's ~ up/down** llevar el pelo recogido/suelto **2.** (*of body*) vello *m* **3.** (*on plant*) pelusa *f* ►**that'll put ~s on your <u>chest</u>** *inf* eso te dejará como nuevo; **to make sb's ~s <u>curl</u>** *inf* poner los pelos de punta a alguien; **to <u>get</u> in sb's ~** poner a alguien nervioso; **to not <u>harm</u> a ~ on sb's head** no tocarle ni un pelo a alguien; **<u>keep</u> your ~ on!** *Brit, Aus, iron, inf* ¡no te sulfures!; **to <u>split</u> ~s** buscarle tres pies al gato; **to not <u>turn</u> a ~** no inmutarse

hairbrush ['heəbrʌʃ, *Am:* 'her-] <-es> *n* cepillo *m* (del pelo) **hair conditioner** *n* acondicionador *m* del cabello **hair curler** *n* tenacilla *f* de rizar **haircut** *n* corte *m* de pelo; **to get a ~** cortarse el pelo **hairdo** *n inf* peinado *m* **hairdresser** *n* peluquero, -a *m, f;* **the ~'s** la peluquería

hairdressing *n* **1.** *no pl* (*profession*) peluquería *f* **2.** (*action of styling hair*) peinado *m* **hairdressing salon** *n* (salón *m* de) peluquería *f*

hair drier *n,* **hair dryer** ['heəˌdraɪeʳ, *Am:* 'herˌdraɪɚ] *n* secador *m* (de pelo) **hairgrip** *n* horquilla *f*

hairless ['heəlɪs, *Am:* 'her-] *adj* (*head*) calvo, -a, pelado, -a *AmS;* (*body*) sin vello; (*face*) lampiño, -a; (*animal*) sin pelo

hairline ['heəlaɪn, *Am:* 'her-] *n* **1.** (*lower edge of the hair*) nacimiento *m* del pelo; **he has a receding ~** tiene entradas **2.** (*fine line*) línea *f* muy fina **hairline crack** *n,* **hairline fracture** *n* grieta *f* fina

hairnet ['heənet, *Am:* 'her-] *n* redecilla *f* **hairpiece** *n* postizo *m*

hairpin ['heəpɪn, *Am:* 'her-] *n* horquilla *f,* gancho *m AmL* **hairpin bend** *n Brit, Aus,* **hairpin curve** *n,* **hairpin turn** *n Am*

H

curva *f* muy cerrada

hair-raising ['heəˌreɪzɪŋ, *Am:* 'her-] *adj inf* espeluznante **hair remover** *n* depilatorio *m* **hair restorer** *n* tónico *m* capilar **hair slide** *n* pasador *m* **hair-splitting** I. *n no pl* sutilezas *fpl* II. *adj* (*argument, remark*) demasiado sutil; (*person*) quisquilloso, -a

hairspray ['heəspreɪ, *Am:* 'her-] *n* laca *f* (para el pelo) **hairstyle** *n* peinado *m*

hairy ['heəri, *Am:* 'heri] <-ier, -iest> *adj* 1. (*having much hair*) peludo, -a 2. *inf* (*frightening*) espeluznante

Haiti ['heɪti, *Am:* -t̬i] *n* Haití *m*

Haitian ['heɪʃən] I. *n* haitiano, -a *m, f* II. *adj* haitiano, -a

hake [heɪk] <-(s)> *n* merluza *f*

hale [heɪl] *adj* robusto, -a; ~ **and hearty** fuerte como un roble

half [hɑːf, *Am:* hæf] I. <halves> *n* 1. (*equal part*) mitad *f;* ~ **an apple** media manzana; **in** ~ por la mitad; ~ **and** ~ mitad y mitad; **to cut sth into halves** partir algo por la mitad; **a kilo and a** ~ un kilo y medio; **to go halves** (**on sth**) *inf* pagar (algo) a medias; **to go halves with sb** ir a medias con alguien; **to do things by halves** hacer las cosas a medias; **my other** ~ *fig* mi media naranja; **first/second** ~ SPORTS primer/segundo tiempo; **the first/second** ~ **of a century** la primera/segunda mitad de un siglo; **that was a game and a** ~! *fig* ¡menudo partido! 2. *Brit, inf* (*of beer*) media pinta *f* ▸ **to be too clever by** ~ pasarse de listo II. *adj* medio, -a; ~ **a pint** media pinta; ~ **an hour, a** ~ **hour** media hora; ~ **the country** medio país; **she's** ~ **the player she used to be** esta jugadora no es ni sombra de lo que era III. *adv* 1. (*almost*) casi; **to be** ~ **sure** estar casi seguro 2. (*partially*) a medias; ~ **asleep** medio dormido; ~ **cooked** medio crudo; ~ **done** a medio hacer; ~ **naked** medio desnudo; ~ **empty/full** medio vacío/lleno 3. (*by fifty percent*) ~ **as many/much** la mitad; ~ **as much again** la mitad más 4. *inf* (*most*) la mayor parte; ~ (**of**) **the time** la mayor parte del tiempo 5. (*thirty minutes after*) ~ **past three** las tres y media; (**at**) ~ **past nine** a las nueve y media; **at** ~ **past** *Brit, inf* a y media 6. *Brit, inf* (*intensifies negative statement*) **not** ~ no poco; **he wasn't** ~ **handsome** era guapísimo; **do you like it? – not** ~! ¿te gusta? – ¡no me gusta, me encanta! IV. *pron* la mitad; ~ **and** ~ mitad y mitad

halfback ['hɑːfbæk, *Am:* 'hæf-] *n* SPORTS medio *m* **half-baked** *adj* 1. (*food*) medio cocido, -a 2. *inf* (*plan*) sin sentido, estúpido, -a **half board** *n no pl* media pensión *f* **half-breed** *n,* **half-caste** *n* mestizo, -a **half-brother** *n* hermanastro *m* **half-crown** *n* HIST media corona *f* **half-dozen** *adj* media docena *f* **half-empty** *adj* medio vacío, -a **half-fare** *n* medio billete *m* **half-full** *adj* medio lleno, -a **half-hearted** *adj* poco entusiasta; **a** ~ **attempt** un intento desganado **half-mast** *n* **at** ~ a media asta **half-moon** *n* media luna *f;* ~ **shaped** en forma de media luna **half note** *n Am* MUS blanca *f* **half-pence** *n inv,* **halfpenny** <-ies> *n* HIST medio penique *m* **half-price** *adj* **at** ~ a mitad de precio **half-sister** *n* hermanastra *f* **half-term** *n no pl, Brit* vacaciones *fpl* de mitad de trimestre **half-timbered** *adj* con entramado de madera **half-time** *n* 1. SPORTS descanso *m;* **at** ~ en el descanso 2. ECON media jornada *f;* **to be on** ~ trabajar media jornada **half-title** *n* 1. (*first printed page*) portadilla *f* 2. (*title*) titulillo *m* **half tone** *n* media tinta *f* **halfway** I. *adj* 1. (*midway*) medio, -a; ~ **point** punto medio; ~ **stage** etapa *f* intermedia 2. (*partial*) parcial II. *adv* 1. (*to or at half the distance*) a mitad de camino; **to be** ~ **between ... and ...** estar entre... y...; **to be** ~ **through sth** ir por la mitad de algo; ~ **through the year** a mediados de año; ~ **up** a media cuesta; **to meet sb** ~ *fig* llegar a un acuerdo con alguien 2. (*nearly, partly*) **to go** ~ **towards** (**doing**) **sth** hacer algo en parte; **the proposals only went** ~ **towards meeting their demands** las propuestas sólo satisfacían en parte sus exigencias **half-wit** *n* imbécil *mf* **half-yearly** I. *adj* semestral II. *adv* semestralmente

halibut ['hælɪbət] <-(s)> *n* halibut *m*

halitosis [ˌhælɪ'təʊsɪs, *Am:* -'toʊ-] *n no pl* halitosis *f inv*

hall [hɔːl] *n* 1. (*room by front door*) vestíbulo *m* 2. (*large public room*) sala *f;* (*in schools*) comedor *m;* **concert** ~ sala *f* de conciertos; **town** ~, **city** ~ *Am* ayuntamiento *m* 3. UNIV colegio *m* mayor; ~ **of residence** residencia *f* universitaria 4. (*corridor*) pasillo *m* 5. (*country house*) casa *f* solariega

hallelujah [ˌhælɪ'luːjə] I. *interj* ¡aleluya! II. *n* aleluya *m*

hallmark ['hɔːlmɑːk, *Am:* -mɑːrk] I. *n* 1. *Brit* (*engraved identifying mark*) contraste *m* 2. (*identifying symbol*) distintivo *m;* **her** ~ su sello personal; **to bear all the** ~**s of ...** *fig* tener todas las características de... II. *vt* contrastar

hallo [hə'ləʊ, *Am:* -'loʊ] <-s> *interj Brit* hola

hallow ['hæləʊ, *Am:* -oʊ] *vt* 1. (*sanctify*) santificar; (*consecrate*) consagrar; **to be** ~**ed** ser sagrado 2. (*venerate*) venerar

hallowed *adj* sagrado, -a

Halloween *n,* **Hallowe'en** [ˌhæləʊ'iːn, *Am:* ˌhæloʊ'-] *n* víspera *f* de Todos los Santos

La fiesta de **Hallowe'en** se celebra el día 31 de octubre, el día antes de **All Saints' Day**, también llamado **All Hallows** (Todos los Santos). Desde hace mucho tiempo en esta festividad cobran un protagonismo destacado los espíritus y las brujas. Los niños hacen **turnip lanterns**, (farolillos hechos con calabazas vaciadas) y en Escocia hacen **guising** (esto es, se disfrazan y van de casa en casa cantando o recitando poemas para que los dueños de la casa les den dinero). En los EE.UU. los niños se difrazan al atardecer y van de puerta en puerta con un saco en la mano. Cuando el dueño de la casa abre la puerta los niños gritan: '**Trick or treat!**'; el inquilino elige entonces entre darles un **treat** (dulce) o sufrir un **trick** (susto). Hoy en día los sustos prácticamente han desaparecido, pues los niños sólo se acercan a aquellas casas en las que las luces de fuera están encendidas, lo cual funciona como señal de bienvenida.

hallucinate [hə'lu:sɪneɪt] *vi a. fig* alucinar
hallucination [hə,lu:sɪ'neɪʃən] *n no pl* alucinación *f*
hallucinogenic [hə,lu:sɪnə'dʒenɪk, *Am:* -noʊ'-] *adj* alucinógeno, -a
halo ['heɪləʊ, *Am:* -loʊ] <-s *o* -es> *n* **1.** *a. fig* ASTR halo *m* **2.** *a. fig* REL aureola *f*
halogen ['hælədʒen, *Am:* 'hæloʊ-] *n* halógeno *m*
halogen bulb *n* bombilla *f* halógena
halogen lamp *n* lámpara *f* halógena
halt [hɒlt, *Am:* hɔ:lt] **I.** *n no pl* **1.** (*standstill, stoppage*) parada *f;* **to bring sth/sb to a ~** detener algo/a alguien; **to call a ~ to sth** poner coto a algo; **to come to a ~** pararse **2.** (*interruption*) interrupción *f* **3.** RAIL apeadero *m* **II.** *vt* (*bring to a permanent stop*) parar; (*bring to a temporary stop*) interrumpir **III.** *vi* (*stop permanently*) parar; (*stop temporarily*) interrumpirse **IV.** *interj* **~!** ¡alto!
halter ['hɔ:ltə^r, *Am:* -t̬ɚ] *n* **1.** (*animals*) ronzal *m* **2.** (*criminals*) soga *f*
halterneck ['hɒltənek, *Am:* -'hɔ:lt̬ɚ-] *n* top *m* con tirante de cuello
halting *adj* (*speech, movement*) vacilante
halve [hɑ:v, *Am:* hæv] **I.** *vt* **1.** (*lessen*) reducir a la mitad; (*number*) dividir por dos **2.** (*cut in two equal pieces*) partir por la mitad **II.** *vi* reducirse a la mitad
halyard ['hæljəd, *Am:* -jɚd] *n* NAUT driza *f*
ham [hæm] **I.** *n* **1.** *no pl* (*cured*) jamón *m* (serrano); (*cooked*) jamón *m* (cocido); **a slice of ~** una loncha de jamón **2.** (*actor*) histrión *m* **3.** (*radio*) radioaficionado, -a *m, f* **II.** *vi* actuar con histrionismo **III.** *vt* **~ up** interpretar con afectación; **to ~ it up** actuar histriónicamente
hamburger ['hæmbɜ:gə^r, *Am:* -bɜ:rgɚ] *n* **1.** (*take-away*) hamburguesa *f* **2.** *no pl, Am* (*chopped beef*) carne *f* picada
ham-fisted [,hæm'fɪstɪd, *Am:* 'hæmfɪstɪd] *adj Brit, Aus,* **ham-handed** [,hæm'hændɪd, *Am:* 'hæm,hændɪd] *adj Am* torpe
hamlet ['hæmlət] *n* aldea *f*
hammer ['hæmə^r, *Am:* -ɚ] **I.** *n* **1.** (*tool*) martillo *m;* **~ blow** *a. fig* martillazo *m;* **the ~ and sickle** POL, HIST la hoz y el martillo; **throwing the ~** SPORTS lanzamiento *m* de martillo; **to go under the ~** *a. fig* (*painting*) salir a subasta **2.** (*part of modern gun*) percutor *m* ▶**to go at it ~ and tongs** *inf* (*do energetically*) echar el resto; (*fight*) luchar a brazo partido **II.** *vt* **1.** (*hit with tool: metal*) martillear; (*nail*) clavar; **to ~ sth (into sth)** clavar algo (en algo); **to ~ sth into sb** *fig* meter algo en la cabeza a alguien **2.** *inf* (*beat easily in sports*) dar una paliza **3.** (*condemn: book, film*) machacar; **to ~ sb for sth** criticar duramente a alguien por algo **4.** FIN, ECON declarar insolvente **5.** *inf* (*become very drunk*) **to get ~ed (on sth)** emborracharse (de algo) **III.** *vi* **1.** (*use a hammer*) martillear; **to ~ at sth** dar martillazos a algo **2.** (*strike as with a hammer*) golpear; (*heart*) latir con fuerza; (*head*) estar a punto de estallar; **to ~ on sth** aporrear algo
◆**hammer in** *vt* clavar
◆**hammer out** *vt* **1.** (*correct*) alisar a martillazos **2.** (*find solution*) negociar; **to ~ a settlement** llegar a un arreglo
hammer drill *n* perforadora *f* de percusión
hammerhead *n* **1.** (*head of a hammer*) cabeza *f* de martillo **2.** ZOOL **~ shark** pez *m* martillo
hammock ['hæmək] *n* hamaca *f*
hamper¹ ['hæmpə^r, *Am:* -pɚ] *vt* (*hinder*) dificultar; **to ~ sb/sth** poner trabas a alguien/algo
hamper² ['hæmpə^r, *Am:* -pɚ] *n* **1.** (*picnic basket*) cesta *f* **2.** *Am* (*for dirty linen*) cesto *m* de la ropa
hamster ['hæmstə^r, *Am:* -stɚ] *n* hámster *m*
hamstring ['hæmstrɪŋ] **I.** *n* ANAT tendón *m* de la corva; ZOOL tendón *m* del corvejón **II.** *vt irr* **1.** (*cut the hamstring*) desjarretar **2.** (*render powerless: thing*) paralizar; (*person*) incapacitar; **to be hamstrung** estar atado de pies y manos
hand [hænd] **I.** *n* **1.** ANAT mano *f;* **to be good with one's ~s** ser mañoso; **to deliver a letter by ~** entregar una carta en mano; **to do sth by ~** hacer algo a mano; **to keep one's ~s off** no tocar; **to shake ~s with sb** estrechar la mano a alguien; **to take sb by the ~** llevar a alguien de la mano; **to tie ~ and foot** *a. fig* atar de pies y manos; **sword in ~** espada en ristre; **~ in ~** de la mano; **get your ~s off!** ¡no toques!; **~s up!** ¡manos arriba! **2.** (*handy, within reach*) **at ~** muy cerca; **to ~** a mano; **to keep sth close at ~** tener algo a mano; **to be at ~** acercarse; **in ~** (*available to use*) disponible; (*being arranged*) entre manos; **preparations are in ~** los preparativos están en marcha **3.** (*what needs doing now*) **the problem in ~** el problema que nos ocupa; **to be on ~** (*object*) estar a mano; (*person*) estar ahí; **to get out of ~** (*things, situation*) irse de las manos; (*person*) descontrolarse **4.** *pl* (*responsiblity, authority, care*) **to be in good ~s** estar en buenas manos; **to fall into the ~s of sb** caer en manos de alguien; **to put sth into the ~s of sb** poner algo en manos de alguien; **at the ~s of sb** (*because of*) a manos de alguien **5.** (*assistance*) **to give (sb) a ~ (with sth)**

echar (a alguien) una mano (con algo); **to keep one's ~ in** no perder la práctica **6.** (*control*) **to have sth in ~** tener algo entre manos; **to have sth well in ~** tener algo bajo control; **to have a ~ in sth** intervenir en algo; **to take sb in ~** apretar las clavijas a alguien **7.** GAMES **to have a good/poor ~** tener una buena/mala mano; **to show one's ~** *a. fig* enseñar las cartas; **a ~ of poker** una mano de póquer **8.** (*pointer on clock*) manecilla *f;* **the hour ~** la aguja de las horas; **the minute ~** el minutero; **the second ~** el segundero **9.** (*manual worker*) obrero, -a *m, f;* (*sailor*) marinero, -a *m, f;* **factory ~** operario, -a *m, f* **10.** (*skilful person*) **old ~** veterano, -a *m, f;* **to be an old ~ at sth** tener mucha experiencia en algo **11.** (*applause*) aplauso *m;* **let's have a big ~ for ...** un gran aplauso para... **12.** (*measurement*) palmo *m* de alzada **13.** (*handwriting*) letra *f;* **in his own ~** de su puño y letra ►**to make money ~ over fist** hacer dinero a espuertas; **to lose money ~ over fist** perder dinero rápidamente; **to be ~ in glove with sb** ser uña y carne con alguien; **to put one's ~ in one's pocket** contribuir con dinero; **to be able to turn one's ~ to anything** saber hacer cualquier cosa; **with a firm ~** con mano dura; **at first ~** de primera mano; **to have one's ~s full** estar muy ocupado; **with a heavy** [*o* **an iron**] **~** con mano dura; **to play a lone ~** actuar solo; **on the one ~ ... on the other** (~) ... por un lado..., por otro (lado)...; **second ~** de segunda mano; **to have one's ~s tied** tener las manos atadas; **to ask for sb's ~ in marriage** *form* pedir la mano de alguien; **to have sb eat out of one's ~** meterse a alguien en el bolsillo; **to force sb's ~** forzar la mano a alguien; **to get one's ~s on sb** atrapar a alguien; **to lay one's ~s on sth** hacerse con algo; **to not soil one's ~s with sth** no mancharse las manos con algo; **to throw in one's ~** darse por vencido **II.** *vt* **1.** (*give*) dar; **will you ~ me my bag?** ¿puedes pasarme mi bolso? **2.** (*give credit to*) **you've got to ~ it to him** hay que reconocer que lo hace muy bien

◆**hand around** *vt* hacer circular

◆**hand back** *vt* devolver

◆**hand down** *vt* **1.** (*knowledge, tradition*) transmitir; (*objects*) pasar; **to hand sth down from one generation to another** transmitir algo de generación en generación **2.** *Am* LAW (*judgement*) pronunciar

◆**hand in** *vt* (*task, document*) entregar; **to ~ one's resignation** presentar la dimisión

◆**hand on** *vt* (*knowledge*) transmitir; (*object*) pasar; **to hand sth on to sb** pasar algo a alguien

◆**hand out** *vt* **1.** (*distribute*) repartir **2.** (*give: advice*) dar; (*punishment*) aplicar

◆**hand over** **I.** *vt* **1.** (*give, submit: money, prisoner*) entregar; (*cheque*) extender **2.** (*pass: power, authority*) transferir; (*property*) ceder **3.** TEL pasar; **to hand sb over to sb** pasar a alguien con alguien **II.** *vi* **to ~ to sb** delegar en alguien; TV pasar la conexión a alguien

◆**hand round** *vt* hacer circular

handbag ['hændbæg] *n* bolso *m,* cartera *f AmL* **handball** *n no pl* SPORTS balonmano *m* **hand-barrow** *n Brit* carretilla *f* **handbill** *n* folleto *m* **handbook** *n* manual *m* **handbrake** *n Brit* AUTO freno *m* de mano **handcart** *n* carretilla *f* **handcuff** *vt* esposar **handcuffs** *npl* esposas *fpl;* **a pair of ~** unas esposas

handful ['hændfʊl] *n no pl* **1.** *a. fig* (*small amount*) puñado *m;* **a ~ of people** un puñado de personas **2.** (*person*) **to be a real ~** (*child*) ser un bicho; (*adult*) ser de armas tomar

hand grenade *n* granada *f* de mano **handgun** *n* pistola *f*

handicap ['hændɪkæp] **I.** *n* **1.** (*disability*) discapacidad *f;* **mental ~** discapacidad *f* mental; **physical ~** invalidez *f* **2.** (*disadvantage*) desventaja *f* **3.** SPORTS hándicap *m* **II.** <-pp-> *vt* perjudicar; **to be ~ped** estar en una situación de desventaja

handicapped **I.** *adj* **physically ~** minusválido, -a; **mentally ~** disminuido psíquico **II.** *n* **the ~** los minusválidos

handicraft ['hændɪkrɑːft, *Am:* -kræft] *n* **1.** (*art*) artesanía *f* **2.** SCHOOL trabajos *mpl* manuales

handiwork ['hændɪwɜːk, *Am:* -wɜːrk] *n no pl* **1.** (*work*) trabajo *m* artesanal **2.** (*product*) artesanía *f;* SCHOOL trabajos *mpl* manuales; **this must be Peter's ~** *iron* esto debe ser obra de Peter

handkerchief ['hæŋkətʃɪf, *Am:* -kɚtʃɪf] *n* pañuelo *m*

handle ['hændl] **I.** *n* **1.** (*of pot, basket, bag*) asa *f;* (*of drawer*) tirador *m;* (*of knife*) mango *m* **2.** (*knob*) pomo *m;* (*lever*) palanca *f* **3.** *inf* (*name*) título *m* ►**to fly off the ~** *inf* perder los estribos **II.** *vt* **1.** (*touch*) tocar; **~ with care** frágil **2.** (*move, transport*) llevar **3.** (*machine, tool, weapon*) manejar; (*chemicals*) manipular; **to ~ a situation well** manejar bien una situación; **she ~s light expertly in her paintings** en sus cuadros maneja la luz con maestría; **I don't know how to ~ her** no sé cómo tratarla **4.** (*direct*) ocuparse de; (*case*) llevar; **I'll ~ this** yo me encargo de esto; **he ~s the márketing** es el responsable de marketing; **he doesn't know how to ~ other people** (*business*) no sabe dirigir; (*socially*) no tiene don de gentes **5.** (*control*) dominar; (*work, difficult situation*) poder con; **to ~ an increase in prices** hacer frente a un aumento de precios **6.** (*discuss, portray: subject*) tratar **7.** (*operate: car*) conducir, manejar *AmL;* (*boat*) dirigir **8.** *Brit* COM comerciar con **III.** *vi* **+ adv/prep** responder; **to ~ poorly** no responder bien

handlebar moustache *n* bigote *m* afilado

handlebars ['hændlbɑːʳz, *Am:* -bɑːrz] *npl* manillar *m*

handler *n* adiestrador(a) *m(f)*

handling *n no pl* **1.** (*management*) manejo *m;* (*of goods*) manipulación *f;* (*of subject*) tratamiento *m;* (*of person*) trato *m;* (*of car*) conducción, manejo *m AmL* **2.** COM porte *m*

hand luggage *n no pl* equipaje *m* de mano **handmade** *adj* hecho, -a a mano

hand-me-down ['hændmidaʊn] *n* prenda *f* heredada

hand-operated *adj* manual

handout ['hændaʊt] *n* **1.** (*leaflet*) folleto *m* **2.** (*press release*) comunicado *m* de prensa **3.** (*written information*) apuntes *mpl* **4.** (*money*) limosna *f*

hand-picked [ˌhænd'pɪkt] *adj* cuidadosamente seleccionado, -a

handrail ['hændreɪl] *n* (*stairs*) pasamanos *m inv;* (*bridge*) barandilla *f* **hand saw** *n* serrucho *m* **handshake** *n* apretón *m* de manos

handsome ['hænsəm] *adj* **1.** (*man*) guapo; (*animal, thing*) bello, -a; **the most ~ man** el hombre más apuesto **2.** (*impressive*) magnífico, -a **3.** (*large*) considerable; (*price, salary*) elevado, -a; (*donation*) generoso, -a; **by a ~ margin** por un amplio margen **4.** (*gracious: gesture*) noble

hands-on [ˌhændz'ɒn, *Am:* -'ɑːn] *adj* **1.** (*instruction*) práctico, -a; **~ approach** enfoque práctico **2.** INFOR manual

handspring ['hændsprɪŋ] *n* salto *m* mortal; **backward ~** salto mortal hacia atrás **handstand** *n* pino *m;* **to do a ~** hacer el pino **hand-to-mouth** *adj* (*salary*) precario, -a; **to lead a ~ existence** tener lo justo para vivir **handwork** *n no pl* trabajo *m* hecho a mano **handwriting** *n no pl* letra *f*

handwritten [ˌhænd'rɪtn] *adj* manuscrito, -a

handy ['hændi] <-ier, -iest> *adj* **1.** (*user-friendly*) manejable; (*form, guide*) sencillo, -a **2.** (*conveniently available*) a mano; (*nearby*) cercano, -a; **to keep sth ~** tener algo a mano; **to be ~ for sth** quedar cerca de algo **3.** (*skilful*) hábil; **to be ~ with sth** ser mañoso para algo; **to be ~ about the house** ser un manitas **4.** (*convenient*) práctico, -a; (*useful*) útil; **to come in ~** venir bien; **to come in ~ for sb** venir muy bien a alguien

handyman ['hændɪmæn] <-men> *n* manitas *m inv*

hang [hæŋ] **I.** <hung, hung> *vi* **1.** (*be suspended*) colgar; (*picture*) estar colgado; **to ~ by/on/from sth** colgar de algo; **to ~ in a gallery** estar expuesto en una galería **2.** (*lean over or forward*) inclinarse **3.** (*float: smoke, fog*) flotar; (*bird*) planear; **to ~ above sb/sth** cernirse sobre alguien/algo; **to leave a question ~ing** dejar una pregunta en el aire **4.** (*be pending*) estar pendiente **5.** (*die*) morir en la horca **6.** (*fit, drape: clothes, fabrics*) caer; **to ~ well** tener buena caída ▸**he can go ~** por mí como si se muere **II.** <hung, hung> *vt* **1.** (*attach*) colgar; (*washing*) tender; (*door*) colocar; **to ~ wallpaper (on a wall)** empapelar (una pared); **to ~ the curtains** colgar las cortinas; **the gallery will ~ many of his paintings** muchas de sus obras se expondrán en la galería **2.** (*decorate*) adornar **3.** (*head*) bajar **4.** (*execute*) ahorcar ▸**I'll be ~ed if ...** que me ahorquen si...; **~ it (all)** ¡caray! **III.** *n no pl* FASHION caída *f* ▸**to get the ~ of sth** *inf* coger el truquillo a algo; **I don't give a ~** *Am, inf* me importa un bledo

◆**hang about, hang around I.** *vi* **1.** *inf* (*waste time*) perder el tiempo **2.** (*wait*) esperar **3.** (*idle*) no hacer nada; **there's a couple of kids hanging around on the street** dos niños andan vagabundeando por la calle **II.** *vt insep* rondar; **I had to ~ the bus station for an hour** tuve que estar una hora de plantón en la estación de autobuses; **to ~ a place** andar rondando por un sitio

◆**hang back** *vi* **1.** (*be reluctant to move forward*) quedarse atrás **2.** (*hesitate*) vacilar

◆**hang behind** *vi* rezagarse

◆**hang on I.** *vi* **1.** (*wait briefly*) esperar; **to keep sb hanging on** hacer esperar a alguien; **~!** *inf* ¡espera un momento!; **she's on the other phone, would you like to ~?** está hablando por la otra línea, ¿quiere esperar? **2.** (*hold on to*) **to ~ to sth** agarrarse a algo; **~ tight** agárrate fuerte **3.** (*persevere*) mantenerse firme; (*resist*) aguantar **II.** *vt insep* **1.** (*depend upon*) depender de **2.** (*give attention*) estar pendiente de; **to ~ sb's every word** estar pendiente de lo que dice alguien

◆**hang out I.** *vt* (*washing*) tender; (*tongue*) sacar; (*flag*) izar **II.** *vi* **1.** (*dangle*) colgar; **with his tongue hanging out** *a. fig* con la lengua fuera; **let it all ~!** *inf* ¡suéltate la melena! *fig* **2.** *inf* (*frequent*) andar; **where does he ~ these days?** ¿por dónde anda estos días? **3.** *inf* (*reside*) vivir

◆**hang over** *vt insep* estar suspendido sobre; *fig* cernirse sobre

◆**hang round** *vi, vt Brit s.* **hang around**

◆**hang together** *vi* **1.** (*make sense*) ser coherente **2.** (*remain associated*) permanecer unidos

◆**hang up I.** *vi* colgar; **to ~ on sb** colgar a alguien **II.** *vt* **1.** (*curtains, receiver*) colgar **2.** (*give up*) **to ~ one's football boots/boxing gloves** *fig* colgar las botas/los guantes **3.** *inf* (*delay*) causar un retraso a

hangar ['hæŋəʳ, *Am:* -ɚ] *n* hangar *m*

hangdog ['hæŋdɒg, *Am:* -dɑːg] *adj* **1.** (*defeated*) abatido, -a **2.** (*ashamed*) avergonzado, -a

hanger ['hæŋəʳ, *Am:* -ɚ] *n* (*clothes*) percha *f*

hanger-on [ˌhæŋər'ɒn, *Am:* -ɚ'ɑːn] <hangers-on> *n a. fig* lapa *f*

hang-glider ['hæŋglaɪdəʳ, *Am:* -dɚ] *n* SPORTS ala *f* delta

hang-gliding ['hæŋglaɪdɪŋ] *n no pl* SPORTS vuelo *m* con ala delta

hanging ['hæŋɪŋ] **I.** *n* **1.** (*act of execution*) ejecución *f* (en la horca) **2.** *no pl* (*system of execution*) horca *f* **3.** *pl* (*curtains*) colgaduras *fpl* **II.** *adj* **1.** (*bridge*) colgante **2.** (*crime*) condenado, -a a la horca

hangman ['hæŋmən] <-men> *n* **1.** (*person*) verdugo *m* **2.** GAMES ahorcado *m* **hangnail** *n* padrastro *m* **hangout** *n inf* guarida *f;* **a favourite ~ of artists** un lugar frecuentado por artistas **hangover** *n* **1.** (*sickness*) resaca *f,* goma *f AmL* **2.** (*left-over*) vestigio *m* **hang-up** *n inf* complejo *m;* **to have a ~ about sth** estar acomplejado por algo

hank [hæŋk] *n* madeja *f*

◆**hanker after** *vt,* **hanker for** *vt* ansiar; **to ~ the past** sentir nostalgia del pasado

hankering *n* anhelo *m;* **to have a ~ for sth** ansiar algo

hankie *n,* **hanky** ['hæŋki] *n inf abbr of* **handkerchief** pañuelo *m*

hanky-panky [ˌhæŋki'pæŋki] *n no pl, inf* (*dishonest behaviour*) tejemanejes *mpl;* (*involving sex*) asunto *m*

hanukkah ['hɑːnəkə] *n* hanukah *m*

haphazard [hæp'hæzəd, *Am:* -ɚd] *adj* **1.** (*badly planned*) hecho, -a de cualquier manera **2.** (*random, arbitrary*) caprichoso, -a

hapless ['hæpləs] *adj* desafortunado, -a

happen ['hæpən] *vi* **1.** (*occur*) pasar; **if anything ~s to me ...** si me ocurre algo...; **these things ~** son cosas que pasan; **whatever ~s** pase lo que pase; **what's ~ed to your hand?** ¿qué te ha pasado en la mano?; **something amazing ~ed to her that day** aquel día le sucedió una cosa asombrosa **2.** (*chance*) **I ~ed to be at home** dio la casualidad de que estaba en casa; **it ~ed (that) ...** resultó que...; **as it ~s ...** da la casualidad de que...; **how does it ~ that ...?** ¿cómo puede ser que...?; **he/it ~s to be my best friend** pues resulta que es mi mejor amigo

happening ['hæpənɪŋ] *n* **1.** (*events*) suceso *m* **2.** (*performance*) happening *m*

happily ['hæpɪli] *adv* **1.** (*contentedly*) felizmente; **they lived ~ ever after** fueron felices y comieron perdices **2.** (*willingly*) con mucho gusto **3.** (*fortunately*) afortunadamente

happiness ['hæpɪnɪs] *n no pl* felicidad *f;* **I wish you every ~** que seas muy feliz

happy ['hæpi] <-ier, -iest> *adj* **1.** (*feeling very good*) feliz; **to be ~ that ...** estar contento de que...; **to be ~ to know that ...** alegrarse de saber que...; **I'm so ~ for you** me alegro mucho por ti; **to be ~ to do sth** estar encantado de hacer algo; **I'll be ~ to see you tomorrow morning** les recibiré con mucho gusto mañana por la mañana; **~ birthday!** ¡feliz cumpleaños!; **many ~ returns (of the day)!** ¡que cumplas muchos más! **2.** (*satisfied*) contento, -a; **to be ~ about sb/sth** estar contento con alguien/algo; **to be ~ doing sth** estar contento de hacer algo; **are you ~ with the idea?** ¿te parece bien la idea? **3.** (*fortunate*) afortunado, -a; **a ~ coincidence** una feliz coincidencia **4.** (*suitable: phrase, behaviour*) acertado, -a; **a ~ thought** una feliz idea

happy-go-lucky [ˌhæpigəʊ'lʌki, *Am:* -goʊ'-] *adj* despreocupado, -a

happy medium *n* justo medio *m*

harass ['hærəs, *Am:* hə'ræs] *vt* **1.** (*persistently annoy*) acosar; (*with cares*) abrumar; (*with troubles*) agobiar; **to ~ sb with questions** acosar a alguien a preguntas **2.** (*torment*) atormentar **3.** (*attack continually*) hostigar

harassed ['hærəst, *Am:* hə'ræst] *adj* agobiado, -a

harassment ['hærəsmənt, *Am:* hə'ræs-] *n no pl* **1.** (*pestering*) acoso *m;* **sexual ~** acoso sexual **2.** (*attack*) hostigamiento *m*

harbinger ['hɑːbɪndʒəʳ, *Am:* 'hɑːrbɪndʒɚ] *n liter* (*person*) precursor(a) *m(f);* (*thing*) presagio *m;* **a ~ of doom** un mal presagio

harbor *Am, Aus,* **harbour** ['hɑːbəʳ, *Am:* 'hɑːrbɚ] **I.** *n* **1.** (*port*) puerto *m;* **fishing ~** puerto pesquero **2.** *fig* (*shelter*) refugio *m* **II.** *vt* **1.** (*give shelter to*) dar cobijo a **2.** (*keep: feelings*) albergar; (*hopes*) abrigar; **to ~ suspicions** tener sospechas; **to ~ a grudge (against sb)** guardar rencor (a alguien) **3.** (*keep in hiding*) esconder; (*criminal*) encubrir **4.** (*contain*) contener

hard [hɑːd, *Am:* hɑːrd] **I.** *adj* **1.** (*firm, rigid*) duro, -a; (*rule*) estricto, -a; (*fate*) cruel; **~ times** malos tiempos; **to have a ~ time** pasarlo mal; **to give sb a ~ time** hacérselo pasar mal a alguien; **the ~ left/right** POL la extrema izquierda/derecha; **~ luck!**, **~ lines!** *Brit* ¡mala suerte! **2.** (*intense, concentrated*) **to take a (good) ~ look at sth** analizar algo detenidamente; **a ~ fight** una lucha encarnizada; **to be a ~ worker** ser muy trabajador **3.** (*forceful*) fuerte **4.** (*difficult, complex*) difícil; **to be ~ work for sb to do sth** ser muy difícil para alguien hacer algo; **to be ~ to please** ser difícil de contentar; **to get ~** complicarse; **a ~ bargain** un trato poco ventajoso; **to learn the ~ way** *fig* aprender a base de errores [*o* palos] **5.** (*severe*) severo, -a **6.** (*hostile, unkind*) **a ~ heart** un corazón de piedra; **to be ~ on sb/sth** ser duro con alguien/algo; **to be (as) ~ as nails** *fig* tener un corazón de piedra **7.** (*extremely cold*) riguroso, -a **8.** (*solid: evidence*) concluyente; (*fact*) innegable; **~ and fast information** información veraz **II.** *adv* **1.** (*forcefully*) fuerte; **to hit sb ~** pegar fuerte a alguien; **to press/pull ~** apretar/estirar con fuerza **2.** (*rigid*) **frozen ~** helado, -a **3.** (*energetically, vigorously*) mucho; **to fight ~** *fig* luchar con todas sus fuerzas; **to study/work ~** estudiar/trabajar mucho; **to try ~ to do sth** esforzarse en hacer algo; **to be ~ at it** trabajar con ahínco; **think ~** concéntrate; **to die ~** *fig* tardar en desaparecer **4.** (*intently*) detenidamente; **to look ~ at sth** estudiar algo con detenimiento **5.** (*closely*) **~ by** muy cerca; **~ upon** muy de cerca; **to be ~ up** no tener ni un céntimo **6.** (*heavy*) mucho; **it rained ~** llovió fuerte; **to take sth ~** tomarse algo muy mal; **I would be ~ pressed to choose one** me costaría mucho decidirme por uno

hardback ['hɑːdbæk, *Am:* 'hɑːrd-] **I.** *n* libro *m* de tapa dura; **in** ~ con tapa dura **II.** *adj* con tapa dura **hard-bitten** *adj* endurecido, -a **hardboard** *n no pl* chapa *m* de madera dura **hard-boiled** *adj* (*egg*) duro, -a; *inf* (*person*) endurecido, -a **hard cash** *n no pl* dinero *m* contante y sonante **hard copy** <-ies> *n* INFOR impresión *f* **hard core** *n* **1.** (*inner circle within group*) núcleo *m* duro **2.** *Brit* (*road foundation mixture*) balasto *m* **3.** (*pornography*) pornografía *f* dura **hard court** *n* pista *f* (de tenis) dura **hard currency** <-ies> *n* moneda *f* fuerte **hard disk** *n* INFOR disco *m* duro **hard drink** *n,* **hard liquor** *n* bebida *f* fuerte **hard drinker** *n* gran bebedor(a) *m(f)* **hard drug** *n* droga *f* dura **hard-earned** *adj* (*money*) ganado, -a con el sudor de la frente; (*rest, holiday*) merecido, -a

harden ['hɑːdn, *Am:* 'hɑːr-] **I.** *vt* **1.** (*make more solid, firmer*) endurecer; (*steel*) templar **2.** (*make tougher*) curtir; **to ~ oneself to sth** acostumbrarse a algo; **to become ~ed** curtirse; **life has ~ed his personality** la vida lo ha endurecido; **to ~ one's heart** *fig* mostrarse inflexible **3.** (*opinions, feelings*) afianzar; (*character*) confirmar **II.** *vi* **1.** (*become firmer: character*) endurecerse **2.** (*become inured*) **to ~ to sth** acostumbrarse a algo **3.** (*attitude*) volverse inflexible **4.** (*become confirmed: idea*) confirmarse; (*feeling, intention*) afianzarse

hard feelings [ˌhɑːd'fiːlɪŋz, *Am:* ˌhɑːrd-] *npl* resentimiento *m;* **no ~!** ¡olvidémoslo! **hard-fought** *adj* reñido, -a **hard hat** *n* casco *m* **hard-headed** *adj* realista **hard-hearted** *adj* duro, -a de corazón **hard-hit** *adj* muy afectado, -a; **to be ~ by sth** ser azotado por algo **hard-hitting** *adj* impactante **hard labor** *n Am,* **hard labour** *n Brit, Aus* LAW trabajos *mpl* forzados **hard line** *n no pl* POL línea *f* dura **hardliner** *n* POL radical

hardly ['hɑːdli, *Am:* 'hɑːrd-] *adv* **1.** (*barely*) apenas; **~ anything** casi nada; **~ ever** casi nunca; **she can ~ ...** apenas puede...; **she can ~ wait until tomorrow** tiene unas ganas locas de que llegue mañana **2.** (*certainly not*) **it's ~ my fault that it's raining** ¿qué culpa tengo de que llueva?; **you can ~ expect him to do that** no puedes esperar que haga eso; **~!** ¡qué va! *inf*

hardness ['hɑːdnɪs, *Am:* 'hɑːrd-] *n no pl* **1.** (*solidity*) dureza *f;* (*unfeelingness*) insensibilidad *f;* **~ of heart** dureza de corazón **2.** (*difficulty*) dificultad *f* **3.** (*of winter*) rigor *m*

hard-nosed [ˌhɑːd'nəʊzd, *Am:* ˌhɑːrd-'noʊzd] *adj* duro, -a **hard-pressed** *n* apurado, -a **hard sell** *n* venta *f* agresiva

hardship ['hɑːdʃɪp, *Am:* 'hɑːrd-] *n* (*suffering*) penas *fpl;* (*adversity*) adversidad *f;* (*deprivation*) penuria *f;* **to suffer great ~** pasar muchos apuros; **to live in ~** pasar privaciones

hard shoulder [ˌhɑːd'ʃəʊldəʳ, *Am:* ˌhɑːrd-'ʃoʊldɚ] *n Brit* arcén *m,* banquina *f Arg, Urug* **hardtop** *n* AUTO coche *m* no descapotable

hardware *n no pl* **1.** (*household articles*) ferretería *f;* **~ dealer** ferretero, -a *m, f* **2.** (*articles of metal*) quincallería *f* **3.** INFOR hardware *m;* **computer ~** soporte *m* físico del ordenador **4.** MIL armamento *m* **hard-wearing** *adj* resistente **hardwood** *n* madera *f* noble **hard-working** *adj* trabajador(a)

hardy ['hɑːdi, *Am:* 'hɑːr-] <-ier, -iest> *adj* (*person, animal*) fuerte; (*plant*) resistente

hare [heəʳ, *Am:* her] *n* liebre *f* ►**to run with the ~ and hunt with the** **hounds** *prov* servir a Dios y al diablo; **to be (as) mad as a (March) ~** *inf* estar más loco que una cabra

harebrained ['heəbreɪnd, *Am:* 'her-] *adj* disparatado, -a **harelip** *n* MED labio *m* leporino

harem ['hɑːriːm, *Am:* 'herəm] *n* HIST harén *m*

hark [hɑːk, *Am:* hɑːrk] *vi* **~!** HIST ¡escucha!; **~ who's talking!** *Brit, iron* ¡mira quién habla!; **to ~ back to sth** *fig* evocar algo

harm [hɑːm, *Am:* hɑːrm] **I.** *n no pl* daño *m;* **to do ~ to sb/sth** hacer daño a alguien/algo; **to do more ~ than good** hacer más mal que bien; **(to put) out of ~'s way** (poner) a salvo; **to see no ~ in sth** no ver nada malo en algo; **I meant no ~** no pretendía hacer daño; **you will come to no ~** no te va a pasar nada; **there's no ~ in trying** no se pierde nada con intentarlo **II.** *vt* **1.** (*hurt, ruin*) hacer daño; **it wouldn't ~ you to stay at home** *iron* no te morirás por quedarte en casa; (*reputation*) perjudicar **2.** (*spoil*) estropear

harmful ['hɑːmfəl, *Am:* 'hɑːrm-] *adj* dañino, -a; (*thing*) nocivo, -a; **to be ~ to sth** ser perjudicial para algo

harmless ['hɑːmlɪs, *Am:* 'hɑːrm-] *adj* (*animal, person*) inofensivo, -a; (*thing*) inocuo, -a; (*fun, joke*) inocente

harmonic [hɑː'mɒnɪk, *Am:* hɑːr'mɑːnɪk] *adj* armónico, -a

harmonica [hɑː'mɒnɪkə, *Am:* hɑːr'mɑːnɪ-] *n* MUS armónica *f,* rondín *m Bol, Ecua, Perú*

harmonious [hɑː'məʊnɪəs, *Am:* hɑːr-'moʊ-] *adj* armonioso, -a

harmonium [hɑː'məʊnɪəm, *Am:* hɑːr-'moʊ-] *n* MUS armonio *m*

harmonization [ˌhɑːmənɪ'zeɪʃən, *Am:* ˌhɑːr-] *n no pl* armonización *f*

harmonize ['hɑːmənaɪz, *Am:* 'hɑːr-] **I.** *vt* armonizar **II.** *vi* **to ~ (with sb/algo)** armonizar (con alguien/algo)

harmony ['hɑːməni, *Am:* 'hɑːr-] <-ies> *n* armonía *f;* **in ~ (with sb/sth)** en armonía (con alguien/algo)

harness ['hɑːnɪs, *Am:* 'hɑːr-] **I.** *n* **1.** (*of animal*) arnés *m;* (*for children*) correas *fpl;* **security ~** arnés de seguridad **2.** (*cooperation*) **to work in ~** trabajar en equipo **3.** (*everyday life*) **to get back in ~** *fig* volver a la rutina **II.** *vt* **1.** (*secure: horse*) poner los arreos a; **to ~ a horse/donkey to a carriage**

enganchar un caballo/burro a un carro **2.** (*exploit: resources*) aprovechar

harp [hɑːp, *Am:* hɑːrp] **I.** *n* arpa *f* **II.** *vi* **to ~ on about sth** (*talk about*) insistir sobre algo; (*complain*) quejarse de algo

harpoon [hɑːˈpuːn, *Am:* hɑːrˈ-] **I.** *n* arpón *m* **II.** *vt* arponear

harpsichord [ˈhɑːpsɪkɔːd, *Am:* ˈhɑːrpsɪkɔːrd] *n* MUS clavicémbalo *m*

harrow [ˈhærəʊ, *Am:* ˈheroʊ] **I.** *n* grada *f* **II.** *vt* **1.** AGR gradar **2.** (*disturb*) atormentar

harrowing *adj* (*story, experience*) desgarrador(a); (*prospect*) angustioso, -a

harsh [hɑːʃ, *Am:* hɑːrʃ] *adj* **1.** (*severe: education, parents*) severo, -a; (*punishment*) duro, -a **2.** (*unfair: criticism*) cruel; (*words, reality*) duro, -a **3.** (*unfriendly*) desabrido, -a **4.** (*uncomfortable: light*) fuerte; (*climate, winter*) riguroso, -a; (*terrain*) desolado, -a; (*contrast*) violento, -a **5.** (*rough*) áspero, -a **6.** (*unaesthetic: colour*) chillón, -ona **7.** (*unpleasant to the ear: sound*) discordante; (*voice*) estridente

hart [hɑːt, *Am:* hɑːrt] *n* HIST ciervo *m*

harum-scarum [ˌheərəmˈskeərəm, *Am:* ˌherəmˈskerəm] **I.** *adv* alocadamente **II.** *adj* atolondrado, -a

harvest [ˈhɑːvɪst, *Am:* ˈhɑːr-] **I.** *n* (*of crops*) cosecha *f;* (*of grape*) vendimia *f;* (*of vegetables*) recolección *f;* **the apple ~** la cosecha de la manzana; **a good ~ of potatoes** una buena cosecha de patatas **II.** *vt a. fig* cosechar; (*grape*) vendimiar; (*vegetables*) recolectar; **to ~ a field** hacer la cosecha en un campo **III.** *vi* cosechar

harvester *n* **1.** (*machine*) **combine ~** cosechadora *f* **2.** (*person*) recolector(a) *m(f);* (*of grain*) segador(a) *m(f);* (*of grape*) vendimiador(a) *m(f)*

harvest festival *n* fiesta *f* de la cosecha

harvest moon *n* luna *f* llena de otoño

has [həz, *stressed:* hæz] *3rd pers sing of* **have**

has-been [ˈhæzbiːn, *Am:* -bɪn] *n inf* vieja gloria *f;* **to be a ~** ser alguien que ya ha pasado a la historia

hash¹ [hæʃ] **I.** *vt* GASTR picar **II.** *n* **1.** GASTR picadillo *m* **2.** *no pl, inf* lío *m;* **to make a ~ of sth** armarse un lío con algo

◆**hash up** *vt* volver a hacer

hash² [hæʃ] *n inf* chocolate *m*

hash browns *npl Am: patatas hervidas y después fritas*

hashish [ˈhæʃiːʃ] *n no pl* hachís *m inv*

hasn't [ˈhæznt] = **has not** *s.* **have**

hassle [ˈhæsl] **I.** *n no pl, inf* (*bother*) lío *m;* **to give sb ~** fastidiar a alguien; **it's such a ~** es un jaleo **II.** *vt inf* fastidiar; **to ~ sb to do sth** estar encima a alguien para que haga algo

hassock [ˈhæsək] *n* **1.** (*tuft of grass*) mata *f* de hierba **2.** (*in church*) cojín *m* (para arrodillarse)

haste [heɪst] *n no pl* prisa *f;* **to make ~** apresurarse; **in ~** de prisa ►**more ~ less speed** *prov* vísteme despacio, que tengo prisa *prov*

hasten [ˈheɪsn] **I.** *vt form* acelerar; **to ~ sb** dar prisa a alguien; **to ~ one's steps** apresurar el paso **II.** *vi* apresurarse; **to ~ to do sth** apresurarse a hacer algo

hasty [ˈheɪsti] <-ier, -iest> *adj* **1.** (*fast*) rápido, -a; **to beat a ~ retreat** *a. fig* retirarse a toda prisa **2.** (*rashly*) precipitado, -a; **to make ~ decisions** tomar decisiones irreflexivamente; **to leap to ~ conclusions** sacar conclusiones precipitadas; **to be ~ in doing sth** precipitarse en algo

hat [hæt] *n* sombrero *m;* **to pass round the ~** pasar la gorra ►**I'll eat my ~ if ...** que me maten si...; **to keep sth under one's ~** no decir ni una palabra sobre algo; **to talk through one's ~** *inf* decir bobadas; **my ~!** ¡caracoles!

hatch¹ [hætʃ] **I.** *vi* salir del cascarón **II.** *vt* **1.** (*chick*) incubar, empollar **2.** (*devise in secret*) tramar; **to ~ a plan** urdir un plan

hatch² [hætʃ] <-es> *n* trampilla *f;* (*between kitchen and dining room*) ventanilla *f;* NAUT escotilla ►**down the ~!** ¡salud!

hatch³ [hætʃ] *vt* sombrear

hatchback [ˈhætʃbæk] *n* AUTO coche *m* con puerta trasera

hatchet [ˈhætʃɪt] *n* hacha *f* (pequeña) ►**to bury the ~** enterrar el hacha de guerra

hatchet-faced *adj inf* de cara chupada

hatchet man *n inf* **1.** (*employee*) *encargado de los trabajos sucios* **2.** (*thug*) matón *m*

hatching [ˈhætʃɪŋ] *n no pl* salida *f* del huevo

hate [heɪt] **I.** *n* odio *m;* **to feel ~ for sb** odiar a alguien; **one of my pet ~s is ...** una de las cosas que más odio es... **II.** *vt* odiar; **to ~ sb's guts** *inf* odiar a alguien a muerte

hateful [ˈheɪtfəl] *adj* odioso, -a

hatpin [ˈhætpɪn] *n* alfiler *m* de sombrero

hatred [ˈheɪtrɪd] *n no pl* odio *m;* **~ of sb/sth** odio a [*o* hacia] alguien/algo

hatstand [ˈhætstænd] *n* percha *f* para sombreros

hatter [ˈhætəʳ, *Am:* ˈhæt̬ɚ] *n* **to be as mad as a ~** estar como una cabra

hat-trick [ˈhættrɪk] *n* SPORTS *tres goles marcados por un mismo jugador;* **to score a ~** marcar tres tantos

haughty [ˈhɔːti, *Am:* ˈhɑːt̬i] <-ier, iest> *adj* altivo, -a

haul [hɔːl, *Am:* hɑːl] **I.** *vt* **1.** (*pull with effort*) arrastrar; **to ~ up the sail** izar la vela; **to ~ a boat out of the water** sacar una barca del agua **2.** (*transport goods*) transportar **II.** *n* **1.** (*distance*) trayecto *m;* **long ~ flight** vuelo *m* intercontinental; **in** [*o* **over**] **the long ~** *fig* a la larga **2.** (*quantity caught: of fish, shrimp*) redada *f;* (*of stolen goods*) botín *m* **3.** (*tug*) tirón *m,* jalón *m CSur;* **to give a ~** dar un tirón

◆**haul down** *vt* (*flag, sail*) arriar

◆**haul off** *vi* NAUT cambiar de rumbo

◆**haul up** *vt inf* **to haul sb up before sb**

hacer que alguien dé explicaciones a alguien

haulage ['hɔːlɪdʒ, *Am:* 'hɑː-] *n no pl* **1.** (*transportation*) transporte *m* **2.** (*costs*) gastos *mpl* de transporte

haulage business *n,* **haulage company** *n* empresa *f* de transportes **haulage contractor** *n* transportista *mf* **haulage firm** *n s.* **haulage company**

hauler ['hɔːləʳ, *Am:* 'hɑːlɚ] *n Am,* **haulier** ['hɔːliəʳ, *Am:* 'hɑːljɚ] *n Brit, Aus* (*business*) empresa *f* de transportes; (*person*) transportista *mf*

haunch [hɔːntʃ, *Am:* hɑːntʃ] <-es> *n* **1.** ANAT cadera *f;* **to sit on one's ~es** ponerse de [*o* en] cuclillas **2.** (*of meat*) pierna *f*

haunt [hɔːnt, *Am:* hɑːnt] **I.** *vt* **1.** (*ghost*) rondar **2.** (*plague, bother*) perseguir; **to be ~ed by memories of an unhappy childhood** perseguir (a alguien) los recuerdos de una infancia infeliz; **to be ~ed by sth** estar obsesionado por algo **3.** (*frequent*) frecuentar; **to ~ a place** rondar un lugar **II.** *n* lugar *m* preferido; **a student ~** un lugar frecuentado por los estudiantes

haunted *adj* **1.** (*frequented by ghosts*) embrujado, -a **2.** (*troubled: look*) angustiado, -a, preocupado, -a

haunting *adj* **1.** (*disturbing*) **a ~ fear/memory** un miedo/recuerdo recurrente e inquietante **2.** (*memorable*) **to have a ~ beauty** tener una belleza evocadora; **a ~ melody** una melodía inolvidable

Havana [hə'vænə] *n* La Habana

have [həv, *stressed:* hæv] **I.** <has, had, had> *vt* **1.** (*own*) tener, poseer; **she's got two brothers** tiene dos hermanos; **~ you got a cold? – no, I've got a headache** ¿estás resfriado? – no, me duele la cabeza; **to ~ sth to do** tener algo que hacer **2.** (*engage in*) **to ~ a walk** pasear; **to ~ a talk with sb** hablar con alguien; **to ~ a bath/shower** bañarse/ducharse; **to ~ a nap** echar una cabezadita; **to ~ a game** echar una partida **3.** (*eat*) **to ~ lunch** comer; **I ~n't had shrimp in ages!** ¡hace años que no como gambas!; **to ~ some coffee** tomar un poco de café **4.** (*give birth to*) **to ~ a child** tener un hijo **5.** (*receive*) tener, recibir; **to ~ news of sb** tener [*o* recibir] noticias de alguien; **to ~ visitors** tener visita **6.** (*prepare*) **to ~ dinner ready** tener la cena preparada **7.** (*cause to occur*) **to not ~ sb/sth doing sth** no dejar que alguien/algo haga algo; **I'll ~ Bob give you a ride home** le pediré [*o* diré] a Bob que te lleve a casa **8.** (*understand*) **I kept telling him you were French, but he wouldn't ~ it** le dije una y otra vez que eras francesa, pero él no bajaba del burro ►**to ~ done with it** acabar con el asunto; **to ~ it in for sb** *inf* tenerla tomada con alguien; **to ~ it in one to do sth** ser capaz de hacer algo; **I didn't think she had it in her!** ¡no pensaba que fuera capaz de eso!; **if she finds out about what you've done, you've ~ it!** *inf* si se entera de lo que has hecho, ¡estás listo!; **to ~ had it with sb/sth** *inf* haber tenido más que suficiente de alguien/algo **II.** <has, had, had> *aux* (*indicates perfect tense*) **he has never been to Scotland** nunca ha estado en Escocia; **we had been swimming** habíamos estado nadando; **to ~ got to do sth** *Brit, Aus* tener que hacer algo; **what time ~ we got to be there?** ¿a qué hora tenemos que estar allí?; **do we ~ to finish this today?** ¿tenemos que acabar esto hoy?; **had I known you were coming, ...** *form* si hubiera sabido que ibas a venir,...

◆**have around** *vt always sep* (*gadget*) tener a mano

◆**have back** *vt always sep* **can I have it back?** ¿me lo devuelves?; **they solved their problems and she had him back** resolvieron sus diferencias y ella le abrió las puertas de casa de nuevo

◆**have in** *vt always sep* invitar; **they had some experts in** llamaron a algunos expertos

◆**have off** *vt* **1.** *Brit, Aus, inf* (*have sexual intercourse*) **to have it off with sb** hacerlo con alguien **2.** (*remove: clothes*) quitar

◆**have on** *vt always sep* **1.** (*wear: clothes*) llevar (puesto); **he didn't have any clothes on** estaba desnudo **2.** (*carry*) **to have sth on oneself** llevar algo encima; **have you got any money on you?** ¿llevas dinero contigo? **3.** *Brit, inf* (*fool*) **to have sb on** tomar el pelo a alguien **4.** (*plan*) **have you got anything on this week?** ¿tienes planes para esta semana?

◆**have out** *vt always sep* **1.** (*remove*) sacar **2.** *inf* (*argue*) **to have it out with sb** tenerla con alguien

◆**have over** *vt always sep* invitar

◆**have up** *vt always sep* **1.** (*invite*) invitar **2.** *Brit, inf* (*take to court for a trial*) llevar a juicio

haven ['heɪvn] *n* refugio *m*

have-nots ['hævnɒts] *npl* **the ~** los pobres

haven't ['hævnt] = **have not** *s.* **have**

haves [hævz] *npl* **the ~ and the have-nots** los ricos y los pobres

havoc ['hævək] *n no pl* estragos *mpl;* **the ~ of the fire/the storm** los estragos del fuego/de la tormenta; **to play ~ with sth** hacer estragos de algo; **to wreak ~ on sth** desbaratar algo

Havre ['hɑːvrə] *n* **Le ~** El Havre

haw [hɔː, *Am:* hɑː] **I.** *interj* (*to horse*) ¡ria! **II.** *vi* **to hem and ~** *Am,* **to hum and ~** *Brit, Aus* vacilar

Hawaii [hə'waɪiː, *Am:* hə'wɑː-] *n* Hawai *m*

Hawaiian [hə'waɪjən, *Am:* hə'wɑː-] **I.** *n* **1.** (*person*) hawaiano, -a *m, f* **2.** LING hawaiano *m* **II.** *adj* hawaiano, -a

hawk [hɔːk, *Am:* hɑːk] **I.** *n* halcón *m* **II.** *vt* (*wares*) pregonar **III.** *vi* carraspear

hawker *n* vendedor(a) *m(f)* ambulante

hawk-eyed [ˌhɔːk'aɪd, *Am:* ˌhɑːk-] *adj* **to be ~** tener ojos de lince

hawk moth *n* esfinge *m*

hawser ['hɔ:zəʳ, *Am:* 'hɑ:zɚ] *n* NAUT guindaleza *f*
hawthorn ['hɔ:θɔ:n, *Am:* 'hɑ:θɔ:rn] *n no pl* BOT espino *m*
hay [heɪ] *n no pl* heno *m* ▸**to make ~ while the sun shines** aprovechar la oportunidad cuando se presenta; **to hit the ~** *inf* acostarse
haycock ['heɪkɒk, *Am:* -kɑ:k, -] *n* montón *m* de heno **hay fever** *n no pl* fiebre *f* del heno **hayrick** *n,* **haystack** *n* almiar *m* **haywire** *adj inf* **to go/be ~** (*person*) volverse/estar loco; (*machine*) estropearse
hazard ['hæzəd, *Am:* -ɚd] **I.** *n* **1.** (*danger*) peligro *m* **2.** *no pl* (*risk*) riesgo *m;* **fire ~** peligro de incendio; **health ~** riesgo para la salud **II.** *vt* **1.** aventurar; **to ~ a guess at sth** aventurar una respuesta a algo **2.** (*risk*) arriesgar
hazardous ['hæzədəs, *Am:* -ɚ-] *adj* (*dangerous*) peligroso, -a; (*risky*) arriesgado, -a
hazard (warning) lights *npl* AUTO luces *fpl* de emergencia
haze [heɪz] **I.** *n* **1.** (*mist*) neblina *f;* **~ of dust** nube *f* de polvo; **heat ~** calina *f* **2.** (*mental*) aturdimiento *m* **II.** *vt Am* hacer novatadas a
hazel ['heɪzl] **I.** *adj* color avellana **II.** *n* BOT avellano *m*
hazelnut ['heɪzlnʌt] *n* BOT avellana *f*
hazy ['heɪzi] <-ier, -iest> *adj* **1.** (*with bad visibility*) neblinoso, -a **2.** (*confused, unclear*) vago, -a
h & c *abbr of* **hot and cold (water)** (agua *f*) caliente y fría
HDTV [ˌeɪtʃdi:ti:'vi:] *n* TV *abbr of* **high-definition television** televisión *f* de alta definición
he [hi:] **I.** *pron pers* **1.** (*male person or animal*) él; **~'s** [*o* **~ is**] **my father** (él) es mi padre; **~'s gone away but ~'ll be back soon** se ha ido, pero volverá pronto; **here ~ comes** ahí viene **2.** (*unspecified sex*) **if somebody comes, ~ will buy it** si alguien viene, lo comprará; **~ who ...** *form* aquél que... **II.** *n* (*of baby*) varón *m;* (*of animal*) macho *m*
head [hed] **I.** *n* **1.** ANAT cabeza *f;* **to nod one's ~** asentir con la cabeza **2.** *no pl* (*unit*) cabeza *f;* **a** [*o* **per**] **~** por cabeza; **a hundred ~ of cattle** cien cabezas de ganado; **to be a ~ taller than sb** sacar una cabeza a alguien **3.** (*mind*) **to clear one's ~** aclararse las ideas; **to get sth/sb out of one's ~** sacarse algo/a alguien de la cabeza; **to have a good ~ for figures** tener cabeza para los números; **to need a clear ~ to do sth** necesitar tener la cabeza clara para hacer algo **4.** *no pl* (*top: of queue*) cabeza *f;* (*of bed, table*) cabecera *f* **5.** BOT cabeza *f;* **a ~ of lettuce** una lechuga **6.** *no pl* (*letter top*) encabezamiento *m* **7.** *pl* FIN (*coin face*) cara *f;* **~s or tails?** ¿cara o cruz? **8.** (*beer foam*) espuma *f* **9.** GEO (*of river*) nacimiento *m* **10.** (*boss*) jefe, -a *m, f* **11.** *Brit* (*headteacher*) director(a) *m(f)* de colegio **12.** TECH (*device*) cabezal *m* **13.** INFOR **read/write ~** cabeza *f* de lectura/escritura ▸**to have one's ~ in the clouds** tener la cabeza llena de pájaros; **to be ~ over heels in love** estar locamente enamorado; **to fall ~ over heels in love with sb** enamorarse locamente de alguien; **to bury one's ~ in the sand** hacer como el avestruz; **to be ~ and shoulders above sb/sth** dar cien vueltas a alguien/algo; **to not be able to make ~ (n)or tail of sth** no entender ni jota de algo; **~s I win, tales you lose** o gano yo o gano yo; **to bang one's ~ against a brick wall** darse de cabeza contra la pared; **to keep one's ~ above water** mantenerse a flote; **to keep one's ~ down** (*to avoid attention*) mantenerse al margen; (*to work hard*) no levantar la cabeza; **to hold one's ~ high** mantener la cabeza alta; **to be off one's ~** *inf* (*crazy*) estar mal de la cabeza; **to be out of one's ~** *inf* (*drunk*) estar pedo; (*stoned*) estar colocado; **to be soft in the ~** estar un poco tocado; **to have one's ~ screwed on (right)** tener la cabeza bien puesta; **to go straight to sb's ~** (*alcohol, wine*) subírse a la cabeza a alguien; **to bite sb's ~ off** echar una bronca a alguien; **to bring sth to a ~** llevar algo a un punto crítico; **to give sb his/her ~** dejar a alguien obrar a su antojo; **to laugh one's ~ off** desternillarse de risa; **~s will roll** van a rodar cabezas; **to scream one's ~ off** gritar a voz en grito **II.** *vt* **1.** (*lead*) encabezar; (*a firm, organization*) dirigir; (*team*) capitanear **2.** PUBL encabezar **3.** SPORTS (*ball*) cabecear **III.** *vi* **to ~ (for) home** dirigirse hacia casa
◆**head back** *vi* volver, regresar
◆**head for** *vt insep* ir rumbo a; **to ~ the exit** dirigirse hacia la salida; **to ~ disaster** ir camino del desastre
◆**head off** **I.** *vt* cortar el paso a **II.** *vi* **to ~ towards** salir hacia
◆**head up** *vt* dirigir
headache ['hedeɪk] *n* dolor *m* de cabeza **headband** *n* cinta *f* de pelo **headbanger** *n inf* heavy *mf* **head cold** *n* resfriado *m* **head cook** *n* jefe, -a *m, f* de cocina **headdress** <-es> *n* tocado *m*
header ['hedəʳ, *Am:* -ɚ] *n* **1.** SPORTS cabezazo *m;* **to take a ~ into the water** tirarse de cabeza al agua **2.** INFOR cabecera *f*
headfirst ['hed'fɜ:st, *Am:* -'fɜ:rst] *adv* de cabeza; **to fall ~** caer de cabeza **headhunt** *vt* ECON cazar talentos **headhunter** *n* **1.** (*warrior*) cazador *m* de cabezas **2.** ECON cazatalentos *mf inv*
heading ['hedɪŋ] *n* (*of chapter*) encabezamiento *m;* (*letterhead*) membrete *m*
headland [ˌhedlænd] *n* cabo *m* **headless** *adj* sin cabeza **headlight** *n,* **headlamp** *n* faro *m* **headline** **I.** *n* titular *m* ▸**to hit the ~s** salir en primera plana **II.** *vt* titular **headlong** *Am, Aus* **I.** *adv* precipitadamente; **to rush ~ into sth** hacer algo de forma precipitada **II.** *adj* precipitado, -a **headmaster** *n* director *m* de colegio **headmistress** <-es> *n* directora *f* de colegio **head office** *n* (oficina *f*) central *f* **head of state** <heads of state> *n* jefe, -a

m, f de Estado **head-on** I. *adj* (*collision*) frontal II. *adv* frontalmente, de frente **headphones** *npl* auriculares *mpl* **headquarters** *n+ sing/pl vb* MIL cuartel *m* general; (*of company*) oficina *f* central; (*of party*) sede *f;* (*of the police*) jefatura *f* de policía **headrest** *n* reposacabezas *m inv* **head restraint** *n* apoyacabezas *m inv* **headroom** *n no pl* altura *f* **headscarf** <-scarves> *n* pañuelo *m* para la cabeza **headset** *n* auriculares *mpl* **headship** *n* 1. ADMIN dirección *f* 2. *Brit* SCHOOL dirección *f* de un colegio **headshrinker** *n inf* (*psychiatrist*) loquero, -a *m, f* **head start** *n* ventaja *f;* **to give sb a ~** dar ventaja a alguien **headstone** *n* lápida *f* **headstrong** *adj* testarudo, -a **headteacher** *n* director(a) *m(f)* de un colegio **head waiter** *n* jefe *m* de comedor, maître *m* **headwaters** *npl* GEO cabecera *f* (de un río) **headway** *n no pl* progreso *m;* **to make ~** hacer progresos **headwind** *n* viento *m* contrario [*o* en contra]; NAUT viento *f* de proa **headword** *n* encabezamiento *m*

heady ['hedi] <-ier, -iest> *adj* 1. (*intoxicating*) embriagador(a) 2. (*exciting*) emocionante

heal [hiːl] I. *vt* (*wound*) curar; (*differences*) salvar II. *vi* (*wound, injury*) cicatrizar

health [helθ] *n no pl* salud *f;* **to be in good/bad ~** estar bien/mal de salud; **to drink to sb's ~** beber a la salud de alguien

healthcare ['helθkeəʳ, *Am:* -ker] *n no pl* asistencia *f* sanitaria [*o* médica] **health center** *n Am,* **health centre** *n Brit* centro *m* médico **health certificate** *n* certificado *m* médico **health club** *n* gimnasio *m* **health farm** *n* balneario *m* **health food** *n no pl* alimentos *mpl* naturales **health food shop** *n,* **health food store** *n* tienda *f* de productos naturales **health hazard** *n* riesgo *m* para la salud **health insurance** *n no pl* seguro *m* médico **health resort** *n Am* (*health farm*) balneario *m* **health service** *n Brit* servicio *m* sanitario **health visitor** *n Brit* MED *enfermera que hace visitas a domicilio para asesorar sobre el cuidado de los niños y de los ancianos*

healthy ['helθi] <-ier, -iest> *adj* 1. MED sano, -a 2. FIN (*strong*) próspero, -a; (*profit*) sustancial 3. (*positive*) positivo, -a

heap [hiːp] I. *n* (*pile*) pila *f,* montón *m;* **to collapse in a ~** *fig* (*person*) caer desplomado; **a (whole) ~ of work** *inf* un montón de trabajo II. *vt* amontonar, apilar; **to ~ sth with sth** llenar algo de algo

hear [hɪəʳ, *Am:* hɪr] <heard, heard> I. *vt* 1. (*perceive*) oír 2. (*be told*) enterarse de; **to ~ that ...** enterarse de que..., oír que... 3. (*listen*) escuchar; **Lord, ~ our prayers** REL escúchanos, Señor II. *vi* 1. (*perceive*) oír; **to ~ very well** oír muy bien 2. (*get news*) enterarse; **to ~ of [*o* about] sth** enterarse de algo ▶**~, ~!** ¡muy bien!

heard [hɜːd, *Am:* hɜːrd] *pt, pp of* **hear**

hearing ['hɪərɪŋ, *Am:* 'hɪr-] *n* 1. *no pl* (*sense*) oído *m* 2. (*act*) audición *f* 3. (*range*) **in sb's ~** en presencia de alguien 4. LAW vista *f*

hearing aid *n* audífono *m*

hearsay ['hɪəseɪ, *Am:* 'hɪr-] *n no pl* habladurías *fpl;* **by ~** de oídas

hearse [hɜːs, *Am:* hɜːrs] *n* coche *m* fúnebre

heart [hɑːt, *Am:* hɑːrt] *n* 1. ANAT corazón *m* 2. (*seat of emotions*) **to break sb's ~** partir el corazón a alguien; **to have a cold ~** ser duro de corazón; **to have a change of ~** cambiar de opinión; **to have a good [*o* kind] ~** tener buen corazón; **to lose ~** desanimarse; **to lose one's ~ (to sb/sth)** enamorarse (de alguien/algo); **to pour one's ~ out to sb** desahogarse con alguien; **to take ~** animarse; **her ~ sank** se le cayó el alma a los pies 3. *no pl* (*centre*) centro *m;* **to get to the ~ of the matter** llegar al fondo de la cuestión 4. GASTR (*of lettuce*) cogollo *m;* **artichoke ~s** corazones *mpl* de alcachofa 5. *pl* (*card suit*) corazones *mpl;* (*in Spanish pack*) copas *fpl* ▶**he had his ~ in his boots** *Brit, inf* tenía el ánimo por los suelos; **to one's ~'s content** hasta quedarse satisfecho; **to have a ~ of gold** tener un corazón de oro, ser todo corazón; **to have one's ~ in the right place** tener buen corazón; **to wear one's ~ on one's sleeve** ir con el corazón en la mano; **to have a ~ of stone** tener un corazón de piedra; **with all one's ~** con toda su alma; **on your own ~ be it** por tu cuenta y riesgo; **she is a girl after my own ~** es una chica de las que a mí me gustan; **to not have the ~ to do sth** no tener el valor para hacer algo; **by ~** de memoria

heartache ['hɑːteɪk, *Am:* 'hɑːrt-] *n no pl* pena *f* **heart attack** *n* ataque *m* al corazón **heartbeat** *n* latido *m* (del corazón) **heartbreak** *n no pl* pena *f* **heartbreaking** *adj* desgarrador(a) **heartbroken** *adj* con el corazón partido **heartburn** *n no pl* acidez *f* de estómago **heart disease** *n no pl* enfermedad *f* coronaria

heartening ['hɑːtənɪŋ, *Am:* 'hɑːrt-] *adj* alentador(a)

heart failure *n no pl* colapso *m* cardíaco

heartfelt ['hɑːtfelt, *Am:* 'hɑːrt-] *adj* sincero, -a; **my ~ condolences** mi más sentido pésame; **~ relief** gran alivio

hearth [hɑːθ, *Am:* hɑːrθ] *n* 1. (*of fire place*) chimenea *f* 2. *liter* (*home*) hogar *m;* **to leave ~ and home** abandonar el hogar

hearth rug *n* alfombrilla *f* (de la chimenea)

heartily *adv* con efusividad; **to dislike sth/sb ~** detestar algo/a alguien; **to eat ~** comer con ganas

heartland ['hɑːtlænd, *Am:* 'hɑːrt-] *n* centro *m;* **the economic ~** el corazón económico

heartless ['hɑːtləs, *Am:* 'hɑːrt-] *adj* sin corazón

heart murmur *n* soplo *m* cardíaco

heartrending ['hɑːtˌrendɪŋ, *Am:* 'hɑːrt-] *adj* desgarrador(a)

heart-searching ['hɑːtˌsɜːtʃɪŋ, *Am:* 'hɑːrt-] *n no pl* examen *m* de conciencia **heart-strings** *npl* **to pull at sb's ~** *fig* tocar la fibra sensible a alguien **heart-throb** *n inf* ídolo *m* **heart-to-heart I.** *n* conversación *f* franca y abierta **II.** *adj* franco, -a y abierto, -a **heart transplant** *n* trasplante *m* de corazón

heartwarming ['hɑːtˌwɔːmɪŋ, *Am:* 'hɑːrt-ˌwɔːr-] *adj* reconfortante

hearty ['hɑːti, *Am:* 'hɑːrt̬i] *adj* <-ier, -iest> **1.** (*enthusiastic*) entusiasta; **~ congratulations** felicidades de todo corazón; **~ welcome** bienvenida calurosa **2.** (*large, strong*) fuerte; **~ appetite** buen apetito; **a ~ breakfast** un desayuno opíparo; **to have a ~ dislike for sth** tener manía a algo; **hale and ~** sano y fuerte

heat [hiːt] **I.** *n no pl* **1.** (*warmth, high temperature*) calor; **in the ~ of the day** cuando más calor hace; **to cook sth on a high/low ~** cocinar algo a fuego rápido/lento **2.** (*heating system*) calefacción *f;* **to turn down the ~** bajar la calefacción **3.** (*emotional state*) acaloramiento *m;* **in the ~ of the argument** en el momento más acalorado de la discusión **4.** (*sports race*) eliminatoria *f* **5.** *no pl* ZOOL celo *m;* **to be on ~** estar en celo ►**if you can't take the ~, get out of the kitchen** *prov* quien no aguante la presión, que no se meta en la olla *prov;* **to put the ~ on sb** presionar a alguien; **to take the ~ off sb** dar un respiro a alguien **II.** *vt* **1.** (*make hot*) calentar **2.** (*excite*) acalorar **III.** *vi* (*become hot*) calentarse; *fig* (*inflame*) acalorarse

◆**heat up I.** *vi* calentarse **II.** *vt* calentar

heated *adj* **1.** (*window*) térmico, -a; (*pool*) climatizado, -a; (*room*) caldeado, -a **2.** (*argument*) acalorado, -a

heatedly *adv* acaloradamente; **to ~ deny sth** negar algo con vehemencia

heater ['hiːtəʳ, *Am:* -t̬ɚ] *n* calefactor *m;* **water ~** calentador *m* de agua

heat exchanger *n* (inter)cambiador *m* térmico **heat gauge** *n* termostato *m*

heath [hiːθ] *n* brezal *m*

heathen ['hiːðn] **I.** *n* pagano, -a *m, f;* **the ~** los infieles **II.** *adj* pagano, -a

heather ['heðəʳ, *Am:* -ɚ] *n no pl* brezo *m*

heating *n no pl* calefacción *f*

heating engineer *n* técnico, -a *m, f* de la calefacción **heating system** *n* sistema *m* de calefacción

heat pump *n* bomba *f* de calor [*o* térmica] **heat rash** <-es> *n* sarpullido *m* **heat-resistant** *adj,* **heat-resisting** *adj* resistente al calor **heat-seeking** *adj* MIL termodirigido, -a **heat shield** *n* blindaje *m* térmico **heat stroke** *n* insolación *f* **heat treatment** *n* termotratamiento *m* **heatwave** *n* ola *f* de calor

heave [hiːv] **I.** *vi* **1.** (*pull*) tirar; (*push*) empujar **2.** (*move up and down*) subir y bajar; **to ~ into view** NAUT aparecer **3.** (*vomit*) tener bascas **II.** *vt* **1.** (*pull*) tirar; (*push*) empujar; **he ~d the door open** abrió la puerta de un empujón; **to ~ a sigh (of relief)** dar un suspiro (de alivio); **to ~ sth at sb** lanzar algo a alguien **2.** (*lift*) levantar **III.** *n* **1.** (*push*) empujón *m;* (*pull*) tirón *m* **2.** (*great effort*) gran esfuerzo *m*

◆**heave to** *vi* <hove to, hoved to> NAUT ponerse al pairo

◆**heave up** *vi* vomitar

heaven ['hevən] *n* cielo *m;* **to go to ~** ir al cielo; **it's ~** *fig, inf* es divino, es fantástico; **to be ~ on earth** *fig* (*place*) ser paradisiaco; **to be in ~** *a. fig* estar en el cielo; **the ~s** (*sky*) el cielo ►**to move ~ and earth** remover Roma con Santiago, mover cielo y tierra; **what/where/when/who/why in ~'s name ...?** ¿qué/dónde/cuándo/quién/por qué demonios...?; **for ~s sake!** ¡por Dios!; **good ~s!** ¡santo cielo!; **to stink to high ~** oler a perro muerto; **~ only knows** sólo Dios lo sabe; **to be in seventh ~** estar en el séptimo cielo; **~ help us** que Dios nos ayude; **thank ~s** gracias a Dios

heavenly ['hevənli] *adj* <-ier, -iest> **1.** (*of heaven*) celestial; **~ body** cuerpo *m* celeste **2.** (*wonderful*) divino, -a

heavens *npl liter* firmamento *m*

heaven-sent [ˌhevən'sent] *adj* caído, -a del cielo

heavy ['hevi] **I.** *adj* <-ier, -iest> **1.** (*weighing a lot*) pesado, -a; **~ food** comida pesada **2.** (*difficult*) difícil; (*schedule*) apretado, -a; **the book was rather ~ going** la lectura del libro era bastante pesada **3.** (*strong*) fuerte; **~ fall** *a.* ECON fuerte descenso **4.** (*not delicate, coarse*) poco delicado, -a; (*features*) basto, -a **5.** (*severe*) severo, -a; (*responsibility*) fuerte; (*sea*) grueso, -a; **~ casualties** muchas bajas; **to be ~ on sb** ser duro con alguien **6.** (*abundant*) abundante; (*investment*) cuantioso, -a; **~ frost/gale** fuertes heladas/chubascos; **to be ~ on sth** consumir mucho de algo; **to be ~ with sth** estar cargado de algo **7.** (*excessive*) **~ drinker/smoker** bebedor/fumador empedernido; **~ sleep** sueño profundo **8.** (*thick*) grueso, -a; (*beard*) denso, -a; (*sky*) encapotado, -a; (*shoe*) resistente **II.** *n* <-ies> *inf* matón *m*

heavy-duty [ˌhevi'djuːti, *Am:* -'duːt̬i] *adj* resistente; (*machine*) resistente; (*vehicle*) (muy) resistente **heavy-going** *adj* dificultoso, -a **heavy goods vehicle** *n* vehículo *m* pesado **heavy-handed** *adj* **1.** (*clumsy*) torpe **2.** (*harsh*) duro, -a **heavy-hearted** *adj* afligido, -a **heavy industry** *n no pl* industria *f* pesada **heavy metal** *n* **1.** (*lead, cadmium*) metal *m* pesado **2.** MUS heavy *m* (metal) **heavy water** *n* agua *f* pesada **heavyweight I.** *adj* **1.** SPORTS (de la categoría) de los pesos pesados **2.** (*cloth*) resistente **3.** (*important*) serio, -a e importante **II.** *n a. fig* peso pesado *m*

Hebrew [hiː'bruː] **I.** *n* **1.** (*person*) hebreo, -a *m, f* **2.** LING hebreo *m* **II.** *adj* hebreo, -a

Hebrides ['hebrɪdiːz] *n* **the** ~ las Hébridas
heck [hek] *interj inf* caramba; **where the ~ have you been?** ¿dónde demonios habéis estado?; **what the ~!** ¿qué más da?
heckle ['hekl] *vi, vt* interrumpir con preguntas [*o* comentarios]
heckler ['heklə^r, *Am:* -ɚ] *n* persona *f* que interrumpe
hectare ['hekteə^r, *Am:* -ter] *n* hectárea *f*
hectic ['hektɪk] **I.** *adj* ajetreado, -a; ~ **fever** fiebre hé(c)tica; ~ **pace** ritmo intenso **II.** *n* MED hé(c)tico, -a *m, f*
hectoliter *n Am,* **hectolitre** ['hektəʊˌliːtə^r, *Am:* -toʊˌliːt̬ɚ] *n* hectolitro *m*
he'd [hiːd] = **he had, he would** *s.* **have, will**
hedge [hedʒ] **I.** *n* **1.** (*line of bushes*) seto *m* vivo **2.** FIN (*protection*) cobertura *f* **II.** *vi* (*avoid action*) dar rodeos; FIN cubrirse **III.** *vt* cercar (con un seto vivo)
◆**hedge about** *vt,* **hedge around** *vt* **1.** (*surround with a hedge*) cercar (con un seto vivo) **2.** (*hinder, hamper*) restringir
◆**hedge in** *vt* rodear; **to ~ an investment** FIN cubrirse contra el riesgo de una inversión
hedgehog ['hedʒhɒg, *Am:* -hɑːg] *n* erizo *m*
hedgerow *n* seto *m* vivo
hedging ['hedʒɪŋ] *n* FIN cobertura *f* de riesgos
heebie-jeebies ['hiːbɪ'dʒiːbɪz] *npl inf* **to give sb the ~** poner a alguien la carne de gallina
heed [hiːd] **I.** *vt form* hacer caso de; **to ~ advice** seguir los consejos **II.** *n* **to pay (no) ~ to sth, to take (no) ~ of sth** (no) prestar atención a algo
heedful ['hiːdfəl] *adj* **to be ~ of sb's advice** prestar atención a los consejos de alguien
heedless ['hiːdlɪs] *adj* irresponsable; ~ **of sth** sin hacer caso a algo; **to be ~ of the risk** no preocuparse del riesgo
hee-haw ['hiːhɔː, *Am:* -hɑː] **I.** *n* rebuzno *m* **II.** *vi* rebuznar
heel [hiːl] **I.** *n* **1.** (*of foot*) talón *m;* **to be at sb's ~s** pisar los talones a alguien **2.** (*of shoe*) tacón *m,* taco *m AmL* **3.** (*of the hand*) base *f* de la mano **4.** (*of loaf of bread*) cuscurro *m* **5.** *inf* (*unfair person*) canalla *m* ▶**to be <u>down</u> at the ~** estar en mal estado; **to follow <u>close</u> on the ~s of sth** seguir inmediatamente a algo; **to be <u>hard</u> on sb's ~s** pisar los talones a alguien; **<u>under</u> the ~ of sb/sth** sometido a alguien/algo; **to <u>bring</u> sb to ~** meter a alguien en cintura; **to <u>come</u> to ~** acceder a obedecer; **to <u>dig</u> one's ~s in** mantenerse en sus trece; **to <u>take</u> to one's ~s** *inf* poner pies en polvorosa; **to <u>turn</u> on one's ~** dar media vuelta; **to <u>walk</u> to ~** andar pegado a alguien **II.** *interj* (*dogs*) ven aquí **III.** *vt* **1.** (*rugby kick*) talonear **2.** (*football kick*) pasar de tacón
heel bar *n* taller *m* de reparación de calzado en el acto
hefty ['hefti] *adj* <-ier, -iest> (*person*) corpulento, -a; (*profit, amount*) cuantioso, -a; (*book*) gordo, -a; (*price rise*) alto, -a
heifer ['hefə^r, *Am:* -ɚ] *n* vaquilla *f*
height [haɪt] *n* **1.** (*of person*) estatura *f;* (*of thing*) altura *f* **2.** *pl* (*high places*) alturas *fpl;* **to be afraid of ~s** tener vértigo; **to attain great ~s** *fig* alcanzar el punto (más) alto; **to rise to giddy ~s** *fig* encumbrarse hasta el puesto más alto; **to scale (new) ~s** *fig* alcanzar (nuevas) cotas **3.** *pl* (*hill*) cerros *mpl* **4.** (*strongest point*) cima *f;* **to be at the ~ of one's career** estar en la cima de su carrera; **the ~ of fashion** el último grito **5.** (*the greatest degree*) cumbre; **the ~ of folly/stupidity** el colmo de la locura/la estupidez; **the ~ of kindness/patience** el súmmum de la amabilidad/la paciencia
heighten ['haɪtn] **I.** *vi* aumentar **II.** *vt* **1.** (*elevate*) elevar **2.** (*increase*) aumentar; **to ~ the effect of sth** acentuar el efecto de algo
heinous ['heɪnəs] *adj form* atroz
heir [eə^r, *Am:* er] *n* heredero *m;* **to be (the) ~ to sth** ser el heredero de algo; ~ **apparent** heredero forzoso; ~ **to the throne** heredero del trono
heiress ['eərɪs, *Am:* 'erɪs] *n* heredera *f*
heirloom ['eəluːm, *Am:* 'er-] *n* reliquia *f;* **family ~** reliquia familiar
heist [haɪst] *n inf* robo *m* a mano armada
held [held] *pt, pp of* **hold**
helicopter ['helɪkɒptə^r, *Am:* -kɑːptɚ] *n* helicóptero *m*
Heligoland ['helɪgəʊlænd, *Am:* -goʊ-] *n* Hel(i)goland *f*
helipad ['helɪpæd] *n* plataforma *f* de aterrizaje de los helicópteros
heliport ['helɪpɔːt, *Am:* -pɔːrt] *n* helipuerto *m*
helium ['hiːlɪəm] *n no pl* helio *m*
hell [hel] **I.** *n no pl* **1.** (*place of punishment*) infierno *m;* ~ **on earth** infierno en vida; **to be (sheer) ~** ser un (auténtico) infierno; **to go to ~** ir al infierno; **to go through ~** pasar un calvario; **to make sb's life ~** *inf* hacer la vida imposible a alguien **2.** *inf* (*as intensifier*) **as cold as ~** un frío de mil demonios; **as hot as ~** un calor infernal; **as hard as ~** duro a más no poder; **to hurt like ~** hacer un daño de mil demonios; **to run like ~** correr (uno) que se las pela; **a ~ of a decision** una decisión muy importante; **a ~ of a noise** un ruido increíble ▶**the road to ~ is paved with good <u>intentions</u>** *prov* el camino que lleva al infierno está lleno de buenas intenciones; **to go ~ for <u>leather</u>** ir como alma que lleva el diablo; **come ~ or high <u>water</u>** contra viento y marea; **to have been to ~ and <u>back</u>** haber pasado un calvario; **I'd see you in ~ <u>first</u>!** *Brit* ¡antes muerto!; **all ~ broke <u>loose</u>** se armó la gorda; **to <u>annoy</u> the ~ out of sb** *inf* molestar horrores a alguien; **to <u>beat</u> the ~ out of sb** dar a alguien una paliza de padre y muy señor mío; **to <u>catch</u> ~** recibir una bronca; **to <u>do</u> sth for**

the ~ of it hacer algo porque sí; **to frighten the ~ out of sb** *inf* dar a alguien un susto de miedo; **to give sb ~ (for sth)** echar un rapapolvo a alguien (por algo); **go to ~!** *inf* (*leave me alone*) ¡déjame en paz!; (*stronger*) ¡vete a la mierda! *vulg;* **to hope to ~** *inf* esperar fervientemente; **to have ~ to pay** *inf* armarse la gorda; **like ~** *inf* y un cuerno; **what the ~** *inf* qué más da **II.** *interj* (*emphasis*) ¡demonios! ►**~'s bells!** ¡por Dios!; **what the ~ ...!** ¡qué diablos...!

he'll [hi:l] = **he will** *s.* **will**

hell-bent [ˌhel'bent, *Am:* '-ˌ-] *adj* **to be ~ on (doing) sth** estar completamente decidido a (hacer) algo **hellfire** *n no pl* fuego *m* del infierno

hellish ['helɪʃ] *adj* infernal; (*experience*) horroroso, -a

hellishly *adv* endemoniadamente

hello [hə'ləʊ, *Am:* -'loʊ] **I.** <hellos> *n* hola *m;* **a big ~** un gran saludo **II.** *interj* **1.** (*greeting*) hola; **to say ~ to sb** saludar a alguien **2.** (*beginning of phone call*) diga, dígame, aló *AmC, AmS* **3.** (*to attract attention*) oiga **4.** (*surprise*) anda; **~,~** pero bueno

helm [helm] *n* timón *m;* **to be at the ~** llevar el timón; *fig* (*lead*) llevar el mando; **to take the ~** (*control*) tomar el mando; *fig* llevar las riendas

helmet ['helmɪt] *n* casco *m;* **crash ~** casco protector

helmsman ['helmzmən] *n* <-men> timonel *m*

help [help] **I.** *vi* **1.** (*assist*) ayudar **2.** (*make easier*) facilitar **3.** (*improve situation*) mejorar **II.** *vt* **1.** (*assist*) ayudar; **nothing can ~ him now** ya no se puede hacer nada por él; **can I ~ you?** (*in shop*) ¿en qué puedo servirle?; **to ~ sb with sth** ayudar a alguien con algo; **to ~ sb with his homework** ayudar a alguien a hacer sus deberes **2.** (*improve*) (ayudar a) mejorar; **this medicine will ~ your headache** esta medicina te aliviará el dolor de cabeza **3.** (*contribute to a condition*) contribuir [*o* ayudar] a **4.** (*prevent*) evitar; **it can't be ~ed** es así y no hay más remedio; **to not be able to ~ doing sth** no poder dejar de hacer algo; **I can't ~ it** no puedo remediarlo; **he can't ~ the way he is** él es así, ¿qué se le va hacer?; **to not be able to ~ but ...** no poder (por) menos de... **5.** (*take sth*) **to ~ oneself to sth** (*at table*) servirse algo **III.** *n* **1.** *no pl* (*assistance*) ayuda *f;* **to be a ~** ser una ayuda; **there'll be no ~ for it but to ...** no habrá más remedio que... **2.** (*servant*) mujer *f* de la limpieza; (*in a shop*) ayudante *mf* **IV.** *interj* **~!** ¡socorro!; **so ~ me God** y que Dios me asista

◆**help out** *vt* ayudar

helper ['helpəʳ, *Am:* -ɚ] *n* ayudante *mf*

helpful ['helpfəl] *adj* **1.** (*willing to help*) servicial **2.** (*useful*) útil

helping ['helpɪŋ] **I.** *n* (*food*) ración *f,* porción *f AmL* **II.** *adj* **to give sb a ~ hand** echar una mano a alguien

helpless ['helplɪs] *adj* indefenso, -a

helpline ['helplaɪn] *n* teléfono *m* de asistencia

helter-skelter [ˌheltə'skeltəʳ, *Am:* -t̬ɚ'skelt̬ɚ] **I.** *adj* caótico, -a **II.** *adv* a la desbandada

hem [hem] **I.** *n* dobladillo *m,* basta *f AmL;* **to take the ~ up/down** meter/sacar el dobladillo **II.** <-mm-> *vt* hacer el dobladillo a **III.** *interj* ejem

◆**hem in** *vt* (*surround*) encerrar; (*constrain*) constreñir

he-man ['hi:mæn] <-men> *n inf* macho *m*

hemisphere ['hemɪsfɪəʳ, *Am:* -sfɪr] *n* hemisferio *m*

hemline ['hemlaɪn] *n* bajo(s) *m(pl)* (del vestido o la falda)

hemlock ['hemlɒk, *Am:* -lɑ:k] *n no pl* cicuta *f*

hemp [hemp] *n no pl* cáñamo *m*

hen [hen] *n* **1.** (*female chicken*) gallina *f;* (*female bird*) hembra *f* **2.** *Scot, inf* (*woman*) guapa *f*

hence [hens] *adv* **1.** (*therefore*) de ahí **2.** *after n* (*from now*) dentro de; **two years ~** de aquí a dos años

henceforth [ˌhens'fɔ:θ, *Am:* -'fɔ:rθ] *adv,* **henceforward** [ˌhens'fɔ:wəd, *Am:* -'fɔ:rwɚd] *adv* de ahora en adelante

henchman ['hentʃmən] <-men> *n* secuaz *m*

hencoop ['henku:p] *n,* **henhouse** ['henhaʊs] *n* gallinero *m*

henna ['henə] **I.** *n* gena *f,* jena *f* **II.** *vt* tintar con gena [*o* jena]

hen night *n,* **hen party** <-ies> *n* (*party*) fiesta *f* para mujeres; (*before wedding*) despedida *f* de soltera

henpecked ['henpekt] *adj* **a ~ husband** un calzonazos

hepatitis [ˌhepə'taɪtɪs, *Am:* -t̬ɪs] *n no pl* hepatitis *f inv*

heptathlon [hep'tæθlɒn, *Am:* -lɑ:n] *n* heptatlón *m*

her [hɜ:ʳ, *Am:* hɜ:r] **I.** *adj pos* su; **~ dress/house** su vestido/casa; **~ children** sus hijos **II.** *pron pers* **1.** (*she*) ella; **it's ~** es ella; **older than ~** mayor que ella; **if I were ~** si yo fuese ella **2.** *direct object* la; *indirect object* le; **look at ~** mírala; **I saw ~** la vi; **he told ~ that ...** le dijo que...; **he gave ~ the pencil** le dio el lápiz (a ella) **3.** *after prep* ella; **it's for/from ~** es para/de ella

herald ['herəld] **I.** *vt* presagiar; **to ~ a new era** anunciar una nueva era; **the much ~ed** el tan anunciado **II.** *n* **1.** (*sign*) presagio *m;* **to be a ~ of sth** ser una señal de algo **2.** HIST (*bringer of news*) heraldo *m*

heraldic [he'rældɪk, *Am:* hə-] *adj* heráldico, -a

heraldry ['herəldri] *n no pl* heráldica *f*

herb [hɜ:b] *n* hierba *f*

herbaceous [hɜ:'beɪʃəs, *Am:* hɚ'-] *adj* herbáceo, -a; ~ **border** arriate *m* de plantas diversas

herbalism ['hɜːbəlɪzəm, *Am:* 'hɜːr-] *n no pl* fitoterapia *f*

herbalist ['hɜːbəlɪst, *Am:* 'hɜːr-] *n* herbolario, -a *m, f,* yerbatero, -a *m, f AmS*

herbicide ['hɜːbɪsaɪd, *Am:* 'hɜːr-] *n* herbicida *m*

herbivorous [hɜː'bɪvərəs, *Am:* hɜːr-] *adj* herbívoro, -a

herculean [ˌhɜːkjʊ'liːən, *Am:* ˌhɜːrkjuː'-] *adj* hercúleo, -a; ~ **task** tarea *f* de romanos

Hercules ['hɛːkjəliːz, *Am:* 'hɛrkjə-] *n* Hércules *m inv*

herd [hɜːd, *Am:* hɜːrd] **I.** *n + sing/pl vb* **1.** (*of animals*) manada *f;* (*of sheep*) rebaño *f;* (*of pigs*) piara *f* **2.** (*of people*) multitud *f;* **the common ~** las masas; **to follow the ~** seguir a la masa **II.** *vt* (*animals*) llevar en manada; (*sheep*) guardar **III.** *vi* ir en manada [*o* rebaño] ◆**herd together** *vt* (*animals*) reunir en una manada [*o* en un rebaño]

herd instinct *n* instinto *m* gregario

herdsman ['hɜːdzmən, *Am:* 'hɜːrdz-] *n* <-men> (*of cattle*) vaquero *m;* (*of sheep*) pastor *m*

here [hɪəʳ, *Am:* hɪr] *adv* **1.** (*in, at, to this place*) aquí; **over ~** acá; **give it ~** *inf* dámelo; **~ and there** aquí y allá **2.** (*introduce*) **here is ...** aquí está... **3.** (*show arrival*) **they are ~** ya han llegado **4.** (*next to*) **my colleague ~** mi colega que está aquí **5.** (*now*) **where do we go from ~?** ¿dónde vamos ahora?; **~ you are** (*giving sth*) aquí tienes; **the ~ and now** el presente; **~ goes** *inf* allá voy; **~ we go** ya estamos otra vez

hereabouts [ˌhɪərə'baʊts, *Am:* ˌhɪrə'bauts] *adv* por aquí

hereafter [hɪər'ɑːftəʳ, *Am:* hɪr'æftɚ] **I.** *adv* en lo sucesivo **II.** *n* **the ~** el más allá

hereby [hɪə'baɪ, *Am:* hɪr'baɪ] *adv form* por la presente

hereditary [hɪ'redɪtri, *Am:* hə'redɪter-] *adj* hereditario, -a

heredity [hɪ'redəti, *Am:* hə'redɪ-] *n no pl* herencia *f*

herein [ˌhɪər'ɪn, *Am:* ˌhɪr-] *adv* en esto

hereof [hɪər'ɒv, *Am:* hɪr'ɑːv] *adv* de esto

heresy ['herəsi] <-ies> *n* herejía *f*

heretic ['herətɪk] *n* hereje *mf*

heretical [hɪ'retɪkl, *Am:* hə'ret̬-] *adj* herético, -a

hereupon [ˌhɪərə'pɒn, *Am:* ˌhɪrə'pɑːn] *adv form* en ese momento

herewith [ˌhɪə'wɪð, *Am:* ˌhɪr'-] *adv form* adjunto, -a

heritage ['herɪtɪdʒ, *Am:* -t̬ɪdʒ] *n no pl* patrimonio *m*

hermaphrodite [hɜː'mæfrədaɪt, *Am:* hɚ-'mæfroʊ-] **I.** *n* hermafrodita *mf* **II.** *adj* hermafrodita

hermetic [hɜː'metɪk, *Am:* hɚ'met̬-] *adj* hermético, -a; ~ **seal** cierre hermético

hermit ['hɜːmɪt, *Am:* 'hɜːr-] *n* eremita *mf*

hermitage ['hɜːmɪtɪdʒ, *Am:* 'hɜːrmɪt̬ɪdʒ] *n* ermita *f*

hermit crab *n* cangrejo *m* ermitaño

hernia ['hɜːnɪə, *Am:* 'hɜːr-] *n* MED hernia *f*

hero ['hɪərəʊ, *Am:* 'hɪroʊ] <heroes> *n* **1.** (*brave man*) héroe *m* **2.** (*main character*) protagonista *m;* **the ~ of a film** el protagonista de una película **3.** (*idol*) ídolo *m* **4.** *Am* (*sandwich*) *sándwich de carne fría, queso y lechuga*

heroic [hɪ'rəʊɪk, *Am:* hɪ'roʊ-] *adj* **1.** (*brave, bold*) heroico, -a; ~ **attempt** intento heroico; ~ **deed** hazaña *f* **2.** (*epic*) heroico, -a; ~ **verse** verso heroico

heroics *n pl* **1.** (*language*) lenguaje *m* grandilocuente **2.** (*action*) acción *f* arriesgada

heroin ['herəʊɪn, *Am:* -oʊ-] *n no pl* heroína *f*

heroin addict *n* MED heroinómano, -a *m, f*

heroine ['herəʊɪn, *Am:* -oʊ-] *n* (*brave woman*) heroína *f;* (*of film*) protagonista *f*

heroism ['herəʊɪzəm, *Am:* -oʊ-] *n no pl* heroísmo *m*

heron ['herən] <-(s)> *n* garza *f* (real)

herpes ['hɜːpiːz] *n* herpes *m inv*

herring ['herɪŋ] <-(s)> *n* arenque *m*

herringbone ['herɪŋbəʊn, *Am:* -boʊn] FASHION **I.** *n no pl* espiga *f* **II.** *adj* de espiga

herring gull *n* gaviota *f* argéntea

hers [hɜːz, *Am:* hɜːrz] *pron pos* (el) suyo, (la) suya, (los) suyos, (las) suyas; **it's not my bag, it's ~** no es mi bolsa, es la de ella; **this house is ~** esta casa es suya; **this glass is ~** este vaso es suyo; **a book of ~** un libro suyo

herself [hɜː'self, *Am:* hɚ-] *pron* **1.** *reflexive* se; *after prep* sí (misma); **she lives by ~** vive sola **2.** *emphatic* ella misma; **she hurt ~** se hizo daño

hertz [hɜːts, *Am:* hɜːrts] *n inv* hercio *m*

he's [hiːz] **1.** = **he is** *s.* **be** **2.** = **he has** *s.* **have**

hesitant ['hezɪtənt] *adj* indeciso, -a; **to be ~ about doing sth** no estar decidido a hacer algo

hesitantly *adv* con indecisión

hesitate ['hezɪteɪt] *vi* vacilar, trepidar *AmL;* **to (not) ~ to do sth** (no) dudar en hacer algo

hesitation [ˌhezɪ'teɪʃən] *n* vacilación *f;* **without ~** sin titubear; **to have no ~ in doing sth** no tener ninguna duda en hacer algo

hessian ['hesɪən, *Am:* 'heʃən] *n no pl, Brit* arpillera *f*

heterogeneous [ˌhetərə'dʒiːnɪəs, *Am:* ˌhet̬əroʊ'-] *adj* heterogéneo, -a

heterosexual [ˌhetərə'sekʃʊəl, *Am:* ˌhet̬əroʊ'-] **I.** *n* heterosexual *mf* **II.** *adj* heterosexual

het up [ˌhet'ʌp, *Am:* ˌhet̬-] *adj inf* alterado, -a

hew [hjuː] <hewed, hewed *o* hewn> **I.** *vt* **1.** (*cut away*) extraer **2.** (*cut into shape*) **to ~ stone/wood** tallar piedra/madera **II.** *vi* **to ~ to sth** *Am* atenerse a algo

hewn ['hjuːn] *pp of* **hew**

hex [heks] *n Am, Aus, inf* maleficio *m;* **to put a ~ on sb/sth** hacer un maleficio a alguien/

algo
hexagon ['heksəgən, *Am:* -gɑːn] *n* hexágono *m*
hexagonal [heks'ægənl] *adv* hexagonal
hexameter [heks'æmɪtəʳ, *Am:* -əṱɚ] *n* hexámetro *m*
hey [heɪ] *interj inf* eh, oye, órale *Méx*
heyday ['heɪdeɪ] *n* apogeo *m;* **in his/her/its ~** en su apogeo
hey presto ['heɪ'prestəʊ, *Am:* -toʊ] *interj Brit, Aus, inf* sorpresa
HGV [ˌeɪtʃdʒiː'viː] *abbr of* **heavy goods vehicle** vehículo *m* pesado
hi [haɪ] *interj* hola
hiatus [haɪ'eɪtəs, *Am:* haɪ'eɪṱəs] <-es> *n* **1.** LING hiato *m* **2.** (*pause*) pausa *f*
hibernate ['haɪbəneɪt, *Am:* -bɚ-] *vi* hibernar
hibernation [ˌhaɪbə'neɪʃən, *Am:* -bɚ'-] *n no pl* hibernación *f*
hibiscus [hɪ'bɪskəs] <-es> *n* BOT hibisco *m*
hiccup, **hiccough** ['hɪkʌp] **I.** *n* hipo *m;* **to have ~s** tener hipo **II.** *vi* <-p(p)-> tener hipo
hid [hɪd] *pt of* **hide²**
hidden ['hɪdn] **I.** *pp of* **hide²** **II.** *adj* (*person, thing*) escondido, -a; (*emotion, information*) oculto, -a; **~ assets** ECON activos ocultos [*o* invisibles]; **~ economy** economía sumergida
hide¹ [haɪd] *n* piel *f* ►**to see neither ~ nor hair of sb** no verle el pelo a alguien
hide² [haɪd] <hid, hidden> **I.** *vi* esconderse, escorarse *Cuba, Hond* **II.** *vt* (*conceal: person, thing*) esconder; (*emotion, information*) ocultar; **to ~ one's face** taparse la cara **III.** *n Brit, Aus* observatorio *m* (*para ver animales salvajes*)
◆**hide away** *vt* esconder
◆**hide out** *vi,* **hide up** *vi* esconderse
hide-and-seek [ˌhaɪdn'siːk] *n* escondite *m;* **to play ~** jugar al escondite
hideaway ['haɪdəweɪ] *n inf* escondite *m*
hideous ['hɪdɪəs] *adj* **1.** (*very unpleasant, ugly*) espantoso, -a **2.** (*terrible*) terrible
hideout ['haɪdaʊt] *n* escondrijo *m;* **secret ~** guarida *f* secreta
hiding¹ ['haɪdɪŋ] *n a. fig* paliza *f;* **to get a real ~** (*defeat*) sufrir una fuerte derrota ►**to be on a ~ to nothing** tener todas las de perder
hiding² ['haɪdɪŋ] *n no pl* **to be in ~** estar escondido; **to go into ~** ocultarse
hierarchic(al) [ˌhaɪə'rɑːkɪk(l), *Am:* ˌhaɪ'rɑːr-] *adj* jerárquico, -a
hierarchy ['haɪərɑːki, *Am:* 'haɪrɑːr-] <-ies> *n* **1.** (*system*) jerarquía *f* **2.** (*upper levels of organization*) cúpula *f*
hieroglyph [ˌhaɪərəʊ'glɪf, *Am:* ˌhaɪroʊ'-] *n* jeroglífico *m*
hieroglyphics *npl* jeroglíficos *mpl*
hi-fi ['haɪfaɪ] **I.** *n abbr of* **high-fidelity** alta fidelidad *f* **II.** *adj abbr of* **high-fidelity** de alta fidelidad; **~ equipment** equipo *m* de alta fidelidad
higgledy-piggledy [ˌhɪgldɪ'pɪgldi] *adj inf* revuelto, -a
high [haɪ] **I.** *adj* **1.** (*elevated*) alto, -a; **one metre ~ and three metres wide** un metro de alto y tres metros de ancho; **knee/waist-~** hasta la rodilla/cintura; **to fly at ~ altitude** volar a gran altitud; **~ cheekbones** pómulos elevados; **to do a ~ dive** lanzarse desde una altura considerable **2.** (*above average*) superior; **to have ~ hopes** (**for sb/sth**) tener grandes esperanzas (puestas en alguien/algo); **to have a ~ opinion of sb** estimar mucho a alguien; **to have ~ praise** (**for sb/sth**) elogiar mucho (a alguien/algo); **of the ~est calibre** de lo mejor; **~ blood-pressure/fever** presión/fiebre alta; **a ~ calibre gun** un arma de gran calibre **3.** (*important, eminent*) elevado, -a; **of ~ rank** de alto rango; **to have sth on the ~est authority** *a. iron* saber algo de buena tinta; **to have friends in ~ places** tener amigos en las altas esferas; (*regarding job*) tener enchufe; **an order from on ~** una orden que viene de arriba; **to be ~ and mighty** ser un engreído **4.** (*under influence of drugs*) colocado, -a **5.** (*of high frequency, shrill: voice*) agudo, -a; **a ~ note** una nota alta **6.** FASHION **with a ~ neckline** con escote a (la) caja **7.** (*beginning to go bad: food*) pasado, -a ►**to leave sb ~ and dry** dejar a alguien colgado **II.** *adv* **1.** (*at or to a great point or height*) a gran altura **2.** (*rough or strong*) con fuerza; **the sea runs ~** la mar está brava ►**to search for sth ~ and low** buscar algo por todas partes **III.** *n* **1.** (*high(est) point*) punto *m* máximo; **an all-time ~** un récord de todos los tiempos; **to reach a ~** alcanzar un nivel récord **2.** *inf* (*trip*) **to be on a ~** estar colocado **3.** (*heaven*) **on ~** en el cielo
highball ['haɪbɔːl] *n Am* whisky *m* con soda
high beam *n Am* luces *fpl* largas **highboy** *n Am* cómoda *f* alta **highbrow** **I.** *adj* culto, -a **II.** *n* intelectual *mf* **highchair** *n* silla *f* alta **High Church** *n no pl sector de la Iglesia anglicana de tendencia conservadora* **high-class** *adj* de alta clase **high court** *n* tribunal *m* superior de justicia **high definition television** *n* televisión *f* de alta definición **high density** *adj a.* INFOR de alta densidad; **~ disk** disco *m* de alta densidad
higher education *n no pl* enseñanza *f* superior

> El **Higher Grade** es el nombre de un examen que hacen los alumnos escoceses que están en el quinto curso (un año después del **GCSE**). Los alumnos pueden elegir examinarse de una única asignatura, aunque lo normal es que ellos prefieran hacer aproximadamente cinco **Highers**.

higher-up ['haɪərʌp, *Am:* 'haɪɚ-] *n inf* superior *m*
highfalutin [ˌhaɪfə'luːtɪn] *adj inf* presuntuoso, -a

high-fibre [ˌhaɪˈfaɪbəʳ] *adj* rico, -a en fibra **high fidelity** *n no pl* alta fidelidad *f* **high-flier** *n* persona *f* de mucho talento **high-flown** *adj* exagerado, -a; ~ **ideas** ideas *fpl* altisonantes **high frequency** *adj* de alta frecuencia **high-handed** *adj* arbitrario, -a; (*treatment*) despótico, -a **high-handedness** *n no pl* arbitrariedad *f* **high heels** *npl* tacones *mpl* altos **highjack** *vt s.* **hijack** **high jinks** *npl* jolgorio *m* **high jump** *n* salto *m* de altura ►**he's for the** ~ *inf* se la va a ganar

> El **Highland dress** o **kilt** es el nombre que recibe el traje tradicional escocés. Procede del siglo XVI y en aquel entonces se componía de una única pieza. A partir del siglo XVII esta pieza única se convierte en dos distintas: el **kilt** (falda escocesa) y el **plaid** (capa de lana). De esta época procede también el **sporran** (una bolsa que cuelga del cinturón). Hasta el siglo XVIII no se diseñan los diferentes **tartans** (modelos de diseños escoceses) para cada familia o clan. Muchos hombres siguen poniéndose el **kilt** en acontecimientos especiales, como por ejemplo, una boda.

highlands *npl Scot* región *f* montañosa; **the Highlands** las Tierras Altas de Escocia **high-level** *adj* de alto nivel **high life** *n* vida *f* de la alta sociedad; **to live the** ~ vivir la buena vida **highlight** I. *n* 1. (*most interesting part*) aspecto *m* interesante 2. *pl* (*bright tint in hair*) mechas *fpl* II. *vt* 1. (*draw attention to*) destacar; (*a problem*) señalar 2. (*mark*) subrayar **highlighter** *n* rotulador *m*

highly [ˈhaɪli] *adv* 1. (*very*) muy 2. (*very well*) **to speak** ~ **of someone** hablar muy bien de alguien; **to think** ~ **of someone** tener muy buen concepto de alguien

highly-educated *adj* de nivel cultural alto **highly-skilled** *adj* con grandes habilidades **highly-strung** *adj* muy excitable

High Mass [ˌhaɪˈmæs] *n* REL misa *f* mayor

highness [ˈhaɪnɪs] <-es> *n* 1. *no pl* (*level*) altura *f* 2. (*prince or princess*) **His/Her/Your Highness** Su Alteza **high-performance** *adj a.* AUTO de gran rendimiento **high-pitched** *adj* 1. (*sloping steeply*) escarpado, -a; ~ **roof** tejado *m* de dos aguas 2. (*sound*) agudo, -a; **a** ~ **voice** una voz aflautada **high point** *n* **the** ~ (*most successful state*) el clímax; (*most enjoyable state*) el punto álgido **high-powered** *adj* 1. (*powerful*) de gran potencia 2. (*influential, important*) poderoso, -a 3. (*advanced*) avanzado, -a **high-pressure** I. *n* METEO presión *f* alta; **a ridge of** ~ una zona de altas presiones II. *adj* enérgico, -a; ~ **sales techniques** ECON técnicas de venta agresivas III. *vt* presionar **high priest** *n* REL sumo sacerdote *m* **high-profile** *adj* ilustre **high-protein** *adj* rico, -a en proteínas **high-ranking** *adj* de categoría **high-resolution** *n* INFOR alta resolución *f* **high-rise** *adj* elevado, -a **high-rise building** *n*, **high-rise flats** *npl* edificio *m* elevado **high-risk** *adj* de alto riesgo; (*investment*) arriesgado, -a **high school** *n Am* ≈ instituto *m*; **junior** ~ centro *m* de enseñanza secundaria

> El término **high school** se utilizaba antiguamente en Gran Bretaña para designar una **grammar school** (escuela secundaria superior), pero hoy en día se emplea con el significado de **secondary school** (escuela secundaria inferior).

high seas *npl* alta mar *f* **high season** *n* temporada *f* alta; **at** ~ en temporada alta **high-security wing** *n* ala *m* de alta seguridad **high society** *n no pl* alta sociedad *f* **high-sounding** *adj* altisonante **high-speed train** *n* tren *m* de alta velocidad **high-spirited** *adj* (*cheerful, lively*) animoso, -a; (*fiery: horse*) fogoso, -a **high spirits** *npl* buen humor *m* **high spot** *n inf* punto *m* culminante; **to be the** ~ **of sth** ser el punto álgido de algo **high street** *n Brit* calle *f* principal **high summer** *n* canícula *f* del verano **hightail** *vi Am, inf* darse el piro **high tea** *n Brit* merienda-cena *f* **high-tech** *adj* de alta tecnología **high technology** *n no pl* alta tecnología *f* **high-tension** *adj* de alta tensión **high tide** *n* 1. (*highest level of the tide*) marea *f* alta 2. *fig* (*highest or most successful point*) apogeo *m* **high treason** *n no pl* alta traición *f* **high-up** I. *adj* importante II. *n* alto cargo *m*

high water *n* marea *f* alta

high water mark *n* 1. (*mark showing water level*) línea *f* de pleamar 2. (*most successful point*) punto *m* culminante

highway [ˈhaɪweɪ] *n* carretera *f*

highway code *n* código *m* de la circulación **highwayman** <-men> *n* HIST salteador *m* de caminos **highway robbery** <-ies> *n* HIST asalto *m*

hijack [ˈhaɪdʒæk] I. *vt* 1. (*take over by force: plane*) secuestrar un avión 2. *fig* (*adopt as one's own*) **to** ~ **sb's ideas/plans** hacer propias las ideas/los planes de alguien II. *n* secuestro *m*

hijacker [ˈhaɪdʒækəʳ, *Am:* -ɚ] *n* secuestrador(a) *m(f)* (aéreo)

hijacking [ˈhaɪdʒækɪŋ] *n no pl* secuestro *m* (aéreo)

hike [haɪk] I. *n* 1. (*long walk*) caminata *f*; **to go on a** ~ dar una caminata 2. *Am, inf* (*increase*) aumento *m* II. *vi* ir de excursión (a pie) III. *vt Am, inf* (*prices, taxes*) aumentar

hiker [ˈhaɪkəʳ, *Am:* -ɚ] *n* excursionista *mf*

hiking [ˈhaɪkɪŋ] *n no pl* excursionismo *m*

hilarious [hɪˈleərɪəs, *Am:* -ˈlerɪ-] *adj* 1. (*very amusing*) divertidísimo, -a 2. (*boisterously merry*) alegre

hilarity [hɪˈlærəti, *Am:* -ˈlerət̬i] *n no pl* hilaridad *f*
hill [hɪl] *n* **1.** colina *f;* **the ~s** la sierra **2.** (*steep slope in road*) cuesta *f* **3.** (*small heap*) montoncito *m* ►**it ain't worth a ~ of beans** *Am, inf* no merece la pena; **as old as the ~s** tan viejo como el mundo; **to be over the ~** *inf* ser demasiado viejo
hillbilly [ˈhɪlbɪli] <-ies> *n Am* palurdo, -a *m, f*
hillock [ˈhɪlək] *n* montículo *m*
hillside [ˈhɪlsaɪd] *n* ladera *f*
hilltop [ˈhɪltɒp, *Am:* -tɑːp] **I.** *n* cumbre *f* **II.** *adj* de la cima
hill-walking [ˈhɪlwɔːkɪŋ] *n no pl* caminatas *fpl*
hilly [ˈhɪli] <-ier, -iest> *adj* montañoso, -a
hilt [hɪlt] *n* (*of a weapon*) empuñadura *f* ►(**up**) **to the ~** totalmente, hasta el cuello *inf;* **to be mortgaged up to the ~** estar completamente hipotecado; **to support sb to the ~** apoyar a alguien incondicionalmente
him [hɪm] *pron pers* **1.** (*he*) él; **it's ~** es él; **older than ~** mayor que él; **if I were ~** yo en su lugar **2.** *direct object* lo, le; *indirect object* le; **she gave ~ the pencil** le dio el lápiz (a él) **3.** *after prep* él; **it's for/from ~** es para/de él **4.** (*unspecified sex*) **if somebody comes, tell ~ that ...** si viene alguien, dile que...
Himalayas [ˌhɪməˈleɪəz] *npl* el Himalaya
himself [hɪmˈself] *pron* **1.** *reflexive* se; *after prep* sí (mismo); **for ~** para él (mismo); **he lives by ~** vive solo **2.** *emphatic* él mismo; **he hurt ~** se hizo daño
hind [haɪnd] **I.** *adj* trasero, -a **II.** <-(s)> *n* cierva *f*
hinder [ˈhɪndəʳ, *Am:* -dɚ] *vt* **1.** (*obstruct*) estorbar; **to ~ progress** frenar el progreso **2.** (*prevent*) **to ~ sb from doing sth** impedir a alguien hacer algo
Hindi [ˈhɪndiː] *n* hindi *m*
hind legs [ˌhaɪndˈlegz] *npl* patas *fpl* traseras ►**to talk the ~ off a donkey** *Brit, inf* hablar por los codos
hindmost [ˈhaɪndməʊst, *Am:* -moʊst] *adj* **1.** (*last*) último, -a **2.** (*rear*) trasero
hindquarters [ˌhaɪndˈkwɔːtəz, *Am:* ˈhaɪndˌkwɔːrt̬ɚz] *npl* ZOOL cuartos *mpl* traseros
hindrance [ˈhɪndrəns] *n* **1.** (*obstruction*) estorbo *m* **2.** (*obstacle*) obstáculo *m;* **to allow sb to enter without ~** dejar que alguien entre sin poner obstáculos
hindsight [ˈhaɪndsaɪt] *n no pl* percepción *f* retrospectiva; **in ~** en retrospectiva; **with the benefit of ~** con la perspectiva del tiempo
Hindu [ˈhɪnduː] **I.** *n* hindú *mf* **II.** *adj* hindú
Hinduism [ˈhɪnduːɪzəm] *n no pl* REL hinduismo *m*
hinge [hɪndʒ] **I.** *n* bisagra *f* **II.** *vi* **to ~ on/upon sb/sth** depender de alguien/algo
hint [hɪnt] **I.** *n* **1.** (*trace*) indicio *m* **2.** (*allusion*) indirecta *f;* **to drop a ~** lanzar una indirecta **3.** (*practical tip*) consejo *m;* **a handy ~** una indicación útil **4.** (*slight amount*) pizca *f* **II.** *vt* **to ~ sth to sb** insinuar algo a alguien **III.** *vi* soltar indirectas; **to ~ at sth** hacer alusión a algo
hip [hɪp] **I.** *n* **1.** ANAT cadera *f;* **to stand with one's hands on (one's) ~s** ponerse en jarras **2.** BOT escaramujo *m* **II.** *adj inf* (*fashionable*) moderno, -a
hipbone [ˈhɪpˌbəʊn, *Am:* -boʊn] *n* hueso *m* de la cadera **hip flask** *n* petaca *m*
hippie [ˈhɪpi] *n* hippy *mf*
hippo [ˈhɪpəʊ, *Am:* -oʊ] *n inf abbr of* **hippopotamus** hipopótamo *m*
hippopotamus [ˌhɪpəˈpɒtəməs, *Am:* -ˈpɑːt̬ə-] <-es *o* -mi> *n* hipopótamo *m*
hippy [ˈhɪpi] <-ies> *n* hippy *mf*
hire [ˈhaɪəʳ, *Am:* ˈhaɪr] **I.** *n no pl* alquiler *m;* **'for ~'** 'se alquila' *m* **II.** *vt* **1.** (*rent*) alquilar, fletar *AmL;* **to ~ sth by the hour/day/week** alquilar algo por horas/días/semanas **2.** (*employ*) contratar, conchabar *AmL;* **to ~ more staff** ampliar la plantilla
◆**hire out** *vt* alquilar; **to ~ sth by the hour/day/week** alquilar algo por horas/días/semanas
hire purchase *n* compra *f* a plazos; **to buy something on ~** comprar algo a plazos **hire purchase agreement** *n* acuerdo *m* de compra a plazos
his [hɪz] **I.** *adj pos* su (de él); **~ car/house** su coche/casa; **~ children** sus hijos **II.** *pron pos* (el) suyo, (la) suya, (los) suyos, (las) suyas, de él; **it's not my bag, it's ~** no es mi bolsa, es la suya; **this house is ~** esta casa es suya; **this glass is ~** este vaso es suyo; **a book of ~** un libro suyo
Hispanic [hɪsˈpænɪk] **I.** *adj* hispánico, -a **II.** *n* hispano, -a *m, f*
hiss [hɪs] **I.** *vi* silbar; **to ~ at sb** silbar a alguien **II.** *vt* silbar **III.** *n* silbido *m*
histamine [ˈhɪstəmiːn] *n* MED histamina *f*
historian [hɪˈstɔːriən] *n* historiador(a) *m(f)*
historic [hɪˈstɒrɪk, *Am:* hɪˈstɔːrɪk] *adj* histórico, -a; **this is a ~ moment ...** es un momento clave...
historical *adj* histórico, -a
history [ˈhɪstəri] *n no pl* historia *f;* **a ~ book** un libro de historia; **sb's life ~** la vida de alguien; **to make ~** hacer época
histrionic [ˌhɪstrɪˈɒnɪk, *Am:* -ˈɑːnɪk] *adj* histriónico, -a
hit [hɪt] **I.** *n* **1.** (*blow, stroke*) golpe *m* **2.** *inf* (*shot*) tiro *m* certero **3.** (*bomb*) impacto *m* **4.** SPORTS punto *m;* **to score a ~** marcar un tanto **5.** (*success*) éxito *m* **II.** <-tt-, hit, hit> *vt* **1.** (*strike*) golpear, pepenar *Méx;* **to ~ sb hard** *a. fig* pegar a alguien con fuerza **2.** (*crash into*) chocar contra; **to ~ a reef/a sandbank** dar contra un arrecife/banco de arena; **to ~ one's head on a shelf** dar con la cabeza contra un estante **3.** (*arrive at, reach target*) alcanzar **4.** (*wound*) herir; *inf* (*kill*) matar

5. (*affect*) afectar; **to ~ sb where it hurts** dar a alguien donde más le duele **6.** (*reach*) tocar; **to ~ rock bottom** *fig* tocar fondo **7.** (*encounter*) tropezar con; **to ~ a lot of resistance/a traffic jam** encontrar mucha resistencia/un atasco **8.** *inf* (*arrive in or at*) llegar a; **to ~ 200 kph** alcanzar los 200 km/h **III.** *vi* **1.** (*strike*) **to ~ against sth** chocar con algo; **to ~ at sb/sth** asestar un golpe a alguien/algo **2.** (*attack*) **to ~ at sth** atacar algo

◆**hit back** *vi* devolver el golpe; **to ~ at sb** defenderse de alguien

◆**hit off** *vt always sep* **to hit it off** (**with sb**) hacer buenas migas (con alguien)

◆**hit on** *vt* **1.** (*think of*) dar con **2.** *Am* (*show sexual interest*) ligar con

◆**hit out** *vi* lanzar un ataque; **to ~ at sb** asestar un golpe a alguien; *fig* tirar pullas a alguien

hit-and-run [ˌhɪtən'rʌn] *adj* **~ accident** accidente de carretera en el que el conductor se da a la fuga; **~ attack** MIL ataque relámpago; **~ driver** conductor que se da a la fuga tras atropellar a alguien

hitch [hɪtʃ] **I.** <-es> *n* **1.** (*obstacle*) obstáculo *m;* **technical ~** problema *m* técnico; **to go off without a ~** salir a pedir de boca **2.** (*sudden pull*) tirón *m* **II.** *vt* **1.** (*fasten*) atar; **to ~ sth to sth** atar algo a algo; **to ~ an animal to sth** amarrar un animal a algo **2.** *inf* (*hitchhike*) **to ~ a lift** hacer dedo **III.** *vi inf* hacer dedo

◆**hitch up** *vt* **1.** (*fasten*) **to hitch sth up to sth** atar algo a algo; **to ~ an animal to sth** amarrar un animal a algo **2.** (*pull up quickly: clothes*) levantar

hitcher ['hɪtʃər] *n* autostopista *mf*

hitchhike ['hɪtʃhaɪk] *vi* hacer autostop, hacer colita *AmS,* pedir aventón *Méx,* pedir chance *Col*

hitchhiker ['hɪtʃhaɪkəʳ, *Am:* -ɚ] *n* autostopista *mf*

hitch-hiking *n no pl* autostop *m*

hi tech [ˌhaɪ'tek] *adj* de alta tecnología

hither ['hɪðəʳ, *Am:* -ɚ] *adv form* acá; **~ and thither** acá y allá

hitherto [ˌhɪðə'tuː, *Am:* -ɚ'-] *adv form* hasta ahora; **~ unpublished** no publicado por ahora; **to reveal ~ unsuspected talents** revelar talentos hasta el momento insospechados

hitman ['hɪtmæn] <-men> *n* pistolero *m*

hit-or-miss *adj* a la buena de Dios

hit parade *n* HIST (*top forty*) lista *f* de éxitos; **to be at the top of the ~** estar en lo más alto de la lista de éxitos

HIV [ˌeɪtʃaɪ'viː] *abbr of* **human immunodeficiency virus** VIH *m*

hive [haɪv] **I.** *n* **1.** (*beehouse*) colmena *f* **2.** + *sing/pl vb* (*swarm*) enjambre *m* **3.** (*busy place*) **to be a ~ of business** ser un punto neurálgico de negocios **II.** *vt* **to ~ sth off** (*separate*) separar algo; (*privatize*) privatizar algo

◆**hive off** *vi* separarse

hives [haɪvz] *n* MED urticaria *f*

hl *abbr of* **hectolitre** hl

HMG [ˌeɪtʃem'dʒiː] *abbr of* **Her/His Majesty's Government** el Gobierno de S.M.

HMI [ˌeɪtʃem'aɪ] *abbr of* **Her/His Majesty's Inspector** (**of schools**) Inspector(a) *m(f)* de S.M.

HMS [ˌeɪtʃem'es] **1.** *abbr of* **Her/His Majesty's Service** el Servicio de S.M. **2.** *abbr of* **Her/His Majesty's Ship** Buque *m* de S.M.

HMSO [ˌeɪtʃemes'əʊ, *Am:* -'oʊ] *abbr of* **Her/His Majesty's Stationery Office** imprenta *f* de S.M.

HNC [ˌeɪtʃen'siː] *abbr of* **Higher National Certificate** HNC *m* (*título nacional de enseñanza superior*)

HND [ˌeɪtʃen'diː] *abbr of* **Higher National Diploma** título *m* nacional de enseñanza superior

ho [həʊ, *Am:* hoʊ] *interj inf* (*expresses scorn, surprise*) oh; (*attracts attention*) oiga; **land ~!** NAUT ¡tierra a la vista!

HO [ˌeɪtʃ'əʊ, *Am:* -'oʊ] **1.** *abbr of* **head office** oficina *f* principal **2.** *abbr of* **Home Office** Ministerio *m* del Interior

hoard [hɔːd, *Am:* hɔːrd] **I.** *n* acumulación *f* **II.** *vt* acumular; (*food*) amontonar

hoarding ['hɔːdɪŋ, *Am:* 'hɔːr-] *n* **1.** *Brit, Aus* (*advertising board*) valla *f* publicitaria **2.** (*temporary fence*) valla *f* de construcción

hoarfrost [ˌhɔː'frɒst, *Am:* ˌhɔːr'frɑːst] *n no pl* escarcha *f*

hoarse [hɔːs, *Am:* hɔːrs] *adj* ronco, -a

hoarseness *n no pl* MED ronquera *f;* (*quality*) ronquedad *f*

hoary ['hɔːri] <-ier, -iest> *adj* **1.** *liter* (*hair*) cano, -a **2.** *fig* (*old*) **~ old joke** chiste *m* viejo; **~ old excuse** excusa *f* de siempre

hoax [həʊks, *Am:* hoʊks] **I.** <-es> *n* (*fraud*) engaño *m;* (*joke*) broma *f* de mal gusto **II.** *vt* engañar

hoaxer *n* (*fraudster*) embaucador(a) *m(f);* (*joke*) gracioso, -a *m, f*

hob [hɒb, *Am:* hɑːb] *n Brit* hornillo *m*

hobble ['hɒbl, *Am:* 'hɑːbl] **I.** *vi* cojear; **to ~ around** ir cojeando **II.** *vt* **1.** *liter* (*hinder*) obstaculizar **2.** (*tie legs: animal*) manear

hobby ['hɒbi, *Am:* 'hɑːbi] <-ies> *n* hobby *m*

hobby-horse ['hɒbɪhɔːs, *Am:* 'hɑːbɪhɔːrs] *n* **1.** (*toy*) caballito *m* **2.** (*topic*) tema *m* preferido (de conversación)

hobgoblin [ˌhɒb'gɒblɪn, *Am:* 'hɑːbˌgɑːb-] *n* duende *m*

hobnailed ['hɒbneɪld, *Am:* 'hɑːb-] *adj* **~ed boots** botas con clavos

hobnob ['hɒbnɒb, *Am:* 'hɑːbnɑːb] <-bb-> *vi inf* alternar; **to ~ with the rich and famous** codearse con los ricos y famosos

hobo ['həʊbəʊ, *Am:* 'hoʊboʊ] <-s *o* -es> *n Am, Aus* **1.** (*tramp*) vagabundo, -a *m, f* **2.** (*itinerant worker*) temporero, -a *m, f*

Hobson's choice [ˌhɒbsnz'tʃɔɪs, *Am:* ˌhɑːb-] *n* opción *f* única

hock[1] [hɒk, *Am:* hɑːk] *n* (*wine*) vino *m* del Rin

hock² [hɒk, *Am:* hɑːk] *Am, inf* **I.** *n* **to be in ~** (**to sb**) (*person*) estar endeudado (con alguien); **to be in ~** (*object*) estar empeñado; **my car is in ~** tengo el coche empeñado **II.** *vt* empeñar; **to be ~ed up to the neck** estar endeudado hasta las orejas

hock³ [hɒk, *Am:* hɑːk] *n* ANAT corvejón *m*

hockey ['hɒki, *Am:* 'hɑːki] *n no pl* hockey *m;* **ice ~** hockey sobre hielo

hockey stick *n* SPORTS stick *m*

hocus-pocus [ˌhəʊkəs'pəʊkəs, *Am:* ˌhoʊkəs'poʊ-] *n no pl* camelo *m*

hodgepodge ['hɒdʒpɒdʒ, *Am:* 'hɑːdʒpɑːdʒ] *n* batiburrillo *m*

hoe [həʊ, *Am:* hoʊ] **I.** *n* azada *f* **II.** *vt* azadonar

hog [hɒg, *Am:* hɑːg] **I.** *n* **1.** *Am* (*pig*) puerco *m,* chancho *m AmS* **2.** *inf* (*person*) egoísta *mf* ►**to live high on the ~** vivir como un rajá; **to go** (**the**) **whole ~** no quedarse a medio camino **II.** <-gg-> *vt inf* (*keep for oneself*) acaparar; (*food*) devorar; **to ~ sb/sth** (**all to oneself**) acaparar a alguien/algo (para uno mismo)

Hogmanay ['hɒgməneɪ, *Am:* 'hɑːg-] *n Scot* Nochevieja *f*

hogshead ['hɒgzhed, *Am:* 'hɑːgz-] *n* **1.** (*barrel*) pipa *f* **2.** (*measurement*) *medida de capacidad de aprox. 240 litros*

hogwash ['hɒgwɒʃ, *Am:* 'hɑːgwɑːʃ] *n no pl, inf* monserga *f*

hoi polloi [ˌhɔɪpə'lɔɪ] *npl inf* **the ~** las masas, el vulgo

hoist [hɔɪst] *vt* (*raise up*) alzar; (*flag*) enarbolar

hoity-toity [ˌhɔɪti'tɔɪti, *Am:* ˌhɔɪt̬i'tɔɪt̬i] *adj inf* repipi

hold [həʊld, *Am:* hoʊld] **I.** *n* **1.** (*grasp, grip*) agarre *m;* **to take ~ of sb/sth** asirse de [*o* a] alguien/algo; **to catch ~ of sb/sth** agarrar a alguien/algo; **to keep ~ of sth** seguir agarrado a algo **2.** (*thing to hold by*) asidero *m* **3.** (*wrestling*) presa *f;* **no ~s barred** *fig* sin restricciones **4.** (*control*) dominio *m;* **to have a** (**strong/powerful**) **~ over sb** tener (mucha/gran) influencia sobre alguien **5.** NAUT, AVIAT bodega *f* **6.** (*delayed*) **to be on ~** estar en espera; TEL estar a la espera; **to put on ~** poner en espera **7.** (*understand*) **to get ~ of sth** comprender algo; **to have a ~ of sth** tener idea de algo; **to get ~ of the wrong idea** hacerse una idea equivocada; **I don't know where you got ~ of that idea** no sé de dónde has sacado esa idea **II.** <held, held> *vt* **1.** (*keep*) tener; (*grasp*) agarrar; **to ~ a gun** sostener un arma; **to ~ hands** agarrarse de la mano; **to ~ sth in one's hand** sostener algo en la mano; **to ~ sb in one's arms** estrechar a alguien entre los brazos; **to ~ sb/sth** (**tight**) sujetar a alguien/algo (con fuerza); **to ~ the door open for sb** aguantar la puerta a alguien **2.** (*support*) soportar; **to ~ one's head high** mantener la cabeza alta **3.** (*keep, retain*) mantener; **to ~ sb's attention/interest** mantener la atención/el interés de alguien; **to ~ sb in custody** LAW mantener a alguien a disposición policial; **to ~ sb hostage** retener a alguien como rehén; **to ~** (**on to**) **the lead** seguir por delante **4.** (*maintain*) **to ~ oneself in readiness** estar listo; **to ~ oneself well** mantenerse en forma **5.** (*make keep to*) **to ~ sb to his/her word** hacer cumplir a alguien su palabra **6.** (*control*) **to ~ sth at the present/last year's level** mantener algo al nivel actual/del año pasado; **to ~ a note** MUS sostener una nota **7.** (*delay, stop*) detener; **~ it!** ¡para!; **to ~ one's breath** contener la respiración; **to ~ one's fire** MIL detener el fuego; **to ~ sb's phone calls** TEL retener las llamadas de alguien **8.** (*contain*) contener; **it ~s many surprises** conlleva muchas sorpresas; **what the future ~s** lo que depara el futuro **9.** (*possess, own*) poseer; (*land, town*) ocupar; **to ~ an account** (**with a bank**) tener una cuenta (en un banco); **to ~ the** (**absolute**) **majority** contar con la mayoría (absoluta); **to ~ a position** (**as sth**) mantener un puesto (como algo); **to ~ the fort** MIL aguantar en su puesto; *fig* hacerse cargo de **10.** (*make happen*) **to ~ a conversation** (**with sb**) mantener una conversación (con alguien); **to ~ an election/a meeting/a news conference** convocar elecciones/una reunión/una rueda de prensa; **to ~ manoeuvres** MIL estar de maniobras; **to ~ talks** dar charlas **11.** (*believe*) creer; **to be held in great respect** ser muy respetado; **to ~ sb responsible for sth** considerar a alguien responsable de algo; **to ~ sth in contempt** despreciar algo **12.** (*postpone*) **to ~ sth in abeyance** dejar algo pendiente **III.** *vi* **1.** (*continue*) seguir; **to ~ still** pararse; **to ~ true** seguir siendo válido; **~ tight!** ¡quieto! **2.** (*stick*) pegarse **3.** (*believe*) sostener

◆**hold against** *vt always sep* **to hold sth against sb** hacerse una mala idea de alguien por algo

◆**hold back** **I.** *vt* (*keep*) retener; **to ~ information** ocultar información; (*stop*) detener; (*impede development*) parar; **to ~ tears** contener las lágrimas ►**there's no holding me** (**back**) nada me retiene **II.** *vi* **1.** (*be unforthcoming*) refrenarse **2.** (*refrain*) **to ~ from doing sth** abstenerse de hacer algo

◆**hold down** *vt* sujetar; (*control, suppress*) oprimir; **to ~ a job** mantener un trabajo

◆**hold forth** *vi* **to ~** (**about sth**) hablar largo y tendido (sobre algo)

◆**hold in** *vt* (*emotion*) contener

◆**hold off** **I.** *vt* (*enemy*) detener **II.** *vi* mantenerse a distancia

◆**hold on** *vi* **1.** (*affix, attach*) agarrarse bien; **to be held on by/with sth** estar sujeto a/con algo **2.** (*manage to keep going*) **to ~** (**tight**) aguantar **3.** (*wait*) esperar

◆**hold onto** *vt insep* **1.** (*grasp*) agarrarse bien a **2.** (*keep*) guardar

◆**hold out** **I.** *vt* extender; **to ~ the hat** *Brit*

pasar el sombrero **II.** *vi* **1.** (*offer, chance*) ofrecer **2.** (*manage to resist*) resistir; **to be unable to ~** no poder aguantar; **to ~ for sth** resistir hasta conseguir algo **3.** (*refuse to give sth*) **to ~ on sb** no acceder a los deseos de alguien

◆**hold over** *vt* **1.** (*defer*) aplazar **2.** *Am* (*extend*) alargar

◆**hold to** *vt insep* atenerse a

◆**hold together I.** *vi* mantenerse unidos; **to be held together with glue** mantenerse pegados **II.** *vt* mantener unidos

◆**hold under** *vt insep* someter

◆**hold up I.** *vt* **1.** (*raise*) levantar; **to ~ one's hand** levantar la mano; **to be held up by (means of)/with sth** ser sostenido por (mediante)/con algo; **to hold up one's head high** *fig* mantener la cabeza alta **2.** (*delay*) atrasar **3.** (*rob with violence*) atracar **4.** (*offer as example*) **to hold sb up as an example of sth** mostrar a alguien como ejemplo de algo **II.** *vi* (*weather*) seguir haciendo bueno; (*material*) durar

◆**hold with** *vt insep* estar de acuerdo con

holdall ['həʊldɔːl, *Am:* 'hoʊld-] *n Brit* bolsa *f* de viaje

holder ['həʊldəʳ, *Am:* 'hoʊldɚ] *n* **1.** (*device*) soporte *m;* **cigarette ~** boquilla *f* **2.** (*person: of shares, of account*) titular *mf;* (*of title*) poseedor(a) *m(f);* **world record ~** plusmarquista *mf* mundial

holding *n* **1.** *pl* (*tenure*) tenencia *f* **2.** (*property*) propiedades *fpl* **3.** ECON participación *f;* **~s** valores *mpl* en cartera

holding company *n* holding *m*

hold-up ['həʊldʌp, *Am:* 'hoʊld-] *n* **1.** (*robbery*) atraco *m* **2.** (*delay*) retraso *m*

hole [həʊl, *Am:* hoʊl] **I.** *n* **1.** (*hollow space*) agujero *m* **2.** (*in golf*) hoyo *m* **3.** (*of mouse*) ratonera *f;* (*of rabbit*) madriguera *f* **4.** *inf* (*jam*) apuro *m;* **to be in a ~** estar en un apuro [*o* aprieto]; **to be in the ~** *Am* estar endeudado ►**to be a round peg in a square ~** estar fuera de lugar **II.** *vt* **1.** (*perforate*) agujerear **2.** (*in golf*) embocar

◆**hole up** *vi inf* esconderse

holiday ['hɒlədeɪ, *Am:* 'hɑːlə-] **I.** *n* **1.** *Brit, Aus* (*vacation*) vacaciones *fpl;* **on ~** de vacaciones; **to take a ~** coger vacaciones **2.** (*public day off*) día *m* festivo ►**a busman's ~** *día de fiesta que uno pasa trabajando* **II.** *vi* pasar las vacaciones; (*in summer*) veranear

holiday camp *n* campamento *f* de verano **holiday entitlement** *n* **he has a ~ of 30 days a year** le corresponden 30 días de vacaciones al año **holiday flat** *n* apartamento *m* de veraneo **holiday house** *n* casa *f* de veraneo **holidaymaker** *n* (*tourist*) turista *mf;* (*in summer*) veraneante *mf* **holiday resort** *n* centro *m* turístico

holiness ['həʊlɪnɪs, *Am:* 'hoʊ] *n no pl* santidad *f;* **His/Your Holiness** Su Santidad

holism ['həʊlɪzəm, *Am:* 'hoʊ-] *n no pl* holismo *m*

holistic [həʊ'lɪstɪk, *Am:* hoʊ-] *adj* holístico, -a

Holland ['hɒlənd, *Am:* 'hɑːlənd] *n* Holanda *f*

holler ['hɒləʳ, *Am:* 'hɑːlɚ] **I.** *vi Am, inf* gritar, chillar **II.** *n Am, inf* chillido *m*

hollow ['hɒləʊ, *Am:* 'hɑːloʊ] **I.** *adj* **1.** (*empty*) hueco, -a **2.** (*worthless, empty: promise*) vano, -a; (*victory*) vacío, -a; (*laughter*) falso, -a **3.** (*sound*) sordo, -a **II.** *n* hueco *m; Am* (*valley*) hondonada *f* **III.** *vt* **to ~ (out)** (*coconut*) vaciar; (*tree trunk*) ahuecar **IV.** *adv* **to sound ~** sonar a hueco ►**to beat sb ~** dar una paliza a alguien

holly ['hɒli, *Am:* 'hɑːli] *n no pl* BOT acebo *m*

hollyhock ['hɒlɪhɒk, *Am:* 'hɑːlɪhɑːk] *n* BOT malvarrosa *f*

holm oak ['həʊmˌəʊk, *Am:* 'hoʊmˌoʊk] *n* BOT encina *f*

holocaust ['hɒləkɔːst, *Am:* 'hɑːləkɑːst] *n* holocausto *m*

hologram ['hɒləgræm, *Am:* 'hɑːlə-] *n* holograma *m*

holster ['həʊlstəʳ, *Am:* 'hoʊlstɚ] *n* pistolera *f,* cañonera *f AmL*

holy ['həʊli, *Am:* 'hoʊ-] <-ier, -iest> *adj* **1.** (*sacred*) santo, -a; (*water*) bendito, -a **2.** *fig* **to be a ~ terror** ser el mismísimo demonio

Holy Communion *n* Sagrada Comunión *f* **Holy Father** *n* Santo Padre *m* **Holy Scripture** *n* **the ~** las Sagradas Escrituras **Holy See** *n* Santa Sede *f* **Holy Spirit** *n* Espíritu *m* Santo **Holy Week** *n* Semana *f* Santa

homage ['hɒmɪdʒ, *Am:* 'hɑːmɪdʒ] *n* homenaje *m;* **to pay ~ to sb** rendir homenaje a alguien

home [həʊm, *Am:* hoʊm] **I.** *n* **1.** (*residence*) casa *f;* **at ~** en casa; **to leave ~** salir [*o* irse] de casa; **away from ~** fuera de casa; **I live in London but my ~ is in Barcelona** vivo en Londres pero soy de Barcelona; **make yourself at ~** ponte cómodo, estás en tu casa **2.** (*family*) hogar *m* **3.** (*institution*) asilo *m;* (*for old people*) residencia *f;* **children's ~** orfanato *m* **II.** *adv* **1.** (*one's place of residence*) **to be ~** estar en casa; **to go/come ~** ir/venir a casa; **to take work ~** llevarse trabajo a casa **2.** (*understanding*) **to bring sth ~ to sb** conseguir que alguien se dé cuenta de algo ►**to be ~ and dry** *Brit,* **to be ~ and hosed** *Aus* tener la victoria asegurada; **this is nothing to write ~ about** esto no es nada del otro mundo **III.** *adj* **1.** (*from own country*) nacional **2.** (*from own area*) local; (*team*) de casa; (*game*) en casa; **the ~ ground** el campo de casa

◆**home in on** *vt insep, inf* **1.** MIL apuntar **2.** (*locate*) localizar y dirigirse hacia

home address *n* dirección *f* particular **home affairs** *npl Brit* POL asuntos *mpl* interiores **home-baked** *adj* casero, -a **homebanking** *n* telebanking *m* **home**

H

brew *n cerveza hecha en casa* **homecoming** *n* regreso *m* (a casa)

> En los EE.UU. se utiliza el término **Homecoming** para referirse a una importante fiesta que tiene lugar en la High School y la universidad. Ese día el equipo de fútbol local juega en su propio campo. Se celebra una gran fiesta y se erige **homecoming queen** a la alumna más popular.

home computer *n* ordenador *m* doméstico **home cooking** *n no pl* cocina *f* casera **Home Counties** *n Brit: condados de los alrededores de Londres* **home economics** *n + sing vb* economía *f* doméstica **home-grown** *adj* **1.** (*vegetables*) de cosecha propia **2.** (*not foreign*) del país **3.** (*local*) local **home help** *n* asistente, -a *m, f* (para las tareas domésticas) **homeland** *n* (*country of birth*) tierra *f* natal **homeless** **I.** *adj* sin hogar **II.** *n + pl vb* **the** ~ los sin techo **homelike** *adj* hogareño, -a **home loan** *n* hipoteca *f*

homely ['həʊmli, *Am:* 'hoʊm-] <-ier, -iest> *adj* **1.** *Brit, Aus* (*plain*) casero, -a **2.** *Am, Aus* (*ugly*) feo, -a

home-made [ˌhəʊm'meɪd, *Am:* ˌhoʊm-] *adj* casero, -a **homemaker** *n Am* ama *f* de casa **home market** *n* mercado *m* nacional **Home Office** *n Brit* Ministerio *m* del Interior **homepage** *n* página *f* inicial, portal *m*

homeopath ['həʊmiəʊpæθ, *Am:* 'hoʊmioʊ-] *n* homeópata *mf*

homeopathic [ˌhəʊmiəʊ'pæθɪk, *Am:* ˌhoʊmioʊ'-] *adj* homeopático, -a

homeopathy [ˌhəʊmi'ɒpəθi, *Am:* ˌhoʊmi'ɒpə-] *n no pl* homeopatía *f*

homeowner ['həʊmˌəʊnəʳ, *Am:* 'hoʊmˌoʊnɚ] *n* propietario, -a *m, f*

home plate *n Am* SPORTS base *f* del bateador **home rule** *n* gobierno *m* autónomo **Home Secretary** <-ies> *n Brit* ministro, -a *m, f* del Interior

homesick ['həʊmsɪk, *Am:* 'hoʊm-] *adj* nostálgico, -a; **to feel** ~ (**for**) tener morriña (de) **homesickness** *n no pl* morriña *f*

homespun ['həʊmspʌn, *Am:* 'hoʊm-] *adj* de andar por casa; (*wisdom*) popular **homestead** *n Am, Aus* finca *f*

home straight *n*, **home stretch** <-es> *n* recta *f* final **home team** *n* equipo *m* local [*o* de casa] **home town** *n* ciudad *f* natal, pueblo *m* natal **home truth** *n* **to tell sb a few ~s** decir a alguien unas cuantas verdades

homeward ['həʊmwəd, *Am:* 'hoʊmwɚd] **I.** *adv* de camino a casa **II.** *adj* (*journey*) de regreso **homewards** *adv s.* **homeward I.**

homework ['həʊmwɜːk, *Am:* 'hoʊmwɜːrk] *n* SCHOOL deberes *mpl* **homeworker** *n* persona *f* que trabaja desde casa

homey ['həʊmi, *Am:* 'hoʊ-] <-ier, -iest> *adj* casero, -a

homicidal [ˌhɒmɪ'saɪdl, *Am:* ˌhɑːmə-] *adj Am, Aus* LAW homicida

homicide ['hɒmɪsaɪd, *Am:* 'hɑːmə-] **I.** *n Am, Aus* **1.** (*crime*) homicidio *m* **2.** (*criminal*) homicida *mf* **II.** *adj* ~ **squad** *Am, Aus* homicidios *mpl*

homing ['həʊmɪŋ, *Am:* 'hoʊ-] *adj* (*instinct*) de volver al hogar; (*device*) buscador(a)

homing pigeon *n* paloma *f* mensajera

homogeneous *adj*, **homogenous** [ˌhɒmə'dʒiːniəs, *Am:* ˌhoʊmoʊ'dʒiː-] *adj* homogéneo, -a

homogenize [hə'mɒdʒənaɪz, *Am:* hə'mɑːdʒə-] *vt* homogeneizar

homograph ['hɒməgrɑːf, *Am:* 'hɑːməgræf] *n* homógrafo *m*

homonym ['hɒmənɪm, *Am:* 'hɑːmə-] *n* homónimo *m*

homophobia [ˌhɒmə'fəʊbiə, *Am:* ˌhoʊmə'foʊ-] *n no pl* homofobia *f*

homophone ['hɒməfəʊn, *Am:* 'hɑːməfoʊn] *n* homófono *m*

homosexual [ˌhɒmə'sekʃʊəl, *Am:* ˌhoʊmoʊ-] **I.** *adj* homosexual **II.** *n* homosexual *mf*

homosexuality [ˌhɒməsekʃʊ'æləti, *Am:* ˌhoʊmoʊsekʃʊ'æləţi] *n no pl* homosexualidad *f*

Hon. *abbr of* **Honorary** Hon.

Honduran [hɒn'djʊərən, *Am:* hɑːn'dʊr-] **I.** *adj* hondureño, -a **II.** *n* hondureño, -a *m, f*

Honduras [hɒn'djʊərəs, *Am:* hɑːn'dʊr-] *n* Honduras *f*

hone [həʊn, *Am:* hoʊn] *vt* (*sharpen*) afilar; *fig* (*refine*) afinar

honest ['ɒnɪst, *Am:* 'ɑːnɪst] *adj* **1.** (*trustworthy*) honesto, -a **2.** (*truthful*) sincero, -a; **to be ~ with oneself** ser sincero consigo mismo; ~ (**to God**) *inf* como Dios manda

honestly *adv* (*truthfully*) sinceramente; (*with honesty*) honradamente

honest-to-goodness ['ɒnɪsttə'gʊdnɪs, *Am:* 'ɑːnɪst-] *adj* como Dios manda

honesty ['ɒnɪsti, *Am:* 'ɑːnɪ-] *n no pl* **1.** (*trustworthiness*) honestidad *f* **2.** (*sincerity*) sinceridad *f*; **in all** ~ para ser sincero

honey ['hʌni] *n no pl* **1.** GASTR miel *f* **2.** *Am* (*sweet person*) encanto *m*; (*sweet thing*) preciosidad *f* **3.** (*darling*) cariño *m* **honeybee** *n* abeja *f* **honeycomb** **I.** *n* panal *m* **II.** *adj* (*pattern*) de panal **honeydew** (**melon**) *n* melón *m* dulce **honeymoon** **I.** *n* luna *f* de miel **II.** *vi* pasar la luna de miel **honeysuckle** *n* BOT madreselva *f*

honk [hɒŋk, *Am:* hɑːŋk] **I.** *vi* **1.** ZOOL graznar **2.** AUTO tocar la bocina **II.** *n* **1.** ZOOL graznido *m* **2.** AUTO bocinazo *m*

honor ['ɑːnɚ] *n Am, Aus s.* **honour**

honorable ['ɑːnɚrəbl] *adj Am, Aus s.* **honourable**

honorary ['ɒnərəri, *Am:* 'ɑːnərer-] *adj* **1.** (*conferred as an honour: title*) honorario, -a; (*president*) de honor **2.** (*without pay*) no remunerado, -a

honors degree *n Am, Aus s.* **honours degree**

honour ['ɒnəʳ] **I.** *n Brit* **1.** (*respect*) honor *m;* **in ~ of sb/sth** en honor de alguien/algo; **to be (in) ~ bound to ...** estar moralmente obligado a... **2.** LAW **Her/His/Your Honour** Su Señoría **3.** *pl* (*distinction*) honores *mpl;* **last ~s** honras *fpl* fúnebres; **to graduate with ~s** licenciarse con matrícula de honor **II.** *vt* **1.** (*fulfil: promise, contract*) cumplir (con) **2.** (*confer honour*) honrar; **to be ~ed** sentirse honrado

honourable ['ɒnərəbl] *adj Brit* **1.** (*worthy of respect: person*) honorable; (*agreement*) honroso, -a **2.** (*honest*) honrado, -a **3.** *Brit* POL **the Honourable member for ...** el Ilustre Señor Diputado de...

honours degree *n Brit* UNIV licenciatura *f* de matrícula de honor

hons *n abbr of* **honours** honores *mpl*

hood¹ [hʊd] *n* **1.** (*covering for head*) capucha *f* **2.** (*on machine*) cubierta *f;* (*on cooker*) campana *f* **3.** *Am* AUTO capó *m* **4.** *Brit* (*folding top*) capota *f*

hood² [hʊd] *n Am, inf* (*gangster*) matón, -ona *m, f*

hoodlum ['hu:dləm] *n* matón, -ona *m, f*

hoodwink ['hʊdwɪŋk] *vt* engañar, emplumar *Guat, Cuba*

hoof [hu:f, *Am:* hʊf] **I.** <hooves *o* hoofs> *n* casco *m*, pezuña *f;* **on the ~** (*cattle*) en pie **II.** *vt inf* **to ~ it** ir a pata

hoo-ha ['hu:hɑ:] *n no pl, inf* jaleo *m*

hook [hʊk] **I.** *n* (*device for holding*) gancho *m;* (*for clothes*) percha *f;* (*fish*) anzuelo *m;* **to leave the phone off the ~** dejar el teléfono descolgado ►**by ~ or by crook** por las buenas o por las malas; **to fall for sth ~, line and sinker** tragárselo [*o* creérselo] todo; **to be off the ~** librarse; **to get one's ~ into sb** tener a alguien en las garras (de uno); **to sling one's ~** *Brit, inf* pirarse **II.** *vt* **1.** (*fasten*) enganchar **2.** (*fish*) pescar **III.** *vi* (*clothes*) abrocharse (con corchetes); (*parts*) engancharse

◆**hook on I.** *vi* conectarse **II.** *vt* enganchar

◆**hook up I.** *vt* **1.** (*hang: curtains*) poner **2.** (*link up*) enganchar; (*connect*) conectar **II.** *vi* **1.** (*connect*) conectarse **2.** (*clothes*) abrocharse

hooked [hʊkt] *adj* **1.** (*nose*) ganchudo, -a **2.** (*addicted*) enganchado, -a

hooker¹ ['hʊkəʳ, *Am:* -ɚ] *n Am, Aus, inf* prostituta *f*

hooker² ['hʊkəʳ, *Am:* -ɚ] *n* SPORTS talonador(a) *m(f)*

hooky ['hʊki] *n no pl, Am, Aus, inf* **to play ~** hacer novillos, capar clase *Col*

hooligan ['hu:lɪgən] *n* hooligan *mf*

hooliganism *n no pl* hooliganismo *m*, gamberrismo *m*

hoop [hu:p] *n* aro *m* ►**to put sb through the ~s** hacérselas pasar negras a alguien

hoopoe ['hu:pu:] *n* abubilla *f*

hoot [hu:t] **I.** *vi* (*owl*) ulular; (*with horn*) tocar la bocina; **to ~ with laughter** desternillarse de risa **II.** *vt* **to ~ sb** tocar la bocina [*o* pitar] a alguien **III.** *n* (*of owl*) ululato *m;* (*of horn*) bocinazo *m;* (*of train*) pitido *m;* **to give a ~ of laughter** soltar una carcajada; **to not give a ~ (about sth)** importar algo un pito a alguien

◆**hoot down** *vt* abuchear

hooter ['hu:təʳ, *Am:* -t̬ɚ] *n* **1.** (*siren*) sirena *f* **2.** *inf* (*nose*) napia *f*

hoover® ['hu:vəʳ, *Am:* -vɚ] **I.** *n Brit, Aus* aspirador *m* **II.** *vt* pasar el aspirador por **III.** *vi* pasar el aspirador

hop¹ [hɒp, *Am:* hɑ:p] *n* BOT lúpulo *m*

hop² [hɒp, *Am:* hɑ:p] <-pp-> **I.** *vi* saltar **II.** *vt Am, inf* (*bus*) subir a; **to ~ it** *Brit, inf* largarse **III.** *n* **1.** (*leap*) salto *m;* (*using only one leg*) salto *m* a la pata coja, brinco *m* de cojito *Méx* **2.** *inf* (*informal dance*) baile *m* **3.** (*short flight*) vuelo *m* corto ►**to catch sb on the ~** *Brit, inf* pillar a alguien desprevenido

◆**hop about** *vi,* **hop around** *vi* saltar; **to ~ from one subject to another** saltar de un tema a otro

◆**hop in** *vt insep* pillar; **to ~ a taxi** *inf* pillar un taxi

◆**hop out** *vi* bajar (de un salto); **to ~ of bed** saltar de la cama

hope [həʊp, *Am:* hoʊp] **I.** *n* esperanza *f;* **to give up ~** perder la(s) esperanza(s); **to pin all one's ~s on sb/sth** poner todas las esperanzas en alguien/algo; **there is still ~** todavía hay esperanzas ►**to not have a ~ in hell** no tener ni la más remota posibilidad **II.** *vi* (*wish*) esperar; **to ~ for the best** esperar que la suerte acompañe a uno

hopeful ['həʊpfəl, *Am:* 'hoʊp-] **I.** *adj* **1.** (*person*) esperanzado, -a; **to be ~** ser optimista **2.** (*promising*) esperanzador(a) **II.** *n pl* candidato, -a *m, f;* **young ~s** jóvenes aspirantes *mfpl*

hopefully *adv* **1.** (*in a hopeful manner*) con ilusión **2.** (*one hopes*) **~!** ¡ojalá!; **~ we'll be in Sweden at 6.00 PM** si todo sale bien estaremos en Suecia a las 6 de la tarde

hopeless ['həʊpləs, *Am:* 'hoʊp-] *adj* (*situation*) desesperado, -a; (*effort*) imposible; **to be ~** *inf* (*person*) ser inútil; (*service*) ser un desastre; **to be ~ at sth** ser negado para algo

hopelessly *adv* **1.** (*without hope*) sin esperanzas **2.** (*totally, completely*) **~ lost** totalmente perdido

hopper ['hɒpəʳ, *Am:* 'hɑ:pɚ] *n* tolva *f*

hopping mad ['hɒpɪŋ 'mæd, *Am:* 'hɑ:p-] *adj inf* furioso, -a; **he is ~** está que trina

hopscotch ['hɒpskɒtʃ, *Am:* 'hɑ:pskɑ:tʃ] *n no pl* **to play ~** jugar a la rayuela

horde [hɔ:d, *Am:* hɔ:rd] *n* multitud *f*

horizon [hə'raɪzn] *n a. fig* horizonte *m*

horizontal [ˌhɒrɪ'zɒntl, *Am:* ˌhɔ:rɪ'zɑ:n-] **I.** *adj* horizontal **II.** *n no pl* horizontal *f*

hormone ['hɔ:məʊn, *Am:* 'hɔ:rmoʊn] *n* hormona *f*

horn [hɔ:n, *Am:* hɔ:rn] *n* **1.** ZOOL cuerno *m*

2. MUS trompa *f* 3. AUTO bocina *f* 4. *no pl* (*material*) cuerno *m* ►**to be on the ~s of a dilemma** estar entre la espada y la pared; **to draw in one's ~s** apretarse el cinturón; **to lock ~s (over sth)** tener un enfrentamiento (por algo)

◆**horn in** *vi Am* **to ~ on sth** entrometerse en algo

hornet ['hɔːnɪt, *Am:* 'hɔːr-] *n* avispón *m*

horn-rimmed ['hɔːnrɪmt, *Am:* 'hɔːrn-] *adj* (*glasses*) de concha

horny ['hɔːni, *Am:* 'hɔːr-] <-ier, -iest> *adj* 1. (*made of horn*) córneo, -a 2. *inf* (*lustful*) cachondo, -a 3. *Am, inf* (*attractive*) macizo, -a

horoscope ['hɒrəskəʊp, *Am:* 'hɔːrəskoʊp] *n* horóscopo *m*

horrendous [hɒ'rendəs, *Am:* hɔː'ren-] *adj* 1. (*crime*) horrendo, -a 2. (*losses*) terrible

horrible ['hɒrəbl, *Am:* 'hɔːr-] *adj* horrible

horrid ['hɒrɪd, *Am:* 'hɔːr-] *adj* (*unpleasant*) horrible; (*unkind*) antipático, -a

horrific [hə'rɪfɪk, *Am:* hɔː'rɪf-] *adj* horroroso, -a

horrify ['hɒrɪfaɪ, *Am:* 'hɔːr-] <-ie-> *vt* horrorizar

horror ['hɒrəʳ, *Am:* 'hɔːrɚ] *n* horror *m*, espantosidad *f AmC, Col, PRico;* **~ film** película *f* de terror

horror-stricken ['hɒrəˌstrɪkən, *Am:* 'hɔː-rɚ-] *adj,* **horror-struck** *adj* horrorizado, -a

hors d'œuvre [ɔː'dɜːv, *Am:* ɔːr'dɜːrv] <hors d'oeuvre *o* hors d'oeuvres> *n* entremés *m*, entremeses *mpl*

horse [hɔːs, *Am:* hɔːrs] *n* 1. ZOOL caballo *m;* **to ride a ~** montar a caballo 2. SPORTS potro *m* ►**to change ~s (in) midstream** cambiar de parecer a mitad de camino; **to get sth straight from the ~'s mouth** saber algo de buena tinta; **don't look a gift ~ in the mouth** *prov* a caballo regalado, no le mires el dentado *prov;* **you can take a ~ to water but you can't make him drink** *prov* puedes darle un consejo a alguien, pero no puedes obligarlo a que lo siga; **to flog a dead ~** perder el tiempo (intentando algo), arar en el mar; **to be on one's high ~** *inf* tener muchos humos; **to eat like a ~** comer como una lima; **to hold one's ~s** *inf* parar el carro

◆**horse about** *vi,* **horse around** *vi* hacer el tonto

horseback ['hɔːsbæk, *Am:* 'hɔːrs-] I. *n* **on ~** a caballo II. *adj* **~ riding** equitación *f* **horsebox** *n,* **horse car** *n Am* remolque *m* para transportar caballos **horse chestnut** *n* (*tree*) castaño *m* de Indias; (*fruit*) castaña *f* de Indias **horse-drawn** *adj* tirado, -a por caballos **horsefly** <-ies> *n* tábano *m* **horsehair** *n no pl* crin *f*

horseman ['hɔːsmən, *Am:* 'hɔːrs-] <-men> *n* jinete *m* **horsemanship** *n no pl* equitación *f*

horseplay ['hɔːspleɪ, *Am:* 'hɔːrs-] *n no pl* juguetecito(s) *m(pl)* **horsepower** *inv n no pl* caballo (*m* de vapor)

horse race *n* carrera *f* de caballos **horse racing** *n* carreras *fpl* de caballos **horseradish** *n* rábano *m* picante **horse riding** *n no pl* equitación *f* **horse sense** *n inf* sentido *m* común **horseshoe** *n* herradura *f* **horse-trading** *n no pl* tira *m* y afloja

horsewhip ['hɔːswɪp, *Am:* 'hɔːrs-] I. <-pp-> *vt* dar latigazos a II. *n* látigo *m*

horsewoman ['hɔːswʊmən, *Am:* 'hɔːrs-] <-women> *n* amazona *f*

hors(e)y ['hɔːsi, *Am:* 'hɔːr-] <-ier, -iest> *adj* 1. (*interested in horses*) aficionado, -a a los caballos 2. (*face*) de caballo

horticultural [ˌhɔːtɪ'kʌltʃərəl, *Am:* ˌhɔːrṭə-'kʌltʃɚ-] *adj no pl* hortícola

horticulture ['hɔːtɪkʌltʃəʳ, *Am:* 'hɔːrṭə-kʌltʃɚ] *n no pl* horticultura *f*

hose [həʊz, *Am:* hoʊz] *n* manguera *f*

hosepipe [həʊzpaɪp, *Am:* hoʊz-] *n Brit s.* **hose**

hosiery ['həʊziəri, *Am:* 'hoʊʒɚi] *n no pl* (*shop*) calcetería *f;* (*goods*) medias *fpl* y calcetines

hospice ['hɒspɪs, *Am:* 'hɑːspɪs] *n* 1. (*house of shelter*) hospicio *m* 2. (*hospital*) residencia *f* para enfermos terminales

hospitable [hɒ'spɪtəbl, *Am:* 'hɑːspɪṭə-] *adj* hospitalario, -a

hospital ['hɒspɪtəl, *Am:* 'hɑːspɪṭəl] *n* hospital *m*

hospitality [ˌhɒspɪ'tæləti, *Am:* ˌhɑːspɪ-'tæləṭi] I. *n no pl* hospitalidad *f* II. *adj* (*food, drinks*) de cortesía

hospitalization [ˌhɒspɪtəlaɪz'eɪʃən, *Am:* ˌhɑːspɪṭəlɪ-] *n no pl* hospitalización *f*

hospitalize ['hɒspɪtəlaɪz, *Am:* 'hɑːspɪṭəl-] *vt* hospitalizar

hospital ship *n* buque *m* hospital

host[1] [həʊst, *Am:* hoʊst] I. *n* 1. (*person who receives guests*) anfitrión, -ona *m, f* 2. (*presenter*) presentador(a) *m(f)* 3. BIO huésped *m* 4. INFOR servidor *m* II. *vt* 1. (*party*) dar; (*event*) ser la sede de 2. (*programme*) presentar

host[2] [həʊst, *Am:* hoʊst] *n* multitud *f;* **a whole ~ of reasons** muchas razones

Host [həʊst, *Am:* hoʊst] *n* REL Hostia *f*

hostage ['hɒstɪdʒ, *Am:* 'hɑːstɪdʒ] *n* rehén *mf;* **to take/hold sb ~** tomar/tener a alguien como rehén ►**to create a ~ to fortune** jugársela

host country <-ies> *n* país *m* anfitrión

hostel ['hɒstl, *Am:* 'hɑːstl] *n* 1. (*cheap hotel*) hostal *m;* **student ~** residencia *f* de estudiantes; **youth ~** albergue *m* juvenil 2. *Brit* (*for homeless*) casa *f* de acogida

hosteller ['hɒstələʳ, *Am:* 'hɑːstəlɚ] *n* alberguista *mf*

hostess ['həʊstɪs, *Am:* 'hoʊ-] <-es> *n* 1. AVIAT azafata *f* 2. (*woman who receives guests*) anfitriona *f* 3. (*presenter*) presentadora *f*

hostile ['hɒstaɪl, *Am:* 'hɑːstl] *adj* hostil; ~

aircraft avión enemigo

hostility [hɒ'stɪləti, *Am:* hɑː'stɪlət̬i] <-ies> *n* hostilidad *f*

hot [hɒt, *Am:* hɑːt] *adj* **1.** (*very warm: food, water*) caliente; (*day, weather*) caluroso, -a; (*climate*) cálido, -a; **it's ~** hace calor **2.** (*spicy*) picante, bravo, -a *AmL* **3.** *inf* (*skilful*) hábil; **to be ~ stuff at (doing) sth** ser un hacha en algo **4.** *inf* (*demanding*) estricto, -a; **to be ~ on sth** dar mucha importancia a algo **5.** (*dangerous*) peligroso, -a; **to be too ~ to handle** *fig* ser demasiado difícil de manejar **6.** *inf* (*sexually attractive*) **to be ~** estar bueno **7.** (*exciting: music, party*) animado, -a; **~ news** noticias frescas ►**to be all ~ and bothered** estar sulfurado

◆**hot up** <-tt-> *vi* (*situation*) calentarse

hot air [ˌhɒt'eəʳ, *Am:* ˌhɑːt'er] *n fig* palabras *fpl* huecas; **to be (just) so much ~ air** ser sólo palabrería **hot-air balloon** *n* globo *m* de aire caliente

hotbed ['hɒtbed, *Am:* 'hɑːt-] *n fig* (*of vice, disease, crime*) caldo *m* de cultivo **hot-blooded** *n* (*easy to anger*) irascible; (*passionate*) apasionado, -a

hotchpotch ['hɒtʃpɒtʃ, *Am:* 'hɑːtʃpɑːtʃ] *n no pl* batiburrillo *m*

hot dog [ˌhɒt'dɒg, *Am:* 'hɑːtdɑːg] *n* **1.** GASTR perrito *m* caliente, pancho *m Arg* **2.** ZOOL perro *m* salchicha

hotel [həʊ'tel, *Am:* hoʊ-] *n* hotel *m*

hotel accommodation *n no pl* alojamiento *m* **hotel bill** *n* factura *f* del hotel

hotelier [həʊ'teliɪ, *Am:* ˌhoʊtel'jeɪ] *n* (*owner*) hotelero, -a *m, f;* (*manager*) director(a) *m(f)* del hotel

hotel industry *n no pl* industria *f* hotelera **hotel staff** *n no pl* personal *m* del hotel

hotfoot ['hɒtfʊt, *Am:* 'hɑːt-] **I.** *adv* a toda prisa **II.** *vt* **to ~ it somewhere** *inf* ir volando a algún sitio **III.** *vi* ir volando

hothead ['hɒthed, *Am:* 'hɑːt-] *n* persona *f* alocada **hotheaded** *adj* impulsivo, -a

hothouse ['hɒthaʊs, *Am:* 'hɑːt-] **I.** *n* invernadero *m* **II.** *adj* de invernadero **hotline** *n* TEL línea *f* directa; **to set up a ~** poner una línea directa

hotly *adv* apasionadamente

hot metal *n* TYPO fundición *f* **hotplate** *n* hornillo *m* **hot potato** <-oes> *n fig* patata *f* caliente **hotrod** *n inf* AUTO coche *m* trucado **hot seat** *n* **1.** (*difficult position*) **to be in the ~** estar en la línea de fuego **2.** (*electric chair*) silla *f* eléctrica **hotshot** *n Am, Aus, inf* hacha *f;* **to be a (real) ~ at sth** *fig* ser un as en algo **hot spot** *n inf* **1.** (*popular place*) lugar *m* concurrido **2.** (*nightclub*) club *m* nocturno **hot stuff** *n* **1.** (*good*) **to be ~ at sth** ser un as en algo **2.** (*sexy*) **to be ~** estar bueno **hot-tempered** *adj* irascible **hot-water bottle** *n* bolsa *f* de agua caliente

hound [haʊnd] **I.** *n* perro *m* de caza **II.** *vt* perseguir

hour ['aʊəʳ, *Am:* 'aʊr] *n* **1.** (*60 minutes*) hora *f;* **to be paid by the ~** cobrar por horas **2.** (*time of day*) **at all ~s of the day and night** noche y día; **ten minutes to the ~** diez minutos para en punto; **till all ~s** hasta muy tarde; **out of ~s, after ~** *Am, Aus* fuera del horario establecido **3.** (*time for an activity*) **lunch ~** hora de comer; **at the agreed ~** a la hora convenida; **opening ~s** horario *m* (comercial) **4.** (*period of time*) momento *m;* **at any ~** en cualquier momento; **to spend long ~s doing sth** pasarse mucho tiempo haciendo algo; **to change from ~ to ~** cambiar cada hora; **to keep irregular/regular ~s** llevar un horario variable/regular; **to work long ~s** trabajar hasta muy tarde; **~ after ~** hora tras hora

hour hand *n* manecilla *f*

hourly *adv* (*every hour*) cada hora; (*pay*) por horas

house [haʊs] **I.** *n* **1.** (*inhabitation*) casa *f;* **to move ~** mudarse; **to set one's ~ in order** *fig* poner sus cosas en orden **2.** (*family*) familia *f;* **the House of Windsor** la casa de Windsor **3.** (*business*) empresa *f;* **it's on the ~** invita la casa **4.** *Brit, Aus* (*school group*) *grupo formado por niños en un colegio internado para juegos y competiciones deportivas* **5.** (*legislative body*) cámara *f* **6.** (*audience*) público *m;* **'~ full'** 'no quedan localidades'; **full ~** (teatro *m*) lleno *m;* **to bring the ~ down** *inf* ser todo un éxito ►**to be as save as ~s** *Brit* ser completamente seguro **II.** *vt* **1.** (*give place to live*) alojar **2.** (*contain*) albergar

house arrest *n no pl* arresto *m* domiciliario **houseboat** *n* casa *f* flotante

housebreaker ['haʊsˌbreɪkəʳ, *Am:* -kɚ] *n* ladrón, -ona *m, f* (que desvalija viviendas) **housebreaking** *n no pl* allanamiento *m* de morada con robo

housecoat ['haʊskəʊt, *Am:* -koʊt] *n* bata *f* **housefly** <-ies> *n* mosca *f* común

household ['haʊshəʊld, *Am:* -hoʊld] **I.** *n* hogar *m* **II.** *adj* doméstico, -a **householder** *n* (*owner*) propietario, -a *m, f* de una casa; (*head*) cabeza *m* de familia

house-hunt ['haʊshʌnt] *vi inf* buscar casa **house husband** *n* amo *m* de casa

housekeeper ['haʊsˌkiːpəʳ, *Am:* -pɚ] *n* ama *f* de llaves **housekeeping** *n no pl* organización *f* doméstica **housekeeping money** *n no pl* dinero *m* para los gastos de la casa

housemaid ['haʊsmeɪd] *n* criada *f* **houseman** *n Brit* mayordomo *m* **house martin** *n* avión *m* común **house physician** *n* médico, -a *m, f* residente **houseplant** *n* planta *f* de interior **houseproud** *adj Brit, Aus* maniático, -a de la limpieza **houseroom** *n* sitio *f* en una casa; **I wouldn't give it ~** no lo permitiría en casa **house rules** *npl* normas *fpl* de la casa **house surgeon** *n Brit* cirujano, -a *m, f* residente **house-to-house** *adj* puerta a puerta **housetrained** *adj Brit, Aus* adiestrado, -a **house-warming** *n,*

house-warming party *n no pl* fiesta *f* de inaguración (de una nueva vivienda) **housewife** <-wives> *n* ama *f* de casa, huarmi *f AmS* **housework** *n no pl* tareas *fpl* del hogar
housing ['haʊzɪŋ] *n* vivienda *f*
housing association *n* cooperativa *f* inmobiliaria **housing benefit** *n Brit* subsidio *m* para la vivienda **housing conditions** *npl* condiciones *fpl* de habitabilidad **housing development** *n Am* urbanización *f* **housing estate** *n Brit* urbanización *f*
hove [həʊv, *Am:* hoʊv] *vi pp of* **heave**
hovel ['hɒvl, *Am:* 'hʌv-] *n* tugurio *m,* sucucho *m AmL*
hover ['hɒvəʳ, *Am:* 'hʌvɚ] *vi* **1.** (*stay in air*) cernerse **2.** (*be in an uncertain state*) estar vacilante **3.** (*wait near*) rondar **4.** (*hesitate*) dudar; **to ~ on the brink of accepting sth** estar casi a punto de aceptar algo
hovercraft ['hɒvəkrɑːft, *Am:* 'hʌvɚkræft] <-(s)> *n* aerodeslizador *m* **hoverport** *n* terminal *f* de aerodeslizadores
how [haʊ] **I.** *adv* **1.** (*in this way*) como; (*in which way?*) cómo; **~ do you mean?** ¿cómo dices?; **~ do you mean you crashed the motorbike?** ¿cómo que te cargaste la moto? **2.** (*in what condition?*) **~ are you?** ¿qué tal?; **~ do you do?** encantado de conocerle **3.** (*for what reason?*) **~ come ...?** *inf* ¿cómo es que...? **4.** (*suggestion*) **~ about ...?** ¿qué tal si... ?; **~ about that!** ¡mira por dónde!; **~'s that for an offer?** ¿trato hecho? **5.** (*intensifier*) **~ pretty she looked!** ¡qué guapa estaba!; **and ~!** ¡ni que lo digas! **II.** *n* modo *m;* **to know the ~(s) and why(s) of sth** saber el cómo y el porqué de algo
how-do-you-do [ˌhaʊdjʊ'duː, *Am:* 'haʊdəjuːduː] *n inf* apuro *m*
however [haʊ'evəʳ, *Am:* -ɚ] **I.** *adv* **1.** (*no matter how*) por más que +*subj;* **~ hard she tries ...** por mucho que lo intente... **2.** (*in whichever way*) como; **do it ~ you like** hazlo como quieras **II.** *conj* (*nevertheless*) sin embargo
howl [haʊl] **I.** *vi* **1.** (*person, animal*) aullar; (*wind*) silbar; **to ~ in** [*o* **with**] **pain** dar alaridos de dolor **2.** (*cry*) chillar; (*child*) berrear **3.** *inf* (*laugh*) morirse de risa **II.** *n* **1.** (*person, animal*) aullido *m* **2.** (*cry*) chillido *m;* (*of child*) berrido *m;* **to give a ~ of pain** soltar un alarido de dolor; **~s of protest** gritos *mpl* de protesta
◆**howl down** *vt* hacer callar a gritos
howler ['haʊləʳ, *Am:* -lɚ] *n* error *m* garrafal; **to make a ~** meter la pata hasta el fondo
howling *adj* aullador(a)
hp [ˌeɪtʃ'piː] *abbr of* **horsepower** CV
HP [ˌeɪtʃ'piː] *n Brit, inf abbr of* **hire purchase** compra *f* a plazos
HQ [ˌeɪtʃ'kjuː] *abbr of* **headquarters** sede *f* central
HRH [ˌeɪtʃɑːʳ'eɪtʃ, *Am:* -ɑːr'-] *abbr of* **Her/His Royal Highness** S.A.R.
ht *abbr of* **height** a
HTML [ˌeɪtʃtiːem'el] *n* INFOR *abbr of* **Hypertext Markup Language** HTML
http *n* INFOR *abbr of* **hypertext transfer protocol** http
hub [hʌb] *n* **1.** (*of wheel*) cubo *m* **2.** *fig* (*centre*) centro *m*
hubbub ['hʌbʌb] *n no pl* barullo *m*
hubcap ['hʌbkæp] *n* tapacubos *m inv*
huckleberry ['hʌklbəri, *Am:* -'ber-] <-ies> *n Am* BOT arándano *m*
huckster ['hʌkstəʳ, *Am:* -stɚ] *n* **1.** (*salesman*) charlatán, -ana *m, f* **2.** *Am* (*writer*) publicista *mf* de pacotilla
huddle ['hʌdl] **I.** *vi* apiñarse **II.** *n* (*close group*) piña *f;* **to go into a ~** hacer grupo aparte
◆**huddle down** *vi* acurrucarse
◆**huddle together** *vi* amontonarse
◆**huddle up** *vi* acurrucarse
hue [hjuː] *n no pl* **1.** (*shade*) tonalidad *f;* **all ~s of ...** *fig* todo tipo de... **2.** (*disapproval*) **~ and cry** protesta *f*
huff [hʌf] **I.** *vi* **to ~ and puff** (*breathe loudly*) jadear; *inf* (*complain*) quejarse **II.** *vt* vociferar **III.** *n inf* enfado *m;* **to be in a ~** estar de morros; **to get into a ~** enfadarse; **to go off in a ~** irse ofendido
huffy ['hʌfi] <-ier, -iest> *adj* **1.** (*offended*) ofendido, -a **2.** (*touchy*) susceptible
hug [hʌg] **I.** <-gg-> *vt* **1.** (*embrace*) abrazar **2.** *fig* (*idea*) aferrarse a **3.** (*not slide on*) **these tyres ~ the road** estos neumáticos se agarran a la carretera **II.** *n* abrazo *m*
huge [hjuːdʒ] *adj* (*extremely big*) enorme; (*impressive*) imponente
hugely *adv* enormemente
hugeness *n no pl* enormidad *f*
hulk [hʌlk] *n* **1.** (*old, large body*) carraca *f;* (*of ship*) casco *m* **2.** (*mass*) mole *f*
hulking *adj* grandote, -a; **~ great** *Brit* descomunal
hull¹ [hʌl] *n* NAUT casco *m*
hull² [hʌl] **I.** *n* (*shell*) cáscara *f;* (*of peas*) vaina *f;* (*of strawberry*) cabito *m* **II.** *vt* pelar
hullabaloo [ˌhʌləbə'luː] *n* barullo *m;* **to make a ~** armar un follón
hullo [hə'ləʊ, *Am:* -'loʊ] *interj Brit s.* **hello**
hum [hʌm] <-mm-> **I.** *vi* **1.** (*bee*) zumbar **2.** (*sing*) tararear **3.** (*be full of activity*) estar animado ►**to ~ and haw** *Brit, Aus* vacilar **II.** *vt* tararear **III.** *n* zumbido *m;* (*of traffic*) murmullo *m*
human ['hjuːmən] *adj* humano, -a
humane [hjuː'meɪn] *adj* humanitario, -a
humanism ['hjuːmənɪzəm] *n no pl* humanismo *m*
humanistic [ˌhjuːmə'nɪstɪk] *adj* humanista
humanitarian [hjuːˌmænɪ'teəriən, *Am:* hjuːˌmænə'teri-] **I.** *n* humanitario, -a *m, f* **II.** *adj* humanitario, -a; **~ aid** ayuda humanitaria
humanities [hjuː'mænətiz, *Am:* -t̬iz] *npl*

humanidades *fpl*
humanity [hjuː'mænəti, *Am:* -t̬i] *n no pl* humanidad *f*
humanize ['hjuːmənaɪz] *vt* humanizar
humanly *adv* humanamente
human nature *n no pl* naturaleza *f* humana **human race** *n no pl* raza *f* humana **human resources** *npl* recursos *mpl* humanos **human rights** *npl* derechos *mpl* humanos
humble ['hʌmbl] I. *adj* humilde; **of ~ birth** de origen humilde; **in my ~ opinion, ...** en mi modesta opinión,... II. *vt* humillar; (*beat*) derrotar
humbleness *n* modestia *f;* (*humility*) humildad *f*
humbug ['hʌmbʌg] *n* 1. *no pl* HIST (*nonsense*) patrañas *fpl;* (*fraud*) engaño *m;* **~!** ¡paparruchas! 2. (*peppermint*) caramelo *m* de menta
humdrum ['hʌmdrʌm] *adj* (*dull*) aburrido, -a; (*lacking excitement*) rutinario, -a
humid ['hjuːmɪd] *adj* húmedo, -a
humidifier [hjuːmɪdɪfaɪəʳ] *n* humidificador *m*
humidify [hjuː'mɪdɪfaɪ] *vt* humidificar
humidity [hjuː'mɪdəti, *Am:* -t̬i] *n no pl* humedad *f*
humiliate [hjuː'mɪlieɪt] *vt* 1. (*shame*) avergonzar, achunchar *AmC;* (*humble*) humillar 2. (*defeat*) derrotar
humiliating *adj* humillante
humiliation [hjuːˌmɪlɪ'eɪʃən] *n* humillación *f*
humility [hjuː'mɪləti, *Am:* -t̬i] *n no pl* humildad *f*
hummingbird ['hʌmɪŋbɜːd, *Am:* -bɜːrd] *n* colibrí *m,* chupaflor *m AmC*
hummock ['hʌmək] *n liter* montículo *m*
humor ['hjuːməʳ, *Am:* -mɚ] *n Am, Aus s.* **humour**
humorist ['hjuːmərɪst] *n* 1. (*writer*) humorista *mf* 2. (*funny person*) cómico, -a *m, f*
humorous ['hjuːmərəs] *adj* (*speech*) humorístico, -a; (*situation*) divertido, -a; **~ story** historia graciosa
humour ['hjuːməʳ, *Am:* -mɚ] *n no pl* 1. (*capacity for amusement*) humor *m;* **sense of ~** sentido *m* del humor 2. *form* (*mood*) talante *m;* **in** (**a**) **good/bad ~** de buen/mal humor
humourless ['hjuːməʳlɪs, *Am:* -mɚ] *adj* sin sentido del humor; **a ~ smile** una sonrisa forzada
hump [hʌmp] I. *n* joroba *f,* petaca *f AmC* ►**to be over the ~** haber pasado lo más difícil; **to get the ~** cabrearse II. *vt* 1. *inf* (*lug, carry*) acarrear 2. *vulg* (*have sex*) follar, coger *AmL*
humpback ['hʌmpbæk] *n* joroba *f*
humpbacked ['hʌmpbækt] *adj* jorobado, -a; **~ bridge** ARCHIT puente peraltado
humph [hʌmpf, mm] *interj* ¡ja!
Hun [hʌn] *n* 1. HIST huno, -a *m, f* 2. *pej* (*German*) alemán, -ana *m, f*
hunch [hʌntʃ] I. <-es> *n* presentimiento *m;* **to have a ~ that ...** tener la corazonada de que...; **to act on a ~** actuar por intuición II. *vi* encorvarse III. *vt* curvar
hunchback ['hʌntʃbæk] *n* (*person*) jorobado, -a *m, f*
hundred ['hʌndrəd] <-(s)> I. *n* cien *m;* **~s of times** cientos de veces II. *adj* ciento; (*before a noun*) cien
hundredfold ['hʌndrədfəʊld, *Am:* -foʊld] *n* cien veces *fpl*
hundredth ['hʌndrədθ] I. *n* centésimo *m* II. *adj* centésimo, -a
hundredweight ['hʌndrədweɪt] <-(s)> *n unidad de peso equivalente a 50,80 kg en Gran Bretaña y 45,36 en los EE.UU.*
hung [hʌŋ] I. *pt, pp of* **hang** II. *adj* colgado, -a; **~ jury** LAW *jurado que se disuelve porque no se llega a ningún acuerdo;* **~ parliament** POL parlamento *m* sin mayoría absoluta
Hungarian [hʌŋ'geərɪən, *Am:* -'gerɪ-] I. *adj* húngaro, -a II. *n* 1. (*person*) húngaro, -a *m, f* 2. LING húngaro *m*
Hungary ['hʌŋgəri] *n* Hungría *f*
hunger ['hʌŋgəʳ, *Am:* -gɚ] I. *n no pl* 1. hambre *f,* filo *m AmC* 2. *fig* (*desire*) ansia *f;* **to have a ~ for sth** estar sediento de algo II. *vi fig* **to ~ after** [*o* **for**] ansiar
hungry ['hʌŋgri] <-ier, -iest> *adj* 1. (*desiring food*) hambriento, -a; **to go ~** pasar hambre 2. *fig* (*wanting badly*) ansioso, -a; **to be ~ for sth** estar ávido de algo
hunk [hʌŋk] *n* 1. (*piece*) trozo *m* 2. *inf* (*man*) cachas *m inv*
hunky dory [ˌhʌŋki'dɔːri] *adj inf* guay
hunt [hʌnt] I. *vt* 1. (*chase to kill*) cazar 2. (*search for*) buscar II. *vi* 1. (*chase to kill*) cazar; **to go ~ing** ir de caza 2. (*search*) **to ~ for** buscar; **to ~ high and low for sth** buscar algo por todas partes III. *n* 1. (*chase*) cacería *f;* **to go on a ~** ir de caza 2. (*search*) búsqueda *f*
hunter *n* 1. (*person*) cazador(a) *m(f)* 2. (*dog*) perro *m* de caza 3. (*horse*) caballo *m* de caza
hunting *n no pl* caza *f*
hunting ground *n* coto *m* de caza **hunting licence** *n Brit, Aus,* **hunting license** *n Am* licencia *f* de caza **hunting-season** *n* temporada *f* de caza
huntress ['hʌntrɪs] *n* cazadora *f*
huntsman ['hʌntsmən] <-men> *n* cazador *m*
hurdle ['hɜːdl, *Am:* 'hɜːr-] I. *n* 1. *a.* SPORTS (*fence*) valla *f* 2. (*obstacle*) obstáculo *m* II. *vi* SPORTS saltar vallas III. *vt* SPORTS saltar
hurdler *n* SPORTS vallista *mf*
hurdle-race *n* SPORTS carrera *f* de vallas
hurdy gurdy ['hɜːdiˌgɜːdi, *Am:* ˌhɜːrdi'gɜːrdi] <-ies> *n* organillo *m*
hurl [hɜːl, *Am:* hɜːrl] *vt* 1. (*throw*) lanzar 2. *fig* (*utter: insults*) soltar
hurly-burly ['hɜːliˌbɜːli, *Am:* 'hɜːrlɪbɜːr-] *n no pl* alboroto *m*
hurrah [hə'rɑː] *interj,* **hurray** [hə'reɪ] *interj*

H

hurra

hurricane ['hʌrɪkən, *Am:* 'hɜːrɪkeɪn] *n* huracán *m*

hurricane lamp *n* farol *m*

hurried ['hʌrɪd, *Am:* 'hɜːr-] *adj* apresurado, -a, apurado, -a *AmL*

hurry ['hʌri, *Am:* 'hɜːr-] <-ie-> **I.** *vi* darse prisa, apurarse *AmL* **II.** *vt* **1.** (*rush*) meter prisas, apurar *AmL* **2.** (*take quickly*) **he was hurried to the hospital** lo llevaron en seguida al hospital **III.** *n* prisa *f*, apuro *m AmL;* **to leave in a ~** irse disparado; **to do sth in a ~** hacer algo de prisa; **what's (all) the ~?** ¿a qué viene tanta prisa?

◆**hurry along** **I.** *vi* apresurarse **II.** *vt always sep* meter prisas

◆**hurry away, hurry off** **I.** *vi* marcharse de prisa **II.** *vt* (*person*) hacer marchar de prisa; (*object*) hacer llevar de prisa

◆**hurry on** *vi* continuar rápidamente

◆**hurry up** **I.** *vi* darse prisa **II.** *vt* meter prisa

hurt [hɜːt, *Am:* hɜːrt] **I.** <hurt, hurt> *vi* doler **II.** *vt* **1.** (*wound*) herir **2.** (*cause pain*) lastimar; **it ~s me** me duele **3.** (*offend*) ofender **4.** (*damage*) dañar **III.** *adj* (*in pain, injured*) dañado, -a; (*grieved, distressed*) dolido, -a **IV.** *n no pl* **1.** (*pain*) dolor *m* **2.** (*injury*) herida *f* **3.** (*offence*) ofensa *f* **4.** (*damage*) daño *m*

hurtful ['hɜːtfəl, *Am:* 'hɜːrt-] *adj* perjudicial

hurtle ['hɜːtl, *Am:* 'hɜːrt-] **I.** *vi* lanzarse; **to ~ along** ir como un rayo **II.** *vt* lanzar

husband ['hʌzbənd] **I.** *n* marido *m* **II.** *vt* economizar

husbandry ['hʌzbəndri] *n no pl* **1.** (*care, management*) cuidado *m* **2.** AGR agricultura *f;* **animal ~** cría *f* de animales

hush [hʌʃ] **I.** *n no pl* silencio *m* **II.** *interj* **~!** ¡chitón! **III.** *vi* callarse **IV.** *vt* (*make silent*) hacer callar; (*soothe*) acallar

◆**hush up** *vt* encubrir

hush-hush [ˌhʌʃ'hʌʃ] *adj inf* secreto, -a

hush money *n inf* unto *m* (*que se utiliza para comprar el silencio de alguien*)

husk [hʌsk] **I.** *n* (*outside covering*) cáscara *f; Am* (*of maize*) farfolla *f* **II.** *vt* descascarillar, destusar *AmC*, despancar *AmS*

husky[1] ['hʌski] <-ier, -iest> *adj* **1.** (*low, rough: voice*) ronco, -a **2.** *Am* (*big, strong*) fornido, -a

husky[2] ['hʌski] <-ies> *n* perro *m* esquimal

hussy ['hʌsi] *n* pendón *m*

hustings ['hʌstɪŋz] *npl* campaña *f* electoral

hustle ['hʌsl] **I.** *vt* **1.** (*hurry*) dar prisa a; (*push*) empujar **2.** (*achieve*) hacerse con **II.** *vi* **1.** (*push for*) moverse *inf* **2.** (*practice prostitution*) prostituirse **III.** *n* ajetreo *m*

hustler ['hʌsləʳ, *Am:* -ɚ] *n* **1.** (*persuader*) camelador(a) *m(f)* **2.** *Am* (*swindler*) estafador(a) *m(f)* **3.** (*prostitute*) puto, -a *m, f*

hustling ['hʌslɪŋ] *n no pl* ajetreo *m*

hut [hʌt] *n* cabaña *f*

hutch [hʌtʃ] <-es> *n* (*box for animals*) jaula *f;* (*for rabbits*) conejera *f*

hyacinth ['haɪəsɪnθ] *n* BOT jacinto *m*

hyaena [haɪ'iːnə] *n* hiena *f*

hybrid ['haɪbrɪd] *n* híbrido, -a *m, f*

hydrangea [haɪ'dreɪndʒə] *n* BOT hortensia *f*

hydrant ['haɪdrənt] *n* boca *f* de riego

hydrate ['haɪdreɪt] *n* hidrato *m*

hydraulic [haɪ'drɒlɪk, *Am:* -'drɑːlɪk] *adj* hidráulico, -a

hydraulics [haɪ'drɒlɪks, *Am:* -'drɑːlɪks] *n* hidráulica *f*

hydrocarbon [ˌhaɪdrə'kɑːbən, *Am:* -droʊ-'kɑːr-] **I.** *n* hidrocarburo *m* **II.** *adj* de hidrocarburo

hydrochloric acid [ˌhaɪdrəʊklɒrɪk'æsɪd, *Am:* -droʊklɔːrɪk'æsɪd] *n no pl* ácido *m* clorhídrico

hydroelectric [ˌhaɪdrəʊɪ'lektrɪk, *Am:* -droʊ-] *adj* hidroeléctrico, -a

hydrofoil ['haɪdrəfɔɪl, *Am:* -droʊ-] *n* hidroala *m*

hydrogen ['haɪdrədʒən] *n no pl* hidrógeno *m*

hydrogen bomb *n* bomba *f* de hidrógeno

hydrophobia [ˌhaɪdrə'fəʊbɪə, *Am:* -droʊ-'foʊ-] *n no pl* hidrofobia *f*

hydroponics [ˌhaɪdrə'pɒnɪks, *Am:* -droʊ-'pɑːnɪks] *n + sing vb* hidroponía *f*

hyena [haɪ'iːnə] *n* hiena *f*

hygiene ['haɪdʒiːn] *n no pl* higiene *f*, salubridad *f AmL*

hygienic [haɪ'dʒiːnɪk, *Am:* ˌhaɪdʒi'enɪk] *adj* higiénico, -a

hygroscope ['haɪgrəskəʊp, *Am:* -groʊs-koʊp] *n* higroscopio *m*

hymn [hɪm] *n* himno *m*

hymnal ['hɪmnəl] *n*, **hymnbook** *n* himnario *m*

hype [haɪp] **I.** *n no pl* COM bombo publicitario **II.** *vt* dar bombo publicitario a

hyperactive [ˌhaɪpə'æktɪv, *Am:* -pɚ-] *adj* hiperactivo, -a

hyperbola [haɪ'pɜːbələ, *Am:* -'pɜːr-] *n* MAT hipérbola *f*

hyperbole [haɪ'pɜːbəli, *Am:* -'pɜːr-] *n no pl* LIT hipérbole *f*

hyperbolic [haɪpə'bɒlɪk, *Am:* -pɚ'bɑːlɪk] *adj* LIT hiperbólico, -a

hyperlink [ˌhaɪpə'lɪŋk] *n* INFOR hiperenlace *m*

hypermarket ['haɪpəmɑːkɪt, *Am:* -pɚ-mɑːr-] *n* hipermercado *m*

hypersensitive [ˌhaɪpə'sensətɪv, *Am:* -pɚ'sensət̬ɪv] *adj* hipersensible

hypertext [ˌhaɪpə'tekst, *Am:* -pɚ-] *n no pl* INFOR hipertexto *m*

hyphen ['haɪfn] *n* guión *m*

hyphenate ['haɪfəneɪt] *vt* separar con guiones

hypnosis [hɪp'nəʊsɪs, *Am:* -'noʊ-] *n no pl* hipnosis *f inv;* **to be under ~** estar hipnotizado

hypnotherapy [ˌhɪpnə'θerəpi, *Am:* -noʊ'-] *n no pl* hipnoterapia *f*

hypnotic [hɪp'nɒtɪk, *Am:* -'nɑːt̬ɪk] *adj* hip-

nótico, -a
hypnotist ['hɪpnətɪst] *n* hipnotizador(a) *m(f)*
hypnotize ['hɪpnətaɪz] *vt* hipnotizar
hypochondria [ˌhaɪpə'kɒndrɪə, *Am:* -poʊ-'kɑːn-] *n no pl* hipocondría *f*
hypochondriac [ˌhaɪpə'kɒn drɪæk, *Am:* -poʊ'kɑːn-] **I.** *n* hipocondríaco, -a *m, f* **II.** *adj* hipocondríaco, -a
hypocrisy [hɪ'pɒkrəsi, *Am:* -'pɑːkrə-] *n no pl* hipocresía *f*
hypocrite ['hɪpəkrɪt] *n* hipócrita *mf*
hypocritical [ˌhɪpə'krɪtɪkl, *Am:* -'krɪt̬-] *adj* hipócrita
hypodermic [ˌhaɪpə'dɜːmɪk, *Am:* -poʊ-'dɜːr-] *adj* hipodérmico, -a
hypotenuse [ˌhaɪ'pɒtənjuːz, *Am:* -'pɑː-tənuːs] *n* hipotenusa *f*
hypothermia [ˌhaɪpə'θɜːmɪə, *Am:* -poʊ-'θɜːr-] *n no pl* hipotermia *f*
hypothesis [haɪ'pɒθəsɪs, *Am:* -'pɑːθə-] *n* <-es> hipótesis *f inv*
hypothetical [ˌhaɪpə'θetɪkl, *Am:* -poʊ-'θet̬-] *adj* hipotético, -a
hysterectomy [ˌhɪstə'rektəmi] *n* MED histerectomía *f*
hysteria [hɪ'stɪərɪə, *Am:* -'sterɪ-] *n no pl* histeria *f*
hysteric [hɪ'sterɪk] **I.** *adj* histérico, -a **II.** *n* histérico, -a *m, f*
hysterical *adj* histérico, -a

I

I, i [aɪ] *n* I, i *f;* ~ **for Isaac** *Brit,* ~ **for Item** *Am* I de Italia
I [aɪ] *pron pers* (*1st person sing*) yo; ~**'m coming** ya voy; ~**'ll do it** (yo) lo haré; **am** ~ **late?** ¿llego tarde?; **she and** ~ ella y yo; **it was** ~ **who did that** fui yo quien lo hizo
IAEA *n abbr of* **International Atomic Energy Agency** OIEA *f*
IATA [aɪ'ɑːtə, *Am:* ˌaɪˌeɪˌtiː'eɪ] *n abbr of* **International Air Transport Association** IATA *f*
ibex ['aɪbeks] <-es> *n* íbice *m,* cabra *f* montesa
ibid. [ɪ'bɪd] *adv abbr of* **ibidem** ibid.
IC [ˌaɪ'siː] *n abbr of* **integrated circuit** CI *m*
i/c *abbr of* **in charge** (**of**) a cargo de
ICBM [ˌaɪsiːbiː'em] *n abbr of* **intercontinental ballistic missile** ICBM *m*
ice [aɪs] **I.** *n* **1.** *no pl* (*frozen water*) hielo *m* **2.** *Brit* (*ice cream*) helado *m,* nieve *f AmC* ▸**to be skating on thin** ~ andar sobre terreno peligroso; **to break the** ~ *inf* romper el hielo; **to cut no** ~ (**with sb**) no tener importancia (para alguien); **to put sth on** ~ posponer algo **II.** *vt* **1.** (*put in fridge*) enfriar **2.** (*put icing on*) escarchar
◆**ice over** *vi* helarse
Ice Age *n* época *f* glacial **ice-axe** *n* piolet *m* **iceberg** *n* iceberg *m;* **the tip of the** ~ *fig* la punta del iceberg **icebound** *adj* bloqueado, -a por el hielo **ice-box** <-es> *n* **1.** *Brit* (*freezer*) congelador *m* **2.** *Am* (*fridge*) nevera *f,* refrigeradora *f AmL* **ice-breaker** *n* rompehielos *m inv* **ice cap** *n* casquete *m* de hielo **ice-cold** *adj* helado, -a
ice cream *n* helado *m,* nieve *f AmC*
ice-cream maker *n* heladero, -a *m, f* **ice--cream parlour** *n* heladería *f*
ice cube ['aɪskjuːb] *n* cubito *m* de hielo
iced [aɪst] *adj* **1.** (*drink*) con hielo **2.** (*covered with icing*) escarchado, -a
ice floe ['aɪsfləʊ, *Am:* -floʊ] *n* témpano *m* de hielo **ice hockey** *n no pl* hockey *m* sobre hielo
Iceland ['aɪslənd] *n* Islandia *f*
Icelander ['aɪsləndəʳ, *Am:* -dɚ] *n* islandés, -esa *m, f*
Icelandic [aɪs'lændɪk] **I.** *adj* islandés, -esa **II.** *n* islandés *m*
ice lolly [ˌaɪs'lɒli, *Am:* -'lɑːli] <-ies> *n Brit* polo *m,* paleta *f AmL* **ice pack** *n* bolsa *f* de hielo **ice rink** *n* pista *f* de patinaje **ice--skate** *vi* patinar sobre hielo **ice-skating** *n no pl* patinaje *m* sobre hielo
icicle ['aɪsɪkl] *n* carámbano *m*
icing ['aɪsɪŋ] *n* glaseado *m* ▸**to be the** ~ **on the cake** ser la guinda del pastel
icing sugar *n no pl* azúcar *m* glas
icon ['aɪkɒn, *Am:* -kɑːn] *n* icono *m*
iconoclast [aɪ'kɒnəklæst, *Am:* -'kɑːnə-] *n* iconoclasta *mf*
iconoclastic [aɪˌkɒnə'klæstɪk, *Am:* -'kɑː-nə-] *adj* iconoclasta
ICU [ˌaɪsiː'juː] *n abbr of* **intensive care unit** UCI *f*
icy ['aɪsi] <-ier, -iest> *adj* **1.** (*with ice*) helado, -a; (*very cold*) glacial **2.** (*unfriendly*) frío, -a
ID [ˌaɪ'diː] *abbr of* **identification** identificación *f*
I'd [aɪd] **1.** = **I would** *s.* **would** **2.** = **I had** *s.* **have**
ID card [aɪ'diːˌkaːd] *n s.* **identity card** carné *m* de identidad
IDDD *Am abbr of* **international direct distance dial**(**ling**) marcación *f* directa internacional
idea [aɪ'dɪə, *Am:* -'diːə] *n* **1.** (*opinion*) idea *f* **2.** (*conception*) concepto *m* **3.** (*notion*) noción *f;* **to get an** ~ **of sth** hacerse una idea de algo
ideal [aɪ'dɪəl, *Am:* -'diː-] **I.** *adj* ideal **II.** *n* ideal *m*
idealise *vt Brit, Aus s.* **idealize**
idealism [aɪ'dɪəlɪzəm, *Am:* aɪ'diːə-] *n no pl* idealismo *m*
idealist [aɪ'dɪəlɪst, *Am:* -'diːə-] *n* idealista *mf*
idealistic [ˌaɪdɪə'lɪstɪk] *adj* idealista

idealize [aɪˈdɪəlaɪz, *Am:* -ˈdiːə-] *vt* idealizar

ideally [aɪˈdɪəli, *Am:* ˈdiːli] *adv* **1.** (*in an ideal way*) inmejorablemente **2.** ~, **we could catch the train** lo mejor sería coger el tren

identical [aɪˈdentɪkl, *Am:* -t̬ə-] *adj* idéntico, -a, individual *CSur*

identifiable [aɪˈdentɪˌfaɪəbl, *Am:* -ˌdent̬əˈ-] *adj* identificable

identification [aɪˌdentɪfɪˈkeɪʃən, *Am:* -t̬ə-] *n no pl* identificación *f*

identification papers *npl* documentación *f*

identifier [aɪˈdentɪfaɪəʳ, *Am:* -t̬əfaɪɚ] *n* INFOR identificador *m*

identify [aɪˈdentɪfaɪ, *Am:* -t̬ə-] <-ie-> *vt* identificar

identikit® [aɪˈdentɪkɪt] *adj Brit, Aus* ~ **picture** retrato *m* robot

identity [aɪˈdentəti, *Am:* -t̬ət̬i] <-ies> *n* identidad *f*

identity card *n* carné *m* de identidad

ideological [ˌaɪdɪəˈlɒdʒɪkl, *Am:* -ˈlɑːdʒɪ-] *adj* ideológico, -a

ideologist [ˌaɪdɪˈɒlədʒɪst, *Am:* -ˈɑːlə-] *n* ideólogo, -a *m, f*

ideology [ˌaɪdɪˈɒlədʒi, *Am:* -ˈɑːlə-] <-ies> *n* ideología *f*

idiocy [ˈɪdɪəsi] <-ies> *n* idiotez *f*, imbecilidad *f*

idiom [ˈɪdɪəm] *n* LING **1.** (*phrase*) modismo *m* **2.** (*style of expression*) lenguaje *m*

idiomatic [ˌɪdɪəˈmætɪk, *Am:* -ˈmæt̬-] *adj* idiomático, -a

idiosyncrasy [ˌɪdɪəʊˈsɪŋkrəsi, *Am:* -oʊˈsɪn-] <-ies> *n* idiosincrasia *f*

idiosyncratic [ˌɪdɪəʊsɪŋˈkrætɪk, *Am:* -oʊsɪnˈkræt̬-] *adj* idiosincrático, -a

idiot [ˈɪdɪət] *n* idiota *mf*

idiotic [ˌɪdɪˈɒtɪk, *Am:* -ˈɑːt̬ɪk] *adj* tonto, -a

idle [ˈaɪdl] **I.** *adj* **1.** (*lazy*) holgazán, -ana **2.** (*with nothing to do*) desocupado, -a; (*machine*) parado, -a **3.** (*unfounded*) vano, -a; (*chatter*) insustancial; (*fear*) infundado, -a **4.** FIN de paro; (*capital*) improductivo, -a **II.** *vi* (*person*) haraganear; (*machine*) marchar al ralentí

idleness [ˈaɪdlnɪs] *n no pl* holgazanería *f*

idler [ˈaɪdləʳ, *Am:* -lɚ] *n* vago, -a *m, f*

idol [ˈaɪdl] *n* ídolo *m*

idolatrous [aɪˈdɒlətrəs, *Am:* -ˈdɑːlə-] *adj* REL idólatra

idolatry [aɪˈdɒlətri, *Am:* -ˈdɑːlə-] *n* idolatría *f*

idolise *vt Brit, Aus*, **idolize** [ˈaɪdəlaɪz] *vt Am* idolatrar

IDP **1.** *abbr of* **integrated data processing** IDP *m* **2.** *abbr of* **International Driving Permit** permiso *m* internacional de conducción

idyll [ˈɪdɪl, *Am:* ˈaɪdəl] *n* idilio *m*

idyllic [ɪˈdɪlɪk, *Am:* aɪ-] *adj* idílico, -a

i.e. [ˌaɪˈiː] *abbr of* **id est** i.e.

if [ɪf] **I.** *conj* **1.** (*supposing that*) si; ~ **it snows** si nieva; ~ **not** si no; **as** ~ **it were true** como si fuera verdad; ~ **they exist at all** si es que en realidad existen; ~ **A is right, then B is wrong** si A es cierto, entonces B es falso; **I'll stay,** ~ **only for a day** me quedaré, aunque sea sólo un día **2.** (*every time that*) ~ **he needs me, I'll help him** si me necesita, le ayudaré **3.** (*whether*) **I wonder** ~ **he'll come** me pregunto si vendrá **4.** (*although*) aunque; **cold** ~ **sunny weather** clima soleado aunque frío **II.** *n* pero *m*; **no** ~**s and buts!** ¡no hay peros que valgan!

iffy [ˈɪfi] <-ier, -iest> *adj inf* dudoso, -a; (*person*) sospechoso, -a

igloo [ˈɪgluː] *n* iglú *m*

igneous [ˈɪgnɪəs] *adj* ígneo, -a

ignite [ɪgˈnaɪt] **I.** *vi* incendiarse **II.** *vt form* incendiar

ignition [ɪgˈnɪʃən] *n no pl* **1.** AUTO encendido *m*; **to switch the** ~ **on** dar al contacto **2.** *form* (*causing to burn*) ignición *f*

ignition coil *n* bobina *f* de encendido **ignition key** *n* llave *f* de contacto, suiche *m Méx* **ignition switch** <-es> *n* interruptor *m* de encendido

ignoble [ɪgˈnəʊbl, *Am:* -ˈnoʊ-] *adj liter* innoble

ignominious [ˌɪgnəˈmɪnɪəs] *adj liter* ignominioso, -a

ignominy [ˈɪgnəmɪni] *n no pl* ignominia *f*

ignoramus [ˌɪgnəˈreɪməs] *n* ignorante *mf*

ignorance [ˈɪgnərəns] *n no pl* ignorancia *f*; **to be left in** ~ **of sth** quedarse sin saber algo ► ~ **is bliss** ojos que no ven corazón que no siente

ignorant [ˈɪgnərənt] *adj* ignorante; **to be** ~ **about sth** desconocer algo

ignore [ɪgˈnɔːʳ, *Am:* -ˈnɔːr] *vt* no hacer caso de, ignorar

iguana [ɪˈgwɑːnə] *n* iguana *f*, basilisco *m Méx*

ilk [ɪlk] *n no pl, liter* calaña *f*

ill [ɪl] **I.** *adj* **1.** (*sick*) enfermo, -a; **to fall** ~ caer enfermo **2.** (*bad*) malo, -a; (*harmful*) nocivo, -a; (*unfavourable*) perjudicial; **an** ~ **omen** un mal presagio **II.** *adv form* (*badly*) mal; **to bode** ~ ser de mal agüero; **to speak** ~ **of sb** hablar mal de alguien

I'll [aɪl] = **I will** *s.* **will**

ill-advised [ˌɪlədˈvaɪzd] *adj* imprudente **ill at ease** *adj* incómodo, -a **ill-bred** *adj* mal educado, -a **ill-conceived** *adj* desacertado, -a

illegal [ɪˈliːgəl] *adj* ilegal

illegal immigrant *n* inmigrante *mf* ilegal

illegality [ˌɪlɪˈgæləti, *Am:* -t̬i] <-ies> *n* ilegalidad *f*

illegible [ɪˈledʒəbl] *adj* ilegible

illegitimate [ˌɪlɪˈdʒɪtɪmət, *Am:* -ˈdʒɪt̬ə-] *adj* ilegítimo, -a

ill-equipped [ˌɪlɪˈkwɪpt] *adj* mal equipado, -a **ill-fated** *adj* (*having bad luck*) desafortunado, -a; (*bringing bad luck*) gafe; **an** ~ **hour** una hora funesta **ill-favored** *adj Am*, **ill-favoured** *adj Brit* feo, -a, poco agraciado, -a

ill-fitting *adj* ~ **clothes** ropa *f* que no queda bien **ill-gotten** *adj* mal habido, -a
illiberal [ɪ'lɪbərəl] *adj form* **1.** (*repressive*) represivo, -a **2.** *Am* (*unaccepting of new ideas*) intolerante
illicit [ɪ'lɪsɪt] *adj* ilícito, -a
illimitable [ɪ'lɪmɪtəbl, *Am:* -t̬ə-] *adj* ilimitado, -a
ill-informed ['ɪlɪnˌfɔːmd] *adj* **1.** (*wrongly informed*) mal informado, -a **2.** (*ignorant*) ignorante
illiteracy [ɪ'lɪtərəsi, *Am:* -'lɪt̬-] *n no pl* analfabetismo *m*
illiterate [ɪ'lɪtərət, *Am:* -'lɪt̬-] **I.** *adj* analfabeto, -a; *pej, fig* inculto, -a **II.** *n* analfabeto, -a *m, f*
ill-mannered [ˌɪl'mænəd, *Am:* -ɚd] *adj* mal educado, -a **ill-natured** *adj* malicioso, -a
illness ['ɪlnɪs] <-es> *n* enfermedad *f*
illogical [ɪ'lɒdʒɪkl, *Am:* -'lɑːdʒɪ-] *adj* ilógico, -a
illogicality [ɪˌlɒdʒɪ'kælɪti, *Am:* -ˌlɑːdʒɪ-'kæləṱi] *n no pl* incongruencia *f*
ill-omened [ˌɪl'əʊmend, *Am:* -'oʊ-] *adj* aciago, -a **ill-starred** *adj* desdichado, -a **ill-tempered** *adj* de mal genio **ill-timed** *adj* inoportuno, -a
ill-treat [ˌɪl'triːt] *vt* maltratar
ill-treatment [ˌɪl'triːtmənt] *n no pl* maltrato *m*
illuminate [ɪ'luːmɪneɪt, *Am:* -mə-] *vt* iluminar; *fig* aclarar
illuminating [ɪ'luːmɪneɪtɪŋ, *Am:* -t̬ɪŋ] *adj form* aclaratorio, -a
illumination [ɪˌluːmɪ'neɪʃən] *n* **1.** *no pl a.* ART iluminación *f* **2.** *pl, Brit* luces *fpl*
illus. *abbr of* **illustrated, illustration** ilus.
illusion [ɪ'luːʒən, *Am:* -'luː-] *n* (*misleading appearance*) apariencia *f;* (*false impression*) ilusión *f;* **to have no ~s** (**about sth**) no tener esperanzas (en algo); **to be under the ~ that ...** estar equivocado creyendo que...
illusionist [ɪ'luːʒənɪst, *Am:* -'luː-] *n* ilusionista *mf*
illusive [ɪ'luːsɪv] *adj,* **illusory** [ɪ'luːsəri] *adj* ilusorio, -a
illustrate ['ɪləstreɪt] *vt* ilustrar; *fig* ejemplificar
illustration [ˌɪlə'streɪʃən] *n* **1.** (*drawing*) ilustración *f* **2.** (*example*) ejemplo *m;* **by way of ~** a modo de ejemplo
illustrative ['ɪləstrətɪv, *Am:* ɪ'lʌstrət̬ɪv] *adj form* ilustrativo, -a
illustrator ['ɪləstreɪtəʳ, *Am:* -t̬ɚ] *n* ilustrador(a) *m(f)*
illustrious [ɪ'lʌstrɪəs] *adj form* ilustre
ill will *n no pl* animadversión *f*
ILO *n abbr of* **International Labour Organisation** OIT *f*
ILS *n abbr of* **instrument landing system** ILS *m*
I'm [aɪm] = **I am** *s.* **am**
image ['ɪmɪdʒ] *n* **1.** (*likeness*) imagen *f;* **to be the living ~ of sb** ser el vivo retrato de alguien **2.** (*picture*) retrato *m* **3.** (*reputation*) reputación *f*
imagery ['ɪmɪdʒəri] *n no pl* LIT imágenes *fpl*
imaginable [ɪ'mædʒɪnəbl] *adj* imaginable
imaginary [ɪ'mædʒɪnəri, *Am:* -əner-] *adj* imaginario, -a
imagination [ɪˌmædʒɪ'neɪʃən] *n* imaginación *f;* (*inventiveness*) inventiva *f*
imaginative [ɪ'mædʒɪnətɪv, *Am:* -t̬ɪv] *adj* imaginativo, -a
imagine [ɪ'mædʒɪn] *vt* **1.** (*form mental image*) imaginar **2.** (*suppose*) figurarse; **~ that!** ¡figúratelo!
imaging *n no pl* INFOR tratamiento *m* de imágenes
imbalance [ˌɪm'bæləns] *n* desequilibrio *m*
imbecile ['ɪmbəsiːl, *Am:* -sɪl] *n* imbécil *mf*
imbecility [ˌɪmbə'sɪləti, *Am:* -t̬i] *n no pl, form* imbecilidad *f*
imbibe [ɪm'baɪb] *vt* beber; *fig* empaparse de
imbroglio [ɪm'brəʊlɪəʊ, *Am:* -'broʊlɪoʊ] *n liter* embrollo *m*
imbue [ɪm'bjuː] *vt form* **1.** (*fill, inspire*) **to ~ sb with sth** imbuir a alguien de algo; **to be ~d with** estar empapado de **2.** (*soak*) empapar
IMF [ˌaɪem'ef] *n no pl abbr of* **International Monetary Fund** FMI *m*
imitate ['ɪmɪteɪt] *vt* imitar; (*copy*) copiar
imitation [ˌɪmɪ'teɪʃən] **I.** *n* **1.** (*mimicry*) imitación *f;* **in ~ of sb/sth** a imitación de alguien/algo **2.** (*copy*) reproducción *f* **II.** *adj* de imitación; (*silk*) sintético, -a; **~ jewels** bisutería *f*
imitative ['ɪmɪtətɪv, *Am:* -teɪt̬ɪv] *adj* imitativo, -a
imitator ['ɪmɪtətəʳ, *Am:* -t̬ɚ] *n* imitador(a) *m(f)*
immaculate [ɪ'mækjʊlət] *adj* **1.** (*spotless, neat*) inmaculado, -a **2.** (*flawless*) impecable
immanence ['ɪmənəns] *n no pl* PHILOS inmanencia *f*
immanent ['ɪmənənt] *adj* inmanente
immaterial [ˌɪmə'tɪərɪəl, *Am:* -'tɪrɪ-] *adj* **1.** (*intangible*) inmaterial **2.** (*not important*) irrelevante
immature [ˌɪmə'tjʊəʳ, *Am:* -'tʊr] *adj* inmaduro, -a; (*people, animals*) joven; (*fruit*) verde
immaturity [ˌɪmə'tjʊərəti, *Am:* -'tʊrət̬i] *n no pl* inmadurez *f*
immeasurable [ɪ'meʒərəbl] *adj* **1.** (*boundless*) inconmensurable **2.** (*vast*) inmenso, -a; (*effect*) incalculable
immediacy [ɪ'miːdɪəsi] *n no pl* inmediatez *f;* (*nearness*) proximidad *f*
immediate [ɪ'miːdɪət, *Am:* -diɪt] *adj* inmediato, -a; **the ~ family** la familia directa; **in the ~ area** en las inmediaciones; **in the ~ future** en un futuro inmediato
immediately **I.** *adv* **1.** (*time*) inmediatamente; **~ after ...** justo después de... **2.** (*place*) **my flat is the one ~ above yours** mi piso es el que se encuentra justo encima del

tuyo **II.** *conj Brit* en cuanto; **call me ~ it is ready** llámame en cuanto esté preparado
immemorial [ˌɪmə'mɔːrɪəl, *Am:* -'mɔːrɪ-] *adj liter* inmemorial, inmemoriable
immense [ɪ'mens] *adj* inmenso, -a; (*importance*) extremo, -a
immensely *adv* enormemente
immensity [ɪ'mensəti, *Am:* -t̬i] *n* inmensidad *f*
immerse [ɪ'mɜːs, *Am:* -'mɜːrs] *vt* sumergir; **to be ~ed in sth** *fig* estar absorto en algo; **to ~ oneself in sth** *fig* sumirse en algo
immersion [ɪ'mɜːʃən, *Am:* -'mɜːr-] *n no pl* **1.** (*putting under water*) inmersión *f* **2.** (*absorption*) sumersión *f*
immersion heater *n* calentador *m* de inmersión
immigrant ['ɪmɪgrənt] *n* inmigrante *mf*
immigrate ['ɪmɪgreɪt] *vi* inmigrar
immigration [ˌɪmɪ'greɪʃən] *n no pl* inmigración *f*
immigration country *n* país *m* receptor de inmigrantes
imminence ['ɪmɪnəns] *n no pl* inminencia *f*
imminent ['ɪmɪnənt] *adj* inminente
immobile [ɪ'məʊbaɪl, *Am:* -'moʊbl] *adj* **1.** (*not moving*) inmóvil **2.** (*rigid*) entumecido, -a
immobilise *vt Brit, Aus,* **immobilize** [ɪ'məʊbəlaɪz, *Am:* -'moʊ-] *vt Am* inmovilizar
immobility [ˌɪmə'bɪləti, *Am:* -moʊ'bɪlət̬i] *n no pl* inmovilidad *f;* (*being still*) entumecimiento *m*
immoderate [ɪ'mɒdərət, *Am:* -'mɑːdɚ-] *adj* excesivo, -a
immodest [ɪ'mɒdɪst, *Am:* -'mɑːdɪst] *adj* **1.** (*conceited*) creído, -a **2.** (*slightly indecent*) descarado, -a
immolate ['ɪməleɪt] *vt form* inmolar
immoral [ɪ'mɒrəl, *Am:* -'mɔːr-] *adj* inmoral
immortal [ɪ'mɔːtl, *Am:* -'mɔːrt̬l] **I.** *adj* **1.** (*undying*) inmortal **2.** (*remembered forever*) imperecedero, -a **II.** *n* inmortal *mf*
immortalise *vt Brit, Aus,* **immortalize** [ɪ'mɔːtəlaɪz, *Am:* -'mɔːrt̬əl-] *vt Am* inmortalizar
immortality [ˌɪmɔː'tæləti, *Am:* -ɔːr'tælət̬i] *n no pl* inmortalidad *f*
immovable [ɪ'muːvəbl] *adj* **1.** (*not moveable*) inamovible **2.** (*not changeable*) inalterable; (*belief*) inquebrantable
immune [ɪ'mjuːn] *adj* **1.** MED inmune **2.** POL, LAW exento, -a
immune system *n* sistema *m* inmunológico
immunise *vt Aus, Brit,* **immunize** ['ɪmjənaɪz] *vt Am* inmunizar
immunity [ɪ'mjuːnəti, *Am:* -t̬i] *n no pl* **1.** MED inmunidad *f* **2.** (*lack of susceptibility*) insensibilidad *f* **3.** LAW exención *f;* **diplomatic ~** inmunidad *f* diplomática
immunological [ˌɪmjʊnəʊ'lɒdʒɪkl, *Am:* -jənoʊ'lɑːdʒɪ-] *adj* inmunológico, -a
immunologist [ˌɪmjʊ'nɒlədʒɪst, *Am:* -'nɑː-lə-] *n* inmunólogo, -a *m, f*
immure [ɪ'mjʊəʳ, *Am:* -'mjʊr] *vt liter* encerrar entre muros
immutable [ɪ'mjuːtəbl, *Am:* -t̬ə-] *adj* **1.** (*unchangeable*) inmutable **2.** (*ever-lasting*) imperecedero, -a **3.** (*eternal*) eterno, -a
imp [ɪmp] *n* **1.** (*small devil*) diablillo, -a *m, f* **2.** (*mischievous child*) pillín, -ina *m, f*
impact ['ɪmpækt] **I.** *n no pl* **1.** (*striking contact*) choque *m;* (*force of striking contact*) impacto *m;* **on ~** por impacto **2.** (*effect*) efecto *m* **II.** *vt Am, Aus* incidir en **III.** *vi Am, Aus* **to ~ on sb/sth** impactar en alguien/algo
impacted [ɪm'pæktɪd] *adj* impactado, -a
impair [ɪm'peəʳ, *Am:* -'per] *vt* **1.** (*weaken*) debilitar **2.** (*damage*) dañar; (*health*) perjudicar
impaired *adj* (*speech, vision, hearing*) dañado, -a; (*weakened*) debilitado, -a; (*health*) perjudicado, -a
impale [ɪm'peɪl] *vt* **to ~ sb/oneself on** atravesar a alguien/atravesarse en
impalpable [ɪm'pælpəbl] *adj liter* impalpable; (*change*) imperceptible
impart [ɪm'pɑːt, *Am:* -'pɑːrt] *vt form* impartir; (*bestow*) conferir; (*secret*) divulgar
impartial [ɪm'pɑːʃl, *Am:* -'pɑːr-] *adj* imparcial
impartiality [ˌɪmˌpɑːʃɪ'æləti, *Am:* -ˌpɑːr-] *n no pl* imparcialidad *f*
impassable [ɪm'pɑːsəbl, *Am:* -'pæsə-] *adj* intransitable; *fig* infranqueable
impasse ['æmpɑːs, *Am:* 'ɪmpæs] *n no pl, a. fig* callejón *m* sin salida
impassioned [ɪm'pæʃnd] *adj form* apasionado, -a
impassive [ɪm'pæsɪv] *adj* impasible
impatience [ɪm'peɪʃns] *n no pl* impaciencia *f*
impatient [ɪm'peɪʃnt] *adj* impaciente; **to be ~ to do sth** impacientarse por hacer algo
impeach [ɪm'piːtʃ] *vt* acusar, (someter a un proceso de incapacitación presidencial)
impeachment *n* acusación *f* (*proceso de incapacitación presidencial*)
impeccable [ɪm'pekəbl] *adj* impecable; (*manners*) intachable
impecunious [ˌɪmpɪ'kjuːnɪəs] *adj form* sin dinero
impede [ɪm'piːd] *vt* impedir
impediment [ɪm'pedɪmənt] *n* **1.** (*hindrance*) impedimento *m* **2.** MED defecto *m*
impel [ɪm'pel] <-ll-> *vt* impeler
impend [ɪm'pend] *vi* avecinarse
impending *adj* inminente
impenetrable [ɪm'penɪtrəbl] *adj* **1.** impenetrable **2.** (*incomprehensible*) incomprensible
impenitent [ɪm'penɪtənt, *Am:* -ətənt] *adj form* impenitente
imperative [ɪm'perətɪv, *Am:* -t̬ɪv] **I.** *adj* **1.** (*urgently essential*) imprescindible **2.** LING imperativo, -a **II.** *n a.* LING imperativo *m*

imperceptible [ˌɪmpəˈseptəbl, *Am:* -pɚ-ˈseptə-] *adj* imperceptible

imperfect [ɪmˈpɜːfɪkt, *Am:* -ˈpɜːr-] **I.** *adj* imperfecto, -a; (*flawed*) defectuoso, -a **II.** *n no pl* LING (pretérito *m*) imperfecto *m*

imperfection [ˌɪmpəˈfekʃən, *Am:* -pɚˈ-] *n* imperfección *f*

imperial [ɪmˈpɪəriəl, *Am:* -ˈpɪr-] *adj* imperial

imperialism [ɪmˈpɪəriəlɪzəm, *Am:* -ˈpɪrɪ-] *n no pl* imperialismo *m*

imperialist [ɪmˈpɪəriəlɪst, *Am:* -ˈpɪri-] **I.** *n* imperialista *mf* **II.** *adj* imperialista

imperil [ɪmˈperəl] <*Brit:* -ll-, *Am:* -l-> *vt form* poner en peligro

imperious [ɪmˈpɪəriəs, *Am:* -ˈpɪrɪ-] *adj* **1.** (*bossy*) imperioso, -a **2.** (*arrogant*) arrogante

imperishable [ɪmˈperɪʃəbl] *adj* imperecedero, -a

impermanent [ɪmˈpɜːmənənt, *Am:* -ˈpɜːr-] *adj* pasajero, -a

impermeable [ɪmˈpɜːmɪəbl, *Am:* -ˈpɜːr-] *adj* impermeable

impersonal [ˌɪmˈpɜːsənl, *Am:* -ˈpɜːr-] *adj a.* LING impersonal

impersonate [ɪmˈpɜːsəneɪt, *Am:* -ˈpɜːr-] *vt* hacerse pasar por; (*imitate*) imitar

impersonator *n* imitador(a) *m(f)*

impertinent [ɪmˈpɜːtɪnənt, *Am:* -ˈpɜːrtn̩-] *adj* impertinente

imperturbable [ˌɪmpəˈtɜːbəbl, *Am:* -pɚˈtɜːr-] *adj form* imperturbable

impervious [ɪmˈpɜːvɪəs, *Am:* -ˈpɜːr-] *adj* impermeable; (*not affected*) inmune

impetuous [ɪmˈpetʃʊəs, *Am:* -ˈpetʃu-] *adj* impetuoso, -a; (*action*) precipitado, -a

impetus [ˈɪmpɪtəs, *Am:* -t̬əs] *n no pl* **1.** (*push*) impulso *m* **2.** (*driving force*) ímpetu *m*

impiety [ɪmˈpaɪəti, *Am:* -t̬i] *n no pl* impiedad *f*

impinge [ɪmˈpɪndʒ] **I.** *vt form* afectar **II.** *vi* **to ~ on sb/sth** afectar a alguien/algo

impious [ˈɪmpɪəs] *adj* impío, -a

impish [ˈɪmpɪʃ] *adj* **1.** (*mischievous*) malicioso, -a **2.** (*cheeky*) pillín, -ina; (*grin*) pícaro, -a

implacable [ɪmˈplækəbl] *adj form* implacable

implacably *adv form* implacablemente

implant [ɪmˈplɑːnt, *Am:* -ˈplænt] **I.** *n* implante *m* **II.** *vt* **1.** (*add surgically*) implantar **2.** (*put in the mind*) inculcar

implausible [ɪmˈplɔːzɪbl, *Am:* -ˈplɑː-] *adj* inverosímil

implement [ˈɪmplɪmənt] **I.** *n* (*tool*) instrumento *m;* (*small tool*) utensilio *m* **II.** *vt* implementar

implementation [ˌɪmplɪmenˈteɪʃən] *n no pl* (*of tools, devices*) puesta *f* en práctica; (*of measures, policies*) implementación *f*

implicate [ˈɪmplɪkeɪt] *vt* (*show sb's involvement*) implicar; (*involve*) involucrar

implication [ˌɪmplɪˈkeɪʃən] *n* **1.** *no pl* (*hinting at*) insinuación *f;* **by ~** implícitamente **2.** (*effect*) consecuencia *f* **3.** (*showing of involvement*) implicación *f*

implicit [ɪmˈplɪsɪt] *adj* **1.** (*suggested*) implícito, -a **2.** (*total*) absoluto, -a; (*faith*) incondicional

implied [ɪmˈplaɪd] *adj* tácito, -a; (*criticism*) implícito, -a

implode [ɪmˈpləʊd, *Am:* -ˈploʊd] *vi* implosionar

implore [ɪmˈplɔːʳ, *Am:* -ˈplɔːr] *vt* implorar; **to ~ sb to do sth** suplicar a alguien que haga algo

imploring [ɪmˈplɔːrɪŋ, *Am:* -ˈplɔːr-] *adj* implorante; (*voice*) suplicante

implosion [ɪmˈpləʊʒən, *Am:* -ˈploʊ-] *n* implosión *f*

imply [ɪmˈplaɪ] <-ie-> *vt* **1.** (*suggest*) sugerir **2.** *form* (*require*) implicar

impolite [ˌɪmpəˈlaɪt] *adj* descortés; (*rude*) grosero, -a

impoliteness *n no pl* descortesía *f*

impolitic [ɪmˈpɒlətɪk, *Am:* -ˈpɑːlə-] *adj form* imprudente

imponderable [ɪmˈpɒndərəbl, *Am:* -ˈpɑːn-] **I.** *adj* imponderable **II.** *n* imponderable *m*

import [ɪmˈpɔːt, *Am:* -ˈpɔːrt] **I.** *vt* **1.** ECON, INFOR importar **2.** *form* (*signify*) significar **II.** *n* **1.** (*good*) producto *m* de importación **2.** *form* (*significance*) importancia *f*

importance [ɪmˈpɔːtns, *Am:* -ˈpɔːr-] *n no pl* importancia *f*

important [ɪmˈpɔːtənt, *Am:* -ˈpɔːr-] *adj* importante

importantly *adv* significativamente

importation [ˌɪmpɔːˈteɪʃən, *Am:* -pɔːrˈ-] *n no pl* ECON importación *f*

import duty <-ies> *n* derecho *m* de aduana

importunate [ɪmˈpɔːtʃʊnət, *Am:* -ˈpɔːrtʃənɪt] *adj form* inoportuno, -a, molesto, -a

importune [ˌɪmpəˈtjuːn, *Am:* ˌɪmpɔːrˈtuːn] *vt form* importunar

impose [ɪmˈpəʊz, *Am:* -ˈpoʊz] **I.** *vt* **1.** (*implement*) imponer **2.** (*force on*) obligar **II.** *vi* aprovecharse; **to ~ on sb** aprovecharse de alguien; **I don't want to ~** no quiero molestar

imposing [ɪmˈpəʊzɪŋ, *Am:* -ˈpoʊ-] *adj* imponente

imposition [ˌɪmpəˈzɪʃən] *n* **1.** *no pl* (*forcing, application*) imposición *f* **2.** (*inconvenience*) molestia *f*

impossibility [ɪmˌpɒsəˈbɪləti, *Am:* -ˌpɑːsəˈbɪlət̬i] *n no pl* imposibilidad *f*

impossible [ɪmˈpɒsəbl, *Am:* -ˈpɑːsə-] **I.** *adj* **1.** (*not possible*) imposible **2.** (*not resolveable*) irresoluble **3.** (*difficult to deal with*) insoportable **II.** *n* **the ~** lo imposible

impossibly *adv* extremadamente

imposter *n,* **impostor** [ɪmˈpɒstəʳ, *Am:* -ˈpɑːstɚ] *n* impostor(a) *m(f)*

imposture [ɪm'pɒstʃəʳ, *Am:* -'pɑːstʃɚ] *n no pl* impostura *f*
impotence ['ɪmpətəns, *Am:* -t̬əns] *n no pl* impotencia *f*
impotent ['ɪmpətənt, *Am:* -t̬ənt] *adj* impotente
impound [ɪm'paʊnd] *vt* incautar
impoverish [ɪm'pɒvərɪʃ, *Am:* -'pɑːvɚ-] *vt* **1.** (*make poor*) empobrecer **2.** (*deplete*) menguar
impoverished *adj* **1.** (*made poor*) empobrecido, -a **2.** (*depleted*) menguado, -a
impracticable [ɪm'præktɪkəbl] *adj* impracticable; (*person*) intratable
impractical [ɪm'præktɪkl] *adj* poco práctico, -a
imprecation [,ɪmprɪ'keɪʃən] *n form* imprecación *f*
imprecise [,ɪmprɪ'saɪs] *adj* impreciso, -a
impregnable [ɪm'pregnəbl] *adj* **1.** (*unable to be taken*) inexpugnable **2.** *Brit, Aus* (*undefeatable*) imbatible
impregnate ['ɪmpregneɪt, *Am:* ɪm'preg-] *vt* **1.** (*make absorb*) impregnar **2.** ZOOL fecundar
impresario [,ɪmprɪ'sɑːrɪəʊ, *Am:* -prə'sɑːrɪoʊ] *n* empresario, -a *m, f*
impress [ɪm'pres] **I.** *vt* **1.** (*affect*) impresionar **2.** (*stamp*) estampar; **to ~ sth on** [*o* **upon**] **sb** (*make realize*) inculcar algo a alguien; (*make remember*) recalcar algo a alguien **II.** *vi* impresionar
impression [ɪm'preʃən] *n* **1.** (*general opinion*) impresión *f;* **to be of** [*o* **under**] **the ~ that ...** tener la impresión de que... **2.** (*feeling*) sensación *f;* **to make an ~ on sb** causar impresión a alguien **3.** (*imitation*) imitación *f* **4.** (*imprint*) impresión *f; fig* huella *f*
impressionable [ɪm'preʃənəbl] *adj* impresionable
impressionism [ɪm'preʃnɪzəm] *n no pl* impresionismo *m*
impressionist [ɪm'preʃnɪst] **I.** *n* **1.** ART impresionista *mf* **2.** (*imitator*) imitador(a) *m(f)* **II.** *adj* impresionista
impressionistic [ɪm,preʃə'nɪstɪk] *adj* impresionista
impressive [ɪm'presɪv] *adj* impresionante
imprint [ɪm'prɪnt] **I.** *vt* **1.** (*stamp*) estampar; (*paper*) imprimir; (*coins*) acuñar; (*leather*) grabar **2.** (*in memory*) grabar **3.** ZOOL marcar **II.** *n* **1.** (*mark*) marca *f; fig* huella *f* **2.** TYPO pie *m* de imprenta
imprison [ɪm'prɪzən] *vt* encarcelar
imprisonment [ɪm'prɪzənmənt] *n no pl* encarcelamiento *m;* **life ~** cadena *f* perpetua
improbability [ɪm,prɒbə'bɪləti, *Am:* ,ɪmprɑːbə'bɪlət̬i] *n no pl* improbabilidad *f*
improbable [ɪm'prɒbəbl, *Am:* -'prɑːbə-] *adj* improbable
impromptu [ɪm'prɒmptjuː, *Am:* -'prɑːmptuː] *adj* de improviso
improper [ɪm'prɒpəʳ, *Am:* -'prɑːpɚ] *adj* **1.** (*incorrect*) incorrecto, -a; (*showing bad judgement*) injusto, -a **2.** (*not socially decent*) indecoroso, -a; (*immoral*) indecente **3.** (*dishonest*) deshonesto, -a
impropriety [,ɪmprə'praɪəti, *Am:* -t̬i] <-ies> *n* **1.** (*improper doings*) incongruencia *f;* (*language*) impropiedad *f* **2.** *no pl* (*indecency*) indecoro *m*
improve [ɪm'pruːv] **I.** *vt* mejorar **II.** *vi* **1.** mejorar; (*progress*) hacer progresos **2.** (*price*) subir
◆**improve on** *vi* superar
improvement [ɪm'pruːvmənt] *n* **1.** (*betterment*) mejora *f;* (*progress*) progreso *m* **2.** *no pl* (*of illness*) mejoría *f* **3.** (*increase in value*) revalorización *f*
improvident [ɪm'prɒvɪdənt, *Am:* -'prɑːvə-] *adj form* **1.** (*not planning*) improvisado, -a **2.** (*imprudent*) imprudente
improvisation [,ɪmprəvaɪ'zeɪʃən, *Am:* ɪm,prɑːvɪ'-] *n* improvisación *f*
improvise ['ɪmprəvaɪz] *vi, vt* improvisar
imprudent [ɪm'pruːdnt] *adj form* imprudente
impudence ['ɪmpjʊdəns] *n no pl* descaro *m*
impudent ['ɪmpjʊdənt] *adj* impertinente
impugn [ɪm'pjuːn] *vt form* impugnar
impulse ['ɪmpʌls] *n,* **impulsion** [ɪm'pʌlʃən] *n* **1.** *a.* ELEC, PHYS, BIO impulso *m;* **to do sth on** (**an**) **~** hacer algo por impulso **2.** (*motive*) incentivo *m*
impulsive [ɪm'pʌlsɪv] *adj* impulsivo, -a
impunity [ɪm'pjuːnəti, *Am:* -t̬i] *n no pl* impunidad *f*
impure [ɪm'pjʊəʳ, *Am:* -'pjʊr] *adj* impuro, -a
impurity [ɪm'pjʊərəti, *Am:* -'pjʊrət̬i] <-ies> *n* impureza *f*
imputation [,ɪmpjʊ'teɪʃən] *n form* imputación *f*
impute [ɪm'pjuːt] *vt* imputar
in[1] [ɪn] **I.** *prep* **1.** (*inside, into*) dentro de; **to be ~ bed** estar en la cama; **gun ~ hand** pistola en mano; **there is sth ~ the drawer** hay algo dentro del cajón; **to put sth ~ sb's hands** poner algo en las manos de alguien; **~ town/jail** en la ciudad/cárcel; **~ the country/hospital** en el país/hospital; **~ France/Peru** en Francia/Perú **2.** (*within*) **~ sb's face/the picture** en el rostro de alguien/la fotografía; **~ the snow/sun** en la nieve/el sol; **the best ~ France/the town** lo mejor de Francia/de la ciudad; **to find a friend ~ sb** encontrar un amigo en alguien **3.** (*position of*) **~ the beginning/end** al principio/final; **right ~ the middle** justo en medio **4.** (*during*) **~ the twenties** en los (años) veinte; **to be ~ one's thirties** estar en los treinta; **~ the reign of Caesar** en el reinado de César; **~ May/spring** en mayo/primavera; **~ the afternoon** por la tarde **5.** (*at later time*) **~ a week/three hours** en una semana/tres horas; **~ (the) future** en el futuro **6.** (*in less than*) **to do sth ~ 4 hours** hacer algo en 4 horas **7.** (*for*) **he**

hasn't done that ~ years/a week no ha hecho eso desde hace años/una semana **8.** (*in situation, state of*) ~ **fashion** de moda; ~ **search of sth/sb** en busca de algo/alguien; ~ **this way** de esta manera; **when ~ doubt** en caso de duda; ~ **anger** enfurecido, alebrestado *Col, Ven;* ~ **fun** de broma, en chanza; ~ **earnest** sinceramente; **to be ~ a hurry** tener prisa; **to be ~ love (with sb)** estar enamorado (de alguien); ~ **alphabetical order** en orden alfabético; **written ~ black and white** *fig* claramente escrito; **dressed ~ red** vestido de rojo **9.** (*concerning*) **deaf ~ one ear** sordo de un oído; **to be interested ~ sth** estar interesado en algo; **to have faith ~ God** tener fe en Dios; **to have confidence ~ sb** tener confianza en alguien; **to have a say ~ the matter** tener algo que decir al respecto; **a change ~ attitude** un cambio de actitud; **a rise ~ prices** un aumento de los precios **10.** (*by*) ~ **saying sth** al decir algo; **to spend one's time ~ doing sth** dedicar el tiempo de uno a hacer algo **11.** (*taking the form of*) **to speak ~ French** hablar en francés; ~ **the form of a request** en forma de petición **12.** (*made of*) ~ **wood/stone** de madera/piedra **13.** (*sound of*) ~ **a whisper** en un murmullo; **to speak ~ a loud/low voice** hablar en voz alta/baja **14.** (*aspect of*) **2 metres ~ length/height** 2 metros de largo/alto; ~ **every respect** en todos los sentidos **15.** (*ratio*) **two ~ six** dos de cada seis; **to buy sth ~ twos** comprar algo de dos en dos; **10 ~ number** 10 en número; ~ **part** en parte; ~ **tens** en grupos de diez **16.** (*substitution of*) ~ **your place** en tu lugar; ~ **lieu of sth** *form* en lugar de algo **17.** (*as conseqence of*) ~ **return** a cambio; ~ **reply** como respuesta ►~ **all** con todo; **all ~ all** en resumen **II.** *adv* **1.** (*inside, into*) dentro, adentro; **to go ~** entrar; **to put sth ~** meter algo **2.** (*to a place*) **to be ~** *inf* estar en casa; **to hand sth ~** entregar algo **3.** (*popular*) **to be ~** estar de moda **4.** SPORTS **to go ~ for sth** lanzarse a por algo **5.** (*up*) **the tide is coming ~** la marea está entrando ►**to be ~ for sth** *inf* estar a punto de recibir algo; **to be ~ on sth** estar enterado de algo **III.** *adj* de moda **IV.** *n* **~s and outs** recovecos *mpl*

in² *abbr of* **inch** pulgada *f*

inability [ˌɪnəˈbɪləti, *Am:* -t̬i] *n no pl* incapacidad *f*, ineptitud *f*

inaccessible [ˌɪnækˈsesəbl] *adj* inaccesible

inaccuracy [ɪnˈækjʊrəsi, *Am:* -jɚə-] <-ies> *n* **1.** (*fact*) error *m* **2.** *no pl* (*quality*) imprecisión *f*, inexactitud *f*

inaccurate [ɪnˈækjərət, *Am:* -jɚət] *adj* **1.** (*inexact*) inexacto, -a **2.** (*wrong*) equivocado, -a

inaction [ɪnˈækʃən] *n no pl* inacción *f*

inactive [ɪnˈæktɪv] *adj* inactivo, -a

inactivity [ˌɪnækˈtɪvəti, *Am:* -t̬i] *n no pl* inactividad *f*

inadequacy [ɪnˈædɪkwəsi] <-ies> *n* **1.** (*insufficiency*) insuficiencia *f* **2.** *no pl* (*quality of being inadequate*) falta *f* de adecuación

inadequate [ɪnˈædɪkwət] *adj* inadecuado, -a; (*inept*) inepto, -a

inadmissible [ˌɪnədˈmɪsəbl] *adj* inadmisible

inadvertent [ˌɪnədˈvɜːtənt, *Am:* -ədˈvɜːr-] *adj* involuntario, -a

inadvisable [ˌɪnədˈvaɪzəbl] *adj* desaconsejable

inalienable [ɪnˈeɪlɪənəbl] *adj form* inalienable

inane [ɪˈneɪn] *adj* estúpido, -a

inanimate [ɪnˈænɪmət] *adj* inanimado, -a

inanity [ɪˈnænəti, *Am:* -t̬i] <-ies> *n* necedad *f*

inapplicable [ɪnˈæplɪkəbl] *adj* inaplicable

inappropriate [ˌɪnəˈprəʊprɪət, *Am:* -ˈproʊ-] *adj* inapropiado, -a; (*not suitable*) inadecuado, -a

inapt [ɪnˈæpt] *adj* inadecuado, -a; (*not skilful*) inhábil, no capacitado, -a

inaptitude [ɪnˈæptɪtjuːd, *Am:* -tətuːd] *n no pl* inhabilidad *f*

inarticulate [ˌɪnɑːˈtɪkjʊlət, *Am:* -ɑːrˈ-] *adj* **1.** (*unable to express*) incapaz de expresarse **2.** (*unclear*) inarticulado, -a

inartistic [ˌɪnɑːˈtɪstɪk, *Am:* -ɑːrˈ-] *adj* poco artístico, -a

inasmuch as [ˌɪnəzˈmʌtʃ əz] *conj form* **1.** (*because*) ya que **2.** (*to the extent that*) en tanto que +*subj*

inattention [ˌɪnəˈtenʃən] *n no pl* inatención *f*

inattentive [ˌɪnəˈtentɪv, *Am:* -t̬ɪv] *adj* distraído, -a; **to be ~ to sb/sth** no prestar atención a alguien/algo

inaudible [ɪnˈɔːdəbl, *Am:* -ˈɑː-] *adj* inaudible

inaugural [ɪˈnɔːgjʊrəl, *Am:* -ˈnɑːg-] *adj* inaugural; (*speech*) de apertura

inaugurate [ɪˈnɔːgjʊreɪt, *Am:* -ˈnɑːg-] *vt* inaugurar

inauguration [ɪˌnɔːgjʊˈreɪʃən, *Am:* -ˌnɑːg-] *n* inauguración *f*

inauspicious [ˌɪnɔːˈspɪʃəs, *Am:* -ɑːˈspɪʃ-] *adj* poco propicio, -a

in-between *adj* intermedio, -a

inboard [ˈɪnbɔːd, *Am:* ˈɪnbɔːrd] *adj* interno, -a

inborn [ˌɪnˈbɔːn, *Am:* ˈɪnbɔːrn] *adj* innato, -a

in-box [ˈɪnbɒks, *Am:* -bɑːks] *n* INFOR buzón *m* de entrada

inbred [ˌɪnˈbred, *Am:* ˈɪnbred] *adj* **1.** (*too closely related*) endogámico, -a **2.** (*inherent*) innato, -a

inbreeding [ˌɪnˈbriːdɪŋ, *Am:* ˈɪnbriːdɪŋ] *n no pl* endogamia *f*

in-built [ˈɪnbɪlt] *adj* integrado, -a; *fig* inherente, innato, -a

Inc. [ɪŋk] *abbr of* **Incorporated** Inc.

incalculable [ɪnˈkælkjʊləbl] *adj* incalculable

incandescent [ˌɪnkænˈdesnt, *Am:* -kenˈ-] *adj* incandescente

I

incantation [ˌɪnkæn'teɪʃən] *n* conjuro *m,* ensalmo *m*

incapability [ɪnˌkeɪpə'bɪləti, *Am:* -t̬i] *n no pl* incapacidad *f*

incapable [ɪn'keɪpəbl] *adj* incapaz; **to be ~ of doing sth** no ser capaz de hacer algo

incapacitate [ˌɪnkə'pæsɪteɪt] *vt* incapacitar

incapacity [ˌɪnkə'pæsəti, *Am:* -t̬i] *n no pl* incapacidad *f*

incarcerate [ɪn'kɑːsəreɪt, *Am:* -'kɑːr-] *vt* encarcelar

incarnate [ɪn'kɑːneɪt, *Am:* -'kɑːr-] *adj* encarnado, -a; **the devil ~** el mismo diablo

incarnation [ˌɪnkɑː'neɪʃən, *Am:* -kɑːr'-] *n* encarnación *f;* **to be the ~ of sth** ser la personificación de algo

incautious [ɪn'kɔːʃəs, *Am:* -'kɑː-] *adj form* imprudente

incendiary [ɪn'sendɪəri, *Am:* -eri] *adj a. fig* incendiario, -a

incense[1] ['ɪnsents] *n* incienso *m*

incense[2] [ɪn'sents] *vt* indignar

incensed *adj* indignado, -a

incentive [ɪn'sentɪv, *Am:* -t̬ɪv] *n* incentivo *m*

incentive scheme *n* plan *m* de incentivos

inception [ɪn'sepʃən] *n no pl* inicio *m*

incertitude [ɪn'sɜːtɪtjuːd, *Am:* -'sɜːrt̬ɪtuːd] *n* incertidumbre *f*

incessant [ɪn'sesnt] *adj* incesante

incest ['ɪnsest] *n no pl* incesto *m*

incestuous [ɪn'sestjuəs, *Am:* -tʃu-] *adj a. fig* incestuoso, -a

inch [ɪntʃ] **I.** <-es> *n* pulgada *f;* **she knows every ~ of Madrid** conoce cada centímetro de Madrid; **she's every ~ a lady** es una señora de pies a cabeza ▸**give someone an ~ and they'll take a mile** *prov* les das la mano y te cogen el brazo *prov;* **to do sth ~ by ~** hacer algo paso a paso **II.** *vi* moverse lentamente
◆**inch forward** *vi* avanzar lentamente

incidence ['ɪntsɪdənts] *n no pl* incidencia *f;* **there is a higher ~ of left-handedness amongst girls than boys** existe un índice mayor de zurdos entre chicas que entre chicos

incident ['ɪntsɪdənt] *n* incidente *m;* **an isolated ~** un episodio aislado

incidental [ˌɪntsɪ'dentəl, *Am:* -t̬əl] *adj* **1.** (*related, of lesser importance*) secundario, -a **2.** (*occuring by chance*) imprevisto, -a

incidentally *adv* por cierto, a propósito

incinerate [ɪn'sɪnəreɪt] *vt* incinerar

incinerator [ɪn'sɪnəreɪtəʳ, *Am:* -t̬ɚ] *n* incinerador *m*

incipient [ɪn'sɪpɪənt] *adj* incipiente; **at an ~ stage** en una etapa naciente

incise *vt Brit, Aus,* **incize** [ɪn'saɪz] *vt Am* cortar; (*in wood*) grabar

incision [ɪn'sɪʒən] *n* MED incisión *f*

incisive [ɪn'saɪsɪv] *adj* **1.** (*clear*) incisivo, -a; (*penetrating*) penetrante **2.** (*keen, acute*) agudo, -a; (*mind*) perspicaz

incisor [ɪn'saɪzəʳ, *Am:* -zɚ] *n* incisivo *m*

incite [ɪn'saɪt] *vt* instigar

incitement [ɪn'saɪtmənt] *n no pl* incitación *f*

incivility [ˌɪnsɪ'vɪləti, *Am:* -t̬i] *n no pl, form* descortesía *f*

inclement [ɪn'klemənt] *adj* inclemente

inclination [ˌɪnklɪ'neɪʃən] *n* **1.** (*tendency*) propensión *f;* **to have an ~ to do sth** tener inclinación a hacer algo **2.** (*slope*) inclinación *f*

incline[1] ['ɪnklaɪn] *n* inclinación *f;* (*of hill, mountain*) pendiente *f*

incline[2] [ɪn'klaɪn] **I.** *vi* **1.** (*tend*) tender **2.** (*lean*) inclinarse **II.** *vt* **1.** (*make sth tend*) predisponer; **to ~ (sb) to do sth** influir (a alguien) para que haga algo **2.** (*make lean*) inclinar

inclined [ɪn'klaɪnd] *adj* predispuesto, -a; **to be ~ to do sth** estar dispuesto a hacer algo

inclose [ɪn'kləʊz, *Am:* -'kloʊz] *vt* encerrar

include [ɪn'kluːd] *vt* incluir; (*in a letter*) adjuntar; **do you ~ that in the service?** ¿lo incluís en el servicio?

including [ɪn'kluːdɪŋ] *prep* incluso; (**not**) **~ tax** impuesto (no) incluido; **up to and ~ 6th June** hasta el 6 de junio inclusive

inclusion [ɪn'kluːʒən] *n no pl* inclusión *f*

inclusive [ɪn'kluːsɪv] *adj* incluido, -a; **all prices are ~ of Value Added Tax** todos los precios llevan incluido el Impuesto sobre el Valor Añadido

incognito [ˌɪnkɒg'niːtəʊ, *Am:* ˌɪnkɑːg'niːtoʊ] *adv* de incógnito, -a

incoherent [ˌɪnkəʊ'hɪərənt, *Am:* -koʊ'hɪrənt] *adj* incoherente

income ['ɪŋkʌm, *Am:* 'ɪn-] *n no pl* ingresos *mpl*

income group *n* tramo *m* de renta **income support** *n no pl, Brit* subsidio *m* otorgado a personas de bajos ingresos **income tax** *n no pl* impuesto *m* sobre la renta; **graduated ~** impuesto *m* proporcional

incoming ['ɪnˌkʌmɪŋ] *adj* entrante

incomings ['ɪnˌkʌmɪŋz] *npl* ECON entradas *fpl*

incommensurate [ˌɪnkə'menʃərət, *Am:* -sɚ-] *adj* desproporcionado, -a; **to be ~ to** no guardar relación con

incommunicado [ˌɪnkəˌmjuːnɪ'kɑːdəʊ, *Am:* -doʊ] *adj* incomunicado, -a; **we wanted to invite you to the party, but you were ~** queríamos invitarte a la fiesta pero estabas ilocalizable

incomparable [ɪn'kɒmprəbl, *Am:* -'kɑːm-] *adj* incomparable

incompatibility [ˌɪnkəmˌpætə'bɪlɪti, *Am:* -ˌpæt̬ə'bɪlət̬i] <-ies> *n no pl* incompatibilidad *f;* **~ with sth** falta de compatibilidad con algo; **Laura left the firm because of her ~ with her workmates** Laura dejó la empresa por falta de entendimiento con sus compañeros

incompatible [ˌɪnkəm'pætəbl, *Am:* -'pæt̬-] *adj* incompatible

incompetence [ɪn'kɒmpɪtənts, *Am:*

-'kaːmpət̬ənts] *n,* **incompetency** *n no pl* incompetencia *f*

incompetent [ɪn'kɒmpɪtənt, *Am:* -'kaːmpət̬ənt] **I.** *adj* incompetente; **mentally** ~ deficiente mental; **she was mentally ~ when she wrote the will** no contaba con plenas facultades mentales cuando redactó el testamento **II.** *n* incompetente *mf*

incomplete [ˌɪnkəm'pliːt] *adj* incompleto, -a; (*not finished*) inacabado, -a

incomprehensible [ˌɪnˌkɒmprɪ'hensəbl, *Am:* ˌɪnkaːm-] *adj* incomprensible

inconceivable [ˌɪnkən'siːvəbl] *adj* inconcebible

inconclusive [ˌɪnkən'kluːsɪv] *adj* **1.** (*not convincing*) inconcluyente **2.** (*without definite results*) no fructífero, -a

incongruous [ɪn'kɒŋgrʊəs, *Am:* -'kaːŋ-] *adj* **1.** (*unsuitable*) inapropiado, -a **2.** (*strange*) fuera de lugar

inconsequent [ɪn'kɒnsɪkwənt, *Am:* -'kaːn-] *adj form* intrascendente

inconsequential [ɪnˌkɒnsɪ'kwenʃl, *Am:* -'kaːn-] *adj* **1.** (*illogical*) inconsecuente **2.** (*unimportant*) intrascendente

inconsiderable [ˌɪnkən'sɪdrəbl] *adj* **a not ~ amount** una suma nada desdeñable

inconsiderate [ˌɪnkən'sɪdərət] *adj* desconsiderado, -a; (*insensitive*) insensible

inconsistency [ˌɪnkən'sɪstəntsi] <-ies> *n* **1.** (*lack of consistency*) falta *f* de coherencia **2.** (*discrepancy*) contradicción *f*

inconsistent [ˌɪnkən'sɪstənt] *adj* **1.** (*changeable*) incoherente **2.** (*lacking agreement*) contradictorio, -a

inconsolable [ˌɪnkən'səʊləbl, *Am:* -'soʊ-] *adj* inconsolable

inconspicuous [ˌɪnkən'spɪkjʊəs] *adj* desapercibido, -a; **highly** ~ imperceptible; **to try to look** ~ tratar de pasar inadvertido

inconstant [ɪn'kɒnstənt, *Am:* -'kaːn-] *adj* **1.** (*changing*) inconstante; (*unpredictable*) imprevisible **2.** (*unfaithful*) infiel

incontestable [ˌɪnkən'testəbl] *adj form* incontestable; **it is ~ that ...** es irrefutable que...

incontinent [ɪn'kɒntɪnənt, *Am:* -'kaːntən-] *adj* MED incontinente

incontrovertible [ɪnˌkɒntrə'vɜːtəbl, *Am:* -ˌkaːntrə'vɜːrt̬ə-] *adj* incontrovertible; **her logic is** ~ su lógica es indiscutible; ~ **proof** prueba *f* irrefutable; **it is ~ that ...** es incuestionable que...

inconvenience [ˌɪnkən'viːnɪəns] **I.** *n* inconveniencia *f* **II.** *vt* causar molestias

inconvenient [ˌɪnkən'viːnɪənt] *adj* inconveniente; (*time*) inoportuno, -a; **it's a very ~ place to hold the party** es un lugar muy poco adecuado para hacer la fiesta

incorporate [ɪn'kɔːpəreɪt, *Am:* -'kɔːr-] *vt* **1.** (*integrate*) incorporar; (*work into*) integrar; (*add*) añadir **2.** (*include*) incluir **3.** *Am* LAW, ECON constituir; **to ~ a company** formar una empresa

incorporation [ɪnˌkɔːpə'reɪʃən, *Am:* -ˌkɔːr-] *n no pl* **1.** (*integration*) incorporación *f;* (*working into*) integración *f* **2.** LAW, ECON constitución *f*

incorporeal [ˌɪnkɔː'pɔːrɪəl, *Am:* -kɔːr'-] *adj form* incorpóreo, -a; **an ~ being** un ser impalpable

incorrect [ˌɪnkə'rekt] *adj* **1.** (*wrong, untrue*) incorrecto, -a; (*diagnosis*) erróneo, -a; **it is ~ that ...** no es cierto que... **2.** (*improper*) inapropiado, -a

incorrigible [ɪŋ'kɒrɪdʒəbl, *Am:* ɪn'kɔːrə-] *adj* incorregible

incorruptible [ˌɪnkə'rʌptəbl] *adj* **1.** (*not able to be corrupted*) incorruptible; (*morally incorruptible*) íntegro, -a **2.** (*not subject to decay*) inalterable

increase[1] ['ɪnkriːs] *n* (*raised amount*) incremento *m;* (*wilful*) subida *f;* (*be getting higher and higher*) crecimiento *m;* **to be on the** ~ ir en aumento

increase[2] [ɪn'kriːs] **I.** *vi* (*become more*) incrementar; (*grow*) crecer; **to ~ dramatically** aumentar espectacularmente; **to ~ tenfold/threefold** multiplicarse por diez/tres **II.** *vt* (*make more*) incrementar; (*make stronger*) intensificar; (*make larger*) aumentar

increasing *adj* creciente

increasingly *adv* cada vez más

incredible [ɪn'kredɪbl] *adj* increíble

incredibly *adv* **1.** (*in an incredible way*) increiblemente **2. ~, nobody was hurt** parece increíble, pero no hubo heridos

incredulity [ˌɪnkrɪ'djuːləti, *Am:* -'duːlət̬i] *n no pl* incredulidad *f;* (*bewilderment*) desconcierto *m*

incredulous [ɪn'kredjʊləs, *Am:* -'kredʒʊ-] *adj* incrédulo, -a

increment ['ɪŋkrəmənt] *n* incremento *m;* (*wilful*) subida *f;* **salary** ~ aumento *m* salarial

incremental [ˌɪŋkrə'məntəl, *Am:* ˌɪŋkrə'mənt̬əl] *adj* ECON incremental

incriminate [ɪn'krɪmɪneɪt] *vt* incriminar; **to ~ oneself** autoinculparse

incriminating *adj* compremetedor(a)

incubate ['ɪnkjʊbeɪt] **I.** *vt* incubar **II.** *vi* incubarse

incubation [ˌɪnkjʊ'beɪʃən] *n no pl* incubación *f*

incubation period *n* período *m* de incubación

incubator ['ɪŋkjʊbeɪtəʳ, *Am:* -t̬ɚ] *n* incubadora *f*

inculcate ['ɪnkʌlkeɪt] *vt* inculcar

incumbent [ɪŋ'kʌmbənt] **I.** *adj* **it is ~ on sb to do sth** incumbe a alguien hacer algo **II.** *n* titular *m*

incur [ɪn'kɜːʳ, *Am:* -'kɜːr] <-rr-> *vt* **1.** FIN, ECON (*debt*) contraer; (*costs*) incurrir en; (*losses*) sufrir **2.** (*bring upon oneself*) acarrear; **to ~ the anger of sb** provocar el enfado de alguien

incurable [ɪn'kjʊərəbl, *Am:* -'kjʊrə-] *adj*

incurable; *fig* incorregible; **he is an ~ romantic** es un romántico empedernido

incursion [ɪn'kɜːʃən, *Am:* -'kɜːr-] *n* **1.** MIL incursión *f* **2.** (*intrusion*) intrusión *f*

indebted [ɪn'detɪd, *Am:* -'det̬-] *adj* **1.** (*obliged*) en deuda; **to be ~ to sb** (**for sth**) estar en deuda con alguien (por algo) **2.** (*having debt*) endeudado, -a

indebtedness *n no pl* **1.** (*state of obligation*) deuda *f* **2.** (*state of debt*) endeudamiento *m*

indecency [ɪn'diːsəntsi] *n no pl* **1.** (*impropriety*) indecencia *f* **2.** LAW abuso *m*

indecent [ɪn'diːsənt] *adj* indecente, indecoroso, -a

indecipherable [ˌɪndɪ'saɪfrəbl] *adj* indescifrable

indecision [ˌɪndɪ'sɪʒən] *n no pl* indecisión *f*, irresolución *f*

indecisive [ˌɪndɪ'saɪsɪv] *adj* **1.** (*unable to make decisions*) indeciso, -a **2.** (*not clear*) irresoluto, -a

indeclinable [ɪndɪ'klaɪnəbl] *adj* LING indeclinable

indecorous [ɪn'dekərəs] *adj form* (*unsuitable*) indecoroso, -a; (*undignified*) indigno, -a

indeed [ɪn'diːd] **I.** *adv* **1.** (*really*) realmente; **this is good news ~!** ¡eso sí que es una buena noticia!; **many people here are very rich ~** mucha gente de aquí es verdaderamente rica **2.** (*expresses affirmation*) en efecto; **yes, he did ~ say that** sí, en efecto dijo eso **II.** *interj* ya lo creo; **he's a lovely boy! – ~!** es un chico encantador – ¡ya lo creo!

indefatigable [ˌɪndɪ'fætɪgəbl, *Am:* -'fæt̬-] *adj form* infatigable

indefensible [ˌɪndɪ'fensəbl] *adj* insostenible; MIL indefendible

indefinable [ˌɪndɪ'faɪnəbl] *adj* indefinible

indefinite [ɪn'defɪnət, *Am:* -ənət] *adj* indefinido, -a; **for an ~ period** por un tiempo indeterminado

indefinite article *n* LING artículo *m* indefinido

indefinitely *adv* indefinidamente

indelible [ɪn'deləbl] *adj* imborrable; (*colours, stains*) indeleble

indemnify [ɪn'demnɪfaɪ] <-ie-> *vt* **1.** (*insure against damage*) asegurar **2.** (*compensate for damage*) indemnizar

indemnity [ɪn'demnəti, *Am:* -t̬i] <-ies> *n form* **1.** *no pl* (*insurance for damage*) indemnidad *f* **2.** (*compensation*) indemnización *f* **3.** (*exemption*) inmunidad *f*

indent [ɪn'dent] **I.** *vi* **1.** TYPO (*make a space*) sangrar **2.** *Brit, Aus* ECON encargar **II.** *vt* marcar; TYPO sangrar; **his footsteps ~ed the sand** sus pasos dejaron marcas en la arena **III.** *n* **1.** *Brit, Aus* ECON pedido *m* **2.** TYPO sangrado *m*

indentation [ˌɪnden'teɪʃən] *n* **1.** TYPO sangría *f* **2.** (*notch*) hendidura *f*; (*cut*) mella *f*

independence [ˌɪndɪ'pendəns] *n no pl* independencia *f*

Independence Day *n Am* día *m* de la Independencia

independent [ˌɪndɪ'pendənt] **I.** *adj* independiente; **to be financially ~** ser económicamente independiente **II.** *n* POL diputado, -a *m, f* independiente

in-depth ['ɪndepθ] *adj* exhaustivo, -a, a fondo

indescribable [ˌɪndɪ'skraɪbəbl] *adj* indescriptible

indestructible [ˌɪndɪ'strʌktəbl] *adj* indestructible; **~ waste products** productos *mpl* no desechables

indeterminable [ˌɪndɪ'tɜːmɪnəbl, *Am:* -'tɜːr-] *adj* indeterminable

indeterminate [ˌɪndɪ'tɜːmɪnət, *Am:* -'tɜːr-] *adj* indeterminado, -a; **to take an ~ stance** adoptar una postura ecléctica

index ['ɪndeks] **I.** *n* **1.** <-es> (*alphabetical list*) índice *m;* **card ~** fichero *m* de tarjetas **2.** <-ices *o* -es> ECON índice *m;* **the Dow Jones Index** el índice Dow Jones; **consumer price ~** índice de precios al consumo **3.** <-ices *o* -es> (*indication*) indicador *m* **4.** <-ices> MAT exponente *m* **II.** *vt* **1.** (*provide with a list*) poner índice a **2.** (*enter in a list*) indexar **3.** ECON **to ~ wages to inflation** equilibrar los sueldos a la inflación; **~ed pension** pensión *f* actualizada al coste de la vida

indexation [ˌindek'seɪʃən] *n no pl* ECON indexación *f*

index card *n* ficha *f*

indexer ['indeksəʳ, *Am:* -sɚ] *n* clasificador *m*

index finger *n* dedo *m* índice **index-linked** *adj Brit* ECON indexado, -a

India ['ɪndɪə] *n no pl* la India *f*

Indian ['ɪndɪən] **I.** *adj* **1.** (*of India*) indio, -a, hindú **2.** (*of America*) indio, -a, indígena **II.** *n* **1.** (*of India*) indio, -a *m, f* **2.** (*of America*) indígena *mf*

Indian club *n* SPORTS bolo *m* **Indian corn** *n no pl, Am* mazorca *f* **Indian file** *n* fila *f* india **Indian ink** *n no pl, Brit, Aus* tinta *f* china **Indian Ocean** *n no pl* Océano *m* Índico **Indian summer** *n* veranillo *m* de San Martín

India paper *n no pl* papel *m* biblia **India rubber** *n* **1.** *no pl* (*substance*) caucho *m* **2.** (*eraser*) goma *f*

indicate ['ɪndɪkeɪt] **I.** *vt* indicar; **to ~ (to sb) that ...** señalar (a alguien) que... **II.** *vi Brit* AUTO poner el intermitente

indication [ˌɪndɪ'keɪʃən] *n* **1.** (*evidence*) indicio *m;* **an ~ of willingness** una muestra de voluntad **2.** *a.* MED indicación *f*

indicative [ɪn'dɪkətɪv, *Am:* -t̬ɪv] **I.** *adj* indicativo, -a **II.** *n* indicativo *m*

indicator ['ɪndɪkeɪtəʳ, *Am:* -t̬ɚ] *n* **1.** (*evidence*) indicador *m* **2.** *Brit* AUTO intermitente *m*

indices ['ɪndɪsiːz] *n pl of* **index**

indict [ɪn'daɪt] *vt* **to ~ sb of sth** LAW acusar a alguien de algo

indictment [ɪn'daɪtmənt] *n* **1.** LAW acusa-

ción *f* **2.** *fig* crítica *f*
indie ['ɪndi] *adj inf* (*album, record company*) independiente
Indies ['ɪndiz] *npl* Indias *fpl;* **the West** ~ Las Antillas
indifference [ɪn'dɪfrəns] *n no pl* indiferencia *f*
indifferent [ɪn'dɪfrənt] *adj* **1.** (*not interested*) indiferente, valemadrista *inv Méx* **2.** (*neither good nor bad*) mediocre
indigenous [ɪn'dɪdʒɪnəs] *adj* indígena
indigestible [ˌɪndɪ'dʒəstəbl] *adj* **1.** (*food*) indigesto, -a **2.** *fig* indigerible
indigestion [ˌɪndɪ'dʒəstʃən] *n no pl* indigestión *f;* **to give oneself** ~ empacharse
indignant [ɪn'dɪgnənt] *adj* indignado, -a; **to become** ~ indignarse; **to be/feel** ~ **about sth** estar/sentirse indignado por algo
indignation [ˌɪndɪg'neɪʃən] *n no pl* indignación *f*
indignity [ɪn'dɪgnɪti, *Am:* -nət̬i] <-ies> *n* **1.** *no pl* (*humiliation*) indignidad *f* **2.** (*sth that humiliates*) afrenta *f*
indirect [ˌɪndɪ'rekt] *adj* indirecto, -a
indirect object *n* LING objeto *m* indirecto
indirect tax <-es> *n* contribución *f* indirecta
indiscernible [ˌɪndɪ'sɜːnəbl, *Am:* -'sɜːr-] *adj* indiscernible; (*not visible*) imperceptible; ~ **to the naked eye** imperceptible a simple vista
indiscipline [ɪn'dɪsɪplɪn] *n no pl, form* falta *f* de disciplina
indiscreet [ˌɪndɪ'skriːt] *adj* indiscreto, -a; (*tactless*) falto, -a de tacto
indiscretion [ˌɪndɪ'skreʃən] *n no pl* (*lack of discretion*) indiscreción *f;* (*lack of tactfulness*) falta *f* de tacto
indiscriminate [ˌɪndɪ'skrɪmɪnət] *adj* **1.** (*uncritical*) sin criterio **2.** (*random*) indiscriminado, -a
indispensable [ˌɪndɪ'spensəbl] *adj* indispensable
indisposed [ˌɪndɪ'spəʊzd, *Am:* -'spoʊzd] *adj* indispuesto, -a; **to be/feel** ~ **to do sth** estar/sentirse indispuesto para hacer algo
indisposition [ˌɪndɪspə'zɪʃən] *n form* **1.** (*illness*) indisposición *f* **2.** *no pl* (*disinclination*) reticencia *f*
indisputable [ˌɪndɪ'spjuːtəbl, *Am:* -t̬ə-] *adj* indiscutible; (*evidence*) incuestionable
indistinct [ˌɪndɪ'stɪŋkt] *adj* indistinto, -a; (*blurred*) borroso, -a
indistinguishable [ˌɪndɪ'stɪŋgwɪʃ əbl] *adj* indistinguible; (*not perceptible*) imperceptible
individual [ˌɪndɪ'vɪdʒuəl] **I.** *n* individuo, -a *m, f* **II.** *adj* individual; (*particular*) particular; **an** ~ **style** un estilo propio
individual case *n* caso *m* particular
individualise *vt Aus, Brit,* **individualize** [ˌɪndɪ'vɪdʒuəlaɪz] *vt Am* individualizar
individualism [ˌɪndɪ'vɪdʒuəlɪzəm] *n no pl* individualismo *m*
individualist *n* individualista *mf*
individualistic [ˌɪndɪˌvɪdʒuə'lɪstɪk] *adj* individualista
individuality [ˌɪndɪˌvɪdʒu'æləti, *Am:* -ˌvɪdʒu'ælət̬i] *n no pl* individualidad *f*
individually *adv* individualmente
indivisible [ˌɪndɪ'vɪzəbl] *adj* indivisible
Indochina [ˌɪdəʊ'tʃaɪnə] *n* Indochina *f*
indoctrinate [ɪn'dɒktrɪneɪt, *Am:* -'dɑːk-] *vt* adoctrinar; **to** ~ **children in sth** adoctrinar a los niños en algo
indoctrination [ɪnˌdɒktrɪ'neɪʃən, *Am:* -ˌdɑːk-] *n no pl* adoctrinamiento *m*
indolent ['ɪndələnt] *adj* indolente
indomitable [ɪn'dɒmɪtəbl, *Am:* -'dɑːmət̬ə-] *adj* indómito, -a; **an** ~ **strength of character** una fuerza de carácter indomable
Indonesia [ˌɪndəʊ'niːzɪə, *Am:* -də'niːʒə] *n* Indonesia *f*
Indonesian **I.** *adj* indonesio, -a **II.** *n* indonesio, -a *m, f*
indoor ['ɪndɔːʳ, *Am:* ˌɪn'dɔːr] *adj* interior; (*pool*) cubierto, -a; (*clothes*) de casa; ~ **plant** planta *f* de interior
indoors [ˌɪn'dɔːz, *Am:* -'dɔːrz] *adv* dentro
indubitable [ɪn'djuːbɪtəbl, *Am:* -'duːbɪt̬ə-] *adj form* indudable
indubitably [ɪn'djuːbɪtəbli, *Am:* -'duːbɪt̬ə-] *adv form* indudablemente
induce [ɪn'djuːs, *Am:* -'duːs] *vt* **1.** (*persuade*) *a.* ELEC, PHYS inducir **2.** (*cause*) provocar
inducement [ɪn'djuːsmənt, *Am:* -'duːs-] *n* incentivo *m*
induct [ɪn'dʌkt] *vt* **1.** (*install*) instalar **2.** (*initiate*) iniciar **3.** (*recruit*) reclutar
induction [ɪn'dʌkʃən] *n* **1.** (*installation*) instalación *f;* (*into organization*) iniciación *f* **2.** (*initiation*) iniciación *f* **3.** *no pl* PHILOS, ELEC inducción *f*
induction coil *n* ELEC bobina *f* de inducción
induction course *n* curso *m* de iniciación
inductive [ɪn'dʌktɪv] *adj* inductivo, -a
indulge [ɪn'dʌldʒ] *vt* (*allow*) consentir; (*desire*) satisfacer; **to** ~ **oneself in ...** darse el lujo de..., permitirse...
indulgence [ɪn'dʌldʒəns] *n* **1.** (*treat*) placer *m;* (*satisfaction*) satisfacción *f;* ~ **in** abandono a **2.** (*tolerance*) tolerancia *f* **3.** REL indulgencia *f*
indulgent [ɪn'dʌldʒənt] *adj* **1.** (*lenient*) indulgente **2.** (*tolerant*) tolerante
industrial [ɪn'dʌstriəl] **I.** *adj* industrial; (*dispute*) laboral; **for** ~ **use** para uso industrial **II.** *npl* FIN acciones *fpl* industriales
industrial estate *n* polígono *m* industrial
industrialise *Brit, Aus,* **industrialize** [ɪn'dʌstriəlaɪz] **I.** *vi* industrializarse **II.** *vt* industrializar
industrialism [ɪn'dʌstriəlɪzəm] *n no pl* industrialismo *m*
industrialist *n* industrial *mf*
industrialization [ɪnˌdʌstriəlaɪ'zeɪʃən, *Am:* -lɪ'-] *n no pl* industrialización *f*
industrial park *n Am* polígono *m* industrial
Industrial Revolution *n* Revolución *f*

Industrial
industrious [ɪn'dʌstrɪəs] *adj* trabajador(a)
industry ['ɪndəstri] *n* **1.** *no pl* (*manufacturing production*) industria *f;* **heavy/light** ~ industria pesada/ligera **2.** <-ies> (*branch*) sector *m* **3.** *no pl* (*diligence*) laboriosidad *f*
inebriate [ɪ'ni:brɪeɪt] *vt form* embriagar
inedible [ɪn'edəbl] *adj* **1.** (*unsuitable as food*) no comestible **2.** (*extremely unpalatable*) incomible
ineducable [ɪn'edʒʊkəbl] *adj* ineducable
ineffable [ɪn'efəbl] *adj* inefable
ineffective [ˌɪnɪ'fektɪv] *adj* ineficaz
ineffectual [ˌɪnɪ'fektʃʊəl] *adj* ineficaz, inútil
inefficiency [ˌɪnɪ'fɪʃənsi] *n no pl* ineficiencia *f*
inefficient [ˌɪnɪ'fɪʃnt] *adj* ineficiente
inelegant [ˌɪn'elɪgənt] *adj* **1.** (*unattractive*) poco elegante **2.** (*unrefined*) tosco, -a; (*gesture, movement*) basto, -a
ineligible [ɪn'elɪdʒəbl] *adj* inelegible; **to be** ~ **for sth** no reunir los requisitos para algo; **to be** ~ **to do sth** no tener derecho a hacer algo
inept [ɪ'nept] *adj* (*unskilled*) inepto, -a; (*inappropriate*) inoportuno, -a; **to be** ~ **at sth** ser inepto para algo; **to be socially** ~ no tener don de gentes
inequality [ˌɪnɪ'kwɒləti, *Am:* -'kwɑ:ləṱi] <-ies> *n* desigualdad *f*
inequitable [ɪn'ekwɪtəbl, *Am:* -wəṱə-] *adj* injusto, -a
inequity [ɪn'ekwəti, *Am:* -ṱi] <-ies> *n* injusticia *f*
ineradicable [ˌɪnɪ'rædɪkəbl] *adj* inextirpable
inert [ɪ'nɜ:t, *Am:* -'nɜ:rt] *adj* **1.** (*not moving*) inerte; *fig* inmóvil **2.** CHEM inactivo, -a
inertia [ɪ'nɜ:ʃə, *Am:* ˌɪn'ɜ:r-] *n no pl* inercia *f; fig* pereza *f*
inertia reel seat belt *n* cinturón *m* de seguridad retráctil
inescapable [ˌɪnɪ'skeɪpəbl] *adj* ineludible
inessential [ˌɪnɪ'senʃl] **I.** *adj* no esencial **II.** *n* cosa *f* no esencial
inestimable [ɪn'estɪməbl] *adj* inestimable; **to be of** ~ **value** ser de valor incalculable
inevitable [ɪn'evɪtəbl, *Am:* -ṱə-] **I.** *adj* inevitable; (*conclusion, consequence*) inexorable **II.** *n no pl* **the** ~ lo inevitable
inexact [ˌɪnɪg'zækt] *adj* inexacto, -a
inexcusable [ˌɪnɪk'skju:zəbl] *adj* imperdonable
inexhaustible [ˌɪnɪg'zɔ:stəbl, *Am:* -'zɔ:s-təbl] *adj* inagotable
inexorable [ˌɪn'eksərəbl] *adj form* inexorable
inexpedient [ˌɪnɪk'spi:dɪənt] *adj form* inapropiado, -a
inexpensive [ˌɪnɪk'spensɪv] *adj* económico, -a; **to be** ~ **to do sth** ser asequible hacer algo
inexperience [ˌɪnɪk'spɪəriənts] *n no pl* falta *f* de experiencia
inexperienced [ˌɪnɪk'spɪərɪənst, *Am:* -'spɪrɪ-] *adj* inexperto, -a; **to be** ~ **with guns** no tener experiencia con armas
inexpert [ɪn'ekspɜ:t, *Am:* -spɜ:rt] *adj* inexperto, -a; (*unskilled*) inhábil
inexplicable [ˌɪnɪk'splɪkəbl, *Am:* ˌɪn'ək-] **I.** *adj* inexplicable **II.** *n no pl* **the** ~ lo inexplicable
inextricable [ˌɪnɪk'strɪkəbl] *adj* inextricable
infallible [ɪn'fæləbl] *adj* indefectible; (*incapable of being wrong*) infalible
infamous ['ɪnfəməs] *adj* **1.** (*shocking*) infame **2.** (*notorious*) de mala fama
infamy ['ɪnfəmi] *n* **1.** <-ies> (*shocking act*) infamia *f* **2.** *no pl* (*notoriety*) mala fama *f*
infancy ['ɪnfəntsi] *n no pl* infancia *f;* **from** ~ desde niño; **to be in its** ~ *fig* estar aún en pañales
infant ['ɪnfənt] *n* (*very young child*) bebé *m;* **a newborn** ~ un recién nacido
infanticide [ɪn'fæntɪsaɪd, *Am:* -ṱə-] *n no pl* infanticidio *m*
infantile ['ɪnfəntaɪl] *adj* infantil
infant mortality *n* mortalidad *f* infantil
infantry ['ɪnfəntri] *n + sing/pl vb* MIL infantería *f*
infantryman <-men> *n* MIL soldado *m* de infantería
infatuated [ɪn'fætʃʊeɪtɪd, *Am:* -ueɪṱɪd] *adj* encaprichado, -a; **to become** ~ **with sb/sth** encapricharse por alguien/algo
infect [ɪn'fekt] *vt* infectar; *a. fig* (*person*) contagiar
infection [ɪn'fekʃən] *n* infección *f; fig* contagio *m;* **risk of** ~ riesgo *m* de contagio
infectious [ɪn'fekʃəs] *adj* infeccioso, -a; *a. fig* contagioso, -a
infelicitous [ˌɪnfɪ'lɪsɪtəs, *Am:* -əṱəs] *adj iron* desafortunado, -a
infer [ɪn'fɜ:ʳ, *Am:* -'fɜ:r] <-rr-> *vt* inferir
inference ['ɪnfərəns] *n form* **1.** (*conclusion*) conclusión *f;* **to draw the** ~ **that ...** sacar la conclusión de que... **2.** *no pl* (*process of inferring*) inferencia *f;* **by** ~ por inferencia
inferior [ɪn'fɪərɪəʳ, *Am:* -'fɪrɪɚ] **I.** *adj* inferior **II.** *n* inferior *mf*
inferiority [ɪnˌfɪəri'ɒrəti, *Am:* -ˌfɪri'ɔ:rəṱi] *n no pl* inferioridad *f*
inferiority complex <-es> *n* complejo *m* de inferioridad
infernal [ɪn'fɜ:nəl, *Am:* -'fɜ:r-] *adj* infernal
inferno [ɪn'fɜ:nəʊ, *Am:* -'fɜ:rnoʊ] *n* infierno *m;* **the building was an** ~ el edificio ardía en llamas
infertile [ɪn'fɜ:taɪl, *Am:* -'fɜ:rṱl] *adj* estéril
infertility [ˌɪnfə'tɪləti, *Am:* -fɚ'tɪləṱi] *n no pl* esterilidad *f*
infest [ɪn'fest] *vt* infestar
infestation [ˌɪnfes'teɪʃən] *n* plaga *f,* infestación *f*
infidel ['ɪnfɪdəl, *Am:* -fədel] *n* infiel *mf*
infidelity [ˌɪnfɪ'deləti, *Am:* -fə'deləṱi] *n no pl* infidelidad *f*
infighting ['ɪnfaɪtɪŋ] *n no pl* lucha *f* interna

infiltrate ['ɪnfɪltreɪt, *Am:* ɪn'fɪl-] *vt* infiltrarse en

infiltration [ˌɪnfɪl'treɪʃən] *n no pl* infiltración *f*

infiltrator *n* infiltrado, -a *m, f*

infinite ['ɪnfɪnət, *Am:* -fənɪt] **I.** *adj* infinito, -a; **with ~ patience** con una paciencia infinita; **to take ~ care** poner sumo cuidado **II.** *n* **the Infinite** el infinito

infinitely *adv* infinitamente

infinitesimal [ˌɪnfɪnɪ'tesɪml] *adj form* infinitesimal

infinitive [ɪn'fɪnətɪv, *Am:* -t̬ɪv] LING **I.** *n* infinitivo *m* **II.** *adj* infinitivo, -a

infinity [ɪn'fɪnəti, *Am:* -t̬i] <-ies> *n* **1.** *no pl* MAT infinito *m*; **to ~** al infinito **2.** (*huge amount*) infinidad *f*

infirm [ɪn'fɜːm, *Am:* -'fɜːrm] *adj* enfermizo, -a; (*weak*) débil

infirmary [ɪn'fɜːməri, *Am:* -'fɜːr-] <-ies> *n* **1.** (*hospital*) hospital *m* **2.** *Am* (*sick room*) enfermería *f*

infirmity [ɪn'fɜːməti, *Am:* -'fɜːrmət̬i] <-ies> *n* **1.** (*illness*) enfermedad *f* **2.** *no pl* (*weakness*) debilidad *f*

inflame [ɪn'fleɪm] *vt* **1.** *a.* MED inflamar **2.** (*stir up*) encender; **to ~ sb with passion** desatar la pasión de alguien

inflammable [ɪn'flæməbl] *adj* inflamable; (*situation*) explosivo, -a

inflammation [ˌɪnflə'meɪʃən] *n* MED inflamación *f*

inflammatory [ɪn'flæmətəri, *Am:* -tɔːr-] *adj* **1.** MED inflamatorio, -a **2.** (*speech*) incendiario, -a

inflatable [ɪn'fleitəbl, *Am:* -t̬ə-] **I.** *adj* hinchable **II.** *n* bote *m* hinchable

inflate [ɪn'fleɪt] **I.** *vt* **1.** (*fill with air*) hinchar, inflar **2.** (*exaggerate*) exagerar **3.** ECON (*prices*) aumentar excesivamente **II.** *vi* hincharse

inflated [ɪn'fleɪtɪd, *Am:* -t̬ɪd] *adj* **1.** (*filled with air*) hinchado, -a **2.** (*exaggerated*) exagerado, -a **3.** ECON (*price*) excesivo, -a

inflation [ɪn'fleɪʃən] *n no pl* inflación *f*

inflationary *adj* FIN inflacionario, -a

inflect [ɪn'flekt] *vt* (*verb*) conjugar; (*noun*) declinar; **to ~ one's voice** modular la voz de uno

inflection *n*, **inflexion** [ɪn'flekʃən] *n* inflexión *f*

inflexibility [ɪnˌfleksə'bɪləti, *Am:* -t̬i] *n no pl* inflexibilidad *f*; (*rigidity*) rigidez *f*

inflexible [ɪn'fleksəbl] *adj* inflexible

inflict [ɪn'flɪkt] *vt* (*wound*) infligir; (*damage*) causar; (*punishment*) imponer

infliction [ɪn'flɪkʃən] *n no pl* imposición *f*

influence ['ɪnfluəns] **I.** *n* influencia *f*; **to exert one's ~** ejercer uno su influencia; **to bring one's ~ to bear on sb** ejercer presión sobre alguien; **to be under the ~** *fig* estar borracho; **to drive under the ~** *fig* conducir bajo los efectos del alcohol **II.** *vt* influir

influential [ˌɪnflʊ'enʃl] *adj* influyente

influenza [ˌɪnflʊ'enzə] *n no pl* gripe *f*

influx ['ɪnflʌks] *n no pl* influjo *m*

inform [ɪn'fɔːm, *Am:* -'fɔːrm] **I.** *vt* informar; **I'm happy to ~ you that …** tengo el placer de comunicarle que…; **to be ~ed about sth** estar enterado de algo **II.** *vi* **to ~ against sb** delatar a alguien

informal [ɪn'fɔːml, *Am:* -'fɔːr-] *adj* informal; (*tone, manner*) familiar; (*person*) afable

informality [ˌɪnfɔː'mæləti, *Am:* -fɔːr'mælət̬i] *n no pl* **1.** (*lack of formality*) informalidad *f* **2.** (*lack of officiality*) falta *f* de ceremonia

informant [ɪn'fɔːmənt, *Am:* -'fɔːr-] *n* informante *mf*; **a reliable ~** una fuente fiable

information [ˌɪnfə'meɪʃən, *Am:* -fɚ'-] *n no pl* **1.** (*data*) información *f*; **a lot of/a little ~** mucha/poca información; **to ask for ~** pedir informes; **for further ~** para más información **2.** INFOR datos *mpl* **3.** (*knowledge*) conocimientos *mpl* **4.** (*enquiry desk*) punto *m* de información **5.** LAW denuncia *f*

information content *n no pl* INFOR contenido *m* de información **information management** *n no pl* gestión *f* de datos **information retrieval** *n no pl* INFOR recuperación *f* de información **information science** *n* ciencias *fpl* de la información **information storage** *n no pl* INFOR almacenaje *m* de información **information superhighway** *n* autopista *f* de la información **information technology** *n no pl* tecnologías *fpl* de la información

informative [ɪn'fɔːmətɪv, *Am:* -'fɔːrmət̬ɪv] *adj* informativo, -a

informed *adj* informado, -a

informer [ɪn'fɔːməʳ, *Am:* -'fɔːrmɚ] *n* denunciante *mf*

infotainment [ɪnfəʊ'teɪnmənt, *Am:* 'ɪnfoʊteɪn-] *n* infotainment *m*

infraction [ɪn'frækʃən] *n* infracción *f*

infra dig [ˌɪnfrə'dɪg] *adj Brit, iron, inf* deshonroso, -a

infrared ['ɪnfrə'red] *adj* infrarrojo, -a

infrastructure ['ɪnfrəˌstrʌktʃəʳ, *Am:* -tʃɚ] *n* infraestructura *f*

infrequent [ɪn'friːkwənt] *adj* poco frecuente

infringe [ɪn'frɪndʒ] *vt* LAW infringir; **to ~ sb's right** vulnerar un derecho de alguien

infringement [ɪn'frɪndʒmənt] *n* LAW infracción *f*; (*of a rule*) violación *f*, vulneración *f*; **copyright ~** violación de los derechos de autor; **~ of a law** violación de una ley

infuriate [ɪn'fjʊərɪeɪt, *Am:* -'fjʊrɪ-] *vt* enfurecer

infuse [ɪn'fjuːz] *vt* **1.** (*fill*) infundir; **to ~ sb with courage** infundir ánimo a alguien **2.** (*tea, herbs*) hacer una infusión de

infusion [ɪn'fjuːʒən] *n a.* MED infusión *f*; ECON inyección *f*

ingenious [ɪn'dʒiːnɪəs, *Am:* -njəs] *adj* **1.** (*creatively inventive*) inventivo, -a; (*idea, method, plan*) ingenioso, -a **2.** (*innovative*) innovador(a)

ingenuity [ˌɪndʒɪˈnjuːəti, *Am:* -t̬i] *n no pl* ingenuidad *f;* **to use one's** ~ utilizar el ingenio
ingenuous [ɪnˈdʒenjʊəs] *adj form* **1.** (*naive*) ingenuo, -a **2.** (*openly honest*) candoroso, -a
ingest [inˈdʒest] *vt form* ingerir
inglenook [ˈɪŋglnʊk] *n* ARCHIT rincón *m* de la chimenea
inglorious [ɪnˈglɔːrɪəs, *Am:* -ˈglɔːrɪ-] *adj* ignominioso, -a; (*dishonourable*) deshonroso, -a
ingoing [ˈɪngəʊɪŋ, *Am:* -goʊ-] *adj* entrante
ingot [ˈɪŋgət] *n* barra *f;* (*of gold, silver*) lingote *m*
ingrained [ˌɪnˈgreɪnd] *adj* **1.** (*embedded: dirt*) incrustrado, -a; **to be/become** ~ **in sth** estar/quedarse incrustrado en algo **2.** (*deep-seated*) arraigado, -a
ingratiate [ɪnˈgreɪʃɪeɪt] *vr* **to** ~ **oneself** (**with sb**) congraciarse (con alguien)
ingratitude [ɪnˈgrætɪtjuːd, *Am:* -ˈgræt̬ə-tuːd] *n no pl* ingratitud *f*
ingredient [ɪnˈgriːdɪənt] *n* **1.** GASTR ingrediente *m* **2.** (*component*) *a.* MED componente *m*
in-group [ˈɪngruːp] *n inf* grupo *m* exclusivista
ingrowing [ɪnˈgrəʊɪŋ, *Am:* ˈɪngroʊ-] *adj,* **ingrown** [ɪnˈgrəʊn, *Am:* ˈɪngroʊn] *adj* que crece hacia dentro (de la piel); ~ **toenail** uñero *m*
inhabit [ɪnˈhæbɪt] *vt* habitar
inhabitable *adj* habitable
inhabitant [ɪnˈhæbɪtənt] *n* habitante *mf*
inhale [ɪnˈheɪl] **I.** *vt* aspirar; MED inhalar **II.** *vi* inhalar
inhaler [ɪnˈheɪləʳ, *Am:* -ɚ] *n* inhalador *m*
inharmonious [ˌɪnhɑːˈməʊnɪəs, *Am:* -hɑːr-ˈmoʊ-] *adj* **1.** (*not peaceful*) poco armonioso, -a **2.** MUS disonante **3.** (*not blending well*) discorde
inhere [ɪnˈhɪəʳ, *Am:* -ˈhɪr] *vi form* **to** ~ **in sth/sb** ser inherente a algo/en alguien
inherent [ɪnˈhɪərənt, *Am:* -ˈhɪr-] *adj* inherente; PHILOS intrínseco, -a; **to be** ~ **in sth** ser inherente a algo
inherit [ɪnˈherɪt] **I.** *vt* heredar **II.** *vi* recibir una herencia
inheritable *adj* heredable
inheritance [ɪnˈherɪtəns] *n* herencia *f; fig* legado *m;* **to come into an** ~ recibir una herencia
inhibit [ɪnˈhɪbɪt] *vt* (*hinder*) impedir; (*impair*) inhibir; **to** ~ **sb from doing sth** impedir a alguien hacer algo
inhibition [ˌɪnɪˈbɪʃən] *n* inhibición *f*
inhospitable [ˌɪnhɒˈspɪtəbl, *Am:* ɪnˈhɑːs-pɪt̬ə-] *adj* inhospitalario, -a; (*attitude*) poco amistoso, -a; (*place*) inhóspito, -a
in-house [ˈɪnhaʊs] COM **I.** *adj* interno, -a **II.** *adv* dentro de la empresa
inhuman [ɪnˈhjuːmən] *adj* (*not human*) inhumano, -a
inhumane [ˌɪnhjuːˈmeɪn] *adj* (*cruel*) inhumano, -a, cruel
inhumanity [ˌɪnhjuːˈmænəti, *Am:* -t̬i] *n no pl* inhumanidad *f*
inimical [ɪˈnɪmɪkl] *adj form* **1.** (*hostile*) contrario, -a; **to be** ~ **to sth** ser contrario a algo **2.** (*harmful*) perjudicial
inimitable [ɪˈnɪmɪtəbl, *Am:* -t̬ə-] *adj* inimitable
iniquitous [ɪˈnɪkwɪtəs, *Am:* -t̬əs] *adj* inicuo, -a
iniquity [ɪˈnɪkwəti, *Am:* -t̬i] <-ies> *n* **1.** *no pl* (*wickedness*) iniquidad *f;* (*sinfulness*) perversidad *f;* (*unfairness*) injusticia *f* **2.** *pl* (*act of wickedness*) iniquidades *fpl;* (*act of unfairness*) injusticias *fpl*
initial [ɪˈnɪʃəl] **I.** *n* inicial *f;* **one's** ~**s** las iniciales de uno **II.** *adj* inicial; (*first*) primero, -a; **in the** ~ **phases** en las primeras etapas **III.** <*Brit* -ll-, *Am* -l-> *vt* marcar con las iniciales
initialise *vt Aus, Brit,* **initialize** [ɪˈnɪʃəlaɪz] *vt Am* INFOR inicializar
initially [ɪˈnɪʃəli] *adv* en un principio
initiate [ɪˈnɪʃɪeɪt] **I.** *vt* **1.** (*start*) iniciar, dar comienzo a; (*proceedings*) entablar **2.** (*admit to group*) admitir (como miembro) **II.** *n* iniciado, -a *m, f*
initiation [ɪˌnɪʃɪˈeɪʃən] *n* **1.** *no pl* (*starting*) inicio *m* **2.** (*introducing*) iniciación *f;* (*as a member*) admisión *f*
initiative [ɪˈnɪʃətɪv, *Am:* -t̬ɪv] *n* iniciativa *f;* **to take the** ~ **in sth** tomar la iniciativa en algo; **to show** ~ demostrar iniciativa; **to use one's** ~ obrar por cuenta propia
inject [ɪnˈdʒekt] *vt* **1.** *a.* MED inyectar **2.** (*introduce*) introducir; (*funds, money*) inyectar; (*invest*) invertir
injection [ɪnˈdʒekʃən] *n* inyección *f*
injection moulding *n* moldura *f* por inyección
injudicious [ˌɪndʒuːˈdɪʃəs] *adj* imprudente
injunction [ɪnˈdʒʌŋkʃən] *n* mandato *m;* LAW auto *m* preventivo
injure [ˈɪndʒəʳ, *Am:* -dʒɚ] *vt* **1.** (*wound*) herir, victimar *AmL* **2.** (*damage*) estropear **3.** (*do wrong to*) perjudicar
injured *adj* **1.** (*wounded*) herido, -a, victimado, -a *AmL* **2.** (*damaged*) estropeado, -a **3.** (*wronged*) perjudicado, -a
injury [ˈɪndʒəri] <-ies> *n* **1.** (*physical*) lesión *f,* herida *f;* **a knee/back** ~ una lesión de rodilla/espalda; **to receive an** ~ ser herido; **to do oneself an** ~ *Brit, Aus, iron* hacerse daño **2.** (*pschological*) daño *m*
injustice [ɪnˈdʒʌstɪs] *n* injusticia *f;* **you do me an** ~ no eres justo conmigo
ink [ɪŋk] **I.** *n* tinta *f;* **to write in** ~ escribir con tinta **II.** *vt* TYPO entintar
ink bottle *n* bote *m* de tinta **ink-jet printer** *n* impresora *f* de chorro de tinta
inkling [ˈɪŋklɪŋ] *n* **1.** (*suspicion*) sospecha *f;* **to have an** ~ **that …** tener la sospecha de que… **2.** (*hint*) indicio *m*

ink-pad ['ɪŋkpæd, *Am:* -pɑːt] *n* almohadilla *f* **inkstain** *n* mancha *f* de tinta

inky ['ɪŋki] <-ier, -iest> *adj* **1.** (*stained*) manchado, -a de tinta **2.** (*black*) negro, -a como la tinta

inlaid [ˌɪn'leɪd, *Am:* 'ɪnleɪd] **I.** *vt pt, pp of* **inlay II.** *adj* taraceado, -a; ~ **work** taracea *f*

inland ['ɪnlənd] **I.** *adj* **1.** (*not coastal: sea, shipping*) interior; (*town, village*) del interior **2.** (*domestic*) nacional; ~ **flight** vuelo *m* nacional **II.** *adv* **1.** (*direction*) tierra adentro **2.** (*place*) hacia el interior

Inland Revenue *n Brit* Hacienda *f*

inland trade *n no pl, Brit* comercio *m* interior

in-laws ['ɪnlɔːz, *Am:* -lɑːz] *npl* suegros *mpl*

inlay [ˌɪn'leɪ] **I.** *n* **1.** *no pl* (*embedded pattern*) incrustración *f* **2.** MED empaste *m* **II.** <inlaid, inlaid> *vt* taracear

inlet ['ɪnlet] *n* **1.** GEO ensenada *f*; (*of sea*) cala *f* **2.** *Brit* TECH entrada *f*; (*pipe*) tubo *m* de admisión

in-line skate *n* patinaje *m* en línea

inmate ['ɪnmeɪt] *n* residente *mf*; (*prison*) preso, -a *m, f*

inn [ɪn] *n* posada *f*

innards ['ɪnədz, *Am:* -ɚdz] *npl inf* **1.** (*entrails*) tripas *fpl* **2.** TECH engranajes *mpl*

innate [ɪ'neɪt] *adj* innato, -a

inner ['ɪnəʳ, *Am:* -ɚ] *adj* **1.** (*located in the interior*) interno, -a, interior; **in the ~ London area** en la zona céntrica de Londres **2.** (*deep*) íntimo, -a; (*secret*) secreto, -a; **one's ~ feelings** los sentimientos más íntimos de uno

inner city *n parte céntrica de la ciudad, habitada con frecuencia por gente pobre y marginada*

innermost ['ɪnəməʊst, *Am:* -ɚmoʊst] *adj* más íntimo, -a; **in his/her ~ being** en lo más profundo de su ser

inner tube *n* cámara *f* de aire

inning ['ɪnɪŋ] *n Am* SPORTS (*baseball game*) inning *m*

innings ['ɪnɪŋz] *n + sing vb Brit* (*cricket*) turno *m* de entrada ►**to have a good ~s** *Brit* tener una vida larga

innocence ['ɪnəsns] *n no pl* inocencia *f*; **to plead one's ~** declararse inocente; **in all ~** inocentemente

innocent ['ɪnəsnt] **I.** *adj* inocente; **to be ~ of sth** ser inocente de algo **II.** *n* inocente *mf*; **to be an ~** ser un inocente; **to come the ~** *inf* hacerse el inocente

innocuous [ɪ'nɒkjʊəs, *Am:* -'nɑːk-] *adj* inocuo, -a

innovate ['ɪnəveɪt] *vi* innovar; (*introduce changes*) introducir novedades

innovation [ˌɪnə'veɪʃən] *n* novedad *f*, innovación *f*

innovative ['ɪnəvətɪv, *Am:* -veɪt̬ɪv] *adj* (*model, product*) novedoso, -a; (*person*) innovador(a)

innovator *n* innovador(a) *m(f)*

innuendo [ˌɪnjuː'endəʊ, *Am:* -doʊ] <-(e)s> *n* **1.** (*insinuation*) insinuación *f*; **to make an ~ (about sth)** hacer una insinuación (sobre algo) **2.** (*suggestive remark*) indirecta *f*

innumerable [ɪ'njuːmərəbl, *Am:* -'nuː-] *adj* innumerable

innumerate [ɪ'njuːmərət, *Am:* -'nuːmɚ-] *adj* **to be ~** ser incompetente en el cálculo

inoculate [ɪ'nɒkjʊleɪt, *Am:* -'nɑːkjə-] *vt* **to ~ sb (against sth)** inocular a alguien (contra algo)

inoculation [ɪˌnɒkjʊ'leɪʃən, *Am:* -ˌnɑːkjə'-] *n* inoculación *f*

inoffensive [ˌɪnə'fensɪv] *adj* inofensivo, -a

inoperable [ˌɪn'ɒpərəbl, *Am:* -'ɑːpɚ-] *adj* inoperable

inoperative [ˌɪn'ɒpərətɪv, *Am:* -'ɑːpɚət̬ɪv] *adj* inoperante

inopportune [ˌɪn'ɒpətjuːn, *Am:* -ˌɑːpɚ'tuːn] *adj* inoportuno, -a; (*inconvenient*) inconveniente

inordinate [ɪ'nɔːdɪnət, *Am:* -'nɔːr-] *adj* desmesurado, -a; **an ~ amount of sth** una cantidad excesiva de algo

inorganic [ˌɪnɔː'gænɪk, *Am:* -ɔːr'-] *adj* inorgánico, -a

in-patient ['ɪnpeɪʃnt] *n* paciente *mf* interno, -a

input ['ɪnpʊt] **I.** *n* **1.** (*contribution*) contribución *f*, aportación *f*; INFOR entrada *f*; **power ~** entrada (de potencia) **2.** *a.* FIN inversión *f* **II.** <-tt-> *vt* INFOR introducir; (*with a scanner*) entrar

input data *npl* INFOR datos *mpl* de entrada

input device *n* INFOR dispositivo *m* de entrada

inquest ['ɪnkwest] *n* **1.** LAW pesquisa *f* judicial; **to hold an ~ (into sth)** llevar a cabo una investigación (sobre algo) **2.** *fig* indagación *f*; **to hold an ~** realizar un análisis

inquire [ɪn'kwaɪəʳ, *Am:* -'kwaɪr] *Brit* **I.** *vi* **1.** (*ask*) preguntar; **to ~ for sb** preguntar por alguien; **to ~ about sth** pedir información sobre algo **2.** (*investigate*) investigar; **to ~ into a matter** indagar en un asunto **II.** *vt* preguntar; **to ~ the reason** preguntar por qué

inquiry [ɪn'kwaɪəri, *Am:* -'kwaɪri] *n Brit* **1.** (*question*) pregunta *f* **2.** (*investigation*) investigación *f*

inquisition [ˌɪnkwɪ'zɪʃən] *n* **1.** (*questioning*) investigación *f*; **to subject sb to an ~** someter a alguien a una investigación **2.** HIST **the Inquisition** la Inquisición

inquisitive [ɪn'kwɪzətɪv, *Am:* -t̬ɪv] *adj* **1.** (*curious*) curioso, -a; (*look, face*) inquiridor(a); (*child*) preguntón, -ona; **to be ~ about sth/sb** sentir curiosidad sobre algo/alguien **2.** (*prying*) fisgón, -ona

inroad ['ɪnrəʊd, *Am:* -roʊd] *n* MIL incursión *f*; *fig* invasión *f*; **to make ~s into one's savings** mermar los ahorros de uno

inrush ['ɪnrʌʃ] <-es> *n* irrupción *f*; (*of people*) afluencia *f*

INS [ˌaɪen'es] *n abbr of* **International News**

Service servicio *m* internacional de noticias

insalubrious [ˌɪnsəˈluːbrɪəs] *adj* (*unpleasant*) insalubre; (*unhealthy*) malsano, -a; (*dirty*) sucio, -a; **an ~ climate** un clima perjudicial para la salud

ins and outs *npl* pormenores *mpl*

insane [ɪnˈseɪn] *adj* demente; *a. fig* (*crazy*) loco, -a; **to be/go ~** estar/volverse loco

insanitary [ɪnˈsænɪtri, *Am:* -teri] *adj* antihigiénico, -a

insanity [ɪnˈsænəti, *Am:* -t̬i] *n no pl* **1.** (*mental illness*) demencia *f* **2.** *a. fig* (*craziness*) locura *f*

insatiable [ɪnˈseɪʃəbl] *adj* insaciable

inscribe [ɪnˈskraɪb] *vt* inscribir; (*engrave*) grabar

inscription [ɪnˈskrɪpʃən] *n* inscripción *f;* (*dedication*) dedicatoria *f*

inscrutable [ɪnˈskruːtəbl, *Am:* -t̬ə-] *adj* (*look, smile*) enigmático, -a; (*person*) insondable

insect [ˈɪnsekt] *n* insecto *m;* **~ bite** picadura *f* de insecto

insecticide [ɪnˈsektɪsaɪd] *n* insecticida *m*

insecure [ˌɪnsɪˈkjʊəʳ, *Am:* -ˈkjʊr] *adj* inseguro, -a; (*future*) incierto, -a

insecurity [ˌɪnsɪˈkjʊərəti, *Am:* -ˈkjʊrət̬i] <-ies> *n* inseguridad *f*

inseminate [ɪnˈsemɪneɪt] *vt* inseminar

insemination [ɪnˌsemɪˈneɪʃən] *n no pl* inseminación *f*

insensible [ɪnˈsensəbl] *adj form* **1.** (*unfeeling*) insensible; (*indifferent*) indiferente; **to be ~ to sth** ser indiferente a algo **2.** (*unaware*) inconsciente; **to be ~ of sth** no ser consciente de algo

insensitive [ɪnˈsensətɪv, *Am:* -t̬ɪv] *adj* insensible; (*indifferent*) indiferente

inseparable [ɪnˈseprəbl] *adj* inseparable, indisoluble

insert[1] [ˈɪnsɜːt, *Am:* -sɜːrt] *n* **1.** (*page*) hoja *f* suelta **2.** (*piece*) material *m* insertado

insert[2] [ɪnˈsɜːt, *Am:* -ˈsɜːrt] *vt* **1.** (*put into*) insertar; (*coins*) introducir **2.** (*add within a text*) intercalar; (*fill in*) añadir

insertion [ɪnˈsɜːʃən, *Am:* -ˈsɜːr-] *n* **1.** *no pl* (*act of inserting*) inserción *f;* (*of coins*) introducción *f* **2.** (*thing inserted*) cosa *f* insertada **3.** (*in a newspaper*) publicación *f*

in-service [ˈɪnsɜvɪs, *Am:* -sɜːr-] *adj* en funcionamiento

inshore [ˌɪnˈʃɔːʳ, *Am:* -ˈʃɔːr] **I.** *adj* cerca de la orilla; **~ waters** aguas *fpl* costeras **II.** *adv* hacia la costa

inside [ɪnˈsaɪd] **I.** *adj* **1.** (*internal*) interno, -a; **the ~ door** la puerta interior **2.** (*from within: information*) confidencial; **the robbery was an ~ job** el robo lo realizaron con ayuda de alguien de dentro **3.** AUTO **~ lane** carril *m* derecho; *Brit, Aus* carril *m* izquierdo **4.** (*inseam*) **~ leg** *Brit, Aus* entrepierna *f* **II.** *n* **1.** (*internal part or side*) interior *m;* **on the ~** por dentro; **to turn sth ~ out** volver algo del revés; **to turn the whole room ~ out** *fig* revolver toda la habitación; **to know a place ~ out** conocer muy bien un lugar; **to know the ~ of sth** conocer los entresijos de algo **2.** *pl, inf* (*entrails*) tripas *fpl* **3.** AUTO **to overtake on the ~** adelantar por la izquierda; *Brit, Aus* adelantar por la derecha **III.** *prep* **1.** (*within*) **~ (of)** dentro de; **to play ~ the house** jugar dentro de casa; **to go ~ the house** entrar en casa **2.** *inf* (*within time of*) **~ three days** en menos de tres días **IV.** *adv* **1.** (*within something*) dentro; **to go ~** entrar **2.** *inf* LAW en chirona, en el bote *Méx* **3.** (*internally*) internamente

insider [ɪnˈsaɪdəʳ, *Am:* ˈɪnˌsaɪdɚ] *n* persona *f* de la casa; (*with special knowledge*) persona *f* enterada

insidious [ɪnˈsɪdɪəs] *adj* insidioso, -a; (*subversive*) subversivo, -a; **~ disease** enfermedad *f* maligna

insight [ˈɪnsaɪt] *n* **1.** *no pl* (*capacity*) perspicacia *f* **2.** (*instance*) nueva percepción *f;* **to gain an ~ into sth/sb** entender mejor algo/a alguien; **the exhibition gave us an ~ into the 19th century** la exposición ha sido una revelación del siglo XIX

insignia [ɪnˈsɪgnɪə] *n* insignia *f*

insignificance [ˌɪnsɪgˈnɪfɪkəns] *n no pl* insignificancia *f;* **to fade into ~** hacerse insignificante

insignificant [ˌɪnsɪgˈnɪfɪkənt] *adj* insignificante; (*trivial*) trivial

insincere [ˌɪnsɪnˈsɪəʳ, *Am:* -ˈsɪr] *adj* poco sincero, -a

insinuate [ɪnˈsɪnjʊeɪt] **I.** *vt* **1.** (*imply sth unpleasant*) insinuar **2.** (*manoeuvre*) introducir **II.** *vr* **to ~ oneself into** introducirse en

insinuation [ɪnˌsɪnjʊˈeɪʃən] *n* **1.** insinuación *f* **2.** (*hint*) indirecta *f*

insipid [ɪnˈsɪpɪd] *adj* **1.** (*food, drink, entertainment*) insípido, -a **2.** (*person*) soso, -a

insist [ɪnˈsɪst] **I.** *vi* insistir; **to ~ on doing sth** obstinarse en hacer algo; **if you ~** si insiste/si insistes **II.** *vt* **1.** (*state*) insistir **2.** (*demand*) exigir

insistence [ɪnˈsɪstəns] *n no pl* insistencia *f;* **her ~ on …** su insistencia en..; **to do sth at sb's ~** hacer algo por insistencia de alguien

insistent [ɪnˈsɪstənt] *adj* insistente; **to be ~ (that) …** insistir (en que)…

insofar as [ˌɪnsəʊˈfɑːr əz, *Am:* -soʊˈfɑːr əz] *adv form* en tanto que +*subj*

insole [ˈɪnsəʊl, *Am:* -soʊl] *n* plantilla *f*

insolence [ˈɪnsələns] *n no pl* insolencia *f*

insolent [ˈɪnsələnt] *adj* insolente

insoluble [ɪnˈsɒljʊbl, *Am:* -ˈsɑːljə-] *adj* insoluble

insolvency [ɪnˈsɒlvəntsi, *Am:* -ˈsɑːl-] *n no pl* insolvencia *f*

insolvent [ɪnˈsɒlvənt, *Am:* -ˈsɑːl-] **I.** *adj* insolvente **II.** *n* insolvente *mf*

insomnia [ɪnˈsɒmnɪə, *Am:* -ˈsɑːm-] *n no pl* insomnio *m;* **to suffer from ~** padecer insomnio

insomniac [ɪnˈsɒmnɪæk, *Am:* -ˈsɑːm-] *n* insomne *mf*

insomuch as [ˌɪnsəʊˈmʌtʃ, *Am:* -soʊˈ-] *conj form* **1.** (*because*) ya que **2.** (*to the extent that*) en tanto que + *subj*

inspect [ɪnˈspekt] *vt* **1.** (*examine carefully*) inspeccionar **2.** (*examine officially*) registrar; **to ~ the books** examinar los libros (de contabilidad) **3.** MIL **to ~ the troops** pasar revista

inspection [ɪnˈspekʃən] *n* inspección *f;* MIL revista *f*

inspector [ɪnˈspektəʳ] *n* inspector(a) *m(f);* **school ~** inspector de enseñanza; **tax ~** inspector fiscal; **ticket ~** revisor(a) *m(f)*

inspiration [ˌɪnspəˈreɪʃən] *n* **1.** *a.* MED inspiración *f* **2.** *no pl* (*source*) fuente *f* de inspiración; **to provide the ~ for sth** servir de inspiración para algo; **to lack ~** tener falta de inspiración

inspire [ɪnˈspaɪəʳ, *Am:* -ˈspaɪr] *vt* **1.** (*stimulate*) inspirar; **to ~ sb with hope** infundir esperanza a alguien **2.** (*cause, lead to*) provocar

inspired *adj* inspirado, -a

instability [ˌɪnstəˈbɪləti, *Am:* -t̬i] *n no pl* inestabilidad *f*

instal <-ll-> *Brit,* **install** [ɪnˈstɔːl] **I.** *vt* **1.** *a.* TECH, INFOR instalar **2.** (*place*) colocar; **to ~ sb** colocar a alguien (en un cargo) **II.** *vr* **to ~ oneself** instalarse

installation [ˌɪnstəˈleɪʃən] *n* instalación *f*

installment *n Am,* **instalment** [ɪnˈstɔːlmənt] *n* **1.** RADIO, TV entrega *f* **2.** COM plazo *m;* **to pay (for sth) by ~s** pagar (algo) a plazos; **to be payable in monthly ~s** ser pagadero a plazos mensuales

instalment plan *n* compra *f* a plazos

instance [ˈɪnstəns] **I.** *n* **1.** (*case*) caso *m;* **in this ~** en este caso; **for ~** por ejemplo; **in the first ~** primero; **in the second ~** en segundo lugar **2.** *form* (*request*) petición *f;* (*order*) pedido *m;* **to do sth at sb's ~** hacer algo a petición de alguien **II.** *vt* poner por caso

instant [ˈɪnstənt] **I.** *n* instante *m,* momento *m;* **at the same ~** al mismo tiempo; **for an ~** por un momento; **in an ~** al instante; **to do sth this ~** hacer algo inmediatamente **II.** *adj* **1.** (*immediate*) inmediato, -a **2.** GASTR instantáneo, -a; **~ coffee** café *m* instantáneo; **~ soup** (*in bags*) sopa *f* de sobre; (*in tins*) sopa *f* en lata **3.** *liter* (*urgent*) urgente

instantaneous [ˌɪnstənˈteɪnɪəs] *adj* instantáneo, -a; (*effect, reaction*) inmediato, -a; (*spontaneous*) espontáneo, -a

instantaneously *adv* instantáneamente; (*spontaneously*) espontáneamente

instantly [ˈɪnstəntli] *adv* al instante

instant replay *n* (*action replay*) repetición *f*

instead [ɪnˈsted] **I.** *adv* en cambio, en lugar de eso **II.** *prep* **~ of** en vez de, en lugar de; **~ of him** en su lugar; **~ of doing sth** en lugar de hacer algo

instep [ˈɪnstep] *n* **1.** (*part of foot*) empeine *m* **2.** (*part of shoe*) lengüeta *f*

instigate [ˈɪnstɪgeɪt] *vt* **1.** (*initiate*) instigar **2.** (*incite*) incitar

instigation [ˌɪnstɪˈgeɪʃən] *n no pl* instigación *f;* **to do sth at the ~ of sb** hacer algo a instigación de alguien

instil [ɪnˈstɪl] <-ll-> *vt,* **instill** *vt Am* **to ~ sth (into sb)** infundir algo (a alguien); (*teach*) inculcar algo (a alguien)

instinct [ˈɪnstɪŋkt] *n* instinto *m;* **to do sth by ~** hacer algo por instinto; **a business/political ~** instinto para los negocios/la política

instinctive [ɪnˈstɪŋktɪv] *adj* instintivo, -a; (*innate*) innato, -a; (*without reflection*) irreflexivo, -a

institute [ˈɪntstɪtjuːt, *Am:* -tuːt] **I.** *n* instituto *m;* (*of education*) escuela *f* **II.** *vt form* **1.** (*establish: system, reform*) instituir **2.** (*initiate: steps, measures*) iniciar; (*legal action*) emprender

institution [ˌɪntstɪˈtjuːʃən, *Am:* -ˈtuː-] *n* **1.** (*act*) institución *f,* establecimiento *m* **2.** (*society*) asociación *f* **3.** (*home*) asilo *m* **4.** *inf* (*person*) mito *m*

institutional [ˌɪntstɪˈtjuːʃənəl, *Am:* -ˈtuː-] *adj* institucional

institutionalise *vt Brit, Aus,* **institutionalize** [ˌɪntstɪˈtjuːʃənəlaɪz, *Am:* -ˈtuː-] *vt Am* institucionalizar; (*person*) ingresar

in-store [ˌɪnˈstɔːʳ] *adj* en el establecimiento; **~ detective** detective *mf* del establecimiento

instruct [ɪnˈstrʌkt] *vt* **1.** (*teach*) instruir **2.** (*order*) ordenar; (*give instructions*) dar instrucciones; **to ~ sb (to do sth)** ordenar a alguien (hacer algo) **3.** *Brit, Aus* LAW dar instrucciones

instruction [ɪnˈstrʌkʃən] *n* **1.** *no pl* (*teaching*) instrucción *f;* **to give sb ~ in sth** enseñar algo a alguien **2.** (*order*) orden *f;* **to give sb ~s** dar órdenes a alguien; **to act on ~s** actuar cumpliendo órdenes; **to carry out ~s** cumplir órdenes **3.** *pl* (*information on method*) instrucciones *fpl*

instruction book *n* manual *m* de instrucciones **instruction leaflet** *n* folleto *m* de instrucciones **instruction manual** *n* manual *m* de instrucciones

instructive [ɪnˈstrʌktɪv] *adj* instructivo, -a

instructor [ɪnˈstrʌktəʳ, *Am:* -tɚ] *n* **1.** (*teacher*) instructor(a) *m(f);* **driving ~** profesor(a) *m(f)* de autoescuela; **ski ~** profesor(a) *m(f)* de esquí **2.** *Am* UNIV profesor(a) *m(f)*

instructress [ɪnˈstrʌktrɪs] *n* instructora *f*

instrument [ˈɪnstrʊmənt, *Am:* -strə-] *n* **1.** MUS instrumento *m* **2.** (*tool*) herramienta *f* **3.** LAW (*document*) documento *m*

instrumental [ˌɪnstrʊˈmentl, *Am:* -strəˈment̬l] **I.** *adj* **1.** MUS instrumental **2.** (*greatly influencial*) **to be ~ to sth** contribuir materialmente a algo; **to be ~ in doing sth** jugar un papel clave en algo **3.** (*relating to tools*)

herramental **II.** *n* MUS pieza *f* instrumental
instrumentation [ˌɪnstrʊmen'teɪʃən, *Am:* -strə-] *n no pl* MUS instrumentación *f*
instrument board *n,* **instrument panel** *n* AUTO salpicadero *m;* AVIAT, NAUT cuadro *m* de mandos
insubordinate [ˌɪnsə'bɔːdɪnət, *Am:* -'bɔːr-dənɪt] *adj* insubordinado, -a; ~ **behaviour** comportamiento *m* desobediente
insubstantial [ˌɪnsəb'stænʃl] *adj* **1.** (*lacking substance*) insustancial **2.** (*lacking significance*) insignificante **3.** (*not real*) irreal
insufferable [ɪn'sʌfrəbl] *adj* insufrible; (*person*) inaguantable; **to be** ~ ser inaguantable
insufficiency [ˌɪnsə'fɪʃəntsi] <-ies> *n* insuficiencia *f*
insufficient [ˌɪnsə'fɪʃənt] *adj* insuficiente
insular ['ɪntsjələʳ, *Am:* -sələ˞] *adj* **1.** GEO insular **2.** (*person*) de miras estrechas
insularity [ˌɪntsj'lærəti, *Am:* -sə'lerət̬i] *n no pl* **1.** GEO insularidad *f* **2.** (*of person*) estrechez *f* de miras
insulate ['ɪntsjəleɪt, *Am:* -sə-] *vt* aislar; **to** ~ **sth** (**against sth**) aislar algo (de algo)
insulating ['ɪnsjʊleɪtɪŋ, *Am:* -t̬ɪŋ] *adj* aislante; (*protective*) protector(a)
insulating tape *n Brit* cinta aislante [*o* aisladora]
insulation [ˌɪntsjə'leɪʃən, *Am:* -sə'-] *n no pl* aislamiento *m*
insulin ['ɪntsjʊlɪn, *Am:* -sə-] *n no pl* insulina *f*
insult ['ɪnsʌlt] **I.** *vt* insultar **II.** *n* insulto *m,* insultada *f AmL* ►**to add** ~ **to** **injury** ... y por si fuera poco...
insuperable [ɪn'sjuːprəbl, *Am:* -'suː-] *adj* insuperable
insupportable [ˌɪnsə'pɔːtəbl, *Am:* -'pɔːr-t̬ə-] *adj form* insoportable
insurance [ɪn'ʃʊərəns, *Am:* -'ʃʊrəns] *n no pl* **1.** (*financial protection*) seguro *m;* **life** ~ seguro de vida; **to have** ~ (**against sth**) tener un seguro (contra algo); **to take out** ~ (**against sth**) hacerse un seguro (contra algo) **2.** (*payment*) indemnización *f;* (*premium*) prima *f* de seguro **3.** (*measure*) medida *f* preventiva
insurance agent *n* agente *mf* de seguros **insurance broker** *n* corredor(a) *m(f)* de seguros **insurance company** <-ies> *n* compañía *f* de seguros **insurance cover** *n no pl* condiciones *fpl* que cubre el seguro **insurance policy** <-ies> *n* póliza *f* de seguros **insurance premium** *n* prima *f* de seguros
insure [ɪn'ʃʊəʳ, *Am:* -'ʃʊr] *vt* asegurar
insured [ɪn'ʃʊəd, *Am:* -'ʃʊrd] **I.** *adj* asegurado, -a **II.** *n* **the** ~ el asegurado, la asegurada
insurer [ɪn'ʃʊərəʳ, *Am:* -'ʃʊrə˞] *n* **1.** (*agent*) asegurador(a) *m(f)* **2.** (*company*) aseguradora *f*
insurmountable [ˌɪnsə'maʊntəbl, *Am:* -sə˞'maʊnt̬ə-] *adj* insuperable
insurrection [ˌɪnsə'rekʃən, *Am:* -sə'rek-] *n* insurrección *f;* **to crush the** ~ acabar con la sublevación
intact [ɪn'tækt] *adj* intacto, -a
intake ['ɪnteɪk] *n* **1.** (*action of taking in*) toma *f;* (*of air, water*) entrada *f;* ~ **of breath** aspiración *f* **2.** (*amount taken in*) consumo *m;* **the recommended daily** ~ **of fibre** la cantidad diaria recomendada de fibra; **food** ~ ración *f* **3.** (*quantity of people*) número *m* de personas admitidas; **the college has increased its** ~ **of students** ha aumentado el número de estudiantes admitidos en la universidad **4.** MIL reemplazo *m* **5.** TECH (*mechanical aperture*) toma *f*
intangible [ɪn'tændʒəbl] **I.** *adj* intangible; ~ **assets** activos *mpl* inmateriales **II.** *n* cosa *f* intangible
integer ['ɪntɪdʒəʳ, *Am:* -dʒə˞] *n* MAT número *m* entero
integral ['ɪntɪgrəl, *Am:* -t̬ə-] *adj* **1.** (*part of the whole*) integrante **2.** (*central, essential*) esencial; **to be** ~ **to sth/sb** ser de vital importancia para algo/alguien **3.** (*complete*) integral **4.** (*built into unit*) incorporado, -a; **the prison has no** ~ **sanitation** la cárcel no dispone de instalaciones de saneamiento **5.** MAT ~ **calculus** cálculo *m* integral
integrate ['ɪntɪgreɪt, *Am:* -t̬ə-] **I.** *vt* (*cause to merge socially*) **to** ~ **sb/sth into sth** integrar a alguien/algo en algo; **to** ~ **oneself into sth** integrarse en algo; **to** ~ **learning with play** mezclar el aprendizaje y los juegos **II.** *vi* integrarse
integrated ['ɪntɪgreɪtɪd, *Am:* -t̬ɪd] *adj* **1.** (*coordinating different elements*) integrado, -a **2.** (*with different ethnic groups*) ~ **school** escuela *f* no segregacionista
integration [ˌɪntɪ'greɪʃən, *Am:* -t̬ə'-] *n no pl* **1.** *a.* MAT integración *f* **2.** (*unification, fusion*) unificación *f*
integrity [ɪn'tegrəti, *Am:* -t̬i] *n no pl* **1.** (*incorruptibility, uprightness*) integridad *f;* **man of** ~ hombre *m* íntegro; **artistic/professional** ~ coherencia *f* artística/profesional **2.** *form* (*unity, wholeness*) totalidad *f*
intellect ['ɪntəlekt, *Am:* -t̬ə-] *n no pl* **1.** (*faculty*) intelecto *m;* **a man/woman of** ~ un hombre/una mujer de gran inteligencia; **powers of** ~ capacidad *f* intelectual **2.** (*thinker, intellectual*) intelectual *mf*
intellectual [ˌɪntə'lektʃʊəl, *Am:* -t̬ə-] **I.** *n* intelectual *mf* **II.** *adj* intelectual
intelligence [ɪn'telɪdʒəns] *n no pl* inteligencia *f;* ~ **agent** agente *mf* secreto, -a; **artificial** ~ inteligencia artificial; **the** ~ **community** los agentes de los servicios secretos; ~ **sources** fuentes *fpl* del servicio de inteligencia
intelligence quotient *n* coeficiente *m* de inteligencia **intelligence service** *n* MIL, POL servicio *m* de inteligencia **intelligence test** *n* test *m* de inteligencia
intelligent [ɪn'telɪdʒənt] *adj* inteligente
intelligentsia [ɪnˌtelɪ'dʒentsɪə] *n* **the** ~ la intelectualidad

intelligible [ɪn'telɪdʒəbl] *adj* inteligible; **this text is hardly** ~ este texto es muy difícil de entender

intend [ɪn'tend] *vt* **1.** (*aim for, plan*) pretender; **to** ~ **doing sth** querer hacer algo; **to** ~ **to do sth** tener la intención de hacer algo; **I'm sure that remark was** ~**ed for me** estoy convencido de que el comentario iba dirigido a mí; **I** ~**ed no harm** no quería hacer daño **2.** (*mean*) querer decir **3.** (*earmark, destine*) **to be** ~**ed for sth** estar destinado a algo; **to be** ~**ed to do sth** estar destinado a hacer algo; **this film is not** ~**ed for children** esta película no es para niños

intended [ɪn'tendɪd] **I.** *adj* **1.** (*planned, intentional*) intencional; (*sought*) deseado, -a **2.** (*husband, wife*) futuro, -a **II.** *n inf* prometido, -a *m, f*

intense [ɪn'tents] *adj* **1.** (*acute, concentrated, forceful*) intenso, -a; (*desire*) ardiente; (*feeling, hatred, friendship*) profundo, -a; (*interest*) sumo, -a; (*love*) apasionado, -a; (*pain, pressure, wind*) fuerte **2.** (*demanding*) nervioso, -a

intensify [ɪn'tentsɪfaɪ] <-ie-> **I.** *vt* intensificar; (*joy, sadness*) aumentar; (*pain*) agudizar **II.** *vi* intensificarse; (*joy, sadness*) aumentar; (*pain*) agudizarse

intensity [ɪn'tentsəti, *Am:* -t̬i] *n no pl* intensidad *f*

intensive [ɪn'tentsɪv] *adj* intensivo, -a

intensive care *n* cuidados *mpl* intensivos

intent [ɪn'tent] **I.** *n* propósito *m;* **a declaration of** ~ una declaración de intenciones; **to all** ~**s and purposes** prácticamente; **with** ~ **to** con el objeto de; **with good/evil** ~ con buenas/malas intenciones **II.** *adj* **1.** (*absorbed, concentrated, occupied*) abstraído, -a; (*look*) atento, -a; **to be** ~ **on sth** estar concentrado en algo **2.** (*decided, set*) decidido, -a; **to be/seem** ~ **on doing sth** estar/parecer resuelto a hacer algo

intention [ɪn'tentʃən] *n* intención *f;* **it is my** ~ **to …** tengo la intención de…; **to have no** ~ **of doing sth** no tener ninguna intención de hacer algo; **with the best of** ~**s** con la mejor intención

intentional [ɪn'tentʃənəl] *adj* intencional; (*insult*) deliberado, -a

interact [ˌɪntər'ækt, *Am:* ɪnt̬ə'ækt] *vi* interaccionar

interaction [ˌɪntər'ækʃən, *Am:* -t̬ə'-] *n* interacción *f;* **non-verbal** ~ comunicación *f* no verbal

interactive [ˌɪntər'æktɪv, *Am:* -t̬ə'æk-] *adj* interactivo, -a

interactive TV [ˌɪntəræktɪvtiː'viː, *Am:* -t̬ə-] *n no pl* televisión *f* interactiva

interbreed [ˌɪntə'briːd, *Am:* -t̬ə'-] *irr* **I.** *vt* cruzar **II.** *vi* cruzarse

intercede [ˌɪntə'siːd, *Am:* -t̬ə'-] *vi* interceder; **to** ~ **for/on behalf of sb** interceder por/en nombre de alguien

intercept [ˌɪntə'sept, *Am:* -t̬ə'-] *vt* interceptar; MAT cortar; **to** ~ **sb** cerrar el paso a alguien

interception [ˌɪntə'sepʃən, *Am:* -t̬ə'-] *n* interceptación *f;* MAT intersección *f*

interceptor [ˌɪntə'septəʳ, *Am:* -t̬ə'septə] *n* MIL interceptador(a) *m(f)*

intercession [ˌɪntə'seʃən, *Am:* -t̬ə'-] *n* intercesión *f;* **through the** ~ **of sb/sth** gracias a la intercesión de alguien/algo; **the** ~ **of human rights organisations** la mediación de organizaciones pro derechos humanos

interchange [ˌɪntə'tʃeɪndʒ, *Am:* -t̬ə-] **I.** *n* **1.** *form* intercambio *m;* ~ **of ideas** cambio *m* de impresiones **2.** *Brit* (*of roads*) enlace *m* **II.** *vt* intercambiar; **to** ~ **letters** cartearse

interchangeable [ˌɪntə'tʃeɪndʒəbl, *Am:* -t̬ə-] *adj* intercambiable

intercity [ˌɪntə'sɪti] <-ies> *Brit* **I.** *n* tren *m* interurbano **II.** *adj* interurbano, -a

intercom ['ɪntəkɒm, *Am:* -t̬əkɑːm] *n* (*on a plane or ship*) intercomunicador *m;* (*on a building*) portero *m* automático; **through (an)** ~ por el interfono; **to speak over the** ~ hablar por el portero automático

intercommunicate [ˌɪntəkə'mjuːnɪkeɪt, *Am:* -t̬ə-] *vi* comunicarse

intercontinental [ˌɪntəˌkɒntɪ'nentl, *Am:* -t̬əˌkɑːntə'nent̬l] *adj* intercontinental; ~ **flight** vuelo *m* intercontinental

intercourse ['ɪntəkɔːs, *Am:* -t̬əkɔːrs] *n no pl* **1. sexual** ~ contacto *m* sexual; **to have sexual** ~ **with sb** tener relaciones sexuales con alguien **2.** *form* **social** ~ trato *m* social; **commercial** ~ relaciones *fpl* comerciales

interdenominational [ˌɪntə dɪˌnɒmɪ'neɪʃənl, *Am:* -t̬ədɪˌnɑːmə'-] *adj* interconfesional

interdepartmental ['ɪntəˌdiːpɑːt'mentl, *Am:* -t̬əˌdiːpɑːrt'ment̬l] *adj* interdepartamental

interdependence [ˌɪntədɪ'pendəns, *Am:* -t̬ədiː'-] *n no pl* interdependencia *f*

interdependent [ˌɪntə dɪ'pendənt, *Am:* -t̬ədiː'-] *adj* interdependiente

interdict [ˌɪntə'dɪkt, *Am:* -t̬ə-] *n Scot* LAW interdicto *m*

interest ['ɪntrəst, *Am:* -trɪst] **I.** *n* **1.** (*hobby*) interés *m;* **to take an** ~ **in sth** interesarse por algo **2.** *no pl* (*curiousity*) **just out of** ~ *inf* por curiosidad; **to lose** ~ **in sb/sth** perder el interés por alguien/algo; **to take no further** ~ **in sth** dejar de interesarse por algo **3.** *pl* (*profit, advantage*) beneficio *m;* **a conflict of** ~**s** un conflicto de intereses; **to look after the** ~**s of sb** velar por los intereses de alguien; **to pursue one's own** ~**s** perseguir los intereses de uno; **in the** ~ **of liberty** en pro de la libertad; **it's in your own** ~ **to do it** te conviene hacerlo por tu propio interés **4.** *no pl* (*power to excite attentiveness*) interés *m;* **to be of** ~ **for sb** interesar a alguien; **this might be of** ~ **to you** esto puede interesarte; **this is of no** ~ **to me** eso no me interesa **5.** *no pl* FIN interés *m;* ~ **rate** tipo *m* de interés; **at 5%** ~ con un interés del 5 %; **to bear** ~ devengar interés; **to earn/pay** ~ **on sth** percibir/pagar intereses por algo; **to pay back with** ~ pagar con intereses; *fig* pagar con creces **6.** (*legal right*) participación *f*; **to have an** ~ **in sth** tener una participación en algo; **to have a controlling** ~ **in a firm** tener una participación mayoritaria en una empresa; **business** ~**s** negocios *mpl*; **the chemicals** ~**s** la industria química; **vested** ~**s** intereses *mpl* creados **II.** *vt* interesar; **may I** ~ **you in this encyclopaedia?** ¿puedo mostrarle esta enciclopedia?

interested [ˈɪntrəstɪd, *Am:* -trɪst-] *adj* interesado, -a; **to be** ~ **in sth/sb** estar interesado en algo/alguien; **I am** ~ **to know more about it** me interesaría saber más sobre eso; **the** ~ **parties** las partes interesadas

interest-free *adj* FIN sin intereses

interesting [ˈɪntrəsˈtɪŋ] *adj* interesante; **it is** ~ **to do sth** resulta interesante hacer algo

interface [ˈɪntəfeɪs, *Am:* -t̬ɚ-] **I.** *n* **1.** (*point of contact*) punto *m* de contacto **2.** PHYS superficie *f* de contacto **3.** INFOR interfaz *f*; **user** ~ interfaz de usuario; **graphic/parallel/serial** ~ interfaz gráfica/en paralelo/en serie **II.** *vi* INFOR **to** ~ **with sth** funcionar conjuntamente con algo **III.** *vt* INFOR conectar

interfere [ˌɪntəˈfɪəʳ, *Am:* -t̬ɚˈfɪr] *vi* **1.** (*become involved*) interferir; **to** ~ **between two people** entrometerse entre dos personas; **to** ~ **in sth** inmiscuirse en algo **2.** (*disturb*) molestar **3.** (*touch*) tocar; **someone has been interfering with my papers** alguien ha estado revolviendo mis papeles **4.** RADIO, TECH (*hamper signals*) producir interferencias **5.** *Brit* (*molest children*) **to** ~ **with** abusar de

interference [ˌɪntəˈfɪərəns, *Am:* -t̬ɚˈfɪr-] *n no pl* **1.** intromisión *f* **2.** RADIO, TECH interferencia *f*

interim [ˈɪntərɪm, *Am:* -t̬ɚ-] **I.** *n no pl* ínterin *m* **II.** *adj* provisional; (*payment*) a cuenta; ~ **dividend** FIN dividendo *m* a cuenta

interior [ɪnˈtɪərɪəʳ, *Am:* -ˈtɪrɪɚ] **I.** *adj* **1.** (*inner, inside, internal*) interno, -a; (*light*) interior; **the** ~ **market** el mercado interior **2.** (*central, inland, remote*) del interior **II.** *n* **1.** (*inside*) interior *m*; **the** ~ **of the country** el interior del país **2.** POL (*home affairs*) **the Ministry of the Interior** el Ministerio de Interior; **the U.S. Interior Department** el departamento de Interior de los Estados Unidos

interior decoration *n no pl* interiorismo *m*

interior designer *n* interiorista *mf*

interject [ˌɪntəˈdʒekt, *Am:* -t̬ɚ-] *vt form* interponer; **to** ~ **a few remarks** hacer algunos comentarios

interjection [ˌɪntəˈdʒekʃən, *Am:* -t̬ɚ-] *n* **1.** *form* (*verbal interruption*) exclamación *f*; ~**s from the audience** interrupciones *fpl* del público **2.** LING interjección *f*

interlace [ˌɪntəˈleɪs, *Am:* -t̬ɚ-] **I.** *vt* entrelazar **II.** *vi* entrelazarse

inter-library loan [ɪntəˈlaɪbrərɪˌləʊn] *n* préstamo *m* interbibliotecario

interlocutor [ˌɪntəˈlɒkjʊtəʳ, *Am:* -t̬ɚˈlɑːkjət̬ɚ] *n form* interlocutor(a) *m(f)*

interloper [ˈɪntələʊpəʳ, *Am:* -t̬ɚloʊpɚ] *n* intruso, -a *m, f*

interlude [ˈɪntəluːd, *Am:* -t̬ɚluːd] *n* **1.** (*interval*) intervalo *m* **2.** THEAT (*intermission*) entreacto *m*; (*short play*) entremés *m* **3.** MUS interludio *m*

intermarry [ˌɪntəˈmæri, *Am:* ˈɪnt̬ɚˌmer-] <-ie-> *vi* (*marry between groups*) casarse (personas de diferentes razas, grupos, clases, etc.); (*marry within family*) casarse (entre sí)

intermediary [ˌɪntəˈmiːdɪəri, *Am:* -t̬ɚˈmiːdɪer-] **I.** *adj* (*between persons*) intermediario, -a; (*intermediate*) intermedio, -a **II.** <-ies> *n* intermediario, -a *m, f*

intermediate [ˌɪntəˈmiːdɪət, *Am:* -t̬ɚ-] **I.** *adj* intermedio, -a; ~ **course** curso *m* de nivel intermedio; ~ **students** estudiantes *mpl* de ciclo medio; ~ **memory** INFOR memoria *f* intermedia **II.** *n* intermediario, -a *m, f*

intermezzo [ˌɪntəˈmetsəʊ, *Am:* -t̬ɚˈmetsoʊ] <-s *o* -zi> *n* MUS intermezzo *m*

interminable [ɪnˈtɜːmɪnəbl, *Am:* -ˈtɜːr-] *adj* interminable

intermission [ˌɪntəˈmɪʃən, *Am:* -t̬ɚ-] *n* **1.** intermedio *m*; **without** ~ sin pausa **2.** CINE, THEAT descanso *m*

intermittent [ˌɪntəˈmɪtnt, *Am:* -t̬ɚ-] *adj* intermitente; ~ **fever** fiebre *f* recurrente

intern¹ [ˈɪntɜːn, *Am:* -tɜːrn] *n Am* estudiante *mf* en prácticas; **hospital** ~ médico *m* asistente; **she worked in the Washington Post as a summer** ~ durante el verano estuvo haciendo prácticas en el Washington Post

intern² [ɪnˈtɜːn, *Am:* -ˈtɜːrn] **I.** *vt* recluir **II.** *vi* MED trabajar como interno, -a; SCHOOL hacer (las) prácticas

internal [ɪnˈtɜːnl, *Am:* -ˈtɜːr-] *adj a.* MED interno, -a; (*trade*) interior; **Internal Revenue Service** *Am* Hacienda *f*; **for** ~ **use only** sólo para uso interno

international [ˌɪntəˈnæʃnəl, *Am:* -t̬ɚ-] **I.** *adj a.* LAW internacional; (*trade*) exterior **II.** *n* **1.** *Brit* SPORTS (*sb on national team*) internacional *mf*; (*sports match*) partido *m* internacional **2.** POL Internacional *f*

International Court of Justice *n* Tribunal *m* Internacional de Justicia **international date line** *n* línea *f* de (cambio de) fecha

internationalise *vt Aus, Brit,* **internationalize** [ˌɪntəˈnæʃənəlaɪz, *Am:* -t̬ɚˈ-] *vt* internacionalizar

International Monetary Fund *n* Fondo *m* Monetario Internacional **International Olympic Committee** *n* Comité *m* Olímpico Internacional

internecine war [ɪntəˈniːsaɪnˌwɔːʳ, *Am:* -t̬ɚˈniːsɪn-] *n* guerra *f* de aniquilación recíproca

internee [ˌɪntɜːˈniː, *Am:* -tɜːrˈ-] *n* interno, -a

m, f

Internet ['ɪntənet, *Am:* -t̬ɚ-] *n* INFOR internet *f;* **to access the ~** entrar en internet; **to do business over the ~** hacer negocios a través de internet

Internet access *n* acceso *m* a internet **Internet-based learning** *n no pl* aprendizaje *m* por Internet [*o* en línea] **Internet café** *n* ciber café *m* **Internet search engine** *n* motor *m* de búsqueda en la red **Internet user** *n* internauta *mf*

internist [ɪn'tɜːnɪst, *Am:* -'tɜːr-] *n Am* internista *mf*

internment [ɪn'tɜːnmənt, *Am:* -'tɜːrn-] *n no pl* internamiento *m*

internment camp *n* campo *m* de internamiento

interpellation [ɪnˌtɜːpə'leɪʃən, *Am:* -ˌtɜːr-] *n* POL interpelación *f*

interphone ['ɪntəfəʊn] *n Am s.* **intercom**

interplanetary [ˌɪntə'plænɪtəri, *Am:* -t̬ɚ-'plænəter-] *adj* interplanetario, -a

interplay ['ɪntəpleɪ, *Am:* -t̬ɚ-] *n no pl* interacción *f*

Interpol ['ɪntəpɒl, *Am:* -t̬ɚpɑːl] *n abbr of* **International Criminal Police Commission** Interpol *f*

interpolate [ɪn'tɜːpəleɪt, *Am:* -'tɜːr-] *vt* interpolar; **to ~ a text** introducir interpolaciones en un texto; **"that happened in Rome, not in Paris!" Sam ~d** *liter* "¡eso ocurrió en Roma, no en París!", puntualizó Sam

interpolation [ɪnˌtɜːpə'leɪʃən, *Am:* -ˌtɜːr-] *n* interpolación *f*

interpret [ɪn'tɜːprɪt, *Am:* -'tɜːrprət] **I.** *vt* **1.** (*decode, construe*) interpretar **2.** (*translate*) traducir **II.** *vi* interpretar; **to ~ from English into Spanish** interpretar del inglés al español

interpretation [ɪnˌtɜːprɪ'teɪʃən, *Am:* -ˌtɜːrprə'-] *n* interpretación *f;* **to put an ~ on sth** interpretar algo; **the rules are open to ~** las normas pueden interpretarse de varias formas

interpreter [ɪn'tɜːprɪtəʳ, *Am:* -'tɜːrprət̬ɚ] *n* **1.** MUS, THEAT, LING intérprete *mf* **2.** INFOR intérprete *m*

interpreting [ɪn'tɜ ːprɪtɪŋ, *Am:* -'tɜːrprət-] *n no pl* interpretación *f*

inter-rail ['ɪntəreɪl] *adj* inter-raíl; **~ ticket** billete *m* inter-raíl

interrelate [ˌɪntərɪ'leɪt, *Am:* -t̬ɚrɪ-] *vi* interrelacionarse; **to ~ with each other** relacionarse entre sí

interrogate [ɪn'terəgeɪt] *vt* interrogar

interrogation [ɪnˌterə'geɪʃən] *n* **1.** *a.* INFOR interrogación *f* **2.** LAW interrogatorio *m;* **police ~** interrogatorio policial; **~ room** sala *f* de interrogatorios

interrogation mark *n,* **interrogation point** *n* interrogante *m*

interrogative [ˌɪntə'rɒgətɪv, *Am:* -t̬ɚ'rɑːgət̬ɪv] **I.** *n* LING (*word*) palabra *f* interrogativa; (*sentence*) oración *f* interrogativa **II.** *adj* **1.** *liter* (*having questioning form*) interrogador(a) **2.** LING interrogativo, -a

interrogator [ɪn'terəgeɪtəʳ, *Am:* -t̬ɚ'rɑːgətɔːr] *n* interrogador(a) *m(f)*

interrogatory [ˌɪntə'rɒgətəri, *Am:* -t̬ɚ'rɑːgətɔːr-] **I.** *adj* interrogador(a) **II.** <-ies> *n* interrogatorio *m*

interrupt [ˌɪntə'rʌpt, *Am:* -t̬ɚ-] *vi, vt* interrumpir

interrupter [ˌɪntə'rʌptəʳ, *Am:* -t̬ɚ'rʌptɚ] *n* ELEC interruptor *m*

interruption [ˌɪntə'rʌpʃən, *Am:* -t̬ɚ-] *n* interrupción *f;* **without ~** sin interrupciones

intersect [ˌɪntə'sekt] **I.** *vt* (*cross at a junction*) cruzar; (*lines*) cortar **II.** *vi* **1.** (*cut, divide*) intersecarse *form;* (*cross at a junction*) cruzarse; **~ing roads** carreteras *fpl* que se cruzan **2.** MAT (*sets*) formar intersección

intersection [ˌɪntə'sekʃən] *n* **1.** (*crossing of lines*) intersección *f* **2.** *Am, Aus* (*junction*) cruce *m*

intersperse [ˌɪntə'spɜːs, *Am:* -t̬ɚ'spɜːrs] *vt* intercalar; **to ~ sth with sth** intercalar algo en algo; **to ~ sth between sth** esparcir algo entre algo; **to ~ anecdotes throughout a speech** salpicar un discurso de anécdotas

interstate [ˌɪntə'steɪt, *Am:* 'ɪnt̬ɚ-] *adj Am* interestatal

interstate highway *n* autopista *f* interestatal **interstate trade** *n* comercio *m* entre estados

interstellar [ˌɪntə'steləʳ, *Am:* -t̬ɚ'stelɚ] *adj form* interestelar

interstice [ɪn'tɜːstɪs, *Am:* -'tɜːr-] *n form* intersticio *m*

intertwine [ˌɪntə'twaɪn, *Am:* -t̬ɚ-] **I.** *vt* entrelazar **II.** *vi* (*flowers, hands*) entrelazarse; (*paths*) entrecruzarse

interurban [ˌɪntə'ɜːbən, *Am:* -t̬ɚ'ɜːr-] *adj Am* interurbano, -a

interval ['ɪntəvl, *Am:* -t̬ɚ-] *n* **1.** *a.* MUS intervalo *m;* **at ~s of five minutes** a intervalos de cinco minutos; **at five-centimetre ~s** con espacios de cinco centímetros; **at regular ~s** a intervalos regulares; **at ~s** de vez en cuando; **sunny ~s** METEO claros *mpl* **2.** THEAT, MUS entreacto *m;* SPORTS descanso *m*

intervene [ˌɪntə'viːn, *Am:* -t̬ɚ-] *vi* **1.** (*involve oneself to help*) intervenir; **to ~ militarily/personally** intervenir militarmente/personalmente; **to ~ on sb's behalf** interceder por alguien **2.** (*meddle unhelpfully*) **to ~ in sth** mezclarse en algo **3.** (*come to pass between*) sobrevenir; **six months ~d before the opening of the swimming-pool** transcurrieron seis meses antes de la inauguración de la piscina

intervening *adj* **in the ~ period** en el ínterin; **in the ~ days** en los días intermedios

intervention [ˌɪntə'venʃən, *Am:* -t̬ɚ'-] *n* intervención *f;* **military ~** MIL intervención militar; **~ price** ECON precio *m* de intervención

interventionist [ˌɪntəˈvenʃənɪst, *Am:* -t̬ɚˈ-] **I.** *n* POL, ECON intervencionista *mf* **II.** *adj* intervencionista

interview [ˈɪntəvjuː, *Am:* -t̬ɚ-] **I.** *n* **1.** (*formal conversation*) entrevista *f*; **telephone ~** encuesta *f* telefónica; **to have a job ~** tener una entrevista de trabajo; **to give an ~** conceder una entrevista **2.** *Brit* LAW interrogatorio *m* **II.** *vt* **1.** entrevistar; **to ~ sb on sth** encuestar a alguien sobre algo **2.** *Brit* LAW interrogar

interviewee [ˌɪntəvjuːˈiː, *Am:* -t̬ɚ-] *n* entrevistado, -a *m, f*

interviewer [ˈɪntəvjuːəʳ, *Am:* -t̬ɚvjuːɚ] *n* entrevistador(a) *m(f)*

interweave [ˌɪntəˈwiːv, *Am:* -t̬ɚ-] *irr* **I.** *vt* entretejer; **to be interwoven with sth** estar estrechamente unido a algo **II.** *vi* (*threads*) entretejerse; (*paths*) entrecruzarse

intestate [ɪnˈtesteɪt] *adj* intestado, -a

intestine [ɪnˈtestɪn] *n* intestino *m*

intimacy [ˈɪntɪməsi, *Am:* -t̬ə-] <-ies> *n* **1.** *no pl* (*familiarity*) intimidad *f*; **to be in terms of ~ with sb** tener intimidad con alguien **2.** *no pl* (*sexual relations*) relaciones *fpl* íntimas **3.** *pl* (*transactions*) gestos *mpl* de complicidad

intimate¹ [ˈɪntɪmət, *Am:* -t̬ə-] **I.** *adj* **1.** (*close, sexual*) íntimo, -a; **~ relationship** relaciones *fpl* íntimas; **to be on ~ terms with sb** tener intimidad con alguien; **to become ~ with sb** intimar con alguien; **to be ~ with sb** tener relaciones sexuales con alguien **2.** (*personal: style*) personal **3.** (*very detailed: knowledge*) profundo, -a; (*link*) estrecho, -a **II.** *n* amigo, -a *m, f* íntimo, -a

intimate² [ˈɪntɪmeɪt, *Am:* -t̬ə-] *vt form* insinuar; **to ~ to sb (that)** … dar a entender a alguien (que)…

intimation [ˌɪntɪˈmeɪʃən, *Am:* -t̬ə-] *n form* (*hint*) insinuación *f*; (*sign*) indicación *f*; **~s** indicios *mpl*

intimidate [ɪnˈtɪmɪdeɪt] *vt* intimidar; **to ~ sb into doing sth** coaccionar a alguien para que haga algo

intimidating *adj* intimidante

intimidation [ɪnˌtɪmɪˈdeɪʃən] *n no pl* intimidación *f*

into [ˈɪntʊ, *Am:* -tə] *prep* **1.** (*to the inside of*) en; (*towards*) hacia; **to walk ~ a place** entrar en un sitio; **to get ~ bed** meterse en la cama; **shall we walk ~ the garden?** ¿vamos a pasear al jardín?; **~ the future** hacia el futuro **2.** (*indicating an extent in time or space*) **deep ~ the forest** en lo más profundo del bosque; **to work late ~ the evening** trabajar hasta tarde **3.** (*against*) contra; **to drive ~ a tree** chocar contra un árbol; **to bump ~ a friend** tropezar con un amigo **4.** (*to the state or condition of*) **to burst ~ tears** echarse a llorar; **to grow ~ a woman** convertirse en una mujer; **to translate from Spanish ~ English** traducir del español al inglés; **to turn sth ~ sth** convertir algo en algo **5.** *inf* (*interested in*) **she's really ~ her new job** está entusiasmada con su nuevo trabajo; **I think they are ~ drugs** creo que andan metidos en drogas **6.** MAT **two ~ ten equals five** diez entre dos es igual a cinco; **two goes ~ five two and a half times** cinco dividido entre dos es igual a dos y medio

intolerable [ɪnˈtɒlərəbl, *Am:* -ˈtɑːlɚ-] *adj* intolerable

intolerance [ɪnˈtɒlərəns, *Am:* -ˈtɑːlɚ-] *n no pl* intolerancia *f*

intolerant [ɪnˈtɒlərənt, *Am:* -ˈtɑːlɚ-] *adj* intolerante; **to be ~ of different opinions** ser intolerante con las opiniones diferentes; **to be ~ of sb** ser intransigente con alguien; **to be ~ of alcohol** MED no tolerar el alcohol

intonation [ˌɪntəˈneɪʃən, *Am:* -toʊˈ-] *n* LING, MUS entonación *f*

intone [ɪnˈtəʊn, *Am:* -ˈtoʊn] *vt form* **1.** (*sing*) entonar **2.** (*say solemnly*) recitar

intoxicant [ɪnˈtɒksɪkənt, *Am:* -ˈtɑːk-] *n* MED (*alcohol*) bebida *f* alcohólica; (*drug*) estupefaciente *m*

intoxicate [ɪnˈtɒksɪkeɪt, *Am:* -ˈtɑːk-] **I.** *vt* **1.** *a. fig* (*induce inebriation*) embriagar **2.** MED intoxicar **II.** *vi* **1.** *a. fig* (*cause intoxication*) embriagar **2.** MED intoxicar

intoxicating [ɪnˈtɒksɪkeɪtɪŋ, *Am:* -ˈtɑːksɪkeɪt̬ɪŋ] *adj* **1.** (*exhilarating, stimulating*) embriagador(a) **2.** (*substance*) estupefaciente; (*causing drunkenness*) alcohólico, -a; **~ drink** bebida *f* alcohólica

intoxication [ɪnˌtɒksɪˈkeɪʃən, *Am:* -ˌtɑːksɪ-] *n no pl* **1.** *a. fig* (*drunkenness*) embriaguez *f*; **in a state of ~** en estado de embriaguez **2.** MED intoxicación *f*

intractable [ˌɪnˈtræktəbl] *adj form* **1.** (*temperament*) obstinado, -a; **an ~ pupil** un alumno incorregible **2.** (*problem*) insoluble; **an ~ situation** una situación difícil de resolver **3.** MED incurable

intracutaneous [ɪntrækjuːˈteɪnəs] *adj* intracutáneo, -a

intramural [ˌɪntrəˈmjʊərəl, *Am:* -ˈmjʊrəl] *adj* **1.** (*within a city or institution*) intramuros *inv* **2.** SCHOOL dentro de la escuela; UNIV dentro de la universidad; **~ contest** campeonato *m* de la escuela/universidad

Intranet [ˌɪntrəˈnet] *n* intranet *f*

intransigence [ɪnˈtrænsɪdʒəns, *Am:* -sə-] *n no pl, form* intransigencia *f*

intransigent [ɪnˈtrænsɪdʒənt, *Am:* -sə-] *adj form* intransigente

intransitive [ɪnˈtrænsətɪv, *Am:* -t̬ɪv] *adj* LING, MAT intransitivo, -a

intrauterine [ˌɪntrəˈjuːtəraɪn, *Am:* -t̬ɚɪn] *adj* MED intrauterino, -a

intravenous [ˌɪntrəˈviːnəs] *adj* MED intravenoso, -a; **~ feeding** alimentación *f* por vía intravenosa

in-tray [ˈɪntreɪ] *n* bandeja *f* de entrada

intrepid [ɪnˈtrepɪd] *adj* intrépido, -a

intricacy [ˈɪntrɪkəsi] <-ies> *n* complejidad *f*

intricate ['ɪntrɪkət] *adj* intrincado, -a; (*mechanism*) complejo, -a; (*problem*) complicado, -a

intrigue [ɪn'tri:g] **I.** *vt* intrigar; **to be ~d by sth** estar intrigado con algo **II.** *vi* **1.** (*plot*) intrigar **2.** (*carry on a secret love affair*) tener una aventura **III.** *n* **1.** (*complications of a plot, machinations*) intriga *f* **2.** (*secret love affair*) aventura *f*

intriguing [ɪn'tri:gɪŋ] *adj* **1.** (*mysterious*) intrigante **2.** (*fascinating*) fascinante; (*smile*) enigmático, -a

intrinsic [ɪn'trɪnsɪk] *adj* intrínseco, -a; **the ~ value of a coin** el valor real de una moneda; **this is ~ to ...** eso es esencial para...

introduce [ˌɪntrə'dju:s, *Am:* -'du:s] *vt* **1.** (*acquaint*) presentar; **allow me to ~ myself** permítame que me presente; **may I ~ you to my husband?** ¿le presento a mi marido?; **they were ~d to each other** les presentaron **2.** (*raise interest in subject*) **to ~ sb to sth** iniciar a alguien en algo **3.** (*bring in*) introducir; (*question*) hacer; (*subject*) abordar; (*bill*) presentar; **to ~ a product into the market** lanzar un producto al mercado **4.** (*insert*) introducir; **to ~ sb into a place** hacer entrar a alguien en un sitio **5.** (*begin, present: book*) prologar; **the second movement is ~d by ...** el segundo movimiento está introducido por...; **the director will ~ the film personally** el director presentará personalmente la película

introduction [ˌɪntrə'dʌkʃən] *n* **1.** (*making first acquaintance*) presentación *f;* **letter of ~** carta *f* de presentación; **to do the ~s** hacer las presentaciones **2.** (*first contact with sth*) iniciación *f;* **my holidays served as an ~ to sailing** mis vacaciones fueron una primera toma de contacto con la navegación **3.** (*establishment*) introducción *f;* (*of a bill*) presentación *f;* **~ into the market** lanzamiento *m* al mercado **4.** (*insertion*) introducción *f* **5.** (*preface*) prólogo *m;* MUS introducción *f*

introductory [ˌɪntrə'dʌktəri] *adj* **1.** (*elementary, preparatory*) de introducción; (*course*) de iniciación **2.** COM (*price*) de lanzamiento **3.** (*beginning*) introductorio, -a; **~ chapter** introducción *f;* **~ remarks** aclaraciones *fpl* preliminares

introspection [ˌɪntrə'spekʃən, *Am:* -troʊ'-] *n no pl* introspección *f*

introspective [ˌɪntrə'spektɪv, *Am:* -troʊ'-] *adj* introspectivo, -a

introvert [ˌɪntrə'vɜ:t, *Am:* -troʊ'vɜ:rt] *n* introvertido, -a *m, f*

introverted *adj* introvertido, -a

intrude [ɪn'tru:d] **I.** *vi* **1.** (*meddle*) entrometerse; **to ~ into sth** inmiscuirse en algo; **to ~ upon sb's privacy** meterse en la vida privada de alguien **2.** (*disturb*) estorbar; **to ~ on sb** importunar a alguien; **am I intruding?** ¿molesto? **II.** *vt* **to ~ sth on sb** importunar a alguien con algo

intruder [ɪn'tru:dəʳ, *Am:* -ɚ] *n* intruso, -a *m, f*

intrusion [ɪn'tru:ʒən] *n* **1.** (*encroachment, infringement*) intrusión *f* **2.** (*meddling*) intromisión *f*

intrusive [ɪn'tru:sɪv] *adj* (*noise*) molesto, -a; (*question*) indiscreto, -a; (*person*) entrometido, -a

intuition [ˌɪntju:'ɪʃən, *Am:* -tu:'-] *n no pl* intuición *f;* **to have an ~ (that) ...** tener la intuición (de que)...

intuitive [ɪn'tju:ɪtɪv] *adj* intuitivo, -a; **an ~ feeling** una intuición

inundate ['ɪnʌndeɪt, *Am:* -ən-] *vt a. fig* inundar; **to ~ sb with sth** inundar a alguien de algo; **to be ~d with presents** verse inundado de regalos; **to be ~d with letters** recibir un aluvión de cartas

inundation [ˌɪnʌn'deɪʃən, *Am:* -ən'-] *n no pl, a. fig* inundación *f*

inure [ɪ'njʊəʳ, *Am:* -'njʊr] *vt form* (*become familiar with*) habituar; (*harden*) curtir, endurecer; **to ~ sb to sth** acostumbrar a alguien a algo; **to ~ oneself against sth** hacerse inmune a algo

invade [ɪn'veɪd] **I.** *vt* invadir; **to ~ the peace** perturbar la paz; **to ~ sb's privacy** invadir la intimidad de alguien; **to ~ sb's rights** usurpar los derechos de alguien **II.** *vi* invadir

invader [ɪn'veɪdəʳ, *Am:* -ɚ] *n* (*aggressive trespasser*) invasor(a) *m(f)*

invalid[1] ['ɪnvəlɪd] **I.** *n* (*incapacitated person*) inválido, -a *m, f;* (*sick person*) enfermo, -a *m, f* **II.** *adj* **1.** (*disabled*) inválido, -a; **~ chair** silla *f* de ruedas **2.** (*sick*) enfermo, -a; **~ diet** dieta *f* para enfermos **III.** *vt* **1.** (*disable*) dejar inválido, -a; (*make sick*) poner enfermo, -a **2.** **to ~ out** *Brit* dar de baja por invalidez; **to ~ sb home** *Brit* repatriar a alguien por invalidez

invalid[2] [ɪn'vælɪd] *adj* **1.** LAW (*not legally binding*) nulo, -a; **legally ~** sin validez legal; **to become ~** caducar **2.** (*unsound*) no válido, -a; **technically ~** técnicamente incorrecto

invalidate [ɪn'vælɪdeɪt] *vt* **1.** (*argument, decision*) invalidar; (*results*) anular **2.** LAW anular; **to ~ a judgement** revocar una sentencia

invalidism [ˌɪnvə'lɪdɪzəm] *n Am,* **invalidity** [ˌɪnvə'lɪdəti, *Am:* -t̬i] *n no pl* **1.** (*convalescent state*) invalidez *f* **2.** (*inadmissibility: of a contract*) nulidad *f;* (*of evidence*) invalidez *f*

invaluable [ɪn'væljʊəbl, *Am:* -juə-] *adj* inapreciable; (*help*) inestimable; **to be ~ to sb** tener un valor inapreciable para alguien

invariable [ɪn'veəriəbl, *Am:* -'verɪ-] *adj form* (*custom*) invariable; (*smile, attitude*) eterno, -a

invariably *adv* invariablemente; **he would ~ be sitting at the bar** siempre se le veía sentado en la barra

invasion [ɪn'veɪʒən] *n* **1.** MIL invasión *f;* **~ by enemy forces** invasión de las tropas enemigas **2.** *no pl* (*interference*) violación *f;* **~ of privacy/of a right** violación de la intimidad/de

I

un derecho
invective [ɪn'vektɪv] *n no pl, form* invectiva *f;* **a stream of** ~ un aluvión de invectivas
inveigle [ɪn'veɪgl] *vt* **to** ~ **sb into sth** embaucar a alguien para algo
invent [ɪn'vent] *vt* inventar
invention [ɪn'venʃən] *n* **1.** (*gadget*) invención *f,* invento *m AmL* **2.** *no pl* (*creativity*) inventiva *f* **3.** (*falsehood*) ficción *f*
inventive [ɪn'ventɪv, *Am:* -t̬ɪv] *adj* inventivo, -a
inventiveness [ɪn'ventɪvnɪs, *Am:* -t̬ɪv-] *n no pl* inventiva *f*
inventor [ɪn'ventəʳ, *Am:* -t̬ɚ] *n* inventor(a) *m(f)*
inventory ['ɪnvəntri, *Am:* -tɔːr-] <-ies> **I.** *n* **1.** (*catalogue*) inventario *m;* **to draw up an** ~ levantar un inventario **2.** *Am* (*stock*) stock *m* **II.** *vt* inventariar **III.** *adj* (*audit, level, number*) de inventario
inverse [ɪn'vɜːs, *Am:* -'vɜːrs] **I.** *adj* inverso, -a **II.** *n no pl* **the** ~ lo inverso; **the** ~ **of sth** lo contrario de algo
inversion [ɪn'vɜːʃən, *Am:* -'vɜːrʒən] *n no pl* inversión *f*
invert [ɪn'vɜːt, *Am:* -'vɜːrt] *vt* invertir; (*reverse*) revertir
invertebrate [ɪn'vɜːtɪbrət, *Am:* -'vɜːrt̬əbrɪt] **I.** *n* invertebrado *m* **II.** *adj* invertebrado, -a
invest [ɪn'vest] **I.** *vt* **1.** (*put in*) invertir; **to** ~ **time and effort in sth** invertir tiempo y dinero en algo **2.** (*bestow attributes*) investir; **to** ~ **sb with sth** investir a alguien de algo **II.** *vi* invertir; **to** ~ **in sth** invertir en algo
investigate [ɪn'vestɪgeɪt] *vt* investigar
investigation [ɪnˌvestɪ'geɪʃən] *n* investigación *f*
investigative [ɪn'vestɪgətɪv, *Am:* -geɪt̬ɪv] *adj* investigador(a); ~ **journalism** periodismo *m* de investigación
investigator [ɪn'vestɪgeɪtəʳ, *Am:* -t̬ɚ] *n* investigador(a) *m(f)*
investment [ɪn'vestmənt] **I.** *n a. fig* inversión *f;* **to be a good** ~ ser una buena inversión; **long-term** ~**s** inversiones *fpl* a largo plazo **II.** *adj* de inversión
investment fund *n* fondo *m* de inversiones **investment income** *n no pl* ingresos *mpl* procedentes de inversiones **investment trust** *n* sociedad *f* de inversiones
investor [ɪn'vestəʳ, *Am:* -tɚ] *n* inversionista *mf*
inveterate [ɪn'vetərət, *Am:* -'vet̬-] *adj* inveterado, -a; (*smoker*) empedernido, -a; (*liar*) incurable
invidious [ɪn'vɪdɪəs] *adj* odioso, -a; (*unfair*) injusto, -a; **to be in an** ~ **position** estar en una posición poco envidiable
invigilate [ɪn'vɪdʒɪleɪt] *vt Brit, Aus* (*in exam*) supervisar
invigorate [ɪn'vɪgəreɪt] *vt* vigorizar; (*stimulate*) estimular
invigorating [ɪn'vɪgəreɪtɪŋ, *Am:* -t̬ɪŋ] *adj* vigorizante
invincible [ɪn'vɪnsəbl] *adj* invencible
invisible [ɪn'vɪzəbl] *adj* invisible; ~ **to sth** invisible a algo
invitation [ˌɪnvɪ'teɪʃən] *n* invitación *f;* **an** ~ **to sth** una invitación a algo
invite[1] ['ɪnvaɪt] *n inf* invitación *f*
invite[2] [ɪn'vaɪt] *vt* **1.** (*request to attend*) invitar; **to** ~ **sb for/to sth** invitar a alguien para/a algo **2.** (*request*) pedir; **to** ~ **offers** solicitar ofertas; **they** ~**d readers to send in their views** pidieron a los lectores sus opiniones; **to** ~ **questions** abrirse a preguntas **3.** (*provoke*) buscarse; **to** ~ **trouble** buscar(se) problemas
inviting [ɪn'vaɪtɪŋ, *Am:* -t̬ɪŋ] *adj* **1.** (*attractive*) atractivo, -a, atrayente **2.** (*tempting*) tentador(a)
in vitro [ɪn'viːtrəʊ, *Am:* -troʊ] *adj, adv* in vitro
in vitro fertilization *n no pl* fecundación *f* in vitro
invocation [ˌɪnvə'keɪʃən] *n* invocación *f*
invoice ['ɪnvɔɪs] **I.** *vt* facturar **II.** *n* factura *f;* ~ **for sth** factura de algo
invoke [ɪn'vəʊk, *Am:* -'voʊk] *vt* invocar
involuntary [ɪn'vɒləntəri, *Am:* -'vɑːlənter-] *adj* involuntario, -a
involve [ɪn'vɒlv, *Am:* -'vɑːlv] *vt* **1.** (*implicate*) implicar, involucrar; **to be** ~**d in sth** estar metido [*o* envuelto] en algo; **to get** ~**d in sth** meterse en algo; **to** ~ **sb in a quarrel** mezclar a alguien en una disputa **2.** (*entail*) comportar; **to** ~ **much expense** causar muchos gastos
involved [ɪn'vɒlvd, *Am:* -'vɑːlvd] *adj* **1.** (*implicated*) involucrado, -a **2.** (*complicated*) complicado, -a
involvement [ɪn'vɒlvmənt, *Am:* -'vɑːlv-] *n no pl* implicación *f*
invulnerable [ɪn'vʌlnərəbl, *Am:* -nɚ-] *adj* invulnerable; **to be** ~ **to sth** ser inmune a algo
inward ['ɪnwəd, *Am:* -wɚd] *adj* **1.** (*trade*) interior; (*investment*) interno, -a **2.** (*inmost*) interior; (*personal*) íntimo, -a
inwardly *adv* interiormente
inwardness *n no pl* interioridad *f*
inwards ['ɪnwədz, *Am:* -wɚds] *adv* hacia adentro, para dentro
I/O INFOR *abbr of* **input/output** E/S
IOC *n abbr of* **International Olympic Committee** COI *m*
iodine ['aɪədiːn, *Am:* -daɪn] *n no pl* yodo *m*
IOM *n abbr of* **Isle of Man** Isla *f* de Man
ion ['aɪən] *n* ión *m*
Ionic [aɪ'ɒnɪk, *Am:* -'ɑːnɪk] *adj* jónico, -a
iota [aɪ'əʊtə, *Am:* -'oʊt̬ə] *n no pl* **1.** (*letter*) iota *f* **2.** *fig* ápice *m;* **there is not one** ~ **of truth in that** no hay ni una pizca de verdad en eso
IOU [ˌaɪəʊ'juː, *Am:* -oʊ'-] *n inf abbr of* **I owe you** pagaré *m*
IOW *n abbr of* **Isle of Wight** Isla *f* de Wight

IPA [ˌaɪpiːˈeɪ] *n* **1.** *abbr of* **International Phonetic Association** AFI *f* **2.** *abbr of* **International Phonetic Alphabet** AFI *m*
IQ [ˌaɪˈkjuː] *n abbr of* **intelligence quotient** CI *m*
IRA [ˌaɪɑːrˈeɪ, *Am:* -ɑːrˈ-] *n no pl abbr of* **Irish Republican Army** IRA *m*
Iran [ɪˈrɑːn, *Am:* -ˈræn] *n* Irán *m*
Iranian [ɪˈreɪnjən] **I.** *n* iraní *mf* **II.** *adj* iraní
Iraq [ɪˈrɑːk] *n* Irak *m*
Iraqi [ɪˈrɑːki] **I.** *n* iraquí *mf* **II.** *adj* iraquí
irascible [ɪˈræsəbl] *adj* irascible
irate [aɪˈreɪt] *adj* airado, -a
IRBM *n abbr of* **intermediate-range ballistic missile** IRBM *m*
Ireland [ˈaɪələnd, *Am:* ˈaɪr-] *n* Irlanda *f;* **Republic of ~** República *f* de Irlanda; **Northern ~** Irlanda del Norte
iridescent [ˌɪrɪˈdesnt] *adj* iridiscente
iris [ˈaɪərɪs, *Am:* ˈaɪ-] <-es> *n* **1.** BOT lirio *m* **2.** ANAT iris *m*
Irish [ˈaɪərɪʃ, *Am:* ˈaɪ-] **I.** *adj* irlandés, -esa **II.** *n* **1.** *pl* (*people*) **the ~** los irlandeses **2.** LING irlandés *m;* **~ Gaelic** gaélico *m* irlandés
Irishman [ˈaɪərɪʃmən, *Am:* ˈaɪ-] <-men> *n* irlandés *m*
Irishwoman [ˈaɪərɪʃwʊmən, *Am:* ˈaɪ-] <-women> *n* irlandesa *f*
irk [ɜːk, *Am:* ɜːrk] *vt* fastidiar
irksome [ˈɜːksəm, *Am:* ˈɜːrk-] *adj* fastidioso, -a
iron [ˈaɪən, *Am:* ˈaɪɚn] **I.** *n* **1.** *no pl* (*metal*) hierro *m,* fierro *m AmL* **2.** (*for pressing clothes*) plancha *f;* **steam ~** plancha de vapor **3.** SPORTS (*golf club*) hierro *m* ►**to have many ~s in the fire** tener muchos asuntos entre manos **II.** *vt* planchar; *fig* allanar **III.** *vi* planchar **IV.** *adj* de hierro; (*discipline*) férreo, -a
Iron Age I. *n* edad *f* de hierro **II.** *adj* de la edad de hierro **Iron Curtain** *n* HIST, POL Telón *m* de Acero
ironic(al) [aɪˈrɒnɪk(el), *Am:* aɪˈrɑːnɪk-] *adj* irónico, -a
ironing [ˈaɪənɪŋ, *Am:* ˈaɪɚn-] *n no pl* planchado *m;* **to do the ~** planchar
ironing board *n* tabla *f* de planchar, burro *m* de planchar *Méx*
iron lung *n* pulmón *m* de acero
ironmonger *n Brit* ferretero *m;* **~'s** *Brit* (*shop*) ferretería *f*
ironmongery *n no pl, Brit* (*goods*) objetos *mpl* de ferretería; (*shop*) ferretería *f*
iron ore *n no pl* mineral *m* de hierro **iron ration** *n* ración *f* de reserva
ironwork *n no pl* herraje *m*
ironworks *n inv* fundición *f,* herrería *f AmL*
irony [ˈaɪərəni, *Am:* ˈaɪ-] <-ies> *n* ironía *f;* **~ of fate** ironía del destino
irradiate [ɪˈreɪdɪeɪt, *Am:* ɪrˈ-] *vt* irradiar
irrational [ɪˈræʃənəl] *adj* irracional
irrational number *n* MAT número *m* irracional
irreconcilable [ɪˌrekənˈsaɪləbl] *adj* (*positions*) inconciliable; (*differences*) irreconciliable
irrecoverable [ˌɪrɪˈkʌvərəbl] *adj* irrecuperable
irredeemable [ˌɪrɪˈdiːməbl] *adj* irredimible
irrefutable [ˌɪrɪˈfjuːtəbl, *Am:* ɪˈrefjəṭə-] *adj* (*evidence*) irrefutable; (*argument, fact, logic*) irrebatible
irregular [ɪˈregjələr, *Am:* -lɚ] *adj* irregular; (*surface*) desigual; (*behaviour*) anómalo, -a; (*life*) desordenado, -a; **~ soldiers** tropas *fpl* irregulares
irregularity [ɪˌregjəˈlærəti, *Am:* ɪˌregjəˈlerəṭi] <-ies> *n* irregularidad *f;* (*of surface*) desigualdad *f;* (*of behaviour*) anormalidad *f*
irrelevance [ɪˈreləvənts, *Am:* ɪrˈ-] *n,* **irrelevancy** <-ies> *n* irrelevancia *f;* **to fade into ~** volverse irrelevante
irrelevant [ɪˈreləvənt, *Am:* ɪrˈ-] *adj* irrelevante; **to be ~ to sth** no ser relevante para algo
irremediable [ˌɪrɪˈmiːdɪəbl] *adj* irremediable; (*damage, loss*) irreparable
irreparable [ɪˈrepərəbl] *adj* irreparable
irreplaceable [ˌɪrɪˈpleɪsəbl] *adj* irreemplazable
irrepressible [ˌɪrɪˈpresəbl] *adj* irrefrenable, incontrolable
irreproachable [ˌɪrɪˈprəʊtʃəbl, *Am:* -ˈproʊ-] *adj* irreprochable; (*past*) intachable
irresistible [ˌɪrɪˈzɪstəbl] *adj* irresistible
irresolute [ɪˈrezəluːt] *adj* irresoluto, -a; (*reply*) indeciso, -a
irrespective [ˌɪrɪˈspektɪv] *prep* **~ of** aparte de; **~ of whether he agrees or not** con independencia de si está de acuerdo; **~ of sth/sb** sin tener en cuenta algo/a alguien
irresponsible [ˌɪrɪˈspɒnsəbl, *Am:* -ˈspɑːn-] *adj* irresponsable
irretrievable [ˌɪrɪˈtriːvəbl] *adj* irrecuperable; (*mistake*) irreparable
irreverence [ɪˈrevərəns] *n no pl* irreverencia *f*
irreverent [ɪˈrevərənt] *adj* irreverente
irreversible [ˌɪrɪˈvɜːsəbl, *Am:* -ˈvɜːr-] *adj* irreversible; (*decision*) irrevocable
irrevocable [ɪˈrevəkəbl] *adj* irrevocable
irrigate [ˈɪrɪgeɪt] *vt* **1.** AGR regar; **to ~ land** regar la tierra **2.** MED irrigar
irrigation [ˌɪrɪˈgeɪʃən] **I.** *n no pl* **1.** AGR riego *m* **2.** MED irrigación *f* **II.** *adj* de riego; **~ canal** acequia *f*
irrigation plant *n* planta *f* de riego
irritable [ˈɪrɪtəbl, *Am:* -ṭə-] *adj* irritable
irritant [ˈɪrɪtənt, *Am:* -ṭənt] *n* irritante *m*
irritate [ˈɪrɪteɪt] *vt* **1.** (*aggravate*) irritar, molestar **2.** MED irritar
irritated *adj* irritado, -a
irritating *adj* irritante
irritation [ˌɪrɪˈteɪʃən] *n* irritación *f*
is [ɪz] *vt, vi 3rd pers sing of* **to be**
ISBN [ˌaɪesbiːˈen] *n abbr of* **International Standard Book Number** ISBN *m*
ISD *n abbr of* **international subscriber dial-**

ling marcación *f* directa internacional
ISDN *n abbr of* **integrated services digital network** RDSI *f*
Islam [ɪz'lɑːm] *n no pl* Islam *m*
Islamic [ɪz'læmɪk, *Am:* -'lɑː-] *adj* islámico, -a; ~ **law** ley islámica
island ['aɪlənd] *n* isla *f;* ~ **of calm** *fig* refugio *m* de paz
islander ['aɪləndəʳ, *Am:* -ɚ] *n* isleño, -a *m, f*
isle *n,* **Isle** [aɪl] *n* ínsula *f*
Isle of Man *n* Isla *f* de Man **Isle of Wight** *n* Isla *f* de Wight
islet ['aɪlɪt] *n liter* islote *m*
isn't ['ɪznt] = **is not**
isobar ['aɪsəbɑːʳ, *Am:* -soʊbɑːr] *n* METEO isobara *f*
isolate ['aɪsəleɪt] *vt* aislar
isolated ['aɪsəleɪtɪd, *Am:* -t̬ɪd] *adj* **1.** (*outlying, disconnected*) aislado, -a **2.** (*lonely*) apartado, -a
isolation [ˌaɪsə'leɪʃən] *n no pl* **1.** (*separation*) aislamiento *m* **2.** (*loneliness*) soledad *f*
isolation hospital *n* hospital *m* de enfermedades contagiosas
isolationism [ˌaɪsə'leɪʃnɪzəm] *n no pl* aislacionismo *m*
isolation ward *n* sala *f* de aislamiento
isosceles triangle [aɪ'sɒsliːzˌtraɪæŋgl, *Am:* -'sɑːsl-] *n* MAT triángulo *m* isósceles
isotherm ['aɪsəθɜːm, *Am:* -soʊθɜːrm] *n* METEO, PHYS isotermo *m*
isotope ['aɪsətəʊp, *Am:* -toʊp] *n* PHYS, ELEC isótopo *m*
Israel ['ɪzreɪl, *Am:* -riəl] *n* Israel *m*
Israeli [ɪz'reɪli] **I.** *n* israelí *mf* **II.** *adj* israelí
Israelite ['ɪzrɪəlaɪt] *n* israelita *mf*
issue ['ɪʃuː] **I.** *n* **1.** (*problem, topic*) cuestión *f;* **family ~s** asuntos *mpl* familiares; **side** ~ asunto *m* menor; **a burning** ~ *fig* un asunto caliente; **the real ~s** las cuestiones de fondo; **the point at** ~ el punto en cuestión; **to force an** ~ forzar una decisión; **to make an ~ of sth** convertir algo en un problema; **at** ~ a debate **2.** PUBL (*copy*) número *m;* **latest** ~ último número **3.** FIN, ECON (*of shares, stamps*) emisión *f;* (*of cheques*) expedición *f* **4.** *form* (*offspring, children*) descendencia *f* **II.** *vt* emitir; (*passport*) expedir; (*patent*) conceder; (*newsletter*) publicar; (*ultimatum*) presentar; **to ~ a statement** hacer una declaración; **to ~ a call for sth** hacer un llamamiento para algo **III.** *vi* **to ~ from** (*born out of*) surgir de; (*come out of*) provenir de
isthmus ['ɪsməs] <-es> *n* istmo *m*
it [ɪt] **I.** *pron dem* la, le, lo (*in many cases, 'it' is omitted when referring to information already known*); **who was ~?** ¿quién era?; **~'s in my bag** está en mi bolso; **~'s Paul who did that** fue Paul quien lo hizo; **~ was in London that ...** fue en Londres donde... **II.** *pron pers* **1.** él, ella, ello; *direct object:* lo, la; *indirect object:* le; **where is your pencil/card? ~ is on my desk** ¿en dónde está tu lápiz/tarjeta? Está encima de mi escritorio; **~ went off badly** aquello fue mal; **your card? I took ~** ¿tu tarjeta? La cogí yo; **~'s your cat, give ~ something to eat** es tu gato, dale algo de comer; **I'm afraid of ~** le tengo miedo; **I fell into ~** caí dentro **2.** (*time*) **what time is ~?** ¿qué hora es? **3.** (*weather*) **~'s cold** hace frío; **~'s snowing** está nevando **4.** (*distance*) **~'s 10 km to the town** hay 10 km hasta el pueblo **5.** (*empty subject*) **~ seems that ...** parece que... **6.** (*passive subject*) **~ is said/hoped that ...** se dice/espera que...
IT [ˌaɪ'tiː] *n no pl* INFOR *abbr of* **Information Technology** tecnología *f* de la información
ITA *n abbr of* **Independent Television Authority** ITA *f*
Italian [ɪ'tæljən] **I.** *adj* italiano, -a **II.** *n* **1.** (*person*) italiano, -a *m, f* **2.** LING italiano *m*
italic [ɪ'tælɪk] *adj* (*of Italy*) itálico, -a
italicise *vt Aus, Brit,* **italicize** [ɪ'tælɪsaɪz] *vt Am* poner en cursiva
italics [ɪ'tælɪks] *npl* cursiva *f;* **in** ~ en cursiva
Italy ['ɪtəli, *Am:* 'ɪt̬-] *n* Italia *f*
itch [ɪtʃ] **I.** *vi* **1.** MED picar **2.** *fig, inf* **to ~ to do sth** morirse por hacer algo **II.** *n* **1.** MED comezón *f,* rasquiña *f Arg* **2.** *fig, inf* inmensas ganas *fpl*
itchy ['ɪtʃi] <-ier, -iest> *adj* que escuece; **my arm feels ~** siento picazón en el brazo; **I've got an ~ feeling** tengo un sentimiento inquietante
item ['aɪtəm, *Am:* -t̬əm] *n* **1.** (*thing*) artículo *m,* objeto *m;* **luxury ~** artículo de lujo; **~ of clothing** prenda *f* de vestir **2.** (*topic*) asunto *m;* **~ on the agenda** asunto a tratar; **~ by ~** punto por punto **3.** COM partida *f;* **~ of expenditure** partida de gasto **4.** PUBL noticia *f;* **news ~** noticia *f* **5.** *inf* (*couple*) pareja *f*
itemise *vt Brit, Aus,* **itemize** ['aɪtəmaɪz] *vt Am* detallar
itinerant [aɪ'tɪnərənt] **I.** *n* viajante *mf* **II.** *adj* intinerante; (*merchant*) ambulante
itinerary [aɪ'tɪnərəri, *Am:* -ərer-] <-ies> *n* itinerario *m*
it'll ['ɪtl, *Am:* 'ɪt̬l] = **it will**
ITN ['aɪtiː'en] *n Brit abbr of* **Independent Television News** ITN *f* (*sociedad por acciones creada y financiada por el conjunto de empresas de televisión que integran la cadena ITV*)
its [ɪts] *adj pos* su; **~ colour/weight** su color/peso; **~ mountains** sus montañas; **the cat hurt ~ head** el gato se lastimó la cabeza
it's [ɪts] **1.** = **it is 2.** = **it has**
itself [ɪt'self] *pron reflexive* él mismo, ella misma, ello mismo; *direct, indirect object:* se; *after prep:* sí mismo, -a; **the place ~** el sitio en sí; **in ~** en sí
ITV ['aɪtiː'viː] *n Brit abbr of* **Independent Television** ITV *f* (*cadena de televisión británica*)
IUD [ˌaɪjuː'diː] *n abbr of* **intrauterine device** DIU *m*

i.v. *abbr of* **intravenous** i.v.
I've [aɪv] = I have *s.* **have**
IVF [ˌaɪviːˈef] *n* MED *abbr of* **in vitro fertilisation** fecundación *f* in vitro
ivory [ˈaɪvəri] <-ies> *n* **1.** *no pl* marfil *m* **2.** *pl, inf* MUS teclas *fpl* (del piano); **to tickle the ivories** *fig* tocar el piano **3.** *pl, inf* ANAT dientes *mpl*
ivory carving *n* talla *f* en marfil **Ivory Coast** *n* Costa *f* de Marfil **ivory tower** *n* *fig* torre *f* de marfil **ivory trading** *n no pl* tráfico *m* de marfil
ivy [ˈaɪvi] <-ies> *n* hiedra *f*

J

J, j [dʒeɪ] *n, n* J, j *f;* ~ **for Jack** *Brit,* ~ **for Jig** *Am* J de Juan
J *n* PHYS *abbr of* **joule** julio *m*
jab [dʒæb] **I.** *n* **1.** (*with a pin*) pinchazo *m;* (*with the elbow*) codazo *m* **2.** (*in boxing*) (golpe *m*) corto *m* **3.** *Brit, Aus, inf* (*injection*) inyección *f* **II.** <-bb-> *vt* **to ~ a needle in sth** pinchar algo con una aguja; **to ~ a finger at sth** señalar algo con el dedo; **to ~ sb in the eye with sth** dar a alguien en el ojo con algo **III.** <-bb-> *vi* **to ~ at sb/sth** (**with sth**) dar a alguien/algo (con algo); **he ~bed at the paragraph with his pen** señaló el párrafo con su bolígrafo
jabber [ˈdʒæbəʳ, *Am:* -ɚ] *vi, vt* farfullar
jabbering *n* farfulla *f*
jack [dʒæk] *n* **1.** AUTO gato *m* **2.** (*in cards*) jota *f;* (*in a Spanish pack*) sota *f* **3.** (*in bowls*) boliche *m*
◆**jack in** *vt Brit, inf* dejar
◆**jack up** *vt* **1.** (*object*) levantar **2.** *inf* (*prices*) aumentar
Jack [dʒæk] *n* **every man** ~ *inf* cada quisque; **before you could say ~ Robinson** en un abrir y cerrar de ojos, en un decir Jesús
jackal [ˈdʒækɔːl, *Am:* -əl] *n* **1.** ZOOL chacal *m* **2.** *pej, inf* (*person*) carroñero, -a *m, f*
jackass [ˈdʒækæs] *n* **1.** ZOOL asno *m* **2.** *pej, inf* (*idiot*) burro, -a *m, f*
jackboot [ˈdʒækbuːt] *n* bota *f* alta ►**under the ~** bajo el yugo
jackdaw [ˈdʒækdɔː, *Am:* -dɑː] *n* grajilla *f*
jacket [ˈdʒækɪt] *n* **1.** (*short coat*) chaqueta *f,* percha *f AmC,* chapona *f RíoPl,* cuácara *f Chile* **2.** (*of a book*) sobrecubierta *f;* (*of a record*) funda *f*
jacket potato *n* patata *f* asada (*con piel*)
jack-in-the-box [ˈdʒækɪnðəbɒks, *Am:* -bɑːks] <-xes> *n* caja *f* de sorpresas
jackknife [ˈdʒæknaɪf] **I.** *n* **1.** (*knife*) navaja *f* **2.** (*dive*) salto *m* de carpa **II.** *vi* plegarse
jack-o'-lantern [ˈdʒækəʊˌlæntən, *Am:* -əˌlæntɚn] *n Am: lámpara hecha con una calabaza ahuecada*
jack plug *n Brit* enchufe *m* de clavija
jackpot [ˈdʒækpɒt, *Am:* -pɑːt] *n* (premio *m*) gordo *m* ►**she's hit the ~** *inf* le ha tocado el gordo
Jacuzzi® [dʒəˈkuːzi] *n* jacuzzi® *m*
jade [dʒeɪd] *no pl n* **1.** (*precious green stone*) jade *m* **2.** (*colour*) verde *m* jade
jaded [ˈdʒeɪdɪd] *adj* **to be ~ with sth** estar harto de algo
jagged [ˈdʒægɪd] *adj* irregular; (*coastline, rocks*) recortado, -a; (*cut, tear*) desigual
jaggy [ˈdʒægi] <-ier, -iest> *adj* irregular
jaguar [ˈdʒægjʊəʳ, *Am:* ˈdʒægwɑːr] *n* jaguar *m*
jail [dʒeɪl] **I.** *n* cárcel *f,* prisión *f;* **to be in ~** (**for sth**) estar en la cárcel (por algo); **to put sb in ~** encarcelar a alguien **II.** *vt* encarcelar; **she was ~ed for life** la condenaron a cadena perpetua
jailbird [ˈdʒeɪlbɜːd, *Am:* -bɜːrd] *n inf* delincuente *mf* habitual **jailbreak** *n* fuga *f*
jailer *n,* **jailor** [ˈdʒeɪləʳ, *Am:* -lɚ] *n* carcelero, -a *m, f*
jalopy [dʒəˈlɒpi, *Am:* -ˈlɑːpi] *n inf* cacharro *m*
jam¹ [dʒæm] *n* GASTR mermelada *f* ►~ **tomorrow** promesas y más promesas
jam² [dʒæm] **I.** *n* **1.** *inf* (*awkward situation*) aprieto *m;* **to get into a ~** meterse en un lío **2.** *no pl* (*crowd*) gentío *m* **3.** AUTO atasco *m;* **paper ~** INFOR atasco de papel **II.** <-mm-> *vt* **1.** (*cause to become stuck*) atascar; (*door*) obstruir; **to ~ sth into sth** embutir algo en algo **2.** (*wheel*) trabar **3.** RADIO interferir **III.** <-mm-> *vi* **1.** (*become stuck*) atrancarse; (*brakes*) bloquearse; (*rifle*) encasquillarse **2.** (*play music*) tocar, improvisar
Jamaica [dʒəˈmeɪkə] *n* Jamaica *f*
Jamaican **I.** *adj* jamaicano, -a **II.** *n* jamaicano, -a *m, f*
jamb [dʒæm] *n* jamba *f*
jamboree [ˌdʒæmbəˈriː] *n* **1.** (*celebration*) juerga *f* **2.** (*scouts' meeting*) congreso *m* de exploradores
jam jar *n* bote *m* para mermelada
jammy [ˈdʒæmi] <-ier, -iest> *adj* **1.** (*covered with jam*) cubierto, -a de mermelada **2.** *Brit, inf* (*lucky*) afortunado, -a; **what a ~ goal!** ¡qué potra de gol! **3.** *Brit, inf* (*easy*) chupado
jam-packed [ˌdʒæmˈpækt] *adj inf* **to be ~** (**with sth**) estar repleto (de algo); **the streets were ~ with people** las calles estaban atestadas de gente
jam session *n inf* jam session *f*
jangle [ˈdʒæŋgl] **I.** *vt* (*coins, keys*) hacer tintinear **II.** *vi* tintinear; **to make sb's nerves ~** crispar los nervios a alguien **III.** *n no pl* sonido *m* metálico
janitor [ˈdʒænɪtəʳ, *Am:* -ət̬ɚ] *n Am, Scot* conserje *mf*
January [ˈdʒænjuəri, *Am:* -jueri] <-ies> *n*

J

enero *m; s. a.* **April**

Jap [dʒæp] *abbr of* **Japanese I.** *n pej, inf* japo *m* **II.** *adj pej, inf* japonés, -esa

japan [dʒəˈpæn] *n no pl* laca *f* japonesa

Japan [dʒəˈpæn] *n* Japón *m*

Japanese [ˌdʒæpəˈniːz] **I.** *adj* japonés, -esa **II.** *n* **1.** (*person*) japonés, -esa *m, f* **2.** *no pl* LING japonés *m*

jar¹ [dʒɑːʳ, *Am:* dʒɑːr] *n* **1.** (*container*) tarro *m* **2.** *inf* (*drink*) **to have a ~** tomar una cerveza

jar² [dʒɑːʳ, *Am:* dʒɑːr] **I.** <-rr-> *vt* (*shake*) sacudir **II.** <-rr-> *vi* **1.** (*cause unpleasant feelings*) **to ~ on sb** crispar los nervios a alguien **2.** (*make unpleasant sound*) chirriar **3.** (*clash: colours, design*) desentonar; **to ~ on the eye** hacer daño a la vista **III.** *n* **1.** (*shake*) sacudida *f* **2.** (*shock*) golpe *m*

jargon [ˈdʒɑːgən, *Am:* ˈdʒɑːr-] *n no pl* jerga *f*

jasmine [ˈdʒæsmɪn] *n no pl* jazmín *m*

jaundice [ˈdʒɔːndɪs, *Am:* ˈdʒɑːn-] *n no pl* MED ictericia *f*

jaundiced [ˈdʒɔːndɪst, *Am:* ˈdʒɑːn-] *adj* **1.** MED ictérico, -a **2.** (*bitter*) negativo, -a; **to look on sth with a ~ eye** ver algo con cierta dosis de cinismo

jaunt [dʒɔːnt, *Am:* dʒɑːnt] *n* excursión *f;* **to go on a ~** salir de excursión

jaunty [ˈdʒɔːnti, *Am:* ˈdʒɑːnt̬i] <-ier, -iest> *adj* desenfadado, -a; **~ step** paso *m* desenvuelto

Java [ˈdʒɑːvə] *n* Java *f*

javelin [ˈdʒævlɪn] *n* **1.** (*spear*) jabalina *f* **2.** *no pl* (*competition*) lanzamiento *m* de jabalina

jaw [dʒɔː, *Am:* dʒɑː] **I.** *n* **1.** ANAT mandíbula *f* **2.** *pl* (*mouth*) boca *f; fig* fauces *fpl* **3.** *pl* TECH mordazas *fpl* ►**to have a ~** *inf* mantener una charla **II.** *vi inf* darle a la sinhueso; **to ~ away to sb** cotorrear con alguien

jawbone [ˈdʒɔːbəʊn, *Am:* ˈdʒɑː-] *n* maxilar *m*

jawbreaker [ˈdʒɔːbreɪkə, *Am:* ˈdʒɑː-] *n* **1.** *Am, Aus* (*sweet*) caramelo *m* duro **2.** *inf* (*tongue twister*) trabalenguas *m inv*

jay [dʒeɪ] *n* arrendajo *m*

jaywalk [ˈdʒeɪwɔːk, *Am:* -wɑːk] *vi* cruzar la calzada imprudentemente

jaywalker [ˈdʒeɪwɔːkəʳ, *Am:* -wɑːkɚ] *n* peatón *m* imprudente

jaywalking *n no pl* cruce *m* de calzada imprudente

jazz [dʒæz] *n no pl* jazz *m;* **~ band/club** grupo *m*/club *m* de jazz ►**and all that ~** *inf* y todo ese rollo

◆**jazz up** *vt inf* animar

jazzy [ˈdʒæzi] <-ier, -iest> *adj* **1.** MUS de jazz **2.** *inf* (*flashy*) llamativo, -a

JCB® [ˌdʒeɪsiːˈbiː] *n Brit: máquina usada para cavar y mover tierra*

jealous [ˈdʒeləs] *adj* **1.** (*envious*) envidioso, -a; **to be ~ of sb** tener celos de alguien; **to feel/be ~** sentir/tener envidia **2.** (*fiercely protective*) celoso, -a; **to be ~ of sth** ser celoso de algo

jealousy [ˈdʒeləsi] <-ies> *n* **1.** (*possessiveness*) celos *mpl;* **to be consumed by ~** estar consumido por los celos **2.** *no pl* (*envy*) envidia *f*

jeans [dʒiːnz] *npl* (pantalones *mpl*) vaqueros *mpl;* **a pair of ~** unos (pantalones) vaqueros

jeep [dʒiːp] *n* jeep *m*

jeer [dʒɪəʳ, *Am:* dʒɪr] **I.** *vt* abuchear **II.** *vi* mofarse; **to ~ at sb** burlarse de alguien **III.** *n* burla *f*

Jehovah [dʒɪˈhəʊvə, *Am:* -ˈhoʊ-] *n no pl* Jehová; **~'s Witness** testigo *m* de Jehová

jell [dʒel] *vi s.* **gel**

jellied *adj* en gelatina; **~ eels** anguilas *fpl* en gelatina

jelly [ˈdʒeli] <-ies> *n* **1.** (*soft transparent substance*) gelatina *f* **2.** *Brit, Aus* (*dessert*) gelatina *f* (*con sabor a frutas*) **3.** (*jam*) mermelada *f* ►**my legs turned to ~** *inf* se me pusieron las piernas como un flan

jellybaby *n* caramelo *m* de goma (*en forma de muñeco*) **jellybean** *n* caramelo *m* de goma (*en forma de judía*) **jellyfish** <-es> *n* medusa *f*

jemmy [ˈdʒemi] <-ies> *n Aus, Brit* palanqueta *f*

jeopardise *vt,* **jeopardize** [ˈdʒepədaɪz, *Am:* ˈ-ɚ-] *vt* poner en peligro

jeopardy [ˈdʒepədi, *Am:* ˈ-ɚ-] *n no pl* peligro *m;* **to put sth in ~** poner algo en peligro

jerk [dʒɜːk, *Am:* dʒɜːrk] **I.** *n* **1.** (*jolt*) sacudida *f;* **with a ~** con un sobresalto **2.** (*movement*) tirón *m;* **to give sth a ~** tirar de algo **3.** *pej, inf* (*person*) estúpido, -a *m, f;* **to feel such a ~** sentirse como un gilipollas **II.** *vi* sacudirse; **to ~ to a halt** detenerse con una sacudida **III.** *vt* **1.** (*shake*) sacudir **2.** (*pull*) tirar bruscamente de

◆**jerk off** *vi vulg* hacerse una paja

jerkin [ˈdʒɜːkɪn, *Am:* ˈdʒɜːr-] *n* chaleco *m*

jerky [ˈdʒɜːki, *Am:* ˈdʒɜːr-] **I.** <-ier, -iest> *adj* (*nervous*) nervioso, -a; (*uneven*) irregular; (*sound, voice*) entrecortado, -a **II.** *n no pl, Am* **beef ~** cecina *f*

jerry-built [ˈdʒerɪˌbɪlt] *adj* mal construido, -a

jerrycan [ˈdʒerɪkæn] *n* bidón *m*

jersey [ˈdʒɜːzi, *Am:* ˈdʒɜːr-] *n* **1.** (*garment*) jersey *m* **2.** (*sports shirt*) camiseta *f* **3.** *no pl* (*cloth*) tejido *m* de punto **4.** (*type of cow*) Jersey *f* (*raza de ganado vacuno*)

jest [dʒest] **I.** *n form* chanza *f;* **to say sth in ~** decir algo en broma ►**many a true word is spoken in ~** *prov* bromeando, bromeando, amargas verdades se van soltando *prov* **II.** *vi form* bromear; **to ~ about sth** burlarse de algo

jester [ˈdʒestəʳ, *Am:* -tɚ] *n* HIST bufón *m*

jesting **I.** *n no pl* gracia *f* **II.** *adj* gracioso, -a

Jesuit [ˈdʒezjʊɪt] **I.** *n* jesuita *m* **II.** *adj* jesuita

Jesuitical [ˌdʒezjʊˈɪtɪkl] *adj* jesuítico, -a

Jesus [ˈdʒiːzəs] **I.** Jesús **II.** *interj inf* ¡por Dios!, ¡híjole! *AmL*

Jesus Christ *n* Jesucristo *m*

jet[1] [dʒet] **I.** *n* **1.** (*aircraft*) avión *m* a reacción, jet *m* **2.** (*stream*) chorro *m* **3.** (*nozzle*) surtidor *m* **II.** <-tt-> *vi* volar; **to ~ off** viajar en avión

jet[2] [dʒet] *n no pl* (*stone*) azabache *m*

jet-black *adj* negro azabache; **~ eyes/hair** ojos/pelo de azabache

jet engine *n* motor *m* a reacción **jet fighter** *n* caza *m* a reacción **jetfoil** *n* hidroala *f* a reacción **jet lag** *n no pl* desfase *m* horario, jet lag *m* **jet plane** *n* avión *m* a reacción **jet-propelled** *adj* a reacción **jet propulsion** *n no pl* propulsión *m* a chorro

jetsam [ˈdʒetsəm] *n no pl s.* **flotsam**

jet set *n inf* **the ~** la jet-set

jettison [ˈdʒetɪsən, *Am:* ˈdʒet̬ə-] *vt* **1.** NAUT echar al mar **2.** (*get rid of: person*) deshacerse de; (*plan*) echar por la borda

jetty [ˈdʒeti, *Am:* ˈdʒet̬-] *n* embarcadero *m*

Jew [dʒuː] *n* judío, -a *m, f*

jewel [ˈdʒuːəl] *n* **1.** (*piece of jewellery*) *a. fig* joya *f;* (*precious stone*) piedra *f* preciosa **2.** (*watch part*) rubí *m*

jeweler *n Am,* **jeweller** [ˈdʒuːələʳ, *Am:* -lɚ] *n* joyero, -a *m, f;* **~'s (shop)** joyería *f*

jewellery *n,* **jewelry** [ˈdʒuːəlri] *n Am no pl* joyas *fpl;* **a piece of ~** una joya

Jewess [ˈdʒuːes, *Am:* -ɪs] *n* judía *f*

Jewish [ˈdʒuːɪʃ] *adj* judío, -a

Jewry [ˈdʒuːri] *n no pl, form* los judíos

Jew's harp *n* birimbao *m*

jib[1] [dʒɪb] *n* (*sail*) foque *m*

jib[2] [dʒɪb] *n* (*of a crane*) brazo *m*

jib[3] [dʒɪb] <-bb-> *vi* **to ~ at doing sth** resistirse a hacer algo

jibe [dʒaɪb] **I.** *n* burla *f;* **to make a ~** hacer una broma **II.** *vi* **to ~ at sth/sb** burlarse de algo/alguien

jiffy [ˈdʒɪfi] *n no pl, inf* **in a ~** en un santiamén

jig [dʒɪg] **I.** <-gg-> *vi* **1.** (*move around*) brincar **2.** (*dance a jig*) bailar la giga **II.** *n* **1.** (*dance*) giga *f* **2.** TECH (*device*) plantilla *f* de guía

jigger [ˈdʒɪgəʳ, *Am:* -ɚ] **I.** *n* medida *f* (*para bebidas alcohólicas*) **II.** *vt Am* (*rearrange*) reorganizar

jiggered [ˈdʒɪgəd, *Am:* -ɚd] *adj* **1.** *Aus, Brit, inf* (*tired*) molido, -a **2.** *Brit, inf* (*broken*) roto, -a

jiggery-pokery [ˌdʒɪgəriˈpəʊkəri, *Am:* -ˈpoʊ-] *n no pl, inf* chanchullos *mpl*

jiggle [ˈdʒɪgl] **I.** *vt* mover; **to ~ sth about** menear algo **II.** *vi* moverse **III.** *n* meneo *m*

jigsaw [ˈdʒɪgsɔː, *Am:* -sɑː] *n* **1.** (*tool*) sierra *f* de vaivén **2.** (*puzzle*) puzzle *m,* rompecabezas *m inv*

jilt [dʒɪlt] *vt* dejar plantado

Jim Crow [ˌdʒɪmˈkrəʊ, *Am:* -ˈkroʊ] *n no pl, Am, pej* racista *mf*

jimjams [ˈdʒɪmdʒæmz] *npl* **1.** *Brit, inf* (*pyjamas*) pijama *m* **2.** *inf* (*shaking*) tembleque *m*

jimmy [ˈdʒɪmi] *n Am* palanqueta *f*

jingle [ˈdʒɪŋgl] **I.** *vt* hacer tintinear **II.** *vi* tintinear **III.** *n* **1.** *no pl* (*noise*) tintineo *m* **2.** (*in advertisments*) jingle *m*

jingoism [ˈdʒɪŋgəʊɪzəm, *Am:* -goʊ-] *n no pl, pej* patriotería *f*

jingoistic [ˌdʒɪŋgəʊˈɪstɪk, *Am:* -goʊˈ-] *adj pej* patriotero, -a

jinx [dʒɪŋks] **I.** *n no pl* gafe *f;* **there's a ~ on this computer** este ordenador está gafado; **to put a ~ on sb/sth** echar una maldición a alguien/algo **II.** *vt* gafar

jitterbug [ˈdʒɪtəbʌg, *Am:* ˈdʒɪt̬ɚ-] **I.** *n* **1.** (*dance*) jitterbug *m* (*baile muy movido*) **2.** (*nervous person*) persona *f* nerviosa **II.** <-gg-> *vi* bailar el jitterbug

jitters [ˈdʒɪtəz, *Am:* ˈdʒɪt̬ɚz] *npl* **1.** *inf* (*nervousness*) nervios *mpl;* **he got the ~** le entró el canguelo **2.** (*shaking*) tembleque *m*

jittery [ˈdʒɪtəri, *Am:* ˈdʒɪt̬-] <-ier, -iest> *adj inf* nervioso, -a; **he felt ~** le dió el tembleque; **he got ~** le entró el canguelo

jive [dʒaɪv] **I.** *n* swing *m* **II.** *vi* bailar el swing

job [dʒɒb, *Am:* dʒɑːb] *n* **1.** (*piece of work, employment*) trabajo *m;* **to make a good/bad ~ of sth** hacer algo bien/mal; **to apply for a ~** presentarse para un trabajo **2.** *no pl* (*duty*) deber *m;* **to do one's ~** cumplir con su deber; **it's not her job** no es asunto suyo **3.** *no pl* (*problem*) tarea *f* difícil; **it's quite a ~ doing that** resulta bastante difícil hacer eso; **I had a ~ doing it** me costó trabajo ►**it's a good ~ that ...** menos mal que...; **to be just the ~** *inf* venir como anillo al dedo; **to do a ~ on sb** *inf* hacer una putada a alguien *vulg*

job advertisement *n* anuncio *m* de trabajo **job analysis** *n* análisis *m inv* del puesto **job application** *n* demanda *f* de empleo

jobber [ˈdʒɒbəʳ, *Am:* ˈdʒɑːbɚ] *n Am* (*wholesaler*) intermediario, -a *m, f*

job centre *n Brit* oficina *f* de empleo **job counsellor** *n* orientador(a) *m(f)* laboral **job creation** *n no pl* creación *f* de empleo **job cuts** *npl* recortes *mpl* laborales **job description** *n* descripción *f* del puesto **job interview** *n* entrevista *f* de trabajo

jobless [ˈdʒɒblɪs, *Am:* ˈdʒɑːb-] **I.** *adj* desocupado, -a **II.** *npl* **the ~** los parados *mpl;* **~ figures** cifras *fpl* de paro

job lot *n* lote *m*

job market *n* mercado *m* de trabajo **job rating** *n* evaluación *f* del lugar de trabajo **job-seeker** *n* demandante *mf* de empleo **job sharing** *n no pl, Brit* jobsharing *m* **job title** *n* título *m* de un puesto de trabajo

Jock [dʒɒk, *Am:* dʒɑːk] *n Brit, inf* escocés *m*

jockey [ˈdʒɒki, *Am:* ˈdʒɑːki] **I.** *n* jockey *mf* **II.** *vi* **to ~ for sth** competir por algo; **to ~ for position** disputarse un puesto

jocose [dʒəʊˈkəʊs, *Am:* dʒoʊˈkoʊs] *adj form* jocoso, -a

jocular [ˈdʒɒkjʊləʳ, *Am:* ˈdʒɑːkjəlɚ] *adj* jocoso, -a

jocund [ˈdʒɒkənd, *Am:* ˈdʒɑːkənd] *adj* jocundo, -a

jodhpurs ['dʒɒdpəz, *Am:* 'dʒɑːdpɚz] *npl* pantalones *mpl* de montar

Joe Bloggs [ˌdʒəʊ'blɒgz, *Am:* ˌdʒoʊ-'blɑːgz] *n Brit, inf* Perico *m* de los Palotes

jog [dʒɒg, *Am:* dʒɑːg] **I.** *n no pl* **1.** (*run*) trote *m;* **to go for a ~** hacer footing **2.** (*knock*) golpe *m;* **to give sth a ~** empujar algo ►**to give sb's memory a ~** refrescar la memoria de alguien **II.** <-gg-> *vi* correr **III.** <-gg-> *vt* empujar; **to ~ sb's elbow** dar a alguien en el codo ►**to ~ sb's memory** refrescar la memoria de alguien

◆**jog along** *vi inf* ir tirando

jogger ['dʒɒgəʳ, *Am:* 'dʒɑːgɚ] *n* persona *f* que hace footing

jogging ['dʒɒgɪŋ, *Am:* 'dʒɑːgɪŋ] *n no pl* footing *m;* **to go (out) ~** hacer footing

joggle ['dʒɒgl, *Am:* 'dʒɑːgl] **I.** *vt* mover **II.** *n* meneo *m*

john [dʒɒn, *Am:* dʒɑːn] *n Am, Aus, inf* (*toilet*) váter *m*

John Bull *n no pl, inf* John Bull *m* (*personificación de todo lo inglés*)

johnnie *n,* **johnny** ['dʒɒni, *Am:* 'dʒɑːni] *n Brit, inf* (*condom*) goma *f*

join [dʒɔɪn] **I.** *vt* **1.** (*connect*) juntar, unir; **to ~ hands** tomarse de la mano; **to ~ sb (together) in marriage** *form* unir a alguien en matrimonio **2.** (*come together with sb*) reunirse [*o* juntarse] con; **they'll ~ us after dinner** vendrán después de cenar **3.** (*become member of: club*) hacerse miembro de; (*society*) ingresar en; (*army*) alistarse en; **to ~ the queue** [*o* **line** *Am*] ponerse en la cola **4.** (*begin to work with*) incorporarse a **II.** *vi* **1.** (*unite*) unirse; **to ~ with sb in doing sth** sumarse a alguien para hacer algo **2.** (*become member*) hacerse socio **III.** *n* unión *f,* juntura *f*

joiner ['dʒɔɪnəʳ, *Am:* -nɚ] *n* carpintero, -a *m, f*

joinery ['dʒɔɪnəri] *n no pl* carpintería *f*

joint [dʒɔɪnt] **I.** *adj* conjunto, -a **II.** *n* **1.** (*connection*) unión *f,* juntura *f* **2.** ANAT articulación *f;* **out of ~** dislocado; **to come out of ~** dislocarse **3.** TECH conexión **4.** BOT nudo *m* **5.** (*meat*) asado *m* **6.** *inf* (*marihuana*) porro *m*

joint account *n* cuenta *f* conjunta **joint committee** *n* comisión *f* mixta **joint debtor** *n* codeudor(a) *m(f)*

jointed *adj* articulado, -a

joint effort *n* trabajo *m* de equipo

jointly *adv* conjuntamente

joint owner *n* copropietario, -a *m, f* **joint ownership** *n no pl* copropiedad *f* **joint property** *n* propiedad comunitaria *f*

joint stock *n* capital *m* social **joint-stock company** *n* sociedad *f* anónima

joint venture *n* empresa *f* conjunta

joist [dʒɔɪst] *n* viga *f*

joke [dʒəʊk, *Am:* dʒoʊk] **I.** *n* **1.** (*amusing story*) chiste *m;* (*trick, remark*) broma *f;* **to get a ~** captar una humorada; **to get beyond a ~** pasarse de castaño oscuro *inf;* **to make a ~** gastar una broma; **to not be able to take a ~** no aceptar una broma; **to do sth for a ~** hacer algo en broma; **to play a ~ on sb** gastar una broma a alguien **2.** *inf* (*easy thing*) **to be no ~** no ser cosa de broma **3.** *no pl, inf* (*ridiculous thing or person*) ridiculez *f;* **what a ~!** ¡qué farsa! ►**the ~ was on me** me salió el tiro por la culata *inf* **II.** *vi* bromear; **to ~ about sth** hacer bromas sobre algo; **you must be ~ing!** ¿lo dices en serio?

joker ['dʒəʊkəʳ, *Am:* 'dʒoʊkɚ] *n* **1.** (*one who jokes*) bromista *mf* **2.** *inf* (*annoying person*) idiota *m* **3.** (*playing card*) comodín *m* ►**to be the ~ in the pack** ser la gran incógnita

joking **I.** *adj* jocoso, -a **II.** *n no pl* bromas *fpl*

jokingly *adv* en broma

jollification [ˌdʒɒlɪfɪ'keɪʃən, *Am:* ˌdʒɑːlə-] *n inf* **1.** *no pl* (*merrymaking*) regocijo *m* **2.** *pl* (*celebratory activities*) festividades *fpl*

jollity ['dʒɒləti, *Am:* 'dʒɑːləṭi] *n no pl* jovialidad *f*

jolly ['dʒɒli, *Am:* 'dʒɑːli] **I.** <-ier, -iest> *adj* **1.** (*happy*) alegre **2.** (*enjoyable*) agradable **II.** *adv Brit, inf* muy; **~ good** estupendo **2.** de verdad; **you'll ~ °well have to!** ¡no te queda más remedio! **III.** *vt* **to ~ sb into doing sth** convencer a alguien para que haga algo; **to ~ sb along** animar a alguien

jolt [dʒəʊlt, *Am:* dʒoʊlt] **I.** *n* **1.** (*sudden jerk*) sacudida *f* **2.** (*shock*) impresión *f* **II.** *vt* **1.** (*jerk*) sacudir **2.** (*shock*) sobresaltar **III.** *vi* dar una sacudida; (*vehicle*) traquetear

Jordan ['dʒɔːdn, *Am:* 'dʒɔːr-] *n* **1.** (*country*) Jordania *f* **2.** (*river*) Jordán *m*

Jordanian [dʒɔː'deɪnɪən, *Am:* dʒɔːr-] **I.** *adj* jordano, -a **II.** *n* jordano, -a *m, f*

josh [dʒɒʃ, *Am:* dʒɑːʃ] *vt, vi inf* tomar el pelo a

joss stick ['dʒɒsˌstɪk, *Am:* 'dʒɑːsˌstɪk] *n* pebete *m*

jostle ['dʒɒsl, *Am:* 'dʒɑːsl] **I.** *vt* empujar **II.** *vi* **1.** (*push*) empujarse **2.** (*compete*) **to ~ for sth** disputarse algo

jot [dʒɒt, *Am:* dʒɑːt] **I.** <-tt-> *vt* **to ~ sth down** apuntar algo **II.** *n no pl* **there's not a ~ of truth in it** eso no tiene ni pizca de verdad

jotter ['dʒɒtəʳ, *Am:* 'dʒɑːtɚ] *n Aus, Brit* cuaderno *m*

jottings *npl* apuntes *mpl*

joule [dʒuːl] *n* PHYS julio *m*

journal ['dʒɜːnəl, *Am:* 'dʒɜːr-] *n* **1.** (*periodical*) revista *f* especializada **2.** (*diary*) diario *m*

journalism ['dʒɜːnlɪzəm, *Am:* 'dʒɜːr-] *n no pl* periodismo *m,* diarismo *m AmL*

journalist ['dʒɜːnlɪst, *Am:* 'dʒɜːr-] *n* periodista *mf*

journalistic [ˌdʒɜːnə'lɪstɪk, *Am:* ˌdʒɜːr-] *adj* periodístico, -a

journey ['dʒɜːni, *Am:* 'dʒɜːr-] **I.** *n* viaje *m* **II.** *vi liter* viajar

journeyman ['dʒɜːnɪmən, *Am:* 'dʒɜːr-] <-men> *n* trabajador *m* calificado

joust [dʒaʊst] **I.** *vi* justar **II.** *n* justa *f*

jovial ['dʒəʊvɪəl, *Am:* 'dʒoʊ-] *adj* jovial

joviality [ˌdʒəʊvɪ'æləti, *Am:* ˌdʒoʊvɪ'æləṭi]

n no pl jovialidad *f*
jowl [dʒaʊl] *n* quijada *f*
joy [dʒɔɪ] *n* **1.** (*gladness*) gozo *m;* **to jump for ~** saltar de alegría **2.** (*cause of joy*) placer *m* **3.** *no pl, Brit, inf* (*success*) **did you have any ~?** ¿tuviste éxito?
joyful ['dʒɔɪfəl] *adj* feliz
joyless ['dʒɔɪləs] *adj* sin alegría; (*face*) triste
joyous ['dʒɔɪəs] *adj liter* de júbilo
joyride ['dʒɔɪraɪd] *n paseo en un coche robado*
joystick ['dʒɔɪstɪk] *n* **1.** AVIAT palanca *f* de mando **2.** INFOR joystick *m*
JP [ˌdʒeɪ'piː] *Brit abbr of* **Justice of the Peace** Juez *mf* de Paz
Jr *abbr of* **Junior** Jr.
jt *abbr of* **joint** adjunto, -a
jubilant ['dʒuːbɪlənt] *adj* jubiloso, -a; (*crowd*) exultante
jubilation [ˌdʒuːbɪ'leɪʃən] *n no pl* júbilo *m*
jubilee ['dʒuːbɪliː] *n* **1.** (*anniversary*) aniversario *m* **2.** REL jubileo *m*
Judaism ['dʒuːdeɪɪzəm] *n no pl* judaísmo *m*
judder ['dʒʌdəʳ, *Am:* -ɚ] *Aus, Brit* **I.** *vi* trepidar **II.** *n no pl* sacudida *f*
judge [dʒʌdʒ] **I.** *n* **1.** LAW juez *mf* **2.** (*referee*) árbitro *m;* (*in a jury*) miembro *m* del jurado; **panel of ~s** jurado *m* **II.** *vi a.* LAW juzgar; (*give one's opinion*) opinar **III.** *vt* **1.** *a.* LAW juzgar; (*question*) decidir; (*assess*) valorar; (*consider*) considerar; **to ~ that ...** opinar que... **2.** (*as a referee*) arbitrar; (*in a jury*) actuar como miembro del jurado de
judg(e)ment ['dʒʌdʒmənt] *n* **1.** LAW fallo *m* **2.** (*opinion*) opinión *f* **3.** (*discernment*) criterio *m*
judg(e)mental [dʒʌdʒ'mentəl, *Am:* -t̬əl] *adj* sentencioso, -a
judicature ['dʒuːdɪkətʃəʳ, *Am:* -tʃɚ] *n no pl* judicatura *f*
judicial [dʒuː'dɪʃl] *adj* judicial
judiciary [dʒuː'dɪʃəri, *Am:* -ier-] *n no pl, form* poder *m* judicial
judicious [dʒuː'dɪʃəs] *adj form* acertado, -a
judo ['dʒuːdəʊ, *Am:* -doʊ] *n no pl* judo *m*
jug [dʒʌg] *n* **1.** *Aus, Brit* (*container*) jarra; (*small: for milk, cream*) jarrita *f* **2.** *no pl, inf* (*prison*) cárcel *f;* **to be in the ~** estar a la sombra
juggernaut ['dʒʌgənɔːt, *Am:* -ɚnɑːt] *n* **1.** AUTO camión *m* grande **2.** (*overwhelming force*) monstruo *m*
juggle ['dʒʌgl] **I.** *vi a. fig* hacer juegos malabares **II.** *vt a. fig* hacer juegos malabares con
juggler *n* malabarista *mf*
jugular ['dʒʌgjələʳ, *Am:* -lɚ] *n* (vena *f*) yugular *f* ▸**to go for the ~** *inf* entrar a degüello
jugular vein *n* vena *f* yugular
juice [dʒuːs] *n* **1.** *no pl* (*drink*) zumo *m* **2.** (*of meat*) jugo *m* **3.** *no pl, Am, inf* (*electricity*) corriente *f;* (*petrol*) combustible *m* ▸**to stew in one's own ~** cocerse en su propia salsa
juicy ['dʒuːsi] <-ier, -iest> *adj* **1.** (*fruit, steak*) jugoso, -a **2.** *inf* (*profit*) sustancioso, -a; (*role*) suculento, -a **3.** *inf* (*scandalous*) escabroso, -a; (*details*) picante
ju-jitsu [ˌdʒuː'dʒɪtsuː] *n no pl* jiujitsu *m*
jukebox ['dʒuːkbɒks, *Am:* -bɑːks] *n* máquina *f* de discos
julep ['dʒuːlɪp, *Am:* -ləp] *n* (*drink*) julepe *m;* **mint ~** julepe de menta
July [dʒuː'laɪ] *n* julio *m; s. a.* **April**
jumble ['dʒʌmbl] **I.** *n no pl* **1.** (*disorderly pile*) revoltijo *m* **2.** *Brit* (*unwanted articles for sale*) cosas *fpl* usadas **II.** *vt* mezclar
jumble sale *n* bazar *m* benéfico
jumbo ['dʒʌmbəʊ, *Am:* -boʊ] **I.** *adj* gigante *m* **II.** *n inf* jumbo *m*
jump [dʒʌmp] **I.** *vi* **1.** (*leap*) saltar; **to ~ up and down** pegar saltos; **to ~ up and down with frustration** *Aus, Brit* subirse por las paredes **2.** (*skip*) brincar; **to ~ for joy** brincar de alegría **3.** (*jerk*) sobresaltarse **4.** (*increase suddenly*) subir de golpe ▸**go ~ in the lake!** *inf* ¡vete a freír espárragos! **II.** *vt* **1.** (*leap across or over*) saltar **2.** (*attack*) atacar **3.** (*disregard*) saltarse ▸**to ~ a queue** colarse **III.** *n* **1.** (*leap*) salto *m* **2.** (*hurdle*) obstáculo *m*
◆**jump about** *vi* dar saltos
◆**jump at** *vt* (*opportunity*) no dejar escapar; (*offer*) aceptar con entusiasmo
◆**jump down** *vi* bajar de un salto
◆**jump in** *vi* entrar de prisa
◆**jump on** *vt* (*criticise*) poner verde
◆**jump out at** *vt* (*error, inconsistency*) saltar a la vista de
◆**jump up** *vi* ponerse de pie de un salto
jumped-up [ˌdʒʌmpt'ʌp] *adj Brit, inf* presuntuoso, -a
jumper ['dʒʌmpəʳ, *Am:* -pɚ] *n* **1.** (*person, animal*) saltador(a) *m(f)* **2.** *Aus, Brit* (*pullover*) suéter *m* **3.** *Am* (*dress*) pichi *m*
jumping jack *n* (*toy*) títere *m*
jump jet *n* avión *m* de despegue vertical
jump lead *n Brit* cable *m* de arranque
jump-start *vt* hacer arrancar (*empujando o haciendo un puente*) **jump suit** *n* mono *m*
jumpy ['dʒʌmpi] <-ier, -iest> *adj inf* nervioso, -a
junction ['dʒʌŋkʃən] *n* (*road ~*) cruce *m;* (*motorway ~*) salida *f*
junction box *n* caja *f* de empalmes
juncture ['dʒʌŋktʃəʳ, *Am:* -tʃɚ] *n no pl, form* coyuntura *f;* **at this ~** en este momento
June [dʒuːn] *n* junio *m; s. a.* **April**
jungle ['dʒʌŋgl] *n* **1.** (*forest*) selva *f* **2.** *fig* (*tangled mass*) maraña *f;* (*of laws*) laberinto *m*
junior ['dʒuːniəʳ, *Am:* '-njɚ] **I.** *adj* **1.** (*younger*) más joven **2.** SPORTS juvenil **3.** (*lower in rank*) subalterno, -a; (*partner*) comanditario, -a **II.** *n* **1.** (*younger person*) **which is the ~?** ¿quién es el más joven? **2.** (*low-ranking person*) subalterno, -a *m, f* **3.** *Brit* SCHOOL alumno, -a *m, f* de primaria **4.** *Am* UNIV estudiante *mf* de tercer año
junior college *n Am: colegio que com-*

J

prende los dos primeros años universitarios
junior high school *n Am* instituto *m* de enseñanza media **junior school** *n Brit* escuela *f* primaria
juniper ['dʒuːnɪpəʳ, *Am:* -pɚ] *n* enebro *m*
junk[1] [dʒʌŋk] I. *n* 1. *no pl* (*objects of no value*) trastos *mpl,* tiliches *mpl AmC, Méx* 2. *Am, inf* (*drugs*) caballo *m* II. *vt inf* tirar a la basura
junk[2] [dʒʌŋk] *n* (*vessel*) junco *m*
junk food *n* comida *f* basura
junkie ['dʒʌŋki] *n inf* yonqui *mf*
junk room *n* trastero *m,* degredo *m Ven*
junk shop *n* tienda *f* de trastos viejos **junkyard** [-jɑːrd] *n* chatarrería *f*
junta ['dʒʌntə, *Am:* 'hʊntə] *n* gobierno *f* dictatorial; (**military**) ~ junta *f* militar
Jupiter ['dʒuːpɪtəʳ, *Am:* -t̬ɚ] *n* Júpiter *m*
juridical [dʒʊə'rɪdɪkəl, *Am:* dʒʊ'-] *adj* jurídico, -a
jurisdiction [ˌdʒʊərɪs'dɪkʃən, *Am:* ˌdʒʊrɪs-] *n no pl* jurisdicción *f;* **to have ~ in sth** tener competencia en algo
jurisprudence [ˌdʒʊərɪs'pruːdənts, *Am:* ˌdʒʊrɪs-] *n no pl* jurisprudencia *f*
jurist ['dʒʊərɪst, *Am:* 'dʒʊrɪst] *n* jurista *mf*
juror ['dʒʊərəʳ, *Am:* 'dʒʊrɚ] *n* miembro *mf* del jurado
jury ['dʒʊəri, *Am:* 'dʒʊri] *n* jurado *m*
juryman ['dʒʊərimən, *Am:* 'dʒʊri-] *n* miembro *m* del jurado
just [dʒʌst] I. *adv* 1. (*very soon*) enseguida; **we're ~ about to leave** estamos a punto de salir 2. (*now*) precisamente; **to be ~ doing sth** estar justamente haciendo algo 3. (*very recently*) ~ **after 10 o'clock** justo después de las 10; **she's ~ turned 15** acaba de cumplir 15 años 4. (*exactly, equally*) exactamente, justo; ~ **like that** exactamente así; ~ **as I expected** tal y como yo esperaba; ~ **now** ahora mismo; **not ~ yet** todavía no 5. (*only*) solamente; ~ **a minute** espera un momento 6. (*simply*) simplemente; ~ **in case it rains** por si llueve 7. (*barely*) ~ (**about**), (**only**) ~ apenas; ~ **in time** justo a tiempo 8. (*very*) muy; **you look ~ wonderful!** ¡estás maravillosa! 9. ~ **about** (*nearly*) casi 10. **it's ~ as well that ...** menos mal que... ►~ **my luck!** ¡que mala suerte tengo!; **isn't it ~?** *inf* ¿verdad? II. *adj* (*fair*) justo, -a ►**to get one's ~ deserts** llevarse su merecido
justice ['dʒʌstɪs] *n* 1. justicia *f;* **to bring sb to ~** llevar a uno ante al tribunal 2. *Am* (*judge*) juez *mf*
justifiable [ˌdʒʌstɪ'faɪəbl, *Am:* ˌdʒʌstə'-] *adj* justificable
justification [ˌdʒʌstɪfɪ'keɪʃən, *Am:* -tə-] *n no pl* justificación *f*
justify ['dʒʌstɪfaɪ] *vt* justificar; **to ~ oneself** disculparse; **to ~ oneself to sb** dar explicaciones a alguien
justly ['dʒʌstli] *adv* justamente
jut [dʒʌt] <-tt-> *vi* **to ~ out** sobresalir
jute [dʒuːt] *n no pl* yute *m*
juvenile ['dʒuːvənaɪl, *Am:* -nl] *adj* 1. *form* (*young*) juvenil 2. *pej* (*childish*) infantil
juvenile court *n* tribunal *m* de menores
juvenile delinquency *n* delincuencia *f* juvenil
juxtapose [ˌdʒʌkstə'pəʊz, *Am:* 'dʒʌkstəpoʊz] *vt* yuxtaponer
juxtaposition [ˌdʒʌkstəpə'zɪʃən] *n no pl* yuxtaposición *f*

K

K, k [keɪ] *n* K, k *f;* ~ **for King** K de Kenia
K INFOR *abbr of* **kilobyte** K *m*
kajal (**eyeliner**) **pencil** [kəˌjel('aɪlaɪnə)-ˌpentsəl] *n* delineador *m* de ojos
kale *n,* **kail** [keɪl] *n* col *f* rizada
kaleidoscope [kə'laɪdəskəʊp, *Am:* -skoʊp] *n* caleidoscopio *m*
kamikaze [ˌkæmɪ'kɑːzi, *Am:* ˌkɑːmə-] *adj* kamikaze *m*
kamikaze attack *n* ataque *m* kamikaze
Kampuchea [ˌkæmpʊ'tʃiːə, *Am:* -puː'-] *n* Kampuchea *f*
Kampuchean I. *adj* kampucheano, -a II. *n* kampucheano, -a *m, f*
kangaroo [ˌkæŋgə'ruː] <-(s)> *n* canguro *m*
kangaroo court *n* tribunal *m* desautorizado
kaolin ['keɪəlɪn] *n no pl* MIN caolín *m*
Kaposi's sarcoma [kæ'pəʊziz sɑː'kəʊmə, *Am:* kə'poʊziz sɑːr'koʊ-] *n* MED sarcoma *m* de Kaposi
karaoke [kæri'əʊki, *Am:* 'kɑːr-] *n* karaoke *m*
karate [kə'rɑːti, *Am:* kæ'rɑːt̬i] *n no pl* kárate *m*
karate chop *n* golpe *m* de kárate
karma ['kɑːmə, *Am:* 'kɑːr-] *n no pl* karma *m*
kayak ['kaɪæk] *n* kayak *m*
kayaking *n no pl* **I love ~** me incanta ir en kayak
Kb, KB [ˌkeɪ'biː] INFOR *abbr of* **kilobyte** Kb
kbyte INFOR *abbr of* **kilobyte** kbyte
kc *abbr of* **kilocycle** kc
KC *n abbr of* **King's Counsel** *abogado de la Corona*
kebab [kə'bæb, *Am:* -'bɑːb] *n* kebab *m*
keel [kiːl] *n* NAUT quilla *f*
◆**keel over** *vi* volcarse; (*person*) desplomarse
keelhaul ['kiːlˌhɔːl, *Am:* -hɑːl] *vt fig, inf* echar un buen rapapolvo
keen [kiːn] I. *adj* 1. (*intent, eager*) entusiasta; (*student*) aplicado, -a; **to be ~ to do sth** tener ganas de hacer algo; **to be ~ on sth** ser aficionado, -a a algo 2. (*perceptive: intelligence*) agudo, -a; (*ear*) fino, -a; **to have ~ eyesight** tener muy buena vista; **to have a ~ sense of smell** tener un agudo sentido del olfato

3.(*extreme*) fuerte; **a ~ interest** un vivo interés; **to have a ~ appetite** tener buen apetito **4.** *liter* (*sharp*) afilado, -a; (*wind*) cortante **5.**(*shrill, piercing*) penetrante **II.** *n* lamento *m* fúnebre **III.** *vi* lamentar; **to ~ for sb** llorar la muerte de alguien

keep [ki:p] **I.** *n* **1.** *no pl* (*livelihood*) subsistencia *f;* **to earn one's ~** ganarse el sustento **2.** HIST (*castle tower*) torre *f* del homenaje ▶**for ~s** para siempre **II.** <kept, kept> *vt* **1.**(*have: shop*) tener; (*guesthouse*) dirigir; (*animals*) criar; *Am* (*children*) cuidar **2.**(*store: silence, secret*) guardar; **~ me a place** guárdame un sitio; **~ the change** quédese con el cambio **3.**(*maintain*) mantener; **to ~ sb under observation** tener a alguien en observación; **to ~ one's eyes fixed on sth/sb** no apartar los ojos de algo/alguien; **to ~ sb awake** no dejar dormir a alguien; **to ~ sth going** mantener algo a flote *fig* **4.**(*detain*) **to ~ sb waiting** hacer esperar a alguien; **to ~ sb in prison** tener a alguien en la cárcel; **he was kept in hospital** se quedó ingresado en el hospital; **what kept you?** ¿por qué tardaste? **5.**(*guard*) guardar; **to ~ one's temper** contener el genio **6.**(*fulfil*) cumplir; **to ~ an appointment** acudir a una cita; **to ~ one's word** cumplir su palabra **7.**(*record: diary*) escribir; (*accounts*) llevar **8.**(*person's expenses*) mantener; **to earn enough to ~ oneself** ganar lo bastante para mantenerse; **to ~ a mistress** mantener a una amante **9.**(*obey, respect*) obedecer; (*law*) observar **10.**(*remain involved*) **to ~ one's hand in** no perder la práctica ▶**to ~ one's balance** mantener el equilibrio; **to ~ time** marcar la hora **III.** <kept, kept> *vi* **1.** *a. fig* (*stay fresh*) conservarse **2.**(*stay*) mantenerse; **to ~ fit** mantenerse en forma; **to ~ silent (about sth)** guardar silencio (sobre algo); **to ~ to the left** circular por la izquierda; **~ quiet!** ¡cállate!; **~ still!** ¡estáte quieto! **3.**(*continue*) **to ~ going** (*person*) seguir tirando; (*machine*) seguir funcionando; **to ~ doing sth** seguir haciendo algo; **he ~s losing his keys** siempre está perdiendo sus llaves ▶**how are you ~ing?** *Brit* ¿cómo estás?

◆**keep ahead** *vi* seguir en cabeza; **to ~ of the others** seguir por delante de los demás

◆**keep at** **I.** *vi* perseverar; **to ~ work** seguir con el trabajo; **~ it!** ¡ánimo! **II.** *vt* **to keep sb at sth** tener a alguien haciendo algo

◆**keep away** **I.** *vi* mantenerse alejado, -a; **keep medicines away from children** mantenga los medicamentos fuera del alcance de los niños; **he can't ~ from it** no puede dejarlo; **~!** ¡no te acerques! **II.** *vt always sep* mantener alejado, -a

◆**keep back** **I.** *vi* (*stay away*) **to ~ from sth/sb** mantenerse alejado de algo/alguien **II.** *vt* **1.** **to ~ one's tears** contener las lágrimas **2.**(*hide*) ocultar; **to keep the truth back from sb** ocultar la verdad a alguien **3.**(*retain sth*) **to keep sth back** quedarse con algo; (*slow down*) retrasar algo

◆**keep down** *vt* **1.** **to keep one's voice down** no levantar la voz; **to keep prices down** controlar los precios **2.**(*suppress*) **to keep sb down** oprimir a alguien **3.**(*not vomit*) retener

◆**keep from** **I.** *vt always sep* **1.**(*prevent*) impedir; **to keep sb from doing sth** impedir que alguien haga algo **2.**(*retain information*) **to keep sth from sb** ocultar algo a alguien **II.** *vi* evitar; **I couldn't ~ laughing** no me podía aguantar la risa

◆**keep in** **I.** *vt* (*person*) no dejar salir; (*emotions*) contener; **to keep a pupil in** retener a un alumno como castigo **II.** *vi* **to ~ line** comportarse bien; **to ~ with sb** tener buena relación con alguien

◆**keep off** **I.** *vi* (*stay off*) mantenerse alejado, -a; **'~'** 'prohibido el paso'; **'~ the grass'** 'prohibido pisar el césped'; **if the rain keeps off ...** si no llueve... **II.** *vt* **1.** mantener alejado, -a; **to keep the rain off sth/sb** resguardar algo/a alguien de la lluvia; **keep your hands off!** ¡no lo toques! **2.**(*avoid*) evitar; **to ~ a subject** *Brit* no mencionar un tema

◆**keep on** **I.** *vi* **1.**(*continue*) seguir; **to ~ doing sth** seguir haciendo algo **2.**(*pester*) **don't ~!** ¡no insistas!; **to ~ about sb/sth** no parar de hablar de alguien/algo; **to ~ at sb** estar siempre encima de alguien **II.** *vt always sep* **1.**(*not to dismiss*) no despedir **2.**(*not to get rid of*) no deshacerse

◆**keep out** **I.** *vi* no entrar; **~!** ¡prohibido el paso!; **to ~ of sth** no meterse en algo; **to ~ of trouble** no meterse en líos **II.** *vt* **to keep sth/sb out (of sth)** no dejar que entre algo/alguien (en algo); **to keep the rain/cold out** resguardar de la lluvia/del frío

◆**keep to** **I.** *vt always sep* (*remain private*) **to keep sth to oneself** guardarse algo para sí; **to keep oneself to oneself** ser poco sociable **II.** *vi* **1.**(*stay in*) **~ the right** seguir hacia la derecha; **to ~ one's bed** quedarse en cama **2.**(*respect*) **to ~ sth** ceñirse a algo; **to keep sb to his/her word** tomar la palabra a alguien

◆**keep together** **I.** *vt* mantener juntos, -as **II.** *vi* mantenerse unidos, -as; **please, ~** por favor, no se separen

◆**keep up** **I.** *vt* **1.**(*trousers*) sujetar; (*ceiling*) sostener; (*prices*) mantener alto, -a **2.**(*continue*) seguir; **to ~ the payments** estar al corriente de los pagos; **~ the good work!** ¡sigue así!; **keep it up!** ¡sigue! **3.**(*maintain*) **to ~ appearances** guardar las apariencias; **to ~ traditions** mantener las tradiciones **4.**(*stop sb sleeping*) tener en vela **II.** *vi* **1.**(*prices*) mantenerse estable; (*moral*) no decaer **2.**(*continue*) seguir; **the rain kept up all night** siguió lloviendo durante toda la noche **3.**(*to stay level with*) **to ~ (with sb/sth)** seguir el ritmo (de alguien/algo); **wages are failing to ~ with inflation** los sueldos no aumentan a la par que la inflación; **I cannot ~ with their conversations** no puedo seguir sus conversaciones; **to ~ with the Joneses** *fig* no ser menos que los demás **4.** (*maintain contact with*) **to ~ with sb** mantener el contacto con alguien **5.** (*remain informed*) **to ~ with sth** mantenerse al tanto de algo; **to ~ with the times** estar al día

keeper ['ki:pəʳ, *Am:* -pɚ] *n* (*in charge*) guarda *mf;* (*museum*) conservador(a) *m(f);* (*jail*) carcelero, -a *m, f*

keeping ['ki:pɪŋ] *n no pl* **1.** (*guarding*) cargo *m;* **to leave sth/sb in sb's ~** dejar algo/a alguien al cuidado de alguien; **to leave sth/sb in safe ~** dejar algo/a alguien en buenas manos **2. in ~ with sth** de acuerdo con algo; **to be out of ~ with sth** desentonar con algo

keepsake ['ki:pseɪk] *n* recuerdo *m*

keg [keg] *n* barril *m*

kelp [kelp] *n no pl tipo de alga marrón usada en comidas*

ken [ken] **I.** *n* **to be beyond sb's ~** ser desconocido para alguien **II.** <-nn-> *vt Scot* (*person*) conocer; (*thing*) saber

kennel ['kenl] *n* **1.** (*doghouse*) perrera *f* **2.** *pl* (*boarding*) residencia *f* canina; (*breeding*) criadero *m* de perros

Kenya ['kenjə] *n* Kenia *f*

Kenyan ['kenjən] **I.** *n* keniano, -a *m, f* **II.** *adj* keniano, -a

kept [kept] **I.** *pt, pp of* **keep II.** *adj* mantenido, -a; **a ~ woman** una amante; **a ~ man** un gigoló

kerb [kɜ:b, *Am:* kɜ:rb] *n Brit, Aus* bordillo *m,* cordón *m CSur*

kerchief ['kɜ:tʃɪf, *Am:* 'kɜ:rtʃɪf] *n* pañoleta *f*

kerfuffle [kə'fʌfl, *Am:* kɚ-] *n Brit, inf* jaleo *m*

kernel ['kɜ:nl, *Am:* 'kɜ:r-] *n* **1.** (*centre of fruit*) almendra *f* **2. maize ~** grano *m* de maíz **3.** (*essential part*) núcleo *m;* **a ~ of truth** una pizca de verdad

kerosene ['kerəsi:n] *n no pl, Am, Aus* queroseno *m*

kestrel ['kestrəl] *n* cernícalo *m*

ketch [ketʃ] <-es> *n* NAUT queche *m*

ketchup ['ketʃəp] *n no pl* ketchup *m*

kettle ['ketl, *Am:* 'keţ-] *n* tetera *f,* pava *f AmL;* **to put the ~ on** poner agua a hervir ►**that's a different ~ of fish** eso es harina de otro costal; **to get into a pretty ~ of fish** meterse en un buen berenjenal *inf*

kettledrum ['ketldrʌm, *Am:* 'keţ-] *n* MUS timbal *m*

key [ki:] **I.** *n* **1.** (*doors*) llave *f;* **master ~** llave maestra **2.** *a.* INFOR tecla *f;* **caps lock ~** tecla de bloqueo de mayúsculas; **to hit a ~** pulsar una tecla **3.** *no pl* (*essential point*) clave *f;* **the ~ to a mystery** la clave de un misterio; **a ~ factor/role** un factor/papel clave **4.** (*list*) clave *f;* (*map*) lista *f* de símbolos convencionales; (*exercises*) soluciones *fpl* **5.** MUS tono *m;* **change of ~** cambio *m* de tono; **in the ~ of C major** en (tono de) do mayor; **to go off ~** desafinar ►**to hold the ~ to sth** tener la clave de algo **II.** *adj* clave **III.** *vt* **1.** (*type*) **to ~ (in)** teclear **2.** (*make appropriate*) adaptar

◆**key in** *vt* INFOR picar, teclear

◆**key up** *vt* emocionar; **to be keyed up** estar emocionado, -a; **to be keyed up for sth** estar listo para algo

keyboard ['ki:bɔ:d, *Am:* -bɔ:rd] **I.** *n* teclado *m* **II.** *vi, vt* teclear

keyboarding *n no pl* introducción *f* desde teclado

keyboard instrument *n* instrumento *m* de teclado

keyhole ['ki:həʊl, *Am:* -hoʊl] *n* ojo *m* de la cerradura **key money** *n no pl* adelanto *m;* **as ~** en concepto de adelanto

keynote ['ki:nəʊt, *Am:* -noʊt] *n* **1.** MUS nota *f* tónica **2.** (*central idea*) idea *f* fundamental; **to be the ~ of sth** ser la piedra angular de algo *fig*

keynoter *n* ponente *mf* del discurso central

keynote speech *n,* **keynote address** *n* discurso *m* central

keypad ['ki:pæd] *n* INFOR teclado *m* numérico

key ring *n* llavero *m* **keystone** *n* **1.** ARCHIT (*centre stone*) clave *f* **2.** (*crucial part*) piedra *f* angular **key stroke** *n* pulsación *f* (de una tecla) **key word** *n* palabra *f* clave

kg *abbr of* **kilogram** kg

khaki ['kɑ:ki, *Am:* 'kæki] **I.** *n no pl* (*colour, cloth*) caqui *m;* **~s** pantalones *mpl* caqui **II.** *adj* caqui

kHz *n abbr of* **kilohertz** KHz *m*

KIA *adj abbr of* **killed in action** fallecido, -a en acto de servicio

kibbutz [kɪ'bʊts] *n* kibbutz *m*

kick [kɪk] **I.** *n* **1.** (*person*) patada *f;* (*horse*) coz *f;* (*in football*) tiro *m;* (*in swimming*) movimiento *m* de las piernas **2.** (*exciting feeling*) placer *m;* **to do sth for ~s** hacer algo para divertirse; **to get a ~ out of sth** encontrar placer en algo; **this drink has a ~ in it** esta bebida es fuerte **3.** (*craze*) **he is on an exercise ~ at the moment** ahora le ha dado por hacer ejercicio **4.** (*gun jerk*) culatazo *m* ►**to be a ~ in the teeth** ser como un jarro de agua fría **II.** *vt* **1.** dar una patada; **to ~ sth open** abrir algo de una patada; **to ~ a ball** chutar una pelota; **to ~ oneself** *fig* darse con la cabeza en la pared **2.** (*stop*) dejar; **to ~ a habit** dejar un vicio ►**to be ~ing one's heels** *Brit* estar de plantón; **to ~ sth into touch** posponer algo; **to ~ sb upstairs** ascender a alguien para librarse de él **III.** *vi* **1.** (*person*) dar patadas a; (*horse*) dar coces; SPORTS chutar **2.** (*gun*) dar culatazo **3.** (*complain*) protestar; **to ~ about sth** quejarse de algo; **to ~ against sth** oponerse a algo **4. to be alive and ~ing** *inf* estar vivito y coleando

◆**kick about, kick around I.** *vi inf* (*hang about*) andar por ahí; (*thing*) andar rodando **II.** *vt* **1.** (*a ball*) dar patadas a **2.** (*treat badly*) maltratar

◆**kick against** *vt insep* protestar contra
◆**kick at** *vt* golpear
◆**kick away** *vt* apartar de un golpe
◆**kick back** I. *vt* (*football*) devolver II. *vi inf* 1. (*recoil*) retroceder; (*gun*) dar culatazo 2. (*give a kickback*) sobornar
◆**kick in** *vt* derribar a patadas; **to kick sb's teeth in** romper la cara a alguien
◆**kick off** I. *vi* (*begin*) empezar; (*in football*) hacer el saque de centro II. *vt* quitar de un puntapié
◆**kick out** I. *vt* **to kick sb out** poner a alguien de patitas en la calle *inf;* **he was kicked out of the party** lo echaron de la fiesta II. *vi* (*person*) dar patadas; (*horse*) dar coces
◆**kick over** *vi* **to ~ the traces** desmandarse
◆**kick up** *vt* **to ~ dust** *a. fig* levantar polvo; **to ~ a fuss/row** armar un escándalo ►**to ~ one's heels** echar una cana al aire
◆**kick upstairs** *vt* ascender

kickback ['kɪkbæk] *n inf* soborno *m*

kicker ['kɪkəʳ, *Am:* -ɚ] *n* 1. (*person who kicks*) pateador(a) *m(f)* 2. *Am, fig* **to be a ~** tener agallas 3. (*surprise*) **it was a real ~ for me** me dejó de piedra *inf* 4. (*sth disadvantageous*) pega *f*

kick-off ['kɪkɒf, *Am:* -ɑːf] *n* SPORTS saque *m* inicial **kick-starter** *n* AUTO pedal *m* de arranque

kid [kɪd] I. *n* 1. (*child*) niño, -a *m, f*, pipiolo, -a *m, f; Am, Aus* (*young person*) chico, -a *m, f;* **~ brother** *Am* hermano *m* pequeño; **as a ~ ...** de niño... 2. ZOOL cría *f;* (*young goat*) cabrito *m* 3. (*goat leather*) cabritilla *f* ►**to treat sb with ~ gloves** tratar a alguien con guante blanco; **that's ~'s stuff** eso está tirado *inf* II. <-dd-> *vi* bromear; **are you ~ing?** ¿bromeas?; **just ~ding** es broma; **no ~ding!** ¡te lo juro! III. *vt* **to ~ sb (about sth)** tomar el pelo a alguien (con algo) IV. *vr* **to ~ oneself that ...** hacerse la ilusión de que...; **stop ~ding yourself!** ¡desengáñate!

kiddie *n*, **kiddy** ['kɪdi] *n inf* crío, -a *m, f*

kidnap ['kɪdnæp] I. <-pp-> *vt* secuestrar, plagiar *AmL* II. *n* secuestro *m*, plagio *m AmL*

kidnapper ['kɪdnæpəʳ, *Am:* -ɚ] *n* secuestrador(a) *m(f)*

kidnapping *n* secuestro *m*

kidney ['kɪdni] *n* riñón *m;* **~ disease** enfermedad *f* renal

kidney bean *n* judía *f*, poroto *m CSur* **kidney donor** *n* donante *mf* de riñón **kidney failure** *n* MED fracaso *m* renal **kidney machine** *n* MED riñón *m* artificial **kidney stone** *n* MED cálculo *m* renal

kidology [kɪ'dɒlədʒi] *n inf* decepción *f*

kill [kɪl] I. *n no pl* 1. (*slaughter*) matanza *f* 2. (*hunting*) pieza *f* ►**to be in at the ~** estar presente en el momento crucial; **to go in for the ~** entrar a matar II. *vi* matar; **thou shalt not ~** (*Bible*) no matarás ►**to be dressed to ~** ir despanpanante III. *vt* 1. (*cause to die*) matar; **to ~ oneself** matarse; **to ~ oneself with laughter** *fig* morirse de risa; **this will ~ you!** *Am, fig* ¡con esto te vas a morir de risa!; **not to ~ oneself trying** *fig, inf* no esforzarse mucho 2. (*destroy*) acabar con; **to ~ the flavour of sth** quitar el gusto a algo; **my feet are ~ing me!** ¡los pies me están matando!; **to ~ sb with kindness** abrumar a alguien con atenciones
◆**kill off** *vt* exterminar; (*a disease*) erradicar

killer ['kɪləʳ, *Am:* -ɚ] *n* 1. (*sb who kills*) asesino, -a *m, f;* **to be a ~** (*person*) ser un asesino; (*disease*) cobrar muchas víctimas; **the test was a real ~** *fig, inf* el test era matador 2. *Am, Aus, inf* (*amusing, talented*) **to be a ~** ser genial; **this joke is a ~** este chiste es para morirse de risa

killer disease *n* enfermedad *f* mortal **killer whale** *n* orca *f*

killing ['kɪlɪŋ] I. *n* (*of a person*) asesinato *m;* (*of an animal*) matanza *f* ►**to make a ~** *inf* hacer su agosto II. *adj* 1. (*murderous*) asesino, -a 2. (*exhausting*) matador(a) 3. (*funny*) para morirse de risa

killjoy ['kɪldʒɔɪ] *n* aguafiestas *mf inv*

kiln ['kɪln] *n* horno *m*

kilo ['kiːləʊ, *Am:* -oʊ] *n* kilo *m*

kilobyte ['kɪləʊbaɪt, *Am:* -oʊ-] *n* INFOR kilobyte *m*

kilocycle ['kɪləʊˌsaɪkl, *Am:* -oʊ-] *n* kilociclo *m*

kilogram *n Am*, **kilogramme** ['kɪləʊgræm, *Am:* -oʊ-] *n* kilogramo *m*

kilojoule ['kɪləʊdʒuːl, *Am:* -oʊ-] *n* kilojoule *m*

kilometre *n Brit, Aus*, **kilometer** [kɪ'lɒmɪtəʳ, *Am:* kɪ'lɑːməţɚ] *n Am* kilómetro *m*

kilowatt ['kɪləʊwɒt, *Am:* -oʊwɑːt] *n* kilovatio *m* **kilowatt hour** *n* kilovatio-hora *m*

kilt [kɪlt] *n* falda *f* escocesa, pollera *f* escocesa *CSur*

kimono [kɪ'məʊnəʊ, *Am:* kə'moʊnə] *n* quimono *m*, kimono *m*

kin [kɪn] *n no pl* **next of ~** parientes *mpl* más cercanos

kind[1] [kaɪnd] *adj* amable; **to be ~ to sb** ser amable con alguien; **he was ~ enough to ...** tuvo la amabilidad de...; **would you be ~ enough/so ~ as to ...?** ¿me haría usted el favor de...?; **with ~ regards** (*in a letter*) muchos recuerdos

kind[2] [kaɪnd] I. *n* 1. (*type*) clase *f;* **sth of the ~** algo por el estilo; **he is not that ~ (of person)** no es de esa clase (de personas); **what ~ of ...?** ¿qué clase de...?; **all ~s of ...** todo tipo de...; **the first of its ~** el primero en su especie; **to hear/say nothing of the ~** no haber oído/dicho nada parecido; **they are two of a ~** son tal para cual 2. (*sth similar to*) especie *f;* **a ~ of soup** una especie de sopa 3. (*sth equal to*) **to do sth in ~** hacer algo de la misma manera; **he swore at me so I answered in ~** me insultó, así que le respondí de igual manera; **he repaid her betrayal in ~** pagó su traición con la misma moneda **4.** (*limited*) **in a ~ of way** en cierta manera; **she has found happiness of a ~ with him** ha encontrado una cierta felicidad junto a él **5.** (*payment*) **to pay sb in ~** pagar a alguien en especias **II.** *adv inf* **I ~ of like it** me gusta en cierta manera; **he was ~ of sad** estaba como triste; **"do you like it?" – "~ of"** "¿te gusta?" – "no está mal"

kindergarten ['kɪndəgɑːtn, *Am:* -dɚgɑːr-] *n* jardín *m* de infancia, jardín *m* infantil *Chile,* jardín *m* de infantes *RíoPl*

kind-hearted [ˌkaɪnd'hɑːtɪd, *Am:* -'hɑːr-t̬ɪd] *adj* bondadoso, -a; **he is very ~** tiene muy buen corazón

kindle ['kɪndl] **I.** *vt a. fig* encender; **to ~ sb's interest** despertar el interés de alguien; **to ~ sb's desire** provocar el deseo en alguien **II.** *vi a. fig* encenderse

kindling ['kɪndlɪŋ] *n no pl* **1.** (*firewood*) leña *f* **2.** *a. fig* (*act of lighting*) encendimiento *m*

kindly ['kaɪndli] **I.** <-ier, -iest> *adj* amable; (*person*) bondadoso, -a **II.** *adv* **1.** (*in a kind manner*) amablemente **2.** (*please*) **you are ~ requested to leave the building** se ruega abandonen el edificio; **~ put that book away!** ¡haz el favor de guardar ese libro! **3.** (*favourably*) **to take ~ to sth** aceptar algo de buen grado

kindness ['kaɪndnɪs] <-es> *n* **1.** *no pl* (*act of being kind*) amabilidad *f* **2.** (*kind act*) favor *m;* **to do sb a ~** hacer un favor a alguien

kindred ['kɪndrɪd] **I.** *n + pl vb* parientes *mpl* **II.** *adj* afín; **~ spirits** almas *fpl* gemelas

kinetic [kɪ'netɪk, *Am:* -'net̬-] *adj* PHYS cinético, -a

kinfolk ['kɪnfəʊk, *Am:* -foʊk] *n + pl vb, Am* parientes *mpl*

king [kɪŋ] *n* **1.** *a.* GAMES rey *m;* **the ~ of beasts** el rey de la selva **2.** (*in draughts*) dama *f*

kingcup ['kɪŋkʌp] *n Brit* BOT botón *m* de oro

kingdom ['kɪŋdəm] *n* reino *m;* **animal/plant ~** reino animal/vegetal; **the ~ of God** REL el Reino de Dios ►**to blow sth to ~ come** hacer saltar algo en pedazos; **(un)til ~ come** hasta el Día del Juicio Final

kingfisher ['kɪŋˌfɪʃəʳ, *Am:* -ɚ] *n* martín *m* pescador

kingly ['kɪŋli] *adj* regio, -a

kingpin ['kɪŋpɪn] *n* TECH pivote *m* central; **to be the ~** (*person*) ser el cerebro; (*thing*) ser la piedra angular

King's Bench *n Brit no pl* LAW Tribunal *m* Supremo

king-size ['kɪŋsaɪz] *adj* gigante; **~ cigarettes** cigarrillos *mpl* largos

kink [kɪŋk] *n* **1.** (*twist: in a pipe, rope*) retorcimiento *m;* (*in hair*) rizo *m* **2.** *Am, Aus* (*sore muscle*) tortícolis *f inv;* **to have a ~ in one's neck** tener tortícolis **3.** (*problem*) fallo *m;* **to iron out (a few) ~s** pulir algunos defectos **4.** (*strange habit*) manía *f*

kinky ['kɪŋki] <-ier, -iest> *adj* **1.** (*twisted*) retorcido, -a **2.** (*with tight curls*) ensortijado, -a **3.** (*unusual*) raro, -a; (*involving unusual sexual acts*) pervertido, -a

kinsfolk ['kɪnzfəʊk, *Am:* -foʊk] *n* HIST *+ pl vb* parientes *mpl* **kinship** *n no pl* (*family relationship*) parentesco *m;* (*similarity*) afinidad *f;* **to feel a ~ with sb** tener afinidad con alguien **kinsman** <-men> *n* HIST pariente *m* **kinswoman** <-women> *n* HIST parienta *f*

kiosk ['kiːɒsk, *Am:* -ɑːsk] *n* **1.** (*stand*) quiosco *m* **2.** *Brit, form* (*telephone box*) cabina *f* (telefónica)

kip [kɪp] *Brit, Aus, inf* **I.** *n no pl, inf* **to get some ~** echar una cabezada, apolillar un rato *RíoPl* **II.** <-pp-> *vi* dormir; **to ~ down** acostarse

kipper ['kɪpəʳ, *Am:* -ɚ] *n* arenque *m* ahumado

Kiribati [ˌkɪrə'bæs, *Am:* 'kɪrəbæs] *n* Kiribati *f*

kirk [kɜːk, *Am:* kɜːrk] *n Scot* iglesia *f;* **the Kirk** *la Iglesia Presbiteriana de Escocia*

kiss [kɪs] **I.** <-es> *n* beso *m;* **~ of life** respiración *f* boca a boca; **~ of death** *fig* beso de la muerte; **to blow sb a ~** lanzar un beso a alguien; **love and ~es** (*at the end of a letter*) muchos besos **II.** *vi* besarse **III.** *vt* besar; **to ~ sb goodnight/goodbye** dar un beso de buenas noches/despedida a alguien

kisser ['kɪsəʳ, *Am:* -ɚ] *n* **1.** (*person*) **he's a wonderful ~!** ¡besa muy bien! **2.** *vulg* (*mouth*) morro *m*

kiss-off ['kɪsɒf, *Am:* -ɑːf] *n Am, inf* **to give the ~** dar calabazas **kiss-proof** *adj* indeleble

kit [kɪt] **I.** *n* **1.** (*set*) utensilios *mpl;* **first aid ~** botiquín *m* de primeros auxilios; **sewing ~** costurero *m;* **tool ~** caja *f* de herramientas **2.** (*parts to put together*) kit *m* **3.** *Brit* MIL, SPORTS (*uniform*) equipo *m* **II.** *vt Brit* **to ~ sb out/up** equipar a alguien

kitbag ['kɪtbæg] *n* macuto *m*

kitchen ['kɪtʃɪn] *n* cocina *f*

kitchenette [ˌkɪtʃɪ'net] *n* cocina *f* pequeña

kitchen foil *n* papel *m* de aluminio **kitchen garden** *n* huerto *m* **kitchen paper** *n no pl* papel *m* de cocina **kitchen range** *n Am,* **kitchen stove** *n* cocina *f* económica **kitchen sink** *n* fregadero *m,* lavaplatos *m inv And,* pileta *f RíoPl* ►**to take everything but the ~** irse con la casa a cuestas **kitchen towel** *n Am* (*tea towel*) paño *m* de cocina **kitchen unit** *n* módulo *m* de cocina

kite [kaɪt] *n* **1.** ZOOL milano *m* **2.** FIN cheque *m* sin fondos **3.** (*toy*) cometa *f,* volantón *m AmL;* **to fly a ~** hacer volar una cometa; *fig* tantear el terreno ►**go fly a ~!** *Am, inf* ¡vete a freír espárragos!

kite-mark ['kaɪtmɑːk, *Am:* -mɑːrk] *n Brit* marchamo *m*

kith [kɪθ] *n + pl vb* **~ and kin** familiares *mpl* y amigos

kitsch [kɪtʃ] **I.** *n no pl* kitsch *m inv* **II.** *adj* kitsch *inv*

kitten ['kɪtn] *n* gatito, -a *m, f* ►**I nearly had**

~**s** casi me da un ataque

kittenish ['kɪtənɪʃ] *adj* coquetón, -ona

kitty ['kɪti, *Am:* 'kɪṭ-] <-ies> *n* **1.** *childspeak* (*kitten or cat*) gatito, -a *m, f* **2.** (*money*) fondo *m*

kiwi ['ki:wi:] *n* **1.** ZOOL, BOT kiwi *m* **2.** *inf* (*New Zealander*) neozelandés, -esa *m, f*

kJ *abbr of* **kilojoule** kJ

KKK [ˌkeɪkeɪ'keɪ] *n abbr of* **Ku Klux Klan** Ku Klux Klan *m*

klaxon ['klæksn] *n* sirena *f,* cláxon *m*

Kleenex® ['kli:neks] *n* kleenex® *m*

kleptomania [ˌkleptə'meɪnɪə, *Am:* -toʊ'-] *n no pl* cleptomanía *f*

kleptomaniac [ˌkleptə'meɪnɪæk, *Am:* -toʊ'-] *n* cleptómano, -a *m, f*

km *abbr of* **kilometre** km

km/h *abbr of* **kilometres per hour** km/h

knack [næk] *n no pl* habilidad *f;* **to have a ~ for sth** tener facilidad para algo; **to get the ~ of sth** coger el tranquillo a algo, tomar la mano a algo *AmL*

knacker ['nækə^r, *Am:* -ɚ] *vt inf* hacer polvo

knackered ['nækəd, *Am:* -ɚd] *adj Brit, Aus, inf* hecho, -a polvo

knapsack ['næpsæk] *n Am* mochila *f,* tamuga *f AmC*

knead [ni:d] *vt* **1.** GASTR amasar; (*clay*) modelar **2.** (*massage*) masajear

knee [ni:] **I.** *n* rodilla *f;* **to be on one's ~s** *a. fig* estar de rodillas; **to get down on one's ~s** arrodillarse; **on your ~s!** ¡de rodillas! ►**to bring sb to their ~s** derrotar a alguien **II.** *vt* **to ~ sb** dar un rodillazo a alguien

kneecap ['ni:ˌkæp] **I.** *n* rótula *f* **II.** <-pp-> *vt* disparar en la rodilla o en las piernas **knee-capping** *n* disparo *m* en la rodilla o en las piernas **knee-deep** *adj* **to be ~ in sth** estar metido hasta las rodillas en algo **knee-high** *adj* **to be ~** llegar hasta las rodillas

knee-jerk ['ni:dʒɜ:k, *Am:* -dʒɜ:rk] *adj* previsible

kneel [ni:l] <knelt *Am:* kneeled, knelt *Am:* kneeled> *vi* arrodillarse

knees-up ['ni:zʌp] *n Brit, inf* fiesta *f;* **to have a ~** correr una juerga

knell [nel] *n* toque *m* de difuntos; **to sound the ~ for sth** *fig* anunciar el fin de algo

knelt [nelt] *pt of* **kneel**

knew [nju:, *Am:* nu:] *pt of* **know**

knickerbockers ['nɪkəbɒkəz, *Am:* -ɚbɑ:kɚz] *npl* pantalón *m* bombacho

knickers ['nɪkəz, *Am:* -ɚz] *npl* **1.** *Brit* (*women's underwear*) bragas *fpl* **2.** *Am* (*knickerbockers*) bombachos *mpl* ►**to get one's ~ in a twist** *Brit, Aus, inf* ponerse nervioso como un flan

knick-knack ['nɪknæk] *n inf* cachivache *m*

knife [naɪf] <knives> *n* **1.** cuchillo *m* **2.** (*dagger*) puñal *m;* **to wield a ~** blandir un puñal *elev* **3.** (*in a machine*) cuchilla *f* ►**the ~s are out for him** *Brit, Aus, inf* se la tienen jurada; **to get one's ~ in(to) sb** ensañarse con alguien; **to turn the ~ (in the wound)** poner el dedo en la llaga; **to be under the ~** MED estar en la mesa de operaciones

knife-edge *n* filo *m;* **to be (balanced) on a ~** *fig* pender de un hilo **knife sharpener** *n* afilador *m*

knifing ['naɪfɪŋ] *n* pelea *f* con navajas

knight [naɪt] **I.** *n* **1.** (*man given honorable rank*) sir *m* **2.** HIST (*man of high social position*) caballero *m* **3.** (*chess figure*) caballo *m* ►**~ in shining armour** príncipe *m* azul **II.** *vt* HIST armar caballero; (*give a honorable title*) conceder el título de sir

knight-errant [ˌnaɪt'erənt] <knights-errant> *n* caballero *m* andante **knighthood** *n* título *m* de Sir; **to give sb a ~** conceder a alguien el título de sir

> En Gran Bretaña, las personas que se han distinguido por sus méritos en favor de su país, son distinguidas con el honor de pasar a formar parte de la **knighthood** (nobleza) y reciben el título de **Sir** delante de su nombre, por ejemplo, **Sir John Smith**. La mujer de un **Sir** recibe el tratamiento de **Lady**, por ejemplo, **Lady Smith** (y se tiene que dirigir uno a ella de esta manera). Si se les quiere nombrar simultáneamente entonces se utilizaría la fórmula de **Sir John and Lady Smith**. A partir del año 1917 también una mujer puede ser distinguida por sus méritos. En ese caso recibe el título de **Dame**, por ejemplo, **Dame Mary Smith**.

knightly ['naɪtli] *adj liter* caballeresco, -a

knit [nɪt] **I.** *vi* (*wool*) hacer punto; (*with a machine*) tejer **II.** *vt* (*wool*) tejer ►**to ~ one's brows** fruncir el ceño

◆**knit together** **I.** *vi* **1.** (*combine or join*) unirse **2.** (*mend*) soldarse **II.** *vt* **1.** (*bones*) soldar **2.** *fig* (*join*) unir

knitter ['nɪtə^r, *Am:* 'nɪṭɚ] *n* **Paula is a wonderful ~** a Paula se le da muy bien hacer punto

knitting *n no pl* **1.** (*the product of knitting*) tejido *m* de punto **2.** (*material being knitted*) labor *f* de punto **3.** (*action of knitting*) **she likes ~** a ella le gusta hacer punto

knitting-needle *n* aguja *f* de hacer punto, aguja *f* de tejer *AmL* **knitting-yarn** *n no pl* lana *f* de tejer

knitwear ['nɪtweə^r, *Am:* -wer] *n no pl* géneros *mpl* de punto

knob [nɒb, *Am:* nɑ:b] *n* **1.** (*round handle: of a door*) pomo *m;* (*of switch*) botón *m;* (*of a drawer*) tirador *m* **2.** (*small amount*) pedazo *m;* (*of butter*) trocito *m* **3.** (*lump*) bulto *m* ►**with (brass) ~s on** *Brit* hasta los tuétanos

knobbly ['nɒbli, *Am:* 'nɑ:bi] <-ier, -iest> *adj,* **knobby** ['nɒbi, *Am:* 'nɑ:bi] *adj Am* nudoso, -a; (*knees*) huesudo, -a

knock [nɒk, *Am:* nɑ:k] **I.** *n* **1.** (*blow*) golpe *m* **2.** (*sound*) llamada *f;* **to give a ~ at the door** llamar a la puerta **3.** *fig, inf* crítica *f;* **to**

take a ~ aguantar un revés **II.** *vi* **1.** (*hit*) golpear; **to ~ on the window/at the door** llamar a la ventana/puerta **2.** TECH (*engine, pipes*) martillear **III.** *vt* **1.** (*hit*) golpear; **to ~ sb** dar un golpe a alguien; **to ~ a hole into the wall** abrir un agujero en la pared; **to ~ the bottom out of sth** *a. fig* desfondar algo **2.** *inf* (*criticize*) criticar

◆**knock about I.** *vi inf* andar vagando, vagabundear; **to ~ in town** andar por la ciudad **II.** *vt* (*person*) pegar; (*ball*) golpear

◆**knock around** *vi, vt s.* **knock about**

◆**knock back** *vt inf* **1.** (*drink quickly*) beber rápidamente; **to knock a beer back** beberse una cerveza de golpe **2.** *Brit, Aus* (*cost a lot*) costar **3.** *Brit, Aus, inf* (*reject advances*) dar calabazas **4.** (*surprise*) pasmar

◆**knock down** *vt* **1.** (*cause to fall*) derribar; (*with a car*) echar por tierra **2.** (*demolish*) demoler; **to ~ every argument** *fig* rebatir todos los argumentos **3.** (*reduce*) rebajar **4.** (*sell at auction*) adjudicar; **the picture was knocked down to Peter** se adjudicó el cuadro a Peter; **to knock sth down to sb for £100** dejar algo a alguien en 100 libras

◆**knock into** *vt* (*make understand*) inculcar; **to knock some sense into sb** hacer entrar en razón a alguien

◆**knock off I.** *vt* **1.** (*cause to fall off*) hacer caer; **to knock sb off his pedestal** *fig* hacer bajar a alguien de su pedestal **2.** (*reduce*) rebajar; **to knock £5 off the price** rebajar 5 libras el precio **3.** *inf* (*steal*) robar **4.** *inf* (*murder*) matar **5.** (*produce easily*) ejecutar prontamente; **to ~ some copies** hacer algunas copias **6.** (*stop*) **to knock it off** dejarlo; **knock it off!** ¡déjalo! **II.** *vi inf* terminar; **to ~ work at 3 p.m.** salir de trabajar a las 3 p.m.; **to ~ for lunch** salir para comer

◆**knock on** *vi* **to be knocking on 40** estar acercándose a los 40

◆**knock out** *vt* **1.** (*render unconscious*) dejar sin sentido; SPORTS dejar K.O.; (*cause to sleep*) hacer dormir; (*exhaust*) agotar **2.** (*remove*) quitar; (*contents in text*) suprimir **3.** (*eliminate*) eliminar; **to be knocked out of a competition** ser eliminado de una competición **4.** (*produce quickly*) hacer, producir **5.** *inf* (*astonish*) pasmar; **to knock sb out** dejar pasmado a alguien

◆**knock over** *vt* atropellar; (*objetos*) volcar

◆**knock together** *vt* construir deprisa; **to ~ something to eat** hacer algo rápido para comer

◆**knock up I.** *vt* **1.** (*make quickly*) construir deprisa **2.** *Brit, Aus, inf* (*awaken*) despertar **3.** *Am, inf* (*impregnate*) dejar encinta; **to get knocked up** quedarse embarazada **II.** *vi* SPORTS pelotear

knockabout ['nɒkəbaʊt, *Am:* 'nɑːk-] *adj* bullicioso, -a; (*comedy, humour*) cómico, -a

knockdown *adj* **1.** (*very cheap*) baratísimo, -a; **~ price** precio *m* de saldo; (*at auction*) precio *m* inicial **2.** (*violent: blow*) duro, -a; (*argument*) arrollador(a); (*fight*) violento, -a

knocker ['nɒkə^r, *Am:* 'nɑːkɚ] *n* (*on door*) aldaba *f; inf* (*person*) detractor(a) *m(f)*

knocking copy *n no pl* ECON contrapublicidad *f*

knocking-off time *n no pl* hora *f* de salir del trabajo

knock-kneed [ˌnɒk'niːd, *Am:* 'nɑːkniːd] *adj* patizambo, -a; *fig* débil **knock-on effect** *n Brit* efecto *m* dominó **knockout I.** *n* **1.** *Brit, Aus* (*competition*) eliminatoria *f* **2.** SPORTS (*boxing*) K.O. *m;* **to win sth by a ~** ganar algo por K.O. **3.** *inf* (*person*) persona *f* estupenda **II.** *adj* **1.** *Brit, Aus* (*competition*) eliminatorio, -a **2.** (*boxing*) **~ blow** golpe *m* duro; *fig* duro revés *m;* **to deal sb's hopes a ~ blow** acabar con las esperanzas de alguien **3.** *inf* (*attractive*) muy atractivo, -a **knock-up** *n* peloteo *m*

knoll [nəʊl, *Am:* noʊl] *n* montículo *m*

knot [nɒt, *Am:* nɑːt] **I.** *n* **1.** (*tied join*) *a.* NAUT nudo *m;* **to tie/untie a ~** hacer/deshacer un nudo **2.** (*bow*) lazo *m* **3.** (*chignon*) moño *m,* chongo *m Méx* **4.** (*small group*) corrillo *m* ►**to tie the ~** *inf* prometerse **II.** <-tt> *vt* anudar; **to ~ sth together** atar algo **III.** <-tt-> *vi* anudarse

knotty ['nɒti, *Am:* 'nɑːt̬i] <-ier, -iest> *adj* **1.** (*full of knots: lumber, wood*) nudoso, -a; (*hair*) enredado, -a **2.** (*difficult*) difícil

know [nəʊ, *Am:* noʊ] **I.** <knew, known> *vt* **1.** (*have information*) saber; **to ~ a bit of English** saber un poco de inglés; **she ~s all of their names** conoce los nombres de todos ellos; **to ~ how to do sth** saber hacer algo; **to ~ all there is to ~ about sth** saber todo lo que hay que saber sobre algo; **to ~ what one is talking about** saber de lo que uno habla; **to ~ sth (off) by heart** saber algo de memoria; **not to ~ the first thing about sth/sb** no saber nada de algo/alguien; **to ~ all the answers** tener todas las respuestas; **if you ~ what I mean** si sabes de qué hablo; **do you ~ what I mean?** ¿entiendes?; **to ~ that ...** saber que...; **to want to ~ sth** querer saber algo; **do you ~ ...?** ¿sabes...?; **you ~ what?** *inf* ¿sabes qué? **2.** (*be acquainted with*) conocer; **to ~ sb by sight/by name/personally** conocer a alguien de vista/por el nombre/personalmente; **(not) to ~ sb to speak to** (no) conocer a alguien como para entablar una conversación; **~ing sb, ...** conociendo a alguien,...; **to get to ~ sb** llegar a conocer a alguien; **to get to ~ each other** llegar a conocerse (bien); **to have ~n sth** haber experimentado algo; **to ~ sth like the back of one's hand** *fig* conocer algo como la palma de la mano **3.** (*recognize*) conocer, reconocer; **to ~ sb/sth by sth** reconocer a alguien/algo por algo; **to ~ sb for sth** reconocer a alguien por algo **II.** <knew, known> *vi* **1.** (*be informed*) saber; **as far as I ~** por lo que sé; **to ~ better (than sb)** saber más (que alguien); **to ~ of** [*o* **about**] **sth** saber de algo, estar enterado de algo; **you** ~ (*you remember*) ya sabes; (*you understand*) entiendes; (**well**) **what do you** ~! *Am, iron* ¡no me digas!; **I** ~! (*I've got an idea!*) ¡lo tengo!; (*said to agree with sb*) ¡lo sé! **2.** (*be certain*) estar seguro; **there's no ~ing** no es seguro; **one never ~s** nunca se sabe **3.** *inf* (*understand*) entender **III.** *n no pl* **to be in the** ~ estar en el ajo; **to be in the ~ about sth** estar enterado de algo

know-all ['nəʊɔːl, *Am:* 'noʊ-] *n Brit, Aus, inf* sabelotodo *mf* **know-how** *n no pl* know-how *m;* **to have ~ about sth** tener el know-how de algo

knowing ['nəʊɪŋ, *Am:* 'noʊ-] **I.** *adj* astuto, -a; (*grins, look, smile*) de complicidad **II.** *n no pl* **there's no** ~ no hay forma de saberlo

knowingly *adv* **1.** (*meaningfully*) con conocimiento **2.** (*with full awareness*) a sabiendas

know-it-all ['nəʊɪtɔːl, *Am:* 'noʊɪt̬-] *n Am s.* **know-all**

knowledge ['nɒlɪdʒ, *Am:* 'nɑːlɪdʒ] *n no pl* **1.** (*body of learning*) conocimiento *m;* **to have** (**some**) **~ of sth** tener (algún) conocimiento de algo; **to have a thorough ~ of sth** conocer algo a fondo **2.** (*acquired information*) saber *m;* **to have** (**no**) **~ about sth/sb** (no) saber de algo/alguien; **to my** ~ que yo sepa; **to be common** ~ ser de dominio público **3.** (*awareness*) conocimiento *m;* **to bring sth to sb's** ~ poner a alguien en conocimiento de algo; **to do sth without sb's** ~ hacer algo sin que alguien lo sepa; **to deny all** ~ (**of sth**) negar cualquier conocimiento (de algo)

knowledgeable ['nɒlɪdʒəbl, *Am:* 'nɑːlɪ-] *adj* entendido, -a; **to be ~ about sth** ser un erudito en algo

known [nəʊn, *Am:* noʊn] **I.** *vt, vi pp of* **know II.** *adj* (*expert*) reconocido, -a; (*criminal*) conocido, -a; **no ~ reason** sin razón aparente; **to make sth** ~ dar a conocer algo; **to make oneself ~ to sb** darse a conocer a alguien

knuckle ['nʌkl] *n* nudillo *m* ▸**to be near the** ~ *Brit, inf* rayar en la indecencia; **to rap sb's ~s** *inf* echar un rapapolvo a alguien

◆**knuckle down** *vi* ponerse a hacer algo con ahinco; **to ~ to work** ponerse a trabajar concienzudamente

◆**knuckle under** *vi* darse por vencido, -a

knuckle-duster ['nʌkldʌstəʳ, *Am:* -tɚ] *n* **1.** (*weapon*) puño *m* de hierro **2.** *inf* (*ring*) aro *m* de hierro

KO [ˌkeɪ'əʊ, *Am:* -'oʊ] *abbr of* **knockout** KO

koala [kəʊ'ɑːlə, *Am:* koʊ-] *n,* **koala bear** *n* coala *m*

kooky ['kuːki] <-ier, -iest> *adj Am, inf* loco, -a

Koran [kə'rɑːn, *Am:* -'ræn] *n no pl* **the** ~ el Corán

Korea [kə'rɪə] *n* Corea *f;* **North/South** ~ Corea del Norte/Sur

Korean [kə'rɪən] **I.** *adj* coreano, -a **II.** *n* **1.** (*person*) coreano, -a *m, f* **2.** LING coreano *m*

kosher ['kəʊʃəʳ, *Am:* 'koʊʃɚ] *adj* autorizado, -a por la ley judía

kowtow [ˌkaʊ'taʊ] *vi inf* saludar humildemente; **to ~ to sb** humillarse ante alguien

Kremlin ['kremlɪn] *n no pl* **the** ~ el Kremlin

krone ['krəʊnə] *n* corona *f*

kudos ['kjuːdɒs, *Am:* 'kuːdoʊz] *n no pl* gloria *f;* **to get ~ for sth** conseguir prestigio por algo

Ku Klux Klan ['kuː'klʌks'klæn] *n no pl* **the** ~ el Ku Klux Klan

kung fu [ˌkʊŋ'fuː] *n no pl* kung fu *m*

Kurd [kɜːd, *Am:* kɜːrd] *n* kurdo, -a *m, f*

Kurdish **I.** *adj* kurdo, -a **II.** *n* **1.** (*person*) kurdo, -a *m, f* **2.** LING kurdo *m*

Kurdistan [ˌkɜːdɪ'stɑːn, *Am:* ˌkɜːrdɪ'stæn] *n* Kurdistán *m*

Kuwait [kʊ'weɪt] *n* Kuwait *m*

Kuwaiti **I.** *adj* kuwaití **II.** *n* **1.** (*person*) kuwaití *mf* **2.** LING kuwaití *m*

kw *abbr of* **kilowatt** KW

kWh *abbr of* **kilowatt hour** kWh

KWIC [kwɪk] INFOR *abbr of* **key word in context** KWIC

KWOC INFOR *abbr of* **key word out of context** KWOC

L

L, l [el] *n* L, l *f;* ~ **for Lucy** *Brit,* ~ **for Love** *Am* L de Lisboa

l *abbr of* **litre** l.

L **1.** *Brit abbr of* **Learner** L **2.** *abbr of* **large** G

LA [ˌel'eɪ] *n abbr of* **Los Angeles** Los Ángeles

lab [læb] *n abbr of* **laboratory** laboratorio *m*

lab coat *n* bata *f* de laboratorio

label ['leɪbəl] **I.** *n* **1.** (*on bottle, clothing*) etiqueta *f* **2.** (*brand name*) marca *f* **3.** (*description*) descripción *f* **II.** <-ll, *Am:* -l> *vt* **1.** (*affix label*) etiquetar **2.** (*categorize*) clasificar

labelling *n Brit,* **labeling** *n no pl, Am, Aus* etiquetado *m*

labor ['leɪbɚ] *Am, Aus s.* **labour**

laboratory [lə'bɒrətəri, *Am:* 'læbrəˌtɔːri] <-ies> *n* laboratorio *m;* **to be still at the ~ stage** estar aún en fase experimental

laboratory assistant *n* auxiliar *mf* de laboratorio **laboratory test** *n* prueba *f* de laboratorio

laborer *n Am, Aus s.* **labourer**

laborious [lə'bɔːrɪəs] *adj* **1.** (*task*) laborioso, -a **2.** (*style*) farragoso, -a

labour ['leɪbəʳ, *Am:* -bɚ] **I.** *n* **1.** (*work*) trabajo *m;* **manual** ~ trabajo manual; **to be a ~ of love** ser una tarea muy grata **2.** *no pl* ECON (*workers*) mano *f* de obra; **skilled** ~ mano de obra cualificada **3.** *no pl* MED (*childbirth*) parto *m;* **to be in** ~ estar de parto **II.** *vi*

1.(*work*) trabajar; **to do ~ing work** trabajar de peón 2.(*do sth with effort*) esforzarse; **to ~ on sth** esforzarse en algo 3.(*move*) moverse penosamente 4.(*act at a disadvantage*) **to ~ under a delusion** estar equivocado III. *vt* insistir en; **to ~ a point** insistir (demasiado) en un punto

labour camp *n* campo *m* de trabajo **labour costs** *npl* costes *mpl* de la mano de obra **Labour Day** *n no pl, Am* Día *m* del Trabajo **labour dispute** *n* conflicto *m* laboral

labourer ['leɪbərəʳ] *n* peón *m*

Labour Exchange *n Brit* HIST bolsa *f* de trabajo **labour force** *n* (*of country*) mano *f* de obra; (*of company*) plantilla *f* **labour-intensive** *adj* que requiere mucha mano de obra

labour market *n* mercado *m* laboral **labour movement** *n* POL movimiento *m* obrero **labour pains** *npl* MED dolores *mpl* de parto **Labour Party** *n no pl, Brit, Aus* POL **the ~** el Partido Laborista **labour relations** *npl* relaciones *fpl* laborales **labour-saving** *adj* que ahorra trabajo **labour shortage** *n* escasez *f* de mano de obra **labour union** *n Am* sindicato *m* **labour ward** *n* sala *f* de partos

Labrador (**retriever**) ['læbrədɔːr (rɪ'triːvəʳ), *Am:* -dɔːr (-ɚ)] *n* labrador *m*

laburnum [lə'bɜːnəm, *Am:* -'bɜːr-] *n* lluvia *f* de oro

labyrinth ['læbərɪnθ, *Am:* -ɚ-] <-es> *n* laberinto *m*

lace [leɪs] I. *n* 1. *no pl* (*cloth*) encaje *m;* (*edging*) puntilla *f* 2.(*cord*) cordón *m;* **shoe ~s** cordones *mpl* de zapatos; **to do up one's ~s** atarse los cordones II. *vt* 1.(*fasten*) atar 2.(*add alcohol to*) echar licor a

◆**lace into** *vt* **to ~ sb** dar una paliza a alguien

◆**lace up** *vt* atar

lacerate ['læsəreɪt] *vt* lacerar

laceration [ˌlæsə'reɪʃən] *n* laceración *f*

lace-ups ['leɪsʌps] *npl* zapatos *mpl* con cordones

lachrymose ['lækrɪməʊs, *Am:* -moʊs] *adj liter* 1.(*tending to cry easily*) llorón, -ona 2.(*sad*) lacrimógeno, -a

lack [læk] I. *n no pl* falta *f;* **~ of funds** escasez *f* de fondos; **for ~ of ...** por falta de... II. *vt* carecer de; **she ~s talent/experience** le falta talento/experiencia; **to ~ the energy to do sth** no tener la fuerza para hacer algo

lackadaisical [ˌlækə'deɪzɪkl] *adj* apático, -a

lackey ['læki] *n a. fig* lacayo, -a *m, f*

lacking ['lækɪŋ] *adj* **he is ~ in talent/experience** le falta talento/experiencia

lackluster *adj Am,* **lacklustre** ['lækˌlʌstəʳ, *Am:* -tɚ] *adj Brit, Aus* 1.(*not shiny*) deslustrado, -a 2.(*dull*) gris

laconic [lə'kɒnɪk, *Am:* -'kɑːnɪk] *adj* lacónico, -a

lacquer ['lækəʳ, *Am:* -ɚ] I. *n* (*for wood, hair*) laca *f;* (*for nails*) esmalte *m* II. *vt* 1.(*coat with varnish*) laquear 2.(*spray hair*) echar laca a

lacrosse [lə'krɒs, *Am:* -'krɑːs] *n no pl* SPORTS lacrosse *m*

lad [læd] *n Brit, inf* (*boy*) chico *m;* **a young ~** un chico; **the ~s** los muchachos; **he's a bit of a ~** le gustan mucho las faldas

ladder ['lædəʳ, *Am:* -ɚ] I. *n* 1.(*for climbing*) escalera *f* (de mano) 2.(*hierarchy*) escala *f;* **to move up the ~** ascender de categoría; (*in company*) ascender en la empresa; **to climb the social ~** subir en la escala social 3. *Brit, Aus* (*in stocking*) carrera *f* II. *vt* hacerse una carrera en III. *vi* **these tights ~ easily** a estas medias se les hacen carreras enseguida

laddie ['lædi] *n Scot, inf* muchacho *m*

laden ['leɪdn] *adj* cargado, -a; **to be ~ with ...** estar cargado de...

la-di-da [ˌlɑːdɪ'dɑː, *Am:* -diː-] *adj inf* repipi

lading ['leɪdɪŋ] *n* NAUT cargamento *m;* **bill of ~** conocimiento *m* de embarque

ladle ['leɪdl] I. *n* cucharón *m,* ramillón *m Col, Ven;* **soup ~** cucharón para la sopa II. *vt* 1.(*soup*) servir (*con cucharón*) 2.(*advice, sympathy*) repartir generosamente

lady ['leɪdi] <-ies> *n* señora *f;* (*aristocratic*) dama *f;* **young ~** señorita *f;* **the ~ of the house** la señora de la casa; **to be a real ~** ser toda una señora; **cleaning ~** mujer de la limpieza; **ladies and gentlemen!** ¡señoras y señores!

ladybird ['leɪdibɜːd, *Am:* -bɜːrd] *n Brit, Aus,* **ladybug** ['leɪdibʌg] *n Am* mariquita *f* **lady-in-waiting** <-ies> *n* dama *f* de honor **ladykiller** *n* casanova *m* **ladylike** *adj* femenino, -a **ladyship** *n form* **her/your ~** Su Señoría **lady's maid** *n* doncella *f*

LAFTA *n abbr of* **Latin American Free Trade Association** ALALC *f*

lag[1] [læg] I. *n* (*lapse*) lapso *m* II. <-gg-> *vi* rezagarse; **to ~ behind** (**sb/sth**) quedarse detrás (de alguien/algo)

lag[2] [læg] <-gg-> *vt* (*insulate*) revestir con aislantes

lag[3] [læg] *n Brit, inf* **old ~** presidiario *m*

lager ['lɑːgəʳ, *Am:* -gɚ] *n no pl* cerveza *f* rubia

lager lout *n Brit, inf* gamberro *m* de litrona

lagging ['lægɪŋ] *n* revestimiento *m*

lagoon [lə'guːn] *n* laguna *f,* cocha *f AmS*

laid [leɪd] *pt, pp of* **lay**[1]

laid-back [ˌleɪd'bæk] *adj inf* tranquilo, -a

lain [leɪn] *pp of* **lie**[2]

lair [leəʳ, *Am:* ler] *n* 1.(*of animal*) cubil *m* 2.(*of criminal*) guarida *f*

laird [leəd, *Am:* lerd] *n Scot* terrateniente *m*

laissez-faire ['leɪseɪ'feəʳ, *Am:* 'leseɪ'fer] *n no pl* laissez-faire *m;* **~ attitude** actitud *f* permisiva

laity ['leɪəti] *n no pl* **the ~** el laicado

lake [leɪk] *n* lago *m*

lam [læm] I. *n Am, inf* **to be on the ~** ser fugitivo de la justicia II. <-mm-> *vt inf* pegar

lama ['lɑːmə] *n* REL lama *m*

lamb [læm] I. *n* 1. (*animal*) cordero *m* 2. *no pl* (*meat*) (carne *f* de) cordero *m* ►**to go like a ~ to the slaughter** ir como borrego al matadero II. *vi* parir

lambast(e) [læm'bæst, *Am:* -'beɪst] *vt* vapulear

lamb chop *n* chuleta *f* de cordero **lambskin** *n* (piel *f* de) cordero *m* **lambswool** *n no pl* lana *f* de cordero

lame [leɪm] *adj* 1. (*person, horse*) cojo, -a; **to go ~** quedarse cojo 2. (*argument*) flojo, -a; (*excuse*) débil

lameness *n no pl* 1. (*of person, horse*) cojera *f* 2. (*of argument*) flojedad *f;* (*of excuse*) debilidad *f*

lament [lə'ment] I. *n* MUS, LIT elegía *f* II. *vt* lamentar; **to ~ sb** llorar a alguien III. *vi* **to ~ over sth** lamentarse de algo

lamentable ['læməntəbl, *Am:* lə'mənt̬ə-] *adj* lamentable

lamentation [ˌlæmen'teɪʃən, *Am:* -ən'-] *n* 1. (*regrets*) lamentos *mpl* 2. *no pl* (*mourning*) lamentación *f*

laminate[1] ['læmɪnət] *n* TECH laminado *m*

laminate[2] ['læmɪneɪt] *vt* (*glass, wood*) laminar; (*document*) plastificar

laminated ['læmɪneɪtɪd, *Am:* -t̬ɪd] *adj* (*glass, wood*) laminado, -a; (*document*) plastificado, -a

lamp [læmp] *n* lámpara *f;* **bedside ~** lamparilla *f* de mesita de noche; **street ~** farola *f*

lampoon [læm'puːn] I. *n* sátira *f* II. *vt* satirizar

lamppost ['læmppəʊst, *Am:* -poʊst] *n* farola *f*

lamprey ['læmpri] *n* lamprea *f*

lampshade ['læmpʃeɪd] *n* pantalla *f* (de lámpara)

LAN [læn] *n* INFOR *abbr of* **local area network** RAL *f*

lance [lɑːns, *Am:* læns] I. *n* MIL lanza *f* II. *vt* MED abrir con lanceta

lancet ['lɑːnsɪt, *Am:* 'lænsɪt] *n* MED lanceta *f*

land [lænd] I. *n* 1. *no pl* GEO, AGR tierra *f;* **on ~** en tierra; **to travel by ~** viajar por tierra; **to work (on) the ~** trabajar (en) el campo; **to have dry ~ under one's feet** pisar tierra firme 2. (*area: for building*) terreno *m* 3. (*country*) país *m* ►**to be in the ~ of the living** *iron* estar despierto; **to see how the ~ lies** tantear el terreno II. *vi* 1. (*plane, bird*) aterrizar; **to ~ on the moon** alunizar; **to come in to ~** aterrizar 2. (*arrive by boat*) llegar en barco 3. (*person, ball*) caer III. *vt* 1. (*bring onto land: aircraft*) hacer aterrizar; (*boat*) amarrar; **to ~ a plane on water** hacer aterrizar un avión en el agua 2. (*unload*) desembarcar 3. (*obtain*) conseguir; (*fish*) pescar; **to ~ a job** conseguir un trabajo 4. (*cause*) **to ~ sb with a problem** endosar un problema a alguien; **to ~ sb in trouble** meter a alguien en un lío

landed ['lændɪd] *adj* que posee tierras; **a ~ family** una familia hacendada; **the ~ gentry** los terratenientes

landfall ['lændfɔːl] *n* vista *f* de tierra; **to make ~** avistar tierra

landfill site ['lændfɪl saɪt] *n* vertedero *m* de basuras

land forces *npl* MIL ejército *m* de tierra

landholder *n* terrateniente *mf*

landing ['lændɪŋ] *n* 1. (*on staircase*) rellano *m* 2. AVIAT aterrizaje *m;* **to make a ~** realizar un aterrizaje 3. NAUT desembarco *m*

landing card *n* tarjeta *f* de desembarque **landing craft** *n* MIL lancha *f* de desembarco **landing field** *n* campo *m* de aterrizaje **landing gear** *n* AVIAT tren *m* de aterrizaje **landing net** *n* salabardo *m* **landing stage** *n* desembarcadero *m* **landing strip** *n* pista *f* de aterrizaje

landlady ['lændˌleɪdi] <-ies> *n* (*of house*) propietaria *f;* (*of pub, hotel*) dueña *f;* (*of boarding house*) patrona *f* **landless** *adj* sin tierras **landlocked** *adj* cercado, -a de tierra; **a ~ country** un país sin acceso al mar **landlord** *n* 1. (*of house*) propietario *m;* (*of pub, hotel*) dueño *m;* (*of boarding house*) patrón *m* 2. (*landowner*) terrateniente *m* **landlubber** *n inf* marinero *m* de agua dulce **landmark** *n* 1. (*object serving as a guide*) mojón *m;* (*point of recognition*) punto *m* destacado 2. (*monument*) monumento *m* histórico 3. (*event*) hito *m* **landmine** *n* mina *f* terrestre **land office** *n Am* HIST oficina *f* del catastro; **to do a ~ business** *Am, inf* hacer un buen negocio **landowner** *n* terrateniente *mf* **land reform** *n* reforma *f* agraria

landscape ['lændskeɪp] I. *n* 1. *no pl* (*scenery, painting*) paisaje *m;* **urban ~** paisaje urbano 2. *fig* panorama *m;* **the political ~** el panorama político 3. INFOR impresión *f* horizontal II. *vt* ajardinar

landscape architect *n,* **landscape gardener** *n* arquitecto, -a *m, f* de jardines **landscape architecture** *n,* **landscape gardening** *n no pl* arquitectura *f* de jardines **landscape painter** *n* paisajista *mf*

landslide ['lændslaɪd] *n* 1. GEO corrimiento *m* de tierras 2. POL victoria *f* arrolladora; **to win by a ~** ganar por mayoría abrumadora **landslip** *n Brit* GEO corrimiento *m* de tierras **land tax** <-es> *n* contribución *f* territorial **landward** I. *adj* de la parte de la tierra; **the ~ side** el lado de la tierra II. *adv* hacia (la) tierra

lane [leɪn] *n* 1. (*narrow road: in country*) vereda *f;* (*in town*) callejón *m* 2. (*marked strip: on road*) carril *m;* SPORTS calle *f;* **bus/cycle ~** carril de autobús/de bicicleta; **to change ~s** cambiar de carril 3. AVIAT vía *f* aérea; NAUT ruta *f* marítima

language ['læŋgwɪdʒ] *n* 1. *no pl* (*system of communication*) lenguaje *m;* **bad ~** palabrotas *fpl;* **formal/spoken/written ~** lengua formal/oral/escrita 2. (*of particular community*) idioma *m;* **native** ~ lengua *f* materna; **the English** ~ la lengua inglesa **3.** (*of specialist group*) lenguaje *m;* **computer programming** ~ lenguaje de programación (de ordenadores); **legal** ~ lenguaje jurídico ►**to speak the same** ~ hablar el mismo idioma

language laboratory *n* laboratorio *m* de idiomas **language learning** *n* aprendizaje *m* de una lengua

languid ['læŋgwɪd] *adj liter* lánguido, -a

languish ['læŋgwɪʃ] *vi* languidecer; **he** ~**ed in bed for weeks** estuvo postrado en la cama durante semanas

languor ['læŋgər, *Am:* -gɚ] *n no pl, liter* languidez *f*

languorous ['læŋgərəs, *Am:* -gɚ-] *adj liter* lánguido, -a

lank [læŋk] *adj* **1.** (*hair*) lacio, -a **2.** (*person*) larguirucho, -a

lanky ['læŋki] *adj* desgarbado, -a

lanolin ['lænəlɪn] *n* lanolina *f*

lantern ['læntən, *Am:* -t̬ɚn] *n* linterna *f;* (*light*) farol *m*

lanyard ['lænjəd, *Am:* -jɚd] *n* **1.** (*short rope or cord*) cordel *m* **2.** NAUT acollador *m*

Laos [laʊs] *n* Laos *m*

lap[1] [læp] *n* falda *f* ►**in the** ~ **of the gods** *Brit* en manos de Dios; **to live in the** ~ **of luxury** vivir a cuerpo de rey

lap[2] [læp] SPORTS **I.** *n* vuelta *f;* ~ **of honour** vuelta de honor **II.** <-pp-> *vt* sacar una vuelta de ventaja a

lap[3] [læp] <-pp-> **I.** *vt* **1.** (*drink*) beber dando lengüetazos **2.** (*waves*) acariciar **II.** *vi* (*hit gently*) **to** ~ **against sth** chocar suavemente contra algo

◆**lap up** *vt* **1.** (*drink*) beber dando lengüetazos **2.** *fig, inf* aceptar entusiasmado; **he lapped up the praise** saboreaba las alabanzas

lapdog ['læpˌdɒg, *Am:* -dɑːg] *n* perro *m* faldero

lapel [lə'pel] *n* solapa *f;* **to grab sb by the** ~**s** agarrar a alguien por las solapas

lapis lazuli [ˌlæpɪs'læzjʊli, *Am:* -'læzə-] *n* **1.** (*blue gemstone*) lapislázuli *m* **2.** (*blue colour*) azul *m* de ultramar

Lapland ['læplænd] *n* Laponia *f*

Laplander ['læplændər, *Am:* -ɚ] *n,* **Lapp** [læp] *n* lapón, -ona *m, f*

lapse [læps] **I.** *n* **1.** *no pl* (*period*) lapso *m* **2.** (*failure*) lapsus *m inv;* ~ **of judgement** desacierto *m;* ~ **of memory** lapsus de memoria **II.** *vi* **1.** (*deteriorate*) deteriorarse **2.** (*end*) terminar; (*contract*) vencer; (*subscription*) caducar **3.** (*revert to*) **to** ~ **into sth** reincidir en algo; **to** ~ **into one's native dialect** recurrir al dialecto nativo; **to** ~ **into silence** quedar(se) en silencio

lapsed [læpst] *adj* (*Catholic*) no practicante

laptop (**computer**) ['æptɒp, *Am:* -tɑːp] *n* (ordenador *m*) portátil *m*

lapwing ['læpwɪŋ] *n* avefría *f*

larceny ['lɑːsəni, *Am:* 'lɑːr-] <-ies> *n Am* hurto *m*

larch [lɑːtʃ, *Am:* lɑːrtʃ] *n* alerce *m*

lard [lɑːd, *Am:* lɑːrd] **I.** *n no pl* manteca *f* de cerdo **II.** *vt* untar (con manteca de cerdo); **to** ~ **with sth** *fig* (*text*) salpicar de algo

larder ['lɑːdər, *Am:* 'lɑːrdɚ] *n* (*room*) despensa *f;* (*cupboard*) alacena *f*

large [lɑːdʒ, *Am:* lɑːrdʒ] *adj* grande; **a** ~ **number of people** un gran número de gente; **a** ~ **family** una familia numerosa ►**to be at** ~ andar suelto; **by and** ~ por lo general

largely ['lɑːdʒli, *Am:* 'lɑːrdʒ-] *adv* en gran parte

largeness *n no pl* (gran) tamaño *m*

large-scale [ˌlɑːdʒ'skeɪl, *Am:* ˌlɑːrdʒ-] *adj* a gran escala

largess *n Am,* **largesse** [lɑː'dʒes, *Am:* lɑːr'-] *n no pl* generosidad *f*

lariat ['lærɪət, *Am:* 'ler-] *n* lazo *m*

lark[1] [lɑːk, *Am:* lɑːrk] *n* (*bird*) alondra *f* ►**to be up with the** ~ levantarse con las gallinas

lark[2] [lɑːk, *Am:* lɑːrk] **I.** *n* **1.** *Brit, inf* (*joke*) broma *f;* **for a** ~ de broma **2.** *Brit, inf* (*business*) asunto *m;* **don't get involved in that** ~**!** ¡no te metas en ese asunto [*o* negocio]!; **sod this for a** ~**!** ¡estoy hasta el gorro de eso! **II.** *vi Brit, inf* **to** ~ **about** hacer tonterías

larkspur ['lɑːkspɜːr, *Am:* 'lɑːrkspɜːr] *n* espuela *f* de caballero

larva ['lɑːvə] <-vae> *n* larva *f*

laryngitis [ˌlærɪn'dʒaɪtɪs, *Am:* ˌlerɪn'dʒaɪt̬ɪs] *n no pl* laringitis *f inv*

larynx ['lærɪŋks, *Am:* 'ler-] <-ynxes *o* -ynges> *n* laringe *f*

lasagne [lə'zænjə, *Am:* -'zɑːnjə] *n* lasaña *f*

lascivious [lə'sɪvɪəs] *adj* lascivo, -a

laser ['leɪzər, *Am:* -zɚ] *n* láser *m*

laser beam *n* rayo *m* láser **laser printer** *n* impresora *f* láser **laser show** *n* espectáculo *m* con láser

lash[1] [læʃ] <-shes> *n* (*eyelash*) pestaña *f*

lash[2] [læʃ] **I.** <-shes> *n* **1.** (*whip*) látigo *m;* (*flexible part of a whip*) tralla *f* **2.** (*stroke of whip*) latigazo *m;* (*of tail*) coletazo *m* ►**to feel the** ~ **of sb's tongue** ser fustigado **II.** *vt* **1.** (*whip*) azotar; (*rain*) golpear **2.** (*criticize*) fustigar

◆**lash about** *vi,* **lash around** *vi* golpear a diestro y siniestro

◆**lash down** *vt* atar firmemente

◆**lash out** *vi* **1.** (*attack*) **to** ~ **at sb** atacar a alguien; (*verbally*) arremeter contra alguien **2.** *inf* (*spend*) **to** ~ **on sth** gastarse mucho dinero en algo

lashing ['læʃɪŋ] *n* **1.** azotaina *f;* **to give sb a tongue** ~ echar un rapapolvo a alguien **2.** *Brit* ~**s of** montones *mpl* de

lass [læs] <-sses> *n,* **lassie** ['læsi] *n Scot, inf* (*girl*) chica *f*

lassitude ['læsɪtjuːd, *Am:* -tuːd] *n no pl, form* lasitud *f*

lasso [læ'suː, *Am:* 'læsoʊ] **I.** <-os *o* -oes> *n*

lazo *m* II. *vt* lazar

last[1] [lɑːst, *Am:* læst] *n* horma *f*

last[2] [lɑːst, *Am:* læst] I. *adj* 1. (*final: time, opportunity*) último, -a; **to have the ~ word** tener la última palabra; **to wait till the ~ minute** (**to do sth**) esperar hasta el último minuto (para hacer algo); **this will be the ~ time** esta será la última vez 2. (*most recent*) último, -a; **~ week** la semana pasada; **~ night** anoche II. *adv* 1. (*coming at the end*) por último; **~ but not least** por último, pero no por eso menos importante 2. (*most recently*) por última vez III. *n* **the ~ to do sth** el último en hacer algo; **the ~ but one** el penúltimo; **that was the ~ of the cake** era todo lo que quedaba de pastel ►**at** (**long**) **~** al fin; **to the ~** *form* hasta el final

last[3] [lɑːst, *Am:* læst] I. *vi* durar II. *vt* **this coat has ~ed me five years** hace cinco años que tengo este abrigo

last-ditch [ˌlɑːstˈdɪtʃ, *Am:* ˌlæst-] *adj*, **last-gasp** [ˌlɑːstˈɡɑːsp, *Am:* ˌlæstˈɡæsp] *adj* desesperado, -a

lasting [ˈlɑːstɪŋ, *Am:* ˌlæst-] *adj* duradero, -a; **to his ~ shame** para su eterna vergüenza

lastly [ˈlɑːstli, *Am:* ˈlæst-] *adv* por último

last-minute [ˌlɑːstˈmɪnɪt, *Am:* ˌlæst-] *adj* de última hora

last name *n* apellido *m*

latch [lætʃ] <-tches> *n* pestillo *m;* **on the ~** cerrado con picaporte

◆**latch on** *vi inf* 1. *Brit* (*understand*) darse cuenta; **to ~ to sth** captar algo 2. (*attach oneself*) **to ~ to sb/sth** agarrarse a alguien/algo

latchkey [ˈlætʃkiː] *n* llave *f* (de la casa)

late [leɪt] I. *adj* 1. (*after appointed time*) retrasado, -a; **you're ~!** ¡llegas tarde!; **the train was an hour ~** el tren llegó con una hora de retraso 2. (*occurring after the usual time*) tardío, -a; **~ developer** estudiante *mf* rezagado; **~ night TV show** programa *m* de televisión de noche; **in the ~ nineteenth-century** a finales del siglo XIX; **in ~ summer** a finales del verano 3. (*deceased*) fallecido, -a 4. (*recent*) reciente; **~ news** noticias *fpl* de última hora II. *adv* 1. (*after usual time*) tarde; **too little, too ~** demasiado poco y demasiado tarde; **to work ~** trabajar hasta (muy) tarde; **it's rather ~ in the day to do sth** es tarde para hacer algo 2. (*at advanced time*) **~ in the day** a última hora del día; **~ at night** muy entrada la noche; **he got his driver's licence ~ in life** se sacó el carnet de conducir de mayor 3. (*recently*) **as ~ as the 1980s** aún en los años ochenta; **of ~** últimamente ►**better ~ than never** *prov* más vale tarde que nunca *prov*

late-breaking *adj* de gran actualidad

latecomer [ˈleɪtˌkʌməʳ, *Am:* -ɚ] *n persona o cosa que llega tarde*

lately [ˈleɪtli] *adv* (*recently*) últimamente, ultimadamente *Méx;* **until ~** hasta hace poco

lateness [ˈleɪtnɪs] *n no pl* retraso *m*

late-night [ˈleɪtˌnaɪt] *adj* nocturno, -a

latent [ˈleɪtnt] *adj* latente

later [ˈleɪtəʳ] I. *adj comp of* **late** posterior; (*version*) más reciente II. *adv comp of* **late** más tarde; **no ~ than nine o'clock** no más tarde de las nueve; **~ on** después; **see you ~!** ¡hasta luego!

lateral [ˈlætərəl, *Am:* ˈlæt̬ɚəl] *adj* lateral; **~ thinking** pensamiento *m* lateral (*manera de solucionar problemas utilizando más la imaginación que el pensamiento lógico*)

latest [ˈleɪtɪst] I. *adj superl of* **late** último, -a; **the ~ …** el más reciente…; **his ~ movie** su última película; **at the ~** a más tardar II. *n* **the ~** las últimas noticias; **have you heard the ~ about them?** ¿te has enterado de lo suyo?; **the ~ in art/physics** lo último en arte/física; **at the** (**very**) **~** a más tardar

latex [ˈleɪteks, *Am:* ˈlæt̬ɪ-] *n* látex *m*

lath [lɑːθ, *Am:* læθ] <-thes> *n* listón *m*

lathe [leɪð] *n* torno *m*

lathe operator *n* tornero, -a *m, f*

lather [ˈlɑːðəʳ, *Am:* ˈlæðɚ] I. *n no pl* 1. (*fine bubbles*) espuma *f* 2. (*sweat*) sudor *m;* **to be in a ~** *fig* estar histérico; **to get** (**oneself**) **into a ~** ponerse histérico II. *vi* hacer espuma III. *vt* enjabonar

Latin [ˈlætɪn, *Am:* -ən] I. *adj* latino, -a II. *n* 1. (*person*) latino, -a *m, f* 2. LING latín *m*

Latin America *n* América *f* Latina

Latin American I. *adj* latinoamericano, -a II. *n* (*person*) latinoamericano, -a *m, f*

Latino [ləˈtiːnəʊ, *Am:* -noʊ] *n* (*person*) latino, -a *m, f*

latish [ˈleɪtɪʃ, *Am:* -t̬ɪʃ] I. *adj* (algo) tardío, -a II. *adv* algo tarde

latitude [ˈlætɪtjuːd, *Am:* ˈlæt̬ətuːd] *n* 1. GEO latitud *f* 2. *form* (*freedom*) libertad *f*

latrine [ləˈtriːn] *n* letrina *f*

latter [ˈlætəʳ, *Am:* ˈlæt̬ɚ] *adj* 1. (*second of two*) **the ~** el último 2. (*near the end*) hacia el final; **in the ~ half of the year** en la segunda mitad del año

latterly *adv* últimamente

lattice [ˈlætɪs, *Am:* ˈlæt̬-] *n* (*framework*) enrejado *m;* (*window*) celosía *f;* **~ screen** pantalla *f* de retícula

Latvia [ˈlætvɪə] *n* Letonia *f*

Latvian I. *adj* letón, -ona II. *n* 1. (*person*) letón, -ona *m, f* 2. LING letón *m*

laudable [ˈlɔːdəbl, *Am:* ˈlɑː-] *adj form* loable

laudanum [ˈlɔːdənəm, *Am:* ˈlɑː-] *n no pl* láudano *m*

laudatory [ˈlɔːdətəri, *Am:* ˈlɑːdətɔːr-] *adj form* laudatorio, -a

laugh [lɑːf] I. *n* 1. (*sound*) risa *f;* **to get a ~** hacer reír; **to do sth for a ~** hacer algo para divertirse 2. *inf* (*activity*) actividad *f* divertida; *Brit* (*person*) persona *f* divertida II. *vi* reír(se); **to ~ aloud** reírse a carcajadas; **to make sb ~** hacer reír a alguien; **to ~ at sb/sth** *a. fig* reírse de alguien/algo; **to ~ till one cries** llorar de la risa; **his threats make me ~** *inf* sus amenazas me hacen gracia ►**he who ~s last ~s longest**

prov quien ríe el último, ríe mejor *prov*
◆**laugh off** *vt* tomar a risa
laughable ['lɑːfəbl, *Am:* 'læfə-] *adj* de risa
laughing I. *n* risas *fpl* II. *adj* de risa; **this is no ~ matter** no es cosa de risa
laughing stock *n* hazmerreír *m*
laughter ['lɑːftəʳ, *Am:* 'læftɚ] *n no pl* risa(s) *f(pl)*; **to roar with ~** echarse a reír ►**~ is the best medicine** *prov* quien canta, sus males espanta *prov*
launch [lɔːntʃ, *Am:* lɑːntʃ] I. <-ches> *n* 1. (*boat*) lancha *f* 2. (*act of setting in the water*) botadura *f* 3. (*act of sending forth: of missile*) lanzamiento *m* 4. (*introduction: of exhibition*) inauguración *f*; (*of book*) presentación *f* II. *vt* 1. (*set in the water*) botar 2. (*send forth: missile*) lanzar 3. (*introduce: book*) presentar 4. (*start: investigation*) emprender; (*exhibition*) inaugurar 5. **to ~ oneself at sb** lanzarse sobre alguien
◆**launch into** *vt* emprender
◆**launch out** *vi Brit* lanzarse
launching ['lɔːntʃɪŋ, *Am:* 'lɑːntʃ-] *n* 1. (*act of setting in the water*) botadura *f* 2. (*act of sending forth: of missile*) lanzamiento *m* 3. (*beginning: of exhibition, campaign*) inauguración *f* 4. (*introduction: of book*) presentación *f*
launching pad *n*, **launch pad** *n* rampa *f* de lanzamiento
launder ['lɔːndəʳ, *Am:* 'lɑːndɚ] *vt* 1. *form* (*wash*) lavar y planchar 2. *fig* (*money*) blanquear, lavar *AmL*
launderette [lɔːn'dret, *Am:* lɑːndə'ret] *n Brit* lavandería *f* (automática)
laundry ['lɔːndri, *Am:* 'lɑːn-] *n* 1. *no pl* (*dirty clothes*) ropa *f* sucia; **to do the ~** hacer la colada 2. *no pl* (*washed clothes*) ropa *f* lavada 3. <-ies> (*place*) lavandería *f*
laundry basket *n* cesto *m* de la ropa sucia **laundry service** *n* servicio *m* de lavandería
laureate ['lɒrɪət, *Am:* 'lɔːriɪt] *n* **Nobel ~** premio *mf* Nobel; **Poet Laureate** poeta *m* laureado (*en Gran Bretaña, poeta elegido por la reina para escribir poemas en ocasiones especiales*)
laurel ['lɒrəl, *Am:* 'lɔːr-] *n* laurel *m* ►**to rest on one's ~s** dormirse en los laureles
lava ['lɑːvə] *n* lava *f*
lavatory ['lævətri, *Am:* -tɔːri] <-ies> *n* lavabo *m*, lavatorio *m AmL*; **public ~** lavabo público; **to go to the ~** ir al baño
lavatory seat *n* taza *f* del váter
lavender ['lævəndəʳ, *Am:* -dɚ] I. *n* lavanda *f* II. *adj* (de) lavanda
lavish ['lævɪʃ] I. *adj* (*banquet*) opíparo, -a; (*party*) espléndido, -a; (*reception*) fastuoso, -a; (*praise*) abundante II. *vt* **to ~ sth on sb** prodigar algo a alguien
law [lɔː, *Am:* lɑː] *n* 1. *a.* PHYS ley *f*; **the ~ of supply and demand** la ley de la oferta y la demanda; **the ~ of averages** (lo que dicen) las estadísticas; **the ~s governing the exportation of paintings** las leyes que regulan la exportación de cuadros; **his word is ~** lo que dice él va a misa; **the first ~ of sth** el principio básico de algo 2. (*legal system*) derecho *m*; (*body of laws*) ley *f*; **~ and order** la ley y el orden; **to be against the ~** ser ilegal; **to take the ~ into one's own hands** tomarse la justicia por su mano 3. (*the police*) policía *f* 4. (*court*) **to go to ~** recurrir a los tribunales ►**the ~ of the jungle** la ley de la selva; **to be a ~ unto oneself** dictar sus propias leyes
law-abiding ['lɔːə'baɪdɪŋ, *Am:* 'lɑː] *adj* observante de la ley **law breaker** *n* transgresor(a) *m(f)* de la ley **law court** *n* tribunal *m* de justicia **law enforcement** *n no pl, Am* aplicación *f* de la ley
lawful ['lɔːfəl, *Am:* 'lɑː-] *adj form* 1. (*legal*) legal; (*demands*) legítimo, -a; **~ owner** propietario, -a *m, f* en derecho 2. (*law-abiding*) observante de la ley
lawgiver ['lɔːˌgɪvəʳ, *Am:* 'lɑːˌgɪvɚ] *n* legislador(a) *m(f)*
lawless ['lɔːlɪs, *Am:* 'lɑː-] *adj* sin leyes; (*country*) anárquico, -a
lawmaker ['lɔːˌmeɪkəʳ, *Am:* 'lɑːˌmeɪkɚ] *n* legislador(a) *m(f)*
lawn [lɔːn, *Am:* lɑːn] *n* (*grass*) césped *m*, pasto *m AmL*
lawnmower *n* cortacésped *m* **lawn tennis** *n* tenis *m* sobre hierba
law school *n Am* facultad *f* de derecho **law student** *n* estudiante *mf* de derecho **lawsuit** *n* proceso *m*; **to bring a ~ against sb** presentar una demanda contra alguien
lawyer ['lɔːjəʳ, *Am:* 'lɑːjɚ] *n* abogado, -a *m, f*
lax [læks] *adj* 1. (*lacking care*) descuidado, -a; **~ security** seguridad *f* poco rigurosa; **to be ~ in doing sth** hacer algo de manera negligente 2. (*lenient*) indulgente; (*rules*) poco severo, -a
laxative ['læksətɪv, *Am:* -t̬ɪv] I. *n* laxante *m* II. *adj* laxante
laxity ['læksəti, *Am:* -t̬i] *n*, **laxness** *n no pl* descuido *m*
lay[1] [leɪ] I. *n* 1. (*situation*) situación *f*; **the ~ of the land** la configuración del terreno; *fig* la situación actual 2. *vulg* **to be a good ~** tener buen polvo II. <laid, laid> *vt* 1. (*place*) poner; **to ~ sth on/over sth** poner algo en/encima de algo; **to ~ sth flat** derribar algo; **to lay stress on sth** poner énfasis en algo; **to lay the blame on sb** echar la culpa a alguien 2. (*install*) colocar; (*cable*) tender; (*carpet*) poner, extender; (*pipes*) instalar; **to ~ the foundations for sth** *a. fig* echar los cimientos de algo 3. (*prepare*) preparar; **to ~ the table** *Brit* poner la mesa 4. (*egg*) poner 5. *vulg* (*have sex with*) follar 6. (*bet*) apostar; **to ~ an amount on sth** apostar una cantidad en algo 7. (*state*) presentar; **to ~ one's case before sb/sth** presentar su caso ante alguien/algo; **to**

~ **a charge against sb** formular una acusación contra alguien; **to ~ claim to sth** reclamar algo **III.** <laid, laid> *vi* poner huevos

◆**lay about** *vt* **to ~ sb** emprenderla a golpes con alguien

◆**lay aside** *vt,* **lay away** *vt* **1.** (*put away*) guardar; **to ~ one's differences** dejar de lado las diferencias **2.** (*save: food*) guardar; (*money*) ahorrar

◆**lay back** *vt* reposar

◆**lay before** *vt* **to lay sth before sb** poner algo frente a alguien; **to lay one's case before sb** presentar su caso ante alguien

◆**lay by** *vt* reservar

◆**lay down** *vt* **1.** (*put down*) poner a un lado; (*arms*) deponer; (*life*) sacrificar **2.** (*establish*) estipular; (*law*) dictar; **it is laid down that ...** está estipulado que...

◆**lay in** *vt* proveerse de

◆**lay into** *vt* **1.** *inf* (*assault*) atacar **2.** (*criticize*) arremeter contra **3.** (*eat*) lanzarse sobre

◆**lay off I.** *vt* despedir (temporalmente) **II.** *vi* dejar; **to ~ sb** dejar en paz a alguien; **to ~ smoking** dejar de fumar

◆**lay on** *vt* **1.** (*instal*) instalar **2.** (*provide: food, drink*) proveer de

◆**lay open** *vt* **1.** (*uncover*) descubrir **2.** (*expose*) exponer; **to lay oneself open** exponerse

◆**lay out** *vt* **1.** (*organize*) organizar **2.** (*spread out*) extender **3.** (*prepare for burial*) amortajar **4.** *inf* (*render unconscious*) dejar fuera de combate **5.** *inf* (*money*) gastar **6.** *Am* (*explain*) presentar

◆**lay to** *vi* llevar a puerto seguro

◆**lay up** *vt* **1.** (*store*) guardar; (*money*) ahorrar **2.** (*ship*) desarmar; (*car*) dejar en el garaje **3.** (*in bed*) **to be laid up** guardar cama

lay[2] [leɪ] *adj* **1.** (*not professional*) lego, -a; **in ~ terms** en términos profanos **2.** (*not of the clergy*) laico, -a

lay[3] [leɪ] *pt of* **lie[2]**

layabout ['leɪəˌbaʊt] *n inf* vago, -a *m, f*

lay-by ['leɪbaɪ] *n* **1.** *Brit* (*stopping place*) apartadero *m* **2.** *no pl, Aus* **to buy/put on ~** comprar a plazos

layer[1] ['leɪəʳ, *Am:* -ɚ] **I.** *n* **1.** capa *f;* **ozone ~** capa de ozono **2.** (*level*) estrato *m* **II.** *vt* acodar

layer[2] ['leɪəʳ, *Am:* -ɚ] *n* (*hen*) gallina *f* ponedora

layered *adj* en capas

layette [leɪ'et] *n* canastilla *f*

layman ['leɪmən] <-men> *n* lego *m*

lay-off ['leɪɒf, *Am:* -ɑːf] *n* despido *m* (*por falta de trabajo*)

layout ['leɪaʊt] *n* **1.** (*of letter, magazine*) diseño *m;* (*of town*) trazado *m* **2.** TYPO maquetación *f*

layover ['leɪəʊvəʳ, *Am:* -oʊvɚ] *n Am* (*on journey*) parada *f;* AVIAT escala *f*

laywoman ['leɪwʊmən] <-women> *n* lega *f*

laze [leɪz] <-zing> *vi* holgazanear

laziness ['leɪzɪnɪs] *n no pl* holgazanería *f*

lazy ['leɪzi] <-ier, -iest> *adj* (*person*) vago, -a; (*day*) perezoso, -a

lb *abbr of* **pound** libra *f* (= *0,45 kg*)

LCD [ˌelsiː'diː] *n abbr of* **liquid crystal display** pantalla *f* de cristal líquido

lead[1] [liːd] **I.** *n* **1.** *no pl* (*front position*) delantera *f;* **to be in the ~** estar a la cabeza; **to hold the ~** llevar la delantera; **to lose one's ~** perder la delantera; **to move into the ~** ponerse a la cabeza; **to take** (**over**) **the lead** tomar la delantera **2.** (*example*) ejemplo *m;* (*guiding*) iniciativa *f;* **to follow sb's ~** seguir el ejemplo de alguien; **to give a ~** dar una indicación **3.** THEAT papel *m* principal; **to play the ~** representar el papel principal **4.** (*clue*) pista *f;* **to get a ~ on sth** recibir una pista acerca de algo **5.** (*connecting wire*) cable *m,* conductor *m* **6.** *Brit, Aus* (*for dog*) correa *f* **II.** <led, led> *vt* **1.** (*be in charge of*) dirigir; (*discussion, inquiry*) conducir **2.** (*conduct*) conducir, llevar; **to ~ the way** ir primero; *fig* mostrar el camino **3.** (*induce*) inducir; **to ~ sb to do sth** llevar a alguien a hacer algo; **to ~ sb to believe that ...** hacer creer a alguien que... **4.** COM, SPORTS (*be ahead of*) encabezar; **to ~ the field** *fig* ir a la cabeza **5.** (*live a particular way: life*) llevar; **to ~ a life of luxury** llevar una vida de lujos; **to ~ a quiet/hectic life** llevar una vida tranquila/ajetreada ►**to ~ sb by the <u>nose</u>** *inf* manejar a alguien fácilmente; **to ~ sb up the garden <u>path</u>** *inf* embaucar a alguien **III.** <led, led> *vi* **1.** (*be in charge*) dirigir **2.** (*guide followers*) guiar **3.** (*conduct*) llevar; **to ~ to/into sth** *a. fig* conducir a/hacia algo **4.** (*be ahead*) liderar; **to ~ by 2 metres** tener una ventaja de 2 metros

◆**lead along** *vt* llevar (de la mano)

◆**lead aside** *vt* llevar a un lado

◆**lead astray** *vt* llevar por mal camino

◆**lead away** *vt* llevar; **he was led away by the police** fue arrestado por la policía

◆**lead back** *vt* hacer volver

◆**lead off I.** *vt* (*person*) llevar afuera; (*room*) comunicar con **II.** *vi* empezar

◆**lead on** *vt* (*trick, fool*) engañar; (*encourage*) incitar a; **she doesn't want to lead him on** no quiere darle falsas expectativas

◆**lead to** *vt* llevar a

◆**lead up to** *vi* **1.** (*cause*) conducir a **2.** (*slowly introduce*) preparar **3.** (*precede*) preceder a

lead[2] [led] *n* **1.** *no pl* (*metal*) plomo *m* **2.** NAUT sonda *f* **3.** (*in pencil*) mina *f*

leaded ['ledəd] **I.** *adj* emplomado, -a; **~ fuel** gasolina *f* con plomo **II.** *n no pl* gasolina *f* con plomo

leaden ['ledn] *adj* **1.** (*dark*) plomizo, -a **2.** (*heavy*) pesado, -a; **~ limbs** pies *mpl* de plomo

leader ['liːdəʳ, *Am:* -dɚ] *n* **1.** (*of group*) líder *mf* **2.** (*guide*) guía *mf* **3.** *Brit* MUS (*first violin*) primer violín *m* **4.** *Am* MUS (*conductor*) director(a) *m(f)* **5.** *Brit* (*in newspaper*) editorial *m*

leadership ['li:dəʃɪp, *Am:* -dɚ-] *n no pl* **1.** (*ability*) liderazgo *m;* ~ **qualities** dotes *fpl* de mando **2.** (*leaders*) dirección *f* **3.** (*function*) mando *m;* **to be under sb's** ~ estar bajo el mando de alguien

lead-free ['ledfri:] *adj* sin plomo

lead guitar *n* **to play** ~ ser el guitarrista principal

leading¹ ['ledɪŋ] *n no pl, Brit* emplomado *m*

leading² ['li:dɪŋ] *n no pl* mando *m*

leading article *n Brit* editorial *m* **leading-edge** *adj* puntero, -a; ~ **technology** tecnología *f* punta **leading lady** *n* actriz *f* principal **leading light** *n inf* **to be a** ~ **in sth** ser una figura de referencia en algo **leading man** *n* actor *m* principal **leading question** *n* pregunta *f* capciosa

lead pencil *n* lápiz *m* de mina **lead poisoning** *n* saturnismo *m*

lead singer *n* cantante *mf* principal **lead story** *n* PUBL artículo *m* principal **lead time** *n* tiempo *m* de entrega

lead up *n* tiempo *m* preparatorio

leaf [li:f] <leaves> *n* **1.** (*of plant*) hoja *f* **2.** *no pl* (*foliage*) follaje *m;* **to be in** [*o* **come into**] ~ echar hojas **3.** (*piece of paper*) hoja *f;* ~ **of paper** hoja de papel **4.** (*of table*) tablero *m* ►**to take a** ~ **from sb's book** seguir el ejemplo de alguien; **to shake like a** ~ temblar como una pluma; **to turn over a new** ~ hacer borrón y cuenta nueva

◆**leaf through** *vt* hojear

leafless ['li:fləs] *adj* deshojado, -a

leaflet ['li:flɪt] *n* folleto *m*

leafy ['li:fi] <-ier, -iest> *adj* frondoso, -a; **a** ~ **suburb** una zona residencial con muchos árboles

league [li:g] *n* **1.** *a.* SPORTS liga *f;* **football** ~ liga de fútbol; **the** ~ **championship** el campeonato de liga; **to be/to be not in the same** ~ **as sb/sth** *fig* estar/no estar a la altura de alguien/algo; **to be out of sb's** ~ no tener comparación con alguien **2.** (*measurement*) legua *f* ►**to be in** ~ **with sb** estar confabulado con alguien

leak [li:k] **I.** *n* (*of gas, water*) fuga *f;* (*of information*) filtración *f;* (*in roof*) gotera *f* **II.** *vi* **1.** (*let escape*) tener una fuga; (*tyre*) perder aire; (*hose, bucket*) perder agua; (*pen*) perder tinta; (*tap*) gotear; **to** ~ **everywhere** chorrear por todos lados **2.** (*information*) filtrarse **III.** *vt* **1.** (*let escape*) derramar; **to** ~ **water** perder agua **2.** (*information*) filtrar

leakage ['li:kɪdʒ] *n* **1.** (*leak*) fuga *f* **2.** *no pl* (*of information*) filtración *f*

leaky ['li:ki] <-ier, -iest> *adj* que tiene fugas

lean¹ [li:n] **I.** <leant *Am:* leaned, leant *Am:* leaned> *vi* inclinarse; **to** ~ **against sth** apoyarse en algo **II.** <leant *Am:* leaned, leant *Am:* leaned> *vt* apoyar; **to** ~ **sth against sth** apoyar algo contra algo

lean² [li:n] *adj* **1.** (*thin*) flaco, -a; (*meat*) magro, -a; (*face*) enjuto, -a **2.** (*efficient: company*) eficiente

◆**lean back** *vi* reclinar(se)

◆**lean forward** *vi* inclinar(se) hacia adelante

◆**lean on** *vt* **1.** (*rely on*) apoyarse en **2.** *inf* (*pressurize*) ejercer presión sobre

◆**lean out** *vi* asomarse

◆**lean over** **I.** *vt* inclinarse sobre **II.** *vi* inclinarse

leaning ['li:nɪŋ] *n* inclinación *f;* **political** ~**s** tendencias *fpl* políticas

leant [lent] *pt, pp of* **lean¹**

lean-to ['li:ntu:] *n* **1.** (*building extension*) anexo *m* **2.** *Am, Aus* (*shack*) cobertizo *m*

leap [li:p] **I.** <leapt *Am:* leaped, leapt *Am:* leaped> *vi* saltar; **to** ~ **forward** saltar hacia adelante; **to** ~ **to do sth** abalanzarse a hacer algo; **to** ~ **with joy** saltar de alegría; **to** ~ **to sb's defence** saltar en defensa de alguien; **his heart** ~**t** le dio un vuelco el corazón; **to** ~ **to mind** venir a la mente **II.** <leapt *Am:* leaped, leapt *Am:* leaped> *vt* saltar **III.** *n* salto *m;* **to take a** ~ dar un salto ►**by** ~**s and bounds** a pasos de gigante; **a** ~ **in the dark** un salto en el vacío

◆**leap at** *vt* **1.** (*jump*) saltar hacia **2.** (*accept*) no dejar pasar; **to** ~ **the chance to do sth** no dejar escapar la oportunidad de hacer algo

◆**leap out** *vi* saltar

◆**leap up** *vi* **1.** (*jump up*) ponerse en pie de un salto; **to** ~ **to do sth** apresurarse a hacer algo **2.** (*rise quickly*) subir de pronto

leapfrog [ˌli:pfrɒg, *Am:* -frɑ:g] **I.** *n no pl* potro *m,* pídola *f;* **to play a game of** ~ jugar a saltar al potro, jugar a la pídola, saltar el burro *Méx* **II.** <-gg-> *vt* pasar por encima de

leapt [lept] *vt, vi pt, pp of* **leap**

leap year *n* año *m* bisiesto

learn [lɜ:n, *Am:* lɜ:rn] **I.** <learnt *Am:* learned, learnt *Am:* learned> *vt* aprender; **to** ~ **to do sth** aprender a hacer algo; **to** ~ **that** enterarse de que **II.** <learnt *Am:* learned, learnt *Am:* learned> *vi* aprender; **to** ~ **from one's mistakes** aprender de los propios errores

learned ['lɜ:nɪd, *Am:* 'lɜ:r-] *adj* erudito, -a

learner ['lɜ:nəʳ, *Am:* 'lɜ:rnɚ] *n* aprendiz *mf;* **to be a quick** ~ aprender rápido

learning ['lɜ:nɪŋ, *Am:* 'lɜ:r-] *n no pl* **1.** (*acquisition of knowledge*) aprendizaje *m* **2.** (*extensive knowledge*) saber *m*

learning disability *n* <-ies> dificultad *f* de aprendizaje

learnt [lɜ:nt, *Am:* lɜ:rnt] *pt, pp of* **learn**

lease [li:s] **I.** *vt* alquilar **II.** *n* (*act*) arrendamiento *m;* (*contract*) contrato *m* de arrendamiento; **to take on** ~ tomar en arriendo

leasehold ['li:shəʊld, *Am:* -hoʊld] COM, FIN, ECON **I.** *n* contrato *m* de arrendamiento; **to hold a** ~ tener un contrato de arrendamiento; **to have sth on** ~ tener algo bajo un contrato de arrendamiento **II.** *adj* **1.** (*kept by lease*) en arrendamiento **2.** (*dealing with leases*) de arrendamiento

leaseholder ['li:shəʊldəʳ, *Am:* -hoʊldɚ] *n* arrendatario, -a *m, f*

leash [li:ʃ] *n Am* correa *f* ►**to keep sb on a tight ~** atar corto a alguien

leasing ['li:sɪŋ] *n no pl* FIN arrendamiento *m* (con opción de compra)

leasing company *n* empresa *f* de arrendamiento

least [li:st] **I.** *adj* mínimo, -a; (*age*) menor **II.** *adv* menos; **the ~ possible** lo menos posible; **she ~ of all** ella menos que nadie **III.** *n* lo menos; **at (the) ~** por lo menos, al menos; **not in the ~!** ¡en absoluto!; **to say the ~** para no decir más

leather ['leðəʳ] *n no pl* cuero *m*

leathering *n* cobertura *f* de cuero

leatherneck ['leðənek] *n Am, inf* soldado *m* de infantería (*de la marina estadounidense*)

leathery ['leðəri] *adj* (*skin*) curtido, -a; (*meat*) correoso, -a

leave[1] [li:v] **I.** <left, left> *vt* **1.** (*depart from*) salir de; (*school, unversity*) abandonar; (*work*) dejar; **to ~ home** irse de casa **2.** (*not take away with*) dejar; (*forget*) olvidar(se); **to ~ sth to sb** dejar algo a alguien; **to ~ sth at home** dejar(se) algo en casa; **to ~ a note/message (for sb)** dejar una nota/un mensaje (para alguien); **to ~ stains** dejar manchas **3.** (*put in a situation*) **to ~ sb alone** dejar en paz a alguien; **to be left homeless** quedarse sin hogar; **to ~ sth open** dejar algo abierto ►**to ~ a lot to be desired** dejar mucho que desear; **to ~ it at that** dejarlo **II.** <left, left> *vi* marcharse, despabilarse *AmL* **III.** *n* partida *f;* **to take (one's) ~ (of sb)** despedirse (de alguien) ►**to take (complete) ~ of one's senses** perder (completamente) la cabeza

◆**leave behind** *vt* **1.** (*not take along*) dejar **2.** (*forget*) olvidar **3.** (*progress beyond*) dejar atrás

◆**leave off** **I.** *vt* **1.** (*give up*) dejar de **2.** (*omit*) omitir **II.** *vi* acabar

◆**leave on** *vt* dejar(se) puesto; (*light*) dejar encendido

◆**leave out** *vt* **1.** (*omit*) omitir **2.** (*exclude*) excluir

◆**leave over** *vt* dejar; **there's nothing left over** no queda nada

leave[2] [li:v] *n* permiso *m;* **to have/get sb's ~ (to do sth)** tener/obtener el permiso de alguien (para hacer algo); **with/without sb's ~** con/sin el permiso de alguien; **to go/be on ~** MIL salir/estar de permiso; **sick ~** baja *f* por enfermedad

leaven ['levn] **I.** *n* levadura *f* **II.** *vt* (a)leudar; *fig* impregnar; **to ~a speech with jokes** aligerar un discurso con bromas

leaves [li:fz] *n pl of* **leaf**

leave-taking ['li:vˌteɪkɪŋ] *n* despedida *f*

leaving ['li:vɪŋ] *n* **1.** *no pl* (*departure*) partida *f* **2.** *pl* (*remaining things*) restos *mpl* **3.** *pl* (*leftovers*) sobras *fpl*

leaving party *n* fiesta *f* de despedida

Lebanese [ˌlebə'ni:z] **I.** *adj* libanés, -esa **II.** *n* libanés, -esa *m, f*

Lebanon ['lebənən, *Am:* -nɑ:n] *n* (**the**) ~ el Líbano

lecher ['letʃəʳ, *Am:* -ɚ] *n* sátiro *m*

lecherous ['letʃərəs] *adj* lascivo, -a

lechery ['letʃəri] *n no pl* lascivia *f,* lujuria *f*

lectern ['lektən, *Am:* -tɚn] *n* atril *m;* REL facistol *m*

lecture ['lektʃəʳ, *Am:* -tʃɚ] **I.** *n a.* UNIV conferencia *f;* **a ~ on sth** una conferencia acerca de algo; **to give sb a ~** *fig* sermonear a alguien **II.** *vi* (*give a lecture*) dar una conferencia; (*teach*) dar clases **III.** *vt* **1.** (*give a lecture*) dar una conferencia a; (*teach*) dar clases a **2.** *fig* (*reprove*) sermonear

lecture notes *npl* apuntes *mpl* de clase

lecturer ['lektʃərəʳ, *Am:* -ɚ] *n* **1.** (*person giving lecture*) conferenciante *mf* **2.** UNIV profesor(a) *m(f)* universitario, -a

lecture room *n* UNIV sala *f* de conferencias **lecture theatre** *n* aula *f* magna **lecture tour** *n* gira *f* de conferencias

led [led] *pt, pp of* **lead**[1]

LED [ˌeli:'di:] *n abbr of* **light-emitting diode** diodo *m* electroluminiscente

ledge [ledʒ] *n* (*shelf*) repisa *f;* (*on building*) cornisa *f;* (*on cliff*) saliente *m;* **window ~** alféizar *m*

ledger ['ledʒəʳ, *Am:* -ɚ] *n* COM libro *m* mayor

lee [li:] *n* sotavento *m*

leech [li:tʃ] <-es> *n* sanguijuela *f,* saguaipé *m Arg* ►**to stick to sb like a ~** pegarse a alguien como una lapa

leek [li:k] *n* puerro *m*

leer [lɪəʳ, *Am:* lɪr] **I.** *vi* mirar lascivamente **II.** *n* mirada *f* lasciva

leeward ['li:wəd, *Am:* -wɚd] METEO **I.** *adj* de sotavento **II.** *adv* a sotavento

leeway ['li:weɪ] *n no pl* flexibilidad *f*

left[1] [left] *pt, pp of* **leave**[1]

left[2] [left] **I.** *n* **1.** *no pl* (*direction, sight*) izquierda *f;* **the ~** la izquierda; **to turn to the ~** girar a la izquierda; **on/to the ~** en/a la izquierda; **on her ~** a su izquierda **2.** *no pl* POL izquierda *f;* **on the ~** de izquierda(s) **II.** *adj* izquierdo, -a **III.** *adv* a [*o* hacia] la izquierda; **to turn ~** girar hacia la izquierda

left hand *n* izquierda *f;* **on the ~** a la izquierda

left-hand [ˌleft'hænd] *adj* a la izquierda; **~ side** lado *m* izquierdo; **~ bend** curva *f* a la izquierda; **~ drive** conducción *f* por la izquierda **left-handed** *adj* zurdo, -a; **~ scissors** tijeras *fpl* para zurdos **left-hander** *n* **1.** (*left-handed*) zurdo, -a *m, f* **2.** SPORTS izquierdazo *m*

leftist ['leftɪst] POL **I.** *adj* izquierdista **II.** *n* izquierdista *mf*

left-luggage office *n Brit* consigna *f,* consignación *f AmC*

leftovers ['left,əʊvəz, *Am:* -,oʊvɚz] *npl* **1.** (*food*) sobras *fpl* **2.** (*remaining things*) restos *mpl*

left wing *n* POL izquierda *f*

left-wing [,left'wɪŋ] *adj* POL de izquierda

left-winger *n* POL izquierdista *mf*

leg [leg] **I.** *n* **1.** (*of person*) pierna *f;* (*of animal, furniture*) pata *f* **2.** (*of trousers*) pernera *f* **3.** GASTR (*of lamb, pork*) pierna *f;* (*of chicken*) muslo *m* **4.** (*segment*) etapa *f* ►**to be on one's last ~s** estar para el arrastre; **to give sb a ~ up** *inf* echar una mano a alguien; **break a ~!** ¡mucha suerte!; **to pull sb's ~** *inf* tomar el pelo a alguien; **to shake a ~** *inf* apresurarse **II.** *vt* <-gg-> *inf* **to ~ it** (*go by foot*) ir a pie; (*run fast*) echar a correr

legacy ['legəsi] <-ies> *n* legado *m;* (*inheritance*) herencia *f*

legal ['liːgl] *adj* **1.** (*in accordance with the law*) legal **2.** (*concerning the law*) jurídico, -a

legal advice *n* consejo *m* jurídico **legal aid** *n derecho a tener un abogado de oficio* **legal fee** *n* honorarios *mpl* de los abogados

legalisation *n s.* **legalization**

legalise *vt Brit, Aus s.* **legalize**

legality [liː'gæləti, *Am:* -t̬i] *n no pl* legalidad *f*

legalization [,liːgəlaɪ'zeɪʃən, *Am:* -ɪ'-] *n no pl* legalización *f*

legalize ['liːgəlaɪz] *vt* legalizar

legally ['liːgəli] *adv* legalmente

legal profession *n* abogacía *f* **legal system** *n* sistema *m* judicial

legate ['legɪt] *n* legado *m*

legation [lɪ'geɪʃən] *n* legación *f*

legend ['ledʒənd] *n* leyenda *f;* **~ has it that ...** dice la leyenda que...; **he was a ~ in his own lifetime** era una leyenda viva

legendary ['ledʒəndri, *Am:* -der-] *adj* legendario, -a; **to be ~ for sth** ser legendario por algo

legerdemain [,ledʒədə'meɪn, *Am:* -ɚdə'-] *n no pl* juego *m* de manos

leggings ['legɪŋz] *npl* mallas *fpl*

leggy ['legi] <-ier, -iest> *adj* patilargo, -a

legible ['ledʒəbl] *adj* legible

legion ['liːdʒən] **I.** *n* **1.** HIST legión *f* **2.** (*many*) multitud *f* **II.** *adj form* **the difficulties are ~** las dificultades son innumerables

legionary ['liːdʒənəri, *Am:* -eri] **I.** *adj* legionario, -a **II.** *n* <-ies> HIST legionario, -a *m, f*

legionnaire [,liːdʒə'neəʳ, *Am:* -'ner] *n* legionario *m*

Legionnaire's disease [,liːdʒə'neəʳz dɪ'ziːz] *n* MED enfermedad *f* del legionario

legislate ['ledʒɪsleɪt] *vi* legislar

legislation [,ledʒɪs'leɪʃən] *n no pl* legislación *f*

legislative ['ledʒɪslətɪv, *Am:* -sleɪt̬ɪv] *adj* legislativo, -a

legislator ['ledʒɪsleɪtəʳ, *Am:* -t̬ɚ] *n* legislador(a) *m(f)*

legislature ['ledʒɪsleɪtʃəʳ, *Am:* -sleɪtʃɚ] *n* cuerpo *m* legislativo

legitimacy [lɪ'dʒɪtɪməsi, *Am:* lə'dʒɪt̬ə-] *n no pl* legitimidad *f*

legitimate¹ [lɪ'dʒɪtɪmət, *Am:* lə'dʒɪt̬ə-] *adj* **1.** (*legal*) legal; **a ~ government** un gobierno legítimo **2.** (*reasonable*) válido, -a **3.** (*born in wedlock*) legítimo, -a

legitimate² [lɪ'dʒɪtəmeɪt, *Am:* lə'dʒɪt̬-] *vt* legitimar

legitimise *vt Brit, Aus,* **legitimize** [lɪ'dʒɪtəmaɪz, *Am:* lə'dʒɪt̬ə-] *vt* **1.** (*make legal*) legitimar **2.** (*justify*) justificar

legless ['legləs] *adj* **1.** (*without legs*) sin piernas **2.** *Brit, inf* (*drunk*) borracho, -a, rascado, -a *Col, Ven,* untado, -a *RíoPl*

legroom ['legrʊm, *Am:* -ruːm] *n no pl* espacio *m* para las piernas

legume ['legjuːm] *n* legumbre *f*

leguminous [lɪ'gjuːmɪnəs, *Am:* lə'gjuː-] *adj* leguminoso, -a

leisure ['leʒəʳ, *Am:* 'liːʒɚ] *n no pl* ocio *m* ►**at one's ~** cuando quiera uno; **call me at your ~** llámame cuando tengas tiempo

leisure activities *n* actividades *fpl* recreativas **leisure centre** *n* centro *m* recreativo

leisured *adj* (*comfortable*) acomodado, -a

leisure hours *n* horas *fpl* libres

leisurely **I.** *adj* pausado, -a **II.** *adv* pausadamente

leisure time *n no pl* tiempo *m* libre **leisure wear** *n* ropa *f* deportiva

lemming ['lemɪŋ] *n* lemming *m;* **like ~s** de una manera suicida

lemon ['lemən] *n* **1.** (*fruit*) limón *m;* **a slice of ~** una rodaja de limón **2.** *no pl* (*colour*) amarillo *m* limón **3.** *Brit, Aus, inf* (*foolish person*) estúpido, -a *m, f,* gafo, -a *m, f Ven* ►**to squeeze sb like a ~** *inf* exprimir a alguien como a un limón

lemonade [,lemə'neɪd] *n* **1.** (*still*) limonada *f* **2.** *Brit* (*fizzy*) gaseosa *f*

lemon juice *n* zumo *m* de limón **lemon peel** *n* corteza *f* de limón **lemon squash** <- -shes> *n Brit, Aus* refresco *m* de limón **lemon tea** *n* té *m* con limón

lend [lend] <lent, lent> **I.** *vt* **1.** (*give temporarily*) prestar; **to ~ money to sb** prestar dinero a alguien **2.** (*impart, grant*) dar; **to ~ colour to sth** dar color a algo; **to ~ support to a view** apoyar una opinión ►**to ~ an ear** prestar atención; **to ~ an ear to sb** prestar oído a alguien; **to ~ a hand to sb** echar una mano a alguien; **to ~ one's name to sth** ofrecer su nombre para algo; **to ~ wings to sb/sth** dar alas a alguien/algo; **to ~ oneself to sth** prestarse uno a algo **II.** *vi* prestar dinero

lender ['lendəʳ, *Am:* -dɚ] *n* FIN prestamista *mf*

lending ['lendɪŋ] *n* préstamo *m*

lending library *n* biblioteca *f* pública

length [leŋθ] *n* **1.** *no pl* (*measurement*) longitud *f;* **it's 3 metres in ~** tiene 3 metros de largo; (**along**) **the** ~ **of sth** a lo largo de algo **2.** (*piece: of pipe, string*) trozo *m* **3.** (*of swimming pool*) largo *m* **4.** *no pl* (*duration*) duración *f;* (**for**) **any** ~ **of time** (por) cualquier lapso de tiempo; **at** ~ al fin, finalmente; **to speak at** ~ hablar largamente; **at great** ~ detalladamente ►**the** ~ **and breadth of** a lo largo y ancho de; **to go to great** ~**s to do sth** dar el máximo para hacer algo

lengthen ['leŋθən] **I.** *vt* **1.** (*in time*) prolongar **2.** (*physically*) alargar **II.** *vi* **1.** (*in time*) prolongarse **2.** (*physically*) alargarse

lengthways ['leŋθweɪz] *adv, adj,* **lengthwise** ['leŋθwaɪz] *adv, adj* a lo largo

lengthy ['leŋθi] <-ier, -iest> *adj* prolongado, -a; ~ **wait** (*speech*) prolijo, -a; **a** ~ **wait** una larga espera

lenience ['liːniənts] *n,* **leniency** *n no pl* indulgencia *f*

lenient ['liːniənt] *adj* (*judge*) indulgente; (*punishment*) poco severo, -a

lens [lenz] <-ses> *n* **1.** (*of glasses*) lente *m o f;* (*of camera*) objetivo *m;* ~**es of glasses** cristales *mpl* de las gafas; (**contact**) ~**es** lentes *fpl* de contacto; **zoom** ~ lente de acercamiento **2.** ANAT cristalino *m*

lent [lent] *pt, pp of* **lend**

Lent [lent] *n no pl* Cuaresma *f*

lentil ['lentl, *Am:* -t̬l] *n* lenteja *f*

Leo ['liːəʊ, *Am:* -oʊ] *n* Leo *m*

leonine ['lɪənaɪn] *adj form* leonino, -a

leopard ['lepəd, *Am:* -ɚd] *n* leopardo *m* ►**a** ~ **can't change its spots** *prov* el árbol que nace torcido jamás sus ramas endereza *prov,* el que nace barrigón ni que lo fajen chiquito *Ven, prov*

leotard ['liːətɑːd, *Am:* -tɑːrd] *n* malla *f*

leper ['lepəʳ, *Am:* -ɚ] *n* **1.** (*leprosy sufferer*) leproso, -a *m, f* **2.** (*disliked person*) marginado, -a *m, f*

leprosy ['leprəsi] *n no pl* lepra *f*

leprous ['leprəs] *adj* leproso, -a

lesbian ['lezbɪən] **I.** *n* lesbiana *f* **II.** *adj* lesbiano, -a

lesbianism *n* lesbianismo *m*

lesion ['liːʒən] *n* lesión *f*

Lesotho [lə'suːtuː, *Am:* lə'soʊtoʊ] *n* Lesoto *m*

less [les] *comp of* **little I.** *adj* (*in degree, size*) menor; (*in quantity*) menos; **sth of** ~ **value** algo de menor valor; ~ **wine/nuts** menos vino/nueces **II.** *adv* menos; **to drink** ~ beber menos; **to see sb** ~ ver menos a alguien; ~ **than 10** menos de [*o* que] 10; **to grow** [*o* **become**] ~ disminuir; **not him, much** [*o* **still**] ~ **her** él no, y mucho menos ella **III.** *pron* menos; ~ **than ...** menos que...; ~ **and** ~ cada vez menos; **to have** ~ **than ...** tener menos que...; **to cost** ~ **than ...** costar menos que...; **the** ~ **you eat, the** ~ **you get fat** mientras menos comas, menos gordo estarás **IV.** *prep* menos; **a month,** ~ **two days** un mes menos dos días

lessen ['lesn] **I.** *vi* (*danger*) reducirse; (*fever*) bajar; (*pain*) aliviarse **II.** *vt* (*diminish*) disminuir; (*risk*) reducir; (*pain*) aliviar

lesser ['lesəʳ, *Am:* -ɚ] *adj comp of* **less** menor; **to a** ~ **extent** en menor grado

lesson ['lesn] *n* **1.** SCHOOL clase *f;* ~**s** lecciones *fpl* **2.** *fig* lección *f;* **to draw a** ~ (**from sth**) aprender una lección (de algo); **to learn one's** ~ aprenderse la lección; **to teach sb a** ~ dar a alguien una lección

lest [lest] *conj liter* **1.** (*for fear that*) no sea que +*subj;* **I didn't do it** ~ **he should come** no lo hice por si venía **2.** (*if*) en caso de que +*subj*

let[1] [let] *n* SPORTS let *m* ►**without** ~ **or hindrance** LAW sin estorbo ni obstáculo

let[2] [let] **I.** *n Brit* alquiler *m* **II.** <let, let> *vt* **1.** (*allow*) dejar; **to** ~ **sb do sth** dejar a alguien hacer algo; **to** ~ **sb know sth** hacer saber algo a alguien; **to** ~ **sth pass** pasar algo por alto; **to** ~ **sb alone** dejar a alguien en paz; ~ **him be!** ¡déjalo en paz! **2.** (*in suggestions*) ~**'s go!** ¡vámonos!; ~**'s say ...** digamos...; ~ **us pray** ¡oremos! **3.** (*filler while thinking*) ~**'s see** veamos; ~ **me think** déjame pensar **4.** MAT ~ **x be y** supongamos que x sea igual a y ►~ **alone ...** (y) menos aún...; **to** ~ **sb have it** decir cuatro verdades a alguien; **to** ~ **sth lie** dejar algo como está; **to** ~ **fly** montar en cólera; **to** ~ **rip** (*become angry*) montar en cólera; (*drive fast*) correr

◆**let by** *vt* dejar pasar

◆**let down** *vt* **1.** (*disappoint*) decepcionar **2.** (*lower*) bajar; (*hair*) soltar; **to let one's hair down** *a. fig* soltarse el pelo **3.** FASHION alargar **4.** *Brit, Aus* (*deflate*) desinflar

◆**let in** *vt* (*person*) dejar entrar; (*light*) dejar pasar ►**to let oneself in for sth** meterse en algo; **to let sb in on sth** revelar un secreto a alguien

◆**let off** *vt* **1.** (*forgive*) perdonar; **to let sb off with a fine** poner sólo una multa a alguien **2.** (*fire: gun*) disparar; (*bomb, firework*) hacer explotar

◆**let on** *vi inf* (*divulge*) **to** ~ **about sth** revelar algo; **to not** ~ **about sth** callarse algo

◆**let out** **I.** *vi Am* (*end*) culminar **II.** *vt* **1.** (*release*) dejar salir; (*prisoner*) poner en libertad; (*laugh*) soltar; **to** ~ **a scream** pegar un grito **2.** FASHION ensanchar **3.** (*reveal: secret*) revelar **4.** (*rent*) alquilar

◆**let up** *vi* **1.** (*become weaker, stop*) debilitarse; (*rain*) amainar; (*cold*) suavizarse; (*fog*) desvanecerse **2.** (*relent*) aflojar; **to** ~ **on sb** ser menos duro con alguien; **to** ~ **on the accelerator** soltar el acelerador

lethal ['liːθl] *adj* letal; (*poison*) mortífero, -a; (*weapon*) mortal; **this brandy's** ~**!** *inf* ¡este brandy es mortal!

lethargic [lɪ'θɑːdʒɪk, *Am:* lɪ'θɑːr-] *adj* **1.** (*lacking energy*) letárgico, -a **2.** (*drowsy*) somnoliento, -a

lethargy ['leθədʒi, *Am:* -ɚ-] *n no pl* **1.** (*lack of* *energy*) letargo *m* **2.** (*drowsiness*) sopor *m*

letter ['letəʳ, *Am:* 'letɚ] *n* **1.** (*message*) carta *f* **2.** (*symbol*) letra *f* ►**to stick to the ~ of the law** aplicar la ley en sentido estricto; **to the ~** al pie de la letra

letter bomb *n* carta *f* bomba **letterbox** *n Brit, Aus* buzón *m* de correos **letterhead** *n* (*at top of letter*) membrete *m;* (*paper*) papel *m* membreteado

lettering ['letərɪŋ] *n no pl* caracteres *mpl*

letterpress *n* TYPO prensa *f* de copiar

lettuce ['letɪs, *Am:* 'let-] *n* lechuga *f*

leucocyte *n,* **leukocyte** ['lu:kəʊsaɪt, *Am:* 'lu:koʊ-] *n* MED leucocito *m*

leukaemia *n,* **leukemia** [lu:'ki:miə] *n Am* leucemia *f*

level ['levəl] **I.** *adj* **1.** (*horizontal*) horizontal; (*flat*) plano, -a; (*spoonful*) raso, -a **2.** (*having same height*) **to be ~ with sth** estar a la misma altura que algo **3.** *Brit, Aus* (*in same position*) **to be ~ with sb/sth** estar a la par de alguien/algo **4.** (*of same amount*) igual **5.** (*calm*) sereno, -a; (*look*) sincero, -a; (*tone*) tranquilo, -a; (*voice*) mesurado, -a; **to keep a ~ head** no perder la cabeza **6.** (*uniform*) uniforme ►**to do one's ~ best** *inf* hacer todo lo posible **II.** *adv* a nivel **III.** *n* **1.** (*position, amount*) nivel *m* **2.** (*height*) altura *f;* **above sea ~** sobre el nivel del mar; **at ground ~** a ras de tierra **3.** *no pl* (*position in hierarchy*) categoría *f;* **at a higher ~** en una categoría superior; **at the (very) highest ~** en el nivel más alto; **to be on a ~ with sb/sth** estar a la misma altura que alguien/algo; **to find one's (own) ~** *inf* encontrar su sitio en la sociedad **4.** (*quality of performance*) nivel *m;* **intermediate ~ students** estudiantes *mfpl* de nivel intermedio **5.** (*meaning*) **on another ~** en otro sentido; **on a serious ~** en un plano serio ►**to be on the ~** (*business, person*) ser serio **IV.** <*Brit:* -ll-, *Am:* -l-> *vt* **1.** (*smoothen, flatten*) nivelar **2.** (*demolish completely*) derribar **3.** (*point*) **to ~ sth at sb** apuntar con algo a alguien

◆**level down** *vt* nivelar (por abajo)

◆**level off** *vi,* **level out** *vi* (*aircraft*) nivelarse; (*inflation*) equilibrarse

◆**level up** *vt* igualar

◆**level with** *vt inf* sincerarse con

level crossing *n Brit, Aus* paso *m* a nivel **level-headed** *adj* sensato, -a **level pegging** *n Brit, Aus* **to be (on) ~** estar en igualdad de condiciones

lever ['li:vəʳ, *Am:* 'levɚ] **I.** *n* palanca *f;* **brake ~** *Brit* freno *m* de mano **II.** *vt* apalancar, palanquear *AmL;* **to ~ sth open** abrir algo con palanca

leverage ['li:vərɪdʒ, *Am:* 'levɚ-] *n no pl* **1.** (*using lever*) apalancamiento *m* **2.** *fig* influencia *f*

leveret ['levərɪt] *n* lebrato *m*

leviathan [lɪ'vaɪəθən] *n* **1.** *liter* (*machine, organization*) gigante *mf* **2.** REL leviatán *m*

levitate ['levɪteɪt] **I.** *vt* mantener en el aire por levitación **II.** *vi* mantenerse en el aire por levitación

levity ['levəti, *Am:* -ti] *n no pl* ligereza *f*

levy ['levi] **I.** <-ies> *n* tasa *f* **II.** <-ie-> *vt* imponer; **to ~ a tax on sth** gravar algo con un impuesto

lewd [lju:d, *Am:* lu:d] *adj* (*person*) lascivo, -a; (*gesture, remark*) obsceno, -a

lewdness *n no pl* (*behaviour*) lascivia *f;* (*of gesture, remark*) obscenidad *f*

lexical ['leksɪkl] *adj* léxico, -a

lexicographer [,leksɪ'kɒgrəfəʳ, *Am:* -kɑ:-'grəfɚ] *n* lexicógrafo, -a *m, f*

lexicography [,leksɪ'kɒgrəfi, *Am:* -kɑ:'grə-] *n no pl* lexicografía *f*

lexicology [,leksɪ'kɒlədʒi, *Am:* -'kɑ:lə-] *n no pl* lexicología *f*

lexicon ['leksɪkən, *Am:* -kɑ:n] *n* **1.** (*vocabulary: of person, subject*) vocabulario *m;* (*of language*) léxico *m,* lexicón *m* **2.** (*dictionary*) diccionario *m*

lexis ['leksɪs] *n no pl* LING vocabulario *m*

LF *abbr of* **low frequency** BF

liability [,laɪə'bɪləti, *Am:* -ti] *n* **1.** *no pl* FIN, LAW responsabilidad *f;* **to accept ~ for sth** hacerse responsable de algo; **limited ~ company** compañía *f* de responsabilidad limitada **2.** *inf* **he's a ~!** ¡es un estorbo!

liable ['laɪəbl] *adj* **1.** (*prone*) propenso, -a; **to be ~ to do sth** ser propenso a hacer algo **2.** LAW responsable; **to be ~ for sth** ser responsable de algo

liaise [lɪ'eɪz] *vi* **to ~ with sb/sth** servir de enlace con alguien/algo

liaison [li'eɪzn, *Am:* 'li:əzɑ:n] *n* **1.** *no pl a.* LING (*contact*) enlace *m;* (*coordination*) coordinación *f* **2.** *Am* (*sb who connects groups*) enlace *mf* **3.** (*sexual affair*) aventura *f*

liaison officer *n* oficial *mf* de enlace

liana *n,* **liane** [li'ɑ:nə] *n* liana *f*

liar ['laɪəʳ, *Am:* -ɚ] *n* mentiroso, -a *m, f*

lib [lɪb] *n no pl, inf abbr of* **liberation** liberación *f*

libel ['laɪbl] **I.** *n* LAW libelo *m;* PUBL difamación *f;* **to sue sb for ~** demandar a alguien por difamación **II.** <*Brit:* -ll-, *Am:* -l-> *vt* LAW, PUBL difamar

libellous *adj,* **libelous** ['laɪbələs] *adj Am* LAW, PUBL difamatorio, -a

liberal ['lɪbərəl] **I.** *adj* **1.** (*tolerant*) *a.* POL liberal **2.** (*generous*) generoso, -a **3.** (*plentiful*) copioso, -a **4.** (*not strict: interpretation*) amplio, -a **II.** *n* liberal *mf*

liberal arts *n Am* humanidades *fpl*

liberalisation *n Brit, Aus s.* **liberalization**

liberalise *vt Brit, Aus s.* **liberalize**

liberalism ['lɪbərəlɪzəm] *n no pl* liberalismo *m*

liberality [,lɪbə'ræləti, *Am:* -ti] *n no pl* **1.** (*tolerance*) liberalidad *f* **2.** (*generosity*) generosidad *f*

liberalization [,lɪbərəlaɪ'zeɪʃən, *Am:* -ɪ'-] *n*

liberalización *f*

liberalize ['lɪbərəlaɪz] *vt* liberalizar

liberate ['lɪbəreɪt] *vt* **1.**(*free*) liberar; (*slaves*) manumitir; **to ~ oneself from sth/sb** librarse de algo/alguien **2.** *fig, iron, inf* (*steal*) robar

liberation [ˌlɪbər'eɪʃən] *n no pl* liberación *f*

liberation organization *n* organización *f* para la liberación

liberator ['lɪbəreɪtəʳ, *Am:* -t̬ɚ] *n* liberador(a) *m(f)*

Liberia [laɪ'bɪəriə] *n* Liberia *f*

Liberian I. *adj* liberiano, -a II. *n* liberiano, -a *m, f*

libertine ['lɪbəti:n, *Am:* -ɚ-] *n* libertino, -a *m, f*

liberty ['lɪbəti, *Am:* -ɚt̬i] *n no pl, form* **1.**(*freedom*) libertad *f;* **to be at ~** estar en libertad; **to be at ~ to do sth** tener el derecho de hacer algo; **to take the ~ of doing sth** tomarse la libertad de hacer algo; **to take liberties with sb** tomarse libertades con alguien; **what a ~!** ¡qué falta de respeto! **2.** *form* (*right*) derechos *mpl*

libidinous [lɪ'bɪdɪnəs, *Am:* lə'bɪdnəs] *adj form* libidinoso, -a

libido [lɪ'bi:dəʊ, *Am:* -doʊ] *n* libido *f*

Libra ['li:brə] *n* Libra *m*

Libran ['li:brən] I. *n* Libra *mf* II. *adj* de Libra

librarian [laɪ'breərɪən, *Am:* -'brer-] *n* bibliotecario, -a *m, f*

library ['laɪbrəri, *Am:* -brer-] *n* <-ies> **1.**(*place*) biblioteca *f;* **film ~** filmoteca *f;* **newspaper ~** hemeroteca *f* **2.**(*collection*) archivo *m*

libretto [lɪ'bretəʊ, *Am:* -'bret̬oʊ] *n* libreto *m*

Libya ['lɪbɪə] *n* Libia *f*

Libyan ['lɪbɪən] I. *adj* libio, -a II. *n* libio, -a *m, f*

lice [laɪs] *npl s.* **louse**

licence ['laɪsənts] *n* **1.**(*document*) licencia *f,* permiso *m;* **driving ~, driver's ~** *Am* carnet *m* de conducir; **gun ~** permiso *m* de armas; **under ~** con licencia **2.** *no pl, form* (*freedom*) libertad *f;* **artistic ~** libertad artística; **to have ~ to do sth** tener libertad para hacer algo

licence number *n* AUTO número *m* de matrícula **licence plate** *n* AUTO matrícula *f*

license ['laɪsənts] I. *vt* autorizar II. *n Am s.* licence

licensed *adj* autorizado, -a; **a ~ restaurant** un restaurante con licencia de licores; **to be ~ to do sth** tener la autorización para hacer algo

licensee [ˌlaɪsənt'si:] *n form* concesionario, -a *m, f*

license fee *n Brit* TV impuesto *m* por el uso de un televisor

licensing ['laɪsəntsɪŋ] I. *n* autorización *f* II. *adj* **~ hours** *horas durante las cuales está permitido la venta y el consumo de alcohol*

licensing laws *n Brit* leyes *fpl* de control de licores

licentious [laɪ'senʃəs] *adj form* licencioso, -a

lichen ['laɪkən] *n* liquen *m*

lick [lɪk] I. *n* **1.**(*with tongue*) lamedura *f* **2.**(*light coating*) **a ~ of paint** una mano de pintura **3.** MUS frase *f* ►**a (cat's) ~ and a promise** *Brit, inf* un lavoteo, un baño de vaquero *Ven* II. *vt* **1.**(*with tongue*) lamer **2.**(*lightly touch*) rozar **3.** *Am, inf* (*defeat*) derrotar **4.** *inf* (*beat*) dar una paliza a

licking *n* **1.** *inf* (*physical beating*) paliza *f* **2.** SPORTS derrota *f*

licorice ['lɪkərɪs, *Am:* -ɚɪʃ] *n no pl, Am* regaliz *f*

lid [lɪd] *n* **1.**(*for container*) tapa *f,* tape *m Cuba, PRico* **2.**(*eyelid*) párpado *m* ►**to keep the ~ on sth** ocultar algo; **to put the ~ on sth** *Brit, Aus* rematar algo; **that puts the ~ on it** *Am* se acabó

lie¹ [laɪ] I. <-y-> *vi* mentir; **to ~ about sth** mentir sobre algo II. <-y-> *vt* **to ~ oneself out of sth** salvarse de algo por una mentira III. *n* mentira *f,* guayaba *f AmL,* boleto *m Arg;* **to be an outright ~** ser de una falsedad total; **to give the ~ to sth** desmentir algo; **to live a ~** vivir en la mentira; **don't tell me ~s!** ¡no me mientas!, ¡no me caigas a cuentos! *Col, Ven*

lie² [laɪ] I. <lay, lain> *vi* **1.**(*be lying down: person*) estar tumbado; **to ~ in bed** estar acostado en la cama; **to ~ on the ground** estar tumbado en el suelo; **to ~ awake** estar despierto; **to ~ still** quedarse inmóvil **2.**(*be positioned*) hallarse; **to ~ off the coast** (*boat*) hallarse lejos de la costa; **to ~ on the route to ...** encontrarse en la ruta de...; **to ~ to the east of ...** quedar al este de...; **to ~ in ruins** estar en ruinas; **to ~ in wait** estar a la espera; **to ~ fallow** AGR, BOT estar en barbecho **3.** *form* (*be buried*) estar enterrado, -a **4. to ~ with sb/sth** (*be responsibility of*) corresponder a alguien/algo; (*be the reason for sth*) ser culpa de alguien/algo **5.** SPORTS ubicarse II. *n no pl, Brit, Aus* posición *f* ►**the ~ of the land** el estado de las cosas

♦**lie about** *vi* **1.**(*be somewhere*) estar por ahí **2.**(*be lazy*) holgazanear

♦**lie back** *vi* recostarse

♦**lie down** *vi* (*act*) acostarse; (*state*) estar acostado ►**to take sth lying down** aceptar algo sin protestar

♦**lie in** *vi inf* quedarse en cama

♦**lie over** *vi Am* quedar aplazado

♦**lie to** *vi* NAUT estar a la capa

♦**lie up** *vi Brit* esconderse, enconcharse *Ven, Perú*

lie detector *n* detector *m* de mentiras

lieu [lu:] *n no pl, form* **in ~ of** en lugar de

Lieut *n abbr of* **Lieutenant 1.** MIL teniente *mf* **2.**(*assistant*) lugarteniente *mf*

lieutenant [lef'tenənt, *Am:* lu:-] *n* **1.** MIL teniente *mf* **2.**(*assistant*) lugarteniente *mf*

life [laɪf] <lives> *n* **1.** vida *f;* **~ after death** vida después de la muerte; **intelligent ~** vida inteligente; **plant ~** vida vegetal; **private ~**

vida privada; **a sign of** ~ una señal de vida; **to be full of** ~ estar lleno de vida; **to draw sth/sb from** ~ ART copiar algo/a alguien del natural; **to lose one's** ~ perder la vida; **to take sb's** ~ matar a alguien; **to take one's (own)** ~ quitarse la vida, suicidarse **2.** *no pl* (*existence*) existencia *f;* **to want sth out of** ~ querer algo de la vida; **to be sb's (whole)** ~ ser la vida (entera) de alguien **3.** *no pl* (*duration*) vida *f* (útil), duración *f* **4.** *inf* (*prison sentence*) cadena *f* perpetua; **to get** ~ ser condenado a cadena perpetua ►**a** ~ **and death struggle** una lucha a vida o muerte; **to be a matter of** ~ **and death** ser un asunto de vida o muerte; **to take one's** ~ **in one's hands** *inf* jugarse la vida; **to risk** ~ **and limb** (**to do sth**) jugarse la vida (para hacer una cosa); **to lay one's** ~ **on the line** poner la vida en peligro; **to be the** ~ **and soul of the party** *Brit* ser el alma de la fiesta; **to do sth for dear** ~ hacer algo desesperadamente; **to live the good** ~ darse la buena vida; **it's a hard** ~! *iron, inf* ¡qué le vamos a hacer!; **as large as** ~ en carne y hueso; **to breathe (new)** ~ **into sth** infundir (nueva) vida a algo; **to bring sth to** ~ animar algo; **to come to** ~ volver a la vida; **to frighten the** ~ **out of sb** dar un susto de muerte a alguien; **to give one's** ~ **for sb/sth** dar la vida por alguien/algo; **to make a new** ~ empezar una nueva vida; **for** ~ de por vida; **I'm not able for the** ~ **of me to ...** *inf* por mucho que lo intente no puedo...; **not on your** ~! *inf* ¡ni hablar!; **that's** ~! ¡así es la vida!; **this is the** ~ **(for me)**! ¡esto sí es vida!

life annuity <-ies> *n* pensión *f* vitalicia **life assurance** *n no pl, Brit* seguro *m* de vida **lifebelt** *n* salvavidas *m inv* **lifeboat** *n* bote *m* salvavidas **life buoy** *n* salvavidas *m inv* **life cycle** *n* ciclo *m* vital **life expectancy** <-ies> *n* esperanza *f* de vida **life form** *n* forma *f* de vida **lifeguard** *n* socorrista *mf,* salvavidas *mf inv AmL* **life imprisonment** *n no pl* cadena *f* perpetua **life insurance** *n no pl* seguro *m* de vida **life jacket** *n* chaleco *m* salvavidas

lifeless [ˈlaɪfləs] *adj* **1.** (*dead*) sin vida **2.** *fig* flojo, -a

lifelike [ˈlaɪflaɪk] *adj* natural

lifeline *n* **1.** NAUT cuerda *f* salvavidas **2.** *fig* cordón *m* umbilical; **to throw sb a** ~ dar una oportunidad a alguien

lifelong [ˌlaɪfˈlɒŋ, *Am:* ˌlaɪfˈlɑːŋ] *adj* de toda la vida

life peer *n Brit: miembro vitalicio de la Cámara de los Lores* **life preserver** *n Am* salvavidas *m inv*

lifer [ˈlaɪfəʳ, *Am:* -fɚ] *n inf* condenado, -a *m, f* a cadena perpetua

life raft *n* bote *m* salvavidas **lifesaver** *n* socorrista *mf* **life sentence** *n* condena *f* a cadena perpetua **life-size** *adj,* **life-sized** *adj* de tamaño natural **lifespan** *n* (*of animals*) tiempo *m* de vida; (*of people*) longevidad *f;* **the average** ~ el promedio de vida; (*of machines*) la vida útil **lifestyle** *n* estilo *m* de vida **life-support system** *n* sistema *m* de respiración artificial **life-threatening** *adj* mortífero, -a **lifetime** *n no pl* **1.** (*of person*) vida *f;* **in my** ~ durante mi vida; **the chance of a** ~ (**for sb**) la oportunidad de su vida; **to happen once in a** ~ suceder una vez en la vida; **to see sth during one's** ~ ver algo en vida; ~ **guarantee** garantía *f* de por vida **2.** (*eternity*) eternidad *f;* **to seem like a** ~ parecer toda una vida **life work** *n no pl* trabajo *m* de toda la vida

lift [lɪft] **I.** *n* **1.** (*upward motion*) elevación *f;* **to give sth a** ~ levantar algo **2.** *no pl* AVIAT fuerza *f* de ascensión **3.** *no pl, fig* (*positive feeling*) ánimos *mpl;* **to give sb a** ~ levantar la moral a alguien **4.** (*hoisting device*) montacargas *m inv* **5.** *Brit* (*elevator*) ascensor *m,* elevador *m AmL;* **to take the** ~ tomar el ascensor **6.** (*car ride*) viaje *m* en coche (*gratuito*), aventón *m Méx;* **to give sb a** ~ llevar (en coche) a alguien; **to hitch a** ~ hacer dedo **II.** *vi* levantarse **III.** *vt* **1.** (*move upwards*) levantar; (*slightly*) alzar; **to** ~ **potatoes** recoger patatas; **to** ~ **fingerprints from sth** sacar las huellas digitales de algo; **to** ~ **one's eyes** alzar los ojos; **to** ~ **one's head** levantar la cabeza; **to** ~ **one's voice** levantar la voz; **to** ~ **one's voice to sb** (*yell at*) levantar la voz a alguien; (*argue with*) discutir con alguien **2.** (*encourage*) animar; **to** ~ **sb's spirits** levantar los ánimos de alguien **3.** (*move by air*) transportar (en avión) **4.** (*stop*) suprimir; **to** ~ **restrictions** levantar las restricciones **5.** *inf* (*steal*) mangar; (*plagiarize*) plagiar; **to** ~ **a tune** copiar una melodía

◆**lift down** *vt Brit, Aus* bajar con cuidado

◆**lift off** *vi* AVIAT despegar

◆**lift up** *vt* alzar; **to** ~ **one's head** levantar la cabeza; **to** ~ **one's voice** alzar la voz

lift-off [ˈlɪftɒf, *Am:* -ɑːf] *n* AVIAT, TECH despegue *m*

ligament [ˈlɪɡəmənt] *n* ligamento *m*

ligature [ˈlɪɡətʃəʳ, *Am:* -tʃɚ] *n* **1.** (*cord*) *a.* MED ligadura *f* **2.** MUS, TYPO ligado *m*

light [laɪt] **I.** *n* **1.** *no pl* (*energy, brightness*) luz *f;* **by the** ~ **of the moon** a la luz de la luna **2.** *no pl* (*daytime*) luz *f* (de día); **first** ~ primera luz del día **3.** (*source of brightness*) luz *f;* (*lamp*) lámpara *f;* **the** ~**s went down** se apagaron las luces; **to put a** ~ **off/on** apagar/encender una luz **4.** *pl* (*traffic light*) semáforo *m* **5.** *no pl* (*clarification, insight*) comprensión *f;* **to cast** [*o* **shed**] ~ **on sth** arrojar luz sobre algo **6.** *no pl* (*perspective*) perspectiva *f;* **to see things in a new** ~ ver las cosas desde otra perspectiva **7.** *no pl* (*joy, inspiration*) sol *m;* **you are the** ~ **of my life** *fig* eres mi sol **8.** *no pl* (*flame*) fuego *m;* **to catch** ~ incendiarse; **to set** ~ **to sth** prender fuego a algo; **do you have a** ~? ¿tienes fuego? **9.** *pl* (*person's abilities*) conocimientos *mpl;* **to do sth according to one's** ~**s** hacer algo como Dios le da a entender a uno ►**to see the ~ at the end of the tunnel** cobrar nuevas esperanza; **to go out like a ~** *inf* (*fall deep asleep quickly*) quedarse dormido enseguida; (*faint suddenly*) perder el conocimiento; **to bring sth to ~** sacar algo a la luz; **to come to ~** salir a la luz **II.** *adj* **1.** (*not heavy*) ligero, -a; **a ~ touch** un pequeño toque **2.** (*not dark: colour*) claro, -a; (*skin*) blanco, -a; (*room*) luminoso, -a **3.** (*not serious*) ligero, -a; **~ opera** opereta *f* **4.** (*not intense: breeze, rain*) leve; **to be a ~ sleeper** tener el sueño ligero; **to be ~ on sth** carecer de algo **5.** GASTR frugal; **a ~ meal** una comida ligera **III.** *adv* ligeramente ►**to get off ~** salir bien parado; **to make ~ of sth** no dar importancia a algo **IV.** *vt* <lit *Am:* lighted, lit *Am:* lighted> **1.** (*illuminate*) iluminar; **to ~ the way** mostrar el camino **2.** (*start burning*) encender, prender *AmL;* **to ~ a cigarette** encender un cigarrillo **V.** *vi* <lit *Am:* lighted, lit *Am:* lighted> (*catch fire*) encenderse

◆**light up I.** *vt* alumbrar, iluminar **II.** *vi* **1.** (*become bright*) iluminarse **2.** (*become animated*) animarse; **his face lights up** se le ilumina la cara **3.** (*start smoking*) encender un cigarrillo

◆**light upon** *vi* caer en la cuenta de; (*suddenly see*) dar con

light bulb ['laɪtbʌlb] *n* bombilla *f,* foco *m AmL*

lighten ['laɪtən] **I.** *vi* **1.** (*become brighter*) clarear **2.** (*become less heavy*) aligerarse; (*mood*) alegrarse **II.** *vt* **1.** (*make less heavy*) aligerar; **to ~ sb's burden** aligerar la carga a alguien **2.** (*bleach, make paler*) aclarar

◆**lighten up** *vi Am, Aus* relajarse

lighter ['laɪtəʳ, *Am:* -t̬ɚ] *n* mechero *m,* encendedor *m AmL*

light-fingered [ˌlaɪt'fɪŋgəd, *Am:* -gɚd] *adj* con las manos largas **light-footed** *adj* ligero, -a de pies **light-headed** *adj* **1.** (*faint*) mareado, -a **2.** (*excited*) delirante **light-hearted** *adj* (*carefree*) despreocupado, -a; (*happy*) alegre; **a ~ look at sth** una mirada alegre a algo **lighthouse** *n* faro *m*

lighting ['laɪtɪŋ, *Am:* -t̬ɪŋ] *n* iluminación *f*

lightly ['laɪtli] *adv* ligeramente; (*to rest, touch*) levemente; **to sleep ~** dormir ligeramente; **to take sth ~** tomar algo a la ligera; **to get off ~** salir bien parado

light meter *n* fotómetro *m;* PHOT exposímetro *m*

lightness ['laɪtnɪs] *n no pl* **1.** (*of thing, touch*) ligereza *f* **2.** (*brightness*) claridad *f*

lightning ['laɪtnɪŋ] *n no pl* relámpago *m;* **a ray of ~** un relámpago; **thunder and ~** rayos y centellas ►**quick as ~** como el relámpago

lightning attack *n* ataque *m* relámpago **lightning conductor** *n Brit,* **lightning rod** *n Am* pararrayos *m inv* **lightning strike** *n Brit, Aus* huelga *f* convocada sin previo aviso

light pen *n* lápiz *m* óptico

lightship *n* buque-faro *m* **lightweight I.** *adj* (*clothing, material*) ligero, -a **II.** *n* **1.** SPORTS peso *m* ligero **2.** (*unimpressive person*) persona *f* de poco peso

light year *n* año *m* luz; **to be ~s away** *inf* estar a años luz de distancia

lignite ['lɪgnaɪt] *n* lignito *m*

likable ['laɪkəbl] *adj Am, Aus s.* **likeable**

like[1] [laɪk] **I.** *vt* **1.** (*find good*) **I ~ it** (esto) me gusta; **she ~s apples** le gustan las manzanas; **I ~ swimming** me gusta nadar; **I ~ her** (ella) me cae bien; **he ~s classical music** le gusta la música clásica; **I like it when/how ...** me gusta cuando/cómo...; **well, how do you ~ that?** (*expressing surprise*) ¿quién lo diría? **2.** (*desire, wish*) querer; **I would ~ to go to ...** me gustaría ir a...; **would you ~ a cup of tea?** ¿quieres un té?; **I should ~ a little bit more time** quisiera tener un poquito más de tiempo; **I should like to know ...** quisiera saber...; **I would ~ a steak** querría un filete **II.** *n pl* gustos *mpl;* **sb's ~s and dislikes** las preferencias de alguien

like[2] [laɪk] **I.** *adj* semejante; **to be of ~ mind** pensar de la misma manera **II.** *prep* **to be ~ sb/sth** ser como alguien/algo; **what was it ~?** ¿cómo fue?; **what does it look ~?** ¿cómo es?; **to work ~ crazy** *inf* trabajar como un burro; **there is nothing ~ ...** no hay nada que se parezca a... ►**~ anything** a más no poder **III.** *conj inf* como si +*subj;* **he speaks ~ he was drunk** habla como si estuviera borracho; **he doesn't do it ~ I do** él no lo hace como yo

likeable ['laɪkəbl] *adj* simpático, -a

likelihood ['laɪklɪhʊd] *n no pl* probabilidad *f;* **in all ~** con toda probabilidad; **there is every/little ~ that ...** hay muchas/pocas probabilidades de que... +*subj*

likely ['laɪkli] **I.** <-ier, -iest> *adj* probable; **it is ~ (that ...)** es probable (que... +*subj*); **to be quite/very ~** ser bastante/muy probable; **to be a ~ story** *iron* ser un cuento chino, ser puro cuento *AmL;* **not ~!** *inf* ¡ni hablar! **II.** *adv* probablemente; **as ~ as not** a lo mejor; **most/very ~** bastante/muy probablemente

like-minded [ˌlaɪk'maɪndɪd, *Am:* '-ˌ-] *adj* del mismo parecer

liken ['laɪkən] *vt* comparar; **to ~ sb to sb** comparar alguien con alguien

likeness ['laɪknɪs] <-es> *n* **1.** (*similarity*) semejanza *f;* **a family ~** un aire de familia; **to bear a ~ to sb** tener parecido con alguien **2.** (*painting*) retrato *m*

likewise ['laɪkwaɪz] *adv* de la misma forma, asimismo; **to do ~** hacer lo mismo

liking ['laɪkɪŋ] *n no pl* afición *f;* (*for particular person*) simpatía *f;* **to develop a ~ for sb** tomar cariño a alguien; **to be to sb's ~** *form* ser del agrado de alguien; **it's too sweet for my ~** es demasiado dulce para mi gusto

lilac ['laɪlək] **I.** *n* **1.** (*bush*) lila *f* **2.** *no pl* (*colour*) lila *m* **II.** *adj* lila

lilo® ['laɪləʊ, *Am:* -loʊ] *n Brit* colchoneta *f*

inflable
lilt ['lɪlt] *n no pl* cadencia *f*
lily ['lɪli] <-ies> *n* lirio *m;* **water** ~ nenúfar *m*
lily-livered ['lɪlɪˌlɪvəd, *Am:* -ɚd] *adj liter* cobarde
lily pad *n* hoja *f* de nenúfar
limb [lɪm] *n* **1.** BOT rama *f* **2.** ANAT miembro *m* ▶**to be/go out on a** ~ (**to do sth**) estar/ponerse en una situación arriesgada (para hacer algo); **to tear sb** ~ **from** ~ despedazar a alguien
limber ['lɪmbəʳ, *Am:* -bɚ] *adj* (*person*) ágil; (*material*) flexible
◆**limber up** *vi* hacer ejercicios de precalentamiento
limbo ['lɪmbəʊ, *Am:* -boʊ] *n no pl* **1.** *a. fig* limbo *m;* **to be in** ~ estar en el limbo **2.** (*dance*) limbo *m;* **to do the** ~ bailar el limbo
lime¹ [laɪm] **I.** *n* **1.** (*fruit*) lima *f* **2.** (*tree*) limero *m* **3.** *no pl* (*juice*) zumo *m* de lima **4.** (*colour*) verde *m* lima **II.** *adj* de color verde lima
lime² [laɪm] **I.** *n no pl* CHEM cal *f* **II.** *vt* abonar con cal
lime³ [laɪm] *n* (*linden tree*) tilo *m*
limelight ['laɪmlaɪt] *n no pl* foco *m* proyector; **to be in the** ~ estar en el candelero; **to hog the** ~ chupar cámara; **to steal the** ~ acaparar la atención del público
limerick ['lɪmərɪk, *Am:* -ɚ-] *n* quintilla *f* humorística
limestone ['laɪmstəʊn, *Am:* -stoʊn] *n no pl* caliza *f*
limit ['lɪmɪt] **I.** *n* límite *m;* (**speed**) ~ AUTO límite *m* de velocidad; **to put a** ~ **on sth** poner un límite a algo; **to overstep the** ~ pasarse del límite; **to know one's** ~**s** conocer los propios límites; **to know no** ~**s** no tener límites; **within** ~**s** dentro de ciertos límites; **to be off** ~**s** (**to sb**) *Am* quedar prohibido el acceso (a alguien); **it's the** ~! ¡es el colmo! **II.** *vt* limitar; **to** ~ **oneself to sth** limitarse a algo
limitation [ˌlɪmɪ'teɪʃən] *n* **1.** *no pl* (*lessening*) restricción *f;* (*of pollution, weapons*) limitación *f* **2.** *pl* limitaciones *fpl;* **she knows her** ~**s** ella sabe sus limitaciones **3.** LAW prescripción *f*
limited ['lɪmɪtɪd, *Am:* -t̬ɪd] *adj* limitado, -a; **to be** ~ **to sth** estar limitado a algo
limited company *n* sociedad *f* (de responsabilidad) limitada
limitless ['lɪmɪtlɪs] *adj* ilimitado, -a
limousine ['lɪməziːn] *n* limusina *f*
limp¹ [lɪmp] **I.** *vi* cojear **II.** *n no pl* cojera *f;* **to walk with a** ~ cojear
limp² [lɪmp] *adj* **1.** (*floppy*) flojo, -a; (*lettuce*) mustio, -a; **to have a** ~ **handshake** dar la mano de forma poco enérgica **2.** (*effort*) débil; (*excuse*) poco convincente
limpet ['lɪmpɪt] *n* lapa *f*
limpid ['lɪmpɪd] *adj liter* límpido, -a; (*air*) diáfano, -a; (*eyes*) claro, -a
limy ['laɪmi] *adj* calizo, -a
linchpin ['lɪntʃpɪn] *n* **1.** TECH pezonera *f* **2.** *fig* eje *m*
linden ['lɪndən] *n Am* BOT tilo *m*
line¹ [laɪn] <-ning> *vt* revestir; (*clothes*) forrar
line² [laɪn] **I.** *n* **1.** (*mark*) *a.* MAT línea *f;* **dividing** ~ línea divisoria; **to be in a** ~ estar en línea; **to form a** ~ formar una línea **2.** *Am* (*queue*) fila *f*, cola *f AmL;* **to get in** ~ ponerse en fila; **to stand in** ~ hacer cola **3.** (*chronological succession*) linaje *m;* **a** (**long**) ~ **of disasters/kings** una (larga) sucesión de desastres/reyes **4.** (*cord*) cuerda *f;* **clothes** ~ cuerda para colgar la ropa **5.** TEL línea *f;* ~**s will be open from ...** las líneas estarán abiertas a partir de...; **to be/stay on the** ~ estar/seguir al habla; **hold the** ~! ¡no cuelgue! **6.** INFOR **on** ~ en línea; **off** ~ desconectado **7.** (*defence*) frente *m;* **front** ~ línea del frente; **to be the last** ~ **of defence** *fig* ser la última línea de defensa; **to be behind enemy** ~**s** estar detrás de las líneas enemigas **8.** (*set of tracks*) vía *f;* (*specific train route*) línea *f;* **the end of the** ~ el final de la línea; **to be at** [*o* **to reach**] **the end of the** ~ *fig* tocar fondo **9.** (*transport company*) línea *f;* **rail/shipping** ~ línea de transporte ferroviario/marítimo **10.** (*of text*) línea *f*, renglón *m;* **to drop sb a** ~ *inf* escribir a alguien **11.** MUS melodía *f* **12.** (*comment*) comentario *m;* **to come up with a** ~ **about sb/sth** salir con un comentario acerca de alguien/algo **13.** (*position, attitude*) línea *f;* ~ **of reasoning** razonamiento *m;* **to be divided along ethnic** ~**s** estar dividido según criterios étnicos; **the official** ~ (**on sth**) la línea oficial (acerca de algo); **to take a** ~ **on sth** tomar posición sobre algo **14.** (*field, pursuit, interest*) especialidad *f;* **what** ~ **are you in?** ¿a qué se dedica? **15.** (*product type*) línea *f;* FASHION línea *f* de moda; **to come out with a new** ~ *Am* sacar una nueva línea **16.** *inf* (*of cocaine*) raya *f;* **to do a** ~ **of cocaine, to do** ~**s** esnifar una raya ▶**somewhere along the** ~ en algún momento; **right down the** ~ *Am* hasta el último momento; **to cross the** ~ salirse de la raya; **to get a** ~ **on sb** obtener información acerca de alguien; **to give sb a** ~ **on sb** dar a alguien información sobre alguien; **to be in** ~ **for sth** tener muchas posibilidades de ascender; **to be in** ~ **with sb/sth** estar de acuerdo con alguien/algo; **to be out of** ~ estar fuera de lugar; **to be out of** ~ **with sb/sth** no estar de acuerdo con alguien/algo **II.** <-ning> *vt* **to** ~ **the streets** ocupar las calles; **to** ~ **the route** alinearse a lo largo de la ruta
◆**line up** **I.** *vt* alinear **II.** *vi* **1.** (*stand in row*) alinearse **2.** *Am* (*wait one behind another*) ponerse en fila, hacer cola **3.** (*oppose*) **to** ~ **against sb/sth** alinearse en contra de alguien/algo
lineage ['lɪnɪɪdʒ] *n* linaje *m*
lineal ['lɪnɪəl] *adj* en línea directa

linear ['lɪnɪəʳ, *Am:* -ɚ] *adj* lineal
linear equation *n* ecuación *f* lineal
linen ['lɪnɪn] *n no pl* lino *m;* **bed** ~ sábanas *fpl;* **table** ~ mantelería *f* ►**to wash one's dirty** ~ **in public** sacar los trapos sucios a relucir
linen basket *n* cesto *m* de la ropa sucia
liner ['laɪnəʳ, *Am:* -nɚ] *n* **1.** (*lining*) forro *m;* **dustbin** ~ bolsa *f* de la basura **2.** (*ship*) transatlántico *m*
linesman ['laɪnzmən] <-men> *n* SPORTS juez *mf* de línea
lineup ['laɪnʌp] *n* **1.** SPORTS (*team*) alineación *f; Am* (*of baseball players*) orden *m* de los bateadores **2.** (*identity parade*) rueda *f* de identificación
linger ['lɪŋgəʳ, *Am:* -gɚ] *vi* entretenerse; (*film*) hacerse largo; **to** ~ **in the memory** perdurar en la memoria; **to** ~ **on** permanecer, perdurar; **to** ~ **on sb/sth** entretenerse con alguien/algo; **to** ~ **over sth** tomarse tiempo para (hacer) algo
lingerie ['lænʒəriː, *Am:* ˌlɑːnʒə'reɪ] *n no pl* lencería *f*
lingering ['lɪŋgərɪŋ] *adj* prolongado, -a; (*doubt*) persistente
lingo ['lɪŋgəʊ, *Am:* -goʊ] <-goes> *n inf* **1.** (*foreign language*) idioma *m* (extranjero) **2.** (*jargon*) jerga *f*
linguist ['lɪŋgwɪst] *n* lingüista *mf*
linguistic [lɪŋ'gwɪstɪk] *adj* lingüístico, -a
linguistics [lɪŋ'gwɪstɪks] *n* lingüística *f*
liniment ['lɪnɪmənt] *n no pl* linimento *m*
lining ['laɪnɪŋ] *n* **1.** (*of boiler, pipes*) revestimiento *m;* (*of coat, jacket*) forro *m* **2.** ANAT pared *f*
link [lɪŋk] **I.** *n* **1.** (*in chain*) eslabón *m* **2.** (*connection*) conexión *f;* **rail** ~ enlace *m* ferroviario **3.** INFOR vínculo *m,* enlace *m* **II.** *vt* **1.** (*connect*) conectar; **to** ~ **hands** darse la mano **2.** (*associate*) relacionar; **to be** ~**ed** (**together**) estar relacionado
linkman ['lɪŋkmæn] <-men> *n Brit* TV, RADIO locutor *m*
links [lɪŋks] *n* **1.** (*golf course*) campo *m* de golf **2.** *Scot* (*dunes*) dunas *fpl*
link-up ['lɪŋkʌp] *n* conexión *f;* (*of spacecraft*) acoplamiento *m;* **satellite** ~ conexión vía satélite
linkwoman ['lɪŋkˌwʊmən] <-women> *n Brit* TV, RADIO locutora *f*
linnet ['lɪnɪt] *n* pardillo *m*
linoleum [lɪ'nəʊlɪəm, *Am:* -'noʊ-] *n,* **lino** ['laɪnəʊ, *Am:* -noʊ] *n no pl* linóleo *m*
linotype® ['laɪnəʊtaɪp] *n* linotipia *f*
linseed ['lɪnsiːd] *n no pl* linaza *f*
linseed oil *n no pl* aceite *m* de linaza
lint [lɪnt] *n no pl, Brit* pelusa *f*
lintel ['lɪntl, *Am:* -t̬l] *n* dintel *m*
lion ['laɪən] *n* león *m* ►**the** ~**'s share** la parte del león
lioness [laɪə'nes] <-sses> *n* leona *f*
lion-hearted ['laɪən'hɑːtɪd, *Am:* -ɑnˌhɑːrt̬ɪd] *adj* valiente
lionize ['laɪənaɪz] *vt* tratar como un personaje importante
lip [lɪp] *n* **1.** ANAT labio *m;* **the question on everyone's** ~**s** la pregunta que se hace todo el mundo; **my** ~**s are sealed** soy una tumba **2.** (*rim: of cup, bowl*) borde *m;* (*of jug*) pico *m* **3.** *no pl, inf* (*impudence*) insolencia *f*
lip gloss *n no pl* brillo *m* de labios
liposuction ['laɪpəʊˌsʌkʃən, *Am:* 'lɪpoʊ-] *n* liposucción *f*
lip-read **I.** *vi* leer los labios **II.** *vt* leer los labios a
lip salve *n no pl* crema *f* de cacao
lip service *n no pl* jarabe *m* de pico; **to pay** ~ **to sth** apoyar algo sólo de boquilla
lipstick *n* barra *f* de labios
liquefy ['lɪkwəfaɪ] <-ie-> **I.** *vt* licuar **II.** *vi* licuarse
liqueur [lɪ'kjʊəʳ, *Am:* -'kɜːr] *n* licor *m*
liquid ['lɪkwɪd] **I.** *n* líquido *m* **II.** *adj* líquido, -a
liquidate ['lɪkwɪdeɪt] *vt a. fig* liquidar
liquidation [ˌlɪkwɪ'deɪʃən] *n* liquidación *f;* **to go into** ~ ECON entrar en liquidación
liquidise ['lɪkwɪdaɪz] *vt Brit, Aus s.* **liquidize**
liquidiser ['lɪkwɪdaɪzəʳ] *n Brit, Aus s.* **liquidizer**
liquidity [lɪ'kwɪdəti, *Am:* -t̬i] *n no pl* liquidez *f*
liquidize ['lɪkwɪdaɪz] *vt* licuar
liquidizer ['lɪkwɪdaɪzəʳ, *Am:* -zɚ] *n* licuadora *f*
liquor ['lɪkəʳ, *Am:* -ɚ] *n no pl* licor *m*
liquorice ['lɪkərɪs, *Am:* -ɚ-] *n no pl* regaliz *m*
Lisbon ['lɪzbən] *n* Lisboa *f*
lisp [lɪsp] **I.** *n no pl* ceceo *m* **II.** *vi* cecear **III.** *vt* pronunciar ceceando
lissom(**e**) ['lɪsəm] *adj liter* grácil
list[1] [lɪst] **I.** *n* lista *f;* ~ **price** precio *m* según catálogo; **shopping** ~ lista de la compra; **to make a** ~ (**of sth**) hacer un listado (de algo) **II.** *vt* **1.** (*make a list*) listar **2.** (*enumerate*) enumerar
list[2] [lɪst] NAUT **I.** *vi* escorar **II.** *n* escora *f*
listen ['lɪsən] **I.** *n inf* **to have a** ~ (**to sth**) *inf* escuchar (algo) **II.** *vi* **1.** (*hear*) escuchar; **to** ~ **to sth/sb** escuchar algo/a alguien; **to** ~ **to reason** atender a razones **2.** (*pay attention*) estar atento; **to** ~ (**out**) **for sth** estar atento para oír algo
◆**listen in** *vi Brit* escuchar (a escondidas); **to** ~ **on sth** escuchar algo (a escondidas)
listener ['lɪsnəʳ, *Am:* -ɚ] *n* oyente *mf*
listeria [lɪ'stɪərɪə, *Am:* -'stɪrɪ-] *npl* listeria *f*
listing ['lɪstɪŋ] *n* **1.** (*list*) lista *f,* listado *m* **2.** (*entry in list*) entrada *f* **3.** *pl, Brit* (*list of shows, films*) guía *f* de espectáculos
listless ['lɪstlɪs] *adj* **1.** (*lacking energy: person*) apagado, -a; (*economy*) débil **2.** (*lacking enthusiasm*) apático, -a; (*performance*) deslucido, -a

lit [lɪt] *pt, pp of* **light**
litany ['lɪtəni] <-ies> *n* letanía *f*
litchi ['laɪtʃiː, *Am:* 'liː-] *n* lichi *m*
liter ['liːtəʳ, *Am:* -t̬ɚ] *n Am* litro *m*
literacy ['lɪtərəsi, *Am:* 'lɪt̬ɚ-] *n no pl* alfabetización *f;* ~ **rate** índice *m* de alfabetización
literal ['lɪtərəl, *Am:* 'lɪt̬ɚ-] *adj* literal; **to take sth in the ~ sense of the word** tomar algo al pie de la letra
literally ['lɪtərəli, *Am:* 'lɪt̬ɚ-] *adv* literalmente; **to take sth/sb ~** tomar algo/a alguien al pie de la letra; **quite ~** literalmente
literary ['lɪtərəri, *Am:* 'lɪt̬ərer-] *adj* literario, -a
literary criticism *n* crítica *f* literaria
literate ['lɪtərət, *Am:* 'lɪt̬ɚ-] *adj* **1.** (*able to read and write*) que sabe leer y escribir; **to be ~** saber leer y escribir **2.** (*well-educated*) culto, -a
literature ['lɪtrətʃəʳ, *Am:* 'lɪt̬ɚətʃɚ] *n no pl* **1.** (*novels, poems*) literatura *f;* **nineteenth-century ~** literatura del siglo XIX **2.** (*promotional material*) material *m* informativo
lithe [laɪð] *adj* ágil
lithium ['lɪθɪəm] *n no pl* litio *m*
lithograph ['lɪθəgrɑːf, *Am:* -græf] **I.** *n* litografía *f* **II.** *vi* litografiar
lithography [lɪ'θɒgrəfi, *Am:* -'θɑːgrə-] *n no pl* litografía *f*
Lithuania [ˌlɪθjʊ'eɪnɪə, *Am:* ˌlɪθʊ-] *n* Lituania *f*
Lithuanian **I.** *n* **1.** (*person*) lituano, -a *m, f* **2.** LING lituano *m* **II.** *adj* lituano, -a
litigant ['lɪtɪgənt, *Am:* 'lɪt̬-] *n* litigante *mf*
litigate ['lɪtɪgeɪt, *Am:* 'lɪt̬-] *vi* litigar
litigation [ˌlɪtɪ'geɪʃən, *Am:* ˌlɪt̬-] *n no pl* litigio *m*
litigious [lɪ'tɪdʒəs] *adj* pleiteador(a)
litmus ['lɪtməs] *n no pl* tornasol *m*
litmus paper *n no pl* papel *m* de tornasol **litmus test** *no pl n* prueba *m* de tornasol; *fig* prueba *f* de fuego
litre ['liːtəʳ, *Am:* -t̬ɚ] *n* litro *m*
litter ['lɪtəʳ, *Am:* 'lɪt̬ɚ] **I.** *n* **1.** *no pl* (*refuse*) basura *f* **2.** ZOOL camada *f* **3.** *no pl* (*bedding for animals*) lecho *m* de paja **4.** MED camilla *f* **II.** *vt* **1.** (*make untidy*) ensuciar (tirando basura) **2.** (*scatter*) esparcir; **the floor was ~ed with clothes** el suelo estaba cubierto de ropa
litter bug *n Am, Aus,* **litter lout** *n Brit: persona que tira basura en un lugar público*
litter tray *n* bandeja *f* para la arena del gato
little ['lɪtl] **I.** *adj* **1.** (*size, age*) pequeño, -a; **a ~ old man/woman** un viejecito/una viejecita; **the ~ ones** *inf* los niños **2.** (*amount*) poco, -a; **a ~ something** alguna cosita; **a ~ bit (of sth)** un poco (de algo); **a ~ something** algo (de comida o de bebida); **~ hope** pocas esperanzas; **~ by ~** poco a poco **3.** (*distance*) corto, -a; **a ~ way** un camino corto **4.** (*duration*) breve; **for a ~ while** durante un ratito; **to have a ~ word with sb** cruzar algunas palabras con alguien **II.** *n* poco *m;* **a ~** un poco; **to know ~** saber poco; **we see ~ of him** lo vemos poco; **to have ~ to say** tener poco que decir **III.** *adv* poco; **~ less than ...** poco menos que...; **~ more than an hour** poco más de una hora; **to make ~ of sth** sacar poco en claro de algo
liturgical [lɪ'tɜːdʒɪkl, *Am:* -'tɜːr-] *adj* litúrgico, -a
liturgy ['lɪtədʒi, *Am:* 'lɪt̬ɚ-] <-ies> *n* REL liturgia *f*
live¹ [laɪv] **I.** *adj* **1.** (*living*) vivo, -a **2.** RADIO, TV en directo; THEAT en vivo **3.** ELEC que lleva corriente; (*wire*) conectado, -a; **to be a (real) ~ wire** *fig* rebosar energía **4.** (*cartridge*) cargado, -a; (*bomb*) con carga explosiva **II.** *adv* RADIO, TV en directo; THEAT en vivo
live² [lɪv] **I.** *vi* vivir; **to ~ above one's means** vivir por encima de las posibilidades de uno; **to ~ in sb's memory** perdurar en la memoria de alguien; **long ~ the king!** ¡viva el rey!; **to ~ off sth/sb** vivir de algo/alguien; **to ~ on sth** (*eat*) alimentarse de algo ►**to ~ and let ~** vivir y dejar vivir **II.** *vt* vivir; **to ~ a happy life** llevar una vida feliz
◆**live down** *vt* lograr superar
◆**live in** *vi vivir en el lugar donde uno trabaja*
◆**live on** *vi* vivir; (*tradition*) seguir vivo
◆**live out** *vt* vivir; (*dreams*) realizar
◆**live through** *vt* (*experience*) vivir
◆**live together** *vi* vivir juntos
◆**live up** *vt* **to live it up** vivir a lo grande
◆**live up to** *vt* vivir conforme a; **to ~ expectations** estar a la altura de lo esperado
livelihood ['laɪvlɪhʊd] *n* sustento *m;* **to earn one's ~** ganarse la vida
liveliness ['laɪvlɪnɪs] *n no pl* viveza *f*
lively ['laɪvli] *adj* (*person, conversation*) animado, -a; (*imagination, interest*) vivo, -a
liven up ['laɪvən ʌp] **I.** *vi* animarse **II.** *vt* animar
liver ['lɪvəʳ, *Am:* -ɚ] *n* hígado *m*
liver complaint *n no pl* afección *f* hepática
liverish ['lɪvərɪʃ] *adj* **1.** (*ill*) enfermo, -a del hígado **2.** (*peevish*) malhumorado, -a
liver sausage *n,* **liverwurst** ['lɪvəwɜːst, *Am:* -ɚwɜːrst] *n no pl, Am, Aus* (embutido *m* de) paté *m* de hígado
livery ['lɪvəri] *n no pl* **1.** FASHION librea *f* **2.** *Brit* (*company colours*) colores *mpl* distintivos (*de una empresa*)
livestock ['laɪvstɒk, *Am:* -stɑːk] *n no pl* ganado *m*
livid ['lɪvɪd] *adj* **1.** (*discoloured*) lívido, -a **2.** (*furious*) furioso, -a
living ['lɪvɪŋ] **I.** *n* **1.** *no pl* (*livelihood*) vida *f;* **to work for one's ~** trabajar para ganarse la vida; **to make a ~** ganarse la vida **2.** *no pl* (*way of life*) (modo *m* de) vida *f* **3.** *pl* (*people*) **the ~** los vivos **II.** *adj* vivo, -a; (*creature*) viviente; **to be the ~ image of sb/sth** ser el vivo retrato de alguien/algo
living conditions *npl* condiciones *fpl* de vida **living quarters** *npl* alojamiento *m* **living room** *n* cuarto *m* de estar, living *m AmL*

living space *no pl n a. fig* espacio *m* vital

living wage *no pl n* salario *m* digno

lizard ['lɪzəd, *Am:* -ɚd] *n* lagarto *m;* (*small*) lagartija *f*

llama ['lɑːmə] *n* llama *f*

load [ləʊd, *Am:* loʊd] **I.** *n* **1.** ELEC *a. fig* carga *f* **2.** (*amount of work*) cantidad *f* (de trabajo); **a heavy/light ~** mucho/poco trabajo **3.** *inf* (*lots*) montón *m;* **~s** [*o* **a ~**] **of ...** un montón de... ▸**to get a ~ of sth** *inf* fijarse en algo **II.** *vt a.* AUTO, PHOT, INFOR cargar **III.** *vi* cargarse

◆**load down** *vt* recargar; *fig* agobiar

◆**load up I.** *vt* cargar **II.** *vi* cargarse

loaded ['ləʊdɪd, *Am:* 'loʊd-] *adj* **1.** (*filled*) cargado, -a **2.** (*unfair: question*) tendencioso, -a; **~ dice** dados *mpl* cargados **3.** *Brit, inf* (*rich*) forrado, -a **4.** *Am, inf* (*drunk*) mamado, -a

loadstone ['ləʊdstəʊn, *Am:* 'loʊdstoʊn] *n* piedra *f* imán

loaf[1] [ləʊf, *Am:* loʊf] <loaves> *n* pan *m;* **a ~ of bread** un pan ▸**half a ~ is better than no bread** *prov* algo es algo; **use your ~!** *Brit* ¡usa la cabeza!

loaf[2] [ləʊf, *Am:* loʊf] *vi* gandulear; **to ~ about** hacer el holgazán

loafer ['ləʊfəʳ, *Am:* 'loʊfɚ] *n* **1.** (*lazy person*) holgazán, -ana *m, f* **2.** *Am* (*shoe*) mocasín *m*

loam [ləʊm, *Am:* loʊm] *n no pl* marga *f*

loan [ləʊn, *Am:* loʊn] **I.** *vt* prestar **II.** *n* préstamo *m,* avío *m AmS*

loanword ['ləʊnwɜːd, *Am:* 'loʊnwɜːrd] *n* LING préstamo *m*

loath [ləʊθ, *Am:* loʊθ] *adj form* reacio, -a; **to be ~ to do sth** resistirse a hacer algo

loathe [ləʊð, *Am:* loʊð] *vt* (*thing*) detestar; (*person*) odiar

loathing *n no pl* odio *m;* **to have a ~ for sb** odiar a alguien; **to have a ~ for sth** tener aversión a algo

loathsome ['ləʊðsəm, *Am:* 'loʊð-] *adj* (*thing*) asqueroso, -a; (*person*) odioso, -a

loaves [ləʊfz, *Am:* loʊfz] *n pl of* **loaf**[1]

lob [lɒb, *Am:* lɑːb] **I.** <-bb-> *vt* lanzar; SPORTS hacer un globo a **II.** *n* SPORTS lob *m*

lobby ['lɒbi, *Am:* 'lɑːbi] **I.** <-ies> *n* **1.** ARCHIT vestíbulo *m* **2.** POL grupo *m* de presión **II.** <-ie-> *vi* **to ~ to have sth done** hacer presión para que se haga algo; **to ~ against/for sth** presionar en contra de/en pro de algo **III.** <-ie-> *vt* presionar

lobbyist ['lɒbiɪst, *Am:* 'lɑːbi-] *n* miembro *m* de un grupo de presión

lobe [ləʊb, *Am:* loʊb] *n* lóbulo *m*

lobster ['lɒbstəʳ, *Am:* 'lɑːbstɚ] *n* (*spiny*) langosta *f;* (*with claws*) bogavante *m*

lobster pot *n* nasa *f*

local ['ləʊkəl, *Am:* 'loʊ-] **I.** *adj* local; (*people*) del lugar; (*official, police*) municipal; TEL urbano, -a; **~ colour** color *m* local **II.** *n* **1.** (*inhabitant*) lugareño, -a *m, f* **2.** *Am* (*bus*) coche *m* de línea; (*train*) tren *m* de cercanías **3.** *Brit* (*pub*) taberna *f* (*del barrio, pueblo, etc.*)

local anaesthetic *n* anestesia *f* local **local authority** *n* municipio *m,* ayuntamiento *m*

local call *n* llamada *f* local

locale [ləʊ'kɑːl, *Am:* loʊ'kæl] *n* escenario *m*

local elections *npl* elecciones *fpl* municipales **local government** *n* administración *f* municipal

locality [ləʊ'kæləti, *Am:* loʊ'kæləṱi] <-ies> *n* localidad *f*

localization [ˌləʊkəlaɪ'zeɪʃən, *Am:* ˌloʊkəlɪ'-] *n no pl* localización *f*

localize ['ləʊkəlaɪz, *Am:* 'loʊ-] *vt* localizar

local paper *n* periódico *m* local **local time** *no pl n* hora *f* local **local train** *n* tren *m* de cercanías

locate [ləʊ'keɪt, *Am:* 'loʊ-] *vt* **1.** (*find*) localizar **2.** (*situate*) situar; **to be ~d near sth** estar situado cerca de algo

location [ləʊ'keɪʃən, *Am:* loʊ'-] *n* **1.** (*place*) posición *f* **2.** (*act of locating*) localización *f* **3.** CINE exteriores *mpl;* **to film sth on ~** rodar algo en exteriores

loc. cit. [ˌlɒk'sɪt, *Am:* ˌlɑːk'sɪt] *abbr of* **loco citato** loc. cit.

loch [lɒk, *Am:* lɑːk] *n Scot* **1.** (*lake*) lago *m* **2.** (*inlet*) brazo *m* de mar

lock[1] [lɒk, *Am:* lɑːk] *n* (*of hair*) mechón *m*

lock[2] [lɒk, *Am:* lɑːk] **I.** *n* **1.** (*fastening device*) cerradura *f,* chapa *f Arg, Méx* **2.** (*on canal*) esclusa *f* **3.** (*in wrestling*) llave *f* **4.** *Aus, Brit* AUTO tope *m* ▸**~, stock and barrel** completamente, por completo; **to be under ~ and key** estar cerrado bajo llave **II.** *vt* **1.** (*fasten with lock*) cerrar con llave; (*confine safely: thing*) guardar bajo llave; (*person*) encerrar; **to be ~ed** (*be held fast*) estar sujeto **2.** (*make immovable*) bloquear; **be ~ed** estar bloqueado; **to be ~ed in(to) discussions** enredarse en discusiones **III.** *vi* cerrase con llave

◆**lock away** *vt* (*jewels, document*) guardar bajo llave; (*person*) encerrar

◆**lock in** *vt* encerrar

◆**lock on** *vi,* **lock onto** *vi* MIL localizar y seguir

◆**lock out** *vt* impedir la entrada a; **to lock oneself out** dejarse las llaves dentro

◆**lock up** *vt* (*jewels, document*) guardar bajo llave; (*person*) encerrar

locker ['lɒkəʳ, *Am:* 'lɑːkɚ] *n* (*at railway station*) consigna *f* automática; (*at school*) taquilla *f*

locket ['lɒkɪt, *Am:* 'lɑːkɪt] *n* guardapelo *m*

lockjaw ['lɒkdʒɔː, *Am:* 'lɑːkdʒɑː] *n no pl* trismo *m*

lockout ['lɒkaʊt, *Am:* 'lɑːk-] *n* cierre *m* patronal

locksmith ['lɒksmɪθ, *Am:* 'lɑːk-] *n* cerrajero, -a *m, f*

lockup ['lɒkʌp, *Am:* 'lɑːk-] *n inf* **1.** (*cell*) calabozo *m* **2.** (*storage space*) garaje *m*

locomotion [ˌləʊkə'məʊʃən, *Am:* ˌloʊkə'moʊ-] *n no pl* locomoción *f*

locomotive [ˌləʊkə'məʊtɪv, *Am:* ˌloʊkə-

'moʊt̬ɪv] I. *n* locomotora *f* II. *adj* locomotor(a); (*force*) locomotriz

locum ['ləʊkəm, *Am:* 'loʊ-] *n Aus, Brit* interino, -a *m, f*

locus ['ləʊkəs, *Am:* 'loʊ-] <-ci> *n* 1. (*exact place*) lugar *m* 2. MAT lugar *m* geométrico 3. BIO locus *m*

locust ['ləʊkəst, *Am:* 'loʊ-] *n* langosta *f*, chapulín *m Méx*

locution [lə'kju:ʃən, *Am:* loʊ'-] *n* locución *f*

lode [ləʊd, *Am:* loʊd] *n* MIN filón *m*

lodestar ['ləʊdstɑ:ʳ, *Am:* 'loʊdstɑ:r] *n* estrella *f* polar

lodestone ['ləʊdstəʊn, *Am:* 'loʊdstoʊn] *n* piedra *f* imán

lodge [lɒdʒ, *Am:* lɑ:dʒ] I. *vi* 1. (*stay in rented room*) alojarse 2. (*become fixed*) quedarse clavado, -a II. *vt* 1. (*accommodate*) alojar 2. (*place*) colocar 3. (*insert*) meter 4. *Brit* (*deposit*) depositar 5. (*bring forward officially: appeal*) interponer; (*objection, protest*) presentar III. *n* 1. (*for hunters*) refugio *m* 2. *Brit* (*at entrance to building*) portería *f*; **porter's** ~ casa *f* del guarda 3. (*of freemasons*) logia *f* 4. (*of beaver*) madriguera *f*

lodger ['lɒdʒəʳ, *Am:* 'lɑ:dʒɚ] *n* inquilino, -a *m, f*; **to take in** ~**s** alquilar habitaciones

lodging ['lɒdʒɪŋ, *Am:* 'lɑ:dʒɪŋ] *n* 1. *no pl* (*accomodation*) alojamiento *m*; **board and** ~ pensión *f* completa 2. *pl, Brit* (*room to rent*) habitación *f* de alquiler

lodging house *n* pensión *f*

loft [lɒft, *Am:* lɑ:ft] I. *n* 1. (*space under roof*) buhardilla *f*; **hay** ~ pajar *m* 2. (*upstairs living space*) loft *m* II. *vt* (*ball*) lanzar por lo alto

lofty ['lɒfti, *Am:* 'lɑ:f-] <-ier, -iest> *adj* 1. *liter* (*tall*) altísimo, -a 2. (*noble: aims, ideals*) noble 3. (*haughty*) altivo, -a

log[1] [lɒg, *Am:* lɑ:g] I. *n* 1. (*tree trunk*) tronco *m* 2. (*firewood*) leño *m* ►**to sleep like a** ~ dormir como un tronco II. <-gg-> *vt* talar III. <-gg-> *vi* talar árboles

log[2] [lɒg, *Am:* lɑ:g] *inf abbr of* **logarithm** log.

log[3] [lɒg, *Am:* lɑ:g] I. *n* registro *m*; **ship's** ~ cuaderno *m* de bitácora II. *vt* 1. (*record*) registrar 2. (*achieve, attain*) alcanzar

◆**log in** *vi* INFOR entrar en el sistema

◆**log off** *vi* INFOR salir del sistema

◆**log on** *vi s.* **log in**

◆**log out** *vi s.* **log off**

loganberry ['ləʊgənberi, *Am:* 'loʊ-] <-ies> *n* frambuesa *f* de Logan

logarithm ['lɒgərɪðəm, *Am:* 'lɑ:gɚ-] *n* logaritmo *m*

logarithmic [ˌlɒgə'rɪðmɪk, *Am:* ˌlɑ:gɚ'rɪθ-] *adj* logarítmico, -a

log book ['lɒgbʊk, *Am:* 'lɑ:gbʊk] *n* NAUT diario *m* de navegación; AVIAT diario *m* de vuelo

log cabin *n* cabaña *f* de troncos **log fire** *n* fuego *m* de leña

logger ['lɒgəʳ, *Am:* 'lɑ:gɚ] *n* leñador(a) *m(f)*

loggerheads ['lɒgəhedz, *Am:* 'lɑ:gɚ-] *npl* **to be at** ~ (**with sb/over sth**) estar en desacuerdo (con alguien/sobre algo)

logic ['lɒdʒɪk, *Am:* 'lɑ:dʒɪk] *n no pl* lógica *f*

logical ['lɒdʒɪkl, *Am:* 'lɑ:dʒɪk-] *adj* lógico, -a

login [lɒgɪn, *Am:* lɑ:g-] *n* INFOR inicio *m* de sesión

logistics [lə'dʒɪstɪks, *Am:* loʊ'-] *n* logística *f*

logjam *n* atolladero *m*

logo ['lɒgəʊ, *Am:* 'loʊgoʊ] *n* logotipo *m*

logoff [lɒgɒf, *Am:* lɑ:gɑ:f] *n* INFOR fin *m* de sesión

logon *n s.* **login**

logrolling ['lɒgrəʊlɪŋ, *Am:* 'lɑ:groʊlɪŋ] *n no pl, Am* amiguismo *m*

loin [lɔɪn] I. *n* 1. *pl* (*body area*) bajo vientre *m* 2. *pl, liter* **the fruit of his** ~**s** su hijo/hija 3. GASTR lomo *m* II. *adj* de lomo

loincloth ['lɔɪnklɒθ, *Am:* '-klɑ:θ] *n* taparrabos *m inv*

loiter ['lɔɪtəʳ, *Am:* -t̬ɚ] *vi* 1. (*linger*) entretenerse 2. *a.* LAW merodear

loiterer ['lɔɪtərəʳ, *Am:* 'lɔɪt̬ɚɚ] *n* 1. *inf* holgazán, -ana *m, f* 2. LAW merodeador(a) *m(f)*

loll [lɒl, *Am:* lɑ:l] *vi* colgar; **to** ~ **about** holgazanear

lollipop ['lɒlipɒp, *Am:* 'lɑ:lipɑ:p] *n* chupachups® *m inv*

lollipop lady, **lollipop man** *n Brit, inf: persona que detiene el tráfico para permitir que los escolares crucen la calle*

lollop ['lɒləp, *Am:* 'lɑ:ləp] *vi* moverse torpemente

lolly ['lɒli, *Am:* 'lɑ:li] <-ies> *n* 1. *Aus, Brit* (*lollipop*) chupachups® *m inv*; **ice** ~ polo *m*, palito *m* (helado) *RíoPl*, chupete *m* (helado) *Chile* 2. *no pl, Brit, inf* (*money*) pasta *f*

London ['lʌndən] *n* Londres *m*

Londoner I. *adj* londinense II. *n* londinense *mf*

lone [ləʊn, *Am:* loʊn] *adj* solitario, -a

loneliness ['ləʊnlɪnɪs, *Am:* 'loʊn-] *n no pl* soledad *f*

lonely ['ləʊnli, *Am:* 'loʊn-] <-ier, -iest> *adj* (*person*) solo, -a; (*life*) solitario, -a; (*place*) aislado, -a

loner ['ləʊnəʳ, *Am:* 'loʊnɚ] *n* solitario, -a *m, f*

lonesome ['ləʊnsəm, *Am:* 'loʊn-] *adj* (*person*) solo, -a; (*place*) aislado, -a

long[1] [lɒŋ, *Am:* lɑ:ŋ] I. *adj* (*distance, time, shape*) largo, -a; **to have a** ~ **way to go** tener mucho camino por recorrer; **it's a** ~ **while since ...** hace mucho tiempo desde que...; ~ **time no see!** *inf* ¡cúanto tiempo (sin verte)! II. *adv* 1. (*a long time*) mucho (tiempo); ~ **after/before** mucho después/antes; ~ **ago** hace mucho (tiempo); **to take** ~ (**to do sth**) tardar mucho (en hacer algo); **to be not** ~ **in doing sth** *form* no tardar en hacer algo; ~ **live the king!** ¡viva el rey! 2. (*for the whole duration*) **all day** ~ todo el día; **as** ~ **as I live** mientras viva 3. *in comparisons* **as** ~ **as** mientras +*subj*; **to no** ~**er do sth** ya no hacer algo ►**so** ~ *inf* ¡hasta luego!; **so** ~ **as** mientras III. *n* mucho tiempo *m* ►**the** ~ **and the short of it**

is that ... en resumidas cuentas...

long² [lɒŋ, *Am:* lɑːŋ] *vi* **to ~ for sb** echar de menos a alguien; **to ~ for sth** estar deseando algo; **to ~ to do sth** anhelar hacer algo

long. *abbr of* **longitude** long.

longboat *n* bote *m*

long-distance [ˌlɒŋˈdɪstənts, *Am:* ˌlɑːŋ-] **I.** *adj* (*bus, flight*) de largo recorrido; (*race, runner*) de fondo; (*negotiations, relationship*) a distancia; **~ call** conferencia *f* **II.** *adv* **to phone ~** hacer una llamada interurbana

longevity [lɒnˈdʒevəti, *Am:* lɑːnˈdʒevət̬i] *n no pl* longevidad *f*

long-haired [ˌlɒŋˈheəd] *adj* (*person*) melenudo, -a; (*animal*) de pelo largo **longhand** *n no pl* escritura *f* normal (*donde las palabras tienen todas sus letras*) **long-haul** *adj* AVIAT de larga distancia

longing [ˈlɒŋɪŋ, *Am:* ˈlɑːŋɪŋ] **I.** *n* **1.** (*nostalgia*) nostalgia *f;* **to feel a ~ for sb** echar de menos a alguien **2.** (*strong desire*) vivo deseo *m;* **to have a ~ to do sth** anhelar hacer algo **II.** *adj* anhelante

longish [ˈlɒŋgɪʃ, *Am:* ˈlɑːŋ-] *adj inf* tirando a largo, -a

longitude [ˈlɒŋgɪtjuːd, *Am:* ˈlɑːndʒətuːd] *n* longitud *f*

longitudinal [ˌlɒŋgɪˈtjuːdɪnl, *Am:* ˌlɑːndʒəˈtuː-] *adj* longitudinal

long johns [ˈlɒŋdʒɒnz, *Am:* ˈlɑːŋdʒɑːnz] *npl inf* calzoncillos *mpl* largos **long jump** *n no pl* salto *m* de longitud, salto *m* largo *AmL* **long-life milk** *n* leche *f* uperizada **long-lived** *adj* **1.** (*person*) longevo, -a **2.** (*feud*) que viene de lejos **long-lost** *adj* perdido, -a hace mucho tiempo **long-range** *adj* (*missile*) de largo alcance; (*aircraft*) transcontinental; (*policy*) a largo plazo **longship** *n* barco *m* vikingo **long shot** *n* **to be a ~** ser una posibilidad muy remota **long-sighted** *adj* **1.** (*having long sight*) hipermétrope **2.** *Am* (*having foresight*) previsor(a) **long-standing** *adj* antiguo, -a **long-suffering** *adj* sufrido, -a **long-term** *adj* (*care*) prolongado, -a; (*loan, memory, strategy*) a largo plazo **long wave** *n* onda *f* larga **long-wave** *adj* de onda larga **longways** *adv,* **longwise** *adv* a lo largo **long-winded** *adj* prolijo, -a

loo [luː] *n Aus, Brit, inf* váter *m*

loofa(h) [ˈluːfə] *n* esponja *f* vegetal

look [lʊk] **I.** *n* **1.** (*act of looking: at person, thing*) mirada *f;* (*examination: of book, face*) ojeada *f;* **to take** [*o* **to have**] **a ~ at sth** echar un vistazo a algo; **to have a ~ for sth/sb** buscar algo/a alguien **2.** (*appearance*) aspecto *m;* **good ~** guapura *f;* **to have the ~ of sb/sth** parecerse a alguien/algo; **by the ~ of things** según parece **3.** (*style*) look *m* **II.** *vi* **1.** (*use sight*) mirar; **to ~ at sth/sb** mirar algo/a alguien; **to ~ at a book** echar una ojeada a un libro; **to ~ out (of) the window** mirar por la ventana; **oh, ~!** ¡mira!; **~ here** ¡oye tú! **2.** (*search*) buscar; **to ~ for sth/sb** buscar algo/a alguien **3.** (*appear, seem*) parecer; **to ~ like sb/sth** parecerse a alguien/algo; **to ~ bad/good** tener mala/buena cara; **to ~ tired** parecer cansado; **to ~ as if ...** parecer como si... +*subj;* **~ alive!** ¡espabila! ►**~ before you leap** *prov* antes de que te cases, mira lo que haces *prov* **III.** *vt* **1.** (*examine*) mirar; **to ~ the other way** *fig* hacer la vista gorda **2.** (*seem*) parecer; **to ~ one's age** aparentar su edad; **to ~ the part** THEAT encajar muy bien en el papel **3.** (*face*) mirar a; **to ~ north** mirar al norte

◆**look about** *vi* mirar alrededor

◆**look after** *vi* **1.** (*tend, care for*) cuidar **2.** (*take responsibility for*) encargarse de

◆**look ahead** *vi* mirar hacia adelante; **looking ahead to ...** de cara a...

◆**look around** *vi s.* **look round**

◆**look away** *vi* apartar la mirada

◆**look back** *vi* **1.** (*look behind oneself*) mirar (hacia) atrás **2.** (*remember*) recordar

◆**look down** *vi* **1.** (*from above*) mirar hacia abajo; (*lower eyes*) bajar la vista **2.** (*feel superior*) **to ~ on sth/sb** menospreciar algo/a alguien

◆**look for** *vt* **1.** (*seek*) buscar **2.** (*expect*) esperar

◆**look forward** *vi* **to ~ to sth** tener muchas ganas de algo; **I ~ to hearing from you** espero tener pronto noticias suyas

◆**look in** *vi Brit, Aus* **to ~ on sb** ir a ver a alguien; **to ~ at the office** pasar por la oficina

◆**look into** *vi* investigar

◆**look on** *vi,* **look upon** *vi* **1.** (*watch*) mirar **2.** (*view*) ver

◆**look onto** *vi* dar a

◆**look out I.** *vt Brit* **to look sth out** buscar algo **II.** *vi* **1.** (*face a particular direction*) **to ~ on** (*window*) dar a **2.** (*watch out*) tener cuidado; **to ~ for** tener cuidado con; (*look for*) buscar

◆**look over** *vt* (*report*) revisar; (*house*) inspeccionar

◆**look round I.** *vi* **1.** (*look behind oneself*) girarse **2.** (*look in all directions*) mirar alrededor **3.** (*search*) **to ~ for** buscar **II.** *vt* (*inspect*) inspeccionar

◆**look through** *vt* **1.** (*look*) mirar por **2.** (*examine*) revisar **3.** (*peruse*) **to ~ sth** echar un vistazo a algo

◆**look to** *vi* **1.** (*attend to*) mirar por **2.** (*depend on*) depender de **3.** (*count on*) contar con

◆**look up I.** *vt* **1.** (*consult*) buscar **2.** (*visit*) ir a ver **II.** *vi* **1.** (*raise one's eyes upward*) mirar hacia arriba; **to ~ to sb** *fig* tener a alguien de [*o* como] ejemplo **2.** (*improve*) mejorar

lookalike [ˈlʊkəˌlaɪk] *n* (*person*) doble *mf;* (*thing*) imitación *f*

looker [ˈlʊkəʳ, *Am:* -ɚ] *n inf* **to be a (real) ~** ser muy guapa

look-in [ˈlʊkɪn] *n Aus, Brit, inf* oportunidad *f;* **I didn't get a ~** no tuve ni la más mínima oportunidad

L

looking glass <-es> *n form* espejo *m*

lookout ['lʊkˌaʊt] *n* **1.** (*observation post*) puesto *m* de observación **2.** (*person*) centinela *mf;* **to be on the** ~ estar alerta **3.** *Brit* (*prospect*) panorama *m* **4.** (*concern*) asunto *m;* **that's his/your** ~ eso es asunto suyo/tuyo

look-over ['lʊkəʊvəʳ] *n* vistazo *m;* **to give sth a** ~ echar un vistazo a algo

loom¹ [lu:m] *n* telar *m*

loom² [lu:m] *vi* **1.** (*come into view*) surgir **2.** (*threaten*) amenazar; **to** ~ **large** cobrar mucha importancia

loony ['lu:ni] **I.** <-ier, -iest> *adj inf* (*person*) chiflado, -a; (*idea*) disparatado, -a **II.** <-ies> *n inf* loco, -a *m, f,* chiflado, -a *m, f*

loop [lu:p] **I.** *n* **1.** (*bend*) curva *f;* (*of string*) lazada *f;* (*of river*) meandro *m* **2.** ELEC circuito *m* cerrado **3.** INFOR bucle *m* **4.** (*contraceptive coil*) espiral *f* ▶**to throw sb for a** ~ *Am, inf* dejar a alguien de piedra **II.** *vi* serpentear **III.** *vt* atar con un lazo; **to** ~ **sth around ...** pasar algo alrededor de... ▶**to** ~ **the** ~ AVIAT rizar el rizo

loophole ['lu:phəʊl, *Am:* -hoʊl] *n fig* escapatoria *f;* **legal** ~ laguna legal

loose [lu:s] **I.** *adj* **1.** (*not tight: clothing*) holgado, -a; (*knot, rope, screw*) flojo, -a; (*skin*) flácido, -a **2.** (*not confined*) suelto, -a; ~ **change** dinero *m* suelto, sencillo *m AmS* **3.** (*not exact: instructions*) poco preciso, -a; (*translation*) libre **4.** (*not strict or controlled: discipline*) relajado, -a; ~ **tongue** lengua *f* desatada **5.** (*sexually immoral*) disoluto, -a **II.** *n* **to be on the** ~ estar en libertad **III.** *vt* soltar

loose-leaf folder *n* carpeta *f* de anillas

loosely ['lu:sli] *adv* **1.** (*not tightly*) sin apretar **2.** (*not exactly: translate*) libremente; (*speak*) en términos generales **3.** (*not strictly: organized*) de forma flexible

loosen ['lu:sn] **I.** *vt* (*belt*) aflojar; (*tongue*) desatar **II.** *vi* aflojarse

loot [lu:t] **I.** *n no pl* **1.** (*plunder*) botín *m* **2.** *inf* (*money*) pasta *f,* lana *f AmL* **II.** *vt, vi* saquear

looting *n no pl* saqueo *m*

lop [lɒp, *Am:* lɑ:p] *vt s.* **lop off**

◆**lop off** <-pp-> *vt* **1.** (*branch*) podar; (*limb*) amputar **2.** (*pages*) eliminar

lope [ləʊp, *Am:* loʊp] *vi* (*person or animal*) andar con paso largo

lopsided [ˌlɒp'saɪdɪd, *Am:* ˌlɑ:p-] *adj* **1.** (*leaning to one side*) torcido, -a, chueco, -a *AmL* **2.** (*biased*) parcial

loquacious [lə'kweɪʃəs, *Am:* loʊ'-] *adj* locuaz

lord [lɔ:d, *Am:* lɔ:rd] *n* **1.** *Brit* (*British peer*) lord *m* **2.** (*aristocrat*) señor *m*

Lord Chancellor *n Brit* Lord *m* Canciller (*presidente de la Cámara de los Lores y máxima autoridad judicial*)

lordly ['lɔ:dli, *Am:* 'lɔ:rd-] <-ier, -iest> *adj* **1.** (*suitable to a lord*) señorial **2.** (*arrogant*) arrogante

Lord Mayor *n Brit* alcalde *m*

lordship ['lɔ:dʃɪp, *Am:* 'lɔ:rd-] *n no pl, form* **His Lordship** *Brit* Su Señoría

lore [lɔ:ʳ, *Am:* lɔ:r] *n no pl* sabiduría *f*

lorry ['lɒri, *Am:* 'lɔ:r-] <-ies> *n Brit* camión *m*

lorry driver *n Brit* camionero(a) *m(f)*

lose [lu:z] <lost, lost> **I.** *vt* perder; **to get lost** (*person*) perderse; (*object*) extraviarse **II.** *vi* perder

loser ['lu:zəʳ, *Am:* -zɚ] *n* perdedor(a) *m(f)*

losing ['lu:zɪŋ] *adj* perdedor(a)

loss [lɒs, *Am:* lɑ:s] <-es> *n* pérdida *f;* **to be at a** ~ no saber cómo reaccionar; **to be at a** ~ **for words** no encontrar palabras con que expresarse

loss leader *n* artículo *m* de gancho **loss-making** *adj* deficitario, -a

lost [lɒst, *Am:* lɑ:st] **I.** *pt, pp of* **lose II.** *adj* **1.** perdido, -a; **to get** ~ perderse; **to give sth/sb up for** ~ dar algo/a alguien por perdido; **to be** ~ **in a book** estar enfrascado en la lectura de un libro **2.** (*preoccupied*) perplejo, -a

lost property *n no pl* objetos *mpl* perdidos

lost property office *n Brit, Aus* oficina *f* de objetos perdidos

lot [lɒt, *Am:* lɑ:t] *n* **1.** (*destiny*) destino *m;* (*fate*) suerte *f* **2.** *Brit* (*large quantity*) **a** ~ **of, lots of** mucho(s); **a** ~ **of wine** mucho vino; ~**s of houses** muchas casas; **I like it a** ~ me gusta mucho; **the whole** ~ todo **3.** (*plot of land*) terreno *m* **4.** (*in auction*) lote *m*

loth [ləʊθ, *Am:* loʊθ] *adj s.* **loath**

lotion ['ləʊʃən, *Am:* 'loʊ-] *n no pl* loción *f*

lottery ['lɒtəri, *Am:* 'lɑ:t̬ɚ-] <-ies> *n* lotería *f,* quiniela *f CSur*

lottery number *n* número *m* de lotería

lotus ['ləʊtəs, *Am:* 'loʊt̬əs] <-es> *n* loto *m*

lotus position *n no pl* posición *f* del loto

loud [laʊd] **I.** *adj* **1.** (*voice*) alto, -a; (*shout*) fuerte **2.** (*colour*) chillón, -ona **3.** (*noisy*) ruidoso, -a **4.** (*vigorous: complaint*) enérgico, -a **II.** *adv* alto; **to laugh out** ~ reír a carcajadas

loudhailer [ˌlaʊd'heɪləʳ, *Am:* -lɚ] *n Brit, Aus* megáfono *m*

loudmouth ['laʊdmaʊθ] *n inf* escandaloso, -a *m, f*

loudness *n no pl* **1.** (*volume*) volumen *m;* (*of explosion*) estruendo *m* **2.** (*of colour*) lo chillón

loudspeaker [ˌlaʊd'spi:kəʳ, *Am:* ˌlaʊd'spi:kɚ] *n* altavoz *m*

Louisiana [luˌi:zi'ænə] *n* Luisiana *f*

lounge [laʊndʒ] **I.** *n* salón *m* **II.** *vi* **1.** (*recline*) repanchigarse **2.** (*be idle*) hacer el vago

◆**lounge about** *vt,* **lounge around** *vt* holgazanear

lounge bar *n Brit* bar *m* **lounge chair** *n* tumbona *f,* reposera *f RíoPl* **lounge lizard** *n hombre que frecuenta bares, salones de hoteles, etc., en busca de mujeres* **lounge suit** *n Brit* traje *m* (de calle)

louse [laʊs] *n* **1.** <lice> (*insect*) piojo *m*

2.<-es> *inf* (*person*) canalla *mf*
◆**louse up** *vt inf* echar a perder
lousy ['laʊzi] <-ier, -iest> *adj inf* 1. (*infested with lice*) piojoso, -a 2. (*of poor quality*) pésimo, -a; **to feel** ~ estar fatal 3. (*contemptible*) asqueroso, -a ▸**to be** ~ **with money** estar podrido de dinero
lout [laʊt] *n* patán *m*, jallán *m AmC*
loutish ['laʊtɪʃ, *Am:* -t̬ɪʃ] *adj* patán
louver *n Am*, **louvre** ['lu:vəʳ, *Am:* -vɚ] *n* persiana *f* de listones
louvred door *n* puerta *f* de persiana
lovable ['lʌvəbl] *adj* adorable
lovage ['lʌvɪdʒ] *n no pl* ligustro *m*
love [lʌv] I. *vt* querer, amar; **I ~ swimming, I ~ to swim** me encanta nadar ▸~ **me,** ~ **my dog** *prov* quien quiere a Beltrán, quiere a su can *prov* II. *n* 1. *no pl* (*affection*) amor *m*; **to be in** ~ (**with sb**) estar enamorado (de alguien); **to fall in** ~ (**with sb**) enamorarse (de alguien); **to make** ~ **to sb** hacer el amor con alguien 2. *no pl, Brit, inf* (*darling*) cariño *m* 3. *no pl* (*in tennis*) cero *m*; ~ **game** *juego en el que quien recibe no ha marcado ningún punto* ▸**not for** ~ (**n**)**or money** por nada del mundo; **there is no** ~ **lost between the two** no se pueden ver III. *vi* querer, amar
love affair *n* aventura *f*, romance *m* **lovebird** *n* periquito *m*; *fig* tortolito *m*
love-hate relationship *n* relación *f* de amor y odio
loveless [lʌvlɪs] *adj* sin amor
love letter *n* carta *f* de amor **love life** *n inf* vida *f* amorosa [*o* sentimental]
loveliness ['lʌvlɪnɪs] *n no pl* (*of scenery*) belleza *f*; (*of person*) encanto *m*
lovely ['lʌvli] <-ier, -iest> *adj* (*house, present*) bonito, -a; (*weather*) precioso, -a; (*person*) encantador(a); **to have a** ~ **time** pasarlo estupendamente
love-making ['lʌvˌmeɪkɪŋ] *n no pl* relaciones *fpl* sexuales
lover ['lʌvəʳ, *Am:* -ɚ] *n* amante *mf*
lovesick ['lʌvsɪk] *adj* locamente enamorado, -a, volado, -a *AmL*
love song *n* canción *f* de amor **love story** *n* historia *f* de amor
lovey [lʌvi] *n no pl, Brit, inf* cariño *m*
loving ['lʌvɪŋ] *adj* cariñoso, -a
low¹ [ləʊ, *Am:* loʊ] I. *adj* 1. (*not high, not loud*) bajo, -a; **to be** ~ (**on sth**) tener poco (de algo); **to cook sth on a** ~ **heat** hacer algo a fuego lento; **stocks are running** ~ las existencias están casi agotadas; **the batteries are running** ~ las baterías se están acabando 2. (*poor: opinion, quality*) malo, -a; (*self-esteem*) bajo, -a; (*visibility*) poco, -a; **a** ~ **trick** una mala jugada II. *adv* bajo, -a; **to feel** ~ estar deprimido III. *n* 1. METEO depresión *f* 2. (*minimum*) mínimo *m*
low² [ləʊ, *Am:* loʊ] I. *vi* mugir II. *n* mugido *m*
low-alcohol *adj* bajo, -a en alcohol **lowborn** *adj* de casa pobre **lowbrow** *adj* poco intelectual **low-calorie** *adj* bajo, -a en calorías **low-cost** *adj* económico, -a **low-cut** *adj* escotado, -a **low demand** *n* baja demanda *f*
lowdown I. *adj inf* bajo, -a; **a** ~ **trick** una mala jugada II. *n inf* **to give sb the** ~ **on sth** poner a alguien al tanto de algo
lower¹ ['ləʊəʳ, *Am:* 'loʊɚ] I. *vt* bajar; (*flag, sails*) arriar; (*lifeboat*) echar al agua; **to** ~ **one's eyes** bajar la vista; **to** ~ **oneself to do sth** rebajarse a hacer algo II. *vi* bajar III. *adj* inferior
lower² [laʊəʳ, *Am:* laʊr] *vi* 1. (*person*) fruncir el ceño 2. (*sky*) encapotarse
lower-case [ˌləʊə'keɪs, *Am:* ˌloʊɚ-] *adj* minúsculo, -a
Lower House *n* **the** ~ la Cámara Baja
low-fat *adj* bajo, -a en calorías; (*milk*) desnatado, -a **low-key** *adj* (*affair*) discreto, -a; (*debate, discussion*) mesurado, -a **lowland** *npl* tierras *fpl* bajas, bajío *m AmL* **low-level** *adj* 1. (*discussion*) a bajo nivel 2. (*bridge*) de poca altura 3. (*radiation*) de baja intensidad
lowly ['ləʊli, *Am:* 'loʊ-] <-ier, -iest> *adj* humilde **low-minded** *adj* vulgar
lowness *n no pl* 1. (*state of being low*) lo bajo 2. MUS gravedad *f* 3. (*baseness*) bajeza *f*, vileza *f* 4. (*humbleness*) humildad *f*
low-pitched *adj* (*voice*) grave **low pressure** *n* baja presión *f* **low profile** *n* **to keep a** ~ tratar de pasar desapercibido **low season** *n* temporada *f* baja **low-spirited** *adj* deprimido, -a **low-tech** *adj* de baja tecnología **low tide** *n*, **low water** *n* marea *f* baja
loyal ['lɔɪəl] *adj* leal; **to remain** ~ (**to sb/sth**) permanecer fiel (a alguien/algo)
loyalist ['lɔɪəlɪst] *n* partidario, -a *m, f* del régimen; **Loyalist** *Brit* unionista *mf*
loyalty ['lɔɪəlti, *Am:* -t̬i] <-ies> *n* lealtad *f*
lozenge ['lɒzɪndʒ, *Am:* 'lɑ:zəndʒ] *n* pastilla *f*
LP [ˌel'pi:] *n abbr of* **long-playing record** LP *m*
LPG *n abbr of* **liquid petroleum gas** GLP *m*
LSD [ˌeles'di:] *n abbr of* **lysergic acid diethylamide** LSD *f*
Ltd ['lɪmɪtɪd, *Am:* -ət̬ɪd] *abbr of* **Limited** SA
lubricant ['lu:brɪkənt] *n no pl* lubricante *m*
lubricate ['lu:brɪkeɪt] *vt* lubricar
lubrication [ˌlu:brɪ'keɪʃən] *n no pl* lubricación *f*
lubricator ['lu:brɪˌkeɪtə, *Am:* -t̬ɚ] *n* lubricador *m*
lucerne [lu:'sɜ:n, *Am:* -'sɜ:rn] *n* alfalfa *f*
lucid ['lu:sɪd] *adj* 1. (*rational*) lúcido, -a 2. (*easily understood*) claro, -a
luck [lʌk] *n no pl* suerte *f*; **good/bad** ~ buena/mala suerte; **a stroke of** ~ un golpe de suerte; **to bring sb** ~ traer suerte a alguien; **to wish sb** (**good**) ~ desear a alguien (buena) suerte; **with** (**any**) ~ con un poco de suerte; **with no** ~ sin éxito; **as** ~ **would have it ...** quiso la suerte que... +*subj*; **to be down on one's** ~ *Brit* estar de mala racha 2. **to be the** ~ **of the °draw** ser cuestión de suerte; **no °such**

L

~! *inf* ¡qué va!; **to press one's** ~ tentar la suerte

luckless [ˈlʌkləs] *adj* desafortunado, -a

lucky [ˈlʌki] <-ier, -iest> *adj* afortunado, -a; **to be ~ in love** tener suerte en el amor; **to be ~ in that** tener la suerte de que +*subj;* **to make a ~ guess** acertar por pura casualidad; ~ **day** día *m* de suerte; ~ **number** número *m* de la suerte

lucrative [ˈluːkrətɪv, *Am:* -t̬ɪv] *adj* lucrativo, -a

lucre [ˈluːkəʳ, *Am:* -kɚ] *n no pl* lucro *m;* (**filthy**) ~ *iron* (cochino) dinero *m*

ludicrous [ˈluːdɪkrəs] *adj* absurdo, -a

ludo [ˈluːdəʊ, *Am:* -doʊ] *n Brit* parchís *m inv*

lug [lʌg] **I.** *vt* <-gg-> *inf* arrastrar **II.** *n Aus, Brit* oreja *f*

luggage [ˈlʌgɪdʒ] *n no pl* equipaje *m*

luggage rack *n Brit* baca *f* **luggage van** *n Aus, Brit* furgón *m* de equipajes

lugger [ˈlʌgəʳ, *Am:* -ɚ] *n* NAUT lugre *m*

lughole *n Brit, inf* oreja *f*

lugubrious [ləˈguːbrɪəs] *adj* lúgubre

lukewarm [ˌluːkˈwɔːm, *Am:* -ˈwɔːrm] *adj* **1.** (*liquid*) tibio, -a **2.** (*unenthusiastic*) poco entusiasta

lull [lʌl] **I.** *vt* calmar; **to ~ sb to sleep** dormir a alguien; **to ~ sb into believing that ...** hacer creer a alguien que... **II.** *n* **1.** (*temporary stillness*) período *m* de calma **2.** (*in conversation*) pausa *f* **3.** (*in fighting*) tregua *f*

lullaby [ˈlʌləbaɪ] <-ies> *n* nana *f*

lumbago [lʌmˈbeɪgəʊ, *Am:* -goʊ] *n no pl* lumbago *m*

lumbar [ˈlʌmbəʳ, *Am:* -bɑːr] *adj* ANAT lumbar

lumbar puncture *n* MED punción *f* lumbar

lumber[1] [ˈlʌmbəʳ, *Am:* -bɚ] *vi* moverse pesadamente

lumber[2] [ˈlʌmbəʳ, *Am:* -bɚ] **I.** *vt Aus, Brit, inf* **to ~ sb with sth** endilgar algo a alguien **II.** *n no pl* **1.** *Am, Aus* madera *f* **2.** (*junk*) trastos *mpl* **III.** *vi* aserrar **lumberjack** *n* leñador *m* **lumberjacket** *n* chaquetón *m* de leñador **lumber room** *n* trastero *m* **lumber trade** *n Am* industria *f* maderera **lumberyard** *n* almacén *m* de maderas

luminary [ˈluːmɪnəri, *Am:* ˈluːmənər-] <-ies> *n fig* lumbrera *f*

luminosity [ˌluːmɪˈnɒsəti, *Am:* ˌluː-məˈnɑːsət̬i] *n no pl* luminosidad *f*

luminous [ˈluːmɪnəs, *Am:* ˈluːmə-] *adj* luminoso, -a

lump [lʌmp] **I.** *n* **1.** (*solid mass*) masa *f;* (*of coal*) trozo *m;* (*of sugar*) terrón *m;* ~ **sum** cantidad *f* única **2.** (*swelling: in breast, on head*) bulto *m* **3.** *inf* (*person*) zoquete *mf* ►**to have a ~ in one's throat** tener un nudo en la garganta **II.** *vt* **1.** (*combine*) agrupar **2.** (*endure*) aguantar; **if you don't like it,** (**you can**) ~ **it** si no te gusta, te aguantas

lump payment *n* pago *m* único **lump sugar** *n* azúcar *m* en terrones

lumpy [ˈlʌmpi] <-ier, -iest> *adj* (*custard, sauce*) grumoso, -a; (*surface*) desigual

lunacy [ˈluːnəsi, *Am:* ˈluː-] *n no pl* locura *f*

lunar [ˈluːnəʳ, *Am:* ˈluːnɚ] *adj* lunar

lunatic [ˈluːnətɪk] **I.** *n* loco, -a *m, f* **II.** *adj* lunático, -a

lunatic asylum *n inf* manicomio *m*

lunch [lʌntʃ] **I.** *n* comida *f;* **to have ~** comer ►**to be out to ~** estar en Babia **II.** *vi* comer

lunch break *n* descanso *m* para comer

luncheon [ˈlʌntʃən] *n form* comida *f*

luncheon meat *n fiambre de cerdo en conserva* **luncheon voucher** *n Brit* vale *m* de comida

lunch hour *n* hora *f* de comer **lunchtime** **I.** *n* hora *f* de comer **II.** *adj* (*concert*) de mediodía

lung [lʌŋ] *n* pulmón *m* ►**to shout at the top of one's ~s** gritar a voz en grito

lung cancer *n* cáncer *m* de pulmón

lunge [lʌndʒ] **I.** *vi* **to ~ at sb** arremeter contra alguien **II.** *n* arremetida *f*

lupin(**e**) [ˈluːpɪn] *n Am* lupino *m,* altramuz *m*

lurch [lɜːtʃ, *Am:* lɜːrtʃ] **I.** *vi* (*people*) tambalearse; (*car, train*) dar sacudidas **II.** <-es> *n* sacudida *f* ►**to leave sb in the ~** *inf* dejar a alguien colgado

lure [lʊəʳ, *Am:* lʊr] **I.** *n* **1.** (*attraction*) atractivo *m* **2.** (*bait*) cebo *m;* (*decoy*) señuelo *m* **II.** *vt* atraer; **to ~ sb into a trap** hacer que alguien caiga en una trampa

lurid [ˈlʊərɪd, *Am:* ˈlʊrɪd] *adj* **1.** (*details*) escabroso, -a; (*language*) morboso, -a **2.** (*extremely bright*) chillón, -ona

lurk [lɜːk, *Am:* lɜːrk] *vi* esconderse

luscious [ˈlʌʃəs] *adj* **1.** (*fruit*) jugoso, -a **2.** *inf* (*girl, curves*) voluptuoso, -a; (*lips*) carnoso, -a

lush [lʌʃ] **I.** *adj* **1.** (*vegetation*) exuberante **2.** (*luxurious*) opulento, -a **II.** *n* <-shes> *Am, inf* borracho, -a *m, f*

lust [lʌst] *n* **1.** (*sexual desire*) lujuria *f* **2.** (*strong desire*) anhelo *m;* ~ **for sth** ansia de algo; ~ **for life** ansias de vivir

luster [ˈlʌstɚ] *n no pl, Am s.* **lustre**

lustful [ˈlʌstfəl] *adj* lujurioso, -a

lustre [ˈlʌstə, *Am:* -tɚ] *n Aus, Brit* lustre *m*

lusty [ˈlʌsti] <-ier, -iest> *adj* (*person*) sano, -a; (*voice*) potente

lute [luːt] *n* laúd *m*

Lutheran [ˈluːθərən] **I.** *adj* luterano, -a **II.** *n* luterano, -a *m, f*

Luxembourg [ˈlʌksəmbɜːg, *Am:* -bɜːrg] *n* Luxemburgo *m*

Luxembourger *n* luxemburgés, -esa *m, f*

luxuriant [lʌgˈʒʊərɪənt, *Am:* -ˈʒʊrɪ-] *adj* (*hair*) abundante; (*vegetation*) exuberante

luxuriate [lʌgˈʒʊərɪeɪt, *Am:* -ˈʒʊrɪ-] *vi* **1.** (*person*) deleitarse; **to ~ in sth** disfrutar con algo **2.** (*plant*) crecer de manera exuberante

luxurious [lʌgˈʒʊərɪəs, *Am:* -ˈʒʊrɪ-] *adj* lujoso, -a

luxury [ˈlʌkʃəri, *Am:* -ʃɚ-] <-ies> *n* lujo *m;* ~ **flat** piso *m* de lujo

LW *n abbr of* **long wave** OL *f*

lychee ['laɪtʃiː, *Am:* 'liːtʃiː] *n* lichi *m*
Lycra® ['laɪkrə] *n* licra® *f*
lye [laɪ] *n* lejía *f*
lying ['laɪɪŋ] **I.** *n* mentiras *fpl* **II.** *adj* mentiroso, -a
lymph [lɪmpf] *n no pl* linfa *f*
lymphatic [lɪm'fætɪk, *Am:* -'fæt̬-] *adj* linfático, -a
lymph gland *n*, **lymph node** *n* ganglio *m* linfático
lynch [lɪntʃ] *vt* linchar
lynx [lɪŋks] <-(es)> *n* lince *m*
lynx-eyed [ˌlɪŋks'aɪd] *adj* con ojos de lince
lyre ['laɪəʳ, *Am:* 'laɪr] *n* lira *f*
lyric ['lɪrɪk] **I.** *adj* lírico, -a **II.** *n* **1.** (*poem*) poema *m* lírico **2.** *pl* (*words for song*) letra *f*
lyrical ['lɪrɪkl] *adj* lírico, -a; **to get ~ about sth** *fig* entusiasmarse por algo
lyricism ['lɪrɪˌsɪzəm] *n no pl* LIT, MUS lirismo *m*
lyricist ['lɪrɪsɪst] *n* letrista *mf*

M

M, m [em] *n* M, m *f*; **~ for Mary** *Brit*, **~ for Mike** *Am* M de María
m **1.** *abbr of* **metre** m **2.** *abbr of* **mile** milla *f* **3.** *abbr of* **million** millón *m* **4.** *abbr of* **minutes** min. **5.** *abbr of* **married** casado, -a
M *n* **1.** *abbr of* **male** H **2.** *abbr of* **medium** M
ma [mɑː] *n inf* mamá *f*
MA [ˌem'eɪ] *n abbr of* **Master of Arts** máster *m* (*de Humanidades o de Filosofía y Letras*); **Louie Sanders, MA** Louie Sanders, licenciado con máster
ma'am [mæm] = **madam** (*form of address*) señora *f*; (*when addressing royalty*) Majestad *f*
mac¹ [mæk] *n Brit, inf* (*coat*) impermeable *m*
mac² [mæk] *n Am, inf* (*form of address*) amigo
Mac [mæk] *n* INFOR *abbr of* **Macintosh** Mac *m*, Mac *f AmL*
macabre [mə'kɑːbrə] *adj* macabro, -a
macadam [mə'kædəm] *n* macadán *m*
macaroni [ˌmækə'rəʊni, *Am:* -ə'roʊ-] *n* macarrones *mpl*
macaroni cheese *n* macarrones *mpl* con queso
mace¹ [meɪs] *n* (*club*) maza *f*
mace² [meɪs] *n* (*spice*) macis *f*
Mace® [meɪs] *n no pl* gas *m* lacrimógeno (*en spray*)
Macedonia [ˌmæsɪ'dəʊniə, *Am:* -ə'doʊni-] *n* Macedonia *f*
Macedonian **I.** *adj* macedonio, -a **II.** *n* **1.** (*person*) macedonio, -a *m, f* **2.** LING macedonio *m*
Mach [mɑːk] *n no pl* PHYS Mach *m*
machete [mə'ʃeti, *Am:* -'ʃet̬-] *n* machete *m*
machine [mə'ʃiːn] **I.** *n* **1.** (*mechanical device*) máquina *f* **2.** (*system*) aparato *m* **II.** *vt* **1.** (*metal*) trabajar a máquina **2.** (*sewing*) coser a máquina
machine gun *n* ametralladora *f* **machine language** *n* INFOR lenguaje *m* máquina **machine-made** *adj* hecho, -a a máquina **machine-readable** *adj* INFOR legible por máquina
machinery [mə'ʃiːnəri] *n no pl* **1.** *a. fig* (*machines*) maquinaria *f* **2.** (*mechanism*) mecanismo *m*
machine tool *n* máquina *f* herramienta
machinist [mə'ʃiːnɪst] *n* maquinista *mf*
macho ['mætʃəʊ, *Am:* 'mɑːtʃoʊ] **I.** *n* machista *m* **II.** *adj* machista
mackerel ['mækrəl] <-(s)> *n* caballa *f*
mackintosh ['mækɪntɒʃ, *Am:* -tɑːʃ] <-es> *n Brit* impermeable *m*
macro ['mækrəʊ, *Am:* -roʊ] *n* INFOR macro *f*
macrobiotic [ˌmækrəʊbaɪ'ɒtɪk, *Am:* -roʊbaɪ'ɑːt̬ɪk] *adj* macrobiótico, -a
macrocosm ['mækrəʊkɒzəm, *Am:* -roʊkɑːzəm] *n* macrocosmos *m inv*
macroeconomics [ˌmækrəʊiːkə'nɒmɪks, *Am:* -roʊˌekə'nɑːmɪks] *n* macroeconomía *f*
mad [mæd] *adj Brit, inf* **1.** (*insane: person*) loco, -a; (*idea*) disparatado, -a; **to go ~** volverse loco; **to drive sb ~** volver loco a alguien **2.** *inf* (*enthusiastic*) **to be ~ about sb** estar loco por alguien; **she's ~ about chocolate** le encanta el chocolate **3.** (*frantic*) frenético, -a
Madagascar [ˌmædə'gæskəʳ, *Am:* -kɚ] *n* Madagascar *m*
madam ['mædəm] *n no pl* señora *f*
madden ['mædən] *vt* enfurecer
maddening *adj* exasperante
made [meɪd] *pp, pt of* **make**
made-to-measure [ˌmeɪdtə'meʒəʳ, *Am:* -ɚ] *adj* (hecho, -a) a medida
made-up ['meɪdʌp] *adj* **1.** (*wearing make-up*) maquillado, -a **2.** (*invented*) inventado, -a
madhouse ['mædhaʊs] *n inf* manicomio *m*
madly ['mædli] *adv* **1.** (*frantically*) frenéticamente **2.** (*intensely*) terriblemente
madman ['mædmən] <-men> *n* loco *m*
madness ['mædnɪs] *n no pl* locura *f*, loquera *f AmL*
madwoman ['mædˌwʊmən] <-women> *n* loca *f*
maelstrom ['meɪlstrəm] *n a. fig* vorágine *f*
maestro ['maɪstrəʊ, *Am:* -stroʊ] *n* maestro *m*
MAFF *n Brit abbr of* **Ministry of Agricultural, Fisheries and Food** *ministerio de agricultura, pesca y alimentación*
Mafia ['mæfiə, *Am:* 'mɑː-] *n* mafia *f*
mag [mæg] *n inf abbr of* **magazine** revista *f*
magazine [ˌmægə'ziːn, *Am:* 'mægəziːn] *n* **1.** (*periodical publication*) revista *f* **2.** MIL (*of gun*) recámara *f* **3.** MIL (*store*) polvorín *m*
maggot ['mægət] *n* gusano *m*

Magi ['meɪdʒaɪ] *npl* **the** ~ los Reyes Magos

magic ['mædʒɪk] **I.** *n no pl* magia *f;* **as if by** ~ como por arte de magia **II.** *adj* mágico, -a

magical *adj* **1.** (*power*) mágico, -a **2.** (*extraordinary, wonderful*) fabuloso, -a

magically *adv* por arte de magia

magic carpet *n* alfombra *f* mágica

magician [mə'dʒɪʃən] *n* mago, -a *m, f*

magisterial [ˌmædʒɪ'stɪərɪəl, *Am:* -'stɪrɪ-] *adj form* **1.** (*having complete authority*) magistral **2.** (*imperious: tone, way*) autoritario, -a

magistrate ['mædʒɪstreɪt] *n Brit: juez que se ocupa de los delitos menores*

magnanimity [ˌmægnə'nɪməti, *Am:* -t̬i] *n no pl, form* magnanimidad *f*

magnanimous [mæg'nænɪməs, *Am:* -əməs] *adj form* magnánimo, -a

magnate ['mægneɪt] *n* magnate *m*

magnesia [mæg'ni:ʃə, *Am:* -ʒə] *n no pl* magnesia *f*

magnesium [mæg'ni:zɪəm] *n no pl* magnesio *m*

magnet ['mægnɪt] *n* imán *m;* **to act as a** ~ **for sth** *fig* atraer como un imán a algo

magnetic [mæg'netɪk, *Am:* -'net̬-] *adj* **1.** (*force*) magnético, -a **2.** (*personality*) atrayente

magnetic field *n* campo *m* magnético **magnetic pole** *n* polo *m* magnético

magnetise ['mægnətaɪz] *vi Brit, Aus s.* **magnetize**

magnetism ['mægnətɪzəm, *Am:* -t̬ɪ-] *n no pl* magnetismo *m*

magnetize ['mægnətaɪz] *vt* magnetizar; **to** ~ **sb** cautivar a alguien

magneto [mæg'ni:təʊ, *Am:* mæg'ni:t̬oʊ] *n* TECH, AUTO magneto *f*

magnification [ˌmægnɪfɪ'keɪʃən] *n no pl* (*lens*) aumento *m;* (*photograph*) ampliación *f*

magnificence [mæg'nɪfɪsəns] *n no pl* magnificencia *f*

magnificent [mæg'nɪfɪsnt] *adj* magnífico, -a

magnify ['mægnɪfaɪ] <-ie-> *vt* **1.** (*make larger*) ampliar; (*voice*) amplificar **2.** (*make worse: problem*) exagerar

magnifying glass *n* lupa *f*

magnitude ['mægnɪtju:d, *Am:* -tu:d] *n no pl* **1.** (*importance*) magnitud *f* **2.** (*large size*) envergadura *f*

magnolia [mæg'nəʊlɪə, *Am:* -'noʊljə] *n* magnolia *f*

magnum opus [ˌmægnəm'əʊpəs, *Am:* -'oʊpəs] *n no pl, form* obra *f* maestra

magpie ['mægpaɪ] *n* (*bird*) urraca *f*

maharaja [ˌmɑ:hə'rɑ:dʒə] *n* HIST maharajá *m*

mahogany [mə'hɒgəni, *Am:* -'hɑ:gən-] **I.** *n no pl* caoba *f* **II.** *adj* de caoba

maid [meɪd] *n* **1.** (*female servant*) criada *f,* mucama *f AmL;* (*in hotel*) camarera *f* **2.** *liter* (*girl, young woman*) doncella *f*

maiden ['meɪdən] **I.** *n liter* doncella *f* **II.** *adj* **1.** (*unmarried*) soltera **2.** (*first: flight*) primero, -a; (*speech*) inaugural

maidenhair fern [ˌmeɪdənheəʳ'fɜ:n, *Am:* -her'fɜ:rn] *n* cabellos *mpl* de Venus

maiden name *n* apellido *m* de soltera **maiden speech** *n* discurso *m* inaugural

mail[1] [meɪl] **I.** *n no pl a.* INFOR correo *m;* **electronic** ~ INFOR correo electrónico; **incoming/outgoing** ~ INFOR correo entrante/saliente; **to send sth through the** ~ mandar [*o* enviar] algo por correo **II.** *vt* mandar [*o* enviar] por correo

mail[2] [meɪl] *n no pl* (*armour*) malla *f*

mailbag ['meɪlbæg] *n* saca *f* de correos **mailbox** *n* **1.** *Am* (*postbox*) buzón *m* **2.** INFOR (**electronic**) ~ buzón *m* electrónico

mailing list *n* lista *f* de direcciones (*a las que se envia publicidad o información*)

mailman *n Am* (*postman*) cartero *m* **mail order** *n* venta *f* por correo **mailshot** *n Brit* mailing *m*

maim [meɪm] *vt* lisiar

main [meɪn] **I.** *adj* (*problem, reason, street*) principal; ~ **cable** cable *m* principal **II.** *n* **1.** TECH (*pipe*) cañería *f* principal **2.** (*cable*) cable *m* principal **3.** *pl, Brit* ELEC, TECH red *f* de suministro ►**in the** ~ en general

mainframe ['meɪnfreɪm] *n* INFOR ordenador *m* central, computadora *f* central *AmL*

mainland ['meɪnlənd] **I.** *n no pl* continente *m* **II.** *adj* ~ **China** China continental; ~ **Spain** España peninsular

mainline ['meɪnlaɪn] *vi, vt inf* chutar(se)

mainly ['meɪnli] *adv* principalmente

main office *n* oficina *f* central **main road** *n* carretera *f* general **mainsail** *n* vela *f* mayor **mainspring** *n* motivo *m* principal **mainstay** *n* pilar *m* **mainstream I.** *n no pl* corriente *f* dominante **II.** *adj* **1.** (*ideology*) dominante **2.** (*film, novel*) comercial

maintain [meɪn'teɪn] *vt* **1.** (*preserve, provide for*) mantener **2.** (*claim*) sostener

maintenance ['meɪntənəns] *n no pl* **1.** (*keeping, preservation*) mantenimiento *m* **2.** (*alimony*) pensión *f* alimenticia

maisonette [ˌmeɪzə'net] *n Brit* dúplex *m*

maize [meɪz] *n no pl* maíz *m,* milpa *f AmL,* capi *m AmS*

Maj. *abbr of* **Major** comandante *mf*

majestic [mə'dʒestɪk] *adj* majestuoso, -a

majesty ['mædʒəsti] <-ies> *n no pl* majestuosidad *f;* **Her/His/Your Majesty** Su Majestad

major ['meɪdʒəʳ, *Am:* -dʒɚ] **I.** *adj* **1.** (*important, significant*) muy importante, fundamental; **a** ~ **problem** un gran problema **2.** (*serious: illness*) grave **3.** MUS mayor; **in C** ~ en do mayor **II.** *n* **1.** MIL comandante *mf* **2.** *Am, Aus* UNIV especialidad *f*

Majorca [mə'jɔ:kə, *Am:* -jɔ:r-] *n* Mallorca *f*

Majorcan I. *adj* mallorquín, -ina **II.** *n* mallorquín, -ina *m, f*

major-general [ˌmeɪdʒə'dʒenərəl, *Am:* -dʒɚ] *n* general *m* de división

majority [mə'dʒɒrəti, *Am:* -'dʒɔ:rət̬i]

<-ies> *n* 1. (*greater part/number*) mayoría *f;* **a narrow/large** ~ POL un margen estrecho/amplio 2. *no pl* (*full legal age*) mayoría *f* de edad; **to reach one's** ~ llegar a la mayoría de edad

make [meɪk] I. *vt* <made, made> 1. (*produce: coffee, soup, supper*) hacer; (*product*) fabricar; (*clothes*) confeccionar; (*record*) grabar; (*film*) rodar; **to make sth out of sth** hacer algo con algo; **to** ~ **time** hacer tiempo 2. (*cause: trouble*) causar; **to** ~ **noise/a scene** hacer ruido/una escena; **to** ~ **oneself look ridiculous** ponerse en ridículo; **to** ~ **a wonderful combination** ser una combinación fabulosa 3. (*cause to be*) **to** ~ **sb sad** poner triste a alguien; **to** ~ **sb happy** hacer feliz a alguien; **to** ~ **oneself heard** hacerse oír; **to** ~ **oneself understood** hacerse entender; **to** ~ **sth easy** hacer que algo sea fácil; **to** ~ **something of oneself** llegar a ser algo 4. (*perform, carry out*) **to** ~ **a call** hacer una llamada; **to** ~ **a decision** tomar una decision; **to** ~ **a reservation** hacer [*o* efectuar] una reserva 5. (*force*) obligar; **to** ~ **sb do sth** hacer que alguien haga algo 6. (*amount to, total*) ser; **two plus two** ~**s four** dos y dos son cuatro 7. (*calculate*) **how much do you** ~ **the total?** ¿cuánto te da? 8. (*earn, get*) **to** ~ **friends** hacer amigos; **to** ~ **money** hacer [*o* ganar] dinero; **to** ~ **profits/losses** tener beneficios/pérdidas; **to** ~ **a living** ganarse la vida 9. *inf* (*get to, reach*) **to** ~ **it to somewhere** llegar a un sitio; **to** ~ **it** alcanzar el éxito 10. (*make perfect*) **that made my day!** ¡eso me alegró el día! ►**to** ~ **or break sth** ser el éxito o la ruina de algo; **to** ~ **do** (**with sth**) arreglárselas (con algo) II. *vi* (*amount to, total*) **today's earthquake** ~**s five since the beginning of the year** el terremoto de hoy es el quinto de este año ►**to** ~ **as if to do sth** fingir hacer algo III. *n* (*brand*) marca *f* ►**to be on the** ~ *inf* (*for money, power*) intentar sacar tajada; (*sexually*) intentar ligar

◆**make away with** *vt* 1. (*kill*) **to** ~ **sb** acabar con alguien 2. (*steal*) **to** ~ **sth** llevarse algo

◆**make for** *vt insep* 1. (*head for*) dirigirse a 2. (*help to promote*) **to** ~ **sth** contribuir a algo

◆**make of** *vt* **what do you** ~ **this book?** ¿qué te parece este libro?

◆**make off** *vi inf* largarse

◆**make out** I. *vi* 1. *inf* (*succeed, cope: person*) arreglárselas 2. *vulg* (*have sex*) **to** ~ **with sb** tirarse a alguien II. *vt* 1. *inf* (*pretend*) **he made himself out to be rich** se hizo pasar por rico 2. (*claim*) **to** ~ **that ...** dar a entender que... 3. (*discern: writing, numbers*) distinguir; (*in the distance*) divisar, visualizar *AmL* 4. (*write out*) **to** ~ **a cheque** extender un cheque

◆**make over** *vt* 1. LAW (*transfer: ownership*) transmitir 2. *Am* (*alter, convert*) **to make sth over into sth** convertir algo en algo

◆**make up** I. *vt* 1. (*invent*) inventar 2. (*prepare*) preparar; (*page*) componer 3. (*produce*) producir 4. (*compensate*) **to** ~ **for sth** compensar algo; **to** ~ **sth by sth** compensar algo con algo 5. *Brit* (*complete*) **to** ~ **the numbers** hacer cuentas 6. (*constitute*) constituir 7. (*decide*) **to** ~ **one's mind** decidirse II. *vi* reconciliarse

◆**make up to** *vt* 1. **to make it up to sb** compensar a alguien 2. *Brit, Aus, inf* (*flatter*) tratar de ganarse el favor de

make-believe [ˈmeɪkbɪˌliːv] I. *n no pl* (*pretence*) fingimiento *m;* **a world of** ~ un mundo de fantasía [*o* de ensueño] II. *adj* imaginario, -a; (*weapon*) de mentira; **a** ~ **world** un mundo de fantasía

maker [ˈmeɪkəʳ, *Am:* -kɚ] *n* 1. (*manufacturer*) fabricante *mf* 2. (*God*) **to meet one's Maker** entregar el alma a Dios

makeshift [ˈmeɪkʃɪft] *adj* provisional

make-up [ˈmeɪkʌp] *n no pl* 1. (*structure*) estructura *f* 2. (*character*) carácter *m* 3. (*cosmetics*) maquillaje *m;* **to put on** ~ maquillarse; **to wear** ~ llevar maquillaje

make-up artist *n* maquillador(a) *m(f)*

making [ˈmeɪkɪŋ] *n* 1. *no pl* (*production*) producción *m;* (*of clothes*) confección *f;* (*of meals*) preparación *f* 2. *pl* (*essential qualities*) **to have the** ~**s of sth** tener madera de algo ►**to be the** ~ **of sb** ser decisivo para alguien

maladjusted [ˌmæləˈdʒʌstɪd] *adj* PSYCH inadaptado, -a

maladministration [ˈmælədˌmɪnɪˈstreɪʃən] *n no pl, form* mala administración *f*

maladroit [ˈmælədrɔɪt] *adj form* torpe

Malagasy [ˌmæləˈgæsi] I. *adj* malgache II. *n a.* LING malgache *m*

malaise [mæˈleɪz] *n no pl* malestar *m*

malapropism [ˈmæləprɒpɪzəm, *Am:* -prɑːpɪ-] *n* LING equivocación *f* de palabras

malaria [məˈleərɪə, *Am:* -ˈlerɪ-] *n no pl* malaria *f*

Malawi [məˈlɑːwi] *n* Malaui *m*

Malawian I. *adj* malauiano, -a II. *n* malauiano, -a *m, f*

Malaysia [məˈleɪzɪə, *Am:* -ʒə] *n* Malaisia *f*

Malaysian [məˈleɪzɪən, *Am:* -ʒən] I. *adj* malaisio, -a II. *n* malaisio, -a *m, f*

malcontent [ˈmælkəntənt] *n form* descontento, -a *m, f*

Maldives [ˈmɔldiːvz, *Am:* ˈmældaɪvz] *npl* Maldivas *fpl*

male [meɪl] I. *adj* (*person, hormone*) masculino, -a; (*animal*) macho; ~ **chauvinism** machismo *m* II. *n* (*person*) varón *m;* (*animal*) macho *m*

malediction [ˌmælɪˈdɪkʃən, *Am:* -əˈ-] *n* maledicción *f*

malevolent [məˈlevəlnt] *adj liter* (*malicious*) malévolo, -a; (*deity, powers*) maligno, -a

malformation [ˌmælfɔːˈmeɪʃən] *n* MED deformación *f*

malfunction [ˌmælˈfʌŋkʃən] I. *vi* 1. (*not*

work properly) funcionar mal **2.** (*stop functioning*) fallar **II.** *n* **1.** (*defective functioning*) mal funcionamiento *m* **2.** (*sudden stop*) fallo *m*

Mali ['mɑːli] *n* Mali *m*

Malian **I.** *adj* malinés, -esa **II.** *n* malinés, -esa *m, f*

malice ['mælɪs] *n no pl* malicia *f;* **with ~ aforethought** con premeditación

malicious [mə'lɪʃəs] *adj* malicioso, -a

malign [mə'laɪn] **I.** *adj form* maligno, -a **II.** *vt* calumniar

malignancy [mə'lɪgnənsi] <-ies> *n a.* MED malignidad *f*

malignant [mə'lɪgnənt] *adj* maligno, -a

malinger [mə'lɪŋgəʳ, *Am:* -gɚ] *vi* fingir estar enfermo

malingerer [mə'lɪŋgərəʳ, *Am:* -ɚɚ] *n persona que finge estar enferma*

mall [mɔːl] *n Am* centro *m* comercial

mallard ['mælɑːd, *Am:* -ɚd] <-(s)> *n* ánade *m* real

malleable ['mælɪəbl] *adj* (*material*) maleable; (*person*) dócil

mallet ['mælɪt] *n* mazo *m*

mallow ['mæləʊ, *Am:* -oʊ] *n* malva *f*

malnutrition [ˌmælnjuː'trɪʃən, *Am:* -nuː'-] *n no pl* desnutrición *f*

malodorous [ˌmæl'əʊdərəs, *Am:* -'oʊ-] *adj form* maloliente

malpractice [ˌmæl'præktɪs] *n* mala práctica *f;* **medical ~** negligencia *f* médica

malt [mɔːlt] **I.** *n no pl* malta *f* **II.** *vt* maltear

Malta ['mɔːltə, *Am:* -t̬ə] *n* Malta *f; s. a.* **Republic of Malta**

Maltese [ˌmɔːl'tiːz] **I.** *adj* maltés, -esa; **~ cross** cruz *f* de Malta **II.** *n* maltés, -esa *m, f*

maltreat [ˌmæl'triːt] *vt form* maltratar

maltreatment *n no pl* malos tratos *mpl*

mamma [mə'mɑː] *n* mamá *f*

mammal ['mæməl] *n* mamífero *m*

mammary gland ['mæmərɪˌglænd] *n* glándula *f* mamaria

mammography [mæ'mɒgrəfi, *Am:* mə'mɑːgrə-] <-ies> *n* mamografía *f*

mammoth ['mæməθ] **I.** *adj* gigantesco, -a **II.** *n* mamut *m*

man [mæn] **I.** *n* <men> **1.** (*male human*) hombre *m* **2.** (*the human race*) ser *m* humano **3.** (*in games*) ficha *f* ►**to talk (as) ~ to ~** hablar de hombre a hombre; **as one ~** unánimamente **II.** *vt* <-nn-> (*operate*) encargarse de; (*ship*) tripular; **to ~ a factory** contratar personal para una fábrica; **some volunteers ~ the phones** algunos voluntarios cogen el teléfono

manacle ['mænəkl] **I.** *n pl* esposas *fpl* **II.** *vt* esposar

manage ['mænɪdʒ] **I.** *vt* **1.** (*accomplish*) lograr; **to ~ to do sth** conseguir hacer algo **2.** *Brit* (*fit into one's schedule*) **to not ~ the time** no tener tiempo **3.** *a.* ECON (*control, be in charge of*) dirigir; (*money, time*) administrar **II.** *vi* **to ~ on sth** arreglárselas con algo

manageable ['mænɪdʒəbl] *adj* (*vehicle*) manejable; (*person, animal*) dócil; (*amount*) razonable

management ['mænɪdʒmənt] *n* **1.** *no pl* (*direction*) manejo *m* **2.** *no pl a.* ECON dirección *f;* **to study ~** estudiar administración de empresas

management buy-out *n* compra *f* de acciones de una empresa por los gerentes **management consultant** *n* consultor(a) *m(f)* gerencial **management negotiator** *n* intermediario, -a *m, f* **management studies** *npl* estudios *mpl* de administración de empresas **management team** *n* equipo *m* directivo

manager ['mænɪdʒəʳ, *Am:* -dʒɚ] *n* **1.** COM (*administrator*) administrador(a) *m(f);* (*of business unit*) gerente *mf* **2.** (*of performer, artist*) representante *mf* artístico, -a

manageress [ˌmænɪdʒə'res, *Am:* 'mæn-] *n* (*woman in charge of a shop*) encargada *f*

managerial [ˌmænə'dʒɪəriəl, *Am:* -'dʒɪri-] *adj* (*relating to a manager*) gerencial; (*directorial*) directivo, -a; **~ position** posición directiva; **~ skills** dotes *fpl* de mando

managing director *n Brit* director(a) *m(f)* general

Mancunian [mæŋ'kjuːniən, *Am:* mæn-] *n* habitante *mf* de Manchester

mandarin ['mændərɪn, *Am:* -dɚ-] *n* mandarín *m*

Mandarin ['mændərɪn, *Am:* -dɚ-] *n no pl* LING mandarín *m*

mandarin (orange) ['mændərɪn, *Am:* 'mændɚɪn] *n* mandarina *f*

mandate ['mændeɪt] **I.** *n* **1.** *a.* POL mandato *m* **2.** (*territory*) territorio *m* bajo mandato **II.** *vt* aprobar oficialmente

mandatory ['mændətri, *Am:* -tɔːri] *adj form* obligatorio, -a; **to make sth ~** imponer algo

mandible ['mændɪbl] *n* mandíbula *f*

mandolin(e) ['mændəlɪn] *n* MUS mandolina *f,* bandolina *f AmL*

mandrake ['mændreɪk] *n* mandrágora *f*

mandrill ['mændrɪl] *n* mandril *m*

mane [meɪn] *n* (*of horse*) crin *f;* (*of person, lion*) melena *f*

man-eater ['mæniːtəʳ, *Am:* -t̬ɚ] *n inf* devorador(a) *m(f)* de hombres

maneuver [mə'nuːvəʳ, *Am:* -vɚ] *n, vi, vt Am s.* **manoeuvre**

maneuverability [məˌnuːvərə'bɪləti, *Am:* -ət̬i] *n Am s.* **manoeuvrability**

maneuverable [mə'nuːvərəbl] *adj Am s.* **manoeuvrable**

manfully ['mænfʊli] *adv* valientemente

manganese ['mæŋgəniːz] *n no pl* manganeso *m*

mange [meɪndʒ] *n no pl* sarna *f,* zarate *f Hond*

mangel ['mæŋgl] *n,* **mangel-wurzel** *n* remolacha *f* forrajera

manger ['meɪndʒəʳ, *Am:* -dʒɚ] *n* pesebre *m*
mangetout [mɑ̃:ʒ'tu:] *n Brit* tirabeque *m*
mangle[1] ['mæŋgl] *vt* (*body, text*) mutilar
mangle[2] ['mæŋgl] *n* **1.** *Brit* (*for wet clothes*) exprimidor *m* **2.** *Am* (*iron*) planchadora *f* mecánica
mango ['mæŋgəʊ, *Am:* -goʊ] *n* <-(e)s> mango *m*
mangrove ['mæŋgrəʊv, *Am:* 'mængroʊv] *n* mangle *m*
mangy ['meɪndʒi] <-ier, -iest> *adj* **1.** (*animal*) sarnoso, -a **2.** *inf* (*carpet, coat*) raído, -a
manhandle ['mænhændl] *vt* **1.** (*treat roughly: person*) maltratar **2.** (*move by hand: heavy object*) empujar
manhole ['mænhəʊl, *Am:* -hoʊl] *n* pozo *m* de visita, boca *f* de visita *Ven*
manhole cover *n* tapa *f* de registro
manhood ['mænhʊd] *n no pl* **1.** (*adulthood*) edad *f* adulta **2.** (*masculinity*) masculinidad *f*
man-hour ['mænaʊəʳ] *n* ECON hora-hombre *f*
manhunt ['mænhʌnt] *n* persecución *f*
mania ['meɪnɪə] *n* (*obsession*) obsesión *f;* PSYCH manía *f*
maniac ['meɪnɪæk] *n* maníaco, -a *m, f;* **football ~** fanático del fútbol
maniacal [mə'naɪəkl] *adj inf* maníaco, -a
manic ['mænɪk] *adj* maníaco, -a
manic depression *n* manía *f* depresiva **manic depressive** *adj* maníaco, -a depresivo, -a **manic psychosis** *n* PSYCH psicosis *f inv* maníaca
manicure ['mænɪkjʊəʳ, *Am:* -kjʊr] **I.** *n* manicura *f* **II.** *vt* **to ~ one's nails** hacerse la manicura
manicure set *n* estuche *m* de manicura
manicurist ['mænɪkjʊərɪst, *Am:* -kjʊr-] *n* manicuro, -a *m, f,* manicurista *mf AmL*
manifest ['mænɪfest] **I.** *adj form* manifiesto, -a; **to make sth ~** poner algo de manifiesto **II.** *vt form* declarar; **to ~ symptoms of sth** manifestar síntomas de algo
manifestation [ˌmænɪfe'steɪʃən] *n form* manifestación *f*
manifestly ['mænɪfestli] *adv form* evidentemente
manifesto [ˌmænɪ'festəʊ, *Am:* -toʊ] <-stos *o* -stoes> *n* manifiesto *m*
manifold ['mænɪfəʊld, *Am:* -foʊld] **I.** *adj liter* múltiple **II.** *n* TECH, AUTO colector *m;* **exhaust ~** colector de gases
manikin ['mænɪkɪn] *n* **1.** (*model*) maniquí *m* **2.** (*dwarf*) enano, -a *m, f*
manil(l)a envelope [mə'nɪlə 'envələʊp, *Am:* -loʊp] *n* sobre *m* manila **manil(l)a paper** *n no pl* papel *m* manila
manioc ['mænɪɒk, *Am:* -ɑ:k] *n* **1.** (*cassava*) yuca *f* **2.** (*flour*) tapioca *f*
manipulate [mə'nɪpjʊleɪt, *Am:* -jə-] *vt* manipular
manipulation [məˌnɪpjʊ'leɪʃən, *Am:* -jə'-] *n* manipulación *f*
manipulative [məˌnɪpjʊ'letɪv, *Am:* -jə'-] *adj* manipulador(a)
manipulator [mə'nɪpjʊleɪtəʳ, *Am:* -jəleɪṱɚ] *n* manipulador(a) *m(f)*
mankind [ˌmæn'kaɪnd] *n no pl* humanidad *f*
manky [ˌmæŋki] <-ier, -iest> *adj Brit, inf* (*clothes*) sobado, -a; (*sofa, carpet*) sucio, -a
manliness ['mænlɪnəs] *n no pl* hombría *f*
manly ['mænli] <-ier, -iest> *adj* varonil
man-made ['mænmeɪd] *adj* (*lake*) artificial; (*fibre*) sintético, -a
manna ['mænə] *n no pl* maná *m*
manned [mænd] *adj* AVIAT tripulado, -a
mannequin ['mænɪkɪn] *n* **1.** (*dummy*) maniquí *m* **2.** (*person*) modelo *mf*
manner ['mænəʳ, *Am:* -ɚ] *n no pl* **1.** (*way, fashion*) manera *f;* **in the ~ of sb** al estilo de alguien; **in a ~ of speaking** por así decirlo **2.** (*behaviour*) **~s** modales *mpl;* **to teach sb ~s** enseñar a alguien a comportarse; **it's bad ~s to ...** es de mala educación... **3.** *form* (*kind, type*) clase *f;* **what ~ of man is he?** ¿qué tipo de hombre es?; **all ~ of ...** toda clase de... ►**as if to the ~ born** como si hubiera nacido para ello; **not by any ~ of means** *Brit* de ningún modo
mannered *adj* amanerado, -a
mannerism ['mænərɪzəm] *n* amaneramiento *m*
mannikin ['mænɪkɪn] *n s.* **manikin**
mannish ['mænɪʃ] *adj* hombruno, -a
manoeuvrability [mə'nu:vrəbɪləti] *n no pl, Brit, Aus* maniobrabilidad *f*
manoeuvrable [mə'nu:vrəbl] *adj Brit, Aus* maniobrable
manoeuvre [mə'nu:vəʳ, *Am:* -vɚ] *Brit, Aus* **I.** *n a.* MIL maniobra *f;* **army ~s** maniobras militares **II.** *vt* hacer maniobrar; **to ~ sb into doing sth** embaucar a alguien para que haga algo **III.** *vi* maniobrar
manometer [mə'nɒmɪteʳ, *Am:* mə'nɑ:məṱɚ] *n* manómetro *m*
manor ['mænəʳ, *Am:* -ɚ] *n* **1.** (*house*) casa *f* solariega **2.** HIST (*territory*) feudo *m*
manpower ['mænpaʊəʳ, *Am:* -ɚ] *n no pl* mano de obra *f*
manqué ['mɑ̃ŋkeɪ] *adj form* frustrado, -a; **a writer ~** un escritor frustrado
manse [mæns] *n Scot: casa de un pastor protestante*
manservant ['mænsɜ:vənt, *Am:* -sɜ:r-] *n* criado *m*
mansion ['mænʃən] *n* mansión *f*
man-sized *adj* muy grande
manslaughter ['mænslɔ:təʳ, *Am:* -slɑ:ṱɚ] *n no pl* homicidio *m* involuntario
mantelpiece ['mæntlpi:s] *n* repisa *f* de la chimenea
mantis ['mæntɪs] *n* mantis *f* religiosa
mantle ['mæntl] *n* **1.** *liter* (*cloak, layer*) manto *m;* **a ~ of snow** un manto de nieve **2.** (*of gas lamp*) camisa *f*
man-to-man *adj* franco, -a
mantra ['mæntrə] *n* mantra *m*

M

manual ['mænjʊəl] I. *adj* manual; ~ **dexterity** habilidad manual II. *n* manual *m;* **instructions** ~ manual de instrucciones
manual labour *n* trabajo *m* manual
manually ['mænjʊəli] *adv* manualmente, con las manos
manual transmission *n* AUTO transmisión *f* manual **manual work** *n* trabajo *m* manual **manual worker** *n* trabajador(a) *m(f)*
manufacture [ˌmænjʊ'fæktʃəʳ, *Am:* -tʃɚ] I. *vt* 1. (*produce*) fabricar; ~**d goods** artículos manufacturados 2. (*invent*) inventar; **to ~ an excuse/a story** inventar una excusa/un cuento II. *n* 1. *no pl* (*production*) manufactura *f* 2. (*product*) producto *m* manufacturado
manufacturer [ˌmænjʊ'fækʃərəʳ, *Am:* -ɚɚ] *n* fabricante *mf;* ~**'s label** etiqueta *f* de fábrica; **to send sth back to the ~** devolver algo a la fábrica
manufacturing [ˌmænjʊ'fæktʃərɪŋ, *Am:* -jə'-] *adj* (*region, firm*) industrial; ~ **industry** industria *f* manufacturera
manure [mə'njʊəʳ, *Am:* -'nʊr] *n no pl* abono *m*
manuscript ['mænjʊskrɪpt] *n* manuscrito *m*
many ['meni] <more, most> I. *adj* muchos, muchas; ~ **flowers** muchas flores; ~ **books** muchos libros; **how ~ bottles?** ¿cuántas botellas?; **too/so ~ people** demasiada/tanta gente; **one too ~** uno de más; ~ **times** muchas veces; **as ~ as ...** tantos como... II. *pron* muchos, muchas; ~ **are here** hay muchos; ~ **think that ...** muchos piensan que...; **so ~** tantos/tantas; **too ~** demasiados/demasiadas III. *n* **the ~** la mayoría; **a good ~** un gran número
many-sided [ˌmenɪ'saɪdɪd] *adj* polifacético, -a
Maoism ['maʊɪzm] *n no pl* maoísmo *m*
Maoist ['maʊɪzt] I. *n* maoísta *mf* II. *adj* maoísta
Maori ['maʊri] I. *n* maorí *mf* II. *adj* maorí
map [mæp] I. *n* 1. (*of region, stars*) mapa *m;* (*of town*) plano *m;* ~ **of the world** mapamundi *m;* **road ~** mapa de carreteras 2. (*simple diagram*) plano *m* ►**to blow** [*o* **wipe**] **sth off the ~** borrar algo del mapa; **to put a town on the ~** dar a conocer a un pueblo II. <-pp-> *vt* trazar un mapa de
◆**map out** *vt* planear, proyectar; **to ~ a route** planear una ruta; **to ~ a course/a plan/a strategy** proyectar un curso/un plan/una estrategia; **his future is all mapped out for him** tiene la vida planificada
maple ['meɪpl] *n* 1. (*tree*) arce *m* 2. *no pl* (*wood*) madera *f* de arce
maple leaf *n* hoja *f* de arce **maple sugar** *n no pl* azúcar *m* de arce **maple syrup** *n no pl* jarabe *m* de arce
map maker *n* cartógrafo, -a *m, f* **map making** *n* cartografía *f*
mar [mɑːʳ, *Am:* mɑːr] <-rr-> *vt* (*ruin*) echar a perder; (*enjoyment, day*) aguar
Mar *n abbr of* March marzo *m*
maraschino cherry [ˌmærə'ʃiːnəʊ-, *Am:* ˌmerə'ʃiːnoʊ-] *n* guinda *f* confitada
marathon ['mærəθən, *Am:* 'merəθɑːn] *n a. fig* maratón *m*
marathon runner *n* maratonista *mf*
maraud [mə'rɔːd, *Am:* -'rɑːd] *vi* merodear
marauder *n* merodeador(a) *m(f)*
marauding *adj* merodeador(a)
marble ['mɑːbl, *Am:* 'mɑːr-] *n* 1. *no pl* (*stone*) mármol *m;* ~ **table** mesa *f* de mármol 2. (*glass ball*) canica *f,* bolita *f CSur,* metra *f Ven;* **to play ~s** jugar a las canicas ►**to lose one's ~s** *inf* perder la cabeza
marble cake *n pastel de molde con chocolate*
marbled *adj* veteado, -a; **to be ~ with sth** estar veteado con algo
march [mɑːtʃ, *Am:* mɑːrtʃ] I. <-es> *n a.* MIL marcha *f;* **funeral ~** marcha fúnebre; **a 20 km ~** una marcha de 20 km; **to be on the ~** estar en marcha; **to be within a day's ~** estar a un día de camino II. *vi a.* MIL marchar; (*parade*) desfilar; **to ~ into a country** invadir un país III. *vt* (*compel to walk*) **to ~ sb off** hacer marchar a alguien
March [mɑːtʃ, *Am:* mɑːrtʃ] *n* marzo *m; s. a.* **April**
marching orders ['mɑːtʃɪŋˌɔːdəz, *Am:* 'mɑːrtʃɪŋˌɔːrdɚz] *n Brit, inf* **to get one's ~** ser despedido; **to give sb his ~** despedir a alguien (del trabajo)
Mardi Gras [ˌmɑːdi'grɑː, *Am:* 'mɑːrdiˌgrɑː] *n* martes *m* de carnaval

> **Mardi Gras** es el equivalente americano del Carnaval. Esta fiesta la trajeron los colonizadores franceses de New Orleans (en lo que posteriormente será el estado de Louisiana). Aunque la mayoría de las personas piensan en New Orleans cuando escuchan la expresión **Mardi Gras**, lo cierto es que también se celebra en otros lugares como Biloxi/Mississippi y Mobile/Alabama. En New Orleans los **krewes** (agrupaciones de carnaval) celebran muchas fiestas y bailes durante estos días y el martes de carnaval salen en cabalgata.

mare ['meəʳ] *n* yegua *f*
mare's nest *n* hallazgo *m* ilusorio
margarine [ˌmɑːdʒə'riːn, *Am:* 'mɑːrdʒɚɪn] *n no pl* margarina *f*
marge [mɑːdʒ, *Am:* mɑːrdʒ] *n Brit, inf abbr of* **margarine** margarina *f*
margin ['mɑːdʒɪn, *Am:* 'mɑːr-] *n a.* TYPO margen *m;* **profit ~** margen de ganancia; **narrow** [*o* **tight**] ~ margen reducido; ~ **of error** margen de error
marginal ['mɑːdʒɪnl, *Am:* 'mɑːr-] *adj* marginal; **to be of ~ interest** ser de interés secundario; **marginal land** tierra *f* marginal; ~ **constituency** *Brit, Aus* POL *circunscripción electoral*

de escasa mayoría
marginalise *vt Brit, Aus,* **marginalize** ['mɑːdʒɪnəlaɪz, *Am:* 'mɑːr-] *vt* marginar
marigold ['mærɪgəʊld, *Am:* 'merɪgoʊld] *n* caléndula *f*
marihuana *n,* **marijuana** [ˌmærɪ'wɑːnə, *Am:* ˌmerɪ'-] *n no pl* marihuana *f*
marina [mə'riːnə] *n* puerto *m* deportivo
marinade [ˌmærɪ'neɪd, *Am:* ˌmer-] *n* escabeche *m*
marinate ['mærɪneɪt, *Am:* 'mer-] *vt* marinar
marine [mə'riːn] **I.** *adj* (*life*) marino, -a; (*insurance*) marítimo, -a; (*engineer*) naval **II.** *n* infante *m* de marina
marine biologist *n* biólogo, -a *m, f* marino, -a **Marine Corps** *n* Infantería *f* de Marina (EE.UU.)
mariner ['mærɪnəʳ, *Am:* 'merɪnɚ] *n liter* marinero, -a *m, f*
marionette [ˌmærɪə'net, *Am:* ˌmer-] *n* marioneta *f*
marital ['mærɪtəl, *Am:* 'merɪt̬əl] *adj* marital; ~ **bliss** felicidad *f* marital; ~ **problems** problemas *mpl* conyugales
marital status *n form* estado *m* civil
maritime ['mærɪtaɪm, *Am:* 'mer-] *adj form* marítimo, -a
maritime law *n* código *m* marítimo
marjoram ['mɑːdʒərəm, *Am:* 'mɑːrdʒɚəm] *n no pl* mejorana *f*
mark¹ [mɑːk, *Am:* mɑːrk] **I.** *n* **1.** (*spot, stain*) mancha *f;* (*scratch*) marca *f;* (*trace*) huella *f;* **to leave one's ~ on sth/sb** *fig* dejar sus huellas en algo/alguien **2.** (*written sign*) raya *f* **3.** SCHOOL nota *f;* **to get full ~s** *Brit, Aus* obtener las máximas calificaciones **4.** *no pl* (*required standard*) norma *f;* **to be up to the ~** ser satisfactorio; **to not feel up to the ~** no sentirse a la altura de las circunstancias **5.** (*target*) blanco *m;* **to hit the ~** dar en el blanco **6.** (*starting line*) línea *f* de partida; **on your ~s, get set, go!** ¡preparados, listos, ya! **7.** LING signo *m;* **punctuation ~** signo de puntuación ▶**there are no ~s for guessing that** no hace falta ser un genio para adivinar eso; **to be quick/slow off the ~** ser rápido/lento de reflejos **II.** *vt* **1.** (*make a spot, stain*) manchar **2.** (*make written sign, indicate*) marcar; **I've ~ed the route on the map** he señalado la ruta en el mapa; **the bottle was ~ed 'poison'** la botella llevaba la etiqueta 'veneno' **3.** (*characterize*) distinguir; **to ~ sb as sth** distinguir a alguien como algo **4.** (*commemorate*) conmemorar; **to ~ the beginning/end of sth** conmemorar el principio/final de algo; **to ~ the 10th anniversary** celebrar el 10° aniversario **5.** SCHOOL puntuar **6.** SPORTS (*opponent*) marcar
◆**mark down** *vt* **1.** (*reduce: prices*) reducir **2.** *Brit* SCHOOL **to mark sb down** bajar las calificaciones de alguien **3.** (*jot down*) apuntar **4.** *fig* (*assess*) **to mark sb down as sth** catalogar a alguien como algo
◆**mark off** *vt* **1.** (*divide land from adjacent areas*) demarcar **2.** (*cross off*) tachar
◆**mark out** *vt* **1.** (*distinguish*) distinguir **2.** *Brit* (*indicate boundary*) trazar
◆**mark up** *vt* aumentar
mark² [mɑːk, *Am:* mɑːrk] *n* FIN marco *m*
marked [mɑːkt, *Am:* mɑːrkt] *adj* **1.** (*improvement, difference*) marcado, -a; (*contrast*) acusado, -a **2.** (*with distinguishing marks*) marcado, -a **3.** (*liable to be attacked*) **to be a ~ man/woman** estar en el punto de mira
markedly ['mɑːkədli, *Am:* 'mɑːrk-] *adv* notablemente
marker ['mɑːkəʳ, *Am:* 'mɑːrkɚ] *n* **1.** (*sign, symbol*) señal *f* **2.** SCHOOL, UNIV corrector(a) *m(f)* **3.** (*pen*) rotulador *m,* marcador *m Arg*
market ['mɑːkɪt, *Am:* 'mɑːr-] **I.** *n* mercado *m,* recova *f And, Urug;* **the coffee ~** el mercado del café; **housing ~** mercado inmobiliario; **job ~** mercado de trabajo; **stock ~** bolsa *f* de valores; **to put sth on the ~** poner algo a la venta; **on the ~** a la venta **II.** *vt* comercializar
marketable *adj* comercial; ~ **commodities** productos *mpl* comerciales
market day *n Brit* día *f* de mercado **market forces** *npl* fuerzas *fpl* del mercado **market garden** *n Brit, Aus* huerto *m* **market gardener** *n Brit, Aus* hortelano, -a *m, f*
marketing *n no pl* **1.** (*discipline*) marketing *m* **2.** (*commercialization*) comercialización *f*
marketing department *n* departamento *m* de marketing **marketing strategy** *n* estrategia *f* de mercado
market leader *n* líder *mf* del mercado **marketplace** *n* **1.** ECON mercado *m* **2.** (*square*) plaza *f* (del mercado) **market price** *n* precio *m* de mercado **market research** *n no pl* estudio *m* de mercado **market researcher** *n* investigador(a) *m(f)* de mercado **market town** *n Brit* población *f* con mercado **market trader** *n* comerciante *mf*
marking *n* (*identification*) señal *f;* (*on animal*) pinta *f*
marking ink *n no pl* tinta *f* indeleble
marksman ['mɑːksmən, *Am:* 'mɑːrks-] <-men> *n* tirador *m*
marksmanship ['mɑːksmənʃɪp, *Am:* 'mɑːrks-] *n no pl* puntería *f*
markswoman ['mɑːkswʊmən, *Am:* 'mɑːrks-] <-women> *n* tiradora *f*
mark-up ['mɑːkʌp, *Am:* 'mɑːrk-] *n* margen *m* de ganancia
marmalade ['mɑːməleɪd, *Am:* 'mɑːr-] *n no pl* mermelada *f* (*de cítricos*)
marmalade cat *n Brit: gato con vetas de color naranja, amarillo y marrón*
marmoset ['mɑːməzet, *Am:* 'mɑːrmə-] *n* tití *m*
maroon¹ [mə'ruːn] **I.** *n no pl* granate *m* **II.** *adj* granate
maroon² [mə'ruːn] *vt* abandonar
marquee [mɑː'kiː, *Am:* mɑːr-] *n* **1.** *Brit, Aus*

M

(*tent*) carpa *f* **2.** *Am* (*rooflike structure*) marquesina *f*
marriage ['mærɪdʒ, *Am:* 'mer-] *n* **1.** (*wedding*) boda *f* **2.** (*relationship, state*) matrimonio *m;* **arranged** ~ matrimonio arreglado; **related by** ~ emparentado por matrimonio; **he is a relative by** ~ es pariente político **3.** *fig* (*of organisations*) unión *f*
marriageable *adj* casadero, -a
marriage broker *n* casamentero, -a *m, f* **marriage bureau** *n Brit* agencia *f* matrimonial **marriage certificate** *n* acta *f* matrimonial **marriage contract** *n* contrato *m* matrimonial **marriage counselling** *n Am, Aus* orientación *f* matrimonial
marriage guidance *n Brit* orientación *f* matrimonial **marriage guidance counsellor** *n Brit* consejero,-a *m, f* matrimonial **marriage guidance office** *n Brit* agencia *f* de orientación matrimonial
marriage licence *n* licencia *f* matrimonial **marriage of convenience** *n* matrimonio *m* de conveniencia **marriage vow** *n* voto *m* matrimonial
married *adj* (*person*) casado, -a; ~ **couple** matrimonio *m;* ~ **life** vida *f* conyugal; **to be** ~ **to sth** *fig* estar atado a algo
married name *n* apellido *m* de casada
marrow¹ ['mærəʊ, *Am:* 'meroʊ] *n Brit, Aus* (*vegetable*) calabacín *m*
marrow² ['mærəʊ, *Am:* 'meroʊ] *n* MED médula *f;* **to the** ~ *fig* hasta los tuétanos
marrow bone *n* hueso *m* medular
marrowfat pea [ˌmærəʊfæt'piː, *Am:* 'meroʊ-] *n* guisante *m* de semilla grande
marry ['mæri, *Am:* 'mer-] <-ie-> **I.** *vt* **1.** (*become husband or wife*) **to** ~ **sb** casarse con alguien; **to get married** (**to sb**) casarse (con alguien) **2.** (*priest*) casar **II.** *vi* casarse; **to** ~ **above/beneath oneself** casarse con alguien de clase superior/inferior; **to** ~ **into a wealthy family** emparentar con una familia rica
Mars [mɑːz, *Am:* mɑːrz] *n no pl* Marte *m*
Marseilles [ˌmɑː'seɪ, *Am:* ˌmɑːr] *n* Marsella *f*
marsh [mɑːʃ, *Am:* mɑːrʃ] <-es> *n* ciénaga *f*
marshal ['mɑːʃl, *Am:* 'mɑːr-] **I.** <*Brit:* -ll-, *Am:* -l-> *vt* ordenar **II.** *n* **1.** (*at public event*) maestro *m* de ceremonias **2.** *Am* LAW alguacil *mf* **3.** MIL mariscal *m;* **field** ~ mariscal de campo **4.** *Am* (*police or fire officer*) comisario *m*
marsh gas *n* metano *m*
marshland ['mɑːʃlænd, *Am:* 'mɑːrʃ-] *n* pantanal *m*
marshmallow ['mɑːʃmæləʊ, *Am:* 'mɑːrʃ-] *n* **1.** (*sweet*) dulce *m* de malvavisco, carlotina *f Ven* **2.** (*plant*) malvavisco *m* **3.** *Am, fig* (*weak person*) blando, -a *m, f*
marshy ['mɑːʃi, *Am:* 'mɑːr-] <-ier, -iest> *adj* pantanoso, -a
marsupial [mɑː'suːpɪəl, *Am:* mɑːr'-] **I.** *n* marsupial *m* **II.** *adj* marsupial
marten ['mɑːtɪn, *Am:* 'mɑːrtn] *n* marta *f*
martial ['mɑːʃəl, *Am:* 'mɑːr-] *adj* marcial
martial arts *n* SPORTS artes *mpl* marciales **martial law** *n* ley *f* marcial; **to impose** ~ **on a country** imponer la ley marcial en un país
Martian ['mɑːʃən, *Am:* 'mɑːr-] **I.** *adj* marciano, -a **II.** *n* marciano, -a *m, f*
martin ['mɑːtɪn, *Am:* 'mɑːrtn] *n* avión *m*
martinet [ˌmɑːtɪ'net, *Am:* ˌmɑːrtə'-] *n form* rigorista *mf*
Martinique [ˌmɑːtɪ'niːk, *Am:* ˌmɑːrtən'iːk] *n* Martinica *f*
martyr ['mɑːtəʳ, *Am:* 'mɑːrt̬ɚ] **I.** *n* mártir *mf;* **to be a** ~ **to arthritis** *fig* estar martirizado por la artritis **II.** *vt* martirizar; ~**ed saint** santo *m* mártir
martyrdom ['mɑːtədəm, *Am:* 'mɑːrt̬ɚ-] *n no pl* martirio *m;* **to suffer** ~ sufrir pena de martirio
marvel ['mɑːvl, *Am:* 'mɑːr-] **I.** *n* maravilla *f;* **it's a** ~ **to me how ...** me maravilla cómo... **II.** <*Brit:* -ll-, *Am:* -l-> *vi* **to** ~ **that ...** maravillarse de que... +*subj;* **to** ~ **at sb/sth** maravillarse de alguien/algo
marvellous *adj Brit,* **marvelous** ['mɑːvələs, *Am:* 'mɑːr-] *adj Am* maravilloso, -a; **to feel** ~ sentirse espléndido
Marxism ['mɑːksizm, *Am:* 'mɑːrk-] *n no pl* marxismo *m*
Marxist ['mɑːksɪstː, *Am:* 'mɑːrk-] **I.** *n* marxista *mf* **II.** *adj* marxista
marzipan ['mɑːzɪpæn, *Am:* 'mɑːr-] *n no pl* mazapán *m*
masc. *adj abbr of* **masculine**
mascara [mæ'skɑːrə, *Am:* -'skerə] *n no pl* rímel *m*
mascot ['mæskət, *Am:* -kɑːt] *n* mascota *f*
masculine ['mæskjəlɪn] *adj a.* LING masculino, -a
masculinity [ˌmæskjə'lɪnəti, *Am:* ˌmæskjə-'lɪnət̬i] *n* masculinidad *f*
mash [mæʃ] **I.** *n no pl* **1.** *Brit, inf* (*mashed potato*) puré *m* de patata **2.** AGR (*animal feed*) afrecho *m* **II.** *vt* machacar; **to** ~ **potatoes** hacer puré de patatas
◆**mash up** *vt* **1.** GASTR triturar **2.** *Am* (*damage*) despachurrar
mask [mɑːsk, *Am:* mæsk] **I.** *n a. fig* máscara *f;* (*only covering eyes*) antifaz *m;* **oxygen** ~ máscara de oxígeno **II.** *vt* enmascarar; **to** ~ **sth with sth** encubrir algo con algo; **to** ~ **the statistics** ocultar las estadísticas
◆**mask out** *vt* PHOT, TYPO ocultar
masked *adj* enmascarado, -a
masked ball *n* baile *m* de máscaras
masking tape *n no pl* cinta *f* adhesiva protectora
masochism ['mæsəkɪzəm] *n no pl* masoquismo *m*
masochist ['mæsəkɪst] *n* masoquista *mf*
masochistic ['mæsəkɪstik] *adj* masoquista
mason ['meɪsn] *n* **1.** (*stone-cutter*) cantero

m **2.** *Am* (*bricklayer*) albañil *m* **3.** (*freemason*) masón, -ona *m, f*
masonic [məˈsɒnɪk, *Am:* -ˈsɑːnɪk] *adj* masónico, -a
masonic lodge *n* logia *f* masónica **masonic order** *n* sociedad *f* de los Masones
masonry [ˈmeɪsnri] *n no pl* **1.** (*occupation*) albañilería *f* **2.** (*stonework*) mampostería *f* **3.** (*freemasonry*) masonería *f*
masquerade [ˌmɑːskəˈreɪd] **I.** *n* mascarada *f* **II.** *vi* **to ~ as sth** hacerse pasar por algo
mass [mæs] **I.** *n no pl* **1.** *a.* PHYS masa *f* **2.** (*formless substance*) bulto *m* **3.** (*large quantity*) montón *m;* **to be a ~ of contradictions** estar lleno de contradicciones; **the ~ of the people** la muchedumbre; **the ~ of the population** la mayoría de la población **II.** *vi* (*gather*) juntarse; (*troops*) concentrarse
Mass [mæs] *n* misa *f;* **to attend ~** ir a misa; **to celebrate a ~** oficiar una misa
massacre [ˈmæsəkəʳ, *Am:* -kɚ] **I.** *n* **1.** (*killing*) masacre *f* **2.** *fig* (*defeat*) aniquilamiento *m* **II.** *vt* **1.** (*kill*) masacrar **2.** *fig* (*defeat*) aniquilar
massage [ˈmæsɑːdʒ, *Am:* məˈ-] **I.** *n* masaje *m;* **water ~** hidromasaje *m;* **to give sb a ~** dar a alguien un masaje **II.** *vt* **1.** dar masajes a **2.** *fig* manipular
massage parlor *n Am,* **massage parlour** *n Brit* salón *m* de relax
masseur [mæˈsɜːʳ, *Am:* -ˈsɜːr] *n* masajista *m*
masseuse [mæˈsɜːz] *n* masajista *f*
mass grave *n* fosa *f* común
massif [ˈmæsɪv] *n* GEO macizo *m*
massive [ˈmæsɪv] *adj* masivo, -a, enorme; **~ amounts of money** grandes cantidades de dinero
mass market *n* mercado *m* de masas **mass-market** *adj* de alto consumo **mass media** *n* **the ~** los medios de comunicación de masas **mass meeting** *n* mitin *m* **mass murder** *n* asesino *m* múltiple **mass murderer** *n* asesino, -a *m, f* múltiple **mass-produce** *vt* fabricar en serie **mass production** *n* fabricación *f* en serie **mass tourism** *n no pl* turismo *m* de masas **mass unemployment** *n no pl* paro *m* masivo
mast [mɑːst, *Am:* mæst] *n* **1.** NAUT mástil *m* **2.** (*flag pole*) asta *m;* **at half ~** a media asta **3.** RADIO, TV antena *f*
mastectomy [ˌmæsˈtekəmi] <-ies> *n* mastectomía *f*
master [ˈmɑːstəʳ, *Am:* ˈmæstɚ] **I.** *n* **1.** (*of house*) señor *m;* (*of slave*) amo *m;* (*of dog*) dueño *m;* **the young ~** el señorito **2.** (*one who excels*) maestro *m;* **~ craftsman** maestro; **to be a ~ of sth** ser experto en algo **3.** (*instructor*) instructor *m;* **dancing/singing ~** instructor de baile/canto; **fencing ~** maestro de esgrima **4.** *Brit* (*schoolteacher*) profesor *m* **5.** (*master copy*) original *m* ►**to be one's own ~** no depender de nadie **II.** *vt* **1.** (*cope with*) vencer; **to ~ one's fear of flying** superar el miedo a volar **2.** (*become proficient at*) dominar
master bedroom *n* dormitorio *m* principal **master class** <-es> *n* clase *f* magistral **master copy** <-ies> *n* original *m*
masterful [ˈmɑːstəfəl, *Am:* ˈmæstɚ-] *adj* **1.** (*authoritative*) autoritario, -a **2.** (*skilful*) magistral
master key *n* llave *f* maestra
masterly [ˈmɑːstəli, *Am:* ˈmæstɚ-] *adj* magistral
mastermind [ˈmɑːstəmaɪnd, *Am:* ˈmæstɚ-] **I.** *n* cerebro *m* **II.** *vt* (*activity*) planear; (*crime*) ser el cerebro de
Master of Arts *n* licenciado, -a *m, f* con máster (*en Humanidades o en Filosofía y Letras*) **Master of Ceremonies** *n* maestro *m* de ceremonias
masterpiece *n* obra *f* maestra **master plan** *n* plan *m* maestro **master race** *n* raza *f* superior
Master's *n,* **Master's degree** *n* máster *m*

> En Gran Bretaña se llama **Master's degree** al grado académico que se obtiene al finalizar una carrera tras la defensa de una tesina (**dissertation**). El **Master's degree** recibe distintos nombres según las disciplinas: **MA** (**Master of Arts**), **MSc** (**Master of Science**), **Mlitt** (**Master of Letters**) y **Mphil** (**Master of Philosohpy**). Sin embargo en Escocia con la expresión **MA** se designa un primer grado académico.

masterstroke *n* toque *m* magistral **master switch** <-es> *n* interruptor *m* principal **masterwork** *n s.* **masterpiece**
mastery [ˈmɑːstəri, *Am:* ˈmæstɚ-] *n no pl* (*skill*) maestría *f;* (*sway*) dominio *m*
masticate [ˈmæstɪkeɪt] *vt* masticar
mastication [ˌmæstɪˈkeɪʃən] *n no pl* masticación *m*
mastiff [ˈmæstɪf] *n* mastín *m*
mastitis [mæˈstaɪtɪs, *Am:* -t̬ɪs] *n no pl* mastitis *f*
masturbate [ˈmæstəbeɪt, *Am:* -tɚ-] **I.** *vi* masturbarse **II.** *vt* masturbar
masturbation [ˌmæstəˈbeɪʃən, *Am:* -tɚˈ-] *n no pl* masturbación *f,* pascuala *f Méx*
mat [mæt] *n* **1.** (*on floor*) estera *f;* (*decorative*) tapiz *m;* **bath ~** alfombra *f* de baño **2.** (*on table*) salvamanteles *m inv* **3.** SPORTS (*in gymnastics*) colchoneta *f* **4.** (*thick layer: of grass, hair*) maraña *f* ►**to be on the ~** estar en apuros
matador [ˈmætədɔːʳ] *n* matador *m*
match[1] [mætʃ] <-es> *n* (*for making fire*) cerilla *f,* fósforo *m,* cerillo *m Méx;* **box of ~es** caja de fósforos
match[2] [mætʃ] **I.** *n* **1.** (*competitor*) contrincante *mf;* **to be a good ~ for sb** poder competir con alguien; **to be no ~ for sb** no poder competir con alguien; **to meet one's ~** encon-

trar la horma de su zapato **2.** SPORTS partido *m* **3.** (*similarity*) **to be a good** ~ combinar bien **4.** (*in marriage*) **to make a good** ~ casarse bien **II.** *vi* (*harmonize: design, colour*) armonizar, pegar; (*description*) coincidir **III.** *vt* **1.** (*have same colour*) hacer juego con **2.** (*equal*) igualar

◆**match against** *vt always sep* enfrentar

◆**match up** **I.** *vi* **1.** (*make sense*) concordar **2.** (*align*) alinear **3. to** ~ **to sth** estar a la altura de algo **II.** *vt* (*put together*) emparejar

matchbox ['mætʃbɒks, *Am:* -bɑːks] <-es> *n* caja *f* de cerillas, cerillero *m AmL*

matching ['mætʃɪŋ] *adj* que hace juego

matchless ['mætʃlɪs] *adv* incomparable

matchmaker ['mætʃmeɪkəʳ, *Am:* -kɚ] *n* casamentero, -a *m, f*

match point *n* SPORTS bola *f* de partido

matchstick ['mætʃˌstɪk] *n* cerilla *f,* fósforo *m,* cerillo *m Méx*

matchstick figure *n,* **matchstick man** *n* monigote *m*

matchwood ['mætʃwʊd] *n no pl* astillas *fpl;* **to be smashed to** ~ hacerse añicos

mate¹ [meɪt] **I.** *n* **1.** (*spouse*) cónyuge *mf* **2.** ZOOL (*male*) macho *m;* (*female*) hembra *f* **3.** *Brit, Aus* (*friend*) amigo, -a *m, f* **4.** *Brit, Aus, inf* (*form of address*) compadre *m* **5.** (*assistant*) ayudante *mf* **6.** *fig* (*one of a pair*) compañero, -a *m, f* **7.** NAUT oficial *m* de abordo; **first/second** ~ primer/segundo oficial **II.** *vi* aparearse **III.** *vt* aparear

mate² [meɪt] **I.** *n* GAMES mate *m* **II.** *vt* dar jaque mate a

material [mə'tɪəriəl, *Am:* -'tɪri-] **I.** *n* **1.** PHILOS, PHYS materia *f* **2.** (*physical substance*) material *m;* **raw** ~ materia *f* prima **3.** *no pl* (*information*) **publicity** ~ material *m* publicitario **4.** *no pl* (*cloth*) tela *f* **5.** (*textile*) tejido *m* **6.** *pl* (*equipment*) materiales *mpl;* **writing** ~**(s)** útiles *mpl* de escritura **II.** *adj* **1.** (*physical*) material; ~ **damage** daño material **2.** (*important*) importante; **to be** ~ **to sth** ser importante para algo

materialise [mə'tɪəriəlaɪz] *vi Brit, Aus s.* **materialize**

materialism [mə'tɪəriəlɪzəm, *Am:* -'tɪri-] *n no pl* materialismo *m*

materialist *n* materialista *mf*

materialistic [məˌtɪəriə'lɪstɪk, *Am:* -ˌtɪri-] *adj* materialista

materialize [mə'tɪəriəlaɪz, *Am:* -'tɪri-] *vi* **1.** (*take physical form*) materializarse **2.** (*hope, idea*) realizarse **3.** (*appear*) aparecer

material witness <-es> *n Brit* testigo *mf* presencial

maternal [mə'tɜːnl, *Am:* -'tɜːr-] *adj* **1.** (*feeling*) maternal **2.** (*relative*) materno, -a

maternity [mə'tɜːnəti, *Am:* -'tɜːrnət̬i] *n no pl* maternidad *f*

maternity clothes *npl* ropa *f* premamá **maternity dress** <-es> *n* vestido *m* premamá **maternity hospital** *n* maternidad *f* **maternity leave** *n* baja *f* por maternidad **maternity ward** *n* sala *f* de maternidad

matey ['meɪti, *Am:* -t̬i] <-ier, -iest> *adj Brit, Aus, inf* amistoso, -a; **to get** ~ **with sb** hacerse amigo de alguien

math [mæθ] *n Am, inf abbr of* **mathematics** mates *fpl*

mathematical [ˌmæθə'mætɪkl, *Am:* -'mæt̬-] *adj* matemático, -a

mathematician [ˌmæθəmə'tɪʃən] *n* matemático, -a *m, f*

mathematics [ˌmæθə'mætɪks, *Am:* -'mæt̬-] *n* matemáticas *fpl*

maths [mæθs] *n Brit, Aus, inf abbr of* **mathematics** mates *fpl*

matinée ['mætɪneɪ, *Am:* -əneɪ] *n* CINE primera sesión *f;* THEAT función *f* de tarde

mating *n* apareamiento *m*

mating season *n* época *f* de celo

matriarchy ['meɪtrɪɑːki, *Am:* -ɑːrk-] *n no pl* matriarcado *m*

matrices ['meɪtrɪsiːz] *n pl of* **matrix**

matriculate [mə'trɪkjʊleɪt, *Am:* -jə-] **I.** *vi* matricularse **II.** *vt* matricular

matriculation [məˌtrɪkjʊ'leɪʃən, *Am:* -jə-] *n* matrícula *f*

matrimonial [ˌmætrɪ'məʊnɪəl, *Am:* -rə'moʊ-] *adj form* matrimonial

matrimony ['mætrɪməni, *Am:* -rəmoʊ-] *n no pl* matrimonio *m*

matrix ['meɪtrɪks] <-ices> *n a.* MAT matriz *f*

matrix printer *n* INFOR impresora *f* de matriz de punto

matron ['meɪtrən] *n* **1.** (*middle-aged woman*) matrona *f* **2.** (*nurse*) enfermera *f* jefe **3.** *Brit* SCHOOL ama *f* de llaves **4.** *Am* (*prison guard*) carcelera *f*

matronly ['meɪtrənli] *adj iron* de matrona; **a** ~ **figure** una persona madura y corpulenta

matt *adj,* **matte** [mæt] *adj Am* mate

matted *adj* enmarañado, -a

matter ['mætəʳ, *Am:* 'mæt̬ɚ] **I.** *n* **1.** (*subject*) materia *f;* (*question, affair*) asunto *m;* **that's another** ~ **altogether** eso es harina de otro costal *fig;* **that's no laughing** ~ no es cosa de risa; **to do sth as a** ~ **of course** hacer algo como parte del procedimiento habitual; **the** ~ **in hand** el asunto del que se trata; **it's a** ~ **of life or death** es un asunto de vida o muerte; **money** ~**s** asuntos financieros; **a** ~ **of opinion** una cuestión de opinión; **the truth of the** ~ la verdad de las cosas; **personal** ~ asunto privado **2.** *pl* (*situation*) situación *f;* **now** ~**s are really bad** ahora han empeorado las circunstancias; **to help** ~**s** mejorar las cosas; **to make** ~**s worse** por si eso fuera poco **3.** (*wrong*) problema *m;* **what's the** ~ **with you?** ¿qué te pasa?; **what's the** ~ **with asking for a pay rise?** ¿qué problema hay en pedir un aumento del sueldo? **4.** (*material*) material *m;* **advertising** ~ material publicitario **5.** (*amount*) **a** ~ **of** ... cosa de...; **in a** ~ **of seconds** en cuestión de segundos **6.** *no pl* (*substance*) materia *f* **II.** *vi* importar; **it really ~s to me** me importa mucho; **no ~ what they say** no importa lo que digan, digan lo que digan; **it doesn't ~ if ...** no importa si...; **it ~s that ...** importa que... +*subj;* **what ~s now is that ...** lo que importa ahora es que...

matter-of-fact [ˌmætəʳəvˈfækt, *Am:* ˌmæt̬ɚ-] *adj* **1.** (*practical*) práctico, -a **2.** (*emotionless*) prosaico, -a

matter-of-factly *adv* **1.** (*practically*) prácticamente **2.** (*emotionlessly*) prosaicamente

matting [ˈmætɪŋ, *Am:* ˈmæt̬-] *n no pl* **1.** (*floor covering*) estera *f* **2.** (*tangling*) enmarañamiento *m*

mattress [ˈmætrɪs] *n* colchón *m*

mature [məˈtjʊəʳ, *Am:* -ˈtʊr] **I.** *adj* **1.** (*person, attitude*) maduro, -a; (*animal*) adulto, -a; **to be ~ beyond one's years** ser muy maduro para su edad; **after ~ reflection** después de una larga reflexión **2.** (*fruit*) maduro, -a; (*wine*) añejo, -a; (*cheese*) curado, -a **3.** FIN vencido, -a **II.** *vi* **1.** *a. fig* madurar **2.** FIN vencer **III.** *vt* **1.** (*cheese, ham*) curar; (*wine*) añejar **2.** (*person*) hacer madurar

maturity [məˈtjʊərəti, *Am:* -ˈtʊrət̬i] *n* <-ies> **1.** *no pl* (*of person, attitude*) madurez *f;* **to come to ~** llegar a la madurez **2.** FIN vencimiento *m;* **to reach ~** tener vencimiento

maudlin [ˈmɔːdlɪn, *Am:* ˈmɑːd-] *adj* **1.** (*sentimental*) sensiblero, -a **2.** (*tearful*) llorón, -ona

maul [mɔːl, *Am:* mɑːl] *vt* **1.** (*wound*) herir **2.** (*criticize*) vapulear

> **Maundy Thursday** es el nombre que recibe el Jueves Santo dentro de la **Holy Week** (Semana Santa). Ese día el monarca reparte a unas cuantas personas pobres previamente escogidas el **Maundy money**. El número de personas a las que se dispensa esta limosna está en relación con la edad del monarca. Cada una de estas personas recibe además un set de monedas de plata acuñadas especialmente para la ocasión.

Mauritania [ˌmɒrɪˈteɪniə, *Am:* ˌmɔːrɪˈ-] *n* Mauritania *f*

Mauritanian **I.** *n* mauritano, -a *m, f* **II.** *adj* mauritano, -a

Mauritian **I.** *n* mauriciano, -a *m, f* **II.** *adj* mauriciano, -a

Mauritius [məˈrɪʃəs, *Am:* mɔːˈrɪʃiəs] *n* Mauricio *m*

mausoleum [ˌmɔːsəˈliːəm, *Am:* ˌmɑː-] *n* mausoleo *m*

mauve [məʊv, *Am:* moʊv] *adj* malva

maverick [ˈmævərɪk, *Am:* ˈmævɚ-] *n* **1.** *Am* ZOOL res *f* sin marcar **2.** (*person*) inconformista *mf*

mawkish [ˈmɔːkɪʃ, *Am:* ˈmɑː-] *adj* (*sentimental*) empalagoso, -a *fig*

max. *inf abbr of* **maximum** máx.

maxim [ˈmæksɪm] *n* máxima *f*

maximal [ˈmæksɪməl] *adj form* máximo, -a

maximise *vt Brit, Aus,* **maximize** [ˈmæksɪmaɪz] *vt* maximizar

maximum [ˈmæksɪməm] **I.** *n* máximo *m;* **to do sth to the ~** hacer algo al máximo; **to reach a ~** llegar al máximo **II.** *adj* máximo, -a; **this car has a ~ speed of 160 km/h** este coche alcanza una velocidad máxima de 160 km/h

maximum security prison *n* prisión *f* de máxima seguridad

may¹ [meɪ] <might, might> *aux* **1.** *form* (*be allowed*) poder; **~ I come in?** ¿puedo pasar?; **~ I ask you a question?** ¿puedo hacerte una pregunta?; **what time will we arrive? – you ~ well ask!** ¿a qué hora llegaremos? – ¡eso quisiera saber yo! **2.** (*possibility*) ser posible; **it ~ rain** puede que llueva; **that's as ~ be, be that as it ~** en cualquier caso **3.** (*hope, wish*) **~ she rest in peace** que en paz descanse

may² [meɪ] *n* (*bush*) espino *m;* (*flower*) flor *f* de espino

May [meɪ] *n* mayo; *s. a.* **April**

maybe [ˈmeɪbiː] **I.** *adv* **1.** (*perhaps*) quizás **2.** (*approximately*) probablemente; **~ as many as two hundred people** unas doscientas personas **II.** *n* quizás *m;* **a definite ~** un quizás definitivo

mayday [ˈmeɪdeɪ] *n* S.O.S. *m*

May Day *n* Primero *m* de mayo

> El **May Day** (1 de mayo) se celebra en algunas partes de Gran Bretaña con el **morris dancing**. En algunos patios de colegios y pueblos se levanta un **maypole** (árbol de mayo) que es adornado con cintas de colores. Cada persona baila cogida a una de esas cintas unos detrás de otros, formándose así un bonito dibujo en torno al árbol.

mayfly [ˈmeɪflaɪ] *n* <-ies> cachipolla *f*

mayhem [ˈmeɪhem] *n no pl* caos *m inv;* **it was ~** era un caos total

mayo [ˈmeɪəʊ, *Am:* -oʊ] *n Am, inf abbr of* **mayonnaise** mayonesa *f*

mayonnaise [ˌmeɪəˈneɪz] *n* mayonesa *f*

mayor [meəʳ, *Am:* meɪɚ] *n* alcalde *m*

mayoress [meəˈres, *Am:* ˈmeɪɚɪs] <-es> *n* alcaldesa *f*

maypole [ˈmeɪpəʊl, *Am:* -poʊl] *n* mayo *m* (*palo*)

may've *inf* = **may have** *s.* **may**

maze [meɪz] *n* laberinto *m*

MB [ˌemˈbiː] *abbr of* **megabyte** MB

MBA [ˌembiːˈeɪ] *n abbr of* **Master of Business Administration** máster *m* en administración de empresas

MC [ˌemˈsiː] *n* **1.** *abbr of* **Master of Ceremonies** maestro, -a *m, f* de ceremonias **2.** *abbr of* **Member of Congress** diputado, -a *m, f* del Congreso (de los Estados Unidos)

MD [ˌem'diː] *n* 1. *abbr of* **managing director** director(a) *m(f)* gerente 2. *abbr of* **Doctor of Medicine** Dr. *m*, Dra. *f*
me [miː] *pron* 1. me; **look at ~** mírame; **she saw ~** me vió; **he told ~ that ...** me dijo que...; **he gave ~ the pencil** me dió el lápiz 2. (*after verb 'to be'*) yo; **it's ~** soy yo; **she is older than ~** ella es mayor que yo 3. (*after prep*) mí; **is this for ~?** ¿es para mí esto?
meadow ['medəʊ, *Am:* -oʊ] *n* pradera *f*
meager *adj Am,* **meagre** ['miːgəʳ, *Am:* -gɚ] *adj* escaso, -a
meal¹ [miːl] *n* comida *f;* **a heavy/light ~** una comida pesada/liviana; **to go out for a ~** comer/cenar fuera; **~s on wheels** *Brit: distribución de comida a domicilio para gente necesitada o imposibilitada* ▸**to make a ~ of sth** hacer una montaña de algo
meal² [miːl] *n* (*flour*) harina *f*
meal ticket *n* 1. *Am, Aus* (*luncheon voucher*) vale *m* de comida 2. *fig* (*means of living*) fuente *f* de ingresos; **he's her latest ~** es el que la mantiene últimamente
mealtime ['miːltaɪm] *n* hora *f* de comer
mealy ['miːli] *adj* <-ier, -iest> harinoso, -a
mealy-mouthed [ˌmiːli'maʊðd, *Am:* 'miːli-maʊðd] *adj* camandulero, -a; **he's too ~** anda con demasiados rodeos
mean¹ [miːn] *adj* 1. (*miserly*) tacaño, -a, amarrado, -a *Arg, Par, PRico, Urug;* **to be ~ with sth** ser mezquino con algo 2. (*unkind*) vil; **to be ~ to sb** tratar mal a alguien; **to have a ~ streak** tener muy mala uva 3. (*bad*) malo, -a; **he's no ~ cook** *inf* es un excelente cocinero 4. (*humble*) pobre 5. *inf* (*excellent*) excelente
mean² [miːn] <meant, meant> *vt* 1. (*signify: word, event*) significar; **does that name ~ anything to you?** ¿te suena ese nombre? 2. (*express, indicate: person*) querer decir; **what do you ~?** ¿a qué te refieres?; **what do you ~, it was my fault?** ¿quieres decir que fue mi culpa?; **I ~ what I say** pienso lo que digo 3. (*intend for particular purpose*) destinar; **to be meant for sth** estar destinado a algo; **to be meant for each other** estar hechos el uno para el otro 4. (*intend*) pretender; **to ~ to do sth** tener la intención de hacer algo; **what do you ~ by arriving so late?** ¿qué te propones al llegar tan tarde?; **to ~ mischief** proponerse alguna travesura; **to ~ well** tener buenas intenciones; **I ~ to say ...** quiero decir...
meander [mɪ'ændəʳ, *Am:* -dɚ] **I.** *n* meandro *m* **II.** *vi* 1. (*flow*) serpentear 2. *fig* (*wander*) vagar; (*digress*) divagar
meandering [mɪ'ændərɪŋ] *adj* 1. (*river*) sinuoso, -a 2. (*explanation*) confuso, -a
meanie [miːni] *n inf* 1. (*miserly person*) avaro, -a *m, f* 2. (*nasty person*) malo, -a *m, f*
meaning ['miːnɪŋ] *n* significado *m;* **to give sth a whole new ~** dar a algo un significado completamente nuevo; **what is the ~ of this?** ¿qué significa esto?; **if you take my ~** *Brit* si entiendes lo que digo, ya me entiendes; **the full ~ of sth** el sentido completo de algo; **to have ~ for sb** tener significado para alguien
meaningful ['miːnɪŋfəl] *adj* 1. (*difference, change*) significativo, -a 2. (*look, smile*) expresivo, -a
meaningless ['miːnɪŋləs] *adj* sin sentido
meanness ['miːnnɪs] *n no pl* 1. (*lack of generosity*) mezquindad *f* 2. (*unkindness*) bajeza *f*
means [miːnz] *n* 1. (*instrument, method*) medio *m;* **~ of communication/transport** medio de comunicación/transporte 2. *pl* (*resources*) medios *mpl;* **~ of support** medios de subsistencia; **ways and ~** medios y arbitrios; **by ~ of sth** por medio de algo; **to try by all (possible) ~ to do sth** intentar hacer algo por todos los medios; **to use all ~ at one's disposal** usar todos los medios a su alcance 3. *pl* (*income*) recursos *mpl;* **a person of ~** una persona acaudalada; **private ~** fondos *mpl* privados; **to be without ~** *form* estar sin recursos; **to live beyond one's ~** vivir por encima de sus posibilidades ▸**by all ~!** ¡por supuesto!; **by no ~** de ninguna manera
means test *n* FIN investigación *f* de los recursos económicos
meant [ment] *pt, pp of* **mean**
meantime ['miːntaɪm] **I.** *adv* mientras tanto **II.** *n* **in the ~** mientras tanto
meanwhile ['miːnwaɪl] *adv* mientras tanto
meany ['miːni] *n inf s.* **meanie**
measles ['miːzlz] *n* sarampión *m*
measly ['miːzli] *adj* <-ier, -iest> miserable
measurable ['meʒərəbl] *adj* 1. (*quantifiable*) medible 2. (*perceptible*) apreciable
measure ['meʒəʳ, *Am:* -ɚ] **I.** *n* 1. (*size*) medida *f;* **to get the ~ of sb** tomar la medida a alguien 2. (*measuring instrument*) metro *m;* (*ruler*) regla *f* 3. (*proof*) medición *f* 4. (*degree, amount*) grado *m;* **there was some ~ of truth in what he said** hubo algo de cierto en lo que él dijo; **in some ~** hasta cierto punto 5. *pl* (*action*) medidas *fpl;* **to take ~s to do sth** tomar medidas para hacer algo 6. LIT metro *m* 7. MUS compás *m* ▸**for good ~** por añadidura; **beyond ~** excesivamente **II.** *vt* medir; **to ~ sth in centimetres/weeks** calcular algo en centímetros/semanas **III.** *vi* medir; **the box ~s 10cm by 10cm by 12cm** la caja mide 10 cm por 10 cm por 12 cm
◆**measure out** *vt* 1. (*weigh*) pesar 2. (*measure length*) medir
◆**measure up** *vi* dar la talla; **to measure up to sth** estar a la altura de algo
measured *adj* (*voice, tone*) comedido, -a; (*response*) moderado, -a
measurement ['meʒəmənt, *Am:* 'meʒɚ-] *n* 1. *no pl* (*act of measuring*) medición *f* 2. (*size*) medida *f;* **to take sb's ~s** tomar a alguien las medidas

measuring cup *n Am, Aus* vaso *m* medidor **measuring jug** *n Brit* jarra *f* graduada **measuring spoon** *n* cuchara *f* medidora

meat [miːt] *n no pl* **1.** carne *f* **2.** *no pl, fig* (*subject matter*) sustancia *f* ►**to be ~ and drink to sb** ser pan comido para alguien; **one man's ~ is another man's poison** *prov* lo que a uno cura a otro mata *prov*

meat-and-potatoes [ˌmiːtəndpəˈteɪtəʊz, *Am:* -pəˈteɪt̬oʊz] *n Am, inf* lo básico **meatball** *n* albóndiga *f* **meat cleaver** *n* cuchilla *f* de carnicero **meat grinder** *n Am* picadora *f* de carne **meat hook** *n* gancho *m* de carnicería **meat loaf** *n* pastel *m* de carne **meat pie** *n* empanada *f* de carne **meat products** *npl* productos *mpl* cárnicos

mecca *n,* **Mecca** [ˈmekə] *n* **1.** REL La Meca **2.** *fig* meca *f*

mechanic [mɪˈkænɪk] *n* mecánico, -a *m, f*

mechanical *adj* **1.** (*relating to machines*) mecánico, -a **2.** (*without thinking*) maquinal

mechanical engineer *n* ingeniero, -a *m, f* mecánico,-a **mechanical engineering** *n no pl* ingeniería *f* mecánica **mechanical pencil** *n Am* portaminas *mpl*

mechanics [mɪˈkænɪks] *npl* **1.** AUTO, TECH mecánica *f* **2.** *inf* (*how things are organized*) mecanismo *m*

mechanise [ˈmekənaɪz] *vt Brit, Aus s.* **mechanize**

mechanism [ˈmekənɪzəm] *n* mecanismo *m*

mechanize [ˈmekənaɪz] *vt* mecanizar

Med [med] *n inf abbr of* **Mediterranean the ~** el Mar Mediterráneo

med. *adj abbr of* **medium** mediano, -a

medal [ˈmedl] *n* medalla *f*

medallion [mɪˈdælɪən, *Am:* məˈdæljən] *n* medallón *m*

medal(l)ist [ˈmedəlɪst] *n* medallista *mf*

meddle [ˈmedl] *vi* **to ~ in sth** meterse en algo

meddlesome [ˈmedlsəm] *adj* entrometido, -a, metiche *Méx,* toposo, -a *Ven*

media [ˈmiːdiə] *n* **1.** *pl of* **medium 2. the ~** los medios; **the mass ~** los medios de comunicación de masas; **a ~ event** un acontecimiento mediático

mediaeval [ˌmediˈiːvəl] *adj s.* **medieval**

median [ˈmiːdiən] *adj* mediano, -a

median strip *n Am, Aus* AUTO raya *f* divisoria

media studies *n* ≈ estudios *mpl* de comunicación audiovisual

mediate [ˈmiːdɪeɪt] **I.** *vi* mediar; **to ~ between two groups** mediar entre dos grupos; **to ~ in sth** mediar en algo **II.** *vt* **to ~ a settlement** hacer de intermediario en un acuerdo

mediation [ˌmiːdɪˈeɪʃən] *n no pl* mediación *f*

mediator [ˈmiːdɪeɪtəʳ, *Am:* -t̬ɚ] *n* mediador(a) *m(f)*

medic [ˈmedɪk] *n* **1.** *inf* (*doctor*) médico, -a *m, f* **2.** (*student*) estudiante *mf* de medicina

Medicaid [ˈmedɪkeɪd] *n no pl, Am: programa de asistencia sanitaria gratuita para personas con pocos ingresos*

medical [ˈmedɪkəl] **I.** *adj* médico, -a **II.** *n inf* reconocimiento *m* médico

medical certificate *n* certificado *m* médico **medical examination** *n* reconocimiento *m* médico **medical history** *n* historial *m* clínico

medicament [mɪˈdɪkəmənt] *n* medicamento *m*

Medicare [ˈmedɪkeəʳ, *Am:* -ker] *n Am: programa de asistencia sanitaria para personas mayores de 65 años*

medicate [ˈmedɪkeɪt] *vt* (*treat medically*) medicar

medicated *adj* (*soap, shampoo*) medicinal

medication [ˌmedɪˈkeɪʃən] <-(s)> *n* medicamento *m*

medicinal [məˈdɪsɪnəl] *adj* medicinal

medicine [ˈmedsən, *Am:* ˈmedɪsən] *n* **1.** (*substance*) medicamento *m;* **to take (one's) ~** tomarse su medicina **2.** *no pl* (*medical knowledge*) medicina *f* **3.** (*remedy*) remedio *m* ►**to give sb a taste of his own ~** pagar a alguien con su misma moneda; **to take one's ~** sufrir las consecuencias

medicine ball *n* balón *m* medicinal **medicine chest** *n* botiquín *m* **medicine man** *n* <-men> hechicero *m*

medieval [ˌmedɪˈiːvl, *Am:* ˌmiːdɪ-] *adj* medieval

mediocre [ˌmiːdɪˈəʊkəʳ, *Am:* -ˈoʊkɚ] *adj* mediocre

mediocrity [ˌmiːdɪˈɒkrəti, *Am:* -ˈɑːkrət̬i] *n no pl* **1.** (*person*) mediocre *mf* **2.** (*quality*) mediocridad *f*

meditate [ˈmedɪteɪt] **I.** *vi* **1.** (*engage in contemplation*) meditar **2.** (*think deeply*) reflexionar; **to ~ on sth** reflexionar sobre algo **II.** *vt* (*plan: revenge*) planear

meditation [ˌmedɪˈteɪʃən] *n no pl* meditación *f*

Mediterranean [ˌmedɪtəˈreɪniən] **I.** *n* Mediterráneo *m* **II.** *adj* mediterráneo, -a

Mediterranean Sea *n* mar *m* Mediterráneo

medium [ˈmiːdiəm] **I.** *adj* mediano, -a **II.** *n* **1.** <media *o* -s> (*method*) medio *m;* **through the ~ of** por medio de **2.** *no pl* INFOR soporte *m;* **data ~** soporte de datos **3.** <-s> (*spiritualist*) médium *mf*

medium-dry *adj* semi seco, -a **medium-rare** *adj* GASTR poco hecho, -a **medium-sized** *adj* mediano, -a **medium-term** *adj* a medio plazo **medium wave** *n Brit* RADIO onda *f* media

medley [ˈmedli] *n* **1.** (*mixture*) mezcla *f* **2.** MUS popurrí *m*

meek [miːk] *adj* manso, -a

meet [miːt] <met, met> **I.** *vt* **1.** (*encounter*) encontrarse con; (*intentionally*) reunirse con; (*for first time*) conocer a; **to arrange to ~ sb** quedar con alguien **2.** (*wait for: at station, airport*) ir a buscar a alguien **3.** (*confront: oppo-*

nent) enfrentarse con; (*problem*) tropezar con **4.** (*fulfil*) reunir; (*cost*) correr con; (*demand*) atender; (*obligation*) cumplir **II.** *vi* **1.** (*encounter*) encontrarse; (*intentionally*) reunirse; (*for first time*) conocerse; **to arrange to ~** quedar **2.** (*join: lines*) unirse; (*rivers*) confluir **3.** SPORTS enfrentarse **III.** *n* **1.** (*sporting event*) encuentro *m* **2.** *Brit* (*fox hunt*) cacería *f*
◆**meet with** *vt insep* reunirse con; **to ~ an accident** sufrir un accidente; **to ~ success** tener éxito; **to meet force with force** combatir la fuerza con la fuerza

meeting ['mi:tɪŋ, *Am:* -t̬ɪŋ] *n* **1.** (*gathering*) reunión *f;* **to call a ~** convocar una reunión **2.** POL mitin *m* **3.** (*casual*) *a.* SPORTS encuentro *m*

meeting point *n* punto *m* de encuentro

megabyte ['megəbaɪt] *n* INFOR megabyte *m*

megahertz ['megəhɜ:ts, *Am:* -hɜ:rts] *n* ELEC megahercio *m*

megalomania [ˌmegələ'meɪnɪə, *Am:* -oʊ'-] *n* megalomanía *f*

megalomaniac [ˌmegələ'meɪnɪæk, *Am:* -oʊ'-] *n* megalómano, -a *m, f*

megaphone ['megəfəʊn, *Am:* -foʊn] *n* megáfono *m*

megastore ['megəstɔ:ʳ, *Am:* -stɔ:r] *n* gran almacén *m*

megawatt ['megəwɒt, *Am:* -wɑ:t] *n* megavatio *m*

melancholia [ˌmelən'kəʊlɪə, *Am:* -'koʊ-] *n no pl* melancolía *f*

melancholic [ˌmeləŋ'kɒlɪk, *Am:* -'kɑ:lɪk] *adj* melancólico, -a

melancholy ['meləŋkɒli, *Am:* -kɑ:li] **I.** *n no pl* melancolía *f* **II.** *adj* melancólico, -a

> La **Melbourne Cup** (Copa), es una de las competiciones hípicas más populares entre los australianos. Siempre tiene lugar el primer martes del mes de noviembre. Las apuestas alcanzan varios millones de dólares. Ese día todo el país se pone sus mejores galas y a mediodía se sirve pollo con champán.

melee ['meleɪ, *Am:* 'meɪleɪ] *n* **1.** (*fight*) riña *f* **2.** (*crowd*) enjambre *m*

mellow ['meləʊ, *Am:* -loʊ] **I.** *adj* <-er, -est> **1.** (*light: voice*) suave; (*flavour*) dulce **2.** (*mature: wine*) añejo, -a **3.** (*relaxed*) tranquilo, -a **II.** *vi* (*person, fruit*) madurar; (*voice, colour*) suavizarse **III.** *vt* **1.** (*wine*) añejar **2.** (*make less severe*) suavizar

melodic [mə'lɒdɪk, *Am:* mə'lɑ:dɪk] *adj* melódico, -a

melodious [mɪ'ləʊdiəs, *Am:* mə'loʊ-] *adj* melodioso, -a

melodrama ['melədrɑ:mə, *Am:* -oʊ-] *n* melodrama *m*

melodramatic [ˌmelədrə'mætɪk, *Am:* -oʊdrə'mæt̬-] *adj* melodramático, -a

melody ['melədi] <-ies> *n* melodía *f*

melon ['melən] *n* melón *m;* (*watermelon*) sandía *f*

melt [melt] **I.** *vt* (*metal*) fundir; (*ice, chocolate*) derretir **II.** *vi* **1.** (*metal*) fundirse; (*ice, chocolate*) derretirse **2.** *fig* enternecerse

meltdown ['meltdaʊn] *n* fusión *f*

melting point *n* punto *m* de fusión **melting pot** *n a. fig* crisol *m*

member ['membəʳ, *Am:* -bɚ] *n* miembro *mf;* (*of society, club*) socio, -a *m, f*

member of parliament *n* POL diputado, -a *m, f*

membership *n* **1.** (*state of belonging*) calidad *f* de miembro; (*to society, club*) calidad *f* de socio; **to apply for ~ of a club** solicitar ingreso en un club; **~ dues** cuotas *fpl* de socio **2.** (*number of members*) número *m* de miembros

membership card *n* carnet *m*

membrane ['membreɪn] *n* membrana *f*

memento [mɪ'mentəʊ, *Am:* mə'mentoʊ] <-s *o* -es> *n* recuerdo *m*

memo ['meməʊ, *Am:* -oʊ] *n abbr of* **memorandum** **1.** (*message*) memorándum *m* **2.** (*note*) nota *f*

memoir ['memwɑ:ʳ, *Am:* -wɑ:r] *n* **1.** (*record of events*) memoria *f* **2.** *pl* (*autobiography*) memorias *fpl*

memo pad *n* bloc *m* de notas

memorabilia [ˌmemərə'bɪlia] *npl* recuerdos *mpl*

memorable ['memərəbl] *adj* memorable

memorandum [ˌmemə'rændəm] <-s *o* -anda> *n form* **1.** (*message*) memorándum *m* **2.** (*note*) nota *f*

memorial [mə'mɔ:riəl] *n* monumento *m* conmemorativo

Memorial Day *n no pl, Am, Can* Día *m* de los Caídos

memorize ['meməraɪz] *vt* memorizar

memory ['meməri] <-ies> *n* **1.** (*ability to remember*) memoria *f;* **to recite sth from ~** recitar algo de memoria; **if my ~ serves me correctly** si la memoria no me falla **2.** (*remembered event*) recuerdo *m;* **to bring back memories** evocar recuerdos **3.** INFOR memoria *f;* **internal/external/core ~** memoria interna/externa/del núcleo; **cache ~** memoria (intermedia) del caché; **read only ~** memoria sólo de lectura; **random access ~** memoria de acceso directo

memory bank *n* INFOR banco *m* de memoria **memory capacity** <-ies> *n* INFOR capacidad *f* de memoria **memory chip** *n* INFOR chip *m* de memoria **memory dump** *n* INFOR vaciado *m* de la memoria **memory expansion card** *n* INFOR tarjeta *f* de expansión de memoria **memory management** *n no pl* INFOR administración *f* de memoria **memory protection** *n no pl* INFOR protección *f* de memoria

men [men] *n pl of* **man**

menace ['menəs] **I.** *n* **1.** (*threat*) amenaza *f* **2.** (*child*) demonio *m*, peligro *m* **II.** *vt* amenazar

menacing *adj* amenazador(a)

menacingly *adv* de modo amenazador

mend [mend] **I.** *n* **1.** (*repair*) reparación *f* **2.** (*patch*) remiendo *m* **3.** *inf* **to be on the ~** ir mejorando **II.** *vt* **1.** (*repair*) reparar **2.** (*darn: socks*) zurcir **III.** *vi* (*improve*) mejorar; (*broken bone*) soldarse

mendacious [men'deɪʃəs] *adj* falso, -a

mendacity [men'dæsəti, *Am:* -t̬i] *n no pl* falsedad *f*

mending ['mendɪŋ] *n no pl* **1.** (*repair*) reparación *f* **2.** (*darning*) zurcido *m* **3.** (*clothes*) ropa *f* por remendar

menial ['miːnɪəl] *adj* de baja categoría

meningitis [ˌmenɪn'dʒaɪtɪs, *Am:* -t̬ɪs] *n no pl* meningitis *f*

menopause ['menəpɔːz, *Am:* -pɑːz] *n no pl* menopausia *f*

men's room ['menzˌruːm] *n Am* lavabo *m* de hombres

menstrual ['menstrʊəl, *Am:* -strəl] *adj* menstrual

menstruate ['menstrʊeɪt, *Am:* -stru-] *vi* menstruar

menstruation [ˌmenstrʊ'eɪʃən, *Am:* -stru'-] *n no pl* menstruación *f*

mental ['mentəl, *Am:* -t̬əl] *adj* **1.** (*of the mind*) mental **2.** *Brit, inf* (*crazy*) chiflado, -a

mental arithmetic *n no pl* cálculo *m* mental **mental hospital** *n* hospital *m* psiquiátrico **mental illness** *n* <-es> enfermedad *f* mental

mentality [men'tæləti, *Am:* -t̬i] <-ies> *n* mentalidad *f*

mentally *adv* mentalmente; **~ disturbed** trastornado, -a

mentally handicapped *adj* **to be ~** tener una minusvalía psíquica

menthol ['menθɒl, *Am:* -θɔːl] *n no pl* mentol *m*

mention ['menʃən] **I.** *n* mención *f;* **to receive a (special) ~** obtener una mención (especial); **to make ~ of sth** mencionar algo **II.** *vt* mencionar; **don't ~ it!** ¡no hay de qué!; **not to ~ ...** sin contar...

mentor ['mentɔːʳ, *Am:* -tɚ] *n* mentor(a) *m(f)*

menu ['menjuː] *n* **1.** (*list of dishes*) carta *f;* (*fixed meal*) menú *m* **2.** INFOR menú *m;* **context/pull-down ~** menú contextual/desplegable

menu-bar *n* barra *f* de menús **menu-driven** *adj* INFOR guiado, -a por menús

MEP [ˌemiː'piː] *n abbr of* **Member of the European Parliament** eurodiputado, -a *m, f*

mercenary ['mɜːsɪnəri, *Am:* 'mɜːrsəner-] **I.** *n* <-ies> mercenario, -a *m, f* **II.** *adj* mercenario, -a

merchandise ['mɜːtʃəndaɪz, *Am:* 'mɜːr-] *n no pl* mercancía *f*

merchant ['mɜːtʃənt, *Am:* 'mɜːr-] *n* comerciante *mf*

merchant bank *n* banco *m* mercantil **merchantman** <-men> *n* buque *m* mercante **merchant navy** *n no pl* marina *f* mercante **merchant ship** *n* mercante *m*

merciful ['mɜːsɪfəl, *Am:* 'mɜːr-] *adj* misericordioso, -a

merciless ['mɜːsɪlɪs, *Am:* 'mɜːr-] *adj* despiadado, -a

mercurial [mɜː'kjʊərɪəl, *Am:* mɜːr'kjʊrɪ-] *adj* **1.** CHEM mercurial **2.** (*changeable*) voluble; (*weather*) cambiante **3.** (*lively*) vivo, -a

mercury ['mɜːkjʊri, *Am:* 'mɜːrkjəri] *n no pl* mercurio *m*

Mercury ['mɜːkjʊri, *Am:* 'mɜːrkjəri] *n no pl* Mercurio *m*

mercy ['mɜːsi, *Am:* 'mɜːr-] *n no pl* **1.** (*compassion*) compasión *f;* **to have ~ on sb** tener compasión de alguien **2.** (*forgiveness*) misericordia *f;* **to be at the ~ of sb** estar a merced de alguien; **to throw oneself upon sb's ~** abandonarse a la merced de uno; **to plead for ~** pedir clemencia

mere [mɪəʳ, *Am:* mɪr] *adj* mero, -a; **a ~ detail** un simple detalle

merely ['mɪəli, *Am:* 'mɪr-] *adv* solamente

merge [mɜːdʒ, *Am:* mɜːrdʒ] **I.** *vi* unirse; ECON, POL fusionarse; **to ~ into sth** fundirse con algo **II.** *vt* unir; ECON, POL, INFOR fusionar

merger ['mɜːdʒəʳ, *Am:* 'mɜːrdʒɚ] *n* ECON fusión *f*

meridian [mə'rɪdɪən] *n* meridiano *m*

meringue [mə'ræŋ] *n* merengue *m,* espumilla *f Ecua, Guat, Hond*

merit ['merɪt] **I.** *n* **1.** (*virtue*) cualidad *f* **2.** (*advantage*) ventaja *f* **3.** *pl* (*commendable quality or act*) mérito *m* **II.** *vt* merecer

meritocracy [ˌmerɪ'tɒkrəsi, *Am:* -ə'tɑːkrə-] <-ies> *n* meritocracia *f*

mermaid ['mɜːmeɪd, *Am:* 'mɜːr-] *n* sirena *f*

merriment ['merɪmənt] *n no pl* **1.** (*laughter and joy*) regocijo *m* **2.** (*amusement*) alegría *f*

merry ['meri] <-ier, -iest> *adj* **1.** (*happy*) alegre **2.** *Brit, inf* (*slightly drunk*) achispado, -a

merry-go-round ['merigəʊˌraʊnd, *Am:* -goʊˌ-] *n* tiovivo *m*

mesh [meʃ] **I.** *n no pl* malla *f;* **wire ~** red *f* de alambrado **II.** *vi* engranar **III.** *vt* hacer engranar

mesmeric [mez'merɪk] *adj* hipnótico, -a

mesmerism ['mezmərɪzəm] *n no pl* hipnosis *f inv*

mesmerize ['mezməraɪz] *vt* hipnotizar

mess [mes] <-es> *n* **1.** *no pl* (*confusion*) confusión *f;* (*disorganized state*) desorden *m;* **to be in a ~** (*things*) estar revuelto; (*person*) estar hecho un lío; **to make a ~ of sth** echar a perder algo; (*things*) desordenar algo **2.** *no pl* (*trouble*) lío *m,* merengue *m Arg* **3.** (*dirt*) suciedad *f* **4.** *no pl, inf* (*animal excrement*) caca *f* **5.** *Brit* MIL (*dining hall*) comedor *m*

◆**mess about** **I.** *vi* hacer el tonto **II.** *vt always sep* tratar mal

◆**mess up** *vt inf* **1.** (*make untidy*) desordenar **2.** (*dirty*) ensuciar **3.** (*botch up*) desarreglar

◆**mess with** *vi inf* **to ~ sb** meterse con alguien; **to ~ sth** interferir con algo

message ['mesɪdʒ] *n* mensaje *m;* **error ~** INFOR mensaje *m* de error

messenger ['mesɪndʒəʳ, *Am:* -dʒɚ] *n* mensajero, -a *m, f*

messenger boy *n* recadero *m*

messiah [mə'saɪə] *n* mesías *m inv*

mess-up ['mesʌp] *n inf* follón *m*

messy ['mesi] <-ier, -iest> *adj* **1.** (*untidy*) desordenado, -a **2.** (*dirty*) sucio, -a **3.** (*unpleasant*) desagradable; **~ business** asunto *m* turbio

met [met] *vi, vt pt of* **meet**

met. *abbr of* **meteorological** meteor.

metabolic [ˌmetə'bɒlɪk, *Am:* ˌmet̬ə'bɑːlɪk] *adj* metabólico, -a

metabolism [mɪ'tæbəlɪzəm] *n* metabolismo *m*

metal ['metl, *Am:* 'met̬-] **I.** *n* **1.** (*element*) metal *m* **2.** *Brit* (*road*) grava *f* **3.** *pl, Brit* RAIL rieles *mpl* **II.** *adj* metálico, -a **III.** *vt* (*road*) engravar

metallic [mɪ'tælɪk, *Am:* mə'-] *adj* metálico, -a

metallurgy [mət'ælədʒi, *Am:* 'mət̬əlɜːr-] *n no pl* metalurgia *f*

metalwork ['metəlwɜːk, *Am:* 'met̬əlwɜːrk] *n no pl* metalistería *f* **metalworker** *n* metalista *mf*

metamorphosis [ˌmetə'mɔːfəsɪs, *Am:* ˌmet̬ə'mɔːrfə-] <-es> *n* metamorfosis *f inv*

metaphor ['metəfəʳ, *Am:* 'met̬əfɔːr] *n* metáfora *f*

metaphorical [ˌmetə'fɒrɪkl, *Am:* ˌmet̬ə-'fɔːr-] *adj* metafórico, -a

metaphysical [ˌmetə'fɪzɪkl, *Am:* ˌmet̬-] *adj* metafísico, -a

metaphysics [ˌmetə'fɪzɪks, *Am:* ˌmet̬-] *n* metafísica *f*

metastasis [mɪ'tæstəsɪs, *Am:* mə'-] <-ses> *n* metástasis *f inv*

mete [ˌmiːt] *vt* **to ~ out** (*punishment*) imponer

meteor ['miːtiəʳ, *Am:* -t̬iɚ] *n* meteoro *m*

meteoric [ˌmiːti'ɒrɪk, *Am:* -t̬i'ɔːr-] *adj a. fig* meteórico, -a

meteorite ['miːtiəraɪt, *Am:* -t̬i-] *n* meteorito *m*

meteorological [ˌmiːtiərə'lɒdʒɪkəl, *Am:* -t̬iɚə'lɑːdʒɪ-] *adj* meteorológico, -a

meteorologist [ˌmiːtiə'rɒlədʒɪst, *Am:* -t̬iə'rɑːl-] *n* meteorólogo, -a *m, f*

meteorology [ˌmiːtiə'rɒlədʒi, *Am:* -ə'rɑːlə-] *n no pl* meteorología *f*

meter¹ ['miːtəʳ, *Am:* -t̬ɚ] *n* contador *m*, medidor *m AmL;* (**parking**) **~** parquímetro *m;* (**taxi**) **~** taxímetro *m*

meter² ['miːtəʳ, *Am:* -t̬ɚ] *n Am s.* **metre**

methane ['miːθeɪn, *Am:* 'meθeɪn] *n* metano *m*

method ['meθəd] *n* método *m;* **there's ~ in his madness** no está tan loco como parece

methodical [mɪ'θɒdɪkl, *Am:* mə'θɑːdɪk-] *adj* metódico, -a

Methodism ['meθədɪzəm] *n* metodismo *m*

Methodist **I.** *n* metodista *mf* **II.** *adj* metodista

methodology [ˌmeθə'dɒlədʒi, *Am:* -'dɑːlə-] *n* metodología *f*

Methuselah [mɪ'θjuːzələ, *Am:* mə'θuː-] *n* Matusalén ►**as old as ~** más viejo que Matusalén

methyl alcohol ['meθɪl'ælkəhɒl, *Am:* -ɑɪl'ælkəhɑːl] *n* metanol *m* **methylated spirits** *n no pl, Aus, Brit* alcohol *m* desnaturalizado

meticulous [mɪ'tɪkjʊləs] *adj* meticuloso, -a, niquitoso, -a *Arg*

metre ['miːtəʳ, *Am:* -t̬ɚ] *n Brit, Aus* metro *m*

metric ['metrɪk] *adj* métrico, -a

metrical ['metrɪkl] *adj* métrico, -a

metro ['metrəʊ, *Am:* -roʊ] *n* RAIL metro *m*

metronome ['metrənəʊm, *Am:* -noʊm] *n* metrónomo *m*

metropolis [mə'trɒpəlɪs, *Am:* -'trɑːpəl-] <-es> *n* metrópoli *f*

metropolitan [ˌmetrə'pɒlɪtən, *Am:* -'pɑːlə-] *adj* metropolitano, -a

mettle ['metl, *Am:* 'met̬-] *n no pl, form* temple *m;* **to show one's ~** demostrar su brío; **to be on one's ~** mostrar todo lo que uno vale

mew [mjuː] **I.** *n* maullido *m* **II.** *vi* maullar

Mexican ['meksɪkən] **I.** *n* mexicano, -a *m, f* **II.** *adj* mexicano, -a

Mexico ['meksɪkəʊ, *Am:* -koʊ] *n no pl* México *m;* **New ~** Nuevo México

Mexico City *n* Ciudad *f* de México

Mg *abbr of* **magnesium** Mg

MHR *n Am abbr of* **Member of the House of Representatives** diputado, -a *m, f* del Congreso (de los Estados Unidos)

Mhz *abbr of* **megahertz** MHz

miaow [miː'aʊ] **I.** *n* miau *m* **II.** *vi* maullar

mica ['maɪkə] *n no pl* mica *f*

mice [maɪs] *n pl of* **mouse**

Michaelmas ['mɪklməs] *n* día *m* de San Miguel

mickey ['mɪki] *n Aus, Brit, inf* **to take the ~ out of sb** tomar el pelo a alguien

Mickey Mouse [ˌmɪki'maʊs] *n* ratoncito *m* Mickey, ratón *m* Miguelito *Méx*

MICR *n* INFOR *abbr of* **magnetic-ink character recognition** reconocimiento *m* de caracteres en tinta magnética

microbe ['maɪkrəʊb, *Am:* -kroʊb] *n* microbio *m*

microbiology [ˌmaɪkrəʊbaɪ'ɒlədʒi, *Am:* -kroʊbaɪ'ɑːlə-] *n no pl* microbiología *f*

microchip ['maɪkrəʊˌtʃɪp, *Am:* -kroʊ-] *n* microchip *m*

microclimate ['maɪkrəʊˌklaɪmɪt, *Am:* -kroʊ-] *n* microclima *m*

microcomputer ['maɪkrəʊkəm'pjuːtəʳ, *Am:* -kroʊkəmˌpjuːt̬ɚ] *n* microordenador *m*, microcomputadora *f AmL*

microcosm ['maɪkrəʊkɒzəm, *Am:* -kroʊkɑːzəm] *n* microcosmos *m inv*
microelectronics [ˌmaɪkrəʊˌɪlek'trɒnɪks, *Am:* -kroʊɪˌlek'trɑːnɪks] *n no pl* microelectrónica *f*
microfiche ['maɪkrəʊfiːʃ, *Am:* -kroʊ-] *n* microficha *f*
microfilm ['maɪkrəʊfɪlm, *Am:* -kroʊ-] *n* microfilm *m*
micrometer [maɪ'krɒmɪtə^r, *Am:* -'krɑːmət̬ɚ] *n* micrómetro *m*
Micronesia [ˌmaɪkrəʊ'niːziə, *Am:* -kroʊ'niʒə] *n* Micronesia *f*
microorganism [ˌmaɪkrəʊ'ɔːgənɪzəm, *Am:* -kroʊ'ɔːr-] *n* microorganismo *m*
microphone ['maɪkrəfəʊn, *Am:* -foʊn] *n* micrófono *m;* **to speak into a ~** hablar por micrófono
microprocessor [ˌmaɪkrə'prəʊsesə^r, *Am:* -kroʊˌprɑːsesɚ] *n* microprocesador *m*
microscope ['maɪkrəskəʊp, *Am:* -skoʊp] *n* microscopio *m*
microscopic [ˌmaɪkrə'skɒpɪk, *Am:* -'skɑːpɪk] *adj* microscópico, -a
microwave ['maɪkrəʊweɪv, *Am:* -kroʊ-] **I.** *n* **1.** (*wave*) microonda *f* **2.** (*oven*) microondas *m inv* **II.** *vt* poner en el microondas
microwave oven *n* microondas *m inv*
mid [mɪd] *prep* en medio de
midday [ˌmɪd'deɪ] **I.** *n no pl* mediodía *m;* **at ~** a mediodía; **~ meal** almuerzo *m*, comida *f* **II.** *adj* de mediodía
middle [mɪdl] **I.** *n* **1.** (*centre*) medio *m;* **in the ~ of sth** en medio de algo; **in the ~ of the night** en plena noche; **to be in the ~ of doing sth** estar ocupado haciendo algo; (**in**) **the ~ of nowhere** donde da la vuelta el viento; **in the ~ of the square** en el centro de la plaza **2.** *inf* (*waist*) cintura *f* **II.** *adj* **1.** (*equidistant*) central **2.** (*medium*) medio, -a
middle age *n* mediana edad *f* **middle-aged** *adj* de mediana edad **Middle Ages** *npl* Edad *f* Media
middlebrow ['mɪdlbraʊ] *adj* (*literature, music*) de nivel cultural medio
middle class *n* clase *f* media
middle-class *adj* de la clase media
middle ear *n* oído *m* medio
Middle East *n* Oriente *m* Medio
middleman ['mɪdlmæn] <-men> *n* intermediario *m*
middle name *n* segundo nombre *m*
middle-of-the-road *adj* moderado, -a
middleweight ['mɪdlweɪt] *n* SPORTS peso *m* medio
middling ['mɪdlɪŋ] **I.** *adj inf* **1.** (*average*) mediano, -a **2.** (*not very good*) regular **II.** *adv* regular
Mideast *n* Oriente *m* Medio
midge [mɪdʒ] *n mosca pequeña de picadura muy irritante*
midget ['mɪdʒɪt] **I.** *adj* en miniatura **II.** *n* enano, -a *m, f*
mid-life crisis [ˌmɪd'laɪf 'kraɪsɪs] *n* crisis *f inv* de los cuarenta
midnight ['mɪdnaɪt] **I.** *n no pl* medianoche *f* **II.** *adj* de medianoche
midpoint ['mɪdpɔɪnt] *n a.* MAT punto *m* medio
midriff ['mɪdrɪf] *n* ANAT diafragma *m*
midshipman ['mɪdʃɪpmən] <-men> *n Brit* guardia *m* marina
midships ['mɪdʃɪps] *adv* en medio del navío
midst [mɪdst] *n no pl* **in the ~ of** en medio de
midsummer [ˌmɪd'sʌmə^r, *Am:* -ɚ] *n no pl* pleno verano *m*
Midsummer('s) Day *n* día *m* de San Juan
midterm [ˌmɪd'tɜːm, *Am:* -'tɜːrm] *adj* UNIV (*exam*) de mitad del trimestre
midway [ˌmɪd'weɪ] **I.** *adv* a mitad del camino **II.** *n Am* avenida *f* central
midweek [ˌmɪd'wiːk] *adv* a mediados de semana
midwife ['mɪdwaɪf] <-wives> *n* comadrona *f*
midwifery ['mɪdwɪfri, *Am:* ˌmɪd'wɪfɚ-] *n no pl* partería *f*
midwinter [ˌmɪd'wɪntə^r, *Am:* -t̬ɚ] *n no pl* pleno invierno *m*
might[1] [maɪt] *pt of* **may it ~ be that ...** podría ser que... +*subj;* **how old ~ she be?** ¿qué edad tendrá?; **~ I open the window?** ¿podría abrir la ventana?
might[2] [maɪt] *n no pl* **1.** (*authority*) poder *m* **2.** (*strength*) fuerza *f;* **military ~** poderío *m* militar; **with all one's ~** con todas sus fuerzas ►**with ~ and main** a más no poder
mightily ['maɪtɪli, *Am:* 'maɪt̬ɪ-] *adv liter* fuertemente
mighty ['maɪti, *Am:* 'maɪt̬i] **I.** <-ier, -iest> *adj* **1.** (*powerful*) fuerte **2.** (*great*) enorme **II.** *adv Am, inf* enormemente
migraine ['miːgreɪn, *Am:* 'maɪ-] <-(s)> *n* migraña *f*
migrant ['maɪgrənt] **I.** *n* **1.** (*person*) emigrante *mf* **2.** ZOOL ave *f* migratoria **II.** *adj* migratorio, -a
migrant worker *n* trabajador(a) *m(f)* emigrante
migrate [maɪ'greɪt, *Am:* '--] *vi* emigrar
migration [maɪ'greɪʃən] <-(s)> *n* emigración *f*
migratory ['maɪgrətri, *Am:* -tɔːr-] *adj* migratorio, -a
mike [maɪk] *n inf abbr of* **microphone** micro *m*
mild [maɪld] **I.** <-er, -est> *adj* **1.** (*not severe*) apacible; (*criticism*) moderado, -a; (*penalty*) leve **2.** (*not strong tasting*) suave **3.** METEO templado, -a **4.** MED (*not serious*) benigno, -a **II.** *n no pl, Brit* cerveza *f* suave
mildew ['mɪldjuː, *Am:* -duː] *n no pl* moho *m*
mildly ['maɪdli] *adv* **1.** (*gently*) suavemente; **to punish sb ~** castigar a alguien de forma poco severa **2.** (*slightly*) ligeramente ►**to put**

M

it ~, that's putting it ~ por no decir algo peor
mildness ['maɪldnɪs] *n no pl* 1. (*placidity*) apacibilidad *f* 2. (*softness*) suavidad *f*
mile [maɪl] *n* milla *f* (*1,61 km*); **to walk for ~s** andar kilómetros y kilómetros; **to be ~s away** *fig* estar fuera de onda ►**to smell sth a ~ off** ver algo a la legua; **to stick** [*o* **stand**] **out a ~** verse a la legua
mileage ['maɪlɪdʒ] *n no pl* AUTO kilometraje *m*
mileometer [maɪ'lɒmɪtəʳ, *Am:* -'lɑːmət̬ɚ] *n Aus, Brit* cuentamillas *m inv*
milepost ['maɪlpəʊst] *n* mojón *m*
milestone ['maɪlstəʊn, *Am:* -stoʊn] *n* 1. (*marker*) mojón *m* 2. *fig* hito *m*
militant ['mɪlɪtənt] I. *adj* militante II. *n* militante *mf*
militarism ['mɪlɪtərɪzəm, *Am:* -tɚ-] *n no pl* militarismo *m*
militarist ['mɪlɪtərɪst, *Am:* -tɚ-] *n* militarista *mf*
militaristic [ˌmɪlɪtə'rɪstɪk] *adj* militarista
militarize ['mɪlɪtəraɪz] *vt* militarizar
military ['mɪlɪtri, *Am:* -ter-] I. *n* **the ~** los militares II. *adj* militar
military academy *n Am* academia *f* militar **military police** *n* policía *f* militar **military service** *n* servicio *m* militar
militia [mɪ'lɪʃə] *n* milicia *f*
milk [mɪlk] I. *n no pl* leche *f* ►**the ~ of human kindness** la compasión personificada; **there's no use crying over spilt ~** a lo hecho pecho II. *vt* 1. ordeñar 2. *fig* **to ~ sb dry** chupar la sangre a alguien
milk bar *n* cafetería *f* **milk chocolate** *n* chocolate *m* con leche **milk float** *n Brit* carro *m* de la leche
milking machine ['mɪlkɪŋməʃiːn] *n* ordeñador *m* automático
milkmaid *n* lechera *f* **milkman** <-men> *n* lechero *m* **milkshake** *n* batido *m* de leche, malteada *f Méx* **milksop** *n* marica *m* **milk tooth** *n* diente *m* de leche
milky ['mɪlki] <-ier, -iest> *adj* 1. (*colour, skin*) lechoso, -a 2. (*tea, coffee*) con mucha leche
Milky Way *n no pl* **the ~** la Vía Láctea
mill [mɪl] I. *n* 1. (*machine: for grain*) molino *m*; (*for coffee*) molinillo *m* 2. (*factory*) fábrica *f* (de tejidos) ►**to go through the ~** pasarlas moradas; **to put sb through the ~** someter a alguien a duras pruebas II. *vt* 1. (*grain, coffee*) moler 2. (*metal*) fresar
millennium [mɪ'lenɪəm] <-s *o* -ennia> *n* milenio *m*
miller ['mɪləʳ, *Am:* -ɚ] *n* molinero, -a *m, f*
millet ['mɪlət] *n no pl* mijo *m*
millibar ['mɪlɪbɑːʳ, *Am:* -bɑːr] *n* milibar *m*
milligram(me) ['mɪlɪgræm] *n* miligramo *m*
millilitre *n Am,* **milliliter** ['mɪlɪˌliːtəʳ, *Am:* -t̬ɚ] *n* mililitro *m*
millimetre *n Am,* **millimeter** ['mɪlɪˌmiːtəʳ, *Am:* -t̬ɚ] *n* milímetro *m*
milliner ['mɪlɪnəʳ, *Am:* -nɚ] *n* sombrerera *f*
millinery ['mɪlɪnəri, *Am:* -ner-] *n* sombrerería *f*
million ['mɪlɪən, *Am:* '-jən] <-(s)> *n* millón *m;* **two ~ people** dos millones de personas; **a ~ times** *inf* una infinidad de veces; **to be one in a ~** ser único
millionaire [ˌmɪlɪə'neəʳ, *Am:* -'ner] *n* millonario, -a *m, f*
millipede ['mɪlɪpiːd] *n* milpiés *m inv*
millpond *n* represa *f* de molino ►**as still as a ~** como una balsa de aceite **millstone** *n* piedra *f* de molino ►**to be a ~ round sb's neck** ser una cruz para alguien **mill wheel** *n* rueda *f* de molino
milt [mɪlt] *n* lecha *f*
mime [maɪm] I. *n* THEAT pantomima *f* II. *vi* actuar de mimo III. *vt* imitar
mime artist *n* mimo *mf*
mimic ['mɪmɪk] I. *vt* <-ck-> imitar II. *n* imitador(a) *m(f)*
mimicry ['mɪmɪkri] *n no pl* 1. (*art*) mímica *f;* (*imitation*) imitación *f* 2. BIO mimetismo *m*
mimosa [mɪ'məʊzə, *Am:* -'moʊsə] *n* mimosa *f*
min. 1. *abbr of* **minute** min. 2. *abbr of* **minimum** mín.
minaret [ˌmɪnə'ret] *n* alminar *m*
mince [mɪns] I. *vt* picar II. *vi* andar con pasos muy cortos III. *n no pl, Aus, Brit* carne *f* picada
mincemeat *n no pl Brit* (*meat*) carne *f* picada; (*fruit*) picadillo *m* de fruta ►**to make ~ of sb** *inf* hacer picadillo a alguien **mince pie** *n* pastel *m* de frutas picadas
mincer ['mɪnsəʳ, *Am:* -ɚ] *n* picadora *f* de carne
mincing ['mɪnsɪŋ] *adj* remilgado, -a, afectado, -a
mind [maɪnd] I. *n* 1. (*brain*) mente *f;* **to be in one's right ~** estar en sus cabales; **to be out of one's ~** estar fuera de juicio 2. (*thought*) pensamiento *m;* **to bear sth in ~** tener algo presente; **to bring sth to ~** recordar algo 3. (*intention*) intención *f;* **to change one's ~** cambiar de parecer; **to have sth in ~** tener pensado algo; **to have half a ~ to ...** estar casi por...; **to know one's own ~** saber lo que uno quiere; **to make up one's ~** decidirse; **to set one's ~ on sth** desear algo con vehemencia; **to set one's ~ to sth** estar resuelto a algo; **to set one's ~ at ease** tranquilizarse 4. (*consciousness*) conciencia *f;* **her mother is on her ~** está preocupada por su madre; **this will take your ~ off it** esto te distraerá 5. (*opinion*) opinión *f;* **to be of the same ~** ser de la misma opinión; **to give sb a piece of one's ~** cantar las cuarenta a alguien; **to be in two ~s** dudar entre dos cosas, estar en un dilema ►**in my ~'s eye** en mi imaginación; **it's a question of ~ over matter** es una cuestión que requiere fuerza de voluntad; **to have a ~ like a sewer** tener una mente cochambrosa II. *vt* 1. (*be careful of*) tener cui-

dado con; ~ **what you're doing!** ¡cuidado lo que haces!; ~ **the step!** ¡cuidado con la escalera! **2.** (*bother*) sentirse molesto por; **I don't ~ the cold** el frío no me molesta; **do you ~ my smoking?** ¿te molesta si fumo?; **would you ~ opening the window?** ¿haces el favor de abrir la ventana?; **I wouldn't ~ a beer** no vendría mal una cerveza **3.** (*look after*) estar al cuidado de; **don't ~ me** no te preocupes por mí ►**to ~ one's p's and q's** tener sumo cuidado en lo que uno dice **III.** *vi* **never ~!** ¡no importa!; **I don't ~** me es igual; **if you don't ~, I prefer ...** si no te importa, prefiero...; **would you ~ if ...** ¿le importa si...?

mind-bending ['maɪndbendɪŋ] *adj* increíble **mind-blowing** *adj inf* alucinante

minded *adj* dispuesto, -a; **to be ~ to** estar dispuesto a

minder ['maɪndəʳ, *Am:* -dɚ] *n* guardaespaldas *mf inv*

mindful ['maɪndfəl] *adj form* cuidadoso, -a; **to be ~ of sth** tener presente algo

mindless ['maɪndlɪs] *adj* **1.** (*job*) mecánico, -a **2.** (*violence*) gratuito, -a **3.** (*heedless*) descuidado, -a

mind reader *n* adivinador(a) *m(f)* de pensamientos

mine¹ [maɪn] *pron pos* (el) mío, (la) mía, (los) míos, (las) mías; **it's not his bag, it's ~** no es su bolsa, es la mía; **this glass is ~** este vaso es mío; **these are his shoes and those are ~** estos zapatos son suyos y estos (son) míos

mine² [maɪn] **I.** *n* MIN, MIL mina *f;* **a ~ of information** *fig* una fuente abundante de información **II.** *vt* **1.** MIN extraer **2.** MIL sembrar minas en

mine detector *n* detector *m* de minas

minefield ['maɪnfi:ld] *n* **1.** campo *m* de minas **2.** *fig* terreno *m* minado

miner ['maɪnəʳ, *Am:* -nɚ] *n* minero, -a *m, f*

mineral ['mɪnərəl] **I.** *n* mineral *m* **II.** *adj* mineral

mineralogical [ˌmɪnərə'lɒdʒɪkl, *Am:* -'lɑ:dʒɪ-] *adj* mineralógico, -a

mineralogist [ˌmɪnə'rælədʒɪst, *Am:* -'rɑ:lə-] *n* mineralogista *mf*

mineralogy [ˌmɪnə'rælədʒi, *Am:* -'rɑ:lə-] *n no pl* mineralogía *f*

mineral water *n* agua *f* mineral

minesweeper ['maɪnˌswi:pəʳ, *Am:* -pɚ] *n inf* dragaminas *m inv*

mingle ['mɪŋgl] **I.** *vt* mezclar; **to be ~d with sth** confundirse con algo **II.** *vi* mezclarse; **to ~ with the guests** mezclarse con los invitados

miniature ['mɪnɪtʃəʳ, *Am:* -iətʃɚ] **I.** *adj* de miniatura **II.** *n* miniatura *f*

miniature camera *n* cámara *f* de bolsillo **miniature railway** *n* ferrocarril *m* miniatura

minibus ['mɪnɪbʌs] *n* microbús *m*

minicab ['mɪnɪkæb] *n Brit* taxi *m*

minim ['mɪnɪm] *n Aus, Brit* MUS corchera *f*

minimal ['mɪnɪml] *adj* mínimo, -a

minimize ['mɪnɪmaɪz] *vt* minimizar; *fig* menospreciar

minimum ['mɪnɪməm] **I.** <-s *o* minima> *n* mínimo *m;* **to reduce sth to a ~** reducir algo al mínimo **II.** *adj* mínimo, -a; **~ requirements** requisitos *mpl* básicos

mining ['maɪnɪŋ] *n no pl* minería *f*

mining engineer *n* ingeniero, -a *m, f* de minas

minion ['mɪnjən] *n* secuaz *mf*

miniskirt ['mɪnɪskɜ:t, *Am:* -skɜ:rt] *n* minifalda *f*

minister ['mɪnɪstəʳ, *Am:* stɚ] *n* **1.** POL ministro, -a *m, f* **2.** REL pastor *m*

ministerial [ˌmɪnɪ'stɪəriəl, *Am:* -'stɪri-] *adj* ministerial

ministrations [ˌmɪnɪ'streɪʃən] *n pl, liter* atenciones *fpl*

ministry ['mɪnɪstri] <-ies> *n* **1.** POL ministerio *m* **2.** REL sacerdocio *m;* **to enter the ~** (*Catholic*) hacerse sacerdote; (*Protestant*) hacerse pastor

mink [mɪŋk] *n no pl* visón *m*

minor ['maɪnəʳ, *Am:* -nɚ] **I.** *adj* (*not great*) pequeño, -a; (*role*) secundario, -a; (*detail*) sin importancia; **~ offence** delito *m* de menor cuantía; **B ~** MUS si *m* menor **II.** *n* **1.** (*person*) menor *mf* de edad **2.** *Am* UNIV asignatura *f* secundaria

Minorca [mɪ'nɔ:ka, *Am:*-'nɔ:r-] *n* Menorca *f*

Minorcan **I.** *adj* menorquín **II.** *n* menorquín, -ina *m, f*

minority [maɪ'nɒrəti, *Am:* -'nɔ:rət̬i] **I.** <-ies> *n* minoría *f;* **to be a ~ of one** ser el único que piensa así; **in a ~ of cases** en muy raros casos **II.** *adj* minoritario, -a; **~ sport** deporte de minorías

minstrel ['mɪnstrəl] *n* HIST juglar *m*

mint¹ [mɪnt] *n* **1.** *no pl* (*herb*) hierbabuena *f* **2.** (*sweet*) caramelo *m* de menta

mint² [mɪnt] **I.** *n* (*coin factory*) casa *f* de la moneda; **to make a ~** *inf* ganar un montón de dinero **II.** *vt* acuñar; **to ~ a word** *fig* acuñar una palabra **III.** *adj* (*coin*) de reciente acuñación; (*stamp*) nuevo, -a; **in ~ condition** en perfecto estado

mint tea *n* té *m* de menta

minuet [ˌmɪnju'et] *n* minué *m*

minus ['maɪnəs] **I.** *prep* **1.** *a.* MAT menos; **5 ~ 2 equals 3** 5 menos 2 igual a 3; **~ ten Celsius** diez grados bajo cero **2.** *inf* (*without*) sin **II.** *adj* MAT menos; (*number*) negativo, -a; **to be in ~ figures** estar en números rojos **III.** *n* signo *m* de menos

minuscule ['mɪnəskju:l, *Am:* -ɪ-] *adj* minúsculo, -a

minute¹ ['mɪnɪt] *n* **1.** (*sixty seconds*) minuto *m* **2.** (*moment*) momento *m;* **any ~** de un momento a otro; **at the last ~** a última hora; **in a ~** ahora mismo; **this very ~** ahora mismo; **to the ~** puntual; **wait a ~** espera un segundo **3.** *pl* (*of meeting*) acta(s) *f(pl)*

minute² [maɪ'nju:t, *Am:* -'nu:t] *adj* dimi-

M

nuto, -a
minute hand *n* minutero *m*
minutely *adv* minuciosamente
minutiae [maɪ'nju:ʃiː, *Am:* mɪ'nu:-] *npl* minucias *fpl*
minx [mɪŋks] *n iron* descarada *f inf*
miracle ['mɪrəkl] *n* milagro *m;* **by a** ~ por milagro
miracle play *n* HIST, THEAT auto *m* sacramental
miraculous [mɪ'rækjʊləs, *Am:* -jə-] *adj* milagroso, -a
mirage ['mɪrɑːʒ] *n* espejismo *m*
mire ['maɪəʳ, *Am:* maɪr] **I.** *n* **1.** (*swamp*) fango *m* **2.** *fig* berenjenal *m* **II.** *vt* **to become ~d in sth** quedar atascado en algo
mirror ['mɪrəʳ, *Am:* -ɚ] **I.** *n* espejo *m* **II.** *vt* reflejar
mirror image *n* contraimagen *f*
mirth [mɜːθ, *Am:* mɜːrθ] *n no pl* regocijo *m*
mirthful ['mɜːθfəl, *Am:* 'mɜːrθ-] *adj* alegre
mirthless ['mɜːθləs, *Am:* 'mɜːrθ-] *adj* **1.** (*joyless*) triste **2.** (*unhappy*) infeliz
misadventure [ˌmɪsəd'ventʃəʳ, *Am:* -tʃɚ] *n* desgracia *f;* **death by** ~ muerte *f* accidental
misalliance [ˌmɪsə'laɪəns] *n* **1.** (*alliance*) alianza *f* inconveniente **2.** (*marriage*) matrimonio *m* desigual
misanthrope ['mɪsnθrəʊp, *Am:* -θroʊp] *n* misántropo, -a *m, f*
misanthropic [ˌmɪsn'θrɒpɪk, *Am:* -ən-'θrɑːpɪk] *adj* misantrópico, -a
misanthropy [mɪs'ænθrəpi] *n no pl* misantropía *f*
misapply [ˌmɪsə'plaɪ] <-ie-> *vt* **to** ~ **sth** hacer un uso indebido de algo
misapprehend [ˌmɪsæprɪ'hend] *vt* comprender mal
misapprehension [ˌmɪsæprɪ'henʃən] *n* mala interpretación *f;* **to be under a** ~ estar equivocado
misappropriate [ˌmɪsə'prəʊprɪeɪt, *Am:* -'proʊ-] *vt* FIN malversar
misappropriation [ˌmɪsəˌprəʊprɪ'eɪʃən, *Am:* -ˌproʊ-] *n no pl* FIN malversación *f*
misbehave [ˌmɪsbɪ'heɪv] *vi* portarse mal
misbehavior *n Am, Aus,* **misbehaviour** [ˌmɪsbɪ'heɪvjəʳ, *Am:* -vjɚ] *n no pl* mala conducta *f*
misc. *adj abbr of* **miscellaneous** diverso, -a
miscalculate [ˌmɪs'kælkjʊleɪt, *Am:* -kjə-] *vt, vi* calcular mal
miscalculation [ˌmɪsˌkælkjʊ'leɪʃən, *Am:* -kjə'-] *n* error *m* de cálculo
miscarriage [ˌmɪs'kærɪdʒ, *Am:* 'mɪsˌker-] *n* aborto *m* (espontáneo)
miscarry [ˌmɪs'kæri, *Am:* 'mɪsˌker-] <-ied, -ying> *vi* **1.** MED abortar **2.** *fig* fracasar
miscellaneous [ˌmɪsə'leɪnɪəs] *adj* diverso, -a; ~ **expenses** gastos *mpl* varios
miscellany [mɪ'seləni, *Am:* 'mɪsəleɪ-] <-ies> *n* miscelánea *f*
mischance [ˌmɪs'tʃɑːns, *Am:* 'tʃæns] *n* (*bad luck*) mala suerte *f;* (*unlucky event*) infortunio *m;* **by some** ~ por desgracia
mischief ['mɪstʃɪf] *n* **1.** (*naughtiness*) travesura *f;* **to keep sb out of** ~ impedir a alguien hacer travesuras **2. to get** (**oneself**) **into** ~ meterse en problemas; **to make** ~ **for sb** amargar la vida a alguien **3.** (*wickedness*) malicia *f*
mischievous ['mɪstʃɪvəs, *Am:* -tʃə-] *adj* **1.** (*naughty*) travieso, -a **2.** (*malicious*) malicioso, -a; ~ **rumours** rumores *mpl* malintencionados
misconceive [ˌmɪskən'siːv] *vt form* malinterpretar
misconceived *adj* mal concebido, -a
misconception [ˌmɪskən'sepʃən] *n* idea *f* equivocada; **a popular** ~ un error común
misconduct [ˌmɪskən'dʌkt, *Am:* -'kɑːn-] **I.** *n no pl* **1.** (*misbehaviour*) mala conducta *f* **2.** (*mismanage*) mala gestión *f* **II.** *vt* **1.** (*behave badly*) **to** ~ **oneself** conducirse mal **2.** (*organize badly*) gestionar mal
misconstruction [ˌmɪskən'strʌkʃən] *n form* mala interpretación *f*
misconstrue [ˌmɪskən'struː] *vt* malinterpretar
misdeed [ˌmɪs'diːd] *n form* fechoría *f*
misdemeanor *n Am,* **misdemeanour** [ˌmɪsdɪ'miːnəʳ, *Am:* -nɚ] *n Brit* **1.** LAW falta *f* **2.** (*bad behaviour*) mala conducta *f*
misdirect [ˌmɪsdɪ'rekt, *Am:* -də'-] *vt* **1.** (*letter*) mandar a una dirección equivocada; (*person*) dar indicaciones equivocadas **2.** LAW instruir mal
miser ['maɪzəʳ, *Am:* -zɚ] *n* avaro, -a *m, f*
miserable ['mɪzrəbl] *adj* **1.** (*unhappy*) triste; **to make life** ~ **for sb** hacer insoportable la vida a alguien **2.** (*poor*) mísero, -a; **a** ~ **amount** una miseria **3.** (*unpleasant*) lamentable
miserably *adv* **1.** (*unhappily*) tristemente **2.** (*completely*) **to fail** ~ fallar del todo
miserly *adj* avaricioso, -a
misery ['mɪzəri] *n* **1.** (*unhappiness*) infelicidad *f* **2.** *no pl* (*suffering*) sufrimiento *m;* **to make sb's life a** ~ amargar la vida a alguien **3.** (*extreme poverty*) miseria *f,* lipidia *f AmC*
misfire [ˌmɪs'faɪəʳ, *Am:* -'faɪɚ] *vi* **1.** (*weapon*) encasquillarse **2.** *fig* (*joke*) no tener éxito **3.** (*engine*) fallar
misfit ['mɪsfɪt] *n* inadaptado, -a *m, f*
misfortune [ˌmɪs'fɔːtʃuːn, *Am:* -'fɔːrtʃən] *n no pl* infortunio *m;* **to suffer** ~ sufrir una desgracia
misgiving [ˌmɪs'gɪvɪŋ] *n* recelo *m;* **to express ~s** recelar; **to be filled with** ~ estar lleno de dudas
misgovern [mɪs'gʌvən, *Am:* -ɚn] *vt* (*country*) gobernar mal; (*business*) gestionar mal
misgovernment *n no pl* (*of country*) mal gobierno *m;* (*of company*) mala gestión *f*
misguided [mɪs'gaɪdɪd] *adj* desencaminado, -a; ~ **idea** desacierto *m*

mishandle [ˌmɪsˈhændl] *vt* **1.** (*handle without care*) manejar mal **2.** (*maltreat*) maltratar **3.** (*deal badly with*) llevar mal

mishap [ˈmɪshæp] *n form* percance *m;* **he had a ~** *iron* tuvo un percance; **a series of ~s** una serie de contratiempos

mishear [ˌmɪsˈhɪəʳ, *Am:* -ˈhɪr] *vt irr* oír mal

mishmash [ˈmɪʃmæʃ] *n* revoltijo *m;* **a ~ of sth** una mezcolanza de algo

misinform [ˌmɪsɪnˈfɔːm, *Am:* -ˈfɔːrm] *vt* informar mal, desinformar *Méx*

misinterpret [ˌmɪsɪnˈtɜːprɪt, *Am:* -ˈtɜːr-] *vt* interpretar mal, malinterpretar *Méx*

misinterpretation [ˌmɪsɪntɜːprɪˈteɪʃən, *Am:* -tɜːr-] *n* interpretación *f* errónea

misjudge [ˌmɪsˈdʒʌdʒ] *vt* juzgar mal

misjudgement [mɪsˈdʒʌdʒmənt] *n* mal cálculo *m*

mislay [ˌmɪsˈleɪ] *vt irr, form* extraviar

mislead [ˌmɪsˈliːd] *vt irr* **1.** (*deceive*) engañar; **to ~ sb about sth** engañar a alguien acerca de algo; **to ~ sb into doing sth** engañar a alguien para que haga algo **2.** (*lead into error*) hacer caer en un error; **to let oneself be misled** dejarse engañar **3.** (*corrupt*) corromper

misleading *adj* engañoso, -a

mismanage [ˌmɪsˈmænɪdʒ] *vt* administrar mal; **to ~ a business** gestionar mal una empresa

mismanagement *n* mala gestión *f*

misname [ˌmɪsˈneɪm] *vt* **to ~ sth** dar un nombre equivocado a algo

misnomer [ˌmɪsˈnəʊməʳ, *Am:* -ˈnoʊmɚ] *n* nombre *m* equivocado

misogynist [mɪˈsɒdʒɪnɪst, *Am:* -ˈsɑːdʒən-] **I.** *n* misógino *m* **II.** *adj* misógino, -a

misplace [ˌmɪsˈpleɪs] *vt* **1.** (*lose*) extraviar **2.** *fig* (*confidence*) dar indebidamente

misprint [ˈmɪsˌprɪnt] *n* errata *f*

mispronounce [ˌmɪsprəˈnaʊns] *vt* pronunciar mal

mispronunciation [ˌmɪsprəˌnʌnsɪˈeɪʃən] *n* mala pronunciación *f*

misread [ˌmɪsˈriːd] *vt irr* **1.** (*read badly*) leer mal **2.** (*interpret badly*) interpretar mal, malinterpretar *Méx*

misrepresent [ˌmɪsˌreprɪˈzent] *vt* tergiversar

misrepresentation [ˌmɪsˌreprɪzenˈteɪʃən] *n* tergiversación *f*

miss¹ [mɪs] *n* (*form of adress*) señorita *f;* **Miss Spain** Miss España

miss² [mɪs] **I.** <-es> *n* fallo *m;* **to give sth a ~** *Brit, Aus, inf* pasar de algo **II.** *vi* fallar **III.** *vt* **1.** (*not hit*) fallar **2.** (*not catch*) perder; **to ~ the bus/train** perder el bus/tren; **to ~ a deadline** no cumplir con una fecha límite **3.** (*avoid*) evitar **4.** (*not notice*) no fijarse en; **to ~ sb** no encontrar a alguien; **you didn't ~ much** no te has perdido nada; **you can't ~ it** no te lo puedes perder **5.** (*not hear*) no oír **6.** (*overlook*) saltarse; **to ~ a meeting** faltar a una reunión **7.** (*not take advantage*) dejar pasar; **to ~ an opportunity** perder una oportunidad **8.** (*regret absence*) echar de menos **9.** (*notice loss*) echar en falta

◆**miss out I.** *vt* **1.** (*omit*) omitir **2.** (*overlook*) saltarse **II.** *vi* **to ~ on sth** perderse algo

misshapen [ˌmɪsˈʃeɪpən] *adj* (*malformed*) deformado, -a

missile [ˈmɪsaɪl, *Am:* ˈmɪsəl] *n* (*rocket*) misil *m;* (*projectile*) proyectil *m*

missile base *n* base *f* de misiles **missile defence system** *n* sistema *m* defensivo de misiles **missile launcher** *n* lanzamisiles *m inv*

missing [ˈmɪsɪŋ] *adj* **1.** (*lost: person*) desaparecido, -a; (*thing or object*) perdido, -a; **~ in combat** desaparecido en combate; **to report sth ~** dar parte de la pérdida de algo **2.** (*absent*) ausente

missing link *n* eslabón *m* perdido **missing person** *n* desaparecido, -a *m, f*

mission [ˈmɪʃən] *n* **1.** *a.* REL (*task*) misión *f;* **peace ~** misión de paz; **rescue ~** operación *f* de rescate; **his ~ in life** su misión en la vida; **~ accomplished** misión cumplida **2.** (*space project*) misión *f* espacial **3.** (*trade centre*) misión *f* comercial **4.** POL delegación *f*

missionary [ˈmɪʃənəri, *Am:* -əner-] **I.** <-ies> *n* misionero, -a *m, f* **II.** *adj* misionero, -a

missionary position *n iron* postura *f* del misionero

mission control *n* centro *m* de control

missis [ˈmɪsɪz] *n inf s.* **missus**

misspell [ˌmɪsˈspel] *vt irr* escribir mal

misspelling *n* falta *f* de ortografía

misspent [ˌmɪsˈspent] *adj* desperdiciado, -a; **a ~ youth** una juventud malgastada

misstate [ˌmɪsˈsteɪt] *vt* sostener erróneamente

missus [ˈmɪsɪz] *n inf* (*wife*) parienta *f*

mist [mɪst] *n* **1.** (*light fog*) neblina *f;* **to be shrouded in ~** estar cubierto por la neblina **2.** *Brit* (*condensation*) vaho *m*

◆**mist up** *vi* empañarse

mistakable [mɪˈsteɪkəbl] *adj* confundible

mistake [mɪˈsteɪk] **I.** *n* error *m;* **typing ~** errata *f;* **to learn from one's ~s** aprender de los propios errores; **to make a ~** cometer un error; **make no ~ about it** no te equivoques; **to repeat past ~s** repetir los errores del pasado; **there must be some ~** tiene que haber un error; **by ~** por error **II.** *vt irr* confundir

mistaken [mɪˈsteɪkən] **I.** *pp of* **mistake** **II.** *adj* (*belief*) equivocado, -a; (*identity*) confundido, -a; **to be** (**very much**) **~** estar (muy) equivocado; **unless I'm very much ~ …** si no me equivoco…

Mister [ˈmɪstəʳ, *Am:* -tɚ] *n* señor *m*

mistime [ˌmɪsˈtaɪm] *vt* hacer algo a destiempo

mistletoe [ˈmɪsltəʊ, *Am:* -toʊ] *n* muérdago *m*

M

mistook [mɪˈstʊk] *pt of* **mistake**
mistranslate [ˌmɪstrænzˈleɪt, *Am:* -ˈtrænzleɪt] *vt* traducir mal
mistreat [ˌmɪsˈtriːt] *vt* maltratar
mistress [ˈmɪstrɪs] *n* **1.** (*sexual partner*) amante *f* **2.** (*woman in charge*) ama *f;* **the ~ of the house** la dueña de la casa **3.** *Brit* SCHOOL maestra *f* **4.** (*owner*) dueña *f*
mistrial [ˌmɪsˈtraɪəl, *Am:* ˈmɪsˌ-] *n* juicio *m* invalidado
mistrust [ˌmɪsˈtrʌst] **I.** *n no pl* desconfianza *f;* **to have a ~ of sb/sth** recelar de alguien/algo **II.** *vt* **to ~ sb/sth** recelar de alguien/algo
mistrustful [ˌmɪsˈtrʌstfəl] *adj* receloso, -a; **to be ~ of sb/sth** recelar de alguien/algo
misty [ˈmɪsti] <-ier, -iest> *adj* **1.** (*foggy*) neblinoso, -a; (*window, glasses*) empañado, -a **2.** *fig* borroso, -a
misunderstand [ˌmɪsˌʌndəˈstænd, *Am:* -dɚˈ-] *vt irr* entender mal
misunderstanding *n* **1.** (*failure to understand*) malentendido *m;* **there must be some ~** debe haber un malentendido **2.** (*disagreement*) desacuerdo *m*
misuse[1] [ˌmɪsˈjuːs] *n* **1.** (*wrong use*) mal uso *m* **2.** (*excessive consumption*) abuso *m*
misuse[2] [ˌmɪsˈjuːz] *vt* **1.** (*handle wrongly*) manejar mal **2.** (*consume to excess*) abusar de
mite [maɪt] *n* **1.** (*insect*) ácaro *m* **2.** *Brit, inf* (*child*) chiquillo, -a *m, f* **3.** (*small amount*) pizca *f*
miter [ˈmaɪt̬ɚ] *n Am s.* **mitre**
mitigate [ˈmɪtɪgeɪt, *Am:* -ˈmɪt̬-] *vt form* mitigar
mitigation [ˌmɪtɪˈgeɪʃən, *Am:* ˌmɪt̬-] *n no pl* atenuación *f;* **in ~** como atenuante
mitre [ˈmaɪtəʳ, *Am:* -t̬ɚ] *n* mitra *f*
mitten [ˈmɪtn] *n* manopla *f*
mix [mɪks] **I.** *n* mezcla *f;* **a ~ of people** una mezcla de gente **II.** *vi* **1.** (*combine*) mezclarse **2.** (*socially*) **to ~ with sb** frecuentar a alguien; **to ~ well** llevarse bien **III.** *vt* **1.** GASTR mezclar; (*dough*) amasar; (*cocktail*) preparar **2.** (*combine*) combinar; **to ~ business with pleasure** combinar el placer con los negocios; **religion and politics don't ~** la religión y la política no hacen buena combinación
◆**mix in** **I.** *vi* convivir **II.** *vt* **to mix sth in with sth** mezclar algo con algo
◆**mix up** *vt* **1.** (*confuse*) confundir **2.** (*put in wrong order*) revolver **3.** GASTR mezclar ►**to mix it up with sb** *Am, inf* pelearse con alguien
◆**mix up in** *vt* **to be mixed up in sth** estar involucrado en algo
◆**mix up with** *vt* **to mix up sth with sth** mezclar algo con algo; **to be mixed up with sth** estar involucrado en algo
◆**mix with** **I.** *vt always sep* confundir ►**to mix it with sb** *Brit, inf* meterse con alguien **II.** *vi* (*associate with*) **to ~ sb** mezclarse con alguien
mixed *adj* **1.** (*containing various elements*) mezclado, -a; (*team*) mixto, -a; **~ marriage** matrimonio mixto; **person of ~ race** mestizo, -a *m, f* **2.** (*contradictory*) contradictorio, -a; **~ feelings** sentimientos contradictorios; **to be a ~ blessing** tener ventajas e inconvenientes
mixed doubles *npl* SPORTS dobles *mpl* mixtos **mixed economy** *n* economía *f* mixta **mixed farming** *n* agricultura *f* mixta **mixed grill** *n* parrillada *f*
mixer [ˈmɪksəʳ, *Am:* -sɚ] *n* **1.** (*machine*) batidora *f* **2.** (*friendly person*) persona *f* sociable; **to be a good ~** tener don de gentes **3.** (*drink*) *bebida que se mezcla con alcohol en cócteles y combinados*
mixer faucet *n,* **mixer tap** *n Am* llave *f* mezcladora
mixture [ˈmɪkstʃəʳ, *Am:* -tʃɚ] *n* mezcla *f*
mix-up [ˈmɪksʌp] *n* confusión *f*
Mk *n abbr of* **mark** **1.** FIN marco *m* **2.** AUTO modelo *m*
ml *n abbr of* **millilitre** ml
MLR *n abbr of* **minimum lending rate** tipo *m* de interés bancario
mm *abbr of* **millimetre** mm
mnemonic [nɪˈmɒnɪk, *Am:* nɪˈmɑːnɪk] *adj* mnemotécnico, -a
mo[1] [moʊ] *n Am abbr of* **month** mes *m*
mo[2] [məʊ, *Am:* moʊ] *inf abbr of* **moment** momento *m*
MO *n* **1.** *abbr of* **modus operandi** procedimiento *m* **2.** *abbr of* **Medical Office** médico *mf* militar **3.** *abbr of* **money order** giro *m*
moan [məʊn, *Am:* moʊn] **I.** *n* **1.** (*sound*) gemido *m* **2.** (*complaint*) quejido *m* **II.** *vi* **1.** (*make a sound*) gemir; **to ~ with pain** gemir de dolor **2.** (*complain*) lamentarse; **to ~ about sth** lamentarse de algo; **to ~ that ...** lamentarse de que... *+subj*
moat [məʊt, *Am:* moʊt] *n* foso *m*
mob [mɒb, *Am:* mɑːb] **I.** *n + sing/pl vb* **1.** (*crowd*) muchedumbre *f;* **angry ~** turba *f;* **~ law** la ley de la calle **2.** *inf* **the Mob** la mafia **3.** *Brit, inf* (*gang*) pandilla *f; iron* banda *f* **4.** *Aus* (*herd*) rebaño *m* **II.** <-bb-> *vt* acosar; **he was ~bed by his fans** sus fans se aglomeraron en torno a él
mobile [ˈməʊbaɪl, *Am:* ˈmoʊbəl] **I.** *n a.* TEL móvil *m* **II.** *adj* **1.** (*able to move*) móvil; (*shop, canteen*) ambulante; **to be ~** *inf* tener coche **2.** (*movable*) movible
mobile home *n* caravana *f* **mobile phone** *n Brit* móvil *m*
mobilisation [ˌməʊbɪlaɪˈzeɪʃən] *n Brit, Aus s.* **mobilization**
mobilise *vt Brit, Aus s.* **mobilize**
mobility [məʊˈbɪləti, *Am:* moʊˈbɪlət̬i] *n no pl* movilidad *f;* **social ~** *Brit* movilidad social
mobilization [ˌməʊbɪlaɪˈzeɪʃən, *Am:* -bəlɪˈ-] *n a.* MIL movilización *f*
mobilize [ˈməʊbɪlaɪz, *Am:* -bə-] *vt* movilizar
moccasin [ˈmɒkəsɪn, *Am:* ˈmɑːkəsən] *n* mocasín *m*

mocha ['mɒkə, *Am:* 'moʊkə] *n no pl* moca *f;* ~ **ice cream** helado *m* de moca
mock [mɒk, *Am:* mɑːk] **I.** *adj* **1.** (*imitation*) artificial; ~ **baroque** que imita el estilo barroco; ~ **leather** polipiel *f* **2.** (*practice*) ~ **exam** examen *m* de prueba **3.** (*fake*) ficticio, -a; ~ **battle** simulacro *m* de batalla; ~ **façade** fachada falsa; ~ **horror** horror fingido **II.** *vi* burlarse; **to** ~ **at sb** burlarse de alguien **III.** *vt* **1.** (*ridicule*) mofarse de **2.** (*imitate*) remedar
mocker ['mɒkəʳ, *Am:* 'mɑːkɚ] *n* **to put the** ~**s on sth** frustrar algo
mockery ['mɒkəri, *Am:* 'mɑːkɚ-] *n* **1.** (*ridicule*) mofa *f* **2.** (*subject of derision*) hazmerreír *mf;* **to make a** ~ **of sb/sth** ridiculizar a alguien/algo **3.** (*ridiculous imitation*) parodia *f*
mocking *n* burla *f*
mockingbird ['mɒkɪŋˌbɜːd, *Am:* 'mɑːkɪŋˌbɜːrd] *n* sinsonte *m,* cenzontle *m Méx*
mock-up ['mɒkʌp, *Am:* 'mɑːk-] *n* réplica *f*
MOD *n Brit s.* **Ministry of Defence** Ministerio *m* de Defensa
modal ['məʊdəl, *Am:* 'moʊ-] *adj* modal
modal verb *n* verbo *m* modal
mode ['məʊd, *Am:* 'moʊd] *n* **1.** *a.* LING, PHILOS (*style*) modo *m;* ~ **of life** modo de vida; ~ **of operation** forma *f* de operar; ~ **of transport** medio *m* de transporte **2.** *no pl, form* (*fashion*) moda *f;* **to be all the** ~ estar a la moda; **in** ~ a la moda
model ['mɒdəl, *Am:* 'mɑːdəl] **I.** *n* (*version, example*) *a.* ART modelo *m;* (*of car, house*) maqueta *f;* **to be the very** ~ **of sth** ser la viva imagen de algo **II.** *adj* modélico, -a; **a** ~ **student** un alumno modelo **III.** <-ll-> *vt* **1.** (*make figure, representation*) modelar; **to** ~ **sth in clay** modelar algo en barro **2.** (*show clothes*) desfilar **3. to** ~ **oneself on sb** tomar a alguien como modelo
model maker *n* maquetista *mf*
modem ['məʊdem, *Am:* 'moʊdəm] *n* INFOR módem *m*
moderate¹ ['mɒdərət, *Am:* 'mɑːdɚ-] **I.** *n* POL moderado, -a *m, f* **II.** *adj* **1.** (*neither large nor small*) mediano, -a **2.** *a.* POL (*not extreme: speed*) moderado, -a; (*increase, means*) mesurado, -a; (*price*) módico, -a
moderate² ['mɒdəreɪt, *Am:* 'mɑːdər-] **I.** *vt* moderar; **to** ~ **a discussion** moderar un debate; **to** ~ **an examination** presidir un examen **II.** *vi* **1.** (*become less extreme*) moderarse **2.** (*act as moderator*) moderar
moderation [ˌmɒdə'reɪʃən, *Am:* ˌmɑːdə-] *n no pl* moderación *f;* **to drink in** ~ beber con moderación
moderator ['mɒdəreɪtəʳ, *Am:* 'mɑːdɚeɪtɚ] *n form* **1.** (*mediator*) mediador(a) *m(f)* **2.** *Am* (*of discussion*) moderador(a) *m(f)* **3.** *Brit* (*of exam*) supervisor(a) *m(f)*
modern ['mɒdən, *Am:* 'mɑːdɚn] *adj* moderno, -a
modernization [ˌmɒdənaɪ'zeɪʃən, *Am:* ˌmɑːdɚnɪ'-] *n* modernización *f*
modernize ['mɒdənaɪz, *Am:* 'mɑːdɚ-] *vt* modernizar
modest ['mɒdɪst, *Am:* 'mɑːdɪst] *adj* **1.** (*not boastful*) modesto, -a; **to be** ~ **about sth** ser modesto en algo **2.** (*moderate*) moderado, -a; **a** ~ **wage** un sueldo modesto
modesty ['mɒdɪsti, *Am:* 'mɑːdɪst-] *n no pl* modestia *f*
modicum ['mɒdɪkəm, *Am:* 'mɑːdɪ-] *n no pl* pizca *f,* pisca *f Méx;* **a** ~ **of truth** una pizca de verdad
modifiable ['mɒdɪfaɪəbl, *Am:* 'mɑːdɪ-] *adj* modificable
modification [ˌmɒdɪfɪ'keɪʃən, *Am:* ˌmɑːdɪ-] *n* modificación *f*
modifier ['mɒdɪfaɪəʳ, *Am:* 'mɑːdɪfaɪɚ] *n* LING modificador *m*
modify ['mɒdɪfaɪ, *Am:* 'mɑːdɪ-] <-ie-> *vt a.* LING modificar
modish ['məʊdɪʃ, *Am:* 'moʊ-] *adj* de moda
modular ['mɒdjʊləʳ, *Am:* 'mɑːdʒələ] *adj* modular; (*construction, degree*) por módulos
modulate ['mɒdjʊleɪt, *Am:* 'mɑːdʒə-] *vt a.* ELEC, RADIO, TV modular
modulation [ˌmɒdjʊ'leɪʃən, *Am:* ˌmɑːdʒə'-] *n* modulación *f*
module ['mɒdjuːl, *Am:* 'mɑːdʒuːl] *n* módulo *m*
mohair ['məʊheəʳ, *Am:* 'moʊher] *n* mohair *m*
moist [mɔɪst] *adj* húmedo, -a
moisten ['mɔɪsn] **I.** *vt* humedecer **II.** *vi* humedecerse
moisture ['mɔɪstʃəʳ, *Am:* -tʃɚ] *n* humedad *f*
moisturise ['mɔɪstʃəraɪz] *vt Brit, Aus s.* **moisturize**
moisturiser *n Aus, Brit s.* **moisturizer**
moisturize ['mɔɪstʃəraɪz] *vt* hidratar
moisturizer *n* hidratante *m*
moisturizing cream *n* crema *f* hidratante
moisturizing lotion *n* loción *f* hidratante
molar¹ ['məʊləʳ, *Am:* 'moʊlɚ] *n* muela *f*
molar² ['məʊləʳ, *Am:* 'moʊlɚ] *adj* CHEM molar
molasses [məʊ'læsɪz, *Am:* moʊ-] *n* melaza *f*
mold [məʊld, *Am:* moʊld] *n, vi Am s.* **mould²**
Moldavia [mɒl'deɪviə, *Am:* mɑːl-] *n s.* **Moldova**
Moldavian **I.** *adj* moldavo, -a **II.** *n* **1.** (*person*) moldavo, -a *m, f* **2.** LING moldavo *m*
molder ['moʊldɚ] *vi Am s.* **moulder**
molding *n Am s.* **moulding**
Moldova [mɒl'dəʊvə, *Am:* mɑːl'doʊ-] *n* Moldavia *f*
Moldovan **I.** *adj* moldavo, -a **II.** *n* moldavo, -a *m, f*
moldy ['moʊldi] *adj Am s.* **mouldy**
mole¹ [məʊl, *Am:* moʊl] *n* ZOOL topo *m*

M

mole² [məʊl, *Am:* moʊl] *n* ANAT lunar *m*

mole³ [məʊl, *Am:* moʊl] *n inf* (*spy*) espía *mf*

molecular [mə'lekjʊləʳ, *Am:* -jələ˞] *adj* molecular

molecule ['mɒlɪkjuːl, *Am:* 'mɑːlɪ-] *n* molécula *f*

molehill ['məʊlhɪl, *Am:* 'moʊl-] *n* topera *f*

molest [mə'lest] *vt* **1.** (*pester*) importunar **2.** (*sexually*) abusar (sexualmente) de

moll [mɒl, *Am:* mɑːl] *n inf* amiga *f* de un gángster

mollify ['mɒlɪfaɪ, *Am:* 'mɑːlə-] <-ie-> *vt* **1.** (*pacify*) apaciguar **2.** (*reduce effect*) aplacar

mollusc *n*, **mollusk** ['mɒləsk, *Am:* 'mɑːləsk] *n* molusco *m*

mollycoddle ['mɒlɪkɒdl, *Am:* 'mɑːlɪkɑːdl] *vt inf* mimar, apapachar *Méx*

Molotov cocktail [ˌmɒlətɒf 'kɒkteɪl, *Am:* ˌmɑːlətɔːf 'kɑːk-] *n* cóctel *m* Molotov

molt [məʊlt, *Am:* moʊlt] *n, vt, vi Am s.* **moult**

molten ['məʊltən, *Am:* 'moʊl-] *adj* fundido, -a

mom [mɒm, *Am:* mɑːm] *n Am, inf* mamá *f*

moment ['məʊmənt, *Am:* 'moʊ-] *n* momento *m;* **at the ~** por el momento; **at any ~** en cualquier momento; **at the last ~** en el último momento; **in a ~** enseguida; **not for a ~** ni por un momento; **the ~ that …** en cuanto… *+subj;* **the ~ of truth** la hora de la verdad; **at the** (**precise**) **~ when …** en el (preciso) momento en que…; **to choose one's ~** escoger el momento; **to leave sth till the last ~** dejar algo hasta el último momento

momentarily ['məʊməntrəli, *Am:* ˌmoʊmən'ter-] *adv* **1.** (*very briefly*) momentáneamente **2.** *Am* (*very soon*) en un momento

momentary ['məʊməntri, *Am:* 'moʊmənter-] *adj* momentáneo, -a

momentous [mə'mentəs, *Am:* moʊ'men̬təs] *adj* (*fact*) trascendental; (*day*) memorable

momentum [mə'mentəm, *Am:* moʊ'men̬təm] *n no pl* PHYS momento *m; fig* impulso *m;* **to gather ~** tomar velocidad

momma ['mɒmə, *Am:* 'mɑːmə] *n,* **mommy** ['mɒmi, *Am:* 'mɑːmi] *n Am, inf* mamá *f*

Monaco ['ɒnəkəʊ, *Am:* 'mɑːnəkoʊ] *n* Mónaco *m*

monarch ['mɒnək, *Am:* 'mɑːnə˞k] *n* monarca *mf*

monarchic(**al**) [mə'nɑːkɪk(l), *Am:* -'nɑːr-] *adj* monárquico, -a

monarchism ['mɒnəkɪzəm, *Am:* 'mɑːnə˞-] *n* monarquismo *m*

monarchist ['mɒnəkɪst, *Am:* 'mɑːnə˞-] *n* monarquista *mf*

monarchy ['mɒnəki, *Am:* 'mɑːnə˞-] <-ies> *n* monarquía *f*

monastery ['mɒnəstri, *Am:* 'mɑːnəster-] <-ies> *n* monasterio *m*

monastic [mə'næstɪk] *adj* **1.** REL monástico, -a **2.** (*ascetic*) monacal

Monday ['mʌndi] *n* lunes *m inv;* **Easter** [*o* **Whit**] **~** lunes de Pascua; *s. a.* **Friday**

monetary ['mʌnɪtəri, *Am:* 'mɑːnəteri] *adj* monetario, -a

monetary fund *n* fondo *m* monetario **monetary policy** *n* política *f* monetaria **Monetary Union** *n* Unión *f* Monetaria

money ['mʌni] *n no pl* dinero *m;* **to be short of ~** ir escaso de dinero; **to change ~** cambiar dinero; **to make ~** hacer dinero; **to raise ~** recolectar fondos; **to throw ~ at sth** malgastar dinero en algo ►**~ is the root of all evil** *prov* el dinero es la fuente de todos los males *prov;* **put your ~ where your mouth is** predica con el ejemplo; **~ doesn't grow on trees** *prov* el dinero no cae del cielo *prov;* **to be made of ~** nadar en la abundancia; **he has ~ to burn** le sobra el dinero; **to marry ~** casarse con alguien rico; **~ talks** *prov* poderoso caballero es don Dinero *prov;* **to be in the ~** estar forrado; **for my ~** en mi opinión

moneybags ['mʌnibægz] *npl inf* ricachón, -ona *m, f* **moneybox** *n* <-es> *Brit* hucha *f* **money-changer** *n* cambista *mf*

moneyed *adj form* adinerado, -a

money-maker *n* mina *f* de dinero *fig* **money-making I.** *adj* muy lucrativo, -a **II.** *n* ganancia *f* **money market** *n* mercado *m* monetario **money order** *n Am, Aus* giro *m* postal **money-spinner** *n* filón *m fig*

mongol ['mɒŋgl, *Am:* 'mɑːŋgəl] *adj* mongólico, -a

Mongol ['mɒŋgl, *Am:* 'mɑːŋgəl] **I.** *adj* mongol(a) **II.** *n* **1.** (*person*) mongol(a) *m(f)* **2.** LING mongol *m*

Mongolia [mɒŋ'gəʊlɪə, *Am:* mɑːŋ'goʊ-] *n* Mongolia *f*

Mongolian [mɒŋ'gəʊlɪən, *Am:* mɑːŋ'goʊ-] **I.** *adj* mongol(a) **II.** *n* **1.** (*person*) mongol(a) *m(f)* **2.** LING mongol *m*

mongolism ['mɒŋgəlɪzəm, *Am:* 'mɑːŋ] *n* mongolismo *m*

mongrel ['mʌŋgrəl, *Am:* 'mɑːŋ-] **I.** *n* perro *m* cruzado; *pej* chucho *m* **II.** *adj* mestizo, -a

monitor ['mɒnɪtəʳ, *Am:* 'mɑːnɪt̬ə˞] **I.** *n* **1.** INFOR monitor *m;* **15-inch ~** monitor de 15 pulgadas **2.** (*person*) supervisor(a) *m(f)* **II.** *vt* controlar; **to ~ sth closely** seguir algo de muy cerca

monk [mʌŋk] *n* monje *m*

monkey ['mʌŋki] **I.** *n* mono, -a *m, f* ►**to make a ~ out of sb** dejar a alguien en ridículo **II.** *vt Am* imitar

◆**monkey about** *vi inf* hacer el indio

monkey business *n* **1.** (*improper conduct*) tejemaneje *m* **2.** (*mischief*) travesura *f* **monkey nut** *n Brit* cacahuete *m*, maní *m AmL* **monkey wrench** *n* <-es> *Am* llave *f* inglesa

mono ['mɒnəʊ, *Am:* 'mɑːnoʊ] **I.** *n no pl* monofonía *f* **II.** *adj* mono

monochrome ['mɒnəʊkrəʊm, *Am:* 'mɑːnoʊkroʊm] *adj* monocromo, -a

monocle ['mɒnəkl, *Am:* 'mɑːnə-] *n* monóculo *m*

monogamous [mə'nɒgəməs, *Am:* mə'nɑːgə-] *adj* monógamo, -a

monogamy [mə'nɒgəmi, *Am:* mə'nɑːgə-] *n no pl* monogamia *f*

monogram ['mɒnəgræm, *Am:* 'mɑːnə-] *n* monograma *m*

monolingual [ˌmɒnəʊ'lɪŋgwəl, *Am:* ˌmɑːnə-] *adj* monolingüe

monolith ['mɒnəlɪθ, *Am:* 'mɑːnə-] *n* monolito *m*

monolithic [ˌmɒnə'lɪθɪk, *Am:* ˌmɑːnə-] *adj* monolítico, -a

monologue ['mɒnəlɒg, *Am:* 'mɑːnəlɑːg] *n* monólogo *m*

monopolize [mə'nɒpəlaɪz, *Am:* -'nɑːpəlaɪz] *vt* monopolizar

monopoly [mə'nɒpəli, *Am:* -'nɑːpəl-] <-ies> *n* monopolio *m*

monorail ['mɒnəʊreɪl, *Am:* 'mɑːnə-] *n* monorraíl *m*

monosyllabic [ˌmɒnəsɪ'læbɪk, *Am:* ˌmɑːnə-] *adj* monosilábico, -a

monotone ['mɒnətəʊn, *Am:* 'mɑːnətoʊn] *n no pl* tono *m* monocorde

monotonous [mə'nɒtənəs, *Am:* -'nɑːtən-] *adj* monótono, -a

monotony [mə'nɒtəni, *Am:* -'nɑːtən-] *n no pl* monotonía *f*

monotype® ['mɒnətaɪp, *Am:* 'mɑːnoʊ-] *n* monotipo *m*

monoxide [mɒ'nɒksaɪd, *Am:* mə'nɑːk-] *n* monóxido *m*

monsoon [mɒn'suːn, *Am:* mɑːn-] *n* monzón *m;* **~s** lluvias *fpl* monzónicas

monster ['mɒnstəʳ, *Am:* 'mɑːnstɚ] **I.** *n* monstruo *m* **II.** *adj inf* enorme

monstrosity [mɒn'strɒsəti, *Am:* mɑːn'strɑːsət̬i] <-ies> *n* monstruosidad *f*

monstrous ['mɒnstrəs, *Am:* 'mɑːn-] *adj* **1.** (*awful*) monstruoso, -a **2.** (*very big*) enorme **3.** (*outrageous*) escandaloso, -a

montage [mɒnt'ɑːʒ, *Am:* 'mɑːntɑːʒ] *n* montaje *m*

month [mʌnθ] *n* mes *m* ►**not in a ~ of Sundays** ni por casualidad

monthly ['mʌnθli] **I.** *adj* mensual **II.** *adv* mensualmente **III.** *n* publicación *f* mensual

monument ['mɒnjʊmənt, *Am:* 'mɑːnjə-] *n* monumento *m*

monumental [ˌmɒnjʊ'mentl, *Am:* ˌmɑːnjə'ment̬l] *adj* (*very big*) monumental; (*error*) garrafal

moo [muː] **I.** <-s> *n* mugido *m* **II.** *vi* mugir

mood[1] [muːd] *n* humor *m;* **in a good/bad ~** de buen/mal humor; **the public ~** el ánimo general; **to be in a talkative ~** estar dispuesto a hablar; **to not be in the ~ to do sth** no tener ganas de hacer algo; **as the ~ takes her** según le da la vena

mood[2] [muːd] *n Am* LING modo *m*

moodiness ['muːdɪnəs] *n no pl* mal humor *m*

moody ['muːdi] <-ier, -iest> *adj* **1.** (*changeable*) voluble **2.** (*bad-tempered*) malhumorado, -a

moon [muːn] *n no pl* luna *f;* **full/new ~** luna llena/nueva ►**once in a blue ~** de Pascua a Ramos; **to be over the ~** estar como un niño con zapatos nuevos

◆**moon about** *vi,* **moon around** *vi* vagar

moonbeam ['muːnbiːm] *n* rayo *m* de luna **moonboots** *npl* botas *fpl* de après-ski **mooncalf** <-ves> *n* imbécil *mf* **moonlight** **I.** *n no pl* luz *f* de la luna **II.** *vi inf* estar pluriempleado **moonlit** *adj* iluminado, -a por la luna **moonshine** *n no pl* **1.** (*moonlight*) claro *m* de luna **2.** *Am, inf* (*alcoholic drink*) *bebida alcohólica destilada ilegalmente* **3.** *inf* (*nonsense*) pamplinas *fpl* **moonstone** *n* labradorita *f*

moony ['muːni] <-ier, -iest> *adj* soñador(a)

moor[1] [mɔːʳ, *Am:* mʊr] *n* (*area*) páramo *m*

moor[2] [mɔːʳ, *Am:* mʊr] *vt* NAUT amarrar

moorhen ['mɔːhen, *Am:* 'mʊr-] *n* polla *f* de agua

mooring ['mʊərɪŋ, *Am:* 'mʊrɪŋ] *n* amarra *f*

moose [muːs] *n* alce *m* americano

moot [muːt] **I.** *vt* **it has been ~ed that ...** se ha sugerido que... **II.** *adj* discutible

mop [mɒp, *Am:* mɑːp] **I.** *n* fregona *f;* **a ~ of hair** una mata de pelo **II.** <-pp-> *vt* fregar

mope [məʊp, *Am:* moʊp] *vi* estar deprimido

◆**mope about** *vi,* **mope around** *vi* andar deprimido

moped ['məʊped, *Am:* 'moʊ-] *n* ciclomotor *m*

moraine [mɒ'reɪn, *Am:* mə'-] *n* morena *f*

moral ['mɒrəl, *Am:* 'mɔːr-] **I.** *adj* moral; **to give sb ~ support** dar apoyo moral a alguien **II.** *n* **1.** (*message*) moraleja *f* **2.** *pl* (*standards*) moralidad *f*

morale [mə'rɑːl, *Am:* -'ræl] *n no pl* moral *f*

moralist ['mɒrəlɪst, *Am:* 'mɔːr-] *n* moralista *mf*

morality [mə'ræləti, *Am:* mɔː'rælət̬i] <-ies> *n* moralidad *f*

moralize ['mɒrəlaɪz, *Am:* 'mɔːr-] *vi* moralizar

morass [mə'ræs] *n* **1.** (*boggy area*) cenagal *m* **2.** *fig* (*complicated situation*) laberinto *m*

moratorium [ˌmɒrə'tɔːrɪəm, *Am:* ˌmɔːr-] <-s *o* -ria> *n form* moratoria *f*

morbid ['mɔːbɪd, *Am:* 'mɔːr-] *adj* **1.** MED mórbido, -a **2.** (*person, interest*) morboso, -a

morbidity [mɔː'bɪdəti, *Am:* mɔːr'bɪdət̬i] *n no pl* morbosidad *f*

more [mɔːʳ, *Am:* mɔːr] *comp of* **much, many** **I.** *adj* más; **~ wine/grapes** más vino/

M

uvas; **a few ~ grapes** unas pocas uvas más; **no ~ wine at all** nada más de vino; **some ~ wine** un poco más de vino **II.** *adv* más; **~ beautiful than me** más bello que yo; **to drink** (**a bit/much**) ~ beber (un poco/mucho) más; **once ~** una vez más; **never ~** nunca más; **to see ~ of sb** volver a ver a alguien; **~ than 10** más de 10 **III.** *pron* más; **~ and ~** más y más; **to have ~ than sb** tener más que alguien; **to cost ~ than sth** costar más que algo; **the ~ you eat, the ~ you get fat** cuanto más comes, más gordo te pones; **what ~ does he want?** ¿qué más quiere?; **many do it but ~ don't** muchos lo hacen, pero la mayoría no ▸**all the** ~ tanto más

morello [mə'reləʊ, *Am:* -oʊ] *n* guinda *f*

moreover [mɔː'rəʊvəʳ, *Am:* -'roʊvɚ] *adv form* además

morgue [mɔːg, *Am:* mɔːrg] *n* depósito *m* de cadáveres, afanaduaría *f Méx*

moribund ['mɒrɪbʌnd, *Am:* 'mɔːr-] *adj form* moribundo, -a

Mormon ['mɔːmən, *Am:* 'mɔːr-] **I.** *n* mormón, -ona *m, f* **II.** *adj* mormónico, -a

morning ['mɔːnɪŋ, *Am:* 'mɔːr-] *n* mañana *f*; **good ~!** ¡buenos días!; **in the ~** por la mañana; **that ~** esa mañana; **the ~ after** la mañana después; **every ~** cada mañana; **every Monday ~** cada lunes por la mañana; **to come in the ~** venir por la mañana; **one July ~** una mañana de julio; **early in the ~** muy por la mañana; **6 o'clock in the ~** las 6 de la mañana; **from ~ till night** de la mañana a la noche

morning-after pill [ˌmɔːnɪŋ'ɑːftəˌpɪl, *Am:* ˌmɔːrnɪŋ'æftɚˌpɪl] *n* píldora *f* del día después **morning coat** *n* chaqué *m* **morning paper** *n* diario *m* **Morning Prayer** *n* maitines *mpl* **morning sickness** *n* náuseas *fpl* matutinas **morning star** *n* lucero *m* del alba

Moroccan [mə'rɒkən, *Am:* -'rɑːkən] **I.** *n* marroquí *mf* **II.** *adj* marroquí

Morocco [mə'rɒkəʊ, *Am:* -'rɑːkoʊ] *n* Marruecos *m*

morocco leather *n* tafilete *m*

moron ['mɔːrɒn, *Am:* 'mɔːrɑːn] *n inf* imbécil *mf*

moronic [mə'rɒnɪk, *Am:* moː'rɑːnɪk] *adj inf* imbécil

morose [mə'rəʊs, *Am:* -'roʊs] *adj* (*person, mood*) taciturno, -a; (*expression*) sombrío, -a

morpheme ['mɔːfiːm, *Am:* 'mɔːr-] *n* LING morfema *m*

morphia ['mɔːfiə, *Am:* 'mɔːr-] *n*, **morphine** ['mɔːfiːn, *Am:* 'mɔːr-] *n* morfina *f*

morphological [ˌmɔːfə'lɒdʒɪkl, *Am:* ˌmɔːrfə'lɑːdʒɪ-] *adj* morfológico, -a

morphology [mɔː'fɒlədʒi, *Am:* mɔːr'fɑːlə-] *n* morfología *f*

> El **Morris dancing** existe desde hace mucho tiempo, pero sus orígenes son desconocidos. El nombre procede de 'Moorish' (árabe). Este baile cobra su principal significado en el **May Day** (1 de mayo) y en **Whitsuntide** (Pentecostés). Los **Morris dancers** son, la mayoría de las veces, grupos de hombres vestidos de blanco; algunos llevan campanillas en las pantorrillas y cada uno de ellos porta un bastón, un pañuelo o una corona en la mano. El baile está lleno de movimiento; los bailarines brincan, dan saltos y golpean el suelo con los pies.

Morse (**code**) [mɔːs, *Am:* mɔːrs-] *n no pl* morse *m*

morsel ['mɔːsl, *Am:* 'mɔːr-] *n* (*of food*) bocado *m*; (*of hope*) brizna *f*

mortal ['mɔːtl, *Am:* 'mɔːrt̬l] **I.** *adj* mortal; **~ danger** peligro *m* de muerte; **to be in ~ fear** estar aterrado **II.** *n liter* mortal *mf*

mortality [mɔː'tæləti, *Am:* mɔːr'tælət̬i] *n no pl, form* mortalidad *f*

mortar ['mɔːtəʳ, *Am:* 'mɔːrtɚ] *n a.* MIL, TECH mortero *m*

mortarboard ['mɔːtəʳbɔːd, *Am:* 'mɔːrtɚ-bɔːrd] *n* birrete *m*, capelo *m Cuba, PRico, Ven*

mortgage ['mɔːgɪdʒ, *Am:* 'mɔːr-] **I.** *n* hipoteca *f* **II.** *vt* hipotecar

mortice ['mɔːtɪs, *Am:* 'mɔːrt̬ɪs] *n s.* **mortise**

mortician [mɔː'tɪʃən, *Am:* mɔːr-] *n Am* director(a) *m(f)* de funeraria

mortification [ˌmɔːtɪfɪ'keɪʃən, *Am:* ˌmɔːrt̬ə-] *n no pl* **1.** (*embarrassment*) humillación *f* **2.** REL mortificación *f*

mortify ['mɔːtɪfaɪ, *Am:* 'mɔːrt̬ə-] *vt* <-ie-> mortificar

mortise ['mɔːtɪs, *Am:* 'mɔːrt̬ɪs] **I.** *n* entalladura *f* **II.** *vt* ensamblar

mortise lock *n* cerradura *f* embutida

mortuary ['mɔːtʃəri, *Am:* 'mɔːrtʃuer-] *n* **1.** *Brit* (*morgue*) depósito *m* de cadávares **2.** *Am* (*funeral parlour*) tanatorio *m*

mosaic [məʊ'zeɪɪk, *Am:* moʊ-] *n* mosaico *m*

Moscow ['mɒskəʊ, *Am:* 'mɑːkaʊ] *n* Moscú *m*

Moses ['məʊzɪz, *Am:* 'moʊ-] *n* Moisés *m*

Moslem ['mɒzləm, *Am:* 'mɑːzlem] **I.** *adj* musulmán, -ana **II.** *n* musulmán, -ana *m, f*

mosque [mɒsk, *Am:* mɑːsk] *n* mezquita *f*

mosquito [mə'skiːtəʊ, *Am:* -t̬oʊ] <-(e)s> *n* mosquito *m*, zancudo *m AmL*

mosquito net *n* mosquitera *f*

moss [mɒs, *Am:* mɑːs] <-es> *n* musgo *m*

mossy ['mɒsi, *Am:* 'mɑːsi] <-ier, -iest> *adj* musgoso, -a

most [məʊst, *Am:* moʊst] *superl of* **many, much I.** *adj* la mayoría de; **~ people** la mayoría de la gente; **to have the ~ grapes/wine** tener más uvas/vino que nadie; **for the ~ part** en su mayor parte **II.** *adv* más; **the ~ beautiful** la más bella, el más bello; **a ~ beautiful even-**

ing una tarde de lo más bella; **what I want** ~ lo que más quiero; ~ **of all** más que nada; ~ **likely** my probablemente **III.** *pron* la mayoría; **at the** (**very**) ~ a lo sumo; ~ **of them/of the time** la mayor parte de ellos/del tiempo; **to make the** ~ **of sth/of oneself** sacar el máximo partido de algo/de sí mismo; **the** ~ **you can have is ...** lo máximo que puedes tener es...

mostly [ˈməʊstli, *Am:* ˈmoʊst-] *adv* **1.** (*usually*) en general **2.** (*nearly all*) casi todo **3.** (*in the majority*) principalmente

MOT [ˌeməʊˈtiː, *Am:* -oʊˈ-] *n abbr of* **Ministry of Transport** Ministerio *m* de Transportes

motel [məʊˈtel, *Am:* moʊ-] *n* motel *m*, hotel-garaje *m AmL*

moth [mɒθ, *Am:* mɑːθ] *n* polilla *f*

mothball [mɒθbɔːl, *Am:* mɑːθbɑːl] **I.** *n* bola *f* de naftalina **II.** *vt* (*idea, plan*) aparcar *fig*

moth-eaten [ˈmɒθˌiːtn, *Am:* ˈmɑːθ-] *adj* apolillado, -a

mother [ˈmʌðəʳ, *Am:* -ɚ] **I.** *n* madre *f* **II.** *vt* mimar

mother country *n* madre patria *f* **motherhood** *n no pl* maternidad *f* **mother-in-law** *n* suegra *f*

motherly [ˈmʌðəli, *Am:* -ɚli] *adj* maternal

mother-of-pearl *n* nácar *m* **Mother's Day** *n no pl* día *m* de la madre **mother tongue** *n* lengua *f* materna

motif [məʊˈtiːf, *Am:* moʊ-] *n* ART motivo *m*

motion [ˈməʊʃən, *Am:* ˈmoʊ-] **I.** *n* **1.** (*movement*) movimiento *m*; **in slow** ~ a cámara lenta; **to put sth in** ~ poner algo en marcha **2.** *Brit, Aus* MED deposición *f* **3.** (*proposal*) moción *f* **II.** *vt* indicar con un gesto; **to** ~ **sb to do sth** indicar a alguien que haga algo **III.** *vi* hacer señas

motionless *adj* inmóvil

motion picture *n Am* película *f*

motivate [ˈməʊtɪveɪt, *Am:* ˈmoʊt̬ə-] *vt* **1.** (*cause*) motivar **2.** (*arouse interest of*) animar

motivation [ˌməʊtɪˈveɪʃən, *Am:* ˌmoʊt̬əˈ-] *n* **1.** (*reason*) motivo *m* **2.** *no pl* (*ambition, drive*) motivación *f*

motive [ˈməʊtɪv, *Am:* ˈmoʊt̬ɪv] **I.** *n* motivo *m* **II.** *adj* PHYS, TECH motriz

motley [ˈmɒtli, *Am:* ˈmɑːt-] <-ier, -iest> *adj pej* variopinto, -a

motor [ˈməʊtəʳ, *Am:* ˈmoʊt̬ɚ] **I.** *n* **1.** *a. fig* motor *m* **2.** *Brit, inf* (*car*) automóvil *m*, carro *m AmL* **II.** *adj a.* PHYS motor, motriz **III.** *vi* **1.** (*drive*) ir en coche **2.** (*go quickly*) ir rápido

motorbike *n inf* moto *f* **motorboat** *n* lancha *f* motora **motor car** *n Brit* automóvil *m* **motorcycle** *n form* motocicleta *f* **motorcycling** *n* motociclismo *m* **motorcyclist** *n* motociclista *mf* **motor-driven** *adj* motorizado, -a

motoring **I.** *adj Brit* automovilístico, -a **II.** *n* automovilismo *m*

motoring school *n* autoescuela *f*

motorist [ˈməʊtərɪst, *Am:* ˈmoʊt̬ɚ-] *n* conductor(a) *m(f)*

motorize [ˈməʊtəraɪz, *Am:* ˈmoʊt̬ə-] *vt* motorizar

motor racing *n Brit* automovilismo *m* **motor scooter** *n* scooter *f* **motor vehicle** *n form* automóvil *m* **motorway** *n Brit* autopista *f*

mottled [ˈmɒtld, *Am:* ˈmɑːt̬ld] *adj* (*leaf, marble*) jaspeado, -a; (*skin*) manchado, -a

motto [ˈmɒtəʊ, *Am:* ˈmɑːt̬oʊ] <-(e)s> *n* lema *m*

mould¹ [məʊld, *Am:* moʊld] *n no pl, Brit* BOT moho *m*

mould² [məʊld, *Am:* moʊld] *Brit* **I.** *n* (*for metal, clay, jelly*) molde *m* ►**to be cast in the same** ~ estar cortado por el mismo patrón **II.** *vt* moldear

moulder [ˈməʊldəʳ, *Am:* ˈmoʊldɚ] *vi Brit* echarse a perder; *fig* desmoronarse

moulding [ˈməʊldɪŋ, *Am:* ˈmoʊld-] *n Brit* ARCHIT moldura *f*

mouldy [ˈməʊldi, *Am:* ˈmoʊl-] <-ier, -iest> *adj Brit* **1.** GASTR (*food*) mohoso, -a **2.** *inf* (*shabby*) gastado, -a

moult [məʊlt, *Am:* moʊlt] *vt Brit* ZOOL mudar

mound [maʊnd] *n* **1.** (*elevation*) montículo *m* **2.** (*heap*) montón *m*

mount [maʊnt] **I.** *n* **1.** (*horse*) montura *f* **2.** (*frame*) marco *m* **II.** *vt* **1.** (*get on: horse*) montar; **to** ~ **a ladder** subirse a una escalera; **to** ~ **the throne** *form* ascender al trono **2.** (*organize*) organizar; **to** ~ **guard** montar guardia **3.** (*fix for display*) fijar **III.** *vi* montarse

mountain [ˈmaʊntɪn, *Am:* -t̬ən] *n* **1.** GEO montaña *f* **2.** *inf* (*amount*) montón *m* ►**to make a** ~ **out of a molehill** ahogarse en un vaso de agua, hacer de la camisa un trapo *Col, Ven;* **to move** ~**s** mover cielo y tierra

mountain chain *n* GEO cordillera *f*

mountaineer [ˌmaʊntɪˈnɪəʳ, *Am:* -tənˈɪr] *n* montañista *mf*

mountaineering *n no pl* montañismo *m*

mountainous [ˈmaʊntɪnəs, *Am:* -tnəs] *adj* **1.** GEO montañoso, -a **2.** (*large and high*) gigantesco, -a

mountain range *n* GEO sierra *f*

mounted [ˈmaʊntɪd, *Am:* -t̬ɪd] *adj* montado, -a; ~ **police** policía *f* montada

mounting *n* (*of machine*) base *f*; (*in frame*) montaje *m*

mourn [mɔːn, *Am:* mɔːrn] **I.** *vi* lamentarse; **to** ~ **for sb** llorar la muerte de alguien **II.** *vt* llorar la muerte de

mourner [ˈmɔːnəʳ, *Am:* ˈmɔːrnɚ] *n* doliente *mf*

mournful [ˈmɔːnfəl, *Am:* ˈmɔːrn-] *adj* **1.** (*grieving*) afligido, -a **2.** (*gloomy*) triste

mourning [ˈmɔːnɪŋ, *Am:* ˈmɔːrn-] *n no pl* luto *m*; **to be in** ~ estar de luto

mouse [maʊs] <mice> *n* ZOOL, INFOR ratón *m* ►**to be as poor as a church** ~ ser más pobre que las ratas

mousehole *n* ratonera *f* **mousemat** *n Brit,* **mousepad** *n Am* INFOR alfombrilla *f* del ratón **mousetrap** *n* ratonera *f*

mousse [muːs] *n* mousse *f*

moustache [mə'stɑːʃ, *Am:* 'mʌstæʃ] *n* bigote *m*

mousy ['maʊsi] *adj* **1.**(*shy*) apocado, -a; **she is very ~** es muy poquita cosa **2.**(*brown*) pardo, -a

mouth¹ [maʊθ] *n* **1.**(*of person, animal*) boca *f;* **to shut one's ~** *inf* callarse **2.**(*opening*) abertura *f;* (*of bottle, jar, well*) boca *f;* (*of cave*) entrada *f;* (*of river*) desembocadura *f* ►**to be born with a silver spoon in one's ~** nacer con un pan debajo del brazo; **it made her ~ water** se le hizo la boca agua con eso; **to be all ~** ser un bocazas; **to be down in the ~** estar deprimido; **to shoot off one's ~ about sth** *Am, inf* hablar más de la cuenta sobre algo

mouth² [maʊð] *vt* **1.**(*form words silently*) articular **2.**(*say insincerely*) soltar; **to ~ an excuse** soltar la excusa de rigor

mouthful ['maʊθfʊl] *n* (*of food*) bocado *m;* (*of drink*) sorbo *m*

mouth organ *n* armónica *f* **mouthpiece** *n* **1.** TEL micrófono *m* **2.**(*of pipe, instrument*) boquilla *f* **3.**(*person*) portavoz *mf* **mouth-to-mouth resuscitation** *n* resucitación *f* boca a boca **mouthwash** *n* enjuague *m* bucal **mouthwatering** *adj* apetitoso, -a

movable ['muːvəbl] *adj* móvil

move [muːv] **I.** *n* **1.**(*movement*) movimiento *m;* **to be on the ~** (*travelling*) estar de viaje; (*very busy*) no parar; **to get a ~ on** darse prisa **2.**(*change of abode*) mudanza *f;* (*change of job*) traslado *m* **3.** GAMES jugada *f;* **it's your ~** te toca a ti **4.**(*action*) paso *m;* **to make the first ~** dar el primer paso **II.** *vi* **1.**(*change position*) moverse; (*advance fast*) avanzar; (*make progress*) hacer progresos **2.**(*in games*) jugar **3.**(*change abode*) mudarse; (*change job*) cambiar de trabajo ►**~ it!** *inf* ¡apúrate! **III.** *vt* **1.**(*change position*) mover; (*make sb change their mind*) hacer cambiar de idea; (*reschedule*) cambiar la fecha de **2.**(*cause emotions*) conmover; **to be ~d by sth** estar afectado por algo **3.**(*propose*) proponer

◆**move about I.** *vi* **1.**(*go around*) ir de un lado a otro **2.**(*travel*) desplazarse **3.**(*change abode*) mudarse; (*change job*) cambiar de trabajo **II.** *vt* (*furniture*) cambiar de sitio

◆**move along I.** *vt* hacer circular **II.** *vi* circular

◆**move away I.** *vi* mudarse de casa **II.** *vt* apartar

◆**move back I.** *vi* retirarse **II.** *vt* colocar más atrás

◆**move down** *vi, vt* bajar

◆**move forward I.** *vi* avanzar **II.** *vt* mover hacia adelante; (*date*) adelantar

◆**move in I.** *vi* **1.**(*move into abode*) instalarse **2.**(*intervene*) intervenir **3.**(*advance to attack*) avanzar; **to ~ on enemy territory** invadir territorio enemigo **II.** *vt* instalar

◆**move off** *vi* marcharse

◆**move on I.** *vi* **1.**(*continue to move*) seguir adelante; **to ~ to another subject** pasar a otro tema **2.**(*make progress*) progresar **3.**(*go forward*) avanzar **II.** *vt* (*disperse*) dispersar

◆**move out** *vi* **1.**(*stop inhabiting*) dejar la casa **2.**(*cease involvement*) **to ~ (of sth)** retirarse (de algo)

◆**move over I.** *vi* **1.**(*make room*) dejar sitio; (*on seat*) correrse hacia un lado **2.**(*switch*) **to ~ towards sth** cambiar a algo **II.** *vt* mover a un lado

◆**move up I.** *vi* **1.**(*make room*) hacer sitio; (*on seat*) correrse hacia un lado **2.**(*increase*) subir **3.** SCHOOL pasar a la clase superior **II.** *vt* **1.**(*person, thing*) subir **2.** SCHOOL pasar a la clase superior

movement ['muːvmənt] *n* **1.** *a.* MUS (*act*) movimiento *m* **2.** *no pl* FIN, COM actividad *f* **3.** *no pl* (*tendency*) tendencia *f*

movie ['muːvi] *n Am, Aus* película *f;* **the ~s** el cine

movie camera *n* cámara *f* cinematográfica **moviegoer** *n* aficionado, -a *m, f* al cine **movie star** *n* estrella *f* de cine **movie theater** *n* cine *m*

moving ['muːvɪŋ] **I.** *adj* **1.**(*that moves*) móvil; **~ stairs** escaleras mecánicas **2.**(*motivating*) motor, motriz; **the ~ force** la fuerza motriz **3.**(*causing emotion*) conmovedor(a) **II.** *n no pl* mudanza *f*

mow [məʊ, *Am:* moʊ] <mowed, mown *o* mowed> *vt* (*grass*) cortar; (*hay*) segar

mower ['məʊəʳ, *Am:* 'moʊɚ] *n* (*for lawn*) cortacésped *m*

mown [məʊn, *Am:* moʊn] *pp of* **mow**

MP [ˌem'piː] *n* **1.** *Brit abbr of* **Member of Parliament** diputado, -a *m, f* **2.** *abbr of* **Military Police** Policía *f* Militar

mpg *n abbr of* **miles per gallon** millas *fpl* por galón

mph [ˌempiː'eɪtʃ] *abbr of* **miles per hour** m/h

Mr ['mɪstəʳ, *Am:* -tɚ] *n abbr of* **Mister** Sr.

Mrs ['mɪsɪz] *n abbr of* **Mistress** Sra.

ms [ˌem'es] *abbr of* **manuscript** ms

Ms [mɪz] *n abbr of* **Miss** *forma de tratamiento que se aplica tanto a mujeres solteras como casadas*

MS [ˌem'es] *abbr of* **multiple sclerosis** esclerosis *f inv* múltiple

MSc [ˌemes'siː] *abbr of* **Master of Science** máster *m* (*de Ciencias*)*;* **Louie Sanders, MSc** Louie Sanders, licenciado con máster

MSG *abbr of* **monosodium glutamate** glutamato *m* monosódico

Mt *abbr of* **Mount** mte.

much [mʌtʃ] <more, most> **I.** *adj* mucho, mucha; **too ~ wine** demasiado vino; **how ~ milk?** ¿cuánta leche?; **too/so ~ water** demasiada/tanta agua; **as ~ as** tanto como; **three times as ~** tres veces más **II.** *adv* mucho; ~

better mucho mejor; **thank you very ~** muchas gracias; **to be ~ surprised** estar muy sorprendido; **~ to my astonishment** para gran sorpresa mía; **not him, ~ less her** él no, y mucho menos ella **III.** *pron* mucho; **~ of the day** la mayor parte del día; **I don't think ~ of it** no le doy mucha importancia; **to make ~ of sb/sth** dar importancia a alguien/algo

muchness ['mʌtʃnəs] *n no pl, inf* **to be much of a ~** ser más o menos lo mismo

muck [mʌk] *n no pl, Brit, inf* **1.** (*dirt*) suciedad *f* **2.** (*manure*) estiércol *m* **3. to make a ~ of sth** echar a perder algo **4.** *pej* (*bad food*) basura *f*

◆muck about I. *vi inf* **1.** (*waste time*) perder el tiempo **2.** (*handle*) **to ~ with sth** manosear algo **II.** *vt always sep* tratar mal

◆muck out *vt* limpiar

◆muck up *vt Brit, inf* estropear

muckheap *n* estercolero, -a *m, f*

muckraker ['mʌkreɪkəʳ, *Am:* -ɚ] *n* revelador(a) *m(f)* de escándalos

muck-up ['mʌkʌp] *n inf* lío *m* grande

mucky ['mʌki] <-ier, -iest> *adj* **1.** (*dirty*) sucio, -a **2.** (*pornographic*) porno

mucous ['mju:kəs] *n* MED mucosa *f*

mucus ['mju:kəs] *n* MED moco *m*

mud [mʌd] *n no pl* **1.** (*wet earth*) barro *m;* **to wallow in ~** revolcarse en el fango **2.** (*insult*) **to hurl ~ at sb** calumniar a alguien ►**to drag sb's name through the ~** ensuciar el nombre de alguien

muddle ['mʌdl] **I.** *n no pl* desorden *m,* desparpajo *m AmL;* **to get in a ~** liarse **II.** *vt* **1.** (*mix up*) desordenar **2.** (*confuse*) confundir **III.** *vi* **to ~ along** ir tirando

muddle-headed ['mʌdlˌhedɪd] *adj* atontado, -a

muddy ['mʌdi] **I.** *vt* **1.** (*make dirty*) manchar de barro **2.** (*confuse*) confundir **II.** <-ier, -iest> *adj* (*dirty*) lleno, -a de barro; (*water*) turbio, -a; (*ground*) fangoso, -a

mudguard ['mʌdgɑ:d, *Am:* -gɑ:rd] *n* guardabarros *m inv,* salpicadera *f Méx* **mudpack** *n* mascarilla *f* de barro **mudslinging** *n inf* calumnia *f*

muff [mʌf] **I.** *n* FASHION manguito *m* **II.** *vt* (*opportunity*) echar a perder

muffin ['mʌfɪn] *n* **1.** *Am: especie de magdalena* **2.** *Brit* ≈ mollete *m*

muffle ['mʌfl] *vt* amortiguar

◆muffle up I. *vi* abrigarse **II.** *vt* abrigar

muffler ['mʌfləʳ, *Am:* -lɚ] *n Am* **1.** AUTO silenciador *m* **2.** (*scarf*) bufanda *f*

mufti ['mʌfti] *n no pl* **in ~** vestido de paisano

mug [mʌg] **I.** *n* **1.** (*for tea, coffee*) tazón *m;* (*for beer*) jarra *m* **2.** *Brit, inf* (*fool*) bobo, -a *m, f* **3.** *pej* (*face*) jeta *f,* escracho *m RíoPl* **II.** <-gg-> *vt* atracar

mugger ['mʌgəʳ, *Am:* -ɚ] *n* atracador(a) *m(f)*

mugging ['mʌgɪŋ] *n* atraco *m*

muggins ['mʌgɪnz] *n no pl, Brit* tonto, -a *m, f,* gafo, -a *m, f Ven*

muggy ['mʌgi] <-ier, -iest> *adj* bochornoso, -a

mugwump ['mʌgwʌmp] *n Am* POL independiente *mf*

mulberry ['mʌlbri, *Am:* -ber-] *n* **1.** (*fruit*) mora *f* **2.** (*tree*) morera *f*

mule [mju:l] *n* (*animal*) mulo, -a *m, f* ►**as stubborn as a ~** terco como una mula

mull [mʌl] *vt* **to ~ sth over** meditar algo

mulled wine [mʌld waɪn] *n vino tinto caliente aromatizado con especias*

mullion ['mʌlɪən, *Am:* -jən] *n* ARCHIT parteluz *m*

multicolo(u)red [ˌmʌlti'kʌləd, *Am:* ˌmʌlt̬i'kʌlɚd] *adj* multicolor

multicultural [ˌmʌltɪ'kʌltʃərəl, *Am:* -t̬ɪ'-] *adj* multicultural

multifarious [ˌmʌltɪ'feərɪəs, *Am:* -t̬ə'ferɪ-] *adj form* diverso, -a

multifunctional [ˌmʌltɪ'fʌnkʃənəl] *adj* multifuncional

multilateral [ˌmʌltɪ'lætərəl, *Am:* -t̬ɪ'læt̬-] *adj* POL multilateral

multilingual [ˌmʌltɪ'lɪŋgwəl, *Am:* -t̬ɪ'-] *adj* plurilingüe

multimedia [ˌmʌltɪmi:diə, *Am:* -t̬ɪ'-] *adj* multimedia *inv*

multimillionaire [ˌmʌltɪmɪljə'neəʳ, *Am:* -t̬ɪmɪljə'ner] *n* multimillonario, -a *m, f*

multinational [ˌmʌltɪ'næʃnəl, *Am:* -t̬ɪ'-] **I.** *n* multinacional *f* **II.** *adj* multinacional

multiple ['mʌltɪpl, *Am:* -t̬ə-] *adj* múltiple

multiplex ['mʌltɪpleks, *Am:* -t̬ə-] *n* multicines *mpl*

multiplication [ˌmʌltɪplɪ'keɪʃən, *Am:* -t̬ə-] *n* multiplicación *f*

multiplicity [ˌmʌltɪ'plɪsəti, *Am:* -t̬ə'plɪsət̬i] *n no pl, form* multiplicidad *f*

multiplier ['mʌltiplaɪəʳ, *Am:* -t̬əplaɪɚ] *n* MAT multiplicador *m*

multiply ['mʌltɪplaɪ, *Am:* -t̬ə-] <-ie-> **I.** *vt* multiplicar **II.** *vi* multiplicarse

multipurpose [ˌmʌltɪ'pɜ:pəs, *Am:* -t̬ɪ'pɜ:r-] *adj* multiuso

multiracial [ˌmʌltɪ'reɪʃl, *Am:* -t̬ɪ-] *adj* multirracial

multistage [ˌmʌltɪ'steɪdʒ, *Am:* -t̬ɪ'-] *adj* de varios escalones

multistor(e)y [ˌmʌltɪstɔ:ri, *Am:* -t̬ɪ'-] *adj* de varios pisos [*o* plantas]

multitasking [ˌmʌltɪ'tɑ:skɪŋ, *Am:* -t̬ɪ'-] *n* INFOR multitarea *f*

multitude ['mʌltɪtju:d, *Am:* -t̬ətu:d] *n* **1.** (*of things, problems*) multitud *f* **2.** (*crowd*) muchedumbre *f;* **the ~s** *liter* las masas

multitudinous [ˌmʌltɪ'tju:dɪnəs, *Am:* -t̬ə'tu:dn-] *adj* multitudinario, -a

multi-user system *n* INFOR sistema *m* multiusuario

mum¹ [mʌm] *n Brit, inf* mamá *f*

mum² [mʌm] *adj* **to keep ~** *inf* guardar silencio

mumble ['mʌmbl] *vi* hablar entre dientes

mumbo jumbo [ˌmʌmbəʊ'dʒʌmbəʊ, *Am:* -boʊ'dʒʌmboʊ] *n no pl, inf* galimatías *m*
mummify ['mʌmɪfaɪ, *Am:* -ə-] <-ie-> *vt* momificar
mummy¹ ['mʌmi] <-ies> *n Brit, inf* (*mother*) mami *f,* mamita *f AmL*
mummy² ['mʌmi] <-ies> *n* (*preserved corpse*) momia *f*
mumps [mʌmps] *n* MED paperas *fpl;* **he's got the ~** tiene paperas
munch [mʌntʃ] *vi, vt* ronzar
mundane [mʌn'deɪn] *adj* prosaico, -a
municipal [mjuː'nɪsɪpl, *Am:* -əpl] *adj* municipal
municipality [mjuːˌnɪsɪ'pæləti, *Am:* -ə'pælət̬i] *n* <-ies> (*city, town*) municipio *m,* comuna *f AmL;* (*local government*) municipalidad *f*
munitions [mjuː'nɪʃənz] *npl* municiones *fpl*
mural ['mjʊərəl, *Am:* 'mjʊrəl] *n* mural *m*
murder ['mɜːdəʳ, *Am:* 'mɜːrdɚ] **I.** *n* (*killing*) asesinato *m;* LAW homicidio *m;* **to commit ~** cometer un asesinato; **this job is ~** *fig* este trabajo es matador; **he gets away with ~** *fig* se le consiente cualquier cosa ►**to scream blue ~** poner el grito en el cielo **II.** *vt* (*kill*) asesinar, ultimar *AmL; fig* (*music, play*) destrozar
murderer ['mɜːdərəʳ, *Am:* 'mɜːrdɚɚ] *n* (*killer*) asesino, -a *m, f;* LAW homicida *mf,* victimario, -a *m, f AmL*
murderess ['mɜːdərɪs, *Am:* 'mɜːrdɚəs] *n* (*killer*) asesina *f;* LAW homicida *f*
murderous ['mɜːdərəs, *Am:* 'mɜːr-] *adj* **1.** (*instinct, look*) asesino, -a; (*plan*) criminal **2.** (*very taxing: heat*) insufrible
murky ['mɜːki, *Am:* 'mɜːr-] <-ier, -iest> *adj* (*water, past*) turbio, -a; (*night*) nublado, -a
murmur ['mɜːməʳ, *Am:* 'mɜːrmɚ] **I.** *vi, vt* murmurar **II.** *n* murmullo *m*
muscle ['mʌsl] *n* **1.** ANAT músculo *m* **2.** *fig* poder *m*
◆**muscle in** *vi* **to ~** (**on sth**) entrometerse (de algo)
muscle-bound ['mʌslˌbaʊnd] *adj* demasiado musculoso, -a
muscleman ['mʌslmæn] <-men> *n* forzudo *m*
muscular ['mʌskjʊləʳ, *Am:* -kjələ˞] *adj* **1.** (*pain, contraction*) muscular **2.** (*arms, legs*) musculoso, -a
muse [mjuːz] **I.** *vi* **to ~** (**on sth**) cavilar [*o* reflexionar] (sobre algo) **II.** *n* musa *f*
museum [mjuː'zɪəm] *n* museo *m;* **~ piece** pieza *f* de museo
mush [mʌʃ] *n no pl* **1.** *inf* (*food*) papilla *f* **2.** (*film, book*) cursilada *f*
mushroom ['mʌʃrʊm, *Am:* -ruːm] **I.** *n* (*wild*) seta *f,* callampa *f Col, Chile, Perú;* (*button mushroom*) champiñón *m* **II.** *vi* (*prices, population*) dispararse; (*town*) crecer de la noche a la mañana
mushy ['mʌʃi] *adj* <-ier, -iest> **1.** (*soft: food*) blando, -a **2.** (*film, book*) sensiblero, -a
music ['mjuːzɪk] *n* **1.** (*art*) música *f;* **it was ~ to her ears** le sonó a música celestial **2.** (*notes*) partitura *f;* **to read ~** leer música
musical ['mjuːzɪkəl] **I.** *adj* musical **II.** *n* musical *m*
music box *n* caja *f* de música **music hall** *n* music hall *m*
musician [mjuː'zɪʃən] *n* músico, -a *m, f*
music stand *n* atril *m*
musk [mʌsk] *n no pl* almizcle *m*
musket ['mʌskɪt] *n* mosquete *m*
musketeer [ˌmʌskɪ'tɪəʳ, *Am:* -kə'tɪr] *n* mosquetero *m*
muskrat ['mʌskræt] *n* almizclera *f,* rata *f* almizclada
Muslim ['mʊzlɪm, *Am:* 'mʌzləm] **I.** *adj* musulmán, -ana **II.** *n* musulmán, -ana *m, f*
muslin ['mʌzlɪn] *n* muselina *f*
muss [mʌs] *vt Am* desordenar
mussel ['mʌsl] *n* mejillón *m*
must [mʌst] **I.** *aux* **1.** (*obligation*) deber; **~ you leave so soon?** ¿tienes que irte tan pronto?; **you ~n't do that** no debes hacer eso **2.** (*probability*) deber de; **I ~ have lost it** debo de haberlo perdido; **you ~ be hungry** supongo que tendrás hambre; **you ~ be joking!** ¡estarás bromeando! **II.** *n* cosa *f* imprescindible; **this book is a ~** este es un libro de lectura obligada
mustache ['mʌstæʃ] *n Am* bigote *m*
mustang ['mʌstæŋ] *n* mustang *m*
mustard ['mʌstəd, *Am:* -tɚd] *n no pl* mostaza *f*
muster ['mʌstəʳ, *Am:* -tɚ] **I.** *vt* **1.** (*gather*) reunir; **to ~ the courage to do sth** armarse de valor para hacer algo **2.** MIL alistar **II.** *vi* congregarse **III.** *n* **to pass ~** ser aceptable
mustn't ['mʌsnt] *must not* **must**
musty ['mʌsti] <-ier, -iest> *adj* (*room*) que huele a humedad; (*book*) que huele a rancio [*o* a viejo]
mutant ['mjuːtənt] **I.** *adj* mutante **II.** *n* mutante *mf*
mutation [mjuː'teɪʃən] *n* mutación *f*
mute [mjuːt] **I.** *n* **1.** (*person*) mudo, -a *m, f* **2.** MUS sordina *f* **II.** *vt* MUS poner sordina a **III.** *adj* mudo, -a; **to remain ~** permanecer mudo
muted *adj* apagado, -a
mutilate ['mjuːtɪleɪt, *Am:* -t̬əl-] *vt* mutilar
mutilation [ˌmjuːtɪ'leɪʃən, *Am:* -t̬l'-] *n* mutilación *f*
mutineer [ˌmjuːtɪ'nɪəʳ, *Am:* -tn'ɪr] *n* amotinador(a) *m(f)*
mutinous ['mjuːtɪnəs, *Am:* -t̬n-] *adj* amotinado, -a
mutiny ['mjuːtɪni] **I.** *n* <-ies> *no pl* motín *m* **II.** *vi* <-ie-> amotinarse
mutter ['mʌtəʳ, *Am:* 'mʌt̬ɚ] **I.** *vi* **1.** (*talk*) murmurar **2.** (*complain*) refunfuñar; **to ~ about sth** refunfuñar por algo **II.** *vt* **1.** (*say*) murmurar **2.** (*complain*) farfullar
mutton ['mʌtən] *n no pl* carne *f* de oveja

►**she's ~ dressed as lamb** es un vejestorio disfrazado de jovencita

muttonchops *n pl,* **muttonchop whiskers** *n pl* patillas *fpl* de boca de hacha

mutual ['mjuːtʃuəl] *adj* (*understanding*) mutuo, -a; (*friend, interest*) común

mutual fund *n Am* fondo *m* de inversión mobiliaria

mutually *adv* mutuamente; **it was ~ agreed** se decidió de común acuerdo

muzak® ['mjuːzæk] *n* hilo *m* musical

muzzle ['mʌzl] **I.** *n* **1.** (*of horse, dog*) hocico *m* **2.** (*for dog*) bozal *m* **3.** (*of gun*) boca *f* **II.** *vt* **1.** (*dog*) poner un bozal a **2.** *fig* (*person, newspaper*) amordazar

muzzy ['mʌzi] <-ier, -iest> *adj* **1.** (*weather*) borroso, -a **2.** (*unable to think clearly*) atontado, -a

MW *abbr of* **medium wave** OM

my [maɪ] **I.** *adj pos* mi; **~ dog/house** mi perro/casa; **~ children** mis hijos; **this car is ~ own** este coche es mío; **I hurt ~ foot/head** me he hecho daño en el pie/la cabeza **II.** *interj* madre mía

myopia [maɪ'əʊpɪə, *Am:* -'oʊ-] *n* miopía *f*

myopic [maɪ'ɒpɪk, *Am:* -'ɑːpɪk] *adj form* **1.** (*shortsighted*) miope **2.** *fig* corto, -a de miras

myriad ['mɪrɪəd] *n* miríada *f*

myrrh [mɜːʳ, *Am:* mɜːr] *n* mirra *f*

myrtle ['mɜːtl, *Am:* 'mɜːrt̬l] *n* mirto *m*

myself [maɪ'self] *pron reflexive* **1.** (*direct, indirect object*) me; **I hurt ~** me hice daño; **I deceived ~** me engañé a mí mismo; **when I express/exert ~** cuando me expreso/esfuerzo; **I bought ~ a bag** me compré una bolsa **2.** *emphatic* yo (mismo, misma); **my brother and ~** mi hermano y yo; **I'll do it ~** lo haré yo mismo; **I did it** (**all**) **by ~** lo hice (todo) yo solo **3.** *after prep* mi (mismo, misma); **I said to ~** me dije (a mí mismo); **I am ashamed at ~** estoy avergonzado de mí mismo; **I live by ~** vivo solo

mysterious [mɪ'stɪərɪəs, *Am:* -'stɪrɪ-] *adj* misterioso, -a

mystery ['mɪstəri] <-ies> *n* misterio *m*

mystic ['mɪstɪk] **I.** *n* místico, -a *m, f* **II.** *adj* místico, -a

mystical ['mɪstɪkl] *adj* místico, -a

mysticism ['mɪstɪsɪzəm] *n no pl* misticismo *m*

mystification [ˌmɪstɪfɪ'keɪʃən] *n* **1.** (*mystery*) misterio *m* **2.** (*confusion*) confusión *f*, perplejidad *f*

mystify ['mɪstɪfaɪ] *vt* <-ie-> desconcertar

mystique [mɪs'tiːk] *n* mística *f*

myth [mɪθ] *n* mito *m*

mythical ['mɪθɪkl] *adj* **1.** (*legendary*) mítico, -a **2.** (*supposed*) supuesto, -a

mythological [ˌmɪθə'lɒdʒɪkl, *Am:* -'lɑːdʒɪk-] *adj* mitológico, -a

mythology [mɪ'θɒlədʒi, *Am:* -'θɑːlə-] *n* <-ies> mitología *f*

N

N, n [en] *n* N, n *f*; **~ for Nelly** *Brit,* **~ for Nan** *Am* N de Navarra

n *abbr of* **noun** n *m*

N *abbr of* **north** N *m*

Naafi ['næfi] *n abbr of* **Navy, Army and Air Force Institutes** **1.** (*shop*) tienda *f* de las Fuerzas armadas británcicas **2.** (*canteen*) cantina *f* de las Fuerzas armadas británcias

nab [næb] <-bb-> *vt inf* (*person*) coger, pescar; (*thing*) coger

nadir ['neɪdɪəʳ, *Am:* -dɚ] *n* nadir *m*

naff [næf] *adj Brit, inf* hortera

nag¹ [næg] *n* (*horse*) jamelgo *m*

nag² [næg] **I.** <-gg-> *vi* regañar; **to ~ at sb** dar la lata a alguien **II.** <-gg-> *vt* regañar, dar la lata a **III.** *n inf* regañón, -ona *m, f,* criticón, -ona *m, f*

nagging ['nægɪŋ] **I.** *n no pl* quejas *fpl* **II.** *adj* **1.** (*criticizing*) criticón, -ona **2.** (*pain, ache*) persistente

nail [neɪl] **I.** *n* **1.** (*tool*) clavo *m* **2.** ANAT uña *f* ►**to hit the ~ on the head** dar en el clavo; **to pay on the ~** pagar a toca teja **II.** *vt* **1.** (*fasten*) clavar **2.** *inf* (*catch: police*) coger; (*lie*) poner al descubierto ►**to ~ one's colours to the mast** mantenerse firme **nail-biting** *adj fig* angustioso, -a **nail brush** <-es> *n* cepillo *m* de uñas **nail clippers** *npl* cortaúñas *m inv* **nail enamel remover** *n Am* quitaesmalte *m* **nail file** *n* lima *f* **nail polish** *n no pl, Am* quitaesmalte *m* **nail scissors** *npl* tijeras *fpl* para uñas **nail varnish** *n no pl* esmalte *m* de uñas

naive, naïve [naɪ'iːv, *Am:* nɑː'-] *adj* ingenuo, -a

naivety [naɪ'iːvəteɪ, *Am:* ˌnɑːiːv'teɪ], **naïveté** [naɪ'iːvəti, *Am:* nɑː'iːvət̬i] *n no pl* ingenuidad *f*

naked ['neɪkɪd] *adj* **1.** (*unclothed*) desnudo, -a, encuerado, -a *Cuba, Méx* **2.** (*uncovered: blade*) desenvainado, -a; (*aggression*) manifiesto, -a; (*ambition*) puro, -a; **to the ~ eye** a simple vista

nakedness *n no pl* desnudez *f*

NALGO ['nælgəʊ, *Am:* -goʊ] *n Brit abbr of* **National and Local Government Officers Association** *sindicato británico de funcionarios*

namby-pamby [ˌnæmbɪ'pæmbi] *adj inf* (*person*) ñoño, -a, remilgado, -a; (*poem*) ñoño, -a

name [neɪm] **I.** *n* **1.** nombre *m;* (*surname*) apellido *m;* **by ~** de nombre; **to know sb by ~** conocer a alguien de oídas; **to go by the ~ of ...** *form* hacerse llamar...; **in ~ only** sólo de nombre; **under the ~ of ...** bajo el seudónimo de...; **in God's ~** en nombre de Dios; **in the ~ of freedom and justice** en nombre de la libertad y de la justicia; **to call sb ~s** llamar a alguien de todo; **in all but ~** en la práctica

2. (*reputation*) fama *f;* **to give sb/sth a good ~** dar buena fama a alguien/algo; **his ~ is mud** *fig* es persona non grata; **to make a ~ for oneself** hacerse un nombre ►**the ~ of the game** lo fundamental; **not to have a penny to one's ~** no tener ni un duro, no tener donde caerse muerto **II.** *vt* **1.** (*call*) poner nombre a, bautizar **2.** (*list*) nombrar **3.** (*choose*) **to ~ the time and the place** fijar la hora y el lugar

name-day *n* santo *m*

name-dropping ['neɪmdrɒpɪŋ, *Am:* -drɑːp-] *n no pl práctica de mencionar gente importante para impresionar*

nameless ['neɪmlɪs] *adj* indescriptible; (*author*) anónimo, -a

namely ['neɪmli] *adv* a saber

nameplate ['neɪmpleɪt] *n* placa *f* con el nombre

namesake ['neɪmseɪk] *n* tocayo, -a *m, f*

Namibia [næ'mɪbiə, *Am:* nə'-] *n* Namibia *f*

Namibian [næ'mɪbɪən, *Am:* nə'-] **I.** *adj* namibio, -a **II.** *n* namibio, -a *m, f*

nan [nɑːn] *n Brit, childspeak, inf* abuela *f*

nanny ['næni] <-ies> *n* niñera *f,* nurse *f AmL*

nanny goat ['nænɪgəʊt, *Am:* -goʊt] *n* cabra *f*

nanosecond ['nɑːnəʊ'sekənd, *Am:* -oʊ,-] *n* nanosegundo *m*

nap¹ [næp] **I.** *n* cabezadita *f;* (*after lunch*) siesta *f;* **to have a ~** echarse un sueñecito [*o* una siesta] **II.** <-pp-> *vi* hacer una cabezadita

nap² [næp] *n* pelo *m*

napalm ['neɪpɑːm] *n no pl* napalm *m*

nape [neɪp] *n* nuca *f,* cogote *m*

napkin ['næpkɪn] *n* servilleta *f*

nappy ['næpi] <-ies> *n* pañal *m*

narcissism ['nɑːsɪsɪzəm, *Am:* 'nɑːrsəsɪ-] *n no pl* narcisismo *m*

narcissus [nɑː'sɪsəs, *Am:* nɑːr'-] <-es *o* narcissi> *n* narciso *m*

narcosis [nɑː'kəʊsɪs, *Am:* nɑːr'koʊ-] *n no pl* narcosis *f inv*

narcotic [nɑː'kɒtɪk, *Am:* nɑːr'kɑːt̬-] **I.** *n* narcótico *m* **II.** *adj* narcótico, -a

nark [nɑːk, *Am:* nɑːrk] **I.** *vt* cabrear **II.** *n inf* soplón, -ona *m, f*

narrate [nə'reɪt, *Am:* 'nereɪt] *vt* **1.** (*tale, story*) narrar, relatar **2.** TV hacer de comentarista de

narration [nə'reɪʃən, *Am:* ner'eɪʃən] *n no pl* (*tale*) narración *f;* TV comentario *m*

narrative ['nærətɪv, *Am:* 'nerət̬ɪv] *n no pl* narración *f,* relato *m*

narrator [nə'reɪtəʳ, *Am:* 'nereɪt̬ɚ] *n* narrador(a) *m(f);* TV comentarista *mf*

narrow ['nærəʊ, *Am:* 'neroʊ] **I.** <-er, -est> *adj* **1.** (*thin*) estrecho, -a **2.** (*limited*) limitado, -a **3.** (*small: margin*) escaso, -a, reducido, -a **II.** *vi* **1.** estrecharse; (*gap*) reducirse **2.** (*field*) limitarse, restringirse **III.** *vt* **1.** (*reduce width of*) estrechar; (*gap*) reducir **2.** (*restrict: field*) limitar, restringir

narrow boat *n* NAUT barcaza *f*

narrow-gauge *n* vía *f* estrecha

narrowly *adv* **1.** (*barely*) por poco, por un escaso margen **2.** (*meticulously*) meticulosamente

narrow-minded [,nærəʊ'maɪndɪd, *Am:* ,neroʊ'-] *adj* de mentalidad cerrada; (*opinions, views*) cerrado, -a

NASA ['næsə] *n Am abbr of* **National Aeronautics and Space Administration** NASA *f*

nasal ['neɪzl] *adj* nasal; (*voice*) gangoso, -a

nascent ['næsənt] *adj* naciente

nastiness ['nɑːstɪnəs, *Am:* 'næstɪ-] *n no pl* **1.** (*wickedness*) maldad *f* **2.** (*of accident*) gravedad *f;* (*of taste*) lo asqueroso; (*odour*) peste *f* **3.** (*dirtiness*) suciedad *f*

nasturtium [nə'stɜːʃəm, *Am:* -'stɜːr-] *n* BOT capuchina *f*

nasty ['nɑːsti, *Am:* 'næsti] <-ier, -iest> *adj* **1.** (*bad*) malo, -a; (*smell, taste*) asqueroso, -a, repugnante; (*surprise*) desagradable **2.** (*dangerous*) peligroso, -a **3.** (*serious*) serio, -a

natal ['neɪtl, *Am:* -t̬l] *adj* natal

natality [nə'tælɪti] *n no pl* natalidad *f*

nation ['neɪʃən] *n* **1.** (*country, state*) nación *f,* país *m;* **to serve the ~** servir a la nación **2.** (*people living in a state*) **the Jewish ~** la nación judía

national ['næʃənəl] **I.** *adj* nacional; **at the ~ level** a nivel nacional **II.** *n* ciudadano, -a *m, f* **foreign ~** extranjero, -a *m, f*

national anthem *n* himno *m* nacional **national assembly** <-ies> *n* asamblea *f* nacional **national bank** *n* banco *m* nacional **national costume** *n* traje *m* nacional **national currency** <-ies> *n* moneda *f* nacional **national debt** *n* deuda *f* nacional

> El **national emblem** (emblema nacional) de Inglaterra es la **Tudor rose**, una rosa blanca y plana de la casa real de York sobre la rosa roja de la casa de Lancaster. El emblema nacional de Irlanda es la **shamrock**, una especio de trébol, que fue utilizado, al parecer, por el patrón de Irlanda, St. Patrick, para ilustrar el misterio de la Santísima Trinidad. El **thistle** (cardo) de Escocia fue elegido por el rey Jaime III en el siglo XV como símbolo nacional. El **dragon** de Gales fue utilizado desde hace mucho tiempo como emblema en las banderas de guerra. Los galos tienen también al **leek** (puerro) como símbolo, el cual, según Shakespeare, fue llevado en la batalla de Poitiers contra los franceses en 1356. La **daffodil** (campana pascual) es un sustituto del siglo XX más bonito.

National Front *n Brit* POL Frente *m* Nacional **national grid** *n Brit, Aus* red *f* eléctrica nacional **National Guard** *n Am* Guardia *f* Nacional **National Health** (**Service**) *n Brit* (servicio *m* de) asistencia *f* sanitaria de la Seguridad Social **national holiday** *n* fiesta *f* nacional **national income** *n no pl* renta *f* nacional **National Insurance** *n no pl, Brit* Seguridad *f* Social

nationalisation [ˌnæʃənəlaɪˈzeɪʃən, *Am:* -ɪˈ-] *n Brit, Aus s.* **nationalization**

nationalise [ˈnæʃənəlaɪz] *vt Brit, Aus s.* **nationalize**

nationalism [ˈnæʃnəlɪzəm] *n no pl* nacionalismo *m*

nationalist [ˈnæʃnəlɪst] **I.** *adj* nacionalista **II.** *n* nacionalista *mf*

nationalistic [ˌnæʃnəˈlɪstɪk] *adj* nacionalista

nationality [ˌnæʃəˈnæləti] <-ies> *n* nacionalidad *f;* **to adopt British/Spanish** ~ adoptar la nacionalidad británica/española

nationalization [ˌnæʃənəlaɪˈzeɪʃən, *Am:* -ɪˈ-] *n* nacionalización *f*

nationalize [ˈnæʃənəlaɪz] *vt* nacionalizar

national park *n,* **National Park** *n* parque *m* nacional **national product** *n* producto *m* interior **national security** *n no pl* seguridad *f* nacional **national service** *n no pl* **1.** *Brit, Aus* (*military service*) servicio *m* militar; **to do** ~ hacer la mili **2.** *Am* (*youth community service*) prestación *f* social sustitutoria (del servicio militar) **national socialism** *n no pl* nacionalsocialismo *m* **national unity** *n no pl* unidad *f* nacional

nation state *n* estado *m* nacional

nationwide [ˌneɪʃənˈwaɪd] **I.** *adv* nacionalmente **II.** *adj* nacional

native [ˈneɪtɪv, *Am:* -t̬ɪv] **I.** *adj* **1.** (*indigenous*) indígena; **to be** ~ **to Ireland** (*plant, animal*) ser originario de Irlanda **2.** (*of place of origin*) nativo, -a, natural; ~ **country** patria *f* **3.** (*indigenous, aboriginal, primitive*) nativo, -a, indígena **4.** (*original*) nativo, -a; (*innate*) innato, -a; (*language*) materno, -a **II.** *n* (*indigenous inhabitant*) nativo, -a *m, f,* natural *mf;* **a** ~ **of Monaco** un nativo de Mónaco; **to speak English like a** ~ hablar el inglés como un nativo

native American **I.** *n* indígena *mf* americano, -a **II.** *adj* indígena **native-born** *adj* nativo, -a; **is he a** ~ **person or did he move there?** ¿es natural de allí o viene de fuera?; ~ **citizen of New York** natural de Nueva York **native speaker** *n* hablante *mf* nativo, -a

nativity [nəˈtɪvəti, *Am:* -t̬i] <-ies> *n* natividad *f;* **the Nativity** la Navidad

nativity play *n* auto *m* de Navidad

NATO [ˈneɪtəʊ, *Am:* -t̬oʊ] *n abbr of* **North Atlantic Treaty Organisation** OTAN *f*

natter [ˈnætəʳ, *Am:* ˈnæt̬ɚ] *inf* **I.** *vi inf* charlar; **to** ~ **away** parlotear **II.** *n* charla *f;* **to have a** ~ (**with sb**) tener una charla (con alguien)

natural [ˈnætʃərəl, *Am:* -ɚəl] **I.** *adj* **1.** (*not artifical, inherent*) natural; ~ **causes** causas *fpl* naturales; **to die from** ~ **causes** morir de causas naturales; ~ **disaster** desastre *m* natural; **to be a** ~ **blonde** ser rubio natural; ~ **father** padre *m* natural **2.** (*usual, to be expected*) normal; **I'm sure there's a** ~ **explanation for it** estoy seguro de que tiene una explicación normal **II.** *n* **1.** *inf* **to be a** ~ **for sth** tener un talento innato para algo **2.** MUS nota *f* natural

natural childbirth *n no pl* parto *m* natural **natural gas** *n no pl* gas *m* natural **natural history** *n no pl* historia *f* natural; ~ **museum** museo *m* de Historia Natural

naturalisation [ˌnætʃərəlaɪˈzeɪʃən, *Am:* -ɚəlɪˈ-] *n no pl, Brit, Aus s.* **naturalization**

naturalise [ˈnætʃərəlaɪz, *Am:* -ɚəl-] *vt Brit, Aus s.* **naturalize**

naturalised *adj Brit, Aus s.* **naturalized**

naturalism [ˈnætʃərəlɪzəm, *Am:* -ɚəl-] *n no pl* naturalismo *m*

naturalist **I.** *n* naturalista *mf* **II.** *adj* naturalista

naturalistic [ˌnætʃərəlˈɪstɪk, *Am:* -ɚəl-] *adj* naturalista

naturalization [ˌnætʃərəlaɪˈzeɪʃən, *Am:* -ɚəlɪˈ-] *n no pl* naturalización *f*

naturalize [ˈnætʃərəlaɪz, *Am:* -ɚəl-] *vt Am* naturalizar

naturalized *adj* naturalizado, -a; ~ **citizen** ciudadano, -a *m, f* naturalizado, -a

natural language *n* lenguaje *m* natural

naturally *adv* naturalmente

natural resources *npl* recursos *mpl* naturales; **to be rich/poor in** ~ ser rico/pobre en recursos naturales **natural science** *n,* **natural sciences** *npl* ciencias *fpl* naturales **natural selection** *n no pl* selección *f* natural **natural wastage** *n no pl, Brit* desechos *mpl* naturales

nature [ˈneɪtʃəʳ, *Am:* -tʃɚ] *n* **1.** *no pl* (*the environment, natural forces*) naturaleza *f;* **to get back to** ~ volver a la naturaleza; **to let** ~ **take its course** dejar que la naturaleza siga su curso **2.** (*essential or innate qualities*) naturaleza *f;* **things of this** ~ cosas de esta índole; **in the** ~ **of things** en la naturaleza de las cosas; **to be in sb's** ~ estar en la naturaleza de alguien ►<u>**second**</u> ~ *hábito muy arraigado en una persona*

nature conservancy *n no pl* conservación *f* natural **nature lover** *n* amante *mf* de la naturaleza **nature reserve** *n* reserva *f* natural **nature study** *n no pl* historia *f* natural **nature trail** *n* ruta *f* ecológica **nature worship** *n no pl* culto *m* a la naturaleza

naturism [ˈneɪtʃərɪzəm] *n no pl* naturismo *m*

naturist [ˈneɪtʃərɪst] *n form* naturista *mf*

naughty [ˈnɔːti, *Am:* ˈnɑːt̬i] <-ier, -iest> *adj* **1.** (*badly behaved: children*) desobediente, travieso, -a **2.** *iron* (*adults*) pícaro, -a **3.** *iron, inf* (*sexually stimulating*) picante; ~ **films** películas *fpl* porno

nausea [ˈnɔːsɪə, *Am:* ˈnɑːzɪə] *n no pl* **1.** náusea *f;* **feeling of** ~ sensación *f* de náusea; **to suffer from** ~ tener náuseas **2.** *fig* repugnancia *f*

nauseate [ˈnɔːsɪeɪt, *Am:* ˈnɑːzɪ-] *vt form* asquear; **to be ~d by sth** tener náuseas por algo

nauseating [ˈnɔːsɪeɪtɪŋ, *Am:* ˈnɑːzɪ-] *adj* repugnante, nauseabundo, -a

nauseous [ˈnɔːsɪəs, *Am:* ˈnɑːʃəs] *adj* nauseabundo, -a; **she is** ~ tiene náuseas

nautical [ˈnɔːtɪkəl, *Am:* ˈnɑːt̬ɪ-] *adj* náutico, -a; ~ **chart** carta *f* náutica

nautical mile *n* milla *f* marina

naval [ˈneɪvəl] *adj* naval; ~ **commander** comandante *mf* naval; ~ **battle/engagement/force** batalla *f*/combate *m*/fuerza *f* naval

naval academy <-ies> *n* academia *f* naval **naval base** *n* base *f* naval **naval power** *n* potencia *f* naval **naval warfare** *n no pl* guerra *f* naval

nave [neɪv] *n* nave *f*

navel [ˈneɪvl] *n* ombligo *m* ►**to contemplate one's** ~ rascarse el ombligo

navigable [ˈnævɪgəbl] *adj* navegable; ~ **waters** aguas *fpl* navegables

navigate [ˈnævɪgeɪt] **I.** *vt* **1.** (*steer*) llevar; AUTO guiar **2.** (*sail*) navegar por; **to** ~ **the ocean/a river** navegar por el océano/un río **3.** (*traverse*) atravesar **4.** INFOR **to** ~ **the Internet** navegar por la red, surfear **II.** *vi* NAUT, AVIAT navegar; AUTO guiar, hacer de copiloto

navigation [ˌnævɪˈgeɪʃən] *n no pl* navegación *f*

navigational [ˌnævɪˈgeɪʃənəl] *adj* de navegación; ~ **error** error *m* de navegación

navigator [ˈnævɪgeɪtəʳ, *Am:* -t̬ɚ] *n* navegante *mf;* AUTO copiloto *mf*

navvy [ˈnævi] <-ies> *n Brit, inf* peón *m*

navy [ˈneɪvi] **I.** <-ies> *n* (*country's military fleet and servicemen*) **the Navy** la Marina; **to be in the Navy** estar en la Marina; **to serve in the** ~ servir en la Marina **II.** *adj* (*dark blue*) azul marino

nay [neɪ] **I.** *adv form* no **II.** *n Am* (*negative vote*) voto *m* en contra

Nazi [ˈnɑːtsi] *n* nazi *mf*

Naziism *n no pl,* **Nazism** [ˈnɑːtsɪzəm] *n no pl* nazismo *m*

NB [ˌenˈbiː] *abbr of* **nota bene** N.B.

NCC [ˈensiːˈsiː] *n Brit abbr of* **Nature Conservancy Council** ≈ ICONA *m*

NCO [ˌensiːˈəʊ, *Am:* -ˈoʊ] *n abbr of* **non commissioned officer** suboficial *mf*

NE [ˌenˈiː] *abbr of* **northeast** NE *m*

neap tide [ˈniːpˌtaɪd] *n* marea *f* muerta

near [nɪəʳ, *Am:* nɪr] **I.** *adj* **1.** (*spatial*) cercano, -a **2.** (*temporal*) próximo, -a; **in the** ~ **future** en un futuro próximo **3.** (*dear*) **a** ~ **and dear friend** un amigo íntimo **4.** (*similar: portrait*) parecido, -a; **the** ~**est thing to sth** lo más parecido a algo **5.** (*almost true*) **to have a** ~ **accident** tener por poco un accidente; **that was a** ~ **miss** [*o* **thing**] faltó poco **II.** *adv* **1.** (*spatial or temporal*) cerca; **to be** ~ estar cerca; **to come** ~ aproximarse, acercarse; **to live quite** ~ vivir bastante cerca; ~ **at hand** a mano; **to come** ~**er to sb/sth** acercarse más a alguien/algo **2.** (*almost*) ~ **to tears** a punto de llorar; **as** ~ **as I can guess** que yo sepa **III.** *prep* **1.** (*in proximity to*) ~ (**to**) cerca de; ~ (**to**) **the house** cerca de la casa; ~ **the end of the film** hacia el final de la película **2.** (*almost*) **it's** ~ **midnight** es casi medianoche; **it's nowhere** ~ **enough** no basta ni con mucho **3.** (*about ready to*) **to be** ~ **to doing sth** estar a punto de hacer algo **4.** (*like*) **the copy is** ~ **to the original** la copia es parecida al original **IV.** *vt* acercarse a; **it is** ~**ing completion** está casi terminado; **he is** ~**ing his goal** está alcanzando su meta

nearby [ˈnɪəbaɪ, *Am:* ˌnɪrˈ-] **I.** *adj* cercano, -a **II.** *adv* cerca; **is it** ~**?** está cerca?

Near East *n* Oriente *m* Próximo

nearly [ˈnɪəli, *Am:* ˈnɪr-] *adv* casi; ~ **certain** casi seguro; **to be not** ~ **as bad** no estar tan mal; **to be** ~ **there** estar casi ahí; **to very** ~ **do sth** estar a punto de hacer algo; **to be** ~ **sth** estar cerca de algo; **that wall is** ~ **three metres high** esa pared tiene casi tres metros; **she's** ~ **as tall as her father** ella es casi tan alta como su padre

nearside [ˈnɪəsaɪd, *Am:* ˌnɪrˈ-] *Brit, Aus* **I.** *n* lado *m* cercano al arcén **II.** *adj* **the** ~ **lane** el lado derecho; *Brit* el lado izquierdo

near-sighted [ˌnɪəˈsaɪtɪd, *Am:* ˌnɪrˈsaɪt̬ɪd] *adj a. fig* miope

nearsightedness [ˌnɪəˈsaɪtɪdnɪs, *Am:* ˌnɪrˈsaɪt̬ɪd-] *n no pl, a. fig* miopía *f*

neat [niːt] *adj* **1.** (*orderly, well-ordered*) cuidado, -a, ordenado, -a; ~ **appearance/beard** apariencia *f*/barba *f* cuidada; **to be** ~ **in one's habits** ser de hábitos ordenados; ~ **and tidy** ordenado **2.** (*deft*) cuidadoso, -a; ~ **answer** respuesta *f* exacta **3.** (*undiluted, pure*) puro, -a; **I'll have a** ~ **gin please** tomaré un gin solo **4.** *Am, Aus, inf* (*fine, good, excellent*) guay *inf;* **a** ~ **guy** un tipo guay

neaten [niːtən] *vt* ordenar; **to** ~ **sth up** poner orden en algo

neatly *adv* **1.** (*with care*) cuidadosamente **2.** (*in orderly fashion*) de forma ordenada **3.** (*deftly*) con estilo

neatness [ˈniːtnəs] *n no pl* pulcritud *f,* limpieza *f*

nebula [ˈnebjələ] <-lae *o* -las> *n* ASTR nebulosa *f*

nebulae *n pl of* **nebula**

nebular *adj* nebular

nebulous [ˈnebjʊləs] *adj* nebuloso, -a; ~ **promise** promesa *f* vaga

necessaries [ˈnesəsəriz] *npl* **the** ~ lo necesario

necessarily [ˈnesəsərəli] *adv* necesariamente; **not** ~ no necesariamente

necessary [ˈnesəsəri, *Am:* -ser-] **I.** *adj* necesario, -a; **to make the** ~ **arrangements** hacer los preparativos necesarios; **a** ~ **evil** un mal necesario; **strictly** ~ estrictamente necesario; **to be** ~ ser necesario; **that won't be** ~ no será necesario; **was it really** ~ **for you to say that?** ¿era necesario que dijeras eso?; **to do**

what is ~ hacer lo que es necesario; **if** ~ cuando sea necesario **II.** *n* **the** ~ lo necesario
necessitate [nɪ'sesɪteɪt, *Am:* nə'-] *vt form* necesitar; **to** ~ **doing sth** necesitar hacer algo
necessity [nɪ'sesəti, *Am:* nə'sesəṱi] <-ies> *n no pl* (*need*) necesidad *f;* **in case of** ~ en caso de necesidad; **when the** ~ **arises** cuando surja la necesidad; ~ **of doing sth** necesidad de hacer algo; ~ **for sb to do sth** necesidad de que alguien haga algo; **there's no** ~ **to pay in advance** no hay necesidad de pagar por adelantado; **by** ~ por necesidad; **bare** ~ primera necesidad ►~ **is the mother of invention** *prov* no hay mejor maestra que el hambre *prov*
neck [nek] **I.** *n* **1.** (*part of body connecting head and shoulders*) cuello *m;* (*nape*) cogote *m;* **to fling one's arms round sb's** ~ abrazar a alguien por el cuello **2.** FASHION cuello *m;* **round** ~ cuello redondo **3.** (*long thin object part*) cuello *m;* ~ **of the bottle/vase/violin** cuello de la botella/del jarrón/del violín ►**to be up to one's** ~ **in sth** *inf* estar (metido) hasta el cuello en algo; **to be breathing down sb's** ~ estar encima de alguien **II.** *vi Am, inf* besuquearse
neckband ['nekbænd] *n* collar *m*
neckerchief ['nekətʃɪf] <neckerchieves> *n* pañuelo *m* atado al cuello
necklace ['neklɪs] *n* collar *m*
necklet ['neklɪt] *n* collar *m;* (*small one*) gargantilla *f*
neckline ['neklaɪn] *n* escote *m* **necktie** *n* corbata *f*
nectar ['nektəʳ, *Am:* -tɚ] *n* néctar *m*
nectarine ['nektərɪn, *Am:* ˌnektə'riːn] *n* nectarina *f*
née [neɪ] *adj* de soltera
need [niːd] **I.** *n no pl* necesidad *f;* **in** ~ necesitado, -a; **basic** ~**s** necesidades básicas; ~ **for sb/sth** necesidad de alguien/algo; **to be in** ~ **of sth** necesitar (de) algo; **to have no** ~ **of sth** no necesitar (de) algo; **as the** ~ **arises** según se sienta la necesidad; **if** ~**(s) be** si es necesario; **no** ~ **to be sth** ninguna necesidad de ser algo; **there's no** ~ **to shout so loud** no hace falta gritar tan alto; **in sb's hour of** ~ (*emergency, crisis*) en un momento de necesidad **II.** *vt* **1.** (*require*) necesitar; **to** ~ **sb to do sth** necesitar que alguien haga algo **2.** (*ought to have*) **to** ~ necesitar; **not to** ~ **sth** no necesitar (de) algo; **to** ~ **(doing) sth** necesitar (hacer) algo; **I** ~ **it like (I** ~**) a hole in the head** *iron* me hace tanta falta como un agujero en la cabeza **3.** (*must, have*) **to** ~ **to do sth** tener que hacer algo; ~ **we/I/you?** ¿nos/me/te hace falta?; **there was no** ~ **to do sth** no había necesidad de hacer algo **4.** (*should*) **you** ~**n't laugh! – you'll be next** ¡no deberías reír! – tú serás el siguiente; **I** ~ **hardly say ...** no hace falta decir que...
needed *adj* necesario, -a
needle ['niːdl] **I.** *n* aguja *f;* **hypodermic needle** jeringa *f;* **knitting** ~ aguja de tejer; ~ **and thread** aguja e hilo; **to thread a** ~ enhebrar una aguja ►**a** ~ **in a haystack** una aguja en un pajar; **to look for a** ~ **in a haystack** buscar una aguja en un pajar **II.** *vt* pinchar, provocar
needle match *n* partido *m* importantísimo
needless ['niːdlɪs] *adj* innecesario, -a; ~ **to say ...** no hace falta decir...; ~ **to say, I didn't reply** ni que decir tiene que no respondí
needlework ['niːdlwɜːk, *Am:* -wɜːrk] *n no pl* labor *f* de aguja
needn't ['niːdənt] = **need not** *s.* **need**
needs [niːdz] *adv* necesariamente; ~ **must** si hace falta; **must** ~ *form* por necesidad
needy ['niːdi] **I.** <-ier, -iest> *adj* necesitado, -a **II.** *npl* **the** ~ los necesitados
nefarious [nɪ'feərɪəs, *Am:* nə'ferɪ-] *adj pej, form* nefario, -a
negate [nɪ'geɪt] *vt* negar
negation [nɪ'geɪʃən] *n no pl* negación *f*
negative ['negətɪv, *Am:* -ṱɪv] **I.** *adj* **1.** (*not positive*) negativo, -a; ~ **answer** respuesta *f* negativa; ~ **clause/form** cláusula *f* negativa; **to be** ~ **about sth/sb** ser negativo respecto a algo/alguien **2.** *a.* MED negativo, -a; ~ **pole** polo *m* negativo; ~ **number** número *m* negativo **II.** *n* **1.** (*rejection*) negativa *f* **2.** (*making use of negation*) negación *f* **3.** PHOT negativo *m* **III.** *vt* negar
negatively *adv* negativamente
negativity [ˌnegə'tɪvəti, *Am:* -əṱi] *n no pl* negatividad
neglect [nɪ'glekt] **I.** *vt* desatender; **to** ~ **one's duties** descuidar los propios deberes; **to** ~ **to do sth** descuidar hacer algo; **I'd** ~**ed to write to him** me olvidé de escribirle **II.** *n no pl* negligencia *f;* (*poor state, unrepaired state*) deterioro *m;* **to be in a state of** ~ estar en un estado de deterioro; **to fall in a state of** ~ deteriorarse
neglected *adj* descuidado, -a; (*undervalued, underappreciated*) desvalorado, -a; ~ **child** niño, -a *m, f* abandonado, -a
neglectful [nɪ'glektfəl] *adj* negligente; ~ **parents** padres *mpl* negligentes; **to be** ~ **of sth/sb** ser negligente respecto a algo/alguien
negligee *n,* **negligée** ['neglɪʒeɪ, *Am:* ˌneglə'ʒeɪ] *n* salto *m* de cama
negligence ['neglɪdʒənts] *n no pl* **1.** (*lack of care, inattention, indifference*) negligencia *f;* (*neglect*) descuido *m,* deterioro **2.** LAW negligencia *f;* **gross** ~ negligencia grave
negligible ['neglɪdʒəbl] *adj* insignificante
negotiable [nɪ'gəʊʃiəbl, *Am:* -'goʊ-] *adj* negociable; ~ **securities** FIN títulos *mpl* negociables; **not** ~ no negociable
negotiate [nɪ'gəʊʃieɪt, *Am:* -'goʊ-] **I.** *vt* **1.** (*discuss*) negociar; **to** ~ **a loan/treaty** negociar un préstamo/tratado **2.** (*convert into money*) **to** ~ **a cheque** cobrar un cheque; **to** ~ **securities** negociar títulos **II.** *vi* negociar; **to** ~ **on sth** negociar algo; **to** ~ **with sb** negociar con alguien

N

negotiating committee *n* comité *m* de negociación

negotiating table *n fig* mesa *f* de negociaciones

negotiation [nɪˌɡəʊʃiˈeɪʃən, *Am:* -ˌɡoʊ-] *n* negociación *f;* ~ **for sth** negociación de algo

negotiator [nɪˈɡəʊʃieɪtəʳ, *Am:* -ˈɡoʊʃieɪt̬ɚ] *n* negociador(a) *m(f)*

Negress [ˈniːɡres, *Am:* -ɡrɪs] *n* negra *f*

negro <-es> *n,* **Negro** [ˈniːɡrəʊ, *Am:* -ɡroʊ] *n* negro *m*

negroid [niːɡrɔɪd] *adj* negroide; ~ **hair** pelo *m* negroide

neigh [neɪ] **I.** *n* relincho *m* **II.** *vi* relinchar

neighbor [ˈneɪbɚ] *n Am s.* **neighbour**

neighborhood [ˈneɪbɚhʊd] *n Am s.* **neighbourhood**

neighboring [ˈneɪbərɪŋ] *adj Am s.* **neighbouring**

neighborliness *n no pl, Am s.* **neighbourliness**

neighborly [ˈneɪbɚli] *adj Am s.* **neighbourly**

neighbour [ˈneɪbəʳ, *Am:* -bɚ] **I.** *n* vecino, -a *m, f;* (*fellow-citizen*) prójimo, -a *m, f* ▶ **love your ~ as you love yourself** ama a tu prójimo como a ti mismo **II.** *vi* **to ~ on sth** lindar con algo

neighbourhood [ˈneɪbəhʊd, *Am:* -bɚ-] *n* **1.** (*smallish localized community*) vecindario *m;* (*people*) vecinos *mpl;* **a closed/friendly ~** un vecindario cerrado/amigable; **the whole ~ is talking about it** todo el vecindario habla de ello; **in the ~** en el vecindario **2.** (*vicinity*) alrededores *mpl,* cercanías *fpl;* **I wouldn't like to live in the ~ of the airport** no me gustaría vivir en los alrededores del aeropuerto **3. in the ~ of** alrededor de; **we're hoping to get something in the ~ of £70,000 for the house** esperamos obtener alrededor de 70.000 libras por la casa

neighbourhood watch *n* vigilancia *f* vecinal

neighbouring [ˈneɪbərɪŋ] *adj* (*nearby*) cercano, -a; (*bordering*) adyacente; ~ **house** casa *f* adyacente; ~ **country** país *m* vecino

neighbourliness *n no pl* convivencia *f;* **an act of ~** un acto de convivencia; **good ~** buena vecindad

neighbourly [ˈneɪbəli, *Am:* -bɚli] *adj* amable

neither [ˈnaɪðəʳ, *Am:* ˈniːðɚ] **I.** *pron* ninguno, -a; **which one? – ~ (of them)** ¿cuál? – ninguno (de los dos) **II.** *adv* ni; **~ … nor …** ni… ni…; **he is ~ wounded nor dead** no está ni herido ni muerto **III.** *conj* tampoco; **if he won't eat, ~ will I** si él no come, yo tampoco **IV.** *adj* ningún, -una; **in ~ case** en ningún caso; **~ book is good** ninguno de los dos libros es bueno

nemesis [ˈneməsɪs] <-ses> *n a. fig* justo castigo *m*

neoclassical [ˌniːəʊˈklæsɪkəl, *Am:* -oʊˈ-] *adj* neoclásico, -a

neocolonialist [ˌniːəʊkəˈləʊniəlɪst, *Am:* -oʊkəˈloʊ-] *adj* neocolonialista

neolithic [ˌniːəˈlɪθɪk, *Am:* -oʊˈ-] *adj* neolítico, -a; ~ **Period** período *m* neolítico

neologism [niːˈɒlədʒɪzəm, *Am:* -ˈɑːlə-] *n form* neologismo *m*

neon [ˈniːɒn, *Am:* -ɑːn] *n no pl* neón *m*

neo-nazi [ˌnɪːəʊˈnɑːtsi] **I.** *n* neonazi *mf* **II.** *adj* neonazi

neon lamp *n,* **neon light** *n* luz *f* de neón

neon sign *n* letrero *m* de neón

nephew [ˈnevjuː, *Am:* ˈnef-] *n* sobrino *m*

nephritis [nɪˈfraɪtɪs, *Am:* -t̬əs] *n no pl* MED nefritis *f inv*

nepotism [ˈnepətɪzəm] *n no pl* nepotismo *m*

Neptune [ˈneptjuːn] *n* Neptuno *m*

nerd [nɜːd, *Am:* nɜːrd] *n Am* lerdo, -a *m, f*

nerdy <-ier, -iest> *adj Am, inf* lerdo, -a

nerve [nɜːv, *Am:* nɜːrv] **I.** *n* **1.** (*fibre*) nervio *m* **2.** (*high nervousness*) **~s** nerviosismo *m;* **to be in a state of ~s** estar nervioso; **to be a bundle of ~s** *fig* ser un puñado de nervios; **to calm one's ~s** calmarse; **to get on sb's ~s** *inf* crispar los nervios a alguien **3.** *no pl* (*courage, bravery*) valor *m;* **to hold/lose one's ~** mantener/perder el valor **4.** (*apprehension*) **~s** ansiedad *f* **5.** (*temerity*) temeridad *f;* **to have the ~ to do sth** *inf* tener el morro de hacer algo; **of all the ~!** *inf* ¡qué morro! ▶ **~s of iron** nervios *mpl* de acero; **to expose** [*o* **to hit**] **a (raw) ~** tocar un tema sensible **II.** *vt* envalentonarse; **to ~ oneself (up) to do sth** *Brit* animarse a hacer algo

nerve cell *n* célula *f* nerviosa **nerve center** *n Am,* **nerve centre** *n Aus, Brit* **1.** (*group of closely connected nerve cells*) centro *m* nervioso **2.** *fig* (*centre of control*) centro *m* neurálgico **nerve gas** <-es> *n* gas *m* nervioso

nerveless [ˈnɜːvlɪs, *Am:* ˈnɜːrv-] *adj* **1.** (*calm*) imperturbable **2.** (*lacking courage*) cobarde

nerve-racking [ˈnɜːvrækɪŋ, *Am:* ˈnɜːrv-] *adj* perturbador(a)

nervous [ˈnɜːvəs, *Am:* ˈnɜːr-] *adj* (*jumpy*) nervioso, -a; (*edgy*) ansioso, -a; **of a ~ disposition** de disposición nerviosa; **to be ~ in sb's presence** estar nervioso en presencia de alguien; **you look a ~ wreck!** ¡pareces un manojo de nervios!; **to make sb ~** poner nervioso a alguien; **to be ~ about sth** estar nervioso por algo

nervous breakdown *n* ataque *m* de nervios; **to have a ~** sufrir un ataque de nervios

nervously *adv* nerviosamente

nervousness *n no pl* (*nervous condition or state*) nerviosismo *m;* (*fearfulness*) ansiedad *f;* **~ about sth** nerviosismo por algo

nervous system *n* sistema *m* nervioso

nervy [ˈnɜːvi, *Am:* ˈnɜːr-] <-ier, -iest> *adj* **1.** *Am* (*rude*) descarado, -a **2.** *Am* (*courageous*) atrevido, -a **3.** *Brit* (*nervous*) nervioso, -a; (*apprehensive*) aprensivo, -a

nest [nest] I. *n* 1. (*animal's home*) nido *m;* (*of hen*) nidal *m* 2. (*cosy domicile*) nido *m;* **to leave the ~** dejar el nido 3. *pej* (*den*) guarida *f* 4. (*location that swarms with sth bad*) cueva *f,* nido *m* 5. (*set, cluster, assemblage*) juego *m* II. *vi* anidar
nest box <-es> *n Am* nido *m* **nest egg** *n* 1. (*egg in a nest*) nidal *m* 2. (*money saved*) ahorros *mpl*
nesting *adj* 1. (*of sets fitting together*) que encaja 2. (*concerning nests*) **~ time** tiempo *m* de anidar
nesting box <-es> *n* nido *m*
nestle ['nesl] I. *vt* arrimar, apoyar; **to ~ sth on sth** apoyar algo contra algo II. *vi* 1. (*snuggle up*) acomodarse; **to ~ up to sb** arrimarse a alguien 2. (*be in sheltered position*) cobijarse
nestling ['nestlɪŋ] *n* pajarito *m*
net¹ [net] I. *n* 1. (*material with spaces*) malla *f;* (*fine netted fabric*) tul *m;* **mosquito ~** mosquitera *f* 2. (*device for trapping fish*) red *f;* **to haul in a ~** pescar con redes; **to fall** [*o* **slip**] **through the ~** *fig* zafarse de las redes de alguien 3. SPORTS red *f* 4. (*final profit*) beneficio *m* neto; (*final amount*) importe *m* neto II. <-tt-> *vt* (*catch: fish*) pescar; (*criminals*) capturar
net² [net] I. *adj* 1. ECON neto, -a; **~ assets** activo *m* neto; **~ income** [*o* **earnings**] beneficio *m* neto 2. (*excluding package: of a weight*) neto, -a; **~ tonnage** tonelaje *m* neto; **~ weight** peso *m* neto II. *vt* **to ~ sth** ganar algo en neto
Net [net] *n* INFOR **the ~** la red; **~ surfer** navegador(a) *m(f)* de la red
netball ['netbɔːl] *n no pl, Brit: juego semejante al baloncesto y practicado mayoritariamente por mujeres* **Net Book Agreement** *n* ≈ acuerdo sobre el precio neto de los libros **net curtain** *n* visillo(s) *m(pl)*
nether ['neðəʳ] *adj iron, liter* de abajo, inferior; **~ regions** *a. fig* infierno *m*
Netherlands ['neðələndz, *Am:* -ɚləndz] *n* **the ~** los Países Bajos, Holanda
netiquette ['netɪket] *n no pl* INFOR etiqueta *f* de la red
Netspeak ['netspiːk] *adj* INFOR lenguaje *m* de internet [*o* de la red]
nett [net] *adj, vt s.* **net¹** II., **net²**
netting ['netɪŋ, *Am:* 'neţɪŋ] *n no pl* 1. (*net*) malla *f;* **you should get some ~ for those windows** deberías comprar un visillo para esas ventanas 2. SPORTS red *f*
nettle ['netl, *Am:* 'neţ-] I. *n* ortiga *f* ►**to grasp the ~** *Aus, Brit* coger el toro por los cuernos II. *vt* provocar, irritar; **to be ~d by sth** estar irritado por algo
nettle rash <-es> *n* urticaria *f*
net weight *n* peso *m* neto
network ['netwɜːk, *Am:* -wɜːrk] I. *n* 1. INFOR, TEL red *f;* **cable ~** cableado *m;* **computer ~** red informática; **telephone ~** red telefónica 2. TV cadena *f* II. *vt* 1. (*link together*) poner en contacto, conectar 2. (*broadcast*) emitir en red III. *vi* interconectar
networking *n* INFOR interconexión *f*
neural ['njʊərəl, *Am:* 'nʊrəl] *adj* neural, del sistema nervioso
neuralgia [njʊə'rældʒə, *Am:* nʊ'-] *n no pl* neuralgia *f*
neuralgic [njuː'rældʒɪk, *Am:* nʊ'-] *adj* neurálgico, -a
neural network *n* INFOR red *f* nerviosa
neurasthenia [ˌnjʊərəs'θiːnɪə, *Am:* ˌnʊræs'-] *n no pl* neurastenia *f*
neuritis [njʊə'raɪtɪs, *Am:* nʊ'raɪţəs] *n no pl* MED neuritis *f inv*
neurological [ˌnjʊərə'lɒdʒɪkəl, *Am:* ˌnʊrə'lɑ-] *adj* neurológico, -a; **~ disorder** trastorno *m* neurológico
neurologist [njʊə'rɒlədʒɪst, *Am:* nʊ'rɑːlə-] *n* neurólogo, -a *m, f*
neurology [njʊə'rɒlədʒi, *Am:* nʊ'rɑːlə-] *n no pl* neurología *f*
neuron ['njʊərɒn, *Am:* 'nʊrɑːn] *n,* **neurone** ['njʊərəʊn, *Am:* 'nʊroʊn] *n* neurona *f*
neuroscience [ˌnjʊə'rəʊ'saɪənts, *Am:* ˌnʊroʊ'saɪ-] *n no pl* neurología *f*
neurosis [njʊə'rəʊsɪs, *Am:* nʊ'roʊ-] <-es> *n* neurosis *f inv*
neurosurgeon [ˌnjʊə'sɜːdʒən, *Am:* ˌnʊroʊ'sɜːr-] *n* neurocirujano, -a *m, f*
neurosurgery [ˌnjʊə'sɜːdʒəri, *Am:* ˌnʊroʊ'sɜːr-] *n no pl* neurocirujía *f*
neurotic [njʊə'rɒtɪk, *Am:* nʊ'rɑːţɪk] I. *n* neurótico, -a *m, f* II. *adj* neurótico, -a
neurotransmitter [ˌnjʊərəʊtrænz'mɪtəʳ, *Am:* ˌnʊroʊtræns'mɪţɚ] *n* MED neurotransmisor *m*
neuter ['njuːtəʳ, *Am:* 'nuːţɚ] I. *adj* neutro, -a; **~ noun** LING sustantivo *m* neutro II. *vt* 1. (*castrate: males*) castrar 2. (*sterilize: females*) esterilizar 3. (*neutralise*) neutralizar
neutral ['njuːtrəl, *Am:* 'nuː-] I. *adj* 1. (*uninvolved*) neutral; **~ country** POL país *m* neutral; **to remain ~** mantenerse al margen 2. *a.* CHEM, ELEC neutro, -a 3. (*unemotional*) objetivo, -a II. *n* 1. (*non-combatant in war*) territorio *m* neutral 2. (*part of gears system*) punto *m* muerto; **in ~** en punto muerto
neutralisation [ˌnjuːtrəlaɪ'zeɪʃən, *Am:* ˌnuːtrəlɪ-] *n Brit, Aus s.* **neutralization**
neutralise ['njuːtrəlaɪz, *Am:* 'nuː-] *vt Brit, Aus s.* **neutralize**
neutrality [njuː'træləti, *Am:* nuː'træləţi] *n no pl* neutralidad *f*
neutralization [ˌnjuːtrəlaɪ'zeɪʃən, *Am:* ˌnuːtrəlɪ'-] *n no pl* neutralización *f*
neutralize ['njuːtrəlaɪz, *Am:* 'nuː-] *vt* neutralizar; **the bomb was ~d by the specialists** los especialistas desactivaron la bomba
neutron ['njuːtrɒn, *Am:* 'nuːtrɑːn] *n* neutrón *m*
neutron bomb *n* bomba *f* de neutrones
never ['nevəʳ, *Am:* -ɚ] *adv* 1. (*at no time, on no occasion*) nunca, jamás; **I ~ forget a face** nunca olvido una cara 2. (*under no circum-*

stances) jamás; ~ **again!** ¡nunca jamás!; ~ **fear!** ¡no te preocupes!; **well I** ~ (**did**) ¡no me digas!, ¿de veras?; **it's** ~ **too late to do sth** nunca es demasiado tarde para hacer algo; ~ **before** nunca antes; ~ **before had I had so much money** jamás había tenido tanto dinero; **as** ~ **before** como nunca; ~ **ever** nunca jamás; **he's** ~ **61, he looks much younger** no aparenta 61, parece mucho más joven; ~ **mind** no importa, tanto da; ~ **say die** *fig* nunca tires la toalla

never-ending [ˌnevər'endɪŋ, *Am:* 'nevɚ-] *adj* interminable **never-failing** *adj* infalible **nevermore** *adv* nunca más **never-never** *n Brit, inf* compra *f* a plazos; **on the** ~ a plazos **never-never land** *n fig, inf* paraíso *m* de irás y no volverás

nevertheless [ˌnevəðə'les, *Am:* ˌnevɚ-] *adv* sin embargo, con todo, no obstante

new [nju:, *Am:* nu:] **I.** *adj* **1.** (*latest, recent*) nuevo, -a, reciente; (*word*) de nuevo cuño; ~ **technology** tecnología *f* punta; **to be the ~est fad** [*o* **craze**] *inf* ser la última moda **2.** (*changed*) nuevo, -a; ~ **boy/girl** *Brit* SCHOOL novato, -a *m, f* **3.** (*inexperienced*) nuevo, -a, novato, -a; **to be a** ~ **one on sb** ser nuevo para alguien; **she's** ~ **to the job** es nueva en el trabajo **4.** (*in new condition*) nuevo, -a; **brand** ~ completamente nuevo **5.** (*fresh*) fresco, -a; ~ **blood** *fig* sangre *f* fresca; **to feel like a** ~ **man/woman** sentirse un hombre nuevo/una mujer nueva **6.** (*freshly found or made public*) fresco, -a, reciente **II.** *n no pl* **the** ~ lo nuevo

New Age *n* **1.** (*movement*) New Age *m* **2.** (*music*) new age *f* **New Ager** *n* seguidor(a) *m(f)* del New Age **New Age Traveller** *n Brit* viajero(a) *m(f)* de la nueva era **newbie** *n* INFOR novato, -a *m, f* (*en la red*) **newborn** **I.** *adj* reciente; ~ **democracy/science** democracia *f* reciente/ciencia *f* reciente; ~ **baby** recién nacido, -a *m, f* **II.** *n* **the** ~ los recién nacidos **New Brunswick** *n* Nueva Brunswick *f* **New Caledonia** *n* Nueva Caledonia *f* **newcomer** *n* **1.** (*person who has just arrived*) recién llegado, -a *m, f* **2.** (*stranger*) nuevo, -a *m, f* **3.** (*beginner, recent starter*) principiante *mf,* novato, -a *m, f;* **I'm a** ~ **to Chester** soy nuevo en Chester

newel ['nju:əl, *Am:* 'nu:-] *n* **1.** (*of a circular staircase*) espigón *m* **2.** (*supporting banister*) poste *m*

New England *n* Nueva Inglaterra *f* **newfangled** *adj* novedoso, -a **new-fashioned** *adj* moderno, -a, a la última (moda)

new-found [ˌnju:'faʊnd, *Am:* ˌnu:-] *adj* recién descubierto; **a** ~ **friend** un amigo nuevo

New Foundland[1] ['nju:fəndlənd, *Am:* 'nu:fəndlənd] *n* Terranova *f*

New Foundland[2] [nju:'faʊndlənd, *Am:* 'nu:fəndlənd], **New Foundland dog** *n* ZOOL perro *m* de Terranova

newish ['nju:ɪʃ, *Am:* 'nu:-] *adj inf* bastante nuevo, -a

new-laid [ˌnju:'leɪd, *Am:* 'nu:-] *adj* ~ **eggs** huevos *mpl* recién puestos

newly ['nju:li, *Am:* 'nu:-] *adv* **1.** (*recently*) recientemente; ~ **married** recién casados **2.** (*freshly*) recién; ~ **painted** recién pintado **3.** (*done differently than before*) nuevamente, de nuevo

newly-wed ['nju:lɪwed, *Am:* 'nu:-] **I.** *npl* recién casados *mpl* **II.** *adj* recién casado, -a

New Man <-men> *n Brit* hombre *m* moderno **new moon** *n* luna *f* nueva **New Orleans** *n* Nueva Orleans *f* **new potatoes** *npl* patatas *fpl* tiernas **New Right** *n* Nueva Derecha *f* (*movimiento político reaccionario a la nueva izquierda*)

news [nju:z, *Am:* nu:z] *n + sing vb* **1.** (*fresh information*) noticias *fpl;* **the** ~ **media** los medios de comunicación; **bad/good** ~ buenas/malas noticias; **he's bad** ~ **for the company** es pájaro de mal agüero para la empresa; **to break the** ~ **to sb** dar la noticia a alguien; **when the** ~ **broke** cuando se supo la noticia; **really! that's** ~ **to me** ¿de veras? no lo sabía **2.** (*broadcast*) noticias *fpl,* informativo *m;* **to be** ~ ser noticia ►**no** ~ **is good** ~ *prov* si no hay noticias, buena señal

news agency <-ies> *n* agencia *f* de noticias **newsagent** *n Brit, Aus* **1.** (*shop*) quiosco *m* **2.** (*person*) vendedor(a) *m(f)* de periódicos **news-boy** *n* **1.** (*seller*) vendedor(a) *m(f)* de periódicos **2.** (*sb delivering papers*) repartidor(a) *m(f)* de periódicos **newscast** *n Am* informativo *m* **newscaster** *n Am* locutor(a) *m(f)* de un informativo **news conference** *n* rueda *f* de prensa **news dealer** *n Am* vendedor(a) *m(f)* de periódicos **newsflash** <-es> *n* ≈ noticia *f* de última hora, flash *m* informativo **newsgroup** *n* INFOR grupo *m* de discusión, grupo *m* de noticias **newshound** *n fig, inf* cazanoticias *mf inv* **news item** *n* noticia *f* **newsletter** *n* nota *f* de prensa **newsmonger** *n* **1.** (*sb gathering news*) chismoso, -a *m, f* **2.** (*a gossip*) cotilleo *m* **newspaper** *n* periódico *m;* ~ **clipping** recorte *m* de periódico **newspeak** *n no pl, pej* lenguaje *m* de los políticos **newsprint** *n no pl* papel *m* de periódico **newsreader** *n Brit, Aus* locutor(a) *m(f)* de un informativo **newsreel** *n* noticiario *m* documental **news release** *n Am* noticiario *m* **news report** *n* informativo *m* **newsroom** *n* sala *f* de redacción **newsstand** *n* quiosco *m* **newsvendor** *n* vendedor(a) *m(f)* de periódicos **newsworthy** *adj* de interés periodístico

newsy ['nju:zi, *Am:* 'nu:-] <-ier, -iest> *adj* lleno, -a de noticias; **a** ~ **letter** una carta cargada de noticias

newt [nju:t, *Am:* nu:t] *n* tritón *m*

New Testament *n* REL Nuevo Testamento *m* **new town** *n Brit: ciudad creada para redistribuir la población* **new wave** *n fig* **1.** (*movement*) new wave *f* **2.** (*fresh outbreak*) nueva ola *f;* **a** ~ **of redundancies/violence**

una nueva ola de despidos/violencia **new world order** *n*, **New World Order** *n* nuevo orden *m* mundial **New Year** *n* **1.** año *m* nuevo; **Happy ~** feliz año nuevo; **to celebrate ~** celebrar el año nuevo **2.** (*opening weeks of year*) principios *mpl* de año **New Year's** *n no pl, Am, inf* (*New Year's Day*) día *f* de año nuevo; (*New Year's Eve*) nochevieja *f* **New Year's Day** *n no pl* día *m* de año nuevo **New Year's Eve** *n no pl* nochevieja *f* **New York** **I.** *n* Nueva York *f* **II.** *adj* neoyorquino, -a **New Yorker** *n* neoyorquino, -a *m, f* **New Zealand** **I.** *n* Nueva Zelanda *f* **II.** *adj* neozelandés, -esa **New Zealander** *n* neozelandés, -esa *m, f*

next [nekst] **I.** *adj* **1.** (*nearest in location*) siguiente **2.** (*following in time*) próximo, -a, que viene; **the ~ day** el día siguiente; **~ month** el mes que viene; **the ~ thing** el siguiente paso; **(the) ~ time** la próxima vez **3.** (*following in order*) siguiente; **to be ~** ser el siguiente; **to be (the) ~ to do sth** ser el próximo en hacer algo; **the ~ sth but one** la siguiente cosa después de ésta; **~ to sth/sb** cerca de algo/alguien **II.** *adv* **1.** (*afterwards, subsequently*) después, luego; **when are you ~ going to London?** ¿cuando vuelves a ir a Londres? **2.** (*almost as much*) **~ to** después de; **cheese is my favourite food and ~ to cheese I like chocolate best** el queso es mi comida preferida y después está el chocolate **3.** (*again, once more*) de nuevo; **when I saw him ~ he had transformed** cuando volví a verlo estaba desconocido **4.** (*almost*) casi; **~ to impossible** casi imposible; **~ to nothing** casi nada **5.** (*second*) **the ~ best thing** lo segundo mejor **III.** *prep* **1.** (*beside*) **~ to** junto a; **~ to the skin** junto a la piel; **my room is ~ to yours** mi habitación está junto a la tuya **2.** (*almost*) casi; **to cost ~ to nothing** no valer casi nada **3.** (*second to*) **~ to last** penúltimo; **~ to Bach, I like Mozart best** después de Bach, Mozart es el que me gusta más

next door [ˌneks'dɔːʳ, *Am:* ˌnekst'dɔːr] **I.** *adv* al lado; **we live ~ to the airport** vivimos al lado del aeropuerto **II.** *adj* de al lado; **to be/feel ~ to sth** *Brit, fig* estar/sentirse cerca de algo **next-door neighbo(u)r** *n* vecino, -a *m, f* de al lado **next of kin** *n no pl* pariente *mf* cercano, -a

nexus ['neksəs] *n inv* nexo *m*

NF [ˌen'ef] *Brit abbr of* **National Front** FN *m*

NHS [ˌenaɪtʃ'es] *Brit abbr of* **National Health Service** servicio *m* de asistencia sanitaria de la Seguridad Social

Niagara Falls [naɪˌægərə'fɔːlz] *n* **the ~** las cataratas del Niágara

nib [nɪb] *n* punta *f;* (*of a pen*) plumilla *f*

nibble ['nɪbl] **I.** *n* **1.** (*a small bite/peck*) mordisco *m*, bocado *m;* **to take a ~ (at sth)** dar un mordisco (a algo) **2.** (*expression of interest*) muestra *f* de interés **3.** *Brit, inf* **~s** tentempié *m* **II.** *vt* **1.** (*bite*) mordisquear; (*rat*) roer **2.** (*pick at*) picar **III.** *vi* **1.** *a. fig* picar **2.** (*purchase little quantities of*) **to ~ at sth** comprar poca cantidad de algo **3.** (*show interest in*) **to ~ at sth** mostrar interés por algo **4.** (*deplete slowly*) **to ~ away at sth** desgastar algo

Nicaragua [ˌnɪkə'rægjʊə, *Am:* -ə'rɑːgwə] *n* Nicaragua *f*

Nicaraguan **I.** *n* nicaragüense *mf* **II.** *adj* nicaragüense

nice [naɪs] **I.** *adj* **1.** (*pleasant, agreeable*) bueno, -a; **~ one!**, **~ work!** *inf* ¡bien hecho!; **~ weather** buen tiempo *m;* **~ work** *inf* buen trabajo *m;* **far ~er** mucho más bonito; **it is ~ to do sth** es agradable hacer algo **2.** (*amiable*) simpático, -a; (*kind*) amable; **to be ~ to sb** ser amable con alguien; **it is/was ~ of sb to do sth** es/fue un detalle por parte de alguien hacer algo; **~ boys** chicos majos **3.** *iron, inf* (*unpleasant*) **that's a ~ thing to say to your brother** vaya cosas de decir a tu hermano **4.** (*subtle*) sutil, delicado, -a; (*fine*) fino, -a **II.** *adv* bien

nice-looking *adj* atractivo, -a

nicely ['naɪsli] *adv* **1.** (*well, satisfactorily*) bien; **to do very ~** quedar muy bonito **2.** (*having success*) espléndidamente **3.** (*in healthy state*) **the princess and the baby were both doing ~** la princesa y el bebé gozaban de buena salud **4.** (*pleasantly, politely*) amablemente

nicety ['naɪsəti, *Am:* -t̬i] <-ies> *n* **1.** *no pl* (*subtle distinction*) sutileza *f* **2.** (*precision*) precisión *f;* **~ of an argument** pormenores *mpl* de una discusión **3.** (*precise differentiations*) **niceties** matices *mpl;* (*in negative sense*) nimiedades *fpl*

niche [niːʃ, *Am:* nɪtʃ] *n* **1.** (*alcove*) nicho *m* **2.** (*desired job*) buen puesto *m;* (*suitable position*) buena posición *f* **3.** (*place suiting a particular group*) refugio *m*

niche market *n* ECON mercado *m* alternativo (especializado)

nick [nɪk] **I.** *n* **1.** (*chip in surface*) mella *f* **2.** *no pl, Brit, inf* (*prison*) **the ~** el trullo **3.** *no pl, Brit, Aus, inf* (*specified state*) **in excellent ~** en perfecto estado *m* ▶**in the ~ of time** por los pelos **II.** *vt* **1.** (*chip*) mellar; (*cut*) cortar **2.** *Brit, Aus, inf* (*steal*) mangar, chingar *Méx*, pispear *Arg* **3.** *Brit, inf* **to ~ sb** (*arrest*) trincar a alguien; (*catch*) echar el guante a alguien **4.** *Am, inf* (*trick*) engañar

nickel ['nɪkl] *n* **1.** *no pl* CHEM níquel *m* **2.** *Am* (*coin*) moneda *f* de cinco centavos

nickel-plated *adj* niquelado, -a

nick-nack ['nɪknæk] *n s.* **knick-knack**

nickname ['nɪkneɪm] **I.** *n* apodo *m* **II.** *vt* apodar

Nicosia [ˌnɪkəʊ'siːə] *n* Nicosia *f*

nicotine ['nɪkətiːn] *n no pl* nicotina *f*

nicotine patch <-es> *n* parche *m* de nicotina

niece [niːs] *n* sobrina *f*

niff [nɪf] *n Brit, inf* tufo *m*

niffy [nɪfi] <-ier, -iest> *adj Brit, inf* apestoso, -a

nifty ['nɪfti] <-ier, -iest> *adj inf* (*stylish, smart*) elegante; (*skilful*) diestro, -a

Niger ['naɪdʒəʳ, *Am:* -dʒɚ] *n* Níger *m*

Nigeria [naɪ'dʒɪəriə, *Am:* -'dʒɪri-] *n* Nigeria *f*

Nigerian I. *adj* nigeriano, -a II. *n* nigeriano, -a *m, f*

niggardly ['nɪgədli, *Am:* -ɚd-] *adj* (*stingy*) tacaño, -a; (*meagre*) miserable

nigger ['nɪgəʳ, *Am:* -ɚ] *n pej* negraco, -a *m, f*

niggle ['nɪgl] I. *vi* fastidiar; **to ~ at sth** preocuparse por algo II. *vt* 1. (*nag pettily*) reparar en minucias 2. (*irritate*) enfurecer, irritar III. *n* 1. (*doubt*) duda *f* 2. (*complaint*) queja *f*

niggling ['nɪglɪŋ] *adj* 1. (*irritating, troubling*) molesto, -a 2. (*needing very precise work*) meticuloso, -a

nigh [naɪ] *adj liter* inminente

night [naɪt] *n* noche *f*; **good ~!** ¡buenas noches!; **last ~** anoche; **10 (o'clock) at ~** las 10 de la noche; **the ~ before** la noche anterior; **open at ~** abierto por la noche; **~ and day** día y noche; **during the ~** durante la noche; **during Tuesday ~** durante la noche del martes; **far into the ~** a altas horas de la noche; **at dead of ~** a mitad de la noche; **wedding ~** noche de bodas; **the Arabian Nights** las mil y una noches; **Twelfth Night** víspera *f* de Reyes; **to work ~s** trabajar de noche

nightbird [naɪtbɜːd, *Am:* naɪtbɜːrd] *n* pájaro *m* nocturno; (*person*) trasnochador(a) *m(f)* **night blindness** *n no pl* ceguera *f* nocturna **nightcap** *n* 1. (*cap*) gorro *m* de dormir 2. (*drink*) bebida *f* (*que se toma antes de acostarse*) **nightclothes** *npl* ropa *f* de dormir **nightclub** *n* club *m* (nocturno) **nightdress** <-es> *n* camisón *m* **nightfall** *n no pl* atardecer *m* **nightgown** *n Am* camisón *m* **nightie** *n inf* camisón *m* **nightingale** *n* ruiseñor *m* **night life** *n no pl* vida *f* nocturna **nightlight** *n* lamparilla *f* **nightlong** *liter* I. *adv* durante toda la noche II. *adj* de toda la noche

nightly ['naɪtli] I. *adv* cada noche II. *adj* 1. (*done or happening each night*) de todas las noches 2. (*nocturnal*) de noche

nightmare ['naɪtmeəʳ, *Am:* -mer] *n* pesadilla *f*

nightmarish ['naɪtmeərɪʃ, *Am:* -mer-] *adj* 1. (*like a horrible dream*) espeluznante 2. (*very distressing*) inquietante

night-night ['naɪtˌnaɪt] *interj inf* buenas noches **night-nurse** *n* enfermera *f* de noche **night owl** *n* lechuza *f*; *fig* noctámbulo, -a *m, f* **night-porter** *n* portero *m* nocturno **nights** *adv* por la noche, de noche **night safe** *n Brit* caja *f* fuerte **night school** *n* escuela *f* nocturna **night shift** *n* turno *m* de noche **nightshirt** *n* camisa *f* de dormir **nightspot** *n inf* club *m* (nocturno) **night stand** *n* mesilla *f* de noche **night stick** *n Am* porra *f* **night table** *n Am* mesilla *f* de noche **night-time** *n no pl* noche *f* **night-watch** <-es> *n* vigilancia *f* nocturna **night watchman** *n* vigilante *m* nocturno, nochero *m CSur* **nightwear** *n no pl* ropa *f* de dormir

nihilism ['naɪɪlɪzəm, *Am:* 'naɪə-] *n no pl* nihilismo *m*

nihilist ['naɪɪlɪst, *Am:* 'naɪə-] *n* nihilista *mf*

nihilistic [ˌnaɪɪ'lɪstɪk, *Am:* 'naɪə-] *adj* nihilista

Nikkei [nɪ'keɪ, *Am:* 'niːkeɪ] *n*, **Nikkei Index** *n no pl* FIN índice *m* Nikkei

nil [nɪl] *n no pl* 1. (*nothing, nought*) nada *f* 2. *Brit* (*no score*) cero *m*

Nile [naɪl] *n* **the ~** el Nilo

nimble ['nɪmbl] *adj* (*agile*) ágil; (*quick and light in movement*) diestro, -a; (*quick-thinking*) listo, -a; **~ mind** mente *f* despierta

nimbus ['nɪmbəs] *n no pl* nimbo *m*

NIMBY, nimby ['nɪmbi] *n abbr of* **not in my back yard** *persona que se opone a que en la zona donde vive se realice cualquier destrozo urbanístico o medioambiental*

nincompoop ['nɪŋkəmpuːp, *Am:* 'nɪn-] *n inf* zoquete *mf*

nine [naɪn] I. *adj* nueve *inv* ►**a ~ days' wonder** la flor de un día; **~ times out of ten** casi siempre II. *n* nueve *m* ►**to be done (up) to the ~s** *inf* ir de punta en blanco; *s. a.* **eight**

ninepins ['naɪnpɪnz] *npl Brit* bolos *mpl*; **to be going down like ~** caer como moscas

nineteen [ˌnaɪn'tiːn] I. *adj* diecinueve II. *n* diecinueve *m*; *s. a.* **eight**

nineteenth I. *adj* decimonoveno, -a II. *n* 1. (*order*) decimonoveno, -a *m, f* 2. (*date*) diecinueve 3. (*fraction*) diecinueveavo *m*; (*part*) diecinueveava parte *f*; *s. a.* **eighth**

nineteenth hole *n inf* (*golf club bar*) bar *m*

nineties *npl* **the ~** los noventa

ninetieth ['naɪntiəθ, *Am:* -t̬ɪ-] I. *adj* nonagésimo, -a II. *n no pl* (*order*) nonagésimo, -a *m, f*; (*fraction*) noventavo *m*; (*part*) noventava parte *f*; *s. a.* **eighth**

nine-to-five I. *adv* de nueve a cinco, en horario de oficina II. *adj* de nueve a cinco; **~ schedule** horario *m* de nueve a cinco

ninety ['naɪnti, *Am:* -t̬i] I. *adj* noventa II. <-ies> *n* noventa *m*; *s. a.* **eighty**

ninja ['nɪndʒə] *n* ninja *mf*

ninjutsu *n no pl* ninjutsu *m*

ninny ['nɪni] <-ies> *n inf* bobo, -a *m, f*

ninth [naɪnθ] I. *adj* noveno, -a II. *n no pl* 1. (*order*) noveno, -a *m, f* 2. (*date*) nueve *m* 3. (*fraction*) noveno *m*; (*part*) novena parte *f*; *s. a.* **eighth**

nip[1] [nɪp] I. <-pp-> *vt* 1. (*bite sharply, bite*) morder; (*insects*) picar 2. (*pinch, squeeze*) pellizcar 3. (*cut*) cortar ►**to ~ sth in the bud** *fig* cortar algo de raíz II. <-pp-> *vi* 1. (*bite*) morder; (*insects*) picar 2. *Brit, Aus, inf* (*hurry*) apresurarse; **to ~ along** correr; **I ~ped round to Bill's to borrow some sugar** me dejé caer por casa de Bill para pedirle un poco de azúcar III. *n* 1. (*pinch, tight squeeze*) pellizco *m*;

(*bite*) mordisco *m;* (*of insects*) picadura *f* **2.** (*sharp cold, chill*) helada *f*

nip² [nɪp] *n Brit, inf* chupito *m*

nipper ['nɪpəʳ, *Am:* -ɚ] *n Brit, inf* chiquillo, -a *m, f*

nipple ['nɪpl] *n* ANAT pezón *m;* (*teat*) tetilla *f,* tetera *f AmL*

nippy ['nɪpi] <-ier, -iest> *adj* **1.** *Brit, Aus, inf* (*quick*) rápido, -a; (*nimble*) ágil **2.** *inf* (*cold*) helado, -a

nirvana [nɪə'vɑnə, *Am:* nɪr-] *n no pl* nirvana *m; fig* perfección *f*

Nissen hut ['nɪsnhʌt] *n* barraca *f* prefabricada (*hecha de metal y cemento*)

nit [nɪt] *n* **1.** *Brit, Aus, pej, inf* (*stupid person*) imbécil *mf* **2.** ZOOL liendre *f*

niter ['naɪtəʳ, *Am:* -t̬ɚ] *n Am* nitro *m*

nitpick ['nɪtpɪk] *vi* criticar

nitpicker ['nɪtpɪkəʳ, *Am:* -ɚ] *n* (*quibbler*) quisquilloso, -a *m, f;* (*petty fault-finder*) criticón, -ona *m, f*

nitpicking ['nɪtpɪkɪŋ] **I.** *adj inf* criticón, -ona; ~ **criticism** crítica *f* mordaz **II.** *n no pl, inf* crítica *f*

nitrate ['naɪtreɪt] *n* nitrato *m*

nitre ['naɪtəʳ, *Am:* -t̬ɚ] *n* nitro *m*

nitric ['naɪtrɪk] *adj* nítrico, -a

nitric acid *n no pl* ácido *m* nítrico

nitrite ['naɪtraɪt] *n* nitrito *m*

nitrogen ['naɪtrədʒən] *n no pl* nitrógeno *m*

nitroglycerin(e) [,naɪtrəʊ'glɪsəri:n, *Am:* -troʊ'-] *n no pl* nitroglicerina *f*

nitrous ['naɪtrəs] *adj* nitroso, -a; ~ **acid** ácido *m* nitroso

nitty-gritty [,nɪti'grɪti, *Am:* ,nɪt̬ɪ'grɪt̬-] *n no pl, inf* **the** ~ lo esencial; **to get down to the** ~ ir al grano

nitwit ['nɪtwɪt] *n inf* idiota *mf*

nix *Am* **I.** *vt inf* rehusar **II.** *adv inf* ¡ni hablar! **III.** *n no pl, inf* nada *f*

NLP [,enel'pi:] *n abbr of* **Neuro-Linguistic Programming** programación *f* neurolingüística

NNE *abbr of* **north-northeast** NNE *m*

NNW *abbr of* **north-northwest** NNO *m*

no [nəʊ, *Am:* noʊ] **I.** *adv* **1.** (*not to any degree*) no; ~ **parking** prohibido estacionar; ~ **way** de ninguna manera; ~ **can do** *inf* no lo puedo hacer; ~ **less than sth/sb** nada menos que algo/alguien **2.** (*equivalent to a negative sentence*) no; (*emphasises previous statement's falsity*) en absoluto **II.** *n* <-(e)s>, *n* (*denial, refusal*) no *m;* **to not take** ~ **for an answer** no admitir un no por respuesta **III.** *interj* (*word used to deny*) no; (*emphasises distress*) qué me dices

no, No. *abbr of* **number** núm., nº

Noah's ark [,nəʊəz'ɑ:k, *Am:* ,noʊəz'ɑ:rk] *n* arca *f* de Noé

nob [nɒb, *Am:* nɑ:b] *n Brit, iron, inf* pez *m* gordo

nobble ['nɒbl] *vt Brit, Aus, inf* **1.** (*tamper with*) **to** ~ **sth** entrometerse en algo **2.** (*successfully bribe*) sobornar; (*spoil*) estropear **3.** (*deliberately grab sb's attention*) **to** ~ **sb** llamar la atención de alguien

Nobel prize [,nəʊbel'praɪz, *Am:* ,noʊbel-'praɪz] *n* premio *m* Nobel

Nobel prize winner *n* ganador(a) *m(f)* del premio Nobel

nobility [nəʊ'bɪləti, *Am:* noʊ'bɪlət̬i] *n no pl* **1.** + *sing/pl vb* (*aristocracy*) nobleza *f;* **the** ~ la aristocracia **2.** (*nobleness of character*) generosidad *f;* (*selflessness*) altruismo *m*

noble ['nəʊbl, *Am:* 'noʊ-] **I.** *adj* **1.** (*of aristocratic or birth*) noble **2.** (*honourable: person*) noble; (*action*) generoso, -a; (*ideas*) grande; ~ **act** acto *m* noble **3.** (*splendid*) majestuoso, -a **4.** (*excellent*) magnífico, -a; (*horse*) noble **II.** *n* noble *mf*

nobleman ['nəʊblmən, *Am:* 'noʊ-] <-men> *n* aristócrata *m* **noble-minded** *adj* honesto, -a **noblewoman** <-women> *n* aristócrata *f*

nobly ['nəʊbli, *Am:* 'noʊ-] *adv* noblemente

nobody ['nəʊbədi, *Am:* 'noʊbɑ:di] **I.** *pron indef, sing* nadie; ~ **speaks** nadie habla; **we saw** ~ **(else)** no vimos a nadie (más); **he told** ~ no se lo dijo a nadie **II.** *n inf* don nadie *m;* **those people are nobodies** esa gente son un cero a la izquierda

nocturnal [nɒk'tɜ:nəl, *Am:* nɑ:k'tɜ:r-] *adj form* nocturno, -a

nocturnally *adv* por la noche

nod [nɒd, *Am:* nɑ:d] **I.** *n* cabezada *f,* inclinación *f* de cabeza ►**a** ~**'s as good as a wink to a blind horse** *prov, inf* a buen entendedor pocas palabras bastan *prov;* **on the** ~ *Brit, inf* sin ser discutido **II.** <-dd-> *vt* **to** ~ **one's head** asentir con la cabeza; **to** ~ **one's head to do sth** dar el visto bueno para hacer algo; **to** ~ **one's head at sth** indicar algo con la cabeza; **to** ~ **a farewell to sb** saludar a alguien con una inclinación de cabeza **III.** <-dd-> *vi* **1.** (*incline head in agreement*) asentir con la cabeza; **to** ~ **to sb** saludar a alguien con una inclinación de cabeza; **to** ~ **at sth** indicar algo con la cabeza **2.** *inf* (*start sleeping, drift off*) dar cabezadas

◆**nod off** *vi* dormirse

nodding ['nɒdɪŋ, *Am:* 'nɑ:dɪŋ] *adj* ~ **acquaintance** conocimiento *f* superficial; **to have only a** ~ **acquaintance with sth** conocer algo sólo por encima

node [nəʊd, *Am:* noʊd] *n* **1.** ANAT (*tissue*) ganglio *m* **2.** BOT (*on a stem*) nódulo *m* **3.** INFOR nodo *m*

nodule ['nɒdju:l, *Am:* 'nɑ:dju:l] *n a.* ANAT, BOT nódulo *m*

no-fault ['noʊfɔ:lt] *adj Am* (*insurance*) con indemnización garantizada

noggin ['nɒgɪn, *Am:* 'nɑ:gɪn] *n* **1.** (*small measure*) vaso *m* pequeño **2.** *Am, Scot, inf* (*head, mind*) coco *m*

no-go area [nəʊgəʊ'eərɪə, *Am:* noʊgoʊ-'erɪ-] *n* MIL zona *f* prohibida

no-hoper [ˌnəʊˈhəʊpəʳ, *Am:* ˌnoʊˈhoʊpɚ] *n Brit, Aus, inf* caso *m* perdido
nohow [ˈnəʊhaʊ, *Am:* ˈnoʊ-] *adv Am* de ninguna manera
noise [nɔɪz] **I.** *n* **1.** (*sound*) ruido *m;* **to make a ~** hacer ruido **2.** *no pl* (*loud, unpleasant sounds*) estruendo *m* **3.** *no pl* ELEC interferencia *f* ►**to make a ~ about sth** *inf* quejarse mucho de algo; **to make** (**the right**) **~s** (*to go along with*) seguir la corriente; (*be polite*) ser muy cortés **II.** *adj* de ruido, ruidoso, -a
noise barrier *n* barrera *f* del sonido
noiseless [ˈnɔɪzləs] *adj* silencioso, -a
noise pollution *n no pl* contaminación *f* acústica **noise prevention** *n no pl* prevención *f* del ruido
noisome [ˈnɔɪsəm] *adj form* asqueroso, -a; (*offensive*) fétido, -a
noisy [ˈnɔɪzi] <-ier, -iest> *adj* **1.** ruidoso, -a; (*very loud, unpleasant*) estrepitoso, -a; (*protest*) escandaloso, -a; **to be ~** ser ruidoso **2.** (*full of loud, unpleasant noise*) bullicioso, -a **3.** ELEC (*signal*) acústico, -a **4.** *fig* (*clothes*) llamativo, -a
no-jump [ˌnəʊˈdʒʌmp] *n* SPORTS salto *m* nulo
nomad [ˈnəʊmæd, *Am:* ˈnoʊ-] *n* nómada *mf*
nomadic [nəʊˈmædɪk, *Am:* noʊ-] *adj* nómada
no-man's-land [ˈnəʊmænzlænd, *Am:* ˈnoʊ-] *n no pl* tierra *f* de nadie
nomenclature [nəˈmenklətʃəʳ, *Am:* ˈnoʊmenkleɪtʃɚ] *n* nomenclatura *f*
nominal [ˈnɒmɪnl, *Am:* ˈnɑːmə-] *adj* **1.** (*in name*) nominal **2.** (*small*) pequeño, -a
nominally [ˈnɒmɪnəli, *Am:* ˈnɑːmə-] *adv* nominalmente
nominate [ˈnɒmɪneɪt, *Am:* ˈnɑːmə-] *vt* **1.** (*propose*) proponer; (*for an award*) nominar **2.** (*appoint*) nombrar
nomination [ˌnɒmɪˈneɪʃən, *Am:* ˌnɑːmə-] *n* **1.** (*proposal*) propuesta *f* **2.** (*appointment*) nombramiento *m;* (*for an award*) nominación *f* **3.** *no pl* (*action of proposing*) proposición *f*
nominative [ˈnɒmɪnətɪv, *Am:* ˈnɑːmənəṱɪv] **I.** *n* nominativo *m* **II.** *adj* nominativo, -a
nominee [ˌnɒmɪˈniː, *Am:* ˌnɑːmə-] *n* candidato, -a *m, f;* (*for an award*) nominado, -a *m, f*
non-acceptance [ˌnɒnəkˈseptənts, *Am:* ˌnɑːnəkˈ-] *n no pl* **1.** (*failure to accept*) rechazo *m* **2.** FIN no aceptación *f*
nonagenarian [ˌnɒnədʒɪˈneərɪən, *Am:* ˌnɑːnədʒəˈnerɪ-] **I.** *n* nonagenario, -a *m, f* **II.** *adj* nonagenario, -a
non-aggression [ˌnɒnəˈgreʃən, *Am:* ˌnɑːnəˈ-] *n no pl* no agresión *f*
non-aggression pact, non-aggression treaty <-ies> *n* pacto *m* de no agresión
non-alcoholic [ˌnɒnælkəˈhɒlɪk, *Am:* ˌnɑːnælkəˈhɑːlɪk] *adj* sin alcohol
non-aligned [ˌnɒnəˈlaɪnd, *Am:* ˌnɑːnə-] *adj* no alineado, -a
non-alignment [ˌnɒnəˈlaɪnmənt, *Am:* ˌnɑːnə-] *n no pl* no alineamiento *m*
non-appearance [ˌnɒnəˈpɪərənts, *Am:* ˌnɑːnəˈpɪrənts] *n no pl* LAW incomparecencia *f*
non-attendance [ˌnɒnəˈtendənts, *Am:* ˌnɑːnəˈ-] *n no pl* ausencia *f*
non-belligerent [ˌnɒnbəˈlɪdʒərənt, *Am:* ˌnɑːn-] *adj* no beligerante
nonce word [ˈnɒnswɜːd, *Am:* ˈnɑːnswɜːrd] *n* palabra *f* creada para una ocasión especial
nonchalant [ˈnɒnʃələnt, *Am:* ˌnɑːnʃəˈlɑːnt] *adj* despreocupado, -a; **to appear ~** mostrarse indiferente; **to be ~ about sth** estar indiferente ante algo
non-com [ˈnɒnkɒm, *Am:* ˈnɑːnkɑːm] *adj inf abbr of* **non-commissioned officer** suboficial *mf*
non-combatant [ˌnɒnˈkɒmbətənt, *Am:* ˌnɑːnkəmˈbætənt] *n* MIL no combatiente *mf*
non-combustible [ˌnɒnkəmˈbʌstəbl, *Am:* ˌnɑːn-] *adj* incombustible
non-commissioned officer [ˌnɒnkəmɪʃəndˈɒfɪsəʳ, *Am:* ˌnɑːnkəmɪʃəndˈɑːfɪsɚ] *n* MIL suboficial *mf*
non-committal [ˌnɒnkəˈmɪtəl, *Am:* ˌnɑːnkəˈmɪṱ-] *adj* evasivo, -a
non-compliance [ˌnɒnkəmˈplaɪənts, *Am:* ˌnɑːn-] *n no pl* incumplimiento *m*
non compos mentis [ˌnɒnˌkɒmpəsˈmentɪs, *Am:* ˌnɑːnˌkɑːmpoʊsˈmenṱɪs] *adj* LAW sin plenas facultades mentales
nonconformist [ˌnɒnkənˈfɔːmɪst, *Am:* ˌnɑːnkənˈfɔːr-] **I.** *adj* inconformista **II.** *n* inconformista *mf*
nonconformity [ˌnɒnkənˈfɔːməti, *Am:* ˌnɑːnkənˈfɔːrməṱi] *n no pl* inconformidad *f*
non-contributory [ˌnɒnkənˈtrɪbjʊtri, *Am:* ˌnɑːnkənˈtrɪbjuːtɔːr-] *adj* sin contribución; **~ pension scheme** plan *m* de pensiones no contributivo
non-cooperation [ˌnɒnkəʊˌɒpərˈeɪʃən, *Am:* ˌnɑːnkoʊˌɑːpəˈreɪ-] *n no pl* no cooperación *f*
non-deposit bottle [ˌnɒndɪˈpɒzɪtˌbɒtl] *n* envase *m* no retornable
nondescript [ˈnɒndɪskrɪpt, *Am:* ˈnɑːndɪ-] *adj* sin nada de particular; (*person*) anodino, -a; (*colour*) indefinido, -a
non-durables [ˌnɒnˈdjʊərəblz] *npl* productos *mpl* deshechables
none [nʌn] **I.** *pron* **1.** (*nobody*) nadie, ninguno, -a; **~ of them** ninguno de ellos; **~ but he saw it** solo lo vio él; **~ of you helped me** ninguno de vosotros me ayudó **2.** (*not any*) ninguno, -a; **~ of my letters arrived** ninguna de mis cartas llegó **3.** (*not any*) nada; **nuts/wine? I've ~** (**at all**) ¿frutos secos/vino? no tengo nada; **~ of your speeches!** ¡nada de sermones!; **~ of that!** ¡déjate de eso! **II.** *adv* **1.** (*not*) **~ the less** sin embargo; **to be ~ the wiser** seguir sin entender nada **2.** (*not very*) **it's ~ too soon** ya era hora; **it's ~ too warm** no hace demasiado calor
nonentity [nɒˈnentəti, *Am:* nɑːˈnenṱəṱi] <-ies> *n* **1.** (*person*) cero *m* a la izquierda

2. *no pl* (*insignificance*) insignificancia *f*

non-essential [nɒnɪ'sentʃəl, *Am:* nɑːnɪ-] I. *adj* secundario, -a II. *n* cosa *f* no esencial

non-event [ˌnɒnɪ'vent, *Am:* ˌnɑːnɪ'vent] *n inf* fiasco *m*

non-existence *n no pl* inexistencia *f*

non-existent [ˌnɒnɪg'zɪstənt, *Am:* ˌnɑːnɪg-'zɪs-] *adj* inexistente

non-fiction [ˌnɒn'fɪkʃən, *Am:* ˌnɑːn-] *n no pl* no ficción *f*

non-flammable [ˌnɒn'flæməbl, *Am:* ˌnɑːn-] *adj* no inflamable

non-infectious [ˌnɒnɪnfekʃəs, *Am:* ˌnɑːn-] *adj* no infeccioso, -a

non-iron [ˌnɒn'aɪən, *Am:* ˌnɑːn'aɪɚn] *adj* que no necesita plancha

non-member country [ˌnɒn'membəʳ 'kʌntri, *Am:* ˌnɑːn'membɚ 'kʌntri] <-ies> *n* POL país *m* no miembro

non-negotiable [ˌnɒnɪ'gəʊʃiəbl, *Am:* ˌnɑːnɪ'goʊ-] *adj* LAW, FIN no negociable

non-pareil ['nɒnpərəl, *Am:* ˌnɑːnpə'rel] I. *adj liter* sin par II. *n liter* cosa *f* sin par

nonplus [ˌnɒn'plʌs, *Am:* ˌnɑːn-] <-ss-> *vt* dejar perplejo; **to be ~sed** quedarse sorprendido

non-polluting [ˌnɒnpə'luːtɪŋ, *Am:* ˌnɑːn-] *adj* no contaminante

non-productive [ˌnɒnprə'dʌktɪv, *Am:* ˌnɑːn-] *adj* improductivo, -a

nonprofit, **non-profit-making** [ˌnɒn'prɒfɪtˌmeɪkɪŋ, *Am:* ˌnɑːn'prɑːfɪt-] *adj Am* no lucrativo, -a

non-proliferation [ˌnɒnprəˌlɪfə'reɪʃən, *Am:* ˌnɑːn-] I. *n no pl* POL no proliferación *f* II. *adj* POL de no proliferación

non-proliferation treaty <-ies> *n* POL tratado *m* de no proliferación

non-refundable [ˌnɒnrɪ'fʌndəbl, *Am:* ˌnɑːn-] *adj* no reembolsable; **~ down payment** pago *m* a fondo perdido

non-resident [ˌnɒn'rezɪdənt, *Am:* ˌnɑːn-] I. *adj* no residente II. *n* transeúnte *mf*

non-returnable [ˌnɒnrɪ'tɜːnəbl, *Am:* ˌnɑːn-rɪ'tɜːr-] *adj* no retornable

non-scheduled [ˌnɒn'ʃedjuːld, *Am:* ˌnɑːn-'skedʒuːld] *adj* no programado, -a

nonsense ['nɒnsənts, *Am:* 'nɑːnsents] I. *n no pl* tonterías *fpl;* **to make (a) ~ of sth** *Brit, Aus* ridiculizar algo; **to talk ~** *inf* decir tonterías II. *adj* 1. LIT (*invented for amusement*) disparatado, -a 2. (*without meaning*) absurdo, -a III. *interj* tonterías

nonsensical [ˌnɒn'sentsɪkl, *Am:* ˌnɑːn-] *adj* absurdo, -a

non-shrink [ˌnɒn'ʃrɪŋk, *Am:* ˌnɑːn-] *adj* que no encoje

non-skid [ˌnɒn'skɪd, *Am:* ˌnɑːn-] *adj* antideslizante

non-smoker [ˌnɒn'sməʊkəʳ, *Am:* ˌnɑːn-'smoʊkɚ] *n* persona *f* que no fuma

non-smoking *adj* no fumador(a)

non-starter [ˌnɒn'stɑːtəʳ, *Am:* ˌnɑːn-'stɑːrt̬ɚ] *n inf* **that proposal is a ~** esa propuesta es imposible

non-stick [ˌnɒn'stɪk, *Am:* ˌnɑːn-] *adj* antiadherente

non-stop [ˌnɒn'stɒp, *Am:* ˌnɑːn'stɑːp] I. *adj* 1. (*without stopping, direct*) sin parar; (*flight*) directo, -a 2. (*uninterrupted*) incesante II. *adv* sin pausa

non-swimmer [ˌnɒn'swɪməʳ, *Am:* ˌnɑːn-'swɪmɚ] *n* no nadador(a) *m(f)*

non-taxable [ˌnɒn'tæksəble] *adj* no impositivo, -a

non-toxic [ˌnɒn'tɒksɪk] *adj* no tóxico, -a

non-verbal [ˌnɒn'vɜːbl, *Am:* ˌnɑːn'vɜːr-] *adj* no verbal

non-violent [ˌnɒn'vaɪələnt, *Am:* ˌnɑːn-] *adj* pacífico, -a

non-voting [ˌnɒn'vəʊtɪŋ] *adj* sin derecho a voto

noodle[1] ['nuːdl] I. *n* fideo *m* II. *adj* de fideos

noodle[2] ['nuːdl] *n Am, inf* 1. (*head*) cabeza *f* 2. (*person*) bobo, -a *m, f*

noodle[3] ['nuːdl] *vi Am, inf* MUS tocar

nook [nʊk] *n liter* rincón *m;* **~s and crannies** todos los rincones

noon [nuːn] *n no pl* mediodía *m;* **at ~** a mediodía; **about ~** alrededor de mediodía

no one ['nəʊwʌn, *Am:* 'noʊ-] *pron s.* **nobody**

noose [nuːs] *n* 1. (*loop of rope*) soga *f* 2. (*loop of rope for trapping*) lazo *m* 3. *fig* (*problem*) aprieto *m* ►**to have a ~ around one's neck** tener la soga al cuello

nope [nəʊp, *Am:* noʊp] *adv inf* no

nor [nɔːʳ, *Am:* nɔːr] *conj* 1. (*and also not*) tampoco; ~ **(do) I** ni yo tampoco 2. (*not either*) ni

Nordic ['nɔːdɪk, *Am:* 'nɔːr-] *adj* nórdico, -a

norm [nɔːm, *Am:* nɔːrm] *n* norma *f*

normal ['nɔːml, *Am:* 'nɔːr-] *adj* 1. (*not out of the ordinary*) normal 2. (*usual*) corriente; **as (is) ~** como es normal

normalcy ['nɔːməlsi, *Am:* 'nɔːr-] *Am,* **normality** [nɔː'mæləti, *Am:* nɔːr'mælət̬i] *n Brit no pl* normalidad *f*

normalize ['nɔːməlaɪz, *Am:* 'nɔːr-] *a.* INFOR I. *vt* normalizar II. *vi* normalizar

normally ['nɔːməli, *Am:* 'nɔːr-] *adv* normalmente

Normandy ['nɔːməndi, *Am:* 'nɔːr-] *n* Normandía *f*

north [nɔːθ, *Am:* nɔːrθ] I. *n* 1. (*cardinal point*) norte *m;* **to lie 5 km to the ~ of sth** quedar a 5 km al norte de algo; **to go/drive to the ~** ir/viajar hacia el norte; **further ~** más al norte 2. GEO Norte *m;* **in the ~ of France** en el norte de Francia; **the Far North** el extremo Norte II. *adj* del norte, septentrional; **~ wind** viento *m* del norte; **~ coast** costa *f* norte; **the North Sea** El Mar del Norte; **North Star** Estrella *f* Polar; **the North Pole** el Polo Norte

North Africa *n* África *f* del Norte **North African** I. *n* norteafricano, -a *m, f* II. *adj* norteafricano, -a

North America *n* América *f* del Norte **North American** I. *n* norteamericano, -a *m, f* II. *adj* norteamericano, -a

North Carolina *n* Carolina *f* del Norte **North Dakota** *n* Dakota *f* del Norte

northeast [ˌnɔːθ'iːst, *Am:* ˌnɔːrθ-] I. *n* nordeste *m* II. *adj* del nordeste

northeastern [ˌnɔːθ'iːstən, *Am:* ˌnɔːrθ-'iːstɚn] *adj* nororiental

northerly ['nɔːðəli, *Am:* 'nɔːrðɚli] *adj* del norte; ~ **direction** dirección *f* norte

northern ['nɔːðən, *Am:* 'nɔːrðɚn] *adj* del norte, norteño, -a, nortino, -a *Chile, Perú;* ~ **hemisphere** hemisferio *m* norte; **the** ~ **part of the country** la parte norte del país; ~ **lights** aurora *f* boreal

northerner ['nɔːðənəʳ, *Am:* 'nɔːrðɚnɚ] *n* norteño, -a *m, f*

Northern Marianas *n* Marianas *fpl* del Norte **northernmost** *adj* más septentrional **Northern Territory** *n* territorio *m* norte

North Pole ['nɔːθpəʊl, *Am:* 'nɔːrθpoʊl] *n* **the** ~ el polo norte **North Sea** I. *n* Mar *m* del Norte II. *adj* del Mar del Norte **North-south divide** *n* ECON división *f* Norte-Sur

northward ['nɔːθwəd, *Am:* 'nɔːrθwɚd] *adv* hacia el norte

northwest [ˌnɔːθ'west, *Am:* ˌnɔːrθ-] I. *n* noroeste *m;* **to the** ~ (**of**) al noroeste (de) II. *adj* del noroeste; ~ **England** el noroeste de Inglaterra III. *adv* en dirección noroeste

northwesterly [ˌnɔːθ'westəli, *Am:* ˌnɔːrθ-'westɚli] *adj* en dirección noroeste; (*from the northwest*) del noroeste; ~ **part** parte *f* noroeste

Northwest Territories *n pl* territorios *mpl* del noroeste

Norway ['nɔːweɪ, *Am:* 'nɔːr-] *n* Noruega *f*

Norwegian [nɔː'wiːdʒən, *Am:* nɔːr'-] I. *adj* noruego, -a II. *n* 1. (*person*) noruego, -a *m, f* 2. LING noruego *m*

nose [nəʊz, *Am:* noʊz] I. *n* 1. (*smelling organ*) nariz *f;* **to blow one's** ~ sonarse la nariz 2. AVIAT (*front*) morro *m* 3. (*smell of wine*) bouquet *m* ►**with one's** ~ **in the air** mirando por encima del hombro; **to put one's** ~ **to the grindstone** *inf* trabajar duro; **to put sb's** ~ **out of joint** *inf* tocar las narices a alguien; **to keep one's** ~ **clean** *inf* no meterse en líos; **to follow one's** ~ *inf* (*trust instincts*) guiarse por su olfato; (*go straight ahead*) seguir adelante; **to get up sb's** ~ *Brit, Aus, inf* poner de los nervios a alguien; **to have a** (**good**) ~ **for sth** tener buen olfato para algo; **to have one's** ~ **in sth** meter las narices en algo; **to keep one's** ~ **out of sth** *inf* no meterse en algo; **to poke one's** ~ **into sth** *inf* entrometerse en algo; **to rub sb's** ~ **in it** restregar algo a alguien por las narices; **to thumb one's** ~ **at sb** hacer un palmo de narices a alguien; (**from**) **under sb's** (**very**) ~ *inf,* **right out from under sb's** ~ *Am, inf* delante de las narices de alguien II. *vi* fisgonear III. *vt* **to** ~ **one's way in/out/up** entrar/salir/pasar lentamente; **to** ~ (**its way**) **through sth** avanzar con precaución a través de algo

◆**nose about, nose around** *vi inf* fisgonear

◆**nose out** I. *vt* descubrir II. *vi* apartarse

nosebag ['nəʊzbæg, *Am:* 'noʊz-] *n* morral *m* **nosebleed** *n* hemorragia *f* nasal **nosecone** *n* AVIAT cabeza *f* **nosedive** I. *n* 1. AVIAT descenso *m* en picado 2. FIN caída *f* en picado II. *vi* 1. AVIAT descender en picado 2. FIN caer en picado **nosegay** *n* ramillete *m* de flores **nose job** *n inf* operación *f* de cirugía plástica de la nariz **nose-wheel** *n* rueda *f* delantera de aterrizaje

nosey ['nəʊzi, *Am:* 'noʊ-] <-ier, -iest> *adj* fisgón, -ona; **to be** ~ ser curioso

nosh [nɒʃ, *Am:* nɑːʃ] I. *n no pl, Brit, Aus, inf* comida *f* II. *vi Brit, Aus, inf* papear

nosh-up ['nɒʃʌp, *Am:* 'nɑːʃ-] *n Brit, Aus, inf* atracón *m*

nostalgia [nɒ'stældʒə, *Am:* nɑː'-] *n no pl* nostalgia *f*

nostalgic [nɒ'stældʒɪk, *Am:* nɑː'-] *adj* nostálgico, -a

no-strike agreement [ˌnəʊstraɪkə'griːmənt] *n* acuerdo *m* de no convocar huelgas

nostril ['nɒstrəl, *Am:* 'nɑːstrəl] *n* ventana *f* de la nariz

nosy ['nəʊzi, *Am:* 'noʊ-] <-ier, -iest> *adj s.* **nosey**

nosy parker ['nəʊzi'pɑːkəʳ, *Am:* 'noʊzi-'pɑːrkɚ] *n inf* fisgón, -ona *m, f*

not [nɒt, *Am:* nɑːt] *adv* no; **it's a woman,** ~ **a man** es una mujer, no un hombre; **he's asked me** ~ **to do it** me ha pedido que no lo haga; ~ **all the children like singing** no les gusta cantar a todos los niños; ~ **me!** ¡yo no!; **why** ~**?** ¿por qué no?; **he is** ~ **ugly** no es feo; **or** ~ o no; ~ **at all** (*nothing*) en absoluto; (*no need to thank*) de nada; ~ **only ... but also ...** no sólo... sino también; ~ **just** [*o* **simply**] no sólo; ~ **much** no demasiado

notable ['nəʊtəbl, *Am:* 'noʊt̬ə-] I. *adj* 1. (*remarkable*) notable 2. (*eminent*) eminente II. *n* persona *f* importante

notably ['nəʊtəbli, *Am:* 'noʊt̬ə-] *adv* notablemente

notary ['nəʊtəri, *Am:* 'noʊt̬ɚ-] <-ies> *n* ~ (**public**) notario, -a *m, f*

notation [nəʊ'teɪʃən, *Am:* noʊ-] *n* MAT, MUS notación *f*

notch [nɒtʃ, *Am:* nɑːtʃ] <-es> I. *vt* 1. (*cut*) hacer una muesca 2. *inf* (*achieve*) conseguir II. *n* 1. (*cut*) muesca *f;* (*hole*) agujero *m* 2. (*degree*) punto *m* 3. *Am* (*narrow valley*) valle *m*

note [nəʊt, *Am:* noʊt] I. *n* 1. (*annotation*) nota *f;* **to take** ~ tomar nota 2. LIT apunte *m* 3. MUS nota *f;* (*sound*) tono *m;* **to strike the right** ~ *fig* dar con el tono apropiado 4. *Brit, Aus* (*piece of paper money*) billete *m*

5. (*importance*) **of ~** *form* notable; **nothing of ~** nada importante **II.** *vt form* anotar; (*mention*) observar; **to ~ (that)** ... hacer notar (que)...

notebook ['nəʊtbʊk, *Am:* 'noʊt-] *n* cuaderno *m*

noted ['nəʊtɪd, *Am:* 'noʊt̬ɪd] *adj* célebre; **to be ~ for sth** ser conocido por algo

notepad ['nəʊtpæd, *Am:* 'noʊt-] *n* bloc *m*

notepaper ['nəʊtˌpeɪpəʳ, *Am:* 'noʊtˌpeɪpɚ] *n no pl* papel *m* de carta

noteworthy ['nəʊtˌwɜːði, *Am:* 'noʊtˌwɜːr-] *adj form* de interés; **nothing/something ~** nada/algo digno de atención

nothing ['nʌθɪŋ] **I.** *pron indef, sing* **1.** (*no objects*) nada; **~ happens** no pasa nada; **we saw ~ (else/more)** no vimos nada (más); **~ new** nada nuevo; **next to ~** casi nada **2.** (*not anything*) **~ came of it** no salió nada (de allí); **~ doing!** *inf* ¡para nada!; **fit for ~** bueno para nada; **to make ~ of it** no darle importancia; **there is ~ to laugh at** no tiene nada de gracioso **3.** (*not important*) **that's ~!** ¡no es nada!; **time is ~ to me** el tiempo no es importante para mí **4.** (*only*) **~ but** tan sólo; **she is ~ if not patient** es paciente por encima de todo; **~ much** no gran cosa **II.** *adv* **~ less than** ni más ni menos que; **~ daunted, I went on** sin flaquear, seguí adelante **III.** *n* **1.** nada *f* **2.** MAT, SPORTS cero *m;* **three to ~** *Am* tres a cero **3.** (*person*) don nadie *m*

nothingness ['nʌθɪŋnɪs] *n no pl* (*emptiness*) vacío *m;* (*worthlessness*) nada *f*

no-throw [ˌnəʊ'θrəʊ] *n* SPORTS lanzamiento *m* nulo

notice ['nəʊtɪs, *Am:* 'noʊt̬ɪs] **I.** *vt* **1.** (*see*) ver; (*perceive*) fijarse en; **to ~ (that)** ... darse cuenta de (que)... **2.** (*recognize*) reconocer **II.** *vi* percatarse **III.** *n* **1.** *no pl* (*attention*) interés *m;* **to take ~ of sb/sth** prestar atención a alguien/algo; **to come to sb's ~ (that ...)** llegar al conocimiento de alguien (que...); **to escape one's ~** no percatarse de algo; **to escape sb's ~ that ...** pasarle a alguien por alto que... **2.** (*display*) letrero *m;* (*in a newspaper, magazine*) anuncio *m* **3.** *no pl* (*warning*) aviso *m;* **to give sb ~ (of sth)** avisar a alguien (de algo); **at short ~** a corto plazo; **at a moment's ~** al momento; **until further ~** hasta nuevo aviso **4.** *no pl* LAW preaviso *m;* **to give (in) one's ~** presentar la dimisión; **to give sb his ~** despedir a alguien

noticeable ['nəʊtɪsəbl, *Am:* 'noʊt̬ɪ-] *adj* evidente; (*difference*) notable

notice board *n Aus, Brit* tablón *m* de anuncios

notifiable ['nəʊtɪfaɪəbl, *Am:* 'noʊt̬ə-] *adj* (*disease*) que hay que notificar

notification [ˌnəʊtɪfɪ'keɪʃən, *Am:* ˌnoʊt̬ə-] *n* notificación *f*

notify ['nəʊtɪfaɪ, *Am:* 'noʊt̬ə-] <-ie-> *vt* informar; **to ~ sb of sth** notificar algo a alguien

notion ['nəʊʃən, *Am:* 'noʊ-] *n* **1.** (*idea*) noción *f;* **to have some ~ of sth** tener algunas nociones de algo; **to have no ~ of sth** no tener ni idea de algo **2.** (*silly idea*) burrada *f;* **to have a ~ to do sth** tener la intención de hacer algo

notional ['nəʊʃənl, *Am:* 'noʊ-] *adj form* teórico, -a

notoriety [ˌnəʊtə'raɪəti, *Am:* ˌnoʊt̬ə'raɪət̬i] *n no pl* mala fama *f*

notorious [nəʊ'tɔːrɪəs, *Am:* noʊ'tɔːrɪ-] *adj* de mala reputación; (*thief*) bien conocido, -a; **she's a ~ liar** tiene fama de mentirosa; **to be ~ for sth** tener mala fama por algo

notwithstanding [ˌnɒtwɪθ'stændɪŋ, *Am:* ˌnɑːt-] *form* **I.** *prep* a pesar de **II.** *adv* no obstante

nougat ['nuːgɑː, *Am:* 'nuːgət] *n no pl* ≈ turrón *m*

nought [nɔːt, *Am:* nɑːt] *n* **1.** *Brit* nada *f* **2.** MAT cero *m*

noun [naʊn] **I.** *n* nombre *m;* LING sustantivo *m* **II.** *adj* nominal

nourish ['nʌrɪʃ, *Am:* 'nɜːr-] *vt* **1.** (*provide with food*) alimentar; **to ~ oneself on sth** alimentarse de algo **2.** *fig, form* (*cherish*) fomentar

nourishing ['nʌrɪʃɪŋ, *Am:* 'nɜːr-] *adj* nutritivo, -a; (*rich*) rico, -a

nourishment *n no pl* **1.** (*food*) alimento *m* **2.** (*providing with food*) nutrición *f*

nous [naʊs, *Am:* nuːs] *n no pl, Aus, Brit, inf* cacumen *m*

Nova Scotia [ˌnəʊvə'skəʊʃə, *Am:* ˌnoʊvə-'skoʊ-] *n* Nueva Escocia *f*

novel¹ ['nɒvl, *Am:* 'nɑːvl] *n* novela *f*

novel² ['nɒvl, *Am:* 'nɑːvl] *adj* nuevo, -a

novelette [ˌnɒvə'let, *Am:* ˌnɑːvə-] *n* novela *f* rosa

novelist ['nɒvəlɪst, *Am:* ˌnɑːvə-] *n* novelista *mf*

novelty ['nɒvəlti, *Am:* 'nɑːvlt̬i] **I.** <-ies> *n* **1.** *no pl* (*newness*) novedad *f* **2.** (*innovation*) innovación *f* **3.** (*cheap trinket*) baratija *f* **II.** *adj* **1.** (*new*) nuevo, -a **2.** (*cheap*) barato, -a

November [nəʊ'vembəʳ, *Am:* noʊ'vembɚ] *n* noviembre *m; s. a.* **April**

novice ['nɒvɪs, *Am:* 'nɑːvɪs] *n* novato, -a *m, f;* REL novicio, -a *m, f*

now [naʊ] **I.** *adv* **1.** (*at the present time*) ahora; **just ~** ahora mismo **2.** (*currently*) actualmente **3.** (*then*) entonces; **any time ~** en cualquier momento; **(every) ~ and then** de vez en cuando **4.** (*give emphasis*) **~, where did I put her book?** ¿se puede saber dónde he puesto su libro?; **~ we're talking!** ahora sí que estamos hablando...; **~ then** ¡vamos a ver! ►**(it's) ~ or never** (es) ahora o nunca **II.** *n* (*present*) presente *m;* **before ~** antes; **by ~** ahora ya; **for ~** por ahora; **as from ~** a partir de ahora **III.** *conj* **~ (that)** ... ahora que...

nowadays ['naʊədeɪz] *adv* hoy en día

nowhere ['nəʊweəʳ, *Am:* 'noʊwer] *adv* en ninguna parte; **to appear from ~** aparecer de

N

la nada; **to be going** ~ *a. fig* no llevar a ninguna parte

nowt [naʊt] *pron Brit* (*nothing*) nada ▶**there's ~ so queer as <u>folk</u>** *prov* hay de todo en la viña del Señor *prov*

noxious ['nɒkʃəs, *Am:* 'nɑːk-] *adj form* nocivo, -a; (*very unpleasant*) desagradable

nozzle ['nɒzl, *Am:* 'nɑːzl] *n* tobera *f;* (*of a petrol pump*) inyector *m;* (*of a gun*) boquilla *f*

NT 1. *abbr of* **New Testament** Nuevo Testamento *m* 2. *abbr of* **National Trust** *instituto del gobierno británico para la conservación del patrimonio histórico-artístico*

nuance ['njuːɑːns, *Am:* 'nuː-] *n* matiz *m*

nub [nʌb] *n* 1. (*point*) quid *m* 2. (*piece*) trozo *m*

nubile ['njuːbaɪl, *Am:* 'nuːbɪl] *adj* núbil

nuclear ['njuːkliəʳ, *Am:* 'nuːkliɚ] *adj* nuclear

nuclear medicine *n no pl* medicina *f* nuclear **nuclear nonproliferation treaty** <-ies> *n* POL, MIL tratado *m* de no proliferación de armas nucleares **nuclear power station** *n* central *f* nuclear **nuclear reactor** *n* reactor *m* nuclear

nucleic acid [njuː'kleɪɪd'æsɪd, *Am:* nuː-'kliː-] *n* ácido *m* nucleico

nucleus ['njuːklɪəs, *Am:* 'nuː-] <-ei *o* -es> *n* núcleo *m*

nude [njuːd, *Am:* nuːd] I. *adj* desnudo, -a II. *n* 1. ART, PHOT desnudo *m* 2. (*naked*) **in the ~** desnudo

nudge [nʌdʒ] I. *vt* dar un codazo a; *fig* empujar; **to ~ sb into doing sth** empujar a alguien a hacer algo II. *vi* codear III. *n* 1. (*push*) codazo *m* 2. (*encouragement*) valor *m*

nudism ['njuːdɪzəm, *Am:* 'nuː-] *n no pl* nudismo *m*

nudist ['njuːdɪst, *Am:* 'nuː-] I. *n* nudista *mf* II. *adj* nudista

nudist beach *n* playa *f* nudista **nudist camp** *n* campamento *m* de nudistas

nudity ['njuːdəti, *Am:* 'nuːdəṱi] *n no pl* desnudez *f*

nugatory ['njuːgətəri, *Am:* 'nuːgətɔːr-] *adj form* insignificante

nugget ['nʌgɪt] *n* MIN pepita *f*

nuisance ['njuːsns, *Am:* 'nuː-] *n* 1. molestia *f*, camote *m AmL;* **to make a ~ of oneself** dar la lata 2. LAW perjuicio *m*

nuke [nuːk, njuːk] *vt inf* 1. MIL bombardear con armas atómicas 2. *Am, Aus, inf* (*cook*) cocinar en el microondas

null [nʌl] *adj* nulo, -a; ~ **and void** sin efecto

nullification [ˌnʌlɪfɪ'keɪʃən] *n* anulación *f*

nullify ['nʌlɪfaɪ] <-ie-> *vt* anular

nullity ['nʌləti, *Am:* -ṱi] *n no pl* nulidad *f*

numb [nʌm] I. *adj* entumecido, -a; **to go ~** entumecerse II. *vt* entumecer; (*desensitize*) insensibilizar

number ['nʌmbəʳ, *Am:* -bɚ] I. *n* 1. MAT número *m;* (*symbol*) cifra *f;* **house ~** número de casa; **telephone ~** número de teléfono 2. (*amount*) cantidad *f;* (**a**) **small/large ~**(**s**) (**of children**) (una) pequeña/gran cantidad (de niños); **for a ~ of reasons** por una serie de razones; **to be 3 in ~** ser 3; **to be few in ~** ser pocos 3. PUBL, MUS, THEAT número *m* ▶**~ <u>one</u>** uno *m* mismo; **to look after ~ <u>one</u>** cuidar de sí mismo; **to be** (**the**) **~ <u>one</u>** ser el mejor; **to <u>have</u> sb's ~** tener calado a alguien; **to be <u>beyond</u> ~** ser tantos que no se pueden contar II. *vt* 1. (*assign a number to*) poner número a; **to ~ sth from ... to ...** numerar algo del... al... 2. (*count*) contar 3. (*amount to*) sumar; **each group ~s 10 members** cada grupo tiene 10 miembros

> El **Number 10 Downing Street** es la residencia oficial del **prime minister** (primer ministro). La casa data del siglo XVII y fue construida por Sir George Downing, político, especulador inmobiliario y espía. El primer ministro vive en el piso más alto y en el resto del edificio se encuentran las oficinas y las salas de reuniones del gabinete de gobierno. El **Chancellor of the Exchequer** (ministro de Hacienda) vive en la casa de al lado, en el **Number 11**. En la misma calle se encuentran además otras dependencias del gobierno.

numbering *n no pl* numeración *f*

numberless *adj* innumerable

number plate *n Brit* matrícula *f*

numbness ['nʌmnɪs] *n no pl* 1. (*on part of body*) entumecimiento *m* 2. (*lack of feeling*) insensibilidad *f*

numeracy ['njuːmərəsi, *Am:* 'nuː-] *n no pl* competencia *f* con los números

numeral ['njuːmərəl, *Am:* 'nuː-] *n* número *m*

numerate ['njuːmərət, *Am:* 'nuː-] *adj* MAT competente en matemáticas

numeration [ˌnjuːmə'reɪʃən, *Am:* ˌnuː-] *n no pl, form* numeración *f*

numerical [njuː'merɪkl, *Am:* nuː-] *adj* numérico, -a; **in ~ order** por orden numérico

numeric keypad [ˌnjuːmerɪk'kiːpæd, *Am:* nuː-] *n* INFOR teclado *m* numérico

numerous ['njuːmərəs, *Am:* 'nuː-] *adj* numeroso, -a

numismatics [ˌnjuːmɪz'mætɪks, *Am:* ˌnuː-mɪz'mæṱ-] *n + sing vb* numismática *f*

numskull ['nʌmskʌl] *n* idiota *mf*

nun [nʌn] *n* monja *f*

nuncio ['nʌnsɪəʊ, *Am:* -oʊ] *n* REL nuncio *m*

nunnery ['nʌnəri] <-ies> *n* convento *m* de monjas

nuptial ['nʌpʃl] *adj* nupcial

nurse [nɜːs, *Am:* nɜːrs] I. *n* 1. MED enfermero, -a *m, f* 2. (*nanny*) niñera *f;* (*wet-nurse*) nodriza *f* II. *vt* 1. (*care for*) cuidar 2. (*nurture*) nutrir 3. (*harbour*) abrigar 4. (*hold carefully*) sostener con cuidado 5. (*breast-feed*) amamantar III. *vi* dar de mamar

nursery ['nɜːsəri, *Am:* 'nɜːr-] I. <-ies> *n* 1. (*school*) guardería *f* 2. (*bedroom*) cuarto *m*

de los niños **3.** BOT vivero *m* **II.** *adj* ~ **education** educación *f* preescolar
nursery rhyme *n* canción *f* infantil **nursery school** *n* parvulario *m* **nursery slopes** *npl Brit* SPORTS pistas *fpl* para principiantes
nursing **I.** *n no pl* enfermería *f* **II.** *adj* de enfermería
nursing home *n* asilo *m* de ancianos
nurture ['nɜːtʃəʳ, *Am:* 'nɜːrtʃɚ] **I.** *vt* alimentar; (*a plant*) cuidar **II.** *n no pl* nutrición *f*
nut [nʌt] *n* **1.** BOT nuez *f* **2.** TECH tuerca *f* **3.** *inf* (*madman*) chiflado, -a *m, f;* (*enthusiast*) entusiasta *mf* **4.** *inf* (*person's head*) coco *m;* **to be off one's** ~ estar grillado ▸**the** ~**s and bolts of sth** los aspectos prácticos de algo; **a hard** ~ **to crack** (*situation*) una situación difícil de llevar; (*person*) un hueso duro de roer
nutcracker ['nʌtˌkrækəʳ, *Am:* -ɚ] *n* cascanueces *m inv* **nuthatch** <-es> *n* trepador *m* **nuthouse** <-s> *n inf* manicomio *m* **nutmeg** *n no pl* nuez *f* moscada
nutrient ['njuːtriənt, *Am:* 'nuː-] **I.** *n* nutriente *m* **II.** *adj* nutritivo, -a
nutrition [njuː'trɪʃən, *Am:* nuː-] **I.** *n no pl* nutrición *f* **II.** *adj* nutricional
nutritionist [njuː'trɪʃənɪst, *Am:* nuː-] *n* nutricionista *mf*
nutritious [njuː'trɪʃəs, *Am:* nuː-] *adj,* **nutritive** ['njuːtrətɪv, *Am:* 'nuːtrət̬ɪv] *adj* nutritivo, -a
nuts [nʌts] **I.** *npl Am, vulg* cojones *mpl* **II.** *adj* **to be** ~ estar chiflado; **to go** ~ volverse loco; **to be** ~ **about sb** estar loco por alguien; **to be** ~ **about sth** pirrarse por algo
nutshell ['nʌtʃel] *n no pl* cáscara *f* de nuez ▸**to put sth in a** ~ decir algo con gran concisión; **in a** ~ en resumidas cuentas
nutty ['nʌti, *Am:* 'nʌt̬-] <-ier, -iest> *adj* **1.** (*cake*) con nueces; (*ice cream*) de nueces; (*taste*) a nueces **2.** *inf* (*crazy*) loco, -a, revirado, -a *Arg, Urug;* **to be** (**as**) ~ **as a fruitcake** estar más loco que una cabra
nuzzle ['nʌzl] **I.** *vt* acariciar con el hocico **II.** *vi* acurrucarse; **to** ~ **closer** arrimarse; **to** ~ (**up**) **against sb/sth** apretarse contra alguien/algo
NW [ˌen'dʌbljuː] *abbr of* **northwest** NO *m*
NY [ˌen'waɪ] *abbr of* **New York** Nueva York *f*
nylon ['naɪlɒn, *Am:* -lɑːn] **I.** *n no pl* nailon *m* **II.** *adj* de nailon
nymph [nɪmf] *n* ninfa *f*
nymphomania [ˌnɪmfə'meɪnɪə, *Am:* -foʊ'-] *n no pl* ninfomanía *f*
nymphomaniac [ˌnɪmfə'meɪnɪæk, *Am:* -foʊ'-] *n* ninfómana *f*
NZ [ˌen'zed, *Am:* -'ziː] *abbr of* **New Zealand** Nueva Zelanda *f*

O

O, o [əʊ] *n* **1.** (*letter*) O, o *f;* ~ **for Oliver** *Brit,* **O for Oboe** *Am* O de Oviedo **2.** (*zero*) cero *m*
oaf [əʊf, *Am:* oʊf] *n inf* (*uncultured*) patán *m;* (*clumsy*) zoquete *mf*
oafish ['əʊfɪʃ, *Am:* 'oʊ-] *adj inf* (*uncultured*) zafio, -a; (*clumsy*) lerdo, -a
oak [əʊk, *Am:* oʊk] *n* (*tree, wood*) roble *m* ▸**mighty** ~**s from little acorns grow** *prov* los grandes logros nacen de pequeñas cosas *prov*
OAP [ˌəʊeɪ'piː, *Am:* ˌoʊ-] *n abbr of* **old-age pensioner** pensionista *mf*
oar [ɔːʳ, *Am:* ɔːr] *n* remo *m* ▸**to stick one's** ~ **in** *inf* meter cuchara
oarsman ['ɔːzmən, *Am:* 'ɔːrz-] <-men> *n* remero *m*
oarswoman ['ɔːzwʊmən, *Am:* 'ɔːrz-] <-women> *n* remera *f*
OAS [ˌəʊeɪ'es, *Am:* ˌoʊ-] *n abbr of* **Organization of American States** OEA *f*
oasis [əʊ'eɪsɪs, *Am:* oʊ-] <-es> *n* oasis *m inv*
oatcake ['əʊtkeɪk, *Am:* 'oʊt-] *n* torta *f* de avena
oath [əʊθ, *Am:* oʊθ] *n* juramento *m;* **to take the** ~ prestar juramento; **under** [*o* **upon**] ~ *Brit* bajo juramento; ~ **of allegiance** juramento de lealtad
oatmeal ['əʊtmiːl, *Am:* 'oʊt-] *n no pl* harina *f* de avena
oats [əʊts, *Am:* oʊts] *n pl* avena *f* ▸**to sow one's wild** ~ andar de picos pardos *inf;* **to feel one's** ~ *Am, inf* sentirse en plena forma; **to get one's** ~ *inf* mojar (con regularidad); **to be off one's** ~ estar desganado
OAU [ˌəʊeɪ'juː, *Am:* ˌoʊ-] *n abbr of* **Organization of African Unity** OUA *f*
obduracy ['ɒbdjʊərəsi, *Am:* 'ɑːbdʊr-] *n no pl* obstinación *f*
obdurate ['ɒbdjʊərət, *Am:* 'ɑːbdʊrɪt] *adj form* obstinado, -a
obedience [ə'biːdɪəns, *Am:* oʊ'-] *n no pl* obediencia *f;* **in** ~ **to** conforme a
obedient [ə'biːdɪənt, *Am:* oʊ'-] *adj* obediente; **to be** ~ **to sb/sth** obedecer a alguien/algo
obelisk ['ɒbəlɪsk, *Am:* 'ɑːbəl-] *n* obelisco *m*
obese [əʊ'biːs, *Am:* oʊ'-] *adj* obeso, -a
obesity [əʊ'biːsəti, *Am:* oʊ'biːsət̬i] *n no pl* obesidad *f*
obey [əʊ'beɪ, *Am:* oʊ'-] *vt* (*person*) obedecer; (*instincts, advice*) hacer caso a; (*order, the law*) cumplir
obituary [əʊ'bɪtʃʊəri, *Am:* oʊ'bɪtʃueri] <-ies> *n,* **obituary notice** *n* necrología *f,* obituario *m AmL*
object[1] ['ɒbdʒɪkt, *Am:* 'ɑːb-] *n* **1.** (*unspecified thing*) objeto *m* **2.** (*purpose, goal*) propósito *m,* objetivo *m;* **the** ~ **of the exercise is ...** el objeto del ejercicio es... **3.** (*obstacle*) **money is no** ~ el dinero no importa **4.** LING complemento *m*

object² [əb'dʒekt] I. *vi* oponerse II. *vt* objetar; **to ~ that ...** objetar que...

objection [əb'dʒekʃən] *n* objeción *f;* **to raise ~s** poner reparos; **to raise ~s to sth** protestar contra algo; **there is no ~** no hay inconveniente

objectionable [əb'dʒekʃənəbl] *adj form* desagradable; (*person*) molesto, -a; (*conduct*) reprensible

objective [əb'dʒektɪv] I. *n* objetivo *m* II. *adj* objetivo, -a

objectivity [ˌɒbdʒɪk'tɪvəti, *Am:* ˌɑːbdʒek-'tɪvət̬i] *n no pl* objetividad *f*

object lesson *n* lección *f* práctica

objector *n* objetor(a) *m(f)*

obligate ['ɒblɪgeɪt, *Am:* 'ɑːblɪ-] *vt* obligar; **to ~ sb to do sth** obligar a alguien a hacer algo

obligation [ˌɒblɪ'geɪʃən, *Am:* ˌɑːblə'-] *n no pl* obligación *f;* **to be under an ~ to do sth** tener la obligación de hacer algo; **to have an ~ to sb** deber favores a alguien

obligatory [ə'blɪgətəri, *Am:* -tɔːri] *adj* obligatorio, -a

oblige [ə'blaɪdʒ] I. *vt* 1. (*force*) obligar 2. (*perform service for*) hacer un favor a; **to ~ sb with sth** hacer a alguien el favor de algo II. *vi* **to be happy to ~** estar encantado de ayudar

obliging [ə'blaɪdʒɪŋ] *adj* servicial, comedido, -a *AmL*

oblique [ə'bliːk, *Am:* oʊ'-] I. *adj* 1. (*indirect*) indirecto, -a 2. (*slanting*) oblicuo, -a II. *n* barra *f* oblicua

obliterate [ə'blɪtəreɪt, *Am:* -'blɪt̬-] *vt* eliminar; (*writing*) borrar; (*town*) arrasar

obliteration [əˌblɪtə'reɪʃən, *Am:* -ˌblɪt̬-] *n no pl* eliminación *f;* (*of writing*) borradura *f;* (*of town*) destrucción *f*

oblivion [ə'blɪvɪən] *n no pl* olvido *m;* **to fall into ~** caer en el olvido

oblivious [ə'blɪvɪəs] *adj* inconsciente; **~ of sth** inconsciente de algo

oblong ['ɒblɒŋ, *Am:* 'ɑːblɑːŋ] I. *n* rectángulo *m,* oblongo *m* II. *adj* rectangular, oblongo, -a

obnoxious [əb'nɒkʃəs, *Am:* -'nɑːk-] *adj* detestable

oboe ['əʊbəʊ, *Am:* 'oʊboʊ] *n* oboe *m*

oboist ['əʊbəʊɪst, *Am:* 'oʊboʊɪst] *n* oboe *mf*

obscene [əb'siːn] *adj* 1. (*indecent*) obsceno, -a, bascoso, -a *Col, Ecua* 2. (*scandalous*) escandaloso, -a

obscenity [əb'senəti, *Am:* -t̬i] <-ies> *n* obscenidad *f,* indecencia *f,* bascosidad *f Col, Ecua*

obscure [əb'skjʊəʳ, *Am:* -'skjʊr] I. *adj* oscuro, -a II. *vt* 1. (*make difficult to see*) oscurecer 2. (*make difficult to understand*) complicar 3. (*hide*) ocultar

obscurity [əb'skjʊərəti, *Am:* -'skjʊrət̬i] *n no pl* oscuridad *f*

obsequious [əb'siːkwɪəs] *adj* servil

observable [əb'zɜːvəbl, *Am:* -'zɜːr-] *adj* observable

observance [əb'zɜːvəns, *Am:* -'zɜːr-] *n* 1. *no pl* (*of laws, rules*) observancia *f;* (*of customs*) cumplimiento *m* 2. REL (*practice*) práctica *f*

observant [əb'zɜːvənt, *Am:* -'zɜːr-] *adj* 1. (*quick to notice things*) observador(a) 2. (*respectful: of rules, laws*) respetuoso, -a; (*of one's duty*) cumplidor(a)

observation [ˌɒbzə'veɪʃən, *Am:* ˌɑːbzɚ'-] *n* 1. (*act of seeing*) observación *f;* LAW vigilancia *f;* **to keep sth/sb under ~** vigilar algo/a alguien; **under ~** MED en observación; **to escape ~** pasar inadvertido 2. (*remark*) comentario *m,* observación *f;* **to make an ~ (about sb/sth)** hacer una observación (sobre alguien/algo)

observation car *n Am* RAIL vagón *m* mirador

observation post *n* MIL puesto *m* de observación **observation tower** *n* atalaya *f*

observatory [əb'zɜːvətri, *Am:* -'zɜːrvətɔːr-] *n* observatorio *m*

observe [əb'zɜːv, *Am:* -'zɜːrv] I. *vt* 1. (*watch closely*) observar; (*notice*) fijarse en; **to ~ sb doing sth** ver a alguien haciendo algo 2. (*remark*) comentar 3. (*obey: rules*) observar; (*silence, religious holiday*) guardar; **to ~ a minute of silence** guardar un minuto de silencio; **to ~ Passover** celebrar la Pascua II. *vi* 1. (*watch*) observar 2. (*remark*) **to ~ (up)on sth** hacer una observación sobre algo

observer [əb'zɜːvəʳ, *Am:* -'zɜːrvɚ] *n* observador(a) *m(f)*

obsess [əb'ses] *vt* obsesionar; **to be ~ed by sb/sth** obsesionarse por alguien/algo; **he is ~ed with being the best** está obsesionado con ser el mejor

obsession [əb'seʃən] *n* obsesión *f;* **to have an ~ with sb/sth** estar obsesionado con alguien/algo

obsessive [əb'sesɪv] *adj* 1. (*person, jealousy*) obsesivo, -a; **to be ~ about sth** estar obsesionado con algo; **to become ~ (about sth)** empezar a obsesionarse (con algo) 2. (*game*) obsesionante

obsolescence [ˌɒbsə'lesənts, *Am:* ˌɑːb-] *n no pl* obsolescencia *f*

obsolescent [ˌɒbsə'lesnt, *Am:* ˌɑːb-] *adj* que está quedando obsoleto, -a

obsolete ['ɒbsəliːt, *Am:* ˌɑːb-] *adj* (*method, design*) obsoleto, -a; (*word, spelling*) caído, -a en desuso

obstacle ['ɒbstəkl, *Am:* 'ɑːbstə-] *n* obstáculo *m;* **an insurmountable ~** un obstáculo insalvable; **to overcome an ~** superar un obstáculo; **to put ~s in the way of sb/sth** poner dificultades a alguien/algo; **to be an ~ to sth** ser un obstáculo para algo

obstacle race *n* carrera *f* de obstáculos

obstetrician [ɒbstə'trɪʃən, *Am:* ɑːbstə-'trɪʃ-] *n* MED obstetra *mf*

obstetrics [ɒb'stetrɪks, *Am:* əb'-] I. *npl* MED obstetricia *f* II. *adj* MED obstétrico, -a

obstinacy ['ɒbstɪnəsi, *Am:* 'ɑːbstə-] *n no pl* obstinación *f*

obstinate ['ɒbstɪnət, *Am:* 'ɑːbstə-] *adj* **1.**(*person, attitude*) obstinado, -a; **to be ~ about sth** ser terco en algo; **an ~ refusal** una negativa rotunda **2.**(*disease*) rebelde; (*problem*) persistente

obstreperous [əb'strepərəs] *adj form* **1.**(*unruly*) rebelde **2.**(*noisy*) ruidoso, -a

obstruct [əb'strʌkt] *vt* **1.**(*block*) obstruir; (*traffic*) bloquear; (*view*) tapar **2.**(*hinder*) dificultar; (*passage*) impedir; (*progress*) obstaculizar; **to ~ the traffic** obstruir el tráfico

obstruction [əb'strʌkʃən] *n* **1.**(*action*) *a.* MED, POL obstrucción *f* **2.**(*impediment*) obstáculo *m;* **an ~ to sth** un obstáculo para algo; **to cause an ~** causar un estorbo; AUTO obstruir el paso

obstructive [əb'strʌktɪv] *adj* (*tactic, attitude*) obstruccionista; (*person*) que pone obstáculos; **don't be so ~** no pongas tantos impedimentos

obtain [əb'teɪn] **I.** *vt* obtener; **to ~ sth from sb/sth** obtener algo de alguien/algo; **to ~ sth for sb** conseguir algo a alguien **II.** *vi form* prevalecer

obtainable [əb'teɪnəbl] *adj* que se puede conseguir; **it is not ~ in this country** no se puede adquirir en este país

obtrude [əb'truːd] **I.** *vt form* (*force*) imponer; **to ~ one's opinion(s) (up)on sb** imponer a alguien las propias opiniones **II.** *vi form* **to ~ upon sth** entrometerse en algo

obtrusive [əb'truːsɪv] *adj form* (*question, presence*) inoportuno, -a; (*noise*) molesto, -a; (*smell*) penetrante; (*colour, design*) (demasiado) llamativo, -a

obtuse [əb'tjuːs, *Am:* ɑːb'tuːs] *adj* obtuso, -a

obviate ['ɒbvɪeɪt, *Am:* 'ɑːb-] *vt* (*necessity, difficulty*) obviar; (*danger*) evitar

obvious ['ɒbviəs, *Am:* 'ɑːb-] *adj* obvio, -a; **a sign of ~ displeasure** un signo de evidente disgusto; **for ~ reasons** por razones obvias; **it is ~ what/where ...** está claro qué/dónde...; **it is ~ to me that ...** me doy perfecta cuenta de que...; **to make sth ~ to sb** hacer algo patente a alguien; **the ~ thing to do** lo que hay que hacer

obviously *adv* obviamente, claramente; **~, ...** como es lógico,...

occasion [ə'keɪʒən] **I.** *n* **1.**(*particular time*) ocasión *f;* **as ~ requires** si la ocasión lo requiere; **on ~** de vez en cuando; **on one ~** en una ocasión; **on several ~s** en varias ocasiones **2.**(*event*) acontecimiento *m;* **on the ~ of ...** con motivo de...; **to dress to suit the ~** vestirse para la ocasión; **to rise to the ~** estar a la altura de las circunstancias **3.**(*reason*) motivo *m;* **to give ~ to sth** dar lugar a algo **4.**(*opportunity*) oportunidad *f;* **should the ~ arise** si se presenta la ocasión; **to have ~ to do sth** tener ocasión de hacer algo; **to take an ~** aprovechar una oportunidad **II.** *vt* ocasionar

occasional [ə'keɪʒənəl] *adj* ocasional; **to pay very ~ visits to sb** visitar rara vez a alguien; **I have the ~ cigarette** fumo un cigarrillo de vez en cuando

occasionally *adv* ocasionalmente, de vez en cuando

occasional table *n* mesa *f* auxiliar

Occident ['ɒksɪdənt, *Am:* 'ɑːksə-] *n no pl* **the ~** Occidente

occidental [ˌɒksɪ'dentəl, *Am:* ˌɑːksə'dentəl] *adj* occidental

occult [ɒ'kʌlt, *Am:* ə'-] **I.** *adj* oculto, -a **II.** *n no pl* **the ~** las ciencias ocultas

occultism ['ɒkʌltɪzəm, *Am:* ə'kʌl-] *n no pl* ocultismo *m*

occupancy ['ɒkjəpəntsi, *Am:* 'ɑːkjə-] *n no pl* (*of building*) ocupación *f;* (*of post*) tenencia *f*

occupancy rate *n* tasa *f* de ocupación

occupant ['ɒkjəpənt, *Am:* 'ɑːkjə-] *n form* **1.**(*of building, vehicle*) ocupante *mf;* (*tenant*) inquilino, -a *m, f* **2.**(*of post*) titular *mf*

occupation [ˌɒkjə'peɪʃən, *Am:* 'ɑːkjə'-] *n* **1.** *a.* MIL ocupación *f;* **to take up ~ of a house** tomar posesión de una vivienda; **~ army** ejército *m* de ocupación **2.**(*profession*) profesión *f* **3.**(*pastime*) pasatiempo *m;* **what's your favourite ~?** ¿a qué prefieres dedicar tu tiempo libre?

occupational [ˌɒkjʊ'peɪʃənəl, *Am:* ˌɑːkjə'-] *adj* profesional

occupational disease *n* enfermedad *f* profesional **occupational hazard** *n* riesgo *m* laboral **occupational pension scheme** *n* plan *m* de pensiones **occupational therapy** *n* terapia *f* ocupacional

occupier ['ɒkjʊpaɪəʳ, *Am:* 'ɑːkjəpaɪɚ] *n* (*of territory, building*) ocupante *mf;* (*tenant*) inquilino, -a *m, f*

occupy ['ɒkjʊpaɪ, *Am:* 'ɑːkjuː-] <-ie-> *vt* **1.**(*room, position*) *a.* MIL ocupar; **to ~ space** ocupar espacio; **the bathroom's occupied** el lavabo está ocupado; **~ing forces** fuerzas *fpl* de ocupación **2.**(*engage*) **to be occupied with sth** estar ocupado con algo; **to keep sb occupied** mantener a alguien ocupado; **to keep one's mind occupied** mantener la mente ocupada; **to ~ oneself** entretenerse; **the whole process occupied a week** todo el proceso llevó una semana **3.**(*hold*) **to ~ a post** ocupar un cargo **4.**(*dwell in*) **the house hasn't been occupied for a long time** nadie ha vivido en la casa durante mucho tiempo **5.**(*employ*) dar trabajo

occur [ə'kɜːʳ, *Am:* -'kɜːr] <-rr-> *vi* **1.**(*happen*) ocurrir; (*change, problem*) producirse; **don't let it ~ again!** ¡que no vuelva a suceder!; **if any of these symptoms ~ consult your doctor** si se presenta alguno de estos síntomas consulte a su médico; **to ~ every two years** tener lugar cada dos años **2.**(*exist*) encontrarse; **the disease does not ~ in this area** la enfermedad no se da en esta zona

O

3. (*come into mind*) **to ~ to sb** ocurrírse a alguien; **it ~d to me that ...** se me ocurrió que...; **did it ever ~ to you that ...?** ¿no se te ha ocurrido nunca que...?

occurrence [ə'kʌrəns, *Am:* -'kɜːr-] *n* **1.** (*event*) acontecimiento *m;* **an unexpected ~** un suceso inesperado; **to be an everyday ~** ser cosa de todos los días; **to be of frequent/rare ~** ser/no ser frecuente **2.** (*case*) caso *m* **3.** *no pl* (*incidence: of disease*) incidencia *f*

ocean ['əʊʃən, *Am:* 'oʊ-] *n* océano *m* ►**~s of ...** un montón de... *inf*

oceangoing ['əʊʃənˌgəʊɪŋ, *Am:* 'oʊʃnˌgoʊ-] *adj* transatlántico, -a

Oceania [ˌəʊʃi'ɑːniə, *Am:* ˌoʊ-] *n* Oceanía *f*

oceanic [ˌəʊʃi'ænɪk, *Am:* ˌoʊʃi'-] *adj* oceánico, -a

ocean liner *n* NAUT transatlántico *m*

oceanography [ˌəʊʃə'nɒgrəfi, *Am:* ˌoʊʃə'nɑːgrə-] *n no pl* oceanografía *f*

ocelot ['əʊsɪlɒt, *Am:* 'ɑːsəlɑːt] *n* ocelote *m,* manigordo *m CRi*

ocher *Am,* **ochre** ['əʊkə^r, *Am:* 'oʊkɚ] **I.** *n no pl* ocre *m* **II.** *adj* ocre

o'clock [ə'klɒk, *Am:* -'klɑːk] *adv* **it's one ~** es la una; **it's two/seven ~** son las dos/las siete

OCR [ˌəʊsiː'ɑː^r, *Am:* ˌoʊ-] *n no pl abbr of* **optical character recognition** ROC *m*

octagon ['ɒktəgən, *Am:* 'ɑktəgɑːn] *n* octógono *m,* octágono *m*

octagonal [ɒk'tægənəl, *Am:* ɑːk-] *adj* octogonal, octagonal

octane ['ɒkteɪn, *Am:* 'ɑːk-] *n* octano *m*

octave ['ɒktɪv, *Am:* 'ɑːk-] *n* LIT, MUS octava *f*

octet [ɒk'tet, *Am:* ɑːk-] *n* MUS octeto *m*

October [ɒk'təʊbə^r, *Am:* ɑːk'toʊbɚ] *n* octubre *m; s. a.* **April**

octogenarian [ˌɒktədʒɪ'neərɪən, *Am:* ˌɑːktoʊdʒɪ'nerɪ-] **I.** *adj* octogenario, -a **II.** *n* octogenario, -a *m, f*

octopus ['ɒktəpəs, *Am:* 'ɑːk-] <-es *o* -pi> *n* pulpo *m*

oculist ['ɒkjʊlɪst, *Am:* 'ɑːkjə-] *n* oculista *mf*

OD [ˌəʊ'diː, *Am:* ˌoʊ-] **I.** *n abbr of* **overdose** sobredosis *f inv* **II.** *vi* **to ~ on sth** tomar una sobredosis de algo; *fig* abusar de algo

odd [ɒd, *Am:* ɑːd] *adj* **1.** (*strange*) extraño, -a; **an ~ person/thing** una persona/cosa rara; **how (very) ~!** ¡qué raro!; **it is ~ that ...** es raro que +*subj;* **to look ~** tener un aspecto extraño **2.** (*not even: number*) impar **3.** (*approximately*) **30 ~ people** 30 y pico personas; **he is about 50 ~** tiene unos 50 y tantos años **4.** (*occasional*) ocasional; **at ~ times** algunas veces; **she does the ~ teaching job** da alguna que otra clase **5.** (*unmatched: glove, sock*) suelto, -a **6.** (*left over*) sobrante; **I've got a few ~ hours** tengo algunas horas libres; **to be the ~ one out** quedar excluido

oddball ['ɒdbɔːl, *Am:* 'ɑːd-] **I.** *n inf* bicho *m* raro **II.** *adj inf* (*sense of humour*) raro, -a; (*idea*) descabellado, -a

oddity ['ɒdəti, *Am:* 'ɑːdəṱi] <-ies> *n* (*person*) excéntrico, -a *m, f;* (*thing*) cosa *f* rara; (*characteristic*) rareza *f*

odd-job man [ˌɒd'dʒɒbmæn, *Am:* 'ɑːddʒɑːb-] *n* hombre *m* que hace pequeñas reparaciones

oddly *adv* **1.** (*in a strange manner*) de forma extraña **2.** (*curiously*) curiosamente; **~ enough** por extraño que parezca

oddments ['ɒdmənts, *Am:* 'ɑːd-] *npl* restos *mpl*

odds [ɒdz, *Am:* ɑːdz] *npl* **1.** (*probability*) probabilidades *fpl;* **the ~ against/on sth** las probabilidades en contra/a favor de algo; **to shorten/lengthen the ~** disminuir/aumentar las posibilidades; **the ~ are against us** tenemos todo en contra; **the ~ are in his favour** tiene todas las de ganar; **the ~ are that ...** lo más seguro es que +*subj* **2.** *Aus, Brit, inf* (*difference*) **it makes no ~ (to me)** (me) da igual; **what's the ~?** ¿qué más da? ►**~ and ends** [*o* **sods**] *Aus, Brit, inf* (*bits*) cosas *fpl* sueltas; (*of fabric*) retales *mpl;* (*of food*) sobras *fpl;* **to pay over the ~** *Aus, Brit, inf* pagar más de la cuenta; **against all (the) ~** a pesar de las circunstancias adversas; **to be at ~ with sb** estar en desacuerdo con alguien

odds-on [ˌɒdz'ɒn, *Am:* ˌɑːdz'ɑːn] *adj* seguro, -a; **it's ~ that ...** lo más probable es que +*subj;* **the ~ favourite to win the race** el gran favorito de la carrera

ode [əʊd, *Am:* oʊd] *n* oda *f*

odious ['əʊdɪəs, *Am:* 'oʊ-] *adj* odioso, -a

odometer [ɒ'dɒmɪtə^r, *Am:* oʊ'dɑːməṱɚ] *n Am* cuentaquilómetros *m inv*

odor *n Am, Aus,* **odour** ['əʊdə^r, *Am:* 'oʊdɚ] *n Brit* (*smell*) olor *m;* (*fragance*) aroma *m;* **to be in good/bad ~ with sb** *fig* estar a bien/mal con alguien

odorless *adj Am, Aus,* **odourless** *adj form* inodoro, -a

odyssey ['ɒdɪsi, *Am:* 'ɑːdɪ-] *n* odisea *f*

OECD [ˌəʊiːsiː'diː, *Am:* ˌoʊ-] *n abbr of* **Organization for Economic Cooperation and Development** OCDE *f*

oecumenical [iːkjʊ'menɪkl, *Am:* ekjə'-] *adj* ecuménico, -a

oesophagus [iː'sɒfəgəs, *Am:* ɪ'sɑːfə-] <-agi *o* -guses> *n* esófago *m*

oestrogen ['iːstrəʊdʒən, *Am:* 'estrə-] *n no pl* estrógeno *m*

of [əv, *stressed:* ɒv] *prep* **1.** de **2.** (*belonging to*) de; **the works ~ Joyce** las obras de Joyce; **a friend ~ mine/theirs** un amigo mío/de ellos **3.** (*done by*) de; **it's kind ~ him** es amable de su parte **4.** (*representing*) de; **a drawing ~ Paul** un dibujo de Paul **5.** (*without*) **a tree bare ~ leaves** un árbol sin hojas; **free ~ charge** sin cargo; **free ~ tax** libre de impuestos; **to cure sb ~ a disease** curar a alguien de una enfermedad **6.** (*with*) **a man ~ courage** un hombre de valor; **a man ~ no importance** un hombre sin importancia; **a city ~ wide avenues** una ciudad con amplias avenidas **7.** (*away from*) **to be north ~ London** estar al norte de Londres **8.** (*temporal*) **the 4th ~ May** el 4 de mayo; **in May ~ 2003** en mayo del 2003 **9.** *Am* (*to*) **it is ten/a quarter ~ two** son las dos menos diez/cuarto **10.** (*consisting of*) de; **a ring ~ gold** un anillo de oro; **to smell/to taste ~ cheese** oler/saber a queso; **to consist ~ six parts** constar de seis partes **11.** (*characteristic*) **with the patience ~ a saint** con la paciencia de un santo; **this idiot ~ a plumber** este idiota del fontanero; **doctor ~ medicine** doctor en medicina **12.** (*concerning*) **his love ~ jazz** su amor por el jazz; **to know sth ~ sb's past** saber algo del pasado de alguien; **to approve ~ sb's idea** estar de acuerdo con la idea de alguien; **what has become ~ him?** ¿qué ha sido de él?; **what I think ~ him** lo que pienso de él **13.** (*cause*) **because ~ sth/sb** a causa de algo/alguien; **to die ~ grief** morir de pena; **it happened ~ itself** sucedió de por sí **14.** (*a portion of*) **there's a lot ~ it** hay mucho de eso; **one ~ the best** uno de los mejores; **the best ~ friends** los mejores amigos; **many ~ them came** muchos de ellos vinieron; **there are five ~ them** hay cinco de ellos; **he knows the five ~ them** los conoce a los cinco; **two ~ the five** dos de los cinco; **he ~ all people knows that** él debería saberlo mejor que nadie; **today ~ all days** hoy precisamente **15.** (*to amount of*) **80 years ~ age** 80 años de edad

off [ɒf, *Am:* ɑ:f] **I.** *prep* **1.** (*close to*) **to be one metre ~ sth/sb** estar a un metro de algo/alguien **2.** (*away from*) **the mill is ~ the road** el molino está algo apartado de la carretera; **to take sth ~ the shelf** coger algo del estante; **keep ~ the grass** mantenerse fuera del césped; **to sing ~ key** cantar fuera de tono; **get ~ me!** *Am, inf* ¡déjame! **3.** (*down from*) **to fall/jump ~ a ladder** caer/saltar de una escalera; **to get ~ the train** bajarse del tren **4.** (*from*) **to eat ~ a plate** comer de un plato; **to cut a piece ~ the cheese** cortar un pedazo del queso; **to take 10 euros ~ the price** rebajar 10 euros del precio **5.** *inf* (*stop liking*) **to go ~ sb/sth** pasar de alguien/algo; **to be ~ smoking/drugs** pasar de fumar/las drogas **6.** (*as source of*) **to run ~ batteries** alimentarse de baterías **II.** *adv* **1.** (*not on*) **to switch/turn sth ~** apagar algo; **it's ~ between them** *fig* lo han dejado **2.** (*away*) **the town is 8 km ~** el pueblo está a 8 km de distancia; **not far ~** faltar poco; **some way ~** a cierta distancia; **to go/run ~** irse/salir corriendo; **~ with him** fuera con él; **it's time I was ~** ya debería haber salido; **to be ~** SPORTS estar fuera de juego **3.** (*removed*) **there is a button ~** le falta un botón; **the lid is ~** la tapa está fuera; **with one's coat ~** con el abrigo quitado; **~ with that hat!** ¡quítate el sombrero! **4.** (*free from work*) **to get ~ at 4:00** salir (del trabajo) a las 4:00; **to get a day ~** tener un día libre **5.** (*completely*) **to kill ~** exterminar; **to pay sth ~** acabar de pagar **6.** COM **5% ~** 5% de descuento **7.** (*bad: food*) **to go ~** pasarse **8.** (*until gone*) **to walk ~ the dinner** caminar para bajar la comida; **to sleep ~ the wine** dormirse para bajar el vino **9.** (*separating*) **to fence sth ~** cercar algo ▶**straight** [*o* **right**] **~** enseguida; **~ and on, on and ~** de cuando en cuando; **it rained ~ and on** llovió intermitentemente **III.** *adj* **1.** (*not on: light*) apagado, -a; (*tap*) cerrado, -a; (*water*) cortado, -a; (*engagement*) suspendido, -a **2.** (*bad: milk*) cortado, -a; (*food*) malo, -a **3.** (*free from work*) **to be ~ at 5:00** salir del trabajo a las 5:00; **I'm ~ on Mondays** los lunes libro **4.** *Aus, Brit* (*provided for*) **to be well ~** tener dinero; **to be badly ~** andar mal de dinero; **to be badly ~ for sugar** andar escaso de azúcar **5.** (*sold out*) **veal is ~ now** ya no queda ternera **6.** *Am, inf* **to go ~ on sb** echar la bronca a alguien **IV.** *n no pl, Brit* salida *f* **V.** *vt Am, inf* **to ~ sb** cargarse a alguien

offal ['ɒfəl, *Am:* 'ɑ:fəl] *n no pl* (*of animal*) despojos *mpl,* achura *f AmS*

offbeat [ˌɒf'bi:t, *Am:* ˌɑ:f-] *adj* poco convencional

off-center *adj Am,* **off-centre** *adj Brit* **1.** (*diverging from the centre*) descentrado, -a **2.** (*unconventional*) poco convencional

off-chance ['ɒftʃɑ:nts, *Am:* 'ɑ:ftʃænts] *n* **on the ~** por si acaso

off-color *adj Am, Aus,* **off-colour** [ˌɒf'kʌlə^{r}, *Am:* ˌɑ:f'kʌlɚ] *adj Brit* **1.** (*unwell*) indispuesto, -a; **to feel ~** encontrarse mal; **to look ~** tener mala cara **2.** (*somewhat obscene: joke*) subido, -a de tono

off day *n* **to have an ~** tener un mal día

off-duty *adj* fuera de servicio

offence [ə'fents] *n* **1.** (*crime*) delito *m;* **minor ~** infracción *f;* **second ~** reincidencia *f;* **traffic ~** infracción de tráfico **2.** (*affront*) atentado *m;* **an ~ against sth** un atentado contra algo; **it is an ~ to the eye** *fig* hace daño a la vista **3.** *no pl* (*upset feeling*) ofensa *f;* **to cause ~ (to sb)** ofender (a alguien); **to take ~ (at sth)** ofenderse (por algo); **no ~ (intended)** *inf* sin ánimo de ofender **4.** REL pecado *m* **5.** *Am* SPORTS ofensiva *f*

offend [ə'fend] **I.** *vi* **1.** (*cause displeasure*) ofender **2.** (*violate*) **to ~ against sth** atentar contra algo; **his remarks ~ against common sense** sus comentarios atentan contra el sentido común **3.** LAW infringir la ley; (*commit a crime*) cometer un delito; **to ~ against a rule** infringir una norma **II.** *vt* **1.** (*upset sb's feelings*) ofender; **to be ~ed at sth** ofenderse por algo; **to be easily ~ed** ser muy susceptible; **she was ~ed that she had not been invited** se ofendió por no haber sido invitada **2.** (*affect disagreeably*) **to ~ the eye** hacer daño a la vista; **to ~ good taste** atentar contra el buen gusto

offender [ə'fendə^{r}, *Am:* -ɚ] *n* infractor(a) *m(f);* (*guilty of crime*) delincuente *mf;* **first ~**

O

delincuente sin antecedentes; **previous** [*o* **repeat**] ~ reincidente *mf;* **young** ~ delincuente juvenil

offense [əˈfens] *n Am s.* **offence**

offensive [əˈfensɪv] **I.** *adj* **1.** (*remark, joke*) ofensivo, -a; (*language, word*) grosero, -a; (*tone*) desagradable; **to be ~ to sb** insultar a alguien **2.** (*disagreeable: smell*) repugnante **II.** *n* MIL ofensiva *f;* **to go on the ~** pasar a la ofensiva; **to launch an ~** (**against sth**) lanzar una ofensiva (contra algo); **to take the ~** tomar la ofensiva

offensive weapon *n* MIL arma *f* ofensiva

offer [ˈɒfəʳ, *Am:* ˈɑːfɚ] **I.** *vt* **1.** (*proffer: help, advice, money*) ofrecer; (*chance*) brindar; **to ~ sb sth** ofrecer algo a alguien; **to ~ an apology** pedir disculpas; **to ~ congratulations to sb** felicitar a alguien; **can I ~ you a drink?** ¿quiere tomar algo?; **to ~ a good price for sth** ofrecer un buen precio por algo; **to ~ information/advice** dar información/consejo; **to ~ a reward** ofrecer una recompensa; **to ~ an explanation** dar una explicación; **to ~ shelter** dar cobijo; **to have much to ~** tener mucho que ofrecer; **to ~ oneself for a post** presentarse para un puesto **2.** (*give: gift*) dar **3.** (*volunteer*) **to ~ to do sth** ofrecerse para hacer algo **4.** (*propose: plan*) proponer; (*excuse*) presentar; (*opinion*) expresar; **to ~ a suggestion** hacer una sugerencia **5.** (*show*) **to ~ resistance** oponer resistencia **II.** *vi* (*present itself: opportunity*) presentarse **III.** *n* (*proposal*) propuesta *f;* (*of help*) ofrecimiento *m;* (*of job*) oferta *f;* **an ~ of marriage** una proposición de matrimonio; **to make sb an ~ they can't refuse** hacer a alguien una oferta muy tentadora; **that's my last ~** es mi última oferta; **to make** [*o* **put in**] **an ~ of £1000 for sth** ofrecer 1000 libras por algo; **to be on ~** *Aus, Brit* estar de oferta

offering [ˈɒfərɪŋ, *Am:* ˈɑːfɚ-] *n* **1.** (*thing given*) ofrecimiento *m;* **as an ~ of thanks** en señal de agradecimiento **2.** (*contribution*) donativo *m* **3.** REL (*sacrifice*) ofrenda *f*

offhand [ˌɒfˈhænd, *Am:* ˌɑːf-] **I.** *adj* **1.** (*uninterested*) brusco, -a; **an ~ reply** una respuesta desabrida; **to be ~ with sb** ser brusco con alguien **2.** (*without previous thought*) improvisado, -a **II.** *adv* de improviso; **to judge sb/sth ~** juzgar algo/a alguien a la ligera

office [ˈɒfɪs, *Am:* ˈɑːfɪs] *n* **1.** (*of company*) oficina *f;* (*room in house*) despacho *m,* archivo *m Col;* **they've got ~s in Paris and Madrid** tienen oficinas en París y Madrid; **to stay at the ~** quedarse en la oficina; **architect's ~** estudio *m* (de arquitecto); **doctor's ~** consultorio *m;* **lawyer's ~** bufete *m* (de abogado) **2.** *Brit* POL **the Foreign Office** *el Ministerio de Relaciones Exteriores de Gran Bretaña;* **the Home Office** *el Ministerio del Interior británico* **3.** POL (*authoritative position*) cargo *m;* **to hold ~** ocupar un cargo; **to be in ~** (*person*) estar en funciones; (*party*) estar en el poder; **to be out of ~** haber dejado el cargo; **to take ~** entrar en funciones **4.** *pl* (*assistance*) mediación *f;* **through the ~s of** gracias a la mediación de **5.** REL oficio *m*

office automation *n* INFOR ofimática *f*

office block *n Aus, Brit* bloque *m* de oficinas **office boy** *n* auxiliar *mf* de oficina **office building** *n Am s.* **office block** **office equipment** *n* material *m* de oficina **office hours** *npl* horas *fpl* de oficina; **to do sth out(side) of ~** hacer algo fuera de las horas de oficina

officer [ˈɒfɪsəʳ, *Am:* ˈɑːfɪsɚ] *n* **1.** MIL oficial *mf;* **naval ~** oficial de marina **2.** (*policeman*) policía *mf;* **police ~** agente *mf* de policía **3.** (*in organization*) directivo, -a *m, f;* (*in political party*) dirigente *mf* **4.** (*official*) funcionario, -a *m, f*

office staff *n no pl* personal *m* de oficina **office supplies** *npl* artículos *mpl* de oficina **office worker** *n* oficinista *mf*

official [əˈfɪʃl] **I.** *n* **1.** POL oficial *mf* **2.** (*civil servant*) funcionario, -a *m, f* **II.** *adj* oficial

officialdom [əˈfɪʃldəm] *n no pl, pej* burocracia *f*

officialese [əˌfɪʃəˈliːz] *n no pl, Am* jerga *f* burocrática

officially [əˈfɪʃəli] *adv* oficialmente

officiate [əˈfɪʃɪeɪt] *vi form* oficiar; **to ~ at a ceremony** oficiar (en) una ceremonia

officious [əˈfɪʃəs] *adj pej* oficioso, -a

offing [ˈɒfɪŋ, *Am:* ˈɑːfɪŋ] *n no pl* **to be in the ~** NAUT estar a la vista; *fig* estar en perspectiva; **good news is in the ~** pronto habrá buenas noticias

off key MUS **I.** *adv* desafinadamente; **to play/sing ~** desafinar **II.** *adj* desafinado, -a

off-licence [ˈɒfˌlaɪsənts, *Am:* ˌɑːfˈlaɪ-] *n Brit* ≈ tienda *f* de licores

off-limits *adj* fuera de los límites (permitidos)

off-line [ˌɒfˈlaɪn, *Am:* ˌɑːf-] *adj* INFOR desconectado, -a, fuera de línea

offload [ˌɒfˈləʊd, *Am:* ˈɑːfloʊd] *vt* **1.** (*unload*) descargar **2.** (*get rid of*) **to ~ sth** deshacerse de algo; **to ~ sth onto sb** endosar algo a alguien; **to ~ work onto sb** descargar trabajo en alguien

off-peak [ˌɒfˈpiːk, *Am:* ˌɑːf-] *adj* (*fare, rate*) fuera de las horas punta; (*phone call*) de tarifa reducida

off-piste [ˌɒfˈpiːst, *Am:* ˌɑːf-] *adj* SPORTS fuera de pista

off-putting [ˌɒfˈpʊtɪŋ, *Am:* ˈɑːfˌpʊt̬-] *adj* **1.** (*smell, manner, appearance*) desagradable; (*person*) antipático, -a **2.** (*experience*) desalentador(a)

off-sales [ˈɒfseɪlz] *n Brit* ≈ tienda *f* de licores

off-season [ˈɒfˌsiːzən, *Am:* ˈɑːf-] **I.** *n* temporada *f* baja **II.** *adj* de temporada baja

offset [ˈɒfset, *Am:* ˈɑːf-] **I.** *n* **1.** TYPO offset *m* **2.** BOT vástago *m* **3.** (*compensation*) compensación *f* **II.** <offset, offset> *vt* **1.** (*compensate*) compensar **2.** TYPO imprimir en offset

offshore [ˌɒfˈʃɔːʳ, *Am:* ˌɑːfˈʃɔːr] **I.** *adj* **1.** (*from the shore: breeze, wind*) terral **2.** (*at sea*) a poca distancia de la costa; ~ **fishing** pesca de bajura; ~ **oilfield** yacimiento *m* petrolífero marítimo **II.** *adv* mar adentro; **to anchor** ~ anclar a cierta distancia de la costa

offside [ˌɒfˈsaɪd, *Am:* ˌɑːf-] **I.** *n* **1.** SPORTS fuera de juego *m* **2.** AUTO lado *m* del conductor; **the** ~ **door** la puerta del conductor **II.** *adv* SPORTS fuera de juego

offspring [ˈɒfsprɪŋ, *Am:* ˈɑːf-] *n inv* **1.** (*animal young*) cría *f* **2.** *pl* (*children*) prole *f*

offstage [ˌɒfˈsteɪdʒ, *Am:* ˌɑːf-] **I.** *adj* de entre bastidores **II.** *adv* entre bastidores

off-street parking [ˌɒfstriːtˈpɑːkɪŋ, *Am:* ˌɑːfstriːtˈpɑːrkɪŋ] *n* aparcamiento *m* fuera de la vía pública, estacionamiento *m* fuera de la vía pública *AmL*

off-the-cuff [ˌɒfðəˈkʌf, *Am:* ˌɑːf-] **I.** *adj* espontáneo, -a **II.** *adv* espontáneamente

off-the-job training *n no pl* formación *f* profesional en un centro especializado

off-the-peg [ˌɒfðəˈpeg, *Am:* ˌɑːf-] *adj Brit,* **off-the-rack** [ˌɒfðəˈræk, *Am:* ˌɑːf-] *adj Am* prêt à porter

off-white [ˌɒfˈhwaɪt, *Am:* ˌɑːf-] *adj* de color hueso

often [ˈɒfən, *Am:* ˈɑːfən] *adv* a menudo; **we** ~ **go there** solemos ir allí; **as** ~ **as** siempre que; **as** ~ **as not** la mitad de las veces; **every so** ~ alguna que otra vez; **how** ~? ¿cuántas veces?; **it's not** ~ **that ...** no es frecuente que +*subj;* **more** ~ **than not** la mayoría de las veces

ogle [ˈəʊgl, *Am:* ˈoʊ-] *vt* **to** ~ **sb** comerse a alguien con los ojos

ogre [ˈəʊgəʳ, *Am:* ˈoʊgɚ] *n* ogro *m*

ogress [ˈəʊgres, *Am:* ˈoʊ-] *n* ogresa *f*

oh [əʊ, *Am:* oʊ] *interj* **1.** (*expressing surprise, disappointment, pleasure*) oh; ~ **dear!** ¡Dios mío!; ~ **no!** ¡ay, no!; ~ **well** bueno; ~ **yes?** ¿ah, sí? **2.** (*by the way*) ah

OHMS [ˌəʊeɪtʃemˈes, *Am:* ˌoʊ-] *abbr of* **On Her/His Majesty's Service** al servicio de Su Majestad

oil [ɔɪl] **I.** *n* **1.** (*lubricant*) aceite *m;* **sunflower** ~ aceite de girasol **2.** *no pl* (*petroleum*) petróleo *m;* **to strike** ~ encontrar petróleo; *fig* encontrar una mina de oro **3.** (*grease*) grasa *f* **4.** *pl* (*oil-based paint*) óleo *m;* **to paint in** ~**s** pintar al óleo ►**to burn the midnight** ~ quemarse las pestañas; **to pour** ~ **on troubled waters** calmar los ánimos, poner paz **II.** *vt* engrasar

oil-based paint *n* pintura *f* al óleo **oilcan** *n* aceitera *f* **oil change** *n* AUTO cambio *m* de aceite **oilcloth** *n* hule *m* **oil company** *n* empresa *f* petroquímica **oil consumption** *n no pl* consumo *m* de petróleo **oil crisis** *n* crisis *f inv* del petróleo **oil-exporting** *adj* exportador(a) de petróleo **oilfield** *n* yacimiento *m* petrolífero **oil-fired** *adj* alimentado, -a a petróleo; ~ **heating system** calefacción *f* a petróleo

oiliness [ˈɔɪlɪnɪs] *n no pl* **1.** (*greasiness: of food*) lo aceitoso; (*of material, skin*) lo grasiento **2.** *fig* lo empalagoso

oil lamp *n* quinqué *m* **oil level** *n* TECH nivel *m* de aceite **oil painting** *n* óleo *m* ►**to be no** ~ *Aus, Brit, iron* no ser ninguna belleza **oil pipeline** *n* oleoducto *m*

oil-producing *adj* productor(a) de petróleo **oil-producing country** *n* país *m* productor de petróleo

oil production *n no pl* producción *f* de petróleo **oilrig** *n* plataforma *f* petrolífera **oil sheik** *n* magnate *m* del petróleo **oilskin** *n* **1.** (*cloth*) hule *m* **2.** *pl* (*clothing*) impermeable *m* **oil slick** *n* marea *f* negra **oil tanker** *n* NAUT petrolero *m* **oil well** *n* pozo *m* de petróleo

oily [ˈɔɪli] <-ier, -iest> *adj* **1.** (*oil-like*) oleoso, -a **2.** (*greasy: hands*) grasiento, -a; (*food*) aceitoso, -a; (*skin, hair*) graso, -a **3.** (*manner*) empalagoso, -a

ointment [ˈɔɪntmənt] *n* MED pomada *f*

OK, okay [ˌəʊˈkeɪ, *Am:* ˌoʊ-] *inf* **I.** *adj* **1.** (*acceptable*) **is it** ~ **with you if ...?** ¿te importa si...?; **it's** ~ **with me** por mí no hay problema; **to be** ~ **for money/work** tener suficiente dinero/trabajo **2.** (*not bad*) **to be** ~ no estar mal; **her voice is** ~**, but it's nothing special** no tiene mala voz, pero tampoco es nada del otro mundo **II.** *interj* vale *inf,* okey *AmL, inf,* órale *Méx* **III.** <OKed, okayed> *vt* **to** ~ **sth** dar el visto bueno a algo **IV.** *n* visto bueno *m;* **to give the** ~ dar el visto bueno **V.** *adv* bastante bien

okra [ˈəʊkrə, *Am:* ˈoʊ-] *n no pl* quingombó *m*

old [əʊld, *Am:* oʊld] **I.** *adj* **1.** (*not young*) viejo, -a; ~ **people** la gente mayor; **to be** ~ **to be doing sth** ser ya muy mayor para hacer algo; **to grow** ~**er** envejecer **2.** (*not new*) viejo, -a; (*food*) pasado, -a; (*wine*) añejo, -a; (*furniture, house*) antiguo, -a **3.** (*denoting an age*) **how** ~ **are you?** ¿cuántos años tienes?; **he's five years** ~ tiene cinco años; **she's three years** ~**er than me** me lleva tres años; **to be** ~ **enough to do sth** tener edad suficiente para hacer algo **4.** (*former: job*) antiguo, -a; ~ **boyfriend** ex-novio *m;* ~ **English** inglés *m* antiguo **5.** (*long known*) de siempre; ~ **friend** viejo amigo; **the same** ~ **faces** las mismas caras de siempre **6.** *inf* (*expression of affection*) **I heard poor** ~ **Frank's lost his job** he oído que el pobre Frank se ha quedado sin trabajo **II.** *n* **1.** (*elderly people*) **the** ~ los viejos, los ancianos *AmL;* **young and** ~ grandes y chicos **2.** *liter* (*past*) **of** ~ antiguamente; **to know sb of** ~ conocer a alguien desde hace tiempo

old age *n* vejez *f;* **to reach** ~ llegar a viejo

old age pensioner *n* pensionista *mf* **old boy** *n* **1.** *Brit, inf* (*old man*) abuelo *m* **2.** *Aus, Brit* (*pupil*) antiguo alumno *m*

old-fashioned [ˌəʊldˈfæʃənd, *Am:* ˌoʊld-]

adj pej **1.** (*not modern: clothes*) pasado, -a de moda; (*views*) anticuado, -a; **to be ~** estar chapado a la antigua **2.** (*traditional*) tradicional; **it has an ~ charm** tiene el encanto de lo antiguo

old girl *n* **1.** *Brit, inf* (*old woman*) viejecita *f* **2.** *Aus, Brit* (*pupil*) antigua alumna *f*

oldish ['əʊldɪʃ, *Am:* 'oʊl-] *adj* algo viejo, -a

old lady *n inf* **my ~** (*mother*) mi vieja; (*wife*) mi parienta **old man** *n inf* **my ~** (*father*) mi viejo; (*husband*) mi marido **old master** *n* ART **1.** (*artist*) gran maestro *m* de la pintura clásica **2.** (*painting*) obra *f* maestra de la pintura clásica **old people's home** *n* residencia *f* de ancianos **old school I.** *adj* de la vieja escuela **II.** *n fig* vieja escuela *f* **old stager** *n* veterano, -a *m, f*

old-style [ˌəʊld'staɪl, *Am:* ˌoʊld-] *adj* a la antigua

Old Testament *n* Antiguo Testamento *m*

old-timer [ˌəʊld'taɪmə^r, *Am:* 'oʊldˌtaɪmɚ] *n inf* **1.** (*old man*) viejo, -a *m, f* **2.** (*long-time worker, resident*) veterano, -a *m, f*

old wives' tale [ˌəʊld'waɪvzˌteɪl, *Am:* ˌoʊld-] *n* cuento *m* de viejas

oleander [ˌəʊli'ændə^r, *Am:* ˌoʊli'ændɚ] *n* adelfa *f*

olfactory [ɒl'fæktəri, *Am:* ɑːl-] *adj* olfativo, -a

olive ['ɒlɪv, *Am:* 'ɑːlɪv] *n* **1.** (*fruit*) oliva *f*, aceituna *f* **2.** (*tree*) olivo *m* **3.** (*colour*) aceituna *m*

olive branch *n* rama *f* de olivo ►**to hold out the ~ to sb** tender a alguien la mano en son de paz **olive grove** *n* olivar *m* **olive oil** *n* aceite *m* de oliva

Olympiad [ə'lɪmpɪæd, *Am:* oʊ'-] *n* SPORTS olimpiada *f*

Olympian [ə'lɪmpɪən, *Am:* oʊ'-] *adj* olímpico, -a

Olympic [ə'lɪmpɪk, *Am:* oʊ'-] *adj* olímpico, -a; **the Olympic Games** SPORTS los Juegos Olímpicos

Oman [əʊ'mɑːn, *Am:* oʊ'-] *n* Omán *m*

Omani [əʊ'mɑːni, *Am:* oʊ'-] **I.** *adj* omaní **II.** *n* omaní *mf*

ombudsman ['ɒmbʊdzmən, *Am:* 'ɑːm-bədz-] <-men> *n* POL defensor(a) *m(f)* del pueblo

omelet(te) ['ɒmlɪt, *Am:* 'ɑːmlət] *n* tortilla *f*

omen ['əʊmen, *Am:* 'oʊ-] *n* indicio *m*, augurio *m*; **to be a good/bad ~ for sth** ser un buen/mal augurio para algo

ominous ['ɒmɪnəs, *Am:* 'ɑːmə-] *adj* (*news*) ominoso, -a; (*implications*) funesto, -a; (*silence*) inquietante

omission [ə'mɪʃən, *Am:* oʊ'-] *n* omisión *f*

omit [ə'mɪt, *Am:* oʊ'-] <-tt-> *vt* (*person, information*) omitir; (*paragraph, passage*) suprimir; **to ~ any reference to sb/sth** evitar toda referencia a alguien/algo; **to ~ to do sth** (*neglect*) dejar de hacer algo; (*forget*) olvidarse de hacer algo

omnibus ['ɒmnɪbəs, *Am:* 'ɑːm-] **I.** <-es> *n* **1.** (*bus*) ómnibus *m* **2.** (*anthology*) antología *f* ►**the man on the Clapham ~** *Brit* el ciudadano de a pie **II.** *adj* **~ edition** antología *f*

omnipotence [ɒm'nɪpətəns, *Am:* ɑːm'nɪpət̬əns] *n no pl* omnipotencia *f*

omnipotent [ɒm'nɪpətənt, *Am:* ɑːm'nɪpət̬ənt] *adj* omnipotente

omnipresent [ˌɒmnɪ'preznt, *Am:* ˌɑːm-] *adj form* omnipresente

omniscient [ɒm'nɪʃnt, *Am:* ɑːm-] *adj form* omnisciente

omnivorous [ɒm'nɪvərəs, *Am:* ɑːm-] *adj* omnívoro, -a; **to be an ~ reader** *fig* ser un lector insaciable

on [ɒn, *Am:* ɑːn] **I.** *prep* **1.** (*place*) sobre, en; **~ the table** sobre la mesa; **~ the wall** en la pared; **to put sth ~ sb's shoulder/finger** poner algo sobre el hombro/en el dedo de alguien; **to be ~ the plane** estar en el avión; **to hang ~ a branch** colgar de una rama; **to have sth ~ one's mind** *fig* tener algo en mente **2.** (*by means of*) **to go ~ the train** ir en tren; **to go ~ foot** ir a pie; **to keep a dog ~ a leash** tener a un perro cogido por la correa **3.** (*source of*) con; **to run ~ gas** funcionar con gasolina; **to live ~ £2,000 a month** vivir con 2,000 libras al mes **4.** MED **to be ~ drugs/cortisone** tomar drogas/cortisona **5.** (*spatial*) **~ the right/left** a la derecha/izquierda; **~ the corner/back of sth** en la esquina/la parte posterior de algo; **a house ~ the river** una casa junto al río **6.** (*temporal*) **~ Sunday** el domingo; **~ Sundays** los domingos; **~ the evening of May the 4th** el cuatro de mayo por la tarde; **at 2:00 ~ the dot** a las 2:00 en punto **7.** (*at time of*) **to leave ~ time** salir a tiempo; **~ her arrival** a su llegada; **~ arriving there** al llegar allí; **to finish ~ schedule** acabar puntualmente **8.** (*about*) sobre; **a lecture ~ Joyce** una conferencia sobre Joyce; **to compliment sb ~ sth** felicitar a alguien por algo; **to be there ~ business** estar ahí por negocios **9.** (*through medium of*) **~ TV/video/CD** en TV/vídeo/CD; **to speak ~ the radio/the phone** hablar en la radio/por teléfono; **to work ~ a computer** trabajar con un ordenador; **to play ~ the flute** tocar la flauta **10.** (*with basis in*) **~ the principle that** en el supuesto de que; **to do sth ~ purpose** hacer algo a propósito **11.** (*in state of*) **~ sale** en venta; **to set sth ~ fire** prender fuego a algo; **to go ~ holiday/a trip** ir de vacaciones/de viaje; **~ the whole** en general **12.** (*involved in*) **to be ~ the committee** estar en el comité; **to work ~ a project** trabajar en un proyecto; **to be ~ page 10** estar en la página 10; **two ~ each side** dos en cada lado **13.** (*because of*) **~ account of sth/sb** a causa de algo/alguien; **to depend ~ sb/sth** depender de alguien/algo **14.** (*against*) **to turn ~ sb** volverse contra alguien; **an attack ~ sb** un ataque contra alguien; **to cheat ~ sb** hacer trampa [*o* engañar] a alguien **15.** (*paid by*) **to buy sth ~ credit** comprar algo a crédito; **this is ~ me** *inf* esto corre por mi cuenta **16.** *Aus, Brit* SPORTS **to be ~ 10 points** tener 10 puntos **II.** *adv* **1.** (*covering one's body*) **to put a hat ~** ponerse un sombrero; **to have sth ~** llevar algo (puesto); **to try ~ sth** probarse algo **2.** (*connected to sth*) **make sure the top's ~ properly** asegúrate de que esté bien tapado; **to screw ~** enroscar **3.** (*aboard*) **to get ~ a train** subir a un tren; **to get ~ a horse** montar en un caballo; **to be ~** (**a horse**) estar montado (en un caballo) **4.** (*not stopping*) **to keep ~ doing sth** seguir haciendo algo; **to get ~ with sth** ponerse a hacer algo **5.** (*in forward direction*) hacia adelante; **to move ~** avanzar; **to urge sb ~** *fig* animar a alguien; **from that day ~** desde aquel día; **later ~** más tarde; **and so ~** y así sucesivamente **6.** (*in operation*) **to turn ~** encender; (*tap*) abrir; **to put the kettle ~** poner agua a calentar **7.** (*performing*) en escena; **to go ~** salir a escena ►**I don't know what he's ~ about** *Aus, Brit* no sé qué está diciendo; **~ and off** de vez en cuando; **well ~ in the night** muy entrada la noche; **to be ~ at sb** (**about sth**) estar encima a alguien (con algo); **~ and ~** sin parar **III.** *adj* **1.** (*functioning: light*) encendido, -a; (*tap*) abierto, -a; (*brake*) puesto, -a; **to leave the light ~** dejar la luz encendida **2.** (*scheduled*) **what's ~ at the cinema this week?** ¿qué dan en el cine esta semana?; **the show will be ~ in Barcelona very soon** el espectáculo estará muy pronto en Barcelona; **have you got anything ~ tomorrow?** ¿tienes algún plan para mañana? **3.** THEAT (*performing*) **to be ~** estar en escena; *Am* (*performing well*) hacerlo muy bien **4.** (*job*) **to be ~ duty** estar de servicio; (*doctor*) estar de guardia **5.** (*good: day*) bueno, -a **6.** (*acceptable*) **that's not ~!** ¡no hay derecho!; **you're ~!** ¡de acuerdo!

once [wʌnts] **I.** *adv* **1.** (*one time*) una vez; **~ a week** una vez por semana; **~ in a lifetime** una vez en la vida; (**every**) **~ in a while** de vez en cuando; **~ again** de nuevo; **~ and for all** de una vez por todas; **just for ~** sólo una vez; **~ more** (*one more time*) otra vez; (*again, as before*) una vez más; **~ or twice** una o dos veces; **at ~** (*simultaneously*) al mismo tiempo; (*immediately*) en seguida **2.** *liter* (*at one time past*) hace tiempo; **~ upon a time there was ...** *liter* érase una vez... **II.** *conj* una vez que *+subj*; **but ~ I'd arrived, ...** pero una vez que llegué... ►**all at ~** todos a la vez; **at ~** en seguida

once-over ['wʌnts,əʊvəʳ, *Am:* 'wʌnts,oʊvɚ] *n inf* **1.** (*examination*) ojeada *f*; **to give sth a ~** dar un vistazo a algo **2.** (*cleaning*) repaso *m*

oncoming ['ɒnkʌmɪŋ, *Am:* 'ɑːn-] *adj* que se aproxima; (*traffic, vehicle*) que viene en dirección contraria

one [wʌn] **I.** *n* (*number*) uno *m* ►**to land sb ~** *inf* dar un golpe a alguien; (**all**) **in ~** todo en uno; **as ~** *form* a la vez; **in ~** de una sola pieza **II.** *adj* **1.** *numeral* un, uno, -a; **~ hundred** cien; **it's ~ o'clock** es la una; **as ~ man** todos a una; **~ man out of** [*o* **in**] **two** uno de cada dos hombres **2.** *indef* un, uno, -a; **we'll meet ~ day** nos veremos un día de estos; **~ winter night** una noche de invierno **3.** (*sole*) único, -a; **her ~ and only hope** su única esperanza **4.** (*single*) mismo, -a, único, -a; **all files on the ~ disk** todos los archivos en un único disco **III.** *pron pers* **1.** *impers, no pl* **what ~ can do** lo que uno puede hacer; **to wash ~'s face** lavarse la cara **2.** (*person*) **no ~** nadie; **every ~** cada uno; **the little ~s** los pequeños; **the ~ who ...** el que...; **I for ~** al menos yo **3.** (*particular thing or person*) **any ~** cualquiera; **this ~** éste; **which ~?** ¿cuál (de ellos)?; **the ~ on the table** el que está en la mesa; **the thinner ~** el más delgado

one-armed [,wʌn'ɑːmd, *Am:* -'ɑːrmd] *adj* manco, -a, sunco, -a *Chile*

one-armed bandit *n Am, Aus* máquina *f* tragaperras, máquina *f* tragamonedas *AmL*

one-eyed [,wʌn'aɪd] *adj* tuerto, -a **one-handed** **I.** *adv* con una sola mano **II.** *adj* manco, -a **one-horse** *adj* **1.** (*using one horse*) de un caballo **2.** (*second-rate*) de poca monta; **a ~ town** un pueblucho **one-legged** *adj* cojo, -a

one-liner [,wʌn'laɪnəʳ, *Am:* -nɚ] *n* frase *f* ingeniosa

one-man [,wʌn'mæn] *adj* **1.** (*consisting of one person*) de un solo hombre; **~ band** hombre *m* orquesta **2.** (*designed for one person*) individual

one-night stand [,wʌnnaɪt'stænd] *n* **1.** MUS, THEAT función *f* única **2.** *inf* (*relationship*) ligue *m* de una noche

one-off [,wʌn'ɒf, *Am:* 'wʌnɑːf] **I.** *n Aus, Brit* **to be a ~** ser un fuera de serie **II.** *adj* excepcional; **~ payment** pago *m* extraordinario

one-piece (**swimsuit**) ['wʌnpiːs] *n* bañador *m*

onerous ['ɒnərəs, *Am:* 'ɑːnɚ-] *adj* oneroso, -a

oneself [wʌn'self] *pron reflexive* **1.** se; *emphatic* sí (mismo, misma); **to deceive ~** engañarse a sí mismo; **to express ~** expresarse **2.** (*same person*) uno mismo

one-sided [,wʌn'saɪdɪd] *adj* (*contest*) desigual; (*decision*) unilateral; (*view, account*) parcial

one-time ['wʌntaɪm] *adj* **1.** antiguo, -a; **~ president** ex-presidente *mf* **2.** (*happening only once*) único, -a

one-track mind [,wʌntræk'maɪnd] *n* **to have a ~** no pensar más que en una cosa

one-upmanship [,wʌn'ʌpmənʃɪp] *n no pl, inf:* arte de estar por encima de los demás

one-way street [,wʌnweɪ'striːt] *n* calle *f* de sentido único **one-way ticket** *n* billete *m* sencillo

O

ongoing ['ɒngəʊɪŋ, *Am:* 'ɑːngoʊ-] *adj* en curso; ~ **state of affairs** situación que sigue en curso

onion ['ʌnɪən] *n* cebolla *f* ►**to know one's ~s** *inf* conocer muy bien su oficio

on-line INFOR **I.** *adj* en línea; ~ **data service** servicio *m* de datos en línea; ~ **information service** servicio *m* de información en línea; ~ **shop** comercio *m* en línea **II.** *adv* en línea

onlooker ['ɒnlʊkəʳ, *Am:* 'ɑːnlʊkɚ] *n* espectador(a) *m(f)*; **there were many ~s at the accident site** había muchos curiosos en el lugar del accidente

only ['əʊnli, *Am:* 'oʊn-] **I.** *adj* único, -a; **the ~ glass he had** el único vaso que tenía; **the ~ way of doing sth** la única manera de hacer algo; **I'm not the ~ one** no soy el único; **the ~ thing is ...** la única cosa es... **II.** *adv* sólo, nomás *AmL*; **not ~ ... but** no solamente...sino; **I can ~ say ...** sólo puedo decir...; **he has ~ two** sólo tiene dos; ~ **Paul can do it** sólo Paul puede hacerlo; **I've ~ just eaten** acabo de comer ahora **III.** *conj inf* sólo que

o.n.o. [ˌəuen'əʊ, *Am:* ˌoʊ-] *adv Aus, Brit abbr of* **or nearest offer** negociable

onrush ['ɒnrʌʃ, *Am:* 'ɑːn-] <-es> *n* **1.** (*of waves*) embate *m* **2.** (*of people*) avalancha *f fig*

onset ['ɒnset, *Am:* 'ɑːn-] *n no pl* comienzo *m*; (*of winter*) llegada *f*; (*of illness*) aparición *f*

onshore ['ɒnʃɔːʳ, *Am:* 'ɑːnʃɔːr] **I.** *adj* (*wind*) del mar **II.** *adv* tierra adentro

onside [ˌɒn'saɪt] SPORTS **I.** *adj* **to be ~** (*player*) estar en posición correcta **II.** *adv* en posición correcta

onslaught ['ɒnslɔːt, *Am:* 'ɑːnslɑːt] *n* ataque *m* violento; *fig* crítica *f* violenta

on-the-job training *n* formación *f* en el puesto de trabajo

onto ['ɒntuː, *Am:* 'ɑːntuː] *prep*, **on to** *prep* **1.** (*in direction of*) sobre; **to put sth ~ the chair** poner algo sobre la silla; **to step ~ the road** pisar la calzada; **to come ~ a subject** llegar a un tema **2.** (*connected to*) **to hold ~ sb's arm** aferrarse al brazo de alguien; **to be ~ sb** ver a alguien su juego

onus ['əʊnəs, *Am:* 'oʊ-] *n* responsibilidad *f*

onward ['ɒnwəd, *Am:* 'ɑːnwɚd] **I.** *adj* hacia adelante; **the ~ march of time** el avance inexorable del tiempo **II.** *adv* hacia adelante; **from today ~** de hoy en adelante

onyx ['ɒnɪks, *Am:* 'ɑːnɪks] *n no pl* GEO ónice *f*, ónix *f*

oodles ['uːdlz] *npl inf* montones *mpl*; ~ **of money** cantidad *f* de dinero

oomph [ʊmf] *n no pl, inf* **1.** (*energy, vitality*) brío *m*; **to have a lot of ~** estar lleno de vida **2.** (*sex appeal*) atractivo *m*

ooze [uːz] **I.** *vi* **1.** (*seep out*) exudar; **to ~ from sth** rezumar(se) de algo; **to ~ with sth** rezumar algo; **to ~ away** acabarse **2.** *fig* (*be full of*) rebosar de; **to ~ with confidence** irradiar seguridad **II.** *vt* rezumar; **to ~ pus** supurar; **to ~ charisma** irradiar simpatía **III.** *n no pl* cieno *m*

opacity [əʊ'pæsəti, *Am:* oʊ'pæsəṱi] *n no pl* **1.** (*non-transparency*) opacidad *f* **2.** (*incomprehensibility*) oscuridad *f*

opal ['əʊpl, *Am:* 'oʊ-] *n* GEO ópalo *m*

opalescent [ˌəʊpə'lesnt, *Am:* ˌoʊ-] *adj* opalescente

opaque [əʊ'peɪk, *Am:* oʊ-] *adj* **1.** (*not transparent*) opaco, -a **2.** (*unintelligible*) oscuro, -a

OPEC ['əʊpek, *Am:* 'oʊ-] *n abbr of* **Organization of Petroleum Exporting Countries** OPEP *f*

open ['əʊpən, *Am:* 'oʊ-] **I.** *adj* **1.** (*not closed*) abierto, -a; **wide ~** completamente abierto; **to push sth ~** abrir algo de un empujón **2.** (*undecided*) sin concretar; **to keep one's options ~** dejar abiertas todas las alternativas **3.** (*not secret, public: scandal*) público, -a; (*hostility*) abierto, -a, manifiesto, -a; **to be an ~ book** *fig* ser un libro abierto; **an ~ secret** una cosa sabida **4.** (*unfolded: map*) desplegado, -a **5.** (*frank: person*) abierto, -a; **to welcome sb with ~ arms** recibir a alguien con los brazos abiertos **6.** (*accessible to all*) abierto, -a; (*discussion*) abierto, -a al público; (*session*) a puertas abiertas; (*trial*) público, -a **7.** (*willing to listen to new ideas*) abierto, -a de mente; **to have an ~ mind** tener una actitud abierta **8.** (*still available: job*) vacante **9.** LING (*vowel*) abierto, -a **II.** *n* **1.** *no pl* (*outdoors, outside*) (**out**) **in the ~** al aire libre **2.** (*not secret*) **to get sth** (**out**) **in the ~** sacar algo a la luz **III.** *vi* **1.** (*door, window, box*) abrirse **2.** (*shop*) abrir **3.** (*start*) comenzar, empezar **IV.** *vt* **1.** (*door, box, shop*) abrir; **to ~ the door to sth** *fig* abrir la puerta a algo; **to ~ sb's eyes** *fig* abrir los ojos a alguien; **to ~ fire** (**on sb**) disparar (a alguien) **2.** (*reveal feelings*) **to ~ one's heart to sb** abrir el corazón a alguien **3.** (*inaugurate*) inaugurar

◆**open onto** *vi* dar a

◆**open out** **I.** *vi* **1.** (*become wider*) ensancharse **2.** (*unfold*) abrirse **II.** *vt* abrir; (*map*) desplegar

◆**open up** **I.** *vi* **1.** (*shop*) abrir **2.** (*shoot*) abrir fuego **II.** *vt* abrir

open-air [ˌəʊpən'eəʳ, *Am:* ˌoʊpən'er] *adj* al aire libre; ~ **swimming pool** piscina *f* descubierta

open-cast mining ['əʊpənkɑːst 'maɪnɪŋ, *Am:* 'oʊpənkæst 'maɪnɪŋ] *n* minería *f* a cielo abierto

open cheque *n* cheque *m* al portador **open credit** *n* crédito *m* abierto

open-ended [ˌəʊpn'endɪd, *Am:* ˌoʊ-] *adj* (*contract*) de duración indefinida; (*question*) abierto, -a

opener ['əʊpənəʳ, *Am:* 'oʊpənɚ] *n* abridor *m*, destapador *m AmL*; **bottle ~** abrebotellas *m inv*; **can ~** abrelatas *m inv*

open-eyed [ˌəʊpən'aɪd, *Am:* ˌoʊ-] *adj* con

los ojos abiertos

open-heart surgery [ˌəʊpənhɑːt'sɜːdʒəri, *Am:* ˌoʊpənhɑːrt'sɜːr-] *n* cirugía *f* a corazón abierto

opening ['əʊpnɪŋ, *Am:* 'oʊp-] *n* **1.** (*gap, hole*) abertura *f;* (*in forest*) claro *m* **2.** (*job opportunity*) vacante *f* **3.** (*beginning*) apertura *f;* (*of book, film*) comienzo *m* **4.** (*ceremony*) inauguración *f;* (*new play, film*) estreno *m*

opening balance *n* FIN saldo *m* de apertura **opening bid** *n* oferta *f* inicial **opening hours** *npl* horario *m* comercial **opening night** *n* THEAT noche *f* del estreno **opening time** *n* hora *f* de apertura

openly ['əʊpənli, *Am:* 'oʊ-] *adv* **1.** (*frankly*) honestamente **2.** (*publicly*) abiertamente

open market *n* mercado *m* abierto

open-minded [ˌəʊpən'maɪndɪd, *Am:* ˌoʊpən'maɪn-] *adj* (*accessible to new ideas*) de actitud abierta; (*unprejudiced*) sin prejuicios **open-mouthed** *adj* boquiabierto, -a

openness ['əʊpənnəs, *Am:* 'oʊ-] *n no pl* franqueza *f*

open-plan [ˌəʊpən'plæn, *Am:* ˌoʊpən-] *adj* de planta abierta

open prison *n Brit* cárcel *f* en régimen abierto **open ticket** *n* billete *m* abierto **Open University** *n Brit* universidad *f* a distancia, universidad *f* abierta *Méx*

opera ['ɒprə, *Am:* 'ɑːpr-] *n* ópera *f*

operable ['ɒpərəbl, *Am:* 'ɑːpər-] *adj* **1.** (*workable: plan*) factible **2.** MED operable

opera glasses *n* gemelos *mpl* de teatro **opera house** *n* ópera *f*

operate ['ɒpəreɪt, *Am:* 'ɑːpər-] **I.** *vi* **1.** (*work, run*) funcionar **2.** (*have or produce an effect*) actuar, surtir efecto **3.** (*perform surgery*) operar; **to** ~ **on sb** operar a alguien **4.** (*do or be in business*) operar **II.** *vt* **1.** (*work*) manejar **2.** (*run, manage*) llevar, tener

operating ['ɒpəreɪtɪŋ, *Am:* 'ɑːpəreɪt̬-] *adj* **1.** ECON (*profit, costs*) de explotación **2.** TECH (*speed*) de funcionamiento **3.** MED de operaciones; ~ **room**, ~ **theatre** [*o* **theater** *Am*] quirófano *m*

operation [ˌɒpə'reɪʃən, *Am:* ˌɑːpə-] *n* **1.** *no pl* (*way of working*) funcionamiento *m;* **to be in** ~ estar en funcionamiento; **to come into** ~ (*machines*) entrar en funcionamiento **2.** *a.* MED, MIL, MAT operación *f;* **rescue** ~ operación de rescate **3.** (*financial transaction*) operación *f* comercial

operational [ˌɒpə'reɪʃənl, *Am:* ˌɑːpə-] *adj* **1.** (*relating to operations*) operativo, -a; ~ **commander** MIL jefe *mf* de operaciones **2.** (*working*) **to be** ~ estar en funcionamiento

operative ['ɒpərətɪv, *Am:* 'ɑːpɚət̬ɪv] **I.** *n* **1.** (*worker*) operario, -a *m, f* **2.** (*detective*) agente *mf* **II.** *adj* **1.** (*rules*) en vigor **2.** MED quirúrgico, -a

operator ['ɒpəreɪtəʳ, *Am:* 'ɑːpəreɪt̬ɚ] *n* **1.** (*person*) operador(a) *m(f);* TEL telefonista *mf;* **machine** ~ maquinista *mf;* **he's a smooth** ~ *inf* sabe conseguir lo que quiere **2.** (*company*) empresa *f*

operetta [ˌɒpə'retə, *Am:* ˌɑːpə'ret̬-] *n* opereta *f*

ophthalmic [ɒf'θælmɪk, *Am:* ɑːf-] *adj* (*clinic*) oftalmológico, -a, de oftalmología; (*surgeon*) oftalmólogo, -a; (*vein*) oftálmico, -a

ophthalmic optician *n* oculista *mf*

ophthalmologist [ˌɒpθə'mɒlədʒɪst, *Am:* ˌɑːfθæl'mɑːlə-] *n* oftalmólogo, -a *m, f*

opiate ['əʊpiət, *Am:* 'oʊpiɪt] *n* opiáceo *m*

opinion [ə'pɪnjən] *n* opinión *f*

opinionated [ə'pɪnjəneɪtɪd, *Am:* -t̬ɪd] *adj pej* dogmático, -a

opinion poll *n* encuesta *f* de opinión

opium ['əʊpiəm, *Am:* 'oʊ-] *n no pl* opio *m*

opium den *n* fumadero *m* de opio

opossum [ə'pɒsəm, *Am:* -'pɑːsəm] *n* zarigüeya *f,* zorro *m Méx*

opponent [ə'pəʊnənt, *Am:* -'poʊ-] *n* **1.** POL opositor(a) *m(f)* **2.** SPORTS contrincante *mf,* rival *mf*

opportune ['ɒpətjuːn, *Am:* ˌɑːpɚ'tuːn] *adj* oportuno, -a

opportunism [ˌɒpə'tjuːnɪzəm, *Am:* ˌɑːpɚ-'tuː-] *n no pl* oportunismo *m*

opportunist [ˌɒpə'tjuːnɪst, *Am:* ˌɑːpɚ'tuː-] **I.** *n* oportunista *mf* **II.** *adj* oportunista

opportunity [ˌɒpə'tjuːnəti, *Am:* ˌɑːpɚ'tuː-nət̬i] <-ies> *n* oportunidad *f;* ~ **to do** [*o* **of doing**] **sth** oportunidad de hacer algo; **at the earliest** ~ lo antes posible

oppose [ə'pəʊz, *Am:* -'poʊz] *vt* **1.** (*be against*) oponerse a, estar en contra de **2.** (*resist*) combatir **3.** (*be on other team, play against*) enfrentarse a

opposed *adj* opuesto, -a; **to be** ~ **to sth** oponerse a algo, estar en contra de algo

opposing *adj* (*opinion*) opuesto, -a, contrario, -a; (*team*) contrario, -a

opposite ['ɒpəzɪt, *Am:* 'ɑːpə-] **I.** *n* contrario *m;* **quite the** ~**!** ¡todo lo contrario! ►~**s attract** los extremos se atraen **II.** *adj* **1.** (*absolutely different*) contrario, -a; **the** ~ **sex** el sexo opuesto **2.** (*facing*) de enfrente; ~ **to/from sth** enfrente a/de algo; **his** ~ **number** su homólogo **III.** *adv* (*facing*) enfrente; **he lives** ~ vive enfrente **IV.** *prep* enfrente de, frente a; ~ **to sth** enfrente de algo; ~ **me** frente a mí; **to sit** ~ (**one another**) estar sentados uno frente al otro

opposition [ˌɒpə'zɪʃən, *Am:* ˌɑːpə-] *n no pl* **1.** POL oposición *f* **2.** (*contrast*) contraposición *f;* **in** ~ **to sth** en contraposición a algo **3.** (*opponent*) adversario, -a *m, f;* ECON competencia *f*

oppress [ə'pres] *vt* oprimir

oppression [ə'preʃən] *n no pl* **1.** (*submission*) opresión *f* **2.** (*feeling*) agobio *m*

oppressive [ə'presɪv] *adj* **1.** (*harsh: regime, measures*) opresivo, -a **2.** (*burdensome*) agobiante; (*heat*) sofocante

oppressor [ə'presəʳ, *Am:* -ɚ] *n* opresor(a)

m(f)
opt [ɒpt, *Am:* ɑːpt] *vi* optar; **to ~ to do sth** optar por hacer algo; **to ~ for sth** optar por algo
◆**opt in** *vi* **to ~** (**to sth**) apuntarse (a algo)
◆**opt out** *vi* **to ~** (**of sth**) borrarse (de algo)
optic ['ɒptɪk, *Am:* 'ɑːp-] **I.** *n inf* ojo *m* **II.** *adj* óptico, -a
optical ['ɒptɪkl, *Am:* 'ɑːp-] *adj* óptico, -a
optician [ɒp'tɪʃən, *Am:* ɑːp-] *n* MED óptico, -a *m, f*
optics ['ɒptɪks, *Am:* 'ɑːp-] *n* óptica *f*
optimal ['ɒptɪml, *Am:* 'ɑːp-] *adj* óptimo, -a
optimism ['ɒptɪmɪzəm, *Am:* 'ɑːptə-] *n no pl* optimismo *m*
optimist ['ɒptɪmɪst, *Am:* 'ɑːptə-] *n* optimista *mf*
optimistic [ˌɒptɪ'mɪstɪk, *Am:* ˌɑːptə-] *adj* optimista
optimize ['ɒptɪmaɪz, *Am:* 'ɑːptə-] *vt* optimizar
optimum ['ɒptɪməm, *Am:* 'ɑːptə-] **I.** *n* <-ma> **the ~** lo ideal **II.** *adj* óptimo, -a
option ['ɒpʃən, *Am:* 'ɑːp-] *n* **1.** (*choice*) *a.* ECON opción *f;* **to have no ~ but to do sth** no tener más remedio que hacer algo; **call ~** opción de compra **2.** (*possibility*) posibilidad *f*
optional ['ɒpʃənl, *Am:* 'ɑːp-] *adj* opcional; (*subject*) optativo, -a
opulence ['ɒpjʊləns, *Am:* 'ɑːpjə-] *n no pl* opulencia *f*
opulent ['ɒpjʊlənt, *Am:* 'ɑːpjə-] *adj* opulento, -a
or [ɔːʳ, *Am:* ɔːr] *conj* o; (*before o, ho*) u; (*between numbers*) ó; **seven ~ eight** siete u ocho; **6 ~ 7** 6 ó 7; **either ... ~ ...** o... o...; **to ask whether ~ not sb is coming** preguntar si alguien viene o no; **I can't read ~ write** no sé leer ni escribir
oracle ['ɒrəkl, *Am:* 'ɔːr-] *n* oráculo *m*
oracular [ə'rækjʊləʳ, *Am:* ɔː'rækjuːlɚ] *adj* del oráculo
oral ['ɔːrəl] *adj* **1.** (*tradition, exam, statement*) oral **2.** (*medication*) por vía oral; (*contraceptive, sex*) oral
orange ['ɒrɪndʒ, *Am:* 'ɔːrɪndʒ] **I.** *n* naranja *f;* **~ drink** naranjada *f* **II.** *adj* naranja
orangeade [ˌɒrɪndʒ'eɪd, *Am:* ˌɔːrɪndʒ'-] *n Am* naranjada *f*
orange grove *n* naranjal *m* **orange juice** *n* zumo *m* de naranja
orange peel *n* piel *f* de naranja **orange tree** *n* naranjo *m*
orang-outan(**g**) *n,* **orang-utan** [ɔːˌræŋuː'tæn, *Am:* ɔː'ræŋətæn] *n* orangután *m*
oration [ɔː'reɪʃən] *n* discurso *m;* **funeral ~** oración *f* fúnebre
orator ['ɒrətəʳ, *Am:* 'ɔːrət̬ɚ] *n* orador(a) *m(f)*
oratorical [ˌɒrə'tɒrɪkl, *Am:* ˌɔːrə'tɔːr-] *adj* oratorio, -a
oratorio [ˌɒrə'tɔːrɪəʊ, *Am:* ˌɔːrə'tɔːrɪoʊ] *n* MUS oratorio *m*
orb [ɔːb, *Am:* ɔːrb] *n liter* esfera *f*
orbit ['ɔːbɪt, *Am:* 'ɔːr-] **I.** *n* **1.** ASTR órbita *f;* **to go into ~** entrar en órbita **2.** (*range of action, field*) campo *m* de influencia **II.** *vi* orbitar **III.** *vt* orbitar alrededor de
orbital ['ɔːbɪtl, *Am:* 'ɔːrbɪt̬l] *adj* orbital; **~ path** camino *m* de circunvalación
orchard ['ɔːtʃəd, *Am:* 'ɔːrtʃɚd] *n* huerto *m;* **cherry ~** cerezal *m*
orchestra ['ɔːkɪstrə, *Am:* 'ɔːrkɪstrə] *n* orquesta *f*
orchestral [ɔː'kestrəl, *Am:* ɔːr'-] *adj* orquestal
orchestra pit *n* foso *m* orquestal **orchestra stalls** *n Brit* platea *f*
orchestrate ['ɔːkɪstreɪt, *Am:* 'ɔːr-] *vt* **1.** MUS orquestar **2.** *fig* (*arrange*) organizar
orchestration [ˌɔːkɪ'streɪʃən, *Am:* ˌɔːr-] *n* **1.** MUS orquestación *f* **2.** *fig* (*arrangement*) organización *f*
orchid ['ɔːkɪd, *Am:* 'ɔːr-] *n* orquídea *f*
ordain [ɔː'deɪn, *Am:* ɔːr'-] *vt* **1.** REL ordenar; **to ~ sb as a priest** ordenar sacerdote a alguien **2.** (*decree, order*) **to ~ that ...** decretar que +*subj*
ordeal [ɔː'diːl, *Am:* ɔːr'-] *n* calvario *m*
order ['ɔːdəʳ, *Am:* 'ɔːrdɚ] **I.** *n* **1.** *no pl* (*sequence*) orden *m;* **to put sth in ~** poner en orden algo; **to leave sth in ~** dejar ordenado algo; **in alphabetical ~** en orden alfabético **2.** (*instruction*) *a.* LAW, REL orden *f;* **to give/receive an ~** dar/recibir una orden; **by ~ of sb** por orden de alguien **3.** (*working condition, satisfactory arrangement*) orden *m;* **to keep ~** mantener el orden; **a new world ~** un nuevo orden mundial; **the car is in perfect working ~** el coche funciona perfectamente bien; **to be out of ~** no funcionar; (*toilet*) estar fuera de servicio; **are your immigration papers in ~?** ¿tienes los papeles de inmigración en regla? **4.** (*appropriate behavior*) **out of ~** improcedente **5.** (*purpose*) **in ~** (**not**) **to** para (no); **in ~ for, in ~ that** para que +*subj* **6.** *Brit* (*social class, rank, kind*) clase *f* **7.** (*request to supply goods or service*) pedido *m;* **made to ~** hecho por encargo **8.** (*architectural style*) orden *m;* **Doric ~** orden dórico **II.** *vi* pedir; **are you ready to ~?** ¿ya han decidido qué van a tomar [*o* pedir]? **III.** *vt* **1.** (*command*) **to ~ sb to do sth** ordenar a alguien que haga algo; **to ~ sb out** echar a alguien **2.** (*request goods or service*) pedir **3.** (*arrange*) ordenar, poner en orden; **to ~ one's thoughts** ordenar los pensamientos de uno **4.** (*arrange according to procedure*) organizar
order book *n* libro *m* de pedidos **order form** *n* hoja *f* de pedidos
orderly ['ɔːdəli, *Am:* 'ɔːrdɚli] <-ies> **I.** *n* **1.** (*hospital attendant*) celador(a) *m(f)* **2.** MIL ordenanza *mf* **II.** *adj* **1.** (*tidy*) ordenado, -a **2.** (*well-behaved*) disciplinado, -a
ordinal ['ɔːdɪnəl, *Am:* 'ɔːrdənəl] *n,* **ordinal number** *n* ordinal *m*
ordinance ['ɔːdənənts, *Am:* 'ɔːrdən-] *n*

ordenanza *f*
ordinary ['ɔːdənəri, *Am:* 'ɔːrdəner-] **I.** *n no pl* **out of the ~** fuera de lo común; **nothing out of the ~** nada excepcional **II.** *adj* normal, corriente; **in the ~ way ...** normalmente...
ordinary seaman <-men> *n* marinero *m* de segunda clase **ordinary share** *n* acción *f* ordinaria
ordnance ['ɔːdnənts, *Am:* 'ɔːrd-] *n* artillería *f*
ordure ['ɔːdjʊə^r, *Am:* 'ɔːrdʒɚ] *n no pl* inmundicia *f*
ore [ɔː^r, *Am:* ɔːr] *n* mena *f*; **iron/copper ~** mineral *m* de hierro/cobre
oregano [ˌɒrɪ'gɑːnəʊ, *Am:* ɔː'regənoʊ] *n no pl* orégano *m*
organ ['ɔːgən, *Am:* 'ɔːr-] *n* órgano *m*
organ donor *n* donante *mf* de órganos **organ grinder** *n* organillero, -a *m, f*
organic [ɔː'gænɪk, *Am:* ɔːr'-] *adj* **1.** (*disease, substance, compound*) orgánico, -a **2.** (*produce, farming method*) biológico, -a **3.** (*fundamental: part*) inherente **4.** (*systematic: change*) sistemático, -a
organisation *n s.* **organization**
organism ['ɔːgənɪzəm, *Am:* 'ɔːr-] *n* organismo *m*
organist ['ɔːgənɪst, *Am:* 'ɔːr-] *n* organista *mf*
organization [ˌɔːgənaɪ'zeɪʃən, *Am:* ˌɔːrgənɪ'-] *n* organización *f*
organizational [ˌɔːgənaɪ'zeɪʃənəl, *Am:* ˌɔːrgənɪ'-] *adj* organizativo, -a
organization chart *n* ECON organigrama *m*
Organization for Economic Cooperation and Development *n* Organización *f* para la Cooperación y el Desarrollo Económico
Organization of African Unity *n no pl* Organización *f* para la Unidad Africana
Organization of Petroleum Exporting Countries *n* Organización *f* de Países Exportadores de Petróleo
organize ['ɔːgənaɪz, *Am:* 'ɔːr-] **I.** *vt* organizar **II.** *vi* organizarse; (*form trade union*) sindicarse
organized *adj* **1.** (*systemized*) ordenado, -a **2.** (*arranged, brought together in a trade union*) organizado, -a
organizer *n* **1.** (*person*) organizador(a) *m(f)* **2.** INFOR agenda *f* electrónica
orgasm ['ɔːgæzəm, *Am:* 'ɔːr-] **I.** *n* orgasmo *m* **II.** *vi* tener un orgasmo
orgasmic [ɔː'gæsmɪk, *Am:* ɔːr'-] *adj* orgásmico, -a
orgy ['ɔːdʒi, *Am:* 'ɔːr-] <-ies> *n* orgía *f*
orient ['ɔːriənt] *vt Am* **to ~ oneself** orientarse
Orient ['ɔːriənt] *n* **the ~** el Oriente
oriental [ˌɔːri'entəl] *adj* oriental
orientate ['ɔːriənteɪt, *Am:* 'ɔːrien-] *vr* **to ~ oneself** orientarse
orientation [ˌɔːriən'teɪʃən, *Am:* ˌɔːrien'-] *n* orientación *f*
orienteering [ˌɔːriən'tɪərɪŋ, *Am:* ˌɔːrien'tɪr-] *n no pl* orientación *f*
orifice ['ɒrɪfɪs, *Am:* 'ɔːrə-] *n form* orificio *m*
origin ['ɒrɪdʒɪn, *Am:* 'ɔːrədʒɪn] *n* origen *m*
original [ə'rɪdʒənəl, *Am:* ə'rɪdʒɪ-] **I.** *n* original *m* **II.** *adj* original, originario, -a; **~ sin** pecado *m* original
originality [əˌrɪdʒən'æləti, *Am:* əˌrɪdʒɪ'næləṭi] *n no pl* originalidad *f*
originally [ə'rɪdʒənəli, *Am:* ə'rɪdʒɪ-] *adv* **1.** (*initially*) originariamente **2.** (*unusually*) con originalidad
originate [ə'rɪdʒəneɪt, *Am:* ə'rɪdʒɪ-] **I.** *vi* originarse **II.** *vt* crear
Orkney Islands ['ɔːkniˌaɪləndz, *Am:* 'ɔːrk-] *n* **the ~** las Órcadas
Orleans ['ɔːliənz, *Am:* 'ɔrliənz] *n* Orleáns *m*
ornament¹ ['ɔːnəmənt, *Am:* 'ɔːr-] *n* adorno *m*
ornament² [ɔːnə'mənt, *Am:* ɔːr-] *vt* adornar
ornamental [ˌɔːnə'mentl, *Am:* ˌɔːrnə'menṭl] *adj* ornamental, decorativo, -a
ornamentation [ˌɔːnəmen'teɪʃən, *Am:* ˌɔːr-] *n no pl, form* ornamentación *f*, decoración *f*
ornate [ɔː'neɪt, *Am:* ɔːr'-] *adj* **1.** (*elaborately decorated*) ornamentado, -a **2.** (*language, style*) florido, -a
ornithologist [ˌɔːnɪ'θɒlədʒɪst, *Am:* ˌɔːrnə'θɑːlə-] *n* ornitólogo, -a *m, f*
ornithology [ˌɔːnɪ'θɒlədʒi, *Am:* ˌɔːrnə'θɑːlə-] *n no pl* ornitología *f*
orphan ['ɔːfn, *Am:* 'ɔːr-] **I.** *n* huérfano, -a *m, f*, guacho, -a *m, f Arg, Chi* **II.** *vt* **to be ~ed** quedar huérfano
orphanage ['ɔːfnɪdʒ, *Am:* 'ɔːr-] *n* orfanato *m*, orfelinato *m*
orthodontist [ˌɔːθəʊ'dɒntɪst, *Am:* ˌɔːrθoʊ'dɑːnṭɪst] *n* ortodoncista *mf*
orthodox ['ɔːθədɒks, *Am:* 'ɔːrθədɑːks] *adj* ortodoxo, -a
orthodoxy ['ɔːθədɒksi, *Am:* 'ɔːrθədɑːk-] <-ies> *n* ortodoxia *f*
orthogonal [ɔː'θɒgənl, *Am:* ɔːr'θɑːgən-] *adj* MAT ortogonal
orthographic(al) [ˌɔːθə'græfɪk(l), *Am:* ˌɔːrθoʊ'-] *adj* ortográfico, -a
orthography [ɔː'θɒgrəfi, *Am:* -'θɑːgrə-] *n no pl* ortografía *f*
orthopaedic [ˌɔːθə'piːdɪk, *Am:* ˌɔːrθoʊ'-] *adj Brit* ortopédico, -a; **~ surgery** ortopedia *f*
orthopaedics [ˌɔːθə'piːdɪks, *Am:* ˌɔːrθoʊ'-] *npl Brit* ortopedia *f*
orthopaedist [ˌɔːθə'piːdɪst, *Am:* ˌɔːrθoʊ'-] *n Brit* ortopedista *mf*
orthopedic [ˌɔːθə'piːdɪk, *Am:* ˌɔːrθoʊ'-] *adj Am s.* **orthopaedic**
orthopedics [ˌɔːθə'piːdɪks, *Am:* ˌɔːrθoʊ'-] *npl Am s.* **orthopaedics**
orthopedist [ˌɔːθə'piːdɪst, *Am:* ˌɔːrθoʊ'-] *n Am s.* **orthopaedist**
OS [ˌəʊ'es, *Am:* ˌoʊ-] **1.** *abbr of* **ordinary seaman** marinero *m* **2.** *abbr of* **Ordnance Sur-**

vey servicio *m* oficial de topografía y cartografía

oscillate ['ɒsɪleɪt, *Am:* 'ɑːsleɪt] *vi a.* PHYS oscilar; (*prices*) fluctuar; **to ~ between hope and despair** moverse entre la esperanza y la resignación

oscillation [ˌɒsɪ'leɪʃən, *Am:* ˌɑːsl'eɪ-] *n a.* PHYS oscilación *f;* (*of prices*) fluctuación *f*

oscilloscope [ə'sɪləskəʊp, *Am:* -skoʊp] *n* osciloscopio *m*

osier ['əʊziəʳ, *Am:* 'oʊʒɚ] *n* **1.** (*tree*) mimbrera *f* **2.** (*branch*) mimbre *m*

osmosis [ɒz'məʊsɪs, *Am:* ɑːz'moʊ-] *n* ósmosis *f inv*

osprey ['ɒsprəɪ, *Am:* 'ɑːspri] *n* águila *f* pescadora

ossify ['ɒsɪfaɪ, *Am:* 'ɑːsə-] <-ie-> **I.** *vi* **1.** (*turn into bone*) osificarse **2.** *fig* (*become rigid*) anquilosarse **II.** *vt* **1.** (*turn into bone*) osificar **2.** *fig* (*cause to be rigid*) anquilosar

ostensible [ɒ'stensəbl, *Am:* ɑː'sten-] *adj* aparente, pretendido, -a

ostentation [ˌɒsten'teɪʃən, *Am:* ˌɑːstən'-] *n no pl, pej* ostentación *f*

ostentatious [ˌɒsten'teɪʃəs, *Am:* ˌɑːstən'-] *adj pej* ostentoso, -a

osteoarthritis [ˌɒstɪəʊɑː'θraɪtɪs, *Am:* ˌɑːstɪoʊɑːr'θraɪt̬ɪs] *n no pl* osteoartritis *f*

osteopath ['ɒstɪəʊpɑːθ, *Am:* 'ɑːstɪoʊpæθ] *n* MED osteópata *mf*

osteoporosis [ˌɒstɪəʊpə'rəʊsɪs, *Am:* ˌɑːstɪoʊpə'roʊ-] *n no pl* osteoporosis *f*

ostracism ['ɒstrəsɪzəm, *Am:* 'ɑːstrə-] *n no pl* ostracismo *m*

ostracize ['ɒstrəsaɪz, *Am:* 'ɑːstrə-] *vt* hacer el vacío a, aislar

ostrich ['ɒstrɪtʃ, *Am:* 'ɑːstrɪtʃ] *n* avestruz *f*

OT *abbr of* **Old Testament** A. T.

other ['ʌðəʳ, *Am:* -ɚ] **I.** *adj* **1.** (*different*) otro, -a; **some ~ way of doing sth** alguna otra forma de hacer algo **2.** (*remaining*) **the ~ one** el otro; **the ~ three** los otros tres; **any ~ questions?** ¿alguna otra pregunta? **3.** (*being vague*) **some ~ time** en algún otro momento; **the ~ day** el otro día; **every ~ day** un día sí y otro no **II.** *pron* **1.** (*people*) **the ~s** los otros; **no ~ than he** *form* nadie excepto él **2.** (*different ones*) **each ~** uno a(l) otro, mutuamente; **some eat, ~s drink** algunos comen, otros beben; **there might be ~s** puede haber otros **3.** *sing* (*either/or*) **to choose one or the ~** escoger uno u otro; **not to have one without the ~** no tener uno sin el otro **4.** (*being vague*) **someone or ~** alguien **III.** *adv* de otra manera; **somehow or ~** de una manera u otra

otherwise ['ʌðəwaɪz, *Am:* '-ɚ-] **I.** *adj form* distinto, -a **II.** *adv* **1.** (*differently: behave, act*) de otro modo **2.** (*in other ways*) **~, ...** por lo demás,... **III.** *conj* si no

OTT [ˌəʊtiː'tiː, *Am:* ˌoʊ-] *Brit abbr of* **over the top** exagerado, -a

otter ['ɒtəʳ, *Am:* 'ɑːt̬ɚ] *n* nutria *f*

OU [ˌəʊ'juː, *Am:* ˌoʊ-] *n Brit abbr of* **Open University** ≈ UNED *f*

ouch [aʊtʃ] *interj* ay

ought [ɔːt, *Am:* ɑːt] *aux* **1.** (*have as duty*) deber; **you ~ to do it** deberías [*o* tendrías que] hacerlo **2.** (*be likely*) tener que; **he ~ to be here** tendría que [*o* debería] estar aquí; **they ~ to win** merecerían ganar **3.** (*probability*) **she ~ to have arrived by now** debe haber llegado ya

ounce [aʊns] *n* **1.** (*weight*) onza *f* (*28,4 g*) **2.** (*of decency, sense*) pizca *f*

our ['aʊəʳ, *Am:* 'aʊɚ] *adj pos* nuestro, -a; **~ house** nuestra casa; **~ children** nuestros hijos

ours ['aʊəz, *Am:* 'aʊɚz] *pron pos* el nuestro, la nuestro; **it's not their bag, it's ~** no es su bolsa, es nuestra; **this house is ~** esta casa es nuestra; **a book of ~** un libro nuestro; **~ is bigger** el nuestro es mayor

ourselves [aʊə'selvz, *Am:* aʊɚ-] *pron reflexive* **1.** nos; *emphatic* nosotros mismos, nosotras mismas; **we hurt ~** nos lastimamos **2.** *after prep* nosotros, -as (mismos, mismas)

oust [aʊst] *vt* (*rival*) desbancar; (*president*) derrocar

out [aʊt] **I.** *vt* **1.** (*eject*) echar **2.** (*reveal homosexuality*) revelar la homosexualidad de **II.** *adj* **1.** (*absent: person*) fuera **2.** (*released: book, news*) publicado, -a **3.** BOT (*flower*) en flor **4.** (*visible*) **the sun/the moon is ~** ha salido el sol/la luna **5.** (*finished*) **before the week is ~** antes de que acabe la semana **6.** (*not functioning: fire, light*) apagado, -a; (*workers*) en huelga **7.** SPORTS (*not playing*) fuera; *a. fig* eliminado, -a; **~ for the count** fuera de combate **8.** (*not possible*) **it is ~** está descartado, eso es imposible **9.** (*unfashionable*) pasado, -a de moda **III.** *adv* **1.** (*not inside*) fuera, afuera; **to go ~** salir fuera; **get ~!** ¡fuera! **2.** (*outside*) afuera; **keep ~!** ¡no entrar!; **to eat ~** comer fuera **3.** (*remove*) **to cross ~ words** tachar palabras; **to get a stain ~** sacar una mancha; **to put ~ a fire** apagar un fuego **4.** (*available*) **the best one ~** el mejor disponible **5.** (*away*) **to be ~** (*person*) no estar; **to go ~ to India** salir para la India; **to be ~ at sea** estar mar adentro; **the tide is going ~** la marea está bajando **6.** (*wrong*) **to be ~ in one's calculations** estar equivocado en los cálculos **7.** (*unconscious*) **to pass ~** perder el conocimiento; **to be ~ cold** estar fuera de combate ▶**to be ~ and about** (*on the road*) estar en camino; (*healthy*) estar repuesto; **~ with it!** ¡desembucha! **IV.** *prep* **1.** (*towards outside*) **~ of** fuera de; **to go ~ of the room** salir de la habitación; **to go ~ of the door** salir por la puerta; **to jump ~ of bed** saltar de la cama; **to take sth ~ of a box** sacar algo de una caja; **to look/lean ~ of the window** mirar por/apoyarse en la ventana **2.** (*outside from*) **~ of sight/of reach** fuera de la vista/del alcance; **to drink ~ of a glass** beber de un vaso; **to be ~ of it** estar en otra honda **3.** (*away from*) **to be ~ of town/the country** estar fuera de la ciudad/del país; **to get ~ of the rain** salir de la lluvia; **~ of the way!** ¡fuera del camino! **4.** (*without*) **to be ~ of money/work** estar sin dinero/trabajo; **~ of breath** sin aliento; **~ of order** averiado, -a **5.** (*not included in*) **to get ~ of the habit of doing sth** quitarse el hábito de hacer algo; **his dog is ~ of control** su perro está fuera de control **6.** (*from*) **made ~ of wood/a blanket** hecho de madera/una manta; **to copy sth ~ of a file** copiar algo de un archivo; **to get sth ~ of sb** sacar algo a alguien; **to read ~ of a novel** leer en una novela; **in 3 cases ~ of 10** en 3 de cada 10 casos **7.** (*because of*) **to do sth ~ of politeness** hacer algo por cortesía

out-and-out [ˌaʊtənd'aʊt] *adj* (*liar, idiot*) consumado, -a, redomado, -a; (*lie*) como una casa; (*disaster*) total, absoluto, -a

outback ['aʊtbæk] *n no pl* **the ~** el interior (*zona despoblada de Australia*)

outbid [ˌaʊt'bɪd] *vt irr* **to ~ sb** (**for sth**) pujar más que alguien (por algo)

outboard ['aʊtbɔːd, *Am:* -bɔːrd] *n*, **outboard motor** *n* fueraborda *m*

outbreak ['aʊtbreɪk] *n* (*of flu, violence*) brote *m;* (*of war*) estallido *m*

outbuilding ['aʊtbɪldɪŋ] *n* dependencia *f*

outburst ['aʊtbɜːst, *Am:* -bɜːrst] *n* arrebato *m*

outcast ['aʊtkɑːst, *Am:* -kæst] **I.** *n* paria *mf;* **social ~** marginado, -a *m, f* de la sociedad **II.** *adj* marginado, -a

outclass [ˌaʊt'klɑːs, *Am:* -'klæs] *vt* superar, aventajar

outcome ['aʊtkʌm] *n* **1.** (*result*) resultado *m* **2.** (*consequence*) consecuencia *f*

outcrop ['aʊtkrɒp, *Am:* -krɑːp] **I.** *n* afloramiento *m* **II.** *vi* aflorar

outcry ['aʊtkraɪ] <-ies> *n* gran protesta *f*

outdated [aʊt'deɪtɪd, *Am:* -t̬ɪd] *adj* anticuado, -a, pasado, -a de moda

outdistance [aʊt'dɪstəns] *vt* dejar atrás

outdo [aʊt'duː] *vt irr* superar, mejorar; **to ~ sb in sth** superar a alguien en algo; **to ~ oneself** mejorarse

outdoor ['aʊtdɔːʳ, *Am:* ˌaʊt'dɔːr] *adj* al aire libre; (*clothes*) de calle; (*plants*) de exterior

outdoors [ˌaʊt'dɔːz, *Am:* ˌaʊt'dɔːrz] *n* **the great ~** el aire libre

outer ['aʊtəʳ, *Am:* -t̬ɚ] *adj* exterior; **~ ear** oído *m* externo

Outer Hebrides ['aʊtəʳ 'hebrɪdiːz, *Am:* -t̬ɚ-] *n* Hébridas *fpl* Exteriores

outermost ['aʊtəməʊst, *Am:* -t̬ɚməst] *n* más exterior

outfield ['aʊtfiːld] *n no pl* (*in cricket, baseball*) parte *f* exterior del campo

outfit ['aʊtfɪt] *n* **1.** (*set of clothes*) conjunto *m* **2.** (*team, organization*) equipo *m;* **research ~** unidad *f* de investigación

outfitter ['aʊtfɪtəʳ, *Am:* -fɪt̬ɚ] *n* **sports ~s** tienda *f* de artículos de deporte

outflow ['aʊtfləʊ, *Am:* -floʊ] *n* (*of liquid*) desagüe *m;* (*of capital*) fuga *f*

outgoing ['aʊtgəʊɪŋ, *Am:* 'aʊtgoʊ-] **I.** *adj* **1.** (*sociable, extrovert*) sociable, extrovertido, -a **2.** (*retiring: President*) saliente **3.** (*ship*) que sale; **~ call** llamada *f* al exterior **II.** *n* **~s** COM salidas *fpl*

outgrow [ˌaʊt'grəʊ, *Am:* -'groʊ] *vt irr* **1.** (*habit*) pasar de la edad de; **to ~ an illness** superar una enfermedad con la edad; **she's ~n her trousers** se le han quedado pequeños los pantalones **2.** (*become bigger than*) crecer más que

outgrowth ['aʊtgrəʊθ, *Am:* -groʊθ] *n* **1.** BOT brote *m* **2.** (*result*) resultado *m*

outhouse ['aʊthaʊs] *n* **1.** *Brit* (*building*) dependencia *f* **2.** *Am* (*toilet*) retrete *m* exterior

outing ['aʊtɪŋ, *Am:* -t̬ɪŋ] *n* excursión *f;* **to go on an ~** ir de excursión

outlandish [aʊt'lændɪʃ] *adj* (*clothes*) estrafalario, -a, extravagante; (*idea*) descabellado, -a

outlast [ˌaʊt'lɑːst, *Am:* -'læst] *vt* **to ~ sth** durar más que algo; **to ~ sb** sobrevivir a alguien

outlaw ['aʊtlɔː, *Am:* -lɑː] **I.** *n* forajido, -a *m, f* **II.** *vt* (*product, practice*) prohibir; (*person*) proscribir

outlay ['aʊtleɪ] *n* desembolso *m*

outlet ['aʊtlet] *n* **1.** (*exit*) salida *f* **2.** (*means of expression*) válvula *f* de escape **3.** ECON punto *m* de venta; **retail ~** tienda *f* al por menor **4.** ELEC toma *f* de corriente

outline ['aʊtlaɪn] **I.** *n* **1.** (*draft*) esbozo *m* **2.** (*shape*) perfil *m* **3.** (*general description*) resumen *m* **II.** *vt* **1.** (*draw outer line of*) perfilar **2.** (*describe*) dar una idea general de; (*summarise*) resumir

outlive [ˌaʊt'lɪv] *vt* sobrevivir a

outlook ['aʊtlʊk] *n* **1.** (*prospects*) perspectivas *fpl* **2.** (*attitude*) punto *m* de vista **3.** (*view*) vista *f*

outlying ['aʊtˌlaɪɪŋ] *adj* distante, alejado, -a

outmaneuver *vt Am*, **outmanoeuvre** [ˌaʊtmə'nuːvəʳ, *Am:* -vɚ] *vt Brit, Aus* (*person*) mostrarse más hábil que; (*car*) ser más maniobrable que

outmoded [ˌaʊt'məʊdɪd, *Am:* -'moʊ-] *adj pej* anticuado, -a, pasado, -a de moda

outmost ['aʊtməʊst, *Am:* -moʊst] *adj* más remoto, -a

outnumber [ˌaʊt'nʌmbəʳ, *Am:* -bɚ] *vt* superar en número a

out-of-court settlement *n* arreglo *m* extrajudicial

out-of-date [ˌaʊtəv'deɪt, *Am:* ˌaʊt̬-] *adj* (*clothes*) anticuado, -a, pasado, -a de moda; (*ticket*) caducado, -a; (*person*) desfasado, -a

out-of-the-way [ˌaʊtəvðə'weɪ, *Am:* ˌaʊt̬əvðə'-] *adj* apartado, -a

outpatient ['aʊtˌpeɪʃənt] *n* paciente *mf* externo, -a

outplay [ˌaʊt'pleɪ] *vt* jugar mejor que

outpost ['aʊtpəʊst, *Am:* -poʊst] *n* **1.** MIL puesto *m* de avanzada **2.** *fig* reducto *m*

O

outpouring ['aʊtˌpɔːrɪŋ] *n* desahogo *m;* ~ **of grief** lamento *m* de dolor
output ['aʊtpʊt] *n no pl* ECON producción *f;* (*of machine*) rendimiento *m*
output device *n* INFOR dispositivo *m* de salida
outrage ['aʊtreɪdʒ] **I.** *n* **1.** (*atrocity*) atrocidad *f;* (*terrorist act*) atentado *m* **2.** (*scandal*) escándalo *m;* **to express** ~ (**at sth**) mostrar indignación (ante algo); **to feel a strong sense of** ~ **at sth** sentirse ultrajado por algo **II.** *vt* (*offend*) ultrajar
outrageous [aʊt'reɪdʒəs] *adj* **1.** (*cruel, violent*) atroz **2.** (*shocking: behaviour*) escandaloso, -a; (*clothes*) extravagante, estrafalario, -a; (*person*) atrevido, -a
outré ['uːtreɪ, *Am:* uː'treɪ] *adj form* extravagante, estrafalario, -a
outrigger ['aʊtrɪgəʳ, *Am:* -ɚ] *n* **1.** (*stabilizer*) balancín *m* **2.** (*boat*) canoa *f* con balancines
outright ['aʊtraɪt] **I.** *adj* (*disaster, defeat*) total; (*winner*) indiscutido, -a; (*hostility*) declarado, -a **II.** *adv* **1.** (*defeat, ignore*) totalmente; (*win*) absolutamente **2.** (*declare, ask*) descaradamente
outrun [ˌaʊt'rʌn] *vt irr* **to** ~ **sb** dejar atrás a alguien
outset ['aʊtset] *n no pl* principio *m;* **from the** ~ de entrada
outshine [ˌaʊt'ʃaɪn] *vt irr* eclipsar
outside [ˌaʊt'saɪd] **I.** *adj* **1.** (*external*) externo, -a, exterior; (*world*) exterior; (*influence, help*) externo, -a; **the** ~ **door** la puerta exterior; ~ **influences** influencias *fpl* exteriores **2.** (*not likely*) **an** ~ **chance that ...** una posibilidad remota de que *+subj* **3.** (*highest*) extremo, -a **II.** *n* **1.** (*external part or side*) exterior *m;* **judging from the** ~ a juzgar por el aspecto exterior **2.** (*at most*) **at the** ~ a lo más **III.** *prep* **1.** (*not within*) fuera de; **from** ~ **sth** desde fuera de algo; **to play** ~ jugar fuera; **to go** ~ **the house** salir de casa **2.** (*next to*) **to wait** ~ **the door** esperar en la puerta **3.** (*not during*) ~ **business hours** fuera de horas de oficina **4.** (*besides*) además de **IV.** *adv* **1.** (*outdoors*) fuera, afuera; **to go** ~ salir afuera; **to live an hour** ~ **Quito** vivir a una hora de Quito **2.** (*beyond*) **to be** ~ **the perimeter** estar afuera del perímetro
outside broadcast *n* transmisión *f* de exteriores **outside lane** *n* AUTO carril *m* de adelantamiento **outside left** *n* extremo *m* izquierdo **outside line** *n* línea *f* exterior
outsider [ˌaʊt'saɪdəʳ, *Am:* -dɚ] *n* **1.** (*person not from a group*) persona *f* de fuera **2.** (*in race, competition*) **to be an** ~ ser un desconocido
outside right *n* extremo *m* derecho
outsize [ˌaʊt'saɪz] *adj* muy grande
outskirts ['aʊtskɜːts, *Am:* -skɜːrts] *npl* afueras *fpl*
outsourcing ['aʊtˌsɔːsɪŋ, *Am:* -ˌsɔːrs-] *n no pl* externalización *f*
outspoken [ˌaʊt'spəʊkən, *Am:* -'spoʊ-] *adj* directo, -a; **to be** ~ no tener pelos en la lengua
outstanding [ˌaʊt'stændɪŋ] *adj* **1.** (*excellent*) destacado, -a **2.** FIN (*account*) por pagar; (*debt*) pendiente (de pago) **3.** (*unsolved*) por resolver
outstay [ˌaʊt'steɪ] *vt* **to** ~ **one's welcome** abusar de la hospitalidad
outstretched [ˌaʊt'stretʃt] *adj* extendido, -a
outstrip [ˌaʊt'strɪp] *vt irr* **1.** (*go faster than*) aventajar **2.** (*be greater than, exceed*) sobrepasar
out-tray ['aʊtˌtreɪ] *n* bandeja *f* de salida
outvote [ˌaʊt'vəʊt, *Am:* -'voʊt] *vt* vencer en unas elecciones; **to be** ~**d** perder en las elecciones
outward ['aʊtwəd, *Am:* -wɚd] **I.** *n no pl* exterior *m* **II.** *adj* **1.** (*exterior: appearance*) exterior; (*sign*) externo, -a **2.** (*voyage*) de ida **3.** (*superficial: similarity, difference*) aparente **III.** *adv* hacia afuera, hacia el exterior
outwardly ['aʊtwədli, *Am:* -wɚd-] *adv* aparentemente
outwards ['aʊtwədz, *Am:* -wɚdz] *adv* hacia afuera, hacia el exterior
outweigh [ˌaʊt'weɪ] *vt* **1.** (*weight*) pesar más que **2.** (*in importance or influence*) tener más peso que
outwit [ˌaʊt'wɪt] <-tt-> *vt* burlar
outwork [ˌaʊt'wɜːk, *Am:* 'aʊtwɜːrk] *n no pl* **1.** MIL defensa *f* (fuera de los límites de la fortificación principal) **2.** ECON trabajo *m* a domicilio
outworker ['aʊtwɜːkəʳ, *Am:* -wɜːrkɚ] *n* trabajador(a) *m(f)* a domicilio
oval ['əʊvəl, *Am:* 'oʊ-] **I.** *n* óvalo *m* **II.** *adj* ovalado, -a, oval
Oval Office *n* **the** ~ el despacho oval
ovary ['əʊvəri, *Am:* 'oʊ-] <-ies> *n* ovario *m*
ovation [əʊ'veɪʃən, *Am:* oʊ-] *n* ovación *f;* **to get an** ~ ser ovacionado
oven ['ʌvən] *n* horno *m*
oven gloves *npl* guantes *mpl* para el horno
ovenproof ['ʌvənpruːf] *adj* refractario, -a
oven-ready [ˌʌvən'redi] *adj* listo, -a para hornear
over ['əʊvəʳ, *Am:* 'oʊvɚ] **I.** *prep* **1.** (*above*) encima de, por encima de; **to hang the picture** ~ **the desk** colgar el cuadro encima del escritorio; **the bridge** ~ **the motorway** el puente sobre la autopista; **to fly** ~ **the sea** volar sobre el mar; **they'll be a long time** ~ **it** estarán mucho tiempo en ello **2.** (*on*) **to hit sb** ~ **the head** golpear a alguien en la cabeza; **to drive** ~ **sth** arrollar algo; **to spread a cloth** ~ **the table** extender un mantel sobre la mesa **3.** (*across*) **to go** ~ **the bridge** cruzar el puente; **the house** ~ **the road** la casa de enfrente; **to come from** ~ **the Rhine** venir de la otra orilla del Rin; **it rained all** ~ **England** llovió por toda Inglaterra; **famous all** ~ **the world** famoso en todo el mundo **4.** (*behind*) **to look** ~ **sb's shoulder** mirar por encima del hombro de alguien; ~ **the dune** detrás de la

duna **5.** (*during*) durante; ~ **the winter** durante el invierno; ~ **time** con el tiempo; ~ **a two year period** durante un período de dos años; **to stay** ~ **the weekend** quedarse a pasar el fin de semana **6.** (*more than*) **to speak for** ~ **an hour** hablar durante una hora; ~ **150** más de 150; **children** ~ **14** niños de más de 14 (años); ~ **and above that** además de eso **7.** (*through*) **I heard it** ~ **the radio** lo oí por la radio; **to hear sth** ~ **the noise** escuchar algo a pesar del ruido; **what came** ~ **him?** ¿qué le picó? *inf* **8.** (*in superiority to*) **to rule** ~ **the Romans** gobernar sobre los romanos; **to have command** ~ **sth** tener mando sobre algo; **to have an advantage** ~ **sb** tener ventaja sobre alguien **9.** (*about*) ~ **sth** acerca de algo; **to puzzle** ~ **a problem** romperse la cabeza sobre un problema **10.** (*for checking*) **to go** ~ **a text** revisar un texto; **to watch** ~ **a child** cuidar a un niño **11.** (*past*) **to be** ~ **the worst** haber pasado lo peor **12.** MAT **4** ~ **12 equals a third** 4 entre 12 es igual a un tercio **II.** *adv* **1.** (*moving above: go, jump*) por encima; **to fly** ~ **the city** volar sobre la ciudad **2.** (*at a distance*) **to move sth** ~ apartar algo; ~ **here** acá; ~ **there** allá; ~ **the road** cruzando la calle **3.** (*moving across*) **to come** ~ **here** venir para acá; **to go** ~ **there** ir para allá; **he has gone** ~ **to France** se ha ido a Francia; **he swam** ~ **to me** nadó hacia mí; **he went** ~ **to the enemy** *fig* se cambió al bando enemigo **4.** (*on a visit*) **come** ~ **tonight** pásate por aquí esta noche **5.** (*changing hands*) **to pass/hand sth** ~ pasar/dar algo **6.** (*downwards*) **to fall** ~ caerse; **to knock sth** ~ tirar algo **7.** (*another way up*) **to turn the page/the pancake** ~ voltear la página/el pastel **8.** (*in exchange*) **to change** ~ intercambiar; **to change** ~ (**from sth**) **to sth else** cambiar (de algo) a otra cosa **9.** (*completely*) **that's her all** ~ eso es muy (típico) de ella; **to look for sb all** ~ buscar a alguien por todos lados; **to turn sth** ~ **and** ~ dar vueltas y vueltas a algo; **to think sth** ~ pensar algo (detalladamente) **10.** (*again*) **to count them** ~ **again** contarlos otra vez; **I repeated it** ~ **and** ~ lo repetí una y otra vez; **to do sth all** ~ *Am* hacer algo desde el principio **11.** (*more*) **children of 14 and** ~ niños de 14 años en adelante; **7 into 30 goes 4 and 2** ~ 30 entre 7 son 4 y nos quedan 2 **12.** (*sb's turn*) **it's** ~ **to him** es su turno; ~ RADIO, AVIAT cambio; ~ **and out** cambio y corto **III.** *adj* **1.** (*finished*) acabado, -a; **it's all** ~ se acabó; **the snow is** ~ se acabó la nieve **2.** (*remaining*) restante; **there are three left** ~ quedan tres

overabundant [ˌəʊvərəˈbʌndənt, *Am:* ˌoʊvɚ-] *adj* superabundante

overact [ˌəʊvərˈækt, *Am:* ˌoʊvɚˈ-] *vi* THEAT sobreactuar

overall[1] [ˌəʊvərˈɔːl, *Am:* ˌoʊ-] *n* **1.** (*protective clothing*) bata *f* **2.** *pl* (*one-piece protective suit*) mono *m;* **a pair of ~s** un peto

overall[2] [ˈəʊvərɔːl, *Am:* ˈoʊ-] **I.** *adj* **1.** (*general*) global **2.** (*above all others*) total; ~ **winner** ganador *m* absoluto **II.** *adv* en conjunto

overanxious [ˌəʊvərˈæŋkʃəs, *Am:* ˌoʊvɚˈ-] *adj* demasiado preocupado, -a

overawe [ˌəʊvərˈɔː, *Am:* ˌoʊvɚˈɑː] *vt* intimidar; **to be ~d** sentirse sobrecogido

overbalance [ˌəʊvəˈbæləns, *Am:* ˌoʊvɚˈ-] *vi* perder el equilibrio

overbearing [ˌəʊvəˈbeərɪŋ, *Am:* ˌoʊvɚˈber-] *adj pej* despótico, -a

overblown [ˌəʊvəˈbləʊn, *Am:* ˌoʊvɚˈbloʊn] *adj* ampuloso, -a

overboard [ˈəʊvəbɔːd, *Am:* ˈoʊvɚbɔːrd] *adv* al agua; **to fall** ~ caer al agua; **man** ~**!** ¡hombre al agua!; **to go** ~ *inf* exagerar; **to go** ~ **for sth** *inf* entusiasmarse locamente por algo

overbook [ˌəʊvəˈbʊk, *Am:* ˌoʊvɚˈ-] *vt* sobrereservar

overbooking *n* AVIAT sobrecontratación *f*

overburden [ˌəʊvəˈbɜːdən, *Am:* ˌoʊvɚˈbɜːr-] *vt* sobrecargar

overcapacity <-ies> *n* sobrecapacidad *f*

overcast [ˌəʊvəˈkɑːst, *Am:* ˈoʊvɚkæst] *adj* nublado, -a

over-cautious [ˌəʊvəˈkɔːʃəs, *Am:* ˌoʊvɚˈkɑː-] *adj* demasiado cauto, -a

overcharge [ˌəʊvəˈtʃɑːdʒ, *Am:* ˌoʊvɚˈtʃɑːrdʒ] **I.** *vt* **to** ~ **sb** cobrar de más a alguien **II.** *vi* cobrar de más

overcoat [ˈəʊvəkəʊt, *Am:* ˈoʊvɚkoʊt] *n* abrigo *m*

overcome [ˌəʊvəˈkʌm, *Am:* ˌoʊvɚˈ-] *irr* **I.** *vt* **1.** (*defeat*) vencer **2.** (*cope with*) superar; (*difficulty*) salvar; **to** ~ **temptation** no sucumbir a la tentación **II.** *vi irr* vencer

overconfident [ˌəʊvəˈkɒnfɪdənt, *Am:* ˌoʊvɚˈkɑːnfə-] *adj* demasiado seguro, -a de sí mismo, -a

overcooked [ˌəʊvəˈkʊkt, *Am:* ˌoʊvɚˈ-] *adj* recocido, -a

overcrowded [ˌəʊvəˈkraʊdɪd, *Am:* ˌoʊvɚˈ-] *adj* abarrotado, -a

overdeveloped [ˌəʊvədɪˈveləpt, *Am:* ˌoʊvɚ-] *adj* superdesarrollado, -a; PHOT sobrerrevelado, -a

overdo [ˌəʊvəˈduː, *Am:* ˌoʊvɚˈ-] *vt* **1.** **to** ~ **things** pasarse; (*work too hard*) trabajar demasiado **2.** *inf* (*exaggerate*) exagerar **3.** (*cook too long*) cocer demasiado

overdone [ˌəʊvəˈdʌn, *Am:* ˌoʊvɚˈ-] *adj* **1.** (*overexaggerated*) exagerado, -a **2.** (*overcooked*) demasiado hecho, -a

overdose [ˈəʊvədəʊs, *Am:* ˈoʊvɚdoʊs] **I.** *n* sobredosis *f inv* **II.** *vi* **to** ~ **on sth** tomar una sobredosis de algo

overdraft [ˈəʊvədrɑːft, *Am:* ˈoʊvɚdræft] *n* FIN descubierto *m;* **to have an** ~ tener un saldo deudor

overdraft facility *n* FIN crédito *m* al descubierto

overdraw [ˌəʊvəˈdrɔː, *Am:* ˌoʊvɚˈdrɑː] *irr vi, vt* girar en descubierto

overdress [ˌəʊvəˈdres, *Am:* ˌoʊvɚˈ-] *vi* vestirse con demasiada elegancia
overdrive [ˈəʊvədraɪv, *Am:* ˈoʊvɚ-] *n no pl, fig* **to go into ~** ir a toda marcha
overdue [ˌəʊvəˈdjuː, *Am:* ˌoʊvɚˈduː] *adj* **1.** (*late*) atrasado, -a; **to be ~** llevar retraso **2.** FIN (*account*) por pagar; (*debt*) pendiente (de pago)
overeat [ˌəʊvərˈiːt, *Am:* ˌoʊvɚˈ-] *irr vi* comer demasiado
overemphasize [ˌəʊvərˈemfəsaɪz, *Am:* ˌoʊvɚˈ-] *vt* sobreenfatizar
overestimate¹ [ˌəʊvərˈestɪmət, *Am:* ˌoʊvɚˈestɪmɪt] *n* sobreestimación *f*
overestimate² [ˌəʊvərˈestɪmeɪt, *Am:* ˌoʊvɚˈestə-] *vt* sobreestimar
overexcited [ˌəʊvərɪkˈsaɪtɪd, *Am:* ˌoʊvɚɪkˈsaɪt̬ɪd] *adj* sobreexcitado, -a
overexert [ˌəʊvəɪgˈzɜːt, *Am:* ˌoʊvɚɪgˈzɜːrt] *vt* **to ~ oneself** hacer un esfuerzo excesivo
overexpose [ˌəʊvərɪkˈspəʊz, *Am:* ˌoʊvɚɪkˈspoʊz] *vt* PHOT sobreexponer
overexposure [ˌəʊvərɪkˈspəʊʒəʳ, *Am:* ˌoʊvɚɪkˈspoʊʒɚ] *n no pl* **1.** PHOT sobreexposición *f* **2.** *fig* aparición *f* excesiva en los medios de comunicación
overextend [ˌəʊvəɪkˈstend] *vt* **to ~ oneself** contraer demasiadas obligaciones financieras
overflow [ˌəʊvəˈfləʊ, *Am:* ˌoʊvɚˈfloʊ] **I.** *n* **1.** (*excess: of liquid*) exceso *m* de líquido; (*of people*) exceso *m* **2.** (*outlet*) rebosadero *m* **II.** *vi* rebosar; (*river*) desbordarse
overfly [ˌəʊvɜˈflaɪ, *Am:* ˌoʊvɚˈ-] <-ie-> *irr vt* sobrevolar
overgrown [ˌəʊvəˈgrəʊn, *Am:* ˌoʊvɚˈgroʊn] *adj* (*garden*) abandonado, -a; **to be ~ with sth** estar cubierto de algo
overhang [ˌəʊvəˈhæŋ, *Am:* ˌoʊvɚˈ-] *irr* **I.** *n* (*cliff*) saliente *m;* ARCHIT alero *m* **II.** *vt* **to ~ sth** sobresalir por encima de algo
overhaul [ˌəʊvəˈhɔːl, *Am:* ˌoʊvɚˈhɑːl] **I.** *n* puesta *f* a punto, revisión *f* **II.** *vt* **1.** (*machine*) poner a punto; (*policy, system*) revisar **2.** (*overtake*) superar
overhead [ˌəʊvəˈhed, *Am:* ˌoʊvɚˈ-] **I.** *n Am* gastos *mpl* generales **II.** *adj* de arriba, encima de la cabeza; **~ cable** cable *m* aéreo; **~ light** luz *f* de techo **III.** *adv* en lo alto, por encima de la cabeza
overheads [ˌəʊvəˈheds, *Am:* ˌoʊvɚˈ-] *npl Brit, Aus s.* **overhead**
overhear [ˌəʊvəˈhɪəʳ, *Am:* ˌoʊvɚˈhɪr] *irr vt* oír por casualidad
overheat [ˌəʊvəˈhiːt, *Am:* ˌoʊvɚˈ-] **I.** *vt* sobrecalentar **II.** *vi* recalentarse
overindulge [ˌəʊvərɪnˈdʌldʒ, *Am:* ˌoʊvɚ-] **I.** *vt* consentir **II.** *vi* **to ~ in sth** abusar de algo
overjoyed [ˌəʊvəˈdʒɔɪd, *Am:* ˌoʊvɚˈ-] *adj* encantado, -a
overkill [ˈəʊvəkɪl, *Am:* ˈoʊvɚ-] *n* **1.** MIL sobrecapacidad *f* de exterminación **2.** *fig* exceso *m* de medios
overland [ˈəʊvəlænd, *Am:* ˈoʊvɚ-] **I.** *adj* terrestre; **~ vehicle** vehículo *m* todoterreno; **by ~ mail** por vía terrestre **II.** *adv* por tierra
overlap¹ [ˈəʊvəlæp, *Am:* ˈoʊvɚ-] *n* (*between tiles, planks*) superposición *f; fig* (*between knowledge, authority*) coincidencia *f* parcial
overlap² [ˌəʊvəˈlæp, *Am:* ˌoʊvɚˈ-] <-pp-> **I.** *vi* (*between tiles, planks*) superponerse; *fig* (*between knowledge, authority*) coincidir en parte **II.** *vt* solapar
overleaf [ˌəʊvəˈliːf, *Am:* ˈoʊvɚliːf] *adv* al dorso
overload¹ [ˈəʊvələʊd, *Am:* ˈoʊvɚloʊd] *n* **1.** ELEC sobrecarga *f* **2.** (*of work*) exceso *m*
overload² [ˌəʊvəˈləʊd, *Am:* ˌoʊvɚˈloʊd] *vt* ELEC sobrecargar; **to be ~ed with sth** *fig* estar agobiado de algo
over-long [ˌəʊvəˈlɒŋ, *Am:* ˌoʊvɚˈlɑːŋ] *adj* demasiado largo, -a
overlook [ˌəʊvəˈlʊk, *Am:* ˌoʊvɚˈ-] **I.** *n Am* vista *f* **II.** *vt* **1.** (*look out onto*) tener vistas a **2.** (*not notice*) pasar por alto; (*deliberately*) no hacer caso de **3.** (*forget*) olvidar
overly [ˈəʊvəli, *Am:* ˈoʊvɚli] *adv* demasiado
overmanning [ˌəʊvəˈmænɪŋ, *Am:* ˌoʊvɚˈ-] *n* exceso *m* de personal
overmuch [ˌəʊvəˈmʌtʃ, *Am:* ˌoʊvɚˈ-] **I.** *adj* excesivo, -a **II.** *adv* en exceso
overnight [ˌəʊvəˈnaɪt, *Am:* ˌoʊvɚˈ-] **I.** *adj* de noche; **~ bag** bolsa *f* de fin de semana; **~ stay** estancia *f* de una noche **II.** *adv* durante la noche; **to stay ~** pasar la noche
overpass [ˈəʊvəpɑːs, *Am:* ˈoʊvɚpæs] *n Am* paso *m* elevado
overpay [ˌəʊvəˈpeɪ, *Am:* ˌoʊvɚˈ-] *irr vt* pagar de más
overpopulated [ˌəʊvəˈpɒpjʊleɪtɪd, *Am:* ˌoʊvɚˈpɑːpjəleɪt̬ɪd] *adj* superpoblado, -a
overpopulation [ˌəʊvəˌpɒpjʊˈleɪʃən, *Am:* ˌoʊvɚˌpɑːpjəˈ-] *n no pl* superpoblación *f*
overpower [ˌəʊvəˈpaʊəʳ, *Am:* ˌoʊvɚˈpaʊɚ] *vt* dominar
overpowering [ˌəʊvəˈpaʊərɪŋ, *Am:* ˌoʊvɚˈpaʊɚ-] *adj* (*person, attack*) abrumador(a); (*taste, smell*) muy fuerte
overproduce [ˌəʊvəprəˈdjuːs, *Am:* ˌoʊvɚproʊˈduːs] **I.** *vi* sobreproducir **II.** *vt* producir en exceso
overrate [ˌəʊvəˈreɪt, *Am:* ˌoʊvɚˈ-] *vt* sobrevalorar
overreach [ˌəʊvəˈriːtʃ, *Am:* ˌoʊvɚˈ-] *vt* **to ~ oneself** extralimitarse
overreact [ˌəʊvəriˈækt, *Am:* ˌoʊvɚriˈ-] *vi* reaccionar de forma exagerada
overreaction [ˌəʊvəriˈækʃən, *Am:* ˌoʊvɚriˈ-] *n* reacción *f* exagerada
override [ˌəʊvəˈraɪd, *Am:* ˌoʊvɚˈ-] **I.** *n* anulación *f* de automatismo **II.** *vt* **1.** (*not accept*) anular **2.** (*interrupt*) cancelar
overriding [ˌəʊvəˈraɪdɪŋ, *Am:* ˌoʊvɚˈ-] *adj* primordial
overrule [ˌəʊvəˈruːl, *Am:* ˌoʊvɚˈ-] *vt* anular; **to ~ an objection** LAW rechazar una objeción

overrun [ˌəʊvəˈrʌn, *Am:* ˌoʊvɚˈ-] **I.** *n* sobrecoste *m* **II.** *vt irr* **1.** (*invade*) invadir; **to be ~ with sth** estar plagado de algo **2.** (*budget*) exceder **III.** *vi irr* prolongarse más de lo previsto; **to ~ on costs** excederse en los costes

overseas [ˌəʊvəˈsiːz, *Am:* ˌoʊvɚˈ-] **I.** *adj* extranjero, -a; (*trade*) exterior **II.** *adv* **to go/travel ~** ir/viajar al extranjero

oversee [ˌəʊvəˈsiː, *Am:* ˌoʊvɚˈ-] *irr vt* supervisar

overseer [ˈəʊvəsɪəʳ, *Am:* ˈoʊvɚˌsiːɚ] *n* supervisor(a) *m(f)*

oversell [ˌəʊvəˈsel, *Am:* -vɚˈ-] *irr vt Am* insistir demasiado en

overshadow [ˌəʊvəˈʃædəʊ, *Am:* ˌoʊvɚˈʃædoʊ] *vt* **1.** (*cast shadow over*) ensombrecer **2.** (*make insignificant*) eclipsar

overshoe [ˈəʊvəʃuː, *Am:* ˈoʊvɚ-] *n* chanclo *m*

overshoot [ˌəʊvəˈʃuːt, *Am:* ˌoʊvɚˈ-] *irr vt* pasar de, ir más allá de; AVIAT aterrizar más allá de ►**to ~ the mark** pasarse de la raya

oversight [ˈəʊvəsaɪt, *Am:* ˈoʊvɚ-] *n* **1.** (*omission*) descuido *m;* **by an ~** por equivocación **2.** (*supervision*) supervisión *f*

oversimplify [ˌəʊvəˈsɪmplɪfaɪ, *Am:* ˌoʊvɚˈsɪmplə-] <-ie-> *vt* simplificar excesivamente

oversize [ˌəʊvəˈsaɪz, *Am:* ˌoʊvɚ-] *adj,* **oversized** *adj* **1.** (*too big*) demasiado grande **2.** *Am* (*clothes*) de talla grande

oversleep [ˌəʊvəˈsliːp, *Am:* ˌoʊvɚˈ-] *irr vi* quedarse dormido

overspend [ˌəʊvəˈspend, *Am:* ˌoʊvɚˈ-] **I.** *vi* gastar demasiado **II.** *vt* **to ~ one's allowance** gastar más de la cuenta

overspill [ˈəʊvəspɪl, *Am:* ˈoʊvɚ-] *n* excedente *m* de población; **~ town** ciudad *f* dormitorio

overstaffed [ˌəʊvəˈstɑːft, *Am:* ˌoʊvɚˈstæft] *adj* con exceso de personal

overstate [ˌəʊvəˈsteɪt, *Am:* ˌoʊvɚˈ-] *vt* exagerar

overstay [ˌəʊvəˈsteɪ, *Am:* ˌoʊvɚˈ-] *vt* **to ~ one's welcome** quedarse más de lo conveniente, abusar de la hospitalidad

overstep [ˌəʊvəˈstep, *Am:* ˌoʊvɚˈ-] *irr vt* sobrepasar ►**to ~ the mark** pasarse de la raya

oversubscribed [ˌəʊvəsəbˈskraɪbd, *Am:* ˌoʊvɚ-] *adj* FIN **the offer was ~** la demanda fue superior a la oferta

oversupply [ˌəʊvəsəˈplaɪ, *Am:* ˌoʊvɚ-] *n* excedente *m*

overt [ˈəʊvɜːt, *Am:* ˈoʊvɜːrt] *adj* (*criticism*) abierto, -a; (*hostility*) declarado, -a

overtake [ˌəʊvəˈteɪk, *Am:* ˌoʊvɚˈ-] *irr* **I.** *vt* **1.** AUTO adelantar; **events have ~n us** los acontecimientos se nos han adelantado **2.** (*in contest*) superar **II.** *vi* adelantar

overtax [ˌəʊvəˈtæks, *Am:* ˌoʊvɚˈ-] *vt* **1.** FIN gravar en exceso (con impuestos) **2.** *fig* poner a prueba

over-the-counter [ˌəʊvəðəˈkaʊntəʳ, *Am:* ˌoʊvɚðəˈkaʊnt̬ɚ] *adj* sin receta

overthrow [ˌəʊvəˈθrəʊ, *Am:* ˌoʊvɚˈθroʊ] **I.** *n* derrocamiento *m* **II.** *vt irr* derrocar

overtime [ˈəʊvətaɪm, *Am:* ˈoʊvɚ-] *n* **1.** (*work*) horas *fpl* extra **2.** *Am* SPORTS prórroga *f*

overtired [ˌəʊvəˈtaɪəd, *Am:* ˌoʊvɚˈtaɪɚd] *adj* rendido, -a

overtone [ˈəʊvətəʊn, *Am:* ˈoʊvɚtoʊn] *n* **1.** (*implication*) trasfondo *m* **2.** MUS armónico *m*

overture [ˈəʊvətjʊəʳ, *Am:* ˈoʊvɚtʃɚ] *n* **1.** MUS obertura *f* **2.** (*show of friendliness*) acercamiento *m;* **to make ~s towards sb** intentar acercarse a alguien

overturn [ˌəʊvəˈtɜːn, *Am:* ˌoʊvɚˈtɜːrn] **I.** *vi* volcar, voltearse *AmL* **II.** *vt* volcar; POL derrumbar

overvalue [ˌəʊvəˈvæljuː, *Am:* ˌoʊvɚˈ-] *vt* sobrevalorar

overview [ˈəʊvəvjuː, *Am:* ˈoʊvɚ-] *n* perspectiva *f* general

overweening [ˌəʊvəˈwiːnɪŋ, *Am:* ˌoʊvɚˈ-] *adj* arrogante

overweight [ˌəʊvəˈweɪt, *Am:* ˌoʊvɚˈ-] *adj* demasiado pesado, -a; **to be ~** pesar demasiado; **to be ~ by a few kilos** tener un sobrepeso de unos quilos

overwhelm [ˌəʊvəˈwelm, *Am:* ˌoʊvɚˈ-] *vt* **1.** (*overcome by force*) abrumar, sobrecoger; **to be ~ed by sth** estar agobiado por algo **2.** (*swamp*) inundar

overwhelming [ˌəʊvəˈwelmɪŋ, *Am:* ˌoʊvɚˈ-] *adj* abrumador(a); **~ grief** dolor inconsolable; **to feel an ~ need to do sth** sentir una necesidad irresistible de hacer algo

overwork [ˌəʊvəˈwɜːk, *Am:* ˌoʊvɚˈwɜːrk] **I.** *n no pl* agotamiento *m* **II.** *vi* trabajar demasiado **III.** *vt* hacer trabajar demasiado

overwrought [ˌəʊvəˈrɔːt, *Am:* ˌoʊvɚˈrɑːt] *adj* **1.** (*person*) alterado, -a **2.** (*style*) recargado, -a

oviduct [ˈəʊvɪdʌkt] *n* oviducto *m*

oviparous [əʊˈvɪpərəs, *Am:* oʊˈ-] *adj* ovíparo, -a

ovulate [ˈɒvjəleɪt, *Am:* ˈɑːvjuː-] *vi* ovular

ovulation [ˌɒvjəˈleɪʃən, *Am:* ˌɑːvjuːˈ-] *n no pl* ovulación *f*

ovum [ˈəʊvəm, *Am:* ˈoʊ-] <ova> *n* óvulo *m*

owe [əʊ, *Am:* oʊ] **I.** *vt* deber **II.** *vi* tener deudas

owing [ˈəʊɪŋ, *Am:* ˈoʊ-] *adj* por pagar

owing to *prep* debido a

owl [aʊl] *n* búho *m,* tecolote *m AmC, Méx;* **barn ~** lechuza *f;* **little ~** mochuelo *m*

owlish [ˈaʊlɪʃ] *adj* sabiondo, -a

own [əʊn, *Am:* oʊn] **I.** *adj* propio, -a; **to see sth with one's ~ eyes** ver algo con los propios ojos ►**to be one's own man/person/woman** ser el jefe de uno mismo; **in one's ~ right** por derecho propio; **to do one's ~ thing** ir a su aire; **in one's ~ time** en su tiempo libre; **to hold one's ~** mantenerse firme **II.** *vt* poseer ►**as if one ~ed the place** como Pedro por su

O

casa **III.** *vt* **to ~ …** confesar que…

◆own up *vi* confesar; **to ~ up to sth** confesar algo

owner ['əʊnəʳ, *Am:* 'oʊnɚ] *n* propietario, -a *m, f;* **to be the ~ of sth** ser el dueño de algo

ownerless ['əʊnələs, *Am:* 'oʊnɚ-] *adj* sin dueño

owner-occupied *adj* ocupado, -a por el dueño

owner-occupier [ˌəʊnəʳ'ɒkjəpaɪəʳ, *Am:* ˌoʊnɚ'ɑːkjuːpaɪɚ] *n* ocupante *mf* propietario, -a

ownership ['əʊnəʃɪp, *Am:* 'oʊnɚ-] *n no pl* posesión *f;* **to claim ~** reclamar la propiedad; **to be under private/public ~** ser de propiedad privada/pública

own goal *n* autogol *m*

own label goods *npl* productos *mpl* con la etiqueta del establecimiento

ox [ɒks, *Am:* ɑːks] <-en> *n* buey *m*

Oxbridge ['ɒksbrɪdʒ, *Am:* 'ɑːks-] *n las universidades de Oxford y Cambridge*

ox cart *n* carro *m* de bueyes

OXFAM ['ɒksfæm, *Am:* 'ɑːks-] *n Brit abbr of* **Oxford Committee for Famine Relief** *organización benéfica contra el hambre*

oxidation [ˌɒksɪ'deɪʃən, *Am:* ˌɑːksɪ'-] *n* oxidación *f*

oxide ['ɒksaɪd, *Am:* 'ɑːk-] *n* óxido *m*

oxidize ['ɒksɪdaɪz, *Am:* 'ɑːk-] **I.** *vi* oxidarse **II.** *vt* oxidar

oxtail ['ɒksteɪl, *Am:* 'ɑːks-] *n* rabo *m* de buey

oxtail soup *n* sopa *f* de rabo de buey

oxyacetylene [ˌɒksiə'setəliːn, *Am:* ˌɑːksiə'seṭəliːn] *n no pl* oxiacetileno *m*

oxygen ['ɒksɪdʒən, *Am:* 'ɑːksɪ-] *n no pl* oxígeno *m*

oxygen cylinder *n* bombona *f* de oxígeno

oxygen mask *n* máscara *f* de oxígeno

oxygen tent *n* cámara *f* de oxígeno

oxymoron [ˌɒksɪ'mɔːrɒn, *Am:* ˌɑːksɪ'mɔːrɑːn] *n* oxímoron *m*

oyster ['ɔɪstəʳ, *Am:* -stɚ] *n* ostra *f*

oyster bank *n,* **oyster bed** *n* banco *m* de ostras

oystercatcher ['ɔɪstəˌkætʃəʳ, *Am:* -stɚˌkætʃɚ] *n* ostrero, -a *m, f*

oz *n abbr of* **ounce** onza *f* (*28,4 g*)

ozone ['əʊzəʊn, *Am:* 'oʊzoʊn] *n no pl* ozono *m*

ozone layer *n* capa *f* de ozono

P

P, p [piː] <-'s> *n* P, p *f;* **~ for Peter** P de París ►**to mind one's ~s and Qs** cuidarse de no meter la pata

p **1.** *abbr of* **page** pág. *f* **2.** *abbr of* **penny** penique *m*

pa [pɑː] *n inf* papá *m*

PA [ˌpiː'eɪ] *n* **1.** *abbr of* **personal assistant** ayudante *mf* personal **2.** *abbr of* **public address system** sistema *m* de megafonía **3.** *Am abbr of* **Pennsylvania** Pensilvania *f*

p.a. [ˌpiː'eɪ] *abbr of* **per annum** por año

pace [peɪs] **I.** *n* **1.** *no pl* (*speed*) velocidad *f;* **to force the ~** forzar el paso; **to quicken one's ~** acelerar el paso; **to set the ~** marcar el ritmo; **to keep ~ with sb** llevar el mismo paso que alguien; **to keep ~ with sth** avanzar al mismo ritmo que algo; **to keep up/to stand the ~** llevar/mantener el ritmo **2.** (*step*) paso *m* ►**to put sb through his/her ~s** poner a alguien a prueba; **to spot sth at 20 ~s** reconocer algo a la milla **II.** <pacing> *vt* **1.** (*walk up and down*) pasearse por **2.** (*measure in strides*) medir a pasos **3.** SPORTS (*set a speed*) marcar el paso para; **to ~ oneself** controlarse el tiempo **III.** <pacing> *vi* **to ~ up and down** pasearse de un lado para otro

pacemaker ['peɪsˌmeɪkəʳ, *Am:* -kɚ] *n* **1.** SPORTS liebre *f* **2.** MED marcapasos *m inv*

pace-setter ['peɪsˌsetəʳ, *Am:* -ˌseṭɚ] *n* SPORTS liebre *f*

pachyderm ['pækɪdɜːm, *Am:* -ədɜːrm] *n* paquidermo *m*

pacific [pə'sɪfɪk] *adj* pacífico, -a

Pacific [pə'sɪfɪk] **I.** *n* **the ~** el Pacífico; **the ~ Ocean** el Océano Pacífico **II.** *adj* del Pacífico

pacification [ˌpæsɪfɪ'keɪʃən, *Am:* -əfɪ'-] *n no pl* pacificación *f*

pacifier ['pæsɪfaɪəʳ, *Am:* -əfaɪɚ] *n* **1.** (*person*) pacificador(a) *m(f)* **2.** *Am* (*baby's dummy*) chupete *m*

pacifism ['pæsɪfɪzəm, *Am:* 'pæsə-] *n no pl* pacifismo *m*

pacifist ['pæsɪfɪst, *Am:* 'pæsə-] **I.** *n* pacifista *mf* **II.** *adj* pacifista

pacify ['pæsɪfaɪ, *Am:* 'pæsə-] <-ie-> *vt* **1.** (*establish peace*) pacificar **2.** (*calm*) calmar

pack [pæk] **I.** *n* **1.** (*bundle*) fardo *m;* (*rucksack*) mochila *f;* (*packet*) paquete *m;* **ice ~** bolsa *f* de hielo **2.** (*group*) grupo *m;* (*of wolves, hounds*) manada *f* **II.** *vi* (*prepare luggage*) hacer las maletas ►**to send sb ~ing** largar a alguien con viento fresco **III.** *vt* **1.** (*fill: box, train*) llenar; **~ed with information** repleto de información **2.** (*wrap*) envasar; (*put in packages*) empaquetar; **to ~ one's suitcase** hacer la maleta **3.** (*compress*) comprimir

◆pack away *vt* **1.** (*put back in place*) guardar **2.** *inf* (*eat*) engullir

◆pack in **I.** *vt* **1.** (*put in*) meter **2.** *inf* (*stop*) dejar; **pack it in!** ¡déjalo! **3.** (*attract audience*) captar **II.** *vi* apiñar

◆pack off *vt inf* **to pack sb off** deshacerse de alguien

◆pack up **I.** *vt* **1.** (*put away*) guardar **2.** *inf* (*finish*) terminar **II.** *vi inf* **1.** (*stop work*) dejar de trabajar **2.** *Brit* (*stop functioning*) averiarse

package ['pækɪdʒ] **I.** *n* paquete *m;* **software ~** paquete de software **II.** *vt* **1.** (*pack*) empaquetar **2.** *fig* echar

package deal *n* acuerdo *m* global con concesiones mutuas **package holiday** *n Brit* viaje *m* organizado **package store** *n Am* licorería *f* **package tour** *n s.* **package holiday**

packaging *n no pl* **1.** (*wrapping*) embalaje *m* **2.** (*action*) envasado *m*

packer ['pækəʳ, *Am:* -ɚ] *n* empaquetador(a) *m(f)*, embalador(a) *m(f)*

packet ['pækɪt] *n* **1.** (*parcel*) paquete *m;* (*of biscuits*) caja *f;* (*of cigarettes*) cajetilla *f* **2.** *inf* (*money*) dineral *m*

packing *n no pl* (*action, material*) embalaje *m;* **to do one's ~** hacer las maletas

packing case *n Brit, Aus* caja *f* de embalaje **packing routine** *n* INFOR rutina *f* de empaquetado

pact [pækt] *n* pacto *m*

pad¹ [pæd] **I.** *n* **1.** (*cushion*) almohadilla *f;* **knee ~** rodillera *f;* **mouse ~** INFOR alfombrilla *f* del ratón; **shin ~** espinillera *f;* **shoulder ~** hombrera *f* **2.** (*of blank*) bloc *m* **3.** (*of animal's foot*) almohadilla *f* (de la pata) **4.** AVIAT plataforma *f* **5.** *inf* (*house, flat*) choza *f* **6.** (*water-lily leaf*) hoja *f* de nenúfar **II.** <-dd-> *vt* acolchar

pad² [pæd] <-dd-> *vi* andar silenciosamente ◆**pad out** *vt* meter paja en; **to ~ a speech/text** inflar un discurso/texto con paja

padded *adj* acolchado, -a; **~ cell** celda *f* de aislamiento

padding *n no pl, a. fig* relleno *m*

paddle ['pædl] **I.** *n* **1.** (*type of oar*) canalete *m* **2.** (*act of paddling*) chapoteo *m;* **to go for a ~** ir a mojarse los pies **II.** *vt* **1.** (*row*) impulsar con canalete **2.** *Am, inf* (*spank*) zurrar **III.** *vi* **1.** (*row*) remar con canalete **2.** (*walk, swim*) chapotear

paddle boat *n* vapor *m* de paletas **paddle steamer** *n* vapor *m* de ruedas

paddling pool *n Brit, Aus* estanque *m* para chapotear

paddock ['pædək] *n* **1.** (*enclosed field*) corral *m;* (*at racecourse*) parque *m* **2.** *Aus* (*open field*) prado *m*

paddy¹ ['pædi] <-ies> *n Brit* rabieta *f;* **to get in(to) a ~** coger una rabieta

paddy² ['pædi] *n,* **paddy field** *n* arrozal *m*

Paddy ['pædi] <-ies> *n pej, inf* irlandés, -esa *m, f*

paddy wagon *n Am, Aus, inf* coche *m* celular

padlock ['pædlɒk, *Am:* -lɑːk] **I.** *n* candado *m* **II.** *vt* cerrar con candado

paediatric [ˌpiːdɪ'ætrik] *adj Brit* pediátrico, -a

paediatrician [ˌpiːdɪə'trɪʃən] *n Brit* MED pediatra *mf*

paediatrics [ˌpiːdɪ'ætrɪks] *n no pl* pediatría *f*

paedophile ['piːdəʊfaɪl] *n* pederasta *m,* pedófilo *m*

pagan ['peɪgən] **I.** *n* pagano, -a *m, f* **II.** *adj* pagano, -a

paganism ['peɪgənɪzəm] *n no pl* paganismo *m*

page¹ [peɪdʒ] *n* (*in book, newspaper*) *a.* INFOR página *f;* (*single sheet of paper*) hoja *f;* **front ~** primera plana *f;* **web ~** página web

page² [peɪdʒ] **I.** *n* **1.** (*knight's attendant*) paje *m* **2.** (*hotel worker*) botones *m inv* **II.** *vt* (*over loudspeaker*) llamar por el altavoz; (*by pager*) buscar llamando por el localizador

pageant ['pædʒənt] *n* (*show, ceremony*) festividades *fpl;* **beauty ~** concurso *m* de belleza

pageantry ['pædʒəntri] *n no pl* pompa *f*

pageboy ['peɪdʒbɔɪ] *n* **1.** (*in hotel*) botones *m inv* **2.** (*at wedding*) paje *m* **3.** (*hairstyle*) peinado *m* de paje

page layout *n* disposición *f* de página **page proof** *n* prueba *f* de plana

pager ['peɪdʒəʳ, *Am:* -dʒɚ] *n* localizador *m*

pagination [ˌpædʒɪ'neɪʃən, *Am:* -ən'eɪʃən] *n no pl* INFOR, TYPO paginación *f*

pagoda [pə'gəʊdə, *Am:* -'goʊ-] *n* pagoda *f*

paid [peɪd] **I.** *pt, pp of* **pay II.** *adj* pagado, -a; **~ holiday** vacaciones *fpl* remuneradas

paid-up *adj* (*member*) que ha pagado una cuota

pail [peɪl] *n Am* cubo *m*

pain [peɪn] **I.** *n* **1.** (*physical suffering*) dolor *m;* **to be in ~** estar sufriendo; **I have a ~ in my foot** me duele el pie **2.** *pl* (*great care*) cuidados *mpl;* **to be at ~s to do sth** esmerarse en hacer algo; **to spare no ~s** no escatimar esfuerzos ►**to be a ~ in the <u>backside</u>** ser un plomo; **to be a ~ in the <u>neck</u>** *inf* ser un coñazo; **<u>on</u>** [*o* **<u>under</u>**] **~ of sth** so pena de algo **II.** *vt* doler; **it ~s me ...** me da lástima (que)...

pain barrier *n* umbral *m* de protección

pained *adj* afligido, -a; **a ~ expression** una cara de disgusto

painful ['peɪnfəl] *adj* **1.** (*causing physical pain*) doloroso, -a **2.** (*emotionally upsetting*) angustioso, -a **3.** (*embarrassing*) desagradable

painfully *adv* **1.** (*with pain*) dolorosamente **2.** (*shy, obvious*) totalmente

painkiller ['peɪnˌkɪləʳ, *Am:* 'peɪnˌkɪlɚ] *n* analgésico *m*

painless ['peɪnləs] *adj* **1.** (*not painful*) indoloro, -a **2.** *fig* (*easy*) fácil

painstaking ['peɪnzˌteɪkɪŋ] *adj* (*research*) laborioso, -a; (*search*) exhaustivo, -a; (*effort*) grande

paint [peɪnt] **I.** *n no pl* pintura *f* **II.** *vi* pintar **III.** *vt* **1.** (*room, picture*) pintar; **to ~ a picture of sth** *fig* describir algo **2.** (*apply make-up*) **to ~ oneself** maquillarse

paint box *n* caja *f* de pinturas

paintbrush ['peɪntbrʌʃ] <-es> *n* (*for pictures*) pincel *m;* (*for walls*) brocha *f*

painted ['peɪntɪd, *Am:* -t̬ɪd] *adj* pintado, -a

painter¹ ['peɪntəʳ, *Am:* -t̬ɚ] *n* **1.** (*artist*) pintor(a) *m(f)* **2.** (*decorator*) pintor(a) *m(f)* (de brocha gorda)

painter² ['peɪntəʳ, *Am:* -t̬ɚ] *n* NAUT (*rope*)

P

amarra *f*
painting *n* 1. (*painted picture*) cuadro *m* 2. *no pl* (*art*) pintura *f;* **19th century French** ~ pintura francesa del siglo XIX
paint pot *n* bote *m* de pintura **paint roller** *n* rodillo *m* **paint stripper** *n* quitapintura *m* **paintwork** *n no pl* pintura *f*
pair [peəʳ, *Am:* per] *n* 1. (*two matching items*) par *m;* **a ~ of gloves/socks** un par de guantes/calcetines; **a ~ of glasses** unas gafas; **a ~ of scissors** unas tijeras; **a ~ of trousers** un pantalón; **a ~ of tweezers** unas pinzas 2. (*group of two people, animals*) pareja *f;* **in ~s** de dos en dos; **a carriage and ~** un landó con dos caballos
◆**pair off** I. *vi* aparearse II. *vt* **to pair sb off (with sb)** emparejar a alguien (con alguien)
pairing *n no pl* apareamiento *m*
pajamas [pəˈdʒɑːməz] *npl Am* pijama *m;* **in (one's) ~** en pijama; **a pair of ~** un pijama
Pakistan [ˌpɑːkɪˈstɑːn, *Am:* ˈpækɪstæn] *n* Paquistán *m*
Pakistani [ˌpɑːkɪˈstɑːni] I. *n* paquistaní *mf* II. *adj* paquistaní
pal [pæl] *n inf* 1. (*friend*) amigo, -a *m, f* 2. (*form of address*) camarada *mf*
◆**pal up** *vi Brit, Aus* hacerse amigos; **to ~ with sb** hacerse amigo de alguien
palace [ˈpælɪs, *Am:* -əs] *n* palacio *m*
palaeography [ˌpælɪˈɒgrəfi, *Am:* ˌpeɪlɪˈɑːgrə-] *n no pl* paleografía *f*
palaeolithic [ˌpælɪəʊˈlɪθɪk, *Am:* ˌpeɪlɪoʊˈ-] I. *adj* paleolítico, -a II. *n* **the Palaeolithic** el Paleolítico
palaeontologist [ˌpælɪɒnˈtɒlədʒɪst, *Am:* ˌpeɪlɪɑːnˈtɑːlə-] *n* paleontólogo, -a *m, f*
palaeontology [ˌpælɪɒnˈtɒlədʒi, *Am:* ˌpeɪlɪɑːnˈtɑːlə-] *n no pl* paleontología *f*
palatable [ˈpælətəbl, *Am:* -ət̬ə-] *adj* 1. (*food*) sabroso, -a 2. (*suggestion*) aceptable
palate [ˈpælət] *n* paladar *m;* **to have a delicate ~** *fig* tener un paladar delicado
palatial [pəˈleɪʃl] *adj* suntuoso, -a
palaver [pəˈlɑːvəʳ, *Am:* -ˈlævɚ] *n inf* lío *m;* **what a ~!** ¡menudo follón!
pale¹ [peɪl] I. *adj* 1. (*lacking colour*) pálido, -a; **to look ~** tener mal color 2. (*not dark*) claro, -a II. *vi* palidecer; **to ~ in comparison with sth** perder en comparación con algo; **to ~ into insignificance** verse insignificante
pale² [peɪl] *n* (*fence post*) estaca *f* ►**to be beyond the ~** ser inaceptable
paleness [ˈpeɪlnɪs] *n no pl* palidez *f*
Palestine [ˈpælɪstaɪn, *Am:* -ə-] *n* Palestina *f*
Palestinian [ˌpæləˈstɪnɪən] I. *n* palestino, -a *m, f* II. *adj* palestino, -a
palette [ˈpælɪt] *n* ART paleta *f*
palisade [ˌpælɪˈseɪd, *Am:* -əˈ-] *n* 1. (*fence*) empalizada *f* 2. *pl, Am* (*cliffs*) acantilados *mpl*
pall¹ [pɔːl] *vi* perder su interés
pall² [pɔːl] *n* 1. (*cloth*) paño *m* mortuorio; **a ~ of smoke** una capa de humo 2. *Am* (*coffin*) féretro *m*
pallbearer [ˈpɔːlˌbeərəʳ, *Am:* -ˌberɚ] *n* portador(a) *m(f)* del féretro
pallet [ˈpælɪt] *n* 1. (*wooden structure*) paleta *f* 2. (*bed*) jergón *m*
palliative [ˈpælɪətɪv, *Am:* -t̬ɪv] I. *n* paliativo *m* II. *adj* paliativo, -a
pallid [ˈpælɪd] *adj* 1. (*very pale*) pálido, -a 2. (*lacking verve*) flojo, -a
pallor [ˈpæləʳ, *Am:* -ɚ] *n* palidez *f*
pally [ˈpæli] <-ier, -iest> *adj inf* afable; **to be ~ with sb** ser muy amigo de alguien
palm¹ [pɑːm] I. *n* (*of hand*) palma *f;* **to read sb's ~** leer la mano a alguien ►**to have sb in the ~ of one's hand** tener a alguien en la palma de la mano; **to have sb eating out of the ~ of one's hand** tener a alguien a su disposición II. *vt* 1. (*hide*) escamotear 2. (*steal*) robar
palm² [pɑːm] *n* (*tree*) palmera *f*
◆**palm off** *vt* **to palm sth off on sb** encajar algo a alguien; **to palm sb off with sth** apartar a alguien con algo
palmist [ˈpɑːmɪst] *n* quiromántico, -a *m, f*
palm leaf <leaves> *n* hoja *f* de palmera **Palm Sunday** *n* Domingo *m* de Ramos
palpable [ˈpælpəbl] *adj* palpable
palpitate [ˈpælpɪteɪt, *Am:* -pə-] *vi* palpitar
palpitations [ˌpælpiˈteɪʃnz, *Am:* -pəˈ-] *npl* MED palpitaciones *fpl;* **to have ~** tener vahídos
palsy [ˈpɔːlzi] *n* MED parálisis *f;* **cerebral ~** parálisis *f* cerebral
paltry [ˈpɔːltri] <-ier, -iest> *adj* insignificante; (*wage*) miserable
pampas [ˈpæmpəs, *Am:* -pəz] *n + sing/pl vb* pampa *f*
pamper [ˈpæmpəʳ, *Am:* -pɚ] *vt* mimar; **to ~ oneself** mimarse
pamphlet [ˈpæmflɪt] *n* (*leaflet*) folleto *m;* POL panfleto *m*
pan¹ [pæn] I. *n* 1. (*cooking container*) cazuela *f;* **frying ~** sartén *f* 2. (*of scales*) platillo *m* 3. (*of lavatory*) taza *f;* **to go down the ~** *fig* irse al traste II. *vt Am* (*gold*) separar en la gamella
pan² [pæn] *vi* CINE panoramizar
pan³ [pæn] *vt inf* dar un palo a; **to ~ a book/a film** dejar por los suelos un libro/una película
◆**pan out** *vi* (*develop*) resultar; **to ~ well** salir bien
panacea [ˌpænəˈsɪə] *n* panacea *f*
panache [pəˈnæʃ] *n no pl* brío *m*
Panama [ˌpænəˈmɑː, *Am:* ˈpænəmɑː] *n* Panamá *m*
Panama Canal *n* Canal *m* de Panamá **Panama City** *n* Ciudad *f* de Panamá
Panamanian [ˌpænəˈmeɪniən] I. *adj* panameño, -a II. *n* panameño, -a *m, f*
Pan-American [ˈpænəˈmerɪkən] *adj* panamericano, -a
pancake [ˈpænkeɪk] *n* crep *m,* panqueque *m AmL*
Pancake Day *n Brit, inf* martes *m inv* de car-

naval

pancreas ['pæŋkriəs] *n* páncreas *m inv*

pancreatic [ˌpæŋkri'ætɪk, *Am:* ˌpænkri'æt̬-] *adj* pancreático, -a

panda ['pændə] *n* panda *m;* **red** ~ panda rojo

panda car *n Brit* coche *m* patrulla

pandemonium [ˌpændə'məʊniəm, *Am:* -də'moʊ-] *n* **1.** (*confusion*) pandemonio *m* **2.** (*noise*) alboroto *m*

pander to ['pædəʳ tʊ, *Am:* -ɚ tə] *vt* consentir

p and p [ˌpiːən'piː] *n abbr of* **postage and packing** correo *m* y embalaje *m*

pane [peɪn] *n* cristal *m;* **window** ~ hoja *f* de cristal de una ventana

panel ['pænəl] **I.** *n* **1.** (*wooden*) tabla *f;* (*metal*) placa *f* **2.** FASHION paño *m* **3.** PUBL tabla *f* **4.** (*team*) panel *m;* (*in exam*) tribunal *m* **5.** (*instrument board*) panel *m;* **control** ~ panel de control; **instrument** ~ AUTO, AVIAT cuadro *m* de mandos **II.** *vt* poner paneles a

panel beater *n* AUTO chapista *mf* **panel discussion** *n* mesa *f* redonda **panel game** *n* TV concurso *m* por equipos

paneling *n no pl* paneles *mpl*

panelist ['pænəlɪst] *n* (*in discussion*) miembro *mf* de una mesa redonda; (*of quiz team*) miembro *mf* de un equipo (de un concurso)

panelling *n s.* **paneling**

panellist ['pænəlɪst] *n s.* **panelist**

pang [pæŋ] *n* punzada *f;* **~s of remorse** remordimientos *mpl;* **~s of guilt** sentimiento *m* de culpabilidad

panhandle ['pænhændl] **I.** *n* GEO *faja angosta de territorio de un estado que entra en el de otro* **II.** *vi* mendigar **III.** *vt* **to** ~ **money** pedir dinero

panhandler ['pænhændləʳ, *Am:* -lɚ] *n inf* pordiosero, -a *m, f*

panic ['pænɪk] **I.** *n* pánico *m;* **to get into a** ~ ponerse nervioso; **to be in a** ~ estar nervioso **II.** <-ck-> *vi* ponerse nervioso

panicky ['pænɪki] <-ier, iest> *adj* (*person*) inquieto, -a; (*feeling*) de pánico

panic-stricken ['pænɪkˌstrɪkən] *adj* preso, -a de pánico

pannier ['pæniəʳ, *Am:* -jɚ] *n* **1.** (*for bicycle*) cesto *m* **2.** (*for horse*) alforja *f*

panorama [ˌpænə'rɑːmə, *Am:* -'ræmə] *n* panorama *m*

panoramic [ˌpænə'ræmɪk] *adj* panorámico, -a; ~ **view** vista *f* panorámica

panpipes ['pænpaɪps] *npl* zampoña *f*

pan scourer *n Brit* estropajo *m*

pansy ['pænzi] <-ies> *n* **1.** (*flower*) pensamiento *m* **2.** *pej* (*homosexual*) marica *m*

pant [pænt] **I.** *vi* jadear; **to be ~ing for** [*o* **after**] **sth** suspirar de [*o* por] algo **II.** *vt* decir jadeando

pantheism ['pæntθiɪzəm] *n no pl* panteísmo *m*

pantheistic [ˌpəntθi'ɪstɪk] *adj* panteístico, -a

pantheon ['pætθiən, *Am:* -ɑːn] *n* panteón *m*

panther ['pæntθəʳ, *Am:* -θɚ] *n* **1.** (*black leopard*) pantera *f* **2.** *Am* (*puma*) puma *m*

panties ['pæntɪz, *Am:* -t̬ɪz] *npl* bragas *fpl*

panto ['pæntəʊ, *Am:* -toʊ] *n Brit, inf abbr of* **pantomime** *s.* **pantomime**

pantomime ['pæntəmaɪm, *Am:* -t̬ə-] *n* **1.** *no pl* (*mime*) pantomima *f* **2.** *Brit* (*play*) *comedia musical navideña basada en cuentos de hadas* **3.** *fig* (*farse*) farsa *f*

pantry ['pæntri] <-ies> *n* despensa *f*

pants [pænts] *npl* **1.** *Brit* (*underpants*) calzoncillos *mpl* **2.** *Am* (*trousers*) pantalones *mpl* ▸**to be caught with one's** ~ **down** *inf* ser cogido con las manos en la masa

pant(s) suit *n Am* traje *m* pantalón (de mujer)

panty-girdle *n* faja *f* pantalón **pantyhose** *npl Am, Aus* medias *fpl* **panty liner** *n* punta *f* del calzón

pap [pæp] *n no pl* **1.** (*food*) papilla *f* **2.** *inf* (*worthless entertainment*) chorrada *f*

papa [pə'pɑː] *n Am, form* papá *m*

papacy ['peɪpəsi] *n no pl* **1.** (*papal office*) pontificado *m* **2.** (*tenure of pope*) papado *m*

papal ['peɪpl] *adj* papal

paparazzo [pæpr'ætsəʊ, *Am:* pɑːpɑː'rɑːtsoʊ] <paparazzi> *n* paparazzo *m*

papaya [pə'paɪə] *n* papaya *f,* lechosa *f Col, PRico, Ven*

paper ['peɪpəʳ, *Am:* -pɚ] **I.** *n* **1.** *no pl* (*for writing*) papel *m;* **a sheet of** ~ una hoja de papel; **to put sth down on** ~ poner algo por escrito; **on** ~ sobre papel **2.** (*newspaper*) periódico *m* **3.** (*wallpaper*) papel *m* para empapelar **4.** (*official document*) documentación *f;* **~s** papeles *mpl* **5.** *no pl, Brit* (*exam*) examen *m* **6.** (*academic discourse*) conferencia *f;* **to give a** ~ dar un discurso **II.** *vt* **to** ~ **the walls** empapelar las paredes

◆**paper over** *vt fig* disimular

paperback ['peɪpəbæk, *Am:* -pɚ-] *n* libro *m* de bolsillo; **in** ~ en rústica

paperback edition *n* edición *f* de bolsillo

paper bag *n* bolsa *f* de papel **paper boy** *n* repartidor *m* de periódicos **paper chase** *n* **1.** (*race*) *carrera por el campo en la que los participantes deben seguir los papelitos que otros han dejado* **2.** (*bureaucracy*) papeleo *m* **paper clip** *n* sujetapapeles *m inv,* clip *m* **paper cup** *n* vaso *m* de papel **paper cutter** *n* guillotina *f* **paper doll** *n* muñeca *f* de papel **paper girl** *n* repartidora *f* de periódicos **paper knife** <knives> *n Brit* abrecartas *m inv* **paper mill** *n* fábrica *f* de papel **paper money** *n no pl* papel *m* moneda **paper napkin** *n* servilleta *f* de papel **paper profit** *n* beneficio *m* ficticio **paper round** *n Brit* ruta *f* del repartidor de periódicos **paper route** *n Am s.* **paper round** **paper'thin** *adj* fino, -a como el papel **paper tiger** *n pej* **he's only a** ~ no es tan bravo el león como lo pintan **paper tissue** *n* pañuelo *m* de papel **paper towel** *n* toallita *f* de papel **paper trail** *n* rastro *m* de documentos **paperweight** *n* pisapapeles *m inv* **paperwork** *n no pl* trabajo *m* administrativo, papeleo *m inf*

papery ['peɪpəri] *adj* de papel

papier-mâché [ˌpæpɪeɪ'mæʃeɪ, *Am:* ˌpeɪpɚmə'ʃeɪ] *n no pl* cartón *m* piedra

papist ['peɪpɪst] **I.** *n pej* papista *mf* **II.** *adj pej* papista

papoose [pə'puːs, *Am:* pæp'uːs] *n* mochila *f* portabebés

pappy¹ ['pæpi] <-ier, -iest> *adj* **1.** (*stodgy*) como papilla **2.** *pej, inf* (*of poor quality*) mediocre

pappy² ['pæpi] *n Am* papá *m*

paprika ['pæprɪkə, *Am:* pæp'riː-] *n no pl* pimentón *m* dulce

Pap smear *n,* **Pap test** *n Am, Aus* MED Papanicolau *m*

Papua New Guinea [ˌpæpuənjuː'gɪni, *Am:* ˌpæpjuənuː'gɪni] *n* Papua-Nueva Guinea *f*

papyrus [pə'paɪərəs, *Am:* -'paɪrəs] <-es *o* -ri> *n* papiro *m*

par [pɑːʳ, *Am:* pɑːr] *n no pl* **1.** (*standard*) **to be on a ~ with sb** estar al mismo nivel que alguien; **below ~** por debajo de la media; **to feel below ~** no sentirse del todo bien; **not to be up to ~** no llegar a la media **2.** SPORTS (*golfing term*) par *m* **3.** FIN valor *m* nominal; **at/above/below ~** a/sobre/bajo la par ►**to be ~ for the course** *inf* ser lo que uno se esperaba

par. *abbr of* **paragraph** párrafo *m*

para ['pærə, *Am:* 'perə] *n* **1.** *Brit, inf* MIL *abbr of* **paratrooper** paracaidista *m* **2.** (*text*) *abbr of* **paragraph** párrafo *m*

parable ['pærəbl, *Am:* 'per-] *n* parábola *f*

parabola [pə'ræbələ] *n* parábola *f*

parabolic [ˌpærə'bɒlɪk, *Am:* ˌperə'bɑːlɪk] *adj* parabólico, -a

paracetamol® [pærə'siːtəmɒl, *Am:* perə'sitəmɑːl] *n no pl* paracetamol *m*

parachute ['pærəʃuːt, *Am:* 'per-] **I.** *n* paracaídas *m inv;* **~ pack** equipo *m* de paracaídas **II.** *vi* lanzarse en paracaídas **III.** *vt* lanzar en paracaídas

parachute jump *n* salto *m* en paracaídas

parachuting *n no pl* paracaidismo *m*

parachutist ['pærəʃuːtɪst, *Am:* 'perəʃuːt̬ɪst] *n* paracaidista *mf*

parade [pə'reɪd] **I.** *n* **1.** (*procession*) *a.* MIL desfile *m;* (*inspection*) revista *f* de tropas **2.** *fig* (*series*) retahíla *f* **II.** *vi* **1.** (*walk in procession*) *a.* MIL desfilar **2.** (*show off*) **to ~ about** jactarse; **to ~ up and down in one's best clothes** pasearse de un lado a otro con sus mejores ropas **III.** *vt* **1.** (*exhibit*) lucir **2.** *fig* (*show off*) ostentar; **to ~ one's knowledge** hacer alarde de erudición

parade ground *n* MIL plaza *f* de armas

paradigm ['pærədaɪm, *Am:* 'per-] *n* paradigma *m*

paradigmatic [ˌpærədɪg'mætɪk, *Am:* ˌperədɪg'mæt̬-] *adj* paradigmático, -a

paradigm shift *n* cambio *m* de paradigma

paradise ['pærədaɪs, *Am:* 'per-] *n* paraíso *m*

paradisiac(al) [ˌpærə'dɪsɪæk(l), *Am:* ˌperə'-] *adj* paradisíaco, -a

paradox ['pærədɒks, *Am:* 'perədɑːks] <-es> *n* paradoja *f*

paradoxical [ˌpærə'dɒksɪkəl, *Am:* ˌperə'dɑːk-] *adj* paradójico, -a

paradoxically *adv* paradójicamente

paraffin ['pærəfɪn, *Am:* 'per-] *n no pl* **1.** *Brit* (*fuel*) queroseno *m* **2.** (*wax*) parafina *f*

paraffin heater *n Brit* estufa *f* de queroseno

paraffin lamp *n Brit* quinqué *m* de petróleo

paraffin wax *n no pl* parafina *f*

paragliding ['pærəˌglaɪdɪŋ, *Am:* 'per-] *n no pl* parapente *m*

paragon ['pærəgən, *Am:* 'perəgɑːn] *n* arquetipo *m;* **a ~ of democracy** un modelo de democracia; **a ~ of virtue** *iron* un ejemplo de virtud

paragraph ['pærəgrɑːf, *Am:* 'perəgræf] *n* **1.** LING párrafo *m* **2.** PUBL (*short article*) breve *m*

Paraguay ['pærəgwaɪ, *Am:* 'perəgweɪ] *n* Paraguay *m*

Paraguayan [ˌpærə'gwaɪən, *Am:* ˌperə'gweɪ-] **I.** *adj* paraguayo, -a **II.** *n* paraguayo, -a *m, f*

parakeet ['pærəkiːt, *Am:* 'per-] *n* periquito *m*

parallel ['pærəlel, *Am:* 'per-] **I.** *adj* **1.** MAT paralelo, -a; **~ to sth** paralelo a algo; **~ experiments** experimentos *mpl* paralelos **2.** ELEC **in ~** en paralelo **II.** *n* **1.** MAT paralela *f* **2.** GEO paralelo *m* **3.** (*similarity*) similitud *f* **4.** **to draw a ~** (*make a comparison*) establecer un paralelismo; **to have no ~** no tener igual; **without ~** sin igual **III.** *vt* ser paralelo a

parallel bars *npl* SPORTS barras *fpl* paralelas

parallel line *n* línea *f* paralela

paralyse ['pærəlaɪz, *Am:* 'per-] *vt Brit, Aus s.* **paralyze**

paralysed *adj Brit, Aus s.* **paralyzed**

paralysis [pə'ræləsɪs] <-ses> *n* parálisis *f inv*

paralytic [ˌpærə'lɪtɪk, *Am:* ˌperə'lɪt̬-] **I.** *adj* **1.** MED paralítico, -a **2.** *inf* (*drunk*) **to be ~** estar como una cuba **II.** *n* paralítico, -a *m, f*

paralyze ['pærəlaɪz, *Am:* 'per-] *vt* **1.** (*render immobile, powerless*) paralizar **2.** (*stupefy*) dejar estupefacto, -a; **to be ~d with fear** estar paralizado de miedo

paralyzed *adj* **1.** (*incapable of movement*) paralizado, -a **2.** *fig* (*incapable of doing anything*) inmovilizado, -a

paramedic [ˌpærə'medɪk, *Am:* ˌper-] *n* paramédico, -a *m, f*

parameter [pə'ræmɪtəʳ, *Am:* -ət̬ɚ] *n* parámetro *m*

paramilitary [ˌpærə'mɪlɪtri, *Am:* ˌperə'mɪləter-] **I.** *adj* paramilitar **II.** *n* paramilitar *mf*

paramount ['pærəmaʊnt, *Am:* 'per-] *adj form* supremo, -a; **of ~ importance** de extrema importancia

paranoia [ˌpærə'nɔɪə, *Am:* ˌper-] *n* paranoia

f

paranoiac [ˌpærə'nɔɪæk, *Am:* ˌper-] **I.** *adj* paranoico, -a **II.** *n* paranoico, -a *m, f*

paranoid ['pærənɔɪd, *Am:* 'perənɔɪd] *adj* **1.** PSYCH paranoico, -a **2.** (*very worried*) **to be ~ about sth** estar obsesionado por algo

paranoid schizophrenia *n* esquizofrenia *f* paranoide

paranormal [pærə'nɔːməl, *Am:* 'perə'nɔːr-] **I.** *adj* paranormal; ~ **powers** poderes *mpl* paranormales **II.** *n no pl* **the** ~ lo paranormal

parapet ['pærəpɪt, *Am:* 'perəpet] *n* parapeto *m*

paraphernalia [ˌpærəfə'neɪlɪə, *Am:* ˌperəfɚ'neɪljə] *npl* parafernalia *f*

paraphrase ['pærəfreɪz, *Am:* 'per-] **I.** *vt* **1.** (*reformulate*) parafrasear **2.** (*humourously imitate*) parodiar **II.** *n* (*reformulation*) paráfrasis *f inv;* **she gave us a quick ~ of what had been said** nos hizo un rápido resumen de lo que se había dicho

paraplegia [ˌpærə'pliːdʒə, *Am:* ˌper-] *n no pl* paraplejía *f*

paraplegic [ˌpærə'pliːdʒɪk, *Am:* ˌper-] **I.** *adj* parapléjico, -a **II.** *n* parapléjico, -a *m, f*

parapsychology [ˌpærəsaɪ'kɒlədʒi, *Am:* ˌperəsaɪ'kɑːlə-] *n no pl* parapsicología *f*

parasite ['pærəsaɪt, *Am:* 'per-] *n a. fig* parásito *m*

parasitic [ˌpærə'sɪtɪk, *Am:* ˌperə'sɪt̬-] *adj a. fig* parásito, -a; ~ **disease** enfermedad *f* parasitaria

parasol ['pærəsɒl, *Am:* 'perəsɔːl] *n* sombrilla *f*

parathyroid (gland) [ˌpærə'θaɪərɔɪd (glænd), *Am:* ˌperə'θaɪ-] *n* paratiroides *f inv*

paratrooper ['pærətruːpəʳ, *Am:* 'perətruːpɚ] *n* paracaidista *mf*

paratroops ['pærətruːps, *Am:* 'per-] *npl* paracaidistas *mpl*

paratyphoid [ˌpærə'taɪfɔɪd, *Am:* ˌper-] *n* MED paratifoidea *f*

parboil ['pɑːbɔɪl, *Am:* 'pɑːr-] *vt* sancochar

parcel ['pɑːsəl, *Am:* 'pɑːr-] **I.** *n* (*packet*) paquete *m;* (*of land*) terreno *m* **II.** <*Brit:* -ll-, *Am:* -l-> *vt* dividir; (*land*) parcelar

◆**parcel out** *vt* repartir en porciones; (*land*) parcelar

◆**parcel up** *vt* empaquetar

parcel bomb *n Brit* paquete-bomba *m* **parcel office** *n* oficina *f* de paquetes postales **parcel post** *n* servicio *m* de paquetes postales

parch [pɑːtʃ, *Am:* pɑːrtʃ] *vt* agostar

parched *adj* **1.** (*dried-out*) seco, -a; **to be ~ with heat** estar agostado por el calor **2.** *fig, inf* (*very thirsty*) **to be ~** estar muerto de sed

parchment ['pɑːtʃmənt, *Am:* 'pɑːrtʃ-] *n* pergamino *m*

pardon ['pɑːdn, *Am:* 'pɑːr-] **I.** *vt* (*forgive*) disculpar; (*prisoner*) indultar; **to ~ (sb) sth** perdonar algo (a alguien); **to ~ sb for sth** perdonar a alguien por algo; ~ **me interrupting** siento interrumpir; **if you'll ~ the expression** si me permite la expresión; (**I beg your**) **~?** (*said to request repetition*) ¿cómo dice?; **~ me!** (*expressing indignation*) ¡usted perdone!; **~ me for breathing!** ¡no hace falta que te pongas así! **II.** *n* indulto *m*

pardonable ['pɑːdnəbl, *Am:* 'pɑːr-] *adj* perdonable

pare [peəʳ, *Am:* per] *vt* **1.** (*fruit*) mondar **2.** (*fingernails*) **to ~ one's nails** cortarse las uñas **3.** *fig* (*costs*) recortar

◆**pare down** *vt* reducir; **to pare sth down to the minimum** reducir algo al mínimo

◆**pare off** *vt* pelar

parent ['peərənt, *Am:* 'perənt] *n* (*father*) padre *m;* (*mother*) madre *f;* **~s** padres *mpl*

parentage ['peərəntɪdʒ, *Am:* 'perənt̬ɪdʒ] *n no pl* familia *f*

parental [pə'rentəl] *adj* de los padres

parental authority *n* patria *f* potestad **parental consent** *n* consentimiento *m* de los padres

parent company <-ies> *n* sociedad *f* matriz

parenthesis [pə'rentθəsɪs] <-ses> *n* **1.** TYPO paréntesis *m inv;* **in parentheses** en paréntesis **2.** (*remark*) inciso *m*

parenthetical [ˌpærən'θetɪkəl, *Am:* ˌperən'θet̬-] *adj form* parentético, -a; ~ **remark** nota *f* explicativa

parenthetically *adv* a modo explicativo

parenthood ['peərənthʊd, *Am:* 'perənt-] *n no pl* (*of man*) paternidad *f;* (*of woman*) maternidad *f*

parenting ['peərntɪŋ, *Am:* 'per-] *n no pl* cuidado *m* de los hijos; ~ **skills** habilidades *fpl* en el cuidado de los hijos

parentless ['peərəntlɪs, *Am:* 'perənt-] *adj* huérfano, -a

Parents and Citizens *n Aus,* **Parent-Teacher Association** *n Brit, Am, Can* asociación *f* de padres y maestros

pariah [pə'raɪə] *n* paria *mf*

paring ['peərɪŋ, *Am:* 'perɪŋ] *n* mondadura *f*

paring knife <knives> *n* cuchillo *m* de mondar

Paris ['pærɪs, *Am:* 'per-] *n* París *m*

parish ['pærɪʃ, *Am:* 'per-] <-es> *n* **1.** REL parroquia *f* **2.** *Brit* POL distrito *m*

parish church <-es> *n* iglesia *f* parroquial **parish clerk** *n* sacristán *m* **parish council** *n* consejo *m* parroquial

parishioner [pə'rɪʃənəʳ, *Am:* -ɚ] *n* feligrés, -esa *m, f*

parish priest *n* párroco *m* **parish-pump politics** *n Brit* parroquialismo *m* **parish register** *n* registro *m* parroquial

Parisian [pə'rɪziən, *Am:* -'rɪʒ-] *n* parisino, -a *m, f*

parity ['pærəti, *Am:* 'perət̬i] <-ies> *n* **1.** (*equality*) igualdad *f* **2.** FIN paridad *f*

park [pɑːk, *Am:* pɑːrk] **I.** *n* parque *m;* (*sur-*

rounding country house) jardines *mpl* **II.** *vt* **1.** (*leave vehicle*) aparcar, estacionar *AmL;* **to ~ a satellite** AVIAT estacionar un satélite **2.** *pej, fig* **to ~ oneself somewhere** arrellanarse en algún sitio; **he ~ed himself in front of the TV** se arrepanchingó delante del televisor **III.** *vi* aparcar, estacionar *AmL*

parka ['pɑːkə, *Am:* 'pɑːr-] *n* parka *f*

park bench *n* banco *m* de un parque

parked *adj* aparcado, -a, estacionado, -a *AmL*

parking *n no pl* aparcamiento *m,* estacionamiento *m AmL*

parking area *n* zona *f* de estacionamiento **parking attendant** *n* guarda *mf* del parking **parking bay** *n* zona *f* de aparcamiento **parking brake** *n Am* freno *m* de mano **parking disc** *n* disco *m* de estacionamiento **parking fine** *n* multa *f* de estacionamiento **parking garage** *n* parking *m* **parking lights** *n Am, Aus* luces *fpl* de estacionamiento **parking lot** *n Am* aparcamiento *m* **parking meter** *n* parquímetro *m* **parking offence** *n* infracción *f* de estacionamiento **parking offender** *n* infractor(a) *m(f)* que paga la multa de estacionamiento **parking permit** *n* permiso *m* de aparcamiento **parking place** *n,* **parking space** *n* aparcamiento *m,* estacionamiento *m AmL* **parking ticket** *n* multa *f* por aparcamiento indebido

Parkinson's disease ['pɑːkɪŋsənzdɪˌziːz, *Am:* 'pɑːr-] *n no pl* enfermedad *f* de Parkinson

Parkinson's law *n no pl, iron* ley *f* de Parkinson

park keeper *n Brit* guardabosque *mf,* guarda *mf* forestal

parkland ['pɑːklænd, *Am:* 'pɑːrk-] *n no pl* zona *f* verde

parkway ['pɑːkweɪ, *Am:* 'pɑːrk-] *n Am, Aus* avenida *f* ajardinada

parky ['pɑːki, *Am:* 'pɑːr-] <-ier, -iest> *adj Brit, inf* (*weather*) glacial

Parl. *abbr of* **Parliament** parlamento *m*

parlance ['pɑːlənts, *Am:* 'pɑːr-] *n no pl, form* lenguaje *m;* **in common ~** en lenguaje corriente; **as it is known in common ~** como se conoce popularmente; **in medical ~** en jerga médica

parley ['pɑːli, *Am:* 'pɑːrleɪ] **I.** *n* parlamento *m* **II.** *vi* parlamentar

parliament ['pɑːləmənt, *Am:* 'pɑːrlə-] *n* (*institution*) parlamento *m;* (*time period*) legislatura *f*

> Las dos **Houses of Parliament** se encuentran en el **Palace of Westminster** de Londres. La cámara baja, elegida por el pueblo, y de la que proceden la mayoría de los ministros, se llama **House of Commons**. Sus diputados reciben el nombre de **members of parliament** o **MPs**. La cámara alta, **House of Lords**, sólo puede aprobar determinadas leyes. Los diputados, **peers of the realm**, se pueden dividir en tres grupos. Los que tienen un escaño en la cámara alta por razón de su trabajo, bien por ser jueces, los **law lords**, o bien por ser obispos de la iglesia anglicana, la **Church of England**. En segundo lugar los que tienen un escaño vitalicio, los **life peers**, y en tercer lugar los que han heredado el escaño junto con su título nobiliario. Un comité de jueces de la **House of Lords** constituye el máximo tribunal de justicia del Reino Unido.

parliamentarian [ˌpɑːləmən'teəriən, *Am:* ˌpɑːrləmən'teri-] *n* (*MP*) diputado, -a *m, f*

parliamentary [ˌpɑːlə'mentəri, *Am:* ˌpɑːrlə'mentɚ-] *adj* parlamentario, -a

parliamentary candidate *n* candidato, -a *m, f* parlamentario, -a **parliamentary chamber** *n* cámara *f* de los diputados **parliamentary debate** *n* debate *m* parlamentario **parliamentary democracy** <-ies> *n* democracia *f* parlamentaria **parliamentary election** *n* elecciones *fpl* parlamentarias **parliamentary government** *n* gobierno *m* parlamentario

parlor *n Am,* **parlour** ['pɑːləʳ, *Am:* 'pɑːrlɚ] *n Brit* **1.** (*shop*) **beauty ~** salón *m* de belleza; **ice-cream ~** heladería *f;* **pizza ~** pizzería *f* **2.** (*room in house*) salón *m*

parlour car *n Am* RAIL coche-salón *m*

parlour game *n* juego *m* de salón

parlourmaid *n* HIST camarera *f*

parlous ['pɑːləs, *Am:* 'pɑːr-] *adj* alarmante; **to be in a ~ state** estar en un estado deplorable

Parmesan (cheese) ['pɑːmɪˌzæn (tʃiːz), *Am:* 'pɑːrməzɑːn (tʃiːz)] *n no pl* queso *m* parmesano

parochial [pə'rəʊkiəl, *Am:* -'roʊ-] *adj* **1.** REL parroquial **2.** (*narrow-minded*) de miras estrechas

parochialism *n no pl, pej* provincialismo *m*

parochial school *n Am* escuela *f* religiosa

parodist ['pærədɪst, *Am:* 'per-] *n* parodista *mf*

parody ['pærədi, *Am:* 'per-] **I.** <-ies> *n* **1.** (*humourous imitation*) parodia *f* **2.** *pej* (*travesty*) burda imitación *f* **II.** <-ie-> *vt* parodiar

parole [pə'rəʊl, *Am:* -'roʊl] **I.** *n no pl* LAW libertad *f* condicional; **to be out on ~** estar en libertad condicional **II.** *vt* **to be ~d** ser puesto en libertad condicional

paroxysm ['pærəksɪzəm, *Am:* 'per-] *n* paroxismo *m;* **~ of joy** exaltación *f* de júbilo; **~ of rage** paroxismo de rabia

parquet ['pɑːkeɪ, *Am:* pɑːr'keɪ] *n no pl* parqué *m;* **~ floor** suelo *m* de parqué

parricide ['pærɪsaɪd, *Am:* 'perə-] *n form* **1.** *no pl* (*murder*) parricidio *m* **2.** (*murderer*) parricida *mf*

parrot ['pærət, *Am:* 'per-] **I.** *n* loro *m,* papagayo *m* ►**to be** **sick as a** ~ *Brit, iron* estar muerto de rabia **II.** *vt pej* repetir como un loro
parrot-fashion *adv* **to repeat sth** ~ repetir algo como un loro
parry ['pæri, *Am:* 'per-] <-ie-> *vt* **1.**(*blow*) desviar **2.**(*question*) eludir
parse [pɑːz, *Am:* pɑːrs] *vt* **to** ~ **a sentence** analizar una frase sintácticamente
Parsee *adj,* **Parsi** [pɑː'siː, *Am:* 'pɑːrsiː] *adj* parsi
parsimonious [ˌpɑːsɪ'məʊniəs, *Am:* ˌpɑːrsə'moʊ-] *adj form* parco, -a; **to be** ~ **with the truth** decir medias verdades
parsimoniously *adv pej, form* escasamente
parsimoniousness *n,* **parsimony** ['pɑːsɪməni, *Am:* 'pɑːrsəmoʊ-] *n no pl, pej, form* tacañería *f*
parsley ['pɑːsli, *Am:* 'pɑːr-] *n no pl* perejil *m*
parsnip ['pɑːsnɪp, *Am:* 'pɑːr-] *n* chirivía *f*
parson ['pɑːsən, *Am:* 'pɑːr-] *n* cura *m;* (*protestant*) pastor *m*
parsonage ['pɑːsənɪdʒ, *Am:* 'pɑːr-] *n* rectoría *f*
parson's nose *n* rabadilla *f*
part [pɑːt, *Am:* pɑːrt] **I.** *n* **1.**(*not the whole*) parte *f;* **the film was good in** ~**s** la película tenía trozos buenos; ~ **of the body** parte del cuerpo; ~ **of the family** parte de la familia; **the easy/hard** ~ lo fácil/lo difícil; **essential/important/integral** ~ parte esencial/importante/integrante; **in** ~ en parte; **in large** ~ en gran parte; **for the most** ~ en la mayor parte **2.**(*component*) componente *m;* **spare** ~**s** piezas *fpl* sueltas **3.**(*area, region*) zona *f;* **in these** ~**s** *inf* en estas zonas **4.**(*measure*) parte *f;* **mix one** ~ **of the medicine with three** ~**s of water** mezclar una parte de la medicina con tres partes de agua **5.**(*role, involvement*) papel *m;* **to want no** ~ **in sth** no querer tener nada que ver en algo; **to do one's** ~ cumplir con su obligación **6.**(*episode in media serial*) capítulo *m* **7.**(*character in film*) papel *m;* **to play the** ~ **of the King** desempeñar el papel del rey **8.** *Am* (*parting of hair*) raya *f* **9.**(*score of particular musician*) parte *f* ►**to be** ~ **and parcel of sth** ser parte esencial de algo; **for my** ~ por mi parte; **to take sb's** ~ tomar partido por alguien; **on sb's** ~ de parte de alguien; **it was a mistake on Julia's** ~ fue un error por parte de Julia **II.** *adv* parcialmente; **to be** ~ **African** ser en parte africano **III.** *vt* **1.**(*detach, split*) separar; **to** ~ **sb from sb/sth** separar a alguien de alguien/algo; **to** ~ **company** tomar direcciones distintas **2.**(*divide*) partir, dividir; **to** ~ **sth in two** partir algo en dos; **to** ~ **sb's hair** hacer la raya a alguien **IV.** *vi* **1.**(*separate*) separarse **2.**(*say goodbye*) despedirse **3.**(*curtains*) correr; **to** ~ **from sb** *form* separarse de alguien; **to** ~ **with one's cash** *inf* desprenderse de su dinero
partake [pɑː'teɪk, *Am:* pɑːr-] *vi irr* **1.** *form* **to** ~ **in sth** tomar parte en algo **2.** *iron* **to** ~ **of sth** (*eat*) comer algo; (*drink*) beber algo
parted *adj* **1.**(*slightly opened*) ~ **lips** labios *mpl* entreabiertos **2.**(*unwillingly separated*) **to be** ~ **from sb** estar separado de alguien
part exchange *n Brit* parte *f* del pago; **to accept/give sth in** ~ aceptar/dar algo como parte del importe
parthenogenesis ['pɑːθənəʊ'dʒenɪsɪs, *Am:* ˌpɑːrθənoʊ'dʒenə-] *n no pl* partenogénesis *f*
partial ['pɑːʃəl, *Am:* 'pɑːr-] *adj* **1.**(*incomplete*) parcial; ~ **recovery** recuperación *f* parcial **2.**(*biased*) parcial **3.**(*fond*) **she is** ~ **to ...** tiene debilidad por...
partial eclipse *n* eclipse *m* parcial
partiality [ˌpɑːʃi'æləti, *Am:* ˌpɑːrʃi'æləṭi] *n no pl* **1.**(*bias*) parcialidad *f* **2.**(*liking*) afición *f*
partially *adv* **1.**(*partly*) parcialmente, en parte; ~ **cooked** medio hecho **2.**(*with bias*) con parcialidad
partially sighted *adj* casi ciego, -a
participant [pɑː'tɪsɪpənt, *Am:* pɑːr'tɪsə-] *n* participante *mf;* (*in contest*) concursante *mf*
participate [pɑː'tɪsɪpeɪt, *Am:* pɑːr'tɪsə-] *vi* participar; (*in contest*) concursar
participation [pɑːˌtɪsɪ'peɪʃən, *Am:* pɑːrˌtɪsə'-] *n no pl* participación *f*
participator [pɑː'tɪsɪpeɪtəʳ, *Am:* pɑːr'tɪsəpeɪṭɚ] *n* participante *mf*
participatory [pɑː'tɪsɪpətəri, *Am:* pɑːr'tɪsəpəˌtɔːr-] *adj* participativo, -a
participatory democracy <-ies> *n* democracia *f* participativa
participle ['pɑːtɪsɪpl, *Am:* 'pɑːrtɪsɪ-] *n* participio *m*
particle ['pɑːtɪkl, *Am:* 'pɑːrṭə-] *n* PHYS, LING partícula *f*
particle accelerator *n* acelerador *m* de partículas **particle physics** *n* física *f* de partículas
particular [pə'tɪkjələʳ, *Am:* pɚ'tɪkjəlɚ] **I.** *adj* **1.**(*special*) particular, especial; (*specific*) concreto, -a, específico, -a; **to be of** ~ **concern to sb** ser de particular interés para alguien; **no** ~ **reason** ninguna razón en concreto; **in** ~ en especial; **nothing in** ~ nada en particular **2.**(*fussy, meticulous*) quisquilloso, -a; (*demanding*) exigente; **he is very** ~ **about his appearance** es muy maniático con su imagen **II.** *n* detalle *m;* **the** ~ las especificidades
particularity [pətɪkjə'lærəti, *Am:* pɚ'tɪkjə'lə-] *n form* particularidad *f*
particularize [pə'tɪkjʊləraɪz, *Am:* pɚ'-] *vt* especificar
particularly [pə'tɪkjʊləli, *Am:* pɚ'tɪkjəlɚ-] *adv* especialmente, particularmente; **I didn't** ~ **want to go but I had to** de hecho no tenía muchas ganas de ir, pero no tuve más remedio
parting ['pɑːtɪŋ, *Am:* 'pɑːrṭɪŋ] **I.** *n* **1.**(*separation*) separación *f* **2.**(*saying goodbye*) despedida *f* **3.** *Brit, Aus* (*in hair*) raya *f;* **centre/side** ~ raya en medio/a un lado **II.** *adj* de des-

P

pedida; ~ **words** palabras *fpl* de despedida
parting shot *n* última palabra *f* (antes de irse)
partisan [ˌpɑːtɪ'zæn, *Am:* 'pɑːrt̬ɪzən] **I.** *adj* partidista; ~ **spirit** partidismo *m* **II.** *n* **1.** (*supporter*) partidario, -a *m, f* **2.** MIL partisano, -a *m, f*
partisanship *n no pl* partidismo *m*
partition [pɑː'tɪʃən, *Am:* pɑːr'-] **I.** *n* **1.** (*wall*) tabique *m* **2.** *no pl* (*of country*) división *f* **3.** INFOR partición *f* **II.** *vt* **1.** (*room*) dividir con un tabique; **to ~ sth off** tabicar algo **2.** (*country*) dividir
partly ['pɑːtli, *Am:* 'pɑːrt-] *adv* en parte, en cierto modo
partner ['pɑːtnə^r, *Am:* 'pɑːrtnɚ] **I.** *n* **1.** COM socio, -a *m, f* **2.** (*accomplice*) ~ **in crime** cómplice *mf* **3.** (*in relationship*) pareja *f* **4.** (*in tennis, dancing*) pareja *f* **II.** *vt* **to ~ sb** asociarse con alguien; **to be ~ed by sb** ir acompañado de alguien
partnership ['pɑːtnəʃɪp, *Am:* 'pɑːrtnɚ-] *n* **1.** (*association*) asociación *f* **2.** COM sociedad *f* (comanditaria); (*of lawyers*) bufete *m;* **to go into ~ with sb** asociarse con alguien
partnership agreement *n* contrato *m* de sociedad
part of speech *n* LING parte *f* de oración
part owner *n* copropietario, -a *m, f* **part ownership** *n* copropiedad *f* **part payment** *n* pago *m* parcial
partridge ['pɑːtrɪdʒ, *Am:* 'pɑːr-] *n* perdiz *f*
part song *n* canción *f* a voces
part-time [ˌpɑːt'taɪm, *Am:* ˌpɑːrt-] **I.** *adj* a tiempo parcial; ~ **worker** trabajador(a) *m(f)* a tiempo parcial **II.** *adv* **to work ~** trabajar a tiempo parcial **part-time job** *n* empleo *m* a tiempo parcial
part-timer *n* (*worker*) empleado, -a *m, f* a tiempo parcial; (*student*) estudiante *mf* a tiempo parcial
part-time staff *n no pl* personal *m* a tiempo parcial **part-time student** *n* estudiante *mf* a tiempo parcial
party ['pɑːti, *Am:* 'pɑːrt̬i] **I.** *n* <-ies> **1.** (*social gathering*) fiesta *f;* **to have a ~** hacer una fiesta **2.** + *sing/pl vb* POL partido *m;* **opposition/ruling ~** partido en la oposición/en el poder **3.** + *sing/pl vb* (*group*) grupo *m;* **coach ~** grupo en autocar; **school ~** grupo de escolares **4.** *a.* LAW parte *f;* **the guilty ~** la parte inculpada; **to be a ~ to sth** ser partícipe en algo; **to be ~ to an arrangement** ser parte implicada en un acuerdo; **to be a ~ to a crime** ser cómplice de un delito **5.** *Am, inf* (*person*) individuo *m* **II.** <-ie-> *vi* ir de fiesta
party conference *n Brit* congreso *m* del partido **party congress** *n Am* congreso *m* del partido **party headquarters** *n* sede *f* del partido **party leader** *n* líder *mf* del partido **party line** *n* **1.** TEL línea *f* de varios abonados **2.** POL política *f* del partido; **to follow the ~** seguir la política del partido **party politics** *npl* política *f* de partidos **party popper** *n Brit* aguafiestas *mf inv*
parvenu ['pɑːvənjuː, *Am:* 'pɑːrvənuː] *n pej, form* advenedizo, -a *m, f*
pass [pɑːs, *Am:* pæs] **I.** <-es> *n* **1.** (*mountain road*) paso *m;* **mountain ~** puerto *m* de montaña **2.** (*in rugby, soccer*) pase *m* **3.** *no pl* (*sexual advances*) **to make a ~ (at sb)** insinuarse (a alguien) **4.** *Brit* (*in exam*) aprobado *m* **5.** (*authorisation*) pase *m;* (*for festival, concert*) entrada *f* **6.** (*public transport*) abono *m* **7.** *Am* UNIV, SCHOOL (*permit to leave class*) permiso *m* ►**to come to a pretty ~** llegar a una situación crítica; **things have come to a pretty ~** las cosas se han puesto feas **II.** *vt* **1.** (*go past*) pasar; (*cross*) cruzar **2.** (*exceed*) sobrepasar; **to ~ a limit** sobrepasar un límite; **to ~ all belief** ser increíble **3.** (*hand to*) **to ~ sth to sb** pasar algo a alguien **4.** (*in rugby, soccer*) pasar **5.** (*exam*) aprobar **6.** (*avoid boredom*) **to ~ the time** pasar el rato **7.** POL (*officially approve*) aprobar; **to ~ sb fit** dar a alguien de alta **8.** (*utter, pronounce*) pronunciar; **to ~ a comment** hacer un comentario; **to ~ sentence** LAW dictar sentencia **9.** MED excretar; **to ~ urine** orinar **III.** *vi* **1.** (*move by*) pasar; **we often ~ed on the stairs** a menudo nos cruzábamos en la escalera; **to ~ unnoticed** pasar desapercibido **2.** (*come to an end*) desaparecer; **it'll soon ~** se olvidará pronto **3.** (*in rugby, soccer*) pasar la pelota **4.** (*in exam*) aprobar **5.** (*elapse: time*) transcurrir **6.** (*not know answer*) pasar; **~!** ¡paso!
◆**pass away** *vi* (*die*) fallecer
◆**pass by I.** *vi* **1.** (*elapse*) pasar **2.** (*go past*) pasar de largo **II.** *vt* pasar algo por alto
◆**pass down** *vt* (*knowledge, beliefs*) transmitir; (*clothes, possessions*) pasar a
◆**pass off I.** *vt* (*treat as unimportant*) disimular **II.** *vi* **1.** (*take place successfully*) tener lugar **2.** (*fade away, wear off*) desaparecer
◆**pass on I.** *vi* **1.** (*continue moving*) seguir su camino; **to ~ to a different topic** pasar a un tema diferente **2.** (*die*) fallecer **II.** *vt* **1.** BIO (*transmit*) contagiar **2.** (*information, advice*) pasar **3.** (*refer*) **to pass sb on to sb** poner a alguien con alguien
◆**pass out I.** *vi* **1.** (*faint*) perder el conocimiento **2.** *Brit, Aus* (*graduate from military college*) graduarse **II.** *vt Am* (*distribute, hand out*) repartir
◆**pass over** *vt* pasar por alto
◆**pass through** *vt* pasar por
◆**pass up** *vt* desperdiciar
passable ['pɑːsəbl, *Am:* 'pæsə-] *adj* **1.** (*unobstructed*) transitable **2.** (*average, fair*) aceptable
passage ['pæsɪdʒ] *n* **1.** (*corridor*) pasillo *m;* (*path*) pasadizo *m* **2.** LIT, MUS pasaje *m* **3.** (*onward journey*) viaje *m* **4.** (*sea voyage*) travesía *f;* **bird of ~** ave *f* de paso; **to work one's ~** pagarse el pasaje trabajando a bordo **5. with the ~ of time** con el transcurso del

tiempo

passageway ['pæsɪdʒweɪ] *n* pasillo *m*

passbook ['pɑːsbʊk, *Am:* 'pæs-] *n* libreta *f* de ahorros

passenger ['pæsəndʒəʳ, *Am:* -əndʒɚ] *n* pasajero, -a *m, f*

passenger list *n* lista *f* de pasajeros

passer-by [ˌpɑːsə'baɪ, *Am:* ˌpæsɚ'-] <passers-by> *n* transeúnte *mf*

passing I. *adj* 1. (*going past*) que pasa 2. (*brief: fad, infatuation*) pasajero, -a; (*glance*) rápido, -a; (*remark*) de pasada; ~ **fancy** capricho *m* II. *n no pl* (*death*) fallecimiento *m* ►**in** ~ al pasar

passing out *n Brit, Aus* MIL, UNIV graduación *f*

passing-out ceremony *n*, **passing-out parade** *n Brit, Aus* MIL, UNIV ceremonia *f* de graduación

passing place *n* apartadero *m*

passion ['pæʃən] *n* (*emotion*) pasión *f;* (*anger*) cólera *f;* **crime of** ~ crimen *m* pasional

passionate ['pæʃənət, *Am:* -ənɪt] *adj* (*emotional*) apasionado, -a; (*angry*) colérico, -a

passionflower ['pæʃənˌflaʊəʳ, *Am:* -ˌflaʊɚ] *n* pasionaria *f*

passion fruit *n* fruta *f* de la pasión

passionless ['pæʃənləs] *adj pej* sin pasión

passion play *n* drama *m* de La Pasión

Passion Week *n* Semana *f* Santa

passive ['pæsɪv] I. *n no pl* LING voz *f* pasiva II. *adj* pasivo, -a

passiveness *n*, **passivity** [pæs'ɪvəti, *Am:* pæs'ɪvət̬i] *n no pl* pasividad *f*

passkey ['pɑːskiː, *Am:* 'pæs-] *n* llave *f* maestra

pass mark *n Brit, Aus* nota *f* mínima para aprobar

Passover ['pɑːsəʊvəʳ, *Am:* 'pæsˌoʊvɚ] *n no pl* Pascua *f* judía

passport ['pɑːspɔːt, *Am:* 'pæspɔːrt] *n* pasaporte *m*

passport control *n*, **passport inspection** *n* control *m* de pasaportes **passport holder** *n* titular *mf* del pasaporte

password ['pɑːswɜːd, *Am:* 'pæswɜːrd] *n* INFOR contraseña *f*

past [pɑːst, *Am:* pæst] I. *n* pasado *m;* **to be a thing of the** ~ ser una cosa del pasado; **sb with a** ~ alguien con historia; **simple** ~ pasado *m* (simple); **to write in the** ~ escribir en pasado II. *adj* pasado, -a; **the** ~ **week** la última semana; **in times** ~ en otros tiempos; **that's** ~ **history** eso pertenece a la historia III. *prep* 1. (*temporal*) después de; **ten/quarter/half** ~ **two** dos y diez/cuarto/media; **it's** ~ **2** son las 2 pasadas 2. (*spatial*) después de 3. (*after*) **I'm** ~ **that** *iron* yo he superado eso 4. (*beyond*) **to be** ~ **thirty** pasar de los treinta; ~ **belief** increíble; ~ **description** indescriptible; **I'm** ~ **caring** ya me trae sin cuidado IV. *adv* por delante; **to go/run/march** ~ (**sb**) ir/correr/pasar por delante (de alguien)

pasta ['pæstə, *Am:* 'pɑːstə] *n no pl* pasta *f*

past continuous *n* pretérito *m* continuo

paste [peɪst] I. *n no pl* 1. (*glue*) engrudo *m*, pegamento *m* 2. (*sticky mixture*) pasta *f;* **meat/fish** ~ paté *m* de carne/pescado; **tomato** ~ concentrado *m* de tomate II. *vt* 1. *a.* INFOR (*stick*) pegar 2. *inf* (*beat*) dar una paliza a

pasteboard ['peɪstbɔːd, *Am:* -bɔːrd] *n no pl* cartón *m*

pastel ['pæstəl, *Am:* pæ'stel] I. *n* 1. ART (*drawing material*) pastel *m;* (*type of drawing*) pintura *f* al pastel 2. (*colour*) tono *m* pastel II. *adj* pastel

paste-up ['peɪstʌp] *n* maqueta *f*

pasteurization [ˌpæstʃəraɪ'zeɪʃən, *Am:* ˌpæstʃɚɪ'-] *n no pl* pasteurización *f*

pasteurize ['pæstʃəraɪz] *vt* pasteurizar

pastime ['pɑːstaɪm, *Am:* 'pæs-] *n* pasatiempo *m*

pastor ['pɑːstəʳ, *Am:* 'pæstɚ] *n* pastor *m*

pastoral ['pɑːstərəl, *Am:* 'pæs-] *adj* 1. REL pastoral 2. LIT, ART pastoril; ~ **scene** escena *f* bucólica

past participle *n* participio *m* pasado **past perfect** *n* pretérito *m* perfecto

pastry ['peɪstri] <-ies> *n* 1. *no pl* (*dough*) masa *f;* ~ **brush** pincel *m* de repostería 2. (*cake*) pastel *m*

pastry chef *n*, **pastry cook** *n* pastelero, -a *m, f*

past tense *n* tiempo *m* pasado

pasture ['pɑːstʃəʳ, *Am:* 'pæstʃɚ] I. *n* 1. AGR pasto *m* 2. *fig* **new** ~**s** nuevos horizontes *mpl;* **to go to** ~**s new** pasar a mejor vida; **to put sb out to** ~ *inf* jubilar a alguien II. *vt* apacentar III. *vi* pacer

pasture land *n* prado *m*

pasty[1] ['pæsti] <-ies> *n* empanada *f;* **Cornish** ~ *empanada de patata, cebolla y carne*

pasty[2] ['peɪsti] <-ier, -iest> *adj* (*texture*) pastoso, -a; (*complexion*) pálido, -a

pat[1] [pæt] I. <-tt-> *vt* (*touch softly*) dar palmaditas a; **to** ~ **sb on the back** *fig* felicitar a alguien II. *n* 1. (*tap*) palmadita *f* 2. (*of butter*) porción *f*

pat[2] [pæt] *pej* I. *adj* (*answer*) fácil II. *adv* **off** ~ *Brit, Aus,* **down** ~ *Am* de memoria

patch [pætʃ] I. *n* 1. (*of land*) parcela *f* de tierra; (*of fog*) zona *f;* **vegetable** ~ huerto *m* 2. *Brit, inf* (*phase*) fase *f* 3. (*of salesman, criminal*) territorio *m* 4. (*piece of cloth*) parche *m;* (*for mending clothes*) remiendo *m;* (*knee*) rodillera *f;* (*elbow*) codera *f* ►**to be not a** ~ **on sb/sth** *Brit, Aus, inf* no tener ni punto de comparación con alguien/algo II. *vt* (*mend: hole, clothes*) remendar

◆**patch up** *vt* 1. (*mend*) hacer un arreglo provisional a 2. *fig* (*friendship*) arreglar; **to patch things up** hacer las paces

patchwork ['pætʃwɜːk, *Am:* -wɜːrk] I. *n no pl* 1. (*needlework*) patchwork *m* 2. *fig* (*mix*) mosaico *m* II. *adj* (*sewed from patches*) de retales; **a** ~ **quilt** un edredón de retazos

patchy ['pætʃi] <-ier, -iest> *adj* (*performance, novel*) desigual; (*weather*) variable; (*results*) irregular

pâté ['pæteɪ, *Am:* pɑː'teɪ] *n* paté *m*

patella [pə'telə] <-e> *n* rótula *f*

patent ['peɪtənt, *Am:* 'pætənt] **I.** *n* LAW patente *f*; **to take out a ~ on sth** patentar algo **II.** *adj* **1.** LAW patentado, -a **2.** *form* (*unconcealed*) evidente **3.** (*handbag, jacket*) de charol **III.** *vt* LAW patentar

patented ['peɪtəntɪd, *Am:* 'pætəntɪd] *adj* LAW patentado, -a

patentee [ˌpeɪtən'tiː, *Am:* ˌpætən'tiː] *n* titular *mf* de una patente

patent leather *n* charol *m*

patent medicine *n* específico *m* **patent office** *n* oficina *f* de patentes

paternal [pə'tɜːnəl, *Am:* -'tɜːr-] *adj* paternal; ~ **grandfather** abuelo paterno; ~ **grandmother** abuela paterna

paternalism [pə'tɜːnəlɪzəm, *Am:* -'tɜːr-] *n no pl* paternalismo *m*

paternalistic [pəˌtɜːnəl'ɪstɪk, *Am:* -ˌtɜːr-] *adj pej* paternalista

paternity [pə'tɜːnəti, *Am:* -'tɜːrnət̬i] *n no pl, form* paternidad *f*

paternity leave *n* permiso *m* de paternidad **paternity suit** *n* litigio *m* por paternidad

path [pɑːθ, *Am:* pæθ] *n* **1.** (*footway, trail*) camino *m*; **to clear a ~** abrir un sendero; **to follow a ~** seguir una senda **2.** (*way*) trayecto *m*; (*of bullet*) trayectoria *f*; **to cross sb's ~** tropezar con alguien **3.** INFOR ruta *f*, localización *f*

pathetic [pə'θetɪk, *Am:* -'θet̬-] *adj* **1.** (*arousing sympathy*) conmovedor(a); **a ~ sight** una escena lastimosa **2.** *pej* (*arousing scorn*) patético, -a; **a ~ performance** una pésima actuación

pathfinder ['pɑːθfaɪndəʳ, *Am:* 'pæθˌfaɪndɚ] *n* explorador(a) *m(f)*; **to be a ~** ser un pionero

pathological [ˌpæθə'lɒdʒɪkl, *Am:* -'lɑːdʒɪk-] *adj inf* patológico, -a

pathologist [pə'θɒlədʒɪst, *Am:* -'θɑːlə-] *n* patólogo, -a *m, f*

pathology [pə'θɒlədʒi, *Am:* -'θɑːlə-] *n no pl* MED patología *f*

pathos ['peɪθɒs, *Am:* -θɑːs] *n* patetismo *m*

pathway ['pɑːθweɪ, *Am:* 'pæθ-] *n* camino *m*, sendero *m*

patience ['peɪʃns] *n no pl* **1.** paciencia *f*; **to have the ~ of a saint** tener más paciencia que un santo **2.** *Brit, Aus* GAMES solitario *m*; **to play ~** hacer solitarios

patient ['peɪʃnt] **I.** *adj* paciente; **to be ~ with sb** tener paciencia con alguien; **just be ~!** ¡ten paciencia! **II.** *n* MED paciente *mf*

patina ['pætɪnə, *Am:* -ənə] *n no pl* pátina *f*

patio ['pætiəʊ, *Am:* 'pæt̬ɪoʊ] <-s> *n* **1.** (*paved area*) *área pavimentada contigua a una casa;* ~ **door** puerta *f* que da al patio **2.** (*courtyard*) patio *m*

patriarch ['peɪtrɪɑːk, *Am:* -ɑːrk] *n* patriarca *m*

patriarchal [ˌpeɪtrɪ'ɑːkl, *Am:* -'ɑːr-] *adj* patriarcal

patriarchy ['peɪtrɪɑːki, *Am:* -ɑːrki] <-ies> *n* patriarcado *m*

patrician [pə'trɪʃən] **I.** *n* patricio *mf* **II.** *adj* patricio, -a

patricide ['pætrɪsaɪd, *Am:* 'pætrə-] *n* (*person*) parricida *mf*; (*crime*) parricidio *m*

patriot ['pætrɪət, 'peɪtrɪət, *Am:* 'peɪ-] *n* patriota *mf*

patriotic [ˌpætrɪ'ɒtɪk, ˌpeɪtrɪ'ɒtɪk, *Am:* ˌpeɪtrɪ'ɑːtɪk] *adj* patriótico, -a

patriotism ['pætrɪətɪzəm, 'peɪtrɪətɪzəm, *Am:* 'peɪtrɪ-] *n no pl* patriotismo *m*

patrol [pə'trəʊl, *Am:* -'troʊl] **I.** <-ll-> *vi* patrullar **II.** <-ll-> *vt* patrullar por **III.** *n* patrulla *f*; **to be on ~** patrullar

patrol car *n* coche *m* patrulla **patrol duty** *n* servicio *m* de patrulla **patrolman** *n* **1.** *Am* policía *m* **2.** *Brit* mecánico *m* del servicio de ayuda en carretera **patrol wagon** *n Am* coche *m* celular

patron ['peɪtrən] *n* **1.** (*benefactor*) patrocinador(a) *m(f)*; (*arts*) mecenas *mf* **2.** REL patron(a) *m(f)*

patronage ['pætrənɪdʒ, *Am:* 'peɪtrən-] *n no pl* **1.** (*support*) patrocinio *m*; ART mecenazgo *m* **2.** ECON clientela *f*

patroness ['peɪtrənɪs] *n* **1.** (*benefactor*) patrocinadora *f*; ART mecenas *f* **2.** REL patrona *f*

patronize ['pætrənaɪz, *Am:* 'peɪtrən-] *vt* **1.** *form* (*be customer*) ser cliente de **2.** (*treat condescendingly*) tratar con condescendencia

patronizing ['pætrənaɪzɪŋ, *Am:* 'peɪtrən-] *adj* condescendiente

> Inglaterra, Irlanda, Escocia y Gales tienen cada una sus propios **patron saints** (santos patrones). La festividad de **St George** de Inglaterra se celebra el 23 de abril; **St Patrick** de Irlanda el 17 de marzo; **St Andrew** de Escocia el 30 de noviembre y **St David** de Gales el 1 de marzo.

patter ['pætəʳ, *Am:* 'pæt̬ɚ] **I.** *n no pl* **1.** (*clever talk*) labia *f* **2.** (*tapping: of rain*) golpeteo *m*; (*of feet*) pasitos *mpl* **II.** *vi* (*make sound*) golpetear; (*walk lightly*) corretear; **to ~ about** andar con pasos ligeros

patter merchant *n inf* charlatán, -ana *m, f*

pattern ['pætən, *Am:* 'pæt̬ɚn] **I.** *n* **1.** (*model*) modelo *m* **2.** ART (*design, motif*) diseño *m*; **floral ~** motivo *m* floral **3.** FASHION (*paper guide*) patrón *m*; ECON (*sample*) muestra *f* **II.** *vt* (*emulate, follow, imitate*) seguir el modelo

pattern book *n* muestrario *m*

patterned *adj* estampado, -a

paunch [pɔːntʃ, *Am:* pɑːntʃ] *n* panza *f*

paunchy <-ier, -iest> *adj* panzudo, -a

pauper ['pɔːpəʳ, *Am:* 'pɑːpɚ] *n* indigente

mf; ~'s **grave** fosa *f* común

pause [pɔːz, *Am:* pɑːz] **I.** *n* pausa *f* ▶**to give sb ~ for thought** *form* dar que pensar a alguien **II.** *vi* hacer una pausa

pave [peɪv] *vt* pavimentar; **to ~ the way for sth** *fig* preparar el terreno para algo

pavement ['peɪvmənt] *n* **1.** *Brit* (*beside road*) acera *f*, vereda *f AmL*, banqueta *f Guat, Méx* **2.** *Am, Aus* (*highway covering*) calzada *f*

pavement artist *n* artista *mf* de la calle

pavilion [pə'vɪljən] *n* pabellón *m*

paving *n no pl* **1.** (*space*) pavimento *m* **2.** (*material*) losas *fpl*

paving stone *n Brit* losa *f*

paw [pɔː, *Am:* pɑː] **I.** *n* pata *f*; (*of cat*) garra *f*; (*of lion*) zarpa *f*; *iron, inf* (*of person*) manaza *f* **II.** *vt* tocar con la pata; **to ~ sb** *pej* manosear a alguien **III.** *vi* **to ~ at sth** tocar algo con la pata

pawn[1] [pɔːn, *Am:* pɑːn] *n* GAMES peón *m*; *fig* títere *m*

pawn[2] [pɔːn, *Am:* pɑːn] **I.** *vt* empeñar **II.** *n* **to be in ~** estar en prenda

pawnbroker ['pɔːnˌbrəʊkəʳ, *Am:* 'pɑːnˌbroʊkɚ] *n* prestamista *mf* (sobre prenda), agenciero, -a *m, f Chile*; **the ~'s** la casa de empeños

pawnbroking *n* empeño *m*

pawn shop *n*, **pawnbroker's shop** *n* casa *f* de empeños

pay [peɪ] **I.** *n* paga *f*; **to be in the ~ of sb** estar a sueldo de alguien **II.** <paid, paid> *vt* **1.** (*redeem with money*) pagar; **to ~ cash** pagar al contado; **to ~ one's debts** liquidar las deudas de uno **2.** (*be worthwhile for*) ser provechoso, -a **3.** (*give, render*) **to ~ attention** (**to sth**) prestar atención (a algo); **to ~ a call** (**on sb**), **to ~** (**sb**) **a call** hacer una visita (a alguien); **to ~ sb a compliment** hacer un cumplido a alguien; **to ~ homage to sb** rendir homenaje a alguien; **to ~ respects to sb** presentar los respetos a alguien **III.** <paid, paid> *vi* **1.** (*settle, recompense*) pagar **2.** (*benefit*) ser provechoso, -a

◆**pay back** *vt* devolver; **I'll pay you back!** ¡me las vas a pagar!; **to pay sb back in the same coin** pagar a alguien con la misma moneda

◆**pay in** *vt* ingresar

◆**pay off I.** *vt* **1.** (*debt*) liquidar **2.** *inf* (*bribe*) sobornar **II.** *vi fig* merecer la pena

◆**pay out I.** *vt* **1.** (*money*) desembolsar **2.** SPORTS **to ~ the rope** dar cuerda **II.** *vi* pagar

◆**pay over** *vt Brit* entregar

◆**pay up** *vi* pagar (lo que se debe)

payable ['peɪəbl] *adj* pagadero, -a; **to make a cheque ~ to sb** extender un cheque a favor de alguien

Pay As You Earn *n no pl, Brit: sistema de recaudación de impuestos por medio de retenciones sobre el salario*

pay award *n* adjudicación *f* de aumento de salario

payback clause ['peɪbæk 'klɔːz] *n* cláusula *f* de restitución **payback period** *n* período *m* de restitución

paycheck *n Am*, **paycheque** ['peɪtʃek] *n Brit* cheque *m* de salario **pay claim** *n Brit, Aus* reivindicación *f* salarial **payday** *n no pl* día *m* de pago **pay deal** *n* acuerdo *m* salarial **pay desk** *n* caja *f* **pay differential** *n* diferencia *f* de salarios

PAYE [ˌpiːeɪwar'iː] *n no pl, Brit abbr of* **Pay As You Earn**

payee [per'iː] *n* beneficiario, -a *m, f*

payer ['peɪəʳ, *Am:* -ɚ] *n* pagador(a) *m(f)*; **bad ~** moroso, -a *m, f*

pay freeze *n* congelación *f* salarial **pay hike** *n Am* aumento *m* de sueldo

paying *adj* rentable

payload ['peɪləʊd, *Am:* -loʊd] *n* **1.** AVIAT carga *f* útil **2.** MIL carga *f* explosiva

paymaster ['peɪmɑːstəʳ, *Am:* -mæstɚ] *n* pagador(a) *m(f)*

payment ['peɪmənt] *n* **1.** (*sum of cash*) pago *m*; **to make a down ~** pagar en efectivo **2.** (*installment*) plazo *m*; (*reward*) recompensa *f*

pay negotiations *npl* negociaciones *fpl* salariales

payoff ['peɪɒf, *Am:* -ɑːf] *n* **1.** (*payment*) pago *m* **2.** *inf* (*bribe*) soborno *m*, coima *f CSur*, mordida *f Méx*; **to make a ~ to sb** sobornar a alguien **3.** *inf* (*positive result*) beneficios *mpl*; (*on bet*) ganacias *fpl* **4.** *Am, inf* (*climax*) clímax *m* **5.** (*debt payment*) liquidación *f*

pay-office *n* caja *f*

payout *n* FIN desembolso *m*

pay packet *n Brit, Aus* sobre *m* de paga **pay-per-view** (**television**) *n no pl* televisión *f* de pago **payphone** *n* teléfono *m* público **pay raise** *n Am*, **pay rise** *n Brit, Aus* aumento *m* de sueldo **payroll** *n* nómina *f*; **~ tax** impuesto *m* sobre salarios **pay round** *n* serie *f* de negociaciones salariales **pay settlement** *n* acuerdo *m* salarial **payslip** *n* nómina *f* **pay station** *n Am* teléfono *m* público **pay talks** *npl* negociaciones *fpl* salariales **pay TV** *n* televisión *f* de pago; **to subscribe to ~** abonarse a la televisión de pago

PBS [ˌpiːbiː'es] *n no pl, Am abbr of* **Public Broadcasting System** *organismo americano de producción audiovisual*

PC [ˌpiː'siː] **I.** *n* **1.** *abbr of* **personal computer** PC *m* **2.** *Brit abbr of* **Police Constable** agente *mf* de policía **II.** *adj abbr of* **politically correct** políticamente correcto, -a

p.c. *abbr of* **per cent** p.c.

PE [ˌpiː'iː] *abbr of* **physical education** educación *f* física

pea [piː] *n* guisante *m*, arveja *f Col, Chile* ▶**to be like two ~s in a pod** ser como dos gotas de agua

peace [piːs] *n no pl* **1.** (*absence of war*) paz *f* **2.** (*social order*) orden *m* público; **to keep the ~** mantener el orden; **to make ~** hacer las paces; **to make one's ~ with sb** hacer las

P

paces con alguien **3.** (*tranquillity*) tranquilidad *f;* ~ **of mind** tranquilidad de ánimo; **to be at ~ about one's situation** estar satisfecho de la propia situación; ~ **and quiet** paz y tranquilidad; **to be at** ~ estar en paz; **to give sb no** ~ no dejar a alguien en paz; **to leave sb in** ~ dejar a alguien en paz **4.** REL ~ **be with you** que la paz sea con vosotros; (**may he**) **rest in** ~ que en paz descanse ►**to be at ~ with the world** estar satisfecho de la vida; **to hold one's** ~ guardar silencio; **speak now or forever hold your** ~ que hable ahora o que calle para siempre

peaceable ['pi:səbl] *adj* pacífico, -a

peace activist *n* pacifista *mf* **peace conference** *n* conferencia *f* de paz **peace enforcement** *n* imposición *f* de la paz

peaceful ['pi:sfəl] *adj* **1.** (*calm, quiet: animal*) manso, -a; (*place, person*) tranquilo, -a **2.** (*non-violent*) pacífico, -a

peace initiative *n* iniciativa *f* de paz

peacekeeping ['pi:sˌki:pɪŋ] *n no pl* mantenimiento *m* de la paz

peacekeeping forces *npl* fuerzas *fpl* de paz

peace-loving *adj* amante de la paz

peacemaker ['pi:sˌmeɪkəʳ, *Am:* -kɚ] *n* (*between countries*) pacificador(a) *m(f);* (*between friends*) conciliador(a) *m(f)*

peacemaking ['pi:sˌmeɪkɪŋ] **I.** *n* (*between countries*) pacificación *f;* (*between friends*) conciliación *f* **II.** *adj* (*between countries*) de pacificación; (*between friends*) de conciliación

peace march <-es> *n* marcha *f* por la paz **peace movement** *n* movimiento *m* pacifista **peace negotiations** *npl* negociaciones *fpl* de paz **peace offer** *n* oferta *f* de paz **peace offering** *n* prenda *f* de paz **peace pipe** *n* pipa *f* de la paz **peace settlement** *n* acuerdo *m* de paz **peace sign** *n* señal *f* de paz **peacetime I.** *n no pl* tiempo *m* de paz **II.** *adj* de tiempo de paz **peace treaty** <-ies> *n* tratado *m* de paz

peach [pi:tʃ] **I.** <-es> *n* **1.** (*fruit*) melocotón *m,* durazno *m Arg, Chile;* ~ **orchard** melocotonar *m* **2.** (*tree*) melocotonero *m,* duraznero *m Arg, Chile* **3.** *fig, inf* (*nice person*) monada *f;* **a ~ of a day** un día encantador **II.** *adj* de color melocotón

peach tree *n* melocotonero *m,* duraznero *m Arg, Chile*

peacock ['pi:kɒk, *Am:* -kɑ:k] *n* **1.** ZOOL pavo *m* real **2.** (*vain person*) engreído, -a *m, f* ►**as proud as a** ~ orgulloso como un pavo real; **to strut like a** ~ pavonearse

pea green I. *n* verde *m* claro **II.** *adj* verde claro

peahen ['pi:hen] *n* pava *f* real

peak [pi:k] **I.** *n* **1.** (*mountain top*) cima *f;* **beat the egg whites until they are stiff enough to form firm ~s** bata las claras de huevo a punto de nieve **2.** (*highest point, summit*) punto *m* máximo; **to be at the ~ of one's career/power** estar en la cúspide de su carrera/poder **3.** *Brit* (*of cap*) visera *f* **II.** *vi* (*career*) alcanzar el apogeo; (*athlete*) alcanzar el mejor rendimiento; (*skill*) alcanzar el nivel más alto; (*figures, rates, production*) alcanzar el máximo **III.** *adj* máximo, -a

peak capacity <-ies> *n* capacidad *f* óptima **peak demand** *n* demanda *f* máxima

peaked *adj Am* (*tired or sick*) enfermizo, -a; (*pale*) pálido, -a

peaked hat *n* gorra *f* con visera

peak hours *npl* horas *fpl* punta **peak level** *n no pl* nivel *m* máximo **peak load** *n* **1.** (*full capacity*) capacidad *f* máxima **2.** ELEC carga *f* máxima **peak period** *n* período *m* de máxima actividad **peak power** *no pl n* rendimiento *m* máximo **peak season** *n* temporada *f* alta **peak speed** *n* velocidad *f* máxima

peaky ['pi:ki] <-ier, -iest> *adj Brit* paliducho, -a

peal [pi:l] **I.** *n* **1.** (*of bell*) repique *m;* (*thunder*) trueno *m;* **a ~ of laughter** una carcajada **2.** (*set*) ~ **of bells** carillón *m* **II.** *vi* (*thunderstorm*) tronar; (*bell*) repiquetear

◆**peal out** *vi* resonar; (*thunder*) tronar

peanut ['pi:nʌt] *n* **1.** (*nut*) cacahuete *m,* maní *m AmL,* cacahuate *m Méx* **2.** *inf* (*very little*) **to pay ~s** pagar una miseria

peanut butter *n no pl* mantequilla *f* de cacahuete

pear [peəʳ, *Am:* per] *n* **1.** (*fruit*) pera *f* **2.** (*tree*) peral *m*

pearl [pɜ:l, *Am:* pɜ:rl] *n* **1.** perla *f;* **to wear ~s** llevar perlas; **a string of ~s** un collar de perlas **2.** *fig* (*a drop*) gota *f;* ~ **of dew** gota de rocío; **~s of sweat** gotas de sudor **3.** *fig* (*a fine example*) joya *f;* **a ~ of a …** una joya de… ►**to cast one's ~s before the swine** *prov* echarles margaritas a los cerdos *prov*

pearl barley *n no pl* cebada *f* perlada **pearl button** *n* botón *m* de perla **pearl diver** *n,* **pearl fisher** *n* pescador(a) *m(f)* de perlas **pearl-fishing I.** *n no pl* pesca *f* de perlas **II.** *adj* de pesca de perlas

pearly ['pɜ:li, *Am:* 'pɜ:r-] <-ier, -iest> *adj* perlino, -a

pear tree *n* peral *m*

peasant ['pezənt] **I.** *n* **1.** (*small farmer*) campesino, -a *m, f* **2.** *pej, inf* (*uncouth person*) paleto, -a *m, f* **II.** *adj* campesino, -a, rural

peasantry ['pezəntri] *n no pl* campesinado *m*

pea-souper [ˌpi:'su:pəʳ, *Am:* 'pi:ˌsu:pɚ] *n* **1.** *Brit, fig, inf* (*fog*) niebla *f* espesa **2.** *Can, pej* (*French Canadian*) canadiense *mf* de habla francesa

peat [pi:t] *n no pl* turba *f*

peat bog *n* turbera *f*

pebble ['pebl] *n* guijarro *m*

pebbly ['pebli] <-ier- iest> *adj* guijarroso, -a

pecan [pɪ'kæn, *Am:* pɪ'kɑ:n] *n* pacana *f*

peccadillo [ˌpekə'dɪləʊ, *Am:* -oʊ] <-(oe)s>

n desliz *m*
peck [pek] **I.** *n* **1.** (*of bird*) picotazo *m* **2.** (*quick kiss*) besito *m* **II.** *vt* **1.** (*bird*) picar, picotear **2.** (*kiss quickly*) besar **III.** *vi* **1.** picar; **eat properly, don't ~!** ¡come bien, no picotees! **2.** (*nag*) **to ~ at sb** fastidiar a alguien
pecker ['pekəʳ, *Am:* -ɚ] *n vulg* (*penis*) polla *f*, verga *f AmL*, pija *f Arg, Urug* ▸**to keep one's ~ up** *Brit, inf* no desanimarse
pecking order *n* orden *m* de picoteo de las gallinas; *fig* jerarquía *f*
peckish ['pekɪʃ] *adj* **1.** *Brit, Aus* hambriento, -a **2.** *Am* (*irritable*) irritable
pectin ['pektɪn] *n no pl* pectina *f*
pectoral ['pektərəl] *adj* pectoral
peculiar [pɪ'kjuːlɪəʳ, *Am:* -'kjuːljɚ] *adj* **1.** (*strange*) extraño, -a, raro, -a **2.** (*sick, nauseous*) **to feel a little ~** no sentirse del todo bien; **to have a ~ feeling** tener malestar **3.** (*belonging to*) propio, -a; **to be ~ to sb** ser propio de alguien
peculiarity [pɪˌkjuːlɪ'ærəti, *Am:* -'erət̬i] <-ies> *n* **1.** (*strangeness*) singularidad *f* **2.** (*strange habit*) rareza *f* **3.** (*idiosyncrasy*) peculiaridad *f*
peculiarly [pɪ'kjuːlɪəli, *Am:* -'kjuːljɚ-] *adv* **1.** (*strangely*) de forma rara **2.** (*especially*) particularmente **3.** (*belonging to*) típicamente
pecuniary [pɪ'kjuːnɪəri, *Am:* -eri] *adj form* **1.** (*motives*) pecuniario, -a **2.** (*problems*) financiero, -a
pedagogic [ˌpedə'gɒdʒɪk, *Am:* -'gɑː-] *adj* pedagógico, -a
pedagogue ['pedəgɒg, *Am:* -gɑːg] *n* pedagogo, -a *m, f*
pedagogy ['pedəgɒdʒi, *Am:* -gɑːdʒi] *n no pl* pedagogía *f*
pedal ['pedəl] **I.** *n* pedal *m* **II.** <*Brit:* -ll-, *Am:* -l-> *vt* **to ~ a bicycle** impulsar una bicicleta pedaleando **III.** <*Brit:* -ll-, *Am:* -l-> *vi* pedalear
pedal bin *n* cubo *m* de la basura (con pedal)
pedal boat *n*, **pedalo** ['pedələʊ, *Am:* -oʊ] *n* patín *m* a pedal
pedant ['pedənt] *n pej* pedante *mf*
pedantic [pɪ'dæntɪk, *Am:* pəd'æn-] *adj pej* pedante
pedantry ['pedəntri] <-ies> *n pej* pedantería *f*
peddle ['pedl] *vt pej* **1.** (*sell*) vender (de puerta en puerta); **to ~ drugs** traficar con drogas **2.** (*idea, lies*) difundir
peddler ['pedləʳ, *Am:* 'pedlɚ] *n Am s.* **pedlar**
pederast ['pedəræst] *n* pederasta *m*
pederasty ['pedəræsti] *n no pl* pederastia *f*
pedestal ['pedɪstəl] *n* pedestal *m* ▸**to knock sb off their ~** bajar los humos a alguien; **to put sb on a ~** poner a alguien en un pedestal
pedestrian [pɪ'destriən, *Am:* pə'-] **I.** *n* peatón, -ona *m, f* **II.** *adj* **1.** (*for walkers*) de peatones **2.** *form* (*uninteresting*) pedestre
pedestrianise *vt Aus, Brit,* **pedestrianize** [pɪ'destriənaɪz, *Am:* pə'-] *vt* convertir en zona peatonal
pedestrian mall *n Am, Aus,* **pedestrian precinct** *n Brit* zona *f* peatonal
pediatric [ˌpiːdi'ætrɪk] *adj Am s.* **paediatric**
pediatrician [ˌpiːdiə'trɪʃən] *n Am s.* **paediatrician**
pedicure ['pedɪkjʊəʳ, *Am:* -kjʊr] *n* pedicura *f*
pedicurist ['pedɪkjʊərɪst] *n* pedicuro, -a *m, f*
pedigree ['pedɪgriː] **I.** *n* **1.** (*genealogy: of animal*) pedigrí *m;* (*of person*) genealogía *f* **2.** (*background*) expediente *m* **II.** *adj* (*animal*) de raza
pedlar ['pedləʳ, *Am:* -lɚ] *n Brit, Aus* **1.** (*travelling salesperson*) vendedor(a) *m(f)* ambulante **2.** (*drug dealer*) traficante *mf* de drogas
pedometer [pɪ'dɒmɪtəʳ, *Am:* pɪ'dɑːmət̬ɚ] *n* podómetro *m*
pedophile ['piːdəʊfaɪl] *n Am s.* **paedophile**
pee [piː] *inf* **I.** *n no pl* pis *m;* **to have a ~** hacer pis **II.** *vi* hacer pis; **to ~ in one's pants** mearse encima **III.** *vt* **to ~ oneself** mearse encima
peek [piːk] **I.** *n* mirada *f* rápida; **to have a ~ at sth** echar una mirada furtiva a algo **II.** *vi* mirar furtivamente; **to ~ at sth** echar una mirada furtiva a algo
◆**peek out** *vi* asomar; (*person*) asomarse
peel [piːl] **I.** *n* (*skin*) piel *f;* (*of fruit*) cáscara *f;* (*peladuras*) mondas *fpl* **II.** *vt* (*fruit*) pelar; (*paper*) despegar; (*bark*) descortezar; (*skin*) levantar **III.** *vi* (*person*) pelarse; (*paint*) desconcharse; (*layer of paper*) despegarse; (*bark*) descortezarse
◆**peel off I.** *vt* (*paper*) despegar; (*paint*) quitar; (*bark*) descortezar; (*clothes*) quitarse **II.** *vi* **1.** (*come off: paper*) despegarse; (*paint*) desconcharse; (*skin*) pelarse **2.** (*veer away: car, motorbike*) desviarse
peeler ['piːləʳ, *Am:* -lɚ] *n* pelapatatas *m inv*
peelings ['piːlɪŋz] *npl* (*of fruit*) peladuras *fpl*
peep¹ [piːp] **I.** *n* (*sound: of bird*) pío *m;* (*of car horn*) pitido *m;* **not to give a ~** no decir ni pío **II.** *vi* piar
peep² [piːp] **I.** *n* (*furtive look*) vistazo *m;* **to have a ~ at sth** echar una ojeada a algo **II.** *vi* **1.** (*look quickly*) mirar rápidamente, vichar *Arg;* **to ~ at sth** echar un vistazo a algo; **to ~ through sth** atisbar a través de algo **2.** (*appear, come partly out*) asomar **III.** *vt* asomar
◆**peep out** *vi* asomar
peephole ['piːphəʊl, *Am:* -hoʊl] *n* mirilla *f*
peeping tom *n* mirón, -ona *m, f*
peepshow ['piːpʃəʊ, *Am:* -ʃoʊ] *n espectáculo de striptease que funciona con monedas*
peer¹ [pɪəʳ, *Am:* pɪr] *vi* **to ~ at sth** escudriñar algo; **to ~ into the distance** fijar la mirada en la distancia; **to ~ over one's glasses** atisbar

por encima de sus gafas

peer² [pɪəʳ, *Am:* pɪr] *n* **1.** (*equal*) igual *mf,* par *mf;* **to have no ~s** no tener par **2.** LAW **to be tried by a jury of one's ~s** ser juzgado por los iguales de uno **3.** *Brit* (*lord*) noble *mf*

peerage ['pɪərɪdʒ, *Am:* 'pɪrɪdʒ] *n* **1.** *no pl, Brit* (*aristocracy*) nobleza *f* **2.** (*title*) **to be given a ~** recibir un título nobiliario **3.** (*book*) guía *f* nobiliaria

peeress ['pɪəres, *Am:* 'pɪrɪs] <-es> *n Brit* paresa *f*

peerless ['pɪəlɪs, *Am:* 'pɪr-] *adj form* sin par, incomparable

peeve [piːv] *vt inf* fastidiar

peeved [piːvd] *adj inf* mosqueado, -a; **to be ~ at sb for sth** estar mosqueado con alguien por algo

peevish ['piːvɪʃ] *adj* malhumorado, -a

peewit ['piːwɪt] *n* avefría *f*

peg [peg] **I.** *n* **1.** (*for coat*) colgador *m* **2.** (*in furniture, for tent*) estaquilla *f;* (*in mountaineering, on guitar*) clavija *f;* **clothes ~** pinza *f* de tender la ropa, broche *m* de tender la ropa *Arg;* **to buy clothes off the ~** comprarse ropa de confección ►**to take sb down a ~ or two** bajar los humos a alguien; **to feel like a square ~ in a round hole** sentirse fuera de lugar; **to use sth as a ~ to hang sth on** usar algo de apoyo para algo **II.** <-gg-> *vt* **1.** (*hold down with pegs*) enclavijar **2.** ECON fijar; **to ~ prices** congelar precios **3.** (*link*) **to ~ sth to sth** vincular algo a algo **4.** *Am* (*throw*) lanzar **5.** *fig* (*guess correctly*) acertar

◆**peg away** *vi inf* darle duro; **to ~ at sth** persistir en algo

◆**peg out I.** *vt* **1.** (*hang out*) tender; **to ~ clothes** tender la ropa **2.** (*mark*) señalar con estacas **II.** *vi Aus, Brit* **1.** *fig, inf* (*die*) palmarla **2.** (*stop working: car, machine*) quedarse, tronarse *Méx*

peg-leg *n inf* pata *f* de palo

pejorative [pɪ'dʒɒrətɪv, *Am:* -'dʒɔːrət̬ɪv] *form* **I.** *adj* despectivo, -a **II.** *n* palabra *f* despectiva

Pekinese [ˌpiːkɪ'niːz, *Am:* -kə'niːz] **I.** *n* **1.** (*person*) pequinés, -esa *m, f* **2.** (*dog*) pequinés *m* **II.** *adj* pequinés, -esa

pelican ['pelɪkən] *n* pelícano *m*

pellet ['pelɪt] *n* (*small, hard ball*) bolita *f;* (*animal excrement*) cagadita *f inf;* (*gunshot*) perdigón *m*

pellet gun *n* pistola *f* de perdigones

pell-mell [ˌpel'mel] *adv* (*hurriedly*) atropelladamente; (*confusedly*) desordenadamente

pelt¹ [pelt] *n* (*animal skin*) pellejo *m;* (*fur*) piel *f*

pelt² [pelt] **I.** *n* **at full ~** a todo correr **II.** *vt* (*throw*) lanzar; **to ~ sb with stones** tirar piedras a alguien **III.** *vi* **1.** *impers* (*rain heavily*) llover a cántaros **2.** (*run, hurry*) apresurarse; **to ~ after sb** salir disparado tras alguien

pelvic ['pelvɪk] *adj* pélvico, -a

pelvis ['pelvɪs] <-es> *n* pelvis *f inv*

pen¹ [pen] **I.** *n* (*fountain pen*) pluma *f* estilográfica, pluma *f* fuente *AmL;* (*ballpoint*) bolígrafo *m,* birome *f Arg,* pluma *f* atómica *Méx,* lápiz *m* de pasta *Chile;* **felt-tip ~** rotulador *m;* **to put ~ to paper** ponerse a escribir ►**the ~ is mightier than the sword** *prov* más puede la pluma que la espada *prov* **II.** <-nn-> *vt* escribir

pen² [pen] *n* **1.** (*enclosure*) corral *m;* **pig ~** pocilga *f* **2.** *Am, inf* (*jail*) talego *m,* tanque *m Méx*

◆**pen in** <-nn-> *vt* (*enclose*) cercar

penal ['piːnəl] *adj* penal

penal code *n* código *m* penal **penal institution** *n* penitenciaría *f*

penalise *vt Brit, Aus,* **penalize** ['piːnəlaɪz] *vt Am* penalizar

penal offense *n Am* delito *m* penal

penalty ['penəlti, *Am:* -t̬i] <-ies> *n* **1.** LAW pena *f;* **death ~** pena de muerte; **to pay a ~ for sth** ser penalizado por algo **2.** (*punishment*) castigo *m* **3.** SPORTS castigo *m;* (*in football*) penalti *m*

penalty area *n* SPORTS área *f* de penalti **penalty box** <-es> *n* (*in ice hockey*) banquillo *m* **penalty clause** *n* cláusula *f* penal **penalty kick** *n* SPORTS tiro *m* de penalti; **to award a ~** señalar un penalti

penance ['penəns] *n no pl* REL penitencia *f;* **to do ~ for sth** hacer penitencia por algo

pence [pens] *n pl of* **penny**

penchant ['pɑːnʃɑːn, *Am:* 'pentʃənt] *n* (*liking*) inclinación *f;* **to have a ~ for sth** tener inclinación por algo

pencil ['pentsəl] **I.** *n* lápiz *m;* **coloured ~** lápiz de color; **a ~ of light** un haz de luz **II.** <*Brit:* -ll-, *Am:* -l-> *vt* dibujar a lápiz

◆**pencil in** *vt* apuntar (de forma provisional)

pencil beam *n* viga *f* delgada **pencil box** <-es> *n* estuche *m* (para lápices), cartuchera *f Arg,* alcancía *f Urug* **pencil case** *n* estuche *m* (para lápices), chuspa *f Col,* cartuchera *f Arg* **pencil sharpener** *n* sacapuntas *m inv,* tajalápiz *m Col* **pencil skirt** *n* falda *f* de tubo

pendant ['pendənt] **I.** *n* (*hanging*) colgante *m* **II.** *adj* colgante

pendant lamp *n* lámpara *f* de techo

pendent ['pendənt] *adj* LAW pendiente

pending ['pendɪŋ] **I.** *adj* pendiente; **~ deal** negocio *m* pendiente; **~ law suit** litigio *m* pendiente **II.** *prep* hasta; **~ further instructions** hasta nuevo aviso

pendulous ['pendjələs, *Am:* -dʒələs] *adj form* colgante

pendulum ['pendjələm, *Am:* -dʒələm] *n* péndulo *m*

penetrate ['penɪtreɪt] *vt* **1.** (*move into or through*) penetrar; **to ~ a market** introducirse en un mercado **2.** (*spread through, permeate*) impregnar, calar en **3.** *fig* (*see through*) entender

penetrating *adj* (*voice, gaze, insight*) penetrante; (*rain*) que cala; (*heat, cold*) agudo, -a

penetration [ˌpenɪ'treɪʃən] *n a. fig* penetra-

ción *f*
pen friend *n Aus, Brit* amigo, -a *m, f* por correspondencia
penguin ['peŋgwɪn] *n* pingüino *m*
penholder ['pen,həʊldəʳ, *Am:* -,hoʊldɚ] *n* (*rack*) portalápices *m inv*
penicillin [,penɪ'sɪlɪn] *n no pl* penicilina *f*
peninsula [pə'nɪnsjʊlə, *Am:* -sələ] *n* península *f*
peninsular [pə'nɪnsjʊləʳ, *Am:* -səlɚ] *adj* peninsular
Peninsular War *n* **the** ~ la Guerra de la Independencia
penis ['piːnɪs] <-nises *o* -nes> *n* pene *m*
penitence ['penɪtəns] *n no pl* REL penitencia *f*; **to perform** ~ hacer penitencia
penitent ['penɪtənt] REL **I.** *n* penitente *mf* **II.** *adj* penitente
penitential [,penɪ'tentʃəl] *adj* penitencial
penitentiary [,penɪ'tentʃəri] *n Am* prisión *f* penitenciaria
penknife ['pennaɪf] <-knives> *n* navaja *f*
pen name *n* seudónimo *m*
pennant ['penənt] *n* banderín *m;* NAUT gallardete *m*
penniless ['penɪlɪs] *adj* **to be** ~ no tener un duro; **to leave sb** ~ dejar a alguien en la miseria
pennon ['penən] *n* pendón *m;* (*on lance*) banderola *f*
Pennsylvania [pensɪl'veɪniə] *n* Pensilvania *f*
penny ['peni] *n* **1.** *Brit* penique *m* **2.** *Am* centavo *m* ►**a** ~ **for your thoughts** ¿en qué piensas?; **to earn/cost a pretty** ~ ganar/costar un dineral; **to earn a quick** ~ ganar dinero fácil; **two** [*o* **ten**] **a** ~ está regalado; **they're ten a** ~ los hay a patadas; **the** ~ (**has**) **dropped!** por fin cayó en cuenta, por fin le cayó el veinte *Méx;* **a** ~ **saved is a** ~ **gained** *prov* muchos pocos hacen un montón *prov*
penny-pinching ['peni,pɪntʃɪŋ] **I.** *n no pl* tacañería *f* **II.** *adj* tacaño, -a
penny whistle *n* flautín *m*
penny-wise *adj* **to be** ~ **and pound-foolish** gastar a manos llenas y hacer economías en nimiedades
pen pal *n* amigo, -a *m, f* por correspondencia
pen pusher *n Aus, Brit, pej, inf* chupatintas *mf inv,* suche *mf Chile*
pension[1] ['pentʃən] **I.** *n* FIN pensión *f;* **to draw a** ~ cobrar una pensión **II.** *vt* **to** ~ **sb off** jubilar a alguien
pension[2] ['pɑ̃nsjɔ̃ːŋ, *Am:* pɑ̃n'sjɔ̃ʊŋ] *n* (*boarding house*) pensión *f*
pensionable ['pentʃənəbl, *Am:* -ʃən-] *adj Brit* de jubilación; **of** ~ **age** de edad de jubilación
pensioner ['pentʃənəʳ, *Am:* -ʃənɚ] *n Brit* pensionista *mf*
pension fund *n* fondo *m* de pensiones **pension plan** *n* plan *m* de pensiones **pension reserves** *npl* reservas *fpl* para pensiones
pension scheme *n Aus, Brit* plan *m* de pensiones
pensive ['pentsɪv] *adj* pensativo, -a; **to be in a** ~ **mood** estar meditabundo, -a
pentagon ['pentəgən, *Am:* -t̬əgɑːn] *n* pentágono *m*
pentameter [pen'tæmɪtəʳ, *Am:* -ət̬ɚ] *n* LIT pentámetro *m*
pentathlete [pen'tæθliːt] *n* pentatleta *mf*
pentathlon [pen'tæθlən, *Am:* -lɑːn] *n* pentatlón *m*
Pentecost ['pentəkɒst, *Am:* -t̬ɪkɑːst] *n no pl* REL Pentecostés *m*
penthouse ['penthaʊs] *n* (*flat*) ático *m* de lujo
pent-up [,pent'ʌp] *adj* **1.** (*emotion*) contenido, -a, reprimido, -a **2.** (*energy*) acumulado, -a
penultimate [pen'ʌltɪmət, *Am:* pɪ'nʌlt̬ə-] *form* **I.** *n* **the** ~ el penúltimo, la penúltima **II.** *adj* penúltimo, -a
penurious [pɪ'njʊərɪəs, *Am:* pə'nʊrɪ-] *adj form* miserable, paupérrimo, -a
penury ['penjʊəri, *Am:* -jʊri] *n no pl, form* penuria *f,* miseria *f*
peony ['piːəni] <-ies> *n* peonía *f*
people ['piːpl] **I.** *n* **1.** *pl* (*plural of person*) gente *f;* **city** ~ gente de ciudad; **country** ~ gente de campo; **the beautiful** ~ la gente guapa, la gente linda *AmL;* **the rich** ~ la gente rica **2.** *no pl* (*nation, ethnic group*) pueblo *m;* ~**'s democracy** democracia *f* popular; ~**'s republic** república *f* popular; **the chosen** ~ REL el pueblo elegido **3.** (*ordinary citizens*) ciudadanos, -as *m, f pl;* ~**'s park** parque *m* público **II.** *vt* ~**d by** poblado de
pep [pep] **I.** *n no pl, inf* empuje *m;* **to be full of** ~ estar lleno de vitalidad **II.** <-pp-> *vt* animar, levantar el ánimo
pepper ['pepəʳ, *Am:* -ɚ] **I.** *n* **1.** *no pl* (*spice*) pimienta *f;* **black/white** ~ pimienta negra/blanca **2.** (*vegetable*) pimiento *m* **II.** *vt* **1.** (*add pepper*) poner pimienta a **2. to** ~ **sb with bullets** acribillar a alguien a balas; **to be** ~**ed with sth** (*speech, comments*) estar acribillado de algo; **to be** ~**ed with mistakes** estar lleno de errores
pepper-and-salt *adj* (*hair*) entrecano, -a
pepper box <-es> *n Am* pimentero *m*
peppercorn ['pepəkɔːn, *Am:* -ɚkɔːrn] *n* grano *m* de pimienta
peppercorn rent *n no pl, Aus, Brit* alquiler *m* nominal
pepper mill *n* molinillo *m* de pimienta
peppermint ['pepəmɪnt, *Am:* -ɚ-] *n* **1.** *no pl* (*mint plant*) menta *f* **2.** (*sweet*) caramelo *m* de menta
peppermint tea *n* té *m* de menta
pepper pot *n Aus, Brit,* **pepper shaker** *n Am* pimentero *m*
peppery ['pepəri] *adj* **1.** GASTR picante **2.** *fig* (*irritable*) cascarrabias *inv*
pep pill *n inf* estimulante *m* **pep talk** *n inf*

to give sb a ~ dar ánimos a alguien

peptic ['peptɪk] *adj* péptico, -a

peptic ulcer *n* úlcera *f* péptica

per [pɜːʳ, *Am:* pɜːr] *prep* **1.** (*for a*) por; **£5 ~ kilo/hour** £5 por kilo/hora **2.** (*in a*) por, a; **100 km ~ hour** 100 km por hora; **~ cent** por ciento **3.** *form* (*as stated in*) (**as**) **~ account** según consta; **as ~ usual** como siempre

perambulator [pə'ræmbjʊleɪtəʳ, *Am:* -t̬ɚ] *n form* cochecito *m,* carriola *f Méx*

per annum *adv form* al año, por año **per capita** *form* **I.** *adv* per cápita **II.** *adj* **~ consumption** consumo *m* per cápita; **~ income** ingresos *mpl* per cápita

perceivable [pə'siːvəbl, *Am:* pɚ'-] *adj* perceptible

perceive [pə'siːv, *Am:* pɚ'-] *vt* **1.** (*see*) ver; (*sense*) percibir, notar; **to ~ that ...** percibir que... **2.** (*view, regard*) considerar; **how do the Spanish ~ the British?** ¿qué piensan los españoles de los británicos? **3.** (*understand*) comprender

percent *n Am,* **per cent** [pə'sent, *Am:* pɚ'-] *n Brit* porcentaje *m;* **25 ~** 25 por ciento; **what ~ ...** ¿qué porcentaje...?

percentage [pə'sentɪdʒ, *Am:* pɚ'sent̬ɪdʒ] *n* **1.** (*proportion*) porcentaje *m;* **what ~ ...?** ¿qué porcentaje...?; **to get a ~ of sth** recibir un tanto por ciento de algo **2.** *Am, Aus* (*advantage*) tajada *f inf* ►**to play the ~s** sopesar las posibilidades

percentage point *n* punto *m* porcentual

perceptible [pə'septəbl, *Am:* pɚ'-] *adj* perceptible

perception [pə'sepʃən, *Am:* pɚ'-] *n* **1.** percepción *f* **2.** (*idea*) idea *f* **3.** (*insight*) perspicacia *f,* agudeza *f*

perceptive [pə'septɪv, *Am:* pɚ'-] *adj* perspicaz, agudo, -a

perch[1] [pɜːtʃ, *Am:* pɜːrtʃ] **I.** <-es> *n* **1.** (*rod for birds*) percha *f* **2.** (*high location or position*) posición *f* privilegiada ►**to come off one's ~** bajarse del burro; **to knock sb off his ~** bajar los humos a alguien **II.** *vi* (*person*) sentarse; (*bird*) posarse

perch[2] [pɜːtʃ, *Am:* pɜːrtʃ] *n* perca *f*

percolate ['pɜːkəleɪt, *Am:* 'pɜːr-] **I.** *vt* filtrar, colar; (*coffee*) preparar **II.** *vi* **1.** (*filter through*) filtrarse **2.** *fig* (*spread*) difundirse

percolator ['pɜːkə leɪtəʳ, *Am:* 'pɜːrkələɪt̬ɚ] *n* cafetera *f* eléctrica

percussion [pə'kʌʃən, *Am:* pɚ'-] **I.** *n no pl* MUS percusión *f;* **to play ~** ser percusionista **II.** *adj* MUS de percusión

percussionist *n* MUS percusionista *mf*

perdition [pə'dɪʃən, *Am:* pɚ'-] *n no pl* **1.** *liter* (*hell*) perdición *f* **2.** *fig* (*state of ruin*) desastre *m*

peregrine ['perɪgrɪn] *n* peregrino, -a *m, f*

peregrine falcon *n* halcón *m* peregrino

peremptorily *adv* en tono perentorio, imperiosamente

peremptory [pə'remptəri] *adj* **1.** (*person*) autoritario, -a; (*order, tone*) perentorio, -a, imperioso, -a **2.** LAW perentorio, -a

perennial [pər'eniəl, *Am:* pə'ren-] **I.** *n* planta *f* perenne **II.** *adj* **1.** BOT perenne **2.** (*constant*) constante

perfect[1] ['pɜːfɪkt, *Am:* 'pɜːr-] **I.** *adj* perfecto, -a; (*calm*) total; (*opportunity*) ideal; (*silence*) absoluto, -a; **in ~ condition** en estado perfecto; **the ~ crime** el crimen perfecto; **a ~ gentleman** todo un señor; **a ~ idiot** un tonto de remate; **to be a ~ stranger** ser completamente desconocido; **to have the ~ right to do sth** tener todo el derecho a hacer algo; **to be far from ~** estar (muy) lejos de ser perfecto; **to be a ~ match for sth** ir de maravilla con algo; **to be a ~ match for sb** ser la pareja perfecta para alguien **II.** *n no pl* LING perfecto *m*

perfect[2] [pə'fekt, *Am:* pɜːr-] *vt* perfeccionar

perfectible [pə'fektəbəl, *Am:* pɚ'-] *adj* perfectible

perfection [pə'fekʃən, *Am:* pɚ'-] *n no pl* perfección *f;* **to do sth to ~** hacer algo a la perfección

perfectionist *n* perfeccionista *mf*

perfectly *adv* perfectamente; **~ clear** completamente claro; **~ happy** absolutamente contento; **to be ~ honest, ...** para serte sincero,...; **to be ~ right** tener toda la razón

perfidious [pə'fɪdiəs, *Am:* pɚ'-] *adj liter* pérfido, -a; **~ attack** ataque *m* a traición

perforate ['pɜːfəreɪt, *Am:* 'pɜːr-] *vt* perforar; (*ticket*) picar

perforated *adj* perforado, -a; **to have a ~ eardrum** tener una perforación de tímpano

perforation [ˌpɜːfər'eɪʃən, *Am:* ˌpɜːfə'reɪ-] *n* perforación *f*

perform [pə'fɔːm, *Am:* pɚ'fɔːrm] **I.** *vt* **1.** MUS, THEAT, TV interpretar **2.** (*do, accomplish*) realizar; **to ~ one's duty/a function** cumplir con su deber/una función; **to ~ miracles/wonders** hacer milagros/maravillas; **to ~ a task** llevar a cabo una tarea; **to ~ a trick** realizar un truco **3.** INFOR ejecutar **4.** MED, SPORTS practicar **II.** *vi* **1.** THEAT actuar; MUS tocar **2.** (*operate*) funcionar

performance [pə'fɔːmənts, *Am:* pɚ'fɔːr-] *n* **1.** (*of play*) representación *f;* (*by individual actor*) actuación *f;* **to give a ~** hacer una representación; **to put on a ~ of a play** poner en escena una representación de una obra **2.** SPORTS actuación *f;* **high/low ~** AUTO alto/bajo rendimiento *m* **3.** *inf* (*fuss*) lío *m;* **to make a ~ about sth** *Brit, fig* montar un jaleo por algo

performance level *n* **1.** (*degree of success*) nivel *m* de rendimiento **2.** ECON (*output*) rendimiento *m;* **a high/low ~** un alto/bajo rendimiento **performance report** *n* informe *m* de rendimiento

performer [pə'fɔːməʳ, *Am:* pɚ'fɔːrmɚ] *n* **1.** THEAT artista *mf* **2.** (*achiever*) **star ~** (*in a show*) estrella *f;* (*at work*) empleado, -a *m, f* modelo; **bad ~** (*at school*) mal(a) estudiante *mf;* (*at work*) mal(a) trabajador(a) *m(f)*

perfume ['pɜːfjuːm, *Am:* 'pɜːr-] **I.** *n* **1.** *no pl* (*scented liquid*) perfume *m;* ~ **maker** perfumista *mf;* **to put on** ~ ponerse perfume **2.** (*fragrance*) fragancia *f* **II.** *vt* perfumar

perfunctory [pə'fʌŋktəri, *Am:* pɚ'-] *adj* (*inspection*) superficial; (*reading*) por encima; (*mention*) de pasada; (*greeting, smile*) forzado, -a; (*examination*) rutinario, -a

pergola ['pɜːgələ, *Am:* 'pɜːr-] *n* pérgola *f*

perhaps [pə'hæps, *Am:* pɚ'-] *adv* quizá(s), tal vez

peril ['perəl] *n form* peligro *m;* **to be in** ~ correr peligro; **at one's** ~ por su cuenta y riesgo; **at** [*o* **in**] ~ **of sth** en peligro por algo; **the ~s of sth** el peligro de algo

perilous ['perələs] *adj form* peligroso, -a

perimeter [pə'rɪmɪtəʳ, *Am:* pə'rɪmət̬ɚ] *n* perímetro *m*

perimeter fence *n* cercado *m*

period ['pɪəriəd, *Am:* 'pɪri-] **I.** *n* **1.** *a.* GEO período *m;* **in/over a** ~ **of sth** en/durante un período de algo **2.** ECON plazo *m;* **a fixed** ~ un plazo fijo; ~ **of grace** plazo *m* de gracia **3.** SCHOOL (*lesson*) hora *f* **4.** (*distinct stage*) época *f* **5.** (*menstruation*) período *m,* regla *f;* **to have one's** ~ tener la regla **6.** *Am* LING punto *m* final **II.** *interj Am* ¡y punto! *inf*

period furniture *n no pl* mobiliario *m* de época

periodic [ˌpɪəri'ɒdɪk, *Am:* ˌpɪri'ɑːdɪk] *adj* periódico, -a

periodical [ˌpɪəri'ɒdɪkl, *Am:* ˌpɪri'ɑːdɪ-] **I.** *n* (*general*) revista *f;* (*specific*) boletín *m* **II.** *adj* periódico, -a

periodic table *n* tabla *f* de elementos

peripheral [pə'rɪfərəl] **I.** *adj* **1.** (*importance, role*) secundario, -a **2.** *a.* ANAT, INFOR periférico, -a **II.** *n* INFOR periférico *m*

periphery [pə'rɪfəri] <-ies> *n* periferia *f;* (*of society*) margen *m*

periscope ['perɪskəʊp, *Am:* -skoʊp] *n* periscopio *m*

perish ['perɪʃ] *vi* **1.** *liter* (*die*) perecer; ~ **the thought!** ¡Dios nos libre! **2.** *Aus, Brit* (*deteriorate: rubber, leather*) deteriorarse; (*vegetables*) estropearse

perishable ['perɪʃəbl] *adj* perecedero, -a

perisher *n Brit, inf* pillo, -a *m, f*

perishing *adj* **1.** (*as intensifier*) dichoso, -a; **I forgot my** ~ **keys** me olvidé las dichosas llaves **2.** *Aus, Brit, inf* (*extremely cold*) **it's ~!** ¡hace un frío que pela!; **I'm** ~ estoy muerto de frío

peritonitis [ˌperɪtə'naɪtɪs, *Am:* -toʊ'naɪt̬ɪs] *n no pl* MED peritonitis *f inv*

perjure ['pɜːdʒəʳ, *Am:* 'pɜːrdʒɚ] *vt* **to** ~ **oneself** perjurar(se)

perjurer ['pɜːdʒərəʳ, *Am:* 'pɜːrdʒɚɚ] *n* perjuro, -a *m, f*

perjury ['pɜːdʒəri, *Am:* 'pɜːr-] *n* perjurio *m*

perk [pɜːk, *Am:* pɜːrk] *n* (*advantage*) ventaja *f*

◆**perk up** **I.** *vi* **1.** (*cheer up*) alegrarse; **to** ~ **at sth** alegrarse por algo **2.** (*improve*) mejorar **II.** *vt* **1.** (*cheer up*) alegrar; (*make more lively*) animar **2.** (*raise*) **to** ~ **one's ears** aguzar las orejas

perky ['pɜːki, *Am:* 'pɜːr-] <-ier, -iest> *adj* alegre

perm[1] [pɜːm, *Am:* pɜːrm] *n* **1.** *inf abbr of* **permanent wave** permanente *f,* permanente *m Méx* **2.** *Brit, inf abbr of* **permutation** combinación *f*

perm[2] [pɜːm, *Am:* pɜːrm] *vt* **to** ~ **one's hair, to have one's hair ~ed** hacerse la permanente

permafrost ['pɜːməfrɒst, *Am:* 'pɜːrməfrɑːst] *n no pl* permafrost *m*

permanence ['pɜːmənənts, *Am:* 'pɜːr-] *n,* **permanency** *n no pl* permanencia *f*

permanent ['pɜːmənənt, *Am:* 'pɜːr-] *adj* (*job*) fijo, -a; (*damage*) irreparable; (*exhibition, situation, position*) permanente; (*ink*) indeleble; (*relationship*) estable; (*tooth*) definitivo, -a

permanent wave *n* permanente *f,* permanente *m Méx*

permanganate [pə'mæŋgəneɪt, *Am:* pɚ'-] *n* permanganato *m*

permeable ['pɜːmɪəbl, *Am:* 'pɜːr-] *adj* permeable

permeate ['pɜːmɪeɪt, *Am:* 'pɜːr-] **I.** *vt* (*liquid, smoke, smell*) impregnar **II.** *vi* **to** ~ **into/through sth** penetrar en/a través de algo

permissible [pə'mɪsəbl, *Am:* pɚ'-] *adj* (*permitted*) permisible; (*acceptable*) tolerable

permission [pə'mɪʃən, *Am:* pɚ'-] *n no pl* permiso *m*

permissive [pə'mɪsɪv, *Am:* pɚ'-] *adj pej* permisivo, -a

permissiveness *n no pl* permisividad *f*

permit[1] ['pɜːmɪt, *Am:* 'pɜːr-] *n* permiso *m* (por escrito); **residence** ~ permiso de residencia; **to hold a** ~ tener un permiso

permit[2] [pə'mɪt, *Am:* pɚ'-] <-tt-> **I.** *vt* permitir; **I will not** ~ **you to go there** no te permito que vayas allí; **to** ~ **oneself sth** permitirse algo **II.** *vi* **weather ~ing** si hace buen tiempo, si el tiempo no lo impide; **if time ~s** si hay tiempo; **the law ~s of no other interpretation** *form* la ley no acepta otra interpretación

permitted [pə'mɪtɪd, *Am:* pɚ'mɪt̬-] *adj* permitido, -a

permutation [ˌpɜːmjuː'teɪʃən, *Am:* ˌpɜːr-] *n form* **1.** MAT permutación *f* **2.** *Brit* SPORTS combinación *f*

pernicious [pə'nɪʃəs, *Am:* pɚ'-] *adj* **1.** *form* (*harmful*) perjudicial **2.** MED pernicioso, -a

pernicious anaemia *n Brit,* **pernicious anemia** *n Am* anemia *f* perniciosa

pernickety [pə'nɪkəti, *Am:* pɚ'nɪkət̬i] *adj Brit, pej* **1.** (*exacting*) puntilloso, -a; **to be** ~ **about sth** ser puntilloso con algo **2.** (*difficult*) que requiere minuciosidad

peroxide [pə'rɒksaɪd, *Am:* -'rɑːk-] **I.** *n no pl* peróxido *m;* **hydrogen** ~ agua *f* oxigenada

P

II. *vt* oxigenar

peroxide blonde *n* rubia *f* teñida

perpendicular [ˌpɜːpənˈdɪkjʊləʳ, *Am:* ˌpɜːrpənˈdɪkjuːlɚ] I. *adj* perpendicular II. *n* perpendicular *f*

perpetrate [ˈpɜːpɪtreɪt, *Am:* ˈpɜːrpə-] *vt form* (*crime*) perpetrar, cometer; (*error*) cometer

perpetration [ˌpɜːpɪˈtreɪʃən, *Am:* ˌpɜːrpəˈ-] *n form* perpetración *f*

perpetrator [ˈpɜːpɪtreɪtəʳ, *Am:* ˈpɜːrpətreɪt̬ɚ] *n form* autor(a) *m(f), de un delito*

perpetual [pəˈpetʃʊəl, *Am:* pɚˈpetʃu-] *adj* 1. (*lasting forever*) perpetuo, -a 2. (*repeated*) continuo, -a

perpetuate [pəˈpetʃʊeɪt, *Am:* pɚˈpetʃu-] *vt* perpetuar

perpetuity [ˌpɜːpɪˈtjuːəti, *Am:* ˌpɜːrpəˈtuːət̬i] *n no pl, form* perpetuidad *f;* **for** [*o* **in**] ~ LAW a perpetuidad

perplex [pəˈpleks, *Am:* pɚˈ-] *vt* desconcertar

perplexed [pəˈplekst, *Am:* pɚˈ-] *adj* perplejo, -a

perplexity [pəˈpleksəti, *Am:* pɚˈpleksət̬i] <-ies> *n* perplejidad *f;* **to look at sth in** ~ mirar algo con perplejidad

perquisite [ˈpɜːkwɪzɪt, *Am:* ˈpɜːr-] *n Brit, form* (beneficio *m*) extra *m*

persecute [ˈpɜːsɪkjuːt, *Am:* ˈpɜːrsɪ-] *vt* 1. *a.* POL perseguir 2. (*harass*) molestar

persecution [ˌpɜːsɪˈkjuːʃən, *Am:* ˌpɜːrsɪˈ-] *n* persecución *f*

persecution complex *n no pl* manía *f* persecutoria

persecutor *n* perseguidor(a) *m(f)*

perseverance [ˌpɜːsɪˈvɪərəns, *Am:* ˌpɜːrsəˈvɪr-] *n no pl* perseverancia *f*

persevere [ˌpɜːsɪˈvɪəʳ, *Am:* ˌpɜːrsəˈvɪr] *vi* perseverar

persevering *adj* perseverante

Persia [ˈpɜːʃə, *Am:* ˈpɜːrʒə] *n no pl* Persia *f*

Persian I. *adj* persa II. *n* 1. (*person*) persa *mf* 2. LING persa *m*

persist [pəˈsɪst, *Am:* pɚˈ-] *vi* 1. (*continue: cold, heat, rain*) continuar; (*habit, belief, doubts*) persistir 2. (*person*) insistir

persistence [pəˈsɪstəns, *Am:* pɚˈ-] *n no pl* 1. (*of cold, belief*) persistencia *f* 2. (*of person*) insistencia *f*

persistent [pəˈsɪstənt, *Am:* pɚˈ-] *adj* 1. (*cold, belief*) persistente 2. (*person*) insistente

persistent offender *n* reincidente *mf*

person [ˈpɜːsən, *Am:* ˈpɜːr-] <people *o form* -s> *n* 1. (*human*) persona *f;* **about** [*o* **on**] **one's** ~ encima; **as a** ~ como persona; **per** ~ por persona 2. LING persona *f;* **first/second** ~ primera/segunda persona

persona [pəˈsəʊnə, *Am:* pɚˈsoʊ-] *n form* 1. (*image*) imagen *f* 2. (*character*) personaje *m*

personable [ˈpɜːsənəbl, *Am:* ˈpɜːr-] *adj* agradable

personage [ˈpɜːsənɪdʒ, *Am:* ˈpɜːr-] *n iron, form* personaje *m*

personal [ˈpɜːsənəl, *Am:* ˈpɜːr-] *adj* 1. (*property*) privado, -a; (*data, belongings, account*) personal 2. (*direct, done in person*) en persona 3. (*private: letter*) personal; (*question*) indiscreto, -a; (*matter*) privado, -a, personal; (*life*) privado, -a 4. (*offensive: comment, remark*) ofensivo, -a; **to get** ~ llevar las cosas al plano personal; **it's nothing** ~ no es nada personal 5. (*bodily, physical: appearance*) personal; (*hygiene*) íntimo, -a 6. (*human*) ~ **quality** calidad *f* humana

personal assistant *n* ayudante *mf* personal **personal computer** *n* ordenador *m* personal, computadora *f* personal *AmL*

personality [ˌpɜːsənˈæləti, *Am:* ˌpɜːr-] *n* <-ies> 1. (*character*) personalidad *f* 2. (*famous person*) personalidad *f,* figura *f*

personally *adv* personalmente; **to take sth** ~ ofenderse con [*o* por] algo

personal pronoun *n* pronombre *m* personal

personalty [ˈpɜːsənəlti, *Am:* ˈpɜːrsənəlt̬i] <-ies> *n* bienes *mpl* muebles

personification [pəˌsɒnɪfɪˈkeɪʃən, *Am:* pɚˌsɑːnɪ-] *n* personificación *f;* **he is the ~ of kindness** es la amabilidad personificada

personify [pəˈsɒnɪfaɪ, *Am:* pɚˈsɑːnɪ-] *vt* personificar

personnel [ˌpɜːsənˈel, *Am:* ˌpɜːr-] *n* 1. *pl* (*staff, employees*) personal *m* 2. *no pl* (*department*) departamento *m* de personal

personnel department *n* departamento *m* de personal **personnel director** *n* director(a) *m(f)* de personal **personnel manager** *n* jefe, -a *m, f* de personal

perspective [pəˈspektɪv, *Am:* pɚˈ-] *n* perspectiva *f;* **you have to keep things in** ~ no tienes que perder de vista la verdadera dimensión de las cosas; **to put a different ~ on things** cambiar el cariz de las cosas

perspicacious [ˌpɜːspɪˈkeɪʃəs, *Am:* ˌpɜːr-] *adj form* perspicaz

perspicacity [ˌpɜːspɪˈkæsəti, *Am:* ˌpɜːrspɪˈkæsət̬i] *n no pl, form* perspicacia *f*

perspicuity [ˌpɜːspɪˈkjuːəti, *Am:* ˌpɜːrspɪˈkjuːət̬i] *n no pl, form* perspicuidad *f*

perspicuous [pəˈspɪkjʊəs, *Am:* pɚˈ-] *adj form* perspicuo, -a

perspiration [ˌpɜːspəˈreɪʃən, *Am:* ˌpɜːr-] *n no pl* transpiración *f;* **beads of** ~ gotas *fpl* de sudor

perspire [pəˈspaɪəʳ, *Am:* pɚˈspaɪɚ] *vi* transpirar

persuade [pəˈsweɪd, *Am:* pɚˈ-] *vt* convencer; **to ~ sb into sth** convencer a alguien de algo; **to ~ sb out of sth** disuadir a alguien de algo; **to ~ sb to do sth** convencer a alguien de que haga algo; **to ~ sb that ...** convencer a alguien de que...

persuasion [pəˈsweɪʒən, *Am:* pɚˈ-] *n* 1. (*act*) persuasión *f* 2. (*conviction*) creencia *f*

persuasive [pəˈsweɪsɪv, *Am:* pɚˈ-] *adj* (*person, manner*) persuasivo, -a; (*argument*) convincente

pert [pɜːt, *Am:* pɜːrt] *adj* **1.** (*nose, buttocks, breasts*) respingón, -ona **2.** (*reply*) descarado, -a **3.** (*hat*) garboso, -a

pertain [pəˈteɪn, *Am:* pɚˈ-] *vi form* **to ~ to sth** concernir algo

pertinent [ˈpɜːtɪnənt, *Am:* ˈpɜːrtnənt] *adj form* pertinente; **to be ~ to sth** guardar relación con algo

perturb [pəˈtɜːb, *Am:* pɚˈtɜːrb] *vt form* perturbar

perturbation [ˌpɜːtəˈbeɪʃən, *Am:* ˌpɜːrt̬ɚˈ-] *n form* perturbación *f*

Peru [pəˈruː] *n* Perú *m*

perusal [pəˈruːzl] *n no pl, form* lectura *f;* **he sent a copy of the report for their ~** envió una copia del informe para que lo examinaran

peruse [pəˈruːz] *vt form* (*read*) leer detenidamente; (*examine*) examinar

Peruvian [pəˈruːvɪən] **I.** *adj* peruano, -a **II.** *n* peruano, -a *m, f*

pervade [pəˈveɪd, *Am:* pɚˈ-] *vt form* (*attitude, idea*) dominar; (*smell, smoke*) invadir

pervasive [pəˈveɪsɪv, *Am:* pɚˈ-] *adj form* (*attitude, idea*) dominante; (*influence*) omnipresente; (*smell*) penetrante

perverse [pəˈvɜːs, *Am:* pɚˈvɜːrs] *adj* **1.** (*stubborn*) obstinado, -a **2.** (*unreasonable, deviant, corrupt*) perverso, -a **3.** (*contrary*) contradictorio, -a

perverseness *n no pl, pej* **1.** (*stubbornness*) obstinación *f* **2.** (*unreasonableness, deviancy*) perversidad *f* **3.** (*contrariness*) contradicción *f*

perversion [pəˈvɜːʃən, *Am:* pɚˈvɜːrʒən] *n* **1.** (*sexual deviance*) perversión *f* **2.** (*corruption*) **~ of justice** deformación *f* de la justicia; **~ of the truth** distorsión *f* de la verdad

perversity [pəˈvɜːsəti, *Am:* pɚˈvɜːrsət̬i] <-ies> *n* **1.** (*stubbornness*) obstinación *f* **2.** (*unreasonableness, wickedness*) perversidad *f*

pervert¹ [ˈpɜːvɜːt, *Am:* ˈpɜːrvɜːrt] *n* (*sexual deviant*) pervertido, -a *m, f*

pervert² [pəˈvɜːt, *Am:* pɚˈvɜːrt] *vt* pervertir; **to ~ the truth** distorsionar la verdad

perverted *adj* (*person, practice*) pervertido, -a

peseta [pəˈseɪtə] *n* peseta *f*

peso [ˈpeɪsəʊ, *Am:* -soʊ] *n* peso *m*

pessary [ˈpesəri] <-ies> *n* **1.** (*device*) pesario *m* **2.** (*vaginal suppository*) supositorio *m* vaginal

pessimism [ˈpesɪmɪzəm, *Am:* ˈpesə-] *n no pl* pesimismo *m*

pessimist *n* pesimista *mf*

pessimistic [ˌpesɪˈmɪstɪk, *Am:* ˌpesəˈ-] *adj* pesimista; **to be ~ about sth** ser pesimista con respecto a algo

pest [pest] *n* **1.** (*destructive insect, animal*) plaga *f* **2.** *inf* (*annoying person*) pesado, -a *m, f*

pest control *n* (*of insects*) fumigación *f;* (*of rats*) desratización *f*

pester [ˈpestəʳ, *Am:* -ɚ] *vt* molestar

pesticide [ˈpestɪsaɪd, *Am:* ˈpestə-] *n* pesticida *m*

pestiferous [peˈstɪfərəs] *adj* pestilente

pestilent [ˈpestɪlənt, *Am:* ˈpestlənt] *adj,* **pestilential** [ˌpestɪˈlentʃəl, *Am:* ˌpestəˈ-] *adj* **1.** (*deadly*) mortal **2.** (*troublesome*) pesado, -a

pestle [ˈpesl] *n* mano *f* de mortero

pet¹ [pet] **I.** *n* **1.** (*house animal*) animal *m* doméstico **2.** *pej* (*favourite person*) mimado, -a *m, f;* **he's the teacher's ~** es el mimado del profesor **3.** *inf* (*nice or thoughtful person*) encanto *m* **4.** *Aus, Brit, inf* (*term of endearment*) cariño *m* **II.** *adj* **1.** (*cat, dog, snake*) doméstico, -a **2.** (*favourite: project, theory*) favorito, -a

pet² [pet] <-tt-> **I.** *vi* acariciarse **II.** *vt* **1.** (*caress*) acariciar **2.** (*pamper*) mimar

petal [ˈpetl, *Am:* ˈpet̬l] *n* **1.** BOT pétalo *m* **2.** *Brit, inf* (*term of endearment*) cariño *m*

petard [peˈtɑːd, *Am:* pɪˈtɑːrd] *n* **he was <u>hoist</u> with his own ~** *prov* le salió el tiro por la culata

peter [ˈpiːtəʳ, *Am:* -t̬ɚ] *vi* **to ~ away** [*o* **out**] (*trail, track, path*) desaparecer; (*conversation, interest*) decaer

Peter [ˈpiːtəʳ, *Am:* -t̬ɚ] **to rob ~ to pay <u>Paul</u>** *prov* desnudar a un santo para vestir a otro *prov*

petite [pəˈtiːt] *adj* menudo, -a

petition [pɪˈtɪʃən, *Am:* pəˈ-] **I.** *n* **1.** POL petición *f* **2.** LAW demanda *f* **II.** *vi* **1.** POL **to ~ for sth** elevar una petición solicitando algo **2.** LAW **to ~ for divorce** presentar una demanda de divorcio **III.** *vt* POL elevar una petición a, peticionar *AmL*

petitioner *n* **1.** POL peticionario, -a *m, f* **2.** LAW demandante *mf*

pet name *n* apodo *m,* sobrenombre *m*

petrel [ˈpetrəl] *n* petrel *m*

Petri dish [ˈpetriˌdɪʃ, *Am:* ˈpiːtriˌdɪʃ] *n* plato *m* de Petri

petrifaction [ˌpetrɪˈfækʃən] *n,* **petrification** [ˌpetrɪfɪˈkeɪʃən] *n* **1.** GEO petrificación *f* **2.** (*terror*) terror *m*

petrified *adj* **1.** GEO petrificado, -a **2.** (*terrified*) aterrorizado, -a

petrify [ˈpetrɪfaɪ] <-ies> **I.** *vi* GEO petrificarse **II.** *vt* **1.** GEO petrificar **2.** (*terrify*) aterrorizar

petrochemical [ˌpetrəʊˈkemɪkəl, *Am:* -roʊˈ-] **I.** *n* producto *m* petroquímico **II.** *adj* petroquímico, -a

petrodollar [ˈpetrəʊˌdɒləʳ, *Am:* -roʊˌdɑːlɚ] *n* petrodólar *m*

petrol [ˈpetrəl] *n no pl, Aus, Brit* gasolina *f,* nafta *f RíoPl,* bencina *f Chile;* **unleaded ~** gasolina sin plomo

petrol can *n Aus, Brit* bidón *m* de gasolina

petrol consumption *n no pl, Aus, Brit* consumo *m* de gasolina

petroleum [pɪˈtrəʊliəm, *Am:* pəˈtroʊ-] *n* petróleo *m,* canfín *m AmC*

petrol gauge *n Aus, Brit* indicador *m* (del nivel) de la gasolina **petrol pipe** *n Aus, Brit*

P

oleoducto *m* **petrol pump** *n Aus, Brit* **1.** (*at garage*) surtidor *m* de gasolina **2.** (*in engine*) bomba *f* de gasolina **petrol station** *n Aus, Brit* gasolinera *f,* bomba *f And, Ven,* estación *f* de nafta *RíoPl,* bencinera *f Chile,* grifo *m Perú*
petrol tank *n Aus, Brit* depósito *m* de gasolina
pet shop *n* ≈ pajarería *f*
petticoat ['petɪkəʊt, *Am:* 'peṱɪkoʊt] *n* enagua *f,* combinación *f,* fondo *m Méx*
pettifogging ['petɪfɒgɪŋ, *Am:* 'peṱɪfɑːgɪŋ] *adj pej* (*person*) puntilloso, -a; (*paper work*) farragoso, -a; (*details*) insignificante
pettiness ['petɪnəs, *Am:* 'peṱ-] *n no pl* **1.** (*triviality, insignificance*) nimiedad *f* **2.** (*small-mindedness*) mezquindad *f*
petting ['petɪŋ, *Am:* 'peṱ-] *n* **1.** (*stroking*) caricias *fpl* **2.** (*sexual fondling and touching*) manoseo *m*
petty ['peti, *Am:* 'peṱ-] <-ier, -iest> *adj* **1.** *pej* (*detail, amount*) trivial, insignificante; (*person, attitude*) mezquino, -a **2.** LAW menor
petty larceny *n* LAW hurto *m* de cosas de poco valor **petty officer** *n* NAUT suboficial *mf* de marina
petulant ['petjələnt, *Am:* 'petʃə-] *adj* enfurruñado, -a
petunia [pɪ'tjuːniə, *Am:* pə'tuːnjə] *n* petunia *f*
pew [pjuː] *n* banco *m* (de iglesia) ▸**take** a ~ *iron* ¡siéntate!
pewter ['pjuːtəʳ, *Am:* -ṱɚ] *n no pl* peltre *m*
PG *n abbr of* **parental guidance** *película para menores acompañados*
pg *Am abbr of* **page** pág. *f*
PGCE *n Brit abbr of* **Postgraduate Certificate in Education** *diploma de postgrado de pedagogía*
pH [ˌpiː'eɪtʃ] pH
phalanx ['fælæŋks, *Am:* 'feɪlæŋks] <-es *o* phalanges> *n form* falange *f*
phallic ['fælɪk] *adj* fálico, -a
phallus ['fæləs] <-es *o* phalli> *n* falo *m*
phantasmal [fæn'tæzməl] *adj liter* **1.** (*imaginary, unreal*) ilusorio, -a **2.** (*ghost-like*) fantasmal
phantom ['fæntəm, *Am:* -ṱəm] **I.** *n* fantasma *m* **II.** *adj* **1.** *iron* (*ghostly*) fantasmal **2.** (*imaginary*) ilusorio, -a
pharaoh ['feərəʊ, *Am:* 'feroʊ] *n* faraón *m*
pharisaic(al) [ˌfærɪ'seɪɪk(əl), *Am:* ˌferɪ'-] *adj* farisaico, -a
Pharisee ['færɪsiː, *Am:* 'ferɪ-] *n* fariseo, -a *m, f*
pharmaceutic [ˌfɑːmə'sjuːtɪk, *Am:* ˌfɑːrmə'suːṱɪ-] *adj* farmacéutico, -a
pharmaceutical **I.** *adj* farmacéutico, -a **II.** *n pl* fármacos *mpl*
pharmaceutics *n no pl* farmacia *f*
pharmaceutics industry *n no pl* industria *f* farmacéutica
pharmacist ['fɑːməsɪst, *Am:* 'fɑːr-] *n* farmacéutico, -a *m, f,* farmaceuta *mf Col, Ven*
pharmacology [ˌfɑːmə'kɒlədʒi, *Am:* ˌfɑːrmə'kɑːlə-] *n no pl* farmacología *f*
pharmacopoeia [ˌfɑːməkə'piːə, *Am:* ˌfɑːrmə'koʊ-] *n* farmacopea *f*
pharmacy ['fɑːməsi, *Am:* 'fɑːr-] <-ies> *n* farmacia *f*
pharyngitis [ˌfærɪn'dʒaɪtɪs, *Am:* ˌferɪn'dʒaɪṱɪs] *n no pl* faringitis *f*
pharynx ['færɪŋks] <pharynges> *n* faringe *f*
phase [feɪz] **I.** *n* (*stage*) fase *f;* (*period*) etapa *f;* **to go through a** ~ pasar por una etapa; **to be in** ~ estar sincronizado; **to be out of** ~ estar desfasado **II.** *vt* **1.** (*do in stages*) realizar por etapas **2.** (*coordinate*) sincronizar
◆**phase in** *vt* introducir paulatinamente
◆**phase out** *vt* (*service*) retirar progresivamente; (*product*) dejar de producir paulatinamente
PhD [ˌpiːeɪtʃ'diː] *n abbr of* **Doctor of Philosophy** **1.** (*award*) doctorado *m* **2.** (*person*) Dr. *m,* Dra. *f*
pheasant ['fezənt] <-(s)> *n* faisán *m*
phenomena *n pl of* **phenomenon**
phenomenal *adj* (*success, achievement*) espectacular; (*strength*) increíble
phenomenon [fɪ'nɒmɪnən, *Am:* fə'nɑːmənɑːn] <phenomena *o* -s> *n* fenómeno *m*
phew [fjuː] *interj inf* ¡uf!
phial ['faɪəl] *n Brit* ampolla *f*
philander [fɪ'lændəʳ, *Am:* -dɚ] *vi pej* ir detrás de las mujeres
philanderer *n pej* mujeriego *m*
philanthropic [ˌfɪlən'θrɒpɪk, *Am:* -æn'θrɑːpɪk-] *adj* filantrópico, -a
philanthropist [fɪ'lænθrəpɪst, *Am:* fə'-] *n* filántropo, -a *m, f*
philanthropy [fɪ'lænθrəpi, *Am:* fə'-] *n no pl* filantropía *f*
philatelic [fɪlə'telɪk] *adj* filatélico, -a
philatelist [fɪ'lætəlɪst, *Am:* -'læṱ-] *n* filatelista *mf*
philately [fɪ'lætəli, *Am:* -'læṱ-] *n no pl* filatelia *f*
philharmonic [ˌfɪlɑː'mɒnɪk, *Am:* ˌfɪlhɑːr'mɑːnɪk] *adj* filarmónico, -a
Philippines ['fɪlɪpiːnz, *Am:* 'fɪlə-] *npl* **the** ~ las Filipinas
philistine ['fɪlɪstaɪn, *Am:* -stiːn] *pej* **I.** *n* ignorante *mf* **II.** *adj* ignorante
philological [ˌfɪlə'lɒdʒɪkl, *Am:* -'lɑːdʒɪk-] *adj* filológico, -a
philologist [fɪ'lɒlədʒɪst, *Am:* fɪ'lɑːlə-] *n* filólogo, -a *m, f*
philology [fɪ'lɒlədʒi, *Am:* fɪ'lɑːlə-] *n no pl* filología *f*
philosopher [fɪ'lɒsəfəʳ, *Am:* -'lɑːsəfɚ] *n* filósofo, -a *m, f*
philosophic(al) [ˌfɪlə'sɒfɪk(əl), *Am:* -ə'sɑːfɪk-] *adj* filosófico, -a
philosophize [fɪ'lɒsəfaɪz, *Am:* -'lɑːsə-] *vi* filosofar
philosophy [fɪ'lɒsəfi, *Am:* -'lɑːsə-] *n no pl* filosofía *f*

philter *n Am,* **philtre** ['fɪltəʳ, *Am:* -t̬ɚ] *n Brit* filtro *m*

phlebitis [flɪ'baɪtɪs, *Am:* fliː'baɪt̬ɪs] *n* MED flebitis *f inv*

phlegm [flem] *n no pl* flema *f*

phlegmatic [fleg'mætɪk, *Am:* -'mæt̬-] *adj* flemático, -a

phobia ['fəʊbiə, *Am:* 'foʊ-] *n* PSYCH fobia *f*

phoenix ['fiːnɪks] *n* fénix *m*

phone [fəʊn, *Am:* foʊn] **I.** *n* teléfono *m;* **to hang up** [*o* **put down**] **the** ~ colgar el teléfono; **to pick up the** ~ coger el teléfono; **by** ~ por teléfono; **to be on the** ~ *Brit* estar hablando por teléfono **II.** *vt* telefonear, llamar (por teléfono) **III.** *vi* telefonear, llamar (por teléfono)

◆**phone back** *vt* volver a telefonear, volver a llamar (por teléfono)

◆**phone in I.** *vi* telefonear, llamar (por teléfono); **to** ~ **sick** telefonear para dar parte de enfermo **II.** *vt* telefonear, llamar por teléfono

◆**phone round** *vi* hacer llamadas

◆**phone up** *vt* telefonear, llamar (por teléfono)

phone book *n* guía *f* telefónica, directorio *m Col, Méx* **phone booth** <-es> *n* cabina *f* telefónica **phone box** <-es> *n Brit* cabina *f* telefónica **phone call** *n Brit* llamada *f* (telefónica) **phonecard** *n* tarjeta *f* telefónica

phone-in *n programa de radio o televisión en el que el público participa por teléfono*

phoneme ['fəʊniːm, *Am:* 'foʊ-] *n* LING fonema *m*

phone number *n* número *m* de teléfono

phonetic [fə'netɪk, *Am:* foʊ'net̬-] *adj* fonético, -a; **the International Phonetic Alphabet** el Alfabeto Fonético Internacional; ~ **transcription** transcripción *f* fonética

phonetician [ˌfəʊnɪ'tɪʃən, *Am:* ˌfoʊnə'-] *n* fonetista *mf*

phonetics [fə'netɪks, *Am:* foʊ'net̬-] *n* fonética *f*

phoney ['fəʊni, *Am:* 'foʊ-] **I.** <-ier, -iest> *adj inf* (*person, address*) falso, -a; (*documents*) falsificado, -a ►**to be as** ~ **as a two-dollar bill** *Am* ser más falso que un duro sevillano, ser más falso que un billete de tres pesos *Méx* **II.** *n* (*person*) farsante *mf*

phonic ['fɒnɪk, *Am:* 'fɑːnɪk] *adj* LING fónico, -a

phonology [fə'nɒlədʒi, *Am:* -'nɑːlə-] *n no pl* fonología *f*

phony ['fəʊni, *Am:* 'foʊ-] *adj Am s.* **phoney**

phooey ['fuːi] *interj iron, inf* ¡bobadas!

phosphate ['fɒsfeɪt, *Am:* 'fɑːs-] *n* fosfato *m*

phosphorescence [ˌfɒsfə'resns, *Am:* ˌfɑːs-] *n no pl* fosforescencia *f*

phosphorescent [ˌfɒsfər'esənt, *Am:* ˌfɑːsfə'res-] *adj* fosforescente

phosphoric [fɒs'fɒrɪk, *Am:* fɑːs'fɔːr-] *adj,* **phosphorous** ['fɒsfərəs, *Am:* 'fɑːs-] *adj* fosfórico, -a

phosphorus ['fɒsfərəs, *Am:* 'fɑːs-] *n no pl* fósforo *m*

photo ['fəʊtəʊ, *Am:* 'foʊt̬oʊ] <-s> *n inf abbr of* **photograph** foto *f*

photo call *n* rueda *f* fotográfica

photocell ['fəʊtəʊsel, *Am:* 'foʊt̬oʊ-] *n* célula *f* fotoeléctrica

photocopier ['fəʊtəʊˌkɒpiəʳ, *Am:* ˌfoʊt̬oʊ'kɑːpiɚ] *n* fotocopiadora *f*

photocopy ['fəʊtəʊˌkɒpi, *Am:* 'foʊt̬oʊˌkɑːpi] **I.** <-ies> *n* fotocopia *f;* **to make a** ~ **of sth** hacer una fotocopia de algo **II.** *vt* fotocopiar

photocopying bureau *n* fotocopistería *f*

photoelectric [ˌfəʊtəʊɪ'lektrɪk, *Am:* ˌfoʊt̬oʊ-] *adj* fotoeléctrico, -a; ~ **cell** célula *f* fotoeléctrica

photo finish *n* SPORTS resultado *m* comprobado por fotocontrol

photoflash ['fəʊtəʊˌflæʃ] *n* flash *m*

photogenic [ˌfəʊtəʊ'dʒenɪk, *Am:* ˌfoʊt̬oʊ'-] *adj* fotogénico, -a

photograph ['fəʊtəgrɑːf, *Am:* 'foʊt̬oʊgræf] **I.** *n* fotografía *f;* **aerial** ~ fotografía aérea; **colour/black-and-white** ~ fotografía en color/blanco y negro; **to take a** ~ **of sb** sacar una fotografía de alguien **II.** *vt* fotografiar **III.** *vi* **to** ~ **well** ser fotogénico

photograph album *n* álbum *m* de fotos

photographer [fə'tɒgrəfəʳ, *Am:* -'tɑːgrəfɚ] *n* fotógrafo, -a *m, f;* **amateur** ~ fotógrafo aficionado; ~**'s model** modelo *mf* fotográfico, -a

photographic [ˌfəʊtə'græfɪk, *Am:* ˌfoʊt̬ə'-] *adj* fotográfico, -a

photography [fə'tɒgrəfi, *Am:* -'tɑːgrə-] *n no pl* fotografía *f*

photojournalism [ˌfəʊtəʊ'dʒɜːnlɪzəm, *Am:* ˌfoʊt̬oʊ'dʒɜːr-] *n no pl* fotoperiodismo *m*

photometer [fəʊ'tɒmɪtəʳ] *n* fotómetro *m*

photomontage ['fəʊtəʊmɒn'tɑːʒ, *Am:* ˌfoʊt̬oʊmɑːn'-] *n* fotomontaje *m*

photon ['fəʊtɒn, *Am:* 'foʊtɑːn] *n* fotón *m*

photo opportunity *n* oportunidad *f* fotográfica

photo reporter *n* reportero, -a *m, f* fotográfico, -a

photosensitive [ˌfəʊtəʊ'sensɪtɪv, *Am:* ˌfoʊt̬oʊ'sensə-] *adj* fotosensible

photosetting ['fəʊtəʊˌsetɪŋ] *n* ART fotocomposición *f*

photostat ['fəʊtəstæt, *Am:* 'foʊt̬oʊ-] <-tt-> *vt* fotostatar

photosynthesis [ˌfəʊtəʊ'sɪntθɪsɪs, *Am:* ˌfoʊt̬oʊ'-] *n no pl* fotosíntesis *f*

phrasal verb [ˌfreɪzəl'vɜːb, *Am:* ˌfreɪzəl'vɜːrb] *n* LING verbo *m* con partícula

phrase [freɪz] **I.** *n* frase *f;* (*idiomatic expression*) expresión *f;* **verb/noun phrase** sintagma verbal/nominal; **to have a good turn of** ~ ser muy elocuente **II.** *vt* **to** ~ **sth well/badly** expresar algo bien/mal

phrasebook ['freɪzbʊk] *n* libro *m* de frases

phraseology [ˌfreɪzi'ɒlədʒi, *Am:* -'ɑːlə-] *n no pl* fraseología *f*

phrenetic [frə'netɪk, *Am:* frɪ'net̬-] *adj s.* **frenetic**

phut [fʌt] *interj* **to go ~** *Brit, Aus, inf* estropearse

pH-value [ˌpiː'eɪtʃ'væljuː] *n* valor *m* del pH

physical ['fɪzɪkəl] **I.** *adj* físico, -a; **~ attraction** atracción *f* física; **to be in a weak ~ condition** estar en bajas condiciones físicas; **to have a ~ disability** sufrir una discapacidad física; **~ exercise** ejercicio *m* físico **II.** *n* MED reconocimiento *m* médico

physical education *n* educación *f* física

physically *adv* (*attractive*) físicamente; (*dangerous*) desde el punto de vista físico

physician [fɪ'zɪʃən] *n Am* médico, -a *m, f*

physicist ['fɪzɪsɪst] *n* físico, -a *m, f;* (*student*) estudiante *mf* de física

physics ['fɪzɪks] **I.** *n no pl* física *f* **II.** *adj* físico, -a

physio ['fɪziəʊ, *Am:* -oʊ] *n* **1.** *abbr of* **physiotherapist** fisioterapeuta *mf* **2.** *no pl abbr of* **physiotherapy** fisioterapia *f*

physiognomy [ˌfɪzi'ɒnəmi, *Am:* -'ɑːgnə-] *n no pl* fisonomía *f*

physiological [ˌfɪziə'lɒdʒɪkəl, *Am:* -'lɑːdʒɪk-] *adj* fisiológico, -a

physiologist *n* fisiólogo, -a *m, f;* (*student*) estudiante *mf* de fisiología

physiology [ˌfɪzi'ɒlədʒi, *Am:* -'ɑːlə-] *n no pl* fisiología *f*

physiotherapist *n* fisioterapeuta *mf*

physiotherapy [ˌfɪziəʊ'θerəpi, *Am:* -oʊ'-] *n no pl* fisioterapia *f*

physique [fɪ'ziːk] *n* físico *m*

pianist ['pɪənɪst, *Am:* 'piːnɪst] *n* pianista *mf*

piano ['pjɑːnəʊ, *Am:* pi'ænoʊ] <-s> *n* piano *m;* **to play the ~** tocar el piano

piazza [pɪ'ætsə, *Am:* -'ɑːt-] *n* plaza *f*

picaresque [ˌpɪkə'resk, *Am:* -ə˞'-] *adj* LIT picaresco, -a

piccaninny [ˌpɪkə'nɪni, *Am:* 'pɪk-] <-ies> *n pej* (*child*) negrito, -a *m, f*

piccolo ['pɪkələʊ, *Am:* -loʊ] <-s> *n* flautín *m*

pick [pɪk] **I.** *vt* **1.** (*select*) elegir; **to ~ sb for sth** elegir a alguien para algo; **to ~ sth at random** elegir algo al azar; **to ~ a fine time to do sth** *iron* escoger un buen momento para hacer algo; **to ~ one's way** moverse con cuidado **2.** (*harvest: fruit, vegetables*) recoger **3.** (*touch*) tocar; **to ~ one's nose** hurgarse la nariz; **to ~ one's teeth** limpiarse los dientes con un mondador; **to ~ holes in sth** *fig* encontrar fallos a algo **4.** MUS (*guitar*) tocar **5.** (*steal*) robar; **to ~ a lock** forzar una cerradura; **to ~ sb's pocket** robar algo del bolsillo de alguien; **to ~ sb's brain** *fig* aprovecharse de los conocimientos de alguien **II.** *vi* **to ~ and choose** tardar en escoger **III.** *n* **1.** (*selection*) elección *f;* (*of people*) selección *f;* **to take one's ~** eligir; **to have one's ~** poder elegir; **the ~ of the bunch** el mejor del grupo **2.** (*pickaxe*) pico *m;* **with ~s and shovels** con pico y pala

◆**pick at** *vt insep* **1.** (*toy with: food*) picotar **2.** (*handle*) manosear; (*scratch*) rascar **3.** (*bother*) **to ~ sb/sth** fastidiar a alguien/algo

◆**pick off** *vt* **1.** (*shoot*) abatir (a tiros) **2.** *fig* (*take the best*) escoger lo mejor **3.** (*pull off*) separar; **to pick an apple off the tree** coger una manzana del árbol

◆**pick on** *vt insep* **1.** (*victimize*) meterse con **2.** (*select*) **to ~ sb for sth** escoger a alguien para algo

◆**pick out** *vt* **1.** (*choose*) elegir **2.** (*recognize*) distinguir

◆**pick over** *vt* ir revolviendo y examinando

◆**pick up** **I.** *vt* **1.** (*lift*) levantar; **to ~ the phone** coger el teléfono; **to pick oneself up** ponerse de pie; **to pick oneself up off the floor** levantarse del suelo; **to ~ the pieces** *fig* empezar de nuevo **2.** (*get*) conseguir; (*conversation*) captar; **to ~ a bargain** conseguir una ganga; **to ~ an illness** contagiarse con una enfermedad; **to ~ speed** coger velocidad; **to ~ the bill** *inf* pagar la cuenta **3.** (*collect*) recoger; **to pick sb up** recoger a alguien **4.** (*buy*) adquirir **5.** (*detect: noise*) detectar **6.** (*learn*) aprender **7.** (*sexually*) **to pick sb up** ligarse a alguien **8.** *Brit, Aus, inf* (*halt*) detener; (*arrest*) arrestar **9.** (*reprimand*) reprender; **to pick sb up on sth** reprender a alguien por algo **10.** *inf* (*earn*) ganar **II.** *vi* **1.** (*improve*) mejorar; (*numbers*) ir a mejor; MED reponerse **2.** (*continue*) continuar; **to ~ where one left off** reanudar donde uno lo dejó

pickaback ['pɪkəbæk] *n inf s.* **piggyback**

pickax *n Am,* **pickaxe** ['pɪkæks] *n Brit, Aus* pico *m*

picker *n* recolector(a) *m(f)*

picket ['pɪkɪt] **I.** *n* **1.** (*striker*) *a.* MIL piquete *m* **2.** (*stake*) estaca *f* **II.** *vt* (*in strike*) formar piquete en

picket fence *n* valla *f* **picket line** *n* piquete *m;* **to be on the ~** participar en un piquete; **to cross the ~** no hacer caso de un piquete

picking *n* selección *f*

picking list *n Am* COM inventario *m* de ganancias

pickings ['pɪkɪŋz] *npl* sobras *fpl*

pickle ['pɪkl] **I.** *n* encurtido *m; Am* (*cucumber*) pepinillo *m* en vinagre al eneldo ▸**to be in a (pretty) ~** *inf* estar en un (buen) berenjenal **II.** *vt* (*vegetables*) conservar en vinagre; (*fish*) conservar en escabeche

pickled *adj* **1.** (*vegetables*) encurtido, -a; (*fish*) en escabeche **2.** *fig, inf* (*drunk*) borracho, -a; **to get ~** emborracharse

picklock ['pɪklɒk, *Am:* -lɑːk] *n* **1.** (*burglar*) ladrón, -ona *m, f* **2.** (*instrument*) ganzúa *f*

pick-me-up ['pɪkmiʌp] *n* tónico *m;* (*drink*) bebida *f* estimulante

pickpocket ['pɪkpɒkɪt, *Am:* -ˌpɑːkɪt] *n* carterista *mf,* bolsista *mf AmC, Méx*

pick-up ['pɪkʌp] *n* **1.** (*part of record player*) brazo *m* del tocadiscos **2.** *inf* (*collection*) recogida *f* **3.** (*vehicle*) camioneta *f* con plataforma

pick-up point *n* punto *m* de recogida

picky ['pɪki] <-ier, -iest> *adj pej, inf* criticón, -ona; **to be a ~ eater** ser caprichoso para comer

picnic ['pɪknɪk] **I.** *n* picnic *m;* **to take a ~** hacer un picnic; **to go on a ~** ir de picnic; **to seem like a ~** parecer agradable; **to be no ~** *fig* no ser nada agradable **II.** <-ck-> *vi* ir de merienda al campo

picnicker *n* excursionista *mf*

picnic lunch *n* picnic *m* **picnic site** *n* lugar *m* para hacer picnics

pictogram ['pɪktəgræm] *n* pictograma *m*

pictorial [pɪk'tɔːriəl] *adj* (*form, method*) pictórico, -a; (*book, brochure*) ilustrado, -a

picture ['pɪktʃəʳ, *Am:* -tʃɚ] **I.** *n* **1.** (*image*) imagen *f;* (*painting*) pintura *f;* (*drawing*) ilustración *f;* **to draw a ~** hacer un dibujo; **to paint a ~** pintar un cuadro; **as pretty as a ~** como de postal **2.** (*photo*) fotografía *f;* **to take a ~** sacar una fotografía; **satellite ~** fotografía por satélite; **wedding ~** fotografía de boda **3.** (*film*) película *f;* **to make a ~** hacer una película; **to go to the ~s** ir al cine **4.** (*mental image*) imagen *f* **5.** *fig* (*depiction*) representación *f;* **to paint a ~ of sth** representar algo ►**a ~ is worth a thousand words** *prov* una imagen vale más que mil palabras; **to paint a very black ~** pintar un panorama muy negro; **to be in the ~** estar al corriente; **to get the ~** entender; **to keep sb in the ~** (**about sth**) mantener a alguien al tanto (de algo); **to put sb in the ~** poner a alguien en antecedentes **II.** *vt* imaginarse; (*depict*) representar; **to ~ oneself ...** imaginarse...

picture book *n* libro *m* ilustrado **picture frame** *n* marco *m* (para cuadro) **picture gallery** *n* galería *f* de arte **picture-goer** *n* cinéfilo, -a *m, f* **picture library** *n* pinacoteca *f* **picture postcard** *n* tarjeta *f* postal **picture puzzle** *n* rompecabezas *m inv*

picturesque [ˌpɪktʃə'resk] *adj* **1.** (*scenic*) pintoresco, -a **2.** *iron* (*language*) vívido, -a

picture tube *n* tubo *m* de imagen **picture window** *n* ventanal *m*

piddle ['pɪdl] *inf* **I.** *n* orina *f* **II.** *interj* ¡mierda! **III.** *vi* mear

piddling ['pɪdlɪŋ] *adj pej, inf* de poca monta; **the ~ sum of £5** la insignificante suma de 5 libras

pidgin ['pɪdʒɪn] *n* **1.** LING *versión simplificada de una lengua* **2.** *inf* **to speak ~ English/French** chapurrear algo de inglés/francés

pie [paɪ] *n* tarta *f,* pay *m AmS* ►**it's ~ in the sky** es como prometer la luna; (**as**) **easy as ~** más fácil imposible; **to eat humble ~** tragarse las palabras

piebald ['paɪbɔːld] *adj* pío, -a

piece [piːs] *n* **1.** (*bit: of wood, metal, food*) trozo *m;* (*of text*) sección *f;* (*of land*) terreno *m;* (*of broken glass*) fragmento *m;* **a ~ of paper** (*scrap*) un trozo de papel; (*sheet*) una hoja; **in one ~** en una sola pieza; **in ~s** en pedazos; **to break sth to/in ~** hacer algo pedazos; **to tear sth into ~s** desgarrar algo; (**all**) **in one ~** (todo) de una pieza; **~ by ~** pieza por pieza; **to come to ~s** (*shatter*) hacerse añicos; (*made to be disassembled*) ser desmontable; **to take sth to ~s** *Brit* desmontar algo; **to go** (**all**) **to ~s** (*trauma*) sufrir un ataque de nervios; (*collapse, break*) venirse abajo **2.** (*item, one of set*) unidad *f;* **~ of luggage** bulto *m;* **~ of clothing** prenda *f* de vestir; **~ of equipment** aparato *m* **3.** (*game*) pieza *f* **4.** (*scrap*) **a ~ of advice** un consejo; **~ of evidence** prueba *f;* **a ~ of information** una información; **a ~ of news** una noticia **5.** ART, MUS pieza *f;* PUBL anuncio *m;* **~ of theatre** obra *f* de teatro; **a ~ of writing** un texto **6.** (*coin*) moneda *f;* **a 50p ~** una moneda de 50 peniques ►**to get a ~ of the action** *Am* (*profits*) obtener una parte del beneficio; (*get excitement*) pasarlo bien; **to be a ~ of cake** *inf* ser pan comido; **to want a ~ of the cake** querer parte del pastel; **to give sb a ~ of one's mind** *inf* decir cuatro verdades a alguien; **to say one's ~** decir lo que uno quiere decir

◆**piece together** *vt* (*reconstruct*) reconstruir; **to ~ evidence** atar cabos

piecemeal ['piːsmiːl] **I.** *adv* poco a poco **II.** *adj* que va poco a poco

piece number *n* número *m* de pieza **piece price** *n* precio *m* por unidad **piece rate** *n* precio *m* por unidad

piecework ['piːswɜːk, *Am:* -wɜːrk] *n no pl* trabajo *m* a destajo; **to do ~** trabajar a destajo

piece-worker *n* destajista *mf*

pied [paɪd] *adj* pío, -a

pie-eyed [ˌpaɪ'aɪd] *adj inf* (*drunk*) **to be ~** estar como una cuba

pier [pɪəʳ, *Am:* pɪr] *n* **1.** (*jetty*) muelle *m,* malecón *m* **2.** ARCHIT (*pillar*) columna *f;* (*bridge support*) pila *f*

pierce [pɪəs, *Am:* pɪrs] **I.** *vt* (*perforate*) perforar; **to ~ a hole in sth** agujerear algo; **to have one's ears ~ed** agujerearse las orejas **II.** *vi* (*drill*) **to ~ into sth** penetrar en algo; **to ~ through sth** atravesar algo

piercing **I.** *adj* **1.** (*wind*) cortante; **it's ~ cold!** ¡hace un frío que pela! **2.** (*eyes, gaze, look*) penetrante; (*question, reply, wit*) punzante; (*sarcasm*) agudo, -a **3.** (*cry*) desgarrador(a) **II.** *n* piercing *m*

piety ['paɪəti, *Am:* -t̬i] *n no pl* piedad *f*

piffle ['pɪfl] *n no pl, inf* disparates *mpl*

piffling ['pɪflɪŋ] *adj inf* insignificante

pig [pɪg] **I.** *n* **1.** ZOOL cerdo *m* **2.** *pej, inf* (*person*) cochino, -a *m, f;* **to be a ~** *Brit* ser un cerdo; **to be a ~ to sb** portarse mal con alguien ►**to make a ~'s ear of sth** *Brit, inf* hacer algo fatal; **to buy a ~ in a poke** cerrar

P

un trato a ciegas; **to sell a ~ in a poke** dar gato por liebre; **~s might fly** *inf* ¡y un jamón!; **to make a ~ of oneself** ponerse como un cerdo **II.** *vt* **to ~ oneself on sth** comer demasido de algo

◆**pig out** *vi inf* ponerse morado

pigeon ['pɪdʒən] *n* paloma *f;* **it's not my ~** eso no me corresponde

pigeon fancier *n Brit, Aus* colombófilo, -a *m, f*

pigeonhole ['pɪdʒənhəʊl, *Am:* -hoʊl] **I.** *n* casilla *f;* **to put sb in a ~** encasillar a alguien **II.** *vt* **to ~ sb** encasillar a alguien; **to ~ sb as sth** poner la etiqueta de algo a alguien

pigeon-toed ['pɪdʒəntəʊd, *Am:* -toʊd] *adj* **to be ~** tener los pies torcidos hacia dentro

piggery ['pɪgəri] <-ies> *n* **1.** AGR pocilga *f* **2.** (*gluttony*) glotonería *f*

piggish ['pɪgɪʃ] *adj pej* puerco, -a

piggy ['pɪgi] **I.** *adj* <-ier, -iest> *inf* **1.** (*pig-like*) con apariencia de cerdo; **~ eyes** ojos *mpl* pequeños **2.** (*greedy*) glotón, -ona **II.** <-ies> *n childspeak* cerdito *m*

piggyback ['pɪgibæk] *n* **to give a child a ~** llevar a un niño a caballito

piggy bank *n* hucha *f*, *en forma de cerdito*

pigheaded [,pɪg'hedɪd] *adj* testarudo, -a

pig iron *n* hierro *m* bruto

piglet ['pɪglət, *Am:* -lɪt] *n* cochinillo *m*

pigment ['pɪgmənt] *n* pigmento *m*

pigmentation [,pɪgmen'teɪʃən] *n no pl* pigmentación *f*

pigmy ['pɪgmi] **I.** <-ies> *n* **1.** (*short person*) pigmeo, -a *m, f* **2.** (*unimportant person*) enano, -a *m, f* **II.** *adj* ZOOL enano, -a

pigskin ['pɪgskɪn] *n* **1.** (*leather*) piel *f* de cerdo **2.** *Am, inf* (*American football ball*) pelota *f* de fútbol americano

pigsty ['pɪgstaɪ] *n a. fig, pej* pocilga *f*

pigswill ['pɪgswɪl] *n no pl* bazofia *f*

pigtail ['pɪgteɪl] *n* (*single*) coleta *f;* (*one of two plaits*) trenza *f;* **to have one's hair in ~s** llevar el pelo trenzado

pike[1] [paɪk] *n* (*fish*) lucio *m*

pike[2] [paɪk] *n* (*weapon*) pica *f*

pike[3] [paɪk] *n Am* autopista *f*

pikestaff ['paɪkstɑːf, *Am:* -stæf] *n no pl* **as plain as a ~** *Brit* claro como la luz del día

pilaster [pɪ'læstəʳ, *Am:* -tɚ] *n* pilastra *f*

pilchard ['pɪltʃəd, *Am:* -tʃɚd] *n* sardina *f*

pile [paɪl] **I.** *n* **1.** (*heap*) montón *m;* **to have ~s of sth** *inf* tener montones de algo; **to make a ~** *fig, inf* hacer fortuna **2.** (*stack*) pila *f* **3.** ELEC pila *f* **4.** ARCHIT pila *f* **5.** (*of carpet*) pelo *m* **II.** *vt* amontonar; **to ~ sth high** apilar algo

◆**pile in** *vi* **~!** ¡todos dentro, que nos vamos!

◆**pile on** *vt* **1.** (*enter*) entrar desordenadamente **2.** (*heap*) amontonar; **to pile sth on sth** amontonar algo encima de algo **3. to pile it on** *inf* exagerar; **to ~ the agony** *Brit, inf* aumentar el dolor

◆**pile up** **I.** *vi* **1.** (*accumulate*) acumularse **2.** (*form a pile*) apilarse **II.** *vt* amontonar

pile-driver ['paɪl,draɪvəʳ, *Am:* -vɚ] *n* martinete *m*

piles *npl inf* almorranas *fpl*

pile-up ['paɪlʌp] *n* accidente *m* múltiple

pilfer ['pɪlfəʳ, *Am:* -fɚ] *vt* ratear

pilfering *n* hurtos *mpl*

pilgrim ['pɪlgrɪm] *n* peregrino, -a *m, f*

pilgrimage ['pɪlgrɪmɪdʒ] *n* peregrinación *f;* **to make a ~** hacer una peregrinación

pill [pɪl] *n* pastilla *f*, píldora *f;* **the ~** (*contraception*) la píldora; **to be on the ~** estar tomando la píldora ►**to be a bitter ~ to swallow** ser un trago amargo; **to pop ~s** drogarse con pastillas; **to sweeten** [*o* **sugar**] **the ~** dorar la píldora

pillage ['pɪlɪdʒ] **I.** *vt form* saquear **II.** *vi* realizar un saqueo **III.** *n no pl, form* saqueo *m*

pillar ['pɪləʳ, *Am:* -ɚ] *n* **1.** ARCHIT pilar *m*, columna *f;* **a ~ of flame/smoke** una columna de fuego/humo **2.** *fig* (*of support*) sostén *m;* **to be a ~ of strength** ser firme como una roca ►**to chase sb from ~ to post** acosar a alguien

pillar box *n Brit* buzón *m*

pillbox ['pɪlbɒks, *Am:* -bɑːks] *n* **1.** (*for tablets*) pastillero *m* **2.** MIL fortín *m*

pillion ['pɪlɪən, *Am:* 'pɪljən] *Brit, Aus* **I.** *n* (*motorbike*) asiento *m* de atrás **II.** *adv* **to ride/sit ~** montarse/sentarse en el asiento de atrás

pillory ['pɪləri] **I.** <-ie-> *vt* **to ~ sb/sth** poner en ridículo a alguien/algo **II.** *n* picota *f*

pillow ['pɪləʊ, *Am:* -oʊ] *n* **1.** (*for bed*) almohada *f* **2.** *Am* (*cushion*) cojín *m*

pillowcase ['pɪləʊkeɪs, *Am:* -oʊ-] *n*, **pillow cover** *n*, **pillowslip** *n* funda *f* de almohada

pilot ['paɪlət] **I.** *n* **1.** AVIAT piloto *mf* **2.** NAUT práctico *mf* **3.** TV programa *m* piloto **4.** TECH (*light*) piloto *m* **II.** *vt* **1.** (*plane*) pilotar **2.** (*boat*) guiar **3.** COM (*product*) desarrollar; **to ~ a bill** encargarse de un proyecto de ley

pilot boat *n* bote *m* del práctico **pilot fish** *n* pez *m* piloto **pilot instructor** *n* instructor(a) *m(f)* de vuelo

pilotless *adj* sin piloto

pilot light *n* piloto *m* **pilot plant** *n* planta *f* piloto **pilot program** *n Am*, **pilot scheme** *n Brit, Aus* programa *m* piloto **pilot's licence** *n* licencia *f* de vuelo **pilot study** *n* estudio *m* piloto **pilot survey** *n* estudio *m* experimental **pilot test** *n* prueba *f* piloto

pimento [pɪ'mentəʊ, *Am:* -toʊ] <-s> *n* pimiento *m*

pimp [pɪmp] **I.** *n* chulo *m* **II.** *vi* hacer de chulo

pimple ['pɪmpl] *n* grano *m*

pimply ['pɪmpli] <-ier, -iest> *adj* lleno, -a de granos

pin [pɪn] **I.** *n* **1.** (*needle*) alfiler *m;* MIL (*on grenade*) arandela *f;* **tie ~** alfiler *m* de corbata **2.** *Am* (*brooch*) prendedor *m* **3.** *pl, iron* patas *fpl* ►**to have ~s and needles** sentir un hormigueo; **as bright as a new ~** brillante como una patena; **you could have heard a ~ drop** se podía oír hasta el vuelo de una mosca II. <-nn-> *vt* (*attach using pin*) **to ~ sth on** prender algo con un alfiler; **to ~ back one's ears** *fig* escuchar atentamente

◆**pin down** *vt* 1. (*define*) precisar 2. (*locate*) concretar 3. (*pressure to decide*) presionar 4. (*restrict movement*) inmovilizar

◆**pin together** *vt* unir; **to pin papers together** grapar papeles

◆**pin up** *vt* (*attach using pins*) recoger con alfileres; (*picture on wall*) fijar con chinchetas; **to ~ one's hair** recogerse el pelo con horquillas

PIN [pɪn] *n abbr of* **personal identification number** PIN *m* (*número de identificación personal*)

pinafore ['pɪnəfɔːʳ, *Am:* -fɔːr] *n* 1. (*apron*) delantal *m* 2. *Brit, Aus* pichi *m*

pinafore dress *n* pichi *m*

pinball ['pɪnbɔːl] *n* **to play ~** jugar al flíper

pinball machine *n* flíper *m*

pincers ['pɪntsəz, *Am:* -sɚz] *npl* 1. ZOOL pinzas *fpl* 2. (*tool*) tenazas *fpl*

pinch [pɪntʃ] I. *vt* 1. (*nip, tweak*) pellizcar; **to ~ oneself** *fig* pellizcarse para ver si no se está soñando 2. (*be too tight*) apretar; **the shoes ~ my feet** los zapatos me aprietan 3. *inf* (*steal*) birlar II. *vi* 1. (*squeeze with fingers*) estrujar 2. (*boots, shoes, slippers*) apretar III. *n* 1. (*nip*) pellizco *m;* **to give sb a ~** dar un pellizco a alguien; **at a ~**, **in a ~** *Am* si realmente es necesario; **to feel the ~** pasar apuros 2. (*small quantity*) pizca *f* ►**to take sth with a ~ of salt** tomar algo con cierto escepticismo

pinched [pɪntʃt] *adj* demacrado, -a

pincushion ['pɪnˌkʊʃən] *n* acerico *m*

pine¹ [paɪn] *n* (*tree, wood*) pino *m*

pine² [paɪn] *vi* **to ~ (away)** languidecer; **to ~ for sb** suspirar por alguien

◆**pine away** *vi* languidecer

pineal ['pɪniəl] *adj* pineal

pineal body *n*, **pineal gland** *n* glándula *f* pineal

pineapple ['paɪnæpl] *n* piña *f;* **tinned ~s** piña *f* en almíbar

pine cone *n* piña *f*

pine grove *n* pinar *m* **pine needle** *n* aguja *f* de pino **pine wood** *n no pl* madera *f* de pino

ping [pɪŋ] I. *n* (*sound: of bell*) tintín *m;* (*of glass, metal*) sonido *m* metálico II. *vi* tintinear; (*click*) hacer clic

ping-pong ['pɪŋˌpɒŋ, *Am:* -ˌpɑːŋ] *n no pl, inf* ping-pong *m*

pinhead ['pɪnhed] *n* 1. (*part of pin*) cabeza *f* de alfiler 2. *pej, inf* (*simpleton*) cabeza *f* de chorlito

pinion¹ ['pɪnjən] *vt* inmovilizar; **she was ~ed against the wall** estaba contra la pared sin poderse mover

pinion² ['pɪnjən] *n* TECH piñón *m*

pink [pɪŋk] I. *n* 1. (*colour*) rosa *m* 2. BOT clavelina *f* ►**to be in the ~** rebosar de salud II. *adj* rosado, -a; **to turn ~ with pleasure/embarrassment** ponerse colorado de placer/vergüenza

pinkie ['pɪŋki] *n Am, Aus, inf* dedo *m* meñique

pinking shears *npl* tijeras *fpl* dentadas

pinko ['pɪŋkəʊ, *Am:* -koʊ] <-s *o* -es> *n pej* POL rojo, -a *m, f*

pinnacle ['pɪnəkl] *n* 1. *pl* (*of mountain*) pico *m* 2. ARCHIT (*tower*) pináculo *m* 3. *no pl, fig* cúspide *f*

pinpoint ['pɪnpɔɪnt] I. *vt* (*location, reason*) indicar con toda precisión; **to ~ the cause of sth** señalar la causa de algo II. *adj* exacto, -a; **~ accuracy** gran precisión *f*

pinprick ['pɪnprɪk] *n pl* pinchazo *m*

pinstripe ['pɪnstraɪp] I. *adj* de raya diplomática II. *n no pl* (*stripe*) raya *f* fina; (*suit*) traje *m* de raya diplomática

pint [paɪnt] *n* pinta *f* (*Aus, Brit = 0,57 l, Am = 0,47 l*); **a ~ of beer/milk** una pinta de cerveza/leche

pinta ['paɪntə, *Am:* -t̬ə] *n Brit, inf* pinta *f* (de leche)

pint-size(d) ['paɪntsaɪz(d)] *adj inf* pequeño, -a

pin-up ['pɪnʌp] *n* 1. (*poster*) póster *m* (*de una celebridad*) 2. (*man*) chico *m* de póster; (*girl*) pin-up *f*

pioneer [ˌpaɪə'nɪəʳ, *Am:* -'nɪr] I. *n* pionero, -a *m, f* II. *vt* hacer los preparativos para

pioneering *adj* innovador(a)

pious ['paɪəs] *adj* 1. REL piadoso, -a 2. *iron* piadoso, -a; **~ intentions** intenciones *fpl* piadosas; **~ hope** *Brit* esperanza *f* piadosa

pip¹ [pɪp] *n* BOT pepita *f*

pip² [pɪp] *n pl, Brit* (*sound*) pitido *m*

pip³ [pɪp] <-pp-> *vt Brit, inf* vencer; **to ~ sb at the post** ganar a alguien en el último momento

pipe [paɪp] I. *n* 1. TECH (*tube*) tubo *m;* (*smaller*) caño *m;* (*for gas, water*) cañería *f* 2. (*for smoking*) pipa *f*, cachimba *f AmL;* **to light one's ~** encenderse la pipa; **put that in your ~ and smoke it** *iron* ¡chúpate eso! 3. MUS (*wind instrument*) caramillo *m;* (*in organ*) cañón *m;* **~s** gaita *f* II. *vt* 1. (*transport*) transportar por tuberías 2. (*speak shrilly, chirping*) decir con voz estridente III. *vi* trinar; (*very loudly*) hablar muy alto

◆**pipe down** *vi inf* (*be quiet*) callarse; (*become quieter*) calmarse

◆**pipe up** *vi* decir inesperadamente

pipe cleaner *n* limpiapipas *m inv*

pipe dream *n* sueño *m* imposible

pipe-fitter *n* fontanero, -a *m, f*

pipeline ['paɪplaɪn] *n* tubería *f;* **to be in the ~** *fig* estar tramitándose

piper ['paɪpəʳ, *Am:* -pɚ] *n* gaitero, -a *m, f* ►**he who pays the ~ calls the tune** *prov* quien paga, manda

piping ['paɪpɪŋ] *n no pl* 1. FASHION ribete *m*

P

2. (*pipes*) tubería *f*

piping hot *adv* bien caliente

pipsqueak ['pɪpskwi:k] *n pej, inf* fantoche *m*

piquant ['pi:kənt] *adj* **1.** (*food*) picante **2.** (*intriguing*) intrigante

pique [pi:k] **I.** *n no pl* resentimiento *m;* **to do sth in a fit of** ~ hacer algo motivado por el rencor **II.** *vt* **1.** (*annoy*) ofender **2.** (*arouse*) **to** ~ **sb's curiosity/interest** despertar la curiosidad/el interés de alguien

piracy ['paɪərəsi, *Am:* 'paɪrə-] *n no pl* NAUT, COM piratería *f;* **software** ~ piratería *f* de software

pirate ['paɪərət, *Am:* 'paɪrət] **I.** *n* pirata *m* **II.** *adj* pirata; ~ **copy** copia *f* pirata; ~ **video** vídeo *m* pirata **III.** *vt* piratear

pirouette [ˌpɪrʊ'et, *Am:* -u'et] **I.** *n* pirueta *f* **II.** *vi* piruetear

Pisces ['paɪsi:z] *n* Piscis *m*

piss [pɪs] *vulg* **I.** *n no pl* meada *f;* **to have a** ~ mear; **to need a** ~ tener ganas de mear ►**to take the** ~ (**out of sb**) *Brit* cachondearse (de alguien) **II.** *vi* **1.** (*urinate*) mear **2.** *Brit, Aus* (*rain*) llover; **it's ~ing with rain** estar lloviendo a cántaros **III.** *vt* **to** ~ **oneself laughing** mearse de risa

◆**piss about, piss around** *Brit, Aus* **I.** *vi inf* **1.** (*act silly*) hacer el burro **2.** (*waste time*) perder el tiempo **II.** *vt inf* **to piss sb about** [*o* **around**] (*waste time*) hacer perder el tiempo a alguien

pissed [pɪst] *adj inf* **to be** ~ **1.** *Brit, Aus* (*drunk*) estar borracho **2.** *Am* (*angry*) estar de mala leche

piss-up ['pɪsʌp] *n Brit, Aus, inf* juerga *f* de borrachera

pistachio [pɪ'stɑ:ʃiəʊ, *Am:* -'stæʃioʊ] <-s> *n* pistacho *m,* pistache *m Méx*

pistil ['pɪstɪl] *n* pistilo *m*

pistol ['pɪstəl] *n* pistola *f;* **to hold a** ~ **to sb's head** *fig* poner a alguien entre la espada y la pared

pistol shot *n* pistoletazo *m*

piston ['pɪstən] *n* TECH pistón *m*

piston engine *n* motor *m* de pistón **piston ring** *n* aro *m* de pistón

pit¹ [pɪt] **I.** *n* **1.** (*in ground*) hoyo *m;* (*on metal*) muesca *f;* (*on face*) marca *f;* **in the** ~ **of the stomach** en la boca del estómago **2.** (*mine*) mina *f;* **to go down the** ~ bajar a las minas; **to work in the ~s** trabajar en las minas **3. the ~s** *pl, fig, inf* lo peor **4.** *inf* (*untidy place*) lobera *f* **5.** THEAT (*seating area*) patio *m* de asientos; (*orchestral area*) platea *f* **6. the ~s** *pl* SPORTS los boxes **II.** <-tt-> *vt* **to be ~ted** (**with sth**) tener marcas (formadas por algo)

pit² [pɪt] <-tt-> *Am* **I.** *n* (*of fruit*) hueso *m* **II.** *vt* GASTR deshuesar

pit-a-pat [ˌpɪtə'pæt, *Am:* 'pɪţəpæt] **I.** *adv* **his heart went** ~ su corazón empezó a palpitar a gran velocidad **II.** *n* (*of feet*) paso *m* ligero; (*of heart*) latido *m*

pitch¹ [pɪtʃ] **I.** *n* **1.** *Brit, Aus* (*playing field*) campo *m;* **football/rugby** ~ campo de fútbol/rugby **2.** *Brit* (*place for camping*) terreno *m* para acampar **3.** *Am* (*baseball*) lanzamiento *m* **4.** MUS, LING tono *m* **5.** (*volume*) volumen *m;* **to be at fever** ~ estar muy emocionado **6.** (*spiel*) rollo *m;* **sales** ~ labia *f* para vender; **to make a** ~ soltar un rollo **7.** (*slope*) grado *m* de inclinación; **low/steep** ~ pendiente *f* suave/pronunciada **II.** *vt* **1.** (*throw*) lanzar; **to** ~ **sb into a situation** meter a alguien en una situación; **to be ~ed** (**headlong**) **into despair** estar sumido en la deseperación **2.** SPORTS (*throw*) tirar **3.** (*fix level of sound*) **this tune is ~ed** (**too**) **high/low** esta afinación es (demasiado) alta/baja **4.** (*aim at*) **to** ~ **sth at sb** diseñar algo para alguien **III.** *vi* **1.** (*thrust*) tirar **2.** *Am* SPORTS (*throw baseball*) lanzar **3.** (*slope*) inclinarse

◆**pitch in** *vi inf* contribuir

◆**pitch into** *vt* **1.** (*attack verbally*) arremeter contra **2.** (*begin enthusiastically*) emprender enérgicamente

◆**pitch out** *vt* tirar

pitch² [pɪtʃ] *n no pl* (*bitumen*) brea *f*

pitch-black [ˌpɪtʃ'blæk] *adj* (*extremely dark*) negro, -a como la boca de un lobo; (*very black*) muy negro, -a

pitched battle *n* batalla *f* campal

pitched roof *n* tejado *m* a dos aguas

pitcher¹ ['pɪtʃəʳ, *Am:* -ɚ] *n* (*large jug*) cántaro *m; Am* (*smaller*) jarra *f*

pitcher² ['pɪtʃəʳ, *Am:* -ɚ] *n* SPORTS (*baseball*) lanzador(a) *m(f)*

pitchfork ['pɪtʃfɔ:k, *Am:* -fɔ:rk] *n* (*for hay*) horca *f*

pitch pine *n* pino *m* tea

piteous ['pɪtiəs, *Am:* 'pɪţ-] *adj* patético, -a; **a** ~ **sight** una escena patética

pitfall ['pɪtfɔ:l] *n pl* escollo *m*

pith [pɪθ] *n no pl* **1.** BOT (*part of plants*) médula *f* **2.** *fig* (*main point*) meollo *m;* (*substance of speech*) esencia *f*

pithead ['pɪtˌhed] **I.** *n no pl* bocamina *f* **II.** *adj* de la bocamina

pith helmet *n* salacot *m*

pithy ['pɪθi] <-ier, -iest> *adj* (*succinct, concise*) sucinto, -a

pitiable ['pɪtiəbl, *Am:* 'pɪţ-] *adj form s.* **pitiful**

pitiful ['pɪtifəl, *Am:* 'pɪţ-] *adj* **1.** (*terrible*) lamentable; ~ **conditions** condiciones *fpl* lamentables; **a** ~ **sight** una escena patética **2.** (*unsatisfactory*) insatisfactorio, -a; ~ **excuse** excusa *f* pobre

pitiless ['pɪtiləs, *Am:* 'pɪţ-] *adj* despiadado, -a

piton ['pi:tɒn, *Am:* -tɑ:n] *n* SPORTS pitón *m*

pitta (**bread**) ['pɪtəˌbred, *Am:* 'pɪţ-] *n no pl* pan *m* de pitta

pittance ['pɪtənts] *n no pl* miseria *f,* pavada *f CSur;* **to live on a** ~ vivir de una renta miserable

pituitary (**gland**) [pɪ'tju:ɪtəri, *Am:* -'tu:-

əter-] *n* glándula *f* pituitaria

pity ['pɪti, *Am:* 'pɪţ-] **I.** *n no pl* **1.** (*compassion*) compasión *f;* **in ~** por piedad; **to feel ~ for sb** compadecerse de alguien; **to take ~ on sb** apiadarse de alguien; **for ~'s sake** ¡por piedad! **2.** (*shame*) **to be a ~** ser una pena; (**it's a**) **~** (es una) lástima; **the ~ of it is that ...** lo lamentable es que...; **more's the ~!** ¡desgraciadamente!; **what a ~!** ¡qué pena! **II.** <-ies, -ied> *vt* compadecerse de

pitying *adj* compasivo, -a

pivot ['pɪvət] **I.** *n* **1.** TECH eje *m* **2.** (*focal point*) punto *m* central; **to be the ~ of sth** ser el eje de algo; (*person*) ser el centro de algo **II.** *vi* **to ~ round** girar; **to ~ around sth** *a. fig* girar en torno a algo; **to ~ through 90 degrees** dar un giro de 90 grados

pivotal ['pɪvətəl, *Am:* -ţəl] *adj* fundamental

pixel [pɪksəl] *n* INFOR pixel *m*

pixie *n*, **pixy** ['pɪksi] <-ies> *n* LIT duende *m*

pizza ['pi:tsə] *n* pizza *f*

placard ['plækɑ:d, *Am:* -ɑ:rd] *n* pancarta *f*

placate [plə'keɪt, *Am:* 'pleɪkeɪt] *vt* **1.** (*soothe*) aplacar **2.** (*appease*) apaciguar

placatory [plə'keɪtəri, *Am:* 'pleɪkətɔ:r-] *adj form* **1.** (*calming*) apaciguador(a) **2.** (*appeasing, conciliatory*) conciliador(a)

place [pleɪs] **I.** *n* **1.** (*location, area*) lugar *m;* **~ of birth** lugar de nacimiento; **~s of interest** lugares de interés; **~ of refuge** refugio *m;* **people in high ~s** gente *f* bien situada; **to be in ~** estar en su sitio; *fig* estar listo; **to do sth in ~** *Am* hacer algo en el acto; **if I were in your ~, ...** yo en tu lugar...; **in ~ of sb/sth** en vez de alguien/algo; **not to be the ~ to do sth** no ser el lugar apropiado para hacer algo; **this is no ~ to bring up your children** éste no es un lugar apropiado para criar a tus hijos; **it is not your ~ to say that** no eres quien para decir eso **2.** *inf* (*house*) casa *f;* **at my ~** en mi casa **3.** (*building*) edificio *m* **4.** (*commercial location*) local *m* **5.** (*position*) posición *f;* **to lose one's ~** (*book*) perder la página; **to take first/second ~** quedar en primer/segundo lugar; **in the first ~** primero; **in the second ~** segundo; **a ~ among the best directors** un lugar entre los mejores directores **6.** (*seat*) sitio *m;* (*in theatre*) localidad *f;* **is this ~ taken?** ¿está libre este sitio?; **to change ~s with sb** cambiar el sitio con alguien; **to save sb a ~** guardar un sitio a alguien; **to lay** [*o* **set**] **a ~ at the table** poner un cubierto en la mesa **7.** (*in organization*) plaza *f;* **she has got a ~ at university** ha obtenido una plaza en la universidad **8.** MAT **decimal ~** decimal *m* ►**a ~ in the sun** una situación ventajosa; **to fall into ~** encajar; **to go ~s** *inf* (*become successful*) llegar lejos; **to know one's ~** saber cuál es el lugar de uno; **to put sb in his ~** poner a alguien en su sitio; **all over the ~** por todas partes; **any ~** *Am, inf* en/a cualquier sitio; **every ~** *Am, inf* en todas partes; **some ~** *Am, inf* (a) algún sitio; **to feel out of ~** sentirse fuera de lugar; **a ~ for everything and everything in its ~** un sitio para cada cosa y cada cosa en su sitio; **no ~** *Am, inf* en ningún sitio **II.** *vt* **1.** (*position, put*) colocar; **to ~ sth somewhere** colocar algo en un sitio; **to ~ an advertisement in the newspaper** poner un anuncio en el periódico; **to ~ a comma/a full stop** poner una coma/un punto; **to ~ sth on the agenda** apuntar algo en la agenda; **we are well ~d to see the match** estamos en un buen sitio para ver el partido; **how are you ~d for money?** ¿cuál es tu situación económica? **2.** (*impose*) imponer; **to ~ an embargo on sth** prohibir algo; **to ~ a limit on sth** poner un límite a algo **3.** (*ascribe*) poner; **to ~ the blame on sb** echar la culpa a alguien; **to ~ one's hopes on sb/sth** poner sus esperanzas en alguien/algo; **to ~ importance on sb/sth** conceder importancia a alguien/algo; **to ~ the emphasis on sth** hacer énfasis en algo; **to ~ one's faith in sb** depositar su confianza en alguien **4.** (*arrange for*) hacer; **to ~ an order for sth** hacer un pedido de algo; **to ~ a bet** hacer una apuesta; **to ~ sth at sb's disposal** poner algo a disposición de alguien **5.** (*appoint to a position*) **to ~ sb in charge** (**of sth**) poner a alguien a cargo (de algo); **to ~ sb under surveillance** poner a alguien bajo vigilancia; **to ~ sth under the control of sb** poner algo bajo el control de alguien; **to ~ sb in jeopardy** poner a alguien en peligro; **to ~ sb under pressure** someter alguien a presión; **to ~ sb on** (**the**) **alert** alertar a alguien; **to ~ sth above sth** poner algo por encima de algo; **to be ~d first/second** SPORTS quedar en primer/segundo lugar **6.** (*employ*) colocar **7.** (*identify*) reconocer; **I can't ~ him** su cara me suena, pero no la puedo situar **III.** *vi Brit* SPORTS clasificarse

placebo [plə'si:bəʊ, *Am:* -boʊ] <-s> *n a. fig* placebo *m*

place card *n* tarjeta *f* (indicadora del puesto que se ocupa)

place kick *n* SPORTS tiro *m* libre **place mat** *n* salvamanteles *m inv*

placement ['pleɪsmənt] *n* colocación *f*

place name *n* topónimo *m*

placenta [plə'sentə, *Am:* -ţə] <-s *o* -ae> *n* MED placenta *f*

placid ['plæsɪd] *adj* plácido, -a

plagiarism ['pleɪdʒərɪzəm, *Am:* -dʒɚɪ-] *n no pl* plagio *m*

plagiarist ['pleɪdʒərɪst, *Am:* -dʒɚ-] *n* plagiario, -a *m, f*

plagiarize ['pleɪdʒəraɪz] **I.** *vt* plagiar; **to ~ sth from sth** plagiar algo de algo **II.** *vi* hacer un plagio; **to ~ from sth** hacer un plagio de algo

plague [pleɪg] **I.** *n* peste *f;* (*infestation of insects*) plaga *f;* (*source of annoyance*) pesadez *f;* **the ~** (*bubonic plague*) la peste; **to avoid sb like the ~** huir de alguien como de la peste **II.** *vt* fastidiar; **to ~ sb for sth** acosar a

alguien por algo
plaice [pleɪs] *inv n* platija *f*
plaid [plæd] I. *n no pl, Am* tela *f* a cuadros II. *adj* de tartán; ~ **skirt** falda *f* escocesa
plain [pleɪn] I. *adj* 1. sencillo, -a; (*one colour*) de un solo color; (*without additions*) sin aditivos; ~ **yoghurt** yogur *m* natural 2. (*uncomplicated*) fácil; **the ~ folks** el pueblo llano; ~ **and simple** liso y llano 3. (*clear, obvious*) evidente; **it is ~ that ...** es evidente que...; **to be ~ enough** estar lo suficientemente claro; **to make sth ~** dejar algo claro; **to make oneself ~ (to sb)** hacerse entender (a alguien); **to be ~ with sb** ser franco con alguien; **to be as ~ as the nose on your face** estar más claro que el agua 4. (*mere, pure*) puro, -a; **the ~ truth** la pura realidad 5. (*not pretty*) sin atractivo; **a ~ girl** una chica más bien fea II. *adv inf* (*downright*) y punto; ~ **awful** horrible III. *n* 1. GEO llanura *f*; **the ~s** *pl* las llanuras; **the great Plains** la grandes llanuras (norteamericanas) 2. (*knitting stitch*) punto *m* de media
plain clothes LAW I. *n* ropa *f* de calle; **in ~** en traje de calle; (*of policeman*) ropa *f* de paisano II. *adj* (*policeman*) de paisano
plainly ['pleɪnli] *adv* 1. (*simply*) simplemente 2. (*clearly*) claramente; (*obviously*) evidentemente; **to be ~ visible** ser muy visible 3. (*undeniably*) sin duda
plainness ['pleɪnnəs] *n no pl* 1. (*simplicity*) sencillez *f* 2. (*obviousness*) evidencia *f* 3. (*unattractiveness*) falta *f* de atractivo
plain sailing *n fig* **to be ~** ser cosa de coser y cantar
plain-spoken [ˌpleɪn'spəʊkən, *Am:* -'spoʊ-] *adj* franco, -a
plaintiff ['pleɪntɪf, *Am:* -t̬ɪf] *n* demandante *mf*
plaintive ['pleɪntɪv, *Am:* -t̬ɪv] *adj* lastimero, -a
plait [plæt] I. *n* trenza *f* II. *vt* trenzar III. *vi* hacer trenzas
plan [plæn] I. *n* 1. (*scheme, programme*) plano *m*; **to draw up a ~** elaborar un plan; **to go according to ~** ir de acuerdo con lo previsto; **to change ~s** cambiar de planes; **to have ~s** tener planes; **to make ~s for sth** hacer planes para algo 2. FIN, ECON (*insurance scheme*) seguro *m*; **healthcare ~** seguro *m* médico; **savings ~** plan *m* de ahorro 3. (*diagram*) plano *m*; **street ~** plano *m* de calles II. <-nn-> *vt* 1. (*work out in detail*) planificar; (*prepare*) preparar; **~ned economy** economía *f* planificada; **to ~ sth for sb** preparar algo para alguien 2. (*intend*) proponerse; **to ~ to do sth** proponerse hacer algo III. *vi* hacer proyectos; **to ~ carefully** hacer proyectos detallados
plane¹ [pleɪn] I. *n* 1. (*level surface*) nivel *m*; MAT plano *m* 2. (*level of thought*) nivel *m* (intelectual) II. *vi* planear III. *adj* plano, -a; MAT llano, -a; ~ **angle** ángulo *m* plano
plane² [pleɪn] *n* (*airplane*) avión *m*; **by ~** en avión
plane³ [pleɪn] I. *n* cepillo *m* II. *vt* cepillar
plane⁴ [pleɪn] *n* (*tree*) plátano *m*
plane crash *n* accidente *m* de aviación
planet ['plænɪt] *n* planeta *m*; ~ **Earth** la Tierra; ~ **Jupiter/Venus** el planeta Júpiter/Venus; **to be on a different ~** *fig* estar en otro mundo
planetarium [ˌplænɪ'teərɪəm, *Am:* -'terɪ-] <-s *o* -ria> *n* planetario *m*
planetary ['plænɪtəri, *Am:* -teri] *adj* planetario, -a; ~ **motion** movimiento *m* planetario
plane tree *n* plátano *m*
plank [plæŋk] *n* 1. (*long board*) tabla *f*; NAUT tablazón *m* 2. (*of policy, ideology*) puntal *m*
planking *n no pl* tablas *fpl*
plankton ['plæŋktən] *n no pl* plancton *m*
planner *n* planificador(a) *m(f)*; **city ~** urbanista *mf*
planning *n no pl* planificación *f*; **city ~** planificación urbanística; **environmental ~** proyectos *mpl* medioambientales; **at the ~ stage** en la etapa de planificación
planning board *n* comisión *f* planificadora
planning permission *n* permiso *m* de construcción
plant [plɑːnt, *Am:* plænt] I. *n* 1. BOT planta *f* 2. (*factory*) fábrica *f* 3. *no pl* (*machinery*) maquinaria *f* 4. *no pl* (*misleading evidence*) **the drugs were a ~** la policía había colocado las drogas para inculparlo II. *vt* 1. AGR (*put in earth*) plantar; **to ~ sth with sth** sembrar algo de algo 2. (*put*) colocar; **to ~ oneself somewhere** *inf* meterse en algún sitio; **to ~ a bomb** poner una bomba; **to ~ a secret agent** introducir a un agente secreto 3. *inf* (*to incriminate*) **to ~ evidence on sb** colocar pruebas para incriminar a alguien III. *adj* vegetal; **the ~ kingdom** el reino vegetal; ~ **life** vida *f* vegetal
plantain ['plæntɪn] *n* (*fruit, tree*) plátano *m*
plantation [plæn'teɪʃən] *n* plantación *f*; (*of trees*) arboleda *f*
planter ['plɑːntəʳ, *Am:* 'plænt̬ɚ] *n* 1. (*owner of plantation*) hacendado, -a *m, f* 2. (*plant holder*) maceta *f*
plaque [plɑːk, plæk, *Am:* plæk] *n* 1. (*on building*) placa *f*; **memorial ~** placa conmemorativa 2. *no pl* MED sarro *m*
plash [plæʃ] I. *n* (*splash*) salpicadura *f*; (*noise*) chapoteo *m* II. *vi* **to ~ about** (*play*) chapotear
plasm ['plæzm] *n* molde *m*
plasma ['plæzmə] *n no pl* plasma *m*
plaster ['plɑːstəʳ, *Am:* 'plæstɚ] I. *n* 1. *no pl* (*used in building*) *a.* MED yeso *m* 2. *Brit* (*sticking plaster*) tirita *f* II. *vt* 1. (*wall, ceiling*) enyesar 2. *inf* (*put all over*) llenar
plasterboard ['plɑːstəbɔːd, *Am:* 'plæstɚ-bɔːrd] *n no pl* cartón *m* de yeso (y fieltro)
plaster cast *n* 1. MED escayola *f* 2. ART vaciado *m*
plastered *adj inf* (*drunk*) borracho, -a; **to get**

~ emborracharse

plasterer *n* yesero, -a *m, f*

plastic ['plæstɪk] **I.** *n* **1.** (*material*) plástico *m* **2.** ~**s** *pl* (*manufacturing sector*) sector *m* de los plásticos **II.** *adj* **1.** (*made from plastic*) de plástico **2.** *pej* (*artifical*) artificial **3.** ART (*malleable*) ~ **arts** artes *fpl* plásticas **4.** *fig* (*impressionable*) influenciable

plastic bag *n* bolsa *f* de plástico **plastic bomb** *n* bomba *f* de goma **plastic bullet** *n* bala *f* de goma **plastic explosive** *n* explosivo *m* plástico

Plasticine® ['plæstɪsi:n] *n no pl* plastilina *f*

plasticity [plæ'stɪsəti, *Am:* -t̬i] *n no pl* plasticidad *f*

plastic money *n no pl* dinero *m* plástico

plastics industry *n* sector *m* de los plásticos

plastic surgery *n* cirugía *f* plástica

plate [pleɪt] **I.** *n* **1.** (*dinner plate*) plato *m* **2.** (*panel, sheet*) lámina *f;* **steel** ~ lámina de acero **3.** AUTO **number** ~ *Brit,* **license** ~ *Am,* **licence** ~ *Can* placa *f* **4.** TYPO lámina *f* **5.** *no pl* (*layer of metal*) capa *f;* **gold** ~ capa de oro **6.** (*silver cutlery*) vajilla *f* de plata **7.** (*picture in book*) ilustración *f* ▸**to have a lot on one's** ~ tener muchos asuntos entre manos; **to give sth to sb on a** ~ servir algo a alguien en bandeja **II.** *vt* **to** ~ **sth with gold/silver** chapar algo con oro/plata

plateau ['plætəʊ, *Am:* plæt'oʊ] <*Brit:* -x, *Am, Aus:* -s> *n* meseta *f*

plated *adj* (*coated in metal*) chapeado, -a; (*jewellery*) chapado, -a

plateful ['pleɪtfʊl] *n* plato *m*

plate glass *n* luna *f*

platelet ['pleɪlət] *n* plaqueta *f*

plate rack *n* portaplatos *m inv* **plate-warmer** *n* calentador *m* de platos

platform ['plætfɔ:m, *Am:* -fɔ:rm] *n* **1.** *a.* INFOR plataforma *f* **2.** *Brit, Aus* RAIL andén *m;* **railway** ~ andén de estación de trenes **3.** (*stage*) escenario *m* **4.** *Brit* (*at meeting*) tribuna *f* **5.** (*political programme*) programa *m* electoral **6.** *pl* (*shoes*) zapatos *mpl* de plataforma

platform shoes *npl* zapatos *mpl* de plataforma

plating *n* (*covering of metal*) enchapado *m;* **gold/silver** ~ chapado *m* de oro/de plata

platinum ['plætɪnəm, *Am:* 'plætnəm] *n no pl* platino *m*

platitude ['plætɪtju:d, *Am:* 'plæt̬ətu:d] *n pej* perogrullada *f*

platonic [plə'tɒnɪk, *Am:* -'tɑ:nɪk] *adj* platónico, -a; ~ **love** amor *m* platónico

platoon [plə'tu:n] *n* MIL pelotón *m*

platter ['plætəʳ, *Am:* 'plæt̬ɚ] *n* **1.** (*large dish*) fuente *f* **2.** (*food*) plato *m* fuerte

platypus ['plætɪpəs, *Am:* 'plæt̬-] <-es> *n* ornitorrinco *m*

plausibility [ˌplɔ:zə'bɪlɪti, *Am:* ˌplɑ:zə'bɪlət̬i] *n no pl* plausibilidad *f*

plausible ['plɔ:zəbl, *Am:* 'plɑ:-] *adj* plausible

play [pleɪ] **I.** *n* **1.** *no pl* (*recreation*) juego *m;* **to be at** ~ estar en juego; **to do sth in** ~ hacer algo en broma; **it's only in** ~ sólo es broma **2.** *no pl* SPORTS juego *m;* **to be in/out of** ~ estar dentro/fuera de juego **3.** SPORTS (*move*) jugada *f;* **foul** ~ juego sucio; **to make a bad/good** ~ hacer una mala/buena jugada **4.** THEAT obra *f* de teatro; **one-act** ~ obra de un acto; **radio** ~ emisión *f* dramática **5.** *no pl* (*free movement*) juego *m;* **to allow** [*o* **give**] **sth full** ~ dar rienda suelta a algo **6.** *no pl* (*interaction*) juego *m;* **to bring sth into** ~ poner algo en juego; **to come into** ~ entrar en juego ▸**to make a** ~ **for sth** intentar conseguir algo **II.** *vi* **1.** *a.* SPORTS jugar; **to** ~ **for a team** jugar en un equipo; **to** ~ **fair/rough** jugar limpio/sucio **2.** (*perform*) actuar **3.** MUS tocar **III.** *vt* **1.** (*participate in game, sport*) jugar; **to** ~ **bridge/football** jugar al bridge/al fútbol; **to** ~ **a card** jugar una carta **2.** (*participate in sport*) jugar a; **to** ~ **football** jugar al fútbol; **to** ~ **a match/a round** jugar un partido/una ronda **3.** (*perform a role*) interpretar, hacer el papel de; **to** ~ **the clown** [*o* **fool**] hacer el payaso; **to** ~ **to a full house** llenar un teatro **4.** MUS tocar; **to** ~ **the piano** tocar el piano **5.** (*operate an audio or video device*) poner; **do you have to play the music so loud?** ¿es necesario que pongas el equipo de música tan alto?; **to** ~ **a CD/video** poner un compact disc/un vídeo **6.** (*perpetrate: joke*) gastar

◆**play about** *vi* jugar

◆**play along** *vi* **to** ~ **with sb** seguir la corriente a alguien

◆**play around** *vi* **1.** (*play*) jugar **2.** *pej* (*commit adultery*) **to** ~ **with sb** tener un lío con alguien **3.** (*experiment*) **to** ~ **with sth** ensayar algo de varias maneras **4.** *pej* (*tamper*) **to** ~ **with sth** manosear algo

◆**play at** *vt* **1.** (*pretend*) **to** ~ (**being**) **sth** jugar a (ser) algo **2.** (*do for amusement*) **to** ~ (**being**) **sth** hacer como que (se es) algo; **she is playing at being a student** hace como que estudia **3.** *pej* (*do*) **what are you playing at?** ¿a qué viene esto?

◆**play back** *vt* poner

◆**play down** *vt* quitar importancia a

◆**play off I.** *vi* jugar un partido de desempate **II.** *vt* **to play sb off against sb** oponer a dos personas

◆**play on I.** *vt* **1.** (*exploit*) **to** ~ **sb's feelings/weakness** aprovecharse de los sentimientos/la debilidad de alguien **2.** (*phrase, word*) jugar con **II.** *vi* (*keep playing*) SPORTS, GAMES seguir jugando; MUS seguir tocando

◆**play out** *vt* representar; **to** ~ **one's fantasies** convertir sus fantasías en realidad

◆**play through** *vt* tocar

◆**play up I.** *vt* **1.** (*exaggerate: problem, difficulty*) exagerar **2.** *Brit* (*cause trouble*) fastidiar **II.** *vi* **1.** *Aus, Brit* (*malfunction*) no marchar bien; (*hurt*) doler **2.** *Brit* (*cause annoyance*) dar guerra

◆**play upon** *vt* 1.(*exploit*) **to ~ sb's feelings/weakness** aprovecharse de los sentimientos/la debilidad de alguien 2.(*phrase, word*) jugar con

◆**play with** *vt* 1.*a. fig* (*play*) jugar 2.(*manipulate nervously*) juguetear; **to ~ one's food** jugar con la comida 3.(*consider, toy with*) **to ~ an idea** dar vueltas a una idea

playable ['pleɪəbl] *adj* (*pitch*) que se puede jugar

play-act ['pleɪækt] *vi* 1. THEAT actuar 2. *fig* hacer teatro

playback ['pleɪbæk] *n* (*of tape*) reproducción *f*

playbill *n* THEAT 1.(*poster*) cartel *m* 2. *Am* (*program*) programa *m*

playboy ['pleɪbɔɪ] *n* playboy *m*

player ['pleɪəʳ, *Am:* -ɚ] *n* 1. SPORTS jugador(a) *m(f)*; **card ~** jugador(a) *m(f)* de cartas; **football ~** futbolista *mf;* **tennis ~** tenista *mf* 2. MUS instrumentista *mf;* **cello ~** violoncelista *mf;* **flute ~** flautista *mf;* **oboe ~** oboísta *mf* 3. THEAT actor *m*, actriz *f* 4.(*playback machine*) **cassette ~** casete *m;* **CD ~** compact disc *m;* **record ~** tocadiscos *m inv*

playfellow ['pleɪˌfeləʊ, *Am:* -oʊ] *n* compañero, -a *m, f* de juego

playful ['pleɪfəl] *adj* 1.(*full of fun*) juguetón, -ona; **the children were in a ~ mood** los niños tenían ganas de jugar 2.(*comment, tone*) de guasa; **he's only being ~** sólo está bromeando

playground ['pleɪgraʊnd] *n* 1.(*of school*) patio *m;* (*in park*) campo *m* de recreo 2. *fig* (*resort*) lugar *m* de recreo

playgroup ['pleɪgru:p] *n* guardería *f*

playhouse ['pleɪhaʊs] *n* 1.(*theatre*) teatro *m* 2.(*miniature house*) casa *f* de muñecas

playing card *n* carta *f*, naipe *m* **playing field** *n* campo *m* de deportes

playmate ['pleɪmeɪt] *n* compañero, -a *m, f* de juego

play-off ['pleɪɒf, *Am:* -ɑ:f] *n* desempate *m;* **~ match** partido *m* de desempate

playpen ['pleɪpen] *n* parque *m*

playroom ['pleɪrʊm, *Am:* -ru:m] *n* cuarto *m* de jugar

playschool ['pleɪsku:l] *n Brit* jardín *m* de infancia

playsuit ['pleɪsu:t] *n* (*for baby*) pelele *m*

plaything ['pleɪθɪŋ] *n a. fig* juguete *m*

playtime ['pleɪtaɪm] *n no pl* SCHOOL recreo *m*

playwright ['pleɪraɪt] *n* dramaturgo, -a *m, f*

plaza ['plɑ:zə] *n* 1.(*open square*) plaza *f* 2.(*shopping centre*) (**shopping**) **~** centro *m* comercial

plc [ˌpi:el'si:] *n Brit abbr of* **public limited company** S.A. *f*

plea [pli:] *n* 1.(*appeal*) petición *f*, súplica *f;* **to make a ~ for help/mercy** pedir ayuda/clemencia; **a ~ that ...** una petición de que... 2. LAW alegato *m;* **to enter a ~ of guilty/not guilty** declararse culpable/inocente 3. *form* (*excuse*) pretexto *m*

plea bargaining *n Am: acuerdo táctico entre fiscal y defensa para agilizar los trámites judiciales*

plead [pli:d] <pleaded *Am:* pled, pleaded *Am:* pled> I. *vi* 1.(*implore, beg*) implorar, suplicar; **to ~ for forgiveness/justice** suplicar perdón/justicia; **to ~ with sb** (**to do sth**) suplicar (hacer algo) a alguien 2. LAW **to ~ guilty/innocent** (**to a charge**) declararse culpable/inocente (de un cargo) II. *vt* 1. LAW **to ~ sb's case** defender el caso de alguien; **to ~ insanity** alegar enajenación mental 2.(*claim as pretext*) pretextar; **to ~ ignorance of sth** pretextar su ignorancia en algo 3.(*argue for*) **to ~ sb's cause** defender la causa de alguien; **to ~ one's suit** *form* pedir la mano de alguien

pleading ['pli:dɪŋ] I. *n* 1.(*entreaty, appeal*) súplicas *fpl* 2. LAW alegato *m* II. *adj* (*look, tone*) suplicante

pleasant ['plezənt] *adj* 1.(*pleasing*) agradable; **it is my ~ duty to inform you that ...** me complace comunicarle que...; **what a ~ surprise!** ¡qué agradable sorpresa!; **have a ~ journey!** ¡buen viaje!; **~ weather** buen tiempo 2.(*friendly*) amable; **to make oneself ~** (**to sb**) procurar ser amable (con alguien); **to be ~** (**to sb**) ser amable (con alguien)

pleasantry ['plezəntri] <-ies> *n* 1.(*joke*) broma *f* 2. *pl* (*remarks*) cumplidos *mpl;* **an exchange of pleasantries** un intercambio de cumplidos

please [pli:z] I. *vt* 1.(*make happy*) gustar; **to be hard to ~** ser difícil de contentar; **she's notoriously hard to ~** es muy difícil complacerla 2. *inf* (*do as one wishes*) **~ yourself** haz lo que te parezca II. *vi* 1.(*be agreeable*) **eager to ~** deseoso de agradar 2.(*think fit, wish*) **to do as one ~s** hacer lo que uno quiera; **you can do as you ~** como usted quiera; **to do whatever one ~s** hacer todo lo que se quiera III. *interj* por favor; **if you ~** *form* con su permiso; **more potatoes? ~** ¿más patatas? Sí, por favor

pleased *adj* 1.(*satisfied, contented*) satisfecho, -a; **to be ~ about sth** estar contento de algo; **to be ~ that ...** estar contento de que +*subj;* **to be ~ with oneself** estar satisfecho de uno mismo 2.(*happy, glad*) contento, -a; **I'm ~ to report that ...** me complace informarle de que...; **I'm very ~ to meet you** encantado de conocerle 3.(*willing*) **to be ~ to do sth** estar encantado de hacer algo ►**to be as ~ as Punch** (**about sth**) estar más contento que unas Pascuas (con algo)

pleasing *adj* agradable; **~ news** buenas noticias *fpl*

pleasurable ['pleʒərəbl] *adj* grato, -a; **a ~ sensation** una agradable sensación

pleasure ['pleʒəʳ, *Am:* -ɚ] *n* 1. *no pl* (*feeling of enjoyment*) placer *m;* **it was such a ~ to meet you** ha sido un placer conocerle; **to take ~ in sth/in doing sth** disfrutar de algo/

haciendo algo; **with** ~ con mucho gusto **2.** (*source of enjoyment*) placer *m;* **the ~s and pains of camping** los pros y los contras de la acampada **3.** *form* (*will, desire*) **what is your ~, Madame?** ¿en qué puedo servirle, señora?

pleasure boat *n* embarcación *f* de recreo **pleasure principle** *n no pl* PSYCH principio *m* del placer **pleasure trip** *n* viaje *m* de recreo

pleat [pliːt] *n* pliegue *m*

pleb [pleb] *n Brit, inf abbr of* **plebian** plebeyo, -a *m, f*

plebeian [plɪ'biːən] **I.** *adj form* plebeyo, -a **II.** *n* HIST plebeyo, -a *m, f*

plebiscite ['plebɪsɪt, *Am:* -əsaɪt] *n* plebiscito *m;* **to hold a ~ (on sth)** someter (algo) a plebiscito

pled [pled] *Am, Scot pt, pp of* **plead**

pledge [pledʒ] **I.** *n* **1.** (*solemn promise*) promesa *f* solemne; **to fulfil a ~** cumplir un compromiso; **to make a ~ that ...** prometer solemnemente que... **2.** (*symbolic sign of a promise*) **as a ~ of sth** en señal de algo; **a ~ of good faith** una garantía de buena fe **3.** (*promised charitable donation*) donativo *m* prometido **4.** (*pawned item*) prenda *f* **II.** *vt* **1.** (*promise*) prometer; **to ~ loyalty** jurar lealtad; **to ~ to do sth** prometer hacer algo; **to ~ that ...** prometer que...; **we've ~d ourselves to fight for justice** nos hemos comprometido a luchar por la justicia; **I've been ~d to secrecy** he jurado guardar el secreto **2.** (*give as security*) **to ~ money** dar dinero como garantía

plenary ['pliːnəri] *adj* plenario, -a

plenary meeting *n* reunión *f* plenaria **plenary powers** *n* plenos poderes *mpl* **plenary session** *n* sesión *f* plenaria

plenipotentiary [ˌplenɪpə'tenʃəri, *Am:* -poʊ'tenʃɪeri] **I.** <-ries> *n* ADMIN, POL plenipotenciario, -a *m, f* **II.** *adj* ADMIN, POL plenipotenciario, -a; **~ power** plenipotencia *f*

plentiful ['plentɪf(ʊ)l, *Am:* -t̬ɪ-] *adj* abundante; **strawberries are ~ in the summer** en verano hay abundancia de fresas

plenty ['plenti, *Am:* -t̬i] **I.** *n no pl* **1.** (*abundance*) abundancia *f;* **land of ~** tierra *f* de abundancia; **food in ~** comida *f* en abundancia **2.** (*a lot*) **~ of money/time** dinero/tiempo de sobra **II.** *adv* suficientemente; **~ more** mucho más; **there's ~ more beer in the fridge** hay mucha más cerveza en la nevera

plenum ['pliːnəm] *n* pleno *m*

plethora ['pleθərə, *Am:* 'pleθɚə] *n* plétora *f*

pleurisy ['plʊərəsi, *Am:* 'plʊrə-] *n no pl* MED pleuresía *f*

plexus ['pleksəs] <-(es)> *n* plexo *m;* **solar ~** plexo solar

pliable ['plaɪəbl] *adj* **1.** (*supple*) flexible **2.** *fig* (*easily influenced*) dócil

pliers ['plaɪəz, *Am:* 'plaɪɚz] *npl* alicates *mpl;* **a pair of ~** unos alicates

plight [plaɪt] **I.** *n* apuro *m;* **to be in a dreadful ~** estar en una terrible situación **II.** *vt form* **to ~ one's troth** prometerse

plimsoll ['plɪmpsəl] *n Brit* zapatilla *f* de deporte

Plimsoll line *n* NAUT línea *f* de máxima carga

PLO [ˌpiːel'əʊ, *Am:* -'oʊ] *n abbr of* **Palestine Liberation Organization** OLP *f*

plod [plɒd, *Am:* plɑːd] **I.** *n* paso *m* lento **II.** <-dd-> *vi* **1.** (*walk heavily*) andar con paso pesado; **to ~ through the mud** andar con dificultad sobre el barro **2.** (*do without enthusiasm*) **to ~ through one's work** trabajar sin ganas; **to ~ through a book** leer un libro lentamente

◆**plod away** *vi* (*continue working*) ir tirando

◆**plod on** *vi* (*continue walking*) caminar penosamente

plodder ['plɒdəʳ, *Am:* 'plɑːdɚ] *n* (*worker*) trabajador(a) *m(f)* más voluntarioso, -a que eficiente; (*student*) empollón, -ona *m, f inf*

plonk[1] [plɒŋk, *Am:* plʌŋk] *n Brit, Aus, inf* vino *m* peleón

plonk[2] [plɒŋk, *Am:* plʌŋk] **I.** *n inf* (*sound*) ruido *m* sordo **II.** *vt inf* (*set down heavily*) dejar caer pesadamente; **she ~ed the books on the table** dejó caer los libros sobre la mesa

◆**plonk down** *vt inf* dejar caer pesadamente; **to plonk oneself down on a chair** dejarse caer en una silla

plop [plɒp, *Am:* plɑːp] **I.** *n* plaf *m;* **to fall with a ~** caerse haciendo plaf **II.** <-pp-> *vi* (*fall*) caerse haciendo plaf

plot [plɒt, *Am:* plɑːt] **I.** *n* **1.** (*conspiracy, secret plan*) conspiración *f;* **to foil a ~** hacer fracasar una conspiración; **to hatch a ~** tramar una intriga **2.** (*story line*) argumento *m* **3.** (*small piece of land*) terreno *m;* **a ~ of land** un terreno; **building ~** solar *m* ▸**the ~ thickens** *iron* el asunto se complica **II.** <-tt-> *vt* **1.** (*conspire*) tramar **2.** (*create*) **to ~ a story line** idear un argumento **3.** (*graph, line*) trazar; (*mark on map*) señalar; **to ~ a course** planear una ruta **III.** <-tt-> *vi* **to ~ against sb** conspirar contra alguien; **to ~ to do sth** planear hacer algo

◆**plot out** *vt* trazar

plotter ['plɒtəʳ, *Am:* 'plɑːt̬ɚ] *n* **1.** (*person*) conspirador(a) *m(f)* **2.** INFOR plotter *m,* tabla *f* trazadora

plough [plaʊ] **I.** *n* arado *m* ▸**to put one's hand to the ~** ponerse manos a la obra **II.** *vt* **1.** AGR arar **2.** (*move through*) **to ~ one's way through sth** abrirse paso por algo; (*work through*) hacer algo sin ganas **3.** (*invest*) **to ~ money into a project** invertir mucho dinero en un proyecto **III.** *vi* **1.** AGR arar **2.** **to ~ through sth** (*move through*) abrirse paso por algo; (*work through*) terminar algo a duras penas

◆**plough back** *vt* **to plough sth back (into sth)** reinvertir algo (en algo); **to plough profits back** reinvertir los beneficios

◆**plough into** *vt insep* chocar contra
◆**plough up** *vt* (*fields, land*) roturar
Plough [plaʊ] *n no pl* **the** ~ ASTR el Carro
plow [plaʊ] *n Am s.* **plough**
ploy [plɔɪ] *n* **1.**(*activity*) actividad *f* **2.**(*tactics*) táctica *f*
PLP *n Brit* POL *abbr of* **Parliamentary Labour Party** *los diputados del Partido Laborista*
pluck [plʌk] **I.** *n* **1.**(*sharp pull*) tirón *m* **2.**(*courage*) valor *m;* **to have a lot of** ~ tener agallas; **it takes a lot of** ~ hace falta mucho valor **II.** *vt* **1.**(*remove quickly*) arrancar **2.**(*remove hair or feathers*) **to** ~ **a chicken** desplumar un pollo; **to** ~ **one's eyebrows** depilarse las cejas **3.** MUS puntear **III.** *vi* **to** ~ **at sb's sleeve** tirar a alguien de la manga
◆**pluck out** *vt* arrancar
◆**pluck up** *vt* **to** ~ **one's courage** armarse de valor; **to** ~ **the courage to do sth** armarse de valor para hacer algo
plucky ['plʌki] <-ier, -iest> *adj* valiente
plug [plʌg] **I.** *n* **1.** ELEC (*connector*) enchufe *m;* (*socket*) toma *f* de corriente **2.**(*stopper*) tapón *m* **3.** *inf* (*publicity*) **to give sth a** ~ dar publicidad a algo **4.**(*spark plug*) bujía *f* **5.**(*chunk*) ~ **of tobacco** tableta *f* de tabaco de mascar **II.**<-gg-> *vt* **1.**(*connect*) conectar; ELEC enchufar **2.**(*stop up, close*) **to** ~ **a hole** tapar un agujero; **to** ~ **a leak** taponar un escape **3.**(*publicize*) anunciar **4.** *Am, inf* (*shoot*) pegar un tiro a
◆**plug away** *vi* **to** ~ (**at sth**) perseverar (en algo)
◆**plug in I.** *vt* conectar; ELEC enchufar **II.** *vi* conectar; ELEC enchufar
◆**plug up** *vt* tapar
plughole ['plʌghəʊl, *Am:* -hoʊl] *n* desagüe *m* ►**to go down the** ~ irse al garete
plug-in *n* INFOR plug-in *m,* enchufe *m*
plum [plʌm] **I.** *n* **1.**(*fruit*) ciruela *f;* (*tree*) ciruelo *m* **2.**(*opportunity*) chollo *m* **3.**(*colour*) color *m* ciruela **II.** *adj* **1.**(*colour*) de color ciruela **2.**(*exceptionally good*) inmejorable; **a** ~ **job** un trabajo fantástico
plumage ['plu:mɪdʒ] *n no pl* plumaje *m*
plumb [plʌm] **I.** *vt a. fig* sondar; **to** ~ **the depth** sondar la profundidad; **to** ~ **the depths** *fig* estar muy deprimido; **to** ~ **the mystery of the universe** plantearse los misterios del universo **II.** *adv* **1.** *inf* (*exactly*) exactamente; **he hit me** ~ **on the nose** me dio de lleno en la nariz **2.** *Am, inf* (*completely*) completamente **III.** *n* plomada *f;* **to be out of** ~ no estar a plomo
◆**plumb in** *vt* **to plumb sth in** instalar algo
plumber ['plʌməʳ, *Am:* -ɚ] *n* fontanero, -a *m, f,* plomero, -a *m, f AmL,* gasfitero, -a *m, f Chile, Perú*
plumbing ['plʌmɪŋ] **I.** *n no pl* fontanería *f* **II.** *adj* ~ **contractor** fontanero, -a *m, f,* gasfitero, -a *m, f Chile, Perú;* ~ **fixture** instalación *f* sanitaria; ~ **work** obra *f* de fontanería
plume [plu:m] **I.** *n* **1.**(*feather*) pluma *f* **2.**(*cloud: of smoke, gas*) nube *f* ►**to be dressed in borrowed** ~**s** *liter* atribuirse honores que no se merecen **II.** *vt* **to** ~ **oneself on sth** vanagloriarse de algo
plummet ['plʌmɪt] *vi* caer en picado
plummy ['plʌmi] <-ier, -iest> *adj* (*voice, tone*) pijo, -a *inf,* popoff *Méx*
plump [plʌmp] *adj* (*person*) rollizo, -a; (*animal*) gordo, -a
◆**plump down** *inf* **I.** *vt* dejar caer **II.** *vi* dejarse caer
◆**plump for** *vt inf* optar por
◆**plump up** *vt* **1.**(*pillow*) sacudir **2.**(*chicken*) cebar
plumpness ['plʌmpnəs] *n no pl* gordura *f*
plum pudding *n Brit* budín *m* de pasas
plum tree *n Brit* ciruelo *m*
plunder ['plʌndəʳ, *Am:* -dɚ] **I.** *n no pl* **1.**(*stolen goods*) botín *m* **2.**(*act of plundering*) saqueo *m* **II.** *vt* **1.**(*steal*) robar **2.**(*loot*) saquear **III.** *vi* robar
plunderer ['plʌndərəʳ, *Am:* -dɚɚ] *n* saqueador(a) *m(f)*
plunge [plʌndʒ] **I.** *n* **1.**(*sharp decline*) caída *f* **2.**(*dive*) zambullida *f* de cabeza ►**to take the** ~ dar el paso decisivo; (*get married*) casarse **II.** *vi* **1.**(*fall suddenly*) precipitarse; **to** ~ **to one's death** tener una caída mortal **2.**(*leap, enter*) **we** ~**d into the sea** nos zambullimos en el mar; **he** ~**d into the forest** se precipitó hacia el bosque **3.**(*begin abruptly*) **to** ~ **into sth** emprender algo **III.** *vt* hundir; **to** ~ **a knife into sth** clavar un cuchillo en algo; **we've** ~**ed ourselves into debt** nos hemos metido en deudas
◆**plunge in** *vi* lanzarse
plunger ['plʌndʒəʳ, *Am:* -dʒɚ] *n* (*of syringe*) émbolo *m;* (*for drain, sink*) desatascador *m*
plunk [plʌŋk] *n Am s.* **plonk[2]**
pluperfect ['plu:ˌpɜ:fɪkt, *Am:* -ˌpɜ:r-] *n* LING pluscuamperfecto *m*
plural ['plʊərəl, *Am:* 'plʊrəl] **I.** *n* plural *m;* **in the** ~ en plural; **second person** ~ segunda persona del plural **II.** *adj* **1.** *a.* LING plural **2.**(*multiple*) múltiple
pluralism ['plʊərəlɪzəm, *Am:* 'plʊrəl-] *n no pl* PHILOS pluralismo *m*
pluralistic [ˌplʊərəl'ɪstɪk, *Am:* ˌplʊrəl'-] *adj* pluralista
plurality [plʊə'ræləti, *Am:* plʊ'rælət̬i] <-ies> *n* **1.** *no pl* (*variety*) pluralidad *f;* ~ **of opinions** diversidad *f* de opiniones **2.**(*largest single share of votes*) mayoría *f* de votos; **to have a** ~ ganar por mayoría
plus [plʌs] **I.** *prep* más; **5** ~ **2 equals 7** 5 más 2 igual a 7 **II.** *conj* además **III.**<-es> *n* **1.**(*mathematical symbol*) signo *m* más **2.**(*advantage*) punto *m* a favor **IV.** *adj* **1.**(*above zero*) positivo, -a; ~ **8** más 8; ~ **two degrees** dos grados positivos **2.**(*more than*) algo más de; **200** ~ más de 200 **3.**(*positive or advantageous*) **the** ~ **side** (**of sth**) el lado positivo (de algo)

plus fours *npl* pantalones *mpl* de golf
plush [plʌʃ] **I.** *adj* **1.** (*luxurious*) lujoso, -a, elegante **2.** (*made of plush*) de felpa **II.** <-es> *n* felpa *f*
plus sign *n* signo *m* más
Pluto ['plu:təʊ, *Am:* -t̬oʊ] *n* Plutón *m*
plutocracy [plu:'tɒkrəsi, *Am:* -'tɑ:krə-] <-ies> *n no pl* plutocracia *f*
plutocrat ['plu:təkræt, *Am:* -t̬ə-] *n* plutócrata *mf*
plutocratic [ˌplu:tə'krætɪk, *Am:* -toʊ'kræt̬-] *adj* plutocrático, -a
plutonium [plu:'təʊniəm, *Am:* -'toʊ-] *n no pl* plutonio *m*
ply¹ [plaɪ] *n no pl* **1.** (*thickness: of cloth, wood*) capa *f* **2.** (*strand of rope*) **two-~ rope** cuerda *f* de dos cabos
ply² [plaɪ] <-ie-> **I.** *vt* **1. to ~ one's trade** ejercer su profesión **2. to ~ sb with questions** acosar a alguien con preguntas; **to ~ sb with wine** no parar de servir vino a alguien **3.** (*sell*) **to ~ drugs** traficar con drogas; **to ~ one's wares** vender su mercancía **4.** (*travel: ship*) navegar por; **to ~ a route** hacer un trayecto **II.** *vi* **1.** *Brit* **to ~ for business** ofrecer sus servicios **2.** (*travel*) **to ~ between Paris and Lyon** hacer regularmente el trayecto entre París y Lyon
plywood ['plaɪwʊd] *n no pl* contrachapado *m*
p.m. [ˌpi:'em] *abbr of* **post meridian** p.m.; **one ~** la una de la tarde; **eight ~** las ocho de la noche
PM [ˌpi:'em] *n* **1.** *abbr of* **Prime Minister** primer ministro *m*, primera ministra *f* **2.** *abbr of* **post mortem** autopsia *f*
PMS [ˌpi:em'es] *n abbr of* **premenstrual syndrome** SPM *m*
pneumatic [nju:'mætɪk, *Am:* nu:'mæt̬-] *adj* neumático, -a
pneumatic brakes *npl* frenos *mpl* neumáticos **pneumatic tyre** *n Brit* neumático *m*
pneumonia [nju:'məʊnɪə, *Am:* nu:'moʊnjə] *n no pl* neumonía *f*
PO [ˌpi:'əʊ, *Am:* -'oʊ] *n Brit abbr of* **Post Office** Correos *m*
poach¹ [pəʊtʃ] *vt* (*eggs*) escalfar; (*fish*) cocer
poach² [pəʊtʃ] **I.** *vt* **1.** (*catch illegally*) cazar en vedado; (*fish*) pescar en vedado **2.** (*appropriate unfairly*) robar; **to ~ someone's ideas** birlar las ideas de alguien; **to ~ a manager from a company** apropiarse de un director de una empresa **II.** *vi* (*catch illegally*) cazar furtivamente; (*fish*) pescar furtivamente; **to ~ on sb's territory** *fig* pisar el terreno a alguien
poacher ['pəʊtʃəʳ, *Am:* 'poʊtʃɚ] *n* (*hunter*) cazador(a) *m(f)* furtivo, -a; (*fisherman*) pescador(a) *m(f)* furtivo, -a
poaching ['pəʊtʃɪŋ, *Am:* 'poʊtʃ-] *n no pl* (*hunting*) caza *f* furtiva; (*fishing*) pesca *f* furtiva
POB *n abbr of* **Post-Office Box** apdo. *m* de correos
PO Box [ˌpi:'əʊbɒks, *Am:* -'oʊbɑ:ks] <-es> *n abbr of* **Post Office Box** apartado *m* de correos
pock [pɒk, *Am:* pɑ:k] *n* (*scar*) picadura *f*; (*pustule*) pústula *f*
pocket ['pɒkɪt, *Am:* 'pɑ:kɪt] **I.** *n* **1.** (*in trousers, jacket*) bolsillo *m*, bolsa *f AmC, Méx;* **~ dictionary** diccionario *m* de bolsillo; **~ edition** edición *f* de bolsillo; **back/breast ~** bolsillo trasero/de pecho; **inside ~** bolsillo interior; **to be in ~/out of ~** salir ganando/perdiendo; **to pay for sth out of one's own ~** pagar algo de su bolsillo **2.** (*isolated group or area*) **~ of greenery** zona *f* verde; **a ~ of resistance** un foco de resistencia; **~ of turbulence** AVIAT, METEO racha *f* de turbulencias **3.** (*in billiard table*) tronera *f* ►**to put one's pride in one's ~** tragarse el orgullo; **to have sth/sb in one's ~** tener algo/a alguien en el bolsillo; **to line one's ~s** forrarse (de dinero); **to live in sb's ~** *pej* estar siempre pegado a alguien **II.** *vt* **1.** (*put in pocket*) **to ~ sth** meterse algo en el bolsillo **2.** (*keep for oneself*) apropiarse de ►**to ~ one's pride** tragarse el orgullo
pocketbook ['pɒkɪtbʊk, *Am:* 'pɑ:kɪtbʊk] *n* **1.** *Am* (*woman's handbag*) bolso *m*, cartera *f AmL* **2.** (*wallet*) monedero *m;* **to vote with one's ~** *Am* votar con el bolsillo **3.** *Am* (*book*) libro *m* de bolsillo
pocket calculator *n* calculadora *f* de bolsillo **pocket camera** *n* cámara *f* de bolsillo
pocketful ['pɒkɪtfʊl, *Am:* 'pɑ:kɪt-] *n* **a ~ of sth** un puñado de algo
pocket handkerchief *n* pañuelo *m* de bolsillo **pocketknife** <-knives> *n* navaja *f* **pocket money** *n no pl* **1.** (*for small personal expenses*) dinero *m* para gastos personales **2.** *Brit* (*from one's parents*) paga *f*
pocket-size(d) ['pɒkɪtsaɪz(d), *Am:* 'pɑ:kɪt-] *adj* de bolsillo
pod [pɒd, *Am:* pɑ:d] *n* **1.** BOT vaina *f* **2.** AVIAT tanque *m*
POD *abbr of* **pay on delivery** pago *m* contra entrega
podgy ['pɒdʒi, *Am:* 'pɑ:dʒi] <-ier, -iest> *adj* gordinflón, -ona
podiatrist [pəʊ'daɪətrɪst, *Am:* pə'daɪ-] *n* pedicuro, -a *m, f*
podium ['pəʊdiəm, *Am:* 'poʊ-] <-dia> *n* podio *m*
poem ['pəʊɪm, *Am:* poʊəm] *n* poema *m*
poet ['pəʊɪt, *Am:* poʊət] *n* poeta *mf*
poetic [pəʊ'etɪk, *Am:* poʊ'et̬-] *adj* poético, -a
poetry ['pəʊɪtri, *Am:* 'poʊə-] *n no pl, a. fig* poesía *f*
pogrom ['pɒgrəm, *Am:* 'poʊgrəm] *n* pogromo *m*
poignant ['pɔɪnjənt] *adj* conmovedor(a)
poinsettia [pɔɪnt'setiə, *Am:* -'set̬-] *n* flor *f* de Pascua
point [pɔɪnt] **I.** *n* **1.** (*sharp end*) punta *f;* **knife ~** punta de un cuchillo; **pencil ~** punta

P

de un lápiz **2.** (*promontory*) cabo *m* **3.** (*particular place*) punto *m* **4.** (*particular time*) momento *m;* **boiling/freezing** ~ punto *m* de ebullición/congelación; **starting** ~ punto de partida; **to do sth up to a** ~ hacer algo hasta cierto punto; **to get to the** ~ **that ...** llegar al extremo de...; **at that** ~ en ese instante; **at this** ~ **in time** en este momento **5.** (*significant idea*) cuestión *f;* **that's just the** ~**!** ¡eso es lo importante!; **to be to the** ~ venir al caso; **to be beside the** ~ no venir al caso; **to get to the** ~ ir al grano; **to get the** ~ (**of sth**) entender (algo); **to make one's** ~ expresar su opinión; **to miss the** ~ no captar lo relevante; **to see sb's** ~ aceptar la opinión de alguien; **to take sb's** ~ aceptar el argumento de alguien; ~ **taken** de acuerdo; ~ **by** ~ punto por punto **6.** (*purpose*) finalidad *f;* **what's the** ~**?** ¿qué sentido tiene? **7.** (*in score, result*) punto *m;* **percentage** ~ puntos *mpl* porcentuales; **to win** (**sth**) **on** ~**s** SPORTS ganar (algo) por puntos **8.** MAT **decimal** ~ coma *f,* punto *m* decimal *AmL* **9.** *a.* TYPO punto *m;* **join** ~**s A and B together** unir los puntos A y B **10.** *Brit, Aus* (*socket*) toma *f* de corriente **11.** *pl* AUTO (*electrical contacts*) platinos *mpl* **12.** *pl, Brit* RAIL agujas *fpl* ▶**to not put too fine a** ~ **on it, ...** hablando en plata...; **to make a** ~ **of doing sth** procurar de hacer algo **II.** *vi* señalar; (*indicate*) indicar; **to** ~ **to an icon** INFOR apuntar a un icono **III.** *vt* **1.** (*aim*) apuntar; **to** ~ **sth at sb** apuntar con algo a alguien; **the man had** ~**ed a knife at him** el hombre le había amenazado con un cuchillo; **to** ~ **a finger at sb** *a. fig* señalar con el dedo a alguien **2.** (*direct, show position or direction*) señalar; **to** ~ **sth toward sth/sb** dirigir algo hacia algo/alguien; **to** ~ **sb toward sth** indicar a alguien el camino hacia algo

◆**point out** *vt* **1.** (*show*) indicar; **if you see her, please point her out to me** si la ves, por favor indícame quién es **2.** (*inform of*) **to point sth out to sb** advertir a alguien de algo; **to** ~ **that ...** señalar que...

◆**point up** *vi form* destacar; **to** ~ **how ...** poner de relieve cómo...

point-blank [ˌpɔɪnt'blæŋk] **I.** *adv* **1.** (*fire*) a quemarropa **2.** (*ask*) a bocajarro; **to refuse** ~ negarse rotundamente **II.** *adj* **1.** (*very close, not far away*) **to shoot sb at** ~ **range** disparar a alguien a quemarropa **2.** (*blunt, direct*) directo, -a

pointed ['pɔɪntɪd, *Am:* -t̬ɪd] *adj* **1.** (*implement, stick*) puntiagudo, -a **2.** *fig* (*criticism*) mordaz; (*question*) directo, -a; (*remark*) intencionado, -a

pointer ['pɔɪntəʳ, *Am:* -t̬ɚ] *n* **1.** (*for blackbord*) puntero *m;* (*of clock*) aguja *f;* (*of scale*) fiel *m* **2.** INFOR puntero *m;* **mouse** ~ puntero del ratón **3.** (*advice, tip*) consejo *m* **4.** (*dog*) perro *m* de muestra

pointless ['pɔɪntləs] *adj* inútil; **it's** ~ **arguing with him** no sirve de nada discutir con él

point of view <points of view> *n* punto *m* de vista; **from a purely practical** ~ desde una perspectiva puramente práctica

pointsman ['pɔɪntsmən] <-men> *n Brit* RAIL guardabarrera *mf*

point-to-point (**race**) [ˌpɔɪnttə'pɔɪnt (reɪs)] *n carrera de caballos a campo traviesa*

poise [pɔɪz] **I.** *n no pl* **1.** (*composure*) aplomo *m;* **to lose/regain one's** ~ perder/recobrar la serenidad **2.** (*elegance*) porte *m* **II.** *vt* **to be** ~**d to do sth** estar a punto de hacer algo

poised *adj* **1.** (*suspended*) suspendido, -a **2.** (*ready*) preparado, -a **3.** (*calm*) sereno, -a

poison ['pɔɪzən] **I.** *n* veneno *m;* **rat** ~ matarratas *m inv;* **to lace sth with** ~ rociar algo con veneno; **to take** ~ envenenarse ▶**what's your** ~**?** *iron* ¿qué tomas? **II.** *vt* **1.** (*administer poison to*) envenenar **2.** (*spoil, corrupt*) emponzoñar; **the long dispute has** ~**ed relations between the two countries** el largo conflicto ha enturbiado las relaciones entre ambos países; **to** ~ **sb's mind** (**against sb**) indisponer a alguien (contra alguien)

poison gas *n no pl* gas *m* tóxico

poisoning *n no pl* envenenamiento *m*

poisonous ['pɔɪzənəs] *adj* venenoso, -a; ~ **atmosphere** *fig* ambiente *m* pernicioso; ~ **remark** comentario *m* malicioso

poke¹ [pəʊk, *Am:* poʊk] *n dial* (*bag*) bolsa *f,* saco *m*

poke² [pəʊk, *Am:* poʊk] **I.** *n* (*push*) empujón *m;* (*with the elbow*) codazo *m;* **to give sb a** ~ dar un codazo a alguien **II.** *vt* (*with finger*) dar con la punta del dedo en, tocar con la punta del dedo; (*with elbow*) dar un codazo a; **to** ~ **a hole in sth** hacer un agujero en algo; **to** ~ **holes in an argument** echar un argumento por tierra; **to** ~ **one's nose into sb's business** meter las narices en los asuntos de alguien **III.** *vi* **to** ~ **at sth/sb** dar a algo/alguien; **to** ~ **through** (**sth**) salirse (de algo)

◆**poke about** *vi,* **poke around** *vi* curiosear

◆**poke out I.** *vi* **to** ~ (**of sth**) salirse (de algo) **II.** *vt* **1.** (*stick out*) **to poke one's head out** asomar la cabeza **2.** (*push out*) **to poke sth out** sacar algo; **to poke sb's eye**(**s**) **out** saltarle los ojos a alguien

◆**poke round** *vi* curiosear

◆**poke up I.** *vi* asomar **II.** *vt* **to** ~ **a fire** atizar el fuego

poker¹ ['pəʊkəʳ, *Am:* 'poʊkɚ] *n* (*card game*) póquer *m*

poker² ['pəʊkəʳ, *Am:* 'poʊkɚ] *n* (*fireplace tool*) atizador *m*

pokey ['pəʊki, *Am:* 'poʊ-] **I.** *adj s.* **poky II.** *n Am, inf* (*prison*) cárcel *f;* **he'll get three years in** ~ le caerán tres años en chirona

poky ['pəʊki, *Am:* 'poʊ-] <-ier, -iest> *adj* **1.** (*uncomfortably small*) diminuto, -a; **a** ~ **little room** un cuartucho **2.** *Am* (*annoyingly slow*) lerdo, -a

Poland ['pəʊlənd, *Am:* 'poʊ-] *n* Polonia *f*

polar ['pəʊlə^r, *Am:* 'poʊlɚ] *adj* GEO, MAT polar; ~ **opposites** polos *mpl* opuestos

polar bear *n* oso *m* polar **polar circle** *n* círculo *m* polar **polar front** *n* METEO frente *m* polar **polar ice cap** *n no pl* casquete *m* polar

polarisation [ˌpəʊləraɪ'zeɪʃən] *n no pl, Brit, Aus s.* **polarization**

polarise ['pəʊləraɪz] *vt, vi Brit, Aus s.* **polarize**

polarity [pəʊ'lærəti, *Am:* poʊ'lerət̬i] *n no pl* polaridad *f*

polarization [ˌpəʊləraɪ'zeɪʃən, *Am:* ˌpoʊlɚɪ'-] *n no pl* polarización *f*

polarize ['pəʊləraɪz, *Am:* 'poʊ-] **I.** *vt* polarizar; **to ~ sth into two groups** polarizar algo en dos grupos **II.** *vi* polarizarse

polar lights *npl* aurora *f* boreal **polar region** *n* región *f* polar **polar zone** *n* región *f* polar

pole¹ [pəʊl, *Am:* poʊl] *n* palo *m;* **electricity ~** poste *m* de electricidad; **flag ~** asta *f* de bandera; **fishing ~** caña *f* de pescar; **telegraph ~** poste *m* telegráfico ▸**to not touch sth with a barge ~** no querer ver algo ni de lejos; **to be up the ~** *Brit* estar como una cabra *inf*

pole² [pəʊl, *Am:* poʊl] *n* **1.** GEO, ELEC polo *m;* **the magnetic ~s** GEO los polos magnéticos; **the minus/positive ~** el polo negativo/positivo **2.** *fig* **to be ~s apart** ser polos opuestos; **political ~s** extremos *mpl* políticos

Pole¹ [pəʊl, *Am:* poʊl] *n* (*person*) polaco, -a *m, f*

Pole² [pəʊl, *Am:* poʊl] *n* GEO **the North/South ~** el Polo Norte/Sur

poleaxe ['pəʊlæks, *Am:* 'poʊl-] **I.** *n* **1.** (*medieval weapon*) hacha *f* de armas **2.** (*axe used in naval warfare*) hacha *f* de abordaje **II.** *vt* (*strike powerfully*) tumbar, noquear; **he was completely ~d when his wife left him** se quedó de una pieza cuando su mujer le dejó

polemic [pə'lemɪk] **I.** *n* polémica *f* **II.** *adj* polémico, -a

polemical *adj* polémico, -a

pole position *n no pl* posición *f* de ventaja; **to be in ~** estar en cabeza

Pole Star *n* estrella *f* polar

pole vault *n* salto *m* con pértiga **pole vaulter** *n* saltador(a) *m(f)* de pértiga

police [pə'liːs] **I.** *n no pl* policía *f* **II.** *vt* **to ~ an area** vigilar una zona; **to ~ a process** supervisar un proceso; **to ~ oneself** controlarse; **to ~ the frontier** patrullar por la frontera

police car *n* coche *m* de policía **police constable** *n Brit* policía *m,* guardia *m* **police court** *n* juzgado *m* de guardia **police department** *n Am* departamento *m* de policía **police dog** *n* perro *m* policía **police escort** *n* escolta *f* policial; **under ~** con escolta policial **police force** *n* cuerpo *m* de policía **police informer** *n* confidente *mf* de la policía **police magistrate** *n* juez(a) *m(f)* de guardia

policeman [pə'liːsmən] <-men> *n* policía *m,* guardia *m*

police officer *n* agente *mf* de policía **police patrol** *n* patrulla *f* policial **police raid** *n* redada *f,* arreada *f Arg* **police record** *n* **1.** (*dossier*) expediente *m* **2.** (*history of convictions*) antecedentes *mpl* penales; **to have a long ~** tener un largo historial delictivo **police reporter** *n* reportero, -a *m, f* de asuntos policiales **police state** *n pej* estado *m* policíaco **police station** *n* comisaría *f*

policewoman [pə'liːsˌwʊmən] <-women> *n* mujer *f* policía

policy¹ ['pɒləsi, *Am:* 'pɑːlə-] <-ies> *n* **1.** POL, ECON política *f;* **a change in ~** un cambio de política; **domestic/economic ~** política interior/económica; **company ~** política de empresa; **to set ~** (**on sth**) establecer una política (en materia de algo) **2.** (*principle*) principio *m;* **my ~ is to tell the truth whenever possible** tengo por norma decir la verdad siempre que sea posible

policy² ['pɒləsi, *Am:* 'pɑːlə-] <-ies> *n* FIN póliza *f;* **to take out a ~** hacerse un seguro

policyholder ['pɒləsiˌhəʊldə^r, *Am:* 'pɑːləsiˌhoʊldɚ] *n* asegurado, -a *m, f* **policy maker** *n* responsable *mf* de los principios políticos de un partido **policy-making** *n no pl* formulación *f* de principios políticos **policy number** *n* número *m* de póliza **policy owner** *n* titular *mf* de una póliza

polio [ˌpəʊliəʊ, *Am:* ˌpoʊlioʊ] *n,* **poliomyelitis** [ˌpəʊliəʊmaɪə'laɪtɪs, *Am:* ˌpoʊlioʊˌmaɪə'laɪt̬əs] *n no pl* MED polio *f,* poliomielitis *f*

polio vaccine *n* vacuna *f* contra la polio

polish ['pɒlɪʃ, *Am:* 'pɑːlɪʃ] **I.** *n no pl* **1.** (*substance: for furniture*) cera *f;* (*for shoes*) betún *m;* (*for silver*) abrillantador *m;* (*for nails*) esmalte *m* **2.** (*action*) pulimento *m;* **to give sth a ~** dar brillo a algo **3.** (*sophisticated or refined style*) refinamiento *m* **II.** *vt* **1.** (*rub to make shine*) sacar brillo a; (*shoes, silver*) limpiar **2.** *fig* (*refine*) pulir

◆**polish off** *vt* (*food*) despacharse; (*work, opponent*) liquidar

◆**polish up** *vt* **1.** (*polish to a shine*) dar brillo **2.** (*improve, brush up*) perfeccionar

Polish ['pəʊlɪʃ, *Am:* 'poʊ-] **I.** *adj* polaco, -a **II.** *n* **1.** (*person*) polaco, -a *m, f* **2.** LING polaco *m*

polished *adj* **1.** (*shiny*) pulido, -a **2.** *fig* (*sophisticated*) distinguido, -a; ~ **manners** modales *mpl* refinados; **a ~ performance** una actuación impecable

polite [pə'laɪt] *adj* **1.** (*courteous*) atento, -a; ~ **refusal** declinación *f* cortés **2.** (*cultured*) educado, -a; (*refined*) fino, -a; ~ **society** buena sociedad *f* **3.** (*superficially courteous*) correcto, -a; **to keep a ~ conversation going**

mantener una conversación por cortesía
politeness *n no pl* **1.** (*good manners*) cortesía *f* **2.** (*consideration*) atenciones *fpl*
politic ['pɒlɪtɪk, *Am:* 'pɑːlə-] *adj* **1.** (*judicious, prudent*) prudente **2.** POL **the body ~** el cuerpo político
political [pə'lɪtɪkəl, *Am:* -'lɪt̬ə-] *adj* político, -a; **~ pundit** experto, -a *m, f* en política; **to make ~ capital (out) of sth** sacar provecho político de algo
politically correct *adj* políticamente correcto, -a *(actitud que refleja una ideología progresista)*
politician [ˌpɒlɪ'tɪʃən, *Am:* ˌpɑːlə'-] *n* político, -a *m, f*
politicize [pe'lɪtɪsaɪz, *Am:* -'lɪt̬ə-] *vt* politizar
politics *n pl* **1.** (*activities of government*) política *f;* **to go into ~** dedicarse a la política; **to talk ~** hablar de política **2.** *Brit* (*political science*) ciencias *fpl* políticas
polka ['pɒlkə, *Am:* 'poʊl-] **I.** *n* polca *f* **II.** *vi* bailar la polca
poll [pəʊl, *Am:* poʊl] **I.** *n* **1.** (*public survey*) encuesta *f;* **opinion ~** sondeo *m* de la opinión pública; **to conduct a ~** hacer una encuesta **2.** *pl* (*elections*) **to go to the ~s** acudir a las urnas **3.** (*results of a vote*) **to head the ~** obtener la mayoría de votos **4.** (*number of votes cast*) votos *mpl;* **there was a heavy/light ~** ha habido una alta/baja participación en las elecciones **II.** *vt* **1.** (*record the opinion*) sondear; **half the people ~ed** la mitad de los encuestados **2.** (*receive*) **to ~ votes** obtener votos
pollard ['pɒləd, *Am:* 'pɑːlɚd] *vt* desmochar
pollen ['pɒlən, *Am:* 'pɑːlən] *n no pl* polen *m*
pollen count *n* índice *m* de polen en el aire
pollinate ['pɒlɪneɪt, *Am:* 'pɑːlə-] *vt* polinizar
polling *n no pl* votación *f*
polling booth *n Brit, Aus* cabina *f* electoral **polling card** *n Brit, Aus* papeleta *f* electoral **polling day** *n no art, Brit, Aus* día *m* de elecciones **polling place** *n Am,* **polling station** *n Brit, Aus* colegio *m* electoral
pollster ['pəʊlstə^r, *Am:* 'poʊlstɚ] *n* encuestador(a) *m(f)*
pollutant [pəl'uːtənt] *n* contaminante *m,* agente *m* contaminador
pollute [pə'luːt] *vt* **1.** (*contaminate*) contaminar **2.** *fig* (*corrupt*) corromper; **to ~ sb's mind** corromper la mente de alguien
polluter [pə'luːtə^r, *Am:* -t̬ɚ] *n* contaminador(a) *m(f)*
pollution [pə'luːʃən] *n no pl* contaminación *f*
polo ['pəʊləʊ, *Am:* 'poʊloʊ] *n no pl* SPORTS polo *m*
polo neck *n* cuello *m* vuelto; **~ sweater** jersey *m* de cuello vuelto, polera *f Arg, Urug* **polo shirt** *n* polo *m*
poly ['pɒli, *Am:* 'pɑːli] *n Brit, inf s.* **polytechnic** escuela *f* politécnica
polyamide ['pɒli'æmaɪd, *Am:* ˌpɑːli-] *n* poliamida *f*
polychrome [ˌpɒlɪ'krəʊm] *adj* polícromo, -a
polyclinic ['pɒlɪklɪnɪk, *Am:* ˌpɑːlɪ'-] *n* policlínica *f,* policlínico *m AmL*
polyester [ˌpɒli'estə^r, *Am:* ˌpɑːli'estɚ] *n no pl* poliéster *m*
polygamist *n* polígamo *m*
polygamous *adj* polígamo, -a
polygamy [pə'lɪgəmi] *n no pl* poligamia *f*
polyglot ['pɒlɪglɒt, *Am:* 'pɑːlɪglɑːt] **I.** *adj* polígloto, -a **II.** *n* políglota *mf*
polygon ['pɒlɪgən, *Am:* 'pɑːlɪgɑːn] *n* polígono *m*
polygonal [pə'lɪgənəl] *adj* poligonal
polygraph ['pɒlɪgrɑːf, *Am:* 'pɑːlɪgræf] *n Am* polígrafo *m,* detector *m* de mentiras
polymeric [ˌpɒlɪ'merɪk, *Am:* ˌpɑːlɪ'-] *adj* polimérico, -a
polymorphous [ˌpɒlɪ'mɔːfəs, *Am:* ˌpɑːlɪ'mɔːr-] *adj* polimorfo, -a
Polynesia [ˌpɒlɪ'niːʒə, *Am:* ˌpɑːlə'niːʒə] *n* Polinesia *f*
Polynesian **I.** *adj* polinesio, -a **II.** *n* polinesio, -a *m, f*
polyp ['pɒlɪp, *Am:* 'pɑːlɪp] *n* MED, ZOOL pólipo *m*
polyphonic [ˌpɒlɪ'fɒnɪk, *Am:* ˌpɑːlɪ'fɑːnɪk] *adj* MUS polifónico, -a
polyphony [pə'lɪfəni] *n no pl* MUS polifonía *f*
polystyrene [ˌpɒlɪ'staɪəriːn, *Am:* ˌpɑːlɪ-] *n no pl, Brit, Aus* poliestireno *m*
polysyllabic [ˌpɒlɪsɪ'læbɪk, *Am:* ˌpɑːlɪsɪ'-] *adj* polisílabo, -a
polysyllable [ˌpɒlɪ'sɪləbəl, *Am:* 'pɑːlɪˌsɪl-] *n* LING polisílabo *m*
polytechnic [ˌpɒlɪ'teknɪk, *Am:* ˌpɑːlɪ-] *n* escuela *f* politécnica
polytheism ['pɒlɪθiːɪzəm, *Am:* 'pɑːlɪ-] *n no pl* politeísmo *m*
polytheistic [ˌpɒlɪθi'ɪstɪk, *Am:* ˌpɑːlɪ-] *adj* politeísta
polythene ['pɒlɪθiːn, *Am:* 'pɑːlɪ-] *n no pl* polietileno *m*
polythene bag *n Brit, Aus* bolsa *f* de polietileno
polyunsaturated [ˌpɒliʌn'sætʃəreɪtɪd, *Am:* ˌpɑːliʌn'sætʃəreɪt̬ɪd] *adj* poliinsaturado, -a
polyunsaturated fats *npl,* **polyunsaturates** [ˌpɒliʌn'sætʃəreɪts, *Am:* ˌpɑːli-] *npl* grasas *fpl* poliinsaturadas
polyurethane [ˌpɒlɪ'jʊərəθeɪn, *Am:* ˌpɑːlɪ'jʊrə-] *n no pl* poliuretano *m*
polyvalent [ˌpɒlɪ'veɪlənt, *Am:* ˌpɑːlɪ'-] *adj* polivalente
pomade [pəʊ'mɑːd, *Am:* pɑː'meɪd] *n no pl* pomada *f*
pomegranate ['pɒmɪgrænɪt, *Am:* 'pɑːmˌgræn-] *n* **1.** (*fruit*) granada *f* **2.** (*tree*) granado *m*
pomp [pɒmp, *Am:* pɑːmp] *n no pl* pompa *f;* **~ and circumstance** pompa y solemnidad
pomposity [pɒm'pɒsəti, *Am:* pɑːm'pɑːsə-

t̬i] *n no pl* pomposidad *f*

pompous ['pɒmpəs, *Am:* 'pɑːm-] *adj* **1.** pomposo, -a **2.** (*pretentious*) ostentoso, -a; ~ **language** lenguaje *m* ampuloso

ponce [pɒns, *Am:* pɑːns] **I.** *n* **1.** *Brit, Aus, pej* (*effeminate man*) mariquita *m* **2.** *Brit, inf* (*pimp*) chulo *m* **II.** *vi* **to ~ about 1.** *Brit, Aus, pej* (*behave in effeminate manner*) mariconear *pey* **2.** *Brit* (*muck about*) perder el tiempo

poncho ['pɒntʃəʊ, *Am:* 'pɑːntʃoʊ] *n* poncho *m*, ruana *f Col, Ven*, zarape *m Guat, Méx*

poncy ['pɒnsi, *Am:* 'pɑːnsi] *adj* <-ier, -iest> *Brit, Aus, pej* de mariquita

pond [pɒnd, *Am:* pɑːnd] *n* **1.** (*natural*) charca *f;* (*artificial*) estanque *m;* **duck ~** estanque de patos; **fish ~** vivero *m* **2.** *iron* (*Atlantic ocean*) **the Pond** el charco

ponder ['pɒndəʳ, *Am:* 'pɑːndɚ] **I.** *vt* considerar, sopesar **II.** *vi* reflexionar; **to ~ on sth** meditar sobre algo; **to ~ whether/why ...** preguntarse si/por qué...

ponderous ['pɒndərəs, *Am:* 'pɑːn-] *adj* **1.** (*movement*) pesado, -a **2.** (*style*) laborioso, -a

pone [pəʊn] *n Am* borona *f;* **corn ~** pan *m* de maíz

pong [pɒŋ, *Am:* pɑːŋ] *inf* **I.** *n Brit, Aus* peste *f;* **what a ~!** ¡qué peste! **II.** *vi Brit, Aus, pej* **to ~ of sth** apestar a algo

pontiff ['pɒntɪf, *Am:* 'pɑːnt̬ɪf] *n* REL **the ~** el pontífice

pontifical [pɒn'tɪfɪkəl, *Am:* pɑːn'-] *adj* pontifical

pontificate¹ [pɒn'tɪfɪkeɪt, *Am:* pɑːn-] *vi pej* pontificar

pontificate² [pɒn'tɪfɪkət, *Am:* pɑːn'tɪfɪkət] *n* pontificado *m*

pontoon [pɒn'tuːn, *Am:* pɑːn-] *n* **1.** (*floating device*) pontón *m* **2.** *no pl, Brit* (*card game*) veintiuna *f*

pontoon bridge *n* puente *m* de pontones

pony ['pəʊni, *Am:* 'poʊ-] <-ies> *n* (*horse*) poni *m*

ponytail ['pəʊnitaɪl, *Am:* 'poʊ-] *n* coleta *f*

pony-trekking *n no pl* excursión *f* en poni; **to go ~** ir de excursión en poni

poo [puː] *s.* **pooh**

poodle ['puːdl] *n* caniche *m;* **to be sb's ~** *Brit, iron* ser el perrito faldero de alguien

poof [puːf] **I.** *n Brit, Aus, pej* maricón *m* **II.** *interj Am, inf* ¡chas!

poofter [puːftə, *Am:* -tɚ] *n Brit, Aus, pej* maricón *m*

pooh [puː] **I.** *n Brit, Aus, childspeak* caca *f;* **to do a ~** hacer caca **II.** *vi Brit, Aus, childspeak* hacer caca **III.** *interj inf* **1.** (*to indicate disgust*) **~! what a ghastly smell!** ¡puf, qué peste! **2.** (*to indicate impatience*) ¡bah!

pooh-pooh [ˌpuː'puː] *vt inf* **to ~ a plan/a proposal** desdeñar un plan/una proposición

pool¹ [puːl] *n* **1.** (*of water*) charca *f;* (*of oil, blood*) charco *f;* **rock ~** piscina *f* de roca; **a ~ of light** un foco de luz **2.** (*artificial*) estanque *m;* **swimming ~** piscina *f*, pileta *f RíoPl*

pool² [puːl] **I.** *n* **1.** (*common fund*) fondo *m* común **2.** (*common supply*) reserva *f;* **car ~** parque *m* de automóviles; **gene ~** acervo *m* genético; **typing ~** servicio *m* de mecanografía **3.** SPORTS billar *m* americano; **to shoot ~** *inf* jugar al billar; **to be dirty ~** *Am, inf* ser un juego sucio **4.** *pl, Brit* (**football**) **~s** quiniela *f;* **to do the ~s** hacer la quiniela **II.** *vt* (*money, resources*) hacer un fondo común; (*information*) compartir

pool hall *n*, **pool room** *n* sala *f* de billar

pool table *n* mesa *f* de billar

poop¹ [puːp] *n* NAUT popa *f;* **~ deck** castillo *m* de popa

poop² [puːp] *n no pl, Am, inf* (*information*) **to get the ~ on sth/sb** ponerse al tanto de algo/alguien

poop³ [puːp] *inf* **I.** *n no pl* caca *f;* **dog ~** caca de perro **II.** *vi* hacerse caca

◆**poop out** *vi Am, Aus, inf* quedar hecho polvo

pooper scooper ['puːpəˌskuːpəʳ, *Am:* -pɚˌskuːpɚ] *n*, **poop scoop** ['puːpskuːp] *n Am* pala *f* para recoger excrementos

poop sheet *n Am, inf* folleto *m*

poor [pʊəʳ, *Am:* pʊr] **I.** *adj* **1.** (*lacking money*) pobre **2.** (*attendance, harvest*) escaso, -a; (*memory, performance*) malo, -a; **~ soil** terreno *m* pobre; **~ visibility** visibilidad *f* escasa; **to be ~ at sth** no estar fuerte en algo; **to be in ~ health** estar mal de salud; **to be a ~ loser** no saber perder; **to be a ~ sailor** marearse fácilmente; **to give a ~ account of oneself** causar mala impresión; **to cut a ~ figure** (**as sth**) hacer un mal papel (como algo); **to be a ~ excuse for sth** ser una mala versión de algo; **to have ~ eyesight** tener mala vista; **to have ~ hearing** ser duro de oído; **to make a ~ job of** (**doing**) **sth** hacer algo mal **3.** (*deserving of pity*) pobre; **you ~ thing!** ¡pobrecito! **II.** *n* **the ~** los pobres

poor box <-es> *n* cepillo *m* de los pobres

poorhouse *n* HIST asilo *m* de los pobres

poorly ['pʊəli, *Am:* 'pʊr-] **I.** *adv* **1.** (*resulting from poverty*) pobremente; **to be ~ off** andar escaso de dinero **2.** (*inadequately*) mal; **~ dressed** mal vestido; **to think ~ of sb** tener mala opinión de alguien **II.** *adj* **to feel ~** encontrarse mal

poorness ['pʊənɪs, *Am:* 'pʊr-] *n no pl* **1.** (*inadequacy*) impropiedad *f;* **the ~ of his judgment** lo inadecuado de su opinión **2.** (*poverty*) pobreza *f*

poor relation *n* pariente *mf* pobre

pop¹ [pɒp, *Am:* pɑːp] **I.** *adj* popular; **~ culture** cultura *f* pop **II.** *n no pl* MUS pop *m*

pop² [pɒp, *Am:* pɑːp] *n inf* (*father*) papá *m*

pop³ [pɒp, *Am:* pɑːp] *n no pl abbr of* **population** hab. *mf*

pop⁴ [pɒp, *Am:* pɑːp] **I.** *n* **1.** (*small explosive noise*) pequeña explosión *f;* **the ~ of a champagne cork** el taponazo de una botella de cava

P

2. (*drink*) gaseosa *f;* **orange** ~ naranjada *f;* **fizzy** ~ bebida *f* gaseosa **II.** <-pp-> *vi* **1.** (*explode*) estallar; (*burst*) reventar; **to let the cork** ~ hacer saltar el tapón **2.** (*go, come quickly*) **to** ~ **upstairs** subir un momento; **to** ~ **out for sth** salir un momento a por algo **III.** <-pp-> *vt* **1.** (*make burst*) hacer estallar **2.** (*put quickly*) meter; **to** ~ **sth on/off** ponerse/quitarse algo

◆**pop in** *vi* entrar un momento en; **we popped in at my brother's on our way home** de vuelta a casa, pasamos por casa de mi hermano

◆**pop off** *vi iron, inf* (*die*) estirar la pata

◆**pop out** *vi* salir; **to** ~ **from somewhere** salir de pronto de un sitio; **to** ~ **for sth** salir un momento a hacer algo

◆**pop up** *vi* (*appear*) aparecer; **to** ~ **out of nowhere** surgir de la nada

pop art *n no pl* pop art *m* **pop concert** *n* concierto *m* pop

popcorn ['pɒpkɔːn, *Am:* 'pɑːpkɔːrn] *n no pl* palomitas *fpl* de maíz, pororó *m CSur,* cacalote *m AmC, Méx*

pope [pəʊp, *Am:* poʊp] *n* REL **1.** (*Catholic*) papa *m* **2.** (*Orthodox priest*) pope *m*

pop-eyed [ˌpɒp'aɪd, *Am:* 'pɑːpˌaɪd] *adj* de ojos saltones; **he looked at me** ~ me miró con los ojos desorbitados

pop group *n* grupo *m* pop

pop gun *n* pistola *f* de juguete

poplar ['pɒpləʳ, *Am:* 'pɑːplɚ] *n* álamo *m*

poplin ['pɒplɪn, *Am:* 'pɑːplɪn] *n no pl* popelín *m*

pop music *n no pl* música *f* pop

popper ['pɒpəʳ, *Am:* 'pɑːpɚ] *n* **1.** *Brit, inf* (*drug*) popper *m* **2.** (*button*) cierre *m* automático

poppet ['pɒpɪt, *Am:* 'pɑːpɪt] *n Aus, Brit, inf* tesoro *m fig*

poppy ['pɒpi, *Am:* 'pɑːpi] <-ies> *n* amapola *f*

poppycock ['pɒpɪkɒk, *Am:* 'pɑːpɪkɑːk] *n no pl, inf* tonterías *fpl*

Poppy Day *n Brit s.* **Remembrance Day**

poppy seeds *npl* semillas *fpl* de amapola

pop singer *n* cantante *mf* pop **pop song** *n* canción *f* pop **pop star** *n* estrella *f* del pop

populace ['pɒpjʊləs, *Am:* 'pɑːpjəlɪs] *n no pl* **the** ~ el pueblo

popular ['pɒpjʊləʳ, *Am:* 'pɑːpjəlɚ] *adj* **1.** (*liked*) popular; **she is very** ~ **among her colleagues** es muy apreciada entre sus compañeros; **he is** ~ **with girls** tiene éxito con las chicas **2.** (*by the people*) popular; ~ **elections** elecciones *fpl* democráticas; ~ **front** frente *m* popular; ~ **support** el apoyo del pueblo; **by** ~ **request** a petición del público **3.** (*widespread*) generalizado, -a **4.** (*cheap*) económico, -a

popularity [ˌpɒpjʊ'lærəti, *Am:* ˌpɑːpjə'lerəṱi] *n no pl* popularidad *f*

popularize ['pɒpjʊləraɪz, *Am:* 'pɑːpjə-] *vt* **1.** (*make known or liked*) popularizar **2.** (*make understood*) divulgar

popularly ['pɒpjʊləli, *Am:* 'pɑːpjəlɚ-] *adv* generalmente; **to be** ~ **known as ...** ser vulgarmente conocido como...

populate ['pɒpjəleɪt, *Am:* 'pɑːpjə-] *vt* poblar

population [ˌpɒpjə'leɪʃən, *Am:* ˌpɑːpjə'-] *n* población *f;* **the working** ~ la población activa; **the dolphin** ~ la población de delfines

population density *n* densidad *f* de población **population explosion** *n* explosión *f* demográfica

populous ['pɒpjʊləs, *Am:* 'pɑːpjə-] *adj form* populoso, -a

porcelain ['pɔːsəlɪn, *Am:* 'pɔːr-] *n no pl* porcelana *f*

porch [pɔːtʃ, *Am:* pɔːrtʃ] *n* **1.** (*over entrance*) porche *m;* (*church*) pórtico *m* **2.** *Am* (*verandah*) veranda *f*

porcupine ['pɔːkjʊpaɪn, *Am:* 'pɔːr-] *n* puercoespín *m*

pore [pɔːʳ, *Am:* pɔːr] *n* poro *m*

◆**pore over** *vi* reflexionar sobre; **to** ~ **a book/map** estudiar detenidamente un libro/mapa

pork [pɔːk, *Am:* pɔːrk] *n no pl* (carne *f* de) cerdo *m,* (carne *f* de) puerco *m Méx,* (carne *f* de) chancho *m Chile, Perú*

pork chop *n* chuleta *f* de cerdo

porker *n* cebón *m*

pork pie *n Brit* empanada *f* de cerdo

porky **I.** <-ier, -iest> *adj pej, inf* gordinflón, -ona **II.** *n* <-ies> *pl, Brit, inf* (*lies*) bola *f;* **to tell porkies** contar mentiras

porn [pɔːn, *Am:* pɔːrn] *n abbr of* **pornography** porno *m*

pornographic [ˌpɔːnə'græfɪk, *Am:* ˌpɔːrnə'-] *adj* pornográfico, -a

pornography [pɔː'nɒgrəfi, *Am:* pɔːr'nɑːgrə-] *n no pl* pornografía *f;* **hard-core** ~ pornografía dura

porous ['pɔːrəs] *adj* poroso, -a

porpoise ['pɔːpəs, *Am:* 'pɔːr-] *n* marsopa *f*

porridge ['pɒrɪdʒ, *Am:* 'pɔːr-] *n no pl* ≈ gachas *fpl* de avena

porridge oats *npl* copos *mpl* de avena

port¹ [pɔːt, *Am:* pɔːrt] *n* **1.** NAUT (*harbour*) puerto *m;* ~ **of call** puerto de escala; **fishing/trading** ~ puerto pesquero/comercial; **to come into** ~ tomar puerto; **to leave** ~ zarpar **2.** INFOR puerto *m;* **parallel/serial/printer/game** ~ puerto paralelo/serial/de impresora/de juegos ►**any** ~ **in a storm** en tiempos de guerrra cualquier hoyo es trinchero

port² [pɔːt, *Am:* pɔːrt] **I.** *n no pl* AVIAT, NAUT (*side*) babor *m;* **to** ~ a babor **II.** *adj* NAUT, AVIAT de babor; **on the** ~ **side** a babor

port³ [pɔːt, *Am:* pɔːrt] *n no pl* (*wine*) oporto *m*

portable ['pɔːtəbl, *Am:* 'pɔːrṱə-] *adj* portátil

portacabin ['pɔːtəˌkæbin, *Am:* 'pɔːrṱə-] *n Brit s.* **Portakabin**

portage ['pɔːtɪdʒ, *Am:* 'pɔːrṱɪdʒ] *n no pl*

porte *m*
Portakabin® ['pɔːtəˌkæbin, *Am:* 'pɔːrt̬ə-] *n Brit* caseta *f* portátil
portal ['pɔːtəl, *Am:* 'pɔːrt̬əl] *n a.* INFOR (*gateway*) portal *m*
port authority *n* autoridad *f* portuaria
port charges *npl,* **port dues** *npl* derechos *mpl* portuarios
portcullis [ˌpɔːt'kʌlɪs, *Am:* ˌpɔːrt-] <-es> *n* rastrillo *m*
portentous [pɔː'tentəs, *Am:* pɔːr'tent̬əs] *adj* **1.** *form* (*signifying something to come*) profético, -a; (*ominous*) de mal agüero **2.** (*too serious*) solemne
porter ['pɔːtəʳ, *Am:* 'pɔːrt̬ɚ] *n* **1.** (*person who carries luggage*) mozo *m* de equipajes; (*in hospital*) camillero *m;* (*on expedition*) porteador *m* **2.** *Brit* (*doorkeeper*) portero *m;* (*in college*) bedel *m;* (*in hotel*) conserje *m;* **~'s lodge** conserjería *f* **3.** *Am* (*attendant on a train*) camarero *m*
portfolio [pɔːt'fəʊlɪəʊ, *Am:* pɔːrt'foʊlɪoʊ] *n* **1.** (*case*) portafolio(s) *m* (*inv*) **2.** (*examples of drawings, designs*) carpeta *f* de trabajos **3.** FIN, POL cartera *f;* **minister without ~** ministro, -a *m, f* sin cartera
porthole ['pɔːthəʊl, *Am:* 'pɔːrthoʊl] *n* portilla *f*
portico ['pɔːtɪkəʊ, *Am:* 'pɔːrt̬ɪkoʊ] <-es *o* -s> *n* pórtico *m*
portion ['pɔːʃən, *Am:* 'pɔːr-] **I.** *n* **1.** (*part*) parte *f;* **to accept one's ~ of the blame** aceptar su parte de culpa **2.** (*serving*) ración *f;* (*of cake, cheese*) trozo *m* **II.** *vt* **to ~ out sth** repartir algo
portly ['pɔːtli, *Am:* 'pɔːrt-] <-ier, -iest> *adj* corpulento, -a
portrait ['pɔːtrɪt, *Am:* 'pɔːrtrɪt] **I.** *n* ART, LIT retrato *m;* **to paint a ~ of sb** retratar a alguien **II.** *adj* TYPO de formato vertical
portraitist *n,* **portrait painter** *n* retratista *mf*
portraiture ['pɔːtrɪtʃəʳ, *Am:* 'pɔːrtrɪtʃɚ] *n no pl* ART, LIT retrato *m*
portray [pɔː'treɪ, *Am:* pɔːr'-] *vt* **1.** ART (*person*) retratar; (*object*) pintar; (*scene, environment*) representar **2.** *fig* describir **3.** THEAT interpretar
portrayal [pɔː'treɪəl, *Am:* pɔːr'-] *n* **1.** ART retrato *m* **2.** *fig* descripción *f* **3.** THEAT interpretación *f*
Portugal ['pɔːtjʊgəl, *Am:* 'pɔːrtʃəgəl] *n* Portugal *m*
Portuguese [ˌpɔːtjʊ'giːz, *Am:* ˌpɔːrtʃə'-] **I.** *adj* portugués, -esa **II.** *n* **1.** (*person*) portugués, -esa *m, f* **2.** LING portugués *m*
POS [ˌpiːəʊ'es] *abbr of* **point of sale** punto *m* de venta
pose¹ [pəʊz, *Am:* poʊz] *vt* (*difficulty, problem*) plantear; (*question*) formular; **to ~ a threat to sb** representar una amenaza para alguien
pose² [pəʊz, *Am:* poʊz] **I.** *vi* **1.** ART, PHOT posar **2.** (*affected behaviour*) darse tono **3.** (*pretend to be*) **to ~ as sb/sth** hacerse pasar por alguien/algo **II.** *n* **1.** (*body position*) pose *f;* **to adopt a ~** adoptar una pose **2.** (*pretence*) afectación *f;* **it's all a ~** es todo fachada
poser ['pəʊzəʳ, *Am:* 'poʊzɚ] *n* **1.** *inf* (*question*) pregunta *f* difícil; (*problem*) dilema *m* **2.** *pej* (*person*) **he's a ~** se hace el interesante
posh [pɒʃ, *Am:* pɑːʃ] *inf* **I.** *adj* **1.** (*stylish: area*) elegante; (*car, hotel, restaurant*) de lujo **2.** *Brit* (*person, accent*) pijo, -a, cheto, -a *CSur* **II.** *adv Brit, inf* **stop acting so ~!** ¡deja de comportarte como un pijo!
posit ['pɒzɪt, *Am:* 'pɑːzɪt] *vt form* postular
position [pə'zɪʃən] **I.** *n* **1.** *a.* MIL, SPORTS posición *f;* **from this ~ you can see the whole beach** desde este lugar se puede ver toda la playa; **the ~ of a house** la ubicación de una casa; **they took up their ~s** ocuparon sus puestos; **to be in ~** estar en su sitio; **to be out of ~** estar fuera de lugar; **yoga ~** postura *f* de yoga **2.** *Brit, Aus* (*rank*) posición *f,* puesto *m;* (*social*) rango *m;* **the ~ of director** el cargo de director; **a ~ of responsibility/trust** un puesto de responsabilidad/confianza **3.** *form* (*opinion*) postura *f;* **to take up a ~ on sth** adoptar una postura sobre algo **4.** (*situation*) situación *f;* **financial ~** situación económica; **to be in the fortunate ~ of ...** tener la suerte de...; **to be in a ~ to do sth** estar en condiciones de hacer algo; **to be in no ~ to do sth** no estar en condiciones de hacer algo; **to put sb in a difficult ~** poner a alguien en un aprieto **II.** *vt* (*place*) colocar; MIL apostar
positive ['pɒzətɪv, *Am:* 'pɑːzət̬ɪv] *adj* **1.** *a.* ELEC, MAT positivo, -a; **~ criticism** crítica *f* constructiva; **to think ~** ser positivo **2.** MED **HIV ~** seropositivo, -a **3.** (*certain*) definitivo, -a; (*proof*) concluyente; **to be ~ about sth** estar seguro de algo; (**absolutely**) **~!** ¡segurísimo! **4.** (*complete*) auténtico, -a; **a ~ miracle** un verdadero milagro
positively *adv* **1.** (*think*) positivamente; **to answer ~** contestar afirmativamente **2.** (*completely*) totalmente; **to ~ refuse to do sth** negarse rotundamente a hacer algo
poss. *abbr of* **possessive** posesivo *m*
posse ['pɒsi, *Am:* 'pɑːsi] *n* banda *f;* **a whole ~ of reporters** una legión de reporteros
possess [pə'zes] *vt* **1.** (*own, have*) poseer **2.** **to ~ sb** (*anger, fear*) apoderarse de alguien; (*evil spirit*) poseer a alguien; **what ~ed you to do that?** ¿cómo se te ocurrió hacer eso?
possessed [pə'zest] *adj* poseso, -a, poseído, -a; **to be ~ with sth** estar obsesionado con algo; **to behave like sb ~** comportarse como un poseso
possession [pə'zeʃən] *n* **1.** *no pl* (*having*) posesión *f;* **illegal ~ of arms** tenencia *f* ilícita de armas; **to take ~ of sth** tomar posesión de algo; **to come into ~ of sth** *form* hacerse con algo; **to gain ~ of sth** apoderarse de algo; **to be in sb's ~** estar en poder de alguien; **to**

P

have sth in one's ~ *form* tener algo en su poder **2.** (*item of property*) bien *m* **3.** POL dominio *m* ►~ **is nine points of the law** la posesión es lo que cuenta

possessive [pəˈzesɪv] *adj* posesivo, -a; **to be** ~ **about sb** comportarse de manera posesiva con alguien

possessor [pəˈzesəʳ, *Am:* -ɚ] *n iron* poseedor(a) *m(f)*

possibility [ˌpɒsəˈbɪləti, *Am:* ˌpɑːsəˈbɪləṱi] *n* <-ies> **1.** (*feasible circumstance or action*) posibilidad *f* **2.** *no pl* (*likelihood*) perspectiva *f*; **within the bounds of** ~ dentro de lo posible; **if by any** ~ **…** si por casualidad…; **is there any** ~ (**that**) …? *form* ¿hay alguna posibilidad de que +*subj*…? **3.** (*potential*) **to have possibilities** tener posibilidades

possible [ˈpɒsəbl, *Am:* ˈpɑːsə-] *adj* posible; **as clean/good as** ~ lo más limpio/lo mejor posible; **as far as** ~ en lo posible; **as soon as** ~ lo antes posible; **if** ~ si es posible

possibly [ˈpɒsəbli, *Am:* ˈpɑːsə-] *adv* **1.** (*perhaps*) quizás; **could you** ~ **help me?** ¿sería tan amable de ayudarme? **2.** (*by any means*) **we did all that we** ~ **could** hicimos todo lo posible; **I couldn't** ~ **do it** me es totalmente imposible hacerlo

possum [ˈpɒsəm, *Am:* ˈpɑːsəm] <-(s)> *n* zarigüeya *f* ►**to play** ~ (*pretend to be asleep*) hacerse el dormido; (*pretend to be ignorant*) hacerse el sueco

post[1] [pəʊst, *Am:* poʊst] **I.** *n no pl, Brit* correo *m*; **by** ~ por correo; **to open the** ~ abrir las cartas; **by return of** ~ a vuelta de correo; **by separate** ~ en sobre aparte; **is there any** ~**?** ¿ha llegado alguna carta? **II.** *vt Brit, Aus* echar (al correo); **to** ~ **sb sth** enviar algo por correo a alguien

post[2] [pəʊst, *Am:* poʊst] **I.** *n* (*job*) puesto *m*; **to apply for a teaching** ~ solicitar un empleo de profesor; **to take up a** ~ entrar en funciones; **to desert one's** ~ MIL desertar del puesto **II.** *vt* **1.** (*send to work*) destinar **2.** MIL (*position*) apostar

post[3] [pəʊst, *Am:* poʊst] **I.** *n* **1.** *a.* SPORTS poste *m*; **starting/finishing** ~ línea *f* de salida/de meta **2.** *inf* (*goalpost*) poste *m* (de portería) **II.** *vt Brit, Aus* **to** ~ **sth** (**on sth**) fijar algo (en algo); **to** ~ **sth on the noticeboard** poner algo en el tablón de anuncios; ~ **no bills** prohibido fijar carteles

postage [ˈpəʊstɪdʒ, *Am:* ˈpoʊ-] *n no pl* franqueo *m*; ~ **and packing** gastos *mpl* de envío

postage meter *n Am* (máquina *f*) franqueadora *f*, estampilladora *f AmL* **postage paid** *adj* con franqueo pagado **postage rate** *n* tarifa *f* postal **postage stamp** *n form* sello *m*, estampilla *f AmL*

postal [ˈpəʊstəl, *Am:* ˈpoʊ-] *adj* postal

postal code *n* código *m* postal **postal order** *n* giro *m* postal **postal vote** *n* voto *m* por correo **postal worker** *n* empleado, -a *m, f* de correos

postbag [ˈpəʊstbæg, *Am:* ˈpoʊst-] *n Brit* **1.** (*bag*) saca *f* (postal) **2.** (*letters*) correspondencia *f* **postbox** <-es> *n Brit, Aus* buzón *m* **postcard** *n* (tarjeta *f*) postal *f* **post-code** *n Brit* código *m* postal

postdate [ˌpəʊstˈdeɪt, *Am:* ˌpoʊst-] *vt* **1.** (*write a later date on*) posfechar **2.** (*happen after*) ocurrir después de

posted [ˈpəʊstɪd, *Am:* ˈpoʊst-] *adj* **to keep sb** ~ tener a alguien al corriente

poster [ˈpəʊstəʳ, *Am:* ˈpoʊstɚ] *n* (*notice*) cartel *m*; (*picture*) póster *m*

poste restante [ˈpəʊstˈrestɑːnt, *Am:* ˌpoʊstresˈtɑːnt] *n Brit* lista *f* de correos, poste *m* restante *AmL*

posterior [pɒˈstɪərɪəʳ, *Am:* pɑːˈstɪrɪɚ] **I.** *adj form* posterior **II.** *n iron* trasero *m inf*

posterity [pɒˈsterəti, *Am:* pɑːˈ-] *n no pl, form* posteridad *f*; **to preserve sth for** ~ guardar algo para la posteridad

postern [ˈpɒstən, *Am:* ˈpoʊstɚn] *n* postigo *m*; MIL poterna *f*

post-free *Brit* **I.** *adj* sin gastos de franqueo **II.** *adv* con porte pagado

postgraduate [ˌpəʊstˈgrædʒuət, *Am:* ˌpoʊstˈgrædʒuwɪt] **I.** *n* postgraduado, -a *m, f* **II.** *adj* de postgrado; ~ **studies** (estudios *mpl* de) postgrado *m*

post-haste [ˌpəʊstˈheɪst, *Am:* ˌpoʊst-] *adv form* con presteza

posthumous [ˈpɒstjəməs, *Am:* ˈpɑːstʃəməs] *adj form* póstumo, -a

posting [ˈpəʊstɪŋ, *Am:* ˈpoʊ-] *n* destino *m*

postman [ˈpəʊstmən, *Am:* ˈpoʊst-] <-men> *n Brit* cartero *m*

postmark [ˈpəʊstmɑːk, *Am:* ˈpoʊstmɑːrk] **I.** *n* matasellos *m inv*; **date as** ~ fecha *f* de timbre **II.** *vt* matasellar; **the letter is** ~**ed Rome** la carta lleva matasellos de Roma

postmaster [ˈpəʊstˌmɑːstəʳ, *Am:* ˈpoʊstˌmæstɚ] *n* jefe *m* de la oficina de correos

post meridiem *adv s.* **p.m.**

post-modern [ˌpəʊstˈmɒdən, *Am:* ˌpoʊstˈmɑːdɚn] *adj* posmoderno, -a

post-modernism *n no pl* posmodernismo *m*

postmortem [ˌpəʊstˈmɔːtəm, *Am:* ˌpoʊstˈmɔːrṱəm] *n* autopsia *f*; **to carry out a** ~ realizar una autopsia

postnatal [ˌpəʊstˈneɪtəl, *Am:* ˌpoʊstˈneɪṱəl] *adj* postnatal; ~ **depression** depresión *f* posparto

Post Office *n* (oficina *f* de) correos *m*; **to take sth to the** ~ llevar algo a correos

post office box *n* apartado *m* de correos, casilla *f* postal *CSur*

post-paid [ˌpəʊstˈpeɪd, *Am:* ˌpoʊst-] **I.** *adj* (*letter*) con franqueo pagado; (*parcel*) sin gastos de franqueo **II.** *adv* (*send: letter*) con franqueo pagado; (*parcel*) con porte pagado

postpone [pəʊstˈpəʊn, *Am:* poʊstˈpoʊn] *vt* aplazar, postergar *AmL*

postponement *n* aplazamiento *m*, postergación *f AmL*

postscript ['pəʊstskrɪp, *Am:* 'poʊs-] *n* **1.** (*at end of letter*) posdata *m* **2.** *fig* epílogo *m;* **as a ~ to sth** como colofón de algo
postulate¹ ['pɒstjəleɪt, *Am:* 'pɑːstʃə-] *vt form* **1.** (*hypothesize*) postular **2.** (*assume*) presuponer
postulate² ['pɒstjələt, *Am:* 'pɑːstʃəlɪt] *n form* postulado *m*
posture ['pɒstʃəʳ, *Am:* 'pɑːstʃɚ] **I.** *n no pl* postura *f,* actitud *f* **II.** *vi* tomar una postura, adoptar una actitud; **to ~ as sth** *pej* dárselas de algo
postwar [ˌpəʊst'wɔːʳ, *Am:* ˌpoʊst'wɔːr] *adj* de la posguerra; **the ~ years** la posguerra; **~ Europe** la Europa de la posguerra
posy ['pəʊzi, *Am:* 'poʊ-] <-ies> *n* ramillete *m*
pot¹ [pɒt, *Am:* pɑːt] **I.** *n* **1.** (*container*) bote *m* **2.** (*for cooking*) olla *f;* **~s and pans** cacharros *mpl* **3.** (*of food*) tarro *m;* (*of drink*) jarro *m;* (*for coffee*) cafetera *f;* (*for tea*) tetera *f* **4.** (*for plants*) maceta *f;* (*for flowers*) tiesto *m* **5.** *inf* GAMES **to win the ~** llevarse el bote **6.** *inf* (*a lot*) montón *m;* **~s of money** montones de dinero **7.** *iron* (*potbelly*) barriga *f inf* ►**it's** (**a case of**) **the ~ calling the kettle black** dijo la sartén al cazo, apártate que me tiznas; **to go to ~** *inf* echarse a perder; (*business, plan*) irse al garete **II.** <-tt-> *vt* **1.** (*put in a pot: food*) conservar en un tarro; **to ~** (**up**) (*plants*) plantar **2.** (*shoot*) cazar **3.** *Brit* SPORTS meter en la tronera
pot² [pɒt, *Am:* pɑːt] *n no pl, inf* (*marijuana*) hierba *f,* mota *f Méx;* **to smoke ~** fumar maría
potash ['pɒtæʃ, *Am:* 'pɑːt-] *n no pl* potasa *f*
potassium [pə'tæsiəm] *n no pl* potasio *m*
potassium chloride *n no pl* cloruro *m* potásico **potassium cyanide** *n no pl* cianuro *m* potásico **potassium permanganate** *n no pl* permanganato *m* potásico
potato [pə'teɪtəʊ, *Am:* -t̬oʊ] <-es> *n* patata *f,* papa *f AmL;* **sweet ~** batata *f;* **baked ~** patata al horno; **mashed ~es** puré *m* de patatas; **fried/roast**(**ed**) **~s** patatas fritas/asadas
potato beetle *n,* **potato bug** *n Am* escarabajo *m* de la patata **potato chips** *npl Am, Aus,* **potato crisps** *npl Brit* patatas *fpl* fritas (en bolsa), papas *fpl* chip *AmL* **potato masher** *n* pasapurés *m inv* **potato peeler** *n* pelapatatas *m inv,* pelapapas *m inv AmL*
potbellied *adj* panzudo, -a
potbelly [pɒt'beli, *Am:* 'pɑːtˌbel-] <-ies> *n* barriga *f,* guata *f Chile*
potboiler ['pɒtˌbɔɪləʳ, *Am:* 'pɑːtˌbɔɪlɚ] *n pej: libro escrito rápidamente para ganar dinero*
poteen [pɒ'tiːn, pɒ'tʃiːn, *Am:* poʊ'tiːn] *n Irish: en Irlanda, whisky destilado ilegalmente*
potency ['pəʊtənsi, *Am:* 'poʊ-] *n no pl* potencia *f;* (*of drink, evil, temptation*) fuerza *f;* (*of spell*) poder *m*
potent ['pəʊtnt, *Am:* 'poʊ-] *adj* potente; (*drink, symbol*) fuerte; (*poison, motive*) poderoso, -a; (*remedy*) eficaz; (*argument*) convincente
potentate ['pəʊtnteɪt, *Am:* 'poʊ-] *n liter* potentado, -a *m, f*
potential [pə'tenʃl, *Am:* poʊ'-] **I.** *adj* **1.** posible **2.** LING, PHYS potencial **II.** *n no pl* potencial *m;* **to have** (**a lot of**) **~** tener (muchas) capacidades
potentiality [pəˌtenʃɪ'æləti, *Am:* poʊˌtenʃɪ'ælət̬i] *n form no pl* posibilidad *f*
potentially [pə'tenʃəli, *Am:* poʊ'-] *adv* potencialmente
potholder ['pɒtˌhəʊldəʳ] *n Am, Aus* agarrador *m*
pothole ['pɒtˌhəʊl, *Am:* 'pɑːtˌhoʊl] *n* **1.** (*in road*) bache *m,* pozo *m CSur* **2.** (*underground hole*) sima *f*
potholer ['pɒtˌhəʊləʳ, *Am:* 'pɑːtˌhoʊlɚ] *n Brit* espeleólogo, -a *m, f*
potion ['pəʊʃən, *Am:* 'poʊ-] *n* poción *f,* pócima *f*
pot luck *n no pl* **to take ~** tomar lo que haya
potpourri [ˌpəʊ'pʊəriː, *Am:* ˌpoʊpʊ'riː] *n* popurrí *m*
pot roast *n* estofado *m*
potshot ['pɒtʃɒt, *Am:* 'pɑːtʃɑːt] *n* tiro *m* al azar; **to take a ~ at sb** disparar al azar contra alguien; *fig* (*criticize*) arremeter contra alguien
potted ['pɒtɪd, *Am:* 'pɑːt̬ɪd] *adj* **1.** (*plant*) en tiesto **2.** (*food*) en conserva; **~ shrimps** pasta *f* de camarones **3.** *Brit, inf* (*shorter*) resumido, -a
potter¹ ['pɒtəʳ, *Am:* 'pɑːt̬ɚ] *n* alfarero, -a *m, f;* **~'s wheel** torno *m* de alfarero
potter² ['pɒtəʳ, *Am:* 'pɑːt̬ɚ] *vi Brit* **1.** (*go along*) **to ~ around the village** pasearse por el pueblo **2.** *fig* entretenerse
pottery ['pɒtəri, *Am:* 'pɑːt̬ɚ-] *n* **1.** *no pl* (*art*) cerámica *f* **2.** <-ies> (*workshop*) alfarería *f*
potty ['pɒti, *Am:* 'pɑːt̬i] **I.** <-ier, -iest> *adj Brit, inf* (*mad*) chiflado, -a; **to go ~** chiflarse; **to drive sb ~** volver loco a alguien; **to be ~ about sb** estar loco por alguien; **it is ~ to do that** es una chifladura hacer eso **II.** <-ies> *n* (*for baby*) orinal *m*
pouch [paʊtʃ] *n* **1.** *a.* ANAT, ZOOL bolsa *f;* **tobacco ~** petaca *f* **2.** (*for mail*) valija *f*
pouf(**fe**) [puːf] *n* puf *m*
poulterer ['pəʊltərəʳ, *Am:* 'poʊlt̬ɚɚ] *n Brit* pollero, -a *m, f;* **~'s** pollería *f*
poultice ['pəʊltɪs, *Am:* 'poʊlt̬ɪs] *n* cataplasma *f*
poultry ['pəʊltri, *Am:* 'poʊl-] *n* **1.** *pl* (*birds*) aves *fpl* de corral **2.** *no pl* (*meat*) carne *f* de ave
poultry farm *n* granja *f* avícola **poultry farming** *n no pl* avicultura *f*
pounce [paʊns] **I.** *n* (*spring*) salto *m* **II.** *vi* **1.** (*jump*) saltar; **to ~ on sth** abalanzarse sobre algo; (*bird of prey*) precipitarse sobre algo **2.** *fig* **to ~ on an opportunity** no dejar escapar una oportunidad

P

pound[1] [paʊnd] *n* **1.** (*weight*) libra *f* (*454 g*); **by the** ~ por libras **2.** (*currency*) libra *f*; ~ **coin** moneda *f* de una libra; ~ **note** billete *m* de una libra; ~ **sterling** libra esterlina

pound[2] [paʊnd] *n* (*for cars*) depósito *m*; (*for dogs*) perrera *f*; (*for sheep*) redil *m*

pound[3] [paʊnd] **I.** *vt* **1.** (*hit repeatedly*) aporrear; (*beat*) golpear; (*with a hammer*) martillear; **the waves ~ed the ship** las olas batían contra el barco **2.** (*walk heavily*) patear; **I could hear him ~ing the floor upstairs** podía oír sus pasos en el piso de arriba **3.** (*crush*) machacar; (*spices*) moler; MIL batir; **to** ~ **sth to rubble** reducir algo a escombros **II.** *vi* **1.** (*beat*) dar golpes; (*on a door, table*) aporrear; (*heart, pulse*) latir con fuerza; (*music*) retumbar; **to** ~ **away on a piano** aporrear un piano; **the waves ~ed against the shore** las olas azotaban la orilla; **my head is ~ing!** ¡me estalla la cabeza! **2.** (*run*) **to** ~ **downstairs** bajar corriendo **3.** *fig* **to** ~ **away at sth** insistir en algo

pounding ['paʊndɪŋ] *n* **1.** *no pl* (*noise*) golpeteo *m*; (*of heart*) fuerte latido *m*; (*of sea*) embate *m*; (*in head*) martilleo *m* **2.** *no pl* (*crushing*) trituración *f*; (*grinding*) molienda *f* **3.** (*attack*) ataque *m*; *a. fig* (*beating*) paliza *f inf*; **to take a** ~ *a. fig* recibir una paliza; **the film took a heavy** ~ la película tuvo muy malas críticas

pour [pɔːʳ, *Am:* pɔːr] **I.** *vt* **1.** (*cause to flow*) vertir; **to** ~ **coffee/wine** echar café/vino; **to** ~ **sb sth** servir algo a alguien; **to** ~ **oneself a glass of wine** echarse un vaso de vino **2.** (*give in large amounts*) vertir; (*money, resources*) invertir; **to** ~ **scorn on sth** burlarse de algo **II.** *vi* **1.** (*flow in large amounts: water*) fluir; (*letters, messages*) llegar en grandes cantidades; **to** ~ **into sth** (*sunshine*) entrar a raudales en algo; (*people*) entrar en tropel en algo; **refugees are ~ing into the country** no cesan de llegar refugiados al país; **to be ~ing with sweat** estar empapado en sudor **2.** *impers* **it's ~ing (with rain)** llueve a cántaros

◆**pour in** *vi* llegar en abundancia

◆**pour out** **I.** *vt* **1.** (*serve from container*) vertir **2.** (*recount*) **to** ~ **sth to sb** revelar algo a alguien **3.** (*cause to flow quickly: smoke, water*) echar; **to** ~ **one's thanks** dar las gracias efusivamente **II.** *vi* (*liquid*) salir; (*people*) salir en tropel

pout [paʊt] **I.** *vi* hacer un mohín **II.** *vt* **to** ~ **one's lips** hacer un mohín **III.** *n* mohín *m*

poverty ['pɒvəti, *Am:* 'pɑːvɚt̬i] *n no pl* **1.** (*lack of money*) pobreza *f*; **extreme** ~ miseria *f* **2.** (*lack of ideas, imagination*) escasez *f*

poverty line *n* mínimo *m* vital; **to live below the** ~ carecer de lo necesario para vivir

poverty-stricken ['pɒvətiˌstrɪkən, *Am:* 'pɑːvɚt̬i-] *adj* muy pobre

POW [ˌpiːəʊ'dʌbljuː, *Am:* -oʊ'-] *n abbr of* **prisoner of war** prisionero *m* de guerra

powder ['paʊdəʳ, *Am:* -dɚ] **I.** *n* **1.** *no pl* (*dust*) polvo *m*; **baking** ~ levadura *f*; **to crush** [*o* **reduce**] **sth to a** ~ reducir algo a polvo **2.** *no pl* (*make-up*) polvos *mpl*; **talcum** ~ polvos de talco **3.** *no pl* (*snow*) nieve *f* en polvo **4.** *Brit* (*washing powder*) detergente *m* en polvo **II.** *vt* **1.** (*cover with powder*) empolvar; **to** ~ **one's face** empolvarse; **to** ~ **one's nose** *fig* ir al servicio **2.** (*sprinkle*) espolvorear

powder compact *n* polvera *f*

powdered *adj* (*in powder form*) en polvo; ~ **sugar** azúcar *m* glas

powder keg *n fig* polvorín *m* **powder puff** *n* borla *f*, cisne *m RíoPl* **powder room** *n* tocador *m*

powdery ['paʊdəri] *adj* como de polvo

power ['paʊəʳ, *Am:* 'paʊɚ] **I.** *n* **1.** *no pl* (*ability to control*) poder *m* **2.** (*country, organization, person*) potencia *f* **3.** (*right*) derecho *m* **4.** *no pl* (*ability*) capacidad *f* **5.** *no pl* (*strength*) fuerza *f* **6.** *no pl* (*electricity*) electricidad *f*; **to cut off the** ~ cortar la corriente **7.** *no pl* (*energy*) energía *f* ►**more** ~ **to your elbow!** ¡que tengas suerte!; **to do sb a** ~ **of good** hacer bien a alguien; **the** ~ **behind the throne** el poder en la sombra; **the ~s that be** las autoridades **II.** *vi* **to** ~ **along the track** ir disparado por el camino **III.** *vt* impulsar

power-assisted steering *n* dirección *f* asistida **powerboat** *n* lancha *f* fuera borda **power brakes** *npl* AUTO frenos *mpl* asistidos **power cable** *n* cable *m* de transmisión **power cut** *n Brit, Aus* apagón *m*

power-driven *adj* eléctrico, -a

powerful ['paʊəfəl, *Am:* 'paʊɚ-] *adj* **1.** (*influential, mighty*) poderoso, -a **2.** (*having great physical strength*) fuerte **3.** (*having a great effect*) convincente **4.** (*affecting the emotions*) intenso, -a; ~ **emotions** emociones *fpl* fuertes **5.** (*able to perform very well*) potente

powerfully ['paʊəfəli, *Am:* 'paʊɚ-] *adv* **1.** (*using great force*) con potencia **2.** (*argue, speak*) de forma convincente

powerhouse ['paʊəˌhaʊs, *Am:* 'paʊɚ-] *n* fuente *f* de energía; **to be a** ~ **of ideas** *fig* ser una fuente inagotable de ideas

powerless ['paʊələs, *Am:* 'paʊɚ-] *adj* impotente; **to be** ~ **against sb** no poder hacer nada contra alguien

power line *n* línea *f* eléctrica **power mower** *n* segadora *f* eléctrica **power plant** *n* central *f* eléctrica **power point** *n Brit, Aus* toma *f* de corriente **power politics** *n* política *f* de fuerza **power station** *n* central *f* eléctrica; **nuclear** ~ central *f* nuclear **power steering** *n* dirección *f* asistida **power tool** *n* herramienta *f* mecánica

powwow ['paʊwaʊ] *n* **1.** asamblea *f* (*de indígenas norteamericanos*) **2.** *fig, inf* discusión *f*

pox [pɒks, *Am:* pɑːks] *n no pl, inf* sífilis *f inv*

poxy ['pɒksi, *Am:* 'pɑːk-] <-ier, -iest> *adj*

Brit, inf insignificante

pp *abbr of* **pages** págs.

PR [piː'ɑːʳ, *Am:* -'ɑːr] *n no pl* **1.** *abbr of* **public relations** relaciones *fpl* públicas **2.** POL *abbr of* **proportional representation** representación *f* proporcional

practicable ['præktɪkəbl] *adj form* factible

practical ['præktɪkl] **I.** *adj* práctico, -a **II.** *n* examen *m* práctico

practicality [ˌpræktɪ'kæləti, *Am:* -t̬i] *n* <-ies> **1.** *no pl* (*feasibility*) viabilidad *f* **2.** (*practical detail*) **the practicalities of sth** los detalles prácticos de algo

practically ['præktɪkəli, *Am:* -kli] *adv* **1.** (*almost*) casi **2.** (*of a practical nature*) **to be ~ based** basarse en la práctica; **to be ~ minded** tener sentido práctico

practice ['præktɪs] **I.** *n* **1.** *no pl* (*act of practising*) práctica *f;* **to be out of ~** estar desentrenado; **~ makes perfect** se aprende con la práctica **2.** (*custom, regular activity*) costumbre *f;* **traditional religious ~s** tradiciones *fpl* religiosas; **standard ~** práctica *f* habitual; **to make a ~ of sth** tener algo como norma **3.** (*training session*) entrenamiento *m* **4.** *no pl* (*of profession*) ejercicio *m* **II.** *vt Am s.* **practise**

practiced ['præktɪst] *adj Am s.* **practised**

practise ['præktɪs] *Brit, Aus* **I.** *vt* **1.** (*do, carry out*) practicar **2.** (*improve skill*) hacer ejercicios de; **to ~ the piano** estudiar el piano **3.** (*work in*) ejercer ►**to ~ what one preaches** predicar con el ejemplo **II.** *vi* **1.** (*improve skill*) practicar; SPORTS entrenar **2.** (*work in profession*) ejercer; **to ~ as a doctor** ejercer de médico

practised ['præktɪst] *adj Brit, Aus* (*experienced, skilled*) experto, -a; **to be ~ in sth** tener experiencia en algo; **a ~ liar** un mentiroso consumado

practising ['præktɪsɪŋ] *adj Brit, Aus* (*doctor, lawyer*) en ejercicio; REL practicante

practitioner [præk'tɪʃənəʳ, *Am:* -ɚ] *n form* (*of a skill*) profesional *mf;* (*doctor*) médico, -a *m, f;* **legal ~** abogado, -a *m, f*

pragmatic [præg'mætɪk, *Am:* -'mæt̬-] *adj* pragmático, -a

pragmatism ['prægmətɪzəm] *n* pragmatismo *m*

prairie ['preəri, *Am:* 'preri] *n* pradera *f*

praise [preɪz] **I.** *vt* **1.** (*express approval*) elogiar; **to ~ sb to the skies** poner a alguien por las nubes **2.** (*worship*) alabar **II.** *n no pl* **1.** (*expression of approval*) elogio *m;* **to heap ~ on sb, to shower sb with ~** cubrir a alguien de alabanzas **2.** *form* (*worship*) alabanza *f;* **~ be** (**to God**)! ¡alabado sea (Dios)!

praiseworthy ['preɪzˌwɜːði, *Am:* -ˌwɜːr-] *adj* loable

pram [præm] *n Brit, Aus* cochecito *m*

prance [prɑːns, *Am:* præns] *vi* (*horse*) hacer cabriolas; (*person*) pavonearse

prang [præŋ] **I.** *vt Brit, Aus, inf* dar un golpe a **II.** *n Brit, Aus, inf* golpe *m*

prank [præŋk] *n* broma *f;* **to play a ~ on sb** gastar una broma a alguien

prat [præt] **I.** *n Brit, inf* imbécil *mf* **II.** <-tt-> *vi Brit, inf* **to ~ about** hacer el imbécil

prate [preɪt] *vi form* parlotear

prattle ['prætl, *Am:* 'præt̬-] **I.** *vi pej* parlotear; (*child*) balbucear **II.** *n no pl, pej* parloteo *m;* (*child*) balbuceo *m*

prawn [prɔːn, *Am:* prɑːn] *n* gamba *f*

prawn cocktail *n* cóctel *m* de gambas

pray [preɪ] **I.** *vi* **1.** REL rezar; **to ~ to sb** (**that**) rogar a alguien (que +*subj*) **2.** (*hope*) **to ~ for sth** rogar algo **II.** *vt form* suplicar; **I ~ you tell me ...** le ruego que me diga...

prayer [preəʳ, *Am:* prer] *n* **1.** REL oración *f;* **to say a ~, to say one's ~s** rezar **2.** *no pl* (*action of praying*) rezo *m* **3.** *fig* (*hope*) súplica *f;* **to not have a ~ of doing sth** *inf* no tener ninguna posibilidad de hacer algo

prayer book *n* devocionario *m* **prayer meeting** *n* reunión *f* de fieles para rezar **prayer rug** *n* alfombra *f* de oración

praying mantis ['preɪɪŋ'mæntɪs, *Am:* -t̬ɪs] *n* mantis *f inv* religiosa

preach [priːtʃ] **I.** *vi* predicar **II.** *vt* **1.** REL predicar; **to ~ a sermon/the Gospel** predicar un sermón/el Evangelio **2.** (*advocate*) abogar por ►**to practise what you ~** predicar con el ejemplo

preacher ['priːtʃəʳ, *Am:* -ɚ] *n* predicador(a) *m(f)*

preamble [priː'æmbl] *n form* preámbulo *m*

prearrange [ˌpriːə'reɪndʒ] *vt* organizar de antemano

prebend ['prebənd] *n Brit* prebenda *f*

precarious [prɪ'keərɪəs, *Am:* -'kerɪ-] *adj* precario, -a

precast [ˌpriː'kɑːst, *Am:* 'priːkæst] *adj* prefabricado, -a

precaution [prɪ'kɔːʃən, *Am:* -'kɑː-] *n* precaución *f*

precautionary [ˌprɪ'kɔːʃənəri, *Am:* -'kɑːʃəner-] *adj* de precaución; **~ measure** medida *f* preventiva

precede [prɪ'siːd] *vt* preceder; **to ~ the report with an introduction** empezar el informe con una introducción

precedence ['presɪdəns, *Am:* 'presə-] *n no pl* **1.** (*priority*) prioridad *f;* **to take ~ over sb** tener prioridad sobre alguien **2.** *form* (*order of priority*) preferencia *f*

precedent ['presɪdent, *Am:* 'presə-] *n* precedente *m;* **to set a ~** (**for sth/doing sth**) sentar un precedente (para algo/hacer algo)

preceding [prɪ'sɪːdɪŋ] *adj* precedente; **the ~ day** el día anterior

precept ['priːsept] *n form* **1.** (*rule*) precepto *m* **2.** (*principle*) principio *m*

precinct ['priːsɪŋkt] *n* **1.** *Brit* (*enclosed area*) recinto *m;* **pedestrian ~** zona *f* peatonal **2.** *Am* (*electoral district*) distrito *m* **3.** *no pl, form* (*environs*) alrededores *mpl*

P

precious ['preʃəs] **I.** *adj* **1.** (*of great value*) precioso, -a; **you can keep your ~ ring!** *iron* ¡guárdate tu maldito anillo! **2.** (*affected*) afectado, -a; (*person*) amanerado, -a **II.** *adv inf* ~ **few** muy pocos; **to be ~ little help** ser de muy poca ayuda

precipice ['presɪpɪs, *Am:* 'presə-] *n* precipicio *m*

precipitate¹ [prɪ'sɪpɪteɪt] **I.** *vt* **1.** *form* (*provoke*) precipitar **2.** *form* (*throw*) arrojar **3.** CHEM precipitar **II.** *vi* precipitar

precipitate² [prɪ'sɪpɪtət, *Am:* prɪ'sɪpɪtɪt] **I.** *adj form* precipitado, -a **II.** *n no pl* precipitado *m*

precipitation [prɪˌsɪpɪ'teɪʃən] *n no pl, form* precipitación *f*

precipitous [prɪ'sɪpɪtəs, *Am:* -t̬əs] *adj* **1.** (*very steep*) empinado, -a **2.** (*rapid*) apresurado, -a **3.** *form* (*precipitate*) precipitado, -a

précis ['preɪsiː, *Am:* preɪ'siː] **I.** *n* resumen *m* **II.** *vt form* resumir

precise [prɪ'saɪs] *adj* **1.** (*moment, measurement*) exacto, -a **2.** (*person*) meticuloso, -a

precisely *adv* **1.** (*exactly*) precisamente; **~!** ¡eso es!; **to do ~ the opposite** hacer justamente lo contrario **2.** (*carefully*) meticulosamente

precision [prɪ'sɪʒən] **I.** *n no pl* **1.** (*accuracy*) precisión *f* **2.** (*meticulous care*) exactitud *f* **II.** *adj* de precisión

preclude [prɪ'kluːd] *vt form* excluir

precocious [prɪ'kəʊʃəs, *Am:* -'koʊ-] *adj* precoz

precociousness *n,* **precocity** [prɪ'kɒsəti, *Am:* prɪ'kɑːsət̬i] *n no pl, form* precocidad *f*

preconceived [ˌpriːkən'siːvd] *adj* preconcebido, -a

preconception [ˌpriːkən'sepʃən] *n* idea *f* preconcebida

precondition [ˌpriːkən'dɪʃən] *n* condición *f* previa

precook ['priːkʊk] *vt* precocinar

precursor [ˌpriː'kɜːsəʳ, *Am:* prɪ'kɜːrsɚ] *n form* precursor(a) *m(f)*

predate [priː'deɪt] *vt form* preceder

predator ['predətəʳ, *Am:* -t̬ɚ] *n* depredador *m*

predatory ['predətri, *Am:* -tɔːri] *adj* depredador(a)

predecessor ['priːdɪsesəʳ, *Am:* 'predəsesɚ] *n* predecesor(a) *m(f)*; (*ancestor*) antepasado, -a *m, f*

predestination [ˌpriːdestɪ'neɪʃən] *n no pl* predestinación *f*

predestine [ˌpriː'destɪn] *vt* predestinar

predetermine [ˌpriːdɪ'tɜːmɪn, *Am:* -'tɜːrmən] *vt form* predeterminar; **to ~ the consequences** determinar de antemano las consecuencias

predicament [prɪ'dɪkəmənt] *n form* apuro *m*

predicate¹ ['predɪkət, *Am:* 'predɪkɪt] *n* LING predicado *m*

predicate² ['predɪkeɪt] *vt form* **to be ~d on sth** estar basado en algo

predicative [prɪ'dɪkətɪv, *Am:* prɪ'dɪkət̬ɪv] *adj* LING predicativo, -a

predict [prɪ'dɪkt] *vt* predecir

predictable [prɪ'dɪktəbl] *adj* previsible

prediction [prɪ'dɪkʃən] *n* **1.** (*forecast*) pronóstico *m* **2.** *no pl* (*act of predicting*) predicción *f*

predilection [ˌpriːdɪ'lekʃən, *Am:* ˌpredəl'ek-] *n form* predilección *f*

predispose [ˌpriːdɪ'spəʊz, *Am:* -'spoʊz] *vt* predisponer

predisposition [ˌpriːdɪspə'zɪʃən] *n* **1.** *form* (*tendency*) predisposición *f* **2.** MED propensión *f*

predominance [prɪ'dɒmɪnəns, *Am:* -'dɑːmə-] *n no pl* predominio *m*

predominant [prɪ'dɒmɪnənt, *Am:* -'dɑːmə-] *adj* predominante

predominate [prɪ'dɒmɪneɪt, *Am:* -'dɑːmə-] *vi* predominar

pre-eminence [ˌpriː'emɪnənts] *n no pl, form* preeminencia *f*

pre-eminent [ˌpriː'emɪnənt] *adj form* preeminente

pre-empt [ˌpriː'empt] *vt form* adelantarse a

pre-emption [ˌpriː'empʃən] *n* apropiación *f* (por derecho preferente)

pre-emptive [priː'emptɪv] *adj* **1.** (*right*) prioritario, -a **2.** (*attack*) preventivo, -a

preen [priːn] **I.** *vi* **1.** (*bird*) arreglarse **2.** *fig* (*congratulate oneself*) pavonearse **II.** *vt* **1.** (*tidy*) arreglar **2.** (*groom*) **to ~ oneself** atildarse; **to ~ oneself on sth** (*congratulate*) enorgullecerse de algo

pre-existing ['priːfæb] *adj* preexistente

prefab ['priːfæb] *inf* **I.** *n abbr of* **prefabricated house** casa *f* prefabricada **II.** *adj abbr of* **prefabricated** prefabricado, -a

prefabricate [ˌpriː'fæbrɪkeɪt] *vt* prefabricar

prefabricated *adj* prefabricado, -a

prefabricated house *n* casa *f* prefabricada

preface ['prefɪs] **I.** *n* prefacio *m* **II.** *vt form* introducir

prefatory ['prefətri, *Am:* -tɔːri] *adj form* preliminar

prefect ['priːfekt] *n* prefecto *m*

prefer [prɪ'fɜːʳ, *Am:* priː'fɜːr] <-rr-> *vt* **1.** (*like better*) preferir **2.** *Brit* LAW **to ~ charges (against sb)** presentar cargos (en contra de alguien)

preferable ['prefrəbl] *adj* preferible

preferably ['prefrəbli] *adv* preferentemente

preference ['prefrəns] *n* **1.** *no pl* (*liking better*) preferencia *f* **2.** (*priority*) prioridad *f*

preferential [ˌprefə'renʃl] *adj* preferente; ECON preferencial

preferred [prɪ'fɜːd, *Am:* priː'fɜːrd] *adj* preferido, -a

prefigure [ˌpriː'fɪgəʳ, *Am:* -'fɪgjɚ] *vt form* prefigurar

prefix ['priːfɪks, *Am:* 'priːfɪks] <-es> *n*

prefijo *m*

pregnancy ['pregnəntsi] *n no pl* (*condition*) embarazo *m;* ZOOL preñez *f*

pregnancy test *n* prueba *f* de embarazo

pregnant ['pregnənt] *adj* **1.**(*woman*) embarazada; (*animal*) preñado; **to be ~ by sb** estar embarazada de alguien; **to become ~** (*woman*) quedarse embarazada; (*animal*) quedarse preñado; **to get sb ~** dejar embarazada a alguien **2.** *fig* (*silence, pause*) muy significativo, -a; **to be ~ with possibilities for sth** tener muchas posibilidades para algo

prehensile [prɪ'hensaɪl, *Am:* priː'hensɪl] *adj* prensil

prehistoric [ˌpriːhɪ'stɒrɪk, *Am:* -'stɔːr-] *adj* prehistórico, -a

prehistory [ˌpriː'hɪstri] *n no pl* prehistoria *f*

prejudge [ˌpriː'dʒʌdʒ] *vt* prejuzgar

prejudice ['predʒʊdɪs] **I.** *n* **1.**(*preconceived opinion*) prejuicio *m* **2.** *no pl* (*bias*) parcialidad *f;* LAW perjuicio *m;* **without ~** sin detrimento de sus propios derechos; **without ~ to sth** LAW sin perjuicio de algo **II.** *vt* **1.**(*bias*) **to ~ sb against sth** predisponer a alguien contra algo **2.**(*damage*) perjudicar

prejudiced ['predʒʊdɪst] *adj* (*person*) lleno, -a de prejuicios; (*attitude, judgment, opinion*) parcial; **to be ~ against sb** estar predispuesto contra alguien; **to be ~ in favour of sb** estar predispuesto a favor de alguien

prejudicial [ˌpredʒə'dɪʃəl] *adj form* perjudicial

preliminary [prɪ'lɪmɪnəri, *Am:* prɪ'lɪmənerˑ] **I.** *adj* preliminar **II.**<-ies> *n* **1.**(*introduction*) preparativos *mpl* **2.** SPORTS (*heat*) preliminares *mpl* **3.** *form* (*preliminary exam*) examen *m* preliminar

prelims ['priːlɪmz, *Am:* 'priːlɪms] *npl inf* **1.**(*exams*) *abbr of* **preliminary exams** exámenes *mpl* preliminares **2.** *abbr of* **preliminary pages** páginas *fpl* preliminares

prelude ['preljuːd] *n* preludio *m*

premarital [ˌpriː'mærɪtl, *Am:* -'merət̬l] *adj* prematrimonial

premature ['premətʃəʳ, *Am:* ˌpriːmə'tʊr] *adj* prematuro, -a

premature ejaculation *n* eyaculación *f* precoz

premeditated [ˌpriː'medɪteɪtɪd, *Am:* -teɪt̬ɪd] *adj* premeditado, -a

premeditation [ˌpriːmedɪ'teɪʃən] *n no pl, form* premeditación *f*

premenstrual [ˌpriː'mentstruəl, *Am:* -strəl] *adj* premenstrual

premenstrual tension *n* síndrome *m* premenstrual

premier ['premiəʳ, *Am:* prɪ'mɪr] **I.** *n* POL primer ministro *m* **II.** *adj* primero, -a

première ['premieəʳ, *Am:* prɪ'mɪr] **I.** *n* estreno *m* **II.** *vt, vi* estrenar

premise ['premɪs] **I.** *n* **1.**(*of argument*) premisa *f;* **on the ~ that ...** en el supuesto de que... **2.** *pl* (*shop*) local *m* **II.** *vt form* **1.**(*base*) basar **2.** *Am* (*preface*) empezar

premium ['priːmiəm] **I.** *n* **1.**(*insurance payment*) prima *f* **2.**(*extra charge*) recargo *m* **3.** *Am* (*petrol*) súper *f* **II.** *adj* de primera calidad

premium bond *n Brit* bono *m* del Estado (*que participa en un sorteo nacional*) **premium price** *n* precio *m* con prima **premium quality** *n* máxima calidad *f*

premonition [ˌpriːmə'nɪʃən] *n* premonición *f;* **to have a ~ that ...** tener el presentimiento de que...

prenatal [ˌpriː'neɪtl, *Am:* -t̬l] *adj* prenatal

preoccupation [ˌpriːɒkjʊ'peɪʃən, *Am:* priːˌɑːkjuː'-] *n* preocupación *f*

preoccupied [prɪː'ɒkjʊpaɪd, *Am:* priː'ɑːkjuː-] *adj* preocupado, -a; **to be ~ about sth** inquietarse por algo; **to be ~ with sth** estar absorto en algo

preoccupy [priː'ɒkjʊpaɪ, *Am:* priː'ɑːkjuː-] <-ie-> *vt* preocupar

preordain [ˌpriːɔː'deɪn, *Am:* -ɔːr'-] *vt form* predeterminar

prep [prep] *n no pl, Brit, inf abbr of* **preparation** deberes *mpl*

prepack [ˌpriː'pæk] *vt Brit* preempaquetar

prepaid [ˌpriː'peɪd] *adj* pagado, -a por adelantado

prepaid postcard *n* postal *f* franqueada **prepaid reply** *n* sobre *m* con el franqueo pagado

preparation [ˌprepə'reɪʃən] **I.** *n* **1.** *no pl* (*getting ready*) preparación *f* **2.**(*substance*) preparado *m* **3.** *pl* (*measures*) preparativos *mpl* **II.** *adj* de preparación

preparatory [prɪ'pærətəri, *Am:* -'perətɔːr-] *adj* preliminar

preparatory course *n* curso *m* preparatorio **preparatory school** *n* **1.** *Brit* escuela *f* privada (*imparte enseñanza primaria*) **2.** *Am* colegio *m* privado (*imparte enseñanza secundaria*)

prepare [prɪ'peəʳ, *Am:* -'per] **I.** *vt* preparar **II.** *vi* prepararse; **to ~ for action** prepararse para actuar

prepared [prɪ'peəd, *Am:* -'perd] *adj* **1.**(*ready*) listo, -a **2.**(*willing*) dispuesto, -a; **to be ~ to do sth** estar preparado para hacer algo **3.**(*food, speech*) preparado, -a de antemano

preparedness [prɪ'peərɪdnɪs, *Am:* -'perd-] *n no pl, form* preparación *f*

prepay [ˌpriː'peɪ] *vt irr* pagar por anticipado; (*letter*) franquear

prepayment [ˌpriː'peɪmənt] *n* anticipo *m;* (*of letter*) franqueo *m*

preponderance [prɪ'pɒndərənts, *Am:* -'pɑːn-] *n no pl, form* predominio *m*

preponderant [prɪ'pɒndərənt, *Am:* -'pɑːn-] *adj form* predominante

preposition [ˌprepə'zɪʃən] *n* preposición *f*

prepossessing [ˌpriːpə'zesɪŋ] *adj* agradable, atractivo, -a

preposterous [prɪ'pɒstərəs, *Am:* -'pɑːstə-] *adj* ridículo, -a

preppie, preppy ['prepi] *Am* **I.** <-ies> *n* pijo, -a *m, f* **II.** *adj* <preppier, preppiest> pijo, -a

prepuce ['pri:pju:s] *n* (*foreskin*) prepucio *m;* (*clitoral foreskin*) prepucio del clítoris

prerequisite [,pri:'rekwɪzɪt] *form* **I.** *adj* fundamental **II.** *n* requisito *m* esencial; **to be a ~ for sth** ser una condición sine qua non para algo

prerogative [prɪ'rɒgətɪv, *Am:* -'rɑ:gət̬ɪv] *n form* (*right, privilege*) prerrogativa *f;* **that's your ~** estás en tu derecho; **skiing used to be the ~ of the rich** antes, esquiar era patrimonio exclusivo de los ricos

presage ['presɪdʒ] **I.** *n liter* **1.** (*sign*) presagio *m* **2.** (*presentiment*) presentimiento *m* **II.** *vt liter* (*have presentiment of*) presentir **III.** *vi liter* **to ~ well/ill** ser buen/mal presagio

Presbyterian [,prezbɪ'tɪəriən, *Am:* -'tɪri-] **I.** *n* presbiteriano, -a *m, f* **II.** *adj* presbiteriano, -a

presbytery ['prezbɪtri, *Am:* -teri] *n* REL **1.** ARCHIT (*part of church*) presbiterio *m* **2.** (*priest's residence*) casa *f* del cura

pre-school ['pri:sku:l] **I.** *n Am, Aus* jardín *m* de infancia **II.** *adj* preescolar; (*child*) en edad preescolar

prescribe [prɪ'skraɪb] **I.** *vt* **1.** MED recetar; (*rest, diet*) recomendar **2.** *form* (*order*) prescribir; **~d by law** establecido por la ley **II.** *vi* MED hacer una receta

prescribed [prɪ'skraɪbd] *adj* prescrito, -a; **in the ~ way** de conformidad con lo prescrito; **in the ~ time** dentro del plazo fijado por la ley

prescription [prɪ'skrɪpʃən] *n* **1.** MED receta *f;* **only available on ~** con receta médica; **to make out a ~** extender una receta **2.** *form* (*act of prescribing*) prescripción *f*

prescription charge *n pago de una parte del coste de las medicinas a cargo del paciente*

prescriptive [prɪ'skrɪptɪv] *adj* preceptivo, -a

prescriptive grammar *n* LING gramática *f* normativa

presence ['prezənts] *n* **1.** (*attendance*) presencia *f;* **military/police ~** presencia militar/policial; **~ of mind** presencia de ánimo; **in sb's ~** en presencia de alguien; **in my ~** delante de mí; **in the ~ of two witnesses** ante dos testigos; **your ~ is requested** se ruega su asistencia; **to feel sb's ~** sentir la presencia de alguien; **to make one's ~ felt** hacerse notar **2.** (*personality*) carisma *m*

present[1] ['prezənt] **I.** *n no pl* presente *m* ▸**at ~** en este momento; **for the ~** por ahora **II.** *adj* **1.** (*current: address, generation*) actual; **at the ~ moment** [*o* **time**] en este momento; **the ~ year** el año en curso; **in the ~ case** en este caso; **up to the ~ time** hasta la fecha; **the ~ writer** quien esto escribe **2.** (*in attendance*) presente; **to be ~ at sth** asistir a algo; **all those ~** todos los presentes; **~ company excepted** exceptuando a los presentes

present[2] ['prezənt] *n* (*gift*) regalo *m;* **to give sb a ~** hacer un regalo a alguien; **I got it as a ~** me lo regalaron; **to make sb a ~ of sth** regalar algo a alguien

present[3] [prɪ'zent] *vt* **1.** (*give*) presentar; **to ~ one's apologies** *form* presentar sus disculpas; **to ~ one's credentials** presentar sus credenciales; **to ~ sth (to sb)** entregar algo (a alguien); **to ~ sb with sth** obsequiar a alguien con algo, obsequiar algo a alguien *AmL* **2.** (*introduce*) presentar; **to ~ sb to sb** presentar alguien a alguien; **may I ~ my wife?** permítame presentarle a mi esposa; **to ~ a bill** presentar un proyecto de ley; **to ~ a programme** *Aus, Brit* presentar un programa; **~ing X as Julius Caesar** con X en el papel de Julio César **3.** (*confront*) **to ~ sb with sth** enfrentar a alguien con algo; **to be ~ed with a complicated situation** verse frente a una situación complicada; **to ~ sb with a problem** plantear un problema a alguien **4.** (*constitute*) constituir; **to ~ a problem for sb** significar un problema para alguien; **to ~ difficulties for sb** plantear dificultades a alguien **5.** (*offer*) ofrecer; (*view, atmosphere*) presentar **6.** (*exhibit: argument, plan, theory*) exponer; (*cheque, passport, ticket*) presentar; **to ~ a petition to sb** elevar una petición a alguien *form* **7.** (*appear*) **to ~ oneself for sth** presentarse a algo

presentable [prɪ'zentəbl, *Am:* prɪ'zent̬ə-] *adj* presentable; **to make oneself ~** arreglarse

presentation [,prezən'teɪʃən] *n* **1.** (*act*) presentación *f;* (*of theory, dissertation*) exposición *f;* (*of thesis*) lectura *f;* **to make a ~** hacer una exposición; **on ~ of this voucher** al presentar este vale **2.** (*of prize, award*) entrega *f*

presentation copy *n* ejemplar *m* de cortesía

present-day [,prezəntdeɪ] *adj* actual; **~ London** el Londres de hoy (en) día

presenter [prɪ'zentəʳ, *Am:* prɪ'zent̬ɚ] *n* presentador(a) *m(f)*

presentiment [prɪ'zentɪmənt] *n form* presentimiento *m;* **to have a ~ of sth** presentir algo; **to have the ~ that ...** tener el presentimiento de que...

presently ['prezəntli] *adv* **1.** (*soon*) pronto; **I'll be there ~** voy enseguida **2.** (*now*) ahora

present participle *n* LING participio *m* presente **present tense** *n* LING tiempo *m* presente

preservation [,prezə'veɪʃən, *Am:* -ɚ'-] *n no pl* **1.** (*of building*) conservación *f;* **to be in a poor/good state of ~** estar en mal/buen estado **2.** (*of species, custom*) preservación *f*

preservative [prɪ'zɜ:vətɪv, *Am:* -'zɜ:rvət̬ɪv] **I.** *adj* preservativo, -a **II.** *n* conservante *m;* **free from artificial ~s** sin conservantes (artificiales)

preserve [prɪ'zɜ:v, *Am:* -'zɜ:rv] **I.** *vt* **1.** (*maintain: customs, peace*) mantener; (*dignity,* *sense of humour*) conservar; (*appearance, silence*) guardar **2.** (*food*) conservar **3.** (*protect*) proteger; **to ~ sb from sth** proteger a alguien de algo; **heaven ~ us!** ¡que Dios nos ampare! **II.** *n* **1.** (*jam*) confitura *f* **2.** (*reserve*) coto *m*, vedado *m*; **game ~** coto de caza; **wildlife ~** reserva *f* de animales **3.** *fig* (*domain*) terreno *m*; **to be the ~ of the rich** ser dominio exclusivo de los ricos; **to be a male ~** estar vedado a las mujeres

preserved *adj* **1.** (*maintained*) conservado, -a; **to be badly ~** estar en mal estado **2.** (*food*) en conserva; **~ food** conservas *fpl*

pre-shrunk [ˌpriːˈʃrʌŋk] *adj* preencogido, -a

preside [prɪˈzaɪd] *vi* presidir; **to ~ at/over sth** presidir algo; **to ~ at a table** ocupar la cabecera de la mesa

presidency [ˈprezɪdənsi] *n* **1.** (*office of president*) POL presidencia *f*; (*of company*) dirección *f*; (*of university*) rectoría *f* **2.** (*tenure as president*) mandato *m* (presidencial)

president [ˈprezɪdənt] *n* POL presidente, -a *m, f*; (*of company*) director(a) *m(f)*; (*of university*) rector(a) *m(f)*

presidential [ˌprezɪˈdentʃəl] *adj* presidencial

presidential address *n* discurso *m* presidencial **presidential candidate** *n* candidato, -a *m, f* a la presidencia **presidential election** *n* elecciones *fpl* presidenciales

President's Day *n no pl, Am* Día *m* del Presidente

press [pres] **I.** *vt* **1.** (*push: button, switch*) pulsar; (*bell*) tocar; (*trigger*) apretar; **to ~ sth down** apretar algo **2.** (*squeeze*) apretar; **the crowd ~ed us against the locked door** la multitud nos apretujaba contra la puerta cerrada **3.** (*flatten: flowers, grapes, olives*) prensar **4.** (*extract juice*) exprimir **5.** (*iron*) planchar **6.** MUS (*album, disk*) imprimir **7.** (*try to force*) presionar; **to ~ sb to do sth** presionar a alguien para que haga algo; **to ~ sb for sth** exigir algo de alguien; **to ~ sb for payment** acosar a alguien para que pague; **to be ~ed for time/money** andar justo de tiempo/dinero; **to ~ sth on sb** imponer algo a alguien **8.** (*pursue*) insistir; **to ~ a claim** insistir en una petición; **to ~ one's case** insistir en sus argumentos **9.** LAW **to ~ charges** presentar cargos **II.** *vi* **1.** (*push*) apretar; **to ~ hard** apretar fuerte; **to ~ on the brake pedal** pisar el freno **2.** (*crowd*) apiñarse; **to ~ through the crowd** abrirse paso entre el gentío; **to ~ down** (**on sth**) hacer presión (sobre algo) **3.** (*be urgent*) urgir; **time is ~ing** el tiempo apremia **4.** (*pressurize*) hacer presión; **to ~ for sth** insistir para conseguir algo **III.** *n* **1.** (*push*) presión *f*; (*of hand*) apretón *m*; **at the ~ of a button** apretando un botón **2.** (*ironing*) planchado *m*; **to give sth a ~** planchar algo **3.** (*crush*) apiñamiento *m* **4.** (*machine*) prensa *f*; (*for racket*) tensor *m*; **printing ~** imprenta *f*; **to be in** [*o* **on** *Am*] **~** estar en prensa; **to go to ~** (*newspaper, book*) ir a imprenta; **hot off the ~** (*news*) de última hora **5.** PUBL **the ~** la prensa; **to have a bad/good ~** (*publicity*) tener buena/mala prensa **6.** (*cupboard*) ropero *m*

◆**press ahead** *vi s.* **press on**

◆**press down on** *vt* **1.** (*force down*) apretar **2.** (*lean on*) apoyarse en

◆**press forward** *vi s.* **press on**

◆**press in** *vt* clavar

◆**press on** *vi* seguir adelante

◆**press upon** *vt* apretar

press agency *n* agencia *f* de prensa **press baron** *n* magnate *m* de la prensa **press-button** *n* botón *m* de control **press campaign** *n* campaña *f* de prensa **press card** *n* acreditación *f* de periodista **press clipping** *n*, **press cutting** *n Brit* recorte *m* de prensa **press conference** *n* rueda *f* de prensa; **to hold a ~** dar una rueda de prensa **press coverage** *n* cobertura *f* periodística **press gallery** *n* tribuna *f* de la prensa

press-gang [ˈpresgæŋ] *vt* **to ~ sb into doing sth** forzar a alguien a hacer algo

pressing I. *adj* (*issue, matter*) urgente; (*need*) apremiante **II.** *n* (*of clothes*) planchado *m*; (*of records, fruits*) prensado *m*

pressman [ˈpresmən] *n* **1.** (*journalist*) periodista *m* **2.** (*printing press operator*) tipógrafo *m* **press office** *n* oficina *f* de prensa **press officer** *n* encargado, -a *m, f* de prensa **press photographer** *n* reportero, -a *m, f* gráfico, -a **press release** *n* comunicado *m* de prensa; **to issue a ~** emitir un comunicado **press report** *n* reportaje *m*

press-stud [ˈpresstʌd] *n Aus, Brit* broche *m* automático

press-up [ˈpresʌp] *n Brit* SPORTS flexión *f* de brazos

pressure [ˈpreʃəʳ, *Am:* -ɚ] **I.** *n* **1.** *a.* PHYS presión *f*; **high/low ~** presión alta/baja; **to put ~ on sth** hacer presión sobre algo; **at full ~** a toda presión; **to be under ~** *a. fig* estar bajo presión **2.** *no pl* (*influence*) **to put ~ on sb** (**to do sth**) presionar a alguien (para que haga algo); **to do sth under ~ from sb** hacer algo presionado por alguien; **to bring ~ to bear on sb** ejercer presión sobre alguien; **under the ~ of circumstances** bajo la presión de las circunstancias **3.** *pl* (*pressure*) tensiones *fpl* **4.** MED tensión *f*; **blood ~** tensión arterial **5.** ELEC voltaje *m* **II.** *vt* **to ~ sb to do sth** presionar a alguien para que haga algo

pressure cabin *n* AVIAT cabina *f* presurizada **pressure cooker** *n* olla *f* a presión, olla *f* presto *Méx* **pressure ga(u)ge** *n* manómetro *m* **pressure group** *n* POL grupo *m* de presión

pressurize [ˈpreʃəraɪz] *vt* **1.** (*control air pressure*) presurizar **2.** (*person, government*) presionar; **to ~ sb into doing sth** forzar a alguien a hacer algo

prestige [preˈstiːʒ] *n no pl* prestigio *m*

prestigious [preˈstɪdʒəs] *adj* prestigioso, -a

P

pre-stressed concrete [ˌpriːˈstrest ˈkɒŋkriːt, *Am:* ˌpriːˈstrest ˈkɑːn-] *n* hormigón *m* pretensado

presumably [prɪˈzjuːməbli, *Am:* prɪˈzuːmə-] *adv* presumiblemente

presume [prɪˈzjuːm, *Am:* prɪˈzuːm] **I.** *vt* **1.** (*suppose*) suponer; **to ~ that ...** imaginarse que...; **~d dead** dado por muerto; **to be ~d innocent** ser presuntamente inocente; **Dr Smith, I ~?** usted debe de ser el Dr. Smith **2.** (*dare*) **to ~ to do sth** atreverse a hacer algo **II.** *vi* **1.** (*be presumptuous*) presumir **2.** (*be rude*) **I don't wish to ~, but ...** no quisiera parecer impertinente, pero... **3.** (*take advantage of*) **to ~ on sb** abusar de alguien

presumption [prɪˈzʌmpʃən] *n* **1.** (*assumption*) suposición *f;* **the ~ is that ...** se supone que...; **the ~ of innocence** LAW la presunción de inocencia **2.** *no pl, form* (*arrogance*) presunción *f* **3.** (*daring*) atrevimiento *m*

presumptive [prɪˈzʌmptɪv] *adj* presunto, -a

presumptuous [prɪˈzʌmptjʊəs, *Am:* -tʃuːəs] *adj* **1.** (*arrogant*) impertinente **2.** (*forward*) osado, -a

presuppose [ˌpriːsəˈpəʊz, *Am:* -ˈpoʊz] *vt form* presuponer

presupposition [ˌpriːsʌpəˈzɪʃən] *n* presuposición *f;* **to be based on false ~s** basarse en suposiciones falsas

pre-tax [ˌpriːˈtæks] *adj* antes de impuestos, bruto, -a

pretence [prɪˈtents, *Am:* ˈpriːtents] *n no pl* **1.** (*claim*) pretensión *f;* **to make no ~ to erudition** no pretender ser erudito **2.** (*simulation*) fingimiento *m;* **to make a ~ of sth** fingir algo; **to make no ~ of sth** no disimular algo **3.** (*pretext*) pretexto *m;* **under (the) ~ of ...** con el pretexto de...

pretend [prɪˈtend] **I.** *vt* **1.** (*make believe*) fingir; **to ~ to be interested** fingir interés; **to ~ to be dead** hacerse el muerto; **to ~ to be sb** hacerse pasar por alguien; **the children ~ed that they were dinosaurs** los niños imaginaban que eran dinosaurios **2.** (*claim*) pretender; **I don't ~ to know** no pretendo saber **II.** *vi* fingir; **he's just ~ing** sólo está fingiendo

pretended *adj* fingido, -a

pretender *n* pretendiente *mf;* **a ~ to the throne** un pretendiente al trono

pretense [prɪˈtents, *Am:* ˈpriːtents] *n no pl, Am s.* **pretence**

pretension [prɪˈtentʃən] *n* **1.** (*claim*) pretensión *f;* **to have ~s to (being/doing) sth** tener pretensiones de (ser/hacer) algo **2.** *no pl s.* **pretentiousness**

pretentious [prɪˈtentʃəs] *adj pej* pretencioso, -a; (*in bad taste*) cursi

pretentiousness *n no pl, pej* pretensión *f;* (*in bad taste*) cursilería *f*

preterit(e) [ˈpretərɪt, *Am:* ˈpreţ̬ɚɪt] LING **I.** *n* pretérito *m* **II.** *adj* pretérito, -a *form*

preternatural [ˌpriːtəˈnætʃərəl, *Am:* -ţ̬ɚˈnætʃɚəl] *adj form* (*exceptional*) prodigioso, -a

pretext [ˈpriːtekst] *n* pretexto *m;* **a ~ for to do sth** un pretexto para hacer algo; **on the ~ that ...** con el pretexto de que...; **under the ~ of doing sth** so pretexto de hacer algo *form*

prettify [ˈprɪtɪfaɪ, *Am:* ˈprɪţ̬-] *vt* (*room, street*) engalanar; (*account, report*) adornar *fig*

pretty [ˈprɪti, *Am:* ˈprɪţ̬-] **I.** *adj* <-ier, -iest> **1.** (*beautiful: thing*) bonito, -a, lindo, -a *AmL;* (*child, woman*) guapo, -a, lindo, -a *AmL;* **not a ~ sight** nada agradable de ver **2.** *inf* (*considerable*) menudo, -a; **~ mess** menudo lío *m* **II.** *adv* (*quite*) bastante **2. ~ much** más o menos; **to be ~ much the same** ser prácticamente lo mismo; **I'm ~ nearly finished** ya casi he terminado; **~ well everything** casi todo

pretzel [ˈpretsl] *n* galleta *f* salada

prevail [prɪˈveɪl] *vi* **1.** (*triumph*) prevalecer; **to ~ over/against sth** prevalecer sobre/contra algo; **to ~ over/against sb** triunfar sobre/contra alguien **2.** (*predominate*) predominar; (*conditions, situation*) imperar **3. to ~ (up)on sb (to do sth)** *form* convencer a alguien (para que haga algo)

prevailing *adj* predominante; (*atmosphere, feelings*) reinante; **under the ~ circumstances** en las circunstancias actuales

prevalence [ˈprevələnts] *n no pl* **1.** (*common occurence*) preponderancia *f;* **the ~ of drugs in some neighbourhoods** la presencia habitual de drogas en algunos barrios **2.** (*predominance*) predominio *m*

prevalent [ˈprevələnt] *adj* **1.** (*common*) corriente; (*disease, opinion*) extendido, -a **2.** (*present-day*) actual **3.** (*predominant*) predominante

prevaricate [prɪˈværɪkeɪt, *Am:* prɪˈverɪ-] *vi form* andarse con rodeos; **to ~ over sth** dar vueltas a algo

prevarication [prɪˌværɪˈkeɪʃən, *Am:* prɪˌver-] *n no pl, form* evasivas *fpl*

prevent [prɪˈvent] *vt* **1.** (*hamper*) impedir; **to ~ sb from doing sth** impedir que alguien haga algo; **the news ~ed his coming** la noticia impidió que viniera **2.** (*avoid*) prevenir; (*confusion, panic, crime*) evitar

preventative [prɪˈventətɪv, *Am:* prɪˈventəţ̬ɪv] *adj s.* **preventive**

prevention [prɪˈventʃən] *n no pl* prevención *f;* **for the ~ of crime** para evitar la delincuencia ▶ **~ is better than <u>cure</u>** *prov,* **an ounce of ~ is worth a pound of <u>cure</u>** *Am, prov* más vale prevenir que curar *prov*

preventive [prɪˈventɪv, *Am:* -ţ̬ɪv] *adj* preventivo, -a

preview [ˈpriːvjuː] **I.** *n* CINE, THEAT preestreno *m;* (*film extract*) tráiler *m;* (*of TV programme, exhibition*) adelanto *m* **II.** *vt* CINE, THEAT preestrenar

previous [ˈpriːviəs] **I.** *adj* **1.** (*former*) anterior; **on the ~ day/week** el día/la semana anterior; **no ~ experience required** no se necesita experiencia **2.** (*prior*) previo, -a; **without ~ notice** sin previo aviso **II.** *adv* **~ to doing sth** antes de hacer algo

previous convictions *npl* antecedentes *mpl* penales

previously *adv* **1.** (*beforehand*) previamente **2.** (*formerly*) anteriormente; **to have met sb ~** haber visto a alguien antes

pre-war [ˌpriːˈwɔːʳ, *Am:* -ˈwɔːr] *adj* de antes de la guerra; **the ~ years** la preguerra

prey [preɪ] *n no pl* **1.** (*animal*) presa *f;* **bird of ~** ave *f* de presa **2.** (*person*) víctima *f;* **to be easy ~ for sb** ser presa [*o* blanco] fácil para alguien; **to fall ~ to** (*animal*) ser presa de; (*person*) ser víctima de

◆**prey on** *vt*, **prey upon** *vt* **1.** (*feed on*) alimentarse de; **fear ~ed on me** *fig* fui preso del miedo **2.** (*exploit*) aprovecharse de

price [praɪs] **I.** *n* **1.** COM precio *m;* **oil ~s, the ~ of oil** el precio del petróleo; **to ask a high/low ~** pedir un precio alto/bajo; **to be the same ~** valer [*o* costar] lo mismo; **to go up/down in ~** subir/bajar de precio; **to name a ~** pedir un precio; **what ~ are apples?** ¿a cuánto están las manzanas? **2.** FIN (*of stocks*) cotización *f,* precio *m* **3.** *fig* precio *m;* **the ~ one has to pay for fame** el precio de la fama; **beyond** [*o* **without**] **~** sin precio; **to set a high ~ on sth** valorar mucho algo ►**to set a ~ on sb's head** poner precio a la cabeza de alguien; **at any ~** a toda costa; **not at any ~** por nada del mundo; **to pay a heavy ~** pagarlo caro; **to pay the ~** pagar caro; **at a ~** a un precio muy alto **II.** *vt* **1.** (*mark with price tag*) poner el precio a **2.** (*fix price*) poner precio a, valorar; **to be reasonably ~d** tener un precio razonable ►**to be ~d out of the market** no poder competir en el mercado por su alto precio

price bracket *n* gama *f* de precios **price control** *n* control *m* de precios **price cut(ting)** *n* recorte *m* de precios **price fixing** *n* fijación *f* de precios **price freeze** *n* congelación *f* de precios **price index** *n* índice *m* de precios

priceless [ˈpraɪslɪs] *adj* **1.** (*invaluable*) incalculable; **to be ~** no tener precio **2.** *fig* (*funny*) divertidísimo, -a; **that's ~!** ¡eso es para partirse de risa! *inf,* ¡eso es un plato! *AmL, inf*

price level *n* nivel *m* de precios **price list** *n* lista *f* de precios **price range** *n* gama *f* de precios **price rise** *n* aumento *m* de precios **price stability** *n* estabilidad *f* de precios **price tag** *n*, **price ticket** *n* **1.** (*label*) etiqueta *f* (del precio) **2.** *inf* (*cost*) precio *m* **price war** *n* guerra *f* de precios

pricey [ˈpraɪsi] *adj* <pricier, priciest> *inf* (*object*) carillo, -a; (*shop*) carero, -a

pricing [ˈpraɪsɪŋ] *n* fijación *f* de precios; **~ policy** política *f* de precios

prick [prɪk] **I.** *vt* **1.** (*jab*) pinchar, picar; **to ~ one's finger with** [*o* **on**] **a needle** pincharse el dedo con una aguja; **to ~ sb's conscience** hacer que a alguien le remuerda la conciencia **2.** (*mark with holes*) agujerear **II.** *vi* **1.** (*pin*) pinchar **2.** (*hurt: eyes, skin*) escocer, arder *CSur* **III.** *n* **1.** (*act, pain*) pinchazo *m;* **to feel the ~ of conscience** tener remordimientos de conciencia **2.** (*mark*) agujero *m* **3.** *vulg* (*penis*) polla *f,* pija *f RíoPl* **4.** *vulg* (*idiot*) gilipollas *m inv*

◆**prick out** *vt* (*flowers*) repicar

◆**prick up** *vt* **to ~ one's ears** (*animal*) erguir las orejas; (*person*) aguzar el oído

prickle [ˈprɪkl] **I.** *n* **1.** (*thorn: of plant*) pincho *m;* (*of animal*) púa *f* **2.** (*tingle*) picor *m;* **to feel a ~ of excitement** sentir un cosquilleo de emoción **II.** *vi* **1.** (*cause prickling sensation*) picar **2.** (*tingle*) sentir picor **3.** (*prick*) pinchar **III.** *vt* (*prick*) pinchar, picar

prickly [ˈprɪkli] <-ier, -iest> *adj* **1.** (*thorny: plant*) espinoso, -a; (*animal*) con púas **2.** (*tingling*) que pica; (*beard*) que pincha; **~ heat** fiebre *f* miliar; **~ sensation** picor *m* **3.** *inf* (*easily offended*) irritable

prickly pear *n* **1.** (*fruit*) higo *m* chumbo **2.** (*plant*) chumbera *f*

pride [praɪd] **I.** *n* **1.** *no pl* (*proud feeling*) orgullo *m;* **to feel great ~** estar muy orgulloso; **to take ~ in sth** enorgullecerse de algo; (*one's work*) esmerarse en algo; **to be sb's ~ and joy** ser el orgullo de alguien **2.** *no pl* (*self-respect*) amor *m* propio; **to hurt sb's ~** herir el orgullo de alguien; **to swallow one's ~** tragarse el orgullo; **false ~** vanidad *f* **3.** *no pl* (*arrogance*) soberbia *f* **4.** (*animal group*) manada *f* ►**~ comes** [*o* **goes**] **before a fall** *prov* más dura será la caída; **to have ~ of place** ocupar el lugar de honor **II.** *vt* **to ~ oneself on (doing) sth** enorgullecerse de (hacer) algo; **to ~ oneself that ...** preciarse de que...

priest [priːst] *n* REL cura *m*

priestess [ˈpriːstes, *Am:* -stɪs] *n* REL sacerdotisa *f*

priesthood [ˈpriːsthʊd] *n no pl* REL **1.** (*position, office*) sacerdocio *m;* **to enter the ~** ser ordenado sacerdote **2.** (*priests in general*) clero *m*

priestly [ˈpriːstli] *adj* sacerdotal

prig [prɪg] *n pej* mojigato, -a *m, f*

priggish [ˈprɪgɪʃ] *adj pej* mojigato, -a

prim [prɪm] <-mer, -mest> *adj* **1.** *pej* remilgado, -a; **~ and proper** remilgado **2.** (*appearance*) escrupuloso, -a

primacy [ˈpraɪməsi] *n no pl, form* primacía *f*

prima donna [priːməˈdɒnə, *Am:* -ˈdɑːnə] *n* **1.** (*opera singer*) prima donna *f* **2.** *pej* (*arrogant person*) diva *f*

primaeval [praɪˈmiːvəl] *adj s.* **primeval**

primal [ˈpraɪməl] *adj* **1.** (*primitive*) primario, -a **2.** (*most important*) primordial

primarily [ˈpraɪmərɪli, *Am:* praɪˈmerəl-] *adv* principalmente, ante todo

primary [ˈpraɪməri, *Am:* -mer-] **I.** *adj* **1.** (*principal*) fundamental; (*aim*) prioritario,

P

-a; **to be of ~ importance** ser de una importancia primordial **2.** (*basic*) primario, -a; (*industry*) de base; ~ **meaning of a word** primer sentido de una palabra; ~ **stress** LING acento *m* primario **II.** <-ies> *n Am* POL elecciones *fpl* primarias

primary colour *n* color *m* primario **primary education** *n no pl* enseñanza *f* primaria

primate ['praɪmeɪt, *Am:* -mɪt] *n* **1.** ZOOL primate *m* **2.** REL primado *m*

prime [praɪm] **I.** *adj* **1.** (*main*) principal; (*objective*) prioritario, -a; **of ~ importance** de importancia primordial **2.** (*first-rate*) excelente; **of ~ quality** de primera calidad; **in ~ condition** en perfecto estado **II.** *n no pl* apogeo *m elev;* **to be in one's ~, to be in the ~ of life** estar en la flor de la vida; **to be past one's ~** no ser ya ningún jovencito; **to be cut off in one's ~** morir en la flor de la vida **III.** *vt* **1.** (*undercoat: surface*) aplicar una capa de base sobre; (*canvas*) aprestar **2.** (*prepare for exploding: gun, pump, motor*) cebar **3.** (*prepare*) **to ~ sb for doing sth** preparar a alguien para hacer algo; **to be well ~d for an interview** ir bien preparado para una entrevista **4.** (*brief*) informar **5.** (*make drunk*) emborrachar; **to be well ~d** estar contentillo

prime cost *n* ECON coste *m* de producción **prime meridian** *n* GEO primer meridiano *m* **prime minister** *n* POL primer(a) ministro, -a *m, f* **prime mover** *n* fuerza *f* motriz; (*person*) promotor(a) *m(f)* **prime number** *n* MAT número *m* primo

primer ['praɪmə^r, *Am:* -mɚ] *n* **1.** (*paint*) (pintura *f* de) imprimación *f;* **a ~ coat** una primera mano **2.** (*explosive*) cartucho *m* **3.** (*textbook*) manual *m;* (*for learning to read*) cartilla *f*

prime time *n* RADIO, TV horas *fpl* de máxima audiencia

primeval [praɪ'miːvəl] *adj* primigenio, -a; (*forest*) virgen

primitive ['prɪmɪtɪv, *Am:* -t̬ɪv] **I.** *adj a.* ART, HIST, ZOOL primitivo, -a; (*method, weapon*) rudimentario, -a **II.** *n* ART, HIST, SOCIOL primitivo, -a *m, f*

primogeniture [ˌpraɪməʊ'dʒenɪtʃə^r, *Am:* -moʊ'dʒenɪtʃɚ] *n no pl* primogenitura *f*

primordial [praɪ'mɔːdiəl, *Am:* -'mɔːr-] *adj form* **1.** (*from beginning*) primigenio, -a **2.** (*basic*) primario, -a

primrose ['prɪmrəʊz, *Am:* -roʊz] **I.** *n* **1.** BOT prímula *f,* primavera *f* **2.** (*colour*) ~ (**yellow**) amarillo *m* pálido **II.** *adj* de color amarillo pálido

primula ['prɪmjələ] *n* prímula *f,* primavera *f*

primus® ['praɪməs] *n* hornillo *m* de queroseno

prince [prɪnts] *n* príncipe *m;* **crown ~** príncipe heredero; **Prince Charming** príncipe azul; **Prince of Wales** Príncipe de Gales; **the Prince of Darkness** el príncipe de las tinieblas

prince consort *n* príncipe *m* consorte

princely ['prɪntsli] *adj fig* magnífico, -a; **the ~ sum of 10 pence** *iron* la bonita suma de 10 peniques

princess [prɪn'ses, *Am:* 'prɪntsɪs] *n* princesa *f*

principal ['prɪntsəpl] **I.** *adj* principal **II.** *n* **1.** *Am, Aus* (*headmaster*) director(a) *m(f);* (*of university*) rector(a) *m(f)* **2.** FIN capital *m*

principality [ˌprɪntsɪ'pæləti, *Am:* -sə'pælət̬i] *n* principado *m*

principally *adv* principalmente

principle ['prɪntsəpl] *n* principio *m*

principle clause *n* cláusula *f* principal

print [prɪnt] **I.** *n* **1.** (*printed lettering*) texto *m* impreso; **bold ~** negrita *f* **2.** (*printed form*) **to rush sth into ~** publicar algo precipitadamente; **to appear in ~** publicarse; **to go out of ~** agotarse **3.** (*engraving*) grabado *m;* PHOT positivo *m* **4.** (*printed pattern*) estampado *m* **5.** *inf* (*fingerprint*) huella *f* **II.** *vt* **1.** (*publish*) publicar **2.** (*put into printed form*) imprimir **3.** INFOR (*make a print-out of*) sacar copias de **4.** PHOT positivar **5.** (*mark fabric*) estampar **6.** (*write in unjoined letters*) escribir con letras de imprenta **III.** *vi* **1.** (*appear in printed form*) imprimirse **2.** (*write in unjoined letters*) escribir con letras de imprenta

printable ['prɪntəbl, *Am:* -t̬ə-] *adj* imprimible

printed circuit board *n* ELEC circuito *m* impreso

printer ['prɪntə^r, *Am:* -t̬ɚ] *n* **1.** (*person*) impresor(a) *m(f)* **2.** INFOR impresora *f;* **inkjet/laser ~** impresora de chorro de tinta/láser

printer driver *n* controlador *m* de impresora

printing *n* **1.** *no pl* (*art*) imprenta *f* **2.** (*action*) impresión *f*

printing ink *n* tinta *f* de imprenta **printing press** *n* prensa *f* **printing works** *npl* imprenta *f*

print-out ['prɪntaʊt] *n* INFOR impresión *f,* listado *m*

print run *n* tirada *f*

print shop *n* imprenta *f*

prior ['praɪə^r, *Am:* 'praɪɚ] **I.** *adv form* (*before*) antes; ~ **to doing sth** antes de hacer algo **II.** *adj form* **1.** (*earlier*) previo, -a **2.** (*preferred*) preferente **III.** *n* REL prior *m*

prioritize [praɪ'ɒrɪtaɪz, *Am:* -'ɔːrə-] *vt* priorizar

priority [praɪ'ɒrəti, *Am:* -'ɔːrət̬i] **I.** <-ies> *n* **1.** *no pl* (*being most important*) prioridad *f;* (*in time*) anterioridad *f* **2.** *pl* (*order of importance*) prioridades *fpl;* **to get one's priorities right** establecer un orden de prioridades **II.** *adj* **1.** (*of utmost importance*) prioritario, -a **2.** (*claim, right*) *a.* FIN preferente

priory ['praɪəri] *n* priorato *m*

prise [praɪz] *vt Brit, Aus s.* **prize²**

prism [prɪzəm] *n* prisma *m*

prismatic [prɪz'mætɪk, *Am:* -'mæt̬-] *adj*

prismático, -a
prison ['prɪzən] *n* prisión *f;* **to go to ~** ir a la cárcel; **to put sb in ~** encarcelar a alguien
prison camp *n* campamento *m* para prisioneros **prison cell** *n* celda *f*
prisoner ['prɪzənəʳ, *Am:* -ɚ] *n* preso, -a *m, f;* MIL prisionero, -a *m, f;* **to hold sb ~** detener a alguien; **to take sb ~** hacer prisionero a alguien
prisoner of war *n* prisionero, -a *m, f* de guerra
prison inmate *n* recluso, -a *m, f* **prison riot** *n* motín *m* carcelero **prison yard** *n* patio *m* de la cárcel
pristine ['prɪsti:n] *adj form* prístino, -a
privacy ['prɪvəsi, *Am:* 'praɪ-] *n no pl* intimidad *f;* **to desire ~** desear estar a solas
private ['praɪvɪt, *Am:* -vət] **I.** *adj* **1.** (*not public*) privado, -a **2.** (*confidential*) confidencial; **sb's ~ opinion** la opinión personal de alguien **II.** *n* **1.** *pl, inf* (*genitals*) partes *fpl;* **~ parts** partes *fpl* pudendas **2.** MIL soldado *m* raso
privateer [ˌpraɪvə'tɪəʳ, *Am:* -'tɪr] *n* NAUT (*vessel*) corsario *m*
privately ['praɪvɪtli, *Am:* -vət-] *adv* **1.** (*in private*) en privado; **to celebrate ~** celebrar a puerta cerrada **2.** (*secretly*) en secreto **3.** (*personally*) personalmente
privation [praɪ'veɪʃən] *n no pl, form* privación *f;* **to live in ~** vivir en la miseria; **to suffer ~** pasar apuros
privatization [ˌpraɪvɪtaɪ'zeɪʃən, *Am:* -vətɪ'-] *n no pl* privatización *f*
privatize ['praɪvɪtaɪz, *Am:* -və-] *vt* privatizar
privet ['prɪvɪt] *n no pl* alheña *f*
privilege ['prɪvəlɪdʒ] **I.** *n* **1.** (*special right*) privilegio *m* **2.** (*honour*) honor *m* **II.** *vt* **to be ~d to do sth** tener el privilegio de hacer algo
privileged ['prɪvəlɪdʒd] *adj* **1.** (*special*) privilegiado, -a **2.** (*confidential*) confidencial
privy¹ ['prɪvi] *adj form* **to be ~ to sth** estar al tanto de algo
privy² ['prɪvi] *n* (*toilet*) retrete *m*
prize¹ [praɪz] **I.** *n* **1.** (*in competition*) premio *m;* **to carry off a ~** ganar un premio **2.** (*reward*) recompensa *f* **II.** *adj* **1.** *inf* (*first-rate*) de primera; **a ~ idiot** un tonto de remate **2.** (*prizewinning*) premiado, -a **III.** *vt* apreciar; **to ~ sth highly** estimar algo mucho
prize² [praɪz] *vt* **to ~ sth off** arrancar algo; **to ~ sth open** abrir algo por la fuerza
prizefight ['praɪzfaɪt] *n* combate *m* de boxeo profesional
prizefighter *n* boxeador(a) *m(f)* profesional
prizefighting *n no pl* boxeo *m* profesional
prize-giving *n* reparto *m* de premios
prize list *n* lista *f* de premiados **prize money** *n* SPORTS premio *m* en metálico
prizewinning ['praɪzˌwɪnɪŋ] *adj* premiado, -a
pro¹ [prəʊ, *Am:* proʊ] *inf* **I.** *n abbr of* **professional** profesional *mf* **II.** *adj abbr of* **professional** profesional
pro² [prəʊ, *Am:* proʊ] **I.** *adv* a favor **II.** *n* pro *m;* **the ~s and cons of sth** los pros y los contras de algo **III.** *prep* pro **IV.** *adj* favorable
proactive [ˌprəʊ'æktɪv, *Am:* ˌproʊ'-] *adj* con iniciativa
probability [ˌprɒbə'bɪləti, *Am:* ˌprɑ:bə'bɪləṱi] *n* probabilidad *f;* **in all ~** sin duda
probable ['prɒbəbl, *Am:* 'prɑ:bə-] *adj* **1.** (*likely*) probable **2.** (*credible*) verosímil
probably *adv* probablemente
probate ['prəʊbeɪt, *Am:* 'proʊ-] *n no pl* **1.** LAW legalización *f* de un testamento **2.** *Aus* FIN derechos *mpl* de sucesión
probation [prəʊ'beɪʃən, *Am:* proʊ'-] *n no pl* **1.** (*in job*) período *m* de prueba; **to be on ~** estar a prueba **2.** LAW libertad *f* condicional
probationary [prəʊ'beɪʃənəri, *Am:* proʊ'-] *adj* de prueba; **~ period** período *m* de prueba
probationer [prəʊ'beɪʃənəʳ, *Am:* proʊ-'beɪʃənɚ] *n* **1.** (*offender on probation*) persona *f* en libertad condicional **2.** (*worker*) trabajador(a) *m(f)* en período de prueba
probation officer *n funcionario que hace el seguimiento de personas en libertad condicional*
probe [prəʊb, *Am:* proʊb] **I.** *vi* (*examine*) investigar; **to ~ into the possibilities** tantear las posibilidades; **to ~ into sb's private life** indagar en la vida privada de alguien **II.** *vt* **1.** (*examine*) investigar **2.** MED sondar **III.** *n* **1.** (*examination, investigation*) investigación *f* **2.** MED, AVIAT sonda *f*
probity ['prəʊbəti, *Am:* 'proʊbəṱi] *n no pl, form* probidad *f*
problem ['prɒbləm, *Am:* 'prɑ:bləm] *n* problema *m*
problematic(al) [ˌprɒblə'mætɪk(əl), *Am:* ˌprɑ:blə'mæṱ-] *adj* **1.** (*creating difficulty*) problemático, -a **2.** (*questionable, disputable*) dudoso, -a
problem child *n* niño, -a *m, f* difícil
proboscis [prəʊ'bɒsɪs, *Am:* proʊ'bɑ:sɪs] *n* **1.** ZOOL probóscide *f* **2.** *iron* (*person's nose*) napia *f*
procedural [prə'si:dʒərəl, *Am:* -dʒɚ-] *adj* de procedimiento; LAW procesal
procedure [prə'si:dʒəʳ, *Am:* -dʒɚ] *n* procedimiento *m*
proceed [prə'si:d, *Am:* proʊ'-] *vi form* **1.** (*move along*) seguir; (*continue*) continuar; (*continue driving*) seguir adelante; **to ~ with sth** avanzar con algo; **to ~ against sb** proceder contra alguien **2.** (*come from*) **to ~ from** provenir de **3.** (*start, begin*) **to ~ with sth** empezar con algo; **to ~ to do sth** ponerse a hacer algo
proceedings [prə'si:dɪŋz, *Am:* proʊ'-] *npl* **1.** LAW proceso *m* **2.** *form* (*events*) actos *mpl* **3.** *form* (*minutes*) actas *fpl*
proceeds ['prəʊsi:dz, *Am:* 'proʊ-] *n* ingresos *mpl*
process¹ ['prəʊses, *Am:* 'prɑ:-] **I.** *n* proceso *m;* **in the ~** mientras tanto; **to be in the ~ of**

P

doing sth estar en vías de hacer algo **II.** *vt* **1.** *a.* TECH, INFOR procesar; (*of raw materials, waste*) tratar **2.** PHOT revelar

process² [prəʊ'ses, *Am:* proʊ-] *vi form* desfilar

process chart *n* diagrama *m* del proceso **process engineering** *n* ingeniería *f* de procesos

processing ['prəʊsesɪŋ, *Am:* 'prɑ:-] *n no pl* **1.** *a.* TECH, INFOR procesamiento *m;* (*of raw materials, waste*) tratamiento *m;* **data** ~ procesamiento de datos; **batch** ~ procesamiento por lotes **2.** PHOT revelado *m*

procession [prə'seʃən] *n* **1.** desfile *m;* **funeral** ~ cortejo *m* fúnebre; **to go in** ~ desfilar **2.** REL procesión *f* **3.** *fig* serie *f*

processor [prəʊ'sesəʳ, *Am:* prɑ:-] *n* INFOR procesador *m*

proclaim [prə'kleɪm, *Am:* proʊ'-] *vt form* proclamar; **to** ~ **war** declarar la guerra

proclamation [ˌprɒklə'meɪʃən, *Am:* ˌprɑ:klə-] *n form* proclamación *f;* **a** ~ **of war** una declaración de guerra

proclivity [prə'klɪvəti, *Am:* proʊ'klɪvəţi] *n form* propensión *f;* **sexual** ~ tendencia *f* sexual; **to have a** ~ **for sth** ser proclive a algo

procrastinate [prəʊ'kræstɪneɪt, *Am:* proʊ'kræstə-] *vi* dejar para más tarde

procrastination [prəʊˌkræstɪ'neɪʃən, *Am:* proʊ'kræstə-] *n no pl* dilación *f*

procreate ['prəʊkrɪeɪt, *Am:* 'proʊ-] *vi form* procrear

procreation [ˌprəʊkrɪ'eɪʃən, *Am:* ˌproʊ-] *n no pl, form* procreación *f*

proctor ['prɒktəʳ, *Am:* 'prɑ:ktɚ] *n* **1.** *Brit* UNIV censor(a) *m(f), persona que cuida de la disciplina* **2.** *Am* UNIV vigilante *mf*

procurable [prə'kjʊrəbl, *Am:* proʊ'-] *adj* asequible

procurator ['prɒkjʊəreɪtəʳ, *Am:* 'prɑ:kjəreɪţɚ] *n* LAW procurador(a) *m(f)*

procurator fiscal *n Scot* LAW fiscal *mf*

procure [prə'kjʊəʳ, *Am:* proʊ'kjʊr] *form* **I.** *vt* (*obtain*) obtener; **to** ~ **sth for sb, to** ~ **sb sth** obtener algo para alguien **II.** *vi* LAW dedicarse al proxenetismo

procurement [prə'kjʊəmənt, *Am:* proʊ'kjʊr-] *n no pl, form* adquisición *f*

prod [prɒd, *Am:* prɑ:d] **I.** *n* (*poke*) golpe *m;* (*with elbow*) codazo *m;* (*with sharp object*) pinchazo *m;* **to give sb a** ~ *fig* dar un empujón a alguien **II.** <-dd-> *vt* **1.** (*poke*) golpear; (*with elbow*) dar un codazo; (*with sharp object*) pinchar **2.** (*encourage, urge on, stimulate*) **to** ~ **sb** (**into doing sth**) estimular a alguien (para que haga algo)

prodigal ['prɒdɪgl, *Am:* 'prɑ:dɪ-] *adj form* pródigo, -a

prodigious [prə'dɪdʒəs] *adj form* (*size, height*) ingente; (*achievement, talent*) prodigioso, -a

prodigy ['prɒdɪdʒi, *Am:* 'prɑ:də-] *n* prodigio *m;* **child** ~ niño, -a *m, f* prodigio

produce¹ [prə'dju:s, *Am:* -'du:s] *vt* **1.** (*create*) producir; (*manufacture*) fabricar **2.** (*give birth to*) dar a luz **3.** CINE, THEAT, TV realizar; (*musical recording*) dirigir **4.** (*show*) mostrar; **to** ~ **a knife** sacar un cuchillo; **to** ~ **one's passport** enseñar el pasaporte; **to** ~ **an alibi** presentar una coartada **5.** (*cause*) causar; **to** ~ **results** producir resultados

produce² ['prɒdju:s, *Am:* 'prɑ:du:s] *n no pl* AGR productos *mpl* agrícolas

producer [prə'dju:səʳ, *Am:* -'du:sɚ] *n* productor(a) *m(f)*

product ['prɒdʌkt, *Am:* 'prɑ:dʌkt] *n* **1.** *a.* MAT producto *m* **2.** (*result*) resultado *m*

production [prə'dʌkʃən] *n* **1.** *no pl* (*of goods*) fabricación *f* **2.** *no pl* CINE, THEAT, TV producción *f* **3.** *no pl, form* (*presentation: of ticket, passport*) presentación *f*

production capacity *n* capacidad *f* de producción **production costs** *npl* costes *mpl* de producción **production director** *n* director(a) *m(f)* de producción **production line** *n* cadena *f* de montaje **production manager** *n* encargado, -a *m, f* de producción **production time** *n* tiempo *m* de producción **production volume** *n* volumen *m* de producción

productive [prə'dʌktɪv] *adj* productivo, -a; (*land, soil*) fértil; (*writer*) prolífico, -a

productivity [ˌprɒdʌk'tɪvəti, *Am:* ˌproʊdək'tɪvəţi] *n no pl* productividad *f*

productivity agreement *n Brit* acuerdo *m* de productividad **productivity bonus** *n* prima *f* de productividad

Prof. [prɒf, *Am:* prɑ:f] *abbr of* **Professor** prof. *m*, profa. *f*

profane [prə'feɪn, *Am:* proʊ'-] *adj* **1.** (*blasphemous*) blasfemo, -a **2.** *form* (*secular*) profano, -a

profanity [prə'fænəti, *Am:* proʊ'fænəţi] *n form* **1.** (*blasphemy*) blasfemia *f* **2.** (*obscene word*) palabrota *f;* **to utter a** ~ soltar un taco

profess [prə'fes] *vt* profesar; **to** ~ **little enthusiasm** manifestar poco entusiasmo; **to** ~ **to be sth** pretender ser algo; **to** ~ **oneself satisfied** (**with sth**) declararse satisfecho (con algo)

professed [prə'fest] *adj* **1.** (*self-acknowledged*) declarado, -a **2.** (*alleged*) supuesto, -a

profession [prə'feʃən] *n* **1.** (*occupation*) profesión *f;* **teaching** ~ docencia *f* **2.** (*declaration*) declaración *f*

professional [prə'feʃənəl] **I.** *adj* **1.** (*relating to profession*) profesional **2.** (*competent*) experto, -a **II.** *n* profesional *mf*

professionalism [prə'feʃənəlɪzəm] *n no pl* **1.** (*attitude*) profesionalidad *f* **2.** SPORTS profesionalismo *m*

professionally [prə'feʃənəli] *adv* **1.** (*by a professional*) profesionalmente **2.** (*in a professional manner*) con profesionalidad

professor [prə'fesəʳ, *Am:* -ɚ] *n Brit* UNIV catedrático, -a *m, f; Am* SCHOOL profesor(a) *m(f)*

professorial [ˌprɒfɪ'sɔːriəl, *Am:* ˌproʊfə'-] *adj* profesoral
professorship [prə'fesəʃɪp, *Am:* '-ɚ-] *n* cátedra *f*
proffer ['prɒfəʳ, *Am:* 'prɑːfɚ] *vt form* ofrecer
proficiency [prə'fɪʃnsi] *n no pl* competencia *f*
proficient [prə'fɪʃnt] *adj* competente
profile ['prəʊfaɪl, *Am:* 'proʊ-] **I.** *n* **1.** (*side view*) perfil *m;* **in** ~ de perfil **2.** (*description*) descripción *f;* **user** ~ INFOR perfil *m* de usuario ►**to keep a low** ~ tratar de pasar inadvertido **II.** *vt* (*describe*) describir
profit ['prɒfɪt, *Am:* 'prɑːfɪt] **I.** *n* **1.** FIN beneficio *m* **2.** (*advantage*) provecho *m* **II.** *vi* **1.** (*benefit*) beneficiarse; **to** ~ **by sth** sacar provecho de algo **2.** (*make a profit*) ganar
profitability [ˌprɒfɪtə'bɪləti, *Am:* ˌprɑːfɪt̬ə-'bɪlət̬i] *n no pl* rentabilidad *f*
profitable ['prɒfɪtəbl, *Am:* 'prɑːfɪt̬ə-] *adj* **1.** FIN rentable; **a** ~ **investment** una inversión lucrativa **2.** (*advantageous*) provechoso, -a
profit-earning *adj* rentable
profiteer [ˌprɒfɪ'tɪəʳ, *Am:* ˌprɑːfɪ'tɪr] *n pej* especulador(a) *m(f)*
profiteering *n no pl, pej* especulación *f*
profit-making *adj* lucrativo, -a; ~ **movie** película *f* rentable
profit margin *n* margen *m* de beneficio **profit maximization** *n* maximización *f* del beneficio **profit-oriented** *adj Am* orientado, -a a la obtención de beneficios **profit--related** *adj* que depende de los beneficios **profit sharing** *n* participación *f* en los beneficions **profit taking** *n* FIN realización *f* de beneficios
profligate ['prɒflɪgət, *Am:* 'prɑːflɪgɪt] *adj form* derrochador(a)
profound [prə'faʊnd] *adj* profundo, -a
profundity [prə'fʌndəti, *Am:* proʊ'-] *n form no pl* profundidad *f*
profuse [prə'fjuːs] *adj* profuso, -a; **to be** ~ **in one's praise of sth** alabar algo con efusión
profusion [prə'fjuːʒən] *n no pl, form* profusión *f;* **in** ~ en abundancia
prog. *n abbr of* **program** progr.
progenitor [prəʊ'dʒenɪtəʳ, *Am:* proʊ'dʒenət̬ɚ] *n form* progenitor(a) *m(f)*
progeny ['prəʊdʒəni, *Am:* 'prɑːdʒə-] *n pl, form* progenie *f*
prognosis [prɒg'nəʊsɪs, *Am:* prɑːg'noʊ-] *n form* pronóstico *m*
prognosticate [prɒg'nɒstɪkeɪt, *Am:* prɑːg'nɑːstɪ-] *vt form* pronosticar
program ['prəʊgræm, *Am:* 'proʊ-] **I.** *n* programa *m* **II.** <-mm-> *vt* programar
programmable [prəʊ'græməbl, *Am:* 'proʊgræmə-] *adj* programable
programme ['prəʊgræm, *Am:* 'proʊ-] *n, vt Aus, Brit s.* **program**
programmer *n* programador(a) *m(f)*
programming *n* programación *f*
programming language *n* lenguaje *m* de programación
progress¹ ['prəʊgres, *Am:* 'prɑː-] *n no pl* progreso *m;* **to make** ~ avanzar; **to be in** ~ estar en curso
progress² [prəʊ'gres, *Am:* proʊ-] *vi* **1.** (*improve*) progresar **2.** (*continue onward*) avanzar; **to** ~ **to sth** evolucionar hacia algo
progression [prə'greʃən] *n no pl* **1.** (*development*) desarrollo *m;* (*of disease*) evolución *f* **2.** MAT (*series*) progresión *f*
progressive [prə'gresɪv] **I.** *adj* **1.** (*by successive stages*) progresivo, -a; (*disease*) degenerativo, -a **2.** POL progresista **3.** (*modern*) moderno, -a **4.** MUS de vanguardia; (*jazz*) experimental **5.** LING continuo, -a **II.** *n* **1.** POL progresista *mf* **2.** LING (*verb form*) tiempo *m* continuo
prohibit [prə'hɪbɪt, *Am:* proʊ'-] *vt* **1.** (*forbid*) prohibir; **to be ~ed by law** estar prohibido por ley **2.** (*prevent*) impedir
prohibition [ˌprəʊɪ'bɪʃən, *Am:* ˌproʊ-] *n* **1.** (*ban*) prohibición *f* **2.** *Brit* LAW acto *m* de inhibición **3.** *Am* HIST **the Prohibition** la Ley Seca
prohibitive [prə'hɪbətɪv, *Am:* proʊ'hɪbət̬ɪv] *adj* prohibitivo, -a
project¹ ['prɒdʒekt, *Am:* 'prɑːdʒekt] *n* **1.** (*undertaking, plan*) proyecto *m* **2.** SCHOOL, UNIV (*essay*) trabajo *m*
project² [prəʊ'dʒekt, *Am:* prə-] **I.** *vt* **1.** (*forecast*) pronosticar; **to be ~ed to do sth** estar previsto para hacer algo **2.** (*propel*) impulsar; **to** ~ **one's mind into the future** lanzar la mente al futuro **3.** PSYCH proyectar; **to** ~ **sth onto sb** proyectar algo en alguien **4.** (*promote*) promover; **to** ~ **oneself** promocionarse **II.** *vi* sobresalir
projectile [prəʊ'dʒektaɪl, *Am:* prə'dʒektəl] *n* proyectil *m*
projection [prəʊ'dʒekʃən, *Am:* prə-] *n* **1.** (*forecast*) pronóstico *m* **2.** (*protrusion*) saliente *m;* (*of rock*) prominencia *f* **3.** *no pl* PSYCH proyección *f*
projectionist *n* proyeccionista *mf*
project management *n* dirección *f* de proyectos **project manager** *n* director(a) de proyectos *m*
projector [prə'dʒektəʳ, *Am:* -'dʒektɚ] *n* proyector *m*
prolapse ['prəʊlæps, *Am:* 'proʊ-] *n* MED prolapso *m*
prole [prəʊl, *Am:* proʊl] *adj, n inf, pej abbr of* **proletarian** proletario, -a *m, f;* **the ~s** el proletariado
proletarian [prəʊlɪ'teərɪən, *Am:* ˌproʊlə-'terɪ-] **I.** *adj* proletario, -a **II.** *n* proletario, -a *m, f*
proletariat [ˌprəʊlɪ'teərɪət, *Am:* ˌproʊlə'terɪ-] *n no pl* proletariado *m*
proliferate [prə'lɪfəreɪt, *Am:* proʊ'-] *vi* proliferar
proliferation [prəˌlɪfə'reɪʃən, *Am:* proʊˌ-] *n no pl* proliferación *f*

P

prolific [prəˈlɪfɪk, *Am:* proʊˈ-] *adj* **1.** (*producing a lot*) prolífico, -a **2.** (*having many offspring*) fecundo, -a

prolix [ˈprəʊlɪks, *Am:* proʊˈlɪks] *adj pej, form* prolijo, -a

prologue *n Brit,* **prolog** [ˈprəʊlɒg, *Am:* ˈproʊlɑːg] *n Am* **1.** (*introduction*) prólogo *m;* (*play*) presentación *f* **2.** *fig, inf* (*preliminary event*) preludio *m;* **to be a ~ to sth** ser un preámbulo de algo

prolong [prəˈlɒŋ, *Am:* proʊˈlɑːŋ] *vt* prolongar; (*agony*) alargar

prolongation [ˌprəʊlɒŋˈgeɪʃən, *Am:* ˌproʊlɑːŋˈ-] *n no pl* prolongación *f*

prom [prɒm, *Am:* prɑːm] *n* **1.** *Am* (*school dance*) baile *m* **2.** *Brit* (*concert*) concierto *m* (*en el que parte del público está de pie*) **3.** *Brit* (*seafront*) paseo *m* marítimo

promenade [ˌprɒməˈnɑːd, *Am:* ˌprɑːməˈneɪd] **I.** *n* **1.** *Brit* (*seafront*) paseo *m* marítimo **2.** *form* (*walk*) paseo *m* **II.** *vi* pasearse

promenade concert *n Brit* concierto *m* (*en el que parte del público está de pie*) **promenade deck** *n* cubierta *f* de paseo

prominence [ˈprɒmɪnəns, *Am:* ˈprɑːmə-] *n no pl* **1.** (*conspicuousness*) prominencia *f;* **to give ~ to sth** hacer resaltar algo **2.** (*importance*) importancia *f;* **to gain ~** ganar trascendencia

prominent [ˈprɒmɪnənt, *Am:* ˈprɑːmə-] *adj* **1.** (*conspicuous*) prominente; **to put sth in a ~ position** poner algo en una buena posición **2.** (*teeth, chin*) saliente **3.** (*distinguished, well-known*) importante; (*position*) destacado, -a; **to be ~ in sth** desempeñar un papel importante en algo

promiscuity [ˌprɒmɪˈskjuːəti, *Am:* ˌprɑːmɪˈskjuːət̬i] *n no pl* promiscuidad *f*

promiscuous [prəˈmɪskjuəs] *adj pej* promiscuo, -a

promise [ˈprɒmɪs, *Am:* ˈprɑːmɪs] **I.** *vt* (*pledge, have potential*) prometer; **to ~ to do sth** prometer hacer algo **II.** *vi* (*pledge*) prometer; **I ~!** ¡lo prometo! **III.** *n* **1.** (*pledge*) promesa *f;* **to make a ~** prometer **2.** *no pl* (*potential*) posibilidad *f;* **a young person of ~** un joven de porvenir; **to show ~** demostrar aptitudes; **to fulfil one's ~** satisfacer las esperanzas

promising *adj* prometedor(a)

promissory note [ˈprɒmɪsəriˌnəʊt, *Am:* ˈprɑːmɪsɔːriˌnoʊt] *n* pagaré *m*

promo [ˈprəʊməʊ, *Am:* ˈproʊmoʊ] *n inf s.* **promotion** promoción *f*

promontory [ˈprɒməntəri, *Am:* ˈprɑːməntɔːr-] <-ies> *n* GEO promontorio *m*

promote [prəˈməʊt, *Am:* -ˈmoʊt] *vt* **1.** (*in army, company, organization*) ascender; (*soccer team*) subir **2.** (*encourage*) promover **3.** (*advertise*) promocionar

promoter *n* promotor(a) *m(f)*

promotion [prəˈməʊʃən, *Am:* -ˈmoʊ-] *n* **1.** (*in army, company, organization*) ascenso *m;* **to get a ~** subir en el escalafón **2.** (*encouragement, advertising*) promoción *f;* **sales ~** promoción de ventas

promotional material [prəˈməʊʃənəl məˈtɪəriəl, *Am:* prəˈmoʊʃənəl məˈtɪriəl] *n* material *m* de promoción

prompt [prɒmpt, *Am:* prɑːmpt] **I.** *vt* **1.** (*spur*) provocar; **to ~ sb to do sth** estimular a alguien para que haga algo **2.** THEAT apuntar **II.** *adj* (*quick*) rápido, -a; (*action*) inmediato, -a; (*delivery*) sin demora; **to be ~** ser puntual **III.** *adv* puntualmente **IV.** *n* **1.** INFOR línea *f* de comandos **2.** THEAT (*prompter*) apuntador(a) *m(f);* **to give sb a ~** apuntar a alguien

prompt box <-es> *n* THEAT concha *f* del apuntador

prompter [ˈprɒmptəʳ, *Am:* ˈprɑːmptɚ] *n* THEAT apuntador(a) *m(f)*

promptitude [ˈprɒmptɪtjuːd, *Am:* ˈprɑːmptɪtuːd] *n no pl, form* prontitud *f*

promptly [ˈprɒmptli, *Am:* ˈprɑːmpt-] *adv* **1.** (*quickly*) rápidamente **2.** *inf* (*immediately afterward*) puntualmente

promptness [ˈprɒmptnɪs, *Am:* ˈprɑːmpt-] *n no pl s.* **promptitude**

promulgate [ˈprɒmlgeɪt, *Am:* ˈprɑːml-] *vt form* **1.** (*theory, belief*) divulgar **2.** LAW promulgar

promulgation [ˌprɒmlˈgeɪʃən, *Am:* ˌprɑːmlˈ-] *n no pl, form* **1.** (*of theory, belief*) divulgación *f* **2.** LAW promulgación *f*

prone [prəʊn, *Am:* proʊn] **I.** *adj* **to be ~ to do sth** ser propenso a hacer algo **II.** *adv form* boca abajo

prong [prɒŋ, *Am:* prɑːŋ] *n* (*of fork*) diente *m;* (*of antler*) punta *f*

pronominal [prəʊˈnɒmɪnl, *Am:* proʊˈnɑːmə-] *adj* LING pronominal

pronoun [ˈprəʊnaʊn, *Am:* ˈproʊ-] *n* LING pronombre *m*

pronounce [prəˈnaʊnts] *vt* **1.** (*speak*) pronunciar **2.** (*declare*) declarar; (*judgement*) dictaminar; **to ~ that ...** afirmar que...

pronounceable *adj* pronunciable

pronounced *adj* pronunciado, -a; (*accent*) marcado, -a

pronouncement [prəʊˈnaʊntsmənt, *Am:* ˈprə-] *n* declaración *f;* **to make a ~** pronunciarse; (*pass judgement*) hacer un dictamen

pronto [ˈprɒntəʊ, *Am:* ˈprɑːnt̬oʊ] *adv inf* enseguida

pronunciation [prəˌnʌntsɪˈeɪʃən] *n* LING *no pl* pronunciación *f*

proof [pruːf] **I.** *n* **1.** *no pl a.* LAW prueba *f;* **~ of sth** comprobación *f* de algo; **the burden of ~** el peso de la demostración **2.** *no pl* (*test*) examen *m* **3.** TYPO prueba *f* de imprenta **4.** MAT prueba *f* matemática ►**the ~ of the pudding is in the eating** *prov* no se sabe si algo es bueno hasta que no se prueba **II.** *adj* **1.** (*impervious*) inmune; **to be ~ against burglars** estar a prueba de ladrones **2.** (*alcoholic strength*) de graduación **III.** *vt* impermeabilizar

proofread ['pru:f,ri:d] *irr* TYPO, PUBL I. *vt* corregir II. *vi* corregir pruebas
proofreader *n* corrector(a) *m(f)* de pruebas
proofreading *n no pl* corrección *f* de pruebas
prop¹ [prɒp, *Am:* prɑ:p] *n* 1. (*support*) apoyo *m* 2. THEAT objeto *m* de atrezzo
prop² [prɒp, *Am:* prɑ:p] *n* 1. ECON *abbr of* **proprietor** propietario, -a *m, f* 2. AVIAT *abbr of* **propeller** hélice *f*
propaganda [,prɒpə'gændə, *Am:* ,prɑ:pə'-] *n no pl* propaganda *f*
propagandist [,prɒpə'gændɪst, *Am:* ,prɑ:pə'-] I. *n* propagandista *mf* II. *adj* propagandístico, -a
propagate ['prɒpəgeɪt, *Am:* 'prɑ:pə-] I. *vt* 1. BOT propagar 2. (*disseminate: lie, rumour*) difundir II. *vi* propagarse
propagation [,prɒpə'geɪʃən, *Am:* ,prɑ:pə'-] *n no pl* 1. BOT propagación *f* 2. (*of lies, rumour*) difusión *f*
propane ['prəʊpeɪn, *Am:* 'proʊ-] *n no pl* propano *m*
propel [prə'pel] <-ll-> *vt* propulsar
propellant [prə'pelənt] *n* propelente *m*
propeller [prə'pelə^r, *Am:* -ɚ] *n* hélice *f*
propeller shaft *n* TECH árbol *m* de transmisión
propelling pencil *n Brit, Aus* (lápiz *m*) portaminas *m inv*
propensity [prə'pensəti, *Am:* -t̬i] *n no pl, form* propensión *f*; **to have a ~ to do sth** tener tendencia a hacer algo
proper ['prɒpə^r, *Am:* 'prɑ:pɚ] I. *adj* 1. (*real*) verdadero, -a; **a ~ job** un trabajo como es debido 2. (*appropriate: time, place, method*) apropiado, -a; (*use*) correcto, -a; **~ meaning** sentido *m* exacto 3. (*socially respectable*) **to be ~ to do sth** ser debido hacer algo 4. *form* (*itself*) verdadero, -a; **it's not in London ~** no está en Londres propiamente dicho 5. *Brit, inf* (*total*) completo, -a; **I felt a ~ idiot** me sentí un verdadero idiota II. *adv Brit, inf* 1. (*very*) muy 2. *iron* (*genteelly*) como Dios manda
proper fraction *n* MAT fracción *f* propia
properly ['prɒpəli, *Am:* 'prɑ:pɚli] *adv* 1. (*correctly*) correctamente; **~ speaking** hablando como es debido; **~ dressed** vestido apropiadamente 2. (*behave*) como es debido 3. (*politely*) educadamente 4. *Brit* (*thoroughly*) completamente
proper name *n*, **proper noun** *n* nombre *m* propio
propertied *adj* ECON adinerado, -a
property ['prɒpəti, *Am:* 'prɑ:pɚt̬i] <-ies> *n* 1. *no pl* (*possession*) propiedad *f*; LAW (*house, land*) bien *m* inmueble; **a man of ~** un hombre adinerado; **private ~** propiedad privada 2. (*house*) inmueble *m*; (*land*) terreno *m* 3. (*attribute*) atributo *m* ►**a <u>hot</u> ~** un gran éxito
property developer *n* ECON promotor(a) *m(f)* inmobiliario **property development** *n* ECON promoción *f* inmobiliaria **property insurance** *n no pl* seguro *m* de la propiedad **property man** *n*, **property manager** *n* THEAT encargado *m* del atrezzo **property market** *n no pl* mercado *m* inmobiliario **property owner** *n* propietario, -a *m, f* **property room** *n* THEAT habitación *f* del atrezzo **property speculation** *n no pl* ECON especulación *f* inmobiliaria **property tax** *n* impuesto *m* sobre la propiedad
prophecy ['prɒfəsi, *Am:* 'prɑ:fə-] <-ies> *pl n* profecía *f*
prophesy ['prɒfɪsaɪ, *Am:* 'prɑ:fə-] <-ie-> I. *vt* (*predict*) predecir; REL profetizar II. *vi* profetizar
prophet ['prɒfɪt, *Am:* 'prɑ:fɪt] *n* 1. REL profeta, -isa *m, f* 2. (*person who foretells events*) adivino, -a *m, f*; **~ of doom** catastrofista *mf*
prophetess ['prɒfɪtes, *Am:* 'prɑ:fɪt̬əs] *n* profetisa *f*
prophetic [prə'fetɪk] *adj* profético, -a
prophylactic [,prɒfɪ'læktɪk, *Am:* ,proʊfə'-] I. *adj* MED profiláctico, -a II. *n* 1. MED (*preventive medicine*) (fármaco *m*) profiláctico *m* 2. (*condom*) condón *m*
prophylaxis [prɒfɪ'læksɪs, *Am:* ,proʊfə'-] *n no pl* MED profilaxis *f*
propinquity [prə'pɪŋkwəti, *Am:* proʊ'pɪŋkwət̬i] *n no pl, form* 1. (*proximity*) proximidad *f* 2. (*kinship*) parentesco *m*
propitious [prə'pɪʃəs] *adj form* favorable
prop jet *n* turbohélice *f*
proponent [prə'pəʊnənt, *Am:* -'poʊ-] *n* defensor(a) *m(f)*
proportion [prə'pɔ:ʃən, *Am:* -'pɔ:r-] *n* 1. (*relationship*) proporción *f*; **the ~ of A to B** el porcentaje entre A y B; **to be out of ~ to sth** estar desproporcionado con algo; **to be in ~ to sth** estar en proporción con algo; **to keep a sense of ~** mantener un sentido de la medida; **to blow sth out of (all) ~** exagerar algo desmesuradamente 2. (*part*) parte *f* proporcional 3. *pl* (*size*) dimensiones *fpl*; **a building of gigantic ~s** un edificio de grandes medidas
proportional [prə'pɔ:ʃənəl, *Am:* -'pɔ:r-] *adj* proporcional; **inversely ~** inversamente proporcional
proportionality [prə,pɔ:ʃənælɪti, *Am:* -,pɔ:rʃənælət̬i] *n no pl* proporcionalidad *f*
proportional representation *n no pl* POL representación *f* proporcional
proportionate [prə'pɔ:ʃənət, *Am:* -'pɔ:rʃənɪt] *adj s.* **proportional**
proportioned *adj* **well ~** bien proporcionado; **to be generously ~** *iron* estar muy bien hecho
proposal [prə'pəʊzəl, *Am:* -'poʊ-] *n* 1. (*firm suggestion*) propuesta *f*; **to put forward a ~** presentar una proposición; **peace ~** propuesta *f* de paz 2. (*offer of marriage*) declaración *f*; **to make a marriage ~** hacer una petición de mano
propose [prə'pəʊz, *Am:* -'poʊz] I. *vt* 1. (*put*

P

forward) proponer; **to ~ a toast** proponer un brindis **2.** (*intend*) **to ~ to do sth** tener la intención de hacer algo **3.** (*nominate*) nombrar **II.** *vi* (*marriage*) **to ~** (**to sb**) declararse (a alguien) ▶**man ~s, God disposes** *prov* el hombre propone y Dios dispone *prov*

proposer [prəˈpəʊzəʳ, *Am:* -ˈpoʊzɚ] *n* **1.** (*suggestor*) autor(a) *m(f)* de una moción **2.** (*nominator*) proponente *mf*

proposition [ˌprɒpəˈzɪʃən, *Am:* ˌprɑːpəˈ-] **I.** *n* **1.** (*theory, argument*) proposición *f* **2.** (*business*) ofrecimiento *m* **3.** (*suggestion*) sugerencia *f* **II.** *vt* hacer proposiciones deshonestas a

propound [prəˈpaʊnd] *vt form* proponer

proprietary [prəˈpraɪətri, *Am:* -teri] *adj* **1.** (*owning property*) propietario, -a **2.** ECON (*name, brand*) registrado, -a; (*article*) patentado, -a

proprietor [prəˈpraɪətəʳ, *Am:* proʊˈpraɪət̬ɚ] *n* propietario, -a *m, f*; (*of business*) dueño, -a *m, f*

proprietorship *n* propiedad *f*

proprietress [prəˈpraɪətrɪs, *Am:* proʊˈ-] *n* propietaria *f*

propriety [prəˈpraɪəti, *Am:* -t̬i] <-ies> *n* **1.** *no pl* (*correctness*) corrección *f* **2.** (*standard of conduct*) **the proprieties** convenciones *fpl* sociales; **to observe the proprieties** atenerse al decoro

propulsion [prəˈpʌlʃən] *n no pl* propulsión *f*

pro rata [ˌprəʊˈrɑːtə, *Am:* ˌproʊˈreɪt̬ə] **I.** *adj* prorrateado, -a **II.** *adv* proporcionalmente

prorate *vt,* **pro-rate** [prəʊˈreɪt] *vt Am* prorratear

prorogation [ˌprəʊrəʊˈgeɪʃən, *Am:* ˌproʊroʊˈ-] *n* POL prorrogación *f*

prorogue [prəʊˈrəʊg, *Am:* proʊˈroʊg] *vt* prorrogar

prosaic [prəˈzeɪɪk, *Am:* proʊˈ-] *adj form* prosaico, -a

proscenium [prəˈsiːnɪəm, *Am:* proʊˈ-] <-s *o* proscenia> *n* THEAT proscenio *m*

proscribe [prəˈskraɪb, *Am:* proʊˈ-] *vt* proscribir

proscription [prəˈskrɪpʃən, *Am:* proʊˈ-] *n no pl, form* proscripción *f*

prose [prəʊz, *Am:* proʊz] *n no pl* prosa *f*

prosecutable [ˌprɒsɪˈkjuːtəbl] *adj* LAW procesable

prosecute [ˈprɒsɪkjuːt, *Am:* ˈprɑːsɪ-] **I.** *vt* **1.** LAW **to ~ sb** (**for sth**) procesar a alguien (por algo) **2.** *form* (*pursue, follow up*) proseguir; (*studies*) sacar adelante **II.** *vi* interponer

prosecuting *adj* acusador(a)

prosecuting attorney *n Am* fiscal *mf*

prosecution [ˌprɒsɪˈkjuːʃən, *Am:* ˌprɑːsɪˈ-] *n* **1.** *no pl* LAW (*proceedings*) proceso *m* **2.** *no pl* LAW (*the prosecuting party*) **the ~** la acusación; **witness for the ~** testigo *mf* de cargo **3.** *form* (*of campaign, inquiry*) seguimiento *m*

prosecutor [ˈprɒsɪkjuːtəʳ, *Am:* ˈprɑːsɪkjuːt̬ɚ] *n* LAW fiscal *mf*

proselyte [ˈprɒsəlaɪt, *Am:* ˈprɑːsə-] *n* REL prosélito, -a *m, f*

proselytise *vi,* **proselytize** [ˈprɒsəlɪtaɪz, *Am:* ˈprɑːsəlɪ-] *vi* hacer proselitismo

prosody [ˈprɒsədi, *Am:* ˈprɑːsə-] *n no pl* prosodia *f*

prospect [ˈprɒspekt, *Am:* ˈprɑːspekt] **I.** *n* **1.** (*possibility*) posibilidad *f;* **the ~ of sth** la probabilidad de algo **2.** *pl* (*chances*) perspectivas *fpl* **3.** *liter* (*view*) panorama *m;* **a ~ of/over sth** una vista de/sobre algo **4.** ECON (*potential customer*) posible cliente *m,* posible clienta *f;* (*potential employee*) candidato, -a *m, f* **II.** *vi* MIN buscar

prospective [prəˈspektɪv] *adj* posible; (*candidat*) futuro, -a

prospector [prɒˈspektəʳ, *Am:* ˈprɑːspektɚ] *n* MIN prospector(a) *m(f);* (*gold*) cateador(a) *m(f)*

prospectus [prəˈspektəs] *n* prospecto *m;* UNIV folleto *m* informativo

prosper [ˈprɒspəʳ, *Am:* ˈprɑːspɚ] *vi* prosperar

prosperity [prɒˈsperəti, *Am:* prɑːˈsperət̬i] *n no pl* prosperidad *f*

prosperous [ˈprɒspərəs, *Am:* ˈprɑːspɚ-] *adj* próspero, -a; (*business*) exitoso, -a

prostate (**gland**) [ˈprɒsteɪt-, *Am:* ˈprɑːsteɪt-] *n* próstata *f*

prostitute [ˈprɒstɪtjuːt, *Am:* ˈprɑːstətuːt] **I.** *n* prostituta *f* **II.** *vt a. fig* **to ~ oneself** prostituirse; **to ~ one's talents** prostituir su talento

prostitution [ˌprɒstɪˈtjuːʃən, *Am:* -ˈtʃuː-] *n no pl* prostitución *f*

prostrate [ˈprɒstreɪt, *Am:* ˈprɑːstreɪt] **I.** *adj a. fig* postrado, -a; **to be ~ with grief** estar abatido por el dolor **II.** *vt* **to ~ oneself** postrarse

protagonist [prəˈtægənɪst, *Am:* proʊˈ-] *n* **1.** (*main character*) protagonista *mf* **2.** (*advocate*) defensor(a) *m(f);* **to be a ~ of sth** luchar por algo

protect [prəˈtekt] *vt* proteger; (*one's interests*) salvaguardar; **to ~ oneself** resguardarse

protection [prəˈtekʃən] *n no pl* protección *f;* **to be under sb's ~** estar bajo la protección de alguien

protection factor *n* factor *m* de protección

protectionism [prəˈtekʃənɪzəm] *n no pl, pej* proteccionismo *m*

protectionist *adj pej* proteccionista

protection racket *n* chantaje *m* (*practicado a propietarios de comercios*)

protective [prəˈtektɪv] *adj* **1.** (*affording protection*) proteccionista; **~ custody** detención *f* preventiva **2.** (*wishing to protect*) protector(a)

protector [prəˈtektəʳ, *Am:* -ɚ] *n* **1.** (*person*) protector(a) *m(f)* **2.** (*device*) aparato *m* protector

protectorate [prəˈtektərət, *Am:* -ɪt] *n* protectorado *m*

protégé(**e**) [ˈprɒtɪʒeɪ, *Am:* ˈproʊt̬əʒeɪ] *n m(f)* protegido, -a *m, f*

protein ['prəʊtiːn, *Am:* 'proʊ-] *n* proteína *f;* ~ **deficiency** deficiencia *f* proteínica
protest¹ ['prəʊtest, *Am:* 'proʊtest] *n* **1.** (*complaint*) protesta *f;* **in** ~ en señal de protesta; **to do sth under** ~ hacer algo que conste como protesta **2.** (*demonstration*) manifestación *f* de protesta
protest² [prə'test, *Am:* proʊ'-] **I.** *vi* protestar; **to** ~ **about/against sth** protestar por/en contra de algo **II.** *vt* **1.** (*solemnly affirm*) **to** ~ **that ...** declarar que...; **to** ~ **one's innocence** afirmar su inocencia **2.** *Am* (*show dissent*) protestar en contra de
Protestant ['prɒtɪstənt, *Am:* 'prɑːt̬ə-] *n* protestante *mf*
Protestantism *n no pl* protestantismo *m*
protestation [ˌprɒtes'teɪʃən, *Am:* ˌprɑːt̬es-'teɪ-] *n pl* **1.** (*strong objection*) protesta *f* **2.** (*strong affirmation*) afirmación *f*
protester *n* manifestante *mf*
protest march *n* marcha *f* de protesta **protest vote** *n* voto *m* de protesta
protocol ['prəʊtəkɒl, *Am:* 'proʊt̬əkɔːl] *n* protocolo *m*
proton ['prəʊtɒn, *Am:* 'proʊtɑːn] *n* protón *m*
protoplasm ['prəʊtəplæzəm, *Am:* 'proʊt̬ə-] *n no pl* protoplasma *m*
prototype ['prəʊtətaɪp, *Am:* 'proʊt̬ə-] *n* prototipo *m*
protozoan [ˌprəʊtə'zəʊən, *Am:* ˌproʊt̬ə-'zoʊ-] <-s *o* -zoa> *n* protozoo *m*
protract [prə'trækt, *Am:* proʊ'-] *vt form* prolongar
protracted [prə'træktɪd, *Am:* proʊ'-] *adj* prolongado, -a
protraction [prə'trækʃən, *Am:* proʊ'-] *n* **1.** *no pl* (*prolonging*) prolongación *f* **2.** ANAT (*muscle action*) extensión *f*
protractor [prə'træktəʳ, *Am:* proʊ'-] *n* (*angle measuring device*) transportador *m*
protrude [prə'truːd, *Am:* proʊ'-] *vi* sobresalir
protruding [prə'truːdɪŋ, *Am:* proʊ'-] *adj* prominente; (*ears*) que sobresale
protrusion [prə'truːʒən, *Am:* proʊ'-] *n* protuberancia *f*
protuberance [prə'tjuːbərəns, *Am:* proʊ-'tuː-] *adj form* protuberancia *f*
protuberant [prə'tjuːbərənt, *Am:* proʊ-'tuː-] *adj form* protuberante; (*eyes*) saltón, -ona
proud [praʊd] **I.** *adj* **1.** (*pleased*) orgulloso, -a; **to be** ~ **of sth/sb** enorgullecerse de algo/alguien; **to be** ~ **to do sth** tener el honor de hacer algo; **to be** ~ **that ...** estar orgulloso de que... **2.** (*having self-respect*) digno, -a **3.** *pej* (*arrogant*) arrogante **4.** *Brit* (*protruding*) **to stand** ~ sobresalir **II.** *adv* **to do sb** ~ *Aus, Brit* ser motivo de orgullo para alguien
proudly *adv* orgullosamente
provable ['pruːvəbl] *adj* demostrable
prove [pruːv] <proved *o Am:* proven> **I.** *vt* (*verify: theory*) probar; (*innocence, loyalty*) demostrar; **to** ~ **oneself** (**to be**) **sth** demostrarse (ser) algo; **to** ~ **sb innocent** probar la inocencia de alguien **II.** *vi* (*be established*) resultar; **to** ~ **to be sth** resultar ser algo
proven ['pruːvən] **I.** *vi, vt Am, Scot pp of* **prove II.** *adj* (*verified*) comprobado, -a
provenance ['prɒvənənts, *Am:* 'prɑːvən-] *n no pl, form* procedencia *f*
provender ['prɒvɪndəʳ, *Am:* 'prɑːvəndɚ] *n* **1.** AGR forraje *m* **2.** *iron, inf* (*sustenance*) provisiones *fpl*
proverb ['prɒvɜːb, *Am:* 'prɑːvɜːrb] *n* refrán *m,* proverbio *m;* **as the** ~ **goes ...** como dice el proverbio...
proverbial [prəʊ'vɜːbiəl, *Am:* prə'vɜːr-] *adj* proverbial
provide [prəʊ'vaɪd, *Am:* prə-] *vt* **1.** proveer; **to** ~ **sb with sth** proporcionar algo a alguien **2.** *form* LAW estipular
provided *conj* ~ **that ...** con tal que... +*subj*
providence ['prɒvɪdənts, *Am:* 'prɑːvə-] *n no pl* providencia *f;* **divine** ~ REL Divina Providencia
providential [ˌprɒvɪ'dentʃəl, *Am:* ˌprɑːvə'-] *adj form* providencial
provider *n* **1.** (*person*) proveedor(a) *m(f)* **2.** INFOR proveedor *m;* **Internet Service** ~ proveedor de servicios Internet
providing *conj* ~ (**that**) ... con tal que... +*subj*
province ['prɒvɪnts, *Am:* 'prɑːvɪnts] *n* **1.** POL, ADMIN provincia *f* **2.** *no pl* (*branch of a subject*) campo *m*
provincial [prəʊ'vɪntʃəl, *Am:* prə'vɪntʃəl] **I.** *adj* **1.** POL, ADMIN provincial **2.** *pej* (*unsophisticated*) provinciano, -a **II.** *n* (*person from provinces*) provinciano, -a *m, f*
proving ground *n* terreno *m* de pruebas
provision [prəʊ'vɪʒən, *Am:* prə-] **I.** *n* **1.** (*act of providing*) suministro *m* **2.** (*thing provided*) provisión *f* **3.** (*preparation*) previsiones *fpl;* **to make** ~ **for sth** tomar medidas de previsión para algo **4.** LAW (*in will, contract*) disposición *f* **II.** *vt* abastecer
provisional [prəʊ'vɪʒənəl, *Am:* prə-] *adj* provisional
provisional driving licence *n Aus, Brit* permiso *m* de conducción provisional
proviso [prə'vaɪzəʊ, *Am:* prə'vaɪzoʊ] <-s> *n* (*stipulation*) condición *f;* **with the** ~ **that ...** con la condición de que +*subj*
provocation [ˌprɒvə'keɪʃən, *Am:* ˌprɑːvə'-] *n* provocación *f*
provocative [prə'vɒkətɪv, *Am:* -'vɑːkət̬ɪv] *adj* **1.** (*causing anger*) provocador(a) **2.** (*sexually*) provocativo, -a
provoke [prə'vəʊk, *Am:* -'voʊk] *vt* **1.** (*make angry*) provocar; **to** ~ **sb into doing sth** provocar a alguien para que haga algo **2.** (*discussion*) motivar; (*interest*) despertar; (*crisis*) causar
provoking *adj* (*irritating*) irritante

P

provost ['prɒvəst, *Am:* 'proʊvoʊst] *n* **1.** *Brit* UNIV rector(a) *m(f)* **2.** *Scot* POL alcalde(sa) *m(f)*
prow [praʊ] *n* NAUT proa *f*
prowess ['praʊɪs] *n no pl, form* destreza *f;* (*sexual, sporting*) proeza *f*
prowl [praʊl] **I.** *n inf* **to be on the ~** estar merodeando **II.** *vt* vagar por; **to ~ the streets for victims** merodear por las calles en busca de víctimas **III.** *vi* **to ~** (**about, around**) rondar (por)
prowl car *n Am* coche-patrulla *m*
prowler *n* merodeador(a) *m(f)*
prowling *n* merodeo *m*
proximity [prɒk'sɪməti, *Am:* prɑːk'sɪmət̬i] *n no pl, form* proximidad *f;* **to be in** (**close**) **~ to sth** estar cerca de algo
proxy ['prɒksi, *Am:* 'prɑːk-] <-ies> *n* apoderado, -a *m, f;* **to do sth by ~** hacer algo por poderes
prude [pruːd] *n pej* mojigato, -a *m, f*
prudence ['pruːdns] *n no pl* prudencia *f*
prudent ['pruːdnt] *adj* prudente
prudery ['pruːdəri] <-ies> *n pej* mojigatería *f*
prudish ['pruːdɪʃ] *adj pej* mojigato, -a
prune¹ [pruːn] *vt* podar; **to ~** (**back**) **costs** reducir gastos
prune² [pruːn] *n* (*dried plum*) ciruela *f* pasa
pruning *n* poda *f*
pruning hook *n* podadera *f* **pruning saw** *n* serrucho *m* de podar **pruning shears** *npl Am* BOT tijeras *fpl* de podar
prurience ['prʊərɪəns, *Am:* 'prʊrɪ-] *n no pl, pej, form* lascivia *f*
prurient ['prʊərɪənt, *Am:* 'prʊrɪ-] *adj pej, form* lascivo, -a
Prussia ['prʌʃə] *n* HIST, POL, GEO Prusia *f*
Prussian ['prʌʃən] **I.** *n* HIST prusiano, -a *m, f* **II.** *adj* prusiano, -a
prussic acid [ˌprʌsɪk'æsɪd] *n no pl* ácido *m* prúsico
pry¹ [praɪ] <pries, pried> *vi pej* (*be nosy*) husmear; **to ~ into sth** entrometerse en algo; **to ~ about** curiosear
pry² [praɪ] *vt s.* **prize²**
prying ['praɪɪŋ] *adj* fisgón, -ona; **~ eyes** miradas *fpl* indiscretas
PS [ˌpiː'es] *abbr of* **postscript** P.D.
psalm [sɑːm] *n* REL salmo *m*
psephology [se'fɒlədʒi, *Am:* siː'fɑːlə-] *n* análisis *m* electoral
pseud [sjuːd, *Am:* suːd] *n Brit, inf* intelectualoide *mf*
pseudo ['sjuːdəʊ, *Am:* 'suːdoʊ] *adj* falso, -a
pseudointellectual **I.** *n* pseudointelectual *mf* **II.** *adj* pseudointelectual
pseudonym ['sjuːdənɪm, *Am:* 'suː-] *n* seudónimo *m*
psittacosis [ˌsɪtə'kəʊsɪs, *Am:* -'koʊ-] *n* psitacosis *f inv*
PSV *n abbr of* **public service vehicle** vehículo *m* de servicio público
psych(**e**) **up** ['saɪk] *vt inf* **to psych**(**e**) **oneself up** mentalizarse; **to psych**(**e**) **sb up** mentalizar a alguien
psyche ['saɪki] *n* psique *f*
psychedelic [ˌsaɪkɪ'delɪk, *Am:* -kə'-] *adj* psicodélico, -a
psychiatric [ˌsaɪkɪ'ætrɪk] *adj* psiquiátrico, -a
psychiatrist [saɪ'kaɪətrɪst] *n* psiquiatra *mf*
psychiatry [saɪ'kaɪətri] *n no pl* psiquiatría *f*
psychic ['saɪkɪk] **I.** *adj* **1.** (*occult powers*) parapsicológico, -a **2.** (*of the mind*) psíquico, -a **II.** *n* vidente *mf*
psychoanalyse [ˌsaɪkəʊ'ænəlaɪz, *Am:* -koʊ'-] *vt* psicoanalizar
psychoanalysis [ˌsaɪkəʊə'næləsɪs, *Am:* -koʊə'-] *n no pl* psicoanálisis *m inv*
psychoanalyst [ˌsaɪkəʊ'ænəlɪst, *Am:* -koʊ'-] *n* psicoanalista *mf*
psychoanalytic(**al**) [ˌsaɪkəʊˌænəl'ɪtɪk(əl), *Am:* -koʊˌænə'lɪt̬ɪk(əl)] *adj* psicoanalítico, -a
psychoanalyze [ˌsaɪkəʊ'ænəlaɪz, *Am:* -koʊ'ænəlaɪz] *vt Am s.* **psychoanalyse**
psychological [ˌsaɪkə'lɒdʒɪkəl, *Am:* -kə'lɑːdʒɪ-] *adj* psicológico, -a
psychologist *n* psicólogo, -a *m, f*
psychology [saɪ'kɒlədʒi, *Am:* -'kɑːlə-] <-ies> *n* (*science, mentality*) psicología *f*
psychopath ['saɪkəʊpæθ, *Am:* -kəpæθ] *n* psicópata *mf*
psychopathic [ˌsaɪkəʊ'pæθɪk, *Am:* ˌsaɪkə'-] *adj* psicopático, -a
psychosis [saɪ'kəʊsɪs, *Am:* -'koʊ-] <-ses> *n* psicosis *f inv*
psychosomatic [ˌsaɪkəʊsə'mætɪk, *Am:* -koʊsoʊ'mæt̬-] *adj* psicosomático, -a
psychotherapist [ˌsaɪkə'θerəpɪst, *Am:* -koʊ'-] *n* psicoterapeuta *mf*
psychotherapy [ˌsaɪkəʊ'θerəpi, *Am:* -koʊ'-] *n no pl* psicoterapia *f*
psychotic [saɪ'kɒtɪk, *Am:* -'kɑːt̬ɪk] **I.** *adj* psicótico, -a **II.** *n* psicótico, -a *m, f*
PT [ˌpiː'tiː] *n* **1.** *abbr of* **physical therapy** fisioterapia *f* **2.** *abbr of* **physical training** educación *f* física
pt *n* **1.** *abbr of* **part** parte *f* **2.** *abbr of* **pint** pinta *f* (≈ *0,67 litros, Am:* ≈ *0,47 litros*) **3.** *abbr of* **point** punto *m*
ptarmigan ['tɑːmɪgən, *Am:* 'tɑːrmɪ-] *n* perdiz *f* blanca
pto *abbr of* **please turn over** ver al dorso
PTO [ˌpiːtiː'əʊ, *Am:* -'oʊ] *n abbr of* **Parent-teacher Organisation** asociación *f* de padres y maestros
pub [pʌb] *n Aus, Brit, inf* bar *m*
pub crawl *n inf* **to go on a ~** ir de bar en bar tomando copas
puberty ['pjuːbəti, *Am:* -bɚt̬i] *n no pl* pubertad *f*
pubic ['pjuːbɪk] *adj* pubiano, -a, púbico, -a
pubis ['pjuːbɪs] <-es> *n* pubis *m inv*
public ['pʌblɪk] **I.** *adj* **1.** (*of/for the people, provided by the state*) público, -a **2.** (*done openly*) abierto, -a; **to go ~ with sth** revelar algo **II.** *n* **1.** (*people collectively, audience*)

público *m;* **in** ~ en público **2.** (*ordinary people*) gente *f* de la calle

public accountant *n Am* contable *mf* público, -a, contador(a) *m(f)* público, -a **public address** (**system**) *n* sistema *m* de megafonía **public affairs** *npl* asuntos *mpl* públicos

publican ['pʌblɪkən] *n Aus, Brit* tabernero, -a *m, f*

public appearance *n* aparición *f* pública **public appointment** *n* designación *f* pública **public assistance** *n Am* ayuda *f* estatal

publication [ˌpʌblɪ'keɪʃən] *n no pl* publicación *f*

public authority *n* **1.** (*state authority*) autoridad *f* estatal **2.** (*department, authority*) departamento *m* público **public bar** *n Brit* bar *m* **public convenience** *n Aus, Brit, form* aseos *mpl* públicos **public defender** *n Am* LAW defensor(a) *m(f)* de oficio **public domain** *n* dominio *m* público **public enemy** *n* enemigo, -a *m, f* público, -a **public expenditure** *n,* **public expense** *n* ADMIN, POL, ECON gastos *mpl* estatales **public funds** *npl* POL, ADMIN, FIN, ECON fondos *mpl* públicos

public health *n no pl* MED, ADMIN sanidad *f* pública **public health service** *n* servicio *m* sanitario

public holiday *n* fiesta *f* oficial **public house** *n Brit, form* bar *m* **public information officer** *n* funcionario, -a *m, f* de información pública **public interest** *n* interés *m* público

publicist ['pʌblɪsɪst] *n* publicista *mf*

publicity [pʌb'lɪsəti, *Am:* -t̬i] *n* **1.** *no pl* publicidad *f* **2.** (*attention*) **to attract** ~ atraer la atención ►**any** ~ **is** <u>**good**</u> ~ cualquier tipo de promoción es buena

publicity agent *n* agente *mf* de publicidad **publicity campaign** *n* ECON campaña *f* de promoción **publicity department** *n* departamento *m* de promoción **publicity material** *n* material *m* publicitario

publicize ['pʌblɪsaɪz] *vt* promocionar

public law *n* LAW derecho *m* público **public library** <- libraries> *n* biblioteca *f* pública **public limited company** *n* sociedad *f* anónima **public loan** *n* empréstito *m* público

publicly *adv* **1.** (*openly*) en público **2.** ~ **owned** de propiedad pública

public nuisance *n* daño *m* público **public opinion** *n* opinión *f* pública **public property** *n* bienes *mpl* públicos **public prosecution** *n* fiscalía *f* **public prosecutor** *n* fiscal *mf* **public records** *npl* documentos *mpl* públicos

public relations *npl* relaciones *fpl* públicas **public-relations officer** *n* secretario, -a *m, f* de relaciones públicas

public school *n* **1.** *Brit* (*private*) colegio *m* privado **2.** *Am, Aus* (*state-funded*) escuela *f* pública **public sector** *n* sector *m* público

public-spirited [ˌpʌblɪk'spɪrɪtɪd, *Am:* -ət̬ɪd] *adj* solidario, -a

public telephone *n* teléfono *m* público **public transport**(**ation**) *n* transporte *m* público **public utility** *n* empresa *f* de servicios públicos **public works** *npl* ADMIN, POL obras *fpl* públicas

publish ['pʌblɪʃ] *vt* **1.** (*book, author, result*) publicar; (*information*) divulgar **2.** REL **to** ~ **the banns** correr las amonestaciones

publisher *n* **1.** (*company*) editorial *f* **2.** (*person*) editor(a) *m(f)*

publishing *n no pl, no art* industria *f* editorial

publishing house *n* editorial *f*

puck [pʌk] *n* SPORTS disco *m*

pucker ['pʌkəʳ, *Am:* -ɚ] *vt* **to** ~ **one's lips/brow** fruncir la boca/la frente

pudding ['pʊdɪŋ] *n* **1.** (*dessert*) postre *m;* (*cooked sweet dish*) pudding *mpl* **2.** (*savoury pastry dish*) budín *m*

puddle ['pʌdl] *n* charco *m*

pudenda [pju:'dendə] *npl form* partes *fpl* pudendas

pudgy ['pʊdʒi] <-ier, -iest> *adj* rechoncho, -a

puerile ['pjʊəraɪl, *Am:* 'pju:ərɪl] *adj form* pueril

puerility [ˌpjʊə'rɪləti, *Am:* ˌpju:ə'rɪlət̬i] *n no pl* puerilidad *f*

Puerto Rican ['pwɜ:təʊ'ri:kən, *Am:* ˌpwert̬ə'-] **I.** *n* portorriqueño, -a *m, f* **II.** *adj* portorriqueño, -a

Puerto Rico ['pwɜ:təʊ'ri:kəʊ, *Am:* ˌpwert̬ə'ri:koʊ] *n* Puerto Rico *m*

puff [pʌf] **I.** *vi* **1.** (*blow*) soplar **2.** (*be out of breath*) jadear **II.** *vt* **1.** (*smoke*) soplar; (*cigarette smoke*) echar **2.** (*praise*) dar bombo a **3.** (*say while panting*) resoplar **III.** *n* **1.** *inf* (*breath, wind*) soplo *m;* (*vapour*) soplido *m;* (*of dust, smoke*) bocanada *f;* (*of air*) ráfaga *f* **2.** *Am, Can* (*quilt*) edredón *m* **3.** *Brit, inf* **to be out of** ~ quedarse sin aliento **4.** calada *f;* **to take** ~**s on a cigarette** dar caladas a un cigarro **5.** *inf* (*speech*) bombo *m*

◆**puff out** *vt* **1.** (*expand*) inflar **2.** (*exhaust*) dejar sin aliento

◆**puff up** **I.** *vt* inflar **II.** *vi* hincharse

puff adder *n* víbora *f* bufadora

puffball ['pʌfbɔ:l] *n* bejín *m*

puffin ['pʌfɪn] *n* frailecillo *m*

puff pastry *n* hojaldre *m*

puffy ['pʌfi] <-ier, -iest> *adj* hinchado, -a

pug [pʌg] *n* doguillo *m*

pugilism ['pju:dʒɪlɪzəm] *n* boxeo *m*

pugilist ['pju:dʒɪlɪst] *n* boxeador *m*

pugnacious [pʌg'neɪʃəs] *adj form* agresivo, -a

pugnacity [pʌg'næsəti, *Am:* -t̬i] *n no pl, form* belicosidad *f*

pug nose *n pej* nariz *f* chata

puke [pju:k] *inf* **I.** *vt* vomitar **II.** *vi* vomitar; **he makes me** (**want to**) ~! ¡me da asco!

◆**puke up** *inf* **I.** *vt* **to puke sth up** vomitar algo **II.** *vi* vomitar
pukka ['pʌkə] *adj* **1.** (*genuine*) genuino, -a **2.** (*of good quality*) auténtico, -a
pull [pʊl] **I.** *vt* **1.** (*draw*) tirar de, jalar *AmL;* (*trigger*) apretar **2.** *inf* (*take out: gun, knife*) sacar **3.** MED (*extract*) sacar; (*tooth*) extraer **4.** SPORTS, MED (*strain*) forzar **5.** (*attract*) atraer **6.** *Aus, Brit, inf* (*sexually*) ligar **7.** *Brit* (*pint*) servir ►**to ~ a fast one** *inf* hacer una jugarreta **II.** *vi* **1.** (*exert pulling force*) tirar **2.** *inf* (*attract sexual partner*) ligar **III.** *n* **1.** (*act of pulling*) tirón *m;* (*stronger*) jalón *m* **2.** *inf* (*influence*) influencia *f* **3.** (*knob, handle*) cuerda *f;* (*of a curtain*) tirador *m* **4.** (*attraction*) atracción *f;* (*power to attract*) atractivo *m* **5.** (*of cigarette, drink*) chupada *f*
◆**pull about** *vt* maltratar
◆**pull ahead** *vi* tomar la delantera
◆**pull apart** *vt insep* **1.** (*break into pieces*) separar **2.** (*separate using force*) hacer pedazos **3.** (*criticize*) poner por el suelo
◆**pull away** **I.** *vi* (*vehicle*) alejarse **II.** *vt* arrancar; **to pull sth away from sth** arrancar algo a algo
◆**pull back** **I.** *vi* **1.** (*move out of the way*) retirarse **2.** (*not proceed, back out*) dar marcha atrás **II.** *vt* retener
◆**pull down** *vt* **1.** (*move down*) bajar **2.** (*demolish*) tirar abajo **3.** (*drag down, hold back*) **to pull sb down** arrastrar a alguien **4.** *Am* (*earn wages*) ganar
◆**pull in** **I.** *vi* (*vehicle*) llegar **II.** *vt* **1.** (*attract*) atraer **2.** *Brit* (*arrest*) detener **3.** *Brit, inf* (*earn wages*) ganar
◆**pull off** *vt* **1.** (*leave*) arrancar **2.** *inf* (*succeed*) lograr; **to pull it off** lograrlo, vencer
pull out **I.** *vi* **1.** (*move out to overtake*) salirse; (*drive onto road*) meterse **2.** (*leave*) dejar **3.** (*withdraw*) retirarse **II.** *vt* (*take out*) sacar
◆**pull over** **I.** *vt* **1.** (*cause to fall*) volcar **2.** (*police*) parar **II.** *vi* hacerse a un lado
◆**pull round**, **pull through** **I.** *vi* reponerse **II.** *vt* **to pull sth round** ayudar a algo a reponerse
◆**pull together** **I.** *vt* **1.** (*regain composure*) **to pull oneself together** recobrar la compostura **2.** (*organise, set up*) organizar **II.** *vi* trabajar conjuntamente
◆**pull up** **I.** *vt* **1.** (*raise*) levantar; (*blinds*) subir **2.** (*plant*) arrancar **3.** *inf* (*reprimand*) reprender **II.** *vi* parar
pull-down menu ['pʊldaʊn 'menju:] *n* INFOR menú *m* desplegable
pullet ['pʊlɪt] *n* polla *f* (*gallina de menos de un año*)
pulley ['pʊli] <-s> *n* TECH polea *f*
Pullman (**car**) ['pʊlmən (kɑ:ʳ)] *n* RAIL vagón *m* de lujo
pull-out **I.** *n* **1.** MIL retirada *f* **2.** PUBL (*part of magazine*) desplegable *m* **II.** *adj* desplegable
pullover ['pʊləʊvəʳ, *Am:* -oʊvɚ] *n* jersey *m,* suéter *m*
pull-up ['pʊlʌp] *n* (*exercise*) presión *f*
pulmonary ['pʌlmənəri, *Am:* -ner-] *adj* pulmonar
pulp [pʌlp] **I.** *n* **1.** (*soft wet mass*) pasta *f;* (*for making paper*) pulpa *f* de papel; **~ mill** fábrica *f* de pasta; **to beat sb to a ~** *inf* hacer papilla a alguien **2.** (*of fruit*) pulpa *f* **3.** (*literature*) literatura *f* barata **II.** *vt* hacer pulpa
pulpit ['pʊlpɪt] *n* REL púlpito *m*
pulsar ['pʌlsɑ:ʳ, *Am:* -sɑ:r] *n* púlsar *m*
pulsate [pʌl'seɪt, *Am:* 'pʌlseɪt] *vi* palpitar
pulsation [pʌl'seɪʃən] *n* pulsación *f*
pulse[1] [pʌls] **I.** *n* **1.** ANAT pulso *m;* (*heartbeat*) latido *m;* **to take sb's ~** tomar el pulso a alguien **2.** (*single vibration*) pulsación *f* **II.** *vi* latir
pulse[2] [pʌls] *n* GASTR legumbre *f*
pulverize ['pʌlvəraɪz] *vt* pulverizar
puma ['pju:mə] *n* puma *m*
pumice ['pʌmis] *n* **~** (**stone**) piedra *f* pómez
pummel ['pʌml] <*Brit:* -ll-, *Am:* -l-> *vt* aporrear
pump [pʌmp] **I.** *n* bomba *f;* (*for fuel*) surtidor *m* **II.** *vt* bombear
pumpernickel ['pʌmpənɪkl, *Am:* -pɚ-] *n no pl* pan *m* integral de centeno
pumping *n* bombeo *m*
pumping station *n* estación *f* de bombeo
pumpkin ['pʌmpkɪn] *n* calabaza *f,* zapallo *m* *CSur, Perú*
pun [pʌn] **I.** *n* juego *m* de palabras, albur *m* *Méx* **II.** <-nn-> *vi* hacer juegos de palabras, alburear *Méx*
punch[1] [pʌntʃ] **I.** *vt* **1.** (*hit*) pegar; **to ~ sb unconscious** dejar a alguien inconsciente de un puñetazo **2.** (*pierce*) perforar, ponchar *Méx;* (*ticket*) picar; **to ~ holes in sth** hacer agujeros a algo; **to ~ the clock** [*o* **card**] fichar **3.** *Am, Can* AGR (*cattle*) aguijonear, picanear *AmL* **II.** *vi* **1.** (*hit*) pegar **2.** (*employee*) **to ~ in/out** fichar **III.** <-es> *n* **1.** (*hit*) puñetazo *m;* (*in boxing*) golpe *m;* **to give sb a ~** dar un puñetazo a alguien **2.** (*tool for puncturing*) punzón *m;* (*for metal, leather*) sacabocados *m inv;* (**hole**) **~** perforadora *f;* (**ticket**) **~** máquina *f* de picar billetes **3.** *fig* (*strong effect*) fuerza *f;* **with ~** con nervio ►**to pull one's ~es** no emplear toda su fuerza; **to roll with the ~es** saber arreglárselas
punch[2] [pʌntʃ] *n* ponche *m*
Punch and Judy show [ˌpʌntʃənd-'dʒu:diʃəʊ, *Am:* ˌpʌntʃənd'dʒu:diʃoʊ] *n* teatro *m* de polichinelas
punch bag *n Brit* saco *m* de arena
punch bowl *n* ponchera *f*
punch card *n* tarjeta *f* perforada
punch-drunk ['pʌntʃdrʌŋk] *adj a. fig* atontado, -a; **to be ~** estar grogui *inf*
punching bag *n Am* saco *m* de arena
punchline ['pʌntʃlaɪn] *n* gracia *f* (de un chiste)
punch-up ['pʌntʃʌp] *n Brit, inf* pelea *f;* **to have a ~** liarse a golpes *inf*

punctilious [pʌŋk'tɪliəs] *adj form* (*with attention to detail*) puntilloso, -a; (*with correct behavior*) formalista

punctual ['pʌŋktʃuəl] *adj* puntual

punctuality [ˌpʌŋktʃu'æləti, *Am:* -ət̬i] *n no pl* puntualidad *f*

punctuate ['pʌŋktʃueɪt] *vt* **1.** LING puntuar **2.** (*appear intermittently*) salpicar *fig;* (*interrupt*) interrumpir

punctuation [ˌpʌŋktʃu'eɪʃən] *n no pl* puntuación *f*

punctuation mark *n* signo *m* de puntuación

puncture ['pʌŋktʃəʳ, *Am:* -tʃɚ] **I.** *vt* **1.** (*pierce*) pinchar, ponchar *Méx;* (*abscess*) reventar; (*lung*) perforar; **to ~ a hole in sth** hacer un agujero a algo **2.** (*confidence*) minar **II.** *vi* (*tyre, ball*) pincharse, poncharse *Méx;* (*car*) pinchar **III.** *n* **1.** (*in tyre, ball*) pinchazo *m,* ponchadura *f Méx;* **to have a ~** (*driver*) pinchar; **to have a slow ~** *Brit* perder aire; **~** (**repair**) **patch** parche *m* **2.** MED (*in skin*) punción *f*

pundit ['pʌndɪt] *n* (*expert*) experto, -a *m, f*

pungent ['pʌndʒənt] *adj* **1.** (*sharp*) punzante; (*smell*) acre; (*taste*) fuerte **2.** (*criticism*) cáustico, -a

punish ['pʌnɪʃ] *vt* castigar; **to ~ oneself** castigarse

punishable *adj liter* punible; **~ by death** penado con la muerte

punishing **I.** *adj* (*difficult*) duro, -a; (*trying*) agotador(a) **II.** *n* **to take a ~** llevarse una paliza; **this car has taken a real ~** este coche está muy castigado

punishment ['pʌnɪʃmənt] *n* **1.** (*punishing*) castigo *m;* **capital ~** pena *f* capital; **to inflict a ~ on sb** castigar a alguien **2.** (*rough use*) maltrato *m;* **to take a lot of ~** estar muy baqueteado

punitive ['pju:nɪtɪv, *Am:* -t̬ɪv] *adj form* punitivo, -a; **~ damages** LAW daños *mpl* ejemplares; **~ expedition** MIL expedición *f* punitiva; **~ sanctions** sanciones *fpl*

punk [pʌŋk] **I.** *n* **1.** (*person*) punk *mf* **2.** *Am, pej* (*troublemaker*) gamberro, -a *m, f* **II.** *adj* **1.** (*music, style*) punk **2.** *Am* (*poor quality*) de pacotilla

punnet ['pʌnɪt] *n Aus, Brit* (*for fruit*) cestito *m*

punt¹ [pʌnt] SPORTS **I.** *vt* (*in rugby, American football*) despejar **II.** *vi* (*in rugby, American football*) despejar **III.** *n* (*kick*) patada *f* de despeje

punt² [pʌnt] **I.** *vt* (*in boat*) **to ~ sb** llevar a alguien en batea **II.** *vi* (*in boat*) ir en batea; **to go ~ing** salir de paseo en batea **III.** *n* (*boat*) batea *f*

punt³ [pʌnt] *vi* GAMES jugar contra la banca

punter ['pʌntəʳ, *Am:* -t̬ɚ] *n Brit, inf* **1.** GAMES (*gambler*) jugador(a) *m(f);* (*at races*) apostante *mf* **2.** (*customer*) cliente *mf*

puny ['pju:ni] <-ier, -iest> *adj* (*person*) enclenque; (*argument*) endeble; (*attempt*) lastimoso, -a

pup [pʌp] **I.** *n* **1.** (*baby dog*) cachorro, -a *m, f;* **to be in ~** estar preñada **2.** (*baby animal*) cría *f* ►**to sell sb a ~** dar gato por liebre a alguien **II.** *vi* <-pp-> parir

pupa ['pju:pə] <pupas *o* pupae> *n* BIO crisálida *f,* pupa *f*

pupate ['pju:peɪt] *vi* BIO convertirse en crisálida

pupil¹ ['pju:pl] *n* SCHOOL alumno, -a *m, f*

pupil² ['pju:pl] *n* ANAT pupila *f*

puppet ['pʌpɪt] *n a. fig* títere *m;* **glove ~** muñeco *m* de guiñol

puppeteer [pʌpɪ'tɪəʳ, *Am:* -ə'tɪr] *n* titiritero, -a *m, f*

puppet government *n pej* gobierno *m* títere **puppet show** *n* THEAT función *f* de marionetas

puppy ['pʌpi] <-ies> *n* cachorro, -a *m, f*

purchase ['pɜ:tʃəs, *Am:* 'pɜ:rtʃəs] **I.** *vt* **1.** *form* (*buy*) comprar, adquirir **2.** NAUT **to ~ the anchor** levar el ancla **II.** *n* **1.** (*act of buying*) compra *f,* adquisición *f;* **to make a ~** hacer una adquisición; **compulsory ~** *Brit* compra forzosa **2.** (*hold*) agarre *m;* **to get a ~ on sth** agarrarse a [*o* de] algo

purchase price *n* precio *m* de compra

purchaser *n* **1.** (*buyer*) comprador(a) *m(f)* **2.** (*at auction*) adjudicatario, -a *m, f*

purchase tax *n* impuesto *m* sobre las ventas

purchasing *n form* compras *fpl*

purchasing department *n* departamento *m* de compras **purchasing manager** *n* director(a) *m(f)* de compras **purchasing power** *n* poder *m* adquisitivo

pure [pjʊəʳ, *Am:* pjʊr] *adj* puro, -a; **~ air** aire *m* puro; **~ gold** oro *m* puro; **~ mathematics** matemáticas *fpl* puras; **~ and simple** simple y llano; **it was ~ accident** fue por pura casualidad; **to be ~ in heart** ser limpio de corazón

purebred ['pjʊəbred, *Am:* 'pjʊr-] **I.** *n* animal *m* de pura raza **II.** *adj* de pura raza; **a ~ horse** un purasangre

purée ['pjʊəreɪ, *Am:* pjʊ'reɪ] **I.** *vt* hacer puré de **II.** *n* puré *m*

purely ['pjʊəli, *Am:* 'pjʊrli] *adv* **1.** (*completely*) puramente; **~ by chance** por pura casualidad **2.** (*simply*) meramente; **~ and simply** simple y llanamente

purgative ['pɜ:gətɪv, *Am:* 'pɜ:rgət̬ɪv] **I.** *n* purga *f* **II.** *adj* MED purgante, purgativo, -a

purgatory ['pɜ:gətri, *Am:* 'pɜ:rgətɔ:ri] *n no pl* **1.** REL **Purgatory** Purgatorio *m;* **to be in Purgatory** estar en el Purgatorio **2.** *fig* (*unpleasant experience*) calvario *m;* **to go through ~** pasar las de Caín

purge ['pɜ:dʒ, *Am:* 'pɜ:rdʒ] **I.** *vt* **1.** MED, POL purgar; **to ~ a group of extremist elements** purgar a un grupo de elementos extremistas; **to ~ sb from a party** expulsar a alguien de un partido **2.** REL (*crime, sin*) expiar **II.** *n* MED, POL purga *f*

purification [ˌpjʊərɪfɪ'keɪʃən, *Am:* ˌpjʊrə-]

n no pl a. REL purificación *f;* (*of water*) depuración *f*

purify ['pjʊərɪfaɪ, *Am:* 'pjʊrə-] *vt* (*cleanse*) purificar; (*language, water*) depurar; REL (*soul, body*) limpiar; **to ~ oneself of sth** purificarse de algo

purist ['pjʊərɪst, *Am:* 'pjʊrɪst] *n* purista *mf*

puritan ['pjʊərɪtən, *Am:* 'pjʊrɪ-] *n a. fig* puritano, -a *m, f*

puritanical [ˌpjʊərɪ'tænɪkəl, *Am:* ˌpjʊrɪ'-] *adj* puritano, -a

Puritanism *n no pl* puritanismo *m*

purity ['pjʊərəti, *Am:* 'pjʊrɪṭi] *no pl n* pureza *f*

purl [pɜːl, *Am:* pɜːrl] **I.** *n* punto *m* al revés **II.** *adj* **~ stitch** punto *m* al revés **III.** *vt* hacer con puntos al revés; (*stitches*) hacer al revés; **knit one, ~ one** uno al derecho, otro al revés **IV.** *vi* tejer al revés

purloin [pɜː'lɔɪn, *Am:* pɚ'-] *vt form* hurtar

purple ['pɜːpl, *Am:* 'pɜːr-] **I.** *adj* (*reddish*) púrpura; (*bluish*) morado, -a; **to be ~ with rage** estar lívido de rabia **II.** *n* (*reddish*) púrpura *m;* (*bluish*) morado *m*

purport ['pɜːpət, *Am:* pɜːr'pɔːrt] **I.** *vi form* (*claim*) **to ~ to be sth** pretender ser algo **II.** *n* **1.** (*meaning*) sentido *m* **2.** (*purpose*) intención *f*

purpose ['pɜːpəs, *Am:* 'pɜːrpəs] *n* **1.** (*goal*) intención *f;* **for the ~** al efecto; **the sole ~ of sth** el único objetivo de algo; **I did that for a ~** por algo hice eso; **for that very ~** precisamente por eso; **for practical ~s** a efectos prácticos; **not to the ~** que no viene al caso; **to have a ~ in life** tener una meta en la vida; **for humanitarian ~s** con fines humanitarios; **for future ~s** para las necesidades futuras **2.** (*motivation*) (**strength of**) **~** resolución *f* **3.** (*use*) utilidad *f;* **to no ~** inútilmente; **to serve a ~** servir de algo; **what's the ~ of ...?** ¿para qué sirve...? ►**on** ~ a propósito

purpose-built [ˌpɜːpəs'bɪlt, *Am:* ˌpɜːr-] *adj* construido, -a al efecto

purposeful ['pɜːpəsfəl, *Am:* 'pɜːr-] *adj* **1.** (*determined*) decidido, -a **2.** (*meaningful*) con sentido **3.** (*intentional*) intencionado, -a

purposeless ['pɜːpəsləs, *Am:* 'pɜːrpəs-] *adj* **1.** (*aimless*) sin sentido; (*utterance, violence*) gratuito, -a **2.** (*useless*) inútil **3.** (*character, person*) irresoluto, -a

purposely ['pɜːpəsli, *Am:* 'pɜːr-] *adv* a propósito

purr [pɜːʳ, *Am:* pɜːr] **I.** *vi* (*cat*) ronronear; (*engine*) zumbar **II.** *n* (*of cat*) ronroneo *m;* (*of engine*) zumbido *m*

purse [pɜːs, *Am:* pɜːrs] **I.** *n* **1.** *Am* (*handbag*) bolso *m,* cartera *f AmL,* bolsa *f Méx* **2.** *Brit* (*wallet*) monedero *m* **3.** (*funds*) **public ~** erario *m* público; **to be beyond one's ~** estar fuera de las posibilidades de uno **4.** (*prize*) premio *m* en efectivo **II.** *vt* (*lips*) apretar

purser ['pɜːsəʳ, *Am:* 'pɜːrsɚ] *n* NAUT contable *mf* de navío

purse strings *npl fig* **to hold the ~** administrar el dinero; **to loosen the ~** aflojar la bolsa

pursuance [pə'sjuːənts, *Am:* pɚ'suː-] *n no pl, form* ejecución *f;* **in ~ of sth** (*in accordance with*) de conformidad con algo; **in ~ of her duty** en cumplimiento de su deber

pursuant [pə'sjuːənt, *Am:* pɚ'suː-] *adv* LAW **~ to** conforme a, de acuerdo con

pursue [pə'sjuː, *Am:* pɚ'suː] *vt* **1.** (*chase*) perseguir **2.** (*seek to find*) buscar; (*dreams, goals*) luchar por; (*rights, peace*) reivindicar **3.** (*follow: plan*) seguir; **to ~ a matter** seguir un caso **4. to ~ a career** dedicarse a una carrera profesional; **to ~ a degree in sth** seguir estudios de algo

pursuer [pə'sjuːəʳ, *Am:* pɚ'suːɚ] *n* perseguidor(a) *m(f)*

pursuit [pə'sjuːt, *Am:* pɚ'suːt] *n* **1.** (*chase*) persecución *f;* **to be in ~ of sth** ir tras algo; (*knowledge, happiness*) ir en busca de algo; (*hunt*) ir a la caza de algo; **to be in hot ~ of sb** pisar los talones a alguien *fig* **2.** (*activity*) actividad *f;* **leisure ~s** pasatiempos *mpl;* **outdoor ~s** actividades al aire libre

purulent ['pjʊərələnt, *Am:* 'pjʊrə-] *adj* purulento, -a

purvey [pə'veɪ, *Am:* pɚ'-] *vt* proveer, suministrar; **to ~ sth to sb** proveer a alguien de algo

purveyor [pə'veɪəʳ, *Am:* pɚ'veɪɚ] *n* ECON proveedor(a) *m(f)*

pus [pʌs] *n* MED *no pl* pus *m,* postema *f Méx*

push [pʊʃ] **I.** *vt* **1.** (*shove*) empujar; **to ~ one's way through sth** abrirse paso a empujones por algo; **to ~ sth to the back of one's mind** intentar no pensar en algo; **to ~ the door open** abrir la puerta de un empujón; **to ~ sb out of sth** echar a alguien de algo a empujones; **to ~ sb out of the way** apartar a alguien a empujones **2.** (*force*) **to ~ one's luck** tentar a la suerte; **to ~ sb too far** sacar a alguien de quicio **3.** (*coerce*) obligar; **to ~ sb to do** [*o* **into doing**] **sth** presionar a alguien para que haga algo; **to ~ oneself** exigirse demasiado; **don't ~ yourself!** *iron* ¡no trabajes tanto! **4.** (*insist*) insistir en; **to ~ sb for sth** apremiar a alguien para algo **5.** (*press: button*) apretar; (*accelerator*) pisar; **to ~ the doorbell** tocar el timbre **6.** (*find sth difficult*) **to be** (**hard**) **~ed to do sth** tener dificultad para hacer algo **7.** (*be short of*) **to be ~ed for money/time** andar escaso de dinero/tiempo **8.** *inf* (*promote*) promover; ECON fomentar **9. to be ~ing 30** rondar los 30 años **II.** *vi* **1.** (*force movement*) empujar **2.** (*press*) apretar **3.** (*insist*) presionar; **to ~ for sth** presionar para (conseguir) algo **III.** <-es> *n* **1.** (*shove*) empujón *m;* (*slight push*) empujoncito *m;* **to give sb a ~** *fig* dar un empujón a alguien; **she got the ~** *inf* (*from boyfriend*) su novio la dejó; (*from employer*) la echaron del trabajo; **to give sb the ~** *inf* (*break up with*) dejar a alguien; (*fire*) echar a alguien **2.** (*press*) **at the ~**

of a button apretando un botón **3.** (*strong action*) impulso *m;* (*will to succeed*) empuje *m* **4.** (*strong effort*) esfuerzo *m;* **to make a ~ for sth** hacer un esfuerzo para algo; **at a ~ ...** si me apuras... **5.** (*publicity*) campaña *f;* **to make a ~** hacer una campaña **6.** MIL (*military attack*) ofensiva *f* ►**if/when ~ comes to shove** en caso de apuro

◆**push along** *vi inf* largarse

◆**push around** *vt* mangonear *inf*

◆**push away** *vt* apartar

◆**push back** *vt* (*move backwards*) hacer retroceder; (*person*) empujar hacia atrás; (*hair*) echar hacia atrás

◆**push down** *vt* **1.** (*knock down*) derribar **2.** (*press down*) apretar **3.** ECON (*price, interest rate*) hacer bajar

◆**push forward** **I.** *vt* **1.** (*force forward*) empujar hacia adelante **2.** (*promote*) promocionar **3.** (*call attention to oneself*) **to push oneself forward** hacerse valer **II.** *vi* **1.** (*advance*) avanzar **2.** (*continue*) **to ~ (with sth)** seguir (con algo)

◆**push in** **I.** *vt* **1.** (*nail*) empujar (hacia adentro) **2.** (*force in*) **to push one's way in** colarse *inf* **II.** *vi* (*force way in*) entrar a empujones

◆**push off** **I.** *vi inf* largarse **II.** *vt* NAUT (*boat*) desatracar

◆**push on** **I.** *vi* **1.** (*continue despite problems*) **to ~ (with sth)** seguir adelante (con algo) **2.** (*continue travelling*) **we pushed on to Madrid** seguimos hasta Madrid **II.** *vt* **1.** (*activate*) apresurar **2.** (*press*) **to push sb on to do sth** empujar a alguien a hacer algo

◆**push out** *vt* **1.** (*force out*) **to push sb out (of sth)** echar a alguien (de algo) **2.** (*get rid of*) eliminar; **to push competitors out of the market** eliminar a los competidores del mercado **3.** (*produce: roots, blossoms*) echar **4.** NAUT (*boat*) echar al agua

◆**push over** *vt always sep* (*thing*) volcar; (*person*) hacer caer

◆**push through** **I.** *vi* abrirse paso entre **II.** *vt* **1.** (*legislation, proposal*) hacer aceptar **2.** (*help to succeed*) llevar a buen término

◆**push up** *vt* **1.** (*move higher*) levantar; *fig* (*help*) dar un empujón **2.** (*price, interest rate*) hacer subir

pushbike ['pʊʃbaɪk] *n Aus, Brit, inf* bici *f*

push-button ['pʊʃˌbʌtən] **I.** *adj* de botones **II.** *n* botón *m* **push-button telephone** *n* teléfono *m* de botones

pushcart ['pʊʃkɑːt, *Am:* -kɑːrt] *n* carretilla *f* de mano

pushchair ['pʊʃtʃeəʳ, *Am:* -tʃer] *n Brit* sillita *f* de paseo

pusher *n inf* camello *mf*

pushover ['pʊʃəʊvəʳ, *Am:* -ˌoʊvɚ] *n* **1.** (*easy success*) **to be a ~** ser pan comido **2.** (*easily influenced*) **to be a ~** ser muy fácil de convencer

pushpin ['pʊʃpɪn] *n Am* chincheta *f*

push start **I.** *vi* arrancar empujando el coche **II.** *n* **to give sb a ~** ayudar a alguien a arrancar empujando el coche

push-up ['pʊʃʌp] *n* SPORTS flexión *f;* **to do ~s** hacer flexiones

pushy ['pʊʃi] *adj pej* **1.** (*ambitious*) ambicioso, -a **2.** (*arrogant*) prepotente

puss [pʊs] <-es> *n* (*cat*) minino, -a *m, f;* **Puss in Boots** el gato con botas

pussy ['pʊsi] <-ies> *n* **1.** (*cat*) **~ (cat)** minino, -a *m, f* **2.** *no pl, vulg* conejo *m,* concha *f AmL*

pussyfoot ['pʊsifʊt] *vi inf* **to ~ around an issue** dar largas a un asunto

pussy willow *n* sauce *m* blanco

pustule ['pʌstjuːl, *Am:* -tʃuːl] *n* pústula *f*

put [pʊt] <-tt-, put, put> **I.** *vt* **1.** (*place*) poner; (*in box, hole*) meter; **~ the spoons next to the knives** coloca las cucharas junto a los cuchillos; **to ~ sth to one's lips** llevarse algo a los labios; **~ it there!** (*shake hands*) ¡chócala!; **to ~ sth in the oven** meter algo en el horno **2.** (*add*) echar; **to ~ sugar/salt in sth** echar azúcar/sal a algo; **to ~ the date on sth** poner la fecha en algo; **to ~ sth on a list** apuntar algo en una lista; **to ~ sth in writing** poner algo por escrito **3.** (*direct*) **to ~ the blame on sb** echar la culpa a alguien; **to ~ pressure on sb** presionar a alguien; **to ~ a spell on sb** echar una maldición a alguien; **to ~ one's heart into sth** poner todo el afán de uno en algo; **to ~ one's mind to sth** poner los cinco sentidos en algo; **to ~ one's trust in sb** depositar la confianza de uno en alguien **4.** (*invest*) **to ~ sth into sth** invertir algo en algo; **to ~ energy/time into sth** dedicar energía/tiempo a algo **5.** (*bet*) apostar; **to ~ money on sth** jugarse dinero a algo; **to ~ sth toward sth** contribuir con algo para algo **6.** (*cause to be*) **to ~ sb in a good mood** poner a alguien de buen humor; **to ~ sb in danger** poner a alguien en peligro; **to ~ oneself in sb's place/shoes** ponerse en el lugar de alguien; **to ~ sb in prison** meter a alguien en la cárcel; **to ~ into practice** poner en práctica; **to ~ sb on the train** acompañar a alguien hasta el tren; **to ~ sth right** arreglar algo; **to ~ sb straight** poner a alguien en el buen camino; **to ~ sb to bed** acostar a alguien; **to ~ to death** ejecutar; **to ~ sth to good use** hacer buen uso de algo; **to ~ to shame** avergonzar; **to ~ sb to trouble** causar molestias a alguien; **to ~ sb under oath** tomar juramento a alguien; **to ~ sb in mind of sth** recordar algo a alguien; **to ~ sb to expense** ocasionar gastos a alguien; **to ~ to flight** poner en fuga; **to ~ a stop to sth** poner fin a algo; **to ~ sb to work** poner a alguien a trabajar **7.** (*impose*) **to ~ an idea in sb's head** meter una idea en la cabeza a alguien; **to ~ a tax on sth** gravar algo con un impuesto **8.** (*attribute*) **to ~ a high value on sth** valorar mucho algo **9.** (*present*) **to ~ one's point of view** exponer el punto de vista de uno; **to ~ a question** plantear una pregunta;

P

to ~ **sth to discussion** someter algo a debate; **to ~ sth to the vote** someter algo a votación; **to ~ a proposal before a committee** presentar una propuesta ante un comité; **I ~ it to you that…** mi opinión es que… **10.** (*express*) decir; **as John ~ it** como dijo John; **to ~ one's feelings into words** expresar sus sentimientos con palabras; **to ~ sth into Spanish** traducir algo al español **11.** (*judge*) **I ~ the number of visitors at 2,000** calculo que debe haber recibido unos 2.000 visitantes; **I'd ~ her at about 35** calculo que tiene unos 35 años; **to ~ sb on a level with sb** poner a alguien al mismo nivel que alguien **12.** SPORTS (*throw*) **to ~ the shot** lanzar el peso **II.** *vi* NAUT **to ~ to sea** zarpar

◆**put about** *irr* **I.** <-tt-> *vt* **1.** (*spread: rumour*) hacer circular; **to put it about that…** hacer correr la voz que… **2.** *inf* (*be promiscuous*) **to put it about** mariposear **3.** NAUT hacer virar **II.** *vi* NAUT virar

◆**put across** <-tt-> *irr vt* (*make understood*) comunicar; **to put sth across to sb** hacer entender algo a alguien; **to put oneself across well** causar buena impresión

◆**put aside** <-tt-> *irr vt* **1.** (*place to one side*) dejar a un lado **2.** (*save*) ahorrar; (*time*) reservar **3.** (*give up*) **to put sth aside** dejar algo **4.** (*reject*) rechazar **5.** (*ignore: fears, differences*) dejar de lado

◆**put away** <-tt-> *irr vt* **1.** (*save*) ahorrar **2.** *inf* (*eat a lot*) zamparse **3.** (*remove*) guardar **4.** *inf* (*imprison*) **to put sb away** encerrar a alguien **5.** *inf* (*kill*) matar

◆**put back** <-tt-> *irr vt* **1.** (*return*) volver a poner en su sitio **2.** (*postpone*) posponer **3.** SCHOOL (*not progress*) **to put sb back a year** hacer repetir curso a alguien **4.** (*set earlier: watch*) atrasar

◆**put by** <-tt-> *irr vt* ahorrar

◆**put down** <-tt-> *irr vt* **1.** (*set down*) dejar; **not to be able to put a book down** no poder parar de leer un libro; **to ~ the (tele)phone** colgar el teléfono **2.** (*lower*) bajar; **to put one's arm/feet down** bajar el brazo/los pies; **to put sb down somewhere** dejar a alguien en un sitio **3.** (*attribute*) **to put sth down to sb** atribuir algo a alguien **4.** (*write*) escribir; **to put sth down on paper** poner algo por escrito **5.** (*assess*) catalogar; **I put her down as 30** le echo 30 años **6.** (*register*) **to put sb down for sth** inscribir a alguien en algo **7.** FIN (*prices*) disminuir **8.** ECON (*leave as deposit*) dejar en depósito **9.** (*stop: rebellion, opposition*) reprimir **10.** *inf* (*humiliate*) menospreciar **11.** (*have killed: animal*) sacrificar

◆**put forward** <-tt-> *irr vt* **1.** (*offer for discussion: subject*) proponer; (*idea, plan*) exponer; (*suggestion*) hacer; **to ~ a proposal** hacer una propuesta **2.** (*advance: event*) adelantar; **to put the clock forward** adelantar el reloj

◆**put in** <-tt-> *irr* **I.** *vt* **1.** (*place inside*) meter **2.** (*add*) poner; **to ~ a comma/a full stop** añadir una coma/un punto **3.** (*say*) decir; (*remark*) hacer; **to put a word in** intervenir en la conversación **4.** AGR (*plant: vegetables*) plantar; (*seeds*) sembrar **5.** TECH (*install*) instalar; **to ~ a shower** poner una ducha **6.** POL (*candidate, party*) elegir **7.** (*invest: money*) poner; (*time*) dedicar; **to ~ a lot of effort on sth** dedicar muchos esfuerzos a algo; **to ~ overtime** hacer horas extras **8.** (*direct*) **to put one's faith in sb** tener fe en alguien; **to put one's hope in sb** poner las esperanzas de uno en alguien **9.** (*submit: claim, request*) presentar; (*candidate*) presentarse; **to put oneself in for sth** inscribirse para algo **10.** (*make*) **to ~ an appearance** hacer acto de presencia **II.** *vi* **1.** (*apply*) **to ~ for sth** solicitar algo **2.** NAUT (*dock*) hacer escala

◆**put into** <-tt-> *irr vt* **1.** (*place inside*) meter **2.** **to put sth into sth** (*add*) añadir algo a algo; GASTR echar algo a algo; (*include*) incluir algo en algo **3.** (*dress in*) **to put sb into sth** vestir a alguien de algo **4.** TECH (*install*) instalar **5.** FIN (*deposit*) **to put money into a bank** ingresar dinero en un banco **6.** (*invest*) **to put sth into sth** (*money*) invertir algo en algo; (*time, effort*) dedicar algo a algo **7.** (*cause to be*) **to put a plan into operation** poner un plan en marcha **8.** (*institutionalize*) **to put sb into sth** meter a alguien en algo; **to put sb into prison** mandar a alguien a la cárcel

◆**put off** <-tt-> *irr vt* **1.** (*turn off*) apagar **2.** (*drop off: passenger*) dejar **3.** (*delay*) posponer; **to put sth off for a week** aplazar algo una semana **4.** (*make wait*) entretener; **to put sb off with excuses** dar largas a alguien *inf* **5.** (*repel*) alejar; (*food, smell*) dar asco a **6.** (*discourage*) desanimar; **to put sb off sth** disuadir a alguien de algo; **to put sb off sb** hacer que alguien le coja antipatía a alguien **7.** (*disconcert*) desconcertar **8.** (*distract*) distraer; **to put sb off sth** distraer a alguien de algo; **to put sb off their stride** *fig* hacer perder el hilo a alguien; **to put sb off the scent** despistar a alguien

◆**put on** <-tt-> *irr vt* **1.** (*place upon*) **to put sth on sth** poner algo sobre algo **2.** (*attach*) **to put sth on sth** poner algo a algo **3.** (*wear*) ponerse; **to ~ make-up** maquillarse **4.** (*turn on*) encender; **to ~ Mozart** poner música de Mozart **5.** (*use*) **to ~ the brakes** frenar; **to put the handbrake on** poner el freno de mano **6.** (*perform: film*) dar; (*show*) presentar; THEAT poner en escena **7.** (*provide: dish*) servir; **to ~ a party** dar una fiesta **8.** (*assume: expression*) adoptar; **to ~ a frown** fruncir el ceño; **to ~ airs** darse tono **9.** (*pretend*) fingir; (*accent*) afectar **10.** (*be joking with*) **to put sb on** tomar el pelo a alguien **11.** (*gain: weight*) engordar; **to ~ 10 years** envejecer 10 años **12.** (*water, soup*) calentar **13.** TEL **to put sb on the (tele)phone** pasar el teléfono a alguien; **to put sb on to sb** poner a alguien con alguien;

I'll put him on le paso con él 14. (*inform*) **to put sb on to sb** hablar a alguien de alguien; **to put sb on to sth** dar a alguien información sobre algo

◆**put out** <-tt-> *irr* I. *vt* 1. (*take outside*) **to put the dog out** sacar al perro 2. (*extend*) extender; **to ~ one's hand** tender la mano; **to ~ one's tongue** sacar la lengua 3. (*extinguish: fire*) extinguir; **to ~ a cigarette** apagar un cigarrillo 4. (*turn off*) apagar 5. (*eject*) expulsar; (*dismiss*) echar 6. (*publish, issue*) publicar; (*announcement*) hacer público 7. (*produce industrially*) producir 8. (*sprout: leaves*) echar 9. (*contract out*) subcontratar; **to put sth out to a company** subcontratar algo con una empresa 10. (*inconvenience*) molestar a; **to put oneself out for sb** molestarse por alguien 11. (*offend*) ofender 12. (*dislocate*) dislocar, zafar *AmL;* **to ~ one's shoulder** dislocarse [*o* zafarse *AmL*] el hombro 13. (*make unconscious*) dejar sin sentido; MED anestesiar 14. NAUT botar II. *vi* NAUT zarpar

◆**put over** <-tt-> *irr vt* 1. (*place higher*) **to put sth over sth** poner algo por encima de algo 2. (*make understood: idea, plan*) comunicar 3. (*fool*) **to put sth over on sb** engañar a alguien

◆**put through** <-tt-> *irr vt* 1. (*insert through*) **to put sth through sth** hacer pasar algo por algo 2. (*process with: proposal*) hacer aceptar; (*bill*) hacer aprobar 3. (*send*) mandar; **to put sb through college** mandar a alguien a la universidad 4. TEL poner; **to ~ a telephone call to Paris** poner una conferencia a París; **to put a call through** pasar una llamada; **to put sb through** (**to sb**) pasar a alguien (con alguien) 5. (*implement*) llevar a cabo 6. (*make endure*) **to put sb through sth** someter a alguien a algo; **to put sb through it** hacer pasar un mal rato a alguien

◆**put together** <-tt-> *irr vt* 1. (*join*) juntar; (*collection*) reunir; (*assemble*) ensamblar; (*machine, model, radio*) montar; (*pieces*) acoplar 2. (*connect: facts, clues*) relacionar 3. (*create*) crear; (*list*) hacer; (*team*) formar; (*meal*) preparar; (*dress*) confeccionar 4. MAT sumar

◆**put up** <-tt-> *irr* I. *vt* 1. (*hang up*) colgar; (*notice*) fijar 2. (*raise*) levantar; (*one's collar*) subirse; (*flag*) izar; **to put one's hair up** recogerse el pelo 3. (*umbrella*) abrir 4. (*build*) construir; (*tent*) armar 5. (*increase: prices*) subir 6. (*make available*) **to put sth up for sale** poner algo en venta; **to put sth up for auction** sacar algo a subasta pública 7. (*give shelter*) alojar; **I can put you up for a week** te puedes quedar una semana en casa 8. (*provide: funds*) aportar; **to ~ the money for sth** poner el dinero para algo 9. (*show opposition*) **to ~ opposition** oponerse; **to ~ a struggle** poner resistencia 10. (*submit: candidate, proposal*) presentar II. *vi* alojarse; **to ~ at a hotel** hospedarse en un hotel; **to ~ at sb's place for the night** pasar la noche en casa de alguien

◆**put up with** <-tt-> *irr vt* soportar

putative ['pju:tətɪv, *Am:* -t̬ət̬ɪv] *adj form* (*reputed*) supuesto, -a; (*father*) putativo, -a

put-off *n Am, inf* aplazamiento *m;* **to give sb a ~** dar largas a alguien

put-on ['pʌtɒn, *Am:* -ɑ:n] *n Am, inf* burla *f;* (*joke*) broma *f*

put option *n* ECON opción *f* de venta

putrefaction [ˌpju:trɪ'fækʃən, *Am:* -trə'-] *n no pl, form* putrefacción *f*

putrefy ['pju:trɪfaɪ, *Am:* -trə-] <-ie-> *vi form* pudrirse

putrid ['pju:trɪd] *adj form* 1. (*decayed*) podrido, -a, putrefacto, -a; (*smell*) pútrido, -a 2. (*very bad*) pésimo, -a

putsch [pʊtʃ] <-tsches> *n* golpe *m* de estado

putt [pʌt] SPORTS I. *vi* tirar al hoyo II. *n* tiro *m* al hoyo, put *m AmL*

puttee ['pʌti, *Am:* pʌt'i:] *n* polaina *f*

putter[1] ['pʌtə^r, *Am:* 'pʌt̬ɚ] *n* (*golf club*) putter *m*

putter[2] ['pʌtə^r, *Am:* 'pʌt̬ɚ] *vi Am s.* **potter**

putty ['pʌti, *Am:* 'pʌt̬-] *n no pl* masilla *f* ►**to be like ~ in sb's hands** ser completamente manejable

putty knife <-knives> *n* espátula *f*

put-up *adj inf* **a ~ job** un asunto fraudulento

put-upon *adj inf* explotado, -a

puzzle ['pʌzl] I. *vt* dejar perplejo, -a II. *vi* **to ~ about sth** dar vueltas a algo III. *n* 1. (*game*) rompecabezas *m inv;* **jigsaw ~** puzzle *m;* **crossword ~** crucigrama *m* 2. (*mystery*) misterio *m*, enigma *m;* **to be a ~ to sb** ser un misterio para alguien; **to solve a ~** resolver un enigma

puzzled *adj* perplejo, -a; **to be ~ about sth** estar desconcertado por algo

puzzler ['pʌzlə^r, *Am:* -lɚ] *n* (*mystery*) enigma *m*

puzzling *adj* desconcertante

PVC [ˌpi:vi:'si:] *n abbr of* **polyvinyl chloride** PVC *m*

pygmy ['pɪgmi] I. *n* <-ies> 1. (*short person*) pigmeo, -a *m, f* 2. *fig* enano, -a *m, f* II. *adj* ZOOL enano, -a

pyjamas [pə'dʒɑ:məz] *npl Aus, Brit* pijama *m;* **in** (**one's**) **~** en pijama; **a pair of ~** un pijama

pylon ['paɪlɒn, *Am:* -lɑ:n] *n* ELEC torre *f* de alta tensión

pyramid ['pɪrəmɪd] *n* pirámide *f*

pyramid selling *n no pl* ECON, LAW venta *f* piramidal

pyre ['paɪə^r, *Am:* 'paɪɚ] *n* pira *f*

Pyrenees [pɪrə'ni:z] *npl* **the ~** los Pirineos

Pyrex® ['paɪəreks, *Am:* 'paɪ-] I. *n* pirex *m* II. *adj* de pirex

pyrites [ˌpaɪə'raɪti:z, *Am:* paɪ'-] <-tae> *n* pirita *f;* **iron ~** pirita de hierro

pyromania [ˌpaɪrəʊ'meɪnɪə, *Am:* ˌpaɪroʊ'-] *n no pl* piromanía *f*

pyrotechnic [ˌpaɪrəʊ'teknɪk, *Am:* ˌpaɪroʊ'-] *adj* **1.** pirotécnico, -a; ~ **display** fuegos pirotécnicos **2.** *fig* (*brilliant*) espectacular
python ['paɪθən, *Am:* -θɑːn] <-(ons)> *n* pitón *f*

Q

Q, q [kjuː] *n* Q, q *f;* ~ **for Queenie** *Brit,* ~ **for Queen** *Am* Q de Quebec
Q *abbr of* **Queen** reina *f*
Qatar [kə'tɑːʳ, *Am:* 'kɑːtɑːr] *n* Qatar *m*
QC [ˌkjuː'siː] *n Brit abbr of* **Queen's Counsel** *título de abogacía de categoría superior*
QED [ˌkjuːiː'diː] *abbr of* **quod erat demonstrandum** Q.E.D.
qtr *abbr of* **quarter** cuarto *m*
qua [kwɑː] *prep form* como
quack¹ [kwæk] **I.** *n* (*duck's sound*) graznido *m* **II.** *vi* graznar
quack² [kwæk] *pej* **I.** *n* **1.** (*unqualified doctor*) curandero, -a *m, f* **2.** *Aus, Brit, iron* (*doctor*) matasanos *m inv* **II.** *adj* falso, -a
quack-quack *n childspeak* cuac cuac *m*
quad [kwɒd, *Am:* kwɑːd] *n* **1.** *inf* (*quadruplet*) cuatrillizo, -a *m, f* **2.** (*quadrangle*) cuadrángulo *m*
quadrangle ['kwɒdræŋgl, *Am:* 'kwɑːdræŋ-] *n form* cuadrángulo *m*
quadrangular [kwɒ'dræŋgjʊləʳ, *Am:* kwɑː'dræŋgjələ˞] *adj* cuadrangular
quadrant ['kwɒdrənt, *Am:* 'kwɑːdrənt] *n* cuadrante *m*
quadraphonic [ˌkwɒdrə'fɒnɪk, *Am:* ˌkwɑːdrə'fɑːnɪk] *adj* MUS cuadrafónico, -a
quadratic [kwɒ'drætɪk, *Am:* kwɑː'dræt̬-] *adj* cuadrático, -a
quadrilateral [ˌkwɒdrɪ'lætərəl, *Am:* ˌkwɑːdrɪ'læt̬-] *n* cuadrilátero *m*
quadripartite ['kwɒdrɪ'pɑːtaɪt] *adj form* cuatripartito, -a
quadruped ['kwɒdrʊped, *Am:* 'kwɑːdrʊ-] *n* cuadrúpedo *m*
quadruple ['kwɒdruːpl, *Am:* 'kwɑːdruː-] **I.** *vt* cuadruplicar **II.** *vi* cuadruplicarse **III.** *adj* cuádruple
quadruplet ['kwɒdruːplət, *Am:* kwɑː'druːplɪt] *n* cuatrillizo, -a *m, f*
quaff [kwɒf, *Am:* kwɑːf] *vt liter* beber; **to ~ one's sorrows away** *fig* ahogar las penas
quagmire ['kwægmaɪəʳ, *Am:* -ə˞] *n* **1.** (*area*) cenagal *m* **2.** (*situation*) atolladero *m*
quail¹ [kweɪl] <-(s)> *n* (*bird*) codorniz *f*
quail² [kweɪl] *vi* (*feel fear*) acobardarse; **to ~ before sb/sth** acobardarse ante alguien/algo
quaint [kweɪnt] *adj* **1.** (*charming*) pintoresco, -a **2.** *pej* (*strange*) extraño, -a **3.** (*pleasantly unusual*) singular
quaintness ['kweɪntnɪs] *n no pl* lo pintoresco *m;* (*strangeness*) lo raro
quake [kweɪk] **I.** *n* **1.** (*shaking*) temblor *m* **2.** *inf* (*earthquake*) terremoto *m* **II.** *vi* **1.** (*move*) estremecerse **2.** (*shake*) temblar; **to ~ with cold/fear** temblar de frío/miedo; **to ~ at sth** temblar ante algo
Quaker ['kweɪkəʳ, *Am:* -kə˞] **I.** *n* Cuáquero, -a *m, f;* **the ~s** los Cuáqueros **II.** *adj* cuáquero, -a
qualification [ˌkwɒlɪfɪ'keɪʃən, *Am:* ˌkwɑːlɪ-] *n* **1.** (*document*) título *m;* (*exam*) calificación *f;* **academic ~** título académico; **her ~s are very good** está muy cualificada **2.** (*limiting criteria*) restricción *f;* (*condition*) reserva *f;* (*change*) matización *f;* **without ~** sin reservas **3.** SPORTS (*preliminary test*) clasificación *f*
qualified ['kwɒlɪfaɪd, *Am:* 'kwɑːlɪ-] *adj* **1.** (*trained*) titulado, -a; (*certified*) certificado, -a; (*by the state*) homologado, -a **2.** (*competent*) capacitado, -a **3.** (*limited*) limitado, -a; **to be a ~ success** tener cierto éxito
qualify ['kwɒlɪfaɪ, *Am:* 'kwɑːlɪ-] <-ie-> **I.** *vt* **1.** (*give credentials*) acreditar **2.** (*make eligible*) habilitar; **to ~ sb to do sth** dar derecho a alguien para hacer algo **3.** (*explain and limit*) limitar; **to ~ a remark** matizar un comentario **4.** LING (*modify*) calificar **II.** *vi* **1.** (*meet standards*) **to ~ for sth** estar habilitado para algo; (*be eligible*) tener derecho a algo; (*have qualifications*) estar acreditado para algo **2.** (*complete training*) titularse, recibirse *AmL* **3.** SPORTS clasificarse
qualifying ['kwɒlɪfaɪɪŋ, *Am:* 'kwɑːlɪ-] *adj* **1.** (*limiting*) matizador(a) **2.** SPORTS (*testing standard*) clasificatorio, -a; ~ **round** eliminatoria *f* **3.** LING (*modifying*) calificativo, -a
qualitative ['kwɒlɪtətɪv, *Am:* 'kwɑːlɪteɪt̬ɪv] *adj* cualitativo, -a; ~ **difference** diferencia cualitativa
quality ['kwɒləti, *Am:* 'kwɑːlət̬i] **I.** <-ies> *n* **1.** *no pl* (*degree of goodness*) calidad *f;* ~ **of life** calidad de vida **2.** (*characteristic*) cualidad *f;* **artistic ~** cualidades *fpl* artísticas **II.** *adj* de calidad
quality control *n* control *m* de calidad
quality time *n no pl* tiempo *m* para relacionarse
qualm [kwɑːm] *n* escrúpulo *m;* **to feel/have ~s (about sth)** sentir/tener escrúpulos (respecto a algo); **to have no ~s about doing sth** no tener escrúpulos para hacer algo; **without the slightest ~** sin el menor remordimiento
quandary ['kwɒndəri, *Am:* 'kwɑːn-] <-ies> *n* dilema *m;* **to be in a ~** estar en un dilema
quango ['kwæŋgəʊ, *Am:* -goʊ] *n Brit abbr of* **quasi-autonomous non-governmental organisation** *organismo no gubernamental semiautónomo*
quantifiable ['kwɒntɪfaɪəbl, *Am:* 'kwɑːnt̬ə-] *adj* cuantificable
quantification [ˌkwɒntɪfɪ'keɪʃən, *Am:* ˌkwɑːnt̬ə-] *n* cuantificación *f*
quantify ['kwɒntɪfaɪ, *Am:* 'kwɑːnt̬ə-]

<-ie-> *vt* cuantificar

quantitative ['kwɒntɪtətɪv, *Am:* 'kwɑːn-t̬əteɪt̬ɪv] *adj* cuantitativo, -a

quantity ['kwɒntəti, *Am:* 'kwɑːnt̬ət̬i] **I.** <-ies> *n* **1.** (*amount*) cantidad *f;* **a large/small ~ of sth** una gran/pequeña cantidad de algo **2.** (*large amounts*) cantidades *fpl;* **to buy in ~** comprar al por mayor **II.** *adj* en cantidad

quantity discount *n* descuento *m* por grandes cantidades **quantity surveyor** *n* *Brit* aparejador(a) *m(f)*

quantum ['kwɒntəm, *Am:* 'kwɑːnt̬əm] <quanta> *n* **1.** *form* (*quantity*) cuantía *f* **2.** PHYS (*unit of radient energy*) cuanto *m*

quantum mechanics *n + sing vb* mecánica *f* cuántica

quarantine ['kwɒrəntiːn, *Am:* 'kwɔːrən-] **I.** *n* cuarentena *f;* **to be/place under ~** estar/poner en cuarentena **II.** *vt* **to ~ sb/an animal** poner en cuarentena a alguien/a un animal

quark [kwɑːk, *Am:* kwɑːrk] *n* PHYS quark *m*

quarrel ['kwɒrəl, *Am:* 'kwɔːr-] **I.** *n* disputa *f;* **to patch up one's ~** arreglar los pleitos **II.** <-ll-> *vi* reñir, pelearse; **to ~ about sth** pelearse por algo

quarrelsome ['kwɒrəlsəm, *Am:* 'kwɔːr-] *adj* **1.** (*belligerent*) pendenciero, -a, peleonero, -a *Méx* **2.** (*grumbly*) enojadizo, -a, enojón, -ona *Méx*

quarry[1] ['kwɒri, *Am:* 'kwɔːr-] **I.** <-ies> *n* (*rock pit*) cantera *f* **II.** <-ie-> *vt* extraer

quarry[2] ['kwɒri, *Am:* 'kwɔːr-] <-ies> *n* presa *f*

quart [kwɔːt, *Am:* kwɔːrt] *n* cuarto *m* de galón

quarter ['kwɔːtəʳ, *Am:* 'kwɔːrt̬ɚ] **I.** *n* **1.** (*one fourth*) cuarto *m;* **three ~s** tres cuartos; **a ~ of the British** una cuarta parte de los británicos; **a ~ of a century/an hour** un cuarto de siglo/de hora; **a ~ to three** las tres menos cuarto, un cuarto para las tres *AmL;* **a ~ past three** las tres y cuarto **2.** *Am* (*25 cents*) un cuarto de dólar **3.** *a.* FIN, SCHOOL trimestre *m* **4.** (*neighbourhood*) barrio *m;* (*area*) zona *f;* **at close ~s** de cerca; **all ~s of the earth** en todos los confines de la tierra **5.** (*mercy*) cuartel *m;* **to give ~** dar cuartel; **to ask for ~** pedir cuartel **6.** *pl* (*unspecified group or person*) círculos *mpl;* **in certain ~s** en ciertos círculos; **in high ~s** en altas esferas **7.** (*area of compass*) cuadrante *m;* **from the north/west ~** desde el cuadrante norte/oeste **II.** *vt* **1.** (*cut into four*) cuartear; **to ~ sb** descuartizar a alguien **2.** (*give housing*) alojar; **to be ~ed with sb** estar alojado en casa de alguien; MIL acuartelar **III.** *adj* cuarto; **~ hour/pound** un cuarto de hora/libra

quarterback ['kwɔːtəbæk, *Am:* 'kwɔːrt̬ɚ-] *n* (*US football*) mariscal *mf* de campo

quarter-day *n Brit* día *m* de liquidación

quarterdeck *n* NAUT alcázar *m* **quarterfinal** *n* SPORTS cuarto *m* de final

quartering *n no pl* **1.** (*dividing into fourths*) corte *m* en cuatro **2.** MIL (*housing*) acuartelamiento *m* **3.** (*emblems on shield*) cuartel *m*

quarterly ['kwɔːtəli, *Am:* 'kwɔːrt̬ɚli] **I.** *adv* trimestralmente **II.** *adj* trimestral

quartermaster ['kwɔːtəˌmɑːstəʳ, *Am:* 'kwɔːrt̬ɚˌmæstɚ] *n* **1.** MIL oficial *m* de intendencia **2.** NAUT cabo *mf* de la marina **quarter-tone** *n* MUS cuarto *m* de tono

quartet *n,* **quartette** [kwɔː'tet, *Am:* kwɔːr-] *n* MUS cuarteto *m*

quartz [kwɔːts, *Am:* kwɔːrts] **I.** *n no pl* cuarzo *m* **II.** *adj* de cuarzo; **~ crystal** cristal de cuarzo

quartz clock *n* reloj *m* de cuarzo

quartz (iodine) lamp *n* lámpara *f* de cuarzo

quasar ['kweɪzɑːʳ, *Am:* -zɑːr] *n* quásar *m*

quash [kwɒʃ, *Am:* kwɑːʃ] *vt* **1.** (*supress*) suprimir; (*rebellion*) sofocar; (*rumour*) acallar; **to ~ sb's dreams/plans** aplastar los sueños/planes de alguien **2.** LAW (*annul: conviction, verdict, sentence*) anular; (*indictment, decision*) invalidar; (*law, bill, writ*) derogar

quasi- ['kwɑːsi, *Am:* 'kweɪsaɪ] cuasi

quatrain ['kwɒtreɪn, *Am:* 'kwɑːtreɪn] *n* LIT cuarteto *m*

quaver ['kweɪvəʳ, *Am:* -vɚ] **I.** *vi* temblar **II.** *n* **1.** (*shake*) temblor *m;* **with a ~ in one's voice** con voz trémula **2.** *Aus, Brit* MUS corchea *f*

quay [kiː] *n* muelle *m*

queasy ['kwiːzi] <-ier, -iest> *adj* **1.** (*nauseous*) mareado, -a; **to have a ~ feeling** sentir náuseas **2.** *fig* (*unsettled*) intranquilo, -a; **with a ~ conscience** con la conciencia intranquila; **to feel ~ about sth** sentir desasosiego acerca de algo

Quebec [kwɪ'bek, *Am:* kwiː'bek] *n* Quebec *m*

queen [kwiːn] **I.** *n* **1.** (*monarch*) reina *f;* **~ of hearts/diamonds** (*cards*) reina de corazones/diamantes **2.** *pej* (*gay man*) loca *f;* **drag ~** drag queen *f* **II.** *vt* **1.** (*make queen*) **to ~ sb** coronar reina a alguien **2.** (*in chess*) coronar

queen bee *n* **1.** ZOOL abeja *f* reina **2.** *pej* (*bossy woman*) mandamás *f inv* **queen dowager** *n* reina *f* viuda

queenly ['kwiːnli] <-ier, iest> *adj* regia

Queen Mother *n* Reina *f* Madre **Queen's Counsel** *n Brit* LAW *título de abogacía de categoría superior* **Queen's English** *n no pl, Brit* inglés *m* correcto; **to speak ~** hablar correctamente

queer [kwɪəʳ, *Am:* kwɪr] **I.** <-er, -est> *adj* **1.** (*strange*) extraño, -a; **to have ~ ideas** tener ideas raras; **to feel rather ~** sentirse algo extraño; **to be a ~ fish** ser un bicho raro; **to be ~ in the head** estar medio loco **2.** *pej, inf* (*homosexual*) maricón **II.** *n pej, inf* maricón *m* **III.** *vt* **to ~ sb's pitch** *Aus, Brit, inf* estropear los planes de alguien

quell [kwel] *vt* (*unrest, rebellion, protest*) sofocar; (*doubts, fears, anxieties*) disipar; **to ~ sb's anger** calmar la rabia de alguien

quench [kwentʃ] *vt* **1.** (*satisfy*) satisfacer; (*thirst*) saciar; **to ~ sb's thirst for knowledge**

fig saciar la curiosidad de alguien **2.** (*put out*) sofocar; **to ~ the fire** apagar el incendio **3.** (*supress*) suprimir; **to ~ sb's desire** apagar el deseo de alguien; **to ~ sb's enthusiasm** contener el entusiasmo de alguien

querulous ['kwerʊləs, *Am:* 'kwerjə-] *adj* (*person*) quejoso, -a; (*voice*) quejumbroso, -a

query ['kwɪəri, *Am:* 'kwɪri] **I.** <-ies> *n* pregunta *f;* **to have a ~ for sb** tener una pregunta para alguien; **to raise a ~** plantear un interrogante; **to settle a ~** resolver un interrogante **II.** <-ie-> *vt* **1.** *form* (*dispute*) cuestionar; (*doubt*) poner en duda **2.** (*ask*) preguntar; **to ~ whether ...** preguntar si...

quest [kwest] *n* búsqueda *f;* **in ~ of sth/sb** en busca de algo/alguien; **the ~ for truth** la búsqueda de la verdad

question ['kwestʃən] **I.** *n* **1.** (*inquiry*) pregunta *f;* **frequently asked ~s** *a.* INFOR preguntas frecuentes; **to put a ~ to sb** hacer una pregunta a alguien; **to pop the ~ to sb** proponer matrimonio a alguien, declarárse a alguien *Méx* **2.** *no pl* (*doubt*) duda *f;* **without ~** sin duda; **to be beyond ~** estar fuera de duda **3.** (*issue*) cuestión *f;* **it's a ~ of life or death** *a. fig* es un asunto de vida o muerte; **to be a ~ of time/money** ser una cuestión de tiempo/dinero; **to raise a ~** plantear un problema; **to be out of the ~** ser totalmente imposible; **there's no ~ of sb doing sth** sería imposible que alguien hiciera algo **4.** SCHOOL, UNIV (*test problem*) pregunta *f;* **to do a ~** resolver una pregunta **II.** *vt* **1.** (*ask*) preguntar **2.** (*interrogate*) interrogar **3.** (*doubt*) cuestionar; (*facts, findings*) poner en duda

questionable ['kwestʃənəbl] *adj* discutible

questioner *n* interrogador(a) *m(f)*

questioning I. *n no pl* interrogatorio *m;* **to be taken in for ~** ser detenido para ser interrogado **II.** *adj* inquisidor(a); **to have a ~ mind** ser inquisitivo

question mark *n* signo *m* de interrogación; **a ~ hangs over sth** *fig* un interrogante se cierne sobre algo

question master *n Brit* presentador(a) *m(f)*

questionnaire [ˌkwestʃə'neəʳ, *Am:* ˌkwestʃə'ner] *n* cuestionario *m*

question time *n Brit* POL turno *m* de preguntas

queue [kju:] **I.** *n Aus, Brit a.* INFOR cola *f;* (*in traffic*) retención *f,* congestionamiento *m Méx;* **to be in a ~ for sth** estar en la cola para algo; **to join a ~** ponerse en la cola; **to stand in a ~** hacer cola **II.** *vi* hacer cola

quibble ['kwɪbl] **I.** *n* **1.** (*petty argument*) pega *f;* **a ~ over sth** una objeción acerca de algo **2.** (*criticism*) sutileza *f* **II.** *vi* poner peros a; **to ~ over sth** quejarse por algo

quibbler ['kwɪbləʳ, *Am:* -lɚ] *n* polemizador(a) *m(f)*

quibbling ['kwɪblɪŋ] **I.** *n no pl* sutilezas *fpl* **II.** *adj* quisquilloso, -a

quiche [ki:ʃ] *n* quiche *f,* quiche *m AmL*

quick [kwɪk] **I.** <-er, -est> *adj* **1.** (*fast*) rápido, -a, veloz; **~ as lightning** (veloz) como un rayo; **in ~ succession** uno detrás del otro; **to be ~ to do sth** hacer algo con rapidez; **to have a ~ one** tomarse una copa rápida; **to have a ~ meal** hacer una comida rápida **2.** (*short*) corto, -a; **the ~est way** el camino más corto; **to give sb a ~ call** hacer una llamada corta a alguien **3.** (*hurried*) apresurado, -a; **to say a ~ good-bye/hello** decir un adiós/hola apresurado **4.** (*smart*) vivo, -a; **~ thinking** pensamiento ágil; **to have a ~ mind** tener una mente vivaz; **to have a ~ temper** tener mal genio **II.** <-er, -est> *adv* rápidamente; **~!** ¡rápido!; **as ~ as possible** tan pronto como sea posible; **to get rich ~** enriquecerse rápidamente **III.** *n* **1.** carne *f* viva; **to bite/cut nails to the ~** dejar las uñas en carne viva **2.** *pl, form* **the ~ and the dead** los vivos y los muertos ►**to** <u>**cut**</u> **sb to the ~** herir a alguien en lo más vivo

quick-acting [ˌkwɪk'æktɪŋ] *adj* de efecto rápido; **to be ~** actuar rápidamente **quick-change artist** *n* transformista *mf*

quicken ['kwɪkən] **I.** *vt* **1.** (*make faster*) apresurar; **to ~ the pace** acelerar el paso **2.** (*awaken*) estimular **II.** *vi* **1.** (*increase speed*) apresurarse **2.** (*become more active*) avivarse

quick-freeze ['kwɪkfri:z] *vt irr* congelar rápidamente

quickie ['kwɪki] *n* **1.** *inf* (*fast thing*) cosa *f* rápida **2.** *inf* (*fast drink*) copa *f* rápida **3.** *inf* (*quick sex*) quiqui *m,* palito *m Méx*

quickly ['kwɪkli] *adv* rápidamente

quickness ['kwɪknɪs] *n no pl* **1.** (*speed*) rapidez *f;* **~ of temper** mal carácter *m* **2.** (*liveliness*) viveza *f;* **~ of mind** mente *f* rápida

quicksand ['kwɪksænd] *n no pl* arenas *fpl* movedizas; **moral ~** *fig* moral *f* escabrosa **quicksilver** *n no pl s.* **mercury** mercurio *m* **quickstep** *n no pl* quickstep *m* (*baile formal a ritmo rápido*) **quick-tempered** *adj* irascible **quick-witted** *adj* perspicaz; **a ~ reply** una respuesta aguda

quid¹ [kwɪd] *inv n Brit, inf* (*money*) libra *f;* **to be ~s in** estar forrado

quid² [kwɪd] *n inf* (*tobacco*) mascada *f* de tabaco

quid pro quo ['kwɪdprəʊ'kwəʊ, *Am:* -proʊ'kwoʊ] *n form* compensación *f*

quiescent [kwɪ'esnt, *Am:* kwaɪ'-] *adj form* inactivo, -a

quiet ['kwaɪət] **I.** *n no pl* **1.** (*silence*) silencio *m* **2.** (*lack of activity*) sosiego *m;* **peace and ~** paz y tranquilidad; **on the ~** a escondidas **II.** <-er, -est> *adj* **1.** (*not loud*) silencioso, -a; **to speak in a ~ voice** hablar en voz baja **2.** (*not talkative*) callado, -a; **to keep ~** mantenerse callado **3.** (*secret*) secreto, -a; **to have a ~ word with sb** hablar en privado con alguien; **to keep ~ about sth** mantenerse callado respecto de algo **4.** (*unostentatious*) discreto, -a **5.** (*unexciting*) tranquilo, -a

quieten ['kwaɪətn] **I.** *vi* **1.** (*quiet*) callarse **2.** (*calm*) calmarse **II.** *vt* **1.** (*make quiet*) hacer callar **2.** (*calm*) calmar

◆quieten down **I.** *vi* **1.** (*quiet*) callarse **2.** (*calm*) calmarse **II.** *vt* **1.** (*silence*) hacer callar **2.** (*calm* (*down*)) calmar

quietly ['kwaɪətli] *adv* **1.** (*not loudly*) silenciosamente; **to speak ~** hablar en voz baja **2.** (*speaking*) calladamente **3.** (*peacefully*) calmadamente

quietness ['kwaɪətnɪs] *n no pl* tranquilidad *f*

quietude ['kwaɪɪtju:d, *Am:* 'kwaɪətu:d] *n no pl, form* quietud *f*

quiff [kwɪf] *n* copete *m,* gallo *m Méx*

quill [kwɪl] *n* **1.** (*feather, pen*) pluma *f; liter* (*pen*) cálamo *m* **2.** (*porcupine*) púa *f*

quilt [kwɪlt] **I.** *n* edredón *m* **II.** *vt* acolchar

quin [kwɪn] *n Brit abbr of* **quintuplet** quintillizo, -a *m, f*

quince [kwɪns] *n no pl* membrillo *m*

quinine [kwɪ'ni:n, *Am:* 'kwaɪnaɪn] *n no pl* quinina *f*

quintessence [kwɪn'tesns] *n no pl* quintaesencia *f*

quintessential [ˌkwɪntə'senʃəl, *Am:* -te'-] *adj form* por antonomasia

quintet(te) [kwɪn'tet] *n* quinteto *m*

quintuple ['kwɪntjʊpl, *Am:* kwɪn'tu:-] *form* **I.** *adj* quíntuplo, -a **II.** *vt* quintuplicar **III.** *vi* quintuplicarse

quintuplet ['kwɪntju:plet, *Am:* kwɪn'tʌplɪt] *n* quintillizo, -a *m, f*

quip [kwɪp] **I.** *n* pulla *f* **II.** *vi* decir humorísticamente

quirk [kwɜ:k, *Am:* kwɜ:rk] *n* **1.** (*habit*) excentricidad *f* **2.** (*oddity*) rareza *f* **3.** (*sudden twist or turn*) **a ~ of fate** un capricho del destino

quirky ['kwɜ:ki, *Am:* 'kwɜ:r-] <-ier, -iest> *adj* **1.** (*original*) original **2.** (*odd*) excéntrico, -a

quit [kwɪt] <quit *o* quitted, quit *o* quitted> **I.** *vi* parar; (*job*) dimitir **II.** *vt* **1.** (*leave*) dejar; (*place*) irse de **2.** *Am* (*stop*) parar; (*smoking*) dejar de **3.** INFOR salir de

quite [kwaɪt] *adv* **1.** (*fairly*) bastante; **~ a bit** considerablemente, bastantito *Méx;* **~ a distance** una distancia considerable; **~ something** una cosa notable **2.** (*completely*) completamente; **~ wrong** totalmente equivocado; **not ~** no tanto; **not ~ as clever/rich as ...** no tan inteligente/rico como...

quits [kwɪts] *adj inf* en paz; **to be ~ (with sb)** estar en paz con alguien; **to call it ~** hacer las paces

quittance ['kwɪtns] *n form* descargo *m*

quiver¹ ['kwɪvəʳ, *Am:* -ɚ] **I.** *n* (*shiver*) estremecimiento *m* **II.** *vi* temblar

quiver² ['kwɪvəʳ, *Am:* -ɚ] *n* aljaba *f*

quixotic [kwɪk'sɒtɪk, *Am:* -'sɑ:t̬ɪk] *adj liter* quijotesco, -a

quiz [kwɪz] **I.** <-es> *n* **1.** (*game*) acertijo *m;* **~ question** pregunta *f* de concurso **2.** (*short test*) encuesta *f* **II.** *vt* interrogar

quizmaster ['kwɪzˌmɑ:stəʳ, *Am:* -ˌmæstɚ] *n* moderador *m*

quiz show *n* programa *m* concurso

quizzical ['kwɪzɪkəl] *adj* **1.** (*questioning*) interrogante **2.** (*teasing*) burlón, -ona

quoit [kɔɪt, *Am:* kwɔɪt] *n Am* tejo *m*

quorate ['kwɔ:rət, *Am:* 'kwɔ:rɪt] *adj form* con quórum

quorum ['kwɔ:rəm] *n form* quórum *m*

quota ['kwəʊtə, *Am:* 'kwoʊt̬ə] *n* **1.** (*fixed amount allowed*) cuota *f;* **export ~** cupo *m* de exportación **2.** (*proportion*) parte *f*

quotable ['kwəʊtəbl, *Am:* 'kwoʊt̬ə-] *adj* citable

quotation [kwəʊ'teɪʃən, *Am:* kwoʊ'-] *n* **1.** (*repeated words*) cita *f* **2.** FIN cotización *f*

quotation marks *npl* comillas *fpl*

quote [kwəʊt, *Am:* kwoʊt] **I.** *n* **1.** *inf* (*quotation*) cita *f* **2.** *pl, inf* (*quotation marks*) comillas *fpl* **3.** *inf* (*estimate*) presupuesto *m* **4.** FIN cotización *f* **II.** *vt* **1.** citar **2.** (*name*) nombrar **3.** FIN cotizar; **a ~d company** una empresa que cotiza en bolsa **III.** *vi* (*repeat exact words*) citar; **to ~ from sb** citar a alguien; **to ~ from memory** citar de memoria

quotidian [kwəʊ'tɪdiən, *Am:* kwoʊ'-] *adj form* cotidiano, -a

quotient ['kwəʊʃənt, *Am:* 'kwoʊ-] *n* **1.** MAT cociente *m* **2.** (*factor*) coeficiente *m;* **intelligence ~** coeficiente de inteligencia

qwerty keyboard [ˌkwɜ:ti'ki:bɔ:dfaɪl, *Am:* ˌkwɜ:rt̬i'ki:bɔ:rd-] *n* teclado *m* qwerty

R

R, r [ɑ:ʳ, *Am:* ɑ:r] r, R *f;* **~ for Roger** R de Ramón

R. **1.** *abbr of* **River** r. **2.** *Am abbr of* **Republican** republicano, -a

rabbi ['ræbaɪ] *n* rabino *m*

rabbit ['ræbɪt] **I.** *n* conejo, -a *m, f* **II.** *vi Brit, Aus, inf* parlotear

rabbit hole *n* conejera *f* **rabbit hutch** *n* conejera *f* **rabbit punch** *n* golpe *m* en la nuca

rabble ['ræbl] *n no pl* muchedumbre *f;* **the ~** el populacho

rabble-rouser ['ræblˌraʊzəʳ, *Am:* -zɚ] *n* agitador(a) *m(f)*

rabble-rousing *adj* agitador(a)

rabid ['ræbɪd] *adj* **1.** (*furious*) furibundo, -a **2.** (*fanatical*) fanático, -a **3.** (*suffering from rabies*) rabioso, -a

rabies ['reɪbi:z] *n* rabia *f;* **to carry ~** tener la rabia

RAC [ˌɑ:ʳeɪ'si:, *Am:* ˌɑ:r-] *n Brit abbr of* **Royal Automobile Club** ≈ Real Automóbil Club *m* de España

raccoon [rəˈkuːn, *Am:* rækˈuːn] *n* mapache *m*
race¹ [reɪs] **I.** *n* carrera *f;* **a ~ against time** una carrera contra reloj; **100-metre ~** carrera de cien metros lisos; **to run a ~** participar en una carrera ▶**slow and steady wins the ~** *prov* despacito y buena letra **II.** *vi* **1.** (*move quickly*) correr; SPORTS competir; **to ~ through one's work** hacer el trabajo a toda prisa **2.** (*engine*) acelerarse **III.** *vt* **1.** (*compete against*) competir con; **to ~ sb home** echar una carrera hasta casa a alguien **2.** (*enter for race: horse*) hacer correr
race² [reɪs] *n no pl* **1.** (*ethnic grouping*) raza *f* **2.** (*species*) especie *f* **3.** (*lineage*) estirpe *f*
race conflict *n no pl* conflicto *m* racial
racecourse [ˈreɪskɔːs, *Am:* -kɔːrs] *n* hipódromo *m*
race hatred *n no pl* odio *m* racial
racehorse [ˈreɪshɔːs, *Am:* -ˌhɔːrs] *n* caballo *m* de carreras
race meet *n Am,* **race meeting** *n* concurso *m* hípico
racer [ˈreɪsəʳ, *Am:* -ɚ] *n* **1.** (*person*) corredor(a) *m(f)* **2.** (*bicycle*) bicicleta *f* de carreras
race relations *npl* relaciones *fpl* interraciales **race riot** *n* disturbio *m* racial
racetrack [ˈreɪstræk] *n* hipódromo *m*
racial [ˈreɪʃəl] *adj* racial
racialism [ˈreɪʃəlɪzəm] *n Brit s.* **racism**
racialist [ˈreɪʃəlɪst] *n, adj Brit s.* **racist**
racing **I.** *n* carreras *fpl* **II.** *adj* de carreras
racing bicycle *n,* **racing bike** *n inf* bicicleta *f* de carreras **racing car** *n* coche *m* de carreras **racing driver** *n* piloto *mf* de carreras, volante *m AmL* **racing yacht** *n* yate *m* de regata
racism [ˈreɪsɪzəm] *n no pl* racismo *m*
racist [ˈreɪsɪst] **I.** *n* racista *mf* **II.** *adj* racista
rack [ræk] **I.** *n* **1.** (*framework, shelf*) estante *m;* **luggage ~** portaequipajes *m inv;* **plate ~** escurreplatos *m inv* **2.** GASTR **~ of lamb/beef** costillar *m* de cordero/ternera **3.** (*torture instrument*) potro *m;* **to be on the ~** *fig* estar en ascuas **II.** *vt* atormentar
racket [ˈrækɪt] *n* **1.** SPORTS raqueta *f;* **~s** frontenis *m; inv* **2.** *no pl, inf* (*loud noise*) barullo *m,* balumba *f AmS;* **to make a ~** armar un alboroto **3.** (*scheme*) chanchullo *m,* transa *f Méx*
racketeer [ˌrækɪˈtɪəʳ, *Am:* -əˈtɪr] *n* timador(a) *m(f)*
rack-rent [ˈrækrent] *n* alquiler *m* exorbitante
racoon [rəˈkuːn, *Am:* rækˈuːn] *n s.* **raccoon**
racy [ˈreɪsi] <-ier, -iest> *adj* (*film, book*) atrevido, -a
radar [ˈreɪdɑːʳ, *Am:* -dɑːr] *n no pl* radar *m*
radar screen *n* pantalla *f* de radar **radar trap** *n* detector *m* de velocidad
radial [ˈreɪdiəl] *adj* radial; TECH en estrella
radiant [ˈreɪdiənt] *adj* radiante
radiate [ˈreɪdieɪt] **I.** *vi* irradiar **II.** *vt* **1.** (*emit*) irradiar **2.** (*display: happiness, enthusiasm*) mostrar
radiation [ˌreɪdiˈeɪʃən] *n no pl* radiación *f*
radiation sickness *n no pl* radiotoxemia *f* **radiation therapy** *n* radioterapia *f*
radiator [ˈreɪdieɪtəʳ, *Am:* -t̬ɚ] *n* radiador *m*
radiator cap *n* tapón *m* del radiador
radical [ˈrædɪkəl] **I.** *n* **1.** *a.* CHEM, MAT radical *m* **2.** POL radical *mf* **II.** *adj* (*change, idea*) radical; (*measures*) drástico, -a
radicalism [ˈrædɪkəlɪzəm] *n no pl* radicalismo *m*
radii [ˈreɪdɪaɪ] *n pl of* **radius**
radio [ˈreɪdiəʊ, *Am:* -oʊ] **I.** *n* radio *f,* radio *m AmC* **II.** *vt* (*information*) radiar; (*person*) llamar por radio
radioactive [ˌreɪdiəʊˈæktɪv, *Am:* -oʊˈ-] *adj* radioactivo, -a
radioactivity [ˌreɪdiəʊəkˈtɪvəti, *Am:* -oʊ-ækˈtɪvət̬i] *n no pl* radiactividad *f*
radio alarm (**clock**) *n* radio *f* despertador **radio beacon** *n* radiofaro *m* **radio button** *n* INFOR botón *m* tipo radio
radiocarbon dating [ˌreɪdiəʊˈkɑːbən ˈdeɪtɪŋ, *Am:* -oʊkɑːr-] *n no pl* fechado *m* por radiocarbono
radio cassette (**recorder**) *n* radiocasete *m*
radiogram [ˈreɪdiəʊgræm, *Am:* -oʊ-] *n* radiograma *m*
radiograph [ˈreɪdiəʊgrɑːf, *Am:* -oʊgræf] *n* radiografía *f*
radiographer *n* radiógrafo, -a *m, f*
radiography [ˌreɪdiˈɒgrəfi, *Am:* -ˈɑːgrə-] *n* radiografía *f*
radio ham *n* radioaficionado, -a *m, f*
radiologist [ˌreɪdiˈɒlədʒɪst, *Am:* -ˈɑːlə-] *n* radiólogo, -a *m, f*
radiology [ˌreɪdiˈɒlədʒi, *Am:* -ˈɑːlə-] *n no pl* radiología *f*
radio microphone *n* micrófono *m* inalámbrico
radio operator *n* radioperador(a) *m(f)* **radiopager** *n* buscapersonas *m inv* **radio play** *n* pieza *f* radiofónica **radio programme** *n* programa *m* de radio
radioscopy [ˌreɪdiˈɒskəpi] *n no pl* MED radioscopia *f*
radio set *n* aparato *m* de radio **radio station** *n* emisora *f* de radio, estación *f* de radio *AmL;* **pirate ~** emisora *f* pirata, estación *f* pirata *AmL*
radiotelephony [ˌreɪdiəʊtɪˈlefəni] *n no pl* radiotelefonía *f*
radio telescope *n* radiotelescopio *m*
radiotherapy [ˌreɪdiəʊˈθerəpi, *Am:* -oʊˈ-] *n no pl* radioterapia *f*
radio wave *n* onda *f* de radio
radish [ˈrædɪʃ] <-es> *n* rábano *m*
radium [ˈreɪdiəm] *n no pl* radio *m*
radium treatment *n* radioterapia *f*
radius [ˈreɪdiəs] <-dii> *n* radio *m*
RAF [ˌɑːʳeɪˈef, *Am:* ˌɑːr-] *n abbr of* **Royal Air Force the ~** la fuerza aérea británica
raffia [ˈræfiə] *n no pl* rafia *f*
raffish [ˈræfɪʃ] *adj* (*appearance*) de pillo, -a

raffle ['ræfl] **I.** *n* rifa *f* **II.** *vt* rifar

raft [rɑːft, *Am:* ræft] **I.** *n* **1.** (*vessel*) balsa *f* **2.** *inf* (*a lot*) montón *m* **II.** *vt* transportar en balsa **III.** *vi* ir en balsa

rafter[1] ['rɑːftəʳ, *Am:* 'ræftɚ] *n* viga *f*

rafter[2] ['rɑːftəʳ, *Am:* 'ræftɚ] *n* (*person*) balsero, -a *m, f*

rafting *n* rafting *m*

rag [ræg] **I.** *n* **1.** (*old cloth*) trapo *m* **2.** *pl* (*worn-out clothes*) harapos *mpl* **3.** *pej* (*newspaper*) periodicucho *m* **4.** MUS ragtime *m* **II.** <-gg-> *vt inf* tomar el pelo a

ragamuffin ['rægəmʌfɪn] *n inf* golfo, -a *m, f*

ragbag ['rægbæg] *n* mezcolanza *f*

rage [reɪdʒ] **I.** *n* **1.** *no pl* (*anger*) furia *f;* **to be in a ~** estar hecho una furia **2.** (*fashion*) **to be all the ~** ser el último grito **II.** *vi* **1.** (*express fury*) enfurecerse; **to ~ at sb/sth** enfurecerse con alguien/algo **2.** (*continue: battle*) continuar con pleno vigor; (*epidemic*) hacer estragos; (*wind, storm*) bramar; (*fire*) arder furiosamente

ragged ['rægɪd] *adj* **1.** (*torn: clothes*) hecho, -a jirones **2.** (*wearing worn clothes*) andrajoso, -a **3.** (*rough*) recortado, -a **4.** (*irregular*) irregular ▶**to run sb ~** agotar a alguien

raging ['reɪdʒɪŋ] *adj a.* METEO furioso, -a; (*blizzard*) violento, -a; (*sea*) embravecido, -a; (*toothache*) intenso, -a

ragout ['rægu:, *Am:* ræg'u:] *n no pl* ragú *m*

rag rug *n* alfombrilla *f* de retazos

ragtag ['rægtæg] *n* chusma *f*

ragtime ['rægtaɪm] *n no pl* ragtime *m*

rag trade *n inf* gremio *m* de la aguja

raid [reɪd] **I.** *n* **1.** MIL incursión *f* **2.** (*attack*) ataque *m* **3.** (*robbery*) asalto *m* **4.** (*by police*) redada *f* **II.** *vt* **1.** MIL invadir **2.** (*attack*) atacar **3.** (*by police*) hacer una redada en

rail [reɪl] **I.** *n* **1.** (*part of fence*) valla *f;* (*bar for supporting people*) barandilla *f;* (*bar for hanging things on*) barra *f;* **towel ~** portatoallas *m inv* **2.** *no pl* (*railway system*) ferrocarril *m* **3.** (*track*) raíl *m,* riel *m AmL;* **by ~** en tren, por ferrocarril; **~ ticket** billete *m* de ferrocarril, boleto *m* de tren *Méx* ▶**to go off the ~s** *Brit, inf* descarrilarse **II.** *vt* **to ~ sth in** [*o* **off**] cercar algo

◆**rail against** *vt* clamar contra

railcard ['reɪlkɑːd, *Am:* -kɑːrd] *n tarjeta para obtener descuentos en el tren*

railhead ['reɪlhed] *n* cabeza *f* de línea

railing ['reɪlɪŋ] *n* **1.** (*post*) valla *f;* **iron ~** verja *f;* **wooden ~** cerco *m* **2.** (*of stairs*) pasamanos *m inv* **rail network** *n* red *f* ferroviaria

railroad ['reɪlrəʊd, *Am:* -roʊd] **I.** *n Am* **1.** (*system*) ferrocarril *m* **2.** (*track*) línea *f* de ferrocarril **II.** *vt fig* **to ~ sb into doing sth** obligar a alguien a hacer algo

rail strike *n* huelga *f* de ferrocarril

railway ['reɪlweɪ] *n Brit* **1.** (*tracks*) vía *f* férrea **2.** (*system*) ferrocarril *m*

railway bridge *n* puente *m* ferroviario **railway carriage** *n* vagón *m* **railway crossing** *n* paso *m* a nivel **railway engine** *n* locomotora *f* **railway line** *n* vía *f* del tren **railwayman** <-men> *n* ferroviario *m,* ferrocarrilero *m Méx* **railway station** *n* estación *f* del ferrocarril

rain [reɪn] **I.** *n no pl* lluvia *f;* **~ shower** chubasco *m;* **the ~s** la temporada de lluvias ▶**come ~ or shine** pase lo que pase; **to be as right as ~** *inf* estar perfectamente **II.** *vi* llover **III.** *vt* llover

◆**rain off** *vt,* **rain out** *vt Am* **to be rained off** [*o* **out**] cancelarse por lluvia

rainbow *n* METEO arco *m* iris **rain cloud** *n* nube *f* de lluvia **raincoat** *n* gabardina *f,* piloto *m Arg* **raindrop** *n* gota *f* de lluvia **rainfall** *n no pl* precipitación *f* **rain forest** *n* selva *f* tropical **rain gauge** *n* pluviómetro *m* **rainproof** **I.** *adj* impermeable **II.** *vt* impermeabilizar **rainstorm** *n* tormenta *f* de lluvia **rainwater** *n no pl* agua *f* de lluvia

rainy ['reɪni] *adj* <-ier, -iest> lluvioso, -a; **the ~ season** la estación de las lluvias

raise [reɪz] **I.** *n Am, Aus* (*of wages, prices*) aumento *m* **II.** *vt* **1.** (*lift*) levantar; (*periscope, window*) subir; (*arm, hand, leg*) levantar; (*flag*) izar; (*anchor*) levar; (*ship*) poner a flote **2.** (*stir up*) provocar; (*doubts*) suscitar **3.** (*increase: wages, awareness*) aumentar; (*bet*) subir; MAT elevar; (*standards*) mejorar **4.** (*promote*) ascender **5.** (*introduce: subject, problem*) plantear **6.** FIN recaudar **7.** (*build*) erigir; (*monument*) levantar **8.** (*bring up, cultivate*) cultivar **9.** (*end: embargo*) levantar **10.** (*contact*) llamar, contactar *Méx;* **to ~ the alarm** dar la voz de alarma ▶**to ~ hell** [*o* **Cain**] poner el grito en el cielo

raisin ['reɪzn] *n* pasa *f*

rake[1] [reɪk] *n* (*dissolute man*) vividor *m*

rake[2] [reɪk] **I.** *n* (*tool*) rastrillo *m* **II.** *vt* rastrillar

◆**rake in** *vt inf* (*money*) amasar; **to be raking it in** estar forrándose

◆**rake up** *vt* **1.** (*gather*) reunir **2.** *fig* (*refer to*) sacar a relucir; (*quarrel*) atizar

rake-off ['reɪkɒf, *Am:* -ɑːf] *n inf* tajada *f*

rakish ['reɪkɪʃ] *adj* **1.** (*jaunty*) desenvuelto, -a **2.** (*dissolute*) disoluto, -a

rally ['ræli] <-ies> **I.** *n* **1.** (*race*) rally *m* **2.** (*in tennis*) peloteo *m* **3.** POL mitin *m* **II.** *vi* **1.** MED mejorar; FIN repuntar **2.** MIL agruparse; **to ~ behind sb** apoyar a alguien **III.** *vt* **1.** MIL reagrupar **2.** (*support*) apoyar

◆**rally round** **I.** *vt* apoyar **II.** *vi* agruparse

rally driver *n* conductor(a) *m(f)* de rallys

ram [ræm] **I.** *n* **1.** (*male sheep*) carnero *m;* (*astrology*) Aries *m* **2.** (*implement*) maza *f;* MIL ariete *m* **II.** *vt* <-mm-> **1.** (*hit*) embestir contra **2.** (*push*) **to ~ sth into sth** embutir algo en algo

RAM [ræm] *n* INFOR *abbr of* **Random Access Memory** RAM *f*

Ramadan [ˌræmə'dæn, *Am:* ˌræmə'dɑːn] *n* Ramadán *m*

ramble ['ræmbl] **I.** *n* (*walk*) caminata *f;* **to go for a** ~ ir de excursión **II.** *vi* **1.** (*person*) pasear; (*river*) serpentear; (*plant*) trepar **2.** (*in speech*) divagar

rambler ['ræmbləʳ, *Am:* -blɚ] *n* **1.** (*walker*) excursionista *mf* **2.** BOT rosa *f* trepadora

rambling ['ræmblɪŋ] **I.** *n* **1.** (*walking*) excursionismo *m* **2.** *pl* (*speech*) divagaciones *fpl* **II.** *adj* **1.** (*building*) laberíntico, -a **2.** (*plant*) trepador(a) **3.** (*talk*) divagante

ramekin ['reɪmkɪn, *Am:* 'ræməkɪn] *n* potecito *m*

ramification [ˌræmɪfɪ'keɪʃən] *n* ramificación *f*

ramify ['ræmɪfaɪ] *vi* ramificarse

ramp [ræmp] *n* **1.** (*sloping way*) rampa *f;* AVIAT escalerilla *f* **2.** *Am* AUTO (*lane to join*) carril *m* de incorporación; (*lane to leave*) carril *m* de salida

rampage [ræm'peɪdʒ, *Am:* 'ræmpeɪdʒ] **I.** *n* destrozos *mpl;* **to be on the** ~ ir arrasando todo **II.** *vi* arrasar

rampant ['ræmpənt] *adj* (*disease, growth*) exhuberante; (*inflation*) galopante

rampart ['ræmpɑːt, *Am:* -pɑːrt] *n* muralla *f*

ramrod ['ræmrɒd, *Am:* -rɑːd] *n* baqueta *f* ►**as stiff as a** ~ más tieso que un ajo

ramshackle ['ræmʃækl] *adj* **1.** (*dilapidated*) desvencijado, -a **2.** (*disorganized*) improvisado, -a

ran [ræn] *pt of* **run**

ranch [rɑːntʃ, *Am:* ræntʃ] **I.** <-es> *n* granja *f,* rancho *m Méx,* estancia *f RíoPl* **II.** *adj* de granja **III.** *vi* (*conduct a ranch*) llevar una granja

rancher ['rɑːntʃəʳ, *Am:* 'ræntʃɚ] *n* **1.** (*owner*) hacendado, -a *m, f,* ranchero, -a *m, f Méx* **2.** (*worker*) granjero, -a *m, f*

rancid ['rænsɪd] *adj* rancio, -a

rancor ['ræŋkəʳ, *Am:* -kɚ] *n Am, Aus s.* **rancour**

rancorous ['ræŋkərəs] *adj* rencoroso, -a

rancour ['ræŋkəʳ, *Am:* -kɚ] *n no pl* rencor *m*

random ['rændəm] **I.** *n no pl* **at** ~ al azar **II.** *adj* aleatorio, -a

randy ['rændi] <-ier, -iest> *adj inf* cachondo, -a, birriondo, -a *Méx*

rang [ræŋ] *pt of* **ring[2]**

range [reɪndʒ] **I.** *n* **1.** (*area*) área *m;* (*for shooting*) campo *m* de tiro **2.** (*row*) hilera *f* **3.** *Am* (*pasture*) pradera *f* **4.** (*field*) ámbito *m,* campo *m* **5.** (*scale*) gama *f;* **the full** ~ **of sth** la gama completa de algo **6.** FASHION **autumn/spring** ~ línea *f* de otoño/primavera **7.** GEO cadena *f* **8.** MUS extensión *f* **9.** (*maximum capability*) alcance *m;* **out of** ~ fuera del alcance; **within** ~ al alcance **II.** *vi* **1.** (*vary*) variar **2.** (*rove*) deambular **3.** (*extend*) extenderse **III.** *vt* alinear; **to** ~ **oneself** alinearse

range finder *n* telémetro *m*

ranger ['reɪndʒəʳ, *Am:* -dʒɚ] *n* guardabosque *mf*

rangy ['reɪndʒi] *adj* <-ier, -iest> larguirucho, -a

rank[1] [ræŋk] *adj* **1.** (*absolute*) total; (*beginner*) absoluto, -a **2.** (*smelling unpleasant*) fétido, -a

rank[2] [ræŋk] **I.** *n* **1.** *no pl* (*status*) rango *m* **2.** MIL graduación *f;* **the** ~**s** las tropas; **to break** ~ romper filas **3.** (*row*) fila *f;* **cab** ~ parada *f* de taxis, sitio *m* de taxis *Méx* **II.** *vi* clasificarse; **to** ~ **as sth** figurar como algo; **to** ~ **above sb** estar por encima de alguien **III.** *vt* **1.** (*classify*) clasificar **2.** (*arrange*) situar

◆**rank among** *vi* situarse entre

ranking ['ræŋkɪŋ] *n* clasificación *f*

rankle ['ræŋkl] *vi* doler; **to** ~ **with sb** estar resentido con alguien; **it** ~**s that ...** duele que... +*subj*

ransack ['rænsæk] *vt* **1.** (*search*) revolver **2.** (*plunder*) saquear

ransom ['rænsəm] **I.** *n* rescate *m;* **to hold sb to** ~ secuestrar a alguien y pedir rescate; *fig* chantajear a alguien **II.** *vt* rescatar

rant [rænt] **I.** *n no pl* despotrique *m* **II.** *vi* despotricar; **to** ~ **and rave** despotricar

rap [ræp] **I.** *n* **1.** (*knock*) golpe *m* seco **2.** MUS rap *m* **II.** *vt* golpear **III.** *vi* **1.** (*talk*) charlar **2.** MUS rapear

rapacious [rə'peɪʃəs] *adj form* codicioso, -a; (*appetite*) voraz

rapacity [rə'pæsəti, *Am:* -t̬i] *n no pl* rapacidad *f*

rape[1] [reɪp] **I.** *n* **1.** (*of person*) violación *f* **2.** (*of city*) saqueo *m* **II.** *vt* **1.** (*person*) violar **2.** (*city*) saquear

rape[2] [reɪp] *n* BOT, AGR colza *f*

rapeseed oil *n* aceite *m* de colza

rapid ['ræpɪd] *adj* **1.** (*quick*) rápido, -a **2.** (*sudden*) súbito, -a

rapidity [rə'pɪdəti, *Am:* -t̬i] *n no pl* rapidez *f*

rapids ['ræpɪdz] *n* rápidos *mpl*

rapier ['reɪpɪəʳ, *Am:* -ɚ] *n* estoque *m*

rapist ['reɪpɪst] *n* violador(a) *m(f)*

rapport [ræ'pɔːʳ, *Am:* -'pɔːr] *n no pl* compenetración *f*

rapprochement [ræ'prɒʃmɒŋ, *Am:* ˌræprɔːʃ-] *n no pl* acercamiento *m*

rapt [ræpt] *adj* (*person*) absorto, -a; (*attention*) completo, -a

rapture ['ræptʃəʳ, *Am:* -tʃɚ] *n no pl* éxtasis *m inv*

rapturous ['ræptʃərəs] *adj* (*expression*) extasiado, -a; (*applause*) entusiasta; (*welcome*) desbordante

rare[1] [reəʳ, *Am:* rer] *adj* (*uncommon*) raro, -a

rare[2] [reəʳ, *Am:* rer] *adj* GASTR poco hecho, -a

rarebit ['reəbɪt, *Am:* 'rer-] *n* **Welsh** ~ pan *m* tostado con queso, mollete *m Méx*

rarefy ['reərɪfaɪ, *Am:* 'rerə-] *vt* enrarecer

rarely ['reəli, *Am:* 'rer-] *adv* raramente, raras veces

raring ['reərɪŋ, *Am:* 'rerɪŋ] *adj inf* **to be** ~ **to do sth** tener muchas ganas de hacer algo

rarity ['reərəti, *Am:* 'rerət̬i] <-ies> *n no pl* rareza *f*

rascal ['rɑːskl, *Am:* 'ræskl] *n* granuja *mf*

rash¹ [ræʃ] *n* **1.** MED sarpullido *m* **2.** *no pl* (*outbreak*) racha *f*
rash² [ræʃ] *adj* (*decision*) precipitado, -a; (*move*) impulsivo, -a
rasher ['ræʃəʳ, *Am:* -ɚ] *n* loncha *f* (de beicon), rebanada *f* (de tocino) *AmC*
rashness ['ræʃnɪs] *n no pl* precipitación *f*
rasp [rɑːsp, *Am:* ræsp] **I.** *n* **1.** (*tool*) escofina *f* **2.** (*sound*) chirrido *m* **II.** *vt* **1.** (*file*) escofinar **2.** (*rub roughly*) raspar **3.** (*say roughly*) espetar **III.** *vi* (*make grating sound*) chirriar
raspberry ['rɑːzbəri, *Am:* 'ræzˌber-] <-ies> *n* **1.** (*fruit*) frambuesa *f* **2.** *inf* (*sound*) pedorreta *f,* trompetilla *f AmL*
rasping ['rɑːspɪŋ, *Am:* 'ræsp-] *adj* áspero, -a
rastafarian [ˌræstə'feərɪən, *Am:* ˌrɑːstə'ferɪ-] **I.** *n* rastafari *mf* **II.** *adj* rastafariano, -a
rat [ræt] *n* **1.** (*animal*) rata *f* **2.** (*person*) canalla *mf* ►**I smell a** ~ aquí hay gato encerrado
ratable ['reɪtəbl, *Am:* -t̬ə-] *adj s.* **rateable**
ratchet ['rætʃɪt] *n* TECH trinquete *m*
◆**ratchet up** *vt* incrementar
rate [reɪt] **I.** *n* **1.** (*speed*) velocidad *f;* **at this** ~ a este ritmo; **at one's own** ~ a su propio ritmo **2.** (*proportion*) índice *m,* tasa *f;* **mortality** ~ tasa *f* de mortalidad; **unemployment** ~ índice *m* de desempleo **3.** (*price*) precio *m;* **interest** ~ tipo *m* de interés **4.** *pl, Aus, Brit* (*local tax*) contribución *f* municipal ►**at any** ~ de todos modos **II.** *vt* **1.** calificar; **to** ~ **sb/sth as sth** considerar algo/a alguien como algo **2.** *Aus, Brit* FIN tasar **III.** *vi* **to** ~ **as** ser considerado como
rateable ['reɪtəbl, *Am:* -t̬ə-] *adj Brit* tasable; ~ **value** valor *m* catastral
rather ['rɑːðəʳ, *Am:* 'ræðɚ] **I.** *adv* **1.** (*somewhat*) ~ **sleepy** medio dormido **2.** (*more exactly*) más bien **3.** (*on the contrary*) más bien **4.** (*very*) bastante **5.** (*in preference to*) **I would** ~ **stay here** prefiero quedarme aquí; ~ **you than me!** ¡no quisiera estar en tu lugar! **II.** *interj* por supuesto
ratification [ˌrætɪfɪ'keɪʃən, *Am:* ˌræt̬ə-] *n no pl* ratificación *f*
ratify ['rætɪfaɪ, *Am:* 'ræt̬ə-] *vt* ratificar
rating ['reɪtɪŋ, *Am:* -t̬ɪŋ] *n* **1.** *no pl* (*estimation*) evaluación *f* **2.** *pl* TV, RADIO índice *m* de audiencia **3.** *Brit* MIL marinero *m*
ratio ['reɪʃiəʊ, *Am:* -oʊ] *n* proporción *f*
ration ['ræʃən] **I.** *n* **1.** (*fixed allowance*) ración *f* **2.** *pl* (*total amount allowed*) raciones *fpl;* **food** ~**s** víveres *mpl* **II.** *vt* racionar
rational ['ræʃənəl] *adj* **1.** (*able to reason*) racional **2.** (*sensible*) razonable
rationale [ˌræʃə'nɑːl, *Am:* -'næl] *n* razón *f* fundamental
rationalism ['ræʃənəlɪzəm] *n no pl* racionalismo *m*
rationalist ['ræʃənəlɪst] PHILOS **I.** *n* racionalista *mf* **II.** *adj* racionalista
rationalistic [ˌræʃənə'lɪstɪk] *adj* racionalista
rationality [ˌræʃə'næləti, *Am:* -t̬i] *n no pl* racionalidad *f*
rationalization [ˌræʃənəlaɪ'zeɪʃən, *Am:* -əlɪ'-] *n no pl* racionalización *f*
rationalize ['ræʃənəlaɪz] *vt* racionalizar
rationing *n no pl* racionamiento *m*
rat poison *n* raticida *m* **rat race** *n* **the** ~ la lucha para sobrevivir
rattle ['rætl, *Am:* 'ræt̬-] **I.** *n* **1.** *no pl* (*noise*) ruido *m;* (*of carriage*) traqueteo *m* **2.** (*for baby*) sonajero *m,* cascabel *m AmL* **II.** *vi* hacer ruido; (*carriage*) traquetear **III.** *vt* **1.** (*making noise*) hacer sonar **2.** (*make nervous*) poner nervioso, -a; (*shock*) desconcertar
rattlesnake ['rætlsneɪk, *Am:* 'ræt̬-] *n* serpiente *f* de cascabel, víbora *f* de cascabel *Méx*
rattling ['rætlɪŋ] *adj* **1.** (*noisy*) ruidoso, -a **2.** (*fast, brisk*) rápido, -a
ratty ['ræti, *Am:* 'ræt̬-] *adj* <-ier, -iest> *inf* malhumorado, -a
raucous ['rɔːkəs, *Am:* 'rɑː-] *adj* (*shout*) estridente; (*crowd*) ruidoso, -a
raunchy ['rɔːntʃi, *Am:* 'rɑːn-] <-ier, -iest> *adj* atrevido, -a
ravage ['rævɪdʒ] *vt* hacer estragos en
rave [reɪv] **I.** *n Brit, inf* juerga *f* **II.** *adj* (*review*) elogioso, -a **III.** *vi* desvariar; **to** ~ **against sb/sth** despotricar contra alguien/algo; **to** ~ **about sth/sb** poner algo/a alguien por las nubes
ravel ['rævl] <-ll-, *Am:* -l-> *vt* enredar
raven ['reɪvn] **I.** *n* cuervo *m* **II.** *adj liter* negro azabache
ravenous ['rævənəs] *adj* (*person, animal*) hambriento, -a; (*appetite*) voraz
ravine [rə'viːn] *n* barranco *m*
raving ['reɪvɪŋ] **I.** *adj* (*success*) total; **a** ~ **madman** un loco de remate **II.** *adv* **to be** ~ **mad** estar como una cabra **III.** *npl* desvaríos *mpl*
ravioli [rævi'əʊli, *Am:* -'oʊ-] *n* ravioles *mpl*
ravish ['rævɪʃ] *vt liter* **1.** (*please greatly*) cautivar **2.** (*rape*) violar
ravishing *adj* encantador(a)
raw [rɔː, *Am:* rɑː] **I.** *n* **in the** ~ en cueros; **to touch sb on the** ~ *Brit, Aus* herir a alguien en lo más vivo **II.** *adj* **1.** (*unprocessed: sewage*) sin tratar; (*silk*) salvaje; (*data*) en sucio; ~ **material** materia prima; **to get a** ~ **deal** sufrir un trato injusto **2.** (*sore*) en carne viva **3.** (*uncooked*) crudo, -a **4.** (*inexperienced*) novato, -a **5.** (*unrestrained*) salvaje **6.** (*weather*) crudo, -a
rawhide ['rɔːhaɪd, *Am:* 'rɑː-] *n* cuero *m* sin curtir
Rawlplug® ['rɔːlplʌg, *Am:* 'rɑːl-] *n Brit* taco *m* (de plástico), taquete *m* (de plástico) *Méx*
rawness ['rɔːnɪs, *Am:* 'rɑː-] *n no pl* **1.** (*harshness*) crudeza *f* **2.** (*inexperience*) inexperiencia *f*
ray¹ [reɪ] *n* **1.** (*of light*) rayo *m* **2.** (*trace*) resquicio *m*
ray² [reɪ] *n* (*fish*) raya *f*
rayon ['reɪɒn, *Am:* -ɑːn] *n* rayón *m*
raze [reɪz] *vt* arrasar

razor ['reɪzəʳ, *Am:* -zɚ] **I.** *n* navaja *f* de afeitar, barbera *f Col;* **electric ~** maquinilla *f* de afeitar, rasuradora *f Méx* **II.** *vt* afeitar
razorback ['reɪzəbæk, *Am:* -zɚ-] *n Am* (*half-wild hog*) ≈ jabalí *m* **razorbill** *n* alca *f* **razor blade** *n* hoja *f* de afeitar **razor-sharp** *adj* **1.** (*knife*) muy afilado, -a **2.** (*person*) agudo, -a **razor wire** *n* alambrado *m* de púas
razzle ['ræzl] *n no pl, Brit, inf* **to go** (**out**) **on the ~** salir de parranda
R & B [ˌɑːʳənd'biː, *Am:* ˌɑr-] *abbr of* **rhythm and blues** rhythm *m* and blues
RC [ˌɑːʳ'siː, *Am:* ˌɑːr-] **1.** *abbr of* **Roman Catholic** católico, -a *m, f* **2.** *abbr of* **Red Cross** Cruz *f* Roja
RCMP *Can abbr of* **Royal Canadian Mounted Police** policía *f* montada del Canadá
Rd *abbr of* **road** c/
R & D [ˌɑːʳənd'diː, *Am:* ˌɑr-] *abbr of* **Research and Development** I+D
RE [ˌɑːʳ'iː, *Am:* ˌɑːr-] *n Brit abbr of* **Religious Education** educación *f* religiosa
re^{1} [riː] *prep* con relación a
re^{2} [reɪ] *n no pl* MUS re *m*
reach [riːtʃ] **I.** *n* **1.** *no pl* (*range*) alcance *m;* **to be within** (**sb's**) **~** *a. fig* estar al alcance (de alguien); **to be out of** (**sb's**) **~** *a. fig* estar fuera del alcance (de alguien); **to have a long ~** tener mucho alcance **2.** (*of river*) tramo *m;* **the upper/lower ~es of the Amazon** la parte alta/baja del Amazonas **II.** *vt* **1.** (*stretch out*) alargar, extender **2.** (*arrive at: city, country*) llegar a; (*land*) tocar; (*finish line*) alcanzar **3.** (*attain*) alcanzar; (*agreement*) llegar a; **to ~ 80** cumplir (los) 80 (años) **4.** (*extend to*) llegar a **5.** (*communicate with*) ponerse en contacto con **III.** *vi* **to ~ for sth** alargar la mano para tomar algo
◆**reach down** *vi* **to ~ to** (*land*) extenderse hasta; (*clothes*) llegar hasta
◆**reach out** *vi* alargar la(s) mano(s); **to ~ for sth** alargar la mano para agarrar algo
react [rɪ'ækt] *vi* reaccionar; **to ~ to sth** reaccionar ante algo; MED reaccionar a algo; **to ~ against sth** reaccionar contra algo; **to ~ on sth** producir una reacción en algo
reaction [rɪ'ækʃən] *n* **1.** *a.* CHEM reacción *f;* **chain ~** reacción en cadena **2.** *pl* MED reflejos *mpl*
reactionary [rɪ'ækʃənri, *Am:* -eri] **I.** *adj* reaccionario, -a **II.** <-ies> *n* reaccionario, -a *m, f*
reactivate [riː'æktɪveɪt, *Am:* -tə-] **I.** *vt* reactivar **II.** *vi* reactivarse
reactive [riː'æktɪv] *adj* reactivo, -a
reactor [rɪ'æktəʳ, *Am:* -tɚ] *n* reactor *m*
read^{1} [riːd] **I.** *n no pl* lectura *f* **II.** *vt* <read, read> **1.** leer; **to ~ sth aloud** leer algo en voz alta; **to ~ sb a lesson** leer la lección a alguien **2.** (*decipher*) descifrar; **to ~ sb's mind** [*o* **thoughts**] adivinar los pensamientos de alguien; **to ~ sb's hand** leer la mano a alguien; **to ~ sb like a book** conocer a alguien como la palma de la mano; **~ my lips!** ¡léeme los labios! **3.** (*interpret*) interpretar **4.** (*inspect*) inspeccionar; (*meter*) leer **5.** (*understand*) entender; **I don't ~ you** no te sigo **6.** *Brit* UNIV estudiar **III.** *vi* <read, read> (*person*) leer; (*book, magazine*) leerse
◆**read off** *vt* leer (de un tirón)
◆**read on** *vi* seguir leyendo
◆**read out** *vt* **1.** (*read aloud*) leer en voz alta **2.** INFOR (*data*) sacar
◆**read over** *vt* releer
◆**read through** *vt* leer de principio a fin
◆**read up** *vi* repasar
read^{2} [red] *adj* leído, -a; **little/widely ~** poco/muy leído ►**to take sth as ~** dar algo por hecho; **to take it as ~ that ...** dar por sentado que... +*subj*
readability [ˌriːdə'bɪləti, *Am:* -əţi] *n no pl* legibilidad *f*
readable ['riːdəbl] *adj* **1.** (*legible*) legible **2.** (*easy to read*) ameno, -a
reader ['riːdəʳ, *Am:* -dɚ] *n* **1.** (*person*) lector(a) *m(f)* **2.** (*book*) libro *m* de lectura **3.** TECH lector *m* **4.** PUBL corrector(a) *m(f)* **5.** *Brit* UNIV profesor(a) *m(f)* adjunto, -a
readership ['riːdəʃɪp, *Am:* -dɚ-] *n no pl* lectores *mpl*
read head *n* INFOR lector
readies ['redɪz] *npl inf* pasta *f*
readily ['redɪli] *adv* **1.** (*promptly*) de buena gana **2.** (*easily*) fácilmente
readiness ['redɪnɪs] *n no pl* **1.** (*willingness*) (buena) disposición *f* **2.** (*preparedness*) preparación *f*
reading ['riːdɪŋ] **I.** *n* **1.** *no pl* lectura *f* **2.** (*interpretation*) interpretación *f* **3.** TECH medición *f* **II.** *adj* de lectura; **to have a ~ age of seven** leer al nivel de un niño de siete años
reading book *n* libro *m* de lectura **reading glasses** *npl* gafas *fpl* para leer **reading lamp** *n* lámpara *f* portátil **reading list** *n* lista *f* de lecturas **reading room** *n* sala *f* de lectura
readjust [ˌriːə'dʒʌst] **I.** *vt a.* TECH reajustar **II.** *vi* (*objects*) reajustarse; (*people*) readaptarse
readjustment [ˌriːə'dʒʌstmənt] *n* TECH reajuste *m*
read only memory *n* INFOR memoria *f* ROM
ready ['redi] **I.** *adj* <-ier, -iest> **1.** (*prepared*) listo, -a, pronto, -a *Urug;* **to be ~** estar listo; **to get ~** (**for sth**) prepararse (para algo); **to get sth ~** preparar algo **2.** (*willing*) dispuesto, -a **3.** (*available*) disponible; **~ cash** dinero *m* en efectivo; **to be a ~ source of sth** ser una fuente fácil de algo; **~ to hand** a mano **4.** (*quick, prompt*) vivo, -a; (*mind*) agudo, -a; (*tongue*) afilado, -a; **to find ~ acceptance** tener inmediata aceptación ►**~, steady, go!** *Brit* SPORTS ¡preparados, listos, ya! **II.** *n* **at the ~** a punto; (**with**) **his pencil at the ~** (con) su lápiz a mano **III.** *vt* preparar

ready-made [ˌredi'meɪd] *adj* hecho, -a; (*meal*) precocinado, -a; (*clothing*) de confección

ready-to-wear [ˌreditə'weə^r, *Am:* -'wer] **I.** *adj* prêt-à-porter **II.** *n no pl* prêt-à-porter *m*

reaffirm [ˌriːə'fɜːm, *Am:* -'fɜːrm] *vt* reafirmar

reafforest [ˌriːə'fɒrɪst, *Am:* -'fɔːr-] *vt Brit, Aus* reforestar

reafforestation [ˌriːəˌfɒrɪ'steɪʃən, *Am:* -'fɔːr-] *n Brit, Aus* reforestación *f*

real [rɪəl, *Am:* riːl] **I.** *adj* **1.** (*actual*) real; (*threat, problem*) verdadero, -a; **for ~** de verdad **2.** (*genuine*) auténtico, -a; **the ~ thing** lo auténtico; **a ~ man** *iron* un hombre como Dios manda ►**the ~ McCoy** *inf* lo realmente genuino **II.** *adv Am, inf* muy

real estate *n no pl, Am, Aus* bienes *mpl* raíces

realignment [ˌriːə'laɪnmənt] *n* reordenamiento *m;* AUTO realineamiento *m*

realism ['rɪəlɪzəm, *Am:* 'riːlɪ-] *n no pl* realismo *m*

realist ['rɪəlɪst, *Am:* 'riːlɪst] *n* realista *mf*

realistic [ˌrɪə'lɪstɪk, *Am:* ˌriːə'-] *adj* realista

reality [rɪ'æləti, *Am:* -t̬i] *n no pl* realidad *f;* **to come back to ~** volver a la realidad; **to face ~** enfrentarse a la realidad; **to become a ~** hacerse realidad; **in ~** en realidad

realizable ['rɪəlaɪzəbl, *Am:* 'riːə-] *adj a.* FIN realizable

realization [ˌrɪəlaɪ'zeɪʃən, *Am:* ˌriːəlɪ'-] *n* **1.** (*awareness*) comprensión *f* **2.** *no pl a.* FIN realización *f*

realize ['rɪəlaɪz, *Am:* 'riːə-] **I.** *vt* **1.** (*be aware of*) ser consciente de; (*become aware of*) darse cuenta de **2.** (*achieve*) realizar **3.** (*fulfill*) cumplir **4.** FIN realizar; (*acquire*) liquidar **II.** *vi* (*notice*) darse cuenta; (*be aware of*) ser consciente

really ['rɪəli, *Am:* 'riːə-] **I.** *adv* **1.** (*genuinely*) de verdad **2.** (*actually*) en realidad **3.** (*very*) muy **II.** *interj* **1.** (*surprise and interest*) ¿ah sí? **2.** (*annoyance*) pero bueno **3.** (*disbelief*) ¿de veras?

realm [relm] *n* **1.** (*kingdom*) reino *m* **2.** (*area of interest*) campo *m*

realtor ['rɪəltə^r, *Am:* 'riːəlt̬ɚ] *n Am, Aus* agente *mf* inmobiliario, -a, corredor(a) *m(f)* de propiedades *Chile*

realty ['rɪəlti, *Am:* 'riːəlt̬i] *n no pl* bienes *mpl* raíces

reanimate [riː'ænɪmeɪt] *vt* reanimar

reap [riːp] *vi, vt* cosechar

reaper ['riːpə^r, *Am:* 'riːpɚ] *n* **1.** (*person*) cosechador(a) *m(f)* **2.** (*machine*) cosechadora *f*

reappear [ˌriːə'pɪə^r, *Am:* -'pɪr] *vi* reaparecer

reapply [ˌriːə'plaɪ] **I.** *vi* **to ~ for sth** volver a presentar una solicitud para algo **II.** *vt* (*paint*) dar otra capa de

reappoint [ˌriːə'pɔɪnt] *vt* volver a nombrar

reappraisal [ˌriːə'preɪzl] *n* FIN revaluación *f*

rear¹ [rɪə^r, *Am:* rɪr] **I.** *adj* (*light*) trasero, -a; (*leg, wheel*) posterior **II.** *n* **1.** (*back part*) parte *f* trasera **2.** *inf* (*buttocks*) trasero *m* **3.** MIL retaguardia *f;* **to bring up the ~** cerrar la marcha

rear² [rɪə^r, *Am:* rɪr] **I.** *vt* **1.** (*bring up: child, animals*) criar **2.** (*raise*) **to ~ one's head** levantar la cabeza **II.** *vi* (*horse*) encabritarse; **to ~ above sth** erguirse por encima de algo

rear admiral *n* MIL contraalmirante *mf*

rearguard ['rɪəgɑːd, *Am:* 'rɪrgɑːrd] *n no pl* retaguardia *f;* **to fight a ~ action** resistir en lo posible

rearm [ˌriː'ɑːm, *Am:* -'ɑːrm] **I.** *vi* rearmarse **II.** *vt* rearmar

rearmament [riː'ɑːməmənt, *Am:* -'ɑːrmə-] *n no pl* rearmamento *m*

rearmost ['rɪəməʊst, *Am:* 'rɪrmoʊst] *adj* último, -a

rearrange [ˌriːə'reɪndʒ] *vt* **1.** (*system*) reorganizar **2.** (*furniture*) colocar de otra manera **3.** (*meeting*) volver a concertar

rear view mirror *n* retrovisor *m*

rearward ['rɪəwəd, *Am:* 'rɪrwɚd] *adj, adv* hacia atrás

rear-wheel drive *n* tracción *f* trasera

reason ['riːzn] **I.** *n* **1.** (*motive*) motivo *m;* **the ~ why ...** el motivo por el que...; **for no particular ~** sin ningún motivo en concreto; **for some ~** por algún motivo **2.** (*common sense*) sensatez *f;* **within ~** dentro de lo razonable; **to listen to ~** atender a razones; **to be beyond all ~** no tener ninguna lógica; **the Age of Reason** HIST el Siglo de las Luces **3.** (*sanity*) razón *f;* **to lose one's ~** perder la razón **II.** *vt* razonar **III.** *vi* razonar; **to ~ from sth** discurrir partiendo de algo

reasonable ['riːznəbl] *adj* **1.** (*sensible*) sensato, -a; (*demand*) razonable **2.** (*fair*) juicioso, -a **3.** (*inexpensive*) moderado, -a

reasonably ['riːznəbli] *adv* **1.** (*fairly*) razonablemente **2.** (*acceptably*) bastante

reasoning ['riːznɪŋ] *n no pl* razonamiento *m*

reassemble [ˌriːə'sembl] **I.** *vt* (*machine*) volver a montar; (*people*) volver a reunir **II.** *vi* volver a reunirse

reassess [ˌriːə'ses] *vt* **1.** (*situation*) volver a valorar [*o* considerar] **2.** FIN (*taxes*) volver a fijar; (*damages*) volver a valorar

reassurance [ˌriːə'ʃʊərəns, *Am:* -'ʃʊrəns] *n* **1.** (*comfort*) palabras *fpl* tranquilizadoras **2.** *no pl* FIN reaseguro *m*

reassure [ˌriːə'ʃʊə^r, *Am:* -'ʃʊr] *vt* tranquilizar

reassuring [ˌriːə'ʃʊərɪŋ, *Am:* -'ʃʊr-] *adj* tranquilizador(a)

reawaken [ˌriːə'weɪkən] *vt* volver a despertar

rebate ['riːbeɪt] *n* **1.** (*refund*) reembolso *m;* **tax ~** devolución *f* de impuestos **2.** (*discount*) rebaja *f*

rebel¹ ['rebl] **I.** *n* rebelde *mf* **II.** *adj* rebelde

rebel² [rɪ'bel] <-ll-> *vi* rebelarse

rebellion [rɪ'belɪən, *Am:* -'beljən] *n no pl* rebelión *f*

rebellious [rɪ'belɪəs, *Am:* -'beljəs] *adj*

R

rebelde; (*child*) revoltoso, -a
rebirth [ˌriː'bɜːθ, *Am:* -'bɜːrθ] *n* renacimiento *m*
reboot [ˌriː'buːt] INFOR **I.** *vt* recargar **II.** *vi* recargarse
rebound [rɪ'baʊnd, *Am:* riː'-] **I.** *vi* rebotar; **to ~ on sb** *fig* volverse en contra de alguien **II.** *n no pl* rebote *m;* **to marry on the ~** casarse por despecho
rebuff [rɪ'bʌf] **I.** *vt* rechazar **II.** *n* rechazo *m;* **to meet with a ~** ser rechazado, -a
rebuild [ˌriː'bɪld] *vt irr* **1.** (*build again*) reconstruir; (*face, life*) rehacer **2.** (*restore*) restablecer **3.** (*replenish: stock*) reponer
rebuke [rɪ'bjuːk] **I.** *vt* reprender **II.** *n* **1.** (*reproof*) reprimenda *f* **2.** *no pl* (*censure*) represión *f*
rebut [rɪ'bʌt] <-tt-> *vt* rebatir
rebuttal [rɪ'bʌtl, *Am:* -'bʌt̬-] *n* refutación *f*
recalcitrant [rɪ'kælsɪtrənt] *adj* recalcitrante
recall [rɪ'kɔːl] **I.** *vt* **1.** (*remember*) recordar **2.** (*call back: ambassador*) retirar; (*troops*) llamar **3.** ECON retirar (del mercado) **II.** *vi* recordar **III.** *n* **1.** (*memory*) memoria *f* **2.** POL retirada *f* **3.** ECON retirada *f* (del mercado) ►**to be lost beyond ~** estar completamente perdido
recant [rɪ'kænt] **I.** *vt* retractarse de; **to ~ one's faith/belief** abjurar de su fe/creencia **II.** *vi* retractarse
recap¹ ['riːkæp] **I.** <-pp-> *vi, vt* recapitular **II.** *n* recapitulación *f*
recap² [ˌriː'kæp] <-pp-> *vt Am* AUTO recauch(ut)ar, reencauchar *AmC*
recapitulate [ˌriːkə'pɪtʃʊleɪt, *Am:* -'pɪtʃə-] *vi, vt* recapitular
recapitulation [ˌriːkəˌpɪtʃʊ'leɪʃən, *Am:* -ˌpɪtʃə'-] *n* **1.** (*summary*) resumen *m* **2.** MUS, THEAT, CINE recapitulación *f*
recapture [ˌriː'kæptʃəʳ, *Am:* -tʃɚ] **I.** *vt* **1.** (*town*) volver a tomar; (*fugitive*) volver a capturar **2.** (*reexperience*) recuperar; (*beauty, feeling*) recobrar **II.** *n* (*of town*) reconquista *f*
recast [ˌriː'kɑːst, *Am:* -'kæst] *vt* **1.** THEAT, CINE cambiar el reparto de **2.** TECH, LIT refundir
recede [rɪ'siːd] *vi* **1.** (*move backward: sea*) retirarse; (*tide*) bajar; (*fog*) desvanecerse; **to ~ into the distance** perderse en la distancia **2.** (*diminish*) disminuir; (*prices*) bajar
receding chin *n* barbilla *f* hundida **receding hairline** *n* entradas *fpl*
receipt [rɪ'siːt] **I.** *n* **1.** (*document*) recibo *m* **2.** *pl* COM ingresos *mpl* **3.** (*act of receiving*) recepción *f;* **payment on ~** pago *m* al recibo; **on ~ of ...** al recibo de... **II.** *vt* acusar recibo de
receipt book *n* libro *m* talonario
receivable *adj* COM por cobrar
receive [rɪ'siːv] **I.** *vt* **1.** (*be given*) *a.* TEL, RADIO recibir; (*pension, salary*) percibir **2.** (*react to: proposal, suggestion*) acoger; **the book was well/bady ~d** el libro tuvo buena/mala acogida **3.** (*injury*) sufrir **4. to ~ sb into the Church** admitir a alguien en el seno de la Iglesia **5.** LAW **to ~ stolen goods** comerciar con bienes robados **II.** *vi Am* SPORTS recibir
received [rɪ'siːvd] *adj* admitido, -a; **~ wisdom** creencia *f* popular
receiver [rɪ'siːvəʳ, *Am:* -ɚ] *n* **1.** TEL auricular *m,* tubo *m AmL,* fono *m Chile* **2.** RADIO receptor *m* **3.** ECON **the official ~** el síndico (de la quiebra) **4.** *Am* SPORTS receptor(a) *m(f);* (*tennis*) jugador(a) *m(f)* que está al resto
recent ['riːsənt] *adj* reciente; **in ~ times** en los últimos tiempos
recently *adv* recientemente
receptacle [rɪ'septəkl] *n* receptáculo *m*
reception [rɪ'sepʃən] *n* **1.** *no pl* (*welcome*) acogida *f* **2.** (*in hotel*) recepción *f*
reception area *n* (zona *f* de) recepción *f* **reception centre** *n Brit* centro *m* educativo (*en el que los niños empiezan la escolarización*) **reception class** *n Brit* clase *f* del primer año **reception desk** *n* (mesa *f* de) recepción *f*
receptionist [rɪ'sepʃənɪst] *n* recepcionista *mf*
receptive [rɪ'septɪv] *adj* receptivo, -a
receptiveness *n,* **receptivity** [ˌriːsep'tɪvəti, *Am:* riːˌsep'tɪvət̬i] *n no pl* receptividad *f*
recess [rɪ'ses, *Am:* 'riːses] **I.** <-es> *n* **1.** POL suspensión *f* de actividades, receso *m AmL* **2.** *Am, Aus* SCHOOL recreo *m* **3.** ARCHIT hueco *m* **4.** *pl* (*place*) lugar *m* recóndito **II.** *vi Am, Aus* prorrogar; (*meeting, session*) suspender **III.** *vt* ARCHIT rebajar
recession [rɪ'seʃən] *n* **1.** (*retreat*) retroceso *m* **2.** ECON recesión *f*
recessive [rɪ'sesɪv] *adj* BIO recesivo, -a
recharge [ˌriː'tʃɑːdʒ, *Am:* -'tʃɑːrdʒ] **I.** *vt* recargar **II.** *vi* recargarse
rechargeable [ˌriː'tʃɑːdʒəbl, *Am:* -'tʃɑːrdʒ-] *adj* recargable
recidivism [rɪ'sɪdɪvɪzəm, *Am:* -'sɪdə-] *n no pl* reincidencia *f*
recidivist [rɪ'sɪdɪvɪst, *Am:* -'sɪdə-] *n* reincidente *mf*
recipe ['resəpi] *n a. fig* receta *f*
recipient [rɪ'sɪpɪənt] *n* (*of letter*) destinatario, -a *m, f;* (*of transplant*) receptor(a) *m(f);* (*of gift*) beneficiario, -a *m, f*
reciprocal [rɪ'sɪprəkl] **I.** *adj* **1.** *a.* LING, MAT recíproco, -a **2.** (*reverse*) mutuo, -a **II.** *n* MAT recíproco *m*
reciprocate [rɪ'sɪprəkeɪt] **I.** *vt* corresponder a, reciprocar *AmL* **II.** *vi* **1.** corresponder **2.** TECH alternar
reciprocity [ˌresɪ'prɒsəti, *Am:* -'prɑːsət̬i] *n no pl* reciprocidad *f*
recital [rɪ'saɪtl, *Am:* -t̬l] *n* **1.** MUS recital *m* **2.** (*description*) relación *f*
recitation [ˌresɪ'teɪʃən] *n* LIT recitación *f*
recitative [ˌresɪtə'tiːv] *n* MUS recitativo *m*
recite [rɪ'saɪt] **I.** *vt* **1.** (*repeat*) recitar **2.** (*list*) enumerar **II.** *vi* dar un recitado
reckless ['rekləs] *adj* imprudente; LAW teme-

rario, -a

recklessness *n no pl* imprudencia *f,* temeridad *f*

reckon ['rekən] **I.** *vt* **1.** (*calculate*) calcular **2.** (*consider*) considerar; **to ~ (that) ...** creer (que)...; **I ~ not** me parece que no; **what do you ~?** ¿qué opinas? **3.** (*judge*) estimar **II.** *vi inf* calcular

◆**reckon in** *vt* tomar en cuenta

◆**reckon on** *vt insep* **1.** (*count on*) contar con **2.** (*expect*) esperar

◆**reckon up** *vt* calcular

◆**reckon with** *vt insep* tener en cuenta; **she is a force to be reckoned with** es alguien a quien hay que tener muy en cuenta

◆**reckon without** *vt insep* no tener en cuenta

reckoning ['rekənɪŋ] *n* **1.** (*calculation*) cálculo *m;* **to be out in one's ~** calcular mal **2.** (*settlement*) ajuste *m* de cuentas

reclaim [rɪ'kleɪm] *vt* **1.** (*claim back: title, rights*) reclamar **2.** (*reuse: land*) recuperar; (*material*) reciclar **3.** (*reform*) regenerar

reclamation [ˌreklə'meɪʃən] *n no pl* **1.** (*of title, rights*) reclamación *f* **2.** (*of land*) recuperación *f;* (*of material*) reciclaje *m* **3.** (*reformation*) regeneración *f*

recline [rɪ'klaɪn] **I.** *vi* apoyarse; **to ~ on** reclinarse contra [*o* en] **II.** *vt* reclinar

recliner [rɪ'klaɪnə^r^, *Am:* -nɚ] *n* asiento *m* reclinable

reclining seat *n,* **reclining chair** *n* asiento *m* reclinable

recluse [rɪ'klu:s, *Am:* 'reklu:s] *n* ermitaño, -a *m, f*

reclusive *adj* solitario, -a

recognition [ˌrekəg'nɪʃən] *n no pl a.* INFOR reconocimiento *m;* **optical character ~** reconocimiento óptico de caracteres; **voice ~** reconocimiento de la voz; **in ~ of** en reconocimiento de

recognizable ['rekəgnaɪzəbl] *adj* reconocible

recognizance [rɪ'kɒgnɪzns, *Am:* -'kɑ:gnɪ-] *n* fianza *f*

recognize ['rekəgnaɪz] *vt* reconocer

recognized ['rekəgnaɪzd] *adj* reconocido, -a

recoil[1] [rɪ'kɔɪl] *vi* **1.** (*draw back*) echarse atrás; **to ~ in horror** retroceder de miedo; **to ~ at sth** sentir repugnancia hacia algo; **to ~ from doing sth** rehuir hacer algo **2.** (*gun*) retroceder

recoil[2] ['ri:kɔɪl] *n* retroceso *m*

recollect [ˌrekə'lekt] *vi, vt* recordar

recollection [ˌrekə'lekʃən] *n* recuerdo *m;* **to have no ~ of sth** no recordar algo

recommend [ˌrekə'mend] *vt* recomendar; **it is not to be ~ed** no es recomendable

recommendable *adj* recomendable

recommendation [ˌrekəmen'deɪʃən, *Am:* -mən'-] *n* **1.** (*suggestion*) recomendación *f;* **on sb's ~** por recomendación de alguien **2.** (*advice*) consejo *m*

recompense ['rekəmpents] **I.** *n no pl* **1.** (*reward*) recompensa *f* **2.** (*compensation*) compensación *f* **II.** *vt* **1.** (*reward*) recompensar **2.** (*make amends*) compensar

reconcile ['rekənsaɪl] *vt* **1.** (*person*) reconciliar; **to become ~d with sb** reconciliarse con alguien **2.** (*difference, fact*) conciliar; **to be ~d to sth** aceptar algo; **to become ~d to sth** resignarse a algo

reconciliation [ˌrekənˌsɪlɪ'eɪʃən] *n* **1.** (*restoration of good relations*) reconciliación *f* **2.** *no pl* (*making compatible*) conciliación *f*

recondition [ˌri:kən'dɪʃən] *vt* reacondicionar

reconnaissance [rɪ'kɒnɪsənts, *Am:* -'kɑ:nə-] *n* reconocimiento *m*

reconnaissance flight *n* vuelo *m* de reconocimiento

reconnoiter *Am,* **reconnoitre** [ˌrekə'nɔɪtə^r^, *Am:* ˌri:kə'nɔɪt̬ɚ] **I.** *vt* reconocer **II.** *vi* reconocer el terreno

reconsider [ˌri:kən'sɪdə^r^, *Am:* -ɚ] **I.** *vt* reconsiderar **II.** *vi* recapacitar

reconstruct [ˌri:kən'strʌkt] *vt* **1.** (*building*) reconstruir **2.** (*life*) rehacer; (*crime, event*) reconstituir

reconstruction [ˌri:kən'strʌkʃən] *n* **1.** *no pl* (*of building*) reconstrucción *f* **2.** (*of crime, event*) reconstitución *f*

record[1] ['rekɔ:d, *Am:* -ɚd] **I.** *n* **1.** (*account*) relación *m;* (*document*) documento *m;* **medical ~** historial *m* médico; **to say sth off the ~** decir algo extraoficialmente; **to put sth on ~** dejar constancia de algo **2.** *no pl* (*sb's past*) antecedentes *mpl;* **to have a good ~** tener un buen historial; **to have a clean ~** no tener antecedentes **3.** *pl* archivos *mpl* **4.** MUS disco *m;* **to make a ~** grabar un disco **5.** SPORTS récord *m;* **to break a ~** batir un récord **6.** LAW acta *f* **7.** INFOR juego *m* de datos **II.** *adj* récord; **to do sth in ~ time** hacer algo en un tiempo récord; **to reach a ~ high** alcanzar un máximo sin precedentes

record[2] [rɪ'kɔ:d, *Am:* -'kɔ:rd] **I.** *vt* **1.** (*store*) archivar **2.** *a.* INFOR registrar; MUS grabar **3.** LAW hacer constar en acta **II.** *vi* grabar

record-breaker ['rekɔ:dˌbreɪkə^r^, *Am:* -ɚdˌbreɪkɚ] *n* SPORTS plusmarquista *mf* **record-breaking** *adj* que bate todos los récords

recorded [rɪ'kɔ:dɪd, *Am:* -'kɔ:rd-] *adj* registrado, -a; (*history*) documentado, -a; (*music*) grabado, -a

recorder [rɪ'kɔ:də^r^, *Am:* -'kɔ:rdɚ] *n* **1.** (*tape recorder*) magnetofón *m* **2.** MUS flauta *f* dulce **3.** *Brit* LAW juez *mf*

record holder *n* SPORTS plusmarquista *mf*

recording *n* (*of sound*) grabación *f*

recording session *n* sesión *f* de grabación **recording studio** *n* estudio *m* de grabación

record label *n* sello *m* discográfico **record library** *n* discoteca *f* **record player** *n* tocadiscos *m inv* **record token** *n* cupón *m* para discos

R

recount¹ [rɪ'kaʊnt] *vt* **1.** (*narrate*) contar **2.** (*count again*) volver a contar
recount² ['riːkaʊnt] *n* POL recuento *m*
recoup [rɪ'kuːp] *vt* (*expenditure, energy*) recuperar; (*losses*) resarcirse de
recourse [rɪ'kɔːs, *Am:* 'riːkɔːrs] *n no pl* recurso *m;* **to have ~ to** recurrir a
recover [rɪ'kʌvəʳ, *Am:* -ɚ] **I.** *vt* **a.** INFOR recuperar; **to ~ one's composure** recobrar su compostura **II.** *vi* **1.** (*regain health*) reponerse **2.** (*return to normal*) recuperarse
re-cover [ˌriː'kʌvəʳ, *Am:* -ɚ] *vt* retapizar
recoverable [rɪ'kʌvərəbl] *adj* **1. a.** INFOR recuperable **2. a.** FIN reactivable
recovery [rɪ'kʌvəri, *Am:* -ɚi] <-ies> *n* **1. a.** MED, ECON recuperación *f;* **to be beyond ~** ser irrecuperable **2.** INFOR reactivación *f*
recovery service *n no pl* servicio *m* de grúa **recovery ship** *n* barco *m* de salvamento **recovery vehicle** *n* vehículo *m* de salvamento
recreate [ˌriːkri'eɪt] *vt* recrear
recreation¹ [ˌriːkri'eɪʃən] *n no pl* (*of conditions, situation*) recreación *f*
recreation² [ˌrekri'eɪʃən] *n* **1. a.** SCHOOL recreo *m* **2.** (*pastime*) diversión *f*
recreational [ˌrekri'eɪʃənəl] *adj* recreativo, -a
recreational vehicle *n Am* roulotte *f*
recreation centre *n* centro *m* recreativo **recreation ground** *n Brit* campo *m* de deportes **recreation room** *n* salón *m* recreativo
recreative ['rekrɪˌeɪtɪv, *Am:* -t̬ɪv] *adj* recreativo, -a
recriminate [rɪ'krɪmɪneɪt, *Am:* -əneɪt] *vi* recriminar
recrimination [rɪˌkrɪmɪ'neɪʃən, *Am:* -ə'-] *n pl* recriminación *f*
recruit [rɪ'kruːt] **I.** *vt* MIL reclutar; (*employee*) contratar **II.** *n* MIL recluta *mf*
recruiting **I.** *n no pl* MIL reclutamiento *m;* ECON contratación *f* **II.** *adj* MIL de reclutamiento; ECON de contratación
recruiting office *n* MIL oficina *f* de reclutamiento
recruitment **I.** *n no pl* MIL reclutamiento *m;* ECON contratación *f;* (*of members*) afiliación *f* **II.** *adj* de reclutamiento
recruitment agency *n* agencia *f* de selección de personal
rectangle ['rektæŋgl] *n* rectángulo *m*
rectangular [rek'tæŋgjʊləʳ, *Am:* -gjəlɚ] *adj* rectangular
rectification [ˌrektɪfɪ'keɪʃən, *Am:* ˌrektə-] *n no pl* rectificación *f*
rectify ['rektɪfaɪ, *Am:* -tə-] *vt* rectificar
rectilinear [ˌrektɪ'lɪnɪəʳ, *Am:* -tə'-] *adj* rectilíneo, -a
rectitude ['rektɪtjuːd, *Am:* -tətuːd] *n no pl* rectitud *f*
rector ['rektəʳ, *Am:* -tɚ] *n* **1.** *Brit* REL ≈ párroco *m* **2.** *Am, Scot* SCHOOL director(a) *m(f)* **3.** *Am, Scot* UNIV rector(a) *m(f)*
rectory ['rektəri] <-ies> *n* rectoría *f*
rectum ['rektəm] *n* ANAT recto *m*
recumbent [rɪ'kʌmbənt] *adj liter* recostado, -a
recuperate [rɪ'kuːpəreɪt] **I.** *vi* recuperarse **II.** *vt* recuperar
recuperation [rɪˌkuːpə'reɪʃən] *n no pl* recuperación *f*
recur [rɪ'kɜːʳ, *Am:* -'kɜːr] *vi* repetirse
recurrence [rɪ'kʌrəns, *Am:* -'kɜːr-] *n* repetición *f*
recurrent [rɪ'kʌrənt, *Am:* -'kɜːr-] *adj* (*dream, motif*) recurrente; (*problem*) repetido, -a; (*costs, expenses*) constante
recurring *adj* recurrente
recurring decimal *n* decimal *m* periódico
recycle [ˌriː'saɪkl] *vt* reciclar
recycling **I.** *n no pl* reciclaje *m* **II.** *adj* de reciclaje
recycling plant *n* planta *f* de reciclaje
red [red] **I.** <-dd-> *adj* rojo, -a; (*wine*) tinto, -a; **to be** [*o* **go**] **~** ruborizarse **II.** *n* rojo *m;* **to be in the ~** FIN estar en números rojos ►**to make sb see ~** sacar a alguien de quicio; **to see ~** salir de sus casillas
Red Army *n* Ejército *m* Rojo
red-blooded [ˌred'blʌdɪd] *adj* fogoso, -a
redcap ['redkæp] *n* **1.** *Brit, inf* MIL policía *mf* militar **2.** *Am* (*railway porter*) mozo *m* de estación **Red Crescent** *n no pl* **the ~** la Media Luna Roja **Red Cross** *n no pl* **the ~** la Cruz Roja **redcurrant** *n* grosella *f* **red deer** *n inv* ciervo *m*
redden ['redn] **I.** *vi* enrojecerse; (*person*) ruborizarse; **to ~ with embarrassment** ponerse colorado de vergüenza **II.** *vt* enrojecer
reddish ['redɪʃ] *adj* rojizo, -a
redecorate [ˌriː'dekəreɪt] *vt* redecorar; (*paint*) volver a pintar; (*wallpaper*) volver a empapelar
redecoration [ˌriːdekə'reɪʃən] *n* (*repainting*) cambio *m* de pintura; (*re-papering*) cambio *m* de papel pintado
redeem [rɪ'diːm] *vt* **1. a.** REL (*person, soul*) redimir; (*situation*) salvar; **to ~ oneself** redimirse **2.** FIN (*policy, share*) liquidar; (*pawned item*) desempeñar; (*debt*) pagar; **to ~ a mortgage** amortizar una hipoteca **3.** (*fulfill: promise*) cumplir
redeemable *adj* FIN reembolsable
Redeemer [rɪ'diːməʳ, *Am:* -mɚ] *n no pl* REL **the ~** el Redentor
redeeming [rɪ'diːmɪŋ] *adj* redentor(a); **he has no ~ features** no tiene ningún punto a su favor
redefine [ˌriːdɪ'faɪn] *vt* redefinir
redemption [rɪ'dempʃən] *n no pl* **1. a.** REL redención *f* **2.** FIN (*of policy, share*) liquidación *f;* (*of mortgage*) amortización *f*
redeploy [ˌriːdɪ'plɔɪ] *vt* (*workers, staff*) reorganizar, reubicar *AmL;* (*soldiers, troops*) cambiar la disposición de

redeployment *n* (*of workers, staff*) reorganización *f*, reubicación *f AmL;* (*of soldiers, troops*) redistribución *f*
redevelop [ˌriːdɪˈveləp] *vt* reurbanizar
redevelopment [ˌriːdɪˈveləpmənt] *n* reurbanización *f*
red-haired [ˌredˈheəʳd] *adj* pelirrojo, -a
red-handed [ˌredˈhændɪd] *adj* **to catch sb ~** pillar a alguien con las manos en la masa
redhead [ˈredhed] *n* pelirrojo, -a *m, f*
red-headed *adj* pelirrojo, -a
red herring *n fig* pista *f* falsa
red-hot [ˌredˈhɒt, *Am:* -hɑːt] *adj* **1.** (*extremely hot*) candente; **to be ~** estar al rojo vivo **2.** (*exciting*) apasionante **3.** (*up-to--the-minute*) de última hora
Red Indian *n* piel *mf* roja
redirect [ˌriːdɪˈrekt] *vt* reorientar; (*letter*) reexpedir; (*traffic*) desviar
redistribute [ˌriːdɪˈstrɪbjuːt] *vt* redistribuir
redistribution [ˌriːdɪstrɪˈbjuːʃən] *n no pl* redistribución *f*
red-letter day [ˌredˈletəˌdeɪ, *Am:* -ˈleṭɚ-] *n* día *m* memorable
red light *n* semáforo *m* en rojo **red-light district** *n* barrio *m* chino
red meat *n no pl* carne *f* roja
redneck [ˈrednek] *n Am: campesino blanco de la clase baja rural, perteneciente de los estados del Sur*
redness [ˈrednɪs] *n no pl* rojez *f*
redo [ˌriːˈduː] *vt irr* rehacer
redolent [ˈredələnt] *adj form* **1.** (*smelling of*) **~ of sth** con olor a algo **2.** (*suggestive of*) **to be ~ of sth** hacer pensar en algo
redouble [rɪˈdʌbl] *vt* redoblar; **to ~ one's efforts** redoblar los esfuerzos
redoubtable [rɪˈdaʊtəbl, *Am:* -ṭə-] *adj* imponente, temible
redound [rɪˈdaʊnd] *vi form* **to ~ to sb's advantage** redundar en beneficio de alguien; **to ~ to sb's credit** aumentar el prestigio de alguien
red pepper *n* pimiento *m* rojo
redraft¹ [ˌriːˈdrɑːft, *Am:* -ˈdræft] *vt* volver a redactar
redraft² [ˈriːdrɑːft, *Am:* -dræft] *n* nuevo borrador *m*
redress [rɪˈdres] **I.** *vt* (*grievance*) reparar; (*fault*) remediar; (*imbalance*) rectificar **II.** *n* (*of grievance, imbalance*) reparación *f;* **to seek ~** exigir reparación
Red Sea *n no pl* **the ~** el Mar Rojo **redskin** *n* piel *mf* roja **red tape** *n no pl* papeleo *m*
reduce [rɪˈdjuːs, *Am:* -ˈduːs] **I.** *vt* **1.** (*diminish*) reducir; (*price*) rebajar; (*wages*) recortar **2.** MIL degradar **3. to ~ sb to tears** hacer llorar a alguien; **to ~ sth to rubble/ashes** reducir algo a escombros/cenizas; **to be ~d to doing sth** verse forzado a hacer algo **4.** MAT (*fraction*) simplificar **II.** *vi Am* adelgazar
reduced [rɪˈdjuːst, *Am:* -ˈduːst] *adj* **1.** (*lower*) reducido, -a; (*price*) rebajado, -a **2.** (*impoverished*) **to be in ~ circumstances** estar pasando estrecheces
reducer [rɪˈdjuːsəʳ, *Am:* -ˈduːsɚ] *n Am* producto *m* adelgazante
reduction [rɪˈdʌkʃən] *n* reducción *f;* (*in price*) rebaja *f*
redundancy [rɪˈdʌndəntsi] <-ies> *n* **1.** *no pl* (*uselessness*) superfluidad *f;* LING redundancia *f* **2.** (*unemployment*) desempleo *m* **3.** *Brit, Aus* ECON despido *m*
redundancy payment *n Brit, Aus* indemnización *f* por despido
redundant [rɪˈdʌndənt] *adj* **1.** (*superfluous*) superfluo, -a; LING redundante **2.** *Brit, Aus* **to be made ~** ser despedido, -a
reduplicate [rɪˈdjuːplɪkeɪt, *Am:* -ˈduːplə-] *vi* reduplicar
reduplication [rɪˌdjuːplɪˈkeɪʃən, *Am:* -ˌduːpləˈ-] *n* reduplicación *f*
red wine *n* vino *m* tinto
redwood [ˈredwʊd] *n* secuoya *f*
re-echo [ˌriːˈekəʊ, *Am:* -oʊ] **I.** *vt* repetir **II.** *vi* resonar
reed [riːd] *n* **1.** (*plant*) junco *m*, totora *f AmS* **2.** *Brit* (*straw*) caña *f* **3.** MUS lengüeta *f*
reed instrument *n* instrumento *m* de lengüeta
re-educate [ˌriːˈedʒʊkeɪt] *vt* reeducar
reedy [ˈriːdi] *adj* **1.** (*full of reeds*) poblado, -a de juncos **2.** MUS (*voice*) aflautado, -a
reef [riːf] **I.** *n* **1.** (*ridge*) arrecife *m* **2.** (*part of sail*) rizo *m* **II.** *vt* NAUT arrizar
reefer [ˈriːfəʳ, *Am:* -fɚ] *n inf* porro *m*
reef knot *n* nudo *m* de rizo
reek [riːk] **I.** *vi* apestar; **to ~ of corruption** apestar a corrupción **II.** *n* hedor *m*
reel¹ [riːl] *n* (*storage or winding device*) carrete *m;* (*for film, yarn, tape*) bobina *f*
reel² [riːl] **I.** *vi* **1.** (*move unsteadily*) tambalearse **2.** (*recoil*) retroceder **II.** *n* reel *m* (*baile escocés*)
re-elect [ˌriːɪˈlekt] *vt* reelegir
re-election [ˌriːɪˈlekʃən] *n* reelección *f*
re-employ [ˌriːɪmˈplɔɪ] *vt* volver a emplear
re-engage [ˌriːɪnˈgeɪdʒ] *vt* volver a contratar
re-enter [ˌriːˈentəʳ, *Am:* -ṭɚ] **I.** *vt* **1.** (*go in again*) volver a entrar en **2.** INFOR teclear de nuevo **II.** *vi* reingresar
re-entry [ˌriːˈentri] <-ies> *n* reingreso *m*
ref [ref] *n* **1.** *inf abbr of* **referee** árbitro, -a *m, f* **2.** *abbr of* **reference** referencia *f*
refectory [rɪˈfektəri] <-ies> *n* refectorio *m*
refer [rɪˈfɜːʳ, *Am:* -ˈfɜːr] <-rr-> *vt* **to refer sth to sb** (*article*) remitir algo a alguien; **to ~ a patient to a specialist** mandar a un paciente a un especialista; **to ~ a case to sb/sth** LAW remitir una causa a alguien/algo
◆**refer back to** *vt* remitir a; **the reader is referred back to the introduction** se remite al lector a la introducción
◆**refer to** *vt* **1.** (*mention, allude*) referirse a; **to never ~ sth** no mencionar nunca algo; **to ~ sb as sth** calificar a alguien de algo; **refering**

R

to your letter/phone call, ... con relación a su carta/llamada,... **2.** (*concern*) concernir; **does this information ~ me?** ¿esta información tiene algo que ver conmigo? **3.** (*consult, turn to*) consultar; **to ~ one's notes** consultar sus apuntes; ~ **page 70** ver página 70; **I ~ the facts** me remito a los hechos

referee [ˌrefəˈriː] **I.** *n* **1.** SPORTS árbitro, -a *m, f,* referí *m AmL* **2.** (*in dispute*) mediador(a) *m(f)* **3.** *Brit* (*for employment*) persona *f* que da referencias del candidato **II.** *vi, vt* arbitrar

reference [ˈrefərənts] *n* **1.** (*consultantion*) consulta *f;* **to make ~ to sth** hacer referencia a algo **2.** (*source*) referencia *f* **3.** (*allusion*) alusión *f;* **with ~ to what was said** en alusión a lo que se dijo **4.** ADMIN (*number*) número *m* de referencia **5.** (*for job application*) referencias *fpl;* **to take up ~s** pedir referencias

reference book *n* libro *m* de consulta **reference library** *n* biblioteca *f* de consulta **reference number** *n* **1.** (*in document, on book*) número *m* de referencia **2.** (*on product*) número *m* de serie

referendum [ˌrefəˈrendəm] <-s *o* -da> *n* referéndum *m*

referral [rɪˈfɜːrəl] *n* remisión *f*

refill[1] [ˌriːˈfɪl] *vt* rellenar

refill[2] [ˈriːfɪl] *n* recambio *m*

refine [rɪˈfaɪn] *vt* **1.** (*oil, sugar*) refinar **2.** (*technique*) perfeccionar

refined [rɪˈfaɪnd] *adj* **1.** (*oil, sugar*) refinado, -a **2.** (*sophisticated*) sofisticado, -a **3.** (*very polite*) fino, -a

refinement [rɪˈfaɪnmənt] *n* **1.** (*improvement*) refinamiento *m* **2.** *no pl* (*purification*) refinación *f* **3.** *no pl* (*good manners*) finura *f*

refinery [rɪˈfaɪnəri] <-ies> *n* refinería *f*

refit[1] [ˌriːˈfɪt] <-tt- *o Am* -t-> *a.* NAUT **I.** *vi* repararse **II.** *vt* reparar

refit[2] [ˈriːfɪt] *n a.* NAUT reparación *f*

reflate [riːˈfleɪt] *vt* reflacionar

reflation [ˌriːˈfleɪʃən] *n* reflación *f*

reflect [rɪˈflekt] **I.** *vt* reflejar **II.** *vi* **1.** (*cast back light*) reflejarse **2.** (*contemplate*) reflexionar **3.** **to ~ badly on sth** no decir mucho de algo

reflecting *adj* reflectante

reflecting telescope *n* telescopio *m* reflector

reflection [rɪˈflekʃən] *n* **1.** (*image*) reflejo *m* **2.** (*thought*) reflexión *f;* **~s on sth** reflexión acerca de algo; **on ~** pensándolo bien **3.** *fig* **to be a fair ~ of sth** ser un fiel reflejo de algo; **to be a poor ~ on sth** no decir mucho de algo

reflective [rɪˈflektɪv] *adj* **1.** (*surface*) reflector(a) **2.** (*thoughtful*) reflexivo, -a

reflector [rɪˈflektəʳ, *Am:* -ɚ] *n* (*mirror*) reflector *m;* (*of bicycle, car*) captafaros *m inv*

reflex [ˈriːfleks] <-es> **I.** *n* reflejo *m* **II.** *adj* reflejo, -a

reflex action *n* acto *m* reflejo **reflex camera** *n* cámara *f* réflex

reflexive [rɪˈfleksɪv] **I.** *adj* **1.** *Am* (*independent of will*) reflejo, -a **2.** LING reflexivo, -a **II.** *n* LING reflexivo *m*

reflexology [ˌriːflekˈsɒlədʒi, *Am:* -ˈsɑːlə-] *n* reflexología *f*

refloat [ˌriːˈfləʊt, *Am:* -ˈfloʊt] *vt* reflotar

reflux [ˌriːˈflʌks] *n* reflujo *m*

reforest [ˌriːˈfɒrɪst, *Am:* -ˈfɔːr-] *vt* reforestar

reform [rɪˈfɔːm, *Am:* -ˈfɔːrm] **I.** *vt* reformar **II.** *vi* reformarse **III.** *n* reforma *f*

re-form [ˌriːˈfɔːm, *Am:* -ˈfɔːrm] **I.** *vt* formar de nuevo **II.** *vi* formarse de nuevo

reformation [ˌrefəˈmeɪʃən, *Am:* -ɚˈ-] *n* reforma *f;* **the Reformation** la Reforma

reformatory [rɪˈfɔːmətəri, *Am:* -ˈfɔːrmətɔːri] <-ies> *n Am* reformatorio *m*

reformer *n* reformador(a) *m(f)*

reform school *n* reformatorio *m*

refract [rɪˈfrækt] *vt* PHYS refractar

refraction [rɪˈfrækʃən] *n* refracción *f*

refractory [rɪˈfræktəri] *adj* refractario, -a

refrain[1] [rɪˈfreɪn] *vi form* abstenerse; **to ~ from doing sth** abstenerse de hacer algo

refrain[2] [rɪˈfreɪn] *n* MUS estribillo *m*

refresh [rɪˈfreʃ] *vt* refrescar; **to ~ oneself** refrescarse

refresher *n* **1.** (*course*) curso *m* de reciclaje **2.** *Brit* LAW honorarios *mpl* suplementarios

refreshing *adj* **1.** (*drink*) refrescante **2.** (*change, difference*) reconfortante

refreshment [rɪˈfreʃmənt] *n* **1.** (*drink*) refresco *m* **2.** (*food*) refrigerio *m*

refrigerant [rɪˈfrɪdʒərənt] *n* refrigerante *m*

refrigerate [rɪˈfrɪdʒəreɪt] *vt* refrigerar

refrigeration [rɪˌfrɪdʒəˈreɪʃən] *n no pl* refrigeración *f*

refrigerator [rɪˈfrɪdʒəreɪtəʳ, *Am:* -t̬ɚ] *n* nevera *f,* refrigerador *m AmL,* frigider *m Chile*

refuel [ˌriːˈfjuːəl] <-ll-, *Am:* -l-> **I.** *vi* repostar combustible **II.** *vt* reabastecer de combustible; *fig* renovar

refuge [ˈrefjuːdʒ] *n* refugio *m;* **to take ~ in sth** refugiarse en algo

refugee [ˌrefjʊˈdʒiː] *n* refugiado, -a *m, f*

refugee camp *n* campo *m* de refugiados

refund[1] [ˌriːˈfʌnd] *vt* reembolsar

refund[2] [ˈriːfʌnd] *n* reembolso *m*

refurbish [ˌriːˈfɜːbɪʃ, *Am:* -ˈfɜːrbɪʃ] *vt* restaurar, refaccionar *AmL*

refusal [rɪˈfjuːzl] *n* negativa *f*

refuse[1] [rɪˈfjuːz] **I.** *vi* negarse **II.** *vt* (*request, gift*) rechazar; (*permission, entry*) denegar; **to ~ sb sth** negar algo a alguien

refuse[2] [ˈrefjuːs] *n form* basura *f;* **garden/kitchen ~** desperdicios *mpl* de jardín/cocina

refuse bin *n* cubo *m* de basura, bote *m* de basura *Méx* **refuse collection** *n* recogida *f* de basuras **refuse collector** *n Brit* basurero, -a *m, f* **refuse disposal** *n* eliminación *f* de basura **refuse dump** *n* vertedero *m,* basurero *m Méx*

refusenik [reˈfjuːznɪk] *n* POL objetor *m*

refutation [ˌrefjuːˈteɪʃən] *n* refutación *f*

refute [rɪˈfjuːt] *vt* refutar

regain [rɪˈgeɪn] *vt* (*freedom, possession*)

recuperar; (*consciousness, health*) recobrar
regal ['riːgl] *adj* regio, -a
regale [rɪ'geɪl] *vt iron* agasajar
regalia [rɪ'geɪlɪə, *Am:* -'geɪljə] *n* **1.** (*clothes*) traje *m* de gala **2.** (*insignia*) insignias *fpl*
regard [rɪ'gɑːd, *Am:* -'gɑːrd] **I.** *vt* **1.** (*consider*) considerar; **to ~ sb highly** tener muy buena opinión de alguien **2.** *form* (*watch*) contemplar **3.** (*concerning*) **as ~s ...** respecto a... **II.** *n form* **1.** (*consideration*) consideración *f*; **to pay no ~ to sth** no prestar atención a algo; **with ~ to ...** en cuanto a... **2.** (*respect*) respeto *m*, estima *f*; **to hold sb/sth in high ~** tener una alta estima por alguien/algo **3.** (*point*) respecto *m*; **in this ~** con respecto a esto **4.** *pl* (*in messages*) recuerdos *mpl*; **with kind ~s** muchos saludos
regardful [rɪ'gɑːdfəl, *Am:* -'gɑːrd-] *adj* atento, -a
regarding *prep* en cuanto a
regardless [rɪ'gɑːdləs, *Am:* -'gɑːrd-] **I.** *adv* a pesar de todo; **to press on ~** seguir cueste lo que cueste **II.** *adj* indiferente; **~ of ...** sin tener en cuenta...
regatta [rɪ'gætə, *Am:* -'gɑːt̬ə] *n* regata *f*
regency ['riːdʒənsi] *n* regencia *f*
regenerate [rɪ'dʒenəreɪt] **I.** *vt* regenerar **II.** *vi* regenerarse
regeneration [rɪˌdʒenə'reɪʃən] *n no pl* regeneración *f*
regent ['riːdʒənt] **I.** *n* regente *mf* **II.** *adj* **Prince Regent** Príncipe *m* Regente
reggae ['regeɪ] *n no pl* reggae *m*
regicide ['redʒɪsaɪd] *n* **1.** (*person*) regicida *mf* **2.** (*action*) regicidio *m*
regime [reɪ'ʒiːm, *Am:* rə'-] *n* régimen *m*
regimen ['redʒɪmen, *Am:* -əmen] *n form* régimen *m*
regiment ['redʒɪmənt, *Am:* -əmənt] **I.** *n* **1.** MIL regimiento *m* **2.** *fig* multitud *f* **II.** *vt* reglamentar
regimentation [ˌredʒɪmen'teɪʃən, *Am:* -əmən'-] *n* reglamentación *f*
region ['riːdʒən] *n* **1.** GEO, ANAT región *f*; **in the ~ of 30** alrededor de 30 **2.** (*administrative area*) provincia *f*
regional ['riːdʒənl] *adj* regional
regionalism ['riːdʒənəˌlɪzəm] *n* regionalismo *m*
register ['redʒɪstəʳ, *Am:* -stɚ] **I.** *n* registro *m*; **class ~** lista *f* de la clase **II.** *vt* registrar; (*car*) matricular; (*voter*) inscribir; (*letter, parcel*) certificar **III.** *vi* **1.** (*record*) inscribirse; UNIV matricularse, inscribirse *AmL* **2.** (*be understood*) **the information didn't ~ with him** no retuvo la información
registered ['redʒɪstəd, *Am:* -ɚd] *adj* registrado, -a; (*nurse*) diplomado, -a; (*student*) matriculado, -a; (*letter, parcel*) certificado, -a
registrar [ˌredʒɪ'strɑːʳ, *Am:* 'redʒɪstrɑːr] *n* **1.** ADMIN secretario, -a *m, f* del registro civil **2.** *Brit* UNIV secretario, -a *m, f* general **3.** *Brit, Aus* MED médico *mf* asistente
registration [ˌredʒɪ'streɪʃən] *n* **1.** (*act*) inscripción *f*; UNIV matriculación *f* **2.** (*number*) matrícula *f*
registration document *n Brit* documento *m* de matriculación **registration fee** *n* cuota *f* de inscripción; UNIV matrícula *f* **registration number** *n* matrícula *f*
registry ['redʒɪstri] *n Brit* registro *m*
regress [rɪ'gres] *vi* retroceder
regression [rɪ'greʃən] *n no pl* regresión *f*
regressive [rɪ'gresɪv] *adj* regresivo, -a
regret [rɪ'gret] **I.** <-tt-> *vt* lamentar; **to ~ doing sth** arrepentirse de haber hecho algo; **we ~ any inconvenience to passengers** lamentamos las molestias para los pasajeros **II.** *n* arrepentimiento *m*; **to have ~** tener remordimientos; **to have no ~s about sth** no arrepentirse de algo; **much to my ~** muy a mi pesar; **to send one's ~s** enviar disculpas
regretful [rɪ'gretfəl] *adj* arrepentido, -a
regretfully *adv* lamentablemente
regrettable [rɪ'gretəbl, *Am:* -'gret̬-] *adj* lamentable
regroup [ˌriː'gruːp] **I.** *vt* reagrupar **II.** *vi* reagruparse
regular ['regjʊləʳ, *Am:* -jəlɚ] **I.** *adj* **1.** (*pattern*) regular; (*appearance, customer*) habitual; (*procedure*) normal; **to have ~ meetings** tener reuniones periódicas **2.** *Am* (*gas*) normal **3.** LING regular **4.** *inf* (*real*) verdadero, -a **II.** *n* **1.** (*customer*) asiduo, -a *m, f* **2.** MIL soldado *m* regular
regularity [ˌregjʊ'lærəti, *Am:* -'lerət̬i] *n no pl* regularidad *f*
regularize ['regjʊləraɪz] *vt* **1.** (*standardize*) normalizar **2.** (*normalize*) regularizar
regularly *adv* con regularidad
regulate ['regjʊleɪt] *vt* **1.** (*supervise*) reglamentar **2.** (*adjust*) regular
regulation [ˌregjʊ'leɪʃən] **I.** *n* **1.** (*rule*) regla *f*; **safety ~s** reglamento *m* de seguridad; **in accordance with the ~s** de acuerdo con el reglamento **2.** *no pl* (*adjustment*) regulación *f* **II.** *adj* reglamentario, -a
regulator ['regjʊleɪtəʳ, *Am:* -t̬ɚ] *n* regulador *m*
regulatory [ˌregjʊ'leɪtri, *Am:* 'regjəleɪtɔːri] *adj* regulador(a)
regurgitate [riː'gɜːdʒɪteɪt, *Am:* -'gɜːrdʒə-] *vt* **1.** (*food*) regurgitar **2.** (*ideas, facts*) repetir maquinalmente
rehabilitate [ˌriːhə'bɪlɪteɪt, *Am:* '-ə-] *vt* rehabilitar
rehabilitation [ˌriːhəˌbɪlɪ'teɪʃən, *Am:* -ə'-] *n no pl* rehabilitación *f*
rehabilitation centre *n* centro *m* de rehabilitación
rehash[1] [ˌriː'hæʃ] *vt* hacer un refrito de
rehash[2] ['riːhæʃ] *n* refrito *m*
rehearsal [rɪ'hɜːsl, *Am:* -'hɜːrsl] *n* ensayo *m*
rehearse [rɪ'hɜːs, *Am:* -'hɜːrs] *vt, vi* ensayar
reign [reɪn] **I.** *vi* **1.** (*be monarch*) reinar **2.** *fig* (*be dominant*) imperar **II.** *n* **1.** (*sovereignty*)

R

reinado *m* **2.** (*rule*) régimen *m*
reimburse [ˌriːɪm'bɜːs, *Am:* -'bɜːrs] *vt* reembolsar
reimbursement *n* reembolso *m*
rein [reɪn] *n* rienda *f* ►**to give free ~ to sb** dar rienda suelta a alguien; **to keep sb on a tight ~** atar corto a alguien, tener a alguien controlado; **to hold the ~s** sujetar las riendas
reincarnation [ˌriːɪnkɑː'neɪʃən, *Am:* -kɑːr'-] *n* reencarnación *f*
reindeer ['reɪndɪəʳ, *Am:* -dɪr] *n inv* reno *m*
reinforce [ˌriːɪn'fɔːs, *Am:* -'fɔːrs] *vt a.* MIL reforzar; (*argument*) fortalecer
reinforcement *n* refuerzo *m*
reinstate [ˌriːɪn'steɪt] *vt form* restituir
reinsure [ˌriːɪn'ʃʊəʳ, *Am:* -'ʃʊr] *vt* reasegurar
reintegrate [ˌriː'ɪntəgreɪt] *vt* reintegrar; (*criminal*) reinsertar
reintegration ['riːˌɪntə'greɪʃən] *n* reintegración *f;* (*of criminal*) reinserción *f*
re-introduce [ˌriːɪntrə'djuːs, *Am:* -'duːs] *vt* reintroducir
reissue [ˌriː'ɪʃuː, *Am:* -'ɪʃjuː] **I.** *vt* volver a emitir **II.** *n* reexpedición *f*
reiterate [ri'ɪtəreɪt, *Am:* -'ɪt̬əreɪt] *vt* reiterar
reiteration [riˌɪtə'reɪʃən, *Am:* -ˌɪt̬ə'reɪ-] *n* reiteración *f*
reject¹ [rɪ'dʒekt] *vt a.* MED, TECH rechazar; (*application, request*) desestimar; (*accusation*) negar; (*bill, motion*) impugnar; (*proposal*) descartar
reject² ['riːdʒekt] *n* **1.** (*cast-off*) artículo *m* defectuoso **2.** (*person*) persona *f* rechazada
rejection [rɪ'dʒekʃən] *n* rechazo *m*
rejoice [rɪ'dʒɔɪs] *vi* regocijarse; **to ~ in doing sth** regocijarse haciendo algo; **I ~d to see that …** me alegré al ver que…
rejoicing *n no pl* regocijo *m*
rejoin¹ [ˌriː'dʒɔɪn] **I.** *vt* (*join again*) volver a unirse con; (*regiment*) reincorporarse a; (*political party*) reintegrarse a **II.** *vi* reunirse
rejoin² [rɪ'dʒɔɪn] *vt* (*reply*) replicar
rejoinder [rɪ'dʒɔɪndəʳ, *Am:* -dɚ] *n* réplica *f*
rejuvenate [riː'dʒuːvəneɪt] *vt* rejuvenecer
rekindle [riː'kɪndl] *vt a. fig* reavivar
relapse [rɪ'læps] **I.** *n* MED recaída *f* **II.** *vi a.* MED recaer
relate [rɪ'leɪt] **I.** *vt* **1.** (*establish connection*) relacionar **2.** (*tell*) contar **II.** *vi* **1.** (*be connected with*) **to ~ to sb/sth** estar relacionado con alguien/algo **2.** (*understand*) **to ~ to sth/sb** comprender algo/a alguien
related *adj* **1.** (*linked*) relacionado, -a **2.** (*in same family*) emparentado, -a; **to be ~ to sb** estar emparentado con alguien; **to be closely/distantly ~** tener parentesco cercano/lejano
relating to *prep* acerca de
relation [rɪ'leɪʃən] *n* **1.** *no pl* (*link*) relación *f;* **in ~ to** en relación a; **to bear no ~ to sb/sth** no tener relación con alguien/algo **2.** (*relative*) pariente *mf* **3.** *pl* (*contact*) relaciones *fpl*
relationship [rɪ'leɪʃənʃɪp] *n* **1.** (*link*) relación *f* **2.** (*family connection*) parentesco *m* **3.** (*between two people*) relaciones *fpl;* **to be in a ~ with sb** tener una relación con alguien; **business ~s** relaciones comerciales
relative ['relətɪv, *Am:* -t̬ɪv] **I.** *adj* relativo, -a **II.** *n* pariente *mf*
relative clause *n* oración *f* relativa
relatively *adv* relativamente
relativity [ˌrelə'tɪvəti, *Am:* -t̬i] *n* relatividad *f*
relaunch¹ [ˌriː'lɔːntʃ] *vt* relanzar
relaunch² ['riːˌlɔːntʃ] *n* relanzamiento *m*
relax [rɪ'læks] **I.** *vi* relajarse; (*restrictions*) mitigarse; (*rules*) suavizarse; (*security*) debilitarse; **relax!** ¡cálmate! **II.** *vt* relajar; (*restrictions*) mitigar; (*rules*) suavizar; (*security*) debilitar; **to ~ one's efforts** disminuir sus esfuerzos; **to ~ one's hold on sth** dejar de agarrarse a algo; *fig* ejercer menos control sobre algo
relaxation [ˌriːlæk'seɪʃən] *n* relajación *f*
relaxed *adj* relajado, -a
relay ['riːleɪ] **I.** *vt* (*information*) pasar; TV retransmitir **II.** *n* **1.** (*group*) turno *m;* **to work in ~s** trabajar por turnos **2.** SPORTS carrera *f* de relevos **3.** ELEC relé *m*
re-lay [ˌriː'leɪ] *vt* volver a colocar
release [rɪ'liːs] **I.** *vt* **1.** (*set free*) poner en libertad **2.** (*cease to hold*) soltar; PHOT disparar **3.** (*allow to escape: gas*) emitir; (*steam*) desprender **4.** (*weaken: pressure*) aliviar **5.** (*make public: information*) anunciar; (*book*) publicar; (*film*) estrenar; (*CD*) poner a la venta **II.** *n no pl* **1.** (*of prisoner*) excarcelación *f;* (*of hostage*) liberación *f* **2.** PHOT disparador *m* **3.** (*relaxation*) aflojamiento *m* **4.** (*escape*) escape *m* **5.** *no pl* (*publication*) publicación *f;* (*of film*) estreno *m;* (*of CD*) puesta *f* a la venta; **press ~** comunicado *m* de prensa
relegate ['relɪgeɪt, *Am:* 'relə-] *vt* relegar
relent [rɪ'lent] *vi* (*person*) ceder; (*wind, rain*) amainar
relentless [rɪ'lentləs] *adj* (*pursuit, opposition*) implacable; (*pressure*) incesante; (*criticism*) despiadado, -a
relevance ['reləvənts] *n,* **relevancy** *n no pl* pertinencia
relevant ['reləvənt] *adj* pertinente
reliability [rɪˌlaɪə'bɪləti, *Am:* -t̬i] *n no pl* **1.** (*dependability*) seguridad *f* **2.** (*trustworthiness*) fiabilidad *f*
reliable [rɪ'laɪəbl] *adj* **1.** (*credible*) fidedigno, -a; (*authority*) serio, -a; (*evidence*) fehaciente; (*statistics*) auténtico, -a; (*testimony*) verídico, -a **2.** (*trustworthy*) de confianza
reliance [rɪ'laɪəns] *n no pl* **1.** (*dependence*) dependencia *f* **2.** (*belief*) confianza *f*
reliant [rɪ'laɪənt] *adj* **to be ~ on sb/sth** depender de alguien/algo
relic ['relɪk] *n a. fig* reliquia *f*
relief [rɪ'liːf] **I.** *n* **1.** *no pl* (*aid*) socorro *m;* **to be on ~** *Am, inf* vivir de la caridad **2.** (*relaxation*) alivio *m;* **it's a ~ that** es un alivio que +*subj;* **that's a ~!** ¡menos mal! **3.** (*replacement*) relevo *m* **4.** MIL descerco *m* **5.** *a.* GEO

relieve *m;* **to throw sth into** ~ hacer resaltar algo **6. tax** ~ desgravación *f* fiscal **II.** *adj* **1.** de relevo; (*driver*) suplente **2.** GEO en relieve

relief worker *n* trabajador(a) *m(f)* de una organización humanitaria

relieve [rɪ'liːv] *vt* **1.** (*assist*) socorrer **2.** (*alleviate: pain*) aliviar; (*suffering*) mitigar; (*feelings*) desahogar; (*one's mind*) tranquilizar **3.** MIL descercar **4.** (*urinate, defecate*) **to** ~ **oneself** hacer sus necesidades

relieved *adj* aliviado, -a

religion [rɪ'lɪdʒən] *n* religión *f*

religious [rɪ'lɪdʒəs] *adj* religioso, -a

relinquish [rɪ'lɪŋkwɪʃ] *vt* (*claim, title*) renunciar a; (*control*) ceder; **to** ~ **one's grip on sth** soltar algo

reliquary ['relɪkwəri, *Am:* -əkwer-] <-ies> *n* relicario *m*

relish ['relɪʃ] **I.** *n* **1.** *no pl* (*enjoyment*) gusto *m;* **with** ~ con gusto **2.** (*enthusiasm*) entusiasmo *m* **3.** GASTR condimento *m* **II.** *vt* deleitarse en; **I don't** ~ **...** no me entusiasma...

reload [ˌriː'ləʊd, *Am:* -'loʊd] **I.** *vt* recargar **II.** *vi* recargarse

relocate [ˌriːləʊ'keɪt, *Am:* -'loʊkeɪt] **I.** *vi* trasladarse **II.** *vt* trasladar

relocation [ˌriːləʊ'keɪʃən, *Am:* -loʊ'-] *n* (*of company*) reubicación *f;* (*of person*) traslado *m*

reluctance [rɪ'lʌktəns] *n no pl* desgana *f;* **with** ~ de mala gana

reluctant [rɪ'lʌktənt] *adj* reacio, -a; **to be** ~ **to do sth** tener pocas ganas de hacer algo, ser reacio a hacer algo

rely [rɪ'laɪ] *vi* **to** ~ **on** [*o* **upon**] (*trust*) confiar en; (*depend on*) depender de; **to** ~ **on** [*o* **upon**] **sb to do sth** contar con alguien para hacer algo

REM [ˌɑːr'iː'em, *Am:* ˌɑːriː'em] *abbr of* **Rapid Eye Movement** movimiento *m* rápido del ojo

remain [rɪ'meɪn] *vi* **1.** (*stay*) quedar(se) **2.** (*continue*) permanecer; **to** ~ **aloof** mantenerse apartado; **to** ~ **seated** quedarse sentado; **to** ~ **unsolved** seguir sin solucionarse; **to** ~ **to be done** estar por hacer; **much** ~**s to be done** queda mucho por hacer; **the fact** ~**s that ...** sigue siendo un hecho que...; **it** (**only**) ~**s for me to ...** sólo me resta...; **it** ~**s to be seen** (**who/what/how**) está por ver (quién/qué/cómo)

remainder [rɪ'meɪndəʳ, *Am:* -dɚ] **I.** *n no pl* *a.* MAT resto *m;* **the** ~ **of sb's life** lo que queda de la vida de alguien **II.** *vt* saldar

remaining [rɪ'meɪnɪŋ] *adj* restante

remains [rɪ'meɪnz] *npl* restos *mpl*

remake¹ [ˌriː'meɪk] <remade> *vt* volver a hacer

remake² ['riːmeɪk] *n* nueva versión *f*

remand [rɪ'mɑːnd, *Am:* -'mænd] **I.** *vt* **to** ~ **sb to prison** [*o* **in custody**] poner a alguien en prisión preventiva; **to** ~ **sb on bail** poner a alguien en libertad bajo fianza **II.** *n* **to be on** ~ estar en prisión preventiva

remand centre *n Brit, Aus* centro *m* de detención preventiva

remark [rɪ'mɑːk, *Am:* -'mɑːrk] **I.** *vi* **to** ~ **on sth** hacer observaciones sobre algo **II.** *n* observación *f;* **to make** ~**s about sb/sth** hacer comentarios sobre alguien/algo

remarkable [rɪ'mɑːkəbl, *Am:* -'mɑːr-] *adj* extraordinario, -a; (*coincidence*) singular; **to be** ~ **for sth** ser notable por algo

remarkably *adj* extraordinariamente

remarry [ˌriː'mæri, *Am:* -'mer-] <-ie-> *vi* volver a casarse

remedial [rɪ'miːdiəl] *adj* (*action*) remediador(a); SCHOOL recuperativo, -a; MED terapéutico, -a

remedy ['remədi] **I.** <-ies> *n* **1.** remedio *m;* **to be beyond** ~ no tener remedio **2.** LAW (**legal**) ~ recurso *m* (legal) **II.** *vt* remediar; (*mistake*) corregir

remember [rɪ'membəʳ, *Am:* -bɚ] **I.** *vt* **1.** (*recall*) recordar; **I can't** ~ **his name** no recuerdo su nombre **2.** (*commemorate*) conmemorar **II.** *vi* acordarse

remembrance [rɪ'membrənts] *n* **1.** *no pl* (*act of remembering*) recuerdo *m;* **in** ~ **of** en conmemoración de **2.** *pl* (*greetings*) recuerdos *mpl*

Remembrance Day *n Brit: día en que se conmemora a los caídos en las guerras mundiales*

> El **Remembrance Day**, **Remembrance Sunday** o **Poppy Day** se celebra el segundo domingo de noviembre en conmemoración del armisticio firmado el 11 de noviembre de 1918. Este día se recuerda especialmente con misas y distintas ceremonias a todos aquellos soldados que murieron en las dos guerras mundiales. Las personas llevan unas amapolas de tela, que simbolizan las amapolas florecientes de los campos de batalla de Flandes después de la I Guerra Mundial. A las 11 de la mañana se guardan dos minutos de silencio.

remind [rɪ'maɪnd] *vt* recordar; **to** ~ **sb to do sth** recordar a alguien que haga algo; **he** ~**s me of you** me recuerda a ti; **that** ~**s me, ...** por cierto,...

reminder [rɪ'maɪndəʳ, *Am:* -ɚ] *n* **1.** (*note*) recordatorio *m* **2.** (*warning*) advertencia *f;* **to give sb a gentle** ~ dar a alguien una advertencia amistosa **3.** (*memento*) recuerdo *m*

reminisce [ˌremɪ'nɪs, *Am:* -ə'-] *vi* narrar reminiscencias

reminiscence [ˌremɪ'nɪsns, *Am:* -ə'-] *n* reminiscencia *f*

reminiscent [ˌremɪ'nɪsnt, *Am:* -ə'-] *adj* **to be** ~ **of sb/sth** hacer pensar en alguien/algo

remiss [rɪ'mɪs] *adj* negligente

remission [rɪ'mɪʃən] *n* remisión *f*

remit¹ [rɪ'mɪt] <-tt-> *vt form* **1.** (*send*) remi-

R

tir; (*money*) enviar **2.** LAW perdonar

remit[2] ['ri:mɪt] *n* competencia *f*

remittance [rɪ'mɪtns] *n* giro *m*

remix ['ri:miks] MUS **I.** *vt* mezclar **II.** <-es> *n* mezcla *f*

remnant ['remnənt] *n* resto *m*

remnant sale *n* venta *f* de saldos

remodel [ˌri:'mɒdəl, *Am:* -'mɑ:dəl] <-ll-, *Am:* -l-> *vt* remodelar

remonstrance [rɪ'mɒntstrənts, *Am:* -'mɑ:nt-] *n form* protesta *f*

remonstrate ['remənstreɪt, *Am:* rɪ'mɑ:nt-] *vi* protestar

remorse [rɪ'mɔ:s, *Am:* -'mɔ:rs] *n no pl* remordimiento *m;* **without** ~ sin remordimientos

remorseful [rɪ'mɔ:sfəl, *Am:* -'mɔ:rs-] *adj* arrepentido, -a

remorseless [rɪ'mɔ:sləs, *Am:* -'mɔ:rs-] *adj* (*merciless*) despiadado, -a; (*attack*) implacable

remote [rɪ'məʊt, *Am:* -'moʊt] *adj* <-er, -est> (*place, possibility*) remoto, -a

remote control *n* mando *m* a distancia **remote-controlled** *adj* teledirigido, -a

remoteness *n no pl* alejamiento *m*

remould ['ri:məʊld, *Am:* -moʊld] **I.** *vt* recauchutar **II.** *n* recauchutado *m*

remount [ˌri:'maʊnt] **I.** *vt* subir de nuevo a **II.** *vi* volverse a montar

removable [rɪ'mu:vəbl] *adj* **1.** (*stain*) que se puede quitar **2.** (*easy to take off*) desmontable; (*sleeves*) de quita y pon

removal [rɪ'mu:vəl] *n* **1.** *no pl* (*of stain, problem*) eliminación *f* **2.** (*extraction*) extracción *f* **3.** *no pl, Brit* (*move*) mudanza *f*

removal expenses *n* gastos *mpl* de mudanza **removal firm** *n* agencia *f* de mudanzas **removal van** *n* camión *m* de mudanzas

remove [rɪ'mu:v] **I.** *vt* **1.** (*take away*) quitar; (*clothes*) quitarse **2.** (*get rid of*) eliminar; (*cork, dent*) sacar; (*entry, name*) borrar; (*doubts, fears*) disipar; (*problem*) solucionar; **to ~ one's hair** depilarse **3.** (*dismiss from job*) destituir **II.** *n form* **to be at one ~ from sth** estar a un paso de algo

remover [rɪ'mu:vəʳ, *Am:* -ɚ] *n* **1.** agente *mf* de mudanzas **2. stain** ~ quitamanchas *m inv*

remunerate [rɪ'mju:nəreɪt] *vt form* remunerar

remuneration [rɪˌmju:nə'reɪʃən] *n form* remuneración *f*

remunerative [rɪ'mju:nərətɪv, *Am:* -nəreɪt̬ɪv] *adj form* lucrativo, -a

Renaissance [rɪ'neɪsns, *Am:* ˌrenə'sɑ:ns] *n* **the** ~ el Renacimiento

renal ['ri:nl] *adj* renal

rename [ˌri:'neɪm] *vt* poner un nuevo nombre a

rend [rend] <rent *o Am* rended> *vt liter* desgarrar

render ['rendəʳ, *Am:* -dɚ] *vt form* **1.** (*make*) hacer; **to ~ sb speechless** dejar a alguien mudo **2.** (*perform*) representar; MUS interpretar **3.** (*give: thanks*) ofrecer; (*aid, service*) prestar; (*judgement*) emitir **4.** (*translate*) traducir **5.** ARCHIT enlucir, frisar *And*

rendering ['rendərɪŋ] *n* **1.** (*performance*) representación *f;* MUS interpretación *f* **2.** (*translation*) traducción *f*

rendezvous ['rɒndɪvu:, 'rɒndɪvu:z, *Am:* 'rɑ:ndeɪ-] **I.** *n inv* **1.** (*meeting*) cita *f* **2.** (*place*) lugar *m* de reunión **II.** *vi* reunirse

rendition [ren'dɪʃən] *n* **1.** (*performance*) interpretación *f* **2.** (*translation*) traducción *f*

renegade ['renɪgeɪd, *Am:* 'renə-] **I.** *n* renegado, -a *m, f* **II.** *adj* renegado, -a

renege [rɪ'neɪg, *Am:* -'nɪg] *vi form* **to ~ on sth** incumplir algo

renew [rɪ'nju:, *Am:* -'nu:] *vt* **1.** (*begin again: membership, passport*) renovar; (*relationship*) reanudar; **to ~ one's efforts to do sth** recobrar fuerzas para hacer algo **2.** (*mend*) recuperar

renewable [rɪ'nju:əbl, *Am:* -'nu:-] *adj* renovable

renewal [rɪ'nju:əl, *Am:* -'nu:-] *n* renovación *f*

renewed [rɪ'nju:d, *Am:* -'nu:d] *adj* renovado, -a

rennet ['renɪt] *n no pl* cuajo *m*

renounce [rɪ'naʊns] *vt* renunciar a

renovate ['renəveɪt] *vt* restaurar, refaccionar *Ven, Col*

renovation [ˌrenə'veɪʃən] *n* renovación *f*

renown [rɪ'naʊn] *n no pl* renombre *m*

renowned [rɪ'naʊnd] *adj* renombrado, -a

rent[1] [rent] **I.** *n* rasgadura *f* **II.** *pt, pp of* **rend**

rent[2] [rent] **I.** *n* alquiler *m;* **for** ~ se alquila **II.** *vt* alquilar; (*land*) arrendar **III.** *vi* alquilarse

rental ['rentəl, *Am:* -t̬əl] **I.** *n* alquiler *m* **II.** *adj* de alquiler

rent boy *n Brit, inf* chico *m* de compañía **rent control** *n* control *m* de rentas **rent-free** *adj* exento, -a de alquiler

renunciation [rɪˌnʌnsɪ'eɪʃən] *n no pl* renuncia *f*

reopen [ri:'əʊpən, *Am:* -'oʊ-] **I.** *vt* reabrir **II.** *vi* reabrirse

reorder [ˌri:'ɔ:dəʳ] **I.** *n* nuevo pedido *m* **II.** *vt* **1.** (*reorganize*) reordenar **2.** COM hacer un nuevo pedido de

reorganize [ri:'ɔ:gənaɪz, *Am:* -'ɔ:rgən-] **I.** *vt* reorganizar **II.** *vi* reorganizarse

rep [rep] *n inf* **1.** *abbr of* **representative** representante *mf* de ventas **2.** THEAT *abbr of* **repertory** repertorio *m*

Rep. **1.** *abbr of* **Republic** Rep. **2.** *abbr of* **Republican** republicano, -a

repaint [ri:'peɪnt] *vt* repintar

repair [ri:'peəʳ, *Am:* -'per] **I.** *vt* **1.** (*machine*) reparar; (*clothes*) arreglar **2.** (*set right: damage*) enmendar; (*friendship*) reestablecer **II.** *n* **1.** (*mending: of machine*) reparación *f;* (*of clothes*) arreglo *m;* **to be beyond** ~ no tener arreglo; **to be under** ~ estar en reparación **2.** (*state*) **to be in good/bad** ~ estar en buen/mal estado

repairable [rɪ'peərəbl, *Am:* -'perə-] *adj* reparable

repair kit *n* caja *f* de herramientas **repairman** <-men> *n* (*for cars*) mecánico *m;* (*for television*) técnico *m* **repair shop** *n* taller *m* de reparaciones

repaper [riː'peɪpəʳ] *vt* empapelar de nuevo

reparable ['repərəbl] *adj* reparable

reparation [ˌrepə'reɪʃən] *n* **1.** (*setting right*) reparación *f* **2.** *pl* FIN indemnización *f*

repartee [ˌrepɑː'tiː, *Am:* -ɑːr'-] *n no pl* réplica *f*

repatriate [riː'pætrɪeɪt, *Am:* -'peɪtrɪ-] *vt* repatriar

repatriation [ˌriːpætri'eɪʃən, *Am:* rɪˌpeɪtri'-] *n no pl* repatriación *f*

repay [rɪ'peɪ] <repaid> *vt* (*money*) devolver; (*debts*) liquidar; (*person*) pagar; **to ~ money to sb** reintegrar dinero a alguien; **to ~ sb for sth** premiar a alguien por algo; **to ~ a kindness** devolver una atención

repayable [rɪ'peɪəbl] *adj* reembolsable

repayment [rɪ'peɪmənt] *n* reembolso *m*

repeal [rɪ'piːl] **I.** *vt* revocar **II.** *n no pl* revocatoria *f*

repeat [rɪ'piːt] **I.** *vt* **1.** (*say or do again*) repetir **2.** (*recite*) recitar **II.** *vi* (*happen again*) repetirse; (*taste*) repetir **III.** *n* **1.** repetición *f* **2.** TV retransmisión *f*

repeated *adj* repetido, -a

repeatedly *adv* repetidas veces

repeat order *n* COM pedido *m* de repitición **repeat performance** *n* repetición *f*

repel [rɪ'pel] <-ll-> *vt* **1.** (*ward off*) rechazar **2.** MIL, PHYS repeler **3.** (*disgust*) repugnar

repellent [rɪ'pelənt] **I.** *n* repelente *m* **II.** *adj* repugnante

repent [rɪ'pent] **I.** *vi form* arrepentirse **II.** *vt* arrepentirse de

repentance [rɪ'pentənts] *n no pl* arrepentimiento *m*

repentant [rə'pentənt] *adj* arrepentido, -a

repercussion [ˌriːpə'kʌʃən, *Am:* -pɚ'-] *n* repercusión *f*

repertoire ['repətwɑːʳ, *Am:* -ɚtwɑːr] *n* repertorio *m*

repertory company ['repətəri'kʌmpəni, *Am:* -ɚtɔːr-] *n Brit* compañía *f* de repertorio **repertory theatre** *n Brit* teatro *m* de repertorio

repetition [ˌrepɪ'tɪʃən, *Am:* -ə'-] *n* repetición *f*

repetitious [ˌrepɪ'tɪʃəs, *Am:* -ə'-] *adj,* **repetitive** [rɪ'petətɪv, *Am:* -'peţəţɪv] *adj* repetitivo, -a

replace [rɪ'pleɪs] *vt* **1.** (*take the place of*) reemplazar; (*person*) sustituir **2.** (*put back*) reponer

replaceable [rɪ'pleɪsəbl] *adj* reemplazable

replacement [rɪ'pleɪsmənt] **I.** *n* **1.** (*person*) sustituto, -a *m, f;* (*part*) recambio *m* **2.** MIL reemplazo *m* **3.** (*act of substituting*) sustitución *f* **II.** *adj* de repuesto

replay[1] [ˌriː'pleɪ] *vt* **1.** SPORTS volver a jugar **2.** MUS volver a tocar **3.** TV repetir

replay[2] ['riːpleɪ] *n* **1.** SPORTS, TV repetición *f* **2.** MUS reproducción *f*

replenish [rɪ'plenɪʃ] *vt* rellenar; (*supplies*) abastecer de nuevo; (*stocks*) reponer

replete [rɪ'pliːt] *adj* repleto, -a

replica ['replɪkə] *n* réplica *f*

replicate ['replɪkeɪt] *vt* replicar

reply [rɪ'plaɪ] **I.** <-ied> *vt* contestar **II.** <-ied> *vi* **1.** (*verbally*) contestar **2.** (*react*) responder **III.** <-ies> *n* respuesta *f*

reply coupon *n* cupón *m* respuesta **reply-paid envelope** *n* sobre *m* prepagado

report [rɪ'pɔːt, *Am:* -'pɔːrt] **I.** *n* **1.** (*account*) informe *m;* PUBL noticia *f;* (*longer*) reportaje *m;* **to give a ~** presentar un informe **2.** (*unproven claim*) rumor *m* **3.** (*explosion*) estallido *m* **II.** *vt* **1.** (*recount*) relatar; (*discovery*) anunciar; **to ~ that ...** informar que...; **nothing to ~** sin novedades **2.** (*denounce*) denunciar **III.** *vi* **1.** (*make results public*) presentar un informe **2.** (*arrive at work*) presentarse; **to ~ sick** dar parte de enfermedad

◆**report back I.** *vt* **to report sth back to sb** relatar algo a alguien **II.** *vi* presentar un informe

report card *n Am* cartilla *f* escolar

reporter [rɪ'pɔːtəʳ, *Am:* -'pɔːrţɚ] *n* reportero, -a *m, f*

repose [rɪ'pəʊz, *Am:* -'poʊz] **I.** *vi* **1.** (*rest*) reposar **2.** (*lie*) descansar **II.** *vt* **1.** (*rest*) reposar **2.** *fig* (*confidence*) depositar **III.** *n no pl* reposo *m;* **in ~** de reposo

repository [rɪ'pɒzɪtəri, *Am:* -'pɑːzɪtɔːri] <-ies> *n* **1.** (*store*) depósito *m* **2.** (*person*) depositario, -a *m, f*

repossess [ˌriːpə'zes] *vt* recobrar

repossession [ˌriːpə'zeʃən] *n* recuperación *f*

reprehensible [ˌreprɪ'hensəbl] *adj* censurable

represent [ˌreprɪ'zent] *vt* **1.** (*act for, depict*) representar **2.** (*state*) declarar

representation [ˌreprɪzen'teɪʃən] *n* **1.** (*acting for, depiction*) representación *f* **2.** (*statement*) declaración *f*

representative [ˌreprɪ'zentətɪv, *Am:* -ţəţɪv] **I.** *adj* **1.** *a.* POL representativo, -a **2.** (*typical*) típico, -a **II.** *n* **1.** *a.* COM representante *mf,* agenciero, -a *m, f Arg* **2.** LAW apoderado, -a *m, f* **3.** POL diputado, -a *m, f*

repress [rɪ'pres] *vt* reprimir

repressed [rɪ'prest] *adj* reprimido, -a

repression [rɪ'preʃən] *n no pl* represión *f*

repressive [rɪ'presɪv] *adj* represivo, -a

reprieve [rɪ'priːv] **I.** *vt* indultar **II.** *n* indulto *m*

reprimand ['reprɪmɑːnd, *Am:* -rəmænd] **I.** *vt* reprender **II.** *n* reprimenda *f*

reprint[1] [ˌriː'prɪnt] *vt* reimprimir

reprint[2] ['riːprɪnt] *n* reimpresión *f*

reprisal [rɪ'praɪzl] *n* represalia *f;* **to take ~s** tomar represalias

reproach [rɪ'prəʊtʃ, *Am:* -'proʊtʃ] I. *vt* reprochar II. *n* reproche *m;* **beyond ~** intachable; **to be a ~ to sb** ser una vergüenza para alguien
reproachful [rɪ'prəʊtʃfəl, *Am:* -'proʊtʃ-] *adj* acusador(a)
reprobate ['reprəbeɪt] I. *n a.* REL réprobo, -a *m, f* II. *adj* 1. (*wicked*) malvado, -a 2. REL réprobo, -a
reprocess [,riː'prəʊses, *Am:* -'prɑːses] *vt* reprocesar
reprocessing *n no pl* reprocesamiento *m*
reprocessing plant *n* ECOL, TECH planta *f* reprocesadora
reproduce [,riːprə'djuːs, *Am:* -'duːs] I. *vi* reproducirse II. *vt* reproducir
reproduction [,riːprə'dʌkʃən] *n* reproducción *f*
reproductive [,riːprə'dʌktɪv] *adj* reproductor(a)
reproof [rɪ'pruːf] I. *n* reprensión *f* II. *vt* reprender
reprove [rɪ'pruːv] *vt* reprender
reproving [rɪ'pruːvɪŋ] *adj* reprobatorio, -a
reptile ['reptaɪl] *n* reptil *m*
reptilian [rep'tɪlɪən] *adj* reptil
republic [rɪ'pʌblɪk] *n* república *f*
republican [rɪ'pʌblɪkən] I. *n* republicano, -a *m, f* II. *adj* republicano, -a
republication [,riː,pʌblɪ'keɪʃən] *n no pl* reedición *f*

La **Republic of Malta** (República de Malta), que durante los años 1814 al 1947 fue una colonia británica y base naval, se ha dado a conocer en los últimos años como **English language learning centre** (centro de enseñanza del inglés). Jóvenes de toda Europa viajan hasta Malta para participar en sus renombradas escuelas de inglés. La mayoría de la veces los estudiantes se alojan con familias maltesas. Durante el verano se celebran un gran número de actividades en la playa en las que los estudiantes que lo desean pueden participar. Además, al anochecer, la ciudad de Paceville ofrece múltiples posibilidades de diversión para gente joven.

repudiate [rɪ'pjuːdɪeɪt] *vt* (*person*) repudiar; (*accusation*) negar; (*suggestion*) rechazar
repugnance [rɪ'pʌgnəns] *n no pl* repugnancia *f*
repugnant [rɪ'pʌgnənt] *adj* repugnante
repulse [rɪ'pʌls] I. *vt* 1. (*disgust*) repulsar 2. (*ward off*) rechazar 3. MIL repeler II. *n* repulsa *f*
repulsion [rɪ'pʌlʃən] *n no pl* repulsión *f*
repulsive [rɪ'pʌlsɪv] *adj* repulsivo, -a
repurchase [,riː'pɜːtʃəs] I. *vt* readquirir II. *n* readquisición *f*
reputable ['repjʊtəbl, *Am:* -t̬əbl] *adj* acreditado, -a
reputation [,repjʊ'teɪʃən] *n* reputación *f;* **to have a good/bad ~** tener buena/mala fama; **to know sb by ~** conocer a alguien de oídas
repute [rɪ'pjuːt] *n no pl* reputación *f*
reputed [rɪ'pjuːtɪd, *Am:* -t̬ɪd] *adj* supuesto, -a; **she is ~ to be rich** tiene fama de rica
request [rɪ'kwest] I. *n* petición *f;* ADMIN solicitud *f;* **on ~** a petición; **to make a ~ for sth** pedir algo II. *vt* pedir; ADMIN solicitar
requiem ['rekwiəm] *n,* **requiem mass** *n* réquiem *m*
require [rɪ'kwaɪə^r, *Am:* -'kwaɪɚ] *vt* 1. (*need*) necesitar 2. (*demand*) exigir; **to ~ sb to do sth** exigir a alguien que haga algo
requirement [rɪ'kwaɪəmənt, *Am:* -'kwaɪɚ-] *n* requisito *m*
requisite ['rekwɪzɪt] I. *adj* indispensable II. *n* requisito *m*
requisition [,rekwɪ'zɪʃən] I. *vt* requisar II. *n* 1. *no pl* (*act of requesting*) requisición *f;* (*written request*) solicitud *f* 2. MIL requisa *f*
reroute [,riː'ruːt] *vt* desviar
rerun¹ [,rɪː'rʌn] *vt irr* CINE, TV repetir; THEAT reestrenar
rerun² ['riːrʌn] *n* CINE, TV repetición *f;* THEAT reestreno *m*
resale ['riːseɪl] *n* reventa *m*
reschedule [,riː'ʃedjuːl, *Am:* -'skedʒuːl] *vt* reprogramar
rescind [rɪ'sɪnd] *vt* rescindir
rescue ['reskjuː] I. *vt* (*save*) rescatar; (*hostage*) liberar II. *n* rescate *m;* **to come to sb's ~** rescatar a alguien
rescuer ['reskjʊə^r, *Am:* -ɚ] *n* salvador(a) *m(f)*
research [rɪ'sɜːtʃ, *Am:* 'riːsɜːrtʃ] I. *n* investigación *f* II. *vi, vt* investigar
researcher *n* investigador(a) *m(f)*
research work *n* trabajos *mpl* de investigación **research worker** *n* investigador(a) *m(f)*
resemblance [rɪ'zembləns] *n no pl* parecido *m*
resemble [rɪ'zembl] *vt* parecerse a
resent [rɪ'zent] *vt* **to ~ sth** sentirse molesto por algo
resentful [rɪ'zentfəl] *adj* (*person*) resentido, -a; (*expression*) de resentimiento
resentment [rɪ'zentmənt] *n* resentimiento *m*
reservation [,rezə'veɪʃən, *Am:* -ɚ'-] *n* (*doubt, booking*) reserva *f;* **to have ~s about sth** tener ciertas dudas sobre algo
reserve [rɪ'zɜːv, *Am:* -'zɜːrv] I. *n* 1. reserva *f;* **to have sth in ~** tener algo en reserva 2. SPORTS suplente *mf* 3. MIL **the ~** la reserva II. *vt* reservar
reserve currency *n* divisa *f* de reserva
reserved *adj* reservado, -a
reserve price *n* precio *m* mínimo
reservist [rɪ'zɜːvɪst, *Am:* -'zɜːr-] *n* MIL reservista *mf*
reservoir ['rezəvwɑː^r, *Am:* -ɚvwɑːr] *n*

1. (*tank*) depósito *m* 2. (*lake*) embalse *m*

reset [ˌriːˈset] *vt irr* 1. (*machine*) reajustar; INFOR reiniciar 2. (*jewel*) reengastar

reset button *n* INFOR, ELEC tecla *f* de reinicio

resettle [ˌriːˈsetl] I. *vi* reasentarse II. *vt* (*person*) asentar; (*area*) repoblar

reshuffle [ˌriːˈʃʌfl] I. *vt* reorganizar II. *n* reorganización *f*

reside [rɪˈzaɪd] *vi form* residir

residence [ˈrezɪdənts] *n* 1. (*home*) domicilio *m* 2. *no pl* (*act*) residencia *f*

residence permit *n* permiso *m* de residencia

resident [ˈrezɪdənt] I. *n* residente *mf* II. *adj* residente

residential [ˌrezɪˈdenʃl] *adj* residencial

residual [rɪˈzɪdjʊəl, *Am:* -ˈzɪdʒu-] *adj* residual

residue [ˈrezɪdjuː, *Am:* -əduː] *n* residuo *m*

resign [rɪˈzaɪn] I. *vi* 1. (*leave job*) renunciar; POL dimitir 2. GAME abandonar II. *vt* (*leave: job*) renunciar a; POL dimitir de; **to ~ oneself to sth** resignarse a algo

resignation [ˌrezɪgˈneɪʃən] *n* 1. (*from job*) renuncia *f;* POL dimisión *f* 2. *no pl* (*conformity*) resignación *f*

resigned [rɪˈzaɪnd] *adj* resignado, -a, botado, -a *Ecua*

resilience [rɪˈzɪlɪəns, *Am:* ˈzɪljəns] *n no pl* (*of material*) elasticidad *f;* (*of person*) resistencia *f*

resilient [rɪˈzɪlɪənt, *Am:* -ˈzɪljənt] *adj* (*material*) elástico, -a; (*person*) resistente

resin [ˈrezɪn] *n no pl* resina *f*

resinous [ˈrezɪnəs] *adj* resinoso, -a

resist [rɪˈzɪst] I. *vt* resistir; **to ~ doing sth** resistirse a hacer algo II. *vi* resistir

resistance [rɪˈzɪstənts] *n* resistencia *f*

resistance fighter *n* miembro *mf* de la resistencia

resistant [rɪˈzɪstənt] *adj* resistente

resistor [rɪˈzɪstəʳ, *Am:* -tɚ] *n* resistencia *f*

resit [ˈriːsɪt] I. *vt irr, Brit* SCHOOL, UNIV presentarse otra vez a II. *n Brit* SCHOOL, UNIV examen *m* de recuperación

resolute [ˈrezəluːt] *adj* resuelto, -a

resolution [ˌrezəˈluːʃən] *n a.* INFOR, PHOT, TV resolución *f*

resolvable [rɪˈzɒlvəbl, *Am:* -ˈzɑːlvə-] *adj* solucionable

resolve [rɪˈzɒlv, *Am:* -ˈzɑːlv] I. *vt* 1. (*solve*) resolver 2. (*settle*) acordar; **to ~ that ...** acordar que... +*subj* II. *n* resolución *f*

resolved [rɪˈzɒlvd, *Am:* -ˈzɑːlvd] *adj* resuelto, -a

resonance [ˈrezənəns] *n no pl* resonancia *f*

resonant [ˈrezənənt] *adj* resonante

resonate [ˈrezəneɪt] *vi* resonar

resort [rɪˈzɔːt, *Am:* -ˈzɔːrt] *n* 1. *no pl* (*use*) recurso *m;* **without ~ to sth** sin recurrir a algo; **as a last ~** como último recurso 2. (*for holidays*) lugar *m* de veraneo; **ski ~** estación *f* de esquí

resound [rɪˈzaʊnd] *vi* resonar

resounding *adj* 1. (*noise*) resonante 2. (*failure, success*) rotundo, -a

resource [rɪˈzɔːs, *Am:* ˈriːsɔːrs] I. *n* 1. (*asset*) recurso *m* 2. *pl* **natural ~s** recursos *mpl* naturales 3. (*resourcefulness*) inventiva *f* ►**to be thrown back on one's own ~s** tener que apañárselas con sus propios recursos II. *vt* financiar

resourceful [rɪˈzɔːsfəl, *Am:* -ˈsɔːrs-] *adj* ingenioso, -a

respect [rɪˈspekt] I. *n* 1. (*relation*) respeto *m* 2. (*esteem*) estima *f;* **with all due ~** con el debido respeto 3. (*point*) respecto *m;* **in all/many/some ~s** desde todos/muchos/algunos puntos de vista; **in every ~** en todos los sentidos; **in ~ of** respecto a; **in this ~** a este respecto; **with ~ to** con respecto a 4. *pl* (*greetings*) recuerdos *mpl* II. *vt* respetar

respectable [rɪˈspektəbl] *adj* 1. (*person*) respetable 2. (*behaviour*) decente 3. (*performance, result*) aceptable

respected [rɪˈspektəd] *adj* respetado, -a

respectful [rɪˈspektfəl] *adj* respetuoso, -a

respectfully [rɪˈspektfəli] *adv* respetuosamente; **Respectfully yours ...** Atentamente...

respecting [rɪˈspektɪŋ] *prep* respecto a

respective [rɪˈspektɪv] *adj* respectivo, -a

respectively *adv* respectivamente

respiration [ˌrespəˈreɪʃen] *n no pl* respiración *f*

respirator [ˈrespəreɪtəʳ, *Am:* -t̬ɚ] *n* respirador *m*

respiratory [rɪˈspaɪərətri, *Am:* ˈrespɚətɔːri] *adj* respiratorio, -a

respite [ˈrespaɪt, *Am:* -pɪt] *n no pl* 1. (*pause*) pausa *f* 2. (*delay*) retraso *m*

resplendent [rɪˈsplendənt] *adj* resplandeciente

respond [rɪˈspɒnd, *Am:* -ˈspɑːnd] *vi* 1. (*answer*) contestar 2. (*react*) responder

respondent [rɪˈspɒndənt, *Am:* -ˈspɑːn-] *n* 1. (*to questionnaire*) encuestado, -a *m, f* 2. LAW demandado, -a *m, f*

response [rɪˈspɒns, *Am:* -ˈspɑːns] *n* 1. (*answer*) respuesta *f* 2. (*reaction*) reacción *f* 3. REL responso *m*

responsibility [rɪˌspɒnsəˈbɪləti, *Am:* -ˌspɑːnsəˈbɪlət̬i] *n* responsabilidad *f*

responsible [rɪˈspɒnsəbl, *Am:* -ˈspɑːn-] *adj* responsable; **to be ~ for sth/to sb** ser responsable de algo/ante alguien

responsive [rɪˈspɒnsɪv, *Am:* -ˈspɑːn-] *adj* (*person*) receptivo, -a; (*mechanism*) sensible; **to be ~ to sth** MED responder a algo

rest[1] [rest] I. *vt* 1. (*cause to repose*) descansar 2. (*support*) apoyar 3. *Am* LAW **to ~ one's case** terminar la presentación de su alegato II. *vi* 1. (*cease activity*) reposar, descansar 2. (*remain*) quedar 3. (*be supported*) apoyarse; **to ~ on sth** (*theory*) basarse en algo 4. *Am* LAW concluir ►**you can ~ assured that**

R

… esté seguro de que… **III.** *n* **1.** (*period of repose*) descanso *m;* **to come to ~** detenerse; **at ~** (*not moving*) en reposo; (*dead*) en paz **2.** MUS pausa *f* **3.** (*support*) apoyo *m*

rest² [rest] *n* resto *m;* **the ~** (*the other people*) los demás; (*the other things*) lo demás; **for the ~** por lo demás

restate [ˌriːˈsteɪt] *vt* exponer de nuevo

restaurant [ˈrestərɔ̃ːŋ, *Am:* -tərɑːnt] *n* restaurante *m*

restaurant car *n Brit* vagón *m* restaurante

restaurateur [ˌrestɒrəˈtɜːʳ, *Am:* -tɚəˈtɜːr] *n* restaurador(a) *m(f)*

rest cure *n* cura *f* de reposo **rest day** *n* día *m* de descanso

restful [ˈrestfəl] *adj* tranquilo, -a, relajante

rest home *n* residencia *f* de ancianos

resting place *n* morada *f*

restitution [ˌrestɪˈtjuːʃən, *Am:* -ˈtuː-] *n no pl* **1.** (*return*) restitución *f* **2.** LAW indemnización *f*

restive [ˈrestɪv] *adj* inquieto, -a

restless [ˈrestlɪs] *adj* **1.** (*agitated*) inquieto, -a **2.** (*impatient*) impaciente **3.** (*wakeful: night*) en blanco

restock [ˌriːˈstɒk, *Am:* -ˈstɑːk] **I.** *vt* reabastecer; (*with animals, plants*) repoblar **II.** *vi* reponer existencias

restoration [ˌrestəˈreɪʃən] *n* **1.** *no pl* (*act of restoring: of building, painting, monarchy*) restauración *f;* (*of communication, peace*) restablecimiento *m* **2.** *no pl* (*return to owner*) restitución *f;* (*of stolen goods*) devolución *f*

restorative [rɪˈstɔːrətɪv, *Am:* -t̬ɪv] *adj* reconstituyente

restore [rɪˈstɔːʳ, *Am:* -ˈstɔːr] *vt* **1.** (*reestablish: building, painting, monarchy*) restaurar; (*communication, peace*) reestablecer; **to ~ sb's sight** hacer que alguien recobre la vista; **to ~ sb's faith in sth** hacer que alguien recupere la fe en algo; **to ~ sb to health** devolver la salud a alguien; **to ~ sb to power** volver a colocar a alguien en el poder **2.** *form* (*return to owner*) restituir

restorer [rɪˈstɔːrəʳ, *Am:* -ɚ] *n* restaurador(a) *m(f)*

restrain [rɪˈstreɪn] *vt* (*person, animal*) contener; (*temper, ambition*) dominar; (*trade*) restringir; (*inflation*) frenar; **to ~ sb from doing sth** impedir que alguien haga algo; **to ~ oneself** contenerse

restrained [rɪˈstreɪnd] *adj* (*person*) comedido, -a; (*style*) sobrio, -a; (*criticism, policy*) moderado, -a

restraint [rɪˈstreɪnt] *n* **1.** *no pl* (*self-control*) dominio *m* de sí mismo; **to exercise ~** *form* mostrarse comedido **2.** (*restriction*) restricción *f*

restrict [rɪˈstrɪkt] *vt* (*limit*) restringir; **to ~ oneself** limitarse

restricted *adj* **1.** (*limited*) restringido, -a; (*document*) confidencial; (*parking*) limitado, -a; **entry is ~ to …** sólo se permite la entrada a… **2.** (*small: space*) reducido, -a; (*existence, horizon*) limitado, -a

restricted area *n* MIL zona *f* restringida

restriction [rɪˈstrɪkʃən] *n* restricción *f;* **speed ~** límite *m* de velocidad; **to impose ~s on sth** imponer restricciones a algo

restrictive [rɪˈstrɪktɪv] *adj* restrictivo, -a

restring [ˌriːˈstrɪŋ] *irr vt* (*instrument, tennis racket*) volver a encordar; (*necklace*) reensartar

rest room *n Am* aseos *mpl*

restructure [ˌriːˈstʌktʃəʳ, *Am:* -tʃɚ] *vt* reestructurar

restructuring *n* reestructuración *f*

result [rɪˈzʌlt] **I.** *n* **a.** MAT, SPORTS, POL resultado *m;* (*of exam*) nota *f;* **to get ~s** obtener buenos resultados; **with no ~** sin resultado; **as a ~ of** a consecuencia de; **as a ~** por consiguiente **II.** *vi* **to ~ from** ser consecuencia de; **to ~ in** ocasionar

resultant [rɪˈzʌltənt] *adj* resultante

resume [rɪˈzjuːm, *Am:* -ˈzuːm] **I.** *vt* **1.** (*start again: work, journey*) reanudar; (*speech*) proseguir con **2.** *form* (*reoccupy: place*) volver a ocupar; (*duties*) volver a asumir **II.** *vi form* proseguir

résumé [ˈrezjuːmeɪ, *Am:* ˈrezʊmeɪ] *n* **1.** (*summary*) resumen *m* **2.** *Am, Aus* (*curriculum vitae*) currículum *m* (vitae)

resumption [rɪˈzʌmpʃən] *n* **1.** *no pl* (*of journey, work*) reanudación *f* **2.** (*of power, duties*) reasunción *f*

resurface [ˌriːˈsɜːfɪs, *Am:* -ˈsɜːrfɪs] **I.** *vi* volver a salir a la superficie; *fig* resurgir **II.** *vt* repavimentar

resurgence [rɪˈsɜːdʒəns, *Am:* -ˈsɜːrdʒəns] *n no pl, form* resurgimiento *m*

resurgent [rɪˈsɜːdʒənt, *Am:* -ˈsɜːrdʒənt] *adj form* renaciente

resurrect [ˌrezəˈrekt] *vt a. fig* resucitar

resurrection [ˌrezəˈrekʃən] *n no pl* resurrección *f*

resuscitate [rɪˈsʌsɪteɪt, *Am:* -əteɪt] *vt* resucitar

retail [ˈriːteɪl] COM **I.** *n no pl* venta *f* al detalle **II.** *vt* vender al detalle **III.** *vi* venderse al detalle; **this product ~s at £5** el precio de venta al público de este producto es de 5 libras **IV.** *adv* al detalle

retail business *n* comercio *m* minorista

retailer *n* minorista *mf,* menorista *mf Chile, Méx*

retailing *n* venta *f* al detalle

retail outlet *n* COM punto *m* de venta

retail price *n* COM precio *m* de venta al público **retail price index** *n* ECON índice *m* de precios al consumo

retail trade *n* ECON comercio *m* minorista

retain [rɪˈteɪn] *vt* **1.** *form* (*keep: power*) retener; (*property*) quedarse con; (*right*) reservarse; (*title*) revalidar **2.** (*not lose: dignity*) mantener; (*colour*) conservar **3.** (*hold in place: water*) contener **4.** (*remember*) retener **5.** (*employ*) contratar

retainer *n* 1. ECON iguala *f* 2. (*servant*) criado, -a *m, f*
retaining wall *n* muro *m* de contención
retake[1] [ˌriːˈteɪk] *vt irr* 1. (*recapture: town*) volver a tomar; (*person*) volver a capturar; **to ~ the lead** recuperar el liderazgo 2. SCHOOL, UNIV (*exam*) volver a presentarse a 3. CINE volver a rodar; PHOT volver a hacer
retake[2] [ˈriːteɪk] *n* 1. *Brit* SCHOOL, UNIV examen *m* de recuperación 2. CINE toma *f* repetida
retaliate [rɪˈtælɪeɪt] *vi* tomar represalias
retaliation [rɪˌtælɪˈeɪʃən] *n no pl* represalias *fpl*
retaliatory [rɪˈtælɪətri, *Am:* -tɔːri] *adj* vengativo, -a; **~ measures** represalias *fpl*
retard [rɪˈtɑːd, *Am:* -ˈtɑːrd] *vt form* (*growth, development*) retardar; (*journey*) retrasar; **mentally ~ed person** retrasado, -a *m, f* mental
retardation [ˌriːtɑːˈdeɪʃən, *Am:* -tɑːrˈ-] *n no pl, form* retraso *m*
retch [retʃ] *vi* tener arcadas
retention [rɪˈtenʃən] *n no pl* 1. *form* (*keeping: of properties, heat*) retención *f;* (*of rules, laws*) mantenimiento *m* 2. *form* (*memory*) retentiva *f* 3. (*of lawyer, consultant*) contratación *f*
retentive [rɪˈtentɪv, *Am:* -t̬ɪv] *adj* retentivo, -a; **he's very ~** tiene muy buena memoria
rethink[1] [ˌriːˈθɪŋk] *vt irr* replantearse
rethink[2] [ˈriːθɪŋk] *n no pl* replanteamiento *m*
reticent [ˈretɪsnt, *Am:* ˈret̬əsnt] *adj* reticente
retina [ˈretɪnə, *Am:* ˈretnə] <-s *o* -nae> *n* retina *f*
retinue [ˈretɪnjuː, *Am:* ˈretnuː] *n inv* séquito *m*
retire [rɪˈtaɪəʳ, *Am:* -ˈtaɪɚ] I. *vi* 1. (*stop working*) jubilarse; (*soldier, athlete*) retirarse 2. *form* (*withdraw*) retirarse; **to ~ to the drawing room** pasar al salón 3. MIL replegarse 4. SPORTS (*from a race*) abandonar II. *vt* 1. (*stop working*) jubilar 2. MIL (*soldier*) retirar 3. FIN (*bond*) redimir
retired *adj* jubilado, -a; (*soldier, athlete*) retirado, -a
retirement [rɪˈtaɪəmənt, *Am:* -ˈtaɪɚ-] *n* 1. (*act of retiring*) retiro *m;* (*from race*) abandono *m* 2. *no pl* (*after working*) jubilación *f;* (*of soldier, athlete*) retiro *m;* **to be in ~** estar jubilado; **to come out of ~** salir de su retiro 3. MIL retirada *f*
retirement age *n* edad *f* de jubilarse **retirement pay** *n*, **retirement pension** *n* pensión *f* de jubilación
retiring *adj* 1. (*reserved*) reservado, -a 2. (*worker, official*) saliente
retort [rɪˈtɔːt, *Am:* -ˈtɔːrt] I. *vt* replicar II. *vi* replicar III. *n* 1. (*reply*) réplica *f* 2. CHEM retorta *f*
retouch [ˌriːˈtʌtʃ] *vt a.* ART, PHOT retocar
retrace [riːˈtreɪs] *vt* repasar; **to ~ one's steps** volver sobre sus pasos
retract [rɪˈtrækt] I. *vt* 1. (*statement, offer*) retirar 2. (*claws*) retraer; (*wheels*) replegar II. *vi* 1. (*withdraw statement, offer*) retractarse 2. (*be withdrawn: claws*) retraerse; (*wheels*) replegarse
retractable [rɪˈtræktəbl] *adj* retráctil
retraction [rɪˈtrækʃən] *n* (*of statement, offer*) retractación *f*
retrain [riːˈtreɪn] I. *vt* reciclar II. *vi* hacer un curso de reciclaje
retread[1] [ˌriːˈtred, *Am:* -ˈtrɑːd] *vt* (*a tyre*) recauchutar, reencauchar *Col, Perú*
retread[2] [ˈriːtred] *n* neumático *m* recauchutado
retreat [rɪˈtriːt] I. *vi* retroceder; MIL batirse en retirada II. *n* 1. (*withdrawal*) *a.* MIL retirada *f;* (*signal*) retreta *f;* **to sound** [*o* **beat**] **the ~** dar el toque de retreta 2. (*safe place*) refugio *m* 3. (*seclusion*) retiro *m;* **to go on a ~** hacer un retiro espiritual
retrench [rɪˈtrentʃ] I. *vi* reducir costes II. *vt* (*reduce: personnel, expenses*) reducir
retrenchment *n* 1. (*spending cut*) reducción *f* de gastos 2. *Aus* (*dismissal*) despido *m* por reducción de plantilla; (*of personnel*) reducción *f* 3. *no pl* (*cutting down*) supresión *f*
retrial [ˌriːˈtraɪəl, *Am:* ˈriːtraɪl] *n* nuevo juicio *m*
retribution [ˌretrɪˈbjuːʃən, *Am:* -rəˈ-] *n no pl, form* castigo *m* justo; **divine ~** justicia *f* divina
retributive [rɪˈtrɪbjʊtɪv] *adj form* punitivo, -a
retrieval [rɪˈtriːvl] *n no pl* (*finding*) *a.* INFOR recuperación *f;* **on-line information ~** recuperación de información en línea
retrieve [rɪˈtriːv] I. *vt* 1. (*get back*) *a.* INFOR recuperar 2. (*make amends for: error*) enmendar 3. (*repair: loss*) reparar; (*situation*) salvar 4. SPORTS (*game*) cobrar; (*in tennis*) devolver II. *vi* SPORTS cobrar
retriever [rɪˈtriːvəʳ, *Am:* -ɚ] *n* perro *m* cobrador
retroactive [ˌretrəʊˈæktɪv, *Am:* -roʊˈ-] *adj* retroactivo, -a
retrograde [ˈretrəgreɪd] *adj* retrógrado, -a
retrogressive [ˌretrəˈgresɪv, *Am:* ˈretrəgres-] *adj form* retrógrado, -a
retrospect [ˈretrəspekt] *n no pl* **in ~** mirando hacia atrás
retrospective [ˌretrəˈspektɪv] I. *adj* 1. (*looking back*) retrospectivo, -a 2. *Brit* LAW retroactivo, -a II. *n* ART exposición *f* retrospectiva
return [rɪˈtɜːn, *Am:* -ˈtɜːrn] I. *n* 1. (*going back*) regreso *m;* (*home, to work, to school*) vuelta *f;* **on his ~** a su regreso 2. (*to previous situation*) retorno *m;* **a ~ to sth** un restablecimiento de algo 3. MED (*of illness*) recaída *f* 4. (*giving back*) devolución *f* 5. (*recompense*) recompensa *f* 6. *Brit, Aus* (*ticket*) billete *m* de ida y vuelta, boleto *m* redondo *Méx* 7. FIN (*proceeds*) ganancia *f;* (*interest*) rédito *m;* **~ on capital** interés *m* del capital 8. *pl* POL resulta-

R

dos *mpl* de las elecciones **9.** *no pl* INFOR (tecla *f* de) retorno *m* **10.** (*report*) informe *m* **11.** FIN declaración *f* ►**many happy ~s (of the day)!** ¡feliz cumpleaños!; **by ~ (of post)** *Brit, Aus* a vuelta de correo; **in ~ for sth** a cambio de algo **II.** *adj* **1.** (*coming back: flight, journey*) de vuelta; (*ticket*) de ida y vuelta, redondo, -a *Méx* **2.** THEAT (*performance*) segundo, -a **3.** SPORTS (*match*) de vuelta **III.** *vi* **1.** (*come back*) volver; (*home*) regresar a; (*to task*) reanudar **2.** (*reappear*) volver a aparecer **IV.** *vt* **1.** (*give back*) devolver **2.** (*reciprocate*) corresponder a; (*compliment, favour, ball*) devolver; **to ~ sb's call** devolver la llamada a alguien; **to ~ good for evil** devolver bien por mal **3.** (*send back*) volver a colocar; **~ to sender** devuélvase al remitente **4.** FIN (*yield*) dar; (*profit*) proporcionar **5.** LAW (*pronounce: verdict*) emitir; (*judgement*) dictar **6.** *Brit* POL (*elect*) elegir **7.** ECON (*income*) declarar

returnable [rɪ'tɜːnəbl, *Am:* -'tɜːrn-] *adj* (*fee*) reembolsable; (*bottle*) retornable

return fare *n* precio *m* del billete de ida y vuelta **return flight** *n* viaje *m* de vuelta

returning officer *n Can* POL escrutador(a) *m(f)*

return journey *n* viaje *m* de vuelta

return key *n* INFOR tecla *f* de retorno **return match** *n* SPORTS partido *m* de vuelta **return ticket** *n* **1.** *Aus, Brit* billete *m* de ida y vuelta, boleto *m* redondo *Méx* **2.** *Am* billete *m* de vuelta

reunification [riːˌjuːnɪfɪ'keɪʃən, *Am:* -nəfɪ'-] *n no pl* reunificación *f*

reunion [ˌriː'juːnɪən, *Am:* -'juːnjən] *n* **1.** (*meeting*) reunión *f* **2.** (*after separation*) reencuentro *m*

reunite [ˌriːjuː'naɪt] **I.** *vt* **1.** (*bring together*) volver a unir **2.** (*friends*) reconciliar **II.** *vi* reunirse

reusable [ˌriː'juːzəbl] *adj* reutilizable

reuse [ˌriː'juːz] *vt* volver a usar

rev [rev] *n* AUTO revolution *f*

◆**rev up** AUTO **I.** *vt* <-vv-> acelerar **II.** *vi* embalarse

revaluation [riːˌvæljʊ'eɪʃən] *n* revaluación *f*

revalue [riː'væljuː] *vt* revaluar

revamp [ˌriː'væmp] *vt inf* modernizar

rev counter *n* cuentarrevoluciones *m inv*

Revd. *abbr of* Reverend Rev.

reveal [rɪ'viːl] *vt* **1.** (*divulge: secret, identity*) revelar; **he ~d his identity** desveló su identidad; **to ~ how/why ...** manifestar cómo/el porqué... **2.** (*uncover*) descubrir

revealing [rɪ'viːlɪŋ] *adj* revelador(a)

reveille [rɪ'væli, *Am:* 'revli] *n no pl, no indef art* MIL diana *f*

revel ['revl] <-ll-, *Am:* -l-> *vi* ir de juerga

◆**revel in** <-ll-, *Am:* -l-> *vi* **to ~ sth** deleitarse con algo

revelation [ˌrevə'leɪʃən] *n* revelación *f;* **the Book of Revelations** el Apocalipsis

reveler *n Brit,* **reveller** *n Am* juerguista *mf*

revelry ['revəlri] <-ies> *n no pl* jolgorio *m*

revenge [rɪ'vendʒ] **I.** *n no pl* **1.** (*retaliation*) venganza *f;* **in ~ (for sth)** como venganza (por algo) **2.** SPORTS revancha *f* **II.** *vt* vengar; **to ~ oneself on sb** vengarse de alguien

revenue ['revənjuː, *Am:* 'revənuː] *n* **1.** (*income*) ingresos *mpl;* (*of government*) rentas *fpl* públicas **2.** (*department*) Hacienda *f* Pública

revenue officer *n* delegado, -a *m, f* de Hacienda **revenue stamp** *n Am* timbre *m* fiscal

reverberate [rɪ'vɜːbəreɪt, *Am:* -'vɜːrbəreɪt] *vi* **1.** (*sound, light, heat*) reverberar **2.** *fig* tener gran repercusión

reverberation [rɪˌvɜːbə'reɪʃən, *Am:* -ˌvɜːrbə'-] *n* **1.** *no pl* (*of sound, heat, light*) reverberación *f* **2.** *fig* repercusión *f*

revere [rɪ'vɪə^r, *Am:* -'vɪr] *vt* venerar

reverence ['revərəns] *n no pl* veneración *f;* **to pay ~ to sth/sb** rendir homenaje a algo/alguien

Reverend ['revərənd] REL **I.** *adj* reverendo, -a; **the Right Reverend** el obispo; **the Most Reverend** el arzobispo **II.** *n* (*Protestant*) pastor *m;* (*Catholic*) sacerdote *m*

reverent ['revərənt] *adj* reverente

reverential [ˌrevə'renʃl] *adj* reverencial

reverie ['revəri] *n liter* ensueño *m;* **to be (lost) in ~** estar absorto

reversal [rɪ'vɜːsl, *Am:* -'vɜːrsl] *n* **1.** (*change: of order, opinion*) inversión *f;* (*of policy*) cambio *m* completo; LAW (*of decision*) revocación *f* **2.** (*setback*) revés *m*

reverse [rɪ'vɜːs, *Am:* -'vɜːrs] **I.** *vt* **1.** (*turn other way*) volver al revés; (*order*) invertir; (*policy, situation*) cambiar radicalmente; (*judgement*) revocar; **to ~ the charges** *Brit, Can* TEL llamar a cobro revertido **2.** *Aus, Brit* AUTO poner en marcha atrás; **to ~ a car into a garage** entrar en un garaje dando marcha atrás **II.** *vi* **1.** *Aus, Brit* AUTO dar marcha atrás; **to ~ into the garage** entrar al garaje dando marcha atrás **2.** (*order, situation*) invertirse **III.** *n* **1.** *no pl* **the ~** lo contrario; **in ~** a la inversa **2.** AUTO (*gear*) marcha *f* atrás; **to go into ~** dar marcha atrás **3.** (*setback*) revés *m* **4.** (*the back*) reverso *m;* (*of cloth*) revés *m;* (*of document*) dorso *m* **IV.** *adj* **1.** (*inverse*) inverso, -a **2.** (*opposite: direction*) contrario, -a

reverse charge call *n* TEL llamada *f* a cobro revertido **reverse gear** *n* AUTO marcha *f* atrás

reversible [rɪ'vɜːsəbl, *Am:* -'vɜːrsə-] *adj* **1.** (*jacket*) reversible **2.** (*decision*) revocable

reversion [rɪ'vɜːʃən, *Am:* -'vɜːrʒən] *n no pl* reversión *f*

revert [rɪ'vɜːt, *Am:* -'vɜːrt] *vi* volver; **to ~ to type** *fig* volver a ser el mismo de siempre

review [rɪ'vjuː] **I.** *vt* **1.** (*consider*) analizar **2.** (*reconsider*) reexaminar; (*salary*) reajustar **3.** (*look over: notes*) revisar **4.** (*criticize: book, play, film*) hacer una crítica [*o* reseña] de **5.** MIL (*inspect*) pasar revista a **6.** *Am* (*study again*) repasar **II.** *n* **1.** (*examination*) análisis *m inv;* **to come under ~** ser examinado; **to hold a ~** MIL pasar revista **2.** (*reconsideration*) revisión *f;* **to come up for ~** estar pendiente de revisión **3.** (*summary*) resumen *m* **4.** (*criticism: of book, play, film*) crítica *f,* reseña *f* **5.** (*magazine*) revista *f* **6.** THEAT revista *f*

reviewer [rɪ'vjuːəʳ, *Am:* -ɚ] *n* crítico, -a *m, f*

revise [rɪ'vaɪz] **I.** *vt* **1.** (*alter: text, law*) revisar; (*proofs*) corregir; (*opinion*) cambiar de **2.** *Brit, Aus* (*study again*) repasar **II.** *vi Aus, Brit* repasar

revision [rɪ'vɪʒən] *n* **1.** *no pl* (*of text, law*) revisión *f;* (*of proofs*) corrección *f;* (*of policy*) modificación *f* **2.** (*book*) edición *f* corregida **3.** *no pl, Brit, Aus* UNIV repaso *m*

revisionist [rɪ'vɪʒənɪst] *n* revisionista *mf*

revitalize [riː'vaɪtəlaɪz, *Am:* -t̬əl-] *vt* revitalizar; (*trade*) reactivar

revival [rɪ'vaɪvəl] *n* **1.** MED reanimación *f* **2.** (*rebirth: of interest*) renacimiento *m;* (*of idea, custom*) restablecimiento *m;* (*of economy*) reactivación *f;* (*of country*) resurgimiento *m* **3.** CINE, THEAT reestreno *m* **4.** REL despertar *m* religioso

revive [rɪ'vaɪv] **I.** *vt* **1.** MED reanimar **2.** (*resurrect: interest*) hacer renacer; (*idea, custom*) restablecer; (*economy*) reactivar; (*conversation*) reanimar **3.** CINE, THEAT reestrenar **II.** *vi* **1.** (*be restored to life*) volver en sí **2.** (*be restored: country, interest*) resurgir; (*tradition*) restablecerse; (*style*) volver a estar de moda; (*trade, economy*) reactivarse

revocation [ˌrevə'keɪʃən] *n* **1.** (*of licence*) suspensión *f* **2.** (*of law, decision*) revocación *f*

revoke [rɪ'vəʊk, *Am:* -'voʊk] **I.** *vt* **1.** (*cancel: decision, order*) revocar **2.** (*licence*) suspender **II.** *vi* GAMES renunciar

revolt [rɪ'vəʊlt, *Am:* -'voʊlt] POL **I.** *vi* rebelarse, alzarse *AmL;* **to ~ against sb/sth** sublevarse contra alguien/algo **II.** *vt* repugnar a; **it ~s me** me da asco **III.** *n* **1.** (*uprising*) revuelta *f;* **to rise in ~ against sb/sth** alzarse contra alguien/algo **2.** *no pl* (*rebelliousness*) rebeldía *f*

revolting [rɪ'vəʊltɪŋ, *Am:* -'voʊlt̬ɪŋ] *adj* (*disgusting*) repugnante; **to look ~** tener un aspecto horrible

revolution [ˌrevə'luːʃən] *n a.* POL revolución *f*

revolutionary [ˌrevə'luːʃənri] **I.** <-ies> *n* revolucionario, -a *m, f* **II.** *adj* revolucionario, -a

revolutionize [ˌrevə'luːʃnaɪz] *vt, vt* revolucionar

revolve [rɪ'vɒlv, *Am:* -'vɑːlv] *vi* girar; **to ~ on an axis** girar en torno a un eje; **that problem was ~ing in his mind** aquel problema le daba vueltas en la cabeza

◆**revolve around** *vi a. fig* girar alrededor

revolver [rɪ'vɒlvəʳ, *Am:* -'vɑːlvɚ] *n* revólver *m*

revolving *adj* giratorio, -a

revolving door *n* puerta *f* giratoria

revue [rɪ'vjuː] *n* THEAT revista *f*

revulsion [rɪ'vʌlʃən] *n no pl* repulsión *f*

reward [rɪ'wɔːd, *Am:* 'wɔːrd] **I.** *n* recompensa *f* **II.** *vt* recompensar

rewarding *adj* gratificante

rewind [ˌriː'waɪnd] *irr* **I.** *vt* (*tape*) rebobinar; (*clock, watch*) dar cuerda a **II.** *vi* rebobinarse

rewire [ˌriː'waɪəʳ, *Am:* -'waɪɚ] *vt* renovar la instalación eléctrica de

reword [ˌriː'wɜːd, *Am:* -'wɜːrd] *vt* **1.** (*rewrite*) volver a redactar **2.** (*say again*) expresar de otra manera

rework [ˌriː'wɜːk] *vt* revisar; (*theme*) adaptar

rewrite¹ [ˌriː'raɪt] *irr vt* volver a redactar

rewrite² ['riːraɪt] *n* nueva versión *f*

RFC [ˌɑːʳef'siː, *Am:* ˌɑːref'siː] *n abbr of* **Rugby Football Club** club *m* de rugby

Rh *abbr of* **rhesus** Rh

rhapsody ['ræpsədi] <-ies> *n* **1.** MUS rapsodia *f* **2.** (*enthusiasm*) éxtasis *m inv*

rhesus factor ['riːsəsˌfæktəʳ, *Am:* -tɚ] *n no pl* MED factor *m* Rhesus

rhetoric ['retərɪk, *Am:* 'ret̬-] *n no pl* retórica *f*

rhetorical [rɪ'tɒrɪkl, *Am:* -'tɔːr-] *adj* retórico, -a

rheumatic [ruː'mætɪk, *Am:* -'mæt̬-] *adj* reumático, -a

rheumatism ['ruːmətɪzəm] *n no pl* reumatismo *m*

rheumatoid arthritis [ˌruːmətɔɪdˌɑː'θraɪtɪs, *Am:* -ˌɑːr'θraɪt̬ɪs] *n no pl* MED artritis *f inv* reumatoidea

Rhine [raɪn] *n* **the ~** el Rin

rhino ['raɪnəʊ, *Am:* -noʊ] *n inf abbr of* **rhinoceros** rinoceronte *m*

rhinoceros [raɪ'nɒsərəs, *Am:* -'nɑːsɚ-] <-(es)> *n* rinoceronte *m*

Rhodes [rəʊdz, *Am:* roʊdz] *n* Rodas *f*

rhododendron [ˌrəʊdə'dendrən, *Am:* ˌroʊ-] *n* rododendro *m*

rhombus ['rɒmbəs, *Am:* 'rɑːm-] <-es *o* -i> *n* rombo *m*

Rhone [rəʊn, *Am:* roʊn] *n* **the ~** el Ródano

rhubarb ['ruːbɑːb, *Am:* -bɑːrb] **I.** *n no pl* ruibarbo *m* **II.** *interj* **~, ~(, ~)!** ¡bla, bla, bla!

rhyme [raɪm] **I.** *n* **1.** (*similar sound*) rima *f;* **in ~** en verso **2.** (*poem*) poesía *f* ►**without ~ or reason** sin ton ni son **II.** *vi* rimar

rhyming couplet [ˌraɪmɪŋ'kʌplɪt] *n* pareado *m*

rhythm ['rɪðəm] *n* ritmo *m*

rhythmic ['rɪðmɪk] *adj,* **rhythmical** *adj* rítmico, -a

RI [ˌɑːʳ'aɪ, *Am:* ˌɑr-] *abbr of* **religious instruction** religión *f*

rib [rɪb] **I.** *n* **1.** (*bone*) costilla *f;* **to dig sb in the ~s** dar a alguien un codazo en el costado **2.** NAUT cuaderna *f* **3.** *no pl* FASHION canalé *m* **II.** <-bb-> *vt inf* tomar el pelo a

ribald ['rɪbld] *adj* picaresco, -a

ribbon ['rɪbən] *n* (*long strip*) cinta *f;* (*on medal*) galón *m;* **to be cut to ~s** estar hecho

R

jirones

rib cage *n* tórax *m*

ribonucleic acid [ˌraɪbəʊnjuːkleɪɪk'æsɪd] *n* ácido *m* ribonucleico

rice [raɪs] *n no pl* arroz *m*

ricefield *n,* **rice paddy** *n* arrozal *m* **rice-growing** *n no pl* arrozal *m* **rice pudding** *n* arroz *m* con leche

rich [rɪtʃ] **I.** <-er, -est> *adj* **1.** (*person*) rico, -a; (*soil*) fértil; (*furnishings*) opulento, -a; ~ **pickings** ganancias *fpl;* **to become** ~ enriquecerse; **to be** ~ **in sth** abundar en algo **2.** (*stimulating: life, experience, history*) rico, -a **3.** (*food*) pesado, -a **4.** (*intense: colour*) brillante; (*flavour*) intenso, -a; (*tone*) profundo, -a **5.** *inf* **that's** ~**!** ¡mira quién habla! **II.** *n* **the** ~ los ricos

richness *n no pl* **1.** (*affluence*) riqueza *f;* (*of soil*) fertilidad *f* **2.** (*of food*) pesadez *f* **3.** (*intensity: of colour*) brillantez *f;* (*of flavour*) intensidad *f*

rick [rɪk] **I.** *n* almiar *m* **II.** *vt Brit, Aus* amontonar

rickets ['rɪkɪts] *n no pl* raquitismo *m*

rickety ['rɪkəti, *Am:* -ṭi] *adj* (*car*) desvencijado, -a; (*steps*) tambaleante; (*person*) raquítico, -a

rickshaw ['rɪkʃɔː, *Am:* -ʃɑː] *n* carro *m* de culí

ricochet ['rɪkəʃeɪ] **I.** *vi* rebotar **II.** *n* rebote *m*

rid [rɪd] <rid *o* ridded, rid> *vt* **to** ~ **sth/sb of sth** librar algo/a alguien de algo; **to** ~ **oneself of sth** librarse de algo; **to be** ~ **of sth/sb** estar libre de algo/alguien; **to get** ~ **of sb/sth** deshacerse de alguien/algo

riddance ['rɪdns] *n inf* **good** ~ **(to bad rubbish)!** ¡vete con viento fresco!; **to bid sb good** ~ desear a alguien un adiós y hasta nunca

ridden ['rɪdn] *pp of* **ride**

riddle¹ ['rɪdl] *n* **1.** (*conundrum*) adivinanza *f* **2.** (*mystery*) misterio *m;* **to speak in** ~**s** hablar en clave

riddle² ['rɪdl] *vt* acribillar; **to be** ~**d with mistakes** estar plagado, -a de errores

ride [raɪd] **I.** *n* (*on horse, motorbike, car*) paseo *m;* **to give sb a** ~ llevar a alguien ►**to take sb for a** ~ *inf* tomar el pelo a alguien **II.** <rode, ridden> *vt* **1.** (*sit on*) **to** ~ **a bike** ir en bici; **to** ~ **a horse** montar a caballo; **can you** ~ **a bike?** ¿sabes montar en bici?; **to** ~ **the waves** surcar las olas **2.** *Am, inf* (*exploit*) explotar **III.** <rode, ridden> *vi* **1.** (*on horse, bicyle*) montar; **to** ~ **on a horse** montar a caballo; **to** ~ **by bicycle** ir en bicicleta **2.** (*do well*) **to** ~ **high** alcanzar popularidad **3.** *inf* (*take no action*) **to let sth** ~ dejar pasar algo

◆**ride down** *vt* atropellar

◆**ride out** *vt a. fig* aguantar

◆**ride up** *vi* (*person*) acercarse; (*dress*) subirse

rider ['raɪdəʳ, *Am:* -dɚ] *n* **1.** (*on horse*) jinete *m,* amazona *f;* (*on bicycle*) ciclista *mf;* (*on motorbike*) motociclista *mf* **2.** LAW cláusula *f* adicional

ridge [rɪdʒ] *n* **1.** GEO cresta *f* **2.** METEO sistema *m* de altas presiones **3.** (*of roof*) caballete *m* ►**to have been around the** ~**s** *Aus* tener muchas tablas

ridgepole ['rɪdʒpəʊl, *Am:* -poʊl] *n* parhilera *f*

ridgeway ['rɪdʒweɪ] *n* ruta *f* de las crestas

ridicule ['rɪdɪkjuːl] **I.** *n no pl* burlas *fpl;* **to be an object of** ~ ser el hazmerreír; **to hold sb/sth up to** ~ ridiculizar a alguien/algo **II.** *vt* ridiculizar

ridiculous [rɪ'dɪkjʊləs] *adj* ridículo, -a

riding *n no pl* equitación *f*

riding breeches *n* pantalones *mpl* de montar **riding crop** *n* fusta *f* **riding school** *n* escuela *f* de equitación **riding whip** *n s.* **riding crop**

rife [raɪf] *adj* extendido, -a; **to be** ~ **with sth** estar plagado, -a de algo

riffle ['rɪfl] *vt* (*cards*) barajar; (*pages*) volver; (*book*) hojear

riff-raff ['rɪfræf] *n no pl* chusma *f*

rifle¹ ['raɪfl] *n* fusil *m,* rifle *m*

rifle² ['raɪfl] **I.** *vt* **1.** (*plunder*) saquear **2.** (*steal*) robar **II.** *vt* revolver **III.** *vi* **to** ~ **through sth** rebuscar en algo

rifle butt *n* culata *f* de rifle **rifleman** <-men> *n* fusilero *m* **rifle range** *n* campo *m* de tiro **rifle shot** *n* tiro *m* de fusil

rift [rɪft] *n* **1.** (*in earth*) fisura *f* **2.** *fig* ruptura *f;* **to heal the** ~ cerrar la brecha

rig [rɪg] <-gg-> **I.** *vt* **1.** (*falsify*) amañar **2.** NAUT aparejar **II.** *n* **1.** TECH **(oil)** ~ plataforma *f* petrolífera **2.** *Am* (*truck*) camión *m* **3.** NAUT aparejo *m* **4.** *inf* (*clothing*) atuendo *m*

rigger ['rɪgəʳ, *Am:* -ɚ] *n* NAUT aparejador(a) *m(f)*

rigging ['rɪgɪŋ] *n no pl* **1.** (*of result*) pucherazo *m;* **ballot** ~ fraude *m* electoral **2.** NAUT jarcia *f*

right [raɪt] **I.** *adj* **1.** (*correct*) correcto, -a; (*ethical*) justo, -a; (*change*) oportuno, -a; **to put sth** ~ poner algo en orden; **it is** ~ **that ...** es justo que...; **to be** ~ **(about sth)** tener razón (en algo), estar en lo cierto (sobre algo) *AmL;* **to do sth the** ~ **way** hacer algo correctamente; **to do the** ~ **thing** hacer lo que se debe hacer; **to be in the** ~ **place at the** ~ **time** estar en el lugar indicado en el momento indicado; **to be on the** ~ **side of forty** tener menos de cuarenta años; **to put a clock** ~ poner el reloj en hora **2.** (*direction*) derecho, -a; **a** ~ **hook** SPORTS un gancho de derecha **3.** POL de derechas **4.** (*well*) bueno, -a; **to be not (quite)** ~ **in the head** *inf* no estar muy bien de la cabeza **5.** *inf* (*complete*) completo, -a; **he's a** ~ **idiot** es un imbécil total **II.** *n* **1.** *no pl* (*entitlement*) derecho *m;* **to have the** ~ **to do sth** tener el derecho de hacer algo **2.** (*morality*) **to be in the** ~ tener razón **3.** (*right side*) derecha *f;* SPORTS derechazo *m* **4.** POL **the Right** la derecha **III.** *adv* **1.** (*correctly*) correctamente; **to do** ~ obrar bien

2. (*straight*) directamente; ~ **away** inmediatamente 3. (*to the right*) hacia la derecha 4. (*precisely*) precisamente; ~ **here** justo aquí; **to be ~ behind sb** estar inmediatamente detrás de alguien IV. *vt* 1. (*rectify*) rectificar; (*mistake*) arreglar 2. (*straighten*) enderezar V. *interj* de acuerdo, órale *Méx*

right angle *n* ángulo *m* recto

right-angled ['raɪtˌæŋgld] *adj* en ángulo recto

righteous ['raɪtʃəs] I. *adj form* 1. (*person*) virtuoso, -a 2. (*indignation*) justificado, -a; (*tone*) de superioridad moral II. *n pl* **the ~** los justos

rightful ['raɪtfəl] *adj* legítimo, -a

right-hand [ˌraɪt'hænd] *adj* **on the ~ side** a la derecha

right-hand drive *adj* con el volante a la derecha

right-handed [ˌraɪt'hændɪd] *adj* diestro, -a

right-hander *n* 1. (*person*) diestro, -a *m, f* 2. (*punch*) derechazo *m*

rightist ['raɪtɪst] POL I. *n* derechista *mf* II. *adj* de derechas

rightly *adv* 1. (*correctly*) correctamente; **if I remember ~** si recuerdo bien 2. (*justifiably*) con razón; (**whether**) **~ or wrongly** con razón o sin ella

right-minded [ˌraɪt'maɪndɪd] *adj* sensato, -a

right of way <-rights> *n* 1. (*over private land*) servidumbre *f* de paso 2. (*on road*) preferencia *f*

rights issue *n Brit* FIN emisión *f* de derechos de suscripción

right-wing [ˌraɪt'wɪŋ] *adj* POL de derechas; **to be ~** ser de derechas

rigid ['rɪdʒɪd] *adj* 1. (*stiff*) rígido, -a; **to be ~ with fear/pain** estar paralizado, -a de miedo/dolor; **to be bored ~** *Brit, inf* aburrirse como una ostra 2. (*inflexible*) inflexible; (*censorship*) estricto, -a 3. (*intransigent*) intransigente

rigidity [rɪ'dʒɪdəti, *Am:* -ṱi] *n no pl* 1. (*hardness*) rigidez *f* 2. (*inflexibility*) inflexibilidad *f* 3. (*intransigence*) intransigencia *f*

rigmarole ['rɪgmərəʊl, *Am:* -məroʊl] *n no pl* galimatías *m inv*

rigor ['rɪgəʳ, *Am:* -ɚ] *n Am, Aus s.* **rigour**

rigor mortis [ˌrɪgə'mɔːtɪs, *Am:* ˌrɪgɚ'mɔːrṱɪs] *n no pl* MED rigidez *f* cadavérica

rigorous ['rɪgərəs] *adj* riguroso, -a

rigour ['rɪgəʳ, *Am:* -ɚ] *n no pl, Brit, Aus* rigor *m*

rig-out ['rigaʊt] *n inf* atuendo *m*

rile [raɪl] *vt inf* irritar

rim [rɪm] I. *n* 1. (*of cup, bowl*) canto *m* 2. (*spectacle frames*) montura *f* 3. GEO borde *m*; **the Pacific ~** los países de la costa del Pacífico 4. (*dirty mark*) cerco *m* II. <-mm-> *vt* 1. (*surround*) bordear 2. (*frame*) enmarcar

rime [raɪm] *n liter* (*frost*) escarcha *f*

rimless ['rɪmlɪs] *adj* (*spectacles*) sin montura

rind [raɪnd] *n no pl* (*of fruit*) cáscara *f*; (*of bacon, cheese*) corteza *f*

ring¹ [rɪŋ] I. *n* 1. (*small circle*) círculo *m*; (*of people*) corro *m*; (*around eyes*) ojera *f* 2. (*jewellery*) anillo *m* 3. *Brit* (*part of cooker*) quemador *m* 4. (*arena*) ruedo *m*; (*in boxing*) cuadrilátero *m*; (*in circus*) pista *f* II. *vt* 1. (*surround*) rodear; **to be ~ed by sth** estar cercado, -a con algo 2. (*bird*) anillar

ring² [rɪŋ] I. *n* 1. *no pl, Brit* (*telephone call*) llamada *f*; **to give sb a ~** llamar a alguien (por teléfono) 2. (*metallic sound*) sonido *m* metálico; (*of bell*) toque *m* II. <rang, rung> *vt* 1. *Brit* (*call on telephone*) llamar (por teléfono) 2. (*bell*) tocar; (*alarm*) hacer sonar III. <rang, rung> *vi* 1. *Brit* (*call on telephone*) llamar 2. (*produce sound: telephone, bell*) sonar; **to ~ false/true** sonar falso/convincente

◆**ring back** *vi, vt* TEL volver a llamar (a)

◆**ring down** *vt* THEAT **to ~ the curtain** bajar el telón

◆**ring in** *vt* **to ~ the New Year** recibir el año nuevo

◆**ring off** *vi Brit* colgar

◆**ring out** *vi* resonar

◆**ring up** I. *vt* 1. (*telephone*) telefonear 2. (*key in sale*) registrar II. *vi* telefonear

ring binder *n* archivador *m* de anillas

ringer ['rɪŋəʳ, *Am:* -ɚ] *n* **to be a dead ~** (**for sb**) *inf* ser el vivo retrato (de alguien)

ring finger *n* dedo *m* anular

ringing I. *n no pl* repique *m* II. *adj* sonoro, -a

ringing tone *n* TEL tono *m* de llamada

ringleader ['rɪŋliːdəʳ, *Am:* -dɚ] *n* cabecilla *mf*

ringlet ['rɪŋlɪt] *n* tirabuzón *m*

ring road *n Brit, Aus* ronda *f* de circunvalación

ringside ['rɪŋsaɪd] I. *n* **to be at the ~** estar junto al cuadrilátero II. *adj* (*seats*) de primera fila

ringworm ['rɪŋwɜːm, *Am:* -wɜːrm] *n* tiña *f*

rink [rɪŋk] *n* pista *f* de patinaje

rinse [rɪns] I. *vt* (*dishes, clothes*) enjuagar; (*hands*) lavar II. *n* 1. *no pl* (*wash*) enjuague *m*; **cold/hot ~** aclarado *m* frío/caliente 2. (*hair colouring*) reflejos *mpl*

riot ['raɪət] I. *n* disturbio *m*; **a ~ of colour** un derroche de color; **to be a ~** *inf* ser la monda II. *vi* causar disturbios III. *adv* **to run ~** *fig* desmandarse; **to let one's imagination run ~** dar rienda suelta a su imaginación

rioter *n* alborotador(a) *m(f)*

riot gear *n* uniforme *m* antidisturbios

rioting *n no pl* disturbios *mpl*

riotous ['raɪətəs, *Am:* -ṱəs] *adj* 1. (*rebellious*) descontrolado, -a 2. (*uproarious*) escandaloso, -a; (*party*) desenfrenado, -a

riot police *n* policía *f* antidisturbios

rip [rɪp] I. <-pp-> *vi* rasgarse II. <-pp-> *vt* rasgar; **to ~ sth open** abrir algo de un rasgón III. *n* rasgón *m*, rajo *m AmC*

◆**rip down** *vt* arrancar

◆**rip off** *vt* 1. (*remove*) arrancar 2. *inf*

(*swindle*) timar

◆**rip out** *vt* arrancar

◆**rip up** *vt* romper

RIP [ˌɑːʳaɪˈpiː, *Am:* ˌɑːr-] *abbr of* **rest in peace** E.P.D., D.E.P

ripcord [ˈrɪpkɔːd, *Am:* -kɔːrd] *n* cordón *m* de apertura

ripe [raɪp] *adj* **1.** (*fruit*) maduro, -a; **at the ~ old age of 80** a la avanzada edad de 80 **2.** (*ready*) **the time is ~ for ...** es el momento oportuno de... **3.** (*language*) atrevido, -a

ripen [ˈraɪpən] **I.** *vt* hacer madurar **II.** *vi* madurar

ripeness [ˈraɪpnɪs] *n no pl* madurez *f*

rip-off [ˈrɪpɒf, *Am:* -ɑːf] *n inf* timo *m*, vacilada *f inf, Méx*

riposte [rɪˈpɒst, *Am:* -ˈpoʊst] *n* réplica *f*

ripple [ˈrɪpl] **I.** *n* onda *f*; **~ of applause** unos cuantos aplausos; **raspberry ~** helado *m* de vainilla con vetas de frambuesa **II.** *vt* rizar **III.** *vi* rizarse

rip-roaring [ˈrɪprɔːrɪŋ, *Am:* ˌrɪpˈ-] *adj inf* animadísimo, -a; **a ~ success** un éxito clamoroso

riptide [ˈrɪptaɪd] *n* corriente *f* de resaca

rise [raɪz] **I.** *n no pl* **1.** (*increase*) subida *f*; **to be on the ~** ir en aumento; **to give ~ to sth** dar lugar a algo; (**pay**) **~** *Brit* incremento *m* salarial; **to get** [*o* **take**] **a ~ out of sb** burlarse de alguien **2.** (*incline*) cuesta *f* **II.** <rose, risen> *vi* **1.** (*arise*) levantarse **2.** (*become higher: ground*) subir (en pendiente); (*temperature*) aumentar; (*river*) crecer **3.** (*go up: smoke*) subir; (*moon, sun*) salir; (*building*) elevarse **4.** (*improve socially*) ascender; (*in the ranks*) ganar; **to ~ to fame** alcanzar la fama **5.** (*be reborn*) resucitar **6.** (*rebel*) sublevarse

◆**rise above** *vt insep* **1.** (*be higher than*) estar por encima de **2.** (*problem, opposition*) superar

◆**rise up** *vi* **1.** (*arise*) levantarse **2.** (*rebel*) alzarse

risen [ˈrɪzn] *pp of* **rise**

riser a\q [ˈraɪzəʳ, *Am:* -zɚ] *n* **1.** (*person*) **early ~** madrugador(a) *m(f)*; **late ~** dormilón, -ona *m, f* **2.** (*part of step*) contrahuella *f* **3.** *pl, Am* (*set of steps*) escaleras *fpl*

risible [ˈrɪzəbl] *adj* risible

rising [ˈraɪzɪŋ] **I.** *n* levantamiento *m* **II.** *adj* (*in number*) creciente; (*in status*) ascendente; (*floodwaters*) en aumento; (*sun*) naciente

risk [rɪsk] **I.** *n* **1.** (*chance*) riesgo *m*; **to run the ~ of sth** correr el riesgo de algo **2.** *no pl* (*danger*) peligro *m*; **at one's own ~** bajo su propia responsabilidad; **to be at ~** correr peligro **II.** *vt* arriesgar; **to ~ doing sth** arriesgarse a hacer algo; **to ~ one's life** poner la propia vida en peligro

risk capital *n* ECON capital *m* de riesgo **risk factor** *n* factor *m* de riesgo

risk-free *adj*, **riskless** *adj Am* sin riesgo

risk liability *n* responsabilidad *f* sobre riesgos

risky [ˈrɪski] <-ier, -iest> *adj* arriesgado, -a, riesgoso, -a *AmL*

risqué [ˈriːskeɪ, *Am:* rɪˈskeɪ] *adj* atrevido, -a

rissole [ˈrɪsəʊl, *Am:* -oʊl] *n* croqueta *f*

rite [raɪt] *n* rito *m*; **last ~s** extremaunción *f*

ritual [ˈrɪtʃʊəl, *Am:* -uəl] **I.** *n* ritual *m* **II.** *adj* ritual

ritzy [ˈrɪtsi] <-ier, -iest> *adj inf* lujoso, -a

rival [ˈraɪvl] **I.** *n* rival *mf* **II.** *adj* competidor(a); **a ~ brand** una marca rival **III.** <-ll-, *Am:* -l-> *vt* competir con

rivalry [ˈraɪvlri] *n* rivalidad *f*

river [ˈrɪvəʳ, *Am:* -ɚ] *n* río *m*

river basin *n* cuenca *f* de río **river bed** *n* lecho *m* de un río **river fish** *n* pez *m* de río **river police** *n* policía *f* fluvial

riverside [ˈrɪvəsaɪd, *Am:* ˈrɪvɚ-] *n no pl* ribera *f*

rivet [ˈrɪvɪt] **I.** *n* remache *m* **II.** *vt* **1.** (*join*) remachar **2.** (*interest*) **to be ~ed by sth** quedar absorto, -a con algo

riveting [ˈrɪvətɪŋ, *Am:* -ɪt̬ɪŋ] *adj inf* fascinante

rivulet [ˈrɪvjʊlɪt] *n* **1.** *liter* (*stream*) arroyo *m* **2.** (*of sweat, blood*) gotas *fpl*

RN [ˌɑːʳˈen, *Am:* ˌɑːrˈen] *n Brit* MIL *abbr of* **Royal Navy** *flota real*

RNA [ˌɑːʳenˈeɪ, *Am:* ˌɑːrenˈeɪ] *n abbr of* **ribonucleic acid** ARN *m*

RNLI [ˌɑːʳenelˈaɪ, *Am:* ˌɑːrenelˈaɪ] *n Brit* NAUT *abbr of* **Royal National Lifeboat Institution** *servicio de lanchas de socorro*

roach [rəʊtʃ, *Am:* roʊtʃ] *n* **1.** (*fish*) rubio *m* **2.** *Am, inf* (*cockroach*) cucaracha *f*

road [rəʊd, *Am:* roʊd] *n* **1.** (*between towns*) carretera *f*; (*in town*) calle *f*; (*route*) camino *m*; **by ~** por carretera; **to be on the ~** (*fit for driving*) estar en circulación; (*travelling by road*) estar en camino; (*performing on tour*) estar de gira **2.** *fig* sendero *m*; **to be on the ~ to recovery** estar reponiéndose; **to be on the right ~** *Brit* ir bien encaminado ►**all ~s lead to Rome** *prov* todos los caminos llevan a Roma *prov*; **let's hit the ~!** *inf* ¡vamos a ponernos en marcha!; **to get sth on the ~** *inf* empezar (con) algo

road accident *n* accidente *m* de circulación **roadblock** *n* control *m* de carretera **road haulage** *n no pl* transporte *m* por carretera **road hog** *n inf* loco, -a *m, f* del volante

roadhouse [ˈrəʊdhaʊs, *Am:* ˈroʊd-] <-houses> *n Am* motel *m*

roadie [ˈrəʊdi, *Am:* ˈroʊ-] *n persona encargada de transportar y montar el equipo de un grupo musical*

road map *n* mapa *m* de carreteras **road rage** *n* furia *f* al volante **road safety** *n no pl* seguridad *f* vial **road sense** *n* instinto *m* del automovilista

roadshow [ˈrəʊdʃəʊ, *Am:* ˈroʊdʃoʊ] *n* gira *f*

roadside [ˈrəʊdsaɪd, *Am:* ˈroʊd-] **I.** *n* borde *m* de la carretera **II.** *adj* de carretera

road sign *n* señal *f* de tráfico

road surface *n* pavimento *m* **road sweeper** *n* barrendero, -a *m, f* **road-test**

vt **to ~ a car** someter un coche a una prueba de carretera **road traffic** *n no pl* tráfico *m* vial **road transport** *n no pl, Brit* transporte *m* por carretera **road user** *n* usuario, -a *m, f* de la vía pública

roadway ['rəʊdweɪ, *Am:* 'roʊd-] *n no pl* calzada *f*

roadworks ['rəʊdwɜːks, *Am:* 'roʊdwɜːrks] *npl* obras *fpl* de carretera

roam [rəʊm, *Am:* roʊm] **I.** *vi* vagar **II.** *vt* vagar por

roan [rəʊn, *Am:* roʊn] *n* ruano *m*

roar [rɔːʳ, *Am:* rɔːr] **I.** *vi* (*lion, person*) rugir; (*cannon*) tronar; **to ~ with laughter** reírse a carcajadas **II.** *vt* vociferar **III.** *n* (*of lion, person*) rugido *m;* (*of engine*) estruendo *m*

roaring I. *adj* rugiente; (*thunder*) estruendoso, -a; (*fire*) furioso, -a; (*success*) clamoroso, -a; (*trade*) tremendo, -a **II.** *adv* completamente

roast [rəʊst, *Am:* roʊst] **I.** *vt* asar; (*coffee*) tostar **II.** *vi* (*food*) asarse; (*person*) achicharrarse **III.** *n* asado *m* **IV.** *adj* (*meat*) asado, -a; (*coffee*) tostado, -a

roaster ['rəʊstəʳ, *Am:* 'roʊstɚ] *n* asador *m*

roasting ['rəʊstɪŋ, *Am:* 'roʊst-] **I.** *n* **1.** (*baking*) asado *m* **2.** *inf* (*telling off*) **to give sb a ~** echar una bronca a alguien **II.** *adj* abrasador(a) **III.** *adv* **~ hot** abrasador(a)

rob [rɒb, *Am:* rɑːb] <-bb-> *vt* **1.** (*person, house*) robar; (*bank*) asaltar; **to ~ sb of sth** robar algo a alguien **2.** (*deprive*) **to ~ sb of sth** privar a alguien de algo

robber ['rɒbəʳ, *Am:* 'rɑːbɚ] *n* ladrón, -ona *m, f;* **bank ~** atracador(a) *m(f)* de bancos

robbery ['rɒbəri, *Am:* 'rɑːbɚi] <-ies> *n* robo *m*

robe [rəʊb, *Am:* roʊb] *n* (*formal*) toga *f;* (*dressing gown*) traje *m*

robin ['rɒbɪn, *Am:* 'rɑːbɪn] *n* ZOOL petirrojo *m;* *Am* (*American songbird*) tordo *m* norteamericano

robot ['rəʊbɒt, *Am:* 'roʊbɑːt] *n* (*machine*) robot *m;* (*person*) autómata *m*

robotics [rəʊ'bɒtɪks, *Am:* roʊ'bɑːt̬ɪks] *npl* robótica *f*

robust [rəʊ'bʌst, *Am:* roʊ'-] *adj* **1.** (*person*) robusto, -a; (*health*) de hierro; (*currency*) fuerte **2.** (*statement*) enérgico, -a

robustness *n no pl* **1.** (*vitality*) robustez *f;* (*long-term strength*) solidez *f* **2.** (*frankness*) vigor *m*

rock[1] [rɒk, *Am:* rɑːk] *n* **1.** GEO roca *f;* (*in sea*) escollo *m* **2.** (*music*) rock *m* ►**to be between a ~ and hard place** estar entre la espada y la pared; **as solid as a ~** duro como una piedra; **to be on the ~s** estar sin blanca; **whisky on the ~s** whisky con hielo

rock[2] [rɒk, *Am:* rɑːk] **I.** *vt* **1.** (*swing*) mecer **2.** (*shock*) sacudir **II.** *vi* balancearse

rock-and-roll [ˌrɒkənd'rəʊl, *Am:* ˌrɑːkənd'roʊl] *n no pl* rock and roll *m* **rock band** *n* grupo *m* de rock **rock bottom** *n* fondo *m;* **to hit ~** tocar fondo; **to be at ~** estar por los suelos **rock bun** *n,* **rock cake** *n Brit, Aus* bollo *m* con frutos secos **rock climber** *n* escalador(a) *m(f)* **rock climbing** *n no pl* escalada *f* en roca

rocker ['rɒkəʳ, *Am:* 'rɑːkɚ] *n* **1.** (*chair*) mecedora *f* **2.** *Brit* (*musician, fan*) roquero, -a *m, f* ►**to be off one's ~** *inf* estar chiflado

rockery ['rɒkri, *Am:* 'rɑːkɚi] <-ies> *n* jardín *m* rocoso

rocket ['rɒkɪt, *Am:* 'rɑːkɪt] **I.** *n* **1.** (*weapon*) misil *m* **2.** (*vehicle for space travel*) cohete *m* espacial **3.** (*firework*) cohete *m* **4.** *no pl* (*reprimand*) bronca *f;* **to give sb a ~** echar un rapapolvo a alguien **II.** *vi* (*costs, prices*) dispararse; **to ~ up** dispararse

rocket launcher *n* lanzacohetes *m inv*

rock face *n* pared *f* rocosa **rock festival** *n* festival *m* de rock **rock garden** *n Am* jardín *m* rocoso

Rockies ['rɒkiz, *Am:* 'rɑːkiz] *n* **the ~** las Rocosas

rocking chair ['rɒkɪŋ, *Am:* 'rɑːk-] *n* mecedora *f,* columpio *m AmL* **rocking horse** *n* caballito *m* mecedor

rock music *n no pl* música *f* rock **rock'n'roll** *n no pl* rock and roll *m* **rock plant** *n* planta *f* rupestre **rock salt** *n no pl* sal *f* gema **rock star** *n* estrella *f* del rock

rocky[1] ['rɒki, *Am:* 'rɑːki] <-ier, -iest> *adj* rocoso, -a; (*ground*) pedregoso, -a

rocky[2] ['rɒki, *Am:* 'rɑːki] <-ier, -iest> *adj* (*unstable*) inestable

Rocky Mountains *n* Montañas *fpl* Rocosas

rococo [rəʊ'kəʊkəʊ, *Am:* rə'koʊkoʊ] **I.** *n no pl* rococó *m* **II.** *adj* rococó

rod [rɒd, *Am:* rɑːd] *n* (*stick*) varilla *f;* (*fishing rod*) caña *f* de pescar

rode [rəʊd, *Am:* roʊd] *pt of* **ride**

rodent ['rəʊdnt, *Am:* 'roʊ-] *n* roedor *m*

rodeo ['rəʊdɪəʊ, *Am:* 'roʊdɪoʊ] <-s> *n* rodeo *m*

roe[1] [rəʊ, *Am:* roʊ] *n* (*fish eggs*) hueva *f*

roe[2] [rəʊ, *Am:* roʊ] <-(s)> *n* (*deer*) corzo, -a *m, f*

roe buck *n,* **roebuck** ['rəʊbʌk, *Am:* 'roʊ-] *n* corzo *m*

roger ['rɒdʒəʳ, *Am:* 'rɑːdʒɚ] *interj* RADIO recibido

rogue [rəʊg, *Am:* roʊg] **I.** *n* **1.** (*rascal*) pícaro, -a *m, f* **2.** (*villain*) bribón, -ona *m, f* **II.** *adj* (*animal*) solitario, -a; (*trader, company*) deshonesto, -a

roguery ['rəʊgəri, *Am:* 'roʊ-] <-ies> *n* (*of child*) pillería *f;* (*of adult*) truhanería *f*

roguish ['rəʊgɪʃ, *Am:* 'roʊ-] *adj* pícaro, -a

ROI [ˌɑːʳəʊ'aɪ, *Am:* ˌɑːroʊ'aɪ] *n abbr of* **return on investment** rendimiento *m* de las inversiones

role *n,* **rôle** [rəʊl, *Am:* roʊl] *n a.* THEAT papel *m;* **to play a ~** THEAT hacer un papel; *fig* desempeñar un papel

role model *n* modelo *m* a imitar **role play** *n* juego *m* de imitación **role reversal** *n* inversión *m* de papeles

roll [rəʊl, *Am:* roʊl] **I.** *n* **1.** (*turning over*) voltereta *f* **2.** *no pl* (*swaying movement*) balanceo *m;* **to be on a ~** *fig* tener buena suerte **3.** (*cylinder: of cloth, paper*) rollo *m;* (*film*) carrete *m* **4.** (*noise: of drum*) redoble *m;* (*of thunder*) retumbo *m* **5.** (*catalogue of names*) padrón *m;* (*for elections*) censo *m;* **to call the ~** pasar lista **6.** (*bread*) panecillo *m* **II.** *vt* **1.** (*push: ball, barrel*) hacer rodar; (*dice*) tirar; **to ~ one's eyes** poner los ojos en blanco **2.** (*form into cylindrical shape*) **to ~ sth into sth** enrollar algo en algo; **all ~ed into one** todo unido en uno **3.** (*make: cigarette*) liar **4.** (*flatten: grass*) allanar **III.** *vi* **1.** (*move*) rodar; (*with undulating motion*) ondular **2.** (*be in operation*) funcionar

◆**roll about** *vi* vagar; (*ship*) balancearse

◆**roll back** *vt* **1.** (*cause to retreat*) hacer retroceder **2.** *Am* ECON reducir **3.** (*return to previous state*) hacer recular

◆**roll by** *vi* (*vehicle, clouds*) avanzar; (*time, years*) pasar

◆**roll down** **I.** *vt* (*sleeve*) desenrollar; (*window*) bajar **II.** *vi* rodar por

◆**roll in** *vi* **1.** llegar en abundancia **2. to be rolling in money** *inf* nadar en dinero

◆**roll off** *vi* caer rodando

◆**roll on** *vi* seguir rodando; (*time*) pasar; **~ Christmas!** *Brit, Aus, inf* ¡que llegue Navidad!

◆**roll out** **I.** *vt* **1.** (*flatten*) estirar; (*pastry*) extender **2.** *Am* ECON transferir **3.** (*unroll*) desenrollar **II.** *vi Am* ECON transferir

◆**roll over** *vi* dar vueltas

◆**roll up** **I.** *vi inf* aparecer; **~!** *Brit, Aus* ¡vengan todos! **II.** *vt* enrollar; (*sleeves*) arremangarse

roll bar *n* AUTO barra *f* protectora antivuelco **roll call** *n* lista *f*

roller ['rəʊləʳ, *Am:* 'roʊlɚ] *n* **1.** TECH rodillo *m* **2.** (*wave*) ola *f* grande **3.** (*for hair*) rulo *m*

roller bearing *n* TECH cojinete *m* de rodillos **rollerblade®** **I.** *n* patín *m* en línea **II.** *vi* patinar en línea **roller blind** *n Brit, Aus* persiana *f* **roller coaster** *n* montaña *f* rusa **roller-skate** **I.** *n* patín *m* de ruedas **II.** *vi* patinar

rollicking ['rɒlɪkɪŋ, *Am:* 'rɑːlɪ-] **I.** *adj* (*amusing*) alegre; (*party*) divertido, -a **II.** *n Brit, inf* **to give sb a ~** echar una bronca a alguien

rolling *adj* rodante; (*hills*) ondulado, -a; (*programme*) continuo, -a

rolling mill *n* **1.** (*machine*) tren *m* de laminación **2.** (*factory*) taller *m* de laminación **rolling pin** *n* rodillo *m* **rolling stock** *n* AUTO material *m* rodante

rollneck ['rəʊlnek, *Am:* 'roʊl-] *n* jersey *m* de cuello vuelto

roll-on ['rəʊlɒn, *Am:* 'roʊlɑːn] *adj* (*deodorant*) de bola

roll-on-roll-off *adj* AUTO ro-ro; (*ferry*) de autotransbordo

roly-poly¹ [ˌrəʊli'pəʊli, *Am:* ˌroʊli'poʊ-] *adj inf* regordete, -a

roly-poly² [ˌrəʊli'pəʊli, *Am:* ˌroʊli'poʊ-] *n,* **roly-poly pudding** *n* GASTR brazo *m* de gitano

ROM [rɒm, *Am:* rɑːm] *n no pl* INFOR *abbr of* **Read Only Memory** ROM *f*

Roman ['rəʊmən, *Am:* 'roʊ-] **I.** *adj* romano, -a; (*alphabet*) latino, -a; (*religion*) católico, -a **II.** *n* romano, -a *m, f*

Roman Catholic **I.** *n* católico, -a *m, f* **II.** *adj* católico, -a; **the ~ Church** la Iglesia católica romana

romance [rəʊ'mænts, *Am:* roʊ'mænts] **I.** *n* **1.** (*love affair*) romance *m* **2.** (*novel*) novela *f* rosa; (*film*) película *f* de amor **3.** (*glamour*) romanticismo *m* **II.** *vi* fantasear

Romanesque [ˌrəʊmə'nesk, *Am:* ˌroʊ-] *adj* románico, -a

Romania [rə'meɪnɪə, *Am:* roʊ'-] *n* Rumanía *f*

Romanian [rə'meɪnɪən, *Am:* roʊ'-] **I.** *adj* rumano, -a **II.** *n* **1.** (*person*) rumano, -a *m, f* **2.** LING rumano *m*

romantic [rəʊ'mæntɪk, *Am:* roʊ'mænt̬ɪk] **I.** *adj a.* LIT, ART romántico, -a **II.** *n* romántico, -a *m, f*

romanticism [rəʊ'mæntɪsɪzəm, *Am:* roʊ'mænt̬ə-] *n no pl* romanticismo *m*

Romany ['rɒməni, *Am:* 'rɑːmə-] *n* **1.** (*ethnic group*) gitano, -a *m, f* **2.** *no pl* (*language*) romaní *m*

Rome ['rəʊm, *Am:* 'roʊm] *n* Roma *f* ►**~ was not built in a day** *prov* no se ganó Zamora en una hora *prov;* **when in ~ (do as the Romans)** *prov* allí donde fueres haz lo que vieres *prov*

romp [rɒmp, *Am:* rɑːmp] **I.** *vi* juguetear; **to ~ home** ganar fácilmente **II.** *n* retozo *m*

rompers ['rɒmpəʳz, *Am:* 'rɑːmpɚz] *npl Am* pelele *m*

roof [ruːf] <-s> **I.** *n* (*of house*) tejado *m;* (*of car*) techo *m;* (*of tree*) punta *f;* (*of mouth*) paladar *m* ►**to go through the ~** (*prices*) estar por las nubes; (*person*) subirse por las paredes; **to hit the ~** subirse por las paredes; **to raise the ~** *inf* armar jaleo **II.** *vt* techar

roofer ['ruːfəʳ, *Am:* -fɚ] *n* techador *m*

roof garden *n* azotea *f* con flores y plantas

roofing *n no pl* techumbre *f*

roofrack *n Brit* baca *f,* parrilla *f AmL*

rooftop ['ruːftɒp, *Am:* -tɑːp] *n* techo *m*

rook [rʊk] **I.** *n* **1.** (*bird*) grajo *m* **2.** (*in chess*) torre *f* **II.** *vt inf* estafar

rookery ['rʊkəri] *n* colonia *f* de grajos

rookie ['rʊki] *n Am, Aus, inf* novato, -a *m, f*

room [ruːm] **I.** *n* **1.** (*in house*) habitación *m,* pieza *f AmL,* ambiente *m CSur;* **~ and board** pensión *f* completa **2.** *no pl* (*space*) espacio *m;* **to make ~ for sb/sth** hacer sitio parar alguien/algo; **there's no more ~ for anything else** ya no cabe nada más; **~ for improvement** posibilidad *f* de mejorar; **there is no ~ for doubt** no cabe duda **II.** *vi Am* **to ~ with sb** compartir alojamiento con alguien

roomful ['ruːmfəl] *n* habitación *f* llena
rooming house *n Am* pensión *f*
roommate ['ruːmmeɪt] *n Am* compañero, -a *m, f* de habitación **room service** *n* servicio *m* de habitaciones **room temperature** *n* temperatura *f* ambiente
roomy ['ruːmi] <-ier, -iest> *adj* amplio, -a
roost [ruːst] **I.** *n* percha *f* ►**to rule the** ~ llevar la voz cantante **II.** *vi* (*bird*) posarse para dormir; *fig* pasar la noche
rooster ['ruːstəʳ, *Am:* -stɚ] *n Am, Aus* gallo *m*
root [ruːt] *n* **1.** *a.* BOT, LING, MAT raíz *f;* **to take** ~ *a. fig* arraigar **2.** (*source*) causa *f;* **the** ~ **of all evil** la esencia de todos los males; **the** ~ **of the problem is that ...** el problema radica en que...
◆**root about** *vi,* **root around** *vi* hozar; **to** ~ **for sth** buscar algo
◆**root out** *vt* arrancar
root beer *n Am: bebida gaseosa hecha con extractos de plantas* **root cause** *n* causa *f* primordial
rootless *adj* desarraigado, -a
root sign *n* MAT raíz *f* **root vegetable** *n* tubérculo *m*
rope [rəʊp, *Am:* roʊp] **I.** *n* **1.** (*cord*) cuerda *f;* (*of garlic*) manojo *m;* (*of pearls*) sarta *f* **2.** *pl* (*in boxing*) cuerdas *fpl* **3.** (*for capital punishment*) soga *f* ►**to know the** ~**s** estar al tanto de todo; **to learn the** ~**s** aprender el oficio; **to show sb the** ~**s** enseñar el oficio a alguien; **to have sb on the** ~**s** tener a alguien contra las cuerdas **II.** *vt* atar con una cuerda
◆**rope in** *vt* **to rope sb in** (**to doing sth**) agarrar a alguien (para que haga algo)
◆**rope off** *vt* acordonar
◆**rope up** *vi* encordarse
rope ladder *n* escalera *f* de cuerda
rop(e)y ['rəʊpi, *Am:* 'roʊ-] <-ier, -iest> *adj Brit, Aus, inf* **1.** (*ill*) pachucho, -a **2.** (*argument*) flojo, -a
ro-ro ['rəʊrəʊ] *n Brit* NAUT *abbr of* **roll-on--roll-off** ro-ro *m*
rosary ['rəʊzəri, *Am:* 'roʊ-] <-ies> *n* rosario *m*
rose¹ [rəʊz, *Am:* roʊz] **I.** *n* **1.** (*flower, colour*) rosa *f* **2.** (*on watering can*) roseta *f;* (*on shower*) alcachofa *f* **3.** ARCHIT rosetón *m* ►**to come up smelling of** ~**s** aparecer contento; **coming up** ~**s** a pedir de boca **II.** *adj* rosa
rose² [rəʊz, *Am:* roʊz] *pt of* **rise**
rosebud ['rəʊzbʌd, *Am:* 'roʊz-] *n* capullo *m* **rosebush** *n* rosal *m* **rose garden** *n* rosaleda *f*
rosehip ['rəʊzhɪp, *Am:* 'roʊz-] *n* escaramujo *m*
rosemary ['rəʊzməri, *Am:* 'roʊzmer-] *n no pl* romero *m*
rosette [rəʊ'zet, *Am:* roʊ'-] *n* ARCHIT rosetón *m;* (*badge*) escarapela *f*
rose water *n no pl* agua *f* de rosas **rose window** *n* ARCHIT rosetón *m*
rosin ['rɒzɪn, *Am:* 'rɑːzən] *n no pl* colofonia *f*
roster ['rɒstəʳ, *Am:* 'rɑːstɚ] *n no pl* lista *f*
rostrum ['rɒstrəm, 'rɒstrə, *Am:* 'rɑːstrəm, 'rɑːstrə] <-s *o* rostra> *n* (*for conductor*) estrado *m;* (*for public speaker*) tribuna *f*
rosy ['rəʊzi, *Am:* 'roʊ-] <-ier, -iest> *adj* **1.** (*rose-colour*) rosado, -a; (*cheek*) sonrosado, -a **2.** (*optimistic: viewpoint*) optimista; (*future*) prometedor(a)
rot [rɒt, *Am:* rɑːt] **I.** *n no pl* putrefacción *f* ►**to stop the** ~ cortar por lo sano; **to talk** ~ decir sandeces **II.** <-tt-> *vi* pudrirse **III.** *vt* pudrir
◆**rot away I.** *vt* pudrir **II.** *vi* pudrirse
rota ['rəʊtə, *Am:* 'roʊt̬ə] *n Brit* lista *f* de turnos
rotary ['rəʊtəri, *Am:* 'roʊt̬ɚ-] *adj* rotatorio, -a; (*pump*) giratorio, -a
rota system *n* sistema *m* de turnos
rotate [rəʊ'teɪt, *Am:* 'roʊteɪt] **I.** *vt* **1.** (*turn round*) dar vueltas a **2.** (*alternate*) alternar; (*duties*) turnarse en; AGR cultivar en rotación **II.** *vi* girar; **to** ~ **around sth** girar alrededor de algo
rotation [rəʊ'teɪʃən, *Am:* roʊ'-] *n* **1.** *a.* ASTR, AGR rotación *f* **2.** (*alternation*) alternación *f;* **in** ~ por turno
rotatory ['rəʊtətəri, *Am:* 'roʊtətɔːr-] *adj* rotativo, -a
rote [rəʊt, *Am:* roʊt] *n no pl* **by** ~ de memoria
rotor ['rəʊtəʳ, *Am:* 'roʊt̬ɚ] *n* rotor *m*
rotten ['rɒtn, *Am:* 'rɑːtn] *adj* **1.** (*food*) podrido, -a; **to go** ~ pudrirse **2.** *inf* (*nasty: behaviour*) despreciable **3.** *inf* (*performance, book*) malísimo, -a
rotund [rəʊ'tʌnd, *Am:* roʊ'-] *adj* redondeado, -a
rotunda [rəʊ'tʌndə, *Am:* roʊ'-] *n* ARCHIT rotonda *f*
rouble ['ruːbl] *n* rublo *m*
rouge [ruːʒ] *n no pl* colorete *m,* rouge *m Arg, Chile*
rough [rʌf] **I.** *adj* **1.** (*uneven: road*) desigual; (*surface*) áspero, -a **2.** (*poorly made: work*) chapucero, -a **3.** (*harsh: voice*) bronco, -a **4.** (*imprecise*) aproximado, -a; (*idea*) impreciso, -a; ~ **work** borrador *m* **5.** (*unrefined: person, manner*) tosco, -a **6.** (*stormy: sea*) agitado, -a; (*weather*) tempestuoso, -a **7.** (*difficult*) difícil; (*treatment*) duro, -a; **to be** ~ **on sb** *inf* ser injusto con alguien **8.** *Brit, inf* (*unwell*) mal **II.** *n* **1.** (*sketch*) borrador *m* **2.** *Brit* (*young man*) gamberro *m* **3.** *no pl* SPORTS **the** ~ el rough ►**to take the** ~ **with the smooth** estar a las duras y a las maduras **III.** *vt* **to** ~ **it** *inf* pasar sin comodidades **IV.** *adv* **to play** ~ jugar duro; **to live** ~ vivir a la intemperie
roughage ['rʌfɪdʒ] *n no pl* fibra *f* (de los alimentos)
rough-and-ready [ˌrʌfənd'redi] *adj* (*primitive*) tosco pero eficaz **rough-and-tumble**

R

n riña *f*; *fig* juegos *mpl* bruscos
rough diamond *n Brit, Aus* diamante *m* en bruto
roughen ['rʌfən] *vt* poner áspero **rough-hewn** *adj* **1.** (*wood*) desbastado, -a **2.** (*features*) tosco, -a
roughhouse ['rʌfhaʊs] **I.** *vi* armar jaleo **II.** *n inf* jaleo *m*
roughly *adv* **1.** (*approximately*) aproximadamente; ~ **speaking** por así decirlo **2.** (*aggressively*) bruscamente
roughneck ['rʌfnek] *n* **1.** *Am, inf* (*oil rig worker*) trabajador *m* de un pozo petrolífero **2.** *Am, Aus, inf* (*violent man*) matón *m*
roughness ['rʌfnɪs] *n no pl* **1.** (*of surface*) aspereza *f*; (*of ground*) desigualdad *f* **2.** (*unfairness*) dureza *f*
roughshod ['rʌfʃɒd, *Am:* -ʃɑːd] *adv* **to ride ~ over sb** no tener la menor consideración con alguien
rough-spoken [ˌrʌf'spəʊkən, *Am:* -'spoʊ-] *adj* malhablado, -a
roulette [ruː'let] *n no pl* ruleta *f*
round [raʊnd] **I.** <-er, -est> *adj* **1.** (*circular: object, number*) redondo, -a; (*arch*) de medio punto; (*dozen*) completo, -a; **could you make it a ~ hundred?** ¿podrían ser cien para redondear? **2.** (*not angular*) arqueado, -a **3.** (*sonorous*) sonoro, -a **II.** *adv* alrededor; **to go ~ and ~** dar muchas vueltas; **to come ~** pasar por casa; ~ (**about**) **10 o'clock** a eso de las 10; **the other way ~** al revés; **all ~** (*everywhere*) por todos lados; (*for everybody*) para todos; **taken all ~** en conjunto **III.** *prep* **1.** (*surrounding*) alrededor de; **to go ~ sth** dar la vuelta a algo; **the earth goes ~ the sun** la tierra da vueltas alrededor del sol; **to find a way ~ a problem** *fig* encontra la vuelta a un problema; **to go ~ the corner** doblar la esquina; **just ~ the corner** justo a la vuelta de la esquina **2.** (*visit*) **to go ~ a museum** visitar un museo; **to go ~ the park** dar una vuelta por el parque **3.** (*here and there*) **all ~ the house** por toda la casa; **to wander ~ the world** viajar por el mundo; **to drive ~ France** conducir por Francia; **to sit ~ the room** estar sentado en la habitación **4.** (*approximately*) alrededor de; ~ **11:00** alrededor de las 11:00; ~ **May 10** alrededor del 10 de mayo; **somewhere ~ here** en algún lugar de por aquí **IV.** *n* **1.** (*circle*) círculo *m* **2.** (*series*) serie *f*; (*of applause*) salva *f*; (*of shots*) descarga *f* **3.** *pl* (*route*) recorrido *m*; MIL ronda *f*; MED visita *f*; **to do one's paper ~** *Aus, Brit* hacer el reparto de los periódicos **4.** (*routine*) rutina *f* **5.** (*time period: of elections*) vuelta *f*; (*in card games*) mano *f*; SPORTS eliminatoria *f*; (*in boxing*) asalto *m* **6.** *Brit* (*slice: of bread*) rodaja *f*; **a ~ of toast** una tostada **7.** (*of drinks*) ronda *f*; **this is my ~** esta ronda la pago yo **8.** (*of ammunition*) bala *f* **9.** MUS canon *m* **V.** *vt* redondear; (*corner*) doblar
◆**round down** *vt* MAT redondear por defecto
◆**round off** *vt* **1.** (*finish*) rematar **2.** (*smooth*) pulir **3.** MAT redondear
◆**round on** *vt* volverse en contra de
◆**round out** *vt s.* **round off**
◆**round up** *vt* **1.** MAT redondear por exceso **2.** (*gather*) reunir; (*cattle*) rodear
roundabout ['raʊndəbaʊt] **I.** *n Aus, Brit* **1.** AUTO rotonda *f* **2.** *Brit* (*ride*) tiovivo *m* **II.** *adj* indirecto, -a; **to take a ~ route** ir dando un rodeo
rounded *adj* redondeado, -a
rounders ['raʊndəz, *Am:* -dɚz] *n no pl, Brit* SPORTS *juego similar al béisbol*
roundly *adv* (*assert, deny*) categóricamente, rotundamente; **to defeat sb ~** derrotar de forma aplastante a alguien
round robin *n* **1.** (*letter*) carta *f* colectiva **2.** (*competition*) torneo *m* (*en el que cada participante se enfrenta con cada uno de los demás*)
round-shouldered [ˌraʊnd'ʃəʊldəd, *Am:* -'ʃoʊldɚd] *adj* encorvado, -a; **to be ~** ser cargado de espaldas
roundsman ['raʊndzmən] *n Brit* repartidor *m*
round-table discussion [ˌraʊnd'teɪbl dɪ'skʌʃən] *n* mesa *f* redonda **round-the-clock** **I.** *adj* (*surveillance*) de veinticuatro horas **II.** *adv* las veinticuatro horas; **to work ~** trabajar día y noche **round trip** *n* viaje *m* de ida y vuelta; ~ **ticket** *Am* billete *m* de ida y vuelta
round-up ['raʊndʌp] *n* **1.** AGR rodeo *m* **2.** (*by police*) redada *f* **3.** (*summary*) resumen *m*
rouse [raʊz] *vt* **1.** (*waken*) despertar **2.** (*activate*) provocar; **to ~ sb to do sth** animar a alguien a hacer algo; **to ~ sb to action** mover a alguien a la acción
rousing ['raʊzɪŋ] *adj* (*welcome*) caluroso, -a; (*speech*) vehemente
roustabout ['raʊstəbaʊt] *n Am* (*labourer*) peón *m*
rout [raʊt] **I.** *vt* **1.** (*defeat*) derrotar **2.** (*put to flight*) poner en fuga **II.** *n* **1.** (*defeat*) derrota *f* aplastante **2.** (*flight*) huida *f* en desbandada
◆**rout out** *vt* **1.** (*make come out*) hacer salir **2.** (*find*) encontrar
route [ruːt, *Am:* raʊt] **I.** *n* **1.** (*way*) ruta *f*; (*of parade, bus*) recorrido *m*; NAUT rumbo *m*; (*to success*) camino *m* **2.** *Am* (*delivery path*) recorrido *m*; **to have a paper ~** hacer un reparto de periódicos **3.** *Am* (*road*) carretera *f* **II.** *vt* **to ~ sth via London** enviar algo vía Londres
routine [ruː'tiːn] **I.** *n* **1.** *a.* INFOR rutina *f*; **he went into his usual ~** *inf* me vino con la misma cantinela de siempre **2.** (*of dancer*) número *m* **II.** *adj* **1.** (*regular*) habitual; (*inspection*) de rutina; (*medical case*) común **2.** (*uninspiring*) rutinario, -a
routinely *adv* habitualmente
roux [ruː] *n no pl mezcla de mantequilla y harina para espesar las salsas*
rove [rəʊv, *Am:* roʊv] **I.** *vi* **to ~ over sth**

recorrer algo **II.** *vt* recorrer

rover ['rəʊvəʳ, *Am:* 'roʊvɚ] *n* trotamundos *m inv*

roving ['rəʊvɪŋ, *Am:* 'roʊv-] *adj* (*animal, thieves*) errante; (*ambassador*) itinerante

row[1] [rəʊ, *Am:* roʊ] *n* **1.** (*line: of houses, cars*) hilera *f;* (*of people, of seats*) fila *f;* **to stand in a ~** estar en la fila **2.** (*succession*) sucesión *f;* **three times in a ~** tres veces consecutivas

row[2] [raʊ] **I.** *n* **1.** (*quarrel*) pelea *f;* **to have a ~** pelearse **2.** (*noise*) escándalo *m;* **to make a ~** armar jaleo **II.** *vi inf* pelearse; **to ~ with sb** reñir con alguien

row[3] [rəʊ, *Am:* roʊ] **I.** *vi* remar **II.** *vt* (*boat*) llevar; **to ~ sb across the lake** llevar a alguien en bote al otro lado del lago **III.** *n* paseo *m* en bote; **to go for a ~** ir a dar un paseo en bote

rowan ['rəʊən, *Am:* 'roʊən] *n* serbal *m*

rowanberry ['rəʊən,beri, *Am:* 'roʊən-] *n* serba *f*

rowboat ['rəʊbəʊt, *Am:* 'roʊboʊt] *n Am* bote *m* de remos

rowdy ['raʊdi] <-ier, -iest> *adj* **1.** (*noisy*) alborotador(a) **2.** (*quarrelsome*) pendenciero, -a

rower ['rəʊəʳ, *Am:* 'roʊɚ] *n* remero, -a *m, f*

rowing *n no pl* SPORTS remo *m*

rowing boat *n Brit* bote *m* de remos **rowing club** *n* club *m* de remo

rowlock ['rɒlək, *Am:* 'rɑːlək] *n* NAUT tolete *m*

royal ['rɔɪəl] **I.** *adj* **1.** (*of monarch*) real; **the ~ we** el plural mayestático **2.** *fig* regio, -a; (*welcome*) espléndido, -a **3.** *inf* (*big*) soberano, -a **II.** *n inf* miembro *m* de la familia real

Royal Highness *n* Alteza *f* Real; **His/Her ~** Su Alteza Real

royalist ['rɔɪəlɪst] **I.** *n* monárquico, -a *m, f* **II.** *adj* monárquico, -a

royal jelly *n* jalea *f* real

royalty ['rɔɪəlti, *Am:* -t̬i] <-ies> *n* **1.** *no pl* (*sovereignty*) realeza *f;* **to treat sb like ~** tratar a alguien a cuerpo de rey **2.** *pl* (*payment*) derechos *mpl* de autor

RP [,ɑːʳ'piː, *Am:* ,ɑːr-] *n no pl abbr of* **received pronunciation** *pronunciación estándar del inglés británico*

RPI [,ɑːʳpiː'aɪ] *n no pl, Brit abbr of* **retail price index** IPC *m*

rpm [,aːʳpiː'em, *Am:* ,ɑːr-] *n abbr of* **revolutions per minute** rpm

RR [,ɑːrɑːr] *n Am abbr of* **Railroad** F.C. *m*

RRP [,ɑːʳɑːʳ'piː] *n no pl, Brit abbr of* **recommended retail price** PVP *m*

RSI [,ɑːʳes'aɪ, *Am:* ,ɑːr-] *n abbr of* **repetitive strain injury** lesión *f* de la tensión repetida

RSPCA [,ɑːʳes,piːsiː'eɪ, *Am:* ,ɑːr-] *n Brit abbr of* **Royal Society for the Prevention of Cruelty to Animals** ≈ asociación *f* protectora de animales

RSVP [,ɑːʳesviː'piː, *Am:* ,ɑːr-] *vi abbr of* **répondez s'il vous plait** s.r.c.

Rt Hon. *n Brit* POL *abbr of* **Right Honourable** ≈ Excelentísimo Señor *m,* ≈ Excelentísima Señora *f* (*tratamiento protocolario que se da a los diputados británicos*)

rub [rʌb] **I.** *n* **1.** (*act of rubbing*) frotamiento *m;* **to give sth a ~** frotar algo **2.** *liter* (*difficulty*) dificultad *f;* **there's the ~** ahí está el quid de la cuestión **II.** <-bb-> *vt* frotar; (*one's eyes*) restregarse; (*one's hands*) frotarse; **to ~ sth clean** lustrar algo **III.** <-bb-> *vi* rozar

◆**rub against** *vi* **to ~ sth** rozar con algo; (*cat*) restregarse contra algo

◆**rub along** *vi Brit, inf* **1.** (*manage*) ir tirando **2. to ~ with sb** llevarse bien con alguien

◆**rub down** *vt* **1.** (*smooth*) pulir; (*horse*) almohazar **2.** (*dry*) secar frotando

◆**rub in** *vt* **1.** (*spread on skin*) aplicar frotando **2.** *inf* (*keep reminding*) reiterar; *pej* insistir en

◆**rub off** **I.** *vi* **1.** (*become clean: stain*) irse **2. to ~ on sb** (*affect*) pegarse a alguien **II.** *vt* (*dirt*) quitar frotando

◆**rub out** *vt* **1.** (*remove: writing*) borrar; (*dirt*) quitar **2.** *Am, inf* (*murder*) liquidar

rubber ['rʌbəʳ, *Am:* -ɚ] *n* **1.** (*material*) goma *f,* hule *m Méx* **2.** *Aus, Brit* (*pencil eraser*) goma *f* (de borrar), borrador *m Col* **3.** *Am, inf* (*condom*) goma *f,* forro *m RíoPl* **4.** *pl, Am* (*shoes*) chanclos *mpl* **5.** (*game*) *serie de tres o cinco partidos;* (*in bridge*) rubber *m*

rubber band *n* goma *f* (elástica) **rubber boots** *npl* botas *fpl* de goma **rubber cheque** *n inf* cheque *m* sin fondos **rubber gloves** *npl* guantes *mpl* de goma

rubberneck ['rʌbənek, *Am:* -ɚ-] **I.** *n* (*tourist*) turista *mf;* (*at accident*) mirón, -ona *m, f* **II.** *vi* (*sightsee*) hacer turismo; (*be nosy*) curiosear

rubber plant *n* planta *f* del caucho **rubber-stamp** **I.** *vt* (*decision*) dar el visto bueno a **II.** *n* (*device*) sello *m* de goma **rubber tree** *n* árbol *m* del caucho

rubbery <-ier, -iest> *adj* (*texture*) parecido a la goma; (*food*) correoso, -a

rubbing *n* frotamiento *m*

rubbish ['rʌbɪʃ] **I.** *n no pl, Brit* **1.** *inf* (*waste*) basura *f* **2.** *inf* (*nonsense*) tonterías *fpl* **II.** *vt Aus, Brit, inf* poner verde

rubbish bin *n* cubo *m* de la basura **rubbish chute** *n* vertedero *m* de basuras **rubbish collection** *n* recogida *f* de basuras **rubbish container** *n* contenedor *m* de basura **rubbish dump** *n,* **rubbish tip** *n* vertedero *m,* tiradero *m Méx*

rubbishy *adj Aus, Brit, inf* de pacotilla

rubble ['rʌbl] *n no pl* escombros *mpl*

rub-down ['rʌbdaʊn] *n* fricción *f*

rubella [ruː'belə] *n no pl* MED rubéola *f*

rubicund ['ruːbɪkənd, *Am:* -bəkʌnd] *adj liter* rubicundo, -a

rubric ['ruːbrɪk] *n* **1.** (*heading*) epígrafe *m* **2.** (*instructions*) normas *fpl* **3.** REL rúbrica *f*

ruby ['ruːbi] **I.** <-ies> *n* rubí *m* **II.** *adj* de color rubí

R

RUC [ˌɑːrˈjuːˈsiː, *Am:* ˌɑːr-] *n abbr of* **Royal Ulster Constabulary** *policía de Irlanda del norte*

ruck [rʌk] **I.** *n* **1.** (*crowd*) melé *f* **2.** (*fold*) arruga *f* **II.** *vt* **to ~ up** (*clothes*) arrugar

rucksack [ˈrʌksæk] *n Brit* mochila *f*

ruckus [ˈrʌkəs] *n Am, inf* jaleo *m*, toletole *m CSur*

ructions [ˈrʌkʃənz] *npl Aus, Brit, inf* **there will be ~** se va a armar una gorda

rudder [ˈrʌdəʳ, *Am:* -ɚ] *n* AVIAT, NAUT timón *m*

rudderless *adj a. fig* sin timón

ruddy [ˈrʌdi] <-ier, -iest> *adj* **1.** *liter* (*cheeks*) rubicundo, -a **2.** (*light*) rojizo, -a **3.** *Aus, Brit, inf* (*bloody*) maldito, -a

rude [ruːd] *adj* **1.** (*impolite*) grosero, -a, meco, -a *Méx* **2.** (*vulgar*) vulgar; (*joke*) verde **3.** (*sudden*) brusco, -a; (*surprise*) desagradable **4.** *liter* (*unrefined*) tosco, -a

rudimentary [ˌruːdɪˈmentəri, *Am:* -dəˈ-] *adj* rudimentario, -a

rudiments [ˈruːdɪmənt, *Am:* -də-] *npl* rudimentos *mpl*

rue [ˈruː] *vt liter* lamentar

rueful [ˈruːfəl] *adj* **1.** (*repentant*) arrepentido, -a **2.** (*sad*) triste

ruff [rʌf] *n* (*collar*) gorguera *f*; (*of an animal*) collar *m*

ruffian [ˈrʌfɪən] *n iron* canalla *mf*

ruffle [ˈrʌfl] **I.** *vt* **1.** (*agitate: hair*) alborotar; (*clothes*) fruncir; (*feathers*) erizar **2.** (*upset*) alterar **II.** *n* volante *m*

rug [rʌg] *n* **1.** (*small carpet*) alfombra *f* **2.** *Brit* (*blanket*) manta *f*

rugby [ˈrʌgbi] *n no pl* rugby *m*

rugged [ˈrʌgɪd] *adj* **1.** (*uneven: cliff, mountains*) escarpado, -a; (*landscape, country*) accidentado, -a; (*ground*) desigual **2.** (*tough: face*) de facciones duras; (*construction, vehicle*) resistente

ruin [ˈruːɪn] **I.** *vt* **1.** (*bankrupt*) arruinar **2.** (*destroy: city, building*) destruir **3.** (*spoil: dress, surprise*) estropear; (*child*) malcriar **II.** *n* **1.** (*bankruptcy, downfall*) ruina *f*; **drugs will be his ~** las drogas serán su ruina **2.** *pl* (*remains*) ruinas *fpl*

ruination [ˌruːɪˈneɪʃən, *Am:* -əˈ-] *n no pl* ruina *f*

ruinous [ˈruːɪnəs, *Am:* ˈruːə-] *adj* ruinoso, -a

rule [ruːl] **I.** *n* **1.** (*law*) regla *f*; (*principle*) norma *f*; **~s and regulations** reglamento *m*; **~s of the road** normas *fpl* de tráfico; **to be the ~** ser la norma; **to break a ~** infringir una norma; **to play (it) by the ~s** obedecer las reglas; **it is against the ~s** va contra las normas; **as a ~** por lo general **2.** *no pl* (*control*) gobierno *m*; **the ~ of Henry VIII** el reinado de Enrique VIII **3.** (*measuring device*) regla *f* ►**a ~ of <u>thumb</u>** una regla general; **~s are made to be <u>broken</u>** las normas están para desobedecerlas **II.** *vt* **1.** (*govern: country*) gobernar; (*company*) dirigir **2.** (*control*) dominar **3.** (*draw*) trazar con una regla; (*paper*) pautar **4.** LAW (*decide*) dictaminar, fallar **III.** *vi* **1.** (*control*) gobernar; (*monarch*) reinar **2.** (*predominate*) imperar **3.** LAW **to ~ for/against sb/sth** fallar a favor/en contra de alguien/algo

◆**rule off** *vt* separar con una línea

◆**rule out** *vt* descartar

rule book *n* reglamento *m*

ruler *n* **1.** (*governor*) gobernante *mf*; (*sovereign*) soberano, -a *m, f* **2.** (*measuring device*) regla *f*

ruling [ˈruːlɪŋ] **I.** *adj* **1.** (*governing*) gobernante; (*class*) dirigente; (*monarch*) reinante **2.** (*primary*) dominante **II.** *n* fallo *m*; **the final ~** la sentencia definitiva

rum¹ [rʌm] *n* ron *m*

rum² [rʌm] <rummer, rummest> *adj Brit, dial, inf* raro, -a

Rumania [rʊˈmeɪnɪə, *Am:* roʊˈ-] *n s.* **Romania**

Rumanian [rʊˈmeɪnɪən, *Am:* roʊˈ-] *s.* **Romanian**

rumba [ˈrʌmbə] *n* rumba *f*

rumble [ˈrʌmbl] **I.** *n no pl* **1.** (*sound*) ruido *m* sordo; (*of thunder*) estruendo *m*; (*of stomach*) borborigmo *m* **2.** *Am, Aus, inf* (*fight*) pelea *f* **II.** *vi* hacer un ruido sordo; (*thunder*) retumbar; **my stomach is ~ing** me suenan las tripas **III.** *vt Brit, inf* (*person*) calar; (*plot, scheme*) descubrir

rumbling **I.** *n* (*sound*) ruido *m* sordo; (*of thunder*) estruendo *m*; **there were ~s of war** se hablaba de una posible guerra **II.** *adj* retumbante

rumbustious [rʌmˈbʌstɪəs, *Am:* -tʃəs] *adj Brit, inf* bullicioso, -a

ruminant [ˈruːmɪnənt, *Am:* -mə-] ZOOL **I.** *n* rumiante *mf* **II.** *adj* rumiante

ruminate [ˈruːmɪneɪt, *Am:* -mə-] *vi* rumiar

ruminative [ˈruːmɪnətɪv, *Am:* -məˌneɪt̬ɪv] *adj form* meditabundo, -a

rummage [ˈrʌmɪdʒ] **I.** *vi* hurgar; (*in drawer*) revolver **II.** *n no pl* (*search*) **to have a ~ around for sth** buscar algo

rummage sale *n mercadillo donde se venden objetos usados*

rummy [ˈrʌmi] *n no pl* GAMES rummy *m*

rumor *Am,* **rumour** [ˈruːməʳ, *Am:* -mɚ] *Brit, Aus* **I.** *n* rumor *m* **II.** *vt* **it is ~ed that ...** se rumorea que...

rump [rʌmp] *n* **1.** (*back end: of horse*) grupa *f*; (*of bird*) rabadilla *f* **2.** (*cut of beef*) cuarto *m* trasero **3.** *iron* (*buttocks*) trasero *m*

rumple [ˈrʌmpl] *vt* arrugar; **to ~ sb's hair** despeinar a alguien

rump steak *n* filete *m* de lomo de ternera

rumpus [ˈrʌmpəs] *n no pl, inf* jaleo *m* ►**to <u>raise</u> a ~** armar un escándalo

run [rʌn] **I.** *n* **1.** (*jog*) **to break into a ~** echar a correr; **to go for a ~** salir a correr; **to do sth at a ~** hacer algo deprisa y corriendo **2.** (*trip*) viaje *m*; (*of train*) trayecto *m*; **to go for a ~ in the car** ir a dar una vuelta en el coche **3.** (*series*) racha *f*; (*of books*) tirada *f*

4. (*demand*) demanda *f;* **a sudden ~ on the dollar** una súbita presión sobre el dólar; **a ~ on the banks** un pánico bancario **5.** (*type*) categoría *f* **6.** (*direction, tendency*) dirección *f;* (*of oppinion*) corriente *f;* **the ~ of events** el curso de los acontecimientos **7.** (*enclosure for animals*) corral *m* **8.** (*hole in tights*) carrera *f* **9.** SPORTS (*in baseball, cricket*) carrera *f;* (*ski slope*) pista *f* de esquí **10.** CINE, THEAT permanencia *f* en cartel **11.** MUS carrerilla *f* **12.** MIL **bombing ~** bombardeo *m* ▶**to give sb a ~ for their money** hacer sudar tinta a alguien; **to have a (good) ~ for one's money** no poder quejarse; **in the long ~** a la larga; **in the short ~** a corto plazo; **on the ~** deprisa y corriendo; **to be on the ~** huir de la justicia **II.** *vi* <ran, run> **1.** (*move fast*) correr; **to ~ for the bus** correr para no perder el autobús; **to ~ for help** correr en busca de ayuda; **~ for your lives!** ¡sálvese quien pueda! **2.** (*operate*) funcionar; **to ~ smoothly** ir sobre ruedas *fig* **3.** (*go, travel*) ir; **to ~ off the road** salirse de la carretera; **to ~ ashore/onto the rocks** NAUT embarrancar **4.** (*extend*) extenderse; **the road ~s along the coast** la carretera bordea la costa **5.** (*last*) **to ~ for two hours** durar dos horas; **to ~ and run** ser el cuento de nunca acabar *inf* **6.** (*be*) existir **7.** (*flow: river*) fluir; (*make-up*) correrse; (*nose*) gotear *inf;* **the tap is ~ning hot** por el grifo sale agua caliente **8.** (*enter election*) presentarse, postularse *AmL;* **to ~ for election/President** presentarse a las elecciones/como candidato a presidente **9.** + *adj* (*be*) **to ~ dry** (*river*) secarse; **to ~ short** (*water*) escasear **10.** (*say*) decir **III.** *vt* <ran, run> **1.** (*move fast*) **to ~ a race** participar en una carrera **2.** (*enter in race: candidate, horse*) presentar **3.** (*drive*) llevar; **to ~ sb home** llevar a alguien a casa; **to ~ a truck into a tree** chocar contra un árbol con un camión; **to ~ a ship ashore** hacer encallar un barco **4.** (*pass*) pasar **5.** (*operate*) poner en marcha; (*car*) llevar; (*computer program*) ejecutar; (*engine*) hacer funcionar; **to ~ a washing machine** poner una lavadora **6.** (*manage, govern*) dirigir, pilotear *AmL;* **to ~ a farm** tener una granja; **to ~ a government** estar al frente de un gobierno; **to ~ a household** llevar una casa **7.** (*conduct*) realizar; (*experiment, test*) llevar a cabo **8.** (*provide: course*) organizar **9.** (*let flow*) dejar correr; (*bath*) preparar **10.** (*show: article*) publicar; (*series*) emitir **11.** (*smuggle*) pasar de contrabando **12.** (*not heed: blockade*) romper; (*red light*) saltar(se) (en rojo) **13.** (*incur*) exponerse a; (*risk*) correr **14.** (*perform tasks*) **to ~ errands** hacer recados

◆**run about** *vi* andar de un lado para otro

◆**run across I.** *vi* cruzar corriendo **II.** *vt* toparse con

◆**run after** *vt* correr tras

◆**run against** *vt* POL ir contra

◆**run along** *vi* marcharse

◆**run away** *vi* escaparse; (*water*) derramarse

◆**run away with** *vt* apoderarse de

◆**run back** *vi* volver corriendo

◆**run down I.** *vi* (*clock*) parar; (*battery*) gastarse **II.** *vt* **1.** (*run over*) atropellar **2.** (*disparage*) hablar mal de **3.** (*capture*) capturar

◆**run in I.** *vi* entrar corriendo **II.** *vt* **1.** AUTO rodar **2.** *inf* (*capture*) detener

◆**run into** *vt* dar con; AUTO chocar con

◆**run off I.** *vi* escaparse; (*water*) derramarse **II.** *vt* **1.** (*water*) dejar correr **2.** TYPO tirar **3.** (*make quickly*) hacer deprisa; (*letter*) escribir deprisa

◆**run on** *vi* **1.** (*continue to run*) seguir corriendo **2.** (*conversation*) continuar; (*words*) estar escritos sin dejar espacio

◆**run out of** *vi* quedarse sin

◆**run over I.** *vi* (*person*) irse; (*fluid*) rebosar **II.** *vt* AUTO atropellar a

◆**run through** *vt* **1.** (*station*) pasar sin parar por **2.** (*money*) derrochar

◆**run up I.** *vi* **1.** subir corriendo **2. to ~ against difficulties** tropezar con dificultades **II.** *vt* **1.** (*flag*) izar **2.** (*make quickly*) hacer deprisa **3.** (*debt*) contraer; **to ~ debts** endeudarse

runabout ['rʌnəbaʊt] *n* AUTO coche *m* pequeño

runaround ['rʌnə'raʊnd] *n no pl* **to give sb the ~** traer a alguien al retortero

runaway ['rʌnəweɪ] **I.** *adj* **1.** (*train*) fuera de control; (*person*) fugitivo, -a; (*horse*) desbocado, -a **2.** (*enormous: success*) arrollador(a) **II.** *n* fugitivo, -a *m, f*

run-down [ˌrʌn'daʊn] **I.** *n* **1.** (*report*) resumen *m;* **to give sb a ~ on sth** poner a alguien al tanto de algo **2.** *no pl* (*reduction*) disminución *f;* (*of staff*) reducción *f* **II.** *adj* **1.** (*building, town*) mal conservado, -a **2.** (*person*) debilitado, -a

rune [ruːn] *n* runa *f*

rung[1] [rʌŋ] *n* **1.** (*ladder*) peldaño *m* **2.** (*level*) nivel *m*

rung[2] [rʌŋ] *pp of* **ring**[2]

run-in ['rʌnɪn] *n* **1.** *inf* (*argument*) altercado *m* **2.** (*prelude*) etapa *f* previa

runner ['rʌnəʳ, *Am:* -ɚ] *n* **1.** SPORTS (*person*) corredor(a) *m(f);* (*horse*) caballo *m* de carreras **2.** (*messenger*) mensajero, -a *m, f* **3.** (*smuggler*) contrabandista *mf;* **drug ~** camello *m* **4.** (*rail*) riel *m;* (*on sledge*) patín *m* **5.** (*stem*) tallo *m* rastrero **6.** (*long rug*) alfombrilla *f* estrecha ▶**to do a ~** *inf* largarse

runner bean *n Brit* habichuela *f*

runner-up [ˌrʌnər'ʌp, *Am:* -ɚ'-] *n* subcampeón, -ona *m, f*

running I. *n no pl* **1.** (*action of a runner*) carrera *f* **2.** (*operation*) acción *f;* (*of a machine*) funcionamiento *m;* **the day-to-day ~ of the business** el día a día del negocio ▶**to be in/out of the ~** tener/no tener posibilidades de ganar **II.** *adj* **1.** (*consecutive*) sucesivo, -a; (*day*) consecutivo, -a **2.** (*ongoing*) continuado,

-a **3.** (*operating*) que está funcionando **4.** (*flowing*) que fluye

running back *n Am* SPORTS running back *m* **running costs** *npl* gastos *mpl* de explotación **running order** *n* buen estado *m*

runny ['rʌni] <-ier, -iest> *adj* líquido, -a; (*sauce*) acuoso, -a

run-off ['rʌnɒf] *n* **1.** POL desempate *m* **2.** SPORTS segunda vuelta *f* **3.** (*rainfall*) escorrentía *f*

run-of-the-mill [ˌrʌnəvðə'mɪl] *adj* corriente y moliente

runt [rʌnt] *n* **1.** ZOOL enano *m* **2.** *inf* (*weakling*) redrojo *m*

run-through ['rʌnθruː] *n* THEAT, MUS ensayo *m* (rápido); **to have a ~ of sth** ensayar algo

run-up ['rʌnʌp] *n* **1.** SPORTS carrerilla *f* **2.** (*prelude*) período *m* previo; **the ~ to sth** el preludio de algo

runway ['rʌnweɪ] *n* pista *f*

rupee [ruː'piː, *Am:* 'ruːpiː] *n* rupia *f*

rupture ['rʌptʃəʳ, *Am:* -tʃɚ] **I.** *vi* romperse **II.** *vt* romper; **to ~ oneself** herniarse **III.** *n* **1.** (*act of bursting*) ruptura *f* **2.** (*hernia*) hernia *f*, relajadura *f Méx*

rural ['rʊərəl, *Am:* 'rʊrəl] *adj* rural

ruse [ruːz] *n* treta *f*

rush¹ [rʌʃ] *n* BOT junco *m*

rush² [rʌʃ] **I.** *n* **1.** (*hurry*) prisa *f*; **to be in a ~** tener prisa; **to leave in a ~** salir corriendo **2.** (*charge, attack*) ataque *m*; (*surge*) ola *f*; (*of air*) corriente *f*; (*of customers*) oleada *f*; **there's been a ~ on oil** ha habido una fuerte demanda de aceite; **gold ~** fiebre *f* del oro **3.** (*dizziness*) mareo *m* **II.** *vi* ir deprisa **III.** *vt* **1.** (*do quickly*) hacer precipitadamente **2.** (*hurry*) apresurar **3.** (*attack*) asaltar

♦**rush about** *vi* correr de acá para allá

♦**rush at** *vt* precipitarse hacia

♦**rush into** *vt* **1. to ~ sth** precipitarse en algo **2. to rush sb into doing sth** presionar a alguien para que haga algo

♦**rush out** **I.** *vi* (*leave*) salir precipitadamente **II.** *vt* (*publish*) publicar con urgencia

♦**rush through** *vt* aprobar urgentemente

♦**rush up** *vi* subir corriendo

rush hour *n* hora *f* punta **rush order** *n* pedido *m* urgente

rusk [rʌsk] *n* bizcocho *m*

russet ['rʌsɪt] *liter* **I.** *adj* bermejo, -a **II.** *n no pl* color *m* bermejo

Russia ['rʌʃə] *n* Rusia *f*

Russian ['rʌʃən] **I.** *adj* ruso, -a **II.** *n* **1.** (*person*) ruso, -a *m, f* **2.** (*language*) ruso *m*

rust [rʌst] **I.** *n no pl* **1.** (*decay*) oxidación *f* **2.** (*substance*) herrumbre *f* **3.** (*colour*) color *m* herrumbre **II.** *vi* oxidarse **III.** *vt* oxidar

rust-coloured *adj* de color herrumbre

rustic ['rʌstɪk] *adj* **1.** (*rural*) rústico, -a **2.** (*simple, plain*) sencillo, -a

rustle ['rʌsl] **I.** *vi* (*leaves*) susurrar; (*paper*) crujir **II.** *vt* **1.** (*leaves*) hacer susurrar; (*paper*) hacer crujir **2.** (*steal: cattle*) robar **III.** *n* (*of leaves*) susurro *m*; (*of paper*) crujido *m*

rustler ['rʌsləʳ, *Am:* -ɚ] *n* ladrón, -ona *m, f* de ganado

rustproof ['rʌstpruːf] *adj* inoxidable

rusty ['rʌsti] <-ier, -iest> *adj* **1.** (*metal*) oxidado, -a **2.** (*in skill*) falto, -a de práctica; **my Spanish is a bit ~** tengo bastante olvidado el castellano

rut¹ [rʌt] *n* bache *m* ►**to be stuck in a ~** estar metido en la rutina

rut² [rʌt] *n no pl* ZOOL celo *m*

rutabaga [ˌruːtə'beɪgə, *Am:* -t̬ə'-] *n Am* nabo *m* sueco

ruthless ['ruːθləs] *adj* (*person*) despiadado, -a; (*ambition*) implacable; **to be ~ in doing sth** hacer algo sin piedad; **to be ~ in enforcing the law** hacer cumplir la ley a raja tabla

ruthlessness *n no pl* crueldad *f*

RV [ˌɑːʳ'viː, *Am:* ˌɑːr-] *Am abbr of* **recreational vehicle** caravana *f* pequeña

Rwanda [rʊ'ændə, *Am:* -'ɑːn-] *n* Ruanda *f*

Rwandan **I.** *adj* ruandés, -esa **II.** *n* ruandés, -esa *m, f*

rye [raɪ] *n no pl* centeno *m*

S

S, s [es] *n* S, s; **~ for Sugar** S de Soria

s [es] *abbr of* **second** s

S [es] *n no pl* **1.** *abbr of* **south** S *m* **2.** *Am abbr of* **satisfactory** suficiente *m*

SA **1.** *abbr of* **South Africa** Sudáfrica *f* **2.** *abbr of* **South America** Sudamérica *f* **3.** *abbr of* **South Australia** sur *m* de Australia

Sabbath ['sæbəθ] *n* sabat *m*

sabbatical [sə'bætɪkl, *Am:* -'bæt̬-] UNIV **I.** *n* año *m* de permiso **II.** *adj* sabático, -a

saber ['seɪbəʳ, *Am:* -bɚ] *n Am s.* **sabre**

sable ['seɪbl] *n no pl* (*fur*) marta *f*

sabotage ['sæbətɑːʒ] **I.** *vt* sabotear **II.** *n* sabotaje *m*

saboteur [ˌsæbə'tɜːʳ, *Am:* -'tɜːr] *n* saboteador(a) *m(f)*

sabre ['seɪbəʳ, *Am:* -bɚ] *n Aus, Brit* sable *m*

sabre-rattling ['seibəˌrætlɪŋ, *Am:* -bɚˌ-] *n pej* patriotería *f*

sac [sæk] *n* BIO, ANAT saco *m*

saccharin ['sækərɪn] *n no pl* sacarina *f*

saccharine ['sækəriːn, *Am:* -ɚɪn] *adj pej* empalagoso, -a

sachet ['sæʃeɪ, *Am:* -'-] *n* bolsita *f*

sack¹ [sæk] **I.** *n* **1.** (*large bag*) saco *m*; (*paper or plastic bag*) bolsa *f* **2.** *Am* (*paper, plastic*) bolsa *f* **3.** *no pl, inf* (*bed*) **to hit the ~** irse al catre *inf* **4.** *no pl, inf* (*dismissal*) **to get the ~** ser despedido; **to give sb the ~** despedir a alguien **II.** *vt* despedir

sack² [sæk] **I.** *n no pl* (*plundering*) saqueo *m* **II.** *vt* (*plunder*) saquear

sackcloth ['sækklɒːθ, *Am:* -klɑːθ] *n no pl* arpillera *f* ►**to be wearing ~ and ashes** llevar el hábito de penitencia
sackful ['sækfʊl] *n* saco *m*
sacking[1] ['sækɪŋ] *n* **1.** *no pl* (*sackcloth*) arpillera *f* **2.** *inf* (*dismissal*) despido *m*
sacking[2] ['sækɪŋ] *n* (*plundering*) saqueo *m*
sack race *n* carrera *f* de sacos
sacrament ['sækrəmənt] *n* (*ceremony*) sacramento *m;* **the ~** (*consecrated bread and wine*) la Eucaristía
sacramental [ˌsækrə'mentl, *Am:* -t̬l] *adj* sacramental
sacred ['seɪkrɪd] *adj* sagrado, -a; **to be ~ to sb** estar consagrado a alguien; **is nothing ~ to you?** ¿no tienes respeto por nada?
sacrifice ['sækrɪfaɪs, *Am:* -rə-] **I.** *vt* **1.** *a.* REL sacrificar **2.** (*give up: time, money*) renunciar a; **to ~ one's free time** privarse de tiempo libre **II.** *vi* **to ~ to the gods** hacer sacrificios a los dioses **III.** *n* sacrificio *m;* **at the ~ of sth** en detrimento de algo
sacrilege ['sækrɪlɪdʒ, *Am:* -rə-] *n* sacrilegio *m*
sacrilegious [ˌsækrɪ'lɪdʒəs, *Am:* -rə'-] *adj* sacrílego, -a
sacristan ['sækrɪstən] *n* sacristán *m*
sacristy ['sækrɪsti] *n* REL sacristía *f*
sacrosanct ['sækrəʊsæŋkt, *Am:* -roʊ-] *adj* sacrosanto, -a
sacrum ['seɪkrəm] <-a> *n* sacro *m*
SAD [ˌeseɪ'diː] *n abbr of* **seasonal affective disorder** trastorno *m* afectivo estacional
sad [sæd] <-dd-> *adj* **1.** (*unhappy*) triste; **it is ~ that** es una pena que *+subj;* **to make sb ~** poner triste a alguien; **to become ~** entristecerse **2.** (*pathetic*) patético, -a **3.** (*deplorable, shameful*) lamentable; **~ to say ...** lamentablemente...
sadden ['sædən] *vt* entristecer; **to be deeply ~ed** estar muy afligido
saddle ['sædl] **I.** *n* **1.** (*seat*) silla *f* de montar **2.** GASTR cuarto *m* trasero ►**to be in the ~** llevar las riendas **II.** *vt* **1.** (*horse*) ensillar **2.** *inf* (*burden*) **to ~ sb with sth** encajar algo a alguien
saddlebag ['sædlbæg] *n* alforja *f*
saddler ['sædləʳ, *Am:* -lɚ] *n* talabartero, -a *m, f*
saddle-sore ['sædlsɔːʳ] *adj* dolorido, -a en las posaderas; **he's ~** le duelen las posaderas de montar
sadism ['seɪdɪzəm, *Am:* 'sædɪ-] *n no pl* sadismo *m*
sadist ['seɪdɪst, *Am:* 'sæd-] *n* sádico, -a *m, f*
sadistic [sə'dɪstɪk] *adj* sádico, -a
sadly *adv* **1.** (*unhappily*) tristemente **2.** (*regrettably*) desgraciadamente; **to be ~ mistaken** estar muy equivocado
sadness ['sædnəs] *n no pl* tristeza *f*
sae, SAE [ˌeseɪ'iː] *n abbr of* **stamped addressed envelope** *sobre con las señas de uno y con sello*
safari [sə'fɑːri] *n* safari *m;* **to go on ~** irse de safari
safari park *n* safari-park *m*
safe [seɪf] **I.** *adj* **1.** (*free of danger*) seguro, -a; (*driver*) prudente; **at a ~ distance** a una distancia prudente; **it is not ~ to ...** es peligroso... *+infin;* **just to be ~** por precaución; **~ journey!** ¡buen viaje! **2.** (*secure*) salvo, -a; **to feel ~** sentirse a salvo; **to keep sth in a ~ place** guardar algo en un lugar seguro; **to put sth somewhere ~** poner algo a buen recaudo; **to win by a ~ margin** ganar con un amplio margen **3.** (*certain*) seguro, -a; **a ~ seat** un escaño fijo; **a ~ bet** una apuesta segura **4.** (*trustworthy*) de fiar ►**to be on the ~ side ...** para mayor seguridad...; **it is better to be ~ than sorry** *prov* más vale prevenir que curar *prov;* **~ and sound** sano y salvo **II.** *n* caja *f* de caudales
safe-blower *n,* **safebreaker** ['seɪfˌbreɪkəʳ, *Am:* -kɚ] *n Aus, Brit* ladrón, -ona *m, f* de cajas fuertes **safe deposit box** *n* caja *f* de seguridad
safeguard ['seɪfgɑːd, *Am:* -gɑːrd] **I.** *vt* salvaguardar **II.** *vi* protegerse; **to ~ against sth** protegerse contra algo **III.** *n* salvaguardia *f;* **as a ~ against sth** para evitar algo
safekeeping [ˌseɪf'kiːpɪŋ] *n no pl* custodia *f;* **to be in sb's ~** estar bajo la custodia de alguien
safely *adv* sin riesgos; **I can ~ say ...** puedo decir sin temor a equivocarme que...
safe sex [seɪf'seks] *n* sexo *m* seguro
safety ['seɪfti] *n no pl* (*being safe*) seguridad *f;* **a place of ~** un lugar seguro; **for sb's ~** para la seguridad de alguien ►**there's ~ in numbers** *prov* cuantos más, menos peligro
safety belt *n* cinturón *m* de seguridad **safety catch** *n* (*on gun*) seguro *m* **safety curtain** *n* THEAT telón *m* de seguridad **safety glass** *n* vidrio *m* inastillable **safety margin** *n* margen *m* de seguridad **safety measures** *npl* medidas *fpl* de seguridad **safety net** *n* **1.** red *f* (de seguridad) **2.** *fig* protección *f* **safety pin** *n* imperdible *m* **safety razor** *n* maquinilla *f* de afeitar **safety regulations** *npl* normas *fpl* de seguridad **safety valve** *n* válvula *f* de seguridad
saffron ['sæfrən] *n no pl* azafrán *m*
sag [sæg] **I.** <-gg-> *vi* **1.** (*droop*) combarse, achiguarse *Arg, Chile* **2.** (*sink*) hundirse; (*spirit*) decaer; (*interest*) decrecer **II.** *n no pl* **1.** (*drooping condition*) bajada *f* **2.** (*fall*) caída *f*
saga ['sɑːgə] *n* saga *f*
sagacious [sə'geɪʃəs] *adj form* sagaz
sagacity [sə'gæsəti, *Am:* -t̬i] *n no pl, form* sagacidad *f*
sage[1] [seɪdʒ] *liter* **I.** *adj* (*wise*) sabio, -a **II.** *n* (*wise man*) sabio *m*
sage[2] [seɪdʒ] *n no pl* (*herb*) salvia *f*
Sagittarius [ˌsædʒɪ'teərɪəs, *Am:* -ə'terɪ-] *n* Sagitario *m*

S

Sahara [sə'hɑːrə, *Am:* -'herə] *n* **the ~ (Desert)** el Sáhara

said [sed] **I.** *pp, pt of* **say II.** *adj* dicho, -a

sail [seɪl] **I.** *n* **1.** (*on boat*) vela *f* **2.** (*windmill blade*) aspa *f* ►**to set ~ (for a place)** zarpar (hacia un lugar); **under full ~** a toda vela **II.** *vi* **1.** (*travel*) navegar; **to ~ around the world** dar la vuelta al mundo en barco **2.** (*start voyage*) zarpar **3.** (*move smoothly*) deslizarse **4.** *fig* (*do easily*) **to ~ through sth** hacer algo con facilidad ►**to ~ against the wind** nadar a contracorriente; **to ~ close to the wind** pisar terreno peligroso **III.** *vt* **1.** (*manage: boat, ship*) gobernar **2.** (*navigate*) cruzar; **to ~ the seas** surcar los mares

sailboard ['seɪlbɔːd, *Am:* -bɔːrd] *n* tabla *f* de windsurf

sailboarding *n* windsurf *m*

sailboat ['seɪlbəʊt, *Am:* -boʊt] *n Am* (*sailing boat*) barco *m* de vela

sailing *n* **1.** NAUT navegación *f* **2.** SPORTS vela *f* **3.** (*departure*) salida *f*

sailing boat *n Aus, Brit* barco *m* de vela **sailing ship** *n,* **sailing vessel** *n* velero *m*

sailor ['seɪləʳ, *Am:* -lɚ] *n* **1.** (*seaman*) marinero, -a *m, f* **2.** SPORTS navegante *mf*

sailor suit *n* traje *m* de marinero

saint [seɪnt, sənt] *n* santo, -a *m, f*

sainted *adj* santo, -a; **my ~ aunt!** *fig* ¡caray!

Saint Kitts and Nevis *n* Islas *fpl* de San Cristóbal y Nevis

saintliness *n* santidad *f*

saintly ['seɪntli] *adj* santo, -a; (*life*) ejemplar

> El **Saint Patrick's Day**, 17 de marzo, es el día en que se celebra el patrón de Irlanda. En los EE.UU., sin embargo, no es día de fiesta oficial. A pesar de ello mucha gente lleva el color verde y se organizan fiestas. En muchas ciudades hay desfiles, de los cuales el más grande y famoso es el que tiene lugar en New York City.

Saint's Day *n* santo *m*

sake¹ [seɪk] *n* **1.** (*purpose*) **for the ~ of sth** por algo **2.** (*benefit*) **for the ~ of sb** por alguien ►**for Christ's ~!** *pej* ¡por Dios!; **for goodness ~!** ¡por el amor de Dios!; **for old times' ~** por los viejos tiempos

sake² *n,* **saki** ['sɑːki] *n* sake *m*

salable ['seɪləbl] *adj Am s.* **saleable**

salacious [sə'leɪʃəs] *adj pej* salaz

salad ['sæləd] *n* ensalada *f,* verde *m CSur*

salad bowl *n* ensaladera *f* **salad cream** *n Brit: aliño para la ensalada parecido a la mayonesa* **salad days** *npl* años *mpl* mozos **salad dressing** *n* aliño *m*

salami [sə'lɑːmi] *n no pl* salami *m,* salame *m CSur*

sal-ammoniac [ˌsælə'məʊnɪæk, *Am:* -'moʊ-] *n* sal *f* amoníaca

salaried ['sælərɪd] *adj* (*employee, staff*) asalariado, -a

salary ['sæləri] *n* sueldo *m*

salary cut *n* reducción *f* salarial **salary review** *n* revisión *f* de sueldos **salary scale** *n* banda *f* salarial

sale [seɪl] *n* **1.** (*act of selling*) venta *f* **2.** (*reduced prices*) saldo *m;* **the ~s** las rebajas; **charity ~** venta *f* benéfica; **end-of-season ~** liquidación *f* de final de temporada **3.** (*auction*) subasta *f* **4.** *pl* (*department that sells*) (departamento *m* de) ventas *fpl* ►**to put sth up for ~** poner algo en venta; **for ~** se vende; **on ~** en venta

saleable ['seɪləbl] *adj* vendible

sale price *n* precio *m* de venta

saleroom ['seɪlruːm] *n Am* sala *f* de subastas

sales analysis *n* análisis *m inv* de las ventas **sales assistant** *n Brit* dependiente, -a *m, f* **sales book** *n* libro *m* de ventas **sales campaign** *n* campaña *f* de ventas **sales-clerk** *n Am* dependiente, -a *m, f* **sales conference** *n* conferencia *f* de ventas **sales department** *n* sección *f* de ventas **sales director** *n* director(a) *m(f)* de ventas **sales drive** *n* promoción *f* de ventas **sales executive** *n* ejecutivo, -a *m, f* de ventas **sales figures** *npl* cifras *fpl* de ventas **sales force** *n* personal *m* de ventas **sales forecast** *n* previsión *f* de ventas **salesgirl** *n,* **saleslady** *n* dependienta *f* **sales invoice** *n* FIN factura *f* de venta(s) **sales ledger** *n* FIN libro *m* de ventas **sales literature** *n* ECON propaganda *f* de venta **salesman** *n* (*in shop*) dependiente *m;* (*for company*) representante *m;* **door-to-door ~** vendedor *m* a domicilio **sales manager** *n* jefe *mf* de ventas **salesmanship** *n no pl* arte *m* de vender **sales meeting** *n* reunión *f* de ventas **salesperson** *n* vendedor(a) *m(f)* **sales pitch** *n* rollo *m* publicitario **sales receipt** *n* comprobante *m* de caja **sales rep** *n inf,* **sales representative** *n* agente *mf* de ventas **sales revenue** *n* facturación *f* **salesroom** *n Brit* sala *f* de subastas **sales talk** *n* palabrería *f* de vendedor **sales tax** *n Am* FIN impuesto *m* sobre las ventas **saleswoman** *n* (*in a shop*) dependienta *f;* (*seller*) vendedora *f*

salient ['seɪlɪənt, *Am:* 'seɪljənt] *adj* **1.** (*angle, structure*) saliente **2.** *fig* sobresaliente

saline ['seɪlaɪn, *Am:* -liːn] **I.** *adj* salino, -a; **~ drip** gota a gota *m* salino **II.** *n* solución *f* salina

saliva [sə'laɪvə] *n no pl* saliva *f*

salivate ['sælɪveɪt, *Am:* 'sælə-] *vi* salivar

sallow ['sæləʊ, *Am:* -oʊ] *adj* <-er, -est> (*skin*) cetrino, -a

sally ['sæli] **I.** <-ies> *n* salida *f* **II.** <-ie-> *vi* MIL hacer una salida; **to ~ forth** ponerse en marcha; *fig* salir resueltamente

salmon ['sæmən] *n* salmón *m;* **smoked ~** salmón ahumado

salmonella [ˌsælmə'nelə] *n no pl* **1.** (*bacteria*) salmonella *f* **2.** (*illness*) salmonelosis *f*

salmon farm *n* piscifactoría *f* de salmón

salmon ladder *n* paso *m* salmonero **salmon trout** *n* trucha *f* asalmonada
salon ['sælɒn, *Am:* se'lɑːn] *n* **1.** (*reception room*) recibidor *m* **2.** (*beauty establishment*) **beauty** ~ salón *m* de belleza; **hairdressing** ~ peluquería *f*
saloon [sə'luːn] *n* **1.** *Brit* (*car*) turismo *m* **2.** *Am* (*bar*) bar *m*
salsify ['sælsɪfaɪ, *Am:* -sə-] *n no pl* salsifí *m*
salt [sɔːlt] **I.** *n* sal *f;* **bath ~s** sales de baño; **smelling ~s** sales aromáticas ►**~ of the earth** sal de la tierra; **to take sth with a grain** [*o* **pinch**] **of ~** creerse la mitad de la mitad de algo; **to rub ~ in the wound** hurgar en la herida; **to be worth one's ~** merecer el pan que se come **II.** *vt* **1.** (*add salt to*) poner sal **2.** (*preserve in salt*) salar **3.** (*sprinkle with salt*) sazonar con sal **III.** *adj* salado, -a
SALT [sɔːlt] *n abbr of* **Strategic Arms Limitation Talks** Conversaciones *fpl* para la limitación de armas estratégicas
salt cellar *n* salero *m* **salt lake** *n* lago *m* de agua salada **salt mine** *n* mina *f* de sal
saltpeter *n*, **saltpetre** [ˌsɔːlt'piːtəʳ, *Am:* 'sɔːltˌpiːt̬ɚ] *n no pl* salitre *m*
salt shaker *n Am, Aus* salero *m* **salt water** *n no pl* **1.** (*sea water*) agua *f* de mar **2.** (*water with salt*) agua *f* salada
saltwater ['sɔːltˌwɔːtəʳ, *Am:* 'sɔːltˌwɑːt̬ɚ] *adj* de agua salada
salty ['sɔːlti, *Am:* 'sɔːlt̬i] *adj* (*taste*) salado, -a
salubrious [sə'luːbriəs] *adj form* salubre
salutary ['sæljətəri, *Am:* -ter-] *adj* saludable
salutation [ˌsælјə'teɪʃən] *n* saludo
salute [sə'luːt] **I.** *vt* **1.** *a.* MIL saludar **2.** *fig* (*honour*) **to ~ sb** rendir homenaje a alguien **II.** *vi a.* MIL saludar **III.** *n* MIL **1.** (*hand gesture*) saludo *m;* **to take the ~** presidir el desfile **2.** (*ceremonial firing of guns*) salva *f*
Salvadorian [ˌsælvə'dɔːrɪən] **I.** *adj* salvadoreño, -a **II.** *n* salvadoreño, -a *m, f*
salvage ['sælvɪdʒ] **I.** *vt* salvar **II.** *n no pl* **1.** (*retrieval*) salvamento *m* **2.** (*things saved*) objetos *mpl* salvados
salvage operation *n* operación *f* de salvamento **salvage value** *n* valor *m* de desecho **salvage vessel** *n* buque *m* de salvamento
salvation [sæl'veɪʃən] *n no pl* salvación *f*
Salvation Army *n no pl* Ejército *m* de Salvación
salve [sælv, *Am:* sæv] **I.** *n* **1.** (*ointment*) ungüento *m* **2.** *fig* bálsamo *m* **II.** *vt* curar; *fig* (*conscience*) tranquilizar
salver ['sælvəʳ, *Am:* -vɚ] *n form* bandeja *f*
salvo ['sælvəʊ, *Am:* -voʊ] <-(e)s> *n* salva *f;* **to fire a ~** disparar una salva; **~ of applause** salva de aplausos
sal volatile [ˌsælvə'lætəli, *Am:* -voʊ'læt̬-] *n no pl* sal *f* de amonio
SAM [sæm] *n abbr of* **surface-to-air missile** proyectil *m* tierra-aire
same [seɪm] **I.** *adj* **1.** (*identical*) igual; **the ~** (**as sb/sth**) igual (que alguien/algo); **to go the ~ way** (**as sb**) llevar el mismo camino (que alguien) **2.** (*not another*) mismo, -a; **the ~** el mismo; **at the ~ time** al mismo tiempo **3.** (*unvarying*) idéntico, -a ►**to be one and the ~** ser lo mismo; **by the ~ token** del mismo modo **II.** *pron* **1.** (*nominal*) **the ~** el mismo, la misma, lo mismo; **she's much the ~** sigue igual; **it's always the ~** siempre es lo mismo **2.** (*adverbial*) **it's all the ~ to me** me da igual; **it's not the ~ as before** ya no es lo mismo; **it comes to the ~** da lo mismo; **all the ~** de todas formas; **~ to you** igualmente **III.** *adv* igual
sameness *n no pl* **1.** (*similarity*) igualdad *f* **2.** (*monotony*) monotonía *f*
Samoa [sə'məʊə, *Am:* sə'moʊə] *n* Samoa *f*
Samoan **I.** *adj* samoano, -a **II.** *n* samoano, -a *m, f*
sample ['sɑːmpl, *Am:* 'sæm-] **I.** *n* muestra *f;* **free ~** muestra gratuita; **urine ~** muestra de orina **II.** *vt* **1.** (*try*) probar **2.** (*survey*) tomar muestras
sample book *n* muestrario *m*
sampler ['sɑːmpləʳ, *Am:* 'sæmplɚ] *n* **1.** (*embroidery*) dechado *m* **2.** *Am* (*collection*) muestra *f* **3.** MUS equipo *m* de grabación
sampling ['sɑːmplɪŋ, *Am:* 'sæm-] *n* muestreo *m*
sanatorium [ˌsænə'tɔːrɪəm] <-s *o* -ria> *n* sanatorio *m*
sanctify ['sæŋktɪfaɪ] <-ie-> *vt* **1.** REL santificar **2.** *fig* (*legitimize*) avalar
sanctimonious [ˌsæŋktɪ'məʊnɪəs, *Am:* -'moʊ-] *adj pej* mojigato, -a
sanction ['sæŋkʃən] **I.** *n* **1.** *no pl* (*approval*) autorización *f;* **to give one's ~ to sth** dar su aprobación a algo **2.** LAW, POL sanción *f* **II.** *vt* **1.** (*authorize*) autorizar **2.** (*approve*) aprobar **3.** (*penalize*) sancionar
sanctity ['sæŋktəti, *Am:* -t̬i] *n no pl* **1.** REL (*holiness*) santidad *f* **2.** (*sacredness*) inviolabilidad *f*
sanctuary ['sæŋktʃʊəri, *Am:* -tʃueri] *n* <-ies> **1.** REL (*holy place*) santuario *m* **2.** (*area around altar*) sagrario *m* **3.** *no pl* (*place of refuge*) refugio *m;* **to seek ~ in sth** refugiarse en algo **4.** (*area for animals*) reserva *f;* **wildlife ~** reserva natural
sand [sænd] **I.** *n no pl* arena *f;* **fine/coarse ~** arena fina/gruesa; **grains of ~** granos *mpl* de arena; **the ~s** (*beach*) la playa ►**the ~s of time are running out** el tiempo se agota **II.** *vt* **1.** (*cover with sand*) enarenar **2.** (*make smooth*) lijar; (*floor*) pulir
sandal ['sændl] *n* sandalia *f*, quimba *f AmL*
sandalwood ['sændlwʊd] *n no pl* sándalo *m*
sandbag ['sændbæg] **I.** *n* saco *m* de arena **II.** <-gg-> *vt* proteger con sacos de arena
sandbank ['sændbæŋk] *n*, **sandbar** ['sændbɑːʳ, *Am:* -bɑːr] *n* banco *m* de arena
sandblast ['sændblɑːst, *Am:* -blæst] *vt* pulir con chorro de arena

S

sandbox *n Am s.* **sandpit**
sandboy ['sændbɔɪ] *n* **to be as happy as a ~** estar como unas pascuas
sandcastle *n* castillo *m* de arena **sand dune** *n* duna *f* **sand flea** *n* pulga *f* de mar **sandglass** *n* reloj *m* de arena **sand martin** *n* avión *m* zapador
sandpaper ['sændpeɪpəʳ, *Am:* -pɚ] **I.** *n no pl* papel *m* de lija **II.** *vt* lijar
sandpiper ['sænd,paɪpəʳ, *Am:* -pɚ] *n* andarríos *m inv*
sandpit *n Brit* cajón *m* de arena (*donde juegan los niños*) **sandshoe** *n* **1.** (*beach shoe*) playera *f* **2.** *Aus* (*sport shoe*) zapatilla *f* **sandstone** *n no pl* piedra *f* arenisca **sandstorm** *n* tormenta *f* de arena
sandwich ['sænwɪdʒ, *Am:* 'sændwɪtʃ] **I.** <-es> *n* bocadillo *m;* (*made with sliced bread*) sándwich *m* **II.** *vt* intercalar
sandwich board *n* cartelón *m* **sandwich counter** *n* merendero *m* **sandwich course** <- -es> *n Brit* UNIV *programa que intercala estudio con prácticas profesionales* **sandwich man** <- -men> *n* hombre-anuncio *m*
sandy ['sændi] *adj* <-ier, -iest> arenoso, -a; (*hair*) rubio, -a rojizo, -a
sane [seɪn] *adj* **1.** (*of sound mind*) cuerdo, -a **2.** (*sensible*) sensato, -a
sang [sæŋ] *pt of* **sing**
sanguine ['sæŋgwɪn] *adj form* optimista
sanitarium [,sænɪ'teərɪəm, *Am:* -'terɪ-] <-s *o* -ria> *n Am* clínica *f*
sanitary ['sænɪtəri, *Am:* -teri] *adj* **1.** (*relating to hygiene*) sanitario, -a **2.** (*clean*) higiénico, -a
sanitary towel *n Brit,* **sanitary napkin** *n Am* compresa *f* (higiénica)
sanitation [,sænɪ'teɪʃən] *n no pl* saneamiento *m*
sanity ['sænəti, *Am:* -t̬i] *n no pl* **1.** (*of person*) cordura *f* **2.** (*of decision*) sensatez *f*
sank [sæŋk] *pt of* **sink**
Santa (**Claus**) [,sæntə('klɔːz), *Am:* 'sænt̬ə-(,klɑːz)] *n no pl* Papá *m* Noel
sap[1] [sæp] *n no pl* **1.** BOT savia *f* **2.** (*vitality*) vitalidad *f*
sap[2] [sæp] <-pp-> *vt* **1.** (*weaken*) socavar **2.** MIL zapar
sap[3] [sæp] *n inf* (*fool*) papanatas *mf*
sapling ['sæplɪŋ] *n* pimpollo *m*
sapper ['sæpəʳ, *Am:* -ɚ] *n Brit* zapador(a) *m(f)*
sapphire ['sæfaɪəʳ, *Am:* -aɪɚ] **I.** *n* **1.** (*stone*) zafiro *m* **2.** (*colour*) azul *m* zafiro **II.** *adj* **1.** (*necklace, ring*) de zafiro **2.** (*colour*) azul zafiro
sarcasm ['sɑːkæzəm, *Am:* 'sɑːr-] *n no pl* sarcasmo *m*
sarcastic [sɑː'kæstɪk, *Am:* sɑːr'-] *adj* sarcástico, -a
sarcophagus [sɑːr'kɑːfə-] <-es *o* -gi> *n* sarcófago *m*
sardine [sɑː'diːn, *Am:* sɑːr'-] *n* sardina *f* ▸**to be packed (in) like ~s** estar como sardinas en lata
Sardinia [sɑː'dɪniə, *Am:* sɑːr-] *n* Cerdeña *f*
Sardinian **I.** *n* sardo, -a *m, f* **II.** *adj* sardo, -a
sardonic [sɑː'dɒnɪk, *Am:* sɑːr'dɑːnɪk] *adj* sardónico, -a
sari ['sɑːri] *n* sari *m*
sartorial [sɑː'tɔːriəl, *Am:* sɑːr'-] *adj* (*elegance*) en el vestir
SAS [,eseɪ'es] *n Brit* MIL *abbr of* **Special Air Service** *comando de operaciones especiales del ejército británico*
SASE [,eseɪes'iː] *n Am abbr of* **self-addressed stamped envelope** *sobre con las señas de uno y con sello*
sash[1] [sæʃ] <-es> *n* faja *f*
sash[2] [sæʃ] <-es> *n* ARCHIT marco *m* corredizo de ventana
sash window *n* ARCHIT ventana *f* de guillotina
sat [sæt] *pt, pp of* **sit**
SAT *n Am abbr of* **scholastic aptitude test** *examen que se realiza al final de la enseñanza secundaria*
Satan ['seɪtən] *n no pl* Satanás *m*
satanic [sə'tænɪk] *adj* **1.** (*evil*) demoníaco, -a **2.** (*relating to Satanism*) satánico, -a
Satanism *n no pl* Satanismo *m*
satchel ['sætʃəl] *n* bolsa *f,* busaca *f Col, Ven*
sate [seɪt] *vt form* saciar; **to ~ sb** (**with sth**) hartar a alguien (con algo); **to be ~d** (**with sth**) estar saciado (de algo)
satellite ['sætəlaɪt, *Am:* 'sæt̬-] **I.** *n* **1.** ASTR, TECH satélite *m* **2.** (*subservient follower*) acólito, -a *m, f* **II.** *adj* TECH por satélite
satellite broadcasting *n no pl* transmisión *f* por satélite **satellite dish** *n* antena *f* parabólica **satellite state** *n* estado *m* satélite **satellite television** *n no pl* televisión *f* por satélite **satellite town** *n* ciudad *f* satélite
satiate ['seɪʃɪeɪt] *vt* saciar
satiety [sə'taɪəti, *Am:* -t̬i] *n no pl, form* saciedad *f*
satin ['sætɪn, *Am:* 'sætn] **I.** *n* raso *m* **II.** *adj* (*finish, paper*) satinado, -a
satire ['sætaɪəʳ, *Am:* -aɪɚ] *n* LIT sátira *f*
satirical [sə'tɪrɪkl] *adj* satírico, -a
satirist ['sætərɪst, *Am:* 'sæt̬ɚ-] *n* escritor(a) *m(f)* satírico, -a
satirize ['sætəraɪz, *Am:* 'sæt̬-] *vt* satirizar
satisfaction [,sætɪs'fækʃən, *Am:* ,sæt̬-] *n no pl* **1.** satisfacción *f;* **to derive ~ from sth** conseguir satisfacción de algo; **to do sth to sb's ~** hacer algo para satisfacción de alguien; **to be a ~** (**to sb**) ser una satisfacción (para alguien) **2.** (*compensation*) compensación *f*
satisfactory [,sætɪs'fæktəri, *Am:* ,sæt̬-] *adj* satisfactorio, -a; SCHOOL suficiente
satisfy ['sætɪsfaɪ, *Am:* -əs-] <-ie-> *vt* **1.** (*person, desire*) satisfacer **2.** (*condition*) cumplir **3.** (*convince*) convencer; **to ~ sb that ...** convencer a alguien de que... **4.** (*debt*) saldar ▸**to ~ the examiners** *Brit* ser aprobado
satisfying *adj* satisfactorio, -a

satsuma [sæt'suːmə, *Am:* 'sætsəmɑː] *n Brit, Am* satsuma *f*

saturate ['sætʃəreɪt] *vt* **1.** (*soak*) empapar; **to be ~d in tradition** estar empapado en la tradición **2.** (*fill to capacity*) saturar; **to ~ the market** saturar el mercado

saturation [ˌsætʃə'reɪʃən] *n no pl* saturación *f*

saturation point *n* punto *m* de saturación; **to reach ~** alcanzar el punto de saturación

Saturday ['sætədeɪ, *Am:* 'sæt̬ɚ-] *n* sábado *m; s. a.* **Friday**

Saturn ['sætən, *Am:* 'sæt̬ɚn] *n no pl* Saturno *m*

satyr ['sætəʳ, *Am:* 'seɪt̬ɚ] *n* sátiro *m*

sauce [sɔːs, *Am:* sɑːs] *n* **1.** salsa *f;* **tomato ~** salsa de tomate **2.** (*impertinence*) frescura *f* ▶**what's ~ for the goose is ~ for the gander** *prov* lo que es bueno para uno es bueno para el otro

sauce boat *n* salsera *f*

saucepan ['sɔːspən, *Am:* 'sɑːs-] *n* cacerola *f*

saucer ['sɔːsəʳ, *Am:* 'sɑːsɚ] *n* platillo *m*

saucily ['sɔːsɪli, *Am:* 'sɑː-] *adv* con frescura

sauciness ['sɔːsɪnəs, *Am:* 'sɑː-] *n no pl* **1.** (*impudence*) desfachatez *f* **2.** *Brit* (*smuttiness*) indecencia *f*

saucy ['sɔːsi, *Am:* 'sɑː-] *adj* <-ier, -iest> **1.** (*impudent*) descarado, -a **2.** *Brit* (*smutty*) indecente; (*underwear*) provocativo, -a

Saudi Arabia [ˌsaʊdiə'reɪbiə] *n no pl* Arabia *f* Saudí [*o* Saudita]

Saudi Arabian [ˌsaʊdiə'reɪbiən] **I.** *n* saudí *mf,* saudita *mf* **II.** *adj* saudí, saudita

sauerkraut ['saʊəkraʊt, *Am:* 'saʊɚ-] *n no pl* chucrú *m*

sauna ['sɔːnə, *Am:* 'saʊ-] *n* sauna *f;* **to have a ~** hacer una sesión de sauna

saunter ['sɔːntəʳ, *Am:* 'sɑːnt̬ɚ] **I.** *vi* pasear **II.** *n no pl* paseo *m*

sausage ['sɒsɪdʒ, *Am:* 'sɑːsɪdʒ] *n* salchicha *f;* (*cured*) salchichón *m* ▶**not a ~** *Brit, inf* ¡nada de nada!

sausage dog *n Brit, inf* perro, -a *m, f* salchicha **sausage meat** *n no pl* carne *f* de salchicha **sausage roll** *n Brit, Aus* empanadilla *f* de salchicha

sauté ['səʊteɪ, *Am:* soʊ'teɪ] *vt* saltear

savage ['sævɪdʒ] **I.** *adj* **1.** (*fierce*) salvaje, feroz **2.** *inf* (*bad-tempered*) de mal carácter **II.** *n pej* salvaje *mf* **III.** *vt* **1.** (*attack*) atacar salvajemente **2.** (*criticize*) criticar con saña

savagely *adv* **1.** (*attack*) salvajemente **2.** (*criticize*) con saña

savagery *n no pl* ferocidad *f*

savanna(h) [sə'vænə] *n* sabana *f*

save¹ [seɪv] **I.** *vt* **1.** (*rescue*) salvar; **to ~ sb's life** salvar la vida a alguien; **to ~ one's soul** salvarse; **to ~ face** salvar las apariencias; **to ~ one's own skin** salvar el pellejo **2.** (*keep for future use*) guardar **3.** (*collect*) coleccionar **4.** (*avoid wasting*) ahorrar **5.** (*reserve*) reservar **6.** (*prevent from doing*) impedir **7.** INFOR guardar **8.** SPORTS parar **II.** *vi* **1.** (*keep for the future*) ahorrar; **to ~ for sth** ahorrar para algo **2.** (*conserve*) **to ~ on sth** guardar algo **III.** *n* SPORTS parada *f*

save² [seɪv] *prep* **~ (for)** salvo; **all ~ the youngest** todos salvo los más jóvenes

saver ['seɪvəʳ] *n* ahorrador(a) *m(f)*

saving ['seɪvɪŋ] **I.** *n* **1.** *pl* (*money*) ahorros *mpl* **2.** (*economy*) ahorro *m* **3.** (*rescue*) rescate *m;* **to be the ~ of sb** ser la salvación de alguien **II.** *adj* **his ~ grace** lo único que lo salva **III.** *prep* excepto

savings account ['seɪvɪŋzəˌkaʊnt] *n* cuenta *f* de ahorros **savings bank** *n* caja *f* de ahorros **savings bonus** *n* bono *m* de ahorro **savings book** *n* libreta *f* de ahorro **savings certificate** *n Brit* bono *m* de caja de ahorros **savings deposits** *npl* depósitos *mpl* de ahorro

savior *n Am,* **saviour** ['seɪvjəʳ, *Am:* -vjɚ] *n* salvador(a) *m(f)*

savor ['seɪvɚ] *n Am s.* **savour**

savory ['seɪvəri] *n Am s.* **savoury**

savour ['seɪvəʳ, *Am:* -vɚ] **I.** *n* **1.** (*taste*) sabor *m* **2.** (*pleasure*) gusto *m* **II.** *vt* saborear

savoury ['seɪvəri] **I.** *adj* **1.** (*salty*) salado, -a **2.** (*appetizing*) sabroso, -a; (*smell, taste*) apetitoso, -a **3.** (*socially acceptable*) respetable **II.** *n Brit* plato *m* salado

Savoy [sə'vɔɪ] *n* Saboya *f*

savoy (cabbage) *n* col *f* rizada

savvy ['sævi] *inf* **I.** *adj* <-ier, -iest> espabilado, -a **II.** *n no pl* inteligencia *f*

saw¹ [sɔː, *Am:* sɑː] *pt of* **see**

saw² [sɔː, *Am:* sɑː] **I.** *n* sierra *f;* **power ~** sierra eléctrica **II.** <-ed, sawn *o* -ed> *vt* serrar

saw³ [sɔː, *Am:* sɑː] *n* refrán *m*

sawdust ['sɔːdʌst, *Am:* 'sɑː-] *n no pl* serrín *m*

sawed-off shotgun *n Am s.* **sawn-off shotgun**

sawmill ['sɔːmɪl, *Am:* 'sɑː-] *n* aserradero *m*

sawn [sɔːn, *Am:* sɑːn] *pp of* **saw**

sawn-off shotgun [ˌsɔːnɒf'ʃɒtgʌn, *Am:* ˌsɑːnɑːf'ʃɑːtgʌn] *n* escopeta *f* de cañones recortados

Saxon [sæksən] **I.** *n* sajón, -ona *m, f* **II.** *adj* sajón, -ona

Saxony ['sæksəni] *n no pl* Sajonia *f*

saxophone ['sæksəfəʊn, *Am:* -foʊn] *n* saxofón *m*

saxophonist [sæk'sɒfənɪst, *Am:* 'sæksəfoʊnɪst] *n* saxofonista *mf*

say [seɪ] **I.** <said, said> *vt* **1.** (*speak*) decir; **to ~ sth to sb's face** decir algo a alguien en su cara; **~ no more!** ¡no diga más! **2.** (*state information*) **to ~ (that) …** decir (que)…; **to have something/nothing to ~ (to sb)** tener algo/no tener nada que decir (a alguien); **to ~ goodbye to sb** despedirse de alguien **3.** (*express*) expresar **4.** (*think*) opinar; **people ~ that …** se dice que…; **to ~ to oneself**

S

decirse a sí mismo **5.** (*recite*) recitar; (*prayer*) rezar **6.** (*indicate*) indicar; **to ~ sth about sb/sth** expresar algo sobre alguien/algo; **the said sb/sth ...** *form* dicha persona/cosa... **7.** (*convey meaning*) significar **8.** *inf* (*suggest*) sugerir **9.** (*tell*) explicar; **to ~ where/when** explicar dónde/cuándo; **it's not for me to ~ ...** no me corresponde decir... **10.** (*for instance*) (**let's**) ~ **...** digamos... ►**when all is said and done** a fin de cuentas; **having said that, ...** una vez dicho eso,...; **to ~ when** decir basta; **you don't ~** (**so**)! ¿de veras?; **you said it!** *inf* ¡dímelo a mí! **II.** <said, said> *vi* **I ~!** *Brit* ¡oiga!; **I'll ~!** *inf* ¡ya lo creo!; **I must ~ ...** debo admitir...; **not to ~ ...** incluso...; **that is to ~ ...** es decir... **III.** *n no pl* parecer *m;* **to have one's ~** expresar su propia opinión; **to have a ~ in sth** tener voz y voto en algo **IV.** *interj Am* (*positive reaction*) caramba; **~, that's a great idea!** ¡perfecto, es una gran idea!

SAYE [ˌeseɪwaɪ'iː] *abbr of* **Save As You Earn** ahorre mientras gane

saying ['seɪɪŋ] *n* **1.** (*proverb*) dicho *m;* **as the ~ goes** como dice el refrán **2. it goes without ~** ni que decir tiene

say-so ['seɪsəʊ, *Am:* -soʊ] *n no pl, inf* **1.** (*approval*) visto bueno *m;* **to have sb's ~** tener la aprobación de alguien **2.** (*assertion*) afirmación *f;* **don't just believe it on my ~** no te lo creas porque yo te lo diga

scab [skæb] *n* **1.** (*over wound*) costra *f* **2.** *inf* (*strikebreaker*) esquirol *mf* **3.** *no pl* BOT, ZOOL roña *f*

scabbard ['skæbəd, *Am:* -ɚd] *n* vaina *f*

scabby ['skæbi] *adj* <-ier, -iest> **1.** (*having scabs*) con costras **2.** ZOOL roñoso, -a **3.** *pej, inf* (*disgusting*) horrible

scabies ['skeɪbiːz] *n no pl* MED sarna *f,* zarate *m Hond*

scabrous ['skeɪbrəs, *Am:* 'skæbrəs] *adj* escabroso, -a

scaffold ['skæfə(ʊ)ld, *Am:* 'skæfld] *n* **1.** (*for execution*) patíbulo *m* **2.** (*for building*) andamio *m*

scaffolding ['skæfəldɪŋ] *n no pl* andamiaje *m*

scalawag ['skæləwæg] *n Am s.* **scallywag**

scald [skɔːld, *Am:* skɑːld] **I.** *vt* **1.** (*burn*) escaldar **2.** (*clean*) esterilizar con agua caliente **3.** (*heat: milk*) calentar **II.** *n* MED escaldadura *f*

scalding ['skɔːldɪŋ, *Am:* 'skɑːld-] *adj* que escalda; **~ hot** hirviendo

scale[1] [skeɪl] **I.** *n* **1.** ZOOL escama *f* **2.** *no pl* TECH, MED sarro *m* **II.** *vt* **1.** (*remove scales*) escamar **2.** TECH, MED quitar el sarro de

scale[2] [skeɪl] *n* (*weighing device*) platillo *m;* **~s** balanza *f;* (*bigger*) báscula *f* ►**to tip the ~s** inclinar la balanza

scale[3] [skeɪl] **I.** *n* (*range, magnitude, proportion*) *a.* MUS escala *f;* **a sliding ~** ECON una banda fluctuante; **on a large/small ~** a gran/pequeña escala; **to draw sth to ~** dibujar algo a escala **II.** *vt* **1.** (*climb*) escalar; **to ~ the heights** (**of sth**) trepar a las alturas (de algo) **2.** TECH, ARCHIT reducir a escala

◆**scale down** *vt* (*demand, expectations*) reducir

scale drawing *n* TECH, ARCHIT dibujo *m* a escala **scale model** *n* modelo *m* a escala

scallop ['skɒləp, *Am:* 'skɑːləp] *n* vieira *f;* **~** (**shell**) venera *f*

scallywag ['skælɪwæg] *n inf* sinvergüenza *mf*

scalp [skælp] **I.** *n* **1.** (*head skin*) cuero *m* cabelludo **2.** (*war trophy*) cabellera *f; fig* persona *f* importante; **to be out after sb's ~** querer acabar con alguien **II.** *vt* **1.** (*in war*) **to ~ sb** arrancar la cabellera a alguien; *iron* cortar el pelo a alguien **2.** *Am, Aus, inf* (*re-sell*) revender

scalpel ['skælpəl] *n* MED escalpelo *m*

scaly ['skeɪli] *adj* <-ier, -iest> **1.** ZOOL escamoso, -a **2.** MED (*skin*) reseco, -a

scam [skæm] *n inf* timo *m*

scamp [skæmp] *n inf* granuja *mf,* mandinga *m Arg*

scamper ['skæmpəʳ, *Am:* -pɚ] *vi* corretear

scampi [skæmpi] *npl* gambas *fpl* rebozadas

scan [skæn] **I.** <-nn-> *vt* **1.** (*scrutinize*) escudriñar **2.** (*look through quickly*) dar un vistazo; (*newspaper*) hojear **3.** MED explorar; (*brain*) hacer un escáner de **4.** LIT medir **5.** INFOR escanear **II.** <-nn-> *vi* medir(se) **III.** *n* INFOR escaneado *m;* MED escáner *m*

scandal ['skændl] *n* **1.** (*public outrage*) escándalo *m;* **to uncover** [*o* **expose**] **a ~** sacar a la luz un escándalo; **to cover up a ~** tapar un escándalo **2.** *no pl* (*gossip*) chismorreo *m;* **to spread ~** difundir habladurías **3.** (*sth bad*) **what a ~!** ¡qué vergüenza!

scandalize ['skændəlaɪz] *vt* escandalizar

scandalmonger ['skændlmʌŋgəʳ, *Am:* -ˌmɑːŋgɚ] *n pej* chismoso, -a *m, f*

scandalous ['skændələs] *adj* **1.** (*spreading scandal*) escandaloso, -a **2.** (*disgraceful*) vergonzoso, -a; **it is ~ that ...** resulta vergonzoso que... *+subj*

Scandinavia [ˌskændɪ'neɪviə] *n* Escandinavia *f*

Scandinavian **I.** *adj* escandinavo, -a **II.** *n* escandinavo, -a *m, f*

scanner ['skænəʳ, *Am:* -ɚ] *n* INFOR escáner *m*

scanning *n* INFOR, MED escaneo *m*

scant [skænt] *adj* escaso, -a; **~ attention** poca atención

scantily *adv* insuficientemente; **~ dressed** [*o* **clad**] ligero de ropa

scanty ['skænti, *Am:* -ţi] *adj* **1.** (*very small*) corto, -a; (*clothing*) ligero, -a **2.** (*insufficient*) insuficiente

scapegoat ['skeɪpgəʊt, *Am:* -goʊt] *n* cabeza *f* de turco; **to be a ~ for sb/sth** ser un chivo expiatorio para alguien/algo

scapula ['skæpjʊlə] <-s *o* -lae> *pl n* omóplato *m*

scar [skɑːʳ, *Am:* skɑːr] **I.** *n* **1.** MED (*on skin*) cicatriz *f;* **to leave a ~** dejar cicatriz **2.** (*mark of damage*) señal *f* **3.** PSYCH trauma *m* **4.** GEO paraje *m* rocoso **II.** <-rr-> *vt* marcar con cicatriz; **to be ~red** (**by sth**) tener una cicatriz (hecha por algo); **to be ~red for life** quedar marcado de por vida **III.** <-rr-> *vi* **to ~** (**over**) cicatrizar(se)

scarab ['skærəb, *Am:* 'sker-] *n* escarabajo *m*

scarce [skeəs, *Am:* skers] *adj* escaso, -a; **to make oneself ~** *inf* largarse

scarcely ['skeəsli, *Am:* 'skers-] *adv* **1.** (*barely*) apenas **2.** (*certainly not*) ni mucho menos

scarcity ['skeəsəti, *Am:* 'skersəṱi] *n no pl* escasez *f*

scare [skeəʳ, *Am:* sker] **I.** *vt* asustar, julepear *Arg, Par, Urug,* acholar *Chile, Perú;* **to ~ sb into/out of doing sth** espantar a alguien para que haga/no haga algo; **to be ~d stiff** estar muerto de miedo; **to ~ sb shitless** *vulg* acojonar a alguien **II.** *vi* asustarse; (**not**) **to ~ easily** (no) asustarse fácilmente **III.** *n* **1.** (*fright*) susto *m,* julepe *m AmL;* **to have a ~** llevarse un sobresalto; **to give sb a ~** dar un susto a alguien **2.** (*panic*) pánico *m;* **~ story** historia *f* alarmista

◆**scare away** *vt,* **scare off** *vt* ahuyentar

scarecrow ['skeəkrəʊ, *Am:* 'skerkroʊ] *n* espantapájaros *m inv*

scaremonger ['skeə,mʌŋgəʳ, *Am:* 'sker-,mɑːŋgɚ] *n pej* alarmista *mf*

scarf [skɑːf, *pl* skɑːvz, *Am:* skɑːrf, *pl* skɑːrvz] <-ves *o* -s> *n* (*round neck*) bufanda *f;* (*round head*) pañuelo *m*

scarlet ['skɑːlət, *Am:* 'skɑːr-] **I.** *n no pl* escarlata *f* **II.** *adj* de color escarlata; **to turn ~** ponerse colorado

scarlet fever *n no pl* MED escarlatina *f*

scarp [skɑːp, *Am:* skɑːrp] *n* declive *m*

scarper ['skɑːpəʳ, *Am:* 'skɑːrpɚ] *vi Brit, Aus, inf* largarse

scary ['skeəri, *Am:* 'skeri] *adj* <-ier, -iest> que da miedo; **~ film** película *f* de miedo

scat [skæt] *interj inf* fuera

scathing ['skeɪðɪŋ] *adj* mordaz; **to be ~ about sb/sth** criticar duramente a alguien/algo

scatological [,skætə'lɒdʒɪkəl, *Am:* ,skæṱə-'lɑːdʒɪ-] *adj form* escatológico, -a

scatter ['skætəʳ, *Am:* 'skæṱɚ] **I.** *vt* esparcir; **to ~ sth with sth** salpicar algo con algo; **to ~ sth to the four winds** esparcir algo a los cuatro vientos **II.** *vi* dispersarse; **to ~ in all directions** desparramarse en todas direcciones

scatterbrain ['skætəbreɪn, *Am:* 'skæṱɚ-] *n pej* cabeza *mf* de chorlito

scatterbrained *adj* atolondrado, -a

scatter cushion *n Brit, Aus* almohadón *m*

scattered *adj* **1.** disperso, -a **2.** (*widely separated*) separado, -a **3.** (*sporadic*) espóradico, -a

scatty ['skæti, *Am:* 'skæṱi] *adj Brit, inf* atolondarado, -a

scavenge ['skævɪndʒ] *vi* **1.** (*search*) buscar cosas en la basura, pepenar *AmC, Méx* **2.** ZOOL buscar comida

scavenger ['skævɪndʒəʳ, *Am:* -ɚ] *n* **1.** ZOOL animal *m* carroñero **2.** (*person*) *persona que hurga en la basura en busca de comida, etc.*

scenario [sɪ'nɑːrɪəʊ, *Am:* sə'nerɪoʊ] *n* **1.** (*situation*) marco *m* hipotético **2.** THEAT, LIT guión *m*

scene [siːn] *n* **1.** THEAT, CINE (*unit of drama*) escena *f;* (*setting*) escenario *m;* **nude ~** escena *f* de desnudo; **behind the ~s** *a. fig* entre bastidores **2.** (*locality*) lugar *m;* **the ~ of the crime** la escena del crimen **3.** (*view*) vista *f* **4.** (*milieu*) mundo *m;* **the art/drugs ~** el mundo del arte/de las drogas; **it is/isn't my ~** *inf* eso es/no es lo mío; **to appear on the ~** presentarse; **to depart from the political ~** desaparecer del escenario político; **to set the ~** crear un ambiente **5.** (*embarrassing incident*) escándalo *m;* **to make a ~** montar un número

scene change *n* cambio *m* de decorado

scene painter *n* escenógrafo, -a *m, f*

scenery ['siːnəri] *n no pl* **1.** (*landscape*) paisaje *m* **2.** THEAT, CINE decorado *m;* **to blend into the ~** conseguir pasar inadvertido

scene shifter *n* tramoyista *mf*

scenic ['siːnɪk] *adj* **1.** THEAT escénico, -a **2.** (*of beautiful scenery*) pintoresco, -a; **~ road** ruta *f* turística

scent [sent] **I.** *n* **1.** (*aroma*) olor *m* **2.** (*in hunting*) rastro *m;* **to be on the ~ of sth/sb** estar sobre la pista de algo/alguien; **to throw sb off the ~** despistar a alguien **3.** *no pl, Brit* (*perfume*) perfume *m* **II.** *vt* **1.** (*smell*) oler **2.** (*sense, detect*) intuir; **to ~ that ...** sospechar que... **3.** (*apply perfume*) perfumar

scent bottle *n* frasco *m* de perfume

scentless *adj* inodoro, -a

scepter ['septɚ] *n Am s.* **sceptre**

sceptic ['skeptɪk] *n* escéptico, -a *m, f*

sceptical *adj* escéptico, -a

scepticism ['skeptɪsɪzəm] *n no pl* escepticismo *m*

sceptre ['septəʳ, *Am:* -tɚ] *n* cetro *m*

schedule ['ʃedjuːl, *Am:* 'skedʒuːl] **I.** *n* **1.** (*timetable*) horario *m;* **bus ~** horario de autobuses; **flight ~** horario de vuelos; **to stick to a ~** seguir un horario; **everything went according to ~** todo fue según lo previsto **2.** (*plan of work*) programa *m* **3.** FIN inventario *m* **II.** *vt* **1.** (*plan*) programar **2.** (*list*) hacer una lista

scheduled *adj* programado, -a

scheduled flight *n* vuelo *m* regular

schematic [skɪ'mætɪk, *Am:* skiː'mæṱ-] *adj* esquemático, -a

scheme [skiːm] **I.** *n* **1.** (*structure*) esquema *m* **2.** *Brit* (*programme*) programa *m;* ECON plan *m* **3.** (*plot*) treta *f* **II.** *vi pej* intrigar; **to ~ to do sth** intrigar para hacer algo

schemer ['skiːməʳ, *Am:* -ɚ] *n* intrigante *mf*

scheming ['skiːmɪŋ] *adj* intrigante

schism ['sɪzəm] *n* cisma *m*

schismatic [sɪz'mætɪk, *Am:* -'mæt̬-] REL I. *adj* cismático, -a II. *n* cismático, -a *m, f*
schist [ʃɪst] *n no pl* GEO esquisto *m*
schizophrenia [ˌskɪtsəʊ'fri:nɪə, *Am:* -sə'-] *n no pl* esquizofrenia *f*
schizophrenic [ˌskɪtsəʊ'frenɪk, *Am:* -sə'-] I. *adj* esquizofrénico, -a II. *n* esquizofrénico, -a *m, f*
scholar ['skɒləʳ, *Am:* 'skɑ:lɚ] *n* 1. (*learned person*) erudito, -a *m, f* 2. (*student*) estudiante *mf* 3. (*scholarship holder*) becario, -a *m, f*
scholarly *adj* erudito, -a
scholarship ['skɒləʃɪp, *Am:* 'skɑ:lɚ-] *n* 1. *no pl* (*learning*) erudición *f* 2. (*grant*) beca *f* **scholarship holder** *n* becario, -a *m, f*
scholastic [skə'læstɪk] *adj* académico, -a
school[1] [sku:l] I. *n* 1. (*institution*) escuela *f;* **primary** ~ colegio *m;* **secondary** ~ instituto *m* de enseñanza secundaria, liceo *m Chile, Méx;* **public** ~ *Brit* escuela privada; *Am* escuela pública; **dancing** ~ escuela de baile; **driving** ~ autoescuela; **to be in** ~ estar en edad escolar; **to go to** ~ ir al colegio; **to start** ~ empezar la escuela; **to leave** ~ terminar el colegio 2. (*buildings*) colegio *m* 3. *no pl* (*classes*) clases *fpl* 4. (*university division*) facultad *f* 5. *Am* (*university*) universidad *f* II. *vt* enseñar III. *adj* escolar
school[2] [sku:l] *n* ZOOL banco *m*
school age ['sku:leɪdʒ] *n* edad *f* escolar **school attendance** *n* asistencia *f* a la escuela **schoolbag** *n* cartera *f* del colegio **school board** *n Am* ADMIN consejo *m* escolar **schoolbook** *n* libro *m* escolar **schoolboy** I. *n* colegial *m,* escolero *m Perú* II. *adj* de colegial **schoolchild** *n* colegial(a) *m(f),* escolero, -a *m, f Perú* **schooldays** *npl* años *mpl* de colegio **school dinner** *n* comida *f* de colegio **school fees** *npl* cuota *f* escolar **schoolgirl** I. *n* colegiala *f,* escolera *f Perú* II. *adj* de colegiala **schoolhouse** <-es> *n Am* escuela *f*
schooling *n no pl* enseñanza *f*
school leaver *n Brit, Aus: alumno que ha finalizado sus estudios* **school-leaving certificate** *n Brit* graduado *m* escolar **school magazine** *n* revista *f* del colegio **schoolmaster** *n* profesor *m* **schoolmate** *n* compañero, -a *m, f* de clase **schoolmistress** *n* profesora *f* **school nurse** *n* enfermera *f* de escuela

> Con la expresión **School of the air** se designa una red de difusión por radio para el **outback** de Australia. Esta red funciona en zonas aisladas del país y tiene como finalidad educar a la población en edad escolar. Una docena de estas escuelas cubren un área de 2,5 millones de km y alcanzan a cientos de niños. Los alumnos reciben material didáctico y envían sus deberes hechos de vuelta, hablan por radio con sus profesores y compañeros de clase y la mayoría de las veces son sus padres o un profesor particular quienes los vigilan en casa.

school report *n* boletín *m* de notas **schoolroom** *n* clase *f*

> El **school system** (sistema escolar) americano comienza con la **elementary school** (que abarca desde el curso primero hasta el sexto u octavo). En algunos lugares después del **sixth grade**, el sexto curso, los alumnos pasan a otra escuela, la **junior high school** (donde se les imparte la docencia correspondiente a los cursos séptimo, octavo y noveno). Después los alumnos acceden a la **high school** donde permanecen por espacio de tres cursos. En aquellos lugares donde no hay **junior high school** los alumnos pasan directamente de la **elementary school** (donde han estado ocho años) a la **high school**, que, en ese caso, comienza con el **ninth grade**, es decir, el noveno curso. Los alumnos finalizan su itinerario escolar cuando han terminado el **twelfth grade**, el curso decimosegundo.

schoolteacher *n* profesor(a) *m(f)* **schoolwork** *n* trabajo *m* escolar **schoolyard** *n Am* patio *m* del colegio
schooner ['sku:nəʳ, *Am:* -nɚ] *n* 1. NAUT goleta *f* 2. *Am, Aus* (*tall glass*) jarra *f* 3. *Brit* (*sherry glass*) copa *f* de jerez
sciatic [saɪ'ætɪk, *Am:* -'æt̬-] *adj* ciático, -a
sciatica [saɪ'ætɪkə, *Am:* -'æt̬-] *n no pl* MED ciática *f*
science ['saɪənts] I. *n no pl* ciencia *f;* **pure/applied** ~ ciencias *fpl* puras/aplicadas; **the wonders of modern** ~ las maravillas de la ciencia moderna II. *adj* de ciencias
science fiction I. *n no pl* ciencia ficción *f* II. *adj* de ciencia ficción **science laboratory** *n* laboratorio *m* de ciencias **science park** *n* parque *m* tecnológico
scientific [ˌsaɪən'tɪfɪk] *adj* científico, -a
scientist ['saɪəntɪst, *Am:* -t̬ɪst] *n* científico, -a *m, f*
sci-fi ['saɪˌfaɪ] *n abbr of* **science fiction** ciencia *f* ficción
Scilly Isles ['sɪli aɪls] *n* **the** ~ las Islas Sorlingas
scintillating ['sɪntɪleɪtɪŋ, *Am:* -t̬leɪt̬ɪŋ] *adj* (*performance*) brillante; (*wit*) chispeante
scion ['saɪən] *n form* 1. (*descendant*) descendiente *mf* 2. BOT injerto *m,* esqueje *m*
scissors ['sɪzəz, *Am:* -ɚz] *npl* tijeras *fpl;* **a pair of** ~ unas tijeras; ~ **kick** SPORTS chilena *f;* **a** ~ **and paste job** un refrito
sclerosis [sklə'rəʊsɪs, *Am:* sklɪ'roʊ-] *n no pl* MED esclerosis *f*
scoff[1] [skɒf, *Am:* skɑ:f] *vi* (*mock*) burlarse; **to** ~ **at sth/sb** reírse de algo/alguien

scoff² [skɒf, *Am:* skɑːf] *vt Brit, inf* (*eat*) engullir
scold [skəʊld, *Am:* skoʊld] *vt* regañar
scolding ['skəʊldɪŋ, *Am:* 'skoʊld-] *n* reprimenda *f*, raspada *f Méx, PRico*, trepe *m CRi*
scone [skɒn, *Am:* skoʊn] *n* bollo *m*
scoop [skuːp] **I.** *n* **1.** (*utensil*) cucharón *m;* **ice-cream** ~ cuchara *f* de helado; **measuring** ~ cuchara de medición **2.** (*amount*) cucharada *f* **3.** PUBL primicia *f* informativa **II.** *vt* **1.** PUBL adelantarse con una exclusiva **2.** (*win*) ganar; **to** ~ **the pool** *Brit, Aus, inf* acaparar todos los premios
◆**scoop up** *vt* recoger
scoot [skuːt] *vi inf* largarse; **to** ~ **over** *Am* escabullirse
scooter ['skuːtəʳ, *Am:* -t̬ɚ] *n* **1.** (*toy*) patinete *m* **2.** (*vehicle*) (**motor**) ~ escúter *m*, Vespa® *f*
scope [skəʊp, *Am:* skoʊp] *n no pl* **1.** (*range*) alcance *m* **2.** (*possibilities*) posibilidades *fpl;* **limited/considerable** ~ campo *m* de acción limitado/considerable
scorch [skɔːtʃ, *Am:* skɔːrtʃ] **I.** *vt* chamuscar **II.** *vi* chamuscarse **III.** *n* <-es> quemadura *f*
scorcher *n inf* día *m* de mucho calor
scorching *adj* abrasador(a); **it's** ~ **hot** hace un calor abrasador
score [skɔːʳ, *Am:* skɔːr] **I.** *n* **1.** SPORTS (*number of points*) puntuación *f;* **to keep** (**the**) ~ llevar la cuenta **2.** SPORTS (*goal, point*) gol *m* **3.** SCHOOL nota *f* **4.** (*twenty*) veintena *f;* ~**s of people** mucha gente **5.** (*reason*) motivo *m* **6.** (*dispute*) rencilla *f;* **to settle a** ~ ajustar cuentas **7.** MUS partitura *f* **8.** (*line*) arañazo *m* ►**to know the** ~ estar al tanto; **what's the** ~**?** *inf* ¿cómo van? **II.** *vt* **1.** (*goal, point*) marcar; (*triumph, victory*) obtener **2.** (*cut*) cortar **3.** *inf* (*buy: drugs*) conseguir **4.** MUS (*arrange*) instrumentar **III.** *vi* **1.** SPORTS (*make a point*) marcar un tanto **2.** *inf* (*succeed*) triunfar **3.** *inf* (*make sexual conquest*) echar un polvo **4.** *inf* (*buy drugs*) comprar droga
◆**score out** *vt* tachar
scoreboard ['skɔːbɔːd, *Am:* 'skɔːrbɔːrd] *n* marcador *m* **scorecard** *n* tarjeta *f* de registro de la puntuación
scorer *n* (*player: in soccer*) goleador(a) *m(f);* (*in basketball*) *jugador que marca uno o más tantos*
scoring *n* puntuación *f*
scorn [skɔːn, *Am:* skɔːrn] **I.** *n* desprecio *m;* **to pour** ~ **on sb/sth** ridiculizar a alguien/algo; **to be the** ~ **of sb** ser despreciado por alguien **II.** *vt* **1.** (*feel contempt*) despreciar, ajotar *Cuba* **2.** (*refuse*) rechazar (por orgullo); **to** ~ **to do sth** no dignarse a hacer algo
scornful ['skɔːnfəl, *Am:* 'skɔːrn-] *adj* desdeñoso, -a
Scorpio ['skɔːpiəʊ, *Am:* 'skɔːrpioʊ] *n* Escorpión *m*
scorpion ['skɔːpiən, *Am:* 'skɔːr-] *n* escorpión *m*
Scot [skɒt, *Am:* skɑːt] *n* escocés, -esa *m, f*
scotch [skɒtʃ, *Am:* skɑːtʃ] *vt* **1.** (*rumour*) acallar **2.** (*plan*) frustrar
Scotch [skɒtʃ, *Am:* skɑːtʃ] **I.** *n* whisky *m* (escocés); **a** ~ **on the rocks** un whisky con hielo, un whisky en las rokas *Méx* **II.** *adj* escocés, -esa
Scotch broth *n no pl* sopa *f* de verduras
scot-free [ˌskɒt'friː, *Am:* ˌskɑːt'-] *adv* **1.** (*without punishment*) impunemente; **to get away** ~ librarse del castigo **2.** (*unharmed*) sin un rasguño
Scotland ['skɒtlənd, *Am:* 'skɑːt-] *n* Escocia *f*
Scots [skɒts, *Am:* skɑːts] *adj s.* **Scottish**
Scotsman ['skɒtsmən, *Am:* 'skɑːts-] <-men> *n* escocés *m*
Scotswoman ['skɒtsˌwʊmən, *Am:* 'skɑːts-] <-women> *n* escocesa *f*
Scottish ['skɒtɪʃ, *Am:* 'skɑːt̬ɪʃ] *adj* escocés, -esa
scoundrel ['skaʊndrəl] *n pej* sinvergüenza *mf*
scour [skaʊəʳ, *Am:* skaʊɚ] **I.** *vt* **1.** (*scrub*) fregar **2.** (*search*) recorrer; **the police are** ~**ing the club** la policía esta haciendo una batida en el club **II.** *n no pl* fregado, -a *m, f;* **to give sth a** ~ fregar algo
scourer *n* estropajo *m*
scourge [skɜːdʒ, *Am:* skɜːrdʒ] **I.** *n a. fig* azote *m* **II.** *vt* **1.** (*inflict suffering*) azotar **2.** (*whip*) flagelar
scouring pad *n* estropajo *m*
scout [skaʊt] **I.** *n* explorador(a) *m(f)*, scout *mf Méx;* **talent** ~ cazatalentos *m* **II.** *vi* **to** ~ **ahead** reconocer el terreno; **to** ~ **around for sth** buscar algo
scoutmaster *n* jefe *m* de exploradores, akela *m Méx*
scowl [skaʊl] **I.** *n* ceño *m* fruncido **II.** *vi* fruncir el ceño
scrabble ['skræbl] *vi* **1.** (*grope*) hurgar **2.** (*claw for grip*) escarbar
scrag [skræg] <-gg-> *vt* **1.** (*kill*) ahorcar **2.** *inf* (*mistreat*) maltratar
scraggy ['skrægi] <-ier, -iest> *adj* flaco, -a
scram [skræm] <-mm-> *vi inf* largarse, rajarse *AmC*
scramble ['skræmbl] **I.** *vi* **1.** (*move hastily*) moverse apresuradamente; **to** ~ **for sth** esforzarse por algo; **to** ~ **through the hedge** arrastrarse por la zanja **2.** (*try to get first*) luchar **3.** (*take off quickly*) despegar **II.** *vt* **1.** (*mix together*) revolver; ~**d eggs** huevos revueltos **2.** (*encrypt*) codificar **3.** (*take off quickly*) hacer despegar **III.** *n* **1.** *no pl* (*rush*) carrera *f;* (*chase*) persecución *f* **2.** *no pl* (*struggle to get*) arrebatiña *f*, rebatinga *f Méx* **3.** (*motorcycle race*) carrera *f* de motocross
scrambler ['skræmbləʳ, *Am:* -blɚ] *n* **1.** (*device*) scrambler *m* **2.** (*motorcycle*) motocicleta *f* de motocross
scrap¹ [skræp] **I.** *n* **1.** (*small piece*) trozo *m;* (*of paper, cloth*) pedazo *m* **2.** (*small amount*)

S

pizca *f;* (*of information*) retazo *m;* **not a ~ of truth** ni un ápice de verdad **3.** *pl* (*leftover food*) sobras *fpl* **4.** *no pl* (*old metal*) chatarra *f* **II.** <-pp-> *vt* **1.** (*get rid of*) desechar; (*abandon*) descartar; (*abolish*) abolir **2.** (*use for scrap metal*) desguazar, deshuesar *Méx*

scrap² [skræp] **I.** *n inf* (*fight*) agarrada *f,* agarrón *m Méx* **II.** <-pp-> *vi* pelearse

scrapbook ['skræpbʊk] *n* álbum *m* de recortes **scrap dealer** *n* chatarrero, -a *m, f*

scrape [skreɪp] **I.** *vt* **1.** (*remove layer*) raspar, rasquetear *Arg;* (*remove: dirt*) limpiar **2.** (*graze*) rozar; (*scratch*) rascar **3.** (*rub against*) rozar **II.** *vi* **1.** (*rub against*) rozar **2.** (*make unpleasant noise*) chirriar **3.** (*economize*) ahorrar **III.** *n* **1.** *no pl* (*act of scraping*) raspado, -a *m, f* **2.** (*graze on skin*) raspadura *f* **3.** (*sound*) chirrido *m* **4.** *inf* (*situation*) lío *m;* **to get into a ~** meterse en un lío

◆**scrape along** *vi s.* **scrape by**

◆**scrape away** *vt* raspar

◆**scrape by** *vi* apañárselas

◆**scrape through** **I.** *vt* pasar por los pelos **II.** *vi* aprobar por los pelos

scraper ['skreɪpəʳ, *Am:* -ɚ] *n* (*tool*) raspador *m;* (*for cleaning shoes*) limpiabarros *m inv*

scrapheap ['skræphiːp] *n* montón *m* de basura; **to end up on the ~** quedarse sin futuro laboral

scrapie ['skreɪpi] *n* escrapie *m*

scrapings *npl* **1.** (*leftovers*) sobras *fpl* **2.** TECH limaduras *fpl*

scrap iron *n no pl* chatarra *f* **scrap merchant** *n Brit* chatarrero, -a *m, f*

scrappy¹ ['skræpi] <-ier, -iest> *adj* **1.** (*knowledge*) superficial **2.** (*performance, game*) irregular

scrappy² ['skræpi] <-ier, -iest> *adj Am* (*ready to fight*) pendenciero, -a, peleonero, -a *Méx*

scratch [skrætʃ] **I.** *n* **1.** (*cut on skin*) rasguño *m,* rayón *m AmL* **2.** (*mark*) raya *f* **3.** *no pl* (*act of scratching*) arañamiento *m* **4.** (*start*) principio *m;* **from ~** desde cero **II.** *vt* **1.** (*cut slightly*) arañar **2.** (*mark*) rayar **3.** (*relieve itch*) rascar **4.** (*erase*) tachar **5.** (*exclude*) retirar **6.** *Am, inf* (*cancel*) cancelar **7.** (*write*) garabatear **III.** *vi* **1.** (*use claws: cat*) arañar **2.** (*relieve itch*) rascarse **3.** *Brit* (*write*) raspear **IV.** *adj* improvisado, -a

◆**scratch about** *vi,* **scratch around** *vi Brit* escarbar

◆**scratch out** *vt* **1.** (*with claws*) arañar; **to scratch sb's eyes out** *fig* sacar los ojos a alguien **2.** (*line, word*) tachar

scratch card ['skrætʃkaːd, *Am:* -kaːrd] *n* tarjeta *f* rasca, raspadita *f Arg* **scratch paper** *n no pl, Am* papel *m* de borrador

scratchy ['skrætʃi] <-ier, -iest> *adj* **1.** (*record*) rayado, -a **2.** (*irritating*) áspero, -a **3.** *Brit* (*pen*) que raspa; (*handwriting*) garabatoso, -a

scrawl [skrɔːl, *Am:* skrɑːl] **I.** *vt* garabatear **II.** *n no pl* garabato *m*

scrawny ['skrɔːni, *Am:* 'skrɑː-] <-ier, -iest> *adj* escuálido, -a, silgado, -a *Ecua*

scream [skriːm] **I.** *n* **1.** (*cry*) grito *m;* (*shrill cry*) chillido *m;* (*shout*) alarido *m* **2.** (*of animal*) chillido *m* ►**to be a ~** ser la monda **II.** *vi* (*shout*) gritar; (*cry shrilly*) chillar; **to ~ with laughter** reír a carcajadas **III.** *vt* (*shout*) gritar; (*abuse, obscenities*) lanzar; **to ~ oneself hoarse** gritar hasta enronquecer

scree [skriː] *n no pl* pedregal *m* (en una ladrera)

screech [skriːtʃ] **I.** *n* chillido *m* **II.** *vi* chillar; **to ~ with pain** lanzar gritos de dolor

screech-owl *n* lechuza *f*

screeds [skriːdz] *npl* páginas *fpl* y páginas

screen [skriːn] **I.** *n* **1.** *a.* TV, CINE, INFOR pantalla *f;* **split/touch ~** pantalla dividida/táctil **2.** (*framed panel*) biombo *m;* (*for protection*) cortina *f;* (*in front of fire*) pantalla *f;* **glass ~** vitral *m* **3.** *no pl* (*thing that conceals*) cortina *f* **II.** *vt* **1.** (*conceal*) ocultar **2.** (*shield*) proteger **3.** (*examine*) examinar; (*revise*) revisar **4.** TV emitir; CINE proyectar **5.** (*put through a sieve*) cribar

◆**screen off** *vt* separar con un biombo

screening *n* **1.** (*showing: in cinema*) proyección *f;* (*on television*) emisión *f* **2.** *no pl* (*testing*) prueba *f* **3.** MED (*examination*) chequeo *m*

screenplay ['skriːnpleɪ] *n* guión *m*

screensaver *n* INFOR salvapantallas *m inv*

screenshot *n* INFOR captura *f* de pantalla

screen test *n* prueba *f* **screenwriter** *n* guionista *mf*

screw [skruː] **I.** *n* **1.** (*small metal fastener*) tornillo *m;* **to tighten (up)/loosen a ~** apretar/aflojar un tornillo **2.** (*turn*) vuelta *f* **3.** (*propeller*) hélice *f* **4.** *Brit, inf* (*prison guard*) carcelero, -a *m, f* **5.** *no pl* (*spin*) efecto *m,* chanfle *m Méx* **6.** (*twisted piece*) rosca *f* ►**he's got a ~ loose** *inf* le falta un tornillo; **to put the ~s on sb** *inf* apretar las tuercas a alguien **II.** *vt* **1.** (*with a screw*) atornillar **2.** (*by twisting*) enroscar **3.** *inf* (*cheat*) timar **4.** *vulg* (*have sex with*) follar con, coger *AmL* **5.** (*make move in a curve*) enroscar; **to ~ the ball** dar efecto a la pelota **III.** *vi* **1.** (*turn like a screw*) enroscarse **2.** (*move in a curve*) dar efecto **3.** *vulg* (*have sex*) echar un polvo, echarse un palo *Méx*

◆**screw down** *vt* enroscar

◆**screw up** **I.** *vt* **1.** (*fasten with screws*) atornillar **2.** (*tighten*) apretar **3.** (*crush*) estrujar **4.** (*twist*) retorcer **5.** *inf* (*make a mess of*) joder **6.** *inf* (*make anxious*) poner neurótico **II.** *vi* cagarla

screwball ['skruːbɔːl] *n Am, inf* (*odd person*) chiflado, -a *m, f;* **~ comedy** comedia *f* disparatada

screwdriver ['skruːˌdraɪvəʳ, *Am:* -vɚ] *n* destornillador *m,* desarmador *m AmL*

screwed *adj inf* jodido, -a *vulg*

screw top *n* tapón *m* de rosca

screwy ['skruːi] <-ier, iest> *adj inf* chalado, -a

scribble ['skrɪbl] **I.** *vt* garabatear **II.** *vi* hacer garabatos **III.** *n* garabatos *mpl*
scribbling block *n,* **scribbling pad** *n* bloc *m* de notas
scrimmage ['skrɪmɪdʒ] *n* **1.** (*fight*) escaramuza *f* **2.** (*in US football*) línea *f* de golpeo
scrimp [skrɪmp] *vi* escatimar; **to ~ and save** apretarse el cinturón *fig*
script [skrɪpt] **I.** *n* **1.** CINE guión *m;* TV, THEAT argumento *m* **2.** (*writing*) escritura *f;* **Arabic ~** escritura árabe **3.** *Brit, Aus* (*exam*) examen *m* **II.** *vt* escribir el guión de
script girl *n* secretaria *f* de rodaje
scriptural ['skrɪptʃərəl, *Am:* -tʃɚ-] *adj* bíblico, -a
Scripture ['skrɪptʃəʳ, *Am:* -tʃɚ] *n* Sagrada Escritura *f*
scriptwriter ['skrɪptraɪtəʳ, *Am:* -t̬ɚ] *n* guionista *mf*
scroll [skrəʊl, *Am:* skroʊl] **I.** *n* **1.** (*roll*) rollo *m* (de papel) **2.** ARCHIT voluta *f* **II.** *vi* INFOR desplazarse; **to ~ (to the) right/left** desplazarse a la derecha/izquierda; **to ~ down/up** desplazarse hacia abajo/arriba
scrooge [skru:dʒ] *n* tacaño, -a *m, f*
scrotum ['skrəʊtəm, *Am:* 'skroʊt̬əm] <-tums *o* -ta> *n* escroto *m*
scrounge [skraʊndʒ] **I.** *vt inf* conseguir gorroneando, manguear *Arg;* **to ~ sth off** [*o* **from**] **sb** sacar algo de gorra a alguien **II.** *vi inf* gorronear **III.** *n inf* **to be on the ~** vivir de gorra
scrounger ['skraʊndʒəʳ, *Am:* -ɚ] *n pej, inf* gorrón, -ona *m, f,* pedinche *mf Méx*
scrub¹ [skrʌb] <-bb-> **I.** *vt* **1.** (*clean*) fregar **2.** (*cancel*) cancelar **II.** *vi* fregar; **to ~ at sth** restregar algo **III.** *n no pl* fregado *m;* **to give sth a (good) ~** fregar algo vigorosamente
scrub² [skrʌb] *n no pl* matorral *m*
scrubber ['skrʌbəʳ, *Am:* -ɚ] *n* **1.** (*person who scrubs*) fregón, -ona *m, f* **2.** *Brit, pej, inf* putona *f*
scrubbing brush ['skrʌbɪŋbrʌʃ] *n* cepillo *m* de fregar
scruff [skrʌf] *n* **1.** (*back of neck*) cogote *m;* **to grab sb by the ~ of the neck** coger a alguien por el cogote **2.** *Brit, inf* (*dirty person*) persona *f* desaliñada, facha *f Méx*
scruffy ['skrʌfi] <-ier, -iest> *adj* (*clothes*) deshilachado, -a; (*person*) desaliñado, -a, fachoso, -a *Méx;* (*area, place*) dejado, -a
scrum ['skrʌm] *n* SPORTS melé *f*
scrum half *n* medio melé *m*
scrummage ['skrʌmɪdʒ] *n s.* **scrum**
scrumptious ['skrʌmpʃəs] *adj Brit, inf* de rechupete
scrumpy ['skrʌmpi] *n no pl, Brit* sidra *f*
scrunch [skrʌntʃ] **I.** *vi* crujir **II.** *vt* ronzar **III.** *n no pl* crujido *m*
scruple ['skru:pl] **I.** *n no pl* escrúpulo *m;* **to have no ~s (about doing sth)** no tener escrúpulos (en hacer algo) **II.** *vi* tener escrúpulos
scrupulous ['skru:pjʊləs] *adj* escrupuloso, -a
scrutineer [ˌskru:tɪ'nɪəʳ, *Am:* -tn'ɪr] *n Brit, Aus* escrutador(a) *m(f)*
scrutinise *vt Brit, Aus,* **scrutinize** ['skru:tɪnaɪz, *Am:* -tənaɪz] *vt* (*examine*) escudriñar; (*votes*) escrutar; (*text*) revisar
scrutiny ['skru:tɪni, *Am:* -təni] *n no pl* escrutinio *m*
scuba diving ['sku:bəˌdaɪvɪŋ] *n* submarinismo *m*
scud [skʌd] <-dd-> *vi* correr
scuff [skʌf] **I.** *vt* **1.** (*roughen surface*) raspar **2.** (*drag along ground*) arrastrar **II.** *n* rozadura *f*
scuffle ['skʌfl] **I.** *n* refriega *f* **II.** *vi* pelearse
scull [skʌl] **I.** *vi* remar **II.** *n* espadilla *f*
scullery ['skʌləri] *n* antecocina *f*
sculpt [skʌlpt] *vt* esculpir
sculptor ['skʌlptəʳ, *Am:* -tɚ] *n* escultor *m*
sculptress ['skʌlptrəs] *n* escultora *f*
sculptural ['skʌlptʃərəl] *adj* escultórico, -a
sculpture ['skʌlptʃəʳ, *Am:* -tʃɚ] **I.** *n* escultura *f* **II.** *vt* esculpir
scum [skʌm] *n no pl* **1.** (*foam*) espumaje *m* **2.** (*evil people*) escoria *f*
scumbag ['skʌmbæg] *n pej* cerdo, -a *m, f*
scupper ['skʌpəʳ, *Am:* -ɚ] *vt* **1.** (*ship*) hundir **2.** *inf* (*plan*) echar por tierra
scurf [skɜ:f, *Am:* skɜ:rf] *n no pl* caspa *f*
scurrilous ['skʌrɪləs, *Am:* 'skɜ:rɪ-] *adj pej* (*damaging*) difamatorio, -a; (*insulting*) calumnioso, -a
scurry ['skʌri, *Am:* 'skɜ:ri] <-ie-> *vi* correr
scurvy ['skɜ:vi, *Am:* 'skɜ:r-] **I.** *n no pl* escorbuto *m,* berbén *m Méx* **II.** *adj* vil; **a ~ trick** un truco ruin
scuttle¹ ['skʌtl, *Am:* 'skʌt̬-] *vi* (*run*) correr
scuttle away *vi,,* **scuttle off** *vi* (*run*) escabullirse
scuttle² ['skʌtl, *Am:* 'skʌt̬-] *vt* **1.** (*sink*) hundir **2.** (*plan*) echar por tierra
scuttle³ ['skʌtl, *Am:* 'skʌt̬-] *n* (*for coal*) cajón *m* para el carbón
scythe [saɪð] **I.** *n* guadaña *f* **II.** *vt* (*with a scythe*) guadañar; (*with swinging blow*) segar
SDI [ˌesdi:'aɪ] *n Am abbr of* **Strategic Defense Initiative** IDE *f*
SE [ˌes'i:] *n abbr of* **southeast** SE *m*
sea [si:] *n* **1.** mar *m o f;* **at the bottom of the ~** en el fondo del mar; **by ~** por mar; **by the ~** junto al mar; **out at ~** en alta mar; **to put (out) to ~** hacerse a la mar; **the open ~, the high ~s** el mar abierto **2.** (*wide expanse*) **a ~ of people** un mar de gente ►**worse things happen at ~!** (*things could be worse*) ¡más se perdió en la guerra!; **to sail the seven ~s** surcar los siete mares; **to be (all) at ~** estar totalmente perdido
sea air *n no pl* aire *m* de mar **sea anemone** *n* anémona *f* de mar **sea bed** *n no pl* lecho *m* marino **sea bird** *n* ave *f* marina
seaboard ['si:bɔ:d, *Am:* -bɔ:rd] *n* litoral *m*
seaborne ['si:bɔ:n, *Am:* -bɔ:rn] *adj* trans-

S

portado, -a por mar
sea breeze *n* brisa *f* marina **sea change** *n* cambio *m* profundo **sea cow** *n* manatí *m* **sea dog** *n* lobo *m* de mar
seafarer ['siː,feərəʳ, *Am:* -,ferɚ] *n liter* marinero, -a *m, f*
seafaring *adj liter* marinero, -a
seafish <-(es)> *n inv* pez *m* marino
seafood ['siːfuːd] *n no pl* marisco *m*
seafront ['siːfrʌnt] *n* **1.** (*promenade*) paseo *m* marítimo, malecón *m Méx* **2.** (*beach*) playa *f*
seagoing ['siː,gəʊɪŋ, *Am:* -,goʊ-] *adj* de altura
seagull ['siːgʌl] *n* gaviota *f*
seahorse *n* caballito *m* de mar
seal[1] [siːl] *n* ZOOL foca *f*
seal[2] [siːl] **I.** *n* **1.** (*wax mark, stamp*) sello *m;* **given under my hand and ~** sellado y firmado de mi puño y letra **2.** (*to prevent opening: on letter*) sello *m;* (*on goods*) precinto *m;* (*on door*) precintado *m* ► **~ of approval** aprobación *f* **II.** *vt* **1.** (*put a seal on*) sellar **2.** (*prevent opening*) precintar **3.** (*block access*) acordonar; (*frontier, port*) cerrar
◆**seal up** *vt* precintar
sealant ['siːlənt] *n* (*substance*) silicona *f* selladora
sea legs *npl* equilibrio *m;* **to get one's ~** acostumbrarse a mantener el equilibrio (en barco) **sea level** *n no pl* nivel *m* del mar
sealing wax *n no pl* lacre *m*
sea lion *n* ZOOL león *m* marino
sealskin ['siːlskɪn] *n no pl* piel *f* de foca
seam [siːm] **I.** *n* **1.** (*stitching*) costura *f;* **to come** [*o* **fall**] **apart at the ~s** descoserse; *fig* rebosar de gente **2.** (*junction*) juntura *f* **3.** (*wrinkle*) arruga *f* **4.** MIN veta *f,* filón *m* **II.** *vt* (*sew*) coser
seaman ['siːmən] <-men> *n* (*sailor*) marinero *m*
sea mile *n* milla *f* marina
seamless *adj* **1.** (*without seam*) sin costuras **2.** (*transition*) perfecto, -a
seamstress ['sempstrɪs, *Am:* 'siːmstrɪs] *n* costurera *f*
seamy ['siːmi] <-ier, -iest> *adj* sórdido, -a
seance ['seɪɑ̃ːnts, *Am:* 'seɪɑːnts] *n* sesión *f* de espiritismo
seaplane ['siːpleɪn] *n* AVIAT hidroavión *m* **seaport** *n* puerto *m* de mar **sea power** *n* **1.** *no pl* (*naval strength*) fuerza *f* naval **2.** (*state*) potencia *f* naval
sear [sɪəʳ, *Am:* sɪr] *vt* **1.** (*scorch*) quemar; (*into memory*) grabar a fuego **2.** (*wither*) secar, marchitar **3.** GASTR brasar (a fuego vivo) **4.** MED cauterizar **5.** (*make numb*) volver insensible
search [sɜːtʃ, *Am:* sɜːrtʃ] **I.** *n a.* INFOR búsqueda *f;* (*of building*) registro *m,* cateo *m Méx,* esculco *m Col, Méx;* (*of person*) cacheo *m;* **to go in ~ of sth** ir en busca de algo **II.** *vi a.* INFOR buscar; **to ~ for** [*o* **after**] **sth** buscar algo; **to ~ high and low (for sth)** buscar (algo) por todas partes; **~ and replace** INFOR buscar y reemplazar **III.** *vt* **1.** *a.* INFOR buscar en; (*building, baggage*) registrar, catear *Méx,* esculcar *Col, Méx;* (*person*) cachear **2.** (*examine*) examinar; **to ~ one's memory** hacer memoria; **to ~ one's conscience** hacer examen de conciencia ► **~ me!** *inf* ¡yo qué sé!
◆**search out** *vt* (*people*) encontrar; (*information*) averiguar
search engine *n* INFOR motor *m* de búsqueda
searcher *n* miembro *m* de un equipo de salvamento
search function *n* INFOR función *f* de búsqueda
searching *adj* **1.** (*penetrating*) inquisitivo, -a; (*look*) penetrante **2.** (*exhaustive*) minucioso, -a
searchlight ['sɜːtʃlaɪt, *Am:* 'sɜːrtʃ-] *n* reflector *m*
search operation *n* operación *f* de búsqueda **search party** <-ies> *n* equipo *m* de salvamento **search warrant** *n* orden *f* de registro [*o* de allanamiento *AmL*]
searing *adj* **1.** (*heat*) abrasador(a) **2.** (*pain*) punzante **3.** (*criticism*) virulento, -a
sea salt *n* sal *f* marina
seascape ['siːskeɪp] *n* **1.** (*picture*) marina *f* **2.** (*view*) vista *f* marina
sea shanty *n* saloma *f*
seashell ['siːʃel] *n* concha *f* (marina)
seashore ['siːʃɔːʳ, *Am:* -ʃɔːr] *n no pl* **1.** (*beach*) playa *f* **2.** (*near sea*) costa *f*
seasick ['siːsɪk] *adj* mareado, -a; **to get ~** marearse
seasickness ['siːsɪknɪs] *n* mareo *m*
seaside ['siːsaɪd] **I.** *n no pl, Brit* **1.** (*beach*) playa *f* **2.** (*coast*) costa *f* **II.** *adj Brit* costero, -a; **a ~ resort** un lugar de veraneo costero, un balneario *AmL*
season ['siːzən] **I.** *n* **1.** (*period of year*) estación *f* **2.** (*epoch*) época *f;* **the Christmas ~** las Navidades; **the ~ of good will** la época navideña; **Season's Greetings** Felices Fiestas; **the (fishing/hunting) ~** la temporada (de pesca/de caza); **the close ~** la veda; **the strawberry/apple ~** la temporada de las fresas/manzanas; **to be in ~** estar en sazón; **to be out of ~** estar fuera de temporada; **high/low ~** temporada alta/baja; **the concert ~** *Brit, Aus* la temporada de conciertos **3.** SPORTS temporada *f* **4.** ZOOL **to be in ~** estar en celo; **the mating ~** la época del celo **5.** *inf* (*ticket*) abono *m* (de temporada) **II.** *vt* **1.** GASTR sazonar; (*add salt and pepper*) salpimentar **2.** (*dry out*) secar **III.** *vi* **1.** (*dry out*) secarse **2.** *fig* **to become ~ed to sth** acostumbrarse a algo
seasonable ['siːzənəbl] *adj* **1.** (*expected*) propio, -a de la estación **2.** *liter* (*appropriate*) oportuno, -a
seasonal ['siːzənəl] *adj* **1.** (*connected with time of year*) estacional **2.** (*temporary*) temporal; **~ worker** temporero, -a *m, f* **3.** (*grown*

in a season: fruits, vegetables) del tiempo

seasoned *adj* **1.** (*experienced*) experimentado, -a **2.** (*dried: wood*) secado, -a **3.** (*spiced*) sazonado, -a

seasoning ['siːzənɪŋ] *n* **1.** *no pl* (*salt and pepper*) condimento *m* **2.** (*herb or spice*) sazón *f*, yuyos *mpl Ecua, Perú*

season ticket *n Brit, Aus* abono *m* (de temporada) **season ticket holder** *n* RAIL persona *f* en posesión de un abono; SPORTS, THEAT abonado, -a *m, f*

seat [siːt] **I.** *n* **1.** (*furniture*) asiento *m;* (*on a bicycle*) sillín *m;* (*in theatre*) butaca *f;* (*in a car, bus*) plaza *f;* **back ~** asiento trasero; **is this ~ free/taken?** ¿está libre/ocupado este asiento?; **to keep a ~ for sb** guardar el asiento a alguien; **to take one's ~** sentarse **2.** (*ticket*) entrada *f;* **to book a ~** reservar una entrada **3.** *no pl* (*part: of chair*) asiento *m;* (*of trousers*) fondillos *mpl* **4.** (*buttocks*) trasero *m inf* **5.** POL escaño *m*, banca *f Arg, Par, Urug;* **to win/lose a ~** ganar/perder un escaño **6.** (*centre*) sede *f;* **~ of learning** *form* centro *m* de enseñanza **7.** (*country residence*) casa *f* solariega **8.** (*riding style*) **to have a good ~** montar bien ►**to fly by the ~ of one's pants** dejarse guiar por el instinto **II.** *vt* **1.** (*place on a seat*) sentar; **to ~ oneself** *form* tomar asiento; (*offer a seat to*) colocar **2.** (*have enough seats for*) tener cabida para; **the bus ~s 20** el autobús tiene 20 plazas **3.** ARCHIT, TECH asentar

seat belt *n* cinturón *m* de seguridad; **to fasten one's ~** abrocharse el cinturón de seguridad

seating *n no pl* **1.** (*seats*) asientos *mpl* **2.** (*number*) número *m* de asientos; **~ capacity** número de plazas; **~ for two thousand** aforo de dos mil personas **3.** (*arrangement*) distribución *f* de los asientos

seating arrangements *npl* distribución *f* de los asientos **seating plan** *n* disposición *f* de los invitados

SEATO ['siːtəʊ, *Am:* -t̬oʊ] *n no pl abbr of* **Southeast Asia Treaty Organization** Organización *f* del Tratado del Sudeste Asiático

sea urchin *n* erizo *m* de mar

seaward ['siːwəd, *Am:* -wɚd] **I.** *adv* hacia el mar **II.** *adj* **1.** (*facing sea*) que da al mar **2.** (*moving towards sea*) que va hacia el mar

seawater ['siːˌwɔːtəʳ, *Am:* -ˌwɑːt̬ɚ] *n no pl* agua *f* de mar

seaway ['siːweɪ] *n* **1.** (*channel*) canal *m* marítimo **2.** (*route*) ruta *f* marítima

seaweed ['siːwiːd] *n no pl* algas *fpl*, huiro *m Chile*

seaworthy ['siːˌwɜːði, *Am:* -ˌwɜːr-] *adj* en condiciones de navegar

sebaceous gland [sɪ'beɪʃəsˌglænd, *Am:* sə'-] *n* glándula *f* sebácea

sec [sek] *n s.* **second** seg. *m*

secateurs [ˌsekə'tɜːz, *Am:* 'sekətɚz] *npl* podadera *f;* **a pair of ~** una podadera

secede [sɪ'siːd] *vi* separarse

secession [sɪ'seʃən] *n no pl* secesión *f;* **War of Secession** Guerra *f* de Secesión

seclude [sɪ'kluːd] *vt liter* recluir

secluded [sɪ'kluːdɪd] *adj* (*place*) aislado, -a; (*life*) solitario, -a

seclusion [sɪ'kluːʒən] *n no pl* aislamiento *m;* **to live in ~** vivir aislado

second¹ ['sekənd] **I.** *adj* **1.** (*after first*) segundo, -a; **every ~ boy/cat** uno de cada dos chicos/gatos; **every ~ year** cada dos años; **every ~ week** una semana sí y otra no; **to be ~** ser el segundo; **the ~ biggest town** la segunda ciudad más grande; **to be ~ only to sb/sth** ser superado únicamente por alguien/algo; **to be ~ to none** no ser inferior a nadie **2.** (*another*) otro, -a; **to be a ~ Mozart** ser otro Mozart; **to give sb a ~ chance** dar a alguien una segunda oportunidad; **to have ~ thoughts about sb/sth** dudar de alguien/algo; **on ~ thoughts** *Brit, Aus,* **on ~ thought** *Am, Aus* pensándolo bien; **to do sth a ~ time** volver a hacer algo; **to get one's ~ wind** recobrar el aliento; **to have a ~ helping** repetir de algo **3.** *Brit, Aus* **the ~ floor** *Brit* el segundo piso, el tercer piso *AmL; Am* el primer piso, el segundo piso *AmL* **II.** *n* **1.** *Brit* (*second-class degree*) *título calificado con la segunda o tercera nota que es posible obtener en el Reino Unido* **2.** *no pl* (*second gear*) segunda *f* **3.** *pl* (*extra helping*) **can I have ~s?** ¿puedo repetir? **4.** COM (*imperfect item*) artículo *m* con defectos de fábrica **5.** (*in duel*) padrino *m* **6.** MUS segunda *f* **7.** (*seconder*) persona *f* que secunda una propuesta **III.** *adv* **1.** (*second place*) en segundo lugar **2.** (*second class*) **to travel ~** viajar en segunda **IV.** *vt* **1.** (*support in debate*) secundar **2.** *form* (*back up*) apoyar

second² ['sekənd] *n* (*unit of time*) segundo *m;* **per ~** por segundo; **at that very ~** en ese preciso instante; **just a ~!** ¡un segundo!; **it won't take a ~!** ¡sólo será un momento!

second³ [sɪ'kɒnd, *Am:* -'kɑːnd] *vt Brit, Aus* (*officer, staff*) destinar

secondary ['sekəndəri, *Am:* -deri] **I.** *adj* **1.** (*not main*) secundario, -a; **to be ~ to sth** ser de menor importancia que algo **2.** SCHOOL (*teacher, pupil*) de enseñanza secundaria; **~ modern** centro *m* de formación profesional **3.** (*industry*) derivado, -a **II.** <-ies> *n* **1.** (*person*) subalterno, -a *m, f* **2.** SCHOOL *s.* **secondary school**

secondary school *n* **1.** (*school*) instituto *m* de enseñanza secundaria, liceo *m Chile, Méx* **2.** *no pl* (*education*) enseñanza *f* secundaria

second-best **I.** *adj* **to be ~** (*person*) ser un segundón; (*option*) ser una segunda alternativa **II.** *n* segundo, -a *m, f* **III.** *adv* **to come off ~** (**to sb**) perder (contra alguien)

second chamber *n* POL cámara *f* alta **second class** **I.** *n no pl* segunda *f* (clase) **II.** *adv* **1.** RAIL (*in the second class*) en segunda (clase) **2.** *Brit* (*by second-class mail*) por correo regular **III.** *adj* **1.** (*in second class*) de segunda clase; ~ **mail** correo *m* regular **2.** *pej* (*inferior: hotel, service*) de segunda categoría; (*goods*) de calidad inferior **second cousin** *n* primo, -a *m, f* segundo, -a **second-degree burn** *n* quemadura *f* de segundo grado

seconder *n* persona *f* que secunda una propuesta

second-guess [ˌsekənd'ges] *vt* anticiparse a

secondhand [ˌsekənd'hænd] **I.** *adj* (*clothes, car, information*) de segunda mano; (*bookshop*) de viejo **II.** *adv* **1.** (*used*) de segunda mano **2.** (*from third party*) por terceros

second hand *n* (*on watch*) segundero *m*

second lieutenant *n* MIL alférez *mf*

secondly *adv* en segundo lugar

secondment [sɪ'kɒndmənt, *Am:* -'kɑːnd-] *n Brit, Aus* **1.** *no pl* (*transfer*) traslado *m* temporal por trabajo **2.** (*period*) estancia *f* en un lugar por motivos de trabajo

second-rate [ˌsekənd'reɪt] *adj* mediocre

secrecy ['siːkrəsi] *n no pl* **1.** (*confidentiality*) secreto *m;* **in** ~ en secreto; **to swear sb to** ~ hacer que alguien jure no revelar algo **2.** (*secretiveness*) misterio *m*

secret ['siːkrɪt] **I.** *n* **1.** (*information*) secreto *m;* **an open** ~ un secreto a voces; **to let sb in on a** ~ revelar un secreto a alguien **2.** (*knack*) truco *m;* (*of success*) secreto *m* **3.** (*mystery*) misterio *m* **II.** *adj* (*known to few*) secreto, -a; **to keep sth** ~ (**from sb**) ocultar algo (a alguien)

secret agent *n* agente *mf* secreto, -a

secretarial [ˌsekrə'teəriəl, *Am:* -'teri-] *adj* administrativo, -a

secretariat [ˌsekrə'teəriət, *Am:* -'teri-] *n* secretaría *f*

secretary ['sekrətəri, *Am:* -rəteri] <-ies> *n* **1.** (*in office*) secretario, -a *m, f* **2.** POL ministro, -a *m, f,* secretario, -a *m, f Méx;* **Secretary of the Treasury** ≈ Ministro, -a *m, f* de Hacienda; **Secretary of State** *Brit* ministro; *Am* secretario de Estado

secretary-general [ˌsekrətəri'dʒenərəl, *Am:* -rəteri'-] <secretaries-general> *n* secretario, -a *m, f* general

secrete[1] [sɪ'kriːt] *vt* (*discharge*) segregar

secrete[2] [sɪ'kriːt] *vt form* (*hide*) ocultar

secretion [sɪ'kriːʃən] *n* (*discharge*) secreción *f*

secretive ['siːkrətɪv, *Am:* -t̬ɪv] *adj* reservado, -a

sect [sekt] *n* secta *f*

sectarian [sek'teərɪən, *Am:* -'terɪ-] **I.** *adj* **1.** (*ideology*) sectario, -a **2.** (*schooling*) confesional **II.** *n* sectario, -a *m, f*

section ['sekʃən] **I.** *n* **1.** (*part*) *a.* MIL, MUS, PUBL sección *f;* (*of object*) parte *f* **2.** (*group*) sector *m* **3.** (*of area*) zona *f;* (*of city*) distrito *m* **4.** (*of document*) párrafo *m;* LAW artículo *m* **5.** (*of road*) tramo *m* **6.** (*cut*) corte *m* **II.** *vt* **1.** (*cut*) seccionar **2.** (*divide*) dividir

◆**section off** *vt* acordonar

sectional ['sekʃənl] *adj* **1.** (*limited to a group: interests*) particular; (*differences*) entre facciones **2.** (*done in section: design, view*) en sección **3.** *Am* (*made in sections: furniture, sofa*) modular

sector ['sektəʳ, *Am:* -tɚ] *n* sector *m;* **public/private** ~ sector público/privado

secular ['sekjʊləʳ, *Am:* -lɚ] *adj* **1.** (*non-religious*) secular; (*education*) laico, -a; (*art*) profano, -a **2.** REL seglar **3.** (*centuries-old*) secular

secularize ['sekjʊləraɪz] *vt* secularizar

secure [sɪ'kjʊəʳ, *Am:* -'kjʊr] **I.** *adj* <-rer, -est> **1.** (*safe*) seguro, -a; **to be** ~ **from sth** estar protegido contra algo; **to make sth** ~ **against attack** proteger algo contra los ataques **2.** (*confident*) **to feel** ~ **about sth** sentirse seguro respecto a algo; **to be** ~ **in the knowledge that ...** tener la certeza de que...; **to feel emotionally** ~ tener estabilidad emocional **3.** (*guarantee*) **to be financially** ~ tener estabilidad económica **4.** (*fixed*) firme; (*foundation*) sólido, -a **II.** *vt* **1.** (*obtain*) obtener **2.** (*make firm*) asegurar; *fig* afianzar; (*door*) cerrar firmemente; (*boat*) amarrar; (*position*) consolidar **3.** (*make safe*) proteger **4.** (*put in safe place*) poner a buen recaudo **5.** (*guarantee repayment*) garantizar; **a** ~**d loan** un préstamo con garantía

securities market *n* mercado *m* de valores

security [sɪ'kjʊərəti, *Am:* 'kjʊrət̬i] <-ies> *n* **1.** *no pl* (*safety*) seguridad *f;* ~ **risk** peligro *m* para la seguridad **2.** *no pl* (*stability*) estabilidad *f;* ~ **of employment** estabilidad laboral **3.** (*safeguard*) salvaguardia *f* **4.** *no pl* (*payment guarantee*) fianza *f;* **to stand** ~ **for sb** salir fiador de alguien **5.** *pl* FIN títulos *mpl* **Security Council** *n* Consejo *m* de Seguridad (de las Naciones Unidas) **security forces** *npl* fuerzas *fpl* de seguridad **security guard** *n* guarda *mf* jurado, -a

sedan [sɪ'dæn] *n Am, Aus* AUTO sedán *m*

sedan chair *n* silla *f* de manos

sedate [sɪ'deɪt] **I.** *adj* (*lifestyle, person*) tranquilo, -a; (*colour, style*) sobrio, -a **II.** *vt* MED sedar

sedation [sɪ'deɪʃən] *n no pl* MED sedación *f;* **under** ~ sedado

sedative ['sedətɪv, *Am:* -t̬ɪv] **I.** *adj* sedante **II.** *n* sedante *m*

sedentary ['sedəntəri, *Am:* -teri] *adj* sedentario, -a

sedge [sedʒ] *n no pl* juncia *f*

sediment ['sedɪmənt, *Am:* 'sedə-] *n no pl* sedimento *m;* (*in wine, coffee*) poso *m*

sedimentary [ˌsedɪ'mentri] *adj* sedimentario, -a

sedition [sɪ'dɪʃən] *n no pl, form* sedición *f*

seditious [sɪ'dɪʃəs] *adj form* sedicioso, -a

seduce [sɪ'djuːs, *Am:* -'duːs] *vt* seducir; **to** ~ **sb into doing sth** inducir a alguien a hacer algo

seducer [sɪ'djuːsəʳ, *Am:* -'duːsɚ] *n* seductor(a) *m(f)*

seduction [sɪ'dʌkʃən] *n* **1.** *no pl* (*act*) seducción *f* **2.** *pl* (*seductive quality*) atractivo *m*

seductive [sɪ'dʌktɪv] *adj* **1.** (*sexy*) seductor(a) **2.** (*attractive*) atrayente; (*offer*) tentador(a)

sedulous ['sedjʊləs, *Am:* 'sedjə-] *adj liter* (*at work*) diligente; (*student*) aplicado, -a

see¹ [siː] <saw, seen> **I.** *vt* **1.** (*perceive*) ver; **to ~ that ...** ver que...; **to ~ sth with one's own eyes** ver algo con sus propios ojos; **it is worth ~ing** vale la pena verlo **2.** (*watch*) ver; **you were ~n to enter the building** se os vio entrar en el edificio **3.** (*inspect*) ver; **may I ~ your driving licence?** ¿me permite (ver) su permiso de conducir? **4.** (*visit*) visitar; **to ~ a little/a lot of sb** ver a alguien poco/a menudo; **~ you around!** ¡nos vemos!; **~ you!** *inf* (*when meeting again later*) ¡hasta luego! **5.** (*have relationship*) **to be ~ing sb** salir con alguien **6.** (*have meeting*) tener una entrevista con **7.** (*talk to*) **I would like to ~ you about that matter** querría hablar contigo sobre ese asunto; **Mr Brown will ~ you now** el Sr. Brown le recibirá ahora **8.** (*accompany*) acompañar a **9.** (*perceive*) darse cuenta de; (*understand*) comprender; **I don't ~ what you mean** no entiendo lo que quieres decir; **to make sb ~ reason** hacer entrar en razón a alguien; **to ~ sth in a new light** cambiar de opinión respecto a algo **10.** (*envisage*) creer; **as I ~ it ...** a mi modo de ver...; **I don't ~ him doing that** no le creo capaz de hacer eso; **I could ~ it coming** lo veía venir **11.** (*witness*) presenciar; **he won't ~ fifty again** ya pasa de los cincuenta **12.** (*investigate*) **to ~ how/what/if ...** averiguar cómo/qué/si... **13.** (*ensure*) **~ that you are ready when we come** procura estar listo cuando vengamos **II.** *vi* **1.** (*use eyes*) ver; **as far as the eye can ~** hasta donde alcanza la vista **2.** (*find out*) descubrir; **~ for yourself!** ¡compruébelo usted mismo!; **let me ~** ¿a ver?; **let's ~** vamos a ver; **we'll/I'll (have to) ~** ya lo veremos/veré; **you'll ~** ya verás **3.** (*understand*) comprender; **I ~** ya veo; **you ~?** ¿entiendes?; **as far as I can ~** por lo que yo veo ►**he can't ~ further than the <u>end</u> of his nose** no puede ver más allá de sus narices

◆**see about** *vt inf* encargarse de; (*consider*) pensarse ►**we'll <u>soon</u> ~ that!** *inf* ¡eso ya lo veremos!

◆**see in** *vt* (*welcome*) hacer pasar; **to see the New Year in** celebrar el Año Nuevo

◆**see off** *vt* **1.** (*say goodbye*) despedir **2.** (*drive away*) deshacerse de **3.** (*defeat*) derrotar

◆**see out** *vt* **1.** (*escort to door*) acompañar hasta la puerta **2.** (*continue to end*) seguir hasta el final de; (*programme, film*) quedarse hasta el final de **3.** (*last until end*) durar hasta el final de; **to see the winter out** resistir el invierno

◆**see through** *vt* **1.** (*look through*) ver a través de **2.** (*not be deceived by*) calar a *inf;* (*mystery*) penetrar en **3.** (*sustain*) **to see sb through (a difficult time)** mantener a alguien a flote (en tiempos difíciles) **4.** (*last*) durar **5.** (*continue to end*) llevar a buen término *form*

◆**see to** *vt* **1.** (*attend to*) encargarse de **2.** (*ensure*) **to ~ it that ...** asegurarse de que...

see² [siː] *n* REL sede *f;* **the Holy See** la Santa Sede

seed [siːd] **I.** *n* **1.** BOT (*source*) semilla *f;* (*of fruit*) pepita *f,* pepa *f AmL* **2.** *no pl* (*seeds*) simiente *f* **3.** (*beginning*) germen *m;* (*of revolution*) semilla *f;* **to sow the ~s of doubt/discord** sembrar la duda/la discordia **4.** *no pl* ANAT semen *m* **II.** *vt* **1.** AGR sembrar; **to ~ itself** (*a plant*) desgranarse **2.** (*help start*) contribuir a la puesta en marcha; **to ~ a project with money** aportar capital a un proyecto **3.** (*remove seeds*) despepitar **4.** SPORTS preseleccionar **III.** *vi* granar

seed bed *n* **1.** AGR semillero *m* **2.** *fig* foco *m*

seed corn *n* **1.** BOT trigo *m* de siembra **2.** *fig* capital *m* simiente

seedless ['siːdləs] *adj* sin pepitas

seedling ['siːdlɪŋ] *n* planta *f* de semillero

seed potato *n* patata *f* de siembra

seedy ['siːdi] <-ier, -iest> *adj* **1.** (*dubious*) sórdido, -a; (*place*) de mala muerte; (*clothing*) raído, -a **2.** (*unwell*) pachucho, -a *inf;* **to feel ~** encontrarse mal

seeing **I.** *conj* **~ (that)** en vista de (que) **II.** *n* visión *f;* **~ is believing** ver para creer

seek [siːk] <sought> **I.** *vt* **1.** (*look for*) buscar; **to ~ one's fortune** probar suerte **2.** (*try to obtain*) procurar obtener; (*solution*) tratar de encontrar; (*shelter*) buscar; (*damages*) reclamar **3.** (*ask for: help, approval*) pedir; (*job*) solicitar **4.** (*attempt*) tratar de **II.** *vi* (*search*) buscar

◆**seek out** *vt* (*person*) ir a buscar; (*information*) averiguar

seeker *n* buscador(a) *m(f)*

seem [siːm] *vi* **1.** (*appear to be*) parecer; **they ~ed to like the idea** parecía que les gustaba la idea; **to ~ as if ...** parecer como si... +*subj;* **it is not all what it ~s** no es lo que parece; **things aren't always what they ~** las apariencias engañan **2.** (*appear*) **it ~s that ...** parece que...; **so it ~s, so would ~** eso parece

seeming *adj form* aparente

seemingly *adv* aparentemente

seemly ['siːmli] <-ier, -iest> *adj* apropiado, -a

seen [siːn] *pp of* **see**

seep [siːp] *vi* filtrarse

◆**seep away** *vi* escurrirse

seepage ['siːpɪdʒ] *n no pl* (*of water*) filtración *f;* (*of gas*) fuga *f*

seer [sɪəʳ, *Am:* sɪr] *n liter* adivino, -a *m, f*

seersucker ['sɪəˌsʌkəʳ, *Am:* 'sɪrˌsʌkɚ] *n* sirsaca *f*

seesaw ['siːsɔː, *Am:* -sɑː] **I.** *n* **1.** (*in play-*

ground) balancín *m* **2.** *fig* vaivén *m* **II.** *vi* **1.** (*play*) columpiarse **2.** *fig* oscilar **III.** *adj* ~ **motion** movimiento *m* oscilante
seethe [siːð] *vi* **1.** (*bubble*) borbotar **2.** *fig* (*be angry*) estar furioso, -a; **to ~ with anger** hervir de cólera **3.** *fig* (*be busy*) bullir; **to ~ with tourists** estar plagado de turistas
see-through ['siːθruː] *adj* transparente
segment[1] ['segmənt] *n* **1.** MAT, ZOOL segmento *m*; (*of orange*) gajo *m* **2.** (*of society*) sector *m*
segment[2] [seg'ment, *Am:* 'segmənt] **I.** *vt* segmentar; (*orange*) dividir en gajos **II.** *vi* segmentarse
segmentation [ˌsegmən'teɪʃən] *n no pl* segmentación *f*
segregate ['segrɪgeɪt, *Am:* -rə-] *vt* (*races*) segregar; (*girls and boys*) separar
segregation [ˌsegrɪ'geɪʃən, *Am:* -rə'-] *n no pl* segregación *f*
seismic ['saɪzmɪk] *adj* GEO sísmico, -a
seismograph ['saɪzməgrɑːf, *Am:* -græf] *n* sismógrafo *m*
seismologist [saɪz'mɒlədʒɪst, *Am:* -'mɑː-lə-] *n* sismólogo, -a *m, f*
seismology [saɪz'mɒlədʒi, *Am:* -'mɑːlə-] *n no pl* sismología *f*
seize [siːz] *vt* **1.** (*grasp*) asir *form*, cachar *Arg, Nic, Urug*, acapillar *Méx*; **to ~ sb by the arm/by the throat** agarrar a alguien del brazo/por el cuello **2.** (*take: opportunity*) no dejar escapar; (*initiative, power*) tomar **3.** (*overcome*) **he was ~d by fear/desire** el miedo/el deseo se apoderó de él; **I was ~d with panic** estaba sobrecogido por el pánico **4.** (*capture: criminal*) detener; (*fortress, town*) tomar **5.** (*confiscate: property*) confiscar; (*drugs, weapons*) incautarse de **6.** (*understand*) captar **7.** (*kidnap*) secuestrar
◆**seize on** *vt* aprovecharse de
◆**seize up** *vi* (*stop*) paralizarse; (*engine, muscles*) agarrotarse; INFOR colgarse *inf*
seizure ['siːʒəʳ, *Am:* -ʒɚ] *n* **1.** *no pl* (*seizing*) asimiento *m* **2.** (*taking possession: of town*) toma *f*; (*of drugs*) incautación *f*; (*of property, contraband*) confiscación *f* **3.** MED (*stroke*) ataque *m* **4.** (*seizing up*) agarrotamiento *m*
seldom ['seldəm] *adv* rara vez
select [sɪ'lekt, *Am:* sə'-] **I.** *vt* (*candidate, player, information*) seleccionar; (*gift, wine*) escoger; **~ed works** obras *fpl* escogidas **II.** *adj* **1.** (*high-class*) selecto, -a; (*club, restaurant*) exclusivo, -a; (*school, university*) elitista; (*product*) de primera calidad **2.** (*exclusive*) **the ~ few** los escogidos
select committee *n Brit* POL comisión *f* investigadora
selection [sɪ'lekʃən, *Am:* sə'-] *n* **1.** (*choosing*) selección *f* **2.** (*range*) gama *f*; (*of food, drink*) surtido *m* **3.** *no pl* (*choice*) elección *f* **4.** (*chosen player*) **this player is a ~ for the team** este jugador ha sido seleccionado para entrar en el equipo
selective [sɪ'lektɪv, *Am:* sə'-] *adj* selectivo, -a
selectivity [ˌsɪlek'tɪvəti, *Am:* ˌsəlek'tɪvət̬i] *n no pl* selectividad *f*
selector [sɪ'lektəʳ, *Am:* sə'lektɚ] *n* **1.** SPORTS (*of team*) seleccionador(a) *m(f)* **2.** TECH selector *m*
selenium [sɪ'liːniəm] *n* selenio *m*
self [self] *n* <selves> uno mismo, una misma; **his better ~** su mejor parte; **one's other ~** su alter ego; **the ~** PSYCH el yo
self-abasement *n no pl* rebajamiento *m* de sí mismo **self-abuse** *n* masturbación *f* **self-addressed** *adj* ~ **envelope** sobre *m* con la dirección de uno mismo **self-adhesive** *adj* autoadhesivo, -a **self-appointed** *adj pej* autoproclamado, -a **self-assurance** *n no pl* seguridad *f* en uno mismo; **to possess ~** tener confianza en uno mismo **self-assured** *adj* seguro, -a de sí mismo, -a **self-catering** *adj Aus, Brit* (*apartment*) con cocina individual; (*holiday*) sin servicio de comidas **self-centered** *adj Am*, **self-centred** *adj Brit, Aus* egocéntrico, -a **self-colored** *adj Am*, **self-coloured** *adj Brit, Aus* **1.** (*natural*) de color natural **2.** (*one colour*) unicolor **self-complacent** *adj pej* engreído, -a **self-composed** *adj* dueño, -a de sí mismo, -a; **to remain ~** no perder la serenidad **self-conceited** *adj pej* vanidoso, -a **self-confessed** *adj* confeso, -a; **she's a ~ coward** se confiesa cobarde **self-confidence** *n no pl* seguridad *f* en uno mismo; **to have ~** confiar en sí mismo **self-conscious** *adj* **1.** (*shy*) tímido, -a; **to feel ~** sentirse cohibido **2.** *pej* (*unnatural*) afectado, -a **self-contained** *adj* **1.** (*self-sufficient: community, village*) autosuficiente; (*apartment*) con cocina y cuarto de baño **2.** *pej* (*reserved*) reservado, -a **self-contradictory** *adj form* contradictorio, -a; **a ~ statement** un contrasentido **self-control** *n no pl* dominio *m* de sí mismo **self-critical** *adj* autocrítico, -a **self-criticism** *n no pl* autocrítica *f* **self-deception** *n no pl* engaño *m* de uno mismo **self-defeating** *adj* contraproducente **self-defence** *n Aus, Brit*, **self-defense** *n Am* **1.** *no pl* (*protection*) defensa *f* personal **2.** *no pl* LAW legítima defensa *f* **self-denial** *n no pl* abnegación *f* **self-destruct** *vi* autodestruirse **self-determination** *n no pl* POL autodeterminación *f* **self-discipline** *n no pl* autodisciplina *f* **self-educated** *adj* autodidacto, -a **self-effacing** *adj* humilde **self-employed** **I.** *adj* **to be ~** trabajar por cuenta propia **II.** *n* **the ~** los trabajadores por cuenta propia **self-esteem** *n no pl* amor *m* propio **self-evident** *adj* evidente **self-explanatory** *adj* que se explica por sí mismo **self-expression** *n no pl* expresión *f* de la propia personalidad **self-fulfilling** *adj* (*prediction*) que tiene como consecuencia su propio cumplimiento **self-governing** *adj* autónomo, -a **self-government** *n no pl* autonomía *f* **self-help** *n* autoayuda *f*; ~

group grupo *m* de apoyo mutuo **self-importance** *n no pl, pej* presunción *f* **self-important** *adj pej* presuntuoso, -a **self-imposed** *adj* (*deadline*) autoimpuesto, -a; (*exile*) voluntario, -a **self-indulgence** *n no pl* indulgencia *f* con uno mismo **self-indulgent** *adj* indulgente consigo mismo, -a **self-inflicted** *adj* autoinfligido, -a **self-interest** *n no pl* interés *m* propio; **to be motivated by** ~ estar motivado por el interés personal

selfish ['selfɪʃ] *adj pej* egoísta

selfishness *n no pl, pej* egoísmo *m*

self-justification *n* autojustificación *f*

selfless ['selfləs] *adj* desinteresado, -a

self-made [ˌself'meɪd] *adj* que se ha hecho a sí mismo, -a **self-opinionated** *adj pej* testarudo, -a **self-pity** *n no pl* lástima *f* de sí mismo **self-portrait** *n* ART autorretrato *m* **self-possessed** *adj* dueño, -a de sí mismo, -a **self-preservation** *n no pl* instinto *m* de conservación **self-raising flour** *n no pl, Brit* harina *f* con levadura incorporada **self-realization** *n* autorealización *f* **self-reliance** *n no pl* independencia *f* **self-reliant** *adj* independiente **self-respect** *n no pl* amor *m* propio; **to lose all** ~ perder la dignidad **self-respecting** *adj* con amor propio; **every** ~ **man ...** todo hombre que se precie... **self-righteous** *adj pej* farisaico, -a; (*tone*) de superioridad moral **self-rising flour** *n no pl, Am* harina *f* con levadura incorporada **self-sacrifice** *n no pl* abnegación *f* **self-sacrificing** *adj* sacrificado, -a **self-satisfaction** *n no pl, pej* satisfacción *f* de sí mismo **self-satisfied** *adj pej* satisfecho, -a de sí mismo, -a **self-seeking** *adj form* egoísta **self-service I.** *n* autoservicio *m* **II.** *adj* ~ **store** autoservicio *m;* ~ **restaurant** self-service *m* **self-sufficiency** *n no pl* autosuficiencia *f* **self-sufficient** *adj* **1.** independiente **2.** ECON autosuficiente; ~ **economy** autarquía *f* **self-taught** *adj* autodidacto, -a; **to be** ~ **in sth** haber aprendido algo por su cuenta **self-willed** *adj* obstinado, -a, voltario, -a *Chile* **self-winding watch** *n* reloj *m* de cuerda automática

sell [sel] **I.** *n no pl* **1.** *a.* FIN (*thing to sell*) venta *f* **2.** *inf* (*deception*) estafa *f* **II.** *vt* <sold, sold> **1.** (*exchange for money*) vender; **to** ~ **sth for £100** vender algo por [*o* en] 100 libras; **to** ~ **sth at half price** vender algo a mitad de precio; **to** ~ **sth at a loss** vender algo perdiendo dinero **2.** *fig* (*make accepted*) hacer aceptar; **I'm sold on your plan** tu plan me ha convencido ►**to** ~ **oneself short** no hacerse valer **III.** *vi* <sold, sold> **1.** (*be exchanged for money: company, shop*) estar en venta; (*product*) venderse; **to** ~ **at** [*o* **for**] **£5** venderse a 5 libras **2.** (*be accepted*) tener aceptación

◆**sell off** *vt* (*shares, property*) liquidar; (*industry*) privatizar

◆**sell out I.** *vi* **1.** COM, FIN agotarse **2.** *fig* venderse **II.** *vt* liquidar

◆**sell up** *Aus, Brit* **I.** *vi* liquidar **II.** *vt* vender

sellable *adj* vendible

sell-by date ['selbaɪˌdeɪt] *n Brit* COM fecha *f* límite de venta

seller *n* **1.** (*person*) vendedor(a) *m(f);* ~**'s market** mercado *m* de vendedores **2.** (*product*) **good/poor** ~ artículo *m* que tiene mucha/poca demanda

selling *n* ventas *fpl*

selling point *n* atractivo *m* para el consumidor **selling price** *n* precio *m* de venta

sell-off *n* (*of shares, property*) liquidación *f;* (*of industry*) privatización *f*

Sellotape® ['selәteɪp, *Am:* -oʊ-] *n no pl, Brit* celo *m*

sell-out ['selaʊt] *n* **1.** THEAT, CINE éxito *f* de taquilla **2.** (*betrayal*) traición *f*

selves [selvz] *n pl of* **self**

semantic [sɪ'mæntɪk, *Am:* sә'mænţɪk] *adj* LING semántico, -a

semantics [sɪ'mæntɪks, *Am:* sә'mænţɪks] *npl* LING semántica *f*

semaphore ['semәfɔːʳ, *Am:* -fɔːr] **I.** *n no pl* semáforo *m* **II.** *vt* transmitir por semáforo **III.** *vi* hacer señales con semáforo

semblance ['sembləns] *n no pl, form* apariencia *f*

semen ['siːmәn] *n no pl* semen *m*

semester [sɪ'mestәʳ, *Am:* sә'mestɚ] *n* UNIV semestre *m* (académico)

semi ['semi] *n* **1.** *Aus, Brit, inf* (*house*) casa *f* pareada **2.** *Am, Aus, inf* (*truck*) trailer *m* **3.** *inf* SPORTS semifinal *f*

semiautomatic [ˌsemiɔːtә'mætɪk, *Am:* -ɑːţә'mæţɪk] *adj* semiautomático, -a

semibreve ['semɪbriːv] *n Aus, Brit* MUS redonda *f*

semicircle ['semɪˌsɜːkl, *Am:* -ˌsɜːrkl] *n* MAT semicírculo *m*

semicircular [ˌsemɪ'sɜːkjʊləʳ, *Am:* 'sɜːrkjәlɚ] *adj* semicircular

semicolon [ˌsemɪ'kəʊ lən, *Am:* 'semɪˌkoʊ-] *n* punto *m* y coma

semiconductor [ˌsemɪkәn'dʌktәʳ, *Am:* -tɚ] *n* ELEC semiconductor *m*

semiconscious [ˌsemɪ'kɒntʃәs, *Am:* -'kɑːn-] *adj* semiconsciente

semi-detached [ˌsemɪdɪ'tætʃt] *adj* ~ **house** casa *f* pareada

semifinal [ˌsemɪ'faɪnәl] *n* SPORTS semifinal *f*

semifinalist [ˌsemɪ'faɪnәlɪst] *n* SPORTS semifinalista *mf*

seminal ['semɪnәl, *Am:* 'semә-] *adj* (*important*) fundamental

seminar ['semɪnɑːʳ, *Am:* -әnɑːr] *n* UNIV seminario *m*

seminary ['semɪnәri, *Am:* -ner-] *n* REL seminario *m*

semiofficial *adj* semioficial

semiotics [ˌsemi'ɒtɪks, *Am:* ˌsiːmi'ɑːţɪks] *n no pl* semiótica *f*

S

semiprecious [ˌsemɪˈpreʃəs] *adj* semiprecioso, -a
semiquaver [ˈsemɪˌkweɪvəʳ, *Am:* -vɚ] *n Aus, Brit* MUS semicorchea *f*
semiskilled [ˌsemɪˈskɪld] *adj* semicualificado, -a
Semite [ˈsiːmaɪt, *Am:* ˈsemaɪt] *n* semita *mf*
Semitic [sɪˈmɪtɪk, *Am:* səˈmɪt̬-] *adj* semítico, -a
semitone [ˈsemɪtəʊn, *Am:* -toʊn] *n* MUS semitono *m*
semitrailer [ˈsemɪˌtreɪləʳ, *Am:* -ɚ] *n Am* tráiler *m*
semitropical [ˌsemɪˈtrɒpɪkəl, *Am:* -ˈtrɑːpɪ-] *adj* subtropical
semivowel [ˈsemɪˌvaʊəl] *n* LING semivocal *f*
semolina [ˌseməˈliːnə] *n no pl* sémola *f*
Sen. *n Am abbr of* **Senator** senador(a) *m(f)*
senate [ˈsenɪt] *n no pl* **1.** POL senado *m* **2.** UNIV consejo *m*
senator [ˈsenətəʳ, *Am:* -t̬ɚ] *n* POL senador(a) *m(f)*
senatorial [ˌsenəˈtɔːriəl] *adj Am* senatorial
send [send] **I.** *vt* <sent, sent> **1.** (*message, letter, flowers*) enviar, mandar; (*telegram*) poner; **to ~ sth by post** enviar algo por correo; **to ~ sb to prison** mandar a alguien a la cárcel; **to ~ one's love to sb** mandar saludos cariñosos a alguien; **~ her my regards** dale recuerdos de mi parte; **Philip ~s his apologies** Philip pide que lo disculpen; **to ~ word (to sb)** *form* informar (a alguien) **2.** (*propel*) lanzar; **to ~ sth flying** hacer saltar algo por los aires **3.** RADIO transmitir **4.** *inf* (*cause*) **to ~ sb to sleep** hacer que alguien se duerma; **to ~ sb crazy** *Brit* volver loco a alguien ►**to ~ sb packing** *inf* mandar a alguien a freír espárragos **II.** *vi* <sent, sent> mandar a alguien
◆**send away** **I.** *vi* **to ~ for sth** pedir algo (por correo) **II.** *vt* **1.** (*dismiss*) despedir **2.** (*send to another place*) enviar
◆**send back** *vt* devolver; (*person*) hacer volver
◆**send down** *vt* **1.** *Brit* UNIV (*expel*) expulsar **2.** LAW (*imprison*) encarcelar **3.** (*cause to drop: prices, temperature*) hacer bajar
◆**send for** *vt* (*person*) llamar; (*assistance*) pedir; (*goods*) encargar
◆**send forth** *vt* **1.** *liter* (*make go*) enviar **2.** (*emit*) emitir; (*smell, heat*) despedir
◆**send in** *vt* **1.** (*application, report*) enviar; (*reinforcements*) mandar **2.** (*let in*) hacer pasar
◆**send off** **I.** *vt* **1.** (*cause to depart*) mandar; (*by post*) enviar por correo **2.** *Aus, Brit* SPORTS expulsar **II.** *vi* **to ~ for sth** pedir algo (por correo)
◆**send on** *vt* **1.** (*send in advance*) mandar por adelantado **2.** (*forward: mail*) remitir; (*order*) transmitir
◆**send out** **I.** *vt* **1.** (*ask to leave*) echar **2.** (*send on errand*) mandar **3.** (*dispatch*) enviar **4.** (*emit: signal, rays*) emitir; (*smell, heat*) despedir **II.** *vi* **to ~ for sth** pedir que traigan algo
◆**send up** *vt* **1.** (*drive up: prices, temperature*) hacer subir **2.** (*caricature*) imitar **3.** *Am* (*put in prison*) meter preso
sender *n* remitente *mf;* **'return to ~'** 'devuélvase al remitente'
send-off [ˈsendɒf, *Am:* -ɑːf] *n* despedida *f;* **to give sb a good ~** dar una buena despedida a alguien **send-up** *n inf* parodia *f*
Senegal [ˌsenɪˈgɔːl] *n* el Senegal
Senegalese [ˌsenɪgəˈliːz] **I.** *adj* senegalés, -esa **II.** *n* senegalés, -esa *m, f*
senile [ˈsiːnaɪl] *adj* senil; **to go ~** chochear
senile dementia *n* demencia *f* senil
senility [sɪˈnɪləti, *Am:* səˈnɪlət̬i] *n no pl* senilidad *f*
senior [ˈsiːniəʳ, *Am:* -njɚ] **I.** *adj* **1.** *form* (*older*) mayor; **James Grafton, Senior** James Grafton, padre **2.** (*higher in rank*) superior; **to be ~ to sb** estar por encima de alguien **3.** (*of earlier appointment*) más antiguo, -a **4.** SCHOOL de los cursos superiores; (*pupil*) de último curso **II.** *n* **1.** (*older person*) mayor *mf;* **she is two years my ~** me lleva dos años **2.** (*of higher rank*) superior *mf* **3.** *Am* SCHOOL estudiante *mf* de último curso
senior citizen *n* jubilado, -a *m, f* **senior high school** *n* instituto *m* de bachillerato
seniority [ˌsiːniˈɒrəti, *Am:* siːˈnjɔːrət̬i] *n no pl* antigüedad *f*
senior officer *n* oficial *mf* de alto rango **senior partner** *n* socio, -a *m, f* mayoritario, -a **senior school** *n* colegio *m* de enseñanza secundaria
sensation [senˈseɪʃən] *n* sensación *f;* **to be ~** ser un éxito; **to cause a ~** hacer furor
sensational [senˈseɪʃənəl] *adj* **1.** (*fabulous*) sensacional **2.** *pej* (*newspaper, disclosure*) sensacionalista
sense [sents] **I.** *n* **1.** (*faculty*) sentido *m;* **~ of hearing** oído *m;* **~ of sight** vista *f;* **~ of smell** olfato *m;* **~ of taste** gusto *m;* **~ of touch** tacto *m* **2.** (*ability*) sentido *m;* **to have no ~ of occasion** ser inoportuno; **to lose all ~ of time** perder la noción del tiempo **3.** (*way*) sentido *m;* **in every ~** en todos los sentidos; **in a ~** en cierto modo; **in no ~** de ninguna manera **4.** (*sensation*) sensación *f* **5.** *pl* (*clear mental faculties*) juicio *m;* **to be in one's (right) ~s** estar en su sano juicio; **to bring sb to his/her ~s, to come to one's ~s** (*recover consciousness*) recobrar el conocimiento; (*see reason*) entrar en razón; **to make sb see ~** hacer entrar en razón a alguien; **to take leave of one's ~s** perder la razón **6.** *no pl* (*good judgment*) **(common) ~** sentido *m* común; **to have enough** [*o* **the good**] **~ to ...** tener la sensatez de...; **to talk ~** decir cosas sensatas **7.** (*feeling*) impresión *f;* **to feel a ~ of belonging** sentirse aceptado **8.** (*meaning*) significado *m,* sentido *m;* **to make ~** tener sentido; **in the full ~ of the word** en el sentido amplio de la

palabra; **there's no ~ in doing ...** no tiene sentido hacer...; **what's the ~ in doing ...?** ¿qué sentido tiene hacer...? **9.** (*opinion*) opinión *f* (general) **II.** *vt* sentir; **to ~ that ...** darse cuenta de que...

senseless ['sentsləs] *adj* **1.** (*pointless*) sin sentido; (*remark*) insensato, -a **2.** MED inconsciente; **to beat sb ~** dejar a alguien sin sentido de una paliza

sense organ *n* órgano *m* sensorial

sensibility [ˌsentsɪ'bɪləti, *Am:* -sə'bɪləṱi] *n no pl* sensibilidad *f;* **to offend sb's sensibilities** herir la sensibilidad de alguien

sensible ['sentsɪbl, *Am:* -sə-] *adj* **1.** (*having good judgement: person, decision*) sensato, -a **2.** (*suitable: clothes, shoes*) práctico, -a **3.** (*aware*) consciente **4.** (*noticeable*) notable

sensibly *adv* **1.** (*wisely*) sensatamente; (*behave*) prudentemente; (*decide*) acertadamente **2.** (*dress*) con ropa cómoda

sensitive ['sentsɪtɪv, *Am:* -səṱɪv] *adj* **1.** (*appreciative*) sensible; **to be ~ to sb's needs** ser consciente de las necesidades de alguien **2.** (*touchy*) susceptible; **to be ~ about sth** ser susceptible a algo **3.** (*touchy: subject, moment*) delicado, -a; (*age*) conflictivo, -a **4.** (*secret: documents, work*) confidencial

sensitiveness *n,* **sensitivity** [ˌsentsɪ'tɪvəti, *Am:* -sətɪvəṱi] *n* **1.** (*touchiness*) susceptibilidad *f* **2.** (*understanding*) sensibilidad *f,* delicadeza *f* **3.** (*secret nature*) confidencialidad *f*

sensitize ['sentsɪtaɪz, *Am:* -sə-] *vt Am* sensibilizar; **to ~ sb to a problem** concienciar a alguien de un problema

sensor ['sentsəʳ, *Am:* -sɚ] *n* TECH, ELEC sensor *m*

sensory ['sentsəri] *adj* sensorial

sensual ['sentsjʊəl, *Am:* -ʃuəl] *adj* sensual

sensuality [ˌsentsju'æləti, *Am:* -ʃu'æləṱi] *n no pl* sensualidad *f*

sensuous ['sentsjʊəs, *Am:* -ʃuəs] *adj* sensual

sent [sent] *pp, pt of* **send**

sentence ['sentəns, *Am:* -ṱəns] **I.** *n* **1.** (*court decision*) sentencia *f;* (*punishment*) condena *f;* **jail ~** condena de encarcelamiento; **life ~** cadena perpetua; **to receive a ~** ser condenado; **to serve a ~** cumplir una condena **2.** LING frase *f* **II.** *vt* condenar

sententious [sen'tenʃəs] *adj form* sentencioso, -a

sentient ['senʃnt] *adj form* sensible

sentiment ['sentɪmənt, *Am:* -ṱə-] *n form* **1.** (*opinion*) opinión *f;* **public/popular ~** opinión pública/popular; **to echo a ~** hacerse eco de una opinión; **to share sb's ~** compartir la opinión de alguien **2.** *no pl* (*emotion*) sentimiento *m*

sentimental [ˌsentɪ'mentəl, *Am:* -ṱə'menṱəl] *adj* **1.** sentimental; **to be ~ about sth** ser sentimental con algo **2.** *pej* sensiblero, -a

sentimentality [ˌsentɪmen'tæləti, *Am:* -ṱəmen'tæləṱi] *n no pl, pej* sentimentalismo *m*

sentimentalize [ˌsentɪ'mentəlaɪz, *Am:* -ṱə'menṱəlaɪz] *vt Am, pej* dar una visión sentimental de

sentry ['sentri] *n* centinela *m;* **to be on ~ duty** estar de guardia

sentry box *n* garita *f* de centinela

separable ['sepərəbl] *adj form* separable

separate¹ ['seprət, *Am:* 'sepɚɪt] **I.** *adj* separado, -a; **to remain a ~ entity** ser una entidad independiente; **a ~ piece of paper** una hoja de papel aparte; **to go one's ~ ways** ir por distintos caminos; **to keep sth ~** mantener algo aparte **II.** *n pl* piezas *fpl* sueltas de ropa

separate² ['sepəreɪt] **I.** *vt* separar; **to ~ two people** separar a dos personas; **to ~ egg whites from yolks** separar las claras de los huevos de las yemas **II.** *vi* separarse

separated *adj* separado, -a

separation [ˌsepə'reɪʃən] *n* separación *f;* (*division*) división *f*

separatism ['sepərətɪzm] *n no pl* separatismo *m*

separatist ['sepərətɪst] **I.** *n* separatista *mf* **II.** *adj* separatista

separator ['sepəreɪtəʳ, *Am:* -ṱɚ] *n* separador *m*

sepia ['siːpɪə] **I.** *n* sepia *f* **II.** *adj* de color sepia

sepsis ['sepsɪs] *n no pl* sepsis *f*

September [sep'tembəʳ, *Am:* -bɚ] *n* septiembre *m; s. a.* **April**

septic ['septɪk] *adj* séptico, -a; **to go** [*o* **turn**] **~** infectarse

septicaemia *n Brit,* **septicemia** [ˌseptɪ'siːmiə, *Am:* -tə'-] *n Am no pl* septicemia *f*

septuagenarian [ˌseptjʊədʒɪ'neəriən, *Am:* -tuədʒə'neri-] **I.** *n* septuagenario, -a *m, f* **II.** *adj* septuagenario, -a

sepulcher *n Am s.* **sepulchre**

sepulchral [sɪ'pʌlkrəl, *Am:* sə'pʌl-] *adj liter* **1.** (*silence*) sepulcral **2.** (*gloomy*) lóbrego, -a

sepulchre ['sepəlkəʳ, *Am:* -kɚ] *n Brit* sepulcro *m*

sequel ['siːkwəl] *n* **1.** continuación *f;* **the ~ of an earlier success** la secuela de un éxito temprano **2.** (*follow-up*) desenlace *m*

sequence ['siːkwəns] *n* **1.** (*order*) orden *m;* (*of events*) sucesión *f* **2.** (*part of film*) secuencia *f*

sequential [sɪ'kwenʃl] *adj form* secuencial

sequestrate [sɪ'kwestreɪt] *vt* (*confiscate*) confiscar; (*property in litigation*) secuestrar

sequestration [ˌsiːkwe'streɪʃən] *n no pl* **1.** (*confiscation*) embargo *m;* (*of property in litigation*) secuestro *m* **2.** *Am* (*isolation*) aislamiento *m*

sequin ['siːkwɪn] *n* lentejuela *f*

sequoia [sɪ'kwɔɪə] *n* secoya *f*

Serb [sɜːb, *Am:* sɜːrb] **I.** *adj* serbio, -a **II.** *n* serbio, -a *m, f*

Serbia ['sɜːbɪə, *Am:* 'sɜːr-] *n* Serbia *f*

Serbian ['sɜːbɪən, *Am:* 'sɜːr-] *n s.* **Serb**

Serbo-Croat [ˌsɜːbəʊ'krəʊæt, *Am:* ˌsɜːrboʊkroʊ'-] *n* LING serbocroata *mf*

serenade [ˌserəˈneɪd] **I.** *vt* **1.** (*sing to*) cantar una serenata a **2.** (*play music for*) dar una serenata a **II.** *n* serenata *f*, mañanita *f Méx*

serene [sɪˈriːn, *Am:* səˈ-] *adj* **1.** (*calm*) sereno, -a; (*sea*) calmado, -a **2.** (*peaceful*) tranquilo, -a **3.** (*cheerful*) feliz

serenity [sɪˈrenəti, *Am:* səˈrenət̬i] *n no pl* **1.** (*calmness*) serenidad *f* **2.** (*tranquility*) tranquilidad *f* **3.** (*cheerfulness*) felicidad *f*

serf [sɜːf, *Am:* sɜːrf] *n* HIST siervo, -a *m, f*

serfdom *n no pl* HIST servidumbre *f*

sergeant [ˈsɑːdʒənt, *Am:* ˈsɑːrdʒənt] *n* sargento *mf;* ~ **at arms** ujier *m*

sergeant major *n* brigada *mf*

serial [ˈsɪəriəl, *Am:* ˈsɪri-] **I.** *n* serial *m;* **TV** ~ telenovela *f* **II.** *adj* **1.** (*in series*) consecutivo, -a **2.** (*shown in parts*) por entregas

serialize [ˈsɪəriəlaɪz, *Am:* ˈsɪri-] *vt* (*in newspaper, magazine*) publicar por entregas; TV, RADIO presentar por capítulos

serial killer *n* asesino, -a *m, f* en serie **serial number** *n* numero *m* de serie **serial port** *n* INFOR puerto *m* en serie

series [ˈsɪəriːz, *Am:* ˈsɪriːz] *n inv* **1.** (*sequence*) serie *f* **2.** (*succession*) sucesión *f;* **in** ~ ELEC en serie **3.** (*set of broadcasts*) ciclo *m*

serious [ˈsɪəriəs, *Am:* ˈsɪri-] *adj* **1.** (*earnest, solemn*) serio, -a **2.** (*problem, injury*) grave **3.** (*not slight*) de consideración; (*argument*) importante **4.** (*determined*) firme; **to be ~ about sb** ir en serio con alguien **5.** *inf* (*significant*) significativo, -a; ~ **money** cantidad de dinero **6.** (*large: debt, amount*) considerable

seriously *adv* **1.** (*in earnest*) seriamente, en serio; **to ~ expect sb to do sth** esperar de verdad que alguien haga algo; **no, ~ ...** no, en serio...; **it would be ~ wrong of him if ...** sería un gran error por su parte si... **2.** (*ill, damaged*) gravemente **3.** *inf* (*very*) extremadamente; **she was ~ drunk** estaba borracha a más no poder

seriousness *n no pl* **1.** (*truthfulness*) seriedad *f;* **in all** ~ en serio **2.** (*serious nature*) gravedad *f*

sermon [ˈsɜːmən, *Am:* ˈsɜːr-] *n a. fig* sermón *m;* **to deliver a** ~ dar un sermón

serpent [ˈsɜːpənt, *Am:* ˈsɜːr-] *n* serpiente *f*

serpentine [ˈsɜːpəntaɪn, *Am:* ˈsɜːr-] *adj liter* **1.** (*snake-like*) serpentino, -a **2.** (*twisting*) serpenteante **3.** (*complicated*) complicado, -a **4.** (*sly*) ingenioso, -a; (*explanation*) artificioso, -a

serrated [sɪˈreɪtɪd, *Am:* ˈsereɪt̬ɪd] *adj* serrado, -a; ~ **knife** cuchillo *m* de sierra

serried [ˈserɪd] *adj liter* apretado, -a; ~ **ranks** filas *fpl* cerradas

serum [ˈsɪərəm, *Am:* ˈsɪrəm] <-s *o* sera> *n* suero *m*

servant [ˈsɜːvənt, *Am:* ˈsɜːr-] *n* criado, -a *m, f*, mucamo, -a *m, f AmL*

serve [sɜːv, *Am:* sɜːrv] **I.** *n* SPORTS saque *m* **II.** *vt* **1.** (*attend*) atender **2.** (*provide*) servir; **to ~ alcohol** servir bebidas alcohólicas **3.** (*be enough for*) ser suficiente **4.** (*work for*) estar al servicio de; **to ~ sb's interests** servir a los intereses de alguien **5.** (*complete: sentence, mandate*) cumplir; **to ~ time** (**for sth**) *inf* cumplir condena (por algo) **6.** (*help achieve*) ser útil a; **if my memory ~s me right** si la memoria no me falla **7.** SPORTS sacar **8.** (*deliver*) entregar; **to ~ sb with papers** proporcionar papeles a alguien ▸**it ~s him/her right!** ¡se lo merece! **III.** *vi* **1.** (*put food on plates*) servir **2.** (*be useful*) servir; **to ~ as sth** servir de algo **3.** (*work for*) prestar servicio; **to ~ in the army** servir en el ejército **4.** (*be acceptable*) ser aceptable; (*suffice*) ser suficiente **5.** SPORTS sacar

◆**serve out** *vt* **1.** GASTR servir **2.** (*sentence, mandate*) cumplir

◆**serve up** *vt* GASTR servir; *fig* ofrecer

server [ˈsɜːvəʳ, *Am:* ˈsɜːrvɚ] *n* **1.** (*spoon*) cuchara *f* de servir; **salad ~s** cubiertos *mpl* para servir ensalada **2.** (*tray*) bandeja *f;* (*dish*) fuente *f* **3.** (*waiter*) camarero, -a *m, f* **4.** INFOR servidor *m* **5.** SPORTS *jugador que tiene el saque*

service [ˈsɜːvɪs, *Am:* ˈsɜːr-] **I.** *n* **1.** *no pl* (*in shop, restaurant*) servicio *m* **2.** (*help, assistance*) asistencia *f*, servicio *m;* **bus/train** ~ servicio de autobuses/trenes; **to be of ~** (**to sb**) ser de utilidad (a alguien); **to operate a ~** llevar a cabo un servicio; **to press sth into ~** recurrir a algo; **to see ~** *fig* prestar servicio **3.** (*department*) servicio *m;* **the Service** MIL el ejército; NAUT la marina; AVIAT la aviación; **to be fit/unfit for ~** ser apto/no apto para el servicio **4.** SPORTS saque *m* **5.** REL oficio *m;* **morning ~** misa matinal; **to hold a ~** celebrar una misa **6.** *Brit* TECH mantenimiento *m;* AUTO revisión *f* **7.** (*set*) vajilla *f;* **tea ~** juego *m* de té **8.** *pl, Brit* área *f* de servicio ▸**to be at sb's ~** *iron* estar al servicio de alguien; **to be in ~** (*employed as servant*) estar empleado como criado; (*be in use*) estar en uso **II.** *vt* **1.** (*car, TV*) revisar **2.** FIN **to ~ a loan** pagar el interés de un préstamo

serviceable [ˈsɜːvɪsəbl, *Am:* ˈsɜːr-] *adj* servible

service area *n* área *f* de servicio **service bus** *n*, **service car** *n Aus* coche *m* de línea **service center** *n Am* **1.** (*on motorway*) área *f* de servicios **2.** (*for repairs*) centro *m* de reparaciones; (*garage*) garaje *m* **service charge** *n* gastos *mpl* de servicio **service department** *n* sección *f* de mantenimiento **service elevator** *n Am* (*for employees*) ascensor *m* para empleados; (*for goods*) montacargas *m inv* **service entrance** *n* entrada *f* de servicio **service hatch** *n* ventanilla *f* para servir **service industry** *n* sector *m* servicios **service lift** *n Brit* (*for employees*) ascensor *m* para empleados; (*for goods*) montacargas *m inv* **serviceman** *n* militar *m* **service road** *n* vía *f* de acceso **service sector** *n* sector *m* (de) servicios **service**

station *n* 1.(*selling gasoline*) estación *f* de servicio 2. *Brit* (*on motorway*) área *f* de servicio **servicewoman** *n* militar *f*
serviette [ˌsɜːvɪˈet, *Am:* ˌsɜːr-] *n Brit* servilleta *f*
servile [ˈsɜːvaɪl, *Am:* ˈsɜːrvl] *adj pej* servil
servility [sɜːˈvɪləti, *Am:* sɜːrˈvɪləţi] *n no pl, pej* servilismo *m*
serving [ˈsɜːvɪŋ, *Am:* ˈsɜːr-] I. *n* (*portion*) ración *f* II. *adj* activo
serving hatch *n* ventanilla *f* para servir **serving spoon** *n* cuchara *f* de servir
servitude [ˈsɜːvɪtjuːd, *Am:* ˈsɜːrvətuːd] *n no pl, form* servidumbre *f*
servo [ˈsɜːvəʊ, *Am:* ˈsɜːrvoʊ] *n* servo *m*
sesame [ˈsesəmi] *n no pl* sésamo *m* ►open ~! ¡ábrete, sésamo!
session [ˈseʃən] *n* 1.(*meeting*) sesión *f*; **to be in** ~ estar reunido; **a drinking** ~ *inf* una borrachera 2. *Am, Scot* SCHOOL clase *f*; (*teaching year*) curso *m*
set [set] I. *adj* 1.(*ready*) listo, -a; **to get** ~ (**to do sth**) prepararse (para hacer algo) 2.(*fixed*) fijo, -a; **to be** ~ **in one's ways** tener costumbres profundamente arraigadas 3.(*assigned*) asignado, -a II. *n* 1.(*group: of people*) grupo *m*; (*of cups, chess*) juego *m*; (*of kitchen utensils*) batería *f*; (*of stamps*) serie *f*; (*of tools*) set *m*; ~ **of glasses** cristalería *f*; ~ **of teeth** dentadura *f* 2.(*collection*) colección *f* 3. CINE plató *m* 4.(*television*) televisor *m* 5.(*in tennis*) set *m* 6.(*musical performance*) actuación *f*; **to play a long/short** ~ tocar durante mucho/poco tiempo III. *vt* <set, set> 1.(*place*) poner, colocar; **a house that is** ~ **on a hill** una casa situada sobre una colina; **to** ~ **a broken bone** colocar bien un hueso roto 2.(*give: task*) imponer; (*problem*) plantear; (*example*) dar 3.(*start*) **to** ~ **a boat afloat** poner una barca a flote; **to** ~ **sth on fire** prender fuego algo; **to** ~ **sth in motion** poner algo en movimiento; **to** ~ **the country on the road to economic recovery** encaminar el país hacia la recuperación económica; **to set a dog on sb** hacer que un perro ataque a alguien 4.(*adjust*) ajustar; (*prepare*) preparar; **to** ~ **the table** poner la mesa 5.(*fix*) fijar; (*record*) establecer; (*date, price*) determinar; **to** ~ **oneself a goal** fijarse un objetivo 6.(*arrange*) acordar 7.(*encrust*) adornar; (*insert*) introducir; **to** ~ **a watch with sapphires** engastar zafiros en un reloj 8.(*provide*) poner; **to** ~ **sth to music** poner música a algo IV. *vi* 1. MED soldarse 2.(*become firm: cement*) endurecerse; (*jelly, cheese*) cuajar 3.(*sink*) hundirse 4.(*sun*) ponerse
◆**set about** *vt* 1.(*begin*) emprender; **to** ~ **doing sth** comenzar a hacer algo 2. *inf* (*attack*) atacar
◆**set against** *vt* 1.(*compare*) comparar; **to set the advantages against the disadvantages** sopesar las ventajas y los inconvenientes 2.(*offset*) compensar 3.(*make oppose*) **to set sb against sb/sth** poner a alguien en contra de alguien/algo
◆**set apart** *vt* 1.(*distinguish*) diferenciar 2.(*reserve*) reservar
◆**set aside** *vt* 1.(*save*) reservar; (*time*) guardar; (*money*) ahorrar 2.(*ignore*) ignorar; **to set one's differences aside** dejar a un lado las diferencias con alguien 3.(*overturn*) desechar 4.(*put to side*) dejar de lado
◆**set back** *vt* 1.(*delay*) retrasar 2.(*place away from*) apartar 3. *inf* (*cost*) costar
◆**set down** *vt* 1.(*land*) poner en tierra; (*aeroplane*) hacer aterrizar 2.(*drop off*) dejar 3.(*write*) poner por escrito; (*record*) registrar
◆**set forth** I. *vt form s.* **set out** II. *vi liter* partir
◆**set off** I. *vi* partir; **to** ~ (**for a place**) ponerse en camino (hacia un lugar) II. *vt* 1. accionar 2.(*detonate*) hacer explotar; (*explosive*) detonar 3.(*cause*) causar 4.(*enhance*) hacer; **to set sb off** (**doing sth**) hacer [*o* provocar] que alguien (haga algo)
◆**set on** *vt* atacar
◆**set out** I. *vt* 1.(*display, arrange*) disponer, colocar 2.(*explain*) exponer II. *vi* 1. *s.* **set off** 2.(*intend*) **to** ~ **to do sth** tener la intención de hacer algo
◆**set to** *vi* 1.(*begin*) ponerse manos a la obra 2. *inf* (*begin fighting*) llegar a las manos; **to** ~ **with sb** empezar a pelearse con alguien
◆**set up** *vt* 1.(*prepare*) poner, construir 2.(*establish*) establecer; (*arrange*) disponer; (*cause*) causar; (*committee*) constituir; (*corporation*) crear; (*dictatorship*) instaurar 3.(*claim*) **to set oneself up as sth** dárselas de algo 4.(*make healthy*) fortalecer 5.(*provide*) proveer 6. *inf* (*deceive*) defraudar
setback [ˈsetbæk] *n* revés *m*; **to experience a** ~ tener un contratiempo
set square *n Aus, Brit* cartabón *m*
settee [seˈtiː] *n* sofá *m*
setter [ˈsetəʳ, *Am:* ˈseţɚ] *n* (*dog*) setter *mf*
setting [ˈsetɪŋ, *Am:* ˈseţ-] *n* 1.(*of sun*) puesta *f* 2.(*scenery*) escenario *m*; (*surroundings*) entorno *m*; (*landscape*) marco *m* 3. TECH ajuste *m* 4.(*frame for jewel*) engaste *m* 5. MUS arreglo *m*
setting lotion *n* fijador *m* (para el pelo)
settle [ˈsetl, *Am:* ˈseţ-] I. *vi* 1.(*take up residence*) instalarse 2.(*get comfortable*) ponerse cómodo, -a 3.(*calm down*) calmarse; (*weather*) serenarse; (*situation*) normalizarse, aconcharse *Chile* 4. *Aus, Brit* (*apply oneself*) aplicarse; **to** ~ **to work** ponerse a trabajar en serio 5.(*reach an agreement*) llegar a un acuerdo 6. *form* (*pay*) pagar; **to** ~ **with sb** saldar las cuentas con alguien 7.(*accumulate*) acumularse; (*snow*) cuajar 8.(*land*) asentarse; (*bird*) posarse 9.(*sink*) hundirse 10.(*food*) asentarse en el estómago II. *vt* 1.(*calm down: stomach*) calmar 2.(*decide*) acordar; **it's been ~d that ...** se ha acordado que... 3.(*conclude*) finalizar; (*resolve*) resolver;

S

(*problem*) solucionar; (*affairs*) arreglar; **to ~ a lawsuit** poner fin a un litigio **4.** (*pay*) pagar; (*an account*) liquidar **5.** (*colonize*) colonizar ►**that ~s it!** ¡ya no hay más que decir!

◆**settle down** **I.** *vi* **1.** (*take up residence*) instalarse **2.** (*get comfortable*) ponerse cómodo, -a **3.** (*adjust*) adaptarse **4.** (*calm down*) calmarse **II.** *vt* **to set oneself down to sth** acostumbrarse a algo

◆**settle for** *vt* contentarse con

◆**settle in** *vi* acostumbrarse

◆**settle on** *vt* **1.** (*decide on*) decidir **2.** (*agree on*) acordar **3.** (*bequeath*) dejar

◆**settle up** *vi* ajustar cuentas

◆**settle upon** *vt form s.* **settle on**

settled ['setld, *Am:* 'set̬-] *adj* **1.** (*established*) establecido, -a; (*in a regular way of life*) instalado, -a; **to feel ~** sentirse cómodo **2.** (*calm*) calmado, -a **3.** (*fixed*) fijo, -a

settlement ['setlmənt, *Am:* 'set̬-] *n* **1.** (*resolution*) resolución *f;* (*of strike*) finalización *f* **2.** (*agreement*) acuerdo *m;* **to negotiate a ~ (with sb)** negociar un acuerdo (con alguien) **3.** FIN, ECON liquidación *f,* pago *m;* **in ~ of sth** para liquidar algo **4.** (*village, town*) asentamiento *m;* (*act of colonization*) colonización *f* **5.** *no pl* (*subsidence*) hundimiento *m*

settlement date *n* FIN fecha *f* de resolución

settler ['setləʳ, *Am:* 'set̬lɚ] *n* colono, -a *m, f*

set-to ['settuː] *n inf* bronca *f;* **to have a ~ (with sb)** tener una bronca (con alguien)

set-up ['setʌp, *Am:* 'set̬-] *n* **1.** (*way things are arranged*) estructura *f;* (*arrangement*) organización *f* **2.** *inf* (*trick*) trampa *f*

seven ['sevn] **I.** *adj* siete *inv* **II.** *n* siete *m; s. a.* **eight**

sevenfold ['sevnfəʊld, *Am:* -foʊld] **I.** *adj* séptuplo, -a **II.** *adv* **to increase ~** aumentar en siete veces

seventeen [ˌsevn'tiːn] **I.** *adj* diecisiete *inv* **II.** *n* diecisiete *m; s. a.* **eight**

seventeenth [ˌsevn'tiːnθ] **I.** *adj* decimoséptimo, -a **II.** *n no pl* **1.** (*order*) decimoséptimo, -a *m, f* **2.** (*date*) diecisiete *m* **3.** (*fraction*) diecisieteavo *m;* (*part*) diecisieteava parte *f; s. a.* **eighth**

seventh ['sevəntθ] **I.** *adj* séptimo, -a **II.** *n no pl* **1.** (*order*) séptimo, -a *m, f* **2.** (*date*) siete *m* **3.** (*fraction*) séptimo *m;* (*part*) octava parte *f; s. a.* **eighth**

seventieth ['sevəntiθ] **I.** *adj* septuagésimo, -a **II.** *n no pl* (*order*) septuagésimo, -a *m, f;* (*fraction*) septuagésimo *m;* (*part*) septuagésima parte *f; s. a.* **eighth**

seventy ['sevənti, *Am:* -t̬i] **I.** *adj* setenta *inv* **II.** *n* <-ies> setenta *m; s. a.* **eighty**

sever ['sevəʳ, *Am:* 'sevɚ] *vt* (*limb, branch*) cortar; (*relationship*) romper

several ['sevərəl] **I.** *adj* **1.** (*some*) varios, -as; (*reasons*) diversos, -as; **~ times** varias veces; (*distinct*) distintos, -as **2.** (*individual*) respectivos, -as **II.** *pron* (*some*) algunos, -as; (*different*) varios, -as; **~ of us** algunos de nosotros; **we've got ~** tenemos varios

severally *adv* **1.** (*individually*) respectivamente **2.** (*separately*) por separado

severance ['sevərənts] *n no pl, form* ruptura *f*

severance pay *n* indemnización *f* por despido

severe [sɪ'vɪəʳ, *Am:* sə'vɪr] *adj* **1.** (*problem, illness*) grave; (*pain*) fuerte; **to be under ~ strain** estar bajo una gran tensión **2.** (*criticism, punishment, person*) severo, -a; (*strict*) estricto, -a; (*rough*) duro, -a **3.** (*weather*) riguroso, -a; **~ frost** fuerte helada *f* **4.** (*austere*) austero, -a

severely *adv* **1.** (*harshly*) con severidad **2.** (*damaged*) seriamente; (*ill*) gravemente

severity [sɪ'verəti, *Am:* sə'verət̬i] *n no pl* **1.** (*of illness, problem*) gravedad *f* **2.** (*of criticism, punishment, person*) severidad *f* **3.** (*austerity*) austeridad *f*

Seville [sə'vɪl] *n* Sevilla *f*

sew [səʊ, *Am:* soʊ] <sewed, sewn *o* sewed> **I.** *vt* coser; **hand ~n** cosido a mano **II.** *vi* coser

◆**sew on** *vt* coser

◆**sew up** *vt* **1.** (*repair*) coser, zurcir **2.** MED suturar **3.** *inf* (*arrange*) arreglar; **to ~ a deal** cerrar un trato

sewage ['suːɪdʒ] *n no pl* aguas *fpl* residuales

sewage farm *n,* **sewage plant** *n* ECOL planta *f* de tratamiento de aguas residuales

sewer ['səʊəʳ, *Am:* 'soʊɚ] *n* alcantarilla *f*

sewerage ['sʊərɪdʒ, *Am:* 'suːɚɪdʒ] *n no pl* alcantarillado *m,* drenaje *m Méx*

sewer rat *n* rata *f* de alcantarilla

sewing ['səʊɪŋ, *Am:* 'soʊ-] **I.** *n no pl* costura *f* **II.** *adj* de costura

sewing basket *n* costurero *m* **sewing machine** *n* máquina *f* de coser

sewn [səʊn, *Am:* soʊn] *pp of* **sew**

sex [seks] **I.** <-es> *n* (*gender, intercourse*) sexo *m;* **to have ~** tener relaciones sexuales **II.** *vt* determinar el sexo de

sex appeal *n no pl* atractivo *m* sexual **sex discrimination** *n no pl* discriminación *f* sexual **sex education** *n no pl* educación *f* sexual

sexism ['seksɪzəm] *n no pl* sexismo *m*

sexist **I.** *adj* sexista **II.** *n* sexista *mf*

sexless ['sekslǝs] *adj* sin sexo

sex life *n no pl* vida *f* sexual **sex symbol** *n* símbolo *m* sexual

sextant ['sekstənt] *n* sextante *m*

sextet [seks'tet] *n* sexteto *m*

sexton ['sekstən] *n* sacristán *m*

sexual ['sekʃʊəl, *Am:* -ʃuəl] *adj* sexual

sexual harassment *n* acoso *m* sexual **sexual intercourse** *n* relaciones *fpl* sexuales

sexuality [ˌsekʃʊ'æləti, *Am:* -ʃu'ælət̬i] *n no pl* sexualidad *f*

sexually *adv* sexualmente; **to be ~ abused** ser víctima de abusos sexuales

sexy ['seksi] <-ier, -iest> *adj inf* **1.** (*physi-*

cally appealing) sexy **2.** (*exciting*) excitante

Seychelles [seɪ'ʃelz] *n* Islas *fpl* Seychelles

SGML *n* INFOR *abbr of* **Standard General Markup Language** SGML *m*

Sgt *n abbr of* **sergeant** Sgto. *m*

shabby ['ʃæbi] <-ier, -iest> *adj* **1.** (*badly maintained*) deteriorado, -a **2.** (*poorly dressed*) desharrapado, -a, encuerado, -a *Méx, Cuba* **3.** (*mean*) mezquino, -a; (*trick*) sucio, -a

shack [ʃæk] *n* choza *f,* ruca *f Arg, Chile,* jacal *m Méx*

◆**shack up** *vi* irse a vivir juntos, arrejuntarse *Méx*

shackle ['ʃækl] **I.** *vt* poner grilletes a, encadenar **II.** *n pl* grilletes *mpl*

shade [ʃeɪd] **I.** *n* **1.** *no pl* (*shadow*) sombra *f;* (*of a painting*) sombreado *m;* **in the ~ of** a [*o* en] la sombra de **2.** (*covering*) pantalla *f* **3.** *pl, Am* (*roller blind*) persiana *f* **4.** (*variation*) matiz *m;* (*of colour*) tono *m;* **pastel ~s** tonos pastel **5.** *no pl* (*small amount*) pizca *f* **6.** *pl, inf* (*glasses*) gafas *fpl* de sol **7.** *inf* (*resemblance*) **~s of Nixon/1989** esto recuerda a Nixon/1989 ►**to leave sb/sth in the ~** eclipsar a alguien/algo **II.** *vt* **1.** (*cast shadow on*) dar sombra a; (*protect*) resguardar (de la luz) **2.** ART sombrear **III.** *vi* (*colours*) fundirse

shading *n no pl* sombreado *m*

shadow ['ʃædəʊ, *Am:* -oʊ] **I.** *n* **1.** *a. fig* sombra *f;* **the ~s** las tinieblas **2.** (*smallest trace*) pizca *f;* **without a ~ of a doubt** sin sombra de duda ►**to have ~s under one's eyes** tener ojeras; **to be a ~ of one's former self** no ser ni la sombra de lo que se era; **to be afraid of one's own ~** tener miedo de la propia sombra; **to cast a ~ over sth** ensombrecer algo; **to wear oneself to a ~** agotarse; **to be under sb's ~** estar a la sombra de alguien **II.** *vt* **1.** ART sombrear **2.** (*darken*) ensombrecer **3.** (*follow*) seguir **4.** FIN seguir

shadow-boxing ['ʃædəʊbɒksɪŋ, *Am:* -oʊbɑːksɪŋ] *n no pl* **1.** SPORTS *boxeo con un adversario imaginario* **2.** *fig* disputa *f* con un adversario imaginario

shadowy <-ier, -iest> *adj* **1.** (*containing darker spaces*) sombreado, -a; (*photograph*) oscuro, -a **2.** (*vague*) impreciso, -a **3.** (*suspicious*) sombrío, -a

shady ['ʃeɪdi] <-ier, -iest> *adj* **1.** (*protected from light*) sombreado, -a **2.** *inf* (*dubious*) turbio, -a; (*character*) sospechoso, -a

shaft [ʃɑːft, *Am:* ʃæft] **I.** *n* **1.** (*of tool*) mango *m;* (*of weapon*) asta *f;* (*of arrow*) venablo *m* **2.** TECH eje *m* **3.** (*ray*) rayo *m* **4.** (*for elevator*) hueco *m;* (*of mine*) pozo *m;* **well ~** pozo ►**to give sb the ~** *Am, inf* joder a alguien **II.** *vt inf* (*have sex with, defeat*) joder

shag[1] [ʃæg] <-gg-> *vi Brit, Aus, vulg* follar, coger *Méx*

shag[2] [ʃæg] *n vulg* polvo *m*

shagged out [ʃægd'aʊt] *adj Brit, Aus, pej, inf* hecho, -a polvo

shaggy ['ʃægi] <-ier, -iest> *adj* peludo, -a; (*coat*) lanudo, -a ►**~ dog story** chiste *m* malo

shah [ʃɑː] *n* sha *m*

shake [ʃeɪk] **I.** *n* **1.** (*wobble*) sacudida *f;* (*vibration*) vibración *f;* (*quiver*) temblor *m;* **with a ~ in one's voice** con la voz temblorosa **2.** *pl* tembleque *m,* temblorina *f Méx;* **to get the ~s** *inf* tener miedo **3.** *Am, inf* (*milk shake*) batido *m,* malteada *f AmL* **4.** *inf* **in two ~s of a duck's tail** en un santiamén; **to be no great ~s** no ser gran cosa; **to be no great ~s (at doing sth)** no ser nada del otro mundo (en algo); **I'm no great ~s as a singer** no se me da muy bien cantar **II.** <shook, shaken> *vt* **1.** (*joggle*) agitar; (*person*) sacudir; (*head*) mover; (*hand*) estrechar; (*house*) hacer temblar; **to ~ one's fist (at sb)** amenazar con el puño (a alguien); **to ~ hands** darse la mano; **to ~ sb by the hand** estrechar la mano de alguien; **to ~ one's head** negar con la cabeza; **to ~ one's hips** mover las caderas **2.** (*unsettle*) debilitar **3.** (*make worried*) desconcertar **III.** <shook, shaken> *vi* temblar; **~ well before opening** agitar bien antes de abrir

◆**shake down** *vt inf* **1.** hacer caer sacudiendo **2.** *Am* (*cheat*) timar

◆**shake off** *vt* **1.** (*agitate to remove*) sacudirse **2.** (*eliminate: cold*) quitarse (de encima); (*pursuer, feeling*) librarse de

◆**shake out** *vt* sacudir

◆**shake up** *vt* **1.** (*jumble*) sacudir, zamarronear *Chile* **2.** (*make worried*) desconcertar **3.** (*reorganize*) reorganizar

shakedown ['ʃeɪkdaʊn] *n inf* **1.** (*bed*) cama *f* improvisada **2.** *Am* (*search*) redada *f,* arreada *f Arg* **3.** *Am* (*extortion*) exacción *f* de dinero

shaken ['ʃeɪkn] *vi, vt pp of* **shake**

shaker ['ʃeɪkə^r, *Am:* -kɚ] *n* (*for cocktails*) coctelera *f;* **salt ~** salero *m*

shake-up ['ʃeɪkʌp] *n* reorganización *f*

shakily ['ʃeɪkɪli] *adv* **1.** (*physically weak*) de modo inestable **2.** (*uncertainly*) con poca firmeza

shaking ['ʃeɪkɪŋ] **I.** *n* temblor *m* **II.** *adj* tembloroso, -a

shaky ['ʃeɪki] <-ier, -iest> *adj* **1.** (*jerky*) tembloroso, -a; **to be ~ on one's feet** estar inseguro al andar **2.** (*wavering*) inseguro, -a **3.** (*unstable*) inestable; (*economy*) débil

shale [ʃeɪl] *n no pl* esquisto *m*

shall [ʃæl] *aux* **1.** (*future*) **I ~ give back the money** devolveré el dinero; **we ~ win the match** ganaremos el partido **2.** (*ought to*) **he ~ call his mother** debería llamar a su madre; **we ~ overcome!** ¡nos sobrepondremos! **3.** (*expresses what is mandatory*) **that ~ be unlawful** eso es ilegal

shallot [ʃə'lɒt, *Am:* -'lɑːt] *n* chalote *m,* cebolleta *f AmL*

shallow ['ʃæləʊ, *Am:* -oʊ] **I.** *adj* **1.** (*not deep*) poco profundo, -a **2.** (*only light*) débil **3.** (*superficial*) superficial **II.** *npl* bajío *m*

shallowness *n no pl* **1.** (*lack of depth*) poca profundidad *f* **2.** (*superficiality*) superficialidad *f*

sham [ʃæm] *pej* **I.** *n* **1.** (*imposture*) impostura *f;* (*fake*) fraude *m* **2.** (*impostor*) impostor(a) *m(f)* **II.** *adj* (*document, trial*) falso, -a; (*deal*) fraudulento, -a; (*sympathy*) hipócrita; (*marriage*) simulado, -a **III.** <-mm-> *vt* fingir **IV.** *vi* fingir

shamble ['ʃæmbl] *vi* arrastrar los pies

shambles ['ʃæmblz] *n inf* (*place*) escombrera *f;* (*situation*) confusión *f*

shambolic [ʃæm'bɒlɪk, *Am:* -'bɑ:lɪk] *adj Brit, inf* caótico, -a

shame [ʃeɪm] **I.** *n no pl* **1.** (*humiliation*) vergüenza *f,* pena *f AmC;* **to die of** ~ morirse de vergüenza; **to feel no** ~ no sentir vergüenza; **to put sb to** ~ avergonzar a alguien; **to my** ~ **...** para vergüenza mía...; ~ **on you!** *a. iron* ¡debería darte vergüenza! **2.** (*discredit*) deshonra *f;* **to bring** ~ **on sb** deshonrar a alguien **3.** (*pity*) pena *f;* **what a** ~**!** ¡qué pena!; **what a** ~ **that ...** qué lástima que *+subj;* **it's a** ~ **to have to** *+infin* es una pena tener que *+infin;* **it's a** ~ **that ...** es una pena que... *+subj;* **it's a crying** ~ es una verdadera lástima **II.** *vt* **1.** (*mortify*) avergonzar **2.** (*discredit*) deshonrar

shamefaced [ˌʃeɪm'feɪst, *Am:* '--] *adj* abochornado, -a, apenado, -a *AmC*

shameful ['ʃeɪmfəl] *adj pej* **1.** (*causing disgrace*) vergonzoso, -a, penoso, -a *AmC* **2.** (*outrageous*) bochornoso, -a; **it's** ~ **that ...** es vergonzoso que... *+subj*

shameless ['ʃeɪmlɪs] *adj pej* descarado, -a, conchudo, -a *AmL,* pechugón, -ona *AmL,* vaquetón, -ona *Méx*

shammy ['ʃæmi] <-ies> *n inf no pl, inf* gamuza *f*

shampoo [ʃæm'pu:] **I.** *n* champú *m;* ~ **and set** lavar y peinar **II.** *vt* lavar con champú

shamrock ['ʃæmrɒk, *Am:* -rɑ:k] *n* trébol *m*

shandy ['ʃændi] <-ies> *n Brit, Aus* clara *f*

shank [ʃæŋk] *n* **1.** TECH mango *m* **2.** (*leg*) pata *f;* (*of bird*) zanca *f* ►**to go on** ~**'s pony** ir en el coche de San Fernando, ir a pata *Méx*

shanty¹ ['ʃænti, *Am:* -t̬i] <-ies> *n* (*shack*) chabola *f,* favela *f AmL,* choza *f Méx*

shanty² ['ʃænti, *Am:* -t̬i] *n* (*song*) saloma *f*

shanty town *n* chabolas *fpl,* favelas *fpl AmL,* barriada *f Perú,* ciudad *f* perdida *Méx,* villa *f* miseria *RíoPl*

shape [ʃeɪp] **I.** *n* **1.** (*form*) forma *f;* **to get out of** ~, **to lose** ~ perder la forma; **to take** ~ adquirir forma; **in the** ~ **of sth** en forma de algo; **the** ~ **of things to come** lo que nos espera **2.** *no pl* (*condition*) condición *f;* **in bad/good** ~ en malas/buenas condiciones; **to get sth into** ~ acondicionar algo; **to get into** ~ ponerse en forma; **to knock** [*o* **lick** *Am*] **sth/sb into** ~ poner algo/a alguien a punto **II.** *vt* **1.** (*form*) **to** ~ **sth into sth** dar a algo la forma de algo **2.** (*influence*) influenciar **3.** (*determine*) condicionar

shapeless ['ʃeɪpləs] *adj* **1.** (*without definite shape*) informe **2.** (*not shapely*) deforme

shapely ['ʃeɪpli] <-ier, -iest> *adj* bien proporcionado, -a; (*leg*) torneado, -a; (*person*) de buen talle

shard [ʃɑ:d, *Am:* ʃɑ:rd] *n* casco *m,* tepalcate *m Guat, Méx*

share [ʃeəʳ, *Am:* ʃer] **I.** *n* **1.** (*part*) parte *f,* porción *f;* **the lion's** ~ la mayor parte; **to go** ~**s on sth** ir a medias en algo, ir a mitas con algo *Méx* **2.** (*participation*) participación *f* **3.** FIN acción *f;* **stocks and** ~**s** acciones y participaciones; **to have** ~**s in sth** tener acciones en algo **II.** *vi* **1.** (*divide*) repartir **2.** (*allow others to use*) compartir ►**to** ~ **and** ~ **alike** compartir las cosas **III.** *vt* **1.** (*divide*) dividir **2.** (*have in common*) compartir; **to** ~ **sb's view** compartir las opiniones de alguien; **to want to** ~ **one's life with sb** querer compartir la vida con alguien

◆**share out** *vt* dividir

share capital *n* capital *m* social **share certificate** *n* título *m* de acción

sharecropper ['ʃeəˌkrɒpəʳ, *Am:* 'ʃerˌkrɑ:pɚ] *n* aparcero, -a *m, f*

shareholder ['ʃeəˌhəʊldəʳ, *Am:* 'ʃerˌhoʊldɚ] *n* accionista *mf*

shareholding *n* participación *f* accionaria

share index *n* índice *m* bursátil **share issue** *n* emisión *f* de acciones **share option** *n* opción *f* de compra de acciones

share-out ['ʃeəraʊt, *Am:* 'ʃeraʊt] *n* reparto *m*

share price *n* FIN cotización *f* de las acciones

shareware ['ʃeəweəʳ, *Am:* 'ʃerwer] *n no pl* INFOR shareware *m,* programa *m* compartido

shark [ʃɑ:k, *Am:* ʃɑ:rk] <-(s)> *n* **1.** (*fish*) tiburón *m* **2.** *pej, inf* (*person*) estafador(a) *m(f)*

sharp [ʃɑ:p, *Am:* ʃɑ:rp] **I.** *adj* **1.** (*cutting*) afilado, -a; (*pointed*) puntiagudo, -a **2.** (*angular: feature*) anguloso, -a; (*corner, edge, angle*) agudo, -a; (*curve*) cerrado, -a **3.** (*severe*) severo, -a; (*pain*) agudo, -a, intenso, -a; (*look*) penetrante; (*reprimand*) violento, -a; **to have a** ~ **tongue** tener una lengua afilada [*o* viperina]; **to be** ~ **with sb** ser mordaz con alguien **4.** (*astute*) astuto, -a; (*perceptive*) perspicaz, alicuz *Hond;* (*mind*) vivo, -a **5.** (*pungent*) acre; (*wine*) ácido, -a **6.** (*sudden*) súbito, -a; (*abrupt*) abrupto, -a; (*marked*) pronunciado, -a **7.** (*penetrating*) penetrante; (*storm*) fuerte; (*sound*) agudo, -a; (*fight*) encarnizado, -a **8.** (*distinct*) nítido, -a **9.** MUS sostenido, -a; **C** ~ do sostenido **II.** *adv* **1.** (*exactly*) en punto; **at ten o'clock** ~ a las diez en punto **2.** (*suddenly*) de repente; **to pull up** ~ frenar en seco **3.** MUS desafinadamente **III.** *n* MUS sostenido *m*

sharpen ['ʃɑ:pən, *Am:* 'ʃɑ:r-] *vt* **1.** (*blade*) afilar; (*pencil*) sacar punta a **2.** (*intensify*) agudizar; (*mind*) aguzar; (*appetite*) abrir

sharpener ['ʃɑ:pənəʳ, *Am:* 'ʃɑ:rpənɚ] *n* afilador *m,* afiladora *f Méx;* **pencil** ~ sacapuntas *m inv*

sharper [ˈʃɑːpəʳ, *Am:* ˈʃɑːrpɚ] *n inf* (*cheat*) estafador(a) *m(f)*; (*at cards*) fullero(a) *m(f)*

sharp-eyed [ʃɑːpˈaɪd, *Am:* ʃɑːrpˈ-] *adj* observador(a)

sharpness *n no pl* **1.** (*of blade*) filo *m;* (*of pencil*) punta *f* **2.** (*of pain*) agudeza *f* **3.** (*of comment*) mordacidad *f* **4.** (*suddenness: of curve*) brusquedad *f* **5.** (*intensity*) intensidad *f;* (*of blow*) violencia *f* **6.** (*clarity*) nitidez *f* **7.** (*perceptiveness*) perspicacia *f;* (*intelligence*) astucia *f* **8.** (*chic*) elegancia *f*

sharp practice *n* artimañas *fpl*

sharpshooter [ˈʃɑːpˌʃuːtəʳ, *Am:* ˈʃɑːrpˌʃuːt̬ɚ] *n* tirador(a) *m(f)* de primera

sharp-sighted [ˌʃɑːpˈsaɪtɪd, *Am:* ˈʃɑːrpˌsaɪt̬ɪd] *adj* **1.** (*very observant*) de vista aguda **2.** (*alert*) sagaz **sharp-tempered** *adj* malhumorado, -a **sharp-tongued** *adj* mordaz **sharp-witted** *adj* agudo, -a

shat [ʃæt] *pt, pp of* **shit**

shatter [ˈʃætəʳ, *Am:* ˈʃæt̬ɚ] **I.** *vi* hacerse añicos **II.** *vt* **1.** (*smash*) hacer añicos, destrozar **2.** (*disturb*) perturbar; (*unity*) destruir **3.** (*exhaust*) cansar; **to be ~ed** estar rendido

shattering *adj* tremendo, -a

shatterproof [ˈʃætəpruːf, *Am:* ˈʃæt̬ɚ-] *adj* inastillable

shave [ʃeɪv] **I.** *n* afeitado *m,* rasurada *f Méx;* **to have a ~** afeitarse ►**to have a close ~** librarse por los pelos **II.** *vi* afeitarse **III.** *vt* **1.** (*remove body hair*) afeitar, rasurar *Méx* **2.** (*brush past*) rozar **3.** (*decrease: budget*) recortar

shaven [ˈʃeɪvən] *adj* (*face, legs*) afeitado, -a; (*head*) rapado, -a

shaver [ˈʃeɪvəʳ, *Am:* -vɚ] *n* maquinilla *f* de afeitar, rasuradora *f Méx*

shaving brush *n* brocha *f* de afeitar **shaving cream** *n* crema *f* de afeitar **shaving foam** *n* espuma *f* de afeitar **shaving mirror** *n* espejo *m* para afeitarse **shaving soap** *n* jabón *m* de afeitar

shawl [ʃɔːl, *Am:* ʃɑːl] *n* chal *m*

she [ʃiː] **I.** *pron pers* (*female person or animal*) ella; **~'s my mother** (ella) es mi madre; **~'s gone away but ~'ll be back soon** se ha ido pero regresará pronto; **here ~ comes** ahí viene; **~ who ...** *form* aquélla quien... **II.** *n* **1.** (*animal*) hembra *f* **2.** *inf* (*person*) fémina *f;* (*baby*) it's a ~, es niña

sheaf [ʃiːf, ʃiːvz] <sheaves> *n* (*of wheat*) gavilla *f;* (*of documents*) fajo *m*

shear [ʃɪəʳ, *Am:* ʃɪr] <sheared, sheared *o* shorn> *vt* **1.** (*sheep*) esquilar **2.** (*person*) rapar; **to be shorn of sth** *fig* ser despojado de algo

◆**shear off** *vi* romperse

shears [ʃɪəz, *Am:* ʃɪrz] *npl* (*for sheep*) tijeras *f* de esquilar *pl;* (*for sheep*) tijeras de podar; (*for metal*) cizalla *f*

sheath [ʃiːθ] *n* **1.** (*covering*) funda *f;* (*for knife*) vaina *f,* funda *f AmL* **2.** *Brit* (*condom*) condón *m* **3.** (*dress*) vestido *m* de tubo

sheathe [ʃiːð] *vt* **1.** (*knife*) envainar, enfundar *AmL* **2.** (*cover*) revestir

sheath knife *n* cuchillo *m* de monte

shebang [ʃɪˈbæŋ] *n no pl, Am, inf* **the whole ~** todo el asunto

shed¹ [ʃed] *n* cobertizo *m,* galera *f AmL,* galpón *m AmC,* galerón *m CRi, ElSal*

shed² [ʃed] <shed, shed> **I.** *vt* **1.** (*cast off*) quitarse; (*clothes*) despojarse de; (*hair, weight*) perder; **to ~ one's skin** mudar la piel **2.** (*eliminate*) deshacerse de; (*jobs*) eliminar **3.** (*blood, tears*) derramar; (*light*) emitir **II.** *vi* (*snake*) mudar de piel; (*cat*) pelechar

sheen [ʃiːn] *n no pl* brillo *m*

sheep [ʃiːp] *n* oveja *f;* (*ram*) carnero *m* ►**to separate the ~ from the goats** separar el grano de la paja; **black ~** oveja negra

sheep-dip [ˈʃiːpdɪp] *n* AGR baño *m* desinfectante

sheepdog [ˈʃiːpdɒg, *Am:* -dɑːg] *n* perro *m* pastor

sheepfold [ˈʃiːpfəʊld, *Am:* -foʊld] *n* redil *m,* majada *f CSur*

sheepish [ˈʃiːpɪʃ] *adj* tímido, -a

sheepskin [ˈʃiːpskɪn] *n* piel *f* de borrego

sheer¹ [ʃɪəʳ, *Am:* ʃɪr] **I.** *adj* **1.** (*unmitigated*) puro, -a; (*bliss*) completo, -a; (*boredom, lunacy*) total; **~ coincidence** pura coincidencia **2.** (*vertical*) escarpado, -a; **~ drop** caída *f* en picado **3.** (*thin*) fino, -a; (*diaphanous*) transparente **II.** *adv liter* absolutamente

sheer² [ʃɪəʳ, *Am:* ʃɪr] *vi* NAUT desviarse

sheet [ʃiːt] *n* **1.** (*for bed*) sábana *f* **2.** (*of paper*) hoja *f;* **~ of paper** hoja de papel **3.** (*plate of material*) placa *f;* (*of glass*) lámina *f* **4.** (*perforated set of stamps*) plancha *f* **5.** (*paper with information on*) folleto *m* **6.** (*layer*) capa *f* **7.** (*broad mass*) cortina *f;* **~ of flame** cortina de llamas; **the rain was coming down in ~s** llovía a cántaros

sheet feed *n* INFOR alimentador *m* de papel

sheet lightning *n no pl* fucilazo *m* **sheet metal** *n* metal *m* en planchas **sheet music** *n* partituras *fpl*

sheik(h) [ʃeɪk, *Am:* ʃiːk] *n* jeque *m*

shelf [ʃelf, *pl* ʃelvz] <shelves> *n* **1.** (*for storage*) estante *m;* **to buy sth off the ~** comprar algo hecho; **to put sth on the ~** *fig* arrinconar algo **2.** GEO arrecife *m* ►**to be (left) on the ~** *Brit, Aus, inf* quedarse para vestir santos

shelf life *n no pl* tiempo *m* de conservación

shell [ʃel] **I.** *n* **1.** (*of nut, egg*) cáscara *f;* (*of shellfish, snail*) concha *f;* (*of crab, tortoise*) caparazón *m* **2.** TECH armazón *m;* (*of house*) estructura *f;* (*of ship*) casco *m* **3.** (*gun*) proyectil *m,* cartucho *m AmL* ►**to come out of one's ~** salir del cascarón; **to crawl into one's ~** meterse en su cascarón **II.** *vt* **1.** (*remove shell*) pelar **2.** MIL bombardear **III.** *vi* bombardear

◆**shell out** *inf* **I.** *vt* soltar **II.** *vi* aflojar; **to ~ for sth** apoquinar para algo

shellac [ʃəˈlæk] *n* laca *f*

shellfish ['ʃelfɪʃ] *n* **1.** GASTR marisco *m* **2.** ZOOL (*crustacean*) crustáceo *m;* (*mollusc*) molusco *m*

shell hole *n hoyo que forma un obús al explotar*

shelling *n no pl* bombardeo *m*

shell-shock *n* neurosis *f* de guerra

shell-shocked *adj* que padece neurosis de guerra; *fig* traumatizado, -a

shelter ['ʃeltəʳ, *Am:* -t̬ɚ] **I.** *n* refugio *m;* **to take ~** refugiarse **II.** *vt* resguardar **III.** *vi* refugiarse

sheltered *adj* **1.** (*protected against weather*) abrigado, -a **2.** *pej* (*overprotected*) sobreprotegido, -a **3.** *Am* (*tax-protected*) protegido, -a

shelve [ʃelv] **I.** *vt* **1.** (*delay, postpone*) posponer; POL postergar **2.** (*erect shelves in*) poner estantes **II.** *vi* descender

shelving *n no pl* estantería *f*

shenanigans [ʃɪ'nænɪgənz] *npl* chanchullos *mpl*

shepherd ['ʃepəd, *Am:* -ɚd] **I.** *n* pastor *m* **II.** *vt* (*sheep*) guiar; (*people*) dirigir

shepherdess [ˌʃepə'des, *Am:* 'ʃepɚdɪs] <-es> *n* pastora *f*

shepherd's pie *n* pastel *m* de carne

sherbet ['ʃɜːbət, *Am:* 'ʃɜːr-] *n* **1.** *no pl, Brit, Aus* (*sweet tasting powder*) sidral® *m* **2.** *Am* (*sorbet*) sorbete *m*

sheriff ['ʃerɪf] *n* **1.** *Am* (*official*) sheriff *mf* **2.** *Brit* (*representative*) representante *mf* de la corona **3.** *Scot* (*judge*) juez *mf* principal de un distrito

sherry ['ʃeri] <-ies> *n* jerez *m*

Shetland Islands *n,* **Shetlands** ['ʃetləndz] *npl* Islas *fpl* Shetland

shield [ʃiːld] **I.** *n* **1.** (*armour*) escudo *m* **2.** (*protective layer*) revestimiento *m; fig* caparazón *m* **3.** (*logo*) insignia *f* **4.** (*prize*) placa *f* **5.** *Am* (*badge*) chapa *f* (de policia) **II.** *vt* proteger

shift [ʃɪft] **I.** *vt* **1.** (*change, rearrange*) mover; (*reposition*) cambiar de sitio; **to ~ the blame onto sb** echar la culpa a alguien; **to ~ one's ground** cambiar de opinion; **~ yourself!** (*hurry up*) ¡date prisa!; (*move*) ¡quítate de ahí! **2.** *Am* (*in mechanics: of gears, lanes*) cambiar **3.** *Brit, Aus, inf* (*dispose of*) sacar; (*stain*) quitar **4.** (*sell*) vender **II.** *vi* **1.** (*change, rearrange position*) moverse; (*wind*) cambiar **2.** *inf* (*move over*) correrse **3.** (*fend*) **to ~ for oneself** arreglárselas solo **4.** *inf* (*move very fast*) volar **III.** *n* **1.** (*alteration, change*) cambio *m;* (*of power*) giro *m* **2.** (*linguistic change*) mutación *f* **3.** (*period of work*) turno *m;* **to work in ~s** trabajar por turnos

shifting *adj* movedizo, -a; (*values*) cambiante

shift key *n* tecla *f* de las mayúsculas

shiftless ['ʃɪftləs] *adj pej* (*idle*) holgazán, -ana; (*lacking purpose*) haragán, -ana

shiftwork ['ʃɪftwɜːk, *Am:* -wɜːrk] *n no pl* trabajo *m* por turnos **shiftworker** *n* trabajador(a) *m(f)* por turnos

shifty ['ʃɪfti] <-ier, -iest> *adj* sospechoso, -a; (*eyes*) furtivo, -a

Shiite ['ʃiːaɪt] **I.** *adj* chiíta **II.** *n* chiíta *mf*

shilling ['ʃɪlɪŋ] *n* HIST chelín *m*

shilly-shally ['ʃɪliʃæli] *vi pej, inf* titubear

shimmer ['ʃɪməʳ, *Am:* -ɚ] **I.** *vi* brillar **II.** *n no pl* resplandor *m*

shin [ʃɪn] **I.** *n* **1.** (*leg below knee*) espinilla *f* **2.** *no pl* (*lower leg of beef*) jarrete *m* **II.** <-nn-> *vi* **to ~ down** deslizarse; **to ~ up sth** trepar a algo

shindig ['ʃɪndɪg] *n inf* **1.** (*party*) juerga *f* **2.** *Brit, Aus* (*argument*) escándalo *m;* **to kick up a ~** armar un lío

shine [ʃaɪn] **I.** *n no pl* brillo *m* ►**to take a ~ to sb** sentir simpatía por alguien **II.** <shone *o* shined, shone *o* shined> *vi* **1.** (*moon, sun, stars*) brillar; (*gold, metal*) relucir; (*light*) alumbrar; (*eyes*) resplandecer **2.** (*be gifted*) destacar **III.** <shone *o* shined, shone *o* shined> *vt* **1.** (*point light*) **to ~ a light at sth/sb** alumbrar algo/a alguien con una luz; **to ~ a torch onto sth** iluminar algo con una linterna **2.** (*brighten by polishing*) sacar brillo a; (*shoes*) lustrar

◆**shine down** *vi* brillar

◆**shine out** *vi* **1.** (*be easily seen*) notarse **2.** (*excel*) brillar

shiner ['ʃaɪnəʳ, *Am:* -nɚ] *n inf* ojo *m* morado

shingle ['ʃɪŋgl] *n* **1.** *no pl* (*pebble mass alongside water*) guijarros *mpl* **2.** (*tiles for roof*) teja *f* (de madera)

shingles ['ʃɪŋglz] *n no pl* MED herpes *m*

shining ['ʃaɪnɪŋ] *adj* **1.** (*gleaming*) reluciente, abrillantado, -a *AmL;* (*eyes*) brillante **2.** (*outstanding*) magnífico, -a; **a ~ example** un ejemplo perfecto

shiny ['ʃaɪni] <-ier, -iest> *adj* brillante

ship [ʃɪp] **I.** *n* barco *m;* **passenger ~** buque *m* de pasajeros; **sailing ~** velero *m;* **to board a ~** subir a una embarcación, embarcar **II.** *vt* <-pp-> **1.** (*send by boat*) mandar por barco; **to ~ freight** enviar mercancías por barco **2.** (*transport*) transportar

◆**ship off** *vt* (*goods*) expedir; (*person*) enviar

◆**ship out** *vi* embarcarse

shipboard ['ʃɪpbɔːd, *Am:* -bɔːrd] *adj* **on ~** a bordo

shipbuilder ['ʃɪpˌbɪldəʳ, *Am:* -dɚ] *n* constructor(a) *m(f)* naval

shipbuilding *n no pl* construcción *f* naval

shipload ['ʃɪpləʊd, *Am:* -loʊd] *n* cargamento *m* **shipmate** *n* camarada *mf* de a bordo

shipment ['ʃɪpmənt] *n* **1.** (*quantity*) remesa *f* **2.** *no pl* (*action*) envío *m*

shipowner *n* **1.** (*person*) armador(a) *m(f)* **2.** (*company*) naviera *f*

shipper *n* consignador(a) *m(f);* **wine ~** (*company*) exportadora *f* de vinos

shipping ['ʃɪpɪŋ] *n no pl* **1.** (*ships*) embarcaciones *fpl* **2.** (*freight dispatch*) transporte *m*

shipping agency *n* agencia *f* marítima **shipping agent** *n* consignatario, -a *m, f* **shipping company** *n* compañía *f* naviera **shipping department** *n* departamento *m* de envíos **shipping lane** *n* ruta *f* de navegación **shipping office** *n* agencia *f* marítima

ship's chandler *n* proveedor(a) *m(f)* de buques

shipshape ['ʃɪpʃeɪp] *adj inf* limpio y ordenado; **to get sth ~** tener algo en orden

shipway ['ʃɪpweɪ] *n* canal *m* **shipwreck** I. *n* 1. (*accident*) naufragio *m* 2. (*remains of ship*) restos *mpl* de un naufragio II. *vt* hacer naufragar; **to be ~ed** naufragar; *fig* estar hundido **shipwright** *n* carpintero *m* de navío **shipyard** *n* astillero *m*

shire ['ʃaɪəʳ, *Am:* 'ʃaɪɚ] *n* condado *m*

shire horse *n* caballo *m* de tiro

shirk [ʃɜːk, *Am:* ʃɜːrk] *pej* I. *vt* eludir II. *vi* escaquearse; **to ~ from sth** escaquearse de algo

shirker ['ʃɜːkəʳ, *Am:* 'ʃɜːrkɚ] *n pej* vago, -a *m, f*

shirt [ʃɜːt, *Am:* ʃɜːrt] *n* (*man's, woman's*) camisa *f;* (*woman's*) blusa *f* ►**to give sb the ~ off one's back** dar hasta la camiseta a alguien; **to have the ~ off sb's back** dejar a alguien sin camisa; **to lose one's ~** perder hasta la camisa; **keep your ~ on!** *Am* ¡no te sulfures!; **to put one's ~ on sth** jugarse hasta la camisa en [*o* por] algo

shirt collar *n* cuello *m* de camisa **shirt front** *n* pechera *f*

shirtsleeve ['ʃɜːtsliːv, *Am:* 'ʃɜːrt-] *n* manga *f* de camisa

shirty ['ʃɜːti, *Am:* 'ʃɜːrt̬i] <-ier, -iest> *adj Brit, Aus, pej, inf* borde; **to get ~ (with sb)** ponerse borde (con alguien)

shit [ʃɪt] *inf* I. *n no pl* 1. (*faeces*) mierda *f* 2. *pej* (*nonsense*) gilipolleces *fpl,* pendejadas *fpl AmL* 3. (*nasty person*) cabrón, -ona *m, f* 4. (*as intensifier*) **I don't give a ~!** ¡me importa un carajo! ►**to beat the ~ out of sb** moler a alguien a palos; **to frighten the ~ out of sb** hacer que alguien se cague de miedo; **to be in the ~** estar jodido; **no ~!** ¡no jodas! II. *interj* mierda III. <shit, shit> *vi* cagar IV. <shit, shit> *vt* cagar; **to ~ oneself** cagarse (encima); *fig* cagarse de miedo; **to ~ bricks** *Am* acojonarse

shite [ʃaɪt] *n Brit s.* **shit**

shitty ['ʃɪti, *Am:* 'ʃɪt̬-] <-ier, -iest> *adj pej, inf* 1. (*unfair, unpleasant*) asqueroso, -a 2. (*sick, ill*) jodido, -a

shiver ['ʃɪvəʳ, *Am:* -ɚ] I. *n* estremecimiento *m;* **to feel a ~** tener un escalofrío; **to give sb the ~s** *inf* dar miedo a alguien II. *vi* temblar; **to ~ with cold** tiritar de frío

shivery ['ʃɪvəri] <-ier, -iest> *adj* estremecido, -a; **to feel ~** tener escalofríos

shoal¹ [ʃəʊl, *Am:* ʃoʊl] *n* 1. (*of fish*) banco *m* 2. *Brit* montón *m;* **~s of** montones *mpl* de

shoal² [ʃəʊl, *Am:* ʃoʊl] *n* 1. (*area of shallow water*) bajío *m* 2. (*sand bank*) banco *m* de arena

shock¹ [ʃɒk, *Am:* ʃɑːk] I. *n* 1. (*unpleasant surprise*) conmoción *f,* batata *f CSur;* **the ~ of my life** *inf* el susto de mi vida; **look of ~** mirada *f* de asombro; **to give sb a ~** dar un disgusto a alguien 2. *inf* (*electric shock*) descarga *f* 3. MED shock *m;* **to die from ~** morir de la impresión 4. (*impact: of explosion, earthquake*) sacudida *f* ►**~, horror!** *iron* ¡qué horror! II. *vt* 1. (*appal*) horrorizar 2. (*scare*) asustar III. *vi* impactar

shock² [ʃɒk, *Am:* ʃɑːk] *n* (*of hair*) mata *f*

shock absorber ['ʃɒkæbˌzɔːbəʳ, *Am:* 'ʃɑːkəbˌsɔːrbɚ] *n* amortiguador *m*

shocker ['ʃɒkəʳ, *Am:* 'ʃɑːkɚ] *n inf* (*unpleasant news*) noticia *f* desagradable; (*surprising news*) bombazo *m*

shocking ['ʃɒkɪŋ, *Am:* 'ʃɑːkɪŋ] *adj* 1. (*causing indignation, distress*) espantoso, -a; (*news*) horrible 2. (*surprising*) chocante 3. (*offensive*) escandaloso, -a; (*crime*) espantoso, -a 4. *Brit, inf* (*terrible*) horroroso, -a

shockproof ['ʃɒkpruːf, *Am:* 'ʃɑːk-] *adj* 1. (*mechanism*) a prueba de choques 2. (*person*) imperturbable **shock therapy** *n,* **shock treatment** *n* terapia *f* de shock **shock troops** *npl* tropas *fpl* de asalto **shock wave** *n* 1. PHYS onda *f* expansiva 2. *fig* conmoción *f*

shod [ʃɒd] *pt, pp of* **shoe**

shoddy ['ʃɒdi, *Am:* 'ʃɑːdi] <-ier, -iest> *adj pej* 1. (*goods*) de muy mala calidad 2. (*treatment*) mezquino, -a

shoe [ʃuː] I. *n* (*for person*) zapato *m;* (*for horse*) herradura *f;* **high-heeled ~** zapatos *mpl* de tacón alto; **training ~** zapatillas *fpl* de deporte ►**to fill sb's ~s** pasar a ocupar el puesto de alguien; **if I were in your ~s** *inf* si estuviera en tu lugar II. <shod *o Am:* shoed, shod *o Am:* shoed> *vt* (*person*) calzar; (*horse*) herrar, encasquillar *AmL*

shoehorn ['ʃuːhɔːn, *Am:* -hɔːrn] *n* calzador *m* **shoelace** *n* cordón *m* (de zapato), pasador *m Perú* **shoemaker** *n* zapatero, -a *m, f* **shoe polish** *n* betún *m,* lustrina *f Chile* **shoe-repair shop** *n* rápido *m*

shoeshine ['ʃuːʃaɪn] *n Am* limpieza *f* de zapatos **shoeshine boy** *n Am* limpiabotas *m inv*

shoeshop *n* zapatería *f* **shoe size** *n* número *m* de zapato **shoestore** *n Am* zapatería *f,* peletería *f Cuba*

shoestring ['ʃuːstrɪŋ] *n Am* cordón *m* (de zapato) ►**to do sth on a ~** *inf* hacer algo con poquísimo dinero; **to start on a ~** comenzar con aprietos **shoe tree** *n* horma *f*

shone [ʃɒn, *Am:* ʃoʊn] *pt, pp of* **shine**

shoo [ʃuː] I. *interj inf* fuera II. *vt inf* ahuyentar

shook [ʃʊk] *n pt of* **shake**

shoot [ʃuːt] I. *n* 1. (*hunt*) cacería *f;* **to go on a ~** ir de caza 2. CINE rodaje *m;* PHOT sesión *f* 3. BOT retoño *m* II. *interj Am* (*shit*) mecachis

S

III. <shot, shot> *vi* 1. (*fire weapon*) disparar; **to ~ to kill** tirar a matar; **to ~ at sth/sb** disparar a algo/alguien 2. *Am* (*aim*) **to ~ for sth** intentar conseguir algo 3. SPORTS chutar 4. CINE rodar; PHOT disparar 5. (*move rapidly*) volar; **to ~ to fame** hacerse famoso de repente; **to ~ past** (*car*) pasar como un rayo ▶**to ~ for** [*o* **at**] **the moon** ir a por todas; **to be shot through with sth** estar repleto de algo IV. <shot, shot> *vt* 1. (*bullet*) disparar; (*missile, arrow*) lanzar 2. (*person*) disparar, abalear *AmS,* balear *AmC,* balacear *Méx;* **to ~ sb dead** matar a alguien a tiros 3. CINE (*film*) rodar; (*scene*) filmar; PHOT tomar 4. (*direct*) **to ~ questions at sb** acribillar a alguien a preguntas; **to ~ a glance at sb** lanzar una mirada a alguien 5. *Am, inf* **to ~ a goal** meter un gol 6. *inf* (*drugs*) **to ~ heroin** chutarse heroína ▶**to ~ the breeze** *Am, inf* cotillear, dar a la sinhueso; **to ~ darts at sb** *Am, inf* lanzar miradas asesinas a alguien; **to ~ the works** *Am, inf* tirar la casa por la ventana

◆**shoot ahead** *vi* tomar la delantera rápidamente

◆**shoot down** *vt* (*aircraft*) derribar; *inf* (*proposal*) rebatir

◆**shoot off** I. *vt* arrancar de un sitio ▶**to shoot one's mouth off** *inf* cotorrear II. *vi* (*vehicle*) salir como un bólido

◆**shoot out** *vi* salir disparado

◆**shoot past** *vi* pasar como una bala

◆**shoot up** *vi* 1. (*expand, increase rapidly*) crecer mucho; (*skyscraper*) aparecer (de la nada); *inf* (*child*) pegar un estirón 2. *inf* (*inject drugs*) chutarse

shooting [ˈʃuːtɪŋ, *Am:* -t̬ɪŋ] I. *n* 1. (*killing*) asesinato *m* 2. *no pl* (*firing of gun*) tiroteo *m* 3. *no pl* (*hunting*) caza *f;* **to go ~** ir de caza 4. *no pl* SPORTS tiro *m* al blanco II. *adj* (*pain*) punzante

shooting gallery *n* barraca *f* de tiro al blanco **shooting jacket** *n* chaquetón *m* **shooting lodge** *n* pabellón *m* de caza **shooting range** *n* campo *m* de tiro **shooting season** *n* temporada *f* de caza **shooting star** *n* estrella *f* fugaz **shooting stick** *n* bastón *m* taburete

shootout [ˈʃuːtaʊt] *n* tiroteo *m*

shop [ʃɒp, *Am:* ʃɑːp] I. *n* 1. (*for sale of goods*) tienda *f;* **betting ~** agencia *f* de apuestas; **book ~** librería *f;* **to go to the ~s** ir de compras 2. (*for manufacture*) taller *m* ▶**to set up ~ as sth** establecerse como algo; **to talk ~** hablar de trabajo; **all over the ~** por todas partes II. <-pp-> *vi* comprar III. <-pp-> *vt* *Brit, inf* (*betray*) chivarse de

shopaholic [ʃɒpəˈhɒlɪk, *Am:* ʃɑːp-] *n* adicto, -a *m, f* a las compras

shop assistant *n Brit* dependiente, -a *m, f* **shopfitter** *n* diseñador(a) *m(f)* de espacios comerciales **shop floor** *n* (*in factory*) taller *m* **shop front** *n* escaparate *m* **shopgirl** *n Brit* dependienta *f* **shopkeeper** *n* comerciante *mf,* despachero, -a *m, f Chile* **shopkeeping** *n no pl* comercio *m*

shoplifter [ˈʃɒplɪftəʳ, *Am:* ˈʃɑːpˌlɪftɚ] *n* ladrón, -ona *m, f* (*que roba en tiendas*) **shoplifting** *n* robo *m* (en tiendas)

shopper *n* comprador(a) *m(f)*

shopping [ˈʃɒpɪŋ, *Am:* ˈʃɑːp-] *n no pl* 1. (*activity*) compra *f;* **to go ~** ir de tiendas 2. (*purchases*) compras *fpl*

shopping arcade *n* galería *f* comercial **shopping bag** *n Brit* bolsa *f* de compras, jaba *f Cuba* **shopping basket** *n* cesta *f* de la compra **shopping cart** *n Am* carrito *m* de la compra **shopping center** *n Am, Aus,* **shopping centre** *n* centro *m* comercial **shopping list** *n* lista *f* de la compra **shopping mall** *n Am, Aus* centro *m* comercial **shopping street** *n* calle *f* comercial **shopping trolley** *n Brit* carrito *m* de la compra

shopsoiled [ˌʃɒpˈsɔɪld, *Am:* ˈʃɑːpˌsɔɪld] *adj Brit, Aus* deteriorado, -a

shop steward *n* enlace *mf* sindical **shoptalk** *n no pl* conversación *f* sobre el trabajo **shopwalker** *n Brit* supervisor(a) *m(f)* **shop window** *n* escaparate *m,* vitrina *f AmL,* vidriera *f AmL*

shopworn [ˈʃɒpwɔːn, *Am:* ˈʃɑːpwɔːrn] *adj* 1. *Am* (*goods*) deteriorado, -a 2. (*cliché*) gastado, -a

shore [ʃɔːʳ, *Am:* ʃɔːr] *n* 1. (*coast*) costa *f* 2. (*beach*) orilla *f;* **on ~** a tierra 3. *pl, fig* (*a country*) **these ~s** estas tierras 4. ARCHIT puntal *m*

◆**shore up** *vt a. fig* apuntalar

shore leave *n* permiso *m* para ir a tierra **shoreline** *n* orilla *f*

shorn [ʃɔːn, *Am:* ʃɔːrn] *pp of* **shear**

short [ʃɔːt, *Am:* ʃɔːrt] I. *adj* 1. (*not long*) corto, -a 2. (*not tall*) bajo, -a, petizo, -a *CSur, Bol* 3. (*brief*) breve; (*memory*) malo, -a 4. (*not enough*) escaso, -a; **to be** [*o* **run**] **~ on sth** andar escaso de algo; **to be ~ on brains** *inf* ser algo corto; **to be ~ of breath** quedarse sin aliento; **to be in ~ supply** escasear 5. LING (*vowel*) breve 6. (*brusque*) brusco, -a; **to be ~ with sb** tratar a alguien con sequedad II. *n* 1. CINE cortometraje *m* 2. *inf* ELEC cortocircuito *m* 3. *Brit, inf* (*drink*) *bebida alcohólica servida sin agua* III. *adv* 1. (*abruptly*) **to cut ~** interrumpir bruscamente; **to go ~ of sth** *Brit* pasar sin algo; **to stop sth/sb ~** parar algo/a alguien en seco 2. (*below the standard*) **in ~** en resumidas cuentas; **to fall ~** quedarse corto; **to fall ~ of sth** no alcanzar algo

shortage [ˈʃɔːtɪdʒ, *Am:* ˈʃɔːrt̬ɪdʒ] *n* falta *f;* (*water*) escasez *f*

shortbread [ˈʃɔːtbred, *Am:* ˈʃɔːrt-] *n no pl* galleta *f* dulce de mantequilla **shortcake** *n* 1. galleta *f* dulce de mantequilla 2. *Am* (*layer cake*) pastel *m* relleno

short-change [ʃɔːtˈtʃeɪndʒ, *Am:* ʃɔːrtˈ-] *vt* dar mal el cambio; *fig* timar

short-circuit [ʃɔːtˈsɜːkɪt, *Am:* ʃɔːrtˈsɜːr-]

I. *n* cortocircuito *m* II. *vi* ponerse en cortocircuito III. *vt* 1. ELEC poner en cortocircuito 2. (*bypass*) saltarse

shortcoming [ˈʃɔːtˌkʌmɪŋ, *Am:* ˈʃɔːrt-] *n* defecto *m*

shortcrust [ˈʃɔːtkrʌst, *Am:* ˈʃɔːrt-] *n*, **shortcrust pastry** *n no pl* pasta *f* quebradiza

short cut *n* atajo *m; fig* fórmula *f* mágica; **keyboard** ~ INFOR tecla *f* aceleradora

shortcut key *n* INFOR tecla *f* aceleradora

short-dated [ˌʃɔːtˈdeɪtɪd, *Am:* ʃɔːrtˈdeɪt̬ɪd] *adj* a corto plazo

shorten [ˈʃɔːtən, *Am:* ˈʃɔːr-] I. *vt* acortar; (*name, title*) abreviar II. *vi* acortarse

shortening [ˈʃɔːtnɪŋ, *Am:* ˈʃɔːrt-] *n no pl* 1. (*reduction*) reducción *f* 2. GASTR manteca *f*

shortfall [ˈʃɔːtfɔːl, *Am:* ˈʃɔːrt-] *n* deficiencia *f;* ECON déficit *m*

shorthand [ˈʃɔːthænd, *Am:* ˈʃɔːrt-] *n no pl, Brit, Aus, Can* taquigrafía *f*

shorthanded [ˌʃɔːtˈhændɪd, *Am:* ʃɔːrtˈ-] *adj* falto, -a de mano de obra

shorthand typist *n Aus, Brit* taquimecanógrafo, -a *m, f*

short-haul [ˈʃɔːthɔːl, *Am:* ˈʃɔːrthɑːl] *adj* de corto recorrido **shortlist** I. *vt* preseleccionar II. *n* lista *f* de candidatos preseleccionados **short-lived** *adj* efímero, -a; (*happiness*) pasajero, -a

shortly [ˈʃɔːtli, *Am:* ˈʃɔːrt-] *adv* dentro de poco; ~ **after ...** poco después...

shortness [ˈʃɔːtnɪs, *Am:* ˈʃɔːrt-] *n no pl* 1. (*condition of being short*) cortedad *f* 2. (*brevity*) brevedad *f* 3. (*insufficiency*) escasez *f;* ~ **of breath** falta *f* de aliento 4. (*brusqueness*) sequedad *f*

short order *n Am* comida *f* rápida; (*order*) pedido *m* de comida rápida; ~ **cook** *cocinero que prepara platos sencillos y rápidos* **short-range** *adj* MIL de corto alcanze

shorts [ʃɔːts, *Am:* ˈʃɔːrts] *npl* 1. *Brit, Aus* (*short trousers*) pantalones *mpl* cortos, shorts *mpl;* **a pair of** ~ unos shorts, unos pantalones cortos 2. *Am* (*underpants*) calzoncillos *mpl*

short-sighted [ˈʃɔːrtˌsaɪt̬ɪd] *adj* 1. (*myopic*) miope 2. (*not prudent*) corto, -a de miras **short-sleeved** *adj* de manga corta **short-staffed** *adj Aus, Brit* falto, -a de personal **short story** *n* narración *m* corta **short-tempered** *adj* irascible **short-term** *adj* a corto plazo **short time** *n* jornada *f* reducida **short wave** *n* onda *f* corta

shot¹ [ʃɒt, *Am:* ʃɑːt] I. *n* 1. (*act of firing weapon*) tiro *m*, disparo *m*, baleo *m AmC;* **to fire a** ~ disparar un tiro 2. *no pl* (*shotgun pellets*) perdigones *mpl* 3. (*person*) tirador(a) *m(f);* **to be a good/poor** ~ ser un buen/mal tirador 4. SPORTS (*football*) tiro *m;* (*tennis*) golpe *m* 5. (*photograph*) foto *f;* CINE toma *f* 6. *inf* (*injection*) inyección *f* 7. *inf* (*try, stab*) intento *m;* **to have a** ~ **at sth** probar suerte con algo; **to give sth one's best** ~ hacerlo lo mejor que se pueda 8. (*small amount of alcohol*) chupito *m* ►~ **in the arm** estímulo *m;* **a** ~ **in the dark** *inf* un palo de ciego; **not by a long** ~ ni por asomo; **to call (all) the** ~**s** cortar el bacalao *fig;* **like a** ~ *inf* como un bólido II. *pp, pt of* **shoot**

shot² [ʃɒt, *Am:* ʃɑːt] *adj* 1. (*woven*) tornasolado, -a 2. *inf* (*worn out*) hecho, -a polvo ►**to get** ~ **of sth/sb** quitarse algo/a alguien de encima

shotgun [ˈʃɒtgʌn, *Am:* ˈʃɑːt-] *n* escopeta *f*

shot put *n* SPORTS lanzamiento *m* de peso **shot putter** *n* lanzador(a) *m(f)* de peso

should [ʃʊd] *aux* 1. (*expression of advisability*) **to insist that sb** ~ **do sth** insistir en que alguien debería hacer algo 2. (*asking for advice*) ~ **I/we ...?** ¿debería/deberíamos...? 3. (*expression of expectation*) **I** ~ **be so lucky!** *inf* ¡ojalá! 4. *form* (*expressing a condition*) **I** ~ **like to see her** me gustaría verla 5. (*rhetorical expression*) **why** ~ **I/you ...?** ¿por qué debería/deberías...? 6. *Brit, form* **I prefer that Anna** ~ **do it** prefiero que lo haga Anna 7. *form* (*would*) **we** ~ **like to invite you** nos gustaría invitarte/invitaros

shoulder [ˈʃəʊldəʳ, *Am:* ˈʃoʊldɚ] I. *n* 1. ANAT hombro *m;* ~ **to** ~ hombro con hombro; **to glance over one's** ~ mirar por encima del hombro; **to sling sth over one's** ~ echarse algo al hombro; **to be sb's** ~ **to cry on** ser el paño de lágrimas de alguien; **to lift a burden from one's** ~**s** *fig* quitarse un peso de encima 2. (*piece of meat*) paletilla *f;* (*of beef*) paleta *f* 3. (*side of road*) arcén *m* 4. (*shoulder-like part of sth*) lomo *m* ►**to rub** ~**s with sb** codearse con alguien; **to stand** ~ **to** ~ **with sb** apoyar a alguien II. *vt* 1. empujar; **to** ~ **one's way** abrirse paso a empujones; **to** ~ **sb aside** empujar a alguien a un lado 2. (*place on one's shoulders*) llevar en los hombros 3. (*accept: responsability*) cargar con

shoulder bag *n* bolso *m* de bandolera **shoulder blade** *n* omóplato *m* **shoulder pad** *n* hombrera *f* **shoulder strap** *n* tirante *m*

shout [ʃaʊt] I. *n* 1. (*loud cry*) grito *m;* **to give sb a** ~ *inf* avisar a alguien 2. *Aus, Brit, inf* (*round of drinks*) **it's my** ~ esta ronda la pago yo II. *vi* gritar; **to** ~ **at sb** gritar a alguien; **to** ~ **for help** pedir auxilio a gritos ►**to give sb sth to** ~ **about** dar una gran alegría a alguien III. *vt* gritar; (*slogans*) corear; **to** ~ **abuse at sb** insultar a alguien a gritos; **to** ~ **oneself hoarse** gritar hasta quedarse ronco

◆**shout down** *vt* hacer callar a gritos

◆**shout out** *vt* gritar

shouting *n no pl* griterío *m* ►**within** ~ **distance** al alcance de la voz; ~ **match** pelea *f* de gallos *fig*

shove [ʃʌv] I. *n* empujón *m*, pechada *f Arg, Chile;* **to give sth a** ~ dar un empujón a algo II. *vt* 1. (*push*) empujar; **to** ~ **one's way through** abrirse paso a empujones; **to** ~ **sb about** [*o* **around**] *fig* abusar de alguien

2. (*place*) meter **III.** *vi* empujar; **to ~ along** *inf* largarse

◆**shove off** *vi* **1.** *inf* (*go away*) largarse **2.** (*launch by foot*) desatracar

shovel ['ʃʌvəl] **I.** *n* **1.** (*tool*) pala *f;* **a ~ of sth** una palada de algo **2.** (*machine*) excavadora *f* **II.** <*Brit:* -ll-, *Am:* -l-> *vt* palear; **to ~ food into one's mouth** engullir comida **III.** <*Brit:* -ll-, *Am:* -l-> *vi* palear

show [ʃəʊ, *Am:* ʃoʊ] **I.** *n* **1.** (*expression*) demostración *f;* **~ of solidarity** muestra *f* de solidaridad **2.** (*exhibition*) exposición *f;* **dog ~** exposición *f* canina; **fashion ~** desfile *m* de modelos; **slide ~** pase *m* de diapositivas; **to be on ~** estar expuesto **3.** (*play*) espectáculo *m;* TV programa *m;* THEAT representación *f;* **quiz ~** concurso *m* **4.** *inf* (*business*) asunto *m* ► **~ of hands** voto a mano alzada; **let's get the ~ on the road** *inf* vamos a ponernos manos a la obra; **to put on a good ~ of sth** hacer ver algo; **the ~ must go on** *prov* hay que seguir adelante; **to run the ~** llevar la voz cantante **II.** <showed, shown> *vt* **1.** (*display*) mostrar; (*slides*) pasar; ART exponer **2.** (*express*) demostrar; (*enthusiasm*) expresar **3.** (*expose*) exponer **4.** (*point out, record*) señalar; (*statistics*) indicar **5.** (*prove*) probar; **to ~ sb that ...** demostrar a alguien que... **6.** (*escort*) guiar; **to ~ sb over a place** *Aus, Brit* enseñar un lugar a alguien; **to ~ sb to the door** acompañar a alguien a la puerta **7.** (*project*) proyectar; (*on television*) poner **III.** *vi* <showed, shown> **1.** (*be visible*) verse **2.** *Am, Aus, inf* (*arrive*) aparecer **3.** (*be shown: film*) proyectarse

◆**show around** *vt* guiar

◆**show in** *vt* hacer pasar

◆**show off** **I.** *vt* lucir **II.** *vi* alardear, compadrear *Arg, Urug*

◆**show out** *vt* acompañar a la puerta

◆**show up** **I.** *vi* **1.** (*be apparent*) ponerse de manifiesto **2.** *inf* (*arrive*) aparecer **II.** *vt* **1.** (*expose*) descubrir; **to show sb up as (being) sth** demostrar que alguien es algo **2.** (*embarrass*) poner en evidencia

showbiz *n no pl, inf s.* **show business** mundo *m* del espectáculo **showboat** *n Am* barco-teatro *m* **show business** *n no pl* mundo *m* del espectáculo **showcase** **I.** *n* escaparate *m* **II.** *vt* exhibir

showdown ['ʃəʊdaʊn, *Am:* 'ʃoʊ-] *n* enfrentamiento *m*

shower ['ʃaʊəʳ, *Am:* 'ʃaʊɚ] **I.** *n* **1.** (*of rain*) chaparrón *m;* (*of sparks, insults*) lluvia *f* **2.** (*for washing*) ducha *f,* lluvia *f Arg, Chile, Nic* **3.** *Am* (*party*) fiesta *f* (*con motivo de un nacimiento, matrimonio, etc.*) **4.** *Brit, inf* (*group*) **a ~ of idiots** una panda de imbéciles **II.** *vt* derramar; **to ~ sb with water** regar a alguien de agua; **to ~ compliments on sb** colmar de cumplidos a alguien **III.** *vi* **1.** (*take a shower*) ducharse **2.** (*spray*) regar

shower cabinet *n* armario *m* de la ducha **shower cap** *n* gorro *m* de ducha **shower curtain** *n* cortina *f* de ducha **shower gel** *n* gel *m* de ducha

showery ['ʃaʊəri, *Am:* 'ʃaʊɚi] *adj* lluvioso, -a

show flat *n* piso *m* de muestra **showgirl** *n* corista *f* **showground** *n* recinto *m* ferial **show home** *n,* **show house** *n Brit* casa *f* de muestra

showing *n* **1.** (*exhibition*) exposición *f* **2.** (*broadcasting*) proyección *f* **3.** (*performance*) actuación *f*

showing-off *n pej* presunción *f*

show jumping ['ʃəʊˌdʒʌmpɪŋ, *Am:* 'ʃoʊˌ-] *n no pl* concurso *m* hípico

showman ['ʃəʊmən, *Am:* 'ʃoʊ-] *n* artista *m,* showman *m*

showmanship ['ʃəʊmənʃɪp, *Am:* 'ʃoʊ-] *n* sentido *m* de la teatralidad

shown [ʃəʊn, *Am:* ʃoʊn] *pp of* **show**

show-off ['ʃəʊɒf, *Am:* 'ʃoʊˌɑːf] *n* fanfarrón, -ona *m, f*

showpiece ['ʃəʊpiːs, *Am:* 'ʃoʊ-] **I.** *n* joya *f* **II.** *adj* excepcional

showroom ['ʃəʊrʊm, *Am:* 'ʃoʊruːm] *n* salón *m* de exposición

show trial *n* juicio *m* (*llevado a cabo como demostración de poderío*)

showy ['ʃəʊi, *Am:* 'ʃoʊ-] <-ier, -iest> *adj* llamativo, -a

shrank [ʃræŋk] *vt, vi pt of* **shrink**

shrapnel ['ʃræpn(ə)l] *n no pl* metralla *f*

shred [ʃred] **I.** <-dd-> *vt* (*cut into shreds*) cortar en tiras; (*document*) triturar **II.** *n* **1.** (*strip*) tira *f;* **to be in ~s** estar hecho jirones; **to tear sb to ~s** hacer trizas a alguien **2.** *no pl, fig* (*of hope, truth*) pizca *f*

shredder ['ʃredəʳ, *Am:* -ɚ] *n* trituradora *f*

shrew [ʃruː] *n* **1.** (*animal*) musaraña *f* **2.** *pej* (*bad-tempered woman*) arpía *f*

shrewd [ʃruːd] *adj* (*person*) astuto, -a, habiloso, -a *Chile,* lépero, -a *Cuba;* (*comment*) hábil; (*decision*) inteligente; (*eye*) agudo, -a

shrewish ['ʃruːɪʃ] *adj pej* regañon, -ona *m, f*

shriek [ʃriːk] **I.** *n* chillido *m* **II.** *vi* chillar; **to ~ with laughter** reírse a carcajadas **III.** *vt* chillar

shrift [ʃrɪft] *n* **to get short ~ from sb** recibir cajas destempladas de alguien; **to give short ~ to sb** echar a alguien con cajas destempladas; **to give short ~ to sth** despachar algo

shrill [ʃrɪl] *adj* agudo, -a

shrimp [ʃrɪmp] *n* <-(s)> **1.** *Brit* camarón *m* **2.** *Am* gamba *f* **3.** *inf* (*person*) renacuajo, -a *m, f*

shrimp cocktail *n Am* cóctel *m* de gambas

shrine [ʃraɪn] *n* **1.** (*tomb*) sepulcro *m* **2.** (*site of worship*) santuario *m;* **a ~ for sb** un altar en honor a alguien

shrink [ʃrɪŋk] **I.** *n inf* loquero, -a *m, f* **II.** <shrank *o Am:* shrunk, shrunk *o Am:* shrunken> *vt* **1.** (*make smaller*) encoger **2.** (*reduce: costs*) reducir **III.** <shrank *o Am:* shrunk, shrunk *o Am:* shrunken> *vi* **1.** (*become smaller: clothes*) encoger

2. (*become reduced*) disminuir 3. *liter* (*cower*) retroceder (por miedo); **to ~ away from sb/sth** echarse atrás ante alguien/algo 4. (*be reluctant to*) **to ~ from** (**doing**) **sth** rehuir (hacer) algo

shrinkage ['ʃrɪŋkɪdʒ] *n no pl* 1. (*of clothes*) encogimiento *m* 2. (*of costs*) reducción *m*

shrink-wrap ['ʃrɪŋkræp] I. *n* envoltura *f* de plástico II. *vt* (*food*) empaquetar en plástico

shrivel ['ʃrɪvəl] <*Brit:* -ll-, *Am:* -l-> I. *vi* (*fruit*) secarse; (*plant*) marchitarse; (*skin*) arrugarse; (*person*) consumirse II. *vt* (*fruit*) secar; (*skin*) arrugar

◆**shrivel up** *vi* (*fruit*) secarse; (*plant*) marchitarse; (*person*) consumirse

shroud [ʃraʊd] I. *n* (*covering*) velo *m;* (*for burial*) sudario *m;* (*of dust, fog*) capa *f* II. *vt* envolver; **to ~ sth in sth** envolver algo con algo; **~ed in mystery** envuelto en un halo de misterio

Shrove Tuesday [ˌʃrəʊv'tjuːzdeɪ, *Am:* ʃroʊv'tuːzdeɪ] *n* martes *m inv* de Carnaval

shrub [ʃrʌb] *n* arbusto *m*

shrubbery ['ʃrʌbəri] *n no pl* arbustos *mpl*

shrug [ʃrʌg] I. *n* encogimiento *m* de hombros II. <-gg-> *vt* **to ~ one's shoulders** encogerse de hombros III. <-gg-> *vi* encogerse de hombros

◆**shrug off** *vt* 1. (*ignore*) negar importancia a 2. (*overcome*) superar

shrunk [ʃrʌŋk] *pp, pt of* **shrink**

shrunken ['ʃrʌŋkən] I. *pp of* **shrink** II. *adj* encogido, -a

shuck [ʃʌk] *vt Am* (*fruits*) pelar; (*beans*) desenvainar; (*clothes*) quitarse

shucks [ʃʌks] *interj Am, inf* caray

shudder ['ʃʌdəʳ, *Am:* -ɚ] I. *vi* (*person*) estremecerse; (*ground, machine*) vibrar; **to ~ at the memory of sth** temblar al recordar algo II. *n* (*of person*) estremecimiento *m;* (*of ground, machine*) vibración *f;* **it sent a ~ down my spine** hizo que me estremeciera

shuffle ['ʃʌfl] I. *n* 1. (*of cards*) **to give the cards a ~** barajar las cartas 2. (*of cabinet, management*) reestructuración *f* 3. *no pl* (*dragging of feet*) arrastre *m* II. *vt* 1. (*papers*) revolver; (*cards*) barajar 2. (*cabinet, management*) reestructurar 3. (*feet*) arrastrar III. *vi* 1. (*mix cards*) barajar 2. (*drag feet*) arrastrar los pies

◆**shuffle off** *vi* alejarse arrastrando los pies

shun [ʃʌn] <-nn-> *vt* rehuir

shunt [ʃʌnt] I. *vt* 1. RAIL cambiar de vía 2. *fig* **to ~ sb aside** relegar a alguien II. *n* RAIL empujón *m*

shunting *n* cambio *m* de vía

shunting engine *n* locomotora *f* de maniobra

shush [ʃʊʃ] I. *interj* silencio II. *vt inf* hacer callar III. *vi inf* callarse

shut [ʃʌt] I. *adj* cerrado, -a; **to slam a door ~** cerrar la puerta de un portazo II. <shut, shut> *vt* cerrar; **to ~ one's ears to sth** hacer oídos sordos a algo; **to ~ one's finger in the door** pillarse el dedo en la puerta III. <shut, shut> *vi* 1. (*door, window*) cerrarse 2. (*shop, factory*) cerrar

◆**shut away** *vt* encerrar; **to shut oneself away** recluirse

◆**shut down** I. *vt* 1. (*shop, factory*) cerrar; (*airport*) paralizar 2. (*turn off*) desconectar II. *vi* (*shop, factory*) cerrar; (*engine*) apagarse

◆**shut in** *vt* encerrar

◆**shut off** *vt* 1. (*isolate*) aislar 2. (*turn off*) desconectar

◆**shut out** *vt* 1. (*block out*) ahuyentar; (*thought*) borrar de la memoria 2. (*exclude*) dejar fuera; **to shut sb out** no dejar entrar a alguien 3. SPORTS dejar a cero

◆**shut up** I. *vt* 1. (*confine*) encerrar 2. *Aus, Brit* (*stop business*) cerrar 3. *inf* (*cause to stop talking*) hacer callar; **to shut sb up for good** *fig* hacer callar a alguien para siempre II. *vi inf* (*stop talking*) callarse

shutdown ['ʃʌtdaʊn] *n* cierre *m*

shuteye ['ʃʌtaɪ, *Am:* 'ʃʌt̬-] *n no pl, inf* sueñecito *m;* **to get some ~** echarse un sueñecito

shut-off I. *n* suspensión *f* II. *adj* (*valve*) de cierre

shutout ['ʃʌtaʊt] *n* victoria *f* abrumadora (*sin que marque el adversario*)

shutter ['ʃʌtəʳ, *Am:* -t̬ɚ] *n* 1. PHOT obturador *m* 2. (*of window*) contraventana *f;* (*of shop*) persiana *f;* **to put up the ~s** cerrar el negocio

shuttle ['ʃʌtl, *Am:* 'ʃʌt̬-] I. *n* 1. (*train*) servicio *m* de enlace; (*plane*) puente *m* aéreo; (*space*) transbordador *m* espacial 2. (*sewing-machine bobbin*) lanzadera *f* II. *vt* transportar III. *vi* AVIAT volar (regularmente); (*travel regularly*) ir y venir

shuttlecock ['ʃʌtlkɒk, *Am:* 'ʃʌt̬lkɑːk] *n* volante *m*

shuttle flight *n* puente *m* aéreo **shuttle service** *n* servicio *m* de enlace

shy[1] [ʃaɪ] I. <-ie-> *vt inf* (*throw*) tirar II. *n* 1. (*throw*) tirada *f;* (*in soccer*) saque *m* de banda 2. *fig* (*attempt*) tentativa *f;* **to have a ~ at sth** probar algo

shy[2] [ʃaɪ] I. <-er, -est> *adj* 1. (*timid*) tímido, -a 2. (*lacking*) escaso, -a; **we're still a few pounds ~** nos faltan todavía unas cuantas libras II. <-ie-> *vi* (*horse*) respingar, bellaquear *Arg, Bol, Urug*

◆**shy away from** *vi* **to ~ sth** asustarse de algo; **to ~ doing sth** evitar hacer algo

shyly *adv* tímidamente

shyness *n no pl* timidez *f*

Siamese [ˌsaɪə'miːz] I. *n inv* 1. (*person*) siamés, -esa *m, f* 2. (*language*) siamés *m* II. *adj* 1. GEO, HIST siamés, -esa 2. (*brothers*) **~ twins** siameses *mpl*

Siberia [saɪ'bɪəriə, *Am:* -'bɪri-] *n no pl* Siberia *f*

sibling ['sɪblɪŋ] *n form* hermano, -a *m, f*

Sicilian [sɪ'sɪljən] I. *adj* siciliano, -a II. *n* (*person*) siciliano, -a *m, f*

Sicily ['sɪsɪli] *n* Sicilia *f*

S

sick [sɪk] I. <-er, -est> *adj* 1. (*ill*) enfermo, -a; **to feel ~** sentirse mal; **to fall ~** caer enfermo; **to be off ~** estar de baja (por enfermedad); **to be ~ at heart** *liter* estar muy deprimido 2. (*about to vomit*) mareado, -a; **to be ~** (*nauseated*) estar mareado (y a punto de vomitar); (*vomit*) vomitar; **to get ~** vomitar; **to feel ~ to one's stomach** tener el estómago revuelto; **too much alcohol makes me ~** el exceso de alcohol me pone fatal 3. *inf* (*car*) averiado, -a 4. *inf* (*disgusted*) asqueado, -a; **to be ~ about sth** estar asqueado de algo 5. (*angry*) furioso, -a; **to be ~ and tired of sth** estar harto de algo 6. *inf* (*cruel*) cruel; (*joke*) de mal gusto II. *n* 1. (*ill people*) **the ~** los enfermos 2. *no pl, Brit, inf* (*vomit*) vómito *m*

◆**sick up** *vt* vomitar, devolver

sick bag *n* bolsa *f* para vomitar **sick bay** *n* enfermería *f* **sickbed** *n* lecho *m* de enfermo

sicken ['sɪkən] I. *vi* (*become sick*) enfermar; **to ~ for sth** *Brit* (*become sick with*) estar incubando algo II. *vt* (*upset*) molestar, estar asqueado de algo; **so much violence in films ~s me** me pone enfermo tanta violencia en las películas

sickening ['sɪkənɪŋ] *adj* 1. (*repulsive*) repugnante 2. (*annoying*) ofensivo, -a

sickle ['sɪkl] *n* hoz *f*

sick leave ['sɪkliːv] *n* baja *f* por enfermedad; **to be on ~** estar de baja por enfermedad **sick list** *n* lista *f* de enfermos

sickly ['sɪkli] <-ier, -iest> *adj* 1. (*not healthy*) enfermizo, -a, apolismado, -a *Col, Méx, PRico,* telenque *Chile* 2. (*pale*) pálido, -a 3. (*very sweet*) empalagoso, -a

sickness ['sɪknəs] *n no pl* 1. (*illness*) enfermedad *f* 2. (*nausea*) mareo *m*

sickness benefit *n Aus, Brit* subsidio *m* por incapacidad

sick note *n* certificado *m* de baja

sick pay *n* subsidio *m* de enfermedad

sickroom ['sɪkrʊm, *Am:* -ruːm] *n* cuarto *m* del enfermo

side [saɪd] *n* 1. (*vertical surface*) lado *m;* **at the ~ of sth** en el lado de algo; **at sb's ~** al lado de alguien; **~ by ~** uno al lado de otro 2. (*flat surface*) superficie *f;* (*of page*) cara *f* 3. (*edge*) límite *m;* (*of river*) ribera *f;* (*of road*) arcén *m;* **on all ~(s)** por todas partes 4. (*half*) parte *f;* **I like to sleep on the right ~ of the bed** me gusta dormir en el lado derecho de la cama; **in Great Britain, cars drive on the left ~ of the road** en Gran Bretaña se conduce por la izquierda 5. (*cut of meat*) costado *m* 6. (*direction*) **from all ~(s)** de todas partes; **from ~ to ~** de lado a lado 7. (*party in dispute*) bando *m;* (*team*) equipo *m;* **to take ~s** tomar partido; **to take sb's ~** ponerse de parte de alguien; **to be on the ~ of sb/sth** ser partidario de alguien/algo; **to have sth on one's ~** tener algo a su favor; **on my father's ~** por parte de mi padre 8. (*aspect*) aspecto *m;* (*of story*) versión *f* 9. (*aside*) **on the ~** aparte; **to leave sth on one ~** dejar algo a un lado ▸**the other ~ of the coin** la otra cara de la moneda; **to come down on one ~ of the fence or other** tomar partido por una postura o por la otra; **to be on the right/wrong ~ of the law** estar dentro/fuera de la ley; **to get on the right/wrong ~ of sb** congraciarse/ponerse a malas con alguien; **to be on the right/wrong ~ of 40** no llegar a/pasar de 40 años; **to be on the save ~ ...** para mayor seguridad...

sidearm *n* pistola *f*

sideboard ['saɪdbɔːd, *Am:* -bɔːrd] *n* 1. (*buffet*) aparador *m,* bufet *m AmL* 2. *pl, Brit, inf* (*sideburns*) patillas *fpl*

sideburns ['saɪdbɜːnz, *Am:* -bɜːrnz] *npl* patillas *fpl*

sidecar ['saɪdkɑːʳ, *Am:* -kɑːr] *n* sidecar *m* **side dish** *n* acompañamiento *m* **side effect** *n* efecto *m* secundario **side issue** *n* tema *m* secundario **sidekick** *n* subordinado, -a *m, f* **sidelight** *n* AUTO luz *f* de posición

sideline ['saɪdlaɪn] I. *n* 1. (*secondary activity*) actividad *f* secundaria 2. *Am* SPORTS (*line*) línea *f* de banda; (*area*) banda *f;* **on the ~s** *fig* al margen; **from the ~s** desde fuera II. *vt* 1. SPORTS (*keep from playing*) dejar sin jugar 2. (*ignore*) marginar

sidelong ['saɪdlɒŋ, *Am:* -lɑːŋ] *adj* (*glance*) de soslayo

side road *n* carretera *f* secundaria

sidesaddle ['saɪdˌsædl] I. *n* silla *f* de amazona II. *adv* **to ride ~** montar a asentadillas

side salad *n* ensalada *f* de acompañamiento **sideshow** *n* caseta *f;* **to be a ~ of sth** *fig* tener una función secundaria respecto a algo **side-slip** *n* AVIAT deslizamiento *m* lateral

sidestep ['saɪdstep] <-pp-> I. *vt a. fig* esquivar II. *vi* dar un paso hacia un lado

side street *n* calle *f* lateral **side table** *n* trinchero *m*

sidetrack ['saɪdtræk] I. *vt* apartar de su propósito, distraer II. *n* vía *f* muerta; *fig* cuestión *f* secundaria

side view *n* perfil *m*

sidewalk ['saɪdwɔːk, *Am:* -wɑːk] *n Am* acera *f,* vereda *f AmL,* banqueta *f Guat, Méx*

sideward ['saɪdwəd], **sideways** ['saɪdweɪz] I. *adv* 1. (*to/from a side*) de lado; (*glance*) de reojo; **to look ~ to the left and right** mirar hacia la izquierda y hacia la derecha 2. (*facing a side*) hacia un lado II. *adj* lateral; (*glance*) de reojo

side whiskers *npl* patillas *fpl* **side wind** *n* viento *m* lateral

sidewinder ['saɪdˌwaɪndəʳ, *Am:* -dɚ] *n* 1. ZOOL crótalo *m* 2. *Am* (*blow*) ráfaga *f* oblicua

siding ['saɪdɪŋ] *n* 1. RAIL vía *f* muerta 2. *no pl, Am* (*wall*) recubrimiento *m* aislante

sidle ['saɪdl] *vi* **to ~ up to sb** acercarse sigilosamente a alguien

siege [siːdʒ] *n* MIL sitio *m;* **to lay ~ to sth** sitiar algo; **to be under ~** estar sitiado

Sierra Leone [sɪ'erəlɪ'əʊn, *Am:* sɪˌerəlɪ'oʊn] *n* Sierra *f* Leona

Sierra Leonean [sɪ'erəlɪ'əʊnɪən] **I.** *adj* sierraleonés, -esa **II.** *n* sierraleonés, -esa *m, f*

sieve [sɪv] **I.** *n* (*for flour*) tamiz *m;* (*for liquid*) colador *m;* **to put sth through a ~** pasar algo por una criba ►**to have a memory like a ~** tener la cabeza como un colador **II.** *vt* (*flour*) tamizar; (*liquid*) colar

sift [sɪft] *vt* **1.** (*pass through sieve*) tamizar **2.** (*examine closely*) escudriñar

sigh [saɪ] **I.** *n* suspiro *m;* **to let out a ~** dejar escapar un suspiro **II.** *vi* suspirar; **to ~ with relief** suspirar aliviado; **to ~ for sb** *form* suspirar por alguien

sight [saɪt] **I.** *n* **1.** (*view, faculty*) vista *f;* **to be out of (one's) ~** no estar a la vista (de uno); **to come into ~** aparecer; **to catch ~ of sth** vislumbrar algo; **to hate the ~ of sth/sb** no poder ver algo/a alguien; **to know sb by ~** conocer a alguien de vista; **to lose ~ of sth** perder algo de vista; (*to forget*) no tener presente algo; **at first ~** a primera vista; **within ~ of sth** a la vista de algo; **I can't bear the ~ of him!** ¡no lo puede ni ver!; **get out of my ~!** *inf* ¡fuera de mi vista!; **at the ~ of ...** al ver... **2.** *pl* (*attractions*) lugares *mpl* de interés **3.** (*on gun*) mira *f;* **to line up the ~s** alinear las miras; **to lower one's ~s** *fig* apuntar más bajo en cuanto a sus ambiciones; **to set one's ~s on sth** *fig* poner la mira en algo **4.** *no pl* **a ~** (*a lot*) un montón; **she's a ~ better than him** ella es mucho mejor que él ►**to be a ~ for sore eyes** *inf* ser una alegría para los ojos; **out of ~, out of mind** *prov* ojos que no ven, corazón que no siente *prov;* **a real ~** *inf* horrible; **you look a real ~ in those trousers!** ¡estás horrible con esos pantalones!; **second ~** clarividencia *f;* **to have second ~** ser clarividente; **~ unseen** sin haber visto; **I never buy anything ~ unseen** nunca compro nada sin verlo bien antes; **out of ~!** *inf* ¡fabuloso! **II.** *vt* ver

sighted *adj* vidente

sightless *adj* invidente

sightly ['saɪtli] *adj* agradable a la vista

sight-read ['saɪtri:d] MUS **I.** *vi* interpretar a primera vista **II.** *vt* ejecutar a primera vista

sightseeing ['saɪtˌsi:ɪŋ] *n no pl* turismo *m;* **to go ~** visitar los lugares de interés

sightseeing tour *n* visita *f* a los lugares de interés

sightseer ['saɪtˌsi:əʳ, *Am:* -ɚ] *n* turista *mf*

sign [saɪn] **I.** *n* **1.** (*gesture*) señal *f;* **to make a ~ (to sb)** hacer un gesto (a alguien); **to make the ~ of the cross** hacer la señal de la cruz; **as a ~ that ...** como señal de que... **2.** (*signpost*) indicador *m;* (*signboard*) letrero *m* **3.** (*symbol*) símbolo *m* **4.** *a.* MAT, ASTR, MUS signo *m;* **a ~ that ...** un signo de que... **5.** (*trace*) rastro *m;* **they could not find any ~ of them** no pudieron encontrar ningún rastro de ellos; **it's a ~ of the times** así son los tiempos actuales **II.** *vt* **1.** (*write signature on*) firmar; **he ~ed himself 'Mark Taylor'** firmó con el nombre de 'Mark Taylor' **2.** (*employ under contract*) contratar; SPORTS fichar **3.** (*gesticulate*) indicar; **to ~ sb to do sth** indicar a alguien que haga algo **4.** (*say in sign language*) decir por señas **III.** *vi* **1.** (*write signature*) firmar; **~ here, please** firme aquí, por favor; **to ~ for sth** firmar el recibo de algo; **to ~ for a team** fichar por un equipo **2.** (*use sign language*) comunicarse por señas **3.** (*gesticulate*) gesticular; **to ~ to sb to do sth** hacer señas a alguien para que haga algo; **to ~ to sb that ...** indicar con señas a alguien que... *+subj*

◆**sign away** *vt* firmar la cesión de; (*land*) abandonar; (*rights*) ceder

◆**sign in I.** *vi* firmar la entrada **II.** *vt* **to sign sb in** firmar por alguien

◆**sign off I.** *vi inf* **1.** RADIO, TV terminar la emisión **2.** (*end*) terminar; **I think I'll ~ early today** creo que hoy acabaré pronto de trabajar **II.** *vt* despedir

◆**sign on I.** *vi* **1.** (*agree to take work*) firmar un contrato; **to sign on as a soldier** enrolarse como soldado; **to ~ for sth** inscribirse en algo; **he has signed on for courses in English** se ha apuntado a clases de inglés **2.** *Brit, inf* (*confirm unemployed status*) sellar (en el paro) **II.** *vt* contratar

◆**sign out I.** *vi* firmar en el registro de salida **II.** *vt* **to ~ sth** firmar para retirar algo; **you must sign all books out** tienes que firmar para sacar libros prestados; **she signed out a company car** firmó para tomar prestado un coche de la empresa

◆**sign over** *vt* firmar un traspaso; **to sign property over to sb** poner algo a nombre de alguien

◆**sign up I.** *vi* apuntarse **II.** *vt* contratar

signal ['sɪgnəl] **I.** *n* **1.** (*particular gesture*) seña *f;* **to give (sb) a ~ (to do sth)** hacer una señal (a alguien) (para que haga algo) **2.** (*indication*) signo *m;* **to be a ~ that ...** ser signo de que... **3.** AUTO, RAIL, INFOR señal *f* **4.** ELEC, RADIO transmisión *f;* (*reception*) recepción *f* **II.** <*Brit:* -ll-, *Am:* -l-> *vt* **1.** (*indicate*) indicar; **to ~ that ...** señalar que... **2.** (*gesticulate*) hacer señas; **he ~led them to be quiet** les hizo señas para que se callaran **III.** <*Brit:* -ll-, *Am:* -l-> *vi* hacer una señal; **the teacher ~led for the examination to begin** el profesor señaló el comienzo del examen; **he ~led right** AUTO puso el intermitente derecho **IV.** *adj form* notable

signal box *n* RAIL garita *f* de señales **signal lamp** *n* lámpara *f* de señales

signally *adv* notablemente

signalman ['sɪgnəlmən] <-men> *n* RAIL guardavía *mf*

signatory ['sɪgnətəri, *Am:* -tɔ:r-] *n* signatario, -a *m, f*

signature ['sɪgnətʃəʳ, *Am:* -nətʃɚ] *n* firma *f*

signboard ['saɪnbɔ:d, *Am:* -bɔ:rd] *n* letrero *m*

S

signet ring ['sɪgnɪtˌrɪŋ] *n* anillo *m* de sello
significance [sɪg'nɪfɪkəns, *Am:* -'nɪfə-] *n no pl* **1.** (*importance*) importancia *f* **2.** (*meaning*) significado *m*
significant [sɪg'nɪfɪkənt, *Am:* -'nɪfə-] *adj* **1.** (*important*) importante; (*improvement*) significativo, -a; (*increase*) considerable; (*difference*) notable **2.** (*meaningful*) con significado
signify ['sɪgnɪfaɪ, *Am:* -nə-] **I.** <-ie-> *vt* **1.** *form* (*mean*) significar; **to ~ that ...** significar que... **2.** (*indicate*) indicar **II.** <-ie-> *vi form* (*matter*) tener importancia
sign language ['saɪnˌlæŋgwɪdʒ] *n* lenguaje *m* de señas **sign painter** *n* rotulista *mf* **signpost I.** *n a. fig* señal *f* **II.** *vt* señalizar
Sikh [si:k] *n no pl* sij *mf*
silage ['saɪlɪdʒ] *n no pl* AGR ensilaje *m*
silence ['saɪləns] **I.** *n* silencio *m* ►**~ is golden** *prov* el silencio es oro **II.** *vt* (*machine, bells*) silenciar; (*person*) hacer callar
silencer ['saɪlənsəʳ, *Am:* -sɚ] *n* silenciador *m*
silent ['saɪlənt] *adj* silencioso, -a; LING mudo, -a; **~ film** película *f* muda; **the ~ majority** la mayoría silenciosa; **~ partner** *Am* ECON socio *m* comanditario; **to be ~ on sth** no decir nada sobre algo; **to fall ~** callarse
silently *adv* silenciosamente, en silencio
silhouette [ˌsɪlu'et] **I.** *n* silueta *f* **II.** *vt* destacar; **to be ~d against sth** perfilarse sobre algo
silica ['sɪlɪkə] *n no pl* sílice *f*
silicate ['sɪlɪkeɪt] *n* silicato *m*
silicon ['sɪlɪkən] *n no pl* silicio *m*
silicon chip *n* INFOR, ELEC chip *m* de silicio
silicone ['sɪlɪkəʊn, *Am:* -koʊn] *n no pl* silicona *f*
silicosis [ˌsɪlɪ'kəʊsɪs, *Am:* -'koʊ-] *n no pl* MED silicosis *f*
silk [sɪlk] *n* **1.** seda *f*; **~ dress** vestido *m* de seda; **~ scarf** pañuelo *m* de seda **2.** *Brit* LAW abogado, -a *m, f* (de categoría superior); **to receive** [*o* **to take**] **~** ser ascendido a la abogacía superior
silken ['sɪlkən] *adj* (*clothing*) de seda; (*hair*) sedoso, -a; (*voice*) suave
silk hat *n* sombrero *m* de copa **silk moth** *n* mariposa *f* de seda **silk paper** *n* papel *m* de seda **silk screen printing** *n* serigrafía *f* **silkworm** *n* gusano *m* de seda
silky ['sɪlki] <-ier, -iest> *adj* sedoso, -a; (*fur, voice*) suave
sill [sɪl] *n* (*of door*) umbral *m*; (*of window*) alféizar *m*
silly ['sɪli] <-ier, -iest> *adj* (*person*) tonto, -a, dundo, -a *AmC, Col,* baboso, -a *AmC*; (*idea*) estúpido, -a; **~ season** *período de verano en que los periódicos llenan sus páginas con noticias triviales.*; **it was ~ of her to ...** fue una estupidez por su parte...; **to look ~** parecer ridículo; **to laugh oneself ~** desternillarse de risa; **to knock sb ~** *inf* dejar a alguien atontado de una paliza
silo ['saɪləʊ, *Am:* -loʊ] *n* silo *m*
silt [sɪlt] *n no pl* sedimento *m*
◆**silt up** *vi* encenagarse
silver ['sɪlvəʳ, *Am:* -vɚ] **I.** *n no pl* **1.** (*metal*) plata *f* **2.** (*coins*) monedas *fpl* de plata **3.** (*cutlery*) cubertería *f* **4.** (*dishes, trays*) vajilla *f* de plata **II.** *adj* **1.** (*made of silver*) de plata **2.** (*silver-coloured*) plateado, -a
silver birch *n* abedul *m* (plateado) **silver fir** *n* abeto *m* blanco
silverfish ['sɪlvəˌfɪʃ, *Am:* -vɚˌ-] *n* **1.** (*fish*) pez *m* plateado **2.** (*insect*) lepisma *m*
silver foil *n* papel *m* de plata **silver jubilee** *n* vigésimo quinto aniversario *m* **silver lining** *n* resquicio *m* de esperanza **silver mine** *n* mina *f* de plata **silver paper** *n* papel *m* de plata **silver plate** *n* **1.** (*dishes, trays*) vajilla *f* de plata **2.** (*coating*) baño *m* de plata **silver-plate** *vt* platear **silver screen** *n* CINE **the ~** la pantalla cinematográfica **silver service** *n* servicio *m* de guante blanco
silverside ['sɪlvəsaɪd, *Am:* -vɚ-] *n no pl, Aus, Brit* cuarto *m* trasero de la ternera
silversmith ['sɪlvəsmɪθ, *Am:* -vɚ-] *n* platero, -a *m, f*
silverware ['sɪlvəweəʳ, *Am:* -vɚwer] *n no pl* **1.** (*cutlery*) cubertería *f* **2.** (*dishes, trays*) vajilla *f* de plata
silver wedding *n* bodas *fpl* de plata
silvery <-ier, -iest> *adj* plateado, -a
simian ['sɪmiən] **I.** *n* simio *m* **II.** *adj* simiesco, -a
similar ['sɪmɪləʳ, *Am:* -əlɚ] *adj* similar
similarity [ˌsɪmə'lærəti, *Am:* -ə'lerət̬i] *n* parecido *m*, semejanza *f*
simile ['sɪmɪli, *Am:* -əli] *n* LIT, LING símil *m*
similitude [sɪ'mɪlɪtju:d, *Am:* sə'mɪlətu:d] *n* **1.** (*quality of being similar*) similitud *f* **2.** (*comparison*) comparación *f*
simmer ['sɪməʳ, *Am:* -ɚ] **I.** *vi* **1.** GASTR hervir a fuego lento **2.** *fig* estar a punto de estallar **II.** *vt* cocer a fuego lento **III.** *n* ebullición *f* lenta; **to bring sth to a ~** poner algo a hervir; **to keep sth at a ~** mantener algo hirviendo a fuego lento
◆**simmer down** *vi inf* tranquilizarse
simper ['sɪmpəʳ, *Am:* -pɚ] **I.** *vi* sonreír como un tonto, sonreír como una tonta **II.** *n* sonrisa *f* afectada
simple ['sɪmpl] *adj* **1.** (*not elaborate, not complex*) sencillo, -a **2.** (*not difficult*) fácil **3.** (*honest*) honesto, -a **4.** (*ordinary*) normal **5.** (*foolish*) simple
simple-minded [ˌsɪmpl'maɪndɪd] *adj inf* **1.** (*dumb*) tonto, -a **2.** (*naive*) ingenuo, -a
simpleton ['sɪmpltən] *n inf* bobalicón, -ona *m, f,* guanaco, -a *AmL*
simplicity [sɪm'plɪsəti, *Am:* -t̬i] *n no pl* **1.** (*plainness*) sencillez *f* **2.** (*ease*) simplicidad *f*
simplification [ˌsɪmplɪfɪ'keɪʃən, *Am:* -plə-] *n* simplificación *f*
simplify ['sɪmplɪfaɪ, *Am:* -plə-] *vt* simplificar
simplistic [sɪm'plɪstɪk] *adj pej* simplista
simply ['sɪmpli] *adv* **1.** (*not elaborately*) sen-

cillamente **2.** (*just*) simplemente **3.** (*absolutely*) completamente **4.** (*naturally*) de forma natural
simulate ['sɪmjʊleɪt] *vt* **1.** (*resemble*) simular **2.** (*feign*) fingir
simulation [ˌsɪmjʊ'leɪʃən] *n* (*imitation*) simulación *f;* (*of feeling*) fingimiento *m*
simulator ['sɪmjʊleɪtəʳ, *Am:* -t̬ɚ] *n* INFOR, TECH simulador *m*
simultaneous [ˌsɪml'teɪnɪəs, *Am:* ˌsaɪml-'teɪnjəs] *adj* simultáneo, -a; ~ **broadcast** retransmisión *f* simultánea
sin [sɪn] **I.** *n* pecado *m;* **to confess a** ~ confesar un pecado ►**to be as ugly as** ~ ser más feo que Picio **II.** *vi* <-nn-> pecar
since [sɪns] **I.** *adv* **1.** (*from then on*) desde entonces; **ever** ~ desde entonces **2.** (*ago*) **long** ~ hace mucho tiempo; **not long** ~ hace poco **II.** *prep* desde; **how long is it** ~ **the crime?** ¿cuánto tiempo ha pasado desde el crimen? **III.** *conj* **1.** (*because*) ya que, puesto que **2.** (*from the time that*) desde que; **it's a week now** ~ **I came back** ya ha pasado una semana desde que llegué
sincere [sɪn'sɪəʳ, *Am:* sɪn'sɪr] *adj* sincero, -a
sincerely *adv* sinceramente; **yours** ~ le saluda atentamente
sincerity [sɪn'serəti, *Am:* sɪn'serət̬i] *n no pl* sinceridad *f;* **in all** ~ con toda franqueza
sine [saɪn] *n* MAT seno *m*
sinecure ['saɪnɪkjʊəʳ, *Am:* 'saɪnəkjʊr] *n* sinecura *f*
sine die [ˌsaɪnɪ'daɪiː, *Am:* ˌsaɪni'daɪi] *adv* LAW sine die
sine qua non [ˌsɪnikwɑː'nəʊn, *Am:* 'sɪneɪ-kwɑː'noʊn] *n form* condición *f* sine qua non
sinew ['sɪnjuː] *n* tendón
sinewy *adj* **1.** (*muscular*) nervudo, -a **2.** (*meat*) con nervios
sinful ['sɪnfəl] *adj* (*person*) pecador(a); (*thought, act*) pecaminoso, -a; (*waste*) inmoral
sing [sɪŋ] <sang, sung> **I.** *vi* (*person, bird*) cantar; (*wind, kettle*) silbar; **to** ~ **to sb** cantar para alguien **II.** *vt* cantar; **to** ~ **sb to sleep** arrullar a alguien
◆**sing out I.** *vi* (*sing*) cantar fuerte **II.** *vt inf* (*call*) **to** ~ **sb's name** llamar a alguien a voces
◆**sing up** *vi Brit, Aus* cantar más fuerte
singalong ['sɪŋəlɒŋ, *Am:* -lɑːŋ] *n* canto *m* a coro
Singapore [ˌsɪŋə'pɔːʳ, *Am:* 'sɪŋəpɔːr] *n* Singapur *m*
Singaporean [sɪŋə'pɔːʳiːən, *Am:* 'sɪŋə-pɔːriːən] **I.** *adj* de Singapur **II.** *n* habitante *mf* de Singapur
singe [sɪndʒ] **I.** *vt* chamuscar; (*hair*) quemar las puntas de **II.** *n* quemadura *f* superficial
singer ['sɪŋəʳ, *Am:* -ɚ] *n* cantante *mf*
singer-songwriter *n* cantautor(a) *m(f)*
singing *n no pl* canto *m* **singing lesson** *n* lección *f* de canto **singing teacher** *n* profesor(a) *m(f)* de canto **singing voice** *n* **to have a good** ~ tener buena voz (para el canto)
single ['sɪŋgl] **I.** *adj* **1.** (*one only*) único, -a; (*blow*) solo, -a; **not a** ~ **person/thing** nadie/nada; **not a** ~ **soul** ni un alma; **every** ~ **thing** cada cosa; **in** ~ **figures** por debajo de diez **2.** (*with one part*) simple **3.** (*unmarried*) soltero, -a **4.** (*ticket*) sencillo, -a **5.** (*bed, room*) individual **II.** *n* **1.** *Brit, Aus* (*one-way ticket*) billete *m* de ida **2.** (*one-dollar note*) billete *m* de un dólar **3.** (*record*) single *m* **4.** SPORTS golpe *m* que marca un tanto; (*in baseball*) primera base *f* **5.** (*single room*) habitación *f* individual
◆**single out** *vt* señalar; **to single sb out for criticism** criticar a alguien en particular
single-breasted *adj* (*suit*) recto, -a, sin cruzar **single currency** *n* moneda *f* única **single-decker** *n* autobús *m* de un piso **single-entry bookkeeping** *n* contabilidad *f* por partida simple **Single European Market** *n* **the** ~ el mercado Único Europeo **single-handed** *adv* sin ayuda de nadie **single-hander** *n* NAUT yate *m* de un solo tripulante **single-lens reflex camera** *n* cámara *f* réflex (monoobjetivo) **single-minded** *adj* resuelto, -a **single-mindedness** *n no pl* firmeza *f* **single mother** *n* madre *f* soltera **single parent** *n* (*father*) padre *m* soltero; (*mother*) madre *f* soltera **single-parent family** <-ies> *n* familia *f* monoparental
singles bar *n* bar *m* de encuentros
single-seater *n* monoplaza *m* **single-sex school** *n* (*for boys*) escuela *f* para niños; (*for girls*) escuela *f* para niñas
singlet ['sɪŋglɪt] *n Brit, Aus* camiseta *f*
single-track *adj* **1.** RAIL de vía única **2.** (*road*) de carril único
singly ['sɪŋgli] *adv* uno por uno
singsong ['sɪŋsɒŋ, *Am:* -sɑːŋ] **I.** *n* **1.** *Brit, Aus* (*singing session*) concierto *m* espontáneo **2.** *no pl* (*way of speaking*) sonsonete *m* **II.** *adj* **to speak in a** ~ **voice** hablar cantando
singular ['sɪŋgjələʳ, *Am:* -lɚ] **I.** *adj* **1.** LING singular; ~ **form** forma *f* de singular; **the third person** ~ la tercera persona del singular **2.** (*notable*) singular; **of** ~ **beauty** de belleza sin par; **a** ~ **lack of tact** una increíble falta de tacto **II.** *n no pl* LING singular *m;* **in the** ~ en singular
singularity [ˌsɪŋgjə'lærəti, *Am:* -'lerət̬i] *n no pl, form* singularidad *f*
singularly *adv form* singularmente
Sinhalese [ˌsɪŋhə'liːz, *Am:* ˌsɪnhə'liːz] **I.** *n* **1.** (*person*) cingalés, -esa *m, f* **2.** (*language*) cingalés *m* **II.** *adj* cingalés, -esa
sinister ['sɪnɪstəʳ, *Am:* -stɚ] *adj* siniestro, -a
sink [sɪŋk] <sank *o* sunk, sunk> **I.** *n* (*in kitchen*) fregadero *m;* (*in bathroom*) lavabo *m* **II.** *vi* **1.** (*in water*) hundirse; **to** ~ **to the bottom** hundirse hasta el fondo **2.** (*price, level*) bajar **3.** (*drop down*) caer; **to** ~ **to the ground** caer al suelo; **to** ~ **to one's knees** hincarse de rodillas **4.** (*decline*) bajar; **to** ~ **in sb's estimation** perder la estima de alguien; **to** ~ **into**

S

depression sumirse en la depresión; **to ~ into oblivion** caer en el olvido; **to be ~ing (fast)** (*in health*) empeorar (rápidamente) ▶**to leave sb to ~ or swim** abandonar a alguien a su suerte **III.** *vt* **1.** (*cause to submerge*) hundir **2.** (*ruin*) destruir **3.** MIN excavar **4.** SPORTS (*ball*) meter **5.** *Brit, Aus, inf* (*drink: bottle*) tragarse **6.** (*invest*) invertir **7.** (*plant, bury: teeth*) hincar; **to ~ one's teeth into sth** hincar los dientes en algo

◆**sink back** *vi* (*lean back*) repantigarse

◆**sink down** *vi* **1.** (*descend*) descender **2.** (*to the ground*) agacharse

◆**sink in** *vi* **1.** (*go into surface*) penetrar **2.** (*be absorbed: liquid*) calar **3.** (*be understood*) entenderse

sinker ['sɪŋkəʳ, *Am:* -kɚ] *n* plomo *m*

sinking ['sɪŋkɪŋ] **I.** *n* hundimiento *m* **II.** *adj* **a ~ feeling** una sensación de que todo se va a pique; **with a ~ heart** con el alma encogida

sink unit ['siŋk͵juːnɪt] *n* lavadero *m*

sinner ['sɪnəʳ, *Am:* -ɚ] *n* pecador(a) *m(f)*

sinuous ['sɪnjʊəs] *adj* sinuoso, -a

sinus ['saɪnəs] *n* seno *m*

sinusitis [͵saɪnə'saɪtɪs, *Am:* -t̬ɪs] *n no pl* MED sinusitis *f*

Sioux [suː] **I.** *adj* sioux **II.** *n* **1.** (*person*) sioux *mf* **2.** (*language*) sioux *m*

sip [sɪp] **I.** <-pp-> *vt* sorber **II.** <-pp-> *vi* sorber **III.** *n* sorbo *m*; **to have a sip** dar un sorbo

siphon ['saɪfən] **I.** *n* sifón *m* **II.** *vt* sacar con sifón

◆**siphon off** *vt* **1.** (*liquid*) sacar con sifón **2.** (*money*) malversar

sir [sɜːʳ, *Am:* sɜːr] *n* señor *m*

sire ['saɪəʳ, *Am:* 'saɪɚ] *n* (*form of address*) señor *m*

siren ['saɪərən, *Am:* 'saɪrən] *n* sirena *f*

sirloin ['sɜːlɔɪn, *Am:* 'sɜːr-] *n no pl* solomillo *m*, diezmillo *m Méx*

sirocco [sɪ'rɒkəʊ, *Am:* sə'rɑːkoʊ] *n* METEO siroco *m*

sis [sɪs] *n Am, inf abbr of* **sister** hermana *f*

sisal ['saɪsəl] *n no pl* **1.** (*plant*) pita *f* **2.** (*fibre*) sisal *m*

sissy ['sɪsi] **I.** <-ies> *n inf* marica *m* **II.** <-ier, -iest> *adj inf* mariquita

sister ['sɪstəʳ, *Am:* -ɚ] *n* **1.** *a.* REL hermana *f*; **Sister Catherine** Sor Caterina; **~ company** empresa *f* asociada; **~ ship** barco *m* gemelo **2.** *Brit, Aus* (*nurse*) enfermera *f*

sisterhood ['sɪstəhʊd, *Am:* -tɚ-] *n no pl* hermandad *f*

sister-in-law ['sɪstərɪnlɔː, *Am:* -tɚɪnlɑː] <sisters-in-law *o* sister-in-laws> *n* cuñada *f*, concuña *f AmL*

sisterly *adj* de hermana

sit [sɪt] <sat, sat> **I.** *vi* **1.** sentarse; (*be in seated position*) estar sentado, -a; **~!** (*to dog*) ¡siéntate! **2.** ART posar; **to ~ for one's portrait** hacerse retratar **3.** (*enter exam*) presentarse; **to ~ for an examination** presentarse a un examen **4.** *inf* (*babysit*) **to ~ for sb** cuidar a alguien **5.** (*perch*) posarse; (*incubate eggs*) empollar **6.** (*be placed*) yacer; (*rest unmoved*) permanecer quieto, estar; **to ~ on the shelf** estar en el estante **7.** (*be in session*) celebrar sesión **8.** POL (*be in office*) **to ~ in parliament/congress** ser diputado **9.** (*fit*) **to ~ well/badly** caer [*o* sentar] bien/mal **10.** (*be agreeable*) **the idea doesn't ~ well with any of them** la idea no les convence a ninguno ▶**to be ~ting pretty** estar bien situado; **to ~ tight** (*not move*) no moverse; (*not change opinion*) no dar el brazo a torcer **II.** *vt* **1.** (*put on seat*) sentar **2.** *Brit* (*take exam*) presentarse a; **to ~ an exam** presentarse a un examen

◆**sit about** *vi Brit*, **sit around** *vi* estar sin hacer nada; **to ~ around the house** vagar por la casa

◆**sit back** *vi* **1.** (*in chair*) sentarse cómodamente **2.** (*do nothing*) cruzarse de brazos

◆**sit down** **I.** *vi* **1.** (*take a seat*) sentarse **2.** (*be sitting*) estar sentado **II.** *vt* sentar; **to sit oneself down** sentarse

◆**sit in** *vi* **1.** (*observe*) asistir como oyente **2.** (*represent*) **to ~ for sb** sustituir a alguien **3.** (*hold sit-in*) hacer una sentada

◆**sit on** *vt inf* **1.** (*withold: information*) guardar para sí; (*secret*) no revelar **2.** (*rebuke: person*) poner en su sitio; (*idea, scheme*) acabar con

◆**sit out** **I.** *vi* (*sit outdoors*) sentarse fuera **II.** *vt* **1.** (*not take part in*) no tomar parte en; **to ~ a dance** no bailar **2.** (*remain until the end of*) aguantar hasta el final

◆**sit through** *vt* aguantar hasta el final

◆**sit up** **I.** *vi* **1.** (*sit erect*) sentarse derecho; **~!** ¡siéntate derecho! **2.** *inf* (*pay attention*) prestar atención **3.** (*not go to bed*) trasnochar **II.** *vt* incorporar

sitcom ['sɪtkɒm, *Am:* -kɑːm] *n inf* TV *abbr of* **situation comedy** comedia *f* de situación

sit-down strike [͵sɪtdaʊn'straɪk] *n* huelga *f* de brazos caídos

site [saɪt] **I.** *n* **1.** (*place*) sitio *m*; (*of battle*) lugar *m* **2.** (*vacant land for building*) solar *m*; **building ~** obra *f* **3.** GEO, HIST yacimiento *m* **4.** INFOR página *f*, sitio *m*; **web ~** página *f* web, sitio *m* web **II.** *vt* situar

sit-in ['sɪtɪn, *Am:* 'sɪt̬-] *n* sentada *f*; **to hold a ~** hacer una sentada

siting *n no pl* situación *f*

sitter *n* **1.** ART modelo *mf* **2.** *Am* (*babysitter*) canguro *mf* **3.** *inf* SPORTS cosa *f* fácil; **to miss a ~** fallar algo de lo más fácil

sitting *n* (*session*) sesión *f*; (*for meal*) turno *m*

sitting duck *n s.* **sitting target** **sitting member** *n Brit* POL miembro *mf* en funciones **sitting room** *n Brit* cuarto *m* de estar **sitting target** *n* blanco *m* fácil **sitting tenant** *n* inquilino, -a *m, f* en posesión

situate ['sɪtʃʊeɪt, *Am:* 'sɪtʃueɪt] *vt form* **1.** (*locate*) colocar, ubicar *Arg* **2.** (*in context*) situar

situated ['sɪtʃʊeɪtɪd, *Am:* 'sɪtʃueɪt̬ɪd] *adj* **1.** (*located*) situado, -a; **to be ~ near the station** estar ubicado cerca de la estación **2.** (*in a state*) **to be well/badly ~** estar bien/mal situado; **to be well ~ to do sth** estar en una buena situación para hacer algo

situation [ˌsɪtʃʊ'eɪʃən, *Am:* ˌsɪtʃu'-] *n* **1.** (*circumstances*) situación *f;* ECON, POL coyuntura *f* **2.** (*location*) colocación *f* **3.** (*job*) puesto *m*

sit-up ['sɪtʌp] *n* **to do ~s** hacer abdominales

six [sɪks] **I.** *adj* seis *inv* **II.** *n* seis *m;* **in ~ figures** por encima de cien mil ►**to give sb ~ of the best** dar a alguien seis azotes; **to be at ~es and sevens** estar hecho un lío; *s. a.* **eight**

six-figure sum *n* cantidad *f* de seis cifras

six-footer [ˌsɪks'fʊtəʳ] *n persona que mide 1,83 metros o más*

six-pack ['sɪkspæk] *n* (*of beer*) paquete *m* de seis cervezas

sixteen [sɪk'stiːn] **I.** *adj* dieciséis *inv* **II.** *n* dieciséis *m; s. a.* **eight**

sixteenth [ˌsɪk'stiːnθ] **I.** *adj* decimosexto, -a **II.** *n no pl* **1.** (*order*) decimosexto, -a *m, f* **2.** (*date*) dieciséis *m* **3.** (*fraction*) dieciseisavoo *m;* (*part*) dieciseisava parte *f; s. a.* **eighth**

sixth [sɪksθ, *Am:* sɪkstθ] **I.** *adj* sexto, -a **II.** *n no pl* **1.** (*order*) sexto, -a *m, f* **2.** (*date*) seis *m* **3.** (*fraction*) sexto *m;* (*part*) sexta parte *f; s. a.* **eighth**

> **Sixth-form college** es el nombre que recibe en Gran Bretaña un college para alumnos de 16-18 años, procedentes de un colegio donde no hay **sixth form** (sexto curso). En el college pueden examinarse de sus **A-levels** (algo parecido a la selectividad) o realizar dos cursos equivalentes que les permiten prepararse al acceso a la universidad.

sixtieth ['sɪkstiθ] **I.** *adj* sexagésimo, -a **II.** *n no pl* (*order*) sexagéximo, -a *m, f;* (*fraction*) sexagésimo *m;* (*part*) sexagésima parte *f; s. a.* **eighth**

sixty ['sɪksti] **I.** *adj* sesenta *inv* **II.** *n* <-ies> sesenta *m; s. a.* **eighty**

size¹ [saɪz] **I.** *n no pl* **1.** (*of person, thing, space*) tamaño *m;* (*of problem, operation*) magnitud *f;* **a company of that ~** una empresa de tal envergadura; **to be the same ~ as ...** ser de las mismas dimensiones que...; **to increase/decrease in ~** aumentar/disminuir de tamaño; **to double in ~** doblar en tamaño; **of any ~** de cualquier tamaño; **the ~ of a thumbnail** la medida de una uña; **economy ~ pack** *fig* tamaño *m* ahorro **2.** (*of clothes*) talla *f;* (*of shoes*) número *m;* **collar ~** talla *f* de cuello **3.** (*of amount, bill*) cantidad *f* **II.** *vt* **1.** (*person, thing, space*) medir **2.** (*clothes*) clasificar según la talla

◆**size up** *vt* evaluar

size² [saɪz] *n* cola *f;* (*for cloth*) apresto *m*

sizeable ['saɪzəbl] *adj* bastante grande; (*sum*) considerable

sizzle ['sɪzl] **I.** *vi* chisporrotear **II.** *n no pl* chisporroteo *m*

sizzler ['sɪzləʳ, *Am:* -lɚ] *n inf* (*day*) día *m* caluroso

skate¹ [skeɪt] *n* (*fish*) raya *f*

skate² [skeɪt] **I.** *n* patín *m* ►**to get one's ~s on** *Brit, inf* darse prisa **II.** *vi* patinar; **to ~ over an issue** tocar un tema muy por encima

skateboard ['skeɪtbɔːd, *Am:* -bɔːrd] *n* monopatín *m*

skateboarder *n* monopatinador(a) *m(f)*

skater *n* patinador(a) *m(f);* **figure ~** patinador(a) *m(f)* artístico, -a

skating *n* patinaje *m*

skating rink *n* pista *f* de patinaje

skedaddle [skɪ'dædl] *vi inf* escabullirse

skein [skeɪn] *n* **1.** (*of wool*) madeja *f* **2.** (*of geese, swans*) bandada *f*

skeleton ['skelɪtən, *Am:* '-ə-] *n* **1.** ANAT esqueleto *m,* cacastle *m AmC, Méx;* **to be reduced to a ~** (*be very skinny*) quedarse en los huesos **2.** (*framework: of boat, plane*) armazón *m;* (*of building*) estructura *f* **3.** (*outline: of book, report*) esquema *m* ►**to have a ~ in the cupboard** tener un secreto vergonzoso

skeleton key *n* llave *f* maestra **skeleton staff** *n* personal *m* mínimo

skeptic ['skeptɪk] *n Am, Aus s.* **sceptic**

skeptical *adj Am, Aus s.* **sceptical**

skepticism ['skeptɪsɪzəm] *n Am, Aus s.* **scepticism**

sketch [sketʃ] **I.** *n* **1.** ART boceto *m;* **to make a ~ of sth** hacer un croquis de algo **2.** (*rough draft*) borrador *m* **3.** (*outline*) esquema *m* **4.** THEAT, TV sketch *m* **II.** *vt* **1.** ART hacer un boceto de **2.** (*write draft of*) hacer un borrador de **III.** *vi* ART dibujar

◆**sketch in** *vt* (*details*) resumir

◆**sketch out** *vt* **1.** ART bosquejar **2.** (*describe*) esbozar

sketchbook ['sketʃbʊk] *n* cuaderno *m* de dibujo

sketchy ['sketʃi] <-ier, -iest> *adj* (*vague*) impreciso, -a; (*incomplete*) incompleto, -a

skew [skjuː] **I.** *vt* (*distort*) distorsionar **II.** *n* oblicuidad *f;* **to be on the ~** estar sesgado

skewbald ['skjuːbɔːld, *Am:* -bɑːld] **I.** *n* caballo *m* pío **II.** *adj* pío

skewed ['skjuːd] *adj* sesgado, -a

skewer ['skjʊəʳ, *Am:* 'skjuːɚ] **I.** *n* pincho *m,* brocheta *f* **II.** *vt* ensartar

skew-whiff [ˌskjuː'wɪf] *adj Brit, Aus, inf* torcido, -a

ski [skiː] **I.** *n* esquí *m;* **on ~s** con esquís **II.** *vi* esquiar; **to ~ down the slope** bajar la pista esquiando

ski boot *n* bota *f* de esquí

skid [skɪd] **I.** <-dd-> *vi* **1.** (*on ice*) patinar, colear *AmC, Ant;* **to ~ to a halt** resbalar hasta detenerse; (*while driving*) derrapar; **to ~ off the road** derrapar y salir de la carretera **2.** (*slide over*) **to ~ along** [*o* **across**] **sth** desli-

S

zarse sobre algo II. *n* 1. (*while driving*) derrape *m;* **to go into a ~** empezar a resbalar 2. AVIAT tren *m* de aterrizaje ►**to put the ~s under sb** *Brit, Aus, inf* hacer la zancadilla a alguien; **to put the ~s under sth** *Brit, Aus, inf* hacer fracasar algo; **to be on the ~s** *inf* andar de capa caída

skidmark *n* AUTO huella *f* de un patinazo

skid row *n no pl, Am* barrio *m* bajo; **to be on ~** pordiosear

skier ['ski:əʳ, *Am:* -ɚ] *n* esquiador(a) *m(f)*

skiff [skɪf] *n* esquife *m*

ski goggles *npl* gafas *fpl* de esquiar

skiing *n no pl* esquí *m;* **~ equipment** equipo *m* de esquiar; **~ lesson** lección *f* de esquí

skiing holiday *n* vacaciones *fpl* de esquí

ski instructor *n* monitor *m* de esquí **ski instructress** *n* monitora *f* de esquí **ski jump** *n* 1. *no pl* (*jump*) salto *m* de esquí 2. (*runway*) pista *f* para saltos de esquí

skilful ['skɪlfəl] *adj Brit, Aus* hábil, tinoso, -a *Col, Ven*

skilfully *adv Brit, Aus* hábilmente

ski lift *n* telesquí *m*

skill [skɪl] *n* 1. *no pl* (*ability*) habilidad *f;* **to involve some ~** requerir cierta destreza 2. (*technique*) técnica *f;* **communication ~s** facilidad *f* de comunicación; **language ~s** habilidad *f* para las lenguas; **negotiating ~s** artes *fpl* de negociación

skilled *adj* 1. (*trained*) preparado, -a; (*skilful*) hábil, habiloso, -a *Chile, Perú* 2. (*requiring skill*) cualificado, -a; **~ labour** mano de obra *f* cualificada

skillet ['skɪlɪt] *n* 1. *Brit* (*saucepan*) cacerola *f* 2. *Am* (*frying pan*) sartén *f*

skillful ['skɪlfəl] *adj s.* **skilful**

skillfully *adv Am s.* **skilfully**

skim [skɪm] <-mm-> I. *vt* 1. (*move above*) rozar 2. GASTR espumar; (*milk*) desnatar II. *vi* **to ~ over sth** pasar rozando algo; **to ~ through sth** *fig* hojear algo

ski mask *n* pasamontañas *m*

skimmed milk *n Brit,* **skim milk** *n Am no pl* leche *f* desnatada

skimmer *n* espumadera *f*

skimp [skɪmp] *vi* escatimar gastos; **to ~ (on sth)** escatimar (algo)

skimpy ['skɪmpi] <-ier, -iest> *adj* 1. (*meal*) escaso, -a; (*knowledge*) superficial 2. (*dress*) corto, -a y estrecho, -a

skin [skɪn] I. *n* 1. (*of person*) piel *f;* (*of animal*) pellejo *m,* piel *f;* **to be soaked to the ~** estar calado hasta los huesos 2. (*of apple, potato, tomato*) piel *f;* (*of melon*) corteza *f;* (*of banana*) cáscara *f* 3. TECH revestimiento *m* 4. (*on milk*) nata *f* ►**to be all ~ and bone(s)** estar en los huesos; **it's no ~ off his/her nose** ni le va ni le viene; **by the ~ of one's teeth** por los pelos; **to have a thick ~** ser insensible a las críticas; **to jump out of one's ~** llevarse un susto tremendo; **to get under sb's ~** (*affect*) afectar a alguien II. <-nn-> *vt* 1. (*remove skin from: animal*) despellejar; **to ~ sb alive** *iron* desollar vivo a alguien 2. (*graze*) despellejar

skin cancer *n* cáncer *m* de piel **skincare** *n* cuidado *m* de la piel **skin-deep** *adj* epidérmico, -a; (*beauty*) superficial **skin disease** *n* enfermedad *f* cutánea **skin diver** *n* submarinista *mf* **skin-diving** *n no pl* submarinismo *m* **skin flick** *n inf* película *f* porno

skinflint ['skɪnflɪnt] *n* tacaño, -a *m, f*

skinful ['skɪnfʊl] *n no pl, inf* **to have had a ~** llevar una copa de más

skin graft *n* MED 1. (*transplant*) injerto *m* de piel 2. (*section*) trozo *m* de piel

skinhead ['skɪnhed] *n* cabeza *mf* rapada

skinny ['skɪni] <-ier, -iest> *adj* flaco, -a, charcón, -ona *Arg, Bol, Urug*

skinny-dip ['skɪnidɪp] <-pp-> *vi inf* bañarse en cueros

skint [skɪnt] *adj* **to be ~** no tener ni un céntimo

skintight [skɪn'taɪt] *adj* muy ceñido, -a

skip¹ [skɪp] *n Brit, Aus* (*container*) contenedor *m* de basura

skip² [skɪp] I. <-pp-> *vi* 1. (*take light steps*) brincar; **to ~ from one subject to another** saltar de un tema a otro; **to ~ across to the shops** ir a las tiendas; **to ~ over to France** hacerse una escapadita a Francia 2. *Brit, Aus* (*with rope*) saltar a la comba II. <-pp-> *vt* 1. (*leave out*) omitir 2. (*not participate in*) saltarse; **to ~ classes** faltar a clase 3. *inf* (*leave*) **to ~ the country** salir del país apresuradamente 4. *Am* (*hop with rope*) **to ~ rope** saltar a la comba III. *n* brinco *m*

ski pants *npl* pantalones *mpl* de esquí **ski pass** *n* forfait *m* **ski-plane** *n* avión *m* que puede aterrizar sobre la nieve **ski pole** *n* palo *m* de esquí

skipper ['skɪpəʳ, *Am:* -ɚ] I. *n* NAUT patrón, -ona *m, f;* (*captain*) capitán, -ana *m, f; inf* (*form of address*) jefe *m* II. *vt* (*ship*) patronear; (*aircraft*) pilotar; (*team*) capitanear

skipping rope *n Brit,* **skip rope** *n Am* comba *f*

ski rack *n* portaesquís *m* **ski resort** *n* estación *f* de esquí

skirmish ['skɜ:mɪʃ, *Am:* 'skɜ:r-] I. *n* 1. MIL escaramuza *f,* entrevero *m Arg, Chile, Urug* 2. (*argument*) roce *m* II. *vi* 1. MIL escaramuzar 2. (*argue*) discutir

skirt [skɜ:t, *Am:* skɜ:rt] I. *n* 1. (*garment*) falda *f,* pollera *f AmL;* (*lower part of coat*) faldón *m* 2. *no pl, pej, inf* (*women*) **a piece of ~** una tía II. *vt* 1. (*path, road*) rodear 2. (*avoid*) evitar

skirting (board) ['skɜ:tɪŋ(bɔ:d), *Am:* 'skɜ:rt̬ɪŋ(bɔ:rd)] *n Brit, Aus* rodapié *m*

ski run *n* pista *f* de esquí **ski school** *n* escuela *f* de esquí **ski slope** *n* pista *f* de esquí **ski stick** *n Brit* palo *m* de esquí **ski suit** *n* mono *m* de esquí

skit [skɪt] *n* sátira *f;* **a ~ on sb/sth** una parodia sobre alguien/algo

ski tow *n* telesquí *m*
skitter about ['skɪtəʳ ə'baʊt, *Am:* 'skɪt̬ɚ ə'baʊt] *vi* pulular
skittish ['skɪtɪʃ, *Am:* 'skɪt̬-] *adj* **1.** (*nervous: horse, person*) nervioso, -a, pajarero, -a *AmL* **2.** (*uncertain*) caprichoso, -a
skittle ['skɪtl, *Am:* 'skɪt̬-] *n* bolo *m;* **a game of ~s** un partido de bolos
skive [skaɪv] *vi Brit, inf* gandulear
♦skive off *vi Brit, inf* **to ~ school** hacer novillos
skiver ['skaɪvəʳ, *Am:* -ɚ] *n Brit, inf* gandul(a) *m(f)*
skivvy ['skɪvi] **I.** <-ies> *n* **1.** *Brit* (*servant*) fregona *f* **2.** *pl, Am, inf* (*men's underwear*) calzoncillos *mpl* **3.** *Aus* (*polo-neck*) *suéter fino de cuello redondo* **II.** *vi* hacer las tareas más pesadas
skulduggery [skʌl'dʌgəri] *n no pl* trampas *fpl*
skulk [skʌlk] *vi* **1.** (*hide*) esconderse **2.** (*move furtively*) merodear
skull [skʌl] *n* calavera *f;* ANAT cráneo *m* ►**the ~ and <u>crossbones</u>** la bandera pirata; **to be <u>bored</u> out of one's ~** *inf* estar aburrido como una ostra
skullcap ['skʌlkæp] *n* (*small cap*) casquete *m;* REL solideo *m*
skunk [skʌŋk] *n* **1.** (*animal*) mofeta *f,* zorrino *m CSur,* mapurite *m AmC,* mapuro *m Col, Ven* **2.** *inf* (*person*) canalla *mf*
sky [skaɪ] <-ies> *n* cielo *m;* **the sunny skies of Spain** el cielo soleado de España; **under blue skies** bajo el cielo azul ►**the ~'s the <u>limit</u>** todo es posible; **red ~ at <u>night</u>, shepherd's delight** *prov* el cielo rojo por la noche anuncia buen tiempo; **to <u>praise</u> sth/sb to the skies** poner algo/a alguien por las nuebes
sky-blue [ˌskaɪblu:] *adj* azul celeste *inv* **sky blue** *n no pl* azul *m* celeste
skydiving ['skaɪˌdaɪvɪŋ] *n* caída *m* libre (*en paracaídas*)
sky-high [ˌskaɪ'haɪ] **I.** *adv a. fig* por las nubes; **to go ~** (*prices*) dispararse **II.** *adj* (*price*) astronómico, -a
skyjack ['skaɪdʒæk] *vt* (*plane*) secuestrar
skylark ['skaɪlɑ:k, *Am:* -lɑ:rk] **I.** *n* alondra *f* **II.** *vi* juguetear
skylight ['skaɪlaɪt] *n* tragaluz *m,* aojada *f Col*
skyline ['skaɪlaɪn] *n* **1.** (*city rooftops*) perfil *m* **2.** (*horizon*) horizonte *m*
skyrocket ['skaɪˌrɒkɪt, *Am:* 'skaɪˌrɑ:kɪt] *vi* subir (como un cohete); (*price*) dispararse
skyscraper ['skaɪskreɪpəʳ, *Am:* -pɚ] *n* rascacielos *m inv*
slab [slæb] *n* **1.** (*flat piece: of stone*) losa *f;* (*of concrete*) bloque *m;* (*of wood*) tabla *f;* (*of marble*) placa *f* **2.** (*slice: of cake, of cheese*) trozo *m;* (*of chocolate*) tableta *f* **3.** (*in mortuary*) mesa *f* de amortajamiento
slack [slæk] **I.** *adj* **1.** (*loose: rope*) flojo, -a; (*muscle*) flácido, -a **2.** *pej* (*lazy: student*) vago, -a; (*piece of work*) flojo, -a; (*writing style*) descuidado, -a; (*discipline*) laxo, -a; (*in paying*) negligente **3.** (*not busy*) de poca actividad; **~ demand** poca demanda **II.** *n no pl* **1.** flojedad; **to take up the ~** (*of rope*) tensar la cuerda; (*compensate*) compensar **2.** COM período *m* de inactividad **III.** *vi* hacer el vago
slacken ['slækən] **I.** *vt* **1.** (*loosen*) aflojar **2.** (*reduce: speed, vigilance*) reducir; (*pace*) aflojar **II.** *vi* **1.** (*loosen*) aflojarse, petaquearse *Col* **2.** (*diminish: demand, intensity*) disminuir
♦slack off *vi,* **slacken off I.** *vi* **1.** (*make less effort*) hacer menos esfuerzo **2.** (*go more slowly*) aflojar el paso **3.** (*diminish: demand, intensity*) disminuir **II.** *vt* reducir
slackening ['slækənɪŋ] *n no pl* **1.** (*loosening*) aflojamiento *m* **2.** (*of speed, intensity*) disminución *f*
slacker ['slækəʳ, *Am:* -ɚ] *n inf* vago, -a *m, f*
slackness ['slæknɪs] *n no pl* **1.** (*looseness*) falta *f* de tensión **2.** (*of discipline*) relajamiento *m;* (*negligence*) negligencia *f* **3.** COM inactividad *f* **4.** (*laziness*) pereza *f*
slacks [slæks] *npl* pantalones *mpl* (de sport)
slag [slæg] **I.** *n* **1.** *no pl* (*waste*) escoria *f* **2.** *Brit, pej* (*slut*) puta *f* **II.** <-gg-> *vt inf* (*criticize*) poner por los suelos
♦slag off *vt inf* poner por los suelos
slag heap *n* escorial *m*
slain [sleɪn] **I.** *pp of* **slay II.** *n* **the ~** los fallecidos
slake [sleɪk] *vt liter* aplacar; **to ~ one's thirst** apagar la sed
slalom ['slɑ:ləm] *n* slalom *m*
slam [slæm] **I.** <-mm-> *vt* **1.** (*strike*) golpear; **to ~ the door** dar un portazo; **to ~ the window/book shut** cerrar la ventana/el libro de un golpe; **to ~ the ball into the net** disparar la pelota a la red; **to ~ the phone down on sb** colgar el teléfono a alguien bruscamente **2.** *inf* (*criticize*) poner por los suelos **II.** <-mm-> *vi* **1.** (*close noisily*) cerrarse de golpe **2.** (*hit hard*) **to ~ against sth** chocar contra algo; **to ~ into sth** chocar con algo **III.** *n* (*of door*) portazo *m;* **to close a book with a ~** cerrar un libro de un golpe
slammer ['ʃlæməʳ, *Am:* -ɚ] *n no pl, inf* chirona *f,* cana *f AmS,* bote *m Méx,* guandoca *f Col*
slander ['slɑ:ndəʳ, *Am:* 'slændɚ] **I.** *n no pl* LAW calumnia *f* **II.** *vt* calumniar
slanderer ['slɑ:ndərəʳ, *Am:* 'slændɚɚ] *n* calumniador(a) *m(f)*
slanderous ['slɑ:ndərəs, *Am:* 'slændɚ-] *adj* calumnioso, -a
slang [slæŋ] **I.** *n no pl* argot *m* **II.** *adj* de argot **III.** *vt Brit, Aus, inf* insultar
slanging match *n Brit, Aus* bronca *f*
slangy <-ier, -iest> *adj inf* argótico, -a
slant [slɑ:nt, *Am:* slænt] **I.** *vi* inclinarse **II.** *vt* **1.** (*make diagonal*) inclinar **2.** (*give bias to*) presentar tendenciosamente **III.** *n* **1.** *no pl* (*slope*) inclinación *f;* **to be on the ~** estar

inclinado, -a **2.** (*perspective*) perspectiva *f;* **to put a favourable ~ on sth** dar un sesgo favorable a algo

slanting *adj* (*roof*) inclinado, -a; (*eyes*) rasgado, -a

slap [slæp] **I.** *n* palmada *f;* **a ~ in the face** una bofetada, una biaba *Arg, Urug,* un bife *Arg, Urug; fig* un insulto; **the ~ of the waves** el rugir de las olas ►**~ and tickle** *Brit, inf* achuchones *mpl* **II.** <-pp-> *vt* **1.** (*hit*) dar una palmada, guantear *AmL* **2.** (*put*) **to ~ the book onto the table** tirar el libro en la mesa; **to ~ paint onto the wall** pintar la pared rápidamente **III.** *adv inf* directamente, de lleno; **to drive ~ into sth** chocar de lleno contra algo; **to leave ~ in the middle of a meeting** marcharse justo en plena reunión

◆**slap down** *vt* **1.** (*put down with slap*) tirar **2.** (*silence rudely*) hacer callar

slap-bang [ˌslæpˈbæŋ] *adv Brit, inf* de golpe y porrazo

slapdash [ˈslæpdæʃ] *adj pej, inf* chapucero, -a

slaphead [ˈslæphed] *n inf* calvorota *mf*

slapjack [ˈslæpˌdʒæk] *n Am* crepe *m*

slapstick [ˈslæpstɪk] *n no pl* payasadas *fpl*

slap-up [ˈslæpʌp] *adj Brit, Aus, inf* **a ~ meal** una comilona

slash [slæʃ] **I.** *vt* **1.** (*cut deeply*) rajar; **to ~ one's wrists** cortarse las venas **2.** (*reduce: prices, spending*) rebajar (drásticamente); (*budget*) recortar (drásticamente) **II.** *n* **1.** (*cut*) corte *m* **2.** (*swinging blow*) latigazo *m* **3.** FASHION raja *f* **4.** TYPO barra *f* **5.** *Brit, Aus, inf* meada *f;* **to go for** [*o* **to have**] **a ~** ir a mear

slat [slæt] *n* (*of wood*) listón *m,* tablilla *f;* (*of plastic*) tira *f*

slate [sleɪt] **I.** *n* **1.** *no pl* (*for roof, writing*) pizarra *f* **2.** *Am, Aus* POL lista *f* de candidatos ►**to have a clean ~** no tener borrones en la hoja de servicios; **to wipe the ~ clean** hacer borrón y cuenta nueva; **to put sth on the ~** apuntar algo en la cuenta **II.** *vt* **1.** (*cover with slates*) empizarrar **2.** *Am, Aus* (*schedule*) programar; POL poner en la lista de canditatos **3.** *Brit, Aus, inf* (*criticize*) poner por los suelos

slattern [ˈslætən, *Am:* ˈslæt̬ɚn] *n pej* puta *f*

slatternly *adj pej* sucio, -a

slaughter [ˈslɔːtəʳ, *Am:* ˈslɑːt̬ɚ] **I.** *vt* **1.** (*kill: animal*) matar, beneficiar *AmL,* carnear *CSur;* (*people*) masacrar **2.** *inf* (*defeat*) dar una paliza a **II.** *n no pl* **1.** (*killing: of animal*) matanza *f,* beneficio *AmL,* carneada *f Arg, Chile, Par, Urug;* (*of people*) masacre *f* **2.** *inf* (*defeat*) paliza *f*

slaughterhouse [ˈslɔːtəhaʊs, *Am:* ˈslɑːt̬ɚ-] *n* matadero *m,* tablada *f Par*

Slav [slɑːv] **I.** *n* eslavo, -a *m, f* **II.** *adj* eslavo, -a

slave [sleɪv] **I.** *n* esclavo, -a *m, f* ►**to be a ~ to fashion** ser un esclavo de la moda **II.** *vi* trabajar como un burro

slave driver *n iron, inf* negrero, -a *m, f*

slaver[1] [ˈslævəʳ, *Am:* -ɚ] **I.** *vi* babear **II.** *n no pl* baba *f*

slaver[2] [ˈsleɪvəʳ, *Am:* -ɚ] *n* HIST **1.** (*ship*) barco *m* que trafica con esclavos **2.** (*slave trader*) traficante *mf* de esclavos

slavery [ˈsleɪvəri] *n no pl* esclavitud *f*

slave trade *n* HIST tráfico *m* de esclavos

Slavic [ˈslɑːvɪk] **I.** *n* eslavo, -a *m, f* **II.** *adj* eslavo, -a

slavish [ˈsleɪvɪʃ] *adj* **1.** (*unoriginal*) poco original **2.** (*servile*) servil

Slavonic [sləˈvɒnɪk, *Am:* -ˈvɑːnɪk] **I.** *n* eslavo, -a *m, f* **II.** *adj* eslavo, -a

slay [sleɪ] <slew, slain> *vt* LIT matar

sleaze [sliːz] *n no pl* sordidez *f;* POL corrupción *f*

sleazy [ˈsliːzi] <-ier, -iest> *adj* (*area, bar, affair*) sórdido, -a; (*person*) con mala pinta; POL corrupto, -a

sled [sled] *Am* **I.** *n s.* **sledge[1]** **II.** <-dd-> *vi s.* **sledge[1]**

sledge[1] [sledʒ] **I.** *n* trineo *m* **II.** *vi* ir en trineo

sledge[2] [sledʒ] *n s.* **sledgehammer**

sledgehammer [ˈsledʒˌhæməʳ, *Am:* -ɚ] *n* almádena *f* ►**to use a ~ to crack a nut** matar moscas a cañonazos

sleek [sliːk] *adj* (*fur, hair*) lacio, -a y brillante; (*car*) de líneas elegantes; (*person*) muy aseado, -a

◆**sleek down** *vt* alisar

sleep [sliːp] **I.** *n* **1.** *no pl* (*resting state*) sueño *m;* **to go** [*o* **get**] **to ~** dormirse; **to fall into a deep ~** caer en un sueño profundo; **to not lose ~ over sth** no perder el sueño por algo; **to put sb to ~** dormir a alguien; **to put an animal to ~** (*kill*) sacrificar un animal; **go back to ~!** *iron* ¡sigue durmiendo! **2.** *no pl* (*substance*) lagañas *fpl;* **to have ~ in one's eyes** tener lagañas; **to rub the ~ from one's eyes** quitarse las lagañas **II.** <slept, slept> *vi* dormir; **to ~ sound(ly)** dormir profundamente; **~ tight!** ¡que duermas bien! ►**to ~ on it** consultarlo con la almohada **III.** *vt* alojar

◆**sleep around** *vi pej, inf* acostarse con cualquiera

◆**sleep in** *vi* **1.** *Brit* (*stay in bed*) dormir hasta tarde **2.** (*live*) vivir en (la) casa (donde uno trabaja)

◆**sleep off** *vt* **to sleep it off** dormir la mona, dormir la cruda *AmL*

◆**sleep out** *vi* (*outside*) dormir al aire libre

◆**sleep through** *vt* **to ~ noise** no despertarse con el ruido; **to ~ the journey** dormir durante todo el viaje

◆**sleep together** *vi* **1.** (*have sex*) acostarse juntos **2.** (*share bed*) dormir juntos

◆**sleep with** *vt* **1.** (*have sex with*) acostarse con **2.** (*share bed with*) dormir con

sleeper [ˈsliːpəʳ, *Am:* -pɚ] *n* **1.** (*person*) persona *f* dormida; **to be a heavy/light ~** tener el sueño profundo/ligero **2.** RAIL (*carriage*) coche *m* cama **3.** *Brit, Aus* RAIL (*blocks*) traviesa *f* **4.** (*earstud*) pendiente *m* (en forma de bolita)

sleepiness *n no pl* somnolencia *f*

sleeping *adj* dormido, -a

sleeping bag *n* saco *m* de dormir **Sleeping Beauty** *n* la Bella Durmiente **sleeping car** *n* coche *m* cama **sleeping partner** *n Brit* COM socio, -a *m, f* comanditario, -a **sleeping pill** *n* somnífero *m* **sleeping policeman** <-men> *n* resalto *m* **sleeping sickness** *n no pl* encefalitis *f* letárgica **sleeping tablet** *n* somnífero *m*

sleepless ['sli:pləs] *adj* (*person*) insomne; (*night*) en vela

sleepwalk ['sli:pˌwɔ:k, *Am:* -ˌwɑ:k] *vi* caminar dormido, -a; **he ~s** es sonámbulo

sleepwalker ['sli:pˌwɔ:kəʳ, *Am:* -ˌwɑ:kɚ] *n* sonámbulo, -a *m, f*

sleepy ['sli:pi] <-ier, -iest> *adj* **1.** (*drowsy*) somnoliento, -a **2.** (*quiet: village*) aletargado, -a

sleepyhead ['sli:pihed] *n inf* dormilón, -ona *m, f*

sleet [sli:t] **I.** *n no pl* aguanieve *f* **II.** *vi* **it is ~ing** cae aguanieve

sleeve [sli:v] *n* **1.** (*of shirt*) manga *f*; **to roll up one's ~s** arremangarse **2.** (*cover*) manguito *m* **3.** (*for record*) funda *f* ►**to <u>have</u> sth up one's ~** tener algo en la manga; **to <u>laugh</u> up one's ~ at sb** reírse de alguien para sus adentros

sleeveless ['sli:vlɪs] *adj* sin mangas

sleigh [sleɪ] *n* trineo *m*

sleight of hand [ˌslaɪtɒf'hænd, *Am:* -ɑ:f-] *n no pl* prestidigitación *f*, juego *m* de manos

slender ['slendəʳ, *Am:* -dɚ] *adj* **1.** (*rod, branch*) fino, -a; (*person*) delgado, -a, silgado, -a *Ecua* **2.** (*majority, resources*) escaso, -a; (*chance*) remoto, -a

slenderize ['slendəraɪz] *vi, vt Am, inf* adelgazar

slept [slept] *pt, pp of* **sleep**

slew [slu:] *pt of* **slay**

slice [slaɪs] **I.** *n* **1.** GASTR (*of bread*) rebanada *f*; (*of ham*) loncha *f*; (*of meat*) tajada *f*; (*of cake, pizza*) trozo *m*; (*of cucumber, lemon*) rodaja *f* **2.** (*part: of credit, profits*) parte *f* **3.** (*tool*) pala *f* **4.** (*tennis*) golpe *m* con efecto; (*golf*) slice *m* ►**to get a ~ of the <u>cake</u>** sacar tajada; **~ of <u>life</u>** estampa *f* realista **II.** *vt* **1.** (*bread*) cortar (en rebanadas); (*ham*) cortar (en lonchas); (*meat*) cortar (en tajadas); (*cake*) cortar (en trozos); (*cucumber, lemon*) cortar en (rodajas) **2.** SPORTS **to ~ the ball** (*in tennis*) dar efecto a la pelota; (*in golf*) golpear la bola de slice ►**any <u>way</u> you ~ it** *Am* lo mires por donde lo mires **III.** *vi* **to ~ easily** ser fácil de cortar

◆**slice off** *vt* **1.** (*bread*) cortar (en rebanadas); (*ham*) cortar (en lonchas); (*meat*) cortar (en tajadas); (*cake*) cortar (en trozos); (*cucumber, lemon*) cortar (en rodajas) **2.** (*reduce by*) reducir en

◆**slice up** *vt* (*bread*) cortar en rebanadas; (*ham*) cortar en lonchas; (*meat*) cortar en tajadas; (*cake*) cortar en trozos; (*cucumber*) cortar en rodajas

sliced *adj* (*bread*) cortado, -a en rebanadas; (*ham*) cortado, -a en lonchas; (*meat*) cortado, -a en tajadas; (*cake*) cortado, -a en trozos; (*cucumber, lemon*) cortado, -a en rodajas

sliced bread *n* pan *m* de molde ►**it's the best <u>thing</u> since ~** es lo mejor del mundo

slicer *n* (*for bread*) (máquina *f*) rebanadora *f* de pan; (*for meat*) máquina *f* de cortar fiambre

slick [slɪk] **I.** <-er, -est> *adj* **1.** (*performance*) pulido, -a **2.** (*person*) hábil; *pej* astuto **II.** *n* **1.** (*oil*) marea *f* negra **2.** *Am* (*magazine*) revista *f* ilustrada

◆**slick back** *vt*, **slick down** *vt* (*hair*) alisar

slicker ['slɪkəʳ, *Am:* -ɚ] *n Am* **1.** (*city slicker*) urbanita *mf* **2.** (*coat*) impermeable *m*

slide [slaɪd] **I.** <slid, slid> *vi* **1.** (*slip*) resbalar **2.** (*glide smoothly*) deslizarse; **the door ~s open/shut** la puerta se abre/se cierra corriéndola; **to ~ back into one's old habits** volver a las viejas costumbres **II.** <slid, slid> *vt* deslizar; **to ~ the door open/shut** correr la puerta; **to ~ sth across the floor** pasar algo deslizándolo por el suelo **III.** *n* **1.** (*act of sliding*) deslizamiento *m* **2.** (*sliding place on ice*) rampa *f* **3.** (*playground structure*) tobogán *m* **4.** GEO desprendimiento *m* **5.** FIN caída *f* **6.** PHOT diapositiva *f* **7.** (*for microscope*) portaobjetos *m inv* **8.** MUS vara *f* corredera **9.** *Brit* (*hair clip*) pasador *m*

slide projector *n* proyector *m* de diapositivas **slide rule** *n* regla *f* de cálculo

sliding *adj* (*sunroof*) corredizo, -a; (*door*) corredero, -a

sliding scale *n* escala *f* móvil

slight [slaɪt] **I.** <-er, -est> *adj* **1.** (*small: chance*) escaso, -a; (*error*) pequeño, -a; **the ~est thing** la menor tontería; **not in the ~est** en absoluto; **not to have the ~est (idea)** no tener ni la menor idea **2.** (*slim: person*) delgado, -a **II.** *n* desaire *m* **III.** *vt* despreciar

slightly *adv* un poco; **to know sb ~** conocer muy poco a alguien

slim [slɪm] **I.** <slimmer, slimmest> *adj* **1.** (*thin: person*) delgado, -a **2.** (*cigarette, book*) fino, -a **3.** (*slight: chance*) escaso, -a **II.** <-mm-> *vi* (*become slim*) adelgazar; (*try to get thinner*) hacer régimen

◆**slim down** *vi* adelgazar

slime [slaɪm] *n no pl* **1.** (*mud*) cieno *m* **2.** (*of fish, slug*) baba *f*

slimebag *n*, **slimeball** *n no pl* asqueroso, -a *m, f*

slimmer *n* persona *f* que está a régimen

slimming **I.** *n no pl* adelgazamiento *m* **II.** *adj* (*pill*) para adelgazar; (*food, drinks*) de bajo contenido calórico

slimy ['slaɪmi] <-ier, -iest> *adj* **1.** (*covered in slime*) viscoso, -a **2.** *pej* (*person*) asqueroso, -a; **~ git** *Brit* imbécil *mf* de mierda

sling [slɪŋ] <slung, slung> **I.** *vt* **1.** (*fling*) lanzar, aventar *Méx* **2.** (*hang*) colgar **II.** *n* **1.** (*for broken arm*) cabestrillo *m*; (*for carrying baby*) canguro *m* **2.** (*for lifting*) eslinga *f*

3.(*weapon*) honda *f*

◆**sling out** *vt inf* (*rubbish*) tirar a la basura; (*person*) echar

slingshot ['slɪŋʃɒt, *Am:* -ʃɑːt] *n Am, Aus* tirachinas *m inv,* honda *f CSur, Perú,* resortera *f Méx*

slink [slɪŋk] <slunk> *vi* **to ~ away** [*o* **off**] escabullirse

slinky ['slɪŋki] <-ier, iest> *adj* (*walk*) sinuoso, -a; (*dress*) ceñido, -a

slip [slɪp] <-pp-> **I.** *n* **1.**(*slipping*) resbalón *m* **2.**(*mistake*) error *m;* **to make a ~** cometer un error; **~ of the pen** lapsus *m* calami; **~ of the tongue** lapsus (linguae) **3.** COM resguardo *m;* **a ~ of paper** un trozo de papel **4.**(*women's underwear*) combinación *f* **5.** BOT esqueje *m* ▸**there's many a ~ (twixt cup and lip)** *prov* de la mano a la boca desaparece la sopa *prov;* **to give sb the ~** darle el esquinazo a alguien **II.** *vi* **1.**(*slide*) resbalarse **2.**(*move quietly*) deslizarse; **to ~ into a pub** colarse en un bar; **to ~ into/out of one's pyjamas** ponerse/quitarse el pijama **3.**(*decline*) decaer; **to ~ into a depression** caer en una depresión **III.** *vt* **1.**(*put smoothly*) deslizar; **to ~ sb a note** pasar una nota a alguien disimuladamente; **to ~ in a comment** dejar caer un comentario; **to ~ some money to sb** pasar dinero a alguien disimuladamente **2.**(*escape from*) escabullirse de; **to ~ sb's attention** pasar desapercibido por alguien; **it ~ped my mind** se me olvidó **3.** NAUT (*anchor*) soltar

◆**slip away** *vi* **1.**(*leave unnoticed*) escabullirse; **to ~ (from sb)** escaparse (de alguien) **2.**(*pass swiftly*) pasar rápidamente **3.**(*be dying*) morirse

◆**slip by** *vi* **1.**(*pass quickly: time*) pasar rápidamente **2.**(*pass unnoticed*) pasar inadvertido, -a

◆**slip down** *vi* dejarse caer

◆**slip in** *vi* colarse

◆**slip off** **I.** *vi* **1.**(*leave unnoticed*) escabullirse **2.**(*fall off*) caerse **II.** *vt* (*clothes*) quitarse

◆**slip on** *vt* (*clothes*) ponerse

◆**slip out** *vi* **1.**(*go out for short time*) salir un momento **2.**(*leave unobtrusively*) escabullirse **3.**(*be spoken accidentally*) escaparse; **the name slipped out** se me escapó el nombre

◆**slip up** *vi* equivocarse

slipcase ['slɪpkeɪs] *n* estuche *m*

slipknot ['slɪpnɒt, *Am:* -nɑːt] *n* nudo *m* corredizo

slip-on ['slɪpɒn, *Am:* -ɑːn] **I.** *adj* (*shoes*) sin cordones **II.** *n pl* zapatos *mpl* sin cordones

slippage ['slɪpɪdʒ] *n* (*in value, standards*) disminución *f*

slipper ['slɪpəʳ, *Am:* -ɚ] *n* zapatilla *f,* pantufla *f AmL*

slippery ['slɪpəri] <-ier, -iest> *adj* **1.**(*not giving firm hold: surface*) resbaladizo, -a; (*soap*) escurridizo, -a **2.**(*untrustworthy: person*) que no es de fiar ▸**to be a ~ customer** ser un pájaro de cuenta; **to be as ~ as an eel** ser escurridizo como una anguila; (**be on**) **the ~ slope** encontrarse en un terreno resbaladizo

slip road ['slɪprəʊd, *Am:* -roʊd] *n Brit* vía *f* de acceso

slipshod ['slɪpʃɒd, *Am:* -ʃɑːd] *adj* chapucero, -a

slipstream ['slɪpstriːm] *n* estela *f*

slip-up ['slɪpʌp] *n* desliz *m*

slipway ['slɪpweɪ] *n* NAUT grada *f*

slit [slɪt] **I.** <slit, slit> *vt* cortar; **to ~ sb's throat** cortar el cuello a alguien; **to ~ one's wrists** cortarse las venas **II.** *n* **1.**(*tear*) raja *f* **2.**(*narrow opening*) rendija *f*

slither ['slɪðəʳ, *Am:* -ɚ] *vi* deslizarse; **to ~ down the slope** deslizarse por la pendiente; **to ~ on the ice** patinar sobre el hielo

sliver ['slɪvəʳ, *Am:* -ɚ] *n* (*of glass, wood*) astilla *f;* (*of cake*) trocito *m;* (*of lemon*) rodaja *f* fina

slob [slɒb, *Am:* slɑːb] *n inf* patán *m*

◆**slob about** *vi inf* holgazanear

slobber ['slɒbəʳ, *Am:* 'slɑːbɚ] *vi* babear

slobbery ['slɒbəri, *Am:* 'slɑːbɚi] *adj* baboso, -a

sloe [sləʊ, *Am:* sloʊ] *n* **1.**(*fruit*) endrina *f* **2.**(*bush*) endrino *m*

slog [slɒg, *Am:* slɑːg] *inf* **I.** *n no pl* esfuerzo *m* **II.** <-gg-> *vi* (*walk*) caminar con gran esfuerzo **III.** <-gg-> *vt* (*hit*) golpear

slogan ['sləʊgən, *Am:* 'sloʊ-] *n* eslogan *m*

sloop [sluːp] *n* balandro *m*

slop [slɒp, *Am:* slɑːp] <-pp-> **I.** *vt inf* derramar **II.** *vi inf* derramarse; **to ~ about** [*o* **around**] salpicarlo todo **III.** *n* **1.** *no pl, inf* (*watery food*) aguachirle *f* **2.** *pl* (*waste liquid*) líquido *m* de desecho

◆**slop out** *vi Brit* vaciar el orinal

slope [sləʊp, *Am:* sloʊp] **I.** *n* inclinación *f;* (*up*) cuesta *f;* (*down*) declive *m;* (*for skiing*) pista *f* **II.** *vi* inclinarse; **to ~ down** descender, bajar; **to ~ up** ascender, subir **III.** *vt* inclinar; **~ arms!** ¡armas al hombro!

◆**slope off** *vi Brit, pej* largarse

sloping *adj* (*roof*) inclinado, -a; (*shoulders*) caído, -a

sloppiness *n no pl, pej* **1.**(*carelessness*) falta *f* de cuidado **2.**(*sentimentality*) sensiblería *f*

sloppy ['slɒpi, *Am:* 'slɑːpi] <-ier, -iest> *adj* **1.**(*careless*) descuidado, -a **2.**(*sentimentally romantic*) sensiblero, -a **3.**(*too wet: kiss*) baboso, -a **4.**(*loose-fitting: jumper*) holgado, -a

slosh [slɒʃ, *Am:* slɑːʃ] **I.** *vt inf* **1.**(*liquid*) echar salpicando **2.** *Brit* (*hit*) cascar **II.** *vi* **1.**(*splash*) chapotear **2.**(*water*) agitarse

◆**slosh about** *vi,* **slosh around** *vi* echar salpicando

sloshed *adj inf* borracho, -a; **to get ~** agarrar una tajada

slot [slɒt, *Am:* slɑːt] **I.** *n* **1.**(*narrow opening*) ranura *f* **2.** TV espacio *m* **3.** AVIAT slot *m* **II.** <-tt-> *vi* **to ~ in** encajar **III.** <-tt-> *vt* **to ~**

sth in hacer encajar

sloth [sləʊθ, *Am:* slɑːθ] *n* **1.** *no pl* (*laziness*) pereza *f* **2.** ZOOL perezoso *m*

slothful ['sləʊθfəl, *Am:* 'slɑːθ-] *adj* perezoso, -a

slot machine ['slɒtməʃiːn, *Am:* 'slɑːt-] *n* **1.** (*fruit machine*) máquina *f* tragaperras **2.** *Brit, Aus* (*vending machine*) máquina *f* expendedora **slot meter** *n* contador *m* (*que funciona con monedas*)

slouch [slaʊtʃ] **I.** *vi* **1.** (*have shoulders bent*) encorvarse **2.** (*walk*) caminar arrastrando los pies **II.** *n* postura *f* encorbada ►**to be no** ~ no ser manco

slough¹ [slʌf] *n* **1.** (*bog*) ciénaga *f* **2.** *liter* (*depressed state*) abismo *m*

slough² [slaʊ, *Am:* sluː] *vt* ZOOL (*skin*) mudar de

Slovak ['sləʊvæk, *Am:* 'sloʊvɑːk-] **I.** *adj* eslovaco, -a **II.** *n* **1.** (*person*) eslovaco, -a *m, f* **2.** LING eslovaco *m*

Slovakia [sləʊ'vækiə, *Am:* sloʊ'vɑːki-] *n no pl* Eslovaquia *f*

Slovakian *n s.* **Slovak**

sloven ['slʌvən] *n* persona *f* dejada

Slovene ['sləʊviːn, *Am:* 'sloʊ-] **I.** *adj* esloveno, -a **II.** *n* **1.** (*person*) esloveno, -a *m, f* **2.** LING esloveno *m*

Slovenia [sləʊ'viːniə, *Am:* sloʊ'-] *n no pl* Eslovenia *f*

Slovenian *n s.* **Slovene**

slovenly ['slʌvənli] *adj* descuidado, -a

slow [sləʊ, *Am:* sloʊ] **I.** *adj* **1.** (*not fast*) lento, -a; (*poison*) de efectos retardados; **to be ~ to do sth** tardar en hacer algo; **to be (10 minutes) ~** ir (10 minutos) retrasado **2.** (*stupid*) torpe, guanaco, -a *AmL* **II.** *vi* ir más despacio; **to ~ to a halt** detenerse gradualmente **III.** *vt* frenar; (*development*) retardar

◆**slow down** **I.** *vt* ralentizar **II.** *vi* **1.** (*reduce speed*) reducir la velocidad **2.** (*be less active*) moderar el ritmo de vida

slowcoach ['sləʊkəʊtʃ, *Am:* 'sloʊkoʊtʃ] *n Brit, Aus, childspeak* tortuga *f*

slowdown ['sləʊdaʊn, *Am:* 'sloʊ-] *n* ECON ralentización *f;* **economic ~** reducción *f* de la actividad económica

slowly *adv* lentamente; **~ but surely** lento pero seguro

slow motion **I.** *n* cámara *f* lenta; **in ~** a cámara lenta **II.** *adj* a cámara lenta **slow-moving** *adj* lento, -a; (*traffic*) denso, -a

slowness *n no pl* **1.** (*lack of speed*) lentitud *f* **2.** (*stupidity*) torpeza *f*

slow train *n* tren *m* lento **slow-witted** *adj* lerdo, -a **slowworm** *n* lución *m*

SLR *n abbr of* **single-lens reflex camera** cámara *f* réflex (monoobjetivo)

sludge [slʌdʒ] *n no pl* lodo *m*

slug¹ [slʌg] *n* ZOOL babosa *f*

slug² [slʌg] <-gg-> **I.** *vi inf* (*hit*) aporrear; **to ~ it out** pegarse **II.** *n inf* **1.** (*bullet*) bala *f* **2.** *Am* (*coin*) ficha *f* **3.** *inf* (*swig*) trago *m*

sluggish ['slʌgɪʃ] *adj* (*person*) perezoso, -a, conchudo, -a *Méx;* (*progress*) lento, -a; (*market*) flojo, -a

sluice [sluːs] **I.** *n* (*gate*) compuerta *f* **II.** *vt* regar; **to ~ sth down** enjuagar algo

sluice gate *n* compuerta *f* **sluiceway** *n* canal *m* de desagüe

slum [slʌm] **I.** *n* (*area*) barrio *m* pobre; (*on outskirts*) suburbio *m;* **to live in ~ conditions** vivir en condiciones de pobreza **II.** <-mm-> *vt* **to ~ it** *iron* vivir como pobres

slumber ['slʌmbəʳ, *Am:* -bɚ] **I.** *vi liter* dormir **II.** *n liter* (*sleep*) sueño *m* ligero; (*inactive state*) marasmo *m elev*

slum clearance *n no pl* demolición *f* de los barrios pobres **slum dweller** *n* habitante *mf* de los barrios bajos **slum landlord** *n* casero *m* de tugurios

slump [slʌmp] **I.** *n* ECON **1.** (*decline*) depresión *f;* **~ in prices** descenso *m* repentino de los precios **2.** (*recession*) recesión *f* **II.** *vi* desplomarse; (*prices*) bajar notablemente

slung [slʌŋ] *pt, pp of* **sling**

slunk [slʌŋk] *pt, pp of* **slink**

slur [slɜːʳ, *Am:* slɜːr] <-rr-> **I.** *vt* pronunciar con dificultad; **to ~ one's words** arrastrar las palabras **II.** *n* **1.** (*insult*) calumnia *f* **2.** (*in speech*) pronunciación *f* incomprensible

slurp [slɜːp, *Am:* slɜːrp] *inf* **I.** *vt, vi* sorber (ruidosamente) **II.** *n* sorbo *m* (ruidoso)

slurry ['slʌri, *Am:* 'slɜːr-] *n no pl* compuesto *m* acuoso

slush [slʌʃ] *n no pl* **1.** (*snow*) nieve *f* medio derretida **2.** *inf* (*sentimentality*) sentimentalismo *m*

slush fund *n pej* fondos *mpl* para sobornar

slushy *adj* <-ier, -iest> **1.** (*snow*) a medio derretir **2.** (*sentimental*) sentimentaloide

slut [slʌt] *n pej* puta *f*

sluttish ['slʌtɪʃ, *Am:* 'slʌt̬-] *adj pej* (*messy*) guarro, -a

sly [slaɪ] *adj* **1.** (*secretive*) sigiloso, -a; (*smile*) sutil; **on the ~** a hurtadillas **2.** (*crafty*) astuto, -a, songo, -a *Col, Méx*

slyly *adv* **1.** (*secretively*) sigilosamente **2.** (*craftily*) con astucia

smack¹ [smæk] **I.** *vt* **1.** (*slap*) dar un manotazo a **2.** (*hit noisily*) golpear; **to ~ one's lips** relamerse los labios **II.** *n* **1.** *inf* (*slap*) bofetada *f;* (*soft blow*) palmada *f* **2.** *inf* (*kiss*) besazo *m* **3.** (*loud noise*) ruido *m* fuerte **III.** *adv* **1.** (*exactly*) exactamente **2.** (*completely*) de lleno

◆**smack of** *vi* oler a

smack² [smæk] *n no pl, inf* (*heroin*) heroína *f*

smacker ['smækəʳ, *Am:* -ɚ] *n inf* **1.** *Brit* (*pound*) libra *f; Am* (*dollar*) dólar *m* **2.** (*loud kiss*) beso *m* sonoro

small [smɔːl] **I.** *adj* **1.** (*not large*) pequeño, -a; (*person*) bajo, -a, petizo, -a *CSur, Bol* **2.** (*young*) joven **3.** (*insignificant*) insignificante; **on a ~ scale** a pequeña escala; **in his/**

her own ~ **way** de forma modesta **4.** TYPO (*letter*) minúscula; **with a** ~ **'c'** con 'c' minúscula ►**to be grateful for** ~ **mercies** *prov* dar las gracias por los pequeños favores; **it's a** ~ **world** *prov* el mundo es un pañuelo *prov* **II.** *n no pl* **the** ~ **of the back** la región lumbar

small ad *n* anuncio *m* breve **small arms** *npl* armas *fpl* de bajo calibre **small beer** *n Brit* poca cosa **small business** <-es> *n* pequeña empresa *f* **small businessman** *n* pequeño empresario *m* **small change** *n no pl* calderilla *f*, chaucha *f Bol, Chile, Perú*, chirolas *fpl Arg* **small claims court** *n Brit* tribunal *m* de primera instancia que se ocupa de delitos menores **small fry** *n inf* **to be** ~ ser poco importante

smallholder ['smɔːlˌhəʊldəʳ, *Am:* -ˌhoʊldɚ] *n Brit* minifundista *mf*

smallholding *n Brit* minifundio *m*

small hours *npl* madrugada *f* **small intestine** *n* intestino *m* delgado

smallish ['smɔːlɪʃ] *adj* más bien pequeño, -a

small-minded [ˌsmɔːl'maɪndɪd] *adj pej* estrecho, -a de miras

smallness ['smɔːlnɪs] *n no pl* pequeñez *f*

smallpox ['smɔːlpɒks, *Am:* -pɑːks] *n no pl* viruela *f*

small print *n no pl* letra *f* menuda **small-scale** *adj* en [*o* a] pequeña escala **small screen** *n no pl* **the** ~ la pequeña pantalla **small talk** *n no pl* conversación *f* sin trascendencia; **to make** ~ estar de cháchara **small-time** *adj* de poca monta

smarmy ['smɑːmi, *Am:* 'smɑːr] *adj pej* zalamero, -a

smart [smɑːt, *Am:* smɑːrt] **I.** *adj* **1.** (*clever*) inteligente; **to make a** ~ **move** dar un paso inteligente; **to be too** ~ **for sb** ser demasiado listo para alguien **2.** (*elegant*) elegante **3.** (*quick*) rápido, -a; **to do sth at a** ~ **pace** hacer algo de forma rápida **II.** *vi* escocer; **my eyes** ~ me pican los ojos **III.** *n* escozor *m*

smart-alec(k) ['smɑːt'ælɪk, *Am:* ˌsmɑːrt'-] *n pej, inf* sabelotodo *mf*

smartarse ['smɑːtɑːs, *Am:* 'smɑːrtɑːrs] *n Brit, Aus,* **smart ass** *n pej, inf* listillo, -a *m, f* **smart bomb** *n* bomba *f* teledirigida **smart card** *n* INFOR tarjeta *f* electrónica

smarten ['smɑːtn, *Am:* 'smɑːr-] **I.** *vt* **to** ~ **sth up** arreglar algo **II.** *vi* **to** ~ **up** arreglarse

smartness ['smɑːtnɪs, *Am:* 'smɑːrt-] *n no pl* **1.** (*elegance*) elegancia *f* **2.** (*intelligence*) inteligencia *f*

smash [smæʃ] **I.** *n* **1.** (*sound*) estruendo *m* **2.** (*accident*) colisión *f* **3.** SPORTS mate *m* **II.** *vt* **1.** (*break*) romper, quebrar *AmL;* (*glass*) hacer pedazos; *fig* destruir; **to** ~ **a rebellion** acabar con una revuelta **2.** SPORTS (*record*) batir **III.** *vi* **1.** (*break into pieces*) romperse, quebrarse *AmL;* (*glass*) hacerse pedazos **2.** (*strike against*) chocar; **to** ~ **into sth** chocar contra algo

◆**smash in** *vt* forzar; **to smash sb's face in** *inf* romperle la cara a alguien

◆**smash up** *vt* hacer pedazos; (*car*) destrozar

smash-and-grab raid [ˌsmæʃəndgræb'reɪd] *n Brit, Aus* robo *m* (*en el que se rompe el escaparate de una tienda*)

smashed *adj inf* (*on alcohol*) borracho, -a; **to get** ~ emborracharse; (*on drugs*) colocado, -a; **to get** ~ colocarse

smasher *n Brit, inf* **to be a** ~ estar como un tren

smash (hit) *n* éxito *m*

smashing *adj Brit, inf* imponente

smash-up *n* choque *m* violento

smattering ['smætərɪŋ, *Am:* 'smæt̬-] *n* nociones *fpl*

smear [smɪəʳ, *Am:* smɪr] **I.** *vt* **1.** (*spread*) untar **2.** (*attack*) desprestigiar; **to** ~ **sb's good name** manchar el buen nombre de alguien **II.** *n* **1.** (*blotch*) mancha *f* **2.** (*accusation*) calumnia *f* **3.** MED frotis *m* **smear campaign** *n* campaña *f* de desprestigio **smear tactics** *n* tácticas *f* difamatorias *pl* **smear test** *n* MED citología *f*

smell [smel] <*Brit, Aus:* smelt, smelt *Am, Aus:* -ed, -ed> **I.** *vi* **1.** (*use sense of smell*) olfatear **2.** (*give off odour*) oler **3.** (*have unpleasant smell*) apestar **II.** *vt* (*person*) oler; (*animal*) olfatear **III.** *n* **1.** (*sense of smelling*) olfato *m* **2.** (*odour*) olor *m* **3.** *pej* (*stink*) hedor *m* **4.** (*sniff*) inhalación *f*

◆**smell out** *vt* olfatear

smelling salts ['smelɪŋsɔːlts] *npl* MED sales *fpl* aromáticas

smelly ['smeli] *adj* <-ier, -iest> apestoso, -a, que huele mal, foche *Chile*

smelt[1] [smelt] *Brit, Aus pt, pp of* **smell**

smelt[2] [smelt] *vt* MIN fundir

smelt[3] [smelt] <-(s)> *n* (*fish*) eperlano *m*

smidgen ['smɪdʒən] *n inf* pizca *f*

smile [smaɪl] **I.** *n* sonrisa *f;* **to be all** ~**s** ser todo sonrisas; **to give sb a** ~ sonreír a alguien; **to raise a** ~ hacer reír **II.** *vi* sonreír; **to** ~ **at** [*o* **about**] **sth** reírse de algo; **to** ~ **on sb/sth** mirar con buenos ojos a alguien/algo

smiley ['smaɪli] *n* INFOR smiley *m*

smiling *adj* sonriente

smirch [smɜːtʃ, *Am:* smɜːrtʃ] *vt liter* mancillar

smirk [smɜːk, *Am:* smɜːrk] **I.** *vi* sonreírse afectadamente **II.** *n* sonrisa *f* afectada

smite [smaɪt] <smote, smitten> *vt liter* golpear

smith [smɪθ] *n* herrero, -a *m, f*

smithereens [ˌsmɪðə'riːnz] *npl* añicos *mpl;* **to smash sth to** ~ hacer algo añicos

smithy ['smɪði, *Am:* 'smɪθ-] <-ies> *n* herrería *f*

smitten ['smɪtən] *adj* **to be** ~ **with sb/sth** estar loco por alguien/algo; **to be** ~ **by sb** estar enamorado de alguien; **she was** ~ **by remorse** le remordía la conciencia

smock [smɒk, *Am:* smɑːk] *n* bata *f* corta

smocking *n no pl* nido *m* de abeja
smog [smɒg, *Am:* smɑ:g] *n no pl* niebla *f* con humo
smoke [sməʊk, *Am:* smoʊk] **I.** *n* **1.** *no pl* (*from fire*) humo *m* **2.** *inf* (*cigarette*) cigarrillo *m* **3.** *Brit, inf* (*London*) **the ~** Londres *m* ▶**there's no ~ without fire** *Brit, Aus, prov,* **where there's ~, there's fire** *Am, prov* cuando el río suena, agua lleva *prov;* **to go up in ~** quedarse en agua de borrajas **II.** *vt* **1.** (*cigarette, tobacco*) fumar, pitar *AmS;* **to ~ a pipe** fumar en pipa **2.** GASTR ahumar ▶**to ~ the peace pipe** *Am* fumar la pipa de la paz; **put that in your pipe and ~ it!** ¡métetelo donde te quepa! **III.** *vi* **1.** (*produce smoke*) echar humo **2.** (*smoke tobacco*) fumar, pitar *AmS*
◆**smoke out** *vt* (*rats, insects*) hacer salir con humo; (*people*) poner al descubierto
smoke bomb *n* bomba *f* de humo
smoked *adj* ahumado, -a
smoke detector *n* detector *m* de humo
smokeless ['sməʊkləs, *Am:* 'smoʊk-] *adj* sin humo
smoker *n* **1.** (*person who smokes*) fumador(a) *m(f);* **to be a heavy ~** fumar mucho **2.** RAIL vagón *m* de fumadores
smokescreen *n a. fig* cortina *f* de humo **smoke signal** *n* señal *f* de humo
smokestack ['sməʊkstæk, *Am:* 'smoʊk-] *n* chimenea *f*
smoking *n no pl* el fumar; **~ ban** prohibición *f* de fumar; **to give up ~** dejar de fumar
smoking car *n Am,* **smoking compartment** *n* RAIL compartimento *m* de fumadores **smoking jacket** *n* batín *m*
smoky ['sməʊki, *Am:* 'smoʊ-] *adj* <-ier, -iest> **1.** (*filled with smoke*) lleno, -a de humo **2.** (*producing smoke*) humeante; (*fire*) que humea **3.** (*tasting of smoke*) ahumado, -a
smolder ['smoʊldɚ] *vi Am s.* **smoulder**
smooch [smu:tʃ] **I.** *vi* (*kiss*) besuquearse **II.** *n* (*kiss*) **to have a ~** besuquearse
smooth [smu:ð] **I.** *adj* **1.** (*not rough*) liso, -a; (*surface*) llano, -a; (*skin, texture*) suave; (*sauce*) sin grumos; (*sea*) tranquilo, -a; **as ~ as silk** tan suave como la seda **2.** (*uninterrupted*) sin dificultades; (*flight*) tranquilo, -a; (*landing*) suave **3.** (*mild: wine, whisky*) suave **4.** (*suave*) zalamero, -a; **to be a ~ talker** tener un pico de oro **II.** *vt* allanar
◆**smooth down** *vt* alisar
◆**smooth over** *vt* (*difficulty*) solucionar
smoothie *n,* **smoothy** ['smu:ði] *n inf* zalamero, -a *m, f*
smoothly *adv* **to go ~** ir bien
smoothness *n no pl* **1.** (*evenness*) lisura *f* **2.** (*lack of difficulty*) fluidez *f* **3.** (*mild taste or texture*) suavidad *f*
smooth-shaven *adj* bien afeitado, -a **smooth talk** *n pej* labia *f* **smooth-talking** *adj pej* zalamero, -a
smote [sməʊt, *Am:* smoʊt] *pt of* **smite**
smother ['smʌðəʳ, *Am:* -ɚ] *vt* **1.** (*suffocate*) ahogar **2.** (*suppress*) contener **3.** (*cover*) **to be ~ed in sth** estar cubierto de algo
smoulder ['sməʊldəʳ, *Am:* 'smoʊldɚ] *vi* **1.** (*burn slowly*) arder sin llama; (*cigarette*) consumirse lentamente **2.** *fig* arder
smudge [smʌdʒ] **I.** *vt* **1.** (*smear*) hacer borroso **2.** (*make dirty*) manchar; (*reputation*) destruir **II.** *vi* mancharse; (*make-up*) correrse **III.** *n* mancha *f*
smudgy ['smʌdʒi] *adj* <-ier, -iest> manchado, -a
smug [smʌg] *adj* <-gg-> presumido, -a; **to be ~ about sth** presumir de algo
smuggle ['smʌgl] *vt* LAW pasar de contrabando
smuggler ['smʌgləʳ, *Am:* -lɚ] *n* contrabandista *mf*
smuggling ['smʌglɪŋ] *n no pl* contrabando *m*
smut [smʌt] *n* **1.** *no pl* (*obscenity*) obscenidades *fpl* **2.** (*soot*) tizne *m*
smutty ['smʌti, *Am:* 'smʌt̬-] *adj* <-ier, -iest> obsceno, -a; (*joke*) verde
snack [snæk] **I.** *n* refrigerio *m,* puntal *m AmL;* **to have a ~** tomarse un tentempié **II.** *vi* picar
snack bar *n* cafetería *f*
snaffle ['snæfl] *vt Brit, Aus, inf* mangar
snag [snæg] **I.** *n* **1.** (*problem*) dificultad *f;* **there's a ~** hay un problema **2.** (*in clothing*) enganchón *m* **II.** <-gg-> *vt* **1.** (*catch and pull*) enganchar **2.** (*cause problems*) causar problemas a **III.** <-gg-> *vi* **to ~ on sth** engancharse en algo
snail [sneɪl] *n* caracol *m* ▶**at a ~'s pace** a paso de tortuga
snail mail *n* INFOR correo *m* tortuga **snail shell** *n* caparazón *m* de caracol
snake [sneɪk] **I.** *n* (*small*) culebra *f;* (*large*) serpiente *f* ▶**~ in the grass** traidor(a) *m(f);* **~s and ladders** ≈ juego *m* de la oca **II.** *vi* serpentear, viborear *Arg, Urug*
snake bite *n* mordedura *f* de serpiente **snake charmer** *n* encantador(a) *m(f)* de serpientes **snakeskin** *n* piel *f* de serpiente **snake venom** *n* veneno *m* de serpiente
snap [snæp] <-pp-> **I.** *n* **1.** (*sound*) chasquido *m* **2.** (*photograph*) foto *f* **3.** *Am* (*snap-fastener*) (cierre *m*) automático *m* **4.** METEO **a cold ~** una ola de frío **II.** *adj* repentino, -a; **~ decision** decisión *f* repentina **III.** *interj inf* GAMES yo también **IV.** *vi* **1.** (*break*) romperse **2.** (*move*) **to ~ back** recolocarse; **to ~ shut** cerrarse de golpe **3.** (*make snapping sound*) hacer un chasquido **4.** (*bite*) **to ~ at sb** intentar morder a alguien **5.** (*speak sharply*) contestar con brusquedad; **to ~ at sb** contestar a alguien de forma brusca **V.** *vt* **1.** (*break*) romper; **to ~ sth shut** cerrar algo de golpe **2.** (*make snapping sound*) chasquear; **to ~ a whip** dar un latigazo; **to ~ one's fingers** chasquear los dedos **3.** PHOT tomar un fotografía de
◆**snap out** *vi* **to ~ of sth** quitarse algo de

S

encima; ~ **of it!** ¡anímate!

◆**snap up** *vt* lanzarse sobre

snapdragon ['snæpˌdrægən] *n* boca *f* de dragón

snap-fastener *n* (cierre *m*) automático *m*

snappish ['snæpɪʃ] *adj* brusco, -a

snappy ['ʃnæpi] *adj* <-ier, -iest> **1.** *inf* FASHION de lo más elegante; **to be a ~ dresser** vestir con elegancia **2.** (*quick*) rápido, -a; **look ~!** ¡date prisa!

snapshot ['snæpʃɒt, *Am:* -ʃɑ:t] *n* foto *f* instantánea

snare [sneəʳ, *Am:* sner] **I.** *n* trampa *f* **II.** *vt* (*catch: animal*) cazar (con trampa); (*person*) atrapar

snare drum *n* tambor *m*

snarl[1] [snɑ:l, *Am:* snɑ:rl] **I.** *vi* gruñir **II.** *n* gruñido *m*

snarl[2] [snɑ:l, *Am:* snɑ:rl] *n* **1.** (*tangle*) enredo *m* **2.** (*traffic jam*) atasco *m*

◆**snarl up** *vi* enmarañarse

snarl-up ['snɑ:lʌp, *Am:* 'snɑ:rl-] *n* atasco *m*

snatch [snætʃ] **I.** <-es> *n* **1.** (*sudden grab*) arrebatamiento *m;* **to make a ~ at sth** intentar arrebatar algo **2.** (*theft*) robo *m* **3.** (*piece: of music, conversation*) retazo *m;* **to do sth in ~es** hacer algo a ratos **4.** *vulg* (*female genitals*) coño *m* **II.** *vt* **1.** (*steal*) robar; (*win*) ganar; **to ~ sth** (**away**) **from sb** arrebatar algo de alguien **2.** (*kidnap*) secuestrar **III.** *vi* quitar algo de las manos; **to ~ at sth** tratar de arrebatar algo

◆**snatch up** *vt* agarrar

snazzy ['snæzi] *adj* <-ier, -iest> *inf* de lo más elegante

sneak [sni:k] *Am* **I.** *vi* **1.** (*move stealthily*) moverse furtivamente; **to ~ in/out** entrar/salir a hurtadillas; **to ~ away** [*o* **off**] escabullirse **2.** *Brit, inf* (*denounce*) **to ~ on sb** delatar a alguien **II.** *vt* hacer furtivamente; **to ~ a look at sth/sb** mirar algo/a alguien con disimulo; **to ~ sth in/out** lograr introducir/sacar algo **III.** *n Brit, childspeak* acusica *mf*

sneaker ['sni:kəʳ, *Am:* -kɚ] *n pl, Am* zapatillas *fpl* de deporte

sneaking *adj* (*secret*) secreto, -a

sneak preview *n* CINE preestreno *m* **sneak-thief** *n* ratero, -a *m, f*

sneaky ['sni:ki] *adj* <-ier, -iest> furtivo, -a

sneer [snɪəʳ, *Am:* snɪr] **I.** *vi* hacer un gesto de burla y desprecio; (*mock*) mofarse; **to ~ at sth/sb** mofarse de algo/alguien **II.** *n* expresión *f* desdeñosa

sneering ['snɪərɪŋ, *Am:* 'snɪr-] *adj* burlón, -ona

sneeze [sni:z] **I.** *vi* estornudar ▶**not to be ~d at** no ser de despreciar **II.** *n* estornudo *m*

snick [snɪk] *vt Brit, Aus* SPORTS (*ball*) golpear con el borde del bate

snicker ['snɪkəʳ, *Am:* -ɚ] *Am* **I.** *vi s.* **snigger** **II.** *n s.* **snigger**

snide [snaɪd] *adj pej* vil

sniff [snɪf] **I.** *n* **1.** (*smell*) husmeo *m;* **to have a ~** oler; **to catch a ~ of sth** captar el olor de algo **2.** (*expression of disdain*) expresión *f* de desdén **II.** *vi* **1.** (*inhale*) sorber; **to ~ at sth** oler algo **2.** (*show disdain*) **to ~ at sth** despreciar algo ▶**not to be ~ed at** no ser de despreciar **III.** *vt* olfatear

◆**sniff out** *vt* (*locate by smelling*) encontrar olfateando; (*discover*) descubrir

sniffer dog ['snɪfəʳˌdɒg, *Am:* 'snɪfɚˌdɑ:g] *n* perro *m* rastreador

sniffle ['snɪfl] **I.** *vi* **1.** (*sniff*) sorberse los mocos **2.** (*cry*) lloriquear **II.** *npl* **to have the ~s** estar un poco acatarrado

sniffy *adj inf* desdeñoso, -a

snifter ['snɪftəʳ, *Am:* -tɚ] *n* **1.** *Am* (*glass*) copa *f* de coñac **2.** *inf* (*small drink*) trago *m*

snigger ['snɪgəʳ, *Am:* -ɚ] **I.** *vi* reírse con disimulo; **to ~ at sth** reírse de algo con disimulo **II.** *n* risa *f* disimulada

snip [snɪp] **I.** *vt* cortar (con tijeras) **II.** *n* **1.** (*cut*) tijeretazo *m* **2.** (*piece of cloth*) recorte *m* **3.** *Brit, inf* (*cheap item*) ganga *f* **4.** *no pl, Brit, iron, inf* (*vasectomy*) vasectomía *f*

snipe[1] [snaɪp] *vi* **1.** MIL tirar (desde un escondite) **2.** *fig* **to ~ at sb** criticar a alguien

snipe[2] [snaɪp] *n* ZOOL agachadiza *f*

sniper ['snaɪpəʳ, *Am:* -ɚ] *n* francotirador(a) *m(f)*

sniping *n* (*criticism*) critiqueo *m*

snippet ['snɪpɪt] *n* (*small piece: of cloth*) retal *m;* (*of paper*) pedazo *m;* (*of cardboard*) trozo *m;* (*of information*) retazo *m;* (*of conversation, text*) fragmento *m*

snitch [snɪtʃ] *inf* **I.** *vt* (*steal*) birlar **II.** *vi pej* chivarse; **to ~ on sb** chivarse de alguien **III.** <-es> *n* **1.** (*thief*) caco *mf* **2.** (*tattle-tale*) soplón, -ona *m, f*

snivel ['snɪvəl] **I.** <*Brit:* -ll-, *Am:* -l-> *vi* (*cry*) lloriquear **II.** *n no pl* lloriqueo *m*

snivel(l)ing **I.** *n no pl* lloriqueo *m* **II.** *adj* llorón, -ona

snob [snɒb, *Am:* snɑ:b] *n* (e)snob *mf,* pituco, -a *m AmS*

snobbery ['snɒbəri, *Am:* 'snɑ:bɚ-] *n* (e)snobismo *m*

snobbish ['snɒbɪʃ, *Am:* 'snɑ:bɪʃ] <more, most> *adj* (e)snob

snob value *n no pl* cachet *m*

snog [snɒg, *Am:* snɑ:g] *Brit* **I.** <-gg-> *vi inf* morrearse **II.** *vt inf* morrear **III.** *n inf* morreo *m;* **to have a ~** morrearse

snook [snu:k, *Am:* snʊk] *n no pl* **to cock a ~ at sth/sb** *Brit, inf* hacer burla a algo/alguien

snooker ['snu:kəʳ, *Am:* 'snʊkɚ] **I.** *vt* **1.** *Am, inf* (*trick*) poner en un aprieto **2.** GAMES (*block*) bloquear; **to be ~ed** *fig, inf* fastidiársele a uno el plan **II.** *n* billar *m* inglés

snoop [snu:p] *pej, inf* **I.** *n* fisgón, -ona *m, f* **II.** *vi* fisgonear

snooper ['snu:pəʳ, *Am:* -ɚ] *n pej, inf* **1.** (*one looking secretly*) fisgón, -ona *m, f* **2.** (*spy*) espía *mf* **3.** (*investigator*) investigador(a) *m(f)*

snooty ['snu:ti, *Am:* -t̬i] <-ier, -iest> *adj* presumido, -a, pituco, -a *AmS*

snooze [snu:z] *inf* **I.** *vi* (*nap*) echar una cabezada; (*nap lightly*) dormitar **II.** *n* cabezada *f*
snooze button *n* botón *m* de alarma de un despertador
snore [snɔ:ʳ, *Am:* snɔ:r] MED **I.** *vi* roncar **II.** *n* ronquido *m*
snorkel ['snɔ:kəl, *Am:* 'snɔ:r-] SPORTS **I.** *n* tubo *m* snorkel (de respiración) **II.** <*Brit:* -ll-, *Am:* -l-> *vi* bucear con tubo
snorkelling *n* SPORTS **to go ~** bucear con tubo
snort [snɔ:t, *Am:* snɔ:rt] **I.** *vi* bufar, resoplar **II.** *vt* **1.** *inf* (*inhale*) inhalar; (*cocaine*) esnifar **2.** (*say with disapproval*) decir bufando **III.** *n* **1.** (*noise*) bufido *m* **2.** *inf* (*small drink*) trago *m*
snot [snɒt, *Am:* snɑ:t] *n no pl, inf* moco *m*
snotrag ['snɒtræg] *n inf* pañuelo *m*
snotty ['snɒti, *Am:* 'snɑ:t̬i] <-ier, -iest> *adj inf* **1.** (*full of mucus*) lleno, -a de mocos **2.** (*rude*) petulante
snout [snaʊt] *n* **1.** ZOOL hocico *m;* (*of pig*) morro *m* **2.** *inf* (*of person*) napia *f*
snow [snəʊ, *Am:* snoʊ] *no pl* **I.** *n* **1.** METEO nieve *f;* **a blanket of ~** un manto de nieve **2.** *inf* (*cocaine*) coca *f* **II.** *vi* nevar
◆**snow in** *vt* **to be snowed in** estar aprisionado por la nieve
◆**snow under** *vt* **to be snowed under** (**with sth**) estar desbordado (de algo)
snowball ['snəʊbɔ:l, *Am:* 'snoʊ-] **I.** *n* bola *f* de nieve ►**not to have a ~'s chance in hell** (**of doing sth**) no tener ninguna posibilidad (de hacer algo) **II.** *vi fig* aumentar progresivamente
snowball effect *n no pl* efecto *m* de bola de nieve
snow bank *n* banco *m* de nieve **snow blindness** *n no pl* ceguera *f* causada por el resplandor de la nieve **snowboard** *n* snowboard *m* **snowboarding** *n* **to go ~** hacer snowboard
snowbound ['snəʊbaʊnd, *Am:* 'snoʊ-] *adj* (*vehicle*) embarrancado, -a en la nieve; (*person*) aprisionado, -a por la nieve
snow-capped ['snəʊkæpt, *Am:* 'snoʊ-] *adj* cubierto, -a de nieve **snow chain** *n* AUTO cadena *f* para la nieve **snowdrift** *n Brit* ventisquero *m* **snowdrop** *n* campanilla *f* de invierno **snowfall** *n* METEO **1.** *no pl* (*amount snowed*) nevada *f* **2.** (*snowstorm*) tormenta *f* de nieve, nevazón *m Arg, Chile, Ecua* **snowflake** *n* copo *m* de nieve **snow goggles** *npl* gafas *fpl* para la nieve **snowline** *n* límite *m* de las nieves perpetuas **snowman** *n* muñeco *m* de nieve **snowmobile** *n* motonieve *f* **snowplough** *n Brit,* **snowplow** *n Am* **1.** (*snow mover*) quitanieves *m inv* **2.** SPORTS (*stop*) cuña *f* **snowshoe** *n* raqueta *f* (de nieve) **snowstorm** *n* tormenta *f* de nieve **snowsuit** *n* mono *m* acolchado (para la nieve) **snow tire** *n Am,* **snow tyre** *n Brit* AUTO neumático *m* antideslizante **snow-white** *adj* blanco, -a como la nieve
Snow White *n no pl* **~ and the Seven Dwarfs** LIT Blancanieves y los siete enanitos
snowy ['snəʊi, *Am:* 'snoʊ-] *adj* **1.** METEO (*region, season*) de mucha nieve; (*street, field*) cubierto, -a de nieve **2.** (*pure white: hair, flowers*) blanco, -a como la nieve; (*clouds*) níveo, -a *form*
SNP [ˌesen'pi:] *n abbr of* **Scottish National Party** Partido *m* Nacional Escocés
snub [snʌb] **I.** <-bb-> *vt* **to ~ sb** hacer el vacío a alguien **II.** *n* desaire *m*
snub nose *n* nariz *f* respingona **snub-nosed** *adj* **1.** (*person*) de nariz respingona **2.** (*gun*) de cañón corto; (*pliers*) de dientes cortos
snuff [snʌf] **I.** *n* rapé *m* **II.** *vt* **1.** (*put out*) apagar **2.** *Aus, Brit, inf* **to ~ it** estirar la pata
◆**snuff out** *vt* **1.** (*candle*) apagar **2.** (*opposition*) sofocar
snuff box *n* tabaquera *f*
snuffle ['snʌfl] **I.** *vi* **1.** (*sniffle*) estar acatarrado; (*breath*) respirar haciendo ruido por la nariz **2.** (*speak nasally*) ganguear **II.** *n* (*sound*) resoplido *m;* **to have the ~s** estar acatarrado
snug [snʌg] **I.** *adj* **1.** (*cozy*) acogedor(a); (*warm*) cómodo, -a y bien caliente **2.** (*tight: dress*) ajustado, -a **II.** *n Brit* salón *m* pequeño
snuggle ['snʌgl] *vi* acurrucarse; **to ~ up to sb** acurrucarse contra alguien
so [səʊ, *Am:* soʊ] **I.** *adv* **1.** (*in the same way*) tan, tanto; **~ did/do I** yo también; **~ to speak** por así decirlo **2.** (*like that*) así; **~ they say** así dicen; **is that ~?** ¿de verdad?; **I hope/think ~** así lo espero/pienso; **just** [*o* **quite**] **~!** ¡eso es! **3.** (*to such a degree*) tan, tanto; **I ~ love him** lo amo tanto; **~ late** tan tarde; **~ many books** tantos libros; **not ~ ugly as that** no tan feo como eso; **would you be ~ kind as to ...?** ¿sería usted tan amable de...? **4.** (*in order that*) para; **I bought the book ~ that he would read it** compré el libro para que él lo leyera **5.** (*as a result*) así; **and ~ she won** y así ganó ►**and ~ on** [*o* **forth**] etcétera; **or ~** más o menos **II.** *conj* **1.** (*therefore*) por (lo) tanto **2.** *inf* (*and afterwards*) **~** (**then**) **he told me ...** y entonces me dijo... **3.** (*summing up*) así que; **~ what?** ¿y qué?; **~ now, ...** entonces...; **~, I was saying ...** entonces, como decía... **III.** *interj* **~ that's why!** ¡es por eso!
soak [səʊk, *Am:* soʊk] **I.** *n* **1.** (*time under water*) remojo *m* **2.** *inf* (*heavy drinker*) borrachín, -ina *m, f* **II.** *vt* **1.** (*keep in liquid*) remojar, ensopar *AmS;* **to ~ sth in liquid** poner algo en remojo **2.** *inf* (*overcharge*) desplumar **III.** *vi* (*lie in liquid*) estar en remojo
◆**soak in** *vi* penetrar
◆**soak off** *vt* despegar
◆**soak up** *vt* **1.** (*absorb*) absorber; (*money, resources*) agotar **2.** (*take in: people*) embelesar; (*information*) absorber **3.** (*bask in: sun*) tomar; (*atmosphere*) disfrutar de
soaked *adj* empapado, -a
soaking **I.** *n* remojo *m;* **to get a ~** calarse hasta los huesos **II.** *adj* **~** (**wet**) (*person, ani-*

S

mal) empapado, -a; (*day*) de muchísima agua
so-and-so ['səʊənsəʊ, *Am:* 'soʊənsoʊ] *n inf* **1.** (*person*) fulano *m;* (*thing*) cosa *f* cualquiera **2.** *pej* (*idiot*) idiota *mf;* **Mr** ~ don *m* Fulano
soap [səʊp, *Am:* soʊp] **I.** *n* **1.** *no pl* (*for washing*) jabón *m* **2.** TV (*soap opera*) telenovela *f* ►**soft** ~ coba *f* **II.** *vt* enjabonar
soapbox ['səʊpbɒks, *Am:* 'soʊpbɑːks] *n* **1.** (*container*) caja *f* de jabón **2.** (*pedestal*) caja *f* vacía empleada como tribuna ►**to get on one's** ~ echar un discurso **soap bubble** *n* burbuja *f* de jabón **soapdish** *n* jabonera *f* **soap dispenser** *n* dispensador *m* de jabón **soap flakes** *npl* jabón *m* en escamas **soap opera** *n* telenovela *f* **soap powder** *n no pl* jabón *m* en polvo **soapsuds** *npl* espuma *f* de jabón
soapy ['səʊpi, *Am:* 'soʊp-] <-ier, -iest> *adj* **1.** (*full of lather*) lleno, -a de jabón **2.** (*like soap*) jabonoso, -a; **to taste** ~ saber a jabón **3.** (*flattering*) zalamero, -a
soar [sɔːʳ, *Am:* sɔːr] *vi* **1.** (*rise*) subir muy alto; (*house*) elevarse mucho **2.** (*increase: temperature*) aumentar bruscamente; (*prices*) ponerse por las nubes; (*awareness*) crecer sensiblemente; (*hopes*) renacer **3.** (*bird, plane*) remontar el vuelo; (*glide*) planear **4.** (*excel*) llegar muy alto
soaring *adj* **1.** (*increasing*) en aumento; (*very high*) altísimo, -a **2.** (*gliding*) planeador, -a
sob [sɒb, *Am:* sɑːb] **I.** *n* sollozo *m* **II.** <-bb-> *vi* sollozar **III.** <-bb-> *vt* decir sollozando
sober ['səʊbəʳ, *Am:* 'soʊbɚ] *adj* **1.** (*not drunk*) sobrio, -a **2.** (*serious: mood, atmosphere, expression*) serio, -a **3.** (*plain: clothes*) sencillo, -a; (*colour*) discreto, -a **4.** (*sensible*) sensato, -a
◆**sober up** **I.** *vi* **1.** (*become less drunk*) espabilar la borrachera **2.** (*become serious*) ponerse serio **II.** *vt* **to sober sb up** (*make less drunk*) quitar la borrachera a alguien; (*make serious*) poner serio a alguien
sobering *adj* que hace pensar
soberness *n no pl* **1.** (*not drunkenness*) sobriedad *f* **2.** (*seriousness*) seriedad *f* **3.** (*plainness*) sencillez *f*
sobriety [səʊ'braɪəti, *Am:* sə'braɪət̬i] *n no pl, form* **1.** (*not drunkenness*) sobriedad *f* **2.** (*seriousness*) seriedad *f*
sobriquet ['səʊbrɪkeɪ, *Am:* 'soʊ-] *n* apodo *m*
sob story *n pej* dramón *m*
so-called [ˌsəʊ'kɔːld, *Am:* ˌsoʊ'kɑːld] *adj* así llamado, -a, presunto, -a
soccer ['sɒkəʳ, *Am:* 'sɑːkɚ] *n no pl, Am* fútbol *m*
soccer player *n* futbolista *mf*
sociability [ˌsəʊʃə'bɪləti, *Am:* ˌsoʊʃə'bɪlət̬i] *n no pl* sociabilidad *f*
sociable ['səʊʃəbl, *Am:* 'soʊ-] *adj* sociable
social ['səʊʃəl, *Am:* 'soʊ-] *adj* social; ~ **drinker** *persona que no bebe a solas, sino en compañía;* **to climb the** ~ **ladder** trepar en la escalera social
social democrat *n* socialdemócrata *mf*
socialism ['səʊʃəlɪzəm, *Am:* 'soʊ-] *n no pl* socialismo *m*
socialist *n* socialista *mf*
socialite ['səʊʃəlaɪt, *Am:* 'soʊ-] *n* persona *f* con mucha vida social
socialize ['səʊʃəlaɪz, *Am:* 'soʊ-] **I.** *vi* alternar con la gente **II.** *vt* **1.** PSYCH socializar **2.** POL, ECON nacionalizar
socially *adv* socialmente
social science *n* ciencia *f* social **social security** *n no pl* **1.** *Aus, Brit* (*welfare*) seguridad *f* social **2.** *Am* (*government pension*) subsidio *m* de la seguridad social **social service** *n* **1.** (*community help*) servicio *m* social **2.** *pl* (*welfare*) servicios *mpl* sociales **social studies** *n Am* SCHOOL estudios *mpl* sociales **social work** *n no pl* asistencia *f* social **social worker** *n* asistente *mf* social
societal [sə'saɪətəl, *Am:* -t̬l] *adj* societal
society [sə'saɪəti, *Am:* -t̬i] *n* **1.** (*all people*) sociedad *f;* (**high**) ~ alta sociedad *f;* **to be a menace to** ~ ser una amenaza para la sociedad **2.** (*organization*) asociación *f*
sociocultural [ˌsəʊʃiəʊ'kʌltʃərəl, *Am:* ˌsoʊsioʊ-] *adj* sociocultural
socioeconomic [ˌsəʊʃiəʊˌiːkə'nɒmɪk, *Am:* ˌsoʊsioʊˌekə'nɑːmɪk] *adj* socioeconómico, -a
sociolinguistics [ˌsəʊʃiəʊlɪŋ'gwɪstɪks, *Am:* ˌsoʊsioʊ-] *n* sociolingüística *f*
sociological [ˌsəʊʃiə'lɒdʒɪkəl, *Am:* ˌsoʊsiə'lɑːdʒɪ-] *adj* sociológico, -a
sociologist [ˌsəʊʃi'ɒlədʒɪst, *Am:* ˌsoʊsi'ɑːlə-] *n* sociólogo, -a *m, f*
sociology [ˌsəʊʃi'ɒlədʒi, *Am:* ˌsoʊsi'ɑːlə-] *n no pl* sociología *f*
sociopolitical [ˌsəʊʃiəʊpəl'ɪtɪkəl, *Am:* ˌsoʊsioʊpə'lɪt̬-] *adj* sociopolítico, -a
sock¹ [sɒk, *Am:* sɑːk] *n* calcetín *m,* media *f AmL;* **knee** ~ calcetín *m* largo ►**to pull one's** ~**s up** *inf* hacer un esfuezo; **put a** ~ **in it!** *inf* ¡a callar!
sock² [sɒk, *Am:* sɑːk] **I.** *vt inf* (*hit*) pegar; **to** ~ **sb in the eye** dar un golpe a alguien en el ojo ►~ **it to 'em!** *Am* ¡a por ellos! **II.** *n inf* tortazo *m*
socket ['sɒkɪt, *Am:* 'sɑːkɪt] *n* **1.** ELEC enchufe *m,* tomacorriente *m Arg, Perú;* **mains** ~ toma *f* de la red; **double/triple** ~ enchufe de dos/tres entradas **2.** (*of eye*) cuenca *f,* órbita *f;* (*of tooth*) alvéolo *m;* (*of knee, arm, hip*) fosa *f*
sod¹ [sɒd, *Am:* sɑːd] *n* césped *m*
sod² [sɒd, *Am:* sɑːd] **I.** *n Brit vulg* cabrón, -ona *m, f;* **the lucky** ~**!** ¡qué suerte tiene el cabrón!; **poor** ~ pobre diablo ►**I don't give a** ~**!** *vulg* ¡me importa un huevo! **II.** *vt Brit, vulg* ~ **it!** ¡mierda!; ~ **him!** ¡que se joda!
◆**sod off** *vi Brit, inf* ~**!** ¡vete a la mierda!
soda ['səʊdə, *Am:* 'soʊ-] *n* **1.** *no pl* CHEM sosa *f* **2.** *Am* (*fizzy drink*) refresco *m* **3.** (*mixer drink*) soda *f*

soda bread *n no pl pan hecho con levadura de bicarbonato* **soda fountain** *n Am* (*pouring device*) surtidor *m* de agua con gas; (*place*) bar *m* de bebidas no alcohólicas **soda siphon** *n* sifón *m* **soda water** *n no pl* soda *f*

sodden ['sɒdn, *Am:* 'sɑ:dn] *adj* empapado, -a

sodding ['sɒdɪŋ, *Am:* 'sɑ:dɪŋ] *adj Brit, vulg* jodido, -a

sodium ['səʊdɪəm, *Am:* 'soʊ-] *n no pl* sodio *m*

sodium bicarbonate *n no pl* bicarbonato *m* sódico **sodium carbonate** *n no pl* carbonato *m* sódico **sodium chloride** *n no pl* cloruro *m* sódico

sodomize ['sɒdəmaɪz, *Am:* 'sɑ:də-] *vt* sodomizar

sodomy ['sɒdəmi, *Am:* 'sɑ:də-] *n no pl, form* sodomía *f*

sod's law *n,* **Sod's law** [ˌsɒdz'lɔ:, *Am:* ˌsɑ:dz'lɑ:] *n no pl* la ley de Murphy

sofa ['səʊfə, *Am:* 'soʊ-] *n* sofá *m*

sofa bed *n* sofá-cama *m*

soft [sɒft, *Am:* sɑ:ft] *adj* **1.** (*not hard: ground, sand, contact lenses*) blando, -a; (*pillow, sofa*) mullido, -a; (*metal*) dúctil; ~ **tissue** MED tejido *m* blando **2.** (*smooth: cheeks, skin, landing*) suave; (*hair*) fino, -a; ~ **as silk** suave como la seda **3.** (*weak*) débil; **to go** ~ debilitarse **4.** (*mild*) ligero, -a; (*wind, rain*) suave; (*climate*) agradable; (*drug*) blando, -a **5.** (*not bright: colour*) delicado, -a; (*glow*) suave; (*lighting, light*) tenue **6.** (*quiet: sound, music*) agradable; (*voice*) dulce **7.** (*lenient*) indulgente; **to be** ~ **with sb** ser demasiado tolerante con alguien **8.** (*easy*) fácil; **the** ~ **option** la opción más sencilla; **a** ~ **target** un blanco fácil **9.** (*compassionate*) compasivo, -a **10.** FIN (*currency*) débil

softball ['sɒftbɔ:l, *Am:* 'sɑ:ft-] *n Am: deporte similar al béisbol sobre un terreno más pequeño y con pelota grande y blanda*

soft-boiled [ˌsɒft'bɔɪld, *Am:* ˌsɑ:ft'-] *adj* pasado, -a por agua

soften ['sɒfən, *Am:* 'sɑ:fən] **I.** *vi* **1.** (*let get soft: butter, ground*) reblandecerse, amelcochar *Méx* **2.** (*become lenient*) ablandarse **II.** *vt* **1.** (*make soft: butter*) reblandecer; (*skin*) suavizar **2.** (*colour, voice*) suavizar **3.** (*make easier to bear: effect*) mitigar; (*opinion, words*) suavizar; (*blow*) amortiguar

◆**soften up** *vt* ablandar; MIL debilitar

softener ['sɒfənəʳ, *Am:* 'sɑ:fənɚ] *n* **1.** (*for clothes*) suavizante *m* **2.** (*for water*) descalcificador *m*

softening **I.** *n no pl* **1.** (*reduction of hardness*) reblandecimiento *m;* (*of voice*) suavización *f* **2.** (*of light*) debilitamiento *m* **II.** *adj* reblandecedor(a); (*agent*) suavizante

soft furnishings *n Aus, Brit,* **soft goods** *npl Am* ropa *f* de casa

soft-headed *adj pej* bobo, -a

soft-hearted [ˌsɒft'hɑ:tɪd, *Am:* 'sɑ:ftˌhɑ:rt̬ɪd] *adj* bondadoso, -a

softie ['sɒfti, *Am:* 'sɑ:f-] *n inf* blandengue *mf*

softly *adv* **1.** (*not hard*) suavemente **2.** (*quietly*) silenciosamente **3.** (*to shine*) tenuemente **4.** (*leniently*) indulgentemente; **to take a** ~, ~ **approach** ser cauteloso

softness ['sɒftnɪs, *Am:* 'sɑ:ft-] *n no pl* **1.** (*not hardness*) blandura *f* **2.** (*smoothness*) suavidad *f;* (*of hair*) finura *f* **3.** (*of light*) debilidad *f* **soft-soap** *vt inf* dar coba a **soft-spoken** *adj* de voz suave **soft toy** *n Brit* (muñeco de) peluche *m*

software ['sɒftweəʳ, *Am:* 'sɑ:ftwer] *n no pl* software *m;* **accounting** ~ programa *m* de contabilidad

software engineer *n* ingeniero, -a *m, f* de software **software package** *n* paquete *m* de programas **software piracy** *n* piratería *f* de software

softwood ['sɒftwʊd, *Am:* 'sɑ:ft-] *n* **1.** *no pl* (*wood*) madera *f* blanda **2.** (*tree*) árbol *m* de hoja perenne

softy ['sɒfti, *Am:* 'sɑ:f-] *n inf* blandengue *mf*

soggy ['sɒgi, *Am:* 'sɑ:gi] <-ier, -iest> *adj* empapado, -a

soh [səʊ, *Am:* soʊ] *n* MUS sol *m*

soil¹ [sɔɪl] **I.** *vt form* (*make dirty*) manchar; (*clothing, shoes*) ensuciar; **to** ~ **sb's reputation** manchar la reputación de alguien **II.** *vi* ensuciarse

soil² [sɔɪl] *n no pl* AGR suelo *m;* **fertile** ~ tierra *f* fértil; **foreign** ~ tierras *fpl* extranjeras

soirée *n,* **soiree** ['swɑ:reɪ, *Am:* swɑ:'reɪ] *n form* velada *f*

sojourn ['sɒdʒɜ:n, *Am:* 'soʊdʒɜ:rn] *n* estancia *f*

solace ['sɒlɪs, *Am:* 'sɑ:lɪs] **I.** *n no pl* consuelo *m* **II.** *vt* consolar

solar ['səʊləʳ, *Am:* 'soʊlɚ] *adj* solar

solar battery *n* pila *f* solar **solar cell** *n* célula *f* solar **solar eclipse** *n* eclipse *m* de sol **solar energy** *n no pl* energía *f* solar

solarium [səʊ'leərɪəm, *Am:* soʊ'leri-] <-s *o* solaria> *n* **1.** (*tanning room*) solárium *m* **2.** *Am* (*conservatory*) invernadero *m*

solar panel *n* placa *f* solar **solar plexus** *n no pl* plexo *m* solar **solar power** *n no pl* energía *f* solar **solar radiation** *n no pl* radiación *f* solar **solar system** *n* sistema *m* solar **solar wind** *n no pl* viento *m* solar

sold [səʊld, *Am:* soʊld] *pt, pp of* **sell**

solder ['sɒldəʳ, *Am:* 'sɑ:dɚ] **I.** *vt* soldar **II.** *n no pl* soldadura *f*

soldering iron ['sɒldərɪŋaɪən, *Am:* 'sɑ:dərɪŋˌaɪɚn] *n* soldador *m*

soldier ['səʊldʒəʳ, *Am:* 'soʊldʒɚ] **I.** *n* **1.** MIL (*military person*) militar *mf;* **old** ~ veterano *m* **2.** (*non officer*) soldado *mf* **II.** *vi* servir como soldado

◆**soldier on** *vi* seguir adelante

sold out [ˌsəʊld'aʊt, *Am:* ˌsoʊld-] *adj* vendido, -a

sole¹ [səʊl, *Am:* soʊl] *adj* (*unique*) único, -a;

S

(*exclusive*) exclusivo, -a; ~ **right** derecho *m* en exclusiva

sole[2] [səʊl, *Am:* soʊl] *n* (*of foot*) planta *f;* (*of shoe*) suela *f*

sole[3] [səʊl, *Am:* soʊl] <-(s)> *n* (*fish*) lenguado *m;* **lemon** ~ mendo *m* limón

solecism ['sɒlɪsɪzəm, *Am:* 'sɑːlə-] *n form* **1.** LING solecismo *m* **2.** (*breach of good manners*) incorrección *f*

solely ['səʊli, *Am:* 'soʊli] *adv* únicamente

solemn ['sɒləm, *Am:* 'sɑːləm] *adj* (*occasion, promise*) solemne; (*person, appearance*) serio, -a

solemnity [sə'lemnəti, *Am:* -t̬i] *n* solemnidad *f*

solemnize ['sɒləmnaɪz, *Am:* 'sɑːləm-] *vt form* solemnizar

solenoid ['səʊlənɔɪd, *Am:* 'soʊ-] *n* ELEC solenoide *m*

sol-fa [ˌsɒl'fɑː, *Am:* ˌsoʊl'fɑː] *n* MUS solfeo *m*

solicit [sə'lɪsɪt] **I.** *vt form* (*ask for*) solicitar **II.** *vi* (*prostitute*) abordar clientes

soliciting *n no pl* LAW ejercicio *m* de la prostitución

solicitor [sə'lɪsɪtəʳ, *Am:* -t̬ɚ] *n* **1.** *Aus, Brit* (*for court case*) procurador(a) *m(f);* (*for legal transactions*) notario, -a *m, f* **2.** *Am* (*city lawyer*) fiscal *mf* general

solicitous [sə'lɪsɪtəs, *Am:* -t̬əs] *adj* solícito, -a

solicitude [səˌlɪsɪ'tjuːd, *Am:* sə'lɪsɪtuːd] *n no pl, form* atención *f*

solid ['sɒlɪd, *Am:* 'sɑːlɪd] **I.** *adj* **1.** (*hard*) sólido, -a; (*rock, silver, wood*) macizo, -a; (*table, door, wall*) robusto, -a; (*meal*) pesado, -a; **to be** (**as**) ~ **as a rock** ser duro como una piedra **2.** (*not hollow*) macizo, -a **3.** (*true*) real; (*facts*) verídico, -a; (*evidence*) sustancial; (*argument*) sólido, -a; (*reasons*) de peso; (*conviction*) firme; (*agreement*) concreto, -a **4.** (*uninterrupted: wall, line*) ininterrumpido, -a; (*hour, day, week*) entero, -a **5.** (*three-dimensional*) tridimensional **6.** (*good: work, picture*) excelente **II.** *adv* **to be packed** ~ estar lleno hasta los topes; **to be frozen** ~ estar completamente helado **III.** *n* **1.** (*shape*) sólido *m* **2.** *pl* GASTR alimentos *mpl* sólidos

solidarity [ˌsɒlɪ'dærəti, *Am:* ˌsɑːlə'derət̬i] *n no pl* solidaridad *f*

solid fuel *n* combustible *m* sólido

solidify [sə'lɪdɪfaɪ, *Am:* -əfaɪ] <-ie-, -ying> **I.** *vi* solidificarse; (*plans, project, idea*) concretarse **II.** *vt* **1.** (*make hard*) solidificar **2.** (*reinforce*) reforzar

solidity [sə'lɪdəti, *Am:* -t̬i] *n* solidez *f*

solidly *adv* **1.** (*robustly*) sólidamente **2.** (*without interruption*) ininterrumpidamente **3.** (*in strong manner*) fuertemente **4.** (*unanimously*) unánimemente

solid-state [ˌsɒlɪdsteɪt, *Am:* ˌsɑːlɪd'-] *adj* de estado sólido

soliloquy [sə'lɪləkwi] *n* soliloquio *m*

solitaire [ˌsɒlɪ'teəʳ, *Am:* 'sɑːləter] *n* solitario *m*

solitary ['sɒlɪtəri, *Am:* 'sɑːləteri] **I.** *adj* **1.** (*alone, single*) solitario, -a **2.** (*isolated*) solo, -a, íngrimo, -a *AmL;* (*unvisited*) apartado, -a; **to go for a** ~ **walk** ir a pasear solo **II.** *n* **1.** *no pl, inf* (*isolation*) incomunicación *f* **2.** (*hermit*) solitario, -a *m, f*

solitary confinement *n* aislamiento *m*

solitude ['sɒlɪtjuːd, *Am:* 'sɑːlətuːd] *n no pl* **1.** (*loneliness*) soledad *f* **2.** (*isolation*) aislamiento *m*

solo ['səʊləʊ, *Am:* 'soʊloʊ] **I.** *adj* solo, -a; ~ **flight** vuelo *m* en solitario **II.** *adv* a solas; MUS solo; **to go** ~ lanzarse como solista; **to fly** ~ AVIAT volar en solitario **III.** *n* MUS solo *m*

soloist ['səʊləʊɪst, *Am:* 'soʊloʊ-] *n* solista *mf*

Solomon Islands ['sɒləmənˌaɪləndz, *Am:* 'sɑːlə-] *n* Islas *fpl* Salomón

solstice ['sɒlstɪs, *Am:* 'sɑːl-] *n* solsticio *m*

soluble ['sɒljəbl, *Am:* 'sɑːl-] *adj* (*substance, problem*) soluble

solution [sə'luːʃən] *n* solución *f*

solve [sɒlv, *Am:* sɑːlv] *vt* resolver

solvency ['sɒlvənsi, *Am:* 'sɑːl-] *n no pl* solvencia *f*

solvent ['sɒlvənt, *Am:* 'sɑːl-] **I.** *n* disolvente *m* **II.** *adj* solvente

solvent abuse *n Brit* inhalación *f* de disolventes

Somali [ˌsə'mɑːli, *Am:* soʊ'-] **I.** <-(s)> *n* **1.** (*person*) somalí *mf* **2.** (*language*) somalí *m* **II.** *adj* somalí

Somalia [ˌsə'mɑːliə, *Am:* soʊ'-] *n* Somalia *f*

somber *adj Am,* **sombre** ['sɒmbəʳ, *Am:* 'sɑːmbɚ] *adj* (*mood*) sombrío, -a; (*colour*) oscuro, -a

some [sʌm] **I.** *adj indef* **1.** *pl* (*several*) algunos, -as; ~ **apples** algunas manzanas; ~ **people think ...** algunos piensan... **2.** (*imprecise*) algún, alguna; (**at**) ~ **place** (en) algún lugar; ~ **day** algún día; (**at**) ~ **time** (en) algún momento; **for** ~ **time** durante cierto tiempo; ~ **other time** en algún otro momento; ~ **time ago** hace algún tiempo; **in** ~ **way or another** de alguna u otra manera; **to have** ~ **idea of sth** tener alguna idea de algo **3.** (*amount*) un poco de, algo de; ~ **more tea** un poco más de té; **to have** ~ **money** tener algo de dinero; **to** ~ **extent** hasta cierto punto **II.** *pron indef* **1.** *pl* (*several*) algunos; **I would like** ~ quisiera algunos; ~ **like it, others don't** a algunos les gusta, a otros no **2.** (*part of it*) algo; **I would like** ~ quisiera algo **III.** *adv* **1.** (*about*) unos, unas; ~ **more apples** unas manzanas más; ~ **more wine** un poco más de vino; ~ **ten of them** unos diez de ellos; ~ **hundred kilos** aproximadamente cien kilos **2.** *Am* (*little*) **to feel** ~ **better** sentirse un poco mejor

somebody ['sʌmbədi, *Am:* -ˌbɑːdi] *pron indef* alguien; ~ **else** otra persona, algún otro; ~ **or other** alguien; ~ **kind** alguien amable; **there is** ~ **Spanish on the phone** hay alguien español al teléfono

somehow ['sʌmhaʊ] *adv* **1.** (*through unknown methods*) de alguna manera **2.** (*for an unclear reason*) por algún motivo **3.** (*come what may*) de un modo u otro

someone ['sʌmwʌn] *pron s.* **somebody**

someplace ['sʌmpleɪs] *adv Am* en algún lugar

somersault ['sʌməsɔːlt, *Am:* -ɚsɑːlt] **I.** *n* salto *m* mortal; **to turn a ~** dar un salto mortal **II.** *vi* (*vehicle*) dar una vuelta de campana; (*person*) dar un salto mortal

something ['sʌmθɪŋ] **I.** *pron indef, sing* **1.** (*some object or concept*) algo; **~ else/nice** algo más/bonito; **~ or other** alguna cosa; **one can't have ~ for nothing** quie algo quiere, algo le cuesta **2.** (*about*) **... or ~** *inf* ...o algo así; **two metres ~** dos metros y pico; **his name is Paul ~** su nombre es Paul no sé qué **II.** *n* **a little ~** una cosita; **a certain ~** cierta cosa ►**that is really ~!** ¡ésa sí que es buena! **III.** *adv* **~ around £10** alrededor de 10 libras; **~ over/under £100** algo más/menos de 100 libras

sometime ['sʌmtaɪm] **I.** *adv* en algún momento; **~ soon** pronto **II.** *adj form* antiguo, -a

sometimes ['sʌmtaɪmz] *adv* a veces

somewhat ['sʌmwɒt, *Am:* -wɑːt] *adv* algo

somewhere ['sʌmweəʳ, *Am:* -wer] *adv* **1.** (*be*) en alguna parte; (*go*) a alguna parte; **to be ~ else** estar en otra parte; **to go ~ else** ir a otra parte; **to get ~** *fig* progresar; **or ~** *inf* o así **2.** (*roughly*) alrededor de; **she is ~ around 40** tiene alrededor de 40 años; **he earns ~ around 40,000 dollars** gana alrededor de 40.000 dólares

somnambulism [sɒm'næmbjʊlɪzəm, *Am:* sɑːm'-] *n no pl* sonambulismo *m*

somnolent ['sɒmnələnt, *Am:* 'sɑːm-] *adj* (*sleepy*) soñoliento, -a

son [sʌn] *n* hijo *m* ►**~ of a bitch** *inf* hijo de puta

sonar ['səʊnɑːʳ, *Am:* 'soʊnɑːr] *n* sónar *m*

sonata [sə'nɑːtə, *Am:* -t̬ə] *n* sonata *f;* **piano ~** sonata para piano

song [sɒŋ, *Am:* sɑːŋ] *n* **1.** MUS (*piece of music*) canción *f;* **to give sb a ~** cantar para alguien **2.** (*action of singing*) canto *m* ►**~ and dance** *Brit, pej, inf* numerito *m; Am, inf* (*untrue justification*) rollo *m;* **to make a ~ and dance about sth** montar un número por algo; (**to go**) **for a ~** venderse a precio de saldo; **to be on ~** estar en forma

songbird ['sɒŋbɜːd, *Am:* 'sɑːŋbɜːrd] *n* pájaro *m* cantor **songbook** *n* cancionero *m* **songwriter** *n* compositor(a) *m(f)*

sonic ['sɒnɪk, *Am:* 'sɑːnɪk] *adj* **1.** (*relating to sound*) acústico, -a **2.** (*at the speed of sound*) sónico, -a

sonic boom *n* AVIAT explosión *f* ultrasónica

son-in-law ['sʌnɪnlɔː, *Am:* -lɑː] <sons-in-law *o* son-in-laws> *n* yerno *m*

sonnet ['sɒnɪt, *Am:* 'sɑːnɪt] *n* soneto *m*

sonny ['sʌni] *n no pl, inf* hijito *m;* (*aggressive*) majo *m*

sonorous [sə'nɔːrəs] *adj* sonoro, -a

soon [suːn] *adv* pronto, mero *AmC, Méx;* **~ after ...** poco después de...; **how ~ ...?** ¿para cuándo...?; **as ~ as possible** tan pronto como sea posible; **as ~ as possible** lo más pronto posible; **I would just as ~ ...** preferiría...

sooner ['suːnəʳ, *Am:* -ɚ] *adv comp of* **soon** más temprano; **~ or later** tarde o temprano; **no ~ ... than** apenas...cuando; **no ~ said than done** dicho y hecho; **I would ~ leave** preferiría irme; **the ~er the better** cuanto antes mejor

soot [sʊt] *n no pl* hollín *m*

soothe [suːð] *vt* **1.** (*make calm*) calmar **2.** (*reduce: pain*) aliviar

soothing *adj* **1.** (*calming*) tranquilizador(a) **2.** (*pain-relieving*) analgésico, -a; (*balsamic: ointment, balm, massage*) reparador(a)

soothsayer ['suːθˌseɪəʳ, *Am:* -ɚ] *n* adivino *m*

sooty ['sʊti, *Am:* 'sʊt̬-] <-ier, -iest> *adj* lleno, -a de hollín

sop [sɒp, *Am:* sɑːp] *n pej* concesión *f*

sophisticated [sə'fɪstɪkeɪtɪd, *Am:* -təkeɪt̬ɪd] *adj* **1.** (*refined*) sofisticado, -a **2.** (*cultured*) culto, -a **3.** (*highly developed*) refinado, -a; (*method*) sofisticado, -a

sophistication [səˌfɪstɪ'keɪʃən, *Am:* -tə'-] *n no pl* **1.** (*refinement*) sofisticación *f* **2.** (*complexity*) complejidad *f*

sophistry ['sɒfɪstri, *Am:* 'sɑːfɪ-] *n no pl* sofistería *f*

sophomore ['sɒfəmɔːʳ, *Am:* 'sɑːfəmɔːr] *n Am* estudiante *mf* de segundo año

soporific [ˌsɒpə'rɪfɪk, *Am:* ˌsɑːpə-] *adj* soporífero, -a

sopping ['sɒpɪŋ, *Am:* 'sɑːpɪŋ] *inf* **I.** *adj* empapado, -a **II.** *adv* **~ wet** empapado

soppy ['sɒpi, *Am:* 'sɑːpi] <-ier, -iest> *adj inf* sensiblero, -a

soprano [sə'prɑːnəʊ, *Am:* -'prænoʊ] *n* **1.** (*vocal range*) soprano *m* **2.** (*singer*) soprano *f*

sorbet ['sɔːbeɪ, *Am:* 'sɔːr-] *n* sorbete *m*

sorcerer ['sɔːsərəʳ, *Am:* 'sɔːrsərɚ] *n liter* hechicero *m*

sorceress ['sɔːsərɪs, *Am:* 'sɔːr-] *n liter* hechicera *f*

sorcery ['sɔːsəri, *Am:* 'sɔːr-] *n liter* hechicería *f*

sordid ['sɔːdɪd, *Am:* 'sɔːr-] *adj* **1.** (*unclean*) sórdido, -a, miserable **2.** *pej* (*base*) sórdido, -a; **all the ~ details** todos los detalles escabrosos

sore [sɔːʳ, *Am:* sɔːr] **I.** *adj* **1.** (*aching*) dolorido, -a; **to be in ~ need of sth** necesitar algo a toda costa; **a ~ point** *fig* un punto delicado **2.** *Am, inf* (*offended*) ofendido, -a; (*aggrieved*) resentido, -a; **~ loser** mal perdedor **II.** *n* MED llaga *f; fig* recuerdo *m* doloroso; **to open an old ~** abrir una vieja herida

sorely ['sɔːli, *Am:* 'sɔːr-] *adv form* muy; **he**

will be ~ missed lo echarán mucho de menos; **to be ~ tempted to do sth** estar casi por hacer algo

sorority [sə'rɒrəti, *Am:* -'rɔːrəţi] *n Am* UNIV club *m* femenino

sorrel ['sɒrəl, *Am:* 'sɔːr-] *n no pl* acedera *f*

sorrow ['sɒrəʊ, *Am:* 'sɑːroʊ] **I.** *n* pena *f;* **to feel ~ over sth** sentirse apenado por algo; **to my ~** *form* a mi pesar **II.** *vi* **to ~ over sth** sentirse afligido por algo

sorrowful ['sɒrəʊfəl, *Am:* 'sɑːrəfəl] *adj* apenado, -a; **with a ~ sigh** con un suspiro de aflicción

sorry ['sɒri, *Am:* 'sɑːr-] **I.** <-ier, -iest> *adj* **1.** triste, apenado, -a; **to be ~ (that)** sentir (que) +*subj;* **to be ~ for oneself** compadecerse de sí mismo; **to feel ~ for sb** tener lástima de alguien **2.** (*regretful*) arrepentido, -a; **to be ~ about sth** estar arrepentido por algo; **to say ~** pedir perdón **3.** (*said before refusing*) **I'm ~ but I don't agree** lo siento, pero no estoy de acuerdo **4.** (*wretched, pitiful*) desgraciado, -a; (*choice*) desafortunado, -a; (*figure*) lastimoso, -a **II.** *interj* **1.** (*expressing apology*) **~!** ¡perdón! **2.** *Brit, Aus* (*requesting repetition*) **~?** ¿cómo dice?; **~ but before continuing ...** disculpen, pero antes de continuar...

sort [sɔːt, *Am:* sɔːrt] **I.** *n* **1.** (*type*) tipo *m;* (*kind*) especie *f;* (*variety*) clase *f;* **flowers of all ~s** toda clase de flores; **something/nothing of the ~** algo/nada por el estilo **2.** INFOR ordenación *f* **3.** (*expressing uncertainty*) **he was a friend of ~s** se le podía considerar amigo **4.** *inf* (*to some extent*) **~ of** en cierto modo; **I ~ of feel that ...** en cierto modo pienso que...; **that's ~ of difficult to explain** es algo difícil de explicar **5.** (*not exactly*) **~ of** más o menos **6.** (*person*) **to not be the ~ to do sth** no ser de los que hacen algo; **to be sb's ~** ser del tipo de alguien; **I know your ~!** ¡sé de qué pie calzas! ►**it takes all ~s to make a world** *prov* hay de todo en la viña del Señor *prov;* **to be/feel out of ~s** estar/encontrarse pachucho **II.** *vt* **1.** (*arrange*) clasificar **2.** INFOR ordenar; **to ~ in ascending/descending order** poner en orden ascendente/descendente **3.** *Brit, inf* (*restore to working order*) arreglar **III.** *vi* **to ~ through sth** revisar algo

◆**sort out** *vt* **1.** (*arrange*) clasificar; (*choose*) separar **2.** (*tidy up*) arreglar **3.** (*resolve*) solucionar; (*details*) aclarar; **to sort oneself out** tomarse un respiro **4.** (*beat up*) **to sort sb out** ajustar las cuentas a alguien

sort code *n* FIN código *m* de clasificación

sorter *n* **1.** (*postal employee sorting mail*) clasificador(a) *m(f)* **2.** (*machine*) clasificadora *f*

sortie ['sɔːtiː, *Am:* 'sɔːr-] *n* **1.** MIL incursión *f* **2.** *iron, inf* (*short trip*) escapada *f* **3.** *inf* (*try*) intento *m*

sorting office *n* oficina *f* de clasificación de correo

SOS [ˌesəʊ'es, *Am:* -oʊ'-] *n* s.o.s. *m*

so-so ['səʊsəʊ, *Am:* 'soʊsoʊ] *inf* **I.** *adj* regular **II.** *adv* ni fu ni fa, así así

soufflé ['suːfleɪ, *Am:* suː'fleɪ] *n* suflé *m*

sought [sɔːt, *Am:* sɑːt] *pt, pp of* **seek**

sought-after ['sɔːtˌɑːftəʳ, *Am:* 'sɑːtˌæftɚ] *adj* solicitado, -a

soul [səʊl, *Am:* soʊl] **I.** *n* **1.** (*spirit*) alma *f;* **to pray for sb's ~** rezar por el alma de alguien; **God rest his/her ~** que en paz descanse **2.** (*person*) alma *f;* **not a ~** ni un alma **3.** *no pl* MUS soul *m* **4.** (*essence*) **to be the ~ of discretion** ser la discreción en persona **II.** *adj Am* **~ food** *comida tradicional de los negros del Sur de los Estados Unidos*

soul-destroying ['səʊldɪˌstrɔɪɪŋ, *Am:* 'soʊl-] *adj* desmoralizador(a)

soulful ['səʊlfəl, *Am:* 'soʊl-] *adj* conmovedor(a)

soulless ['səʊlləs, *Am:* 'soʊl-] *adj pej* (*person*) desalmado, -a; (*building, town*) impersonal; (*work*) mecánico, -a

soul mate *n* amigo, -a *m, f* del alma **soul music** *n* (música *f*) soul *m* **soul-searching** *n no pl* examen *m* de conciencia; **after much ~** después de mucha reflexión **soul-stirring** *adj* conmovedor(a)

sound¹ [saʊnd] **I.** *n* **1.** (*noise*) ruido *m;* **there wasn't a ~ to be heard** no se oía nada **2.** LING, PHYS sonido *m* **3.** (*radio, TV*) volumen *m;* **to turn the ~ down/up** bajar/subir el volumen **4.** (*idea expressed in words*) **by the ~ of it** según parece; **I don't like the ~ of that** no me huele nada bien **II.** *vi* **1.** (*make noise*) sonar **2.** (*seem*) parecer **III.** *vt* (*alarm*) hacer sonar; (*bell, car horn*) tocar; **to ~ the retreat** MIL tocar la retirada

sound² [saʊnd] **I.** *adj* **1.** (*healthy*) sano, -a; (*robust*) fuerte; **to be of ~ mind** estar en su sano juicio **2.** (*good: character, health*) bueno, -a; (*basis*) sólido, -a **3.** (*trustworthy*) digno, -a de confianza; (*competent*) competente **4.** (*thorough*) profundo, -a **5.** (*undisturbed: sleep*) profundo, -a; **to be a ~ sleeper** tener el sueño profundo **II.** *adv* **to be ~ asleep** estar profundamente dormido

sound³ [saʊnd] *vt* **1.** NAUT sondear **2.** MED auscultar

sound⁴ [saʊnd] *n* (*channel*) estrecho *m;* (*inlet*) brazo *m* de mar

◆**sound off** *vi inf* **to ~ about sb/sth** sentar cátedra sobre algo/alguien

◆**sound out** *vt* tantear

sound archives *npl* archivos *mpl* de sonido **sound barrier** *n* barrera *f* del sonido **soundbite** *n* frase *f* lapidaria **soundboard** *n* MUS tabla *f* armónica **soundbox** *n* caja *f* de resonancia **sound card** *n* tarjeta *f* de sonido **sound effects** *n* efectos *mpl* de sonido **sound engineer** *n* técnico *m* de sonido

sounding *n* NAUT sondeo *m;* **to take ~s** *fig* tantear el terreno

sounding board *n* tabla *f* armónica

soundless ['saʊndləs] *adj* silencioso, -a

soundly *adv* **1.** (*completely*) **to sleep** ~ dormir profundamente **2.** (*strongly*) **to thrash sb** ~ dar una buena paliza a alguien

soundness *n no pl* **1.** (*firmness*) firmeza *f* **2.** (*good sense*) sensatez *f*

soundproof ['saʊndpru:f] **I.** *vt* insonorizar **II.** *adj* insonorizado, -a

sound system *n* equipo *m* de sonido **soundtrack** *n* CINE banda *f* sonora **sound wave** *n* onda *f* sonora

soup [su:p] *n no pl* sopa *f;* (*clear*) caldo *m;* **home-made** ~ sopa casera; **instant** ~ sopa instantánea ►**to be in the** ~ *inf* estar con el agua al cuello

soupçon ['su:psɒn, *Am:* su:p'sɑ:n] *n no pl* pizca *f*

souped-up *adj* AUTO trucado, -a

soup kitchen *n* comedor *m* de beneficencia **soup plate** *n* plato *m* sopero **soup spoon** *n* cuchara *f* sopera

sour ['saʊəʳ, *Am:* 'saʊɚ] **I.** *adj* **1.** (*fruit, wine*) agrio, -a; (*milk*) cortado, -a; **to go** ~ agriarse; (*milk*) cortarse **2.** (*character, person*) agrio, -a **II.** *n Am* **whisky** ~ *combinado de whisky, zumo de limón y azúcar* **III.** *vt* agriar; *fig* amargar **IV.** *vi* agriarse; (*milk*) cortarse; *fig* (*person*) amargarse

source [sɔ:s, *Am:* sɔ:rs] **I.** *n* **1.** *a. fig* fuente *f;* **according to Government** ~**s** según fuentes gubernamentales; **from a reliable** ~ de una fuente fiable; **to list one's** ~**s** hacer la bibliografía **2.** (*origin*) origen *m;* **a** ~ **of inspiration** una fuente de inspiración; ~ **text** texto *m* original **3.** *Brit, Aus* FIN **to tax sth at** ~ cobrar los impuestos de algo en el origen **II.** *vt* seleccionar

sourpuss ['saʊəpʊs, *Am:* 'saʊɚ-] *n inf* amargado, -a *m, f*

souse [saʊs] *vt* (*food*) macerar

south [saʊθ] **I.** *n* sur *m;* **to lie 5 km to the** ~ **of sth** quedar a 5 km al sur de algo; **to go/drive to the** ~ ir hacia el sur; **further** ~ más al sur; **in the** ~ **of France** en el sur de Francia **II.** *adj* del sur, meridional; ~ **wind** viento *m* del sur; ~ **coast** costa *f* sur

South Africa *n* Sudáfrica *f* **South African** **I.** *adj* sudafricano, -a **II.** *n* sudafricano, -a *m, f* **South America** *n* América *f* del Sur **South American** **I.** *adj* sudamericano, -a **II.** *n* sudamericano, -a *m, f*

southbound ['saʊθbaʊnd] *adj* hacia el sur

South Carolina *n* Carolina *f* del Sur **South Dakota** *n* Dakota *f* del Sur

south-east [ˌsaʊθ'i:st] **I.** *n no pl* sureste *m* **II.** *adj* del sureste; **Southeast Asia** el sureste asiático **III.** *adv* al sureste **south-easterly** **I.** *adj* **in a** ~ **direction** hacia el sureste **II.** *n* (*wind*) viento *m* del sureste **south-eastern** *adj* sureste **south-eastwards** *adv* hacia el sureste

southerly ['sʌðəli, *Am:* -ɚli] **I.** *adj* (*location*) en el sur; **in a** ~ **direction** en dirección sur; ~ **wind** viento *m* meridional [*o* sur] **II.** *n* viento *m* meridional

southern ['sʌðən, *Am:* -ɚn] *adj* del sur; **the** ~ **part of the country** la parte sur del país

Southern Cross *n* Cruz *f* del Sur

southerner ['sʌðənəʳ, *Am:* -ɚnɚ] *n* sureño, -a *m, f*

southern hemisphere *n* hemisferio *m* sur **southern lights** *npl* aurora *f* austral

southernmost *adj* más al sur

south-facing *adj* orientado, -a al sur

South Korea *n* Corea *f* del Sur **South Korean** **I.** *adj* surcoreano, -a **II.** *n* surcoreano, -a *m, f*

southpaw ['saʊθpɔ:, *Am:* -pɑ:] *n Am* zurdo, -a *m, f*

South Pole *n* Polo *m* Sur

southward(s) ['saʊθwəd(z), *Am:* -wɚd(z)] *adv* hacia el sur

south-west [ˌsaʊθ'west] **I.** *n no pl* suroeste *m* **II.** *adj* del suroeste **III.** *adv* al suroeste **south-westerly** **I.** *adj* **in a** ~ **direction** hacia el suroeste **II.** *n* (*wind*) viento *m* del suroeste **south-western** *adj* del suroeste **south-westward(s)** *adv* hacia el suroeste

souvenir [ˌsu:və'nɪəʳ, *Am:* -'nɪr] *n* recuerdo *m*

sou'wester [ˌsaʊ'westəʳ, *Am:* -tɚ] *n* sueste *m*

sovereign ['sɒvrɪn, *Am:* 'sɑ:vrən] **I.** *n* **1.** (*ruler*) soberano, -a *m, f* **2.** (*coin*) soberano *m* **II.** *adj* (*self-governing*) soberano, -a; ~ **state** estado *m* soberano

sovereignty ['sɒvrənti, *Am:* 'sɑ:vrənt̬i] *n no pl* soberanía *f*

soviet ['səʊviət, *Am:* 'soʊviet] **I.** *n* soviet *m* **II.** *adj* soviético, -a

Soviet Union *n* HIST Unión *f* Soviética

sow¹ [səʊ, *Am:* soʊ] <sowed, *o* sowed sown> **I.** *vt* sembrar **II.** *vi* sembrar ►**as you** ~, **so shall you reap** lo que siembres cosecharás

sow² [saʊ] *n* (*pig*) cerda *f* ►**you can't make a silk purse out of a** ~**'s ear** *prov* no se le puede pedir peras al olmo

sowing machine ['səʊɪŋmə'ʃi:n, *Am:* 'soʊ-] *n* sembradora *f*

sown [səʊn, *Am:* soʊn] *pp of* **sow**

sox [sɔks, *Am:* sɑ:ks] *npl Am* calcetines *mpl*

soy [sɔɪ] *n Am,* **soya** ['sɔɪə] *n Brit* soja *f*

soya bean *n Brit,* **soybean** ['sɔɪbi:n] *n Am* soja *f* **soya sauce** *n Brit,* **soy sauce** *n Am* salsa *f* de soja

sozzled ['sɒzld, *Am:* 'sɑ:zld] *adj Brit, Aus, inf* **to be** ~ estar mamado, -a; **to get** ~ agarrar una trompa

spa [spɑ:] *n* **1.** (*mineral spring*) manantial *m* de agua mineral **2.** (*town*) ciudad *f* balnearia **3.** *Am* (*health centre*) balneario *m*

space [speɪs] **I.** *n* espacio *m;* **parking** ~ plaza *f* de aparcamiento; **in a short** ~ **of time** en un breve espacio de tiempo; **leave some** ~ **for dessert** deja espacio para el postre **II.** *vt* espaciar

◆**space out** *vt* espaciar
space age *n* era *f* espacial
space bar *n* barra *f* espaciadora
space capsule *n* cápsula *f* espacial **space centre** *n* centro *m* espacial **spacecraft** *n* nave *f* espacial **spaceman** <-men> *n* astronauta *m,* cosmonauta *m* **space probe** *n* sonda *f* espacial
spacer *n* espaciador *m*
space-saving *adj* que ocupa poco espacio
spaceship ['speɪsʃɪp] *n* nave *f* espacial, astronave *f* **space shuttle** *n* transbordador *m* espacial **space station** *n* estación *f* espacial **spacewoman** <-women> *n* astronauta *f*
spacing ['speɪsɪŋ] *n no pl* **1.** (*arrangement of spaces*) espaciamiento *m* **2.** TYPO espacio *m;* **double ~** doble espacio
spacious ['speɪʃəs] *adj* espacioso, -a
spade [speɪd] *n* **1.** (*tool*) pala *f* **2.** (*playing card*) pica *f* ▶**to call a ~ a ~** llamar al pan, pan y al vino, vino
spadework ['speɪdwɜːk, *Am:* -wɜːrk] *n no pl* trabajo *m* preparatorio
spaghetti [spə'geti, *Am:* -'geţ-] *n* espaguetis *mpl*
spaghetti western *n* CINE spaghetti western *m*
Spain [speɪn] *n* España *f*
Spam® [spæm] *n no pl fiambre enlatado hecho con carne de cerdo*
span¹ [spæn] *pt of* **spin**
span² [spæn] **I.** *n* **1.** (*of time*) lapso *m,* espacio *m;* (*of project*) duración *f* **2.** ARCHIT (*of bridge, arch*) luz *f* **3.** AVIAT, NAUT (*of wing, sail*) envergadura *f* **II.** <-nn-> *vt* **1.** (*cross*) atravesar **2.** (*include*) abarcar
spangle ['spæŋgl] *n* lentejuela *f*
spangled *adj* con lentejuelas; **to be ~ with sth** *fig* estar salpicado de algo
Spaniard ['spænjəd, *Am:* -jɚd] *n* español(a) *m(f)*
spaniel ['spænjəl, *Am:* -jəl] *n* perro *m* de aguas
Spanish ['spænɪʃ] **I.** *adj* español(a); **~ speaker** hispanohablante *mf* **II.** *n* **1.** (*people*) español(a) *m(f);* **the ~** los españoles **2.** LING español *m*
spank [spæŋk] *vt* dar unos cachetes (en el trasero)
spanking ['spæŋkɪŋ] **I.** *n* zurra *f,* fleta *f AmC;* **to give sb a ~** zurrar a alguien **II.** *adj inf* **~ new** nuevo y flamante; **at a ~ pace** a paso ligero
spanner ['spænəʳ, *Am:* -ɚ] *n Brit, Aus* llave *f;* **adjustable ~** llave inglesa ▶**to throw a ~ in the works** fastidiarlo todo
spar¹ [spɑːʳ, *Am:* spɑːr] *n* NAUT palo *m*
spar² [spɑːʳ, *Am:* spɑːr] *vi* <-rr-> **1.** (*in boxing*) entrenar **2.** (*argue*) discutir
spar³ [spɑːʳ, *Am:* spɑːr] *n* MIN espato *m*
spare [speəʳ, *Am:* sper] **I.** *vt* **1.** (*pardon*) perdonar; **to ~ sb's feelings** no herir los sentimientos de alguien; **to ~ sb sth** ahorrar algo a alguien; **to ~ no effort** no escatimar esfuerzos **2.** (*do without*) prescindir de; (*time*) disponer de **II.** *adj* **1.** (*additional: key*) de repuesto; (*room, minute*) libre **2.** (*remaining*) sobrante **3.** *liter* (*gaunt: build*) enjuto, -a; (*meal*) frugal, austero, -a ▶**to go ~** *Brit, inf* volverse loco **III.** *n* repuesto *m*
spare part *n* repuesto *m* **spare ribs** *n pl* costillas *fpl* (de cerdo) **spare time** *n no pl* tiempo *m* libre **spare tire** *n Am,* **spare tyre** *n* **1.** AUTO rueda *f* de recambio **2.** *iron* michelín *m*
sparing ['speəʳɪŋ, *Am:* 'sperɪŋ] *adj* moderado, -a; **to be ~ with one's praise** escatimar los elogios
spark [spɑːk, *Am:* spɑːrk] **I.** *n* **1.** (*from fire, electrical*) chispa *f* **2.** (*small amount*) pizca *f;* **not even a ~ of interest/intelligence** ni una pizca de interés/inteligencia **II.** *vt* (*debate, protest, problems*) desencadenar; (*interest*) despertar, suscitar; (*riot*) hacer estallar; **to ~ sb into action** hacer que alguien se mueva
◆**spark off** *vt* desencadenar
sparking plug ['spɑːkɪŋplʌg, *Am:* 'spɑːrk-] *n Am* bujía *f*
sparkle ['spɑːkl, *Am:* 'spɑːr-] **I.** *n no pl* destello *m,* brillo *m* **II.** *vi* (*fire*) chispear; (*sea*) destellar, centellear; (*eyes*) brillar
sparkler ['spɑːkləʳ, *Am:* 'spɑːrklɚ] *n* **1.** (*firework*) bengala *f* **2.** *inf* (*diamond*) diamante *m*
sparkling ['spɑːklɪŋ, *Am:* 'spɑːrkl-] *adj* **1.** (*light, diamond*) brillante **2.** (*conversation, wit*) chispeante
spark plug ['spɑːkplʌg, *Am:* 'spɑːrk-] *n Brit* bujía *f*
sparring match ['spɑːrɪŋ] *n* combate *m* de entrenamiento **sparring partner** *n* **1.** SPORTS sparring *m* **2.** *fig* antagonista *mf*
sparrow ['spærəʊ, *Am:* 'speroʊ] *n* gorrión *m*
sparrowhawk ['spærəʊhɔːk, *Am:* 'speroʊhɑːk] *n* gavilán *m*
sparse [spɑːs, *Am:* spɑːrs] *adj* escaso, -a
sparsely *adv* escasamente
Spartan ['spɑːtən, *Am:* 'spɑːr-] *adj* espartano, -a
spasm ['spæzəm] *n* MED espasmo *m;* (*of anger*) arrebato *m;* (*of coughing, pain*) ataque *m;* **to go into ~** *Brit, Aus* contraerse espasmódicamente
spasmodic [spæz'mɒdɪk, *Am:* -'mɑːdɪk] *adj* **1.** (*interest*) ocasional; (*activity*) irregular **2.** MED espasmódico, -a
spastic ['spæstɪk] *n pej* espástico, -a *m, f*
spat¹ [spæt] *pt, pp of* **spit**
spat² [spæt] **I.** *n inf* (*quarrel*) rencilla *f* **II.** <-tt-> *vi Am, Aus* (*quarrel*) reñir
spat³ [spæt] *n pl* (*overshoe*) polaina *f*
spate [speɪt] *n no pl* (*of letters, inquiries*) aluvión *m;* (*of burglaries*) racha *f,* serie *f;* **to be in full ~** *Brit* (*river*) estar crecido
spatial ['speɪʃəl] *adj* espacial

spatter ['spætəʳ, *Am:* 'spæţɚ] **I.** *vt* salpicar; **to ~ sb with mud/water** salpicar de barro/agua a alguien **II.** *vi* salpicar **III.** *n* salpicadura *f*, salpicada *f Méx;* **~ of rain** cuatro gotas *fpl*

spatula ['spætjʊlə, *Am:* 'spætʃə-] *n* espátula *f*

spawn [spɔːn, *Am:* spɑːn] **I.** *n* **1.** *no pl* ZOOL hueva(s) *f(pl)* **2.** *pej* (*offspring*) prole *f* **II.** *vt* generar, producir **III.** *vi* desovar

spay [speɪ] *vt* (*animal*) esterilizar (*extirpando los ovarios*)

speak [spiːk] <spoke, spoken> **I.** *vi* **1.** hablar; **to ~ to sb** hablar con alguien; **to ~ in riddles** hablar en clave; **to ~ on behalf of sb** hablar por alguien; **so to ~** por así decirlo; **~ when you're spoken to** contesta cuando te pregunten **2.** + *adv* **broadly ~ing** en términos generales; **scientifically ~ing** desde el punto de vista científico; **strictly ~ing** en realidad **II.** *vt* decir, hablar; **to ~ dialect/a foreign language** hablar dialecto/un idioma extranjero; **to ~ one's mind** hablar claro [*o* con franqueza]; **to ~ the truth** decir la verdad; **to not ~ a word** no decir ni una palabra

◆**speak for** *vi* **1.** (*represent*) hablar por; **speaking for myself …** en cuanto a mí…; **it speaks for itself** habla por sí solo; **to be old enough to ~ oneself** ser lo bastante mayorcito para defenderse **2.** (*advocate, support*) hablar en favor de

◆**speak out** *vi* expresarse; **to ~ against sth** denunciar algo

◆**speak up** *vi* **1.** (*state views*) decir lo que se piensa; **to ~ for sth** hablar a favor de algo **2.** (*talk more loudly*) hablar más alto

speaker *n* **1.** hablante *mf* **2.** (*orator*) orador(a) *m(f)* **3.** *Brit, Can* POL presidente, -a *m, f* (*de la cámara*); **Madame ~** Señora Presidenta **4.** (*loudspeaker*) altavoz *m*

speaking **I.** *n no pl* **1.** (*action*) habla *f* **2.** (*public speaking*) oratoria *f* **II.** *adj* hablante; (*tour*) comentado, -a; **to be on ~ terms with sb** estar en buenas relaciones con alguien; **not to be on ~ terms** no hablarse, no dirigirse la palabra

speaking clock *n Brit* servicio *m* telefónico de información horaria **speaking part** *n* THEAT, CINE papel *m* hablado

spear [spɪəʳ, *Am:* spɪr] **I.** *n* lanza *f*; (*for throwing*) jabalina *f*; (*for fishing*) arpón *m* **II.** *vt* atravesar (con una lanza); (*with fork*) pinchar

spearhead ['spɪəhed, *Am:* 'spɪr-] **I.** *vt* encabezar **II.** *n a. fig* punta *f* de lanza

spearmint ['spɪəmɪnt, *Am:* 'spɪr-] *n no pl* menta *f* verde

special ['speʃəl] **I.** *adj* (*attention, case, diet*) especial; (*aptitude, character*) excepcional; **nothing ~** *inf* nada en particular **II.** *n* **1.** TV programa *m* especial **2.** RAIL tren *m* especial **3.** GASTR especialidad *f* del día **4.** *pl, Am* COM ofertas *fpl* especiales

Special Branch *n Brit: departamento policial encargado de velar por la seguridad del Estado* **special delivery** *n* correo *m* urgente **special edition** *n* número *m* extraordinario **special effects** *n* efectos *mpl* especiales

specialism ['speʃəlɪzm] *n* especialidad *f*

specialist ['speʃəlɪst] *n* especialista *mf*

speciality [ˌspeʃɪ'æləti, *Am:* -ţi] *n* <-ies> especialidad *f*

specialization [ˌspeʃəlaɪ'zeɪʃən, *Am:* -ɪ'-] *n* especialización *f*

specialize ['speʃəlaɪz] **I.** *vt* especializar **II.** *vi* especializarse

specialized *adj* especializado, -a

specially *adv* especialmente; **a ~ good wine** un vino especialmente bueno

special offer *n* oferta *f* especial **special pleading** *n* argucias *fpl*

specialty ['speʃəlti, *Am:* -ţi] *n Am, Aus s.* **speciality**

species ['spiːʃiːz] *n inv* especie *f*

specific [spə'sɪfɪk] **I.** *adj* específico, -a; **to be ~ to sth** ser propio de algo; **to be ~** dar detalles **II.** *npl* datos *mpl* específicos

specifically *adv* **1.** (*expressly*) expresamente; (*ask, mention*) explícitamente **2.** (*particularly*) específicamente

specification [ˌspesɪfɪ'keɪʃən, *Am:* -əfɪ'-] *n* especificación *f*

specify ['spesɪfaɪ, *Am:* -əfaɪ] <-ie-> *vt* especificar

specimen ['spesɪmɪn, *Am:* -əmən] *n* **1.** (*of blood, urine*) muestra *f*; (*example*) ejemplar *m;* **a ~ copy** un ejemplar de muestra **2.** *inf* (*person*) espécimen *m*

specious ['spiːʃəs] *adj form* engañoso, -a

speck [spek] *n* punto *m;* (*of paint*) manchita *f*; (*of dust*) mota *f*; **not a ~ of sth** ni pizca de algo

speckle ['spekl] *n* motita *f*

speckled *adj* con motitas, moteado, -a

specs [speks] *npl Brit, inf abbr of* **spectacles** gafas *fpl*

spectacle ['spektəkl] *n* **1.** espectáculo *m;* **to make a real ~ of oneself** dar el espectáculo **2.** *pl, Brit* (*glasses*) gafas *fpl*, anteojos *mpl AmL*, lentes *fpl AmL;* **a pair of ~** unas gafas

spectacle case *n* estuche *m* de gafas

spectacled *adj* con gafas

spectacular [spek'tækjʊləʳ, *Am:* -lɚ] **I.** *adj* espectacular **II.** *n* programa *m* especial

spectator [spek'teɪtəʳ, *Am:* -ţɚ] *n* espectador(a) *m(f)*

specter *n Am s.* **spectre**

spectral ['spektrəl] *adj* espectral

spectre ['spektəʳ, *Am:* -tɚ] *n* espectro *m*, fantasma *m*

spectroscope ['spektrəʊskəʊp, *Am:* -skoʊp] *n* PHYS espectroscopio *m*

spectrum ['spektrəm] <-ra *o* -s> *n* **1.** PHYS espectro *m* **2.** (*range*) gama *f*; **the political ~** el espectro político

speculate ['spekjʊleɪt] *vi* **1.** **to ~ about sth** (*hypothesize*) especular acerca de algo; (*con-*

jecture) hacer conjeturas acerca de algo **2.** (*buy and sell*) especular

speculation [ˌspekjʊ'leɪʃən] *n* especulación *f*, conjetura *f*; **stock-market** ~ especulación bursátil

speculative ['spekjʊlətɪv, *Am:* leɪt̬ɪv] *adj* especulativo, -a

speculator ['spekjʊleɪtəʳ, *Am:* -t̬ɚ] *n* especulador(a) *m(f)*; **property** ~ especulador en bienes raíces

speculum ['spekjələm] *n* espéculo *m*

sped [sped] *pt, pp of* **speed**

speech [spi:tʃ] <-es> *n* **1.** *no pl* (*capacity to speak*) habla *f*; **to lose the power of** ~ perder el habla **2.** (*words*) palabras *fpl* **3.** (*public talk*) discurso *m*; **to make** [*o* **give**] **a** ~ pronunciar un discurso

speech act *n* LING acto *m* de habla **speech day** *n Brit* día *m* de entrega de premios **speech defect** *n* defecto *m* del habla

speechify ['spi:tʃɪfaɪ, *Am:* -tʃə-] *vi* perorar

speech impediment *n* defecto *m* del habla

speechless ['spi:tʃləs] *adj* mudo, -a; **to be** ~ **with indignation** enmudecer de indignación; **to leave sb** ~ dejar a alguien sin palabras

speech recognition *n no pl* INFOR, LING reconocimiento *m* de la voz **speech therapist** *n* logopeda *mf* **speech therapy** *n* logopedia *f* **speech writer** *n* escritor(a) *m(f)* (*que escribe discursos para políticos*)

speed [spi:d] **I.** *n* **1.** (*velocity*) velocidad *f*; **at a** ~ **of ...** a una velocidad de... **2.** (*quickness*) rapidez *f* **3.** (*gear*) marcha *f* **4.** PHOT sensibilidad *f* **5.** *inf* (*amphetamine*) anfetas *fpl* **II.** *vi* <sped, sped> **1.** (*go fast*) ir de prisa; **to** ~ **by** pasar volando **2.** (*hasten*) apresurarse **3.** (*exceed speed restrictions*) ir a exceso de velocidad **III.** *vt* <-ed, -ed *o* sped, sped> acelerar; **to** ~ **sb on their way** despedir a alguien

◆**speed off** <-ed, -ed> *vi* salir disparado

◆**speed up** <-ed, -ed> **I.** *vt* (*process*) acelerar, expeditar *AmL*; (*person*) apresurar **II.** *vi* (*car*) acelerar; (*process*) acelerarse; (*person*) darse prisa, apurarse *AmL*

speedboat ['spi:dbəʊt, *Am:* -boʊt] *n* lancha *f* motora **speed bump** *n* banda *f* rugosa **speed cop** *n Am, inf* policía *mf* de tráfico

speeding *n no pl* exceso *m* de velocidad

speed limit *n* velocidad *f* máxima

speedometer [spi:'dɒmɪtəʳ, *Am:* -'dɑ:mət̬ɚ] *n* velocímetro *m*

speed skater *n* patinador(a) *m(f)* de velocidad **speed skating** *n no pl* patinaje *m* de velocidad **speed trap** *n* control *m* de velocidad

speedway ['spi:dweɪ] *n* **1.** *no pl* SPORTS carreras *fpl* **2.** (*track*) pista *f* de carreras

speedy ['spi:di] <-ier, -iest> *adj* veloz

speleologist [ˌspi:lɪ'ɒlədʒɪst, *Am:* -'ɑ:lə-] *n* espeleólogo, -a

speleology [ˌspi:lɪ'ɒlədʒi, *Am:* -'ɑ:lə-] *n no pl* espeleología *f*

spell¹ [spel] *n a. fig* encanto *m*; **to be under a** ~ estar hechizado

spell² [spel] **I.** *n* **1.** (*period*) temporada *f* **2.** (*turn*) turno *m* **II.** *vt Am, Aus* relevar

spell³ [spel] <spelled, spelled *o Brit:* spelt, spelt> **I.** *vt* **1.** (*form using letters*) deletrear; **how do you** ~ **it?** ¿cómo se deletrea? **2.** (*signify*) significar; **this** ~**s trouble** esto significa problemas **II.** *vi* escribir; **to** ~ **well** escribir sin faltas de ortografía

◆**spell out** *vt* deletrear; **to spell sth out for sb** *fig* explicar algo a alguien de un modo sencillo

spellbinding ['spelbaɪndɪŋ] *adj* cautivador(a)

spellbound ['spelbaʊnd] *adj* hechizado, -a; *fig* fascinado, -a

spell checker *n* INFOR corrector *m* ortográfico

speller *n* **to be a good/poor** ~ tener buena/mala ortografía

spelling *n no pl* ortografía *f*; ~ **mistake** falta *f* de ortografía

spelt [spelt] *pp, pt of* **spell**

spend [spend] <spent, spent> **I.** *vt* **1.** (*money*) gastar **2.** (*time*) pasar; **to** ~ **time** (**doing sth**) dedicar tiempo (a hacer algo) **3.** (*use up*) agotar **II.** *vi* gastar

spending *n no pl* gasto *m*; **public** ~ el gasto público

spending cut *n* FIN recorte *m* presupuestario **spending money** *n* dinero *m* para gastos personales **spending power** *n* ECON poder *m* adquisitivo **spending spree** *n* derroche *m* de dinero; **to go on a** ~ gastar dinero a lo loco

spendthrift ['spendθrɪft] *inf* **I.** *adj* derrochador(a), botado, -a *AmC* **II.** *n* derrochador(a) *m(f)*, botador(a) *m(f) AmL*

spent [spent] **I.** *pp, pt of* **spend** **II.** *adj* **1.** (*used*) gastado, -a; **to be a** ~ **force** haber perdido su vigor **2.** *liter* (*very tired*) agotado, -a

sperm [spɜ:m, *Am:* spɜ:rm] <-(s)> *n* esperma *m o f*

sperm count *n* recuento *m* de espermatozoides **sperm donor** *n* donante *m* de esperma

spermicide ['spɜ:mɪsaɪd, *Am:* 'spɜ:rmə-] *n* espermicida *m*

sperm whale ['spɜ:mweɪl, *Am:* 'spɜ:rm-] *n* cachalote *m*

spew [spju:] *vi, vt* vomitar

sphere [sfɪəʳ, *Am:* sfɪr] *n* esfera *f*; ~ **of influence** ámbito *m* de influencia

spherical ['sferɪkl, *Am:* 'sfɪr-] *adj* esférico, -a

spice [spaɪs] **I.** *n* **1.** GASTR especia *f*, olor *m Chile* **2.** *no pl* (*excitement*) picante *m*; **to give** ~ **to sth** dar sabor a algo; **the** ~ **of life** la sal de la vida **II.** *vt* condimentar

spick and span [ˌspɪkən'spæn] *adj inf* impecable

spicy ['spaɪsi] <-ier, -iest> *adj* **1.** (*seasoned*) condimentado, -a **2.** (*sensational*) picante

spider ['spaɪdəʳ, *Am:* -dɚ] *n* araña *f*

spider's web *n Brit,* **spiderweb** ['spaɪdə-web, *Am:* -dɚ-] *n Am, Aus* telaraña *f*

spidery *adj* delgado, -a; ~ **handwriting** letra *f* de trazos largos e inseguros

spiel [ʃpi:l] *n inf* rollo *m*

spigot ['spɪgət] *n* **1.** (*stopper*) espita *f* **2.** *Am* (*tap*) grifo *m*

spike [spaɪk] **I.** *n* **1.** (*pointed object*) pincho *m* **2.** (*on shoes*) clavo *m* **3.** *pl* (*running shoes*) zapatillas *fpl* con clavos **II.** *vt* clavar

spiky ['spaɪki] <-ier, -iest> *adj* **1.** (*sharp*) puntiagudo, -a; (*hair*) de punta **2.** (*irritable*) susceptible

spill [spɪl] **I.** *n* **1.** (*act of spilling*) derrame *m;* **petrol** ~ vertido *m* de petróleo **2.** *inf* (*fall*) caída *f;* **to have a** ~ tener un accidente **II.** *vt* <spilt, spilt *o Am, Aus:* spilled, spilled> derramar **III.** *vi* derramarse

◆**spill over** *vi* derramarse

spillage ['spɪlɪdʒ] *n* derrame *m*

spilt [spɪlt] *pp, pt of* **spill**

spin [spɪn] **I.** *n* **1.** (*rotation*) vuelta *f* **2.** (*in washing machine*) revolución *f* **3.** (*drive*) **to go for a** ~ dar un paseo (en coche) **II.** *vi* <spun *Brit:* span, spun> **1.** (*rotate*) girar **2.** (*make thread*) hilar **III.** *vt* <spun *Brit:* span, spun> **1.** (*rotate*) girar; (*clothes*) centrifugar; **to** ~ **a ball** dar efecto a una pelota; **to** ~ **a coin for sth** echar algo a cara o cruz **2.** (*make thread out of*) hilar **3.** (*tell: story, tale*) contar

◆**spin out** *vt* prolongar

◆**spin round** *vi* girar

spina bifida [ˌspaɪnə'bɪfɪdə] *n no pl* MED espina *f* bífida

spinach ['spɪnɪtʃ] *n no pl* BOT espinaca *f;* GASTR espinacas *fpl*

spinal ['spaɪnəl] *adj* espinal

spinal column *n* columna *f* vertebral **spinal cord** *n* médula *f* espinal

spindle ['spɪndl] *n* huso *m*

spindly <-ier, -iest> *adj* larguirucho, -a

spin doctor *n* POL asesor(a) *m(f)*

spin-dry [ˌspɪn'draɪ, *Am:* 'spɪndraɪ] *vt* centrifugar

spin-dryer *n* secador *m* centrífugo

spine [spaɪn] *n* **1.** (*spinal column*) columna *f* vertebral **2.** (*spike*) púa *f* **3.** BOT espina *f* **4.** (*of book*) lomo *m*

spine-chilling ['spaɪnˌtʃɪlɪŋ] *adj* escalofriante

spineless ['spaɪnləs] *adj* (*weak*) blando, -a

spinner *n* **1.** (*person*) hilandero, -a *m, f* **2.** (*machine*) máquina *f* de hilar

spinney ['spɪni] *n Brit* bosquecillo *m*

spinning *n* rotación *f*

spinning top *n* peonza *f* **spinning wheel** *n* rueca *f*

spin-off ['spɪnɒf, *Am:* -ɑ:f] *n* **1.** (*by-product*) subproducto *m* **2.** (*consequence*) efecto *m* indirecto

spinster ['spɪnstəʳ, *Am:* -stɚ] *n a. pej* solterona *f*

spiny ['spaɪni] <-ier, -iest> *adj a. fig* espinoso, -a

spiny lobster *n* langosta *f*

spiral ['spaɪərəl, *Am:* 'spaɪ-] **I.** *n* espiral *f* **II.** *adj* espiral; ~ **staircase** escalera *f* de caracol **III.** *vi* <*Brit:* -ll-, *Am:* -l-> **1.** (*travel in a spiral*) dar vueltas en espiral; **to** ~ **downwards** bajar en espiral **2.** (*increase*) aumentar

spire ['spaɪəʳ, *Am:* -ɚ] *n* ARCHIT aguja *f*

spirit ['spɪrɪt] *n* **1.** (*soul*) espíritu *m* **2.** (*ghost*) espíritu *m* **3.** *pl* (*mood*) ánimo *mpl;* **to be in high/low ~s** estar animado/desanimado **4.** (*character*) carácter *m* **5.** (*alcoholic drink*) licor *m* **6.** (*attitude or principle*) **the** ~ **of the age** el espíritu de la época; **that's the** ~**!** ¡muy bien!

◆**spirit away** *vt* hacer desaparecer

spirited *adj* (*energetic*) enérgico, -a; (*discussion*) animado, -a; (*person*) animoso, -a, entrador(a) *AmS*

spiritless ['spɪrɪtləs] *adj pej* **1.** (*downhearted*) desanimado, -a **2.** (*irresolute*) indeciso, -a

spirit-level *n* nivel *m* de burbuja

spiritual ['spɪrɪtʃuəl] **I.** *adj* espiritual **II.** *n* MUS espiritual *m* negro

spiritualism ['spɪrɪtʃuəlɪzəm] *n no pl* espiritismo *m*

spit[1] [spɪt] *n* **1.** GASTR asador *m* **2.** (*sandbar*) banco *m* de arena

spit[2] [spɪt] **I.** *n inf* saliva *f* **II.** *vi* <spat, spat> **1.** (*expel saliva*) escupir; **it is ~ting (with rain)** *inf* caen cuatro gotas **2.** (*crackle*) chisporrotear **III.** *vt* escupir

◆**spit out** *vt* **1.** (*expel from mouth*) escupir **2.** (*say angrily*) soltar; **to spit it out** *inf* desembuchar

spite [spaɪt] **I.** *n no pl* rencor *m;* **to do sth from** ~ hacer algo por despecho; **in** ~ **of** a pesar de; **in** ~ **of everyone** a despecho de todos; **in** ~ **of the fact that he is rich** a pesar (del hecho) de que sea rico **II.** *vt* fastidiar

spiteful ['spaɪtfəl] *adj pej* rencoroso, -a

spitting image *n* vivo *m* retrato

spittle ['spɪtl, *Am:* 'spɪṱ-] *n* escupitajo *m,* desgarro *m AmL*

spittoon [spɪ'tu:n] *n* escupidera *f,* salivadera *f Arg, Urug*

splash [splæʃ] **I.** *n* **1.** (*sound*) chapoteo *m* **2.** (*small drops*) salpicadura *f;* **a** ~ **of colour** una mancha de color ►**to make a** ~ causar sensación **II.** *vt* salpicar; **to** ~ **across the front page** poner algo en primera plana **III.** *vi* salpicar

◆**splash down** *vi* amerizar

◆**splash out** *Aus, Brit* **I.** *vi inf* derrochar el dinero; **to** ~ **on sth/sb** gastarse un dineral en algo/alguien **II.** *vt inf* derrochar

splashboard ['splæʃbɔ:d, *Am:* -bɔ:rd] *n* (*on vehicle*) guardabarros *m inv;* (*on boat, in kitchen*) alero *m*

splashdown ['splæʃdaʊn] *n* amerizaje *m*

splat [splæt] *n no pl, inf* plaf *m*

splatter ['splætəʳ, *Am:* 'splæt̬ɚ] *vi, vt* salpicar

splay [spleɪ] I. *vt* extender II. *vi* extenderse

spleen [spli:n] *n* 1. ANAT bazo *m* 2. *no pl, Aus, Brit* (*anger*) mal humor *m;* **to vent one's ~** descargar la rabia de uno

splendid ['splendɪd] *adj* espléndido, -a

splendiferous [splen'dɪfərəs] *adj inf* espléndido, -a

splendo(u)r ['splendəʳ, *Am:* -dɚ] *n* 1. *no pl* (*grandness*) esplendor *m* 2. *pl* (*beautiful things*) maravillas *fpl*

splice [splaɪs] *vt* (*join*) juntar; **to get ~d** *inf* pasar por la vicaría

splint [splɪnt] I. *n* tablilla *f* II. *vt* entablillar

splinter ['splɪntəʳ, *Am:* -t̬ɚ] I. *n* astilla *f* II. *vi* astillarse

splinter group *n* POL grupo *m* disidente

split [splɪt] I. *n* 1. (*crack*) grieta 2. (*in clothes*) desgarrón 3. (*division*) división *f* II. *vt* <split, split> 1. (*divide*) dividir; (*atom*) desintegrar; **to ~ sth between two people** repartir algo entre dos personas 2. (*crack*) agrietar; **to ~ one's head open** abrirse la cabeza ►**to ~ one's sides laughing** partirse de risa III. *vi* <split, split> 1. (*divide*) dividirse 2. (*form cracks*) agrietarse 3. *inf* (*leave*) largarse

◆**split off** I. *vt* separar II. *vi* separarse

◆**split up** I. *vt* partir II. *vi* **to ~ with sb** separarse de alguien

split infinitive *n* LING *infinitivo con un complemento adverbial intercalado entre la partícula 'to' y el verbo* **split-level** *adj* de varios niveles **split pea** *n* guisante *m* seco **split personality** *n* PSYCH doble personalidad *f* **split-screen** *n* pantalla *f* dividida

splitting headache *n inf* dolor *m* de cabeza atroz

split-up ['splɪtʌp] *n* ruptura *m*

splodge [splɒdʒ, *Am:* splɑ:dʒ] *n,* **splotch** [splɒtʃ, *Am:* splɑ:tʃ] *n Brit, inf* mancha *f*

splurge [splɜ:dʒ, *Am:* splɜ:rdʒ] *inf* I. *vt* derrochar II. *vi* derrochar dinero III. *n* derroche *m*

splutter ['splʌtəʳ, *Am:* 'splʌt̬ɚ] I. *vi* (*person*) farfullar; (*candle, engine*) chisporrotear II. *n* (*of person*) farfulla *f;* (*of candle, engine*) chisporroteo *m*

spoil [spɔɪl] I. *n* 1. (*debris*) escombros *mpl* 2. *pl* (*profits*) botín *m* II. *vt* <spoilt, spoilt *Am:* spoiled, spoiled> 1. (*ruin*) estropear, salar *AmL;* (*party*) aguar 2. (*child*) mimar, engreír *AmL,* papachar *Méx* III. *vi* <spoilt, spoilt *Am:* spoiled, spoiled> estropearse

spoiler *n* alerón *m*

spoilsport ['spɔɪlspɔ:t, *Am:* -spɔ:rt] *n inf* aguafiestas *mf inv*

spoilt I. *pp, pt of* **spoil** II. *adj* mimado, -a, engreído, -a *AmL*

spoke¹ [spəʊk, *Am:* spoʊk] *pt of* **speak**

spoke² [spəʊk, *Am:* spoʊk] *n* (*of wheel*) radio *m;* **to put a ~ in sb's wheel** *fig* poner trabas a alguien

spoken *pp of* **speak**

spokesman ['spəʊksmən, *Am:* 'spoʊks-] *n* portavoz *m,* vocero *m AmL*

spokesperson ['spəʊksˌpɜ:sən, *Am:* 'spoʊksˌpɜ:r-] *n* portavoz *mf,* vocero, -a *m, f AmL*

spokeswoman ['spəʊksˌwʊmən, *Am:* 'spoʊks-] *n* portavoz *f,* vocera *f AmL*

sponge [spʌndʒ] I. *n* 1. (*cloth*) esponja *f* 2. GASTR bizcocho *m* ►**to throw in the ~** tirar la toalla II. *vt* limpiar con una esponja

◆**sponge down** *vt,* **sponge off** *vt* limpiar con una esponja

◆**sponge on** *vt inf* vivir a costa de

sponge bag *n Aus, Brit* neceser *m* **sponge bath** *n* lavado *m* con esponja **sponge cake** *n* bizcocho *m*

sponger *n pej* gorrón, -ona *m, f,* sablero, -a *m, f Chile*

spongy ['spʌndʒi] <-ier, -iest> *adj* esponjoso, -a

sponsor ['spɒntsəʳ, *Am:* 'spɑ:ntsɚ] I. *vt* patrocinar II. *n* patrocinador(a) *m(f),* propiciador(a) *m(f) AmL*

sponsorship *n no pl* patrocinio *m*

spontaneity ['spɒntə'neɪəti, *Am:* ˌspɑ:ntə'neɪət̬i] *n no pl* espontaneidad *f*

spontaneous [spɒn'teɪniəs, *Am:* spɑ:n'-] *adj* espontáneo, -a

spoof [spu:f] *n* parodia *f;* **to do a ~ on sth** parodiar algo

spook [spu:k] I. *n* 1. *inf* (*ghost*) espectro *m* 2. *Am* (*spy*) espía *mf* II. *vt Am* asustar

spooky ['spu:ki] <-ier, -iest> *adj inf* espectral

spool [spu:l] *n* (*of thread*) bobina *f;* (*of film*) carrete *m*

spoon [spu:n] I. *n* 1. (*utensil*) cuchara *f* 2. (*amount*) cucharada *f* II. *vt* servir con cuchara

spoonbill ['spu:nbɪl] *n* espátula *f*

spoon-feed ['spu:nfi:d] *vt* 1. (*feed*) dar de comer con cuchara 2. *pej* **to ~ sb** dar todo hecho a alguien

spoonful ['spu:nfʊl] <-s *o* spoonsful> *n* cucharada *f*

sporadic [spə'rædɪk] *adj* esporádico, -a

spore [spɔ:ʳ, *Am:* spɔ:r] *n* espora *f*

sporran ['spɒrən, *Am:* 'spɔ:r-] *n Scot: bolsa que llevan los escoceses sobre la falda*

sport [spɔ:t, *Am:* spɔ:rt] I. *n* 1. (*activity*) deporte *m* 2. *inf* (*person*) **to be a (good) ~** ser buena gente II. *vt* llevar

sporting *adj* deportivo, -a, esportivo, -a *AmL*

sports car *n* coche *m* deportivo

sportscast ['spɔ:tsˌkɑ:st, *Am:* 'spɔ:rtskæst] *n Am* programa *m* deportivo

sportscaster *n Am* locutor(a) *m(f)* deportivo, -a

sports day *n* día *m* de competiciones deportivas (en un colegio) **sports field** *n* campo *m* de deportes **sports jacket** *n* chaqueta *f* de sport

sportsman ['spɔːtsmən, *Am:* 'spɔːrts-] *n* deportista *m*

sportsmanlike ['spɔːtsmənlaɪk, *Am:* 'spɔːrts-] *adj* de espíritu deportivo

sportsmanship *n no pl* deportividad *f*

sports page *n* página *f* de deportes **sportswear** *n no pl* ropa *f* de deporte

sportswoman ['spɔːtsˌwʊmən, *Am:* 'spɔːrts-] *n* deportista *f*

sports writer *n* cronista *mf* deportivo, -a

sporty ['spɔːti, *Am:* 'spɔːrt̬i] <-ier, -iest> *adj* deportivo, -a

spot [spɒt, *Am:* spɑːt] **I.** *n* **1.** (*mark*) mancha *f* **2.** (*pattern*) lunar *m* **3.** *Brit* (*on skin*) grano *m* **4.** *Brit* (*little bit*) poquito *m;* **a ~ of rain** una gota de lluvia; **to be in a ~ of trouble** tener cierta dificultad **5.** (*place*) lugar *m;* **on the ~** (*at the very place*) in situ; (*at once*) en el acto **6.** (*part of TV, radio show*) espacio *m* **7.** *inf* foco *m* ▸**to really hit the ~** venir de perlas; **to have a soft ~ for sb** tener debilidad por alguien; **to knock (the) ~s off sb/sth** dar ciento y raya a alguien/algo; **to put sb on the ~** poner a alguien en un aprieto **II.** *vi* <-tt-> *impers, Brit* **it's ~ting (with rain)** están cayendo cuatro gotas **III.** <-tt-> *vt* **1.** (*see*) divisar **2.** (*speckle*) manchar

spot cash *n* dinero *m* contante **spot check** *n* control *m* al azar

spotless ['spɒtləs, *Am:* 'spɑːt-] *adj* **1.** (*very clean*) inmaculado, -a **2.** (*unblemished*) sin manchas

spotlight ['spɒtlaɪt, *Am:* 'spɑːt-] **I.** *n* foco *m* ▸**to turn the ~ on sb/sth** dejar a alguien/algo en evidencia **II.** <spotlighted, spotlighted *o* spotlit, spotlit> *vt* iluminar

spot market *n* FIN mercado *m* al contado

spot-on [spɒt'ɒn, *Am:* spɑːt'ɑːn] *adj Aus, Brit, inf* **1.** (*exact*) exacto, -a **2.** (*exactly on target*) acertado, -a

spot price *n* precio *m* al contado

spotted *adj* manchado, -a; **a ~ dress** un vestido de lunares

spotter *n* SPORTS, AVIAT observador(a) *m(f)*

spotty ['spɒti, *Am:* 'spɑːt̬i] <-ier, -iest> *adj* **1.** *Aus, Brit* (*having blemished skin*) con granos **2.** *Am, Aus* (*inconsistent*) irregular

spouse [spaʊz] *n form* cónyuge *mf*

spout [spaʊt] **I.** *n* **1.** (*of kettle*) pitorro *m;* (*of jar*) pico *m;* (*tube*) caño *m* **2.** (*jet*) chorro *m* ▸**to be up the ~** *Aus, Brit, inf* estar en una situación desesperada **II.** *vt* **1.** (*send out: flames, water*) echar **2.** *pej* **to ~ sth** perorar sobre algo; **to ~ facts and figures** soltar una retahíla de datos y cifras **III.** *vi* **1.** *pej* (*speechify*) perorar **2.** (*gush*) chorrear

sprain [spreɪn] **I.** *vt* torcer **II.** *n* torcedura *f*

sprang [spræŋ] *vi, vt pt of* **spring**

sprat [spræt] *n* espadín *m*

sprawl [sprɔːl, *Am:* sprɑːl] *pej* **I.** *vi* **1.** (*spread out*) tumbarse; **to send sb ~ing** derribar a alguien **2.** (*town*) extenderse **II.** *n* (*of town*) extensión *f*

sprawling *adj pej* **1.** (*town*) de crecimiento desordenado **2.** (*handwriting*) irregular

spray¹ [spreɪ] **I.** *n* **1.** (*mist*) rocío *m* **2.** (*device*) atomizador *m* **II.** *vt* (*cover in a spray*) rociar **III.** *vi* (*gush*) chorrear

spray² [spreɪ] *n* rama *f;* **a ~ of flowers** un ramo de flores

spray gun *n* pistola *f* pulverizadora

spread [spred] **I.** *n* **1.** (*act of spreading*) propagación *f* **2.** (*range*) gama *f* **3.** (*article*) reportaje *m* a toda página **4.** GASTR pasta *f* **5.** *Am* (*ranch*) hacienda *f,* rancho *m AmL* **6.** *Aus, Brit, inf* (*meal*) comilona *f* **II.** <spread, spread> *vi* (*liquid*) extenderse; (*disease*) propagarse; (*news*) difundirse **III.** <spread, spread> *vt* **1.** (*disease*) propagar; (*news*) difundir **2.** (*butter*) untar **3.** (*payments, work*) distribuir **4.** (*unfold: map, blanket*) extender

spread-eagled [ˌspred'iːgld, *Am:* 'spredˌiː-] *adj* despatarrado, -a

spreadsheet ['spredʃiːt] *n* INFOR hoja *f* de cálculo

spree [spriː] *n* parranda *f,* tambarria *f AmC;* **to go (out) on a drinking ~** ir de juerga

sprig [sprɪg] *n* ramita *f*

sprightly ['spraɪtli] <-ier, -iest> *adj* vivaz

spring [sprɪŋ] **I.** *n* **1.** (*season*) primavera *f* **2.** (*jump*) salto *m* **3.** (*metal coil*) muelle *m;* (*in watch, toy*) resorte *m* **4.** (*elasticity*) elasticidad *f* **5.** (*source of water*) manantial *m,* yurro *m CRi* **II.** <sprang, sprung> *vi* saltar; **to ~ to one's feet** levantarse de un salto; **to ~ shut/open** cerrarse/abrirse de golpe **III.** <sprang, sprung> *vt* **to ~ sth on sb** soltar algo a alguien

◆**spring back** *vi* saltar para atrás

spring balance *n* peso *m* de muelle

springboard ['sprɪŋbɔːd, *Am:* -bɔːrd] *n* trampolín *m*

spring-clean [ˌsprɪŋ'kliːn] *vt* limpiar a fondo **spring-cleaning** *n* limpieza *f* a fondo **spring onion** *n Aus, Brit* cebolleta *f* **spring roll** *n* rollito *m* de primavera

springtime ['sprɪŋtaɪm] *n no pl* primavera *f*

springy ['sprɪŋi] <-ier, -iest> *adj* elástico, -a

sprinkle ['sprɪŋkl] **I.** *vt* salpicar **II.** *n* salpicadura *f*

sprinkler ['sprɪŋkləʳ, *Am:* -ɚ] *n* aspersor *m*

sprinkling ['sprɪŋklɪŋ] *n* **a ~ of sth** unas gotas de algo

sprint [sprɪnt] SPORTS **I.** *vi* esprintar **II.** *n* **1.** (*race*) esprint *m* **2.** *Aus, Brit* (*burst of speed*) carrera *f* corta

sprinter ['sprɪntəʳ, *Am:* -t̬ɚ] *n* velocista *mf*

sprite [spraɪt] *n liter* duende *m*

sprocket ['sprɒkɪt, *Am:* 'sprɑːkɪt] *n,* **sprocket wheel** *n* rueda *f* de espigas

sprog [sprɒg, *Am:* sprɑːg] *n Aus, Brit, inf* bebé *m*

sprout [spraʊt] **I.** *n* **1.** (*of plant*) brote *m* **2.** *pl, Brit* (*brussels sprout*) coles *mpl* de Bruse-

S

las **II.** *vi* (*begin to grow*) brotar **III.** *vt* (*grow: leaves*) echar
◆sprout up *vi* (*plant, child*) crecer rapidamente; (*building*) aparecer
spruce¹ [spru:s] *n* BOT picea *f*
spruce² [spru:s] *adj* aseado, -a
◆spruce up *vt* **to spruce oneself up** arreglarse
sprung [sprʌŋ] **I.** *adj Brit* de muelles **II.** *pp, Am: pt of* **spring**
spry [spraɪ] *adj* ágil
spud [spʌd] *n Brit, inf* patata *f*, papa *f AmL*
spun [spʌn] *pp, pt of* **spin**
spunk [spʌŋk] *n inf* **1.** *no pl* (*bravery*) agallas *fpl* **2.** *Brit, vulg* (*semen*) leche *f*
spur [spɜːʳ, *Am:* spɜːr] **I.** <-rr-> *vt* (*horse*) espolear, talonear *Arg; fig* estimular **II.** *n* **1.** (*device*) espuela *f* **2.** GEO espolón *m* **3.** (*encouragement*) estímulo *m* ►**on the ~ of the moment** *inf* sin pensarlo
spurious [ˈspjʊərɪəs, *Am:* ˈspjʊrɪ-] *adj* falso, -a
spurn [spɜːn, *Am:* spɜːrn] *vt form* desdeñar
spurt [spɜːt, *Am:* spɜːrt] **I.** *n* esfuerzo *m* supremo; **to put on a ~** acelerar **II.** *vt* (*liquid*) echar **III.** *vi* **1.** *Am* (*accelerate*) acelerar **2.** (*gush*) salir a chorros
sputter [ˈspʌtəʳ, *Am:* ˈspʌt̬ɚ] **I.** *vi* (*person*) farfullar; (*candle, engine*) chisporrotear **II.** *n* (*of person*) farfulla *m;* (*of candle, engine*) chisporroteo *m*
sputum [ˈspjuːtəm, *Am:* -t̬əm] *n no pl* esputo *m*
spy [spaɪ] **I.** *n* espía *mf* **II.** *vi* espiar; **to ~ on sb** espiar a alguien **III.** *vt* divisar
spyglass [ˈspaɪglɑːs, *Am:* -glæs] *n* catalejo *m*
spyhole [ˈspaɪhəʊl, *Am:* -hoʊl] *n Aus, Brit* mirilla *f*
spy satellite *n* satélite *m* espía
Sq. *abbr of* **square** Pza.
squabble [ˈskwɒbl, *Am:* ˈskwɑːbl] **I.** *n* riña *f* **II.** *vi* reñir
squad [skwɒd, *Am:* skwɑːd] *n* **1.** (*group*) pelotón *m;* (*of police*) brigada *f;* **anti-terrorist ~** brigada antiterrorista **2.** (*sports team*) equipo *m*
squad car *n Am, Brit* coche-patrulla *m*
squaddie [ˈskwɔdi, *Am:* ˈskwɑːdi] *n Brit, inf* soldado *m* raso
squadron [ˈskwɒdrən, *Am:* ˈskwɑːdrən] *n* escuadrón *m*
squalid [ˈskwɒlɪd, *Am:* ˈskwɑːlɪd] *adj* **1.** *pej* (*dirty*) asqueroso, -a **2.** (*sordid*) sórdido, -a
squall [skwɔːl] **I.** *n* ráfaga *f* **II.** *vi* chillar
squally [ˈskwɔːli] *adj* turbulento, -a
squalor [ˈskwɒləʳ, *Am:* ˈskwɑːlɚ] *n no pl* miseria *f*
squander [ˈskwɒndəʳ, *Am:* ˈskwɑːndɚ] *vt* malgastar, botar *AmL*, fundir *AmL;* **to ~ an opportunity** desperdiciar una oportunidad
square [skweəʳ, *Am:* skwer] **I.** *n* **1.** (*shape*) cuadrado *m* **2.** (*in town*) plaza *f* **3.** (*on chessboard*) casilla *f* **4.** *Am, Aus* (*tool*) escuadra *f* ►**to go back to ~ one** volver al punto de partida **II.** *adj* **1.** (*square-shaped*) cuadrado, -a; **four ~ metres** cuatro metros cuadrados **2.** *inf* (*level*) igual; **to be (all) ~** SPORTS estar (todos) empatados **3.** *inf* (*unfashionable*) carca **III.** *adv* **1.** (*exactly*) exactamente **2.** MAT en ángulo recto; **~ to [o with] the street** en ángulo recto con la calle **IV.** *vt* **1.** (*align*) cuadrar **2.** *inf* (*settle*) acomodar; **I can't ~ this with my principles** no puedo encajar esto con mis principios **3.** MAT elevar al cuadrado
◆square up *vi* **to ~ with sb** ajustar cuentas con alguien
square bracket *n* corchete *m* **square dance** *n* baile *m* de figuras

> **Square dance** es el nombre que recibe un popular baile americano. Grupos de cuatro parejas bailan en círculo, en cuadrado o formando dos líneas. Todos ellos llevan a cabo los movimientos que les va indicando un **caller**. El **caller** puede dar las indicaciones cantando o hablando. Estos bailarines suelen bailar acompañados de músicos con violines, bajos o guitarras.

squarely *adv* directamente
square root *n* raíz *f* cuadrada
squash¹ [skwɒʃ, *Am:* skwɑːʃ] *n Am* (*vegetable*) calabaza *f*
squash² [skwɒʃ, *Am:* skwɑːʃ] **I.** *n* **1.** (*dense pack*) apiñamiento *m* **2.** *no pl* SPORTS squash *m* **3.** *Aus, Brit* (*drink*) zumo *m* **II.** *vt* aplastar
squash court *n* pista *f* de squash **squash racket** *n Brit*, **squash racquet** *n Am, Aus* raqueta *f* de squash
squashy [ˈskwɒʃi, *Am:* ˈskwɑːʃi] <-ier, -iest> *adj* blando, -a
squat [skwɒt, *Am:* skwɑːt] **I.** <-tt-> *vi* **1.** (*crouch down*) agacharse, ñangotarse *PRico, RDom* **2.** (*in property*) ocupar una vivienda sin permiso **II.** *n* (*house*) casa *f* ocupada **III.** <-tt-> *adj* (*person*) rechoncho, -a
squatter [ˈskwɒtəʳ, *Am:* ˈskwɑːt̬ɚ] *n* ocupa *mf*
squaw [skwɔː, *Am:* skwɑː] *n a. pej: mujer india norteamericana*
squawk [skwɔːk, *Am:* skwɑːk] **I.** *vi* graznar **II.** *n* (*sharp cry*) graznido *m*
squeak [skwiːk] **I.** *n* chirrido *m* **II.** *vi* chirriar
squeaky [ˈskwiːki] <-ier, -iest> *adj* chirriante
squeaky-clean [ˌskwiːkiˈkliːn] *adj* relimpio, -a
squeal [skwiːl] **I.** *n* chillido *m* **II.** *vi* (*person, animal*) chillar; (*brakes, car*) chirriar
squeamish [ˈskwiːmɪʃ] *adj* remilgado, -a; **to feel ~** sentir náuseas
squeegee [ˌskwiːˈdʒiː, *Am:* ˈskwiːdʒiː] *n* escobilla *f* de goma
squeeze [skwiːz] **I.** *n* **1.** (*pressing action*) estrujón *m* **2.** ECON (*limit*) restricción *f* **II.** *vt*

1. (*press together*) estrujar; **freshly ~d orange juice** zumo de naranja recién exprimido 2. (*force*) presionar; **to ~ sth out of sb** sacarle algo a alguien

squeezer ['skwiːzəʳ, *Am:* -ɚ] *n* exprimidor *m*

squelch [skweltʃ] I. *vi* chapotear II. *vt Am* aplastar III. *n* chapoteo *m*

squib [skwɪb] *n* sátira *f* ►**a damp** ~ un fiasco

squid [skwɪd] <-(s)> *n* calamar *m*

squiggle ['skwɪgl] *n* garabato *m*

squint [skwɪnt] I. *vi* 1. (*be cross-eyed*) bizquear 2. (*look from corner of eye*) mirar de reojo II. *n* 1. (*eye condition*) estrabismo *m*, bizquera *f AmL* 2. (*quick look*) mirada *f* furtiva

squire ['skwaɪəʳ, *Am:* 'skwaɪɚ] *n* 1. HIST escudero *m* 2. *Brit* (*landowner*) propietario *m*

squirm [skwɜːm, *Am:* skwɜːrm] *vi* retorcerse; **to ~ with embarrassment** avergonzarse mucho

squirrel ['skwɪrəl, *Am:* 'skwɜːr-] *n* ardilla *f*

squirt [skwɜːt, *Am:* skwɜːrt] I. *vt* (*liquid*) echar un chorro de; **to ~ sb with sth** echar un chorro de algo a alguien II. *vi* salir a chorros III. *n* 1. (*small quantity*) chorrito *m* 2. *pej* (*person*) farsante *mf*

Sr *n abbr of* **senior** padre; **George Bush, Sr** George Bush, padre

Sri Lanka [ˌsriː'læŋkə, *Am:* -'lɑːŋ-] *n* Sri Lanka *m*

Sri Lankan [ˌsriː'læŋkən, *Am:* -'lɑːŋ-] I. *adj* esrilanqués, -esa II. *n* esrilanqués, -esa *m, f*

SSW [ˌeses'dʌbljuː] *abbr of* **south-southwest** SSO

st. *n abbr of* **stone** *unidad de peso equivalente a 6,35 kg*

St *n* 1. *abbr of* **saint** (*man*) S., Sto.; (*woman*) Sta.; ~ **Thomas** Sto. Tomás 2. *abbr of* **street** c/

stab [stæb] I. <-bb-> *vt* apuñalar, achurar *CSur*, carnear *Méx*; **to ~ sb to death** matar a alguien de una puñalada; **to ~ sb in the back** *fig* dar a alguien una puñalada trapera II. <-bb-> *vi* señalar III. *n* 1. (*blow*) puñalada *f* 2. (*sudden pain*) punzada *f* 3. (*attempt*) **to have a ~ at** (**doing**) **sth** intentar (hacer) algo

stabbing I. *n* apuñalamiento *m* II. *adj* punzante

stability [stə'bɪləti, *Am:* -t̬i] *n no pl* estabilidad *f*

stabilization [ˌsteɪbəlaɪ'zeɪʃən, *Am:* -blɪ'-] *n no pl* estabilización *f*

stabilize ['steɪbəlaɪz] I. *vt* estabilizar II. *vi* estabilizarse

stabilizer ['steɪbəlaɪzəʳ, *Am:* -ɚ] *n* 1. (*on ship, bicycle*) estabilizador *m* 2. CHEM estabilizante *m*

stable¹ ['steɪbl] *adj* 1. *a.* ECON estable 2. (*structure*) firme 3. MED estacionario, -a

stable² ['steɪbl] I. *n* cuadra *f* II. *vt* guardar en la cuadra

stable lad *n Brit* mozo *m* de cuadra

stack [stæk] I. *vt* 1. (*arrange in a pile*) apilar 2. (*fill: shelves*) llenar ►**the cards are ~ed against us** la suerte está en contra de nosotros II. *n* 1. (*pile*) pila *f* 2. *inf* (*large amount*) montón *m*, ponchada *f CSur* 3. *pl* (*bookcase*) estantería *f*

stadium ['steɪdɪəm] <-s *o* -dia> *n* estadio *m*

staff [stɑːf, *Am:* stæf] I. *n* 1. (*employees*) personal *m*, elenco *m AmL;* **the editorial ~** la redacción 2. SCHOOL, UNIV profesorado *m* 3. MIL Estado *m* Mayor 4. (*stick*) bastón *m;* ~ **of office** bastón de mando 5. (*flagpole*) asta *f* 6. <staves> *Am* MUS pentagrama *m* II. *vt* dotar de personal

staff association *n* asociación *f* de empleados **staff nurse** *n Brit* (*regular nurse*) enfermero, -a *m, f* jefe **staff officer** *n* oficial *m* del Estado Mayor **staffroom** *n* sala *f* de profesores

stag [stæg] *n* ZOOL ciervo *m*

stag beetle *n* ciervo *m* volante

stage [steɪdʒ] I. *n* 1. (*period*) etapa *f*, pascana *f AmS;* **to do sth in ~s** hacer algo por etapas 2. THEAT escena *f;* **the ~** el teatro; **to be on the ~** ser actor/actriz; **to go on the ~** hacerse actor/actriz; **to hold the ~** tener al público pendiente de su palabra II. *vt* 1. (*produce on stage*) representar 2. (*organize*) organizar

stagecoach ['steɪdʒkəʊtʃ, *Am:* -koʊtʃ] *n* diligencia *f*

stage direction *n* acotación *f* **stage door** *n* entrada *f* de artistas **stage fright** *n no pl* pánico *m* escénico

stagehand ['steɪdʒhænd] *n* THEAT tramoyista *mf*

stage-manage [ˌsteɪdʒ'mænɪdʒ, *Am:* 'steɪdʒˌmæn-] *vt* 1. THEAT dirigir la tramoya de 2. *fig* orquestar **stage manager** *n* THEAT director(a) *m(f)* de escena; CINE director(a) *m(f)* de producción **stage name** *n* nombre *m* artístico

stager ['steɪdʒəʳ, *Am:* -dʒɚ] *n* **to be an old ~** ser perro viejo

stage whisper *n* THEAT aparte *m*

stagflation [ˌstæg'fleɪʃən] *n no pl* ECON estagflación *f*

stagger ['stægəʳ, *Am:* -ɚ] I. *vi* tambalearse II. *vt* 1. (*amaze*) asombrar 2. (*work, payments*) escalonar III. *n* tambaleo *m*

staggering *adj* (*amazing*) sorprendente

staging ['steɪdʒɪŋ] *n* THEAT puesta *f* en escena

stagnant ['stægnənt] *adj a. fig* estancado, -a

stagnate [stæg'neɪt, *Am:* 'stægneɪt] *vi* estancarse

stagnation [stæg'neɪʃən] *n no pl* estancamiento *m*

stag night *n,* **stag party** *n Brit* despedida *f* de soltero

stagy ['steɪdʒi] *adj pej* teatral

staid [steɪd] *adj* serio, -a

stain [steɪn] I. *vt* 1. (*mark*) manchar 2. (*dye*) teñir II. *vi* (*become marked*) mancharse III. *n* 1. (*mark*) mancha *f;* **blood/grease/red wine**

~ mancha *f* de sangre/grasa/vino tinto **2.** (*dye*) tinte *m*

stained *adj* (*marked*) manchado, -a

stained glass *n* vidrio *m* de colores **stained glass window** *n* vidriera *f*

stainless ['steɪnləs] *adj* (*immaculate*) inmaculado, -a; (*that cannot be stained*) que no se mancha

stainless steel *n* acero *m* inoxidable

stain remover *n* quitamanchas *m inv*

stair [steəʳ, *Am:* ster] *n* **1.** (*rung*) peldaño *m* **2.** *pl* (*set of steps*) escalera *f*

staircase ['steəkeɪs, *Am:* 'ster-] *n*, **stairway** ['steəweɪ, *Am:* 'ster-] *n* escalera *f*

stairwell ['steəwel, *Am:* 'ster-] *n* hueco *m* de la escalera

stake [steɪk] **I.** *n* **1.** (*stick*) estaca *f*; **to be burnt at the ~** HIST morir en la hoguera **2.** (*share*) participación *f*; **to have a ~ in sth** tener interés en algo **3.** (*bet*) apuesta *f*; **to play for high ~s** arriesgar mucho; **to be at ~** estar en juego **II.** *vt* **1.** (*mark with stakes*) marcar con estacas **2.** (*bet*) apostar; **to ~ one's life on sth** poner la mano en el fuego por algo; **to ~ a claim to sth** reivindicar algo

◆**stake out** *vt Am, inf* poner bajo vigilancia

stakeholder ['steɪkˌhəʊldəʳ, *Am:* -ˌhoʊldɚ] *n* tenedor(a) *m(f)* de apuestas

stalactite ['stæləktaɪt, *Am:* stə'læk-] *n* estalactita *f*

stalagmite ['stæləgmaɪt] *n* estalagmita *f*

stale [steɪl] *adj* **1.** (*not fresh*) pasado, -a; (*bread*) duro, -a; (*air*) viciado, -a; (*joke*) viejo, -a **2.** (*tired*) cansado, -a

stalemate ['steɪlmeɪt] *n* **1.** (*deadlock*) punto *m* muerto **2.** GAMES tablas *fpl*

stalk¹ [stɔːk] *n* (*of plant*) tallo *m*; **her eyes were out on ~s** *Brit, Aus* se le salían los ojos de las órbitas

stalk² [stɔːk] **I.** *vt* (*follow*) acechar **II.** *vi* **to ~ off** marcharse airadamente

stalker *n persona que sigue obsesivamente a otra*

stalking horse ['stɔːkɪŋˌhɔːs, *Am:* -ˌhɔːrs] *n* POL *candidato que se presenta para favorecer a otro*

stall [stɔːl] **I.** *n* **1.** (*for animal*) establo *m* **2.** *Brit, Aus* CINE, THEAT **the ~s** el patio de butacas **3.** (*in market*) puesto *m*, tarantín *m Ven* **II.** *vi* **1.** (*stop running: engine, vehicle*) calarse **2.** *fig, inf* (*delay*) ir con rodeos **III.** *vt* **1.** (*engine, vehicle*) calar **2.** *fig, inf* (*keep waiting*) retener

stallholder ['stɔːlˌhəʊldəʳ, *Am:* -ˌhoʊldɚ] *n* dueño, -a *m, f* de un puesto

stallion ['stælɪən, *Am:* -jən] *n* semental *m*, padrón *m AmL*, padrote *m AmC, Méx*

stalwart ['stɔːlwət, *Am:* -wɚt] *form* **I.** *adj* **1.** (*strong*) fornido, -a **2.** (*loyal*) leal **II.** *n* partidario, -a *m, f* leal

stamen ['steɪmen] <-s *o* -mina> *n* estambre *m*

stamina ['stæmɪnə, *Am:* -ənə] *n no pl* resistencia *f*

stammer ['stæməʳ, *Am:* -ɚ] **I.** *vi* tartamudear **II.** *vt* decir tartamudeando **III.** *n* tartamudeo *m*

stammerer ['stæmərəʳ, *Am:* -ɚɚ] *n* tartamudo, -a *m, f*

stamp [stæmp] **I.** *n* **1.** (*postage stamp*) sello *m*, estampilla *f AmL*; (*device*) tampón *m*; (*mark*) sello *m* **2.** (*characteristic quality*) impronta *f* **3.** (*with foot*) patada *f* **II.** *vt* **1.** (*place postage stamp on*) pegar un sello en **2.** (*impress a mark on*) estampar **3. to ~ one's foot** patear **III.** *vi* patalear

stamp album *n* álbum *m* de sellos **stamp collector** *n* coleccionista *mf* de sellos **stamp duty** *n* LAW impuesto *m* del timbre

stampede [stæm'piːd] **I.** *n* (*of animals*) estampida *f*; (*of people*) desbandada *f* **II.** *vi* huir en desbandada **III.** *vt* **1.** (*cause to stampede*) provocar la desbandada de **2.** (*frighten*) infundir pánico **3.** (*force*) empujar; **to ~ sb into (doing) sth** empujar a alguien a (hacer) algo

stamping ground *n* lugar *m* predilecto

stance [stɑːnts, *Am:* stænts] *n* postura *f*

stand [stænd] **I.** *n* **1.** (*position*) posición *f*; **to take a ~ on (doing) sth** adoptar una postura con respecto a (hacer) algo; **to make a ~ against sth** oponer resistencia a algo **2.** *pl* (*in stadium*) tribuna *f* **3.** (*support, frame*) soporte *m*; **music ~** atril *m* **4.** (*market stall*) puesto *m*, trucha *f AmC* **5.** (*for vehicles*) parada *f*; **taxi ~** parada de taxis **6.** (*witness box*) estrado *m*; **to take the ~** subir al estrado **7.** (*group*) **a ~ of trees** una hilera de árboles **II.** <stood, stood> *vi* **1.** (*be upright*) estar de pie; **to ~ two metres tall** medir dos metros; **to ~ still** estarse quieto, -a **2.** (*be located*) encontrarse **3.** (*remain unchanged: decision, law*) mantenerse en vigor **III.** <stood, stood> *vt* **1.** (*place*) poner (de pie), colocar **2.** (*bear*) aguantar; **I can't ~ her** no la puedo ver **3.** (*pay for*) **to ~ sb a drink** invitar a alguien a una copa; **to ~ a round** *inf* pagar una ronda **4.** LAW (*undergo*) sufragar

◆**stand about** *vi*, **stand around** *vi* esperar

◆**stand aside** *vi* **1.** (*move*) apartarse **2.** (*stay*) mantenerse aparte

◆**stand back** *vi* **1.** (*move backwards*) retroceder **2.** (*be objective*) distanciarse

◆**stand by** **I.** *vi* **1.** (*observe*) quedarse sin hacer nada **2.** (*be ready to take action*) estar alerta **II.** *vt* (*support*) apoyar

◆**stand down** *vi Brit, Aus* renunciar

◆**stand for** *vt* **1.** (*represent*) representar **2.** (*mean*) significar **3.** *Brit, Aus* (*be a candidate*) presentarse a **4.** (*tolerate*) aguantar

◆**stand in** *vi* **to ~ for sb** suplir a alguien

◆**stand out** *vi* destacar

◆**stand over** *vt* vigilar

◆**stand up** **I.** *vi* **1.** (*be upright*) levantarse, arriscarse *Col* **2.** (*evidence, argument*) ser convincente ►**to ~ and be counted** declararse abiertamente **II.** *vt* **to stand sb up** dar un plan-

tón a alguien
stand-alone ['stændəˌləʊn, *Am:* -əˌloʊn] *n* INFOR sistema *m* autónomo
standard ['stændəd, *Am:* -dɚd] **I.** *n* **1.** (*level*) nivel *m;* (*quality*) clase *f* **2.** (*norm*) norma *f* **3.** (*flag*) estandarte *m* **4.** MUS clásico *m* **II.** *adj* **1.** (*normal*) normal; (*procedure*) habitual **2.** LING estándar
standard-bearer ['stændədˌbeərəʳ, *Am:* -dɚdˌberɚ] *n* abanderado, -a *m, f*
standardization [ˌstændədaɪ'zeɪʃən, *Am:* -dɚdɪ'-] *n no pl* estandarización *f;* TECH normalización *f*
standardize ['stændədaɪz, *Am:* -dɚ-] *vt* estandarizar; TECH normalizar
standard lamp ['stændədlæmp, *Am:* -dɚd-] *n Brit, Aus* (*floor lamp*) lámpara *f* de pie **standard size** *n* talla *f* corriente
standby ['stændbaɪ] **I.** *n* **1.** (*of money, food*) reserva *f* **2.** AVIAT lista *f* de espera; **to be** (**put**) **on** ~ estar sobre aviso; **to be on 24-hour** ~ estar listo para partir dentro de 24 horas **II.** *adj* de reserva
stand-in ['stændɪn] *n* suplente *mf;* CINE doble *mf*
standing ['stændɪŋ] **I.** *n* **1.** (*status*) posición *f* **2.** (*duration*) duración *f;* **of long** ~ desde hace mucho tiempo **II.** *adj* **1.** (*upright*) vertical **2.** (*permanent*) permanente **3.** (*water*) estancado, -a
standing order *n* pedido *m* regular **standing ovation** *n* ovación *f* en pie **standing start** *n* **to do sth from a** ~ hacer algo partiendo de cero
standoffish [ˌstænd'ɒfɪʃ, *Am:* -'ɑːfɪʃ] *adj pej, inf* distante, estirado, -a
standpipe ['stændpaɪp] *n* fuente *f* provisional
standpoint ['stændpɔɪnt] *n* punto *m* de vista
standstill ['stændstɪl] *n no pl* paralización *f;* **to be at a** ~ estar parado
stand trial *vi* estar acusado
stand-up ['stændˌʌp] *adj* **1.** (*upright*) ~ **buffet** comida *f* tomada de pie **2.** (*cabaret*) ~ **comedian** cómico, -a *m, f* de micrófono **3.** (*unrestrained*) ~ **fight** pelea *f* violenta; ~ **argument** altercado *m* **4.** FASHION **a** ~ **collar** un cuello alto
stank [stæŋk] *pt of* **stink**
stanza ['stænzə] *n* LIT estrofa *f*
staple[1] ['steɪpl] **I.** *n* **1.** (*product, article*) producto *m* principal **2.** (*basic food*) alimento *m* de primera necesidad **3.** (*important component*) elemento *m* esencial **II.** *adj* **1.** (*principal*) principal **2.** (*standard*) corriente
staple[2] ['steɪpl] **I.** *n* (*fastener*) grapa *f* **II.** *vt* grapar
staple gun *n* grapadora *f* industrial
stapler ['steɪpləʳ, *Am:* -plɚ] *n* grapadora *f*
star [stɑːʳ, *Am:* stɑːr] **I.** *n* **1.** (*heavenly body*) estrella *f* **2.** (*asterisk*) asterisco *m* ▸**to thank one's <u>lucky</u>** ~**s** dar las gracias a Dios; **to be <u>written</u> in the** ~**s** estar escrito en las estrellas; **to <u>reach</u> for the** ~**s** apuntar a lo más alto; **to <u>see</u>** ~**s** ver las estrellas **II.** *vt* <-rr-> **1.** THEAT, CINE tener como protagonista **2.** (*mark with asterisk*) señalar con un asterisco
star billing [ˌstɑː'bɪlɪŋ, *Am:* ˌstɑːr'-] *n no pl* **to get** ~ aparecer con letras grandes en los carteles
starboard ['stɑːbəd, *Am:* 'stɑːrbɚd] **I.** *n* NAUT estribor *m* **II.** *adj* de estribor
starch [stɑːtʃ, *Am:* stɑːrtʃ] **I.** *n* **1.** *no pl* (*stiffening agent*) almidón *m* **2.** GASTR fécula *f* **II.** *vt* almidonar
starchy ['stɑːtʃi, *Am:* 'stɑːrtʃ-] <-ier, -iest> *adj* **1.** (*food*) feculento, -a **2.** *pej, inf* (*person*) estirado, -a
stardom ['stɑːdəm, *Am:* 'stɑːr-] *n no pl* estrellato *m,* estelaridad *f Chile*
stare [steəʳ, *Am:* ster] **I.** *vi* mirar fijamente **II.** *vt* mirar fijamente; **to** ~ **sb in the face** *fig* saltar a la vista; **the answer was staring us in the face** la respuesta era evidente **III.** *n* mirada *f* fija
starfish ['stɑːfɪʃ, *Am:* 'stɑːr-] <-(es)> *n* estrella *f* de mar
stargazer ['stɑːˌgeɪzəʳ, *Am:* 'stɑːrˌgeɪzɚ] *n* (*astronomer*) astrónomo, -a *m, f;* (*astrologer*) astrólogo, -a *m, f*
staring ['steərɪŋ, *Am:* 'ster-] *adj* que mira fijamente; ~ **eyes** ojos desorbitados
stark [stɑːk, *Am:* stɑːrk] **I.** *adj* **1.** (*desolate*) severo, -a; **a** ~ **landscape** un paisaje inhóspito **2.** (*austere*) austero, -a **3.** (*complete*) completo, -a **II.** *adv* ~ **naked** en cueros, empelotado, -a *AmL;* ~ **raving mad** loco de atar
starkers ['stɑːkəʳs, *Am:* 'stɑːrkɚz] *adj Brit, Aus, inf* (*naked*) en cueros
starless ['stɑːlɪs, *Am:* 'stɑːr-] *adj* sin estrellas
starlet ['stɑːlɪt, *Am:* 'stɑːr-] *n* actriz *f* que aspira al estrellato
starlight ['stɑːlaɪt, *Am:* 'stɑːr-] *n no pl* luz *f* de las estrellas
starling ['stɑːlɪŋ, *Am:* 'stɑːr-] *n* estornino *m*
starlit ['stɑːˌlɪt, *Am:* 'stɑːr-] *adj* iluminado, -a por las estrellas
starry ['stɑːri] <-ier, -iest> *adj* estrellado, -a
starry-eyed [ˌstɑːri'aɪd, *Am:* 'stɑːriˌaɪd] *adj* soñador(a)
Stars and Stripes *n no pl* **the** ~ la bandera de las barras y las estrellas
star sign *n* signo *m* del zodiaco
Star-Spangled Banner *n no pl* (*flag*) bandera *f* de las barras y las estrellas; (*anthem*) himno *m* nacional de EE.UU.
star-studded *adj* **1.** (*sky*) estrellado, -a **2.** (*film*) lleno, -a de estrellas; **a** ~ **cast** un reparto estelar
start [stɑːt, *Am:* stɑːrt] **I.** *vi* **1.** (*begin*) comenzar; **to** ~ **to do sth** empezar a hacer algo **2.** (*begin journey*) salir; **the bus** ~**s from the main square** el autobús sale de la plaza principal **3.** (*begin to operate: vehicle, motor*) arrancar **4.** (*make sudden movement*) sobre-

S

saltarse; **to ~ out of sleep** despertarse sobresaltado **II.** *vt* **1.** (*begin*) comenzar; **we ~ work at 6:30 every morning** entramos a trabajar a las 6:30 cada mañana **2.** (*set in operation*) poner en marcha; (*car*) arrancar **3.** COM (*establish: business*) abrir **III.** *n* **1.** (*beginning*) principio *m;* **to make an early/late ~** empezar temprano/tarde; **to make a fresh ~** comenzar de nuevo; **to have a good ~ in life** tener una infancia fácil **2.** SPORTS (*beginning place*) salida *f;* **false ~** salida en falso **3.** (*sudden movement*) sobresalto *m;* **to give a ~** dar un respingo; **to give sb a ~** dar un susto a alguien

◆**start back** *vi* **1.** (*jump back suddenly*) retroceder **2.** (*begin return journey*) emprender el regreso

◆**start in** *vi* poner manos a la obra

◆**start off** **I.** *vi* **1.** (*begin*) empezar **2.** (*begin journey*) partir; (*train, plane*) salir **II.** *vt* empezar; **to start sb off (on sth)** ayudar a alguien (a empezar algo)

◆**start out** *vi* **1.** (*begin*) empezar; **to ~ to do sth** ponerse a hacer algo **2.** (*begin journey*) partir; (*train, plane*) salir

◆**start up** **I.** *vt* **1.** (*organization, business*) fundar **2.** (*vehicle, motor*) arrancar **II.** *vi* **1.** (*jump up*) incorporarse bruscamente **2.** (*begin happening*) empezar **3.** (*begin running: vehicle, motor*) arrancar

START [stɑːt, *Am:* stɑːrt] *abbr of* **Strategic Arms Reduction Talks** START

starter *n* **1.** AUTO arranque *m* **2.** *Brit, inf* GASTR entrante *m* ▶**for ~s** *inf* para empezar

starting *adj* de comienzo

starting line *n* línea *m* de salida **starting point** *n* punto *m* de partida

startle ['stɑːtl, *Am:* 'stɑːrt̬l] *vt* sobresaltar

startling *adj* (*surprising*) asombroso, -a; (*alarming*) alarmante

start-up ['stɑːtʌp, *Am:* 'stɑːrt-] *n* puesta *f* en marcha

start-up capital *n* capital *m* inicial

start-up costs *n* gastos *mpl* de puesta en marcha

starvation [stɑː'veɪʃən, *Am:* stɑːr'-] *n no pl* hambre *m o f;* **to die of ~** morir de hambre

starvation diet *n* régimen *m* de hambre

starve [stɑːv, *Am:* stɑːrv] **I.** *vi* **1.** pasar hambre, hambrear *AmL;* (*die of hunger*) morir de hambre; **to ~ to death** morir de hambre **2.** *inf* (*be very hungry*) morirse de hambre **II.** *vt* **1.** (*deprive: of food*) privar de alimentos; **to ~ sb to death** matar a alguien de inanición **2.** (*deprive: of love, support*) privar

starving *adj* hambriento, -a

stash [stæʃ] **I.** *vt* ocultar **II.** *n* <-es> *inf* **1.** (*hiding place*) escondite *m* **2.** (*cache*) alijo *m*

state [steɪt] **I.** *n* **1.** (*condition*) estado *m;* **~ of siege/war** estado de sitio/guerra; **solid/liquid ~** estado sólido/líquido; **~ of mind** estado de ánimo; **to be in a ~** *inf* estar nervioso **2.** (*nation*) estado *m* **3.** *pl, inf* (*USA*) **the States** los Estados Unidos **4.** (*pomp*) **to lie in ~** yacer en la capilla ardiente **II.** *adj* (*pertaining to a nation*) estatal; **~ secret** secreto *m* de Estado **III.** *vt* **1.** (*express*) declarar **2.** (*specify, fix*) exponer

state-controlled *adj* controlado, -a por el Estado; (*business*) estatal

statecraft ['steɪtkrɑːft, *Am:* -kræft] *n no pl* arte *m* de gobernar

stated *adj* (*specified*) indicado, -a

State Department *n no pl, Am* Departamento *m* de Estado, ≈ Ministerio *m* de Asuntos Exteriores **state education** *n no pl* enseñanza *f* pública

stateless ['steɪtləs] *adj* apátrida

stately ['steɪtli] *adj* majestuoso, -a; **~ home** casa *f* solariega

statement ['steɪtmənt] *n* **1.** (*declaration*) declaración *f;* **to make a ~** LAW prestar declaración **2.** (*bank statement*) extracto *m* de cuenta

state-of-the-art [ˌsteɪtəvðiˈɑːt, *Am:* -'ɑːrt] *adj* moderno, -a; **~ technology** tecnología punta **state-owned** *adj* nacional **state prison** *n Am* prisión *f* estatal

stateroom ['steɪtrʊm, *Am:* -ruːm] *n* **1.** (*in palace, hotel*) salón *m* principal **2.** NAUT camarote *m*

state school *n* escuela *f* pública

stateside ['steɪtsaɪd] *adv Am, inf* en los Estados Unidos

statesman ['steɪtsmən] <-men> *n* estadista *m*

statesmanship *n no pl* arte *m* de gobernar

stateswoman ['steɪtsˌwʊmən] <-men> *n* estadista *f*

state visit *n* visita *f* oficial

static ['stætɪk, *Am:* 'stæt̬-] **I.** *adj* estático, -a; **to remain ~** permanecer inmóvil **II.** *n* PHYS *no pl* electricidad *f* estática

static electricity *n no pl* electricidad *f* estática

station ['steɪʃən] **I.** *n* **1.** RAIL estación *f* **2.** (*place*) sitio *m;* **research ~** centro *m* de investigación; **police ~** comisaría *f;* **petrol** [*o* **gas**] **~** gasolinera *f* **3.** RADIO emisora *f;* TV canal *m* **4.** (*position*) puesto *m;* **action ~s!** MIL ¡a sus puestos! **5.** (*social position*) clase *f* social **6.** *Aus* AGR explotación *f;* **sheep ~** explotación de ganado ovino **II.** *vt* **1.** (*place*) colocar **2.** MIL destinar

stationary ['steɪʃənəri, *Am:* 'steɪʃəner-] *adj* (*not moving*) inmóvil

stationer ['steɪʃənəʳ, *Am:* -ʃənɚ] *n Brit* dueño, -a *m, f* de una papelería; **~'s** papelería *f*

stationery ['steɪʃənəri, *Am:* 'steɪʃəner-] *n no pl* artículos *mpl* de papelería

station house *n Am* comisaría *f* **station master** *n* jefe, -a *m, f* de estación **station wagon** *n Am, Aus* furgoneta *m*

statistical [stə'tɪstɪkl] *adj* estadístico, -a

statistician [ˌstætɪ'stɪʃən] *n* estadístico, -a *m, f*

statistics [stə'tɪstɪks] *n* **1.** (*science*) estadística *f* **2.** *pl* (*data*) estadísticas *fpl*

statuary ['stætʃuəri, *Am:* 'stætʃuer-] *n no pl, form* (*statues*) estatuas *fpl*

statue ['stætʃuː] *n* estatua *f*

Statue of Liberty *n* **the** ~ la Estatua de la Libertad

statuesque [ˌstætju'esk, *Am:* ˌstætʃu'-] *adj form* escultural

statuette [ˌstætju'et, *Am:* ˌstætʃu'-] *n* estatuilla *f*

stature ['stætʃəʳ, *Am:* -ɚ] *n* **1.** (*height*) estatura *f* **2.** (*reputation*) talla *f*

status ['steɪtəs, *Am:* -ţəs] *n no pl* **1.** (*official position*) estatus *m* **2.** (*prestige*) prestigio *m* **status bar** *n,* **status line** *n* INFOR barra *f* de estado **status quo** *n no pl* statu quo *m* **status report** *n* INFOR informe *m* de situación **status symbol** *n* signo *m* de prestigio social

statute ['stætjuːt, *Am:* 'stætʃuːt] *n* LAW ley *f;* **by** ~ de acuerdo con la ley

statute book *n* código *m* de leyes **statute law** *n* derecho *m* escrito **statute of limitations** *n* ley *f* de prescripción

statutory ['stætjətəri, *Am:* 'stætʃətɔːr-] *adj* legal

staunch¹ [stɔːntʃ] *adj* incondicional

staunch² [stɔːntʃ] *vt* restañar

stave [steɪv] *n* **1.** MUS pentagrama *m* **2.** (*piece of wood*) duela *f*

◆**stave in** <stove in, stove in> *vt* romper

◆**stave off** <staved off, staved off> *vt* (*postpone*) aplazar; (*prevent*) evitar

staves *n* **1.** *pl of* **staff I.6. 2.** *pl of* **stave**

stay¹ [steɪ] *n* **1.** NAUT estay *m* **2.** *pl* (*corset*) corsé *m*

stay² [steɪ] **I.** *n* estancia *f,* estada *f AmL* **II.** *vi* **1.** (*remain present*) quedarse; **to** ~ **in bed** guardar cama **2.** (*reside temporarily*) alojarse **3.** (*remain*) permanecer; **to** ~ **friends** seguir siendo amigos **III.** *vt* **1.** (*assuage: hunger, thirst*) aplacar **2.** *liter* (*stop*) parar **3.** (*endure*) resistir; **to** ~ **the course** [*o* **distance**] aguantar hasta el final

◆**stay away** *vi* ausentarse; **to** ~ **from sth** mantenerse alejado de algo

◆**stay behind** *vi* quedarse

◆**stay in** *vi* quedarse en casa

◆**stay on** *vi* quedarse

◆**stay out** *vi* no volver a casa; **to** ~ **all night** pasar toda la noche fuera

◆**stay up** *vi* no acostarse; **to** ~ **late** acostarse tarde

stay-at-home ['steɪəthəʊm, *Am:* -hoʊm] **I.** *n* persona *f* hogareña **II.** *adj* hogareño, -a

stayer *n* (*person*) persona *f* perseverante; (*horse*) caballo *m* apto para carreras de distancia

staying power *n no pl* resistencia *f*

STD [ˌestiː'diː] *n* **1.** MED *abbr of* **sexually transmitted disease** ETS *f* **2.** *Brit, Aus* TECH *abbr of* **subscriber trunk dialling** ~ **code** prefijo *m* de transferencias interurbanas

stead [sted] *n no pl* lugar *m;* **in his/her** ~ en su lugar ►**to stand sb in good** ~ (**for sth**) ser útil a alguien (para algo)

steadfast ['stedfɑːst, *Am:* -fæst] *adj* firme

steady ['stedi] **I.** <-ier, -iest> *adj* **1.** (*stable*) estable; (*job, employment*) fijo, -a; (*temperature*) constante **2.** (*regular*) regular; (*speed*) constante **3.** (*not wavering: hand*) firme **4.** (*calm*) sereno, -a **5.** (*regular: boyfriend*) formal **II.** *vt* **1.** (*stabilize*) estabilizar **2.** (*make calm*) calmar **III.** *adv* **to be going** ~ ser novios formales **IV.** *interj* cuidado

steak [steɪk] *n* **1.** (*for frying, grilling*) bistec *m,* bife *m AmL;* (*for stew, mince*) carne *f* de ternera **2.** (*of lamb, fish*) filete *m*

steal [stiːl] **I.** <stole, stolen> *vt* robar, cachar *AmC,* apachar *Perú;* **to** ~ **sb's heart** robar el corazón a alguien; **to** ~ **a glance** (**at sb/sth**) echar una mirada furtiva (a alguien/algo) ►**to** ~ **the show** llevarse todos los aplausos **II.** <stole, stolen> *vi* **1.** (*take things illegally*) robar **2.** (*move surreptitiously*) **to** ~ **in** entrar a hurtadillas; **to** ~ **away** escabullirse **III.** *n Am, inf* ganga *f;* **to be a** ~ ser una ganga

stealth [stelθ] *n no pl* sigilo *m;* **by** ~ con sigilo

stealthy ['stelθi] *adj* sigiloso, -a

steam [stiːm] **I.** *n no pl* (*water vapour*) vapor *m;* **full** ~ **ahead!** ¡a todo vapor!; **to run out of** ~ *fig* perder vigor ►**to do sth under one's own** ~ hacer algo por sus propios medios; **to let off** ~ desahogarse **II.** *adj* de vapor **III.** *vi* (*produce steam*) echar vapor **IV.** *vt* cocer al vapor

◆**steam off** *vi* NAUT zarpar

◆**steam up** *vi* **1.** (*become steamy*) empañarse **2.** *inf* **to get steamed up** (**about sth**) acalorarse (por algo)

steambath *n* baño *m* turco **steamboat** *n* vapor *m* **steam engine** *n* máquina *f* de vapor

steamer ['stiːməʳ, *Am:* -ɚ] *n* **1.** (*boat*) vapor *m* **2.** GASTR vaporera *f*

steam iron *n* plancha *f* de vapor **steam-roller** **I.** *n* apisonadora *f* **II.** *vt a. fig* aplastar **steamship** **I.** *n* vapor *m* **II.** *adj* ~ **line** compañía *f* naviera

steamy ['stiːmi] <-ier, -iest> *adj* **1.** (*full of steam*) lleno, -a de vapor **2.** (*very humid*) húmedo, -a **3.** *inf* (*sexy*) erótico, -a

steed [stiːd] *n liter* corcel *m*

steel [stiːl] **I.** *n* **1.** *no pl* (*metal*) acero *m;* **nerves of** ~ nervios *mpl* de acero **2.** (*knife sharpener*) afilador *m* **II.** *adj* de acero **III.** *vt* **to** ~ **oneself for sth** armarse de valor para algo

steel band *n banda de percusión típica del Caribe* **steel grey** *n* gris *m* metálico **steel industry** *n* industria *f* siderúrgica **steel mill** *n* planta *f* de laminación de acero **steel wool** *n no pl* lana *f* de acero

steelworker ['stiːlˌwɜːkəʳ, *Am:* -ˌwɜːrkɚ] *n* obrero, -a *m, f* siderúrgico, -a

steelworks ['stiːlwɜːks, *Am:* -wɜːrks] *n inv*

planta *f* siderúrgica

steely ['sti:li] <-ier, -iest> *adj* (*determination*) férreo, -a; (*gaze*) duro, -a

steep¹ [sti:p] *adj* **1.** (*sharply sloping*) empinado, -a **2.** (*dramatic: increase, fall*) pronunciado, -a; **that's a bit ~!** ¡no hay derecho! +*subj* **3.** (*expensive*) exorbitante

steep² [sti:p] **I.** *vt* **1.** (*soak*) remojar **2.** *fig* **to be ~ in tradition/history** tener mucha tradición/la historia **II.** *vi* **to leave sth to ~** dejar algo en remojo

steepen ['sti:pən] *vi* **1.** (*become steeper*) empinarse **2.** *inf* (*become more expensive*) aumentar

steeple ['sti:pl] *n* ARCHIT torre *f*; **church ~** campanario de una iglesia

steeplechase ['sti:pltʃeɪs] *n* carrera *f* de obstáculos

steeplejack ['sti:pldʒæk] *n* reparador(a) *m(f)* de torres

steer¹ [stɪəʳ, *Am:* stɪr] **I.** *vt* **1.** (*direct*) dirigir; (*car*) conducir, manejar *AmL* **2.** (*guide*) guiar **II.** *vi* (*person*) conducir, manejar *AmL*; (*vehicle*) manejarse; **to ~ for sth** NAUT poner rumbo a algo; **to ~ clear of sth/sb** evitar algo/a alguien

steer² [stɪəʳ, *Am:* stɪr] *n* (*young bull*) novillo *m*; (*castrated bull*) buey *m*

steerage ['stɪərɪdʒ, *Am:* 'stɪrɪdʒ] *n no pl* NAUT **to travel ~** viajar en tercera clase

steering *n no pl* dirección *f*

steering committee *n inv, Brit* comité *m* directivo **steering lock** *n* dispositivo *m* antirrobo **steering wheel** *n* (*of car*) volante *m*, guía *f PRico*; (*of ship*) timón *m*

steersman ['stɪəzmən, *Am:* 'stɪrz-] <-men> *n* timonel *m*

stellar ['steləʳ, *Am:* -ɚ] *adj* estelar

stem [stem] **I.** *n* **1.** (*of plant*) tallo *m*; (*of leaf*) pedúnculo *m* **2.** (*part of glass*) pie *m* **3.** LING raíz *f* **4.** NAUT proa *f* ►**from ~ to stern** de proa a popa **II.** <-mm-> *vt* (*stop*) detener; (*blood*) restañar **III.** <-mm-> *vi* **to ~ from** resultar de

stench [stentʃ] *n no pl* hedor *m*

stencil ['stensl] **I.** *n* **1.** (*cut-out pattern*) plantilla *f* **2.** (*picture drawn*) patrón *m* **II.** *vt* dibujar utilizando una plantilla

stenographer [stə'nɒgrəfəʳ, *Am:* -'nɑ:grəfɚ] *n* estenógrafo, -a *m, f*

stenography [stə'nɒgrəfi, *Am:* -'nɑ:grə-] *n no pl* estenografía *f*

step [step] **I.** *n* **1.** (*foot movement*) paso *m*; (*foot print*) huella *f*; **to take a ~** dar un paso; **~ by ~** paso a paso; **to follow in sb's ~s** *fig* seguir el ejemplo de alguien; **to take a ~ towards sth** *fig* dirigirse hacia algo; **to be in/out of ~** llevar/no llevar el paso; *fig* estar/no estar al tanto; **to watch one's ~** andar con cuidado **2.** (*of stair, ladder*) peldaño *m* **3.** (*measure*) medida *f*; **to take ~s (to do sth)** tomar medidas (para hacer algo) **4.** *pl, Brit* (*stepladder*) escalera *f* **5.** *Am* MUS **whole ~** tono *m*; **half ~** semitono *m* **II.** <-pp-> *vi* **1.** (*tread*) pisar **2.** (*walk*) caminar

◆**step aside** *vi* hacerse a un lado

◆**step back** *vi* **1.** (*move back*) retroceder **2.** (*gain new perspective*) distanciarse

◆**step down I.** *vi* (*resign*) dimitir; **to ~ from sth** renunciar a algo **II.** *vt* (*reduce*) reducir

◆**step in** *vi* intervenir

◆**step up** *vt* aumentar

stepbrother *n* hermanastro *m* **stepchild** *n* hijastro, -a *m, f* **stepdaughter** *n* hijastra *f* **stepfather** *n* padrastro *m*

stepladder ['step,lædəʳ, *Am:* -ɚ] *n* escalera *f* de mano

stepmother ['step,mʌðəʳ, *Am:* -ɚ] *n* madrastra *f*

steppe [step] *n* estepa *f*

stepping stone ['stepɪŋstəʊn, *Am:* -stoʊn] *n* **1.** (*stone*) pasadera *f* **2.** *fig* trampolín *m*

stepsister ['step,sɪstəʳ, *Am:* -tɚ] *n* hermanastra *f*

stepson ['stepsʌn] *n* hijastro *m*

stereo ['steriəʊ, *Am:* 'sterioʊ] **I.** *n* **1.** *no pl* **in ~** en estéreo **2.** (*hi-fi system*) equipo *m* (estéreo) **II.** *adj* estéreo

stereophonic [,steriəʊ'fɒnɪk, *Am:* -ə'fɑ:nɪk] *adj* MUS estereofónico, -a

stereoscopic [,steriə'skɒpɪk, *Am:* -'skɑ:pɪk] *adj* estereoscópico, -a

stereotype ['steriətaɪp] **I.** *n pej* estereotipo *m* **II.** *vt pej* estereotipar

sterile ['steraɪl, *Am:* 'sterəl] *adj* estéril

sterility [stə'rɪləti, *Am:* -t̬i] *n no pl* esterilidad *f*

sterilization [,sterəlaɪ'zeɪʃən, *Am:* ,sterəlɪ'-] *n no pl* esterilización *f*

sterilize ['sterəlaɪz] *vt* esterilizar

sterling ['stɜ:lɪŋ, *Am:* 'stɜ:r-] **I.** *n no pl* **1.** FIN libra *f* esterlina **2.** (*metal*) plata *f* de ley **II.** *adj* **1.** FIN **pound ~** libra esterlina **2.** (*of high standard*) excelente

stern¹ [stɜ:n, *Am:* stɜ:rn] *adj* **1.** (*severe*) severo, -a; (*warning*) terminante **2.** (*strict*) estricto, -a **3.** (*difficult: test*) duro, -a ►**to be made of ~er stuff** tener mucho carácter

stern² [stɜ:n, *Am:* stɜ:rn] *n* NAUT popa *f*

sternness ['stɜ:nnɪs, *Am:* 'stɜ:rn-] *n no pl* serveridad *f*

sternum ['stɜ:nəm, *Am:* 'stɜ:r-] <-s *o* -na> *n* esternón *m*

steroid ['stɪərɔɪd, *Am:* 'sterɔɪd] *n* esteroide *m*

stethoscope ['steθəskəʊp, *Am:* -skoʊp] *n* MED estetoscopio *m*

stevedore ['sti:vədɔ:ʳ, *Am:* -dɔ:r] *n* estibador(a) *m(f)*

stew [stju:, *Am:* stu:] **I.** *n* estofado *m*, hervido *m AmS* ►**to be in a ~** sudar la gota gorda **II.** *vt* (*meat*) estofar; (*fruit*) hacer compota de **III.** *vi* cocer

steward ['stjʊəd, *Am:* 'stu:ɚd] *n* **1.** AVIAT auxiliar *m* de vuelo **2.** (*at concert, demonstration*) auxiliar *mf* **3.** (*estate administrator*)

administrador(a) *m(f)*
stewardess [ˌstjʊəˈdes, *Am:* ˈstuːɚdɪs] <-es> *n* azafata *f*, aeromoza *f Méx, AmS*
stick[1] [stɪk] *n* **1.** (*of wood*) vara *f*, palo *m;* (*of celery, rhubarb*) tallo *f;* (*of dynamite*) cartucho *m;* (*of chalk*) tiza *f;* (*of deodorant, glue*) barra *f* **2.** *a.* SPORTS (*for hockey*) palo *m;* **walking ~** bastón *m* **3.** MUS batuta *f* **4.** MIL porra *f* **5.** AUTO palanca *f;* **gear ~** palanca de cambio, palanca de velocidades *Méx* **6.** *inf* (*person*) **old ~** tío *m* **7.** *inf* (*remote area*) **in the ~s** en el quinto pino **8.** *inf* (*criticism*) **to give sb ~** (**about sth**) criticar a alguien (por algo); **to take a lot of ~** llevarse muchos palos ►**to get the wrong end of the ~** coger el rábano por las hojas; **~s and stones may break my bones, but words can never hurt me** *prov* a palabras necias, oídos sordos *prov;* **to be in a cleft ~** estar entre la espada y la pared; **to up ~s** *Brit, inf* levantar campamento
stick[2] [stɪk] <stuck, stuck> **I.** *vi* **1.** (*adhere*) pegarse **2.** (*be unmovable: person*) quedarse parado; (*car, door, window*) atascarse; (*mechanism*) bloquearse **3.** (*endure*) **to ~ in sb's mind** grabarse a alguien (en la mente) **4.** GAMES plantarse **II.** *vt* **1.** (*affix*) pegar **2.** *inf* (*tolerate*) aguantar **3.** *inf* (*put*) poner; **to ~ one's head around the door** asomar la cabeza por la puerta
◆**stick around** *vi inf* quedarse
◆**stick at** *vt* seguir con
◆**stick by** *vt* **1.** (*continue to support: friend*) no abandonar **2.** (*not change: opinion*) mantener **3.** (*comply with: rules*) respetar
◆**stick down** *vt* **1.** (*fix*) pegar **2.** *inf* (*put*) poner **3.** *inf* (*write hastily*) apuntar rápidamente
◆**stick in I.** *vt* **1.** (*put*) poner, meter **2.** (*add*) añadir **3.** (*knife, needle*) clavar **II.** *vi* **to get stuck in** *inf* (*start*) poner manos a la obra; *Brit, inf* (*start eating*) atacar
◆**stick on** *vt* **1.** (*affix: stamp, label*) pegar **2.** *inf* **to be stuck on sb** estar loco por alguien
◆**stick out I.** *vt* asomar; **to stick one's tongue out** sacar la lengua ►**to stick one's neck out** arriesgarse **II.** *vi* **1.** (*protrude: nail, ears*) sobresalir **2.** (*be obvious*) ser evidente; **to ~ a mile** verse [*o* notarse] a la legua, saltar a la vista **3.** (*endure*) **to stick it out** aguantar
◆**stick to** *vt* **1.** (*adhere to: rules*) ceñirse a; (*plan, idea*) seguir con; (*promise*) cumplir; (*principles*) mantener **2.** (*restrict oneself to*) limitarse a
◆**stick together I.** *vt* juntar **II.** *vi* **1.** (*adhere*) juntarse **2.** (*not separate*) no separarse **3.** (*remain loyal*) mantenerse unidos
◆**stick up I.** *vt inf* **1.** (*attach: poster, sign*) colocar **2.** (*raise*) **stick 'em up!** ¡manos arriba! **3.** (*rob*) atracar **II.** *vi* sobresalir; (*hair*) estar de punta
◆**stick up for** *vt* defender
◆**stick with** *vt* **1.** (*not give up*) seguir con; (*thought, idea, memory*) no abandonar **2.** (*persevere in*) seguir adelante con **3.** (*stay near*) no separarse de
sticker [ˈstɪkəʳ, *Am:* -ɚ] *n* **1.** (*label*) pegatina *f* **2.** (*person*) persona *f* tenaz
sticking plaster *n Brit* **1.** (*adhesive dressing*) tirita® *f*, curita® *f AmL* **2.** (*temporary measure*) apaño *m*
stick insect *n* insecto *m* palo **stick-in-the--mud** *n inf: persona rutinaria e inflexible*
stickleback [ˈstɪklbæk] *n* espinoso *m*
stickler [ˈstɪkləʳ, *Am:* -lɚ] *n* **to be a ~ for sth** insistir mucho en algo
stick-on [ˈstɪkɒn, *Am:* -ɑːn] *adj* adhesivo, -a
stickpin [ˈstɪkˌpɪn] *n Am* aguja *f* de corbata
stick-up [ˈstɪkʌp] *n inf* atraco *m*
sticky [ˈstɪki] <-ier, -iest> *adj* **1.** (*label*) adhesivo, -a; (*surface, hands*) pegajoso, -a **2.** (*weather*) bochornoso, -a
stiff [stɪf] **I.** *n inf* (*corpse*) fiambre *m* **II.** *adj* **1.** (*rigid: paper*) rígido, -a; (*brush*) duro, -a; (*shirt*) tieso, -a; (*paste, dough*) consistente; **to be** (**as**) **~ as a board** estar más tieso que un palo **2.** (*not supple: joints*) entumecido, -a **3.** (*difficult to move: muscles*) agarrotado, -a; **to have a ~ neck** tener tortícolis **4.** (*very formal*) encorsetado, -a **5.** (*not friendly*) estirado, -a; (*smile*) forzado, -a **6.** (*strong: competition, test*) duro, -a; (*opposition, drink, wind*) fuerte; (*resistance*) férreo, -a, tenaz; (*punishment, criticism*) fuerte, severo, -a **7.** (*strenuous: climb*) agotador(a) **8.** (*very expensive: price*) exorbitante **III.** *adv* **to be bored ~** estar aburrido como una ostra; **to be scared ~** estar muerto de miedo
stiffen [ˈstɪfn] **I.** *vi* **1.** (*become tense: person*) ponerse tenso; (*muscles*) agarrotarse **2.** (*become dense*) espesarse **3.** (*become stronger: competition*) hacerse más duro **II.** *vt* **1.** (*make rigid: collar, cuff*) almidonar **2.** (*make more dense*) espesar **3.** (*make more difficult, severe: exam*) hacer más difícil; (*penalty*) endurecer **4.** (*strengthen: moral*) fortalecer
stiffening [ˈstɪfnɪŋ] *n no pl* **1.** (*becoming immobile*) entumecimiento *m* **2.** (*rigid material*) entretela *f*
stiff-necked [ˌstɪfˈnekt, *Am:* ˈstɪfnekt] *adj* **1.** (*stubborn: person*) terco, -a; (*resistance*) obstinado, -a **2.** (*proud*) estirado, -a
stifle [ˈstaɪfl] **I.** *vi* **1.** (*suffocate*) sofocarse **2.** (*suffer lack of air*) ahogarse **II.** *vt* **1.** (*suffocate*) sofocar **2.** (*suppress: yawn, scream, desire*) contener; (*initiative, opposition*) reprimir
stifling [ˈstaɪflɪŋ] *adj* (*day, heat*) sofocante; (*room*) agobiante
stigma [ˈstɪgmə] *n* estigma *m*
stigmatize [ˈstɪgmətaɪz] *vt* estigmatizar
stile [staɪl] *n escalones que permiten pasar por encima de una cerca*
stiletto [stɪˈletəʊ, *Am:* -ˈleţoʊ] <-s> *n* **1.** (*dagger*) estilete *m* **2.** *pl* (*shoes*) zapatos *mpl* de tacón de aguja
stiletto heel *n* tacón *m* de aguja

still[1] [stɪl] I. *n* 1. *no pl* (*peace*) quietud *f* 2. CINE, PHOT fotograma *m* II. *adj* 1. (*calm*) tranquilo, -a 2. (*peaceful*) quieto, -a; (*wind, water*) en calma; **to keep ~** quedarse quieto 3. (*not fizzy: water*) sin gas III. *vt* 1. (*calm*) calmar 2. *liter* (*quieten*) acallar

still[2] [stɪl] *adv* 1. aún, todavía; **to be ~ alive** seguir vivo; **to want ~ more** querer todavía [*o* aún] más; **better ~** todavía mejor 2. (*nevertheless*) sin embargo; **~ and all** *Am* aún así

still[3] [stɪl] *n* (*distillery*) destilería *f*

stillbirth ['stɪlbɜːθ, *Am:* -bɜːrθ] *n* nacimiento *m* de un bebé muerto

stillborn ['stɪlˌbɔːn, *Am:* 'stɪlbɔːrn] *adj* 1. (*born dead*) nacido, -a muerto, -a 2. (*unsuccessful*) malogrado, -a

still life *n* ART naturaleza *f* muerta

stillness *n* 1. (*tranquility*) tranquilidad *f* 2. (*lack of movement*) quietud *f* 3. (*calm*) calma *f*

stilt [stɪlt] *n pl* zanco *m*

stilted ['stɪltɪd, *Am:* -t̬ɪd] *adj* (*manner, style*) forzado, -a

stimulant ['stɪmjələnt] *n* 1. (*boost*) estímulo *m* 2. MED estimulante *m*

stimulate ['stɪmjəleɪt] *vt* 1. (*encourage*) estimular; (*economy*) potenciar, estimular; (*discussion*) fomentar 2. MED estimular

stimulating *adj* estimulante

stimulation [ˌstɪmjə'leɪʃən] *n no pl* 1. (*boost*) estimulación *f* 2. (*thought, reaction*) estímulo *m*

stimulus ['stɪmjələs] <-li> *n* estímulo *m*

sting [stɪŋ] I. *n* 1. ZOOL (*organ*) aguijón *m;* (*injury*) picada *f* 2. BOT pelo *m* urticante 3. (*pain*) escozor *m;* **~ of remorse** gusanillo *m* de la conciencia 4. *Am, inf* (*swindle*) estafa *f* II. <stung, stung> *vi* 1. (*injure with poison: insect*) picar 2. (*be painful: cut*) arder; (*eyes*) escocer; (*criticism*) herir III. *vt* 1. (*inject with poison*) picar 2. (*cause pain: eyes*) hacer escocer; (*criticism*) herir profundamente 3. *Brit, Aus* (*goad*) incitar 4. (*swindle*) estafar

stinginess ['stɪndʒɪnɪs] *n no pl* tacañería *f*

stinging nettle [ˌstɪŋɪŋ'netl, *Am:* -'net̬l] *n* ortiga *f*

stingray ['stɪŋreɪ] *n* ZOOL raya *f* venenosa

stingy ['stɪndʒi] <-ier, -iest> *adj inf* (*person*) tacaño, -a, pijotero, -a *AmL,* amarrado, -a *Arg, Par, PRico, Urug,* coñete *Chile, Perú;* (*amount*) mísero, -a

stink [stɪŋk] I. *n* 1. (*smell*) mal olor *m* 2. *fig* escándalo *m;* **to create a ~** montar un escándalo II. <stank *Am, Aus:* stunk, stunk> *vi* 1. (*smell*) apestar, bufar *AmL;* **to ~ of money** *inf* estar podrido de dinero 2. *inf* (*be very bad*) ser pésimo, -a 3. *inf* (*be suspicious: business, situation*) oler mal

stink bomb *n* bomba fétida *f*

stinker ['stɪŋkəʳ, *Am:* -kɚ] *n inf* 1. (*bad person*) canalla *mf* 2. (*unpleasant thing*) asco *m*

stint[1] [stɪnt] *n* período *m*

stint[2] [stɪnt] *vt* (*funds, money*) escatimar; **to ~ oneself of sth** privarse de algo

stipulate ['stɪpjəleɪt] *vt* estipular

stipulation [ˌstɪpjə'leɪʃən] *n* estipulación *f;* **with the ~ that** con la condición de que +*subj*

stir [stɜːʳ, *Am:* stɜːr] I. *n* 1. (*agitation*) **to give sth a ~** remover algo 2. (*excitement*) conmoción *f;* **to cause a ~** causar revuelo II. <-ring, -red> *vt* 1. (*agitate: coffee, sauce, mixture*) remover; (*fire*) atizar, avivar 2. (*arouse: imagination*) estimular; **to ~ sb to do sth** mover alguien a hacer algo; **to ~ trouble** *Am* provocar problemas III. *vi* 1. (*move*) moverse, agitarse 2. (*awake*) despertarse 3. (*venture out*) salir 4. *Brit, Aus* (*cause trouble*) armar follón

stir-fry ['stɜːfraɪ, *Am:* 'stɜːr-] <-ied, -ies> *vt* *freír en poco aceite y removiendo constantemente*

stirring I. *n* (*of envy*) principio *m;* (*of interest*) primeros indicios *mpl* II. *adj* conmovedor(a)

stirrup ['stɪrəp, *Am:* 'stɜːr-] *n* estribo *m*

stitch [stɪtʃ] I. <-es> *n* 1. (*in knitting*) punto *m;* (*in sewing*) puntada *f;* **cross ~** punto de cruz; **to not have a ~ on** *inf* estar en cueros, estar calato *Perú* 2. MED punto *m* (de sutura) 3. (*pain*) flato *m;* **to have a ~** tener flato; **to have sb in ~es** hacer que alguien se tronche de risa ►**a ~ in time saves nine** *prov* una puntada a tiempo ahorra ciento *prov* II. *vi* coser III. *vt* coser

stoat [stəʊt, *Am:* stoʊt] *n* armiño *m*

stock [stɒk, *Am:* stɑːk] I. *n* 1. (*reserves*) reserva *f* 2. COM, ECON existencias *fpl;* **to have sth in ~** tener algo en stock; **to be out of ~** estar agotado; **to take ~** hacer el inventario; *fig* hacer un balance 3. (*share*) FIN acción *f* 4. AGR, ZOOL ganado *m* 5. *no pl* (*line of descent*) linaje *m;* ZOOL, BIO raza *f* 6. (*popularity*) prestigio *m;* **her ~ had fallen/risen** había ganado/perdido prestigio 7. (*belief*) **to put (no) ~ by sth** (no) dar crédito a algo II. *adj* (*model*) estándar; (*response*) típico, -a III. *vt* 1. (*keep in supply: goods*) vender 2. (*supply goods to: shop*) suministrar 3. (*fill: shelves*) llenar

stockade [stɒ'keɪd, *Am:* stɑː'-] *n* 1. (*wooden fence*) empalizada *f* 2. *Am* (*prison*) prisión *f* militar

stockbroker ['stɒkˌbrəʊkəʳ, *Am:* 'stɑːkˌbroʊkɚ] *n* corredor(a) *m(f)* de bolsa

stockbroking *n* correduría *f* de bolsa

stockcar *n* 1. AUTO stock car *m* 2. *Am* RAIL vagón *m* para el ganado **stock company** *n* *Am* 1. FIN sociedad *f* anónima 2. THEAT compañía *f* de repertorio **stock control** *n* control *m* de existencias **stock cube** *n* cubito *m* de caldo **stock exchange** *n* bolsa *f* **stock farmer** *n* ganadero, -a *m, f*

stockfish ['stɒkfɪʃ, *Am:* 'stɑːk-] *n* bacalao *m* seco

stockholder ['stɒkˌhəʊldəʳ, *Am:* 'stɑːkˌhoʊldɚ] *n Am* accionista *mf*

stocking ['stɒkɪŋ, *Am:* 'stɑːkɪŋ] *n* media *f*

stock-in-trade [ˌstɒkɪnˈtreɪd, *Am:* ˌstɑːk-] *n* existencias *fpl*
stockist [ˈstɒkɪst, *Am:* ˈstɑːkɪst] *n Aus, Brit* distribuidor(a) *m(f)*
stock market *n* mercado *m* bursátil
stockpile [ˈstɒkpaɪl, *Am:* ˈstɑːk-] **I.** *n* reservas *fpl;* (*of weapons, ammunition*) arsenal *m* **II.** *vt* almacenar
stock price *n Am* cotización *f* de las acciones
stockroom [ˈstɒkrʊm, *Am:* ˈstɑːkruːm] *n* almacén *m,* bodega *f Méx*
stock-still [ˌstɒkˈstɪl, *Am:* ˌstɑːk-] *adv* **to stand** ~ quedarse inmóvil
stocktaking [ˈstɒkteɪkɪŋ, *Am:* ˈstɑːk-] *n* inventario *m*
stocky [ˈstɒki, *Am:* ˈstɑːki] <-ier, -iest> *adj* bajo, -a y fornido, -a
stockyard [ˈstɒkjɑːd] *n* corral *m*
stodge [stɒdʒ, *Am:* stɑːdʒ] *n Brit, Aus, inf* comida *f* pesada
stodgy [ˈstɒdʒi, *Am:* ˈstɑːdʒi] <-ier, -iest> *adj* **1.** (*food*) pesado, -a **2.** (*person, book*) aburrido, -a
stoic [ˈstəʊɪk, *Am:* ˈstoʊ-] *n* estoico, -a *m, f*
stoical [ˈstəʊɪk(l), *Am:* ˈstoʊ-] *adj* estoico, -a
stoicism [ˈstəʊɪsɪzəm, *Am:* ˈstoʊɪ-] *n no pl* estoicismo *m*
stoke [stəʊk, *Am:* stoʊk] *vt* (*fire*) atizar; (*furnace*) echar carbón [*o* leña] a; *fig* avivar
stoker [ˈstəʊkəʳ, *Am:* ˈstoʊkɚ] *n* RAIL, NAUT fogonero, -a *m, f*
stole[1] [stəʊl, *Am:* stoʊl] *pt of* **steal**
stole[2] [stəʊl, *Am:* stoʊl] *n* estola *f*
stolid [ˈstɒlɪd, *Am:* ˈstɑːlɪd] *adj* impasible
stomach [ˈstʌmək] **I.** *n* **1.** (*internal organ*) estómago *m;* **to have an upset** ~ tener mal el estómago; **to have a strong** ~ tener estómago **2.** (*belly*) vientre *m* **II.** *vt inf* (*drink, food*) tolerar; **to be hard to** ~ (*person, insult*) ser difícil de soportar
stomach ache *n no pl* dolor *m* de estómago
stomach upset *n* problema *m* estomacal
stomp [stɒmp, *Am:* stɑːmp] *vi* pisar fuerte
stone [stəʊn, *Am:* stoʊn] **I.** *n* **1.** GEO piedra *f;* **to be a ~'s throw** (**away**) estar a tiro de piedra **2.** MED cálculo *m* **3.** (*jewel*) piedra *f* preciosa **4.** (*of fruit*) hueso *m,* carozo *m CSur* **5.** *Brit* (*14 lbs*) *unidad de peso equivalente a 6,35 kg* ▸**a rolling** ~ **gathers no moss** *prov* piedra movediza nunca moho la cobija *prov;* **to cast the first** ~ tirar la primera piedra; **to leave no** ~ **unturned** no dejar piedra por mover **II.** *adv* **1.** (*like a stone*) ~ **hard** duro, -a como una piedra **2.** *inf* (*completely*) ~ **crazy** loco de remate **III.** *vt* **1.** (*throw stones at*) apedrear **2.** (*fruit, olives*) deshuesar
Stone Age *n* Edad *f* de Piedra **stone-broke** *adj Am* sin blanca **stone-cold** *adj* helado, -a; **to be** ~ **sober** no haber bebido ni una gota
stoned *adj inf* colocado, -a
stone-deaf [ˌstəʊnˈdef, *Am:* ˌstoʊn-] *adj* sordo, -a como una tapia
stonemason [ˈstəʊnˌmeɪsən, *Am:* ˈstoʊn-] *n* cantero, -a *m, f*
stonewall [ˌstəʊnˈwɔːl, *Am:* ˈstoʊn-] *fig* **I.** *vi* andarse con evasivas **II.** *vt* bloquear
stoneware [ˈstəʊnweəʳ, *Am:* ˈstoʊnwer] *n no pl* cerámica *f* de gres
stonework [ˈstəʊnwɜːk, *Am:* ˈstoʊnwɜːrk] *n no pl* cantería *f*
stony [ˈstəʊni, *Am:* ˈstoʊ-] <-ier, -iest> *adj* **1.** (*beach, ground*) pedregoso, -a **2.** (*expression*) frío, -a; (*silence*) sepulcral; (*heart*) de piedra
stony-broke *adj Brit, Aus, inf* sin blanca
stood [stʊd] *pt, pp of* **stand**
stooge [stuːdʒ] *n* **1.** THEAT compañero *m* **2.** *fig* (*puppet*) títere *m* **3.** *Am, inf* (*informer*) soplón, -ona *m, f*
stool [stuːl] *n* **1.** (*seat*) taburete *m* **2.** *pl* MED deposición *f* ▸**to fall between two ~s** nadar entre dos aguas
stool pigeon *n Am, inf* soplón, -ona *m, f*
stoop[1] [stuːp] **I.** *n no pl* **to have a** ~ ser cargado de espaldas **II.** *vi* inclinarse; **to** ~ **to sth** *pej* rebajarse a algo
stoop[2] [stuːp] *n Am* pórtico *m*
stop [stɒp, *Am:* stɑːp] **I.** *n* **1.** (*break in activity*) pausa *f;* **to come to a** ~ detenerse; **to put a** ~ **to sth** poner fin a algo **2.** (*halting place*) parada *f* **3.** *Brit* LING punto *m* **4.** MUS registro *m* ▸**to pull** (**all**) **the ~s out** desplegar todos los recursos **II.** <-pping, -pped> *vt* **1.** (*cause to cease*) parar **2.** (*refuse payment: wages*) suspender; **to** ~ **a cheque** dar orden de no pagar un cheque **3.** (*switch off*) apagar **4.** (*block*) rellenar; (*hole, ones ears*) tapar **5.** *Brit* (*fill*) empastar **III.** <-pping, -pped> *vi* **1.** (*cease moving*) pararse; (*car*) detenerse **2.** (*cease an activity*) **to** ~ **doing sth** dejar de hacer algo **3.** *Brit* (*stay*) quedarse
◆**stop by** *vi* pasar por
◆**stop in** *vi* quedarse en casa
◆**stop off** *vi* detenerse un rato
◆**stop out** *vi* quedarse fuera
◆**stop over** *vi* pasar la noche, hacer noche
◆**stop up** *vt* (*block*) atascar; (*hole*) tapar; (*gap*) rellenar
stopcock [ˈstɒpkɒk, *Am:* ˈstɑːpkɑːk] *n* llave *f* de paso
stopgap [ˈstɒpgæp, *Am:* ˈstɑːp-] **I.** *n* medida *f* provisional **II.** *adj* provisional
stoplight [ˈstɒplaɪt, *Am:* ˈstɑːp-] *n Am* semáforo *m* rojo
stopover [ˈstɒpəʊvəʳ, *Am:* ˈstɑːpoʊvɚ] *n* (*on journey*) parada *f;* AVIAT escala *f*
stoppage [ˈstɒpɪdʒ, *Am:* ˈstɑːpɪdʒ] *n* **1.** (*cessation of work*) interrupción *f* **2.** FIN, ECON retención *f* **3.** MED oclusión *f*
stopper [ˈstɒpəʳ, *Am:* ˈstɑːpɚ] **I.** *n* tapón *m* **II.** *vt* taponar
stopping train *n tren que para en todas las estaciones*
stop press *n* PUBL noticias *fpl* de última hora
stop sign *n* AUTO, LAW stop *m* **stopwatch**

n cronómetro *m*

storage [ˈstɔːrɪdʒ] *n no pl* **1.** (*of goods, possessions*) almacenaje *m;* **to put sth in ~** almacenar algo **2.** INFOR almacenamiento *m*

storage battery *n* acumulador *m* **storage capacity** *n* capacidad *f* de almacenaje **storage heater** *n Brit* acumulador *m* (de calor) **storage space** *n* espacio *m* para guardar cosas **storage tank** *n* tanque *m* de almacenamiento

store [stɔːʳ, *Am:* stɔːr] **I.** *n* **1.** *Brit* (*storehouse*) almacén *m;* (*department store*) grandes almacenes *mpl,* emporio *m AmC;* **to be in ~** estar en almacén; **what is in ~ for us?** ¿qué nos espera en el futuro? **2.** *Am, Aus* (*shop*) tienda *f* **3.** (*supply: of wine*) reserva *f;* (*of food*) provisión *f* **4.** (*place for keeping supplies*) almacén *m,* depósito *m;* (*for weapons*) arsenal *m* **5.** *no pl* (*importance*) valor *m;* **to set ~ by sth** dar valor a algo **II.** *vt* **1.** (*put into storage*) almacenar **2.** (*keep for future use*) guardar **3.** INFOR (*file*) guardar; (*data*) almacenar

store detective *n* guarda *mf* de seguridad de una tienda

storefront [ˈstɔːfrʌnt, *Am:* ˈstɔːr-] *n Am* escaparate *m*

storehouse [ˈstɔːhaʊs, *Am:* ˈstɔːr-] *n Am* almacén *m; fig* mina *f*

storekeeper [ˈstɔːˌkiːpəʳ, *Am:* ˈstɔːrˌkiːpɚ] *n* tendero, -a *m, f,* comerciante *mf*

storeroom [ˈstɔːrʊm, *Am:* ˈstɔːrruːm] *n* depósito *m,* bodega *f Méx;* (*for food*) despensa *f*

storey [ˈstɔːri] *n Brit, Aus* piso *m*

storeyed *adj,* **storied** *adj Am* **two/three-~** de dos/tres pisos

stork [stɔːk, *Am:* stɔːrk] *n* cigüeña *f*

storm [stɔːm, *Am:* stɔːrm] **I.** *n* **1.** METEO tormenta *f* **2.** *fig* (*argument*) trifulca *f;* (*of protest*) ola *f;* (*of criticism*) vendaval *f;* (*of applause*) salva *f;* **political ~** revuelo *m* político **3. to take sth by ~** asaltar algo; **to take sb by ~** cautivar a alguien ►**a ~ in a teacup** mucho ruido y pocas nueces; **to ride out** [*o* **to weather**] **the ~** capear el temporal **II.** *vi* **1.** *Am* METEO haber tormenta; (*winds*) soplar con fuerza **2.** (*speak angrily*) bramar **III.** *vt* (*town, castle*) asaltar; (*house*) irrumpir en

◆**storm into** *vi* irrumpir en

◆**storm out** *vi* salir airadamente

storm cloud *n* nubarrón *m* **storm door** *n* contrapuerta *f*

storm-tossed *adj* (*boat*) sacudido, -a por la tormenta

stormy [ˈstɔːmi, *Am:* ˈstɔːr-] <-ier, -iest> *adj* (*weather*) tormentoso, -a; (*sea, relationship*) tempestuoso, -a; (*argument*) violento, -a

story[1] [ˈstɔːri] <-ies> *n* **1.** (*account*) historia *f;* (*fictional*) cuento *m;* **to tell a ~** contar un cuento; **to tell stories** (*lie*) contar cuentos; **so the ~ goes** eso dicen **2.** (*news report*) artículo *m* ►**that's another ~** eso es harina de otro costal; **it's the same old ~** es la historia de siempre; **a tall ~** un cuento chino

story[2] [ˈstɔːri] *n Am s.* **storey**

storybook [ˈstɔːribʊk] **I.** *n* libro *m* de cuentos **II.** *adj* **a ~ romance** un romance de cuento de hadas **storyline** *n* (*plot*) argumento *m* **storyteller** *n* narrador(a) *m(f)*

stout [staʊt] **I.** *n* (*beer*) cerveza *f* negra **II.** *adj* (*person*) robusto, -a; (*shoes, boots*) fuerte; (*defender*) firme; (*resistance*) tenaz

stouthearted [ˌstaʊtˈhɑːtɪd, *Am:* -ˈhɑːrt̬ɪd] *adj* (*support*) incondicional; (*defender*) acérrimo, -a; (*resistance*) firme

stoutly [ˈstaʊtli] *adv* **1.** (*strongly*) sólidamente **2.** (*firmly*) con firmeza

stove [stəʊv, *Am:* stoʊv] *n* **1.** (*heater*) estufa *f* **2.** *Am, Aus* cocina *f*

stovepipe [ˈstəʊvpaɪp, *Am:* ˈstoʊv-] *n* conducto *m* de estufa

stow [stəʊ, *Am:* stoʊv] *vt* guardar

◆**stow away** **I.** *vt* esconder **II.** *vi* viajar de polizón

stowage [ˈstəʊɪdʒ, *Am:* ˈstoʊ-] *n no pl* NAUT estiba *f*

stowaway [ˈstəʊəweɪ, *Am:* ˈstoʊ-] *n* polizón *m*

straddle [ˈstrædl] *vt* (*horse*) sentarse a horcajadas sobre

straggle [ˈstrægl] *vi* **1.** (*move in a disorganised group*) avanzar desordenadamente **2.** (*hang untidily: hair*) caer en desorden **3.** (*come in small numbers*) llegar poco a poco **4.** (*lag behind*) rezagarse

straggler [ˈstrægləʳ, *Am:* -lɚ] *n* rezagado, -a *m, f*

straggly [ˈstrægli] <-ier, -iest> *adj* (*hair*) desordenado, -a

straight [streɪt] **I.** *n* (*straight line*) recta *f;* **the finishing ~** la recta final **II.** *adj* **1.** (*not bent*) recto, -a **2.** (*honest*) honrado, -a; (*answer*) franco, -a; **to be ~ with sb** ser sincero con alguien **3.** (*plain*) sencillo, -a; (*undiluted: gin, vodka*) solo, -a **4.** (*clear*) claro, -a **5.** (*consecutive*) seguido, -a; **she won in ~ sets** ganó sin perder ningún set **6.** THEAT (*not comic*) serio, -a **7.** (*traditional*) convencional **8.** *inf* (*heterosexual*) heterosexual **III.** *adv* **1.** (*in a direct line*) en línea recta; **to go ~ ahead** ir todo recto; **to come ~ at sb** ir derecho a alguien **2.** (*at once*) **to get ~ to the point** ir directo al grano **3.** *inf* (*honestly*) honestamente **4.** (*clearly: see, think*) con claridad **5.** (*tidy*) en orden; **to put sth ~** ordenar algo

straightaway [ˌstreɪtəˈweɪ, *Am:* ˌstreɪt̬ə-] **I.** *adv* enseguida **II.** *n Am* SPORTS recta *f*

straighten [ˈstreɪtn] *vt* **1.** (*make straight: hair*) alisar; (*wire*) enderezar **2.** (*unbend: arm, body, leg*) estirar **3.** (*make level: hem*) igualar **4.** (*make tidy: room*) ordenar

◆**straighten out** **I.** *vt* **1.** (*make straight*) estirar **2.** (*make level*) igualar **3.** (*solve: problem*) resolver; (*situation*) arreglar **4.** (*clarify*) aclarar; **to straighten sb out** aclarar algo a alguien **II.** *vi* (*road*) hacerse recto, -a

◆**straighten up** **I.** *vi* (*stand upright*) ponerse derecho, arriscarse *Col* **II.** *vt* **1.** (*make level*) igualar **2.** (*make tidy*) ordenar

straightforward [ˌstreɪtˈfɔːwəd, *Am:* -ˈfɔːrwɚd] *adj* **1.** (*honest*) honesto, -a **2.** (*easy*) sencillo, -a

straight-out [ˌstreɪtˈaʊt] *adj Am, inf* (*outright*) redomado, -a, consumado, -a; (*refusal*) tajante

strain[1] [streɪn] **I.** *n no pl* **1.** *no pl* (*pressure*) presión *f*; **to be under a lot of ~** tener mucho estrés; **to put a ~ on a relationship** crear tensiones en una relación **2.** *no pl* PHYS deformación *f* **3.** MED torcedura *f* **II.** *vi* (*try hard*) esforzarse; **to ~ for effect** utilizar recursos efectistas **III.** *vt* **1.** (*stretch*) estirar; **to ~ a rope** tirar de una cuerda **2.** (*overexert*) **to ~ one's eyes** forzar la vista; **to ~ one's ears** aguzar el oído **3.** (*put stress on: relationship*) crear tensiones en; (*credulity*) poner a prueba **4.** GASTR (*coffee*) filtrar; (*vegetables*) escurrir

strain[2] [streɪn] *n* **1.** (*variety: of animal*) raza *f*; (*of virus*) cepa *f* **2.** (*tendency or trait*) **~ of eccentricity** vena *f* excéntrica; **~ of puritanism** nota *f* de puritanismo **3.** MUS tono *m*

strained [streɪnd] *adj* (*relation*) tenso, -a; (*smile*) forzado, -a

strainer *n* colador *m*

strait [streɪt] *n* **1.** GEO estrecho *m*; **the Straits of Gibraltar** el estrecho de Gibraltar **2.** (*bad situation*) apuro *m*; **to be in a ~** estar en apuros; **to be in dire ~s** estar en grandes apuros

straitened *adj* **in ~ circumstances** en apuros económicos

straitjacket [ˈstreɪtˌdʒækɪt] *n* PSYCH, MED camisa *f* de fuerza

straitlaced [ˌstreɪtˈleɪst, *Am:* ˈstreɪtleɪst] *adj* mojigato, -a

strand[1] [strænd] *n* **1.** (*thread: of wool*) hebra *f*; (*of rope, string*) ramal *m*; **a ~ of hair** un mechón de pelo **2.** (*string: of pearls*) sarta *f*; (*of plot*) hilo *m*

strand[2] [strænd] **I.** *n liter* (*shore*) ribera *f* **II.** *vt* varar; **to be ~ed** quedarse desamparado

strange [streɪndʒ] *adj* **1.** (*peculiar*) extraño, -a, raro, -a; **I felt ~** me sentía raro; **it's ~ that** es raro que *+subj*; **~r things have happened** cosas más raras han pasado; **~ to say** aunque parezca mentira **2.** (*unfamiliar: face*) desconocido, -a; (*bed*) ajeno, -a

strangely *adv* (*behave, dress*) de una manera rara; **~ enough ...** aunque parazca mentira...

stranger [ˈstreɪndʒəʳ, *Am:* -dʒɚ] *n* desconocido, -a *m, f*; **he is no ~ to controversy** la polémica no le es ajena

strangle [ˈstræŋgl] *vt* (*person*) estrangular; (*cry*) ahogar

stranglehold [ˈstræŋglhəʊld, *Am:* -hoʊld] *n* (*control*) dominio *m* total; (*on market*) monopolio *m*; **to have sb in a ~** tener a alguien dominado

strangulation [ˌstræŋgjʊˈleɪʃən] *n* estrangulación *f*

strap [stræp] **I.** *n* (*of bag*) correa *f*; (*of dress*) tirante *m* **II.** <-pp-> *vt* atar [*o* sujetar] con una correa

strapless [ˈstræplɪs] *adj* sin tirantes

strapping [ˈstræpɪŋ] **I.** *n* (*bandage*) esparadrapo *m* **II.** *adj inf* robusto, -a

stratagem [ˈstrætədʒəm, *Am:* ˈstræt̬-] *n* estratagema *f*

strategic [strəˈtiːdʒɪk] *adj* estratégico, -a

strategist [ˈstrætədʒɪst, *Am:* ˈstræt̬-] *n* estratega *mf*

strategy [ˈstrætədʒi, *Am:* ˈstræt̬-] <-ies> *n* estrategia *f*

stratify [ˈstrætɪfaɪ, *Am:* ˈstræt̬ə-] *vt* estratificar

stratosphere [ˈstrætəsfɪəʳ, *Am:* ˈstræt̬əsfɪr] *n* estratosfera *f*; **to go into the ~** (*prices*) irse por las nubes

stratum [ˈstreɪtəm, *Am:* ˈstreɪt̬əm] <strata> *n* estrato *m*

straw [strɔː, *Am:* strɑː] *n* **1.** *no pl* (*dry stems*) paja *f* **2.** (*for drinking*) pajita *f*, popote *m Méx*, pitillo *m And* ▸**a ~ in the wind** un indicio de cómo andan las cosas; **to be the last ~** ser el colmo; **to draw the short ~** tocarle a uno la china; **to clutch at ~s** agarrarse a un clavo ardiendo

strawberry [ˈstrɔːbəri, *Am:* ˈstrɑːˌberi] <-ies> *n* fresa *f*, frutilla *f AmL*

straw-coloured [ˈstrɔːkʌləd] *adj* pajizo, -a

straw man *n* hombre *m* de paja **straw poll** *n* sondeo *m* informal

stray [streɪ] **I.** *n* (*dog*) perro *m* callejero; (*cat*) gato *m* callejero **II.** *adj* **1.** (*homeless: dog, cat*) callejero, -a, realengo, -a *Méx, PRico* **2.** (*loose: hair*) suelto, -a; (*bullet*) perdido, -a **III.** *vi* (*wander*) errar; (*become lost*) perderse; **to ~ from** alejarse de; **to ~ off course** apartarse del camino; **they were warned not to stray beyond the garden** se les advirtió que no salieran del jardín; **to ~ from the point** divagar

streak [striːk] **I.** *n* **1.** (*stripe*) raya *f*; (*in hair*) mechón *m*; (*of light*) rayo *m*; (*of lightning*) relámpago *m* **2.** (*tendency*) vena *f*; **an aggressive ~** una vena agresiva; **to have a ~ of cowardice** tener algo de cobarde **3.** (*spell*) racha *f*; **to be on a winning ~** tener una buena racha ▸**like a ~ of lightning** como un rayo; **to talk a blue ~** *Am* hablar más que un loro agarrado por el rabo **II.** *vt* rayar; **to have one's hair ~ed** hacerse mechas; **to be ~ed with sth** estar manchado de algo **III.** *vi* **1.** (*move very fast*) ir rápido **2.** (*run naked in public*) correr desnudo en un lugar público

streaker *n persona que corre desnuda en un lugar público*

streaky [ˈstriːki] <-ier, -iest> *adj* rayado, -a; **~ bacon** *Brit* bacon *m* entreverado

stream [striːm] **I.** *n* **1.** (*small river*) arroyo *m*, estero *m Chile, Ecua* **2.** (*current*) corriente *f*; **to go against the ~** *fig* ir a contracorriente; **to**

S

come on ~ (*factory*) entrar en funcionamiento **3.** (*flow: of oil, water*) chorrito *m;* (*of people*) torrente *m;* (*of insults*) sarta *f* **4.** *Brit, Aus* SCHOOL *grupo de escolares con la misma aptitud académica* **II.** *vi* **1.** (*flow*) fluir; (*water*) chorrear; (*blood*) manar; (*tears*) caer; **tears ~ed down her face** lloraba a lágrima viva; **blood ~ed from his head** le chorreaba sangre de la cabeza **2.** (*move in numbers*) afluir en masa **3.** (*shine: light, sun*) entrar a raudales **4.** (*run: nose*) gotear; (*eyes*) llorar **III.** *vt Brit, Aus* SCHOOL *dividir en grupos de acuerdo con su aptitud académica*

streamer ['stri:məʳ, *Am:* -mɚ] *n* serpentina *f*

streamline ['stri:mlaɪn] *vt* (*vehicle*) aerodinamizar; (*method*) racionalizar

streamlined *adj* (*vehicle*) aerodinámico, -a; (*method*) racionalizado, -a

street [stri:t] *n* (*road*) calle *f;* **in** [*o* **on**] **the** ~ en la calle ►**to be ~s ahead of sb** estar muy por delante de alguien; **to be on the ~s** hacer la calle; **to be up sb's** ~ ser ideal para alguien; **to walk the ~s** (*wander*) deambular por las calles; (*be a prostitute*) hacer la calle

street battle *n* pelea *f* callejera **streetcar** *n Am* tranvía *m* **street credibility** *n,* **street-cred** *n imagen moderna y urbana* **street directory** *n* guía *f* de calles **street-lamp** *n,* **street light** *n* farola *f* **street lighting** *n no pl* alumbrado *m* (público) **street value** *n no pl* valor *m* de reventa **streetwalker** *n* prostituta *f* que hace la calle

streetwise ['stri:twaɪz] *adj* (*person*) espabilado, -a; (*politician*) astuto, -a

strength [streŋθ] *n* **1.** *no pl* (*power*) fuerza *f,* ñeque *m Chile, Ecua, Perú;* (*of feeling, light*) intensidad *f;* (*of alcohol*) graduación *f;* (*of economy*) solidez *f;* (*mental firmness*) fortaleza *f* **2.** (*number of members*) número *m;* **to be at full** ~ tener el cupo completo; **to be below** ~ (*office*) estar corto de personal **3.** (*strong point*) punto *m* fuerte; **one's ~s and weaknesses** sus virtudes y defectos ►**to go from ~ to ~** ir cada vez mejor

strengthen ['streŋθən] **I.** *vt* **1.** (*make stronger: muscles*) fortalecer; (*wall*) reforzar; (*financial position*) consolidar **2.** (*increase: chances*) aumentar **3.** (*intensify: relations*) intensificar; (*links*) estrechar **II.** *vi* fortalecerse

strenuous ['strenjʊəs, *Am:* -juəs] *adj* (*exercise, sport*) agotador(a); (*supporter*) acérrimo, -a; (*denial*) rotundo, -a

streptococcus [ˌstreptə'kɒkəs, *Am:* -'kɑ:kəs] <-ci> *n* estreptococo *m*

stress [stres] **I.** *n no pl* **1.** (*mental strain*) estrés *m* **2.** (*emphasis*) énfasis *m inv* **3.** LING acento *m* **4.** PHYS tensión *f* **II.** *vt* **1.** (*emphasise*) recalcar **2.** LING acentuar

stressed *adj,* **stressed out** *adj inf* estresado, -a

stress fracture *n* fractura *f* de fatiga **stress-free** *adj* sin estrés

stressful ['stresfʊl] *adj* estresante

stress mark *n* LING acento *m*

stretch [stretʃ] **I.** <-es> *n* **1.** *no pl* (*elasticity*) elasticidad *f* **2.** SPORTS estiramiento *m* **3.** GEO trecho *m* **4.** (*piece*) trozo *m;* (*of road*) tramo *m;* (*of time*) período *m* **5.** (*stage of a race*) recta *f;* **the final** ~ la recta final **6.** (*exertion*) **at full** ~ a todo gas; **to work at full** ~ trabajar al máximo de su capacidad; **not by any ~ of the imagination** ni por asomo **II.** *adj* elástico, -a **III.** *vi* **1.** (*become bigger*) estirarse; (*clothes*) dar de sí **2.** (*extend muscles*) estirarse **3.** (*in time*) **to ~ back to ...** remontarse a... **4.** (*cover an area: sea, influence*) extenderse **IV.** *vt* **1.** (*extend: muscles*) estirar; (*tendon*) distender; **to ~ one's legs** estirar las piernas **2.** (*make go further*) estirar **3.** (*demand a lot of*) **to ~ sb's patience** poner a prueba la paciencia de alguien; **my present job doesn't ~ me** mi trabajo actual no me exige lo suficiente; **his nerves are ~ed to breaking point** tiene los nervios a punto de estallar **4.** (*go beyond*) **to ~ a point** hacer una excepción; **to ~ it a bit** exagerar un poco **5.** LAW sobrepasar los límites de **6.** MUS tensar

stretcher ['stretʃəʳ, *Am:* -ɚ] *n* camilla *f*

stretcher bearer *n* camillero, -a *m, f*

strew [stru:] <strewn, strewn *o* strewed> *vt* esparcir

stricken ['strɪkən] *adj* **1.** (*distressed*) afligido, -a **2.** (*wounded*) herido, -a **3.** (*afflicted*) **to be stricken with illness** estar enfermo; **she was stricken with remorse** le remordía la conciencia **4.** (*damaged: tanker*) siniestrado, -a

strict [strɪkt] *adj* (*person*) severo, -a, fregado, -a *AmC;* (*control, orders, sense*) estricto, -a; (*deadline*) inamovible; (*neutrality*) total; (*secrecy*) completo, -a; (*confidence*) absoluto, -a; **to be ~ with sb** ser severo con alguien

strictly ['strɪktli] *adv* **1.** (*exactly*) estrictamente; **not ~ comparable** no del todo comparable; **~ speaking** en rigor **2.** (*harshly*) severamente; **~ forbidden** terminantemente prohibido

stride [straɪd] **I.** <strode> *vi* andar a trancos; **to ~ ahead** andar dando zancadas; **to ~ across sth** cruzar algo de una zancada **II.** *n* **1.** (*long step*) zancada *f* **2.** (*progress*) progreso *m;* **to make ~s forward** hacer grandes progresos; **to make ~s towards sth** acercarse a algo ►**to get into one's ~, to hit one's ~** coger el ritmo; **to put sb off his/her ~** *Brit* distraer a alguien; **to take sth in one's ~** tomarse algo con calma

strident ['straɪdnt] *adj* estridente

strife [straɪf] *n no pl* lucha *f;* (*verbal*) disputa *f;* **domestic ~** riñas *fpl* domésticas

strike [straɪk] **I.** *n* **1.** (*military attack*) ataque *m* **2.** (*withdrawal of labour*) huelga *f* **3.** (*discovery*) descubrimiento *m* **4.** *Am* (*in baseball*) golpe *m* **5.** *Am* LAW fallo *m* de culpabilidad **II.** <struck *Am:* stricken, struck> *vt* **1.** (*collide with*) golpear; **to ~ a match** encender una cerilla; **to be struck by lightning** ser alcanzado por un rayo; **to ~ a blow against sb** asestar un golpe a alguien **2.** (*achieve*) conseguir; **to ~ a balance** encontrar un equilibrio; **to ~ a bargain with sb** hacer un trato con alguien **3.** (*manufacture: coin*) acuñar **4.** (*seem*) parecer; **it ~s me that ...** se me ocurre que... **5.** (*impress*) impresionar **6.** (*engender*) **to ~ fear into sb** infundir miedo a alguien **7.** (*discover*) descubrir; (*find*) encontrar; **to ~ gold** (*win gold medal*) ganar el oro; (*have financial fortune*) descubrir un filón **8.** (*adopt*) **to ~ an attitude** adoptar una actitud **9.** (*sound the time: clock*) marcar; **the clock struck three** el reloj dio las tres **10.** (*remove: flag*) arriar **11.** (*delete*) borrar, tachar ►**to ~ a chord with sb** llegar a entenderse con alguien; **to ~ the right note** dar con el tono justo; **to ~ sb dumb** dejar a alguien sin habla **III.** <struck, struck> *vi* **1.** (*hit hard*) golpear; (*attack*) atacar; **to ~ at sth** asestar un golpe contra algo; **to ~ at the heart of sth** atacar directamente a algo; **to ~ home** dar en el blanco **2.** (*withdraw labour*) declararse en huelga; **the right to ~** el derecho a la huelga; **to ~ for sth** hacer una huelga para conseguir algo

◆**strike back** *vi* devolver el golpe; **to ~ at sb** tomar represalias contra alguien

◆**strike down** *vt* **1. she was struck down by cancer** fue abatida por el cáncer **2.** *Am* LAW revocar

◆**strike off** *vt Brit, Aus* (*lawyer, doctor*) inhabilitar; **to strike sb off a list** tachar a alguien de una lista

◆**strike out I.** *vt* **1.** (*delete*) borrar **2.** *Am* SPORTS eliminar **II.** *vi* **1.** (*move off*) andar resueltamente; **to ~ on one's own** hacerse independiente **2.** (*hit out*) empezar a repartir golpes **3.** *Am* SPORTS hacer un strike; *fig* fallar

◆**strike up** *vt* (*conversation*) entablar; (*relationship*) iniciar; (*friendship*) trabar

strike action *n* huelga *f*

strikebound ['straɪkbaʊnd] *adj* paralizado, -a por la huelga

strikebreaker ['straɪkˌbreɪkəʳ, *Am:* -kɚ] *n* esquirol *mf*

strike committee *n* comité *m* de huelga **strike fund** *n* fondo *m* de huelga **strike pay** *n* subsidio *m* de huelga

striker ['straɪkəʳ, *Am:* -kɚ] *n* **1.** SPORTS ariete *mf* **2.** (*strike participant*) huelguista *mf*

striking ['straɪkɪŋ] *adj* notable; (*result, beauty*) impresionante; (*resemblance*) sorprendente; (*change*) considerable; (*contrast*) acusado, -a; (*difference*) gran; **visually ~** llamativo

string [strɪŋ] **I.** *n* **1.** (*twine*) *a.* MUS cuerda *f;* (*on puppet*) hilo *m;* **to pull ~s** *fig* mover hilos; **with no ~s attached** sin compromiso alguno **2.** *pl* MUS (*section*) (instrumentos *mpl* de) cuerda *f;* (*players*) (instrumentistas *mpl* de) cuerda **3.** (*chain*) cadena *f;* (*of pearls*) collar *m* **4.** (*sequence: of scandals*) serie *f;* (*of lies*) sarta *f;* (*of people*) hilera *f;* (*of oaths*) retahíla *f* **5.** INFOR secuencia *f* **II.** <strung, strung> *vt* poner una cuerda a; (*instrument*) encordar; (*beads*) ensartar

◆**string along** *inf* **I.** *vi* ir/venir también **II.** *vt Brit* **to string sb along** embaucar a alguien

◆**string out** *vt* **1.** (*extend*) espaciar **2.** (*protract: activity*) prolongar

◆**string up** *vt inf* colgar

string bag *n* bolsa *f* de red **string band** *n* banda *f* de cuerda **string bean** *n Am, Aus* habichuela *f* **stringed instrument** *n* instrumento *m* de cuerda

stringency ['strɪndʒənsi] *n no pl* **1.** (*of measure*) severidad *f;* (*of test*) rigor *m* **2.** FIN dificultad *f*

stringent ['strɪndʒənt] *adj* **1.** (*measure*) severo, -a; (*rigorous: test*) riguroso, -a; (*law, requirement*) estricto, -a **2.** FIN restrictivo, -a

stringer ['strɪŋəʳ, *Am:* -ɚ] *n inf* corresponsal *mf* local

string quartet *n* cuarteto *m* de cuerda

stringy ['strɪŋi] *adj* (*meat*) correoso, -a; (*person*) delgado, -a pero fuerte

strip [strɪp] **I.** *vt* **1.** (*lay bare*) dejar sin cubierta; **to ~ sb of sth** quitarle algo a alguien **2.** (*unclothe*) desnudar **3.** (*dismantle*) desmontar **II.** *vi* desnudarse **III.** *n* **1.** (*ribbon*) tira *f;* (*of metal*) lámina *f;* (*of land*) franja *f* **2.** *Brit, Aus* SPORTS camiseta *f* **3.** (*striptease*) striptease *m* **4.** (*landing area*) pista *f*

strip cartoon *n Brit* historieta *f*

stripe [straɪp] *n* **1.** (*coloured band*) raya *f;* **of every ~** de todo tipo; **governments of every ~** gobiernos de todos los colores **2.** MIL galón *m;* **a man of that ~** *Am, fig* un hombre de esa clase

striped *adj,* **stripey** *adj* rayado, -a; (*shirt*) a rayas

strip light *n Brit* tubo *m* fluorescente **strip lighting** *n* alumbrado *m* fluorescente **strip mining** *n Am* minería *f* a cielo abierto

stripper ['strɪpəʳ, *Am:* -ɚ] *n* persona *f* que hace striptease

strip-search [ˌstrɪ'sɜːtʃ, *Am:* 'strɪpsɜːrtʃ] **I.** *n* registro *m* en el que la persona tiene que desnudarse **II.** *vt* **to ~ sb** hacer desnudar a alguien para registrarle **strip show** *n* espectáculo *m* de striptease

striptease ['strɪptiːz] *n* striptease *m*

stripy *adj* rayado, -a; (*shirt*) a rayas

strive [straɪv] <strove, striven *o* strived, strived> *vi* esforzarse; **to ~ to do sth** esmerarse en hacer algo; **to ~ after sth** luchar por conseguir algo; **to ~ for sth** afanarse para conseguir algo

strobe [strəʊb, *Am:* stroʊb] *n inf* luz *f* estroboscópica

strobe light *n* luz *f* estroboscópica

stroboscope ['strəʊbəskəʊp, *Am:* 'stroʊbəskoʊp] *n* estroboscopio *m*

strode [strəʊd, *Am:* stroʊd] *pt of* **stride**

stroke [strəʊk, *Am:* stroʊk] I. *vt* 1. (*caress*) acariciar 2. SPORTS (*hit smoothly*) golpear suavemente II. *n* 1. (*caress*) caricia *f* 2. MED derrame *m* cerebral; **to have a ~** tener una apoplejía 3. (*of pencil*) trazo *m;* (*of brush*) pincelada *f* 4. (*style of hitting ball*) golpe *m;* (*billiards*) tacada *f;* **at a** (**single**) **~**, **in one ~** de (un solo) golpe 5. *form* (*lash with whip*) latigazo *m* 6. (*in swimming: style*) estilo *m;* (*single movement*) brazada *f* 7. (*bit*) **by a ~ of fate** por cosas del destino; **a ~ of genius** una genialidad; **a ~ of luck** un golpe de suerte; **to not do a ~ of work** *inf* no dar golpe 8. (*of clock*) campanada *f*

stroll [strəʊl, *Am:* stroʊl] I. *n* paseo *m;* **to go for a ~** dar una vuelta II. *vi* dar un paseo; **to ~ along the river bank** pasearse por el lado del río

stroller ['strəʊləʳ, *Am:* 'stroʊlɚ] *n* 1. (*person*) paseante *mf* 2. *Am, Aus* (*pushchair*) cochecito *m*

strong [strɒŋ, *Am:* strɑːŋ] I. *adj* 1. (*powerful*) fuerte; (*coffee*) cargado, -a; (*competition*) duro, -a; (*condemnation*) severo, -a; (*doubt, incentive, influence*) gran, grande; (*protest, measure*) enérgico, -a; (*reason*) de peso; (*wind*) recio, -a; **to produce ~ memories** traer muchos recuerdos 2. (*capable*) competente 3. (*physically powerful*) robusto, -a; **to be as ~ as a horse** ser tan fuerte como un toro 4. (*fit*) sano, -a; (*constitution*) fuerte 5. (*durable*) sólido, -a; (*will, conviction*) firme; (*nerves*) de acero 6. (*staunch*) arraigado, -a; (*antipathy*) gran; (*believer*) fervoroso, -a; (*bond*) fuerte; (*character*) enérgico, -a; (*emotion*) intenso, -a; (*friend*) íntimo, -a; (*friendship*) estrecho, -a; (*objection, opponent*) duro, -a; (*supporter*) acérrimo, -a 7. (*tough*) resistente 8. (*very likely*) muy probable; **~ chances of success** muchas posibilidades de éxito 9. (*marked*) marcado, -a; (*colour*) llamativo, -a; (*light, flavour*) intenso, -a; (*fragrance*) penetrante; (*language*) vulgar 10. (*bright*) brillante 11. (*having high value*) de gran valor II. *adv inf* **to come on ~ to sb** (*show sexual interest in*) ir por alguien; **to be still going ~** ir todavía bien

strong-arm ['strɒŋɑːm, *Am:* 'strɑːŋɑːrm] I. *adj* (*method*) de mano dura II. *vt* utilizar la fuerza física con

strongbox ['strɒŋbɒks, *Am:* 'strɑːŋbɑːks] *n* caja *f* fuerte

stronghold ['strɒŋhəʊld, *Am:* 'strɑːŋhoʊld] *n* (*fortified place*) fortaleza *f; fig* baluarte *m*

strongly *adv* 1. (*powerfully*) fuertemente; (*advise*) fervorosamente; (*condemn*) con dureza; (*criticize, force*) enérgicamente; **to smell ~ of sth** tener un fuerte olor a algo; **to be ~ opposed to sth** estar muy en contra de algo; **to be ~ biased against sb** tener una fuerte predisposición contra algo 2. (*sturdily*) sólidamente

strong-minded [ˌstrɒŋ'maɪndɪd, *Am:* ˌstrɑːŋ-] *adj* resuelto, -a

strongroom ['strɒŋrʊm, *Am:* 'strɑːŋruːm] *n* cámara *f* acorazada

strong-willed [ˌstrɒŋ'wɪld, *Am:* ˌstrɑːŋ-] *adj* resuelto, -a

strontium ['strɒntiəm, *Am:* 'strɑːntʃiəm] *n no pl* estroncio *m*

strop [strɒp, *Am:* strɑːp] *n Brit, Aus, inf* **to be in a ~** estar de mal humor

stroppy ['strɒpi, *Am:* 'strɑːpi] *adj Brit, Aus, inf* enfadado, -a

strove [strəʊv, *Am:* stroʊv] *pt of* **strive**

struck [strʌk] *pt, pp of* **strike**

structural ['strʌktʃərəl] *adj* estructural

structural unemployment *n* ECON, SOCIOL paro *m* estructural

structure ['strʌktʃəʳ, *Am:* -tʃɚ] I. *n* estructura *f;* (*building*) construcción *f* II. *vt* estructurar

struggle ['strʌgl] I. *n* 1. (*effort*) esfuerzo *m;* **to be a real ~** suponer un gran esfuerzo; **to give up the ~ to do sth** dejar de esmerarse en hacer algo 2. (*skirmish*) lucha *f* II. *vi* 1. (*make an effort*) esforzarse 2. (*fight*) luchar

strum [strʌm] <-mm-> *vt* MUS rasguear

strung [strʌŋ] *pt, pp of* **string**

strut¹ [strʌt] I. <-tt-> *vi* **to ~ about** pavonearse II. *vt inf* **to ~ one's stuff** *iron* (*dance*) contonearse

strut² [strʌt] *n* (*in building, plane*) puntal *m*

strychnine ['strɪkniːn, *Am:* -naɪn] *n no pl* estricnina *f*

stub [stʌb] I. *n* (*of cheque*) talón *m;* (*of cigarette*) colilla *f;* (*of pencil*) cabo *m* II. <-bb-> *vt* **to ~ one's toe against sth** tropezar con algo

◆**stub out** *vt* (*cigarette*) apagar

stubble ['stʌbl] *n no pl* 1. (*beard growth*) barba *f* de tres días 2. AGR rastrojo *m*

stubbly ['stʌbli] *adj* (*bristly*) con barba de tres días

stubborn ['stʌbən, *Am:* -ɚn] *adj* (*person, animal*) terco, -a; (*insistence*) tenaz; (*problem*) persistente; (*refusal*) rotundo, -a; (*resistence*) inquebrantable

stubby ['stʌbi] *adj* (*person*) achaparrado, -a; (*finger*) corto, -a

stucco ['stʌkəʊ, *Am:* -oʊ] *n no pl* estuco *m*

stuck [stʌk] I. *pt, pp of* **stick** II. *adj* 1. (*jammed*) atascado, -a 2. *inf* (*crazy about*) **to be ~ on sb** estar loco por alguien 3. *Brit, Aus, inf* (*persevere*) **to get ~ into sth** ponerse en serio con algo

stuck-up [ˌstʌk'ʌp] *adj inf* engreído, -a

stud¹ [stʌd] *n* 1. (*horse*) semental *m,* garañón *m AmL* 2. (*establishment*) caballeriza *f*

stud² [stʌd] *n* 1. (*small metal item*) tachón *m;* (*decorative nail*) clavo *m;* **collar ~** gemelo *m* 2. *Brit, Aus* (*on shoe*) taco *m*

student ['stjuːdənt, *Am:* 'stuː-] *n* estudiante *mf;* **the ~ body** el alumnado

student teacher *n* profesor(a) *m(f)* en prácticas **student union** *n* (*organization*) asociación *f* de estudiantes; (*meeting place*) club *m* de estudiantes universitarios

stud farm ['stʌdfɑːm, *Am:* -fɑːrm] *n* caballeriza *f* **stud horse** *n* semental *m*, garañón *m AmL*

studied ['stʌdɪd] *adj* estudiado, -a; (*answer*) pensado, -a; (*insult*) premeditado, -a

studio ['stjuːdiəʊ, *Am:* 'stuːdioʊ] <-s> *n* **1.** (*of artist*) taller *m* **2.** CINE estudio *m*

studio apartment *n* estudio *m* **studio audience** *n* público *m* en estudio **studio couch** *n* sofá-cama *m*

studious ['stjuːdiəs, *Am:* 'stuː-] *adj* estudioso, -a

study ['stʌdi] **I.** *vt* (*subject*) estudiar; (*evidence*) examinar **II.** *vi* estudiar **III.** <-ies> *n* **1.** (*of subject*) estudio *m;* (*of evidence*) investigación *f* **2.** (*room*) despacho *m*

study group *n* grupo *m* de estudio **study visit** *n* viaje *m* de estudios

stuff [stʌf] **I.** *n no pl* **1.** *inf* (*things*) materia *f;* **to know one's** ~ conocer su oficio **2.** (*belongings*) cosas *fpl* **3.** (*material*) material *m;* (*cloth*) tela *f;* **to be the** ~ **of which heroes are made** tener madera de héroe; **the** (**very**) ~ **of sth** la esencia de algo **II.** *vt* **1.** (*fill*) llenar; **to** ~ **sth into sth** meter algo en algo; **to** ~ **sb's head with sth** llenarle a alguien la cabeza de algo; **to** ~ **oneself** *inf* darse un atracón **2.** (*preserve: animal*) disecar

stuffed shirt *n inf* persona *f* estirada

stuffing ['stʌfɪŋ] *n no pl* relleno *m* ►**to knock the** ~ **out of sb** *inf* dar una paliza a alguien

stuffy ['stʌfi] *adj pej* **1.** (*room*) mal ventilado, -a; (*atmosphere*) cargado, -a **2.** (*person*) tieso, -a

stultifying ['stʌltɪˌfaɪɪŋ, *Am:* -t̬ə-] <-ie-> *adj* embrutecedor(a)

stumble ['stʌmbl] *vi* **1.** (*trip*) tropezar; **to** ~ **on sth** tropezar con algo **2.** (*while talking*) balbucear; **to** ~ **over sth** tropezar en algo

stumbling block *n* obstáculo *m*

stump [stʌmp] **I.** *n* **1.** (*of plant*) tocón *m;* (*of arm*) muñón *m;* (*of tooth*) raigón *m* **2.** *Am* POL **to go on the** ~ hacer campaña **II.** *vt* **1.** *inf* (*baffle*) desconcertar **2.** *Am* POL **to** ~ **the country** viajar por todo el país pronunciando discursos **III.** *vi* **to** ~ **about** andar pisando fuerte

stumpy ['stʌmpi] *adj inf* achaparrado, -a; (*tail*) corto, -a

stun [stʌn] <-nn-> *vt* **1.** (*stupefy*) dejar pasmado **2.** (*render unconscious*) dejar sin sentido

stung [stʌŋ] *pp, pt of* **sting**

stun grenade *n* MIL granada *f* detonadora

stunk [stʌŋk] *pt, pp of* **stink**

stunned *adj* aturdido, -a

stunner ['stʌnəʳ, *Am:* -ɚ] *n inf* **1.** (*surprise*) sorpresa *f;* (*person*) **2.** **she's a** ~ es un bombón

stunning ['stʌnɪŋ] *adj* **1.** (*surprising*) aturdidor(a) **2.** (*impressive*) maravilloso, -a; (*dress*) estupendo, -a; (*view*) espléndido, -a

stunt[1] [stʌnt] *n* **1.** (*acrobatics*) acrobacia *f* **2.** (*feat*) hazaña *f;* **to pull a** ~ *inf* hacer una proeza **3.** (*publicity action*) truco *m* publicitario; **advertising** ~ treta *f* publicitaria **4.** CINE toma *f* peligrosa

stunt[2] [stʌnt] *vt* (*plant*) atrofiar; (*growth*) impedir

stunted *adj* enano, -a; (*child*) poco desarrollado, -a; **emotionally** ~ poco maduro emocionalmente

stuntman ['stʌntmæn] *n* especialista

stupefaction [ˌstjuːpɪ'fækʃən, *Am:* ˌstuːpə'-] *n no pl, form* estupefacción *f*

stupefy ['stjuːpɪfaɪ, *Am:* 'stuːpə-] <-ie-> *vt* atontar; *fig* dejar estupefacto

stupendous [stjuː'pendəs, *Am:* stuː-] *adj* estupendo, -a

stupid ['stjuːpɪd, *Am:* 'stuː-] *adj* estúpido, -a, cojudo, -a *AmL,* zonzo, -a *AmL;* (*mistake*) tonto, -a

stupidity [stjuː'pɪdəti, *Am:* stuː'pɪdət̬i] *n no pl* estupidez *f,* dundera *f AmL*

stupor ['stjuːpəʳ, *Am:* 'stuːpɚ] *n* estupor *m*

sturdy ['stɜːdi, *Am:* 'stɜːr-] *adj* **1.** (*robust*) robusto, -a; (*person*) fuerte **2.** (*resolute*) decidido, -a

sturgeon ['stɜːdʒən, *Am:* 'stɜːr-] *n* esturión *m*

stutter ['stʌtəʳ, *Am:* 'stʌt̬ɚ] **I.** *vi* (*stammer*) tartamudear, cancanear, AmL **II.** *vt* decir algo tartamudeando **III.** *n* tartamudeo *m;* **to have a** ~ tartamudear

stutterer ['stʌtərəʳ, *Am:* 'stʌt̬ɚɚ] *n* tartamudo, -a *m, f*

sty[1] [staɪ] *n* (*pigsty*) pocilga *f*

sty[2] *n,* **stye** [staɪ] *n* MED orzuelo *m*

style [staɪl] **I.** *n* **1.** *a.* ART, ARCHIT estilo *m;* (*of management*) modo *f;* (*of teaching*) forma *f* **2.** (*elegance*) elegancia *f;* **to have no** ~ no ser elegante; **to do things in** ~ hacer las cosas como se debe; **in** ~ de forma elegante; **to live in** (**grand**) ~ vivir a lo grande; **to travel in** ~ viajar con todo el confort **3.** (*fashion*) moda *f;* **in** ~ de moda **4.** (*type*) normas *fpl* de estilo **II.** *vt* **1.** (*design*) diseñar; (*hair*) peinar **2.** (*label*) **to** ~ **oneself as ...** hacerse llamar...

style sheet *n* INFOR hoja *f* de estilo

styling *n* estilización *f*

stylish ['staɪlɪʃ] *adj* **1.** (*fashionable*) a la moda **2.** (*elegant*) garboso, -a

stylist ['staɪlɪst] *n* estilista *mf*

stylistic [staɪ'lɪstɪk] *adj* estilístico, -a

stylize ['staɪəlaɪz, *Am:* 'staɪlaɪz] *vt* estilizar

stylus ['staɪləs] <-es> *n* estilete *m*

stymie ['staɪmi] <-(y)ing> *vt inf* (*person*) poner obstáculos infranqueables ante; (*project*) bloquear

suave [swɑːv] *adj* cortés; *pej* zalamero, -a

sub[1] [sʌb] *n* **1.** *Brit, Aus, inf abbr of* **substitute** sustituto, -a *m, f* **2.** *inf abbr of* **submarine** submarino *m* **3.** *Am, inf abbr of* **sandwich**

sandwich *m* mixto **4.** *Brit, Aus, inf abbr of* **subscription** suscripción *f*
sub² [sʌb] <-bb-> *vi abbr of* **substitute** sustituir
subagency [ˌsʌb'eɪdʒənsi] *n* <-ies> *Am* sucursal *f*
subagent [ˌsʌb'eɪdʒənt] *n* subagente *mf*
subaltern ['sʌbltən, *Am:* səb'ɔːltɚn] *n Brit* MIL alférez *m*
subatomic [ˌsʌbə'tɒmɪk, *Am:* -'tɑːmɪk] *adj* PHYS subatómico, -a
subclass ['sʌbklɑːs, *Am:* -klæs] *n* BIO subclase *f*
subcommittee ['sʌbkəˌmɪti, *Am:* ˌsʌbkə'-] *n* subcomisión *f*
subconscious [ˌsʌb'kɒnʃəs, *Am:* -'kɑːnʃəs] **I.** *n no pl* subconsciente *m* **II.** *adj* subconsciente
subcontinent [ˌsʌb'kɒntɪnənt, *Am:* 'sʌbˌkɑːntnənt] *n* GEO subcontinente *m;* **the** ~ el subcontinente de la India
subcontract [ˌsʌb'kɒntrækt, *Am:* 'sʌbˌkɑːn-] *vt* subcontratar
subcontractor [ˌsʌbkən'træktəʳ] *n* subcontratista *mf*
subculture [ˌsʌb'kʌltʃəʳ, *Am:* 'sʌbˌkʌltʃɚ] *n* subcultura *f*
subcutaneous [ˌsʌbkjuː'teɪnɪəs] *adj* subcutáneo, -a
subdivide [ˌsʌbdɪ'vaɪd] *vt* subdividir
subdivision [ˌsʌbdɪ'vɪʒən] *n* **1.** (*division*) subdivisión *f* **2.** *Am, Aus* (*housing estate*) urbanización *f*
subdue [səb'djuː, *Am:* -'duː] *vt* (*tame*) controlar; (*repress*) reprimir
subdued *adj* (*colour*) suave; (*person*) apagado, -a
sub-edit [ˌsʌb'edɪt] *vt* PUBL corregir
sub-editor [ˌsʌb'edɪtəʳ, *Am:* -t̬ɚ] *n* redactor(a) *m(f)*
subgroup ['sʌbgruːp] *n* subgrupo *m*
subheading ['sʌbˌhedɪŋ, *Am:* 'sʌbˌ-] *n* subtítulo *m*
subject¹ ['sʌbdʒɪkt] **I.** *n* **1.** (*theme*) tema *m;* **to change the** ~ cambiar de tema; **to wander off the** ~ salirse del tema; **on the** ~ **of sb/sth** a propósito de alguien/algo **2.** SCHOOL, UNIV asignatura *f; Brit* (*research area*) ámbito *m* **3.** POL súbdito, -a *m, f;* (*citizen*) ciudadano, -a *m, f* **4.** LING sujeto *m* **5.** (*in experiment*) sujeto *m* de experimentación **II.** *adj* **1.** POL subyugado, -a **2.** (*exposed to*) **to be** ~ **to sth** estar sujeto a algo; **to be** ~ **to colds** ser propenso a acatarrarse; **to be** ~ **to many dangers** estar expuesto a muchos peligros; **to be** ~ **to a high tax** estar sujeto a impuestos elevados; ~ **to prosecution** sujeto a persecución **3.** (*contingent on*) ~ **to approval** pendiente de aprobación
subject² [səb'dʒekt] *vt* dominar
subject catalogue *n* catálogo *m* por temas
subject index *n* índice *m* de materias
subjection [səb'dʒekʃən] *n no pl* POL sometimiento *m*
subjective [səb'dʒektɪv] *adj* subjetivo, -a
subject matter *n* (*of meeting, book*) tema *m;* (*of letter*) contenido *m*
sub judice [ˌsʌb'dʒuːdɪsi, *Am:* -dəsi] *adj* LAW sub júdice
subjugate ['sʌbdʒəgeɪt] *vt form* **1.** (*control*) subyugar **2.** (*make submissive*) someter; **to** ~ **sth to sth** supeditar algo a algo
subjugation [ˌsʌbdʒə'geɪʃən] *n form* subyugación
subjunctive [səb'dʒʌŋktɪv] *n no pl* LING subjuntivo *m*
sublease [ˌsʌb'liːs] *vt* subarrendar
sublet [sʌb'let] <sublet, sublet> *vt* subarrendar
sublieutenant [ˌsʌblə'tenənt, *Am:* -luː'-] *n Brit* MIL alférez *m* de fragata
sublimate ['sʌblɪmeɪt] *vt* PSYCH sublimar
sublime [sə'blaɪm] *adj* **1.** (*glorious*) sublime **2.** *iron* (*absolute*) absoluto, -a; ~ **ignorance** ignorancia *f* supina
subliminal [ˌsʌb'lɪmɪnl, *Am:* -'lɪmənl] *adj* PSYCH subliminal
submachine gun [ˌsʌbmə'ʃiːnˌgʌn] *n* metralleta *f*
submarine [ˌsʌbmə'riːn, 'sʌbməˌriːn, *Am:* 'sʌbməriːn] **I.** *n* **1.** NAUT, MIL submarino *m inv* **2.** *Am, inf* (*sandwich*) sandwich *m* mixto **II.** *adj* submarino, -a
submenu [ˌsʌb'menjuː] *n* INFOR submenú *m*
submerge [səb'mɜːdʒ, *Am:* -'mɜːrdʒ] **I.** *vt* sumergir; **to** ~ **oneself in sth** *fig* dedicarse de lleno a algo **II.** *vi* sumergirse
submersible [səb'mɜːsɪbl, *Am:* -'mɜːrsəbl] *n* sumergible
submersion [səb'mɜːʒən, *Am:* -'mɜːrʒən] *n no pl* sumersión *f*
submission [səb'mɪʃən] *n no pl* **1.** (*acquiescence*) sumisión *f* **2.** *no pl* (*of proposal*) presentación *f;* (*of document*) entrega *f* **3.** (*argument*) argumento *m* **4.** LAW alegato *m;* **in my** ~ *form* en mi opinión
submissive [səb'mɪsɪv] *adj* sumiso, -a
submit [səb'mɪt] <-tt-> **I.** *vt* **1.** (*hand in: proposal*) presentar; (*document*) entregar **2.** *form* (*propose*) proponer **II.** *vi* (*yield*) someterse
subnormal [ˌsʌb'nɔːml, *Am:* -'nɔːrml] *adj* subnormal
subordinate¹ [sə'bɔːdənət, *Am:* -'bɔːrdənɪt] **I.** *n* subordinado, -a *m, f* **II.** *adj* (*secondary*) secundario, -a; (*lower in rank*) subordinado, -a
subordinate² [sə'bɔːdɪnəɪt, *Am:* -'bɔːrdənəɪt] *vt* subordinar
subordinate clause *n* LING frase *f* subordinada
subordination [səˌbɔːdɪ'neɪʃən, *Am:* -ˌbɔːrdən'eɪʃən] *n no pl* subordinación *f*
suborn [sə'bɔːn, *Am:* -'bɔːrn] *vt* LAW sobornar
subplot ['sʌbplɒt, *Am:* -plɑːt] *n* argumento *m* secundario

subpoena [sə'pi:nə] LAW I. *vt* citar; **to ~ sb to testify** mandar comparecer a alguien para testificar II. *n* citación *f* (judicial)

sub-post office [ˌsʌbpəʊst'ɒfɪs, *Am:* -'poʊstˌɑ:fɪs] *n* subdelegación *f* de correos

subscribe [səb'skraɪb] I. *vt* 1. (*contribute*) donar 2. (*sign*) firmar II. *vi* 1. (*agree*) **to ~ to sth** suscribir algo 2. (*make susbscription*) suscribirse

subscriber [səb'skraɪbə^r^, *Am:* -ɚ] *n* (*to magazine*) suscriptor(a) *m(f)*; (*to phone service*) abonado, -a *m, f*

subscript [sʌb'skrɪpt] *n no pl* TYPO subíndice *m*

subscription [səb'skrɪpʃən] *n* suscripción *f*; **to take out a ~ to sth** suscribirse a algo

subsection ['sʌbˌsekʃən] *n* 1. (*part*) subdivisión *f* 2. LAW apartado *m*

subsequent ['sʌbsɪkwənt] *adj* posterior; **~ to ...** después de...

subsequently *adv* después; **~ to ...** después de...

subservient [səb'sɜ:viənt, *Am:* -'sɜ:r-] *adj* 1. *pej* (*servile*) servil 2. (*secondary*) subordinado, -a

subset ['sʌbset] *n* MAT subconjunto *m*

subside [səb'saɪd] *vi* 1. (*lessen*) disminuir 2. (*sink: building*) hundirse; (*water*) bajar

subsidence [səb'saɪdns] *n no pl* (*of building*) hundimiento *m*; (*of water*) bajada *f*

subsidiary [səb'sɪdɪəri, *Am:* -əri] I. *adj* subsidiario, -a; (*reason*) secundario, -a; ECON filial II. <-ies> *n* ECON filial *f*

subsidize ['sʌbsɪdaɪz, *Am:* -sə-] *vt* subvencionar

subsidy ['sʌbsədi, *Am:* -sə-] <-ies> *n* subvención *f*, subsidio *m*; **unemployment ~** subsidio de desempleo

subsist [səb'sɪst] *vi form* subsistir; **to ~ on sth** sustentarse con algo

subsistence [səb'sɪstəns] *n* subsistencia *f*; **means of ~** medios *mpl* de subsistencia; **enough for a bare ~** suficiente para subsistir

subsistence allowance *n Brit* dietas *fpl*
subsistence level *n* nivel *m* de subsistencia **subsistence wage** *n* salario *m* de subsistencia

substance ['sʌbstəns] *n* 1. *no pl* (*matter*) sustancia *f* 2. (*essence*) esencia *f* 3. *no pl* (*significance*) valor *m*; **a film of real ~** una película de gran valor *f* 4. (*main point*) punto *m* más importante; **the ~ of the conversation** el punto esencial de la conversación; **in ~** en esencia 5. (*posessions*) riqueza *f*; **a man of ~** un hombre acaudalado

substandard [ˌsʌb'stændəd, *Am:* -dɚd] *adj* inferior

substantial [səb'stænʃl] *adj* 1. (*important*) sustancial; (*difference, improvement*) notable; **to be in ~ agreement** estar de acuerdo en gran parte 2. (*large*) grande; (*meal*) copioso, -a; (*sum, damage*) considerable 3. (*sturdy*) sólido, -a

substantially [səb'stænʃəli] *adv* 1. (*significantly*) considerablemente 2. (*in the main*) esencialmente

substantiate [səb'stænʃɪeɪt] *vt* corrobar

substantive ['sʌbstəntɪv, *Am:* -t̬ɪv] I. *n* sustantivo *m* II. *adj form* de peso

substation ['sʌbsteɪʃən] *n* 1. ADMIN subdelegación *f*; **police ~** *Am* comisaría *f* de policía 2. ELEC subestación *f*

substitute ['sʌbstɪtju:t, *Am:* -stətu:t] I. *vt* sustituir; **to ~ sb with sb** *inf* reemplazar a alguien por alguien; **to ~ margarine for butter, to ~ butter by** [*o* **with**] **margarine** sustituir la mantequilla por la margarina II. *vi* **to ~ for sb** suplir a alguien III. *n* 1. (*equivalent*) sustituto *m*; (*alternative: for milk, coffee*) sucedáneo *m*; **there's no ~ for him** no hay nadie como él 2. *a.* SPORTS suplente *mf*; **to come on as a ~** sustituir a alguien

substitution [ˌsʌbstɪ'tju:ʃən, *Am:* -stə'tu:-] *n* sustitución *f*

substratum ['sʌbˌstreɪt̬əm] <-ta> *n* sustrato *m*

subsume [səb'sju:m, *Am:* -'su:m] *vt form* subsumir; **to ~ sth under a category** subsumir algo dentro de una categoría

subtenant [ˌsʌb'tenənt, *Am:* 'sʌbˌten-] *n* subarrendatario, -a *m, f*

subterfuge ['sʌbtəfju:dʒ, *Am:* -tɚ-] *n* subterfugio *m*; **by ~** por subterfugio

subterranean [ˌsʌbtə'reɪniən] *adj* subterráneo, -a

subtext ['sʌbtekst] *n* subtexto *m*

subtitle ['sʌbˌtaɪtl, *Am:* 'sʌbˌtaɪt̬l] I. *vt* subtitular II. *n* subtítulo *m*

subtle ['sʌtl, *Am:* 'sʌt̬-] *adj* 1. (*delicate*) sutil; (*flavour*) suave; (*nuance*) tenue 2. (*slight: difference*) sutil 3. (*astute: person*) astuto, -a; (*question, suggestion*) inteligente; (*humour*) fino, -a

subtlety ['sʌtlti, *Am:* 'sʌt̬lt̬i] <-ies> *n* 1. (*delicacy: of flavour, smell*) delicadeza *f* 2. (*of person, argument*) sutileza *f*

subtotal ['sʌbˌtəʊtl, *Am:* -ˌtoʊt̬l] *n* subtotal *m*

subtract [səb'trækt] *vt* sustraer; **to ~ 3 from 5** restar 3 a 5

subtraction [səb'trækʃən] *n no pl* resta *f*, sustracción *f*

subtropical [ˌsʌb'trɒpɪkl, *Am:* -'trɑ:pɪ-] *adj* subtropical

suburb ['sʌbɜ:b, *Am:* -ɜ:rb] *n* barrio *m* periférico; **the ~s** la periferia; **to live in the ~s** vivir en las afueras

suburban [sə'bɜ:bən, *Am:* -'bɜ:r-] *adj* 1. (*area*) periférico, -a; (*train*) de cercanías 2. (*lifestyle*) aburguesado, -a

suburbia [sə'bɜ:bɪə, *Am:* -'bɜ:r-] *n no pl* barrios *mpl* periféricos

subvention [səb'venʃən] *n form* subvención *f*

subversion [səb'vɜ:ʃən, *Am:* -'vɜ:rʒən] *n no pl, form* subversión *f*

subversive [səb'vɜːsɪv, *Am:* -'vɜːr-] *form* I. *adj* subversivo, -a II. *n* persona *f* subversiva
subvert [sʌb'vɜːt, *Am:* -'vɜːrt] *vt* (*authority*) minar; (*principle*) debilitar
subway ['sʌbweɪ] *n* 1. *Brit, Aus* (*walkway*) paso *m* subterráneo 2. *Am* (*railway*) metro *m*, subte *m Arg*
sub-zero [ˌsʌb'zɪərəʊ, *Am:* -'zɪroʊ] *adj* bajo cero
succeed [sək'siːd] I. *vi* 1. (*be successful*) tener éxito; **to ~ in doing sth** lograr hacer algo; **the plan ~ed** el plan salió bien 2. (*follow*) suceder ▶**if at first you don't ~, then try, try and try again** *prov* si no lo consigues a la primera, vuelve a intentarlo una y otra vez II. *vt* (*follow*) suceder a
succeeding *adj* 1. (*next in line*) sucesor(a) 2. (*following*) siguiente; (*generation*) venidero, -a; **in the ~ weeks** en las próximas semanas
success [sək'ses] *n* 1. *no pl* (*outcome*) éxito *m*; **to meet with ~** tener éxito; **to be a big ~ with sb/sth** tener gran éxito con alguien/algo; **to have ~ in doing sth** conseguir hacer algo; **to make a ~ of sth** tener éxito en algo; **to wish sb ~ with sth** desear a alguien que le vaya bien algo; **to be a great ~** ser un gran éxito; **to enjoy ~** tener éxito; **~ story** éxito *m* 2. (*successful person, thing*) éxito *m*; **he was a ~ with my children** les cayó muy bien a mis hijos
successful [sək'sesfəl] *adj* exitoso, -a; (*business*) próspero, -a; (*candidate*) electo, -a; (*solution*) eficaz; **to be ~** (*person*) tener éxito; (*business*) prosperar; **commercially ~** con éxito comercial
succession [sək'seʃən] *n no pl* sucesión *f*; **~ rights** derechos *mpl* de sucesión; **in ~** sucesivamente; **a ~ of** una serie de; **an endless ~ of** un sinfín de
successive [sək'sesɪv] *adj* sucesivo, -a; **six ~ weeks** seis semanas seguidas; **the third ~ defeat** la tercera derrota consecutiva
successor [sək'sesəʳ, *Am:* -ɚ] *n* sucesor(a) *m(f)*
succinct [sək'sɪŋkt] *adj* sucinto, -a
succour ['sʌkəʳ, *Am:* -ɚ] *Brit, Aus,* **succor** *Am, Aus* I. *n* socorro *m*; **to bring ~ to sb** socorrer a alguien II. *vt* socorrer
succulent ['sʌkjʊlənt] I. *adj* (*steak, fruit*) suculento, -a; (*plant*) carnoso, -a II. *n* planta *f* carnosa
succumb [sə'kʌm] *vi form* 1. (*surrender*) sucumbir; **to ~ to pressure/to temptation** sucumbir ante la presión/a la tentación 2. (*die*) morir; **to ~ to one's injuries** morir a causa de las heridas
such [sʌtʃ] I. *adj* tal, semejante; **~ great weather/a good book** un tiempo/un libro tan bueno; **~ an honour** tanto honor; **to earn ~ a lot of money** ganar tanto dinero; **or some ~ remark** o un comentario del estilo; **to buy some fruit ~ as apples** comprar fruta como manzanas II. *pron* **~ is life** así es la vida; **people ~ as him** las personas que son como él; **~ as it is** tal como es; **as ~** propiamente dicho
such-and-such ['sʌtʃənsʌtʃ] *adj inf* tal o cual; **to arrive at ~ a time** llegar a tal o cual hora; **to meet sb in ~ a place** encontrarse con alguien en tal o cual lugar
suchlike ['sʌtʃlaɪk] *pron* **cookies, chocolates and ~** galletas, bombones y cosas por el estilo; **businessmen, politicians and ~** hombres de negocios, políticos y gente de ese tipo
suck [sʌk] I. *vt* succionar; (*with straw*) sorber; (*air*) aspirar; (*breast*) mamar; (*sweets*) chupar; **to ~ one's thumb** chuparse el dedo II. *vi* 1. (*with mouth*) chupar 2. *Am, inf* **this ~s!** ¡esto es una mierda! III. *n* chupada *f*; (*with straw*) sorbo *m*
◆**suck up to** *vt* dar coba a
sucker ['sʌkəʳ, *Am:* -ɚ] I. *n* 1. *Am, pej* (*stupid person*) bobo, -a *m, f* 2. (*device*) *a.* ZOOL ventosa *f* II. *vt Am* timar; **to ~ sb out of sth** estafar algo a alguien
suckle ['sʌkl] I. *vt* amamantar II. *vi* mamar
suckling-pig ['sʌklɪŋˌpɪg] *n* lechón *m*
sucrose ['suːkrəʊs, *Am:* -kroʊs] *n no pl* sacarosa *f*
suction ['sʌkʃən] *n no pl* succión *f*
suction pump *n* bomba *f* de succión
Sudan [suː'dæn] *n* Sudán *m*
Sudanese [ˌsuːdə'niːz] I. *n* sudanés, -esa *m, f* II. *adj* sudanés, -esa
sudden ['sʌdən] *adj* (*immediate*) repentino, -a, sorpresivo, -a *AmL*; (*death*) súbito, -a; (*departure*) imprevisto, -a; (*movement, drop*) brusco, -a; **to put a ~ stop to sth** detener algo de forma repentina; **all of a ~** *inf* de repente
suddenly *adv* de repente
suds [sʌdz] *npl* 1. jabonaduras *fpl* 2. *Am* cerveza *f*
sue [sjuː, *Am:* suː] <suing> I. *vt* demandar; **to ~ sb for damages** demandar a alguien por daños y perjuicios; **to ~ sb for divorce** ponerle a alguien una demanda de divorcio II. *vi* presentar demanda; **to ~ for peace** pedir la paz
suede [sweɪd] *n* ante *m*
suet ['suːɪt] *n no pl* sebo *m*
suffer ['sʌfəʳ, *Am:* -ɚ] I. *vi* sufrir; **the economy ~ed from ...** la economía se vio afectada por...; **to ~ for sth** ser castigado por algo II. *vt* 1. (*undergo: defeat, setback*) sufrir; **to ~ the consequences** sufrir las consecuencias; **to ~ the misfortune** tener mala suerte 2. (*allow*) permitir; **to ~ sth to be done** permitir que algo suceda; (*bear*) aguantar; **to not ~ fools gladly** no tener paciencia con los imbéciles 3. MED padecer
sufferance ['sʌfərəns] *n* tolerancia *f*; **on ~** de mala gana
sufferer ['sʌfərəʳ, *Am:* -ɚɚ] *n* enfermo, -a *m, f*; **AIDS ~** enfermo de SIDA

suffering ['sʌfərɪŋ] *n* sufrimiento *m;* **years of** ~ *no pl* años *mpl* de penurias

suffice [sə'faɪs] *vi* bastar; ~ (**it**) **to say that ...** basta decir que...

sufficiency [sə'fɪʃnsi] *n no pl* cantidad *f* suficiente

sufficient [sə'fɪʃnt] *adj* suficiente; **to have** ~ tener bastante; **to be** ~ **for sth** ser suficiente para algo

suffix ['sʌfɪks] *n* LING sufijo *m*

suffocate ['sʌfəkeɪt] **I.** *vi* asfixiarse **II.** *vt* **1.** (*asphixiate*) asfixiar **2.** *fig* sofocar

suffocating *adj* **1.** (*heat, fumes*) asfixiante **2.** *fig* sofocante

suffrage ['sʌfrɪdʒ] *n no pl* sufragio *m;* **universal** ~ sufragio universal

suffragette [ˌsʌfrə'dʒet] *n* POL, HIST sufragista *f*

sugar ['ʃʊgəʳ, *Am:* -ɚ] **I.** *n* **1.** *no pl* GASTR azúcar *m* **2.** *Am, inf* (*term of affection*) cariño **3.** (*euphemistic*) ¡mecachis! **II.** *vt* echar azúcar a

sugar beet *n* remolacha *f* azucarera **sugar bowl** *n* azucarera *f* **sugar cane** *n* caña *f* de azúcar

sugar-coated [ˌsʊgə'kəʊtɪd] *adj* cubierto, -a de azúcar

sugar daddy *n hombe rico y mayor que da regalos o dinero a una mujer con el objetivo de tener relaciones sexuales con ella* **sugar loaf** *n* pan *m* de azúcar **sugar lump** *n* terrón *m* de azúcar

sugary ['ʃʊgəri] *adj* **1.** (*sweet*) azucarado, -a **2.** *fig, pej* (*insincere*) meloso, -a

suggest [sə'dʒest, *Am:* səg'-] *vt* **1.** (*propose*) proponer, sugerir; **to** ~ (**to sb**) **that ...** sugerirle a alguien que... *+subj;* **to** ~ **doing sth** sugerir hacer algo; **an idea ~ed itself** (**to him**) se le ocurrió una idea **2.** (*indicate*) indicar **3.** (*hint*) insinuar; **what are you trying to ~?** ¿qué insinúas?

suggestible [sə'dʒestəbl, *Am:* səg'dʒestə-] *adj pej, form* sugestionable; **highly** ~ muy influenciable

suggestion [sə'dʒestʃən, *Am:* səg'dʒes-] *n* **1.** (*proposed idea*) sugerencia *f;* **to make the** ~ **that ...** sugerir que... *+subj;* **to be open to new ~s** estar abierto a nuevas sugerencias; **at Ann's** ~ a petición de Ann **2.** (*very small amount*) pizca *f;* **there was a** ~ **of a smile on his face** esbozó una sonrisa **3.** (*insinuation*) insinuación *f*

suggestion box *n* buzón *m* de sugerencias

suggestive [sə'dʒestɪv, *Am:* səg'-] *adj* **1.** (*lewd*) indecente **2.** (*evocative*) sugestivo, -a

suicidal [ˌsjuːɪ'saɪdl, *Am:* ˌsuːə'-] *adj* suicida; **to feel** ~ tener ganas de suicidarse; *fig* tener el ánimo por los suelos

suicide ['sjuːɪsaɪd, *Am:* 'suːə-] *n* **1.** (*act*) suicidio *m;* **to commit** ~ suicidarse **2.** *form* (*person*) suicida *mf*

suit [suːt] **I.** *vt* **1.** (*be convenient*) convenir; **to** ~ **sb** convenirle a alguien; **that ~s me fine** eso me viene bien **2.** (*be right*) ir [*o* sentar] bien; **they are well ~ed** (**to each other**) hacen (una) buena pareja; **this lifestyle seems to** ~ **her** parece ser que este clase de vida le sienta bien **3.** (*look attractive with*) quedar bien; **this dress ~s you** este vestido te sienta bien **4.** (*choose at will*) **to** ~ **oneself** hacer lo que uno quiere; ~ **yourself!** ¡haz lo que quieras! **II.** *n* **1.** (*jacket and trousers*) traje *m,* terno *m Chile,* flus *m Ant, Col, Ven;* (*jacket and skirt*) traje *m* de chaqueta; **bathing** [*o* **swim**] ~ traje *m* de baño **2.** LAW pleito *m;* **to bring a** ~, **to file a** ~ *Am* entablar un pleito **3.** GAMES palo *m;* **to follow** ~ seguir el palo; *fig* seguir el ejemplo

suitable ['suːtəbl, *Am:* -t̬əbl] *adj* apropiado, -a; **to be** ~ **for sb** ser apropiado [*o* adecuado] para alguien; **not** ~ **for chidren under 14** no apto para niños menores de 14 años

suitcase ['suːtkeɪs] *n* maleta *f,* valija *f RíoPl,* petaca *f Méx*

suite [swiːt] *n* **1.** (*set of rooms*) suite *f;* **bridal** ~ suite nupcial **2.** (*set of furniture*) juego *m* **3.** MUS suite *f*

suitor ['suːtəʳ, *Am:* 'suːt̬ɚ] *n* **1.** *a. iron* (*potential husband*) pretendiente *m* **2.** *Am* LAW demandante *mf*

sulfate ['sʌlfeɪt] *n Am s.* **sulphate**

sulfide ['sʌlfaɪd] *n Am s.* **sulphide**

sulfonamide [sʌl'fɑːnəmaɪd] *n Am s.* **sulphonamide**

sulfur ['sʌlfɚ] *n Am s.* **sulphur**

sulfuric [sʌl'fjʊrɪk] *adj Am s.* **sulphuric**

sulfurous ['sʌlfɚəs] *adj Am s.* **sulphurous**

sulk [sʌlk] **I.** *vi* enfurruñarse, alunarse *RíoPl,* amurrarse *Chile* **II.** *n* mal humor *m;* **to be in a** ~ estar enfurruñado, -a, estar alunado, -a *RíoPl,* estar amurrado, -a *Chile*

sulky ['sʌlki] <-ier, -iest> *adj* enfurruñado, -a

sullen ['sʌlən] *adj* **1.** *pej* (*person*) malhumorado, -a **2.** *liter* (*sky*) sombrío, -a

sully ['sʌli] <-ied, -ied> *vt* mancillar, manchar

sulphate ['sʌlfeɪt] *n* sulfato *m*

sulphide ['sʌlfaɪd] *n* sulfuro *m*

sulphonamide [sʌl'fɒnəmaɪd, *Am:* -'fɑːnə-] *n* sulfamida *f*

sulphur ['sʌlfəʳ, *Am:* -fɚ] *n no pl* azufre *m*

sulphur dioxide ['sʌlfəʳdaɪ'ɒksaɪd, *Am:* -fɚdaɪ'ɑːk-] *n* dióxido *m* de azufre

sulphuric [sʌl'fjʊərɪk, *Am:* -'fjʊrɪk] *adj* sulfúrico, -a

sulphuric acid *n* ácido *m* sulfúrico

sulphurous ['sʌlfərəs, *Am:* -fɚ-] *adj* (*solution*) de azufre; (*smell*) a azufre

sultan ['sʌltən] *n* sultán *m*

sultana [sʌl'tɑːnə, *Am:* -'tænə] *n* pasa *f* de Esmirna

sultry ['sʌltri] <-ier, -iest> *adj* **1.** (*weather*) bochornoso, -a **2.** (*sensual*) sensual

sum [sʌm] *n* **1.** (*amount*) cantidad *f* **2.** (*calculation*) cuenta *f;* **to do ~s** hacer cuentas **3.** (*addition*) suma *f* **4.** (*total*) total *m;* **in** ~ en resumen

summarize ['sʌməraɪz] *vt* resumir

summary ['sʌməri] **I.** *n* resumen *m* **II.** *adj* (*dismissal, execution*) inmediato, -a; LAW sumario, -a

summation [sʌ'meɪʃən, *Am:* sə'-] *n* **1.** MAT suma *f* **2.** LAW escrito *m* de conclusiones

summer ['sʌməʳ, *Am:* -ɚ] **I.** *n* verano *m;* **a ~'s day** un día de verano, un dia veraniego **II.** *adj* de verano, veraniego, -a **III.** *vi* veranear, pasar el verano

summer holiday(s) *n* vacaciones *fpl* de verano [*o* estivales]

summerhouse ['sʌməhaʊs, *Am:* '-ɚ-] *n* cenador *m*

summertime ['sʌmətaɪm, *Am:* '-ɚ-] *n no pl* (*season*) verano *m;* **in the ~** en verano

summery ['sʌməri] *adj* veraniego, -a

summing-up [ˌsʌmɪŋ'ʌp] *n* LAW recapitulación *f*

summit ['sʌmɪt] *n* **1.** (*top of mountain*) cima *f* **2.** *fig* (*of career, power*) cumbre *f* **3.** POL cumbre *f;* **to hold a ~** celebrar una cumbre; **~ conference** (conferencia *f*) cumbre

summon ['sʌmən] *vt* (*people*) llamar; (*meeting*) convocar; LAW citar

◆**summon up** *vt* (*countable*) reunir; **to ~ the courage/strength to do sth** armarse de valor/fuerzas para hacer algo

summons ['sʌmənz] *npl* llamamiento *m;* LAW citación *f;* **to issue a ~** despachar una citación; **to serve sb with a ~** entregarle una citación a alguien

sump [sʌmp] *n* **1.** AUTO cárter *m* **2.** MIN sumidero *m* **3.** (*cesspit*) pozo *m* negro

sumptuous ['sʌmptʃʊəs] *adj* suntuoso, -a

sun [sʌn] **I.** *n* sol *m;* **the ~'s rays** los rayos del sol; **the rising/setting ~** el sol naciente/poniente; **to sit in the ~** sentarse al sol ►**to call sb every name under the ~** decir a alguien de todo; **to do/try everything under the ~** hacer/probar de todo **II.** <-nn-> *vt* **to ~ oneself** tomar el sol

sunbaked ['sʌnbeɪkt] *adj* secado, -a al sol; (*earth, street*) calcinado, -a **sunbath** *n* baño *m* de sol

sunbathe ['sʌnbeɪð] *vi* tomar el sol

sunbeam ['sʌnbi:m] *n Brit* rayo *m* de sol **sunbed** *n* **1.** (*in garden*) tumbona *f* **2.** (*with sunray lamp*) cama *f* de rayos UVA

sunblind ['sʌnblaɪnd] *n Brit* toldo *m*

sunblock ['sʌnblɒk, *Am:* 'sʌnblɑ:k] *n* filtro *m* solar

sunburn ['sʌnbɜ:n, *Am:* 'sʌnbɜ:rn] *n* quemadura *f* de sol

sunburned *adj,* **sunburnt** *adj* quemado, -a (por el sol)

sundae ['sʌndeɪ, *Am:* -di] *n helado con trozos de fruta, frutos secos, crema, etc.*

Sunday ['sʌndəɪ] *n* domingo *m;* **Palm/Easter ~** domingo de Ramos/de Resurrección; *s. a.* **Friday**

Sunday best *n,* **Sunday clothes** *npl* vestido *m* de domingo **Sunday school** *n* REL ≈ catequesis *f inv*

sun deck *n* **1.** (*on ship*) cubierta *f* superior **2.** *Am* (*balcony*) solario *m* **sundial** *n* reloj *m* de sol **sundown** *n Am, Aus s.* **sunset** **sun-dried** *adj* secado, -a al sol

sundry ['sʌndri] *adj* varios, -as; **all and ~** *inf* todo el mundo

sunflower ['sʌnˌflaʊəʳ, *Am:* -ˌflaʊɚ] *n* girasol *m,* maravilla *f Chile*

sunflower oil *n* aceite *m* de girasol **sunflower seed** *n* pipa *f*

sung [sʌŋ] *pp of* **sing**

sunglasses ['sʌnˌglɑ:sɪz, *Am:* 'sʌnˌglæsɪs] *npl* gafas *fpl* de sol **sunhat** *n* pamela *f*

sunk [sʌŋk] *pp of* **sink**

sunken ['sʌŋkən] *adj* **1.** (*ship, treasure*) sumergido, -a **2.** (*cheeks, eyes*) hundido, -a

sun lamp *n* **1.** (*ultraviolet*) lámpara *f* de rayos UVA **2.** CINE foco *m*

sunlight ['sʌnlaɪt] *n no pl* luz *f* del sol

sunlit ['sʌnlɪt] *adj* soleado, -a

sunny ['sʌni] <-ier, -iest> *adj* **1.** (*day*) soleado, -a; **she likes her eggs ~ side up** *Am* le gustan los huevos fritos sólo por un lado **2.** (*personality*) alegre

sun protection factor *n* factor *m* de protección solar **sunray** *n Am* rayo *m* de sol

sunrise ['sʌnraɪz] *n* amanecer *m;* **at ~** al amanecer, al alba

sunrise industry *n* industria *f* del porvenir

sunroof ['sʌnru:f] *n* techo *m* corredizo **sunroom** *n Am* solario *m* **sunscreen** *n* filtro *m* solar

sunset ['sʌnset] *n* puesta *f* de sol; **at ~** al atardecer

sunshade ['sʌnʃeɪd] *n* **1.** (*umbrella*) sombrilla *f* **2.** *Am* (*awning*) toldo *m*

sunshine ['sʌnʃaɪn] *n* **1.** *no pl* (*light*) sol *m;* **in the ~** al sol **2.** *Brit* (*friendly*) nene, -a *m, f;* (*to show irritation*) majo, -a *m, f,* guapo, -a *m, f*

sunspot ['sʌnspɒt, *Am:* -spɑ:t] *n* mancha *f* solar **sunstroke** *n no pl* insolación *f,* asoleada *f Col, Chile, Guat;* **to have ~** tener una insolación

suntan ['sʌntæn] *n* bronceado *m;* **to get a ~** broncearse

suntan cream *n,* **suntan lotion** *n* crema *f* bronceadora

suntanned *adj* bronceado, -a

suntan oil *n* aceite *m* bronceador

suntrap ['sʌntræp] *n Brit, Aus* lugar *m* resguardado y soleado

sun-up ['sʌnʌp] *n Am s.* **sunrise**

sun visor *n* AUTO visera *f* **sun-worshipper** *n iron* fanático, -a *m, f* del sol

sup [sʌp] <-pp-> **I.** *vt Brit* beber **II.** *vi liter* **to ~ on sth** cenar algo

super¹ ['su:pəʳ, *Am:* -pɚ] **I.** *adj inf* genial **II.** *n* AUTO (gasolina *f*) súper *f*

super² *n* **1.** *Brit, Am abbr of* **superintendent** superintendente *mf* **2.** *Aus, inf abbr of* **superannuation** jubilación *f*

superabundant [ˌsu:pərə'bʌndənt] *adj*

superabundante, sobreabundante
superannuated [ˌsuːpərˈænjʊeɪtɪd, *Am:* -jueɪt̬ɪd] *adj iron* anticuado, -a
superannuation [ˈsuːpərˌænjʊˈeɪʃən, *Am:* ˌsuːpərˌænjuˈ-] *n Brit, Aus* **1.** (*payment*) inversión *f* en un plan de pensiones **2.** *no pl* (*pension*) pensión *f* (de jubilación)
superb [suːˈpɜːb, *Am:* səˈpɜːrb] *adj* magnífico, -a
supercharged [ˈsuːpətʃɑːdʒd, *Am:* -pɚtʃɑːrdʒd] *adj* **1.** (*engine*) sobrealimentado, -a **2.** (*atmosphere*) cargado, -a de emotividad
supercharger [ˈsuːpəˌtʃɑːdʒəʳ, *Am:* -pɚˌtʃɑːrdʒɚ] *n* TECH sobrealimentador *m*
supercilious [ˈsuːpəˈsɪlɪəs, *Am:* ˌsuːpɚˈsɪlɪəs] *adj pej* altanero, -a
superego [ˈsuːpəregəʊ, *Am:* ˌsuːpɚˈiːgoʊ] *n* PSYCH superego *m*
superficial [ˌsuːpəˈfɪʃl, *Am:* ˌsuːpɚˈ-] *adj* superficial
superficiality [ˌsuːpəˌfɪʃɪˈæləti, *Am:* -pɚˌfɪʃɪˈælət̬i] *n no pl* superficialidad *f*
superfluous [suːˈpɜːflʊəs, *Am:* -ˈpɜːr-] *adj* superfluo, -a; **to be ~** estar de más
superglue® [ˈsuːpəgluː, *Am:* -pɚ-] *n* superglue® *m;* **to stick like ~ to sb** pegarse a alguien como una lapa
supergrass [ˈsuːpəgrɑːs, *Am:* -pɚgræs] *n Brit, inf* soplón, -ona *m, f*
superhero [ˈsuːpəˌhɪərəʊ, *Am:* -pɚˌ-] <-heroes> *n inf* superhéroe *m*
superhighway [ˌsuːpəˈhaɪweɪ, *Am:* ˈsuːpɚˈ-] *n Am* autopista *f* (de varios carriles)
superhuman [ˌsuːpəˈhjuːmən, *Am:* -pɚˈ-] *adj* sobrehumano, -a
superimpose [ˌsuːpərɪmˈpəʊz, *Am:* -pɚɪmˈpoʊz] *vt* PHOT superponer
superintend [ˌsuːpərɪnˈtend, *Am:* ˌsuːpɚ-] *vt* supervisar
superintendent [ˌsuːpərɪnˈtendənt, *Am:* ˌsuːpɚ-] *n* **1.** (*person in charge: of school, department*) director(a) *m(f)* **2.** *Am* (*of building*) portero, -a *m, f* **3.** *Brit* LAW (*police officer*) comisario, -a *m, f* de policía **4.** *Am* LAW (*head of police department*) superintendente *mf*
superior [suːˈpɪəriəʳ, *Am:* səˈpɪriɚ] **I.** *adj* **1.** (*better, senior*) superior; **to be ~ (to sb/sth)** estar por encima de alguien/algo **2.** (*arrogant*) de superioridad **II.** *n* superior *mf*
superiority [suːˌpɪəriˈɒrəti, *Am:* səˌpɪriˈɔːrət̬i] *n no pl* superioridad *f*
superiority complex *n inf* complejo *m* de superioridad
superlative [suːˈpɜːlətɪv, *Am:* səˈpɜːrlət̬ɪv] **I.** *adj* **1.** (*best*) excepcional **2.** LING superlativo, -a **II.** *n* LING superlativo *m*
superman [ˈsuːpəmæn, *Am:* -pɚ-] *n* superhombre *m;* CINE Supermán *m*
supermarket [ˈsuːpəmɑːkɪt, *Am:* -pɚˌmɑːr-] *n* supermercado *m*
supermarket trolley *n Brit* carrito *m* de supermercado
supermodel [ˈsuːpəˌmɒdəl, *Am:* ˈsuːpɚˌmɑːdəl] *n* supermodelo *f*
supernatural [ˌsuːpəˈnætʃərəl, *Am:* -pɚˈnætʃɚəl] **I.** *adj* sobrenatural **II.** *n* **the ~** lo sobrenatural
supernumerary [ˌsuːpəˈnjuːmərəri, *Am:* -pɚˈnuːmərer-] **I.** *adj form* supernumerario, -a **II.** <-ies> *n form* supernumerario, -a *m, f;* THEAT figurante *mf*
superpower [ˌsuːpəˈpaʊəʳ, *Am:* ˈsuːpɚˌpaʊɚ] *n* POL superpotencia *f*
superscript [ˈsuːpəskrɪpt, *Am:* -pɚ-] *n no pl* TYPO superíndice *m*
supersede [ˌsuːpəˈsiːd, *Am:* -pɚˈ-] *vt* sustituir
supersonic [ˌsuːpəˈsɒnɪk, *Am:* -pɚˈsɑːnɪk] *adj* AVIAT supersónico, -a
superstar [ˈsuːpəstɑʳ, *Am:* ˈsuːpɚstɑːr] *n* superestrella *f*
superstition [ˌsuːpəˈstɪʃən, *Am:* -pɚˈ-] *n* superstición *f*
superstitious [ˌsuːpəˈstɪʃəs, *Am:* -pɚˈ-] *adj* supersticioso, -a
superstore [ˈsuːpəstɔːʳ, *Am:* -pɚstɔːr] *n* hipermercado *m*
superstructure [ˈsuːpəstrʌktʃəʳ, *Am:* -pɚˌstrʌktʃɚ] *n* superestructura *f*
supertanker [ˈsuːpəˌtæŋkəʳ, *Am:* -pɚˌtæŋkɚ] *n* superpetrolero *m*
supervene [ˌsuːpəˈviːn, *Am:* -pɚˈ-] *vi form* sobrevenir
supervise [ˈsuːpəvaɪz, *Am:* -pɚ-] *vt* (*watch over*) supervisar; (*thesis*) dirigir
supervision [ˌsuːpəˈvɪʒən, *Am:* -pɚˈ-] *n no pl* supervisión *f;* **under the ~ of sb** bajo la supervisión de alguien
supervisor [ˌsuːpəˈvaɪzəʳ, *Am:* ˈsuːpɚvaɪzɚ] *n* **1.** (*person in charge*) supervisor(a) *m(f)* **2.** UNIV director(a) *m(f)* de tesis **3.** *Am* POL alcalde, -esa *m, f*
supervisory [ˌsuːpəˈvaɪzəri, *Am:* -pɚˈvaɪzɚ-] *adj* de supervisor
supine [ˈsuːpaɪn, *Am:* suːˈ-] **I.** *adj* **1.** (*lying down*) supino, -a; **to be ~** estar tumbado de espaldas **2.** (*weak*) lánguido, -a **II.** *adv* **to lie ~** estar tumbado de espaldas
supper [ˈsʌpəʳ, *Am:* -ɚ] *n* cena *f;* **to have ~** cenar
suppertime *n no pl* hora *f* de cenar
supplant [səˈplɑːnt, *Am:* -ˈplænt] *vt* sustituir
supple [ˈsʌpl] *adj* (*person*) ágil; (*leather, skin*) flexible
supplement [ˈsʌplɪmənt, *Am:* -lə-] **I.** *n* **1.** (*something extra*) complemento *m* **2.** (*part of newspaper*) suplemento *m* **3.** (*of book*) apéndice *m* **II.** *vt* complementar
supplementary [ˌsʌplɪˈmentəri, *Am:* -ləˈment̬ɚi] *adj* adicional, suplementario, -a
suppleness [ˈsʌplnɪs] *n* (*person*) agilidad *f;* (*of leather, skin*) flexibilidad *f*
supplicant [ˈsʌplɪkənt, *Am:* -lə-] *n* suplicante *mf*
supplication [ˌsʌplɪˈkeɪʃən, *Am:* -ləˈ-] *n* súplica *f*

S

supplier [sə'plaɪəʳ, *Am:* -ɚ] *n* proveedor(a) *m(f)*

supply [sə'plaɪ] **I.** <-ie-> *vt* **1.** (*provide: electricity, food, money*) suministrar; (*information*) proporcionar, facilitar; **to be accused of ~ing drugs** ser acusado de tráfico de drogas **2.** COM proveer **II.** *n* **1.** (*act of providing: of electricity, water*) suministro *m* **2.** *no pl* ECON oferta *f;* **~ and demand** oferta y demanda; **to be in short ~** escasear

supply-side economics [sə'plaɪsaɪd ˌiːkə'nɒmɪks, *Am:* -'nɑːmɪks] *npl* economía *f* de la oferta **supply teacher** *n Brit, Aus* suplente *mf*

support [sə'pɔːt, *Am:* -'pɔːrt] **I.** *vt* **1.** (*hold up: roof*) sostener; (*weight*) aguantar, resistir; **to ~ oneself on sth** apoyarse en algo **2.** (*provide for*) mantener; **to ~ four children** mantener a cuatro hijos; **to ~ oneself** ganarse la vida **3.** (*provide with money*) financiar **4.** (*encourage*) apoyar **5.** *Brit* SPORTS (*follow*) ser un seguidor de **6.** (*show to be true*) confirmar **II.** *n* **1.** *no pl* (*backing, help*) apoyo *m;* **to give sb moral ~** darle apoyo moral a alguien **2.** (*structure*) soporte *m; fig* (*person*) sostén *m* **3.** FIN ayuda económica **4.** (*knee protector*) protector *m;* **~ stockings** medias *fpl* elásticas **5.** (*confirmation*) confirmación *f;* **to lend ~ to sth** respaldar algo; **in ~ of sth** en apoyo de algo

supporter *n* **1.** (*of cause, candidate*) partidario, -a *m, f* **2.** *Brit* SPORTS (*fan*) seguidor(a) *m(f)*

supporting *adj Brit* (*film, role*) secundario, -a

supportive [sə'pɔːtɪv, *Am:* -'pɔːrt̬ɪv] *adj* comprensivo, -a; **to be ~ of sth/sb** apoyar algo/a alguien

suppose [sə'pəʊz, *Am:* -'poʊz] *vt* **1.** suponer; **to ~ (that) ...** suponer que...; **I ~ not/so** supongo que no/que sí; **I don't ~ so** supongo que no; **let's ~ that** en el caso de que +*subj* **2.** (*believe, think*) creer **3.** (*obligation*) **to be ~d to do sth** tener que hacer algo; **he was ~d to collect the money** tenía que ir a recoger el dinero; **you are not ~d to know that** no deberías saber eso **4.** (*opinion*) **the book is ~d to be very good** dicen que el libro es muy bueno; **she is ~d to be intelligent** dicen que es inteligente

supposed *adj* (*killer*) presunto, -a; (*date*) supuesto, -a

supposedly [sə'pəʊzɪdli, *Am:* -'poʊ-] *adv* supuestamente

supposing *conj* **~ that ...** suponiendo que...

supposition [ˌsʌpə'zɪʃən] *n* suposición *f*

suppository [sə'pɒzɪtəri, *Am:* -'pɑːzətɔːri] <-ies> *n* supositorio *m*

suppress [sə'pres] *vt* **1.** (*criticism, revolt, terrorism*) reprimir, sofocar **2.** (*sneeze, yawn, emotion*) reprimir; (*evidence, information*) ocultar **3.** MED inhibir

suppression [sə'preʃən] *n no pl* **1.** (*of criticism, revolt*) represión *f* **2.** (*of anger, emotion*) represión *f;* (*of evidence*) ocultación *f* **3.** MED inhibición *f* **4.** PSYCH (*of memories*) represión *f*

suppurate ['sʌpjʊreɪt] *vi* MED supurar

supremacy [sʊ'preməsi, *Am:* sə'-] *n no pl* supremacía *f*

supreme [suː'priːm, *Am:* sə'-] **I.** *adj* **1.** (*authority*) supremo, -a; (*commander*) en jefe; **Supreme Court** Tribunal *m* Supremo **2.** (*achievement, sacrifice*) mayor; **to show ~ courage** mostrar una gran valentía **II.** *adv* **to reign ~** estar en la cumbre, no tener ningún rival

surcharge ['sɜːtʃɑːdʒ, *Am:* 'sɜːrtʃɑːrdʒ] **I.** *n* recargo *m* **II.** *vt* aplicar un recargo a

sure [ʃʊəʳ, *Am:* ʃʊr] **I.** *adj* **1.** (*certain*) seguro, -a; **to be ~ of sth** estar seguro de algo; **to be ~ (that) ...** estar seguro de que...; **to make ~ (that) ...** asegurarse de que...; **(not) to be ~ if ...** (no) estar seguro de si...; **she is ~ to come** vendrá seguro; **are you ~ you won't come?** ¿estás seguro de que no vendrás?; **I'm not ~ why/how** no sé muy bien por qué/cómo; **~ thing!** *Am* ¡claro!; **for ~** seguro **2.** (*confident*) **to be ~ of oneself** estar seguro de sí mismo **II.** *adv* seguro; **~ I will!** *Am, inf* ¡seguro!; **for ~** a ciencia cierta; **~ enough** en efecto ►**as ~ as I'm standing here** como me llamo...

surefooted [ˌʃɔː'fʊtɪd, *Am:* ʃʊrˌfʊːt̬ɪd] *adj* **1.** (*when walking, climbing*) de pie firme **2.** (*confident*) seguro, -a de sí mismo, -a

surely ['ʃɔːli, *Am:* 'ʃʊrli] *adv* **1.** (*certainly*) sin duda **2.** (*to show astonishment*) por supuesto; **~ you don't expect me to believe that?** ¿no esperarás que me lo crea? **3.** *Am* (*yes, certainly*) ¡claro!

surety ['ʃʊərəti, *Am:* 'ʃʊrət̬i] <-ies> *n* LAW **1.** (*person*) fiador(a) *m(f);* **to stand ~ (for sb)** ser fiador de alguien **2.** (*guarantee*) fianza *f*

surf [sɜːf, *Am:* sɜːrf] **I.** *n* olas *fpl* **II.** *vi* SPORTS hacer surf **III.** *vt* INFOR **to ~ the internet** navegar por internet

surface ['sɜːfɪs, *Am:* 'sɜːr-] **I.** *n* superficie *f;* **on the ~** *fig* a primera vista; **to scratch the ~ of sth** tratar algo superficialmente [*o* por encima] **II.** *vi* salir a la superficie **III.** *vt* (*road, wall*) revestir; (*with asphalt*) asfaltar

surface mail *n* **by ~** (*land*) por vía terrestre; (*sea*) por vía marítima **surface tension** *n* PHYS tensión *f* superficial **surface-to-air missile** *n* MIL misil *m* tierra-aire

surfboard ['sɜːfbɔːd, *Am:* 'sɜːrfbɔːrd] *n* tabla *f* de surf

surfeit ['sɜːfɪt, *Am:* 'sɜːr-] *n no pl, form* exceso *m*

surfer ['sɜːfəʳ, *Am:* 'sɜːrfɚ] *n* **1.** surfista *mf* **2.** INFOR internauta *mf*

surfing ['sɜːfɪŋ, *Am:* 'sɜːr-] *n no pl* surf *m*

surge [sɜːdʒ, *Am:* sɜːrdʒ] **I.** *vi* **1.** (*move forward*) abalanzarse; (*waves*) levantarse **2.** (*increase*) aumentar vertiginosamente **II.** *n* (*of waves*) oleaje *m;* (*of anger*) arranque *m;* (*of indignation*) ola *f;* (*of price, support*) aumento *m* repentino; **power ~** sobrecarga *f*

surgeon ['sɜːdʒən, *Am:* 'sɜːr-] *n* cirujano, -a

m, f

surgery ['sɜːdʒəri, *Am:* 'sɜːr-] *n* **1.** *Brit, Aus* (*medical practice*) consulta *f;* **to hold a ~** tener consulta; **~hours** horario *m* de consulta **2.** *no pl* (*medical operation*) cirugía *f;* **to perform ~** practicar una intervención quirúrgica; **to undergo ~** someterse a una intervención quirúrgica **3.** *Brit* POL *sesión durante la que un parlamentario atiende las consultas de sus electores*

surgical ['sɜːdʒɪkl, *Am:* 'sɜːr-] *adj* (*procedure*) quirúrgico, -a; (*collar, stocking*) ortopédico, -a

Surinam(e) ['sʊəˌnæm, *Am:* ˌsʊrɪ'nɑːm] *n* Surinam *m*

Surinamese [ˌsʊənæ'miːz] **I.** *adj* surinamés, -esa **II.** *n* surinamés, -esa *m, f*

surly ['sɜːli, *Am:* 'sɜːr-] <-ier, -iest> *adj* hosco, -a

surmise ['sɜːmaɪz, *Am:* sɚ'maɪz] *vt form* conjeturar

surmount [sə'maʊnt, *Am:* sɚ'-] *vt* **1.** (*overcome*) superar **2.** *form* (*be on top*) coronar

surname ['sɜːneɪm, *Am:* 'sɜːr-] *n* apellido *m*

surpass [sə'pɑːs, *Am:* sɚ'pæs] *vt* sobrepasar; **to ~ oneself** superarse

surplus ['sɜːpləs, *Am:* 'sɜːr-] **I.** *n* (*of product*) excedente *m;* FIN superávit *m* **II.** *adj* sobrante; **to be ~ to requirements** *Brit* estar de más

surprise [sə'praɪz, *Am:* sɚ'-] **I.** *n* sorpresa *f;* **in ~** con sorpresa; **to sb's ~** para sorpresa de alguien **II.** *vt* sorprender; **it ~d her that ...** le sorprendió que... *+subj;* **to ~ sb doing sth** sorprender a alguien haciendo algo

surprised *adj* sorprendido, -a

surprising *adj* sorprendente, sorpresivo, -a *AmL*

surprisingly *adv* sorprendentemente

surreal [sə'rɪəl, *Am:* sə'riːəl] *adj* surrealista

surrealism [sə'rɪəlɪzəm, *Am:* -'riːə-] *n* ART surrealismo *m*

surrealist [sə'rɪəlɪst, *Am:* -'riːə-] ART **I.** *n* surrealista *mf* **II.** *adj* surrealista

surrender [sə'rendəʳ, *Am:* -dɚ] **I.** *vi* rendirse; **to ~ to sb** entregarse a alguien **II.** *vt form* entregar **III.** *n* **1.** (*giving up*) rendición *f* **2.** *no pl, form* (*of document*) entrega *f*

surreptitious [ˌsʌrəp'tɪʃəs, *Am:* ˌsɜːr-] *adj* subrepticio, -a, furtivo, -a

surrogacy ['sʌrəgəsi] *n no pl* alquiler *m* de madres

surrogate ['sʌrəgɪt, *Am:* 'sɜːr-] **I.** *adj* (*substitute*) sucedáneo, -a **II.** *n* sustituto, -a *m, f*

surrogate mother *n* madre *f* de alquiler

surround [sə'raʊnd] **I.** *vt* rodear **II.** *n* (*frame*) marco *m*

surrounding *adj* de alrededor

surroundings *npl* alrededores *mpl*

surtax ['sɜːtæks, *Am:* 'sɜːr-] *n* FIN, POL sobretasa *f*

surveillance [sɜː'veɪləns, *Am:* sɚ'-] *n no pl* vigilancia *f;* **to be under ~** estar bajo vigilancia

survey [sə'veɪ, *Am:* sɚ'-] **I.** *vt* **1.** (*research*) investigar **2.** (*look at carefully*) contemplar **3.** *Brit* (*examine*) examinar **4.** GEO medir **5.** (*poll*) encuestar **II.** *n* **1.** (*poll*) encuesta *f* **2.** (*report*) informe *m* **3.** (*examination*) examen *m* **4.** GEO medición *f*

surveyor [sə'veɪəʳ, *Am:* sɚ'veɪɚ] *n* **1.** GEO topógrafo, -a *m, f* **2.** *Brit* (*property assessor*) tasador(a) *m(f)*

survival [sə'vaɪvl, *Am:* sɚ'-] *n* **1.** *no pl* supervivencia *f* **2.** (*relic*) reliquia *f* ►**the ~ of the fittest** la ley del más fuerte

survive [sə'vaɪv, *Am:* sɚ'-] **I.** *vi* (*stay alive: person*) sobrevivir; (*book*) conservarse; **to ~ on sth** *inf* vivir [*o* alimentarse] a base de algo **II.** *vt* sobrevivir a; **to ~ an accident** salir con vida de un accidente

surviving *adj* superviviente

survivor [sə'vaɪvəʳ, *Am:* sɚ'vaɪvɚ] *n* superviviente *mf*

susceptible [sə'septəbl] *adj* susceptible; MED propenso, -a

suspect¹ [sə'spekt] *vt* **1.** (*think likely*) sospechar, imaginar; **to ~ sth** sospechar [*o* imaginarse] algo **2.** (*consider guilty*) sospechar de, cachar *Chile;* **to ~ sb's motives** dudar de los motivos de alguien

suspect² ['sʌspekt] **I.** *n* sospechoso, -a *m, f* **II.** *adj* sospechoso, -a

suspend [sə'spend] *vt* **1.** (*stop temporarily*) suspender; (*judgement, proceedings*) posponer **2.** SCHOOL, UNIV expulsar temporalmente **3.** (*hang*) colgar

suspender [sə'spendəʳ, *Am:* -dɚ] *n* **1.** *Brit* (*strap*) liga *f* **2.** *pl, Am* (*braces*) tirantes *mpl,* suspensores *mpl AmL,* calzonarias *fpl Col*

suspender belt *n Brit, Aus* liguero *m,* portaligas *m inv AmL*

suspense [sə'spens] *n* **1.** (*uncertainty*) incertidumbre *f;* **to keep sb in ~** mantener a alguien sobre ascuas [*o* en vilo] **2.** CINE suspense *m*

suspension [sə'spentʃən] *n no pl* **1.** suspensión *f* **2.** SCHOOL, UNIV expulsión *f* temporal

suspension bridge *n* puente *m* colgante

suspension points *npl* puntos *mpl* suspensivos

suspicion [sə'spɪʃən] *n* **1.** (*belief*) sospecha *f;* **to arrest sb on ~ of sth** arrestar a alguien como sospechoso de algo; **to be above ~** estar por encima de toda sospecha **2.** *no pl* (*mistrust*) recelo *m,* desconfianza *f* **3.** (*small amount*) pizca *f*

suspicious [sə'spɪʃəs] *adj* **1.** (*arousing suspicion*) sospechoso, -a, emponchado, -a *Arg, Bol, Perú* **2.** (*lacking trust*) desconfiado, -a

◆**suss out** [sʌs] *vt Brit, Aus, inf* calar

sustain [sə'steɪn] *vt* **1.** (*maintain*) sostener **2.** (*withstand*) aguantar **3.** (*uphold: conviction*) confirmar; (*objection*) admitir

sustainable [sə'steɪnəbl] *adj* sostenible

sustained [sə'steɪnd] *adj* continuo, -a; (*applause*) prolongado, -a

sustenance ['sʌstɪnənts, *Am:* -tnəns] *n no*

pl sustento *m;* **to give sb ~** sustentar a alguien
suture ['su:tʃəʳ, *Am:* -tʃɚ] MED **I.** *n* (*stitch*) sutura *f;* (*thread*) hilo *m* de sutura **II.** *vt* suturar
svelte [svelt] *adj* esbelto, -a
SW [ˌes'dʌblju:] *abbr of* **southwest** SO
swab [swɒb, *Am:* swɑ:b] **I.** *n* **1.** MED (*pad*) tapón *m;* (*for examination*) frotis *m inv* **2.** NAUT fregona *f* **II.** <-bb-> *vt* **1.** MED limpiar (con algodón) **2.** (*wash*) fregar
swaddle ['swɒdl, *Am:* 'swɑ:dl] *vt* envolver
swaddling clothes *n* pañales *mpl*
swagger ['swægəʳ, *Am:* -ɚ] **I.** *vi* pavonearse **II.** *n no pl* arrogancia *f*
swallow¹ ['swɒləʊ, *Am:* 'swɑ:loʊ] **I.** *vt* tragar, engullir, tambar *Ecua, inf* **II.** *vi* tragar saliva **III.** *n* trago *m*
◆**swallow down** *vt* tragar
◆**swallow up** *vt* (*absorb*) tragar
swallow² ['swɒləʊ, *Am:* 'swɑ:loʊ] *n* ZOOL golondrina *f* ►**one ~ doesn't make a summer** *prov* una golondrina no hace verano *prov*
swam [swæm] *vi pt of* **swim**
swamp [swɒmp, *Am:* swɑ:mp] **I.** *n* pantano *m,* suampo *m AmC,* wampa *f Méx* **II.** *vt* (*flood*) inundar; **to ~ sb** (**with sth**) abrumar a alguien (con algo); **to be ~ed with sth** estar agobiado de algo
swamp fever *n no pl* MED paludismo *m,* fiebre *f* palúdica
swampland ['swɒmpˌlænd, *Am:* 'swɑ:mp-lænd] *n* pantano *m*
swampy ['swɒmpi, *Am:* 'swɑ:mp-] <-ier, -iest> *adj* pantanoso, -a
swan [swɒn, *Am:* swɑ:n] **I.** *n* cisne *m* **II.** <-nn-> *vi Brit, Aus, inf* **to ~ about** pavonearse
swank [swæŋk] **I.** *vi inf* fanfarronear **II.** *n no pl, inf* fanfarronada *f*
swanky ['swæŋki] *adj inf* **1.** (*luxurious*) pijo, -a **2.** (*boastful*) fanfarrón, -ona
swansong *n* canto *m* del cisne
swap [swɒp, *Am:* swɑ:p] **I.** <-pp-> *vt* cambiar; **to ~ sth** (**for sth**) cambiar algo (por algo); **to ~ sth with sb** cambiarle algo a alguien **II.** <-pp-> *vi* cambiar **III.** *n* cambio *m*
swarm [swɔ:m, *Am:* swɔ:rm] **I.** *vi* **1.** ZOOL, BIO (*bees*) enjambrar **2.** (*move in large group*) aglomerarse **3.** (*be full*) **to be ~ing with sth** estar plagado [*o* atestado] de algo **II.** *n* **1.** (*of bees*) enjambre *m* **2.** *fig* (*of people*) multitud *f*
swarthy ['swɔ:ði, *Am:* 'swɔ:r-] <-ier, -iest> *adj* moreno, -a
swashbuckling ['swɒʃˌbʌklɪŋ, *Am:* 'swɑ:ʃˌ-] *adj* de capa y espada
swastika ['swɒstɪkə, *Am:* 'swɑ:stɪ-] *n* cruz *f* gamada
swat [swɒt, *Am:* swɑ:t] <-tt-> *vt* (*insect*) aplastar
swatch [swɒtʃ, *Am:* swɑ:tʃ] *n* (*sample*) muestra *f;* (*sample book*) muestrario *m*
swathe [sweɪð] **I.** *vt* (*wrap round*) envolver; (*with bandages*) vendar **II.** *n* **1.** (*long strip*) ringlera *f* **2.** (*area*) extensión *f*
sway [sweɪ] **I.** *vi* balancearse **II.** *vt* **1.** (*move from side to side*) balancear **2.** (*persuade*) persuadir **III.** *n no pl* **1.** (*influence*) influencia *f;* **under the ~ of sb/sth** bajo el influjo de alguien/algo **2.** *form* (*control*) control *m;* **to hold ~ over sth/sb** dominar algo/a alguien
Swazi ['swɑ:zi] **I.** *adj* swazilandés, -esa **II.** *n* swazilandés, -esa *m, f*
Swaziland ['swɑ:zilænd] *n* Swazilandia *f*
swear [sweəʳ, *Am:* swer] <swore, sworn> **I.** *vi* **1.** (*take oath*) jurar; **to ~ on the Bible** jurar sobre la Biblia; **I couldn't ~ to it** *inf* no pondría la mano en el fuego **2.** (*curse*) decir palabrotas **II.** *vt* jurar; **to ~ blind** *Brit, inf* jurar y perjurar; **they swore us to secrecy** nos hicieron jurar que guardaríamos el secreto
◆**swear by** *vt* **to ~ sth** tener una fe ciega a algo
◆**swear in** *vt* LAW **to ~ sb** tomar juramento a alguien
◆**swear off** *vt* **to ~ sth** renunciar a algo
swearing *n* palabrotas *mpl*
swearword ['sweəwɜ:d, *Am:* 'swerwɜ:rd] *n* taco *m,* brulote *m AmS,* garabato *m Chile*
sweat [swet] **I.** *n no pl* **1.** (*perspiration*) sudor *m;* **to get into a ~** empezar a sudar; **to be/get in a ~** (**about sth**) *fig, inf* preocuparse (por algo) **2.** (*effort*) esfuerzo *m;* **no ~** *inf* ningún problema **II.** *vi* (*perspire*) sudar; **to ~ with sth** sudar de algo **III.** *vt* sudar
◆**sweat out** *vt* **to sweat it out** (*do physical exercise*) sudar la gota gorda; (*suffer*) pasar un mal rato
sweat band *n* (*for head*) cinta *f;* (*for wrists*) muñequera *f*
sweated *adj* explotado, -a
sweater ['swetəʳ, *Am:* 'sweţɚ] *n* jersey *m*
sweatshirt ['swetʃɜ:t, *Am:* -ʃɜ:rt] *n* sudadera *f*
sweatshop ['swetʃɒp, *Am:* -ʃɑ:p] *n pej: fábrica donde se explota a los trabajadores*
sweaty ['sweti, *Am:* 'sweţ-] <-ier, -iest> *adj* sudado, -a
swede [swi:d] *n Brit, Aus* GASTR colinabo *m*
Swede [swi:d] *n* sueco, -a *m, f*
Sweden ['swi:dn] *n* GEO Suecia *f*
Swedish ['swi:dɪʃ] **I.** *adj* sueco, -a **II.** *n* **1.** (*person*) sueco, -a *m, f* **2.** LING Sueco *m*
sweep [swi:p] <swept, swept> **I.** *n* **1.** *no pl* (*cleaning action*) barrida *f;* **to give sth a ~** barrer algo **2.** (*chimney cleaner*) deshollinador(a) *m(f)* **3.** (*movement*) **with a ~ of her arm** con un amplio movimiento del brazo **4.** (*area*) extensión *f* **5.** (*range: of weapons, telescope*) alcance *m* **6.** (*search*) **to make a ~ of an area** rastrear una zona **7.** *inf* (*bet*) *s.* **sweepstake** ►**to make a clean ~** hacer tabla rasa **II.** *vt* **1.** (*clean with broom: floor*) barrer; (*chimney*) deshollinar **2.** (*remove*) quitar **3.** (*search*) rastrear **4.** *Am, inf* (*win*) ganar de manera aplastante ►**she swept him off his**

feet se enamoró de ella perdidamente **III.** *vi* **1.** (*clean with broom*) barrer **2.** (*move*) **to ~ into a room** entrar en una habitación majestuosamente; **to ~ into power** llegar al poder fácilmente **3.** (*look round*) mirar alrededor **4.** (*follow path*) **the road ~s round the lake** la carretera rodea el lago **5.** (*extend*) extenderse

◆**sweep aside** *vt* **1.** (*cause to move*) apartar **2.** (*dismiss*) desechar

◆**sweep away** *vt* **1.** (*remove*) erradicar **2.** (*carry away*) arrastrar

◆**sweep out** *vt* barrer

◆**sweep up** *vt* **1.** (*brush*) barrer **2.** (*gather*) recoger

sweeper *n* **1.** (*device*) barredera *f* **2.** (*person*) barrendero, -a *m, f*

sweeping **I.** *adj* (*gesture*) amplio, -a; (*victory*) aplastante **II.** *npl* basura *f*; **the ~s of society** la escoria de la sociedad

sweepstake ['swi:psteɪk] *n apuesta, especialmente en carreras de caballos, en la que la persona que gana se lleva el dinero apostado por todos los demás*

sweet [swi:t] **I.** <-er, -est> *adj* **1.** (*like sugar*) dulce **2.** (*pleasant*) agradable; (*sound*) melodioso -a; **to go one's own ~ way** hacer lo que a uno le da la gana **3.** (*cute*) mono, -a **4.** (*kind: smile*) encantador(a); (*person*) amable; **to keep sb ~** tener contento a alguien; **to be ~ on sb** estar enamorado de alguien **II.** *n* **1.** *Brit, Aus* (*candy*) caramelo *m*, dulce *m Chile* **2.** *Brit, Aus* (*dessert*) postre *m* **3.** *inf* (*term of endearment*) cariño *m*

sweet-and-sour [ˌswi:tən'saʊəʳ, *Am:* -ˌsaʊɚ] *adj* agridulce

sweetbread ['swi:tbred] *n pl* GASTR lechecillas *fpl*

sweet chestnut *n* (*fruit*) castaña *f* (dulce); (*tree*) castaño *m* (dulce)

sweetcorn ['swi:tkɔ:n, *Am:* -kɔ:rn] *n Am* maíz *m* (tierno)

sweeten ['swi:tən] *vt* endulzar; **to ~ sb up** ablandar a alguien

sweetener *n* **1.** GASTR sacarina *f* **2.** *inf* (*incentive*) incentivo *m*

sweetheart ['swi:thɑ:t, *Am:* -hɑ:rt] *n* **1.** (*kind person*) encanto *m* **2.** (*term of endearment*) cariño *m* **3.** (*boyfriend, girlfriend*) novio, -a *m, f*

sweetness *n no pl* dulzor *m*; **to be all ~ and light** *fig* estar de lo más amable

sweet pea *n* guisante *m* de olor **sweet potato** *n* boniato *m* **sweet-talk** *vt* camelar **sweet william** *n* minutisa *f*

swell [swel] <swelled, swollen *o* swelled> **I.** *vt* **1.** (*size*) hinchar **2.** (*number*) engrosar **II.** *vi* **1.** (*get bigger*) hincharse **2.** (*get louder: sound*) subir **3.** (*increase*) aumentar **III.** *n no pl* (*of sea*) oleaje *m*; **a heavy ~** un fuerte oleaje **IV.** <-er, -est> *adj Am, inf* genial

swellhead ['swelhed] *n Am* engreído, -a *m, f*

swelling *n* hinchazón *m*

swelter ['sweltəʳ, *Am:* -ţɚ] *vi* morirse de calor

sweltering *adj* (*heat, weather*) sofocante

swept [swept] *vt, vi pt of* **sweep**

swerve [swɜ:v, *Am:* swɜ:rv] **I.** *vi* **1.** (*car*) virar bruscamente; (*person*) hurtar el cuerpo **2.** (*not uphold*) **to ~ from sth** desviarse de algo **II.** *n* (*of car*) viraje *m* brusco; (*of person*) finta *f*

swift¹ [swɪft] *adj* (*fast-moving*) rápido, -a; (*occurring quickly*) súbito, -a

swift² [swɪft] *n* ZOOL vencejo *m*

swiftly *adv* rápidamente

swiftness *n no pl* rapidez *f*

swig [swɪg] **I.** <-gg-> *vt inf* beber a tragos **II.** *n inf* trago *m*; **to take a ~** tomar un trago

swill [swɪl] **I.** *n no pl* **1.** (*pig feed*) comida *f* para cerdos; *fig, iron* bazofia *f* **2.** (*rinse*) enjuague *m* **II.** *vt* **1.** (*swirl: liquid*) remover **2.** (*rinse*) baldear **3.** (*drink*) beber a tragos

◆**swill down** *vt inf* **to swill sth down** beber algo a tragos

swim [swɪm] **I.** <swam, swum> *vi* **1.** (*in water*) nadar; **the meat was ~ming in grease** *pej* la carne estaba cubierta de grasa **2.** (*be full of water*) estar inundado, -a; **to ~ with tears** deshacerse en un mar de lágrimas **3.** (*whirl*) **her head was ~ming** la cabeza le daba vueltas **II.** <swam *Aus:* swum, swum> *vt* **1.** (*cross*) cruzar a nado **2.** (*do*) **to ~ a few strokes** dar cuatro brazadas **III.** *n* nado *m*; **I'm going to have a ~** voy a nadar ▸**to be in the ~** estar en la onda

swimmer ['swɪməʳ, *Am:* -ɚ] *n* **1.** (*person*) nadador(a) *m(f)* **2.** *pl, Aus, inf* (*swimming costume*) bañador *m*

swimming *n no pl* natación *f*

swimming bath *n* piscina *f*, alberca *f Méx*, pileta *f Arg* **swimming cap** *n* gorro *m* de natación **swimming costume** *n Brit, Aus* traje *m* de baño

swimmingly *adv inf* **to go ~** ir sobre ruedas

swimming pool *n* piscina *f*, alberca *f Méx*, pileta *f Arg* **swimming trunks** *npl* traje *m* de baño (de caballero)

swimsuit ['swɪmsu:t] *n Am* bañador *m*

swindle ['swɪndl] **I.** *vt* estafar **II.** *n* estafa *f*

swindler ['swɪndləʳ, *Am:* -ɚ] *n pej* timador(a) *m(f)*

swine [swaɪn] *n* **1.** *liter* (*pig*) cerdo *m* **2.** <-(s)> *pej, inf* (*mean person*) cabrón, -ona *m, f*

swing [swɪŋ] **I.** *n* **1.** (*movement*) vaivén *m* **2.** (*punch*) golpe *m*; **to take a ~ at sb** (intentar) pegar a alguien **3.** (*hanging seat*) columpio *m*, burro *m AmC* **4.** (*sharp change*) cambio *m* en redondo; POL viraje *m* **5.** *Am* (*quick trip*) viaje *m* **6.** *no pl* MUS swing *m* ▸**what you lose on the ~s, you gain on the roundabouts** *Brit, prov* lo que se pierde por un lado, se gana por otro; **to get (back) into the ~ of things** *inf* cogerle el tranquillo a algo; **to go with a ~** *Brit, inf* (*party*) estar muy animado

S

II. <swung, swung> *vi* **1.** (*move back and forth*) oscilar; (*move circularly*) dar vueltas **2.** (*hit*) **to ~ at sb** (intentar) dar un golpe a alguien **3.** (*on hanging seat*) columpiarse **4.** (*alter*) cambiar; **to ~ between two things** oscilar entre dos cosas **5.** (*be exciting*) ser animado **6.** *Am* (*hang*) colgar **III.** <swung, swung> *vt* **1.** (*move back and forth*) balancear, chilinguear *Col* **2.** *inf* (*influence*) influir
◆**swing around** *vi,* **swing round** *vi* dar un giro

swing bridge *n* puente *m* giratorio **swing door** *n Brit, Aus* (*door that opens in both directions*) puerta *f* de vaivén; (*door that revolves*) puerta *f* giratoria

swingeing ['swɪndʒɪŋ] *adj Brit* (*cut*) salvaje; (*criticism*) feroz

swinging ['swɪŋɪŋ] *adj inf* (*lively*) con mucha marcha; **the ~ 60s** los alegres sesenta

swinish ['swaɪnɪʃ] *adj pej, inf* bellaco, -a

swipe [swaɪp] **I.** *vt* **1.** *Brit* (*swat*) abofetear **2.** *Am* (*graze: car*) dar un golpe a **3.** *inf* (*steal*) robar **4.** (*pass: card*) pasar **II.** *n* (*blow*) golpe *m; fig* (*criticism*) crítica *f;* **to take a ~ at sth** (*hit*) (intentar) pegar a alguien; (*criticize*) criticar a alguien

swirl [swɜːl, *Am:* swɜːrl] **I.** *vi* arremolinarse **II.** *vt* arremolinar **III.** *n* remolino *m*

swish [swɪʃ] **I.** *vi* (*cane*) silbar; (*dress*) hacer frufrú; (*water*) borbotear **II.** *vt* (*cane*) hacer silbar **III.** <-er, -est> *adj inf* elegante **IV.** *n* (*of cane*) silbido *m;* (*of dress*) frufrú *m*

Swiss [swɪs] **I.** *adj* suizo, -a; **~ German/French** alemán/francés suizo **II.** *n* suizo, -a *m, f*

switch [swɪtʃ] **I.** <-es> *n* **1.** ELEC interruptor *m,* suiche *m Méx* **2.** (*substitution*) remplazamiento *m* **3.** (*change*) cambio *m* **4.** (*thin whip*) látigo *m* **5.** *pl, Am* (*points*) puntos *mpl* **II.** *vi* cambiar; **to ~ with sb** cambiarse con alguien **III.** *vt* cambiar; **to ~ sth for sth** cambiar algo por algo
◆**switch off I.** *vt* (*machine, engine*) apagar; (*water, electricity*) cortar **II.** *vi* **1.** (*machine, engine*) apagarse **2.** (*lose attention*) desconectar
◆**switch on I.** *vt* (*machine, engine*) encender; **to ~ the charm** ponerse encantador **II.** *vi* encenderse
◆**switch over** *vi* cambiar; **to ~ to another channel** poner otro canal
◆**switch round** *vt* cambiar

switchback ['swɪtʃbæk] *n* carretera *f* en zigzag

switchblade ['swɪtʃbleɪd] *n Am* navaja *f* automática

switchboard ['swɪtʃbɔːd, *Am:* -bɔːrd] *n* **1.** ELEC conmutador *m* **2.** TEL centralita *f*

switchboard operator *n* telefonista *mf*

switchman <-men> *n Am* guardagujas *m inv*

switchyard *n Am* patio *m* de maniobras

Switzerland ['swɪtsələnd, *Am:* -sɚlənd] *n* Suiza *f*

swivel ['swɪvəl] **I.** *n* plataforma *f* giratoria **II.** <*Brit:* -ll-, *Am:* -l-> *vt* girar

swivel chair *n* silla *f* giratoria

swizzle stick *n* agitador *m*

swollen ['swəʊlən, *Am:* 'swoʊ-] **I.** *pp of* **swell II.** *adj* hinchado, -a

swollen-headed *adj* engreído, -a

swoon [swuːn] **I.** *vi* **1.** (*be in state of ecstasy*) estar embelesado; **to ~ over sb** derretirse por alguien **2.** *liter* (*faint*) desvanecerse **II.** *n liter* desvanecimiento *m*

swoop [swuːp] **I.** *n* **1.** (*dive*) caída *f* en picado **2.** *inf* (*surprise attack*) redada *f* **II.** *vi* **1.** (*dive*) bajar en picado **2.** *inf* (*make sudden attack*) abatirse; (*police*) hacer una redada

swop [swɒp, *Am:* swɑːp] <-pp-> *vt, vi Brit, Can s.* **swap**

sword [sɔːd, *Am:* sɔːrd] *n* espada *f;* **to draw a ~** desenfundar una espada ►**to have a ~ of Damocles hanging over one's head** tener la espada de Damocles suspendida sobre la cabeza de uno

sword dance *n* danza *f* de las espadas **swordfish** <-(es)> *n* pez *m* espada **swordplay** *n* esgrima *f;* **verbal ~** enfrentamiento *m* dialéctico **swordpoint** *n no pl* **to do sth at ~** hacer algo por obligación

swordsman ['sɔːdzmən, *Am:* 'sɔːrdz-] <-men> *n* **1.** HIST espadachín *m* **2.** (*fencer*) esgrimidor *m*

swordsmanship *n no pl* destreza *f* en el manejo de la espada

swore [swɔː, *Am:* swɔːr] *pt of* **swear**

sworn [swɔːn, *Am:* swɔːrn] **I.** *pp of* **swear II.** *adj* jurado, -a

swot [swɒt, *Am:* swɑːt] <-tt-> *vi Brit, Aus, inf* hacer codos, machetearse *Méx;* **to ~ for an exam** empollar para un examen

swum [swʌm] *pp, a. Aus pt of* **swim**

swung [swʌŋ] *pt, pp of* **swing**

sycamore ['sɪkəmɔːʳ, *Am:* -mɔːr] *n* **1.** *Brit* plátano falso *m* **2.** *Am* plátano *m*

sycophant ['sɪkəfænt, *Am:* -fənt] *n pej* adulador(a) *m(f)*

sycophantic [ˌsɪkəʊ'fæntɪk, *Am:* -t̬ɪk] *adj pej* adulador(a)

syllable ['sɪləbl] *n* sílaba *f;* **stressed/unstressed ~** sílaba tónica/átona; **not a ~** *fig* ni media palabra

syllabus ['sɪləbəs] <-es, *form:* syllabi> *n* (*in general*) plan *m* de estudios; (*for specific subject*) programa *m*

sylph [sɪlf] *n* sílfide *f*

symbiosis [ˌsɪmbɪ'əʊsɪs, *Am:* -'oʊ-] *n no pl* simbiosis *f*

symbiotic [ˌsɪmbɪ'ɒtɪk, *Am:* -'ɑːt̬ɪk] *adj* BIO simbiótico, -a

symbol ['sɪmbl] *n* símbolo *m*

symbolic(al) [sɪm'bɒlɪk(l), *Am:* -'bɑːlɪk-] *adj* simbólico, -a

symbolism ['sɪmbəlɪzəm] *n no pl* simbolismo *m*

symbolize ['sɪmbəlaɪz] *vt* simbolizar
symmetrical [sɪ'metrɪkl] *adj* simétrico, -a
symmetry ['sɪmətri] *n no pl* simetría *f*
sympathetic [ˌsɪmpə'θetɪk, *Am:* -'θet̬-] *adj* **1.**(*understanding*) comprensivo, -a; (*sympathizing*) receptivo, -a; **to lend a ~ ear to sb** estar dispuesto a escuchar a alguien **2.** POL simpatizante; **to be ~ towards sb/sth** apoyar a alguien/algo
sympathize ['sɪmpəθaɪz] *vi* **1.**(*understand*) mostrar comprensión; (*feel compassion for*) compadecerse de **2.**(*agree*) estar de acuerdo; **to ~ with sb/sth** simpatizar con alguien/algo
sympathizer *n* simpatizante *mf*
sympathy ['sɪmpəθi] *n no pl* **1.**(*compassion*) compasión *f*; (*understanding*) comprensión *f*; **you have my deepest ~** le acompaño en el sentimiento **2.**(*solidarity*) solidaridad *f*
symphonic [sɪm'fɒnɪk, *Am:* -'fɑːnɪk] *adj* sinfónico, -a
symphony ['sɪmfəni] *n* **1.**(*piece of music*) sinfonía *f* **2.**(*orchestra*) orquesta *f* sinfónica
symphony concert *n* concierto *m* sinfónico **symphony orchestra** *n* orquesta *f* sinfónica
symposium [sɪm'pəʊziəm, *Am:* -'poʊ-] <-s *o* -sia> *n form* simposio *m*
symptom ['sɪmptəm] *n* síntoma *m*
symptomatic [ˌsɪmptə'mætɪk, *Am:* -'mæt̬-] *adj* sintomático, -a
synagogue ['sɪnəgɒg, *Am:* -gɑːg] *n* sinagoga *f*
synchronize ['sɪŋkrənaɪz] **I.** *vt* sincronizar **II.** *vi* sincronizarse
synchronous ['sɪŋkrənəs] *adj* sincrónico, -a
syncopate ['sɪŋkəpeɪt] *vt* MUS sincopar
syndicate¹ ['sɪndɪkət, *Am:* -dəkɪt] *n* **1.** ECON consorcio *m* **2.** PUBL agencia *f* de noticias
syndicate² ['sɪndɪkeɪt, *Am:* -də-] *vt* **1.** ECON agrupar **2.** PUBL vender
syndication [ˌsɪndɪ'keɪʃən, *Am:* -də'-] *n no pl* **1.** ECON agrupación *f* **2.** PUBL venta *f*
syndrome ['sɪndrəʊm, *Am:* -droʊm] *n* síndrome *m*; **acquired immune deficiency ~** síndrome de la inmunodeficiencia adquirida
synergy ['sɪnədʒi, *Am:* -ɚdʒi] *n no pl* sinergía *f*
synod ['sɪnəd] *n* sínodo *m*
synonym ['sɪnənɪm] *n* sinónimo *m*
synonymous [sɪ'nɒnɪməs] *adj* sinónimo, -a
synopsis [sɪ'næpsɪs] <-es> *n* sinopsis *f inv*
syntactic(al) [sɪn'tæktɪk(əl)] *adj* sintáctico, -a
syntax ['sɪntæks] *n no pl* sintaxis *f inv*
synthesis ['sɪntθəsɪs] <-es> *n* síntesis *f inv*
synthesize ['sɪnθəsaɪz] *vt* sintetizar
synthesizer *n* sintetizador *m*
synthetic [sɪn'θetɪk, *Am:* -'θet̬-] *adj* **1.**(*man-made*) sintético, -a **2.** *pej* (*fake*) artificial
syphilis ['sɪfɪlɪs, *Am:* 'sɪflɪs] *n no pl* sífilis *f inv*
syphilitic [ˌsɪfɪ'lɪtɪk, *Am:* -ə'lɪt̬-] *adj* sifilítico, -a
syphon ['saɪfn] *n* sifón *m*
Syria ['sɪrɪə] *n* Siria *f*
Syrian ['sɪrɪən] **I.** *adj* sirio, -a **II.** *n* sirio, -a *m, f*
syringe [sɪ'rɪndʒ, *Am:* sə'-] **I.** *n* jeringuilla *f* **II.** *vt* **to ~ sb's ears** destaponarle los oídos a alguien
syrup ['sɪrəp] *n no pl* **1.** GASTR almíbar *m*, sirope *m AmC, Col* **2.** MED jarabe *m*; **cough ~** jarabe para la tos
syrupy ['sɪrəpi] *adj pej* empalagoso, -a
system ['sɪstəm] *n* **1.**(*set*) sistema *m*; **music ~** equipo *m* de música **2.**(*method of organization*) método *m*; POL régimen *m* **3.**(*order*) método *m* ▸**to get something out of one's ~** *inf* quitarse algo de encima
systematic [ˌsɪstə'mætɪk, *Am:* -'mæt̬-] *adj* sistemático, -a
systematize ['sɪstəmətaɪz] *vt* sistematizar
system check *n* verificación *f* del sistema **system crash** <-es> *n* fallo *m* en el sistema **system disk** *n* disco *m* del sistema **system error** *n* error *m* en el sistema **system registry** *n* registro *m* del sistema
systems analysis *n* análisis *m inv* de sistemas **systems analyst** *n* analista *mf* de sistemas
system software *n* software *m* de sistema

T

T, t [tiː] *n* T, t *f*; **~ for Tommy** *Brit*, **~ for Tare** *Am* T de Tarragona
t *abbr of* **tonne** t (*Brit: 1,016 kilos; Am: 907 kilos*)
ta [tɑː] *interj Brit, inf* (*thanks*) gracias
TA *n Brit abbr of* **Territorial Army** *ejército voluntario de reservistas británico*
tab [tæb] *n* **1.**(*flap*) solapa *f*; (*on file*) lengüeta *f*; **write-protect ~** INFOR lengüeta *f* protectora **2.**(*label*) etiqueta *f* **3.** *inf* (*bill*) cuenta *f*; **to put sth on the ~** cargar algo en la cuenta **4.** *Am* (*ringpull*) anilla *f* **5.** *Brit, dial* (*cigarette*) cigarrillo *m* **6.** MED **a ~ of acid** una tableta de LSD ▸**to keep ~s on sth/sb** no perder de vista algo/a alguien
tabby ['tæbi] **I.** *adj* atigrado, -a **II.** *n* gato *m* atigrado
tabernacle ['tæbənækl, *Am:* 'tæbɚ-] *n* **1.** *form* (*place*) tabernáculo *m* **2.**(*container*) sagrario *m*
tab key *n* tabulador *m*
table ['teɪbl] **I.** *n* **1.** mesa *f*; **to clear/set the ~** recoger/poner la mesa **2.** MATH tabla *f*; **multiplication ~** tabla de multiplicar **3.**(*list*) lista *f*; **~ of contents** índice *m* ▸**the ~s have turned** han cambiado las tornas **II.** *vt* **1.** *Brit, Aus* (*pro-*

T

pose discussion of) poner sobre la mesa **2.** *Am* (*postpone discussion of*) posponer

tablecloth ['teɪblklɒθ, *Am:* -klɑːθ] *n* mantel *m* **table land** *n* meseta *f* **table linen** *n no pl* mantelería *f* **table manners** *npl* modales *mpl* en la mesa **table mat** *n* salvamanteles *m inv* **tablespoon** *n* **1.** (*spoon*) cucharón *m* **2.** (*amount*) cucharada *f*

tablet ['tæblɪt] *n* **1.** (*pill*) comprimido *m* **2.** (*of stone*) lápida *f;* ~ **of soap** *Brit* pastilla *f* de jabón **3.** *Scot* GASTR dulce *m* de azúcar

table-talk *n* sobremesa *f* **table tennis** *n no pl* ping-pong *m* **tableware** *n no pl, form* servicio *m* de mesa **table wine** *n* vino *m* de mesa

tabloid ['tæblɔɪd] *n* diario *m* sensacionalista; **the** ~ **press** la prensa amarilla

taboo, **tabu** [tə'buː] **I.** *n* tabú *m* **II.** *adj* tabú

tabular ['tæbjʊlə^r, *Am:* -lɚ] *adj form* tabular

tabulate ['tæbjʊleɪt] *vt* disponer en tablas; INFOR tabular

tabulator ['tæbjʊleɪtə^r, *Am:* -t̬ɚ] *n form* tabulador *m*

tachograph ['tækəgrɑːf] *n* tacógrafo *m*

tacit ['tæsɪt] *adj* tácito, -a

taciturn ['tæsɪtɜːn, *Am:* -ətɜːrn] *adj* taciturno, -a, soturno, -a *Ven*

taciturnity [ˌtæsɪ'tɜːnəti, *Am:* -ə'tɜːrnət̬i] *n no pl, form* taciturnidad *f*

tack [tæk] **I.** *n* **1.** (*short nail*) tachuela *f* **2.** *no pl* (*riding gear*) montura *f* **3.** NAUT amura *f* **4.** (*approach*) política *f;* **to try a different** ~ intentar un enfoque distinto **II.** *vt* **1.** (*nail down*) clavar con tachuelas **2.** (*sew loosely*) hilvanar **III.** *vi* NAUT virar

tackle ['tækl] **I.** *vt* **1.** (*in soccer*) entrar a; (*in rugby, US football*) placar **2.** (*deal with: issue*) abordar; (*job*) emprender; (*problem*) atacar; **to** ~ **sb about sth** enfrentarse con alguien por algo **II.** *n no pl* **1.** (*in soccer*) entrada *f;* (*in rugby, US football*) placaje *m* **2.** *Am* (*line position*) atajo *m* **3.** (*equipment*) equipo *m* **4.** NAUT aparejo *m*

tacky ['tæki] <-ier, -iest> *adj* **1.** (*sticky*) pegajoso, -a **2.** *inf* (*showy*) vulgar; (*shoddy*) de mala calidad, de pacotilla *AmL*

tact [tækt] *n no pl* tacto *m*

tactful ['tæktfəl] *adj* discreto, -a

tactic ['tæktɪk] *n* ~(**s**) táctica *f*

tactical ['tæktɪkl] *adj* táctico, -a

tactician [tæk'tɪʃən] *n* táctico, -a *m, f*

tactile ['tæktaɪl, *Am:* -tl] *adj form* táctil

tactless ['tæktləs] *adj* falto, -a de tacto

tactlessness *n no pl* falta *f* de tacto

tad [tæd] *n* **a** ~ un poquitín

tadpole ['tædpəʊl, *Am:* -poʊl] *n* renacuajo *m*

taffeta ['tæfɪtə, *Am:* -t̬ə] *n no pl* tafetán *m*

tag [tæg] **I.** *n* **1.** *a.* INFOR (*label*) etiqueta *f;* (*metal*) herrete *m* **2.** *no pl* (*game*) **to play** ~ jugar al pillapilla **3.** LING **question** ~ cláusula *f* final interrogativa **II.** <-gg-> *vt* (*label*) etiquetar; **to** ~ **sth onto sth** añadir algo a algo

◆**tag along** *vi inf* seguir; **to** ~ **with sb** ir detrás de alguien

tail [teɪl] **I.** *n* **1.** ANAT, AVIAT cola *f;* (*of dog, bull*) rabo *m* **2.** *pl, inf* (*tail coat*) frac *m* **3.** *pl* (*side of coin*) cruz *f* **4.** *inf* (*person*) perseguidor(a) *m(f)* **5.** *inf* (*bottom*) trasero *m* ►**to chase one's** ~ pillarse los dedos; **to turn** ~ **and run** huir **II.** *vt* seguir

◆**tail away** *vi* ir disminuyendo; (*get worse*) ir empeorando

◆**tail back** *vi Brit* (*traffic*) extenderse

◆**tail off** *vi* disminuir; (*sound*) desvanecerse

tailback ['teɪlbæk] *n Brit* caravana *f* de coches **tailboard** *n Brit* compuerta *f* trasera **tail end** *n* extremo *m* **tailgate I.** *n Am, Aus* (*of car*) puerta *f* de atrás; (*of truck*) compuerta *f* **II.** *vt Am* perseguir **tailless** *adj* sin cola **taillight** *n* AUTO luz *f* trasera

tailor ['teɪlə^r, *Am:* -lɚ] **I.** *n* sastre *m* **II.** *vt* **1.** (*clothes*) confeccionar **2.** (*adapt*) adaptar

tailor-made [ˌteɪlə'meɪd, *Am:* -lɚ'-] *adj* **1.** (*custom-made*) hecho, -a a medida **2.** (*perfect*) perfecto, -a

tailpiece ['teɪlpiːs] *n* **1.** (*part added*) añadidura *f* **2.** AVIAT cola *f* **3.** TYPO viñeta *f* **tailpipe** *n Am* tubo *m* de escape **tailspin** *n* barrena *f* picada; **to go into a** ~ caer en picado **tail wind** *n* viento *m* de cola

taint [teɪnt] **I.** *vt* (*food*) contaminar; (*reputation*) manchar **II.** *n no pl* mancha *f*

taintless *adj liter* incorrupto, -a

Taiwan [ˌtaɪ'wɑːn] *n* Taiwán *m*

Taiwanese [ˌtaɪwə'niːz] **I.** *adj* taiwanés, -esa **II.** *n* taiwanés, -esa *m, f*

Tajikistan [tɑː'dʒiːkɪˌstɑːn] *n* Tayikistán *m*

take [teɪk] **I.** *n* **1.** *no pl* (*receipts*) ingresos *mpl* **2.** PHOT, FILM toma *f* ►**to be on the** ~ *Am, inf* dejarse sobornar **II.** <took, taken> *vt* **1.** (*accept*) aceptar; (*advice*) seguir; (*criticism*) soportar; (*responsibility*) asumir; **to** ~ **sth seriously** tomar algo en serio; **to** ~ **one's time** tomarse su tiempo; **to** ~ **sth as it comes** aceptar algo tal y como es **2.** (*hold*) coger, agarrar *AmL* **3.** (*eat*) comer; (*medicine*) tomar **4.** (*use*) necesitar **5.** (*receive*) recibir **6.** *Brit* (*rent*) alquilar **7.** (*capture: prisoners*) prender; (*city*) conquistar; (*power*) tomar **8.** (*assume*) **to** ~ **office** entrar en funciones **9.** (*bring*) llevar **10.** (*require*) exigir, requerir; **this shirt** ~**s a lot of ironing** esta camisa ha de plancharse mucho **11.** (*do*) REL oficiar; UNIV cursar **12.** (*have: decision, bath, holiday*) tomar; (*walk*) dar; (*trip*) hacer; (*ticket*) sacar; (*census*) levantar; **to** ~ **a rest** descansar **13.** *Brit* (*score*) obtener **14.** *Brit, Aus* (*teach*) enseñar **15.** (*feel, assume*) **to** ~ (**an**) **interest in sb/sth** interesarse por alguien/algo; **to** ~ **offence** ofenderse; **to** ~ **pity on sb/sth** apiadarse de alguien/algo; **to** ~ **the view that ...** adoptar la opinión de que... **16.** (*make money*) ganar **17.** (*photograph*) sacar **18.** (*use for travel: bus, train*) coger, tomar *AmL* **19.** (*regard as*) tener; **to** ~ **sb for sth** tener a alguien por algo ►~ **it**

or leave it ¡tómalo o déjalo!; **what do you ~ me for?** ¿por quién me has tomado?; ~ **it from me** puedes creerme; **I ~ it that ...** supongo que...; ~ **that!** ¡toma! **III.**<took, taken> *vi* tener efecto; (*plant*) prender; (*dye*) pegar; **to ~ against sb** *Brit* encontrar a alguien antipático

◆**take aback** *vt* (*suprise*) sorprender; (*shock*) abatir

◆**take after** *vt* parecerse a

◆**take along** *vt* (*take*) llevar (consigo); (*bring*) traer (consigo)

◆**take apart I.** *vt* **1.** (*disassemble*) desmontar **2.** (*analyse*) reseñar **3.** (*destroy*) despedazar **II.** *vi* desmontarse

◆**take away I.** *vt* **1.** (*remove*) quitar **2.** (*go away with*) llevar(se) **3.** (*lessen*) disminuir **4.** (*subtract from*) restar **II.** *vi* quitarse; **to ~ from the importance/worth of sth** restar importancia/mérito a algo

◆**take back** *vt* **1.** (*return*) devolver **2.** (*accept back*) aceptar; (*employee*) volver a emplear; (*spouse*) reconciliarse con **3.** (*repossess*) recobrar **4.** (*retract*) retractar **5.** (*carry to past time*) evocar **6.** (*remind*) recordar

◆**take down** *vt* **1.** (*remove*) quitar; (*from high place*) bajar **2.** (*disassemble*) desmontar **3.** (*write down*) apuntar **4.** *inf* (*diminish the pride of*) **to take sb down** bajar los humos a alguien; (*humble*) humillar a alguien

◆**take in** *vt* **1.** (*bring inside*) recoger, acoger (en casa); (*admit*) aceptar **2.** (*hold*) **to take sb in one's arms** sostener a alguien entre sus brazos; **to take sth in hand** *fig* hacerse cargo de algo **3.** (*accommodate*) alojar; (*for rent*) hospedar **4.** (*bring to police*) entregar **5.** (*deceive*) estafar; **to be taken in (by sb/sth)** ser engañado (por alguien/algo) **6.** *Am, Aus* (*go to see*) ir a ver **7.** (*understand*) comprender; **to take sth in at a glance** asimilar algo en un abrir y cerrar de ojos **8.** (*include*) incluir **9.** FASHION estrechar

◆**take off I.** *vt* **1.** (*remove from*) retirar; **to take sb off a list** tachar a alguien de una lista **2.** (*clothes*) quitarse **3.** (*bring away*) llevarse **4.** (*subtract*) descontar **5.** (*stop showing*) descontinuar **6.** *Brit* (*imitate*) imitar **II.** *vi* **1.** AVIAT despegar **2.** *inf* (*leave*) salir; *inf* (*flee*) huir **3.** (*have success*) empezar a tener éxito

◆**take on I.** *vt* **1.** (*agree to try*) aceptar **2.** (*acquire*) adoptar **3.** (*hire*) contratar **4.** (*fight*) enfrentarse a **5.** (*stop for loading: passengers*) cargar; (*fuel*) abastecerse de; (*goods*) tomar **II.** *vi* apurarse

◆**take out** *vt* **1.** (*remove*) quitar; (*extract*) extraer; (*withdraw*) retirar **2.** (*bring outside*) llevar fuera; (*garbage*) tirar, botar *Col, Ven* **3.** (*for walk*) llevar de paseo **4.** *inf* (*kill*) eliminar; (*destroy*) destruir **5.** (*arrange to get: licence*) obtener **6.** (*borrow*) tomar prestado **7.** (*vent anger*) **to take sth out on sb** desahogarse riñendo a alguien **8.** *inf* (*tire*) **to take it out of sb** agotar a alguien

◆**take over I.** *vt* **1.** (*buy out*) comprar **2.** (*seize control*) tomar el control de **3.** (*assume*) asumir **4.** (*possess*) tomar posesión de; **to be taken over by one's work** estar dominado por su trabajo **5.** (*start using*) comenzar a usar **II.** *vi* tomar posesión

◆**take to** *vt* **1.** (*start to like*) coger simpatía a, encariñarse con *AmL* **2.** (*begin as a habit*) **to ~ doing sth** aficionarse a hacer algo; **to ~ drink/drugs** darse a la bebida/las drogas **3.** (*go to*) dirigirse a; **to ~ the streets (in protest)** tomar las calles (para protestar); **to ~ one's bed** meterse en la cama

◆**take up I.** *vt* **1.** (*bring up*) subir **2. to ~ arms (against sth)** tomar las armas (contra algo) **3.** (*start doing*) comenzar; (*job*) empezar; (*piano*) iniciarse en; (*fishing*) dedicarse a **4.** (*discuss*) tratar **5.** (*accept*) aceptar **6.** (*adopt*) adoptar **7.** (*continue doing*) proseguir **8.** (*join in*) participar **9.** (*occupy*) ocupar **10.** (*pull up*) alzar **11.** (*shorten*) coger a **12.** (*patronise*) patrocinar **13.** (*absorb*) absorber **II.** *vi* **to ~ with sb** relacionarse con alguien; **to ~ with sth** familiarizarse con algo

takeaway ['teɪkəweɪ] *n Brit, Aus* comida *f* para llevar

take-home pay ['teɪkhəʊmˌpeɪ, *Am:* 'teɪkhoʊmˌpeɪ] *n no pl* salario *m* neto

taken *vi, vt pp of* **take**

take-off ['teɪkɒf, *Am:* -ɑːf] *n* **1.** AVIAT despegue *m* **2.** *Brit, Aus* (*imitation*) imitación *f*

take-out ['teɪkaʊt] *n Am* comida *f* para llevar

takeover ['teɪkˌəʊvəʳ, *Am:* -ˌoʊvɚ] *n* POL toma *f* del poder; ECON adquisición *f*

takeover bid *n* oferta *f* pública de adquisición de acciones

taker ['teɪkəʳ, *Am:* -kɚ] *n* **the suggestion had no ~s** nadie aceptó la propuesta

take-up ['teɪkʌp] *n* **1.** TECH compensación *f* **2.** (*of scheme, suggestion*) aceptación *f*

taking ['teɪkɪŋ] **I.** *n* **1.** *no pl* (*capture*) toma *f;* **it's yours for the ~** es tuyo si lo quieres **2.** *pl* (*receipts*) ingresos *mpl* **II.** *adj* atractivo, -a

talc [tælk] *n,* **talcum (powder)** ['tælkəm(ˌpaʊdəʳ)] *n no pl* **1.** CHEM talco *m* **2.** MED polvos *mpl* de talco

tale [teɪl] *n* **1.** (*story*) historia *f;* LIT cuento *m* **2.** (*lie*) mentira *f;* **dead men tell no ~s** los muertos no mienten ►**to tell ~s** chivarse

talent ['tælənt] *n* **1.** (*ability*) talento *m* **2.** *Brit, Aus, iron* (*attractive girls*) bombones *fpl*, buenonas *fpl Col*, mamacitas *fpl Méx;* (*boys*) bombones *mpl,* mangos *mpl Ven,* bizcochos *mpl Col,* papacitos *mpl Méx*

talented *adj* talentoso, -a

talisman ['tælɪzmən] *n* talismán *m*

talk [tɔːk] **I.** *n* **1.** (*conversation*) conversación *f,* plática *f Méx* **2.** (*lecture*) charla *f* **3.** *no pl* (*things said*) chisme *m;* **big ~** jactancia *f* **4.** *pl* (*formal discussions*) negociaciones *fpl* ►**to be the ~ of the town** andar de boca en boca; **to be all ~ (and no action)** hablar mucho (y no hacer nada) **II.** *vi* (*speak*) hablar; **to ~ about sb behind their back** murmurar de alguien a sus espaldas; **to give sb something to ~ about** dar a alguien motivos para hablar; **~ing of holidays, ...** hablando de las vacaciones,... ►**to ~ dirty** decir obscenidades; **look who's ~ing** *inf,* **you're a fine one to ~** *inf* ¡mira quién habla!; **to set sb ~ing** *Brit* dar que hablar a alguien **III.** *vt* **1.** (*utter*) decir **2.** (*discuss*) hablar de

◆**talk back** *vi* replicar

◆**talk down I.** *vt* (*speak louder than*) apabullar **II.** *vi pej* **to ~ to sb** hablar a alguien con condescendencia

◆**talk out** *vt* **1.** (*discuss*) discutir **2.** (*convince not to*) **to talk sb out of sth** disuadir a alguien de algo

◆**talk over** *vt* **to talk sth over** (**with sb**) hablar algo (con alguien)

◆**talk round I.** *vt* **to talk sb round** convencer a alguien **II.** *vi* (*avoid*) **to ~ sth** dar vueltas a algo

◆**talk through** *vt* **1.** (*discuss*) discutir **2.** (*explain*) explicar

talkative ['tɔːkətɪv, *Am:* -t̬ɪv] *adj* locuaz

talker *n* hablador(a) *m(f)*

talking I. *adj* parlante **II.** *n no pl* habla *f;* **"no ~"** "prohibido hablar"

talking shop *n inf* ≈ mentidero *m*

talking-to ['tɔːkɪŋtuː] *n* sermón *m;* **to give sb a ~** echar un sermón a alguien

talk show *n* programa *m* de entrevistas

tall [tɔːl] *adj* alto, -a; **to grow ~(er)** crecer

tallboy ['tɔːlbɔɪ] *n* cómoda *f* alta

tallness ['tɔːlnɪs] *n no pl* altura *f*

tallow ['tæləʊ, *Am:* -oʊ] *n no pl* sebo *m*

tally[1] ['tæli] <-ie-> *vi* concordar; **to ~ with sth** coincidir con algo

tally[2] ['tæli] <-ies> **I.** *n* cuenta *f;* **to keep a ~ (of sth)** llevar la cuenta (de algo) **II.** *vt* llevar la cuenta de

◆**tally up** *vt* llevar la cuenta de

tally-ho [ˌtælɪ'həʊ, *Am:* -'hoʊ] *interj* hala

talon ['tælən] *n* garra *f*

tamarind ['tæmərɪnd] *n* tamarindo *m*

tamarisk ['tæmərɪsk] *n* tamarisco *m*

tambour ['tæmbʊəʳ, *Am:* -bʊr] *n* tambor *m*

tambourine [ˌtæmbə'riːn] *n* pandereta *f*

tame [teɪm] **I.** *adj* **1.** (*domesticated*) doméstico, -a; (*not savage*) manso, -a **2.** (*unexciting*) soso, -a **II.** *vt* (*feelings*) dominar; (*animal*) domesticar, aguachar *Chile*

tamer ['teɪməʳ, *Am:* -ɚ] *n* domador(a) *m(f)*

tamp [tæmp] *vt* apisonar

tamper ['tæmpəʳ, *Am:* -ɚ] *vi* entrometerse

◆**tamper with** *vt* manosear; (*document*) falsificar; (*witness*) sobornar; (*lock*) tratar de forzar

tamper-proof ['tæmpəpruːf, *Am:* -pɚ-] *adj,* **tamper-resistant** *adj* no manipulable

tampon ['tæmpən, *Am:* -pɑːn] *n* MED tapón *m;* (*for absorbing menstrual blood*) tampón *m*

tan[1] [tæn] **I.** <-nn-> *vi* broncearse **II.** <-nn-> *vt* **1.** (*make brown*) broncear; **to be ~ned** estar moreno **2.** (*leather*) curtir ►**to ~ sb's hide** *inf* dar una paliza a alguien **III.** *n* bronceado *m;* **to get a ~** ponerse moreno **IV.** *adj* marrón claro

tan[2] MAT *abbr of* **tangent** tg

tandem ['tændəm] **I.** *n* tándem *m;* **to work in ~** trabajar conjuntamente **II.** *adv* en tándem; **to ride ~** montar en tándem

tang [tæŋ] *n* olor *m* penetrante

tangent ['tændʒənt] *n* tangente *f;* **to go off at a ~** salirse por la tangente

tangential [tæn'dʒenʃl] *adj* tangencial

tangerine [ˌtændʒə'riːn] *n* mandarina *f*

tangible ['tændʒəbl] *adj* tangible; (*benefit*) palpable; **~ asset** bien *m* material

Tangier ['tændʒɪəʳ, *Am:* tæn'dʒɪr] *n* Tánger *m*

tangle ['tæŋgl] **I.** *n* **1.** (*in hair, string*) maraña *f* **2.** *fig* (*confusion*) enredo *m* **II.** *vt* enredar **III.** *vi* enredarse

◆**tangle with** *vi* (*quarrel*) meterse con

tango ['tæŋgəʊ, *Am:* -goʊ] **I.** *n* tango *m* ►**it takes two to ~** *prov* es cosa de dos **II.** *vi* bailar un tango

tangy ['tæŋi] <-ier, -iest> *adj* fuerte

tank [tæŋk] *n* **1.** (*container*) depósito *m* **2.** (*aquarium*) acuario *m* **3.** MIL tanque *m*

tanked up *adj* **to be ~** ir como una cuba

tankard ['tæŋkəd, *Am:* -kɚd] *n* jarra *f*

tanker ['tæŋkəʳ, *Am:* -ɚ] *n* **1.** (*lorry*) camión *m* cisterna **2.** (*ship*) buque *m* cisterna; **oil ~** petrolero *m* **3.** (*aircraft*) avión *m* cisterna

tanned [tænd] *adj* bronceado, -a

tanner ['tænəʳ, *Am:* -ɚ] *n* curtidor(a) *m(f)*

tannery ['tænəri] *n* curtiduría *f*

tannic acid [ˌtænɪk'æsɪd] *n* ácido *m* tánico

tannin ['tænɪn] *n* tanino *m*

tanning ['tænɪŋ] *n* **1.** (*of leather*) curtido *m* **2.** *inf* (*beating*) paliza *f*

tannoy® *n Brit,* **Tannoy®** ['tænɔɪ] *n Brit* sistema *m* de megafonía

tantalize ['tæntəlaɪz, *Am:* -t̬əlaɪz] *vt* **1.** (*torment*) atormentar **2.** (*tempt*) tentar

tantalizing *adj* tentador(a); (*smile*) seductor(a)

tantamount ['tæntəmaʊnt, *Am:* -t̬ə-] *adj* equivalente; **to be ~ to sth** equivaler a algo

tantrum ['tæntrəm] *n* berrinche *m,* dengue *m Méx;* **to have** [*o* **throw**] **a ~** coger [*o* agarrar *AmL*] una rabieta

Tanzania [ˌtænzə'nɪə, *Am:* -'niːə] *n* Tanzania *f*

Tanzanian [ˌtænzə'nɪən, *Am:* -'niːən] **I.** *adj* tanzano, -a **II.** *n* tanzano, -a *m, f*

tap[1] [tæp] **I.** *n* **1.** *Brit* (*for water*) grifo *m,* canilla *f Arg, Par, Urug;* **beer on ~** cerveza *f* de barril; **to turn the ~ on/off** abrir/cerrar el grifo; **on ~** *fig* al alcance de la mano **2.** TEL micrófono *m* de escucha **II.** <-pp-> *vt* **1.** TEL intervenir; (*conversation*) interceptar; (*phone*) pinchar *inf* **2.** (*make use of*) utilizar; (*sources*) explotar **3.** (*let out*) espitar

tap[2] [tæp] **I.** *n* **1.** (*light knock*) golpecito *m* **2.** (*tap-dancing*) claqué *m* **II.** <-pp-> *vt* golpear suavemente; **to ~ one's fingers on the table** tamborilear con los dedos sobre la mesa **III.** <-pp-> *vi* dar golpecitos

tap dance ['tæp,dɑːnts, *Am:* -,dænts] *n* claqué *m*

tape [teɪp] **I.** *n* **1.** (*adhesive strip*) cinta *f* adhesiva; MED esparadrapo *m;* **masking ~** cinta adhesiva protectora; **Scotch ~®** *Am* celo *m,* durex *m AmL* **2.** (*measure*) cinta *f* métrica **3.** SPORTS cinta *f* de llegada **4.** (*cassette*) cinta *f,* tape *m RíoPl;* **to get sth on ~** grabar algo **II.** *vt* **1.** (*fasten with tape*) poner una cinta a **2.** (*record*) grabar; **to have** (**got**) **sb ~d** *Brit, Aus, inf* tener a alguien calado

tape cassette *n* casete *f* **tape deck** *n* platina *f* **tape measure** *n* metro *m*

taper ['teɪpəʳ, *Am:* -pɚ] **I.** *n* (*slim candle*) candela *f;* (*wax-coated wick*) cerilla *f* **II.** *vt* afilar **III.** *vi* afilarse

◆**taper off** *vi* disminuir

tape-record *vt* grabar (en cinta) **tape recorder** *n* grabadora *f* **tape recording** *n* grabación *f* (en cinta)

tapered wing [,teɪpəd'wɪŋ, *Am:* -ɚd'-] *n* AVIAT ala *f* ahusada

tapestry ['tæpɪstri, *Am:* -əstri] *n* **1.** (*art form*) tapicería *f* **2.** (*object*) tapiz *m* **3.** *fig* collage *m*

tapeworm ['teɪpwɜːm, *Am:* -wɜːrm] *n* tenia *f,* solitaria *f*

tapioca [,tæpɪ'əʊkə, *Am:* -'oʊ-] *n* tapioca *f*

tapir ['teɪpəʳ, *Am:* -pɚ] *n* tapir *m*

tappet ['tæpət] *n* alzaválvulas *m inv*

taproom ['tæprʊm, *Am:* -ruːm] *n* cervecería *f*

tap water *n* agua *f* corriente

tar [tɑːʳ, *Am:* tɑːr] **I.** *n no pl* alquitrán *m* **II.** <-rr-> *vt* alquitranar; **to ~ and feather sb** emplumar a alguien

tarantula [tə'ræntjʊlə, *Am:* -tʃələ] *n* tarántula *f*

tardy ['tɑːdi, *Am:* 'tɑːr-] <-ier, -iest> *adj liter* tardío, -a; *pej* (*sluggish*) lento, -a

tare [teəʳ, *Am:* ter] *n* ECON tara *f*

target ['tɑːgɪt, *Am:* 'tɑːr-] **I.** *n* **1.** (*mark aimed at*) objetivo *m;* **to hit the ~** dar en el blanco **2.** ECON objetivo *m;* **to be on ~** ir de acuerdo con lo previsto **II.** <*Brit* -tt- *o Am* -t-> *vt* centrarse en; **to ~ sth on sth** (*missile*) apuntar algo a algo; (*campaign*) destinar algo a algo

target date *n* fecha *f* límite **target language** *n* LING lengua *m* de destino; INFOR lenguaje *m* objeto **target practice** *n* prácticas *fpl* de tiro **target price** *n* precio *m* indicativo

targetted ['tɑːgɪtəd, *Am:* 'tɑːrgɪt̬ɪd] *adj Brit* elegido, -a como objetivo

tariff ['tærɪf, *Am:* 'ter-] *n* **1.** *Brit* (*list of charges*) tarifa *f* **2.** (*customs duty*) arancel *m*

tariff barrier *n* ECON barrera *f* arancelaria

tarmac® ['tɑːmæk, *Am:* 'tɑːr-], **tarmacadam®** **I.** *n no pl* **1.** *Brit* (*paving material*) asfalto *m* **2.** AVIAT pista *f* de despegue **II.** <-ck-> *vt Brit* asfaltar

tarn [tɑːn, *Am:* tɑːrn] *n* lago *m* de montaña

tarnish ['tɑːnɪʃ, *Am:* 'tɑːr-] **I.** *vi* deslustrarse **II.** *vt* deslustrar; (*reputation*) manchar **III.** *n* mancha *f*

tarpaulin [tɑː'pɔːlɪn, *Am:* tɑːr'pɑː-] *n* lona *f* impermeabilizada

tarragon ['tærəgən, *Am:* 'terəgɑːn] *n no pl* estragón *m*

tarsus ['tɑːsəs, *Am:* 'tɑːr-] *n* ANAT tarso *m*

tart¹ [tɑːt, *Am:* tɑːrt] *adj* **1.** (*sharp*) agrio, -a; (*acid*) ácido, -a **2.** (*caustic*) cortante

tart² [tɑːt, *Am:* tɑːrt] *n* **1.** GASTR tarta *f* **2.** *Brit, pej, inf* (*woman of questionable morals*) pendón *m;* (*prostitute*) fulana *f*

◆**tart up** *vt Brit, pej, inf* remodelar; **to tart oneself up** emperifollarse

tartan ['tɑːtn, *Am:* 'tɑːrtn] *n* **1.** *no pl* (*cloth*) tela *f* a cuadros escoceses **2.** (*design*) tartán *m*

Tartar ['tɑːtəʳ, *Am:* 'tɑːrt̬ɚ] *n* (*bad-tempered person*) persona *f* intratable

tartar ['tɑːtəʳ, *Am:* 'tɑːrt̬ɚ] *n no pl* **1.** MED sarro *m* **2.** CHEM tártaro *m*

tartar(e) sauce *n no pl* salsa *f* tártara

tartaric [tɑː'tærɪk, *Am:* tɑːr-] *n* ácido *m* tartárico

task [tɑːsk, *Am:* tæsk] **I.** *n* tarea *f,* tonga *f Col;* **to take sb to ~** llamar la atención a alguien **II.** *vt* imponer una tarea; **to be ~ed with sth** estar encargado de algo

taskforce *n* MIL destacamento *m;* (*team*) equipo *m* de trabajo **taskmaster** *n* capataz *m;* **to be a hard ~** ser un tirano

Tasmania [tæz'meɪniə] *n* Tasmania *f*

Tasmanian [tæz'meɪniən] **I.** *adj* tasmano, -a **II.** *n* tasmano, -a *m, f*

tassel ['tæsl] *n* borla *f*

taste [teɪst] **I.** *n* **1.** *no pl* sabor *m;* **sense of ~** sentido *m* del gusto **2.** (*small portion*) bocado *m;* **to have a ~ of sth** probar algo **3.** (*liking*) gusto *m;* **to lose the ~ for sth** perder el gusto por algo; **to have different ~s** tener gustos distintos; **to get a ~ for sth** tomar el gusto a algo **4.** *no pl* (*experience*) experiencia *f* ▶**to leave a bad ~** (**in one's mouth**) dejar un mal sabor de boca **II.** *vt* **1.** (*food, drink*) saborear **2.** (*experience*) experimentar; (*luxury*) probar **III.** *vi* saber; **to ~ bitter/sweet** tener un sabor amargo/dulce; **to ~ of** [*o* **like**] **sth** saber a algo

tastebud ['teɪstbʌd] *n* papila *f* gustativa

tasteful ['teɪstfəl] *adj* con gusto; (*decorous*) con delicadeza

tasteless ['teɪstləs] *adj* **1.** (*without flavour*) soso, -a **2.** (*clothes, remark*) de mal gusto

taster ['teɪstəʳ, *Am:* -ɚ] *n* **1.** (*person*) catador(a) *m(f)* **2.** *Brit* (*sample*) muestra *f*

tasty ['teɪsti] *adj* **1.** (*tasting good*) sabroso, -a **2.** *Brit, inf* (*attractive*) buenísimo, -a

tat [tæt] *n no pl, pej, inf* porquería *f*

tattered ['tætəd, *Am:* 'tæt̬ɚd] *adj* (*clothes*) hecho jirones; (*person*) harapiento, -a; (*reputation*) destrozado, -a

tatters ['tætəʳz, *Am:* 'tæt̬ɚz] *npl* jirones *fpl;*

T

to be in ~ estar hecho jirones

tattle ['tætl, *Am:* 'tæţ-] *n* chismorreo *m*

tattler ['tætləʳ, *Am:* 'tæţlɚ] *n* cotilla *mf*

tattoo [tə'tu:, *Am:* tæt'u:] **I.** *n* **1.** MIL espectáculo *m* militar **2.** (*marking on skin*) tatuaje *m* **II.** *vt* tatuar

tatty ['tæti, *Am:* 'tæţ-] <-ier, -iest> *adj pej* estropeado, -a

taught [tɔ:t, *Am:* tɑ:t] *pt, pp of* **teach**

taunt [tɔ:nt, *Am:* tɑ:nt] **I.** *vt* burlarse de **II.** *n* insulto *m*

Taurus ['tɔ:rəs] *n* Tauro *m*

taut [tɔ:t, *Am:* tɑ:t] *adj* (*wire, string*) tensado, -a; (*skin*) terso, -a; (*nerves*) tenso, -a

tautological [ˌtɔ:tə'lɒdʒɪkəl, *Am:* ˌtɑ:ţə'lɑ:dʒɪk-] *adj,* **tautologous** [tɔ:'tɒləgəs, *Am:* tɑ:'tɑ:lə-] *adj* tautológico, -a

tautology [tɔ:'tɒlədʒi, *Am:* tɑ:'tɑ:lə-] <-ies> *n* tautología *f*

tavern ['tævən, *Am:* -ɚn] *n* taberna *f,* estanquillo *m Ecua*

tawdry ['tɔ:dri, *Am:* 'tɑ:-] <-ier, -iest> *adj pej* (*vulgar*) hortera; (*pompous*) de relumbrón

tawny ['tɔ:ni, *Am:* 'tɑ:-] <-ier, -iest> *adj* de color ambar ocuro

tawny owl *n* cárabo *m*

tax [tæks] **I.** <-es> *n* **1.** FIN impuesto *m;* **hidden ~es** *Am* impuestos encubiertos; **to collect ~es** recaudar impuestos; **to increase ~es** subir los impuestos; **to put a ~ on sth** gravar algo con un impuesto; **free of ~** exento de impuestos **2.** *fig* (*burden*) carga *f;* **to be a ~ on sb** ser una carga para alguien **II.** *vt* **1.** FIN gravar con un impuesto **2.** (*accuse*) acusar **3.** *fig* (*need effort*) exigir un esfuerzo

taxable ['tæksəbl] *adj* imponible

tax allowance *n* desgravación *f* fiscal

taxation [tæk'seɪʃən] *n no pl* (*taxes*) impuestos *mpl;* (*system*) sistema *m* impositivo

tax avoidance *n* evasión *f* de impuestos **tax base** *n* base *f* imponible **tax bracket** *n* categoría *f* impositiva **tax collector** *n* recaudador(a) *m(f)* de impuestos **tax consultant** *n* asesor(a) *m(f)* fiscal **tax-deductible** *adj* deducible (a efectos impositivos) **tax disc** *n* *Brit: adhesivo que se engancha en la ventanilla del coche y certifica que se ha satisfecho el impuesto de circulación* **tax dodger** *n,* **tax evader** *n* evasor(a) *m(f)* de impuestos **tax evasion** *n* evasión *f* de impuestos **tax exemption** *n* exención *f* fiscal **tax-free** *adj* libre de impuestos **tax haven** *n* paraíso *m* fiscal

taxi ['tæksi] **I.** *n* taxi *m* **II.** *vi* ir en taxi; AVIAT rodar

taxidermist ['tæksɪˌdɜ:mɪst, *Am:* -dɜ:r-] *n* taxidermista *mf*

taxidermy ['tæksɪˌdɜ:mi, *Am:* -dɜ:r-] *n* taxidermia *f*

taxi driver *n* taxista *mf,* ruletero, -a *m, f AmC, Méx*

taximeter ['tæksɪmi:təʳ, *Am:* -ţɚ] *n* taxímetro *m*

taxing *adj* difícil

taxiplane *n* avión *m* para vuelos no regulares

taxi rank *n Brit,* **taxi stand** *n Am* parada *f* de taxis

taxman ['tæksmæn] *n no pl* recaudador(a) *m(f)* de impuestos; **the ~** Hacienda *f*

taxonomy [tæk'sɒnəmi, *Am:* -'sɑ:nə-] *n* taxonomía *f*

taxpayer ['tæksˌpeɪəʳ, *Am:* -ɚ] *n* contribuyente *mf* **tax rebate** *n* devolución *f* de impuestos **tax relief** *n* exención *f* de impuestos **tax return** *n* declaración *f* de renta **tax revenues** *n* ingresos *mpl* fiscales **tax system** *n* sistema *m* impositivo **tax year** *n* año *m* fiscal

TB [ˌti:'bi:] *n abbr of* **tuberculosis** tuberculosis *f inv*

T-bar ['ti:bɑ:ʳ, *Am:* -bɑ:r] *n,* **T-bar lift** *n* barra *f* en forma de T

tbs(p) *abbr of* **tablespoonful** cucharada *f* sopera

tea [ti:] *n* **1.** *no pl* (*plant, drink*) té *m;* **a cup of ~** una taza de té; **strong/weak ~** té fuerte/flojo; **camomile ~** infusión *f* de manzanilla **2.** *Brit* (*afternoon meal*) merienda *f; Aus* (*evening meal*) cena *f* ►**not for all the ~ in China** ni por todo el oro del mundo

tea bag *n* bolsita *f* de té **tea break** *n Brit* descanso *m* (para el té) **tea caddy** *n* caja *f* para té

teacake ['ti:keɪk] *n* bollito *m* con pasas

teach [ti:tʃ] <taught, taught> **I.** *vt* enseñar; **to ~ oneself sth** aprender algo por su propia cuenta; **to ~ sb a lesson** *fig* dar una lección a alguien **II.** *vi* dar clases

teacher ['ti:tʃəʳ, *Am:* -tʃɚ] *n* profesor(a) *m(f)*

teacher training *n* formación *f* de profesorado **teacher training college** *n Brit* instituto *f* de ciencias de la educación

tea chest *n* caja *f* de embalaje

teaching **I.** *n* **1.** *no pl* (*profession*) docencia *f* **2.** *pl* (*doctrine*) enseñanza *f* **II.** *adj* didáctico, -a

teaching staff *n* profesorado *m*

tea cloth *n Brit* paño *m* de cocina **tea cosy** *n* cubretetera *m* **teacup** *n* taza *f* de té **tea house** *n* salón *m* de té

teak [ti:k] *n no pl* teca *f*

tea leaves *npl* hojas *fpl* de té

team [ti:m] **I.** *n* (*group*) equipo *m;* (*of oxen*) yunta *f;* (*of horses*) tiro *m;* (*of dogs*) traílla *f* **II.** *adj* de equipo **III.** *vt* asociar; (*match*) combinar

◆**team up** *vi* agruparse; **to ~ with** asociarse con

team captain *n* capitán, -ana *m, f* de equipo **team effort** *n* esfuerzo *m* conjunto **team-mate** *n* compañero, -a *m, f* **team play** *n* juego *m* de equipo **team spirit** *n* espíritu *m* de equipo **teamwork** *n* trabajo *m* en equipo

teapot ['ti:pɒt, *Am:* -pɑ:t] *n* tetera *f*

tear¹ [tɪəʳ, *Am:* tɪr] **I.** *n* lágrima *f;* **to bring ~s to sb's eyes** hacer que a alguien se le salten las lágrimas; **to burst into ~s** echarse a llorar; **to have ~s in one's eyes** tener los ojos llenos de lágrimas; **to not shed (any) ~s** no derramar una (sola) lágrima **II.** *vi* llorar

tear[2] [teə^{r}, *Am:* ter] **I.** *n* rotura *f* **II.** <tore, torn> *vt* **1.** (*rip*) rasgar; (*ruin*) romper; **to ~ a hole in sth** hacer un agujero en algo; **to be torn between two possibilities** no saber qué posibilidad elegir **2.** (*strain: muscle*) distender **III.** <tore, torn> *vi* **1.** (*rip*) rasgarse **2.** (*rush wildly*) lanzarse; **to ~ down the stairs** precipitarse escaleras abajo

◆**tear apart** *vt* destrozar; *fig* dividir

◆**tear at** *vt* quitar precipitadamente

◆**tear away** **I.** *vi* salir disparado **II.** *vt* **1.** (*make depart*) **to tear sb away** sacar a alguien; **to tear oneself away** irse de mala gana **2.** (*pull*) arrancar

◆**tear down** *vt* derribar

◆**tear into** *vt* (*verbally*) arremeter contra; (*physically*) lanzarse sobre

◆**tear off** **I.** *vt* (*remove*) arrancar; **to ~ one's clothes** quitarse la ropa de un tirón **II.** *vi* (*leave quickly*) salir disparado

◆**tear out** *vt* arrancar de cuajo; **to tear one's hair out over sth** *fig* subirse por las paredes por algo

◆**tear up** *vt* despedazar; *fig* (*agreement*) anular

tearaway ['teərəweɪ, *Am:* 'terə-] *n Brit, Aus, inf* gamberro, -a *m, f*

teardrop ['tɪədrɒp, *Am:* 'tɪrdrɑːp] *n* lágrima *f*

tearful ['tɪəfəl, *Am:* 'tɪrfəl] *adj* lloroso, -a

tear gas *n* gas *m* lacrimógeno **tear jerker** *n inf* (*film*) película *f* lacrimógena; (*song*) canción *f* lacrimógena

tea room *n* salón *m* de té

tease [tiːz] **I.** *vt* **1.** (*make fun of*) tomar el pelo a; **to ~ sb about sth** tomar el pelo a alguien por algo **2.** (*provoke*) provocar; (*sexually*) tentar **3.** TECH cardar **II.** *n* bromista *mf;* (*sexually*) provocador(a) *m(f)*

teaser ['tiːzə^{r}, *Am:* -ɚ] *n* rompecabezas *m inv*

tea service *n,* **tea set** *n* juego *m* de té **teashop** *n Brit* salón *m* de té **teaspoon** *n* **1.** (*spoon*) cucharita *f* **2.** (*amount*) cucharadita *f*

teaspoonful ['tiːspuːnfʊl] *n* cucharadita *f*

tea-strainer ['tiːˌstreɪnə^{r}, *Am:* -ɚ] *n* colador *m* para el té

teat [tiːt] *n* (*nipple: of animal*) teta *f;* (*of bottle*) tetina *f*

teatime ['tiːtaɪm] *n Brit* hora *f* del té **tea towel** *n Brit* paño *m* de cocina **tea tray** *n* bandeja *f* del té **tea trolley** *n* carrito *m* del té **tea urn** *n* tetera *f* grande **tea wagon** *n Am s.* **tea trolley**

technical ['teknɪkəl] *adj* técnico, -a; **~ term** tecnicismo *m*

technical college *n Brit* HIST escuela *f* politécnica

technicality [ˌteknɪ'kæləti, *Am:* -nə'kæləṭi] <-ies> *n* **1.** (*detail*) detalle *m* técnico; **to be acquitted on a ~** ser absuelto por un defecto de forma **2.** (*technical matter*) carácter *m* técnico

technical school *n* escuela *f* de artes y oficios

technician [tek'nɪʃən] *n* técnico, -a *m, f*

technique [tek'niːk] *n* técnica *f*

technological [ˌteknə'lɒdʒɪkl, *Am:* -'lɑːdʒɪ-] *adj* tecnológico, -a

technology [tek'nɒlədʒi, *Am:* -'nɑːlə-] *n* tecnología *f*

technophile [ˌteknəʊ'faɪl] *n* tecnófilo, -a *m, f*

technophobe [ˌteknəʊ'fəʊb, *Am:* -nə'foʊ-] *n* tecnófobo, -a *m, f*

tectonics [tek'tɒnɪks, *Am:* -tɑːnɪks] *n* tectónica *f*

teddy[1] ['tedi] *n* (*underwear*) camiseta *f* interior

teddy[2] ['tedi] <-ies> *n,* **teddy bear** *n* osito *m* de peluche

tedious ['tiːdiəs] *adj* aburrido, -a, tedioso, -a

tediousness *n no pl* pesadez *f*

tedium ['tiːdɪəm] *n no pl* tedio *m*

tee [tiː] *n* SPORTS tee *m*

◆**tee off** **I.** *vi* **1.** SPORTS dar el primer golpe **2.** *inf* (*start*) empezar **II.** *vt Am, inf* **to tee sb off** cabrear a alguien

teem [tiːm] *vi* rebosar; **to ~ with sth** estar repleto de algo; **to be ~ing with rain** estar diluviando

teeming *adj* muy numeroso, -a

teen ['tiːn] *n* adolescente *mf*

teenage(d) ['tiːneɪdʒ(d)] *adj* adolescente

teenager ['tiːneɪdʒə^{r}, *Am:* -dʒɚ] *n* adolescente *mf*

teens [tiːnz] *npl* adolescencia *f;* **to be in one's ~** no haber cumplido los veinte años

teensy [tiːnzi] *adj,* **teensy weensy** *adj,* **teeny** ['tiːni] *adj* chiquitín, -ina

teenybopper ['tiːniˌbɒpə^{r}, *Am:* -ˌbɑːpɚ] *n inf* quinceañero, -a *m, f*

teeny weeny [ˌtiːni'wiːni] *adj inf s.* **teensy**

tee-shirt ['tiːʃɜːt, *Am:* -ʃɜːrt] *n* camiseta *f*

teeter ['tiːtə^{r}, *Am:* -ṭɚ] *vi* **to ~ (around)** tambalearse; **to ~ on the brink of sth** estar a punto de algo

teeth [tiːθ] *pl of* **tooth**

teethe [tiːð] *vi* echar los dientes

teething problems *n,* **teething troubles** *n Brit, Aus, fig* problemas *mpl* de partida

teetotal [ˌtiː'təʊtəl, *Am:* -'toʊṭəl] *adj* abstemio, -a

teetotaler *n Am,* **teetotaller** [ˌtiː'təʊtələ^{r}, *Am:* -'toʊṭəlɚ] *n* abstemio, -a *m, f*

tel. *abbr of* **telephone** tel.

telecast ['telɪkɑːst, *Am:* -kæst] *n Am* transmisión *f* por televisión

telecommunications ['telɪkəˌmjuːnɪ'keɪʃnz] *npl* telecomunicaciones *fpl*

telecommuting ['telɪkɒˌmjuːtɪŋ] *n* INFOR

T

teletrabajo *m*
teleconference ['telɪˌkɒnfərəns, *Am:* -ˌkɑːn-] *n* teleconferencia *f*
telecopier® ['telɪkɒpɪə] *n Am* fotocopiadora *f*
telecopy ['telɪkɑpi] *n Am* fotocopia *f*
telefax® ['telɪfæks] *n* telefax *m*
telegenic [ˌtelɪ'dʒenɪk, *Am:* -ə'-] *adj* telegénico, -a
telegram ['telɪgræm] *n* telegrama *m*
telegraph ['telɪgrɑːf, *Am:* -græf] **I.** *n no pl* telégrafo *m* **II.** *vt* telegrafiar; **to ~ sb** mandar un telegrama a alguien **III.** *adj* telegráfico, -a
telegraphese [ˌtelɪgrə'fiːz, *Am:* -græf'iːz] *n no pl* estilo *m* telegráfico
telegraphic [ˌtelɪ'græfɪk, *Am:* -ə'-] *adj* telegráfico, -a
telegraph pole *n*, **telegraph post** *n Brit, Aus* poste *m* telegráfico
telegraphy [tɪ'legrəfi, *Am:* tə'leg-] *n no pl* telegrafía *f*
telemessage ['telɪˌmesɪdʒ] *n Brit* telegrama *m*
telepathic [ˌtelɪ'pæθɪk, *Am:* -ə'-] *adj* telepático, -a; **to be ~** tener telepatía
telepathy [tɪ'lepəθi, *Am:* tə'-] *n no pl* telepatía *f*
telephone ['telɪfəʊn, *Am:* -əfoʊn] **I.** *n* teléfono *m*; **mobile ~** (teléfono *m*) móvil *m* **II.** *vt* llamar por teléfono **III.** *vi* telefonear; **to ~ long-distance** hacer una llamada de larga distancia **IV.** *adj* telefónico, -a; (*booking*) por teléfono
telephone book *n* guía *f* telefónica **telephone booth** *n*, **telephone box** *n Am* cabina *f* telefónica **telephone call** *n* llamada *f* telefónica; **to make a ~** llamar por teléfono **telephone connection** *n* conexión *f* telefónica **telephone conversation** *n* conversación *f* telefónica **telephone directory** *n* guía *f* telefónica **telephone exchange** *n Brit* central *f* telefónica **telephone information service** *n form* servicio *m* de información telefónica **telephone message** *n form* mensaje *m* telefónico **telephone number** *n* número *m* de teléfono **telephone operator** *n Am* operador(a) *m(f)* telefónico, -a **telephone rates** *n* tarifa *f* telefónica
telephonist [tɪ'lefənɪst, *Am:* tə'-] *n Brit* telefonista *mf*
telephony [tɪ'lefəni, *Am:* tə'-] *n no pl* telefonía *f*; **digital mobile ~** telefonía móvil digital
telephoto lens [ˌtelɪfəʊtəʊ'lens, *Am:* 'teləfoʊt̬oʊ-] *n* teleobjetivo *m*
teleprinter ['telɪprɪntəʳ, *Am:* -əˌprɪnt̬ɚ] *n* teletipo *m*
teleprocessing ['telɪprəʊˌsesɪŋ] *n* INFOR teleproceso *m*
TelePrompter® ['telɪprɒmptəʳ, *Am:* -əˌprɑːmptɚ] *n Am, Aus* teleprompter® *m*
telesales ['telɪseɪls] *n no pl* ventas *fpl* por teléfono
telescope ['telɪskəʊp, *Am:* -əskoʊp] **I.** *n* telescopio *m* **II.** *vi* plegarse
telescopic [ˌtelɪ'skɒpɪk, *Am:* -ə'skɑːpɪk] *adj* **1.** (*vision, sight*) telescópico, -a **2.** (*folding*) plegable
teleshopping ['telɪʃɒpɪŋ, *Am:* 'teləʃɑːpɪŋ] *n* telecompra *f*; (*shop*) teletienda *f*
teletex® *n*, **Teletex®** ['telɪteks] *n no pl, Brit* teletexto *m*
teletype® *n*, **Teletype®** ['telɪtaɪp, *Am:* 'telə-] *n* teletipo *m*
teletypewriter [ˌtelɪ'taɪpraɪtəʳ] *n Am* teletipo *m*
televangelist [ˌtelɪ'vændʒəlɪst] *n Am* predicador(a) *m(f)* de la tele
televiewer ['telɪˌvjuːəʳ, *Am:* -əˌvjuːɚ] *n* telespectador(a) *m(f)*
televise ['telɪvaɪz, *Am:* 'telə-] *vt* televisar; **to ~ sth live** transmitir algo en directo
television ['telɪˌvɪʒən, *Am:* 'teləvɪʒ-] *n* televisión *f*; **to watch ~** ver la televisión; **to turn the ~ on/off** encender/apagar la televisión
television announcer *n* locutor(a) *m(f)* de televisión **television camera** *n* cámara *f* de televisión **television program** *n Am, Aus*, **television programme** *n Brit* programa *m* de televisión **television set** *n* televisor *m* **television studio** *n* estudio *m* de televisión
teleworking ['telɪˌwɜːkɪŋ, *Am:* -ˌwɜːr-] *n* teletrabajo *m*
telex ['teleks] **I.** *n* <-es> télex *m* **II.** *adj* por télex **III.** *vt* enviar por télex; **to ~ sb sth** comunicar algo por télex a alguien
tell [tel] **I.** <told, told> *vt* **1.** (*say*) decir; **to ~ sb of sth** comunicar algo a alguien; **to ~ sb whether ...** informar a alguien de si...; **I told you so** te avisé **2.** (*narrate*) contar; **~ me another (one)** *inf* cuéntame otra **3.** (*command*) mandar; **to ~ sb to do sth** ordenar a alguien hacer algo; **do as you're told** *inf* haz lo que te mandan **4.** (*make out*) reconocer **5.** (*distinguish*) distinguir; **to ~ sth from sth** distinguir algo de algo **6.** (*know*) saber; **there is no telling** no hay manera de saberlo **7.** (*count*) contar; (*add up*) sumar; **all told** en total ►**to ~ it <u>like</u> it is** *inf* decir las cosas claras; **that <u>would</u> be ~ing** eso podría ser cierto; **you're ~ing <u>me</u>!** *inf* ¡a mí me lo vas a contar! **II.** <told, told> *vi* **1.** hablar; **to ~ of sth/sb** hablar de algo/alguien **2.** (*know*) saber; **you never can ~** nunca se sabe; **how can I ~?** ¡yo qué se!; **who can ~?** ¿quién sabe? **3.** (*have an effect*) tener efecto
◆**tell against** *vt Brit* **to ~ sb/sth** obrar en contra de alguien/algo
◆**tell apart** *vt* distinguir
◆**tell off** *vt* regañar; **to tell sb off for sth** reñir a alguien por algo
◆**tell on** *vt* **to ~ sb** chivarse de alguien
teller ['teləʳ, *Am:* -ɚ] *n* **1.** (*vote counter*) escrutador(a) *m(f)* **2.** (*bank employee*) cajero,

-a *m, f*

telling [ˈtelɪŋ] **I.** *adj* **1.** (*revealing*) revelador(a) **2.** (*significant*) contundente **II.** *n* narración *f*

telling-off [ˈtelɪŋˈɒf, *Am:* ˌtelɪŋˈɑːf] <tellings-off> *n* bronca *f;* **to give sb a ~ for** (**doing**) **sth** echar una bronca a alguien por (hacer) algo

telltale [ˈtelteɪl] **I.** *n pej* chivato, -a *m, f* **II.** *adj* revelador(a)

telly [ˈteli] *n Brit, Aus, inf* tele *f*

temerity [tɪˈmerəti, *Am:* təˈmerəţi] *n no pl, form* temeridad *f;* **to have the ~ to do sth** atreverse a hacer algo

temp [temp] **I.** *vi* trabajar temporalmente **II.** *n* trabajador(a) *m(f)* temporal

temp. *abbr of* **temperature** temperatura

temper [ˈtempəʳ, *Am:* -pɚ] **I.** *n* (*temperament*) temperamento *m;* (*mood*) humor *m;* (*tendency to become angry*) genio *m;* **good ~** buen humor; **bad ~** mal genio; **to get into a ~** ponerse como una fiera; **to keep one's ~** no perder la calma; **to lose one's ~** perder los estribos; **~s were getting** (**rather**) **frayed** el ambiente se estaba cargando **II.** *vt* **1.** (*mitigate*) mitigar, atenuar; **to ~ one's criticism** suavizar las críticas **2.** (*make hard*) templar

temperament [ˈtemprəmənt] *n* (*character*) temperamento *m;* (*moodiness*) genio *m;* **a fit of ~** un ataque de furia

temperamental [ˌtemprəˈmentl, *Am:* -ţl] *adj* **1.** (*relating to mood*) temperamental **2.** (*unpredictable*) caprichoso, -a

temperance [ˈtempərəns] *n no pl, form* (*moderation*) moderación *f;* (*abstinence*) abstinencia *f*

temperate [ˈtempərət] *adj* (*moderate*) moderado, -a; (*climate*) templado, -a

temperature [ˈtemprətʃəʳ, *Am:* -pɚətʃɚ] *n* temperatura *f;* MED fiebre *f;* **to run a ~** tener fiebre

tempest [ˈtempɪst] *n liter* tempestad *f*

tempestuous [temˈpestjʊəs, *Am:* -tʃuəs] *adj* tempestuoso, -a

template [ˈtemplɪt] *n* plantilla *f*

temple[1] [ˈtempl] *n* REL templo *m*

temple[2] [ˈtempl] *n* ANAT sien *f*

tempo [ˈtempəʊ, *Am:* -poʊ] <-s *o* -pi> *n* **1.** MUS tempo *m* **2.** (*pace*) ritmo *m*

temporal [ˈtempərəl] *adj form* temporal

temporarily [ˈtemprərəli, *Am:* ˈtempərerəli] *adv* temporalmente

temporary [ˈtemprəri, *Am:* ˈtempəreri] *adj* (*improvement*) pasajero, -a; (*staff, accommodation*) temporal; (*relief*) momentáneo, -a

temporize [ˈtempəraɪz] *vi* tratar de ganar tiempo

tempt [tempt] *vt* **1.** tentar; **to ~ sb into doing sth** tentar a alguien a hacer algo **2.** (*persuade*) convencer; **to ~ sb into doing sth** incitar a alguien a hacer algo

temptation [tempˈteɪʃən] *n* **1.** *no pl* (*attraction*) tentación *f;* **to resist ~** (**to do sth**) resistir la tentación (de hacer algo); **to succumb to ~** ceder a la tentación **2.** (*tempting thing*) aliciente *m*

tempting [ˈtemptɪŋ] *adj* atractivo, -a; (*offer*) tentador(a)

temptress [ˈtemptrɪs] <-es> *n* tentadora *f*

ten [ten] **I.** *adj* diez *inv* **II.** *n* diez *m;* **~ to one he comes** seguro que viene; **~s of thousands** decenas *fpl* de miles; *s. a.* **eight**

tenable [ˈtenəbl] *adj* defendible

tenacious [tɪˈneɪʃəs, *Am:* təˈ-] *adj* (*belief*) firme; (*person*) tenaz

tenacity [tɪˈnæsəti, *Am:* təˈnæsəţi] *n no pl* tenacidad *f*

tenancy [ˈtenənsi] <-ies> *n* **1.** (*status*) inquilinato *m* **2.** (*right*) arrendamiento *m*

tenant [ˈtenənt] *n* (*of land*) arrendatario, -a *m, f;* (*of house*) inquilino, -a *m, f*

tenant farmer *n* (*of land*) agricultor(a) *m(f)* arrendatario, -a

tench [ten(t)ʃ] *n* tenca *f*

tend[1] [tend] *vi* **1.** (*have tendency*) tender; **to ~ to do sth** tender a hacer algo; **I ~ to disagree** *Brit* no comparto completamente su opinión **2.** (*usually do*) soler

tend[2] [tend] *vt* (*look after*) ocuparse de; (*a person*) cuidar de

◆**tend to** *vt* (*look after*) ocuparse de

tendency [ˈtendənsi] <-ies> *n* tendencia *f;* MED propensión *f*

tendentious [tenˈdenʃəs] *adj* tendencioso, -a

tender[1] [ˈtendəʳ, *Am:* -dɚ] *adj* **1.** (*not tough*) vulnerable **2.** (*easily damaged*) débil **3.** *liter* (*youthful: age*) tierno, -a **4.** (*painful*) doloroso, -a; (*part of the body*) sensible; (*subject*) delicado, -a **5.** (*affectionate*) cariñoso, -a; **to have a ~ heart** tener buen corazón

tender[2] [ˈtendəʳ, *Am:* -dɚ] **I.** *n* COM oferta *f;* **to put in a ~** hacer una oferta; **to put sth out for ~** *Brit* sacar algo a concurso **II.** *vt* (*offer*) ofrecer; (*apology*) presentar **III.** *vi* **to ~ for sth** hacer una oferta para algo

tender[3] [ˈtendəʳ, *Am:* -dɚ] *n* RAIL ténder *m;* NAUT gabarra *f*

tenderfoot [ˈtendəfʊt, *Am:* -dɚ-] <-s *o* -feet> *n Am* principiante *mf*

tender-hearted [ˌtendəˈhɑːtɪd, *Am:* ˈtendɚˌhɑːrţɪd] *adj* bondadoso, -a; **to be ~** tener buen corazón

tenderize [ˈtendəraɪz] *vt* ablandar

tenderizer *n* ablandador *m* de carne

tenderloin [ˈtendəlɔɪn, *Am:* -dɚ-] *n no pl* lomo *m*

tenderly *adv* cariñosamente

tenderness [ˈtendənɪs, *Am:* -ɚ-] *n no pl* **1.** (*softness*) blandura *f* **2.** (*affection*) ternura *f* **3.** (*sensitivity*) sensibilidad *f*

tendon [ˈtendən] *n* tendón *m*

tendril [ˈtendrəl] *n* zarcillo *m*

tenement [ˈtenəmənt] *n* bloque *m* de pisos

Tenerife [ˌtenəˈriːf] *n* Tenerife *m*

tenet [ˈtenɪt] *n* principio *m*

tenfold ['tenfəʊld, *Am:* -foʊld] **I.** *adj* décuplo, -a **II.** *adv* diez veces
tenner ['tenəʳ, *Am:* -ɚ] *n Brit, inf* billete *m* de diez libras
tennis ['tenɪs] *n no pl* tenis *m*
tennis ball *n* pelota *f* de tenis **tennis court** *n* pista *f* de tenis **tennis elbow** *n* codo *m* de tenista **tennis player** *n* tenista *mf* **tennis racket** *n* raqueta *f* de tenis
tenon ['tenən] *n* espaldón *m*
tenor ['tenəʳ, *Am:* -ɚ] **I.** *n* **1.** *a.* MUS tenor *m* **2.** (*character*) tono *m;* (*of events*) curso *m* **II.** *adj* MUS de tenor
tenpin bowling [ˌtenpɪn'bəʊlɪŋ, *Am:* -'boʊ-] *n* bolos *mpl*
tense¹ [tents] *n* LING tiempo *m*
tense² [tents] **I.** *adj* (*wire, person, atmosphere*) tenso, -a **II.** *vt* tensar **III.** *vi* ponerse tenso
◆**tense up** *vi* ponerse tenso
tension ['tentʃən] *n no pl* tensión *f*
tent [tent] *n* (*for camping*) tienda *f* de campaña, carpa *f AmL;* (*in circus*) carpa *f*
tentacle ['tentəkl, *Am:* -t̬ə-] *n* tentáculo *m*
tentative ['tentətɪv, *Am:* -t̬ət̬ɪv] *adj* **1.** (*person*) vacilante **2.** (*decision*) provisional
tentatively *adv* **1.** (*suggest*) con vacilación **2.** (*decide*) provisionalmente
tenterhooks ['tentəhʊks, *Am:* -t̬ɚ-] *npl* **to be on ~** tener el alma en vilo; **to keep sb on ~** tener a alguien en ascuas
tenth [tenθ] **I.** *adj* décimo, -a **II.** *n no pl* **1.** (*order*) décimo, -a *m, f* **2.** (*date*) diez *m* **3.** (*fraction*) décimo *m;* (*part*) décima parte *f; s. a.* **eighth**
tent peg *n* estaquilla *f* de tienda **tent pole** *n* mástil *m* de tienda
tenuous ['tenjʊəs] *adj* tenue; (*connection*) sutil; (*argument*) poco sólido, -a
tenure ['tenjʊəʳ, *Am:* -jɚ] *n no pl* **1.** (*possession*) posesión *f,* tenencia *f* **2.** (*period of holding sth*) ejercicio *m*
tepee ['ti:pi:] *n* tipi *m*
tepid ['tepɪd] *adj* tibio, -a
term [tɜ:m, *Am:* tɜ:rm] **I.** *n* **1.** (*label, word*) término *m;* **~ of abuse** insulto *m;* **~ of endearment** expresión *f* afectuosa; **in glowing ~s** con gran admiración; **in no uncertain ~s** en términos claros; **in simple ~s** en palabras sencillas **2.** *pl* (*conditions*) condiciones *fpl;* **to offer easy ~s** ofrecer facilidades de pago **3.** (*limit*) límite *m;* COM plazo *m;* **~ of delivery** plazo de entrega; **~ of notice** plazo de despido **4.** (*period*) período *m;* (*duration*) duración *f;* (*of contract*) vigencia *f;* (*of office*) mandato *m;* **prison ~** sentencia *f* de prisión; **in the short/long ~** a corto/largo plazo **5.** (*category*) término *m;* **to think in ~s of sth** pensar en términos de algo **6.** *Brit* UNIV, SCHOOL trimestre *m* **7.** *pl* relaciones *fpl;* **to be on good/bad ~s with sb** llevarse bien/mal con alguien **II.** *vt* llamar; (*label*) calificar de
terminal ['tɜ:mɪnl, *Am:* 'tɜ:r-] **I.** *adj* terminal; (*extreme*) absoluto, -a; (*boredom*) mortal **II.** *n* **1.** RAIL, AVIAT, INFOR terminal *f* **2.** ELEC polo *m*
terminate ['tɜ:mɪneɪt, *Am:* 'tɜ:r-] *form* **I.** *vt* (*finish*) poner fin a; (*contract*) rescindir; (*pregnancy*) interrumpir **II.** *vi* terminarse
termination [ˌtɜ:mɪ'neɪʃən, *Am:* ˌtɜ:r-] *n no pl* (*ending*) fin *m;* (*of contract*) rescisión *f;* (*of pregnancy*) interrupción *f*
terminological [ˌtɜ:mɪnə'lɒdʒɪkl, *Am:* ˌtɜ:rmɪnə'lɑ:dʒɪ-] *adj* terminológico, -a
terminology [ˌtɜ:mɪ'nɒlədʒi, *Am:* ˌtɜ:r-mɪ'nɑ:lə-] *n* terminología *f*
terminus ['tɜ:mɪnəs, *Am:* 'tɜ:r-] <-es *o* -i> *n* (*station*) estación *f* terminal; (*bus stop*) última parada *f*
termite ['tɜ:maɪt, *Am:* 'tɜ:r-] *n* termita *f*
tern [tɜ:n, *Am:* tɜ:rn] *n* golondrina *f* de mar
terrace ['terəs] **I.** *n* **1.** *a.* AGR terraza *f* **2.** *pl, Brit* SPORTS gradas *fpl* **3.** *Brit, Aus* (*row of houses*) hilera *f* de casas adosadas **II.** *vt* formar terrazas en **III.** *adj* en terrazas
terraced house *n* casa *f* adosada
terrain [te'reɪn] *n* terreno *m*
terrapin ['terəpɪn] <-(s)> *n* galápago *m*
terrestrial [tɪ'restrɪəl, *Am:* tə'-] *adj form* terrestre
terrible ['terəbl] *adj* **1.** (*shocking*) terrible **2.** (*very bad*) espantoso, -a **3.** *inf* (*as intensifier*) fatal
terribly ['terəbli] *adv* **1.** (*very badly*) terriblemente **2.** (*very*) tremendamente
terrier ['terɪəʳ, *Am:* -ɚ] *n* terrier *m*
terrific [tə'rɪfɪk] *adj* **1.** (*terrifying*) terrorífico, -a **2.** (*excellent*) tremendo, -a **3.** *as intensifier* (*very great*) estupendo, -a
terrified *adj* aterrorizado, -a
terrify ['terəfaɪ] <-ie-> *vt* aterrar
terrifying *adj* aterrador(a)
territorial [ˌterɪ'tɔ:rɪəl, *Am:* -ə'-] **I.** *n* MIL reservista *m* **II.** *adj* territorial
territory ['terɪtəri, *Am:* 'terətɔ:ri] <-ies> *n* **1.** (*area of land*) territorio *m;* **forbidden ~** zona *f* prohibida **2.** (*activity*) terreno *m*
terror ['terəʳ, *Am:* -ɚ] *n no pl* terror *m;* **to have a ~ of sth** tener miedo a algo; **to strike ~** infundir terror; **to be in ~ of one's life** temer por la vida de uno; **a ~ of a child** *inf* un niño terrible
terrorism ['terərɪzəm] *n no pl* terrorismo *m*
terrorist ['terərɪst] **I.** *n* terrorista *mf* **II.** *adj* terrorista
terrorize ['terəraɪz] *vt* aterrorizar
terror-stricken ['terəˌstrɪkən, *Am:* -ɚˌ-] *adj,* **terror-struck** ['terəstrʌk, *Am:* '-ɚ-] *adj* aterrorizado, -a
terry cloth [ˌteri'klɒθ, *Am:* -'klɑ:θ] *n no pl* felpa *f*
terse [tɜ:s, *Am:* tɜ:rs] *adj* lacónico, -a
tertiary ['tɜ:ʃəri, *Am:* 'tɜ:rʃɪeri] **I.** *adj form* terciario, -a **II.** <-ies> *n* **the Tertiary** GEO el Terciario
tessellated ['tesəleɪtɪd, *Am:* -t̬ɪd] *adj* teselado, -a

test [test] I. *n* 1. SCHOOL, UNIV examen *m;* **to pass/fail a ~** aprobar/suspender un examen; **driving ~** examen de conducir 2. MED prueba *f;* **blood ~** análisis *m inv* de sangre 3. (*trial*) **to be a ~ of endurance** ser una prueba de resistencia; **to put sth to the ~** poner algo a prueba II. *vt* 1. (*examine*) examinar 2. MED analizar; (*hearing*) examinar; **to ~ sb for sth** hacer a alguien una prueba de algo 3. (*measure*) comprobar 4. (*try to prove*) someter a prueba 5. (*try with senses*) tocar; (*by tasting*) probar

testament ['testəmənt] *n* 1. *form* (*will*) testamento *m;* **last will and ~** testamento y últimas voluntades 2. *form* (*evidence*) testimonio *m* 3. REL **the Old/New ~** el Antiguo/Nuevo Testamento

test ban *n* prohibición *f* de ensayos nucleares **test bench** *n* banco *m* de pruebas **test card** *n* carta *f* de ajuste **test case** *n* causa *f* que sienta jurisprudencia **test drive** *n* prueba *f* de carretera

tester ['testəʳ, *Am:* -ɚ] *n* 1. (*person*) examinador(a) *m(f)* 2. (*sample*) frasco *m* de muestra

test flight *n* vuelo *m* de ensayo

testicle ['testɪkl] *n* testículo *m*

testify ['testɪfaɪ] <-ie-> I. *vi* 1. (*give evidence*) testificar 2. *form* (*prove*) **to ~ to sth** atestiguar algo II. *vt* 1. (*bear witness to*) demostrar 2. (*declare under oath*) testificar; **to ~ that ...** declarar que...

testimonial [ˌtestɪ'məʊnɪəl, *Am:* -'moʊ-] *n form* 1. (*character reference*) referencias *fpl* 2. (*tribute*) homenaje *m*

testimony ['testɪməni, *Am:* -moʊni] <-ies> *n* testimonio *m;* **to give ~** dar testimonio

testing I. *n no pl* experiencia *f* II. *adj* duro, -a; **~ times** tiempos *mpl* difíciles

testing ground *n* zona *f* de pruebas

test match *n* partido *m* internacional **test piece** *n* MUS obra *f* elegida para un certamen **test pilot** *n* piloto *mf* de pruebas **test stage** *n* período *m* de pruebas

test tube *n* probeta *f* **test-tube baby** *n* bebé *m* probeta

testy ['testi] <-ier, -iest> *adj* irritable

tetanus ['tetənəs] *n no pl* tétano *m;* **~ injection** vacuna *f* contra el tétano

tetchy ['tetʃi] <-ier, -iest> *adj* irritable

tether ['teðəʳ, *Am:* -ɚ] I. *n* cuerda *f* ►**to be at the end of one's ~** no aguantar más II. *vt* amarrar; **to be ~ed to sth** *fig* estar atado a algo

Teutonic [tjuː'tɒnɪk, *Am:* tuː'tɑːnɪk] *adj* teutónico, -a

Texan ['teksən] I. *n* tejano, -a *m, f* II. *adj* tejano, -a

Texas ['teksəs] *n* Tejas *m*

text [tekst] *n* texto *m*

textbook ['tekstbʊk] I. *n* libro *m* de texto II. *adj* de manual

text editor *n* INFOR editor *m* de textos

textile ['tekstaɪl] I. *n pl* tejidos *mpl* II. *adj* textil

textile mill *n* fábrica *f* de tejidos

text processing *n* INFOR procesamiento *m* de textos

textual ['tekstʃʊəl, *Am:* -tʃu-] *adj* textual

texture ['tekstʃəʳ, *Am:* -tʃɚ] *n* 1. (*feel*) textura *f* 2. (*consistency*) estructura *f*

Thai [taɪ] I. *adj* tailandés, -esa II. *n* 1. (*person*) tailandés, -esa *m, f* 2. LING tailandés *m*

Thailand ['taɪlənd] *n* Tailandia *m*

thalidomide [θə'lɪdəʊmaɪd] *n* talidomida *f*

Thames [temz] *n no pl* **the (River) ~** el Támesis

than [ðən, ðæn] *conj* que; **you are taller ~ she (is)** eres más alto que ella; **more ~ 60** más de 60; **more ~ once** más de una vez; **nothing else ~ ...** nada más que...; **no other ~ you** nadie más que tú; **no sooner had she told him, ~ ...** en cuanto se lo dijo...

thank [θæŋk] *vt* agradecer; **to ~ sb (for sth)** dar las gracias a alguien (por algo); **~ you** gracias; **~ you very much!** ¡muchas gracias!; **no, ~ you** no, gracias

thankful ['θæŋkfəl] *adj* 1. (*pleased*) satisfecho, -a; **to be ~ that ...** alegrarse de que... +*subj* 2. (*grateful*) agradecido, -a

thankfully *adv* afortunadamente

thankless ['θæŋkləs] *adj* desagradecido, -a; (*task*) ingrato, -a

thanks [θæŋks] *npl* gracias *fpl;* **~ very much** muchísimas gracias; **~ to** gracias a; **in ~ for ...** en recompensa por...; **no ~ to him** no fue gracias a él

thanksgiving [ˌθæŋks'gɪvɪŋ] *n no pl* acción *f* de gracias

> **Thanksgiving** (Acción de Gracias) es una de las fiestas más importantes de los EE.UU. Se celebra el cuarto jueves del mes de noviembre. El primer **Thanksgiving Day** fue celebrado en 1621 por los **Pilgrims** en **Plymouth Colony**. Habían sobrevivido a grandes dificultades y querían dar las gracias a Dios por ello. Es costumbre que las familias se reúnan para celebrar este día. La comida principal consiste en **stuffed turkey** (pavo relleno), **cranberry sauce** (salsa de arándanos), **yams** (patatas dulces) y **corn** (maíz).

Thanksgiving Day *n* Día *m* de Acción de Gracias (*en Estados Unidos se celebra el último martes de noviembre, en Canadá el segundo lunes de octubre*)

that [ðæt, ðət] I. *adj dem* <those> ese, esa, eso; (*more remote*) aquel, aquella, aquello; **~ table** esa mesa; **~ book** ese libro II. *pron* 1. *rel* que; **the woman ~ told me ...** la mujer que me dijo...; **all ~ I have** todo lo que tengo 2. *dem* **what is ~?** ¿eso qué es?; **who is ~?** ¿ése/ésa quién es?; **like ~** así; **after ~** después de eso; **~'s it!** ¡eso es! III. *adv* tan; **it was ~ hot** hacía tanto calor IV. *conj* 1. que; **I told you ~ I couldn't come** te he dicho que no puedo ir; **~ I should live to see this!** ¡que tenga que vivir para ver algo así! **2.** (*in order that*) para que +*subj*

thatch [θætʃ] **I.** *n no pl* **1.** (*roof*) techo *m* de paja **2.** (*hair*) mata *f* (de pelo) **II.** *vt* poner un techo de paja a

thatched roof *n* techo *m* de paja

thaw [θɔː, *Am:* θɑː] **I.** *n* **1.** (*weather*) deshielo *m* **2.** (*in relations*) distensión *f* **II.** *vi* **1.** (*weather*) deshelar; (*food*) descongelarse **2.** (*relations*) volverse más cordial **III.** *vt* derretir

the [ðə, *stressed, before vowel* ðiː] **I.** *def art* el *m,* la *f,* los *mpl,* las *fpl;* **from ~ garden** del jardín; **at ~ hotel** en el hotel; **at ~ door** a la puerta; **to ~ garden** al jardín; **in ~ winter** en invierno **II.** *adv* (*in comparison*) **~ more one tries, ~ less one succeeds** cuanto más se esfuerza uno, menos lo logra; **~ sooner ~ better** cuanto antes mejor

theater *n Am,* **theatre** [ˈθɪətəʳ, *Am:* ˈθiːət̬ɚ] *n Brit, Aus* **1.** THEAT (*place, art*) teatro *m;* (*company*) compañía *f* de teatro **2.** *Am, Aus* CINE cine *m* **3.** UNIV aula *f* **4.** *Brit* (*in hospital*) **operating ~** quirófano *m* **5.** *fig* (*scene*) escenario *m*

theatre company *n* compañía *f* de teatro **theatre critic** *n* crítica *f* teatral **theatregoer** *n* aficionado, -a *m, f* al teatro

theatrical [θɪˈætrɪkl] *adj* teatral; **don't be so ~ about it** no hagas tanto teatro por eso

thee [ðiː] *pron pers* HIST te; **with ~** contigo

theft [θeft] *n* robo *m;* **petty ~** hurto *m*

their [ðeəʳ, *Am:* ðer] *adj pos* su(s); **~ house** su casa; **~ children** sus hijos

theirs [ðeəz, *Am:* ðerz] *pron pos* (el) suyo *m,* (la) suya *f,* (los) suyos *mpl,* (las) suyas *fpl;* **this house is ~** esta casa es suya; **they aren't our bags, they are ~** no son nuestras bolsas, son suyas; **a book of ~** un libro suyo

theism [ˈθiːɪzəm] *n no pl* teísmo *m*

them [ðem, ðəm] *pron pers pl* **1.** (*they*) ellos, -as; **older than ~** mayor que ellos; **if I were ~** si yo fuese ellos **2.** *direct object* los, las; *indirect object* les; **look at ~** míralos; **I saw ~** yo los vi; **he gave ~ the pencil** les ha dado el lápiz **3.** *after prep* ellos, -as; **it's from/for ~** es de/para ellos

thematic [ˌθiːmˈætɪk, *Am:* θiːˈmæt̬-] *adj* temático, -a

theme [θiːm] *n a.* MUS tema *m;* **on the ~ of** sobre el tema de

theme music *n no pl* sintonía *f* **theme park** *n* parque *m* temático **theme song** *n,* **theme tune** *n no pl* sintonía *f*

themselves [ðəmˈselvz] *pron* **1.** *subject* ellos mismos, ellas mismas **2.** *object, reflexive* se; **the children behaved ~** los niños se portaron bien **3.** *after prep* sí mismos, sí mismas; **by ~** solos, -as

then [ðen] **I.** *adj form* (de) entonces; **the ~ chairman** el entonces presidente **II.** *adv* **1.** (*at aforementioned time*) entonces; **before ~** hasta entonces; **from ~ on**(**wards**) a partir de entonces; **since ~** desde entonces; **until ~** hasta aquel momento; (**every**) **now and ~** de vez en cuando **2.** (*after that*) después; **what ~?** ¿y qué? **3.** (*additionally*) además; **but ~** (**again**) pero también, y además **4.** (*as a result*) por tanto, así pues; **~ he must be there** entonces debe estar ahí **5.** (*that being the case*) en ese caso **6.** (*agreement*) **all right ~** de acuerdo pues

thence [ðens] *adv form* de ahí

thenceforth [ˌðensˈfɔːθ, *Am:* -ˈfɔːrθ] *adv form,* **thenceforward** [ˌðensˈfɔːwəd, *Am:* -ˈfɔːrwɚd] *adv form* a partir de entonces

theocracy [θɪˈɒkrəsi, *Am:* -ˈɑːkrə-] <-ies> *n no pl* teocracia *f*

theodolite [θɪˈɒdəlaɪt, *Am:* -ˈɑːdəlaɪt] *n* teodolito *m*

theologian [ˌθɪəˈləʊdʒən, *Am:* ˌθiːəˈloʊ-] *n* teólogo, -a *m, f*

theological [ˌθɪəˈlɒdʒɪkl, *Am:* ˌθiːəˈlɑːdʒɪ-] *adj* teológico, -a

theology [θɪˈɒlədʒi, *Am:* -ˈɑːlə-] <-ies> *n* teología *f*

theorem [ˈθɪərəm, *Am:* ˈθiːɚəm] *n* MAT teorema *m;* **Pythagoras's ~** el teorema de Pitágoras

theoretical [θɪəˈretɪkəl, *Am:* ˌθiːəˈret̬-] *adj* teórico, -a

theoretically *adv* teóricamente

theorist [ˈθɪərɪst, *Am:* ˈθiːɚɪst] *n* teórico, -a *m, f*

theorize [ˈθɪəraɪz, *Am:* ˈθiːə-] *vi* teorizar

theory [ˈθɪəri, *Am:* ˈθiːə-] <-ies> *n* teoría *f;* **in ~** en teoría

therapeutic(**al**) [ˌθerəˈpjuːtɪk(əl), *Am:* -t̬ɪk-] *adj* terapéutico, -a

therapeutics [ˌθerəˈpjuːtɪks, *Am:* -t̬ɪks] *n* terapéutica *f*

therapist [ˈθerəpɪst] *n* terapeuta *mf*

therapy [ˈθerəpi] <-ies> *n* terapia *f*

there [ðeəʳ, *Am:* ðer] **I.** *adv* allí, allá; **here and ~** aquí y allá; **~ is/are** hay; **~ will be** habrá; **~ you are!** ¡ahí lo tienes!; **~'s the train** ahí está el tren; **~ is no one** no hay nadie; **~ and then** en el acto **II.** *interj* vaya; **~, take this** toma esto; **~, that's enough!** ¡bueno, basta ya!

thereabouts [ˈðeərəbaʊts, *Am:* ˈðerə-] *adv* (*approximately*) más o menos; (*near*) por ahí

thereafter [ðeərˈɑːftəʳ, *Am:* ðerˈæftɚ] *adv* a partir de entonces

thereby [ðeəˈbaɪ, *Am:* ðerˈ-] *adv form* por eso ►**~ hangs a tale** *iron* es una larga historia

therefore [ˈðeəfɔːʳ, *Am:* ˈðerfɔːr] *adv* por (lo) tanto; **to decide ~ to do sth** decidir hacer algo por consiguiente

therein [ðeərˈɪn, *Am:* ðerˈ-] *adv form* ahí dentro; *fig* en eso

thereof [ðeərˈɒv, *Am:* ðerˈɑːv] *adv form* de eso

thereupon [ˌðeərəˈpɒn, *Am:* ˌðerəˈpɑːn]

adv acto seguido

therm [θɜːm, *Am:* θɜːrm] *n* termia *f*

thermal ['θɜːməl, *Am:* 'θɜːr-] I. *n* 1. (*air current*) corriente *f* térmica 2. *pl* (*underwear*) ropa *f* interior térmica II. *adj* PHYS, INFOR térmico, -a; (*water*) termal

thermal underwear *n* ropa *f* interior térmica

thermodynamic [ˌθɜːməʊdaɪ'næmɪk, *Am:* ˌθɜːrmoʊ-] *adj* termodinámico, -a

thermoelectric [ˌθɜːməʊɪ'lektrɪk, *Am:* ˌθɜːrmoʊɪ'-] *adj* termoeléctrico, -a

thermometer [θə'mɒmɪtəʳ, *Am:* θɚ'mɑːməṭɚ] *n* termómetro *m*

thermonuclear [ˌθɜːməʊ'njuːklɪəʳ, *Am:* ˌθɜːrmoʊ'nuːklɪɚ] *adj* termonuclear

Thermos® (**bottle**) ['θɜːmɒs(ˌbɒtl), *Am:* 'θɜːrməs(ˌbɑːṭl)] *n*, **Thermos® flask** *n* termo *m*

thermostat ['θɜːməʊstæt, *Am:* 'θɜːrməstæt] *n* termostato *m*

thermostatic [ˌθɜːməʊ'stætɪk, *Am:* ˌθɜːrmə'stæṭ-] *adj* termostático, -a

thesaurus [θɪ'sɔːrəs] <-es *o* -ri> *n* diccionario *m* de sinónimos

these [ðiːz] *pl of* **this**

thesis ['θiːsɪs] <-ses> *n* tesis *f inv*

they [ðeɪ] *pron pers* 1. (*3rd person pl*) ellos, -as; ~ **are my parents/sisters** (ellos/ellas) son mis padres/hermanas 2. (*people in general*) ~ **say that ...** dicen que...

they'll [ðeɪl] = **they will** *s.* **will**

they're [ðeɪr, *Am:* ðer] = **they are** *s.* **be**

they've [ðeɪv] = **they have** *s.* **have**

thick [θɪk] I. *adj* 1. (*not thin: wall*) grueso, -a; (*coat*) gordo, -a 2. (*dense: hair*) abundante; (*forest*) denso, -a; (*liquid*) espeso, -a 3. (*extreme: darkness*) profundo, -a; (*accent*) marcado, -a 4. (*stupid*) corto, -a; **to be as ~ as two short planks** *inf* no tener dos dedos de frente 5. (*very friendly*) **to be ~ with sb** ser muy amigo de alguien 6. *Brit, inf* (*plentiful*) atestado, -a 7. *Brit* (*not right*) **to be a bit ~** ser injusto ►**through ~ and thin** a las duras y a las maduras II. *n no pl, inf* **to be in the ~ of sth** estar de lleno en algo

thicken ['θɪkən] I. *vt* espesar II. *vi* espesarse

thickener *n*, **thickening** *n* espesante *m*

thicket ['θɪkɪt] *n* matorral *m*

thick-headed [ˌθɪk'hedɪd, *Am:* 'θɪkˌhedɪd] *adj* ceporro, -a

thickness ['θɪknɪs] *n* 1. *no pl* (*size*) grosor *m* 2. (*of hair*) abundancia *f*; (*of sauce*) consistencia *f*

thickset [ˌθɪk'set, *Am:* 'θɪkset] *adj* rechoncho, -a

thick-skinned [ˌθɪk'skɪnd, *Am:* 'θɪkskɪnd] *adj* insensible; **he is ~** todo le resbala

thief [θiːf, *s* 'θiːvz] <thieves> *n* ladrón, -ona *m, f*

thieve [θiːv] *vi, vt liter* robar

thieving ['θiːvɪŋ] I. *n liter* robo *m* II. *adj* de dedos largos

thigh [θaɪ] *n* muslo *m*

thigh bone *n* fémur *m*

thimble ['θɪmbl] *n* dedal *m*

thin [θɪn] <-nn-> I. *adj* 1. (*not thick: clothes*) fino, -a; (*person*) delgado, -a; (*very slim*) flaco, -a 2. (*soup, sauce*) claro, -a; (*wine*) aguado, -a 3. (*sparse: hair*) ralo, -a; **to be ~ on top** ser calvo 4. (*voice*) débil; (*excuse*) poco convincente II. <-nn-> *vt* (*dilute*) aclarar

◆**thin down** I. *vi* adelgazar II. *vt* aclarar

◆**thin out** I. *vt* hacer menos denso; (*plants*) entresacar II. *vi* disminuir

thine [ðaɪn] *pron pos* HIST (el) tuyo *m*, (la) tuya *f*, (lo) tuyo *neuter*, (los) tuyos *mpl*, (las) tuyas *fpl*

thing [θɪŋ] *n* 1. (*object, action*) cosa *f*; **the lucky/best/main ~** lo bueno/mejor/principal; **sweet ~s** pasteles *mpl*; **one ~ after another** una cosa después de otra; **to be a ~ of the past** ser algo del pasado; **the last ~ she wants to do is ...** lo último que quiere hacer es... 2. (*matter*) **to know a ~ or two** saber algo; **above all ~s** por encima de todo; **another ~** otra cosa; **and another ~, ...** y por otra parte,...; **if it's not one ~ it's another** cuando no es una cosa es otra 3. (*social behaviour*) **it's the done ~** es lo que hay que hacer 4. (*fashion*) **the latest ~ in shoes** el último grito en zapatos 5. *fam* (*the important point*) **the real ~** lo auténtico; **the very ~** lo importante 6. *pl* (*possessions*) pertenencias *fpl*; **all his ~s** todas sus cosas 7. *pl* (*the situation*) **as ~s stand, the way ~s are** tal como están las cosas; **the shape of ~s to come** lo que se avecina 8. *inf* (*term of affection*) **the poor ~!** ¡el pobre!; (*children, animals*) ¡pobrecito!; **you lucky ~!** ¡qué suerte tienes!; **¡lazy ~!** ¡vago!; **¡stupid ~!** ¡imbécil! ►**to be all ~s to all men** actuar según sopla el viento; **it's just one of those ~s** es una de esas cosas que pasan; **he won but it was a close ~** ganó por un pelo; **all ~s being equal** si no sale ningún imprevisto; **first ~s first** lo primero es lo primero; **to not know the first ~ about sth** no tener ni la remota idea de algo; **to be onto a good ~** *inf* tener un chollo; **to do one's own ~** hacer la suya; **to have a ~ about sth** *inf* tener asco a algo; **to be hearing ~s** oír campanas; **to make a** (**big**) **~ out of sth** armar un escándalo por algo

thingamabob ['θɪŋəməˌbɒb, *Am:* -bɑːb] *n*, **thingamajig** ['θɪŋəməˌdʒɪg] *n*, **thingy** ['θɪŋi] *n* (*object*) cosa *f*; (*person*) ése, ésa

think [θɪŋk] <thought, thought> I. *n* **to have a ~ about sth** pensarse algo II. *vt* 1. (*believe*) pensar, creer; **who would have thought it!** ¡quien lo hubiese pensado! 2. (*consider*) considerar; **to ~ sb** (**to be**) **sth** considerar a alguien como algo; **to ~ nothing of sb** no tener ninguna fe en alguien; **~ nothing of it!** ¡no merece la pena mencionarlo! III. *vi* pensar; **to ~ aloud** pensar en voz alta; **to ~ for oneself** pensar por sí mismo; **to ~ to oneself**

pensar para sí mismo; **to ~ of doing sth** pensar en hacer algo; **to ~ about/of sb/sth** pensar en alguien/algo

◆**think ahead** *vi* pensar de cara al futuro

◆**think back** *vi* **to ~ to sth** recordar algo; **to ~ over sth** hacer memoria de algo

◆**think of** *vi* pensar en

◆**think out** *vt* **1.** (*consider*) pensar muy bien **2.** (*plan*) planear cuidadosamente

◆**think over** *vt* reflexionar sobre

◆**think through** *vt* estudiar detenidamente

◆**think up** *vt* inventar

thinker *n* pensador(a) *m(f)*

thinking I. *n no pl* **1.** (*thought process*) pensamiento *m* **2.** (*reasoning*) razonamiento *m* **3.** (*opinion*) opinión *f* **II.** *adj* inteligente

think tank *n* gabinete *m* estratégico

thinner *n* disolvente *m*

thinness *n no pl* delgadez *f*

thin-skinned [ˌθɪn'skɪnd, *Am:* 'θɪnskɪnd] *adj* sensible

third [θɜːd, *Am:* θɜːrd] **I.** *adj* tercero, -a **II.** *n no pl* **1.** (*order*) tercero, -a *m, f* **2.** (*date*) tres *m* **3.** (*fraction*) tercio *m* **4.** MUS, AUTO tercera *f* **5.** *Brit* UNIV *cuarta nota de la escala de calificaciones del título universitario; s. a.* **eighth**

third degree *n* **to give sb the ~** someter a alguien al tercer grado **third-degree burns** *npl* quemaduras *fpl* de tercer grado

thirdly *adv* en tercer lugar

third party *n* tercero *m* **third-party insurance** *n*, **third-party liability** *n* seguro *m* a terceros

third person *n* LING tercera persona *f* **third-rate** *adj* de baja categoría **Third World** *n* **the ~** el Tercer Mundo

thirst [θɜːst, *Am:* θɜːrst] *n* sed *f;* **to die of ~** morir de sed; **to quench one's ~** apagar la sed; **~ for power** ansias *fpl* de poder

thirsty ['θɜːsti, *Am:* 'θɜːr-] <-ier, -iest> *adj* sediento, -a; **to be ~** tener sed; **to be ~ for sth** *fig* estar ansioso por algo

thirteen [ˌθɜː'tiːn, *Am:* θɜːr'-] **I.** *adj* trece **II.** *n* trece *m; s. a.* **eight**

thirteenth [ˌθɜː'tiːnθ, *Am:* θɜːr'-] **I.** *adj* decimotercero, -a **II.** *n no pl* **1.** (*order*) decimotercero, -a *m, f* **2.** (*date*) trece *m* **3.** (*fraction*) decimotercero *m;* (*part*) decimotercera parte *f; s. a.* **eighth**

thirtieth ['θɜːtɪəθ, *Am:* 'θɜːrt̬ɪ-] **I.** *adj* trigésimo, -a **II.** *n* **1.** (*order*) trigésimo, -a *m, f* **2.** (*date*) treinta *m* **3.** (*fraction*) trigésimo *m;* (*part*) trigésima parte *f; s. a.* **eighth**

thirty ['θɜːti, *Am:* 'θɜːrt̬i] <-ies> **I.** *adj* treinta **II.** *n* treinta *m; s. a.* **eighty**

this [ðɪs] **I.** <these> *adj det* este, -a; **~ car** este coche; **~ house** esta casa; **~ one** éste, -a; **~ day** hoy; **~ morning/evening** esta mañana/tarde; **~ time** esta vez; **~ time last month** hoy hace un mes; **these days** hoy en día **II.** <these> *pron dem* éste *m,* ésta *f,* esto *neuter;* **what is ~?** ¿esto qué es?; **who is ~?** ¿éste/ésta quién es?; **~ and that** esto y aquello; **~ is Ana (speaking)** (*on the phone*) soy Ana **III.** *adv* así; **~ late** tan tarde; **~ much** tanto; **~ big** así de grande

thistle ['θɪsl] *n* cardo *m*

tho' [ðəʊ, *Am:* ðoʊ] *conj s.* **though**

thong [θɒŋ, *Am:* θɑːŋ] *n* **1.** (*strip of leather*) correa *f* **2.** (*G-string*) tanga *m* **3.** *pl, Am, Aus* (*sandal*) chanclas *fpl*

thorax ['θɔːræks] <-es *o* -aces> *n* tórax *m*

thorn [θɔːn, *Am:* θɔːrn] *n* espina *f* ►**that's a ~ in my flesh** es una espina que tengo clavada

thorny ['θɔːni, *Am:* 'θɔːr-] <-ier, -iest> *adj* espinoso, -a, espinudo, -a *AmC, CSur;* (*issue*) peliagudo, -a

thorough ['θʌrə, *Am:* 'θɜːroʊ] *adj* **1.** (*complete*) absoluto, -a **2.** (*detailed*) exhaustivo, -a **3.** (*careful*) minucioso, -a

thoroughbred ['θʌrəbred, *Am:* 'θɜːroʊ-] **I.** *n* pura sangre *mf* **II.** *adj* de alcurnia

thoroughfare ['θʌrəfeər, *Am:* 'θɜːroʊfer] *n form* vía *f* pública

thoroughgoing ['θʌrəˌgəʊɪŋ, *Am:* ˌθɜːroʊ'goʊ-] *adj form* **1.** (*conscientious: analysis*) riguroso, -a **2.** (*complete: reform*) profundo, -a

thoroughly *adv* **1.** (*in detail*) a fondo **2.** (*completely*) completamente

thoroughness *n no pl* meticulosidad *f*

those [ðəʊz, *Am:* ðoʊz] *pl of* **that**

thou[1] [ðaʊ] *pron pers, liter* tú

thou[2] [θaʊ] *abbr of* **thousand** mil

though [ðəʊ, *Am:* ðoʊ] **I.** *conj* aunque; **as ~** como si *+subj;* **even ~** aunque; **even ~ it's cold** aunque hace frío **II.** *adv* sin embargo; **he did do it, ~** sin embargo, él sí lo hizo

thought [θɔːt, *Am:* θɑːt] *n* **1.** *no pl* (*process*) reflexión *f;* **on second ~s** tras madura reflexión; **without ~** sin pensar; **after much ~** tras mucho reflexionar; **to be deep in ~** estar ensimismado; **lost in ~** absorto [*o* sumido] en sus pensamientos **2.** (*idea, opinion*) pensamiento *m;* **that's a ~** es posible ►**a penny for your ~s** *prov* ¿en qué piensas?

thoughtful ['θɔːtfəl, *Am:* 'θɑːt-] *adj* **1.** (*pensive*) pensativo, -a **2.** (*careful*) cuidadoso, -a **3.** (*considerate*) amable

thoughtless ['θoːtləs] *adj* (*not thinking enough*) irreflexivo, -a; (*tactless*) desconsiderado, -a; (*careless*) descuidado, -a

thought-out [ˌθoːt'aʊt, *Am:* ˌθɑːt̬-] *adj* planeado, -a **thought-provoking** *adj* que hace pensar

thousand ['θaʊznd] **I.** *adj* mil **II.** *n* mil *m*

thousandth ['θaʊzntθ] **I.** *n* milésimo *m* **II.** *adj* **1.** (*being one of a thousand*) milésimo, -a **2.** (*in a series*) **the ~** el número mil

thrash [θræʃ] *vt* **1.** (*beat*) apalear **2.** *inf* (*defeat*) dar una paliza a

◆**thrash out** *vt inf* (*problem*) discutir; (*agreement*) llegar a

thrashing *n* paliza *f,* batida *f AmL*

thread [θred] **I.** *n* **1.** *no pl* (*for sewing*) hilo *m* **2.** (*of screw*) rosca *f* ►**to hang by a ~** pender de un hilo **II.** *vt* (*needle*) enhebrar; **to**

~ **sth through sth** pasar algo por algo; **to ~ sth onto sth** ensartar algo en algo
threadbare ['θredbeə^r, *Am:* -ber] *adj* **1.** (*worn*) raído, -a **2.** (*argument, excuse*) trillado, -a
threat [θret] *n* amenaza *f*
threaten ['θretən] **I.** *vt* amenazar; **to ~ to do sth** amenazar con hacer algo **II.** *vi* amenazar
threatening *adj* amenazador(a)
three [θriː] **I.** *adj* tres **II.** *n* tres *m; s. a.* **eight**
three-cornered [ˌθriː'kɔːnəd, *Am:* -'kɔːrnəd] *adj* triangular; **~ hat** tricornio *m*
three-D *adj inf abbr of* **three-dimensional** tridimensional **three-dimensional** *adj* tridimensional
threefold ['θriːfəʊld, *Am:* -foʊld] **I.** *adj* triple **II.** *adv* por triplicado
three-part *adj* de tres partes
threepenny bit ['θrepəni bɪt] *n Brit* moneda *f* de tres peniques
three-piece [ˌθriː'piːs] *adj* de tres piezas **three-piece suit** *n* terno *m*
three-ply ['θriːplaɪ] *adj* de tres capas; (*wood*) contrachapado, -a; (*wool*) de tres hebras **three-quarter** (**length**) *adj* tres cuartos
threesome ['θriːsəm] *n* trío *m*
three-wheeler [θrɪ'wiːlə^r] *n* vehículo *m* de tres ruedas
thresh [θreʃ] *vt* trillar
threshing machine ['θreʃɪŋ mə'ʃiːn] *n* trilladora *f*
threshold ['θreʃhəʊld, *Am:* -hoʊld] *n* **1.** (*doorway*) umbral *m* **2.** (*limit*) límite *m;* **pain ~** umbral de dolor; **tax ~** nivel *m* mínimo de tributación
threw [θruː] *pt of* **throw**
thrice [θraɪs] *adv* tres veces
thrift [θrɪft] *n no pl* ahorro *m*
thrifty ['θrɪfti] <-ier, -iest> *adj* ahorrador(a)
thrill [θrɪl] **I.** *n* estremecimiento *m* **II.** *vt* estremecer, emocionar **III.** *vi* estremecerse
thriller ['θrɪlə^r, *Am:* -ɚ] *n* (*book*) novela *f* de suspense; (*film*) película *f* de suspense
thrilling ['θrɪlɪŋ] *adj* emocionante
thrive [θraɪv] <thrived *o* throve, thrived *o* thriven> *vi* (*person, plant*) crecer mucho; (*business*) prosperar
thriving *adj* próspero, -a
throat [θrəʊt, *Am:* θroʊt] *n* **1.** (*internal*) garganta *f;* **sore ~** dolor *m* de garganta **2.** (*external*) cuello *m;* **to grab sb by the ~** agarrar a alguien por el cuello ►**to <u>stick</u> in sb's ~** (*proposal*) no ser aceptable para alguien; (*words*) quedárse atragantado a alguien; **to be at <u>each</u> other's ~s** estar como el perro y el gato
throaty ['θrəʊti, *Am:* 'θroʊt̬i] <-ier, -iest> *adj* (*voice*) ronco, -a; (*laugh*) gutural
throb [θrɒb, *Am:* θrɑːb] **I.** *n* (*of engine*) vibración *f;* (*of heart*) palpitación *f* **II.** <-bb-> *vi* (*engine*) vibrar; (*heart*) palpitar
throes [θrəʊz, *Am:* θroʊz] *npl* angustia *f;* (*of death*) agonía *f;* **to be in the ~ of sth** estar de lleno en algo
thrombosis [θrɒm'bəʊsɪs, *Am:* θrɑːm'boʊ-] <-es> *n* trombosis *f inv*
throne [θrəʊn, *Am:* θroʊn] *n* trono *m*
throng [θrɒŋ, *Am:* θrɑːŋ] **I.** *n* multitud *f* **II.** *vt* atestar; **to be ~ed** estar abarrotado **III.** *vi* ir en tropel; **to ~ to do sth** acudir en masa a hacer algo
throttle ['θrɒtl, *Am:* 'θrɑːt̬l] **I.** *n* acelerador *m;* **to open the ~** acelerar; **at full ~** a todo gas *inf* **II.** <-ll-> *vt* estrangular
◆**throttle back** *vi* reducir (la velocidad)
through [θruː] **I.** *prep* **1.** (*spatial*) a través de, por; **to go right ~ sth** traspasar algo; **to go ~ the door** pasar por la puerta; **to walk ~ a room** atravesar una habitación; **to walk ~ a village** caminar por un pueblo **2.** (*temporal*) durante; **all ~ my life** durante toda mi vida; **to be ~ sth** acabar de (hacer) algo **3.** *Am* (*until*) hasta; **open Monday ~ Friday** abierto de lunes a viernes **4.** MAT **6 ~ 3 is 2** 6 entre 3 da 2 **5.** (*by means of*) por (medio de) **II.** *adv* **1.** (*of place*) de un lado a otro; **I read the book ~** leí el libro entero; **to go ~ to sth** ir directo a algo **2.** (*of time*) **all day ~** de la mañana a la noche; **halfway ~** a medio camino **3.** TEL **to put sb ~ to sb** poner a alguien con alguien **4.** (*completely*) completamente; **to think sth ~** pensarse algo detenidamente ►**~ <u>and</u> ~** de cabo a rabo **III.** *adj* **1.** (*finished*) terminado, -a; **we are ~** hemos terminado **2.** (*direct*) directo, -a **3.** SCHOOL **to get ~** aprobar
through flight *n* vuelo *m* directo
throughout [θruː'aʊt] **I.** *prep* **1.** (*spatial*) por todas partes de; **~ the town** por toda la ciudad **2.** (*temporal*) a lo largo de; **~ his stay** durante toda su estancia **II.** *adv* **1.** (*spatial*) por [*o* en] todas partes **2.** (*temporal*) todo el tiempo
throughput ['θruːpʊt] *n no pl* producción *f;* INFOR procesamiento *m*
through ticket *n* pase *m* **through traffic** *n* (tráfico *m* de) tránsito *m* **through train** *n* tren *m* directo
throughway ['θruːweɪ] *n Am* autopista *f* de peaje
throve [θrəʊv, *Am:* θroʊv] *pt of* **thrive**
throw [θrəʊ, *Am:* θroʊ] **I.** *n* **1.** (*act of throwing*) lanzamiento *m* **2.** SPORTS derribo *m* **3.** *inf* (*chance*) oportunidad *f;* **his last ~** su última oportunidad **II.** <threw, thrown> *vi* lanzar **III.** <threw, thrown> *vt* **1.** (*propel*) tirar; (*ball, javelin*) lanzar; **to ~ oneself into sb's arms** echarse a los brazos de alguien; **to ~ oneself at sb** echar los tejos a alguien **2.** (*cause to fall: rider*) desmontar; (*opponent*) derribar **3.** (*dedicate*) **to ~ oneself into sth** entregarse de lleno a algo **4.** (*direct: glance*) echar; (*remark*) dejar caer; (*kiss*) lanzar **5.** *inf* (*confuse*) desconcertar **6.** TECH tornear **7.** (*turn on*) dar a; **to ~ the switch** pulsar el interruptor **8.** (*have*) **to ~ a tantrum** coger [*o* agarrar *AmL*] una rabieta **9.** (*give*) **to ~ a party** dar una fiesta **10.** (*cast off*) soltar
◆**throw away** *vt* **1.** (*discard*) tirar

T

2. (*waste*) malgastar; **to throw money away on sth** despilfarrar dinero en algo; **to throw oneself away** sacrificarse inútilmente 3. (*speak casually*) soltar
◆throw back *vt* 1. (*return*) devolver 2. (*open: curtains*) correr; (*blanket*) apartar 3. (*remind unkindly*) echar en cara; (*retort angrily*) replicar; **to throw sth back in sb's face** echar algo en cara a alguien
◆throw down *vt* 1. (*throw from above*) tirar 2. (*deposit forcefully*) dejar; (*weapons*) abandonar 3. (*drink quickly*) engullir
◆throw in I. *vt* 1. (*put into*) arrojar 2. (*include*) agregar; (*comment*) soltar II. *vi* (*propel*) lanzar
◆throw off *vt* 1. (*remove*) quitarse 2. (*escape from*) librarse de 3. (*rid oneself of*) zafarse de 4. (*write quickly*) improvisar
◆throw on *vt* 1. (*clothes*) ponerse 2. (*pounce upon*) **to throw oneself on sb** abalanzarse sobre alguien
◆throw out *vt* 1. (*eject: person*) echar; (*thing*) tirar; (*case*) rechazar; (*suggestion*) despreciar 2. (*emit: heat, light*) despedir
◆throw over *vt* (*lover*) abandonar
◆throw together *vt* 1. *inf* (*make quickly*) hacer en un momento 2. (*cause to meet*) juntar
◆throw up I. *vt* 1. (*project upwards*) lanzar al aire 2. (*bring to light*) revelar 3. (*build quickly*) levantar 4. *inf* (*give up*) dejar 5. *inf* (*vomit*) vomitar, buitrear *CSur,* revulsar *Méx* II. *vi inf* vomitar, buitrear *CSur,* revulsar *Méx*
throwaway ['θrəʊəweɪ, *Am:* 'θroʊ-] *adj* desechable; ~ **razor** maquinilla *f* de usar y tirar; ~ **remark** comentario *m* hecho de paso
throwback ['θrəʊbæk, *Am:* 'θroʊ-] *n* vuelta *f;* BIO atavismo *m*
thrower *n* lanzador(a) *m(f)*
throw-in ['θrəʊɪn, *Am:* 'θroʊ-] *n* (*in soccer*) saque *m* de banda; (*in baseball*) lanzamiento *m*
throwing *n* lanzamiento *m*
thrown *pp of* **throw**
thru [θruː] *prep, adj Am s.* **through**
thrum [θrʌm] I. <-mm-> *vt* (*guitar*) rasguear II. *vi* (*engine*) vibrar III. *n* (*of engine*) vibración *f*
thrush[1] [θrʌʃ] *n* tordo *m*
thrush[2] [θrʌʃ] *n* MED afta *f*
thrust [θrʌst] I. <-, -> *vi* 1. (*shove*) empujar; **to ~ at sb with sth** asestar un golpe a alguien con algo 2. (*force one's way*) abrirse paso II. <-, -> *vt* (*push*) empujar; (*insert*) clavar; **to ~ one's hands into one's pockets** meterse las manos en los bolsillos III. *n* 1. (*shove*) empujón *m;* **sword ~** estocada *f* 2. *no pl* (*impetus*) empuje *m;* **the main ~ of an argument** la idea central de una discusión 3. *no pl* TECH (*propulsion*) propulsión *f*
thrusting ['θrʌstɪŋ] *adj* arribista
thruway ['θruːweɪ] *n Am* autopista *f* de peaje
thud [θʌd] I. <-dd-> *vi* dar un golpe sordo; **to ~ on the table with one's fist** pegar un puñetazo encima de la mesa II. *n* golpe *m* sordo
thug [θʌg] *n* matón *m*
thumb [θʌm] I. *n* pulgar *m* ►**to be all fingers and ~s, to be all ~s** ser un manazas; **to stand out like a sore ~** cantar como una almeja; **to be under sb's ~** estar dominado por alguien II. *vt* 1. (*hitchhike*) **to ~ a lift** hacer dedo 2. (*soil with the thumbs*) manosear 3. (*glance through: book*) hojear
thumb-index *n* índice *m* recortado
thumbnail ['θʌmneɪl] *n* uña *f* del pulgar
thumbnail sketch *n* pequeña reseña *f*
thumbscrew ['θʌmskruː] *n* empulgueras *fpl*
thumbtack *n Am, Aus* tachuela *f*
thump [θʌmp] I. *vt* golpear; **to ~ sth down** dejar caer algo II. *vi* 1. (*heart*) latir fuertemente 2. (*beat*) **to ~ on sth** aporrear algo III. *n* 1. (*blow*) porrazo *m;* **to give sb a ~** dar un mamporro a alguien 2. (*noise*) golpe *m* sordo
thumping *adj inf* descomunal; **I've got a ~ headache** me va a estallar la cabeza
thunder ['θʌndəʳ, *Am:* -dɚ] I. *n no pl* 1. METEO trueno *m,* pillán *m Chile;* **a clap of ~** un trueno 2. (*sound*) estruendo *m* ►**to look like ~** tener cara de pocos amigos; **to steal sb's ~** quitar las primicias a alguien II. *vi* hacer gran estruendo; (*shout*) gritar III. *vt* bramar
thunderbolt ['θʌndəbəʊlt, *Am:* -dɚboʊlt] *n* 1. METEO rayo *m* 2. *fig* bomba *f* ►**to drop a ~ on sb** dejar a alguien fulminado **thunderclap** *n* trueno *m* **thundercloud** *n pl* nubarrón *m*
thundering ['θʌndərɪŋ] I. *n no pl* estruendo *m* II. *adj inf* (*very noisy*) estruendoso, -a; *fig* (*very great*) enorme
thunderous ['θʌndərəs] *adj* estruendoso, -a
thunderstorm ['θʌndəstɔːm, *Am:* -dɚstɔːrm] *n* tormenta *f*
thunderstruck ['θʌndəstrʌk, *Am:* -dɚ-] *adj form* estupefacto, -a
thundery ['θʌndəri] *adj* <-ier, -iest> tormentoso, -a
Thursday ['θɜːzdeɪ, *Am:* 'θɜːrz-] *n* jueves *m inv;* **Maundy ~** Jueves Santo; *s. a.* **Friday**
thus [ðʌs] *adv form* 1. (*therefore*) por lo tanto 2. (*like this*) de este modo; ~ **far** hasta aquí
thwart [θwɔːt, *Am:* θwɔːrt] *vt* frustrar; (*plan*) desbaratar
thy [ðaɪ] *pron pos, liter* tu(s)
thyme [taɪm] *n no pl* tomillo *m*
thyroid ['θaɪrɔɪd] *adj* tiroides *f inv*
tiara [tɪ'ɑːrə, *Am:* -'erə] *n* diadema *f*
tibia ['tɪbɪə] <-iae> *n* tibia *f*
tic [tɪk] *n* tic *m*
tick[1] [tɪk] *n* garrapata *f*
tick[2] [tɪk] *n Brit, inf* (*credit*) crédito *m;* **on ~** de fiado
tick[3] [tɪk] I. *n* 1. (*sound*) tic-tac *m* 2. (*mark*) visto *m* II. *vi* hacer tic-tac; **I don't know what makes her ~** no acabo de entender su manera

de ser **III.** *vt* marcar

◆**tick off** *vt* **1.** (*mark off*) marcar **2.** *Brit, Aus, inf* (*scold*) echar una bronca a **3.** *Am, inf* (*exasperate*) dar la lata a

◆**tick over** *vi* **1.** TECH ir al ralentí **2.** *fig* ir tirando

ticker ['tɪkəʳ, *Am:* -ɚ] *n* **1.** TEL teletipo *m* **2.** (*watch*) reloj *m* **3.** *inf* (*heart*) corazón *m*

ticker tape *n no pl* cinta *f* de teletipo

ticker-tape parade *n Am* desfile *m* triunfal

ticket ['tɪkɪt] *n* **1.** (*for bus, train*) billete *m*, boleto *m AmL;* (*for cinema, concert*) entrada *f;* (*for cloakroom*) ticket *m;* (*for lottery*) boleto *m;* **return** ~ billete *m* de vuelta **2.** (*price, information tag*) etiqueta *f* **3.** AUTO multa *f* **4.** *Brit* POL programa *m* electoral ►**just the** ~ justo lo que hacía falta

ticket agency *n* taquilla *f* **ticket collector** *n* revisor(a) *m(f)* **ticket counter** *n* mostrador *m* de venta de entradas **ticket holder** *n* persona *f* que tiene entrada **ticket machine** *n* dispensador *m* de billetes **ticket office** *n* RAIL ventanilla *f* de venta de billetes; THEAT taquilla *f*

ticking[1] ['tɪkɪŋ] *n no pl* (*sound*) tic-tac *m*

ticking[2] ['tɪkɪŋ] *n no pl* (*textile*) terliz *m*

ticking-off [ˌtɪkɪŋ'ɒf, *Am:* -'ɑːf] <tickings-off> *n Brit, inf* rapapolvo *m*, jalada *f Méx*

tickle ['tɪkl] **I.** *vi* hacer cosquillas; (*clothes*) picar **II.** *vt* **1.** hacer cosquillas **2.** (*amuse*) hacer gracia ►**to be ~d pink** *inf* estar encantado **III.** *n* cosquilleo *m;* (*tingling*) picor *m*

ticklish ['tɪklɪʃ] *adj* que tiene cosquillas; (*delicate*) delicado, -a

tidal ['taɪdəl] *adj* de la marea

tidal wave *n* maremoto *m*

tidbit ['tɪdbɪt] *n Am s.* **titbit**

tiddly ['tɪdli] *adj* <-ier, -iest> **1.** *inf* (*tiny*) diminuto, -a **2.** *Brit, Aus, inf* (*tipsy*) alegre

tiddlywink ['tɪdlɪwɪŋk] *n* pulga *f;* **~s** juego *m* de las pulgas

tide [taɪd] *n* **1.** (*of sea*) marea *f;* **high** ~ pleamar *f;* **low** ~ bajamar *f* **2.** (*of opinion*) corriente *f;* **to go against the** ~ ir contracorriente; **to swim with the** ~ seguir la corriente

◆**tide over** *vt always sep* **to tide sb over** sacar a alguien de un apuro

tideland ['taɪdlænd] *n Am* marisma *f* **tidemark** *n* **1.** (*mark left by high tide*) marca *f* que deja la marea **2.** *Brit, iron* (*on bath*) marca *f* de mugre

tidiness ['taɪdɪnɪs] *n no pl* orden *m*

tidy ['taɪdi] **I.** *adj* <-ier, -iest> **1.** (*orderly*) ordenado, -a; **to have a ~ mind** ser metódico **2.** *inf* (*considerable*) considerable **II.** *n* organizador(a) *m(f);* **the garage needs a** ~ hay que arreglar el garaje **III.** *vt* ordenar

tie [taɪ] **I.** *n* **1.** (*necktie*) corbata *f* **2.** (*cord*) atadura *f* **3.** *pl* (*bond*) lazos *mpl;* (*diplomatic*) relaciones *fpl* **4.** (*equal ranking*) empate *m* **5.** *Brit* SPORTS partido *m* **II.** *vi* **1.** (*fasten*) atarse **2.** SPORTS empatar **III.** *vt* **1.** (*fasten*) atar; (*knot*) hacer **2.** (*restrict*) limitar; **to be ~d by/to sth** estar limitado por/a algo

◆**tie back** *vt* atar

◆**tie down** *vt* atar; **to tie sb down to sth** *inf* comprometer a alguien a algo

◆**tie in I.** *vt* relacionar **II.** *vi* coincidir

◆**tie up** *vt* **1.** (*bind*) atar; (*hair*) recogerse; **to ~ some loose ends** *fig* atar cabos sueltos **2.** (*delay*) obstruir **3.** (*be busy*) **to be tied up** estar ocupado **4.** FIN, ECON (*capital*) inmovilizar; **to be tied up in sth** estar invertido en algo **5.** *Brit* (*connect with*) relacionar; **to be tied up with sth** estar ligado a algo

tie-break ['taɪbreɪk] *n Brit,* **tie-breaker** *n* desempate *m*

tie clip *n* aguja *f* de corbata

tie-in ['taɪɪn] *n* **1.** (*agreement*) acuerdo *m* **2.** (*connection*) relación *f*

tie-on *adj* para atar

tiepin ['taɪpɪn] *n* aguja *f* de corbata

tier [tɪəʳ, *Am:* tɪr] *n* (*row*) hilera *f;* (*level*) grada *f;* (*in a hierarchy*) nivel *m*

tie-up ['taɪʌp] *n* conexión *f*

tiff [tɪf] *n inf* pelea *f;* **to have a** ~ tener un altercado

tiger ['taɪgəʳ, *Am:* -gɚ] *n* tigre *m* ►**to have a ~ by the tail** tener el toro por los cuernos

tight [taɪt] **I.** *adj* **1.** (*screw, knot*) apretado, -a; (*clothing*) ceñido, -a **2.** (*rope, skin*) tirante **3.** (*condition, discipline*) estricto, -a, riguroso, -a; (*budget*) restringido, -a; (*situation*) difícil; (*schedule*) apretado, -a; **to keep a ~ hold on sth** mantener un control riguroso de algo; **to be ~ for money/time** ir escaso de dinero/tiempo **4.** (*bend*) cerrado, -a **5.** (*hard-fought*) reñido, -a **6.** *inf* (*drunk*) como una cuba **II.** *adv* fuerte; **to close sth** ~ cerrar bien algo; **sleep ~!** ¡que duermas bien!

tighten ['taɪten] **I.** *vt* **1.** (*make tight*) apretar; (*rope*) tensar **2.** (*restrictions*) intensificar **II.** *vi* apretarse; (*restrictions*) intensificarse

tight-fisted [ˌtaɪt'fɪstɪd] *adj inf* agarrado, -a

tight-fitting *adj* ajustado, -a

tight-lipped [ˌtaɪt'lɪpt] *adj* callado, -a; **to be ~ about sth** no abrir boca sobre algo

tightness *n no pl* **1.** (*of clothing*) lo ajustado **2.** (*of discipline*) lo estricto; (*of budget*) lo restringido; (*of schedule*) lo apretado **3.** PSYCH tensión *f*

tightrope ['taɪtrəʊp, *Am:* -roʊp] *n* cuerda *f* floja; **to walk a ~** *a. fig* caminar en la cuerda floja

tightrope walker *n* funámbulo, -a *m, f*

tights [taɪts] *npl* **1.** *Brit* (*leggings*) medias *fpl;* **to have a ladder in one's** ~ tener una carrera en las medias **2.** *Am, Aus* (*for dancing*) mallas *fpl*

tightwad ['taɪtwɒd, *Am:* -wɑːd] *n Am, Aus, inf* tacaño, -a *m, f*

tigress ['taɪgrɪs] *n* tigresa *f*

tike [taɪk] *n s.* **tyke**

tile [taɪl] **I.** *n* (*for roof*) teja *f;* (*for walls, floors*) azulejo *m* ►**to have a night (out) on the ~s, to be (out) on the ~s** ir de farra **II.** *vt* (*roof*)

T

tejar; (*wall*) poner azulejos a, alicatar; (*floor*) embaldosar

tiler ['taɪləʳ, *Am:* -ɚ] *n* albañil *m* (especializado en recubrimientos)

till[1] [tɪl] **I.** *prep* hasta **II.** *conj* hasta (que)

till[2] [tɪl] *n* caja *f* ►**he was caught with his hand in the ~** lo pillaron con las manos en la masa

till[3] [tɪl] *vt* cultivar

tiller ['tɪləʳ, *Am:* -ɚ] *n* barra *f* del timón; **at the ~** al timón

tilt [tɪlt] **I.** *n* inclinación *f* ►**(at) full ~** a toda máquina **II.** *vt* inclinar; **to ~ sth back** inclinar algo hacia atrás **III.** *vi* inclinarse; **to ~ back** inclinarse hacia atrás; **to ~ over** volcarse

timber ['tɪmbəʳ, *Am:* -bɚ] *n* **1.** *no pl, Brit* (*wood*) madera *f* **2.** (*beam*) viga *f*, madero *m* **3.** (*trees*) árboles *mpl;* **~!** ¡árbol va!

timbered *adj* de madera

timberline ['tɪmbəlaɪn, *Am:* -bɚ-] *n Am* límite *m* forestal **timber merchant** *n* maderero *m*

time [taɪm] **I.** *n* **1.** tiempo *m;* **to kill ~** matar el tiempo; **to make ~** hacer tiempo; **to spend ~** pasar el tiempo; **(how) ~ flies** el tiempo vuela; **~ passes** el tiempo apremia; **as ~ goes by** con el paso del tiempo; **in the course of ~** con el paso del tiempo; **to be a matter of ~** ser cuestión de tiempo; **(only) ~ can tell** (sólo) el tiempo lo dirá; **of all ~** de todos los tiempos; **in ~** a tiempo; **over ~** con el tiempo **2.** *no pl* (*period*) período *m;* **access ~** INFOR tiempo de acceso; **extra ~** SPORTS prórroga *f;* **free ~** tiempo libre; **after a ~** al cabo de un tiempo; **all the ~** continuamente; **a long ~ ago** hace mucho tiempo; **some ~ ago** hace algún tiempo; **for the ~ being** por ahora; **given ~** con el tiempo; **to have a good ~** pasárselo bien; **to have all the ~ in the world** tener todo el tiempo del mundo; **to run out of ~, to be (all) out of ~** *Am, Aus, inf* acabarse el tiempo; **to save ~** ganar tiempo; **to waste ~** perder el tiempo; **most of the ~** la mayor parte del tiempo; **in one week's ~** dentro de una semana; **for a short/long period of ~** durante un corto/largo período de tiempo; **there's no ~ to lose** no hay tiempo que perder; **can I have ~ off to go to the dentist?** ¿puedo salir (del trabajo) para ir al dentista?; **to take one's ~ in doing sth** tomarse uno su tiempo para hacer algo; **it takes a long/short ~** se tarda mucho/poco; **to give sb a hard ~** *inf* hacerlas pasar canutas a alguien; **I (don't) have a lot of ~ for him** (no) me cae bien **3.** (*clock*) hora *f;* **arrival/departure ~** hora *f* de llegada/salida; **bus/train ~s** horario *m* de autobús/tren; **to have the ~** tener hora exacta **4.** (*moment*) momento *m;* **the best ~ of day** el mejor momento del día; **this ~ tomorrow** mañana a esta hora; **at all ~s** a todas horas; **at a different ~** en otro momento; **each ~** cada vez; **the right ~** el momento oportuno **5.** *no pl* (*specific point in time*) hora *f;* **at any ~** a cualquier hora; **at any given ~, at (any) one ~** en un momento dado; **the last/next ~** la última/próxima vez; **at other ~s** en otros tiempos; **at the present ~** actualmente; **it is about ~ that ...** ya es hora de que... +*subj;* **~ and (~) again** una y otra vez; **ahead of ~** con antelación; **to know at the ~** saber en su momento; **to remember the ~ ...** recordar cuando... **6.** (*occasion*) vez *f;* **three ~s champion** *Brit, Aus,* **three ~ champion** *Am* tricampeón, -ona *m, f;* **lots of ~s** muchas veces; **for the hundredth ~** por centésima vez; **from ~ to ~** de vez en cuando **7.** *no pl* (*right moment*) hora *f;* **breakfast ~** hora *f* de desayunar; **it's high ~ that ...** ya es hora de que... +*subj;* **ahead of ~** antes de tiempo; **to do sth dead on ~** hacer algo en el momento preciso; **the ~ comes** llega el momento **8.** (*epoch*) época *f;* **at one ~** en una época; **from [*o* since] ~ immemorial** desde tiempos inmemoriales; **to be behind the ~s** estar anclado en el pasado; **in ~s gone by** en tiempos pasados; **to keep up with the ~s** estar al día **9.** SPORTS tiempo *m;* **record ~** tiempo récord **10.** *no pl* MUS tiempo *m* **11.** ECON horas *fpl* de trabajo; **to work full/part ~** trabajar a jornada completa/tiempo parcial; **to be on short ~** estar en jornada reducida ►**~ is of the essence** no hay tiempo que perder; **to have ~ on one's hands** tener tiempo de sobra; **~ is a great healer** *prov* el tiempo lo cura todo; **~ is money** *prov* el tiempo es oro; **there's a ~ and a place (for everything)** *prov* todo a su debido tiempo; **a week is a long ~ in politics** *prov* aún puede pasar de todo; **there's no ~ like the present** *prov* no dejes para mañana lo que puedas hacer hoy *prov;* **~ and tide wait for no man** *prov* el tiempo no perdona; **~ heals all wounds** *prov* el tiempo lo cura todo; **in less than no ~** en menos (de lo) que canta un gallo; **to buy ~** ganar tiempo; **~s are changing** los tiempos cambian; **to do ~** *inf* estar a la sombra; **~ moves on** la vida sigue **II.** *vt* **1.** SPORTS cronometrar, relojear *Arg* **2.** (*choose best moment for*) elegir el momento para **III.** *adj* SPORTS **~ trial** prueba *f* contrarreloj

time and motion study *n* COM estudio *m* de la racionalización del trabajo

time bomb *n* bomba *f* de relojería **time card** *n Am* tarjeta *f* de registro horario **time clock** *n* reloj *m* de control de asistencia

time-consuming ['taɪmkən,sju:mɪŋ, *Am:* -,su:-] *adj* que exige mucho tiempo

time difference *n* diferencia *f* horaria

timekeeper *n* **1.** (*device*) cronómetro *m* **2.** (*person*) cronometrista *mf;* **to be a poor ~** no ser muy puntual **time lag** *n* retraso *m* **time-lapse photography** *n* fotografía *m* de lapso de tiempo

timeless ['taɪmləs] *adj* eterno, -a

time limit *n* límite *m* de tiempo **time lock** *n* cerradura *f* de tiempo

timely ['taɪmli] *adj* <-ier, -iest> oportuno,

-a; **in a ~ fashion** *Brit* a tiempo
time-out [ˌtaɪm'aʊt] *n* **1.** SPORTS tiempo *m* muerto **2.** (*rest*) descanso *m*
timer ['taɪmə^r, *Am:* -ɚ] *n* temporizador *m;* GASTR reloj *m* avisador
timesaving ['taɪmˌseɪvɪŋ] *adj* que ahorra tiempo
timescale ['taɪmskeɪl] *n* escala *f* de tiempo
timeshare *n* multipropiedad *f* **time-sharing** *n no pl* **1.** (*on holiday*) multipropiedad *f* **2.** INFOR tiempo *m* compartido **time sheet** *n* hoja *f* de asistencia **time switch** *n Brit, Aus* interruptor *m* horario **timetable I.** *n* (*for bus, train*) horario *m;* (*for project, events*) programa *m* **II.** *vt* programar
timeworn ['taɪmwɔːn, *Am:* -wɔːrn] *adj* usado, -a; (*excuse*) trillado, -a
time zone *n* huso *m* horario
timid ['tɪmɪd] *adj* <-er, -est> tímido, -a
timidity [tɪ'mɪdəti, *Am:* -t̬i] *n no pl* timidez *f*
timing ['taɪmɪŋ] *n no pl* **1.** cronometraje *m;* **that was perfect ~** ha sido el momento oportuno **2.** (*rhythm*) compás *m*
timorous ['tɪmərəs] *adj* temeroso, -a
timpani ['tɪmpəni] *npl* MUS tímpanos *mpl*
tin [tɪn] **I.** *n* **1.** *no pl* (*metal*) estaño *m;* (*tinplate*) hojalata *f* **2.** (*container*) lata *f* **3.** (*for baking*) molde *m* **II.** *vt* enlatar
tin can *n* lata *f*
tincture ['tɪŋktʃə^r, *Am:* -tʃɚ] *n* tintura *f*
tinder ['tɪndə^r, *Am:* -dɚ] *n no pl* yesca *f*
tin foil *n* papel *m* de aluminio
ting [tɪŋ] *n* tilín *m*
tinge [tɪndʒ] **I.** *n* **1.** (*of colour*) tinte *m* **2.** (*of emotion*) dejo *m* **II.** *vt* **1.** (*dye*) teñir **2.** *fig* matizar
tingle ['tɪŋgl] **I.** *vi* estremecerse **II.** *n no pl* estremecimiento *m*
tin god *n pej, inf* héroe *m* de cartón **tin hat** *n* casco *m* de acero **tinhorn** *n Am, inf* petulante *mf*
tinker ['tɪŋkə^r, *Am:* -kɚ] **I.** *n* **1.** HIST hojalatero *m* **2.** *Brit* gitano, -a *m, f* **II.** *vi* **to ~ with sth** tratar de reparar algo
tinkle ['tɪŋkl] **I.** *vi* tintinear **II.** *vt* hacer tintinear **III.** *n* tintineo *m;* **to give sb a ~** *inf* llamar a alguien (por teléfono)
tinned [tɪnd] *adj Brit, Aus* en lata; (*fruit*) en conserva
tinny ['tɪni] *adj* <-ier, -iest> (*sound*) metálico, -a; (*taste*) que sabe a lata
tin-opener *n Brit, Aus* abrelatas *m inv* **tinplate** *n no pl* hojalata *f*
tinpot ['tɪnpɒt, *Am:* 'tɪnpɑːt] *adj pej, inf* de pacotilla
tinsel ['tɪnsl] *n no pl* oropel *m*
tint [tɪnt] **I.** *n* (*colour*) tono *m;* (*for hair*) tinte *m* **II.** *vt* teñir
tiny ['taɪni] *adj* <-ier, -iest> menudo, -a, chingo, -a *Col, Cuba*
tip¹ [tɪp] **I.** <-pp-> *vt* cubrir **II.** *n* punta *f;* **from ~ to toe** de pies a cabeza; **the southern ~ of Florida** el cabo sur de Florida; **it's on the ~ of my tongue** lo tengo en la punta de la lengua
tip² [tɪp] **I.** <-pp-> *vt* **1.** *Brit, Aus* (*empty out*) verter; **it's ~ping it down** *inf* está lloviendo a cántaros **2.** (*incline*) inclinar; **to ~ the balance against/in favour of sb** inclinar la balanza en contra/a favor de alguien **II.** *vi* inclinarse **III.** *n Brit* **1.** (*for rubbish*) basurero *m;* **rubbish ~** vertedero *m* de basura **2.** *inf* (*mess*) desorden *m*
tip³ [tɪp] **I.** *n* **1.** (*for service*) propina *f,* yapa *f Méx;* **10 per cent ~** el diez por ciento de propina **2.** (*hint*) aviso *m;* **to give sb a ~** dar a alguien un consejo; **to take a ~ from sb** seguir el consejo de alguien **II.** <-pp-> *vt* **1.** (*give money*) dar una propina a **2.** *Brit* (*predict*) pronosticar ►**to ~ sb the wink** dar el soplo a alguien **III.** <-pp-> *vi* dar propina
◆**tip off** *vt* avisar
◆**tip out I.** *vt* verter **II.** *vi* caer
◆**tip over I.** *vt* volcar **II.** *vi* volcarse
◆**tip up I.** *vt* inclinar **II.** *vi* inclinarse
tip-off ['tɪpɒf, *Am:* -ɑːf] *n inf* soplo *m*
tipple ['tɪpl] **I.** *vi* (*drink*) beber **II.** *vt* beber **III.** *n inf* bebida *f;* **favourite ~** trago *m* favorito
tipster ['tɪpstə^r, *Am:* -stɚ] *n* SPORTS pronosticador(a) *m(f)*
tipsy ['tɪpsi] *adj* <-ier, -iest> bebido, -a, achispado, -a *AmL*
tiptoe ['tɪptəʊ, *Am:* -toʊ] **I.** *n* punta *f* del pie; **on ~(s)** de puntillas **II.** *vi* ponerse de puntillas
tiptop [ˌtɪp'tɒp, *Am:* 'tɪptɑːp] *adj inf* de primera
tip-up seat ['tɪpʌp'siːt] *n* asiento *m* reclinable
tirade [taɪ'reɪd, *Am:* 'taɪreɪd] *n* diatriba *f*
tire¹ ['taɪə^r, *Am:* 'taɪɚ] *n Am s.* **tyre**
tire² ['taɪə^r, *Am:* 'taɪɚ] **I.** *vt* cansar **II.** *vi* cansarse
tired ['taɪəd, *Am:* 'taɪɚd] *adj* <-er, -est> (*person*) cansado, -a; (*excuse*) trillado, -a; **to be sick and ~ of sth** estar aburrido de algo; **the same ~ old faces** las mismas caras de siempre
tiredness *n no pl* cansancio *m*
tireless ['taɪələs, *Am:* 'taɪɚ-] *adj* incansable
tiresome ['taɪəsəm, *Am:* 'taɪɚ-] *adj* molesto, -a; (*person*) pesado, -a, molón, -ona *Guat, Ecua, Méx*
tiring ['taɪrɪŋ] *adj* agotador(a), cansador(a) *Arg*
'tis [tɪz] = **it is** *s.* **be**
tissue ['tɪʃuː] *n* **1.** *no pl* (*paper*) papel *m* de seda **2.** (*handkerchief*) pañuelo *m* de papel, Kleenex® *m* **3.** *no pl* ANAT, BIOL tejido *m;* **a ~ of lies** una sarta de mentiras
tit¹ [tɪt] *n* paro *m;* **blue ~** herrerillo *m;* **coal ~** carbonero *m*
tit² [tɪt] *n* **1.** *vulg* teta *f* **2.** *Brit, inf* estúpido, -a *m, f*
titanic [taɪ'tænɪk] *adj* titánico, -a
titanium [taɪ'teɪnɪəm] *n no pl* titanio *m*
titbit ['tɪtbɪt] *n Brit* **1.** (*delicacy*) golosina *f*

2. (*piece: of information*) noticia *f;* (*of gossip*) cotilleo *m*

titillate ['tɪtɪleɪt, *Am:* -əleɪt] *vt* excitar

titillation [ˌtɪtɪ'leɪʃən, *Am:* -əl'eɪ-] *n no pl* excitación *f*

titivate ['tɪtɪveɪt, *Am:* 'tɪt̬ə-] *vt* adornar; **to ~ oneself** arreglarse

title ['taɪtl, *Am:* -t̬l] **I.** *n* **1.** (*name*) título *m* **2.** (*championship*) campeonato *m* **3.** *no pl* LAW derecho *m* **II.** *vt* titular

title deed *n* título *m* de propiedad **title-holder** *n* titular *mf* **title page** *n* portada *f* **title role** *n* papel *m* principal **title track** *n* canción *f* que da nombre a un álbum

titter ['tɪtə^r, *Am:* 'tɪt̬ɚ] **I.** *vi* reírse disimuladamente **II.** *n* risa *f* disimulada

tittle-tattle ['tɪtltætl, *Am:* 'tɪt̬lˌtæt̬l] *n no pl, inf* chismorreo *m*

tizz [tɪz] *n,* **tizzy** ['tɪzi] *n inf* excitación *f;* **to be in a ~** estar aturdido

TNT [ˌtiːen'tiː] *n abbr of* **trinitrotoluene** TNT *m*

to [tuː] **I.** *prep* **1.** (*in direction of*) a; **to go ~ France/Oxford** ir a Francia/Oxford; **to go ~ town** ir a la ciudad; **to go ~ the dentist('s)** ir al dentista; **to go ~ the cinema/theatre** ir al cine/teatro; **to go ~ bed** irse a la cama; **to go ~ the south** ir al sur, ir hacia el sur; **~ the left/right** a la izquierda/derecha; **to fall ~ the ground** caerse al suelo; **the path ~ the lake** el camino que lleva al lago **2.** (*before*) a **quarter ~ five** las cinco menos cuarto **3.** (*until*) hasta; **to count up ~ 10** contar hasta 10; **~ this day** hasta el día de hoy; **frightened ~ death** muerto de miedo; **done ~ perfection** hecho a la perfección; **~ some extent** hasta cierto punto **4.** *with indirect object* **to talk ~ sb** hablar con alguien; **to show sth ~ sb** mostrar algo a alguien; **I said ~ myself ...** me dije a mí mismo...; **this belongs ~ me** esto es mío **5.** (*towards*) con; **to be kind/rude ~ sb** ser amable/grosero con alguien **6.** (*against*) contra; **elbow ~ elbow** codo con codo; **close ~ sth** cerca de algo; **to clasp sb ~ one's bosom** estrechar a alguien contra su pecho; **to fix sth ~ the wall** fijar algo en la pared; **5 added ~ 10 equals 15** 5 más 10 son 15 **7.** (*in comparison*) a; **3 (goals) ~ 1** 3 (goles) a 1; **superior ~ sth/sb** superior a algo/alguien **8.** (*from opinion of*) **to sound strange ~ sb** sonar extraño a alguien; **it doesn't make any sense ~ me** no tiene sentido para mí; **what's it ~ them?** *inf* ¿qué les importa a ellos?; **~ all appearances** al parecer **9.** (*proportion*) **one litre ~ one person** un litro por persona; **by a majority of 5 ~ 1** por una mayoría de 5 a 1; **the odds are 3 ~ 1** las probabilidades son de 3 a 1 **10.** (*causing*) **much ~ my surprise** para mi sorpresa **11.** (*by*) por; **known ~ sb** conocido de [*o* por] alguien **12.** (*matching*) de; **the top ~ this jar** la tapa de este tarro **13.** (*of*) de; **the secretary ~ the boss** la secretaria del jefe **14.** (*for purpose of*) para ►**that's all there is ~ it** eso es todo **II.** *infinitive particle* **1.** (*infinitive: not translated*) **~ do/walk/put** hacer/caminar/poner **2.** (*in command*) **I told him ~ eat** le dije que comiera **3.** (*after interrogative words*) **I know what ~ do** sé qué hacer; **she didn't know how ~ say it** no sabía como decirlo **4.** (*wishes*) **he wants ~ listen** quiere escuchar; **she wants ~ go** quiere irse **5.** (*purpose*) **he comes ~ see me** viene a verme; **to phone ~ ask sth** llamar para preguntar algo **6.** (*attitude*) **she seems ~ enjoy it** parece que disfruta; **~ be honest ...** (dicho) sinceramente... **7.** (*future intention*) **the work ~ be done** el trabajo que hay que hacer; **sth ~ buy** algo que hay que comprar **8.** (*in consecutive acts*) para; **I came back ~ find she had left Madrid** volví para descubrir que se había ido de Madrid **9.** (*introducing a complement*) **he wants me ~ tell him a story** quiere que le cuente un cuento; **to be too tired ~ do sth** estar demasiado cansado para hacer algo **10.** (*in general statements*) **it is easy ~ do it** es fácil hacerlo **11.** (*in ellipsis*) **he doesn't want ~ eat, but I want ~** él no quiere comer, pero yo sí **III.** *adv* **to push the door ~** cerrar la puerta empujándola

toad [təʊd, *Am:* toʊd] *n* **1.** (*animal*) sapo *m* **2.** (*person*) esperpento *m*

toad-in-the-hole [ˌteʊdɪnðə'həʊl, *Am:* ˌtoʊdɪnðə'hoʊl] *n Brit* salchichas *fpl* empanizadas

toadstool ['təʊdstuːl, *Am:* 'toʊd-] *n* seta *f* venenosa

toady ['təʊdi, *Am:* 'toʊ-] **I.** <-ies> *n* adulador(a) *m(f),* jalamecate *mf Ven* **II.** *vi* adular, jalar mecate *Ven*

to and fro *adv* de un lado a otro

toast [təʊst, *Am:* toʊst] **I.** *n* **1.** *no pl* (*bread*) tostada *f;* **a piece of ~** una tostada **2.** (*drink*) brindis *m inv* **II.** *vt* **1.** (*cook*) tostar **2.** (*drink*) brindar **III.** *vi* tostarse

toaster *n* tostadora *f*

toastmaster ['təʊstmɑːstə^r, *Am:* 'toʊstˌmæstɚ] *n* maestro, -a *m, f* de ceremonias

toast rack *n* portatostadas *m inv*

tobacco [tə'bækəʊ, *Am:* -oʊ] *n no pl* tabaco *m*

tobacconist [tə'bækənɪst] *n* estanquero, -a *m, f*

to-be [tə'biː] *adj* futuro, -a

toboggan [tə'bɒgən, *Am:* -'bɑːgən] **I.** *n* tobogán *m* **II.** *vi* deslizarse por el tobogán

toboggan run *n,* **toboggan slide** *n* pista *f* de tobogán

toby (jug) ['təʊbi(dʒʌg), *Am:* 'toʊ-] *n* pichel *m* (*en forma de hombre*)

tod [tɒd, *Am:* tɑːd] *n no pl, Brit, inf* **to be on one's ~** estar a solas

today [tə'deɪ] **I.** *adv* **1.** (*this day*) hoy **2.** (*nowadays*) hoy día **II.** *n no pl* **1.** (*this day*) hoy *m* **2.** (*nowadays*) actualidad *f*

toddle ['tɒdl, *Am:* 'tɑːdl] *vi* **1.** (*walk*) andar

tambaleándose; (*child*) dar los primeros pasos **2.** *inf* (*go*) **to ~ (off)** marcharse, irse

toddler ['tɒdləʳ, *Am:* 'tɑːdlɚ] *n* niño, -a *m, f* que empieza a caminar

toddy ['tɒdi, *Am:* 'tɑːdi] <-ies> *n* (**hot**) ~ ponche *m*

to-do [tə'duː] *n inf* lío *m*

toe [təʊ, *Am:* toʊ] **I.** *n* **1.** ANAT dedo *m* del pie; **on one's ~s** de puntillas **2.** (*of sock*) punta *f;* (*of shoe*) puntera *f* ▶**to keep sb on their ~s** mantener a alguien en estado de alerta; **to step on sb's ~s** pisotear a alguien **II.** *vt* **to ~ the line** conformarse

toecap *n* puntera *f* **toehold** *n* **1.** (*when climbing*) punto *m* de apoyo para el pie **2.** *fig* trampolín *m* **toenail** *n* uña *f* del dedo del pie

toffee ['tɒfi, *Am:* 'tɑːfi] *n* toffee *m*

toffee apple *n* manzana *f* acaramelada **toffee-nosed** *adj Brit, pej, inf* engreído, -a

toffy ['tɒfi, *Am:* 'tɑːfi] *n s.* **toffee**

together [tə'geðəʳ, *Am:* -ɚ] **I.** *adv* **1.** (*jointly*) juntos, juntas; **all ~** todos juntos, todas juntas; **~ with sb/sth** junto con alguien/algo; **to live ~** vivir juntos; **to get ~** juntarse; **to get it ~** *inf* organizarse **2.** (*at the same time*) a un tiempo, a la vez **II.** *adj inf* equilibrado, -a

togetherness *n no pl* compañerismo *m*

toggle ['tɒgl, *Am:* 'tɑːgl] **I.** *n* **1.** INFOR tecla *f* de conmutación **2.** TECH palanca *f* acodada **II.** *vt* pulsar

toggle switch *n* interruptor *m* de palanca

Togo ['təʊgəʊ, *Am:* 'toʊgoʊ] *n* Togo *f*

Togolese [ˌtəʊgəʊ'liːz, *Am:* ˌtoʊgoʊ'liːs] **I.** *adj* togolés, -esa **II.** *n* togolés, -esa *m, f*

toil [tɔɪl] **I.** *n no pl* labor *f* **II.** *vi* **1.** (*work hard*) afanarse **2.** (*move*) moverse con gran dificultad

toilet ['tɔɪlɪt] *n* **1.** (*room*) cuarto *m* de baño **2.** (*appliance*) váter *m,* inodoro *m* **3.** *form* (*process*) aseo *m*

toilet bag *n* neceser *m* **toilet paper** *n* papel *m* higiénico

toiletries ['tɔɪlɪtriz] *npl* artículos *mpl* de tocador

toiletries bag *n Am* neceser *m*

toilet roll *n Brit, Aus* rollo *m* de papel higiénico **toilet soap** *n* jabón *m* de tocador, jabón *m* de olor *Col, Ven* **toilet water** *n* colonia *f*

to-ing and fro-ing [ˌtuːɪŋən'frəʊɪŋ, *Am:* -'froʊ-] <to-ings and fro-ings> *n no pl* trajín *m*

token ['təʊkən, *Am:* 'toʊ-] **I.** *n* **1.** (*sign*) señal *f;* (*of affection*) muestra *f;* **by the same ~** por la misma razón; **in ~ of** *form* en señal de **2.** *Brit, Aus* (*coupon*) bono *m* **3.** (*for machines*) ficha *f* **II.** *adj* (*symbolic*) simbólico, -a

told [təʊld, *Am:* toʊld] *pt, pp of* **tell**

tolerable ['tɒlərəbl, *Am:* 'tɑːlɚ-] *adj* soportable, tolerable

tolerably ['tɒlərəbli, *Am:* 'tɑːlɚ-] *adv form* pasablemente

tolerance ['tɒlərəns, *Am:* 'tɑːlɚ-] *n no pl* tolerancia *f*

tolerant ['tɒlərənt, *Am:* 'tɑːlɚ-] *adj* tolerante

tolerate ['tɒləreɪt, *Am:* 'tɑːləreɪt] *vt* **1.** (*accept*) *a.* MED tolerar **2.** (*endure*) soportar

toleration [ˌtɒlə'reɪʃən, *Am:* ˌtɑːlə'reɪ-] *n no pl* tolerancia *f*

toll¹ [təʊl, *Am:* toʊl] *n* **1.** AUTO peaje *m* **2.** *Am* TEL tarifa *f* **3.** *no pl* (*damage*) número *m* de víctimas

toll² [təʊl, *Am:* toʊl] **I.** *vt* tañer; **to ~ the knell** *fig* doblar las campanas por un difunto **II.** *vi* doblar

toll bridge *n* puente *m* de peaje **toll call** *n Am* conferencia *f* **toll-free** *adv Am* gratis **tollhouse** *n* HIST cabina *f* de peaje **toll road** *n* autopista *f* de peaje

tom [tɒm, *Am:* tɑːm] *n* (*cat*) gato *m* macho

tomato [tə'mɑːtəʊ, *Am:* -'meɪt̬oʊ] <-es> *n* tomate *m*

tomato ketchup *n* salsa *f* de tomate

tomb [tuːm] *n* tumba *f,* guaca *f AmL*

tombola [tɒm'bəʊlə, *Am:* 'tɑːmblə] *n Brit, Aus* tómbola *f*

tomboy ['tɒmbɔɪ, *Am:* 'tɑːm-] *n* marimacho *m,* marimacha *f Ven*

tombstone ['tuːmstəʊn, *Am:* 'tuːmstoʊn] *n* lápida *f* sepulcral

tomcat ['tɒmkæt, *Am:* 'tɑːm-] *n* (gato *m*) macho

tome [təʊm, *Am:* toʊm] *n* librote *m*

tomfoolery [tɒm'fuːləri, *Am:* ˌtɑːm'fuːlɚi] *n no pl* tontería *f*

tommy gun ['tɒmigʌn, *Am:* 'tɑmi-] *n* metralleta *f*

tomograph ['tɒməgrɑːf] *n* MED tomógrafo *m*

tomography [tə'mɒgrəfi, *Am:* toʊ-'mɑːgrə-] *n* MED tomografía *f*

tomorrow [tə'mɒrəʊ, *Am:* -'mɑːroʊ] **I.** *adv* mañana; **the day after ~** pasado mañana; **all (day) ~** todo el día de mañana; **a week from ~** de mañana en una semana; **~ morning/evening** mañana por la mañana/tarde; **see you ~!** ¡hasta mañana!; **~ is another day!** ¡mañana será otro día! **II.** *n* mañana *m* ▶**~ is another day** *prov* mañana es otro día; **never put off until ~ what you can do today** *prov* nunca dejes para mañana lo que puedas hacer hoy *prov;* **who knows what ~ will bring?** ¿quién sabe qué nos depara el mañana?

tom-tom ['tɒmtɒm, *Am:* 'tɑːmtɑːm] *n* tantán *m*

ton [tʌn] *n* tonelada *f* (*Brit: 1,016 kilos; Am: 907 kilos*)*;* **~s of** *inf* montones de

tone [təʊn, *Am:* toʊn] **I.** *n* **1.** (*sound*) tono *m;* (*of instrument*) tonalidad *f;* (*of voice*) timbre *m* **2.** (*style*) clase *f* **3.** (*of colour*) matiz *f,* tono *m* **4.** *no pl* (*condition*) tono *m* **II.** *vt* (*muscles, skin*) tonificar

◆**tone down** *vt* moderar

◆**tone in** *vi* armonizar

◆**tone up** *vt* poner en forma

tone control *n* control *m* de tonalidad

tone-deaf [ˌtəʊn'def, *Am:* 'toʊn-] *adj* falto,

-a de oído musical
toneless ['təʊnləs, *Am:* 'toʊn-] *adj* monótono, -a
tone poem *n* poema *m* sinfónico
toner ['təʊnəʳ, *Am:* 'toʊnɚ] *n* **1.** (*for skin*) tonificante *m* **2.** (*for printer*) tóner *m;* PHOT virador *m*
Tonga ['tɒŋə, *Am:* 'tɑːŋ-] *n* Tonga *f*
Tongan **I.** *adj* tongano, -a **II.** *n* **1.** (*person*) tongano, -a *m, f* **2.** LING tongano *m*
tongs [tɒŋz, *Am:* tɑːŋz] *npl* tenazas *fpl*
tongue [tʌŋ] **I.** *n* **1.** ANAT lengua *f;* **to bite one's ~** morderse la lengua; **to find one's ~** recobrar el habla; **to hold one's ~** callarse; **to stick one's ~ out** (**at sb**) sacar la lengua (a alguien); **to get one's ~ around a word** pronunciar una palabra **2.** (*language*) idioma *m;* **to speak in ~s** hablar en lenguas desconocidas **3.** *no pl* (*expressive style*) expresión *f;* **to have a sharp ~** tener una lengua afilada ►**to say sth ~ in cheek** decir algo irónicamente; **to give sb the rough side of one's ~** *inf,* **to speak with a forked ~** hablar con lengua bífida, criticar a alguien severamente; **have you lost your ~?** ¿se te ha comido la lengua el gato?; **to set ~s wagging** dar que hablar **II.** *vt* MUS tocar
tongue-tied ['tʌŋtaɪd] *adj fig* **to be ~** cortarse
tongue twister *n* trabalenguas *m inv*
tonic[1] ['tɒnɪk, *Am:* 'tɑːnɪk] *n* (*stimulant*) tónico *m,* estimulante *m*
tonic[2] ['tɒnɪk, *Am:* 'tɑːnɪk] *n* MUS tónica *f*
tonic[3] ['tɒnɪk, *Am:* 'tɑːnɪk] *n,* **tonic water** *n* tónica *f*
tonight [tə'naɪt] *adv* (*evening*) esta tarde; (*night*) esta noche
tonnage ['tʌnɪdʒ] *n no pl* tonelaje *m*
tonne [tʌn] *n no pl* tonelada *f* (métrica)
tonsil ['tɒnsl, *Am:* 'tɑːn-] *n* MED amígdala *f*
tonsillitis [ˌtɒnsɪ'laɪtɪs, *Am:* ˌtɑːnsə'laɪt̬ɪs] *n no pl* amigdalitis *f*
too [tuː] *adv* **1.** (*overly*) demasiado; **~ right!** ¡muy bien dicho! **2.** (*very*) mucho **3.** (*also*) también; **me ~!** *inf* ¡y yo! **4.** (*moveover*) además **5.** *Am, inf* (*for emphasis*) ya lo creo
took [tʊk] *vt, vi pt of* **take**
tool [tuːl] **I.** *n* **1.** (*implement*) herramienta *f,* implemento *m AmL* **2.** (*instrument*) instrumento *m* **II.** *vt* (*shape with a tool*) trabajar
tool bag *n* bolsa *f* de herramientas **tool bar** *n* INFOR barra *f* de herramientas **tool box** *n,* **tool chest** *n* caja *f* de herramientas **tool kit** *n* juego *m* de herramientas **tool-maker** *n* fabricante *m* de herramientas **tool shed** *n* cobertizo *m* para herramientas
toot [tuːt] **I.** *n* toque *m* suave (de bocina); **to give a ~** tocar el claxon **II.** *vt* (*sound*) sonar **III.** *vi* pitar
tooth [tuːθ] <teeth> *n* **1.** ANAT (*of person, animal*) diente *m;* (*molar*) muela *f;* **to bare one's teeth** enseñar los dientes; **he's cutting a ~** le está saliendo un diente **2.** (*of comb*) púa *f;* (*of saw*) diente *m* ►**to set sb's teeth on edge** dar dentera a alguien; **to fight ~ and nail** (**to do sth**) luchar a brazo partido (para hacer algo); **to be long in the ~** ser entrado en años; **to have a sweet ~** ser goloso; **to cut one's teeth on sth** adquirir experiencia en algo; **to get one's teeth into sth** hincar el diente a algo; **to give sth teeth** dar efectividad a algo; **to grit one's teeth** aguantarse; **to lie through one's teeth** mentir descaradamente; **in the ~ of sth** (*straight into*) en medio de algo; (*despite*) a pesar de algo
toothache ['tuːθeɪk] *n* dolor *m* de muelas
toothbrush ['tuːθbrʌʃ] *n* cepillo *m* de dientes
toothed *adj* dentado, -a
toothpaste ['tuːθpeɪst] *n no pl* pasta *f* dentífrica [*o* de dientes]
toothpick *n* palillo *m,* pajuela *f Bol, Col*
toothsome ['tuːθsəm] *adj* sabroso, -a
toothy [tuːθi] <-ier, -iest> *adj* dentudo, -a; **to give a ~ smile** sonreír enseñando los dientes
tootle ['tuːtl, *Am:* -t̬l] *vi inf* **to ~ along** ir sin prisas
toots ['tʊts] *n Am, inf* chica *f*
top[1] [tɒp, *Am:* tɑːp] *n* (*spinning top*) peonza *f*
top[2] [tɒp, *Am:* tɑːp] **I.** *n* **1.** (*highest part*) parte *f* superior; (*of mountain*) cima *f;* (*of tree*) copa *f;* (*of head*) coronilla *f;* **to get on ~ of sth** *a. fig* llegar a lo más alto de algo; **from ~ to bottom** de arriba a abajo; **from ~ to toe** de pies a cabeza; **to feel on ~ of the world** estar contentísimo **2.** (*surface*) superficie *f;* **on ~ of** encima de **3.** *no pl* (*highest rank*) lo mejor; **to be at the ~** estar en la cima; **to be at the ~ of the class** ser el primero de la clase; **to go to the ~** ir a la cima **4.** (*clothing*) top *m* **5.** (*end*) punta *f* superior; (*of street*) final *m;* (*of table, list*) cabeza *f* **6.** (*lid: of bottle*) tapón *m* ►**at the ~ of one's voice** a grito pelado; **to be off one's ~** *Brit, inf* no estar en su sano juicio; **to go over the ~** exagerar **II.** *adj* **1.** (*highest, upper*) más alto **2.** (*best*) de primera calidad **3.** (*most successful*) exitoso, -a **4.** (*most important*) mejor **5.** (*maximum*) máximo, -a **III.** <-pp-> *vt* **1.** (*be at top of*) encabezar **2.** (*provide topping*) coronar **3.** (*surpass*) superar **4.** *Brit, inf* (*kill*) matar
◆**top off** *vt* **1.** GASTR coronar **2.** (*conclude*) rematar
◆**top up** *vt* **1.** (*fill up again*) recargar; **to top sb up with sth** *inf* servir algo más a alguien **2.** (*add to*) completar
topaz ['təʊpæz, *Am:* 'toʊ-] *n* topacio *m*
topcoat ['tɒpkəʊt, *Am:* 'tɑːpkoʊt] *n* sobretodo *m* **top copy** *n* original *m* **top dog** *n inf* **1.** (*boss*) alto cargo *m* **2.** (*victor*) vencedor(a) *m(f)* **top drawer** *adj* de alta sociedad **top executive** *n* ejecutivo, -a *m, f* superior **top-flight** *adj* de primera clase **top hat** *n* sombrero *m* de copa, galera *f AmL* **top-**

-heavy *adj* inestable
topic ['tɒpɪk, *Am:* 'tɑːpɪk] *n* tema *m*
topical ['tɒpɪkl, *Am:* 'tɑːpɪ-] *adj* de interés actual
topicality [ˌtɒpɪ'kæləti, *Am:* ˌtɑːpɪ'kæləṱi] *n no pl* actualidad *f*
topless ['tɒplɪs, *Am:* 'tɑːp-] **I.** *adj* que deja el busto al descubierto **II.** *adv* **to go ~** ir en topless
top-level [ˌtɒp'levəl, *Am:* 'tɑːpˌlev-] *adj* **1.** (*of highest rank*) de alto nivel **2.** (*of highest importance*) de primera categoría
top loader *n* lavadora *f* de carga superior
top management *n* altos cargos *mpl*
topmost ['tɒpməʊst, *Am:* 'tɑːp-] *adj* más alto, -a
top-notch [ˌtɒp'nɒtʃ, *Am:* ˌtɑːp'nɑːtʃ] *adj inf* de primera
topographer [tə'pɒgrəfəʳ, *Am:* -'pɑːgrəfɚ] *n* topógrafo, -a *m, f*
topographical [ˌtɒpə'græfɪkl, *Am:* ˌtɑːpə'-] *adj* topográfico, -a
topography [tə'pɒgrəfi, *Am:* -'pɑːgrə-] *n no pl* topografía *f*
topper ['tɒpəʳ, *Am:* 'tɑːpɚ] *n inf s.* **top hat**
topping ['tɒpɪŋ, *Am:* 'tɑːpɪŋ] *n* GASTR cobertura *f*
topple ['tɒpl, *Am:* 'tɑːpl] **I.** *vt a.* POL derribar **II.** *vi* **to ~ (down)** caerse
◆**topple over** *vi* volcarse
top price *n* precio *m* máximo **top priority** *n* prioridad *f* máxima **top quality** *n* máxima calidad *f* **top-ranking** *adj* importante; (*university*) de alto nivel **topsail** *n* gavia *f* **top salary** *n* salario *m* máximo **top secret** *adj* confidencial **top-selling** *adj* de mayor venta **topsoil** *n no pl* capa *f* superior del suelo **top speed** *n* velocidad *f* máxima **topspin** *n no pl* SPORTS efecto *m* topspin
topsy-turvy [ˌtɒpsi'tɜːvi, *Am:* ˌtɑːpsɪ'tɜːr-] *inf* **I.** *adj* desordenado, -a **II.** *adv* patas arriba
torch [tɔːtʃ, *Am:* tɔːrtʃ] <-es> *n* **1.** *Aus, Brit* (*electric*) linterna *f* **2.** (*burning stick*) antorcha *f;* **to carry a ~ for sb** estar enamorado de alguien; **to put sth to the ~** prender fuego a algo **3.** *Am* (*blowlamp*) soplete *m*
torchlight ['tɔːtʃlaɪt, *Am:* 'tɔːrtʃ-] *n no pl* (*electric*) luz *f* de linterna; (*burning*) luz *f* de antorcha
torchlight procession *n* desfile *m* con antorchas
tore [tɔːʳ, *Am:* tɔːr] *vi, vt pt of* **tear**
torment ['tɔːment, *Am:* 'tɔːr-] **I.** *n* **1.** (*suffering*) tormento *m;* **to be in ~** sufrir mucho; **to go through ~s** sufrir lo indecible **2.** (*physical pain*) suplicio *m* **3.** (*torture*) tortura *f* **4.** (*annoying thing*) angustia *f* **II.** *vt* atormentar
tormentor [tɔː'mentəʳ, *Am:* tɔːr'menṱɚ] *n* atormentador(a) *m(f)*
torn [tɔːn, *Am:* tɔːrn] *vi, vt pp of* **tear**
tornado [tɔː'neɪdəʊ, *Am:* tɔːr'neɪdoʊ] *n* <-(e)s> tornado *m*
torpedo [tɔː'piːdəʊ, *Am:* tɔːr'piːdoʊ] MIL, NAUT **I.** <-es> *n* torpedo *m* **II.** *vt* torpedear
torpid ['tɔːpɪd, *Am:* 'tɔːr-] *adj form* aletargado, -a
torpor ['tɔːpəʳ, *Am:* 'tɔːrpɚ] *n no pl, form* sopor *m*, letargo *m*
torque [tɔːk, *Am:* tɔːrk] *n no pl* PHYS par *m* de torsión
torrent ['tɒrənt, *Am:* 'tɔːr-] *n* **1.** (*large amount of water*) torrente *m;* **to rain in ~s** llover a cántaros **2.** (*of complaints, abuse*) carga *f*
torrential [tə'renʃl, *Am:* tɔː'-] *adj* torrencial, torrentoso, -a *AmL*
torsion ['tɔːʃən, *Am:* 'tɔːr-] *n no pl* TECH, MED torsión *f*
torso ['tɔːsəʊ, *Am:* 'tɔːrsoʊ] *n* torso *m*
tortoise ['tɔːtəs, *Am:* 'tɔːrṱəs] *n* tortuga *f*
tortoiseshell ['tɔːtəsʃel, *Am:* 'tɔːrṱəs-] *n no pl* concha *f*
tortuous ['tɔːtjʊəs, *Am:* 'tɔːrtʃuəs] *adj* (*complicated, indirect*) tortuoso, -a; (*reasoning*) enrevesado, -a
torture ['tɔːtʃəʳ, *Am:* 'tɔːrtʃɚ] **I.** *n* **1.** *no pl* (*cruelty*) tortura *f;* (*mental*) tormento *m* **2.** (*suffering*) suplicio *m* **II.** *vt* **1.** (*cause suffering to*) torturar **2.** (*disturb*) atormentar; **to ~ oneself with sth** martirizarse con algo
torturer ['tɔːtʃərəʳ, *Am:* 'tɔːrtʃɚɚ] *n* torturador(a) *m(f)*
Tory ['tɔːri] *Brit* **I.** <-ies> *n miembro o partidario de los conservadores británicos* **II.** *adj* del partido conservador británico
tosh [tɒʃ, *Am:* tɑːʃ] *n no pl, inf* tonterías *fpl;* **to talk ~** decir tonterías
toss [tɒs, *Am:* tɑːs] **I.** *n* **1.** (*throw*) lanzamiento *m;* (*of head*) movimiento *m* brusco **2.** (*throwing of a coin*) sorteo *m* a cara o cruz; **to win/lose the ~** ganar/perder a cara o cruz ►**to argue the ~** *inf* discutir insistentemente; **I don't give a ~** *inf* me importa un pepino **II.** *vt* **1.** (*throw*) lanzar; (*pancake*) dar la vuelta; **to ~ a coin** echar una moneda a cara o cruz **2.** (*shake: head*) sacudir **III.** *vi* **to ~ for sth** echar algo a cara o cruz ►**to ~ and turn** dar vueltas en la cama
◆**toss about** *vt,* **toss around** *vt* **1.** (*move roughly*) zarandear; (*head, hair*) agitar **2.** (*consider*) considerar
◆**toss away** *vt* tirar
◆**toss off** **I.** *vt* **1.** *inf* (*do quickly*) hacer rápidamente; (*write*) escribir rápidamente **2.** (*drink quickly*) beber de un trago **II.** *vi Aus, Brit, vulg* hacerse una paja
◆**toss out** *vt* tirar
◆**toss up** *vi* **to ~ for sth** echar algo a cara o cruz
toss-up ['tɒsʌp, *Am:* 'tɑːs-] *n* **it's a ~ between …** la cosa está entre…
tot [tɒt, *Am:* tɑːt] *n* **1.** *inf* (*child*) niño, -a *m, f* pequeño, -a **2.** (*alcohol*) dedo *m*
◆**tot up** **I.** *vt inf* sumar **II.** *vi* **to ~ to (an amount)** sumar (una cantidad)

T

total ['təʊtl, *Am:* 'toʊt̬l] **I.** *n* (*sum, cost*) total *m* **II.** *adj* **1.** (*entire: sum, cost*) total **2.** (*absolute*) total, absoluto, -a; **a ~ failure** un fracaso total **III.** *vt* <*Brit:* -ll-, *Am:* -l-> **1.** (*count*) sumar **2.** (*amount to*) ascender a

totalitarian [ˌtəʊtælɪ'teəriən, *Am:* toʊˌtælə'teri-] *adj* POL totalitario, -a

totalitarianism *n no pl* POL totalitarismo *m*

totality [təʊ'tæləti, *Am:* toʊ'tælət̬i] *n no pl* totalidad *f;* **in its ~** en total

totally ['təʊtəli, *Am:* 'toʊt̬əl-] *adv* totalmente

tote[1] [təʊt, *Am:* toʊt] *n no pl* SPORTS totalizador *m*

tote[2] [təʊt, *Am:* toʊt] *vt inf* llevar

tote bag *n* bolsa *f* grande

totem (**pole**) ['təʊtəm(ˌpəʊl), *Am:* 'toʊt̬əm (ˌpoʊl)] *n* tótem *m*

totter ['tɒtəʳ, *Am:* 'tɑːt̬ɚ] *vi* tambalearse

tottery ['tɒtəri, *Am:* 'tɑːt̬-] *adj* tambaleante

toucan ['tuːkæn] *n* tucán *m*

touch [tʌtʃ] <-es> **I.** *n* **1.** *no pl* (*sensation*) tacto *m* **2.** (*act of touching*) toque *m* **3.** *no pl* (*communication*) **to be/get/keep in ~** (**with sb/sth**) estar/ponerse/mantenerse en contacto (con alguien/algo); **to be out of ~ with sb** no tener contacto con alguien; **to lose ~ with sb** perder el contacto con alguien **4.** *no pl* (*skill*) habilidad *f;* **to lose one's ~** perder la destreza **5.** *no pl* (*small amount*) poquito *m;* (*of bitterness, irony*) pizca *f;* **a ~ of genius** un punto de genialidad **6.** (*detail*) toque *m;* **the human ~** el toque humano **7.** SPORTS **to go into ~** salir del campo ►**to be a soft ~** *inf* ser demasiado blando **II.** *vt* **1.** (*feel*) tocar; **to ~ the brake** pisar el freno **2.** (*brush against*) rozar **3.** (*reach*) alcanzar **4.** (*eat, drink*) probar; **he didn't ~ it** no lo probó **5.** (*move emotionally*) conmover, enternecer **6.** (*equal*) **there's no painter to ~ him** no existe pintor que le iguale **III.** *vi* tocarse

◆**touch at** *vi* NAUT hacer escala en

◆**touch down** *vi* AVIAT aterrizar

◆**touch in** *vt* ART esbozar

◆**touch off** *vt* hacer estallar; (*protest*) provocar

◆**touch on** *vt* tocar

◆**touch up** *vt* **1.** (*improve*) mejorar; PHOT retocar **2.** *Brit, inf* (*sexually*) **to touch sb up** magrear a alguien

◆**touch upon** *vt* tocar

touch and go *adj* **to be ~ whether ...** no estar claro si...

touchdown ['tʌtʃdaʊn] *n* **1.** AVIAT aterrizaje *m* **2.** SPORTS (*American football*) touchdown *m;* (*rugby*) ensayo *m*

touched [tʌtʃt] *adj* **1.** (*moved*) conmovido, -a **2.** *inf* (*crazy*) chiflado, -a

touchiness ['tʌtʃɪnəs] *n no pl, inf* **1.** (*of person*) susceptibilidad *f* **2.** (*of issue*) delicadeza *f*

touching ['tʌtʃɪŋ] *adj* conmovedor(a)

touch-sensitive *adj* INFOR sensible al tacto

touchstone ['tʌtʃstəʊn, *Am:* -stoʊn] *n* piedra *f* de toque

touch-type ['tʌtʃtaɪp] *vi* mecanografiar al tacto

touchy ['tʌtʃi] <-ier, -iest> *adj* **1.** (*person*) susceptible; **she's very ~ about her work** es muy susceptible cuando se trata de su trabajo **2.** (*issue*) delicado, -a

tough [tʌf] **I.** *adj* **1.** (*fabric, substance*) fuerte; (*meat, skin*) duro, -a; **to be ~ as old boots** (*meat*) estar más duro que una suela **2.** (*hardy: person*) resistente **3.** (*strict*) estricto, -a; (*negotiator*) implacable; **to be ~ on sb** ser severo con alguien **4.** (*difficult*) difícil; (*exam, question*) peliagudo, -a **5.** (*violent*) violento, -a; (*neighbourhood*) peligroso, -a **6.** *inf* (*unlucky*) **~ luck** mala suerte **II.** *n Am, inf* matón, -ona *m, f*

◆**tough out** *vt* **to tough it out** (*endure*) no ceder; (*face up to*) afrontar

toughen ['tʌfən] **I.** *vt* endurecer **II.** *vi* endurecerse

toughness *n no pl* **1.** (*strength*) resistencia *f* **2.** (*hardness: of meat*) dureza *f* **3.** (*difficulty*) dificultad *f*

toupée ['tuːpeɪ, *Am:* tuː'peɪ] *n* peluquín *m*

tour [tʊəʳ, *Am:* tʊr] **I.** *n* **1.** (*journey*) viaje *m;* **guided ~** excursión *f* guiada; **sightseeing ~** paseo *m* por los lugares de interés **2.** (*of factory*) visita *f* **3.** MUS gira *f;* **to be/go on ~** estar/ir de gira **II.** *vt* **1.** (*travel around*) recorrer **2.** (*visit professionally*) visitar **3.** (*perform*) ir de gira por **III.** *vi* ir de viaje

touring company *n* compañía *f* teatral itinerante

tourism ['tʊərɪzəm, *Am:* 'tʊrɪ-] *n no pl* turismo *m*

tourist ['tʊərɪst, *Am:* 'tʊrɪst] *n* **1.** (*traveller*) turista *mf* **2.** *Aus, Brit* SPORTS visitante *mf*

tourist agency *n* agencia *f* de viajes **tourist bureau** *n* oficina *f* de viajes **tourist class** *n* clase *f* turista **tourist guide** *n* **1.** (*book*) guía *f* turística **2.** (*person*) guía *mf* **tourist industry** *n* industria *f* turística **tourist information office** *n* oficina *f* de turismo **tourist season** *n* temporada *f* turística **tourist ticket** *n* pasaje *m* de turista **tourist visa** *n* visado *m* turístico

tournament ['tɔːnəmənt, *Am:* 'tɜːr-] *n* SPORTS torneo *m*

tour operator *n* operador *m* turístico

tousle ['taʊzl] *vt* revolver

tousled ['taʊzlt] *adj* despeinado, -a

tout [taʊt] **I.** *n* revendedor(a) *m(f)* **II.** *vt* **1.** (*try to sell*) tratar de vender **2.** *Brit* (*ticket*) revender **III.** *vi* **to ~ for custom** buscar clientes

tow [təʊ, *Am:* toʊ] **I.** *n* remolque *m;* **to give sb/sth a ~** remolcar a alguien/algo; **to have sb in ~** *fig* llevar a alguien a cuestas **II.** *vt* remolcar; **to ~ a vehicle** llevarse un coche a remolque

toward(**s**) [tə'wɔːd(z), *Am:* tɔːrd(z)] *prep* **1.** (*in direction of*) hacia; (*of time*) hacia, cerca de **2.** (*for*) por **3.** (*in respect of*) respecto a; **to feel sth ~ sb** sentir algo por alguien

tow bar *n* barra *f* de tracción **tow boat** *n* NAUT remolcador *m*

towel ['taʊəl] **I.** *n* toalla *f* ►**to throw in the ~** tirar la toalla **II.** *vt* <-ll-> **to ~ sth dry** secar algo con toalla

towel(l)ing *n no pl* felpa *f*

towel rack *n Am,* **towel rail** *n Aus, Brit* toallero *m*

tower ['taʊəʳ, *Am:* 'taʊɚ] *n* torre *f* ►**a ~ of strength** un gran apoyo

◆**tower above** *vi,* **tower over** *vi* **to ~ sth/sb** ser mucho más alto que algo/alguien

tower block *n Brit* edificio *m* de apartamentos

towering *adj* **1.** (*very high*) altísimo, -a **2.** (*very large*) inmenso, -a; (*temper*) intenso, -a

town [taʊn] *n* (*large*) ciudad *f;* (*small*) pueblo *m;* **the ~** el centro ►**to go out on the ~** salir de juerga; **to paint the ~ red** irse de juerga

town centre *n Brit* centro *m* de la ciudad **town clerk** *n Brit* secretario, -a *m, f* del ayuntamiento **town council** *n Brit* ayuntamiento *m* **town councillor** *n* concejal(a) *m(f)* **town hall** *n* POL ayuntamiento *m* **town house** *n* **1.** (*residence in town*) casa *f* de la ciudad **2.** (*part of terrace*) casa *f* unifamiliar **town planning** *n* urbanismo *m*

townscape ['taʊnskeɪp] *n* paisaje *m* urbano

townsfolk ['taʊnzfəʊk, *Am:* -foʊk] *npl* ciudadanos *mpl*

township ['taʊnʃɪp] *n* **1.** *Am, Can* municipio *m* **2.** (*in South Africa*) distrito *m* segregado

townspeople ['taʊnz,piːpl] *npl* ciudadanos *mpl*

tow truck *n Am* grúa *f*

toxaemia *n,* **toxemia** [tɒk'siːmiə, *Am:* tɑːk-] *n Am no pl* toxemia *f*

toxic ['tɒksɪk, *Am:* 'tɑːk-] *adj* tóxico, -a

toxicology [,tɒksɪ'kɒlədʒi, *Am:* ,tɑːksɪ'kɑːlə-] *n no pl* toxicología *f*

toxic waste *n* residuos *mpl* tóxicos

toxin ['tɒksɪn, *Am:* 'tɑːk-] *n* toxina *f*

toy [tɔɪ] *n* juguete *m;* **cuddly ~** muñeco *m* de peluche

◆**toy with** *vt* jugar con; **to ~ an idea** dar vueltas a una idea; **to ~ sb's affections** jugar con los sentimientos de alguien

toy car *n* coche *m* de juguete **toy dog** *n* perro *m* faldero **toyshop** *n* juguetería *f*

trace[1] [treɪs] *n* (*for horse*) correa *f;* **to kick over the ~s** sacar los pies del plato

trace[2] [treɪs] **I.** *n* **1.** (*sign*) rastro *m;* **to leave a ~ of sth** dejar indicios de algo; **to disappear without ~** desaparecer sin dejar rastro **2.** (*slight amount*) pizca *f;* **~s of a drug/poison** pequeñas cantidades de droga/veneno; **without any ~ of sarcasm/humour** sin nada de sarcasmo/humor **II.** *vt* **1.** (*locate*) localizar; **to ~ sb to somewhere** localizar a alguien en algún sitio; **it can be ~d back to the Middle Ages** se remonta a la Edad Media **2.** (*draw outline of*) trazar; (*with tracing paper*) calcar

traceable ['treɪsəbl] *adj* rastreable; **an easily ~ reference** una referencia fácil de encontrar

trace element *n* oligoelemento *m*

tracer ['treɪsəʳ, *Am:* -ɚ] *n* MIL bala *m* trazadora

tracery ['treɪsəri] *n* tracería *f*

trachea [trə'kɪə, *Am:* 'treɪkɪə] <-s *o* -chae> *n* tráquea *f*

tracing *n* calco *m*

tracing paper *n* papel *m* de calco

track [træk] **I.** *n* **1.** (*path*) senda *f* **2.** (*rails*) vía *f* **3.** *Am* (*in station*) andén *m* **4.** (*mark*) pista *f;* (*of animal*) huella *f;* (*of bullet*) trayectoria *f;* **to cover one's ~s** borrar las huellas; **to leave ~s** dejar huellas; **to be on the ~ of sb** seguir la pista a alguien **5.** (*path*) camino *m;* **to be on the right ~** *a. fig* ir por buen camino; **to be on the wrong ~** *fig* estar equivocado **6.** (*logical course*) curso *m;* **the ~ of an argument** el hilo de un argumento; **to get off the ~** salirse del tema; **to be on ~ (to do sth)** estar en camino (de hacer algo) **7.** (*career path*) rumbo *m;* **to change ~** cambiar de rumbo **8.** SPORTS pista *f* **9.** (*song*) canción *f* ►**to live on the wrong side of the ~s** *inf* vivir en los barrios pobres; **to keep ~ (of sb/sth)** no perder de vista (a alguien/algo); **to lose ~ (of sb/sth)** perder de vista (a alguien/algo); **to make ~s** *inf* largarse; **to stop sb (dead) in his ~s** parar los pies a alguien; **to throw sb off the ~** despistar a alguien **II.** *vt* **1.** (*pursue*) seguir la pista de; **to ~ sth/sb** seguir algo/a alguien **2.** (*trace*) trazar **III.** *vi* CINE avanzar

◆**track down** *vt* localizar

track-and-field *n* atletismo *m*

trackball *n* INFOR trackball *f*

tracker dog *n* perro *m* rastreador

track event *n* SPORTS carrera *f* de atletismo

tracking station ['trækɪŋ'steɪʃən] *n* AVIAT, TECH centro *m* de seguimiento

track record *n* historial *m* **track shoe** *n* zapatilla *f* de atletismo **tracksuit** *n* chándal *m*

tract[1] [trækt] *n* (*leaflet*) folleto *m*

tract[2] [trækt] *n* **1.** (*of land*) tramo *m* **2.** ANAT, MED sistema *m;* **digestive ~** tubo *m* digestivo; **respiratory ~** aparato *m* respiratorio

tractable ['træktəbl] *adj* (*person, animal*) dócil; (*problem*) soluble

traction ['trækʃən] *n no pl* **1.** (*grip*) adherencia *f* **2.** MED tracción *f*

traction engine *n* máquina *f* de tracción

tractor ['træktəʳ, *Am:* -tɚ] *n* tractor *m*

trad [træd] *adj Aus, Brit, inf abbr of* **traditional** tradicional

trade [treɪd] **I.** *n* **1.** *no pl* (*buying and selling*) comercio *m;* **~ in sth** comercio de algo **2.** *no pl* (*business activity*) negocio *m* **3.** (*type of business*) industria *f;* **building ~** sector *m* de la construcción; **fur ~** comercio *m* de pieles **4.** (*profession*) oficio *m;* **to learn a ~** aprender

T

un oficio; **to be a baker by** ~ ser panadero de profesión **5.** (*swap*) intercambio *m* **II.** *vi* **1.** (*exchange goods*) comerciar; **to ~ with sb** tener relaciones comerciales con alguien **2.** (*do business*) negociar; **to ~ in sth** dedicarse al negocio de algo **III.** *vt* **1.** (*swap, exchange*) intercambiar; **to ~ sth for sth** cambiar algo por algo **2.** (*sell*) vender

◆**trade in** *vt* aportar como parte del pago

◆**trade on** *vt* aprovecharse de

trade agreement *n* acuerdo *m* comercial **trade association** *n* asociación *f* mercantil **trade balance** *n* balanza *f* comercial **trade barrier** *n* barrera *f* arancelaria **trade cycle** *n* ciclo *m* mercantil **trade directory** *n* guía *f* mercantil **trade discount** *n* descuento *m* comercial **trade fair** *n* COM feria *f* de muestras **trade gap** *n* déficit *m inv* de la balanza comercial

trade-in ['treɪdɪn] *n* COM permuta *f*

trade-in value *n* valor *m* de un artículo usado descontado de otro nuevo

trade journal *n* periódico *m* gremial **trademark** *n* **1.** COM marca *f;* **registered** ~ marca *f* registrada **2.** *fig* distintivo *m* **trade name** *n* (*of a firm*) razón *f* social; (*trademark*) marca *f*

trade-off ['treɪdɒf, *Am:* -ɑːf] *n* **1.** (*exchange*) intercambio *m;* **to make a ~ between things** hacer un intercambio de cosas **2.** *fig* (*inconvenience*) precio *m*

trade policy *n* política *f* comercial **trade press** *n no pl* prensa *f* especializada **trade price** *n Brit* precio *m* de mayorista; **to buy sth at** ~ comprar algo a precio de mayorista

trader ['treɪdəʳ, *Am:* -ɚ] *n* comerciante *mf*

trade register *n* registro *m* mercantil **trade route** *n* ruta *f* comercial **trade secret** *n* secreto *m* profesional

tradesman ['treɪdzmən] <-men> *n* tendero *m*

tradespeople ['treɪdzˌpiːpl] *npl* tenderos *mpl*

trade surplus *n* excedente *m* comercial **trade union** *n* sindicato *m* **trade unionism** *n no pl* sindicalismo *m* **trade unionist** *n* sindicalista *mf* **trade war** *n* guerra *f* comercial **trade wind** *n* viento *m* alisio

trading ['treɪdɪŋ] *n no pl* comercio *m;* **insider** ~ uso *m* de información confidencial

trading area *n* zona *f* comercial **trading estate** *n Brit* zona *f* industrial **trading licence** *n* licencia *f* comercial **trading volume** *n* volumen *m* comercial

tradition [trə'dɪʃən] *n* tradición *f;* **by** ~ por tradición; **to be in the ~ of sb/sth** ser del estilo de alguien/algo

traditional [trə'dɪʃənəl] *adj* **1.** (*customary*) tradicional **2.** (*conventional*) clásico, -a

traditionalism [trə'dɪʃənəlɪzəm] *n no pl* tradicionalismo *m*

traditionalist [trə'dɪʃənəlɪst] *n* tradicionalista *mf*

traffic ['træfɪk] **I.** *n no pl* **1.** (*vehicles*) tráfico *m;* **heavy** ~ tráfico *m* denso; **air/rail** ~ tráfico *m* aéreo/ferroviario; **commercial** ~ tráfico *m* comercial; **passenger** ~ tráfico *m* de pasajeros; **to get stuck in** ~ quedarse atrapado en un atasco **2.** (*movement: of goods, passengers*) tránsito *m;* **drug** ~ tráfico *m* de drogas **3.** *form* (*dealings*) **to have ~ with sb** tener relaciones comerciales con alguien **II.** <trafficked, trafficked> *vi pej* **to ~ in sth** traficar con algo

traffic accident *n* accidente *m* de tráfico **traffic calming** *n* reducción *f* de tráfico **traffic circle** *n Am* rotonda *f* **traffic island** *n Brit* isleta *f* **traffic jam** *n* atasco *m*

trafficker ['træfɪkəʳ, *Am:* -ɚ] *n pej* traficante *mf;* **drug/arms** ~ traficante de drogas/de armas

traffic light *n* semáforo *m* **traffic regulation** *n* normas *fpl* de circulación **traffic sign** *n* señal *f* de tráfico **traffic warden** *n Brit* controlador(a) *m(f)* de estacionamientos

tragedy ['trædʒədi] <-ies> *n* tragedia *f*

tragic ['trædʒɪk] *adj* trágico, -a

tragicomedy [ˌtrædʒɪ'kɒmədi, *Am:* -'kɑːmə-] <-ies> *n* tragicomedia *f*

trail [treɪl] **I.** *n* **1.** (*path*) camino *m* **2.** (*track*) pista *f;* (*of aeroplane*) estela *f;* **a ~ of destruction** una estela de destrucción; **to be on the ~ of sth/sb** seguir la pista de algo/alguien; **to be hot on the ~ of sb** estar muy cerca de encontrar a alguien; **to follow a** ~ (*in hunting*) seguir un rastro **II.** *vt* **1.** (*follow*) seguir la pista de; **to ~ an animal** seguir el rastro de un animal **2.** (*drag*) arrastrar **3.** (*be losing to*) **to ~ sb/sth** estar perdiendo a alguien/algo **III.** *vi* **1.** (*drag*) **to ~ (somewhere)** arrastrarse (a algún sitio) **2.** SPORTS ir perdiendo; **to ~ by 6 points** ir perdiendo por 6 puntos; **to ~ behind sth/sb** ir por detrás de algo/alguien

◆**trail along I.** *vi* arrastrarse **II.** *vt* arrastrar

◆**trail away** *vi* esfumarse

◆**trail behind** *vi* ir detrás

◆**trail off** *vi* esfumarse

trailblazer ['treɪlˌbleɪzəʳ, *Am:* -zɚ] *n* pionero, -a *m, f*

trailer *n* **1.** (*wheeled container*) remolque *m* **2.** *Am* (*mobile home*) caravana *f* **3.** (*advertisement*) avance *m* publicitario; CINE tráiler *m*

trailer camp *n,* **trailer park** *n Am* cámping *m* de caravanas

train [treɪn] **I.** *n* **1.** (*railway*) tren *m;* **to travel by** ~ viajar en tren **2.** (*series*) serie *f;* **~ of thought** hilo *m* del pensamiento; **to put sth in** ~ poner algo en movimiento **3.** (*retinue*) séquito *m* **4.** (*procession: of animals, things*) recua *f* **5.** (*of dress*) cola *f* **II.** *vi* entrenarse; **to ~ to be sth** prepararse para ser algo **III.** *vt* formar; (*animal*) amaestrar; **to ~ sb in the use of sth** adiestrar a alguien en el uso de algo; **to ~ sb for sth** entrenar a alguien para algo

train accident *n* accidente *m* ferroviario **train connection** *n* conexión *f* ferroviaria **train driver** *n* maquinista *mf*

trained ['treɪnd] *adj* **1.** (*educated*) formado,

-a; (*animal*) amaestrado, -a; **to be ~ in sth** estar formado en algo **2.** (*expert*) cualificado, -a
trainee [treɪ'ni:] *n* aprendiz(a) *m(f)*
traineeship *n* aprendizaje *m*
trainee teacher *n* estudiante *mf* de magisterio
trainer *n* **1.** (*person*) entrenador(a) *m(f)* **2.** *Brit* (*shoe*) zapatilla *f* de deporte
training *n no pl* **1.** (*education*) formación *f*; **~ on-the-job** formación *f* laboral **2.** SPORTS entrenamiento *m*; **to be in ~ for sth** estar entrenando para algo; **to be good ~ for sth** ser un buen entrenamiento para algo
training camp *n* SPORTS campamento *m* de instrucción **training college** *n Brit* escuela *f* normal **training course** *n* curso *m* de formación **training programme** *n* programa *m* de entrenamiento **training ship** *n* buque-escuela *m*
train schedule *n* horario *m* de trenes **train service** *n* servicio *m* de trenes
traipse [treɪps] *vi pej* andar sin ganas; **to ~ around the shops** patearse las tiendas
trait [treɪt] *n* rasgo *m*
traitor ['treɪtəʳ, *Am:* -t̬ɚ] *n* traidor(a) *m(f)*; **to turn ~** volver la casaca
traitorous ['treɪtərəs, *Am:* -t̬ɚ-] *adj pej, form* traicionero, -a
trajectory [trə'dʒektəri, *Am:* -tɚi] *n* **1.** PHYS trayectoria *f* **2.** *fig* (*path*) camino *m*; **to be on a downward/an upward ~** ir descendiendo/ascendiendo
tram [træm] *n Brit, Aus* tranvía *m*; **to go by ~** viajar en tranvía
tramline ['træmlaɪn] *n* **1.** (*track, route*) carril *m* del tranvía **2.** *pl* (*in tennis*) líneas *fpl* laterales
trammel ['træml] *liter* **I.** *n pl* trabas *fpl* **II.** *vt* <-ll-> poner trabas a
tramp [træmp] **I.** *vi* **1.** (*walk heavily*) andar con pasos pesados **2.** (*go on foot*) ir a pie **II.** *vt* pisar con fuerza **III.** *n* **1.** *no pl* (*sound*) pisada *m* fuerte **2.** *no pl* (*walk*) caminata *f*; **to go for a ~** ir de caminata **3.** (*down-and-out*) vagabundo *m* **4.** *Am, pej* (*woman*) fulana *f*
trample ['træmpl] **I.** *vt* pisar; **to ~ sb's foot** pisar el pie a alguien; **to be ~d to death** ser pisoteado hasta la muerte; **to ~ sth underfoot** pisotear algo **II.** *vi* **to ~ on sth** pisar algo
trampoline ['træmpəli:n] *n* trampolín *m*
tramway ['træmweɪ] *n* **1.** (*rails*) raíles *mpl* del tranvía **2.** (*system*) tranvía *m*
trance [trɑ:ns, *Am:* træns] *n* trance *m*; **to be in a ~** estar en trance
tranny ['træni] *n Brit, inf* transistor *m*
tranquil ['træŋkwɪl] *adj* tranquilo, -a
tranquility [træŋ'kwɪləti, *Am:* -ət̬i] *n Am s.* **tranquillity**
tranquilize ['træŋkwɪlaɪz] *vt Am s.* **tranquillize**
tranquilizer *n Am s.* **tranquillizer**
tranquillity [træŋ'kwɪləti, *Am:* -t̬i] *n no pl* tranquilidad *f*
tranquillize ['træŋkwɪlaɪz] *vt* MED tranquilizar
tranquillizer *n* tranquilizante *m*; **to be on ~s** estar tomando tranquilizantes
transact [træn'zækt] *vt* tramitar; **to ~ a business** despachar un negocio
transaction [træn'zækʃən] *n* COM transacción *f*, transa *f RíoPl*; **business ~** transacción *f* comercial
transalpine [træn'zælpaɪn] *adj* transalpino, -a
transatlantic *adj*, **trans-Atlantic** [ˌtrænzət'læntɪk, *Am:* ˌtræntsæt'-] *adj* transatlántico, -a
transceiver [træn'si:vəʳ] *n* transmisor-receptor *m*
transcend [træn'send] *vt* **1.** (*go beyond*) trascender; **to ~ barriers/limitations** traspasar las barreras/los límites **2.** (*surpass*) exceder
transcendent [træn'sendənt] *adj* trascendente; (*superior*) supremo, -a
transcendental [ˌtræntsen'dentəl, *Am:* -t̬əl] *adj* trascendental
transcontinental [ˌtrænsˌkɒntɪ'nentəl, *Am:* ˌtræntsˌkɑ:ntən'en-] *adj* transcontinental
transcribe [træn'skraɪb] *vt* transcribir
transcript ['træntskrɪpt] *n* transcripción *f*
transcription [træn'skrɪpʃən] *n* transcripción *f*
transducer [trænz'dju:səʳ, *Am:* trænts'du:sɚ] *n* ELEC transductor *m*
transept ['træntsept] *n* ARCHIT crucero *m*
transfer¹ [trænts'fɜ:, *Am:* -'fɜ:r] **I.** <-rr-> *vt* **1.** (*move*) trasladar **2.** (*reassign: power*) transferir **3.** COM (*shop*) traspasar **4.** SPORTS (*sell*) traspasar **II.** <-rr-> *vi* **1.** (*move*) trasladarse **2.** (*change train, plane*) hacer transbordo
transfer² ['træntsfɜ:ʳ, *Am:* 'træntsfɜ:r] *n* **1.** (*process of moving*) traslado *m*; **~ of information** transmisión *f* de información **2.** (*reassignment*) transferencia *f* **3.** COM (*of a shop*) traspaso *m* **4.** SPORTS traspaso *m* **5.** *Am* (*ticket*) billete *m* de transbordo **6.** (*picture*) cromo *m*
transferable [trænts'fɜ:rəbl] *adj* transferible
transference ['træntsfɜ:rəns] *n no pl, form a.* PSYCH transferencia *f*
transfigure [trænts'fɪgəʳ, *Am:* trænts'fɪgjɚ] *vt* transfigurar
transfix [trænts'fɪks] *vt form* traspasar; **to be ~ed by sb/sth** estar totalmente paralizado por alguien/algo
transform [trænts'fɔ:m, *Am:* trænts'fɔ:rm] *vt* transformar
transformation [ˌtræntsfə'meɪʃən, *Am:* ˌtræntsfɚ'-] *n* transformación *f*
transformer *n* ELEC transformador *m*
transfuse [trænts'fju:z] *vt* MED hacer una transfusión de
transfusion [trænts'fju:ʒən] *n* transfusión *f*; **blood ~** transfusión de sangre; **to give sb a ~** hacer a alguien una transfusión de sangre
transgress [trænz'gres, *Am:* trænts-] *form*

T

I. *vt* transgredir; **to ~ a law** infringir una ley II. *vi* cometer una transgresión

transgression [trænz'greʃən, *Am:* trænts-] *n form* transgresión *f*

transgressor *n* transgresor(a) *m(f)*; REL pecador(a) *m(f)*

transient ['trænziənt, *Am:* 'træntʃənt] *form* I. *adj* pasajero, -a II. *n* residente *mf* temporal

transistor [træn'zɪstəʳ, *Am:* træn'zɪstɚ] *n* ELEC transistor *m*

transistorize [træn'zɪstəraɪz] *vt* transistorizar

transit ['træntsɪt] *n no pl* tránsito *m;* **in ~** de paso

transit business *n* negocio *m* de tránsito **transit camp** *n Brit* campamento *m* provisional **transit desk** *n* AVIAT cabina *f* de tránsito

transition [træn'zɪʃən] *n* transición *f*

transitional [træn'zɪʃənəl] *adj* (*period*) transitorio, -a; (*government*) de transición

transitive ['træntsətɪv, *Am:* 'træntsət̬ɪv] *adj* LING transitivo, -a

transit lounge *n* sala *f* de tránsito

transitory ['træntsɪtəri, *Am:* 'træntsətɔːri] *adj* pasajero, -a

transit passenger *n* pasajero, -a *m, f* de tránsito **transit visa** *n* visado *m* de tránsito

translatable *adj* traducible

translate [trænz'leɪt, *Am:* træn'sleɪt] I. *vt* 1. LING traducir; **to ~ sth from English into Spanish** traducir algo del inglés al español 2. (*adapt*) adaptar; **to ~ a play for the cinema** adaptar una obra de teatro para el cine 3. (*transform*) **to ~ a plan into action** llevar a cabo un plan II. *vi* LING traducir; **to ~ from English into Spanish** traducir del inglés al español

translation [trænz'leɪʃən, *Am:* træn'sleɪ-] *n* traducción *f*

translator *n* traductor(a) *m(f)*

transliterate [trænz'lɪtəreɪt, *Am:* træn'slɪt̬əreɪt] *vt* transliterar

transliteration [ˌtrænzlɪtər'eɪʃən, *Am:* trænˌslɪt̬ə'reɪ-] *n* LING *no pl* transliteración *f*

translucent [trænz'luːsənt, *Am:* træn'sluː-] *adj,* **translucid** *adj* translúcido, -a

transmigration [ˌtrænzmaɪ'greɪʃən, *Am:* ˌtræntsmaɪ'-] *n* transmigración *f*

transmissible [trænz'mɪsəbl, *Am:* træn'smɪs-] *adj* transmisible

transmission [trænz'mɪʃən, *Am:* træn'smɪʃ-] *n* transmisión *f;* **data ~** INFOR transmisión de datos

transmission speed *n* INFOR velocidad *f* de transmisión (de datos)

transmit [trænz'mɪt, *Am:* træn'smɪt] <-tt-> *vt* transmitir

transmitter *n* 1. (*apparatus*) transmisor *m* 2. (*station*) emisora *f*

transmitting station *n* emisora *f*

transmogrify [trænz'mɒgrɪfaɪ, *Am:* træn'smɑːgrə-] *vt* transformar completamente

transmutation [ˌtrænzmjuː'teɪʃən, *Am:* ˌtrænts-] *n form* transmutación *f*

transmute [trænz'mjuːt, *Am:* ˌtrænts-] *form* I. *vt* transmutar; **to ~ sth into sth** transmutar algo en algo II. *vi* **to ~ into sth** transmutarse en algo

transoceanic ['trænzˌəʊʃi'ænɪk, *Am:* ˌtræntsoʊʃi'-] *adj* transoceánico, -a

transom ['træntsəm] *n* 1. (*horizontal bar*) travesaño *m* 2. *Am* (*window*) montante *m*

transparency [træn'spærəntsi, *Am:* træn'sperənt-] *n* <-ies> transparencia *f*

transparent [trænt'spærənt, *Am:* træn'sperənt-] *adj* transparente

transpiration [ˌtræntspɪ'reɪʃən] *n no pl* transpiración *f*

transpire [træn'spaɪəʳ, *Am:* træn'spaɪɚ] *vi* 1. (*happen*) tener lugar; **it ~ed that ...** ocurrió que... 2. (*come to be known*) saberse 3. (*emit water vapour*) transpirar

transplant¹ [træn'splɑːnt, *Am:* træn'splænt] *vt* 1. MED, BOT trasplantar 2. (*relocate*) trasladar

transplant² ['træntsplɑːnt, *Am:* 'træntsplænt] *n* trasplante *m*

transplantation [ˌtræntsplɑːn'teɪʃən, *Am:* ˌtræntsplæn'-] *n no pl* trasplante *m*

transport¹ [træn'spɔːt, *Am:* træn'spɔːrt] *vt* 1. (*people, goods*) transportar 2. *Brit* HIST (*to penal colony*) deportar 3. *liter* (*fill with emotion*) arrebatar; **to be ~ed with joy/grief** estar lleno de alegría/pena

transport² ['træntspɔːt, *Am:* 'træntspɔːrt] *n* 1. *no pl* (*means of conveyance*) transporte *m;* **public ~** transporte *m* público; **~ costs** gastos *mpl* de transporte 2. (*plane*) avión *m* de transporte; (*ship*) buque *m* de transporte 3. *form* (*strong emotion*) arrebato *m;* **to be in ~s of joy** estar lleno de alegría

transportable *adj* transportable

transportation [ˌtræntspɔː'teɪʃən, *Am:* ˌtræntspɚː'-] *n no pl* 1. (*of people, goods*) transporte *m* 2. (*of a convict*) deportación *f*

transport café <- -s> *n Brit* cafetería *f* de carretera

transporter [træn'spɔːtəʳ, *Am:* træn'spɔːrt̬ɚ] *n* transportador *m*

transpose [træn'spəʊz, *Am:* træn'spoʊz] *vt* 1. (*reverse position of*) transponer 2. (*change location*) trasladar 3. MUS, MATH transportar

transsexual [træn'sekʃʊəl, *Am:* træn'sekʃuəl] I. *n* transexual *mf* II. *adj* transexual

transverse ['trænzvɜːs, *Am:* 'trænts-] *adj* transversal

transvestite [træns'vestaɪt, *Am:* 'trænts-] *n* travestido *m*

trap [træp] I. *n* 1. (*device*) trampa *f;* **to set a ~** poner una trampa 2. (*dangerous situation*) encerrona *f;* (*ambush*) emboscada *f;* **to fall into a ~** caer en una emboscada 3. *Brit, inf* (*mouth*) boca *f;* **to shut one's ~** cerrar el pico; **to keep one's ~ shut** mantener la boca cerrada **4.** (*curve in pipe*) sifón *m* **5.** HIST (*carriage*) tartana *f* **6.** (*for clay pigeons*) lanzaplatos *m inv* **II.** *vt* <-pp-> atrapar; **to feel ~ped** sentirse encerrado

trapdoor [ˌtræp'dɔːʳ, *Am:* 'træpdɔːr] *n* escotillón *m*

trapeze [trə'piːz, *Am:* træp'iːz] *n* trapecio *m*

trapezium [trə'piːziəm] <-s *o* -zia> *pl n Brit, Aus,* **trapezoid** ['træpɪzɔɪd] *n Am* MAT trapecio *m*

trapper ['træpəʳ, *Am:* -ɚ] *n* trampero, -a *m, f;* **fur ~** cazador(a) *m(f)* de animales de piel

trappings ['træpɪŋz] *npl* arreos *mpl;* **the ~ of power** el boato del poder

Trappist ['træpɪst] **I.** *adj* trapense **II.** *n* trapense *m*

trap shooting *n no pl* tiro *m* al plato

trash [træʃ] **I.** *n no pl* **1.** *Am* (*rubbish*) basura *f;* **to take the ~ out** sacar la basura **2.** *inf* (*people*) gentuza *f;* (*book, film*) basura *f* **3.** *inf* (*nonsense*) tonterías *fpl;* **to talk ~** decir tonterías **II.** *vt inf* **1.** (*wreck*) destrozar **2.** (*criticize*) poner por los suelos

trashcan ['træʃkæn] *n Am* cubo *m* de la basura

trashy ['træʃi] *adj inf* malo, -a

trauma ['trɔːmə, *Am:* 'traːmə] *n* PSYCH, MED trauma *m*

traumatic [trɔː'mætɪk, *Am:* traː'mæt̬-] *adj* traumático, -a

traumatise *vt Aus, Brit,* **traumatize** ['trɔːmətaɪz] *vt* traumatizar; **to be ~d by sth** estar traumatizado por algo

travel ['trævəl] **I.** <*Brit:* -ll-, *Am:* -l-> *vi* **1.** (*make journey*) viajar; **to ~ by air/car/train** viajar en avión/coche/tren; **to ~ first-class** viajar en primera clase; **to ~ light** viajar con poco equipaje **2.** (*light, sound*) propagarse **3.** (*be away*) estar de viaje **4.** *inf* (*go fast*) ir rápido **II.** <*Brit:* -ll-, *Am:* -l-> *vt* viajar por; **to ~ a country/the world** viajar por un país/el mundo; **to ~ the length and breadth of a country** viajar a lo largo y ancho de un país **III.** *npl* viajes *mpl*

travel agency *n* agencia *f* de viajes **travel agent** *n* agente *mf* de viajes **travel bureau** *n* agencia *f* de viajes **travel card** *n* bono *m* de transporte **travel cot** *n* cama *f* plegable de viaje

traveled *adj Am s.* **travelled**

traveler ['trævləʳ, *Am:* -lɚ] *n Am s.* **traveller**

travel expenses *n* gastos *mpl* de viaje **travel guide** *n* (*person, book*) guía *f* turística

traveling *n no pl, Am s.* **travelling**

travel insurance *n* seguro *m* de viaje

travelled *adj Brit* que ha viajado

traveller ['trævələʳ, *Am:* -əlɚ] *n Brit* viajero, -a *m, f;* **commercial ~** *Brit* viajante *mf* comercial

traveller's cheque *n Brit,* **traveler's check** *n Am* cheque *m* de viaje

travelling *n no pl, Brit* viajar *m*

travelling allowance *n* dietas *fpl* **travelling bag** *n* bolsa *f* de viaje **travelling circus** *n* circo *m* ambulante **travelling crane** *n* grúa *f* de corredera **travelling exhibition** *n* exposición *f* ambulante **travelling salesman** *n* viajante *mf* de comercio

travelog *n Am,* **travelogue** ['trævəlɒg, *Am:* -əlaːg] *n Brit, Aus* TV documental *m* de interés turístico; CINE película *f* de viajes

travel-sick *adj* mareado, -a

travel sickness *n no pl* mareo *m*

traverse ['trævɜːs, *Am:* -ɚs] *vt* **1.** (*cross*) atravesar **2.** (*move along*) recorrer

travesty ['trævəsti, *Am:* -ɪsti] <-ies> *n pej* parodia *f*

trawl [trɔːl, *Am:* traːl] **I.** *vi* **1.** (*fish*) pescar al arrastre **2.** (*search*) **to ~ through sth** rastrear algo **II.** *vt* (*fish: sea*) hacer pesca al arrastre en **III.** *n* **1.** (*net*) red *f* barredera **2.** (*search*) rastreo *m*

trawler ['trɔːləʳ, *Am:* 'traːlɚ] *n* pesquero *m* de arrastre

tray [treɪ] *n* bandeja *f,* charola *f AmS*

treacherous ['tretʃərəs] *adj* **1.** (*disloyal*) traicionero, -a **2.** (*dangerous: road, weather*) peligroso, -a

treachery ['tretʃəri] *n no pl* traición *f*

treacle ['triːkl] *n no pl, Brit* melaza *f*

treacly ['triːkli] *adj* **1.** (*thick and sticky*) meloso, -a **2.** (*sentimental*) empalagoso, -a

tread [tred] **I.** <trod *Am:* treaded, trodden *Am:* trod> *vi* pisar; **to ~ on** [*o* **in**] **sth** pisar algo **II.** *vt* pisar; **to ~ one's weary way** andar a paso cansino **III.** *n* **1.** (*manner of walking*) paso *m;* **a heavy ~** un paso fuerte **2.** (*step*) escalón *m* **3.** AUTO dibujo *m*

treadle ['tredl] *n* pedal *m*

treadmill ['tredmɪl] *n* **1.** (*wheel, exercise machine*) rueda *f* de andar **2.** *fig* rutina *f*

treason ['triːzn] *n no pl* traición *f;* **high ~** *form* alta traición

treasonable ['triːzənəbl] *adj,* **treasonous** ['triːzənəs] *adj* traidor(a)

treasure ['treʒəʳ, *Am:* -ɚ] **I.** *n* **1.** *no pl* (*precious items*) tesoro *m* **2.** (*highly valued thing, person*) joya *f;* **my assistant is a ~** mi ayudante es una joya **II.** *vt* atesorar; **to ~ the memories of sb** guardar los recuerdos de alguien como un tesoro

treasure house *n* sala *f* del tesoro **treasure hunt** *n* caza *f* del tesoro

treasurer ['treʒərəʳ, *Am:* -ɚ] *n* tesorero, -a *m, f*

treasure trove *n* tesoro *m* hallado

treasury ['treʒəri] <-ies> *n* tesorería *f;* **the Treasury** Hacienda *f*

treasury bill *n Am* letra *f* del Tesoro **treasury bond** *n Am* bono *m* del Tesoro **treasury note** *n Am* pagaré *m* del Tesoro **Treasury Secretary** *n Am* ≈ Ministro, -a *m, f* de Hacienda

treat ['triːt] I. *vt* 1. (*deal with, handle*) *a.* MED tratar; **to ~ sb/sth badly** tratar mal a alguien/algo; **to ~ sb/sth as if ...** tratar a alguien/algo como si +*subj* 2. (*process*) tratar; **to ~ a substance with acid** tratar una sustancia con ácido 3. (*discuss*) tratar 4. (*pay for*) invitar; **to ~ sb to an ice cream** invitar a alguien a un helado II. *vi* **to ~ with sb** negociar con alguien III. *n* 1. (*pleasurable event*) convite *m;* (*present*) regalo *m;* **it's my ~** invito yo 2. (*pleasure*) placer *m;* **it was a real ~** ha sido un auténtico placer ►**to work a ~** *Brit, inf* funcionar muy bien

treatise ['triːtɪz, *Am:* -t̬ɪs] *n* tratado *m*

treatment ['triːtmənt] *n* 1. *no pl* trato *m;* **to get rough ~ from sb** recibir un mal trato de alguien; **to give sb the ~** *inf* hacer sufrir a alguien; **special ~** tratamiento *m* especial 2. MED tratamiento *m;* **to respond to ~** responder al tratamiento

treaty ['triːti, *Am:* -t̬i] <-ies> *n* tratado *m;* **peace ~** tratado de paz

treble ['trebl] I. *adj* 1. (*three times greater*) triple 2. MUS de tiple II. *n* MUS tiple *mf* III. *vt* triplicar IV. *vi* triplicarse

treble clef *n* clave *f* de sol

tree [triː] I. *n* árbol *m;* **to climb a ~** trepar a un árbol; **the Tree of Knowledge** el árbol de la ciencia ►**you can't see the forest** *Brit, Aus* [*o* **wood** *Am*] **for the ~s** los árboles no te dejan ver el bosque; **to bark up the wrong ~** *inf* tomar el rábano por las hojas; **to grow on ~s** caer del cielo; **money doesn't grow on ~s** el dinero no cae del cielo; **that doesn't grow on ~s** eso no se encuentra a la vuelta de la esquina II. *vt* (*animal*) hacer refugiarse en un árbol

tree frog *n* rana *f* de San Antonio **tree house** *n* cabaña *f* en un árbol **treeless** *adj* sin árboles **treeline** *n* límite *m* forestal

tree-lined ['triːlaɪnd] *adj* arbolado, -a; **a ~ street** una calle bordeada de árboles

tree surgeon *n* arboricultor(a) *m(f)* **treetop** *n* copa *f* del árbol; **in the ~s** en lo alto de los árboles **tree trunk** *n* tronco *m* del árbol

trefoil ['trefɔɪl, *Am:* 'triːfɔɪl] *n* trébol *m*

trek [trek] I. <-kk-> *vi* caminar II. *n* 1. (*walk*) caminata *f* (larga) 2. (*migration*) migración *f*

trekking ['trekɪŋ] *n* trekking *m;* **to go ~** hacer senderismo

trellis ['trelɪs] <-es> *n* espaldera *f;* (*for plants*) enrejado *m*

tremble ['trembl] I. *vi* temblar; **to ~ with cold** tiritar de frío; **to ~ like a leaf** temblar como un azogado II. *n* temblor *m;* **to be all of a ~** *Brit, inf* estar como un flan

tremendous [trɪ'mendəs] *adj* 1. (*enormous*) enorme; (*crowd, scope*) inmenso, -a; (*help*) grande; (*success*) contundente 2. *inf* (*extremely good*) estupendo, -a

tremolo ['treməlәʊ, *Am:* -əloʊ] *n* MUS trémolo *m*

tremor ['treməʳ, *Am:* -ɚ] *n* 1. (*shake*) vibración *f;* (*earthquake*) temblor *m* 2. (*of fear, excitement*) estremecimiento *m*

tremulous ['tremjʊləs] *adj* trémulo, -a

trench [trentʃ] <-es> *n* zanja *f;* MIL trinchera *f*

trenchant ['trentʃənt] *adj* mordaz

trench coat *n* trinchera *f* **trench warfare** *n* guerra *f* de trincheras

trend [trend] I. *n* 1. (*tendency*) tendencia *f;* **downward/upward ~** tendencia *f* a la baja/alcista; **a ~ toward(s) ...** una tendencia hacia... 2. (*fashion*) moda *f;* **the latest ~** las últimas tendencias; **to set a new ~** fijar una nueva moda II. *vi* tender; **to ~ to sth** tender a algo

trendsetter ['trend,setəʳ, *Am:* -,set̬ɚ] *n* persona *f* que inicia una moda

trendy ['trendi] I. <-ier, -iest> *adj* (*clothes, bar*) de moda; (*person*) moderno, -a II. <-ies> *n* persona *f* de tendencias ultramodernas

trepidation [,trepɪ'deɪʃən] *n no pl* ansiedad *f;* **to do sth with ~** hacer algo inquietamente

trespass ['trespəs] *vi* 1. LAW entrar ilegalmente 2. REL pecar

trespasser ['trespəsəʳ, *Am:* -pæsɚ] *n* intruso, -a *m, f*

trestle ['tresl] *n* caballete *m*

trestle table *n* mesa *f* de caballete

triad ['traɪæd] *n* tríada *f*

trial ['traɪəl] *n* 1. LAW proceso *m;* **~ by jury** juicio *m* con jurado; **to stand ~** ser procesado; **to be on ~ for one's life** ser acusado de un crimen capital 2. (*test*) prueba *f;* **clinical ~s** ensayos *mpl* clínicos; **~ of strength** prueba de fuerza; **to give sb a ~** poner a alguien a prueba; **to have sth on ~** tener algo a prueba 3. (*source of problems*) suplicio *m;* **~s and tribulations** tribulaciones *fpl* 4. (*competition*) competición *f*

trial flight *n* vuelo *m* de prueba **trial period** *n* período *m* de prueba **trial separation** *n* separación *f* de prueba

triangle ['traɪæŋgl] *n* triángulo *m*

triangular [traɪ'æŋgjʊləʳ, *Am:* -lɚ] *adj* triangular

tribal ['traɪbl] *adj* tribal

tribalism ['traɪblɪzəm] *n no pl* tribalismo *m*

tribe [traɪb] *n* tribu *f;* **the twelve ~s of Israel** HIST las doce tribus de Israel

tribesman ['traɪbzmən] <-men> *n* miembro *m* de una tribu

tribulation [,trɪbjʊ'leɪʃən, *Am:* -jə'-] *n form* tribulación *f*

tribunal [traɪ'bjuːnl] *n* tribunal *m;* (*investigative body*) comisión *f* de investigación

tribune[1] ['trɪbjuːn] *n* HIST tribuno *m*

tribune[2] ['trɪbjuːn] *n* ARCHIT tribuna *f*

tributary ['trɪbjətəri, *Am:* -teri] I. <-ies> *n* 1. (*river*) afluente *m* 2. HIST (*person*) contribuyente *mf;* (*state*) estado *m* tributario II. *adj form* 1. (*river*) afluyente 2. HIST (*state*) tributario, -a

tribute ['trɪbjuːt] *n* 1. (*token of respect*)

homenaje *m;* **to pay ~ to sb/sth** rendir tributo a alguien/algo; **floral ~** *form* ofrenda *f* floral **2.** (*sign of sth positive*) elogio *m;* **to be a ~ to sth/sb** hacer honor a algo/alguien **3.** HIST (*money paid to a superior power*) tributo *m*

trice [traɪs] *n inf* **in a ~** en un santiamén

trick [trɪk] **I.** *n* **1.** (*ruse*) truco *m,* trampa *f;* **a dirty ~** *inf* una mala pasada; **to play a ~ on sb** tender una trampa a alguien; **to be up to one's (old) ~s again** volver a hacer de las suyas **2.** (*of magician*) truco *m* **3.** (*technique*) truquillo *m* **4.** (*illusion*) ilusión *f;* **a ~ of the light** una ilusión óptica; **his eyes are playing ~s on him** ve visiones **5.** GAME mano *f;* **to take all the ~s** ganar todas las bazas ►**to try every ~ in the book** intentar todos los trucos habidos y por haber; **the ~s of the trade** los trucos del oficio; **that'll do the ~** con eso solucionamos el tema; **to not miss a ~** no perder ripio **II.** *adj* **1.** (*deceptive*) **a ~ question** una pregunta con trampa **2.** *Am, inf* (*weak*) débil **III.** *vt* (*deceive*) engañar; (*fool*) burlar; (*swindle*) timar

trickery ['trɪkəri] *n no pl* artimañas *fpl;* **to resort to ~** recurrir a engaños

trickle ['trɪkl] **I.** *vi* **1.** (*flow slowly*) salir en un chorro fino; (*in drops*) gotear **2.** *fig* (*people*) **to ~ in/out** entrar/salir poco a poco; **to ~ out** (*information*) difundirse poco a poco **II.** *n* **1.** (*of liquid*) hilo *m;* (*drops*) goteo *m* **2.** (*of people, information*) goteo *m*

◆**trickle away** *vi* consumirse poco a poco

trickster ['trɪkstəʳ, *Am:* -stɚ] *n pej* estafador(a) *m(f),* trácala *f Méx*

tricksy ['trɪksi] *adj* (*playful*) juguetón, -ona

tricky ['trɪki] <-ier, -iest> *adj* **1.** (*crafty*) astuto, -a **2.** (*difficult*) complicado, -a; (*situation*) delicado, -a; **to be ~ to do** ser difícil de hacer

tricycle ['traɪsɪkl] *n* triciclo *m*

trident ['traɪdnt] *n* tridente *m*

tried [traɪd] **I.** *vi, vt pt, pp of* **try II.** *adj* probado, -a; **~ and tested** probado con toda garantía

triennial [traɪ'enɪəl] *adj* trienal

trier ['traɪəʳ, *Am:* -ɚ] *n inf* persona *f* que se esfuerza mucho

trifle ['traɪfəl] *n* **1.** (*insignificant thing*) bagatela *f* **2.** (*small amount*) insignificancia *f;* **a ~** un poquito **3.** *Brit* (*dessert*) dulce *m* de bizcocho borracho

◆**trifle away** *vt* malgastar; **to trifle one's time away** perder el tiempo

◆**trifle with** *vt* jugar con; **to ~ sb's affections** jugar con los sentimientos de alguien

trifling *adj* insignificante

trig. *abbr of* **trigonometry** trigonometría *f*

trigger ['trɪgəʳ, *Am:* -ɚ] **I.** *n* **1.** (*of gun*) gatillo *m;* **to pull the ~** apretar el gatillo; **~ mechanism** mecanismo *m* disparador **2.** *fig* detonante *m* **II.** *vt* **1.** (*reaction*) provocar; (*revolt*) hacer estallar **2.** (*start*) accionar; **to ~ an alarm** disparar una alarma

trigger-happy ['trɪgəˌhæpi, *Am:* -ɚˌ-] *adj* de gatillo fácil

trigonometry [ˌtrɪgə'nɒmətri, *Am:* -'nɑːmə-] *n no pl* MAT trigonometría *f*

trike [traɪk] *n inf abbr of* **tricycle** triciclo *m*

trilateral [ˌtraɪ'lætərəl, *Am:* traɪ'læt̬ɚ-] *adj* **1.** (*involving three parties*) trilateral **2.** MAT trilátero, -a

trilby ['trɪlbi] <-ies> *n Brit* sombrero *m* de fieltro

trilingual [ˌtraɪ'lɪŋgwəl] *adj* trilingüe

trill [trɪl] **I.** *n* **1.** (*birdsong*) trino *m* **2.** (*quavering note*) quiebro *m* **II.** *vi* **1.** (*bird*) trinar **2.** (*speak*) hablar de forma afectada **III.** *vt* **to ~ one's r's** pronunciar la r con vibración

trillion ['trɪlɪən, *Am:* -jən] *n* billón *m*

trilogy ['trɪlədʒi] <-ies> *n* trilogía *f*

trim [trɪm] **I.** *n* **1.** (*state*) (buen) estado *m;* **to be in ~ (for sth)** estar listo (para algo); **to be in fighting ~** estar listo para entrar en combate **2.** (*hair*) **to give sb a ~** cortar las puntas del pelo a alguien; **to give sth a ~** dar un recorte a algo **3.** *no pl* (*decorative edge*) borde *m* **II.** *adj* **1.** (*attractively thin, compact*) en buen estado **2.** (*neat*) aseado, -a; (*lawn*) cuidado, -a **III.** <-mm-> *vt* **1.** (*cut*) cortar; **to ~ one's beard** cortarse la barba **2.** (*reduce*) reducir

◆**trim down** *vt* recortar

◆**trim off** *vt* cortar

trimming *n* **1.** (*decoration*) adorno *m* **2.** *pl* GASTR guarnición *f*

Trinidad ['trɪnɪdæd] *n* Trinidad *f;* **~ and Tobago** Trinidad y Tobago

Trinidadian ['trɪnɪdædiən] **I.** *adj* de Trinidad **II.** *n* habitante *mf* de Trinidad

Trinity ['trɪnəti, *Am:* -t̬i] *n no pl* Trinidad *f;* **the (holy) ~** la (Santísima) Trinidad

trinket ['trɪŋkɪt] *n* baratija *f*

trio ['triːəʊ, *Am:* -oʊ] *n a.* MUS trío *m;* **string ~** trío *m* de cuerda

trip [trɪp] **I.** *n* **1.** (*journey*) viaje *m;* (*shorter*) excursión *f;* **business ~** viaje de negocios; **to go on a ~** irse de viaje **2.** *inf* (*effect of drugs*) viaje *m* **3.** (*fall*) tropezón *m* **II.** <-pp-> *vi* **1.** (*stumble*) tropezar; **to ~ on sth** tropezar con algo **2.** (*move lightly*) andar con paso ligero **III.** <-pp-> *vt* **1.** (*cause to stumble*) **to ~ sb (up)** hacer tropezar a alguien **2.** (*switch on*) encender

◆**trip over** *vi* dar un tropezón

◆**trip up I.** *vi* **1.** (*stumble*) tropezar **2.** (*verbally*) equivocarse **II.** *vt* **1.** (*cause to stumble*) hacer tropezar **2.** (*cause to fail*) confundir

tripartite [ˌtraɪ'pɑːtaɪt, *Am:* -'pɑːr-] *adj* tripartito, -a

tripe [traɪp] *n no pl* **1.** GASTR callos *mpl,* guata *f Méx* **2.** *pej, inf* (*nonsense, rubbish*) tonterías *fpl;* **to talk ~** decir bobadas

triple ['trɪpl] **I.** *adj* triple **II.** *vt* triplicar **III.** *vi* triplicarse

triple jump *n* triple salto *m*

triplet ['trɪplɪt] *n* **1.** (*baby*) trillizo, -a *m, f;* **to have ~s** tener trillizos **2.** MUS tresillo *m*

T

triplicate ['trɪplɪkət, *Am:* -kɪt] *adj* triplicado, -a; **in** ~ por triplicado

tripod ['traɪpɒd, *Am:* -pɑːd] *n* trípode *m*

tripper ['trɪpəʳ, *Am:* -ɚ] *n Brit, inf* excursionista *mf*

tripping ['trɪpɪŋ] *adj* ligero, -a

triptych ['trɪptɪk] *n* (*art*) tríptico *m*

trisect [traɪ'sekt] *vt* trisecar

trite [traɪt] *adj* tópico, -a

triumph ['traɪʌmf] **I.** *n* **1.** (*success*) triunfo *m;* **a ~ over sb** un triunfo sobre alguien; **to do sth in** ~ hacer algo triunfalmente; **to hail sth as a** ~ clamar algo como un triunfo **2.** (*supreme example*) éxito *m;* **a ~ of engineering/medicine** un éxito de la ingeniería/medicina **II.** *vi* **1.** (*achieve success*) triunfar; **to ~ over sth/sb** triunfar sobre algo/alguien **2.** (*exult excessively*) mostrarse triunfante

triumphal [traɪ'ʌmfəl] *adj* triunfal

triumphant [traɪ'ʌmfnt] *adj* **1.** (*victorious*) triunfante; (*return*) triunfal; **to emerge ~ from sth** salir triunfante de algo **2.** (*successful*) exitoso, -a

trivia ['trɪvɪə] *npl* trivialidades *fpl*

trivial ['trɪvɪəl] *adj* **1.** (*unimportant*) irrelevante; (*dispute, matter*) trivial **2.** (*insignificant*) insignificante

triviality [ˌtrɪvi'æləti, *Am:* -t̬i] *n* <-ies> **1.** *no pl* (*unimportance*) trivialidad *f* **2.** (*unimportant thing*) nimiedad *f*

trivialize ['trɪvɪəlaɪz] *vt* trivializar

trod [trɒd, *Am:* trɑːd] *pt, pp of* **tread**

trodden ['trɒdn, *Am:* 'trɑːdn] *pp of* **tread**

troglodyte ['trɒglədaɪt, *Am:* 'trɑːglə-] *n* troglodita *mf*

Trojan ['trəʊdʒən, *Am:* 'troʊ-] **I.** *n* troyano, -a *m, f* ►**to work like a** ~ trabajar como un esclavo **II.** *adj* troyano, -a; **~ Horse** caballo *m* de Troya; **the ~ War** la Guerra de Troya

trolley ['trɒli, *Am:* 'trɑːli] *n* **1.** *Brit, Aus* (*small cart*) carretilla *f;* **drinks** ~ carrito *m* de bebidas; **luggage** ~ carrito *m* para el equipaje; **shopping** ~ carrito *m* de la compra **2.** *Am* (*trolleycar*) tranvía *m* ►**to be off one's** ~ estar chiflado

trolleybus ['trɒlibʌs, *Am:* 'trɑːli-] *n* trolebús *m* **trolleycar** *n Am* tranvía *m*

trollop ['trɒləp, *Am:* 'trɑːləp] *n pej, inf* marrana *f,* tusa *f Cuba*

trombone [trɒm'bəʊn, *Am:* trɑːm'boʊn] *n* trombón *m*

trombonist [trɒm'bəʊnɪst, *Am:* trɑːm'boʊ-] *n* trombón *mf*

troop [truːp] **I.** *n* **1.** *pl* MIL tropas *fpl;* **cavalry** ~ escuadrón *m* de caballería **2.** (*of people*) grupo *m* **II.** *vi* **to ~ in/out** entrar/salir en tropel **III.** *vt* **to ~ the colour** *Brit* presentar la bandera

troop carrier *n* avión *m* de transporte de tropas

trooper ['truːpəʳ, *Am:* -ɚ] *n* **1.** MIL soldado *m* de caballería **2.** *Am* (*state police officer*) policía *mf;* **state** ~ policía *f* estatal ►**to swear like a** ~ soltar tacos como un carretero

trophy ['trəʊfi, *Am:* 'troʊ-] *n* <-ies> trofeo *m*

tropic ['trɒpɪk, *Am:* 'trɑːpɪk] *n* (*latitude*) trópico *m;* **the ~s** los trópicos; **Tropic of Cancer/Capricorn** Trópico de Cáncer/Capricornio

tropical ['trɒpɪkl, *Am:* 'trɑːpɪk-] *adj* tropical

troposphere ['trəʊpəsfɪəʳ] *n no pl* troposfera *f*

trot [trɒt, *Am:* trɑːt] **I.** *n* **1.** (*of horse*) trote *m* **2.** *pl, inf* (*diarrhoea*) **to have the ~s** tener diarrea, tener obradera *Col, Guat, Pan* ►**on the** ~ seguidos **II.** *vi* **1.** (*horse*) trotar; (*person*) andar trotando **2.** (*run at moderate pace*) ir al trote **3.** (*go busily*) ir apresurado **III.** <-tt-> *vt* (*horse*) hacer trotar

◆**trot along** *vi,* **trot off** *vi* marcharse

◆**trot out** *vt* (*excuse, explanation*) soltar; **to ~ arguments** sacar a relucir argumentos

trotter ['trɒtəʳ, *Am:* 'trɑːt̬ɚ] *n* manita *f* de cerdo

trouble ['trʌbl] **I.** *n* **1.** (*difficulty*) dificultad *f,* problema *m;* **to have** ~ tener dificultades; **to ask for** ~ buscarse problemas; **to spell** ~ *inf* suponer problemas; **to store up** ~ ir haciendo algo que traerá problemas; **to be in/get into** ~ estar/meterse en un lío; **to be in serious** ~ estar metido en serios problemas; **to be in ~ with sb** tener problemas con alguien; **to land sb in** ~ meter en un lío a alguien; **to stay out of** ~ mantenerse al margen de los problemas **2.** *pl* (*series of difficulties*) problemas *mpl;* **to be the least of sb's ~s** ser el menor de los males de alguien **3.** *no pl* (*inconvenience*) molestia *f;* **to go to the** ~ (**of doing sth**) darse la molestia (de hacer algo); **to go to a lot of ~ for sb** tomarse muchas molestias por alguien; **to put sb to the ~ of doing sth** molestar a alguien pidiéndole que haga algo; **to be** (**not**) **worth the** ~ (**of doing sth**) (no) merecer la pena (hacer algo) **4.** *no pl* (*physical ailment*) enfermedad *f;* **stomach** ~ dolor *m* de estómago **5.** *no pl* (*malfunction*) avería *f;* **engine** ~ avería del motor **6.** (*strife*) conflictos *mpl;* **to stir up** ~ crear conflictos **II.** *vt* **1.** *form* (*cause inconvenience*) molestar; **to ~ sb for sth** molestar a alguien por algo; **to ~ sb to do sth** molestar a alguien para que haga algo **2.** (*make an effort*) **to ~ oneself about sth** esforzarse en algo **3.** (*cause worry*) preocupar; (*cause pain*) afligir; **to be ~d by sth** verse en problemas por algo **III.** *vi* esforzarse; **to ~ to do sth** molestarse en hacer algo

troubled *adj* **1.** (*period*) turbulento, -a; (*water*) revuelto, -a **2.** (*worried*) preocupado, -a; (*look*) de preocupación

trouble-free [ˌtrʌbl'friː] *adj* sin problemas

troublemaker ['trʌblˌmeɪkəʳ, *Am:* -kɚ] *n* alborotador(a) *m(f)*

troubleshooting ['trʌblʃuːtɪŋ] *n* localización *f* de problemas

troublesome ['trʌblsəm] *adj* molesto, -a

trouble spot *n* centro *m* de fricción
trough [trɒf, *Am:* trɑːf] *n* 1.(*receptacle*) abrevadero *m;* **feeding** ~ comedero *m;* **to feed at the public** ~ *fig* malversar los fondos públicos 2.(*low point*) punto *m* bajo 3. METEO zona *f* de bajas presiones
troupe [truːp] *n* THEAT compañía *f*
trouper ['truːpəʳ, *Am:* -pɚ] *n* artista *mf* veterano, -a
trouser clip *n* pinza *f* (para ir en bicicleta)
trouser leg *n* pernera *f*
trousers ['traʊzəz, *Am:* -zɚz] *n pl* pantalones *mpl;* **a pair of** ~ un pantalón ▶**to wear the** ~ llevar los pantalones
trouser suit *n Brit* traje-pantalón *m*
trousseau ['truːsəʊ, *Am:* -soʊ] *n* ajuar *m*
trout [traʊt] *n* <-(s)> 1.(*fish*) trucha *f* 2. *Brit, inf* (*woman*) bruja *f*
trout farm *n* criadero *m* de truchas
trowel ['traʊəl] *n* (*for building*) llana *f;* (*for gardening*) desplantador *m*
Troy [trɔɪ] *n no pl* HIST Troya *f*
troy ounce *n* onza *f* troy
truancy ['truːənsi] *n no pl* falta *f* a clase
truant ['truːənt] I. *n* persona *f* que hace novillos; **to play** ~ *Brit, Aus* hacer novillos II. *vi Brit, Aus* hacer novillos
truce [truːs] *n* tregua *f;* **to call a** ~ acordar una tregua
truck[1] [trʌk] I. *n* 1.(*lorry*) camión *m;* **pickup** ~ camioneta *f* de plataforma 2. *Brit* (*train*) vagón *m* de mercancías II. *vt Am* transportar
truck[2] [trʌk] *n no pl, inf* (*dealings*) trato *m;* **to have no** ~ **with sb/sth** no tratar con alguien/algo
truck driver *n* camionero, -a *m, f*
trucker *n* camionero, -a *m, f*
truck farming *n no pl, Am, Can* horticultura *f*
trucking *n no pl* transporte *m* por carretera
trucking company *n* empresa *f* transportista
truculence ['trʌkjʊləns] *n no pl* agresividad *f;* (*rebelliousness*) rebeldía *f*
truculent ['trʌkjʊlənt] *adj* agresivo, -a; (*rebellious*) rebelde
trudge [trʌdʒ] I. *vi* caminar penosamente II. *vt* recorrer penosamente III. *n* caminata *f* penosa
true [truː] I. *adj* 1.(*not false*) cierto, -a; **to be** ~ ser verdad [*o* cierto]; **to be** ~ **that ...** ser cierto que...; **to hold sth to be** ~ creer que algo es verdad; **to ring** ~ sonar convincente 2.(*genuine, real*) auténtico, -a; ~ **love** amor *m* verdadero; **the** ~ **faith** la fe verdadera; **sb's** ~ **self** la verdadera personalidad de alguien; **to come** ~ hacerse realidad; **in the** ~ **sense of the word** en el sentido real de la palabra 3.(*faithful, loyal*) fiel; **to be/remain** ~ **to sth/sb** ser/mantenerse fiel a algo/alguien; **to be** ~ **to one's word** mantener su palabra; **to be** ~ **to oneself** ser fiel a sí mismo 4.(*accurate*) exacto, -a II. *adv* 1.(*truly*) verdaderamente 2.(*accurately*) de forma precisa; **to aim** ~ apuntar bien III. *n* **to be out of** ~ no estar a nivel
◆**true up** *vt* corregir
true-blue [ˌtruː'bluː] *adj Brit, inf* leal
trueborn ['truːbɔːn, *Am:* -bɔːrn] *adj form* legítimo, -a
true-hearted [ˌtruː'hɑːtɪd, *Am:* 'truːˌhɑːrt̬ɪd] *adj form* fiel
true-life [ˌtruː'laɪf] *adj* verdadero, -a
truelove ['truːlʌv] *n liter* fiel amante *mf*
truffle ['trʌfl] *n* trufa *f*
truism ['truːɪzəm] *n* (*obviously true*) perogrullada *f;* (*cliché*) tópico *m*
truly ['truːli] *adv* 1.(*accurately*) verdaderamente 2.(*sincerely*) sinceramente 3.(*as intensifier*) realmente ▶**yours** ~ (*at end of letter*) un saludo; (*the speaker*) su seguro servidor *form*
trump [trʌmp] I. *n* (*in cards*) triunfo *m;* **what's ~s?** ¿qué triunfa? ▶**to turn up ~s** *Brit* salvar la situación II. *vt* 1.(*in cards*) fallar 2.(*surpass*) superar
◆**trump up** *vt* falsificar; **to** ~ **an accusation** inventar una acusación
trumpet ['trʌmpɪt, *Am:* -pət] I. *n* trompeta *f* ▶**to blow one's own** ~ *inf* tirarse flores II. *vi* (*elephant*) barritar III. *vt* (*news, success*) proclamar
trumpeter ['trʌmpɪtəʳ, *Am:* -pət̬ɚ] *n* trompetista *mf*
truncate [trʌŋ'keɪt] *vt* truncar
truncheon ['trʌntʃən] *n Brit, Aus* porra *f,* macana *f AmL*
trundle ['trʌndl] I. *vi* rodar II. *vt* hacer rodar
trunk [trʌŋk] *n* 1. ANAT, BOT tronco *m* 2.(*of elephant*) trompa *f* 3.(*for storage*) baúl *m* 4. *Am* (*of car*) maletero *f,* baúl *m AmL* 5. *pl* bañador *m;* **a pair of swimming ~s** un traje de baño
trunk call *n Brit* conferencia *f* **trunk road** *n Brit* carretera *f* nacional
truss [trʌs] I. *n* 1.(*bundle*) lío *m;* (*of hay*) haz *m* 2. MED braguero *m* II. *vt* atar
◆**truss up** *vt* atar
trust [trʌst] I. *n* 1. *no pl* (*belief*) confianza *f;* **to gain sb's** ~ ganarse la confianza de alguien; **to place one's** ~ **in sb/sth** depositar su confianza en alguien/algo; **to take sth on** ~ aceptar algo con los ojos cerrados; **to betray sb's** ~ traicionar la confianza de alguien 2. *no pl* (*responsibility*) responsabilidad *f;* **a position of** ~ un puesto de responsabilidad 3. FIN, COM consorcio *m;* **investment** ~ grupo *m* de inversión 4. LAW **to hold sth in** ~ tener algo en fideicomiso 5.(*association*) asociación *f;* **brains** ~ *Brit,* **brain** ~ *Am* grupo *m* de peritos II. *vt* 1.(*place trust in*) confiar en; **to** ~ **sb to do sth** confiar a alguien el hacer algo 2.(*rely on*) dar responsabilidad a; **to** ~ **sb with sth** confiar la responsabilidad de algo a alguien 3.(*hope*) **to** ~ **that ...** esperar que +*subj* III. *vi* confiar; **to** ~ **in sth/sb** confiar en algo/alguien

T

trusted ['trʌstɪd] *adj* (*friend, servant*) leal; (*method, remedy*) comprobado, -a

trustee [trʌs'tiː] *n* fideicomisario, -a *m, f;* **board of ~s** consejo *m* de administración

trustful ['trʌstfəl] *adj* confiado, -a

trust fund *n* FIN fondo *m* de fideicomiso

trusting *adj* confiado, -a

trustworthiness ['trʌstˌwɜːðɪnɪs, *Am:* -ˌwɜːr-] *n no pl* (*of person*) honradez *f;* (*of data*) fiabilidad *f*

trustworthy ['trʌstˌwɜːði, *Am:* -ˌwɜːr-] *adj* (*person*) honrado, -a; (*data*) fiable

trusty ['trʌsti] <-ier, -iest> *adj* leal

truth [truːθ] *n* verdad *f;* **a grain of ~** una pizca de verdad; **in ~** en realidad; **the ~ about sth/sb** la verdad sobre algo/alguien; **to tell the ~** a decir verdad

truthful ['truːθfəl] *adj* **1.** (*true*) veraz; (*sincere*) sincero, -a; **to be ~ with sb** ser sincero con alguien **2.** (*accurate*) preciso, -a

truthfulness *n no pl* **1.** (*veracity*) veracidad *f;* (*sincerity*) sinceridad *f* **2.** (*accuracy*) exactitud *f*

try [traɪ] **I.** *n* **1.** (*attempt*) intento *m;* **to give sth a ~** intentar algo **2.** (*in rugby*) ensayo *m* **II.** <-ie-> *vi* esforzarse; **to ~ and do sth** *inf* intentar hacer algo **III.** <-ie-> *vt* **1.** (*attempt*) intentar; **to ~ one's best** esforzarse al máximo; **to ~ one's luck** probar suerte **2.** (*test*) experimentar **3.** (*sample*) probar **4.** (*annoy*) cansar; **his demands would ~ the patience of a saint** sus peticiones acabarían con la paciencia de un santo **5.** LAW juzgar

◆**try for** *vt insep, Brit, Aus* tratar de obtener

◆**try on** *vt* **1.** (*put on*) probar; **to try sth on for size** probar algo para ver la talla **2.** *Brit, Aus, inf* **to try it on** ver hasta dónde se puede llegar; **don't try it on with me** no trates de embaucarme

◆**try out** *vt* probar; **to try sth out on sb** dar a probar algo a alguien

trying *adj* (*exasperating*) molesto, -a; (*difficult*) difícil

try-out ['traɪaʊt] *n* prueba *f*

tsar [zɑːʳ, *Am:* zɑːr] *n* zar *m*

tsarina [zɑː'riːnə] *n* zarina *f*

tsarist ['zɑːrɪst] **I.** *adj* zarista **II.** *n* zarista *mf*

tsetse fly ['tetsiˌflaɪ, *Am:* 'tsetsiˌflaɪ] *n* mosca *f* tsetsé

T-shirt ['tiːʃɜːt, *Am:* -ʃɜːrt] *n* camiseta *f,* playera *f Guat, Méx,* polera *f Chile*

tsp *abbr of* **teaspoon** (*amount*) cucharadita *f*

T-square ['tiːskweəʳ, *Am:* -skwer] *n* TECH escuadra *f* en forma de T

tub [tʌb] *n* **1.** (*container*) cubo *m* **2.** (*bathtub*) bañera *f* **3.** (*carton*) tarrina *f;* **a ~ of ice-cream** una tarrina de helado

tuba ['tjuːbə] *n* tuba *f*

tubby ['tʌbi] <-ier, -iest> *adj inf* rechoncho, -a, requenete *Ven*

tube [tjuːb, *Am:* tuːb] *n* **1.** (*hollow cylinder*) tubo *m* **2.** ANAT trompa *f;* **Fallopian ~** trompa de Falopio **3.** *no pl, Brit, inf* (*underground*) metro *m* **4.** *Am, inf* TV tele *f* ►**to go down the ~s** echarse a perder

tuber ['tjuːbəʳ, *Am:* 'tuːbɚ] *n* tubérculo *m*

tubercular [tjuː'bɜːkjʊləʳ, *Am:* tuː'bɜːrkjəlɚ] *adj* MED tuberculoso, -a

tuberculosis [tjuːˌbɜːkjʊ'ləʊsɪs, *Am:* tuːˌbɜːrkjə'loʊ-] *n no pl* tuberculosis *f inv*

tuberculous [tjuː'bɜːkjʊləs, *Am:* tuː'bɜːr-] *adj* tuberculoso, -a

tube station *n* estación *f* de metro

tub-thumper ['tʌbˌθʌmpəʳ, *Am:* -ɚ] *n pej, inf* orador(a) *m(f)* demagógico, -a

TUC [ˌtiːjuː'siː] *n Brit abbr of* **Trades Union Congress** congreso *m* sindical

tuck [tʌk] **I.** *n* **1.** (*fold*) pliegue *m* **2.** *no pl, Brit* (*sweets*) golosinas *fpl* **II.** *vt* (*fold*) plegar

◆**tuck away** *vt* (*hide*) poner a buen recaudo; **to be tucked away** estar en un sitio seguro

◆**tuck in** **I.** *vt* **1.** (*push into position*) colocar en su sitio; **to tuck one's shirt in** meterse la camisa **2.** (*settle in bed*) arropar **II.** *vi* comer con apetito

tucker ['tʌkəʳ, *Am:* -ɚ] *vt Am, inf* cansar

tuck shop *n Brit* tienda *f* de dulces

Tuesday ['tjuːzdəɪ, *Am:* 'tuːz-] *n* martes *m inv;* **Shrove ~** martes de carnaval; *s. a.* **Friday**

tuft [tʌft] *n* (*of hair*) mechón *m;* (*of feathers*) penacho *m;* (*of grass*) mata *f*

tug [tʌg] **I.** *n* **1.** (*pull*) tirón *m;* **to give sth a ~** dar un tirón a algo **2.** NAUT remolcador *m* **II.** <-gg-> *vt* **1.** (*pull*) tirar de **2.** NAUT remolcar

tuition [tjuː'ɪʃən] *n no pl* **1.** (*teaching*) enseñanza *f* **2.** *Am* (*fee*) tasas *fpl*

tuition fees *n* tasas *fpl*

tulip ['tjuːlɪp, *Am:* 'tuː-] *n* tulipán *m*

tumble ['tʌmbl] **I.** *n* caída *f;* **to take a ~** caerse **II.** *vi* **1.** (*fall*) caerse **2.** *fig* (*decline*) descender

◆**tumble down** *vi* desplomarse

◆**tumble over** *vi* caerse

◆**tumble to** *vt* caer en la cuenta de

tumbledown ['tʌmblˌdaʊn] *adj* en ruinas

tumble drier *n,* **tumble dryer** *n* secadora *f*

tumbler ['tʌmbləʳ, *Am:* -blɚ] *n* vaso *m*

tumbleweed ['tʌblwiːd] *n* planta *f* rodadora

tumescent [tuː'mesnt] *adj* tumescente

tummy ['tʌmi] <-ies> *n childspeak* barriguita *f*

tummy ache *n childspeak* dolor *m* de tripa

tumor *n Am,* **tumour** ['tjuːməʳ, *Am:* 'tuːmɚ] *n Brit, Aus* tumor *m;* **brain ~** tumor *m* cerebral; **malignant ~** tumor *m* maligno

tumult ['tjuːmʌlt, *Am:* 'tuː-] *n no pl* **1.** (*uproar*) tumulto *m* **2.** (*emotional confusion*) agitación *f*

tumultuous [tjuː'mʌltʃʊəs, *Am:* tuː'mʌltʃuːəs] *adj* **1.** (*uproariously noisy*) tumultuoso, -a; (*applause*) apoteósico, -a **2.** (*disorderly*) agitado, -a

tun [tʌn] *n* (*large vat*) tonel *m;* (*in brewery*) barril *m*

tuna ['tjuːnə, *Am:* 'tuː-] *n* <-(s)> atún *m*

tundra ['tʌndrə] *n no pl* tundra *f*

tune [tjuːn, *Am:* tuːn] I. *n* 1. MUS melodía *f;* **a catchy** ~ una tonada pegajosa 2. *no pl* (*pitch*) **to be in** ~ estar afinado; **to be out of** ~ estar desafinado; **to be in** ~ **with sth** *fig* armonizar con algo; **to be out of** ~ **with sth** *fig* desentonar con algo ►**to change one's** ~ cambiar de parecer; **to sing another** ~ cambiar de parecer; **to the** ~ **of 100 euros** por valor de 100 euros II. *vt* 1. MUS afinar 2. AUTO poner a punto

◆**tune in** I. *vi* 1. RADIO, TV **to** ~ **to a station** sintonizar una emisora 2. *fig, inf* sintonizar con II. *vt Am, Aus* RADIO, TV sintonizar

◆**tune up** *vt* AUTO poner a punto

tuneful ['tjuːnfəl] *adj* MUS melódico, -a

tuneless ['tjuːnləs] *adj* MUS disonante

tuner *n* 1. MUS (*person*) afinador(a) *m(f)* 2. (*radio*) sintonizador *m*

tune-up ['tjuːnʌp] *n* 1. MUS afinado *m* 2. AUTO puesta *f* a punto

tungsten ['tʌŋstən] *n* tungsteno *m*

tunic ['tjuːnɪk, *Am:* 'tuː-] *n* FASHION casaca *f;* HIST túnica *f*

tuning *n no pl* 1. MUS afinación *f* 2. RADIO sintonización 3. AUTO puesta *f* a punto

tuning fork *n* MUS diapasón *m*

Tunisia [tjuː'nɪzɪə, *Am:* tuː'niːʒə] *n* Túnez *m*

Tunisian [tjuː'nɪzɪən, *Am:* tuː'niːʒən] I. *n* tunecino, -a *m, f* II. *adj* tunecino, -a

tunnel ['tʌnl] I. *n* 1. ARCHIT túnel *m* 2. MIN galería *f* II. <*Brit:* -ll-, *Am:* -l-> *vi* hacer un túnel III. <*Brit:* -ll-, *Am:* -l-> *vt* cavar; **to** ~ **one's way out** escapar haciendo un túnel

tunny ['tʌni] *n* <-(ies)> *Brit, inf* atún *m*

tuppence ['tʌpəns] *n no pl, Brit, inf* dos peniques *mpl* ►**I don't care** ~ me importa un rábano; **to not give** ~ **for sth** no dar ni un duro por algo

tuppenny ['tʌpəni] *adj Brit, inf* de dos peniques

turban ['tɜːbən, *Am:* 'tɜːr-] *n* turbante *m*

turbid ['tɜːbɪd, *Am:* 'tɜːr-] *adj* (*water*) turbio, -a

turbine ['tɜːbaɪn, *Am:* 'tɜːrbɪn] *n* turbina *f*

turbocharged ['tɜːbəʊˌtʃɑːdʒd, *Am:* 'tɜːrboʊtʃɑːrdʒd] *adj* ELEC, TECH turboalimentado, -a

turbocharger ['tɜːbəʊˌtʃɑːdʒəʳ, *Am:* 'tɜːrboʊtʃɑːrdʒɚ] *n* ELEC, TECH turbocompresor *m* **turbo engine** *n* motor *m* turbo **turbojet** *n* turborreactor *m*

turbot ['tɜːbət, *Am:* 'tɜːr-] *n* <-(s)> rodaballo *m*

turbulence ['tɜːbjʊləns, *Am:* 'tɜːr-] *n no pl* turbulencia *f*

turbulent ['tɜːbjʊlənt, *Am:* 'tɜːr-] *adj* turbulento, -a

turd [tɜːd, *Am:* tɜːrd] *n vulg* 1. (*excrement*) zurullo *m* 2. (*person*) cerdo, -a *m, f*

tureen [tjʊ'riːn, *Am:* tʊ'-] *n* sopera *f*

turf [tɜːf, *Am:* tɜːrf] <-s *o* -ves> *n* 1. *no pl* BOT césped *m;* **a** (**piece of**) ~ un tepe; **the** ~ (*horse racing*) las carreras de caballos 2. (*territory*) territorio *m*

turf accountant *n Brit, form* corredor(a) *m(f)* de apuestas

turgid ['tɜːdʒɪd, *Am:* 'tɜːr-] *adj form* 1. *pej* (*style*) ampuloso, -a 2. (*swollen*) hinchado, -a

Turk [tɜːk, *Am:* tɜːrk] *n* turco, -a *m, f*

turkey ['tɜːki, *Am:* 'tɜːr-] *n* 1. ZOOL pavo *m* 2. *Am, Aus, inf* THEAT fiasco *m* 3. *Am, Aus, inf* (*stupid person*) papanatas *mf inv* ►**to talk** ~ *Am, inf* hablar claro

Turkey ['tɜːki, *Am:* 'tɜːr-] *n* Turquía *f*

Turkish ['tɜːkɪʃ, *Am:* 'tɜːr-] I. *adj* turco, -a II. *n* 1. (*person*) turco, -a *m, f* 2. LING turco *m*

turmoil ['tɜːmɔɪl, *Am:* 'tɜːr-] *n* 1. *no pl* (*state of chaos*) caos *m inv;* **to be thrown into** ~ estar sumido en el caos 2. (*of mind*) trastorno *m;* **to be in a** ~ estar desconcertado

turn [tɜːn, *Am:* tɜːrn] I. *vi* 1. (*rotate*) girar, dar vueltas; **to** ~ **on sth** girar sobre algo 2. (*switch direction*) volver; (*tide*) cambiar; (*car*) girar; **to turn around** dar media vuelta, voltearse *AmL;* **to** ~ **right/left** torcer a la derecha/izquierda 3. (*change*) cambiar, transformarse; (*for worse*) volverse; **to** ~ **traitor** volver la casaca; **to** ~ **grey** (**overnight**) quedar canoso (de la noche a la mañana) 4. (*change colour: leaves*) cambiar de color 5. (*feel nauseous: stomach*) retorcerse 6. (*spoil: cream, milk*) agriarse II. *vt* 1. (*rotate*) hacer girar; (*key*) dar vuelta a; (*screw on*) atornillar; (*unscrew*) desatornillar 2. (*switch direction*) volver, voltear *AmL;* **to** ~ **one's head** volver la cabeza; **to** ~ **a page** pasar una página; **to** ~ **the coat inside out** volver el abrigo del revés 3. (*attain a particular age*) cumplir 4. (*pass a particular hour*) dar; **it has** ~**ed three o'clock** dieron las tres 5. (*cause to feel nauseated*) **it** ~**ed my stomach** se me revolvió el estómago ►**to** ~ **sth upside down** dejar algo patas arriba III. *n* 1. (*change in direction*) cambio *m* de dirección; **to make a** ~ **to the right** girar hacia la derecha; **to take a** ~ **for the worse/better** mejorar/empeorar 2. (*changing point*) giro *m;* **the** ~ **of the century** el cambio de siglo 3. (*period of duty*) turno *m;* **to be sb's** ~ **to do sth** ser el turno de alguien para hacer algo; **it's your** ~ te toca a ti; **to do sth in** ~ hacer algo por turnos; **to miss a** ~ estar una vuelta sin jugar; **to speak out of** ~ hablar fuera de lugar 4. (*rotation, twist*) rotación *f* 5. (*service*) favor *m,* servicio *m;* **to do sb a good** ~ hacer un favor a alguien; **one good** ~ **deserves another** *prov* favor con favor se paga 6. (*shock*) susto *m;* **to give sb a** ~ dar un susto a alguien 7. (*queasiness*) desmayo *m;* **to have** ~**s** tener ataques 8. THEAT número *m*

◆**turn against** *vt* volverse en contra de

◆**turn away** I. *vi* apartarse; **to** ~ **from sb/sth** alejarse de alguien/algo II. *vt* 1. (*refuse entry*) no dejar entrar 2. (*deny help*) rechazar

◆**turn back** I. *vi* (*return to starting point*) retroceder II. *vt* 1. (*send back*) hacer regresar

2. (*fold towards itself: bedcover*) remangar; (*corner of paper*) doblar
◆**turn down** *vt* **1.** (*reject*) rechazar **2.** (*reduce volume*) bajar **3.** (*fold*) doblar
◆**turn in I.** *vt* (*hand over*) entregar **II.** *vi inf* (*go to bed*) acostarse
◆**turn into** *vt* transformar en
◆**turn off I.** *vt* **1.** ELEC, TECH desconectar; (*light*) apagar; (*motor*) parar; (*gas*) cerrar **2.** *inf* (*be unappealing*) repugnar **II.** *vi* (*leave path*) desviarse
◆**turn on** *vt* **1.** ELEC, TECH conectar; (*light*) encender, prender *AmL;* (*gas*) abrir **2.** (*excite*) excitar; (*attract*) gustar **3.** (*show, demonstrate*) poner en juego; **to ~ the charm** desplegar el encanto **4.** (*attack*) atacar
◆**turn out I.** *vi* **1.** (*end up, work out*) salir **2.** (*be revealed*) **it turned out to be true** resultó ser cierto **II.** *vt* **1.** (*light*) apagar **2.** (*kick out*) echar; **to turn sb out on the street** echar a alguien a la calle **3.** (*empty*) vaciar
◆**turn over I.** *vi* (*start, operate: engine*) hacer funcionar **II.** *vt* **1.** (*change the side*) dar la vuelta a, volver **2.** (*criminal*) entregar **3.** (*control*) ceder; (*possession*) traspasar **4.** (*facts*) meditar; **to ~ an idea** dar vueltas a una idea **5.** COM, FIN mover, facturar **6.** *Brit, inf* (*steal from*) robar; (*search*) saquear
◆**turn round I.** *vi* volverse **II.** *vt* **1.** (*move*) girar **2.** (*change*) cambiar, transformar; (*reform*) reformar
◆**turn to** *vt* **1.** (*face*) volverse hacia **2.** (*request aid*) **to ~ sb** (**for sth**) recurrir a alguien (para algo)
◆**turn up I.** *vi* **1.** (*arrive*) llegar **2.** (*become available*) aparecer **3.** (*point upwards*) doblarse hacia arriba **II.** *vt* **1.** (*volume*) subir **2.** (*shorten*) acortar **3.** (*point upwards*) doblar hacia arriba **4.** (*find*) encontrar; (*locate*) localizar

turnabout ['tɜːnəˌbaʊt, *Am:* 'tɜːrn-] *n*, **turnaround** ['tɜːnərˌaʊnd, *Am:* 'tɜːrnɚ-] *n* **1.** (*change*) giro *m* en redondo **2.** (*improvement*) mejora *f* **3.** COM procesamiento *m*
turnabout time *n*, **turnaround time** *n* AVIAT, NAUT tiempo *m* en puerto
turncoat ['tɜːnkəʊt, *Am:* 'tɜːrnkoʊt] *n* chaquetero, -a *m, f*
turner ['tɜːnəʳ, *Am:* 'tɜːrnɚ] *n inf* tornero, -a *m, f*
turning ['tɜːnɪŋ, *Am:* 'tɜːr-] *n* **1.** (*road*) bocacalle *f* **2.** (*act of changing direction*) vuelta *f*
turning point *n* momento *m* decisivo; **a ~ in one's career** un cambio decisivo en su carrera
turnip ['tɜːnɪp, *Am:* 'tɜːr-] *n* nabo *m*
turnkey operation [ˌtɜːnkiː ˌɒpər'eɪʃən, *Am:* ˌtɜːrnkiː ˌɑːpə'reɪ-] *n* proyecto *m* listo para empezar a funcionar
turn-off ['tɜːnɒf, *Am:* 'tɜːrnɑːf] *n* **1.** AUTO salida *f* de una calle **2.** *inf* (*something unappealing*) **to be a real ~** ser repugnante
turnout ['tɜːnaʊt, *Am:* 'tɜːrn-] *n* **1.** (*attendance*) número *m* de asistentes **2.** POL número *m* de votantes **3.** ECON producción *f* **4.** FASHION atuendo *m*
turnover ['tɜːnˌəʊvəʳ, *Am:* 'tɜːrnˌoʊvɚ] *n* **1.** COM, FIN volumen *m* de negocios; (*sales*) facturación *f* **2.** (*in staff*) rotación *f* **3.** GASTR empanada *f*
turnpike ['tɜːnpaɪk, *Am:* 'tɜːrn-] *n Am* AUTO autopista *f* de peaje
turnround ['tɜːnraʊnd, *Am:* 'tɜːrn-] *n no pl, Brit s.* **turnaround**
turnstile ['tɜːnstaɪl, *Am:* 'tɜːrn-] *n* SPORTS torniquete *m*
turntable ['tɜːnˌteɪbl, *Am:* 'tɜːrn-] *n* **1.** MUS (*record player*) plato *m* giratorio **2.** RAIL plataforma *f* giratoria
turn-up ['tɜːnʌp, *Am:* 'tɜːrn-] *n Brit* vuelta *f;* **trouser ~** dobladillo *m* del pantalón, valenciana *f Méx* ►**to be a ~ for the book**(**s**) ser una gran sorpresa
turpentine ['tɜːpəntaɪn, *Am:* 'tɜːr-] *n no pl* trementina *f*
turpitude ['tɜːpɪtjuːd, *Am:* 'tɜːrpɪtuːd] *n no pl, form* vileza *f;* **moral ~** inmoralidad *f*
turps [tɜːps, *Am:* tɜːrps] *n no pl, inf abbr of* **turpentine** trementina *f*
turquoise ['tɜːkwɔɪz, *Am:* 'tɜːr-] *n* **1.** (*stone*) turquesa *f* **2.** (*color*) azul *m* turquesa
turret ['tʌrɪt, *Am:* 'tɜːr] *n* **1.** (*tower*) torreón *m* **2.** (*of tank, ship*) torreta *f*
turtle ['tɜːtl, *Am:* 'tɜːrtl̬] <-(s)> *n* tortuga *f*
turtledove ['tɜːtldʌv, *Am:* 'tɜːrtl̬-] *n* tórtola *f*
turtleneck ['tɜːtlnek, *Am:* 'tɜːrtl̬-] *n Brit* cuello *m* de cisne
tusk [tʌsk] *n* colmillo *m*
tussle ['tʌsl] **I.** *vi* pelearse **II.** *n* (*physical struggle*) pelea *f;* (*quarrel*) riña *f*
tussock ['tʌsək] *n* mata *f* de hierba
tut [tʌt] *interj* **~ ~!** ¡vaya, vaya!
tutelage ['tjuːtɪlɪdʒ, *Am:* 'tuːt̬lɪdʒ] *n no pl* tutela *f*
tutor ['tjuːtəʳ, *Am:* 'tuːt̬ɚ] **I.** *n* SCHOOL, UNIV **1.** (*private teacher*) profesor(a) *m(f)* particular; (*at home*) preceptor(a) *m(f)* **2.** *Brit* (*supervising teacher*) tutor(a) *m(f)* **II.** *vt* SCHOOL, UNIV **to ~ sb** (**in sth**) dar clases particulares a alguien (de algo)
tutorial [tjuː'tɔːrɪəl, *Am:* tuː'-] *n* clase *f* en grupo reducido
tuxedo [tʌk'siːdəʊ, *Am:* -doʊ] *n Am* esmoquin *m*
TV [ˌtiː'viː] *n abbr of* **television** TV *f*
twaddle ['twɒdl, *Am:* 'twɑːdl] *n no pl, inf* estupideces *fpl;* **to talk ~** decir tonterías
twang [twæŋ] **I.** *n* **1.** MUS tañido *m* **2.** LING gangueo *m* **II.** *vt* hacer vibrar; (*strings*) puntear; **to ~ someone's nerves** crispar los nervios a alguien **III.** *vi* vibrar
tweak [twiːk] **I.** *vt* pellizcar **II.** *n* pellizco *m*
twee [twiː] *adj Brit, inf* cursi
tweed [twiːd] *n* **1.** *no pl* (*textile*) tweed *m* **2.** *pl* (*suit*) traje *m* de tweed
tweedy ['twiːdi] *adj* <-ier, -iest> *fig* de clase alta rural

tweet [twiːt] **I.** *n* pío *m* **II.** *vi* piar
tweeter ['twiːtəʳ, *Am:* -t̬ɚ] *n* altavoz *m* para altas frecuencias
tweezers ['twiːzəz, *Am:* -zɚz] *npl* (**a pair of**) ~ (unas) pinzas
twelfth [twelfθ] **I.** *adj* duodécimo, -a **II.** *n no pl* **1.** (*order*) duodécimo, -a *m, f* **2.** (*date*) doce *m* **3.** (*fraction*) duodécimo *m;* (*part*) duodécima parte *f; s. a.* **eighth**
twelve [twelv] **I.** *adj* doce **II.** *n* doce *m; s. a.* **eight**
twentieth ['twentɪəθ, *Am:* -t̬ɪ-] **I.** *adj* vigésimo, -a **II.** *n* **1.** (*order*) vigésimo, -a *m, f* **2.** (*date*) veinte *m* **3.** (*fraction*) vigésimo *m;* (*part*) vigésima parte *f; s. a.* **eighth**
twenty ['twenti, *Am:* -t̬i] <-ies> **I.** *adj* veinte **II.** *n* veinte *m; s. a.* **eighty**
twerp [twɜːp, *Am:* twɜːrp] *n inf* imbécil *mf*
twice [twaɪs] *adv* dos veces
twiddle ['twɪdl] **I.** *vt a.* TECH, ELEC (hacer) girar ▸**to ~ one's thumbs** estar mano sobre mano **II.** *vi* **to ~ with sth** juguetear con algo **III.** *n* giro *m*
twig [twɪg] **I.** *n* ramita *f* **II.** *vi inf* darse cuenta
twilight ['twaɪlaɪt] *n* crepúsculo *m*
twin [twɪn] **I.** *n* gemelo, -a *m, f;* **identical ~s** gemelos idénticos **II.** *adj* gemelo, -a **III.** *vt* <-nn-> hermanar **IV.** *vi* <-nn-> hermanarse
twin bed *n* cama *f* gemela **twin brother** *n* hermano *m* gemelo
twine [twaɪn] **I.** *vt* **1.** (*wind up*) enrollar **2.** (*encircle*) rodear **II.** *n no pl* cordel *m*
twinge [twɪndʒ] *n* **1.** MED punzada *f* **2.** *fig* arrebato *m;* **a ~ of conscience** un remordimiento de conciencia
twinkle ['twɪŋkl] **I.** *vi* (*diamond, eyes*) brillar; (*star*) centellear **II.** *n* (*of stars*) centelleo *m;* (*of jewels, light, eye*) brillo *m* ▸**to be just a ~ in sb's father's eye** no haber nacido; **to do sth in a ~** hacer algo en un abrir y cerrar de ojos
twinkling ['twɪŋklɪŋ] **I.** *adj* (*diamond, eyes*) brillante; (*star*) centelleante **II.** *n* parpadeo *m;* **in the ~ of an eye** en un abrir y cerrar de ojos
twinning ['twɪnɪŋ] *n no pl* hermanamiento *f* de dos ciudades
twin room *n* habitación *f* con camas gemelas
twin set *n Brit, Aus* conjunto *m* (de suéter y rebeca para mujer) **twin sister** *n* hermana *f* gemela **twin town** *n Brit* ciudad *f* hermanada
twirl [twɜːl, *Am:* twɜːrl] **I.** *vi* girar; **to ~ around sth** dar vueltas alrededor de algo **II.** *vt* (*whirl*) dar vueltas a; (*moustache*) retorcer **III.** *n* pirueta *f*
twist [twɪst] **I.** *vt* **1.** (*turn*) dar vueltas a, girar **2.** (*wind around*) enroscar; **to ~ sth around sth** enrollar algo alrededor de algo **3.** MED torcer **4.** (*distort: truth*) tergiversar ▸**to ~ sb's arm** presionar a alguien; **to ~ sb round one's little finger** manejar a alguien a su antojo **II.** *vi* **1.** (*squirm around*) (re)torcerse **2.** (*curve: path, road*) serpentear; **to ~ and turn** dar vueltas **3.** (*dance*) bailar el twist **III.** *n* **1.** (*turn*) vuelta *f;* **to give sth a ~** dar un giro a algo **2.** (*unexpected change*) giro *m* **3.** (*curl: of hair*) mecha *f;* (*of lemon*) rodajita *f;* (*of paper*) cucurucho *m;* (*of coil*) vuelta *f* **4.** (*dance*) twist *m* ▸**to go round the ~** *Brit, inf* volverse loco; **to be in a ~** *inf* estar aturdido
◆**twist off** *vt* desenroscar
twisted ['twɪstɪd] *adj* **1.** (*cable, metal*) retorcido, -a; (*ankle*) torcido, -a **2.** (*perverted*) pervertido, -a; (*logic, humour*) retorcido, -a
twister ['twɪstəʳ, *Am:* -ɚ] *n* **1.** METEO tornado *m* **2.** *inf* (*swindler*) tramposo, -a *m, f*
twisty ['twɪsti] *adj* <-ier, -iest> *inf* (*road*) sinuoso, -a
twit [twɪt] *n inf* imbécil *mf*
twitch [twɪtʃ] **I.** *vi* ANAT, MED moverse (nerviosamente); (*face*) contraerse **II.** *vt* **1.** ANAT, MED mover nerviosamente **2.** (*pull*) tirar de **III.** *n* <-es> **1.** ANAT, MED movimiento *m* espasmódico; **to have a (nervous) ~** tener un tic (nervioso) **2.** (*pull*) tirón *m*
twitter ['twɪtəʳ, *Am:* 'twɪt̬ɚ] **I.** *vi* **1.** ZOOL gorjear **2.** (*talk*) parlotear **II.** *n* gorjeo *m*
two [tuː] **I.** *adj* dos **II.** *n* dos *m* ▸**that makes ~ of us** *inf* ya somos dos; **to put ~ and ~ together** *inf* sacar conclusiones; *s. a.* **eight**
two-bit [tuː'bɪt] *adj Am, inf* insignificante
two-dimensional [ˌtuːdɪ'mentʃənəl] *adj* **1.** bidimensional **2.** *fig* superficial **two-door** *adj* AUTO de dos puertas **two-edged** *adj* de doble filo **two-faced** *adj pej* falso, -a, falluto, -a *RíoPl*
twofold ['tuːfəʊld, *Am:* -foʊld] **I.** *adv* dos veces **II.** *adj* doble
two-part *adj* de dos partes **two-party system** *n* sistema *f* bipartidista
twopence ['tʌpəns] *n Brit* FIN dos peniques *mpl* ▸**I don't care ~** me importa un rábano; **to not give ~ for sth** no dar ni un duro por algo
twopenny ['tʌpəni] *adj Brit, inf* (*worthless*) insignificante
two-phase *adj* ELEC bifásico, -a **two-piece** *n* **1.** (*suit*) conjunto *m* de dos piezas **2.** (*bikini*) bañador *m* de dos piezas **two-seater** AUTO **I.** *n* biplaza *m* **II.** *adj* de dos plazas
twosome ['tuːsəm] *n* (*duo*) dúo *m;* (*couple*) pareja *f*
two-stroke AUTO **I.** *n* motor *m* de dos tiempos **II.** *adj* de dos tiempos **two-tiered** *adj* de dos pisos **two-time** *vt inf* poner los cuernos a
two-way [ˌtuː'weɪ, *Am:* 'tuː-] *adj* de dos sentidos; (*tunnel, bridge*) de doble sentido; (*process*) recíproco, -a; (*conversation*) bilateral; (*switch*) de dos direcciones
two-way radio *n* transmisor *m* receptor
tycoon [taɪ'kuːn] *n* FIN magnate *m*
tyke [taɪk] *n* **1.** (*child*) chiquillo, -a*m, f* travieso, -a **2.** (*dog*) perro *m* callejero
tympanum ['tɪmpənəm] *n* tímpano *m*
type [taɪp] **I.** *n* **1.** (*sort, kind: style, print, language*) tipo *m;* (*of machine*) modelo *m*

2. (*class: animal, person, skin*) clase *f* **3.** *inf* (*person*) tipo *m,* sujeto *m;* **he's not her** ~ no es su tipo **4.** TYPO tipo *m* (de letra) **II.** *vt* **1.** (*write with machine*) escribir a máquina **2.** (*categorize*) clasificar **III.** *vi* escribir a máquina

◆**type out** *vt* escribir a máquina

◆**type up** *vt* pasar a máquina

typecast ['taɪpkɑːst, *Am:* -kæst] <typecast, typecast> *vt* encasillar

typeface ['taɪpfeɪs] *n no pl* tipografía *f*

typescript ['taɪpskrɪpt] *n* texto *m* mecanografiado **typesetter** *n* **1.** (*machine*) máquina *f* de componer **2.** (*person*) tipógrafo, -a *m, f*

typesetting ['taɪpˌsetɪŋ, *Am:* -ˌset̬-] *n no pl* composición *f* tipográfica

typewrite ['taɪpraɪt] *irr vt* mecanografiar

typewriter ['taɪpˌraɪtəʳ, *Am:* -t̬ɚ] *n* máquina *f* de escribir

typewriter ribbon *n* cinta *f* para máquina de escribir

typewritten *adj* escrito, -a a máquina

typhoid ['taɪfɔɪd] *n,* **typhoid fever** *n no pl* fiebre *f* tifoidea

typhoon [taɪ'fuːn] *n* METEO tifón *m*

typhus ['taɪfəs] *n no pl* tifus *m inv*

typical ['tɪpɪkəl] *adj* típico, -a; (*symptom*) característico, -a; **to be** ~ **of sb to do sth** ser típico de alguien el hacer algo

typically *adv* típicamente

typify ['tɪpɪfaɪ] <-ie-> *vt* simbolizar

typing ['taɪpɪŋ] *n no pl* mecanografía *f*

typist ['taɪpɪst] *n* mecanógrafo, -a *m, f*

typographer [taɪ'pɒgrəfəʳ, *Am:* -'pɑːgrəfɚ] *n* tipógrafo, -a *m, f*

typographic(al) [ˌtaɪpəʊ'græfɪk(əl), *Am:* -pə'-] *adj* tipográfico, -a

typographic(al) error *n* errata *f* de imprenta

typography [taɪ'pɒgrəfi, *Am:* -'pɑːgrə-] *n no pl* tipografía *f*

tyrannical [tɪ'rænɪkəl] *adj pej* tiránico, -a

tyrannize ['tɪrənaɪz] *vt* tiranizar

tyranny ['tɪrəni] *n no pl* tiranía *f*

tyrant ['taɪərənt, *Am:* 'taɪrənt] *n* tirano, -a *m, f*

tyre ['taɪəʳ, *Am:* 'taɪɚ] *n Aus, Brit* neumático *m,* llanta *f Méx,* caucho *m Col, Ven;* **spare** ~ neumático de repuesto

tyre gauge *n Aus, Brit* medidor *m* de presión **tyre pressure** *n no pl* presión *f* del neumático

tzar [zɑːʳ, *Am:* zɑːr] *n* zar *m*

tzetze fly ['tetsiˌflaɪ] *n* mosca *f* tsetsé

U

U, u [juː] *n* U, u *f;* ~ **for Uncle** U de Uruguay

U¹ **1.** *Brit* CINE *abbr of* **universal** para todos los públicos **2.** *abbr of* **uranium** uranio *m* **3.** *Am, Aus, inf abbr of* **university** universidad *f*

U² *adj Aus, Brit, inf* de la clase alta

UAE [ˌjuːeɪ'iː] *npl abbr of* **United Arab Emirates** EAU *mpl*

ubiquitous [juː'bɪkwɪtəs, *Am:* -wət̬əs] *adj* omnipresente

ubiquity [juː'bɪkwəti, *Am:* -t̬i] *n no pl* ubicuidad *f,* omnipresencia *f*

U-boat ['juːbəʊt, *Am:* -boʊt] *n* submarino *m* alemán

UCCA ['ʌkə] *n Brit abbr of* **Universities Central Council for Admissions** *consejo de admisión a la universidad*

UDA [ˌjuːdiː'eɪ] *n abbr of* **Ulster Defence Association** *asociación de defensa del Ulster*

udder ['ʌdəʳ, *Am:* -ɚ] *n* ubre *f*

UDI [ˌjuːdiː'aɪ] *n abbr of* **unilateral declaration of independence** declaración *f* unilateral de independencia

UDR [ˌjuːdiː'ɑːʳ, *Am:* -'ɑːr] *n abbr of* **Ulster Defence Regiment** *regimiento de defensa del Ulster*

UEFA [juː'eɪfə] *n abbr of* **Union of European Football Associations** UEFA *f*

UFO [ˌjuːef'əʊ, *Am:* -'oʊ] *n abbr of* **unidentified flying object** OVNI *m*

Uganda [juː'gændə] *n* Uganda *f*

Ugandan **I.** *adj* ugandés, -esa **II.** *n* ugandés, -esa *m, f*

ugh [ɜːh] *interj inf* uf

ugliness ['ʌglɪnɪs] *n no pl* **1.** (*unattractiveness*) fealdad *f* **2.** (*nastiness*) repugnancia *f*

ugly ['ʌgli] <-ier, iest> *adj* **1.** (*not attractive*) feo, -a, macaco, -a *Arg, Méx, Cuba, Chile;* ~ **duckling** patito *m* feo; **to be** ~ **as sin** ser más feo que Picio **2.** (*angry: mood*) peligroso, -a; (*look*) repugnante **3.** (*violent*) violento, -a; **to turn** ~ ponerse violento **4.** (*harsh*) desagradable; (*story*) fastidioso, -a; (*truth*) terrible; (*weather*) horroroso, -a; (*clouds*) amenazante; ~ **rumours** calumnias *fpl*

UHF [ˌjuːeɪtʃ'ef] *n abbr of* **ultrahigh frequency** UHF *f*

UHT [ˌjuːeɪtʃ'tiː] *adj abbr of* **ultra heat treated** UHT

UK [ˌjuː'keɪ] *n abbr of* **United Kingdom** RU *m*

ukelele [ˌjuːkəl'eɪli] *n* ukelele *m*

Ukraine [juː'kreɪn] *n* Ucrania *f*

Ukrainian **I.** *adj* ucraniano, -a **II.** *n* **1.** (*person*) ucraniano, -a *m, f* **2.** LING ucraniano *m*

ulcer ['ʌlsəʳ, *Am:* -sɚ] *n* **1.** MED úlcera *f,* chácara *f Col* **2.** *fig* llaga *f*

ulcerate ['ʌlsəreɪt] *vi* ulcerarse

ulcerous ['ʌlsərəs] *adj* ulceroso, -a

ullage ['ʌlɪdʒ] *n no pl* **1.** (*shortage*) escasez *f* **2.** (*liquid loss*) merma *f*

ulna ['ʌlnə] <ulnae *o* s> *n* cúbito *m*

Ulster ['ʌlstəʳ, *Am:* -stɚ] *n no pl* Ulster *m*
ulterior [ʌl'tɪərɪəʳ, *Am:* -'tɪrɪɚ] *adj* **1.** (*secret*) secreto, -a; (*motive*) oculto, -a **2.** (*beyond scope*) ulterior
ultimate ['ʌltɪmət, *Am:* -t̬əmɪt] **I.** *adj* **1.** (*best*) máximo, -a; (*experience, feeling*) extremo, -a **2.** (*highest degree of*) máximo, -a; (*accolade, praise*) supremo, -a; (*honor, sacrifice*) altísimo, -a **3.** (*maximum: authority*) máximo, -a **4.** (*final*) final; (*cost, consequences, effect*) definitivo, -a **5.** (*fundamental*) fundamental; (*cause, goal, responsibility*) primordial **II.** *n* (*the best*) **the ~** lo máximo; (*bad taste, vulgarity*) el colmo; **the ~ in fashion** el último grito en moda; **the ~ in stupidity** el colmo de la estupidez
ultimately ['ʌltɪmətli, *Am:* -t̬əmɪt-] *adv* **1.** (*in the end*) finalmente **2.** (*fundamentally*) fundamentalmente
ultimatum [ˌʌltɪ'meɪtəm, *Am:* -t̬ə'meɪt̬əm] <ultimata *o* -tums> *n* ultimátum *m*
ultimo ['ʌltɪməʊ, *Am:* -t̬ɪmoʊ] *adv* ECON, COM del mes pasado
ultrahigh frequency [ˌʌltrəˌhaɪ'friːkwəntsi] *n no pl* frecuencia *f* ultraalta
ultramarine [ˌʌltrəmə'riːn] **I.** *adj* ultramarino, -a **II.** *n no pl* azul *m* de ultramar
ultramodern [ˌʌltrə'mɒdən, *Am:* -'mɑːdɚn] *adj* ultramoderno, -a
ultra-short wave [ˌʌltrəʃɔːt'weɪv, *Am:* -ʃɔːrt'weɪv] *n* onda *f* ultracorta
ultrasonic [ˌʌltrə'sɒnɪk, *Am:* -'sɑːnɪk] *adj* ultrasónico, -a
ultrasound ['ʌltrəsaʊnd] *n* ultrasonido *m*
ultrasound picture *n* imagen *f* por ultrasonido
ultraviolet [ˌʌltrə'vaɪələt, *Am:* -lɪt] *adj* ultravioleta
Ulysses ['juːlɪsiːz, *Am:* juː'lɪs-] *n* Ulises *m*
umbel ['ʌmbəl] *n* umbela *f*
umber ['ʌmbəʳ, *Am:* -bɚ] **I.** *adj* de color ocre oscuro **II.** *n no pl* ocre *m* oscuro
umbilical [ʌm'bɪlɪkl] *adj* umbilical
umbilical cord *n* cordón *m* umbilical
umbrage ['ʌmbrɪdʒ] *n no pl, form* resentimiento *m;* **to take ~ at sth** ofenderse por algo
umbrella [ʌm'brelə] *n* **1.** (*rain*) paraguas *m inv;* (*sun*) sombrilla *f;* **beach ~** parasol *m* **2.** (*protection*) cobertura *f;* MIL cortina *f* de fuego antiaéreo; **to do sth under the ~ of sth** hacer algo bajo el amparo de algo
umbrella case *n,* **umbrella cover** *n* funda *f* de paraguas **umbrella organization** *n* POL, ADMIN organización *f* paraguas **umbrella stand** *n* paragüero *m*
umpire ['ʌmpaɪəʳ, *Am:* -paɪɚ] SPORTS **I.** *n* árbitro *mf* **II.** *vt* arbitrar
umpteen ['ʌmptiːn] *adj inf* incontable; **~ reasons** múltiples razones *fpl;* **to do sth ~ times** hacer algo innumerables veces
umpteenth ['ʌmptiːnθ] *adj* enésimo, -a
UN [ˌjuː'en] *n abbr of* **United Nations** ONU *f*
unabashed [ˌʌnə'bæʃt] *adj* desenvuelto, -a; (*behaviour*) atrevido, -a
unabated [ˌʌnə'beɪtɪd, *Am:* -t̬ɪd] *adj* continuado, -a; (*hurricane, storm*) persistente; (*fighting, rioting, energy*) constante; (*interest, enthusiasm*) vivo, -a; (*curiosity*) incesante
unable [ʌn'eɪbl] *adj* incapaz
unabridged [ˌʌnə'brɪdʒd] *adj* **1.** LIT, PUBL no abreviado, -a **2.** (*whole*) completo, -a
unacceptable [ˌʌnək'septəbl] *adj* **1.** (*not good enough*) inaceptable; (*conditions*) inadmisible **2.** (*intolerable*) intolerable; **the ~ face of sth** *Aus, Brit* el lado oscuro de algo
unaccompanied [ˌʌnə'kʌmpənɪd] *adj* **1.** (*without companion*) solo, -a, sin compañía **2.** MUS sin acompañamiento
unaccountable [ˌʌnə'kaʊntəbl, *Am:* -t̬ə-] *adj* **1.** (*not responsible*) irresponsable **2.** (*inexplicable*) inexplicable
unaccounted for [ˌʌnə'kaʊntɪd'fɔːʳ, *Am:* -t̬ɪdˌfɔːr] *adj* **1.** (*unexplained*) inexplicado, -a **2.** (*not included in count*) sin contar
unaccustomed [ˌʌnə'kʌstəmd] *adj* **1.** (*seldom seen*) raro, -a **2.** (*something new*) inusual; **to be ~ to doing sth** no tener la costumbre de hacer algo
unacknowledged [ˌʌnək'nɒlɪdʒd, *Am:* -'nɑːlɪdʒd] *adj* ignorado, -a; (*author, scientist*) no reconocido, -a; **to remain ~** permanecer en el anonimato
unaddressed [ˌʌnə'drest] *adj* sin señas
unadorned [ˌʌnə'dɔːnd, *Am:* -'dɔːrnd] *adj* **1.** (*plain*) sin adorno; (*story*) simple; (*fashion, style*) sencillo, -a **2.** (*pure*) puro, -a; **the ~ truth** la pura verdad
unadulterated [ˌʌnə'dʌltəreɪtɪd, *Am:* -t̬əreɪt̬ɪd] *adj* **1.** (*not changed*) sin mezcla **2.** (*pure: substance*) puro, -a; (*alcohol, wine*) no adulterado, -a; **~ nonsense** completo disparate *m*
unadventurous [ˌʌnəd'ventʃərəs] *adj* poco atrevido, -a; (*style*) poco llamativo, -a
unadvisable [ˌʌnəd'vaɪzəbl] *adj* poco aconsejable
unaffected [ˌʌnə'fektɪd] *adj* **1.** (*not changed*) inalterado, -a **2.** (*not influenced*) espontáneo, -a **3.** (*down to earth*) sencillo, -a; (*manner, speech*) natural
unafraid [ˌʌnə'freɪd] *adj* sin temor; **to be ~ of sb/sth** no tener miedo de alguien/algo
unaided [ʌn'eɪdɪd] *adj* sin ayuda; **to do sth ~** hacer algo por sí solo
unalike [ˌʌnə'laɪk] *adj* disímil
unalloyed [ˌʌnə'lɔɪd] *adj liter* puro, -a; (*happiness, pleasure*) absoluto, -a
unaltered [ʌn'ɔːltəd, *Am:* -t̬ɚd] *adj* inalterado, -a; **to leave sth ~** dejar algo tal como estaba
unambiguous [ˌʌnæm'bɪgjʊəs] *adj* inequívoco, -a; (*statement*) incuestionable; (*language, terms*) unívoco, -a
un-American [ˌʌnə'merɪkən] *adj* antiamericano, -a (*término empleado por los propios estadounidenses*)

unanimity [ˌjuːnəˈnɪməti, *Am:* -t̬i] *n no pl, form* unanimidad *f*

unanimous [juːˈnænɪməs, *Am:* -əməs] *adj* unánime; (*support*) total

unannounced [ˌʌnəˈnaʊnst] **I.** *adj* **1.** (*without warning*) sin aviso; (*arrival, appearance*) imprevisto, -a; (*visitor, guest*) inesperado, -a **2.** (*not made known*) fortuito, -a; (*act*) repentino, -a **II.** *adv* de repente; (*arrive, visit*) sin aviso

unanswerable [ˌʌnˈɑːnsərəbl, *Am:* -ˈæn-] *adj* **1.** (*without an answer*) incontestable **2.** *form* (*irrefutable*) irrefutable; (*proof*) irrebatible

unanswered [ˌʌnˈɑːnsəd, *Am:* -ˈænsɚd] *adj* sin contestar

unappetizing [ˌʌnˈæpɪtaɪzɪŋ, *Am:* -ˈæpə-] *adj* poco apetitoso, -a

unapproachable [ˌʌnəˈprəʊtʃəbl, *Am:* -ˈproʊ-] *adj* **1.** (*building*) inaccesible **2.** (*person*) intratable

unarmed [ˌʌnˈɑːmd, *Am:* -ˈɑːrmd] *adj* desarmado, -a

unashamed [ˌʌnəˈʃeɪmd] *adj* desvergonzado, -a; (*greed, hypocrisy, selfishness*) descarado, -a; **to be ~ of sth** (*guilt*) no tener remordimiento por algo; (*shame*) no avergonzarse por algo

unasked [ˌʌnˈɑːskt, *Am:* -ˈæskt] *adj* **1.** (*not questioned*) no solicitado, -a; (*spontaneous*) **2.** espontáneo, -a

unassignable [ˌʌnəˈsaɪnəbl] *adj* LAW intrasferible

unassuming [ˌʌnəˈsjuːmɪŋ, *Am:* -ˈsuː-] *adj* modesto, -a

unattached [ˌʌnəˈtætʃt] *adj* **1.** (*not connected*) suelto, -a; (*part*) separable **2.** (*independent*) libre **3.** (*unmarried*) soltero, -a

unattainable [ˌʌnəˈteɪnəbl] *adj* inasequible; (*goal, ideal*) inalcanzable

unattended [ˌʌnəˈtendɪd] *adj* **1.** (*alone*) sin compañía; **to leave the children ~** dejar a los niños sin vigilancia **2.** (*unmanned*) desatendido, -a **3.** (*not taken care of*) descuidado, -a

unattractive [ˌʌnəˈtræktɪv] *adj* **1.** (*quite ugly*) feo, -a; (*place, town*) poco atractivo, -a **2.** (*unpleasant*) desagradable; (*personality, character*) antipático, -a

unauthorized [ˌʌnˈɔːθəraɪzd, *Am:* -ˈɑː-] *adj* no autorizado, -a

unavailable [ˌʌnəˈveɪləbl] *adj* inasequible; (*article*) agotado, -a; (*man, woman*) ocupado, -a

unavailing [ˌʌnəˈveɪlɪŋ] *adj form* (*denial*) inútil; (*effort, attempt*) vano, -a

unavoidable [ˌʌnəˈvɔɪdəbl] *adj* ineludible; (*accident, fate*) inevitable

unaware [ˌʌnəˈweəʳ, *Am:* -ˈwer] *adj* **to be ~ of sth** ignorar algo

unawares [ˌʌnəˈweəz, *Am:* -ˈwerz] *adv* **to catch sb ~** coger a alguien desprevenido

unbalanced [ˌʌnˈbælənst] *adj* **1.** (*uneven*) desnivelado, -a; (*account*) desequilibrado, -a **2.** (*mental state*) trastornado, -a

unbar [ˌʌnˈbɑːʳ, *Am:* -ˈbɑːr] *vt* desatrancar

unbearable [ˌʌnˈbeərəbl, *Am:* -ˈberə-] *adj* **1.** (*painful*) insoportable, inaguantable **2.** (*person*) insufrible

unbeatable [ˌʌnˈbiːtəbl, *Am:* -ˈbiːt̬ə-] *adj* **1.** (*team, record*) imbatible; (*army*) invencible **2.** (*pizza, shirt*) insuperable; (*value, quality*) inmejorable

unbeaten [ˌʌnˈbiːtn] *adj* (*team, player*) invicto, -a; (*record*) imbatible

unbecoming [ˌʌnbɪˈkʌmɪŋ] *adj* **1.** (*dress, suit*) que sienta mal **2.** (*attitude, manner*) impropio, -a

unbeknown(**st**) [ˌʌnbɪˈnəʊn, *Am:* -ˈnoʊn] *adv form* **~ to her** sin saberlo ella

unbelief [ˌʌnbɪˈliːf] *n no pl* **1.** incredulidad *f* **2.** REL escepticismo *m*

unbelievable [ˌʌnbɪˈliːvəbl] *adj* increíble

unbeliever [ˌʌnbɪˈliːvəʳ, *Am:* -vɚ] *n* REL no creyente *mf*

unbelieving [ˌʌnbɪˈliːvɪŋ] *adj* incrédulo, -a

unbend [ʌnˈbend] **I.** *vt* enderezar; (*wire*) desdoblar **II.** *vi irr* **1.** (*straighten out*) enderezarse **2.** (*relax*) relajarse

unbending *adj* firme; (*will, determination*) inquebrantable; (*attitude*) rígido, -a

unbiased [ʌnˈbaɪəst] *adj* imparcial; (*judge*) justo, -a; (*opinion, report, advice*) objetivo, -a

unbidden [ˌʌnˈbɪdən] *liter* **I.** *adv* espontáneamente, sin ser llamado, -a **II.** *adj* espontáneo, -a

unbind [ʌnˈbaɪnd] *irr vt* desatar

unbleached [ʌnˈbliːtʃt] *adj* sin blanquear; **~ flour** harina *f* integral

unblinking [ʌnˈblɪnkɪŋ] *adj* (*gaze, look*) imperturbable; (*devotion, help*) resuelto, -a

unblushing [ʌnˈblʌʃɪŋ] *adj* desvergonzado, -a

unbolt [ʌnˈbəʊlt, *Am:* -ˈboʊlt] *vt* desatrancar

unborn [ʌnˈbɔːn, *Am:* -ˈbɔːrn] *adj* **1.** (*not yet born: baby*) no nacido, -a; (*foetus*) nonato, -a **2.** (*future*) venidero, -a, por venir

unbosom [ʌnˈbʊzəm] *vt form* **1.** (*reveal*) revelar **2.** (*confide in*) **to ~ oneself to sb** abrirse a alguien

unbounded [ʌnˈbaʊndɪd] *adj* (*optimism, enthusiasm, passion*) ilimitado, -a; (*hope*) infinito, -a; (*love, desire, joy*) inmenso, -a; (*ambition*) desmedido, -a

unbowed [ʌnˈbaʊd] *adj* **1.** (*erect*) erguido, -a **2.** (*not submitting*) orgulloso, -a

unbreakable [ʌnˈbreɪkəbl] *adj* (*material*) irrompible, indestructible; (*rule, promise, faith*) inquebrantable; (*record*) imbatible

unbribable [ʌnˈbraɪbəbl] *adj* insobornable

unbridled [ʌnˈbraɪdld] *adj* desenfrenado, -a

un-British [ʌnˈbrɪtɪʃ] *adj* antibritánico, -a (*término empleado por los propios británicos*)

unbroken [ʌnˈbrəʊkən, *Am:* -ˈbroʊ-] *adj* **1.** (*not broken*) no roto, -a; **an ~ promise** una promesa no rota **2.** (*uncrushed*) intacto, -a **3.** (*continuous, without a break*) ininterrumpido, -a **4.** (*unsurpassed: record*) imbatible **5.** (*not tamed*) no domesticado, -a; **an ~ horse** un caballo salvaje

unbuckle [ʌn'bʌkl] *vt* deshebillar; **to ~ a seatbelt** desabrochar el cinturón de seguridad

unburden [ʌn'bɜːdən, *Am:* -'bɜːr-] *vt* **1.** (*unload*) aliviar **2.** (*relieve oneself*) **to ~ oneself** (**of sth**) desahogarse (de algo); **to ~ oneself** (**to sb**) deshogarse (con alguien); **to ~ one's sorrows** contar las penas

unbusinesslike [ʌn'bɪznɪslaɪk] *adj* poco profesional

unbutton [ʌn'bʌtən] **I.** *vt* desabrochar **II.** *vi* desabrocharse

uncalled-for [ʌn'kɔːldfɔːʳ, *Am:* -fɔːr] *adj* gratuito, -a, impropio, -a; **an ~ remark** un comentario fuera de lugar; **to be ~ to do sth** ser gratuito el hacer algo

uncanny [ʌn'kæni] *adj* <-ier, -iest> **1.** (*mysterious*) misterioso, -a **2.** (*remarkable*) extraordinario, -a; **to be ~ how ...** ser sorprendente cómo...; **an ~ knack** una destreza extraordinaria

uncared-for [ʌn'keədfɔːʳ, *Am:* -'kerdfɔːr] *adj,* **uncared for** *adj* descuidado, -a

uncarpeted *adj* no enmoquetado, -a

unceasing [ʌn'siːsɪŋ] *adj form* incesante; **~ support** apoyo *m* incondicional

unceremonious [ʌnˌserɪ'məʊniəs, *Am:* -'moʊ-] *adj* **1.** (*abrupt*) brusco, -a **2.** (*informal*) informal

uncertain [ʌn'sɜːtən, *Am:* -'sɜːr-] *adj* **1.** (*unsure*) dudoso, -a; **to be ~ of sth** no estar seguro de algo; **to be ~ whether/when ...** no estar seguro de si/cuándo...; **in no ~ terms** claramente **2.** (*unpredictable, chancy*) incierto, -a; **an ~ future** un futuro incierto **3.** (*volatile*) volátil; **an ~ temper** un temperamento volátil

uncertainty [ʌn'sɜːtənti, *Am:* -'sɜːrtənt̬i] <-ies> *n* **1.** (*unpredictability*) incerteza *f* **2.** *no pl* (*unsettled state*) incertidumbre *f;* **~ about sth/sb** incertidumbre sobre algo/alguien **3.** *no pl* (*hesitancy*) indecisión *f*

unchallenged [ʌn'tʃælɪndʒd] *adj* **1.** (*not questioned or doubted*) incontestado, -a **2.** (*not opposed*) no protestado, -a; **to go ~** pasar sin protesta

unchanged [ʌn'tʃeɪndʒd] *adj* **1.** (*unaltered*) inalterado, -a **2.** (*not replaced*) no sustituido, -a

uncharacteristic [ˌʌnkærəktə'rɪs tɪk, *Am:* -ˌkerɪktə'-] *adj* poco característico, -a; **to be ~ of sb/sth** no ser típico de alguien/algo

uncharitable [ˌʌn'tʃærɪtəbl, *Am:* -'tʃerət̬ə-] *adj* **1.** (*severe*) duro, -a; **to be ~ in sth** ser severo en algo; **to be ~** (**of sb**) **to do sth** ser duro (por parte de alguien) el hacer algo **2.** (*ungenerous*) poco caritativo, -a

unchecked [ˌʌn'tʃekt] *adj* **1.** (*unrestrained*) desenfrenado, -a; **~ passion/violence** pasión *f*/violencia *f* desenfrenada **2.** (*not examined or verified*) no examinado, -a **3.** (*not checked*) no comprobado, -a

unchristian [ˌʌn'krɪstʃən] *adj* indigno, -a de un cristiano

uncivil [ˌʌn'sɪvl] *adj form* grosero, -a; **to be ~ to sb** ser grosero con alguien

unclad [ˌʌn'klæd] *adj form* desnudo, -a

unclaimed [ˌʌn'kleɪmd] *adj* **1.** (*not claimed*) sin reclamar **2.** (*not reclaimed*) no reclamado, -a

unclassified [ˌʌn'klæsɪfaɪd] *adj* ADMIN sin clasificar

uncle ['ʌŋkl] *n* tío *m* ►**to say ~** *Am, childspeak* rendirse

unclean [ˌʌn'kliːn] *adj* **1.** (*unhygienic*) sucio, -a **2.** *form* (*taboo*) tabú **3.** (*soiled, impure*) impuro, -a

unclear [ˌʌn'klɪəʳ, *Am:* -'klɪr] *adj* **1.** (*not certain*) nada claro, -a; **to be ~ about sth** no estar seguro de algo **2.** (*vague*) vago, -a; **an ~ statement** una afirmación vaga

uncluttered [ˌʌn'klʌtəd, *Am:* -'klʌt̬ɚd] *adj* **1.** (*not messily crowded*) no muy concurrido, -a **2.** (*simple*) simple; **an ~ mind** una mente sencilla

uncollected [ˌʌnkə'lektɪd] *adj* **1.** (*not reclaimed*) no reclamado, -a **2.** (*unincluded in collected works*) no incluido, -a

uncolored *adj Am, Aus,* **uncoloured** [ʌn'kʌləd, *Am:* ʌn'kʌlɚd] *adj Brit* **1.** (*having no colour*) incoloro, -a **2.** (*impartial*) imparcial

uncomfortable [ʌn'kʌmpftəbl, *Am:* ʌn-'kʌmpfɚt̬ə-] *adj* **1.** (*situation*) molesto, -a; **an ~ silence** un silencio molesto **2.** (*person ill at ease*) incómodo, -a; **it makes sb ~ to do sth** le hacer sentir incómodo a alguien el hacer algo

uncommitted [ˌʌnkə'mɪtɪd, *Am:* -'mɪt̬-] *adj* **1.** (*non-aligned*) no alineado, -a **2.** (*not committed*) no comprometido, -a; **to be ~ to sth** no estar comprometido con algo

uncommon [ʌn'kɒmən, *Am:* ʌn'kɑːmən] *adj* **1.** (*rare*) extraño, -a; **to be not ~ for sb/sth** no ser raro para alguien/algo **2.** *form* (*exceptional*) extraordinario, -a; **with ~ interest** con un especial interés

uncommonly *adv* **1.** (*unusually*) raramente **2.** *form* (*extremely*) excepcionalmente

uncommunicative [ˌʌnkə'mjuːnɪkətɪv, *Am:* ˌʌnkə'mjuːnɪkət̬ɪv] *adj* poco comunicativo, -a; **to be ~ about sth/sb** ser reservado respecto a algo/alguien

uncompromising [ʌn'kɒmprəmaɪzɪŋ, *Am:* ʌn'kɑːm-] *adj* intransigente; **to take an ~ stand** adoptar una postura intransigente

unconcerned [ˌʌnkən'sɜːnd, *Am:* -'sɜːrnd] *adj* **1.** (*not worried*) despreocupado, -a; **to be ~ about sth/sb** no preocuparse por algo/alguien **2.** (*indifferent*) indiferente; **to be ~ with sth/sb** ser indiferente con algo/alguien

unconditional [ˌʌnkən'dɪʃənl] *adj* incondicional; **~ love** amor *m* incondicional

unconfirmed [ˌʌnkən'fɜːmd, *Am:* -'fɜːrmd] *adj* no confirmado, -a

U

uncongenial [ˌʌnkən'dʒiːnɪəl] *adj* **1.** (*unfriendly*) antipático, -a **2.** (*not pleasant*) desfavorable; ~ **conditions** condiciones *fpl* adversas
unconnected [ˌʌnkə'nektɪd] *adj* desconectado, -a; **to be ~ to sth** estar desconectado de algo
unconscionable [ʌn'kɒntʃənəbl, *Am:* -'kɑːn-] *adj form* desmedido, -a
unconscious [ʌn'kɒntʃəs, *Am:* ʌn'kɑːn-] **I.** *adj* **1.** (*not conscious*) inconsciente; **to knock sb ~** dejar a alguien inconsciente; ~ **state** estado *m* de inconsciencia **2.** PSYCH (*subconscious*) subconsciente **3.** (*unaware*) no intencional; **to be ~ of sth** *form* no ser consciente de algo **II.** *n no pl* PSYCH **the ~** el inconsciente
unconsciously *adv* inconscientemente
unconsciousness *n no pl* **1.** (*loss of consciousness*) pérdida *f* de conocimiento **2.** *form* (*unawareness*) inconsciencia *f*
unconsidered [ˌʌnkən'sɪdəd, *Am:* ˌʌnkən-'sɪdɚd] *adj form* desconsiderado, -a
unconstitutional [ʌnˌkɒntstɪ'tjuːʃənəl, *Am:* ʌnˌkɑːntstə'tuː-] *adj* inconstitucional
unconsummated [ʌn'kɒntsəmeɪtɪd, *Am:* ʌn'kɑːntsəmeɪt̬ɪd] *adj* no consumado, -a
uncontested [ˌʌnkən'testɪd] *adj* **1.** (*unquestioned*) incontestable **2.** LAW (*not disputed*) sin oposición; **an ~ divorce** un divorcio sin oposición de ninguna de las partes
uncontrollable [ˌʌnkən'trəʊləbl, *Am:* -'troʊ-] *adj* **1.** (*irresistible*) irrefrenable **2.** (*frenzied*) incontrolable; **an ~ child** un niño ingobernable
uncontrolled [ˌʌnkən'trəʊld, *Am:* -'troʊld] *adj* descontrolado, -a
uncontroversial [ˌʌnkɒntrə'vɜːʃl] *adj* no controvertido, -a
unconvinced [ˌʌnkən'vɪnst] *adj* **to be ~ of sth** no estar convencido de algo
unconvincing [ˌʌnkən'vɪnsɪŋ] *adj* **1.** (*not persuasive*) nada convincente; **rather ~** poco convincente **2.** (*not credible*) nada creíble
uncooked [ˌʌn'kʊkt] *adj* crudo, -a
uncooperative [ˌʌnkəʊ'ɒpərətɪv, *Am:* -koʊ'ɑːpɚət̬ɪv] *adj* poco cooperativo, -a
uncork [ˌʌn'kɔːk, *Am:* -'kɔːrk] *vt* **1.** (*extract cork from bottle*) descorchar **2.** *inf* (*let out sth repressed*) **to ~ one's feelings** dejar aflorar los sentimientos; **to ~ a surprise** destapar una sorpresa
uncorroborated [ˌʌnkər'ɒbəreɪtɪd, *Am:* -'rɑːbəreɪt̬ɪd] *adj* no corroborado, -a
uncountable noun [ʌn'kaʊntəbl naʊn, *Am:* ʌn'kaʊnt̬əbl naʊn] *n* LING substantivo *m* incontable
uncouple [ˌʌn'kʌpl] *vt* **to ~ sth (from sth) 1.** TECH desacoplar algo (de algo) **2.** (*separate*) separar algo (de algo)
uncouth [ʌn'kuːθ] *adj* basto, -a
uncover [ʌn'kʌvəʳ, *Am:* -'kʌvɚ] *vt* dejar al descubierto, desvelar; **to ~ a wound** *a. fig* dejar descubierta una herida; **to ~ a secret** desvelar un secreto
uncritical [ˌʌn'krɪtɪkl, *Am:* -'krɪt̬-] *adj* falto, -a de sentido crítico; **to be ~ of sth/sb** no criticar algo/a alguien
uncrowned [ˌʌn'kraʊnd] *adj* sin corona
UNCTAD *n abbr of* **United Nations Commission for Trade and Development** UNCTAD *f*
unction ['ʌŋkʃən] *n* **1.** *form* unción *f* **2.** *s.* **unctuousness**
unctuous ['ʌŋktʃuəs] *adj* **1.** *form* (*obsequious*) zalamero, -a **2.** (*oily*) untuoso, -a
uncut [ʌn'kʌt] *adj* **1.** (*not cut*) sin cortar; **an ~ diamond** un diamante en bruto **2.** (*not shortened*) sin cortes
undated [ʌn'deɪtɪd, *Am:* -t̬ɪd] *adj* sin fecha
undaunted [ʌn'dɔːntɪd, *Am:* -'dɑːnt̬ɪd] *adj* impertérrito, -a; **to be ~ by sth** quedarse impávido ante algo
undeceive [ˌʌndɪ'siːv] *vt liter* **to ~ sb (of sth)** desengañar a alguien (de algo)
undecided [ˌʌndɪ'saɪdɪd] *adj* **1.** (*unresolved*) indeciso, -a; **to be ~ about sth** estar indeciso ante algo; **to be ~ as to what to do** no saber qué hacer **2.** (*not settled*) no decidido, -a; **an ~ vote** un voto indeciso
undeclared [ˌʌndɪ'kleəd, *Am:* -'klerd] *adj* **1.** FIN (*kept secret*) no declarado, -a; ~ **income** ingresos *mpl* no declarados; ~ **goods** bienes *mpl* no declarados **2.** (*not official*) no oficial; **an ~ war** *a. fig* una guerra no oficial
undefined [ˌʌndɪ'faɪnd] *adj* **1.** (*not defined*) indefinido, -a **2.** (*lacking clarity*) no claro, -a
undeliverable [ˌʌndɪ'lɪvrəbl] *adj* que no puede ser entregado, -a
undelivered [ˌʌndɪ'lɪvəd, *Am:* -ɚd] *adj* sin entregar
undemanding [ˌʌndɪ'mɑːndɪŋ] *adj* **1.** (*requiring little effort*) que exige poco esfuerzo **2.** (*easy-going*) **to be ~** ser poco exigente
undemocratic [ˌʌndemə'krætɪk] *adj* antidemocrático, -a
undemonstrative [ˌʌndɪ'mɒnstrətɪv, *Am:* -'mɑːnstrət̬ɪv] *adj form* reservado, -a
undeniable [ˌʌndɪ'naɪəbl] *adj* innegable; ~ **evidence** prueba *f* irrefutable
undeniably *adv* indudablemente
under ['ʌndəʳ, *Am:* -dɚ] **I.** *prep* **1.** (*below*) debajo de; ~ **the bed** debajo de la cama; ~ **there** ahí debajo **2.** (*supporting*) bajo; **to break ~ the weight** romperse bajo el peso **3.** (*less than*) **to cost ~ £10** costar menos de £10; **those ~ the age of 30** aquellos con menos de 30 años de edad **4.** (*governed by*) ~ **Charles X** bajo Carlos X; **to be ~ sb's influence** estar bajo la influencia de alguien **5.** (*in state of*) ~ **the circumstances** en esas circumstancias; ~ **repair** en reparación **6.** (*in category of*) **to classify the books ~ author** clasificar los libros por autor **7.** LAW ~ **the treaty** conforme al Tratado **II.** *adv* debajo; **as ~** como abajo

underachieve [ˌʌndərəˈtʃiːv, *Am:* -dɚ-] *vi* no rendir lo suficiente
underact [ˌʌndərˈækt, *Am:* -dɚ-] **I.** *vi actuar sin suficiente brío* **II.** *vt* **to ~ a part** *representar un papel sin suficiente brío*
underage [ˌʌndərˈeɪdʒ, *Am:* -dɚˈ-] *adj,* **under age** *adj* menor de edad
underbid [ˌʌndəˈbɪd, *Am:* -dɚˈ-] *irr* **I.** *vi* declarar menos de lo que uno tiene **II.** *vt* **to ~ sb/sth** ofrecer un precio más bajo que alguien/algo
undercapitalized [ˌʌndəˈkæpɪtəlaɪzd, *Am:* -dɚˈ-] *adj* subcapitalizado, -a; **to be ~** estar descapitalizado
undercarriage [ˈʌndəˌkærɪdʒ, *Am:* -dɚˌker-] *n Brit* AVIAT tren *m* de aterrizaje
undercharge [ˌʌndəˈtʃɑːdʒ, *Am:* -dɚˈtʃɑːrdʒ] **I.** *vt* **to ~ sb** cobrar de menos a alguien **II.** *vi* cobrar menos; **to ~ for sth** cobrar menos de lo que vale por algo
underclothes [ˈʌndəkləʊðz, *Am:* -dɚkloʊðz] *npl,* **underclothing** [ˈʌndəˌkləʊðɪŋ, *Am:* -dɚˌkloʊ-] *n no pl* ropa *f* interior
undercoat [ˈʌndəkəʊt, *Am:* -dɚkoʊt] *n no pl* primera capa *f* de pintura
undercover [ˌʌndəˈkʌvər, *Am:* -dɚˈkʌvɚ] **I.** *adj* secreto, -a; **~ agent** agente *mf* secreto **II.** *adv* clandestinamente
undercurrent [ˈʌndəkʌrənt, *Am:* -dɚkɜːr-] *n* **1.** (*undertow*) corriente *f* submarina **2.** (*underlying influence*) tendencia *f* oculta
undercut [ˌʌndəˈkʌt, *Am:* -dɚˈ-] *irr vt* **1.** (*charge less than competitors*) vender más barato **2.** (*undermine*) socavar
underdeveloped [ˌʌndədɪˈveləpt, *Am:* -dɚdɪˈ-] *adj* **1.** (*below its economic potential*) subdesarrollado, -a; **~ country** país *m* subdesarrollado; **an ~ resource** un recurso infradesarrollado **2.** PHOT insuficientemente revelado, -a **3.** (*insufficiently mature*) inmaduro, -a
underdog [ˈʌndədɒg, *Am:* -dɚdɑːg] *n* desvalido, -a *m, f;* **to side with the ~** estar del lado de los perdedores
underdone [ˌʌndəˈdʌn, *Am:* -dɚˈ-] *adj* (*cooked less than necessary*) poco hecho, -a
underemployed [ˌʌndərɪmˈplɔɪd, *Am:* -dɚɪmˈplɔɪd] *adj* **1.** (*having too little work*) subempleado, -a **2.** ECON (*insufficiently used*) **to be ~** ser poco utilizado, -a
underequipped [ˌʌndərɪˈkwɪpt] *adj* mal equipado, -a; **an ~ expedition** una expedición con un equipamiento insuficiente
underestimate [ˌʌndərˈestɪmeɪt, *Am:* -dɚˈestə-] **I.** *vt* **to ~ sth/sb** subestimar algo/a alguien **II.** *n* infravaloración *f*
underexpose [ˌʌndərɪkˈspəʊz, *Am:* -dɚɪkˈspoʊz] *vt* PHOT **to ~ a film/photo** subexponer una película/foto
underexposure [ˌʌndərɪkˈspəʊʒər, *Am:* -dɚɪkˈspoʊʒɚ] *n no pl* PHOT subexposición *f*
underfed [ˌʌndəˈfed, *Am:* -dɚˈ-] *n* desnutrido, -a *m, f*
underfelt [ˈʌndəfelt, *Am:* -dɚ-] *n no pl* arpillera *f*
underfloor heating [ˌʌndəˈflɔːhiːtɪŋ, *Am:* -dɚflɔːrˈhiːt̬ɪŋ] *n* calefacción *f* por suelo
underfoot [ˌʌndəˈfʊt, *Am:* -dɚˈ-] *adv* (*below one's feet*) debajo de los pies; **to trample sb/sth ~** *a. fig* pisar a alguien/algo
underfund [ˌʌndəˈfʌnd, *Am:* -dɚˈ-] *vt* **to ~ sth** infradotar algo
underfunding [ˌʌndəˈfʌndɪŋ] *n no pl* infradotación *f*
undergarment [ˈʌndəgɑːmənt, *Am:* -dɚgɑːr-] *n form* prenda *f* de ropa interior
undergo [ˌʌndəˈgəʊ, *Am:* -dɚˈgoʊ] *irr vt* **to ~ sth** experimentar algo; **to ~ a change** sufrir un cambio
undergraduate [ˌʌndəˈgrædʒʊət, *Am:* -dɚˈgrædʒuət] *n* estudiante *mf* no licenciado, -a; **~ program** programa *m* para no licenciados
underground [ˈʌndəgraʊnd, *Am:* -dɚ-] **I.** *adj* **1.** (*below earth surface*) subterráneo, -a **2.** (*clandestinely anti-government*) clandestino, -a; **~ movement** movimiento *m* clandestino **3.** (*relating to subway system*) de metro **II.** *adv* **1.** (*below earth surface*) bajo tierra **2. to go ~** pasar a la clandestinidad; **to drive sb ~** meter a alguien en la clandestinidad **III.** *n* **1.** *no pl, Brit* (*subway train*) metro *m;* **by ~** en metro **2.** (*movement*) **the ~** POL la resistencia; (*lifestyle*) el underground
underground railway *n* ferrocarril *m* subterráneo **underground station** *n* estación *f* de metro
undergrowth [ˈʌndəgrəʊθ, *Am:* -dɚgroʊθ] *n no pl* maleza *f;* **dense ~** maleza espesa
underhand [ˈʌndəhænd, *Am:* ˌʌndɚˈ-] **I.** *adj Brit* turbio, -a, solapado, -a **II.** *adv Am* (*underarm*) por debajo del hombro
underinsure [ˌʌndərɪnˈʃʊər, *Am:* -dɚɪnˈʃʊr] *vt* **to ~ sth** asegurar algo por debajo del valor real
underlay [ˌʌndəˈleɪ, *Am:* -dɚˈ-] **I.** *n no pl, Brit, Aus* refuerzo *m;* **carpet ~** refuerzo *m* de alfombra **II.** *vt pt of* **underlie**
underlie [ˌʌndəˈlaɪ, *Am:* -dɚˈ-] *irr vt* **to ~ sth** subyacer a algo
underline [ˌʌndəˈlaɪn, *Am:* -dɚˈ-] *vt* **1.** (*draw a line beneath*) subrayar; **to ~ sth in red** subrayar algo en rojo **2.** (*emphasize*) enfatizar; **to ~ that ...** subrayar que...
underling [ˈʌndəlɪŋ, *Am:* -dɚlɪŋ] *n pej* subordinado, -a
underlying [ˌʌndəˈlaɪɪŋ, *Am:* -dɚˈ-] *adj* subyacente; **the ~ reason for sth** la razón que subyace a algo
undermanned [ˌʌndəˈmænd, *Am:* -dɚˈ-] *adj* sin plantilla suficiente
undermanning [ˌʌndəˈmænɪŋ, *Am:* -dɚˈ-] *n no pl* escasez *f* de personal
undermentioned [ˌʌndəˈmenʃnd, *Am:* -dɚˈ-] *adj Brit, form* abajo citado, -a
undermine [ˌʌndəˈmaɪn, *Am:* -dɚˈ-] *vt*

U

1. (*tunnel under*) socavar; **to ~ a river bank** socavar la orilla de un río **2.** (*damage, sap, weaken*) arruinar; **to ~ hopes** desalentar; **to ~ a currency** debilitar una divisa; **to ~ sb's confidence** bajar la confianza de alguien; **to ~ sb's health** perjudicar a la salud de alguien

undermost ['ʌndəməʊst, *Am:* -dɚmoʊst] *adj* **the ~ ...** el más bajo...

underneath [ˌʌndə'niːθ, *Am:* -dɚ'-] **I.** *prep* debajo de **II.** *adv* por debajo **III.** *n no pl* **the ~** la superficie inferior **IV.** *adj* inferior

undernourished [ˌʌndə'nʌrɪʃt, *Am:* -dɚ'nɜːr-] *adj* desnutrido, -a

underpaid [ˌʌndə'peɪd, *Am:* -dɚ'-] *adj* mal pagado, -a

underpants ['ʌndəpænts, *Am:* -dɚ-] *npl* calzoncillos *mpl*

underpass ['ʌndəpɑːs, *Am:* -dɚpæs] <-es> *n* paso *m* subterráneo

underpay [ˌʌndə'peɪ, *Am:* -dɚ'-] *irr vt* pagar un sueldo insuficiente

underperform [ˌʌndəpə'fɔːm] *vi* rendir por debajo de lo suficiente

underplay ['ʌndəpleɪ, *Am:* ˌʌndɚ'pleɪ] **I.** *vt* **1.** (*play down*) subestimar; **to ~ the importance/seriousness of sth** subestimar la importancia/gravedad de algo **2.** (*act with restraint*) actuar con contención **II.** *vi* no actuar demasiado en un papel

underpopulated [ˌʌndə'pɒpjʊleɪtɪd, *Am:* -dɚ'pɑːpjə-] *adj* poco poblado, -a

underprivileged [ˌʌndə'prɪvəlɪdʒd, *Am:* -dɚ'-] **I.** *adj* sin privilegios; **the ~ class** la clase no privilegiada **II.** *n* **the ~** *pl* los no privilegiados

underrate [ˌʌndə'reɪt, *Am:* -dɚ'-] *vt* **to ~ sth/sb** subestimar algo/a alguien; **to ~ the difficulty/importance of sth** infravalorar la dificultad/importancia de algo

underrepresented [ˌʌndəreprɪ'zentɪd, *Am:* -dɚreprɪ'zenṭɪd] *adj* con mala representación

underscore [ˌʌndə'skɔːʳ, *Am:* -dɚ'skɔːr] *vt* **1.** (*put a line under*) subrayar **2.** (*emphasize*) recalcar; **to ~ a point** recalcar un punto

underseal ['ʌndəsiːl, *Am:* -dɚ-] *Brit* **I.** *n* impermeable *m* **II.** *vt* impermeabilizar

undersell [ˌʌndə'sel, *Am:* -dɚ'-] *irr vt* **1.** (*offer goods cheaper*) **to ~ goods** vender mercancias a un precio más bajo; **to ~ the competition** vender a precios más bajos que la competencia **2.** (*undervalue*) **to ~ sth/sb** no hacer la suficiente publicidad de algo/alguien; **to ~ oneself** no saber venderse uno mismo

undershirt ['ʌndəʃɜːt, *Am:* -dɚʃɜːrt] *n Am* camiseta *f*

underside ['ʌndəsaɪd, *Am:* -dɚ-] *n* superficie *f* inferior

undersigned ['ʌndəsaɪnd, *Am:* 'ʌndɚsaɪnd] *n form* **the ~** el/la abajofirmante

undersize *adj*, **undersized** [ˌʌndə'saɪzd, *Am:* 'ʌndɚsaɪzd] *adj* de tamaño insuficiente

underskirt ['ʌndəskɜːt, *Am:* -dɚskɜːrt] *n* enaguas *fpl*

understaffed [ˌʌndə'stɑːft, *Am:* -dɚ'stæft] *adj* falto, -a de personal

understand [ˌʌndə'stænd, *Am:* -dɚ'-] *irr* **I.** *vt* **1.** (*perceive meaning*) **to ~ sth/sb** comprender algo/a alguien; **to make oneself understood** hacerse entender; **not to ~ a word** no entender ni una palabra; **to ~ that ...** entender que... **2.** (*sympathize with*) **to ~ sb's doing sth** entender que alguien haga algo **3.** (*feel empathetic insight*) **to ~ sb/an animal** ponerse en la piel de alguien/de un animal **4.** *form* (*be informed*) **to ~ that ...** quedar informado de que...; **to ~ from sb that ...** saber por alguien que...; **to give sb to ~ that ...** dar a alguien a entender que... **5.** (*believe*) creer; (*infer*) sobreentender; **to ~ that ...** sobreentender que...; **to ~ sb to mean/do sth** inferir que alguien quiere decir/hacer algo; **as I ~ it** según tengo entendido; **it is understood that ...** se sobreentiende que... **6.** (*interpret*) interpretar; **to ~ from sth that ...** inferir a partir de algo que... **II.** *vi* entender; **to ~ about sth** entender de algo

understandable [ˌʌndə'stændəbl, *Am:* -dɚ'-] *adj* comprensible; **to be ~ that ...** ser comprensible que...

understanding **I.** *n* **1.** *no pl* (*comprehension, grasp*) entendimiento *m;* **to not have any ~ of sth** no tener ni idea de algo; **to come to an ~** llegar a entender; **sb's ~ of sth** la interpretación de alguien de algo **2.** (*entente, agreement*) acuerdo *m;* **to come to an ~** llegar a un acuerdo; **a tacit ~** un acuerdo tácito **3.** *no pl* (*harmony, rapport*) comprensión *f;* **a spirit of ~** un espíritu de comprensión **4.** *no pl* (*condition*) condición *f;* **to do sth on the ~ that ...** hacer algo a condición de que... **5.** *no pl, form* (*intellectual ability*) inteligencia *f* **II.** *adj* comprensivo, -a

understate [ˌʌndə'steɪt, *Am:* -dɚ'-] *vt* minimizar; **to ~ sb's viewpoint** quitar importancia a la opinión de alguien

understated *adj* sencillo, -a

understatement [ˌʌndə'steɪtmənt, *Am:* ˌʌndɚ'steɪt-] *n* atenuación *f;* **to be the ~ of the year** *fig, iron* el eufemismo del año

understocked [ˌʌndə'stɒkt, *Am:* -dɚ'stɑːkt] *adj* con pocas existencias; **~ shelves** estanterías *fpl* con pocas existencias

understood [ˌʌndə'stʊd, *Am:* -dɚ'-] *vt, vi pt, pp of* **understand**

understorey [ˌʌndə'stɔːri] *n* capa *f* inferior de plantas (*en un bosque*)

understudy ['ʌndəˌstʌdi, *Am:* -dɚˌ-] THEAT **I.** <-ies> *n* suplente *mf;* **to be the ~ for sb/sth** ser el suplente de alguien/algo **II.** <-ie-> *vt* **to ~ sb** doblar a alguien

undertake [ˌʌndə'teɪk, *Am:* -dɚ'-] *irr vt* **1.** (*set about, take on*) establecer; **to ~ a journey** emprender un viaje **2.** *form* (*commit oneself to*) **to ~ to do sth** comprometerse a hacer algo; **to ~ (that) ...** comprometerse a (que)...

undertaker ['ʌndəˌteɪkəʳ, *Am:* -dɚˌteɪkɚ] *n* **1.** (*mortician*) director(a) *m(f)* de pompas fúnebres **2.** (*institute*) **the ~'s** la funeraria
undertaking [ˌʌndə'teɪkɪŋ, *Am:* ˌʌndɚ'teɪ-] *n* **1.** (*professional project*) empresa *f;* **noble ~** noble empresa **2.** *form* (*pledge*) promesa *f;* **an ~ to do sth** una promesa de hacer algo; **to give an ~ that ...** prometer que...
under-the-counter [ˌʌndəðə'kaʊntəʳ, *Am:* -dɚðə'kaʊn t̬ɚ] **I.** *adj* (*deal*) poco limpio, -a **II.** *adv* ilícitamente
undertone ['ʌndətəʊn, *Am:* -dɚtoʊn] *n* **1.** *no pl* (*low voice*) voz *f* baja; **to say sth in an ~** decir algo en voz baja **2.** (*undercurrent, insinuation*) insinuación *f*
underused [ˌʌndə'ju:zd, *Am:* -dɚ'-] *adj,* **underutilized** [ˌʌndə'ju:tɪlaɪzd, *Am:* -dɚ-'ju:t̬əlaɪzd] *adj* infrautilizado, -a
undervalue [ˌʌndə'vælju:, *Am:* -dɚ'-] *vt* subvalorar
underwater [ˌʌndə'wɔ:təʳ, *Am:* -dɚ'wɑ:-t̬ɚ] **I.** *adj* submarino, -a **II.** *adv* por debajo del agua
underwear ['ʌndəweəʳ, *Am:* -dɚwer] *n no pl* ropa *f* interior
underweight [ˌʌndə'weɪt, *Am:* -dɚ'-] *adj* de peso insuficiente
underworked *adj* **1.** (*insufficiently used*) poco utilizado, -a **2.** (*insufficiently challenged*) sin dificultades
underworld ['ʌndəwɜ:ld, *Am:* -dɚwɜ:rld] *n* **1.** *no pl* (*criminal milieu*) hampa *m* **2.** ART, LIT (*afterworld*) **the Underworld** el infierno
underwrite [ˌʌndər'aɪt, *Am:* 'ʌndɚraɪt] *irr vt* **1.** (*sign*) firmar; **to ~ a contract** firmar un contrato **2.** FIN, ECON (*guarantee share issues*) garantizar una emisión de acciones **3.** (*provide insurance for*) asegurar
underwriter ['ʌndərˌaɪtəʳ, *Am:* -dɚˌraɪt̬ɚ] *n* asegurador(a) *m(f)*
undesirable [ˌʌndɪ'zaɪərəbl, *Am:* -'zaɪrəbl] **I.** *adj* indeseable; **to be ~ that ...** no ser recomendable que...; **an ~ character** un carácter difícil **II.** *n* indeseable *mf*
undetected [ˌʌndɪ'tektɪd] *adj* no descubierto, -a; **to go ~** pasar inadvertido, -a
undeveloped [ˌʌndɪ'veləpt] *adj* **1.** POL, ECON subdesarrollado, -a **2.** (*not built on or used*) poco utilizado, -a **3.** PHOT no revelado, -a **4.** BIO, PSYCH no desarrollado, -a
undid [ʌn'dɪd] *vt, vi pt of* **undo**
undies ['ʌndɪz] *npl inf* paños *mpl* menores
undischarged bankrupt [ˌʌndɪstʃɑ:dʒd-'bæŋkrʌpt, *Am:* -tʃɑ:rdʒd'-] *n* COM quebrado, -a *m, f* no rehabilitado, -a
undisclosed [ˌʌndɪs'kləʊzd, *Am:* -'kloʊzd] *adj* no revelado, -a; **an ~ amount** una cantidad no desvelada; **an ~ location** una ubicación sin desvelar; **an ~ source** una fuente no revelada
undiscovered [ˌʌndɪs'kʌvəd, *Am:* -ɚd] *adj* no descubierto, -a; **to go ~** ir de incógnito
undisputed [ˌʌndɪ'spju:tɪd, *Am:* -t̬ɪd] *adj* incontestable
undistinguished [ˌʌndɪ'stɪŋgwɪʃt] *adj* mediocre
undisturbed [ʌndɪ'stɜ:bd, *Am:* -stzɜ:rbd] *adj* **they were ~ by the noise** el ruido no les molestaba
undivided [ˌʌndɪ'vaɪdɪd] *adj* **1.** (*not split*) íntegro, -a **2.** (*intense*) intenso, -a; **sb's ~ attention** toda la atención de alguien
undo [ʌn'du:] *irr vt* **1.** (*unfasten*) soltar; **to ~ buttons** desabrochar botones; **to ~ a zipper** bajar una cremallera **2.** (*cancel*) anular; **to ~ the damage** reparar el daño; **to ~ the good work** deshacer el trabajo bueno **3.** (*cause ruin*) arruinar; **to ~ sb's good name** perjudicar el buen nombre de alguien ►**what's done cannot be undone** *prov* lo hecho, hecho está *prov*
undoing *n no pl, form* ruina *f*
undone [ʌn'dʌn] **I.** *vt pp of* **undo** **II.** *adj* **1.** (*not fastened*) desatado, -a; **to come ~** deshacerse **2.** (*uncompleted*) por hacer; **to leave sth ~** dejar algo sin hacer
undoubted [ʌn'daʊtɪd, *Am:* -t̬ɪd] *adj* indudable
undoubtedly *adv* indudablemente
undreamed-of [ʌn'dri:mdˌɒv, *Am:* -ˌɑ:v] *adj,* **undreamt-of** [ʌn'dremtˌɒv, *Am:* -ˌɑ:v] *adj* inimaginable
undress [ʌn'dres] **I.** *vt* desnudar, desvestir *AmL;* **to ~ sb with one's eyes** *fig* desnudar a alguien con la mirada **II.** *vi* desvestirse **III.** *n no pl* ropa *f* informal
undressed *adj* desvestido, -a; **to get ~** desnudarse
undue [ˌʌn'dju:, *Am:* -'du:] *adj form* indebido, -a; **~ pressure** presión *f* excesiva
undulate ['ʌndjəleɪt, *Am:* -dʒə-] *vi form* ondular
undulating *adj form* **1.** (*moving like a wave*) ondulante **2.** (*shaped like waves*) ondulado, -a
unduly [ʌn'dju:li, *Am:* -'du:-] *adv* indebidamente
undying [ˌʌn'daɪɪŋ] *adj liter* imperecedero, -a; **~ love** amor *m* eterno
unearned [ˌʌn'ɜ:nd, *Am:* -'ɜ:rnd] *adj* **1.** (*undeserved*) inmerecido, -a **2.** (*not worked for*) no ganado, -a
unearth [ʌn'ɜ:θ, *Am:* -'ɜ:rθ] *vt* **1.** (*dig up*) desenterrar **2.** (*discover with difficulty*) sacar a la luz; **to ~ the truth** descubrir la verdad
unearthly [ʌn'ɜ:θli, *Am:* -'ɜ:rθ-] *adj* **1.** (*unsettling*) sobrenatural; **~ noise/scream** ruido *m*/grito *m* aterrador **2.** *inf* (*inconvenient*) intempestivo, -a **3.** (*not from the earth*) sobrenatural
unease [ʌn'i:z] *n no pl* malestar *m;* **with growing ~** con creciente inquietud
uneasiness *n no pl* inquietud *f*
uneasy [ʌn'i:zi] *adj* <-ier, -iest> **1.** (*uncertain*) intranquilo, -a; **to be/feel ~ about sth/sb** estar/sentirse inquieto por algo/alguien **2.** (*causing anxiety*) ansioso, -a; (*suspicion*) inquietante; (*relationship*) inestable **3.** (*inse-*

U

cure) dudoso, -a

uneconomic [ʌnˌiːkəˈnɒmɪk, *Am:* -ˌekəˈnɑːmɪk] *adj* poco lucrativo, -a

uneducated [ʌnˈedʒʊkeɪtɪd, *Am:* -ˈedʒʊkeɪt̬ɪd] I. *adj* inculto, -a II. *n* **the** ~ los ignorantes

unemotional [ˌʌnɪˈməʊʃənəl, *Am:* -ˈmoʊ-] *adj* 1. (*not feeling emotions*) impasible 2. (*not revealing emotions*) reservado, -a

unemployable [ˌʌnɪmˈplɔɪəbl] *adj* incapacitado, -a para trabajar

unemployed [ˌʌnɪmˈplɔɪd] I. *n pl* **the** ~ los desempleados II. *adj* parado, -a

unemployment [ˌʌnɪmˈplɔɪmənt] *n no pl* 1. (*condition of lacking work*) desempleo *m* 2. (*rate of joblessness*) desocupación *f*

unemployment benefit *n* subsidio *m* de paro

unending [ʌnˈendɪŋ] *adj* interminable

unenlightened [ˌʌnɪnˈlaɪtənd] *adj* 1. (*not wise or insightful*) poco instruido, -a 2. (*lack of insight*) ignorante 3. *a. iron* (*not informed*) desinformado, -a

unenviable [ʌnˈenviəbl] *adj* poco envidiable

unequal [ʌnˈiːkwəl] *adj* 1. *form* (*different*) diferente; ~ **triangle** triángulo *m* de lados desiguales 2. (*unjust, inequitable*) desigual 3. (*unable*) **to be** ~ **to sth** no estar a la altura de algo

unequaled *adj Am,* **unequalled** *adj Brit* sin igual

unequivocal [ˌʌnɪˈkwɪvəkəl] *adj* inequívoco, -a; **an** ~ **success** un éxito indudable; **to be** ~ **in sth** ser claro en algo

unerring [ʌnˈɜːrɪŋ] *adj* infalible

UNESCO *n,* **Unesco** [juːˈneskəʊ, *Am:* -koʊ] *n no pl abbr of* **United Nations Educational, Scientific and Cultural Organization** UNESCO *f*

unethical [ʌnˈeθɪkəl] *adj* poco ético, -a

uneven [ˌʌnˈiːvən] *adj* 1. (*not flat or level*) desnivelado, -a 2. (*unequal*) desigual 3. (*different*) distinto, -a 4. (*of inadequate quality*) irregular 5. (*erratic, fluctuating*) cambiante 6. MED anormal

uneventful [ˌʌnɪˈventfəl] *adj* sin acontecimientos; (*unexciting*) tranquilo, -a

unexampled [ˌʌnɪgˈzɑːmpld, *Am:* -ɪgˈzæm-] *adj form* único, -a

unexceptionable [ˌʌnɪkˈsepʃənəbl] *adj form* intachable

unexceptional [ˌʌnɪkˈsepʃənəl] *adj* corriente

unexciting *adj* 1. (*commonplace*) trivial 2. (*uneventful*) aburrido, -a

unexpected [ˌʌnɪkˈspektɪd] I. *adj* inesperado, -a II. *n no pl* **the** ~ lo inesperado

unexplained [ˌʌnɪkˈspleɪnd] *adj* inexplicado, -a; **her absence was** ~ su ausencia era inexplicable

unexploded [ˌʌnɪkˈspləʊdɪd] *adj* sin explotar

unexploited *adj* inexplotado, -a

unexpressed *adj* sobreentendido, -a

unexpressive [ˌʌnɪkˈspresɪv] *adj* inexpresivo, -a

unexpurgated [ˌʌnˈekspɜːgeɪtɪd, *Am:* -spɚgeɪt̬ɪd] *adj* íntegro, -a

unfailing [ʌnˈfeɪlɪŋ] *adj* 1. (*always present when needed*) indefectible 2. (*not running out*) incansable

unfair [ˌʌnˈfeəʳ, *Am:* -ˈfer] *adj* injusto, -a; (*advantage, disadvantage*) desfavorable

unfaithful [ˌʌnˈfeɪθfʊl] *adj* 1. (*adulterous*) infiel 2. (*disloyal*) desleal 3. *form* (*not accurate*) inexacto, -a

unfaltering [ʌnˈfɔːltərɪŋ, *Am:* -ˈfɑːlt̬ɚɪŋ] *adj* 1. (*without hesitation*) resuelto, -a; **with** ~ **steps** con pasos firmes 2. (*decided*) decidido, -a

unfamiliar [ˌʌnfəˈmɪljəʳ, *Am:* -jɚ] *adj* 1. (*new, not familiar*) desconocido, -a; **to be** ~ **to sb** resultar desconocido a alguien 2. (*unacquainted*) ajeno, -a

unfashionable [ʌnˈfæʃənəbl] *adj* pasado, -a de moda

unfasten [ˌʌnˈfɑːsən, *Am:* -ˈfæsn] I. *vt* desatar II. *vi* soltarse

unfathomable [ʌnˈfæðəməbl] *adj* 1. *a. fig* (*too deep to measure*) insondable 2. (*inexplicable*) inexplicable

unfavorable *adj Am,* **unfavourable** [ˌʌnˈfeɪvərəbl] *adj Brit, Aus* 1. (*adverse*) adverso, -a 2. (*disadvantagous*) desfavorable

unfeeling [ʌnˈfiːlɪŋ] *adj* insensible

unfeigned [ʌnˈfeɪnd] *adj* verdadero, -a

unfettered [ʌnˈfetəd, *Am:* -ˈfet̬ɚd] *adj* sin ataduras

unfilled *adj* vacío, -a

unfinished [ʌnˈfɪnɪʃt] *adj* inacabado, -a

unfit [ʌnˈfɪt] I. *adj* 1. (*unhealthy*) **I'm** ~ no estoy en forma; **to be** ~ **for sth** no estar en condiciones para algo 2. (*incompetent*) incapaz 3. (*unsuitable*) no apto, -a; **to be** ~ **for sth** ser no apto para algo; **to be** ~ **for (human) habitation** ser inhabitable (para el ser humano) II. *vt* <-tt-> *form* inhabilitar

unflagging [ʌnˈflægɪŋ] *adj* incansable

unflappable [ʌnˈflæpəbl] *adj inf* imperturbable

unflinching [ʌnˈflɪntʃɪŋ] *adj* intrépido, -a; (*report*) atrevido, -a; (*support, honesty*) resuelto, -a

unfold [ʌnˈfəʊld, *Am:* -ˈfoʊld] I. *vt* 1. (*open out sth folded*) desenvolver; **to** ~ **one's arms** extender sus brazos 2. *form* (*make known*) **to** ~ **one's ideas/plans** exponer sus ideas/planes II. *vi* 1. (*develop, evolve*) desarrollarse 2. (*become revealed*) revelarse 3. (*become unfolded*) extenderse

unforeseeable [ˌʌnfɔːˈsiːəbl, *Am:* -fɔːrˈ-] *adj* imprevisible

unforeseen [ˌʌnfɔːˈsiːn, *Am:* -fɔːrˈ-] *adj* imprevisto, -a

unforgettable [ˌʌnfəˈgetəbl, *Am:* -fɚˈget̬-] *adj* inolvidable

unforgivable [ˌʌnfəˈgɪvəbl, *Am:* -fɚˈ-] *adj* imperdonable

unfortunate [ʌnˈfɔːtʃənət, *Am:* -ˈfɔːrtʃnət] **I.** *adj* **1.** (*luckless*) desafortunado, -a; **to be ~ that ...** ser lamentable que... +*subj* **2.** *form* (*regrettable*) deplorable **3.** (*inopportune*) inoportuno, -a **4.** (*adverse*) funesto, -a **II.** *n* desgraciado, -a *m, f*

unfortunately *adv* por desgracia

unfounded [ʌnˈfaʊndɪd] *adj* infundado, -a

unfreeze [ʌnˈfriːz] *irr* **I.** *vt* descongelar **II.** *vi* descongelarse

unfrequented [ˌʌnfrɪˈkwentɪd, *Am:* ʌnˈfriːkwent̬ɪd] *adj* solitario, -a

unfriendly [ʌnˈfrendli] *adj* <-ier, -iest> **1.** (*unsociable*) insociable **2.** *fig* (*hard to use*) complicado, -a **3.** (*inhospitable*) hostil

unfulfilled [ˌʌnfʊlˈfɪld] *adj* **1.** (*not carried out*) incumplido, -a **2.** (*unsatisfied*) insatisfecho, -a **3.** (*frustrated*) frustrado, -a

unfulfilled order *n* orden *f* incumplida

unfurl [ʌnˈfɜːl, *Am:* -ˈfɜːrl] **I.** *vt* desplegar; **to ~ an umbrella** abrir un paraguas; **to ~ a sail** largar una vela **II.** *vi* desplegarse

unfurnished [ˌʌnˈfɜːnɪʃt, *Am:* -ˈfɜːr-] *adj* desamueblado, -a

ungainly [ʌnˈgeɪnli] *adj* <-ier, -iest> torpe

ungenerous [ʌnˈdʒenərəs] *adj* tacaño, -a

ungentlemanly [ʌnˈdʒentlmənli] *adj* poco cortés

unget-at-able [ˌʌngetˈætəbl, *Am:* ˌʌnget̬ˈæt̬-] *adj inf* inaccesible

ungodly [ʌnˈgɒdli, *Am:* ʌnˈgɑːdli] *adj* <-ier, -iest> **1.** *inf* (*unreasonable*) atroz **2.** (*impious*) impío, -a

ungovernable [ʌnˈgʌvənəbl, *Am:* ʌnˈgʌvɚnə-] *adj* ingobernable

ungraceful [ʌnˈgreɪsfəl] *adj* chabacano, -a

ungracious [ˌʌnˈgreɪʃəs] *adj form* descortés

ungrateful [ʌnˈgreɪtfəl] *adj* ingrato, -a

ungrudging [ʌnˈgrʌdʒɪŋ] *adj* **1.** (*without reservation*) generoso, -a **2.** (*not resentful or envious*) incondicional

ungrudgingly *adv* de buena gana

unguarded [ʌnˈgɑːdɪd, *Am:* ʌnˈgɑːr-] *adj* **1.** (*not defended or watched*) sin vigilancia **2.** (*careless*) desprevenido, -a; **in an ~ moment** en un momento de descuido

unguent [ˈʌŋgwənt] *n liter* ungüento *m*

unhallowed [ʌnˈhæləʊd, *Am:* -oʊd] *adj* **1.** (*not consecrated*) profano, -a **2.** (*unholy*) sacrílego, -a

unhappy [ʌnˈhæpi] *adj* <-ier, -iest> **1.** (*sad*) infeliz; **to make sb ~** hacer desdichado a alguien **2.** (*unfortunate*) desafortunado, -a

unharmed [ʌnˈhɑːmd, *Am:* -ˈhɑːrmd] *adj* ileso, -a

UNHCR [ˌjuːeneɪtʃsiːˈɑːʳ] *n no pl abbr of* **United Nations High Commission for Refugees** ACNUR *f*

unhealthy [ʌnˈhelθi] *adj* <-ier, -iest> **1.** (*sick*) enfermizo, -a **2.** (*unwholesome*) nocivo, -a **3.** *inf* (*dangerous*) arriesgado, -a **4.** PSYCH (*morbid*) morboso, -a

unheard [ʌnˈhɜːd, *Am:* -ˈhɜːrd] *adj* **1.** (*not heard*) desoído, -a **2.** (*ignored*) desatendido, -a

unheard-of [ʌnˈhɜːdˌɒv, *Am:* -ˈhɜːrdˌɑːv] *adj* **1.** (*incredible*) sin precedente **2.** (*impossible*) inaudito, -a

unhelpful [ʌnˈhelpfʊl] *adj* de poca ayuda

unhinge [ʌnˈhɪndʒ] *vt* **1.** (*take off hinges*) desgoznar **2.** (*make crazy*) desquiciar

unholy [ʌnˈhəʊli, *Am:* -ˈhoʊ-] <-ier, -iest> *adj* **1.** (*wicked*) impío, -a **2.** REL (*profane*) profano, -a **3.** (*outrageous*) atroz; **to get up at some ~ hour** levantarse a una hora infame

unhook [ʌnˈhʊk] *vt* **1.** (*remove hooks*) desenganchar **2.** (*unfasten*) soltar

unhoped-for [ʌnˈhəʊptˌfɔːʳ, *Am:* -ˈhoʊptˌfɔːr] *adj* inesperado, -a

unhorse [ˌʌnˈhɔːs, *Am:* -ˈhɔːrs] *vt* desmontar

unhurt [ʌnˈhɜːt, *Am:* -ˈhɜːrt] *adj* ileso, -a

UNICEF *n*, **Unicef** [ˈjuːnɪsef] *n no pl abbr of* **United Nations International Children's Emergency Fund** UNICEF *f*

unicorn [ˈjuːnɪkɔːn, *Am:* -kɔːrn] *n* unicornio *m*

unidentified [ˌʌnaɪˈdentɪfaɪd, *Am:* -t̬ə-] *n* **1.** (*unknown*) desconocido, -a **2.** (*not yet made public*) no identificado, -a

unification [ˌjuːnɪfɪˈkeɪʃən] *n no pl* unificación *f*

uniform [ˈjuːnɪfɔːm, *Am:* -nəfɔːrm] **I.** *n* uniforme *m* **II.** *adj* **1.** (*same or similar*) uniforme **2.** (*constant*) constante

uniformity [ˌjuːnɪˈfɔːməti, *Am:* -nəˈfɔːrmət̬i] *n no pl* (*sameness*) uniformidad *f*

unify [ˈjuːnɪfaɪ, *Am:* -nə-] *vt* unificar

unilateral [ˌjuːnɪˈlætrəl, *Am:* -nəˈlæt̬-] *adj* unilateral

unimaginable [ˌʌnɪˈmædʒnəbl] *adj* inimaginable

unimpeachable [ˌʌnɪmˈpiːtʃəbl] *adj form* intachable; **an ~ source** una fuente fidedigna

unimportant [ˌʌnɪmˈpɔːtənt, *Am:* -ˈpɔːr-] *adj* sin importancia

uninformed [ˌʌnɪnˈfɔːmd, *Am:* -ˈfɔːrmd] *adj* desinformado, -a

uninhabitable [ˌʌnɪnˈhæbɪtəbl, *Am:* -t̬əbl] *adj* inhabitable

uninhabited [ˌʌnɪnˈhæbɪtɪd] *adj* **1.** (*not lived in*) deshabitado, -a **2.** (*deserted*) desierto, -a

uninhibited [ˌʌnɪnˈhɪbɪtɪd, *Am:* -t̬ɪd] *adj* desinhibido, -a

uninjured [ˌʌnˈɪndʒəd, *Am:* -dʒɚd] *adj* ileso, -a

uninsured [ˌʌnɪnˈʃʊəd, *Am:* -ˈʃʊrd] *adj* no asegurado, -a

unintelligent [ˌʌnɪnˈtelɪdʒənt] *adj* poco inteligente

unintelligible [ˌʌnɪnˈtelɪdʒəbl] *adj* **1.** (*not comprehensible*) incomprensible **2.** (*unreadable*) ininteligible

unintentional [ˌʌnɪnˈtentʃənəl] *adj* involuntario, -a

U

unintentionally *adv* sin intención
uninterested [ʌn'ɪntrəstɪd] *adj* indiferente
uninteresting *adj* aburrido, -a
uninterrupted [ʌn,ɪntər'ʌptɪd] *adj* ininterrumpido, -a
union ['juːnjən] *n* **1.** *no pl* (*act of becoming united*) unión *f* **2.** (*instance of becoming united*) asociación *f* **3.** + *sing/pl vb* (*organization representing employees*) sindicato *m;* **the ~ demands** las exigencias gremiales **4.** *form* (*marriage*) enlace *m* **5.** (*harmony, concord*) **to live in perfect ~** vivir en perfecta armonía
unionise ['juːnjənaɪz] *Brit, Aus* **I.** *vt* agremiar **II.** *vi* agremiarse
unionist ['juːnjənɪst] *n* unionista *mf*
unionize *vt, vi s.* **unionise**
Union Jack *n* (*British national flag*) *bandera del Reino Unido*
union member *n* sindicalista *mf*
unique [juː'niːk] *adj* **1.** (*only one*) único, -a; **a ~ characteristic** una característica exclusiva **2.** (*exceptional*) excepcional
uniqueness *n no pl* unicidad *f*
uniqueness theorem *n* MAT teorema *m* de la unicidad
unisex ['juːnɪseks, *Am:* -nə-] *adj* unisex
unison ['juːnɪsən, *Am:* -nə-] **I.** *n* **1.** *no pl* MUS **to sing in ~** cantar al unísono **2.** (*in agreement*) **to act in ~ with sb** obrar de acuerdo con alguien **II.** *adj* MUS unísono, -a
unit ['juːnɪt] *n* **1.** *a.* INFOR, COM unidad *f;* **central processing ~** unidad de procesamiento central; **tape backup/output ~** unidad de respaldo/de salida en cinta; **~ of currency** unidad monetaria **2.** + *sing/pl vb* (*organized group of people*) brigada *f* **3.** (*element of furniture*) elemento *m*
unit cost *n* COM coste *m* unitario
unite [juː'naɪt] **I.** *vt* **1.** (*join together*) juntar; (*bring together*) unir **2.** LAW (*join in marriage*) casar **II.** *vi* **1.** POL, SOCIOL (*join in common cause*) **to ~ against sb** unirse para hacer frente a alguien **2.** (*join together*) juntarse
united *adj* unido, -a
United Arab Emirates *npl* **the ~** los Emiratos Arabes Unidos **United Kingdom** *n no pl* **the ~** el Reino Unido **United Nations** *n no pl* **the ~** las Naciones Unidas **United States** *n + sing vb* Estados *mpl* Unidos; **the ~ of America** los Estados Unidos América
unit price *n* COM precio *m* por unidad **unit trust** *n Brit* fondo *m* de inversión inmobiliaria
unity ['juːnəti, *Am:* -t̬i] *n no pl* **1.** (*oneness*) unidad *f;* **~ of a film/novel** continuidad *f* de una película/novela **2.** (*harmony, consensus*) consenso *m*
Univ. *abbr of* **University** Univ.
universal [,juːnɪ'vɜːsəl, *Am:* -nə'vɜːr-] **I.** *adj* universal; **~ agreement** acuerdo *m* global **II.** *n* universal *m*
universe ['juːnɪvɜːs, *Am:* -nəvɜːrs] *n* **the ~** el universo
university [,juːnɪ'vɜːsəti, *Am:* -nə'vɜːrsət̬i] <-ies> *n* universidad *f;* **the ~ community** la comunidad universitaria
university education *n no pl* educación *f* universitaria **university lecturer** *n* profesor(a) *m(f)* universitario, -a **university town** *n* ciudad *f* universitaria
unjust [ʌn'dʒʌst] *adj* injusto, -a
unjustifiable [ʌn,dʒʌstɪ'faɪəbl] *adj* injustificable
unjustified [ʌn'dʒʌstɪfaɪd] *adj* injustificado, -a; (*complaint*) no justificado, -a
unjustly *adv* **1.** (*in an unjust manner*) inmerecidamente **2.** (*wrongfully*) injustamente
unkempt [ʌn'kempt] *adj* descuidado, -a; (*appearance*) desarreglado, -a; (*hair*) despeinado, -a
unkind [ʌn'kaɪnd] *adj* **1.** (*not kind*) desagradable; **to be ~ to sb** tratar mal a alguien; **to be ~ to animals** ser cruel con los animales **2.** (*not gentle*) **to be ~ to hair/hands/skin** estropear el pelo/las manos/la piel
unkindly *adv* cruelmente; **to take sth ~** tomarse algo mal
unknowing [,ʌn'nəʊɪŋ, *Am:* -'noʊ-] *adj* no consciente
unknown [,ʌn'nəʊn, *Am:* -'noʊn] **I.** *adj* **1.** (*not known*) desconocido, -a; **~ to me ...** sin saberlo yo... **2.** (*not widely familiar*) ignorado, -a **II.** *n* **1.** (*thing*) **the ~** lo desconocido; MAT la incógnita **2.** (*person*) desconocido, -a *m, f*
unlawful [,ʌn'lɔːfəl, *Am:* -'lɑː-] *adj* ilegal; (*possession, association*) ilícito, -a
unleaded [ʌn'ledɪd] *adj* sin plomo
unlearn [ʌn'lɜːn, *Am:* -'lɜːrn] *vt* **to ~ sth** (*intentionally forget*) olvidar algo; (*intentionally stop doing sth*) acostumbrarse a no hacer algo
unleash [ʌn'liːʃ] *vt* (*a dog*) soltar; *fig* (*passions*) desatar; (*a war*) desencadenar
unleavened [ʌn'levənd] *adj* (*bread*) sin levadura
unless [ən'les] *conj* a no ser que +*subj,* a menos que +*subj;* **he'll buy it ~ she already has it** lo comprará a menos que ella ya lo tenga; **I don't say anything ~ I'm sure** yo no digo nada a menos que esté seguro; **he won't come ~ he has time** no vendrá a menos que tenga tiempo; **~ I'm mistaken** si no me equivoco
unlicensed [ʌn'laɪsəntst] *adj* sin patente; (*restaurant*) no autorizado, -a; *Brit* sin permiso
unlike [ʌn'laɪk] **I.** *adj* diferente, distinto, -a **II.** *prep* **1.** (*different from*) diferente; **to be ~ sth/sb** ser distinto de algo/alguien **2.** (*in contrast to*) a diferencia de **3.** (*not characteristic of*) **it's ~ sb/sth** no es característico de alguien/algo
unlikely [ʌn'laɪkli] <-ier, -iest> *adj* **1.** (*improbable*) improbable; **(sth) seems ~** (algo) parece poco probable; **it's ~ that ...** es difícil que... **2.** (*unconvincing*) inverosímil
unlimited [ʌn'lɪmɪtɪd, *Am:* -t̬ɪd] *adj* **1.** (*not

limited) ilimitado, -a; (*access, visibility*) sin límite **2.** (*very great*) impresionante
unlisted [ʌn'lɪstɪd] *adj* **1.** FIN (*stock market*) no cotizado, -a; ~ **securities** valores *mpl* no inscritos en bolsa **2.** *Am, Aus* (*not in the phone book*) no incluido, -a en la guía telefónica
unload [ʌn'ləʊd, *Am:* -'loʊd] **I.** *vt* **1.** (*remove the contents*) **to ~ sth** descargar algo **2.** (*remove film: a camera*) vaciar **3.** *inf* (*get rid of*) **to ~ sth** deshacerse de algo **4. to ~ one's worries on sb** vaciar las preocupaciones con alguien **II.** *vi* **1.** AUTO (*remove the contents*) descargar **2.** (*be emptied*) vaciar **3.** *inf* (*relieve stress*) tranquilizarse
unlock [ʌn'lɒk, *Am:* -'lɑːk] *vt* **1.** (*release a lock*) liberar **2.** (*release*) abrir **3.** (*solve*) solucionar; (*mystery, riddle*) resolver
unlocked *adj* abierto, -a; *fig* resuelto, -a
unlooked-for [ʌn'lʊktˌfɔːʳ, *Am:* -ˌfɔːr] *adj form* inesperado, -a; (*problem*) inopinado, -a
unlucky [ʌn'lʌki] *adj* **1.** (*unfortunate*) desgraciado, -a; (*at cards, in love*) desafortunado, -a; **to be ~ enough to get a cold** tener la mala suerte de coger un resfriado **2.** *form* (*bringing bad luck*) **to be ~** ser nefasto, -a; (*day*) ser funesto, -a
unman [ʌn'mæn] <-nn-> *vt* **to ~ sb** acobardar a alguien
unmanageable [ʌn'mænɪdʒəbəl] *adj* **1.** (*unwieldy: vehicle, boat*) difícil de manejar, ingobernable **2.** (*incontrollable: person, situation*) incontrolable
unmanned *adj* AVIAT, TECH no tripulado, -a
unmannerly [ʌn'mænəli, *Am:* -ɚli] *adj form* (*behaviour*) desconsiderado, -a; **to be ~** ser descortés
unmarked [ʌn'mɑːkt, *Am:* -mɑːrkt] *adj* **1.** SCHOOL, UNIV (*exam*) sin corregir **2.** (*without mark, stain*) sin marcas
unmarried [ʌn'mærɪd, *Am:* -'mer-] *adj* soltero, -a; ~ **mother** madre *f* soltera
unmask [ʌn'mɑːsk, *Am:* -'mæsk] *vt* **to ~ sb/sth** (**as sb/sth**) *a. fig* desenmascarar a alguien/algo (como alguien/algo)
unmatched [ʌn'mætʃt] *adj* **1.** (*unequalled*) inigualable; **to be ~ by sb** no ser igualado por alguien **2.** (*extremely great*) sin par
unmentionable [ʌn'mentʃənəbl] *adj* inmencionable; (*disease*) indescriptible
unmentioned [ʌn'mentʃənd] *adj* indecible
unmindful [ʌn'maɪndfəl] *adj* **to be ~ of sth** hacer caso omiso de algo
unmistak(e)able [ˌʌnmɪ'steɪkəbl] *adj* inconfundible; (*symptom*) inequívoco, -a
unmitigated [ʌn'mɪtɪgeɪtɪd, *Am:* -'mɪṭəgeɪṭɪd] *adj* (*total*) absoluto, -a; (*disaster*) total; (*contempt*) rotundo, -a; (*evil*) implacable
unmoved [ʌn'muːvd] *adj* impasible
unnamed [ʌn'neɪmd] *adj* no nombrado, -a
unnatural [ʌn'nætʃərəl, *Am:* -ɚəl] *adj* **1.** (*contrary to nature*) poco natural; (*affected*) afectado, -a; (*sexual practices*) perverso, -a **2.** (*not normal*) anormal
unnecessarily [ˌʌn'nesəsərəli, *Am:* -ˌnesə'ser-] *adv* innecesariamente
unnecessary [ʌn'nesəsəri, *Am:* -seri] *adj* **1.** (*not necessary*) innecesario, -a **2.** (*uncalled for*) superfluo, -a
unnerve [ʌn'nɜːv, *Am:* -'nɜːrv] *vt* **to ~ sb** poner nervioso a alguien
unnerving *adj* enervante
unnoticed [ˌʌn'nəʊtɪst, *Am:* -'noʊṭɪst] *adj* desapercibido, -a; **to go ~ that ...** pasar inadvertido que…
unnumbered [ˌʌn'nʌmbəd, *Am:* -bɚd] *adj* **1.** (*not marked with a number: house, page*) sin numerar **2.** *form* (*too many to be counted*) innumerable
UNO ['juːnəʊ, *Am:* -noʊ] *n no pl abbr of* **United Nations Organization** ONU *f*
unobtainable [ˌʌnəb'teɪnəbl] *adj* inalcanzable
unobtrusive [ˌʌnəb'truːsɪv] *adj* (*people*) modesto, -a; (*things*) discreto, -a
unoccupied [ˌʌn'ɒkjəpaɪd, *Am:* -'ɑːkjə-] *adj* **1.** (*uninhabited*) deshabitado, -a **2.** MIL desocupado, -a **3.** (*chair, table*) libre
unofficial [ˌʌnə'fɪʃəl] *adj* no oficial; (*figures*) oficioso, -a; (*capacity*) extraoficial
unorganized [ˌʌn'ɔːgənaɪzd, *Am:* -'ɔːr-] *adj* desorganizado, -a
unorthodox [ʌn'ɔːθədɒks, *Am:* -'ɔːrθədɑːks] *adj* poco ortodoxo, -a; (*approach*) poco convencional
unpack [ʌn'pæk] **I.** *vt* (*a car*) descargar; **to ~ sth** sacar algo **II.** *vi* deshacer el equipaje
unpaid [ʌn'peɪd] *adj* **1.** (*not remunerated*) no remunerado, -a; (*services*) sin sueldo **2.** (*not paid*) pendiente
unpalatable [ʌn'pælətəbl, *Am:* -ṭəbl] *adj a. fig* desagradable
unparalleled [ʌn'pærəleld, *Am:* ʌn'per-] *adj form* sin precedentes
unparliamentary [ʌnˌpɑːlə'mentəri, *Am:* ʌnˌpɑːrlə'menṭɚ-] *adj* impropio, -a de un parlamentario; (*language*) antiparlamentario, -a
unperturbed [ˌʌnpə'tɜːbd, *Am:* ˌʌnpɚ'tɜːrbd] *adj* impasible; **to be ~ by sth** quedarse impertérrito ante algo
unpick [ʌn'pɪk] *vt* **1.** (*undo sewing*) descoser **2.** *fig* (*painstakingly destroy*) deshacer
unplaced [ʌn'pleɪst] *adj* SPORTS no clasificado, -a
unplanned [ʌn'plænd] *adj* espontáneo, -a
unpleasant [ʌn'plezənt] *adj* **1.** (*not pleasing*) desagradable; (*sensation*) repugnante **2.** (*unfriendly*) antipático, -a
unpleasantness *n no pl* **1.** (*quality of being unpleasant*) **the ~** lo desagradable **2.** (*unfriendly feelings*) antipatía *f*
unplug [ʌn'plʌg] <-gg-> *vt* **1.** (*disconnect an electric plug*) desconectar **2.** (*unstop: drain, pipe*) destapar
unplumbed [ʌn'plʌmd] *adj* **1.** (*not understood*) insondable **2.** (*without plumbing*) sin

U

fontanería

unpolished [ʌn'pɒlɪʃt, *Am:* ʌn'pɑːlɪʃt] *adj* **1.** (*not polished*) sin pulir **2.** (*not refined*) poco refinado, -a

unpolluted [ˌʌnpə'luːtɪd, *Am:* ˌʌnpə'luːt̬ɪd] *adj* impoluto, -a; (*water*) no contaminado, -a

unpopular [ʌn'pɒpjələʳ, *Am:* ʌn'pɑːpjələ˞] *adj* **1.** (*not liked*) que gusta poco **2.** (*not widely accepted*) que cae mal; **to be ~ with sb** caer mal a alguien

unpopularity [ʌnˌpɒpjə'lærəti, *Am:* ʌnˌpɑːpjə'lerət̬i] *n no pl* impopularidad *f*

unpractical [ʌn'præktɪkəl] *adj* **1.** (*impractical*) poco práctico, -a **2.** (*lacking skill in practical matters*) desmañado, -a

unpracticed *adj Am*, **unpractised** [ʌn'præktɪst] *adj Brit, form* inexperto, -a; **to be ~ in sth** no tener práctica en algo

unprecedented [ʌn'presɪdentɪd, *Am:* -ədent̬ɪd] *adj* sin precedentes; (*action*) inaudito, -a

unpredictable [ˌʌnprɪ'dɪktəbl] *adj* **1.** (*not predictable*) imprevisible **2.** (*moody*) temperamental

unprejudiced [ʌn'predʒədɪst] *adj* **1.** (*not prejudiced*) imparcial; (*opinion*) objetivo, -a **2.** (*not prejudiced against race*) sin prejuicios

unpremeditated [ˌʌnpriː'medɪteɪtɪd, *Am:* ˌʌnpriː'medɪteɪt̬ɪd] *adj* no planeado, -a; LAW (*crime, murder*) no premeditado, -a

unpretentious [ˌʌnprɪ'tentʃəs] *adj* sin pretensiones

unprincipled [ʌn'prɪntsəpld] *adj* sin principios; (*person*) sin escrúpulos

unproductive [ˌʌnprə'dʌktɪv] *adj* (*business, land*) improductivo, -a; (*negotiations*) infructuoso, -a

unprofessional [ˌʌnprə'feʃənəl] *adj* **1.** (*not meeting professional standards*) indigno, -a de su profesión **2.** (*not to be taken seriously*) poco profesional **3.** (*not conforming to professional ethics*) contrario, -a a la ética profesional; (*conduct*) inexperto, -a

unprofitable [ʌn'prɒfɪtəbl, *Am:* ʌn'prɑːfɪt̬ə-] *adj* **1.** (*not making a profit*) no rentable; (*investment*) infructuoso, -a **2.** (*unproductive*) inútil; (*a day*) improductivo, -a

unprompted [ʌn'prɒmptɪd, *Am:* ʌn'prɑːmp-] *adj* espontáneo, -a; **to do sth ~** hacer algo sin ayuda de nadie

unprovided for [ˌʌnprə'vaɪdɪdˌfɔː, *Am:* -ˌfɔːr] *adj* sin medios de subsistencia; **to leave sb ~** dejar a alguien desamparado

unprovoked [ˌʌnprə'vəʊkt, *Am:* ˌʌnprə'voʊkt] *adj* no provocado, -a

unpublished [ˌʌn'pʌblɪʃt] *adj* inédito, -a

unpunctual [ʌn'pʌŋktʃuəl] *adj* impuntual; (*start*) con retraso

unqualified [ʌn'kwɒlɪfaɪd, *Am:* ʌn'kwɑːlə-] *adj* **1.** (*without qualifications*) sin título; **to be ~ for sth** no estar cualificado para algo **2.** (*unlimited, unreserved*) incondicional; (*denial*) sin restricciones; (*disaster*) absoluto, -a; (*success*) rotundo, -a; (*support*) total

unquestionable [ʌn'kwestʃənəbl] *adj* incuestionable; (*evidence*) inapelable; (*fact*) innegable

unquestionably *adv* indudablemente

unquestioning [ʌn'kwestʃənɪŋ] *adj* incondicional; (*obedience*) ciego, -a

unquote [ʌn'kwəʊt, *Am:* ʌn'kwoʊt] *vi indicar que una cita o otra cosa entre comillas se acaba*

unquoted *adj* FIN que no cotiza en bolsa

unravel [ʌn'rævəl] <-ll-, *Am:* -l-> **I.** *vt* **1.** (*unknit, undo*) deshacer; (*a knot*) desenredar; (*a mystery, secret*) aclarar **2.** (*destroy*) destruir **II.** *vi* deshacerse

unreadable [ʌn'riːdəbl] *adj* **1.** (*illegible*) ininteligible **2.** LIT (*badly written*) ilegible **3.** (*heavy going*) de lectura muy pesada

unreal [ʌn'rɪəl, *Am:* -'riːl] *adj* **1.** (*not real*) irreal **2.** *inf* (*astonishingly good*) impresionante

unrealistic [ʌnˌrɪə'lɪstɪk] *adj* **1.** (*not realistic*) poco realista **2.** LIT, THEAT, CINE (*not appearing convincingly real*) inverosímil

unrealized *adj* **1.** (*not realized*) sin explotar **2.** FIN (*not turned into money*) no realizado, -a

unreasonable [ʌn'riːzənəbl] *adj* **1.** (*not showing reason*) poco razonable **2.** (*unfair*) injusto, -a; (*demands*) excesivo, -a

unreasoning [ʌn'riːzənɪŋ] *adj* irracional

unrecognised [ʌn'rekəgnaɪzd] *adj* no reconocido, -a

unredeemed [ˌʌnrɪ'diːmd] *adj* absoluto, -a; REL irredento, -a

unrefined [ˌʌnrɪ'faɪnd] *adj* **1.** (*not refined: sugar, oil*) sin refinar **2.** (*not socially polished*) poco refinado, -a

unreflecting [ˌʌnrɪ'flektɪŋ] *adj form* irreflexivo, -a

unregistered [ʌn'redʒɪstəd, *Am:* -stə˞d] *adj* (*birth, person*) no registrado, -a; (*mail*) sin certificar

unrelated [ˌʌnrɪ'leɪtɪd, *Am:* -rɪ'leɪt̬ɪd] *adj* no relacionado, -a

unrelenting [ˌʌnrɪ'lentɪŋ, *Am:* -rɪ'lent̬ɪŋ] *adj* **1.** (*not yielding*) implacable; **to be ~ in sth** ser inexorable en algo **2.** (*incessant, not easing: pain, pressure*) incesante; (*rain*) imparable **3.** *form* (*unmerciful*) despiadado, -a

unreliability [ˌʌnrɪlaɪə'bɪlɪti, *Am:* -rɪlaɪə'bɪlət̬i] *n no pl* informalidad *f*

unreliable [ˌʌnrɪ'laɪəbl] *adj* informal

unrelieved [ˌʌnrɪ'liːvd] *adj* **1.** (*depressingly unvarying*) total; (*poverty*) absoluto, -a; (*pressure, stress*) sin alivio; (*tedium*) monótono, -a **2.** (*not helped*) desprovisto, -a de ayuda

unremarkable [ˌʌnrɪ'mɑːkəbl, *Am:* -rɪ'mɑːrk-] *adj* normal

unremitting [ˌʌnrɪ'mɪtɪŋ, *Am:* -rɪ'mɪt̬-] *adj form* sin tregua; (*determination*) incesante; **to be ~ in sth** ser infatigable en algo

unrepeatable [ˌʌnrɪ'piːtəbl, *Am:* -t̬ə-] *adj* (*shocking*) irrepetible; (*sale price*) inmejorable

unrepentant [ˌʌnrɪˈpentənt] *adj* impenitente

unrequited [ˌʌnrɪˈkwaɪtɪd, *Am:* -rɪˈkwaɪṭɪd] *adj* (*love*) no correspondido, -a

unreserved [ˌʌnrɪˈzɜːvd, *Am:* -rɪˈzɜːrvd] *adj* **1.** (*absolute*) incondicional; (*support*) sin reservas **2.** (*not having been reserved: tickets, seats*) no reservado, -a **3.** (*not aloof*) abierto, -a; (*friendliness*) franco, -a

unreservedly *adv* sin reservas; **to apologize** ~ disculparse profusamente

unresolved [ˌʌnrɪˈzɒlvd, *Am:* -rɪˈzɑːlvd] *adj* sin resolver

unrest [ʌnˈrest] *n no pl* descontento *m;* (*ethnic, social*) malestar *m*

unrestrained [ˌʌnrɪˈstreɪnd] *adj* incontrolado, -a; (*criticism, consumerism*) desenfrenado, -a; (*laughter*) desmedido, -a

unrestricted [ˌʌnrɪˈstrɪktɪd] *adj* ilimitado, -a; (*access*) libre

unripe [ʌnˈraɪp] *adj* **1.** (*not ripe*) verde; **to pick sth** ~ recoger algo que no está en su punto **2.** *form* (*immature*) inmaduro, -a

unrivaled *adj Am,* **unrivalled** [ʌnˈraɪvəld] *adj* incomparable

unroll [ʌnˈrəʊl, *Am:* -ˈroʊl] **I.** *vt* **to** ~ **sth** desenrollar algo **II.** *vi* desenrollarse

unruffled [ʌnˈrʌfld] *adj* **1.** (*not nervous, disturbed*) sereno, -a; **to be** ~ **by sb/sth** no inmutarse ante alguien/algo **2.** (*not ruffled up: feathers, fur, hair*) liso, -a

unruly [ʌnˈruːli] <-ier, -iest> *adj* **1.** (*disorderly*) indisciplinado, -a; (*crowd*) difícil de controlar **2.** (*difficult to control: hair*) rebelde; (*children*) revoltoso, -a

unsaddle [ʌnˈsædl] *vt* **1.** (*remove a saddle: a horse*) desensillar **2.** (*unseat: a rider*) derribar

unsafe [ʌnˈseɪf] *adj* **1.** (*dangerous*) inseguro, -a; (*animal*) peligroso, -a; **to declare sth** ~ declarar algo arriesgado **2.** (*in danger*) en peligro **3.** *Brit* LAW (*likely not to stand*) no válido, -a

unsaid [ʌnˈsed] **I.** *vt pt, pp of* **unsay II.** *adj form* sin decir; **to leave sth** ~ callarse algo; **to be better left** ~ mejor no hablar

unsalaried *adj* sin sueldo; (*position*) no remunerado, -a

unsaleable [ˌʌnˈseɪləbl] *adj* invendible

unsatisfactory [ʌnˌsætɪsˈfæktəri, *Am:* ʌnˌsæṭ-] *adj* **1.** (*not satisfactory*) insatisfactorio, -a; (*answer*) poco convincente; (*service*) poco satisfactorio, -a **2.** SCHOOL (*grade*) deficiente

unsatisfied [ʌnˈsætɪsfaɪd, *Am:* -ˈsæṭ-] *adj* **1.** (*not content*) insatisfecho, -a **2.** (*not convinced*) no convencido, -a; **sth leaves sb** ~ algo deja a alguien descontento **3.** (*not sated*) no saciado, -a

unsavory *adj Am, Aus,* **unsavoury** [ʌnˈseɪvəri] *adj Brit, Aus* **1.** (*unpleasant to the taste, smell*) desagradable **2.** (*disgusting*) repugnante **3.** (*socially offensive*) repulsivo, -a; (*reputation*) indeseable

unsay [ʌnˈseɪ] *irr vt* **to** ~ **sth** desdecirse de algo ►**what's said cannot be unsaid** *prov* lo dicho dicho está *prov*

unscathed [ʌnˈskeɪðd] *adj* ileso, -a

unscheduled [ʌnˈʃedjuːld, *Am:* -ˈskedʒʊld] *adj* no programado, -a; (*train*) no previsto, -a

unschooled [ʌnˈskuːld] *adj form* **1.** (*uninstructed*) no instruido, -a; **to be** ~ **in sth** *fig* no estar cultivado en algo **2.** (*untrained: horse*) no entrenado, -a

unscreened *adj* **1.** (*not checked*) sin revisar **2.** (*not shown on a screen*) sin aparecer en pantalla

unscrew [ʌnˈskruː] **I.** *vt* **1.** (*screw*) destornillar **2.** (*lid*) desenroscar **II.** *vi* (*screw*) destornillarse

unscripted [ʌnˈskrɪptɪd] *adj* espontáneo, -a; (*speech*) improvisado, -a

unscrupulous [ʌnˈskruːpjələs] *adj* sin escrúpulos; (*dealings, methods*) poco honesto, -a

unseal [ʌnˈsiːl] *vt* **1.** (*open: a letter*) abrir **2.** (*tell: a secret*) desvelar

unsealed *adj* **1.** (*not sealed*) desellado, -a **2.** (*open*) abierto, -a

unseat [ʌnˈsiːt] *vt* **1.** (*remove from power*) derrocar **2.** (*throw: a rider*) derribar

unsecured [ˌʌnsɪˈkjʊəd, *Am:* -ˈkjʊrd] *adj* **1.** FIN (*stock*) no garantizado, -a; (*loan*) sin aval **2.** (*unfastened*) no sujeto, -a

unseeing [ʌnˈsiːɪŋ] *adj form* ciego, -a; **to look at sb with** ~ **eyes** *fig* mirar a alguien sin verlo

unseemly [ʌnˈsiːmli] *adj form* impropio, -a; (*behaviour*) indecoroso, -a

unseen [ʌnˈsiːn] *adj* (*not seen by sb*) sin ser visto, -a; **to do sth** ~ hacer algo inadvertidamente; **sight** ~ a ciegas

unselfish [ʌnˈselfɪʃ] *adj* generoso, -a

unserviceable [ʌnˈsɜːvɪsəbl, *Am:* -ˈsɜːr-] *adj* inservible; (*appliances*) inutilizable

unsettle [ʌnˈsetl, *Am:* -ˈseṭ-] *vt* **1.** (*make nervous*) **to** ~ **sb** alterar a alguien **2.** COM (*make unstable: the market*) desestabilizar

unsettled [ˌʌnˈsetld, *Am:* -ˈseṭ-] *adj* **1.** (*changeable*) cambiante; (*period*) agitado, -a; (*weather*) inestable **2.** (*troubled*) inquieto, -a **3.** (*unresolved: issue, question*) no resuelto, -a **4.** (*queasy, nauseaus: stomach*) revuelto, -a **5.** (*without settlers*) no colonizado, -a

unsettling *adj* **1.** (*causing nervousness*) inquietante; CINE (*image*) desestabilizador(a) **2.** (*causing disruption*) perturbador(a); COM variable

unshak(e)able [ʌnˈʃeɪkəbl] *adj* inquebrantable

unshaved *adj,* **unshaven** [ʌnˈʃeɪvən] *adj* sin afeitar

unshod [ʌnˈʃɒd, *Am:* -ˈʃɑːd] *adj form* descalzo, -a

unshrinkable [ʌnˈʃrɪŋkəbl] *adj* que no encoge

unshrinking [ʌnˈʃrɪŋkɪŋ] *adj fig* impávido, -a; ~ **courage** valor *m* impávido; **to be** ~ **in the face of sth** quedarse impávido ante algo

unsightly [ʌn'saɪtli] <-ier, -iest> *adj* feo, -a

unsigned [ʌn'saɪnd] *adj* sin firmar

unskilled [ʌn'skɪld] *adj* **1.** (*not skilled*) no cualificado, -a; **to be ~ in** (**doing**) **sth** no estar cualificado para (hacer) algo **2.** (*not requiring skill*) no especializado, -a; **~ job** puesto *m* de trabajo no especializado

unsociable [ʌn'səʊʃəbl, *Am:* -'soʊ-] *adj* insociable

unsocial [ʌn'səʊʃəl, *Am:* -'soʊ-] *adj* **1.** (*unsociable*) insociable **2.** *Brit* (*outside of the standard working day*) fuera del horario laboral; **~ hours** horas *fpl* extras

unsold [ʌn'səʊld, *Am:* -'soʊld] *adj* sin vender

unsolicited [ˌʌnsə'lɪsɪtɪd, *Am:* -t̬ɪd] *adj* no solicitado, -a

unsolved [ʌn'sɒlvd, *Am:* -'sɑːlvd] *adj* sin resolver

unsophisticated [ˌʌnsə'fɪstɪkeɪtɪd, *Am:* -təkeɪt̬ɪd] *adj* **1.** (*simple*) sencillo, -a; **~ pleasure** placer *m* sencillo **2.** (*simple: a person*) ingenuo, -a; (*a taste*) cándido, -a **3.** (*uncomplicated: a machine*) simple

unsound [ʌn'saʊnd] *adj* **1.** (*weak, unstable*) débil **2.** (*unreliable*) de no fiar; **to be ~ on sth** no ser de fiar en algo **3.** (*not financially stable*) inestable **4.** (*not valid*) erróneo, -a; **~ argument** argumento *m* no válido; **~ judgement** juicio *m* equivocado; **~ police evidence** prueba *f* policial falsa **5.** (*unhealthy*) no sano, -a; **to be of ~ mind** ser de mente enfermiza

unsparing [ʌn'speərɪŋ, *Am:* -'sper-] *adj* **1.** (*merciless*) despiadado, -a **2.** *form* (*lavish*) pródigo, -a; **to be ~ in one's efforts** no escatimar en esfuerzos

unspeakable [ʌn'spiːkəbl] *adj* indecible; **~ atrocities** atrocidades *fpl* incalificables

unspecified [ʌn'spesɪfaɪd] *adj* **1.** (*not specified*) no especificado, -a **2.** (*not named*) sin nombre

unspoiled [ʌn'spɔɪlt, *Am:* -'spɔɪld] *adj* natural

unspoken [ʌn'spəʊkən, *Am:* -spoʊ-] *adj* tácito, -a

unstable [ʌn'steɪbl] *adj* **1.** (*not stable*) inestable; *fig* voluble; **~ chair** silla *f* poco firme **2.** (*not emotionally stable*) volátil; **emotionally ~** no estable emocionalmente

unsteady [ʌn'stedi] *adj* (*chair*) poco firme; (*hand*) tembloroso, -a

unstressed [ʌn'strest] *adj* LING átono, -a

unstuck [ʌn'stʌk] *adj* **to come ~** (*be no longer stuck*) despegarse; *inf* (*fail*) fracasar

unstudied [ʌn'stʌdɪd] *adj form* natural; **~ naturalness** naturalidad *f* sin afectación; **~ response** respuesta *f* no estudiada

unsubstantial [ˌʌnsəb'stæntʃəl] *adj* **1.** (*not substantial*) insustancial; **~ improvements** mejoras *fpl* no sustanciales **2.** (*not significant*) insignificante

unsubstantiated [ˌʌnsəb'stæntʃieɪtɪd, *Am:* -'stæntʃieɪt̬ɪd] *adj* no probado, -a

unsuccessful [ˌʌnsək'sesfəl] *adj* fracasado, -a; **~ candidate** candidato, -a *m, f* fracasado, -a; **to be ~ in sth** fracasar en algo

unsuitable [ʌn'suːtəbl, *Am:* -'suːt̬ə-] *adj* inapropiado, -a; **~ clothes** ropa *f* inapropiada; **~ moment** momento *m* inoportuno; **to be ~ for sth** ser inapropiado para algo; **to be ~ to the occasion** no ajustarse a la ocasión

unsuited [ʌn'suːtɪd, *Am:* -'suːt̬ɪd] *adj* inapropriado, -a; **to be ~ to** [*o* **for**] **sth** no ser apropiado para algo; **to be ~ to each other** ser incompatibles

unsullied [ʌn'sʌlɪd] *adj form* inmaculado, -a; **to be ~ by sth** no estar corrompido por algo

unsung [ʌn'sʌŋ] *adj* olvidado, -a; **the ~ hero** el héroe desconocido

unsure [ʌn'ʃʊəʳ, *Am:* -'ʃʊr] *adj* inseguro, -a; **to be ~ how/what ...** no ser seguro cómo/qué...; **to be ~ about sth** no estar seguro de algo; **to be ~ of oneself** no estar seguro de uno mismo

unsuspecting [ˌʌnsə'spektɪŋ] *adj* confiado, -a; **all ~** nada suspicaz

unsustainable [ˌʌnsə'steɪnəbl] *adj* insostenible

unswerving [ˌʌn'swɜːvɪŋ, *Am:* -'swɜːr-] *adj* (*unshakeable*) inquebrantable; **to be ~ in sth** ser firme en algo

unsympathetic [ˌʌnsɪmpə'θetɪk, *Am:* -'θet̬-] *adj* poco comprensivo, -a

untangle [ʌn'tæŋgl] *vt* **1.** (*hair*) desenredar **2.** (*mystery*) desentrañar

untapped [ˌʌn'tæpt] *adj* **1.** (*not yet tapped*) sin explotar **2.** (*not bugged: line, telephone*) no intervenido, -a **3.** (*not tapped: a keg*) no abierto, -a

untaxed [ˌʌn'tækst] *adj* libre de impuestos; **~ income** FIN ingresos *mpl* no sujetos a contribuciones

untenable [ˌʌn'tenəbl] *adj* insostenible

untenanted [ˌʌn'tenəntɪd, *Am:* -t̬ɪd] *adj* desocupado, -a

untested [ʌn'testɪd] *adj* no probado, -a

unthinkable [ʌn'θɪŋkəbl] **I.** *adj* **1.** (*unimaginable*) inconcebible **2.** (*shocking*) impensable **II.** *n no pl* **the ~** lo inconcebible

unthinking [ʌn'θɪŋkɪŋ] *adj* **1.** (*thoughtless*) irreflexivo, -a **2.** (*unintentional*) no intencionado, -a

unthought-of [ʌn'θɔːtɒv, *Am:* -'θɑːtɑːv] *adj* inimaginable

untidiness [ʌn'taɪdɪnɪs] *n no pl* desorden *m*

untidy [ʌn'taɪdi] <-ier, -iest> *adj* **1.** (*not neat*) desaseado, -a; (*room*) desordenado, -a; (*appearance*) desaliñado, -a **2.** (*not orderly*) sin método; **~ thesis** tesis *f* carente de método; **to have an ~ mind** tener una mente caótica

untie [ˌʌn'taɪ] <-y-> *vt* desatar; **to ~ a boat** desamarrar un bote; **to ~ a knot** deshacer un nudo; **to ~ one's shoelaces** desatarse los cordones

until [ən'tɪl] **I.** *adv temporal* hasta; **~ then**

hasta entonces; ~ **such time as sb does sth** hasta el momento en que alguien haga algo **II.** *conj* hasta que *+subj;* ~ **he comes** hasta que venga; **not ~ sb does sth** no hasta que alguien haga algo; **not ~ he's here** no antes de que él esté aquí

untimely [ʌn'taɪmli] *adj* **1.**(*premature*) prematuro, -a; **sb's ~ death** la muerte prematura de alguien **2.**(*inopportune*) inoportuno, -a

unto ['ʌntuː] *prep* HIST *s.* **to**

untold [ˌʌn'təʊld, *Am:* -'toʊld] *adj* **1.**(*immense*) incalculable; ~ **damage** daños *mpl* incalculables; **in ~ misery** en la más pura miseria **2.**(*not told*) inédito, -a, nunca contado, -a

untouched [ˌʌn'tʌtʃt] *adj* **1.**(*not affected*) intacto, -a; **to leave sth ~** dejar algo intacto **2.**(*not touched*) no tocado, -a; ~ **by human hands** no manipulado **3.**(*not eaten*) no comido, -a; **to leave a meal ~** dejar una comida sin tocar **4.**(*not emotionally moved*) insensible

untoward [ˌʌntə'wɔːd, *Am:* ˌʌn'tɔːrd] *adj form* desfavorable; ~ **side effects** efectos *mpl* secundarios adversos

untrained [ʌn'treɪnd] *adj* **1.**(*skill*) no formado, -a **2.**(*animals*) no adiestrado, -a

untransferable [ˌʌntrænts'fɜːrəbl] *adj* LAW intransferible

untranslat(e)able [ˌʌntrænt'sleɪtəbl, *Am:* -træn'sleɪt̬əbl] *adj* intraducible

untreated [ʌn'triːtɪd, *Am:* -'triːt̬ɪd] *adj* no tratado, -a; ~ **sewage** aguas *fpl* residuales no tratadas; **to remain ~** MED seguir sin estar tratado

untried [ʌn'traɪd] *adj* **1.**(*not tested*) no probado, -a **2.** LAW no procesado, -a

untroubled [ʌn'trʌbld] *adj* tranquilo, -a; **they seemed ~ about her decision** su decisión no parecía preocuparles

untrue [ʌn'truː] *adj* **1.**(*not true*) falso, -a **2.**(*not faithful*) infiel; **to be ~ to sb/sth** ser infiel a alguien/a algo

untrustworthy [ʌn'trʌstˌwɜːði, *Am:* -ˌwɜːr-] *adj* indigno, -a de confianza

untruth [ʌn'truːθ] *n* **1.**(*lie*) mentira *f;* **to tell an ~** contar una mentira **2.** *no pl* (*quality of being untrue*) falsedad *f*

untruthful [ʌn'truːθfəl] *adj* **1.**(*not truthful*) falso, -a **2.**(*tending to tell lies*) mentiroso, -a

unturned [ˌʌn'tɜːnd, *Am:* -'tɜːrnd] *adj* inamovible; (*soil*) inclinado, -a

untutored [ˌʌn'tjuːtəd, *Am:* -'tuːt̬ɚd] *adj form* indocto, -a; **to be ~ in sth** estar poco instruido en algo

unused [ʌn'juːzd] *adj* **1.**(*not in use*) no usado, -a; (*talent, energy*) malgastado, -a; ~ **good** bien *m* sin estrenar **2.**(*never having been used: clothes*) nuevo, -a

unused to [ʌn'juːst tʊ] *adj* (*not accustomed*) **to be ~ sth** no estar acostumbrado a algo; **to be ~ sb doing sth** no estar acostumbrado a que alguien haga algo

unusual [ʌn'juːʒəl, *Am:* -ʒuəl] *adj* **1.**(*atypically positive*) inusitado, -a **2.**(*not usual*) inusual; **to be ~ for sb** ser poco usual en alguien **3.**(*atypically negative*) insólito, -a; ~ **taste** gusto *m* extraño

unusually *adv* extraordinariamente; ~ **for sb** inusual para alguien

unutterable [ʌn'ʌtərəbl, *Am:* -'ʌt̬-] *adj form* indecible; ~ **suffering** sufrimento *m* indecible

unvarnished [ʌn'vɑːnɪʃt, *Am:* -'vɑːr-] *adj* sin barnizar; ~ **furniture** muebles *mpl* sin barnizar; **the ~ truth** *fig* la pura verdad

unveil [ˌʌn'veɪl] **I.** *vt fig* **1.**(*expose*) quitar el velo **2.**(*present to the public*) presentar **II.** *vi* quitarse el velo

unversed [ˌʌn'vɜːst, *Am:* -'vɜːrst] *adj* **to be ~ in sth** ser poco versado en algo

unwaged [ʌn'weɪdʒd] **I.** *adj Brit* sin sueldo; ~ **work** trabajo *m* no remunerado **II.** *n* **the ~** *no pl, Brit* los que no tienen sueldo

unwanted [ʌn'wɒntɪd, *Am:* -'wɑːnt̬ɪd] *adj* no deseado, -a

unwarranted [ʌn'wɒrəntɪd, *Am:* -'wɔːrənt̬ɪd] *adj* **1.**(*not justified*) injustificado, -a; ~ **criticism** crítica *f* injustificada **2.**(*not authorized*) no autorizado, -a

unwavering [ʌn'weɪvərɪŋ] *adj* inquebrantable; **to be ~ in one's support for sb** dar apoyo incondicional a alguien

unwed [ʌn'wed] *adj form* soltero, -a

unwelcome [ʌn'welkəm] *adj* (*guest*) importuno, -a; (*visit*) inoportuno, -a; (*information*) desagradable; **we were made to feel rather ~** nos hicieron sentir que molestábamos

unwell [ʌn'wel] *adj* indispuesto, -a; **to feel ~** sentirse mal

unwieldy [ʌn'wiːldi] *adj* **1.**(*cumbersome*) abultado, -a **2.**(*difficult to manage*) difícil de manejar; ~ **system** sistema *m* difícil de manejar

unwilling [ʌn'wɪlɪŋ] *adj* no dispuesto, -a; **to be ~ to do sth** no estar dispuesto a hacer algo; **to be ~ for sb to do sth** no querer que alguien haga algo

unwillingly *adv* de mala gana

unwind [ʌn'waɪnd] *irr* **I.** *vt* desenrollar **II.** *vi* **1.**(*unroll*) desenrollarse **2.** *fig* (*relax*) relajarse

unwise [ʌn'waɪz] *adj* imprudente

unwitting [ʌn'wɪtɪŋ, *Am:* -'wɪt̬-] *adj* **1.**(*unaware*) inconsciente **2.**(*unintentional*) no intencional

unwittingly *adv* **1.**(*without realizing*) inconscientemente **2.**(*unintentionally*) de forma no intencionada

unwonted [ʌn'wəʊntɪd, *Am:* -'wɔːnt̬ɪd] *adj form* insólito, -a

unworkable [ʌn'wɜːkəbl, *Am:* -'wɜːr-] *adj* impracticable

unworldly [ʌn'wɜːldli, *Am:* -'wɜːrld-] *adj* **1.**(*spiritually-minded*) espiritual **2.**(*naive*) ingenuo, -a **3.**(*unearthly*) poco mundano, -a

unworthy [ʌn'wɜːði, *Am:* -'wɜːr-] <-ier, -iest> *adj* **1.**(*not worthy*) que no merece la pena; **to be ~ of interest** no ser merecedor de la mínima atención **2.** (*discreditable, contemptible*) indigno, -a

unwrap [ʌn'ræp] <-pp-> *vt* **1.** (*remove wrapping*) desenvolver **2.** *fig* (*open, reveal*) sacar a la luz

unwritten [ʌn'rɪtən] *adj* **1.** (*not official*) ~ **agreement** pacto *m* verbal; ~ **law** LAW ley *f* basada en el derecho consuetudinario **2.** (*not written down*) no escrito, -a; ~ **traditions** tradiciones *fpl* no escritas

unyielding [ʌn'ji:ldɪŋ] *adj* **1.** (*stubborn, obstinate*) inflexible; ~ **opposition** oposición *f* firme; **to be ~ in sth** ser inflexible en algo **2.** (*physically hard, firm*) ~ **ground** terreno *m* firme; **to be ~** ser duro

unzip [ʌn'zɪp] <-pp-> *vt* abrir la cremallera de

up [ʌp] **I.** *adv* **1.** (*movement*) (hacia) arriba; ~ **here/there** aquí/allí arriba; **to look ~** mirar (hacia) arriba; **to stand/get ~** ponerse de pie/levantarse; **to go ~** ir hacia arriba; **to throw sth ~** lanzar algo hacia arriba; **to jump ~** saltar hacia arriba; (**stand**) **~!** ¡levántate!; **on the way ~** de subida **2.** (*to another point*) ~ **in Dublin** allá en Dublin; **to go ~ to Scotland** irse a Escocia **3.** (*more volume or intensity*) **apples are ~** han subido las manzanas; **the river is ~** ha subido el río; **the tide is ~** la marea está alta; **to come ~** subir **4.** (*position*) **to be ~ all night** no dormir en toda la noche; **to jump ~ on sth** saltar sobre algo; **with one's head ~** con la cabeza en alto **5.** *fig* (*state*) **to be well ~ in sth** estar fuerte en algo; **to be ~ at the top of sth** estar en lo más alto de algo; **to feel ~ to sth** sentirse capaz de algo; **this isn't ~ to much** esto no vale gran cosa **6.** (*limit*) ~ **to** hasta; ~ **to here** hasta aquí; ~ **to now** hasta ahora; ~ **to £100** hasta £100; **time's ~** se acabó el tiempo; **when 5 hours were ~** cuando pasaron 5 horas; **from the age of 18 ~** a partir de los 18 años (de edad); **to have it ~ to one's ears** (**with sth**) *fig* estar hasta la coronilla (de algo) **7.** (*responsibility of*) **it's ~ to you** tú decides; **it's ~ to me to decide** me toca a mí decidir **8.** SPORTS **to be 2 goals ~** ir ganando por 2 goles **9.** INFOR, TECH en función ►**to be ~ against sth/sb** habérselas con algo/alguien; ~ **and down** arriba y abajo; **to walk ~ and down** caminar de arriba a abajo; **what's ~?** ¿qué hay de nuevo?; **what's ~ with him?** ¿qué le pasa?; ~ **with the king!** ¡viva el rey! **II.** *prep* **1.** (*at top of*) encima de; **to climb ~ a tree** subir arriba de un árbol **2.** (*higher*) **to go ~ the stairs** subir las escaleras; **to run ~ the slope** correr cuesta arriba; **to row ~ the river** remar río arriba; **to go ~ and down sth** ir de arriba a abajo de algo **3.** (*along*) **to go ~ the street** ir por la calle **III.** *n* **~s and downs** altibajos *mpl;* **to be on the ~ and ~** *Brit* estar cada vez mejor **IV.** <-pp-> *vi inf* **to ~ and** +*infin* ponerse de repente a +*infin* **V.** <-pp-> *vt* subir **VI.** *adj* **1.** (*position: building*) levantado, -a; (*tent*) montado, -a; (*flag*) izado, -a; (*curtains, picture*) colgado, -a; (*hand*) alzado, -a; (*blinds*) subido, -a; (*person*) levantado, -a, a pie **2.** (*under repair: road*) abierto, -a **3.** (*healthy*) bien; **to be ~ and about** [*o* **around**] estar en buena forma **4.** (*ready*) **to be ~ for** (**doing**) **sth** estar listo para (hacer) algo; ~ **for sale/discussion/trial** a la venta/a discusión/en juicio

up-and-coming ['ʌpən'kʌmɪŋ] *adj* joven y prometedor(a)

upbeat ['ʌpbi:t] **I.** *n* MUS tiempo *m* débil **II.** *adj inf* optimista; **to be ~ about sth** ser optimista respecto a algo

upbraid [ˌʌp'breɪd] *vt form* **to ~ sb** (**for sth**) reprender a alguien (por algo)

upbringing ['ʌpbrɪŋɪŋ] *n no pl* educación *f;* **to have some kind of ~** tener algún tipo de educación

upcoming ['ʌpˌkʌmɪŋ] *adj* venidero, -a

up-country [ˌʌp'kʌntri, *Am:* 'ʌpkʌn-] **I.** *adv* tierra adentro **II.** *adj* del interior; ~ **tribesmen** tribus *fpl* del interior **III.** *n* interior *m*

update¹ [ʌp'deɪt] *vt* (*bring up to date*) poner al día; INFOR actualizar

update² ['ʌpdeɪt] *n* (*instance of updating*) puesta *f* al día; INFOR actualización *f;* **to give sb an ~** (**on sth**) poner a alguien al día (en algo)

updating *n* actualización *f*

updraught ['ʌpdrɑ:ft] *n* corriente *f* ascendiente

upend [ʌp'end] *vt* **to ~ sb** volcar a alguien; **to ~ sth** poner vertical algo

upfront ['ʌpfrʌnt] *adj inf* **1.** (*open, frank*) abierto, -a; **to be ~ and honest** ser franco y sincero; **to be ~ about sth** ser franco sobre algo **2.** (*advance*) por adelantado; ~ **payment** pago *m* por adelantado

upgrade¹ [ʌp'greɪd] *vt* **1.** (*improve quality*) mejorar la calidad de; INFOR mejorar; (*hardware, software*) modernizar **2.** (*raise in rank*) **to ~ sb** (**to sth**) ascender a alguien (a algo); **to ~ sth** valorar en más algo; **to ~ a job** asignar un grado más alto a un puesto de trabajo

upgrade² ['ʌpgreɪd] *n* **1.** INFOR, TECH, COM (*instance of upgrading*) mejora *f;* **a software ~** una modernización del software **2.** *Am* (*slope*) cuesta *f* **3.** *Am* (*be improving*) **to be on the ~** estar progresando; (*business, sales*) ir mejorando; MED ir recuperándose

upgradeable *adj* modernizable

upgrading *n* **1.** *no pl* (*act of improvement*) mejoramiento *m;* INFOR modernización *f* **2.** (*raising of rank*) subida *f* de rango

upheaval [ʌp'hi:vəl] *n* **1.** *no pl* (*condition of violent change*) sacudida *f;* **political ~** convulsión *f* política **2.** (*instance of violent change*) cataclismo *m* **3.** GEO (*violent upward push*) solevamiento *m;* ~ **of the earth's crust** solevamiento *m* de la corteza terrestre

uphill [ʌp'hɪl] **I.** *adv* (*in an ascending direction*) cuesta arriba; **to run/walk ~** correr/

caminar cuesta arriba II. *adj* 1. (*sloping upward*) ascendente 2. (*difficult*) difícil; ~ **battle** *fig* batalla *f* ardua

uphold [ʌp'həʊld, *Am:* -'hoʊld] *irr vt* 1. (*support, maintain*) sostener; **to ~ the law** defender la ley; **to ~ the principle that ...** defender el principio de que...; **to ~ traditions** apoyar las tradiciones 2. LAW (*confirm*) **to ~ a verdict** confirmar un veredicto

upholster [ʌp'həʊlstəʳ, *Am:* -'hoʊlstɚ] *vt* **to ~ sth** (**in sth**) tapizar algo (de algo)

upholsterer *n* tapicero, -a *m, f*

upholstery *n no pl* 1. (*covering for furniture*) tapizado *m;* **leather ~** tapizado de piel 2. (*act of upholstering*) tapicería *f*

UPI *n Am abbr of* **United Press International** UPI *f*

upkeep ['ʌpki:p] *n no pl* 1. (*maintain in good condition*) conservación *f* 2. (*cost*) gastos *mpl* de mantenimiento 3. (*maintenance*) mantenimiento *m*

upland ['ʌplənd] I. *adj* de la meseta; ~ **plain** llanura *f* de la meseta; ~ **village** pueblo *m* de la meseta II. *n* **the ~s** las tierras altas

uplift¹ [ʌp'lɪft] *vt* 1. (*raise up*) elevar 2. (*inspire*) inspirar; **to ~ sb's heart** edificar el alma de uno

uplift² ['ʌplɪft] *n* 1. GEO (*raising*) sustentación *f* 2. (*spiritual/mental elevation, inspiration*) inspiración *f;* **moral ~** edificación *f* moral; **to give moral ~ to sb** edificar moralmente a alguien

uplifting [ʌp'lɪftɪŋ] *adj* positivo, -a

upload ['ʌpləʊd, *Am:* -oʊd] *vt* INFOR subir

up-market ['ʌp'mɑ:kɪt, *Am:* 'ʌpˌmɑ:r-] I. *adj* (*goods*) superior; ~ **consumers** consumidores *mpl* con poder adquisitivo; ~ **products** productos *mpl* de categoría II. *adv* en la selección superior; **to go ~** buscar clientela de poder adquisitivo

upon [ə'pɒn, *Am:* -'pɑ:n] *prep form* 1. (*on top of*) sobre, encima de 2. (*around*) en; **a ring ~ the finger** un anillo en el dedo 3. (*hanging on*) **to hang ~ the wall** colgar en la pared 4. (*at time of*) ~ **her arrival** a su llegada; ~ **this** a continuación, acto seguido 5. (*long ago*) **once ~ a time** érase una vez

upper ['ʌpəʳ, *Am:* -ɚ] I. *adj* (*further up*) superior; **the Upper House** POL la Cámara Alta II. *n* 1. (*of shoe*) pala *f;* **leather ~s** palas *fpl* de piel 2. *inf* (*drug*) estimulante *m*

upper case *n no pl* TYPO letra *f* mayúscula **upper class** <-es> *n* clase *f* alta **upper-class** *adj* de clase alta; **in ~ circles** en círculos de la alta sociedad **upper-cut** *n* SPORTS gancho *m* **upper deck** *n* (*of ship*) cubierta *f* superior; (*of bus*) piso *m* superior **uppermost** I. *adj* (*highest*) más alto, -a; **to be ~ in one's mind** ocupar el primer lugar en sus pensamientos II. *adv* boca arriba; **to put sth ~** poner algo cara arriba

uppish ['ʌpɪʃ] *adj,* **uppity** ['ʌpəti, *Am:* -t̬i] *adj inf* chulo, -a; **to get ~** ponerse chulo

upright ['ʌpraɪt] I. *adj* 1. (*post, rod*) vertical 2. (*upstanding*) recto, -a; (*citizen*) honrado, -a II. *adv* verticalmente; **to stand ~** permanecer erguido; **to sit bolt ~** estar muy derecho en la silla III. *n* 1. (*upright piano*) piano *m* vertical 2. TECH montante *m* 3. SPORTS poste *m*

uprising ['ʌpraɪzɪŋ] *n* alzamiento *m;* **to crush an ~** aplastar una sublevación

uproar ['ʌprɔ:ʳ, *Am:* -rɔ:r] *n no pl* alboroto *m,* batifondo *m CSur,* tinga *f Méx;* **to cause an ~** provocar un escándalo

uproarious [ʌp'rɔ:rɪəs] *adj* tumultoso, -a; (*joke*) divertidísimo, -a; **to laugh ~ly** morirse de risa

uproot [ˌʌp'ru:t] *vt* 1. (*extract from ground*) arrancar de raíz 2. (*remove from one's home*) desarraigar; **to ~ oneself** perder las raíces

upset¹ [ʌp'set] I. *vt irr* 1. (*overturn*) derrumbar; (*boat, canoe*) volcar 2. (*unsettle*) trastornar; (*distress*) afligir; **to ~ oneself** afligirse 3. (*throw into disorder*) alborotar 4. (*cause pain*) hacer daño a, trastornar II. *adj* 1. (*overturned, up-ended*) trastornado, -a 2. (*disquieted*) perturbado, -a; (*distressed*) acongojado, -a; (*sad*) apenado, -a; **to get ~ about sth** enfadarse por algo; **to be ~ (that) ...** estar enfadado (porque)...; **don't be ~** no te enfades 3. *inf* (*bilious*) **to have an ~ stomach** tener el estómago revuelto

upset² ['ʌpset] *n* 1. *no pl* (*trouble*) problema *m;* (*argument, quarrel*) discusión *f;* (*psychological problems*) trastorno *m;* **to have an ~** tener una discusión; **to be an ~ to sb** ser un contratiempo para alguien 2. (*great surprise*) gran sorpresa *f* 3. *inf* (*disorder*) **stomach ~** trastorno *m* estomacal

upset price *n Am* COM precio *m* mínimo

upsetting *adj* triste; **an ~ piece of news** una noticia desagradable

upshot ['ʌpʃɒt, *Am:* -ʃɑ:t] *n no pl* resultado *m;* **the ~ (of it all) is that ...** el resultado (de todo eso) es que...

upside down [ˌʌpsaɪd 'daʊn] I. *adj* 1. (*reversed in vertical axis*) al revés; **to be ~** (*pictures*) estar al revés 2. (*confused*) muy confuso, -a; **an ~ world** un mundo al revés; **the house was ~** la casa estaba patas arriba II. *adv* al revés; **to turn sth ~** poner algo del revés

upstage¹ ['ʌpsteɪdʒ] I. *adj* THEAT del fondo de la escena; ~ **position** posición *f* al fondo de la escena II. *adv* en el fondo de la escena; **to go ~** ir hacia el fondo de la escena

upstage² [ˌʌp'steɪdʒ] *vt* eclipsar

upstairs [ˌʌp'steəz, *Am:* -'sterz] I. *adj* de arriba; **the ~ rooms** las habitaciones del piso de arriba; **the ~ windows** las ventanas de arriba II. *adv* arriba; **to go ~** ir arriba; **the people who live ~** la gente que vive en el piso de arriba III. *n no pl* (**the**) ~ el piso de arriba

upstanding [ˌʌp'stændɪŋ] *adj form* 1. (*honest*) íntegro, -a 2. (*strong*) **a fine ~ young woman** una mujer de buena apariencia

U

upstart ['ʌpstɑːt, *Am:* -stɑːrt] *n* arribista *mf*
upstate ['ʌpsteɪt] *Am* **I.** *adj* del norte; **in ~ New York** en el norte de Nueva York **II.** *adv* en el norte
upstream [ˌʌp'striːm] **I.** *adj* de las aguas de arriba; **~ pollution** contaminación *f* de las aguas de la zona alta de un río **II.** *adv* aguas arriba; **to swim ~** nadar contra la corriente
upsurge ['ʌpsɜːdʒ, *Am:* -sɜːrdʒ] *n* aumento *m;* **an ~ in sth** un aumento de algo; **the ~ of violence** el resurgir de la violencia; **the ~ of attention** el aumento de la atención
upswing ['ʌpswɪŋ] *n* movimiento *m* hacia arriba; **an ~ in sth** un auge en algo; **an ~ in the economy** una mejora en la economía; **an ~ in exports** un aumento de las exportaciones; **to be on the ~** ir al alza; (*crime, violence*) ir en aumento
uptake ['ʌpteɪk] *n no pl* (*level of absorption*) absorción *f; Brit, Aus* (*level of usage*) consumo *m* ►**to be quick on the ~** *inf* cogerlas al vuelo; **to be slow on the ~** *inf* ser algo torpe
uptight [ʌp'taɪt] *adj inf* tenso, -a; **to be/get ~ (about sth)** estar/ponerse nervioso (por algo)
up-to-date [ˌʌptə'deɪt] *adj* **1.** (*contemporary*) moderno, -a; (*book*) actualizado, -a **2.** (*informed*) al día; **the ~ news** las noticias del día; **to bring sb ~** poner a alguien al corriente
up-to-the-minute ['ʌptəðə'mɪnɪt] *adj* de última hora
uptown [ˌʌp'taʊn, *Am:* 'ʌptaʊn] *Am* **I.** *adj* (*suburbs: north*) del norte; (*suburbs: general*) residencial; **in ~ Manhattan** en los barrios del norte de Manhattan; **an ~ shop** una tienda en los barrios periféricos de la ciudad **II.** *adv* hacia el norte/los barrios periféricos
uptrend ['ʌptrend] *n Am* tendencia *f* al alza; **an ~ in sth** una tendencia alcista en algo
upturn ['ʌptɜːn, *Am:* -tɜːrn] *n* mejora *f;* **the ~ in consumer confidence** ECON el aumento de la confianza del consumidor; **an ~ in the economy** ECON un repunte en la economía
upturned [ˌʌp'tɜːnd, *Am:* -'tɜːrnd] *adj* vuelto, -a hacia arriba; **~ nose** nariz *f* respingona; **with ~ palms** con las palmas hacia arriba
upward ['ʌpwəd, *Am:* -wɚd] **I.** *adj* **1.** (*going upwards in direction*) ascendente; **~ movement** movimiento *m* ascendente; **~ mobility** SOCIOL ascenso *m* social **2.** (*going higher in number*) al alza; **to go ~** ir en aumento **II.** *adv* (hacia) arriba
upwardly *adv* en alza; **~ mobile** que escala posiciones sociales
upwards *adv Brit* (hacia) arriba; **and ~** y más
upward trend *n* tendencia *f* alcista; **~ trend in inflation** ECON tendencia *f* alcista de la inflación
uraemia [jʊə'riːmiə, *Am:* juː'riː-] *n no pl* MED uremia *f*
uranium [jʊə'reɪniəm, *Am:* jʊ-] *n no pl* uranio *m*
Uranus ['jʊərənəs, *Am:* 'jʊrənəs] *n* Urano *m*
urban ['ɜːbən, *Am:* 'ɜːr-] *adj* urbano, -a; **~ area** zona *f* urbana; **~ sprawl** urbanización *f* caótica
urbane [ɜː'beɪn, *Am:* ɜːr-] *adj* fino, -a
urbanise ['ɜːbənaɪz, *Am:* 'ɜːr-] *vt* urbanizar
urbanity [ɜː'bænəti, *Am:* ɜːr'bænət̬i] *n no pl* cortesía *f*
urbanization [ˌɜːbənaɪ'zeɪʃən, *Am:* ˌɜːrbənɪ'-] *n no pl* urbanización *f*
urbanize *vt s.* **urbanise**
urchin ['ɜːtʃɪn, *Am:* 'ɜːr-] *n iron* pilluelo, -a *m, f;* **street ~** golfillo, -a *m, f* callejero, -a
urethra [ˌjʊə'riːθrə, *Am:* ˌjʊ'-] <-s *o* -e> *n* uretra *f*
urge [ɜːdʒ, *Am:* ɜːrdʒ] **I.** *n* (*strong desire*) ansia *f;* (*compulsion*) impulso *m;* PSYCH instinto *m;* **an ~ to do sth** un impulso de hacer algo; **the ~ to express oneself** el deseo de expresarse; **an ~ for power/recognition** un afán de poder/reconocimiento; **an instinctive/irresistible ~** un impulso instintivo/irresistible; **to feel an irresistible ~ to do sth** sentir un deseo irrefrenable de hacer algo; **an uncontrollable ~** un deseo incontrolable; **to control/repress an ~** controlar/reprimir un impulso; **sexual ~** deseo *m* sexual **II.** *vt* **1.** (*push, speed up, move*) empujar; **to ~ sb/sth away from sth** apartar a alguien/algo de algo **2.** (*strongly encourage*) fomentar; **to ~ sb to do sth** instar a alguien a hacer algo; **to ~ sb into sth** incitar a alguien a algo **3.** (*recommend*) recomendar; **to ~ caution on sb** recomendar precaución a alguien
◆**urge on** *vt* **1.** (*encourage*) **to urge sb on (to do sth)** animar a alguien (a hacer algo) **2.** (*persuade*) **to urge self-discipline on sb** recomendar a alguien autodisciplina
◆**urge upon** *vt form s.* **urge on**
urgency ['ɜːdʒənsi, *Am:* 'ɜːr-] *n no pl* **1.** (*top priority, imperativeness*) urgencia *f;* **to be a matter of (great) ~** ser un asunto de (gran) prioridad; **to realize/stress the ~ of sth** darse cuenta de/remarcar la prioridad de algo; **to show a sense of ~** mostrar un sentido de perentoriedad **2.** (*insistence, clamouressness*) insistencia *f*
urgent ['ɜːdʒənt, *Am:* 'ɜːr-] *adj* **1.** (*imperative, crucial: appeal, plea*) urgente; **~ need** necesidad *f* perentoria; **an ~ request** una petición urgente; **to be in ~ need of sth** necesitar algo urgentemente **2.** *form* (*insistent, pleading*) insistente
urgently *adv* **1.** (*very necessarily*) urgentemente **2.** (*earnestly pleading, beggingly*) insistentemente
urinal [jʊə'raɪnel, *Am:* 'jʊrənəl] *n* **1.** urinario *m* **2.** (*vessel*) orinal *m*
urinary ['jʊərɪnəri, *Am:* 'jʊrəneri] *adj* urinario, -a; **~ diseases** enfermedades *fpl* urinarias; **~ incontinence** incontinencia *f* urinaria
urinate ['jʊərɪneɪt, *Am:* 'jʊrəneɪt] *vi* ori-

nar(se)

urine ['jʊərɪn, *Am:* 'jʊrɪn] *n no pl* orina *f*

URL *n* INFOR *abbr of* **universal resource locator** URL *f*

urn [ɜːn, *Am:* ɜːrn] *n* **1.** urna *f* **2.** (*for tea*) tetera *f*

Uruguay ['jʊərəgwaɪ, *Am:* 'jʊrəgweɪ] *n* Uruguay *m*

Uruguayan [ˌjʊərə'gwaɪən, *Am:* ˌjʊrə-'gweɪ-] **I.** *adj* uruguayo, -a **II.** *n* uruguayo, -a *m, f*

us [əs, *stressed:* ʌs] *pron pers* nos; *after prep* nosotros, -as; **it's ~** somos nosotros; **older than ~** mayores que nosotros; **look at ~** míranos; **he saw ~** (él) nos vió; **he gave the pencil to ~** nos dio el lápiz; **it's for/from ~** es para/de nosotros

USA [ˌjuːes'eɪ] *n* **1.** *abbr of* **United States of America** EE.UU. *mpl* **2.** *abbr of* **United States Army** *ejército de los EE.UU.*

USAF [ˌjuːeseɪ'ef] *n abbr of* **United States Air Force** *Fuerza Aérea de los EE.UU.*

usage ['juːzɪdʒ] *n* **1.** *no pl, form* (*treatment*) tratamiento *m* **2.** (*how sth is used*) uso *m;* **in common ~** de uso común; **in general ~** de uso general **3.** LING utilización *f;* **the earliest recorded ~ of the word X** la primera utilización documentada de la palabra X

use¹ [juːs] *n* **1.** (*practical application*) uso *m* **2.** *no pl* (*possibility of applying*) empleo *m;* **in ~** en uso; **to be of ~ to sb** ser de utilidad para alguien; **a ban on the ~ of chemical weapons** una prohibición sobre el uso de armas químicas; **the ~ of drugs** el consumo de drogas; **the correct ~** (**of language**) el uso correcto (de la lengua); **to make ~ of sth** utilizar algo; **to put sth to ~** poner algo en servicio; **to be out of ~** estar fuera de servicio; **to come into ~** empezar a utilizarse; **to go out of ~** quedar en desuso **3.** *no pl* (*purpose*) **to be no ~** no ser de utilidad; **there's no ~ doing sth** no sirve de nada hacer algo; **that's a fat lot of ~** *iron, inf* pues sí que ha valido de mucho; **it's no ~** es inútil; **what's the ~ of doing sth?** ¿de qué sirve hacer algo?; **what ~ is doing sth?** ¿de qué sirve hacer algo? **4.** (*consumption*) consumo *m*

use² [juːz] **I.** *vt* **1.** (*make use of*) usar; (*one's skills, training*) hacer uso de; **to ~ logic** emplear la lógica; **to ~ a name/pseudonym** utilizar un nombre/pseudónimo; **to ~ sth to do sth** utilizar algo para hacer algo; **to ~ sth against sb/sth** utilizar algo en contra de alguien/algo; **to ~ chemical products** emplear productos químicos; **to ~ drugs** consumir drogas; **I could ~ some help** *inf* podría ayudarme **2.** (*employ*) emplear; **to ~ common sense** emplear el sentido común; **to ~ discretion** ser discreto; **~ your head** utilizar la cabeza **3.** (*consume*) utilizar, consumir; **to ~ energy** consumir energía **4.** (*manipulate*) utilizar; (*exploit*) explotar **5.** *form* (*treat in stated way*) **to ~ sb badly/well** tratar mal/bien a alguien **II.** *vi* **he ~d to be/do ...** solía ser/hacer...; **they ~d not to enjoy horror films** no les gustaba ver películas de terror; **did you ~ to work in banking?** ¿trabajabas en la banca?

◆**use up** *vt* agotar

used [juːzd] *adj* (*second-hand*) usado, -a; (*clothes*) de segunda mano; **~ notes** viejas notas

used to [juːst tʊ] *adj* (*familiar with*) acostumbrado, -a; **to be ~ sth** estar acostumbrado a algo; **to become ~ sth** acostumbrarse a algo; **to be ~ the cold/heat** estar acostumbrado al frío/calor; **to be ~ doing sth** tener la costumbre de hacer algo

useful ['juːsfəl] *adj* **1.** (*convenient*) útil; **a ~ thing** una cosa útil; **to be ~** (**for sth**) ser útil (para algo) **2.** (*beneficial*) beneficioso, -a; **a ~ experience** una experiencia útil **3.** (*effective*) eficaz; (*competent*) competente; **to be ~ with sth** *inf* ser competente en algo; **to do sth ~** hacer algo útil

usefulness *n no pl* utilidad *f;* (*applicability*) aplicabilidad *f;* (*relevance*) relevancia *f;* **to outlive one's ~** dejar de tener utilidad

useless ['juːsləs] *adj* **1.** (*in vain*) inútil; (*unusable*) inservible; **to be ~ doing sth** ser inútil hacer algo; **to be ~ for sb/sth** no ser de utilidad para alguien/algo; **to become ~ for sb/sth** dejar de ser útil para alguien/algo; **to be ~ to do sth** no servir de nada el hacer algo; **~ details** detalles *mpl* sin importancia; **~ information** información *f* inútil **2.** *inf* (*incompetent*) incompetente; **to be worse than ~** *inf* no servir para nada

user *n* usuario, -a *m, f;* (*of gas, electricity*) consumidor(a) *m(f);* **drug ~** drogadicto, -a *m, f*

user-friendly *adj* INFOR fácil de utilizar

user interface *n,* **user-interface** *n* INFOR interfaz *f* de usuario **user name** *n* INFOR nombre *m* del usuario **user program** *n* INFOR programa *m* del usuario **user software** *n no pl* INFOR software *m* del usuario

usher ['ʌʃəʳ, *Am:* -ɚ] **I.** *n* ujier *m* **II.** *vt* **to ~ sb into the office** hacer pasar a alguien a la oficina; **to ~ sb out** acompañar a alguien a la puerta

usherette [ˌʌʃə'ret] *n* acomodadora *f*

USM [ˌjuːes'em] *n* **1.** *abbr of* **underwater-to--surface missile** misil *m* agua-tierra **2.** *abbr of* **United States Mail** *correo de los EE.UU.*

USP [ˌjuːes'piː] *n* ECON *abbr of* **unique selling proposition** *característica única de un producto para promocionar su venta*

USS [ˌjuːes'es] *n* **1.** *abbr of* **United States Ship** *barco de los EE.UU.* **2.** *abbr of* **United States Senate** *Senado de los EE.UU.*

usual ['juːʒəl, *Am:* -ʒuəl] **I.** *adj* usual; (**the**) **~ problems** los problemas corrientes; **to find sth in its ~ place** hallar algo en el lugar en que acostumbra a estar; **as ~** como de costumbre; **to be ~ for sb** ser habitual para alguien; **to be ~ for sb to do sth** ser habitual para alguien hacer algo **II.** *n* **the ~** *inf* (*regular drink*) lo de

U

siempre
usually *adv* normalmente; **more than ~** más que de costumbre
usufruct ['ju:sjʊfrʌkt, *Am:* -zʊ-] *n form* LAW usufructo *m*
usurer ['ju:ʒərəʳ, *Am:*-ɚ] *n* LAW usurero, -a *m, f*
usurious [ju:'zjʊəriəs, *Am:* ju:'ʒʊri-] *adj form* LAW usurario, -a
usurp [ju:'zɜ:p, *Am:* -'sɜ:rp] *vt* usurpar
usurper [ju:'zɜ:pəʳ, *Am:* -'sɜ:rpɚ] *n* usurpador(a) *m(f)*
usury ['ju:ʒəri, *Am:* -ʒɚi] *n no pl* LAW usura *f*
USW *n abbr of* **ultrashort waves** ondas *fpl* ultracortas
utensil [ju:'tensl] *n* utensilio *m;* **kitchen ~s** utensilios *mpl* de cocina
uterine ['ju:tərain, *Am:* -t̬ɚɪn] *adj* uterino, -a
uterus ['ju:tərəs, *Am:* -t̬ɚ-] <-ri *o* -es> *n* útero *m*
utilise ['ju:tɪlaɪz, *Am:* -t̬əlaɪz] *vt* utilizar
utilitarian [ju:ˌtɪlɪ'teəriən, *Am:* -ə'terɪ-] *adj* utilitario, -a
utility [ju:'tɪləti, *Am:* -t̬i] <-ies> *n* **1.** *form* (*usefulness*) utilidad *f;* **~ room** office *m* **2.** (*public service*) empresa *f* de servicio público **3.** INFOR herramienta *f*
utilization [ˌju:təlaɪ'zeɪʃən, *Am:* -t̬əlɪ'-] *n no pl* utilización *f*
utilize *vt s.* **utilise**
utmost ['ʌtməʊst, *Am:* -moʊst] **I.** *adj* mayor; **of the ~ brilliance** (*person, mind*) de una inteligencia suprema; **with the ~ care** con sumo cuidado; **with the ~ caution** con toda precaución; **the ~ difficulty** la dificultad máxima; **a matter of ~ importance** un asunto de primerísima importancia **II.** *n no pl* **the ~** lo máximo; **to offer the ~ in power** otorgar el máximo poder; **to be the ~** ser lo máximo; **to the ~** al máximo; **to try sb's patience to the ~** poner a prueba la paciencia de alguien al máximo; **to live life to the ~** vivir la vida al máximo; **to try one's ~** hacer todo lo que se puede
utopia [ju:'təʊpiə, *Am:* -'toʊ-] *n* utopía *f*
utopian *adj* utópico, -a
utter¹ ['ʌtəʳ, *Am:* 'ʌt̬ɚ] *adj* completo, -a; **in ~ despair** en la más absoluta desesperación; **~ nonsense** completa estupidez *f;* **an ~ fool** un completo idiota
utter² ['ʌtəʳ, *Am:* 'ʌt̬ɚ] *vt* **1.** (*emit noise orally*) proferir; **without ~ing a word** sin mediar palabra **2.** (*express*) pronunciar; **to ~ blasphemy against sb/sth** proferir una blasfemia contra alguien/algo; **to ~ a threat** amenazar; **to ~ an oath** hacer una promesa; **to ~ a prayer** decir una oración; **to ~ a warning** dar un aviso
utterance ['ʌtərənts, *Am:* 'ʌt̬-] *n* **1.** (*speech act*) enunciado *m* **2.** *no pl* (*style of delivery*) expresión *f;* **to give ~ to sth** expresar algo; **to give ~ to a feeling** manifestar un sentimiento
utterly *adv* completamente; **to be ~ convinced that ...** estar completamente convencido de que...; **to ~ despise/hate sb** despreciar/odiar profundamente a alguien; **~ irresistible** totalmente irresistible
uttermost ['ʌtəməʊst, *Am:* 'ʌt̬ɚmoʊst] *adj, n s.* **utmost**
U-turn ['ju:tɜ:n, *Am:* 'ju:tɜ:rn] *n* giro *m* de ciento ochenta grados; **to do a ~** hacer un giro completo; **to make a ~** realizar un giro de 180 grados
UV [ˌju:'vi:] *abbr of* **ultraviolet** UV
UVF [ˌju:vi:'ef] *n abbr of* **Ulster Volunteer Force** *ejército de voluntarios del Ulster*
uvula ['ju:vjələ] *n* úvula *f*
uxorious [ʌk'sɔ:riəs] *adj form* muy enamorado de su mujer
Uzbek ['ʊzbək] **I.** *adj* uzbeko, -a **II.** *n* uzbeko, -a *m, f*
Uzbekistan [ʌzˌbekɪ'stɑ:n, *Am:* -'stæn] *n* Uzbekistán *m*

V

V, v [vi:] *n* **1.** (*letter*) V, v *f;* **~ for Victor** V de Valencia **2.** (*Roman numeral five*) V *m*
V **1.** *abbr of* **volume** vol. **2.** *abbr of* **volt** V
vac [væk] **I.** *n* **1.** *Brit, inf abbr of* **vacation** vacaciones *fpl;* **the long ~** las vacaciones de verano **2.** *inf abbr of* **vacuum** vacío *m* **3.** *abbr of* **vacuum cleaner** aspirador *m,* aspiradora *f;* **to give sth a ~** limpiar algo con aspirador **II.** <-cc-> *vt inf abbr of* **vacuum clean** pasar el aspirador **III.** *vi abbr of* **vacuum clean** pasar el aspirador
vac. *adj abbr of* **vacant** vacante
vacancy ['veɪkəntsi] <-ies> *n* **1.** (*room*) cuarto *m* vacío; **'vacancies'** 'habitaciones *fpl* libres'; **'no vacancies'** 'no quedan habitaciones disponibles' **2.** (*time*) tiempo *m* libre **3.** (*employment opportunity*) vacante *f;* **to fill a ~** ocupar una vacante; **to have a ~** ofrecer un puesto de trabajo **4.** *no pl* (*lack of expression*) vacuidad *f*
vacant ['veɪkənt] *adj* **1.** (*empty, void, not filled*) vacío, -a; (*seat*) desocupado, -a; **~ lot** solar *m* libre; **to leave sth ~** dejar algo vacante; **'~'** 'libre' **2.** (*unoccupied job situation*) vacante; **to fall ~** producirse una vacante; **to fill the ~ post** ocupar una vacante **3.** (*expressionless, deadpan*) de bobo
vacate [və'keɪt, *Am:* 'veɪkeɪt] *vt form* (*place, seat*) desocupar; (*a room, offices, house, building*) salir de; (*a job, position, post*) dejar vacante
vacation [və'keɪʃən, *Am:* veɪ-] **I.** *n Am* (*holiday*) vacaciones *fpl;* **to take a ~** tomarse unas vacaciones; **on ~** de vacaciones; **paid ~** vacaciones *fpl* pagadas **II.** *vi Am* estar de vacaciones
vacationer *n Am* veraneante *mf*

vaccinate ['væksɪneɪt, *Am:* -səneɪt-] *vt* MED vacunar; **to be ~ed against measles** estar vacunado contra el sarampión
vaccination [ˌvæksɪ'neɪʃən, *Am:* -sə'neɪ-] *n* MED vacunación *f;* **a ~ against measles** una vacuna contra el sarampión; **oral ~** vacunación *f* oral
vaccine ['væksi:n, *Am:* væk'si:n] *n* MED vacuna *f*
vacillate ['væsəleɪt] *vi* dudar; **to ~ between ... and ...** dudar entre... y...; **to ~ between hope and despair** oscilar entre la esperanza y la desesperación
vacillation [ˌvæsəl'eɪʃən] *n* vacilación *f;* (*indecisiveness*) indecisión *f*
vacuity [və'kju:əti, *Am:* -əţi] *n no pl* vacuidad *f*
vacuous ['vækjuəs] *adj* bobo, -a; **a ~ remark** un comentario necio
vacuum ['vækju:m] **I.** *n* **1.** PHYS (*area without gas, air*) vacío *m;* **perfect ~** vacío *m* perfecto **2.** (*absence of direction*) **to fill/leave a ~** llenar/dejar un vacío **3.** (*isolated from influences, people*) **in a ~** en un vacío **4.** (*hoover*) aspiradora *f* **II.** *vt* limpiar con la aspiradora; **to ~ sth up** pasar la aspiradora a algo
vacuum bottle *n,* **vacuum flask** *n Brit* botella *f* al vacío **vacuum cleaner** *n* aspiradora *f*
vacuum-packaged *adj,* **vacuum-packed** [ˌvækju:m'pækt, *Am:* -juəm'-] *adj* empaquetado, -a al vacío
vacuum suction *n* succión *f* al vacío
vagabond ['vægəbɒnd, *Am:* -ba:nd] **I.** *n* vagabundo, -a *m, f* **II.** *adj* vagabundo, -a
vagary ['veɪgəri, *Am:* 'veɪgɚi] <-ies> *n* **1.** (*caprice, whimsy*) capricho *m* **2.** *pl* (*unpredictable whimsical developments*) impredecibilidad *f;* **the vagaries of the weather** las irregularidades del tiempo; **the vagaries of fashion** la variación de la moda
vagina [və'dʒaɪnə] *n* vagina *f*
vagrancy ['veɪgrənsi] *n no pl* vagabundeo *m*
vagrant ['veɪgrənt] **I.** *n* vagabundo, -a *m, f* **II.** *adj* **1.** vagabundo, -a **2.** *fig* errabundo, -a
vague [veɪg] *adj* **1.** (*imprecise: promise, pain*) vago, -a; (*word*) impreciso, -a; (*outline*) borroso, -a; **I have not the ~st idea** no tengo la más mínima idea **2.** (*absent-minded: expression*) distraído, -a; (*person*) despistado, -a
vagueness *n no pl* **1.** (*imprecision*) vaguedad *f* **2.** (*absent-mindedness*) distracción *f*
vain [veɪn] *adj* **1.** (*conceited, self-admiring*) vanidoso, -a **2.** (*fruitless: attempt, hope*) vano, -a; **it is ~ to ...** +*infin* es inútil... +*infin* **3. in ~** en vano; **it was all in ~** todo fue en vano
vainglorious [ˌveɪn'glɔ:riəs] *adj form* vanaglorioso, -a, jactancioso, -a
valance ['væləntsˌ] *n* **1.** (*textile surrounding for bed*) volante *m* **2.** *Am* (*cloth covering curtain rail*) bastidor *m*
vale *n,* **Vale** [veɪl] *n liter* (*valley*) valle *m;* **this ~ of tears** *fig* este valle de lágrimas
valediction [ˌvælɪ'dɪkʃən, *Am:* ˌvælə'dɪkʃən] *n form* **1.** (*farewell*) adiós *m* **2.** (*speech given when taking leave*) discurso *m* de despedida
valedictory [ˌvælɪ'dɪktəri, *Am:* ˌvælə'dɪktɚ-] *adj Am* (*bidding farewell*) de despedida; **~** (**address**) discurso *m* de despedida
valence ['veɪlənts], **valency** ['veɪləntsi] <-ies> *n* valencia *f*
Valencia [və'lentʃiə] *n* Valencia *f*
Valencian **I.** *adj* valenciano, -a **II.** *n* valenciano, -a *m, f*
valentine ['væləntaɪn] *n* **1.** (*card*) *tarjeta que se manda el día de los enamorados* **2.** (*sweetheart*) enamorado, -a *m, f*
Valentine's Day *n no pl* día *m* de los enamorados, día *m* de San Valentín
valerian [və'lɪəriən, *Am:* -'lɪri-] *n* valeriana *f*
valet ['væleɪ, *Am:* 'vælɪt] **I.** *n* **1.** HIST (*male's private servant*) ayuda *mf* de cámara **2.** (*in a hotel*) mozo *m* de hotel **3.** (*professional car parker*) aparcacoches *m inv* **II.** *vt Brit* (*car*) limpiar
valet service *n* servicio *m* de lavandería
valetudinarian [ˌvælɪtju:dɪ'neəriən, *Am:* -ətu:də'neri-] **I.** *adj* **1.** (*invalid*) inválido, -a **2.** (*hypochondriac*) hipocondríaco, -a **II.** *n* **1.** (*invalid*) inválido, -a *m, f* **2.** (*hypochondriac*) hipocondríaco, -a *m, f*
valiant ['væliənt, *Am:* -jənt] *adj* valiente
valid ['vælɪd] *adj* **1.** (*worthwhile, weighty*) válido, -a; **no longer ~** caducado, -a **2.** (*reasonable because well-founded*) legítimo, -a **3.** LAW (*still in force*) vigente; (*contractually binding*) vinculante
validate ['vælɪdeɪt, *Am:* 'vælə-] *vt* **1.** (*ratify, officially approve*) dar validez a **2.** *a.* INFOR (*verify, authenticate: document*) validar; (*ticket*) sellar
validity [və'lɪdəti, *Am:* -ţi] *n no pl* **1.** (*soundness, weight*) legitimidad *f* **2.** (*legal force*) validez *f;* (*of a law*) vigencia *f*
valley ['væli] *n* valle *m*
valor *n no pl, Am,* **valour** ['vælər, *Am:* -ɚ] *n no pl, Brit, Aus, form* valor *m*
valuable ['væljuəbl] **I.** *adj* (*help, information*) valioso, -a; (*time*) precioso, -a; **this ring is very ~** este anillo tiene mucho valor **II.** *n pl* objetos *mpl* de valor
valuation [ˌvælju'eɪʃən] *n* **1.** (*estimation of financial value*) tasación *f* **2.** *no pl* (*estimated value*) valor *m* **3.** (*acknowledgement of the excellence of sth*) valoración *f*
valuator *n* FIN tasador(a) *m(f)*
value ['vælju:] **I.** *n* **1.** *no pl a.* MAT, MUS (*worth, significance*) valor *m;* **~ judgement** juicio *m* de valor; **to be of ~ to sb** ser valioso para alguien; **to be of little ~** ser de poco valor; **to place a high ~ on sth** dar mucha importancia a algo; **to be good ~** (**for money**) estar bien de precio; **to be of great ~** ser muy valioso; **to**

V

get good ~ for one's money sacar partido al dinero; to increase (in) ~ aumentar de valor; to lose (in) ~ depreciarse; market ~ valor de mercado; to put a ~ on sth poner precio a algo; to the ~ of por valor de 2. *pl* (*moral ethics, standards*) valores *mpl;* set of ~s escala *f* de valores II. *vt* 1. (*think to be significant*) apreciar; to ~ sb as a friend valorar a alguien como amigo 2. (*estimate financial worth*) tasar; to ~ sth at sth valorar algo en algo

value-added tax [ˌvæljuːˈædɪd-] *n Brit* impuesto *m* sobre el valor añadido

valued *adj form* apreciado, -a; ~ customer cliente *mf* valioso, -a

valueless [ˈvæljuːləs] *adj* sin valor

valuer *n Brit* FIN tasador(a) *m(f)*

valve [vælv] *n* 1. AUTO, ANAT válvula *f;* inlet ~ válvula de admisión 2. ELEC lámpara *f* 3. MUS pistón *m*

vamp¹ [væmp] I. *n* 1. (*of a shoe*) empeine *m* 2. MUS acompañamiento *m* improvisado II. *vt* 1. (*shoe*) poner el empeine a 2. MUS improvisar un acompañamiento para III. *vi* MUS improvisar un acompañamiento

vamp² [væmp] *n* vampiresa *f*

vampire [ˈvæmpaɪəʳ, *Am:* -paɪɚ] *n* vampiro *m*

van¹ [væn] *n* 1. (*commercial vehicle*) furgoneta *f;* delivery ~ furgoneta de reparto; removal ~ camión *m* de mudanzas 2. *Brit* (*rail carriage for goods*) furgón *m;* luggage ~ furgón de equipajes

van² [væn] *n no pl abbr of* vanguard vanguardia *f*

van³ [væn] *n Brit, inf* SPORTS *abbr of* advantage ventaja *f*

vandal [ˈvændəl] *n* vándalo *m*

vandalise [ˈvændəlaɪz] *vt s.* **vandalize**

vandalism [ˈvændəlɪzəm] *n no pl* vandalismo *m*

vandalize [ˈvændəlaɪz] *vt* destrozar

vane [veɪn] *n* 1. (*weathercock*) veleta *f* 2. (*of windmill*) aspa *f* 3. (*of propeller*) paleta *f*

vanguard [ˈvæŋgɑːd, *Am:* -gɑːrd] *n no pl* vanguardia *f*

vanilla [vəˈnɪlə] *n no pl* vainilla *f*

vanish [ˈvænɪʃ] *vi* to ~ (from sth) desaparecer (de algo); to ~ into thin air *fig* esfumarse; (*fear, hopes*) desvanecerse; (*cease to exist: era, race*) extinguirse

vanishing cream *n* crema *f* de día **vanishing point** *n* punto *m* de fuga

vanity [ˈvænəti, *Am:* -ət̬i] <-ies> *n* 1. *no pl* (*self-satisfaction*) vanidad *f* 2. *Am* (*dressing table*) tocador *m* 3. *Aus* (*vanitory unit*) mueble *m* de baño (*con lavabo empotrado*)

vanity bag *n,* **vanity case** *n* neceser *m*

vanquish [ˈvæŋkwɪʃ] *vt* derrotar

vantage [ˈvɑːntɪdʒ, *Am:* ˈvænt̬ɪdʒ] *n* ventaja *f*

vantage point *n* 1. (*place with good view*) mirador *m* 2. (*position which gives an advantage*) posición *f* de ventaja

Vanuatu [ˌvænuˈɑːtuː, *Am:* vænˈwɑːtuː] *n* Vanuatu *m*

vapid [ˈvæpɪd] *adj* insulso, -a

vapor [ˈveɪpəʳ, *Am:* -pɚ] *n Am, Aus s.* **vapour**

vaporisation *n,* **vaporization** [ˌveɪpəraɪˈzeɪʃən, *Am:* -ɪˈ-] *n s.* **vapourisation**

vaporize [ˈveɪpəraɪz] I. *vt* vaporizar II. *vi* vaporizarse

vaporizer *n* vaporizador *m*

vapour [ˈveɪpəʳ, *Am:* -pɚ] *n* 1. (*steam*) vapor *m;* water ~ vapor de agua 2. (*on glass*) vaho *m,* vaporizo *m Méx, PRico*

vapourisation [ˌveɪpəraɪˈzeɪʃən, *Am:* -ɪˈ-] *n no pl* vaporización *f*

vapour pressure *n* presión *f* del vapor

vapour trail *n* AVIAT estela *f*

variability [ˌveəriəˈbɪləti, *Am:* ˌveriəˈbɪlət̬i] *n no pl* variabilidad *f*

variable [ˈveəriəbl, *Am:* ˈveri-] I. *n* MAT variable *f* II. *adj* variable

variance [ˈveəriənts, *Am:* ˈveri-] *n* 1. *no pl* (*disagreement, difference*) discrepancia *f;* at ~ en contradicción; to be at ~ with sth discrepar en algo; to set two people at ~ sembrar la discordia entre dos personas 2. *no pl* (*variation*) variación *f* 3. (*in statistics*) variancia *f*

variant [ˈveəriənt, *Am:* ˈveri-] I. *n* variante *f* II. *adj* 1. (*different*) divergente; ~ spelling variante *f* ortográfica 2. (*tending to change*) variable

variation [ˌveəriˈeɪʃən, *Am:* ˌveriˈ-] *n no pl* 1. *a.* BIO, MUS variación *f;* a ~ on sth una variación de algo 2. (*varying, difference, dissimilarity*) diferencia *f;* wide ~s in sth grandes diferencias de algo

varicose [ˈværɪkəʊs, *Am:* ˈverəkoʊs] *adj* MED varicoso, -a; ~ veins varices *fpl*

varied [ˈveərɪd, *Am:* ˈverɪd] *adj* 1. (*altered, diverse*) variado, -a 2. (*having different colours*) multicolor

variegated [ˈveərɪgeɪtɪd, *Am:* ˈveriəgeɪt̬ɪd] *adj* multicolor

variety [vəˈraɪəti, *Am:* -t̬i] <-ies> *n* 1. *no pl* (*diversity*) variedad *f;* to lend ~ to sth variar algo 2. (*assortment*) surtido *m;* for a ~ of reasons por varias razones; in a ~ of ways de diversas formas 3. (*sort, category*) tipo *m;* a ~ of communism una forma de comunismo; a new ~ of tulip una nueva variedad de tulipán 4. *no pl* THEAT variedades *fpl* ► ~ is the spice of life *prov* en la variedad está el gusto *prov*

variety show *n* 1. THEAT espectáculo *m* de variedades 2. RADIO, TV programa *m* de variedades **variety theatre** *n* THEAT teatro *m* de variedades

various [ˈveəriəs, *Am:* ˈveri-] *adj* 1. (*numerous*) varios, -as; for ~ reasons por diversas razones 2. (*diverse*) diferentes

varmint [ˈvɑːmɪnt, *Am:* ˈvɑːr-] *n* 1. ZOOL alimaña *f* 2. *Am* (*person*) sinvergüenza *mf*

varnish [ˈvɑːnɪʃ, *Am:* ˈvɑːr-] I. *n no pl*

1. (*liquid used to protect a surface*) barniz *m* 2. (*nail polish*) (**nail**) ~ esmalte *m* de uñas II. *vt* barnizar

varsity ['vɑːsəti, *Am:* 'vɑːrsəṱi] <-ies> *n Brit* 1. *inf* (*university*) universidad *f* 2. (*team*) equipo *m* universitario

vary ['veəri, *Am:* 'veri] <-ie-> I. *vi* 1. (*change, be different*) variar; **opinions** ~ hay diversidad de opiniones; **to** ~ **between ... and ...** oscilar entre... y...; **to** ~ **from ...** diferenciarse de... 2. (*diverge*) desviarse; **to** ~ **from sth** apartarse de algo II. *vt* 1. (*change*) variar 2. (*diversify*) dar variedad a

varying *adj* variable

vascular ['væskjələʳ, *Am:* -kjələ˞] *adj no pl* vascular

vase [vɑːz, *Am:* veɪs] *n* 1. (*for flowers*) florero *m* 2. (*ornamental*) jarrón *m* 3. (*receptacle*) vasija *f*

vassal ['væsəl] *n* HIST vasallo, -a *m, f*

vassalage ['væsəlɪdʒ] *n no pl* HIST vasallaje *m*

vast [vɑːst, *Am:* væst] *adj* 1. (*of great extent: area, region*) vasto, -a; **a** ~ **country** un extenso país 2. (*of great size*) enorme; **the** ~ **majority** la gran mayoría; **a** ~ **amount of money** una considerable suma de dinero 3. (*great in degree: importance*) considerable; **his** ~ **knowledge of ...** sus amplios conocimientos en el campo de (la)...

vastly *adv* (*very*) sumamente; ~ **superior** infinitamente superior

vastness *n no pl* inmensidad *f*

vat [væt] *n* tanque *m;* (*for wine or oil*) cuba *f*

VAT [ˌviːeɪ'tiː] *n no pl, Brit abbr of* **value added tax** IVA *m*

Vatican ['vætɪkən, *Am:* 'væṱ-] I. *n no pl* **the** ~ el Vaticano; ~ **City** Ciudad *f* del Vaticano II. *adj* vaticano, -a

vaudeville ['vɔːdəvɪl, *Am:* 'vɑːdvɪl] *n no pl, Am* (*variety theatre*) vodevil *m*

vault[1] [vɔːlt, *Am:* vɑːlt] *n* 1. ARCHIT (*arched structure*) bóveda *f;* (*under churches*) cripta *f;* (*at cemeteries*) panteón *m;* **family** ~ panteón familiar 2. (*underground chamber*) sótano *m;* (*secure repository*) cámara *f;* (*in a bank*) cámara *f* acorazada

vault[2] [vɔːlt, *Am:* vɑːlt] I. *n* salto *m* II. *vi, vt* saltar

vaulted *adj* ARCHIT abovedado, -a

vaulting I. *n no pl* ARCHIT bóveda *f* II. *adj* (*exaggerated*) desmesurado, -a; (*ambition*) desmedido, -a

vaulting horse *n* potro *m* **vaulting pole** *n* pértiga *f*

vaunt [vɔːnt, *Am:* vɑːnt] *vt* jactarse de

VC [ˌviː'siː] *n* 1. *abbr of* **Victoria Cross** *la más alta condecoración militar británica* 2. *abbr of* **Vice-Chairman** vicepresidente, -a *m, f*

VCR [ˌviːsiː'ɑːʳ, *Am:* -'ɑːr] *n Am abbr of* **videocassette recorder** vídeo *m*

VD [ˌviː'diː] *n no pl* MED *abbr of* **venereal disease** enfermedad *f* venérea

VDU [ˌviːdiː'juː] *abbr of* **visual display unit** UDV

VE [ˌviː'iː] *abbr of* **Victory in Europe** *día de la victoria aliada en Europa en la Segunda Guerra Mundial*

veal [viːl] *n no pl* ternera *f*

veal cutlet *n* chuleta *f* de ternera

vector ['vektəʳ, *Am:* -tə˞] I. *n* 1. MAT vector *m* 2. BIO, MED portador(a) *m(f)* II. *adj* MAT vectorial

veer [vɪəʳ, *Am:* vɪr] I. *vi* 1. (*alter course: vehicle*) virar; (*wind*) cambiar de dirección; (*road, way*) torcer 2. (*alter attitude, goal*) cambiar bruscamente; **to** ~ **from sb's usual opinions** desviarse de las opiniones habituales de alguien; **to** ~ **towards sth** dar un giro hacia algo II. *n* (*character, plan*) viraje *m;* (*movement*) cambio *m* de dirección

◆**veer (a)round** *vt* AUTO cambiar de dirección; *fig* cambiar bruscamente

veg [vedʒ] *n no pl, inf* verdura *f;* **fruit and** ~ frutas *fpl* y verduras

vegan ['viːgən] *n vegetariano que no come ni huevos ni productos lácteos*

vegetable ['vedʒtəbl] *n* 1. (*plant*) vegetal *m* 2. (*edible plant*) hortaliza *f;* (**green**) ~ verdura *f;* ~ **soup** sopa *f* de verduras; **root** ~ tubérculo *m;* **seasonal** ~ verdura del tiempo

vegetable butter *n no pl,* **vegetable fat** *n no pl* margarina *f* **vegetable garden** *n* huerto *m* **vegetable kingdom** *n no pl* reino *m* vegetal **vegetable oil** *n no pl* aceite *m* vegetal

vegetarian [ˌvedʒɪ'teəriən, *Am:* -ə'teri-] I. *n* vegetariano, -a *m, f* II. *adj* vegetariano, -a; **to go** ~ hacerse vegetariano

vegetate ['vedʒɪteɪt, *Am:* '-ə-] *vi a. fig* vegetar

vegetation [ˌvedʒɪ'teɪʃən, *Am:* -ə'-] *n no pl* vegetación *f*

vehemence ['viːəmənts] *n no pl* vehemencia *f*

vehement ['viːəmənt] *adj* vehemente

vehicle ['vɪəkl, *Am:* 'viːə-] *n* 1. (*method of transport*) vehículo *m;* **motor** ~ vehículo motorizado 2. (*channel, means of expression*) medio *m;* **to be a** ~ **for sth** servir de vehículo para algo

vehicle registration centre *n Brit* centro *m* de matriculación **vehicle registration number** *n Brit* número *m* de matrícula

vehicular [vi'ɪkjələʳ, *Am:* viː'hɪkjələ˞] *adj form* de vehículos; (*accident*) de circulación; ~ **traffic** tráfico *m* rodado

veil [veɪl] I. *n* velo *m;* (*of smoke*) cortina *f* de humo; **bridal** ~ velo de novia; **a** ~ **of secrecy** un halo de misterio; **under the** ~ **of sth** *fig* con el pretexto de algo; **to draw a** ~ **over sth** *fig* correr un tupido velo sobre algo II. *vt* velar; (*disguise*) disimular; **to** ~ **one's face** taparse con un velo; **to be** ~**ed** estar cubierto con un velo; **the mist** ~**ed the mountains** *fig, liter* la bruma envolvía las montañas

veiled *adj* 1. (*wearing a veil*) cubierto, -a con

velo **2.** (*indirect, masked, concealed: criticism*) velado, -a; **thinly** ~ apenas disimulado
vein [veɪn] *n* **1.** ANAT, BOT vena *f;* GEO veta *f,* sirca *f Chile;* **a quartz** ~ una veta de cuarzo **2.** (*trait, element of stated feeling*) disposición *f;* **a** ~ **of madness** una vena de loco; **to talk in a more serious** ~ hablar más en serio **3.** (*frame of mind, temperament*) estilo *m;* **in (a) similar** ~ del mismo estilo; **in the** ~ **of sth** a la manera de algo
veined *adj* **1.** (*stone, wood*) veteado, -a **2.** (*hand, leaf*) que tiene nervios
velar ['viːləʳ, *Am:* -lɚ] **I.** *adj* LING velar **II.** *n* LING sonido *m* velar
Velcro® ['velkrəʊ, *Am:* -kroʊ] *n no pl* velcro® *m*
veld *n,* **veldt** [velt] *n* veld *m* (*meseta seca característica de Sudáfrica*)
velocity [vɪ'lɒsəti, *Am:* və'lɑːsət̬i] <-ies> *n form* velocidad *f;* **at the** ~ **of** a la velocidad de; **sound/light** ~ velocidad del sonido/de la luz
velvet ['velvɪt] **I.** *n no pl* terciopelo *m* **II.** *adj* **1.** (*made of velvet*) de terciopelo **2.** *fig* (*smooth: voice*) aterciopelado, -a
velveteen [ˌvelvɪ'tiːn] *n* pana *f*
velvety ['velvɪti, *Am:* -vət̬i] *adj fig* aterciopelado, -a
venal ['viːnəl] *adj* **1.** (*that can be purchased*) venal **2.** (*corrupt: regime, ruler*) corrupto, -a
venality [viː'næləti, *Am:* vɪ'nælət̬i] *n no pl* **1.** (*corruptibility*) venalidad *f* **2.** (*corruption*) corrupción *f*
vend [vend] *vt* vender
vendetta [ven'detə, *Am:* -'det̬-] *n* vendetta *f*
vending machine *n* máquina *f* expendedora
vendor ['vendɔːʳ, *Am:* -dɚ] *n* vendedor(a) *m(f)*
vendue ['vendjuː] *n Am* subasta *f*
veneer [və'nɪəʳ, *Am:* -'nɪr] **I.** *vt* chapar **II.** *n* **1.** chapado *m* **2.** *no pl, fig* apariencia *f*
venerable ['venərəbl] *adj* **1.** (*person*) venerable **2.** (*tradition*) ancestral; (*building, tree*) centenario, -a; ~ **ruins** ruinas *fpl* milenarias
venerate ['venəreɪt] *vt* venerar
veneration [ˌvenə'reɪʃen] *n no pl* veneración *f;* **to hold sb in** ~ venerar a alguien
venereal [və'nɪəriəl, *Am:* və'nɪri-] *adj* MED venéreo, -a; ~ **disease** enfermedad *f* venérea
venetian blind [vəˌniːʃən'blaɪnd] *n* persiana *f* veneciana
Venezuela [ˌvenɪ'zweɪlə, *Am:* -ə'zweɪ-] *n* Venezuela *f*
Venezuelan **I.** *adj* venezolano, -a **II.** *n* venezolano, -a *m, f*
vengeance ['vendʒənts] *n no pl* venganza *f;* **to take** ~ **(up)on sb** vengarse de alguien; **with a** ~ con ganas
venial ['viːniəl] *adj form* venial; (*offence*) leve; (*error*) sin importancia; ~ **sin** pecado *m* venial
venison ['venɪsən] *n no pl* (carne *f* de) venado *m*
venom ['venəm] *n no pl* veneno *m; fig* malevolencia *f*
venomous ['venəməs] *adj* venenoso, -a; (*malicious*) maligno, -a; (*tongue*) viperino, -a
venous ['viːnəs] *adj* venoso, -a
vent [vent] **I.** *n* **1.** (*small outlet for gas: of a building*) conducto *m* de ventilación; (*of a volcano*) chimenea *f;* **air** ~ respiradero *m* **2.** FASHION abertura *f* **3.** (*release of feelings*) **to give** ~ **to sth** dar rienda suelta a algo; **to give** ~ **to one's feelings** desahogarse **II.** *vt* (*feelings*) dar rienda suelta a; (*opinion*) expresar; **to** ~ **one's anger on sb** desahogarse con alguien
ventilate ['ventɪleɪt, *Am:* -t̬əleɪt-] *vt* **1.** (*oxygenate a space*) ventilar; **artificially** ~**d** MED con respiración asistida **2.** (*give utterance to, verbalize*) expresar
ventilation [ˌventɪ'leɪʃən, *Am:* -t̬ə'leɪ-] *n no pl* ventilación *f*
ventilation duct *n* conducto *m* de ventilación
ventilator ['ventɪleɪtəʳ, *Am:* -t̬əleɪt̬ɚ] *n* **1.** (*device*) ventilador *m* **2.** MED respirador *m*
ventricle ['ventrɪkl] *n* ventrículo *m*
ventriloquist [ven'trɪləkwɪst] *n* ventrílocuo, -a *m, f*
venture ['ventʃəʳ, *Am:* -tʃɚ] **I.** *n* **1.** (*endeavour*) aventura *f* **2.** COM empresa *f;* **joint** ~ empresa conjunta **II.** *vt* **1.** (*dare*) **to** ~ **to do sth** atreverse a hacer algo; **may I** ~ **a suggestion?** ¿me permite hacer una sugerencia? **2.** (*dare to express: an opinion*) aventurar **3.** (*put at risk, endanger*) **to** ~ **sth (on sth)** arriesgar algo (en algo) ►**nothing** ~**d, nothing gained** *prov* quien no se arriesga, no pasa la mar *prov* **III.** *vi* aventurarse
◆**venture on** *vt* emprender, embarcarse en
◆**venture out** *vi* atreverse a salir
venture capital *n* FIN capital *m* de riesgo
venturesome ['ventʃəsəm, *Am:* -tʃɚ-] *adj form* **1.** (*adventurous: person*) atrevido, -a; (*enterprising*) emprendedor(a) **2.** (*risky, not safe*) arriesgado, -a
venue ['venjuː] *n* (*of meeting*) lugar *m* (de reunión); (*of concert*) lugar *m* (de celebración); (*of match*) campo *m*
Venus ['viːnəs] *n no pl* Venus *m*
veracious [və'reɪʃəs] *adj form* **1.** (*honest*) honesto, -a **2.** (*accurate and precise*) veraz
veracity [və'ræsəti, *Am:* və'ræsət̬i] *n no pl* **1.** (*truthfulness*) honestidad *f* **2.** (*accuracy*) veracidad *f*
veranda *n,* **verandah** [və'rændə] *n* veranda *f*
verb [vɜːb, *Am:* vɜːrb] *n* verbo *m;* **intransitive/transitive** ~ verbo intransitivo/transitivo
verbal ['vɜːbəl, *Am:* 'vɜːr-] *adj* **1.** (*oral, unwritten*) verbal; ~ **agreement** acuerdo *m* verbal; ~ **facility** facilidad *f* de palabra **2.** (*word for word: translation*) literal
verbalise, verbalize ['vɜːbəlaɪz, *Am:* 'vɜːr-] *vt* expresar con palabras, verbalizar
verbally *adv* verbalmente

verbatim [vɜːˈbeɪtɪm, *Am:* vɚˈbeɪt̬ɪm] **I.** *adj* literal **II.** *adv* literalmente

verbiage [ˈvɜːbiɪdʒ, *Am:* ˈvɜːr-] *n no pl* verborrea *f*

verbose [vɜːˈbəʊs, *Am:* vɚˈboʊs] *adj* verboso, -a; (*speech*) prolijo, -a

verbosity [vɜːˈbɒsəti, *Am:* vɚˈbɑːsət̬i] *n no pl* verbosidad *f*

verdant [ˈvɜːdənt, *Am:* ˈvɜːr-] *adj liter* verde

verdict [ˈvɜːdɪkt, *Am:* ˈvɜːr-] *n* **1.** LAW (*of jury*) veredicto *m;* (*of magistrate, judge*) fallo *m;* ~ **of guilty/not guilty** veredicto de culpabilidad/inocencia; **to bring in** [*o* **to return**] **a** ~ (*jury*) emitir un veredicto; (*magistrate, judge*) dictar sentencia **2.** (*opinion after consideration, conclusion*) juicio *m;* **to give a** ~ **on sth/sb** dar una opinión sobre algo/alguien; **what is your** ~**?** ¿qué opinas?

verdigris [ˈvɜːdɪgrɪs, *Am:* ˈvɜːrdɪgriːs] *n no pl* verdín *m*

verge [vɜːdʒ, *Am:* vɜːrdʒ] *n* **1.** (*physical edge, margin*) margen *m* **2.** *Brit* (*part next to road or way*) arcén *m* **3.** *fig* (*brink*) borde *m;* **to be on the** ~ **of ...** estar al borde de...; **to be on the** ~ **of a solution** estar a punto de encontrar una solución; **to be on the** ~ **of doing sth** estar a punto de hacer algo; **to be on the** ~ **of tears** estar a punto de llorar

◆**verge on** *vt* rayar en; **to** ~ **the ridiculous** rayar en lo ridículo; **she is verging on fifty** ronda los cincuenta años

verger [ˈvɜːdʒəʳ, *Am:* ˈvɜːrdʒɚ] *n* sacristán *m*

verifiable [ˈverɪfaɪəbl, *Am:* ˈverəfaɪ-] *adj* comprobable

verification [ˌverɪfɪˈkeɪʃən, *Am:* ˌ-ə-] *n no pl* **1.** (*checking*) verificación *f* **2.** (*confirmation*) confirmación *f*

verify [ˈverɪfaɪ, *Am:* ˈ-ə-] <-ie-> *vt* **1.** (*corroborate*) confirmar; (*suspicions, theory*) corroborar **2.** (*authenticate*) verificar

verisimilitude [ˌverɪsɪˈmɪlɪtjuːd, *Am:* -əsəˈmɪlətuːd] *n no pl* verosimilitud *f*

veritable [ˈverɪtəbl, *Am:* -ət̬ə-] *adj* auténtico, -a

vermicelli [ˌvɜːmɪˈtʃeli, *Am:* ˌvɜːrməˈtʃel-] *n no pl* cabello *m* de ángel

vermicide [ˈvɜːmɪsaɪd, *Am:* ˈvɜːrmə-] *n no pl* vermicida *m*

vermiform [ˈvɜːmɪfɔːm, *Am:* ˈvɜːrməfɔːrm] *adj* vermiforme

vermilion [vəˈmɪljən, *Am:* vɚˈmɪljən], **vermillion** **I.** *n* bermellón *m* **II.** *adj* bermellón *inv*

vermin [ˈvɜːmɪn, *Am:* ˈvɜːr-] *n* **1.** *pl* (*animals*) alimañas *fpl;* (*insects*) bichos *mpl* **2.** *pej* (*people*) gentuza *f*

verminous *adj* **1.** (*dog*) pulgoso, -a; (*person*) piojoso, -a **2.** (*disease*) verminoso, -a

vermouth [ˈvɜːməθ, *Am:* vɚˈmuːθ] *n no pl* vermut *m,* vermú *m*

vernacular [vəˈnækjələʳ, *Am:* vɚˈnækjəlɚ] *n* **1.** (*local language*) lengua *f* vernácula **2.** (*everyday language*) lengua *f* coloquial

vernal equinox [ˌvɜːnəlˈiːkwɪnɒks, *Am:* ˌvɜːrnəlˈiːkwɪnɑːks] <-es> *n* equinoccio *m* vernal

veronica [vəˈrɒnɪkə, *Am:* vəˈrɑːnɪ-] *n* verónica *f*

verruca [vəˈruːkə] <-s *o* -ae> *n* verruga *f*

versatile [ˈvɜːsətaɪl, *Am:* ˈvɜːrsət̬əl] *adj* **1.** (*flexible*) versátil; (*mind*) ágil **2.** (*multifaceted*) polifacético, -a **3.** (*multipurpose: material*) polivalente

versatility [ˌvɜːsəˈtɪləti, *Am:* ˌvɜːrsəˈtɪlət̬i] *n no pl* (*flexibility*) versatilidad *f;* (*of mind*) agilidad *f*

verse [vɜːs, *Am:* vɜːrs] *n* **1.** LIT verso *m* **2.** MUS estrofa *f* **3.** REL versículo *m*

versed *adj* **to be** (**well**) ~ **in sth** estar (muy) versado en algo

versify [ˈvɜːsɪfaɪ, *Am:* ˈvɜːrsə-] <-ie-> **I.** *vi* versificar **II.** *vt* poner en verso

version [ˈvɜːʃən, *Am:* ˈvɜːrʒən] *n* versión *f*

verso [ˈvɜːsəʊ, *Am:* ˈvɜːrsoʊ] *n form* **1.** (*of printed page*) dorso *m* **2.** (*of a coin, medal*) reverso *m*

versus [ˈvɜːsəs, *Am:* ˈvɜːr-] *prep* **1.** (*in comparison*) frente a **2.** SPORTS, LAW contra

vertebra [ˈvɜːtɪbrə, *Am:* ˈvɜːrt̬ə-] <-ae> *n* vértebra *f*

vertebral [ˈvɜːtɪbrəl, *Am:* ˈvɜːrt̬ə-] *adj* vertebral

vertebrate [ˈvɜːtɪbreɪt, *Am:* ˈvɜːrtəbrɪt] **I.** *n* vertebrado *m* **II.** *adj* vertebrado, -a

vertex [ˈvɜːteks, *Am:* ˈvɜːr-] <-es *o* -tices> *n* vértice *m*

vertical [ˈvɜːtɪkəl, *Am:* ˈvɜːrt̬ə-] *adj* vertical; ~ **drop** caída *f* en picado

vertiginous [vɜːˈtɪdʒɪnəs, *Am:* vɚˈtɪdʒə-] *adj form* vertiginoso, -a

vertigo [ˈvɜːtɪgəʊ, *Am:* ˈvɜːrt̬əgoʊ] *n no pl* vértigo *m*

verve [vɜːv, *Am:* vɜːrv] *n no pl* ímpetu *m;* **with** ~ con brío; **to give sth** (**added**) ~ dar un toque a algo

very [ˈveri] **I.** *adv* **1.** (*extremely*) muy; ~ **much** mucho; **not** ~ **much** no mucho; **to feel** ~ **much at home** sentirse como en casa; **I am** ~**,** ~ **sorry** de veras lo siento **2.** (*expression of emphasis*) **the** ~ **best** lo mejor de lo mejor; **the** ~ **first** el primerísimo; **at the** ~ **most** como mucho; **at the** ~ **least** por lo menos; **the** ~ **same** justo lo mismo ►~ __**well**__ muy bien; **to be all** ~ __**fine**__ **..., but ...** estar todo eso muy bien..., pero... **II.** *adj* **at the** ~ **bottom** al final del todo; **the** ~ **next day** justo al día siguiente; **the** ~ **fact** el mero hecho; **the** ~ **man** el mismísimo

Very light *n* bengala *f* **Very pistol** *n* pistola *f* para disparar bengalas

vesicle [ˈvesɪkl] *n* vesícula *f*

vespers [ˈvespəz, *Am:* -pɚz] *npl* REL (*evensong*) vísperas *fpl*

vessel [ˈvesəl] *n* **1.** (*any kind of boat*) embarcación *f;* (*large boat*) navío *m* **2.** (*container*) recipiente *m* **3.** (*person*) baza *f* **4.** ANAT, BOT vaso *m*

vest[1] [vest] *n* **1.** *Brit* (*undergarment*) camiseta *f;* **thermal** ~ camiseta térmica **2.** *Am, Aus* (*outergarment*) chaleco *m;* **bullet-proof** ~ chaleco antibalas

vest[2] [vest] *vt* **to ~ sb with sth** investir a alguien con algo; **to ~ sth in sb** conferir algo a alguien; **to ~ one's hopes in sb/sth** poner sus esperanzas en alguien/algo; **~ed interests** intereses *mpl* creados

vestibule ['vestɪbju:l, *Am:* -tə-] *n* vestíbulo *m*

vestige ['vestɪdʒ] *n* vestigio *m;* **a ~ of truth** un asomo de verdad; **to show a ~ of sth** mostrar un resquicio de algo

vestments ['vestmənts] *npl* vestiduras *fpl*

vest-pocket [ˌvest'pɒkɪt, *Am:* -'pɑ:kɪt] *n Am, Aus* bolsillo *m* del chaleco; ~ **camera** cámara *f* de bolsillo

vestry ['vestri] <-ies> *n* sacristía *f*

vet[1] [vet] *n* **1.** (*animal doctor*) veterinario, -a *m, f* **2.** *a. fig* MIL veterano, -a *m, f*

vet[2] [vet] *vt* <-tt-> **1.** (*examine carefully*) examinar **2.** (*screen*) someter a investigación

vetch [vetʃ] <-es> *n* algarroba *f*

veteran ['vetərən, *Am:* 'veţɚn] **I.** *n a. fig* MIL veterano, -a *m, f* **II.** *adj a. fig* MIL veterano, -a

veteran car *n Brit* coche *m* antiguo (*fabricado antes de 1905*)

Veterans Day *n no pl, Am* día *m* de los Veteranos

> La fiesta del **Veterans Day**, que se celebra el 11 de noviembre, fue creada, en un principio, para conmemorar el armisticio alcanzado entre Alemania y los EE.UU. en el año 1918. En realidad, ese día se honra a todos los veteranos de todas las guerras americanas.

veterinarian [ˌvetərɪ'neəriən, *Am:* -'neri-] *n Am* (*vet*) veterinario, -a *m, f*

veterinary ['vetərɪnəri, *Am:* -ner-] *adj* veterinario, -a; ~ **surgeon** médico *mf* veterinario, -a

veto ['vi:təʊ, *Am:* -ţoʊ] **I.** *n* <-es> veto *m;* **to put a ~ on sth** *Brit* vetar algo; **to have a ~ over sth** tener derecho a veto en algo **II.** *vt* <vetoed> **1.** (*exercise a veto against*) vetar **2.** (*forbid*) prohibir

vex [veks] *vt* **1.** (*cause trouble for*) sacar de quicio **2.** (*upset*) afligir; **he is ~ed by computer problems** los problemas informáticos le enojan

vexation [vek'seɪʃən] *n* disgusto *m;* **to be a ~ to sb** ser una vejación para alguien

vexatious [vek'seɪʃəs] *adj* fastidioso, -a; ~ **child** niño(a) *m(f)* irritante; ~ **problem** problema *m* engorroso

v. g. *abbr of* **very good** m. b.

VHF [ˌvi:eɪtʃ'ef] *abbr of* **very high frequency** VHF

via ['vaɪə] *prep* por; ~ **London/the bridge** por Londres/el puente

viability [ˌvaɪə'bɪləti, *Am:* -əţi] *n no pl* viabilidad *f*

viable ['vaɪəbl] *adj* viable

viaduct ['vaɪədʌkt] *n* viaducto *m*

vibes [vaɪbz] *npl inf* **1.** (*feeling*) **good/bad ~** buenas/malas vibraciones **2.** (*vibraphone*) vibráfono *m*

vibrant ['vaɪbrənt] *adj* **1.** (*lively: person*) enérgico, -a; (*music*) vibrante; ~ **performance** espectáculo *m* contundente **2.** (*bustling*) efervescente; (*economy*) en ebullición **3.** (*bright and strong: colour, light*) radiante

vibraphone ['vaɪbrəfəʊn, *Am:* -foʊn] *n* vibráfono *m*

vibrate [vaɪ'breɪt, *Am:* 'vaɪbreɪt] **I.** *vi* **1.** (*shake quickly, oscillate*) vibrar; **to ~ with enthusiasm** estremecerse de entusiasmo **2.** (*continue to be heard: sound*) hacer vibrar **II.** *vt* hacer vibrar

vibration [vaɪ'breɪʃən] *n* vibración *f*

vibrator [vaɪ'breɪtəʳ, *Am:* 'vaɪbreɪţɚ] *n* TECH vibrador *m;* (*sexual stimulation*) consolador *m*

vicar ['vɪkəʳ, *Am:* -ɚ] *n* vicario *m*

vicarage ['vɪkərɪdʒ] *n* vicaría *f* ►**to look like a ~ tea-party** parecer una tertulia de jubilados

vicarious [vɪ'keəriəs, *Am:* -'keri-] *adj* (*thrill*) indirecto, -a; (*authority*) delegado, -a

vice[1] [vaɪs] *n* vicio *m;* ~ **squad** brigada *f* antivicio

vice[2] [vaɪs] *n Brit, Aus* (*tool*) torno *m* de banco

vice-chairman [ˌvaɪs'tʃeəmən, *Am:* -'tʃer-] <-men> *n* vicepresidente, -a *m, f* **vice--chancellor** *n Brit* UNIV rector(a) *m(f)* **Vice President, vice-president** *n* **1.** (*deputy president*) presidente, -a *m, f* en funciones **2.** (*title*) vicepresidente, -a *m, f*

vice versa [ˌvaɪsi'vɜ:sə, *Am:* -sə'vɜ:r-] *adv* viceversa

vicinity [vɪ'sɪnəti, *Am:* və'sɪnəţi] <-ies> *n* inmediaciones *fpl;* **in the ~ of ...** en los alrededores de...

vicious ['vɪʃəs] *adj* **1.** (*malicious*) malo, -a; (*fighting*) salvaje; (*gossip*) malicioso, -a **2.** (*cruel, violent*) despiadado, -a **3.** (*able to cause pain: animal*) feroz **4.** (*extremely powerful: pain*) atroz; (*wind*) devastador(a)

vicious circle *n* círculo *m* vicioso

vicissitudes [vɪ'sɪsɪtju:dz, *Am:* vɪ'sɪsətu:dz] *n form pl* vicisitudes *fpl;* **the ~s of life** los avatares de la vida

victim ['vɪktɪm] *n* víctima *f;* **to be the ~ of sth** ser víctima de algo ►**to fall ~ to sb/sth** sucumbir a alguien/algo

victimize ['vɪktɪmaɪz, *Am:* -tə-] *vt* discriminar; **to be ~d by law** ser víctima de la ley

victor ['vɪktəʳ, *Am:* -tɚ] *n* vencedor(a) *m(f);* **to emerge (as) the ~** salir victorioso

La **Victoria Cross** fue creada en el año 1856 por la reina Victoria durante la guerra de Crimea como la condecoración militar más alta de la **Commonwealth**. Se concede a quien haya destacado por su valentía. La inscripción reza: '**For valour**' (Por el valor).

Victorian [vɪk'tɔːriən] **I.** *adj* victoriano, -a **II.** *n* victoriano, -a *m, f*
victorious [vɪk'tɔːriəs] *adj* victorioso, -a; ~ **team** equipo *m* ganador
victory ['vɪktəri] <-ies> *n* victoria *f;* **to clinch a** ~ (**over sb**) conseguir una victoria (sobre alguien); **to win a** ~ (**in sth**) obtener una victoria (en algo)
victualler ['vɪtələʳ, *Am:* 'vɪt̬ələ˞] *n* ≈ encargado, -a *m, f* de una bodega
victuals ['vɪtəlz, *Am:* 'vɪt̬-] *n pl, a. iron* vituallas *fpl*
videlicet [vɪ'diːlɪset, *Am:* vɪ'deləsɪt] *adv form* a saber
video ['vɪdiəʊ, *Am:* -oʊ] **I.** *n* **1.** vídeo *m;* **to come out on** ~ salir en vídeo **2.** (*tape*) cinta *f* de vídeo; **blank** ~ cinta de vídeo virgen **II.** *vt* grabar en vídeo
video camera *n* videocámara *f* **video cassette** *n* videocasete *m* **video conference** *n* videoconferencia *f* **video game** *n* videojuego *m* **videophone** *n* videoteléfono *m* **video recorder** *n* magnetoscopio *m* **video set** *n* equipo *m* de vídeo **video surveillance** *n no pl* vigilancia *f* con cámaras de vídeo **videotape I.** *n* cinta *f* de vídeo **II.** *vt* grabar en vídeo **videotex**(**t**) *n* videotexto *m* **video transmission** *n no pl* transmisión *f* por vídeo **video transmitter** *n* transmisor *m* de señales de vídeo
vie [vaɪ] <vying> *vi* **to** ~ (**with sb**) **for sth** competir (con alguien) por algo
Vienna [vi'enə] *n* Viena *f*
Viennese [ˌvɪə'niːz, *Am:* ˌviːə'-] **I.** *n inv* vienés, -esa *m, f* **II.** *adj* vienés, -esa
Vietcong [ˌvjet'kɒŋ, *Am:* ˌviːet'kɑːŋ] *n inv* vietcong *m*
Vietnam [ˌvjet'næm, *Am:* ˌviːet'nɑːm] *n* Vietnam *m*
Vietnamese [ˌvjetnə'miːz, *Am:* viˌet-] **I.** *adj* vietnamita **II.** *n* **1.** (*person*) vietnamita *mf* **2.** LING vietnamita *m*
view [vjuː] **I.** *n* **1.** (*opinion*) punto *m* de vista; **exchange of** ~**s** intercambio *m* de opiniones; **conflicting** ~**s** opiniones *fpl* contrapuestas; **prevailing** ~ opinión *f* dominante; **to express a** ~ expresar un parecer; **to have an optimistic** ~ **of life** ver la vida con optimismo; **to hold strong** ~**s about sth** mantener una postura fuerte sobre algo; **to share a** ~ compartir un punto de vista; **a long** ~ **of sth** una visión amplia de algo; **in her** ~ **...** a su modo de ver... **2.** (*perspective*) perspectiva *f;* **long-term** ~ perspectiva a largo plazo; **to take the long** ~ **of sth** considerar algo a largo plazo **3.** (*sight*) vista *f;* **to afford a panoramic** ~ permitir una vista panorámica; **to block sb's** ~ estar tapando a alguien (la vista); **to come into** ~ aparecer ante la vista; **to disappear from** ~ perderse de vista; **to keep sb/sth in** ~ mantener a alguien/algo en el punto de mira **4.** (*opportunity to observe*) panorama *m* ▸**to take a poor** ~ **of sth** ver algo con malos ojos, tener un concepto desfavorable de algo; **to have sth in** ~ tener algo en mente; **in** ~ **of sth** en vista de algo; **to be on** ~ estar expuesto; **to be on** ~ **to the public** estar abierto al público; **with a** ~ **to sth** con vistas a algo; **with this in** ~ con este fin **II.** *vt* **1.** (*consider*) considerar; **to** ~ **sth from a different angle** enfocar algo desde un ángulo distinto; **to** ~ **sth with reluctance** tomarse algo con reticencia **2.** (*watch*) ver **3.** (*take a look at*) mirar
viewer *n* **1.** (*person*) telespectador(a) *m(f)* **2.** (*device*) proyector *m* de diapositivas **3.** INFOR visor *m,* visualizador *m*
viewfinder ['vjuːˌfaɪndəʳ, *Am:* -də˞] *n* visor *m*
viewing *n no pl* visita *f;* **a second** ~ **of the film is also frightening** ver la película por segunda vez también da miedo; ~ **figures** índice *m* de audiencia
viewpoint ['vjuːpɔɪnt] *n* **1.** (*point of view*) punto *m* de vista **2.** (*vista point*) mirador *m*
vigil ['vɪdʒɪl, *Am:* 'vɪdʒəl] *n* vela *f;* **to keep** ~ mantenerse alerta; **to hold a** ~ velar
vigilance ['vɪdʒɪləns] *n no pl* vigilancia *f;* **to relax** ~ bajar la guardia
vigilant ['vɪdʒɪlənt] *adj* vigilante; **to be** ~ **in doing sth** estar atento al hacer algo
vignette [vɪ'njet] *n* estampa *f*
vigor *n Am, Aus,* **vigour** ['vɪgəʳ, *Am:* -ə˞] *n no pl* vigor *m;* (*energy*) energía *f;* **to do sth with** ~ hacer algo con energía
vigorous ['vɪgərəs] *adj* **1.** (*energetic*) enérgico, -a; (*protest*) rotundo, -a **2.** (*flourishing: growth*) pujante
vile [vaɪl] *adj* **1.** (*disgusting, shameful*) vil **2.** *inf* (*very bad*) vomitivo, -a; (*weather*) asqueroso, -a; ~ **mood** humor *m* de perros; **to be** ~ **to sb** portarse como un cerdo con alguien; **to smell** ~ apestar
vilify ['vɪlɪfaɪ, *Am:* '-ə-] <-ie-> *vt form* envilecer
village ['vɪlɪdʒ] **I.** *n* **1.** (*small settlement*) aldea *f* **2.** + *pl/sing vb* (*populace*) pueblo *m* **II.** *adj* de pueblo
village community <-ies> *n* pueblo *m* de organización comunal **village green** *n* prado *m* comunal **village inn** *n* taberna *f* de pueblo
villager ['vɪlɪdʒəʳ, *Am:* -ədʒə˞] *n* aldeano, -a *m, f*
villain ['vɪlən] *n* **1.** (*evil person*) villano, -a *m, f;* **small-time** ~ maleante *mf;* **to cast sb as a** ~ quedar alguien como el malo **2.** (*bad guy*) granuja *mf* ▸**the** ~ **of the piece** *inf* el malo/la mala de la obra

V

villainous [vɪlənəs] *adj* infame
villainy ['vɪləni] *n no pl* vileza *f*
vim [vɪm] *n no pl* brío *m*
vinaigrette [ˌvɪnɪ'gret, *Am:* -ə'-] *n no pl* vinagreta *f*
vindicate ['vɪndɪkeɪt, *Am:* -də-] *vt* **1.** (*justify*) justificar **2.** (*support*) reivindicar **3.** (*clear of blame, suspicion*) vindicar
vindication [ˌvɪndɪ'keɪʃən, *Am:* -də'-] *n no pl* **1.** (*justification*) justificación *f* **2.** (*act of clearing blame*) vindicación *f*
vindictive [vɪn'dɪktɪv] *adj* vengativo, -a
vine [vaɪn] *n* **1.** (*grape plant*) vid *f* **2.** (*climbing type*) parra *f*
vinegar ['vɪnɪgəʳ, *Am:* -əgɚ] *n no pl* vinagre *m*
vinegary *adj* avinagrado, -a; **to be ~** estar aliñado con vinagre
vineyard ['vɪnjəd, *Am:* -jɚd] *n* viñedo *m*
vintage ['vɪntɪdʒ, *Am:* -t̬ɪdʒ] **I.** *n* **1.** (*wine from a particular year*) cosecha *f* **2.** (*harvest season*) vendimia *f* **II.** *adj* **1.** GASTR añejo, -a **2.** (*high and classic quality*) excelente; **~ music of the sixties** clásicos *mpl* de la música de los sesenta **3.** *Aus, Brit* AUTO antiguo, -a; **~ car** coche *m* de época
vintner ['vɪntnəʳ, *Am:* -nɚ] *n* vinatero, -a *m, f*
vinyl ['vaɪnəl] **I.** *n no pl* vinilo *m* **II.** *adj* de vinilo
viola¹ [vi'əʊlə, *Am:* vi'oʊ-] *n* MUS viola *f*
viola² ['vaɪələ, *Am:* 'viːələ] *n* BOT viola *f*
violate ['vaɪəleɪt] *vt* **1.** (*break, not comply with*) violar; **to ~ a cease-fire agreement** romper un acuerdo de alto al fuego **2.** (*disturb*) perturbar; (*tomb*) profanar; **to ~ sb's privacy** entrometerse en la privacidad de alguien
violation [ˌvaɪə'leɪʃən] *n* violación *f;* **traffic ~** infracción *f* de tráfico
violence ['vaɪələnts] *n no pl* violencia *f*
violent ['vaɪələnt] *adj* **1.** (*cruel*) violento, -a; (*argument*) duro, -a **2.** (*very powerful*) fuerte; (*clothes*) chillón, -ona
violet ['vaɪələt, *Am:* -lɪt] **I.** *n* **1.** BOT violeta *f* **2.** (*colour*) violeta *m* **II.** *adj* violeta
violin [ˌvaɪə'lɪn] *n* MUS violín *m*
violinist [vaɪə'lɪnɪst] *n* MUS violinista *mf*
violoncellist [ˌvaɪələn'tʃelɪst, *Am:* ˌviːəlɑːn'-] *n* MUS violoncelista *mf*
violoncello [ˌvaɪələn'tʃeləʊ, *Am:* ˌviːəlɑːn'tʃeloʊ] *n* violoncelo *m*
VIP [ˌviːaɪ'piː] *s.* **very important person** VIP *mf*
viper ['vaɪpəʳ, *Am:* -pɚ] *n a. fig* víbora *f*
virago [vɪ'rɑːgəʊ, *Am:* və'rɑːgoʊ] <-(e)s> *n* arpía *f*
virgin ['vɜːdʒɪn, *Am:* 'vɜːr-] *n* virgen *f;* **the Blessed ~** la Santísima Virgen
virginal ['vɜːdʒɪnəl, *Am:* 'vɜːr-] *n* virginal
virgin forest *n* bosque *m* virgen
Virginia [və'dʒɪnjə, *Am:* vɚ-] *n* Virginia *f*
Virgin Islands *n* Islas *fpl* Vírgenes
virginity [və'dʒɪnəti, *Am:* vɚ'dʒɪnət̬i] *n no pl* virginidad *f;* **to lose one's ~** perder uno la virginidad
Virgo ['vɜːgəʊ, *Am:* 'vɜːrgoʊ] *n* Virgo *mf*
virile ['vɪraɪl, *Am:* -əl] *adj* viril
virility [vɪ'rɪləti, *Am:* və'rɪlət̬i] *n no pl* **1.** (*sexual vigour*) virilidad *f* **2.** (*forcefulness*) fuerza *f*
virology [vaɪə'rɒlədʒi, *Am:* vaɪ'rɑːlə-] *n no pl* virología *f*
virtual ['vɜːtʃuəl, *Am:* 'vɜːrtʃu-] *adj* virtual; **to provoke a ~ collapse of the economy** provocar prácticamente un colapso de la economía; **to be a ~ unknown** ser en efecto un desconocido
virtually *adv* prácticamente
virtual office *n* oficina *f* virtual **virtual reality** *n* realidad *f* virtual **virtual shopping mall** *n* centro *m* comercial virtual **virtual storage** *n no pl* almacenamiento *m* virtual
virtue ['vɜːtjuː, *Am:* 'vɜːrtʃuː] *n* **1.** (*good moral quality*) virtud *f* **2.** (*advantage, benefit*) ventaja *f* ▸**to make a ~ of necessity** hacer de la necesidad virtud; **to make a ~ (out) of sth** convertir algo en virtud; **by ~ of** *form* en virtud de
virtuosity [ˌvɜːtju'ɒsəti, *Am:* ˌvɜːrtʃu'ɑːsət̬i] *n no pl, form* virtuosidad *f*
virtuoso [ˌvɜːtju'əʊsəʊ, *Am:* ˌvɜːrtʃu'oʊsoʊ] <-s *o* -osi> **I.** *n* virtuoso, -a *m, f* **II.** *adj* virtuoso, -a; **a ~ display of diplomacy** un magnífico despliegue de habilidad diplomática
virtuous ['vɜːtʃuəs, *Am:* 'vɜːrtʃu-] *adj* **1.** (*morally good*) virtuoso, -a **2.** (*chaste*) casto, -a
virulence ['vɪrʊlənts, *Am:* -jə-] *n no pl* virulencia *f*
virulent ['vɪrʊlənt, *Am:* -jə-] *adj* **1.** MED virulento, -a **2.** *form* (*hateful and fierce*) violento, -a
virus ['vaɪərəs, *Am:* 'vaɪ-] <-es> *n* INFOR, MED virus *m inv*
visa ['viːzə] **I.** *n* visado *m* **II.** *adj* de visado
vis-à-vis [ˌviːzɑː'viː, *Am:* ˌviːzə'viː] **I.** *prep* con relación a; (*compared to*) en comparación con **II.** *n* cara a cara *m*
viscera ['vɪsərə] *npl* vísceras *fpl*
viscose ['vɪskəʊs, *Am:* -koʊs] *n no pl* viscosa *f*
viscosity [vɪ'skɒsəti, *Am:* -'skɑːsət̬i] *n no pl* viscosidad *f*
viscount ['vaɪkaʊnt] *n* vizconde *m*
viscountess [ˌvaɪkaʊn'təs, *Am:* 'vaɪkaʊnt̬ɪs] *n* vizcondesa *f*
viscous ['vɪskəs] *adj* viscoso, -a
vise [vaɪs] *n Am s.* **vice²**
visibility [ˌvɪzə'bɪləti, *Am:* -əbɪlət̬i] *n no pl* **1.** (*clearness of view*) visibilidad *f;* **poor ~** poca visibilidad **2.** (*public awareness*) notoriedad *f*
visible ['vɪzəbl] *adj* **1.** (*able to be seen, noticeable*) visible; **to be barely ~** ser a penas perceptible **2.** (*in the public eye*) notorio, -a
vision ['vɪʒən] *n* **1.** *no pl* (*sight*) vista *f;*

blurred ~ visión *f* borrosa **2.** (*mental image*) *a.* REL visión *f* **3.** *fig* (*beautiful sight*) imagen *f;* **to have ~s of fame** soñar con ser famoso
visionary ['vɪʒənəri, *Am:* -əneri] **I.** *n* visionario, -a *m, f* **II.** *adj* **1.** (*hallucinatory*) utópico, -a **2.** (*future-orientated*) con visión de futuro
visit ['vɪzɪt] **I.** *n* visita *f;* **to have a ~ from sb** recibir una visita de alguien; **to pay a ~ to sb** ir a ver a alguien **II.** *vt* visitar **III.** *vi* ir de visita
visitation [ˌvɪzɪ'teɪʃən, *Am:* -ə'-] *n* **1.** (*act of visiting*) visita *f* **2.** *iron* (*official visit*) inspección *f* **3.** REL visión *f* **4.** *Am* (*time*) tiempo *m* de visita
visiting hours *npl* horario *m* de visita **visiting professor** *n* profesor(a) *m(f)* visitante
visitor ['vɪzɪtə^r, *Am:* -t̬ɚ] *n* visitante *mf;* **~s' book** libro *m* de visitas
visor ['vaɪzə^r, *Am:* -zɚ] *n* visera *f*
vista ['vɪstə] *n* **1.** (*splendid view*) vista *f* **2.** *fig* perspectiva *f;* **to open up a ~** abrir una perspectiva; **to raise a ~** levantar perspectivas
visual ['vɪʒuəl] *adj* visual; **~ sense** sentido *m* estético; **~ aid** soporte *m* visual
visualize ['vɪʒuəlaɪz] *vt* visualizar
vital ['vaɪtəl, *Am:* -t̬əl] *adj* vital; **~ ingredient** ingrediente *m* esencial; **~ organs** órganos *mpl* vitales; **~ part** parte *f* crucial; **~ statistics** estadísticas *fpl* demográficas; **it is ~ to do ...** es fundamental hacer...
vitality [vaɪ'tæləti, *Am:* -ət̬i] *n no pl* vitalidad *f*
vitalize ['vaɪtəlaɪz, *Am:* -t̬əlaɪz-] *vt* **1.** (*give life to*) vivificar **2.** (*animate*) dar vida; *fig* vitalizar
vitamin ['vɪtəmɪn, *Am:* 'vaɪt̬ə-] *n* vitamina *f*
vitamin deficiency *n no pl* avitaminosis *f inv* **vitamin tablets** *n* comprimidos *mpl* vitamínicos
vitreous ['vɪtriəs] *adj* vítreo, -a
vitrify ['vɪtrɪfaɪ, *Am:* -trə-] <-ie-> **I.** *vt* vitrificar **II.** *vi* vitrificarse
vitriol ['vɪtriəl] *n no pl* vitriolio *m*
vitriolic [ˌvɪtri'ɒlɪk, *Am:* -'ɑːlɪk] *adj* vitriólico, -a
vituperate [vɪ'tjuːpəreɪt, *Am:* vaɪ'tuːpəreɪt] *form* **I.** *vt* vituperar **II.** *vi* vituperarse
vituperation [vɪˌtjuːpə'reɪʃən, *Am:* vaɪˌtuːpəreɪ-] *n no pl, form* vituperio *m*
vivacious [vɪ'veɪʃəs] *adj* vivaz; **a ~ blonde** una rubia llena de vida; **a ~ life** una vida animada
vivacity [vɪ'væsəti, *Am:* -ət̬i] *n no pl* vivacidad *f*
vivarium [vaɪ'veəriəm, *Am:* vaɪ'veri-] <-s *o* vivaria> *n* vivero *m*
viva voce [ˌvaɪvə'vəʊsi, *Am:* -'voʊsiː] **I.** *n* examen *m* oral **II.** *adj* oral **III.** *adv* a viva voz
vivid ['vɪvɪd] *adj* (*colour*) vivo, -a; (*language*) vívido, -a; (*imagination*) fértil
viviparous [vɪ'vɪpərəs, *Am:* vaɪ'-] *adj* vivíparo, -a
vivisect [ˌvɪvɪ'sekt, *Am:* 'vɪvəsekt] *vt* viviseccionar
vivisection [ˌvɪvɪ'sekʃən, *Am:* -ə'-] *n no pl* vivisección *f*
vixen ['vɪksən] *n* **1.** ZOOL zorra *f* **2.** *pej* (*woman*) arpía *f*
viz [vɪz] *adv abbr of* **videlicet** (**namely**) a saber
vocabulary [vəʊ'kæbjələri, *Am:* voʊ'kæbjəler-] *n* vocabulario *m;* **limited ~** vocabulario limitado; **to widen one's ~** ampliar el vocabulario de uno; **the word 'politeness' isn't in his ~** *iron* la palabra 'modales' no entra en su vocabulario
vocal ['vəʊkəl, *Am:* 'voʊ-] **I.** *adj* **1.** (*of the voice*) oral; **~ communication** comunicación *f* oral; **~ cords** cuerdas *fpl* vocales **2.** (*outspoken*) vehemente; **a ~ minority** una minoría que se hace oír; **to be ~** (**about sth**) armar revuelo (acerca de algo) **II.** *n* voz *f,* vocalista *mf;* **lead ~** voz principal; **to be on ~s** cantar
vocalist ['vəʊkəlɪst, *Am:* 'voʊ-] *n* vocalista *mf*
vocalize ['vəʊkəlaɪz, *Am:* 'voʊ-] **I.** *vi* vocalizar **II.** *vt* vocalizar
vocation [vəʊ'keɪʃən, *Am:* voʊ'-] *n* vocación *f;* **to miss one's ~** equivocarse de carrera
vocational [vəʊ'keɪʃənəl, *Am:* voʊ'-] *adj* vocacional; **~ counselling** orientación *f* profesional; **~ training** formación *f* profesional
vociferate [vəʊ'sɪfəreɪt, *Am:* voʊ'-] **I.** *vi* quejarse a gritos **II.** *vt* vociferar
vociferation [vəʊˌsɪfə'reɪʃən, *Am:* voʊˌ-] *n form* vocerío *m*
vociferous [vəʊ'sɪfərəs, *Am:* voʊ'-] *adj* vociferante
vogue [vəʊg, *Am:* voʊg] *n* moda *f* ▶ **to have a ~** estar de moda; **in ~** de moda; **to be back in ~** ponerse de moda de nuevo; **out of ~** pasado de moda
voice [vɔɪs] **I.** *n* voz *f;* **in a loud ~** en voz alta; **to raise/lower one's ~** levantar/bajar la voz; **to lose one's ~** quedarse afónico; **to listen to the ~ of reason** atender a razones; **to make one's ~ heard** hacerse escuchar; **with one ~** a coro; **to give ~ to sth** expresar algo; **the ~ within sb** la voz de la conciencia de alguien **II.** *vt* expresar
voice box <-es> *n inf* laringe *f*
voiced *adj* sonoro, -a
voiceless ['vɔɪsləs] *adj* **1.** LING sordo, -a **2.** *liter* sin voz
voice over *n* TV, CINE voz *f* en off
void [vɔɪd] **I.** *n* **1.** (*empty space*) hueco *m* **2.** (*feeling of emptiness*) vacío *m* **II.** *adj* inválido, -a; **to be ~ of sth** estar falto de algo **III.** *vt* anular
vol *abbr of* **volume** vol.
volatile ['vɒlətaɪl, *Am:* 'vɑːlət̬əl] *adj* volátil; (*situation*) inestable; (*person*) voluble
volcanic [vɒl'kænɪk, *Am:* vɑːl'-] *adj* volcánico, -a
volcano [vɒl'keɪnəʊ, *Am:* vɑːl'keɪnoʊ] <-(e)s> *n* volcán *m*
vole [vəʊl, *Am:* voʊl] *n* ratón *m* de campo

V

volition [vəʊ'lɪʃən, *Am:* voʊ'-] *n no pl, form* voluntad *f;* **to do sth (out) of one's own ~** hacer algo por voluntad propia
volley ['vɒli, *Am:* 'vɑ:li] **I.** *n* **1.** (*salvo*) descarga *f;* **to discharge ~s** descargar salvas **2.** (*onslaught*) lluvia *f;* **a ~ of enquiries** una retahíla de preguntas; **a ~ of insults** una sarta de insultos **3.** SPORTS volea *f* **II.** *vi* SPORTS volear **III.** *vt* **to ~ a ball** sacar una pelota
volleyball ['vɒlibɔ:l, *Am:* 'vɑ:li-] *n no pl* voleibol *m*
volt [vəʊlt, *Am:* voʊlt] *n* voltio *m*
voltage ['vəʊltɪdʒ, *Am:* 'voʊlt̬ɪdʒ] *n* voltaje *m*
voltage detector *n* ELEC voltímetro *m* **voltage drop** *n* ELEC caída *f* de tensión
volte-face [ˌvɒlt'fɑ:s, *Am:* ˌvɑ:lt'fɑ:s] *n* cambio *m* radical (de opinión)
voluble ['vɒljəbl, *Am:* 'vɑ:l-] *adj form* **1.** (*loquacious*) locuaz **2.** (*wordy*) extenso, -a
volume ['vɒlju:m, *Am:* 'vɑ:lju:m] *n no pl* (*all senses*) volumen *m;* **~ of sales** COM volumen de ventas; **to turn the ~ up/down** subir/bajar el volumen ►**to speak ~s for sth** ser muy indicativo de algo
volume control, **volume regulator** *n* control *m* del volumen **volume discount** *n* rappel *m*
voluminous [və'lu:mɪnəs, *Am:* və'lu:mə-] *adj form* **1.** (*extensive*) exhaustivo, -a **2.** (*very large*) voluminoso, -a; (*clothes*) amplísimo, -a
voluntary ['vɒləntəri, *Am:* 'vɑ:lənteri] *adj* voluntario, -a
voluntary organization *n* organización *f* de voluntariado **voluntary redundancy** <-ies> *n* baja *f* incentivada
volunteer [ˌvɒlən'tɪəʳ, *Am:* ˌvɑ:lən'tɪr] **I.** *n* voluntario, -a *m, f* **II.** *vt* **to ~ oneself for sth** ofrecerse (voluntario) para algo; **to ~ information** dar información por iniciativa propia **III.** *vi* ofrecerse; (*willingly join*) presentarse voluntario, -a **IV.** *adj* de voluntarios; **~ army** ejército *m* de voluntarios
voluptuous [və'lʌptʃuəs] *adj* **1.** (*sexually appealing*) voluptuoso, -a **2.** (*epicurean*) placentero, -a
volute [vəʊ'lu:t, *Am:* və'lu:t] *n* **1.** ARCHIT voluta *f* **2.** ZOOL (*marine gastropod*) concha *f;* (*snail's shell*) caparazón *m*
vomit ['vɒmɪt, *Am:* 'vɑ:mɪt] **I.** *vi* vomitar; **it makes me want to ~** *a. fig* me produce náuseas **II.** *vt* vomitar **III.** *n no pl* vómito *m*
voodoo ['vu:du:] *n no pl* **1.** (*black magic*) vudú *m* **2.** *inf* (*jinx*) **there is (some sort of) ~ on this castle** este castillo está hechizado
voracious [və'reɪʃəs, *Am:* vɔ:'reɪ-] *adj* voraz
voracity [və'ræsəti, *Am:* vɔ:'ræsət̬i] *n no pl* voracidad *f*
vortex ['vɔ:teks, *Am:* 'vɔ:r-] <-es *o* vortices> *n* vórtice *m;* **~ of emotion** torbellino *m* de emociones
vote [vəʊt, *Am:* voʊt] **I.** *vi* **1.** (*elect*) votar; **to ~ for/against sb/sth** votar a favor/en contra de alguien/algo **2.** (*formally decide*) **to ~ on sth** someter algo a votación **II.** *vt* **1.** (*elect*) elegir por votación **2.** (*propose*) **to ~ that ...** votar que... +*subj* **3.** (*declare*) considerar **III.** *n* **1.** (*formally made choice*) voto *m* **2.** (*election*) votación *f;* **to put sth to the ~** someter algo a votación **3.** (*right to elect*) **to have the ~** tener derecho al voto
◆**vote down** *vt* rechazar (por votación)
◆**vote in** *vt* elegir (por votación)
◆**vote on** *vt* aprobar (por votación)
◆**vote out** *vt* **to vote sb out (of sth)** no reelegir a alguien (en algo)
voter *n* votante *mf*
voting **I.** *adj* de votos **II.** *n* votación *f*
voting booth <-es> *n* cabina *f* de votación **voting box** <-es> *n* urna *f* de votos **voting machine** *n* máquina *f* de recuento de votos
vouch [vaʊtʃ] **I.** *vi* **to ~ for sth/sb** responder de algo/por alguien **II.** *vt* **to ~ that ...** confirmar que...
voucher ['vaʊtʃəʳ, *Am:* -tʃɚ] *n Aus, Brit* **1.** (*coupon*) vale *m* **2.** (*receipt*) comprobante *m*
vouchsafe [ˌvaʊtʃ'seɪf] *vt form* **to ~ (sb) sth** dignarse a dar algo (a alguien); **to ~ to do sth** dignarse a hacer algo
vow [vaʊ] **I.** *vt* jurar; **to ~ chastity** hacer voto de castidad **II.** *n* **to take a ~** hacer los votos
vowel ['vaʊəl] *n* vocal *f*
voyage ['vɔɪɪdʒ] **I.** *n* viaje *m* **II.** *vi* viajar; **to ~ across sth** viajar por algo
voyager ['vɔɪɪdʒəʳ, *Am:* 'vɔɪɪdʒɚ] *n* navegante *mf*
voyeur [vwɑ:'jɜ:ʳ, *Am:* vɔɪ'jɜ:r] *n* mirón, -ona *m, f*
VTOL ['vi:tɒl, *Am:* -tɑ:l] AVIAT *abbr of* **vertical take-off and landing** despegue *m* y aterrizaje vertical
VTR [ˌvi:ti:'ɑ:ʳ, *Am:* -'ɑ:r] *n abbr of* **videotape recorder** vídeo *m*
vulcanite ['vʌlkənaɪt] *n no pl* vulcanita *f*
vulcanization [ˌvʌlkənaɪ'zeɪʃən] *n no pl* vulcanización *f*
vulcanize ['vʌlkənaɪz] *vt* vulcanizar
vulgar ['vʌlgəʳ, *Am:* -gɚ] *adj* **1.** (*crude*) ordinario, -a **2.** (*commonplace*) vulgar; **~ accent** acento *m* chabacano
vulgarity [vʌl'gærəti, *Am:* -'gerət̬i] *n no pl* **1.** (*crudeness*) vulgaridad *f* **2.** (*ordinariness*) chabacanería *f*
vulgarize ['vʌlgəraɪz] *vt* vulgarizar
Vulgate ['vʌlgeɪt] *n* **the ~** la Vulgata
vulnerable ['vʌlnərəbl, *Am:* 'vʌlnɚə-] *adj* vulnerable
vulture ['vʌltʃəʳ, *Am:* -tʃɚ] *n a. fig* buitre *m*
vulva ['vʌlvə] <-s *o* -e> *n* vulva *f*
vying ['vaɪɪŋ] *pres p of* **vie**

W

W, w ['dʌblju:] *n* W, w *f;* ~ **for William** W de Washington
w *abbr of* **watt** W
W *n abbr of* **west** O
wack [wæk] *n Brit, inf* amigo, -a *m, f,* pipe *m AmC*
wacko ['wækəʊ, *Am:* -oʊ] *n Am* bicho *m* raro
wacky ['wæki] <-ier, -iest> *adj inf* (*person*) chiflado, -a; (*thing*) estrambótico, -a
wad [wɒd, *Am:* wɑ:d] *n* (*of straw*) manojo *m;* (*of cotton*) bola *f;* (*of banknotes*) fajo *m;* (*of forms*) montón *m*
wadding ['wɒdɪŋ, *Am:* 'wɑ:d-] *n no pl* relleno *m*
waddle ['wɒdl, *Am:* 'wɑ:dl] **I.** *vi* anadear **II.** *n* andares *mpl* de pato
wade [weɪd] **I.** *vi* caminar por el agua; **to ~ across** vadear; **to ~ into sth** adentrarse en algo caminando; **to ~ into sb** *inf* tomarla con alguien; **to ~ through a book** leerse un libro con dificultad **II.** *vt* vadear **III.** *n Am* chapoteo *m*
wader ['weɪdəʳ, *Am:* -dɚ] *n* **1.** (*bird*) ave *m* zancuda **2.** *pl* (*boots*) botas *fpl* de pescador
wafer ['weɪfəʳ, *Am:* -fɚ] *n* **1.** (*biscuit*) galleta *f* de barquillo; (*for ice cream*) barquillo *m* **2.** REL hostia *f*
wafer-thin [ˌweɪfə'θɪn, *Am:* -fɚ'-] *adj* finísimo, -a
waffle¹ ['wɒfl, *Am:* 'wɑ:fl] *Brit* **I.** *vi* (*to talk*) **to ~ (on)** parlotear; (*in an essay*) meter paja *fig* **II.** *n no pl* palabrería *f;* (*in an essay*) paja *f fig*
waffle² ['wɒfl, *Am:* 'wɑ:fl] *n* GASTR gofre *m,* waffle *m AmL*
waffle iron *n Am* plancha *f* para gofres [*o* waffles *AmL*]
waft [wɒft, *Am:* wɑ:ft] *liter* **I.** *vi* (*scent, sound*) llegar (flotando); **a delicious smell ~ed in from the kitchen** un delicioso aroma llegaba (flotando) de la cocina **II.** *vt* llevar por el aire
wag¹ [wæg] **I.** <-gg-> *vt* menear; **to ~ one's finger at sb** amenazar a alguien con el dedo; **the dog ~ged its tail** el perro meneaba el rabo **II.** <-gg-> *vi* menearse **III.** *n* meneo *m*
wag² [wæg] *n inf* bromista *mf*
wage [weɪdʒ] **I.** *vt* (*war*) hacer; **to ~ war against sth/sb** librar una batalla contra algo/alguien; **to ~ a campaign for/against sth** emprender una campaña por/contra algo **II.** *n* sueldo *m;* **living ~** salario mínimo vital; **minimum ~** salario mínimo; **real ~s** salario real; **to earn a ~** percibir un salario; **to get a good ~** tener un buen sueldo
wage adjustment *n* ajuste *m* salarial **wage bill** *n* nómina *f* **wage claim** *n,* **wage demand** *n Brit* reivindicación *f* salarial **wage costs** *npl* costes *mpl* salariales **wage differentials** *npl* disparidades *fpl* salariales **wage dispute** *n* disputa *f* salarial **wage earner** *n* asalariado, -a *m, f* **wage freeze** *n* congelación *f* salarial **wage increase** *n* aumento *m* salarial **wage level** *n* nivel *m* de salarios **wage negotiation** *n* negociación *f* salarial **wage packet** *n Brit* **1.** (*pay*) sueldo *m* (neto) **2.** (*envelope*) sobre *m* de la paga
wager ['weɪdʒəʳ, *Am:* -dʒɚ] **I.** *n* apuesta *f;* **to lay a ~** hacer una apuesta **II.** *vt* apostar; **to ~ one's reputation/life** jugarse la reputación/vida
wage scale *n* escala *f* de salarios
wages clerk *n* administrativo, -a *m, f* del área de personal
wage settlement *n* fijación *f* de salarios **wage slip** *n* recibo *m* de sueldo
wages policy <-ies> *n* política *f* salarial
wage worker *n Am* asalariado, -a *m, f*
waggish ['wægɪʃ] *adj inf* bromista
waggle ['wægl] **I.** *vt* mover **II.** *vi* moverse
waggly ['wægli] <-ier, -iest> *adj* tambaleante; (*tooth*) flojo, -a
waggon *n Brit,* **wagon** ['wægən] *n* **1.** (*horse-drawn*) carro *m* **2.** *Brit* RAIL vagón *m* **3.** (*truck*) camión *m* ▸**to be on the ~** *inf* no beber; **to fall off the ~** *inf* volver a darse a la bebida; **to go on the ~** *inf* dejar la bebida
waif [weɪf] *n liter* **1.** (*child*) niño, -a *m, f* sin techo **2.** (*animal*) animal *m* callejero ▸**the ~s and strays** los sin techo
wail [weɪl] **I.** *vi* gemir; (*wind*) silbar **II.** *vt* lamentar **III.** *n* lamento *m*
wailing *n* gemidos *mpl*
Wailing Wall *n* Muro *m* de las Lamentaciones
waist [weɪst] *n* cintura *f*
waistband ['weɪstbænd] *n* cinturilla *f* **waistcoat** *n Brit* chaleco *m*
waist-deep [ˌweɪst'di:p] *adj* hasta la cintura
waistline ['weɪstlaɪn] *n* cintura *f;* **to watch the ~** guardar la línea
wait [weɪt] **I.** *vi* esperar; **to ~ for sth/sb** esperar algo/a alguien; **to keep sb ~ing** hacer esperar a alguien; **he cannot ~ to see her** está ansioso por verla; **~ and see** espera y verás; **(just) you ~!** ¡vas a ver!; **~ for it!** *inf* ¡espera el momento! **II.** *vt* esperar; **to ~ one's turn** esperar su turno **III.** *n no pl* espera *f;* **to lie in ~ for sb** estar al acecho de alguien
◆**wait about** *vi,* **wait around** *vi* **to ~ for sth** estar a la espera de algo
◆**wait behind** *vi* quedarse
◆**wait in** *vi* **to ~ for sb** quedarse en casa esperando a alguien
◆**wait on** *vt* **1.** (*serve*) servir **2.** *form* (*expect*) **to ~ sth** esperar a algo
◆**wait up** *vi* **to ~ for sb** esperar a alguien levantado

El **Waitangi Day** o **New Zealand Day** se celebra el 6 de enero. Ya que fue en ese día del año 1840 cuando 512 jefes de la tribu

W

de los **Maori** firmaron un acuerdo con el gobierno británico que significó el comienzo de Nueva Zelanda como nación.

waiter ['weɪtəʳ, *Am:* -t̬ɚ] *n* camarero *m,* garzón *m AmL,* mesero *m Méx*
waiting *n no pl* **1.** (*time spent waiting*) **the** ~ la espera **2.** *Brit* (*parking*) estacionamiento *m*
waiting game *n* **to play a** ~ dejar pasar el tiempo **waiting list** *n* lista *f* de espera **waiting room** *n* sala *f* de espera
waitress ['weɪtrɪs] *n* camarera *f,* garzona *f AmL,* mesera *f Méx*
waive [weɪv] *vt form* (*right*) renunciar a; (*rule*) no aplicar; (*charge*) cancelar
waiver ['weɪvəʳ, *Am:* -vɚ] *n* renuncia *f*
wake¹ [weɪk] *n* NAUT estela *f;* **in the** ~ **of** tras, después de
wake² [weɪk] *n* velatorio *m*
wake³ [weɪk] <woke *o* waked, woken *o* waked> **I.** *vi* despertarse **II.** *vt* despertar
◆**wake up** *vi, vt* despertar
wakeful ['weɪkfəl] *adj form* **1.** (*sleepless*) desvelado, -a; ~ **night** noche *f* en vela **2.** (*vigilant, alert*) alerta; **to feel** ~ sentirse despierto
waken ['weɪkən] *vt form* despertar
wakey ['weɪki] *interj iron* ~ ~**!** ¡venga, despierta!
Wales ['weɪlz] *n* Gales *m;* **North/South** ~ Gales del Norte/Sur; **New South** ~ Nueva *f* Gales del Sur
walk [wɔːk, *Am:* wɑːk] **I.** *n* **1.** (*stroll*) paseo *m;* **to take a** ~ ir a dar un paseo; **to take sb out for a** ~ sacar a alguien a pasear; **it's a five minute** ~ está a cinco minutos a pie **2.** (*gait*) andar *m* **3.** (*walking speed*) paso *m* ►~ **of life** condición *f;* **people from all** (**different**) ~**s of life** gente de todas las profesiones y condiciones sociales **II.** *vt* **1.** (*go on foot*) andar; (*distance*) recorrer a pie **2.** (*accompany*) **to** ~ **sb home** acompañar a alguien a su casa **3.** (*take for a walk*) **to** ~ **the dog** sacar a pasear el perro **4.** *Brit, inf* (*pass easily*) superar fácilmente; **she'll** ~ **the interview** la entrevista es pan comido para ella **III.** *vi* (*go on foot*) andar, caminar; (*stroll*) pasear ►**to** ~ **on air** no caber en sí de gozo
◆**walk about** *vi,* **walk around** *vi* dar una vuelta
◆**walk away** *vi form* irse; **to** ~ **from sb** alejarse de alguien; **to** ~ **from sth** desentenderse de algo; **to** ~ **from an accident** salir ileso de un accidente
◆**walk back** *vi* volver a pie
◆**walk in** *vi* entrar; **to** ~ **on sb** (**doing sth**) sorprender a alguien (haciendo algo) al entrar
◆**walk off** **I.** *vt* **to** ~ **the meal** salir a dar un paseo para bajar la comida **II.** *vi* marcharse
◆**walk on** *vi* seguir andando
◆**walk out** *vi* **1.** (*leave*) salir **2.** (*go on strike*) ir a la huelga
◆**walk over** *vt* (*rights*) pisotear; **to walk** (**all**) **over sb** machacar a alguien
◆**walk through** *vt insep* (*part*) ensayar
◆**walk up** *vi* **1.** (*go up*) subir **2.** (*approach*) **to** ~ **to sb** acercarse a alguien
walkabout ['wɔːkəbaʊt, *Am:* 'wɑː-] *n inf* paseo *m;* **to go** ~ pasearse entre el público
walkaway ['wɔːkəweɪ, *Am:* 'wɑː-] *n Am* victoria *f* fácil, pan *m* comido *inf;* **to win in a** ~ ganar sin problemas
walker ['wɔːkəʳ, *Am:* 'wɑːkɚ] *n* **1.** (*stroller*) paseante *mf* **2.** SPORTS marchista *mf* **3.** (*sb whose hobby is walking*) excursionista *mf*
walker-on *n* THEAT figurante, -a *m, f;* CINE extra *mf*
walkie-talkie [ˌwɔːki'tɔːki, *Am:* ˌwɑːki'tɑː-] *n* walkie-talkie *m*
walk-in ['wɔːkɪn, *Am:* 'wɑːk-] *adj Am* (*furniture*) empotrado, -a; ~ **wardrobe** vestidor *m*
walking **I.** *n no pl* paseo *m;* SPORTS marcha *f* atlética; **to do a lot of** ~ andar mucho **II.** *adj* **1.** **it is within** ~ **distance** se puede ir a pie **2.** (*human*) ambulante; **to be a** ~ **encyclopaedia** ser una enciclopedia ambulante
walking frame *n* andador *m* **walking-shoes** *npl* zapatos *mpl* para caminar **walking-stick** *n* bastón *m* **walking-tour** *n* excursión *f* a pie; (*guided trip*) paseo *m* guiado
walkman® ['wɔːkmən, *Am:* 'wɑːk-] <-s> *n* walkman® *m*
walk-on ['wɔːkɒn, *Am:* 'wɑːkɑːn] *adj* ~ **part** THEAT papel *m* de figurante; CINE papel *m* de extra
walk-out ['wɔːkaʊt, *Am:* 'wɑːk-] *n* salida *f;* (*strike*) huelga *f;* **to stage a** ~ salir; (*strike*) declarar la huelga
walk-over ['wɔːkˌəʊvəʳ, *Am:* 'wɑːkˌoʊvɚ] *n inf* victoria *f* fácil; **it was a** ~ fue pan comido
walk-through ['wɔːkˌθruː, *Am:* 'wɑːk-] *n* ensayo *m*
walkway ['wɔːkweɪ, *Am:* 'wɑːk-] *n* pasarela *m*
wall [wɔːl] **I.** *n* **1.** muro; (*in the interior*) *a.* ANAT pared *f;* (*enclosing town*) muralla *f;* (*enclosing house*) tapia *f;* **artery** ~ pared arterial; **the city** ~**s** las murallas de la ciudad; **the Great Wall of China** la Gran Muralla China; **dry-stone** ~ muro de piedra **2.** (*barrier*) barrera *f;* **a** ~ **of silence** un muro de silencio; **a** ~ **of water** una cortina de agua **3.** AUTO valla *f* ►**to have one's back to the** ~ estar entre la espada y la pared; ~**s have ears** *prov* las paredes oyen *prov;* **to go to the** ~ (*fail*) fracasar; (*go bankrupt*) quebrar; **to go up** [*o* **to climb**] **the** ~ subirse por las paredes **II.** *vt* (*garden*) cercar con un muro; (*town*) amurallar
◆**wall in** *vt* **1.** (*garden*) cercar con un muro; (*town*) amurallar **2.** *fig* encerrar
◆**wall off** *vt* separar con un muro; **to wall oneself off** *fig* encerrarse en sí mismo
◆**wall up** *vt* (*person*) emparedar; (*opening*) cerrar con un muro
wall bars *npl* espalderas *fpl* **wall chart** *n*

gráfico *m* de pared **wall clock** *n* reloj *m* de pared

wallet ['wɒlɪt, *Am:* 'wɑːlɪt] *n* cartera *f,* billetera *f AmL*

wallflower ['wɔːlˌflaʊəʳ, *Am:* -ˌflaʊɚ] *n* 1. BOT al(h)elí *m* 2. *fig* ≈ patito *m* feo

wallhanging *n* tapiz *m*

Wallis and Futuna [ˌwɒlɪsəndfuː'tjuːnə, *Am:* ˌwɑːlɪs-] *n* ~ **Islands** Islas *fpl* Wallis y Fortuna

wall map *n* mapa *m* mural

Wallonia [wə'ləʊniə, *Am:* wɑː'loʊ-] *n* Valonia *f*

Walloon [wɒ'luːn, *Am:* wɑː-] I. *adj* valón, -ona II. *n* 1. (*person*) valón, -ona *m, f* 2. LING valón *m*

wallop ['wɒləp, *Am:* 'wɑːləp] I. *vt inf* 1. (*hit hard*) dar un golpetazo 2. (*punish*) dar una paliza, zurrar II. *n* golpetazo *f;* **to give sb a** ~ pegar a alguien

walloping I. *adj* 1. *inf* (*very big*) enorme 2. *Am, inf* (*very good*) estupendo II. *n inf* paliza *f;* **to give sb a** ~ dar una paliza a alguien

wallow ['wɒləʊ, *Am:* 'wɑːloʊ] I. *n* revolcón *m* II. *vi* 1. (*lie in earth*) revolcarse 2. (*remain in negative state*) sumirse; **to** ~ **in self-pity** sumirse en la autocompasión 3. (*revel*) regodearse; **to** ~ **in wealth** nadar en la abundancia

wallpaper ['wɔːlˌpeɪpəʳ, *Am:* -pɚ] I. *n* papel *m* pintado; **a roll of** ~ un rollo de papel pintado; **to hang** ~ empapelar II. *vt* empapelar

wall socket *n* enchufe *m* de pared

Wall Street *n* 1. (*street*) *calle bursátil y financiera en Nueva York* 2. *fig* mundo *m* bursátil

wall-to-wall ['wɔltə'wɔːl, *Am:* -t̬ə'-] *adj* ~ **carpets** moqueta *f*

walnut ['wɔːlnʌt] *n* 1. (*nut*) nuez *f* 2. (*tree*) nogal *m*

walrus ['wɔːlrəs] <walruses *o* walrus> *n* morsa *f*

waltz [wɔːls, *Am:* wɔːlts] <-es> I. *n* vals *m* II. *vi* 1. (*dance*) valsar 2. *inf* (*walk confidently*) ir tan fresco III. *vt* **to** ~ **sb** bailar el vals con alguien

◆**waltz about** *vi,* **waltz around** *vi* dar vueltas despreocupado

◆**waltz in** *vi inf* entrar como si nada

◆**waltz off** *vi inf* **to** ~ **with sth** robar algo

◆**waltz out** *vi inf* salir como si nada

wan [wɒn, *Am:* wɑːn] <-nn> *adj liter* macilento, -a

wand [wɒnd, *Am:* wɑːnd] *n* (*conjuror's stick*) varita *f* mágica; **to wave one's magic** ~ agitar la varita mágica

wander ['wɒndəʳ, *Am:* 'wɑːndɚ] I. *vt* vagar por; **to** ~ **the streets** deambular por las calles, callejear II. *vi* (*roam*) vagar; (*stroll*) pasearse; **to let one's thoughts** ~ dejar volar la imaginación III. *n inf* paseo *m;* **to go for a** ~ **around the city** dar una vuelta por la ciudad

wanderer ['wɒndərəʳ, *Am:* 'wɑːndɚɚ] *n* hombre *m* errante, mujer *f* errante; *pej* vagabundo, -a *m, f*

wandering ['wɒndərɪŋ, *Am:* 'wɑːn-] *adj* 1. (*nomadic*) errante; (*salesman*) ambulante; ~ **tribe** tribu nómada 2. (*not concentrating*) divagante

wanderings ['wɒndərɪŋz, *Am:* 'wɑːn-] *n* andanzas *fpl; pej* vagabundeo *m*

wane [weɪn] I. *vi* menguar; **to wax and** ~ crecer y menguar II. *n* mengua *f;* **to be on the** ~ menguar

wangle ['wæŋgl] *vt inf* conseguir; **to** ~ **one's way into sth** arreglárselas para entrar en algo

want [wɒnt, *Am:* wɑːnt] I. *vt* 1. (*wish*) querer; **to** ~ **to do sth** querer hacer algo; **to** ~ **sb to do sth** querer que alguien haga algo; **to** ~ **sth done** querer que se haga algo; **you're** ~**ed on the phone** te llaman al teléfono; **I was** ~**ing to leave** estaba deseando marcharme 2. (*need*) necesitar; **he is** ~**ed by the police** lo busca la policía; **'**~**ed'** 'se busca'; **this soup** ~**s a bit of salt** a esta sopa le falta sal; **this** ~**s a lot of time** esto exige mucho tiempo II. *n* 1. (*need*) necesidad *f;* **to be in** ~ **of sth** necesitar algo 2. (*lack*) falta *f;* **for** ~ **of sth** por falta de algo; **to live in** ~ *form* vivir necesitado

◆**want in** *vi inf* **to** ~ **sth** querer participar en algo

◆**want out** *vi inf* **to** ~ (**of sth**) querer salirse (de algo)

wantage ['wɒntɪdʒ, *Am:* 'wɑːnt̬ɪdʒ] *n Am* deficiencia *f*

wanting *adj* deficiente; **to be** ~ **in sth** estar falto de algo; **there is sth** ~ falta algo

wanton ['wɒntən, *Am:* 'wɑːntən] *adj* 1. (*extreme*) desenfrenado, -a 2. (*mindless*) sin razón; ~ **destruction** destrucción sin sentido; ~ **disregard** desatención injustificada; ~ **waste** dispendio gratuito 3. (*licentious*) lascivo, -a 4. (*capricious*) caprichoso, -a; (*playful*) juguetón, -ona

WAP TEL, INFOR *abbr of* **wireless application protocol** WAP

wapiti ['wɒpɪti, *Am:* 'wɑːpət̬i] *n inv* wapití *m*

war [wɔːʳ, *Am:* wɔːr] *n* guerra *f;* **civil** ~ guerra civil; **the Great War** la Primera Guerra Mundial; **the Second World War** la Segunda Guerra Mundial; **a holy** ~ una guerra santa; **the horrors of** ~ los horrores de la guerra; **in time of** ~ en tiempo(s) de guerra; **to be at** ~ estar en guerra; **to declare** ~ **on sb** declarar la guerra a alguien; *fig* hacer la vida imposible a alguien; **to go to** ~ entrar en guerra; **to make** ~ **on sb** hacer la guerra a alguien

war atrocities *npl* crímenes *fpl* de guerra

war baby *n* niño, -a *m, f* nacido, -a durante la guerra

warble ['wɔːbl, *Am:* 'wɔːr-] *vi* (*bird*) trinar; (*lark*) gorjear; *iron* (*person*) hacer gorgoritos

warbler ['wɔːbləʳ, *Am:* 'wɔːrblɚ] *n* curruca *f*

war bond *n* bono *m* de guerra **war bulletin** *n* boletín *m* de guerra **war correspondent** *n* corresponsal *mf* de guerra **war crime** *n*

crimen *m* de guerra **war criminal** *n* criminal *mf* de guerra **war cry** *n* grito *m* de guerra
ward [wɔːd, *Am:* wɔːrd] *n* **1.** (*wardship*) tutela *f*; **in** ~ bajo tutela **2.** (*person*) pupilo, -a *m, f* **3.** (*in hospital*) sala *f*; **geriatric/psychiatric** ~ pabellón *m* geriátrico/psiquiátrico; **maternity** ~ sala *f* de maternidad **4.** *Brit* (*political area*) distrito *m* electoral
◆**ward off** *vt* evitar
warden ['wɔːdn, *Am:* 'wɔːr-] *n* guardián, -ana *m, f*; (*of a college*) director(a) *m(f)*; (*of a prison*) alcaide *m*
warder ['wɔːdəʳ, *Am:* 'wɔːrdɚ] *n* celador *m*
wardress ['wɔːdrɪs, *Am:* 'wɔːr-] *n* celadora *f*
wardrobe ['wɔːdrəʊb, *Am:* 'wɔːrdroʊb] *n* **1.** (*cupboard*) (armario *m*) ropero *m* **2.** *no pl* (*clothes*) vestuario *m*
wardrobe trunk *n* baúl *m* ropero
wardship ['wɔːdʃɪp, *Am:* 'wɔːrd-] *n no pl* tutela *f*
war effort *n* esfuerzo *m* bélico
warehouse ['weəhaʊs, *Am:* 'wer-] *n* almacén *m*
warehouse keeper *n* almacenista *mf*
wares [weəz, *Am:* werz] *npl inf* mercancías *fpl*
warfare ['wɔːfeəʳ, *Am:* 'wɔːrfer] *n no pl* guerra *f*
war game *n* juego *m* de guerra
warhead ['wɔːhed, *Am:* 'wɔːr-] *n* (*of rocket*) cabeza *f* de guerra
warily ['weərɪli, *Am:* 'wer-] *adv* (*expecting danger*) cautamente; (*suspiciously*) recelosamente
warlike ['wɔːlaɪk, *Am:* 'wɔːr-] *adj* **1.** (*of war*) bélico, -a **2.** (*belligerent*) belicoso, -a; ~ **speech** discurso beligerante
warlord ['wɔːlɔːd, *Am:* 'wɔːrlɔːrd] *n* jefe *m* militar
warm [wɔːm, *Am:* wɔːrm] **I.** *adj* **1.** (*comfortably hot*) caliente; (*clothes*) de abrigo; **nice and** ~ a gusto y calentito; **as** ~ **as toast** *inf* bien calentito; **to be** ~ (*person*) tener calor; (*thing*) estar caliente; (*weather*) hacer calor **2.** (*affectionate*) afectuoso; ~ **welcome** calurosa bienvenida; **to be** ~ ser [*o* estar] efusivo **3.** (*suggesting heat: day*) caluroso, -a; (*climate, wind*) cálido, -a **4.** (*fresh*) fresco, -a; ~ **track** huella fresca ►**you're getting** ~ ¡caliente, caliente! **II.** *n no pl* **the** ~ el calor **III.** *vt* calentar; **to** ~ **one's feet** calentarse los pies; **to** ~ **the soup** calentar la sopa; **to** ~ **sb's heart** reconfortar a alguien
◆**warm up** **I.** *vi* calentarse **II.** *vt* **1.** (*make hot*) calentar; **to warm sb up** hacer entrar en calor a alguien **2.** (*food*) recalentar
warm-blooded [ˌwɔːm'blʌdɪd, *Am:* ˌwɔːrm'-] *adj* de sangre caliente
warm front *n* frente *m* cálido
warm-hearted [ˌwɔːm'hɑːtɪd, *Am:* ˌwɔːrm-'hɑːrt̬ɪd] *adj* bondadoso, -a; (*affectionate*) cariñoso, -a
warmly *adv* **1.** (*of heat*) **wrap up** ~**!** ¡abrígate bien! **2.** (*enthusiasm*) calurosamente; **she shook my hand** ~ me estrechó la mano afectuosamente
warm start *n* arranque *m* en caliente
warmth [wɔːmθ, *Am:* wɔːrmθ] *n no pl* **1.** (*heat*) calor *m* **2.** (*affection*) calidez *f*
warm-up ['wɔːmʌp] *n* SPORTS (pre)calentamiento *m*
warn [wɔːn, *Am:* wɔːrn] *vt* **1.** (*make aware*) avisar, advertir; **to** ~ **sb not to do sth** advertir a alguien que no haga algo; **to** ~ **sb of a danger** prevenir a alguien contra un peligro **2.** LAW poner sobre aviso
◆**warn off** *vt* **to warn sb off sth** apercibir a alguien de algo; **to warn sb off doing sth** advertir a alguien de que no haga algo
warning [wɔːnɪŋ, *Am:* wɔːrnɪŋ] **I.** *n* aviso *m*, advertencia *f*; **a word of** ~ una advertencia; **to give sb a** ~ advertir a alguien; **give me some days'** ~ avísame von unos días de antelación; **to issue a** ~ (**about sth**) hacer una advertencia (acerca de algo); **to sound a note of** ~ dar la voz de alarma; **without** ~ sin previo aviso **II.** *adj* de advertencia
warning light *n* luz *f* de advertencia **warning shot** *n* disparo *m* de advertencia **warning sign** *n* señal *f* de peligro
warp [wɔːp, *Am:* wɔːrp] **I.** *vi* torcerse, deformarse **II.** *vt* **1.** (*wood*) torcer, deformar **2.** (*mind*) pervertir; **to** ~ **sb's mind** (re)torcer la mente de alguien **III.** *n* deformación *f*; **to have a ~ed way of looking at things** tener una manera retorcida de ver las cosas
warpaint ['wɔːpeɪnt, *Am:* 'wɔːr-] *n* pintura *f* de guerra
war-path ['wɔːʳpɑːθ, *Am:* 'wɔːrpæθ] *n no pl* **to be on the** ~ estar en pie de guerra; *fig* tener ganas de pelea
warped *adj* deformado, -a; (*mind*) pervertido, -a
warrant ['wɒrənt, *Am:* 'wɔːr-] **I.** *n* **1.** COM garantía *f* **2.** LAW orden *f*; **arrest** ~ orden de detención; **search** ~ orden de registro; **to execute a** ~ ejecutar una orden judicial **3.** *no pl* (*justification*) justificación *f* **II.** *vt* **1.** (*promise*) garantizar **2.** (*justify*) justificar
warrantee [ˌwɒrən'tiː, *Am:* ˌwɔːr-] *n* beneficiario, -a *m, f* de una garantía
warrant officer *n* **1.** MIL brigada *m* **2.** NAUT contramaestre *m*
warrantor ['wɒrəntɔːʳ, *Am:* 'wɔːrəntɔːr] *n* garante *mf*
warranty ['wɒrənti, *Am:* 'wɔːrənt̬i] <-ies> *n* garantía *f*
warren ['wɒrən, *Am:* 'wɔːr-] *n* **1.** ZOOL conejera *f* **2.** *fig* laberinto *m*
warring *adj* en guerra; ~ **factions** facciones beligerantes
warrior ['wɒriəʳ, *Am:* 'wɔːrjɚ] *n* guerrero, -a *m, f*
Warsaw ['wɔːsɔː, *Am:* 'wɔːrsɑː] *n* Varsovia *f*
Warsaw Pact *n*, **Warsaw Treaty** *n* HIST Pacto *m* de Varsovia

warship ['wɔːʃɪp, *Am:* 'wɔːr-] *n* barco *m* de guerra

wart [wɔːt, *Am:* wɔːrt] *n* verruga *f;* **~s and all** *inf*(*description, portrait*) con sus virtudes y defectos

warthog ['wɔːthɒg, *Am:* 'wɔːrthɑːg] *n* jabalí *m* verrugoso

wartime ['wɔːtaɪm, *Am:* 'wɔːr-] *n no pl* tiempo *m* de guerra; **in ~** en tiempos de guerra

wartorn ['wɔːtɔːn] *adj* destrozado, -a por la guerra

war-weary ['wɔːˌwɪəri, *Am:* 'wɔːrˌwɪri] *adj* cansado, -a por la guerra

wary ['weəri, *Am:* 'weri] <-ier, -iest> *adj* (*not trusting*) receloso, -a; (*watchful*) cauteloso, -a; **to be ~ of sth/sb** recelar de algo/alguien; **to be ~ about (doing) sth** dudar sobre (si hacer) algo; **with a ~ note in one's voice** con una nota de alerta en la voz

war zone ['wɔːzəʊn, *Am:* 'wɔːrzoʊn] *n* zona *f* de guerra

was [wɒz, *Am:* wɑːz] *pt of* **be**

wash [wɒʃ, *Am:* wɑːʃ] **I.** *vt* **1.** (*clean*) lavar; (*dishes*) fregar; **to ~ one's hair/hands** lavarse la cabeza/las manos; **to ~ the floor** fregar el suelo **2.** (*waves*) bañar **3.** (*river, sea*) llevar, arrastrar; **to ~ overboard** arrastrar fuera de la cubierta **II.** *vi* **1.** (*person*) lavarse; (*cloth*) poderse lavar; **that excuse won't ~ with me** *inf* esa excusa conmigo no cuela **2.** (*do the washing*) lavar la ropa **3.** (*sea*) chapotear **III.** *n* **1.** (*cleaning with water*) lavado *m;* **to have a ~** darse un baño **2.** *no pl* (*clothes for cleaning*) **the ~** la ropa para lavar; **to be in the ~** estar en la lavandería **3.** *no pl, liter* (*sound of water*) chapoteo *m* **4.** NAUT remolinos *mpl;* AVIAT disturbios *mpl* aerodinámicos **5.** (*thin layer*) capa *f,* baño *m;* (*painting*) mano *f* **6.** (*even situation*) empate *m* ▶**to come out in the ~** *prov* arreglarse todo

◆**wash away** *vt* **1.** (*clean*) quitar **2.** (*carry elsewhere*) llevar, arrastrar

◆**wash down** *vt* **1.** (*clean*) lavar **2.** (*carry elsewhere*) llevar, arrastrar **3.** *fig* **~ the pill with water** trágate la pastilla con agua

◆**wash off** *vi, vt* quitar(se)

◆**wash out** **I.** *vi* quitarse **II.** *vt* **1.** (*clean*) lavar; (*remove*) quitar **2.** *fig* **our party was washed out** la fiesta fue cancelada

◆**wash over** *vt* **1.** (*flow over*) pasar por encima de **2.** (*have no effect on*) no afectar

◆**wash up** **I.** *vt* **1.** (*dishes*) fregar **2. the sea washed it up** el mar lo arrojó sobre la playa **II.** *vi* **1.** (*clean dirty dishes*) fregar los platos **2.** *Am* (*wash*) lavarse (las manos y la cara)

washable *adj* lavable

wash-and-wear *adj* de lava y pon

wash basin *n Brit* (*basin*) lavabo *m;* (*bowl*) palangana *m* **wash board** *n* tabla *f* de lavar **wash-bowl** *n Am s.* **wash basin** **wash cloth** *n Am* manopla *f* **washday** *n* día *m* de colada **wash-down** *n* (*of oneself*) baño *m;* (*of sth*) lavado *m;* **to give sth a ~** dar a algo una lavada

washed-out [ˌwɒʃt'aʊt, *Am:* ˌwɑːʃt-] *adj* **1.** (*bleached*) desteñido, -a; **~ jeans** tejanos descoloridos **2.** (*pale*) demacrado, -a **3.** (*tired*) cansado, -a

washer ['wɒʃəʳ, *Am:* 'wɑːʃɚ] *n* **1.** *Am* (*washing-machine*) lavadora *f* **2.** (*plastic ring*) arandela *f*

wash-hand-basin *n* (*basin*) lavabo *m;* (*bowl*) palangana *m* **wash-house** *n* lavadero *m*

washing ['wɒʃɪŋ, *Am:* 'wɑːʃɪŋ] *n no pl* **1.** (*clothes for cleaning*) ropa *f* sucia **2.** (*act*) lavado *f;* (*of clothes*) colada *f;* **to do the ~** hacer la colada

washing machine *n* lavadora *f,* lavarropas *f inv Arg* **washing powder** *n no pl, Brit* detergente *m* en polvo **washing soda** *n no pl* sosa *f*

Washington [ˌwɒʃɪŋtən, *Am:* ˌwɑːʃɪŋ-] *n* Washington *m*

Washington D.C. *n* Washington D.C.

> **Washington's Birthday** es un día de fiesta oficial en los EE.UU. Aunque George Washington en realidad nació el 22 de febrero de 1732, su cumpleaños se celebra desde hace algunos años siempre el tercer lunes del mes de febrero, para que se produzca así un fin de semana largo.

washing-up [ˌwɒʃɪŋ'ʌp, *Am:* ˌwɑːʃɪŋ'-] *n Brit* platos *mpl* sucios; **to do the ~** fregar los platos

washing-up basin *n,* **washing-up bowl** *n* fregadero *m* **washing-up liquid** *n* detergente *m* líquido

wash-leather ['wɒʃleðəʳ] *n* gamuza *f*

washout ['wɒʃaʊt, *Am:* 'wɑːʃ-] *n inf* desastre *m*

washroom ['wɒʃrʊm, *Am:* 'wɑːʃruːm] *n Am* aseos *mpl,* sanitarios *mpl AmL*

wasn't [wɒznt, *Am:* wɑːznt] = **was not** *s.* **be**

wasp [wɒsp, *Am:* wɑːsp] *n* avispa *f*

WASP [wɒsp, *Am:* wɑːsp] *n Am abbr of* **White Anglo-Saxon Protestant** *persona de la clase privilegiada de los EE.UU., blanca, anglosajona y protestante*

waspish ['wɒspɪʃ, *Am:* 'wɑːspɪʃ] *adj* mordaz

wasp's nest *n* avispero *m*

wasp-waisted *adj* con cintura de avispa

wastage ['weɪstɪdʒ] *n no pl* **1.** (*waste*) desgaste *m* **2.** (*loss*) merma *f* **3.** (*byproduct of process*) residuos *mpl*

waste [weɪst] **I.** *adj* sobrante; (*material*) de desecho; (*land*) yermo, -a; **to lay ~** devastar; **to lie ~** quedar sin cultivar **II.** *n* **1.** *no pl* (*misuse*) derroche *m;* **it's a ~ of energy/money** es un derroche de energía/dinero; **it's a ~ of time** es una pérdida de tiempo; **to lay ~ to the land** devastar la tierra; **to go to ~** echarse a perder; **what a ~!** ¡qué pena! **2.** *no pl* (*unwanted matter*) desechos *mpl;* **household/industrial** ~ residuos *mpl* domésticos/industriales; **nuclear** ~ residuos *mpl* nucleares; **toxic** ~ residuos *mpl* tóxicos; **to recycle** ~ reciclar la basura **III.** *vt* malgastar; (*time*) perder; (*opportunity*) desaprovechar; **to ~ one's breath** *fig* hablar inútilmente; **to ~ no time in doing sth** apresurarse a hacer algo; **to not ~ words** no gastar saliva inútilmente **IV.** *vi* agotarse ►**~ not, want not** *prov* quien guarda, halla *prov*

♦**waste away** *vi* consumirse

wastebasket ['weɪstˌbɑːskɪt, *Am:* -ˌbæskət] *n Am,* **wastebin** ['weɪstbɪn] *n Brit* papelera *m* **waste disposal** *n* eliminación *f* de desperdicios **waste-disposal unit** *n* triturador *m* de basuras

wasteful ['weɪstfəl] *adj* derrochador(a); **to be ~ with electricity** gastar mucha electricidad

waste heat *n* calor *m* residual **wasteland** *n* yermo *m* **waste management** *n no pl* gestión *f* de residuos **wastepaper** *n no pl* papel *m* usado; (*recyclable*) papel *m* reciclable **wastepaper basket** *n* papelera *f* **waste pipe** *n* tubo *m* de desagüe **waste product** *n* residuos *mpl* **waster** *n* **1.** (*person*) derrochador(a) *m(f);* **a money** ~ un manirroto **2.** (*good-for-nothing*) perdido, -a *m, f*

waste reprocessing *n no pl* reciclado *m* de residuos **waste separation** *n no pl* separación *f* de residuos **waste steam** *n no pl* vapor *m* de escape **waste water** *n* aguas *fpl* residuales

wasting ['weɪstɪŋ] *adj* (*disease*) debilitante

wastrel ['weɪstrəl] *n* **1.** (*wasteful person*) derrochador(a) *m(f)* **2.** (*good-for-nothing*) perdido, -a *m, f*

watch [wɒtʃ, *Am:* wɑːtʃ] **I.** *n* **1.** *no pl* (*act of observation*) vigilancia *f;* **to be on the ~ for sth** estar a la mira de algo; **to be under ~** estar bajo vigilancia; **to keep a close ~ on sb/sth** vigilar a alguien/algo con mucho cuidado; **to put a ~ on sb** poner a alguien bajo vigilancia **2.** (*period of duty*) guardia *f;* **to be on ~, to keep ~** estar de guardia **3.** (*group of guards*) guardia *f;* HIST ronda *f* **4.** (*clock on wrist*) reloj *m* de pulsera; (*clock on chain*) reloj *m* de bolsillo **II.** *vt* **1.** (*observe*) mirar; **to ~ the clock** mirar el reloj; **to ~ a film** ver una película; **to ~ TV** ver la televisión; **to ~ the world go by** mirar cómo pasa la gente; **to ~ sb/sth do sth** mirar a alguien/algo hacer algo; **to ~ how sb does sth** mirar cómo alguien hace algo **2.** (*keep vigil*) vigilar; **to ~ sth/sb like a hawk** vigilar algo/a alguien como un perro guardián; **to ~ the kids** vigilar a los niños **3.** (*mind*) fijarse en; **to ~ every penny (one spends)** estar pendiente de cada peseta (que se gasta); **to ~ one's weight** cuidar el peso; **~ it!** ¡cuidado!, ¡aguas! *Méx;* **to ~ it (with sb)** tener cuidado (con alguien); **~ yourself** cuídate **III.** *vi* fijarse; **to ~ as sb/sth does sth** fijarse en cómo alguien/algo hace algo

♦**watch out** *vi* tener cuidado; **~!** ¡cuidado!

watchband ['wɒtʃbænd] *n Am s.* **watchstrap**

watchdog ['wɒtʃdɒg, *Am:* 'wɑːtʃdɑːg] *n* **1.** *Am* perro *m* guardián **2.** (*keeper of standards*) guardián, -ana *m, f;* (*official organization*) organismo *m* de vigilancia; **a ~ on sth** un guardián de algo

watcher ['wɒtʃəʳ, *Am:* 'wɑːtʃɚ] *n* observador(a) *m(f)*

watchful ['wɒtʃfəl, *Am:* 'wɑːtʃ-] *adj* vigilante; **to keep a ~ eye on sb/sth** estar pendiente de alguien/algo; **under the ~ eye of sb** bajo la atenta mirada de alguien

watch-maker ['wɒtʃˌmeɪkəʳ, *Am:* 'wɑːtʃ-meɪkɚ] *n* relojero, -a *m, f*

watchman ['wɒtʃmən, *Am:* 'wɑːtʃ-] <-men> *n* guardián *m;* **night** ~ vigilante *m* nocturno

watchstrap ['wɒtʃstræp] *n Brit* correa *f* de reloj

watchtower ['wɒtʃtaʊəʳ, *Am:* 'wɑːtʃtaʊɚ] *n* atalaya *f*

watchword ['wɒtʃwɜːd, *Am:* 'wɑːtʃwɜːrd] *n* **1.** (*symbol*) consigna *f* **2.** (*password*) contraseña *f*

water ['wɔːtəʳ, *Am:* 'wɑːt̬ɚ] **I.** *n* **1.** *no pl* (*liquid*) agua *f;* **bottled** ~ agua embotellada; **a bottle of** ~ una botella de agua; **a drink/a glass of** ~ un trago/un vaso de agua; **hot and cold running** ~ agua corriente fría y caliente; **under** ~ bajo agua **2.** (*area of water*) **the ~s of the Rhine** las aguas del Rin; **coastal ~s** aguas costeras; **territorial ~s** aguas jurisdiccionales; **unchartered ~s** *fig* territorio *m* desconocido; **by** ~ por mar **3.** (*urine*) aguas *mpl* menores; **to pass** ~ orinar **4.** MED ~ **on the brain** hidrocefalia *f;* ~ **on the knee** derrame *m* sinovial; **to take the ~s** tomar las aguas ►**to be ~ under the bridge** ser agua pasada; **like ~ off a duck's back** como si oyera llover; **to spend money like** ~ gastar el dinero como si creciera en los árboles; **to pour cold ~ on sth** echar agua fría a algo; **to be in deep** ~ estar metido en un lío; **still ~s run deep** *prov* no te fíes del agua mansa *prov;* **of the first** ~ (*excellent*) de primera; (*extremely bad*) ínfimo, -a; **to get into hot** ~ meterse en honduras; **to fish in troubled ~s** pescar en río revuelto; **to hold** ~ (*explanation*) ser consistente; **to muddy the ~s** enmarañar las cosas **II.** *vt* (*plants*) regar; (*livestock*) dar de beber a **III.** *vi* **1.** (*produce tears*) lagrimear **2.** (*salivate*) salivar; **it makes my mouth** ~ se me hace la boca agua

waterbird *n* ave *f* acuática **water boatman** *n* hidrómetra *m*

water-borne ['wɔːtəbɔːn, *Am:* 'wɑːt̬ɚ-bɔːrn] *adj* por mar; ~ **attack** ataque por agua; **a ~ disease** enfermedad propagada por el agua

water bottle *n* botellón *m* de agua; (*for soldiers, travellers*) cantimplora *f* **water butt** *n* tinaja *f* **water cannon** *n inv* cañón *m* de agua **water carrier** *n* aguador(a) *m(f)* **water cart** *n* HIST cuba *f* de agua **water closet** *n* retrete *m,* excusado *m AmL* **watercolor** *Am,* **watercolour** I. *n* acuarela *f* II. *adj* de [*o* en] acuarela **water content** *n* contenido *m* de agua

water-cooled ['wɔ:təku:ld, *Am:* 'wɑ:t̬ɚ-] *adj* refrigerado, -a por agua

water-cooling *n* refrigeración *f* por agua **watercourse** *n* cauce *m* **watercraft** *n liter* embarcación *f* **watercress** *n no pl* berro *m* **water cure** *n* MED cura *f* de agua

water-driven *adj* movido, -a por agua

waterfall *n* cascada *f* **waterfowl** *n inv* ave *f* acuática **waterfront** *n* (*harbour*) puerto *m* **water gauge** *n* medidor *m* de agua; **to read the** ~ leer el medidor de agua **water heater** *n* calentador *m* de agua **water hole** *n* abrevadero *m* **water hose** *n* manguera *f* de agua **water ice** *n Brit* sorbete *m*

watering *n* 1. (*of plants*) riego *m* 2. (*tears*) lagrimeo *m*

watering can ['wɔ:tərɪŋkæn, *Am:* 'wɑ:t̬ɚ-] *n* regadera *f* **watering place** *n* 1. (*for animals*) abrevadero *m* 2. *Brit* (*sea-side resort*) balneario *m*

waterless ['wɔ:tələs, *Am:* 'wɑ:t̬ɚləs] *adj* árido, -a; ~ **desert/wasteland** desierto/páramo árido

water level *n* nivel *m* del agua **water lily** <-ies> *n* nenúfar *m* **water line** *n no pl* línea *f* de flotación

water-logged ['wɔ:təlɒgd, *Am:* 'wɑ:t̬ɚlɑ:gd] *adj* anegado, -a

Waterloo [ˌwɔ:tə'lu:, *Am:* 'wɑ:t̬ɚ-] *n* **to meet one's** ~ llegar a uno su San Martín

water main *n* cañería *f* principal **waterman** <-men> *n* barquero *m* **watermark** *n* 1. (*river or tide level*) línea *f* del agua 2. (*on paper*) filigrana *f* **watermelon** *n* sandía *f* **water meter** *n* contador *m* de agua **water pipe** *n* 1. (*for transporting water*) cañería *f* 2. (*hookah*) pipa *f* de agua **water pistol** *n* pistola *f* de agua **water pollution** *n no pl* contaminación *f* del agua **water polo** *n* waterpolo *m,* polo *m* acuático **water power** *n no pl* fuerza *f* hidráulica **water pressure** *n no pl* presión *f* del agua

waterproof ['wɔ:təpru:f, *Am:* 'wɑ:t̬ɚ-] I. *adj* impermeable II. *n Brit* impermeable *m* III. *vt* impermeabilizar

water-repellent *adj* hidrófugo, -a

watershed ['wɔ:təʃed, *Am:* 'wɑ:t̬ɚ-] *n* 1. (*high ground*) divisoria *m* de aguas 2. *no pl, fig* (*great change*) punto *m* de inflexión; **to mark a** ~ marcar un punto decisivo

water shortage *n* escasez *f* de agua **waterside** *n no pl* orilla *f,* ribera *f*

water-ski ['wɔ:təski:, *Am:* 'wɑ:t̬ɚ-] I. *vi* esquiar en el agua; **to go** ~**ing** hacer esquí acuático II. <-s> *n* esquí *m* acuático

water-skiing *n no pl* esquí *m* acuático

water softener *n* ablandador *m* de agua

water-soluble *adj* soluble en agua

water spout *n Am* METEO tromba *f*

water supply *n* suministro *m* de agua **water supply pipe** *n* tubería *f* del suministro de agua **water supply point** *n* punto *m* de suministro de agua

watertable *n* capa *f* freática **water tank** *n* cisterna *f;* (*smaller one*) aljibe *m*

watertight ['wɔ:tətaɪt, *Am:* 'wɑ:t̬ɚ-] *adj* 1. (*not allowing water in*) hermético, -a; *fig* (*separate*) estanco, -a 2. *fig* (*not allowing doubt*) irrecusable; (*agreement*) a toda prueba

water tower *n* depósito *f* elevado de agua **water vapor** *n Am,* **water vapour** *n* vapor *m* de agua **water vole** *n* rata *f* de agua **water wave** *n* ola *f* (de agua) **waterway** *n* canal *m* **waterwings** *npl* flotadores *mpl;* **to wear** ~ usar flotadores **waterworks** *n pl* 1. (*where public water is stored*) reserva *f* de abastecimiento de agua 2. *inf* (*body organs*) vías *fpl* urinarias ►**to turn on the** ~ echar a llorar

watery ['wɔ:təri, *Am:*'wɑ:t̬ɚ-] <-ier, -iest> *adj* 1. (*bland*) aguado, -a; **a** ~ **soup** una sopa aguada 2. (*weak in colour*) deslavado, -a; (*weak in strength*) diluido, -a; **a** ~ **sun** un sol pálido

watt [wɒt, *Am:* wɑ:t] *n* ELEC vatio *m*

wattage ['wɒtɪdʒ, *Am:* 'wɑ:t̬ɪdʒ] *n no pl* ELEC vatiaje *m*

wave ['weɪv] I. *n* 1. (*of water*) ola *f;* (*on surface, of hair*) ondulación *f;* **to make** ~**s** *fig* causar problemas; **to be on the crest of the** ~ *fig* estar en la cumbre 2. PHYS onda *f* 3. (*hand movement*) **to give sb a** ~ saludar a alguien con la mano II. *vi* 1. (*make hand movement*) **to** ~ **at** [*o* **to**] **sb** saludar a alguien con la mano; **to** ~ **goodbye** decir adiós con la mano 2. (*move from side to side: field of corn*) mecerse con el viento; (*flag*) ondear III. *vt* 1. (*move to signal*) **to** ~ **sb goodbye** decir adiós con la mano a alguien 2. (*move from side to side*) agitar 3. (*hair*) ondular; **to have one's hair** ~**d** rizarse el pelo

◆**wave aside** *vt fig* rechazar; **to** ~ **an idea/objection/suggestion** rechazar una idea/objeción/sugerencia

◆**wave down** *vt* **to wave sb/sth down** hacer señales a alguien/algo para que pare

◆**wave on** *vt* **to wave sb/sth on** hacer señales a alguien/algo para que siga adelante

◆**wave through** *vt* hacer señales para dejar pasar

wave-band *n* RADIO banda *f* de frecuencias **wave-length** *n* longitud *f* de onda; **on a** ~ en una onda; **to be on the same** ~ *fig* estar en la misma onda **wave power** *n* energía *f* de las ondas

waver ['weɪvəʳ, *Am:* -vɚ] *vi* 1. (*lose determination*) vacilar 2. (*be unable to decide*) titubear; **to** ~ **between ... and ...** dudar entre... o...; **to** ~ **over sth** titubear acerca de algo 3. (*lose strength*) desfallecer

waverange ['weɪvreɪndʒ] *n* amplitud *f* de onda

waverer ['weɪvərəʳ, *Am:* -ɚɚ] *n* indeciso, -a *m, f*

wavering *adj* vacilante; (*between two options*) titubeante

wavy ['weɪvi] <-ier, -iest> *adj* (*hair*) ondulado, -a; (*pattern*) ondulante

wax¹ [wæks] **I.** *n no pl* **1.** (*fatty substance*) cera *f;* **candle ~** vela *f* de cera; (*for polishing*) cera lustradora **2.** (*inside ear*) cerumen *m,* cerilla *f* **II.** *vt* **1.** (*polish: floor, furniture*) encerar; (*shoes*) lustrar **2.** (*remove hair from*) depilar con cera

wax² [wæks] *vi liter* **1.** (*moon*) crecer; **to ~ and wane** crecer y descrecer; *fig* tener altibajos **2.** (*become*) ponerse; **she ~ed lyrical about her holiday** se entusiasmó mucho con sus vacaciones

wax paper *n* papel *m* encerado **waxwork** *n* figura *f* de cera

waxy ['wæksi] <-ier, -iest> *adj* **1.** (*oily, shiny*) lustroso, -a **2.** (*apparently of wax*) ceroso, -a

way [weɪ] **I.** *n* **1.** (*route*) camino *m;* **to be (well) on the ~ to doing sth** *fig* ir camino de hacer algo; **to be on the ~** estar en camino; **to be out of the ~** estar en un lugar remoto; **to be under ~** estar en curso; **on the ~ to sth** de camino a algo; **to elbow one's ~ somewhere** abrirse camino (a codazos) hasta algún lugar; **to find one's ~ around sth** encontrar el camino alrededor de algo; *fig* encontrar una manera de evitar algo; **to find one's ~ into/out of sth** encontrar la manera de entrar/salir de algo; **to find one's ~ through sth** encontrar el camino a través de algo; **to go out of one's ~ to do sth** *fig* tomarse la molestia de hacer algo; **to go one's own ~** *fig* irse por su lado; **(to go) by ~ of sth** (ir) por vía de algo; **to know one's ~ around sth** saber cómo moverse en algo; **to know one's ~ around the town** conocer el pueblo; **to lead the ~** mostrar el camino; **to lose one's ~** equivocar el camino; **to make one's ~** (*make progress*) progresar; (*move*) abrirse camino; **to make one's ~ through the crowd** abrirse camino a través de la muchedumbre; **to pay one's ~** *fig* ser solvente; **to talk one's ~ out of sth** *fig* salvarse de algo con labia; **to see the error of one's ~s** darse cuenta de sus errores; **to work one's ~ up** *fig* ascender con el trabajo personal **2.** (*road*) camino *m;* (*small one*) sendero *m;* **Way** (*name of road*) Vía *f;* **cycle ~** carril *m* bici **3.** (*facing direction*) dirección *f;* **the right/wrong ~ round** del derecho/del revés; **to show the ~ forward** señalar el camino; **this ~ on** *Aus, Brit* siga en esta dirección **4.** (*distance*) trayecto *m;* **all the ~** (*the whole distance*) todo el trayecto; (*completely*) completamente; **to be a long ~ off** estar muy alejado; **to have a (long) ~ to go** tener aún un (largo) trayecto por recorrer; **to have come a long ~** *fig* haber llegado lejos; **to go a long ~** *fig* ir lejos **5.** (*fashion*) manera *f;* **in many ~s** de muchas maneras; **in some ~s** en cierto modo; **there are no two ~s about it** no hay otra posibilidad; **the ~ to do sth** la manera de hacer algo; **the ~s and means of doing/to do sth** los medios (y arbitrios) para hacer algo; **by ~ of** a modo de **6.** *no pl* (*manner*) modo *m;* (*customs*) costumbres *fpl;* **sb's ~ of life** el estilo de vida de alguien; **to my ~ of thinking** tal como lo veo yo; **she wouldn't have it any other ~** no lo aceptaría de ninguna otra manera; **in a big ~** en gran escala; **either ~** de cualquier forma; **no ~!** *inf* (*impossible*) ¡de ninguna manera!; *inf* (*definitely no!*) ¡ni hablar!; **in no ~** ¡para nada!; **to get one's own ~** salirse con la suya; **it's always the ~** siempre es de esa manera; **in a ~** en cierto modo **7.** *no pl* (*free space*) paso *m;* **to be in sb's ~** estorbar a alguien; **in the ~** en el paso; **to get out of sb's/sth's ~** dejar el camino libre a alguien/algo; **to give ~** dar paso; *fig* dejar hacer; **to give ~ to sth** dar paso a algo; **to make ~ (for sb/sth)** hacer lugar (para alguien/algo); **to stand in sb's ~** ir contra los deseos de alguien **8.** *no pl* (*condition*) estado *m;* **to be in a bad ~** estar en mala forma; **to be in a terrible ~** estar terriblemente mal; **to be in the family ~** *inf* estar embarazada ►**to go the ~ of all flesh** sucumbir a la inevitable muerte; **the ~ to a man's heart is through his stomach** *prov* el camino al corazón de un hombre pasa por el estómago *prov;* **to want things both ~s** querer estar en misa y repicando; **to see/find out which ~ the wind blows** ver/descubrir por donde van los tiros; **to rub sb up the wrong ~** caer mal a alguien; **by the ~** por cierto **II.** *adv inf* mucho; **to be ~ past sb's bedtime** haber pasado con mucho de la hora de dormir

way-bill ['weɪbɪl] *n* hoja *f* de ruta

waylay [ˌweɪ'leɪ, *Am:* 'weɪleɪ] <waylaid, waylaid> *vt* acechar

way of thinking *n* forma *f* de pensar

way out [ˌweɪ'aʊt] *n* salida *f*

way-out [ˌweɪ'aʊt] *adj inf* (*very modern*) ultramoderno, -a; (*unusual or amazing*) fuera de serie

wayside ['weɪsaɪd] *n* borde *m* del camino; **to fall by the ~** *fig* quedarse en el camino

wayside inn *n* parador *m* de carretera

wayward ['weɪwəd, *Am:* -wɚd] *adj* díscolo, -a

WBT *abbr of* **Web Based Training** WBT

WC [ˌdʌblju:'si:] *n abbr of* **water closet** WC *m*

we [wi:] *pron pers* nosotros, -as; **~'re going to Paris and ~'ll be back here tomorrow** iremos a París y volveremos mañana; **as ~ say** como nosotros decimos

weak [wi:k] *adj* **1.** (*not strong*) débil; (*coffee, tea*) claro, -a; **to be ~ with desire/love** languidecer de deseo/amor; **to be ~ with**

hunger/thirst estar sin fuerzas por el hambre/la sed; **to be ~ at the knees** temblarle a uno las piernas; **the ~ link** *fig* el punto débil; ~ **spot** *fig* flaqueza *f* **2.** (*below standard*) flojo, -a; **to be ~** (**at sth**) estar flojo (en algo)

weaken [ˈwiːkən] **I.** *vi* (*become less strong*) debilitarse; (*diminish*) disminuir **II.** *vt* (*make less strong*) debilitar; (*diminish*) disminuir

weakling [ˈwiːklɪŋ] *n* enclenque *mf*

weakly [ˈwiːkli] *adv* **1.** (*without strength*) débilmente **2.** (*unconvincingly*) sin convicción

weak-minded [ˌwiːkˈmaɪndɪd] *adj* **1.** (*lacking determination*) indeciso, -a; (*weak-willed*) pusilánime **2.** (*stupid*) tonto, -a

weakness [ˈwiːknɪs] <-es> *n* **1.** *no pl* (*lack of strength*) debilidad *f;* **to have a ~ for sth** tener debilidad por algo **2.** (*area of vulnerability*) punto *m* débil; (*flaw in artistic work*) imperfección *f;* (*flaw in character*) flaqueza *f*

weal [wiːl] *n* cardenal *m*

wealth [welθ] *n no pl* **1.** (*money*) riqueza *f;* (*fortune*) fortuna *f* **2.** (*large amount*) abundancia *f*

wealth creation *n,* **wealth generation** *n no pl* generación *f* de riqueza **wealth tax** <-es> *n* impuesto *m* sobre el patrimonio

wealthy [ˈwelθi] **I.** <-ier, -iest> *adj* rico, -a **II.** *n* **the ~** *no pl* los ricos

wean [wiːn] *vt* (*animal, baby*) destetar; **to ~ sb** (**off sth**) *fig* desenganchar a alguien (de algo), quitar a alguien la costumbre (de algo)

weapon [ˈwepən] *n* arma *f*

weaponry [ˈwepənri] *n no pl* armamento *m*

wear [weəʳ, *Am:* wer] <wore, worn> **I.** *vt* **1.** (*have on body: clothes, jewellery*) llevar; **to ~ one's hair loose/tied back** llevar el pelo suelto/recogido **2.** (*deteriorate*) desgastar **3.** *Brit, Aus, inf* (*permit*) permitir **II.** *vi* (*spoil: clothes, machine parts*) desgastarse; **to ~ thin** raerse; *fig* desgastarse **III.** *n* **1.** (*clothing*) ropa *f;* **casual/sports ~** ropa informal/deportiva **2.** (*amount of use*) desgaste *m;* **to be the worse for ~** (*person*) estar desmejorado; (*thing*) estar desgastado; **to take some/a lot of ~ and tear** soportar algo de/mucho desgaste

◆**wear away** **I.** *vt* desgastar **II.** *vi* desgastarse; (*person*) consumirse

◆**wear down** *vt* **1.** (*reduce*) gastar; *fig* (*tire*) desgastar; **to ~ sb's resistance** desgastar la resistencia de alguien **2.** (*make weak and useless*) agotar

◆**wear off** *vi* desaparecer

◆**wear on** *vi* (*time*) pasar lentamente

◆**wear out** **I.** *vi* gastarse **II.** *vt* gastar; (*patience*) agotar

wearable [ˈweərəbl, *Am:* ˈwerə-] *adj* que se puede llevar

wearing [ˈweərɪŋ, *Am:* ˈwer-] *adj* agotador(a)

wearisome [ˈwɪərɪsəm, *Am:* ˈwɪrɪ-] *adj form* (*causing boredom*) aburrido; (*causing tiredness*) extenuante

weary [ˈwɪəri, *Am:* ˈwɪri] **I.** <-ier, -iest> *adj* **1.** (*very tired*) extenuado, -a **2.** (*tiring*) agotador(a) **3.** (*bored*) aburrido, -a; (*unenthusiastic*) desanimado, -a; **to be ~ of sth** estar harto de algo; **a ~ joke** un chiste viejo **II.** *vt* (*make tired*) **to ~ sb with sth** fatigar a alguien con algo; (*make bored*) aburrir a alguien con algo **III.** *vi* (*become tired*) cansarse; (*become bored*) aburrirse

weasel [ˈwiːzl] *n* comadreja *f*

weather [ˈweðəʳ, *Am:* -ɚ] **I.** *n no pl* tiempo *m;* (*climate*) clima *m;* **~ permitting** si lo permite el tiempo ►**to make heavy ~ of sth** complicar algo; **to be under the ~** estar indispuesto **II.** *vi* aguantar **III.** *vt* **1.** (*wear*) desgastar **2.** (*endure*) resistir; **to ~ sth** hacer frente a algo; **to ~ the storm** *fig* capear el temporal

weather-beaten [ˈweðəˌbiːtən, *Am:* -ɚˌ-] *adj* deteriorado, -a por la intemperie; **~ face** cara *f* curtida

weatherboard [ˈweðəbɔːd, *Am:* -ɚbɔːrd], **weather boarding** **I.** *n* tabla *f* de chilla; **~ house** *Am* casa *f* de madera **II.** *vt* cubrir con tablas

weather-bound *adj* bloqueado, -a por el mal tiempo

weather bureau <-s *o* -x> *n Am* servicio *m* meteorológico **weather chart** *n* mapa *m* meteorológico **weathercock** *n* veleta *f* **weather conditions** *npl* condiciones *fpl* atmosféricas **weather forecast** *n* previsión *f* meteorológica

weathering [ˈweðərɪŋ] *n no pl* deterioro *m* por la intemperie

weatherman [ˈweðəmæn, *Am:* ˈweðɚ-] *n* hombre *m* del tiempo

weatherproof [ˈweðəpruːf, *Am:* ˈweðɚ-] *adj* a prueba de la intemperie

weave [wiːv] **I.** <wove *Am:* weaved, woven *Am:* weaved> *vt* **1.** (*produce cloth*) tejer; **to ~ sth into sth** entrelazar algo con algo **2.** (*intertwine things*) entretejer; *fig* tramar; **to ~ sth together** entrelazar algo **3.** (*move back and forth*) **to ~ one's way through sth** abrirse paso entre algo **II.** <wove *Am:* weaved, woven *Am:* weaved> *vi* **1.** (*produce cloth*) tejer **2.** (*move by twisting and turning*) serpentear ►**let's get weaving** *Brit, inf* ¡vámonos! **III.** *n* tejido *m;* **striped ~** tejido a rayas; **loose/tight ~** tejido amplio/ajustado

weaver [ˈwiːvəʳ, *Am:* -vɚ] *n* tejedor(a) *m(f);* **basket ~** canastero *m*

weaver bird *n* ZOOL tejedor *m*

web[1] [web] *n* **1.** (*woven net*) tela *f;* **spider('s) ~** telaraña *f;* **to spin a ~** hacer una telaraña **2.** *fig* (*complex network*) trama *f;* **a ~ of intrigue** una trama de intrigas; **a ~ of lies** una sarta de mentiras **3.** *fig* (*trap*) trampa *f* **4.** (*connective tissue*) membrana *f*

web[2] [web] **I.** *n* INFOR web *f;* **on the ~** en la red **II.** *adj inv* INFOR de internet

webaddict *n* INFOR ciberadicto, -a *m, f* **web browser** *n* INFOR navegador *m* de internet

webfooted [ˌweb'fʊtɪd, *Am:* 'webˌfʊt̬ɪd] *adj* palmípedo, -a

webmaster *n* INFOR administrador(a) *m(f)* de web **web-offset** (**printing**) *n* web offset *m* **web page** *n* INFOR página *f* web; ~ **wizard** asistente *mf* para páginas web **website** *n* INFOR sitio *m* web; **sports ~s** webs *fpl* de deporte; **to visit a ~** visitar un sitio web **web surfer** *n* INFOR internauta *mf* **webzine** *n* INFOR revista *f* electrónica

wed [wed] <wedded *o* wed, wedded *o* wed> *form* **I.** *vt* **1.** (*marry*) **to ~ sb** casarse con alguien **2.** *fig* (*join closely*) casar; **to ~ sth and sth** unir algo a algo **II.** *vi* casarse

we'd [wiːd] **1.** = **we had** *s.* **have 2.** = **we would** *s.* **would**

wedded ['wedɪd] *adj* **1.** (*married*) casado, -a; **lawful ~ wife** *form* legítima esposa **2.** (*united*) **to be ~ to sth** estar unido a algo; **to be ~ to a habit** tener una costumbre; **to be ~ to an opinion** aferrarse a una opinión

wedding ['wedɪŋ] *n* boda *f*

wedding anniversary <-ies> *n* aniversario *m* de bodas **wedding breakfast** *n* banquete *m* de boda **wedding cake** *n no pl* tarta *f* nupcial **wedding day** *n* día *m* de la boda **wedding dress** *n* traje *m* de novia **wedding guest** *n* invitado , -a *m, f* de boda **wedding night** *n* noche *f* de bodas **wedding present** *n* regalo *m* de boda **wedding ring** *n* alianza *f*

wedge [wedʒ] **I.** *n* **1.** (*tapered block*) cuña *f* **2.** *fig* (*triangular piece*) porción; **a ~ of cake/pie** un trozo de pastel/tarta **II.** *vt* poner una cuña a; **to ~ the door open** mantener la puerta abierta (con una cuña); **to be ~d between sth** (*people*) estar apretado entre algo; (*object*) quedar encajado entre algo

wedlock ['wedlɒk, *Am:* -lɑːk] *n no pl* matrimonio *m;* **out of ~** fuera del matrimonio; **sex out of ~** sexo *m* extraconyugal; **to be born in/out of ~** nacer dentro/fuera del matrimonio

Wednesday ['wenzdeɪ] *n* miércoles *m inv;* **Ash ~** Miércoles de Ceniza; *s. a.* **Friday**

wee [wiː] **I.** *adj Scot, a. inf* pequeñito, -a; **a ~ bit** un poquito **II.** *n no pl, childspeak, inf* pipí *m;* **to have to go ~** tener que ir a hacer pipí **III.** *vi childspeak, inf* hacer pipí; **I want to ~!** ¡quiero hacer pipí!

weed [wiːd] **I.** *n* **1.** (*plant*) mala hierba *f* **2.** *Brit, pej, inf* (*person*) enclenque *mf* **3.** *no pl, inf* (*tobacco*) **the ~** el tabaco **4.** *no pl, inf* (*marijuana*) marihuana *f* ►**to grow like a ~** crecer como la mala hierba **II.** *vt* desherbar **III.** *vi* arrancar las malas hierbas

weedkiller ['wiːdkɪləʳ, *Am:* -ɚ] *n no pl* herbicida *m*

weedy ['wiːdi] *adj* <-ier, iest> **1.** (*full of weeds*) lleno, -a de malas hierbas **2.** *Brit, pej, inf* (*very thin*) flaco, -a; (*underdeveloped*) esmirriado, -a

week [wiːk] *n* **1.** (*seven days*) semana *f;* **it'll be ~s before ...** pasarán semanas antes de que... +*subj;* **a few ~s ago** hace pocas semanas; **last ~** la semana pasada; **once a ~** una vez por semana; **during the ~** durante la semana; **~ after ~** semana tras semana; **~ by ~** semana a semana **2.** (*work period, working days*) semana *f* laboral; **a thirty-seven-and-a-half hour ~** una semana laboral de trenta y siete horas y media

weekday ['wiːkdeɪ] *n* día *m* laborable; **on ~s** en días laborables

weekend [ˌwiːk'end, *Am:* 'wiːkend] *n* fin *m* de semana; **at the ~**(**s**) *Brit, Aus,* **on the ~**(**s**) *Am* el fin de semana; **~ cottage** casita *f* de fin de semana

weekender [ˌwiːk'endəʳ, *Am:* 'wiːkˌendɚ] *n* *persona que se va de casa durante el fin de semana*

weekly ['wiːkli] **I.** *adj* semanal; **~ magazine** revista *f* semanal **II.** *adv* semanalmente; **to meet/publish ~** reunirse/publicar semanalmente **III.** *n* <-ies> semanario *m*

weeny ['wiːni] *adj* <-ier, -iest> *inf* chiquitito, -a; **a ~ bit** un poquitín

weep [wiːp] **I.** *vi* <wept, wept> **1.** (*cry*) llorar; **to ~ like a baby** lloriquear como un bebé; **to ~ with joy/rage** llorar de alegría/rabia; **to ~ inconsolably** llorar desconsoladamente **2.** (*secrete liquid*) supurar **II.** *vt* <wept, wept> (*tears*) derramar; **to ~ tears of joy/rage** (**over sb/sth**) llorar de alegría/rabia (por alguien/algo) **III.** *n* llanto *m;* **to have a** (**good**) **~** desahogarse llorando

weeping **I.** *adj* lloroso, -a **II.** *n no pl* llanto *m*

weeping willow *n* sauce *m* llorón

w.e.f. *abbr of* **with effect from** válido, -a a partir de

weigh [weɪ] **I.** *vi* pesar **II.** *vt* **1.** (*measure weight*) pesar; **to ~ oneself** pesarse **2.** (*consider carefully*) sopesar; **to ~ one's words** medir las palabras; **to ~ sth against sth** contraponer algo a algo **3.** NAUT (*pull up*) **to ~ anchor** levar el ancla

◆**weigh down** *vt* **1.** (*cause to bend*) doblar bajo un peso **2.** *fig* (*depress*) abrumar; **to weigh sb down with sth** cargar a alguien con algo

◆**weigh in** *vi* **1.** (*be weighed*) pesarse; **to ~ at 80 kilos** pesar 80 kilos **2.** *inf* (*enter into, take part*) intervenir; **to ~** (**to sth**) **with sth** intervenir (en algo) afirmando algo; **to ~ to a discussion with one's opinion** intervenir en una discusión dando su opinión

◆**weigh out** *vt* pesar

◆**weigh up** *vt* (*calculate*) calcular; (*judge*) juzgar

weighbridge ['weɪbrɪdʒ] *n* báscula *f* de puente

weigh-in ['weɪɪn] *n* pesaje *m*

weight [weɪt] **I.** *n* **1.** *no pl* (*amount weighed*) peso *m;* **a decrease/an increase in ~** una disminución/un aumento de peso; **to lift a heavy ~** levantar un peso pesado; **to put on ~**

engordar; **what a** ~ ¡qué pesado! **2.** (*metal specific weight*) pesa *f;* **to lift** ~**s** levantar pesas **3.** *no pl* (*value, importance*) valor *m;* **to attach** ~ **to sth** dar importancia a algo; **to carry** ~ tener mucho peso ►**to take the** ~ **off one's feet** sentarse y descansar; **to be a** ~ **off sb's mind** ser un alivio para alguien; **it's a great** ~ **off my mind** es un peso que me quito de encima; **to pull one's** ~ *inf* poner de su parte **II.** *vt* cargar; **to** ~ **sth with stones** cargar algo de piedras

◆**weight down** *vt* **1.** (*overload*) sobrecargar **2.** (*make heavy*) sujetar con un peso **3.** *fig* (*strain*) apretar

weighting *n no pl, Brit* **1.** (*paid to employee*) plus *m* por el coste de la vida **2.** MAT ponderación *f*

weightless ['weɪtləs] *adj* ingrávido, -a

weightlessness *n no pl* ingravidez *f*

weightlifter *n* levantador(a) *m(f)* de pesas

weight-lifting ['weɪtˌlɪftɪŋ] *n no pl* levantamiento *m* de pesas; **to do** ~ hacer pesas

weighty ['weɪti, *Am:* -t̬i] *adj* <-ier, -iest> **1.** (*heavy*) pesado, -a **2.** (*important*) importante; ~ **matters** asuntos *mpl* de peso

weir [wɪəʳ, *Am:* wɪr] *n* presa *f*

weird [wɪəd, *Am:* wɪrd] *adj* misterioso, -a; **how** ~ ¡qué raro!; ~ **and wonderful** extraordinario

weirdie ['wɪədi, *Am:* 'wɪrdi] *n,* **weirdo** ['wɪədəʊ, *Am:* 'wɪrdoʊ] *n inf* bicho *m* raro

welcome ['welkəm] **I.** *vt* **1.** (*greet kindly*) dar la bienvenida a; **to** ~ **sb warmly** acoger a alguien calurosamente **2.** (*support*) aprobar **II.** *n* **1.** (*friendly reception*) bienvenida *f;* **speech of** ~ discurso *m* de bienvenida **2.** *no pl* (*period of being wanted*) aceptación *f* **3.** (*expression of approval*) aprobación *f;* **to give sth a cautious** ~ dar una acogida contenida a algo **III.** *adj* **1.** (*gladly received*) grato, -a; **a non** ~ **guest** un invitado no grato; **to be** ~ ser bienvenido **2.** (*gladly received*) deseado, -a; **a** ~ **break** una ruptura deseada; **a** ~ **change** un cambio esperado ►**you are** ~ de nada; **to be** ~ **to do sth** *inf* poder hacer algo; **you are** ~ **to use it** está a su disposición **IV.** *interj* ¡bienvenido!; ~ **aboard** NAUT bienvenidos a bordo

welcoming *adj* acogedor(a); ~ **arms** brazos abiertos; ~ **smile** sonrisa *f* agradable

weld [weld] **I.** *vt* **1.** (*join metal*) soldar; **to** ~ **sth** (**together**) soldar algo **2.** (*unite*) unir; **to** ~ **players into a team** unir a jugadores en un equipo **II.** *n* soldadura *f*

welder *n* soldador(a) *m(f)*

welding *n no pl* soldadura *f*

welding torch <-es> *n* soplete *m* soldador

welfare ['welfeəʳ, *Am:* -fer] *n no pl* **1.** (*health, happiness*) bienestar *m* **2.** (*state aid*) asistencia *f* social; ~ **policy** política *f* de asistencia social; ~ **system** sistema *m* asistencial; **social** ~ asistencia *f* social; **to be on** ~ vivir a cargo de la asistencia social

welfare payments *npl Am* pensión *f* de asistencia social **welfare services** *npl* servicios *mpl* de asistencia social **welfare state** *n* estado *m* del bienestar **welfare work** *n no pl* trabajos *mpl* de asistencia social **welfare worker** *n* asistente, -a *m, f* social

we'll [wiːl] = **we will** *s.* **will**

well¹ [wel] **I.** *adj* <better, best> bien; **to feel** ~ sentirse bien; **to get** ~ recuperarse; **to look** ~ tener buen aspecto **II.** <better, best> *adv* **1.** (*in a satisfactory manner*) bien; ~ **enough** suficientemente bien; ~ **done** bien hecho; **to do sth as** ~ **as ...** hacer algo tan bien como...; ~ **put** bien expresado; (**time/money**) ~ **spent** (tiempo/dinero) bien gastado **2.** (*thoroughly, fully, extensively*) completamente; ~ **east/west** bien hacia el este/oeste; ~ **enough** suficiente; **pretty** ~ bastante a fondo; **to know sb pretty** ~ conocer a alguien bastante bien; ~ **and truly** de verdad; **it costs** ~ **over...** cuesta tranquilamente más de... **3.** (*very, completely*) muy; **to be** ~ **pleased with sth** estar muy satisfecho con algo **4.** (*fairly, reasonably*) justamente; **he couldn't very** ~ **refuse their kind offer** no podía rechazar su amable oferta; **you may** ~ **think it was his fault** bien podrías pensar que tiene la culpa; **he might** ~ **be the best person to ask** puede que sea la persona idónea a quien preguntar; **you might** (**just**) **as** ~ **tell her the truth** más valdría que le dijeras la verdad ►**to leave** ~ **alone** no meterse en algo; **to be** ~ **away** *Brit, inf* (*completely absorbed*) estar completamente absorto; (*asleep*) estar profundamente dormido; (*drunk*) estar borracho como una cuba; **all** ~ **and good** muy bien; **that's all very** ~**, but ...** todo eso está muy bien, pero...; **as** ~ *Brit* (*also*) también; **as** ~ **as** así como; **just as** ~ menos mal; **to be** ~ **in with sb** *Brit, inf,* **to be in** ~ **with sb** *Am, inf* estar a bien con alguien; **to be** ~ **in with sth** *Brit, inf,* **to be in** ~ **with sth** *Am, inf* estar metido en algo; **to be** ~ **out of it** *Brit, Aus* librarse de una buena **III.** *interj* (*exclamation*) vaya; ~, ~ ¡vaya, vaya!; **very** ~**!** ¡muy bien!

well² [wel] **I.** *n* (*hole for water etc.*) pozo *m;* **water** ~ manantial *m* de agua; **to drill a** ~ perforar un pozo **II.** *vi* (*flow*) manar; **to** ~ **up in sth** brotar en algo; **to** ~ (**up**) **out of sth** (*water*) emanar de algo

◆**well up** *vi a. fig* (*rise*) brotar

well-advised [ˌweləd'vaɪzd] *adj form* bien asesorado, -a; **he would be** ~ **to stay at home** haría bien en quedarse en casa

well-appointed [ˌwelə'pɔɪntɪd, *Am:* -t̬ɪd] *adj form* bien amueblado, -a

well-balanced [ˌwel'bæləntst] *adj* bien equilibrado, -a; ~ **diet** dieta equilibrada; ~ **children** niños equilibrados

well-behaved [ˌwelbɪ'heɪvd] *adj* bien educado, -a; (*child*) formal; (*dog*) manso, -a

well-being ['welˌbiːɪŋ] *n no pl* bienestar *m;* **a feeling of** ~ una sensación de bienestar

well-bred [ˌwelˈbred] *adj* (*well brought up*) bien educado, -a; (*classy, refined*) refinado, -a; **a ~ voice** una voz educada

well-chosen [ˌwelˈtʃəʊzən, *Am:* -ˈtʃoʊ-] *adj* elegido, -a con cuidado; **to say a few ~ words** decir unas palabras acertadas

well-connected [ˌwelkəˈnektɪd] *adj* **to be ~** tener contactos; **a ~ family** una familia influyente

well-deserved [ˌweldɪˈsɜːvd] *adj* merecido, -a

well-developed [ˌweldɪˈveləpt] *adj* bien desarrollado, -a; **~ area** zona desarrollada; **physically ~** físicamente desarrollado; **a ~ sense of humour** un agudo sentido del humor

well-disposed [ˌweldɪˈspəʊzd, *Am:* -ˈspoʊzd] *adj* favorable; **to be ~ towards sth** ser favorable a algo; **to feel ~ towards sb** tener una disposición favorable hacia alguien

well-done [ˌwelˈdʌn] *adj* (*meat*) muy hecho, -a

well-dressed [ˌwelˈdrest] *adj* bien vestido, -a

well-earned [ˌwelˈɜːnd, *Am:* -ˈɜːrnd] *adj* merecido, -a

well-educated [ˌwelˈedʒʊkeɪtɪd, *Am:* -ˈedʒʊkeɪt̬ɪd] *adj* culto, -a

well-fed [ˌwelˈfed] *adj* (*full of food*) lleno, -a; (*from good feeding*) bien alimentado, -a

well-founded [ˌwelˈfaʊndɪd] *adj* fundado, -a; **~ suspicions** sospechas bien fundadas

well-groomed [ˌwelˈgruːmd] *adj* acicalado, -a

well-heeled [ˌwelˈhiːld] **I.** *adj inf* ricacho, -a **II.** *npl* **the ~** los ricos

wellies [ˈweliz] *n pl, Brit, inf* botas *fpl* de goma

well-informed [ˌwelɪnˈfɔːmd, *Am:* -ˈfɔːrmd] *adj* enterado, -a; **to be ~ about sb/sth** estar bien informado sobre alguien/algo; **to be ~ on a particular topic** conocer a fondo un tema concreto

wellington (**boot**) [ˈwelɪŋtən (buːt)] *n* bota *f* de goma

well-intentioned [ˌwelɪnˈtentʃənd] *adj* bienintencionado, -a

well-kept [ˌwelˈkept] *adj* (muy) cuidado, -a

well-knit [ˌwelˈnɪt] *adj* (*body*) robusto, -a; *fig* (*scheme, idea*) lógico, -a; **a ~ plot/story** una trama/historia bien construida

well-known [ˌwelˈnəʊn, *Am:* -ˈnoʊn] *adj* conocido, -a; **to be ~ for sth** ser conocido por algo; **it is ~ that ...** es bien sabido que...

well-mannered [ˌwelˈmænəd, *Am:* -ɚd] *adj* con buenos modales; **a ~ child** un niño educado

well-meaning [ˌwelˈmiːnɪŋ] *adj* bienintencionado, -a; **~ comments** comentarios *mpl* sin malicia

well-meant [ˌwelˈment] *adj* bienintencionado, -a

well-nigh [ˈwelnaɪ] *adv* casi; **to be ~ impossible** ser casi imposible

well-off [ˌwelˈɒf, *Am:* -ˈɑːf] **I.** *adj* **1.** (*wealthy*) acomodado, -a **2.** (*having a lot*) que tiene mucho; **the city is ~ for parks** la ciudad tiene muchos parques; **to not know when one is ~** no saber la suerte que se tiene **II.** *npl* **the ~** los ricos

well-oiled [ˌwelˈɔɪld] *adj* **1.** (*functioning smoothly*) eficaz **2.** *inf* (*inebriated, drunk*) hecho, -a una cuba

well-organised [ˌwelˈɔːgənaɪzd, *Am:* -ˈɔːr-] *adj* bien organizado, -a

well-paid [ˌwelˈpeɪd] *adj* bien pagado, -a

well-placed [ˌwelpleɪst] *adj* bien situado, -a

well-proportioned [ˌwelprəˈpɔːʃənd, *Am:* -ˈpɔːr-] *adj* bien proporcionado, -a

well-read [ˌwelˈred] *adj* **1.** (*knowledgeable*) instruido, -a **2.** (*read frequently*) muy leído, -a

well-spoken [ˌwelˈspəʊkən, *Am:* -ˈspoʊ-] *adj* **1.** (*polite*) bienhablado, -a **2.** (*refined*) con acento culto

well-thought-of [ˌwelˈθɔːtəv, *Am:* -ˈθɑːt̬əːv] *adj* (*person*) de buena reputación; (*school*) de prestigio

well-timed [ˌwelˈtaɪmd] *adj* oportuno, -a

well-to-do [ˌweltəˈduː] *inf* **I.** *adj* acaudalado, -a **II.** *n* **the ~** la gente adinerada

well-turned [ˌwelˈtɜːnd, *Am:* -ˈtɜːrnd] *adj* **1.** (*gracefully shaped*) elegante **2.** (*cleverly expressed: phrase*) bien construido, -a

well-wisher [ˈwelˌwɪʃəʳ, *Am:* ˈwelˌwɪʃɚ] *n* simpatizante *mf*

well-worn [ˌwelˈwɔːn, *Am:* -ˈwɔːrn] *adj* **1.** (*damaged by wear*) raído, -a **2.** *fig* (*over-used*) trillado, -a

welly [ˈweli] *n inf abbr of* **wellington** bota *f* de goma

Welsh [welʃ] **I.** *adj* galés, -esa **II.** *n* **1.** (*person*) galés, -esa *m, f* **2.** LING galés *m*

Welshman [ˈwelʃmən] <-men> *n* galés *m*

Welshwoman [ˈwelʃˌwʊmən] <-women> *n* galesa *f*

welt [welt] *n* **1.** (*from blow*) cardenal *f* **2.** (*in shoe*) vira *f*

welter-weight [ˈweltəweɪt, *Am:* -t̬ɚ-] *n* welter *m*

wend [wend] *vt liter* **to ~ one's way to town** dirigir sus pasos hacia la cuidad

went [went] *pt of* **go**

wept [wept] *pt, pp of* **weep**

were [wɜːʳ, *Am:* wɜːr] *pt of* **be**

we're [wɪəʳ, *Am:* wɪr] = **we are** *s.* **be**

weren't [wɜːnt, *Am:* wɜːrnt] = **were not** *s.* **be**

west [west] **I.** *n* **1.** (*cardinal point*) oeste *m;* **in the ~ of Spain** en el oeste de España; **to lie 5 km to the ~ of ...** quedar a 5 km al oeste de...; **to go/drive to the ~** ir/conducir hacia el oeste **2.** (*part of the world*) **the West** el mundo occidental **3.** (*part of the US*) **the Far West** el Lejano Oeste; **the Wild West** el Oeste Americano **II.** *adj* occidental; **~ wind** viento *m* del oeste; **~ coast** costa *f* oeste; **West African** de África Occidental; **West Berlin** Berlín Occi-

dental; **West Indies** Antillas *fpl* **III.** *adv* al oeste; **further** ~ más al oeste ▸**to go** ~ (*thing*) estropearse; (*person*) irse al otro mundo
westbound ['westbaʊnd] *adj* que va hacia el oeste
West End **I.** *n* **the** ~ el West End de Londres **II.** *adj* **the** ~ **theatres** los teatros del West End
westerly ['westəli, *Am:* -tɚli] *adj* del oeste; **the** ~ **part of the site** la zona oeste del lugar; ~ **winds** vientos *mpl* del oeste
western ['westən, *Am:* -tɚn] **I.** *adj* del oeste; **the** ~ **part of the country** la parte occidental del país **II.** *n* CINE western *m*
westerner *n* **1.** (*person from the west*) occidental *mf* **2.** (*person from the western US*) norteamericano, -a *m, f* del oeste
westernize ['westənaɪz, *Am:* -tɚ-] *vt* occidentalizar
Western Samoa *n* Samoa *f* Occidental
West Germany *n* HIST Alemania *f* Occidental
Westminster Abbey [ˌwestmɪntstəʳ'æbi, *Am:* -stɚ'æbi] *n* Abadía *f* de Westminster **Westminster City** *n* Ciudad *f* de Westminster
West Virginia *n* Virginia *f* Occidental
westward(s) ['westwəd(z), *Am:* -wɚd(z)] *adj* hacia el oeste
wet [wet] **I.** *adj* <-tt-> **1.** (*soaked*) mojado, -a; **to get** ~ mojarse; **to get sth** ~ mojar algo; ~ **through** mojado hasta los huesos **2.** (*not yet dried*) húmedo, -a; ~ **paint** pintura fresca **3.** (*rainy*) lluvioso, -a; ~ **weather** tiempo lluvioso ▸**to be a** ~ **blanket** ser un aguafiestas; **to be** ~ **behind the ears** estar con la leche en los labios; **to be all** ~ *Am* ser tonto **II.** <wet, wet> *vt* **1.** (*make damp*) humedecer **2.** (*urinate on*) **to** ~ **oneself** orinarse; **to** ~ **the bed** mojar la cama; **to** ~ **one's pants** mearse **III.** *n* **1.** *no pl* **the** ~ (*rain*) la lluvia **2.** *Am* POL antiprohibicionista *mf*
wether ['weðəʳ, *Am:* -ɚ] *n* ZOOL carnero *m* castrado
wet-nurse **I.** *n* HIST nodriza *f* **II.** *vt* criar **wet season** *n* estación *f* de las lluvias
wetsuit *n* traje *m* de neopreno
wetting *n no pl* mojada *f*
we've [wi:v] = **we have** *s.* **have**
whack [hwæk] **I.** *vt* golpear **II.** *n* **1.** (*blow*) golpe *m;* **to give sth (a good)** ~ golpear algo ruidosamente **2.** *no pl* (*share, part*) parte *f;* **a fair** ~ una parte justa; **to pay full** ~ pagarlo todo ▸**to be out of** ~ *Am* estar fastidiado; **to have a** ~ **at sth** *inf* intentar algo
whacked *adj inf* hecho, -a polvo
whacking **I.** *adj* grandote, -a **II.** *adv* muy; **a** ~ **big kiss** un beso muy grande **III.** *n Brit, Aus* zurra *f;* **a real** ~ una verdadera tunda
whale [hweɪl] *n* ballena *f;* **a beached** ~ una ballena varada ▸**to have a** ~ **of a time** pasarlo bomba; **a** ~ **of a ...** *Am* un(a) enorme…; **a** ~ **of a difference** una gran diferencia
whaling *n no pl* pesca *f* de ballenas
wham [hwæm] *interj inf* **1.** (*sound-effect for blow*) zas **2.** (*describes action*) y zas
whang [hwæŋ] *interj inf* zas
wharf [hwɔ:f, *Am:* hwɔ:rf] <-ves> *n* muelle *m;* **price ex** ~ precio *m* franco de muelle
wharfage ['wɔ:fɪdʒ, *Am:* 'wɔ:r-] *n* muellaje *m*
what [hwɒt, *Am:* hwʌt] **I.** *adj interrog* qué; ~ **kind of book?** ¿qué tipo de libro?; ~ **time is it?** ¿qué hora es?; ~ **men is he talking about?** ¿de qué hombres está hablando?; ~ **an idiot!** ¡qué idiota!; ~ **a fool I am!** ¿qué tonto soy! **II.** *pron* **1.** *interrog* qué; ~ **can I do?** ¿qué puedo hacer?; ~ **does it matter?** ¿qué importa?; ~**'s on** ¿qué ponen?; ~**'s up?** ¿qué hay?; ~ **for?** ¿para qué?; ~ **is he like?** ¿cómo es (él)?; ~**'s his name?** ¿cómo se llama?; ~**'s it called?** ¿cuál es su nombre?, ¿cómo se llama?; ~ **about Paul?** ¿y Paul?; ~ **about a walk?** ¿te va un paseo?; ~ **if it snows?** *inf* ¿y si nieva? **2.** *rel* lo que; ~ **I like is** ~ **he says/is talking about** lo que me gusta es lo que dice/lo que está hablando; ~ **is more** lo que es más; **he knows** ~**'s** ~**!** sabe cuántas son cinco **III.** *interj* ~**!** ¡qué!; **so** ~**?** ¿y qué?; **is he coming, or** ~**?** ¿viene, o qué?
whatever [hwɒt'evəʳ, *Am:* hwʌt'evɚ] **I.** *pron* **1.** (*anything*) (todo) lo que; ~ **happens** pase lo que pase **2.** (*any of them*) cualquier(a); ~ **you pick is fine** cualquiera (de los) que elijas está bien; **nothing** ~ nada de nada **II.** *adj* **1.** (*being what it may be*) cualquiera que; ~ **the reason** sea cual sea la razón **2.** (*of any kind*) de ningún tipo; **there is no doubt** ~ no hay ningún tipo de duda
whatnot ['hwɒtnɒt, *Am:* 'hwʌtnɑ:t] *n no pl* chisme *m;* **and** ~ *inf* y demás
whatsit ['hwɒtsɪt, *Am:* 'hwʌt-] *n inf* chisme *m*
whatsoever [ˌhwɒtsəʊ'evəʳ, *Am:* ˌhwʌtsoʊ'evɚ] *adv* sea cual sea; **to have no interest** ~ **in sth** no tener interés alguno en algo
wheat [hwi:t] *n no pl* trigo *m;* ~ **field** campo *m* de trigo; ~ **price** precio *m* del trigo ▸**to separate the** ~ **from the chaff** separar la cizaña del buen grano
wheat belt *n Am* zona *f* de cultivo de trigo **wheatgerm** *n no pl* germen *m* de trigo
wheel [hwi:l] **I.** *n* **1.** (*of vehicle*) rueda *f;* **alloy** ~**s** llantas *fpl* de aleación; **front/rear** ~ rueda *f* delantera/trasera; **big** ~ noria *f;* **to be on** ~**s** ir sobre ruedas **2.** TECH torno *m;* **spinning** ~ rueca *f* **3.** AUTO volante *m;* **to be at the** ~ ir al volante; **to take the** ~ tomar el volante; **to get behind the** ~ ponerse al volante **4.** *pl, inf* (*vehicle, car*) carro *m* **5.** NAUT timón *m* ▸**to be hell on** ~**s** *Am, inf* ser un peligro (al volante); **to set one's shoulder to the** ~ arrimar el hombro; **to spin one's** ~**s** *Am* no hacer progresos; **to have** ~**s within** ~**s** *Brit* ser más complicado de lo que parece **II.** *vt* hacer girar; **to** ~ **a pram along** empujar un carrito de niño **III.** *vi* girar ▸**to** ~ **and deal** *inf* hacer negocios sucios

◆**wheel around** *vi s.* **wheel round**
◆**wheel in** *vt* **1.**(*roll in*) rodar **2.***fig, inf* (*introduce*) traer
◆**wheel round** *vi* dar media vuelta
wheelbarrow ['hwi:lˌbærəʊ, *Am:* -ˌberoʊ] *n* carretilla *f*
wheel brace *n* llave *f* de ruedas en cruz
wheelchair *n* silla *f* de ruedas **wheel clamp** **I.** *n* cepo *m* **II.** *vt* poner cepo a
wheeler-dealer [ˌhwi:lə'di:ləʳ, *Am:* -lɚ'di:-lɚ] *n pej, inf* comerciante *mf* poco escrupuloso, -a
wheelhouse ['hwi:lhaʊs] *n* timonera *f*
wheeling ['hwi:lɪŋ] *n no pl* ~ **and dealing** *pej, inf* negocios *mpl* sucios
wheeze [hwi:z] **I.** <-zing> *vi* resollar **II.** *n* **1.** *no pl* (*of breath*) resuello *m* **2.** *Brit, inf* (*clever scheme*) treta *f;* **a good** ~ una buena idea; **to have a** ~ tener una buena ocurrencia
wheezy *adj* <-ier, -iest> jadeante
whelp [hwelp] **I.** *n* cachorro *m* **II.** *vt* parir
when [hwen] **I.** *adv* cuándo; **since** ~? ¿desde cuándo?; **I'll tell him** ~ **to go** yo le diré cuándo ir **II.** *conj* **1.**(*at which time*) cuando; **at the moment** ~ **he came** en el momento en que vino **2.**(*during the time that*) ~ **singing that song** cuando cantaba esa canción **3.**(*every time that*) ~ **it snows** cuando nieva **4.**(*although*) **he buys it** ~ **he could borrow it** lo compra cuando podría pedirlo prestado **5.**(*considering that*) si; **how can I listen** ~ **I can't hear?** ¿cómo puedo escuchar si no puedo oír?
whence [hwents] *adv form* por lo cual; (*interrogative*) ¿de dónde?
whenever [hwen'evəʳ, *Am:* -ɚ] **I.** *conj* **1.**(*every time that*) siempre que; ~ **I can** siempre que puedo **2.**(*at any time that*) **he can come** ~ **he likes** puede venir cuando quiera **II.** *adv* ~ **did I say that?** ¿cuándo fue que dije yo eso?; **I can do it tomorrow or** ~ puedo hacerlo mañana o un día de estos
where [hweəʳ] *adv* **1.** *interrog* dónde; ~ **does he come from?** ¿de dónde es?; ~ **does he live?** ¿dónde vive?; ~ **is he going** (**to**)? ¿a dónde va? **2.** *rel* donde; **I'll tell him** ~ **to go** yo le diré a dónde ir; **the box** ~ **he puts his things** la caja donde pone sus cosas; **this is** ~ **my horse was found** aquí es donde se encontró mi caballo; **London,** ~ **Paul comes from, is ...** Londres, de donde viene Paul, es...
whereabout(**s**) ['hweərəbaʊt(s), *Am:* 'hwerə-] **I.** *n + sing/pl vb* paradero *m;* **do you know the** ~ **of my book?** *form* ¿sabes dónde está mi libro? **II.** *adv inf* dónde; ~ **in Barcelona do you live?** ¿en qué zona de Barcelona vives?
whereas [hweər'æz, *Am:* hwer'-] *conj* **1.**(*while*) mientras que **2.** LAW considerando que
whereby [hweə'baɪ, *Am:* hwer'-] *conj form* por lo cual
wherein [hweər'ɪn, *Am:* hwer'-] *conj form* en donde
wheresoever [ˌhweəsəʊ'evəʳ, *Am:* ˌhwer-soʊevɚ] *adv, conj form s.* **wherever**
whereupon [ˌhweərə'pɒn, *Am:* 'hwerə-ˌpɑ:n] *conj form* con lo cual
wherever [ˌhweər'evəʳ, *Am:* ˌhwer'evɚ] **I.** *conj* dondequiera que; ~ **I am/I go** dondequiera que esté/vaya; ~ **there is sth** dondequiera que haya algo; ~ **he likes** donde le plazca **II.** *adv* ~ **did she find that?** ¿dónde demonios encontró eso?; **... or** ~ ...o donde sea
wherewithal ['hweəwɪðɔ:l, *Am:* 'hwer-] *n no pl, liter* recursos *mpl;* **to lack the** ~ (**to do sth**) no tener los medios (para hacer algo)
whet [hwet] <-tt-> *vt* **1.**(*sharpen*) afilar **2.** *fig* (*increase, stimulate*) estimular; **to** ~ **sb's appetite** (**for sth**) aguzar el deseo de alguien (por algo)
whether ['hweðəʳ, *Am:* -ɚ] *conj* **1.**(*if*) si; **to tell/ask** ~ **it's true** (**or not**) decir/preguntar si es verdad (o no); **she doesn't know** ~ **to buy it or not** no sabe si comprarlo o no; **I doubt** ~ **he'll come** dudo que venga **2.**(*all the same*) sea; ~ **rich or poor...** sean ricos o pobres...; ~ **it rains or thunders ...** aunque llueva o truene...; ~ **I go by bus or bike ...** vaya en autobos o en bicicleta...
whetstone ['hwetstəʊn, *Am:* -stoʊn] *n* piedra *f* de afilar
whew [fju:] *interj inf* uf
whey [hweɪ] *n no pl* suero *m*
which [hwɪtʃ] **I.** *adj interrog* qué; ~ **one/ones?** ¿cuál/cuáles? **II.** *pron* **1.** *interrog* cuál, qué; ~ **is his?** ¿cuál es el suyo? **2.** *rel* que, el que, la que, los que, las que; **the book** ~ **I read/of** ~ **I'm speaking** el libro que leí/del que estoy hablando; **he said he was there,** ~ **I believed** dijo que estaba ahi, lo cual creí
whichever [hwɪtʃ'evəʳ, *Am:* -ɚ] **I.** *pron* cualquiera que; **you can choose** ~ **you like** puedes escoger el que quieras **II.** *adj* cualquier, el que; **you can take** ~ **book you like** puedes coger el libro que quieras
whiff [hwɪf] *n* **1.**(*quick smell*) olor *m;* **to catch a** ~ **of sth** percibir un olorcillo a algo **2.** *fig* (*slight trace*) indicio *m;* **a** ~ **of corruption** una sospecha de corrupción
whiffy ['hwɪfi] *adj* <-ier, -iest> *Brit, inf* apestoso, -a
Whig [hwɪg] *n* HIST *miembro del partido liberal;* **the** ~**s** los liberales
while [hwaɪl] **I.** *n* rato *m;* **a short** ~ un ratito; **quite a** ~ bastante tiempo; **after a** ~ después de un tiempo; **for a** ~ durante un rato; **once in a** ~ de vez en cuando **II.** *conj* **1.**(*during which time*) mientras; **I did it** ~ **he was sleeping** lo hice mientras él dormía; ~ **I live** mientras viva **2.**(*although*) aunque; ~ **I like it, I won't buy it** aunque me guste, no lo compraré; ~ **I know it's true ...** a pesar de que sé que es verdad...
◆**while away** *vt* pasar; **to** ~ **the time** hacer tiempo

whilst [hwaɪlst] *conj Brit s.* **while**
whim [hwɪm] *n* capricho *m;* **to do sth on a ~** hacer algo por capricho; **as the ~ takes him** según se le antoja
whimper ['hwɪmpə^r, *Am:* -pɚ] **I.** *vi* quejarse; (*child*) lloriquear; (*dog*) gemir **II.** *n* quejido *m;* **a ~ of protest** un gemido de protesta; **to give a ~** dar un gemido
whimsical ['hwɪmzɪkəl] *adj* **1.** (*odd*) peregrino, -a **2.** (*capricious*) caprichoso, -a
whimsicality [ˌhwɪmzɪ'kæləti, *Am:* -ţi] *n no pl* **1.** (*odd character*) extravagancia *f* **2.** (*caprice*) capricho *m*
whimsy ['hwɪmzi] <-ies> *n pej* **1.** *no pl* (*odd fancifulness*) extravagancia *f* **2.** (*odd, fanciful thing or work*) fantasía *f* **3.** (*whim*) capricho *m*
whin [hwɪn] *n* tojo *m*
whine [hwaɪn] **I.** <-ning> *vi* **1.** (*complaining noise*) gemir; (*cry*) lloriquear **2.** (*engine*) zumbar **II.** *n* (*of a person or animal*) quejido *m;* (*of an engine*) zumbido *m*
whinge [hwɪndʒ] *Brit, Aus* **I.** <whingeing *o* whinging> *vi inf* quejarse **II.** *n inf* quejido *m;* **to have a ~** (**about sb/sth**) quejarse (de alguien/algo)
whinny ['hwɪni] **I.** <-ied, -ing> *vi* relinchar **II.** *n* <-ies> relincho *m*
whip [hwɪp] **I.** *n* **1.** (*lash*) látigo *m,* chicote *m AmL,* fuete *m AmL;* **to crack a ~** hacer restallar un látigo **2.** (*person*) *persona encargada de la disciplina de partido;* **chief ~** diputado *m* jefe encargado de la disciplina de partido **3.** *Brit* (*call*) llamada *f;* **a three-line ~** llamada apremiante **II.** <-pp-> *vt* **1.** (*strike with whip*) azotar **2.** *fig* (*force fiercely*) fustigar **3.** GASTR batir **4.** *Am, fig, inf* (*defeat*) **to ~ sb at** [*o* **in**] **sth** dar una paliza a alguien en algo **III.** <-pp-> *vi* restallar
◆**whip away** *vt* arrebatar
◆**whip back** *vi* **1.** (*bounce back*) rebotar de repente hacia atrás **2.** *fig* (*return*) volverse de golpe
◆**whip off** *vt* (*clothes*) quitarse con un movimiento brusco; (*tablecloth*) sacar de un tirón
◆**whip on** *vt* **1.** (*urge on*) animar **2.** (*put on quickly*) ponerse rápidamente
◆**whip out** *vt* **1.** (*take out*) sacar de repente **2.** (*produce*) hacer rápidamente
◆**whip round** *vi* volverse de repente; **to ~ the corner** (*car*) doblar la esquina a toda velocidad
◆**whip up** *vt* **1.** (*encourage*) avivar; **to ~ support** conseguir apoyo **2.** *inf* (*prepare quickly*) preparar rápidamente **3.** GASTR **to ~ eggs** batir huevos
whipcord ['hwɪpkɔːd, *Am:* -kɔːrd] *n* tralla *f*
whip hand *n* **the ~** el mando; **to hold the ~** llevar la batuta **whip-lash** *n* <-es> **1.** (*whip part*) tralla *f* **2.** (*blow from whip*) latigazo *m* **3.** *no pl* (*injury*) traumatismo *m* cervical
whipped cream *n* nata *f* para montar
whipper-in [ˌhwɪpə^r'ɪn, *Am:* -ɚ'-] *n* (*in hunting*) perrero *m*
whipper-snapper ['hwɪpəˌsnæpə^r, *Am:* -ɚˌsnæpɚ] *n iron* mequetrefe *m*
whippet ['hwɪpɪt] *n* lebrel *m*
whipping I. *n* **1.** (*punishment*) azotaina *f;* **to be given a** (**good**) **~** dar una (buena) azotaina a alguien **2.** *Am* (*physical beating*) paliza *f;* **to give/get a ~** dar/llevarse una paliza **3.** *no pl* (*gusting*) azote *m;* **the ~ of the wind** el azote del viento **II.** *adj* (*gusty*) racheado, -a; **a ~ wind** un golpe de viento
whipping-boy ['hwɪpɪŋbɔɪ] *n* cabeza f de turco *m* **whipping cream** *n no pl* nata *f* para montar **whipping top** *n* peonza *f*
whip-round ['hwɪpraʊnd] *n Brit, inf* colecta *f;* **to have a ~ for sb** hacer una colecta para alguien
whirl [hwɜːl, *Am:* hwɜːrl] **I.** *vi* girar rápidamente; **my head ~s** *fig* la cabeza me da vueltas **II.** *vt* hacer girar; **to ~ sb** (**a**)**round** dar vueltas a alguien **III.** *n* torbellino *m;* **a ~ of dust** una polvareda ►**to have one's head in a ~** dar vueltas la cabeza a uno; **to give sth a ~** probar algo
whirligig ['hwɜːlɪgɪg, *Am:* 'hwɜːr-] *n* **1.** (*toy*) molinete *m* **2.** *fig* vicisitudes *fpl*
whirlpool ['hwɜːlpuːl, *Am:* 'hwɜːrl-] *n* remolino *m* **whirlwind** *n* torbellino *m;* **a ~ romance** un idilio relámpago
whirlybird ['hwɜːlɪˌbɜːd, *Am:* 'hwɜːrlɪˌbɜːrd] *n Am* (*helicopter*) helicóptero *m*
whirr [hwɜː^r, *Am:* hwɜːr] **I.** *vi* hacer ruido **II.** *n* ruido *m;* (*of bird's wings*) aleteo *m*
whisk [hwɪsk] **I.** *vt* **1.** GASTR batir **2.** (*take quickly*) llevar rápidamente; **to ~ sb off somewhere** llevar a alguien a toda prisa a algún sitio **3.** (*with sweeping movement: tail*) sacudir **II.** *n* **1.** (*kitchen tool*) batidora *f;* **electric ~** batidora eléctrica; **hand-held ~** batidora de mano **2.** (*sweeping motion*) sacudida *f*
whisker ['hwɪskə^r, *Am:* -kɚz] *n* **1.** **~s** (*facial hair*) pelo *m* de la barba **2.** (*on side of face*) patilla *f* **3.** *pl* (*of animal*) bigotes *mpl* ►**by a ~** por un pelo; **within a ~** (**of sth**) a dos dedos (de algo)
whiskey *n Irish, Am,* **whisky** ['hwɪski] *n* <-ies> *Brit, Aus no pl* whisky *m*
whisper ['hwɪspə^r, *Am:* -pɚ] **I.** *vi* cuchichear **II.** *vt* **1.** (*speak softly*) susurrar; **to ~ sth in sb's ear** decir algo al oído a alguien **2.** *fig* (*gossip, speak privately*) rumorear; **it is ~ed that ...** se rumorea que... **III.** *n* **1.** (*soft sound or speech*) cuchicheo *m;* **to lower one's voice to a ~** bajar la voz y hablar en un susurro; **to speak in a ~** hablar muy bajo **2.** *fig* (*rumour*) rumor *m* **3.** *fig, liter* (*soft rustle*) susurro *m;* **the ~ of the leaves** el rumor de las hojas
whispering *n no pl* **1.** (*talking very softly*) susurro *m* **2.** *fig* (*gossiping*) chismes *mpl*
whispering campaign *n* campaña *f* de rumores
whist [hwɪst] *n no pl* whist *m;* **a game of ~**

una partida de whist

whistle ['hwɪsl] I. <-ling> *vi* 1. (*of person*) silbar; **to ~ at sb/sth** silbar a alguien/ algo; **to ~ in admiration** silbar de admiración 2. (*of bird*) trinar II. <-ling> *vt* silbar III. *n* 1. *no pl* (*blowing sound*) silbido *m*; **the ~ of the wind** el silbido del viento 2. (*musical device*) pito *m*; **referee's ~** silbato *m* del árbitro; **to blow a ~** pitar ▶**to blow the ~ on sb** llamar al orden a alguien; **to wet one's ~** remojar el gaznate

whit [hwɪt] *n no pl, form* pizca *f*; **not a ~** ni pizca; **to not care a ~ (about sth)** no preocuparse en absoluto (por algo)

white [hwaɪt] I. *adj* blanco, -a; **~ sauce** besamel *f*; **~ wedding** boda *f* tradicional; **to turn [*o* go] ~ with fear** palidecer de miedo ▶**to fly into a ~ rage** ponerse lívido de rabia II. *n* 1. (*colour*) blanco *m*; **~ of an egg** clara *f* de huevo; **the ~ of the eye** el blanco del ojo 2. (*person*) blanco, -a *m, f*

white-bait ['hwaɪtbeɪt] *n inv* chanquetes *mpl*

white-collar [ˌhwaɪt'kɒləʳ, *Am:* -'kɑːlɚ] *adj* **~ worker** oficinista *mf*

white corpuscle *n* MED glóbulo *m* blanco **white elephant** *n* objeto *m* grande e inútil **white ensign** *n* NAUT enseña *f* blanca **white feather** *n* **to show the ~** mostrarse cobarde **white flag** *n* bandera *f* blanca; **to fly [*o* raise] a ~** alzar una bandera blanca **white goods** *npl* 1. (*major household appliances*) electrodomésticos *mpl* 2. (*household linen*) ropa *f* blanca

Whitehall ['hwaɪthɔːl] *n* 1. (*offices of Britain's government*) *calle de Londres donde se encuentran los ministerios* 2. *fig* (*government of Britain*) *gobierno británico*

white heat *n no pl* 1. (*of metal*) candencia *f* 2. *fig* (*passion*) apasionamiento *m* **white horses** *npl Brit* (*olas*) cabrillas *mpl*

White House *n no pl* **the ~** la Casa Blanca

white lead *n no pl* albayalde *m* **white lie** *n* mentira *f* piadosa **white man** <-men> *n* hombre *m* blanco **white meat** *n no pl* carne *f* blanca

whiten ['hwaɪtən] I. *vt* blanquear II. *vi* blanquear; (*go pale*) palidecer

whitener ['hwaɪtnəʳ, *Am:* 'hwaɪtnɚ] *n* blanqueador *m*

whiteness *n* blancura *f*

whitening *n no pl s.* **whitener**

white-out *n* 1. (*dense blizzard*) ventisca *f* 2. *no pl, Am* TYPO líquido *m* corrector **white paper** *n Brit, Aus* POL libro *m* blanco **white sale** *n* quincena *f* blanca **white slave** *n pej* blanca *f* prostituida; **~ trade** trata *f* de blancas **white spirit** *n no pl, Brit* trementina *f*

whitethorn ['hwaɪtθɔːn, *Am:* -θɔːrn] *n* espino *m*

white tie I. *adj* **~ dinner** cena *f* de etiqueta II. *n* corbatín *m* blanco

whitewash ['hwaɪtwɒʃ, *Am:* -wɑːʃ] I. <-es> *n* 1. *no pl* (*for whitening walls*) enjalbegue *m* 2. (*coverup*) blanqueo *m* 3. *inf* (*overwhelming victory*) paliza *f* II. *vt* 1. (*cover in white solution*) encalar 2. (*conceal negative side of*) blanquear 3. *inf* SPORTS (*defeat completely*) dar un baño a

whitewater rafting [ˌhwaɪtwɔːtəʳ'rɑːftɪŋ, *Am:* -wɑt̬ɚ'ræftɪŋ] *n no pl* rafting *m* de aguas bravas

white wine *n no pl* vino *m* blanco

whither ['hwɪðəʳ, *Am:* -ɚ] *adv form* adónde

whiting[1] ['hwaɪtɪŋ, *Am:* -t̬ɪŋ] *n* (*fish*) pescadilla *f*

whiting[2] ['hwaɪtɪŋ, *Am:* -t̬ɪŋ] *n no pl* (*white substance*) tiza *f*

Whit Monday [ˌhwɪt'mʌndeɪ] *n* Lunes *m inv* de Pentecostés

Whitsun ['hwɪtsən] I. *n no pl* Pentecostés *m*; **at ~** en Pentecostés II. *adj* de Pentecostés

Whit Sunday [ˌhwɪt'sʌndeɪ] *n no pl* Domingo *m* de Pentecostés

Whitsuntide ['hwɪtsəntaɪd] *n no pl s.* **Whitsun**

whittle ['hwɪtl, *Am:* 'hwɪt̬-] <-ling> *vt* tallar
◆**whittle away at** *vt* 1. (*take little bits off*) cortar pedazos de 2. *fig* (*decrease*) reducir poco a poco
◆**whittle down** *vt* reducir gradualmente

whizz [hwɪz] I. *n* 1. (*brilliant person*) genio *m* 2. (*noise*) silbido *m* II. *vi* silbar; **to ~ along** *inf* ir a toda pastilla; **to ~ by** *inf* pasar como una bala

whiz(z) kid *n inf* joven genio *m*

who [huː] *pron* 1. *interrog* quién, quiénes; **~ broke the window?** ¿quién rompió la ventana?; **~ were they?** ¿quiénes eran? 2. *rel* que; **they have a daughter ~ works in Paris** tienen una hija que trabaja en París; **the people ~ work here** la gente que trabaja aquí; **all those ~ know her** todos los que la conozcan; **it was your sister ~ did it** fue tu hermana quien lo hizo

WHO [ˌdʌbljuːˌeɪtʃ'əʊ, *Am:* -'oʊ] *n abbr of* **World Health Organization** OMS *f*

whoa [hwəʊ, *Am:* hwoʊ] *interj* 1. (*command to stop a horse*) so 2. *fig, inf* (*to stop something*) vale

whodunit *n*, **whodunnit** [ˌhuː'dʌnɪt] *n inf* novela *f* policíaca

whoever [huː'evəʳ, *Am:* -ɚ] *pron* 1. *rel* (*who*) quien, quienquiera que; **they didn't write to me, ~ they were** no me escribieron, quienesquiera que fuesen; **~ said that doesn't know me** el que dijo eso no me conoce 2. *interrog, inf* (*angry*) quién (diablos); **~ said that?** ¿quién diablos dijo eso?

whole [həʊl, *Am:* hoʊl] I. *adj* 1. (*entire*) todo, -a; **the ~ world** el mundo entero 2. (*in one piece*) entero, -a; **to swallow sth ~** tragarse algo entero 3. (*intact: thing*) intacto, -a; (*person*) ileso, -a 4. *inf* (*big*) **a ~ lot of people** mucha gente; **to be a ~ lot faster** ser mucho más rápido II. *n* 1. (*a complete thing*) todo *m*; **as a ~** (*concept*) en su totalidad; **taken as a ~**

en conjunto; **on the** ~ en general **2.** *no pl* (*entirety*) totalidad *f;* **the** ~ la totalidad; **the** ~ **of Barcelona** toda Barcelona; **the** ~ **of next week** toda la semana que viene **III.** *adv* completamente; ~ **new** completamente nuevo

wholefood ['həʊlfu:d, *Am:* 'hoʊl-] *n Brit* **1.** *no pl* (*unprocessed food*) comida *f* naturista; ~ **diet** alimentación *f* naturista **2.** *pl* (*unprocessed food products*) alimentos *mpl* integrales

wholefood shop *n Brit* tienda *f* de comida naturista

wholegrain ['həʊlgreɪn, *Am:* 'hoʊl-] *adj* integral; ~ **bread** pan *m* integral; ~ **food products** productos *mpl* integrales

whole-hearted [ˌhəʊl'hɑ:tɪd, *Am:* ˌhoʊl-'hɑ:rt̬ɪd] *adj* entusiasta; (*completely sincere*) completamente sincero, -a; ~ **thanks** agradecimiento *m* de todo corazón

wholemeal ['həʊlmi:l, *Am:* 'hoʊl-] *adj Brit* integral; ~ **bread** pan *m* integral

wholesale ['həʊlseɪl, *Am:* 'hoʊl-] **I.** *n* venta *f* al por mayor **II.** *adj* **1.** al por mayor; ~ **business** negocio *m* mayorista; ~ **prices** precios *mpl* al por mayor; ~ **supplier** proveedor *m* mayorista **2.** (*on a large scale*) a gran escala; ~ **reform** reforma *f* a gran escala **III.** *adv* **1.** COM al por mayor **2.** (*in bulk*) en masa

wholesaler ['həʊlseɪləʳ, *Am:* 'hoʊlseɪlɚ] *n* mayorista *mf;* **furniture** ~ mayorista *m* de muebles

wholesome ['həʊlsəm, *Am:* 'hoʊl-] *adj* sano, -a; **the** ~ **outdoor life** la vida sana al aire libre; (**good**) ~ **fun** diversión *f* saludable; (**good**) ~ **food** comida *f* sana

whole-tone scale *n* MUS escala *f* completa

whole wheat **I.** *adj* de trigo integral **II.** *n* trigo *m* integral

who'll [hu:l] = **who will** *s.* **will**

wholly ['həʊli, *Am:* 'hoʊ-] *adv* enteramente; **to be** ~ **aware of sth** ser totalmente consciente de algo; ~ **different** completamente diferente

whom [hu:m] *pron* **1.** *interrog* a quién, a quiénes; *after prep* quién, quiénes; ~ **did he see?** ¿a quién ha visto?; **to** ~ **did he talk?** ¿con quién ha hablado? **2.** *rel* a quien, que; *after prep* quien, que; **those** ~ **I love** aquellos a quienes amo; **with** ~ con quien

whoop [hu:p] **I.** *vi* gritar **II.** *vt* **to** ~ **it up** echar una cana al aire **III.** *n* grito *m;* ~ **of triumph** grito *m* de victoria; **to give a loud** ~ dar un grito muy fuerte

whoopee ['hwʊpi, *Am:* 'hwu:pi] **I.** *interj* estupendo **II.** *n no pl* juerga *f;* **to make** ~ divertirse una barbaridad

whooping cough ['hu:pɪŋkɒf, *Am:* -kɑ:f] *n no pl* tos *f* ferina

whoops [hwʊps] *interj inf* epa

whop [hwɒp, *Am:* hwɑ:p] *inf* **I.** <-pp-> *vt* **1.** (*strike*) pegar **2.** (*in competition*) derrotar **II.** *n* zurra *f*

whopper ['hwɒpəʳ, *Am:* 'hwɑ:pɚ] *n iron* **1.** (*huge thing*) cosa *f* muy grande; **a** ~ **of a fish** un pez enorme **2.** (*lie*) embuste *m;* **to tell a** ~ contar una mentira muy gorda

whopping ['hwɒpɪŋ, *Am:* 'hwɑ:pɪŋ] *adj inf* enorme; **a** ~ **lie** una mentira muy grande; ~ **great** grandísimo

whore [hɔ:ʳ, *Am:* hɔ:r] *n pej* puta *f*

whorl [hwɜ:l, *Am:* hwɜ:rl] *n liter* espira *f*

whortleberry ['hwɜ:tlˌberi, *Am:* 'hwɜ:rt̬l-] <-ies> *n* arándano *m*

who's [hu:z] **1.** = **who is** *s.* **is** **2.** = **who has** *s.* **has**

whose [hu:z] **I.** *adj* **1.** *interrog* de quién, de quiénes; ~ **book is this?** ¿de quién es este libro?; ~ **son is he?** ¿de quién es hijo? **2.** *rel* cuyo, cuya, cuyos, cuyas; **the girl** ~ **brother I saw** la chica cuyo hermano vi **II.** *pron pos* de quién, de quiénes; ~ **is this pen?** ¿de quién es esta pluma?; **I know** ~ **this is** sé de quién es esto

why [hwaɪ] **I.** *adv* por qué; ~ **didn't you tell me about that?** ¿por qué no me dijiste nada sobre eso?; **that's** ~ **I didn't tell you** por eso no te dije nada; **I want to know** ~ **you came late** quiero saber por qué llegaste tarde; ~ **not?** ¿por qué no?; ~**'s that?** ¿y eso por qué? **II.** *n* porqué *m;* **the** ~**s and wherefores of sth** las razones de algo, el porqué de algo **III.** *interj* ¡cómo!

wick [wɪk] *n* mecha *f* ►**to get on sb's** ~ *Brit, inf* hacer subir a alguien por las paredes

wicked ['wɪkɪd] **I.** *adj* **1.** (*evil*) malvado, -a **2.** (*playfully malicious*) malo, -a; **a** ~ **sense of humor** un sentido del humor mordaz **3.** (*likely to cause pain*) inicuo, -a **4.** *inf* (*great fun*) de puta madre **II.** *n* **the** ~ los malos

wicker ['wɪkəʳ, *Am:* -ɚ] *n no pl* mimbre *m*

wicker basket *n* cesta *f* de mimbre **wicker bottle** *n* recipiente *m* de mimbre **wicker chair** *n* silla *f* de mimbre **wicker furniture** *n no pl* muebles *mpl* de mimbre **wickerwork** *n no pl* **1.** (*material*) artículo *m* de mimbre **2.** (*art*) cestería *f*

wicket ['wɪkɪt] *n Brit* **1.** (*cricket target*) palos *mpl* **2.** (*ground*) área *f;* **to be on a sticky** ~ estar en una situación difícil

wicket-keeper ['wɪkɪtˌki:pəʳ, *Am:* -pɚ] *n Brit* guardameta *m*

wide [waɪd] **I.** *adj* **1.** (*broad*) extenso, -a; (*as a measurement*) ancho, -a; **it is 3 m** ~ mide 3 m de ancho; **the** (**great**) ~ **world** el ancho mundo; **to search** (**for sb/sth**) **the** ~ **world over** buscar (a alguien/algo) por todo el mundo **2.** (*very open*) vasto, -a; **eyes** ~ **with fear/surprise** ojos *mpl* muy abiertos de miedo/sorpresa **3.** (*varied*) amplio, -a; **a** ~ **range** una amplia gama; **to have a** ~ **experience in sth** tener una amplia experiencia en algo **4.** (*extensive*) grande; ~ **support** gran apoyo *m* ►**to be** ~ **of the mark** no acertar **II.** *adv* extensamente; **to be** ~ **apart** estar muy lejos (el uno del otro); **to open** ~ abrir mucho; ~ **open** (*eyes*) muy abierto; (*door*) abierto de

W

par en par

wide-angle [ˌwaɪd'æŋgl] *adj* (*lente*) gran angular

wide-awake [ˌwaɪdə'weɪk] *adj* completamente despierto, -a

wide boy *n Brit, inf* tramposo *m*

wide-eyed [ˌwaɪd'aɪd, *Am:* 'waɪdaɪd] *adj fig* inocente

widely *adv* **1.**(*broadly*) extensamente; **to gesture ~** gesticular mucho; **to smile ~ at sb** sonreír ampliamente a alguien **2.**(*extensively*) ampliamente; **~ accepted/admired** muy aceptado/admirado **3.**(*to a large degree*) considerablemente; **~ differing aims** objetivos *mpl* muy diferentes

widen ['waɪdən] **I.** *vt* extender; (*discussion*) ampliar **II.** *vi* ensancharse

wide-open ['waɪdˌəʊpən, *Am:* ˌoʊ-] *adj* **1.**(*undecided*) abierto, -a **2.**(*vulnerable, exposed*) expuesto, -a; **to be ~ to comments** estar expuesto a comentarios

wide-range filter *n* filtro *m* de gama amplia

widespread ['waɪdspred] *adj* extendido, -a; *fig* general; **~ speculation** especulación difundida; **there is ~ speculation that ...** se especula mucho que...

widow ['wɪdəʊ, *Am:* -oʊ] **I.** *n* viuda *f;* **to be left a ~** enviudar **II.** *vt* **to ~ sb** dejar viuda a alguien; **to be ~ed** enviudar

widowed *adj* viudo, -a

widower ['wɪdəʊəʳ, *Am:* oʊɚ] *n* viudo *m;* **to be left a ~** enviudar

widowhood ['wɪdəʊhʊd, *Am:* -oʊ-] *n no pl* viudez *f*

widow's allowance *n* subsidio *m* de viudedad **widow's peak** *n* pico *m* que forma el pelo entre las entradas **widow's pension** *n* pensión *f* de viudedad

width [wɪdθ] *n* **1.** *no pl* (*distance across*) extensión *f;* (*of wallpaper*) anchura *f;* **to be 3 cm in ~** medir 3 cm de ancho **2.** (*full extent of sth: of clothes*) ancho *m;* **to swim two ~s** nadar dos anchos **3.** *no pl* (*amount, size*) amplitud *f*

wield [wiːld] *vt* **1.**(*hold*) manejar **2.**(*weapon*) empuñar **3.**(*power*) ejercer

wife [waɪf] <wives> *n* esposa *f;* **my ~** mi mujer

wifely ['waɪfli] *adj* de esposa; (*duties*) conyugal

wig [wɪg] *n* peluca *f*

wiggle ['wɪgl] **I.** *vt* menear; (*toes*) mover; (*one's hips*) contonear **II.** *vi* contonearse **III.** *n* (*movement*) meneo *m;* (*when walking*) contoneo *m*

wigwam ['wɪgwæm, *Am:* -wɑːm] *n* wigwam *m*

wild [waɪld] **I.** *adj* **1.**(*not domesticated: animal, man*) salvaje; (*flower*) silvestre; (*horse*) no domesticado, -a **2.**(*uncultivated: country, landscape*) agreste **3.**(*undisciplined*) indisciplinado, -a; (*party*) loco, -a **4.**(*not sensible*) insensato, -a; (*scheme, plan*) estrafalario, -a; (*behaviour, remarks*) delirante **5.**(*not accurate: blow, punch, shot*) errado, -a; (*estimate, guess*) disparatado, -a **6.**(*extreme*) absurdo, -a **7.**(*stormy*) tormentoso, -a; (*wind, weather*) furioso, -a **8.** *inf*(*angry*) furioso, -a; **to drive sb ~** sacar de quicio a alguien; **to go ~** ponerse loco **9.** *inf*(*very enthusiastic*) emocionado, -a; (*applause*) entusiasta **10.**(*untidy: hair*) descuidado, -a **11.** GAMES, INFOR (*substitutable*) comodín **12.** *inf*(*wonderful*) maravilloso, -a **II.** *adv* silvestre; **to grow ~** crecer libre ►**to run ~** (*child*) crecer como un salvaje; (*horse*) desbocarse; **to let one's imagination run ~** dejar volar la imaginación **III.** *n* **1.** *no pl* **the ~** (*natural environment*) la naturaleza; **to survive in the ~** (*animals*) sobrevivir en libertad **2.** *pl* **the ~s** la tierra virgen; (**out**) **in the ~s** en el quinto pino *inf*

wild beast *n* bestia *f* salvaje; **~ show** espectáculo *m* de fieras **wild boar** *n* jabalí *m* **wild card** *n a.* INFOR comodín *m* **wildcat I.** *n* **1.** ZOOL (*wild cat*) gato *m* montés **2.** *fig* (*fierce woman*) fiera *f* **II.** *adj* **1.**(*very risky*) arriesgado, -a **2.**(*unofficial: strike*) salvaje **3.**(*exploratory: drilling, well*) exploratorio, -a

wilderness ['wɪldənəs, *Am:* -dɚ-] *n no pl* **1.**(*desert tract*) páramo *m* **2.**(*unspoilt land*) tierra *f* virgen **3.** *fig* (*uncultivated garden*) selva *f irón* ►**to be in the ~** *Brit* estar marginado

wildfire ['waɪldˌfaɪəʳ, *Am:* -faɪɚ] *n* fuego *m* arrasador ►**to spread like ~** extenderse como un reguero de pólvora

wildfowl ['waɪldfaʊl] *inv n* ave *f* de caza **wild goose** <- geese> *n* ganso *m* salvaje **wild-goose chase** *n* empresa *f* desatinada; (*hopeless search*) búsqueda *f* inútil; **to send sb** (**off**) **on a ~** mandar a alguien a buscar una aguja en un pajar **wildlife** *n no pl* fauna *f* y flora

wildly *adv* **1.**(*in an uncontrolled way*) como loco; (*to gesticulate*) con furia, violentamente; **to behave ~** portarse como un salvaje; **to talk ~** hablar sin ton ni son **2.**(*haphazardly*) a lo loco; (*shoot, guess*) a tontas y a locas **3.** *inf* (*very*) muy; **~ exaggerated** superexagerado; **~ expensive** carísimo; **~ improbable** totalmente improbable

wildness *n no pl* **1.**(*natural state*) estado *m* salvaje; (*of a country*) estado *m* agreste **2.**(*uncontrolled behaviour*) desenfreno *m* **3.**(*haphazardness*) insensatez *f*

wiles [waɪlz] *npl* artimañas *fpl;* **to use all one's ~** usar todas sus tretas

wilful ['wɪlfəl] *adj Brit* **1.**(*deliberate*) deliberado, -a; (*disobedience of orders*) intencionado, -a; (*murder*) premeditado, -a **2.**(*self-willed*) testarudo, -a; (*obstinate*) obstinado, -a

wiliness ['waɪlɪnəs] *n no pl* astucia *f*

will[1] [wɪl] <would, would> **I.** *aux* **1.**(*to form future tense*) **they'll be delighted** estarán encantados; **I'll be with you in a minute** estaré contigo en un minuto; **I expect they'll**

come by car supongo que vendrán en coche; **I'll answer the telephone** contesto yo al teléfono; **she ~ have received the letter by now** ya debe haber recibido la carta **2.** (*with tag question*) **you won't forget to tell him, ~ you?** no te olvidarás decírselo, ¿verdad?; **they ~ accept this credit card in France, won't they?** aceptarán esta tarjeta de crédito en Francia, ¿no? **3.** (*to express immediate future*) **we'll be off now** ahora nos vamos; **I'll be going then** me voy entonces; **there's someone at the door – I'll go** llaman a la puerta – voy yo **4.** (*to express an intention*) **sb ~ do that** alguien hará eso; **I'll not be spoken to like that!** ¡no consiento que se me hable así! **5.** (*in requests and instructions*) **~ you let me speak!** ¡déjame hablar!; **just pass me that knife, ~ you?** pásame ese cuchillo, ¿quieres?; **give me a hand, ~ you?** me ayudas, ¿quieres? **6.** (*in polite requests*) **~ you sit down?** ¿pueden hacer el favor de sentarse?; **~ you be having a slice of cake?** ¿quiere un pedazo de tarta? **7.** (*used to express willingness*) **who'll post this letter for me? – I ~** ¿quién me echa esta carta al buzón? – lo haré yo; **~ you do that for me? – of course I ~** ¿harás eso por mí? – claro que sí **8.** (*used to express a fact*) **eat it now, it won't keep** cómetelo ahora, después se pondrá malo; **the car won't run without petrol** el coche no funciona sin gasolina **9.** (*to express persistence*) **he ~ keep doing that** se empeña en hacer eso; **they ~ keep sending me those brochures** no dejan de mandarme estos folletos; **the door won't open** no hay manera de que se abra esta puerta **10.** (*to express likelihood*) **they'll be tired** estarán cansados; **as you ~ all probably know already...** como todos sabrán... **II.** *vi form* disponer; **as you ~** como quieras

will² [wɪl] **I.** *n* **1.** *no pl* (*faculty*) voluntad *f;* (*desire*) deseo *m;* **the ~ of the people** la voluntad del pueblo; **to have the ~ to do sth** tener la voluntad de hacer algo; **to lose the ~ to live** perder las ganas de vivir; **to do sth with a ~** hacer algo con empeño; **at ~** a voluntad **2.** (*testament*) testamento *m* ▸**where there's a ~, there's a way** *prov* querer es poder *prov;* **with the best ~ in the world** con la mejor voluntad del mundo; **to have a ~ of one's own** ser cabezón **II.** *vt* **1.** (*try to cause by will-power*) sugestionar; **to ~ sb to do sth** sugestionar a alguien para que haga algo **2.** *form* (*ordain*) ordenar; **God ~ed it and it was so** Dios así lo quiso **3.** (*bequeath*) legar

willful ['wɪlfəl] *adj Am s.* **wilful**

William ['wɪljəm] *n* Guillermo *m;* **~ Tell** LIT Guillermo Tell; **~ the Conqueror** HIST Guillermo el Conquistador

willies ['wɪliz] *npl inf* **to have the ~** horrorizarse; **to give sb the ~** poner los pelos de punta a alguien

willing ['wɪlɪŋ] *adj* **1.** (*not opposed*) dispuesto, -a; **to be ~ to do sth** estar dispuesto a hacer algo; **to lend a ~ hand** dar una mano; **God ~** si Dios quiere; **to show ~** *Brit* dar muestras de buena voluntad **2.** (*compliant*) servicial

willingness *n no pl* **1.** (*readiness*) disposición *f;* **to show a ~ to do sth** mostrar buena voluntad para hacer algo **2.** (*enthusiasm*) entusiasmo *m;* **lack of ~** falta *f* de ánimo

will-o'-the-wisp [ˌwɪləðə'wɪsp] *n* **1.** (*ghostly light*) fuego *m* fatuo **2.** *fig* (*elusive thing*) quimera *f*

willow ['wɪləʊ, *Am:* -oʊ] *n* sauce *m*

willowy ['wɪləʊi, *Am:* -oʊ-] *adj* esbelto, -a

willpower ['wɪlˌpaʊəʳ, *Am:* -paʊɚ] *n no pl* fuerza *f* de voluntad

willy-nilly [ˌwɪli'nɪli] *adv* **1.** (*like it or not*) sea como sea **2.** *Am* (*in disorder*) de cualquier manera

wilt [wɪlt] *vi* **1.** (*droop: plants*) marchitarse **2.** (*feel weak: person*) languidecer; (*lose confidence*) desanimarse

wily ['waɪli] <-ier, -iest> *adj* astuto, -a

wimp [wɪmp] *n inf* endeble *mf*

win [wɪn] **I.** *n* victoria *f* **II.** <won, won> *vt* **1.** (*be victorious in: lawsuit, competition*) ganar; MIL vencer; **to ~ first prize** llevarse el primer premio **2.** (*obtain*) obtener; (*promotion, contract*) conseguir; (*recognition, popularity*) ganarse; **to ~ a reputation as a writer** lograr ser reconocido como escritor; **to ~ sb's heart** conquistar el corazón de alguien ▸**to ~ the day** prevalecer; **you can't ~ them all** no se puede pretender ganarlas todas; **you ~ some, you lose some** no se puede ganar todo **III.** <won, won> *vi* ganar; **to ~ easily** ganar con facilidad ▸**to ~ hands down** ganar con mucha facilidad; **you (just) can't ~ with him/her** con él/ella, siempre llevas las de perder, ¡no hay caso!; **you ~!** ¡como tú digas!

◆**win back** *vt* recuperar

◆**win over** *vt* **to win sb over to sth** (*persuade to change mind*) convencer a alguien para algo; (*persuade to transfer allegiance*) ganarse a alguien para algo

◆**win round** *vt s.* **win over**

◆**win through** *vi* salir adelante; SPORTS triunfar al fin

wince [wɪns] **I.** *vi* **1.** (*with pain*) hacer un gesto de dolor **2.** (*with embarrassment*) estremecerse **II.** *n* mueca *f* de dolor; **to give a ~** crispársele el rostro a uno

winch [wɪntʃ] **I.** <-es> *n* torno *m* **II.** *vt* levantar con un torno

wind¹ [wɪnd] **I.** *n* **1.** (*current of air*) viento *m;* **a breath of ~** un poco de aire; **gust of ~** ráfaga *f;* **to run before the ~** navegar viento en popa **2.** *no pl* (*breath*) aliento *m;* **to get one's ~** recobrar el aliento **3.** *no pl, Brit, Aus* MED gases *mpl;* **to break ~** ventosear; **to suffer from ~** tener gases ▸**to take the ~ out of sb's sails** desanimar a alguien; **he who sows the ~ shall reap the whirlwind** *prov* quien siembra vientos recoge tempestades *prov;* **to sail close**

W

to the ~ estar a punto de pasarse de la raya; **to get ~ of sth** enterarse de algo; **to go** [*o* **run**] **like the ~** correr como el viento; **to put the ~ up** *Brit, Aus* asustarse; **to put the ~ up sb** *Brit, Aus* asustar a alguien; **there's sth in the ~** se está tramando algo **II.** *vt* dejar sin aliento

wind² [waɪnd] <wound, wound> **I.** *vt* **1.** (*coil*) enrollar; (*wool*) ovillar; **to ~ sth around sth** enrollar algo alrededor de algo **2.** (*wrap*) envolver **3.** (*turn: handle*) hacer girar; (*clock, watch*) dar cuerda a **4.** (*film*) hacer correr **II.** *vi* serpentear

◆**wind back** *vt* (*film, tape*) rebobinar

◆**wind down I.** *vt* **1.** (*lower*) bajar **2.** (*gradually reduce*) disminuir progresivamente; (*activities, operations, production*) reducir; (*business*) limitar **II.** *vi* **1.** (*become less active*) limitarse; (*business*) tocar a su fin **2.** (*relax after stress*) desconectar **3.** (*need rewinding: clock, spring*) pararse

◆**wind forward** *vt* (*film, tape*) hacer correr

◆**wind on** *vt Brit, Aus* (*film*) enrollar

◆**wind up I.** *vt* **1.** (*bring to an end*) acabar; (*debate, meeting, speech*) concluir **2.** *Brit, Aus* ECON (*close down: company*) liquidar **3.** (*raise*) levantar **4.** (*tension spring*) dar cuerda a **5.** *Brit, inf* (*tease*) **to wind sb up** tomar el pelo a alguien **II.** *vi* **1.** (*come to an end*) finalizar **2.** *inf* (*end up*) **to ~ in prison** ir a parar a a la carcel

windbag ['wɪndbæg] *n inf* charlatán, -ana *m, f*

windbreak ['wɪndbreɪk] *n* barrera *f* contra el viento **wind cone** *n* manga *f* de viento **wind energy** *n no pl* energía *f* eólica

winder ['waɪndəʳ, *Am:* -ɚ] *n* **1.** *Brit* (*on watch*) cuerda *f* **2.** (*on toy*) manivela *f*

windfall ['wɪndfɔːl] *n* **1.** (*fruit*) fruta *f* caída **2.** *fig* (*money*) ganancia *f* imprevista **wind farm** *n* ECOL granja *f* con energía eólica **wind generator** *n* ECOL generador *m* eólico

winding ['waɪndɪŋ] *adj* sinuoso, -a

winding rope *n* cuerda *f* ondulada **winding sheet** *n* mortaja *f* **winding staircase** *n* escalera *f* de caracol

winding-up [ˌwaɪndɪŋ'ʌp] *n no pl* **1.** (*conclusion*) conclusión *f* **2.** *Brit, Aus* ECON (*of a company*) disolución *f*; (*of company's affairs*) liquidación *f*

winding-up sale *n* liquidación *f* total

wind instrument *n* instrumento *m* de viento **windjammer** *n* NAUT velero *m* grande **windlass** *n* torno *m* **windmill** *n* **1.** (*wind-powered mill*) molino *m* de viento **2.** (*toy*) molinete *m*

window ['wɪndəʊ, *Am:* -doʊ] *n* **1.** (*in building*) ventana *f*; (*bedroom*) vitrina *f*; **~ ledge** alféizar *m*; **a ~ on the world** *fig* una ventana abierta al mundo **2.** (*of shop*) vidriera *f*; (*window display*) escaparate *m* **3.** (*side windows*) ventanilla *f*; (*of vehicle*) luna *f*; **rear ~** luna trasera **4.** INFOR ventana *f*; **~ separator** separador *m* de ventana; **pop-up ~** ventana emergente **5.** (*in envelope*) ventanilla *f* **6.** *fig* (*time period*) ocasión *f*; **a ~ of opportunity** una oportunidad ►**to go out** (**of**) **the ~** *inf* (*plan*) venirse abajo

window box <-es> *n* jardinera *f* **window cleaner** *n* **1.** (*person*) limpiacristales *mf inv* **2.** *no pl* (*product*) limpiacristales *m inv* **window display** *n* escaparate *m* **window display competition** *n* competición *f* de escaparates **window dressing** *n no pl* **1.** (*in shop*) escaparatismo *m* **2.** *fig* fachada *f*; (*effort*) esfuerzo *m* por aparentar **window envelope** *n* sobre *m* de ventanilla **window frame** *n* marco *m* de la ventanta **window pane** *n* cristal *m* (de la ventana) **window--shopping** *n no pl* **to go ~** ir a mirar escaparates **windowsill** *n* repisa *f* de la ventana

windpipe ['wɪndpaɪp] *n* tráquea *f* **wind power** *n no pl* **1.** (*electricity*) energía *f* eólica **2.** (*force of wind*) impulso *m* por viento

windscreen ['wɪndskriːn] *n Brit, Aus* parabrisas *m inv*

windscreen wiper *n* limpiaparabrisas *m inv*

windshield ['wɪndʃiːld] *n Am* (*windscreen*) parabrisas *m inv* **windsock** *n* manga *f* de viento

windsurfer ['wɪndsɜːfəʳ, *Am:* -sɜːrfɚ] *n* surfista *mf*

windsurfing ['wɪndsɜːfɪŋ, *Am:* -sɜːrf-] *n no pl* windsurf *m*

windswept ['wɪndswept] *adj* **1.** (*exposed to wind*) azotado, -a por el viento **2.** (*looking wind-blown*) despeinado, -a

wind tunnel *n* TECH túnel *m* aerodinámico **wind turbine** *n* turbina *f* eólica

windward ['wɪndwəd, *Am:* -wɚd] NAUT **I.** *adj* de barlovento **II.** *n* barlovento *m*; (**to**) **~** a barlovento

windy¹ ['wɪndi] <-ier, -iest> *adj* ventoso, -a

windy² ['wɪndi] <-ier, -iest> *adj* sinuoso, -a

wine [waɪn] **I.** *n no pl* vino *m* **II.** *vt* **to ~ and dine sb** dar a alguien muy bien de comer y de beber

wine bottle *n* botella *f* de vino **wine cooler** *n* recipiente *m* para mantener fresco el vino **wine glass** <-es> *n* copa *f* para vino **wine-grower** *n* viticultor(a) *m(f)*

wine-growing I. *n no pl* viticultura *f* **II.** *adj* vinícola

wine list *n* carta *f* de vinos **wine merchant** *n* **1.** (*seller of wines*) vinatero, -a *m, f* **2.** (*shop*) vinatería *f*

winepress ['waɪnpres] <-es> *n* prensa *f* de uvas

winery ['waɪnəri] <-ies> *n* bodega *f*

wine-tasting *n* **1.** *no pl* (*activity*) catadura *f* de vinos **2.** (*event*) degustación *f* de vinos

wine waiter *n* sommelier *m*

wing [wɪŋ] **I.** *n* **1.** ZOOL, AVIAT ala *f*; **to take ~** *liter* alzar el vuelo **2.** ARCHIT ala *f*; **the west ~ of the house** el ala oeste de la casa **3.** SPORTS (*side of field: left, right*) ala *f* exterior; (*player*) extremo, -a *m, f* **4.** POL ala *f*; **left ~** ala izquierda **5.** *pl* THEAT bastidores *mpl;* **to be waiting in the ~s** *fig* estar esperando su oportunidad **6.** *Brit* AUTO aleta *f* **7.** *pl* MIL (*pilot's badge*) insignia *f* ►**to spread one's ~s** desplegar las alas; **to stretch one's ~s** extender las alas; **to take sb under one's ~** hacerse cargo de alguien **II.** *vt* **1.** (*wound, in hunting: bird*) herir en el ala; (*person*) herir superficialmente **2.** (*fly*) volar **III.** *vi* volar

wing chair *n* sillón *m* de orejas **wing commander** *n Brit* teniente *m* coronel de aviación

winged ['wɪŋd] *adj* alado, -a; (*seed*) con alas

winger ['wɪŋəʳ, *Am:* -ɚ] *n* SPORTS extremo, -a *m, f*

wing nut *n* TECH palomilla *f*

wingspan ['wɪŋspæn] *n,* **wingspread** ['wɪŋspred] *n* envergadura *f*

wink [wɪŋk] **I.** *n* guiño *m;* **to give sb a ~** guiñar el ojo a alguien ►**to have forty ~s** *inf* echarse una siestecita; **not to sleep a ~** no pegar ojo; **in a ~** en un abrir y cerrar de ojos **II.** *vi* **1.** (*close one eye*) guiñar el ojo; **to ~ at sb** guiñar el ojo a alguien **2.** (*flash: a light*) parpadear

winker *n Brit* AUTO intermitente *m*

winner ['wɪnəʳ, *Am:* -ɚ] *n* **1.** (*person*) ganador(a) *m(f)* **2.** *inf* SPORTS tanto *m* decisivo **3.** *inf* (*success*) éxito *m;* (*book*) obra *f* premiada; **to be on to a ~ with sth** tener mucho éxito con algo

winning ['wɪnɪŋ] **I.** *adj* **1.** (*that wins*) ganador(a); (*ticket*) premiado, -a; (*point*) decisivo, -a; (*team*) vencedor(a) **2.** (*charming*) encantador(a) **II.** *n* **1.** *no pl* (*act of achieving victory*) triunfo *m* **2.** *pl* (*money*) ganancias *fpl*

winnow ['wɪnəʊ, *Am:* -oʊ] *vt* **1.** (*grain*) aventar **2.** (*select*) seleccionar; **to ~ the list down to 8** seleccionar 8 de la lista

winsome ['wɪnsəm] *adj liter* atractivo, -a; (*charm, smile*) encantador(a)

winter ['wɪntəʳ, *Am:* -t̬ɚ] **I.** *n* invierno *m* **II.** *vi* (*animals*) invernar; (*person*) pasar el invierno

winter coat *n* chaqueta *f* de invierno; (*of animal*) pelaje *m* de invierno **winter season** *n* invierno *m* **winter solstice** *n* solsticio *m* de invierno **winter sports** *npl* deportes *mpl* de invierno **wintertime** *n no pl* invierno *m;* **in (the) ~** en invierno

wint(e)ry ['wɪntri] *adj* **1.** (*typical of winter*) invernal **2.** *fig* (*cold, unfriendly*) frío, -a

WIP [ˌdʌbljuːaɪ'piː] *n abbr of* **work in progress** trabajo *m* en curso de ejecución

wipe [waɪp] **I.** *n* **1.** (*act of wiping*) limpieza *f;* **to give sth a ~** pasar un trapo a algo, limpiar algo; **to give the floor a ~** limpiar el suelo **2.** (*tissue*) toallita *f* **II.** *vt* **1.** (*remove dirt*) limpiar; (*floor*) fregar; (*one's nose*) sonarse; (*dishes*) secar; **to ~ sth dry** secar algo **2.** (*erase material from: disk, a tape*) borrar **III.** *vi* secar

◆**wipe down** *vt* pasar un trapo a; (*floor*) limpiar

◆**wipe off** *vt* **1.** (*remove by wiping*) quitar con un trapo **2.** (*erase: data, programme*) borrar **3.** ECON reducir ►**to wipe the smile off sb's face** borrar la sonrisa de la cara de alguien

◆**wipe out** **I.** *vt* **1.** (*clean*) limpiar **2.** (*destroy: population, village*) exterminar; (*sb's profits*) acabar con **3.** (*cancel: debt*) liquidar **4.** *inf* (*tire out*) dejar hecho polvo **5.** *inf* (*economically*) arruinar **II.** *vi inf* (*driving, skiing*) perder el control

◆**wipe up** **I.** *vt* limpiar **II.** *vi* secar

wire ['waɪəʳ, *Am:* 'waɪɚ] **I.** *n* **1.** *no pl* (*metal thread*) alambre *m* **2.** ELEC cable *m* **3.** (*telegram*) telegrama *m* **4.** *Am* (*hidden microphone*) micrófono *m* escondido **5.** (*prison camp fence*) alambrada *f* ►**to get one's ~s crossed** *inf* tener un malentendido; **to get (sth) in under the ~** *Am, inf* conseguir algo justo a tiempo; **to go (down) to the ~** *inf* ir hasta el último momento; **to pull ~s** utilizar las influencias **II.** *vt* **1.** (*fasten with wire*) sujetar con alambre; **to ~ sth to the door** sujetar algo a la puerta con alambre **2.** ELEC conectar; **to be ~d for cable TV** tener instalación de televisión por cable **3.** *Am* (*fit with concealed microphone*) colocar un micrófono oculto en; **to be ~d** (*person*) llevar un micrófono oculto **4.** (*send telegram to*) **to ~ sb** poner un telegrama a alguien; **to ~ sb money** enviar un giro telegráfico a alguien

wire-cutters ['waɪəˌkʌtəʳz, *Am:* 'waɪɚˌkʌt̬ɚz] *npl* cortaalambres *m inv,* pinzas *fpl* de corte *Méx* **wire fence** *n* alambrada *f*

wire-haired terrier [ˌwaɪəheəd'teriəʳ, *Am:* ˌwaɪɚherd'teriɚ] *n* terrier *m* de pelo duro

wireless ['waɪələs, *Am:* 'waɪɚ-] *n Brit* **1.** *no pl* radio *f;* **on the [*o* by] ~** por radio **2.** (*set*) receptor *m* de radio

wireless operator *n* radiotelegrafista *mf;* AVIAT radio *mf* **wireless set** *n Brit* receptor *m* de radio

wirephoto *n* telefotografía *f*

wirepuller *n inf* enchufista *mf*

wirepulling *n no pl, inf* enchufismo *m*

wiretapping ['waɪəˌtæpɪŋ, *Am:* 'waɪɚ-] *n no pl* escuchas *fpl* telefónicas

wire transfer *n Am* transferencia *f* por cable

wiring ['waɪərɪŋ, *Am:* 'waɪɚ-] *n no pl* ELEC **1.** (*system of wires*) cableado *m* **2.** (*electrical installation*) instalación *f* eléctrica

wiring diagram *n* ELEC diagrama *m* de la instalación eléctrica

wiry ['waɪəri, *Am:* 'waɪɚ-] <-ier, -iest> *adj* **1.** (*rough-textured: hair*) áspero, -a, tieso, -a **2.** (*lean and strong: build, person*) enjuto, -a y fuerte

wisdom ['wɪzdəm] *n no pl* **1.** (*state of being wise*) sabiduría *f;* **with the ~ of hindsight** con la sabiduría que da la experiencia; **~ comes with age** la madurez llega con la edad **2.** (*sensibleness*) prudencia *f*

wisdom tooth <- teeth> *n* muela *f* del juicio

wise[1] [waɪz] *adj* **1.** (*having knowledge and sagacity*) sabio, -a; **the Three Wise Men** los Reyes Magos; **it's easy to be ~ after the event** es muy fácil criticar a posteriori **2.** (*showing sagacity*) acertado, -a; (*advice, saying*) adecuado, -a; (*words*) juicioso, -a **3.** (*sensible*) sensato, -a; (*decision, choice*) inteligente **4.** *inf* (*aware*) consciente; **to be ~ to sb** tener calado a alguien; **to be ~ to sth** estar al tanto de algo; **to get ~ to sth** caer en la cuenta de algo; **to get ~ to sb's game** enterarse del juego de alguien; **to be none the ~r for sth** seguir sin enterarse de algo **5.** *inf* (*cheeky*) pícaro, -a; **to get ~ with sb** insolentarse con alguien

◆**wise up I.** *vi* **to ~ to sth** ponerse al tanto de algo **II.** *vt* **to wise sb up about sth** poner a alguien al tanto de algo

wise[2] [waɪz] *n form* manera *f*, modo *m;* **in any/no ~** en modo alguno/de ninguna manera

wiseacre ['waɪzˌeɪkər, *Am:* -kɚ] *n* sabelotodo *mf*

wisecrack ['waɪzkræk] **I.** *n* broma *f;* **to make a ~ about sth** hacer un chiste sobre algo **II.** *vi* bromear

wise guy *n inf* gracioso, -a *m, f*

wish [wɪʃ] **I.** <-es> *n* **1.** (*desire*) deseo *m;* **against my ~es** en contra de mi voluntad; **to express a ~ that ...** rogar que...; **to have no ~ to do sth** no tener ganas de hacer algo; **to make a ~** expresar un deseo **2.** *pl* (*friendly greetings*) recuerdos *mpl;* **give him my best ~es** dale muchos recuerdos de mi parte; (**with**) **best ~es** (*at end of letter*) un abrazo **II.** *vt* **1.** (*feel a desire*) desear; **I ~ he hadn't come** ojalá no hubiera venido; **I ~ you'd told me** (*expressing annoyance*) me lo podrías haber dicho **2.** *form* (*want*) **to ~ to do sth** querer hacer algo; **I ~ to be alone** deseo estar solo **3.** (*hope*) **to ~ sb luck** desear suerte a alguien; **to ~ sb happy birthday** felicitar a alguien por su cumpleaños; **to ~ sb good night** dar las buenas noches a alguien **III.** *vi* **1.** (*want*) desear; **as you ~** como usted mande; **if you ~** como quieras; **to ~ for sth** anhelar algo **2.** (*make a wish*) **to ~ for sth** desear algo; **everything one could ~ for** todo lo que uno podría desear

wishbone ['wɪʃbeʊn, *Am:* -boʊn] *n* espoleta *f*

wishful thinking *n no pl* ilusión *f*

wishy-washy ['wɪʃiwɒʃi, *Am:* -ˌwɑːʃi] *adj pej* **1.** (*indeterminate and insipid*) insípido, -a; (*argument*) flojo, -a **2.** (*weak and watery: coffee, drink, soup*) aguado, -a; (*food*) soso, -a

wisp [wɪsp] *n* (*of hair*) mechón *m;* (*of straw*) brizna *f;* (*of smoke*) voluta *f;* (*of cloud*) jirón *m;* **a little ~ of a boy** un chico menudito

wispy ['wɪspi] <-ier, -iest> *adj* (*hair*) ralo, -a; (*person*) menudo, -a; (*clouds*) tenue

wisteria [wɪ'stɪərɪə, *Am:* -'stɪrɪ-] *n no pl* glicina *f*

wistful ['wɪstfəl] *adj* (*melancholy, nostalgic*) nostálgico, -a; (*longing*) añorado, -a

wit [wɪt] **I.** *n* **1.** *no pl* (*clever humour*) ingenio *m;* **to have a dry ~** ser mordaz **2.** (*practical intelligence*) inteligencia *f;* **to be at one's ~s' end** estar para volverse loco; **to gather one's ~s** poner las ideas en orden; **to frighten sb out of his/her ~s** dar a alguien un susto de muerte; **to have/keep one's ~s about one** andar con mucho ojo; **to live off one's ~s** vivir del cuento **3.** (*witty person*) chistoso, -a *m, f;* (*quick-witted person*) persona *f* ocurrente **II.** *vi form* **to ~** a saber

witch [wɪtʃ] <-es> *n* **1.** (*woman with magic powers*) bruja *f* **2.** *pej, inf* (*ugly or unpleasant woman*) arpía *f*

witchcraft ['wɪtʃkrɑːft, *Am:* -kræft] *n no pl* brujería *f*, payé *m CSur*

witch doctor *n* brujo *m*, payé *m CSur*

witchery ['wɪtʃəri] *n no pl s.* **witchcraft**

witch-hunt ['wɪtʃhʌnt] *n pej* caza *f* de brujas

witching hour ['wɪtʃɪŋˌaʊər, *Am:* 'wɪtʃɪŋˌaʊr] *n liter* medianoche *f*

with [wɪð, wɪθ] *prep* **1.** (*accompanied by*) con; (**together**) **~ sb** (junto) con alguien **2.** (*by means of*) con; **to take sth ~ one's fingers/both hands** tomar algo con los dedos/las dos manos; **to replace sth ~ something else** reemplazar algo por otra cosa **3.** (*having*) **the man ~ the umbrella** el hombre del paraguas; **~ no hesitation at all** sin ningún titubeo **4.** (*on one's person*) **he took it ~ him** lo llevó consigo [*o* encima] **5.** (*manner*) **~ all speed** a toda velocidad; **~ one's whole heart** de todo corazón **6.** (*in addition to*) **and ~ that he went out** y a continuación salió **7.** (*despite*) **~ all his faults** a pesar de todos sus defectos **8.** (*caused by*) **to cry ~ rage** llorar de rabia; **to turn red ~ anger** ponerse rojo de cólera **9.** (*full of*) **black ~ flies** negro de moscas; **to fill up ~ fuel** llenar de gasolina **10.** (*opposing*) **a war ~ Italy** una guerra contra Italia; **to be angry ~ sb** estar enfadado con alguien **11.** (*supporting*) **to be ~ sb/sth** estar de acuerdo con alguien/algo; **popular ~ young people** popular entre los jóvenes **12.** (*concerning*) **to be pleased ~ sth** estar satisfecho con algo; **what's up** [*o* **what's the matter**] **~ him?** ¿qué le pasa? **13.** (*understanding*) **I'm not ~ you** *inf* no te sigo; **to be ~ it** *inf* estar al tanto; **to get ~ it** ponerse al día ►**away ~ him!** ¡llévenselo!

withdraw [wɪð'drɔː, *Am:* -'drɑː] *irr* **I.** *vt* **1.** (*take out*) quitar; (*money*) sacar **2.** (*take back*) retirar **3.** (*cancel*) cancelar; (*motion, action*) anular; (*charge*) apartar; **to ~ one's labour** *Brit, form* ir a la huelga **II.** *vi* **1.** *form a.* MIL (*leave*) marcharse, retirarse; **to ~ from public life** retirarse de la vida pública; SPORTS abandonar **2.** *fig* (*become quiet and unsociable*) recluirse; (*into silence*) retraerse

withdrawal [wɪð'drɔːəl, *Am:* -'drɑː-] *n* **1.** *a.* MIL retirada *f;* **to make a** ~ FIN sacar dinero **2.** *no pl* LAW retracto *m;* (*of consent, support*) supresión *f* **3.** *no pl* (*sports*) abandono *m* **4.** *no pl* (*distancing from others*) retraimiento *m*

withdrawal symptoms *npl* síndrome *m* de abstinencia; **to suffer** (**from**) ~ *a. fig* tener el mono *inf*

wither ['wɪðəʳ, *Am:* -ɚ] **I.** *vi* **1.** (*plants*) marchitarse **2.** *fig* (*lose vitality*) debilitarse; **to allow sth to** ~ dejar que algo pierda vida ►**to** ~ **on the vine** desaparecer poco a poco **II.** *vt* **1.** (*plant*) marchitar **2.** *fig* (*strength*) mermar

withering ['wɪðərɪŋ] *adj* **1.** (*fierce and destructive*) destructivo, -a; (*heat*) abrasador(a); (*fire*) arrollador(a) **2.** (*contemptuous: criticism*) hiriente

withhold [wɪð'həʊld, *Am:* -'hoʊld] *irr vt* **1.** (*not give: information*) **to** ~ **sth** (**from sb**) ocultar algo (a alguien); (*one's support*) negar; (*evidence*) no revelar **2.** (*not pay: benefits, rent*) retener

within [wɪð'ɪn] **I.** *prep* **1.** *form* (*inside of*) dentro de; ~ **the country/town** dentro del país/de la ciudad **2.** (*in limit of*) ~ **sight/hearing** al alcance de la vista/del oído; ~ **easy reach** al alcance de la mano **3.** (*in less than*) en (el transcurso de); ~ **one hour** en una hora; ~ **3 days** en el plazo de tres días; ~ **2 km of the town** a menos de 2 km de la ciudad **4.** (*in accordance to*) de acuerdo a; ~ **the law** dentro de la ley **II.** *adv* dentro; **from** ~ desde adentro

without [wɪð'aʊt] **I.** *prep* sin; ~ **warning** sin previo aviso; **to be** ~ **relatives** no tener parientes; **to do** ~ **sth** apañárselas sin algo **II.** *adv liter* fuera; **from** ~ desde fuera

withstand [wɪð'stænd] *irr vt* resistir; (*heat, pressure*) soportar

witness ['wɪtnəs] **I.** *n* **1.** *a.* LAW testigo *mf;* ~ **for the defence** testigo de descargo; **according to** ~**es** según testigos; **to be** (**a**) ~ **to sth** presenciar algo **2.** *no pl, form* (*testimony*) testimonio *m;* **to bear** ~ **to sth** dar fe de algo **II.** *vt* **1.** (*see*) ser testigo de; **to** ~ **sb doing sth** observar a alguien haciendo algo **2.** (*be there during*) vivir; (*changes*) presenciar **3.** (*attest authenticity of*) atestiguar la veracidad de **III.** *vi Brit* LAW dar fe de; **to** ~ **to sth** dar fe de algo; **to** ~ **to have done sth** demostrar haber hecho algo

witness box <-es> *n Brit,* **witness stand** *n Am* tribuna *f* (de los testigos)

witty ['wɪti, *Am:* 'wɪt̬-] <-ier, -iest> *adj* (*possessing or showing wit*) ingenioso, -a; (*funny*) gracioso, -a

wizard ['wɪzəd, *Am:* -ɚd] **I.** *n* **1.** (*magician*) mago, -a *m, f* **2.** (*expert*) genio *m;* **to be a** ~ **at sth** ser un genio haciendo algo **II.** <-er, -est> *adj Brit, inf* fantástico, -a

wizardry ['wɪzədri, *Am:* -ɚd-] *n no pl* magia *f*

wizened ['wɪznd] *adj* marchito, -a; (*face, skin*) arrugado, -a

WNW *abbr of* **west-northwest** ONO

w/o *prep abbr of* **without** sin

wobble ['wɒbl, *Am:* 'wɑːbl] **I.** *vi* **1.** (*move unsteadily*) tambalearse; (*wheel*) bailar; (*jelly, fat*) moverse; (*rock*) balancearse **2.** (*tremble: voice*) temblar **3.** *fig* (*fluctuate: prices, shares*) fluctuar **II.** *vt* hacer tambalearse; (*camera*) mover **III.** *n* **1.** (*wobbling movement*) tambaleo *m* **2.** (*quavering sound*) temblor *m* **3.** ECON fluctuación *f*

wobbly ['wɒbli, *Am:* 'wɑːbli] **I.** <-ier, -iest> *adj* **1.** (*unsteady*) tambaleante; (*line*) zigzagueante; (*chair*) cojo, -a **2.** (*wavering: a note, a voice*) tembloroso, -a **II.** <-ies> *n Brit, inf* pataleta *f;* **to throw a** ~ poner el grito en el cielo

woe [wəʊ, *Am:* woʊ] *n* **1.** *no pl, liter* (*unhappiness*) desgracia *f;* **a tale of** ~ tragedia *f;* ~ **betide you!** ¡maldito seas! **2.** *pl, form* (*misfortunes*) males *mpl;* **to pour out one's** ~**s** contar a alguien sus penas

woebegone ['wəʊbɪgɒn, *Am:* 'woʊbɪgɑːn] *adj liter* angustiado, -a

woeful ['wəʊfəl, *Am:* 'woʊ-] *adj* **1.** (*deplorable*) deplorable; (*ignorance, incompetence*) lamentable **2.** *liter* (*sad*) afligido, -a

wog [wɒg, *Am:* wɑːg] *n Brit, Aus, pej, inf* **1.** (*dark-skinned person*) negro, -a *m, f* **2.** *Aus* (*non-English-speaking immigrant*) extranjero, -a *m, f*

wok [wɒk, *Am:* wɑːk] *n* puchero *m* chino de metal

woke [wəʊk, *Am:* woʊk] *vt, vi pt of* **wake**

woken ['wəʊkən, *Am:* 'woʊ-] *vt, vi pp of* **wake**

wolf [wʊlf] **I.** <wolves> *n* **1.** (*animal*) lobo *m* **2.** *inf* (*seducer*) don Juan *m* ►**to keep the** ~ **from the door** no pasar miseria; **a** ~ **in sheep's clothing** un lobo disfrazado de cordero; **to cry** ~ dar una falsa alarma; **to throw sb to the wolves** arrojar a alguien a los lobos **II.** *vt inf* engullir

wolf cub *n* lobato *m* **wolfhound** *n* perro *m* lobo **wolf whistle** *n* silbido *m* de admiración

woman ['wʊmən] <women> *n* **1.** (*female human*) mujer *f;* **the other** ~ la querida; ~ **candidate** candidata *f;* ~ **president** presidenta *f;* **women's libber** defensor(a) *m(f)* de los derechos de la mujer **2.** *inf* (*man's female partner*) esposa *f*

woman doctor *n* doctora *f* **woman driver** *n* conductora *f*

womanhood ['wʊmənhʊd] *n no pl* **1.** (*female adulthood*) condición *f* de mujer; **to reach** ~ hacerse adulta **2.** (*women as a group*) mujeres *fpl*

womanish ['wʊmənɪʃ] *adj pej* afeminado

womanize ['wʊmənaɪz] *vi inf* andar detrás de las mujeres

womanizer *n* mujeriego *m*

womankind [ˌwʊmən'kaɪnd, *Am:* 'wʊmənkaɪnd] *n no pl, form* sexo *m* femenino; **all ~** todas las mujeres

womanly ['wʊmənli] *adj* **1.** (*not manly*) femenino, -a; (*wiles*) de mujer **2.** (*not girlish*) de mujer adulta

womb [wu:m] *n* útero *m;* **in the ~** en el seno materno

womenfolk ['wɪmɪnfəʊk, *Am:* -foʊk] *npl* mujeres *fpl*

women's centre *n* centro *m* para mujeres **women's lib** *n no pl, inf abbr of* **women's liberation** liberación *f* de la mujer **women's refuge** *n Brit, Aus,* **women's shelter** *n Am* centro *m* de acogida para mujeres

won [wʌn] *vt, vi pt, pp of* **win**

wonder ['wʌndəʳ, *Am:* -dɚ] **I.** *vt* **1.** (*ask oneself*) preguntarse; **to make sb ~** hacer pensar a alguien **2.** (*feel surprise*) **I ~ why he said that** me extraña que dijera eso **II.** *vi* **1.** (*ask oneself*) preguntarse; **to ~ about sth** preguntarse algo; **to ~ about doing sth** pensar si hacer algo **2.** (*feel surprise*) sorprenderse; **to ~ at sth/sb** maravillarse de algo/alguien; **I don't ~** (**at it**) no me extraña **III.** *n* **1.** (*marvel*) maravilla *f;* **to do ~s** hacer maravillas; **the ~s of modern technology** los prodigios de la tecnología moderna; **it's a ~** (**that**) ... es un milagro que ...; **~s** (**will**) **never cease!** *iron* ¡eso sí es increíble! **2.** *no pl* (*feeling*) asombro *m;* **in ~** con estupefacción; **to listen in ~** escuchar con estupor ►**to be a nine-days' ~** ser un prodigio efímero

wonder boy *n iron, inf* joven *m* prodigio **wonder drug** *n* remedio *m* milagroso

wonderful ['wʌndəfəl, *Am:* -dɚ-] *adj* maravilloso, -a

wonderland ['wʌndəlænd, *Am:* -dɚlænd] *n* país *m* de las maravillas **wonderment** *n no pl* admiración *f*

wonky ['wɒŋki, *Am:* 'wɑ:ŋ-] <-ier, -iest> *adj Brit, Aus, inf* **1.** (*unsteady*) poco firme; (*feeling*) débil **2.** (*askew*) torcido, -a

wont [wəʊnt, *Am:* wɔ:nt] **I.** *adj form* acostumbrado, -a; **to be ~ to do sth** soler hacer algo **II.** *n no pl, form* costumbre *f;* **as is her ~** como suele hacer

won't [wəʊnt, *Am:* woʊnt] = **will not** *s.* **will**

woo [wu:] *vt* **1.** (*try to attract*) **to ~ sb** (*customers, investors*) buscar atraer a alguien; (*voters*) buscar el apoyo de alguien **2.** (*court*) cortejar

wood [wʊd] *n* **1.** *no pl* (*material*) madera *f;* (*to build a fire*) leña *f* **2.** (*group of trees*) bosque *m* **3.** SPORTS (*golf*) palo *m* de madera **4.** *no pl, Brit* (*wooden container*) barril *m;* **beer from the ~** cerveza *f* de barril ►(**to**) **touch ~**, (**to**) **knock on ~** *Am* tocar madera; **to be out of the ~** estar a salvo

wood alcohol *n no pl* metanol *m* **woodbine** *n* BOT **1.** (*wild honeysuckle*) madreselva *f* **2.** *Am* (*Virginia creeper*) parra *f* virgen **woodcarver** *n* tallista *mf* de madera **woodcraft** *n no pl* **1.** (*outdoor skills*) conocimiento *m* de la vida del bosque **2.** (*artistic skill*) artesanía *f* en madera **woodcut** *n* ART grabado *f* en madera **woodcutter** *n* leñador(a) *m(f)*

wooded ['wʊdɪd] *adj* boscoso, -a

wooden ['wʊdn] *adj* **1.** (*made of wood*) de madera; **~ leg** pata *f* de palo **2.** (*awkward*) rígido, -a; (*smile*) inexpresivo, -a

woodland ['wʊdlənd] **I.** *n* bosque *m* **II.** *adj* de los bosques

wood panelling *n no pl* paneles *mpl* de madera **woodpecker** *n* pájaro *m* carpintero **woodpile** *n* montón *m* de leña **wood preservative** *n* conservante *m* de la madera **wood pulp** *n no pl* TECH pulpa *f* de madera

woodshed ['wʊdʃed] **I.** *n* leñera *f* **II.** <-dd-> *vi Am, inf* tocar un instrumento musical

woodwind ['wʊdwɪnd] MUS **I.** *n* instrumentos *mpl* de viento (de madera) **II.** *adj* de viento

woodwork ['wʊdwɜ:k, *Am:* -wɜ:rk] *n no pl* **1.** (*wooden parts of building*) carpintería *f* **2.** *Brit* (*carpentry*) ebanistería *f;* (*craftsmanship*) artesanía *f* en madera **3.** *inf* SPORTS los postes y el travesaño ►**to come out of the ~** salir de quién sabe dónde **woodworm** *n inv* **1.** (*larva that attacks wood*) carcoma *f* **2.** *no pl* (*damage*) madera *f* carcomida

woody ['wʊdi] <-ier, -iest> *adj* **1.** (*tough like wood: plant, stem, tissue*) leñoso, -a **2.** (*like wood: flavour*) amaderado, -a **3.** (*wooded*) boscoso, -a

woof [wu:f] **I.** *n* (*dog*) ladrido *m;* **to give a loud ~** ladrar **II.** *vi* ladrar; **to ~ at sb** gritar fuertemente a alguien

woofer ['wu:fəʳ, *Am:* -ɚ] *n* bafle *m*

wool [wʊl] *n no pl* lana *f* ►**to pull the ~ over sb's eyes** dar a alguien gato por liebre

woolen ['wʊlən] *adj Am s.* **woollen**

wool-gathering ['wʊlˌgæðərɪŋ] *n* **to be ~** andar distraído

woollen ['wʊlən] *adj* de lana

woolly ['wʊli] **I.** <-ier, -iest> *adj* **1.** (*made of wool*) de lana **2.** (*wool-like*) lanoso, -a **3.** (*vague*) vago, -a; (*idea, thinking*) impreciso, -a **II.** <-ies> *n Brit, inf* prenda *f* de lana

wool trade *n* comercio *m* de lana

wooly ['wʊli] <-ier, -iest> *adj Am s.* **woolly**

woozy ['wu:zi] <-ier, -iest> *adj inf* indispuesto, -a

wop [wɒp, *Am:* wɑ:p] *n pej, inf* italiano, -a *m, f*

word [wɜ:d, *Am:* wɜ:rd] **I.** *n* **1.** (*unit of language*) palabra *f;* **a ~ of Hebrew origin** una voz de origen hebreo; **to be a man/woman of few ~s** ser hombre/mujer de pocas palabras; **to not breathe a ~ of sth** no decir ni pío de algo; **to be too ridiculous for ~s** ser tremendamente ridículo; **in other ~s** en otros términos; **~ for ~** literalmente **2.** *no pl* (*news*) noticia *f;* (*message*) mensaje *m;* **to get ~ of**

sth enterarse de algo; **to have ~ from sb** tener un recado de alguien; **to have ~ that ...** tener conocimiento de que... **3.** *no pl* (*order*) orden *f;* **a ~ of advice** un consejo; **a ~ of warning** una advertencia; **to say the ~** dar la orden; **just say the ~** sólo tienes que pedirlo **4.** *no pl* (*promise*) palabra *f* de honor; **to be a man/woman of one's ~** ser un hombre/una mujer de palabra; **to keep one's ~** cumplir su promesa; **take my ~ for it!** ¡acepta mi palabra! **5.** *no pl* (*statement of facts*) explicación *f* **6.** *pl* MUS (*lyrics*) letra *f* **7.** REL **the Word of God** la palabra de Dios ►**to have a quick ~ in sb's ear** hablar en privado con alguien; **to not be able to get a ~ in edgeways** *inf* no poder meter baza; **by ~ of mouth** de viva voz; **to put ~s in(to) sb's mouth** atribuir a alguien algo que no dijo; **to take the ~s (right) out of sb's mouth** quitar la palabra de la boca a alguien; **famous last ~s!** *inf* ¡y yo me lo creo!; **to not have a good ~ to say about sb/sth** no poder decir nada bueno sobre alguien/algo; **to put in good ~ for sb** interceder por alguien; **~s fail me!** ¡no tengo palabras!; **from the ~ go** desde el primer momento; **to have ~s with sb** (*quarrel*) discutir con alguien; **mark my ~s!** ¡acuérdate de lo que te digo!; **to mince one's ~s** medir sus palabras; **to not mince one's ~s** no tener pelos en la lengua; **my ~!** ¡caramba! **II.** *vt* expresar

word break *n* LING separación *f* de palabra **word division** *n no pl* LING división *f* de palabra

wording *n no pl* **1.** (*words used*) términos *mpl* **2.** (*style*) estilo *m*

wordless ['wɜːdləs, *Am:* 'wɜːrd-] *adj* mudo, -a

word order *n no pl* LING orden *m* de las palabras

word-perfect [ˌwɜːd'pɜːfɪkt, *Am:* ˌwɜːrd-'pɜːrfɪkt] *adj* **to be ~** saber perfectamente su papel

wordplay ['wɜːdpleɪ, *Am:* 'wɜːrdpleɪ] *n no pl* juego *m* de palabras

word processing *n no pl* INFOR tratamiento *m* de textos **word processor** *n* INFOR procesador *m* de textos **word wrap** *n no pl* INFOR salto *m* de línea automático

wordy ['wɜːdi, *Am:* 'wɜːr-] <-ier, iest> *adj pej* farragoso, -a

wore [wɔː^r, *Am:* wɔːr] *vt, vi pt of* **wear**

work [wɜːk, *Am:* wɜːrk] **I.** *n* **1.** *no pl* (*useful activity*) trabajo *m;* **to be hard ~ (doing sth)** (*strenuous*) ser un gran esfuerzo (hacer algo); (*difficult*) ser una tarea difícil (hacer algo); **to set sb to ~** poner a trabajar a alguien; **good ~!** ¡bien hecho! **2.** *no pl* (*employment*) empleo *m;* **to be in/out of ~** estar en activo/en paro **3.** *no pl* (*place of employment*) lugar *m* de trabajo **4.** (*product*) *a.* ART, MUS obra *f;* **~ of reference** libro *m* de consulta **5.** *pl + sing/pl vb* (*factory*) fábrica *f;* **steel ~s** fundición *f* de acero **6.** *pl* TECH (*of a clock*) mecanismo *m* **7.** *no pl* PHYS esfuerzo *m* ►**to have one's ~ cut out to do sth** costarle trabajo a uno hacer algo; **to make short ~ of sb** hacer trizas a alguien; **to make short ~ of sth** despachar algo rápidamente; **to get to ~ on sb** *inf* ponerse a convencer a alguien; **to give sb the ~s** *inf* tratar duro a alguien **II.** *vi* **1.** (*do job*) trabajar; **to ~ abroad** trabajar en el extranjero; **to ~ as sth** trabajar de algo; **to ~ to rule** ECON hacer huelga de celo **2.** (*be busy*) estar ocupado; **to get ~ing** poner manos a la obra; **to ~ hard** ser aplicado; **to ~ to do sth** dedicarse a hacer algo **3.** TECH funcionar; **to get sth to ~** conseguir que algo funcione **4.** (*be successful*) salir adelante; (*plan, tactics*) llevarse a cabo **5.** MED hacer efecto **6.** (*have an effect*) **to ~ against sb/sth** obrar en contra de alguien/algo; **to ~ against a candidate** resultar negativo para un candidato; **to ~ for sb** ser eficaz para alguien; **to ~ both ways** ser un arma de doble filo **7.** (*move*) **to ~ (somewhere)** moverse (hacia algún sitio) **8.** + *adj* (*become*) **to ~ free** soltarse; **to ~ loose** desprenderse **9.** *liter* (*change expression: sb's face*) moverse; (*contort*) contraerse; (*twitch*) temblar ►**to ~ like a charm** funcionar de maravilla; **to ~ like a dog** *Am,* **to ~ like a slave** trabajar como un esclavo; **to ~ like a Trojan** *Brit* trabajar como un demonio; **to ~ round to sth** prepararse con tranquilidad para algo **III.** *vt* **1.** (*make sb work*) **to ~ sb hard** hacer trabajar duro a alguien; **to ~ oneself to death** matarse trabajando; **to ~ a forty--hour week** tener una semana laboral de cuarenta horas **2.** TECH (*operate*) hacer funcionar; **to be ~ed by sth** ser accionado por algo **3.** (*move back and forward*) mover; **to ~ sth backwards and forwards** tirar algo hacia adelante y hacia atrás; **to ~ sth free** liberar algo; **to ~ sth loose** desprender algo; **to ~ one's way along sth** abrirse camino por algo **4.** (*bring about*) producir; (*a cure*) efectuar; (*a miracle*) lograr; **to ~ it** [*o* **things**] **so that ...** arreglárselas para que... *+subj* **5.** (*shape*) tallar; (*bronze, iron*) trabajar **6.** FASHION (*embroider*) bordar **7.** MIN explotar; AGR cultivar **8.** (*pay for by working*) **to ~ one's passage** NAUT costear el viaje trabajando; **to ~ one's way through university** pagarse la universidad trabajando

◆**work away** *vi* trabajar sin parar

◆**work in** *vt* **1.** (*mix in: into a dough*) añadir; (*on one's skin*) penetrar poco a poco **2.** (*include*) introducir; (*fit in*) colocar

◆**work off** **I.** *vt* **1.** (*counter effects of*) contrarrestar; (*one's anger, frustration*) desahogar; (*stress*) aliviar **2.** (*pay by working*) pagar con el trabajo; (*a debt, loan*) amortizar **II.** *vi* TECH separarse

◆**work on** *vt* (*a car, project*) trabajar sobre; (*accent, fitness, skills*) esforzarse para mejorar; (*assumption, hypothesis*) partir de; (*person*) intentar persuadir a

◆**work out** **I.** *vt* **1.** (*solve*) resolver; **to work**

things out arreglárselas **2.** (*calculate*) calcular **3.** (*develop*) desarrollar; (*a settlement, solution*) elaborar; (*decide*) determinar **4.** (*understand*) comprender **5.** (*complete*) completar; (*one's contract*) cumplir con **6. to be worked out** (*lode, mine, quarry*) estar agotado **II.** *vi* **1.** (*give a result: a calculation, sum*) resultar; (*cheaper, more expensive*) salir **2.** (*be resolved*) resolverse **3.** (*be successful*) acabar bien; **to ~ for the best** salir perfectamente **4.** (*do exercise*) entrenarse

◆**work over** *vt inf* dar una paliza a

◆**work up** *vt* **1.** (*generate: courage, energy, enthusiasm*) estimular **2.** (*arouse strong feelings*) excitar; **to work oneself up** emocionarse; **to ~ into a frenzy** emocionar hasta el frenesí; **to work sb up into a rage** sacar a alguien de quicio **3.** (*develop*) desarrollar; (*idea, plan, sketch*) llevar a cabo; (*business*) fomentar; **to work one's way up through the firm** ir ascendiendo en la empresa

workable ['wɜːkəbl, *Am:* 'wɜːr-] *adj* **1.** (*feasible*) factible; (*compromise, plan*) viable **2.** (*able to be manipulated*) que se puede trabajar; AGR (*ground, land*) explotable

workaday ['wɜːkədeɪ, *Am:* 'wɜːr-] *adj* de todos los días

workbag ['wɜːkbæg, *Am:* 'wɜːrk-] *n* bolsa *f* de herramientas **workbench** <-es> *n* mesa *f* de trabajo **workbook** *n* cuaderno *m* de ejercicios **work camp** *n* campo *m* de trabajo **workday** *n Am s.* **working day**

worker ['wɜːkəʳ, *Am:* 'wɜːrkɚ] *n* trabajador(a) *m(f)*; (*in factory*) obrero, -a *m, f*

work ethic *n* ética *f* del trabajo **workforce** *n + sing/pl vb* población *f* activa **workhorse** *n* bestia *f* de carga **work-in** *n* ECON ocupación *f* laboral

working **I.** *adj* **1.** (*employed*) empleado, -a; (*population*) activo, -a **2.** (*pertaining to work*) de trabajo; (*control*) efectivo, -a; (*day, hour, week*) laboral **3.** (*functioning*) que funciona; (*moving: model*) móvil; (*part of a machine*) operativo, -a **4.** (*used as basis: theory, hypothesis*) de base; **to have a ~ knowledge of sth** tener conocimientos básicos de algo **II.** *n no pl* **1.** (*activity*) actividad *f* **2.** (*employment*) trabajo *m*

working class [ˌwɜːkɪŋ'klɑːs, *Am:* 'wɜːrkɪŋˌklæs] <-es> *n* **the ~** la clase obrera **working-class** *adj* obrero, -a; (*background*) humilde **working day** *n Brit* (*weekday*) día *m* laborable; (*time*) jornada *f* laboral

working-out ['wɜːkɪŋˌaʊt, *Am:* 'wɜːrk-] *n* solución *f*

working-over ['wɜːkɪŋˌəʊvəʳ, *Am:* 'wɜːrkɪŋˌoʊvɚ] *n inf* paliza *f*; **to get a good ~** recibir una buena paliza

workload ['wɜːkləʊd, *Am:* 'wɜːrkloʊd] *n* (volumen *m* de) trabajo *m*; **to have a heavy/light/unbearable ~** tener mucho/poco/demasiado trabajo

workman ['wɜːkmən, *Am:* 'wɜːrk-] <-men> *n* obrero *m*

workmanlike ['wɜːkmənlaɪk, *Am:* 'wɜːrk-] *adj* **1.** (*showing skill: performance, job*) profesional **2.** (*technically sufficient: performance*) correcto, -a

workmanship ['wɜːkmənʃɪp, *Am:* 'wɜːrk-] *n no pl* **1.** (*skill in working*) destreza *f* **2.** (*work executed*) trabajo *m* **3.** (*quality of work*) confección *f*; **shoddy ~** mala calidad; **of fine ~** de excelente factura

work of art *n* obra *f* de arte

workout ['wɜːkaʊt, *Am:* 'wɜːrk-] *n* SPORTS entrenamiento *m*

work permit *n* permiso *m* de trabajo **workplace** *n* COM lugar *m* de trabajo; **safety in the ~** seguridad *f* en el trabajo

works committee *n*, **works council** *n* comité *m* de empresa

work-sharing ['wɜːkˌʃeərɪŋ, *Am:* 'wɜːrkˌʃerɪŋ] *n sistema en el cual dos personas comparten un puesto de trabajo*

worksheet ['wɜːkʃiːt, *Am:* 'wɜːrk-] *n* hoja *f* de trabajo

workshop ['wɜːkʃɒp, *Am:* 'wɜːrkʃɑːp] *n* **1.** (*repair place*) taller *m* **2.** (*meeting for learning*) seminario *m*; **drama ~** taller de arte dramático

work-shy ['wɜːkʃaɪ, *Am:* 'wɜːrk-] *adj Brit* perezoso, -a

works manager *n* gerente *mf* de fábrica **works outing** *n* excursión *f* del personal

workspace ['wɜːkspeɪs, *Am:* 'wɜːrk-] *n* INFOR área *f* de trabajo **work station** *n* INFOR estación *f* de trabajo

work-study program *n* SCHOOL, UNIV, COM programa *m* de estudio del trabajo

worktable ['wɜːkˌteɪbl, *Am:* 'wɜːrk-] *n* mesa *f* de trabajo **worktop** *n Brit* (*surface in kitchen*) encimera *f*

work-to-rule [ˌwɜːktə'ruːl, *Am:* ˌwɜːrk-] *n* huelga *f* de celo

workweek ['wɜːkwiːk, *Am:* 'wɜːrk-] *n Am* semana *f* laborable

world [wɜːld, *Am:* wɜːrld] *n* **1.** *no pl* GEO mundo *m*; **the ~'s population** la población mundial; **a ~ authority** una autoridad mundial; **the ~ champion** el campeón del mundo; **the best/worst in the ~** el mejor/peor del mundo; **the tallest man in the ~** el hombre más alto del mundo; **the (whole) ~ over** en el mundo entero; **to see the ~** ver mundo; **to travel all over the ~** viajar por todo el mundo **2.** (*defined group*) **the ~ of dogs/horses** el mundo de los perros/caballos; **the animal ~** el mundo animal; **the Christian/Muslim ~** el mundo cristiano/musulmán; **the New/Old/Third ~** el Nuevo/Viejo/Tercer Mundo ►**to be a ~ of difference between ...** existir una enorme diferencia entre...; **to have the ~ at one's feet** tener el mundo a sus pies; **all the ~ and her husband/his wife** *Brit, inf* ciento y la madre; **the ~ at large** el mundo en general; **the ~ is his/her oyster** tiene el mundo a sus pies; **to feel on top of the ~** estar en el séptimo cielo; **that's the way of the ~** ¡así es la vida!; **to be for all the ~ like …** ser exactamente como…; **to be ~s apart** ser como la noche y el día; **to have the best of both ~s** nadar y guardar la ropa; **to be dead to the ~** dormir como un tronco; **to be out of this ~** *inf* ser fantástico; **it's a small ~!** ¡el mundo es un pañuelo!; **I wouldn't do such a thing for (all) the ~** no haría algo así por nada del mundo; **to go up in the ~** *Brit, inf* prosperar; **the ~ to come** REL el más allá; **to come down in the ~** *Brit, inf* venir a menos; **to live in a ~ of one's own** vivir en su mundo; **to mean (all) the ~ to sb** serlo todo para alguien; **to think the ~ of sb/sth** tener un alto concepto de alguien/algo; **what/who/how in the ~ …?** ¿qué/quién/cómo demonios…?

World Bank *n* **the ~** el Banco Mundial **world beater** *n* SPORTS campeón, -ona *m, f* mundial **world-class** *adj* de clase mundial **world congress** *n* congreso *m* mundial **World Cup** *n* SPORTS **the ~** la Copa del Mundo; **the ~ Finals** la final de la Copa del Mundo **World Fair** *n* feria *f* mundial

world-famous [ˌwɜːld'feɪməs, *Am:* 'wɜːrld-ˌfeɪ-] *adj* de fama mundial

world language *n* lengua *f* universal

worldly ['wɜːldli, *Am:* 'wɜːrld-] *adj* **1.** (*of physical, practical matters*) material; **~ goods** posesiones materiales **2.** (*having experience*) mundano, -a; (*manner*) sofisticado, -a; **(~) wise** (*person*) con mucho mundo

world opinion *n* opinión *f* mundial **world population** *n* **the ~** la población mundial **world power** *n* potencia *f* mundial **world record** *n* SPORTS récord *m* mundial

world-shaking *adj*, **world-shattering** *adj* **a ~ piece of news** una noticia que ha conmocionado al mundo **world view** *n* visión *f* del mundo **world war** *n* HIST guerra *f* mundial

world-weary [ˌwɜːld'wɪəri, *Am:* 'wɜːrldˌwɪ-ri] *adj* hastiado, -a; **to be [*o* feel] ~** estar cansado de la vida

world-wide [ˌwɜːld'waɪd, *Am:* 'wɜːrld-ˌwaɪd] **I.** *adj* mundial **II.** *adv* por todo el mundo

World Wide Web *n* INFOR Red *f* Mundial

worm [wɜːm, *Am:* wɜːrm] **I.** *n* gusano *m*; (*insect larva*) oruga *f*; **earth ~** lombriz *f* ►**the ~ turns** la paciencia tiene un límite **II.** *vt* **1.** (*treat for worms*) desparasitar **2.** (*squeeze slowly through*) **to ~ one's way through people** colarse entre la gente; **to ~ oneself under sth** deslizarse por debajo de algo **3.** (*gain trust dishonestly*) **to ~ oneself into someone's trust** ganarse la confianza de alguien con artimañas **4.** (*obtain dishonestly*) **to ~ a secret out of sb** sonsacar un secreto a alguien **III.** *vi* **to ~ through the crowd** colarse entre el gentío

worm-eaten ['wɜːmˌiːtən, *Am:* 'wɜːrm-] *adj* (*beam, table, wood*) carcomido, -a; (*fruit*) picado, -a por los gusanos; (*cloth*) apolillado, -a

worm-hole ['wɜːmhəʊl, *Am:* 'wɜːrmhoʊl] *n* agujero *m* de lombriz; **the cupboard was full of ~s** el armario estaba todo carcomido

wormy ['wɜːmi, *Am:* 'wɜːr-] <-ier, -iest> *adj* (*full of worms: fruit*) agusanado, -a; (*wood*) carcomido, -a

worn [wɔːn, *Am:* wɔːrn] **I.** *vt, vi pp of* **wear** **II.** *adj* **1.** (*shabby, deteriorated*) desgastado, -a; (*clothing*) raído, -a **2.** (*exhausted: person*) ojeroso, -a **3.** (*overused: expression, news, story*) tópico, -a

worn-out [ˌwɔːn'aʊt, *Am:* ˌwɔːrn-] *adj* **1.** (*exhausted: person, animal*) rendido, -a **2.** (*used up: clothing*) raído, -a; (*wheel bearings*) desgastado, -a

worried *adj* preocupado, -a; **to be ~ about [*o* by] sth** estar preocupado por algo; **I am ~ that he may be angry** tengo miedo de que esté enfadado; **to be ~ sick about [*o* by] sb/sth** estar preocupadísimo por alguien/algo; **with a ~ expression** con semblante preocupado

worrisome ['wʌrɪsəm, *Am:* 'wɜːri-] *adj form* preocupante

worry ['wʌri, *Am:* 'wɜːr-] **I.** <-ies> *n* **1.** (*anxiety, concern*) preocupación *f*; **to be a cause of ~ to sb** dar problemas a alguien; **to have a ~ (about sth)** estar preocupado (por algo); **do you really have no ~s about the future?** ¿no te preocupa el futuro de verdad? **2.** (*trouble*) problema *m*; **financial worries** problemas *fpl* económicos; **it is a great ~ to me** me preocupa mucho **II.** *vt* <-ie-, -ing> **1.** (*preoccupy, concern*) preocupar; **she is worried that she might not be able to find another job** tiene miedo de no encontrar otro trabajo; **that doesn't ~ me** eso me tiene sin cuidado **2.** (*bother*) molestar **3.** (*pursue and scare*) perseguir; **to ~ an animal** correr tras un animal **4.** (*shake around*) **to ~ sth** juguetear con algo; **the dog worries the bone** el perro mordisquea el hueso **III.** <-ie-, -ing> *vi* (*be preoccupied, concerned*) **to ~ (about sth)** preocuparse (por algo); **don't ~!** ¡no te preocupes!; **not to ~!** *inf* ¡no pasa nada!

worrying *adj* preocupante

worse [wɜːs, *Am:* wɜːrs] **I.** *adj comp of* **bad** peor; **to be ~ than …** ser peor que…; **to be even/much ~** ser aún/mucho peor; **he was none the ~ for it** no le había pasado nada; **from bad to ~** de mal en peor; **to get ~ and ~** ser cada vez peor; **it could have been ~** podría haber sido peor; **to make matters ~ …** por si fuera poco…; **so much the ~ for her!** ¡tanto peor para ella!; **~ luck** *inf* (por) mala suerte; **to get ~** empeorar; **if he gets any ~ …** si se pone peor… **II.** *n no pl* **the ~** el/la peor; **to change for the ~** cambiar para mal; **to have seen ~** haber visto cosas peores; **I don't think any the ~ of her** mi opinión sobre ella no ha cambiado; **~ was to follow** todavía faltaba lo peor **III.** *adv comp of* **badly** peor; **to do sth ~ than …** hacer algo peor que…; **he did**

~ **than he was expecting in the exams** los exámenes le fueron peor de lo que esperaba; **to be** ~ (**off**) estar peor

worsen ['wɜːsən, *Am:* 'wɜːr-] *vi, vt* empeorar

worship ['wɜːʃɪp, *Am:* 'wɜːr-] **I.** *vt* <-pp-, *Am:* -p-> **1.** *a.* REL adorar; **to** ~ **God** rendir culto a Dios; **to** ~ **money/sex** tener obsesión por el dinero/sexo **2.** (*feel great admiration for*) idolatrar ►**to** ~ **the ground sb walks on** besar el suelo que alguien pisa **II.** *vi* <-pp-, *Am:* -p-> REL hacer sus devociones **III.** *n no pl* **1.** (*adoration*) adoración *f;* (*reverence*) veneración *f* **2.** *a.* REL culto *m;* (*religious service*) oficio *m* **3.** POL, LAW **his Worship the Mayor ...** el Excelentísimo Señor alcalde ...; **Your Worship** Su Señoría

worshipper *n* REL adorador(a) *m(f);* **hundreds of ~s attended the ceremony** cientos de fieles asistieron a la ceremonia; **devil** ~ satanista *mf*

worst [wɜːst, *Am:* wɜːrst] **I.** *adj superl of* **bad the** ~ el/la peor; **the** ~ **soup I've ever eaten** la peor sopa que he comido (nunca); **the** ~ **mistake** el error más grave **II.** *adv superl of* **badly** peor; **to be** ~ **hit/affected by sth** ser los más azotados/afectados por algo **III.** *n no pl* (*most terrible one, time, thing*) **the** ~ lo peor; **the** ~ **of it is that ...** lo peor de todo es que ...; **the** ~ **is over now** ya ha pasado lo peor; **at** ~ en el peor de los casos; **at her** ~ en su peor momento; **this problem has shown him at his** ~ este problema ha sacado a relucir lo peor de él; **to fear the** ~ temerse lo peor; ~ **of all** lo peor de todo ►**if** (**the**) ~ **comes to** (**the**) ~ en el peor de los casos; **to get the** ~ **of it** (*suffer the worst*) llevarse la peor parte

worsted ['wʊstɪd] *n no pl* (*fabric*) estambre *m*

worth [wɜːθ, *Am:* wɜːrθ] **I.** *n no pl* **1.** (*excellence, importance: of a person*) valía *f;* (*of a thing*) valor *m;* **to prove one's** ~ demostrar su valía; **to be of great/little** ~ **to sb** tener gran/poco valor para alguien **2.** (*monetary value*) **a pound's** ~ **of apples** una libra de manzanas; **4 million pounds** ~ **of gift items** objetos de regalo por valor de 4 millones de libras; **to get one's money's** ~ **from sth** sacar partido a algo; **of comparable** ~ de precio similar; **a month's/three hour's** ~ **of work** un mes/tres horas de trabajo **3.** (*wealth*) fortuna *f* **II.** *adj* **1.** *a.* COM, FIN, ECON **to be** ~ **...** valer...; **it is** ~ **about £200 000** está valorado en unas 200 000 libras; **it's** ~ **a lot to me** tiene mucho valor para mí; **to be** ~ **millions** *inf* ser millonario **2.** (*significant enough, useful*) **to be** ~ **...** merecer...; **to be** ~ **a mention** ser digno de mención; **it's not** ~ **arguing about!** ¡no vale la pena discutir por eso!; **it is** ~ **seeing** es digno de ver; **it's** ~ **remembering that ...** conviene recordar que...; **it is** (**well**) ~ **a listen/visit** merece la pena escucharlo/visitarlo; **it's** ~ **a try** vale la pena intentarlo ►**to be** ~ **sb's while it isn't** ~ **my while** no me compensa; **to make sth** ~ **sb's while** compensar a alguien por algo; **if a thing is** ~ **doing, it's** ~ **doing well** *prov* lo que se hace hay que hacerlo bien *prov;* **to do sth for all one's** ~ hacer algo con todas sus fuerzas; **for what it's** ~ *inf* por si sirve de algo; **to be** (**well**) ~ **it** valer la pena

worthless ['wɜːθləs, *Am:* 'wɜːrθ-] *adj* **1.** (*of no monetary value*) sin ningún valor **2.** (*of no significance, use*) inútil

worthwhile [ˌwɜːθ'hwaɪl, *Am:* ˌwɜːrθ-] *adj* **1.** (*profitable, beneficial*) que vale la pena; **it's not** ~ **making such an effort** no merece la pena esforzarse tanto; **it isn't financially** ~ **for me** no me compensa económicamente **2.** (*useful*) útil

worthy ['wɜːði, *Am:* 'wɜːr-] **I.** <-ier, -iest> *adj* **1.** *form* (*admirable*) encomiable; (*principles*) loable; **a** ~ **cause** una noble causa **2.** (*appropriate for, to*) digno, -a; **to be** ~ **of sth** ser merecedor de algo; **to be** ~ **of attention** merecer atención **II.** <-ies> *n iron* (*important person*) personaje *m* ilustre; **the local worthies** las personalidades más destacadas del lugar

would [wʊd] *aux pt of* **will 1.** (*future in the past*) **he said he** ~ **do it later on** dijo que lo haría más tarde **2.** (*future seeing past in the past*) **we thought they** ~ **have done it before** pensamos que lo habrían hecho antes **3.** (*intention in the past*) **he said he** ~ **always love her** dijo que siempre la querría **4.** (*shows possibility*) **I'd go myself, but I'm too busy** iría yo mismo, pero estoy demasiado ocupado; **it** ~ **have been very boring to do that** habría sido muy aburrido hacer eso **5.** (*conditional*) **what** ~ **you do if you lost your job?** ¿qué harías si te quedaras sin trabajo?; **I** ~ **have done it if you'd asked** lo habría hecho si me lo hubieras pedido **6.** (*polite request*) **if you** ~ **just wait a moment, I'll see if I can find her** espere un momento, por favor, que voy a buscarla; ~ **you phone him, please?** ¿me harías el favor de llamarle?; ~ **you mind saying that again?** ¿te importaría repetir eso?; ~ **you like ...?** ¿te gustaría...?; ~ **you like me to come with you?** ¿quieres que vaya contigo? **7.** (*regularity in past*) **they** ~ **help each other with their homework** solían ayudarse con los deberes **8.** (*stresses as being typical*) **the bus** ~ **be late when I'm in a hurry** por supuesto, el autobos siempre llega tarde cuando tengo prisa; **he** ~ **say that, wouldn't he?** era de esperar que lo dijera, ¿no? **9.** (*courteous opinion*) **I** ~ **imagine that ...** me imagino que...; **I ~n't have thought that ...** nunca habría pensado que... **10.** (*probably*) **the guy on the phone had an Australian accent – that** ~ **be Tom, I expect** el chico con quien hablé por teléfono tenía acento australiano – debía de ser Tom **11.** (*shows preference*) **I** ~ **rather have beer** prefiero beber cerveza; **I** ~ **rather die than do**

that antes morir que hacer eso **12.** (*offering polite advice*) **I ~n't worry, if I were you** yo que tú no me preocuparía **13.** (*asking motives*) **why ~ anyone want to do something like that?** ¿por qué nadie querría hacer algo así? **14.** (*shows a wish*) **ah, ~ I were richer and younger!** ¡ojalá fuera más rico y más joven!; **~ that he were here!** ¡ojalá estuviera aquí!

would-be [ˈwʊdbiː] *adj* **1.** (*wishing to be*) aspirante; **a ~ politician** un aspirante a político **2.** (*pretending to be*) supuesto, -a

wouldn't [wʊdənt] = **would not** *s.* **would**

wound[1] [waʊnd] *vi, vt pt, pp of* **wind[2]**

wound[2] [wuːnd] **I.** *n* herida *f;* **a gunshot/war ~** una herida de bala/guerra; **a leg ~** una herida en la pierna **II.** *vt a. fig* herir

wounded I. *adj a. fig* herido, -a **II.** *npl* **the ~** los heridos

wove [wəʊv, *Am:* woʊv] *vt, vi pt of* **weave**

woven [ˈwəʊvən, *Am:* ˈwoʊv-] **I.** *vt, vi pp of* **weave II.** *adj* (*made by weaving*) tejido, -a

wow [waʊ] *inf* **I.** *interj* (*demonstrates surprise, excitement*) ¡caray! **II.** *n* (*hit, popular item*) exitazo *m;* **to be a ~ with the public** ser un exitazo con el público; **I had a ~ of a time** me lo pasé en grande **III.** *vt* (*delight*) **to ~ sb** volver loco a alguien

WPC [dʌbljuːˌpiːˈsiː] *Brit abbr of* **Woman Police Constable** *mujer policía*

wpm *abbr of* **words per minute** ppm

wraith [reɪθ] *n liter* espectro *m*

wrangle [ˈræŋgl] **I.** <-ling> *vi* **1.** (*argue, debate angrily*) discutir; **to ~ (with sb) about sth** discutir (con alguien) por algo **2.** *Am* (*round up cattle*) arrear ganado **II.** *vt Am* (*round up: horses, cattle*) arrear, rodear *CSur, Cuba, Nic, Col, Perú* **III.** *n* (*intricate argument*) riña *f;* **a ~ about sth** una disputa sobre algo

wrap [ræp] **I.** *n* **1.** (*robe-like covering*) bata *f* **2.** (*shawl*) chal *m* **3.** *no pl* (*protective covering material*) envoltorio *m;* **foil ~** papel *m* de aluminio ▸**to keep sth under ~s** mantener algo en secreto; **to take the ~s off sth** sacar algo a la luz **II.** *vt* <-pp-> **to ~ sth (up) (in a blanket)** envolver algo (con una manta); **~ the glasses in plenty of paper** envuelve bien los vasos con papel; **to ~ sth around sth/sb** envolver algo/a alguien con algo; **he ~ped a scarf around his neck** se puso una bufanda; **to ~ one's fingers around sth** agarrar algo con las manos; **to ~ one's arms around sb** estrechar a alguien entre sus brazos; **a matter ~ped in secrecy** un asunto rodeado de misterio ▸**to ~ sb (up) in cotton wool** *Brit* tener a alguien entre algodones

wraparound [ˈræpəˌraʊnd] *adj* (*skirt, dress*) cruzado, -a; (*sunglasses*) envolvente

◆**wrap up I.** *vt* <-pp-> **1.** (*completely cover*) envolver; **to wrap oneself/sb up (against the cold)** (*dress warmly*) abrigarse (para protegerse del frío) **2.** *inf* (*finish well*) poner fin a; (*deal*) cerrar; (*problem*) acabar con; **that wraps it up for today** eso es todo por hoy **II.** *vi* **1.** (*dress warmly*) abrigarse; **to ~ well/warm** abrigarse bien **2.** (*be absorbed in*) **to be wrapped up in sth** estar absorto en algo; **to be wrapped up in one's work** vivir para el trabajo **3.** (*finish*) terminar **4.** *pej, inf* (*shut up*) cerrar el pico

wrapper [ˈræpəʳ, *Am:* -ɚ] *n* **1.** (*packaging*) envoltorio *m;* (*for a book*) sobrecubierta *f* **2.** *Am* (*robe-like covering*) bata *f*

wrapping paper *n* (*plain*) papel *m* de embalar; (*for presents*) papel *m* de regalo

wrath [rɒθ, *Am:* ræθ] *n no pl, liter* (*fury, anger*) ira *f*

wrathful [ˈrɒθfəl, *Am:* ˈræθ-] *adj liter* iracundo, -a

wreak [riːk] <-ed, -ed *o* wrought, wrought> *vt form* **1.** (*forcefully cause*) causar; **to ~ damage/havoc (on sth)** hacer estragos (de algo) **2.** (*anger*) descargar; **to ~ vengeance on sb** vengarse de alguien

wreath [riːθ] <wreaths> *pl n* (*of flowers, greenery*) corona *f;* (*of smoke*) espiral *f*

wreathe [riːð] *vt liter* **1.** (*gather around*) **to be ~d in sth** estar rodeado de algo; **~d in clouds** envuelto en nubes; **to be ~d in melancholy** estar sumido en la melancolía; **to be ~d in smiles** no dejar de sonreír **2.** (*crown as with a wreath*) coronar **3.** (*intertwine*) entretejer

wreck [rek] **I.** *vt* **1.** (*damage*) destrozar; (*ship*) hundir; (*train*) hacer descarrilar **2.** (*demolish*) derribar **3.** (*hopes, plan*) arruinar; (*chances*) echar por tierra; **to ~ sb's life** destrozar la vida de alguien **II.** *n* **1.** NAUT naufragio *m;* AUTO accidente *m; fig* hundimiento *m;* **the ~ of one's hopes** el fin de las esperanzas **2.** (*ship*) barco *m* hundido; **a ~ of a car/a plane** un coche/un avión siniestrado; **an old ~** un cacharro **3.** *inf* (*any derelict thing*) ruina *f;* (*mess*) caos *m;* **to feel a complete ~** estar hecho polvo; **to be a nervous ~** tener los nervios destrozados

wreckage [ˈrekɪdʒ] *n no pl* (*of ship, car, plane*) restos *mpl;* (*of building*) escombros *mpl*

wrecker [ˈrekəʳ, *Am:* -ɚ] *n* **1.** *Am* (*breakdown truck*) camión-grúa *m* **2.** (*person who causes shipwrecks*) provocador(a) *m(f)* de naufragios **3.** (*worker who demolishes houses*) obrero, -a *m, f* de demolición **4.** (*hooligan*) gamberro, -a *m, f*

wren [ren] *n* chochín *m*

Wren [ren] *n Brit, inf: mujer que pertenece a la marina británica*

wrench [rentʃ] **I.** *vt* **1.** (*jerk and twist out*) arrancar; **to ~ sth from sb** arrancar algo a alguien; **to ~ oneself away** soltarse de un tirón **2.** (*injure*) **to ~ one's ankle** torcerse el tobillo; **to ~ one's shoulder** dislocarse el hombro **3.** *fig* (*forcefully take from*) separar; **to ~ sb from sb** separar a alguien de alguien **II.** *n* **1.** (*twisting jerk*) tirón *m,* jalón *m CSur;* **to**

give sb a ~ dar un tirón a alguien **2.** (*injury*) torcedura *f;* **to give one's ankle a ~** torcerse el tobillo **3.** (*pain caused by a departure*) dolor *m* (*causado por una separación*)*;* **what a ~, seeing you board the plane!** ¡qué doloroso verte subir al avión! **4.** *Am* TECH (*spanner*) llave *f* inglesa

wrestle ['resl] SPORTS **I.** <-ling> *vt* **1.** *a.* SPORTS luchar; **to ~ sb** forcejear con alguien; **to ~ sb to the ground** luchar con [*o* contra] alguien hasta derribarlo **2.** *fig* lidiar con **II.** <-ling> *vi* luchar; **to ~ professionally** dedicarse profesionalmente a la lucha **III.** *n* lucha *f*

wrestler *n* luchador(a) *m(f)*

wrestling *n no pl* SPORTS lucha *f;* **freestyle ~** lucha libre

wrestling bout *n,* **wrestling match** *n* SPORTS combate *m* de lucha

wretch [retʃ] <-es> *n* **1.** (*unfortunate person*) infeliz *mf;* **a poor ~** un pobre diablo **2.** (*mean person*) miserable *mf;* (*mischievous person*) sinvergüenza *mf inf*

wretched ['retʃɪd] *adj* **1.** (*miserable, pitiable: life, person*) desdichado, -a; **to be in a ~ state** estar en un estado lamentable; (*house, conditions*) miserable **2.** (*despicable*) despreciable **3.** (*expressing annoyance*) **my ~ car's broken down again!** ¡este maldito coche se me ha vuelto a estropear! **4.** (*very bad, awful: weather*) horrible; **to feel ~** (*sick*) estar muy mal; (*depressed*) estar muy abatido

wriggle ['rɪgl] **I.** <-ling> *vi* **1.** (*squirm around*) retorcerse **2.** (*move forward by twisting*) serpentear; **to ~ through sth** deslizarse por algo; **to ~ out of sth** *fig, inf* escapar de un apuro **II.** <-ling> *vt* (*jiggle back and forth*) menear; (*body, hand, toes*) mover; **to ~ one's way along** avanzar serpenteando; **to ~ oneself into sth** introducirse con dificultad en algo; **to ~** (**one's way**) **out of sth** escaquearse de algo **III.** *n* meneo *m;* **with a ~, she managed to crawl through the gap** logró deslizarse por el agujero serpenteando

wring [rɪŋ] <wrung, wrung> *vt* **1.** (*twist forcibly*) retorcer; **to ~ one's hands** retorcerse las manos; **to ~ sb's neck** *inf* retorcer el cuello a alguien **2.** (*twist to squeeze out*) escurrir; **to ~ water out of sth** escurrir el agua de algo **3.** (*extract forcibly*) **to ~ the truth out of sb** sacar la verdad a alguien **4.** (*cause pain to*) **to ~ sb's heart** partirle el corazón a alguien

wringer ['rɪŋəʳ, *Am:* -ɚ] *n* rodillo *m* para escurrir la ropa ►**to <u>put</u> sb through the ~** *inf* someter a alguien al tercer grado

wrinkle ['rɪŋkl] **I.** *n* (*fold, crease*) arruga *f* ►**to <u>iron</u> the ~s out** limar asperezas **II.** <-ling> *vi* (*form folds, creases*) arrugarse; (*apple, fruit*) pasarse **III.** <-ling> *vt* (*make have folds, creases*) arrugar ►**to ~ one's <u>brow</u>** fruncir el ceño

wrinkled *adj,* **wrinkly** ['rɪŋkli] *adj* (*clothes, face, skin*) arrugado, -a; (*apple, fruit*) pasado, -a

wrist [rɪst] *n* **1.** ANAT muñeca *f;* **to slash one's ~s** cortarse las venas **2.** (*of a garment*) puño *m*

wrist-band ['rɪstbænd] *n* **1.** (*end of sleeve*) puño *m* **2.** (*strap*) correa *f* **3.** (*sweatband*) muñequera *f*

wristlet *n* muñequera *f*

wrist-watch <-es> *n* reloj *m* de pulsera

writ [rɪt] *n* orden *f* judicial; **~ of summons** notificación *f* de emplazamiento; **to issue a ~ against sb** expedir un mandato judicial contra alguien; **to serve a ~ on sb** notificar un mandato judicial a alguien

write [raɪt] <wrote, written, writing> **I.** *vt* **1.** escribir; **to ~ sth in capital letters** escribir algo con mayúsculas; **to ~ a book/a thesis** escribir un libro/una tesis; **he wrote me a poem** me dedicó un poema; **to ~ sb a cheque** extender un cheque a alguien **2.** MUS componer; **to ~ a song** escribir una canción **3.** INFOR (*save*) guardar; **to ~ sth to a disk** grabar algo en un disco ►**to be nothing to ~ <u>home</u> about** no ser nada del otro mundo *inf* **II.** *vi* **1.** escribir; **to ~ clearly/legibly** escribir con letra clara/legible; **to ~ to sb** *Brit,* **to ~ sb** *Am* escribir a alguien; **to ~ about sth** escribir sobre algo; **to ~ for a newspaper** escribir en un periódico **2.** INFOR (*save*) **to ~ to sth** grabar en algo

◆**write away** *vi* **to ~ for sth** (*brochures, information*) escribir pidiendo algo

◆**write back I.** *vt* **to write** (**sb/sth**) **back** contestar (a alguien/algo) **II.** *vi* contestar

◆**write down** *vt* apuntar

◆**write in I.** *vi* (*send a letter to*) escribir **II.** *vt* **1.** (*insert*) escribir; **to write sth in a space** escribir algo en un espacio; **just write your name in – you can fill the rest of the form in later** escriba sólo su nombre – después podrá rellenar el resto del formulario **2.** LAW (*put in: clause*) incluir **3.** TV, CINE (*character*) añadir

◆**write off I.** *vi* (*send away to ask for*) **to ~ for** (*brochures, information*) solicitar por escrito **II.** *vt* **1.** (*give up doing: attempt*) abandonar; (*project*) dar por perdido **2.** (*abandon as no good*) **to write sth/sb off as useless** descartar algo/a alguien como inútil **3.** FIN (*debt*) cancelar **4.** *Brit* AUTO (*destroy beyond repair*) destrozar; (*consider beyond repair*) declarar siniestro total

◆**write out** *vt* **1.** (*put into writing*) escribir **2.** (*copy*) copiar **3.** (*fill in*) rellenar; **to write a cheque out to sb** extender un cheque a alguien **4.** (*remove from*) suprimir; **to write sb out of a will** desheredar a alguien

◆**write up** *vt* poner por escrito; (*article, report, thesis*) redactar; **to ~ a concert** escribir una crítica sobre un concierto

write-in ['raɪtɪn] *adj Am* POL **a ~ candidate** *un candidato cuyo nombre debe añadir el votante en la papeleta*

write-off ['raɪtɒf] *n* **1.** *Brit* **to be a complete ~** (*car*) ser declarado siniestro total; (*project,* *marriage*) ser un fracaso **2.** FIN cancelación *f* de una deuda

write-protected ['raɪtprə'tektəd] *adj* INFOR protegido, -a contra escritura

writer ['raɪtəʳ, *Am:* -t̬ɚ] *n* **1.** (*person*) escritor(a) *m(f);* ~ **of children's books** autor(a) *m(f)* de libros infantiles **2.** INFOR **CD-ROM/DVD** ~ grabador *m* de CD-ROM/DVD

write-up ['raɪtʌp] *n* ART, THEAT, MUS crítica *f*

writhe [raɪð] <writhing> *vi* **1.** (*squirm and twist around*) retorcerse; **to** ~ (**around**) **in pain** retorcerse de dolor **2.** (*be uncomfortable: with horror*) estremecerse; (*with embarrassment*) sentirse violento; **to make sb** ~ hacer pasar a alguien por una situación incómoda

writing ['raɪtɪŋ, *Am:* -t̬ɪŋ] *n no pl* **1.** (*handwriting*) letra *f;* **in** ~ por escrito; **to put sth in** ~ poner algo por escrito; **there was some** ~ **in the margin of the page** había algo escrito en el margen de la página **2.** *a.* LIT el escribir; **she likes** ~ le encanta escribir **3.** LIT, THEAT (*process*) redacción *f;* **creative** ~ escritura *f* creativa **4.** LIT, THEAT (*written work*) obra *f;* **women's** ~ literatura *f* escrita por mujeres **5.** LIT (*style*) estilo *m* ▶**the** ~ **is on the wall** (**for the campaign**) (la campaña) tiene los días contados

writing desk *n* escritorio *m* **writing-pad** *n* bloc *m* **writing-paper** *n* papel *m* de carta

written I. *vt, vi pp of* **write** II. *adj* (*recorded in writing*) escrito, -a ▶**to have guilt** ~ **all over one's face** llevar la culpa escrita en la cara; **the** ~ **word** la palabra escrita

wrong [rɒŋ, *Am:* rɑːŋ] **I.** *adj* **1.** (*not right: answer*) incorrecto, -a; **to be** ~ **about sth** equivocarse en algo; **to be** ~ **about sb** juzgar mal a alguien; **he is** ~ **in thinking that ...** se equivoca si piensa que...; **to be in the** ~ **place** estar mal colocado; **to be plainly** ~ estar completamente equivocado; **to get the** ~ **number** equivocarse de número; **sorry,** ~ **number!** lo siento, se ha equivocado (de número); **to go the** ~ **direction** tomar el camino equivocado; **to prove sb** ~ demostrar que alguien se equivoca **2.** (*not appropriate*) inoportuno, -a; **to do/say the** ~ **thing** hacer/decir lo que no se debe; **she's the** ~ **person for the job** no es la persona adecuada para el trabajo; **this is the** ~ **time to ...** no es el momento oportuno para...; **the** ~ **side of town** una mala zona de la ciudad; **she got in with the** ~ **crowd** se juntó con quien no le convenía **3.** (*bad*) **is there anything** ~**?** ¿te pasa algo?; **what's** ~ **with you today?** ¿qué te pasa hoy?; **there's nothing** ~ **with your stomach** su estómago está perfectamente; **something's** ~ **with the television** el televisor no funciona bien **4.** LAW, REL mal; **it is** ~ **to do that** está mal hacer eso; **it was** ~ **of him** (**to do that**) ha hecho muy mal (en hacer eso); **what's** ~ **with that?** ¿qué hay de malo en ello? ▶**to fall into the** ~ **hands** caer en manos equivocadas; **the** ~ **side** el revés; **to go down the** ~ **way** (*food, drink*) bajar por mal sitio **II.** *adv* **1.** (*incorrectly*) incorrectamente; **to do sth** ~ hacer algo mal; **to get sth** ~ equivocarse en algo; **to get it** ~ comprender mal; **you got it** ~ **– it's Maria who's coming, not Marina** no lo has entendido – es María quien viene, no Marina; **don't get me** ~ no me malinterpretes; **to go** ~ equivocarse; (*stop working*) estropearse, descomponerse *Méx;* (*fail*) salir mal; **after 500 m turn to the left, you can't go** ~ siga recto 500 m y gire a la izquierda, no tiene pérdida **2.** (*in a morally reprehensible way*) mal; **to do sth** ~ hacer algo mal **III.** *n* **1.** *no pl a.* LAW, REL mal *m;* (**to know**) **right from** ~ saber distinguir entre lo que está bien y lo que está mal; **to put sb in the** ~ echar la culpa a alguien; **to do sb no** ~ no hacer nada malo a alguien **2.** (*unjust action*) injusticia *f;* **to do sb** (**a**) ~ (**in doing sth**) portarse mal con alguien (al hacer algo); **to right a** ~ enderezar un entuerto; **to suffer a** ~ sufrir una injusticia ▶**to do** ~ obrar mal; **he can do no** ~ es incapaz de hacer nada malo; **to be in the** ~ (*not right, mistaken*) estar equivocado; (*do something bad*) actuar mal **IV.** *vt form* **to** ~ **sb** (*treat unjustly*) ser injusto con alguien; (*judge unjustly*) juzgar mal a alguien

wrongdoer ['rɒŋˌduːəʳ, *Am:* 'rɑːŋˌduːɚ] *n* malhechor(a) *m(f)* **wrongdoing** *n no pl* maldad *f;* LAW delito *m;* **to accuse sb of** ~ acusar a alguien de comportamiento ilícito

wrongful *adj* **1.** (*unfair*) injusto, -a **2.** LAW (*unlawful: arrest*) ilegal; (*dismissal*) improcedente

wrong-headed *adj pej* (*person*) cerril; (*concept, idea, plan*) desatinado, -a

wrongly *adv* mal; (*spell*) incorrectamente; (*believe, state*) erróneamente; (*accuse, convict*) injustamente

wrote [rəʊt, *Am:* roʊt] *vi, vt pt of* **write**

wrought [rɔːt, *Am:* rɑːt] **I.** *vt pt, pp of* **work III.4., 5., wreak II.** *adj form* (*crafted*) trabajado, -a; (*metal*) labrado, -a

wrought iron *n no pl* hierro *m* forjado

wrought-up [rɔːt'ʌp] *adj* nervioso, -a; **to be/get** ~ (**about sth/sb**) estar/ponerse nervioso (por algo/alguien)

wrung [rʌŋ] *vt pt, pp of* **wring**

wry [raɪ] <wrier, wriest *o* wryer, wryest> *adj* **1.** (*dry and ironic: comments, humour*) cáustico, -a; **a** ~ **smile** una sonrisa irónica **2.** (*showing dislike*) **to make a** ~ **face** torcer el gesto

WSW *abbr of* **west-southwest** OSO

wt *n abbr of* **weight** peso *m*

WW *n abbr of* **World War** Guerra *f* Mundial

WWF *n abbr of* **World Wildlife Fund** Fundación *f* Mundial para la Naturaleza

WWW *n abbr of* **World Wide Web** INFOR WWW *f*

X

X, **x** [eks] I. *n* 1. X, x *f;* ~ **for Xmas** *Brit,* ~ **for X** *Am* X de xilófono 2. MAT (*unknown number*) x *f* 3. (*used in place of name*) **Mr/Mrs/Ms** ~ el Sr./la Sra. X 4. (*symbol for kiss*) un beso; **all my love, Katy** ~~~ besos, Katy 5. (*cross symbol*) cruz *f;* ~ **marks the spot** el punto está marcado con una cruz II. *vt Am* (*delete*) **to** ~ (**out**) **sth** tachar algo

X-certificate ['ekssə,tɪfɪkət, *Am:* ,ekssɚ-'tɪf-] *adj* **an** ~ **film** una película X

X-chromosome ['eks,krəʊməsəʊm] *n* cromosoma *m* X

xenophobia [,zenəʊ'fəʊbiə, *Am:* -ə'foʊ-] *n no pl* xenofobia *f*

xenophobic [,zenəʊ'fəʊbɪk, *Am:* -ə'foʊ-] *adj* xenófobo, -a

Xerox®, **xerox** ['zɪərɒks, *Am:* 'zɪrɑːks] I. *n* (*photocopy*) fotocopia *f* II. *vt* (*photocopy*) fotocopiar; **a ~ed copy of the document** una fotocopia del documento

XL *adj abbr of* **extra large** XL

Xmas ['krɪstməs, 'eksməs, *Am:* 'krɪs-] *n abbr of* **Christmas** Navidad *f*

X-rated ['eks,reɪtɪd, *Am:* -t̬ɪd] *adj Am s.* **X-certificate**

X-ray ['eksreɪ] I. *n* 1. (*photo*) radiografía *f;* **~s** rayos *mpl* X 2. *no pl* (*hospital department*) radiología *f* II. *vt* radiografiar; **to** ~ **sth/sb** hacer una radiografía de algo/a alguien

xylophone ['zaɪləfəʊn, *Am:* -foʊn] *n* MUS xilófono *m*

Y

Y, **y** [waɪ] *n* 1. Y, y *f;* ~ **for Yellow** *Brit,* ~ **for Yoke** *Am* Y de yema 2. MAT (*unknown quantity*) y *f*

y. *abbr of* **year** a.

yacht [jɒt, *Am:* jɑːt] I. *n* 1. (*for pleasure*) yate *m* 2. (*for racing*) velero *m;* ~ **club** club *m* náutico; ~ **race** regata *f* II. *vi* 1. (*sail in a yacht*) navegar 2. (*race in a yacht*) participar en una regata

yachting *n no pl* 1. (*sailing in yachts*) navegación *f* de recreo 2. (*racing in yachts*) navegación *f* a vela; **to go** ~ navegar

yachtsman ['jɒtsmən, *Am:* 'jɑːts-] <-men> *n* (*yacht owner*) dueño *m* de un yate; (*yacht sailor*) regatista *m*

yack [jæk] *vi inf* cotorrear

yak [jæk] I. *n* yak *m* II. *vi* cotorrear

yam [jæm] *n* 1. (*plant, vegetable*) ñame *m* 2. *Am* (*sweet potato*) batata *f,* camote *m AmL*

yank [jæŋk] I. *vt inf* **to** ~ **sth** tirar de algo, jalar de algo *AmL* II. *vi inf* **to** ~ (**on sth**) tirar (de algo), jalar (de algo); **she ~ed at his hair** le tiró del pelo III. *n inf* tirón *m,* jalón *m AmL;* **to give sth a** ~ dar un tirón [*o* jalón *AmL*] a algo

◆**yank out** *vt* (*remove forcefully*) sacar de un tirón; **to** ~ **a tooth** arrancar un diente

Yank [jæŋk] *n,* **Yankee** ['jæŋki] *n pej, inf* yanqui *mf,* gringo, -a *m, f AmL*

yap [jæp] I. <-pp-> *vi* 1. (*bark*) ladrar 2. *inf* (*talk continuously*) cotorrear II. *n* 1. (*bark*) ladrido *m* 2. *pej, inf* (*foolish talk*) cotorreo *m*

yard[1] [jɑːd, *Am:* jɑːrd] *n* 1. (*3 feet*) yarda *f* (*0,91 m*)*;* **square** ~ yarda cuadrada; **it's about a hundred ~s down the road** está a unas cien yardas de aquí; **~s long** *fig* muy largo 2. NAUT verga *f*

yard[2] [jɑːd, *Am:* jɑːrd] *n* 1. (*enclosed paved area: of a house, school, prison*) patio *m* 2. *Am* (*garden*) jardín *m* 3. (*work area*) taller *m;* **shipbuilding** ~ astillero *m* 4. (*outside area used for storage*) almacén *m;* **wood** ~ depósito *m* de madera 5. (*enclosure for livestock*) corral *m* 6. **the Yard** Scotland Yard *m*

yardstick ['jɑːdstɪk, *Am:* 'jɑːrd-] *n* 1. (*measuring tool*) vara *f* que mide una yarda 2. (*standard*) criterio *m*

yarn [jɑːn, *Am:* jɑːrn] I. *n* 1. *no pl* (*thread*) hilo *m* 2. (*story*) cuento *m;* **to spin a** ~ inventarse una historia II. *vi* inventar historias

yaw [jɔː, *Am:* jɑː] AVIAT, NAUT, TECH I. *vi* (*move sideways: car*) dar bandazos; (*boat*) guiñar II. *n* (*sideways movement: of a car*) bandazo *m;* (*of a boat*) guiñada *f*

yawl [jɔːl, *Am:* jɑːl] *n* yola *f*

yawn [jɔːn, *Am:* jɑːn] I. *vi* 1. (*show tiredness*) bostezar 2. *fig, liter* (*open wide*) abrirse II. *n* 1. (*sign of tiredness*) bostezo *m* 2. *inf* (*boring thing*) plomo *m fig;* **it was a** ~ fue un rollo

yawning *adj* 1. (*bored: audience*) que bosteza 2. (*wide and deep: chasm, crater*) enorme; **there's a** ~ **gap between … and …** hay un abismo entre… y…

yd *abbr of* **yard**(**s**) yarda *f*

yea [jeɪ] I. *adv* HIST (*yes*) sí II. *n* voto *m* a favor; **the ~s and the nays** los votos a favor y los votos en contra

yeah [jeə] *adv inf* (*yes*) sí; **oh ~!** *iron* (*indicating disbelief*) ¡no me digas!; **~, ~, we've heard that one before** ¡sí, sí, eso ya lo hemos oído otras veces!

year [jɪəʳ, *Am:* jɪr] *n* 1. (*twelve months*) año *m;* ~ **of birth** año de nacimiento; ~ **in,** ~ **out** año tras año; **fiscal** ~ FIN ejercicio *f* fiscal; **leap** ~ año bisiesto; **all** (**the**) ~ **round** (durante) todo el año; **every other** ~ cada dos años; **happy new ~!** ¡feliz año nuevo!; **last/next** ~ el año pasado/que viene; **£5000 a year** 5000 libras al año; **the** ~ **when …** el año en que…; **this** ~ este año; **for his ~s** para su edad; **I'm eight ~s old** tengo ocho años; **~s ago** hace años; **I haven't seen her for ~s** hace muchísimo que no la veo; **it's taken me ~s to …** he tardado años en…; **it's been ~s since we had a summer as good as this one** hacía años que no teníamos tan buen tiempo en verano; **it'll be ~s before...** pasarán años hasta que...; **over the ~s** con el tiempo **2.** SCHOOL, UNIV curso *m;* **the academic** ~ el año académico; **she was in my ~ at college** estaba en mi promoción en la universidad ►**(since) the ~ dot** *Brit, Aus* (desde) el año de la pera; **to put ~s on sb** avejentar a alguien; **to take ~s off sb** quitar años (de encima) a alguien

yearbook ['jɪəbʊk, *Am:* 'jɪr-] *n* anuario *m*

yearling ['jɪəlɪŋ, *Am:* 'jɪr-] **I.** *adj* (*colt*) de un año; (*calf, goat, sheep*) añal **II.** *n* (*colt*) potro *m* de un año; (*year-old calf, goat, sheep*) añal *m*

year-long [ˌjɪə'lɒŋ, *Am:* 'jɪrlɑːŋ] *adj* que dura un año

yearly **I.** *adj* (*happening every year*) anual; **on a ~ basis** cada año **II.** *adv* (*every year*) anualmente; **to take place** ~ tener lugar cada año; **twice** ~ dos veces al año

yearn [jɜːn, *Am:* jɜːrn] *vi* (*long*) **to ~ to do sth** ansiar hacer algo; **to ~ after sth** anhelar algo; **to ~ for sth/sb** añorar algo/a alguien

yearning *n no pl* anhelo *m;* ~ **for sth** anhelo de algo; **to have a ~ to do sth** tener ansias de hacer algo

yeast [jiːst] *n no pl* levadura *f*

yeasty <-ier, -iest> *adj* de levadura

yell [jel] **I.** *n* **1.** (*loud shout*) chillido *m;* **to give a ~** dar un grito; **a ~ of laughter** una carcajada **2.** *Am* (*chant*) *grito para animar a un equipo* **II.** *vi* (*shout loudly*) chillar; **to ~ at sb (to do sth)** gritar a alguien (que haga algo); **to ~ for sb** llamar a alguien a gritos; **to ~ for help** pedir ayuda a gritos **III.** *vt* (*shout loudly*) gritar

yellow ['jeləʊ, *Am:* -oʊ] **I.** *adj* **1.** (*colour*) amarillo; **golden ~** amarillo canario; **to turn** [*o* **go**] ~ ponerse amarillo **2.** *pej, inf* (*cowardly*) cobarde **II.** *n* amarillo *m;* ~ **of an egg** *Am* yema *f* de huevo **III.** *vi, vt* amarillear(se)

yellow-belly ['jeləʊˌbeli, *Am:* -oʊ-] <-ies> *n pej, inf* gallina *mf* **yellow dog** *n Am, pej* canalla *mf* **yellow fever** *n* MED fiebre *f* amarilla

yellowish ['jeləʊɪʃ, *Am:* -oʊ-] *adj* amarillento, -a

yellow jack *n* **1.** *Am* (*yellow fever*) fiebre *f* amarilla **2.** NAUT bandera *f* amarilla

yellowness ['jeləʊnəs, *Am:* -oʊ-] *n* amarillez *f*

Yellow Pages® *npl* **the ~** las páginas amarillas

yellowy *adj* amarillento, -a

yelp [jelp] **I.** *vi* (*cry: a dog*) aullar; (*a person*) gritar; **to ~ with pain** gritar de dolor **II.** *n* (*cry: of animal*) aullido *m;* (*of person*) grito *m*

Yemen ['jemən] *n* Yemen *m*

Yemeni ['jeməni] **I.** *adj* yemení **II.** *n* yemení *mf*

yen¹ [jen] *inv n* FIN yen *m*

yen² [jen] *n inf* (*strong desire*) deseo *m;* **(to have) a ~ for sth/sb** morirse por algo/alguien; **(to have) a ~ to do sth** tener unas ganas locas de hacer algo

yeoman ['jəʊmən, *Am:* 'joʊ-] <-men> *n Brit* HIST **1.** (*freeholder*) pequeño terrateniente *m* **2.** MIL soldado *m* de caballería; **Yeoman of the Guard** alabardero *m* de la Casa Real ►**to do ~('s) service** prestar valiosos servicios

yeomanry ['jəʊmənri, *Am:* 'joʊ-] *n no pl* HIST **1.** (*freeholders collectively*) **the ~** los pequeños terratenientes **2.** MIL (*cavalry*) cuerpo *m* voluntario de caballería

yep [jep] *adv inf* (*yes*) sí

Yerevan [jerəvɑːn] *n* Yerevan *m*

yes [jes] **I.** *adv* **1.** (*affirmative answer*) sí; **~, sir/madam** sí, señor/señora; **~ please** sí, por favor; **to answer ~ to sth** contestar que sí a algo; **I'm not a very good cook – ~ you are** no soy muy buen cocinero – sí que lo eres; **~ indeed** por supuesto que sí; **~, of course!** ¡claro que sí! **2.** (*as question*) **~?** TEL ¿sí?; **Johnny? – yes? – can I have a word?** Johnny – ¿qué? – ¿puedo hablar contigo? **3.** (*indicating doubt*) **oh ~?** ¿de verdad? **II.** <yeses> *n* (*statement in favour*) sí *m* **III.** <-ss-> *vt Am* (*say yes to*) **to ~ sb** decir que sí a alguien

yes-man ['jesmæn] <-men> *n pej* servil *m inf*

yesterday ['jestədeɪ, *Am:* -tɚ-] **I.** *adv* ayer; **~ morning** ayer por la mañana, ayer en la mañana *AmL,* ayer a la mañana *CSur;* **the day before ~** anteayer **II.** *n no pl* **1.** el día de ayer **2.** (*the past*) el pasado

yet [jet] **I.** *adv* **1.** (*up to a particular time*) todavía; **it's too early ~ to ...** aún es muy pronto para...; **not ~** aún no; **she hasn't told him ~** todavía no se lo ha contado; **as ~** hasta ahora; **the issue is as ~ undecided** todavía no se ha decidido la cuestión; **her best/worst film ~** la mejor/peor película que ha dirigido hasta ahora; **have you finished ~?** ¿ya has terminado?; **isn't supper ready ~?** ¿aún no está lista la cena?; **can you see the lighthouse ~?** ¿ya ves el faro?; **the best is ~ to come** aún queda lo mejor; **there's a great deal of work ~ to be done** todavía queda mucho por hacer **2.** (*in addition*) **~ more food** todavía más comida; **~ again** otra vez más **3.** + *comp* (*even*) **~ bigger/more beautiful** aún más grande/bonito **4.** (*despite that*) sin embargo **5.** (*in spite of everything*) a pesar de todo; **you wait, I'll get you ~, you bastard!** ¡ya te atraparé, canalla!; **you'll do it ~** algún día lo conseguirás; **we're not giving up, we'll get there ~** no nos hemos rendido, llegaremos allí a pesar de todo **II.** *conj* con todo, a pesar de todo

yew [juː] *n* (*tree and wood*) tejo *m*

YHA *n abbr of* **Youth Hostel Association** *Asociación de Albergues Juveniles*

Yiddish ['jɪdɪʃ] **I.** *adj* yiddish **II.** *n no pl* yiddish *m*

yield [jiːld] **I.** *n* **1.** (*amount produced*) rendimiento *m;* AGR producción *f* **2.** COM, FIN (*profits*) beneficio *m;* (*interest*) interés *m;* **fixed/variable ~** renta *f* fija/variable **II.** *vt* **1.** (*provide: results*) dar; (*information*) proporcionar **2.** AGR (*produce*) producir **3.** COM, FIN (*profit*) proporcionar; (*interest*) devengar *form;* **to ~ 8 %** dar un (interés del) 8 % **4.** (*give up*) **to ~ ground** ceder terreno; **to ~ responsibility** delegar responsabilidades; **to ~ sth to the enemy** entregar algo al enemigo **III.** *vi* **1.** AGR, COM, FIN ser productivo **2.** (*give way*) **to ~ to sth/sb** ceder ante algo/alguien; **to ~ to temptation** ceder a la tentación; **it ~ed because of the weight** cedió al peso **3.** (*surrender*) rendirse **4.** (*give priority*) **to ~ to sth/sb** dar prioridad a algo/alguien **5.** AUTO ceder el paso

◆**yield up** *vt* (*give up*) entregar; (*secret*) revelar

yielding *adj* **1.** (*pliable: a material, a substance*) flexible; (*soft*) blando, -a **2.** *fig* (*compliant*) complaciente

yippee [jɪˈpiː, *Am:* ˈjɪpiː] *interj inf* yupi

YMCA [ˌwaɪemsiːˈeɪ] *abbr of* **Young Men's Christian Association** *Asociación Cristiana de Jóvenes*

yob [jɒb, *Am:* jɑːb] *n,* **yobbo** [ˈjɒbəʊ, *Am:* ˈjɑːboʊ] <-s> *n Brit, Aus, inf* gamberro, -a *m, f*

yodel, **yodle** [ˈjəʊdəl, *Am:* ˈjoʊ-] MUS **I.** <-ll-, *Am:* -l-> *vi* (*sing*) cantar al estilo tirolés **II.** *vt* (*sing*) cantar al estilo tirolés **III.** *n* (*yodelled song*) canción *f* tirolesa

yoga [ˈjəʊgə, *Am:* ˈjoʊ-] *n no pl* yoga *m*

yoghourt [ˈjɒgət, *Am:* ˈjoʊgɚt] *n* yogur *m*

yogi [ˈjəʊgi, *Am:* ˈjoʊ-] *n* yogui *mf*

yogurt [ˈjɒgət, *Am:* ˈjoʊgɚt] *n s.* **yoghourt**

yoke [jəʊk, *Am:* joʊk] **I.** *n* **1.** *a. fig* AGR yugo *m;* **to throw off the ~** liberarse del yugo **2.** FASHION canesú *m* **II.** *vt* **1.** AGR (*fit with yoke*) uncir; **to ~ an animal (to sth)** enyuntar un animal (a algo) **2.** *fig* (*combine*) **to ~ two things together** ligar una cosa a otra

yokel [ˈjəʊkl, *Am:* ˈjoʊ-] *n iron, pej* (*country person*) paleto, -a *m, f,* pajuerano, -a *m, f Arg, Bol, Urug*

yolk [jəʊk, *Am:* joʊk] *n* yema *f* (de huevo)

Yom Kippur [ˌjɒmkɪˈpʊəʳ, *Am:* ˌjɑːmˈkɪpɚ] *n* Yom Kip(p)ur *m*

yonder [ˈjɒndəʳ, *Am:* ˈjɑːndɚ] *dial* **I.** *adv* (*over there*) allá **II.** *adj* (*situated over there*) aquel, aquella; *pl:* aquellos, aquellas

yore [jɔːʳ, *Am:* jɔːr] *n no pl, liter* **in (the) days of ~** antaño

you [juː] *pron pers* **1.** *2nd pers sing* tu, vos *CSur; pl:* vosotros, -as, ustedes *AmL;* **I see ~** te/os veo; **do ~ see me?** ¿me ves/veis?; **I love ~** te/os amo; **it is for ~** es para ti/vosotros; **older than ~** mayor que tú/vosotros; **if I were ~** si yo fuera tú/vosotros; **~'re my brother** tú eres mi hermano **2.** (*2nd person sing, polite form*) usted; *pl:* ustedes; **~'ve a car** usted tiene/ustedes tienen un coche; **~'re going to Paris** va/van a París; **older than ~** mayor que usted/ustedes

you'd [juːd] = **you would** *s.* **would**

you'll [juːl] = **you will** *s.* **will**

young [jʌŋ] **I.** *adj* **1.** *a.* GEO (*not old*) joven; **~ children** niños *mpl* pequeños; **a ~ man** un joven; **sb's ~er brother/son** el hermano/hijo menor de alguien; **the ~er generation** la nueva generación; **the night is still ~** la noche es joven **2.** (*junior*) **old Mr Brown and ~ Mr Brown** el Sr. Brown padre y el Sr. Brown hijo **3.** (*young-seeming: appearance, clothes*) juvenil; **to be ~ at heart** ser joven de espíritu; **she is ~ for her age** parece más joven de lo que es; **to be ~ looking** tener un aspecto juvenil **4.** (*pertaining to youth: love*) de juventud; **in my ~(er) days** cuando era joven ►**you're only ~ once!** ¡sólo se es joven una vez! **II.** *n pl* **1.** (*young people*) **the ~** los jóvenes **2.** ZOOL (*offspring*) crías *fpl;* **with ~** preñada

young people *npl,* **young persons** *npl* los jóvenes

youngster [ˈjʌŋkstəʳ, *Am:* -stɚ] *n* joven *mf*

your [jɔːʳ, *Am:* jʊr] *adj pos* **1.** *2nd pers sing* tu(s); *pl:* vuestro(s), vuestra(s) **2.** (*2nd pers sing and pl: polite form*) su(s)

you're [jɔːʳ, *Am:* jʊr] = **you are** *s.* **be**

yours [jɔːz, *Am:* jʊrz] *pron pos* **1.** *sing:* (el) tuyo, (la) tuya, (los) tuyos, (las) tuyas; *pl:* (el) vuestro, (la) vuestra, (los) vuestros, (las) vuestras, el de ustedes *AmL,* la de ustedes *AmL;* **this glass is ~** este vaso es tuyo/vuestro **2.** *polite form* (el) suyo, (la) suya, (los) suyos, (las) suyas; **~ faithfully** le saluda atentamente

yourself [jɔːˈself, *Am:* jʊr-] *pron reflexive* **1.** *sing:* te; *emphatic:* tú (mismo, misma); *after prep:* ti (mismo, misma) **2.** *polite form:* se; *emphatic:* usted (mismo, misma); *after prep:* sí (mismo, misma)

yourselves *pron reflexive* **1.** os, se *AmL; emphatic, after prep:* vosotros (mismos), vosotras (mismas), ustedes (mismos, mismas) *AmL* **2.** *polite form:* se; *emphatic:* ustedes (mismos/mismas); *after prep:* sí (mismos, mismas)

youth [juːθ] *n* **1.** *no pl* (*period when young*) juventud *f;* **during her (early) ~** en su (primera) juventud; **he is a friend of my ~** es un amigo de juventud **2.** (*young man*) joven *m* **3.** *no pl* (*young people*) jóvenes *mpl;* **the ~** la juventud; **~ culture** cultura *f* juvenil

youth centre *n,* **youth club** *n* club *m* juvenil

youthful [ˈjuːθfəl] *adj* **1.** (*young-looking*) juvenil; **~ appearance** aspecto *m* juvenil **2.** (*typical of the young*) de la juventud **3.** (*young*) joven

youth hostel *n* albergue *m* juvenil **Youth Training Scheme** *n Brit* POL plan *m* de empleo juvenil **youth unemployment** *n* paro *m* juvenil

you've [juːv] = **you have** *s.* **have**

yowl [jaʊl] **I.** *vi* (*howl: dog*) aullar; (*cat*) maullar; (*person*) dar alaridos **II.** *n* (*howl: of a dog*) aullido *m;* (*of a cat*) maullido *m;* (*of a person*)

alarido *m*
yo-yo ['jəʊjəʊ, *Am:* 'joʊjoʊ] *n* (*toy*) yo-yo *m*
yr *pron abbr of* **your**
yuan [ˌjuː'æn] *n* FIN yuan *m*
yucky [jʌki] *adj inf* asqueroso, -a
Yugoslav ['juːgəʊslɑːv, *Am:* 'juːgoʊslɑːv] *adj, n s.* **Yugoslavian**
Yugoslavia ['juːgəʊ'slɑːviə, *Am:* -goʊ'-] *n* HIST Yugoslavia *f*
Yugoslavian I. *adj* yugoslavo, -a II. *n* yugoslavo, -a *m, f*
yukky ['jʌki] <-ier, -iest> *adj s.* **yucky**
Yukon Territory ['juːkɒn 'terɪtəri, *Am:* 'juːkɑːn 'terətɔːri] *n* Territorio *m* del Yukón
yule log ['juːlˌlɒg, *Am:* 'juːlˌlɑːg] *n* 1. (*log*) *tronco que se quema en la chimenea en Navidad* 2. GASTR tronco *m* de Navidad
Yuletide ['juːltaɪd] *n liter* Navidades *fpl*
yummy ['jʌmi] *adj* de rechupete
yuppie ['jʌpi] *n* yuppy *mf*

Z

Z, z [zed, *Am:* ziː] *n* Z, z *f;* ~ **for Zebra** Z de Zaragoza ►**to** <u>**catch**</u> **some** ~**s** *Am, inf* echar una cabezada, apolillar un poco *RíoPl*
Zaire [zaɪ'ɪə, *Am:* -'ɪr] *n* Zaire *m*
Zairean [zaɪ'ɪən] I. *adj* zaireño, -a II. *n* zaireño, -a *m, f*
Zambia ['zæmbɪə] *n* Zambia *f*
Zambian ['zæmbɪən] I. *adj* zambiano, -a II. *n* zambiano, -a *m, f*
zany ['zeɪni] <-ier, -iest> *adj inf* (*person*) chiflado, -a; (*clothing*) estrafalario, -a; (*idea*) loco, -a
zap [zæp] I. <-pp-> *vt* 1. *inf* (*destroy*) liquidar 2. *inf* (*send fast*) enviar rápidamente II. <-pp-> *vi inf* 1. **to** ~ **somewhere** ir a un sitio en un momento; **to** ~ **through sth** despachar algo 2. (*change channels*) hacer zapping III. *interj inf* zas
zapping [zæpɪŋ] *n inf* zapping *m*
zeal [ziːl] *n no pl* celo *m;* **religious** ~ fervor *m* religioso; **reforming** ~ afán *m* reformista
zealot ['zelət] *n* fanático, -a *m, f*
zealous ['zeləs] *adj* ferviente; **to be** ~ **in sth** poner gran celo en algo
zebra ['zebrə, *Am:* 'ziːbrə] *n* cebra *f*
zebra crossing *n Brit, Aus* (*pedestrian crossing*) paso *m* de cebra
zenith ['zenɪθ, *Am:* 'ziːnɪθ] <-es> *n* 1. ASTR (*highest point*) cenit *m* 2. (*most successful point*) apogeo *m;* **to be at the** ~ **of sth** estar en el apogeo de algo
zero ['zɪərəʊ, *Am:* 'zɪroʊ] I. <-s *o* -es> *n* cero *m;* **below** ~ METEO bajo cero; **to be a** ~ ser un cero a la izquierda II. *adj* cero *inv;* ~ **growth** crecimiento *m* cero; ~ **hour** hora *f* cero; ~ **visibility** visibilidad *f* nula; **my chances are** ~ no tengo ninguna posibilidad III. *vt* (*return to zero: device*) poner a cero
◆**zero in on** *vi* 1. (*aim precisely*) apuntar a 2. (*focus on*) **to** ~ **sth** centrarse en algo
zero-rated *adj* FIN no sujeto a IVA **zero tolerance** *n* **policy of** ~ política *f* de mano dura
zest [zest] *n no pl* 1. (*enthusiastic energy*) entusiasmo *m;* **to do sth with** ~ hacer algo con brío; ~ **for life** ganas *fpl* de vivir 2. (*charm, interest*) gracia *f;* **the story lacks** ~ a la historia le falta garra 3. (*rind*) corteza *f;* **lemon/orange** ~ corteza de limón/naranja; **grated lemon** ~ raspadura *f* de limón
zigzag ['zɪgzæg] I. *n* (*crooked line*) zigzag *m* II. *adj* (*crooked*) zigzagueante; (*pattern*) en zigzag III. <-gg-> *vi* zigzaguear
Zimbabwe [zɪm'bɑːbweɪ] *n* Zimbabue *m*
Zimbabwean [zɪm'bɑːbwiən] I. *adj* zimbabuo, -a II. *n* zimbabuo, -a *m, f*
zinc [zɪŋk] *n no pl* cinc *m,* zinc *m*
zip [zɪp] I. *n* 1. (*fastener*) cremallera *f,* cierre *m* relámpago *Arg;* **to do up a** ~ subir una cremallera 2. *no pl, inf* (*vigour*) brío *m* 3. (*whistle*) silbido *m* 4. *no pl, Am, inf* (*nothing*) nada; **I know** ~ **about that** no tengo ni idea de eso II. <-pp-> *vt* **to** ~ **a bag** cerrar la cremallera de un bolso; **to** ~ **a dress** subir la cremallera de un vestido; **to** ~ **sth open** abrir la cremallera de algo; **to** ~ **sth shut** cerrar la cremallera de algo; **to** ~ **sth up** subir la cremallera de algo; **will you** ~ **me up?** ¿me subes la cremallera? III. <-pp-> *vi* **to** ~ **in/past** entrar/pasar volando; **the days** ~**ped by** los días pasaron volando
zip code *n Am* código *m* postal
zip-fastener *n Brit,* **zipper** ['zɪpəʳ, *Am:* -ɚ] *n Am* cremallera *f,* cierre *m* relámpago *Arg*
zippy ['zɪpi] <-ier, -iest> *adj inf* (*fast: car*) veloz; (*energetic*) enérgico, -a
zither ['zɪðəʳ, *Am:* -ɚ] *n* cítara *f*
zloty ['zlɒti, *Am:* 'zlɔːt̬i] *n* zloty *m*
zodiac ['zəʊdiæk, *Am:* 'zoʊ-] *n no pl* zodíaco *m*
zombie ['zɒmbi, *Am:* 'zɑːm-] *n* zombi *mf*
zonal ['zəʊnəl, *Am:* 'zoʊ-] *adj* zonal; **a** ~ **division** una división en zonas
zone [zəʊn, *Am:* zoʊn] I. *n* zona *f;* **nuclear-free** ~ zona desnuclearizada; **time** ~ zona *f* horaria; **frigid/temperate/torrid** ~ METEO zona glacial/templada/tórrida II. *vt* 1. (*divide*) dividir en zonas 2. ADMIN, LAW (*designate*) **to** ~ **an area for residential use** declarar un lugar zona residencial
zoning *n no pl* ADMIN, LAW zonificación *f*
zoo [zuː] *n* zoo *m*
zoological [ˌzəʊəʊ'lɒdʒɪkəl, *Am:* ˌzoʊə'lɑːdʒɪ-] *adj* zoológico, -a; ~ **gardens** (parque *m*) zoológico *m*
zoologist [zu'ɒlədʒɪst, *Am:* zoʊ'ɑːlə-] *n* zoólogo, -a *m, f*
zoology [zu'ɒlədʒi, *Am:* zoʊ'ɑːlə-] *n no pl* zoología *f*
zoom [zuːm] I. *n* 1. PHOT zoom *m* 2. AVIAT su-

bida *f* vertical **3.** (*buzz*) zumbido *m* **II.** *vt* **1.** AVIAT (*plane*) hacer subir verticalmente **2.** PHOT enfocar con el zoom **III.** *vi* **1.** *inf* (*move very fast*) ir zumbando; **to ~ away** salir pitando; **to ~ past** pasar volando **2.** (*plane*) elevarse abruptamente; (*costs, sales*) dispararse *inf*

◆**zoom in** *vi* PHOT enfocar en primer plano; **to ~ on sth/sb** enfocar algo/a alguien en primer plano

◆**zoom out** *vi* PHOT cambiar a un plano general

zoom lens *n* zoom *m*

zucchini [zʊ'ki:ni, *Am:* zu:-] <-(s)> *n inv, Am* calabacín *m*, calabacita *f AmL*

Apéndice II

Supplement II

Los verbos regulares e irregulares españoles
Spanish regular and irregular verbs

Abreviaturas:

pret. ind.	pretérito indefinido
subj. fut.	subjuntivo futuro
subj. imp.	subjuntivo imperfecto
subj. pres.	subjuntivo presente

Verbos regulares que terminan en *-ar, -er* e *-ir*

hablar

presente	imperfecto	pret. ind.	futuro	
hablo	hablaba	hablé	hablaré	**gerundio**
hablas	hablabas	hablaste	hablarás	hablando
habla	hablaba	habló	hablará	
hablamos	hablábamos	hablamos	hablaremos	**participio**
habláis	hablabais	hablasteis	hablaréis	hablado
hablan	hablaban	hablaron	hablarán	

condicional	subj. pres.	subj. imp.	subj. fut.	imperativo
hablaría	hable	hablara/-ase	hablare	
hablarías	hables	hablaras/-ases	hablares	habla
hablaría	hable	hablara/-ase	hablare	hable
hablaríamos	hablemos	habláramos /-ásemos	habláremos	hablemos
hablaríais	habléis	hablarais/-aseis	hablareis	hablad
hablarían	hablen	hablaran/-asen	hablaren	hablen

comprender

presente	imperfecto	pret. ind.	futuro	
comprendo	comprendía	comprendí	comprenderé	**gerundio**
comprendes	comprendías	comprendiste	comprenderás	comprendiendo
comprende	comprendía	comprendió	comprenderá	
comprendemos	comprendíamos	comprendimos	comprenderemos	**participio**
comprendéis	comprendíais	comprendisteis	comprenderéis	comprendido
comprenden	comprendían	comprendieron	comprenderán	

condicional	subj. pres.	subj. imp.	subj. fut.	imperativo
comprendería	comprenda	comprendiera /-iese	comprendiere	
comprenderías	comprendas	comprendieras/ -ieses	comprendieres	comprende
comprendería	comprenda	comprendiera /-iese	comprendiere	comprenda
comprenderíamos	comprendamos	comprendiéramos /-iésemos	comprendiéremos	comprendamos
comprenderíais	comprendáis	comprendierais /-ieseis	comprendiereis	comprended
comprenderían	comprendan	comprendiera /-iesen	comprendieren	comprendan

recibir

presente	imperfecto	pret. ind.	futuro	
recibo	recibía	recibí	recibiré	**gerundio**
recibes	recibías	recibiste	recibirás	recibiendo
recibe	recibía	recibió	recibirá	
recibimos	recibíamos	recibimos	recibiremos	**participio**
recibís	recibíais	recibisteis	recibiréis	recibido
reciben	recibían	recibieron	recibirán	

condicional	subj. pres.	subj. imp.	subj. fut.	imperativo
recibiría	reciba	recibiera/-iese	recibiere	
recibirías	recibas	recibieras/-ieses	recibieres	recibe
recibiría	reciba	recibiera/-iese	recibiere	reciba
recibiríamos	recibamos	recibiéramos /-iésemos	recibiéremos	recibamos
recibiríais	recibáis	reciebierais/-ieseis	recibiereis	recibid
recibirían	reciban	recibieran/-iesen	recibieren	reciban

Verbos con cambios vocálicos

<e → ie> pensar

presente	imperfecto	pret. ind.	futuro	
pienso	pensaba	pensé	pensaré	**gerundio**
piensas	pensabas	pensaste	pensarás	pensando
piensa	pensaba	pensó	pensará	
pensamos	pensábamos	pensamos	pensaremos	**participio**
pensáis	pensabais	pensasteis	pensaréis	pensado
piensan	pensaban	pensaron	pensarán	

condicional	subj. pres.	subj. imp.	subj. fut.	imperativo
pensaría	piense	pensara/-ase	pensare	
pensarías	pienses	pensaras/-ases	pensares	piensa
pensaría	piense	pensara/-ase	pensare	piense
pensaríamos	pensemos	pensáramos /-ásemos	pensáremos	pensemos
pensaríais	penséis	pensarais /-aseis	pensareis	pensad
pensarían	piensen	pensaran/-asen	pensaren	piensen

<o → ue> contar

presente	imperfecto	pret. ind.	futuro	
cuento	contaba	conté	contaré	**gerundio**
cuentas	contabas	contaste	contarás	contando
cuenta	contaba	contó	contará	
contamos	contábamos	contamos	contaremos	**participio**
contáis	contabais	contasteis	contaréis	contado
cuentan	contaban	contaron	contarán	

condicional	subj. pres.	subj. imp.	subj. fut.	imperativo
contaría	cuente	contara/-ase	contare	
contarías	cuentes	contaras/-ases	contares	cuenta
contaría	cuente	contara/-ase	contare	cuente
contaríamos	contemos	contáramos /-ásemos	contáremos	contemos
contaríais	contéis	contarais/-aseis	contareis	contad
contarían	cuenten	contaran	contaren	cuenten

<u → ue> jugar

presente	imperfecto	pret. ind.	futuro	
juego	jugaba	jugé	jugaré	**gerundio**
juegas	jugabas	jugaste	jugarás	jugando
juega	jugaba	jugó	jugará	
jugamos	jugábamos	jugamos	jugaremos	**participio**
jugáis	jugabais	jugasteis	jugaréis	jugado
juegan	jugaban	jugaron	jugarán	

condicional	subj. pres.	subj. imp.	subj. fut.	imperativo
jugaría	juegue	jugara/-ase	jugare	
jugarías	juegues	jugaras/-ases	jugares	juega
jugaría	juegue	jugara/-ase	jugare	juegue
jugaríamos	juguemos	jugáramos/-ásemos	jugáremos	juguemos
jugaríais	juguéis	jugarais/-aseis	jugareis	jugad
jugarían	jueguen	jugaran/-asen	jugaren	jueguen

<e → i> pedir

presente	imperfecto	pret. ind.	futuro	
pido	pedía	pedí	pediré	**gerundio**
pides	pedías	pediste	pedirás	pidiendo
pide	pedía	pidió	pedirá	
pedimos	pedíamos	pedimos	pediremos	**participio**
pedís	pedíais	pedisteis	pediréis	pedido
piden	pedían	pidieron	pedirán	

condicional	subj. pres.	subj. imp.	subj. fut.	imperativo
pediría	pida	pidiera/-iese	pidiere	
pedirías	pidas	pidieras/-ieses	pidieres	pide
pediría	pida	pidiera/-iese	pidiere	pida
pediríamos	pidamos	pidiéramos /-iésemos	pidiéremos	pidamos
pediríais	pidáis	pidierais/-ieseis	pidiereis	pedid
pedirían	pidan	pidieran/-iesen	pidieren	pidan

Verbos con cambios ortográficos

<c → qu> atacar

presente	imperfecto	pret. ind.	futuro	
ataco	atacaba	ataqué	atacaré	**gerundio**
atacas	atacabas	atacaste	atacarás	atacando
ataca	atacaba	atacó	atacará	
atacamos	atacábamos	atacamos	atacaremos	**participio**
atacáis	atacabais	atacasteis	atacaréis	atacado
atacan	atacaban	atacaron	atacarán	

condicional	subj. pres.	subj. imp.	subj. fut.	imperativo
atacaría	ataque	atacara/-ase	atacare	
atacarías	ataques	atacaras/-ases	atacares	ataca
atacaría	ataque	atacara/-ase	atacare	ataque
atacaríamos	ataquemos	atacáramos/-ásemos	atacáremos	ataquemos
atacaríais	ataquéis	atacarais/-aseis	atacareis	atacad
atacarían	ataquen	atacaran/-asen	atacaren	ataquen

<g → gu> pagar

presente	imperfecto	pret. ind.	futuro	
pago	pagaba	pagué	pagaré	**gerundio**
pagas	pagabas	pagaste	pagarás	pagando
paga	pagaba	pagó	pagará	
pagamos	pagábamos	pagamos	pagaremos	**participio**
pagáis	pagabais	pagasteis	pagaréis	pagado
pagan	pagaban	pagaron	pagarán	

condicional	subj. pres.	subj. imp.	subj. fut.	imperativo
pagaría	pague	pagara/-ase	pagare	
pagarías	pagues	pagaras/-ases	pagares	paga
pagaría	pague	pagara/-ase	pagare	pague
pagaríamos	paguemos	pagáramos/-ásemos	pagáremos	paguemos
pagaríais	paguéis	pagarais/-aseis	pagareis	pagad
pagarían	paguen	pagaran/-asen	pagaren	paguen

<z → c> cazar

presente	imperfecto	pret. ind.	futuro	
cazo	cazaba	cacé	cazaré	**gerundio**
cazas	cazabas	cazaste	cazarás	cazando
caza	cazaba	cazó	cazará	
cazamos	cazábamos	cazamos	cazaremos	**participio**
cazáis	cazabais	cazasteis	cazaréis	cazado
cazan	cazaban	cazaron	cazarán	

condicional	subj. pres.	subj. imp.	subj. fut.	imperativo
cazaría	cace	cazara/-ase	cazare	
cazarías	caces	cazaras/-ases	cazares	caza
cazaría	cace	cazara/-ase	cazare	cace
cazaríamos	cacemos	cazáramos/-ásemos	cazáremos	cacemos
cazaríais	cacéis	cazarais/-aseis	cazareis	cazad
cazarían	cacen	cazaran/-asen	cazaren	cacen

<gu → gü> averiguar

presente	imperfecto	pret. ind.	futuro	
averiguo	averiguaba	averigüé	averiguaré	**gerundio**
averiguas	averiguabas	averiguaste	averiguarás	averiguando
averigua	averiguaba	averiguó	averiguará	
averiguamos	averiguábamos	averiguamos	averiguaremos	**participio**
averiguáis	averiguabais	averiguasteis	averiguaréis	averiguado
averiguan	averiguaban	averiguaron	averiguarán	

condicional	subj. pres.	subj. imp.	subj. fut.	imperativo
averiguaría	averigüe	averiguara/-ase	averiguare	
averiguarías	averigües	averiguaras/-ases	averiguares	averigua
averiguaría	averigüe	averiguara/-ase	averiguare	averigüe
averiguaríamos	averigüemos	averiguáramos /-ásemos	averiguáremos	averigüemos
averiguaríais	averigüéis	averiguarais/-aseis	averiguareis	averiguad
averiguarían	averigüen	averiguaran/-asen	averiguaren	averigüen

<c → z> vencer

presente	imperfecto	pret. ind.	futuro	
venzo	vencía	vencí	venceré	**gerundio**
vences	vencías	venciste	vencerás	venciendo
vence	vencía	venció	vencerá	
vencemos	vencíamos	vencimos	venceremos	**participio**
vencéis	vencíais	vencisteis	venceréis	vencido
vencen	vencían	vencieron	vencerán	

condicional	subj. pres.	subj. imp.	subj. fut.	imperativo
vencería	venza	venciera/-iese	venciere	
vencerías	venzas	vencieras/-ieses	vencieres	vence
vencería	venza	venciera/-iese	venciere	venza
venceríamos	venzamos	venciéramos /-iésemos	venciéremos	venzamos
venceríais	venzáis	vencierais/-ieseis	venciereis	venced
vencerían	venzan	vencieran/-iesen	vencieren	venzan

<g → j> coger

presente	imperfecto	pret. ind.	futuro	
cojo	cogía	cogí	cogeré	**gerundio**
coges	cogías	cogiste	cogerás	cogiendo
coge	cogía	cogió	cogerá	
cogemos	cogíamos	cogimos	cogeremos	**participio**
cogéis	cogíais	cogisteis	cogeréis	cogido
cogen	cogían	cogieron	cogerán	

condicional	subj. pres.	subj. imp.	subj. fut.	imperativo
cogería	coja	cogiera/-iese	cogiere	
cogerías	cojas	cogieras/-ieses	cogieres	coge
cogería	coja	cogiera/-iese	cogiere	coja
cogeríamos	cojamos	cogiéramos /-iésemos	cogiéremos	cojamos
cogeríais	cojáis	cogierais/-ieseis	cogiereis	coged
cogerían	cojan	cogieran/-iesen	cogieren	cojan

<gu → g> distinguir

presente	imperfecto	pret. ind.	futuro	
distingo	distinguía	distinguí	distinguiré	**gerundio**
distingues	distinguías	distinguiste	distinguirás	distinguiendo
distingue	distinguía	distinguió	distinguirá	
distinguimos	distinguíamos	distinguimos	distinguiremos	**participio**
distinguís	distinguíais	distinguisteis	distinguiréis	distinguido
distinguen	distinguían	distinguieron	distinguirán	

condicional	subj. pres.	subj. imp.	subj. fut.	imperativo
distinguiría	distinga	distinguiera/-iese	distinguiere	
distinguirías	distingas	distinguieras/-ieses	distinguieres	distingue
distinguiría	distinga	distinguiera/-iese	distinguiere	distinga
distinguiríamos	distingamos	distinguiéramos /iésemos	distinguiéremos	distingamos
distinguiríais	distingáis	distinguierais/-ieseis	distinguiereis	distinguid
distinguirían	distingan	distinguieran/-iesen	distinguieren	distingan

<qu → c> delinquir

presente	imperfecto	pret. ind.	futuro	
delinco	delinquía	delinquí	delinquiré	**gerundio**
delinques	delinquías	delinquiste	delinquirás	delinquiendo
delinque	delinquía	delinquió	delinquirá	
delinquimos	delinquíamos	delinquimos	delinquiremos	**participio**
delinquís	delinquíais	delinquisteis	delinquiréis	delinquido
delinquen	delinquían	delinquieron	delinquirán	

condicional	subj. pres.	subj. imp.	subj. fut.	imperativo
delinquiría	delinca	delinquiera/-iese	delinquiere	
delinquirías	delincas	delinquieras/-ieses	delinquieres	delinque
delinquiría	delinca	delinquiera/-iese	delinquiere	delinca
delinquiríamos	delincamos	delinquiéramos /-iésemos	delinquiéremos	delincamos
delinquiríais	delincáis	delinquierais/-ieseis	delinquiereis	delinquid
delinquirían	delincan	delinquieran/-iesen	delinquieren	delincan

Verbos con desplazamiento en la acentuación

<1. pres: envío> enviar

presente	imperfecto	pret. ind.	futuro	
envío	enviaba	envié	enviaré	**gerundio**
envías	enviabas	enviaste	enviarás	enviando
envía	enviaba	envió	enviará	
enviamos	enviábamos	enviamos	enviaremos	**participio**
enviáis	enviabais	enviasteis	enviaréis	enviado
envían	enviaban	enviaron	enviarán	

condicional	subj. pres.	subj. imp.	subj. fut.	imperativo
enviaría	envíe	enviara/-iase	enviare	
enviarías	envíes	enviaras/-iases	enviares	envía
enviaría	envíe	enviara/-iase	enviare	envíe
enviaríamos	enviemos	enviáramos /-iásemos	enviáremos	enviemos
enviaríais	enviéis	enviarais/-iaseis	enviareis	enviad
enviarían	envíen	enviaran/-iasen	enviaren	envíen

<1. pres: continúo> continuar

presente	imperfecto	pret. ind.	futuro	
continúo	continuaba	continué	continuaré	**gerundio**
continúas	continuabas	continuaste	continuarás	continuando
continúa	continuaba	continuó	continuará	
continuamos	continuábamos	continuamos	continuaremos	**participio**
continuáis	continuabais	continuasteis	continuaréis	continuado
continúan	continuaban	continuaron	continuarán	

condicional	subj. pres.	subj. imp.	subj. fut.	imperativo
continuaría	continúe	continuara/-ase	continuare	
continuarías	continúes	continuaras/-ases	continuares	continúa
continuaría	continúe	continuara/-ase	continuare	continúe
continuaríamos	continuemos	continuáramos /-ásemos	continuáremos	continuemos
continuaríais	continuéis	continuarais/-aseis	continuareis	continuad
continuarían	continúen	continuaran/-asen	continuaren	continúen

Verbos que pierden la *i* átona

<3. pret: tañó> tañer

presente	imperfecto	pret. ind.	futuro	
taño	tañía	tañí	tañeré	**gerundio**
tañes	tañías	tañiste	tañerás	tañendo
tañe	tañía	tañó	tañerá	
tañemos	tañíamos	tañimos	tañeremos	**participio**
tañéis	tañíais	tañisteis	tañeréis	tañido
tañen	tañían	tañeron	tañerán	

condicional	subj. pres.	subj. imp.	subj. fut.	imperativo
tañería	taña	tañera/-ese	tañere	
tañerías	tañas	tañeras/-eses	tañeres	tañe
tañería	taña	tañera/-ese	tañere	taña
tañeríamos	tañamos	tañéramos/-ésemos	tañéremos	tañamos
tañeríais	tañáis	tañerais/-eseis	tañereis	tañed
tañerían	tañan	tañeran/-esen	tañeren	tañan

<3. pret: gruñó> gruñir

presente	imperfecto	pret. ind.	futuro	
gruño	gruñía	gruñí	gruñiré	**gerundio**
gruñes	gruñías	gruñiste	gruñirás	gruñendo
gruñe	gruñía	gruñó	gruñirá	
gruñimos	gruñíamos	gruñimos	gruñiremos	**participio**
gruñís	gruñíais	gruñisteis	gruñiréis	gruñido
gruñen	gruñían	gruñeron	gruñirán	

condicional	subj. pres.	subj. imp.	subj. fut.	imperativo
gruñiría	gruña	gruñera/-ese	gruñere	
gruñirías	gruñas	gruñeras/-eses	gruñeres	gruñe
gruñiría	gruña	gruñera/-ese	gruñere	gruña
gruñiríamos	gruñamos	gruñéramos /-ésemos	gruñéremos	gruñamos
gruñiríais	gruñáis	gruñerais/-eseis	gruñereis	gruñid
gruñirían	gruñan	gruñeran/-esen	gruñeren	gruñan

Los verbos irregulares

abolir

presente	subj. pres.	imperativo	
–	–		**gerundio**
–	–	–	aboliendo
–	–	–	
abolimos	–	–	**participio**
abolís	–	abolid	abolido
–	–	–	

abrir

participio:	abierto

adquirir

presente	imperativo	
adquiero		**gerundio**
adquieres	adquiere	adquiriendo
adquiere	adquiera	
adquirimos	adquiramos	**participio**
adquirís	adquirid	adquirido
adquieren	adquieran	

agorar

presente	
agüero	**gerundio**
agüeras	agorando
agüera	
agoramos	**participio**
agoráis	agorado
agüeran	

ahincar

presente	imperfecto	pret. ind.	imperativo	
ahínco	ahincaba	ahinqué		**gerundio**
ahíncas	ahincabas	ahincaste	ahínca	ahincando
ahínca	ahincaba	ahincó	ahinque	
ahincamos	ahincábamos	ahincamos	ahinquemos	**participio**
ahincáis	ahincabais	ahincasteis	ahincad	ahincado
ahíncan	ahincaban	ahincaron	ahinquen	

airar

presente	
aíro	**gerundio**
aíras	airando
aíra	
airamos	**participio**
airáis	airado
aíran	

andar

presente	pret. ind.	
ando	anduve	**gerundio**
andas	anduviste	andando
anda	anduvo	
andamos	anduvimos	**participio**
andáis	anduvisteis	andado
andan	anduvieron	

asir

presente	imperativo	
asgo		**gerundio**
ases	ase	asiendo
ase	asga	
asimos	asgamos	**participio**
asís	asid	asido
asen	asgan	

aullar

presente	imperativo	
aúllo		**gerundio**
aúllas	aúlla	aullando
aúlla	aúlle	
aullamos	aullemos	**participio**
aulláis	aullad	aullado
aúllan	aúllen	

avergonzar

presente	pret. ind.	imperativo	
avergüenzo	avergoncé		**gerundio**
avergüenzas	avergonzaste	avergüenza	avergonzando
avergüenza	avergonzó	avergüence	
avergonzamos	avergonzamos	avergüencemos	**participio**
avergonzáis	avergonzasteis	avergonzad	avergonzado
avergüenzan	avergonzaron	avergüencen	

caber

presente	pret. ind.	futuro	condicional	
quepo	cupe	cabré	cabría	**gerundio**
cabes	cupiste	cabrás	cabrías	cabiendo
cabe	cupo	cabrá	cabría	
cabemos	cupimos	cabremos	cabríamos	**participio**
cabéis	cupisteis	cabréis	cabríais	cabido
caben	cupieron	cabrán	cabrían	

caer

presente	pret. ind.	
caigo	caí	**gerundio**
caes	caíste	cayendo
cae	cayó	
caemos	caímos	**participio**
caéis	caísteis	caído
caen	cayeron	

ceñir

presente	pret. ind.	imperativo	
ciño	ceñí		**gerundio**
ciñes	ceñiste	ciñe	ciñendo
ciñe	ciñó	ciña	
ceñimos	ceñimos	ciñamos	**participio**
ceñís	ceñisteis	ceñid	ceñido
ciñen	ciñieron	ciñan	

cernir

presente	imperativo	
cierno		**gerundio**
ciernes	cierne	cerniendo
cierne	cierna	
cernimos	cernamos	**participio**
cernís	cernid	cernido
ciernen	ciernan	

cocer

presente	imperativo	
cuezo		**gerundio**
cueces	cuece	cociendo
cuece	cueza	
cocemos	cozamos	**participio**
cocéis	coced	cocido
cuecen	cuezan	

colgar

presente	pret. ind.	imperativo	
cuelgo	colgué		**gerundio**
cuelgas	colgaste	cuelga	colgando
cuelga	colgó	cuelgue	
colgamos	colgamos	colgamos	**participio**
colgáis	colgasteis	colgad	colgado
cuelgan	colgaron	cuelguen	

crecer

presente	imperativo	
crezco		**gerundio**
creces	crece	creciendo
crece	crezca	
crecemos	crezcamos	**participio**
crecéis	creced	crecido
crecen	crezcan	

dar

presente	pret. ind.	subj. pres.	subj. imp.	subj. fut.
doy	di	dé	diera/-ese	diere
das	diste	des	dieras/-eses	dieres
da	dio	dé	diera/-ese	diere
damos	dimos	demos	diéramos/-ésemos	diéremos
dais	disteis	deis	dierais/-eseis	diereis
dan	dieron	den	dieran/-esen	dieren

imperativo	
da	**gerundio**
dé	dando
demos	
dad	**participio**
den	dado

decir

presente	imperfecto	pret. ind.	futuro	
digo	decía	dije	diré	**gerundio**
dices	decías	dijiste	dirás	diciendo
dice	decía	dijo	dirá	
decimos	decíamos	dijimos	diremos	**participio**
decís	decíais	dijisteis	diréis	dicho
dicen	decían	dijeron	dirán	

condicional	subj. pres.	subj. imp.	subj. fut.	imperativo
diría	diga	dijera/-ese	dijere	
dirías	digas	dijeras/-eses	dijeres	di
diría	diga	dijera/-ese	dijere	diga
diríamos	digamos	dijéramos/-ésemos	dijéremos	digamos
diríais	digáis	dijerais/-eseis	dijereis	decid
dirían	digan	dijeran/-esen	dijeren	digan

desosar

presente	imperativo	
deshueso		**gerundio**
deshuesas	deshuesa	desosando
deshuesa	deshuese	
desosamos	desosemos	**participio**
desosáis	desosad	desosado
deshuesan	deshuesen	

dormir

presente	pret. ind.	imperativo	
duermo	dormí		**gerundio**
duermes	dormiste	duerme	durmiendo
duerme	durmió	duerma	
dormimos	dormimos	durmamos	**participio**
dormís	dormisteis	dormid	dormido
duermen	durmieron	duerman	

elegir

presente	pret. ind.	imperativo	
elijo	elegí		**gerundio**
eliges	elegiste	elige	eligiendo
elige	eligió	elija	
elegimos	elegimos	elijamos	**participio**
elegís	elegisteis	elegid	elegido
eligen	eligieron	elijan	

empezar

presente	pret. ind.	imperativo	
empiezo	empecé		**gerundio**
empiezas	empezaste	empieza	empezando
empieza	empezó	empiece	
empezamos	empezamos	empecemos	**participio**
empezáis	empezasteis	empezad	empezado
empiezan	empezaron	empiecen	

enraizar

presente	pret. ind.	imperativo	
enraízo	enraicé		**gerundio**
enraízas	enraizaste	enraíza	enraizando
enraíza	enraizó	enraíce	
enraizamos	enraizamos	enraicemos	**participio**
enraizáis	enraizasteis	enraizad	enraizado
enraízan	enraizaron	enraícen	

erguir

presente	pret. ind.	subj. pres	subj. imp.	subj. fut.
yergo	erguí	irga/yerga	irguiera/-ese	irguiere
yergues	erguiste	irgas/yergas	irguieras/-eses	irguieres
yergue	irguió	irga/yerga	irguiera/-ese	irguiere
erguimos	erguimos	irgamos	irgiéramos /-ésemos	irguiéremos
erguís	erguisteis	irgáis	irguierais/-eseis	irguiereis
yerguen	irguieron	irgan/yergan	irguieran/-esen	irguieren

imperativo	
yergue	**gerundio**
yerga	irguiendo
yergamos	
erguid	**participio**
yergan	erguido

errar

presente	pret. ind.	imperativo	
yerro	erré		**gerundio**
yerras	erraste	yerra	errando
yerra	erró	yerre	
erramos	erramos	erremos	**participio**
erráis	errasteis	errad	errado
yerran	erraron	yerren	

escribir

participio :	escrito

estar

presente	imperfecto	pret. ind.	futuro	
estoy	estaba	estuve	estaré	**gerundio**
estás	estabas	estuviste	estarás	estando
está	estaba	estuvo	estará	
estamos	estábamos	estuvimos	estaremos	**participio**
estáis	estabais	estuvisteis	estaréis	estado
están	estaban	estuvieron	estarán	

condicional	subj. pres.	subj. imp.	subj. fut.	imperativo
estaría	esté	estuviera/-ese	estuviere	
estarías	estés	estuvieras/-eses	estuvieres	está
estaría	esté	estuviera/-ese	estuviere	esté
estaríamos	estemos	estuviéramos /-ésemos	estuviéremos	estemos
estaríais	estéis	estuvierais/-eseis	estuviereis	estad
estarían	estén	estuvieran/-esen	estuvieren	estén

forzar

presente	pret. ind.	imperativo	
fuerzo	forcé		**gerundio**
fuerzas	forzaste	fuerza	forzando
fuerza	forzó	fuerce	
forzamos	forzamos	forcemos	**participio**
forzáis	forzasteis	forzad	forzado
fuerzan	forzaron	fuercen	

fregar

presente	pret. ind.	imperativo	
friego	fregué		**gerundio**
friegas	fregaste	friega	fregando
friega	fregó	friegue	
fregamos	fregamos	freguemos	**participio**
fregáis	fregasteis	fregad	fregado
friegan	fregaron	frieguen	

freír

presente	pret. ind.	imperativo	
frío	freí		**gerundio**
fríes	freíste	fríe	friendo
fríe	frió	fría	
freímos	freímos	friamos	**participio**
freís	freísteis	freíd	freído
fríen	frieron	fríán	frito

haber

presente	pret. ind.	futuro	condicional	subj. pres.
he	hube	habré	habría	haya
has	hubiste	habrás	habrías	hayas
ha	hubo	habrá	habría	haya
hemos	hubimos	habremos	habríamos	hayamos
habéis	hubisteis	habréis	habríais	hayáis
han	hubieron	habrán	habrían	hayan

subj. imp.	subj. fut.	imperativo	
hubiera/-iese	hubiere		**gerundio**
hubieras/-ieses	hubieres	he	habiendo
hubiera/-iese	hubiere	haya	
hubiéramos /-iésemos	hubiéremos	hayamos	**participio** habido
hubierais/-ieseis	hubiereis	habed	
hubieran/-iesen	hubieren	hayan	

hacer

presente	pret. ind.	futuro	imperativo	
hago	hice	haré		**gerundio**
haces	hiciste	harás	haz	haciendo
hace	hizo	hará	haga	
hacemos	hicimos	haremos	hagamos	**participio**
hacéis	hicisteis	haréis	haced	hecho
hacen	hicieron	harán	hagan	

hartar

participio :	hartado – *saturated* harto (*only as attribute*): estoy harto – *I've had enough*

huir

presente	pret. ind.	imperativo	
huyo	huí		**gerundio**
huyes	huiste	huye	huyendo
huye	huyó	huya	
huimos	huimos	huyamos	**participio**
huís	huisteis	huid	huido
huyen	huyeron	huyan	

imprimir

participio :	impreso

ir

presente	indefinido	pret. ind.	subj. pres.	subj. imp.
voy	iba	fui	vaya	fuera/-ese
vas	ibas	fuiste	vayas	fueras/-eses
va	iba	fue	vaya	fuera/-ese
vamos	íbamos	fuimos	vayamos	fuéramos/-ésemos
vais	ibais	fuisteis	vayáis	fuerais/-eseis
van	iban	fueron	vayan	fueran/-esen

subj. fut.	imperativo	
fuere		**gerundio**
fueres	ve	yendo
fuere	vaya	
fuéremos	vayamos	**participio**
fuereis	id	ido
fueren	vayan	

jugar

presente	pret. ind.	subj. pres.	imperativo	
juego	jugé	juegue		**gerundio**
juegas	jugaste	juegues	juega	jugando
juega	jugó	juegue	juegue	
jugamos	jugamos	juguemos	juguemos	**participio**
jugáis	jugasteis	juguéis	jugad	jugado
juegan	jugaron	jueguen	jueguen	

leer

presente	pret. ind.	
leo	leí	**gerundio**
lees	leíste	leyendo
lee	leyó	
leemos	leímos	**participio**
leéis	leísteis	leído
leen	leyeron	

lucir

presente	imperativo	
luzco		**gerundio**
luces	luce	luciendo
luce	luzca	
lucimos	luzcamos	**participio**
lucís	lucid	lucido
lucen	luzcan	

maldecir

presente	pret. ind.	imperativo		
maldigo	maldije		**gerundio**	
maldices	maldijiste	maldice	maldiciendo	
maldice	maldijo	maldiga		
maldecimos	maldijimos	maldigamos	**participio**	
maldecís	maldijisteis	maldecid	maldecido	*cursed*
maldicen	maldijeron	maldigan	maldito	*noun, adjective*

morir

presente	pret. ind.	imperativo	
muero	morí		**gerundio**
mueres	moriste	muere	muriendo
muere	murió	muera	
morimos	morimos	muramos	**participio**
morís	moristeis	morid	muerto
mueren	murieron	mueran	

oír

presente	pret. ind.	imperativo	subj. imp.	subj. fut.
oigo	oí		oyera/-ese	oyere
oyes	oiste	oye	oyeras/-eses	oyeres
oye	oyó	oiga	oyera/-ese	oyere
oímos	oímos	oigamos	oyéramos/-ésemos	oyéremos
oís	oísteis	oid	oyerais/-eseis	oyéreis
oyen	oyeron	oigan	eyeran/-esen	oyeren

gerundio	participio
oyendo	oído

oler

presente	imperativo	
huelo		**gerundio**
hueles	huele	oliendo
huele	huela	
olemos	olamos	**participio**
oléis	oled	olido
huelen	huelan	

pedir

presente	pret. ind.	imperativo	
pido	pedí		**gerundio**
pides	pediste	pide	pidiendo
pide	pidió	pidas	
pedimos	pedimos	pidamos	**participio**
pedís	pedisteis	pedid	pedido
piden	pidieron	pidan	

poder

presente	pret. ind.	futuro	condicional	
puedo	pude	podré	podría	**gerundio**
puedes	pudiste	podrás	podrías	pudiendo
puede	pudo	podrá	podría	
podemos	pudimos	podremos	podríamos	**participio**
podéis	pudisteis	podréis	podríais	podido
pueden	pudieron	podrán	podrían	

podrir (pudrir)

presente	imperfecto	pret. ind.	futuro	condicional
pudro	pudría	pudrí	pudriré	pudriría
pudres	pudrías	pudriste	pudrirás	pudrirías
pudre	pudría	pudrió	pudrirá	pudriría
pudrimos	pudríamos	pudrimos	pudriremos	pudriríamos
pudrís	pudríais	pudristeis	pudriréis	pudriríais
pudren	pudrían	pudrieron	pudrirán	pudrirían

imperativo	
	gerundio
pudre	pudriendo
pudra	
pudramos	**participio**
pudrid	podrido
pudran	

poner

presente	pret. ind.	futuro	condicional	imperativo
pongo	puse	pondré	pondría	
pones	pusiste	pondrás	pondrías	pon
pone	puso	pondrá	pondría	ponga
ponemos	pusimos	pondremos	pondríamos	pongamos
ponéis	pusisteis	pondréis	pondríais	poned
ponen	pusieron	pondrán	pondrían	pongan

gerundio	participio
poniendo	puesto

prohibir

presente	imperativo	
prohíbo		**gerundio**
prohíbes	prohíbe	prohibiendo
prohíbe	prohíba	
prohibimos	prohibamos	**participio**
prohibís	prohibid	prohibido
prohíben	prohíban	

proveer

presente	pret. ind.	
proveo	proveí	**gerundio**
provees	proveíste	proveyendo
provee	proveyó	
proveemos	proveímos	**participio**
proveéis	proveísteis	provisto
proveen	proveyeron	proveído

querer

presente	pret. ind.	futuro	condicional	imperativo
quiero	quise	querré	querría	
quieres	quisiste	querrás	querrías	quiere
quiere	quiso	querrá	querría	quiera
queremos	quisimos	querremos	querríamos	queramos
queréis	quisisteis	querréis	querríais	quered
quieren	quisieron	querrán	querrían	quieran

gerundio	participio
queriendo	querido

raer

presente	pret. ind.	
raigo/rao/rayo	raí	**gerundio**
raes	raíste	rayendo
rae	rayó	
raemos	raímos	**participio**
raéis	raísteis	raído
raen	rayeron	

reír

presente	pret. ind.	imperativo	
río	reí		**gerundio**
ríes	reíste	ríe	riendo
ríe	rió	ría	
reímos	reímos	riamos	**participio**
reís	reísteis	reíd	reído
ríen	rieron	rían	

reunir

presente	imperativo	
reúno		**gerundio**
reúnes	reúne	reuniendo
reúne	reúna	
reunimos	reunamos	**participio**
reunís	reunid	reunido
reúnen	reúnan	

roer

presente	pret. ind.	subj. pres.	subj. imp.	subj. fut.
roo/roigo	roí	roa/roiga	royera/-ese	royere
roes	roíste	roas/roigas	royeras/-eses	royeres
roe	royó	roa/roiga	royera/-ese	royere
roemos	roímos	roamos /roigamos /royamos	royéramos /-ésemos	royéremos
roéis	roísteis	roáis/roigáis /royáis	royerais /-eseis	royereis
roen	royeron	roan/roigan	royeran/-esen	royeren

imperativo	
	gerundio
roe	royendo
roa/roiga	
roamos/roigamos roed roan/roigan	**participio** roído

saber

presente	pret. ind.	futuro	condicional	subj. pres.
sé	supe	sabré	sabría	sepa
sabes	supiste	sabrás	sabrías	sepas
sabe	supo	sabrá	sabría	sepa
sabemos	supimos	sabremos	sabríamos	sepamos
sabéis	supisteis	sabréis	sabríais	sepáis
saben	supieron	sabrán	sabrían	sepan

imperativo

	gerundio
sabe	sabiendo
sepa	
sepamos	**participio**
sabed	sabido
sepan	

salir

presente	futuro	condicional	imperativo	
salgo	saldré	saldría		**gerundio**
sales	saldrás	saldrías	sal	saliendo
sale	saldrá	saldría	salga	
salimos	saldremos	saldríamos	salgamos	**participio**
salís	saldréis	saldríais	salid	salido
salen	saldrán	saldrían	salgan	

seguir

presente	pret. ind.	subj. pres.	subj. imp.	subj. fut.
sigo	seguí	siga	siguiera/-ese	siguiere
sigues	seguiste	sigas	siguieras/-eses	siguieres
sigue	siguió	siga	siguiera/-ese	siguiere
seguimos	seguimos	sigamos	siguéramos /-ésemos	siguiéremos
seguís	seguisteis	sigáis	siguierais/-eseis	siguiereis
siguen	siguieron	sigan	siguieran/-esen	siguieren

imperativo

	gerundio
sigue	siguiendo
siga	
sigamos	**participio**
seguid	seguido
sigan	

sentir

presente	pret. ind.	subj. pres.	subj. imp.	subj. fut.
siento	sentí	sienta	sintiera/-ese	sintiere
sientes	sentiste	sientas	sintieras/-eses	sintieres
siente	sintió	sienta	sintiera/-ese	sintiere
sentimos	sentimos	sintamos	sintiéramos /-ésemos	sintiéremos
sentís	sentisteis	sintáis	sintierais/-eseis	sintiereis
sienten	sintieron	sientan	sintieran/-esen	sintieren

imperativo	
	gerundio
siente	sintiendo
sienta	
sintamos	**participio**
sentid	sentido
sientan	

ser

presente	imperfecto	pret. ind.	futuro	
soy	era	fui	seré	**gerundio**
eres	eras	fuiste	serás	siendo
es	era	fue	será	
somos	éramos	fuimos	seremos	**participio**
sois	erais	fuisteis	seréis	sido
son	eran	fueron	serán	

condicional	subj. pres.	subj. imp.	subj. fut.	imperativo
sería	sea	fuera/-ese	fuere	
serías	seas	fueras/-eses	fueres	sé
sería	sea	fuera/-ese	fuere	sea
seríamos	seamos	fuéramos/-ésemos	fuéremos	seamos
seríais	seáis	fuerais/-eseis	fuereis	sed
serían	sean	fueran/-esen	fueren	sean

soltar

presente	imperativo	
suelto		**gerundio**
sueltas	suelta	soltando
suelta	suelte	
soltamos	soltemos	**participio**
soltáis	soltad	soltado
sueltan	suelten	

tener

presente	pret. ind.	futuro	condicional	imperativo
tengo	tuve	tendré	tendría	
tienes	tuviste	tendrás	tendrías	ten
tiene	tuvo	tendrá	tendría	tenga
tenemos	tuvimos	tendremos	tendríamos	tengamos
tenéis	tuvisteis	tendréis	tendríais	tened
tienen	tuvieron	tendrán	tendrían	tengan

gerundio	participio
teniendo	tenido

traducir

presente	pret. ind.	imperativo	
traduzco	traduje		**gerundio**
traduces	tradujiste	traduce	traduciendo
traduce	tradujo	traduzca	
traducimos	tradujimos	traduzcamos	**participio**
traducís	tradujisteis	traducid	traducido
traducen	tradujeron	traduzcan	

traer

presente	pret. ind.	imperativo	
traigo	traje		**gerundio**
traes	trajiste	trae	trayendo
trae	trajo	traiga	
traemos	trajimos	traigamos	**participio**
traéis	trajisteis	traed	traído
traen	trajeron	traigan	

valer

presente	futuro	imperativo	
valgo	valdré		**gerundio**
vales	valdrás	vale	valiendo
vale	valdrá	valga	
valemos	valdremos	valgamos	**participio**
valéis	valdréis	valed	valido
valen	valdrán	valgan	

venir

presente	pret. ind.	futuro	condicional	imperativo
vengo	vine	vendré	vendría	
vienes	viniste	vendrás	vendrías	ven
viene	vino	vendrá	vendría	venga
venimos	vinimos	vendremos	vendríamos	vengamos
venís	vinisteis	vendréis	vendríais	venid
vienen	vinieron	vendrán	vendrían	vengan

gerundio	participio
viniendo	venido

ver

presente	imperfecto	pret. ind.	subj. imp.	subj. fut.
veo	veía	vi	viera/-ese	viere
ves	veías	viste	vieras/-eses	vieres
ve	veía	vio	viera/-ese	viere
vemos	veíamos	vimos	viéramos/-ésemos	viéremos
veis	veíais	visteis	vierais/-eseis	viereis
ven	veían	vieron	vieran/-esen	vieren

gerundio	participio
viendo	visto

volcar

presente	pret. ind.	imperativo	
vuelco	volqué		**gerundio**
vuelcas	volcaste	vuelca	volcando
vuelca	volcó	vuelque	
volcamos	volcamos	volquemos	**participio**
volcáis	volcasteis	volcad	volcado
vuelcan	volcaron	vuelquen	

volver

presente	imperativo	
vuelvo		**gerundio**
vuelves	vuelve	volviendo
vuelve	vuelva	
volvemos	volvamos	**participio**
volvéis	volved	volvido
vuelven	vuelvan	

yacer

presente	subj. pres.	imperativo	
yazco/yazgo /yago	yazca/yazga /yaga		**gerundio** yaciendo
yaces	yazcas/yazgas /yagas	yace/yaz	
yace	yazca/yazga /yaga	yazca/yazga /yaga	
yacemos	yazcamos /yazgamos /yagamos	yazcamos /yazgamos /yagamos	**participio** yacido
yacéis	yazcáis/yazgáis yagáis	yaced	
yacen	yazcan/yazgan /yagan	yazcan/yazgan /yagan	

Verbos ingleses irregulares
English irregular verbs

Infinitive	Past	Past Participle
abide	abode, abided	abode, abided
arise	arose	arisen
awake	awoke	awaked, awoken
be	was *sing*, were *pl*	been
bear	bore	borne
beat	beat	beaten
become	became	become
beget	begot	begotten
begin	began	begun
behold	beheld	beheld
bend	bent	bent
beseech	besought	besought
beset	beset	beset
bet	bet, betted	bet, betted
bid	bade, bid	bid, bidden
bind	bound	bound
bite	bit	bitten
bleed	bled	bled
blow	blew	blown
break	broke	broken
breed	bred	bred
bring	brought	brought
build	built	built
burn	burned, burnt	burned, burnt
burst	burst	burst
buy	bought	bought
can	could	–
cast	cast	cast
catch	caught	caught
chide	chided, chid	chided, chidden, chid
choose	chose	chosen
cleave[1] *(cut)*	clove, cleaved	cloven, cleaved, cleft
cleave[2] *(adhere)*	cleaved, clave	cleaved
cling	clung	clung
come	came	come
cost	cost, costed	cost, costed
creep	crept	crept
cut	cut	cut

Infinitive	Past	Past Participle
deal	dealt	dealt
dig	dug	dug
do	did	done
draw	drew	drawn
dream	dreamed, dreamt	dreamed, dreamt
drink	drank	drunk
drive	drove	driven
dwell	dwelt	dwelt
eat	ate	eaten
fall	fell	fallen
feed	fed	fed
feel	felt	felt
fight	fought	fought
find	found	found
flee	fled	fled
fling	flung	flung
fly	flew	flown
forbid	forbad(e)	forbidden
forget	forgot	forgotten
forsake	forsook	forsaken
freeze	froze	frozen
get	got	got, gotten *Am*
gild	gilded, gilt	gilded, gilt
gird	girded, girt	girded, girt
give	gave	given
go	went	gone
grind	ground	ground
grow	grew	grown
hang	hung, JUR hanged	hung, JUR hanged
have	had	had
hear	heard	heard
heave	heaved, hove	heaved, hove
hew	hewed	hewed, hewn
hide	hid	hidden
hit	hit	hit
hold	held	held
hurt	hurt	hurt
keep	kept	kept
kneel	knelt	knelt
know	knew	known

Infinitive	Past	Past Participle
lade	laded	laden, laded
lay	laid	laid
lead	led	led
lean	leaned, leant	leaned, leant
leap	leaped, leapt	leaped, leapt
learn	learned, learnt	learned, learnt
leave	left	left
lend	lent	lent
let	let	let
lie	lay	lain
light	lit, lighted	lit, lighted
lose	lost	lost
make	made	made
may	might	–
mean	meant	meant
meet	met	met
mistake	mistook	mistaken
mow	mowed	mown, mowed
pay	paid	paid
put	put	put
quit	quit, quitted	quit, quitted
read [ri:d]	read [red]	read [red]
rend	rent	rent
rid	rid	rid
ride	rode	ridden
ring	rang	rung
rise	rose	risen
run	ran	run
saw	sawed	sawed, sawn
say	said	said
see	saw	seen
seek	sought	sought
sell	sold	sold
send	sent	sent
set	set	set
sew	sewed	sewed, sewn
shake	shook	shaken
shave	shaved	shaved, shaven
stave	stove, staved	stove, staved
steal	stole	stolen

Infinitive	Past	Past Participle
shear	sheared	sheared, shorn
shed	shed	shed
shine	shone	shone
shit	shit, *iron* shat	shit, *iron* shat
shoe	shod	shod
shoot	shot	shot
show	showed	shown, showed
shrink	shrank	shrunk
shut	shut	shut
sing	sang	sung
sink	sank	sunk
sit	sat	sat
slay	slew	slain
sleep	slept	slept
slide	slid	slid
sling	slung	slung
slink	slunk	slunk
slit	slit	slit
smell	smelled, smelt	smelled, smelt
smite	smote	smitten
sow	sowed	sowed, sown
speak	spoke	spoken
speed	speeded, sped	speeded, sped
spell	spelled, spelt	spelled, spelt
spend	spent	spent
spill	spilled, spilt	spilled, spilt
spin	spun	spun
spit	spat	spat
split	split	split
spoil	spoiled, spoilt	spoiled, spoilt
spread	spread	spread
spring	sprang	sprung
stand	stood	stood
stick	stuck	stuck
sting	stung	stung
stink	stank	stunk
strew	strewed	strewed, strewn
stride	strode	stridden
strike	struck	struck
string	strung	strung

Infinitive	Past	Past Participle
strive	strove	striven
swear	swore	sworn
sweep	swept	swept
swell	swelled	swollen
swin	swam	swum
swing	swung	swung
take	took	taken
teach	taught	taught
tear	tore	torn
tell	told	told
think	thought	thought
thrive	throve, thrived	thriven, thrived
throw	threw	thrown
thrust	thrust	thrust
tread	trod	trodden
wake	woke, waked	woken, waked
wear	wore	worn
weave	wove	woven
weep	wept	wept
win	won	won
wind	wound	wound
wring	wrung	wrung
write	wrote	written

Falsos amigos

Para más información el usuario debe de consultar la entrada en el diccionario. En los casos en los que la palabra inglesa está fuera del orden alfabético ésta aparece en ***cursiva***.

False friends

Readers should consult the main section of the dictionary for more complete translation information. When the English term appears out of alphabetical order, it is shown in ***italics***.

Meaning(s) of the Spanish word:	falso amigo false friend español	 English	Significado(s) de la palabra inglesa:
1) enormous	**abismal**	**abysmal**	pésimo
1) present 2) current	**actual**	**actual**	verdadero
at the moment	**actualmente**	**actually**	en realidad
1) appropriate 2) fitting, suitable	**adecuado, -a**	**adequate**	1) suficiente 2) idóneo
1) diary 2) notebook 3) agenda	**agenda**	**agenda**	1) orden del día 2) agenda
bedroom	**alcoba**	**alcove**	nicho
1) entertainment 2) enjoyment	**amenidad**	**amenities**	comodidades
1) to attend (*vi*) 2) to help (*vt*)	**asistir**	**to assist**	ayudar
1) audience 2) (JUR) hearing, courtroom	**audiencia**	**audience**	1) público 2) audiencia
1) to notify 2) to warn 3) to call	**avisar**	***to advise***	aconsejar, asesorar
billion	**billón**	**billion**	mil millones
1) white 2) light 3) pale	**blanco, -a**	**blank**	1) en blanco 2) vacío 3) absoluto, completo
1) soft 2) mild 3) weak 4) gentle	**blando, -a**	**bland**	1) suave, blando 2) afable 3) insípido, insulso
1) excellent 2) brave 3) wild 4) rough	**bravo, -a**	**brave**	valiente
1) countryside 2) field 3) camp	**campo**	**camp**	1) campamento 2) grupo
1) shameless 2) cynical	**cínico, -a (adj)**	***cynical***	1) escéptico 2) cínico
1) shamelessness 2) cynicism	**cinismo**	**cynicism**	1) escepticismo 2) cinismo
1) understanding 2) tolerant 3) comprehensive	**comprensivo, -a**	**comprehensive**	exhaustivo, completo

Meaning(s) of the Spanish word:	falso amigo español	false friend English	Significado(s) de la palabra inglesa:
1) commitment 2) promise 3) agreement 4) awkward situation	**compromise**	**compromise**	1) transigencia 2) arreglo
1) leader 2) driver	**conductor**	**conductor**	1) (MUS) director 2) (PHYS, ELEC) conductor 3) cobrador, interventor
1) lecture 2) conference 3) talk 4) call	**conferencia**	**conference**	congreso
estar constipado: to have a cold	**constipado, -a**	**constipated**	estreñido
1) to build 2) to construe	**construir**	**to construe**	interpretar
1) to check 2) to control	**controlar**	**to control**	1) dominar 2) controlar 3) erradicar
1) habit 2) custom	**costumbre**	**costume**	traje
disappointment	**decepción**	**deception**	1) engaño 2) fraude
to disappoint	**decepcionar**	***to deceive***	engañar
1) request 2) (COM) demand 3) (JUR) action	**demanda**	**demand**	1) exigencia 2) reclamación de un pago 3) demanda
1) to ask for 2) (JUR) to sue	**demandar**	**to demand**	1) reclamar 2) requerir 3) preguntar
1) to displease 2) to anger, to offend	**disgustar**	**to disgust**	1) dar asco 2) repugnar
1) displeasure 2) suffering 3) quarrel	**disgusto**	**disgust**	1) repugnancia 2) indignación
1) to divert 2) to entertain 3) to embezzle	**distraer**	**to distract**	distraer
1) pregnant 2) awkward	**embarazado, -a**	**embarassed**	avergonzado
1) escape 2) excursion	**escapada**	**escapade**	aventura
1) stage 2) scene	**escenario**	***scenery***	1) paisaje 2) decorado
1) possible 2) extra	**eventual**	**eventual**	1) final 2) posible
fortuitously, possibly	**eventualmente**	**eventually**	1) finalmente 2) con el tiempo
1) to incite 2) to irritate 3) to arouse	**excitar**	***to excite***	1) emocionar 2) estimular

Meaning(s) of the Spanish word:	falso amigo false friend español	 English	Significado(s) de la palabra inglesa:
success	**éxito**	**exit**	1) salida 2) desvío
1) strangeness 2) eccentricity	**extravagancia**	**extravagance**	1) derroche 2) lujo 3) prodigalidad 4) extravagancia
1) odd 2) eccentric	**extravagante**	**extravagant**	1) despilfarrador 2) lujoso 3) excesivo 4) extravagante
1) factory 2) masonry 3) building	**fábrica**	**fabric**	1) tejido 2) estructura
1) to manufacture 2) to build 3) to fabricate	**fabricar**	**to fabricate**	1) inventar 2) fabricar 3) falsificar
crème caramel	**flan**	**flan**	1) (*Brit*) tartaleta de frutas 2) (*Am*) flan
1) sentence 2) expression, saying 3) style 4) (MÚS) phrase	**frase**	***phrase***	1) locución 2) expresión
1) study 2) dressing room 3) office 4) (POL) cabinet	**gabinete**	***cabinet***	1) armario, vitrina 2) gabinete de ministros
1) brilliant 2) funny 3) great	**genial**	**genial**	afable
1) genius 2) stroke of genius	**genialidad**	**geniality**	afabilidad
1) pagan 2) dashing, elegant 3) considerate	**gentil (adj)**	**genteel**	distinguido
1) to be ignorant of 2) to ignore	**ignorar**	**to ignore**	no hacer caso a
uninhabitable	**inhabitable**	**inhabitable**	habitable
uninhabited	**inhabitado, -a**	**inhabited**	habitado
insult, harm	**injuria**	**injury**	1) lesión 2) herida
to insult, to injure	**injuriar**	***to injure***	1) herir 2) estropear 3) perjudicar
poisoning	**intoxicación**	**intoxication**	1) embriaguez 2) (MED) intoxicación
to poison	**intoxicar**	***to intoxicate***	1) embriagar 2) (MED) intoxicar
1) to insert 2) to put in	**introducir**	**to introduce**	1) presentar 2) iniciar 3) abordar 4) introducir

Meaning(s) of the Spanish word:	falso amigo / false friend: español	English	Significado(s) de la palabra inglesa:
1) long 2) lengthy 3) shrewd	**largo, -a**	**large**	grande
1) reading 2) reading material 3) knowledge 4) interpretation	**lectura**	**lecture**	1) discurso, conferencia 2) sermón 3) consejo
1) bookshop 2) stationer's 3) library 4) bookcase	**librería**	**library**	1) biblioteca 2) collección
1) mask 2) fancy dress party 3) masquerade	**máscara**	**mascara**	rímel
1) poverty 2) pittance 3) stinginess 4) misfortune	**miseria**	**misery**	tristeza
to inconvenience, to annoy	**molestar**	**to molest**	1) atacar 2) agredir
1) slow to pay up 2) slow	**moroso, -a**	**morose**	taciturno, malhumorado
piece of news	**noticia**	**notice**	1) interés 2) letrero, anuncio 3) aviso
1) well-known 2) obvious	**notorio, -a**	**notorious**	de mala reputación
obvious	**ostensible**	**ostensible**	aparente
relative	**pariente**	**parent**	padre, madre
pretentious	**pedante**	**pedantic**	puntilloso
newspaper	**periódico**	**periodical**	1) boletín 2) revista
1) arrogant, conceited 2) insolent	**petulante**	**petulant**	enfurruñado
condom	**preservativo**	**preservative**	conservante
conceited	**presuntuoso, -a**	**presumptuous**	1) impertinente 2) osado
to aspire to to expect to mean to to try	**pretender**	**to pretend**	1) fingir 2) pretender
teacher	**profesor**	**professor**	1) (*Brit*) catedrático 2) (*Am*) profesor de universidad
1) to make real, to fulfil 2) to carry out, to make 3) (ECON) to realize 4) to produce	**realizar**	**to realize**	1) ser consciente de 2) realizar 3) cumplir
container, vessel	**recipiente**	**recipient**	destinatario
1) to remember 2) to remind	**recordar**	**to record**	1) archivar 2) registrar, grabar

Meaning(s) of the Spanish word:	falso amigo español	false friend English	Significado(s) de la palabra inglesa:
saying	**refrán**	**refrain**	estribillio
importance	**relevancia**	**relevance**	1) pertinencia 2) importancia
1) important 2) outstanding	**relevante**	**relevant**	1) pertinente 2) importante 3) oportuno
to summarize	**resumir**	**to resume**	1) reanudar, proseguir con 2) volver a ocupar
1) insinuating 2) reluctant	**reticente**	**reticent**	reservado
reward, remuneration	**retribución**	**retribution**	castigo justo
health	**sanidad**	**sanity**	cordura
1) healthy 2) intact 3) wholesome	**sano, -a**	***sane***	1) cuerdo 2) sensato
1) sensitive 2) noticeable	**sensible**	**sensible**	1) sensato, prudente 2) práctico 3) consciente 4) notable
1) liking 2) friendliness	**simpatía**	***sympathy***	1) compasión, comprensión 2) simpatía
friendly	**simpático, -a**	***sympathetic***	1) comprensivo, receptivo 2) cordial 3) simpatizante
1) to stand 2) to support	**soportar**	**to support**	1) sostener, aguantar 2) ayudar 3) mantener
1) smooth 2) soft 3) gentle 4) mild	**suave**	**suave**	afable, cortés
1) poor suburb 2) slum area	**suburbio**	**suburb**	barrio periférico
1) to happen (*vi*) 2) to succeed (*vi*) 3) to follow on (*vi*) 4) to inherit (*vt*)	**suceder**	**to succeed**	1) tener éxito 2) suceder
1) event, incident 2) outcome	**suceso**	**success**	éxito
1) evocative 2) thought-provoking 3) attractive	**sugestivo, -a**	**suggestive**	1) indecente 2) sugestivo
1) commonplace 2) cliché	**tópico**	**topic**	tema
1) cruel 2) gruesome	**truculento, -a**	**truculent**	agresivo
1) dissolute 2) habit-forming 3) defective 4) spoilt	**vicioso, -a**	**vicious**	1) malo, salvaje 2) despiadado 3) feroz 4) atroz

Los numerales / Numerals

Los numerales cardinales / Cardinal numbers

cero	0	zero
uno (*apócope* un), una	1	one
dos	2	two
tres	3	three
cuatro	4	four
cinco	5	five
seis	6	six
siete	7	seven
ocho	8	eight
nueve	9	nine
diez	10	ten
once	11	eleven
doce	12	twelve
trece	13	thirteen
catorce	14	fourteen
quince	15	fifteen
dieciséis	16	sixteen
diecisiete	17	seventeen
dieciocho	18	eighteen
diecinueve	19	nineteen
veinte	20	twenty
veintiuno (*apócope* veintiún), -a	21	twenty-one
veintidós	22	twenty-two
veintitrés	23	twenty-three
veinticuatro	24	twenty-four
veinticinco	25	twenty-five
treinta	30	thirty
treinta y uno (*apócope* treinta y un) -a	31	thirty-one
treinta y dos	32	thirty-two
treinta y tres	33	thirty-three
cuarenta	40	forty
cuarenta y uno (*apócope* cuarenta y un) -a	41	forty-one
cuarenta y dos	42	forty-two
cincuenta	50	fifty
cincuenta y uno (*apócope* cincuenta y un) -a	51	fifty-one
cincuenta y dos	52	fifty-two
sesenta	60	sixty
sesenta y uno (*apócope* sesenta y un) -a	61	sixty-one
sesenta y dos	62	sixty-two
setenta	70	seventy
setenta y uno (*apócope* setenta y un) -a	71	seventy-one
setenta y dos	72	seventy-two

setenta y cinco	75	seventy-five
setenta y nueve	79	seventy-nine
ochenta	80	eighty
ochenta y uno (*apócope* ochenta y un) -a	81	eighty-one
ochenta y dos	82	eighty-two
ochenta y cinco	85	eighty-five
noventa	90	ninety
noventa y uno (*apócope* noventa y un) -a	91	ninety-one
noventa y dos	92	ninety-two
noventa y nueve	99	ninety-nine
cien	100	one hundred
ciento uno (*apócope* ciento un) -a	101	one hundred and one
ciento dos	102	one hundred and two
ciento diez	110	one hundred and ten
ciento veinte	120	one hundred and twenty
ciento noventa y nueve	199	one hundred and ninety-nine
dos cientos, -as	200	two hundred
dos cientos uno (*apócope* doscientos un) -a	201	two hundred and one
dos cientos veintidós	222	two hundred and twenty-two
tres cientos, -as	300	three hundred
cuatro cientos, -as	400	four hundred
quinientos, -as	500	five hundred
seiscientos, -as	600	six hundred
sietecientos, -as	700	seven hundred
ochocientos, -as	800	eight hundred
nuevecientos, -as	900	nine hundred
mil	1 000	one thousand
mil uno (*apócope* mil un) -a	1 001	one thousand and one
mil diez	1 010	one thousand and ten
mil cien	1 100	one thousand one hundred
dos mil	2 000	two thousand
diez mil	10 000	ten thousand
cien mil	100 000	one hundred thousand
un millón	1 000 000	one million
dos millones	2 000 000	two million
dos millones quinientos, -as mil	2 500 000	two million, five hundred thousand
mil millones	1 000 000 000	one billion
un billón	1 000 000 000 000	one thousand billion

Los numerales ordinales / Ordinal numbers

primero (*apócope* primer), -a	1º, 1ª	1st	first
segundo, -a	2º, 2ª	2nd	second
tercero (*apócope* tercer), -a	3º, 3ª	3rd	third
cuarto, -a	4º, 4ª	4th	fourth
quinto, -a	5º, 5ª	5th	fifth
sexto, -a	6º, 6ª	6th	sixth
séptimo, -a	7º, 7ª	7th	seventh
octavo, -a	8º, 8ª	8th	eighth
noveno, -a	9º, 9ª	9th	ninth
décimo, -a	10º, 10ª	10th	tenth
undécimo, -a	11º, 11ª	11th	eleventh
duodécimo, -a	12º, 12ª	12th	twelfth
decimotercero, -a	13º, 13ª	13th	thirteenth
decimocuarto, -a	14º, 14ª	14th	fourtheenth
decimoquinto, -a	15º, 15ª	15th	fifteenth
decimosexto, -a	16º, 16ª	16th	sixteenth
decimoséptimo, -a	17º, 17ª	17th	seventeenth
decimoctavo, -a	18º, 18ª	18th	eighteenth
decimonoveno, -a	19º, 19ª	19th	nineteenth
vigésimo, -a	20º, 20ª	20th	twentieth
vigésimo, -a primero, -a (o vigesimoprimero, -a)	21º, 21ª	21st	twenty-first
vigésimo, -a segundo, -a (o vigesimosegundo, -a)	22º, 22ª	22nd	twenty-second
vigésimo, -a tercero, -a (o vigesimotercero, -a)	23º, 23ª	23rd	twenty-third
trigésimo, -a	30º, 30ª	30th	thirtieth
trigésimo, -a primero, -a	31º, 31ª	31st	thirty-first
trigésimo, -a segundo, -a	32º, 32ª	32nd	thirty-second
cuadragésimo, -a	40º, 40ª	40th	fortieth
quincuagésimo, -a	50º, 50ª	50th	fiftieth
sexagésimo, -a	60º, 60ª	60th	sixtieth
septuagésimo, -a	70º, 70ª	70th	seventieth
septuagésimo, -a primero, -a	71º, 71ª	71st	seventy-first
septuagésimo, -a segundo, -a	72º, 72ª	72nd	seventy-second
septuagésimo, -a noveno, -a	79º, 79ª	79th	seventy-ninth
octogésimo, -a	80º, 80ª	80th	eightieth
octogésimo, -a primero, -a	81º, 81ª	81st	eighty-first
octogésimo, -a segundo, -a	82º, 82ª	82nd	eighty-second
nonagésimo, -a	90º, 90ª	90th	nintieth
nonagésimo, -a primero, -a	91º, 91ª	91st	ninety-first
nonagésimo, -a noveno, -a	99º, 99ª	99th	ninety-ninth
centésimo, -a	100º, 100ª	100th	one hundredth
centésimo, -a primero, -a	101º, 101ª	101st	one hundred and first
centésimo, -a décimo, -a	110º, 110ª	110th	one hundred and tenth
centésimo, -a nonagésimo, -a quinto, -a	195º, 195ª	195th	one hundred and ninety-ninth

ducentésimo, -a	200º, 200ª	200th	two hundredth
tricentésimo, -a	300º, 300ª	300th	three hundredth
quingentésimo, -a	500º, 500ª	500th	five hundredth
milésimo, -a	1 000º, 1 000ª	1 000th	one thousandth
dosmilésimo, -a	2 000º, 2 000ª	2 000th	two thousandth
millonésimo, -a	1 000 000º, 1 000 000ª	1 000 000th	one millionth
diezmillonésimo, -a	10 000 000º, 10 000 000ª	10 000 000th	ten millionth

Numeros fraccionarios (o quebrados)

Fractional numbers

mitad; medio, -a	$^1/_2$	one half
un tercio	$^1/_3$	one third
un cuarto	$^1/_4$	one quarter
un quinto	$^1/_5$	one fifth
un décimo	$^1/_{10}$	one tenth
un céntesimo	$^1/_{100}$	one hundredth
un milésimo	$^1/_{1000}$	one thousandth
un millonésimo	$^1/_{1\,000\,000}$	one millionth
dos tercios	$^2/_3$	two thirds
tres cuartos	$^3/_4$	three quarters
dos quintos	$^2/_5$	two fifths
tres décimos	$^3/_{10}$	three tenths
uno y medio	$1\,^1/_2$	one and a half
dos y medio	$2\,^1/_2$	two and a half
cinco tres octavos	$5\,^3/_8$	five and three eighths
uno coma uno	1,1	one point one

Medidas y pesos

Weights and measures

Sistema (de numeración) decimal

Decimal system

mega-	1 000 000	M	mega
hectokilo	100 000	hk	hectokilo
miria-	10 000	ma	myria
kilo	1 000	k	kilo
hecto-	100	h	hecto
deca- (o decá-)	10	da	deca
deci- (o decí-)	0,1	d	deci
centi- (o centí-)	0,01	c	centi
mili-	0,001	m	milli
decimili-	0,000 1	dm	decimilli
centimili-	0,000 01	cm	centimilli
micro-	0,000 001	µ	micro

Tablas de equivalencia

Damos el llamado **imperial system** en los casos en los que en el lenguaje cotidiano éste todavía se sigue usando. Para convertir una medida métrica en la imperial, se debe multiplicar por el factor en **negrita**. Asimismo dividiendo la medida imperial por ese mismo factor se obtiene el equivalente métrico.

Conversion tables

Only imperial measures still in common use are given here. To convert a metric measurement to imperial, multiply by the conversion factor in **bold**. Likewise dividing an imperial measurement by the same factor will give the metric equivalent.

Sistema métrico
Metric measurement

Sistema imperial
Imperial measures

milla marina	1 852 m	–	nautical mile			
kilómetro	1 000 m	km	kilometre *(Brit)*, kilometer *(Am)*	0,62	mile (=1760 yards)	m, mi
hectómetro	100 m	hm	hectometre *(Brit)*, hectometer *(Am)*			
decámetro	10 m	dam	decametre *(Brit)*, decameter *(Am)*			
metro	1 m	m	metre *(Brit)*, meter *(Am)*	1,09 3,28	yard (= 3 feet) foot (= 12 inches)	yd ft
decímetro	0,1 m	dm	decimetre *(Brit)*, decimeter *(Am)*			
centímetro	0,01 m	cm	centimetre *(Brit)*, centimeter *(Am)*	0,39	inch	in
milímetro	0,001 m	mm	millimetre *(Brit)*, millimeter *(Am)*			
micrón, micra	0,000 001 m	µ	micron			
milimicrón	0,000 000 001 m	mµ	millimicron			
ángstrom	0,000 000 000 1 m	Å	angstrom			

Medidas de superficie

Surface measure

kilómetro cuadrado	1 000 000 m²	km²	square kilometre	0,386	square mile (= 640 acres)	sq. m., sq. mi.
hectómetro cuadrado hectárea	10 000 m²	hm² ha	square hectometre hectare	2,47	acre (= 4840 square yards)	a.
decámetro cuadrado área	100 m²	dam² a	square decametre are			
metro cuadrado	1 m²	m²	square metre	1.196 10,76	square yard (9 square feet) square feet (= 144 square inches)	sq. yd sq. ft
decímetro cuadrado	0,01 m²	dm²	square decimetre			
centímetro cuadrado	0,000 1 m²	cm²	square centimetre	0,155	square inch	sq. in.
milímetro cuadrado	0,000 001 m²	mm²	square millimetre			

Medidas de volumen y capacidad — Volume and capacity

kilómetro cúbico	1 000 000 000 m³	km³	cubic kilometre			
metro cúbico estéreo	1 m³	m³ st	cubic metre stere	1,308 35,32	cubic yard (= 27 cubic feet) cubic foot (= 1728 cubic inches)	cu. yd cu. ft
hectolitro	0,1 m³	hl	hectolitre *(Brit)*, hectoliter *(Am)*			
decalitro	0,01 m³	dal	decalitre *(Brit)*, decaliter *(Am)*			
decímetro cúbico litro	0,001 m³	dm³ l	cubic decimetre litre *(Brit)*, liter *(Am)*	0,22 1,76 0,26 2,1	UK gallon UK pint US gallon US pint	gal. pt gal. Pt
decilitro	0,000 1 m³	dl	decilitre *(Brit)*, deciliter *(Am)*			
centilitro	0,000 01 m³	cl	centilitre *(Brit)*, centilter *(Am)*	0,352 0,338	UK fluid ounce US fluid ounce	fl. Oz
centímetro cúbico	0,000 001 m³	cm³	cubic centimetre	0,061	cubic inch	cu. in.
mililitro	0,000 001 m³	ml	millilitre *(Brit)*, milliliter *(Am)*			
milímetro cúbico	0,000 000 001 m³	mm³	cubic millimetre			

Pesos — Weight

tonelada	1 000 kg	t	tonne	0,98 1,1	[long] ton *(Brit)* (= 2240 pounds) [short] ton *(Am)* (= 2000 pounds)	t.
quintal métrico	100 kg	q	quintal			
kilogramo	1 000 g	kg	kilogram	2,2	pound (= 16 ounces)	lb
hectogramo	100 g	hg	hectogram			
decagramo	10 g	dag	decagram			
gramo	1 g	g	gram	0,035	ounce	oz
quilate	0,2 g	–	carat			
decigramo (o decagramo)	0,1 g	dg	decigram			
centigramo	0,01 g	cg	centigram			
miligramo	0,001 g	mg	milligram			
microgramo	0,000 001 g	µg, g	microgram			

Para convertir una temperatura indicada en grados centígrados a Fahrenheit se deben restar 32 y multiplicar por $^5/_9$. Para convertir una temperatura indicada en Fahrenheit a centígrados se debe multiplicar por $^9/_5$ y añadir 32.

To convert a temperature in degrees Celsius to Fahrenheit, deduct 32 and multiply by $^5/_9$. To convert Fahrenheit to Celsius, multiply by $^9/_5$ and add 32.

España
Spain

comunidades autónomas ***autonomous regions***	**capitales** ***capital cities***
Andalucía *Andalusia*	Sevilla *Seville*
Aragón	Zaragoza
Asturias	Oviedo
Baleares *Balearic Islands*	Palma de Mallorca
Canarias *Canary Islands*	Santa Cruz de Tenerife
Cantabria	Santander
Castilla y León	Valladolid
Castilla-La Mancha	Toledo
Cataluña *Catalonia*	Barcelona
Extremadura	Mérida
Galicia	Santiago de Compostela
La Rioja	Logroño
Madrid	**Madrid**
Murcia	Murcia
Navarra	Pamplona
País Vasco *Basque Country*	Vitoria
Valencia	Valencia

Hispanoamérica
Spanish America

países ***countries***	**capitales** ***capital cities***
Argentina	Buenos Aires
Bolivia	La Paz
Chile	Santiago
Colombia	Bogotá
Costa Rica	San José
Cuba	La Habana *Havana*
Ecuador	Quito
El Salvador	San Salvador
Guatemala	Guatemala *Guatemala City*

Honduras	Tegucigalpa
México *Mexico*	Ciudad de México D.F. *Mexico City*
Nicaragua	Managua
Panamá *Panama*	Panamá *Panama City*
Paraguay	Asunción
Perú *Peru*	Lima
Puerto Rico	San Juan
República Dominicana *Dominican Republic*	Santo Domingo
Uruguay	Montevideo
Venezuela	Caracas

Canada
El Canadá

Capital: Ottawa

provinces ***provincias***	**capital cities** ***capitales***
Alberta	Edmonton
British Colombia	Victoria
Manitoba	Winnipeg
New Brunswick *Nuevo Brunswick*	Fredericton
Newfoundland *Terranova*	St. John's
Nova Scotia *Nueva Escocia*	Halifax
Ontario	Toronto
Prince Edward Island *Isla del Príncipe Eduardo*	Charlottetown
Québec	Québec
Saskatchewan	Saskatchewan

territories ***capital cities***	**territorios** ***capitales***
North West Territories *Territorio del Noroeste*	Yellowknife
Nunavut Territory (*since 1st April 1999*) *Territorio del Nunavut*	Iqaluit
Yukon Territory *Territorio del Yukon*	Whitehorse

United Kingdom
Reino Unido

countries *países*	**capital cities** *capitales*
England *Inglaterra*	London *Londres*
Scotland *Escocia*	Edinburgh *Edinburgo*
Wales *País de Gales*	Cardiff
Northern Ireland *Irlanda del Norte*	Belfast

England
Inglaterra

counties *condados*	**abbreviations** *abreviaciones*	**administrative centres** *centros administrativos*
Bedfordshire	Beds	Bedford
Berkshire	Berks	Reading
Buckinghamshire	Bucks	Aylesbury
Cambridgeshire	Cambs	Cambridge
Cheshire	Ches	Chester
Cornwall	Corn	Truro
Cumbria		Carlisle
Derbyshire	Derbs	Matlock
Devon		Exeter
Dorset		Dorchester
Durham	Dur	Durham
East Sussex *Sussex Oriental*	E. Sussex	Lewes
Essex		Chelmsford
Gloucestershire	Glos	Gloucester
Greater London *Gran Londres*		**London** ***Londres***
Greater Manchester *Gran Manchester*		Manchester
Hampshire	Hants	Winchester
Hertfordshire	Herts	Hertford
Kent		Maidstone
Lancashire	Lancs	Preston
Leicestershire	Leics	Leicester
Lincolnshire	Lincs	Lincoln
Merseyside		Liverpool

Norfolk		Norwich
Northamptonshire	Northants	Northampton
Northumberland	Northd	Morpeth
North Yorkshire	N. Yorks	Northallerton
Nottinghamshire	Notts	Nottingham
Oxfordshire	Oxon	Oxford
Shropshire	Salop	Shrewsbury
Somerset	Som	Taunton
South Yorkshire	S. Yorks	Barnsley
Staffordshire	Staffs	Stafford
Suffolk	Suff	Ipswich
Surrey		Kingston upon Thames
Tyne & Wear		Newcastle upon Tyne
Warwickshire	Warks	Warwick
West Midlands	W. Midlands	Birmingham
West Sussex *Sussex Occidental*	W. Sussex	Chichester
West Yorkshire	W. Yorks	Wakefield
Wiltshire	Wilts	Trowbridge
Worcestershire	Worcs	Worcester

Wales, *Welsh:* Cymru
País de Gales

unitary authorities ***unidades administrativas***	**administrative headquarters** ***centros administrativos***
Anglesey	Llangefni
Blaenau Gwent	Ebbw Vale
Bridgend	Bridgend
Caerphilly	Hengoed
Cardiff	**Cardiff**
Carmarthenshire	Carmarthen
Ceredigion	Aberaeron
Conwy	Conwy
Denbighshire	Ruthin
Flintshire	Mold
Gwynedd	Caernarfon
Merthyr Tydfil	Merthyr Tydfil
Monmouthshire	Cwmbran
Neath Port Talbot	Port Talbot
Newport	Newport

Pembrokeshire	Haverfordwest
Powys	Llandrindod Wells
Rhondda Cynon Taff	Clydach Vale
Swansea	Swansea
Torfaen	Pontypool
Vale of Glamorgan	Barry
Wrexham	Wrexham

Scotland
Escocia

unitary authorities *unidades administrativas*	administrative headquarters *centros administrativos*
Aberdeen City	
Aberdeenshire	Aberdeen
Angus	Forfar
Argyll and Bute	Lochgilphead
Clackmannanshire	Alloa
Dumfries and Galloway	Dumfries
Dundee City	
East Ayrshire	Kilmarnock
East Dunbartonshire	Kirkintilloch
East Lothian	Haddington
East Renfrewshire	Giffnock
Edinburgh City	
Falkirk	Falkirk
Fife	Glenrothes
Glasgow City	
Highland	Inverness
Inverclyde	Greenock
Midlothian	Dalkeith
Moray	Elgin
North Ayrshire	Irvine
North Lanarkshire	Motherwell
Orkney Islands *Islas Orcadas*	Kirkwall
Perth and Kinross	Perth
Renfrewshire	Paisley
Scottish Borders	Melrose
Shetland Islands *Islas Shetland*	Lerwick
South Ayrshire	Ayr

South Lanarkshire	Hamilton
Stirling	Stirling
West Dunbartonshire	Dunbarton
Western Isles *Islas Hébridas*	Stornoway
West Lothian	Livingston

Northern Ireland
Irlanda del Norte

counties ***condados***	**principal towns** ***ciudades principales***
Antrim	**Belfast**
Armagh	Armagh
Down	Downpatrick
Fermanagh	Enniskillen
Londonderry	Londonderry
Tyrone	Omagh

Republic of Ireland or Irish Republic, *Gaelic:* Èire
República de Irlanda

provinces
provincias

counties ***condados***	**principal towns** ***ciudades principales***
Connacht, *formerly:* **Connaught**	
Galway, *Gaelic:* Gaillimh	Galway
Leitrim, *Gaelic:* Liathdroma	Carrick-on-Shannon
Mayo, *Gaelic:* Mhuigheo	Castlebar
Roscommon, *Gaelic:* Ros Comáin	Roscommon
Sligo, *Gaelic:* Sligeach	Sligo

Leinster	
Carlow, *Gaelic:* Cheatharlach	Carlow
Dublin, *Gaelic:* Baile Átha Cliath	**Dublin**
Kildare, *Gaelic:* Chill Dara	Naas
Kilkenny, *Gaelic:* Chill Choinnigh	Kilkenny
Laois/Laoighis/Leix	Portlaoise
Longford, *Gaelic:* Longphuirt	Longford

Louth, *Gaelic:* Lughbhaidh	Dundalk
Meath, *Gaelic:* na Midhe	Navan
Offaly, *Gaelic:* Ua bhFailghe	Tullamore
Westmeath, *Gaelic:* na h-Iarmhidhe	Mullingar
Wexford, *Gaelic:* Loch Garman	Wexford
Wicklow, *Gaelic:* Cill Mhantáin	Wicklow

Munster	
Clare, *Gaelic:* An Cláir	Ennis
Cork, *Gaelic:* Chorcaigh	Cork
Kerry, *Gaelic:* Chiarraighe	Tralee
Limerick, *Gaelic:* Luimneach	Limerick
Tipperary, *Gaelic:* Thiobrad Árann	Clonmel
Waterford, *Gaelic:* Phort Láirge	Waterford

Ulster	
Cavan, *Gaelic:* Cabháin	Cavan
Donegal, *Gaelic:* Dún na nGall	Lifford
Monaghan, *Gaelic:* Mhuineachain	Monaghan

Channel Islands ***Islas Anglonormandas***	**principal towns** ***ciudades principales***
Alderney	St. Anne
Guernsey *Isla Guernesey*	St. Peter Port
Jersey	St. Hellier
Sark	Sercq

Australia

Capital: Canberra

states ***estados***	**capital cities** ***capitales***
New South Wales *Nueva Gales del Sur*	Sydney
Queensland	Brisbane
South Australia *Australia-Meridional*	Adelaide
Victoria	Melbourne
Western Australia *Australia Occidental*	Perth
Tasmania	Hobart

territories *territorios*	capital cities *capitales*
Australian Capital Territory *Territorio de la Capital Australiana*	Canberra
Northern Territory *Territorio del Norte*	Darwin

New Zealand
Nueva Zelanda

Capital: Wellington

North Island *Isla del Norte*
South Island *Isla del Sur*
Stewart Island *Isla Stewart*
Chatham Islands *Islas Chatham*

small outlying islands
pequeñas islas periféricas

Auckland Islands *Islas Auckland*
Kermadec Islands *Islas Kermadec*
Campbell Island *Isla Campbell*
the Antipodes *(Islas) Antipodes*
Three Kings Islands *Islas Three Kings*
Bounty Island *Isla Bounty*
Snares Island *Isla Snares*
Solander Island *Isla Solander*

Dependencies
Dependencias

Tokelau Islands *Islas Tokelau*
Ross Dependency *Dependencia Ross*
Niue Island (free associate) *Isla Niue*
Cook Islands (free associate) *Islas Cook*

The United States of America
Estados Unidos de América

Capital: Wahington, DC.

Federal States *Estados Federales*	**abbreviations** *abreviaciones*	**capital cities** *capitales*
Alabama	AL	Montgomery
Alaska	AK	Juneau
Arizona	AZ	Phoenix
Arkansas	AR	Little Rock
California	CA	Sacramento
Colorado	CO	Denver
Connecticut	CT	Hartford
Delaware	DE	Dover
Florida	FL	Tallahassee
Georgia	GA	Atlanta
Hawaii *Hawai*	HI	Honolulu
Idaho	ID	Boise
Illinois	IL	Springfield
Indiana	IN	Indianapolis *Indianápolis*
Iowa	IA	Des Moines
Kansas	KS	Topeka
Kentucky	KY	Frankfort
Louisiana	LA	Baton Rouge
Maine	ME	Augusta
Maryland	MD	Annapolis
Massachusetts	MA	Boston
Michigan	MI	Lansing
Minnesota	MN	St. Paul
Mississippi *Misisipí*	MS	Jackson
Missouri	MO	Jefferson City
Montana	MT	Helena
Nebraska	NB	Lincoln
Nevada	NV	Carson City
New Hampshire *Nueva Hampshire*	NH	Concord
New Jersey *Nueva Jersey*	NJ	Trenton)
New Mexico *Nuevo México*	NM	Santa Fe
New York *Nueva York*	NY	Albany

North Carolina *Carolina del Norte*	NC	Raleigh
North Dakota *Dakota del Norte*	ND	Bismarck
Ohio	OH	Columbus
Oklahoma	OK	Oklahoma City
Oregon *Oregón*	OR	Salem
Pennsylvania *Pensilvania*	PA	Harrisburg
Rhode Island	RI	Providence
South Carolina *Carolina del Sur*	SC	Columbia
South Dakota *Dakota del Sur*	SD	Pierre
Tennessee	TN	Nashville
Texas *Tejas*	TX	Austin
Utah	UT	Salt Lake City
Vermont	VT	Montpelier
Virginia	VA	Richmond
Washington	WA	Olympia
West Virginia *Virginia Occidental*	WV	Charleston
Wisconsin	WI	Madison
Wyoming	WY	Cheyenne

Condiciones de uso

Instalación del Diccionario Cambridge Klett Compact

Terms and conditions of use

How to install Diccionario Cambridge Klett Compact

Este diccionario se puede adquirir en dos versiones: sólo como libro o como libro con CD-ROM complementario. Si ha adquirido esta última versión, se aplicarán la licencia y las instrucciones que siguen.

Condiciones de uso

Éste es un acuerdo legal entre usted ('el cliente') y Cambridge University Press y Ernst Klett Verlag ('la editorial'):

1. Licencia

(a) La editorial otorga al cliente la licencia de uso de un ejemplar de este CD-ROM (i) en un solo ordenador que pueden utilizar uno o varios usuarios de modo no simultáneo, o (ii) por una sola persona en uno o varios ordenadores (siempre y cuando el CD-ROM lo use el cliente en un solo ordenador en un momento dado), pero no en ambos casos.

(b) El cliente no puede: (i) copiar ni autorizar la copia del CD-ROM, (ii) traducir el CD-ROM, (iii) invertir la ingeniería, desensamblar ni descompilar el CD-ROM, (iv) transferir, vender, asignar ni traspasar ninguna porción del CD-ROM, ni (v) utilizar el CD-ROM desde un sistema ni una red.

2. Copyright

Todo el contenido del CD-ROM está protegido por derechos de autor y otras leyes de propiedad intelectual. El cliente adquiere únicamente el derecho de uso del CD-ROM, sin más derechos, explícitos ni implícitos, que los expresados en la licencia.

3. Responsabilidad

En la medida permitida por la ley aplicable, la editorial no se hace responsable de ningún daño directo ni pérdida de cualquier tipo como consecuencia del uso de este producto o de errores o fallos en él contenidos y en cualquier caso la responsabilidad de la editorial se limitará a la cantidad abonada por el cliente para adquirir el producto.

This dictionary is available in two versions, either as a book or as a book plus CD-ROM. If you have the book plus CD-ROM, then the following licence and instructions apply.

Terms and conditions of use

This is a legal agreement between you ('the customer') and Cambridge University Press and Ernst Klett Verlag ('the publisher'):

1. Licence

(a) The publisher grants the customer the licence to use one copy of this CD-ROM (i) on a single computer for use by one or more people at different times, or (ii) by a single person on one or more computers (provided the CD-ROM is only used on one computer at one time and is only used by the customer), but not both.

(b) The customer shall not: (i) copy or authorise copying of the CD-ROM, (ii) translate the CD-ROM, (iii) reverse-engineer, disassemble or decompile the CD-ROM, (iv) transfer, sell, assign or otherwise convey any portion of the CD-ROM, or (v) operate the CD-ROM from a network or mainframe system.

2. Copyright

All material contained within the CD-ROM is protected by copyright and other intellectual property laws. The customer acquires only the right to use the CD-ROM and does not acquire any rights, express or implied, other than those expressed in the licence.

3. Liability

To the extent permitted by applicable law, the publisher is not liable for direct damages or loss of any kind resulting from the use of this product or from errors or faults contained in it and in every case the publisher's liability shall be limited to the amount actually paid by the customer for the product.

Instalación del Diccionario Cambridge Klett Compact

1. Encienda el ordenador e inicie Windows.
2. Introduzca el CD en la unidad de CD-ROM y siga las instrucciones en pantalla. Es aconsejable aceptar las sugerencias de instalación, haciendo clic en el botón SIGUIENTE de cada cuadro de diálogo.
3. Cuando se haya completado la instalación, haga clic en el botón FINALIZAR.

IMPORTANTE

Si la instalación no se inicia automáticamente, es debido a que la función de inicio automático del CD se ha desactivado desde Windows; debe realizar el siguiente procedimiento para comenzar la instalación:

i. Haga clic en el botón INICIO de Windows, sitúe el puntero sobre CONFIGURACIÓN y haga clic en PANEL DE CONTROL.
   Se abrirá la ventana Panel de control.

ii. Haga doble clic en AGREGAR O QUITAR PROGRAMAS.
   Se abrirá el cuadro de diálogo Agregar o quitar programas.

iii. Haga clic en INSTALAR. Siga las instrucciones en pantalla.

Inicio del diccionario

- Haga doble clic en el icono Diccionario, situado en el escritorio.

o

- Haga clic en el botón INICIO de Windows, sitúe el puntero sobre PROGRAMAS, CAMBRIDGE y, por último, seleccione DICCIONARIO CAMBRIDGE KLETT COMPACT.

Para recibir asistencia o consultar las respuestas a las preguntas más habituales, visite la página www.cambridge.org/elt/cdrom

How to install Diccionario Cambridge Klett Compact

1. Turn on your computer and start Windows.
2. Insert the CD into the CD-ROM drive and follow the instructions. We recommend that you follow the suggested installation by clicking NEXT for each dialog box.
3. When the installation is finished, click FINISH.

IMPORTANT

If the CD does not begin installation automatically, the Autorun function on the CD has been turned off by Windows and you will need to do the following steps to start installation:

i. Click and hold the Windows START button, point to SETTINGS, then select CONTROL PANEL.
   The Control panel window opens.

ii. Double-click ADD/REMOVE PROGRAMS.
   The Add/Remove Programs dialog box appears.

iii. Click INSTALL. Follow the instructions.

How to start the dictionary

- Double-click the Diccionario icon on your desktop.

or

- Click and hold the Windows START button, select PROGRAMS, then CAMBRIDGE, then DICCIONARIO CAMBRIDGE KLETT COMPACT.

For support and frequently asked questions, go to www.cambridge.org/elt/cdrom

Símbolos y abreviaturas

Symbols and abbreviations

bloque fraseológico	►	idiom bloc
contracción	=	contraction
corresponde a	≈	equivalent to
cambio de interlocutor	–	change of speaker
marca registrada	®	trademark
	◆	phrasal verb
	1st pers	1st person
	3rd pers	3rd person
	a.	also
abreviación de	*abr de, abbr of*	abbreviation of
adjetivo	*adj*	adjective
administración	ADMIN	administration
adverbio	*adv*	adverb
agricultura	AGR	agriculture
	Am	American English
América Central	*AmC*	
América Latina	*AmL*	
América del Sur	*AmS*	
anatomía	ANAT	anatomy
Zona Andina	*And*	
Antillas	*Ant*	
arquitectura	ARCHIT, ARQUIT	architecture
República Argentina	Arg	
artículo	*art*	article
arte	ART	art
astronomía, astrología	ASTR	astronomy, astrology
automóvil y tráfico	AUTO	automobile, transport
verbo auxiliar	*aux*	auxiliary verb
aviación, tecnología espacial	AVIAT	aviation, aerospace, space technology
biología	BIO	biology
Bolivia	*Bol*	
botánica	BOT	botany
	Brit	British English
	Can	Canadian English
	CHEM	chemistry
Chile	*Chile*	
cine	CINE	cinema
Colombia	*Col*	
comercio	COM	commerce
comparativo	*comp*	comparative
conjunción	*conj*	conjunction
Costa Rica	*CRi*	

Cono Sur (República Argentina, Chile, Paraguay, Uruguay)	*CSur*	
Cuba	*Cuba*	
definido	*def*	definite
deporte	DEP	
	dial	dialect
República Domenicana	*DomR*	
ecología	ECOL	ecology
economía	ECON	economics
Ecuador	*Ecua*	
electrotécnica, electrónica	ELEC	electricity, electronics
lenguaje elevado, literario	*elev*	
El Salvador	*ElSal*	
enseñanza	ENS	
	EU	European Union
femenino	*f*	feminine
	FASHION	fashion and sewing
ferrocarril	FERRO	
figurativo	*fig*	figurative
Filipinas	*Fili*	
filosofía	FILOS	
finananzas, bolsa	FIN	finance, banking, stock exchange
física	FÍS	
lenguaje formal	*form*	formal language
fotografía	FOTO	
	GAMES	games
gastronomía	GASTR	gastronomy
geografía, geología	GEO	geography, geology
Guatemala	*Guat*	
Guayana	*Guay*	
Guinea Ecuatorial	*GuinEc*	
historia, histórico	HIST	history, historical
Honduras	*Hond*	
imperativo	*imper*	imperative
impersonal	*impers*	impersonal
indefinido	*indef*	indefinite
lenguaje informal	*inf*	informal language
infinitivo	*infin*	infinitive
informática	INFOR	computing
	insep	inseparable
interjección	*interj*	interjection
interrogativo	*interrog*	interrogative